Goldmine

THE ULTIMATE GUIDE TO VALUING YOUR VINYL

RECORD ALBUM PRICE GUIDE

3rd Edition

TIM NEELY

Published by

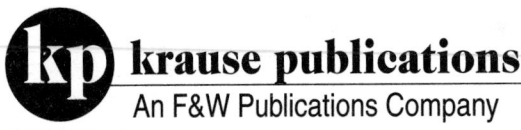
krause publications
An F&W Publications Company

700 East State Street • Iola, WI 54990-0001
715-445-2214 • 888-457-2873
www.krause.com

Please call or write for our free catalog of publications.
Our toll-free number to place an order or obtain a free catalog is 800-258-0929
or please use our regular business telephone 715-445-2214.

Library of Congress Catalog Number: 99-63746
ISBN: 0-87349-671-X

Printed in the United States of America

Edited by Tim Neely
Designed by Patsy Howell

CONTENTS

Introduction to the Third Edition

Welcome to the third edition of the *Goldmine Record Album Price Guide.* We continue to refine and expand what we include in the book, based on market conditions and your input.

As we did in the second edition of the book, we still are using the $20 near-mint value as a minimum for inclusion in the book. Some name artists are in so little demand, or their albums are so common, that none of their U.S.-released catalog meets that criterion. But otherwise, even if an artist has only *one* album that hits that $20 mark, *all* of their known American LP releases are listed.

For example, because a couple of the Eagles' albums – basically, those that were geared toward audiophiles – have a current market value of $20 or more, we've included *all* their albums, even the common ones. This also allows us to include complete album discographies for many acts who have never had such a listing in any price guide before.

Removing the absolute $20 minimum also allows us to include complete album discographies for the most collectible artists, such as the Beatles, Elvis Presley and the Rolling Stones. Yes, all three still have LPs available in the secondary market for under $20, and in some cases for under $10!

We've done a similar expansion in the original cast, soundtrack, television and various artists section that appears in the back of the book. As some of you no doubt know, many of these albums stayed in print on vinyl for years and went through many label changes. Because of the $20 floor, we did not list all the label variations for most of these, as most of the later versions still sell for well under that $20. We have continued to rectify that in this edition. Our ever-alert readers made us aware of some oddities that could make a difference in collectibility. Did you know that the 1980s MCA reissue of *The Glenn Miller Story* soundtrack was in *true stereo?* Neither did I. All prior "stereo" issues on Decca, and earlier MCA reissues as well, were – as Decca called it – "enhanced for stereo." In other words, they were rechanneled.

At the same time we've increased the number of listings in the most popular genres, *we've kept the $20 minimum in place for two major types of music – jazz and classical.*

Even with a cursory glance through the pages of this book, you'll see that we have a *lot* of jazz artists in this book. Part of the reason is because we now have reasonably accurate data available to us, thanks to the 2000 publication of the *Goldmine Jazz Album Price Guide.* We also have not always been consistent in deciding which jazz artists were included and which ones were not. Yes to Cal Tjader and no to Art Blakey? Yes to Duke Ellington and no to Dizzy Gillespie? So in this edition, we've expanded the jazz section to include as many of the major names as would fit within our page-count parameters.

Our survey of classical music, a first for a readily-available price guide, continues in this edition. The price fluctuations we noted in the second edition don't appear in this third edition.

Most of the significant additions in this third edition fall under two categories:

- Soul LPs on obscure (and not-so-obscure) labels.
- Vinyl LPs of the 1990s and beyond.

Each of these has seen occasionally dramatic price increases since the last edition of the book. We also continue to discover things we previously did not know about. Compiling the *Goldmine Record Album Price Guide* is, as much as anything else, a continual learning process.

Market trends

There is no longer any doubt: Online auctions have had a significant effect on the record album market. And not all of it is positive.

Some say that eBay and its cousins, Yahoo! and Amazon, have served to deflate the market significantly. Still others say that online auctions have revitalized the album market. And still others say that it hasn't made a difference one way or another.

And, in their own ways, all are correct. We have dropped some prices in this book based in part on what we see online; we've also raised others; but most remain about the same.

Continuing the trend we first noted several years ago, more albums are being bought and sold on the Internet than ever before. On eBay, there are often over 100,000 albums for sale at a time. The largest dealers' collective, gemm.com (short for Global Electronic Music Marketplace), is said to have several *million* records, tapes and CDs for sale! Several other dealers have hundreds of thousands of records available through their Web sites. For many dealers whose reach used to encompass, say, a 25- or 50-mile radius of their storefront or flea market stand, the Internet has allowed them to expand their customer base worldwide. With those kinds of numbers, and with good search engines that help you find what you're seeking that much more easily, it's no wonder that a lot more records are changing hands via online sales, and that many collectors are filling in decades-old gaps from their want lists.

At the same time, though, a large percentage – perhaps as high as 90 percent – of all records for auction on eBay have no bids! And a recent survey of other collectibles conducted by a company called Auction Watch indicates that the "sell-through rate" – the percentage of items listed on eBay that actually get sold – has dropped significantly, from 72 percent in 2000 to 45 percent in 2003. Is that because no one wants these items? Probably not. It could be because the minimum bid is too high, or that the seller is new or didn't post a picture or claimed that the record was in "good" condition – a grade that is pretty low in record collecting terminology. Or it could be that the people who are most interested in those records weren't bidding that particular week. Or it could be that the sheer number of items for sale makes it impossible for the collector to purchase everything he or she wants at any given time. Consider that, as of the time I write this, eBay has had roughly 2.5 *billion* sale listings in its relatively short history.

Even today, there remain dealers who do no trading over the Internet. Some sell everything face to face; after all, there's no better way of knowing whether a particular record for sale meets your criteria for purchase than to actually see it, hold it in your hands, and even play parts of it. Recent reports from major record conventions have been encouraging, with better attendance and more buying and selling than was true several years ago. Some use the tried-and-true method of mail-order catalogs with no Web element. Others advertise only in the collector's magazines such as *Goldmine.*

The one comment I've heard about online selling that is obviously wrong is this, and I've heard it more than once: "I can see what my records are worth by checking eBay's results from the past month." Why is this wrong? In the grand scheme of things, *a small minority of all records that are sold in the United States and elsewhere are traded on eBay.* It would be as if you determined the state of the U.S. economy by looking only at the price of gasoline. Sure, it means something. But there are a lot of other things that mean something, too, and it's by taking everything together that you get a clearer picture of the way things are.

So what else is going on?

- The audiophile market continues to be turbulent. Since the last edition went to press, the DCC label has, for all practical purposes, gone out of business. The vinyl LPs that came out on DCC are hailed as among the best records ever made in any country at any time, and the prices of some of them reflect that demand. Some of them, which sold for $25 or so when new, have skyrocketed over the $100 mark for near-mint copies.
- It's still true: More younger collectors are discovering the joys of vinyl. And their interest in the format has spurred the sale of new records: Today, while the sales of CDs continue to slide, vinyl sales are increasing, though still a fraction of what they were in their heyday. And while records from the 1950s and 1960s are still the most in demand, more of the younger buyers are discovering more recent music. The 1970s

has seen an increase in interest because of the younger collector, as has out-of-print vinyl from the 1990s. Several "modern" artists who have never appeared in a price guide before have reached that magic $20 floor and have their vinyl LPs listed in this book.

- Whether it's a search for the perfect beat or the deepest groove, soul records have seen a significant increase in interest over the past two years. Even a few relatively common LPs have crept up in value. But for the most part, the more obscure, the better.

- Finally, to get the most for your records, three things matter: Condition, condition and condition! Many of the newer vinyl collectors grew up hearing compact discs, both at home and on the radio. Surface noise is more distracting to these people than it is to people who grew up listening to records. I've seen some seemingly outrageous prices for sealed copies (which, at least in theory, have a mint or near-mint disc inside) of even common LPs. Would you believe someone paid $23 for a sealed vinyl copy of the thrift-shop staple *Whipped Cream And Other Delights* by Herb Alpert and the Tijuana Brass? Well, it happened in 2001!

Grading your records

When it comes to records, and how much you'll get for them, remember this above all:

Condition is (almost) everything!

Yes, it's possible to get a high price for a beat-up record, if it's exceptionally rare. But for common material, if it's not in at least Very Good condition – and preferably closer to Near Mint – you won't get many buyers. Or at least you won't the second time around. So accurately grading your discs is important, whether you're selling your records to a dealer or selling them to another collector.

Visual or play grading? In an ideal world, every record would be played before it is graded. But the time involved makes it impractical for most dealers, and anyway, it's rare that you get a chance to hear a record before you buy through the mail. Some advertisers play-grade everything and say so. But unless otherwise noted, records are visually graded.

How to grade. Look at everything about a record – its playing surface, its label, its edges – under a strong light. Then, based on your overall impression, give it a grade based on the following criteria:

Mint (M): Absolutely perfect in every way – certainly never played, possibly even still sealed. (More on still sealed under "Other considerations.") Should be used sparingly as a grade, if at all.

Near Mint (NM or M-): A nearly perfect record. Many dealers won't give a grade higher than this, implying (perhaps correctly) that no record is ever truly perfect.

The record should show no obvious signs of wear. An LP jacket should have no creases, folds, seam splits or any other noticeable similar defect. No cut-out holes, either. And of course, the same should be true of any other inserts, such as posters, lyric sleeves and the like.

Basically, an LP in Near Mint condition looks as if you just got it home from a retail record store and removed the shrink wrap.

Near Mint is the highest price listed in all *Goldmine* price guides. Anything that exceeds this grade, in the opinion of both buyer and seller, is worth significantly more than the highest *Goldmine* book value.

Very Good Plus (VG+): Generally worth 50 percent of the Near Mint value.

A Very Good Plus record will show some signs that it was played and otherwise handled by a previous owner who took good care of it.

Record surfaces may show some slight signs of wear and may have slight scuffs or very light scratches that don't affect one's listening experience. Slight warps that do not affect the sound are OK.

The label may have some ring wear or discoloration, but it should be barely noticeable. The center hole will not have been misshapen by repeated play.

LP inner sleeves will have some slight ring wear, lightly turned-up corners, or a slight seam split. An LP jacket may also have slight signs of wear and may be marred by a cut-out hole, indentation or corner indicating it was taken out of print and sold at a discount.

In general, if not for a couple minor things wrong with it, this would be Near Mint. All but the most mint-crazy collectors will find a Very Good Plus record highly acceptable.

A synonym used by some collectors and dealers for "Very Good Plus" is "Excellent."

Very Good (VG): Generally worth 25 percent of the Near Mint value.

Many of the defects found in a VG+ record will be more pronounced in a VG disc.

Surface noise will be evident upon playing, especially in soft passages and during a song's intro and fade, but will not overpower the music otherwise. Groove wear will start to be noticeable, as will light scratches (deep enough to feel with a fingernail) that will affect the sound.

Labels may be marred by writing, or have tape or stickers (or their residue) attached. The same will be true of picture sleeves or LP covers. However, it will not have all of these problems at the same time, only two or three of them.

This *Goldmine* price guide lists Very Good as the lowest price. This, *not* the Near Mint price, should be your guide when determining how much a record is worth, as that is the price a dealer will normally pay you for a Near Mint record.

Good (G), Good Plus (G+): Generally worth 10-15 percent of the Near Mint value.

Good does not mean Bad! A record in Good or Good Plus condition can be put onto a turntable and will play through without skipping. But it will have significant surface noise and scratches and visible groove wear (on a styrene record, the groove will be starting to turn white).

A jacket or sleeve will have seam splits, especially at the bottom or on the spine. Tape, writing, ring wear or other defects will start to overwhelm the object.

If it's a common item, you'll probably find another copy in better shape eventually. Pass it up. But if it's something you have been seeking for years, and the price is right, get it ... but keep looking to upgrade.

Poor (P), Fair (F): Generally worth 0-5 percent of the Near Mint price.

The record is cracked, badly warped, and won't play through without skipping or repeating. The LP jacket barely keeps the LP inside it. Inner sleeves are fully seam split, crinkled, and written upon.

Except for impossibly rare records otherwise unattainable, records in this condition should be bought or sold for no more than a few cents each.

Other grading considerations. Most dealers give a separate grade to the record and its cover. In an ad, a record's grade is listed first, followed by that of the jacket, unless noted otherwise.

With **Still Sealed (SS)** records, let the buyer beware, unless it's a U.S. pressing from the last 10-15 years or so. It's too easy to re-seal one. Yes, some legitimately never-opened LPs from the 1960s still exist, and some of them bring rather fancy prices. But if you're looking for a specific pressing, the only way you can know for sure is to open the record. Also, European imports are not factory-sealed, so if you see them advertised as sealed, someone other than the manufacturer sealed them.

Common collecting abbreviations

In addition to the letters used to designate a record's grade, it's not uncommon to see other abbreviations used in dealer

advertisements. Knowing the more common ones helps to prevent confusion. Here are some that pertain to albums:

boot: bootleg (illegal pressing)

cc: cut corner

co: cutout

coh: cut-out hole

cov, cv, cvr: cover

dh: drill hole

dj: disc jockey (promotional) record

gf: gatefold (cover)

imp: import

ins: insert

lbl: label

m, mo: monaural (mono)

nap: (does) not affect play

noc: number on cover

nol: number on label

obi: not actually an abbreviation, "obi" is the Japanese word for "sash" and is used to describe the strip of paper usually wrapped around Japanese (and occasional US) pressings of LPs

orig: original

pr, pro, promo: promotional record

q: quadraphonic

re: reissue

rec: record

ri: reissue

rw: ring wear

s: stereo

sl: slight

sm: saw mark

soc: sticker on cover

sol: sticker on label

ss: still sealed

s/t: self-titled

st: stereo

sw: shrink wrap

toc: tape on cover

tol: tape on label

ts: taped seam

w/: with

wlp: white label promo

wobc: writing on back cover

woc: writing on cover

wofc: writing on front cover

wol: writing on label

wr: wear

wrp: warp

xol: "x" on label

Some notes on the pricing

The prices listed in here were determined from many sources.

The more common items reflect a consensus of used record shops and collectors, plus prices in ads and online over the past few months. In some ways, these items are more difficult to get a handle on; they sell without much publicity because of their low value, thus they aren't reported as often.

The rarer items are often the matter of conjecture because they so rarely come up for public sale. A high auction price for a truly rare piece can be the only way such an item's "worth" can be gauged, no matter what someone says about the value being inflated. Records, as with all collectibles, are only worth what someone will pay for them.

Because of the inexact nature of this undertaking, that's why we always urge you to use a book such as this as a guide and not as the final word on pricing.

We, too, can always use more input on the subject. See the **How you can help** section for more information.

And by the way, the publisher of the book does not engage in the buying and selling of records. So the prices listed in here should not be construed as "offers to buy" or "offers to sell" from Krause Publications.

Some notes on promotional records

To list every promotional version of every album in this book would be a consumption of space better used for unique listings. It would come close to doubling the length of the book. Some selected promos are listed, either because they are unique – in other words, the only version of the album is promotional – or because there is a significant, verifiable price difference between the promo and stock copies.

That said, however, we have noticed in recent years a growth in the collectibility of certain promo albums, especially of hit albums. I've heard of cases where promo versions of, say, Carole King's *Tapestry* or Ted Nugent's *Cat Scratch Fever* have gone for twice as much as the stock copy!

Not all promos are created equal, however.

It's probably easier to say which promotional copies are *not* going to fetch that kind of premium. Those are copies that are otherwise identical to stock copies – the same label, the same number, the same everything – but are merely stamped on the front or back cover with (usually) a gold "For Promotion Only" indicator. There's nothing special about these records for the most part; any time the record company wants to create a promo, it can take a stock copy and gold-stamp it!

These are known as "designate promos" and rarely get more than 10 percent above the price of a regular stock copy, if that. For some sought-after rare items, such as Tori Amos' early album *Y Kant Tori Read,* designate promos go for significantly *less* than copies not so designated.

Some albums that appear to be "designate promos" do have collector value. These are copies pressed on special "audiophile vinyl," the most notable of which are the "Quiex II" pressings from the Warner-Reprise-Geffen family. Some of these fetch as much as 4-5 times the regular editions! These will *always* be marked on the cover with a sticker advertising the "Quiex II" record within. Capitol also did some promo-only audiophile vinyl, which is distinguishable because it altered the covers on most of these. Elektra did some in the late 1980s also, most notably on a couple 10,000 Maniacs albums. These could become more collectible as their presence becomes more known.

Other promos of little collector value are those with a hole punch in the corner. This was Capitol's preferred method of creating promos during much of the 1970s. These are never worth more than the stock copy, and usually go for less.

Also, Columbia for a time merely used a "timing strip" on the front or back cover to designate a promo; these, too, also have little extra value above the stock copy. There is a major exception, though: The earliest promos for Bruce Springsteen's *Greetings From Asbury Park, N.J.* included both an attached timing strip *and* a glossy 8 1/2 x 11 "Bruce Springsteen Fact Sheet" glued to the back cover along the top. By the way, no white-label promos were ever pressed of this title.

Promos that *do* attract interest are those with custom promotional labels. Most of the time, these are white versions of the regular label, thus the term "white label promo." Of course, the label isn't always white; sometimes it's yellow or blue or pink or some other color. But it will always have as part of the label typesetting, "Promotional Copy" or "Audition Copy" or "Demonstration" or some other such term. Sometimes, the label will be almost identical to the

stock versions, but some sort of words alluding to the promotional nature of the record will have been added to the typeset copy.

What makes these promos special? They are far more likely to have been mastered from the actual master mixdown tape, rather than a several-generations-removed copy, thus making them of higher sonic quality than later editions. They are among the first to come off the presses – after all, promos get sent out before stock copies Sometimes they are specially mastered to sound better over the air or through a store's loudspeakers. Regardless, they are sought after, and their value ranges from the same as a stock copy to as much as twice that of a stock copy.

Some notes on imports

If you think adding a lot of promotional listings would make this book unwieldy, think about all the non-U.S. pressings of the albums in this book!

(First, a clarification. In the 1980s, it was not uncommon for American record companies, especially independent ones such as Enigma, to have their LPs pressed in Canada. In fact, every BMG Direct Marketing, i.e., record club, album pressed after 1987 was made in Canada, and they say so on the jacket. Because these albums were designed to be sold in the U.S., we don't consider them imports.)Imports first became an attractive collecting area to Americans in the 1970s. As the sales of U.S. albums increased, the quality control decreased, and the record companies seemed not to care. Meanwhile, overseas, pressings were smaller and done with more care. Often, too, the covers were better and more informative, and the albums had extra goodies not found in the domestic counterparts. With some artists, a record released outside the States might never be released here, or would show up in a radically different form. (Elvis Costello's early catalog is an example.) Import sales have directly led to U.S. releases of several albums, most notably *Cheap Trick At Budokan,* which originally was not going to be released outside Japan! Most imports, by definition, are scarce. Few other countries have the size of market that the United States does. A "gold" record in other countries requires much fewer sales than the same award in the U.S. Imports manufactured before the 1970s, when they started to appear more often in specialty shops in the States, are almost impossible to find here.

But just because the scarcity is there doesn't mean that the demand is. The collecting market for imports is much smaller than the market for domestic records. It is generally true that, in any given country, most of the collecting interest is in records manufactured and/ or marketed in the homeland. That said, though, records from other countries can often bring much more in another country than in the originating country!

As much as a certain minority of readers would like to see them, long listings of imports likely will remain outside the scope of the *Goldmine Record Album Price Guide.*

Selling your records

At some point, perhaps after looking through this book, you may decide that you want to sell your collection. Good for you! And you want to take them to your local used record store with the idea that you'll get the prices you see in this book. Bad for you!

What the values in here reflect are **retail** prices – what a collector might pay for the item from a dealer, and **not** what a dealer will pay a collector for resale. Too many non-collectors (and even some collectors) don't understand that.

I know one dealer who has told me that he won't buy records from someone who tells him they consulted a price guide first. While that is extreme, it shows the distrust some dealers have for books like this and how the public uses (and abuses) them.

Just as importantly, the highest values are for records in the best condition (re-read the section on **Grading your records**). And there is a reason for that: Truly pristine records are very difficult to find! Many

collectors are willing to pay handsomely for them – but for many of the records in this book, Near Mint examples aren't even known to exist!

One reason we've expanded the price listing to three grades of condition is to reflect that. There's a tendency to look at the highest price listed for something and assume that's what your record is worth. More realistically, though, such a small percentage of records are truly Near Mint – especially from the 1950s and 1960s – that your own records, if you were a typical accumulator and not a collector, are considerably less than Near Mint.

Even if you do end up trying to sell to a dealer, choose him or her carefully. It's always best to find someone who has a customer base for your kind of LP.

There is only one way you'll be able to get anything close to the prices listed for most items, and that's to sell them direct to the collector.

The "old-fashioned" way is through record collecting magazines. The oldest and most widely read remains *Goldmine,* which was founded in 1974. Published every two weeks, the magazine is loaded with ads from people selling records of all kinds and from all eras. *Goldmine* has advertising salespeople who will help you put your ad together for maximum impact. To see what *Goldmine* is about, pick up a copy. It is available at all Tower Records stores in the U.S., most Barnes and Noble and Borders bookstores, and hundreds of independent record dealers. If you still can't find a copy, call 1-800-258-0929.

The "newer" way to sell records and other memorabilia is over the Internet. The most popular method is through the online auction, and the most popular of these sites is eBay (www.ebay.com).

Online selling seems to draw two widely different audiences. One is very much the same audience as a stand-alone record store, except on a global scale rather than a regional one. Browsers who know next to nothing about record collecting and the relative scarcity of the listed pieces are common. These are people who can sometimes be fooled into paying too much for a common piece, especially certain million-selling compact discs, because of three magic letters: "OOP," short for "out of print." Just because something's out of print doesn't mean it has vanished off the face of the earth!

The other audience drawn to online sales are the hyper-specialists, and this is often where items can justifiably go for much larger sums than in a retail store. Thanks to search engines on most of the better sites, a fan of, say, the Grateful Dead can type in the words "Grateful Dead" and find nothing but the Grateful Dead-related material. People who specialize in one artist will usually pay more – sometimes a *lot* more – than someone who collects a more broad range of artists. But because they are specialists, they also know which items are common, so they don't get taken on the easy stuff.

I have bought records over the Web, and have yet to have significant problems. It's faster than "snail mail" and less expensive than a long-distance telephone call. But it's not perfect. Just as in real life, it pays to be wary.

As a seller, you are reaching a larger audience than you would in a record collecting magazine, but also a much less targeted one. Also, many sellers have found that eBay overreacts if you say you are selling a promo. Promos are an accepted part of record collecting; entire books have been written on the subject. Despite that, eBay can, and does, remove these items, almost at random, for no good reason, yet does nothing to stop the rampant sale of counterfeits, bootlegs, and CD-R copies of out-of-print LPs or CDs. (It's one thing if you're selling an advance copy of a CD that hasn't been issued to the general public yet. It's another to try to sell a 25-year-old vinyl promo.) So if you're selling promos, use synonyms or code words to keep the eBay police away.

As a buyer, you have to watch out for overgraded, under-described items. Photos of the items help. Also, buying from someone who deals in records as a primary area rather than as an obvious sideline to his/her antiques business is recommended. Look for dealers with strong feedback ratings; that is a sign of satisfied customers. Also, check for use of something resembling the *Goldmine* grading system. People who say their albums are in "good condition" don't know

record collecting, because "good" is a low grade in the world of records (as it is in some other collecting areas, such as coins).

Also as a buyer, don't be afraid to e-mail the seller if you have any questions about the item. If you don't get a satisfactory answer, or get no answer at all, don't bid.

Making sense of the main listings

We've told you about most of the features in the book. Let's break down a listing to see what a line means.

The artist's name is in bold, all capital letters. They are mostly alphabetized the way our computer did, so blame any things that seem out of order on it. I think we caught most of the way-out things, but if not, let us know and we'll get 'em the next time.

A number in parentheses follows some artists' names. This indicates that we have more than one different artist by this name in our database. If numbers are missing – for example, if the first artist listed with a certain name has a (2) after its name – then artist (1) with that name in our database either has no albums or has none that reach our $20 floor for making the book.

Underneath some artists are cross-references or other information we feel is helpful. Cross-references to other artists in the book are in all capital letters.

Then we have grouped the discographies by record label. Under each record label are individual listings in numerical order, ignoring prefixes. This may result in some things appearing to be way out of order. For example, because they have numbers approximately 6,800 apart, mono and stereo versions of the same albums on Columbia will rarely be adjacent to each other. This is also true of other labels with separate mono and stereo numbering systems, such as Mercury, Liberty, Imperial, London, and many more. However, as the RCA Victor label used the same numbers for mono and stereo, those versions are usually listed next to each other.

Each line starts with a check box, which you can use to keep track of what you have. Then comes the record number. You'll also find the title of the record as best as we can determine (you'd be surprised how often the title differs between the record and the jacket!); the year of release; and the value in Very Good, Very Good-Plus and Near Mint condition.

For many listings, you'll see a letter or two in brackets after the record number. These designate something special about the listing as follows:

B: the album is listed as stereo, but some of the tracks are in mono (the "B" means "both" stereo and mono)

DJ: some sort of promotional copy, usually for radio stations, and not meant for public sale

EP: a 12-inch extended play album, usually with only four to six tracks. It normally is no more than half the length of a regular album. Rarely used to describe 12-inch records until the 1980s; before that, it refers to similar 7-inch records.

M: mono record (all 12-inch albums released either in mono only or in both mono and stereo before 1968)

P: the album is listed as stereo, but only part of it is "true" two-channel stereo

PD: picture disc (graphics actually appear as part of the record; these were popular in the late 1970s to early 1980s and, for some artists, are their only valuable albums today)

Q: quadraphonic record (mostly from the years 1972-76, these were usually remixed, sometimes radically, to play on systems with four separate speakers)

R: the album is listed as stereo, but actually is all, or almost all, rechanneled stereo (called "Duophonic" by Capitol or "Enhanced for Stereo" or "Simulated Stereo" by Decca); these almost always are less sought-after than the same material in "true mono"

S: stereo record (again, when the record was pressed both in mono and stereo). If we're not sure of an album's "true" stereo content, or if we know an album is all, or almost all, true stereo, we use "S."

10: a 10-inch album, most of which are from the early years of LPs, 1948-54, and quite difficult to find in top condition

(x) where x is a number: the number of records in a set

Finally, some items have lines in italics following them. That defines something about the item listed above, such as who also is on the record, or a color of label or vinyl.

Making sense of the listings in back

Because of the nature of these items, we've used a slightly different format for the four sections that appear after the letter Z. These four sections are "Original Cast Recordings," "Soundtracks," "Television Albums" and "Various Artists Collections."

Within each category, these are arranged alphabetically by the **title** of the release, again as our computer did them, and ignoring the words "A," "An" or "The." Alas, if the title begins with a number, computers have this nasty tendency to put these first, before things beginning with "A." Unfortunately, because of a different program we're using for this edition, we've had to leave these at the start of the alphabet. We hope to fix this problem for the third edition.

Underneath each title are the applicable releases, arranged alphabetically and numerically by label. Those lines start with a check box, then are followed by the label and number listed together; any applicable abbreviations in brackets (which are the same as in the rest of the book – M for mono, S for stereo, etc.); the year of release; and the prices in three grades of condition.

Why some artists are not listed

As I complete this introduction, I have a list of albums that a well-intentioned reader sent me. None of the albums he listed are in the second edition of this book, and odds are that – even though I know about them – they won't be included in this book, either.

Why is this?

If you read the first introductory page, you'll recall that I mentioned that, in order for an artist to be listed in this book, that artist must have *at least one album released in the United States worth $20 or more in Near Mint condition*. No artist on this reader's list has even one album that reaches that level, unless we haven't yet discovered that LP.

Most likely, if a popular artist began recording in the 1970s or later, but has no listing in this book, that is why. Before writing the author about these albums, please examine our two books that do *not* have a price floor on their listings first. These are the *Goldmine Standard Catalog of American Records 1950-1975* and the *Goldmine Standard Catalog of American Records 1976-Present*. Both are available from fine bookstores everywhere or directly from Krause Publications.

If your albums are not listed in either of those books, and they are not by a jazz or classical artist, then read on and lend us a hand.

How you can help

Conservatively speaking, this book has roughly 60,000 listings by thousands of artists. All of this information is located in a growing database of records, which will make both future price guides and *Goldmine* magazine better products in the long run.

But as you look through this third edition of the *Goldmine Record Album Price Guide,* you'll see that we need help in several areas. We've received invaluable help from dozens of readers, but certain parts of this book aren't as good as they could be, and we know you can help.

We want to know about any missing or incorrect information, but here are some areas with special emphasis:

Late mono LPs. In 1967 and 1968, record companies somewhat abruptly stopped making monaural albums. Some of the mono albums are quite rare now. We're interested in what might exist that we don't

have listed. We're also interested in deleting listings of mono albums that really don't exist. Several collectors of "late mono" have been helpful at filling in holes, but we can always use more.

Private label LPs. In the process of researching this book, we came upon listings for many private label albums. These usually fit in the categories of garage, psychedelic, progressive or punk; all of these, by definition, are rare, and many are highly collectible. As we couldn't confirm the existence of every such LP title we came upon, we can use help with adding more titles, and appropriate pricing, to the list.

Pop albums of the 1950s. We list a lot of albums by non-rock performers of the 1950s that you won't find in any other price guide. But we're sure that we didn't find them all. If, for example, you have a 1950s album by Doris Day or Percy Faith or Vaughn Monroe that's not listed – say, we list two different numbers but it falls in between them – we *do* want to know about that. Especially if it's an early 10-inch album. (That is, one record with four or so songs on each side, not four records with one song on each side. The latter are 78s and outside the scope of this book.)

American pressings meant for other markets. Just as some albums on the London label proudly claim to be "Made in England," even though they were meant for sale in the United States, the opposite is true of some albums meant for sale overseas. Though sold in places like England and Germany, they will say on the labels "Made in U.S.A." We need to know more about these.

On a related subject, we found out quite by accident a few years ago that some labels made special, often unique, compilations that were meant for sale only on military bases overseas. (The At Ease label, manufactured by ABC in the 1970s, was one such imprint.) We'd like to know more about these American albums, too.

And finally, some of the larger American record companies had (and still have) separate divisions that market Spanish-language music to areas with large Hispanic populations, both in the United States and in Latin America. Most of these albums, too, are U.S. pressings, on labels such as CBS International, and some of these can be highly collectible. (Check the listings for Miami Sound Machine or Selena.) We can use more information on this little-known area of album collecting.

The Capitol Record Club. It existed from 1964 to about 1973, and in that time the Capitol Record Club (later the Longines Record Club) issued several thousand LPs. All of them that were not on Capitol or an affiliate had a unique number in the 90000 series. Record collectors usually pay more – sometimes a *lot* more – for a Capitol Record Club edition because they're harder to find than the usual 1960s and early 1970s pressings.

We'd like to document every album that ever came out with a Capitol Record Club number, both by major collectible artists (Jimi Hendrix, Led Zeppelin, the Beach Boys) and by others. This is quite an ambitious project, but we're sure you can help us. The best sources are the LPs themselves, as they had not only a number, but the Capitol-style prefix. Copies of ads for the Capitol Record Club (they often appeared in *TV Guide* and other magazines), or the member booklets that were sent out every few weeks, also would help, though they usually omitted the prefix in their listings.

Later pressings. Many albums stayed in print for years with the same catalog number. In most cases, all we have acknowledged is the original pressing. But we're interested in confirming the existence of later editions. In almost all cases, the reissues are not worth as much as the originals, thus the importance of noting those albums that exist in second and third label variations. Most significantly, we want to know about:

- Early-1960s Capitol albums, originally issued with the Capitol logo at 9 o'clock, that also exist with the logo at 12 o'clock (these are reissues for anything that originally came out before mid-1962).
- Columbia albums that were originally issued with the black and red "6-eye" label that later came out with plain red labels that say "Guaranteed High Fidelity," "360 Sound Stereo" in black with or without arrows,

"360 Sound Stereo" in white, and/or "360 Sound Mono."

- RCA Victor albums with "RCA Victor" in white at the top (rather than silver) with the dog underneath, with various colors (orange or tan, for two examples), or with simply "RCA" and the Nipper logo at 1 o'clock.
- Also, any other label that had variations – did the listed albums stay in print long enough to show up on a later version of the label?

Photos. Sending us photos, photocopies or computer scans of items helps us, as these serve to prove the existence of the item in question.

We hope that future editions of this, and all, *Goldmine* price guides can have some cool photos of rarities. We also can accept computer scans e-mailed to us as attachments or sent on a disc (300 dpi or a very large photo of lower resolution that will resolve at 300 dpi at a smaller size). Some of our photos in this book and others came from computer scans. You can contact us for more information if you think you have something that might be worth putting in a future edition of any of our books.

Anything else that may be of help. Don't assume that someone else already caught that error or made us aware of that missing album. Even if more than one person independently sends the same item or correction, that's more confirmation that it belongs in the next edition.

You may contact the author by mail:
Tim Neely
Goldmine Record Album Price Guide
700 E. State St.
Iola, WI 54990-0001

or by phone:
(715) 445-2214 or 4612, ext. 782

or by e-mail:
neelyt@krause.com

If you write or e-mail, enclose a **daytime** phone number or return e-mail where I can reply in case I have any questions.

Because of the volume of correspondence I receive, and because of deadlines, I can answer only a small percentage of all inquiries. But rest assured that your contribution, whether it be one correction or hundreds of suggestions, is read and considered carefully. Sometimes, your inquiry will be researched and verified on the same day I receive it. Others take longer to research; don't be surprised if it might take some time for them to appear.

I also can be reached via fax at (715) 445-4087, but I prefer that you write or call before faxing me any large contributions.

Acknowledgments

As always, though the book has one author, it has many people behind the scenes helping the author. Without them, this book would not be anywhere near what it is.

First, I'd like to thank everyone who bought the first and/or second editions of the *Goldmine Record Album Price Guide*. I'd especially like to thank all those people who were inspired enough to send their feedback, both positive and negative, and their additions and corrections. I always appreciate hearing from our readers. In addition to many of the 50 states, I heard from people in Canada, England, Australia, Italy and Norway, just to name several. It's gratifying to know that we reach a worldwide record collecting community that cares about getting it right.

I'd also like to thank the readers of a companion volume, the *Goldmine Standard Catalog of American Records 1950-1975*. Many of the items that were submitted in response to that book also applied to this one. I thanked all of you (more than 150!) in the acknowledgments of the second edition of that book; I thank all of you again.

Special thanks go to several people, without whose help this would be a lesser volume:

Bruce Spizer, of the amazing books *The Beatles on Vee-Jay, The Beatles' Story on Capitol Records (2 volumes),* and *The Beatles on Apple Records,* contributed some photos of rare Beatles albums to our color section. His books are *the* references that show how the Beatles were marketed and sold in the United States, and they are loaded with beautiful photographs and reproductions of original documents. You can buy them at www.beatle.net.

Dave Eckstrom of Forever Young Records in Texas, who had one of the two known copies of the stereo *The Freewheelin' Bob Dylan* and supplied photos of this extremely rare artifact.

Steve Schroeder of Albuquerque, N.M., who, every three months or so, sends a packet full of album photocopies, which contain both additions and corrections.

Ernie Mabrey, "Mr. Mono," who collects 1967 and later mono discs; when he finds one I haven't listed, he sends the information to us.

Thomas Grosh of Very English and Rolling Stone in Lancaster, Pa. He has supported our efforts from the very beginning and continues to do so.

Michael Sharritt of Alabama. He, too, has been supplying information and suggestions since some of my earliest price guides, and he continues to aid the cause.

Here at Krause Publications, I'd like to thank Greg Loescher, editor of *Goldmine* magazine, for his continued aid and guidance. In the Krause Publications book department, my thanks go to Debbie Bradley and Paul Kennedy for their suggestions and support.

For this edition, we drew the information from a brand-new (and I hope the last new!) database, which we had to convert from a format we no longer use. It's been in the works for almost two years and has gone through much testing, but I think we've finally got it. Once all the bugs are fixed, you'll see a book where things are sorted more accurately than ever before. I want to thank Tammy Kuhnle of the Krause IT department for finally making it happen, and to Sandy Morrison and Steve Duberstein for getting the information out of the database and onto the printed page.

I'd also like to thank various family members – my mom and my sisters especially – for their constant encouragement, even if I'm not in touch as much as I could be.

Tim Neely
June 2003

Record Label Identifier

For the most part, the most collectible records are original pressings. Those are the ones that presumably were available at the time the album was first issued.

Of course, not every copy of *Elvis' Golden Records* is created equal, no matter how similar the covers may look from pressing to pressing. Copyright dates on liner notes are meaningless. A 1958 date on the cover can be attached to a pressing from the 1980s!

To tell for sure, you have to know the labels.

As opposed to 45s, which often were deleted quickly and replaced by "golden oldies" reissues, albums could stay in print in covers looking ostensibly the same for years, sometimes decades! With only some superficial differences, the same album cover can contain a copy of *Meet The Beatles!* that was pressed in 1964, 1974 or 1984. The same is true of an album such as *Johnny's Greatest Hits* by Johnny Mathis; it was in print from 1958 until vinyl was phased out. In that time, Columbia went through several different label designs. It's only the originals that are most sought after.

Thus this rough guide to many of the most common and collectible labels.

Eventually, with your help, we'd like this to be even more thorough. Instead of listing label variations by approximate year of changeover, we'd like to nail down exact numbers where a label changed from one to another. Sometimes, because of printing plant overlap, this will not be possible. But the closer we get, the better the guide gets.

We'd also like information on labels we chose to omit this time around, either because we don't know or because the information we do have is confusing.

By the way, this guide does not attempt to delve into the various promotional labels record companies used. Most of the time, though, they are white versions of the labels that were in use at the time. Not every label used promo labels; others used them at some times, but not at all times. Columbia, for example, went through a period in the mid 1970s where it had no white-label promos. (Bruce Springsteen's *Greetings From Asbury Park, N.J.,* for example, was never issued as a white label promo.)

Enough ado, let's go:

A&M

1963 (101 only?): Yellowish label, brown print, "A&M Records" logo at top, unboxed.

1963-64 (102?-at least 106): Brown label, "A&M Records" logo at top, now in familiar white box with red "A&M."

1965-73: (starting at 107?): Brown label, "A&M Records" logo at left.

1974-86: Silver gray label with fading A&M logo.

1986-end: Black label with five gold, black and white rounded squares across the center and A&M logo at right.

ABC; ABC-PARAMOUNT

1956-61: Black label, "ABC-Paramount" multicolor logo at top, "A Product of Am-Par Record Corp." in white at bottom.

1962-66: Black label, "ABC-Paramount" multicolor logo at top, "A Product of ABC-Paramount Records Inc." in white at bottom.

1966-67: Possible transition label with "abc" in a white circle at top of label, but not in a multicolored box.

1967-72: "abc" in a white circle at top of label surrounded by a multicolored box.

1973: "ABC" in a white triangle spelled out in children's blocks. Very short-lived label. Quickly replaced by 1967-72 label again until another new label was created.

1974-77: Multicolored (yellow, orange, purple) "target" label with "abc Records" at top of label between two lines.

1977-79: Multicolored (yellow, orange, purple) "target" label with "abc" in an eighth note at top of label. In 1979, the label was bought by MCA, which gradually replaced ABC albums with MCA pressings.

ABC DUNHILL – See DUNHILL.

ABKCO

Allan Klein's reissue label, albums have light blue labels with a darker blue logo above the center hole.

ABNER

Only three albums came out on Abner, and all three exist on three different labels. One label is black with a logo of a falcon on a glove; the other is maroon with the same logo of a falcon on a glove. Abner records also were released on Vee Jay with the same catalog numbers in Abner jackets.

ACE

1958-62: Black label, silver print.

1962: Dark blue label, white at top, "ACE" in blue oval.

1971 (2020-21): Yellow label, black print.

1975 (2022): Red label, black print.

Custom labels were used on 1007 and 1008.

APPLE

1968-75: Green "Granny Smith" apple label on one side, sliced apple on the other. Some, though not all, albums from 1968-70 had a line of small white print on the sliced side with "A Subsidiary of Capitol Industries, Inc." along the bottom and a tiny Capitol logo. The

small print appears only to have been used at one Capitol pressing plant, so two albums could both be originals, yet one will have the "Capitol logo" and the other won't.

1975: "All Rights Reserved" disclaimer added to the label print.

Apple 34001 was originally issued with a red apple label. Custom labels exist on many numbers.

ARGO

Early mono editions had a greenish label, some with gold print, some with silver print, with "ULTRA HIGH FIDELITY" adjacent to the vertical "ARGO." Later mono editions are known to have a silver label with black print or a black label with silver print, also with "ULTRA HIGH FIDELITY."

Early stereo editions have dark blue labels with silver print.

The next label was silver with black print, but without the words "ULTRA HIGH FIDELITY."

The final Argo label (to the end of 1965) was a brown label with a pink and white "ARGO" in an oval at left. The Argo label was replaced by Cadet in 1965.

ARISTA

1975-76 (AL 4001 to 4105?): Light blue label, white Arista logo with "Arista Records" beneath.

1976-77: Light blue label, white Arista logo with "Arista" beneath.

1977-79: Black label, light blue Arista logo, "Arista" underneath.

1979-84: Fading blue label, three-dimensional Arista logo at top, "Arista" at left side of logo slanting upward.

1984-90: Black label, "ARISTA" above multicolor mountain skyline.

1990-end: Black label, "ARISTA" above white mountain skyline.

Custom labels were used on some releases.

ASYLUM

1972-73 (SD 5051 to SD 5066?): White label, "door-in-a-circle" logo at top of label.

1973-84: "Clouds" label. Around 1975, a small "W" (Warner Communications) logo was added to the label print.

1976: Some 45s in this era were issued with a solid blue label with a small "a" at the top. It's unknown if any LPs exist with this label.

1985-end: Split black and yellow label.

Custom labels were used on some releases.

ATCO

1958-61 (33-101 to 33-138): Yellow label with a harp at the upper left.

1961-68 mono: Gold and gray label, "AT" to left of center hole, "CO" to right of center hole in white background.

1961-68 stereo (SD 33-139 to SD 33-256): Purple and brown label, "AT" to left of center hole, "CO" to right of center hole in white background.

1969-77: Yellow label, "Atco" logo at left. Earlier labels have a "1841 Broadway" address, later ones have a "75 Rockefeller Plaza" address and add a small "W" (Warner Communications) logo in the small print.

1978-84: Gray label, logo at top.

1985-end: Whitish label, "ATCO" in different colored letters at an angle at top with many smaller "ATCO"s in the background.

ATLANTIC

1950-60 mono: Black label, silver print.

1959-60 stereo: Green label, silver print.

1960: So-called "bullseye" label. Monos have orange, purple and black fan around the center hole and "Atlantic" in orange and purple band at top; stereos have blue and green fan around the center hole and "Atlantic" in blue and green band at top.

1960-61: "White fan logo" issues. Monos were orange and purple, stereos were green and blue. Through the center hole is a white

strip; on the right side of the center hole, a white "fan" in a black background can be found.

1961-68: "Black fan logo" issues. The "fan" at right switches to a black logo inside a white box.

1969-end: Red and green label with Atlantic logo at top. Early editions have an "1841 Broadway" address along the lower rim; later on, the address was changed and a small "W" (Warner Communications) logo was added.

Custom labels were used for some releases.

AUDIO LAB

A budget label created by Syd Nathan of King Records, all Audio Lab LPs have blue labels with silver print.

B.T. PUPPY

Black label, silver print, "B.T. Puppy Records" in red at top with cocker spaniel head underneath.

BANG

1966-73 (211-227): Mostly red label, white at top, with "BANG records" gun logo centered in a yellow background.

1974-78 (400-410): Sky blue label with clouds and stylized "BANG" curving around the top.

1979-82 (Columbia distribution): Light brown label, red logo on top.

BARNABY

1970-73 (CBS distribution): Light blue label, treble clef logo at left.

1973 (15007-15008, MGM distribution): White label with line drawing.

1974-79 (4000, 5000, 6000 series, distributed by GRT/Janus): Multicolor label, yellow rim, vinyl record hanging limply from tree.

BEARSVILLE

The label had the same basic design throughout its history; only the distribution changed.

1971: "Distributed by Ampex" at the bottom.

1972-76: "Distributed by Warner Bros. Records" at the bottom.

1976-81: No distribution notice at bottom of label.

1981-82: "3300 Warner Blvd." address added to bottom of label.

BELL

1965-69: Blue label, silver print.

1970-74: Silver label, black print.

BELTONE

Only one album was released on the label, and it is mostly orange with black printing.

BIG TREE

1970-71: Red and yellow label.

1971-74: Red and white label.

1974-76: Light blue and red label.

1976-80: Multicolor label.

BIG TOP

All releases have a black label with silver print.

BLUE THUMB

1969 (first four LPs): Black label.

1969-74 (Gulf & Western distribution): Off-white, almost gray label, with blue thumb print at upper left.

1974-end: Multicolored (yellow, orange, purple) "target" label with "abc Blue Thumb" at top of label between two lines and a blue thumb print at upper left.

BLUESVILLE

1960-63: Bright blue label with silver print.

1964-end: Lighter blue label with Prestige trident logo at right side.

BLUESWAY

1967-68: Blue label.
1968-74: Black label, blue rim around outside.

BROTHER

1967 (9001): Brown label with large horseman and "Brother records" at top.
1970-75: Light yellow label, yellow rim around outside, "A Licensee of Warner Bros. Inc." at bottom.
1976-78: Same as 1970-75, but print changes to "A Division of Warner Bros. Records Inc."

BRUNSWICK

1950-63: Black label, silver print.
1963-72: Black label, color band through center, "A Division of Decca Records" in fine print.
1972-end: Black label, color band through center, "Manufactured by Brunswick Record Corp." along rim.

BUDDAH

1967-72: Multicolor kaleidoscope label with black drawing of Buddha at bottom and "BUDDAH RECORDS" on either side of drawing.
1972-76: Maroon label with smiling Buddha figure, "BUDDAH RECORDS" in white at top.
1977-end: Black label with Arista logo added at bottom.

BUENA VISTA

Best known as the label of Annette, it actually predates her hits slightly.
The first series was BV-1300; these have turquoise labels with silver print.
The BV-3300 series, where the Annette records are, were first issued with a black label, silver print. Later ones were issued with a half black, half mostly yellow label with a slight rainbow effect, "Buena Vista" in black over the yellow section.
The BV-4000 series was a continuation of the Disneyland WDL-4000 series (see Disneyland listing for more detail). 4022-4025 were originally issued on black labels, silver print; 4026-4048 first came out on the half black, half yellow label mentioned in the BV-3300 series.
The 1980s issues in the 62000 series have a blue and red label with a white strip just above the center hole that goes through the middle of the center hole. The "Buena Vista" logo is in red at the upper left.

CADENCE

1954-61 (1000 series, 3000-3051?, 4000s, 5000s, 25000 series to 25051?): Maroon lower two-thirds of label; upper third is silver with "cadence" in lowercase and a metronome logo.
1961-64 (3052?-3068, 25052?-25068): Red label, black rim with "CADENCE RECORDS" inside in white.

CADET

Cadet replaced the Argo label in 1965. Many Argo titles were reissued in Argo covers with Cadet labels.
The first label was an all light blue label with "CADET" across the top in black.
The second label was a fading blue label with "CADET" across the top in fading red, white and blue letters.
1971-end (50000 and 60000 series, GRT distribution): Yellow label, red rim, horizontal red stripe through center hole, "CADET" at left.

CADET CONCEPT

All issues have a gray label with black print, "CADET" in pink, "CONCEPT" in orange (red).

CAMDEN – See RCA CAMDEN.

CAMEO

1958 (1001): Black label, brown print, cameo at top.
1958-60 (1002-1007?): Orange label, black print, cameo at top.
1960-68: Red and black label, white cameo in yellow border at left.
1968 (20,000): Purple label, white at top, "Cameo" across the top in an arc, cameo logo inside "o."

CANADIAN-AMERICAN

1959-61 (1001-1005?): Black label, silver print.
1961-65 (1006?-1018): Black label, five color bars across top of label.

CAPITOL

As you might gather, Capitol is at times a confusing label. For now, we're sticking to the regular pop series in this label roundup. Especially in the 1980s, the budget labels used different color schemes; for now, we're ignoring them, but we would appreciate more information.
1949-54 (10-inch albums, most with "H" prefix): Purple label with silver print. Some labels have a silver ring near the outer rim, some do not. Also, some exist with a red label and gold print and/or an "L" prefix.
1954-58 (12-inch mono albums): On albums with a "T" prefix, turquoise label, with or without silver ring near outer rim. Some albums, those with a "W" prefix, were issued with a gray label.
1958-59 (mono and stereo, approx. 1021-1225): Black label, rainbow ring around outside rim (usually called the "black colorband label") with white Capitol logo and "Long Playing High Fidelity" at the left of the label.
1959-62 (mono and stereo, approx. 1226-1660?): Same as 1958-59, except a white line replaces the words "Long Playing High Fidelity."
1962-68 (approx. 1660-2999): Black colorband label, Capitol logo moved to top of label.
1968-69 (approx. 101-200s in new numbering system): Black colorband label, Capitol logo at top, with extra print along the edge of the colorband "A Subsidiary of Capitol Industries, Inc." added to "Mfd. By Capitol Records Inc."
1969-71 (200s into the 700s?): Lime green label, "Capitol" at upper left, new Capitol "target" logo at top.
1971-72 (700s into early 11000s): Red label, "Capitol" at upper left, purple Capitol "target" logo at top. Sometimes assumed to be a country label only, it was used on all Capitol releases for this short period.
1972-78 (Early 11000s into 11800s): Orange label, "Capitol" in greenish letters across bottom of label. Some issues geared toward the R&B market have a red label with "Capitol" in black letters across the bottom.
1978-83 (11800s into 12200s): Purple label with huge white "Capitol" logo dominating the top third of the label.
1983-88: The black colorband label, logo at top, returns, except that the perimeter print is in black, inside the color ring, instead of outside it in white as in the 1960s.
1988-present: Purple label with much smaller Capitol logo at top of label and a long ring of unbroken type around the outer rim.
Custom labels were used on many titles, and especially from 1978 to the present, older labels were often used out of sequence to create a nostalgic feel.

CAPRICORN

1970: Yellow Atco label with "Capricorn Series" at bottom.
1970-71: Pink label.
1972-74: Plain tan label, "CAPRICORN RECORDS" across the top.
1975-78: Light brown label, large goat facing right.

1978-end (Polygram distribution): Light brown label, large goat facing left.

CARLTON

All labels are tan with a black "C" around the center ring and a white strip to the right with a black "Carlton" in it.

CASABLANCA

1974 (9000 series): Dark blue label with Bogart mug and "Manufactured and Distributed by Warner Bros. Records Inc." in white along the bottom.

1974-76 (7000-7020s): Dark blue label with Bogart mug, "Manufactured and Distributed by Casablanca Records Inc." in white along the bottom.

1976-77 (7020s-7050?): Tan label, desert scene at top, "Casablanca" at top.

1977-81 (7050?-7100s): Tan label, desert scene at top, "Casablanca Record and FilmWorks" at top.

1981-end (7100s into six-digit numbers): "Manufactured and Distributed by Polygram" at bottom.

CHALLENGE

1958-63 mono (600-617): Blue label, silver print, "Challenge" logo in oval at top.

1960-65 stereo (2500-2521): Black label, silver print, "Challenge" logo in oval at top.

1963-65 mono (618-621): Blue-green label, silver print, "Challenge" logo in oval at top.

1966-67 (622-624, 2522-2524): Black label, silver print, "CHALLENGE" in block letters across the top.

1969-end (2000 series): Black label, white coat of arms logo at top, "Challenge" in red.

CHANCELLOR

1958-59 (5001-5003): Pink label, black print.

1959-63 (5004-5032): Black label, silver print, "Chancellor" in red across top of label.

CHECKER

1957-65 (1400s and 2971-2995): Black label, silver print, "CHECKER" at left of center hole in vertical block letters. Some issues have maroon label with silver print that are otherwise identical to the black label versions.

1965-66 (2996-3001): Light blue label with alternating red and black checkers at top of label.

1966-71 (3002-3017): Fading blue label with "CHECKER" across the top in fading red, white and blue letters.

1971-end (reissues): Blue label, purple rim, purple stripe through center hole, "CHECKER" at left.

CHESS

1956-1963 (1425-1482): Black label, silver print, "CHESS" at left of center hole in vertical block letters. Some issues have blue label with silver print that are otherwise identical to the black label versions. Those few stereo releases in this time had gold labels with black print.

1963-65 (1483?-1500?): Black label, "CHESS" across the top in gold with a four-color knight chess piece in back. This basic label design also exists on a blue label with all-silver print and no four-color graphics.

1965 (1490s): Fading blue label, "CHESS" across the top in all white letters.

1965-71 (1500-1553 and 400 series): Fading blue label with "CHESS" across the top in fading red, white and blue letters.

1971-76 (50000 and 60000 series, later 200, 400 and 700 series): Orange label, light blue rim, light blue stripe through center hole, "CHESS" at left.

1982-89 (8200, 8300, 8400, 8500, 9000 series): Dark blue label, silver print, "CHESS RECORDS" in arc at top, checkerboard motif around lower edge.

CHRYSALIS

1972-77: Green label, red butterfly at lower left, "Chrysalis" in red along bottom.

1977-87: White label fading to blue at bottom, white butterfly at lower left, "Chrysalis" in white along bottom. During this time, distribution changed from independent to the CBS family of labels; reissues of 1300-series albums have a new prefix, usually "PV," and the number "4" before the four digits.

1987-89: White label, colored butterfly at left.

1989-end: Off-white label, different butterfly logo.

CLASS

1957-58 (5001-5002): Black label, silver print.

1959 (5003-5004): Maroon label, silver print.

CO & CE

Three albums came out on this label, two by the Vogues and one by Lou Christie, all in mono only. The labels are yellow with a white hourglass at left.

COED

1960 (901): Yellow label, black print.

1960 (902): Black label, silver print.

1961-63 (903-906): Red label, black and white print.

COLGEMS

1966-67: Red label, white area at top in which "COLGEMS" appears in red, "TM of Colgems Records" appears underneath the top logo.

1967-70: Same as above, "TM of Colgems Records" is deleted.

COLPIX

1958-62?: Gold label, "COLPIX" in red curving around top of label with line drawing of Statue of Liberty underneath.

1962?-64?: Gold label, strip of movie film with "COLPIX RECORDS" in white background within.

1964?-66?: Light blue label, strip of movie film with "COLPIX RECORDS" in light blue background within.

1966 (4001, stereo only): Dark blue label, silver print, no strip of movie film.

COLUMBIA (pop)

Another long and storied label, its history is less confusing if you break it into its pop and "Masterworks" divisions. The below apply only to pop (GL, CL, CS series before 1970, prefixes ending in "C" after 1970) releases.

10-Inch LPs:

1948-54 (6000 series): Maroon label, gold print, "Long Playing" at bottom.

1955 (10-inch LPs, 2500 House Party Series): Red and black label with six white "eye" logos, three at left, three at right.

12-Inch Mono LPs:

1951-53 (501-525): Black label, silver print, "Long Playing" at bottom. Originals have a "GL" prefix.

1953-55 (525-600s): Maroon label, gold print, "Long Playing" at bottom.

1955-62 (600s-no earlier than 1779): Red and black label with six white "eye" logos, three at left, three at right.

1962-65 (1780?-2300s): Red label, "COLUMBIA" in white along the top, "GUARANTEED HIGH FIDELITY" in black along bottom.

1965-68 (2300s-2800s): Red label, "COLUMBIA" in white along the top, "360 SOUND MONO 360 SOUND" in white along the bottom. Some of the 1968 issues simply say "MONO" along the bottom.

12-Inch Stereo LPs:

1958-62 (8000-no earlier than 8579): Red and black label with six white "eye" logos, three at left, three at right, "STEREO FIDELITY" in white along the bottom.

1962-63 (8580?-unknown): Red label, "COLUMBIA" in white along the top, "360 SOUND STEREO 360 SOUND" in black along bottom, no arrows.

1963-65 (range unknown): Red label, "COLUMBIA" in white along the top, "360 SOUND STEREO 360 SOUND" in black along bottom, arrows added to left of first "360" and right of second "SOUND."

1965-70 (9100s-9999, CS 1000 series, 30000-30050?): Red label, "COLUMBIA" in white along the top, "360 SOUND STEREO 360 SOUND" in white along the bottom.

1970-90: Orange label, gold "COLUMBIA" six times in ring along outer edge.

1990-present: Red label, "COLUMBIA" in white along top, all other label print in black.

Custom labels were used for some releases.

COLUMBIA MASTERWORKS (classical, shows)

Before 1970, classical releases had an "ML" or "MS" prefix; movie and stage play releases had "OL" and "OS" prefixes (sometimes with a "K" before the first two letters).

10-Inch LPs:

Two different labels exist: Some have a green label, gold print, "Long Playing" at bottom, and others have a dark blue label, gold print, "Long Playing" at bottom.

12-Inch Mono LPs:

1948-54 (4001-?): Dark blue label, gold print, "Long Playing" at bottom. Some also have green labels with gold print and "Long Playing" at bottom.

1955-62: Gray and black label with six white "eye" logos, three at left, three at right.

1962-65: Gray label, "COLUMBIA" in white along the top, "GUARANTEED HIGH FIDELITY" in black along bottom.

1965-68: Gray label, "COLUMBIA" in white along the top, "360 SOUND MONO 360 SOUND" in white along the bottom.

12-Inch Stereo LPs:

1958-62: Gray and black label with six white "eye" logos, three at left, three at right, "STEREO FIDELITY" in white along the bottom.

1962-63: Gray label, "COLUMBIA" in white along the top, "360 SOUND STEREO 360 SOUND" in black along bottom, no arrows.

1963-65: Gray label, "COLUMBIA" in white along the top, "360 SOUND STEREO 360 SOUND" in black along bottom, arrows added to left of first "360" and right of second "SOUND."

1965-70: Gray label, "COLUMBIA" in white along the top, "360 SOUND STEREO 360 SOUND" in white along the bottom.

1970-early 1980s: Olive label, gold "COLUMBIA" six times in ring along outer edge.

Later variations include the "COLUMBIA" being replaced by "CBS," a large "FM" on labels, a special label for digital recordings, and a green label with "CBS" around the outer rim in white. By the end of the 1980s, no more vinyl was coming out in this series. Today this label is known as Sony Classical.

COLUMBIA SPECIAL PRODUCTS (CSP)

Late 1950s-1970: Red label, black strip curving along the top of the label, "COLUMBIA SPECIAL PRODUCTS" in white over the black.

1971-82?: Orange label, "CSP" in yellow at top of label, "COLUMBIA SPECIAL PRODUCTS" in smaller print beneath.

1982?-early 1990s: Orange label, "CBS SPECIAL PRODUCTS" in three lines to the left of the center hole.

Early 1990s: Orange label, "Sony Music Special Products" in two lines to the left of the center hole.

CORAL

1950s-1963: Maroon label, silver print.

1963-68: Black label, rainbow ring near center, "A Subsidiary of Decca Records" in fine print.

1968-70: Black label, rainbow ring near center, "A Division of MCA Records" in fine print.

COTILLION

1969-72: Grayish label, "Cotillion" in box at top.

1976-80s: Reactivated label; purple with a round "C" logo at top.

CROWN

This was a budget label. It began by putting some rare R&B and blues sides on LP, but eventually its issues became cheesier and cheesier.

1950s-60: Black label, gold or silver print. Some of the early Crown titles also exist on red vinyl.

1960-mid 60s: Gray label, black print.

Mid 60s-late 60s: Black label, each letter of "CROWN" in a different color.

DAKAR

1969-70 (9000s): Black label with wide rainbow colorband along the edge.

1972-76 (76900s): White label, black print.

DECCA

1949-54 (10-inch LPs in the 5000 series plus 12-inch LPs in the 8000 series): Black label, gold print. Earliest pressings have a "DLP" prefix, which was quickly replaced by "DL."

1954-60 (later 10-inch LPs and 12-inch LPs from around 8100 to 8981): Black label, silver print. Stereo pressings, which added a "7" to the mono number, had maroon labels with silver print.

1960-66 (4000-4830s, 74000-74830s): Black label with rainbow stripe through center hole and "Mfrd. By Decca Records" in the fine print.

1967-71 (4830s to end of mono, 74830 into some 75000s and 79000s): Black label with rainbow stripe through center hole and "A Division of MCA" in the fine print.

1972-73: Black label with rainbow stripe through center hole and "Mfrd. By MCA" in the fine print.

In addition to the regular series, Decca had a "Gold Label Series" of classical music; these have gold labels with black print.

MCA merged Decca, Uni and Kapp in January 1973 and closed down all three.

DEL-FI

1959 (1201): Light blue, black printing, blue circles on a black background around the outside of the label.

1959 (1202-1204): Light blue label, gold and black diamonds around the outside of the label.

1959-64 (1205-1249): Black label, blue and gold diamonds around the outside of the label.

DERAM

The basic label is white at the bottom, brown at the top with "DERAM" in white letters over the brown background.

DIONN

The only album on this label has an orange label with black print.

DISNEYLAND

One of the most confusing labels out there. Albums were issued in several numerical series, sometimes simultaneously.

The first LPs on the label were in the WDL-4000 series. Early pressings have yellow labels and black print with "A Disneyland Record" underneath the center hole. Later editions have red labels with silver print and "Disneyland" in an arc above the center hole.

The WDL-3000 series came next. 3001 was issued with the above yellow label; it was reissued, and all others had their original issue, with a purple label, silver print, and "Disneyland" along the upper edge of the label.

Next were the ST-3900 series. Original editions were issued with purple labels, silver print. Some were reissued in the 1970s with a yellow label, a rainbow band curving along the top edge and "Disneyland" in white on the rainbow.

The next series was in the ST-1900 range. Original editions of these have light blue labels with black print; some later originals and first reissues have a darker blue label; the final reissues have green labels.

The next, and most common, series was the DQ-1200 and 1300 series. Original issues have yellow labels with black print, "Disneyland" curving along the top. Reissues from the 1970s and 1980s have the yellow rainbow label and usually omit the "DQ."

A 1970s and 1980s line was the 2500 series; all of these come with the yellow rainbow label.

Further clarifications are welcome.

DOLTON

1959-62: Light blue label, dark blue print with fish logos at left of center hole.

1962-65: Darker blue label, multicolor fish logo to the left of the center hole.

1966-68: Mostly black label, blue section to left of center hole with stylized red-and-black "D" in white background.

DORE

1960s: Light blue label, feather at top.

1970s: Dark blue label, larger feather on top.

1970s: Black label, multicolor logo.

DOT

1954-56: Maroon label with "Gallatin, Tennessee" in fine print. A possible transition label, maroon with "Hollywood, Cal." in fine print, may exist. (45s exist with this label.)

1956-68: Black label, multicolored cursive "Dot" logo at top.

1968-70: Black label, both "DOT" and Paramount logos appear at top of label.

1971-74: Purple and orange label, "DOT" in box at top of label.

1974-75: Multicolored (yellow, orange, purple) "target" label with "abc Dot Records" at top of label between two lines.

1976-77: Multicolored (yellow, orange, purple) "target" label with "abc Dot" at top of label between two lines.

DUKE

1955 (70): Yellow and purple label, "DUKE" in yellow on purple background.

1957-62 (71-75): Yellow and purple label, "DUKE" in yellow on purple background, purple stripe around the outside of the yellow part of the label.

1963-70 (76-92): Orange label, fading to yellow toward the center hole.

1970s (reissues): Green label.

DUNHILL

1965-68 (50000-50030s): Black label, "DUNHILL" in white with gold border at top.

1968-72 (50030s-50170s): Black label, "DUNHILL" and "abc" in multicolored boxes at top.

1973: "DUNHILL" in a white rectangle spelled out in children's blocks. Very short-lived label. Quickly replaced by 1968-72 label again until another new label was created.

1974-75: Multicolored (yellow, orange, purple) "target" label with "abc Dunhill" at top of label between two lines.

ELEKTRA

1950s: White label with "electron" logo.

Late 1950s-1961?: Gray label, small guitar player at top.

1961?-1966?: Gold label, large guitar player at top.

1966-69: Gold (tan) label with large stylized "E" at top.

1969-70: Red label with large stylized "E" at top.

1971-74: Dark greenish label with butterfly holding white stylized "E" at left, "13 Columbus Circle" address along outer edge.

1975-79: Lighter greenish label with butterfly holding white stylized "E" at left, "W" (Warner Communications) logo added to the fine print.

1980-83: Red label, small white stylized "E" logo at top.

1984-89: Black and red label, "ELEKTRA" across top.

1989-91: Gray label.

1991-present: Tan label.

Custom labels were used for some releases.

EMBER

1958 (100, 200, 300, 400): Red label, black print.

1959 (401, reissues of earlier titles): White label, black print, eight circles around the outside of the label. The word "EMBER" is depicted in burning logs.

1960s (reissues): Black label, silver print.

1960s (800 series): Black label, "EMBER" logo at left with red flames emanating from it.

END

All End LPs (301-316) were issued with a gray label, a front end of a dog at top left, the back end of a dog at top right, and "end" in red letters. The words "A Product of End Music Inc., New York, N.Y." is at the bottom.

Reissues have the same basic label design, but "A Division of Roulette Records, Inc." is the new fine print.

Still later reissues have a light blue label with an orange band through the center hole and the word "END" in blue on either end of the band.

ENJOY

The only album issued on this label has a gold label with blue print.

ENTERPRISE

1967-68 (13-100 series): Blue label, rainbow at top with "Enterprise" in black over the rainbow. These were distributed by Atlantic.

1968-72 (1001-1024, 5000-5002): Black label, "ENTERPRISE" in yellow at top.

1972-74 (1025-1038, 5003-5007, 7501-7510): Black label, "ENTERPRISE" in white directly above center hole, large rainbow-colored stylized "E" above that.

EPIC

1955-62: Yellow label with series of short black lines around the perimeter and "Epic" on top. Some early labels also are gold with a similar design. Stereo issues (1959-62) have the same label but with "Stereorama" above the word "Epic" on the top of the label.

1962-63: Yellow label with "Epic" appearing eight times around the perimeter (mono); yellow label with "Epic Stereo" appearing three times around the perimeter (stereo)

1963-65 (24040s-24160s mono, 26040s-26160s stereo): Yellow label, "A Product of CBS" as part of the fine print.

1965-73 (all later monos, stereos into the 31000s): Yellow label, no "A Product of CBS" at bottom.

1973-79: Orange label with white concentric circles, Epic logo in white at top.

1979-present: Dark blue label, "Epic" in cursive letters across top.

EXCELLO

1960-mid 1960s (8000-8005?): Orange label, blue print.

Mid 1960s-early 1970s: White label, black print, pink and green arrows at top of label.

Early 1970s-1976: Light blue label, "excello" in white background in box.

FAMOUS

A reissue label for Keen material, the label was blue with silver print.

FEDERAL

Early 10-inch albums have all-green labels, "Federal" in silver across the top.

Albums in the 500 series have black labels with silver print and the word "Federal" straight across the top of the label. These are among the rarest and most valuable albums in all of record collecting. Federal albums with green labels and silver top appear to be bootlegs.

FELSTED

All Felsted albums have orange labels with black print.

FIRE

1959-60 (100-101): White label, red print.
1960-62 (102-105): Red label, black print.

FLIP

Two albums, both various artists sets, were released on Flip. Both are blue labels with silver print.

FORUM/FORUM CIRCLE

This budget label reissued material that first appeared on the Roulette label.

1960 (16000 series): Black label, gold print.
1961-63 (9000 series): Mono issues have maroon labels; stereo issues have red labels.
1964 (Forum Circle series): Mono issues have light blue labels, stereo issues have yellow labels.

FRATERNITY

1950s (1001-1012?): Light blue label.
Early 1960s (1013?-1018?): Red label, black print.
Mid to late 1960s and beyond (1019?-1028): Maroon label, silver print.

FURY

Two albums were issued on this label. Both have yellow labels with black print and a horse-in-a-tornado logo.

GEE

1956-59 (701-704): Red label, black print, "GEE" in large red letters in a black background at top.
1961-62 (705-707): Gray label, "GEE RECORDS" across the bottom.

GEFFEN

1980-85: White label with horizontal pinstripes.
1985-1990s: Black label.

GOLDEN WORLD

One album was issued on this label; it has a yellow label with black print.

GOLDWAX

Only two albums are known to have been released on this label in the U.S. Both are yellow with black print.

GONE

All albums on this label, which had LP releases from 1958-61, have pink and tan labels.

GORDY

1962-67 (901-927?): Purple label, "Gordy" in cursive yellow letters at top superimposed over an oval with the slogan "IT'S WHAT'S IN THE GROOVES THAT COUNT."

1968-1980s (928? forward): Purple label, "GORDY" in purple to left of center hole, yellow wedge going through center hole from left to right.

GUARANTEED

The only album issued on this label has a white label with black print and "GUARANTEED" in red, arc-shaped, at the top of the label.

GUYDEN

Three albums on this label, all with purple labels with silver strip at the top, in which "Guyden Records" appears in purple print next to a torch.

HARMONY

This was Columbia's budget label from the mid 1950s until the early 1970s.

1957-early 1960s: Maroon label, silver print.
Early 1960s-late 1960s: Black label, silver print.
Late 1960s-early 1970s: Brown label.
Early 1970s: Gold label, Harmony logo in red.

HERALD

1955-58 (0100-0111): "Spokes label": Multicolored spokes emanate from the center hole to the outside. Above the center hole is a yellow trumpet with a yellow banner and "HERALD" in black print.
1960 (1012): Black label, silver print.
1960-62 (1013-1015): Yellow label, silver print.

HICKORY

1960-62 (100-110?): Black label, silver print, "Hickory" slants upward at top of label.
1963-73 (111?-168): Black label, rainbow at upper left.1973-75 (4501-4524): Brown label, rainbow at upper left, "MGM Records" lion at right of center hole.
1976-77 (44001-44009?): Multicolored (yellow, orange, purple) "target" label with "abc Records" at top of label between two lines and the "Hickory" logo at left of center hole.
1977-79 (44010?-44017): Multicolored (yellow, orange, purple) "target" label with "abc" in an eighth note at top of label, and "Hickory" logo to the right of the note.

HIFI

Standard issues had silver labels with "HIFIRECORD" three times around the perimeter. The word "HIFI" was in silver, "RECORD" was in red.
Also see LIFE.

HIP

Four albums came out on this label from 1969-72. The label is red and pink with "Hip" in blue print bordered in black.

HORIZON

The folk music label of 1961-64 issued its mono albums on black labels with silver print (sometimes white print) and its stereo albums on dark blue labels with silver print.

HULL

Exactly three albums came out on this label, all of them highly desirable. Each had a different label thus:
1000: Dark red label, black print.
1001: Light blue label, black print.
1002: Red label, black print, "Hull Records Inc." in gold above the center hole.

IMPACT

Exactly one album was released on Impact. Its label is red with black print.

IMPERIAL

1950-56 (10-inch LPs; 12-inch LPs in the 100 series): Blue label, "IMPERIAL" in script print at top.

1956-57 (9001-9041?): Maroon label, "IMPERIAL" in silver block letters at top.

1957-64 (9042?-9267?, mono): Black label with colored rays emanating from Imperial logo at top.

1959-64 (12001-12267?, stereo): Black label, silver print, with "IMPERIAL STEREO" directly above the center hole. Some of the later 12250-12267 issues had the mono "colored rays" label with the word "Stereo" added.

1964-66 (9268?-9320s?, 12268?-12320s?): Black label, "IR/Imperial" to left of center hole, white area above logo, pink area below logo.

1966-70 (9320s? to end of monos, 12320s?-12457): Black label, "IR/Imperial" logo to left of center hole in white with red background; green areas above and below logo, which has been enlarged.

INTERPHON

Exactly one label came out on this label. It has a light blue label with red logo to the left of the center hole.

INDIGO

Black label, silver print, the word "Indigo" in indigo (purple) and "Records" next to it in blue.

INFINITY (pop)

In business for just over a year (late 1978 to late 1979), it lasted long enough to have two label variations. The earliest LPs have a primarily white label with "optical illusion" logo at the top. Later LPs have a primarily brown label with a slightly different rendering of the optical illusion logo.

ISLAND

Since the label was first set up as a U.S. entity in 1972, it's been distributed by Capitol, independently, by Warner Bros. and Atco (at the same time for different artists!) and PolyGram. The labels have changed even more often than the distribution, and it's possible we missed a variation or two.

1972-74: Sunray label, "ISLAND" along bottom of label in stylized letters.

1974-75: Yellow background on label, "water skier" offshore, "island" along top.

1975-77: Black label with "I" logo at bottom and "Island Records" underneath.

1977-80: Orange and blue label.

1981-82: Light blue label with darker blue ring around the outside.

1982-83: Dark purple label with skyscraper at left and "Island" slanting upward.

1983-84: Light blue label, "Island" in red across top.

1985-90: Black label.

Custom labels were used for some issues.

JAMIE

1958: Yellow label.

1959-67: White and gold label.

1970 (3034): Orange and black label.

JANUS

1970-76 (3000s, early 7000s): Brownish gold label.

1977-78 (later 7000s): Reddish orange label.

JOSIE

The first label was cream colored with blue print and "josie" at the top of the label in a blue oval.

The second label was tan with black print with the "josie" logo in a black oval. The logo sits atop a group of multicolored stripes emanating vertically from a horizontal white line that goes through the center hole.

The third label was tan with black print, "JOSIE" spelled in five different colors vertically to the left of the center hole.

JUBILEE

1950s (10-inch LPs from 1-25, 12-inch LPs from 1000-1014?): Pink label, black print.

1956-59 (1015?-1104?): Blue label, silver print.

1959-61 (1105?-1121?): Flat black label, silver print, "jubilee" in silver spiked oval at top of label.

1961-64 (5001-5055): Glossy black label, silver print, "jubilee" in large colored spiked oval at top of label.

1965-69 (8001-8031): Glossy black label, silver print, "jubilee" in much smaller colored spiked oval at top of label.

JUDD

The one album on this label has a purple label with silver print.

KAMA SUTRA

1965-69: Yellow label.

1970-71: Pink label.

1972-74: Light blue label, Garden of Eden scene at top.

KAPP

1955-59: Maroon label, silver print. Some issues have a blue label, silver print.

1959-62: Black and blue label with red "K" at top of label and "KAPP" underneath.

1962-64: Black and blue label with white major's hat and "KAPP" underneath.

1964-71: Black label with major's hat and "KAPP" underneath.

1971-73: Orange and purple label.

MCA merged Decca, Uni and Kapp in January 1973 and closed down all three.

Custom labels were used on some issues. For example, there are some early Christmas releases with silver labels and red and green holly leaves adorning the label.

KEEN

1958-59 (2000 series): Colored vertical stripes with letters of "KEEN" in individual gray circles.

1959-60 (86100 series): Black label, "KEEN" to left of center hole, five-color vertical stripe next to it.

KING

One of the most confusing labels at first glance, it's made even more so because of the often wide disparity in asking prices for what appear to be insignificant differences in the size and style of logo. Read on.

Early to mid 1950s (10-inch LPs): Maroon label, silver print. "KING" is in a straight line at the top of the label.

1955-early 1960s (500-late 600s): Black label, silver print, "KING" curves along the outside and is about two inches wide at the top of the label.

Early 1960s-mid 1960s (late 600s-unknown): Black label, silver print, "KING" curves along the outside and is about three inches wide at the top of the label (the letters are thicker and more stretched out than the earlier version).

Late 1950s-mid 1960s (stereo releases): Blue label, silver print, "KING" curves along the outside and is about three inches wide at the top of the label.

Mid 1960s-early 1970s: Blue label, silver print, "KING" straight across the top with a crown centered above the "I" and "N."

Late 1960s: James Brown LPs had a custom brown and orange label with his face on it.

Early 1970s (1146-1154): Yellow label with sitting king right of the center hole.

Mid 1970s (16000 series): Yellow label with "KING" vertically at top of label and two protrusions to form a stylized letter "K" coming from it.

Late 1970s (5000 series): Restores blue crowned King label of the mid- to late-1960s.

KIRSHNER

Successor to Calendar Records.

1969-mid 1970s: Orange label, "KIRSHNER" in individual boxes across the top.

Mid 1970s-early 1980s (CBS distribution): White label with multicolor top.

Custom labels were used on some CBS albums.

KOKO

Mostly a custom label for Luther Ingram, these albums have white labels with the word "KOKO" on both sides of the center hole in alternating yellow, red, purple and blue letters.

LAURIE

1959 (1000-1002): Gold label, black print.

1960-1980s (1003-1010, 2002-2052, 4000 series): Gold "pentagram" in center of label with black background surrounding it. Early pressings tend to be quite firm and substantial, and some seem to be almost brittle; later pressings tend to have glossier labels and flimsier wax.

LEGRAND

Original issues have red and gold labels with no crown on top. LeGrand reissued most of its LPs in the 1980s, and these are easily distinguishable by the white band through the center hole and the crown on the label.

LIBERTY

1956-60 (3001-3140? mono): Turquoise label, silver print, "LIBERTY" at top of label with drawing of Statue of Liberty above.

1958-60 (early 7000s stereo to 7140?): Black label, silver print, "LIBERTY" at top of label with drawing of Statue of Liberty above, huge word "STEREO" just below the logo.

1960-66 (3141?-3420?, 7141?-7420?): Black label, rainbow colored area left of center hole, "LIBERTY" in white over a gold crest left of center hole.

1960-69 (12000 and 14000 "Premier Series"): Gold label, black print, design similar to above except that black lines replace the rainbow area.

1966-69 (3421?-end of mono, 7421?-7620?): Black label, rainbow colored area left of center hole, white vertical line abutting rainbow area, "LIBERTY" in black inside a rounded white box with a Statue of Liberty graphic.

1970-71 (7620?-end of original series): Black label, rainbow colored area left of center hole, white vertical line abutting rainbow area, "LIBERTY" in black inside a squared-off white box with a Statue of Liberty graphic, "Liberty/UA Inc." at bottom of label.

1980-86 (reactivated label, 1000-51100 series and 10000 reissue series): Gray label, multicolored "Liberty" across top.

Custom labels were used for some issues, most notably 1960s issues by the Chipmunks, which have black labels with cartoon renditions of Alvin, Theodore, Simon and David Seville.

LIFE (HIFI)

Actually the "Hifi Life Series," but because of the prominence of the word "Life" on the label, most collectors call this the Life label.

Original issues have a red label with the word "Life" in cursive white letters. Later issues have either yellow or gold labels with a smaller "Life" in black letters.

LONDON (pop)

London releases can be quite confusing. At times, its records for release in the U.S. were pressed both in the U.S. and in England, and different labels were used in each country. The following applies to pop issues only – classical releases are another ballgame entirely. By the 1980s, almost all, if not all, London classical releases were being pressed in Europe, even those meant for sale in the U.S.

10-Inch Albums

Early to mid 1950s: Some have deep blue labels with gold print; some have red labels with gold print.

12-Inch Mono Albums

Mid 1950s-1964 ("LL" prefix until about 3380): Deep red label, silver print, "LONDON" in cursive capital letters across the top with an "ffrr" ear above the "LONDON." Two horizontal silver lines go through the center hole; between these lines are the words "Full Frequency Range Recording."

1964-65 (about 3380-3430): Deep red label, silver print, "LONDON" in a box with the "ffrr" ear logo to the right of this. All of these pressings have print that says "Made in England by the Decca Record Co., Ltd." and will have upside-down matrix numbers on the label.

1964-65 (about 3380-3460): Deep red label, silver print, "LONDON" stands alone, unboxed, above the center hole. All these labels have print that says "Made in U.S.A." Both the above two series ran at the same time, and neither is more "original" than the other, but the "ffrr" pressings are much more rare.

1966-68 (about 3460 to end): Varying shades of red labels (1966s tend to be bright red, 1967s almost maroon) with "LONDON" in a box at the top of the label.

Stereo Albums

1959-64 (PS series to about 379): Deep blue label, silver print, "LONDON" in cursive capital letters across the top with an "ffss" ear above the "LONDON." Underneath this, in a silver box with blue type, are the words "Full Frequency Stereophonic Sound." The earliest stereos have blue shaded back covers; these are known among audiophiles as "blue backs" and demand a premium.

1964-65 (about 380-430): Deep blue label, silver print, "LONDON" in a box with the "ffss" ear logo to the right of this. All of these pressings have print that says "Made in England by the Decca Record Co., Ltd." and will have upside-down matrix numbers on the label.

1964-65 (about 380-460): Deep blue label, silver print, "LONDON" stands alone, unboxed, above the center hole. All these labels have print that says "Made in U.S.A." Both the above two series ran at the same time, and neither is more "original" than the other, but the "ffss" pressings are much more rare.

1966-78 (about 460-early 700s): Varying shades of blue labels (earlier ones are much richer blue than later ones) with "LONDON" in a box at the top of the label.

A "sunrise" label was used on 45s starting around 1976 until about 1983; it's unknown if this was used on LPs, but if it was, it certainly wasn't used until after 1978. Later London pop labels are white with red trim and "LONDON" in white inside a black upside-down triangle.

LUCKY ELEVEN

One album was issued on this label. It has a yellowish label with a greenish horseshoe in the background.

LUNIVERSE

One album was issued on this label. It has a yellow label with black print.

MAINSTREAM

1960s: Silvery-blue label.

1970s: Red and black label, "Red Lion Productions" at upper right, "Mainstream" at upper left.

MCA

1973 (2100): All-black label, white print; appears to have been used only on this number.

1973-77: Black label, silver print, rainbow at upper left.

1977-79: Tan label, darker tan ring around rim.

1980-late 1990s: Blue label, black print, rainbow at upper left.

Late 1990s: White label, new "MCA/Music Corporation of America" logo left of center hole.

Custom labels were used on some releases.

MERCURY (pop)

1949-1955 (25000 series, all 10-inch LPs): Black label, silver print, "MERCURY" curving around outside of top of label.

1955-early 1960s (12-inch mono, 20000-20700s, also stereo from 60000 to 60700s): Black label, silver print, "MERCURY" stands alone at top, no print along lower edge of label.

Early 1960s-1965 (20700s-20900s; 60700s-60900s): Black label, silver print, "Mercury" in an oval. Some of these issues add "Vendor: Mercury Record Corporation" along lower edge of label.

1965-68 (20900s-end, 60900s-61200?): Red label, "MERCURY" in all capital letters across top with Mercury head at upper left.

1968-72 (61200?-61300s? and early SRM-1 series to 670 or so): Bright red label, twelve "Mercury" logos along the outer rim of the label.

1973-74 (SRM-1-670 to 999?): Bright red label, seven "Mercury" logos along the outer rim of the label.

1974-83: Chicago skyline label.

1983-90s: Black label, "Mercury" in glowing red letters across the top.

1990s: Black label, "Mercury" logo in white inside a red diamond at top of label.

Custom labels exist for some issues.

MERCURY (classical Living Presence)

1950s-early 1960s: Flat maroon label, "MERCURY" stands alone, no print along lower rim of label.

Early 1960s-mid 1960s: Flat maroon label, "MERCURY" stands alone, "Vendor: Mercury Record Corporation" added to label print.

Mid 1960s-early 1970s: Glossy maroon label, "Mercury" in oval logo at top of label.

MGM

1949-59 (10-inch LPs and 12-inch LPs to approximately 3770): Yellow label, black trim and print.

1960-68 (3771?-4515?): Black label, multicolor letters across top.

1968-76 (4516? into 5000s): Blue and gold swirl label.

Except for a very few releases, MGM ceased to exist as a record label in 1976; its material became part of the growing PolyGram empire.

MINIT

1961-63 (0001-0004): Orange label, black print.

1964-68 (24005-24023?, 40005-40023?): Black label, silver print, "MINIT" logo to left of center hole, "A Product of Liberty Records" along bottom.

1968-89 (40024?-40028): Same as above, but "Liberty/UA Records" is the new perimeter print.

MONUMENT

1959 (4000 and 14000 only): White label, gray to black vertical stripes, "MONUMENT" above center hole in black with gold trim.

1960-62 (4001-4009, 14001-14009): White and copper swirl label, "Monument" at top, Washington Monument right of center hole.

1963 (8000-8004?, 18000-18004?): White and multicolor swirl label, "Monument" at top, Washington Monument right of center hole.

1963-71 (8005?-end, 18005?-18147): Light green label, gold band around rim, stylized blue, pink and yellow Washington monument above "monument" at top of label.

1971-76 (30000 series, CBS distribution): Dark orange, almost brown, label.

1977-81 (6600, 7600, 8600 series): Black label with "MONUMENT" spelled out in simulated stone-carved letters across the top.

1982-83 (38000 series): Silver label.

MOTOWN

1961 (1000): White label, blue print, large blue "M" at top center that serves to turn the two O's in "MOTOWN" on their sides.

1961-62 (1001-1006): Blue label with map on upper half of the label. The original map stretches from western Kansas to the Atlantic coast with a red star over Detroit.

1962-1980s (1007 on): Blue label with map on upper half of the label. This map stretches only from mid-Indiana to mid-Pennsylvania. This design remained basically unchanged into the 1980s, with only changes in perimeter print. There is also more yellow in the word "MOTOWN" in 1970s and 1980s pressings than in 1960s pressings, where the letters fade from red to yellow to blue. Later pressings never make it all the way to the same rich blue as earlier versions.

MOWEST

A short-lived Motown label of the early 1970s, all of its LPs have a beach-at-sunset label with the top and bottom parts in orange and the middle in light blue.

MUSE

From the Ember-Herald family, this one-off label was black with silver print.

MUSICOR

1962: Brown label.

1962-69: Black label.

1970-75?: Tan label.

1976?-end: Green and yellow label.

MUSTANG

Red label, black print. Two albums were issued on this label, both by the Bobby Fuller Four.

NASCO

This label apparently didn't issue LPs until the late 1960s; several of these are sought after by psychedelic music collectors. The label is black with silver print.

ODE

1967-70: Yellow label, "Ode" logo in black print left of the center hole.

1970-71: White and silver label, "Ode 70" at upper right.

1971-75: White and silver label, "Ode Records Inc." at upper right.

1975-78: Tan label with both Ode and Epic logos.

OKEH

Although active for a long time, Okeh LPs were only issued from 1962 through 1969. All labels are purple with the familiar "Okeh" logo in gold above the center hole.

PARAMOUNT

Not to be confused with ABC-Paramount, this was an entirely different label established around 1969.

Most, if not all, original issues have a gray label with Paramount logo to the left of the center hole in black. Some 1970s reissues, after ABC bought the rights to the label, have a blue label with a white "Paramount" logo at the top.

PARKWAY

1960-61 (7001-7005?): Orange label, "PARKWAY" in uneven black letters across the top.

1961-67 (7006?-7057): Orange and yellow label, "PARKWAY" in white letters straight across the top.

1967 (50,000): Gold label.

PARROT

Except for some subtle perimeter print changes, this label was the same from 1964-76: Black with a colored bird left of center hole and the word "parrot" in yellow at the upper right.

PEACOCK

Almost entirely a gospel label, it had three distinct label designs. The first label was black with silver print, "PEACOCK" in silver above the center hole, a drawing of a peacock in black over the logo. The second label, after ABC picked up distribution, was also black with silver print, but "PEACOCK" was now in white and the peacock drawing was in color.

In 1974, the label changed to an unknown design with "abc Peacock" at top of label between two lines.

PHIL-L.A. OF SOUL

Two albums were issued, both with light yellow labels and black print.

PHILIPS (pop)

The below does not apply to classical LPs issued on the Philips label in the 1980s. Most of those were pressed overseas, usually in The Netherlands, then exported to the U.S. for sale.

The basic label stayed the same from 1962 through the early 1970s: It was black with the "PHILIPS" shield above the center hole. The changes all had to do with the perimeter print, as follows:

1962-63: "Chicago 1, Illinois" at the bottom
1963-66: "Vendor: Mercury Record Corporation" at the bottom.
1966-70: No perimeter print at bottom.
1970-74: "Manufactured and Distributed by Mercury" at the bottom.

PHILLES

1962-63 (4001-4005): Light blue label with black print1964-66 (4006-4011): Yellow and red label, black print.

PHILLIPS INTERNATIONAL

All the LPs issued on this label have a blue world map with a red, white and blue banner across the top. Over the banner it says "Sam C. Phillips International Corp."

PICKWICK

A budget label, most of the albums on this label are common and rarely fetch more than single digits in any condition – and that includes the Elvis ones! The biggest exception is a 1967 Simon and Garfunkel compilation.

From the mid-1960s to about 1976, the label was silver with black print. Starting around 1976 into the early 1980s, the label was black with a multicolored Pickwick logo.

POLYDOR

Labels are red from 1969 into the 1990s, with the only changes taking place in the perimeter print.

PORTRAIT

1976-early 80s: Gray label.
1980s: Black label.
Custom labels were used on some releases.

RAMA

Labels are dark blue with silver print.

RARE EARTH

1969 (505-509): The lower half of the label is white. The upper half has an orange background, a drawing of a tree and the words "RARE EARTH" in white. This label was later used as the promo label, but for the first editions of these early LPs, it also was the stock label.

1970-76 (511-550): All-orange label with a drawing of a tree and the words "RARE EARTH" in white.

RCA CAMDEN

This was RCA Victor's budget label.
1954-57: Pink label.
1957-64: Blue label, purple perimeter.
1964-68: Light blue label, dark blue perimeter.

1969-75: All-blue label with "RCA" turned on its side at left and "Camden" right of the center hole.

Most Camden titles still in print in 1975 were reissued with the same number on Pickwick.

RCA SPECIAL PRODUCTS

Before 1973, there was no label with this official name. Special-products issues on RCA were easily identifiable by the prefix "PR," "PRM" or "PRS" and a three-digit number.

The earliest of these (early 1960s-1968) have a flat black label and silver print, "RCA Victor" in silver and an outline of the Nipper logo in silver underneath.

The next series of these (1968-73) have a tan, almost maize, label, with "RCA" on its side at the left of the center hole, "Victor" to the right of the center hole, and no dog.

When the entire RCA catalog began using alphanumeric prefixes in 1973, RCA Special Products got its own series beginning, for the most part, with "DPL1." Early label colors vary; some are green, some are light blue. By 1977 the label was black with the dog near top, "RCA Special Products" on two lines in white to the left of the dog.

RCA VICTOR (pop)

Another long and involved label with sometimes overlapping label designs. We welcome any corrections and clarifications. The below apply only to pop albums; Red Seal records are treated elsewhere.

10-Inch Albums

1951-55: Most pop albums have black labels with silver print. A silver ring goes all the way around the label. The words "RCA VICTOR" are along the upper edge above the silver ring. An outline of Nipper is under the silver ring at top. Some albums of this period also had green labels with silver print; reissues of older material had silver-gray labels with red print.

Mono 12-Inch Albums

Before 1955 (early 1000s): Black labels with silver print; silver ring all the way around the label; "RCA VICTOR" along upper edge above the ring; outline of Nipper at top under ring.

1955-63 (mid 1000s-2700s): Shiny black label, "RCA VICTOR" in silver with full-bodied Nipper logo underneath. The bottom of the label says "LONG 33 1/3 PLAY."

1963-64 (2700s-2999): Shiny black label, "RCA VICTOR" in white with full Nipper logo. The bottom of the label says "MONO" in some cases; others have an extra-bold "DYNAGROOVE" across the bottom with the word "MONO" in much smaller print on either side.

1965-68 (3300-3900s): Shiny black label, "RCA VICTOR" is much larger along top of label, the Nipper logo is slightly smaller underneath. Along the bottom is either "MONAURAL" or "MONO DYNAGROOVE."

Stereo 12-Inch Albums

1958-63 (2000s-2700s): Shiny black label, "RCA VICTOR" in silver with full-bodied Nipper logo underneath. The bottom of the label says "LIVING STEREO."

1963-64 (2700s-2999): Shiny black label, "RCA VICTOR" in white with full-bodied Nipper logo underneath. The bottom of the label says "STEREO" in some cases; others have an extra-bold "DYNAGROOVE" across the bottom with the word "STEREO" in much smaller print on either side. This series also had the first rechanneled stereo releases, all of which had numbers before 2000; these have the extra bold word "STEREO" at the bottom with "Electronically Reprocessed" underneath.

1965-68 (3300s-early 4000s): Shiny black label, "RCA VICTOR" is much larger along top of label, the Nipper logo is slightly smaller underneath. Along the bottom is either "STEREO," "STEREO DYNAGROOVE" or "STEREO Electronically Reprocessed."

1969-71 (early 4000s-about 4460): Orange label on rigid, non-flexible vinyl, "RCA" on its side to left of center hole, "Victor" to right of center hole, no dog logo.

1971-76 (4460?-APL1-1000 or so): Orange label on so-called "Dynaflex" vinyl, "RCA" on its side to left of center hole, "Victor" to right of center hole, no dog logo.

1974-76 (early APL1 series): Tan label, released simultaneously with above orange label. Tan labels were used in Indianapolis, which explains why more of these are found in the East, and the orange labels were used in Hollywood, which explains why more of these are found in the West.

1976-late 1980s: Black label, Nipper logo is restored and added to upper right. "RCA" is now above the center hole to the left of Nipper, "Victor" is on its side to the left of the center hole.

Late 1980s-1990s: Mostly red label with circular "RCA" logo in black background at top. There are other variations of this label as well. It was not until this label that the word "Victor" was dropped from pop LPs.

RCA VICTOR RED SEAL (classical)

10-Inch Albums

1951-55: Red labels with silver print. A silver ring goes all the way around the label. The words "RCA VICTOR" are along the upper edge above the silver ring. Just under the silver ring are the words "RED SEAL RECORD." Under that is an outline of Nipper.

Mono 12-Inch Albums

Before 1955: Red labels with silver print; silver ring all the way around the label; "RCA VICTOR" along upper edge above the ring; "RED SEAL RECORD" just under the ring; outline of Nipper at top under those words.

1955-63: Deep red label, "RCA VICTOR" in white with full-bodied Nipper logo underneath. Behind the Nipper logo is a darker red area, thus lending the nickname "shaded dog" to these pressings. The bottom of the label says "LONG 33 1/3 PLAY."

1963-64: Deep red label, "RCA VICTOR" in white with full Nipper logo. The bottom of the label says "MONO" in some cases; others have an extra-bold "DYNAGROOVE" across the bottom with the word "MONO" in much smaller print on either side.

1965-68: Red label, "RCA VICTOR" is much larger along top of label, the Nipper logo is slightly smaller underneath, and there is no shading behind it. Along the bottom is either "MONAURAL" or "MONO DYNAGROOVE." Collectors call these "white dog" pressings.

Stereo 12-Inch Albums

1958-63: Shiny red label, "RCA VICTOR" in white with full-bodied Nipper logo underneath. The bottom of the label says "LIVING STEREO." Behind the Nipper logo is a darker red area, thus lending the nickname "shaded dog" to these pressings. Some of these stereo pressings are among the most collected stereo albums in the world!

1963-64: Shiny red label, "RCA VICTOR" in white with full-bodied Nipper logo underneath. The bottom of the label says "STEREO" in some cases; others have an extra-bold "DYNAGROOVE" across the bottom with the word "STEREO" in much smaller print on either side. This series also had the first rechanneled stereo releases, all of which had numbers before 2000; these have the extra bold word "STEREO" at the bottom with "Electronically Reprocessed" underneath. Although these still have the "shaded dog" motif, they are not as collectible as the "LIVING STEREO" originals.

1965-68: Shiny black label, "RCA VICTOR" is much larger along top of label, the Nipper logo is slightly smaller underneath, and there is no shading behind it. Along the bottom is either "STEREO," "STEREO DYNAGROOVE" or "STEREO Electronically Reprocessed." Collectors call these "white dog" pressings.

1969-71: Red label on rigid, non-flexible vinyl, "RCA" on its side to left of center hole, "Red Seal" to right of center hole, no dog logo. This and the next variation are known as "no dog" pressings.

1971-76: Red label on so-called "Dynaflex" vinyl, "RCA" on its side to left of center hole, "Red Seal" to right of center hole, no dog logo.

1976-late 1980s: Black label, Nipper logo is restored and added to upper right. "RCA" is now above the center hole to the left of Nipper, "Red Seal" is on its side to the left of the center hole. These are known as "late dog" pressings.

RED BIRD

A short-lived label, Red Bird released albums from 1964 to 1966. All have yellow labels with black print. A red bird is above the center hole, and the words "Red" and "Bird" are on either side of it in black.

RENDEZVOUS

1958-60 (1301-1310?): Brown label, silver print.

1960-end (1311?-1314): Black label, silver print, "rendezvous records" in white above center hole.

REPRISE

1961-67 (6001-6280?, 1000-1022?; 2000-2015?): Pink, gold and green label with a large steamboat at the upper left corner and the word "reprise:" on the label at upper right. Albums in the 1000 series, which were Frank Sinatra issues, had his photo on the label instead of the steamboat.

1968-70 (6281?-6400s; 1024-1029; 2016?-2025?): Two-tone orange label (rich orange at top, duller orange on bottom) with a smaller steamboat, an "r:" logo in a red circle with a "W7" logo overlapping it at its left.

1970-early 1980s (6400s on, 2026?-2200s): All-tan (dull orange) label with steamboat, the "W7" logo is gone, though the "r:" remains, this time in a box rather than a circle.

Mid 1980s: Black and red label.

Late 1980s-present: Light blue and maize label.

RIC-TIC

Exactly one album was released on this Detroit label. It has a red label with black print.

RISING SONS

A short-lived subsidiary of Monument, this label was black with silver print and four colored arrows at upper left.

ROLLING STONES

1971 (59100): Earliest stock copies of the first album on the label have white labels.

1971-84 (all others): Yellow label with red "lips and tongue" logo left of the center hole.

Custom labels exist for some releases.

ROULETTE

1957 (25001-25003): Black label, silver print, "ROULETTE" in silver along top, silver roulette wheel underneath label name.

1957-59 (25004-25045?): Black label, silver print, "ROULETTE" in white along top, red roulette wheel underneath label name.

1959-62 (25046?-25180s?): White label, black print, "ROULETTE" in black along top, blue, red, yellow and green "spokes" through center hole.

1962-63 (25180s?-25230s?): Left side of label is orange, right side is pink, black print, "ROULETTE" in white to left of center hole between two white lines.

1963-1970s (25230-25361; 42000 and 3000 series): Alternating orange and yellow label in the pattern of a roulette wheel, "ROULETTE" in black near the top of the label.

1980s (59000 series): Alternating orange and yellow label in the pattern of a roulette wheel, "ROULETTE" in green near the top of the label.

Roulette had many other numbering systems, most notably the 52000 series for jazz. We'd appreciate help in placing those series within the above time frame.

RSO

1973-75: Peach label, distributed by Atco.

1976-78: Tan label, distributed by Polydor (has Polydor logo in fine print).

1978-81: Tan label, distributed by Polygram (no Polydor logo in fine print).

1981-83: Silver label.

SAVOY

1950-1960s: Maroon label.

1970s (reissues): Brown label, "Distributed by Arista."

SCEPTER

1961 (501): Red label, "Scepter" in black script and a silver outline.

1962-71: Red label, black wedge through center hole, "SCEPTER RECORDS" in white in two lines at the left of the center hole.

Late 1960s-1973: Kaleidoscopic label, "SCEPTER RECORDS" in black inside white oval at top of label. There may be some overlap between this label and the earlier one, as there also was in 45s.

1974-76: Dark blue label, "SCEPTER" in white.

SCORE

A reissue label for Aladdin material, many of these are quite rare, though not nearly as rare as the Aladdin originals. All of these have maroon labels with "SCORE" above the center hole in an oval.

SHELTER

1971-72 (8900-8910?): Red label with an upside-down Superman logo at left.

1972-73: Red label with blacked-out upside-down Superman logo on top.

1974-76 (MCA distribution): Yellow label.

1977-78 (ABC distribution): Orange label with crescent moon at left.

SIRE

1968-70 (97000 series): White label, both Sire and London logos at top of label.

1970-71: Yellow label, blue stylized "S" at top, "Distributed by Polydor Records" in fine print.

1972-74: Yellow label, blue stylized "S" at top, "Distributed by Famous Music, A G+W Company" in fine print.

1974-76: Yellow label, blue stylized "S" at top, "Distributed by ABC Records Inc." in fine print.

1977-1980s: Yellow label, blue stylized "S" at top, makes reference to distribution by Warner Bros.

SMASH

1961-68: Flat red label, "SMASH" at top of label.

1968-71: Red label, both "SMASH" and Mercury logos at top of label.

SOUL

1965-66 (701-702): White label, black print, "SOUL" printed vertically in purple to the left of the center hole in a light purple background.

1966-78 (703-751): Label has three circles with three shades of purple. The "SOUL" logo is in white, centered at the top of the label.

SOUND STAGE 7

1963-66 (5000-5003?, 15000-15003?): Red label, black print, "SOUND 7 STAGE" above center hole.

1968-70 (15004?-15009): Black label, "SOUND STAGE" in two rows in white print over a blue "7."

1972-75 (30000 series): Gold label.

SPECIALTY

1957 (100): White label with wide black ring around the outside and a narrow yellow ring between the white and black areas. "Specialty" is in cursive letters in yellow over the black ring at the top of the label.

1957-70 (2100-2140s?): Gold label, black print, "Specialty" in gold letters across the top over a black background.

1971-89 (2140s-end): Black and white label, "Specialty" in large yellow letters over the black part of the label. Similar in spirit to the design of 1950s 45 rpm labels.

STAX

1962-68 (701-726): Mono releases have light blue labels with black "Stax" logo at top and stack of records over it. Stereo releases have yellow labels with the same "Stax" records logo.

1968-72 (2000-2045, 3001): Yellow label with "finger-snapping" logo in blue tint at the left of center hole.

1972-75 (2046-2047; 3002-3024, 5500 series): Yellow label with "finger-snapping" logo in brown at left of center hole.

1976-late 1980s (4100 and 8500 series): Purple fading to white label, "finger-snapping" logo in black at left of center hole.

STRAND

Mostly a budget label, its labels were orange with black print.

SUE

Early 1960s: Orange label, black print, "Sue RECORDS" in white print left of center hole.

Mid 1960s: Orange label, black print, "Sue RECORDS" in black print left of center hole.

1969 (8801): Red label, black print.

SUN

1956-65 (1220-1275): Yellow label, brown print. Musical notes ring the outer edge of the label. Alternating brown and yellow rays emanate from the center hole area. The letters "SUN" are in yellow over the rays. At the bottom of the label, in yellow print with brown background, are the words "Memphis, Tennessee."

1969-86 (100-148, 1000-1035): Yellow label, brown print. Four "targets" are visible in the lower half of the label. The music notes only go around half the label instead of nearly all of it, and at the bottom is "Sun International Corp., A Division of the Shelby Singleton Corp., Nashville, U.S.A."

SUNSET

This was Liberty Records' budget label. It has a black label with a light blue area at the left of the label; the "SUNSET" logo is to the left of the center hole.

SWAN

1959-63 (501-512?): White label, red print.

1964-end (513?-517): Black label, silver print.

TAMLA

1961-62 (220-231?): White label, black print. Above the center hole is an overlapping globe-record logo with "TAMLA" in an arc above the globe. The oceans of the world and center hole of the record are colored purple.

1962 (229?-233?): Yellow label, black print, same as above except that the oceans and record hole are colored brown.

1963-67 (236?-280?): Yellow label, black print, side-by-side record and globe at top of label, "TAMLA" in yellow over the globe.

1968-1980s (281?-end): Yellow label, black print, brown areas at upper left and upper right of label, "TAMLA" logo, with flattened globe above, in box centered at top.

TEEM

Ace imprint; purple label with silver print.

THREE BROTHERS

A short-lived label, its only release was a 1973 Lou Christie album. It was mostly blue with yellow and white circles that share the same border.

THRESHOLD

1970-73 (1-10?): White label, purple logo.

1974-83 (11?-end): Dark blue label.

TOP RANK

On mono labels, the upper left quadrant of the label is white with a drawing in gold of a man hitting a gong; the other three quadrants of the label are red.

On stereo labels, the upper left quadrant of the label is white with a drawing in red of a man hitting a gong; the other three quadrants of the label are gold.

TOWER

1965-68: Orange label.
1968-69: Multicolored, striped label.

TRACK

1970-71: Black label, distributed by Atlantic.
1972: Silver label with Decca logo.
1973-75: Brown label, distributed by MCA.

20TH CENTURY/20TH FOX

1958-early 1960s: Light blue "clouds" label, "20th Fox" logo in red at top of label.

Mid 1960s-early 1970s: Black label with gold border, "20th Century Fox Records" logo at top of label. Most of these issues were distributed by ABC.

1972-77: Light blue label, "20th Century" logo in white at top of label.

1978-early 1980s: Light brown label with added spotlights, logo again changes to "20th Century Fox."

UNI

This label had two distinct incarnations.

From 1967-72 it was a quasi-independent division of the MCA family of labels. Labels are yellow with several colored stripes and "uni" at the upper right. Uni, Kapp and Decca were folded at the end of 1972 into the new, all-encompassing MCA label.

In the mid-1980s, MCA briefly reactivated Uni. These labels are blue with "uni RECORDS" in two lines in black above the center hole.

UNITED ARTISTS

1958-59: Red and black label, "UNITED" to left of center hole, "ARTISTS" to right of center hole.

1959: Mono albums had an all-red label; stereo albums had blue labels.

1960: Black label, large "UA" logo on top.

1960-68: Black label, blue, gold, white and red circles along upper edge of label, "UNITED" in gold, "ARTISTS" underneath in white, both words in a rounded-off rectangle.

1968-70: Pink and orange label.

1970-71: Black label, orange area at left of center hole, "UA/ United Artists" logo in box directly left of center hole.

1971-77: Tan label with "UA" in brown at top.

1977-80: Multicolored "sunrise" label.

UNIVERSAL

A country label that lasted for exactly one year (1989). The earliest albums had black and pale yellow labels; later albums have black and red labels.

V.I.P.

This Motown label had a brown, tan, orange, yellow and white label. The "V.I.P." logo is printed vertically to the left of the center hole, inside an oval with an orange background.

VALIANT

Early 1960s: Purple label.
Mid 1960s: Red and black label.

VANGUARD

Early years through 1963: Mono issues were maroon with silver print.

Late 1958s-mid 1960s: Stereo issues were black with silver print.

Mid 1960s-early 1970s: Silvery gray to bronze label with white horseman logo on bottom.

Other labels also existed; we appreciate more information, as many Vanguard releases stayed in print for two decades or more.

VEE JAY

Pre-bankruptcy issues:

1957-60 (1001-1016; 1022; 5001-5005?): Maroon label, silver print with a squiggly line under the words "Vee-Jay RECORDS." A silver band is around the outside of the label. In this number range, stereo issues were gray with black print with otherwise identical graphics.

1960-64 (1019-21; 1023-1070s?, 5006?-5053?, 3004-3037): Black label, silver print, "Vee Jay" logo in white with a treble clef between the two words, surrounded by a red oval. The outer rim of the label has a rainbow band.

1964-65 (1070s-1154; 5054?-5083; 2501-2509): Black label, silver print, "VJ" in white, "VEE-JAY RECORDS" underneath that in two lines in white, all surrounded by two white brackets. The outer rim of the label has a rainbow band.

1964-65 (various, as needed): Black label, silver print, no rainbow band. The letters "VJ" stand alone with "VEE JAY RECORDS" underneath, all in silver print, no brackets.

Post-bankruptcy issues:

Late 1960s-early 1970s: Black label, silver print. Most have the "VJ" and "VEE-JAY RECORDS" in brackets, all in silver print. Some have "VJ" on one line and "RECORDS" on another with no brackets, still all in silver print. Although these records were issued in stereo jackets, they generally play mono!

(This may be the source and time period of most of the "best" illegitimate *Introducing The Beatles* albums, as they match this description. The Beatles albums are considered "counterfeits" because Vee-Jay did not have the rights to reproduce them after 1964. The material Vee-Jay actually owned and reissued at this time, such as *Duke Of Earl* by Gene Chandler, is considered legitimate product, though less valuable than the originals.)

1972-74 (1001-1011 and 2-1000 to 2-1008): Red label, silver print, similar to original maroon Vee-Jay label. At least one of these (1002) was issued on a pink label with black print.

1977 (VJ International): Orange label, black "VJ International" logo in white circle.

VERVE

1956-60 (8000 series mono, 6000 series stereo): Black label, silver print, "Verve Records, Inc." at bottom, "MGV" prefix. Early copies have the famous "trumpet player" logo at the left; these command a premium over those with the large "T" logo.

1961-early 1970s (8000 series): Black label, silver print, "MGM Records" at bottom, "V" prefix for mono, "V6" for stereo.

1966-early 1970s (5000 series): Dark blue label, silver print, "V" prefix for mono, "V6" for stereo.

Early 1970s-1975: White label with both "Verve" and "MGM" logos at top of label.

Various labels were used after Verve was reactivated in the early 1980s.

VIK

A 1950s RCA subsidiary, its issues were black with a multicolor "Vik" logo across the top.

VIRGIN

Virgin's American history is spotty at times; for some years there was no Virgin Records in America, but material that came out on Virgin U.K. was leased to other labels.

1973-75: White label, "two virgins" painting at top of label, distributed by Atlantic.

1976-78: Unknown label design, distributed by CBS.

1979-80: White label, "Virgin" in red letters, again distributed by Atlantic.

1981: Unknown design, distributed by RSO.

1983-86: Black label, "Virgin" and "Epic" logos on label. (All of these were Culture Club albums.)

1987-89: Black label, blue upside-down triangle logo at top of label.

VOLT

1965-68 (411-419): Yellow label, black print, "VOLT RECORDS" above center hole, yellow lightning bolt in black background beneath that.

1969-72 (6001-6017): Dark blue label, black print.

1972-74 (6018-6023 and 9500 series): Orange label, black print.

WAND

1960s: White with black top.

Early 1970s: Kaleidoscope label, "Wand" in black across top of label.

WARNER BROS.

Mono Albums

1958-62 (1200-1470?): Gray label, black "WB" shield at top, "WB" letters in shield are in gold print.

1962-66 (1470?-1620?): Gray label, black "WB" shield at top, "WB" letters in shield are in white print.

1966-67 (1620?-1700s): Gold label.

Stereo Albums

1958-67 (1200-1730?): Gold label.

1968-70 (1730?-1840?): Green label, "Warner Bros.-Seven Arts Records" along top edge, "W7" logo boxed underneath that.

1970-73 (1840?-1890?; 2500-2700?): Green label, "Warner Bros. Records" along top edge, "WB" shield logo underneath that.

1973-78 (2700?-3150?): So-called "Burbank palm trees" label. "Burbank, Home of Warner Bros. Records" along top edge, black "WB" shield underneath that, lined boulevard of palm trees comprises the label design.

1978-83? (3150?-25000?): Tan label, narrow horizontal lines every quarter inch or so, large "WB" shield at top of label.

1983?-present (25000?-on): White label, no horizontal lines, large "WB" shield remains at top.

WARWICK

Original mono labels were white with a green filled-in circle in the middle of the label. Four yellow circles are on the left of the label; four blue circles tend toward the right of the label. At the top is a Warwick crest logo with a green shield. Original stereo labels were also white, but instead of the green filled-in circle, a blue dot is to the right of the center hole and a yellow dot to the left of the center hole. Concentric like-colored circles surround each dot.

The second version of the mono label was plain white with black print and the Warwick logo in black. Stereo labels were purple with silver print and the Warwick logo in silver.

WEED

Exactly one album came out on this short-lived Motown imprint. The label is black with silver print with "WEED" in yellow and two fingers giving the peace sign above that. The label's slogan, which, alas, is not on the record, was "Your Favorite Artists Are On Weed."

WHITE WHALE

1965-67 (100-120?, 7100-7120?): Dark blue label.

1967-70 (7120?-end): Lighter blue label with concentric white circles.

"X"

This subsidiary of RCA Victor released albums from 1954 through 1956. The label is white with red print and a big red "X" at the top of the label.

Dating RCA albums

On all albums pressed by RCA Victor from the early 1950s through 1972, there is an eight-digit master number, four of which are to the left of a hyphen, four of which are to the right.

For albums first released before 1955, you can tell what year the record was mastered by looking at the first two digits. For albums mastered from 1955-72, you can tell the year by looking at the first digit, which will always be a letter.

This list won't tell you what year the album was actually *pressed*; for that, you still need to see the label guide.

The following works on all RCA family albums, including Red Seal, Camden, Bluebird and Victrola. It also works on non-RCA albums that were pressed at the RCA plants, including custom pressings. So you might want to check some albums on such labels as 20th Fox, Cadence and Motown, just to name three, to see if they have RCA-style master numbers.

Here is the RCA code.

1951-54: The first two digits of the master number correspond to the following years.

E1: 1951
E2: 1952
E3: 1953
E4: 1954

1955-72: RCA altered the code so that only the first digit corresponded to the year.

F: 1955
G: 1956
H: 1957
J: 1958
K: 1959
L: 1960
M: 1961
N: 1962
P: 1963
R: 1964
S: 1965
T: 1966
U: 1967
W: 1968
X: 1969
Z: 1970
A: 1971
B: 1972

After 1972: RCA changed its published master numbers to the same number as the record number, with an added "A" for side 1 and a "B" for side 2. You can no longer tell the year based on the master number.

Number	Title (A Side/B Side)	Yr	VG	VG+	NM

A

A.F.O. EXECUTIVES WITH TAMI LYNN
A.F.O.

Number	Title (A Side/B Side)	Yr	VG	VG+	NM
❑ 5002 [M]	A Compendium	1962	37.50	75.00	150.00

ABBA
ATLANTIC

❑ PR 300 [DJ]	Abba	1978	7.50	15.00	30.00
❑ PR 432 [DJ]	A Collection of Hits	1982	7.50	15.00	30.00
❑ PR 436 [(2)DJ]	The Abba Special	1983	12.50	25.00	50.00
❑ SD 16000	Voulez-Vous	1979	2.50	5.00	10.00
❑ SD 16009	Greatest Hits, Vol. 2	1979	3.00	6.00	12.00
❑ SD 16023	Super Trouper	1980	2.50	5.00	10.00
❑ SD 18101	Waterloo	1974	3.00	6.00	12.00
❑ SD 18146	Abba	1975	3.00	6.00	12.00
❑ SD 18189	Greatest Hits	1976	3.00	6.00	12.00
❑ SD 18207	Arrival	1977	3.00	6.00	12.00
❑ SD 19114	Greatest Hits	1977	2.50	5.00	10.00
❑ SD 19115	Arrival	1977	2.50	5.00	10.00
❑ SD 19164	The Album	1978	2.50	5.00	10.00
❑ SD 19332	The Visitors	1981	2.50	5.00	10.00
❑ 80036 [(2)]	The Singles — The First Ten Years	1982	3.75	7.50	15.00
❑ 80142	I Love Abba	1984	2.50	5.00	10.00
❑ 81675	Abba Live	1986	3.00	6.00	12.00

CBS INTERNATIONAL

| ❑ DAL 40301 | Gracias Por La Musica | 1980 | 10.00 | 20.00 | 40.00 |

—Spanish-language versions of some of their hits, this LP was pressed in the U.S.

K-TEL

| ❑ NU 9510 | The Magic of Abba | 1978 | 3.75 | 7.50 | 15.00 |

NAUTILUS

| ❑ NR-20 | Arrival | 1981 | 7.50 | 15.00 | 30.00 |

—Audiophile vinyl

ABBEY TAVERN SINGERS, THE
V.I.P.

| ❑ 402 [M] | We're Off to Dublin in the Green | 1966 | 10.00 | 20.00 | 40.00 |
| ❑ S-402 [S] | We're Off to Dublin in the Green | 1966 | 12.50 | 25.00 | 50.00 |

ABDUL-MALIK, AHMED
NEW JAZZ

| ❑ NJLP-8266 [M] | The Music of Ahmed Abdul-Malik | 1961 | 10.00 | 20.00 | 40.00 |

—Purple label

| ❑ NJLP-8266 [M] | The Music of Ahmed Abdul-Malik | 1965 | 6.25 | 12.50 | 25.00 |

—Blue label, trident logo at right

| ❑ NJLP-8282 [M] | Sounds of Africa | 1962 | 10.00 | 20.00 | 40.00 |

—Purple label

| ❑ NJLP-8282 [M] | Sounds of Africa | 1965 | 6.25 | 12.50 | 25.00 |

—Blue label, trident logo at right

PRESTIGE

| ❑ PRLP-16003 [M] | Eastern Moods | 1963 | 7.50 | 15.00 | 30.00 |

RCA VICTOR

| ❑ LPM-2015 [M] | East Meets West | 1959 | 7.50 | 15.00 | 30.00 |
| ❑ LSP-2015 [S] | East Meets West | 1959 | 10.00 | 20.00 | 40.00 |

RIVERSIDE

| ❑ RLP 12-287 [M] | Jazz Sahara | 1958 | 12.50 | 25.00 | 50.00 |
| ❑ RLP-1121 [S] | Jazz Sahara | 1959 | 10.00 | 20.00 | 40.00 |

STATUS

| ❑ ST-8303 [M] | Spellbound | 1965 | 7.50 | 15.00 | 30.00 |

ABRAMS, MUHAL RICHARD
DELMARK

| ❑ DS-413 | Levels and Degrees of Light | 1968 | 5.00 | 10.00 | 20.00 |
| ❑ DS-423 | Young at Heart, Wise in Time | 1970 | 5.00 | 10.00 | 20.00 |

ABSTRACTS, THE
POMPEII

| ❑ 6002 [M] | The Abstracts | 1968 | 20.00 | 40.00 | 80.00 |

—Stereo cover with "DJ Copy Monaural" sticker; white label promo record

| ❑ SD 6002 [S] | The Abstracts | 1968 | 10.00 | 20.00 | 40.00 |

AC/DC
ATCO

❑ SD 36-142	High Voltage	1976	2.50	5.00	10.00
❑ SD 36-151	Let There Be Rock	1977	2.50	5.00	10.00
❑ 91413	The Razors Edge	1990	3.75	7.50	15.00

ATLANTIC

| ❑ LAAS-001 [DJ] | Live at the Atlantic Studios | 1977 | 15.00 | 30.00 | 60.00 |

—This album has been counterfeited

❑ PR 562 [DJ]	Flick of the Switch Interview Album	1983	10.00	20.00	40.00
❑ SD 11111	For Those About to Rock We Salute You	1981	2.50	5.00	10.00
❑ SD 16018	Back in Black	1980	2.50	5.00	10.00
❑ SD 16033	Dirty Deeds Done Dirt Cheap	1981	2.50	5.00	10.00
❑ SD 19180	Powerage	1978	2.50	5.00	10.00
❑ SD 19212	If You Want Blood You've Got It	1978	2.50	5.00	10.00
❑ SD 19244	Highway to Hell	1979	2.50	5.00	10.00
❑ 80100	Flick of the Switch	1983	2.50	5.00	10.00
❑ 80178 [EP]	'74 Jailbreak	1984	—	3.00	6.00
❑ 81263	Fly on the Wall	1985	2.50	5.00	10.00
❑ 81650	Who Made Who	1986	2.50	5.00	10.00
❑ 81828	Blow Up Your Video	1988	2.50	5.00	10.00

EASTWEST

| ❑ 61780 | Ballbreaker | 1995 | 3.75 | 7.50 | 15.00 |

ACE, JOHNNY
ABC DUKE

| ❑ DLPX-71 | Memorial Album | 1974 | 5.00 | 10.00 | 20.00 |

DUKE

| ❑ DLP-70 [10] | Memorial Album for Johnny Ace | 1955 | 400.00 | 800.00 | 1200. |
| ❑ DLP-71 [M] | Memorial Album for Johnny Ace | 1956 | 125.00 | 250.00 | 500.00 |

—With no playing card on front cover

| ❑ DLP-71 [M] | Memorial Album for Johnny Ace | 1961 | 50.00 | 100.00 | 200.00 |

—With playing card on front cover

| ❑ DLP-71 [M] | Memorial Album for Johnny Ace | 1961 | 2000. | 3000. | 4000. |

—Playing card cover; red vinyl

MCA

| ❑ 27014 | Memorial Album | 1983 | 2.00 | 4.00 | 8.00 |

ACKLIN, BARBARA
BRUNSWICK

❑ BL 754129	Great Soul Hits	1967	6.25	12.50	25.00
❑ BL 754137	Love Makes a Woman	1968	5.00	10.00	20.00
❑ BL 754148	Seven Days of Night	1969	5.00	10.00	20.00
❑ BL 754156	Someone Else's Arms	1970	5.00	10.00	20.00
❑ BL 754166	I Did It	1971	5.00	10.00	20.00
❑ BL 754187	I Call It Trouble	1972	5.00	10.00	20.00

CAPITOL

| ❑ ST-11377 | A Place in the Sun | 1975 | 3.00 | 6.00 | 12.00 |

ACUFF, ROY
CAPITOL

❑ T 617 [M]	Songs of the Smoky Mountains	1955	15.00	30.00	60.00
❑ DT 1870 [R]	The Best of Roy Acuff	1963	5.00	10.00	20.00
❑ T 1870 [M]	The Best of Roy Acuff	1963	7.50	15.00	30.00
❑ DT 2103 [R]	The Great Roy Acuff	1964	3.75	7.50	15.00
❑ T 2103 [M]	The Great Roy Acuff	1964	6.25	12.50	25.00
❑ ST 2276 [S]	The Voice of Country Music	1965	10.00	20.00	40.00
❑ T 2276 [M]	The Voice of Country Music	1965	7.50	15.00	30.00

COLUMBIA

❑ CL 9004 [10]	Songs of the Smoky Mountains	1949	50.00	100.00	200.00
❑ CL 9010 [10]	Old Time Barn Dance	1949	37.50	75.00	150.00
❑ CL 9013 [10]	Songs of the Saddle	1950	37.50	75.00	150.00
❑ FC 39998	Columbia Historic Edition	1985	2.50	5.00	10.00

ELEKTRA

| ❑ E-C 10-1-78 [DJ] | An Interview with Roy Acuff | 1978 | 6.25 | 12.50 | 25.00 |

HARMONY

❑ HL 7082 [M]	Great Speckled Bird	1958	6.25	12.50	25.00
❑ HL 7294 [M]	That Glory Bound Train	1961	5.00	10.00	20.00
❑ HL 7342 [M]	The Great Roy Acuff	196?	3.75	7.50	15.00
❑ HL 7376 [M]	Waiting for My Call to Glory	196?	3.75	7.50	15.00

HICKORY

❑ LPM-H-101 [M]	Once More It's Roy Acuff	1961	7.50	15.00	30.00
❑ LPM-109 [M]	King of Country Music — All-Time Greatest Hits	1962	6.25	12.50	25.00
❑ LPM-113 [M]	Roy Acuff — Star of the Grand Ole Opry	1963	6.25	12.50	25.00
❑ LPM-114 [M]	The World Is His Stage	1963	6.25	12.50	25.00
❑ LPM-115 [M]	Roy Acuff Sings American Folk Songs	1963	6.25	12.50	25.00
❑ LPM-117 [M]	Hand-Clapping Gospel Songs	1963	6.25	12.50	25.00
❑ LPM-119 [M]	Country Music Hall of Fame	1964	5.00	10.00	20.00
❑ LPM-125 [M]	Great Train Songs	1965	5.00	10.00	20.00
❑ LPM-134 [M]	Roy Acuff Sings Hank Williams	1966	10.00	20.00	40.00
❑ LPS-134 [S]	Roy Acuff Sings Hank Williams	1966	10.00	20.00	40.00
❑ LPS-139	Famous Opry Favorites	1967	5.00	10.00	20.00
❑ LPS-145	Living Legend	1968	5.00	10.00	20.00
❑ LPS-147	Treasury of Country Hits	1969	5.00	10.00	20.00
❑ LPS-156	Roy Acuff Time	1970	5.00	10.00	20.00
❑ DT-90698 [R]	Great Train Songs	1965	6.25	12.50	25.00

—Capitol Record Club edition

METRO

| ❑ M 508 [M] | Roy Acuff | 1965 | 3.75 | 7.50 | 15.00 |
| ❑ MS 508 [R] | Roy Acuff | 1965 | 2.50 | 5.00 | 10.00 |

MGM

❑ E-3707 [M]	Favorite Hymns	1958	12.50	25.00	50.00
❑ E-4044 [M]	Hymn Time	1962	6.25	12.50	25.00
❑ SE-4044 [R]	Hymn Time	196?	5.00	10.00	20.00

ROUNDER

| ❑ SS-23 | 1936-1939: Steamboat Whistle Blues | 1985 | 2.50 | 5.00 | 10.00 |
| ❑ SS-24 | 1939-1941: Fly Birdie Fly | 1985 | 2.50 | 5.00 | 10.00 |

ADAMS, BRYAN
A&M

| ❑ SP-3100 | Bryan Adams | 198? | 2.00 | 4.00 | 8.00 |

—Budget-line reissue of 4800

| ❑ SP-3154 | You Want It, You Got It | 198? | 2.00 | 4.00 | 8.00 |

—Budget-line reissue of 4864

❑ SP-3907	Into the Fire	1987	2.00	4.00	8.00
❑ SP-4800	Bryan Adams	1980	3.00	6.00	12.00
❑ SP-4864	You Want It, You Got It	1981	3.00	6.00	12.00
❑ SP-6-4919	Cuts Like a Knife	1983	2.00	4.00	8.00
❑ SP-5013	Reckless	1984	2.00	4.00	8.00
❑ SP-5327 [(2)]	Waking Up the Neighbours	1991	5.00	10.00	20.00

—Columbia House edition; the only U.S. vinyl of this LP

ADAMS, EDIE
DECCA

| ❑ DL 4488 [M] | Behind Those Swingin' Doors | 1964 | 5.00 | 10.00 | 20.00 |
| ❑ DL 74488 [S] | Behind Those Swingin' Doors | 1964 | 6.25 | 12.50 | 25.00 |

MGM

| ❑ E-3751 [M] | Music to Listen to Records To | 1959 | 10.00 | 20.00 | 40.00 |
| ❑ SE-3751 [S] | Music to Listen to Records To | 1959 | 15.00 | 30.00 | 60.00 |

ADAMS, FAYE
COLLECTABLES

| ❑ COL-5122 | Golden Classics | 1988 | 2.50 | 5.00 | 10.00 |

WARWICK

| ❑ W 2031 [M] | Shake a Hand | 1961 | 150.00 | 300.00 | 600.00 |

ADAMS, JERRI
COLUMBIA

| ❑ CL 916 [M] | It's Cool Inside | 1956 | 10.00 | 20.00 | 40.00 |

Number	Title (A Side/B Side)	Yr	VG	VG+	NM
❑ CL 1258 [M]	Play for Keeps	1958	10.00	20.00	40.00

ADAMS, JOHNNY
ANALOGUE PRODUCTIONS

❑ APP 028	Johnny Adams Sings Doc Pomus — The Real Me	199?	5.00	10.00	20.00

ARIOLA AMERICA

❑ SW 50038	After All the Good Is Gone	1978	3.75	7.50	15.00

CHELSEA

❑ CHL 525	Stand By Me	1977	6.25	12.50	25.00

HEP ME

❑ 159	Christmas in New Orleans	197?	3.75	7.50	15.00

ROUNDER

❑ 2044	From the Heart	1984	3.00	6.00	12.00

SSS INTERNATIONAL

❑ 5	Heart and Soul	1969	5.00	10.00	20.00

ADAMS, KAY
TOWER

❑ ST 5033 [S]	Wheels & Tears	1966	7.50	15.00	30.00
❑ T 5033 [M]	Wheels & Tears	1966	6.25	12.50	25.00
❑ ST 5069	Make Mine Country	1967	5.00	10.00	20.00
❑ T 5069 [M]	Make Mine Country	1967	6.25	12.50	25.00
❑ ST 5087	Alcohol & Tears	1968	5.00	10.00	20.00

ADAMS, MIKE, AND THE RED JACKETS
CROWN

❑ CST-255 [S]	Twist Contest	1962	7.50	15.00	30.00
❑ CST-312 [S]	Surfer's Beat	1963	7.50	15.00	30.00
—Black vinyl					
❑ CST-312 [S]	Surfer's Beat	1963	25.00	50.00	100.00
—Red vinyl					
❑ CLP-5255 [M]	Twist Contest	1962	6.25	12.50	25.00
❑ CLP-5312 [M]	Surfer's Beat	1963	6.25	12.50	25.00

ADAMS, PEPPER
INTERLUDE

❑ MO-502 [M]	Pepper Adams 5	1959	12.50	25.00	50.00
—Reissue of Mode 112					
❑ ST-1002 [S]	Pepper Adams 5	1959	10.00	20.00	40.00
—Reissue of Mode 112; remixed into stereo					

MODE

❑ LP-112 [M]	Pepper Adams 5	1957	20.00	40.00	80.00
—With Mel Lewis					

PRESTIGE

❑ PRST-7677	Encounter	1969	5.00	10.00	20.00
—With Zoot Sims					

REGENT

❑ MG-6066 [M]	The Cool Sound of Pepper Adams	1958	17.50	35.00	70.00

RIVERSIDE

❑ RLP 12-265 [M]	10 to 4 at the 5 Spot	1958	12.50	25.00	50.00
❑ RLP-1104 [S]	10 to 4 at the 5 Spot	1959	10.00	20.00	40.00

SAVOY

❑ MG-12211 [M]	The Cool Sound of Pepper Adams	196?	5.00	10.00	20.00
—Reissue of Regent 6066					

WARWICK

❑ W-2041 [M]	Out of This World	1961	10.00	20.00	40.00
—With Donald Byrd					

WORKSHOP JAZZ

❑ WSJ-219 [M]	Pepper Adams Plays the Compositions of Charles Mingus	1964	15.00	30.00	60.00
❑ WSJS-219 [M]	Pepper Adams Plays the Compositions of Charles Mingus	1964	17.50	35.00	70.00

WORLD PACIFIC

❑ PJM-407 [M]	Critic's Choice	1957	20.00	40.00	80.00
—With Mel Lewis					
❑ WPM-407 [M]	Critic's Choice	1958	17.50	35.00	70.00
—With Mel Lewis; reissue with new prefix					

ADAMS, PEPPER, AND JIMMY KNEPPER
METROJAZZ

❑ E-1004 [M]	The Pepper-Knepper Quartet	1958	20.00	40.00	80.00
❑ SE-1004 [S]	The Pepper-Knepper Quartet	1959	15.00	30.00	60.00

ADDEO, LEO
RCA CAMDEN

❑ CAL-510 [M]	Hawaii in Hi-Fi	1960	3.75	7.50	15.00
❑ CAS-510 [S]	Hawaii in Stereo	1960	5.00	10.00	20.00
❑ CAL-594 [M]	More Hawaii in Hi-Fi	1961	3.75	7.50	15.00
❑ CAS-594 [S]	More Hawaii in Hi-Fi	1961	5.00	10.00	20.00
❑ CAL-672 [M]	Great Standards with a Hawaiian Touch	1962	3.00	6.00	12.00
❑ CAS-672 [S]	Great Standards with a Hawaiian Touch	1962	3.75	7.50	15.00
❑ CAL-726 [M]	Organ and Chimes Play Christmas Carols	1962	3.00	6.00	12.00
❑ CAS-726 [S]	Organ and Chimes Play Christmas Carols	1962	3.75	7.50	15.00
❑ CAL-759 [M]	Songs of Hawaii	1963	3.00	6.00	12.00
❑ CAS-759 [S]	Songs of Hawaii	1963	3.75	7.50	15.00
❑ CAL-807 [M]	Calypso and Other Island Favorites	1963	3.00	6.00	12.00
❑ CAS-807 [S]	Calypso and Other Island Favorites	1963	3.75	7.50	15.00
❑ CAL-828 [M]	"Hello Dolly" and Other Favorites	1964	3.00	6.00	12.00
❑ CAS-828 [S]	"Hello Dolly" and Other Favorites	1964	3.75	7.50	15.00
❑ CAL-853 [M]	Hawaiian Paradise	1964	3.00	6.00	12.00
❑ CAS-853 [S]	Hawaiian Paradise	1964	3.75	7.50	15.00
❑ CAL-901 [M]	Far Away Places	1965	3.00	6.00	12.00
❑ CAS-901 [S]	Far Away Places	1965	3.75	7.50	15.00
❑ CAL-977 [M]	Musical Orchids from Hawaii	1966	3.00	6.00	12.00
❑ CAS-977 [S]	Musical Orchids from Hawaii	1966	3.75	7.50	15.00
❑ CAL-2134 [M]	"Love Is a Hurtin' Thing" and Other Favorites	1966	3.00	6.00	12.00
❑ CAS-2134 [S]	"Love Is a Hurtin' Thing" and Other Favorites	1966	3.75	7.50	15.00
❑ CAL-2211 [M]	The Magic of Hawaii	1967	3.00	6.00	12.00
❑ CAS-2211 [S]	The Magic of Hawaii	1967	3.75	7.50	15.00

RCA VICTOR

Number	Title (A Side/B Side)	Yr	VG	VG+	NM
❑ LPM-2414 [M]	Paradise Regained	1961	3.75	7.50	15.00
❑ LSA-2414 [S]	Paradise Regained	1961	7.50	15.00	30.00

ADDERLEY, CANNONBALL
BLUE NOTE

❑ BLP-1595 [M]	Somethin' Else	1958	25.00	50.00	100.00
—Regular version with W. 63rd St. address on label					
❑ BLP-1595 [M]	Somethin' Else	1958	37.50	75.00	150.00
—"Deep groove" version (deep indentation under label on both sides)					
❑ BLP-1595 [M]	Somethin' Else	1963	6.25	12.50	25.00
—With New York, USA address on label					
❑ BST-1595 [S]	Somethin' Else	1959	18.75	37.50	75.00
—Regular version with W. 63rd St. address on label					
❑ BST-1595 [S]	Somethin' Else	1959	25.00	50.00	100.00
—"Deep groove" version (deep indentation under label on both sides)					
❑ B1-46338	Somethin' Else	1997	5.00	10.00	20.00
—Audiophile reissue					
❑ BST-81595	Somethin' Else	199?	6.25	12.50	25.00
—Classic Records reissue					
❑ BST-81595 [S]	Somethin' Else	1963	5.00	10.00	20.00
—With New York, USA address on label					

CAPITOL

❑ ST 2203 [S]	Domination	1964	5.00	10.00	20.00
❑ ST 2216 [S]	Fiddler on the Roof	1965	5.00	10.00	20.00
❑ ST 2284 [S]	Live Session	1965	5.00	10.00	20.00
❑ ST 2399 [S]	Cannonball Adderley — Live!	1965	5.00	10.00	20.00
❑ ST 2531 [S]	Great Love Themes	1966	5.00	10.00	20.00
❑ ST 2617 [S]	Why Am I Treated So Bad?	1966	5.00	10.00	20.00
❑ ST-8-2663 [S]	Mercy, Mercy, Mercy!	1967	5.00	10.00	20.00
—Capitol Record Club edition					
❑ T 2663 [M]	Mercy, Mercy, Mercy!	1967	6.25	12.50	25.00
❑ T 2822 [M]	74 Miles Away — Walk Tall	1967	6.25	12.50	25.00

EMARCY

❑ MG-36043 [M]	Julian "Cannonball" Adderley	1955	15.00	30.00	60.00
❑ MG-36063 [M]	Julian "Cannonball" Adderley and Strings	1956	15.00	30.00	60.00
❑ MG-36077 [M]	In the Land of Hi-Fi	1956	15.00	30.00	60.00
❑ MG-36110 [M]	Sophisticated Swing	1957	15.00	30.00	60.00
❑ MG-36135 [M]	Cannonball's Sharpshooters	1958	15.00	30.00	60.00
❑ MG-36146 [M]	Jump for Joy	1958	15.00	30.00	60.00

FANTASY

❑ FSP 2 [DJ]	Big Man Sampler	1975	5.00	10.00	20.00

LIMELIGHT

❑ LM 82009 [M]	Cannonball and Coltrane	1964	6.25	12.50	25.00
—Reissue of Mercury 20449					
❑ LS 86009 [S]	Cannonball and Coltrane	1964	5.00	10.00	20.00
—Reissue of Mercury 60449					

MERCURY

❑ MG-20449 [M]	Cannonball Adderley Quintet in Chicago	1959	12.50	25.00	50.00
❑ MG-20530 [M]	Jump for Joy	1960	10.00	20.00	40.00
—Reissue of EmArcy 36146					
❑ MG-20531 [M]	Cannonball's Sharpshooters	1960	10.00	20.00	40.00
—Reissue of EmArcy 36135					
❑ MG-20616 [M]	Cannonball En Route	1961	10.00	20.00	40.00
❑ MG-20652 [M]	The Lush Side of Cannonball Adderley	1961	10.00	20.00	40.00
—Reissue of EmArcy 36063					
❑ SR-60449 [S]	Cannonball Adderley Quintet in Chicago	1960	10.00	20.00	40.00
❑ SR-60530 [S]	Jump for Joy	1960	7.50	15.00	30.00
❑ SR-60531 [S]	Cannonball's Sharpshooters	1960	7.50	15.00	30.00
❑ SR-60616 [S]	Cannonball En Route	1961	7.50	15.00	30.00
❑ SR-60652 [R]	The Lush Side of Cannonball Adderley	1961	7.50	15.00	30.00

RIVERSIDE

❑ RLP 12-269 [M]	Portrait of Cannonball	1958	12.50	25.00	50.00
❑ RLP 12-286 [M]	Things Are Getting Better	1959	12.50	25.00	50.00
❑ RLP 12-303 [M]	Cannonball Takes Charge	1959	12.50	25.00	50.00
❑ RLP 12-311 [M]	Cannonball Adderley Quintet in San Francisco	1959	12.50	25.00	50.00
❑ RLP 12-322 [M]	Them Dirty Blues	1960	12.50	25.00	50.00
❑ RLP 344 [M]	Cannonball Adderley Quintet at the Lighthouse	1960	10.00	20.00	40.00
❑ RLP 355 [M]	Cannonball Adderley and the Poll-Winners	1960	10.00	20.00	40.00
❑ RLP 377 [M]	African Waltz	1961	10.00	20.00	40.00
❑ RLP 388 [M]	Cannonball Adderley Quintet Plus	1961	10.00	20.00	40.00
❑ RLP 404 [M]	Cannonball Adderley Sextet In New York	1962	7.50	15.00	30.00
❑ RLP 416 [M]	Cannonball's Greatest Hits	1962	10.00	20.00	40.00
❑ RLP 433 [M]	Know What I Mean?	1962	7.50	15.00	30.00
❑ RLP 444 [M]	Jazz Workshop Revisited	1963	7.50	15.00	30.00
❑ RLP 455 [M]	Cannonball's Bossa Nova	1963	7.50	15.00	30.00
❑ RLP 477 [M]	Nippon Soul — Recorded in Concert in Tokyo	1964	6.25	12.50	25.00
❑ RM 499 [M]	Cannonball in Europe	1967	5.00	10.00	20.00
❑ RLP 1128 [S]	Things Are Getting Better	1959	10.00	20.00	40.00
❑ RLP 1148 [S]	Cannonball Takes Charge	1959	10.00	20.00	40.00
❑ RLP 1157 [S]	Cannonball Adderley Quintet in San Francisco	1959	10.00	20.00	40.00
❑ RLP 1170 [S]	Them Dirty Blues	1960	10.00	20.00	40.00
❑ RS 9344 [S]	Cannonball Adderley Quintet at the Lighthouse	1960	7.50	15.00	30.00
❑ RS 9355 [S]	Cannonball Adderley and the Poll-Winners	1960	7.50	15.00	30.00
❑ RS 9377 [S]	African Waltz	1961	7.50	15.00	30.00
❑ RS 9388 [S]	Cannonball Adderley Quintet Plus	1961	7.50	15.00	30.00
❑ RS 9404 [S]	Cannonball Adderley Sextet In New York	1962	7.50	15.00	30.00
❑ RS 9416 [S]	Cannonball's Greatest Hits	1962	7.50	15.00	30.00
❑ RS 9433 [S]	Know What I Mean?	1962	7.50	15.00	30.00
❑ RS 9444 [S]	Jazz Workshop Revisited	1963	7.50	15.00	30.00
❑ RS 9455 [S]	Cannonball's Bossa Nova	1963	7.50	15.00	30.00
❑ RS 9477 [S]	Nippon Soul — Recorded in Concert in Tokyo	1964	6.25	12.50	25.00

SAVOY

❑ MG-12018 [M]	Presenting Cannonball	1955	20.00	40.00	80.00
—Band pictured on cover					
❑ MG-12018 [M]	Presenting Cannonball	196?	10.00	20.00	40.00
—Cannonballs pictured on cover with band members merely listed					

A

Number	Title (A Side/B Side)	Yr	VG	VG+	NM
WONDERLAND/RIVERSIDE					
❑ RLP 1435 [M]	A Child's Introduction to Jazz	196?	12.50	25.00	50.00

—Adderley narrates an album introducing the works of such artists as Armstrong, Monk, Waller, etc.

ADDERLEY, CANNONBALL AND NAT
LIMELIGHT

Number	Title (A Side/B Side)	Yr	VG	VG+	NM
❑ LM 82032 [M]	Them Adderleys	1964	6.25	12.50	25.00
❑ LS 86032 [S]	Them Adderleys	1964	5.00	10.00	20.00

ADDERLEY, NAT
A&M

Number	Title (A Side/B Side)	Yr	VG	VG+	NM
❑ LP-2005 [M]	You, Baby	1968	6.25	12.50	25.00

—Mono is promo only

ATLANTIC

Number	Title (A Side/B Side)	Yr	VG	VG+	NM
❑ SD 1439 [S]	Autobiography	1965	5.00	10.00	20.00
❑ SD 1460 [S]	Sayin' Something	1966	5.00	10.00	20.00
❑ 1475 [M]	Live at Memory Lane	1967	5.00	10.00	20.00

CAPITOL

Number	Title (A Side/B Side)	Yr	VG	VG+	NM
❑ SVBB-11025 [(2)]	Cannonball Adderley Presents Soul Zodiac	1972	10.00	20.00	40.00

EMARCY

Number	Title (A Side/B Side)	Yr	VG	VG+	NM
❑ MG-36091 [M]	Introducing Nat Adderley	1955	20.00	40.00	80.00
❑ MG-36100 [M]	To the Ivy League from Nat	1956	20.00	40.00	80.00

JAZZLAND

Number	Title (A Side/B Side)	Yr	VG	VG+	NM
❑ JLP-47 [M]	Naturally!	1961	7.50	15.00	30.00
❑ JLP-75 [M]	In the Bag	1962	7.50	15.00	30.00
❑ JLP-947 [S]	Naturally!	1961	10.00	20.00	40.00
❑ JLP-975 [S]	In the Bag	1962	10.00	20.00	40.00

RIVERSIDE

Number	Title (A Side/B Side)	Yr	VG	VG+	NM
❑ RLP 12-285 [M]	Branching Out	1958	12.50	25.00	50.00
❑ RLP 12-301 [M]	Much Brass	1959	12.50	25.00	50.00
❑ RLP 12-318 [M]	The Work Song	1960	10.00	20.00	40.00
❑ RLP-330 [M]	That's Right!	1960	7.50	15.00	30.00
❑ RM-474 [M]	Little Big Horn!	1964	7.50	15.00	30.00
❑ RLP-1143 [S]	Much Brass	1959	12.50	25.00	50.00
❑ RLP-1167 [S]	The Work Song	1960	12.50	25.00	50.00
❑ RS-9330 [S]	That's Right!	1960	10.00	20.00	40.00
❑ RS-9474 [S]	Little Big Horn!	1964	10.00	20.00	40.00

SAVOY

Number	Title (A Side/B Side)	Yr	VG	VG+	NM
❑ MG-12021 [M]	That's Nat	1955	20.00	40.00	80.00

WING

Number	Title (A Side/B Side)	Yr	VG	VG+	NM
❑ MGW-60000 [M]	Introducing Nat Adderley	1956	12.50	25.00	50.00

ADRIAN AND THE SUNSETS
SUNSET

Number	Title (A Side/B Side)	Yr	VG	VG+	NM
❑ 63-601 [M]	Breakthrough	1963	20.00	40.00	80.00

—Black vinyl

| ❑ 63-601 [M] | Breakthrough | 1963 | 37.50 | 75.00 | 150.00 |

—Multi-color vinyl

| ❑ SD 63-601 [S] | Breakthrough | 1963 | 37.50 | 75.00 | 150.00 |

—Black vinyl

| ❑ SD 63-601 [S] | Breakthrough | 1963 | 75.00 | 150.00 | 300.00 |

—Multi-color vinyl

ADVANCEMENT, THE
PHILIPS

Number	Title (A Side/B Side)	Yr	VG	VG+	NM
❑ PHS 600328	The Advancement	1969	10.00	20.00	40.00

ADVENTURERS, THE (1)
COLUMBIA

Number	Title (A Side/B Side)	Yr	VG	VG+	NM
❑ CL 1747 [M]	Can't Stop Twistin'	1961	15.00	30.00	60.00
❑ CS 8547 [S]	Can't Stop Twistin'	1961	20.00	40.00	80.00

AEROSMITH
COLUMBIA

Number	Title (A Side/B Side)	Yr	VG	VG+	NM
❑ A3S 187 [DJ]	Pure Gold from Rock 'n' Roll's Golden Boys	1976	12.50	25.00	50.00

—Promo-only compilation of the first three albums

| ❑ JC 32005 | Aerosmith | 1977 | 2.00 | 4.00 | 8.00 |
| ❑ KC 32005 | Aerosmith | 1973 | 3.00 | 6.00 | 12.00 |

—Light blue cover, most (if not all) of which say "Featuring 'Dream On'" on front

| ❑ KC 32005 | Aerosmith | 1973 | 3.75 | 7.50 | 15.00 |

—Orange cover with correct title "Walking The Dog"

| ❑ KC 32005 | Aerosmith | 1973 | 5.00 | 10.00 | 20.00 |

—Orange cover with back cover typo "Walking The Dig"

| ❑ PC 32005 | Aerosmith | 1976 | 2.50 | 5.00 | 10.00 |

—Without bar code

| ❑ PC 32005 | Aerosmith | 1984 | 2.00 | 4.00 | 8.00 |

—With bar code

❑ JC 32847	Get Your Wings	1977	2.00	4.00	8.00
❑ KC 32847	Get Your Wings	1974	3.00	6.00	12.00
❑ KCQ 32847 [Q]	Get Your Wings	1974	6.25	12.50	25.00
❑ PC 32847	Get Your Wings	1976	2.50	5.00	10.00

—Without bar code

| ❑ PC 32847 | Get Your Wings | 1984 | 2.00 | 4.00 | 8.00 |

—With bar code

| ❑ JC 33479 | Toys in the Attic | 1977 | 2.50 | 5.00 | 10.00 |
| ❑ PC 33479 | Toys in the Attic | 1975 | 3.00 | 6.00 | 12.00 |

—Without bar code

| ❑ PC 33479 | Toys in the Attic | 1984 | 2.00 | 4.00 | 8.00 |

—With bar code

| ❑ PCQ 33479 [Q] | Toys in the Attic | 1975 | 6.25 | 12.50 | 25.00 |
| ❑ JC 34165 | Rocks | 1976 | 2.50 | 5.00 | 10.00 |

—Some copies have "Rocks" in quotes on the cover, others don't; no difference in value

| ❑ PC 34165 | Rocks | 1976 | 3.00 | 6.00 | 12.00 |

—Without bar code. Some copies have "Rocks" in quotes on the cover, others don't; no difference in value

| ❑ PC 34165 | Rocks | 1984 | 2.00 | 4.00 | 8.00 |

—With bar code

❑ PCQ 34165 [Q]	Rocks	1976	6.25	12.50	25.00
❑ JC 34856	Draw the Line	1977	3.00	6.00	12.00
❑ PC 34856	Draw the Line	198?	2.00	4.00	8.00
❑ PC2 35564 [(2)]	Live! Bootleg	1978	3.75	7.50	15.00
❑ FC 36050	Night in the Ruts	1979	2.50	5.00	10.00

Number	Title (A Side/B Side)	Yr	VG	VG+	NM
❑ PC 36050	Night in the Ruts	1984	2.00	4.00	8.00
❑ FC 36865	Aerosmith's Greatest Hits	1980	2.50	5.00	10.00
❑ PC 36865	Aerosmith's Greatest Hits	1984	2.00	4.00	8.00
❑ FC 38061	Rock in a Hard Place	1982	2.50	5.00	10.00
❑ PC 38061	Rock in a Hard Place	1984	2.00	4.00	8.00
❑ FC 40329	Classics Live	1986	2.50	5.00	10.00
❑ FC 40855	Classics Live, Vol. 2	1987	2.50	5.00	10.00
❑ FC 44487	Gems (1973-1982)	1989	2.50	5.00	10.00
❑ C 62088	Just Push Play	2001	2.50	5.00	10.00

GEFFEN

Number	Title (A Side/B Side)	Yr	VG	VG+	NM
❑ GHS 24091	Done with Mirrors	1985	2.50	5.00	10.00
❑ GHS 24162	Permanent Vacation	1987	2.50	5.00	10.00
❑ GHS 24254	Pump	1989	2.50	5.00	10.00

AESOP'S FABLES
CADET CONCEPT

Number	Title (A Side/B Side)	Yr	VG	VG+	NM
❑ LPS-323	In Due Time	1969	5.00	10.00	20.00

AFDEM, JEFF, AND THE SPRINGFIELD FLUTE
BURDETTE

Number	Title (A Side/B Side)	Yr	VG	VG+	NM
❑ 5162	Something	1969	10.00	20.00	40.00

AFFECTION COLLECTION, THE
EVOLUTION

Number	Title (A Side/B Side)	Yr	VG	VG+	NM
❑ 2007	The Affection Collection	1969	5.00	10.00	20.00

AFFINITY
PARAMOUNT

Number	Title (A Side/B Side)	Yr	VG	VG+	NM
❑ PAS-5027	Affinity	1970	6.25	12.50	25.00

AFGHAN WHIGS
COLUMBIA

Number	Title (A Side/B Side)	Yr	VG	VG+	NM
❑ C 69450	1969	1998	3.00	6.00	12.00

SUB POP

Number	Title (A Side/B Side)	Yr	VG	VG+	NM
❑ 60	Up In It	1990	3.00	6.00	12.00
❑ 60	Up In It	1990	6.25	12.50	25.00

—First pressings have orange vinyl and a different sleeve than the black vinyl version

| ❑ 130 | Congregation | 1992 | 5.00 | 10.00 | 20.00 |

—Import only; made in Germany (no U.S. vinyl)

| ❑ 238 | Gentlemen | 1993 | 3.00 | 6.00 | 12.00 |
| ❑ 353 | Black Love | 1996 | 3.00 | 6.00 | 12.00 |

ULTRASUEDE

Number	Title (A Side/B Side)	Yr	VG	VG+	NM
❑ 001	Big Top Halloween	1988	12.50	25.00	50.00

—Approximately 2,000 copies were made

AFRIKA CORPS
IRON CROSS/DACOIT

Number	Title (A Side/B Side)	Yr	VG	VG+	NM
❑ (# unknown)	Music to Kill By	1977	15.00	30.00	60.00

KLEEN KUT/LIMP

Number	Title (A Side/B Side)	Yr	VG	VG+	NM
❑ (# unknown)	Hello World!	1978	5.00	10.00	20.00

—As "The Korps"; blue vinyl

AGAPE
MARK

Number	Title (A Side/B Side)	Yr	VG	VG+	NM
❑ MRS-2170	Gospel Hard Rock	1971	30.00	60.00	120.00

RENRUT

Number	Title (A Side/B Side)	Yr	VG	VG+	NM
❑ 101	Victims of Tradition	1972	30.00	60.00	120.00

AGE OF REASON, THE
GEORGETOWNE

Number	Title (A Side/B Side)	Yr	VG	VG+	NM
❑ (no #)	The Age of Reason	1969	37.50	75.00	150.00

AGGREGATION, THE
LHI

Number	Title (A Side/B Side)	Yr	VG	VG+	NM
❑ 12008	Mind Odyssey	1967	100.00	200.00	400.00

AHBEZ, EDEN
DEL-FI

Number	Title (A Side/B Side)	Yr	VG	VG+	NM
❑ DFLP-1211 [M]	Eden's Island	1960	37.50	75.00	150.00
❑ DFST-1211 [S]	Eden's Island	1960	50.00	100.00	200.00

AIR SUPPLY
ARISTA

Number	Title (A Side/B Side)	Yr	VG	VG+	NM
❑ AL-4268	Lost in Love	1980	2.00	4.00	8.00
❑ AL-8024	Greatest Hits	1983	2.00	4.00	8.00
❑ AL-8283	Air Supply	1985	2.00	4.00	8.00
❑ AL-8292	Now and Forever	1985	—	3.00	6.00

—Budget-line reissue of 9587

| ❑ AL-8311 | Lost in Love | 1985 | — | 3.00 | 6.00 |

—Budget-line reissue of 4268

| ❑ AL-8312 | The One That You Love | 1985 | — | 3.00 | 6.00 |

—Budget-line reissue of 9551

❑ AL-8426	Hearts in Motion	1986	2.00	4.00	8.00
❑ AL-8528	The Christmas Album	1987	2.50	5.00	10.00
❑ AL-9551	The One That You Love	1981	2.00	4.00	8.00
❑ AL-9587	Now and Forever	1982	2.00	4.00	8.00

COLUMBIA

Number	Title (A Side/B Side)	Yr	VG	VG+	NM
❑ JC 35047	Love and Other Bruises	1977	3.75	7.50	15.00
❑ PC 35047	Love and Other Bruises	1981	2.00	4.00	8.00

—Budget-line reissue; much more common than the original "JC" version

MOBILE FIDELITY

Number	Title (A Side/B Side)	Yr	VG	VG+	NM
❑ 1-113	The One That You Love	1983	5.00	10.00	20.00

—Audiophile vinyl

NAUTILUS

Number	Title (A Side/B Side)	Yr	VG	VG+	NM
❑ NR-31	Lost in Love	1982	5.00	10.00	20.00

—Audiophile vinyl

AIRTO
CTI

Number	Title (A Side/B Side)	Yr	VG	VG+	NM
❑ CTSQ-6028 [Q]	Fingers	1974	5.00	10.00	20.00

Number	Title (A Side/B Side)	Yr	VG	VG+	NM

AKENS, JEWEL
ERA
| ❏ EL-110 [M] | The Birds and the Bees | 1965 | 7.50 | 15.00 | 30.00 |
| ❏ ES-110 [S] | The Birds and the Bees | 1965 | 25.00 | 50.00 | 100.00 |

AKIYOSHI, TOSHIKO
CANDID
❏ CD-8012 [M]	Toshiko Mariano Quartet	1960	10.00	20.00	40.00
❏ CD-8015 [M]	Toshiko Mariano	1960	10.00	20.00	40.00
❏ CS-9012 [S]	Toshiko Mariano Quartet	1960	12.50	25.00	50.00
❏ CS-9015 [S]	Toshiko Mariano	1960	12.50	25.00	50.00
DAUNTLESS
| ❏ DM-4308 [M] | The Country and Western Sounds of Jazz | 1963 | 10.00 | 20.00 | 40.00 |
| ❏ DS-6308 [S] | The Country and Western Sounds of Jazz | 1963 | 12.50 | 25.00 | 50.00 |
METROJAZZ
| ❏ E-1001 [M] | United Notions | 1958 | 12.50 | 25.00 | 50.00 |
| ❏ SE-1001 [S] | United Notions | 1959 | 10.00 | 20.00 | 40.00 |
NORGRAN
| ❏ MGN-22 [10] | Toshiko's Piano | 1954 | 37.50 | 75.00 | 150.00 |
STORYVILLE
| ❏ STLP-912 [M] | The Toshiko Trio | 1956 | 15.00 | 30.00 | 60.00 |
| ❏ STLP-918 [M] | Toshiko Akiyoshi, Her Trio, Her Quartet | 1957 | 15.00 | 30.00 | 60.00 |
VEE JAY
| ❏ LP-2505 [M] | Jazz in Japan | 1964 | 7.50 | 15.00 | 30.00 |
| —As "Toshiko Mariano and Her Big Band" | | | | | |
VERVE
| ❏ MGV-8273 [M] | The Many Sides of Toshiko | 1958 | 15.00 | 30.00 | 60.00 |
| ❏ V-8273 [M] | The Many Sides of Toshiko | 1961 | 6.25 | 12.50 | 25.00 |

AKIYOSHI, TOSHIKO, AND LEON SASH
VERVE
| ❏ MGV-8236 [M] | Toshiko and Leon Sash at Newport | 1958 | 15.00 | 30.00 | 60.00 |
| ❏ V-8236 [M] | Toshiko and Leon Sash at Newport | 1961 | 6.25 | 12.50 | 25.00 |

AKIYOSHI, TOSHIKO-LEW TABACKIN BIG BAND
RCA VICTOR
| ❏ CPL-2-2242 [(2)] | Road Time | 1977 | 5.00 | 10.00 | 20.00 |

ALABAMA
ACCORD
| ❏ SN-7132 | Pride of Dixie | 1981 | 2.50 | 5.00 | 10.00 |
ALABAMA
| ❏ ALA-78-9-01 | The Alabama Band | 1978 | 100.00 | 200.00 | 400.00 |
HEARTLAND
| ❏ HL 1186/7 [(2)] | The Very Best of Alabama | 1992 | 3.75 | 7.50 | 15.00 |
LSI
❏ 0177	Deuces Wild	1977	300.00	600.00	1200.
—As "Wild Country"					
❏ 0275	Wild Country	1975	750.00	1125.	1500.
—As "Wild Country"					
PLANTATION
| ❏ 44 | Wild Country | 1981 | 15.00 | 30.00 | 60.00 |
RCA
❏ 5649-1-R	The Touch	1986	2.00	4.00	8.00
❏ 6495-1-R	Just Us	1987	2.00	4.00	8.00
❏ 6825-1-R	Alabama Live	1988	2.00	4.00	8.00
❏ 8587-1-R	Southern Star	1989	2.00	4.00	8.00
❏ 9574-1-RDJ [DJ]	Open-Ended Interview	1988	7.50	15.00	30.00
RCA VICTOR
❏ AHL1-3644	My Home's in Alabama	1980	3.75	7.50	15.00
❏ AYL1-3644	My Home's in Alabama	1986	2.00	4.00	8.00
—"Best Buy Series" reissue					
❏ AHL1-3930	Feels So Right	1981	2.00	4.00	8.00
❏ AHL1-4229	Mountain Music	1982	2.00	4.00	8.00
❏ AHL1-4663	The Closer You Get	1983	2.00	4.00	8.00
❏ AHL1-4939	Roll On	1984	2.00	4.00	8.00
❏ AHL1-5339	40 Hour Week	1985	2.00	4.00	8.00
❏ ASL1-7014	Christmas	1985	3.00	6.00	12.00
—Original copies have gold embossed letters on cover					
❏ ASL1-7014	Christmas	1986	2.50	5.00	10.00
—Later copies have white non-embossed letters on cover					
❏ AHL1-7170	Greatest Hits	1986	2.00	4.00	8.00
SOUTHWAYS
| ❏ 101 | Pride of Dixie | 1981 | 2.50 | 5.00 | 10.00 |
| —Same album as on Accord | | | | | |

ALAIMO, STEVE
ABC-PARAMOUNT
❏ 501 [M]	Starring Steve Alaimo	1965	10.00	20.00	40.00
❏ S-501 [S]	Starring Steve Alaimo	1965	12.50	25.00	50.00
❏ 531 [M]	Where the Action Is	1965	10.00	20.00	40.00
❏ S-531 [S]	Where the Action Is	1965	12.50	25.00	50.00
❏ 551 [M]	Steve Alaimo Sings and Swings	1966	10.00	20.00	40.00
❏ S-551 [S]	Steve Alaimo Sings and Swings	1966	12.50	25.00	50.00
CHECKER
❏ LP-2981 [M]	Twist with Steve Alaimo	1962	37.50	75.00	150.00
❏ LP-2983 [M]	Mashed Potatoes	1962	37.50	75.00	150.00
❏ LP-2986 [M]	Every Day I Have to Cry	1963	37.50	75.00	150.00
CROWN
| ❏ CST-382 [R] | Steve Alaimo | 1963 | 3.75 | 7.50 | 15.00 |
| ❏ CLP-5382 [M] | Steve Alaimo | 1963 | 6.25 | 12.50 | 25.00 |

ALAN, BUDDY
CAPITOL
| ❏ ST-592 | Whole Lot of Somethin' | 1970 | 5.00 | 10.00 | 20.00 |

ALAN, BUDDY, AND DON RICH
CAPITOL
| ❏ ST-769 | We're Real Good Friends | 1971 | 5.00 | 10.00 | 20.00 |

ALBAM, MANNY
CORAL
❏ CRL 57142 [M]	The Jazz Greats of Our Time	1957	10.00	20.00	40.00
❏ CRL 57173 [M]	The Jazz Greats of Our Time, Volume 2	1957	10.00	20.00	40.00
❏ CRL 57207 [M]	West Side Story	1958	10.00	20.00	40.00
❏ CRL 57231 [M]	Sophisticated Lady — The Songs of Duke Ellington	1958	10.00	20.00	40.00
❏ CRL 59101 [M]	The Blues Is Everybody's Business	195?	10.00	20.00	40.00
❏ CRL 59102 [M]	A Gallery of Gershwin	1958	10.00	20.00	40.00
DECCA
| ❏ DL 74517 [S] | Music from West Side Story | 1964 | 5.00 | 10.00 | 20.00 |
DOT
| ❏ DLP-9004 [M] | Jazz New York | 1958 | 10.00 | 20.00 | 40.00 |
| ❏ DLP-9008 [M] | Steve's Song | 1958 | 10.00 | 20.00 | 40.00 |
IMPULSE!
| ❏ A-19 [M] | Jazz Goes to the Movies | 1962 | 6.25 | 12.50 | 25.00 |
| ❏ AS-19 [S] | Jazz Goes to the Movies | 1962 | 7.50 | 15.00 | 30.00 |
MERCURY
| ❏ MG-20325 [M] | With All My Love | 1958 | 10.00 | 20.00 | 40.00 |
RCA VICTOR
❏ LPM-1211 [M]	The RCA Victor Jazz Workshop	1956	12.50	25.00	50.00
❏ LPM-1279 [M]	The Drum Suite	1956	12.50	25.00	50.00
❏ LPM-2432 [M]	More Double Exposure	1961	5.00	10.00	20.00
❏ LSA-2432 [S]	More Double Exposure	1961	7.50	15.00	30.00
❏ LPM-2508 [M]	I Had the Craziest Dream	1962	5.00	10.00	20.00
❏ LSA-2508 [S]	I Had the Craziest Dream	1962	6.25	12.50	25.00
SOLID STATE
| ❏ SM-17009 [M] | The Soul of the City | 1966 | 5.00 | 10.00 | 20.00 |
| ❏ SS-18000 [S] | Brass on Fire | 1966 | 5.00 | 10.00 | 20.00 |
TOP RANK
| ❏ RM-313 [M] | Double Exposure | 1960 | 10.00 | 20.00 | 40.00 |
UNITED ARTISTS
| ❏ UAL-3079 [M] | Drum Feast | 1959 | 7.50 | 15.00 | 30.00 |
| ❏ UAS-6079 [S] | Drum Feast | 1959 | 10.00 | 20.00 | 40.00 |

ALBANY, JOE, AND WARNE MARSH
RIVERSIDE
| ❏ RLP 12-270 [M] | The Right Combination | 1958 | 20.00 | 40.00 | 80.00 |

ALBERGHETTI, ANNA MARIA
CAPITOL
❏ T 887 [M]	I Can't Resist You	1957	7.50	15.00	30.00
❏ ST 1379 [S]	Warm and Willing	1960	7.50	15.00	30.00
❏ T 1379 [M]	Warm and Willing	1960	5.00	10.00	20.00
CELEBRITY HOUSE
| ❏ TW 2001 | Christmas with Anna Maria Alberghetti | 1984 | 3.00 | 6.00 | 12.00 |
| —B-side by Reino Moisio | | | | | |
MERCURY
| ❏ MG-20056 [M] | Songs by Anna Maria Alberghetti | 1955 | 7.50 | 15.00 | 30.00 |
MGM
| ❏ E-4001 [M] | Love Makes the World Go 'Round | 1962 | 5.00 | 10.00 | 20.00 |
| ❏ SE-4001 [S] | Love Makes the World Go 'Round | 1962 | 6.25 | 12.50 | 25.00 |

ALBERT, EDDIE
COLUMBIA
| ❏ CL 2599 [M] | The Eddie Albert Album | 1967 | 5.00 | 10.00 | 20.00 |
| ❏ CS 9399 [S] | The Eddie Albert Album | 1967 | 5.00 | 10.00 | 20.00 |
DOT
| ❏ DLP-3109 [M] | High Upon a Mountain | 1958 | 5.00 | 10.00 | 20.00 |
| ❏ DLP-25109 [S] | High Upon a Mountain | 1958 | 6.25 | 12.50 | 25.00 |
KAPP
❏ KL-1000 [M]	One God	1954	7.50	15.00	30.00
❏ KL-1017 [M]	Eddie Albert and Margo	1956	7.50	15.00	30.00
❏ KL-1083 [M]	September Song	1958	6.25	12.50	25.00

ALBERT, THE
PERCEPTION
| ❏ 9 | The Albert | 1971 | 5.00 | 10.00 | 20.00 |

ALBERTS, AL
CORAL
| ❏ CRL 57259 [M] | A Man Has Got to Sing | 1959 | 6.25 | 12.50 | 25.00 |
| ❏ CRL 757259 [S] | A Man Has Got to Sing | 1959 | 7.50 | 15.00 | 30.00 |

ALBRIGHT, LOLA
COLUMBIA
❏ CL 1327 [M]	Dreamsville	1959	7.50	15.00	30.00
❏ CL 1327 [M]	Dreamsville	1959	10.00	20.00	40.00
❏ CS 8133 [S]	Dreamsville	1959	10.00	20.00	40.00
❏ CS 8133 [S]	Dreamsville	1959	12.50	25.00	50.00

ALBRIGHT, MAX
MOTIF
| ❏ 502 [M] | Mood for Max | 1956 | 15.00 | 30.00 | 60.00 |

ALCATRAZZ
CAPITOL
| ❏ ST-12385 | Disturbing the Peace | 1985 | 5.00 | 10.00 | 20.00 |
| ❏ ST-12477 | Dangerous Games | 1986 | 5.00 | 10.00 | 20.00 |
ROCSHIRE
| ❏ 22016 | No Parole from Rock 'n' Roll | 1983 | 6.25 | 12.50 | 25.00 |
| ❏ 22020 | Live Sentence | 1984 | 5.00 | 10.00 | 20.00 |

ALDA, ROBERT
ROULETTE
| ❏ R-25006 [M] | Robert Alda | 1959 | 6.25 | 12.50 | 25.00 |
| ❏ SR-25006 [S] | Robert Alda | 1959 | 7.50 | 15.00 | 30.00 |

A

Number	Title (A Side/B Side)	Yr	VG	VG+	NM
ALEONG, ALI, AND THE NOBLES					
REPRISE					
❏ R-6011 [M]	Twistin' the Hits	1962	6.25	12.50	25.00
❏ R9-6011 [S]	Twistin' the Hits	1962	7.50	15.00	30.00
❏ R-6020 [M]	C'mon Baby, Let's Dance	1962	6.25	12.50	25.00
❏ R9-6020 [S]	C'mon Baby, Let's Dance	1962	7.50	15.00	30.00
VEE JAY					
❏ LP-1060 [M]	Come Surf with Me	1963	7.50	15.00	30.00
❏ SR-1060 [S]	Come Surf with Me	1963	12.50	25.00	50.00
ALESS, TONY					
ROOST					
❏ RST-2202 [M]	Tony Aless and His Long Island Suite	1955	20.00	40.00	80.00
ALEXANDER, ARTHUR					
DOT					
❏ DLP 3434 [M]	You Better Move On	1962	25.00	50.00	100.00
❏ DLP 25434 [S]	You Better Move On	1962	40.00	80.00	160.00
WARNER BROS.					
❏ BS 2592	Arthur Alexander	1972	6.25	12.50	25.00
ALEXANDER, BOB					
See AL KLINK AND BOB ALEXANDER.					
ALEXANDER, JOE, AND BOBBY TIMMONS					
JAZZLAND					
❏ JLP-23 [M]	Blue Jubilee	1960	7.50	15.00	30.00
❏ JLP-923 [S]	Blue Jubilee	1960	10.00	20.00	40.00
ALEXANDER, MONTY					
PACIFIC JAZZ					
❏ PJ-86 [M]	Alexander the Great	1966	5.00	10.00	20.00
❏ ST-86 [S]	Alexander the Great	1966	6.25	12.50	25.00
❏ PJ-10094 [M]	Spooky	1966	5.00	10.00	20.00
❏ ST-20094 [S]	Spooky	1966	6.25	12.50	25.00
RCA VICTOR					
❏ LPM-3930 [M]	Zing	1968	6.25	12.50	25.00
ALEXANDER, ROLAND					
NEW JAZZ					
❏ NJLP-8267 [M]	Pleasure Bent	1962	12.50	25.00	50.00
—Purple label					
❏ NJLP-8267 [M]	Pleasure Bent	1965	6.25	12.50	25.00
—Blue label, trident at right					
ALEXANDER'S TIMELESS BLOOZBAND					
SMASK					
❏ 1001 [M]	Alexander's Timeless Bloozband	1967	50.00	100.00	200.00
UNI					
❏ 73021	For Sale	1968	6.25	12.50	25.00
ALEXANDRIA, LOREZ					
ARGO					
❏ LP-663 [M]	Early in the Morning	1960	10.00	20.00	40.00
❏ LPS-663 [S]	Early in the Morning	1960	12.50	25.00	50.00
—With the Ramsey Lewis Trio					
❏ LP-682 [M]	Sing No Sad Songs for Me	1961	10.00	20.00	40.00
❏ LPS-682 [S]	Sing No Sad Songs for Me	1961	12.50	25.00	50.00
❏ LP-694 [M]	Deep Roots	1962	10.00	20.00	40.00
❏ LPS-694 [S]	Deep Roots	1962	12.50	25.00	50.00
❏ LP-720 [M]	For Swingers Only	1963	10.00	20.00	40.00
❏ LPS-720 [S]	For Swingers Only	1963	12.50	25.00	50.00
CADET					
❏ LPS-682	Sing No Sad Songs for Me	1966	5.00	10.00	20.00
—Reissue of Argo 682					
IMPULSE!					
❏ A-62 [M]	Alexandria the Great	1964	6.25	12.50	25.00
❏ AS-62 [S]	Alexandria the Great	1964	7.50	15.00	30.00
❏ A-76 [M]	More of the Great Lorez Alexandria	1965	6.25	12.50	25.00
❏ AS-76 [S]	More of the Great Lorez Alexandria	1965	7.50	15.00	30.00
KING					
❏ 542 [M]	This Is Lorez	1956	25.00	50.00	100.00
—Black label, crownless "King"					
❏ 565 [M]	Lorez Sings Prez	1956	25.00	50.00	100.00
—Black label, crownless "King"					
❏ 657 [M]	The Band Swings, Lorez Sings	1959	25.00	50.00	100.00
—Black label, crownless "King"					
❏ S-657 [S]	The Band Swings, Lorez Sings	1959	37.50	75.00	150.00
—Dark blue label, crownless "King"					
❏ 676 [M]	Singing Songs Everyone Knows	1959	25.00	50.00	100.00
—Black label, crownless "King"					
ALFRED, CHUZ					
SAVOY					
❏ MG-12030 [M]	Jazz Young Blood	1955	15.00	30.00	60.00
—With Ola Hanson and Chuck Lee					
ALICE IN CHAINS					
COLUMBIA					
❏ CAS 2192 [EP]	We Die Young	1990	5.00	10.00	20.00
—Five-song promo-only issue predating their first LP					
❏ C2 57804 [(2)]	Jar of Flies/Sap	1994	5.00	10.00	20.00
—Two cassette/CD EP releases in one vinyl package					
❏ C2 67248 [(2)]	Alice in Chains	1995	3.75	7.50	15.00
ALIOTTA-HAYNES-JEREMIAH					
AMPEX					
❏ A-10108	Aliotta-Haynes Music	1970	5.00	10.00	20.00
—As "Aliota-Haynes"					
❏ A-10119	Aliotta-Haynes-Jeremiah	1970	5.00	10.00	20.00
BIG FOOT					
❏ 714	Lake Shore Drive	1978	6.25	12.50	25.00
LITTLE FOOT					
❏ 711	Slippin' Away	1977	5.00	10.00	20.00
ALIVE AND KICKING					
ROULETTE					
❏ SR 42052	Alive and Kicking	1970	5.00	10.00	20.00
ALL AMERICAN RUMBLERS, THE					
GONE					
❏ LP-5006 [M]	Destination Dixie	1959	12.50	25.00	50.00
ALL STARS, THE					
GRAMOPHONE					
❏ 20192	Boogie Woogie	196?	12.50	25.00	50.00
ALLAN, DAVIE, AND THE ARROWS					
TOWER					
❏ DT 5002 [R]	Apache '65	1965	7.50	15.00	30.00
❏ T 5002 [M]	Apache '65	1965	10.00	20.00	40.00
❏ DT 5043 [R]	The Wild Angels	1966	5.00	10.00	20.00
❏ T 5043 [M]	The Wild Angels	1966	7.50	15.00	30.00
❏ DT 5056 [R]	The Wild Angels, Vol. II	1967	5.00	10.00	20.00
❏ T 5056 [M]	The Wild Angels, Vol. II	1967	7.50	5.00	30.00
❏ DT 5074 [R]	Devil's Angel	1967	5.00	10.00	20.00
❏ T 5074 [M]	Devil's Angel	1967	7.50	15.00	30.00
❏ DT 5078 [R]	Blues Theme	1967	10.00	20.00	40.00
❏ T 5078 [M]	Blues Theme	1967	12.50	25.00	50.00
❏ DT 5083 [R]	Mondo Hollywood	1968	5.00	10.00	20.00
❏ T 5083 [M]	Mondo Hollywood	1968	7.50	15.00	30.00
❏ DT 5094 [R]	Cycle-Delic Sounds	1968	12.50	25.00	50.00
❏ T 5094 [M]	Cycle-Delic Sounds	1968	25.00	50.00	100.00
ALLEN, BYRON, TRIO					
ESP-DISK'					
❏ 1005 [M]	The Byron Allen Trio	1965	5.00	10.00	20.00
❏ S-1005 [S]	The Byron Allen Trio	1965	6.25	12.50	25.00
ALLEN, DAVE					
INTERNATIONAL ARTISTS					
❏ 11	Color Blind	1969	15.00	30.00	60.00
—Original pressing					
❏ 11	Color Blind	1979	5.00	10.00	20.00
—Repressing with "RE2" and "Masterfonics" in dead wax					
ALLEN, DAVID					
EVEREST					
❏ SD-1224 [S]	David Allen	1964	5.00	10.00	20.00
PACIFIC JAZZ					
❏ PJM-408 [M]	A Sure Thing	1957	15.00	30.00	60.00
❏ ST-1006 [S]	A Sure Thing	1959	15.00	30.00	60.00
WORLD PACIFIC					
❏ WP-1250 [M]	Let's Face the Music and Dance	1958	10.00	20.00	40.00
❏ ST-1295 [S]	David Allen Sings the Jerome Kern Songbook	1960	7.50	15.00	30.00
❏ WP-1295 [M]	David Allen Sings the Jerome Kern Songbook	1960	7.50	15.00	30.00
ALLEN, DAYTON					
GRAND AWARD					
❏ GA 33-424 [M]	Why Not?	1960	6.25	12.50	25.00
ALLEN, HENRY "RED"					
AMERICAN RECORDING SOCIETY					
❏ G-436 [M]	Traditional Jazz	195?	10.00	20.00	40.00
COLUMBIA					
❏ CS 9247 [S]	Feelin' Good	1966	5.00	10.00	20.00
RCA VICTOR					
❏ LPM-1509 [M]	Ride, Red, Ride in Hi-Fi	1957	12.50	25.00	50.00
SWINGVILLE					
❏ SWLP-2034 [M]	Mr. Allen	1962	10.00	20.00	40.00
—Purple label					
❏ SWLP-2034 [M]	Mr. Allen	1965	5.00	10.00	20.00
—Blue label, trident logo at right					
❏ SWST-2034 [S]	Mr. Allen	1962	12.50	25.00	50.00
—Red label					
❏ SWST-2034 [S]	Mr. Allen	1965	6.25	12.50	25.00
—Blue label, trident logo at right					
VERVE					
❏ MGV-1025 [M]	Red Allen Plays King Oliver	1959	12.50	25.00	50.00
❏ V-1025 [M]	Red Allen Plays King Oliver	1961	5.00	10.00	20.00
❏ V6-1025 [S]	Red Allen Plays King Oliver	1961	6.25	12.50	25.00
"X"					
❏ LVA-3033 [M]	Ridin' with Red	1955	12.50	25.00	50.00
ALLEN, HENRY "RED", AND RED NORVO					
BRUNSWICK					
❏ BL 58044 [10]	Battle of Jazz, Vol. 6	1953	15.00	30.00	60.00
ALLEN, HENRY "RED", AND KID ORY					
VERVE					
❏ MGV-1018 [M]	Henry "Red" Allen Meets Kid Ory	1957	12.50	25.00	50.00
❏ V-1018 [M]	Henry "Red" Allen Meets Kid Ory	1961	5.00	10.00	20.00
❏ V6-1018 [S]	Henry "Red" Allen Meets Kid Ory	1961	5.00	10.00	20.00
❏ MGV-1020 [M]	We've Got Rhythm	1958	12.50	25.00	50.00
❏ V-1020 [M]	We've Got Rhythm	1961	5.00	10.00	20.00
❏ V6-1020 [S]	We've Got Rhythm	1961	5.00	10.00	20.00
❏ MGVS-6076 [S]	Henry "Red" Allen Meets Kid Ory	1959	10.00	20.00	40.00
❏ MGVS-6121 [S]	We've Got Rhythm	1959	10.00	20.00	40.00
ALLEN, HENRY "RED"; JACK TEAGARDEN; KID ORY					
VERVE					
❏ MGV-8233 [M]	Red Allen, Jack Teagarden & Kid Ory at Newport	1958	12.50	25.00	50.00
❏ V-8233 [M]	Red Allen, Jack Teagarden & Kid Ory at Newport	1961	5.00	10.00	20.00

Number	Title (A Side/B Side)	Yr	VG	VG+	NM
ALLEN, LEE					
EMBER					
❑ ELP-200 [M]	Walkin' with Mr. Lee	1958	125.00	250.00	500.00
—Red label					
❑ ELP-200 [M]	Walkin' with Mr. Lee	1959	50.00	100.00	200.00
—White "logs" label					
❑ ELP-200 [M]	Walkin' with Mr. Lee	1961	25.00	50.00	100.00
—Red and black label					
ALLEN, PHYLICIA					
CASABLANCA					
❑ NBLP-7108	Josephine Superstar	1978	6.25	12.50	25.00
ALLEN, RAY, AND THE UPBEATS					
BLAST					
❑ BLP-6804 [M]	A Tribute to Six	1962	30.00	60.00	120.00
ALLEN, REX					
BUENA VISTA					
❑ BV-3307 [M]	Rex Allen Sings 16 Golden Hits	1961	10.00	20.00	40.00
DECCA					
❑ DL 8402 [M]	Under Western Skies	1956	12.50	25.00	50.00
❑ DL 8776 [M]	Mister Cowboy	1959	10.00	20.00	40.00
❑ DL 75011 [S]	The Smooth Country Sound of Rex Allen	1968	5.00	10.00	20.00
❑ DL 75205	The Touch of God's Hand	1970	5.00	10.00	20.00
❑ DL 78776 [S]	Mister Cowboy	1959	15.00	30.00	60.00
HACIENDA					
❑ WWLP-101 [M]	Rex Allen Sings	1960	50.00	100.00	200.00
MERCURY					
❑ MG-20719 [M]	Faith of a Man	1962	6.25	12.50	25.00
❑ MG-20752 [M]	Rex Allen Sings and Tells Tales	1963	6.25	12.50	25.00
❑ SR-60719 [S]	Faith of a Man	1962	7.50	15.00	30.00
❑ SR-60752 [S]	Rex Allen Sings and Tells Tales	1963	7.50	15.00	30.00
ALLEN, RICHIE					
IMPERIAL					
❑ LP-9212 [M]	Stranger from Durango	1962	10.00	20.00	40.00
❑ LP-9229 [M]	The Rising Surf	1963	20.00	40.00	80.00
❑ LP-9243 [M]	Surfer's Slide	1963	20.00	40.00	80.00
❑ LP-12212 [S]	Stranger from Durango	1962	12.50	25.00	50.00
❑ LP-12229 [S]	The Rising Surf	1963	37.50	75.00	150.00
❑ LP-12243 [S]	Surfer's Slide	1963	37.50	75.00	150.00
ALLEN, ROSALIE					
GRAND AWARD					
❑ GA-33-330 [M]	Songs of the Golden West	1957	10.00	20.00	40.00
RCA VICTOR					
❑ LPM-2313 [M]	Rosalie Allen	1961	5.00	10.00	20.00
❑ LSP-2313 [S]	Rosalie Allen	1961	6.25	12.50	25.00
WALDORF					
❑ 150 [10]	Rosalie Allen Sings Country and Western	1955	20.00	40.00	80.00
ALLEN, STEVE					
CASABLANCA					
❑ 811366-1	Funny Fone Calls	1983	2.00	4.00	8.00
—Reissue of Dot 3472					
❑ 811367-1	More Funny Fone Calls	1983	2.00	4.00	8.00
—Reissue of Dot 3517					
CORAL					
❑ CRL 57004 [M]	Music for Tonight	1955	6.25	12.50	25.00
❑ CRL 57015 [M]	Tonight at Midnight	1956	6.25	12.50	25.00
❑ CRL 57018 [M]	Jazz for Tonight	1956	6.25	12.50	25.00
❑ CRL 57019 [M]	Steve Sings	1956	6.25	12.50	25.00
❑ CRL 57028 [M]	Let's Dance	1956	6.25	12.50	25.00
❑ CRL 57048 [M]	Allen Plays Allen	1956	6.25	12.50	25.00
❑ CRL 57070 [M]	The Steve Allen Show	1957	6.25	12.50	25.00
❑ CRL 57138 [M]	Romantic Rendezvous	1957	5.00	10.00	20.00
❑ CRL 57442 [M]	Songs Everybody Knows	1964	3.75	7.50	15.00
❑ CRL 757442 [R]	Songs Everybody Knows	1964	3.00	6.00	12.00
DECCA					
❑ DL 8151 [M]	Steve Allen's All Star Jazz Concert, Vol. 1	1955	7.50	15.00	30.00
❑ DL 8152 [M]	Steve Allen's All Star Jazz Concert, Vol. 2	1955	7.50	15.00	30.00
DOT					
❑ DLP 3472 [M]	Funny Fone Calls	1963	5.00	10.00	20.00
❑ DLP 3473 [M]	12 Greatest Hits	1963	5.00	10.00	20.00
❑ DLP 3480 [M]	Bossa Nova Jazz	1963	3.75	7.50	15.00
❑ DLP 3515 [M]	Gravy Waltz and 11 Current Hits!	1963	3.75	7.50	15.00
❑ DLP 3517 [M]	More Funny Fone Calls	1963	5.00	10.00	20.00
❑ DLP 3519 [M]	Steve Allen Plays the Piano Greats	1963	3.75	7.50	15.00
❑ DLP 3530 [M]	Steve Allen Sings	1963	3.75	7.50	15.00
❑ DLP 3538 [M]	Cuano Caliente El Sol and More	1963	3.75	7.50	15.00
❑ DLP 3560 [M]	Great Ragtime Hits	1963	3.75	7.50	15.00
❑ DLP 3587 [M]	Songs from the Steve Allen TV Show	1964	3.00	6.00	12.00
❑ DLP 3597 [M]	Steve Allen, His Piano and Orchestra	1964	3.00	6.00	12.00
❑ DLP 3624 [M]	I Play for You	1965	3.00	6.00	12.00
❑ DLP 3683 [M]	Rhythm and Blues	1966	3.00	6.00	12.00
❑ DLP 25380 [S]	Bossa Nova Jazz	1963	5.00	10.00	20.00
❑ DLP 25515 [S]	Gravy Waltz and 11 Current Hits!	1963	5.00	10.00	20.00
❑ DLP 25519 [S]	Steve Allen Plays the Piano Greats	1963	5.00	10.00	20.00
❑ DLP 25530 [S]	Steve Allen Sings	1963	5.00	10.00	20.00
❑ DLP 25538 [S]	Cuano Caliente El Sol and More	1963	5.00	10.00	20.00
❑ DLP 25560 [S]	Great Ragtime Hits	1963	5.00	10.00	20.00
❑ DLP 25587 [S]	Songs from the Steve Allen TV Show	1964	3.75	7.50	15.00
❑ DLP 25597 [S]	Steve Allen, His Piano and Orchestra	1964	3.75	7.50	15.00
❑ DLP 25624 [S]	I Play for You	1965	3.75	7.50	15.00
❑ DLP 25683 [S]	Rhythm and Blues	1966	3.75	7.50	15.00
FORUM					
❑ F-9014 [M]	Steve Allen at the Round Table	196?	5.00	10.00	20.00
❑ FS-9014 [S]	Steve Allen at the Round Table	196?	3.75	7.50	15.00

Number	Title (A Side/B Side)	Yr	VG	VG+	NM
HAMILTON					
❑ HLP 132 [M]	Some of My Favorites	196?	3.00	6.00	12.00
❑ HLP 12132 [S]	Some of My Favorites	196?	3.75	7.50	15.00
ROULETTE					
❑ R-25053 [M]	Steve Allen at the Round Table	1959	6.25	12.50	25.00
❑ SR-25053 [S]	Steve Allen at the Round Table	1959	5.00	10.00	20.00
SIGNATURE					
❑ SM 1004 [M]	Man in the Street	1959	7.50	15.00	30.00
❑ SM 1021 [M]	Monday Nights	1960	7.50	15.00	30.00
ALLEN, STEVE, AND MANNY ALBAM					
DOT					
❑ DLP 3194 [M]	...And All That Jazz	1959	6.25	12.50	25.00
❑ DLP 25194 [S]	...And All That Jazz	1959	5.00	10.00	20.00
ALLEN, TONY					
CROWN					
❑ CST-240 [S]	Rock and Roll with Tony Allen	1961	25.00	50.00	100.00
❑ CLP-5231 [M]	Rock and Roll with Tony Allen	1960	25.00	50.00	100.00
—Black label					
❑ CLP-5231 [M]	Rock and Roll with Tony Allen	1961	15.00	30.00	60.00
—Gray label					
ALLEN, WOODY					
BELL					
❑ 6008	The Wonderful Wacky World of Woody Allen	1967	5.00	10.00	20.00
CAPITOL					
❑ ST 2986	The Third Woody Allen Album	1968	6.25	12.50	25.00
CASABLANCA					
❑ NBLP2-7145 [(2)]	Woody Allen: Stand-Up Comic 1964-1968	1979	3.75	7.50	15.00
—Compilation of material from Colpix and Capitol LPs (different from either UA collection)					
COLPIX					
❑ CP 488 [M]	Woody Allen 2	1965	7.50	15.00	30.00
❑ SCP 488 [R]	Woody Allen 2	1965	6.25	12.50	25.00
❑ CP 518 [M]	Woody Allen	1964	7.50	15.00	30.00
UNITED ARTISTS					
❑ UA-LA849-J2 [(2)]	Woody Allen: Stand-Up Comic 1964-1968	1977	5.00	10.00	20.00
—Compilation of material from Colpix and Capitol LPs (different from UA 9968)					
❑ UAS 9968 [(2)]	Woody Allen: The Nightclub Years	1972	5.00	10.00	20.00
—Compilation of material from Colpix and Capitol LPs					
ALLEN AND ROSSI					
ABC-PARAMOUNT					
❑ ABC-270 [M]	Hello Dere	1962	5.00	10.00	20.00
❑ ABC-445 [M]	One More Time Hello Dere	1963	5.00	10.00	20.00
MERCURY					
❑ MG-21077 [M]	The Adventures of Batman and Rubin	1966	10.00	20.00	40.00
❑ SR-61077 [S]	The Adventures of Batman and Rubin	1966	12.50	25.00	50.00
—The above LP was written by "Batman" creator Bob Kane as a parody of his own comic book					
REPRISE					
❑ R-6104 [M]	Too Funny for Words	1964	5.00	10.00	20.00
ROULETTE					
❑ R-507 [M]	The Truth About the Green Hornet	1966	5.00	10.00	20.00
❑ R-508 [M]	Dedicated to Our Armed Forces	1967	5.00	10.00	20.00
ALLIN, GG					
ALIVE					
❑ 0001	Brutality and Bloodshed for All	199?	2.50	5.00	10.00
❑ 0012	Terror in America	199?	2.50	5.00	10.00
BLACK & BLUE					
❑ (# unknown)	Eat My Fuc	1988	3.00	6.00	12.00
—Reissue of Blood LP of the same name					
❑ (# unknown)	Banned in Boston	1989	3.00	6.00	12.00
❑ 006053-X	Always Was, Is and Always Shall Be	1985	12.50	25.00	50.00
—Reissue of Orange original					
BLOOD					
❑ (# unknown)	Eat My Fuc	198?	12.50	25.00	50.00
—Hand-decorated plain cover					
HOMESTEAD					
❑ HMS-069	You Give Love a Bad Name	1987	3.00	6.00	12.00
ORANGE					
❑ (# unknown)	Always Was, Is and Always Shall Be	1980	25.00	50.00	100.00
ALLISON, GENE					
VEE JAY					
❑ LP-1009 [M]	Gene Allison	1959	75.00	150.00	300.00
—Maroon label					
❑ LP-1009 [M]	Gene Allison	196?	25.00	50.00	100.00
—Black label, oval or brackets logo					
ALLISON, KEITH					
COLUMBIA					
❑ CL 2641 [M]	Keith Allison In Action	1967	6.25	12.50	25.00
❑ CS 9441 [S]	Keith Allison In Action	1967	6.25	12.50	25.00
ALLISON, LUTHER					
DELMARK					
❑ DS-625	Love Me, Mama	1969	6.25	12.50	25.00
GORDY					
❑ G-964	Bad News Is Coming	1973	2.50	5.00	10.00
❑ G-967	Luther's Blues	1974	2.50	5.00	10.00
❑ G-974	Night Life	1976	2.50	5.00	10.00
ALLISON, MOSE					
ATLANTIC					
❑ SD 1389 [S]	I Don't Worry About a Thing	1962	5.00	10.00	20.00
❑ SD 1398 [S]	Swingin' Machine	1963	5.00	10.00	20.00
COLUMBIA					
❑ CL 1444 [M]	The Transfiguration of Hiram Brown	1960	5.00	10.00	20.00

Number	Title (A Side/B Side)	Yr	VG	VG+	NM
❏ CL 1565 [M]	I Love the Life I Live	1960	5.00	10.00	20.00
—Red and black label with six "eye" logos					
❏ CS 8240 [S]	The Transfiguration of Hiram Brown	1960	6.25	12.50	25.00
❏ CS 8365 [S]	I Love the Life I Live	1960	6.25	12.50	25.00
—Red and black label with six "eye" logos					
EPIC					
❏ BA 17031 [S]	Take to the Hills	1962	5.00	10.00	20.00
PRESTIGE					
❏ PRLP-7091 [M]	Back Country Suite	1957	15.00	30.00	60.00
—With "W. 50th St., NYC" address on label					
❏ PRLP-7121 [M]	Local Color	1958	15.00	30.00	60.00
—With "W. 50th St., NYC" address on label					
❏ PRLP-7137 [M]	Young Man Blues	1958	15.00	30.00	60.00
—With "W. 50th St., NYC" address on label					
❏ PRLP-7152 [M]	Creek Bank	1959	10.00	20.00	40.00
—Yellow label with Bergenfield, NJ address on label					
❏ PRLP-7189 [M]	Autumn Song	1960	10.00	20.00	40.00
—Yellow label with Bergenfield, NJ address on label					
❏ PRLP-7215 [M]	Ramblin' with Mose	1961	10.00	20.00	40.00
—Yellow label with Bergenfield, NJ address on label					
❏ PRLP-7279 [M]	Mose Allison Sings (The Seventh Son)	1963	10.00	20.00	40.00
—Yellow label with Bergenfield, NJ address on label					
❏ PRST-7279 [S]	Mose Allison Sings (The Seventh Son)	196?	6.25	12.50	25.00
—Blue label, trident logo at right					
❏ PRST-7279 [S]	Mose Allison Sings (The Seventh Son)	1963	12.50	25.00	50.00
—Silver label					
❏ PRLP-7423 [M]	Down Home Piano	1966	5.00	10.00	20.00
—Blue label, trident logo at right					
❏ PRST-7423 [S]	Down Home Piano	1966	6.25	12.50	25.00
—Blue label, trident logo at right					
❏ PRLP-7446 [M]	Mose Allison Plays for Lovers	1967	6.25	12.50	25.00
❏ PRST-7446 [S]	Mose Allison Plays for Lovers	1967	5.00	10.00	20.00

ALLMAN, DUANE
CAPRICORN

❏ 2CP 0108 [(2)]	An Anthology	1972	5.00	10.00	20.00
❏ 2CP 0139 [(2)]	An Anthology, Vol. II	1974	5.00	10.00	20.00
POLYDOR					
❏ PD-1-6338	The Best of Duane Allman	1981	3.00	6.00	12.00
❏ 827563-1	The Best of Duane Allman	1984	2.00	4.00	8.00

ALLMAN, DUANE AND GREGG
BOLD

❏ 33-301	Duane and Gregg Allman	197?	3.00	6.00	12.00
—Non-gatefold cover					
❏ 33-301	Duane and Gregg Allman	1972	6.25	12.50	25.00
—Gatefold cover					

ALLMAN, SHELDON
DEL-FI

❏ DFLP-1213 [M]	Sing Along with Drac	1961	10.00	20.00	40.00
HIFI					
❏ R-415 [M]	Folk Songs for the 21st Century	1960	10.00	20.00	40.00

ALLMAN BROTHERS BAND, THE
ARISTA

❏ AL 9535	Reach for the Sky	1980	2.50	5.00	10.00
❏ AL 9564	Brothers of the Road	1981	2.50	5.00	10.00
ATCO					
❏ SD 33-308	The Allman Brothers Band	1969	3.75	7.50	15.00
❏ SD 33-342	Idlewild South	1970	3.75	7.50	15.00
❏ SD 2-805 [(2)]	Beginnings	1973	5.00	10.00	20.00
CAPRICORN					
❏ 2CP 0102 [(2)]	Eat a Peach	1972	3.75	7.50	15.00
❏ CPN2 0102 [(2)]	Eat a Peach	198?	3.00	6.00	12.00
❏ CX4 0102 [(2)Q]	Eat a Peach	1974	7.50	15.00	30.00
❏ CP 0111	Brothers and Sisters	1973	3.00	6.00	12.00
❏ CPN 0111	Brothers and Sisters	198?	2.00	4.00	8.00
❏ 2CP 0131 [(2)]	The Allman Brothers Band at Fillmore East	1974	3.75	7.50	15.00
❏ CPN2 0131 [(2)]	The Allman Brothers Band at Fillmore East	198?	3.00	6.00	12.00
❏ CX4 0131 [(2)Q]	The Allman Brothers Band at Fillmore East	1974	7.50	15.00	30.00
❏ 2CX 0132 [(2)]	Beginnings	1974	3.75	7.50	15.00
❏ CPN2 0132 [(2)]	Beginnings	198?	3.00	6.00	12.00
❏ CP 0156	Win, Lose or Draw	1975	2.50	5.00	10.00
❏ CPN 0156	Win, Lose or Draw	198?	2.00	4.00	8.00
❏ 2CX 0164 [(2)]	The Road Goes On Forever	1975	3.00	6.00	12.00
❏ 2CX 0177 [(2)]	Wipe the Windows, Check the Oil, Dollar Gas	1976	3.00	6.00	12.00
❏ CPN 0196	The Allman Brothers Band	1978	2.50	5.00	10.00
❏ CPN 0197	Idlewild South	1978	2.50	5.00	10.00
❏ CPN 0218	Enlightened Rogues	1979	2.50	5.00	10.00
❏ 2-802 [(2)M]	The Allman Brothers Band at Fillmore East	1971	20.00	40.00	80.00
—Promo only; sticker on front cover says "Promotional DJ Copy Monaural Not for Sale"					
❏ SD 2-802 [(2)S]	The Allman Brothers Band at Fillmore East	1971	5.00	10.00	20.00
EPIC					
❏ E 46144	Seven Turns	1990	3.75	7.50	15.00
MOBILE FIDELITY					
❏ 1-157 [(2)]	Eat a Peach	1984	50.00	100.00	200.00
—Audiophile vinyl					
❏ 1-213	Brothers and Sisters	1994	7.50	15.00	30.00
—Audiophile vinyl					
NAUTILUS					
❏ NR-30 [(2)]	The Allman Brothers Band at Fillmore East	1982	25.00	50.00	100.00
—Audiophile vinyl					
POLYDOR					
❏ PD-1-6339	The Best of the Allman Brothers Band	1981	2.50	5.00	10.00
❏ 823273-1 [(2)]	The Allman Brothers Band at Fillmore East	1984	2.50	5.00	10.00
❏ 823653-1	The Allman Brothers Band	1984	2.00	4.00	8.00
❏ 823654-1 [(2)]	Eat a Peach	1984	2.50	5.00	10.00
❏ 823708-1	The Best of the Allman Brothers Band	1984	2.00	4.00	8.00
—Reissue of PD-1-6339					
❏ 825092-1	Brothers and Sisters	1985	2.00	4.00	8.00

Number	Title (A Side/B Side)	Yr	VG	VG+	NM
❏ 839417-1 [(6)]	Dreams	1989	10.00	20.00	40.00

ALLSUP, TOMMY
GRT

❏ 20004	Tommy Allsup and the Tennessee Saxes Play the Hits of Tammy Wynette	1970	5.00	10.00	20.00
METROMEDIA					
❏ MM 1004	Tommy Allsup and the Nashville Survey Play the Hits of Charley Pride	1969	6.25	12.50	25.00
REPRISE					
❏ R 6182 [M]	Tommy Allsup Plays the Buddy Holly Songbook	1965	10.00	20.00	40.00
❏ RS 6182 [S]	Tommy Allsup Plays the Buddy Holly Songbook	1965	12.50	25.00	50.00

ALMEIDA, LAURINDO
CAPITOL

❏ H-193 [10]	Guitar Concert	1950	20.00	40.00	80.00
❏ ST 1759 [S]	Viva Bossa Nova!	1962	5.00	10.00	20.00
❏ ST 1872 [S]	Ole! Bossa Nova	1963	5.00	10.00	20.00
❏ ST 1946 [S]	It's a Bossa Nova World	1963	5.00	10.00	20.00
❏ SP 8482 [S]	Songs of Enchantment	196?	5.00	10.00	20.00
CORAL					
❏ CRL 56049 [10]	A Guitar Recital of Famous Serenades	1952	20.00	40.00	80.00
❏ CRL 56086 [10]	Latin Melodies	1952	20.00	40.00	80.00
❏ CRL 57056 [M]	A Guitar Recital of Famous Serenades	1956	12.50	25.00	50.00
CRYSTAL CLEAR					
❏ CCS-8001	Virtuoso Guitar	1978	6.25	12.50	25.00
—Direct-to-disc recording; plays at 45 rpm					
❏ CCS-8007	New Directions	1979	6.25	12.50	25.00
—Direct-to-disc recording					
PACIFIC JAZZ					
❏ PJLP-7 [10]	Laurindo Almeida Quartet	1953	30.00	60.00	120.00
❏ PJLP-13 [10]	Laurindo Almeida Quartet, Vol. 2	1954	30.00	60.00	120.00
❏ PJ-1204 [M]	Laurindo Almeida Quartet Featuring Bud Shank	1955	20.00	40.00	80.00
—Reissue of 10-inch Pacific Jazz LPs					
WORLD PACIFIC					
❏ WP-1204 [M]	Laurindo Almeida Quartet Featuring Bud Shank	1958	12.50	25.00	50.00
—Reissue of Pacific Jazz 1204					
❏ WP-1412 [M]	Brazilliance, Vol. 1	1962	7.50	15.00	30.00
—Reissue of World Pacific 1204					
❏ ST-1419 [S]	Brazilliance, Vol. 2	1962	6.25	12.50	25.00
❏ WP-1419 [M]	Brazilliance, Vol. 2	1962	7.50	15.00	30.00
❏ ST-1425 [S]	Brazilliance, Vol. 3	1962	6.25	12.50	25.00
❏ WP-1425 [M]	Brazilliance, Vol. 3	1962	7.50	15.00	30.00

ALMERICO, TONY
IMPERIAL

❏ LP-9151 [M]	French Quarter Jazz	1961	5.00	10.00	20.00
❏ LP-12072 [S]	French Quarter Jazz	1961	6.25	12.50	25.00

ALPERT, HERB
A&M

❏ SP-3714	Rise	1980	2.00	4.00	8.00
—Reissue of 4790					
❏ SP-3717	Beyond	1980	2.00	4.00	8.00
❏ SP-3728	Magic Man	1981	2.00	4.00	8.00
❏ SP-3731	Fandango	1982	2.00	4.00	8.00
❏ SP-4591	Just You and Me	1976	2.50	5.00	10.00
❏ SP-4790	Rise	1979	2.50	5.00	10.00
❏ SP-4949	Blow Your Own Horn	1983	2.00	4.00	8.00
❏ SP-5082	Wild Romance	1985	2.00	4.00	8.00
❏ SP-5125	Keep Your Eye on Me	1987	2.00	4.00	8.00
❏ SP-5209	Under a Spanish Moon	1988	2.00	4.00	8.00
❏ SP-5273	My Abstract Heart	1989	2.00	4.00	8.00
❏ 75021 5345 1	North on South Street	1991	3.00	6.00	12.00
MOBILE FIDELITY					
❏ 1-053	Rise	1981	6.25	12.50	25.00
—Audiophile vinyl					

ALVIN, DANNY
JAZZOLOGY

❏ 8 [M]	Danny Alvin and the Kings of Dixieland	1964	5.00	10.00	20.00
❏ S-8 [S]	Danny Alvin and the Kings of Dixieland	1964	5.00	10.00	20.00
STEPHENY					
❏ MF-4002 [M]	Club Basin Street	1957	12.50	25.00	50.00

AMAZING RHYTHM ACES
ABC

❏ D-913	Stacked Deck	1975	5.00	10.00	20.00
❏ D-940	Too Stuffed to Jump	1976	3.75	7.50	15.00
❏ AB-1005	Toucan Do It Too	1977	3.75	7.50	15.00
❏ AA-1063	Burning the Ballroom Down	1978	3.75	7.50	15.00
❏ AA-1123	The Amazing Rhythm Aces	1979	5.00	10.00	20.00
COLUMBIA					
❏ JC 36083	The Amazing Rhythm Aces	1979	3.00	6.00	12.00
—Reissue of ABC 1123					
WARNER BROS.					
❏ BSK 3476	How the Hell Do You Spell Rythum?	1980	3.00	6.00	12.00

AMBASSADORS, THE (1)
ARCTIC

❏ ALPS-1005	Soul Summit	1969	6.25	12.50	25.00

AMBER
TOMMY BOY

❏ 1424 [(3)]	The Hits Remixed	2000	5.00	10.00	20.00

Number	Title (A Side/B Side)	Yr	VG	VG+	NM

AMBOY DUKES, THE
DISCREET
❏ DS 2181	Call of the Wild	1974	3.75	7.50	15.00

—As "Ted Nugent and the Amboy Dukes"
❏ DS 2203	Tooth, Fang and Claw	1974	3.75	7.50	15.00

—As "Ted Nugent and the Amboy Dukes"
MAINSTREAM
❏ S-414	Dr. Slingshot	1975	3.75	7.50	15.00
❏ S-421	Ted Nugent and the Amboy Dukes	1976	7.50	15.00	30.00

—Reissue of early material
❏ S-2-801 [(2)]	Journeys and Migrations	1974	7.50	15.00	30.00

—Reissue of 6112 and 6118
❏ S-6104 [S]	The Amboy Dukes	1967	10.00	20.00	40.00
❏ S-6112	Journey to the Center of the Mind	1968	10.00	20.00	40.00
❏ S-6118	Migration	1968	10.00	20.00	40.00
❏ S-6125	The Best of the Original Amboy Dukes	1969	7.50	15.00	30.00
❏ 56104 [M]	The Amboy Dukes	1967	20.00	40.00	80.00

POLYDOR
❏ 24-4012	Marriage on the Rocks/Rock Bottom	1970	6.25	12.50	25.00
❏ 24-4035	Survival of the Fittest/Live	1971	6.25	12.50	25.00

—As "Ted Nugent and the Amboy Dukes"

AMBROSE, AMANDA
DUNWICH
❏ 668 [M]	Amanda	1966	3.75	7.50	15.00
❏ S-668 [S]	Amanda	1966	5.00	10.00	20.00

AMBROSE SLADE
See SLADE.

AMBROSIA
NAUTILUS
❏ NR-23	Life Beyond L.A.	1981	7.50	5.00	30.00

—Audiophile vinyl
20TH CENTURY
❏ T-434	Ambrosia	1975	2.50	5.00	10.00

—New cover without black border
❏ T-434	Ambrosia	1975	3.00	6.00	12.00

—Original cover with black border
❏ T-510	Somewhere I've Never Traveled	1976	2.50	5.00	10.00

—Standard cover
❏ T-510	Somewhere I've Never Traveled	1976	3.00	6.00	12.00

—Fold-open cover in the shape of a pyramid
WARNER BROS.
❏ BSK 3135	Life Beyond L.A.	1978	2.50	5.00	10.00
❏ BSK 3181	Ambrosia	1978	2.00	4.00	8.00

—Reissue of 20th Century 434
❏ BSK 3368	One Eighty	1980	2.50	5.00	10.00
❏ BSK 3638	Road Island	1982	2.50	5.00	10.00

AMECHE, DON, AND FRANCES LANGFORD
COLUMBIA
❏ CL 1692	The Bickersons	1962	5.00	10.00	20.00

—Live-in-the-studio recordings from 1961
❏ CL 1883	The Bickersons Fight Back	1962	5.00	10.00	20.00

—More live-in-the-studio recordings from 1961
❏ G 30523 [(2)]	The Bickersons Rematch	1970	3.75	7.50	15.00

—Compilation of the earlier Columbia LPs
RADIOLA
❏ MR 1115	The Bickersons	198?	3.00	6.00	12.00

—Compilation of radio shows
RADIOLA/MURRAY HILL
❏ 3MH 36721 [(3)]	Return of the Bickersons	1987	5.00	10.00	20.00

—Compilation of radio shows

AMERICA
CAPITOL
❏ SO-11950	Silent Letter	1979	2.50	5.00	10.00
❏ SOO-12098	Alibi	1980	2.50	5.00	10.00
❏ ST-12209	View from the Ground	1982	2.50	5.00	10.00
❏ ST-12277	Your Move	1983	2.50	5.00	10.00
❏ ST-12370	Perspective	1984	2.50	5.00	10.00
❏ ST-12422	In Concert	1985	2.50	5.00	10.00
❏ SN-16275	Alibi	1982	2.00	4.00	8.00
❏ SN-16350	View from the Ground	1985	2.00	4.00	8.00
❏ SN-16361	Your Move	1985	2.00	4.00	8.00

WARNER BROS.
❏ BS 2576	America	1971	6.25	12.50	25.00

—First pressings omit "A Horse with No Name"
❏ BS 2576	America	1972	3.00	6.00	12.00

—With "A Horse with No Name"; green label
❏ BS 2655	Homecoming	1972	3.00	6.00	12.00
❏ BS 2728	Hat Trick	1973	3.00	6.00	12.00
❏ BS 2808	Holiday	1974	3.00	6.00	12.00
❏ BS4 2808 [Q]	Holiday	1974	5.00	10.00	20.00
❏ BS 2852	Hearts	1975	3.00	6.00	12.00
❏ BS4 2852 [Q]	Hearts	1975	5.00	10.00	20.00
❏ BS 2894	History/America's Greatest Hits	1975	3.00	6.00	12.00
❏ BS 2932	Hideaway	1976	3.00	6.00	12.00
❏ BSK 3017	Harbor	1977	3.00	6.00	12.00
❏ BSK 3110	History/America's Greatest Hits	1977	2.50	5.00	10.00

—Reissue of BS 2894 with "Burbank" palm trees label (later white labels are $8 NM)
❏ BSK 3136	America/Live	1977	3.00	6.00	12.00

AMERICAN BLUES, THE
Early incarnation of ZZ TOP.
KARMA
❏ 1001	The American Blues Is Here	1967	100.00	200.00	400.00

UNI
❏ 73044	The American Blues Do Their Thing	1968	15.00	30.00	60.00

Number	Title (A Side/B Side)	Yr	VG	VG+	NM

AMERICAN BLUES EXCHANGE, THE
TAYL
❏ TLS-1	Blueprint	1969	100.00	200.00	400.00

AMERICAN BREED, THE
ACTA
❏ 8002 [M]	The American Breed	1967	5.00	10.00	20.00
❏ 8003 [M]	Bend Me, Shape Me	1968	5.00	10.00	20.00
❏ 8006 [M]	Pumpkin, Powder, Scarlet & Green	1968	12.50	25.00	50.00

—Stock label; the cover is the same as stereo but with a "Monaural" sticker attached
❏ 8008 [M]	Lonely Side of the City	1969	10.00	20.00	40.00

—In stereo cover with "Monaural" sticker; record is regular yellow label
❏ 38002 [S]	The American Breed	1967	6.25	12.50	25.00
❏ 38003 [S]	Bend Me, Shape Me	1968	6.25	12.50	25.00
❏ 38006 [S]	Pumpkin, Powder, Scarlet & Green	1968	5.00	10.00	20.00
❏ 38008 [S]	Lonely Side of the City	1969	5.00	10.00	20.00

AMERICAN DREAM, THE
AMPEX
❏ A-10101	The American Dream	1970	5.00	10.00	20.00

—Produced by Todd Rundgren

AMERICAN EAGLE
DECCA
❏ DL 75258	American Eagle	1971	5.00	10.00	20.00

AMERICAN JAZZ ENSEMBLE, THE
EPIC
❏ LA 16040 [M]	New Dimensions	1962	5.00	10.00	20.00
❏ BA 17040 [S]	New Dimensions	1962	6.25	12.50	25.00

RCA VICTOR
❏ LPM-2557 [M]	The American Jazz Ensemble in Rome	1962	5.00	10.00	20.00
❏ LSP-2557 [S]	The American Jazz Ensemble in Rome	1962	6.25	12.50	25.00

AMERICAN REVOLUTION, THE
FLICK DISC
❏ FL-45,002 [M]	The American Revolution	1968	12.50	25.00	50.00

—White label promo in stereo cover with "Not for Sale DJ Monaural" sticker on front
❏ FLS-45,002 [S]	The American Revolution	1968	6.25	12.50	25.00

AMES, ED
RCA CAMDEN
❏ ACL1-0244	Do You Hear What I Hear?	1973	3.00	6.00	12.00
❏ CAS-2536	Ed Ames	1972	3.00	6.00	12.00
❏ CAS-2598	Somewhere, My Love	1972	3.00	6.00	12.00

RCA VICTOR
❏ ANL1-1780	Pure Gold	1976	2.50	5.00	10.00
❏ LPM-2781 [M]	Opening Night	1963	3.00	6.00	12.00
❏ LSP-2781 [S]	Opening Night	1963	3.75	7.50	15.00
❏ ANL1-2891	The Impossible Dream	1978	2.50	5.00	10.00
❏ LPM-2944 [M]	The Ed Ames Album	1964	3.00	6.00	12.00
❏ LSP-2944 [S]	The Ed Ames Album	1964	3.75	7.50	15.00
❏ LPM-3390 [M]	My Kind of Songs	1965	3.00	6.00	12.00
❏ LSP-3390 [S]	My Kind of Songs	1965	3.75	7.50	15.00
❏ LPM-3460 [M]	It's a Man's World	1965	3.00	6.00	12.00
❏ LSP-3460 [S]	It's a Man's World	1965	3.75	7.50	15.00
❏ LPM-3636 [M]	More I Cannot Wish You	1966	2.50	5.00	10.00
❏ LSP-3636 [S]	More I Cannot Wish You	1966	3.00	6.00	12.00
❏ LPM-3774 [M]	My Cup Runneth Over	1967	2.50	5.00	10.00
❏ LSP-3774 [S]	My Cup Runneth Over	1967	3.00	6.00	12.00
❏ LPM-3834 [M]	Time, Time	1967	3.00	6.00	12.00
❏ LSP-3834 [S]	Time, Time	1967	2.50	5.00	10.00
❏ LPM-3838 [M]	Christmas with Ed Ames	1967	3.75	7.50	15.00
❏ LSP-3838 [S]	Christmas with Ed Ames	1967	3.00	6.00	12.00
❏ LPM-3913 [M]	When the Snow Is On the Roses	1967	3.00	6.00	12.00
❏ LSP-3913 [S]	When the Snow Is On the Roses	1967	2.50	5.00	10.00
❏ LPM-3961 [M]	Who Will Answer? And Other Songs of Our Time	1968	3.75	7.50	15.00
❏ LSP-3961 [S]	Who Will Answer? And Other Songs of Our Time	1968	2.50	5.00	10.00
❏ LPM-4028 [M]	Apologize	1968	5.00	10.00	20.00
❏ LSP-4028 [S]	Apologize	1968	2.50	5.00	10.00
❏ LSP-4079	The Hits of Broadway and Hollywood	1968	2.50	5.00	10.00
❏ LSP-4128	A Time for Living, A Time for Hope	1969	2.50	5.00	10.00
❏ LSP-4172	The Windmills of Your Mind	1969	2.50	5.00	10.00
❏ LSP-4184	The Best of Ed Ames	1969	2.50	5.00	10.00
❏ LSP-4249	Love of the Common People	1969	2.50	5.00	10.00
❏ LSP-4381	Sing Away the World	1970	2.50	5.00	10.00
❏ LSP-4385	Christmas Is the Warmest Time of the Year	1970	5.00	10.00	20.00
❏ LSP-4453	The Songs of Bacharach and David	1971	2.50	5.00	10.00
❏ LSP-4634	Ed Ames	1972	3.75	7.50	15.00
❏ LSP-4683	Ed Ames Remembers Jim Reeves	1972	3.75	7.50	15.00
❏ LSP-4808	Songs from "Lost Horizon"	1973	3.75	7.50	15.00
❏ VPS-6023 [(2)]	This Is Ed Ames	1970	5.00	10.00	20.00

AMES, NANCY
EPIC
❏ LN 24189 [M]	Latin Pulse	1966	3.00	6.00	12.00
❏ LN 24197 [M]	As Time Goes By	1967	3.00	6.00	12.00
❏ LN 24238 [M]	Spiced with Brazil	1967	3.00	6.00	12.00
❏ BN 26189 [S]	Latin Pulse	1966	3.75	7.50	15.00
❏ BN 26197 [S]	As Time Goes By	1967	3.75	7.50	15.00
❏ BN 26238 [S]	Spiced with Brazil	1967	3.75	7.50	15.00
❏ BN 26378	Nancy Ames at the Americana	1968	3.00	6.00	12.00

LIBERTY
❏ LRP-3276 [M]	The Incredible Nancy Ames	1963	3.75	7.50	15.00
❏ LRP-3299 [M]	Portrait of Nancy	1963	3.75	7.50	15.00
❏ LRP-3329 [M]	I Never Will Marry	1964	3.75	7.50	15.00
❏ LRP-3369 [M]	This Is the Girl That Is	1964	3.75	7.50	15.00
❏ LRP-3400 [M]	Let It Be Me	1965	3.75	7.50	15.00
❏ LST-7276 [S]	The Incredible Nancy Ames	1963	5.00	10.00	20.00
❏ LST-7299 [S]	Portrait of Nancy	1963	5.00	10.00	20.00

Number	Title (A Side/B Side)	Yr	VG	VG+	NM
❏ LST-7329 [S]	I Never Will Marry	1964	5.00	10.00	20.00
❏ LST-7369 [S]	This Is the Girl That Is	1964	5.00	10.00	20.00
❏ LST-7400 [S]	Let It Be Me	1965	5.00	10.00	20.00

SUNSET

Number	Title (A Side/B Side)	Yr	VG	VG+	NM
❏ SUM-1109 [M]	The Versatile Nancy Ames	196?	3.00	6.00	12.00
❏ SUS-5109 [S]	The Versatile Nancy Ames	196?	3.75	7.50	15.00

AMES BROTHERS, THE
CORAL

Number	Title (A Side/B Side)	Yr	VG	VG+	NM
❏ CRL 56014 [10]	Sing a Song of Christmas	1950	12.50	25.00	50.00
❏ CRL 56017 [10]	In the Evening by the Moonlight	1951	12.50	25.00	50.00
❏ CRL 56024 [10]	Sentimental Me	1951	12.50	25.00	50.00
❏ CRL 56025 [10]	Hoop-De-Hoo	1951	12.50	25.00	50.00
❏ CRL 56042 [10]	Sweet Leilani	1951	12.50	25.00	50.00
❏ CRL 56050 [10]	Favorite Spirituals	1952	12.50	25.00	50.00
❏ CRL 56079 [10]	Home on the Range	1952	12.50	25.00	50.00
❏ CRL 56080 [10]	Merry Christmas	1952	12.50	25.00	50.00
❏ CRL 56097 [10]	Favorite Songs	1954	12.50	25.00	50.00
❏ CRL 57031 [M]	Ames Brothers Concert	1956	7.50	15.00	30.00
❏ CRL 57054 [M]	Love's Old Sweet Song	1956	7.50	15.00	30.00
❏ CRL 57166	Sounds of Christmas Harmony	1957	7.50	15.00	30.00
❏ CRL 57176 [M]	Love Serenade	1958	7.50	15.00	30.00
❏ CRL 57338 [M]	Our Golden Favorites	1960	7.50	15.00	30.00

EPIC

Number	Title (A Side/B Side)	Yr	VG	VG+	NM
❏ LN 24036 [M]	Hello Italy	1962	3.75	7.50	15.00
❏ LN 24069 [M]	Knees Up Mother Brown	1963	3.75	7.50	15.00
❏ BN 26036 [S]	Hello Italy	1962	5.00	10.00	20.00
❏ BN 26069 [S]	Knees Up Mother Brown	1963	5.00	10.00	20.00

MCA

Number	Title (A Side/B Side)	Yr	VG	VG+	NM
❏ 1510 [R]	The Ames Brothers	197?	2.50	5.00	10.00

RCA CAMDEN

Number	Title (A Side/B Side)	Yr	VG	VG+	NM
❏ CAL-571 [M]	The Ames Brothers — Sweet and Swing	1958	3.75	7.50	15.00

RCA SPECIAL PRODUCTS

Number	Title (A Side/B Side)	Yr	VG	VG+	NM
❏ DVL2-0207 [(2)]	All Their Greatest Hits	1976	3.75	7.50	15.00

RCA VICTOR

Number	Title (A Side/B Side)	Yr	VG	VG+	NM
❏ ANL1-1095e	The Best of the Ames Brothers	1975	2.50	5.00	10.00
❏ LPM-1142 [M]	Exactly Like You	1955	7.50	15.00	30.00
❏ LPM-1157 [M]	Four Brothers	1955	7.50	15.00	30.00
❏ LPM-1228 [M]	The Ames Brothers with Hugo Winterhalter	1956	7.50	15.00	30.00
❏ LPM-1487 [M]	Sweet Seventeen	1957	7.50	15.00	30.00
❏ LPM-1541 [M]	There'll Always Be a Christmas	1957	7.50	15.00	30.00
❏ LPM-1680 [M]	Destination Moon	1958	6.25	12.50	25.00
❏ LSP-1680 [S]	Destination Moon	1958	7.50	15.00	30.00
❏ LPM-1855 [M]	Smoochin' Time	1958	6.25	12.50	25.00
❏ LSP-1855 [S]	Smoochin' Time	1958	7.50	15.00	30.00
❏ LPM-1859 [M]	The Best of the Ames Brothers	1958	6.25	12.50	25.00
❏ LSP-1859(e) [R]	The Best of the Ames Brothers	196?	5.00	10.00	20.00
❏ LPM-1954 [M]	Famous Hits of Famous Quartets	1959	5.00	10.00	20.00
❏ LSP-1954 [S]	Famous Hits of Famous Quartets	1959	6.25	12.50	25.00
❏ LPM-1998 [M]	The Ames Brothers Sing the Best in the Country	1959	5.00	10.00	20.00
❏ LSP-1998 [S]	The Ames Brothers Sing the Best in the Country	1959	6.25	12.50	25.00
❏ LPM-2009 [M]	Words and Music	1959	5.00	10.00	20.00
❏ LSP-2009 [S]	Words and Music	1959	6.25	12.50	25.00
❏ LPM-2100 [M]	Hello, Amigos	1960	5.00	10.00	20.00
❏ LSP-2100 [S]	Hello, Amigos	1960	6.25	12.50	25.00
❏ LPM-2182 [M]	The Blend and the Beat	1960	5.00	10.00	20.00
❏ LSP-2182 [S]	The Blend and the Beat	1960	6.25	12.50	25.00
❏ LPM-2273 [M]	The Best of the Bands	1960	5.00	10.00	20.00
❏ LSP-2273 [S]	The Best of the Bands	1960	6.25	12.50	25.00
❏ LPM-2876 [M]	For Sentimental Reasons	1964	3.00	6.00	12.00
❏ LSP-2876 [S]	For Sentimental Reasons	1964	3.75	7.50	15.00
❏ LPM-2981 [M]	Down Memory Lane with the Ames Brothers	1964	3.00	6.00	12.00
❏ LSP-2981 [S]	Down Memory Lane with the Ames Brothers	1964	3.75	7.50	15.00
❏ LPM-3186 [10]	It Must Be True	1954	12.50	25.00	50.00

READER'S DIGEST

Number	Title (A Side/B Side)	Yr	VG	VG+	NM
❏ RDA-160 [(6)]	Sentimentally Yours	1981	6.25	12.50	25.00

VOCALION

Number	Title (A Side/B Side)	Yr	VG	VG+	NM
❏ VL 3617 [M]	The Ames Brothers	196?	3.75	7.50	15.00
❏ VL 73788 [R]	Christmas Harmony	196?	3.00	6.00	12.00
—Reissue of some Coral tracks					
❏ VL 73818	The Ames Brothers Featuring Ed Ames	196?	2.50	5.00	10.00

AMISH, THE
SUSSEX

Number	Title (A Side/B Side)	Yr	VG	VG+	NM
❏ SUX-7016	The Amish	1972	6.25	12.50	25.00

AMMONS, ALBERT
BLUE NOTE

Number	Title (A Side/B Side)	Yr	VG	VG+	NM
❏ BLP-7017 [10]	Boogie Woogie Classics	1951	75.00	150.00	300.00

MERCURY

Number	Title (A Side/B Side)	Yr	VG	VG+	NM
❏ MG-25012 [10]	Boogie Woogie Piano	1950	37.50	75.00	150.00

AMMONS, ALBERT, AND PETE JOHNSON
RCA VICTOR

Number	Title (A Side/B Side)	Yr	VG	VG+	NM
❏ LPT-9 [10]	8 to the Bar	1952	25.00	50.00	100.00

AMMONS, ALBERT / MEADE LUX LEWIS
MOSAIC

Number	Title (A Side/B Side)	Yr	VG	VG+	NM
❏ M3-103 [(3)]	The Complete Blue Note Recordings of Albert Ammons and Meade Lux Lewis	198?	12.50	25.00	50.00

AMMONS, GENE
ARGO

Number	Title (A Side/B Side)	Yr	VG	VG+	NM
❏ 697 [M]	Dig Him	1962	7.50	15.00	30.00
❏ S-697 [S]	Dig Him	1962	6.25	12.50	25.00
❏ 698 [M]	Just Jug	1962	7.50	15.00	30.00
❏ S-698 [S]	Just Jug	1962	6.25	12.50	25.00

CADET

Number	Title (A Side/B Side)	Yr	VG	VG+	NM
❏ LP-783 [M]	Make It Happen	1967	6.25	12.50	25.00

CHESS

Number	Title (A Side/B Side)	Yr	VG	VG+	NM
❏ LP 1442 [M]	Soulful Saxophone	1959	10.00	20.00	40.00

EMARCY

Number	Title (A Side/B Side)	Yr	VG	VG+	NM
❏ MG-26031 [10]	With or Without	1954	30.00	60.00	120.00

MOODSVILLE

Number	Title (A Side/B Side)	Yr	VG	VG+	NM
❏ MVLP-18 [M]	Nice and Cool	1961	12.50	25.00	50.00
—Originals have green label					
❏ MVLP-18 [M]	Nice and Cool	1965	6.25	12.50	25.00
—Second editions have blue label with trident at right					
❏ MVLP-28 [M]	The Soulful Moods of Gene Ammons	1963	12.50	25.00	50.00
—Originals have green label					
❏ MVLP-28 [M]	The Soulful Moods of Gene Ammons	1965	6.25	12.50	25.00
—Second editions have blue label with trident at right					
❏ MVST-28 [S]	The Soulful Moods of Gene Ammons	1963	10.00	20.00	40.00

PRESTIGE

Number	Title (A Side/B Side)	Yr	VG	VG+	NM
❏ PRLP-107 [10]	Gene Ammons	1951	50.00	100.00	200.00
❏ PRLP-112 [10]	Tenor Sax Favorites, Volume 1	1951	50.00	100.00	200.00
❏ PRLP-127 [10]	Gene Ammons Favorites, Volume 2	1952	50.00	100.00	200.00
❏ PRLP-149 [10]	Gene Ammons Favorites, Volume 3	1953	50.00	100.00	200.00
❏ PRLP-211 [10]	Gene Ammons Jazz Session	1955	50.00	100.00	200.00
❏ PRLP-7039 [M]	Hi Fidelity Jam Session	1956	25.00	50.00	100.00
❏ PRLP-7039 [M]	The Happy Blues	1960	12.50	25.00	50.00
—Retitled version of "Hi Fidelity Jam Session"					
❏ PRLP-7050 [M]	Gene Ammons All Star Session	1956	25.00	50.00	100.00
—Compilation of Prestige 107 and 127					
❏ PRLP-7050 [M]	Woofin' and Tweetin'	1960	12.50	25.00	50.00
—Retitled version of "Gene Ammons All Star Session"					
❏ PRLP-7060 [M]	Jammin' with Gene	1956	25.00	50.00	100.00
❏ PRLP-7060 [M]	Not Really the Blues	1960	12.50	25.00	50.00
—Retitled version of "Jammin' with Gene"					
❏ PRLP-7083 [M]	Funky	1957	25.00	50.00	100.00
—Originals have yellow label, "W. 50th St., NYC" address					
❏ PRLP-7110 [M]	Jammin' in Hi-Fi with Gene Ammons	1957	25.00	50.00	100.00
—Originals have yellow label, "W. 50th St., NYC" address					
❏ PRLP-7132 [M]	The Big Sound	1958	25.00	50.00	100.00
—Originals have yellow label, "W. 50th St., NYC" address					
❏ PRLP-7146 [M]	Blue Gene	1958	12.50	25.00	50.00
—Originals have yellow label, Bergenfield, N.J. address					
❏ PRLP-7176 [M]	The Twister	1960	12.50	25.00	50.00
—Originals have yellow label, Bergenfield, N.J. address; reissue of 7110					
❏ PRLP-7180 [M]	Boss Tenor	1960	12.50	25.00	50.00
—Originals have yellow label, Bergenfield, N.J. address					
❏ PRST-7180 [S]	Boss Tenor	1960	10.00	20.00	40.00
—Originals have silver label					
❏ PRLP-7192 [M]	Jug	1960	12.50	25.00	50.00
—Originals have yellow label, Bergenfield, N.J. address					
❏ PRST-7192 [S]	Jug	1960	10.00	20.00	40.00
—Originals have silver label					
❏ PRLP-7201 [M]	Groove Blues	1961	12.50	25.00	50.00
—Originals have yellow label, Bergenfield, N.J. address					
❏ PRLP-7208 [M]	Up Tight!	1961	12.50	25.00	50.00
—Originals have yellow label, Bergenfield, N.J. address					
❏ PRST-7208 [S]	Up Tight!	1961	10.00	20.00	40.00
—Originals have silver label					
❏ PRLP-7238 [M]	Twistin' the Jug	1962	12.50	25.00	50.00
—Originals have yellow label, Bergenfield, N.J. address					
❏ PRST-7238 [S]	Twistin' the Jug	1962	10.00	20.00	40.00
—Originals have silver label					
❏ PRLP-7257 [M]	Bad! Bossa Nova	1962	7.50	15.00	30.00
—Originals have yellow label, Bergenfield, N.J. address; some copies have a cover calling this "Jungle Soul! (ca' purange)					
❏ PRST-7257 [S]	Bad! Bossa Nova	1962	10.00	20.00	40.00
—Originals have silver label					
❏ PRLP-7270 [M]	Preachin'	1963	7.50	15.00	30.00
—Originals have yellow label, Bergenfield, N.J. address					
❏ PRST-7270 [S]	Preachin'	1963	10.00	20.00	40.00
—Originals have silver label					
❏ PRLP-7275 [M]	Soul Summit, Volume 2	1963	7.50	15.00	30.00
—Originals have yellow label, Bergenfield, N.J. address					
❏ PRST-7275 [S]	Soul Summit, Volume 2	1963	10.00	20.00	40.00
—Originals have silver label					
❏ PRLP-7287 [M]	Late Hour Special	1964	7.50	15.00	30.00
—Originals have yellow label, Bergenfield, N.J. address					
❏ PRST-7287 [S]	Late Hour Special	1964	10.00	20.00	40.00
—Originals have silver label					
❏ PRLP-7320 [M]	Velvet Soul	1964	7.50	15.00	30.00
—Originals have yellow label, Bergenfield, N.J. address					
❏ PRST-7320 [S]	Velvet Soul	1964	10.00	20.00	40.00
—Originals have silver label					
❏ PRLP-7369 [M]	Angel Eyes	1965	6.25	12.50	25.00
—Originals have blue label with trident at right					
❏ PRST-7369 [S]	Angel Eyes	1965	7.50	15.00	30.00
—Originals have blue label with trident at right					
❏ PRLP-7400 [M]	Sock!	1966	6.25	12.50	25.00
—Originals have blue label with trident at right					
❏ PRST-7400 [S]	Sock!	1966	7.50	15.00	30.00
—Originals have blue label with trident at right					
❏ PRLP-7445 [M]	Boss Soul!	1967	6.25	12.50	25.00
—Originals have blue label with trident at right					
❏ PRST-7445 [S]	Boss Soul!	1967	7.50	15.00	30.00
—Originals have blue label with trident at right					
❏ PRLP-7495 [M]	Gene Ammons Live in Chicago	1967	5.00	10.00	20.00
—Originals have blue label with trident at right					
❏ PRST-7495 [S]	Gene Ammons Live in Chicago	1967	6.25	12.50	25.00
—Originals have blue label with trident at right					
❏ PRLP-7534 [M]	Boss Tenor	1967	6.25	12.50	25.00
—Originals have blue label with trident at right					
❏ PRST-7534 [S]	Boss Tenor	1967	5.00	10.00	20.00
—Originals have blue label with trident at right					
❏ PRST-7552	Jungle Soul	1968	5.00	10.00	20.00
—Reissue of 7257					
❏ PRST-7774	The Best of Gene Ammons	1970	5.00	10.00	20.00

Number	Title (A Side/B Side)	Yr	VG	VG+	NM
SAVOY					
❏ MG-14033 [M]	Golden Saxophone	1961	7.50	15.00	30.00
VEE JAY					
❏ LP-3024 [M]	Juggin' Around	1961	10.00	20.00	40.00
❏ LPS-3024 [S]	Juggin' Around	1961	7.50	15.00	30.00

AMMONS, GENE, AND RICHARD "GROOVE" HOLMES

Number	Title (A Side/B Side)	Yr	VG	VG+	NM
PACIFIC JAZZ					
❏ PJ-32 [M]	Groovin' with Jug	1961	10.00	20.00	40.00
❏ ST-32 [S]	Groovin' with Jug	1961	7.50	15.00	30.00

AMMONS, GENE, AND SONNY STITT

Number	Title (A Side/B Side)	Yr	VG	VG+	NM
CADET					
❏ LP-785 [M]	Jug and Sonny	1967	5.00	10.00	20.00
CHESS					
❏ LP 1455 [M]	Jug and Sonny	1960	10.00	20.00	40.00
PRESTIGE					
❏ PRLP-7234 [M]	Soul Summit	1962	12.50	25.00	50.00
❏ PRST-7234 [S]	Soul Summit	1962	10.00	20.00	40.00
❏ PRLP-7454 [M]	Soul Summit	1967	5.00	10.00	20.00
VERVE					
❏ V-8426 [M]	Boss Tenors	1962	5.00	10.00	20.00
❏ V6-8426 [S]	Boss Tenors	1962	6.25	12.50	25.00
❏ V-8468 [M]	Boss Tenors in Orbit	1962	5.00	10.00	20.00
❏ V6-8468 [S]	Boss Tenors in Orbit	1962	6.25	12.50	25.00

AMON DUUL

Number	Title (A Side/B Side)	Yr	VG	VG+	NM
PROPHESY					
❏ PHS-1003	Amon Duul	1969	6.25	12.50	25.00

AMOS, TORI
See Y KANT TORI READ.

AMRAM-BARROW QUARTET, THE

Number	Title (A Side/B Side)	Yr	VG	VG+	NM
DECCA					
❏ DL 8558 [M]	Jazz Studio No. 6	1957	12.50	25.00	50.00

AMY, CURTIS

Number	Title (A Side/B Side)	Yr	VG	VG+	NM
PACIFIC JAZZ					
❏ PJ-62 [M]	Tippin' On Through — Recorded "Live" at the Lighthouse	1962	6.25	12.50	25.00
❏ ST-62 [S]	Tippin' On Through — Recorded "Live" at the Lighthouse	1962	7.50	15.00	30.00
PALOMAR					
❏ GS-34003 [S]	Sounds of Hollywood and Broadway	1965	5.00	10.00	20.00
VERVE					
❏ V6-8684 [S]	Mustang	1966	5.00	10.00	20.00

AMY, CURTIS, AND DUPREE BOLTON

Number	Title (A Side/B Side)	Yr	VG	VG+	NM
PACIFIC JAZZ					
❏ PJ-70 [M]	Katanga!	1963	6.25	12.50	25.00
❏ ST-70 [S]	Katanga!	1963	7.50	15.00	30.00
—Black vinyl					
❏ ST-70 [S]	Katanga!	1963	15.00	30.00	60.00
—Red vinyl					

AMY, CURTIS, AND PAUL BRYANT

Number	Title (A Side/B Side)	Yr	VG	VG+	NM
KIMBERLY					
❏ 2020 [M]	This Is the Blues	1963	5.00	10.00	20.00
❏ 11020 [S]	This Is the Blues	1963	6.25	12.50	25.00
PACIFIC JAZZ					
❏ PJ-9 [M]	The Blues Message	1960	7.50	15.00	30.00
❏ ST-9 [S]	The Blues Message	1960	10.00	20.00	40.00
❏ PJ-26 [M]	Meetin' Here	1961	7.50	15.00	30.00
❏ ST-26 [S]	Meetin' Here	1961	10.00	20.00	40.00

AMY, CURTIS, AND FRANK BUTLER

Number	Title (A Side/B Side)	Yr	VG	VG+	NM
PACIFIC JAZZ					
❏ PJ-19 [M]	Groovin' Blue	1961	7.50	15.00	30.00
❏ ST-19 [S]	Groovin' Blue	1961	10.00	20.00	40.00

AMY, CURTIS, AND VICTOR FELDMAN

Number	Title (A Side/B Side)	Yr	VG	VG+	NM
PACIFIC JAZZ					
❏ PJ-46 [M]	Way Down	1962	6.25	12.50	25.00
❏ ST-46 [S]	Way Down	1962	7.50	15.00	30.00

ANCIENT GREASE

Number	Title (A Side/B Side)	Yr	VG	VG+	NM
MERCURY					
❏ SR-61305	Women and Children First	1970	7.50	15.00	30.00

ANDERS & PONCIA

Number	Title (A Side/B Side)	Yr	VG	VG+	NM
WARNER BROS.					
❏ WS 1778	The Anders & Poncia Album	1969	7.50	15.00	30.00

ANDERSEN, ERIC

Number	Title (A Side/B Side)	Yr	VG	VG+	NM
ARISTA					
❏ AL 4033	Be True to You	1975	2.50	5.00	10.00
❏ AL 4075	Sweet Surprise	1976	2.50	5.00	10.00
❏ AL 4128	The Best Songs	1977	2.50	5.00	10.00
COLUMBIA					
❏ KC 31062	Blue River	1972	2.50	5.00	10.00
❏ PC 31062	Blue River	197?	2.00	4.00	8.00
—Reissue					
VANGUARD					
❏ VSD 7/8 [(2)]	The Best of Eric Andersen	1971	3.75	7.50	15.00
❏ VSD 6540	A Country Dream	1969	3.75	7.50	15.00
❏ VRS 9157 [M]	Today Is the Highway	1965	3.75	7.50	15.00
❏ VRS 9206 [M]	'Bout Changes and Things	1966	3.75	7.50	15.00
❏ VSD 79157 [S]	Today Is the Highway	1965	5.00	10.00	20.00
❏ VSD 79206 [S]	'Bout Changes and Things	1966	5.00	10.00	20.00
❏ VSD 79236	'Bout Changes and Things, Take 2	1968	3.75	7.50	15.00
❏ VSD 79271	More Hits from Tin Can Alley	1969	3.75	7.50	15.00
WARNER BROS.					
❏ WS 1748	Avalanche	1968	3.75	7.50	15.00
❏ WS 1806	Eric Andersen	1969	3.75	7.50	15.00

ANDERSON, AL
Also see NRBQ; THE WILDWEEDS.

Number	Title (A Side/B Side)	Yr	VG	VG+	NM
TWIN/TONE					
❏ TTR 88110	Party Favors	1989	3.00	6.00	12.00
VANGUARD					
❏ VSD-79324	Al Anderson	1973	5.00	10.00	20.00

ANDERSON, BILL

Number	Title (A Side/B Side)	Yr	VG	VG+	NM
DECCA					
❏ DL 4192 [M]	Bill Anderson Sings Country Songs	1962	5.00	10.00	20.00
❏ DL 4427 [M]	Still	1963	5.00	10.00	20.00
❏ DL 4499 [M]	Bill Anderson Sings	1964	3.75	7.50	15.00
❏ DL 4600 [M]	Bill Anderson Showcase	1964	3.75	7.50	15.00
❏ DL 4646 [M]	From This Pen	1965	3.75	7.50	15.00
❏ DL 4686 [M]	Bright Lights and Country Music	1965	3.75	7.50	15.00
❏ DL 4771 [M]	I Love You Drops	1966	3.75	7.50	15.00
❏ DL 4855 [M]	Get While the Gettin's Good	1967	3.75	7.50	15.00
❏ DL 4859 [M]	Bill Anderson's Greatest Hits	1967	5.00	10.00	20.00
❏ DL 4886 [M]	I Can Do Nothing Alone	1967	6.25	12.50	25.00
❏ DXSA 7198 [(2)]	The Bill Anderson Story	1969	3.75	7.50	15.00
❏ DL 74192 [S]	Bill Anderson Sings Country Songs	1962	6.25	12.50	25.00
❏ DL 74427 [S]	Still	1963	6.25	12.50	25.00
❏ DL 74499 [S]	Bill Anderson Sings	1964	5.00	10.00	20.00
❏ DL 74600 [S]	Bill Anderson Showcase	1964	5.00	10.00	20.00
❏ DL 74646 [S]	From This Pen	1965	5.00	10.00	20.00
❏ DL 74686 [S]	Bright Lights and Country Music	1965	5.00	10.00	20.00
❏ DL 74771 [S]	I Love You Drops	1966	5.00	10.00	20.00
❏ DL 74855 [S]	Get While the Gettin's Good	1967	5.00	10.00	20.00
❏ DL 74859 [S]	Bill Anderson's Greatest Hits	1967	5.00	10.00	20.00
❏ DL 74886 [S]	I Can Do Nothing Alone	1967	5.00	10.00	20.00
❏ DL 74998	Wild Weekend	1968	3.75	7.50	15.00
❏ DL 75056	Happy State of Mind	1968	3.75	7.50	15.00
❏ DL 75142	My Life/But You Know I Love You	1969	3.75	7.50	15.00
❏ DL 75161	Bill Anderson's Christmas	1969	3.75	7.50	15.00
❏ DL 75206	Love Is a Sometimes Thing	1970	3.00	6.00	12.00
❏ DL 75254	Where Have All Our Heroes Gone?	1971	3.00	6.00	12.00
❏ DL 75275	Always Remember	1971	3.00	6.00	12.00
❏ DL 75315	Bill Anderson's Greatest Hits, Vol. 2	1971	3.00	6.00	12.00
❏ DL 75339	Singing His Praise	1972	3.00	6.00	12.00
❏ DL 75344	Bill Anderson Sings For "All the Lonely Women in the World"	1972	3.00	6.00	12.00
❏ DL 75383	Don't She Look Good	1972	3.00	6.00	12.00
MCA					
❏ 13	Bill Anderson's Greatest Hits	1973	2.50	5.00	10.00
—Reissue of Decca 74859					
❏ 320	Bill	1973	3.00	6.00	12.00
❏ 416	"Whispering" Bill Anderson	1974	3.00	6.00	12.00
❏ 454	Every Time I Turn the Radio On/Talk to Me Ohio	1974	2.50	5.00	10.00
❏ 693	Love and Other Sad Stories	198?	2.00	4.00	8.00
—Reissue					
❏ 694	Ladies' Choice	198?	2.00	4.00	8.00
—Reissue					
❏ 766	Nashville Mirrors	198?	2.00	4.00	8.00
—Reissue					
❏ 2222	Peanuts & Diamonds & Other Jewels	1975	2.50	5.00	10.00
❏ 2264	Scorpio	1976	2.50	5.00	10.00
❏ 2371	Love and Other Sad Stories	1977	2.50	5.00	10.00
❏ 3075	Ladies' Choice	1979	2.50	5.00	10.00
❏ 3214	Nashville Mirrors	1980	2.50	5.00	10.00
❏ 4001 [(2)]	The Bill Anderson Story	1973	3.00	6.00	12.00
—Reissue of Decca 7198					
❏ 35032	Whispering	197?	2.50	5.00	10.00
MCA CORAL					
❏ 20002	I Can Do Nothing	1973	2.50	5.00	10.00
VOCALION					
❏ VL 3835 [M]	Bill Anderson's Country Style	196?	3.00	6.00	12.00
❏ VL 73835 [S]	Bill Anderson's Country Style	196?	3.75	7.50	15.00
❏ VL 73927	Just Plain Bill	197?	2.50	5.00	10.00

ANDERSON, BILL, AND JAN HOWARD

Number	Title (A Side/B Side)	Yr	VG	VG+	NM
DECCA					
❏ DL 4959 [M]	For Loving You	1967	6.25	12.50	25.00
❏ DL 74959 [S]	For Loving You	1967	5.00	10.00	20.00
❏ DL 75184	If It's All the Same to You	1970	5.00	10.00	20.00
❏ DL 75293	Bill & Jan (Or Jan & Bill)	1972	5.00	10.00	20.00

ANDERSON, CASEY

Number	Title (A Side/B Side)	Yr	VG	VG+	NM
ATCO					
❏ 33-149 [M]	The Bag I'm In	1962	5.00	10.00	20.00
❏ SD 33-149 [S]	The Bag I'm In	1962	6.25	12.50	25.00
❏ 33-166 [M]	More Pretty Girls Than One	1964	5.00	10.00	20.00
❏ SD 33-166 [S]	More Pretty Girls Than One	1964	6.25	12.50	25.00
❏ 33-172 [M]	Live at the Ice House	1965	5.00	10.00	20.00
❏ SD 33-172 [S]	Live at the Ice House	1965	6.25	12.50	25.00
❏ 33-176 [M]	Blues Is a Woman Gone	1965	5.00	10.00	20.00
❏ SD 33-176 [S]	Blues Is a Woman Gone	1965	6.25	12.50	25.00
ELEKTRA					
❏ EKL-192 [M]	Goin' Places	1960	5.00	10.00	20.00
❏ EKS-7192 [S]	Goin' Places	1960	6.25	12.50	25.00

ANDERSON, CAT

Number	Title (A Side/B Side)	Yr	VG	VG+	NM
EMARCY					
❏ MG-36142 [M]	Cat on a Hot Tin Roof	1958	12.50	25.00	50.00
MERCURY					
❏ MG-20522 [M]	Cat on a Hot Tin Roof	1959	10.00	20.00	40.00
❏ SR-60199 [S]	Cat on a Hot Tin Roof	1959	10.00	20.00	40.00

After his death, Duke Records compiled an LP that collected Johnny Ace's top singles in one place. It was issued with two different covers; this one is the somewhat easier to find.

Alexander's Timeless Bloozband made this rare self-titled album as a private pressing in 1967 before getting signed to Uni and having an additional album in 1968.

This rare album by Lee Allen features his biggest hit, "Walking with Mr. Lee."

Before she became a renowned poet, Maya Angelou attempted a singing career. This collectible album, *Miss Calypso,* was the result.

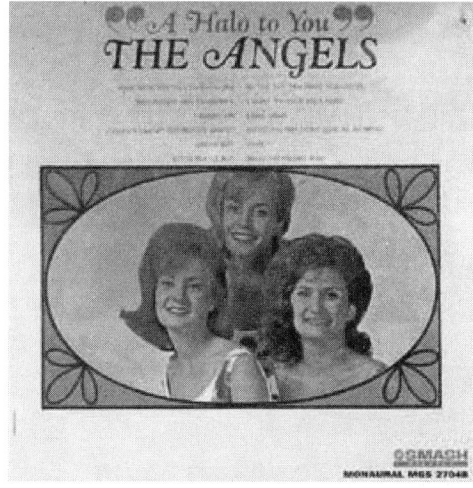

The Angels' album *A Halo to You* was their second for the Smash label; it came out in 1964.

Collectors of Disneyana, early-1960s pop-rock, and cheesecake covers covet Annette (Funicello) records. One of her many LPs was *Bikini Beach.*

Number	Title (A Side/B Side)	Yr	VG	VG+	NM

ANDERSON, CHRIS
JAZZLAND

Number	Title (A Side/B Side)	Yr	VG	VG+	NM
❏ JLP-57 [M]	Inverted Images	1961	7.50	15.00	30.00
❏ JLP-957 [S]	Inverted Images	1961	10.00	20.00	40.00

ANDERSON, ERNESTINE
MERCURY

❏ MG-20354 [M]	Hot Cargo	1958	10.00	20.00	40.00
❏ MG-20400 [M]	Ernestine Anderson	1959	10.00	20.00	40.00
❏ MG-20492 [M]	Fascinating Ernestine	1959	10.00	20.00	40.00
❏ MG-20496 [M]	My Kinda Swing	1959	10.00	20.00	40.00
❏ MG-20582 [M]	Moanin'	1960	10.00	20.00	40.00
❏ SR-60074 [S]	Ernestine Anderson	1959	12.50	25.00	50.00
❏ SR-60171 [S]	Fascinating Ernestine	1959	12.50	25.00	50.00
❏ SR-60175 [S]	My Kinda Swing	1959	12.50	25.00	50.00
❏ SR-60242 [S]	Moanin'	1960	12.50	25.00	50.00

SUE

❏ LP 1015 [M]	The New Sound of Ernestine Anderson	1963	5.00	10.00	20.00

ANDERSON, HERB OSCAR
VERVE

❏ V-5021 [M]	What Would I Be	1967	5.00	10.00	20.00
❏ V6-5021 [S]	What Would I Be	1967	6.25	12.50	25.00

ANDERSON, IVIE, AND LENA HORNE
JAZZTONE

❏ J-1262 [M]	Lena and Ivie	1956	10.00	20.00	40.00

ANDERSON, LAURIE
WARNER BROS.

❏ WBMS-134-2 [(2)DJ]	Home of the Brave Interview	1986	7.50	15.00	30.00
—Part of the Warner Bros. Music Show series					
❏ PRO-A-2123 [EP]	Selections from Mister Heartbreak	1984	2.00	4.00	8.00
—Promo-only sampler with three songs (Excellent Birds/Sharkey's Day/Sharkey's Night)					
❏ PRO-A-2229 [DJ]	Selections from United States Live	1984	3.00	6.00	12.00
—Promo-only sampler with eight tracks					
❏ BSK 3674	Big Science	1982	2.50	5.00	10.00
❏ 25077	Mister Heartbreak	1984	2.50	5.00	10.00
❏ 25077 [DJ]	Mister Heartbreak	1984	3.75	7.50	15.00
—"Quiex II" audiophile pressing					
❏ 25192 [(5)]	United States Live	1984	10.00	20.00	40.00
—Boxed set					
❏ 25400	Home of the Brave (Soundtrack)	1986	2.50	5.00	10.00
❏ 25900	Strange Angels	1989	3.00	6.00	12.00

ANDERSON, LEROY
DECCA

❏ DL 4335 [M]	New Music of Leroy Anderson	1962	3.75	7.50	15.00
❏ DL 7509 [10]	Leroy Anderson, Volume 1	195?	7.50	15.00	30.00
❏ DL 7519 [10]	Leroy Anderson, Volume 2	195?	7.50	15.00	30.00
❏ DL 8121 [M]	Blue Tango and Other Favorites	1955	5.00	10.00	20.00
❏ DL 8193 [M]	Christmas Carols	1955	5.00	10.00	20.00
❏ DL 8865 [M]	Leroy Anderson Conducts Leroy Anderson	1958	3.75	7.50	15.00
❏ DL 8925 [M]	Christmas Festival	1959	3.00	6.00	12.00
❏ DL 8954 [M]	Leroy Anderson Conducts His Music	1959	5.00	10.00	20.00
❏ DL 9749 [M]	Leroy Anderson "Pops" Concert	195?	5.00	10.00	20.00
❏ DL 74335 [S]	New Music of Leroy Anderson	1962	5.00	10.00	20.00
❏ DL 78865 [S]	Leroy Anderson Conducts Leroy Anderson	1958	5.00	10.00	20.00
❏ DL 78925 [S]	Christmas Festival	1959	3.75	7.50	15.00
❏ DL 78954 [S]	Leroy Anderson Conducts His Music	1959	6.25	12.50	25.00

ANDERSON, LIZ
RCA VICTOR

❏ LPM-3769 [M]	Liz Anderson Sings	1967	7.50	15.00	30.00
❏ LSP-3769 [S]	Liz Anderson Sings	1967	5.00	10.00	20.00
❏ LPM-3852 [M]	Cookin' Up Hits	1967	7.50	15.00	30.00
❏ LSP-3852 [S]	Cookin' Up Hits	1967	5.00	10.00	20.00
❏ LPM-3908 [M]	Liz Anderson Sings Her Favorites	1968	10.00	20.00	40.00
❏ LSP-3908 [S]	Liz Anderson Sings Her Favorites	1968	5.00	10.00	20.00
❏ LSP-4014	Like a Merry-Go-Round	1968	5.00	10.00	20.00
❏ LSP-4222	If the Creek Don't Rise	1969	5.00	10.00	20.00
❏ LSP-4346	Husband Hunting	1970	5.00	10.00	20.00

ANDERSON, LYNN
CHART

❏ CHM-1001 [M]	Ride, Ride, Ride	1967	5.00	10.00	20.00
❏ CHS-1001 [S]	Ride, Ride, Ride	1967	3.75	7.50	15.00
❏ CHM-1004 [M]	Promises, Promises	1968	5.00	10.00	20.00
❏ CHS-1004 [S]	Promises, Promises	1968	3.75	7.50	15.00
❏ CHS-1008	Big Girls Don't Cry	1969	3.75	7.50	15.00
❏ CHS-1009	The Best of Lynn Anderson	1969	3.75	7.50	15.00
❏ CHS-1013	With Love, From Lynn	1969	3.75	7.50	15.00
❏ CHS-1017	At Home with Lynn	1969	3.75	7.50	15.00
❏ CHS-1022	Songs That Made Country Girls Famous	1970	3.00	6.00	12.00
❏ CHS-1028	Uptown Country Girl	1970	3.00	6.00	12.00
❏ CHS-1032	Songs My Mother Wrote	1970	3.00	6.00	12.00
❏ CHS-1037	I'm Alright	1970	3.00	6.00	12.00
❏ CHS-1040	Lynn Anderson's Greatest Hits	1971	3.00	6.00	12.00
❏ CHS-1043	Lynn Anderson with Strings	1971	3.00	6.00	12.00
❏ CHS-1050 [(2)]	Lynn Anderson	1972	3.75	7.50	15.00

COLUMBIA

❏ CS 1025	Stay There 'Til I Get There	1970	3.00	6.00	12.00
❏ C 30099	No Love at All	1970	3.00	6.00	12.00
❏ C 30411	Rose Garden	1970	2.50	5.00	10.00
❏ PC 30411	Rose Garden	197?	2.00	4.00	8.00
—Reissue					
❏ C 30793	You're My Man	1971	2.50	5.00	10.00
❏ CG 30902 [(2)]	The World of Lynn Anderson	1971	3.00	6.00	12.00
❏ C 30925	How Can I Unlove You	1971	2.50	5.00	10.00
❏ 3C 30957	Christmas Album	198?	2.00	4.00	8.00
—Reissue of KC 30957					
❏ KC 30957	Christmas Album	1971	3.00	6.00	12.00
❏ KC 31316	Cry	1972	2.50	5.00	10.00

❏ KC 31641	Lynn Anderson's Greatest Hits	1972	2.50	5.00	10.00
❏ PC 31641	Lynn Anderson's Greatest Hits	197?	2.00	4.00	8.00
—Reissue					
❏ KC 31647	Listen to a Country Song	1972	2.50	5.00	10.00
❏ KC 32078	Keep Me in Mind	1973	2.50	5.00	10.00
❏ KC 32429	Top of the World	1973	2.50	5.00	10.00
❏ KC 32719	Queens of Country	1974	2.50	5.00	10.00
❏ KC 32941	Smile for Me	1974	2.50	5.00	10.00
❏ KC 33293	What a Man, My Man Is	1974	2.50	5.00	10.00
❏ KC 33691	I've Never Loved Anyone More	1975	2.50	5.00	10.00
❏ PC 34089	All the King's Horses	1976	2.50	5.00	10.00
❏ PC 34308	Lynn Anderson's Greatest Hits Volume II	1976	2.50	5.00	10.00
❏ PC 34439	Wrap Your Love All Around Your Man	1977	2.50	5.00	10.00
❏ JC 34871	I Love What Love Is Doing to Me/He Ain't You	1977	2.50	5.00	10.00
❏ KC 35445	From the Inside	1978	2.50	5.00	10.00
❏ JC 35776	Outlaw Is Just a State of Mind	1979	2.50	5.00	10.00
❏ JC 36568	Even Cowgirls Get the Blues	1980	2.50	5.00	10.00
❏ FC 37354	Encore	1981	2.50	5.00	10.00
❏ PC 37354	Encore	1983	2.00	4.00	8.00
—Budget-line reissue					

HARMONY

❏ KH 32433	Singing My Song	1973	2.00	4.00	8.00

MERCURY

❏ 834625-1	What She Does Best	1988	2.00	4.00	8.00

MOUNTAIN DEW

❏ 7047	Lynn Anderson	197?	2.50	5.00	10.00

PERMIAN

❏ 8205	Back	1983	2.50	5.00	10.00

PICKWICK

❏ PTP-2049 [(2)]	Lynn Anderson	1973	3.00	6.00	12.00
❏ SPC-3267	Flower of Love	197?	2.00	4.00	8.00
❏ SPC-3296	It Makes You Happy	197?	2.00	4.00	8.00

ANDERSON, MARIAN
RCA VICTOR RED SEAL

❏ LM-110 [10]	Spirituals	195?	12.50	25.00	50.00
❏ LM-2032 [M]	Spirituals	195?	10.00	20.00	40.00
❏ LSC-2592 [S]	He's Got the Whole World in His Hands	1962	5.00	10.00	20.00
—Originals with "shaded dog" label					
❏ LSC-2613 [S]	Marian Anderson Sings Christmas Carols	1961	5.00	10.00	20.00
—Originals with "shaded dog" label					
❏ LSC-2613 [S]	Marian Anderson Sings Christmas Carols	1965	6.25	12.50	25.00
—Second pressings with "white dog" label					
❏ LRM-7006 [10]	Eleven Great Sprituals	1951	12.50	25.00	50.00
❏ LM 7008 [10]	Marian Anderson Sings Christmas Carols	1954	12.50	25.00	50.00

ANDERSON, MILDRED
BLUESVILLE

❏ BVLP-1004 [M]	Person to Person	1960	12.50	25.00	50.00
—Blue and silver label					
❏ BVLP-1004 [M]	Person to Person	1964	6.25	12.50	25.00
—Blue label with trident logo					
❏ BVLP-1017 [M]	No More in Life	1961	12.50	25.00	50.00
—Blue and silver label					
❏ BVLP-1017 [M]	No More in Life	1964	6.25	12.50	25.00
—Blue label with trident logo					

ANDERSON, PINK
BLUESVILLE

❏ BVLP-1038 [M]	Carolina Blues Man	1961	30.00	60.00	120.00
—Blue label, silver print					
❏ BVLP-1038 [M]	Carolina Blues Man	1964	7.50	15.00	30.00
—Blue label with trident logo					
❏ BVLP-1051 [M]	Medicine Show Man	1962	25.00	50.00	100.00
—Blue label, silver print					
❏ BVLP-1051 [M]	Medicine Show Man	1964	7.50	15.00	30.00
—Blue label with trident logo					
❏ BVLP-1071 [M]	Ballad and Folk Singer	1963	25.00	50.00	100.00
—Blue label, silver print					
❏ BVLP-1071 [M]	Ballad and Folk Singer	1964	7.50	15.00	30.00
—Blue label with trident logo					

ANDERSON, PINK, AND REV. GARY DAVIS
RIVERSIDE

❏ RLP 12-611 [M]	Carolina Street Ballads/Harlem Street Spirituals	196?	15.00	30.00	60.00

ANDERZA, EARL
PACIFIC JAZZ

❏ PJ-65 [M]	Outa Sight	1963	6.25	12.50	25.00
❏ ST-65 [S]	Outa Sight	1963	7.50	15.00	30.00

ANDRE'S CUBAN ALL-STARS
CLEF

❏ MGC-515 [10]	Cubano	1954	25.00	50.00	100.00
—This was reissued on 12-inch as part of a JACK COSTANZO album.					

ANDREWS, ERNIE
GENE NORMAN PRESENTS

❏ GNP-28 [M]	In the Dark	1957	10.00	20.00	40.00
❏ GNP-42 [M]	Ernie Andrews	1959	10.00	20.00	40.00
❏ GNP-43 [M]	Travelin' Light	1959	10.00	20.00	40.00
❏ GNPS-10008 [S]	Travelin' Light	1959	10.00	20.00	40.00

ANDREWS, GAYLE
HI-LIFE

❏ HL-54 [M]	Love's a Snap	195?	7.50	15.00	30.00

ANDREWS, JULIE
COLUMBIA

❏ CL 1712 [M]	Broadway's Fair Julie	1962	5.00	10.00	20.00
—Red and black label with six "eye" logos					
❏ CL 1886 [M]	Don't Go In the Lion's Cage Tonight	1963	5.00	10.00	20.00

Number	Title (A Side/B Side)	Yr	VG	VG+	NM
❑ CS 8512 [S]	Broadway's Fair Julie	1962	6.25	12.50	25.00
—Red and black label with six "eye" logos					
❑ CS 8686 [S]	Don't Go In the Lion's Cage Tonight	1963	6.25	12.50	25.00
RCA VICTOR					
❑ LPM-1403 [M]	The Lass with the Delicate Air	1957	10.00	20.00	40.00
—With pale blue jacket and the words "Julie Andrews" in a picture frame					
❑ LPM-1403 [M]	The Lass with the Delicate Air	1958	7.50	15.00	30.00
—With altered cover; "RE" on jacket					
❑ LSP-1403 [S]	The Lass with the Delicate Air	1958	15.00	30.00	60.00
❑ LPM-1681 [M]	Julie Andrews Sings	1958	7.50	15.00	30.00
❑ LSP-1681 [S]	Julie Andrews Sings	1958	12.50	25.00	50.00
❑ LPM-3829 [M]	A Christmas Treasure	1967	3.75	7.50	15.00
❑ LSP-3829 [S]	A Christmas Treasure	1967	3.75	7.50	15.00

ANDREWS, LEE, AND THE HEARTS
COLLECTABLES

Number	Title (A Side/B Side)	Yr	VG	VG+	NM
❑ COL-5003	Gotham Recording Sessions	1982	3.00	6.00	12.00
❑ COL-5028	Biggest Hits	198?	3.00	6.00	12.00
LOST-NITE					
❑ LLP-1 [10]	The Best of Lee Andrews and the Hearts, Volume 1	1981	3.00	6.00	12.00
—Red vinyl; in die-cut cover with sticker					
❑ LLP-2 [10]	The Best of Lee Andrews and the Hearts, Volume 2	1981	3.00	6.00	12.00
—Red vinyl; in die-cut cover with sticker					
❑ LP-101 [M]	Biggest Hits	1964	12.50	25.00	50.00
—Black vinyl					
❑ LP-101 [M]	Biggest Hits	1964	25.00	50.00	100.00
—Yellow vinyl					
❑ LP-113 [M]	Lee Andrews and the Hearts Live	1965	12.50	25.00	50.00

ANDREWS, RUBY
ABC

Number	Title (A Side/B Side)	Yr	VG	VG+	NM
❑ AB-1002	Genuine Ruby	1977	3.75	7.50	15.00
ICHIBAN					
❑ 1104	Kiss This	1991	3.75	7.50	15.00
ZODIAC					
❑ ZS 1001	Everybody Saw You	1970	20.00	40.00	80.00

ANDREWS SISTERS, THE
Also see BING CROSBY.
ABC

Number	Title (A Side/B Side)	Yr	VG	VG+	NM
❑ 4003	Sixteen Great Performances	1975	3.00	6.00	12.00
CAPITOL					
❑ T 790 [M]	The Andrews Sisters in Hi-Fi	1957	7.50	15.00	30.00
❑ T 860 [M]	Fresh and Fancy Free	1957	7.50	15.00	30.00
❑ T 973 [M]	The Dancing Twenties	1957	7.50	15.00	30.00
❑ DT 1924 [R]	The Hits of the Andrews Sisters	1963	3.00	6.00	12.00
❑ T 1924 [M]	The Hits of the Andrews Sisters	1963	5.00	10.00	20.00
DECCA					
❑ DL 4019 [M]	Curtain Call	1956	7.50	15.00	30.00
❑ DL 5065 [10]	Tropical Songs	1950	10.00	20.00	40.00
❑ DL 5120 [10]	The Andrews Sisters	1951	10.00	20.00	40.00
❑ DL 5155 [10]	Club 15	1951	10.00	20.00	40.00
❑ DL 5264 [10]	Berlin Songs	1951	10.00	20.00	40.00
❑ DL 5282 [10]	Christmas Cheer	1950	10.00	20.00	40.00
—Also see "Crosby, Bing"					
❑ DL 5306 [10]	I Love to Tell the Story	1952	10.00	20.00	40.00
❑ DL 5423 [10]	My Isle of Golden Dreams	1953	10.00	20.00	40.00
❑ DL 5438 [10]	Sing, Sing, Sing	1953	10.00	20.00	40.00
❑ DL 8354 [M]	Jingle Bells	1956	7.50	15.00	30.00
❑ DL 8360 [M]	The Andrews Sisters — By Popular Demand	1957	7.50	15.00	30.00
DOT					
❑ DLP 3406 [M]	The Andrews Sisters' Greatest Hits	1962	3.75	7.50	15.00
❑ DLP 3452 [M]	Great Golden Hits	1962	3.75	7.50	15.00
❑ DLP 3529 [M]	Present	1963	3.00	6.00	12.00
❑ DLP 3567 [M]	Great Country Hits	1963	3.00	6.00	12.00
❑ DLP 3632 [M]	The Andrews Sisters Go Hawaiian	1964	3.00	6.00	12.00
❑ DLP 25406 [S]	The Andrews Sisters' Greatest Hits	1962	5.00	10.00	20.00
❑ DLP 25452 [S]	Great Golden Hits	1962	5.00	10.00	20.00
❑ DLP 25529 [S]	Present	1963	3.75	7.50	15.00
❑ DLP 25567 [S]	Great Country Hits	1963	3.75	7.50	15.00
❑ DLP 25632 [S]	The Andrews Sisters Go Hawaiian	1964	3.75	7.50	15.00
HAMILTON					
❑ HLP 124 [M]	Pennsylvania Polka	196?	3.00	6.00	12.00
❑ HLP 12124 [S]	Pennsylvania Polka	196?	3.75	7.50	15.00
MCA					
❑ 739	Near You	198?	2.00	4.00	8.00
—Reissue of Vocalion album					
❑ 908	Rarities	198?	2.00	4.00	8.00
❑ 2-4024	The Best of the Andrews Sisters	1973	3.75	7.50	15.00
❑ 2-4093 [(2)]	The Best of the Andrews Sisters, Vol. 2	197?	3.75	7.50	15.00
❑ 24015	Christmas	1987	2.00	4.00	8.00
❑ 27081	Sixteen Great Performances	1980	2.00	4.00	8.00
—Reissue of ABC 4003					
❑ 27082	Boogie Woogie Bugle Girls	1980	2.00	4.00	8.00
—Reissue of Paramount 6075					
PARAMOUNT					
❑ PAS-1023	In the Mood	1974	3.75	7.50	15.00
❑ PAS-6075	Boogie Woogie Bugle Girls	1973	3.00	6.00	12.00
PICKWICK					
❑ PC-3094 [M]	Don't Sit Under the Apple Tree	196?	3.75	7.50	15.00
❑ SPC-3094 [S]	Don't Sit Under the Apple Tree	196?	3.00	6.00	12.00
❑ SPC-3382	Sing! Sing! Sing!	197?	2.50	5.00	10.00
VOCALION					
❑ VL 3611 [M]	Near You	196?	3.00	6.00	12.00

ANDY AND THE BEY SISTERS
PRESTIGE

Number	Title (A Side/B Side)	Yr	VG	VG+	NM
❑ PRLP-7346 [M]	Now! Hear!	1964	10.00	20.00	40.00
❑ PRST-7346 [S]	Now! Hear!	1964	12.50	25.00	50.00
❑ PRLP-7411 [M]	'Round About Midnight	1965	10.00	20.00	40.00
❑ PRST-7411 [S]	'Round About Midnight	1965	12.50	25.00	50.00

ANGELI, PIER
ROULETTE

Number	Title (A Side/B Side)	Yr	VG	VG+	NM
❑ R-25051 [M]	Italia Con Pier Angeli	1959	6.25	12.50	25.00
❑ SR-25051 [S]	Italia Con Pier Angeli	1959	7.50	15.00	30.00

ANGELOU, MAYA
LIBERTY

Number	Title (A Side/B Side)	Yr	VG	VG+	NM
❑ LRP-3028 [M]	Miss Calypso	1958	12.50	25.00	50.00

ANGELS, THE (1)
ASCOT

Number	Title (A Side/B Side)	Yr	VG	VG+	NM
❑ AM 13009 [M]	The Angels Sing — Twelve of Their Greatest Hits	1964	6.25	12.50	25.00
❑ ALS 16009 [S]	The Angels Sing — Twelve of Their Greatest Hits	1964	7.50	15.00	30.00
CAPRICE					
❑ LP 1001 [M]	...And the Angels Sing	1962	30.00	60.00	120.00
❑ SLP 1001 [S]	...And the Angels Sing	1962	50.00	100.00	200.00
COLLECTABLES					
❑ COL-5085	My Boyfriend's Back: Golden Classics	198?	2.50	5.00	10.00
SMASH					
❑ MGS-27039 [M]	My Boyfriend's Back	1963	10.00	20.00	40.00
❑ MGS-27048 [M]	A Halo to You	1964	10.00	20.00	40.00
❑ SRS-67039 [S]	My Boyfriend's Back	1963	15.00	30.00	60.00
❑ SRS-67048 [S]	A Halo to You	1964	15.00	30.00	60.00

ANGRY SAMOANS
BAD TRIP

Number	Title (A Side/B Side)	Yr	VG	VG+	NM
❑ (# unknown)	Back from Samoa	1982	7.50	15.00	30.00
❑ 001 [EP]	Different World/Unhinged + 4	1986	12.50	25.00	50.00
❑ 002	The Mistaken	1987	12.50	25.00	50.00
—As "The Mistaken"; 1,000 copies made					
❑ 201 [EP]	Inside My Brain	1981	6.25	12.50	25.00
❑ 201 [EP]	Inside My Brain	1981	12.50	25.00	50.00
—Original with heavy gray cardboard cover					
PVC					
❑ 6915	Yesterday Started Tomorrow	1987	3.75	7.50	15.00
❑ 8955	Inside My Brain	1987	3.75	7.50	15.00
—Reissue					
❑ 8965	STP Not LSD	1988	3.00	6.00	12.00

ANIMALS, THE
Includes "Eric Burdon and the Animals." Also see ERIC BURDON; ERIC BURDON AND WAR; ALAN PRICE.
ABKCO

Number	Title (A Side/B Side)	Yr	VG	VG+	NM
❑ AB-4226 [(2)]	The Best of the Animals	1973	3.00	6.00	12.00
❑ AB-4324 [M]	The Best of the Animals	1987	2.50	5.00	10.00
—With alternate version of "We Gotta Get Out of This Place"					
ACCORD					
❑ SN-7193	Looking Back	1981	2.00	4.00	8.00
❑ SN-7235	The Animals with Eric Burdon	1982	2.00	4.00	8.00
I.R.S.					
❑ SP 70037	The Ark	1983	2.50	5.00	10.00
❑ SP 70043	Rip It to Shreds: Their Greatest Hits Live	1984	2.50	5.00	10.00
JET/UA					
❑ JT-LA790-H	Before We Were So Rudely Interrupted	1977	2.50	5.00	10.00
—As "The Original Animals"					
MGM					
❑ E-4264 [M]	The Animals	1964	7.50	15.00	30.00
—"The House of the Rising Sun" is the edited 45 version					
❑ E-4264 [M]	The Animals	1964	25.00	50.00	100.00
—Yellow label promo					
❑ SE-4264 [R]	The Animals	1964	6.25	12.50	25.00
—"The House of the Rising Sun" is the edited 45 version (rechanneled, like the rest of the LP)					
❑ E-4281 [M]	The Animals On Tour	1965	7.50	15.00	30.00
❑ E-4281 [M]	The Animals On Tour	1965	25.00	50.00	100.00
—Yellow label promo					
❑ SE-4281 [R]	The Animals On Tour	1965	6.25	12.50	25.00
❑ E-4305 [M]	Animal Tracks	1965	10.00	20.00	40.00
❑ E-4305 [M]	Animal Tracks	1965	37.50	75.00	150.00
—Yellow label promo					
❑ SE-4305 [R]	Animal Tracks	1965	7.50	15.00	30.00
❑ E-4324 [M]	The Best of the Animals	1966	5.00	10.00	20.00
—This album was the first to contain the full-length version of "House of the Rising Sun."					
❑ E-4324 [M]	The Best of the Animals	1966	20.00	40.00	80.00
—Yellow label promo					
❑ SE-4324 [R]	The Best of the Animals	1966	6.25	12.50	25.00
❑ E-4384 [M]	Animalization	1966	6.25	12.50	25.00
❑ E-4384 [M]	Animalization	1966	25.00	50.00	100.00
—Yellow label promo					
❑ SE-4384 [P]	Animalization	1966	7.50	15.00	30.00
—All stereo except "Inside Looking Out," which is rechanneled.					
❑ E-4414 [M]	Animalism	1966	6.25	12.50	25.00
❑ E-4414 [M]	Animalism	1966	25.00	50.00	100.00
—Yellow label promo					
❑ SE-4414 [S]	Animalism	1966	7.50	15.00	30.00
❑ E-4433 [M]	Eric Is Here	1967	3.75	7.50	15.00
❑ SE-4433 [S]	Eric Is Here	1967	5.00	10.00	20.00
❑ E-4454 [M]	The Best of Eric Burdon and the Animals, Vol. 2	1967	5.00	10.00	20.00
❑ SE-4454 [P]	The Best of Eric Burdon and the Animals, Vol. 2	1967	5.00	10.00	20.00
❑ E-4484 [M]	Winds of Change	1967	5.00	10.00	20.00
❑ SE-4484 [S]	Winds of Change	1967	6.25	12.50	25.00
❑ E-4537 [M]	The Twain Shall Meet	1968	5.00	10.00	20.00
❑ SE-4537 [S]	The Twain Shall Meet	1968	6.25	12.50	25.00

Number	Title (A Side/B Side)	Yr	VG	VG+	NM
❑ E-4553 [M]	Every One of Us	1968	12.50	25.00	50.00
—Mono is promo only (yellow label)					
❑ SE-4553 [S]	Every One of Us	1968	6.25	12.50	25.00
❑ SE-4591 [(2)]	Love Is	1968	12.50	25.00	50.00
❑ SE-4602	Greatest Hits of Eric Burdon and the Animals	1969	3.75	7.50	15.00
❑ ST 90414 [R]	The Animals On Tour	1965	10.00	20.00	40.00
—Capitol Record Club edition					
❑ T 90414 [M]	The Animals On Tour	1965	12.50	25.00	50.00
—Capitol Record Club edition					
❑ T 90571 [M]	Animal Tracks	1965	12.50	25.00	50.00
—Capitol Record Club edition					
❑ KAO 90622 [M]	The Best of the Animals	1966	10.00	20.00	40.00
—Capitol Record Club edition					
❑ SKAO 90622 [R]	The Best of the Animals	1966	10.00	20.00	40.00
—Capitol Record Club edition; black label					
❑ SKAO 90622 [R]	The Best of the Animals	1969	7.50	15.00	30.00
—Capitol Record Club edition; blue and gold label					
❑ T 90687 [M]	The Animals	1966	12.50	25.00	50.00
—Capitol Record Club edition					
❑ ST 90923 [P]	Animalization	1966	12.50	25.00	50.00
—Capitol Record Club edition					
❑ T 90923 [M]	Animalization	1966	12.50	25.00	50.00
—Capitol Record Club edition					
❑ ST-91550 [S]	Every One of Us	1968	10.00	20.00	40.00
—Capitol Record Club edition; black label					
PICKWICK					
❑ SPC-3330	The Early Animals with Eric Burdon	1971	2.00	4.00	8.00
POLYDOR					
❑ 829091-1 [M]	Animalization	1986	2.00	4.00	8.00
SCEPTER CITATION					
❑ 18026	The Best of the Animals	1972	2.00	4.00	8.00
SPRINGBOARD					
❑ SPB-4025	The Best of the Animals	1972	2.00	4.00	8.00
❑ SPB-4065	The Night Time Is the Right Time	1973	2.00	4.00	8.00
WAND					
❑ WDS-690	In the Beginning	1970	2.50	5.00	10.00

ANIMATED EGG, THE
ALSHIRE

Number	Title (A Side/B Side)	Yr	VG	VG+	NM
❑ SF-32700	The Animated Egg	1967	12.50	25.00	50.00

ANKA, PAUL
ABC-PARAMOUNT

Number	Title (A Side/B Side)	Yr	VG	VG+	NM
❑ 240 [M]	Paul Anka	1958	12.50	25.00	50.00
❑ 296 [M]	My Heart Sings	1959	7.50	15.00	30.00
❑ S-296 [S]	My Heart Sings	1959	12.50	25.00	50.00
❑ 323 [M]	Paul Anka Sings His Big 15	1960	12.50	25.00	50.00
❑ S-323 [R]	Paul Anka Sings His Big 15	196?	7.50	15.00	30.00
❑ 347 [M]	Paul Anka Swings for Young Lovers	1960	7.50	15.00	30.00
❑ S-347 [S]	Paul Anka Swings for Young Lovers	1960	10.00	20.00	40.00
❑ 353 [M]	Anka at the Copa	1960	7.50	15.00	30.00
❑ S-353 [S]	Anka at the Copa	1960	10.00	20.00	40.00
❑ ABC 360 [M]	It's Christmas Everywhere	1960	7.50	15.00	30.00
❑ ABCS 360 [S]	It's Christmas Everywhere	1960	10.00	20.00	40.00
❑ 371 [M]	Strictly Instrumental	1961	7.00	15.00	30.00
❑ S-371 [S]	Strictly Instrumental	1961	10.00	20.00	40.00
❑ 390 [M]	Paul Anka Sings His Big 15, Vol. 2	1961	7.50	15.00	30.00
❑ S-390 [S]	Paul Anka Sings His Big 15, Vol. 2	1961	10.00	20.00	40.00
❑ 409 [M]	Paul Anka Sings His Big, Big 15, Volume III	1962	6.25	12.50	25.00
❑ S-409 [S]	Paul Anka Sings His Big, Big 15, Volume III	1962	7.50	15.00	30.00
❑ 420 [M]	Diana	1962	6.25	12.50	25.00
❑ S-420 [S]	Diana	1962	7.50	15.00	30.00
ACCORD					
❑ SN-7117	She's a Lady	1981	2.00	4.00	8.00
BUDDAH					
❑ BDS 5093	Paul Anka	1971	3.00	6.00	12.00
❑ BDS 5114	Jubilation	1972	3.00	6.00	12.00
❑ BDS 5622 [(2)]	This Is Anka	1974	3.75	7.50	15.00
❑ BDS 5667 [(2)]	The Essential Paul Anka	1974	3.75	7.50	15.00
COLUMBIA					
❑ FC 38442	Walk a Fine Line	1983	2.00	4.00	8.00
❑ FC 39323	Paul Anka Live	1984	2.00	4.00	8.00
LIBERTY					
❑ LN-10000	Paul Anka: His Best	1980	2.00	4.00	8.00
—Budget-line reissue					
❑ LN-10001	The Times of Your Life	1980	2.00	4.00	8.00
—Budget-line reissue					
❑ LN-10149	Feelings	1982	2.00	4.00	8.00
—Budget-line reissue					
❑ LN-10220	The Painter	1983	2.00	4.00	8.00
—Budget-line reissue					
PAIR					
❑ PDL2-1129 [(2)]	Songs I Write and Sing	1986	3.00	6.00	12.00
PICKWICK					
❑ PTP-2087 [(2)]	Paul Anka Way	197?	2.50	5.00	10.00
❑ SPC-3508	Puppy Love	1975	2.00	4.00	8.00
❑ SPC-3523	She's a Lady	1975	2.00	4.00	8.00
RANWOOD					
❑ 8203	The Very Best of Paul Anka	1981	2.00	4.00	8.00
RCA CAMDEN					
❑ ACL1-0616	My Way	1974	2.00	4.00	8.00
RCA VICTOR					
❑ ANL1-0896	Remember Diana	1975	2.50	5.00	10.00
❑ ANL1-1054	She's a Lady	1975	2.50	5.00	10.00
❑ ANL1-1584	Paul Anka Sings His Favorites	1976	2.50	5.00	10.00
❑ ANL1-2482	Songs I Wish I'd Written	1977	2.50	5.00	10.00
❑ LPM-2502 [M]	Young, Alive and In Love!	1962	3.75	7.50	15.00
—With portrait of Paul Anka on back cover					

Number	Title (A Side/B Side)	Yr	VG	VG+	NM
❑ LPM-2502 [M]	Young, Alive and In Love!	1962	6.25	12.50	25.00
—With portrait of Paul Anka on front cover					
❑ LSP-2502 [S]	Young, Alive and In Love!	1962	5.00	10.00	20.00
—With portrait of Paul Anka on back cover					
❑ LSP-2502 [S]	Young, Alive and In Love!	1962	7.50	15.00	30.00
—With portrait of Paul Anka on front cover					
❑ LPM-2575 [M]	Let's Sit This One Out	1962	5.00	10.00	20.00
❑ LSP-2575 [S]	Let's Sit This One Out	1962	6.25	12.50	25.00
❑ LPM-2614 [M]	Our Man Around the World	1963	5.00	10.00	20.00
❑ LSP-2614 [S]	Our Man Around the World	1963	6.25	12.50	25.00
❑ LPM-2691 [M]	Paul Anka's 21 Golden Hits	1963	5.00	10.00	20.00
❑ LSP-2691 [S]	Paul Anka's 21 Golden Hits	1963	6.25	12.50	25.00
—LPM/LSP-2691 has re-recorded versions of ABC-Paramount hits					
❑ LPM-2744 [M]	Songs I Wish I'd Written	1963	3.75	7.50	15.00
❑ LSP-2744 [S]	Songs I Wish I'd Written	1963	5.00	10.00	20.00
❑ AFL1-2892	Listen to Your Heart	1978	2.50	5.00	10.00
❑ LPM-2996 [M]	Excitement on Park Avenue	1964	3.75	7.50	15.00
❑ LSP-2996 [S]	Excitement on Park Avenue	1964	5.00	10.00	20.00
❑ AFL1-3382	Headlines	1979	2.50	5.00	10.00
❑ LPM-3580 [M]	Strictly Nashville	1966	3.75	7.50	15.00
❑ LSP-3580 [S]	Strictly Nashville	1966	5.00	10.00	20.00
❑ AYL1-3808	Paul Anka's 21 Golden Hits	1980	2.00	4.00	8.00
—"Best Buy Series" reissue					
❑ LPM-3875 [M]	Paul Anka Live	1967	3.75	7.50	15.00
❑ LSP-3875 [S]	Paul Anka Live	1967	5.00	10.00	20.00
❑ AFL1-3926	Both Sides of Love	1981	2.50	5.00	10.00
❑ LSP-4142	Goodnight My Love	1969	3.75	7.50	15.00
❑ LSP-4203	Sincerely	1969	3.75	7.50	15.00
❑ LSP-4250	Life Goes On	1969	3.75	7.50	15.00
❑ LSP-4300	Paul Anka 70s	1970	3.75	7.50	15.00
RHINO					
❑ RNLP-70220	The Best of Paul Anka (14 Original Hits, 1957-1961)	1986	2.50	5.00	10.00
RIVIERA					
❑ 0047 [M]	Paul Anka and Others	1959	37.50	75.00	150.00
—With Paul Anka's RPM recordings plus tracks by other artists					
SIRE					
❑ SASH-3704 [(2)]	Paul Anka Gold	1974	3.75	7.50	15.00
❑ SBK 6043 [(2)]	The Vintage Years 1957-1961	1978	3.00	6.00	12.00
UNITED ARTISTS					
❑ UA-LA314-G	Anka	1974	2.50	5.00	10.00
❑ UA-LA367-G	Feelings	1975	2.50	5.00	10.00
❑ UA-LA569-G	Times of Your Life	1975	2.50	5.00	10.00
❑ UA-LA653-G	The Painter	1976	2.50	5.00	10.00
❑ UA-LA746-H	The Music Man	1977	2.50	5.00	10.00
❑ UA-LA922-H	Paul Anka: His Best	1978	2.50	5.00	10.00

ANN-MARGRET
Also see AL HIRT.
MCA

Number	Title (A Side/B Side)	Yr	VG	VG+	NM
❑ 3226	Ann-Margret	1980	3.00	6.00	12.00
RCA VICTOR					
❑ LPM-2399 [M]	And Here She Is…	1961	7.50	15.00	30.00
❑ LSP-2399 [S]	And Here She Is…	1961	10.00	20.00	40.00
❑ LPM-2453 [M]	On the Way Up	1961	7.50	15.00	30.00
❑ LSP-2453 [S]	On the Way Up	1961	10.00	20.00	40.00
❑ LPM-2551 [M]	The Vivacious One	1962	7.50	15.00	30.00
❑ LSP-2551 [S]	The Vivacious One	1962	10.00	20.00	40.00
❑ LPM-2659 [M]	Bachelor's Paradise	1963	7.50	15.00	30.00
❑ LSP-2659 [S]	Bachelor's Paradise	1963	10.00	20.00	40.00
❑ LPM-3710 [M]	Songs from The Swinger and Others	1966	15.00	30.00	60.00
❑ LSP-3710 [S]	Songs from The Swinger and Others	1966	20.00	40.00	80.00

ANNA MARIE
Possibly Anna Marie Wooldridge, who later recorded as ABBEY LINCOLN.
VESTA

Number	Title (A Side/B Side)	Yr	VG	VG+	NM
❑ LP-101 [10]	Anna Marie	1955	20.00	40.00	80.00

ANNETTE
BUENA VISTA

Number	Title (A Side/B Side)	Yr	VG	VG+	NM
❑ BV-3301 [M]	Annette	1959	30.00	60.00	120.00
❑ BV-3302 [M]	Annette Sings Anka	1960	25.00	50.00	100.00
❑ BV-3303 [M]	Hawaiiannette	1960	18.75	37.50	75.00
❑ BV-3304 [M]	Italiannette	1960	18.75	37.50	75.00
❑ BV-3305 [M]	Dance Annette	1961	18.75	37.50	75.00
❑ BV-3312 [M]	The Story of My Teens	1962	18.75	37.50	75.00
❑ BV-3313 [M]	Teen Street	1962	18.75	37.50	75.00
❑ BV-3314 [M]	Muscle Beach Party	1963	18.75	37.50	75.00
❑ STER-3314 [S]	Muscle Beach Party	1963	37.50	75.00	150.00
❑ BV-3316 [M]	Beach Party	1963	15.00	30.00	60.00
❑ STER-3316 [S]	Beach Party	1963	25.00	50.00	100.00
❑ BV-3320 [M]	Annette on Campus	1964	12.50	25.00	50.00
❑ STER-3320 [S]	Annette on Campus	1964	25.00	50.00	100.00
❑ BV-3324 [M]	Annette at Bikini Beach	1964	12.50	25.00	50.00
❑ STER-3324 [S]	Annette at Bikini Beach	1964	25.00	50.00	100.00
❑ BV-3325 [M]	Annette's Pajama Party	1964	10.00	20.00	40.00
❑ STER-3325 [S]	Annette's Pajama Party	1964	25.00	50.00	100.00
❑ BV-3327 [M]	Annette Sings Golden Surfin' Hits	1964	25.00	50.00	100.00
❑ STER-3327 [S]	Annette Sings Golden Surfin' Hits	1964	37.50	75.00	150.00
❑ BV-3328 [M]	Something Borrowed, Something Blue	1964	15.00	30.00	60.00
❑ STER-3328 [S]	Something Borrowed, Something Blue	1964	25.00	50.00	100.00
❑ BV-4037	Annette Funicello	1972	12.50	25.00	50.00
RHINO					
❑ RNDF-206	The Best of Annette	1984	3.00	6.00	12.00
❑ RNLP-702 [PD]	The Best of Annette	1984	6.25	12.50	25.00

Number	Title (A Side/B Side)	Yr	VG	VG+	NM

ANNETTE / HAYLEY MILLS
Also see each artist's individual listings.
DISNEYLAND

❏ DL-3508 [M]	Annette and Hayley Mills (Singing 10 of Their Greatest All-Time Hits)	1964	250.00	500.00	1000.

—TV offer; issued with paper jacket. Though the cover says "Buena Vista Records Presents," the label is the yellow Disneyland label

ANONYMOUS
A-MAJOR

❏ AMLS-1002	Inside the Shadow	1976	62.50	125.00	250.00

ANT TRIP CEREMONY
C.R.C.

❏ 2129	24 Hours	1970	150.00	300.00	600.00

ANTHEM
BUDDAH

❏ BDS-5071	Anthem	1971	5.00	10.00	20.00

ANTHONY, RAY
CAPITOL

❏ H 258 [10]	Fox Trots	195?	10.00	20.00	40.00
❏ H 292 [10]	Houseparty Hop	195?	10.00	20.00	40.00

—Reissue of L 292; purple label; "This Album Contains 8 Selections" on upper right back cover

❏ L 292 [10]	Houseparty Hop	195?	12.50	25.00	50.00

—Original issue; maroon label; "In addition to the selections listed, this long playing record contains: PERDIDO - WAGON WHEELS" under the title on back cover

❏ H 476 [10]	I Remember Glenn Miller	1954	10.00	20.00	40.00
❏ T 749 [M]	Jam Session at the Tower	1956	10.00	20.00	40.00

AORTA
COLUMBIA

❏ CS 9785	Aorta	1969	7.50	15.00	30.00

HAPPY TIGER

❏ HT-1010	Aorta 2	1970	10.00	20.00	40.00

APHRODITE'S CHILD
VERTIGO

❏ VEL-2-500 [(2)]	666 (The Apocalypse of John)	1972	5.00	10.00	20.00

APPLE PIE MOTHERHOOD BAND, THE
ATLANTIC

❏ SD 8189	The Apple Pie Motherhood Band	1968	6.25	12.50	25.00
❏ SD 8233	Apple Pie	1969	6.25	12.50	25.00

APPLEJACKS, THE (1)
CAMEO

❏ C-1004 [M]	Alone Together	1958	12.50	25.00	50.00

—As "Dave Appell"

APPLETREE THEATRE CO.
VERVE FORECAST

❏ FTS-3042	Playback	1968	7.50	15.00	30.00

—RICK NELSON appears on this album

APPLEYARD, PETER
AUDIO FIDELITY

❏ AFLP-1901 [M]	The Vibe Sound of Peter Appleyard	1958	10.00	20.00	40.00
❏ AFSD-5901 [S]	The Vibe Sound of Peter Appleyard	1958	10.00	20.00	40.00

APRIL WINE
AQUARIUS

❏ AQR 504	Electric Jewels	1973	3.75	7.50	15.00
❏ AQR 505	Live	1974	3.75	7.50	15.00

ATLANTIC

❏ SD 19303	Stand Back	1981	2.50	5.00	10.00

—Reissue of Big Tree 89506
BIG TREE

❏ BTS 2012	April Wine	1972	5.00	10.00	20.00
❏ 89506	Stand Back	1975	3.75	7.50	15.00

CAPITOL

❏ SPRO-9632/3 [DJ]	Summer Tour 1981	1981	5.00	10.00	20.00

—Promo-only sampler

❏ ST-11852	First Glance	1979	3.00	6.00	12.00
❏ ST-12013	Harder...Faster	1979	2.50	5.00	10.00
❏ SOO-12125	The Nature of the Beast	1981	2.50	5.00	10.00
❏ ST-12218	Power Play	1982	2.50	5.00	10.00
❏ ST-12311	Animal Grace	1984	2.50	5.00	10.00
❏ SN-16245	First Glance	1982	2.00	4.00	8.00

—Budget-line reissue

❏ SN-16322	Harder...Faster	1984	2.00	4.00	8.00

—Budget-line reissue

❏ SN-16344	Power Play	1984	2.00	4.00	8.00

—Budget-line reissue

❏ SN-16379	The Nature of the Beast	1986	2.00	4.00	8.00

—Budget-line reissue

❏ C1-48418	Walking Through Fire	1988	3.00	6.00	12.00

LONDON

❏ PS 675	The Whole World's Goin' Crazy	1976	3.75	7.50	15.00
❏ PS 699	Live at the El Mocambo	1977	3.75	7.50	15.00

AQUATONES, THE
FARGO

❏ 3001 [M]	The Aquatones Sing	1964	125.00	250.00	500.00

RELIC/FARGO

❏ 5033 [M]	The Aquatones Sing	198?	2.00	4.00	8.00

ARBORS, THE
DATE

❏ TEM 3003 [M]	A Symphony for Susan	1967	3.75	7.50	15.00
❏ TEM 3011 [M]	Valley of the Dolls	1967	5.00	10.00	20.00
❏ TES 4003 [S]	A Symphony for Susan	1967	3.75	7.50	15.00
❏ TES 4011 [S]	Valley of the Dolls	1967	3.75	7.50	15.00
❏ TES 4017	The Arbors Featuring I Can't Quit Her and The Letter	1969	3.75	7.50	15.00

ARCHER, FRANCES, AND BEVERLY GILE
DISNEYLAND

❏ WDL-1008 [M]	A Child's Garden of Verses	1959	5.00	10.00	20.00

—Reissue of 3004

❏ DQ-1226 [M]	Songs from All Around the World	1962	5.00	10.00	20.00

—Black and white back cover (original)

❏ DQ-1241 [M]	A Child's Garden of Verses	1964	5.00	10.00	20.00

—Reissue of 1008

❏ EB-1347/8 [10]	A Child's Garden of Verses	1955	37.50	75.00	150.00

—The very first LP released on Disneyland Records

❏ WDL-3004 [M]	A Child's Garden of Verses	1956	6.25	12.50	25.00

—Reissue of 1347/8

❏ WDL-3006 [M]	Folk Songs from the Far Corners	1957	6.25	12.50	25.00
❏ WDL-3023 [M]	Community Concert	1958	7.50	15.00	30.00
❏ ST-3802 [M]	A Child's Garden of Verses	1971	6.25	12.50	25.00

—Reissue of 1241

ARCHIES, THE
ACCORD

❏ SN-7149	Straight A's	1981	2.50	5.00	10.00

CALENDAR

❏ KES-101	The Archies	1968	6.25	12.50	25.00
❏ KES-103	Everything's Archie	1969	6.25	12.50	25.00

51 WEST

❏ 16002	The Archies	1979	2.50	5.00	10.00

KIRSHNER

❏ KES-103 [DJ]	Everything's Archie Box	1969	25.00	50.00	100.00

—Box with LP, photos, press kit and buttons

❏ KES-105	Jingle Jangle	1969	6.25	12.50	25.00
❏ KES-107	Sunshine	1970	6.25	12.50	25.00
❏ KES-109	The Archies Greatest Hits	1970	6.25	12.50	25.00
❏ KES-110	This Is Love	1971	7.50	15.00	30.00

ARDEN, TONI
DECCA

❏ DL 4375 [M]	Italian Gold	196?	3.00	6.00	12.00
❏ DL 8651 [M]	Miss Toni Arden	1957	7.50	15.00	30.00

—Black label, silver print

❏ DL 8765 [M]	Sing a Song of Italy	1958	6.25	12.50	25.00

—Black label, silver print

❏ DL 8875 [M]	Besame	1959	5.00	10.00	20.00

—Black label, silver print

❏ DL 74375 [S]	Italian Gold	196?	3.75	7.50	15.00
❏ DL 78765 [S]	Sing a Song of Italy	1959	7.50	15.00	30.00

—Maroon label, silver print

❏ DL 78875 [S]	Besame	1959	7.50	15.00	30.00

—Maroon label, silver print
HARMONY

❏ HL 7212 [M]	Exciting Toni Arden	196?	5.00	10.00	20.00

AREA CODE 615
POLYDOR

❏ 24-4002	Area Code 615	1969	5.00	10.00	20.00
❏ 24-4025	A Trip in the Country	1970	5.00	10.00	20.00

ARGENT
EPIC

❏ BN 26525	Argent	1970	5.00	10.00	20.00

—Yellow label

❏ BN 26525	Argent	1973	3.00	6.00	12.00

—Orange label

❏ E 30128	A Ring of Hands	1971	5.00	10.00	20.00

—Yellow label

❏ KE 30128	A Ring of Hands	1973	3.00	6.00	12.00

—Orange label

❏ KE 31556	All Together Now	1972	5.00	10.00	20.00

—Yellow label

❏ KE 31556	All Together Now	1973	3.00	6.00	12.00

—Orange label

❏ KE 32195	In Deep	1973	5.00	10.00	20.00

—Orange label

❏ KE 32195	In Deep	1973	6.25	12.50	25.00

—Yellow label

❏ PEQ 32195 [Q]	In Deep	1974	7.50	15.00	30.00
❏ PE 32573	Nexus	1974	5.00	10.00	20.00

—Orange label

❏ PEG 33079 [(2)]	Encore — Live in Concert	1975	5.00	10.00	20.00

—Orange labels

❏ PE 33422	Circus	1975	5.00	10.00	20.00

—Orange label

❏ PE 33955	Anthology	1976	3.75	7.50	15.00

—Orange label

❏ PE 33955	Anthology	1979	2.50	5.00	10.00

—Dark blue label
UNITED ARTISTS

❏ UA-LA560-G	Counterpoint	1975	3.00	6.00	12.00

ARGO, TONY
SAVOY

❏ MG-12157 [M]	Jazz Argosy	1960	10.00	20.00	40.00

ARISTOCATS, THE
HIFI

❏ J-610 [M]	Boogie and Blues	1959	7.50	15.00	30.00
❏ JS-610 [S]	Boogie and Blues	1959	10.00	20.00	40.00

Number	Title (A Side/B Side)	Yr	VG	VG+	NM

ARLEN, HAROLD, AND "FRIEND"
The "Friend" is BARBRA STREISAND.
COLUMBIA MASTERWORKS
❏ OS 2920 [S]	Harold Sings Arlen	1966	10.00	20.00	40.00
—Gray label with "360 Sound" in white					
❏ OL 6520 [M]	Harold Sings Arlen	1966	7.50	15.00	30.00

ARMAGEDDON (1)
AMOS
❏ 73075	Armageddon	1970	6.25	12.50	25.00

ARMAGEDDON (2)
With KEITH RELF, ex-member of THE YARDBIRDS; his last material before his death.
A&M
❏ SP-4513	Armageddon	1975	5.00	10.00	20.00

ARMEN, KAY
DECCA
❏ DL 78835 [S]	Golden Songs of Tin Pan Alley	1959	7.50	15.00	30.00
MGM
| ❏ E-277 [10] | Kay Armen Sings "For No One But You" | 1955 | 10.00 | 20.00 | 40.00 |
| ❏ E-3276 [M] | If You Believe | 1955 | 7.50 | 15.00 | 30.00 |

ARMORED SAINT
CHRYSALIS
❏ FV 41476	March of the Saint	1984	2.00	4.00	8.00
❏ BFV 41516	Delirious Nomad	1985	2.00	4.00	8.00
❏ BFV 41601	Raising Fear	1987	2.00	4.00	8.00
ENIGMA/METAL BLADE
| ❏ 72301 [EP] | Live: Saints Will Conquer | 1988 | 2.00 | 4.00 | 8.00 |
METAL BLADE
| ❏ MBR 1009 [EP] | Armored Saint | 1983 | 12.50 | 25.00 | 50.00 |

ARMS, RUSSELL
ERA
❏ EL-20013 [M]	Where Can a Wanderer Go	1957	6.25	12.50	25.00

ARMSTRONG, LIL HARDIN
RIVERSIDE
❏ RLP 12-120 [M]	Satchmo and Me	195?	10.00	20.00	40.00
—Blue label with microphone logo at top					
❏ RLP 12-120 [M]	Satchmo and Me	1956	15.00	30.00	60.00
—White label, blue print					
❏ RLP-401 [M]	Lil Armstrong and Her Orchestra	1962	7.50	15.00	30.00

ARMSTRONG, LOUIS
ABC
❏ S-650	What a Wonderful World	1968	7.50	15.00	30.00
ACCORD
| ❏ SN-7161 | Mr. Music | 1982 | 2.50 | 5.00 | 10.00 |
AMSTERDAM
| ❏ AMS 12009 | Louis Armstrong and His Friends | 1970 | 3.75 | 7.50 | 15.00 |
ARCHIVE OF FOLK AND JAZZ
| ❏ 258 | Louis "Satchmo" Armstrong | 197? | 3.00 | 6.00 | 12.00 |
| ❏ 312 | Louis Armstrong, Vol. 2 | 197? | 2.50 | 5.00 | 10.00 |
AUDIO FIDELITY
❏ AFLP-1930 [M]	Louis Armstrong Plays King Oliver	1960	7.50	15.00	30.00
❏ AFLP-2128 [M]	Ain't Gonna Give Nobody None of My Jelly Roll	1964	3.75	7.50	15.00
❏ AFLP-2132 [M]	The Best of Louis Armstrong	1964	3.75	7.50	15.00
❏ AFSD-5930 [S]	Louis Armstrong Plays King Oliver	1960	10.00	20.00	40.00
❏ AFSD-6128 [S]	Ain't Gonna Give Nobody None of My Jelly Roll	1964	5.00	10.00	20.00
❏ AFSD-6132 [S]	The Best of Louis Armstrong	1964	5.00	10.00	20.00
❏ AFSD-6241	Louis Armstrong	196?	3.75	7.50	15.00
BIOGRAPH
| ❏ C-5 | Great Soloists | 1973 | 3.00 | 6.00 | 12.00 |
| ❏ C-6 | Louis Armstrong Plays the Blues | 1973 | 3.00 | 6.00 | 12.00 |
BLUEBIRD
❏ AXM2-5519 [(2)]	Young Louis (1932-1933)	1984	3.00	6.00	12.00
❏ 5920-1-RB [(2)]	Pops: The 1940s Small Band Sides	1987	3.75	7.50	15.00
❏ 8310-1-RB	What a Wonderful World	1988	2.50	5.00	10.00
❏ 9759-1-RB	Louis Armstrong & His Orchestra 1932-33: Laughin' Louie	1989	3.00	6.00	12.00
BRUNSWICK
| ❏ BL 58004 [10] | Armstrong Classics | 1950 | 25.00 | 50.00 | 100.00 |
| ❏ BL 754136 | I Will Wait for You | 1968 | 3.75 | 7.50 | 15.00 |
BUENA VISTA
| ❏ BV-4044 | Disney Swings the Satchmo Way | 1968 | 10.00 | 20.00 | 40.00 |
CHIAROSCURO
❏ 2002	Snake Rag	1977	3.00	6.00	12.00
❏ 2003	Great Alternatives	1977	3.00	6.00	12.00
❏ 2006	Sweetheart	1977	3.00	6.00	12.00
COLUMBIA
❏ CL 591 [M]	Louis Armstrong Plays W.C. Handy	1954	10.00	20.00	40.00
❏ CL 708 [M]	Satch Plays Fats	1955	10.00	20.00	40.00
❏ CL 840 [M]	Ambassador Satch	1956	10.00	20.00	40.00
❏ CL 851 [M]	The Louis Armstrong Story, Volume 1	1956	7.50	15.00	30.00
❏ CL 852 [M]	The Louis Armstrong Story, Volume 2	1956	7.50	15.00	30.00
❏ CL 853 [M]	The Louis Armstrong Story, Volume 3	1956	7.50	15.00	30.00
❏ CL 854 [M]	The Louis Armstrong Story, Volume 4	1956	7.50	15.00	30.00
❏ CL 1077 [M]	Satchmo the Great	1957	7.50	15.00	30.00
❏ CL 2638 [M]	Louis Armstrong's Greatest Hits	1967	5.00	10.00	20.00
❏ ML 4383 [M]	The Louis Armstrong Story, Volume 1	1951	12.50	25.00	50.00
❏ ML 4384 [M]	The Louis Armstrong Story, Volume 2	1951	12.50	25.00	50.00
❏ ML 4385 [M]	The Louis Armstrong Story, Volume 3	1951	12.50	25.00	50.00
❏ ML 4386 [M]	The Louis Armstrong Story, Volume 4	1951	12.50	25.00	50.00
❏ CL 6335 [10]	Louis Armstrong Plays W.C. Handy, Volume 2	1955	10.00	20.00	40.00
❏ CS 9438 [R]	Louis Armstrong's Greatest Hits	1967	3.00	6.00	12.00
❏ PC 9438 [R]	Louis Armstrong's Greatest Hits	198?	2.00	4.00	8.00
—Budget-line reissue					
❏ G 30416 [(2)]	The Genius of Louis Armstrong, Vol. 1	1971	3.75	7.50	15.00

Number	Title (A Side/B Side)	Yr	VG	VG+	NM

COLUMBIA MUSICAL TREASURIES
❏ P4M 5676 [(4)]	40 Greatest Hits	197?	5.00	10.00	20.00
DECCA
❏ DX 108 [(2)M]	Satchmo at Symphony Hall	1954	18.75	37.50	75.00
—Black labels, silver print					
❏ DX 155 [(4)M]	Satchmo, A Musical Autobiography	1956	25.00	50.00	100.00
—Black labels, silver print					
❏ DXM 155 [(4)M]	Satchmo, A Musical Autobiography	1960	10.00	20.00	40.00
—Black labels with color bars					
❏ DXB 183 [(2)M]	The Best of Louis Armstrong	196?	7.50	15.00	30.00
❏ DL 4137 [M]	Satchmo's Golden Favorites	1961	5.00	10.00	20.00
❏ DL 4227 [M]	I Love Jazz	1962	5.00	10.00	20.00
❏ DL 4230 [M]	Satchmo, A Musical Autobiography, 1926-1927	1962	6.25	12.50	25.00
❏ DL 4245 [M]	King Louis	1962	5.00	10.00	20.00
❏ DL 4330 [M]	Satchmo, A Musical Autobiography, 1928-1930	1962	6.25	12.50	25.00
❏ DL 4331 [M]	Satchmo, A Musical Autobiography, 1930-1934	1962	6.25	12.50	25.00
❏ DL 5225 [10]	New Orleans to New York	1950	18.75	37.50	75.00
❏ DL 5279 [10]	New Orleans Days	1950	18.75	37.50	75.00
❏ DL 5280 [10]	Jazz Concert	1950	18.75	37.50	75.00
❏ DL 5401 [10]	Satchmo Serenades	1952	18.75	37.50	75.00
❏ DL 5532 [10]	Latter-Day Louis	1954	18.75	37.50	75.00
❏ DL 5536 [10]	Louis Armstrong-Gordon Jenkins	1954	18.75	37.50	75.00
❏ DXSB 7183 [(2)R]	The Best of Louis Armstrong	196?	3.75	7.50	15.00
❏ DL 8037 [M]	Satchmo at Symphony Hall, Volume 1	1954	10.00	20.00	40.00
—Black label, silver print					
❏ DL 8037 [M]	Satchmo at Symphony Hall, Volume 1	1960	3.75	7.50	15.00
—Black label with color bars					
❏ DL 8038 [M]	Satchmo at Symphony Hall, Volume 2	1954	10.00	20.00	40.00
—Black label, silver print					
❏ DL 8038 [M]	Satchmo at Symphony Hall, Volume 2	1960	3.75	7.50	15.00
—Black label with color bars					
❏ DL 8041 [M]	Satchmo at Pasadena	1954	10.00	20.00	40.00
—Black label, silver print					
❏ DL 8041 [M]	Satchmo at Pasadena	1960	3.75	7.50	15.00
—Black label with color bars					
❏ DL 8126 [M]	Satchmo Sings	1955	10.00	20.00	40.00
—Black label, silver print					
❏ DL 8126 [M]	Satchmo Sings	1960	3.75	7.50	15.00
—Black label with color bars					
❏ DL 8168 [M]	Louis Armstrong at the Crescendo, Volume 1	1955	10.00	20.00	40.00
—Black label, silver print					
❏ DL 8169 [M]	Louis Armstrong at the Crescendo, Volume 2	1955	10.00	20.00	40.00
—Black label, silver print					
❏ DL 8211 [M]	Satchmo Serenades	1956	10.00	20.00	40.00
—Black label, silver print					
❏ DL 8211 [M]	Satchmo Serenades	1960	3.75	7.50	15.00
—Black label with color bars					
❏ DL 8283 [M]	New Orleans Jazz	1956	10.00	20.00	40.00
—Black label, silver print					
❏ DL 8283 [M]	New Orleans Jazz	1960	3.75	7.50	15.00
—Black label with color bars					
❏ DL 8284 [M]	Jazz Classics	1956	10.00	20.00	40.00
—Black label, silver print					
❏ DL 8284 [M]	Jazz Classics	1960	3.75	7.50	15.00
—Black label with color bars					
❏ DL 8327 [M]	Satchmo's Collector's Items	1957	10.00	20.00	40.00
—Black label, silver print					
❏ DL 8327 [M]	Satchmo's Collector's Items	1960	3.75	7.50	15.00
—Black label with color bars					
❏ DL 8329 [M]	New Orleans Nights	1957	10.00	20.00	40.00
—Black label, silver print					
❏ DL 8329 [M]	New Orleans Nights	1960	3.75	7.50	15.00
—Black label with color bars					
❏ DL 8330 [M]	Satchmo on Stage	1957	10.00	20.00	40.00
—Black label, silver print					
❏ DL 8330 [M]	Satchmo on Stage	1960	3.75	7.50	15.00
—Black label with color bars					
❏ DL 8488 [M]	Louis and the Angels	1957	10.00	20.00	40.00
—Black label, silver print					
❏ DL 8488 [M]	Louis and the Angels	1960	3.75	7.50	15.00
—Black label with color bars					
❏ DL 8741 [M]	Louis and the Good Book	1960	3.75	7.50	15.00
—Black label with color bars					
❏ DL 8781 [M]	Louis and the Good Book	1958	10.00	20.00	40.00
—Black label, silver print					
❏ DL 8840 [M]	Satchmo in Style	1958	10.00	20.00	40.00
—Black label, silver print					
❏ DL 8840 [M]	Satchmo in Style	1960	3.75	7.50	15.00
—Black label with color bars					
❏ DL 8963 [M]	Satchmo, A Musical Autobiography, 1923-1925	1960	6.25	12.50	25.00
❏ DL 9225 [M]	Rare Items (1935-1944)	196?	5.00	10.00	20.00
❏ DL 9233 [M]	Young Louis the Sideman (1924-1927)	196?	5.00	10.00	20.00
❏ DL 74137 [R]	Satchmo's Golden Favorites	1961	3.00	6.00	12.00
❏ DL 74227 [R]	I Love Jazz	1962	3.00	6.00	12.00
❏ DL 74245 [R]	King Louis	1962	3.00	6.00	12.00
❏ DL 74330 [R]	A Musical Autobiography, 1928-1930	1962	3.00	6.00	12.00
❏ DL 78963 [R]	Satchmo, A Musical Autobiography, 1923-1925	196?	3.00	6.00	12.00
❏ DL 79225 [R]	Rare Items (1935-1944)	196?	3.00	6.00	12.00
❏ DL 79233 [R]	Young Louis the Sideman (1924-1927)	196?	3.00	6.00	12.00
DISNEYLAND
❏ STER-1341	The Wonderful World of Walt Disney	1971	5.00	10.00	20.00
—Reissue of Buena Vista 4044					
GNP CRESCENDO
| ❏ 9050 | Pasadena Concert, Vol. II | 1987 | 2.50 | 5.00 | 10.00 |
| ❏ 11001 [(2)] | An Evening with Louis Armstrong | 1977 | 3.75 | 7.50 | 15.00 |
HARMONY
| ❏ HS 11316 | Louis Armstrong | 197? | 3.00 | 6.00 | 12.00 |

Number	Title (A Side/B Side)	Yr	VG	VG+	NM
☐ KH 31236	The Louis Armstrong Saga	1971	3.00	6.00	12.00
JOLLY ROGER					
☐ 5009 [10]	Louis Armstrong	1954	12.50	25.00	50.00
KAPP					
☐ KL-1364 [M]	Hello, Dolly!	1964	3.00	6.00	12.00
☐ KS-3364 [S]	Hello, Dolly!	1964	3.75	7.50	15.00
MCA					
☐ 538	Hello, Dolly!	197?	2.50	5.00	10.00
—Reissue of Kapp LP					
☐ 1300	Louis and the Good Book	197?	2.50	5.00	10.00
—Reissue of Decca 8741					
☐ 1301	Young Louis the Sideman	197?	2.50	5.00	10.00
—Reissue of Decca 9233					
☐ 1304	Back in New York	197?	2.50	5.00	10.00
☐ 1306	Louis with Guest Stars	197?	2.50	5.00	10.00
☐ 1312	Swing That Music!	197?	2.50	5.00	10.00
☐ 1316	Satchmo Serenades	197?	2.50	5.00	10.00
—Reissue of Decca 8211					
☐ 1322	Satchmo's Collector's Items	197?	2.50	5.00	10.00
—Reissue of Decca 8327					
☐ 1334	Satchmo For Ever!	197?	2.50	5.00	10.00
☐ 1335	Old Favorites	197?	2.50	5.00	10.00
☐ 2-4013 [(2)]	Louis Armstrong at the Crescendo	197?	3.00	6.00	12.00
—Reissue of Decca 8168/8169 in one sleeve					
☐ 2-4035 [(2)]	The Best of Louis Armstrong	197?	3.00	6.00	12.00
—Reissue of Decca 7183					
☐ 2-4057 [(2)]	Satchmo at Symphony Hall	197?	3.00	6.00	12.00
—Reissue of Decca 108					
☐ 10006 [(4)]	Satchmo, A Musical Autobiography	197?	6.25	12.50	25.00
—Reissue of Decca 155					
☐ 25204	What a Wonderful World	1988	2.50	5.00	10.00
—Reissue of ABC 650					
☐ 42328	Louis Armstrong of New Orleans	1990	3.00	6.00	12.00
MERCURY					
☐ MG-21081 [M]	Louis Armstrong Sings Louis Armstrong	1965	3.00	6.00	12.00
☐ SR-61081 [S]	Louis Armstrong Sings Louis Armstrong	1965	3.75	7.50	15.00
METRO					
☐ M-510 [M]	Hello, Louis	1965	3.00	6.00	12.00
☐ MS-510 [S]	Hello, Louis	1965	3.75	7.50	15.00
MILESTONE					
☐ 2010	Early Portrait	197?	2.50	5.00	10.00
☐ 47017 [(2)]	Louis Armstrong and King Oliver	197?	3.00	6.00	12.00
MOSAIC					
☐ MQ8-146 [(8)]	The Complete Decca Studio Recordings of Louis Armstrong and the All-Stars	199?	37.50	75.00	150.00
PABLO					
☐ 2310941	Mack the Knife	1990	3.00	6.00	12.00
PAIR					
☐ PDL2-1042 [(2)]	The Jazz Legend	1986	3.00	6.00	12.00
PAUSA					
☐ 9018	The Greatest of Louis Armstrong	1983	2.50	5.00	10.00
RCA VICTOR					
☐ LPT 7 [10]	Louis Armstrong Town Hall Concert	1951	20.00	40.00	80.00
☐ LJM-1005 [M]	Louis Armstrong Sings the Blues	1954	12.50	25.00	50.00
☐ LPM-1443 [M]	Town Hall Concert Plus	1957	12.50	25.00	50.00
☐ LPM-2322 [M]	A Rare Batch of Satch	1961	6.25	12.50	25.00
☐ LPM-2971 [M]	Louis Armstrong in the '30s/in the '40s	1964	5.00	10.00	20.00
☐ LSP-2971(e) [R]	Louis Armstrong in the '30s/in the '40s	1964	3.00	6.00	12.00
☐ VPM-6044 [(2)]	July 4, 1900/July 6, 1971	1971	5.00	10.00	20.00
RIVERSIDE					
☐ RLP 12-101 [M]	The Young Louis Armstrong	195?	10.00	20.00	40.00
—Blue label					
☐ RLP 12-101 [M]	The Young Louis Armstrong	1956	20.00	40.00	80.00
—White label, blue print					
☐ RLP 12-122 [M]	Louis Armstrong 1923	195?	10.00	20.00	40.00
—Blue label					
☐ RLP 12-122 [M]	Louis Armstrong 1923	1956	20.00	40.00	80.00
—White label, blue print					
☐ RLP-1001 [10]	Louis Armstrong Plays the Blues	1953	25.00	50.00	100.00
☐ RLP-1029 [10]	Louis Armstrong with King Oliver's Creole Jazz Band 1923	1953	25.00	50.00	100.00
SEAGULL					
☐ LG-8206	Greatest Hits: Live in Concert	198?	3.00	6.00	12.00
STORYVILLE					
☐ 4012	Louis Armstrong and His All-Stars	1980	2.50	5.00	10.00
SWING					
☐ SW-8450	Louis and the Big Bands	1984	2.50	5.00	10.00
VANGUARD					
☐ VSD 91/92 [(2)]	Essential Louis Armstrong	1977	3.75	7.50	15.00
☐ VMS 73129	Essential Louis Armstrong, Vol. 1	1986	2.00	4.00	8.00
VERVE					
☐ MGV-4012 [M]	Louis Under the Stars	1957	12.50	25.00	50.00
☐ MGVS-4012	Louis Under the Stars	199?	6.25	12.50	25.00
—Classic Records reissue					
☐ V-4012 [M]	Louis Under the Stars	1961	5.00	10.00	20.00
☐ V6-4012 [S]	Louis Under the Stars	1961	3.75	7.50	15.00
☐ MGV-4035 [M]	I've Got the World on a String	1959	12.50	25.00	50.00
☐ MGVS-4035	I've Got the World on a String	199?	6.25	12.50	25.00
—Classic Records reissue					
☐ V-4035 [M]	I've Got the World on a String	1961	5.00	10.00	20.00
☐ V6-4035 [S]	I've Got the World on a String	1961	3.75	7.50	15.00
☐ MGVS-6044 [S]	Louis Under the Stars	1960	10.00	20.00	40.00
☐ MGVS-6101 [S]	I've Got the World on a String	1960	10.00	20.00	40.00
☐ V-8569 [M]	The Essential Louis A.	1963	3.00	6.00	12.00
☐ V6-8569 [S]	The Essential Louis A.	1963	3.75	7.50	15.00
☐ V-8595 [M]	The Best of Louis Armstrong	1964	3.00	6.00	12.00
☐ V6-8595 [S]	The Best of Louis Armstrong	1964	3.75	7.50	15.00

Number	Title (A Side/B Side)	Yr	VG	VG+	NM
VOCALION					
☐ VL 3851 [M]	Here's Louis Armstrong	196?	3.75	7.50	15.00
☐ VL 73851 [R]	Here's Louis Armstrong	196?	2.50	5.00	10.00
☐ VL 73871 [R]	The One and Only Louis Armstrong	1968	2.50	5.00	10.00
WING					
☐ SR-16381	Great Louis	196?	2.50	5.00	10.00

ARMSTRONG, LOUIS, AND SIDNEY BECHET

JOLLY ROGER

Number	Title (A Side/B Side)	Yr	VG	VG+	NM
☐ 5029 [M]	Louis Armstrong and Sidney Bechet	195?	10.00	20.00	40.00

ARMSTRONG, LOUIS, AND DUKE ELLINGTON

MOBILE FIDELITY

Number	Title (A Side/B Side)	Yr	VG	VG+	NM
☐ 2-155 [(2)]	The Great Reunion	1984	20.00	40.00	80.00
—Audiophile vinyl					
ROULETTE					
☐ R 52074 [M]	Together for the First Time	1961	6.25	12.50	25.00
☐ SR 52074 [S]	Together for the First Time	1961	5.00	10.00	20.00
☐ R 52103 [M]	The Great Reunion	1963	5.00	10.00	20.00
☐ SR 52103 [S]	The Great Reunion	1963	6.25	12.50	25.00

ARMSTRONG, LOUIS/AL HIRT

MURRAY HILL

Number	Title (A Side/B Side)	Yr	VG	VG+	NM
☐ 930633 [(4)]	Louis Armstrong and Al Hirt Play Dixieland Trumpet	197?	5.00	10.00	20.00

ARMSTRONG, LOUIS, AND THE MILLS BROTHERS

DECCA

Number	Title (A Side/B Side)	Yr	VG	VG+	NM
☐ DL 5509 [10]	Louis Armstrong and the Mills Brothers	1954	15.00	30.00	60.00

ARMSTRONG, LOUIS, AND OSCAR PETERSON

VERVE

Number	Title (A Side/B Side)	Yr	VG	VG+	NM
☐ MGVS-6062 [S]	Louis Armstrong Meets Oscar Peterson	1960	10.00	20.00	40.00
☐ MGV-8322 [M]	Louis Armstrong Meets Oscar Peterson	1959	12.50	25.00	50.00
☐ V-8322 [M]	Louis Armstrong Meets Oscar Peterson	1961	5.00	10.00	20.00

ARNAZ, DESI

RCA VICTOR

Number	Title (A Side/B Side)	Yr	VG	VG+	NM
☐ LPM-3096 [10]	Babalu!	1954	30.00	60.00	120.00

ARNOLD, BILLY BOY
See BILLY BOY.

ARNOLD, BUDDY

ABC-PARAMOUNT

Number	Title (A Side/B Side)	Yr	VG	VG+	NM
☐ ABC-114 [M]	Wailing	1956	15.00	30.00	60.00

ARNOLD, EDDY

MGM

Number	Title (A Side/B Side)	Yr	VG	VG+	NM
☐ SE-4878	So Many Ways/If the Whole World Stopped Lovin'	1973	3.00	6.00	12.00
☐ SE-4912	She's Got Everything I Need	1974	3.00	6.00	12.00
☐ SE-4916	I Wish I Had Loved You Better	1974	3.00	6.00	12.00
☐ MG-1-4992	The Wonderful World of Eddy Arnold	1975	3.00	6.00	12.00
☐ MJB-5107 [(2)]	World of Hits	1976	3.00	6.00	12.00
PAIR					
☐ PDL2-1000 [(2)]	The Mellow Side of Eddy Arnold	1986	3.00	6.00	12.00
RCA					
☐ 9963-1-R	Hand-Holdin' Songs	1990	3.75	7.50	15.00
RCA CAMDEN					
☐ CAL-471 [M]	Eddy Arnold (That's How Much I Love You)	1959	5.00	10.00	20.00
☐ CAS-471(e) [R]	Eddy Arnold (That's How Much I Love You)	1966	2.50	5.00	10.00
☐ CAL-563 [M]	More Eddy Arnold	1960	5.00	10.00	20.00
☐ CAS-563(e) [R]	More Eddy Arnold	1966	2.50	5.00	10.00
☐ CAL-741 [M]	Country Songs I Love to Sing	1963	3.75	7.50	15.00
☐ CAS-741(e) [R]	Country Songs I Love to Sing	1966	2.50	5.00	10.00
☐ CAL-799 [M]	Eddy's Songs	1964	3.75	7.50	15.00
☐ CAS-799(e) [R]	Eddy's Songs	1966	2.50	5.00	10.00
☐ CAL-897 [M]	I'm Throwing Rice (At the Girl That I Love) And Other Favorites	1966	3.75	7.50	15.00
☐ CAS-897(e) [R]	I'm Throwing Rice (At the Girl That I Love) And Other Favorites	1966	2.50	5.00	10.00
☐ CAS-2501	Then You Can Tell Me Goodbye	197?	2.50	5.00	10.00
RCA VICTOR					
☐ DPL2-0051 [(2)]	The Greatest of Eddy Arnold	1973	3.75	7.50	15.00
—Special products issue; "Tele House Inc. Presents" on labels					
☐ APL1-0239	The World of Eddy Arnold	1973	3.00	6.00	12.00
☐ PRS-346	Christmas with Eddy Arnold	1971	3.75	7.50	15.00
—Special-products issue					
☐ ANL1-1078	Pure Gold	1975	2.50	5.00	10.00
☐ LPM-1111 [M]	Wanderin' with Eddy Arnold	1955	12.50	25.00	50.00
☐ LPM-1223 [M]	All-Time Favorites	1955	12.50	25.00	50.00
—New version of LPM 3117					
☐ LPM-1224 [M]	Anytime	1955	12.50	25.00	50.00
—New version of LPM 3027					
☐ LPM-1225 [M]	The Chapel on the Hill	1955	12.50	25.00	50.00
—New version of LPM 3031					
☐ LPM-1293 [M]	A Dozen Hits	1956	12.50	25.00	50.00
☐ LPM-1377 [M]	A Little on the Lonely Side	1956	12.50	25.00	50.00
☐ LPM-1484 [M]	When They Were Young	1956	12.50	25.00	50.00
☐ LPM-1575 [M]	My Darling, My Darling	1957	10.00	20.00	40.00
☐ LPM-1733 [M]	Praise Him, Praise Him	1958	10.00	20.00	40.00
☐ APL1-1817	Eddy	1976	3.00	6.00	12.00
☐ LPM-1928 [M]	Have Guitar, Will Travel	1959	6.25	12.50	25.00
☐ LSP-1928 [S]	Have Guitar, Will Travel	1959	7.50	15.00	30.00
☐ LPM-2036 [M]	Thereby Hangs a Tale	1959	6.25	12.50	25.00
☐ LSP-2036 [S]	Thereby Hangs a Tale	1959	7.50	15.00	30.00
☐ LPM-2185 [M]	Eddy Arnold Sings Them Again	1960	6.25	12.50	25.00
☐ LSP-2185 [S]	Eddy Arnold Sings Them Again	1960	7.50	15.00	30.00
☐ LPM-2268 [M]	You Gotta Have Love	1960	6.25	12.50	25.00
☐ LSP-2268 [S]	You Gotta Have Love	1960	7.50	15.00	30.00
☐ APL1-2277	I Need You All the Time	1977	3.00	6.00	12.00

Number	Title (A Side/B Side)	Yr	VG	VG+	NM
❑ LPM-2337 [M]	Let's Make Memories Tonight	1961	5.00	10.00	20.00
❑ LSP-2337 [S]	Let's Make Memories Tonight	1961	6.25	12.50	25.00
❑ LPM-2471 [M]	One More Time	1961	5.00	10.00	20.00
❑ LSP-2471 [S]	One More Time	1961	6.25	12.50	25.00
❑ LPM-2554 [M]	Christmas with Eddy Arnold	1962	5.00	10.00	20.00
❑ LSP-2554 [S]	Christmas with Eddy Arnold	1962	6.25	12.50	25.00
❑ LPM-2578 [M]	Cattle Call	1962	6.25	12.50	25.00
❑ LSP-2578 [S]	Cattle Call	1962	7.50	15.00	30.00
❑ LPM-2596 [M]	Our Man Down South	1962	6.25	12.50	25.00
❑ LSP-2596 [S]	Our Man Down South	1962	7.50	15.00	30.00
❑ LPM-2629 [M]	Faithfully Yours	1963	6.25	12.50	25.00
❑ LSP-2629 [S]	Faithfully Yours	1963	7.50	15.00	30.00
❑ LPM-2811 [M]	Folk Song Book	1964	5.00	10.00	20.00
❑ LSP-2811 [S]	Folk Song Book	1964	6.25	12.50	25.00
❑ LPM-2909 [M]	Sometimes I'm Happy, Sometimes I'm Blue	1964	5.00	10.00	20.00
❑ LSP-2909 [S]	Sometimes I'm Happy, Sometimes I'm Blue	1964	6.25	12.50	25.00
❑ LPM-2951 [M]	Pop Hits from the Country Side	1964	5.00	10.00	20.00
❑ LSP-2951 [S]	Pop Hits from the Country Side	1964	6.25	12.50	25.00
❑ LPM-3027 [10]	Anytime	1952	30.00	60.00	120.00
—Label calls this "Country Classics"					
❑ LPM-3031 [10]	All-Time Hits from the Hills	1952	25.00	50.00	100.00
❑ LPM-3117 [10]	All-Time Favorites	1953	25.00	50.00	100.00
❑ LPM-3219 [10]	When It's Roundup Time in Heaven	1954	25.00	50.00	100.00
❑ LPM-3230	An American Institution Booklet	1954	12.50	25.00	50.00
❑ LPM-3230 [10]	An American Institution	1954	25.00	50.00	100.00
❑ AHL1-3358	Somebody	1979	2.50	5.00	10.00
❑ LPM-3361 [M]	The Easy Way	1965	3.75	7.50	15.00
❑ LSP-3361 [S]	The Easy Way	1965	5.00	10.00	20.00
❑ LPM-3466 [M]	My World	1965	3.00	6.00	12.00
❑ LSP-3466 [S]	My World	1965	3.75	7.50	15.00
❑ LPM-3507 [M]	I Want to Go with You	1966	3.00	6.00	12.00
❑ LSP-3507 [S]	I Want to Go with You	1966	3.75	7.50	15.00
❑ LPM-3565 [M]	The Best of Eddy Arnold	1967	5.00	10.00	20.00
❑ LSP-3565 [S]	The Best of Eddy Arnold	1967	3.75	7.50	15.00
❑ AHL1-3606	A Legend and His Lady	1980	2.50	5.00	10.00
❑ LPM-3622 [M]	The Last Word in Lonesome	1966	3.00	6.00	12.00
❑ LSP-3622 [S]	The Last Word in Lonesome	1966	3.75	7.50	15.00
❑ AYL1-3675	The Best of Eddy Arnold	1980	2.00	4.00	8.00
—"Best Buy Series" reissue					
❑ LPM-3715 [M]	Somebody Like Me	1966	3.00	6.00	12.00
❑ LSP-3715 [S]	Somebody Like Me	1966	3.75	7.50	15.00
❑ LPM-3753 [M]	Lonely Again	1967	5.00	10.00	20.00
❑ LSP-3753 [S]	Lonely Again	1967	3.75	7.50	15.00
❑ LPM-3869 [M]	Turn the World Around	1967	5.00	10.00	20.00
❑ LSP-3869 [S]	Turn the World Around	1967	3.75	7.50	15.00
❑ AHL1-3914	A Man for All Seasons	1980	2.50	5.00	10.00
❑ LPM-3931 [M]	The Everlovin' World of Eddy Arnold	1968	10.00	20.00	40.00
❑ LSP-3931 [S]	The Everlovin' World of Eddy Arnold	1968	3.75	7.50	15.00
❑ AYL1-3937	The Best of Eddy Arnold, Volume II	1981	2.00	4.00	8.00
—"Best Buy Series" reissue					
❑ LPM-4009 [M]	The Romantic World of Eddy Arnold	1968	37.50	75.00	150.00
❑ LSP-4009 [S]	The Romantic World of Eddy Arnold	1968	3.75	7.50	15.00
❑ LSP-4089	Walkin' in Love Land	1968	3.75	7.50	15.00
❑ LSP-4110	Songs of the Young World	1969	3.75	7.50	15.00
❑ LSP-4179	The Glory of Love	1969	3.75	7.50	15.00
❑ LSP-4231	The Warmth of Eddy	1969	3.75	7.50	15.00
❑ AHL1-4263	Don't Give Up on Me	1981	2.50	5.00	10.00
❑ LSP-4304	Love & Guitars	1970	3.00	6.00	12.00
❑ LSP-4320	The Best of Eddy Arnold, Volume II	1970	3.00	6.00	12.00
❑ LSP-4471	Portrait of My Woman	1971	3.00	6.00	12.00
❑ LSP-4625	Loving Her Was Easier	1971	3.00	6.00	12.00
❑ AHL1-4661	Close Enough to Love	1983	2.50	5.00	10.00
❑ LSP-4738	Eddy Arnold Sings for Housewives and Other Ladies	1972	3.00	6.00	12.00
❑ CPL2-4885 [(2)]	The Legendary Performances (1945-1971)	1983	3.00	6.00	12.00
❑ AHL1-5467	Collector's Series	1985	2.50	5.00	10.00
❑ VPS-6032 [(2)]	This Is Eddy Arnold	1972	3.75	7.50	15.00

ARNOLD, HARRY
ATCO

Number	Title (A Side/B Side)	Yr	VG	VG+	NM
❑ 33-120 [M]	I Love Harry Arnold (And All That Jazz)	1960	10.00	20.00	40.00

EMARCY

| ❑ MG-36139 [M] | Harry Arnold and His Orchestra | 1958 | 12.50 | 25.00 | 50.00 |
| ❑ SR-80006 [S] | Harry Arnold and His Orchestra | 1958 | 10.00 | 20.00 | 40.00 |

JAZZLAND

| ❑ JLP-65 [M] | Harry Arnold's Great Big Band and Friends | 1962 | 6.25 | 12.50 | 25.00 |
| ❑ JLP-965 [S] | Harry Arnold's Great Big Band and Friends | 1962 | 7.50 | 15.00 | 30.00 |

JAZZTONE

| ❑ J-1270 [M] | The Jazztone Mystery Band | 1958 | 10.00 | 20.00 | 40.00 |

RIVERSIDE

❑ RM-7526 [M]	Let's Dance on Broadway	196?	5.00	10.00	20.00
❑ RM-7536 [M]	Dancing on Broadway to the Music of Cole Porter	196?	5.00	10.00	20.00
❑ RS-97526 [S]	Let's Dance on Broadway	196?	6.25	12.50	25.00
❑ RS-97536 [S]	Dancing on Broadway to the Music of Cole Porter	196?	6.25	12.50	25.00

ART BEARS
RALPH

| ❑ RR 7905 | Winter Songs | 1979 | 5.00 | 10.00 | 20.00 |

ART ENSEMBLE OF CHICAGO
Also see LESTER BOWIE; ROSCOE MITCHELL.
NESSA

❑ N-3	People in Sorrow	1969	6.25	12.50	25.00
❑ N-4	Les Stances a Sophie	1970	6.25	12.50	25.00
—With Fontella Bass					
❑ N-5	Old/Quartet	1975	5.00	10.00	20.00

ART OF LOVIN'
MAINSTREAM

| ❑ S-6113 | Art of Lovin' | 1968 | 50.00 | 100.00 | 200.00 |

ARTHUR
LHI

Number	Title (A Side/B Side)	Yr	VG	VG+	NM
❑ 12000	Dreams and Images	1968	10.00	20.00	40.00

ARTISTICS, THE
BRUNSWICK

❑ BL 54123 [M]	I'm Gonna Miss You	1967	6.25	12.50	25.00
❑ BL 754123 [S]	I'm Gonna Miss You	1967	6.25	12.50	25.00
❑ BL 754139	The Articulate Artistics	1968	6.25	12.50	25.00
❑ BL 754153	What Happened	1969	6.25	12.50	25.00
❑ BL 754168	I Want You to Make My Life Over	1970	6.25	12.50	25.00
❑ BL 754195	Look Out	1973	5.00	10.00	20.00

OKEH

| ❑ OKM-12119 [M] | Get My Hands on Some Lovin' | 1967 | 20.00 | 40.00 | 80.00 |
| ❑ OKS-14119 [S] | Get My Hands on Some Lovin' | 1967 | 20.00 | 40.00 | 80.00 |

ARTISTS UNITED AGAINST APARTHEID
MANHATTAN

❑ SPRO-9538 [DJ]	Voices of Sun City	1985	6.25	12.50	25.00
—Promo album of interviews with participants in the benefit LP					
❑ ST-53019	Sun City	1985	3.00	6.00	12.00

ARZACHEL
ROULETTE

| ❑ SR 42036 | Arzachel | 1969 | 37.50 | 75.00 | 150.00 |

ASGAERD
THRESHOLD

| ❑ THS 6 | In the Realm of Asgaerd | 1972 | 5.00 | 10.00 | 20.00 |

ASH, MARVIN
CAPITOL

| ❑ H 188 [10] | Honky Tonk Piano | 1950 | 15.00 | 30.00 | 60.00 |

DECCA

| ❑ DL 8346 [M] | New Orleans at Midnight | 1957 | 10.00 | 20.00 | 40.00 |

JAZZ MAN

| ❑ LPJM-335 [10] | Marvin Ash | 1954 | 12.50 | 25.00 | 50.00 |

JUMP

| ❑ JL-4 [10] | Marvin Ash | 1954 | 12.50 | 25.00 | 50.00 |

ASHBY, DOROTHY
ARGO

| ❑ LP-690 [M] | Dorothy Ashby | 1962 | 6.25 | 12.50 | 25.00 |
| ❑ LPS-690 [S] | Dorothy Ashby | 1962 | 7.50 | 15.00 | 30.00 |

ATLANTIC

| ❑ SD 1447 [S] | The Fantastic Jazz Harp of Dorothy Ashby | 1966 | 5.00 | 10.00 | 20.00 |

JAZZLAND

| ❑ JLP-61 [M] | Soft Winds | 1961 | 6.25 | 12.50 | 25.00 |
| ❑ JLP-961 [S] | Soft Winds | 1961 | 7.50 | 15.00 | 30.00 |

NEW JAZZ

❑ NJLP-8209 [M]	In a Minor Groove	1958	15.00	30.00	60.00
—Purple label					
❑ NJLP-8209 [M]	In a Minor Groove	1965	6.25	12.50	25.00
—Blue label, trident logo at right					

PRESTIGE

| ❑ PRLP-7140 [M] | Hip Harp | 1958 | 15.00 | 30.00 | 60.00 |

REGENT

| ❑ MG-6039 [M] | Dorothy Ashby — Jazz Harpist | 1957 | 15.00 | 30.00 | 60.00 |

ASHES
VAULT

| ❑ 125 | Ashes | 1968 | 12.50 | 25.00 | 50.00 |

ASHKAN
SIRE

| ❑ SES-97107 | In from the Cold | 1970 | 6.25 | 12.50 | 25.00 |

ASHLEY, LEON
RCA VICTOR

| ❑ LPM-3900 [M] | Laura (What's He Got That I Ain't Got) | 1967 | 7.50 | 15.00 | 30.00 |
| ❑ LSP-3900 [S] | Laura (What's He Got That I Ain't Got) | 1967 | 5.00 | 10.00 | 20.00 |

ASHWORTH, ERNEST
HICKORY

| ❑ LPM-118 [M] | Hits of Today and Tomorrow | 1964 | 6.25 | 12.50 | 25.00 |

ASIA
Includes members of KING CRIMSON and YES.
GEFFEN

❑ GHS 2008	Asia	1982	2.00	4.00	8.00
—White label with pinstripes					
❑ GHS 2008 [DJ]	Asia	1982	5.00	10.00	20.00
—Promo on "Quiex II" vinyl					
❑ GHS 4008	Alpha	1983	2.00	4.00	8.00
—White label with pinstripes					
❑ GHS 4008 [DJ]	Alpha	1983	5.00	10.00	20.00
—Promo on "Quiex II" vinyl					
❑ GHS 24072	Astra	1985	2.00	4.00	8.00
❑ GHS 24298	Then and Now	1990	3.00	6.00	12.00

ASLEEP AT THE WHEEL
ARISTA

| ❑ AL-8550 | Keepin' Me Up Nights | 1990 | 3.00 | 6.00 | 12.00 |

CAPITOL

❑ ST-11441	Texas Gold	1975	3.00	6.00	12.00
❑ ST-11548	Wheelin' and Dealin'	1976	3.00	6.00	12.00
❑ ST-11620	The Wheel	1977	3.00	6.00	12.00
❑ SW-11726	Collision Course	1978	3.00	6.00	12.00
❑ ST-11945	Served Live	1979	3.00	6.00	12.00
❑ SN-16306	Served Live	1984	2.00	4.00	8.00
—Budget-line reissue					

Number	Title (A Side/B Side)	Yr	VG	VG+	NM
CAPITOL SPECIAL MARKETS					
❏ SL-8138	Drivin'	1980	3.00	6.00	12.00
DOT/MCA					
❏ 39036	Asleep at the Wheel	1985	2.50	5.00	10.00
EPIC					
❏ KE 33097	Asleep at the Wheel	1974	3.75	7.50	15.00
❏ PE 33097	Asleep at the Wheel	197?	2.00	4.00	8.00
—*Reissue*					
❏ BG 33782 [(2)]	Fathers and Sons	1974	6.25	12.50	25.00
—*With Bob Wills*					
❏ EG 33782 [(2)]	Fathers and Sons	197?	3.00	6.00	12.00
—*Reissue*					
❏ BFE 40681	10	1987	2.00	4.00	8.00
❏ FE 44213	Western Standard Time	1988	2.00	4.00	8.00
LIBERTY					
❏ LN-10296	Comin' Right At Ya!	1986	2.00	4.00	8.00
—*Budget-line reissue*					
MCA					
❏ 742	Framed	1982	2.00	4.00	8.00
—*Reissue of 5131*					
❏ 5131	Framed	1980	2.50	5.00	10.00
UNITED ARTISTS					
❏ UA-LA038-F	Comin' Right At Ya!	1973	5.00	10.00	20.00

ASMUSSEN, SVEND

Number	Title (A Side/B Side)	Yr	VG	VG+	NM
ANGEL					
❏ ANG.60000 [10]	Svend Asmussen and His Unmelancholy Danes	1955	15.00	30.00	60.00
❏ ANG.60010 [10]	Rhythm Is Our Business	1955	15.00	30.00	60.00
BRUNSWICK					
❏ BL 58051 [10]	Hot Fiddle	1953	20.00	40.00	80.00
EPIC					
❏ LN 3210 [M]	Skol!	1955	12.50	25.00	50.00

ASSOCIATION, THE

Number	Title (A Side/B Side)	Yr	VG	VG+	NM
COLUMBIA					
❏ KC 31348	Waterbeds in Trinidad	1972	2.50	5.00	10.00
HITBOUND/REALISTIC					
❏ 51-3022	New Memories	1983	3.00	6.00	12.00
PAIR					
❏ PDL2-1061 [(2)]	Songs That Made Them Famous	1986	3.00	6.00	12.00
VALIANT					
❏ VLM-5002 [M]	And Then…Along Comes The Association	1966	5.00	10.00	20.00
❏ VLM-5004 [M]	Renaissance	1966	5.00	10.00	20.00
—*With no blurb for "No Fair at All" on cover*					
❏ VLM-5004 [M]	Renaissance	1967	3.75	7.50	15.00
—*With blurb for "No Fair at All" on cover*					
❏ VLS-25002 [S]	And Then…Along Comes The Association	1966	6.25	12.50	25.00
❏ VLS-25004 [S]	Renaissance	1966	6.25	12.50	25.00
—*With no blurb for "No Fair at All" on cover*					
❏ VLS-25004 [S]	Renaissance	1967	5.00	10.00	20.00
—*With blurb for "No Fair at All" on cover*					
WARNER BROS.					
❏ W 1696 [M]	Insight Out	1967	3.75	7.50	15.00
❏ WS 1696 [S]	Insight Out	1967	5.00	10.00	20.00
—*Gold label*					
❏ WS 1696 [S]	Insight Out	1968	3.00	6.00	12.00
—*With "W7" logo on green label*					
❏ W 1702 [M]	And Then…Along Comes The Association	1967	5.00	10.00	20.00
❏ WS 1702 [S]	And Then…Along Comes The Association	1967	3.00	6.00	12.00
—*With "W7" logo on green label*					
❏ WS 1702 [S]	And Then…Along Comes The Association	1967	5.00	10.00	20.00
—*Gold label*					
❏ WS 1704	Renaissance	1967	3.00	6.00	12.00
❏ WS 1733	Birthday	1968	3.00	6.00	12.00
—*With "W7" logo on green label*					
❏ WS 1767	Greatest Hits	1968	3.00	6.00	12.00
—*With "W7" logo on green label*					
❏ WS 1767	Greatest Hits	197?	2.00	4.00	8.00
—*Any later pressing (LP in print until the late 1980s)*					
❏ WS 1786	Goodbye Columbus	1969	3.00	6.00	12.00
—*With "W7" logo on green label*					
❏ WS 1800	The Association	1969	3.00	6.00	12.00
—*With "W7" logo on green label*					
❏ 2WS 1868 [(2)]	The Association "Live"	1970	3.75	7.50	15.00
❏ WS 1927	Stop Your Motor	1971	3.00	6.00	12.00
❏ ST-91317 [S]	Insight Out	1967	6.25	12.50	25.00
—*Capitol Record Club edition*					
❏ ST-91586	Greatest Hits	1968	5.00	10.00	20.00
—*Capitol Record Club edition*					
❏ STBO-93249 [(2)]	The Association "Live"	1970	5.00	10.00	20.00
—*Capitol Record Club edition*					

ASTRONAUTS, THE (1)

Number	Title (A Side/B Side)	Yr	VG	VG+	NM
RCA VICTOR					
❏ PRM-183 [M]	Rockin' with the Astronauts	1965	7.50	15.00	30.00
❏ LPM-2760 [M]	Surfin' with the Astronauts	1963	15.00	30.00	60.00
❏ LSP-2760 [S]	Surfin' with the Astronauts	1963	20.00	40.00	80.00
❏ LSP-2782 [S]	Everything Is A-OK!	1964	15.00	30.00	60.00
❏ LPM-2858 [M]	Competition Coupe	1964	15.00	30.00	60.00
❏ LSP-2858 [S]	Competition Coupe	1964	20.00	40.00	80.00
❏ LPM-2903 [M]	The Astronauts Orbit Kampus	1964	10.00	20.00	40.00
❏ LSP-2903 [S]	The Astronauts Orbit Kampus	1964	12.50	25.00	50.00
❏ LPM-3307 [M]	The Astronauts Go, Go, Go	1965	7.50	15.00	30.00
❏ LSP-3307 [S]	The Astronauts Go, Go, Go	1965	10.00	20.00	40.00
❏ LPM-3359 [M]	Favorites for You from Us	1965	7.50	15.00	30.00
❏ LSP-3359 [S]	Favorites for You from Us	1965	10.00	20.00	40.00
❏ LPM-3454 [M]	Down the Line	1966	7.50	15.00	30.00
❏ LSP-3454 [S]	Down the Line	1966	10.00	20.00	40.00
❏ LPM-3733 [M]	Travelin' Men	1967	12.50	25.00	50.00
❏ LSP-3733 [S]	Travelin' Men	1967	7.50	15.00	30.00

ASTRONAUTS, THE (1) / THE LIVERPOOL FIVE

Number	Title (A Side/B Side)	Yr	VG	VG+	NM
RCA VICTOR					
❏ PRS-251 [S]	Stereo Festival	1967	25.00	50.00	100.00
—*Special-prodcuts edition*					

ASYLUM CHOIR

LEON RUSSELL and MARC BENNO.

Number	Title (A Side/B Side)	Yr	VG	VG+	NM
MCA					
❏ 684	Asylum Choir II	1979	2.00	4.00	8.00
—*Reissue of Shelter 52010*					
SHELTER					
❏ SR 2120	Asylum Choir II	1974	3.00	6.00	12.00
—*Reissue of 8910*					
❏ SW-8910	Asylum Choir II	1971	3.75	7.50	15.00
❏ 52010	Asylum Choir II	1977	2.50	5.00	10.00
—*Reissue of 2120*					
SMASH					
❏ SRS-67107	Look Inside the Asylum Choir	1968	7.50	15.00	30.00
—*Front cover has a roll of toilet paper*					
❏ SRS-67107	Look Inside the Asylum Choir	197?	3.75	7.50	15.00
—*Front cover has a photo of Leon and Marc*					

ATCHER, BOB

Number	Title (A Side/B Side)	Yr	VG	VG+	NM
COLUMBIA					
❏ CL 2232 [M]	The Dean of Cowboy Singers	1964	6.25	12.50	25.00
❏ HL 9006 [10]	Early American Folk Songs	1949	20.00	40.00	80.00
❏ HL 9013 [10]	Songs of the Saddle	1949	20.00	40.00	80.00
❏ CS 9032 [R]	The Dean of Cowboy Singers	1964	3.75	7.50	15.00
HARMONY					
❏ HL 7313 [M]	Bob Atcher's Best	1964	5.00	10.00	20.00

ATKINS, CHET

Number	Title (A Side/B Side)	Yr	VG	VG+	NM
COLUMBIA					
❏ FC 38536	Work It Out with Chet Atkins C.G.P.	1983	2.50	5.00	10.00
❏ PC 38536	Work It Out with Chet Atkins C.G.P.	1985	2.00	4.00	8.00
—*Budget-line reissue*					
❏ PC 39003	East Tennessee Christmas	1983	2.50	5.00	10.00
❏ FC 39591	Stay Tuned	1985	2.50	5.00	10.00
❏ FC 40256	Street Dreams	1986	2.00	4.00	8.00
❏ FC 40593	Sails	1987	2.00	4.00	8.00
❏ FC 44323	Chet Atkins, C.G.P.	1989	2.00	4.00	8.00
DOLTON					
❏ BLP-16506 [M]	Play Guitar with Chet Atkins	1967	6.25	12.50	25.00
❏ BST-17506 [S]	Play Guitar with Chet Atkins	1967	7.50	15.00	30.00
PAIR					
❏ PDL2-1047 [(2)]	Tennessee Guitar Man	1985	3.00	6.00	12.00
❏ PDL2-1115 [(2)]	Guitar for All Seasons	1986	3.00	6.00	12.00
RCA CAMDEN					
❏ CAL-659 [M]	Chet Atkins and His Guitar	196?	3.75	7.50	15.00
❏ CAS-659(e) [R]	Chet Atkins and His Guitar	1964	3.00	6.00	12.00
❏ CAL-753 [M]	Guitar Genius	196?	3.75	7.50	15.00
❏ CAS-753(e) [R]	Guitar Genius	196?	3.00	6.00	12.00
❏ CAL-981 [M]	Music from Nashville, My Home Town	1966	3.00	6.00	12.00
❏ CAS-981 [S]	Music from Nashville, My Home Town	1966	3.75	7.50	15.00
❏ CAL-2182 [M]	Chet	196?	3.00	6.00	12.00
❏ CAS-2182 [S]	Chet	196?	3.75	7.50	15.00
❏ CAS-2296	Relaxin' with Chet	1969	3.00	6.00	12.00
❏ CAS-2523	Chet 'n Boots	1972	3.00	6.00	12.00
❏ CAS-2555	Nashville Gold	1972	3.00	6.00	12.00
❏ CAS-2600	Finger Pickin' Good	1973	2.50	5.00	10.00
❏ ACL1-7042	Love Letters	197?	2.50	5.00	10.00
RCA RED SEAL					
❏ LM-2870 [M]	The "Pops" Goes Country	1966	3.75	7.50	15.00
❏ LSC-2870 [S]	The "Pops" Goes Country	1966	5.00	10.00	20.00
—*Above two with the Boston Pops Orchestra, Arthur Fiedler, conductor*					
❏ LSC-3104	Chet Picks On the Pops	1969	3.75	7.50	15.00
—*With the Boston Pops Orchestra, Arthur Fiedler, conductor*					
RCA VICTOR					
❏ APL1-0159	Alone	1973	3.00	6.00	12.00
❏ APL1-0329	Superpickers	1974	3.00	6.00	12.00
❏ APL1-0545	Chet Atkins Picks On Jerry Reed	1974	3.00	6.00	12.00
❏ APL1-0645	Chat Atkins Goes to the Movies	1973	3.00	6.00	12.00
❏ ANL1-0981	Chet Atkins Picks the Best	1975	2.50	5.00	10.00
❏ LPM-1090 [M]	A Session with Chet Atkins	1954	15.00	30.00	60.00
—*Red cover*					
❏ LPM-1090 [M]	A Session with Chet Atkins	1961	5.00	10.00	20.00
—*Woman and guitars cover*					
❏ LSP-1090(e) [R]	A Session with Chet Atkins	1967	2.50	5.00	10.00
❏ LPM-1197 [M]	Chet Atkins in Three Dimensions	1956	12.50	52.00	50.00
—*Black-and-white guitar cover*					
❏ LPM-1197 [M]	Chet Atkins in Three Dimensions	1961	5.00	10.00	20.00
—*Red guitar cover*					
❏ LSP-1197(e) [R]	Chet Atkins in Three Dimensions	1967	2.50	5.00	10.00
❏ APL1-1233	The Night Atlanta Burned	1975	3.00	6.00	12.00
❏ LPM-1236 [M]	Stringin' Along with Chet Atkins	1956	12.50	25.00	50.00
—*Orange cover*					
❏ LPM-1236 [M]	Stringin' Along with Chet Atkins	1961	5.00	10.00	20.00
—*Full-color cover*					
❏ LSP-1236(e) [R]	Stringin' Along with Chet Atkins	1967	2.50	5.00	10.00
❏ LPM-1383 [M]	Finger Style Guitar	1956	12.50	25.00	50.00
—*Chet's face not visible on cover*					
❏ LPM-1383 [M]	Finger Style Guitar	1961	5.00	10.00	20.00
—*Chet's face visible on cover*					
❏ LSP-1383(e) [R]	Finger Style Guitar	1962	3.00	6.00	12.00
❏ LPM-1544 [M]	Chet Atkins at Home	1957	12.50	25.00	50.00
—*Title in block letters on cover*					
❏ LPM-1544 [M]	Chet Atkins at Home	1961	5.00	10.00	20.00
—*Title in script on cover*					
❏ LSP-1544(e) [R]	Chet Atkins at Home	1967	2.50	5.00	10.00

Number	Title (A Side/B Side)	Yr	VG	VG+	NM
❑ LPM-1577 [M]	Hi-Fi in Focus	1957	5.00	10.00	20.00
—Guitar on cover					
❑ LPM-1577 [M]	Hi-Fi in Focus	1957	12.50	25.00	50.00
—No guitars on cover					
❑ LSP-1577(e) [R]	Hi-Fi in Focus	196?	2.50	5.00	10.00
❑ ANL1-1935	Christmas with Chet Atkins	1976	2.00	4.00	8.00
—Reissue of LSP-2423					
❑ APL1-1985	The Best of Chet Atkins	1975	3.00	6.00	12.00
❑ LPM-1993 [M]	Chet Atkins in Hollywood	1959	7.50	15.00	30.00
—Night-time cover					
❑ LPM-1993 [M]	Chet Atkins in Hollywood	1961	5.00	10.00	20.00
—Daylight "blonde" cover					
❑ LSP-1993 [S]	Chet Atkins in Hollywood	1959	12.50	25.00	50.00
—Night-time cover					
❑ LSP-1993 [S]	Chet Atkins in Hollywood	1961	7.50	15.00	30.00
—Daylight "blonde" cover					
❑ LPM-2025 [M]	Hum & Strum Along	1959	6.25	12.50	25.00
—Add $10 NM if instruction book is included					
❑ LSP-2025 [S]	Hum & Strum Along	1959	10.00	20.00	40.00
—Add $10 NM if instruction book is included					
❑ LPM-2103 [M]	Mister Guitar	1959	7.50	15.00	30.00
—Lone guitar on cover					
❑ LPM-2103 [M]	Mister Guitar	1961	5.00	10.00	20.00
—Guitar and woman on cover					
❑ LSP-2103 [S]	Mister Guitar	1959	12.50	25.00	50.00
—Lone guitar on cover					
❑ LSP-2103 [S]	Mister Guitar	1961	7.50	15.00	30.00
—Guitar and woman on cover					
❑ LPM-2161 [M]	Teensville	1960	7.50	15.00	30.00
—Title overlaps cover photo					
❑ LPM-2161 [M]	Teensville	1961	5.00	10.00	20.00
—Title in black strip at top of cover photo					
❑ LSP-2161 [S]	Teensville	1960	12.50	25.00	50.00
—Title overlaps cover photo					
❑ LSP-2161 [S]	Teensville	1961	7.50	15.00	30.00
—Title in black strip at top of cover photo					
❑ LPM-2175 [M]	The Other Chet Atkins	1960	5.00	10.00	20.00
❑ LSP-2175 [S]	The Other Chet Atkins	1960	7.50	15.00	30.00
❑ LPM-2232 [M]	Chet Atkins' Workshop	1961	5.00	10.00	20.00
❑ LSP-2232 [S]	Chet Atkins' Workshop	1961	7.50	15.00	30.00
❑ LPM-2346 [M]	The Most Popular Guitar	1961	5.00	10.00	20.00
❑ LSP-2346 [S]	The Most Popular Guitar	1961	7.50	15.00	30.00
❑ AHL1-2405	My Guitar	1977	3.00	6.00	12.00
❑ LPM-2423 [M]	Christmas with Chet Atkins	1961	5.00	10.00	20.00
❑ LSP-2423 [S]	Christmas with Chet Atkins	1961	7.50	15.00	30.00
❑ LPM-2450 [M]	Down Home	1962	5.00	10.00	20.00
❑ LSP-2450 [S]	Down Home	1962	6.25	12.50	25.00
❑ CPL1-2503	A Legendary Performer	1977	3.00	6.00	12.00
❑ LPM-2549 [M]	Caribbean Guitar	1962	5.00	10.00	20.00
❑ LSP-2549 [S]	Caribbean Guitar	1962	6.25	12.50	25.00
❑ LPM-2601 [M]	Back Home Hymns	1962	5.00	10.00	20.00
❑ LSP-2601 [S]	Back Home Hymns	1962	6.25	12.50	25.00
❑ LPM-2616 [M]	Our Man in Nashville	1963	5.00	10.00	20.00
❑ LSP-2616 [S]	Our Man in Nashville	1963	6.25	12.50	25.00
❑ LPM-2678 [M]	Travelin'	1963	5.00	10.00	20.00
❑ LSP-2678 [S]	Travelin'	1963	6.25	12.50	25.00
❑ LPM-2719 [M]	Teen Scene	1963	5.00	10.00	20.00
❑ LSP-2719 [S]	Teen Scene	1963	6.25	12.50	25.00
❑ LPM-2783 [M]	Guitar Country	1964	3.75	7.50	15.00
❑ LSP-2783 [S]	Guitar Country	1964	5.00	10.00	20.00
❑ LPM-2887 [M]	The Best of Chet Atkins	1964	3.75	7.50	15.00
❑ LSP-2887 [S]	The Best of Chet Atkins	1964	5.00	10.00	20.00
❑ LPM-2908 [M]	Progressive Pickin'	1964	3.75	7.50	15.00
❑ LSP-2908 [S]	Progressive Pickin'	1964	5.00	10.00	20.00
❑ LPM-3079 [10]	Chet Atkins' Gallopin' Guitar	1952	37.50	75.00	150.00
❑ LPM-3169 [10]	Stringin' Along with Chet Atkins	1953	25.00	50.00	100.00
❑ AHL1-3302	The First Nashville Guitar Quartet	1979	3.00	6.00	12.00
❑ LPM-3316 [M]	My Favorite Guitars	1965	3.75	7.50	15.00
❑ LSP-3316 [S]	My Favorite Guitars	1965	5.00	10.00	20.00
❑ LPM-3429 [M]	More of That "Guitar Country"	1965	3.75	7.50	15.00
❑ LSP-3429 [S]	More of That "Guitar Country"	1965	5.00	10.00	20.00
❑ AHL1-3505	The Best of Chet On The Road…Live	1980	3.00	6.00	12.00
❑ LPM-3531 [M]	Chet Atkins Picks On the Beatles	1966	6.25	12.50	25.00
❑ LSP-3531 [S]	Chet Atkins Picks On the Beatles	1966	7.50	15.00	30.00
❑ LPM-3558 [M]	The Best of Chet Atkins, Volume 2	1966	3.00	6.00	12.00
❑ LSP-3558 [S]	The Best of Chet Atkins, Volume 2	1966	3.75	7.50	15.00
❑ LPM-3647 [M]	From Nashville with Love	1966	3.00	6.00	12.00
❑ LSP-3647 [S]	From Nashville with Love	1966	3.75	7.50	15.00
❑ LPM-3728 [M]	It's a Guitar World	1967	7.50	15.00	30.00
❑ LSP-3728 [S]	It's a Guitar World	1967	3.00	6.00	12.00
❑ AYL1-3741	The First Nashville Guitar Quartet	1981	2.00	4.00	8.00
—"Best Buy Series" reissue					
❑ LPM-3818 [M]	Chet Atkins Picks the Best	1967	7.50	15.00	30.00
❑ LSP-3818 [S]	Chet Atkins Picks the Best	1967	3.00	6.00	12.00
❑ LPM-3885 [M]	Class Guitar	1967	7.50	15.00	30.00
❑ LSP-3885 [S]	Class Guitar	1967	3.00	6.00	12.00
❑ LPM-3992 [M]	Solo Flights	1968	12.50	25.00	50.00
❑ LSP-3992 [S]	Solo Flights	1968	3.00	6.00	12.00
❑ LPM-4017 [M]	Hometown Guitar	1968	20.00	40.00	80.00
❑ LSP-4017 [S]	Hometown Guitar	1968	3.75	7.50	15.00
❑ AHL1-4044	Still Country — After All These Years	1981	2.50	5.00	10.00
❑ LSP-4061	Solid Gold '68	1968	3.75	7.50	15.00
❑ LSP-4135	Lover's Guitar	1968	3.75	7.50	15.00
❑ LSP-4244	Solid Gold '69	1969	3.00	6.00	12.00
❑ LSP-4331	Yestergroovin'	1970	3.00	6.00	12.00
❑ LSP-4396	Me & Jerry	1971	3.75	7.50	15.00
—With Jerry Reed					
❑ LSP-4464	For the Good Times	1971	3.75	7.50	15.00
❑ AHL1-4724	Great Hits of the Past	1983	2.50	5.00	10.00
❑ LSP-4754	Chet Atkins Picks the Hits	1973	3.75	7.50	15.00
❑ AHL1-5495	Collector's Series	1985	2.50	5.00	10.00
❑ VPS-6030 [(2)]	This Is Chet Atkins	1972	3.75	7.50	15.00

Number	Title (A Side/B Side)	Yr	VG	VG+	NM
❑ VPXS-6079 [(2)]	Now & Then	1972	3.75	7.50	15.00
TIME-LIFE					
❑ 117	Country Music	1981	3.00	6.00	12.00

ATLANTA RHYTHM SECTION
COLUMBIA

Number	Title (A Side/B Side)	Yr	VG	VG+	NM
❑ FC 37550	Quinella	1981	2.50	5.00	10.00
❑ PC 37550	Quinella	1982	2.00	4.00	8.00
—Budget-line reissue					

DECCA

Number	Title (A Side/B Side)	Yr	VG	VG+	NM
❑ DL 75265	Atlanta Rhythm Section	1972	6.25	12.50	25.00
❑ DL 75390	Back Up Against the Wall	1973	6.25	12.50	25.00

MCA

Number	Title (A Side/B Side)	Yr	VG	VG+	NM
❑ 2-4114 [(2)]	Atlanta Rhythm Section	1977	3.00	6.00	12.00
—Combines the two Decca LPs into one package					

MOBILE FIDELITY

Number	Title (A Side/B Side)	Yr	VG	VG+	NM
❑ 1-038	Champagne Jam	1981	10.00	20.00	40.00
—Audiophile vinyl					

POLYDOR

Number	Title (A Side/B Side)	Yr	VG	VG+	NM
❑ PD 6027	Third Annual Pipe Dream	1974	2.50	5.00	10.00
❑ PD 6041	Dog Days	1975	2.50	5.00	10.00
❑ PD-1-6060	Red Tape	1976	2.50	5.00	10.00
❑ PD-1-6080	A Rock and Roll Alternative	1977	2.50	5.00	10.00
❑ PD-1-6134	Champagne Jam	1978	2.50	5.00	10.00
❑ PD-1-6200	Underdog	1979	2.50	5.00	10.00
❑ PD-2-6236 [(2)]	Are You Ready!	1979	3.00	6.00	12.00
❑ PD-1-6285	The Boys from Doraville	1980	2.50	5.00	10.00

ATOMIC ROOSTER
ELEKTRA

Number	Title (A Side/B Side)	Yr	VG	VG+	NM
❑ EKS-74094	Death Walks Behind You	1971	5.00	10.00	20.00
❑ EKS-74109	In Hearing Of Atomic Rooster	1971	5.00	10.00	20.00
❑ EKS-75039	Made in England	1972	5.00	10.00	20.00
❑ EKS-75074	Atomic Rooster IV	1973	3.75	7.50	15.00

ATTILA
BACK-TRAC

Number	Title (A Side/B Side)	Yr	VG	VG+	NM
❑ P 18808	Attila	1985	2.50	5.00	10.00
EPIC					
❑ E 30030	Attila	1970	7.50	15.00	30.00

AU GO-GO SINGERS, THE
With Stephen Stills and Richie Furay, later of BUFFALO SPRINGFIELD.
ROULETTE

Number	Title (A Side/B Side)	Yr	VG	VG+	NM
❑ R 25280 [M]	They Call Us the Au Go-Go Singers	1964	12.50	25.00	50.00
❑ SR 25280 [S]	They Call Us the Au Go-Go Singers	1964	17.50	35.00	70.00

AUDIO TWO
FIRST PRIORITY

Number	Title (A Side/B Side)	Yr	VG	VG+	NM
❑ 90907	What More Can I Say?	1988	20.00	40.00	80.00
❑ 91358	I Don't Care — The Album	1990	20.00	40.00	80.00

AUGER, BRIAN, TRINITY
ATCO

Number	Title (A Side/B Side)	Yr	VG	VG+	NM
❑ 33-258 [M]	Open	1968	5.00	10.00	20.00
—White label promo; no stock copies were issued in mono					
❑ SD 33-258 [S]	Open	1968	3.00	6.00	12.00
❑ SD 33-273	Definitely What!	1969	3.00	6.00	12.00
❑ SD 2-701 [(2)]	Streetnoise	1969	5.00	10.00	20.00
CAPITOL					
❑ DT-136 [R]	Jools & Brian	1969	3.00	6.00	12.00
—American issue of pre-Atco material					
HEADFIRST					
❑ 9702	Search Party	1981	3.75	7.50	15.00
POLYDOR					
❑ PD-1-6505	Genesis	1975	3.00	6.00	12.00
RCA VICTOR					
❑ AFL1-0140	Closer To It	197?	2.00	4.00	8.00
—Reissue					
❑ APL1-0140	Closer To It	1973	2.50	5.00	10.00
❑ AFL1-0454	Straight Ahead	197?	2.00	4.00	8.00
—Reissue					
❑ CPL1-0454	Straight Ahead	1974	2.50	5.00	10.00
❑ CPL1-0645	Live Oblivion	1974	2.50	5.00	10.00
❑ APL1-1210	Reinforcements	1975	2.50	5.00	10.00
❑ CPL2-1230 [(2)]	Live Oblivion, Vol. 2	1976	3.75	7.50	15.00
❑ AFL1-2249	The Best of Brian Auger	1977	2.50	5.00	10.00
❑ ANL1-2481	Live Oblivion	1977	2.00	4.00	8.00
—Reissue					
❑ LSP-4372	Befour	1970	2.50	5.00	10.00
❑ AFL1-4462	Brian Auger's Oblivion Express	197?	2.00	4.00	8.00
—Reissue					
❑ LSP-4462	Brian Auger's Oblivion Express	1971	2.50	5.00	10.00
—Starting here, group is "Oblivion Express"					
❑ LSP-4540	A Better Land	1971	2.50	5.00	10.00
❑ AFL1-4703	Second Wind	197?	2.00	4.00	8.00
—Reissue					
❑ LSP-4703	Second Wind	1972	2.50	5.00	10.00
SPRINGBOARD					
❑ SPB-4044	Brian Auger	1973	2.00	4.00	8.00
—Reissue of early material					
WARNER BROS.					
❑ BS 2981	Happiness Heartaches	1977	2.50	5.00	10.00
❑ BSK 3153	Encore	1978	2.50	5.00	10.00

AUGUST, JAN
MERCURY

Number	Title (A Side/B Side)	Yr	VG	VG+	NM
❑ MG 20072 [M]	Jan August Plays Songs to Remember	1955	6.25	12.50	25.00
❑ MG 20078 [M]	Music for the Quiet Hour	1955	6.25	12.50	25.00
❑ MG 20147 [M]	Piano Roll Blues	1955	6.25	12.50	25.00
❑ MG 20160 [M]	Christmas Favorites	1955	6.25	12.50	25.00

Number	Title (A Side/B Side)	Yr	VG	VG+	NM
❑ MG 20272 [M]	Cocktails and Conversation	195?	5.00	10.00	20.00
❑ MG 20273 [M]	Keyboard Waltzes	195?	5.00	10.00	20.00
❑ MG 20274 [M]	Latin Rhythms	195?	5.00	10.00	20.00
❑ MG 20408 [M]	Cha Cha Charm	1959	3.75	7.50	15.00
❑ MG 20513 [M]	Jan August Plays Great Piano Hits	195?	3.75	7.50	15.00
❑ MG 20618 [M]	Accent!	1961	3.75	7.50	15.00
❑ MG 20659 [M]	Jan August Styles the Great Pop Piano Classics	196?	3.75	7.50	15.00
❑ MG 20667 [M]	Jan August Styles the Great International Hits	196?	3.75	7.50	15.00
❑ MG 20744 [M]	Jan August Plays a Collection of 27 Popular Classical Melodies	196?	3.75	7.50	15.00
❑ MG 25087 [10]	Piano Favorites	195?	7.50	15.00	30.00
❑ MG 25136 [10]	Piano Poetry	195?	7.50	15.00	30.00
❑ SR 60082 [S]	Cha Cha Charm	1959	5.00	10.00	20.00
❑ SR 60189 [S]	Jan August Plays Great Piano Hits	195?	5.00	10.00	20.00
❑ SR 60618 [S]	Accent!	1961	5.00	10.00	20.00
❑ SR 60659 [S]	Jan August Styles the Great Pop Piano Classics	196?	5.00	10.00	20.00
❑ SR 60667 [S]	Jan August Styles the Great International Hits	196?	5.00	10.00	20.00
❑ SR 60744 [S]	Jan August Plays a Collection of 27 Popular Classical Melodies	196?	5.00	10.00	20.00

WING

❑ MGW 12129 [M]	Music for the Quiet Hour	196?	3.00	6.00	12.00
❑ MGW 12175 [M]	Christmas Favorites	196?	3.00	6.00	12.00
❑ MGW 12254 [M]	The Piano Wizardry of Jan August	196?	3.00	6.00	12.00
❑ SRW 16129 [R]	Music for the Quiet Hour	196?	2.50	5.00	10.00
❑ SRW 16254 [R]	The Piano Wizardry of Jan August	196?	2.50	5.00	10.00

AUGUST SONS
EYES IN THE WOODS

❑ (# unknown) [EP]	I Am Not a Vampire	1989	10.00	20.00	40.00

AULD, GEORGIE
ABC-PARAMOUNT

❑ ABC-287 [M]	Georgie Auld Plays for Melancholy Babies	1958	10.00	20.00	40.00
❑ ABCS-287 [S]	Georgie Auld Plays for Melancholy Babies	1959	7.50	15.00	30.00

ALLEGRO

❑ 3102 [M]	Jazz Concert	1953	10.00	20.00	40.00

APOLLO

❑ LAP-102 [10]	Concert in Jazz	1951	20.00	40.00	80.00

CORAL

❑ CRL 56060 [10]	Tenderly	1952	20.00	40.00	80.00
❑ CRL 56085 [10]	Manhattan	1953	20.00	40.00	80.00
❑ CRL 57029 [M]	Lullaby of Broadway	1956	10.00	20.00	40.00
❑ CRL 57032 [M]	Misty	1956	10.00	20.00	40.00

DISCOVERY

❑ DL 3007 [10]	That's Auld	1950	20.00	40.00	80.00

EMARCY

❑ MG-36060 [M]	In the Land of Hi-Fi	1955	10.00	20.00	40.00
❑ MG-36090 [M]	Dancing in the Land of Hi-Fi	1956	10.00	20.00	40.00

JARO

❑ JAM-5003 [M]	Hawaii on the Rocks	1959	7.50	15.00	30.00

PHILIPS

❑ PHS 600096 [S]	Georgie Auld Plays to the Winners	1963	5.00	10.00	20.00
❑ PHS 600116 [S]	Here's to the Losers	1963	5.00	10.00	20.00

ROOST

❑ RST-403 [10]	Georgie Auld Quintet	1951	20.00	40.00	80.00

TOP RANK

❑ RM-306 [M]	The Melody Lingers On	1959	10.00	20.00	40.00
❑ RM-333 [M]	Good Enough to Keep	1960	10.00	20.00	40.00

UNITED ARTISTS

❑ UAL-3068 [M]	Manhattan with Strings	1959	10.00	20.00	40.00
❑ UAS-6068 [S]	Manhattan with Strings	1959	7.50	15.00	30.00

AUM
FILLMORE

❑ Z 30002	Resurrection	1970	7.50	15.00	30.00

SIRE

❑ SES-97007	Bluesvibes	1969	10.00	20.00	40.00

AUSTIN, BOBBY
CAPITOL

❑ ST 2773 [S]	Apartment No. 9	1967	5.00	10.00	20.00
❑ T 2773 [M]	Apartment No. 9	1967	6.25	12.50	25.00
❑ ST 2915	Old Love Never Dies	1968	5.00	10.00	20.00

AUSTIN, CLAIRE
CONTEMPORARY

❑ C-5002 [M]	When Your Lover Has Gone	1956	12.50	25.00	50.00

GOOD TIME JAZZ

❑ L-24 [10]	Claire Austin Sings the Blues	1954	30.00	60.00	120.00

AUSTIN, DONALD
EASTBOUND

❑ EB-9005	Crazy Legs	1973	7.50	15.00	30.00

AUSTIN, GENE
DECCA

❑ DL 8433 [M]	My Blue Heaven	1957	10.00	20.00	40.00

DOT

❑ DLP 3300 [M]	Great Hits	1960	5.00	10.00	20.00
❑ DLP 25300 [S]	Great Hits	1960	6.25	12.50	25.00

FRATERNITY

❑ F-1006 [M]	Gene Austin and His Lonesome Road	1957	5.00	10.00	20.00

RCA VICTOR

❑ LPM-1549 [M]	Restless Heart	1957	10.00	20.00	40.00
❑ LPM-2490 [M]	My Blue Heaven	1961	6.25	12.50	25.00
❑ LPM-3200 [10]	My Blue Heaven	1953	15.00	30.00	60.00
❑ VPM-6065 [(2)]	This Is Gene Austin	1972	5.00	10.00	20.00

"X"

Number	Title (A Side/B Side)	Yr	VG	VG+	NM
❑ LVA-1007 [M]	Gene Austin Sings All-Time Favorites	1954	10.00	20.00	40.00

AUSTIN, SIL
MERCURY

❑ MG-20237 [M]	Slow Walk Rock	1957	17.50	35.00	70.00
❑ MG-20320 [M]	Everything's Shakin'	1958	17.50	35.00	70.00
❑ MG-20424 [M]	Sil Austin Plays Pretty for the People	1959	10.00	20.00	40.00
❑ MG-20576 [M]	Soft, Plaintive and Moody	1960	10.00	20.00	40.00
❑ MG-20663 [M]	Golden Saxophone Hits	1961	6.25	12.50	25.00
❑ MG-20755 [M]	Folk Songs	1963	3.75	7.50	15.00
❑ MG-20925 [M]	Sil Austin Plays Pretty Melodies of the World	1964	5.00	10.00	20.00
❑ MG-21126 [M]	Sil Austin Plays Pretty for the People Again	1967	5.00	10.00	20.00
❑ SR-60096 [S]	Sil Austin Plays Pretty for the People	1959	15.00	30.00	60.00
—Black label					
❑ SR-60096 [S]	Sil Austin Plays Pretty for the People	1965	5.00	10.00	20.00
—Red label, white "MERCURY" at top					
❑ SR-60096 [S]	Sil Austin Plays Pretty for the People	1974	2.50	5.00	10.00
—"Chicago styline" label					
❑ SR-60236 [S]	Soft, Plaintive and Moody	1960	15.00	30.00	60.00
❑ SR-60663 [S]	Golden Saxophone Hits	1961	7.50	15.00	30.00
❑ SR-60755 [S]	Folk Songs	1963	5.00	10.00	20.00
❑ SR-60925 [S]	Sil Austin Plays Pretty Melodies of the World	1964	6.25	12.50	25.00
❑ SR-61126 [S]	Sil Austin Plays Pretty for the People Again	1967	5.00	10.00	20.00

SSS INTERNATIONAL

❑ 4	Honey Sax	1969	3.75	7.50	15.00
❑ 8	Soft Soul with Strings	1970	3.75	7.50	15.00
❑ 14	Sil and Silver Screen	1971	3.75	7.50	15.00
❑ 23	Songs of Gold	1971	3.75	7.50	15.00

WING

❑ SRW-16227 [S]	Everything's Shakin'	196?	3.75	7.50	15.00
❑ SRW-16369 [S]	Sil Austin Again Plays Pretty for the People	196?	3.75	7.50	15.00

AUSTRALIAN ALL STARS, THE
BETHLEHEM

❑ BCP-6070 [M]	Jazz for Beach-Niks	1963	10.00	20.00	40.00
❑ BCP-6073 [M]	Jazz for Surf-Niks	1963	10.00	20.00	40.00

AUSTRALIAN JAZZ QUARTET, THE
BETHLEHEM

❑ BCP-1031 [10]	The Australian Jazz Quartet	195?	15.00	30.00	60.00
❑ BCP-6002 [M]	The Australian Jazz Quartet/Quintet	1955	10.00	20.00	40.00
❑ BCP-6012 [M]	The Australian Jazz Quartet at the Varsity Drag	1956	10.00	20.00	40.00
❑ BCP-6015 [M]	The Australian Jazz Quartet Plus One	1957	10.00	20.00	40.00
❑ BCP-6022 [M]	The Australian Jazz Quartet Plays the Best of Broadway Musical Hits	1957	10.00	20.00	40.00
❑ BCP-6029 [M]	The Australian Jazz Quartet In Free Style	1959	10.00	20.00	40.00
❑ BCP-6030 [M]	Three Penny Opera	1959	10.00	20.00	40.00

AUTOSALVAGE
RCA VICTOR

❑ LPM-3940 [M]	Autosalvage	1968	10.00	20.00	40.00
❑ LSP-3940 [S]	Autosalvage	1968	10.00	20.00	40.00

AUTRY, GENE
CBS SPECIAL PRODUCTS

❑ P 18737	Golden Hits	1985	2.50	5.00	10.00
❑ P 18963	His Golden Hits	1985	2.50	5.00	10.00
❑ P 18964	Famous Favorites	1985	2.50	5.00	10.00

CHALLENGE

❑ CHL-600 [M]	Christmas with Gene Autry	1958	12.50	25.00	50.00

COLUMBIA

❑ CL (# unk) [10]	Easter Favorites	1949	37.50	75.00	150.00
❑ CL 677 [M]	Gene Autry and Champion — Western Adventures	1955	30.00	60.00	120.00
❑ CS 1035	Gene Autry's Country Music Hall of Fame Album	1970	3.75	7.50	15.00
❑ CL 1575 [M]	Gene Autry's Greatest Hits	1961	7.50	15.00	30.00
—Red and black label with six "eye" logos					
❑ CL 2547 [10]	Merry Christmas with Gene Autry	1954	30.00	60.00	120.00
—"House Party Series" release					
❑ CL 2568 [10]	Easter Favorites	1955	30.00	60.00	120.00
—"House Party Series" issue					
❑ CL 6020 [10]	Gene Autry's Western Classics	1949	37.50	75.00	150.00
❑ CL 6137 [10]	Merry Christmas	1950	37.50	75.00	150.00
❑ JL 8001 [10]	Gene Autry at the Rodeo	1949	37.50	75.00	150.00
❑ JL 8009 [10]	Stampede	1949	37.50	75.00	150.00
❑ JL 8012 [10]	Champion	1950	37.50	75.00	150.00
❑ HL 9001 [10]	Gene Autry's Western Classics, Volume 1	1949	37.50	75.00	150.00
❑ HL 9002 [10]	Gene Autry's Western Classics, Volume 2	1949	37.50	75.00	150.00

COLUMBIA SPECIAL PRODUCTS

❑ P 15766	Christmas Favorites	1981	3.00	6.00	12.00
❑ P 15767	Everyone's a Child at Christmas	1981	3.00	6.00	12.00

GRAND PRIX

❑ KS-X11 [S]	The Original Gene Autry Sings Rudolph the Red-Nosed Reindeer and Other Christmas Favorites	1961	5.00	10.00	20.00
❑ KX-11 [M]	The Original Gene Autry Sings Rudolph the Red-Nosed Reindeer and Other Christmas Favorites	1961	3.75	7.50	15.00

GUSTO

❑ 1038	Christmas Classics	1978	2.50	5.00	10.00

HARMONY

❑ HL 7332 [M]	Gene Autry's Great Western Hits	1965	7.50	15.00	30.00
❑ HL 7376 [M]	Back in the Saddle Again	1966	5.00	10.00	20.00
❑ HL 7399 [M]	Gene Autry Sings	1966	5.00	10.00	20.00
❑ HL 9505 [M]	Gene Autry and Champion — Western Adventures	1959	7.50	15.00	30.00
❑ HL 9550 [M]	The Original Rudolph the Red-Nosed Reindeer and Other Children's Christmas Favorites	1964	6.25	12.50	25.00

Number	Title (A Side/B Side)	Yr	VG	VG+	NM
❏ HS 11199 [R]	Gene Autry Sings	1966	3.75	7.50	15.00
❏ HS 11276 [R]	Back in the Saddle Again	1966	3.75	7.50	15.00
❏ HS 14450 [R]	The Original Rudolph the Red-Nosed Reindeer and Other Children's Christmas Favorites	1964	3.00	6.00	12.00

MELODY RANCH

Number	Title (A Side/B Side)	Yr	VG	VG+	NM
❏ 101 [M]	Melody Ranch	1965	10.00	20.00	40.00

MURRAY HILL

Number	Title (A Side/B Side)	Yr	VG	VG+	NM
❏ 897296 [(4)]	Melody Ranch Radio Show	197?	15.00	30.00	60.00

—Compilation of some of Gene's radio shows in a box set

RCA VICTOR

Number	Title (A Side/B Side)	Yr	VG	VG+	NM
❏ LPM-2623 [M]	Gene Autry's Golden Hits	1962	7.50	15.00	30.00
❏ LSP-2623 [S]	Gene Autry's Golden Hits	1962	10.00	20.00	40.00

REPUBLIC

Number	Title (A Side/B Side)	Yr	VG	VG+	NM
❏ 6011	South of the Border, All American Cowboy	1976	5.00	10.00	20.00
❏ 6012	Cowboy Hall of Fame	1976	5.00	10.00	20.00
❏ RLP 6018 [M]	Christmas with Gene Autry	1976	3.00	6.00	12.00

AVALANCHES, THE
WARNER BROS.

Number	Title (A Side/B Side)	Yr	VG	VG+	NM
❏ W 1525 [M]	Ski Surfin'	1963	10.00	20.00	40.00
❏ WS 1525 [S]	Ski Surfin'	1963	15.00	30.00	60.00

AVALON, FRANKIE
ABC

Number	Title (A Side/B Side)	Yr	VG	VG+	NM
❏ ABCX-805 [R]	16 Greatest Hits	1974	3.00	6.00	12.00

CHANCELLOR

Number	Title (A Side/B Side)	Yr	VG	VG+	NM
❏ CHL 5001 [M]	Frankie Avalon	1958	12.50	25.00	50.00
—Pink label					
❏ CHL 5001 [M]	Frankie Avalon	1959	10.00	20.00	40.00
—Black label					
❏ CHL 5002 [M]	The Young Frankie Avalon	1959	10.00	20.00	40.00
—Black label					
❏ CHL 5002 [M]	The Young Frankie Avalon	1959	12.50	25.00	50.00
—Pink label					
❏ CHLS 5002 [S]	The Young Frankie Avalon	1959	12.50	25.00	50.00
—Black label					
❏ CHLS 5002 [S]	The Young Frankie Avalon	1959	15.00	30.00	60.00
—Pink label					
❏ CHLX 5004 [M]	Swingin' on a Rainbow	1959	10.00	20.00	40.00
❏ CHLXS 5004 [S]	Swingin' on a Rainbow	1959	12.50	25.00	50.00
❏ CHL 5011 [M]	Summer Scene	1960	7.50	15.00	30.00
❏ CHLS 5011 [S]	Summer Scene	1960	10.00	20.00	40.00
❏ CHL 5018 [M]	A Whole Lotta Frankie	1961	7.50	15.00	30.00
❏ CHL 5022 [M]	And Now About Mr. Avalon	1961	7.50	15.00	30.00
❏ CHLS 5022 [S]	And Now About Mr. Avalon	1961	10.00	20.00	40.00
❏ CHL 5025 [M]	Italiano	1962	7.50	15.00	30.00
❏ CHLS 5025 [S]	Italiano	1962	10.00	20.00	40.00
❏ CHL 5027 [M]	You're Mine	1962	7.50	15.00	30.00
❏ CHLS 5027 [S]	You're Mine	1962	10.00	20.00	40.00
❏ CHL 5031 [M]	Frankie Avalon's Christmas Album	1962	7.50	15.00	30.00
❏ CHLS 5031 [S]	Frankie Avalon's Christmas Album	1962	10.00	20.00	40.00
❏ CHL 5032 [M]	Cleopatra Plus 13 Other Great Hits	1963	7.50	15.00	30.00
❏ CHLS 5032 [S]	Cleopatra Plus 13 Other Great Hits	1963	10.00	20.00	40.00
❏ 69801 [M]	Young and In Love	1960	10.00	20.00	40.00
—LP without the box					
❏ 69801 [M]	Young and In Love	1960	20.00	40.00	80.00
—LP in felt cover and 3-D portrait, all in box					

DE-LITE

Number	Title (A Side/B Side)	Yr	VG	VG+	NM
❏ 2020	Venus	1976	3.75	7.50	15.00
❏ 9504	You're My Life	1977	3.75	7.50	15.00

EVEREST

Number	Title (A Side/B Side)	Yr	VG	VG+	NM
❏ 4187	Greatest Hits	1982	2.50	5.00	10.00

LIBERTY

Number	Title (A Side/B Side)	Yr	VG	VG+	NM
❏ LN-10193	Songs from Muscle Beach Party	1981	2.00	4.00	8.00
—Budget-line reissue					

MCA

Number	Title (A Side/B Side)	Yr	VG	VG+	NM
❏ 27096	The Best of Frankie Avalon	1985	2.00	4.00	8.00

METROMEDIA

Number	Title (A Side/B Side)	Yr	VG	VG+	NM
❏ MD-1034	I Want You Near Me	1970	3.75	7.50	15.00

SUNSET

Number	Title (A Side/B Side)	Yr	VG	VG+	NM
❏ SUS-5244	Frankie Avalon	1969	3.75	7.50	15.00

TRIP

Number	Title (A Side/B Side)	Yr	VG	VG+	NM
❏ 1621	16 Greatest Hits of Frankie Avalon	1977	2.50	5.00	10.00

UNITED ARTISTS

Number	Title (A Side/B Side)	Yr	VG	VG+	NM
❏ UA-LA450-F	The Very Best of Frankie Avalon	1975	3.00	6.00	12.00
❏ UAL-3371 [M]	Songs from Muscle Beach Party	1964	6.25	12.50	25.00
❏ UAL-3382 [M]	Frankie Avalon's 15 Greatest Hits	1964	5.00	10.00	20.00
❏ UAS-6371 [S]	Songs from Muscle Beach Party	1964	7.50	15.00	30.00
❏ UAS-6382 [S]	Frankie Avalon's 15 Greatest Hits	1964	6.25	12.50	25.00

AVENGERS
CD PRESENTS

Number	Title (A Side/B Side)	Yr	VG	VG+	NM
❏ 007	Avengers	1983	5.00	10.00	20.00
—Black vinyl					
❏ 007	Avengers	1983	7.50	15.00	30.00
—Red vinyl					

GO

Number	Title (A Side/B Side)	Yr	VG	VG+	NM
❏ 005	Avengers	1983	30.00	60.00	120.00

LOOKOUT!

Number	Title (A Side/B Side)	Yr	VG	VG+	NM
❏ 217	The Avengers Died for Your Sins	1999	2.50	5.00	10.00

WHITE NOISE

Number	Title (A Side/B Side)	Yr	VG	VG+	NM
❏ 002 [EP]	Avengers	1978	12.50	25.00	50.00

AVENGERS VI, THE
MARK 56

Number	Title (A Side/B Side)	Yr	VG	VG+	NM
❏ (# unknown)	Good Humor Presents Real Cool Hits	1966	62.50	125.00	250.00
—Custom pressing for the Good Humor ice cream company					

AVERAGE WHITE BAND
ARISTA

Number	Title (A Side/B Side)	Yr	VG	VG+	NM
❏ AB 9523	Shine	1980	2.50	5.00	10.00
❏ AB 9594	Cupid's in Fashion	1981	2.50	5.00	10.00

ATLANTIC

Number	Title (A Side/B Side)	Yr	VG	VG+	NM
❏ SD 2-1002 [(2)]	Person to Person	1977	3.00	6.00	12.00
❏ QD 7308 [Q]	Average White Band	1975	5.00	10.00	20.00
❏ SD 7308	Average White Band	1974	2.50	5.00	10.00
❏ SD 18140	Cut the Cake	1975	2.50	5.00	10.00
❏ SD 18179	Soul Searching	1976	2.50	5.00	10.00
❏ SD 19105	Benny and Us	1977	2.50	5.00	10.00
—With Ben E. King					
❏ SD 19116	Average White Band	1977	2.00	4.00	8.00
—Reissue					
❏ SD 19162	Warmer Communications	1978	2.50	5.00	10.00
❏ SD 19207	Feel No Fret	1979	2.50	5.00	10.00
❏ SD 19266	Volume VIII	1980	2.50	5.00	10.00

MCA

Number	Title (A Side/B Side)	Yr	VG	VG+	NM
❏ 345	Show Your Hands	1973	6.25	12.50	25.00
❏ 475	Put It Where You Want It	1975	2.50	5.00	10.00
—Reissue of MCA 345					

MOBILE FIDELITY

Number	Title (A Side/B Side)	Yr	VG	VG+	NM
❏ 1-245	Average White Band	1996	5.00	10.00	20.00
—Audiophile vinyl					

TRACK

Number	Title (A Side/B Side)	Yr	VG	VG+	NM
❏ 58830	Aftershock	1988	2.50	5.00	10.00

AVONS, THE (1)
HULL

Number	Title (A Side/B Side)	Yr	VG	VG+	NM
❏ HLP-1000 [M]	The Avons	1960	175.00	350.00	700.00

AWESOME DRE AND THE HARDCORE COMMITTEE
BENTLEY

Number	Title (A Side/B Side)	Yr	VG	VG+	NM
❏ 12001	You Can't Hold Me Back	1989	5.00	10.00	20.00

AXTON, HOYT
A&M

Number	Title (A Side/B Side)	Yr	VG	VG+	NM
❏ SP-3155	Life Machine	198?	2.00	4.00	8.00
—Budget-line reissue					
❏ SP-3182	Road Songs	198?	2.00	4.00	8.00
—Budget-line reissue					
❏ SP-4376	Less Than a Song	1973	2.50	5.00	10.00
❏ SP-4402	Life Machine	1974	2.50	5.00	10.00
❏ SP-4510	Southbound	1975	2.50	5.00	10.00
❏ SP-4571	Fearless	1976	2.50	5.00	10.00
❏ SP-4669	Road Songs	1977	2.50	5.00	10.00

ACCORD

Number	Title (A Side/B Side)	Yr	VG	VG+	NM
❏ SN-7197	Heartbreak Hotel	1982	2.50	5.00	10.00

ALLEGIANCE

Number	Title (A Side/B Side)	Yr	VG	VG+	NM
❏ AV-5023	Down and Out	1984	2.50	5.00	10.00

BRYLEN

Number	Title (A Side/B Side)	Yr	VG	VG+	NM
❏ BN 4400	Double Dare	1982	3.00	6.00	12.00

CAPITOL

Number	Title (A Side/B Side)	Yr	VG	VG+	NM
❏ ST-788	Joy to the World	1971	3.00	6.00	12.00
❏ SMAS-850	Country Anthem	1971	3.00	6.00	12.00

COLUMBIA

Number	Title (A Side/B Side)	Yr	VG	VG+	NM
❏ CS 9766	My Griffin Is Gone	1969	3.75	7.50	15.00
❏ KC 33103	My Griffin Is Gone	1975	2.50	5.00	10.00
❏ PC 33103	My Griffin Is Gone	1979	2.00	4.00	8.00
—Budget-line reissue					

EXODUS

Number	Title (A Side/B Side)	Yr	VG	VG+	NM
❏ EX-301 [M]	Hoyt Axton Sings Bessie Smith	1966	5.00	10.00	20.00
❏ EXS-321 [M]	Saturday's Child	1966	5.00	10.00	20.00
—Cover says stereo, record plays mono					

HORIZON

Number	Title (A Side/B Side)	Yr	VG	VG+	NM
❏ WP-1601 [M]	The Balladeer	1962	6.25	12.50	25.00
—Black label					
❏ WP-1601 [M]	Greenback Dollar	1963	5.00	10.00	20.00
—Black label; two fewer songs than "The Balladeer"					
❏ WP-1601 [S]	The Balladeer	1962	7.50	15.00	30.00
—Same number as mono, but with blue label					
❏ WP-1601 [S]	Greenback Dollar	1963	6.25	12.50	25.00
—Blue label; two fewer songs than "The Balladeer"					
❏ SWP-1613 [S]	Thunder 'N Lightnin'	1963	7.50	15.00	30.00
❏ WP-1613 [M]	Thunder 'N Lightnin'	1963	6.25	12.50	25.00
❏ SWP-1621 [S]	Saturday's Child	1963	7.50	15.00	30.00
❏ WP-1621 [M]	Saturday's Child	1963	6.25	12.50	25.00

JEREMIAH

Number	Title (A Side/B Side)	Yr	VG	VG+	NM
❏ JH-5000	A Rusty Old Halo	1979	3.00	6.00	12.00
❏ JH-5001	Where Did the Money Go?	1980	3.00	6.00	12.00

MCA

Number	Title (A Side/B Side)	Yr	VG	VG+	NM
❏ 647	Snow Blind Friend	198?	2.00	4.00	8.00
—Budget-line reissue					
❏ 648	Free Sailin'	198?	2.00	4.00	8.00
—Budget-line reissue					
❏ 2263	Snow Blind Friend	1977	2.50	5.00	10.00
❏ 2319	Free Sailin'	1978	2.50	5.00	10.00

SURREY

Number	Title (A Side/B Side)	Yr	VG	VG+	NM
❏ S-1005 [M]	Mr. Greenback Dollar Man	1965	5.00	10.00	20.00
❏ SS-1005 [S]	Mr. Greenback Dollar Man	1965	6.25	12.50	25.00

VEE JAY

Number	Title (A Side/B Side)	Yr	VG	VG+	NM
❏ LP-1098 [M]	Hoyt Axton Explodes!	1964	6.25	12.50	25.00
❏ LPS-1098 [R]	Hoyt Axton Explodes!	1964	5.00	10.00	20.00
❏ LP-1118 [M]	The Best of Hoyt Axton	1965	5.00	10.00	20.00
❏ LPS-1118 [S]	The Best of Hoyt Axton	1965	6.25	12.50	25.00
❏ LP-1126 [M]	Greenback Dollar	1965	5.00	10.00	20.00
❏ LPS-1126 [S]	Greenback Dollar	1965	6.25	12.50	25.00
❏ LP-1127 [M]	Saturday's Child	1965	5.00	10.00	20.00

Number	Title (A Side/B Side)	Yr	VG	VG+	NM
❑ LPS-1127 [S]	Saturday's Child	1965	6.25	12.50	25.00
—Reissue of Horizon 1621					
❑ LP-1128 [M]	Thunder 'N Lightnin'	1965	5.00	10.00	20.00
❑ LPS-1128 [S]	Thunder 'N Lightnin'	1965	6.25	12.50	25.00
—Reissue of Horizon 1613					

VEE JAY INTERNATIONAL

❑ VJS-2-1005 [(2)]	Gold	1974	5.00	10.00	20.00
—Compilation of older Vee Jay material					
❑ LP-6001	Long Old Road	1977	3.75	7.50	15.00

VEE JAY/DYNASTY

❑ VJS-7306	Bessie Smith… My Way	1974	3.75	7.50	15.00

AYCOCK, EARL
MERCURY

❑ MG-20282 [M]	Earl Aycock	1958	6.25	12.50	25.00

AYERS, ROY
ATLANTIC

❑ 1488 [M]	Virgo Vibes	1967	5.00	10.00	20.00
❑ SD 1514	Stoned Soul Picnic	1968	5.00	10.00	20.00
❑ SD 1538	Daddy Bug	1969	5.00	10.00	20.00

UNITED ARTISTS

❑ UAL-3325 [M]	West Coast Vibes	1964	5.00	10.00	20.00
❑ UAS-6325 [S]	West Coast Vibes	1964	6.25	12.50	25.00

AYLER, ALBERT
ABC IMPULSE!

❑ AS-9165	Love Cry	1968	5.00	10.00	20.00
❑ AS-9175	New Grass	1969	5.00	10.00	20.00
❑ AS-9191	Music Is the Healing Force of the Universe	1969	5.00	10.00	20.00
❑ AS-9208	The Last Album	1971	5.00	10.00	20.00

ESP-DISK'

❑ 1002 [M]	Spiritual Unity	1965	6.25	12.50	25.00
❑ 1010 [M]	Bells	1965	6.25	12.50	25.00
—Black vinyl					
❑ 1010 [M]	Bells	1965	12.50	25.00	50.00
—Yellow vinyl					
❑ S-1010 [S]	Bells	1965	5.00	10.00	20.00
❑ 1016 [M]	New York Eye and Ear Control	1966	6.25	12.50	25.00
❑ S-1016 [S]	New York Eye and Ear Control	1966	5.00	10.00	20.00
❑ 1020 [M]	Spirits Rejoice	1966	6.25	12.50	25.00
❑ S-1020 [S]	Spirits Rejoice	1966	5.00	10.00	20.00

FANTASY

❑ 6016 [M]	My Name Is Albert Ayler	196?	5.00	10.00	20.00
❑ 86016 [S]	My Name Is Albert Ayler	196?	6.25	12.50	25.00

IMPULSE!

❑ A-9155 [M]	Live at the Village Vanguard	1967	7.50	15.00	30.00
❑ AS-9155 [S]	Live at the Village Vanguard	1967	6.25	12.50	25.00

AZAMA, ETHEL
LIBERTY

❑ LRP-3104 [M]	Exotic Dreams	1959	5.00	10.00	20.00
❑ LRP-3142 [M]	Cool Heat	1960	10.00	20.00	40.00
❑ LST-7104 [S]	Exotic Dreams	1959	7.50	15.00	30.00
❑ LST-7142 [S]	Cool Heat	1960	12.50	25.00	50.00

AZITIS
ELCO

❑ SC-EC-5555	Help!	197?	125.00	250.00	500.00

AZTECA
COLUMBIA

❑ CQ 31776 [Q]	Azteca	1974	5.00	10.00	20.00
❑ KC 31776	Azteca	1972	3.00	6.00	12.00
❑ KC 32451	Pyramid of the Sun	1973	3.00	6.00	12.00

AZTECS, THE
WORLD ARTISTS

❑ WAM-2001 [M]	Live at the Ad Lib Club of London	1964	15.00	30.00	60.00

BABASIN, HARRY
MODE

❑ LP-119 [M]	Jazz Pickers	1957	25.00	50.00	100.00

NOCTURNE

❑ NLP-3 [10]	Harry Babasin Quartet	1954	37.50	75.00	150.00

BABY
LONE STARR

❑ 9782	Baby	1974	6.25	12.50	25.00

BABY GRAND
ARISTA

❑ AL 4148	Baby Grand	1977	5.00	10.00	20.00

BABY HUEY
CURTOM

❑ CRS-8007	The Living Legend	1970	10.00	20.00	40.00

BABY RAY
IMPERIAL

❑ LP-9335 [M]	Where Soul Lives	1967	6.25	12.50	25.00
❑ LP-12335 [S]	Where Soul Lives	1967	7.50	15.00	30.00

BACHAUER, GINA
MERCURY LIVING PRESENCE

❑ SR 90301 [S]	Brahms: Piano Concerto No. 2	196?	7.50	15.00	30.00
—With Stanislaw Skrowaczewski/London Symphony Orchestra; maroon label, no "Vendor: Mercury Record Corporation"					
❑ SR 90321 [S]	Beethoven: Piano Concerto No. 5 "Emperor"	196?	15.00	30.00	60.00
—With Stanislaw Skrowaczewski/London Symphony Orchestra; maroon label, no "Vendor: Mercury Record Corporation"					
❑ SR 90368 [S]	Chopin: Piano Concerto No. 1; Nocturne; Three Etudes	196?	7.50	15.00	30.00
—Maroon label, with "Vendor: Mercury Record Corporation"					
❑ SR 90368 [S]	Chopin: Piano Concerto No. 1; Nocturne; Three Etudes	196?	10.00	20.00	40.00
—Maroon label, no "Vendor: Mercury Record Corporation"					
❑ SR 90381 [S]	Beethoven: Piano Concerto No. 4; Piano Sonata in E	196?	10.00	20.00	40.00
—With Antal Dorati/London Symphony Orchestra; maroon label, no "Vendor: Mercury Record Corporation"					
❑ SR 90432 [S]	Chopin: Piano Concerto No. 2 in F; Fantasy in F	1965	10.00	20.00	40.00
—Maroon label, no "Vendor: Mercury Record Corporation"					

BACHAUER, GINA, AND SIR JOHN GIELGUD
MERCURY LIVING PRESENCE

❑ SR 90391 [S]	Collaboration in Poetry and Music	196?	7.50	15.00	30.00
—Maroon label, no "Vendor: Mercury Record Corporation"					

BACHELORS, THE (1)
LONDON

❑ PS 353 [S]	Presenting the Bachelors	1964	5.00	10.00	20.00
❑ PS 393 [P]	Back Again	1964	5.00	10.00	20.00
—"I Wouldn't Trade You for the World" is rechanneled.					
❑ PS 418 [S]	No Arms Can Ever Hold You	1965	5.00	10.00	20.00
❑ PS 435 [P]	Marie	1965	5.00	10.00	20.00
—"Marie" is rechanneled					
❑ PS 460 [S]	Hits of the 60's	1966	5.00	10.00	20.00
❑ PS 491 [P]	The Bachelors' Girls	1966	3.75	7.50	15.00
—"Marie" is rechanneled					
❑ PS 518 [P]	Golden All Time Hits	1967	3.75	7.50	15.00
❑ PS 528 [S]	Bachelors '68	1968	3.00	6.00	12.00
❑ PS 611	Under and Over	1972	2.50	5.00	10.00
❑ LL 3353 [M]	Presenting the Bachelors	1964	3.75	7.50	15.00
❑ LL 3393 [M]	Back Again	1964	3.75	7.50	15.00
❑ LL 3418 [M]	No Arms Can Ever Hold You	1965	3.75	7.50	15.00
❑ LL 3435 [M]	Marie	1965	3.75	7.50	15.00
❑ LL 3460 [M]	Hits of the 60's	1966	3.75	7.50	15.00
❑ LL 3491 [M]	The Bachelors' Girls	1966	3.00	6.00	12.00
❑ LL 3518 [M]	Golden All Time Hits	1967	3.75	7.50	15.00
❑ LL 3528 [M]	Bachelors '68	1968	5.00	10.00	20.00

BACHS, THE
RAIO

❑ (no #)	Out of the Bachs	1967	2000.	3000.	4000.

BACK PORCH MAJORITY, THE
EPIC

❑ LN 24134 [M]	Live from Ledbetter's	1965	3.75	7.50	15.00
❑ LN 24149 [M]	Riverboat Days	1965	3.75	7.50	15.00
❑ LN 24184 [M]	That's the Way It's Gonna Be	1966	3.75	7.50	15.00
❑ LN 24319 [M]	Willy Nilly Wonder of Illusion	1967	5.00	10.00	20.00
❑ BN 26134 [S]	Live from Ledbetter's	1965	5.00	10.00	20.00
❑ BN 26149 [S]	Riverboat Days	1965	5.00	10.00	20.00
❑ BN 26184 [S]	That's the Way It's Gonna Be	1966	5.00	10.00	20.00
❑ BN 26319 [S]	Willy Nilly Wonder of Illusion	1967	3.75	7.50	15.00

BACKUS, JIM
RCA VICTOR

❑ LPM-1362 [M]	Mr. Magoo in Hi-Fi	1957	12.50	25.00	50.00

BACON FAT
BLUE HORIZON

❑ BH-4807	Grease One for Me	1970	6.25	12.50	25.00

BAD BRAINS
BAD BRAINS

❑ 003 [EP]	I and I Survive/Destroy Babylon	1983	10.00	20.00	40.00

CAROLINE

❑ CAROL-1375	Quickness	1989	3.00	6.00	12.00

B

Number	Title (A Side/B Side)	Yr	VG	VG+	NM
❑ CAROL-1613	Rock for Light	1990	3.00	6.00	12.00
—Reissue of PVC 8917 with three bonus tracks					
❑ CAROL-1617	The Youth Are Getting Restless	1990	3.00	6.00	12.00
IMPORTANT					
❑ 003 [EP]	I and i Survive/Destroy Babylon	1983	5.00	10.00	20.00
MAVERICK					
❑ 45882	God of Love	1995	2.50	5.00	10.00
PVC					
❑ 8917	Rock for Light	1983	3.75	7.50	15.00
ROIR					
❑ 8223	Bad Brains	1997	3.75	7.50	15.00
—First issued in the early 1980s on cassette only, this is a limited vinyl reissue					
SST					
❑ 065	I Against I	1986	3.75	7.50	15.00
—No back cover bar code					
❑ 065	I Against I	199?	2.50	5.00	10.00
—With back cover bar code					
❑ 160	Live	1988	3.00	6.00	12.00
❑ 228 [10]	Spirit Electricity	1991	2.50	5.00	10.00
VICTORY					
❑ VR 64 [10]	The Omega Sessions	1997	2.50	5.00	10.00

BAD RELIGION
ATLANTIC

Number	Title (A Side/B Side)	Yr	VG	VG+	NM
❑ 82658	Stranger Than Fiction	1994	3.75	7.50	15.00
❑ 82870	The Gray Race	1996	3.00	6.00	12.00
❑ 83094	No Substance	1998	3.00	6.00	12.00
❑ 83303	The New America	2000	2.50	5.00	10.00
EPITAPH					
❑ EPI-BRLP-1	How Could Hell Be Any Worse?	1982	7.50	15.00	30.00
—Original edition with lyric sheet. Some copies have personal notes or autographs scribbled on the inner sleeves by the band members; these can bring significantly more than this.					
❑ EPI-BRLP-2	Into the Unknown	1983	30.00	60.00	120.00
❑ 86404	Suffer	1988	3.00	6.00	12.00
❑ 86406	No Control	1989	3.00	6.00	12.00
❑ 86407	How Could Hell Be Any Worse?	1989	3.00	6.00	12.00
—Reissue of Epitaph BRLP-1					
❑ 86409	Against the Grain	1990	3.00	6.00	12.00
❑ 86416	Generator	1992	3.00	6.00	12.00
❑ 86420	Recipe for Hate	1993	3.00	6.00	12.00
❑ 86443	All Ages	1995	3.00	6.00	12.00

BADFINGER
APPLE

Number	Title (A Side/B Side)	Yr	VG	VG+	NM
❑ ST-3355	Maybe Tomorrow	1969	500.00	1000.	2000.
—As "The Iveys"; album not released in US; price is for an LP slick, which does exist					
❑ ST 3364	Magic Christian Music	1970	5.00	10.00	20.00
❑ ST 3364	Magic Christian Music	1970	7.50	15.00	30.00
—With Capitol logo on Side 2 bottom					
❑ SKAO 3367	No Dice	1970	7.50	15.00	30.00
❑ SW 3387	Straight Up	1971	15.00	30.00	60.00
❑ SW 3411	Ass	1973	5.00	10.00	20.00
ELEKTRA					
❑ 6E-175	Airwaves	1979	3.00	6.00	12.00
RADIO					
❑ RR 16030	Say No More	1981	2.50	5.00	10.00
RYKO ANALOGUE					
❑ RALP 10189	Day After Day	1990	5.00	10.00	20.00
—Limited edition on clear vinyl with obi					
WARNER BROS.					
❑ BS 2762	Badfinger	1974	3.75	7.50	15.00
❑ BS 2827	Wish You Were Here	1974	3.75	7.50	15.00

BAEZ, JOAN
A&M

Number	Title (A Side/B Side)	Yr	VG	VG+	NM
❑ SP-3103	Come From the Shadows	198?	2.00	4.00	8.00
—Budget-line reissue					
❑ SP-3233	Diamonds and Rust	198?	2.00	4.00	8.00
—Budget-line reissue					
❑ SP-3234	The Best of Joan C. Baez	198?	2.00	4.00	8.00
—Budget-line reissue					
❑ SP-3614	Gracias A La Vida	1974	3.00	6.00	12.00
❑ SP-3704 [(2)]	From Every Stage	1976	3.00	6.00	12.00
❑ SP-4339	Come From the Shadows	1972	2.50	5.00	10.00
❑ SP-4390	Where Are You Now, My Son?	1973	2.50	5.00	10.00
❑ SP-4527	Diamonds and Rust	1975	2.50	5.00	10.00
❑ SP-4603	Gulf Winds	1976	2.50	5.00	10.00
❑ SP-4668	The Best of Joan C. Baez	1977	2.50	5.00	10.00
❑ SP-6506 [(2)]	From Every Stage	198?	2.50	5.00	10.00
—Reissue					
❑ QU-54339 [Q]	Come From the Shadows	1974	5.00	10.00	20.00
❑ QU-54527 [Q]	Diamonds and Rust	1975	5.00	10.00	20.00
GOLD CASTLE					
❑ D1-71309	Recently	1989	3.00	6.00	12.00
—Reissue of 171 009					
❑ D1-71321	Diamonds and Rust in the Castle	1989	3.00	6.00	12.00
❑ D1-71324	Speaking of Dreams	1989	3.00	6.00	12.00
❑ 171009	Recently	1988	2.50	5.00	10.00
MOBILE FIDELITY					
❑ 1-238	Diamonds and Rust	1996	15.00	30.00	60.00
—Audiophile vinyl					
NAUTILUS					
❑ NR-12	Diamonds and Rust	1980	10.00	20.00	40.00
—Audiophile vinyl					
PORTRAIT					
❑ PR 34697	Blowin' Away	1977	2.50	5.00	10.00
❑ JR 35766	Honest Lullaby	1979	2.50	5.00	10.00
SQUIRE					
❑ SQ-33001 [M]	The Best of Joan Baez	1963	5.00	10.00	20.00

VANGUARD

Number	Title (A Side/B Side)	Yr	VG	VG+	NM
❑ VSD-41/42 [(2)]	The Joan Baez Ballad Book	1972	3.00	6.00	12.00
❑ VSD-49/50 [(2)]	The Contemporary Ballad Book	1974	3.00	6.00	12.00
❑ VSD-79/80 [(2)]	The Love Song Album	197?	3.00	6.00	12.00
❑ VSD-105/6 [(2)]	The Country Music Album	1979	3.00	6.00	12.00
❑ VSD-2077 [S]	Joan Baez	1960	6.25	12.50	25.00
❑ VSD-2097 [S]	Joan Baez, Vol. 2	1961	6.25	12.50	25.00
❑ VSD-2122 [S]	Joan Baez In Concert	1962	6.25	12.50	25.00
❑ VSD-2123 [S]	Joan Baez In Concert, Part 2	1963	6.25	12.50	25.00
❑ VSD-6560/1 [(2)]	The First 10 Years	1970	3.75	7.50	15.00
❑ VSD-6570/1 [(2)]	Blessed Are...	1971	3.75	7.50	15.00
—Add 50 percent if bonus 7-inch single, "Maria Dolores"/"Plane Wreck at Los Gatos (Deportee)," and its special sleeve are still in the package					
❑ VRS-9078 [M]	Joan Baez	1960	5.00	10.00	20.00
❑ VRS-9094 [M]	Joan Baez, Vol. 2	1961	5.00	10.00	20.00
❑ VRS-9112 [M]	Joan Baez In Concert	1962	5.00	10.00	20.00
❑ VRS-9113 [M]	Joan Baez In Concert, Part 2	1963	5.00	10.00	20.00
❑ VRS-9160 [M]	Joan Baez/5	1964	3.75	7.50	15.00
❑ VRS-9200 [M]	Farewell, Angelina	1965	3.75	7.50	15.00
❑ VRS-9230 [M]	Noel	1966	3.75	7.50	15.00
❑ VRS-9240 [M]	Joan	1967	3.75	7.50	15.00
❑ VSQ-40001/2 [(2)Q]	Blessed Are	1973	6.25	12.50	25.00
❑ VSQ-40032 [Q]	Hits/Greatest & Others	1973	5.00	10.00	20.00
❑ VMS-73107	The Joan Baez Ballad Book, Vol. 1	1985	2.50	5.00	10.00
❑ VMS-73115	The Joan Baez Ballad Book, Vol. 2	1985	2.50	5.00	10.00
❑ VMS-73119	The Night They Drove Old Dixie Down	198?	2.50	5.00	10.00
❑ VSD-79160 [S]	Joan Baez/5	1964	5.00	10.00	20.00
❑ VSD-79200 [S]	Farewell, Angelina	1965	5.00	10.00	20.00
❑ VSD-79230 [S]	Noel	1966	5.00	10.00	20.00
❑ VSD-79240 [S]	Joan	1967	5.00	10.00	20.00
❑ VSD-79275	Baptism	1968	5.00	10.00	20.00
❑ VSD-79306/7 [(2)]	Any Day Now	1969	6.25	12.50	25.00
❑ VSD-79308	David's Album	1969	3.00	6.00	12.00
❑ VSD-79310	One Day at a Time	1970	3.00	6.00	12.00
❑ VSD-79313	Carry It On	1971	6.25	12.50	25.00
—Soundtrack album					
❑ VSD-79332	Hits/Greatest & Others	1973	2.50	5.00	10.00
❑ VSD-79446/7	Very Early Joan	1981	3.00	6.00	12.00

BAGDASARIAN, ROSS
LIBERTY

Number	Title (A Side/B Side)	Yr	VG	VG+	NM
❑ LRP-3451 [M]	The Crazy, Mixed-Up World of Ross Bagdasarian	1966	10.00	20.00	40.00
❑ LST-7451 [S]	The Crazy, Mixed-Up World of Ross Bagdasarian	1966	12.50	25.00	50.00

BAGLEY, DON
DOT

Number	Title (A Side/B Side)	Yr	VG	VG+	NM
❑ DLP-3070 [M]	Basically Bagley	1957	12.50	25.00	50.00
❑ DLP-9007 [M]	The Soft Sell	1959	12.50	25.00	50.00
❑ DLP-25070 [S]	Basically Bagley	1959	10.00	20.00	40.00
❑ DLP-29007 [S]	The Soft Sell	1959	10.00	20.00	40.00
REGENT					
❑ MG-6061 [M]	Jazz on the Rocks	1957	15.00	30.00	60.00
SAVOY					
❑ MG-12210 [M]	Jazz on the Rocks	196?	5.00	10.00	20.00

BAILES BROTHERS, THE
AUDIO LAB

Number	Title (A Side/B Side)	Yr	VG	VG+	NM
❑ AL-1511 [M]	Avenues of Prayer	1959	50.00	100.00	200.00

BAILEY, BENNY
ARGO

Number	Title (A Side/B Side)	Yr	VG	VG+	NM
❑ LP-668 [M]	The Music of Quincy Jones	1961	6.25	12.50	25.00
❑ LPS-668 [S]	The Music of Quincy Jones	1961	7.50	15.00	30.00
CANDID					
❑ CD-8011 [M]	Big Brass	1960	7.50	15.00	30.00
❑ CS-9011 [S]	Big Brass	1960	10.00	20.00	40.00

BAILEY, BUSTER
FELSTED

Number	Title (A Side/B Side)	Yr	VG	VG+	NM
❑ SJA-2003 [S]	All About Memphis	1959	10.00	20.00	40.00
❑ FAJ-7003 [M]	All About Memphis	1959	10.00	20.00	40.00

BAILEY, DAVE
EPIC

Number	Title (A Side/B Side)	Yr	VG	VG+	NM
❑ LA 16008 [M]	One Foot in the Gutter	1960	7.50	15.00	30.00
❑ LA 16011 [M]	Gettin' Into Something	1960	7.50	15.00	30.00
❑ LA 16021 [M]	Two Feet in the Gutter	1961	7.50	15.00	30.00
❑ BA 17008 [S]	One Foot in the Gutter	1960	12.50	25.00	50.00
❑ BA 17008 [S]	One Foot in the Gutter	199?	6.25	12.50	25.00
—Classic Records reissue					
❑ BA 17011 [S]	Gettin' Into Something	1960	10.00	20.00	40.00
❑ BA 17021 [S]	Two Feet in the Gutter	1961	10.00	20.00	40.00
JAZZ LINE					
❑ 33-01 [M]	Bash!	1961	10.00	20.00	40.00
JAZZTIME					
❑ JS-003 [S]	Reaching Out	1961	10.00	20.00	40.00
—Reissued under GRANT GREEN's name					
❑ JT-003 [M]	Reaching Out	1961	7.50	15.00	30.00

BAILEY, MILDRED
ALLEGRO

Number	Title (A Side/B Side)	Yr	VG	VG+	NM
❑ 3119 [M]	Mildred Bailey Sings	1955	15.00	30.00	60.00
❑ 4009 [10]	Mildred Bailey Songs	1952	20.00	40.00	80.00
❑ 4040 [10]	Mildred Bailey Songs	1954	20.00	40.00	80.00
COLUMBIA					
❑ C3L 22 [(3)]	Her Greatest Performances	1962	12.50	25.00	50.00
—With booklet; originals have red labels with "Guaranteed High Fidelity" at bottom					
❑ CL 6094 [10]	Serenade	1950	15.00	30.00	60.00
DECCA					
❑ DL 5133 [10]	Mildred Bailey Memorial Album	1950	15.00	30.00	60.00

Number	Title (A Side/B Side)	Yr	VG	VG+	NM
❑ DL 5387 [10]	The Rockin' Chair Lady	195?	15.00	30.00	60.00
REGENT					
❑ MG-6032 [M]	Me and the Blues	1957	12.50	25.00	50.00
ROYALE					
❑ VLP 6078 [10]	Mildred Bailey Sings	195?	20.00	40.00	80.00
SAVOY					
❑ MG-12219 [M]	Me and the Blues	196?	5.00	10.00	20.00

BAILEY, PEARL
COLUMBIA

Number	Title (A Side/B Side)	Yr	VG	VG+	NM
❑ CL 6099 [10]	Pearl Bailey Entertains	1950	12.50	25.00	50.00
CORAL					
❑ CRL 56068 [10]	Say Si Si	1953	12.50	25.00	50.00
❑ CRL 56078 [10]	I'm with You	1954	12.50	25.00	50.00
❑ CRL 57037 [M]	Pearl Bailey	1957	10.00	20.00	40.00
❑ CRL 57162 [M]	Cultured Pearl	1958	10.00	20.00	40.00
MERCURY					
❑ MG-20187 [M]	The One and Only Pearl Bailey Sings	1956	10.00	20.00	40.00
❑ MG-20277 [M]	The Intoxicating Pearl Bailey	1957	10.00	20.00	40.00
ROULETTE					
❑ R-25012 [M]	Pearl Bailey A Broad	1957	7.50	15.00	30.00
—Black label original					
❑ R-25016 [M]	Pearl Bailey Sings for Adults Only	1959	5.00	10.00	20.00
—Originals have a white label with colored spokes					
❑ SR-25016 [S]	Pearl Bailey Sings for Adults Only	1959	6.25	12.50	25.00
—Originals have a white label with colored spokes					
❑ R-25037 [M]	St. Louis Blues	1958	7.50	15.00	30.00
—Black label original					
❑ SR-25037 [S]	St. Louis Blues	1959	7.50	15.00	30.00
—Originals have a white label with colored spokes					
❑ R-25063 [M]	Pearl Bailey Sings Porgy and Bess and Other Gershwin Melodies	1959	5.00	10.00	20.00
—Originals have a white label with colored spokes					
❑ SR-25063 [S]	Pearl Bailey Sings Porgy and Bess and Other Gershwin Melodies	1959	6.25	12.50	25.00
—Originals have a white label with colored spokes					
❑ R-25101 [M]	More Songs for Adults Only	1960	5.00	10.00	20.00
—Originals have a white label with colored spokes					
❑ SR-25101 [S]	More Songs for Adults Only	1960	6.25	12.50	25.00
—Originals have a white label with colored spokes					
❑ R-25116 [M]	Songs of the Bad Old Days	1960	5.00	10.00	20.00
—Originals have a white label with colored spokes					
❑ SR-25116 [S]	Songs of the Bad Old Days	1960	6.25	12.50	25.00
—Originals have a white label with colored spokes					
❑ R-25125 [M]	Naughty But Nice	1960	5.00	10.00	20.00
—Originals have a white label with colored spokes					
❑ SR-25125 [S]	Naughty But Nice	1960	6.25	12.50	25.00
—Originals have a white label with colored spokes					
❑ R-25144 [M]	The Best of Pearl Bailey	1961	5.00	10.00	20.00
—Originals have a white label with colored spokes					
❑ SR-25144 [S]	The Best of Pearl Bailey	1961	6.25	12.50	25.00
—Originals have a white label with colored spokes					
❑ R-25155 [M]	Pearl Bailey Sings Songs of Harold Arlen	1961	5.00	10.00	20.00
—Originals have a white label with colored spokes					
❑ SR-25155 [S]	Pearl Bailey Sings Songs of Harold Arlen	1961	6.25	12.50	25.00
—Originals have a white label with colored spokes					
❑ R-25167 [M]	Happy Sounds	1962	5.00	10.00	20.00
—Originals have a white label with colored spokes					
❑ SR-25167 [S]	Happy Sounds	1962	6.25	12.50	25.00
—Originals have a white label with colored spokes					
❑ R-25181 [M]	Come On, Let's Play with Pearlie Mae	1962	5.00	10.00	20.00
—Originals have a white label with colored spokes					
❑ SR-25181 [S]	Come On, Let's Play with Pearlie Mae	1962	6.25	12.50	25.00
—Originals have a white label with colored spokes					
❑ R-25195 [M]	All About Good Little Girls and Bad Little Boys	1963	5.00	10.00	20.00
—Originals have a pink and orange label					
❑ SR-25195 [S]	All About Good Little Girls and Bad Little Boys	1963	6.25	12.50	25.00
—Originals have a pink and orange label					
❑ R-25222 [M]	C'est La Vie	1963	5.00	10.00	20.00
—Originals have a pink and orange label					
❑ SR-25222 [S]	C'est La Vie	1963	6.25	12.50	25.00
—Originals have a pink and orange label					
❑ SR-25259 [S]	The Risque World of Pearl Bailey	1964	5.00	10.00	20.00
❑ SR-25271 [S]	Songs by James Van Heusen	1964	5.00	10.00	20.00
❑ SR-25300 [S]	For Women Only	1965	5.00	10.00	20.00
VOCALION					
❑ VL 3621 [M]	Gems by Pearl Bailey	1958	6.25	12.50	25.00

BAILLARGEON, HELENE
FOLKWAYS

Number	Title (A Side/B Side)	Yr	VG	VG+	NM
❑ FW 829 [10]	Christmas Songs of French Canada	195?	12.50	25.00	50.00
❑ FC 7229	Christmas Songs of French Canada	195?	12.50	25.00	50.00

BAIN, BOB
CAPITOL

Number	Title (A Side/B Side)	Yr	VG	VG+	NM
❑ T 965 [M]	Rockin', Rollin' and Strollin'	1958	20.00	40.00	80.00
❑ ST 1201 [S]	Latin Love	1959	10.00	20.00	40.00
❑ T 1201 [M]	Latin Love	1959	7.50	15.00	30.00
❑ ST 1500 [S]	Guitar De Amor	1961	10.00	20.00	40.00
❑ T 1500 [M]	Guitar De Amor	1961	7.50	15.00	30.00

BAKER, BUDDY
VERVE

Number	Title (A Side/B Side)	Yr	VG	VG+	NM
❑ MGV-2006 [M]	Two in Love	1956	12.50	25.00	50.00
❑ V-2006 [M]	Two in Love	1961	5.00	10.00	20.00

BAKER, CHET
ANALOGUE PRODUCTIONS

Number	Title (A Side/B Side)	Yr	VG	VG+	NM
❑ AAPJ-016	Chet	199?	6.25	12.50	25.00
—Audiophile reissue					
COLPIX					
❑ CP-476 [M]	Chet Baker Sings and Plays	1964	10.00	20.00	40.00

Number	Title (A Side/B Side)	Yr	VG	VG+	NM
❑ SCP-476 [S]	Chet Baker Sings and Plays	1964	12.50	25.00	50.00
COLUMBIA					
❑ CL 549 [M]	Chet Baker and Strings	1954	20.00	40.00	80.00
—Maroon label, gold print					
❑ CL 549 [M]	Chet Baker and Strings	1955	12.50	25.00	50.00
—Red and black label with six "eye" logos					
CROWN					
❑ CLP-5317 [M]	Chet Baker Quintette	196?	5.00	10.00	20.00
HARMONY					
❑ HL 7320 [M]	Love Walked In	1962	5.00	10.00	20.00
JAZZLAND					
❑ JLP-11 [M]	Chet Baker and Orchestra	1960	10.00	20.00	40.00
❑ JLP-18 [M]	Chet Baker in Milan	1960	10.00	20.00	40.00
❑ JLP-21 [M]	Chet Baker with Fifty Italian Strings	1960	10.00	20.00	40.00
❑ JLP-911 [S]	Chet Baker and Orchestra	1960	10.00	20.00	40.00
❑ JLP-918 [S]	Chet Baker in Milan	1960	10.00	20.00	40.00
❑ JLP-921 [S]	Chet Baker with Fifty Italian Strings	1960	10.00	20.00	40.00
LIMELIGHT					
❑ LM-82003 [M]	Baby Breeze	1964	6.25	12.50	25.00
❑ LM-82019 [M]	Baker's Holiday	1965	6.25	12.50	25.00
❑ LS-86003 [S]	Baby Breeze	1964	7.50	15.00	30.00
❑ LS-86019 [S]	Baker's Holiday	1965	7.50	15.00	30.00
MOSAIC					
❑ MR4-113 [(4)]	The Complete Pacific Jazz Live Recordings of the Chet Baker Quartet with Russ Freeman	199?	20.00	40.00	80.00
❑ MR4-122 [(4)]	The Complete Pacific Jazz Studio Recordings of the Chet Baker Quartet with Russ Freeman	199?	20.00	40.00	80.00
PACIFIC JAZZ					
❑ PJLP-3 [10]	Chet Baker Quartet	1953	50.00	100.00	200.00
❑ PJLP-6 [10]	Chet Baker Quartet Featuring Russ Freeman	1953	50.00	100.00	200.00
❑ PJLP-9 [10]	Chet Baker Ensemble	1954	50.00	100.00	200.00
❑ PJLP-11 [10]	Chet Baker Sings	1954	50.00	100.00	200.00
❑ PJLP-15 [10]	Chet Baker Sextet	1954	50.00	100.00	200.00
❑ PJ-1202 [M]	Chet Baker Sings and Plays with Bud Shank, Russ Freeman and Strings	1955	30.00	60.00	120.00
❑ PJ-1203 [M]	Jazz at Ann Arbor	1955	30.00	60.00	120.00
❑ PJ-1206 [M]	The Trumpet Artistry of Chet Baker	1955	30.00	60.00	120.00
❑ PJ-1218 [M]	Chet Baker in Europe	1956	30.00	60.00	120.00
❑ PJ-1222 [M]	Chet Baker Sings	1956	30.00	60.00	120.00
❑ PJ-1224 [M]	Chet Baker and Crew	1956	30.00	60.00	120.00
❑ PJ-1229 [M]	Chet Baker Big Band	1957	30.00	60.00	120.00
PRESTIGE					
❑ PRLP-7449 [M]	Smokin' with the Chet Baker Quintet	1966	5.00	10.00	20.00
❑ PRST-7449 [S]	Smokin' with the Chet Baker Quintet	1966	6.25	12.50	25.00
❑ PRLP-7460 [M]	Groovin' with the Chet Baker Quintet	1966	5.00	10.00	20.00
❑ PRST-7460 [S]	Groovin' with the Chet Baker Quintet	1966	6.25	12.50	25.00
❑ PRLP-7478 [M]	Comin' On with the Chet Baker Quintet	1967	6.25	12.50	25.00
❑ PRST-7478 [S]	Comin' On with the Chet Baker Quintet	1967	5.00	10.00	20.00
❑ PRLP-7496 [M]	Cool Burnin' with the Chet Baker Quintet	1967	7.50	15.00	30.00
❑ PRST-7496 [S]	Cool Burnin' with the Chet Baker Quintet	1967	5.00	10.00	20.00
❑ PRLP-7512 [M]	Boppin' with the Chet Baker Quintet	1967	7.50	15.00	30.00
❑ PRST-7512 [S]	Boppin' with the Chet Baker Quintet	1967	5.00	10.00	20.00
RIVERSIDE					
❑ RLP 12-278 [M]	It Could Happen to You — Chet Baker Sings	1958	12.50	25.00	50.00
❑ RLP 12-281 [M]	Chet Baker in New York	1958	12.50	25.00	50.00
❑ RLP 12-299 [M]	Chet	1959	12.50	25.00	50.00
❑ RLP 12-307 [M]	Chet Baker Plays Lerner and Loewe	1959	12.50	25.00	50.00
❑ RLP-1119 [S]	Chet Baker in New York	1959	10.00	20.00	40.00
❑ RLP-1120 [S]	It Could Happen to You — Chet Baker Sings	1959	10.00	20.00	40.00
❑ RLP-1135 [S]	Chet	1959	10.00	20.00	40.00
❑ RLP-1152 [S]	Chet Baker Plays Lerner and Loewe	1959	10.00	20.00	40.00
SCEPTER					
❑ 540 [M]	Angel Eyes	1966	5.00	10.00	20.00
❑ S-540 [S]	Angel Eyes	1966	6.25	12.50	25.00
WORLD PACIFIC					
❑ ST-1004 [S]	Chet Baker and Crew	1959	15.00	30.00	60.00
❑ WP-1202 [M]	Chet Baker Sings and Plays with Bud Shank, Russ Freeman and Strings	1958	20.00	40.00	80.00
—Reissue of Pacific Jazz 1202					
❑ WP-1203 [M]	Jazz at Ann Arbor	1958	20.00	40.00	80.00
—Reissue of Pacific Jazz 1203					
❑ WP-1206 [M]	The Trumpet Artistry of Chet Baker	1958	20.00	40.00	80.00
—Reissue of Pacific Jazz 1206					
❑ WP-1218 [M]	Chet Baker in Europe	1958	20.00	40.00	80.00
—Reissue of Pacific Jazz 1218					
❑ WP-1222 [M]	Chet Baker Sings	1958	20.00	40.00	80.00
—Reissue of Pacific Jazz 1222					
❑ WP-1224 [M]	Chet Baker and Crew	1958	20.00	40.00	80.00
—Reissue of Pacific Jazz 1224					
❑ WP-1229 [M]	Chet Baker Big Band	1958	20.00	40.00	80.00
—Reissue of Pacific Jazz 1229					
❑ WP-1249 [M]	Pretty/Groovy	1958	25.00	50.00	100.00
❑ ST-1826 [R]	Chet Baker Sings	1964	5.00	10.00	20.00
❑ WP-1826 [M]	Chet Baker Sings	1964	7.50	15.00	30.00
—Reissue of World Pacific 1222					
❑ WP-1842 [M]	Hat's Off	1966	5.00	10.00	20.00
❑ WP-1847 [M]	Quietly, There	1966	5.00	10.00	20.00
❑ WP-1852 [M]	Double Shot	1967	5.00	10.00	20.00
❑ WP-1858 [M]	Into My Life	1967	6.25	12.50	25.00
❑ WPS-21842 [S]	Hat's Off	1966	6.25	12.50	25.00
❑ WPS-21847 [S]	Quietly, There	1966	6.25	12.50	25.00
❑ WPS-21852 [S]	Double Shot	1967	6.25	12.50	25.00
❑ WPS-21858 [S]	Into My Life	1967	5.00	10.00	20.00
❑ WPS-21859 [S]	In the Mood	1968	5.00	10.00	20.00
WORLD PACIFIC JAZZ					
❑ ST-21852 [R]	Chet Baker Plays and Sings	1968	3.00	6.00	12.00
—Compilation of 1950s Pacific Jazz material					

Number	Title (A Side/B Side)	Yr	VG	VG+	NM
BAKER, CHET, AND ART PEPPER					
PACIFIC JAZZ					
❏ PJ-18 [M]	Picture of Health	1961	12.50	25.00	50.00
❏ PJ-1234 [M]	Playboys	1957	37.50	75.00	150.00
—Pacific Jazz records come in World Pacific covers					
WORLD PACIFIC					
❏ PJ-1234 [M]	Playboys	1958	30.00	60.00	120.00
❏ WP-1234 [M]	Playboys	1958	20.00	40.00	80.00
BAKER, GEORGE, SELECTION					
COLOSSUS					
❏ CS-1002	Little Green Bag	1970	5.00	10.00	20.00
WARNER BROS.					
❏ BS 2905	Paloma Blanca	1975	3.75	7.50	15.00
BAKER, GINGER, 'S AIR FORCE					
ATCO					
❏ SD 33-343	Ginger Baker's Air Force 2	1971	3.00	6.00	12.00
❏ SD 2-703 [(2)]	Ginger Baker's Air Force	1970	5.00	10.00	20.00
❏ SD 7012	Stratavarious	1972	3.00	6.00	12.00
AXIOM					
❏ 539864-1	Middle Passage	1990	3.75	7.50	15.00
CELLULOID					
❏ CEL-6126	Horses and Trees	1986	2.50	5.00	10.00
POLYDOR					
❏ 3504 [(2)]	Ginger Baker At His Best	1973	3.75	7.50	15.00
SIRE					
❏ SASD-7532	Eleven Sides of Baker	1977	2.50	5.00	10.00
BAKER, JOSEPHINE					
COLUMBIA					
❏ FL 9532 [10]	Josephine Baker	1951	25.00	50.00	100.00
❏ FL 9533 [10]	Chansons Americaines	1951	25.00	50.00	100.00
COLUMBIA MASTERWORKS					
❏ ML 2608 [10]	Josephine Baker Sings	1952	20.00	40.00	80.00
❏ ML 2609 [10]	Chansons Americaines	1952	20.00	40.00	80.00
❏ ML 2613 [10]	Encores Americaines	1952	20.00	40.00	80.00
JOLLY ROGER					
❏ 5015 [10]	Josephine Baker	1951	12.50	25.00	50.00
MERCURY					
❏ MG-25105 [10]	The Inimitable Josephine Baker	1952	20.00	40.00	80.00
❏ MG-25151 [10]	Avec Josephine Baker	1952	20.00	40.00	80.00
RCA VICTOR RED SEAL					
❏ LM-2427 [M]	The Fabulous Josephine Baker	1960	3.75	7.50	15.00
—Original with "shaded dog" label					
❏ LSC-2427 [S]	The Fabulous Josephine Baker	1960	12.50	25.00	50.00
—Original with "shaded dog" label					
BAKER, LAVERN					
ATCO					
❏ SD 33-372	Her Greatest Recordings	1971	3.00	6.00	12.00
ATLANTIC					
❏ 1281 [M]	LaVern Baker Sings Bessie Smith	1958	30.00	60.00	120.00
—Black label					
❏ 1281 [M]	LaVern Baker Sings Bessie Smith	1960	7.50	15.00	30.00
—Red and purple label, "fan" logo in white					
❏ 1281 [M]	LaVern Baker Sings Bessie Smith	1963	5.00	10.00	20.00
—Red and purple label, "fan" logo in black					
❏ SD 1281 [S]	LaVern Baker Sings Bessie Smith	1959	37.50	75.00	150.00
—Green label					
❏ SD 1281 [S]	LaVern Baker Sings Bessie Smith	1960	10.00	20.00	40.00
—Green and blue label, "fan" logo in white					
❏ SD 1281 [S]	LaVern Baker Sings Bessie Smith	1963	6.25	12.50	25.00
—Green and blue label, "fan" logo in black					
❏ 8002 [M]	LaVern	1956	62.50	125.00	250.00
—Black label					
❏ 8002 [M]	LaVern	1960	7.50	15.00	30.00
—Red and purple label, "fan" logo in white					
❏ 8002 [M]	LaVern	1963	5.00	10.00	20.00
—Red and purple label, "fan" logo in black					
❏ 8007 [M]	LaVern Baker	1957	62.50	125.00	250.00
—Black label					
❏ 8007 [M]	LaVern Baker	1960	7.50	15.00	30.00
—Red and purple label, "fan" logo in white					
❏ 8007 [M]	LaVern Baker	1963	5.00	10.00	20.00
—Red and purple label, "fan" logo in black					
❏ 8030 [M]	Blues Ballads	1959	50.00	100.00	200.00
—Black label					
❏ 8030 [M]	Blues Ballads	1960	7.50	15.00	30.00
—Red and purple label, "fan" logo in white					
❏ 8030 [M]	Blues Ballads	1960	37.50	75.00	150.00
—White "bullseye" label					
❏ 8030 [M]	Blues Ballads	1963	5.00	10.00	20.00
—Red and purple label, "fan" logo in black					
❏ 8036 [M]	Precious Memories	1959	50.00	100.00	200.00
—Black label					
❏ 8036 [M]	Precious Memories	1960	7.50	15.00	30.00
—Red and purple label, "fan" logo in white					
❏ 8036 [M]	Precious Memories	1960	37.50	75.00	150.00
—White "bullseye" label					
❏ 8036 [M]	Precious Memories	1963	5.00	10.00	20.00
—Red and purple label, "fan" logo in black					
❏ SD 8036 [S]	Precious Memories	1959	75.00	150.00	300.00
—Green label					
❏ SD 8036 [S]	Precious Memories	1960	10.00	20.00	40.00
—Green and blue label, "fan" logo in white					
❏ SD 8036 [S]	Precious Memories	1960	50.00	100.00	200.00
—White "bullseye" label					
❏ SD 8036 [S]	Precious Memories	1963	6.25	12.50	25.00
—Green and blue label, "fan" logo in black					

Number	Title (A Side/B Side)	Yr	VG	VG+	NM
❏ 8050 [M]	Saved	1961	25.00	50.00	100.00
—Red and purple label, "fan" logo in white					
❏ 8050 [M]	Saved	1963	5.00	10.00	20.00
—Red and purple label, "fan" logo in black					
❏ SD 8050 [S]	Saved	1961	37.50	75.00	150.00
—Green and blue label, "fan" logo in white					
❏ SD 8050 [S]	Saved	1963	6.25	12.50	25.00
—Green and blue label, "fan" logo in black					
❏ 8071 [M]	See See Rider	1962	25.00	50.00	100.00
—Red and purple label, "fan" logo in white					
❏ 8071 [M]	See See Rider	1963	5.00	10.00	20.00
—Red and purple label, "fan" logo in black					
❏ SD 8071 [S]	See See Rider	1962	37.50	75.00	150.00
—Green and blue label, "fan" logo in white					
❏ SD 8071 [S]	See See Rider	1963	6.25	12.50	25.00
—Green and blue label, "fan" logo in black					
❏ 8078 [M]	The Best of LaVern Baker	1963	37.50	75.00	150.00
—Red and purple label, "fan" logo in black					
❏ 90980	LaVern Baker Sings Bessie Smith	1989	3.00	6.00	12.00
—Reissue of SD 1281					
BRUNSWICK					
❏ BL 754160	Let Me Belong to You	1970	5.00	10.00	20.00
BAKER, MICKEY "GUITAR"					
Also see MICKEY AND SYLVIA.					
ATLANTIC					
❏ 8035 [M]	The Wildest Guitar	1959	37.50	75.00	150.00
—Black label					
❏ 8035 [M]	The Wildest Guitar	1960	12.50	25.00	50.00
—Red and purple label, "fan" logo in white					
❏ SD 8035 [S]	The Wildest Guitar	1959	62.50	125.00	250.00
—Green label					
❏ SD 8035 [S]	The Wildest Guitar	1960	20.00	40.00	80.00
—Green and blue label, "fan" logo in white					
KICKING MULE					
❏ 140	The Jazz Rock Guitar of Mickey Baker	1978	3.00	6.00	12.00
❏ 142	The Blues and Jazz Guitar of Mickey Baker	1978	3.00	6.00	12.00
KING					
❏ 839 [M]	But Wild	196?	20.00	40.00	80.00
—Blue label with crown					
❏ 839 [M]	But Wild	1963	100.00	200.00	400.00
—Black label, no crown					
❏ S-839 [R]	But Wild	196?	10.00	20.00	40.00
BAKER, RONNIE					
WARNER BROS.					
❏ W 1212 [M]	Oh, Johnny!	1958	7.50	15.00	30.00
❏ WS 1212 [S]	Oh, Johnny!	1959	12.50	25.00	50.00
BAKER, SHORTY					
KING					
❏ 608 [M]	Broadway Beat	1958	20.00	40.00	80.00
BAKER, SHORTY, AND DOC CHEATHAM					
SWINGVILLE					
❏ SVLP-2021 [M]	Shorty & Doc	1961	12.50	25.00	50.00
—Purple label					
❏ SVLP-2021 [M]	Shorty & Doc	1965	6.25	12.50	25.00
—Blue label with trident logo at right					
BALDRY, LONG JOHN					
ASCOT					
❏ AM-13022 [M]	Long John's Blues	1965	12.50	25.00	50.00
❏ AS-16022 [R]	Long John's Blues	1965	10.00	20.00	40.00
CASABLANCA					
❏ NBLP 7012	Good to Be Alive	1975	3.00	6.00	12.00
❏ NBLP 7035	Welcome to the Club	1976	3.00	6.00	12.00
EMI AMERICA					
❏ SW-17015	Baldry's Out	1979	2.50	5.00	10.00
❏ SW-17038	Long John Baldry	1980	2.50	5.00	10.00
UNITED ARTISTS					
❏ UAS-5543 [M]	Long John's Blues	1971	3.00	6.00	12.00
—Reissue of Ascot 13022					
WARNER BROS.					
❏ WS 1921	It Ain't Easy	1971	3.75	7.50	15.00
❏ BS 2614	Everything Stops for Tea	1973	3.00	6.00	12.00
BALES, BURT					
ABC-PARAMOUNT					
❏ ABC-181 [M]	Jazz from the San Francisco Waterfront	1957	10.00	20.00	40.00
CAVALIER					
❏ 5007 [10]	On the Waterfront	195?	15.00	30.00	60.00
EUPHONIC					
❏ ESR-1210 [M]	New Orleans Ragtime	196?	7.50	15.00	30.00
GOOD TIME JAZZ					
❏ L-19 [10]	New Orleans Joys	1954	12.50	25.00	50.00
BALES & LINGLE					
GOOD TIME JAZZ					
❏ L-12025 [M]	They Tore My Playhouse Down	1955	10.00	20.00	40.00
BALIN, MARTY					
EMI AMERICA					
❏ SPRO-9673 [DJ]	Balin	1981	5.00	10.00	20.00
—Red vinyl					
❏ ST-17054	Balin	1981	2.50	5.00	10.00
❏ ST-17088	Lucky	1983	2.50	5.00	10.00
BALL, KENNY					
KAPP					
❏ KL-1276 [M]	Midnight in Moscow	1962	5.00	10.00	20.00
❏ KL-1285 [M]	It's Trad	1962	5.00	10.00	20.00

Number	Title (A Side/B Side)	Yr	VG	VG+	NM
❏ KL-1294 [M]	Recorded Live	1962	5.00	10.00	20.00
❏ KS-3276 [S]	Midnight in Moscow	1962	5.00	10.00	20.00
❏ KS-3285 [S]	It's Trad	1962	5.00	10.00	20.00
❏ KS-3294 [S]	Recorded Live	1962	5.00	10.00	20.00
❏ KS-3314 [S]	More	1963	5.00	10.00	20.00
❏ KS-3340 [S]	Big Ones	1963	5.00	10.00	20.00
❏ KS-3348 [S]	Washington Square and the Best of Kenny Ball	1964	5.00	10.00	20.00
❏ KS-3392 [S]	For the Jet Set	1964	5.00	10.00	20.00

BALL, RONNIE
SAVOY

| ❏ MG-12075 [M] | All About Ronnie | 1956 | 10.00 | 20.00 | 40.00 |

BALLADEERS, THE
DEL-FI

| ❏ DFLP-1204 [M] | Alive-O! | 1959 | 10.00 | 20.00 | 40.00 |
| ❏ DFST-1204 [S] | Alive-O! | 1959 | 15.00 | 30.00 | 60.00 |

BALLARD, FRANK
PHILLIPS INTERNATIONAL

| ❏ 1985 [M] | Rhythm-Blues Party | 1962 | 2500. | 3750. | 5000. |

BALLARD, HANK, AND THE MIDNIGHTERS
KING

❏ 618 [M]	Singin' and Swingin'	1959	62.50	125.00	250.00
❏ 674 [M]	The One and Only Hank Ballard	1959	62.50	125.00	250.00
—Brown cover					
❏ 674 [M]	The One and Only Hank Ballard	1960	37.50	75.00	150.00
—Green cover					
❏ 700 [M]	Mr. Rhythm and Blues	1960	37.50	75.00	150.00
❏ 740 [M]	Spotlight on Hank Ballard	1961	37.50	75.00	150.00
❏ KS-740 [S]	Spotlight on Hank Ballard	1961	75.00	150.00	300.00
❏ 748 [M]	Let's Go Again	1961	30.00	60.00	120.00
❏ 759 [M]	Dance Along	1961	30.00	60.00	120.00
❏ 781 [M]	The Twistin' Fools	1962	25.00	50.00	100.00
❏ 793 [M]	Jumpin' Hank Ballard	1962	25.00	50.00	100.00
❏ 815 [M]	The 1963 Sound of Hank Ballard	1963	25.00	50.00	100.00
❏ 867 [M]	Biggest Hits	1963	25.00	50.00	100.00
❏ 896 [M]	A Star in Your Eyes	1964	25.00	50.00	100.00
❏ 913 [M]	Those Lazy, Lazy Days	1965	17.50	35.00	70.00
❏ 927 [M]	Glad Songs, Sad Songs	1965	17.50	35.00	70.00
❏ 950 [M]	24 Hit Tunes	1966	15.00	30.00	60.00
❏ 981 [M]	24 Great Songs	1968	10.00	20.00	40.00
❏ KSD-1052	You Can't Keep a Good Man Down	1969	12.50	25.00	50.00

BALLARD, KAYE
UNITED ARTISTS

❏ UAL-3043 [M]	Kaye Ballard Swings	1959	5.00	10.00	20.00
❏ UAL-3155 [M]	Kaye Ballard Live?	1960	5.00	10.00	20.00
❏ UAL-3165 [M]	Ha-Ha Boo-Hoo	1960	5.00	10.00	20.00
❏ UAS-6043 [S]	Kaye Ballard Swings	1959	6.25	12.50	25.00
❏ UAS-6155 [S]	Kaye Ballard Live?	1960	6.25	12.50	25.00
❏ UAS-6165 [S]	Ha-Ha Boo-Hoo	1960	6.25	12.50	25.00

BANANA SPLITS, THE
DECCA

| ❏ DL 75075 | We're the Banana Splits | 1969 | 50.00 | 100.00 | 200.00 |

BANCHEE
ATLANTIC

| ❏ SD 8240 | Banchee | 1969 | 5.00 | 10.00 | 20.00 |

POLYDOR

| ❏ 24-4066 | Thinkin' | 1971 | 12.50 | 25.00 | 50.00 |

BAND, THE
CAPITOL

❏ STAO-132	The Band	1969	3.75	7.50	15.00
—Lime green label					
❏ STAO-8-0132	The Band	1969	25.00	50.00	100.00
—Capitol Record Club edition with black rainbow label; we don't know if any standard versions of this album exist with this label					
❏ SW-425	Stage Fright	1970	2.50	5.00	10.00
—Without tear-off wraparound cover					
❏ SW-425	Stage Fright	1970	3.75	7.50	15.00
—Includes tear-off wraparound cover					
❏ SMAS-651	Cahoots	1971	3.75	7.50	15.00
❏ SKAO 2955	Music from Big Pink	1968	6.25	12.50	25.00
—Black label with colorband					
❏ SKAO 2955	Music from Big Pink	1969	3.75	7.50	15.00
—Lime green label					
❏ SKAO 2955	Music from Big Pink	1971	3.75	7.50	15.00
—Red label, purple "C" logo at top					
❏ SABB-11045 [(2)]	Rock of Ages	1972	5.00	10.00	20.00
❏ SW-11214	Moondog Matinee	1973	2.50	5.00	10.00
—Without tear-off wraparound cover					
❏ SW-11214	Moondog Matinee	1973	3.75	7.50	15.00
—Includes tear-off wraparound cover					
❏ ST-11440	Northern Lights-Southern Cross	1975	3.00	6.00	12.00
❏ ST-11553	The Best of the Band	1976	3.00	6.00	12.00
❏ SO-11602	Islands	1977	3.00	6.00	12.00
❏ SKBO-11856 [(2)]	Anthology	1978	3.75	7.50	15.00
❏ SN-16003	Cahoots	1980	2.00	4.00	8.00
—Budget-line reissue					
❏ SN-16004	Moondog Matinee	1980	2.00	4.00	8.00
—Budget-line reissue					
❏ SN-16005	Northern Lights-Southern Cross	1980	2.00	4.00	8.00
—Budget-line reissue					
❏ SN-16006	Stage Fright	1980	2.00	4.00	8.00
—Budget-line reissue					
❏ SN-16007	Islands	1980	2.00	4.00	8.00
—Budget-line reissue					
❏ SN-16008	Rock of Ages, Volume 1	1980	2.00	4.00	8.00
—Budget-line reissue					

Number	Title (A Side/B Side)	Yr	VG	VG+	NM
❏ SN-16009	Rock of Ages, Volume 2	1980	2.00	4.00	8.00
—Budget-line reissue					
❏ SN-16010	Anthology, Volume 1	1980	2.00	4.00	8.00
—Budget-line reissue					
❏ SN-16011	Anthology, Volume 2	1980	2.00	4.00	8.00
—Budget-line reissue					
❏ SN-16296	The Band	198?	2.00	4.00	8.00
—Budget-line reissue					
❏ SN-16331	The Best of the Band	198?	2.00	4.00	8.00
—Budget-line reissue					

MOBILE FIDELITY

| ❏ 1-039 | Music from Big Pink | 1981 | 12.50 | 25.00 | 50.00 |
| —Audiophile vinyl | | | | | |

WARNER BROS.

| ❏ PRO-A-737 [DJ] | The Last Waltz Sampler | 1978 | 5.00 | 10.00 | 20.00 |
| ❏ 3WS 3146 [(3)] | The Last Waltz | 1978 | 5.00 | 10.00 | 20.00 |

BANDITS, THE
WORLD PACIFIC

| ❏ ST-1833 [S] | The Electric 12 String | 1964 | 6.25 | 12.50 | 25.00 |
| ❏ T-1833 [M] | The Electric 12 String | 1964 | 5.00 | 10.00 | 20.00 |

BANDWAGON, THE
EPIC

| ❏ BN 26426 | Johnny Johnson and the Bandwagon | 1969 | 5.00 | 10.00 | 20.00 |

BANG
CAPITOL

❏ ST-11015	Bang	1972	3.75	7.50	15.00
❏ SMAS-11110	Mother/Bow to the Music	1972	3.75	7.50	15.00
❏ ST-11190	Music	1973	5.00	10.00	20.00

BANGLES
COLUMBIA

❏ CAS 2270 [DJ]	Interchords	1986	6.25	12.50	25.00
—Promo-only interview album					
❏ BFC 39220	All Over the Place	1984	3.00	6.00	12.00
❏ PC 39220	All Over the Place	1986	2.00	4.00	8.00
—Reissue with new prefix and longer bar code					
❏ BFC 40039	Different Light	1986	3.00	6.00	12.00
❏ FC 40039	Different Light	1986	2.00	4.00	8.00
—Reissue with new prefix; "02" added to bar code on back cover					
❏ OC 44056	Everything	1988	2.50	5.00	10.00

FAULTY PRODUCTS

| ❏ FEP 1302 [EP] | Bangles | 1982 | 5.00 | 10.00 | 20.00 |

I.R.S.

| ❏ SP-70506 [EP] | Bangles | 1983 | 3.00 | 6.00 | 12.00 |
| —Reissue of Faulty Products EP | | | | | |

BANJO KINGS, THE
GOOD TIME JAZZ

❏ L-15 [10]	The Banjo Kings	1953	12.50	25.00	50.00
❏ L-25 [10]	The Banjo Kings, Vol. 2	1954	12.50	25.00	50.00
❏ L-12015 [M]	The Banjo Kings	1955	10.00	20.00	40.00
❏ L-12029 [M]	Nostalgia Revisited	1956	10.00	20.00	40.00
❏ L-12036 [M]	The Banjo Kings Go West	1957	10.00	20.00	40.00
❏ L-12047 [M]	The Banjo Kings Enjoy the Good Old Days	1958	10.00	20.00	40.00
❏ S-12047 [S]	The Banjo Kings Enjoy the Good Old Days	1959	7.50	15.00	30.00

BANKS, DARRELL
ATCO

| ❏ 33-216 [M] | Darrell Banks Is Here | 1967 | 6.25 | 12.50 | 25.00 |
| ❏ SD 33-216 [S] | Darrell Banks Is Here | 1967 | 7.50 | 15.00 | 30.00 |

VOLT

| ❏ VOS-6002 | Here to Stay | 1969 | 6.25 | 12.50 | 25.00 |

BANTAMS, THE
WARNER BROS.

| ❏ W 1625 [M] | Beware the Bantams | 1966 | 5.00 | 10.00 | 20.00 |
| ❏ WS 1625 [S] | Beware the Bantams | 1966 | 6.25 | 12.50 | 25.00 |

BAR-KAYS, THE
ATCO

| ❏ SD 33-289 | Soul Finger | 1968 | 6.25 | 12.50 | 25.00 |

MERCURY

❏ SRM-1-1099	Too Hot to Stop	1976	2.50	5.00	10.00
❏ SRM-1-1181	Flying High on Your Love	1977	2.50	5.00	10.00
❏ SRM-1-3732	Light of Life	1978	2.50	5.00	10.00
❏ SRM-1-3781	Injoy	1979	2.50	5.00	10.00
❏ SRM-1-3844	As One	1980	2.50	5.00	10.00
❏ SRM-1-4028	Nightcruising	1981	2.50	5.00	10.00
❏ SRM-1-4065	Propositions	1982	2.50	5.00	10.00
❏ 818478-1	Dangerous	1984	2.50	5.00	10.00
❏ 824727-1	Banging the Wall	1985	2.50	5.00	10.00
❏ 830305-1	Contagious	1987	2.50	5.00	10.00
❏ 836774-1	Animal	1989	2.50	5.00	10.00

STAX

❏ 4106	Money Talks	1978	2.50	5.00	10.00
❏ 4130	Gotta Groove	1979	2.50	5.00	10.00
❏ MPS-8510	Cold Blooded	1981	2.50	5.00	10.00
❏ MPS-8542	The Best of the Bar-Kays	1988	2.50	5.00	10.00

VOLT

❏ 417 [M]	Soul Finger	1967	10.00	20.00	40.00
❏ S-417 [S]	Soul Finger	1967	10.00	20.00	40.00
❏ 6004	Gotta Groove	1969	7.50	15.00	30.00
❏ 6011	Black Rock	1971	6.25	12.50	25.00
❏ VOS-8001	Do You See What I See	1972	6.25	12.50	25.00
❏ 9504	Cold Blooded	1974	6.25	12.50	25.00

BARBARIANS, THE
LAURIE

| ❏ LLP-2033 [M] | Are You a Boy or Are You a Girl? | 1966 | 37.50 | 75.00 | 150.00 |

Number	Title (A Side/B Side)	Yr	VG	VG+	NM
❑ SLP-2033 [S]	Are You a Boy or Are You a Girl?	1966	50.00	100.00	200.00

RHINO

Number	Title (A Side/B Side)	Yr	VG	VG+	NM
❑ RNLP 008	The Barbarians	1979	3.00	6.00	12.00

BARBARIN, PAUL
ATLANTIC

Number	Title (A Side/B Side)	Yr	VG	VG+	NM
❑ 1215 [M]	New Orleans Jazz	1955	12.50	25.00	50.00
—Black label					
❑ 1215 [M]	New Orleans Jazz	1961	5.00	10.00	20.00
—Multi-color label, white "fan" logo at right					
❑ SD 1215 [S]	New Orleans Jazz	1959	12.50	25.00	50.00
—Green label					
❑ SD 1215 [S]	New Orleans Jazz	1961	5.00	10.00	20.00
—Multi-color label, white "fan" logo at right					

CONCERT HALL JAZZ

Number	Title (A Side/B Side)	Yr	VG	VG+	NM
❑ 1006 [10]	New Orleans Jamboree	1954	12.50	25.00	50.00

GHB

Number	Title (A Side/B Side)	Yr	VG	VG+	NM
❑ GHB-2 [M]	Paul Barbarin and His New Orleans Jazz Band	1962	5.00	10.00	20.00

JAZZTONE

Number	Title (A Side/B Side)	Yr	VG	VG+	NM
❑ J-1205 [M]	New Orleans Jamboree	1955	10.00	20.00	40.00

NOBILITY

Number	Title (A Side/B Side)	Yr	VG	VG+	NM
❑ 708	Last Journey of a Jazzman	196?	5.00	10.00	20.00

SOUTHLAND

Number	Title (A Side/B Side)	Yr	VG	VG+	NM
❑ SLP-237 [M]	Bourbon St. Beat	195?	10.00	20.00	40.00

BARBARIN, PAUL / SHARKEY BONANO
RIVERSIDE

Number	Title (A Side/B Side)	Yr	VG	VG+	NM
❑ RLP 12-217 [M]	New Orleans Contrasts	195?	10.00	20.00	40.00
—Blue label with microphone logo					
❑ RLP 12-217 [M]	New Orleans Contrasts	1955	15.00	30.00	60.00
—White label, blue print					

BARBARIN, PAUL, AND PUNCH MILLER
ATLANTIC

Number	Title (A Side/B Side)	Yr	VG	VG+	NM
❑ 1410 [M]	Paul Barbarin and Punch Miller	1963	5.00	10.00	20.00
❑ SD 1410 [S]	Paul Barbarin and Punch Miller	1963	6.25	12.50	25.00

BARBARIN, PAUL / JOHNNY ST. CYR
SOUTHLAND

Number	Title (A Side/B Side)	Yr	VG	VG+	NM
❑ SLP-212 [M]	Paul Barbarin and His Jazz Band/Johnny St. Cyr and His Hot Five	1955	10.00	20.00	40.00

BARBARY, RICHARD
A&M

Number	Title (A Side/B Side)	Yr	VG	VG+	NM
❑ SP-3010	Soul Machine	1969	5.00	10.00	20.00

BARBER, CHRIS
ATLANTIC

Number	Title (A Side/B Side)	Yr	VG	VG+	NM
❑ 1292 [M]	Here Is Chris Barber	1959	10.00	20.00	40.00

COLPIX

Number	Title (A Side/B Side)	Yr	VG	VG+	NM
❑ CP-404 [M]	Petite But Great	1959	7.50	15.00	30.00

LAURIE

Number	Title (A Side/B Side)	Yr	VG	VG+	NM
❑ 1001 [M]	Petite Fleur	1959	10.00	20.00	40.00
❑ LLP-1003 [M]	Trad Jazz Volume 1	1960	7.50	15.00	30.00
❑ LLP-1009 [M]	Chris Barber's "American" Jazz Band	1962	7.50	15.00	30.00

BARBER, PATRICIA
PREMONITION

Number	Title (A Side/B Side)	Yr	VG	VG+	NM
❑ PREM 737-1	Café Blue	199?	7.50	15.00	30.00
—Audiophile vinyl					
❑ PREM 747-1	Modern Cool	1998	6.25	12.50	25.00
—Audiophile vinyl					
❑ 27290	Nightclub	2000	6.25	12.50	25.00
—Audiophile vinyl					
❑ 90747	Companion	1999	6.25	12.50	25.00
—Audiophile vinyl					

BARBIERI, GATO
ESP-DISK'

Number	Title (A Side/B Side)	Yr	VG	VG+	NM
❑ 1049	In Search of the Mystery	1968	5.00	10.00	20.00

BARBOUR, KEITH
EPIC

Number	Title (A Side/B Side)	Yr	VG	VG+	NM
❑ BN 26485	Echo Park	1969	5.00	10.00	20.00

BARCLAY JAMES HARVEST
HARVEST

Number	Title (A Side/B Side)	Yr	VG	VG+	NM
❑ SW-11145	Baby James Harvest	1973	3.75	7.50	15.00

MCA

Number	Title (A Side/B Side)	Yr	VG	VG+	NM
❑ 2234	Octoberon	1976	2.50	5.00	10.00
❑ 2302	Gone to Earth	1977	2.50	5.00	10.00

POLYDOR

Number	Title (A Side/B Side)	Yr	VG	VG+	NM
❑ PD-1-6173	XII	1978	2.50	5.00	10.00
❑ PD-1-6267	Eyes of the Universe	1980	2.50	5.00	10.00
❑ PD-6508	Everyone Is Everybody Else	1974	3.00	6.00	12.00
❑ PD-6517	Time Honoured Ghosts	1975	3.00	6.00	12.00

SIRE

Number	Title (A Side/B Side)	Yr	VG	VG+	NM
❑ SI-4904	Back Again	1971	3.75	7.50	15.00
❑ SI-5904	Other Short Stories	1972	3.75	7.50	15.00
❑ SES-97026	Barclay James Harvest	1970	5.00	10.00	20.00

BARDOT, BRIGITTE
DOT

Number	Title (A Side/B Side)	Yr	VG	VG+	NM
❑ DLP-3120 [M]	La Belle Bardot	1958	25.00	50.00	100.00

PHILIPS

Number	Title (A Side/B Side)	Yr	VG	VG+	NM
❑ PCC 204 [M]	Brigitte Bardot Sings	1963	7.50	15.00	30.00
❑ PCC 604 [S]	Brigitte Bardot Sings	1963	10.00	20.00	40.00

BARE, BOBBY
COLUMBIA

Number	Title (A Side/B Side)	Yr	VG	VG+	NM
❑ KC 35314	Bare	1977	2.50	5.00	10.00
❑ JC 36323	Down & Dirty	1978	2.50	5.00	10.00

Number	Title (A Side/B Side)	Yr	VG	VG+	NM
❑ PC 36323	Down & Dirty	198?	2.00	4.00	8.00
—Budget-line reissue					
❑ JC 36785	Drunk & Crazy	1980	2.50	5.00	10.00
❑ FC 37157	As Is	1981	2.50	5.00	10.00
❑ FC 37351	Encore	1981	2.50	5.00	10.00
❑ PC 37351	Encore	198?	2.00	4.00	8.00
—Budget-line reissue					
❑ FC 37719	Ain't Got Nothin' to Lose	1982	2.50	5.00	10.00
❑ FC 38311	Biggest Hits	1982	2.50	5.00	10.00
❑ FC 38670	Drinkin' from the Bottle, Singin' from the Heart	1983	2.50	5.00	10.00

HILLTOP

Number	Title (A Side/B Side)	Yr	VG	VG+	NM
❑ 6026	Tender Years	196?	3.00	6.00	12.00

MERCURY

Number	Title (A Side/B Side)	Yr	VG	VG+	NM
❑ SR-61290	This Is Bare Country	1970	5.00	10.00	20.00
❑ SR-61316	Where Have All the Seasons Gone	1971	5.00	10.00	20.00
❑ SR-61363	What Am I Gonna Do?	1972	5.00	10.00	20.00

RCA CAMDEN

Number	Title (A Side/B Side)	Yr	VG	VG+	NM
❑ ACL1-0150	Memphis, Tennessee	1973	3.00	6.00	12.00
❑ CAS-2290	Folsom Prison Blues	1969	3.00	6.00	12.00
❑ CAS-2465	I'm a Long Way from Home	1971	3.00	6.00	12.00

RCA VICTOR

Number	Title (A Side/B Side)	Yr	VG	VG+	NM
❑ APL1-0040	I Hate Goodbyes/Ride Me Down Easy	1973	3.75	7.50	15.00
❑ CPL2-0290 [(2)]	Bobby Bare Sings Lullabys, Legends and Lies	1973	5.00	10.00	20.00
❑ ANL1-0560	Sunday Morning	1974	2.50	5.00	10.00
❑ APL1-0700	Singin' in the Kitchen	1974	3.75	7.50	15.00
❑ APL1-0906	Hard Time Hungrys	1975	3.00	6.00	12.00
❑ APL1-1222	Cowboys and Daddys	1975	3.00	6.00	12.00
❑ APL1-1786	The Winner and Other Losers	1976	3.00	6.00	12.00
❑ APL1-2179	Me and McDill	1977	3.00	6.00	12.00
❑ LPM-2776 [M]	"Detroit City" and Other Hits	1963	5.00	10.00	20.00
❑ LSP-2776 [S]	"Detroit City" and Other Hits	1963	6.25	12.50	25.00
❑ LPM-2835 [M]	500 Miles Away from Home	1964	5.00	10.00	20.00
❑ LSP-2835 [S]	500 Miles Away from Home	1964	6.25	12.50	25.00
❑ LPM-2955 [M]	The Travelin' Bare	1964	5.00	10.00	20.00
❑ LSP-2955 [S]	The Travelin' Bare	1964	6.25	12.50	25.00
❑ LPM-3395 [M]	Constant Sorrow	1965	5.00	10.00	20.00
❑ LSP-3395 [S]	Constant Sorrow	1965	6.25	12.50	25.00
❑ LPM-3479 [M]	The Best of Bobby Bare	1965	5.00	10.00	20.00
❑ LSP-3479 [S]	The Best of Bobby Bare	1965	6.25	12.50	25.00
❑ LPM-3515 [M]	Talk Me Some Sense	1966	5.00	10.00	20.00
❑ LSP-3515 [S]	Talk Me Some Sense	1966	6.25	12.50	25.00
❑ LPM-3618 [M]	The Streets of Baltimore	1966	5.00	10.00	20.00
❑ LSP-3618 [S]	The Streets of Baltimore	1966	6.25	12.50	25.00
❑ LPM-3688 [M]	This I Believe	1966	5.00	10.00	20.00
❑ LSP-3688 [S]	This I Believe	1966	6.25	12.50	25.00
❑ LPM-3831 [M]	A Bird Named Yesterday	1967	6.25	12.50	25.00
❑ LSP-3831 [S]	A Bird Named Yesterday	1967	5.00	10.00	20.00
❑ LPM-3896 [M]	The English Country Side	1967	10.00	20.00	40.00
❑ LSP-3896 [S]	The English Country Side	1967	5.00	10.00	20.00
❑ LPM-3994 [M]	The Best of Bobby Bare — Volume 2	1968	10.00	20.00	40.00
❑ LSP-3994 [S]	The Best of Bobby Bare — Volume 2	1968	5.00	10.00	20.00
❑ AYL1-4118	Greatest Hits	1982	2.00	4.00	8.00
❑ LSP-4177	(Margie's At) The Lincoln Park Inn (And Other Controversial Country Songs)	1969	5.00	10.00	20.00
❑ LSP-4422	Real Thing	1970	3.75	7.50	15.00
❑ AHL1-5469	Collector's Series	1985	2.50	5.00	10.00
❑ VPS-6090 [(2)]	This Is Bobby Bare	1972	5.00	10.00	20.00

UNITED ARTISTS

Number	Title (A Side/B Side)	Yr	VG	VG+	NM
❑ UA-LA621-G	Bare Country	1977	3.00	6.00	12.00

BARE, BOBBY, AND SKEETER DAVIS
RCA VICTOR

Number	Title (A Side/B Side)	Yr	VG	VG+	NM
❑ LPM-3336 [M]	Tunes for Two	1965	5.00	10.00	20.00
❑ LSP-3336 [S]	Tunes for Two	1965	6.25	12.50	25.00
❑ LSP-4335	Your Husband, My Wife	1970	3.75	7.50	15.00

BARE, BOBBY, NORMA JEAN, & LIZ ANDERSON
RCA VICTOR

Number	Title (A Side/B Side)	Yr	VG	VG+	NM
❑ LPM-3764 [M]	The Game of Triangles	1967	6.25	12.50	25.00
❑ LSP-3764 [S]	The Game of Triangles	1967	5.00	10.00	20.00

BARGE, GENE
CHECKER

Number	Title (A Side/B Side)	Yr	VG	VG+	NM
❑ LP-2994 [M]	Dance with Daddy G	1965	12.50	25.00	50.00

BARKER, WARREN
WARNER BROS.

Number	Title (A Side/B Side)	Yr	VG	VG+	NM
❑ W 1205 [M]	"The King and I" for Orchestra	1958	5.00	10.00	20.00
❑ WS 1205 [S]	"The King and I" for Orchestra	1958	6.25	12.50	25.00
❑ W 1290 [M]	TV Guide — Top TV Themes	1959	7.50	15.00	30.00
❑ WS 1290 [S]	TV Guide — Top TV Themes	1959	10.00	20.00	40.00
❑ B 1308 [M]	William Holden Presents a Musical Touch of Far Away Places	1959	7.50	15.00	30.00
❑ BS 1308 [S]	William Holden Presents a Musical Touch of Far Away Places	1959	10.00	20.00	40.00

BARNES, EMIL
AMERICAN MUSIC

Number	Title (A Side/B Side)	Yr	VG	VG+	NM
❑ LP-641 [10]	New Orleans Trad Jazz	1952	12.50	25.00	50.00

BARNES, GEORGE
DECCA

Number	Title (A Side/B Side)	Yr	VG	VG+	NM
❑ DL 8658 [M]	Guitars — By George	1957	10.00	20.00	40.00
—Black label, silver print					

GRAND AWARD

Number	Title (A Side/B Side)	Yr	VG	VG+	NM
❑ GA 33-358 [M]	Guitar in Velvet	195?	6.25	12.50	25.00

MERCURY

Number	Title (A Side/B Side)	Yr	VG	VG+	NM
❑ PPS-2011 [M]	Guitar Galaxies	196?	7.50	15.00	30.00
❑ PPS-6011 [S]	Guitar Galaxies	196?	10.00	20.00	40.00
❑ MG-20956 [M]	Guitar Galaxies	1962	6.25	12.50	25.00
❑ SR-60956 [S]	Guitar Galaxies	1962	7.50	15.00	30.00

Number	Title (A Side/B Side)	Yr	VG	VG+	NM

BARNES, J.J.
VOLT
| ❑ VOS-6001 | Rare Stamps | 1969 | 7.50 | 15.00 | 30.00 |

—With Steve Mancha

BARNES, MAE
ATLANTIC
| ❑ ALS-404 [10] | Fun with Mae Barnes | 1953 | 100.00 | 200.00 | 400.00 |
VANGUARD
| ❑ VRS-9036 [M] | Meet Mae Barnes | 1958 | 12.50 | 25.00 | 50.00 |

BARNET, CHARLIE
AVA
| ❑ A-10 [M] | Charlie Barnet !?!?!?!?!?!?! | 1962 | 6.25 | 12.50 | 25.00 |
| ❑ AS-10 [S] | Charlie Barnet !?!?!?!?!?!?! | 1962 | 7.50 | 15.00 | 30.00 |
CAPITOL
❑ H 235 [10]	Big Bands	195?	15.00	30.00	60.00
❑ H 325 [10]	The Modern Idiom	195?	15.00	30.00	60.00
❑ T 624 [M]	Classics in Jazz	1955	12.50	25.00	50.00
❑ ST 1403 [S]	Jazz Oasis	1960	6.25	12.50	25.00
❑ T 1403 [M]	Jazz Oasis	1960	5.00	10.00	20.00
CHOREO
❑ A-10 [M]	Charlie Barnet !?!?!?!?!?!?!	196?	5.00	10.00	20.00
❑ AS-10 [S]	Charlie Barnet !?!?!?!?!?!?!	196?	6.25	12.50	25.00

—Some copies have Choreo logo on front cover, but Ava labels and back cover

CLEF
❑ MGC-114 [10]	Charlie Barnet Plays Charlie Barnet	1953	25.00	50.00	100.00
❑ MGC-139 [10]	Dance with Charlie Barnet	1953	25.00	50.00	100.00
❑ MGC-164 [10]	Charlie Barnet Dance Session, Vol. 1	1954	25.00	50.00	100.00
❑ MGC-165 [10]	Charlie Barnet Dance Session, Vol. 2	1954	25.00	50.00	100.00
❑ MGC-638 [M]	One Night Stand	1955	20.00	40.00	80.00
COLUMBIA
❑ CL 639 [M]	Town Hall Jazz Concert	195?	10.00	20.00	40.00

—Black and red label with six "eye" logos

| ❑ CL 639 [M] | Town Hall Jazz Concert | 1955 | 12.50 | 25.00 | 50.00 |

—Maroon label, gold print

CROWN
❑ CLP-5114 [M]	A Tribute to Harry James	195?	5.00	10.00	20.00
❑ CLP-5127 [M]	Charlie Barnet Presents a Salute to Harry James	195?	5.00	10.00	20.00
❑ CLP-5134 [M]	On Stage with Charlie Barnet	1959	5.00	10.00	20.00
DECCA
❑ DL 8098 [M]	Hop on the Skyliner	195?	12.50	25.00	50.00
EVEREST
❑ SDBR-1008 [S]	Cherokee	1959	5.00	10.00	20.00
❑ LPBR-5008 [M]	Cherokee	1958	6.25	12.50	25.00
❑ LPBR-5059 [M]	More Charlie Barnet	196?	5.00	10.00	20.00
❑ SDBR-5059 [S]	More Charlie Barnet	196?	6.25	12.50	25.00
MERCURY
❑ MGC-114 [M]	Charlie Barnet Plays Charlie Barnet	1952	37.50	75.00	150.00
RCA VICTOR
❑ LPV-551 [M]	Charlie Barnet (Volume 1)	1968	5.00	10.00	20.00
❑ LPV-567 [M]	Charlie Barnet (Volume 2)	1969	5.00	10.00	20.00
❑ LPM-1091 [M]	Redskin Romp	1955	12.50	25.00	50.00
❑ LPM-2081 [M]	The Great Dance Bands	1960	5.00	10.00	20.00
❑ LPT-3062 [10]	Rockin' in Rhythm	195?	20.00	40.00	80.00
SWING
❑ 103 [M]	Charlie Barnet and His Orchestra	195?	10.00	20.00	40.00
VAULT
❑ LP-9004 [M]	Charlie Barnet Big Band 1967	1967	5.00	10.00	20.00
VERVE
❑ MGV-2007 [M]	Dance Bash	1956	12.50	25.00	50.00
❑ V-2007 [M]	Dance Bash	1961	5.00	10.00	20.00
❑ MGV-2027 [M]	Dancing Party	1956	12.50	25.00	50.00
❑ V-2027 [M]	Dancing Party	1961	5.00	10.00	20.00
❑ MGV-2031 [M]	For Dancing Lovers	1956	12.50	25.00	50.00
❑ V-2031 [M]	For Dancing Lovers	1961	5.00	10.00	20.00
❑ MGV-2040 [M]	Lonely Street	1957	12.50	25.00	50.00
❑ V-2040 [M]	Lonely Street	1961	5.00	10.00	20.00

BARNETT, BOBBY
SIMS
| ❑ LP-198 [M] | Bobby Barnett at the World Famous Crystal Palace, Tombstone, Arizona | 1964 | 6.25 | 12.50 | 25.00 |

BARNUM, H.B.
CAPITOL
❑ ST 2278 [S]	Golden Boy	1965	5.00	10.00	20.00
❑ T 2278 [M]	Golden Boy	1965	3.75	7.50	15.00
❑ ST 2289 [S]	Big Hits of Detroit	1965	5.00	10.00	20.00
❑ T 2289 [M]	Big Hits of Detroit	1965	3.75	7.50	15.00
❑ ST 2583 [S]	Pop and Ice Cream Sodas	1966	5.00	10.00	20.00
❑ T 2583 [M]	Pop and Ice Cream Sodas	1966	3.75	7.50	15.00

BAROQUE ENSEMBLE OF THE MERSEYSIDE KAMMERMUSIKGESELLSCHAFT, THE
ELEKTRA
| ❑ EKL-306 [M] | The Baroque Beatles Book | 1966 | 6.25 | 12.50 | 25.00 |
| ❑ EKS-7306 [S] | The Baroque Beatles Book | 1966 | 7.50 | 15.00 | 30.00 |

BAROQUES, THE
CHESS
| ❑ LP-1516 [M] | The Baroques | 1967 | 20.00 | 40.00 | 80.00 |
| ❑ LPS-1516 [S] | The Baroques | 1967 | 25.00 | 50.00 | 100.00 |

BARRACUDAS, THE
JUSTICE
| ❑ JLP-143 | A Plane View | 1968 | 125.00 | 250.00 | 500.00 |

BARRETT, EMMA
NOBILITY
| ❑ 711 [M] | The Bell Gal and Her New Orleans Jazz | 196? | 5.00 | 10.00 | 20.00 |
RIVERSIDE
| ❑ RLP-364 [M] | Sweet Emma | 1960 | 10.00 | 20.00 | 40.00 |
| ❑ RS-9364 [R] | Sweet Emma | 196? | 5.00 | 10.00 | 20.00 |
SOUTHLAND
| ❑ 241 [M] | Sweet Emma Barrett and Her New Orleans Music | 1964 | 5.00 | 10.00 | 20.00 |
| ❑ 242 [M] | Emma Barrett at Disneyland | 1967 | 5.00 | 10.00 | 20.00 |

BARRETT, RONA
MISS RONA
| ❑ MRR 1001 | Miss Rona Sings Hollywood's Greatest Hits | 1974 | 10.00 | 20.00 | 40.00 |

BARRETT, SUSAN
CAPITOL
| ❑ T 1266 [M] | Mixed Emotions | 1959 | 12.50 | 25.00 | 50.00 |
RCA VICTOR
| ❑ LPM-3738 [M] | Susan Barrett | 1967 | 10.00 | 20.00 | 40.00 |
| ❑ LSP-3738 [S] | Susan Barrett | 1967 | 7.50 | 15.00 | 30.00 |

BARRETT, SYD
CAPITOL
| ❑ C1-91206 | Opel | 1989 | 5.00 | 10.00 | 20.00 |
HARVEST
| ❑ SABB-11314 [(2)] | The Madcap Laughs/Barrett | 1974 | 6.25 | 12.50 | 25.00 |

BARRETTO, RAY
FANIA
❑ SLP-346	Acid	196?	5.00	10.00	20.00
❑ SLP-362	Hard Hands	1970	5.00	10.00	20.00
❑ SLP-378	Together	197?	5.00	10.00	20.00
❑ SLP-388	Barretto Head Sounds	197?	5.00	10.00	20.00
❑ SLP-391	Power	197?	5.00	10.00	20.00
❑ SLP-403	The Message	197?	5.00	10.00	20.00
❑ SLP-410	From the Beginning	197?	5.00	10.00	20.00
TICO
❑ LP-1087 [M]	Charanga Moderna	1962	5.00	10.00	20.00
❑ SLP-1087 [S]	Charanga Moderna	1962	6.25	12.50	25.00
❑ LP-1099 [M]	The Hit Latin Style of Ray Barretto	1963	5.00	10.00	20.00
❑ SLP-1099 [S]	The Hit Latin Style of Ray Barretto	1963	6.25	12.50	25.00
❑ LP-1102 [M]	La Moderna De Siempre	1963	5.00	10.00	20.00
❑ SLP-1102 [S]	La Moderna De Siempre	1963	6.25	12.50	25.00
❑ LP-1114 [M]	Guajira y Guaguanco	1964	5.00	10.00	20.00
❑ SLP-1114 [S]	Guajira y Guaguanco	1964	6.25	12.50	25.00

BARRON, BILL
AUDIO FIDELITY
| ❑ AFLP-2123 [M] | Now Hear This! | 1964 | 5.00 | 10.00 | 20.00 |
| ❑ AFSD-6123 [S] | Now Hear This! | 1964 | 6.25 | 12.50 | 25.00 |
DAUNTLESS
| ❑ DM-4312 [M] | West Side Story Bossa Nova | 1963 | 6.25 | 12.50 | 25.00 |
| ❑ DS-6312 [S] | West Side Story Bossa Nova | 1963 | 7.50 | 15.00 | 30.00 |
SAVOY
❑ MG-12160 [M]	The Tenor Stylings of Bill Barron	1961	10.00	20.00	40.00
❑ MG-12163 [M]	Modern Windows	1962	10.00	20.00	40.00
❑ MG-12183 [M]	Hot Line	1965	6.25	12.50	25.00

BARRY, GENE
RCA VICTOR
| ❑ LPM-2975 [M] | The Star of "Burke's Law" Sings of Love and Things | 1964 | 6.25 | 12.50 | 25.00 |
| ❑ LSP-2975 [S] | The Star of "Burke's Law" Sings of Love and Things | 1964 | 7.50 | 15.00 | 30.00 |

BARRY, JOHN
BULLDOG
| ❑ BDL-1036 | Bond by Barry | 198? | 2.50 | 5.00 | 10.00 |
COLUMBIA
❑ C 1003	Ready When You Are, Mr. J.B.	1970	2.50	5.00	10.00
❑ CL 2493 [M]	Great Movie Sounds of John Barry	1966	3.75	7.50	15.00
❑ CL 2708 [M]	You Only Live Twice	1967	3.75	7.50	15.00
❑ CS 9293 [S]	Great Movie Sounds of John Barry	1966	5.00	10.00	20.00
❑ CS 9508 [S]	You Only Live Twice	1967	5.00	10.00	20.00
UNITED ARTISTS
❑ UAL 3424 [M]	Goldfinger and Other Favorites	1965	3.00	6.00	12.00
❑ UAS 6424 [S]	Goldfinger and Other Favorites	1965	3.75	7.50	15.00

BARRY, LEN
BUDDAH
| ❑ BDS-5105 | Ups & Downs | 1972 | 3.75 | 7.50 | 15.00 |
DECCA
| ❑ DL 4720 [M] | 1-2-3 | 1965 | 7.50 | 15.00 | 30.00 |
| ❑ DL 74720 [P] | 1-2-3 | 1965 | 10.00 | 20.00 | 40.00 |

—"Lip Sync" is rechanneled

RCA VICTOR
| ❑ LPM-3823 [M] | My Kind of Soul | 1967 | 6.25 | 12.50 | 25.00 |
| ❑ LSP-3823 [S] | My Kind of Soul | 1967 | 5.00 | 10.00 | 20.00 |

BARRY AND BARRY
See BARRY McGUIRE AND BARRY KANE.

BARRY AND THE TAMERLANES
VALIANT
| ❑ LP-406 [M] | I Wonder What She's Doing Tonight | 1963 | 37.50 | 75.00 | 150.00 |
| ❑ LPS-406 [S] | I Wonder What She's Doing Tonight | 1963 | 75.00 | 150.00 | 300.00 |

BARRYMORE, LIONEL, AS EBENEZER SCROOGE
MGM
| ❑ CH 112 [10] | A Christmas Carol | 1952 | 10.00 | 20.00 | 40.00 |

B

Number	Title (A Side/B Side)	Yr	VG	VG+	NM

BARTHOLOMEW, DAVE
BROADMOOR
| ❏ BR-1201 | Dave Bartholomew's New Orleans Jazz Band | 1981 | 3.75 | 7.50 | 15.00 |
IMPERIAL
❏ LP-9162 [M]	Fats Domino Presents Dave Bartholomew	1961	25.00	50.00	100.00
❏ LP-9217 [M]	New Orleans House Party	1963	25.00	50.00	100.00
❏ LP-12076 [S]	Fats Domino Presents Dave Bartholomew	1961	37.50	75.00	150.00
❏ LP-12217 [S]	New Orleans House Party	1963	37.50	75.00	150.00

BARTLEY, CHARLENE
RCA VICTOR
| ❏ LPM-1478 [M] | Weekend of a Private Secretary | 1957 | 12.50 | 25.00 | 50.00 |

BARTZ, GARY
MILESTONE
❏ 9006	Libra	1968	5.00	10.00	20.00
❏ 9018	Another Earth	1969	5.00	10.00	20.00
❏ 9027	Home!	1970	5.00	10.00	20.00
❏ 9031	Harlem Bush Music — Taifa	1971	5.00	10.00	20.00
❏ 9032	Harlem Bush Music — Uhuru	1972	5.00	10.00	20.00
PRESTIGE
| ❏ 66001 [(2)] | I've Known Rivers | 197? | 5.00 | 10.00 | 20.00 |

BASIE, COUNT
ABC
| ❏ 570 [M] | Basie's Swingin' — Voices Singin' | 1966 | 5.00 | 10.00 | 20.00 |
| ❏ S-570 [S] | Basie's Swingin' — Voices Singin' | 1966 | 6.25 | 12.50 | 25.00 |
AMERICAN RECORDING SOCIETY
❏ G-401 [M]	Count Basie	1956	10.00	20.00	40.00
❏ G-402 [M]	The Band That Swings the Blues	1956	10.00	20.00	40.00
❏ G-422 [M]	Basie's Best	1957	10.00	20.00	40.00
❏ G-435 [M]	Mainstream Jazz Swing	1957	10.00	20.00	40.00
BRIGHT ORANGE
| ❏ XBO-702 | Count Basie Featuring B.B. King | 196? | 5.00 | 10.00 | 20.00 |
BRUNSWICK
| ❏ BL 54012 [M] | Count Basie | 1957 | 10.00 | 20.00 | 40.00 |
CLEF
❏ MCG-120 [10]	Count Basie and His Orchestra Collates	1953	50.00	100.00	200.00
❏ MCG-146 [10]	Count Basie Sextet	1954	50.00	100.00	200.00
❏ MGC-148 [10]	Count Basie Big Band	1954	50.00	100.00	200.00
❏ MGC-626 [M]	Count Basie Dance Session #1	1954	25.00	50.00	100.00
❏ MGC-633 [M]	Basie Jazz	1954	25.00	50.00	100.00
❏ MGC-647 [M]	Count Basie Jazz Session #2	1955	25.00	50.00	100.00
❏ MGC-666 [M]	Basie	1955	25.00	50.00	100.00
❏ MGC-685 [M]	The Count	1956	20.00	40.00	80.00
❏ MGC-706 [M]	The Swinging Count	1956	15.00	30.00	60.00
❏ MGC-722 [M]	The Band of Distinction	1956	15.00	30.00	60.00
❏ MGC-723 [M]	Basie Roars Again	1956	15.00	30.00	60.00
❏ MGC-724 [M]	The King of Swing	1956	15.00	30.00	60.00
❏ MGC-729 [M]	Basie Rides Again!	1956	15.00	30.00	60.00
COLUMBIA
❏ CL 754 [M]	Classics	1955	10.00	20.00	40.00
❏ CL 901 [M]	Blues By Basie	1956	10.00	20.00	40.00
❏ CL 997 [M]	One O'Clock Jump	1956	10.00	20.00	40.00
❏ CL 2560 [10]	Basie Bash	1956	20.00	40.00	80.00
❏ CL 6079 [10]	Dance Parade	1949	25.00	50.00	100.00
COMMAND
| ❏ CQ-40004 [Q] | Broadway Basie's…Way | 1972 | 5.00 | 10.00 | 20.00 |
DECCA
❏ DXB 170 [(2)M]	The Best of Count Basie	196?	6.25	12.50	25.00
❏ DL 5111 [10]	Count Basie at the Piano	1950	25.00	50.00	100.00
❏ DL 8049 [M]	Count Basie and His Orchestra	1954	12.50	25.00	50.00
EMARCY
| ❏ MG-26023 [10] | Jazz Royalty | 1954 | 17.50 | 35.00 | 70.00 |
EPIC
❏ LG 1021 [10]	The Old Count and the New Count — Basie	1954	17.50	35.00	70.00
❏ LN 1117 [10]	Rock the Blues	1955	17.50	35.00	70.00
❏ LN 3107 [M]	Lester Leaps In	1955	12.50	25.00	50.00
—With Lester Young					
❏ LN 3168 [M]	Let's Go to Prez	1955	12.50	25.00	50.00
—With Lester Young					
❏ LN 3169 [M]	Basie's Back in Town	1955	12.50	25.00	50.00
HAPPY TIGER
| ❏ 1007 | Basie on the Beatles | 196? | 6.25 | 12.50 | 25.00 |
IMPULSE!
| ❏ A-15 [M] | Count Basie and the Kansas City Seven | 1962 | 7.50 | 15.00 | 30.00 |
| ❏ AS-15 [S] | Count Basie and the Kansas City Seven | 1962 | 10.00 | 20.00 | 40.00 |
JAZZ PANORAMA
| ❏ 1803 [10] | Count Basie and Lester Young | 1951 | 25.00 | 50.00 | 100.00 |
MERCURY
| ❏ MGC-120 [10] | Count Basie and His Orchestra Collates | 1952 | 55.00 | 110.00 | 220.00 |
| ❏ MG-25105 [10] | Count Basie and His Kansas City Seven | 1952 | 25.00 | 50.00 | 100.00 |
MOBILE FIDELITY
❏ 1-129	Basie Plays Hefti	1985	20.00	40.00	80.00
—Audiophile vinyl					
❏ 1-237	April in Paris	1995	10.00	20.00	40.00
—Audiophile vinyl					
MOSAIC
| ❏ MR12-135 [(12)] | The Complete Roulette Live Recordings of Count Basie and His Orchestra | 199? | 50.00 | 100.00 | 200.00 |
| ❏ M15Q-149 [(15)] | The Complete Roulette Studio Recordings of Count Basie and His Orchestra | 199? | 62.50 | 125.00 | 250.00 |
RCA CAMDEN
❏ CAL-395 [M]	The Count	1958	6.25	12.50	25.00
❏ CAL-497 [M]	Basie's Basement	1959	6.25	12.50	25.00
❏ CAL-514 [M]	Count Basie in Kansas City	1959	6.25	12.50	25.00
RCA VICTOR
| ❏ LPM-1112 [M] | Count Basie | 1955 | 12.50 | 25.00 | 50.00 |

Number	Title (A Side/B Side)	Yr	VG	VG+	NM

REPRISE
❏ R-6070 [M]	This Time by Basie! Hits of the 50's and 60's	1963	5.00	10.00	20.00
❏ R9-6070 [S]	This Time by Basie! Hits of the 50's and 60's	1963	6.25	12.50	25.00
❏ RS-6153 [S]	Pop Goes the Basie	1965	5.00	10.00	20.00
ROULETTE
❏ RB-1 [(2)M]	The Count Basie Story	1960	10.00	20.00	40.00
❏ SRB-1 [(2)S]	The Count Basie Story	1960	12.50	25.00	50.00
❏ R 52003 [M]	Basie	1958	7.50	15.00	30.00
❏ SR 52003 [S]	Basie	1958	7.50	15.00	30.00
—Black vinyl					
❏ SR 52003 [S]	Basie	1958	25.00	50.00	100.00
—Red vinyl					
❏ R 52011 [M]	Basie Plays Hefti	1958	7.50	15.00	30.00
❏ SR 52011 [S]	Basie Plays Hefti	1958	7.50	15.00	30.00
❏ R 52024 [M]	One More Time	1959	7.50	15.00	30.00
❏ SR 52024 [S]	One More Time	1959	7.50	15.00	30.00
❏ R 52028 [M]	Breakfast, Dance & Barbeque	1959	7.50	15.00	30.00
❏ SR 52028 [S]	Breakfast, Dance & Barbeque	1959	7.50	15.00	30.00
❏ R 52032 [M]	Chairman of the Board	1959	7.50	15.00	30.00
❏ SR 52032 [S]	Chairman of the Board	1959	7.50	15.00	30.00
❏ R 52036 [M]	Dance Along with Basie	1959	7.50	15.00	30.00
❏ SR 52036 [S]	Dance Along with Basie	1959	7.50	15.00	30.00
❏ R 52044 [M]	Not Now — I'll Tell You When	1960	6.25	12.50	25.00
❏ SR 52044 [S]	Not Now — I'll Tell You When	1960	7.50	15.00	30.00
❏ R 52051 [M]	String Along with Basie	1960	6.25	12.50	25.00
❏ SR 52051 [S]	String Along with Basie	1960	7.50	15.00	30.00
❏ R 52056 [M]	Benny Carter's Kansas City Suite	1960	6.25	12.50	25.00
❏ SR 52056 [S]	Benny Carter's Kansas City Suite	1960	7.50	15.00	30.00
❏ R 52065 [M]	Basie at Birdland	1961	6.25	12.50	25.00
❏ SR 52065 [S]	Basie at Birdland	1961	7.50	15.00	30.00
❏ SR 52081 [S]	The Best of Basie	1962	5.00	10.00	20.00
❏ R 52086 [M]	The Legend	1962	5.00	10.00	20.00
❏ SR 52086 [S]	The Legend	1962	6.25	12.50	25.00
❏ SR 52089 [S]	The Best of Basie, Volume 2	1962	5.00	10.00	20.00
❏ R 52099 [M]	Count Basie in Sweden	1963	5.00	10.00	20.00
❏ SR 52099 [S]	Count Basie in Sweden	1963	6.25	12.50	25.00
❏ R 52106 [M]	Easin' It	1963	5.00	10.00	20.00
❏ SR 52106 [S]	Easin' It	1963	6.25	12.50	25.00
❏ R 52111/3 [(2)M]	The World of Count Basie	1964	10.00	20.00	40.00
❏ SR 52111/3 [(2)S]	The World of Count Basie	1964	12.50	25.00	50.00
❏ R 52113 [M]	Back with Basie	1964	5.00	10.00	20.00
❏ SR 52113 [S]	Back with Basie	1964	6.25	12.50	25.00
UNITED ARTISTS
| ❏ UAL-3480 [M] | Basie Meets Bond | 1966 | 6.25 | 12.50 | 25.00 |
| ❏ UAS-6480 [S] | Basie Meets Bond | 1966 | 7.50 | 15.00 | 30.00 |
VERVE
❏ VSPS-12 [S]	Inside Basie, Outside	1966	5.00	10.00	20.00
❏ MGVS-6024 [S]	Count Basie at Newport	1960	12.50	25.00	50.00
❏ MGV-8012 [M]	April in Paris	1957	12.50	25.00	50.00
❏ V-8012 [M]	April in Paris	1961	5.00	10.00	20.00
❏ MGV-8018 [M]	Basie Roars Again	1957	12.50	25.00	50.00
—Reissue of Clef 723					
❏ V-8018 [M]	Basie Roars Again	1961	5.00	10.00	20.00
❏ MGV-8070 [M]	The Count	1957	12.50	25.00	50.00
—Reissue of Clef 120					
❏ V-8070 [M]	The Count	1961	5.00	10.00	20.00
❏ MGV-8090 [M]	The Swinging Count!	1957	12.50	25.00	50.00
—Reissue of Clef 706					
❏ V-8090 [M]	The Swinging Count!	1961	5.00	10.00	20.00
❏ MGV-8103 [M]	The Band of Distinction	1957	12.50	25.00	50.00
—Reissue of Clef 722					
❏ V-8103 [M]	The Band of Distinction	1961	5.00	10.00	20.00
❏ MGV-8104 [M]	The King of Swing	1957	12.50	25.00	50.00
—Reissue of Clef 724					
❏ V-8104 [M]	The King of Swing	1961	5.00	10.00	20.00
❏ MGV-8108 [M]	Basie Rides Again!	1957	12.50	25.00	50.00
—Reissue of Clef 729					
❏ V-8108 [M]	Basie Rides Again!	1961	5.00	10.00	20.00
❏ MGV-8199 [M]	Basie in London	1957	12.50	25.00	50.00
❏ V-8199 [M]	Basie in London	1961	5.00	10.00	20.00
❏ MGV-8243 [M]	Count Basie at Newport	1958	12.50	25.00	50.00
❏ V-8243 [M]	Count Basie at Newport	1961	5.00	10.00	20.00
❏ V6-8243 [S]	Count Basie at Newport	1961	5.00	10.00	20.00
❏ MGV-8291 [M]	Hall of Fame	1958	12.50	25.00	50.00
❏ V-8291 [M]	Hall of Fame	1961	5.00	10.00	20.00
❏ V6-8407 [S]	The Essential Count Basie	1961	5.00	10.00	20.00
❏ V6-8511 [S]	On My Way and Shoutin' Again!	1963	5.00	10.00	20.00
❏ V6-8549 [S]	Li'l Ol' Groovemaker…Basie!	1963	5.00	10.00	20.00
❏ V6-8563 [S]	More Hits of the 50's and 60's	1963	5.00	10.00	20.00
❏ V6-8596 [S]	Verve's Choice — Best of Count Basie	1964	5.00	10.00	20.00
❏ V6-8597 [S]	Basie Land	1964	5.00	10.00	20.00
❏ V6-8616 [S]	Basie Picks the Winners	1965	5.00	10.00	20.00
❏ V-8659 [M]	Basie's Beatle Bag	1966	7.50	15.00	30.00
❏ V6-8659 [S]	Basie's Beatle Bag	1966	10.00	20.00	40.00
❏ V-8687 [M]	Basie's Beat	1967	5.00	10.00	20.00

BASIE, COUNT, AND SAMMY DAVIS, JR.
VERVE
| ❏ V6-8605 [S] | Our Shining Hour | 1965 | 5.00 | 10.00 | 20.00 |

BASIE, COUNT, AND BILLY ECKSTINE
ROULETTE
| ❏ R 52029 [M] | Basie/Eckstine, Incorporated | 1959 | 6.25 | 12.50 | 25.00 |
| ❏ SR 52029 [S] | Basie/Eckstine, Incorporated | 1959 | 7.50 | 15.00 | 30.00 |

BASIE, COUNT, AND MAYNARD FERGUSON
ROULETTE
| ❏ R 52117 [M] | Big Band Scene '65 | 1965 | 5.00 | 10.00 | 20.00 |
| ❏ SR 52117 [S] | Big Band Scene '65 | 1965 | 6.25 | 12.50 | 25.00 |

Number	Title (A Side/B Side)	Yr	VG	VG+	NM

BASIE, COUNT, AND DIZZY GILLESPIE
VERVE

Number	Title (A Side/B Side)	Yr	VG	VG+	NM
❑ V-8560 [M]	The Count Basie Band and the Dizzy Gillespie Band at Newport	1963	5.00	10.00	20.00
❑ V6-8560 [S]	The Count Basie Band and the Dizzy Gillespie Band at Newport	1963	6.25	12.50	25.00

BASIE, COUNT, AND JOE WILLIAMS
CLEF

❑ MGC-678 [M]	Count Basie Swings/Joe Williams Sings	1955	12.50	25.00	50.00

ROULETTE

❑ R 52021 [M]	Memories Ad Lib	1959	7.50	15.00	30.00
❑ SR 52021 [S]	Memories Ad Lib	1959	10.00	20.00	40.00
❑ R 52033 [M]	Everyday I Have the Blues	1959	7.50	15.00	30.00
❑ SR 52033 [S]	Everyday I Have the Blues	1959	10.00	20.00	40.00
❑ R 52054 [M]	Just the Blues	1960	7.50	15.00	30.00
❑ SR 52054 [S]	Just the Blues	1960	10.00	20.00	40.00
❑ R 52093 [M]	Back to Basie and Blues	1963	6.25	12.50	25.00
❑ SR 52093 [S]	Back to Basie and Blues	1963	7.50	15.00	30.00

VANGUARD

❑ VRS-8508 [M]	A Night at Count Basie's	1955	12.50	25.00	50.00

VERVE

❑ MGV-2016 [M]	The Greatest! Count Basie Swings/Joe Williams Sings Standards	1956	12.50	25.00	50.00
❑ MGVS-6006 [S]	The Greatest! Count Basie Swings/Joe Williams Sings Standards	1960	10.00	20.00	40.00
❑ MGV-8063 [M]	Count Basie Swings/Joe Williams Sings	1957	10.00	20.00	40.00
—Reissue of Clef 678					
❑ V-8488 [M]	Count Basie Swings/Joe Williams Sings	1962	6.25	12.50	25.00
—Reissue of 8063					

BASIE, COUNT; JOE WILLIAMS; LAMBERT, HENDRICKS AND ROSS
ROULETTE

❑ R 52018 [M]	Sing Along with Basie	1959	5.00	10.00	20.00
❑ SR 52018 [S]	Sing Along with Basie	1959	6.25	12.50	25.00

BASIN STREET SIX, THE
CIRCLE

❑ L-403 [10]	Dixieland from New Orleans	1951	12.50	25.00	50.00

EMARCY

❑ MG-26012 [10]	The Basin Street Six	1954	12.50	25.00	50.00

MERCURY

❑ MG-20151 [M]	Strictly Dixie	195?	10.00	20.00	40.00
❑ MG-25111 [10]	The Basin Street Six	1951	12.50	25.00	50.00

BASKERVILLE HOUNDS, THE
DOT

❑ DLP-3823 [M]	The Baskerville Hounds (Featuring Space Rock, Part 2)	1967	12.50	25.00	50.00
❑ DLP-25823 [S]	The Baskerville Hounds (Featuring Space Rock, Part 2)	1967	20.00	40.00	80.00

BASS, FONTELLA
CHECKER

❑ LP-2997 [M]	The "New" Look	1966	15.00	30.00	60.00
—Blue label with red and black checkers					
❑ LP-2997 [M]	The "New" Look	1967	7.50	15.00	30.00
—Blue and white label					
❑ LPS-2997 [S]	The "New" Look	1966	20.00	40.00	80.00
—Blue label with red and black checkers					
❑ LPS-2997 [S]	The "New" Look	1967	10.00	20.00	40.00
—Blue and white label					

PAULA

❑ LPS-2203	Free	1971	3.00	6.00	12.00

BASSEY, SHIRLEY
EPIC

❑ LN 3834 [M]	The Bewitching Shirley Bassey	1962	5.00	10.00	20.00

LIBERTY

❑ LWB-111 [(2)]	Live at Carnegie Hall	198?	2.50	5.00	10.00
❑ LWB-715 [(2)]	Greatest Hits	198?	2.50	5.00	10.00
❑ LW-847	Yesterdays	198?	2.00	4.00	8.00
❑ LM-1013	Something Else	198?	2.00	4.00	8.00
❑ LN-10012	The Magic Is You	1980	2.00	4.00	8.00
❑ LN-10104	The Best of Shirley Bassey	1980	2.00	4.00	8.00
❑ LN-10180	I, Capricorn	198?	2.00	4.00	8.00
❑ LN-10252	Greatest Hits	198?	2.00	4.00	8.00
❑ LN-10262	Shirley Means Bassey	198?	2.00	4.00	8.00

MERCURY

❑ 838033-1	La Mujer	1989	3.00	6.00	12.00

MGM

❑ E-3862 [M]	The Fabulous Shirley Bassey	1960	5.00	10.00	20.00
❑ SE-3862 [S]	The Fabulous Shirley Bassey	1960	6.25	12.50	25.00
❑ E-4301 [M]	Golden Sound	1965	3.00	6.00	12.00
❑ SE-4301 [S]	Golden Sound	1965	3.75	7.50	15.00

PAIR

❑ PDL2-1057 [(2)]	Sassy Bassey	1986	3.00	6.00	12.00

PHILIPS

❑ PHM 200168 [M]	Spectacular Shirley Bassey	1965	3.00	6.00	12.00
❑ PHS 600168 [S]	Spectacular Shirley Bassey	1965	3.75	7.50	15.00

UNITED ARTISTS

❑ UA-LA055-F	Never, Never, Never	1973	2.50	5.00	10.00
❑ UA-LA111-H2 [(2)]	Live at Carnegie Hall	1973	3.75	7.50	15.00
❑ UA-LA214-G	Nobody Does It Like Me	1974	2.50	5.00	10.00
❑ UA-LA542-G	Good, Bad But Beautiful	1975	2.50	5.00	10.00
❑ UA-LA605-G	Love, Life and Feelings	1976	2.50	5.00	10.00
❑ UA-LA715-H2 [(2)]	Greatest Hits	1976	3.75	7.50	15.00
❑ UA-LA751-H	You Take My Heart Away	1977	2.50	5.00	10.00
❑ UA-LA847-H	Yesterdays	1977	2.50	5.00	10.00
❑ LM-1013	Something Else	1979	2.50	5.00	10.00

Number	Title (A Side/B Side)	Yr	VG	VG+	NM
❑ UAL 3169 [M]	Shirley Bassey	1962	3.75	7.50	15.00
❑ UAL 3237 [M]	Shirley Bassey Sings the Hits from "Oliver"	1962	3.75	7.50	15.00
❑ UAL 3419 [M]	Shirley Bassey Belts the Best	1965	3.00	6.00	12.00
❑ UAL 3463 [M]	In Person	1965	3.00	6.00	12.00
❑ UAL 3545 [M]	Shirley Means Bassey	1966	3.00	6.00	12.00
❑ UAL 3565 [M]	And We Were Lovers	1967	3.00	6.00	12.00
❑ UAS 5565	I, Capricorn	1971	2.50	5.00	10.00
❑ UAS 5643	And I Love You So	1972	2.50	5.00	10.00
❑ UAS 6169 [S]	Shirley Bassey	1962	5.00	10.00	20.00
❑ UAS 6237 [S]	Shirley Bassey Sings the Hits from "Oliver"	1962	5.00	10.00	20.00
❑ UAS 6419 [S]	Shirley Bassey Belts the Best	1965	3.75	7.50	15.00
❑ UAS 6463 [S]	In Person	1965	3.75	7.50	15.00
❑ UAS 6545 [S]	Shirley Means Bassey	1966	3.75	7.50	15.00
❑ UAS 6565 [S]	And We Were Lovers	1967	3.75	7.50	15.00
❑ UAS 6675	This Is My Life	1969	3.00	6.00	12.00
❑ UAS 6713	Does Anybody Miss Me?	1969	3.00	6.00	12.00
❑ UAS 6765	Shirley Bassey Is Really "Something"	1970	2.50	5.00	10.00
❑ UAS 6797	Something Else	1971	2.50	5.00	10.00

BASSO-VALDAMBRINI OCTET, THE
VERVE

❑ MGVS-6152 [S]	The New Sound from Italy	1960	10.00	20.00	40.00
❑ MGV-20009 [M]	Jazz Festival, Milan	1960	10.00	20.00	40.00
❑ V-20009 [M]	Jazz Festival, Milan	1961	5.00	10.00	20.00
❑ MGV-20011 [M]	The New Sound from Italy	1960	10.00	20.00	40.00
❑ V-20011 [M]	The New Sound from Italy	1961	5.00	10.00	20.00
❑ V6-20011 [S]	The New Sound from Italy	1961	5.00	10.00	20.00

BASTARDS, THE
TREEHOUSE

❑ 016	Monticallo	1989	3.00	6.00	12.00

BATTERED ORNAMENTS
HARVEST

❑ SKAO-422	Mantle-Piece	1970	10.00	20.00	40.00

BAUDUC, RAY, AND NAPPY LAMARE
CAPITOL

❑ T 877 [M]	Riverboat Dandies	1957	10.00	20.00	40.00

MERCURY

❑ MG-(# unknown) [M]	On a Swinging Date	1960	7.50	15.00	30.00
❑ SR-60186 [S]	On a Swinging Date	1960	6.25	12.50	25.00

BAUER, BILLY
AD LIB

❑ AAL-5501 [10]	Let's Have a Session	1955	50.00	100.00	200.00

NORGRAN

❑ MGN-1082 [M]	Billy Bauer Plectrist	1956	20.00	40.00	80.00

VERVE

❑ MGV-8172 [M]	Billy Bauer Plectrist	1957	12.50	25.00	50.00
❑ V-8172 [M]	Billy Bauer Plectrist	1961	5.00	10.00	20.00

BAUGH, PHIL
ERA

❑ ES-801	California Guitar	1969	6.25	12.50	25.00

LONGHORN

❑ LP-02 [M]	Country Guitar	1965	12.50	25.00	50.00

TORO

❑ T-502 [M]	Country Guitar II	1965	10.00	20.00	40.00

BAUHAUS
A&M

❑ SP 4918	The Sky's Gone Out	1982	5.00	10.00	20.00
❑ SP-4953	Burning from the Inside	1983	5.00	10.00	20.00

BEGGARS BANQUET

❑ 9804-1-H [(2)]	Swing the Heartache/The BBC Sessions	1989	5.00	10.00	20.00

BAXTER
PARAMOUNT

❑ PAS-6050	Baxter	1973	5.00	10.00	20.00

BAXTER, LES
CAPITOL

❑ H (# unknown) [10]	Music for Peace of Mind	1953	20.00	40.00	80.00
❑ DT 288 [R]	Ritual of the Savage (Le Sacre Du Sauvage)	196?	3.00	6.00	12.00
❑ H 288 [10]	Le Sacre Du Sauvage	1952	20.00	40.00	80.00
❑ T 288 [M]	Le Sacre Du Sauvage	1954	10.00	20.00	40.00
❑ T 390 [M]	Music Out of the Moon/Music for Peace of Mind	1954	10.00	20.00	40.00
❑ H 474 [10]	Thinking of You	1954	12.50	25.00	50.00
❑ T 474 [M]	Thinking of You	1954	10.00	20.00	40.00
❑ LAL 486 [M]	The Passions	1954	10.00	20.00	40.00
❑ T 594 [M]	Kaleidoscope	1955	10.00	20.00	40.00
❑ T 655 [M]	Tamboo!	1955	10.00	20.00	40.00
❑ T 733 [M]	Caribbean Moonlight	1956	10.00	20.00	40.00
❑ T 774 [M]	Skins!	1957	10.00	20.00	40.00
❑ T 780 [M]	'Round the World	1957	10.00	20.00	40.00
❑ T 843 [M]	Midnight on the Cliffs	1957	10.00	20.00	40.00
❑ T 868 [M]	Ports of Pleasure	1957	10.00	20.00	40.00
❑ T 968 [M]	Space Escapade	1958	10.00	20.00	40.00
❑ T 1012 [M]	Selections from "South Pacific"	1958	10.00	20.00	40.00
❑ T 1088 [M]	Love Is a Fabulous Thing	1958	10.00	20.00	40.00
❑ DT 1388 [R]	Baxter's Best	1960	3.75	7.50	15.00
❑ SM-1388	Baxter's Best	197?	2.00	4.00	8.00
❑ T 1388 [M]	Baxter's Best	1960	7.50	15.00	30.00
❑ ST 1537 [S]	Jewels of the Sea	1961	7.50	15.00	30.00
❑ T 1537 [M]	Jewels of the Sea	1961	6.25	12.50	25.00
❑ ST 1661 [S]	The Sensational Les Baxter	1962	7.50	15.00	30.00
❑ T 1661 [M]	The Sensational Les Baxter	1962	6.25	12.50	25.00
❑ ST 1846 [S]	The Original Quiet Village	1963	6.25	12.50	25.00
❑ T 1846 [M]	The Original Quiet Village	1963	5.00	10.00	20.00
❑ H 2000 [10]	Music Out of the Moon	1953	20.00	40.00	80.00
❑ T 10015 [M]	La Femme	1956	10.00	20.00	40.00

Number	Title (A Side/B Side)	Yr	VG	VG+	NM
❑ M-11702	Ritual of the Savage	1977	2.50	5.00	10.00
❑ SQBO-90984 [(2)]	The Sounds of Adventure	1967	7.50	15.00	30.00
—Capitol Record Club exclusive					
GNP CRESCENDO					
❑ GNP-2036 [M]	Brazil Now	1967	3.75	7.50	15.00
❑ GNPS-2036 [S]	Brazil Now	1967	3.00	6.00	12.00
❑ GNPS-2042	Love Is Blue	1968	3.00	6.00	12.00
❑ GNPS-2047	Aftrican Blue	1969	3.00	6.00	12.00
❑ GNPS-2053	Moon Rock	1969	3.00	6.00	12.00
PICKWICK					
❑ PC-3011 [M]	The Fabulous Sounds of Les Baxter	196?	3.75	7.50	15.00
❑ SPC-3011 [S]	The Fabulous Sounds of Les Baxter	196?	3.75	7.50	15.00
❑ PC-3048 [M]	I Could Have Danced All Night	196?	3.75	7.50	15.00
❑ SPC-3048 [S]	I Could Have Danced All Night	196?	3.00	6.00	12.00
REPRISE					
❑ R-6036 [M]	Voices in Rhythm	1961	3.75	7.50	15.00
❑ R9-6036 [S]	Voices in Rhythm	1961	5.00	10.00	20.00
❑ R-6048 [M]	The Primitive and the Passionate	1962	3.75	7.50	15.00
❑ R9-6049 [S]	The Primitive and the Passionate	1962	5.00	10.00	20.00
❑ R-6079 [M]	Academy Award Winners '63	1963	3.75	7.50	15.00
❑ R9-6079 [S]	Academy Award Winners '63	1963	5.00	10.00	20.00
❑ R-6100 [M]	The Soul of the Drums	1963	3.75	7.50	15.00
❑ R9-6100 [S]	The Soul of the Drums	1963	5.00	10.00	20.00

BAY CITY JAZZ BAND, THE

Number	Title (A Side/B Side)	Yr	VG	VG+	NM
GOOD TIME JAZZ					
❑ L-12017 [M]	The Bay City Jazz Band	1955	7.50	15.00	30.00
❑ L-12053 [M]	Golden Days	1957	7.50	15.00	30.00

BAYETE

Number	Title (A Side/B Side)	Yr	VG	VG+	NM
PRESTIGE					
❑ 10045	Worlds Around the Sun	1972	7.50	15.00	30.00
❑ 10062	Seeking Other Beauty	1973	7.50	15.00	30.00

BAYSIDERS, THE

Number	Title (A Side/B Side)	Yr	VG	VG+	NM
EVEREST					
❑ BRST-1124 [S]	Over the Rainbow	1961	75.00	150.00	300.00
❑ LPBR-5124 [M]	Over the Rainbow	1961	50.00	100.00	200.00

BBC SYMPHONY ORCHESTRA (ANTAL DORATI, CONDUCTOR)

Number	Title (A Side/B Side)	Yr	VG	VG+	NM
MERCURY LIVING PRESENCE					
❑ SR 90416 [S]	Bartok: The Miraculous Mandarin	196?	6.25	12.50	25.00
—Maroon label, with "Vendor: Mercury Record Corporation"					
❑ SR 90416 [S]	Bartok: The Miraculous Mandarin	196?	12.50	25.00	50.00
—Maroon label, no "Vendor: Mercury Record Corporation"					

BE-BOP DELUXE

Number	Title (A Side/B Side)	Yr	VG	VG+	NM
CAPITOL					
❑ SPRO-8486 [DJ]	Sunburst Finish	1975	6.25	12.50	25.00
—Specially banded version for radio					
❑ SN-16022	Sunburst Finish	1980	2.00	4.00	8.00
—Reissue of Harvest 11478					
❑ SN-16023	Drastic Plastic	1980	2.00	4.00	8.00
—Reissue of Harvest 11750					
❑ SN-16024	Futurama	1980	2.00	4.00	8.00
—Reissue of Harvest 11432					
❑ SN-16025	Axe Victim	1980	2.00	4.00	8.00
—Reissue of Harvest 11689					
❑ SN-16026	Modern Music	1980	2.00	4.00	8.00
—Reissue of Harvest 11575					
HARVEST					
❑ SPRO-8531 [DJ]	Be-Bop's Biggest	1978	7.50	15.00	30.00
—Promo-only compilation					
❑ ST-11432	Futurama	1975	2.50	5.00	10.00
❑ ST-11478	Sunburst Finish	1975	2.50	5.00	10.00
❑ ST-11575	Modern Music	1976	2.50	5.00	10.00
❑ SKBB-11666 [(2)]	Live! In the Air Age	1977	3.00	6.00	12.00
❑ SM-11689	Axe Victim	1977	2.50	5.00	10.00
—Their first UK album; first US issue has "SM" prefix					
❑ SW-11750	Drastic Plastic	1978	2.50	5.00	10.00
❑ SKBO-11870 [(2)]	The Best Of & The Rest Of Be-Bop Deluxe	1979	3.00	6.00	12.00

BEACH BOYS, THE

Also see GLEN CAMPBELL; BRUCE JOHNSTON; MIKE LOVE; BRIAN WILSON; CARL WILSON; DENNIS WILSON.

Number	Title (A Side/B Side)	Yr	VG	VG+	NM
ASYLUM					
❑ R 113793	Surf's Up	1972	37.50	75.00	150.00
—RCA Record Club edition, pressed with wrong labels					
BROTHER					
❑ ST 9001 [R]	Smiley Smile	1967	3.75	7.50	15.00
—"Title for this album by Barry Turnbull" on back cover					
❑ ST 9001 [R]	Smiley Smile	1967	5.00	10.00	20.00
—No mention of Barry Turnbull on cover					
❑ T 9001 [M]	Smiley Smile	1967	7.50	15.00	30.00
—"Title for this album by Barry Turnbull" on back cover					
❑ T 9001 [M]	Smiley Smile	1967	10.00	20.00	40.00
—No mention of Barry Turnbull on cover					
BROTHER/REPRISE					
❑ 2MS 2083 [(2)]	Carl and the Passions "So Tough"/Pet Sounds	1972	7.50	15.00	30.00
❑ 2MS 2083 [(2)DJ]	Carl and the Passions "So Tough"/Pet Sounds	1972	12.50	25.00	50.00
—White label promo					
❑ MS 2118	Holland	1973	3.75	7.50	15.00
—Includes bonus stock-copy EP, "Mount Vernon and Fairway," in picture sleeve, taped to back cover					
❑ MS 2118 [DJ]	Holland	1973	10.00	20.00	40.00
—White label promo; includes bonus white-label promo EP, "Mount Vernon and Fairway," in picture sleeve, taped to back cover					
❑ MS 2118 [DJ]	Holland	1973	125.00	250.00	500.00
—Test pressing with "We Got Love," deleted from promos and stock copies					
❑ 2MS 2166 [(2)]	Wild Honey & 20/20	1974	3.75	7.50	15.00
❑ 2MS 2167 [(2)]	Friends & Smiley Smile	1974	3.75	7.50	15.00
❑ MS 2197 [M]	Pet Sounds	1974	5.00	10.00	20.00
❑ MS 2223	Good Vibrations — Best of the Beach Boys	1975	3.00	6.00	12.00

Number	Title (A Side/B Side)	Yr	VG	VG+	NM
❑ MS 2251	15 Big Ones	1976	3.00	6.00	12.00
❑ MSK 2258	Love You	1977	3.00	6.00	12.00
❑ MSK 2268	M.I.U. Album	1978	3.00	6.00	12.00
❑ MSK 2280	Good Vibrations — Best of the Beach Boys	1978	2.50	5.00	10.00
❑ RS-6382	Sunflower	1970	6.25	12.50	25.00
❑ RS-6382 [DJ]	Sunflower	1970	12.50	25.00	50.00
—White label promo					
❑ RS 6453	Surf's Up	1971	5.00	10.00	20.00
❑ RS 6453 [DJ]	Surf's Up	1971	10.00	20.00	40.00
—White label promo					
❑ 2RS 6484 [(2)]	The Beach Boys In Concert	1973	5.00	10.00	20.00
❑ 2RS 6484 [(2)DJ]	The Beach Boys In Concert	1973	10.00	20.00	40.00
—White label promo					
❑ SKAO-93352	Sunflower	1970	50.00	100.00	200.00
—Capitol Record Club edition					
❑ R 113793	Surf's Up	1972	6.25	12.50	25.00
—RCA Record Club edition					
❑ R 130223	15 Big Ones	1976	3.75	7.50	15.00
—RCA Record Club edition					
❑ R 223569 [(2)]	The Beach Boys In Concert	1973	6.25	12.50	25.00
—RCA Record Club edition					
CAPITOL					
❑ SKAO-133	20/20	1969	3.75	7.50	15.00
—"Starline" label					
❑ SKAO-133	20/20	1969	5.00	10.00	20.00
—Black label with colorband					
❑ SKAO-8-0133	20/20	1969	7.50	15.00	30.00
—Capitol Record Club edition; black label					
❑ SKAO-8-0133	20/20	1970	10.00	20.00	40.00
—Capitol Record Club edition; lime label					
❑ SWBB-253 [(2)]	Close-Up	1969	7.50	15.00	30.00
—Reissue of "Surfin' U.S.A." and "All Summer Long" in one package; black labels with colorband					
❑ SWBB-253 [(2)]	Close-Up	1970	10.00	20.00	40.00
—Lime labels					
❑ ST-442	Good Vibrations	1970	5.00	10.00	20.00
—Lime label (original)					
❑ ST-442	Good Vibrations	1972	6.25	12.50	25.00
—Red or orange label					
❑ ST-8-0442	Good Vibrations	1970	7.50	15.00	30.00
—Capitol Record Club edition					
❑ STBB-500 [(2)]	All Summer Long/California Girls	1970	5.00	10.00	20.00
—Lime labels; "Special Double Play" pack; two separate LPs (abridged versions of "All Summer Long" and "Summer Days [And Summer Nights!!]") bound together					
❑ STBB-500 [(2)]	All Summer Long/California Girls	1971	6.25	12.50	25.00
—Red labels; "Special Double Play" pack; two separate LPs (abridged versions of "All Summer Long" and "Summer Days [And Summer Nights!!]") bound together					
❑ SF-501	All Summer Long	1970	2.50	5.00	10.00
—Individual record from above set					
❑ SF-8-0501	All Summer Long	1971	2.50	5.00	10.00
—Capitol Record Club edition					
❑ SF-502	California Girls	1970	2.50	5.00	10.00
—Individual record from above set					
❑ SF-8-0502	California Girls	1971	2.50	5.00	10.00
—Capitol Record Club edition					
❑ STBB-701 [(2)]	Fun, Fun, Fun/Dance, Dance, Dance	1970	5.00	10.00	20.00
—Lime labels; "Special Double Play" pack; two separate LPs (abridged versions of "Shut Down, Volume 2" and "The Beach Boys Today!") bound together					
❑ STBB-701 [(2)]	Fun, Fun, Fun/Dance, Dance, Dance	1971	6.25	12.50	25.00
—Red labels; "Special Double Play" pack; two separate LPs (abridged versions of "Shut Down, Volume 2" and "The Beach Boys Today!") bound together					
❑ SF-702	Fun, Fun, Fun	1971	2.50	5.00	10.00
—Individual record from above set					
❑ SF-8-0702	Fun, Fun, Fun	1971	2.50	5.00	10.00
—Capitol Record Club edition					
❑ SF-703	Dance, Dance, Dance	1971	2.50	5.00	10.00
—Individual record from above set					
❑ SF-8-0703	Dance, Dance, Dance	1971	2.50	5.00	10.00
—Capitol Record Club edition					
❑ DT 1808 [R]	Surfin' Safari	1962	6.25	12.50	25.00
—With only the "Duophonic" banner at top					
❑ DT 1808 [R]	Surfin' Safari	1962	20.00	40.00	80.00
—With "Capitol Full Dimensional Stereo" banner under the "Duophonic" banner					
❑ SM-1808 [R]	Surfin' Safari	197?	2.50	5.00	10.00
❑ T 1808 [M]	Surfin' Safari	1962	10.00	20.00	40.00
❑ SM-1890 [S]	Surfin' U.S.A.	197?	2.50	5.00	10.00
❑ ST 1890 [S]	Surfin' U.S.A.	1963	12.50	25.00	50.00
❑ T 1890 [M]	Surfin' U.S.A.	1963	10.00	20.00	40.00
❑ SM-1981 [S]	Surfer Girl	197?	2.50	5.00	10.00
❑ ST 1981 [S]	Surfer Girl	1963	12.50	25.00	50.00
—With reference to "their other new single record, 'Little Deuce Coupe'" in liner notes					
❑ ST 1981 [S]	Surfer Girl	1963	12.50	25.00	50.00
—With reference to The Four Freshmen in liner notes					
❑ T 1981 [M]	Surfer Girl	1963	10.00	20.00	40.00
—With reference to "their other new single record, 'Little Deuce Coupe'" in liner notes					
❑ T 1981 [M]	Surfer Girl	1963	10.00	20.00	40.00
—With reference to The Four Freshmen in liner notes					
❑ SM-1998 [S]	Little Deuce Coupe	197?	2.50	5.00	10.00
❑ ST 1998 [S]	Little Deuce Coupe	1963	10.00	20.00	40.00
❑ T 1998 [M]	Little Deuce Coupe	1963	10.00	20.00	40.00
❑ ST 2027 [P]	Shut Down, Volume 2	1964	10.00	20.00	40.00
❑ T 2027 [M]	Shut Down, Volume 2	1964	10.00	20.00	40.00
❑ ST 2110 [S]	All Summer Long	1964	7.50	15.00	30.00
—With "Don't Back Down" correctly listed on front cover					
❑ ST 2110 [S]	All Summer Long	1964	12.50	25.00	50.00
—With "Don't Break Down" erroneously listed on front cover					
❑ T 2110 [M]	All Summer Long	1964	7.50	15.00	30.00
—With "Don't Back Down" correctly listed on front cover					
❑ T 2110 [M]	All Summer Long	1964	12.50	25.00	50.00
—With "Don't Break Down" erroneously listed on front cover					
❑ SM-2164	The Beach Boys' Christmas Album	197?	2.50	5.00	10.00
❑ ST 2164 [S]	The Beach Boys' Christmas Album	1964	12.50	25.00	50.00
❑ T 2164 [M]	The Beach Boys' Christmas Album	1964	12.50	25.00	50.00
❑ SM-2198	Beach Boys Concert	197?	2.50	5.00	10.00

B

Number	Title (A Side/B Side)	Yr	VG	VG+	NM
❑ STAO 2198 [S]	Beach Boys Concert	1964	7.50	15.00	30.00
—With bound-in booklet					
❑ STAO-8-2198 [S]	Beach Boys Concert	196?	20.00	40.00	80.00
—Capitol Record Club edition					
❑ TAO 2198 [M]	Beach Boys Concert	1964	7.50	15.00	30.00
—With bound-in booklet					
❑ DT 2269 [R]	The Beach Boys Today!	1965	6.25	12.50	25.00
❑ DT-8-2269 [R]	The Beach Boys Today!	1965	20.00	40.00	80.00
—Capitol Record Club edition					
❑ T 2269 [M]	The Beach Boys Today!	1965	7.50	15.00	30.00
❑ DT 2354 [R]	Summer Days (And Summer Nights!!)	1965	6.25	12.50	25.00
—With "Duophonic" banner					
❑ DT 2354 [R]	Summer Days (And Summer Nights!!)	1965	12.50	25.00	50.00
—With "New Improved Full Dimensional Stereo" banner					
❑ T 2354 [M]	Summer Days (And Summer Nights!!)	1965	7.50	15.00	30.00
❑ DMAS 2398 [R]	Beach Boys Party!	1965	6.25	12.50	25.00
—Without sheet of photos					
❑ DMAS 2398 [R]	Beach Boys Party!	1965	7.50	15.00	30.00
—With sheet of photos					
❑ MAS 2398 [M]	Beach Boys Party!	1965	7.50	15.00	30.00
—Without sheet of photos					
❑ MAS 2398 [M]	Beach Boys Party!	1965	10.00	20.00	40.00
—With sheet of photos					
❑ DT 2458 [R]	Pet Sounds	1966	7.50	15.00	30.00
❑ T 2458 [M]	Pet Sounds	1966	10.00	20.00	40.00
❑ DT 2545 [P]	Best of the Beach Boys	1966	3.00	6.00	12.00
—Black "The Star Line" label					
❑ DT 2545 [P]	Best of the Beach Boys	1966	3.75	7.50	15.00
—Black label with colorband					
❑ DT 2545 [P]	Best of the Beach Boys	1967	3.75	7.50	15.00
—Red and white "Starline" label					
❑ DT 2545 [P]	Best of the Beach Boys	1970	3.00	6.00	12.00
—Green "Starline" label					
❑ DT 2545 [P]	Best of the Beach Boys	1973	2.50	5.00	10.00
—Orange label, "Capitol" on bottom					
❑ DT 2545 [P]	Best of the Beach Boys	1978	2.50	5.00	10.00
—Purple label, large Capitol logo					
❑ DT 2545 [P]	Best of the Beach Boys	1983	2.50	5.00	10.00
—Black label, print in colorband					
❑ T 2545 [M]	Best of the Beach Boys	1966	3.75	7.50	15.00
—Black "The Star Line" label					
❑ T 2545 [M]	Best of the Beach Boys	1966	5.00	10.00	20.00
—Black label with colorband					
❑ T 2545 [M]	Best of the Beach Boys	1967	7.50	15.00	30.00
—Red and white "Starline" label					
❑ T/DT 2580	Smile Booklet	1966	75.00	150.00	300.00
—Printed for insertion into unreleased "Smile" LP; counterfeits exist					
❑ T/DT 2580	Smile	1966	250.00	500.00	1000.
—Unreleased; price is for cover slick, which has been counterfeited					
❑ DT 2706 [P]	Best of the Beach Boys, Vol. 2	1967	3.75	7.50	15.00
—Red and while "Starline" label					
❑ DT 2706 [P]	Best of the Beach Boys, Vol. 2	1970	3.00	6.00	12.00
—Green "Starline" label					
❑ DT 2706 [P]	Best of the Beach Boys, Vol. 2	1973	2.50	5.00	10.00
—Orange label, "Capitol" on bottom					
❑ DT 2706 [P]	Best of the Beach Boys, Vol. 2	1978	2.50	5.00	10.00
—Purple label, large Capitol logo					
❑ T 2706 [M]	Best of the Beach Boys, Vol. 2	1967	6.25	12.50	25.00
❑ DTCL 2813 [(3)R]	The Beach Boys Deluxe Set	1967	12.50	25.00	50.00
—Maroon border on box; custom pressings of LPs with "DTCL" prefixes					
❑ DTCL-8-2813 [(3)R]	The Beach Boys Deluxe Set	1967	37.50	75.00	150.00
—Capitol Record Club edition; blue border on box; custom pressings of LPs with "DTCL" prefixes					
❑ TCL 2813 [(3)M]	The Beach Boys Deluxe Set	1967	62.50	125.00	250.00
—Black border on box; albums have "T" prefixes					
❑ ST 2859 [S]	Wild Honey	1967	5.00	10.00	20.00
❑ T 2859 [M]	Wild Honey	1967	10.00	20.00	40.00
❑ ST-8-2891 [R]	Smiley Smile	1968	75.00	150.00	300.00
—Capitol Record Club edition					
❑ DKAO 2893	Stack-o-Tracks	1968	12.50	25.00	50.00
—Without sheet music booklet					
❑ DKAO 2893	Stack-o-Tracks	1968	25.00	50.00	100.00
—With sheet music booklet					
❑ DKAO-8-2893	Stack-o-Tracks	1968	50.00	100.00	200.00
—Capitol Record Club edition					
❑ ST 2895	Friends	1968	6.25	12.50	25.00
❑ DKAO 2945 [P]	The Best of the Beach Boys, Vol. 3	1968	3.75	7.50	15.00
—Black label with colorband					
❑ DKAO 2945 [P]	The Best of the Beach Boys, Vol. 3	1969	5.00	10.00	20.00
—"Starline" label					
❑ PRO 3133 [DJ]	Silver Platter Service from Hollywood: The Beach Boys Christmas Special	1964	50.00	100.00	200.00
❑ SVBB-11307 [(2)]	Endless Summer	1974	5.00	10.00	20.00
—Orange labels, "Capitol" on bottom; with poster					
❑ SVBB-11307 [(2)]	Endless Summer	1978	3.75	7.50	15.00
—Purple labels, large Capitol logo					
❑ SVBB-11307 [(2)]	Endless Summer	1983	3.00	6.00	12.00
—Black labels, print in colorband					
❑ SVBB-11307 [(2)]	Endless Summer	1988	3.00	6.00	12.00
—Purple labels, small Capitol logo					
❑ SVBB-11384 [(2)]	Spirit of America	1975	3.75	7.50	15.00
—Orange labels, "Capitol" on bottom					
❑ SVBB-11384 [(2)]	Spirit of America	1978	3.00	6.00	12.00
—Purple labels, large Capitol logo					
❑ SVBB-11384 [(2)]	Spirit of America	1983	2.50	5.00	10.00
—Black labels, print in colorband					
❑ SVBB-11384 [(2)]	Spirit of America	1988	2.50	5.00	10.00
—Purple labels, small Capitol logo					
❑ ST-11584	Beach Boys '69 (The Beach Boys Live in London)	1976	3.00	6.00	12.00
❑ SN-12011	Beach Boys '69 (The Beach Boys Live in London)	1979	2.50	5.00	10.00
❑ SVBB-12220 [(2)]	Sunshine Dream	1982	3.00	6.00	12.00
❑ ST-12293	Rarities	1983	3.75	7.50	15.00

Number	Title (A Side/B Side)	Yr	VG	VG+	NM
❑ STBK-12396 [(2)]	Made in U.S.A.	1986	3.00	6.00	12.00
❑ N-16012 [M]	Surfin' Safari	1980	2.00	4.00	8.00
❑ SN-16013 [S]	Little Deuce Coupe	1980	2.00	4.00	8.00
❑ SN-16014 [S]	Surfer Girl	1980	2.00	4.00	8.00
❑ SN-16015 [S]	Surfin' U.S.A.	1980	2.00	4.00	8.00
❑ SN-16016 [S]	All Summer Long	1980	2.00	4.00	8.00
❑ DN-16017 [S]	California Girls	1980	2.00	4.00	8.00
❑ SN-16018 [P]	Fun, Fun, Fun	1980	2.00	4.00	8.00
—Reissue of "Shut Down, Vol. 2"					
❑ DN-16019 [R]	Dance, Dance, Dance	1981	2.00	4.00	8.00
❑ SN-16134	Beach Boys '69 (The Beach Boys Live in London)	1981	2.00	4.00	8.00
❑ SN-16156 [M]	Pet Sounds	1981	2.00	4.00	8.00
❑ SN-16157	Friends	1981	2.00	4.00	8.00
❑ SN-16158 [M]	Smiley Smile	1981	2.00	4.00	8.00
❑ SN-16159 [S]	Wild Honey	1981	2.00	4.00	8.00
❑ DN-16272 [R]	Beach Boys Party!	1982	2.00	4.00	8.00
❑ N-16273	Be True to Your School	1983	2.00	4.00	8.00
❑ DN-16318 [R]	Best of the Beach Boys, Vol. 2	1984	2.00	4.00	8.00
❑ C1-21241 [S]	Pet Sounds	1999	3.75	7.50	15.00
—True stereo version on heavyweight vinyl					
❑ C1-29628 [S]	Surfer Girl	1994	3.75	7.50	15.00
❑ C1-29629 [M]	Shut Down, Volume 2	1994	3.75	7.50	15.00
❑ C1-29630 [S]	Little Deuce Coupe	1994	3.75	7.50	15.00
❑ C1-29631 [S]	All Summer Long	1994	3.75	7.50	15.00
❑ C1-29632 [M]	The Beach Boys Today!	1994	3.75	7.50	15.00
❑ C1-29633 [M]	Summer Days (And Summer Nights!!)	1994	3.75	7.50	15.00
❑ C1-29634	Beach Boys '69 (The Beach Boys Live in London)	1994	3.75	7.50	15.00
❑ C1-29635 [M]	Smiley Smile	1994	3.75	7.50	15.00
❑ C1-29636 [S]	Wild Honey	1994	3.75	7.50	15.00
❑ C1-29637	Friends	1994	3.75	7.50	15.00
❑ C1-29638	20/20	1994	3.75	7.50	15.00
❑ C1-29640 [M]	Beach Boys Party!	1994	3.75	7.50	15.00
❑ C1-29641	Stack-o-Tracks	1994	3.75	7.50	15.00
❑ C1-29661 [M]	Surfin' Safari	1994	3.75	7.50	15.00
❑ C1-48421 [M]	Pet Sounds	1994	3.75	7.50	15.00
❑ C1-48422 [S]	Surfin' U.S.A.	1994	3.75	7.50	15.00
❑ C1-90427	Beach Boys Concert	1994	3.75	7.50	15.00
❑ C1-91318 [R]	Best of the Beach Boys	1988	3.00	6.00	12.00
—Purple label, small Capitol logo					
❑ C1-92639	Still Cruisin'	1989	3.00	6.00	12.00
❑ R 123946	Best of the Beach Boys	197?	3.75	7.50	15.00
—RCA Music Service edition					
❑ R 133854	The Beach Boys' Christmas Album	197?	3.75	7.50	15.00
—RCA Music Service edition					
❑ R 223559 [(2)]	Endless Summer	197?	6.25	12.50	25.00
—RCA Music Service edition					
❑ R 233593 [(2)]	American Summer	1975	6.25	12.50	25.00
—RCA Music Service exclusive					
❑ SF-500501	All Summer Long	1971	2.50	5.00	10.00
—Columbia Record Club edition					
❑ SF-500502	California Girls	1971	2.50	5.00	10.00
—Columbia Record Club edition					
❑ DT-502545 [P]	Best of the Beach Boys	197?	3.75	7.50	15.00
—Columbia Record Club edition					
❑ DT-502706 [P]	Best of the Beach Boys, Vol. 2	197?	3.75	7.50	15.00
—Columbia Record Club edition					
❑ SVBB-511307 [(2)]	Endless Summer	197?	6.25	12.50	25.00
—Columbia Record Club edition					
❑ SVBB-511384 [(2)]	Spirit of America	1975	5.00	10.00	20.00
—Columbia Record Club edition					
CAPITOL SPECIAL MARKETS					
❑ SLB-6994 [(2)]	Golden Years of the Beach Boys	1975	5.00	10.00	20.00
❑ SL-8114	Beach Boys Super Hits	1978	2.50	5.00	10.00
❑ SLB-8134 [(2)]	The Beach Boys	1980	5.00	10.00	20.00
❑ SL-9431	Good Vibrations from the Beach Boys	1986	3.75	7.50	15.00
—Special issue for Sunkist					
CARIBOU					
❑ JZ 35752	L.A. (Light Album)	1979	2.50	5.00	10.00
❑ JZ 35752 [DJ]	L.A. (Light Album)	1979	3.75	7.50	15.00
—White label promo					
❑ PZ 35752	L.A. (Light Album)	1980	2.00	4.00	8.00
—Budget-line reissue					
❑ FZ 36283	Keepin' the Summer Alive	1980	2.50	5.00	10.00
❑ FZ 36283 [DJ]	Keepin' the Summer Alive	1980	3.75	7.50	15.00
—White label promo					
❑ Z2X 37445 [(2)]	Ten Years of Harmony (1970-1980)	1981	3.00	6.00	12.00
❑ BFZ 39946	The Beach Boys	1985	2.50	5.00	10.00
❑ PZ 39946	The Beach Boys	1988	2.00	4.00	8.00
—Budget-line reissue					
DCC COMPACT CLASSICS					
❑ LPZ-2006 [M]	Pet Sounds	1995	30.00	60.00	120.00
—Audiophile vinyl					
ERA					
❑ HTE-805 [M]	The Beach Boys' Biggest Beach Hits	1969	3.75	7.50	15.00
—Also contains non-Beach Boys filler					
EVEREST					
❑ 4108 [M]	Rare Early Recordings	1981	2.00	4.00	8.00
GATEWAY					
❑ GSLP-10104 [M]	Surfing with the Beach Boys, the Marketts and the Frogmen	1979	2.00	4.00	8.00
MOBILE FIDELITY					
❑ 1-116	Surfer Girl	1984	7.50	15.00	30.00
—Audiophile vinyl					
ORBIT					
❑ OR 688 [M]	The Beach Boys' Greatest Hits 1961-1963	1972	3.00	6.00	12.00
—Also contains non-Beach Boys filler					
PAIR					
❑ PDL2-1068 [(2)]	For All Seasons	1986	3.75	7.50	15.00

Number	Title (A Side/B Side)	Yr	VG	VG+	NM
❑ PDL2-1084 [(2)]	Golden Harmonies	1986	3.75	7.50	15.00

PICKWICK

Number	Title (A Side/B Side)	Yr	VG	VG+	NM
❑ PTP-2059 [(2)]	High Water	1973	3.00	6.00	12.00
❑ SPC-3221	Summertime Blues	1970	2.50	5.00	10.00
❑ SPC-3269	Good Vibrations	1971	2.50	5.00	10.00
❑ SPC-3309	Wow! Great Concert!	1972	2.50	5.00	10.00
❑ SPC-3351	Surfer Girl	1973	2.50	5.00	10.00
❑ SPC-3562	Little Deuce Coupe	1975	2.50	5.00	10.00

READER'S DIGEST

❑ RBA-178 [(4)]	Their Greatest Hits and Finest Performances	1989	12.50	25.00	50.00

—Box set

SCEPTER

❑ CTN-18004 [M]	The Best of the Beach Boys (1961-1963)	1972	3.00	6.00	12.00

—Also contains non-Beach Boys filler

SEARS

❑ SPS-609	Summertime Blues	1970	12.50	25.00	50.00

SPRINGBOARD

❑ SPB-4021 [M]	The Beach Boys 1961	1977	2.00	4.00	8.00

—Also contains non-Beach Boys filler

SUNDAZED

❑ LP 5005 [B]	Lost & Found!	1991	3.00	6.00	12.00

—Colored vinyl (red, yellow and light blue are known); first LP issue of the 1961 sessions from the master tapes; three tracks are stereo

TIME-LIFE

❑ SRNR-03 [(2)]	The Beach Boys: 1963-1967	1986	3.75	7.50	15.00

—2 LPs in box with fold-open liner notes; second cover has a portrait of the Beach Boys

❑ SRNR-03 [(2)]	The Beach Boys: 1963-1967	1986	6.25	12.50	25.00

—2 LPs in box with fold-open liner notes; original cover portrays the Beach Boys surfing

WAND

❑ WDS-688 [M]	The Beach Boys' Greatest Hits 1961-1963	1972	3.00	6.00	12.00

—Also contains non-Beach Boys filler

BEACON STREET UNION, THE
MGM

❑ E-4517 [M]	The Eyes of the Beacon Street Union	1967	7.50	15.00	30.00
❑ SE-4517 [S]	The Eyes of the Beacon Street Union	1967	6.25	12.50	25.00
❑ E-4568 [M]	The Clown Died in Marvin Gardens	1968	12.50	25.00	50.00

—May be promo only (yellow label)

❑ SE-4568 [S]	The Clown Died in Marvin Gardens	1968	6.25	12.50	25.00

BEAN, BILLY
RIVERSIDE

❑ RLP-380 [M]	The Trio	1961	10.00	20.00	40.00
❑ RS-9380 [S]	The Trio	1961	12.50	25.00	50.00

BEANS
AVALANCHE

❑ 9200	Beans	1971	5.00	10.00	20.00

BEASLEY, JIMMY
CROWN

❑ CLP-5014 [M]	The Fabulous Jimmy Beasley	1957	37.50	75.00	150.00

—Black label

❑ CLP-5247 [M]	Twist with Jimmy Beasley	1962	10.00	20.00	40.00

—Gray label

MODERN

❑ MLP-1214 [M]	The Fabulous Jimmy Beasley	1956	100.00	200.00	400.00

BEASTIE BOYS
CAPITOL

❑ C1-22940 [(4)]	The Sounds of Science	2000	30.00	60.00	120.00

—Boxed set with hardbound booklet; released a year after a similar CD compilation

❑ C1 37716 [(2)]	Hello Nasty	1998	3.75	7.50	15.00
❑ SPRO 79461 [(2)DJ]	Hip Hop Sampler	1994	15.00	30.00	60.00

—Promo-only compilation of remixes and rarities; 1,250 copies were pressed; only the Side 1 number is listed above (the other three sides are numbered SPRO-79463, SPRO-79472 and SPRO-79473)

❑ C1-91743	Paul's Boutique	1989	3.00	6.00	12.00

—Single gatefold edition

❑ C1-92844	Paul's Boutique	1989	5.00	10.00	20.00

—Multi-gatefold edition (number on record is 91743, the same as single gatefold edition)

❑ C1-98938 [(2)]	Check Your Head	1992	5.00	10.00	20.00

DEF JAM

❑ BFC 40238	Licensed to Ill	1986	3.75	7.50	15.00
❑ FC 40238	Licensed to Ill	1986	2.50	5.00	10.00

—Second pressing, with "02" added to bar code on back cover

GRAND ROYAL

❑ GR 003	Some Old Bullshit	1994	2.50	5.00	10.00
❑ GR 006 [(2)]	Ill Communication	1994	3.75	7.50	15.00
❑ GR 013	The In Sound from Way Out!	1996	5.00	10.00	20.00

—Original editions were limited to 5,000 and have a sticker indicating this on the back cover

❑ GR 013	The In Sound from Way Out!	1999	2.50	5.00	10.00

—Second editions were not limited and have no sticker on the back cover

❑ GR 018 [EP]	Root Down	1995	—	3.00	6.00

—Black vinyl

❑ GR 018 [EP]	Root Down	1995	3.00	6.00	12.00

—Blue vinyl

❑ GR 026 [EP]	Aglio E Olio	1995	—	3.00	6.00
❑ GR 061 [(2)]	Hello Nasty	1998	5.00	10.00	20.00

—Limited edition on yellow vinyl

❑ GR 065 [(2)]	Paul's Boutique	1999	3.75	7.50	15.00

—Reissue of original multi-gatefold edition

❑ GR 066 [(2)]	Check Your Head	1998	3.75	7.50	15.00

—Vinyl reissue of Capitol 98938

❑ GR 071 [(2)]	Scientists of Sound	2000	2.00	4.00	8.00

—Remix album

RAT CAGE

❑ 026 [EP]	Cookypuss	1983	10.00	20.00	40.00

BEAT FARMERS
MCA CURB

❑ 5759	Van Go	1986	3.00	6.00	12.00

Number	Title (A Side/B Side)	Yr	VG	VG+	NM
❑ 5993	The Pursuit of Happiness	1987	3.00	6.00	12.00
❑ 6296	Poor and Famous	1989	3.00	6.00	12.00
❑ L33-17381 [EP]	Home of Country Dick	1987	6.25	12.50	25.00

—Promo-only compilation with four non-LP songs

RHINO

❑ RNOR-021 [EP]	Bigger Stones	1985	3.75	7.50	15.00

—Promo-only four-song sampler from RNLP-853

❑ RNLP-853	Tales of the New West	1985	3.00	6.00	12.00

BEAT OF THE EARTH, THE
ARDISH

❑ AS-001	The Beat of the Earth	1968	75.00	150.00	300.00
❑ AS-0001	The Beat of the Earth	1968	100.00	200.00	400.00

BEATLE BUDDIES, THE
DIPLOMAT

❑ D-2313 [M]	The Beatle Buddies	1964	3.75	7.50	15.00
❑ DS-2313 [S]	The Beatle Buddies	1964	5.00	10.00	20.00

BEATLES, THE
Also see PETE BEST; GEORGE HARRISON; JOHN LENNON; PAUL McCARTNEY; RINGO STARR.

APPLE

❑ SBC-100 [M]	The Beatles' Christmas Album	1970	100.00	200.00	400.00

—Fan club issue of the seven Christmas messages; very good counterfeits exist

❑ SWBO-101 [(2)]	The Beatles	1968	37.50	75.00	200.00

—Numbered copy; includes four individual photos and large poster (included in value); because the white cover shows ring wear so readily, this is an EXTREMELY difficult album to find in near-mint condition

❑ SWBO-101 [(2)]	The Beatles	197?	15.00	30.00	60.00

—Un-numbered copy; includes four individual photos and large poster (included in value)

❑ SWBO-101 [(2)]	The Beatles	1975	17.50	35.00	70.00

—With "All Rights Reserved" on labels; title in black on cover; photos and poster of thinner stock than originals

❑ SW-153 [P]	Yellow Submarine	1969	12.50	25.00	50.00

—With Capitol logo on Side 2 bottom. "Only a Northern Song" is rechanneled.

❑ SW-153 [P]	Yellow Submarine	1971	5.00	10.00	20.00

—With "Mfd. by Apple" on label

❑ SW-153 [P]	Yellow Submarine	1975	6.25	12.50	25.00

—With "All Rights Reserved" on label

❑ SO-383	Abbey Road	1969	5.00	10.00	20.00

—With "Mfd. by Apple" on label; "Her Majesty" IS listed on the label

❑ SO-383	Abbey Road	1969	5.00	10.00	20.00

—With "Mfd. by Apple" on label; "Her Majesty" is NOT listed on the label

❑ SO-383	Abbey Road	1969	10.00	20.00	40.00

—With Capitol logo on Side 2 bottom; "Her Majesty" IS listed on both the jacket and the label

❑ SO-383	Abbey Road	1969	18.75	37.50	75.00

—With Capitol logo on Side 2 bottom; "Her Majesty" is NOT listed on either the jacket or the label

❑ SO-383	Abbey Road	1975	6.25	12.50	25.00

—With "All Rights Reserved" on label, either in black print or in light print along label edge (both versions exist)

❑ SO-385 [DJ]	The Beatles Again	1970	4000.	6000.	8000.

—Prototype covers with "The Beatles Again" on cover; not released to the general public. This is NOT a standard issue!

❑ SW-385	Hey Jude	1970	5.00	10.00	20.00

—With "Mfd. by Apple" on label; label calls the LP "Hey Jude"

❑ SW-385	Hey Jude	1970	6.25	12.50	25.00

—Label calls the LP "The Beatles Again"; record is "SW-385"

❑ SW-385	Hey Jude	1970	10.00	20.00	40.00

—Label calls the LP "The Beatles Again"; record is "SO-385" (this could be found in retail stores as late as 1973)

❑ SW-385	Hey Jude	1970	18.75	37.50	75.00

—With Capitol logo on Side 2 bottom; label calls the LP "Hey Jude"

❑ SW-385	Hey Jude	1975	6.25	12.50	25.00

—With "All Rights Reserved" on label; label calls the LP "Hey Jude"

❑ SKBO-3403 [P]	The Beatles 1962-1966	1973	7.50	15.00	30.00

—Custom red Apple labels. "Love Me Do" and "I Want to Hold Your Hand" are rechanneled; "She Loves You," "A Hard Day's Night," "I Feel Fine" and "Ticket to Ride" are mono; "From Me to You," "Can't Buy Me Love" and everything else is stereo.

❑ SKBO-3403 [P]	The Beatles 1962-1966	1975	12.50	25.00	50.00

—Custom red Apple labels with "All Rights Reserved" on labels

❑ SKBO-3404 [B]	The Beatles 1967-1970	1973	7.50	15.00	30.00

—Custom blue Apple labels. "Hello Goodbye" and "Penny Lane" are mono, all others stereo.

❑ SKBO-3404 [B]	The Beatles 1967-1970	1975	12.50	25.00	50.00

—Custom blue Apple labels with "All Rights Reserved" on labels

❑ SPRO 11206/7 [EP]	Anthology 2 Sampler	1996	37.50	75.00	150.00

—Promo-only collection sent to college radio stations

❑ C1-8-31796 [(2)]	Live at the BBC	1994	12.50	25.00	50.00
❑ AR-34001	Let It Be	1970	6.25	12.50	25.00

—Red Apple label; originals have "Bell Sound" stamped in trail-off area, counterfeits do not

❑ C1-8-34445 [(3)]	Anthology 1	1995	10.00	20.00	40.00

—All copies distributed in the U.S. were manufactured in the U.K. with no distinguishing marks (some LPs imported directly from the U.K. have "Made in England" stickers, which can be removed easily)

❑ C1-8-34448 [(3)]	Anthology 2	1996	10.00	20.00	40.00
❑ C1-8-34451 [(3)]	Anthology 3	1996	7.50	15.00	30.00
❑ C1-97036 [B]	The Beatles 1962-1966	1993	6.25	12.50	25.00

—Custom red Apple labels; red vinyl; all copies pressed in U.K; U.S. versions have a bar-code sticker over the international bar code on back cover. "Love Me Do," "Please Please Me," "From Me to You" and "She Loves You" are mono; all others are stereo.

❑ C1-97039	The Beatles 1967-1970	1993	6.25	12.50	25.00

—Custom blue Apple labels; blue vinyl; all copies pressed in U.K.; U.S. versions have a bar-code sticker over the international bar code on back cover

APPLE FILMS

❑ KAL 004 [DJ]	The Yellow Submarine (A United Artists Release)	1969	1000.	1500.	2000.

—One-sided LP with radio spots for movie

APPLE/CAPITOL

❑ (no #) [(10)]	The Beatles Special Limited Edition	1974	300.00	600.00	1200.
❑ (no #) [(17)]	The Beatles 10th Anniversary Box Set	1974	1000.	1500.	2000.
❑ ST 2047 [P]	Meet the Beatles!	1968	10.00	20.00	40.00

—With Capitol logo on Side 2 bottom

❑ ST 2047 [P]	Meet the Beatles!	1971	5.00	10.00	20.00

—With "Mfd. by Apple" on label

Number	Title (A Side/B Side)	Yr	VG	VG+	NM
❑ ST 2047 [P]	Meet the Beatles!	1975	6.25	12.50	25.00

—With "All Rights Reserved" on label

| ❑ ST 2080 [P] | The Beatles' Second Album | 1968 | 10.00 | 20.00 | 40.00 |

—With Capitol logo on Side 2 bottom

| ❑ ST 2080 [P] | The Beatles' Second Album | 1971 | 5.00 | 10.00 | 20.00 |

—With "Mfd. by Apple" on label

| ❑ ST 2080 [P] | The Beatles' Second Album | 1975 | 6.25 | 12.50 | 25.00 |

—With "All Rights Reserved" on label

| ❑ ST 2108 [S] | Something New | 1968 | 10.00 | 20.00 | 40.00 |

—With Capitol logo on Side 2 bottom

| ❑ ST 2108 [S] | Something New | 1971 | 5.00 | 10.00 | 20.00 |

—With "Mfd. by Apple" on label

| ❑ ST 2108 [S] | Something New | 1975 | 6.25 | 2.50 | 25.00 |

—With "All Rights Reserved" on label

| ❑ STBO 2222 [(2)P] | The Beatles' Story | 1968 | 12.50 | 25.00 | 50.00 |

—With Capitol logo on bottom of B-side of both records

| ❑ STBO 2222 [(2)P] | The Beatles' Story | 1971 | 7.50 | 15.00 | 30.00 |

—With "Mfd. by Apple" on labels

| ❑ STBO 2222 [(2)P] | The Beatles' Story | 1975 | 10.00 | 20.00 | 40.00 |

—With "All Rights Reserved" on labels

| ❑ ST 2228 [P] | Beatles '65 | 1968 | 10.00 | 20.00 | 40.00 |

—With Capitol logo on Side 2 bottom

| ❑ ST 2228 [P] | Beatles '65 | 1971 | 5.00 | 10.00 | 20.00 |

—With "Mfd. by Apple" on label

| ❑ ST 2228 [P] | Beatles '65 | 1975 | 6.25 | 12.50 | 25.00 |

—With "All Rights Reserved" on label

| ❑ ST 2309 [P] | The Early Beatles | 1969 | 10.00 | 20.00 | 40.00 |

—With Capitol logo on Side 2 bottom

| ❑ ST 2309 [P] | The Early Beatles | 1971 | 5.00 | 10.00 | 20.00 |

—With "Mfd. by Apple" on label

| ❑ ST 2309 [P] | The Early Beatles | 1975 | 6.25 | 12.50 | 25.00 |

—With "All Rights Reserved" on label

| ❑ ST 2358 [P] | Beatles VI | 1969 | 10.00 | 20.00 | 40.00 |

—With Capitol logo on Side 2 bottom

| ❑ ST 2358 [P] | Beatles VI | 1971 | 5.00 | 10.00 | 20.00 |

—With "Mfd. by Apple" on label

| ❑ ST 2358 [P] | Beatles VI | 1975 | 6.25 | 12.50 | 25.00 |

—With "All Rights Reserved" on label

| ❑ SMAS 2386 [P] | Help! | 1969 | 10.00 | 20.00 | 40.00 |

—With Capitol logo on Side 2 bottom

| ❑ SMAS 2386 [P] | Help! | 1971 | 5.00 | 10.00 | 20.00 |

—With "Mfd. by Apple" on label

| ❑ SMAS 2386 [P] | Help! | 1975 | 6.25 | 12.50 | 25.00 |

—With "All Rights Reserved" on label

| ❑ ST 2442 [S] | Rubber Soul | 1969 | 10.00 | 20.00 | 40.00 |

—With Capitol logo on Side 2 bottom

| ❑ ST 2442 [S] | Rubber Soul | 1971 | 5.00 | 10.00 | 20.00 |

—With "Mfd. by Apple" on label

| ❑ ST 2442 [S] | Rubber Soul | 1975 | 6.25 | 12.50 | 25.00 |

—With "All Rights Reserved" on label

| ❑ ST 2553 [P] | Yesterday and Today | 1969 | 10.00 | 20.00 | 40.00 |

—With Capitol logo on Side 2 bottom

| ❑ ST 2553 [P] | Yesterday and Today | 1971 | 5.00 | 10.00 | 20.00 |

—With "Mfd. by Apple" on label

| ❑ ST 2553 [P] | Yesterday and Today | 1975 | 6.25 | 12.50 | 25.00 |

—With "All Rights Reserved" on label

| ❑ ST 2553 [S] | Yesterday and Today | 1971 | 6.25 | 12.50 | 25.00 |

—With "Mfd. by Apple" on label; all 11 tracks are in true stereo. Check for a triangle in the record's trail-off area.

| ❑ ST 2576 [S] | Revolver | 1969 | 10.00 | 20.00 | 40.00 |

—With Capitol logo on Side 2 bottom

| ❑ ST 2576 [S] | Revolver | 1971 | 5.00 | 10.00 | 20.00 |

—With "Mfd. by Apple" on label

| ❑ ST 2576 [S] | Revolver | 1975 | 6.25 | 12.50 | 25.00 |

—With "All Rights Reserved" on label

| ❑ SMAS 2653 [S] | Sgt. Pepper's Lonely Hearts Club Band | 1969 | 10.00 | 20.00 | 40.00 |

—With Capitol logo on Side 2 bottom

| ❑ SMAS 2653 [S] | Sgt. Pepper's Lonely Hearts Club Band | 1971 | 6.25 | 12.50 | 25.00 |

—With "Mfd. by Apple" on label

| ❑ SMAS 2653 [S] | Sgt. Pepper's Lonely Hearts Club Band | 1975 | 6.25 | 12.50 | 25.00 |

—With "All Rights Reserved" on label

| ❑ SMAL 2835 [P] | Magical Mystery Tour | 1969 | 10.00 | 20.00 | 40.00 |

—With Capitol logo on Side 2 bottom; with 24-page booklet

| ❑ SMAL 2835 [P] | Magical Mystery Tour | 1971 | 5.00 | 10.00 | 20.00 |

—With "Mfd. by Apple" on label; with 24-page booklet

| ❑ SMAL 2835 [P] | Magical Mystery Tour | 1975 | 6.25 | 12.50 | 25.00 |

—With "All Rights Reserved" on label; with 24-page booklet

ATCO

| ❑ 33-169 [M] | Ain't She Sweet | 1964 | 50.00 | 100.00 | 200.00 |
| ❑ 33-169 [M] | Ain't She Sweet | 1964 | 250.00 | 500.00 | 1000. |

—White label promo

| ❑ SD 33-169 [P] | Ain't She Sweet | 1964 | 100.00 | 200.00 | 400.00 |

—Tan and purple label; all four Beatles tracks are rechanneled

| ❑ SD 33-169 [P] | Ain't She Sweet | 1969 | 125.00 | 250.00 | 500.00 |

—Yellow label

AUDIO RARITIES

| ❑ AR-2452 [M] | The Complete Silver Beatles | 1982 | 3.75 | 7.50 | 15.00 |

—Contains 12 Decca audition tracks

AUDIOFIDELITY

| ❑ PD-339 [M] | First Movement | 1982 | 7.50 | 15.00 | 30.00 |

—Contains eight Decca audition tracks; picture disc

| ❑ PHX-339 [M] | First Movement | 1982 | 3.00 | 6.00 | 12.00 |

—Contains eight Decca audition tracks

BACKSTAGE

| ❑ 2-201 [(2)M] | Like Dreamers Do | 1982 | 10.00 | 20.00 | 40.00 |

—Gatefold package, individually numbered (numbers under 100 increase value significantly)

| ❑ 2-201 [(2)M] | Like Dreamers Do | 1982 | 12.50 | 25.00 | 50.00 |

—Non-gatefold package

| ❑ BSR-1111 [DJ] | Like Dreamers Do | 1982 | 12.50 | 25.00 | 50.00 |

—Gray vinyl promo in white sleeve

| ❑ BSR-1111 [DJ] | Like Dreamers Do | 1982 | 12.50 | 25.00 | 50.00 |

—White vinyl promo in white sleeve

Number	Title (A Side/B Side)	Yr	VG	VG+	NM
❑ BSR-1111 [(3)M]	Like Dreamers Do	1982	15.00	30.00	60.00

—Two picture discs (10 of 15 Decca audition tracks on one, interviews on the other) and one white-vinyl record (same contests as musical picture disc)

| ❑ BSR-1111 [(3)M] | Like Dreamers Do | 1982 | 25.00 | 50.00 | 100.00 |

—Same as above, except colored-vinyl LP is gray

| ❑ BSR-1165 [PD] | The Beatles Talk with Jerry G. | 1982 | 6.25 | 12.50 | 25.00 |

—Picture disc

| ❑ BSR-1175 [PD] | The Beatles Talk with Jerry G., Vol. 2 | 1983 | 6.25 | 12.50 | 25.00 |

—Picture disc

CAPITOL

| ❑ (no #) [(18)] | The Beatles Collection Platinum Series | 1984 | 200.00 | 400.00 | 800.00 |
| ❑ BC-13 [(14)] | The Beatles Collection | 1978 | 62.50 | 125.00 | 250.00 |

—American versions have "EMI" and "BC-13" on box spine; imports go for less

| ❑ SWBO-101 [(2)] | The Beatles | 1976 | 7.50 | 15.00 | 30.00 |

—Orange label; with photos and poster

| ❑ SWBO-101 [(2)] | The Beatles | 1978 | 7.50 | 15.00 | 30.00 |

—Purple label, large Capitol logo; with photos and poster (some copies have four photos as one perforated sheet)

| ❑ SWBO-101 [(2)] | The Beatles | 1983 | 10.00 | 20.00 | 40.00 |

—Black label, print in colorband; with photos and poster (some copies have four photos as one perforated sheet)

| ❑ SW-153 [P] | Yellow Submarine | 1976 | 3.00 | 6.00 | 12.00 |

—Orange label

| ❑ SW-153 [P] | Yellow Submarine | 1978 | 2.50 | 5.00 | 10.00 |

—Purple label, large Capitol logo

| ❑ SW-153 [P] | Yellow Submarine | 1983 | 3.75 | 7.50 | 15.00 |

—Black label, print in colorband

| ❑ SJ-383 | Abbey Road | 1984 | 7.50 | 15.00 | 30.00 |

—New prefix; black label, print in colorband

| ❑ SO-383 | Abbey Road | 1976 | 3.00 | 6.00 | 12.00 |

—Orange label

| ❑ SO-383 | Abbey Road | 1978 | 2.50 | 5.00 | 10.00 |

—Purple label, large Capitol logo

| ❑ SO-383 | Abbey Road | 1983 | 3.75 | 7.50 | 15.00 |

—Black label, print in colorband

| ❑ SJ-385 | Hey Jude | 1984 | 7.50 | 15.00 | 30.00 |

—New prefix; black label, print in colorband

| ❑ SW-385 | Hey Jude | 1976 | 3.00 | 6.00 | 12.00 |

—Orange label (all Capitol label versions call the LP "Hey Jude")

| ❑ SW-385 | Hey Jude | 1978 | 2.50 | 5.00 | 10.00 |

—Purple label, large Capitol logo

| ❑ SW-385 | Hey Jude | 1983 | 12.50 | 25.00 | 50.00 |

—Black label, print in colorband

| ❑ ST 2047 [P] | Meet the Beatles! | 1964 | 37.50 | 75.00 | 150.00 |

—Black label with colorband; "Beatles!" on cover in tan to brown print; label has "ASCAP" after every title except "I Want to Hold Your Hand" (BMI); no producer credit on back cover (this is the second edition of this LP)

| ❑ ST 2047 [P] | Meet the Beatles! | 1964 | 100.00 | 200.00 | 400.00 |

—Black label with colorband; "Beatles!" on cover in tan to brown print; "ASCAP" and "BMI" credits are missing on the label; no producer credit on back cover (this is the first edition of the LP)

| ❑ ST 2047 [P] | Meet the Beatles! | 1965 | 18.75 | 37.50 | 75.00 |

—Black label with colorband; "Beatles!" on cover in green print; most of these have "Produced by George Martin" on lower left of back cover; many of these have a label giving "BMI" credit to every song except "Don't Bother Me" and "Till There Was You"

| ❑ ST 2047 [P] | Meet the Beatles! | 1968 | 12.50 | 25.00 | 50.00 |

—Black colorband label; border print adds "A Subsidiary of Capitol Industries Inc."

| ❑ ST 2047 [P] | Meet the Beatles! | 1969 | 10.00 | 20.00 | 40.00 |

—Lime green label

| ❑ ST 2047 [P] | Meet the Beatles! | 1976 | 3.00 | 6.00 | 12.00 |

—Orange label

| ❑ ST 2047 [P] | Meet the Beatles! | 1978 | 2.50 | 5.00 | 10.00 |

—Purple label, large Capitol logo

| ❑ ST 2047 [P] | Meet the Beatles! | 1983 | 3.75 | 7.50 | 15.00 |

—Black label, print in colorband

| ❑ ST 2047 [P] | Meet the Beatles! | 1964 | 30.00 | 60.00 | 120.00 |

—Black label with colorband; "Beatles!" on cover in tan to brown print; some labels have "ASCAP" after every title except "I Want to Hold Your Hand"; other labels have "ASCAP" after every title except "I Want to Hold Your Hand," "I Saw Her Standing There" and "I Wanna Be Your Man"; still other labels have "ASCAP" after every title except "I Want to Hold Your Hand" and "I Wanna Be Your Man"; back cover adds "Produced by George Martin" to lower left

| ❑ ST-8-2047 [P] | Meet the Beatles! | 1969 | 50.00 | 100.00 | 200.00 |

—Capitol Record Club edition; lime green label

| ❑ ST-8-2047 [P] | Meet the Beatles! | 1969 | 125.00 | 250.00 | 500.00 |

—Capitol Record Club edition; black label with colorband

| ❑ T 2047 [M] | Meet the Beatles! | 1964 | 50.00 | 100.00 | 200.00 |

—Black label with colorband; "Beatles!" on cover in tan to brown print; label has "ASCAP" after every title except "I Want to Hold Your Hand" (BMI); no producer credit on back cover (this is the second edition of this LP)

| ❑ T 2047 [M] | Meet the Beatles! | 1964 | 100.00 | 200.00 | 400.00 |

—Black label with colorband; "Beatles!" on cover in tan to brown print; no producer credit on back cover; "ASCAP" and "BMI" credits are missing on the label (this is the first edition of the LP)

| ❑ T 2047 [M] | Meet the Beatles! | 1965 | 25.00 | 50.00 | 100.00 |

—Black label with colorband; "Beatles!" on cover in green print; most of these have "Produced by George Martin" on lower left of back cover; many of these have a label giving "BMI" credit to every song except "Don't Bother Me" and "Till There Was You"

| ❑ T 2047 [M] | Meet the Beatles! | 1964 | 37.50 | 75.00 | 150.00 |

—Black label with colorband; "Beatles!" on cover in tan to brown print; some labels have "ASCAP" after every title except "I Want to Hold Your Hand"; other labels have "ASCAP" after every title except "I Want to Hold Your Hand," "I Saw Her Standing There" and "I Wanna Be Your Man"; still other labels have "ASCAP" after every title except "I Want to Hold Your Hand" and "I Wanna Be Your Man"; back cover adds "Produced by George Martin" to lower left

| ❑ ST 2080 [P] | The Beatles' Second Album | 1964 | 25.00 | 50.00 | 100.00 |

—Black label with colorband. "She Loves You," "I'll Get You" and "You Can't Do That" are rechanneled

| ❑ ST 2080 [P] | The Beatles' Second Album | 1968 | 12.50 | 25.00 | 50.00 |

—Black colorband label; border print adds "A Subsidiary of Capitol Industries Inc."

| ❑ ST 2080 [P] | The Beatles' Second Album | 1969 | 10.00 | 20.00 | 40.00 |

—Lime green label

| ❑ ST 2080 [P] | The Beatles' Second Album | 1976 | 3.00 | 6.00 | 12.00 |

—Orange label

| ❑ ST 2080 [P] | The Beatles' Second Album | 1978 | 2.50 | 5.00 | 10.00 |

—Purple label, large Capitol logo

| ❑ ST 2080 [P] | The Beatles' Second Album | 1983 | 3.75 | 7.50 | 15.00 |

—Black label, print in colorband

Number	Title (A Side/B Side)	Yr	VG	VG+	NM
❑ ST-8-2080 [P]	The Beatles' Second Album	1964	125.00	250.00	500.00

—*Capitol Record Club edition; black label with colorband*

❑ ST-8-2080 [P]	The Beatles' Second Album	1969	75.00	150.00	300.00

—*Capitol Record Club edition; lime green label*

❑ T 2080 [M]	The Beatles' Second Album	1964	45.00	90.00	180.00
❑ ST 2108 [S]	Something New	1964	20.00	40.00	80.00

—*Black label with colorband*

❑ ST 2108 [S]	Something New	1968	12.50	25.00	50.00

—*Black colorband label; border print adds "A Subsidiary of Capitol Industries Inc."*

❑ ST 2108 [S]	Something New	1969	10.00	20.00	40.00

—*Lime green label*

❑ ST 2108 [S]	Something New	1976	3.00	6.00	12.00

—*Orange label*

❑ ST 2108 [S]	Something New	1978	2.50	5.00	10.00

—*Purple label, large Capitol logo*

❑ ST 2108 [S]	Something New	1983	3.75	7.50	15.00

—*Black label, print in colorband*

❑ ST-8-2108 [S]	Something New	1964	75.00	150.00	300.00

—*Capitol Record Club edition; black label with colorband*

❑ ST-8-2108 [S]	Something New	1969	37.50	75.00	150.00

—*Capitol Record Club edition; lime green label*

❑ ST-8-2108 [S]	Something New	1969	75.00	150.00	300.00

—*Longines Symphonette edition (will be stated on label); lime green label*

❑ T 2108 [M]	Something New	1964	37.50	75.00	150.00
❑ STBO 2222 [(2)P]	The Beatles' Story	1964	37.50	75.00	150.00

—*Black label with colorband. Some of the musical snippets are rechanneled.*

❑ STBO 2222 [(2)P]	The Beatles' Story	1968	20.00	40.00	80.00

—*Black colorband label; border print adds "A Subsidiary of Capitol Industries Inc."*

❑ STBO 2222 [(2)P]	The Beatles' Story	1969	12.50	25.00	50.00

—*Lime green label*

❑ STBO 2222 [(2)P]	The Beatles' Story	1976	5.00	10.00	20.00

—*Orange label*

❑ STBO 2222 [(2)P]	The Beatles' Story	1978	5.00	10.00	20.00

—*Purple label, large Capitol logo*

❑ STBO 2222 [(2)P]	The Beatles' Story	1983	10.00	20.00	40.00

—*Black label, print in colorband*

❑ TBO 2222 [(2)M]	The Beatles' Story	1964	50.00	100.00	200.00
❑ ST 2228 [P]	Beatles '65	1964	20.00	40.00	80.00

—*Black label with colorband. "She's a Woman" and "I Feel Fine" are rechanneled.*

❑ ST 2228 [P]	Beatles '65	1968	12.50	25.00	50.00

—*Black colorband label; border print adds "A Subsidiary of Capitol Industries Inc."*

❑ ST 2228 [P]	Beatles '65	1969	10.00	20.00	40.00

—*Lime green label*

❑ ST 2228 [P]	Beatles '65	1976	3.00	6.00	12.00

—*Orange label*

❑ ST 2228 [P]	Beatles '65	1978	2.50	5.00	10.00

—*Purple label, large Capitol logo*

❑ ST 2228 [P]	Beatles '65	1983	3.75	7.50	15.00

—*Black label, print in colorband*

❑ T 2228 [M]	Beatles '65	1964	30.00	60.00	120.00
❑ ST 2309 [P]	The Early Beatles	1965	25.00	50.00	100.00

—*Black label with colorband. "Love Me Do" and "P.S. I Love You" are rechanneled.*

❑ ST 2309 [P]	The Early Beatles	1968	12.50	25.00	50.00

—*Black colorband label; border print adds "A Subsidiary of Capitol Industries Inc."*

❑ ST 2309 [P]	The Early Beatles	1969	10.00	20.00	40.00

—*Lime green label*

❑ ST 2309 [P]	The Early Beatles	1976	3.00	6.00	12.00

—*Orange label*

❑ ST 2309 [P]	The Early Beatles	1978	2.50	5.00	10.00

—*Purple label, large Capitol logo*

❑ ST 2309 [P]	The Early Beatles	1983	6.25	12.50	25.00

—*Black label, print in colorband*

❑ T 2309 [M]	The Early Beatles	1965	50.00	100.00	200.00
❑ ST 2358 [M]	Beatles VI	1983	3.75	7.50	15.00

—*Black label, print in colorband; plays in mono despite label designation*

❑ ST 2358 [M]	Beatles VI	1988	20.00	40.00	80.00

—*Purple label, small Capitol logo; plays in mono despite label designation*

❑ ST 2358 [P]	Beatles VI	1965	18.75	37.50	75.00

—*Black label with colorband; with song titles listed in correct order on back cover. "Yes It Is" is rechanneled.*

❑ ST 2358 [P]	Beatles VI	1965	20.00	40.00	80.00

—*Black label with colorband; with "See label for correct playing order" on back cover*

❑ ST 2358 [P]	Beatles VI	1968	12.50	25.00	50.00

—*Black colorband label; border print adds "A Subsidiary of Capitol Industries Inc."*

❑ ST 2358 [P]	Beatles VI	1969	10.00	20.00	40.00

—*Lime green label*

❑ ST 2358 [P]	Beatles VI	1976	3.00	6.00	12.00

—*Orange label*

❑ ST 2358 [P]	Beatles VI	1978	2.50	5.00	10.00

—*Purple label, large Capitol logo*

❑ ST-8-2358 [P]	Beatles VI	1965	125.00	250.00	500.00

—*Capitol Record Club edition; black label with colorband*

❑ ST-8-2358 [P]	Beatles VI	1969	100.00	200.00	400.00

—*Capitol Record Club edition; lime green label*

❑ T 2358 [M]	Beatles VI	1965	25.00	50.00	100.00

—*With song titles listed in correct order on back cover*

❑ T 2358 [M]	Beatles VI	1965	30.00	60.00	120.00

—*With "See label for correct playing order" on back cover*

❑ MAS 2386 [M]	Help!	1965	37.50	75.00	150.00
❑ SMAS 2386 [P]	Help!	1965	18.75	37.50	75.00

—*Black label with colorband. Has incidental music by George Martin. "Ticket to Ride" is rechanneled.*

❑ SMAS 2386 [P]	Help!	1968	12.50	25.00	50.00

—*Black colorband label; border print adds "A Subsidiary of Capitol Industries Inc."*

❑ SMAS 2386 [P]	Help!	1969	10.00	20.00	40.00

—*Lime green label*

❑ SMAS 2386 [P]	Help!	1976	3.00	6.00	12.00

—*Orange label*

❑ SMAS 2386 [P]	Help!	1978	2.50	5.00	10.00

—*Purple label, large Capitol logo*

❑ SMAS 2386 [P]	Help!	1983	3.75	7.50	15.00

—*Black label, print in colorband*

❑ SMAS-8-2386 [P]	Help!	1965	100.00	200.00	400.00

—*Capitol Record Club edition; black label with colorband; no "8" on cover*

Number	Title (A Side/B Side)	Yr	VG	VG+	NM
❑ SMAS-8-2386 [P]	Help!	1965	150.00	300.00	600.00

—*Capitol Record Club edition; black label with colorband; with "8" on cover*

❑ SMAS-8-2386 [P]	Help!	1969	50.00	100.00	200.00

—*Capitol Record Club edition; lime green label; no "8" on cover*

❑ SMAS-8-2386 [P]	Help!	1969	100.00	200.00	400.00

—*Capitol Record Club edition; lime green label; with "8" on cover*

❑ SMAS-8-2386 [P]	Help!	197?	175.00	350.00	700.00

—*Longines Symphonette edition; with "Mfd. by Longines" and "8" on cover*

❑ ST 2442 [S]	Rubber Soul	1965	15.00	30.00	60.00

—*Black label with colorband*

❑ ST 2442 [S]	Rubber Soul	1968	12.50	25.00	50.00

—*Black colorband label; border print adds "A Subsidiary of Capitol Industries Inc."*

❑ ST 2442 [S]	Rubber Soul	1969	10.00	20.00	40.00

—*Lime green label*

❑ ST 2442 [S]	Rubber Soul	1976	3.00	6.00	12.00

—*Orange label*

❑ ST-8-2442 [S]	Rubber Soul	1965	75.00	150.00	300.00

—*Capitol Record Club edition; black label with colorband*

❑ ST-8-2442 [S]	Rubber Soul	1969	50.00	100.00	200.00

—*Capitol Record Club edition; lime green label*

❑ ST-8-2442 [S]	Rubber Soul	1969	62.50	125.00	250.00

—*Longines Symphonette edition (will be stated on label); lime green label*

❑ SW 2442 [S]	Rubber Soul	1978	2.50	5.00	10.00

—*Purple label, large Capitol logo*

❑ SW 2442 [S]	Rubber Soul	1983	3.75	7.50	15.00

—*Black label, print in colorband*

❑ T 2442 [M]	Rubber Soul	1965	30.00	60.00	120.00
❑ ST 2553 [P]	Yesterday and Today	1966	20.00	40.00	80.00

—*Trunk cover; black label with colorband (all later variations have the trunk cover). "I'm Only Sleeping," "Dr. Robert" and "And Your Bird Can Sing" are rechanneled.*

❑ ST 2553 [P]	Yesterday and Today	1966	500.00	750.00	1000.

—*"Second state" butcher cover (trunk cover pasted over original cover)*

❑ ST 2553 [P]	Yesterday and Today	1966	375.00	750.00	1500.

—*"Third state" butcher cover (trunk cover removed, leaving butcher intact); cover will be about 3/16-inch narrower than other Capitol Beatles LPs; value is highly negotiable depending upon the success of removing the paste-over*

❑ ST 2553 [P]	Yesterday and Today	1966	4000.	6000.	8000.

—*"First state" butcher cover (never had other cover on top); cover will be the same size as other Capitol Beatles LPs*

❑ ST 2553 [P]	Yesterday and Today	1968	12.50	25.00	50.00

—*Black colorband label; border print adds "A Subsidiary of Capitol Industries Inc."*

❑ ST 2553 [P]	Yesterday and Today	1969	10.00	20.00	40.00

—*Lime green label*

❑ ST 2553 [P]	Yesterday and Today	1976	3.00	6.00	12.00

—*Orange label; it's possible that this and all future pressings have all 11 tracks in true stereo, but we don't know.*

❑ ST 2553 [P]	Yesterday and Today	1978	2.50	5.00	10.00

—*Purple label, large Capitol logo*

❑ ST 2553 [P]	Yesterday and Today	1983	3.75	7.50	15.00

—*Black label, print in colorband*

❑ ST-8-2553 [P]	Yesterday and Today	1966	75.00	150.00	300.00

—*Capitol Record Club edition; black label with colorband*

❑ ST-8-2553 [P]	Yesterday and Today	1969	37.50	75.00	150.00

—*Capitol Record Club edition; lime green label; all 11 tracks are in true stereo! (We don't know if the same is true of the black label version.)*

❑ T 2553 [M]	Yesterday and Today	1966	37.50	75.00	150.00

—*Trunk cover*

❑ T 2553 [M]	Yesterday and Today	1966	250.00	500.00	1000.

—*"Second state" butcher cover (trunk cover pasted over original cover)*

❑ T 2553 [M]	Yesterday and Today	1966	400.00	800.00	1200.

—*"Third state" butcher cover (trunk cover removed, leaving butcher intact); cover will be about 3/16-inch narrower than other Capitol Beatles LPs; value is highly negotiable depending upon the success of removing the paste-over*

❑ T 2553 [M]	Yesterday and Today	1966	2000.	3000.	4000.

—*"First state" butcher cover (never had other cover on top); cover will be the same size as other Capitol Beatles LPs*

❑ ST 2576 [S]	Revolver	1966	25.00	50.00	100.00

—*Black label with colorband*

❑ ST 2576 [S]	Revolver	1968	12.50	25.00	50.00

—*Black colorband label; border print adds "A Subsidiary of Capitol Industries Inc."*

❑ ST 2576 [S]	Revolver	1969	10.00	20.00	40.00

—*Lime green label*

❑ ST 2576 [S]	Revolver	1970	75.00	150.00	300.00

—*Red label with "target" Capitol at top (same design as lime green label)*

❑ ST 2576 [S]	Revolver	1976	3.00	6.00	12.00

—*Orange label*

❑ ST-8-2576 [S]	Revolver	1966	100.00	200.00	400.00

—*Capitol Record Club edition; black label with colorband*

❑ ST-8-2576 [S]	Revolver	1969	30.00	60.00	120.00

—*Capitol Record Club edition; lime green label*

❑ ST-8-2576 [S]	Revolver	1973?	50.00	100.00	200.00

—*Capitol Record Club edition; orange label (a very late issue, as Capitol Record Club closed in 1973)*

❑ SW 2576 [S]	Revolver	1978	2.50	5.00	10.00

—*Purple label, large Capitol logo*

❑ SW 2576 [S]	Revolver	1983	3.75	7.50	15.00

—*Black label, print in colorband*

❑ T 2576 [M]	Revolver	1966	50.00	100.00	200.00
❑ 2653	Sgt. Pepper's Lonely Hearts Club Band Cut-Out Inserts	1967	—	—	3.00
❑ 2653	Sgt. Pepper's Lonely Hearts Club Band Special Inner Sleeve	1967	3.75	7.50	15.00

—*Red-pink psychedelic sleeve only issued with 1967 (mono and stereo) editions*

❑ MAS 2653 [M]	Sgt. Pepper's Lonely Hearts Club Band	1967	75.00	150.00	300.00
❑ SMAS 2653 [S]	Sgt. Pepper's Lonely Hearts Club Band	1967	25.00	50.00	100.00

—*Black label with colorband*

❑ SMAS 2653 [S]	Sgt. Pepper's Lonely Hearts Club Band	1968	15.00	30.00	60.00

—*Black colorband label; border print adds "A Subsidiary of Capitol Industries Inc."*

❑ SMAS 2653 [S]	Sgt. Pepper's Lonely Hearts Club Band	1969	12.50	25.00	50.00

—*Lime green label*

❑ SMAS 2653 [S]	Sgt. Pepper's Lonely Hearts Club Band	1976	3.00	6.00	12.00

—*Orange label*

Number	Title (A Side/B Side)	Yr	VG	VG+	NM
❑ SMAS 2653 [S]	Sgt. Pepper's Lonely Hearts Club Band	1978	2.50	5.00	10.00

—Purple label, large Capitol logo. Many copies from 1978 had a "The Original Classic" sticker on shrink wrap; it was added at the time of the release of the bomb movie version of Sgt. Pepper. Double the value if the sticker is still there.

❑ SMAS 2653 [S]	Sgt. Pepper's Lonely Hearts Club Band	1983	3.75	7.50	15.00

—Black label, print in colorband; some of these had "The Original Classic" stickers, too. Add $10 to value if it is there.

❑ MAL 2835 [M]	Magical Mystery Tour	1967	75.00	150.00	300.00

—With 24-page book bound into center of gatefold

❑ SMAL 2835 [P]	Magical Mystery Tour	1967	25.00	50.00	100.00

—Black label with colorband; with 24-page booklet. "Penny Lane," "Baby You're a Rich Man" and "All You Need Is Love" is rechanneled, as is the second half of "I Am the Walrus" (every "stereo" version of "Walrus" is this way)

❑ SMAL 2835 [P]	Magical Mystery Tour	1968	15.00	30.00	60.00

—Black colorband label; border print adds "A Subsidiary of Capitol Industries Inc."; with 24-page booklet

❑ SMAL 2835 [P]	Magical Mystery Tour	1969	12.50	25.00	50.00

—Lime green label; with 24-page booklet

❑ SMAL 2835 [P]	Magical Mystery Tour	1976	3.00	6.00	12.00

—Orange label; with 24-page booklet

❑ SMAL 2835 [P]	Magical Mystery Tour	1978	2.50	5.00	10.00

—Purple label, large Capitol logo; this edition did not come with booklet

❑ SMAL 2835 [P]	Magical Mystery Tour	1983	3.75	7.50	15.00

—Black label, print in colorband; no booklet

❑ SKBO-3403 [P]	The Beatles 1962-1966	1976	5.00	10.00	20.00

—Red labels

❑ SKBO-3403 [P]	The Beatles 1962-1966	1976	7.50	15.00	30.00

—Blue labels (error pressing)

❑ SKBO-3404 [B]	The Beatles 1967-1970	1976	5.00	10.00	20.00

—Blue labels

❑ SPRO-8969	Rarities	1978	12.50	25.00	50.00

—Purple label, large Capitol logo; part of the U.S. box set The Beatles Collection (BC-13)

❑ SKBO-11537 [(2)]	Rock 'n' Roll Music	1976	6.25	12.50	25.00
❑ SMAS-11638	The Beatles at the Hollywood Bowl	1977	5.00	10.00	20.00

—Originals with embossed title and ticket on front cover

❑ SMAS-11638	The Beatles at the Hollywood Bowl	1980	3.75	7.50	15.00

—Second pressing without embossed title and ticket

❑ SMAS-11638	The Beatles at the Hollywood Bowl	1989	10.00	20.00	40.00

—With UPC code on back cover

❑ SMAS-11638 [DJ]	The Beatles at the Hollywood Bowl	1977	125.00	250.00	500.00

—Advance tan label promo in plain white jacket

❑ SKBL-11711 [(2)P]	Love Songs	1977	5.00	10.00	20.00

—With booklet and embossed, leather-like cover. "P.S. I Love You" and "Yes It Is" are rechanneled.

❑ SKBL-11711 [(2)P]	Love Songs	1988	7.50	15.00	30.00

—With booklet, but without embossed cover

❑ SEAX-11840 [PD]	Sgt. Pepper's Lonely Hearts Club Band	1978	5.00	10.00	20.00

—Picture disc; deduct 25% for cut-outs

❑ SEBX-11841 [(2)]	The Beatles	1978	12.50	25.00	50.00

—White vinyl; with photos and poster (with number "SEBX-11841" on each)

❑ SEBX-11842 [P]	The Beatles 1962-1966	1978	10.00	20.00	40.00

—Red vinyl

❑ SEBX-11843 [B]	The Beatles 1967-1970	1978	10.00	20.00	40.00

—Blue vinyl

❑ SEAX-11900 [PD]	Abbey Road	1978	10.00	20.00	40.00

—Picture disc; deduct 25% for cut-outs

❑ SW-11921 [P]	A Hard Day's Night	1979	3.00	6.00	12.00

—Purple label, large Capitol logo

❑ SW-11921 [P]	A Hard Day's Night	1983	3.75	7.50	15.00

—Black label, print in colorband

❑ SW-11921 [P]	A Hard Day's Night	1988	6.25	12.50	25.00

—Purple label, small Capitol logo

❑ SW-11922	Let It Be	1979	3.75	7.50	15.00

—Purple label, large Capitol logo; with poster and custom innersleeve

❑ SW-11922	Let It Be	1983	3.75	7.50	15.00

—Black label, print in colorband; add 33% if poster is included

❑ SW-11922	Let It Be	1988	6.25	12.50	25.00

—Purple label, small Capitol logo; add 20% if poster and custom innersleeve are included

❑ SN-12009 [DJ]	Rarities	1979	75.00	150.00	300.00

—Green label; withdrawn before official release; all known copies have a plain white sleeve

❑ SHAL-12060 [B]	Rarities	1980	3.75	7.50	15.00

—Same as above, with errors deleted and "Produced by George Martin" added to back cover

❑ SHAL-12060 [B]	Rarities	1980	5.00	10.00	20.00

—Black label with colorband. First pressing says that "There's a Place" debuts in stereo (false) and that the screaming at the end of "Helter Skelter" was a "classic Lennon statement" (it's actually Ringo).

❑ SV-12199	Reel Music	1982	2.50	5.00	10.00

—Standard issue with 12-page booklet

❑ SV-12199 [DJ]	Reel Music	1982	5.00	10.00	20.00

—Yellow vinyl promo; plain white cover with 12-page booklet

❑ SV-12199 [DJ]	Reel Music	1982	10.00	20.00	40.00

—Yellow vinyl promo; numbered back cover with 12-page booklet

❑ SV-12245 [P]	20 Greatest Hits	1982	5.00	10.00	20.00

—Purple label, large Capitol logo. "Love Me Do" and "She Loves You" are rechanneled, the other 18 tracks are stereo

❑ SV-12245 [P]	20 Greatest Hits	1983	5.00	10.00	20.00

—Black label, print in colorband

❑ SV-12245 [P]	20 Greatest Hits	1988	6.25	12.50	25.00

—Purple label, small Capitol logo

❑ SN-16020	Rock 'n' Roll Music, Volume 1	1980	2.50	5.00	10.00
❑ SN-16021	Rock 'n' Roll Music, Volume 2	1980	2.50	5.00	10.00
❑ C1-46435 [M]	Please Please Me	1995	3.00	6.00	12.00

—New prefix; Apple logo on back cover

❑ CLJ-46435 [M]	Please Please Me	1987	5.00	10.00	20.00

—Black label, print in colorband; first Capitol version of original British LP

❑ CLJ-46435 [M]	Please Please Me	1988	6.25	12.50	25.00

—Purple label, small Capitol logo

❑ C1-46436 [M]	With the Beatles	1995	3.00	6.00	12.00

—New prefix; Apple logo on back cover

❑ CLJ-46436 [M]	With the Beatles	1987	5.00	10.00	20.00

—Black label, print in colorband; first Capitol version of original British LP

❑ CLJ-46436 [M]	With the Beatles	1988	6.25	12.50	25.00

—Purple label, small Capitol logo

❑ C1-46437 [M]	A Hard Day's Night	1995	3.00	6.00	12.00

—New prefix; Apple logo on back cover

Number	Title (A Side/B Side)	Yr	VG	VG+	NM
❑ CLJ-46437 [M]	A Hard Day's Night	1987	5.00	10.00	20.00

—Black label, print in colorband; first Capitol version of original British LP

❑ CLJ-46437 [M]	A Hard Day's Night	1988	6.25	12.50	25.00

—Purple label, small Capitol logo

❑ C1-46438 [M]	Beatles for Sale	1995	3.00	6.00	12.00

—New prefix; Apple logo on back cover

❑ CLJ-46438 [M]	Beatles for Sale	1987	5.00	10.00	20.00

—Black label, print in colorband; first Capitol version of original British LP

❑ CLJ-46438 [M]	Beatles for Sale	1988	6.25	12.50	25.00

—Purple label, small Capitol logo

❑ C1-46439 [S]	Help!	1995	3.00	6.00	12.00

—New prefix; Apple logo on back cover

❑ CLJ-46439 [S]	Help!	1987	5.00	10.00	20.00

—Black label, print in colorband; first Capitol version of original British LP

❑ CLJ-46439 [S]	Help!	1988	6.25	12.50	25.00

—Purple label, small Capitol logo

❑ C1-46440 [S]	Rubber Soul	1995	3.00	6.00	12.00

—New prefix; Apple logo on back cover

❑ CLJ-46440 [S]	Rubber Soul	1987	5.00	10.00	20.00

—Black label, print in colorband; first Capitol version of original British LP

❑ CLJ-46440 [S]	Rubber Soul	1988	6.25	12.50	25.00

—Purple label, small Capitol logo

❑ C1-46441 [S]	Revolver	1995	3.00	6.00	12.00

—New prefix; Apple logo on back cover

❑ CLJ-46441 [S]	Revolver	1987	5.00	10.00	20.00

—Black label, print in colorband; first Capitol version of original British LP

❑ CLJ-46441 [S]	Revolver	1988	6.25	12.50	25.00

—Purple label, small Capitol logo

❑ C1-46442 [S]	Sgt. Pepper's Lonely Hearts Club Band	1988	6.25	12.50	25.00

—New number; purple label, small Capitol logo

❑ C1-46442 [S]	Sgt. Pepper's Lonely Hearts Club Band	1995	3.00	6.00	12.00

—With Apple logo on back cover

❑ C1-46443 [(2)]	The Beatles	1988	12.50	25.00	50.00

—New number; purple label, small Capitol logo; with photos and poster (some copies have four photos as one perforated sheet)

❑ C1-46443 [(2)]	The Beatles	1995	5.00	10.00	20.00

—With Apple logo on back cover

❑ C1-46445 [P]	Yellow Submarine	1988	6.25	12.50	25.00

—New number; purple label, small Capitol logo

❑ C1-46445 [P]	Yellow Submarine	1995	3.00	6.00	12.00

—Reissue has the British liner notes, which include a review of the White Album.

❑ C1-46446	Abbey Road	1988	6.25	12.50	25.00

—New number; purple label, small Capitol logo

❑ C1-46446	Abbey Road	1995	3.00	6.00	12.00

—Apple logo restored on back cover on reissue

❑ C1-46447	Let It Be	1995	3.00	6.00	12.00

—New number (the only 1995 reissue with a completely new number)

❑ C1-48062 [P]	Magical Mystery Tour	1988	6.25	12.50	25.00

—New number; purple label, small Capitol logo; no booklet

❑ C1-48062 [P]	Magical Mystery Tour	1992	3.00	6.00	12.00

—With Apple logo on back cover; reissue restores booklet to package

❑ C1-90435 [P]	The Beatles 1962-1966	1988	7.50	15.00	30.00

—New number; purple labels, small Capitol logo

❑ C1-90438 [B]	The Beatles 1967-1970	1988	7.50	15.00	30.00

—New number; purple labels, small Capitol logo

❑ C1-90441 [P]	Meet the Beatles!	1988	6.25	12.50	25.00

—New number; purple label, small Capitol logo

❑ C1-90442	Hey Jude	1988	6.25	12.50	25.00

—New number; purple label, small Capitol logo

❑ C1-90443 [S]	Something New	1988	6.25	12.50	25.00

—New number; purple label, small Capitol logo

❑ C1-90444 [P]	The Beatles' Second Album	1988	6.25	12.50	25.00

—New number; purple label, small Capitol logo

❑ C1-90445 [M]	Beatles VI	1988	6.25	12.50	25.00

—New number; purple label, small Capitol logo; plays in mono despite label designation

❑ C1-90446 [P]	Beatles '65	1988	6.25	12.50	25.00

—New number; purple label, small Capitol logo

❑ C1-90447 [P]	Yesterday and Today	1988	6.25	12.50	25.00

—New number; purple label, small Capitol logo; stereo content uncertain

❑ C1-90452 [S]	Revolver	1988	6.25	12.50	25.00

—New number; purple label, small Capitol logo

❑ C1-90453 [S]	Rubber Soul	1988	6.25	12.50	25.00

—New number; purple label, small Capitol logo

❑ C1-90454 [P]	Help!	1988	6.25	12.50	25.00

—New number; purple label, small Capitol logo

❑ C1-91135 [(2)B]	Past Masters Volume 1 and 2	1988	6.25	12.50	25.00

—Some early tracks are in mono, but "This Boy," "She's a Woman," "Yes It Is," and "The Inner Light" are in stereo.

❑ BBX1-91302 [(14)]	The Beatles Deluxe Box Set	1988	75.00	150.00	300.00

CICADELIC

❑ 1960	Moviemania	1987	3.00	6.00	12.00
❑ 1961	Not a Second Time	1987	3.00	6.00	12.00
❑ 1962	Things We Said Today	1986	3.00	6.00	12.00
❑ 1963	All Our Loving	1986	3.00	6.00	12.00
❑ 1964	East Coast Invasion	1985	3.00	6.00	12.00
❑ 1965	Round the World	1986	3.00	6.00	12.00
❑ 1966	West Coast Invasion	1985	3.00	6.00	12.00
❑ 1967	From Britain with Beat!	1987	3.00	6.00	12.00
❑ 1968	Here, There and Everywhere	1988	3.00	6.00	12.00

CLARION

❑ 601 [M]	The Amazing Beatles and Other Great English Group Sounds	1966	25.00	50.00	100.00
❑ SD 601 [P]	The Amazing Beatles and Other Great English Group Sounds	1966	50.00	100.00	200.00

—All four Beatles tracks are rechanneled

GREAT NORTHWEST

❑ GNW 4007	Beatle Talk	1978	2.50	5.00	10.00
❑ GNW 4007	Beatle Talk	1978	12.50	25.00	50.00

—Columbia Record Club edition; "CRC" on spine

B

Number	Title (A Side/B Side)	Yr	VG	VG+	NM

HALL OF MUSIC

❑ HM-1-2200 [(2)M] Live 1962, Hamburg, Germany — 1981 — 12.50 — 25.00 — 50.00
—Only American LP with the original Eurpoean contents -- "I Saw Her Standing There," "Twist and Shout," "Ask Me Why" and "Reminiscing" replace the four songs listed with the Lingasong issue

I-N-S RADIO NEWS

❑ DOC-1 [DJ] Beatlemania Tour Coverage — 1964 — 750.00 — 1125. — 1500.
—Promo-only open-end interview with script in plain white jacket

LINGASONG

❑ LS-2-7001 [(2)DJ] Live at the Star Club in Hamburg, Germany, 1962 — 1977 — 10.00 — 20.00 — 40.00
—Promo on black vinyl; "D.J. Copy Not for Sale" on labels

❑ LS-2-7001 [(2)DJ] Live at the Star Club in Hamburg, Germany, 1962 — 1977 — 50.00 — 100.00 — 200.00
—Promo only on red vinyl

❑ LS-2-7001 [(2)DJ] Live at the Star Club in Hamburg, Germany, 1962 — 1977 — 75.00 — 150.00 — 300.00
—Promo only on blue vinyl

❑ LS-2-7001 [(2)R] Live at the Star Club in Hamburg, Germany, 1962 — 1977 — 5.00 — 10.00 — 20.00
—American version contains "I'm Gonna Sit Right Down and Cry," "Where Have You Been All My Life," "Till There Was You," and "Sheila," not on imports

LLOYDS

❑ ER-MC-LTD The Great American Tour — 1965 Live Beatlemania Concert — 1965 — 150.00 — 300.00 — 600.00
—Another interview album from the Ed Rudy people, with a live Beatles show in the background and the songs poorly overdubbed by the Liverpool Lads

METRO

❑ M-563 [M] This Is Where It Started — 1966 — 25.00 — 50.00 — 100.00
—Reissue of MGM album with two of the "others" tracks deleted

❑ MS-563 [R] This Is Where It Started — 1966 — 37.50 — 75.00 — 150.00
—In stereo cover

❑ MS-563 [R] This Is Where It Started — 1966 — 50.00 — 100.00 — 200.00
—In mono cover with "Stereo" sticker

MGM

❑ E-4215 [M] The Beatles with Tony Sheridan and Their Guests — 1964 — 50.00 — 100.00 — 200.00
—Without "And Guests" on cover

❑ E-4215 [M] The Beatles with Tony Sheridan and Their Guests — 1964 — 62.50 — 125.00 — 250.00
—With "And Guests" on cover

❑ SE-4215 [R] The Beatles with Tony Sheridan and Their Guests — 1964 — 150.00 — 300.00 — 600.00
—With "And Guests" on cover

❑ SE-4215 [R] The Beatles with Tony Sheridan and Their Guests — 1964 — 200.00 — 400.00 — 800.00
—Without "And Guests" on cover

MOBILE FIDELITY

❑ BC-1 [(13)] The Beatles Collection — 1982 — 125.00 — 250.00 — 500.00

❑ 1-023 Abbey Road — 1979 — 12.50 — 25.00 — 50.00
—Audiophile vinyl

❑ 1-047 [P] Magical Mystery Tour — 1980 — 15.00 — 30.00 — 60.00
—Audiophile vinyl; yes, this contains the rechanneled stereo versions of "Penny Lane," "Baby You're a Rich Man" and "All You Need Is Love"

❑ 2-072 [(2)] The Beatles — 1982 — 12.50 — 25.00 — 50.00
—Audiophile vinyl; not issued with photos or poster

❑ 1-100 [S] Sgt. Pepper's Lonely Hearts Club Band — 1985 — 10.00 — 20.00 — 40.00
—Audiophile vinyl

❑ UHQR 1-100 [S] Sgt. Pepper's Lonely Hearts Club Band — 1982 — 75.00 — 150.00 — 300.00
—Ultra High Quality release with special cover; numbered edition of 5,000; numbers under 100 fetch even more

❑ 1-101 [P] Please Please Me — 1986 — 10.00 — 20.00 — 40.00
—Audiophile vinyl; British version of album. "Love Me Do" and "P.S. I Love You" are rechanneled.

❑ 1-102 [S] With the Beatles — 1986 — 37.50 — 75.00 — 150.00
—Audiophile vinyl; British version of album. Limited run because of a damaged stamper that was not replaced.

❑ 1-103 [S] A Hard Day's Night — 1987 — 10.00 — 20.00 — 40.00
—Audiophile vinyl; British version of album

❑ 1-104 [S] Beatles for Sale — 1986 — 10.00 — 20.00 — 40.00
—Audiophile vinyl; British version of album

❑ 1-105 [S] Help! — 1985 — 10.00 — 20.00 — 40.00
—Audiophile vinyl; British version of album

❑ 1-106 [S] Rubber Soul — 1985 — 10.00 — 20.00 — 40.00
—Audiophile vinyl; British version of album

❑ 1-107 [S] Revolver — 1986 — 10.00 — 20.00 — 40.00
—Audiophile vinyl; British version of album

❑ 1-108 [P] Yellow Submarine — 1987 — 15.00 — 30.00 — 60.00
—Audiophile vinyl

❑ 1-109 Let It Be — 1987 — 10.00 — 20.00 — 40.00
—Audiophile vinyl; gatefold cover

❑ 1-109 Let It Be — 1987 — 50.00 — 100.00 — 200.00
—Audiophile vinyl; regular cover

ORANGE

❑ ORC-12880 [DJ] The Silver Beatles — 1985 — 75.00 — 150.00 — 300.00
—Test pressing; white cover with title sticker

❑ ORC-12880 [DJ] The Silver Beatles — 1985 — 100.00 — 200.00 — 400.00
—Test pressing; full cover cover slick folded around a white cover. Both contain all 15 Decca audition tracks

PBR INTERNATIONAL

❑ 7005/6 [(2)] The David Wigg Interviews (The Beatles Tapes) — 1978 — 20.00 — 40.00 — 80.00
—Blue vinyl

❑ 7005/6 [(2)] The David Wigg Interviews (The Beatles Tapes) — 1980 — 15.00 — 30.00 — 60.00
—Black vinyl

PHOENIX

❑ PHX-352 [M] Silver Beatles, Volume 1 — 1982 — 3.00 — 6.00 — 12.00
—Contains seven Decca audition tracks

❑ PHX-353 [M] Silver Beatles, Volume 2 — 1982 — 3.00 — 6.00 — 12.00
—Contains seven Decca audition tracks (different seven than Phoenix 352)

❑ P20-623 20 Hits, Beatles — 1983 — 5.00 — 10.00 — 20.00
—With 12 Decca audition tracks, four Beatles/Tony Sheridan tracks, and four Tony Sheridan solo tracks

❑ P20-629 20 Hits, Beatles — 1983 — 5.00 — 10.00 — 20.00
—With 20 live Hamburg tracks

PICKWICK

❑ PTP-2098 [(2)M] The Historic First Live Recordings — 1980 — 4.50 — 9.00 — 18.00
—Same contents as Lingasong LP, plus "Hully Gully"

❑ SPC-3661 [M] The Beatles' First Live Recordings, Volume 1 — 1979 — 3.00 — 6.00 — 12.00

❑ SPC-3662 [M] The Beatles' First Live Recordings, Volume 2 — 1979 — 3.00 — 6.00 — 12.00

❑ BAN-90051 [M] Recorded Live in Hamburg, Vol. 1 — 1978 — 7.50 — 15.00 — 30.00

❑ BAN-90061 [M] Recorded Live in Hamburg, Vol. 2 — 1978 — 7.50 — 15.00 — 30.00

❑ BAN-90071 [M] Recorded Live in Hamburg, Vol. 3 — 1978 — 10.00 — 20.00 — 40.00

POLYDOR

❑ 24-4504 [P] The Beatles — Circa 1960 — In the Beginning Featuring Tony Sheridan — 197? — 10.00 — 20.00 — 40.00
—Some copies of the record contain only the title "The Beatles -- In the Beginning"

❑ 24-4504 [P] The Beatles — Circa 1960 — In the Beginning Featuring Tony Sheridan — 1970 — 6.25 — 12.50 — 25.00
—Originals have gatefold cover

❑ PD-4504 [P] The Beatles — Circa 1960 — In the Beginning Featuring Tony Sheridan — 1981 — 3.00 — 6.00 — 12.00
—Reissue without gatefold cover

❑ SKAO-93199 [P] The Beatles — Circa 1960 — In the Beginning Featuring Tony Sheridan — 1970 — 10.00 — 20.00 — 40.00
—Capitol Record Club edition

❑ 825073-1 [P] The Beatles — Circa 1960 — In the Beginning Featuring Tony Sheridan — 1988 — 5.00 — 10.00 — 20.00
—Reissue with new number

RADIO PULSEBEAT NEWS

❑ 2 The American Tour with Ed Rudy — 1964 — 25.00 — 50.00 — 100.00
—Yellow label; some copies came with a special edition of Teen Talk magazine (add 50%)

❑ 2 The American Tour with Ed Rudy — 1980 — 6.25 — 12.50 — 25.00
—Blue label; authorized reissue with Beatles' photo on cover

❑ 3 1965 Talk Album — Ed Rudy with New U.S. Tour — 1965 — 37.50 — 75.00 — 150.00
—"The Beatles" in black print under front cover photo (other versions appear to be bootlegs)

RAVEN/PVC

❑ 8911 Talk Downunder — 1981 — 2.50 — 5.00 — 10.00

❑ 8911 [DJ] Talk Downunder — 1981 — 20.00 — 40.00 — 80.00
—Promo only in white cover with title sticker. Label reads "For Radio Play Only"

SAVAGE

❑ BM-69 [M] The Savage Young Beatles — 1964 — 37.50 — 75.00 — 150.00
—Orange label; no legitimate copy says "Stereo" on cover

❑ BM-69 [M] The Savage Young Beatles — 1964 — 375.00 — 750.00 — 1500.
—Yellow label, glossy orange cover

SILHOUETTE

❑ SM-10004 [PD] Timeless — 1981 — 5.00 — 10.00 — 20.00
—Picture disc with all interviews

❑ SM-10004 [PD] Timeless — 1981 — 6.25 — 12.50 — 25.00
—Picture disc with interviews plus remakes of "Imagine" and "Let It Be" (by non-Beatles)

❑ SM-10010 [PD] Timeless II — 1982 — 5.00 — 10.00 — 20.00
—Picture disc with mostly interviews

❑ SM-10013 The British Are Coming — 1984 — 3.75 — 7.50 — 15.00
—Interview album with numbered sticker (very low numbers increase the value)

❑ SM-10013 The British Are Coming — 1984 — 20.00 — 40.00 — 80.00
—Same as above, but on red vinyl

❑ SM-10013 [DJ] The British Are Coming — 1984 — 10.00 — 20.00 — 40.00
—White label promo; no numbered sticker

❑ SM-10015 Golden Beatles — 1985 — 3.75 — 7.50 — 15.00

❑ SM-10015 Golden Beatles — 1985 — 20.00 — 40.00 — 80.00
—Gold vinyl

❑ PD-83010 [PD] The British Are Coming — 1985 — 7.50 — 15.00 — 30.00
—Picture disc

STERLING

❑ 8895-6481 I Apologize — 1966 — 75.00 — 150.00 — 300.00
—Same as above, but without photo

❑ 8895-6481 I Apologize — 1966 — 100.00 — 200.00 — 400.00
—One-sided LP with John Lennon's "apology" for supposed anti-Christian remarks; includes photo

UNITED ARTISTS

❑ UA-Help-A/B [DJ] United Artists Presents Help! — 1965 — 500.00 — 1000. — 1500.
—Radio spots for movie

❑ UA-Help-INT [DJ] United Artists Presents Help! — 1965 — 1000. — 1500. — 2000.
—Open-end interview with script (red label)

❑ UA-Help-Show [DJ] United Artists Presents Help! — 1965 — 1500. — 2250. — 3000.
—One-sided interview with script (blue label)

❑ SP-2359/60 [DJ] United Artists Presents A Hard Day's Night — 1964 — 1000. — 1500. — 2000.
—Open-end interview with script

❑ SP-2362/3 [DJ] United Artists Presents A Hard Day's Night — 1964 — 375.00 — 750.00 — 1500.
—Radio spots for movie

❑ UAL 3366 [M] A Hard Day's Night — 1964 — 50.00 — 100.00 — 200.00
—With "I Cry Instead" listing

❑ UAL 3366 [M] A Hard Day's Night — 1964 — 62.50 — 125.00 — 250.00
—With "I'll Cry Instead" listing

❑ UAL 3366 [M] A Hard Day's Night — 1964 — 750.00 — 1500. — 3000.
—White label promo

❑ UAS 6366 [P] A Hard Day's Night — 1964 — 50.00 — 100.00 — 200.00
—With "I Cry Instead" listing

❑ UAS 6366 [P] A Hard Day's Night — 1964 — 62.50 — 125.00 — 250.00
—With "I'll Cry Instead" listing. Has incidental music by George Martin. All eight Beatles tracks are rechanneled; Martin's are in true stereo.

❑ UAS 6366 [P] A Hard Day's Night — 1964 — 6000. — 9000. — 12000.
—Pink vinyl; only one copy known, probably privately (and secretly) done by a pressing-plant employee

❑ UAS 6366 [P] A Hard Day's Night — 1968 — 12.50 — 25.00 — 50.00
—Pink and orange label

❑ UAS 6366 [P] A Hard Day's Night — 1970 — 12.50 — 25.00 — 50.00
—Black and orange label

❑ UAS 6366 [P] A Hard Day's Night — 1971 — 5.00 — 10.00 — 20.00
—Tan label

Number	Title (A Side/B Side)	Yr	VG	VG+	NM
❏ UAS 6366 [P]	A Hard Day's Night	1975	5.00	10.00	20.00

—Tan label with "All Rights Reserved" in perimeter print

Number	Title (A Side/B Side)	Yr	VG	VG+	NM
❏ UAS 6366 [P]	A Hard Day's Night	1977	5.00	10.00	20.00

—Sunrise label. Note: Any of the variations from 1968 on can have titles of songs incorrectly listed as "I Cry Instead" and "Tell Me Who," or only one can be wrong, or neither can be wrong. No difference in value at this time.

❏ ST-90828 [P]	A Hard Day's Night	1964	187.50	375.00	750.00

—Capitol Record Club edition

❏ T-90828 [M]	A Hard Day's Night	1964	750.00	1125.	1500.

—Capitol Record Club edition

UNITED DISTRIBUTORS

❏ UDL-2333 [M]	Dawn of the Silver Beatles	1981	12.50	25.00	50.00

—With numbered registration card (deduct 20% if missing)

❏ UDL-2333 [M]	Dawn of the Silver Beatles	1981	15.00	30.00	60.00

—Hand-stamped numbers on back cover and label; contains 10 Decca audition tracks

❏ UDL-2382	Lightning Strikes Twice	1981	15.00	30.00	60.00

—Side 1 has five Beatles' Decca audition tracks; Side 2 has live Elvis Presley performances from 1955

VEE JAY

❏ DX(S)-30	The Beatles vs. The Four Seasons Poster	1964	75.00	150.00	300.00
❏ DX-30 [(2)M]	The Beatles vs. The Four Seasons	1964	200.00	400.00	800.00

—Combines "Introducing the Beatles" with "Golden Hits of the Four Seasons" (Vee Jay 1065)

❏ DXS-30 [(2)S]	The Beatles vs. The Four Seasons	1964	1500.	2250.	3000.

—Combines "Introducing the Beatles" with "Golden Hits of the Four Seasons" (Vee Jay 1065)

❏ 202 [M]	Hear the Beatles Tell All	1964	75.00	150.00	300.00

—Without "PRO" prefix on label

❏ PRO 202 [DJ]	Hear the Beatles Tell All	1964	6000.	12000.	18000.

—White label promo with blue print

❏ PRO 202 [M]	Hear the Beatles Tell All	1964	50.00	100.00	200.00

—With "PRO" prefix on label

❏ PRO 202 [PD]	Hear the Beatles Tell All	1987	5.00	10.00	20.00

—Shaped picture disc with same recordings as the black vinyl versions

❏ PRO 202 [S]	Hear the Beatles Tell All	1979	2.50	5.00	10.00

—Authorized reissue in stereo

❏ LP 1062 [M]	Introducing the Beatles	1964	62.50	125.00	250.00

—Song titles cover; with "Please Please Me" and "Ask Me Why"; plain Vee Jay logo on solid black label

❏ LP 1062 [M]	Introducing the Beatles	1964	62.50	125.00	250.00

—Song titles cover; with "Please Please Me" and "Ask Me Why"; brackets Vee Jay logo with colorband (most common authentic version)

❏ LP 1062 [M]	Introducing the Beatles	1964	75.00	150.00	300.00

—Song titles cover; with "Please Please Me" and "Ask Me Why"; oval Vee Jay logo on solid black label

❏ LP 1062 [M]	Introducing the Beatles	1964	75.00	150.00	300.00

—Song titles cover; with "Please Please Me" and "Ask Me Why"; oval Vee Jay logo with colorband

❏ LP 1062 [M]	Introducing the Beatles	1964	200.00	400.00	800.00

—Song titles cover; with "Love Me Do" and "P.S. I Love You"; oval Vee Jay logo with colorband only!

❏ LP 1062 [M]	Introducing the Beatles	1964	250.00	500.00	1000.

—Blank back cover; with "Please Please Me" and "Ask Me Why"; oval Vee Jay logo with colorband only!

❏ LP 1062 [M]	Introducing the Beatles	1964	250.00	500.00	1000.

—Song titles cover; with "Please Please Me" and "Ask Me Why"; brackets Vee Jay logo on solid black label

❏ LP 1062 [M]	Introducing the Beatles	1964	400.00	800.00	1200.

—Blank back cover; with "Love Me Do" and "P.S. I Love You"; oval Vee Jay logo with colorband only!

❏ LP 1062 [M]	Introducing the Beatles	1964	1500.	2750.	4000.

—"Ad back" cover; with "Love Me Do" and "P.S. I Love You"; oval Vee Jay logo with colorband only!

❏ SR 1062 [B]	Introducing the Beatles	1964	625.00	1250.	2500.

—Blank back cover; with "Love Me Do" and "P.S. I Love You"; oval Vee Jay logo with colorband only!

❏ SR 1062 [B]	Introducing the Beatles	1964	4000.	8000.	12000.

—"Ad back" cover; with "Love Me Do" and "P.S. I Love You" (both mono); oval Vee Jay logo with colorband only!

❏ SR 1062 [S]	Introducing the Beatles	1964	375.00	750.00	1500.

—Song titles cover; with "Please Please Me" and "Ask Me Why"; brackets Vee Jay logo with colorband

❏ SR 1062 [S]	Introducing the Beatles	1964	400.00	800.00	1600.

—Song titles cover; with "Please Please Me" and "Ask Me Why"; oval Vee Jay logo with colorband

❏ SR 1062 [S]	Introducing the Beatles	1964	400.00	800.00	1600.

—Song titles cover; with "Please Please Me" and "Ask Me Why"; plain Vee Jay logo on solid black label

❏ SR 1062 [B]	Introducing the Beatles	1964	3000.	5500.	8000.

—Song titles cover; with "Love Me Do" and "P.S. I Love You"; oval Vee Jay logo with colorband only! This album has been heavily counterfeited; please check the label of your copy before contacting the author. If the words "Introducing the Beatles" are above the center hole of the record, and the words "The Beatles" are below, it is automatically a counterfeit and almost worthless.

❏ LP 1085 [M]	Jolly What! The Beatles and Frank Ifield on Stage	1964	62.50	125.00	250.00

—Man in Beatle wig cover; originals have printing on spine and a dark blue/purple background (counterfeits have a black background and no spine print)

❏ LP 1085 [M]	The Beatles and Frank Ifield on Stage	1964	2000.	3500.	5000.

—Portrait of Beatles cover; counterfeits are poorly reproduced and have no spine print

❏ SR 1085 [B]	Jolly What! The Beatles and Frank Ifield on Stage	1964	125.00	250.00	500.00

—Man in Beatle wig cover; "Stereo" on both cover and label. "From Me to You" is mono.

❏ SR 1085 [B]	The Beatles and Frank Ifield on Stage	1964	4000.	8000.	12000.

—Portrait of Beatles cover; "Stereo" on both cover and label

❏ LP 1092 [M]	Songs, Pictures and Stories of the Fabulous Beatles	1964	125.00	250.00	500.00

—See above; brackets Vee Jay logo with colorband

❏ LP 1092 [M]	Songs, Pictures and Stories of the Fabulous Beatles	1964	125.00	250.00	500.00

—See above; oval Vee Jay logo on solid black label

❏ LP 1092 [M]	Songs, Pictures and Stories of the Fabulous Beatles	1964	125.00	250.00	500.00

—See above; plain Vee Jay logo on solid black label

❏ LP 1092 [M]	Songs, Pictures and Stories of the Fabulous Beatles	1964	125.00	250.00	500.00

—All copies have gatefold cover with 2/3 width on front; also, all copies have "Introducing the Beatles" records. Oval Vee Jay logo with colorband.

❏ VJS 1092 [S]	Songs, Pictures and Stories of the Fabulous Beatles	1964	800.00	1600.	2400.

—See above; brackets Vee Jay logo with colorband

❏ VJS 1092 [S]	Songs, Pictures and Stories of the Fabulous Beatles	1964	800.00	1600.	2400.

—See above; plain Vee Jay logo on solid black label. NOTE: Any non-gatefold copy or any copy called "Songs and Pictures of the Fabulous Beatles" is a counterfeit.

❏ VJS 1092 [S]	Songs, Pictures and Stories of the Fabulous Beatles	1964	800.00	1600.	2400.

—All copies have gatefold cover with 2/3 width on front; also, all copies have "Introducing the Beatles" records. Oval Vee Jay logo with colorband.

BEAU BRUMMELS, THE

ACCORD

❏ SN-7175	Just a Little	1982	2.50	5.00	10.00

AUTUMN

❏ LP 103 [M]	Introducing the Beau Brummels	1965	12.50	25.00	50.00
❏ SLP 103 [S]	Introducing the Beau Brummels	1965	15.00	30.00	60.00
❏ LP 104 [M]	The Beau Brummels, Volume 2	1965	10.00	20.00	40.00
❏ SLP 104 [S]	The Beau Brummels, Volume 2	1965	12.50	25.00	50.00

JAS

❏ 5000	Original Hits of the Beau Brummels	1976	3.75	7.50	15.00

POST

❏ 6000	The Beau Brummels Sing	196?	3.75	7.50	15.00

RHINO

❏ RNLP-101	The Best of the Beau Brummels	1981	2.50	5.00	10.00
❏ RNLP-102	Introducing the Beau Brummels	1981	2.50	5.00	10.00
❏ RNLP-104	From the Vaults	1981	3.00	6.00	12.00
❏ RNLP-70171	The Best of the Beau Brummels (Golden Archive Series)	1986	2.50	5.00	10.00

SUNDAZED

❏ LP 5088	North Beach Legends	2001	3.00	6.00	12.00
❏ LP 5089	Gentle Wanderin' Ways	2001	3.00	6.00	12.00

VAULT

❏ LP-114 [M]	Best of the Beau Brummels	1967	6.25	12.50	25.00
❏ SLP-114 [S]	Best of the Beau Brummels	1967	6.25	12.50	25.00
❏ SLP-121	Beau Brummels, Vol. 44	1968	6.25	12.50	25.00

WARNER BROS.

❏ W 1644 [M]	Beau Brummels '66	1966	5.00	10.00	20.00
❏ WS 1644 [S]	Beau Brummels '66	1966	6.25	12.50	25.00
❏ W 1692 [M]	Triangle	1967	5.00	10.00	20.00
❏ WS 1692 [S]	Triangle	1967	6.25	12.50	25.00
❏ WS 1760	Bradley's Barn	1968	6.25	12.50	25.00
❏ BS 2842	The Beau Brummels	1975	5.00	10.00	20.00

BEAU COUP

AMHERST

❏ AMH 3316	Born and Raised on Rock-n-Roll	1987	3.75	7.50	15.00

BEAUREGARDE

EMPIRE

❏ (no #)	Beauregarde	1969	25.00	50.00	100.00

SOUND

❏ 7104	Beauregarde	1969	20.00	40.00	80.00

BEAVER, PAUL

RAPTURE

❏ 11111	Perchance to Dream	196?	12.50	25.00	50.00

BEAVER AND KRAUSE

LIMELIGHT

❏ 86069	Ragnarok — Electronic Funk	1969	7.50	15.00	30.00

WARNER BROS.

❏ WS 1850	In a Wild Sanctuary	1969	3.75	7.50	15.00
❏ WS 1909	Gandharva	1970	3.75	7.50	15.00
❏ BS 2624	All Good Men	1972	3.75	7.50	15.00

BECHET, SIDNEY

ATLANTIC

❏ ALS-118 [10]	Sidney Bechet Solos	1952	30.00	60.00	120.00
❏ 1206 [M]	Sidney Bechet Duets	1956	20.00	40.00	80.00

—With Muggsy Spanier

BLUE NOTE

❏ BLP-1201 [M]	Jazz Classics, Volume 1	1955	25.00	50.00	100.00

—Regular edition, Lexington Ave. address on label

❏ BLP-1201 [M]	Jazz Classics, Volume 1	1955	37.50	75.00	150.00

—"Deep groove" version (deep indentation under label on both sides)

❏ BLP-1202 [M]	Jazz Classics, Volume 2	1955	25.00	50.00	100.00

—Regular edition, Lexington Ave. address on label

❏ BLP-1202 [M]	Jazz Classics, Volume 2	1955	37.50	75.00	150.00

—"Deep groove" version (deep indentation under label on both sides)

❏ BLP-1203 [M]	Giant of Jazz, Volume 1	1955	25.00	50.00	100.00

—Regular edition, Lexington Ave. address on label

❏ BLP-1203 [M]	Giant of Jazz, Volume 1	1955	37.50	75.00	150.00

—"Deep groove" version (deep indentation under label on both sides)

❏ BLP-1204 [M]	Giant of Jazz, Volume 2	1955	25.00	50.00	100.00

—Regular edition, Lexington Ave. address on label

❏ BLP-1204 [M]	Giant of Jazz, Volume 2	1955	37.50	75.00	150.00

—"Deep groove" version (deep indentation under label on both sides)

❏ BLP-1207 [M]	The Fabulous Sidney Bechet	1956	20.00	40.00	80.00

—Regular edition, Lexington Ave. address on label

❏ BLP-1207 [M]	The Fabulous Sidney Bechet	1956	30.00	60.00	120.00

—"Deep groove" version (deep indentation under label on both sides)

❏ BLP-7001 [10]	Sidney Bechet's Blue Note Jazz Men	1950	100.00	200.00	400.00
❏ BLP-7002 [10]	Jazz Classics, Volume 1	1950	62.50	125.00	250.00
❏ BLP-7003 [10]	Jazz Classics, Volume 2	1950	62.50	125.00	250.00
❏ BLP-7008 [10]	Days Beyond Recall	1951	62.50	125.00	250.00
❏ BLP-7009 [10]	Sidney Bechet with the Blue Note Jazz Men	1951	62.50	125.00	250.00
❏ BLP-7014 [10]	Sidney Bechet's Blue Note Jazz Men, Volume 2	1951	62.50	125.00	250.00
❏ BLP-7020 [10]	The Fabulous Sidney Bechet and His Hot Six	1952	62.50	125.00	250.00
❏ BLP-7022 [10]	The Port of Harlem Six	1952	62.50	125.00	250.00
❏ BLP-7024 [10]	Jazz Festival Concert, Paris 1952 — Volume 1	1953	62.50	125.00	250.00
❏ BLP-7025 [10]	Jazz Festival Concert, Paris 1952 — Volume 2	1953	62.50	125.00	250.00

Number	Title (A Side/B Side)	Yr	VG	VG+	NM
❑ BLP-7026 [10]	Dixie by the Fabulous Sidney Bechet	1953	62.50	125.00	250.00
❑ BLP-7029 [10]	Olympia Concert, Paris 1954 — Volume 1	1954	62.50	125.00	250.00
❑ BLP-7030 [10]	Olympia Concert, Paris 1954 — Volume 2	1954	62.50	125.00	250.00
BRUNSWICK					
❑ BL 54037 [M]	Sidney Bechet in Paris	1958	12.50	25.00	50.00
❑ BL 54048 [M]	The Sidney Bechet Story	1959	10.00	20.00	40.00
COLUMBIA					
❑ CL 836 [M]	Grand Master of the Soprano Sax and Clarinet	1956	12.50	25.00	50.00
—Red and black label with six "eye" logos					
❑ CL 1410 [M]	Sidney Bechet In Concert at the Brussels Fair	1960	7.50	15.00	30.00
—Red and black label with six "eye" logos					
COMMODORE					
❑ FL-20020 [10]	New Orleans Style, Old and New	1952	30.00	60.00	120.00
DIAL					
❑ LP-301 [10]	Black Stick	195?	75.00	150.00	300.00
❑ LP-302 [10]	Sidney Bechet with Wally Bishop's Orchestra	195?	75.00	150.00	300.00
GOOD TIME JAZZ					
❑ L-12013 [M]	King of the Soprano Saxophone	1955	12.50	25.00	50.00
JAZZ PANORAMA					
❑ 1801 [10]	Sidney Bechet, Vol. 1	1951	25.00	50.00	100.00
❑ 1809 [10]	Sidney Bechet, Vol. 2	1951	25.00	50.00	100.00
JOLLY ROGER					
❑ 5028 [10]	Sidney Bechet	1954	12.50	25.00	50.00
LONDON					
❑ WV 91050 [10]	La Nuit Est Une Sorciere	1955	15.00	30.00	60.00
MOSAIC					
❑ MR6-110 [(6)]	The Complete Blue Note Recordings of Sidney Bechet	199?	25.00	50.00	100.00
RCA VICTOR					
❑ LPT-22 [10]	Sidney Bechet	1951	37.50	75.00	150.00
❑ LPT-31 [10]	Treasury of Immortal Performances	1951	37.50	75.00	150.00
❑ LPV-510 [M]	Bechet of New Orleans	1965	5.00	10.00	20.00
❑ LPV-535 [M]	Blue Bechet	1966	5.00	10.00	20.00
REPRISE					
❑ R-6076 [M]	The Immortal Sidney Bechet	1963	6.25	12.50	25.00
❑ R9-6076 [R]	The Immortal Sidney Bechet	1963	5.00	10.00	20.00
RIVERSIDE					
❑ RLP-2516 [10]	Sidney Bechet and His Soprano Sax	1955	62.50	125.00	250.00
RONDO-LETTE					
❑ A 24 [M]	Jam Session Vintage 1946	1953	7.50	15.00	30.00
SAVOY					
❑ MG-15013 [10]	Sidney Bechet	1952	50.00	100.00	200.00
STORYVILLE					
❑ STLP-301 [10]	Sidney Bechet at Storyville, Vol. 1	1954	50.00	100.00	200.00
❑ STLP-306 [10]	Sidney Bechet at Storyville, Vol. 2	1954	50.00	100.00	200.00
❑ STLP-902 [M]	Sidney Bechet at Storyville	1955	12.50	25.00	50.00
"X"					
❑ LVA-3024 [10]	Sidney Bechet and the New Orleans Feetwarmers	1954	25.00	50.00	100.00

BECHET, SIDNEY, AND EDDIE CONDON

Number	Title (A Side/B Side)	Yr	VG	VG+	NM
SAVOY					
❑ MG-12208 [M]	We Dig Dixieland	196?	5.00	10.00	20.00

BECHET, SIDNEY / OMER SIMEON

Number	Title (A Side/B Side)	Yr	VG	VG+	NM
JAZZTONE					
❑ J-1213 [M]	Jazz A La Creole	1955	10.00	20.00	40.00

BECHET, SIDNEY, AND MARTIAL SOLAL

Number	Title (A Side/B Side)	Yr	VG	VG+	NM
WORLD PACIFIC					
❑ PJ-1236 [M]	Young Ideas	1957	20.00	40.00	80.00
❑ WP-1236 [M]	Young Ideas	1957	12.50	25.00	50.00
—Reissue with new prefix					

BECHET, SIDNEY, AND MUGGSY SPANIER

Number	Title (A Side/B Side)	Yr	VG	VG+	NM
ALLEGRO ELITE					
❑ 4123 [10]	Bechet-Spanier Quartet	1956	10.00	20.00	40.00

BECK

Number	Title (A Side/B Side)	Yr	VG	VG+	NM
BONG LOAD					
❑ BL 12	Mellow Gold	1993	3.00	6.00	12.00
❑ BL 30	Odelay	1996	3.00	6.00	12.00
❑ BL 39	Mutations	1999	3.75	7.50	15.00
—Includes bonus 7-inch single with sleeve					
❑ BL 46	Midnite Vultures	2000	3.75	7.50	15.00
FINGERPAINT					
❑ 02 [10]	A Western Harvest Field by Moonlight	1992	5.00	10.00	20.00
—First 3,000 contain a unique insert fingerpainted by Beck and friends at the record release party					
❑ 02 [10]	A Western Harvest Field by Moonlight	1995	2.50	5.00	10.00
—Later pressings do not contain a fingerpainted insert					
FLIPSIDE					
❑ 660 [(2)]	Stereopathetic Soulmanure	2000	3.00	6.00	12.00
—Vinyl issue of 1994 CD compilation					
K					
❑ KLP 28	One Foot in the Grave	1994	2.50	5.00	10.00

BECK, JEFF

Includes the Jeff Beck Group, of whom ROD STEWART was lead singer. Also see BECK, BOGERT AND APPICE; THE YARDBIRDS.

Number	Title (A Side/B Side)	Yr	VG	VG+	NM
ACCORD					
❑ SN-7141	Early Anthology	1981	2.50	5.00	10.00
EPIC					
❑ AS 151 [DJ]	Everything You Always Wanted to Hear by Jeff Beck But Were Afraid to Ask For	1977	5.00	10.00	20.00
—Promo-only sampler					
❑ A2S 850 [(2)DJ]	Then and Now	1981	6.25	12.50	25.00
—Promo-only sampler					
❑ BN 26413	Truth	1973	2.50	5.00	10.00
—Orange label					

Number	Title (A Side/B Side)	Yr	VG	VG+	NM
❑ BN 26413 [M]	Truth	1968	10.00	20.00	40.00
—Mono is promo only with stereo number; cover has "Mono" sticker covering the word "Stereo"					
❑ BN 26413 [S]	Truth	1968	3.75	7.50	15.00
—Yellow label					
❑ PE 26413	Truth	198?	2.00	4.00	8.00
—Reissue with new prefix					
❑ BN 26478	Beck-Ola	1969	3.75	7.50	15.00
—Yellow label					
❑ BN 26478	Beck-Ola	1973	2.50	5.00	10.00
—Orange label					
❑ PE 26478	Beck-Ola	197?	2.00	4.00	8.00
—Reissue with new prefix					
❑ PE 30973	Rough and Ready	198?	2.00	4.00	8.00
—Budget-line reissue					
❑ EQ 30993 [Q]	Rough and Ready	1972	5.00	10.00	20.00
❑ KE 30993	Rough and Ready	1971	3.75	7.50	15.00
—Yellow label					
❑ KE 30993	Rough and Ready	1973	2.50	5.00	10.00
—Orange label					
❑ EQ 31331 [Q]	Jeff Beck Group	1972	5.00	10.00	20.00
❑ KE 31331	Jeff Beck Group	1972	3.75	7.50	15.00
—Yellow label					
❑ KE 31331	Jeff Beck Group	1973	2.50	5.00	10.00
—Orange label					
❑ PE 31331	Jeff Beck Group	198?	2.00	4.00	8.00
—Budget-line reissue					
❑ PE 33409	Blow by Blow	1975	2.50	5.00	10.00
—Orange label, no bar code on cover					
❑ PE 33409	Blow by Blow	198?	2.00	4.00	8.00
—Reissue with dark blue label and bar code on cover					
❑ PEQ 33409 [Q]	Blow by Blow	1975	5.00	10.00	20.00
❑ BG 33779 [(2)]	Truth/Beck-Ola	1975	3.00	6.00	12.00
❑ PE 33849	Wired	1976	2.50	5.00	10.00
—Orange label, no bar code on cover					
❑ PE 33849	Wired	1979	2.00	4.00	8.00
—Reissue with dark blue label; with or without bar code on cover					
❑ PEQ 33849 [Q]	Wired	1976	5.00	10.00	20.00
❑ PE 34433	Jeff Beck with the Jan Hammer Group Live	1977	2.50	5.00	10.00
—Orange label, no bar code on cover					
❑ PE 34433	Jeff Beck with the Jan Hammer Group Live	198?	2.00	4.00	8.00
—Reissue with dark blue label and bar code on cover					
❑ FE 35684	There and Back	1980	2.50	5.00	10.00
❑ PE 35684	There and Back	1985	2.00	4.00	8.00
—Budget-line reissue					
❑ FE 39483	Flash	1985	2.50	5.00	10.00
❑ HE 43409	Blow by Blow	1980	7.50	15.00	30.00
—Half-speed mastered edition					
❑ HE 43849	Wired	198?	7.50	15.00	30.00
—Half-speed mastered edition					
❑ FE 44313	Jeff Beck's Guitar Shop	1989	3.75	7.50	15.00

BECK, PIA

Number	Title (A Side/B Side)	Yr	VG	VG+	NM
EPIC					
❑ LN 3269 [M]	Dutch Treat	1956	10.00	20.00	40.00

BECK, BOGERT & APPICE

Number	Title (A Side/B Side)	Yr	VG	VG+	NM
EPIC					
❑ CQ 32140 [Q]	Beck, Bogert & Appice	1973	5.00	10.00	20.00
❑ KE 32140	Beck, Bogert & Appice	1973	2.50	5.00	10.00
—Orange label					
❑ KE 32140	Beck, Bogert & Appice	1973	3.75	7.50	15.00
—Yellow label					
❑ PE 32140	Beck, Bogert & Appice	198?	2.00	4.00	8.00
—Budget-line reissue					

BEDIENT, JACK

Number	Title (A Side/B Side)	Yr	VG	VG+	NM
EXECUTIVE PRODUCTIONS					
❑ (no #) [M]	Jack Bedient	196?	20.00	40.00	80.00
FANTASY					
❑ 3365 [M]	Live at Harvey's	1965	15.00	30.00	60.00
SATORI					
❑ LP 1001 [M]	Where Did She Go?	1966	15.00	30.00	60.00
TROPHY					
❑ 101 [M]	Two Sides of Jack Bedient	1964	15.00	30.00	60.00

BEDLAM

Number	Title (A Side/B Side)	Yr	VG	VG+	NM
CHRYSALIS					
❑ CHR-1048	Bedlam	1973	6.25	12.50	25.00

BEE, DAVID

Number	Title (A Side/B Side)	Yr	VG	VG+	NM
BALLY					
❑ BAL-12005 [M]	Belgian Jazz	1956	7.50	15.00	30.00
JUBILEE					
❑ JLP-1076 [M]	Dixieland at the World's Fair	1958	6.25	12.50	25.00

BEE, MOLLY

Number	Title (A Side/B Side)	Yr	VG	VG+	NM
ACCORD					
❑ 7901	Sounds Fine to Me	1982	2.50	5.00	10.00
CAPITOL					
❑ T 1097 [M]	Young Romance	1958	10.00	20.00	40.00
GRANITE					
❑ 1002	Good Golly Ms. Molly	1974	3.00	6.00	12.00
MGM					
❑ E-4303 [M]	It's Great, It's Molly Bee	1965	5.00	10.00	20.00
❑ SE-4303 [S]	It's Great, It's Molly Bee	1965	6.25	12.50	25.00
❑ E-4423 [M]	Swingin' Country	1967	5.00	10.00	20.00
❑ SE-4423 [S]	Swingin' Country	1967	6.25	12.50	25.00

BEE GEES

Also see ROBIN GIBB.

Number	Title (A Side/B Side)	Yr	VG	VG+	NM
ATCO					
❑ 33-223 [M]	Bee Gees' 1st	1967	7.50	15.00	30.00

B

Number	Title (A Side/B Side)	Yr	VG	VG+	NM
❑ SD 33-223	Bee Gees' 1st	1969	2.50	5.00	10.00
—Yellow label reissue					
❑ SD 33-223 [S]	Bee Gees' 1st	1967	5.00	10.00	20.00
—Brown and purple label original					
❑ 33-233 [M]	Horizontal	1968	7.50	15.00	30.00
❑ SD 33-233	Horizontal	1969	2.50	5.00	10.00
—Yellow label reissue					
❑ SD 33-233 [S]	Horizontal	1968	5.00	10.00	20.00
—Brown and purple label original					
❑ 33-253 [M]	Idea	1968	12.50	25.00	50.00
—White label promo only					
❑ SD 33-253	Idea	1969	2.50	5.00	10.00
—Yellow label reissue					
❑ SD 33-253 [S]	Idea	1968	5.00	10.00	20.00
—Brown and purple label original					
❑ 33-264 [M]	Rare, Precious & Beautiful	1968	7.50	15.00	30.00
—White label promo only					
❑ SD 33-264	Rare, Precious & Beautiful	1969	2.50	5.00	10.00
—Yellow label reissue					
❑ SD 33-264 [R]	Rare, Precious & Beautiful	1968	3.75	7.50	15.00
—Brown and purple label original					
❑ 33-292 [M]	Best of Bee Gees	1969	7.50	15.00	30.00
—White label promo only					
❑ SD 33-292	Best of Bee Gees	1969	3.00	6.00	12.00
❑ 33-321 [M]	Rare, Precious & Beautiful, Volume 2	1970	7.50	15.00	30.00
—White label promo only					
❑ SD 33-321 [R]	Rare, Precious & Beautiful, Volume 2	1970	3.00	6.00	12.00
❑ SD 33-327	Cucumber Castle	1970	3.00	6.00	12.00
❑ 33-353 [M]	2 Years On	1971	7.50	15.00	30.00
—White label promo only; "DJ Copy Monaural" sticker on cover					
❑ SD 33-353 [S]	2 Years On	1971	3.00	6.00	12.00
❑ SD 2-702 [(2)]	Odessa	1969	10.00	20.00	40.00
—Red felt cover					
❑ SD 2-702 [(2)]	Odessa	1969	20.00	40.00	80.00
—Record club editions with plain red cover					
❑ SD 7003	Trafalgar	1971	3.00	6.00	12.00
❑ SD 7012	To Whom It May Concern	1972	3.00	6.00	12.00

MOBILE FIDELITY

Number	Title (A Side/B Side)	Yr	VG	VG+	NM
❑ 1-263	Trafalgar	1996	10.00	20.00	40.00
—Audiophile vinyl					

NAUTILUS

Number	Title (A Side/B Side)	Yr	VG	VG+	NM
❑ NR-17	Spirits Having Flown	1981	7.50	15.00	30.00
❑ NR-42	Living Eyes	1982	25.00	50.00	100.00
—Record was never released; value is for test pressings					

PICKWICK

Number	Title (A Side/B Side)	Yr	VG	VG+	NM
❑ BAN-90011 [R]	Turn Around, Look at Me	1978	2.00	4.00	8.00
—Reissue of Australian recordings					
❑ BAN-90021 [R]	Monday's Rain	1978	2.00	4.00	8.00
—Reissue of Australian recordings					
❑ BAN-90031 [R]	Take Hold of That Star	1978	2.00	4.00	8.00
—Reissue of Australian recordings					
❑ BAN-90041 [R]	Peace of Mind	1978	2.00	4.00	8.00
—Reissue of Australian recordings; tracks on this LP were making their first appearance in the U.S.					

RSO

Number	Title (A Side/B Side)	Yr	VG	VG+	NM
❑ SMP-1 [DJ]	The Words and Music of Maurice, Barry and Robin Gibb	1979	12.50	25.00	50.00
—Promo-only publisher's sampler					
❑ PRO 033 [DJ]	Saturday Night Fever Special Disco Versions	1978	12.50	25.00	50.00
—Promo-only sampler; contains an otherwise unavailable extended version of "Stayin' Alive"					
❑ SO 870	Life in a Tin Can	1973	2.50	5.00	10.00
❑ SO 874	Best of Bee Gees	1973	2.50	5.00	10.00
—Reissue of Atco SD 33-292					
❑ SO 875	Best of Bee Gees, Vol. 2	1973	2.50	5.00	10.00
❑ PUB-1000 [DJ]	Unichappell Publisher's Sampler	1980	12.50	25.00	50.00
❑ RPO 1008 [DJ]	Select Disco Cuts from "Spirits Having Flown"	1979	7.50	15.00	30.00
❑ RS-1-3003	Children of the World	1976	2.50	5.00	10.00
❑ RS-1-3006	Bee Gees Gold, Volume One	1976	2.50	5.00	10.00
❑ RS-1-3007	Odessa	1976	2.50	5.00	10.00
—Condensed version of Atco original					
❑ RS-1-3024	Main Course	1977	2.00	4.00	8.00
❑ RS-1-3041	Spirits Having Flown	1979	2.50	5.00	10.00
—Some pressings have a cardboard innersleeve, others a paper innersleeve. No difference in value.					
❑ RS-1-3042 [PD]	Spirits Having Flown	1979	3.75	7.50	15.00
❑ RS-1-3098	Living Eyes	1981	2.50	5.00	10.00
❑ RS-2-3901 [(2)]	Here At Last...Bee Gees...Live	1977	3.00	6.00	12.00
❑ RS-2-4200 [(2)]	Bee Gees' Greatest	1979	3.00	6.00	12.00
❑ SO 4800	Mr. Natural	1974	2.50	5.00	10.00
❑ SO 4807	Main Course	1975	2.50	5.00	10.00
❑ 823274-1 [(2)]	Here At Last...Bee Gees...Live	1984	2.50	5.00	10.00
❑ 823658-1	Children of the World	1984	2.00	4.00	8.00
❑ 823659-1	Bee Gees Gold, Volume One	1984	2.00	4.00	8.00
❑ 825390-1 [(2)]	Bee Gees' Greatest	1984	2.50	5.00	10.00
—Gatefold replaced by single-pocket cover					

WARNER BROS.

Number	Title (A Side/B Side)	Yr	VG	VG+	NM
❑ 25541	E.S.P.	1987	2.50	5.00	10.00
❑ 25887	One	1989	3.00	6.00	12.00

BEETHOVEN SOUL
DOT

Number	Title (A Side/B Side)	Yr	VG	VG+	NM
❑ DLP-3821 [M]	Beethoven Soul	1967	6.25	12.50	25.00
❑ DLP-25821 [S]	Beethoven Soul	1967	6.25	12.50	25.00

BEGINNING OF THE END, THE
ALSTON

Number	Title (A Side/B Side)	Yr	VG	VG+	NM
❑ SD 33-379	Funky Nassau	1971	5.00	10.00	20.00

BEIDERBECKE, BIX
COLUMBIA

Number	Title (A Side/B Side)	Yr	VG	VG+	NM
❑ CL 507 [M]	The Bix Beiderbecke Story, Volume 1: Bix and His Gang	1953	10.00	20.00	40.00
—Maroon label, gold print					
❑ GL 507 [M]	The Bix Beiderbecke Story, Volume 1: Bix and His Gang	1952	12.50	25.00	50.00
—Black label, silver print					
❑ CL 508 [M]	The Bix Beiderbecke Story, Volume 2: Bix and Tram	1953	10.00	20.00	40.00
—Maroon label, gold print					
❑ GL 508 [M]	The Bix Beiderbecke Story, Volume 2: Bix and Tram	1952	12.50	25.00	50.00
—Black label, silver print					
❑ CL 509 [M]	The Bix Beiderbecke Story, Volume 3: The Whiteman Years	1953	10.00	20.00	40.00
—Maroon label, gold print					
❑ GL 509 [M]	The Bix Beiderbecke Story, Volume 3: The Whiteman Years	1952	12.50	25.00	50.00
—Black label, silver print					
❑ CL 844 [M]	The Bix Beiderbecke Story, Volume 1: Bix and His Gang	1956	7.50	15.00	30.00
—Red and black label with six "eye" logos					
❑ CL 844 [M]	The Bix Beiderbecke Story, Volume 1: Bix and His Gang	1963	5.00	10.00	20.00
—"Guaranteed High Fidelity" label					
❑ CL 845 [M]	The Bix Beiderbecke Story, Volume 2: Bix and Tram	1956	7.50	15.00	30.00
—Red and black label with six "eye" logos					
❑ CL 845 [M]	The Bix Beiderbecke Story, Volume 2: Bix and Tram	1963	5.00	10.00	20.00
—"Guaranteed High Fidelity" label					
❑ CL 846 [M]	The Bix Beiderbecke Story, Volume 3: The Whiteman Years	1956	7.50	15.00	30.00
—Red and black label with six "eye" logos					
❑ CL 846 [M]	The Bix Beiderbecke Story, Volume 3: The Whiteman Years	1963	5.00	10.00	20.00
—"Guaranteed High Fidelity" label					

COLUMBIA MASTERWORKS

Number	Title (A Side/B Side)	Yr	VG	VG+	NM
❑ ML 4811 [M]	The Bix Beiderbecke Story, Volume 1	1950	17.50	35.00	70.00
❑ ML 4812 [M]	The Bix Beiderbecke Story, Volume 2	1950	17.50	35.00	70.00
❑ ML 4813 [M]	The Bix Beiderbecke Story, Volume 3	1950	17.50	35.00	70.00

JOLLY ROGER

Number	Title (A Side/B Side)	Yr	VG	VG+	NM
❑ 5010 [10]	Bix Beiderbecke	1954	12.50	25.00	50.00

RCA VICTOR

Number	Title (A Side/B Side)	Yr	VG	VG+	NM
❑ LPM-2323 [M]	The Bix Beiderbecke Legend	1961	6.25	12.50	25.00
—"Long Play" on label					

RIVERSIDE

Number	Title (A Side/B Side)	Yr	VG	VG+	NM
❑ RLP 12-123 [M]	Bix Beiderbecke and the Wolverines	195?	7.50	15.00	30.00
—Blue label with microphone logo					
❑ RLP 12-123 [M]	Bix Beiderbecke and the Wolverines	1956	12.50	25.00	50.00
—White label, blue print					
❑ RLP-1023 [10]	Early Bix	1954	20.00	40.00	80.00
❑ RLP-1050 [10]	Bix Beiderbecke and the Wolverines	1954	20.00	40.00	80.00

BEL-AIRE GIRLS, THE
EVEREST

Number	Title (A Side/B Side)	Yr	VG	VG+	NM
❑ STBR-1081 [S]	The Bel-Aire Girls Sing Along with the Teen-Agers	1960	20.00	40.00	80.00
❑ LPBR-5081 [M]	The Bel-Aire Girls Sing Along with the Teen-Agers	1960	15.00	30.00	60.00

BEL-AIRE POPS ORCHESTRA, THE
LIBERTY

Number	Title (A Side/B Side)	Yr	VG	VG+	NM
❑ LRP-3414 [M]	Jan and Dean's Pop Symphony No. 1	1965	30.00	60.00	120.00
❑ LST-7414 [S]	Jan and Dean's Pop Symphony No. 1	1965	50.00	100.00	200.00

BELAFONTE, HARRY
COLUMBIA

Number	Title (A Side/B Side)	Yr	VG	VG+	NM
❑ FC 37489	Loving You Is Where I Belong	1981	2.50	5.00	10.00

DCC COMPACT CLASSICS

Number	Title (A Side/B Side)	Yr	VG	VG+	NM
❑ LPZ-2039	Jump Up Calypso	1997	15.00	30.00	60.00
—Audiophile vinyl					

EMI

Number	Title (A Side/B Side)	Yr	VG	VG+	NM
❑ E1-92247	Belafonte '89	1989	3.00	6.00	12.00

EMI MANHATAN

Number	Title (A Side/B Side)	Yr	VG	VG+	NM
❑ E1-46971	Paradise in Gazankulu	1988	3.00	6.00	12.00

PAIR

Number	Title (A Side/B Side)	Yr	VG	VG+	NM
❑ PDL2-1060 [(2)]	The Belafonte Song Book	1986	3.00	6.00	12.00

RCA CAMDEN

Number	Title (A Side/B Side)	Yr	VG	VG+	NM
❑ ACL1-0502	Abraham, Martin and John	1974	2.50	5.00	10.00
❑ CAS-2599	Harry	1972	2.50	5.00	10.00

RCA CUSTOM EDITION

Number	Title (A Side/B Side)	Yr	VG	VG+	NM
❑ DRL1-0068	I Wish You a Merry Christmas	1973	3.75	7.50	15.00
—Reissue of LSP-2424 with two tracks deleted					

RCA VICTOR

Number	Title (A Side/B Side)	Yr	VG	VG+	NM
❑ APL1-0094	Play Me	1973	3.00	6.00	12.00
❑ ANL1-0979	Pure Gold	1975	2.50	5.00	10.00
❑ LPM-1006 [M]	Belafonte Sings the Blues	1954	12.50	25.00	50.00
—Reissued in 1958 with the same number, then re-recorded in 1959					
❑ LPM-1022 [M]	"Mark Twain" and Other Folk Favorites	1954	12.50	25.00	50.00
❑ LSP-1022(e) [R]	"Mark Twain" and Other Folk Favorites	196?	3.00	6.00	12.00
❑ LPM-1150 [M]	Belafonte	1955	12.50	25.00	50.00
❑ LSP-1150(e) [R]	Belafonte	196?	3.00	6.00	12.00
❑ AFL1-1248	Calypso	1977	2.50	5.00	10.00
—Reissue with new prefix					
❑ LPM-1248 [M]	Calypso	1956	7.50	15.00	30.00
❑ LSP-1248(e) [R]	Calypso	196?	3.00	6.00	12.00
❑ LPM-1402 [M]	An Evening with Belafonte	1957	6.25	12.50	25.00
❑ LSP-1402(e) [R]	An Evening with Belafonte	1960	3.00	6.00	12.00
—Dog on top					
❑ LSP-1402(e) [R]	An Evening with Belafonte	1969	2.50	5.00	10.00
—Orange label					
❑ ANL1-1434	An Evening with Belafonte	1976	2.50	5.00	10.00
—Reissue of LSP-1402					

Number	Title (A Side/B Side)	Yr	VG	VG+	NM
❏ LPM-1505 [M]	Belafonte Sings of the Caribbean	1957	7.50	15.00	30.00
❏ LSP-1505(e) [R]	Belafonte Sings of the Caribbean	196?	3.00	6.00	12.00
❏ LOC-1507 [M]	Porgy and Bess	1959	5.00	10.00	20.00
❏ LSO-1507 [S]	Porgy and Bess	1959	6.25	12.50	25.00
—With Lena Horne					
❏ LPM-1887 [M]	To Wish You a Merry Christmas	1958	6.25	12.50	25.00
❏ LSP-1887 [S]	To Wish You a Merry Christmas	1958	10.00	20.00	40.00
❏ LPM-1927 [M]	Love Is a Gentle Thing	1959	5.00	10.00	20.00
❏ LSP-1927 [S]	Love Is a Gentle Thing	1959	6.25	12.50	25.00
❏ LPM-1972 [M]	Belafonte Sings the Blues	1959	5.00	10.00	20.00
❏ LSP-1972	Belafonte Sings the Blues	199?	6.25	12.50	25.00
—Classic Records reissue on audiophile vinyl					
❏ LSP-1972 [S]	Belafonte Sings the Blues	1959	6.25	12.50	25.00
❏ LPM-2022 [M]	My Lord What a Mornin'	1960	5.00	10.00	20.00
❏ LSP-2022 [S]	My Lord What a Mornin'	1960	6.25	12.50	25.00
❏ LPM-2194 [M]	Swing Dat Hammer	1961	5.00	10.00	20.00
❏ LSP-2194 [S]	Swing Dat Hammer	1961	6.25	12.50	25.00
❏ LPM-2309 [M]	At Home and Abroad	1961	5.00	10.00	20.00
❏ LSP-2309 [S]	At Home and Abroad	1961	6.25	12.50	25.00
❏ ANL1-2324	The Midnight Special	1976	2.50	5.00	10.00
—Reissue of LSP-2449					
❏ LPM-2388 [M]	Jump Up Calypso	1961	5.00	10.00	20.00
❏ LSP-2388 [S]	Jump Up Calypso	1961	6.25	12.50	25.00
❏ LPM-2449 [M]	The Midnight Special	1962	7.50	15.00	30.00
❏ LSP-2449 [S]	The Midnight Special	1962	10.00	20.00	40.00
—The above LP features Bob Dylan on harmonica on the title track, his first appearance on record					
❏ CPL1-2469	A Legendary Performer	1977	2.50	5.00	10.00
❏ LPM-2574 [M]	The Many Moods of Belafonte	1962	5.00	10.00	20.00
❏ LSP-2574 [S]	The Many Moods of Belafonte	196?	5.00	10.00	20.00
—"Stereo" on black label, "RCA Victor" in white					
❏ LSP-2574 [S]	The Many Moods of Belafonte	1962	6.25	12.50	25.00
—"Living Stereo" on label, "RCA Victor" in silver					
❏ LSP-2574 [S]	The Many Moods of Belafonte	1969	3.00	6.00	12.00
—Orange label					
❏ LPM-2626 [M]	To Wish You a Merry Christmas	1962	5.00	10.00	20.00
—Reissue of LPM-1887 with new cover and one additional track					
❏ LSP-2626 [S]	To Wish You a Merry Christmas	1962	6.25	12.50	25.00
❏ LPM-2695 [M]	Streets I Have Walked	1963	5.00	10.00	20.00
❏ LSP-2695 [S]	Streets I Have Walked	1963	6.25	12.50	25.00
❏ LPM-2953 [M]	Ballads, Blues and Boasters	1964	3.75	7.50	15.00
❏ LSP-2953 [S]	Ballads, Blues and Boasters	1964	5.00	10.00	20.00
❏ LPM-3415 [M]	An Evening with Belafonte/Mouskouri	1966	3.75	7.50	15.00
❏ LSP-3415 [S]	An Evening with Belafonte/Mouskouri	1966	5.00	10.00	20.00
—With Nana Mouskouri					
❏ LPM-3420 [M]	An Evening with Belafonte/Makeba	1965	3.75	7.50	15.00
❏ LSP-3420 [S]	An Evening with Belafonte/Makeba	1965	5.00	10.00	20.00
—With Miriam Makeba					
❏ LPM-3571 [M]	In My Quiet Room	1966	3.00	6.00	12.00
❏ LSP-3571 [S]	In My Quiet Room	1966	3.75	7.50	15.00
❏ LPM-3658 [M]	Calypso in Brass	1967	3.00	6.00	12.00
❏ LSP-3658 [S]	Calypso in Brass	1967	3.75	7.50	15.00
❏ LPM-3779 [M]	Belafonte on Campus	1967	3.00	6.00	12.00
❏ LSP-3779 [S]	Belafonte on Campus	1967	3.75	7.50	15.00
❏ AYL1-3801(e) [R]	Calypso	1980	2.00	4.00	8.00
❏ AYL1-3860(e) [R]	Pure Gold	1980	2.00	4.00	8.00
❏ LPM-3938 [M]	Belafonte Sings of Love	1968	3.75	7.50	15.00
❏ LSP-3938 [S]	Belafonte Sings of Love	1968	3.75	7.50	15.00
❏ LSP-4255	Homeward Bound	1969	3.75	7.50	15.00
❏ LSP-4301	By Request	1970	3.00	6.00	12.00
❏ LSP-4481	Warm Touch	1971	3.00	6.00	12.00
❏ LSP-4521	Calypso Carnival	1971	3.00	6.00	12.00
❏ LOC-6006 [(2)M]	Belafonte at Carnegie Hall	1959	6.25	12.50	25.00
❏ LSO-6006 [(2)S]	Belafonte at Carnegie Hall	1959	25.00	50.00	100.00
❏ LSO-6006 [(2)S]	Belafonte at Carnegie Hall	1996	10.00	20.00	40.00
—Classic Records reissue on audiophile vinyl					
❏ LOC-6007 [(2)M]	Belafonte Returns to Carnegie Hall	1960	5.00	10.00	20.00
❏ LSO-6007 [(2)]	Belafonte Returns to Carnegie Hall	1996	10.00	20.00	40.00
—Classic Records reissue on audiophile vinyl					
❏ LSO-6007 [(2)S]	Belafonte Returns to Carnegie Hall	1960	12.50	25.00	50.00
—The above LP also has tracks by Odetta, Miriam Makeba and The Chad Mitchell Trio (the latter for the first time on record)					
❏ LOC-6009 [(2)M]	Belafonte at the Greek Theatre	1964	5.00	10.00	20.00
❏ LSO-6009 [(2)S]	Belafonte at the Greek Theatre	1964	12.50	25.00	50.00
❏ VPS-6024 [(2)]	This Is Harry Belafonte	1970	3.75	7.50	15.00
❏ VPSX-6077 [(2)]	Belafonte Live	1972	3.75	7.50	15.00

BELEW, CARL
BUCKBOARD

Number	Title (A Side/B Side)	Yr	VG	VG+	NM
❏ BBS 1014	Singing My Song	197?	2.50	5.00	10.00

DECCA

❏ DL 4074 [M]	Carl Belew	1960	6.25	12.50	25.00
❏ DL 74074 [S]	Carl Belew	1960	7.50	15.00	30.00

HILLTOP

❏ JM-6013 [M]	Another Lonely Night	1965	5.00	10.00	20.00
❏ JS-6013 [S]	Another Lonely Night	1965	5.00	10.00	20.00

PICCADILLY

❏ 3356	Big Time Gambling Man	198?	2.50	5.00	10.00

RCA VICTOR

❏ LPM-2848 [M]	Hello Out There	1964	5.00	10.00	20.00
❏ LSP-2848 [S]	Hello Out There	1964	6.25	12.50	25.00
❏ LPM-3381 [M]	Am I That Easy to Forget?	1965	5.00	10.00	20.00
❏ LSP-3381 [S]	Am I That Easy to Forget?	1965	6.25	12.50	25.00
❏ LPM-3919 [M]	Twelve Shades of Belew	1968	12.50	25.00	50.00
❏ LSP-3919 [S]	Twelve Shades of Belew	1968	5.00	10.00	20.00

VOCALION

❏ VL 3774 [M]	Country Songs	196?	3.00	6.00	12.00
❏ VL 3791 [M]	Lonely Street	1967	3.75	7.50	15.00
❏ VL 73774 [S]	Country Songs	196?	3.00	6.00	12.00
❏ VL 73791 [S]	Lonely Street	1967	3.00	6.00	12.00

WRANGLER

❏ WR 1007 [M]	Carl Belew	1962	7.50	15.00	30.00

Number	Title (A Side/B Side)	Yr	VG	VG+	NM
❏ WRS 31007 [S]	Carl Belew	1962	10.00	20.00	40.00

BELL, AARON
HERALD

❏ HLP-0100 [M]	Three Swinging Bells	1955	15.00	30.00	60.00

LION

❏ L-70111 [M]	Music from "77 Sunset Strip"	1959	6.25	12.50	25.00
❏ L-70112 [M]	Music from "Peter Gunn"	1959	6.25	12.50	25.00
❏ L-70113 [M]	Music from "Victory at Sea"	1959	6.25	12.50	25.00

RCA VICTOR

❏ LPM-1876 [M]	After the Party's Over	1958	12.50	25.00	50.00

BELL, ARCHIE, AND THE DRELLS
ATLANTIC

❏ 8181 [M]	Tighten Up	1968	12.50	25.00	50.00
❏ SD 8181 [S]	Tighten Up	1968	7.50	15.00	30.00
❏ SD 8204	I Can't Stop Dancing	1968	7.50	15.00	30.00
❏ SD 8226	There's Gonna Be a Showdown	1969	7.50	15.00	30.00

PHILADELPHIA INT'L.

❏ PZ 34323	Where Will You Go When the Party's Over	1976	2.50	5.00	10.00
❏ PZ 34855	Hard Not to Like It	1977	2.50	5.00	10.00
❏ JZ 36096	Strategy	1979	2.50	5.00	10.00

TSOP

❏ PZ 33844	Dance Your Troubles Away	1975	2.50	5.00	10.00

BELL, CHARLES
ATLANTIC

❏ SD 1400 [S]	Another Dimension	1963	5.00	10.00	20.00

COLUMBIA

❏ CL 1582 [M]	The Charles Bell Contemporary Jazz Quartet	1961	5.00	10.00	20.00
❏ CS 8382 [S]	The Charles Bell Contemporary Jazz Quartet	1961	6.25	12.50	25.00

GATEWAY

❏ S-7012 [S]	Charles Bell in Concert	1964	5.00	10.00	20.00

BELL, FREDDIE, AND THE BELL BOYS
MERCURY

❏ MG-20289 [M]	Rock and Roll... All Flavors	1957	50.00	100.00	200.00

20TH FOX

❏ TF-4146 [M]	Bells Are Swinging	1964	6.25	12.50	25.00
❏ TFS-4146 [S]	Bells Are Swinging	1964	7.50	15.00	30.00

BELL, GRAEME
ANGEL

❏ ANG.60002 [10]	Inside Jazz Down Under	1954	15.00	30.00	60.00

BELL, MARTY
RIVERSIDE

❏ RLP 12-206 [M]	The Voice of Marty Bell	1956	15.00	30.00	60.00
—White label, blue print					
❏ RLP 12-206 [M]	The Voice of Marty Bell	1957	10.00	20.00	40.00
—Blue label, microphone logo					

BELL, VINCENT
DECCA

❏ DL 4938 [M]	Pop Goes the Electric Sitar	1967	5.00	10.00	20.00
❏ DL 74938 [S]	Pop Goes the Electric Sitar	1967	3.75	7.50	15.00
❏ DL 75212	Airport Love Theme	1970	3.75	7.50	15.00

MUSICOR

❏ MM-3009 [M]	51 Motion Picture Favorites	1963	3.75	7.50	15.00
❏ MS-3009 [S]	51 Motion Picture Favorites	1963	5.00	10.00	20.00
❏ MM-3047 [M]	Big 16 Guitar Favorites	1965	3.75	7.50	15.00
❏ MS-3047 [S]	Big 16 Guitar Favorites	1965	5.00	10.00	20.00

VERVE

❏ V-8574 [M]	Whistle Stop	1964	3.75	7.50	15.00
❏ V6-8574 [S]	Whistle Stop	1964	5.00	10.00	20.00

BELL, WILLIAM
KAT FAMILY

❏ FZ 38643	Survivor	1983	2.50	5.00	10.00

MERCURY

❏ SRM-1-1146	Coming Back for More	1977	2.50	5.00	10.00
❏ SRM-1-1193	It's Time You Took Another Listen	1978	2.50	5.00	10.00

STAX

❏ 719 [M]	Soul of a Bell	1967	10.00	20.00	40.00
❏ S-719 [S]	Soul of a Bell	1967	12.50	25.00	50.00
❏ ST-2014 [M]	Bound to Happen	1969	12.50	25.00	50.00
—Mono is promo only					
❏ STS-2014 [S]	Bound to Happen	1969	7.50	15.00	30.00
❏ STS-2037	Wow...	1971	7.50	15.00	30.00
❏ STS-3005	Phases of Reality	1973	5.00	10.00	20.00
❏ STS-5502	Relating	1974	5.00	10.00	20.00
❏ MPS-8541	The Best of William Bell	1988	2.50	5.00	10.00

WRC

❏ WL-3007	On a Roll	1986	3.00	6.00	12.00

BELLETTO, AL
CAPITOL

❏ T 751 [M]	Half and Half	1956	12.50	25.00	50.00
❏ T 901 [M]	Whisper Not	1957	12.50	25.00	50.00
❏ T 6506 [M]	The Al Belletto Sextette	1955	15.00	30.00	60.00
❏ T 6514 [M]	Sounds and Songs	1955	15.00	30.00	60.00

KING

❏ 716 [M]	The Big Sound	1961	12.50	25.00	50.00

BELLSON, LOUIS
CAPITOL

❏ H 348 [10]	Just Jazz All-Stars	1952	50.00	100.00	200.00

DISCWASHER

❏ 002	Note Smoking	1979	6.25	12.50	25.00
—Direct-to-disc recording					

Number	Title (A Side/B Side)	Yr	VG	VG+	NM
IMPULSE!					
❏ A-9107 [M]	Thunderbird	1966	6.25	12.50	25.00
❏ AS-9107 [S]	Thunderbird	1966	7.50	15.00	30.00
NORGRAN					
❏ MGN-7 [10]	The Amazing Artistry of Louis Bellson	1954	50.00	100.00	200.00
❏ MGN-14 [10]	The Exciting Mr. Bellson (And His Big Band)	1954	50.00	100.00	200.00
❏ MGN-1007 [M]	Journey Into Love	1954	37.50	75.00	150.00
❏ MGN-1011 [M]	Louis Bellson and His Drums	1954	37.50	75.00	150.00
❏ MGN-1020 [M]	The Driving Louis Bellson	1955	25.00	50.00	100.00
❏ MGN-1046 [M]	Skin Deep	1955	25.00	50.00	100.00
❏ MGN-1099 [M]	The Hawk Talks	1956	20.00	40.00	80.00
—Reissue of 1020					
ROULETTE					
❏ R-52087 [M]	Big Band Jazz from the Summit	1962	5.00	10.00	20.00
❏ SR-52087 [S]	Big Band Jazz from the Summit	1962	6.25	12.50	25.00
❏ R-65002 [M]	Around the World in Percussion	1962	5.00	10.00	20.00
❏ SR-65002 [S]	Around the World in Percussion	1962	6.25	12.50	25.00
VERVE					
❏ MGV-2123 [M]	The Brilliant Bellson Sound	1960	12.50	25.00	50.00
❏ V-2123 [M]	The Brilliant Bellson Sound	1960	5.00	10.00	20.00
❏ V6-2123 [S]	The Brilliant Bellson Sound	1960	5.00	10.00	20.00
❏ MGV-2131 [M]	Louis Bellson Swings Jules Styne	1960	12.50	25.00	50.00
❏ V-2131 [M]	Louis Bellson Swings Jules Styne	1960	5.00	10.00	20.00
❏ V6-2131 [S]	Louis Bellson Swings Jules Styne	1960	5.00	10.00	20.00
❏ MGVS-6093 [S]	The Brilliant Bellson Sound	1960	10.00	20.00	40.00
❏ MGVS-6138 [S]	Louis Bellson Swings Jules Styne	1960	10.00	20.00	40.00
❏ MGV-8016 [M]	Concerto for Drums	1957	12.50	25.00	50.00
—Reissue of Norgran 1011					
❏ V-8016 [M]	Concerto for Drums	1961	5.00	10.00	20.00
❏ MGV-8137 [M]	Skin Deep	1957	12.50	25.00	50.00
—Reissue of Norgran 1046					
❏ V-8137 [M]	Skin Deep	1957	5.00	10.00	20.00
❏ MGV-8186 [M]	The Hawk Talks	1957	12.50	25.00	50.00
—Reissue of Norgran 1099					
❏ V-8186 [M]	The Hawk Talks	1957	5.00	10.00	20.00
❏ MGV-8193 [M]	Drumorama!	1957	12.50	25.00	50.00
❏ V-8193 [M]	Drumorama!	1957	5.00	10.00	20.00
❏ MGV-8256 [M]	Louis Bellson at the Flamingo	1958	12.50	25.00	50.00
❏ V-8256 [M]	Louis Bellson at the Flamingo	1958	5.00	10.00	20.00
❏ MGV-8258 [M]	Let's Call It Swing	1958	12.50	25.00	50.00
❏ V-8258 [M]	Let's Call It Swing	1958	5.00	10.00	20.00
❏ MGV-8280 [M]	Music, Romance and Especially Love	1958	12.50	25.00	50.00
❏ V-8280 [M]	Music, Romance and Especially Love	1958	5.00	10.00	20.00
❏ MGV-8354 [M]	Drummer's Holiday	1959	12.50	25.00	50.00
❏ V-8354 [M]	Drummer's Holiday	1959	5.00	10.00	20.00

BELLSON, LOUIS, AND GENE KRUPA
ROULETTE

Number	Title (A Side/B Side)	Yr	VG	VG+	NM
❏ R-52098 [M]	The Mighty Two	1962	5.00	10.00	20.00
❏ SR-52098 [S]	The Mighty Two	1962	6.25	12.50	25.00

BELLSON, LOUIS, AND LALO SCHIFRIN
ROULETTE

Number	Title (A Side/B Side)	Yr	VG	VG+	NM
❏ SR-52120 [S]	Explorations	1964	5.00	10.00	20.00

BELLUS, TONY
NRC

Number	Title (A Side/B Side)	Yr	VG	VG+	NM
❏ LPA-8 [M]	Robbin' the Cradle	1960	25.00	50.00	100.00
—Black label					
❏ LPA-8 [M]	Robbin' the Cradle	1960	50.00	100.00	200.00
—Blue label					

BELMONTS, THE
BUDDAH

Number	Title (A Side/B Side)	Yr	VG	VG+	NM
❏ BDS-5123	Cigars, Acapella, Candy	1972	12.50	25.00	50.00
DOT					
❏ DLP-25949	Summer Love	1969	7.50	15.00	30.00
SABINA					
❏ SALP-5001 [M]	The Belmonts' Carnival of Hits	1962	37.50	75.00	150.00
STRAWBERRY					
❏ 6001	Cheek to Cheek	1978	3.75	7.50	15.00

BELVIN, JESSE
CROWN

Number	Title (A Side/B Side)	Yr	VG	VG+	NM
❏ CLP-5145 [M]	The Casual Jesse Belvin	1959	17.50	35.00	70.00
—Black label					
❏ CLP-5145 [M]	The Casual Jesse Belvin	196?	3.75	7.50	15.00
—Gray label					
❏ CLP-5187 [M]	The Unforgettable Jesse Belvin	1959	17.50	35.00	70.00
—Black label					
❏ CLP-5187 [M]	The Unforgettable Jesse Belvin	196?	3.75	7.50	15.00
—Gray label					
RCA CAMDEN					
❏ CAL-960 [M]	Jesse Belvin's Best	1966	3.00	6.00	12.00
❏ CAS-960 [S]	Jesse Belvin's Best	1966	3.75	7.50	15.00
RCA VICTOR					
❏ LPM-2089 [M]	Just Jesse Belvin	1959	10.00	20.00	40.00
❏ LSP-2089 [S]	Just Jesse Belvin	1959	15.00	30.00	60.00
❏ LPM-2105 [M]	Mr. Easy	1960	7.50	15.00	30.00
❏ LSP-2105 [S]	Mr. Easy	1960	10.00	20.00	40.00
SPECIALTY					
❏ SP-7003	The Blues Balladeer	1990	3.75	7.50	15.00

BENATAR, PAT
CHRYSALIS

Number	Title (A Side/B Side)	Yr	VG	VG+	NM
❏ CHR 1236	In the Heat of the Night	1979	2.00	4.00	8.00
❏ CHE 1275	Crimes of Passion	1980	2.00	4.00	8.00
❏ CHE 1275	Crimes of Passion	1980	7.50	15.00	30.00
—Error pressing: White label (not a promo) with photo of Pat leaning on a barre, as on regular copies, but with no blue at all, and with no butterfly or "Chrysalis" on label					
❏ CHR 1346	Precious Time	1981	2.00	4.00	8.00

— second column —

Number	Title (A Side/B Side)	Yr	VG	VG+	NM
❏ CHR 1396	Get Nervous	1982	2.00	4.00	8.00
❏ F1-21715	Best Shots	1989	3.00	6.00	12.00
❏ FV 41236	In the Heat of the Night	1983	—	3.00	6.00
—Reissue of 1236					
❏ FV 41275	Crimes of Passion	1983	—	3.00	6.00
—Reissue of 1275					
❏ FV 41346	Precious Time	1983	—	3.00	6.00
—Reissue of 1346					
❏ FV 41396	Get Nervous	1983	—	3.00	6.00
—Reissue of 1396					
❏ FV 41444	Live from Earth	1983	2.00	4.00	8.00
❏ FV 41471	Tropico	1984	2.00	4.00	8.00
❏ FV 41507	Seven the Hard Way	1985	2.00	4.00	8.00
❏ FV 41628	Wide Awake in Dreamland	1988	2.00	4.00	8.00
MOBILE FIDELITY					
❏ 1-057	In the Heat of the Night	1981	6.25	12.50	25.00
—Audiophile vinyl					

BENAY, BEN
CAPITOL

Number	Title (A Side/B Side)	Yr	VG	VG+	NM
❏ ST 2484 [S]	The Big Blues Harmonica of Ben Benay	1966	6.25	12.50	25.00
❏ T 2484 [M]	The Big Blues Harmonica of Ben Benay	1966	5.00	10.00	20.00

BENDIX, WILLIAM
CRICKET

Number	Title (A Side/B Side)	Yr	VG	VG+	NM
❏ CR-30 [M]	William Bendix Sings and Tells Famous Pirate Stories	1959	10.00	20.00	40.00

BENET, VICKI
DECCA

Number	Title (A Side/B Side)	Yr	VG	VG+	NM
❏ DL 8233 [M]	Woman of Paris	1956	10.00	20.00	40.00
❏ DL 8381 [M]	The French Touch	1957	10.00	20.00	40.00
❏ DL 8987 [M]	Vicki Benet a Paris	1959	7.50	15.00	30.00
❏ DL 78987 [S]	Vicki Benet a Paris	1959	10.00	20.00	40.00
LIBERTY					
❏ LRP-3103 [M]	Sing to Me of Love	1960	6.25	12.50	25.00
❏ LST-7103 [S]	Sing to Me of Love	1960	7.50	15.00	30.00

BENNETT, BETTY
ATLANTIC

Number	Title (A Side/B Side)	Yr	VG	VG+	NM
❏ 1226 [M]	Nobody Else But Me	1956	25.00	50.00	100.00
—Black label					
❏ 1226 [M]	Nobody Else But Me	1961	10.00	20.00	40.00
—Multicolor label, white "fan" logo					
KAPP					
❏ KL-1052 [M]	Blue Sunday	1957	10.00	20.00	40.00
TREND					
❏ TL-1006 [10]	Betty Bennett Sings Previn Arrangements	1954	30.00	60.00	120.00
UNITED ARTISTS					
❏ UAL-3070 [M]	I Love to Sing	1959	10.00	20.00	40.00
❏ UAS-6070 [S]	I Love to Sing	1959	12.50	25.00	50.00

BENNETT, BOYD
KING

Number	Title (A Side/B Side)	Yr	VG	VG+	NM
❏ 395-594 [M]	Boyd Bennett	1955	1500.	2750.	4000.

BENNETT, CONNIE, WITH BILL SMITH AND THE HARLEM-AIRES
HOLLYWOOD

Number	Title (A Side/B Side)	Yr	VG	VG+	NM
❏ LPH-30 [M]	Rhythm 'N Blues in the Night	1957	125.00	250.00	500.00
—Photo of Julie "Catwoman" Newmar on front cover					

BENNETT, MAX
BETHLEHEM

Number	Title (A Side/B Side)	Yr	VG	VG+	NM
❏ BCP-48 [M]	Johnny Jaguar	1957	17.50	35.00	70.00
❏ BCP-50 [M]	Max Bennett Plays	1957	17.50	35.00	70.00
❏ BCP-1028 [10]	Max Bennett Quintet	1955	30.00	60.00	120.00

BENNETT, TONY
COLUMBIA

Number	Title (A Side/B Side)	Yr	VG	VG+	NM
❏ GP 14 [(2)]	Love Songs	1969	3.75	7.50	15.00
❏ C2L 23 [(2)M]	Tony Bennett at Carnegie Hall	1962	5.00	10.00	20.00
❏ CL 621 [M]	Cloud Seven	1955	10.00	20.00	40.00
❏ C2S 823 [(2)S]	Tony Bennett at Carnegie Hall	1962	6.25	12.50	25.00
❏ CL 938 [M]	Tony	1956	7.50	15.00	30.00
❏ CL 1079 [M]	The Beat of My Heart	1957	7.50	15.00	30.00
❏ CL 1186 [M]	Long Ago and Far Away	1958	7.50	15.00	30.00
❏ CL 1229 [M]	Tony's Greatest Hits	1958	7.50	15.00	30.00
❏ CL 1292 [M]	Blue Velvet	1958	7.50	15.00	30.00
❏ CL 1301 [M]	Hometown, My Hometown	1959	6.25	12.50	25.00
❏ CL 1429 [M]	To My Wonderful One	1960	6.25	12.50	25.00
❏ CL 1446 [M]	Tony Sings for Two	1960	6.25	12.50	25.00
❏ CL 1471 [M]	Alone Together	1960	6.25	12.50	25.00
❏ CL 1535 [M]	More Tony's Greatest Hits	1961	5.00	10.00	20.00
❏ CL 1559 [M]	A String of Harold Arlen	1961	5.00	10.00	20.00
❏ CL 1658 [M]	My Heart Sings	1961	5.00	10.00	20.00
❏ CL 1763 [M]	Mr. Broadway	1962	3.75	7.50	15.00
❏ CL 1869 [M]	I Left My Heart in San Francisco	1962	3.75	7.50	15.00
❏ CL 1905 [M]	Tony Bennett at Carnegie Hall Vol. 1	1963	3.75	7.50	15.00
❏ CL 2000 [M]	I Wanna Be Around	1963	3.75	7.50	15.00
❏ CL 2056 [M]	This Is All I Ask	1963	3.75	7.50	15.00
❏ CL 2141 [M]	The Many Moods of Tony	1964	3.75	7.50	15.00
❏ CL 2175 [M]	When Lights Are Low	1964	3.75	7.50	15.00
❏ CL 2285 [M]	Who Can I Turn To	1964	3.75	7.50	15.00
❏ CL 2343 [M]	If I Ruled the World — Songs for the Jet Set	1965	3.00	6.00	12.00
❏ CL 2373 [M]	Tony's Greatest Hits, Volume III	1965	3.00	6.00	12.00
❏ CL 2472 [M]	The Movie Song Album	1966	3.00	6.00	12.00
❏ CL 2507 [10]	Alone at Last with Tony Bennett	1955	15.00	30.00	60.00
❏ CL 2550 [10]	Because of You	1956	15.00	30.00	60.00
❏ CL 2560 [M]	A Time for Love	1966	3.00	6.00	12.00
❏ CL 2653 [M]	Tony Makes It Happen!	1967	3.75	7.50	15.00
❏ CL 2773 [M]	For Once in My Life	1967	7.50	15.00	30.00
❏ CL 6221 [10]	Because of You	1952	20.00	40.00	80.00
❏ CS 8107 [S]	Hometown, My Hometown	1959	10.00	20.00	40.00

Number	Title (A Side/B Side)	Yr	VG	VG+	NM
❏ CS 8226 [S]	To My Wonderful One	1960	10.00	20.00	40.00
❏ CS 8242 [S]	Tony Sings for Two	1960	10.00	20.00	40.00
❏ CS 8262 [S]	Alone Together	1960	10.00	20.00	40.00
❏ CS 8335 [S]	More Tony's Greatest Hits	1961	6.25	12.50	25.00
❏ CS 8359 [S]	A String of Harold Arlen	1961	6.25	12.50	25.00
❏ CS 8458 [S]	My Heart Sings	1961	6.25	12.50	25.00
❏ CS 8563 [S]	Mr. Broadway	1962	5.00	10.00	20.00
❏ CS 8652 [R]	Tony's Greatest Hits	1962	3.75	7.50	15.00
❏ CS 8669 [S]	I Left My Heart in San Francisco	1962	5.00	10.00	20.00
❏ PC 8669	I Left My Heart in San Francisco	198?	2.00	4.00	8.00
—Reissue with new prefix					
❏ CS 8705 [S]	Tony Bennett at Carnegie Hall Vol. 1	1963	5.00	10.00	20.00
❏ CS 8800 [S]	I Wanna Be Around	1963	6.25	12.50	25.00
❏ CS 8856 [S]	This Is All I Ask	1963	5.00	10.00	20.00
❏ CS 8941 [S]	The Many Moods of Tony	1964	5.00	10.00	20.00
❏ CS 8975 [S]	When Lights Are Low	1964	5.00	10.00	20.00
❏ CS 9085 [S]	Who Can I Turn To	1964	5.00	10.00	20.00
❏ CS 9143 [S]	If I Ruled the World — Songs for the Jet Set	1965	3.75	7.50	15.00
❏ CS 9173 [S]	Tony's Greatest Hits, Volume III	1965	3.75	7.50	15.00
❏ CS 9272 [S]	The Movie Song Album	1966	3.75	7.50	15.00
❏ CS 9360 [S]	A Time for Love	1966	3.75	7.50	15.00
❏ CS 9453 [S]	Tony Makes It Happen!	1967	3.75	7.50	15.00
❏ CS 9573 [S]	For Once in My Life	1967	3.75	7.50	15.00
❏ CS 9678	Yesterday I Heard the Rain	1968	3.75	7.50	15.00
❏ CS 9739	Snowfall: The Tony Bennett Christmas Album	1968	3.00	6.00	12.00
❏ CS 9814	Tony Bennett's Greatest Hits, Volume IV	1969	3.75	7.50	15.00
❏ CS 9882	I've Gotta Be Me	1969	3.75	7.50	15.00
❏ CS 9980	Tony Sings the Great Hits of Today!	1970	3.00	6.00	12.00
❏ C 30240	All Time Hall of Fame Hits	1971	3.00	6.00	12.00
❏ PC 30240	All Time Hall of Fame Hits	197?	2.50	5.00	10.00
—Reissue with new prefix					
❏ C 30280	Tony Bennett's "Something"	1971	3.00	6.00	12.00
❏ C 30558	Love Story	1971	3.00	6.00	12.00
❏ C 31216	Summer of '42	1972	3.00	6.00	12.00
❏ KC 31460	With Love	1972	3.00	6.00	12.00
❏ KG 31494 [(2)]	Tony Bennett's All-Time Greatest Hits	1972	3.75	7.50	15.00
❏ CG 33612 [(2)]	I Left My Heart in San Francisco/Tony Sings the Great Hits of Today!	1975	3.75	7.50	15.00
❏ FC 40344	The Art of Excellence	1986	2.50	5.00	10.00
❏ CG 40424 [(2)]	Tony Bennett Jazz	1987	3.00	6.00	12.00
❏ FC 44029	Bennett/Berlin	1987	2.50	5.00	10.00
❏ C 63668	Bennett Sings Ellington — Hot and Cool	1999	3.00	6.00	12.00
COLUMBIA LIMITED EDITION					
❏ LE 10057	For Once in My Life	197?	2.50	5.00	10.00
COLUMBIA SPECIAL PRODUCTS					
❏ CSM 552 [M]	Singer Presents Tony Bennett	1966	3.75	7.50	15.00
❏ CSS 552 [S]	Singer Presents Tony Bennett	1966	5.00	10.00	20.00
❏ C 11264	This Is All I Ask	1972	3.00	6.00	12.00
—"Distributed by Arc-Jay-Kay Distributing Co." on upper back cover					
DRG					
❏ MRS-910	Make Magnificent Music	1985	2.50	5.00	10.00
❏ DARC-2-2102 [(2)]	The Rodgers and Hart Songbook	1986	3.75	7.50	15.00
HARMONY					
❏ HS 11340	Just One of Those Things	1969	2.50	5.00	10.00
❏ KH 32171	Tony	1973	2.50	5.00	10.00
IMPROV					
❏ 7112	Life Is Beautiful	197?	3.00	6.00	12.00
❏ 7113	Tony Bennett Sings Rodgers and Hart	197?	3.00	6.00	12.00
❏ 7120	Tony Bennett Sings More Rodgers and Hart	1978	3.00	6.00	12.00
❏ 7123	Beautiful Music	1979	3.00	6.00	12.00
MGM					
❏ SE-4929	Greatest Hits, Vol. 7	1973	3.00	6.00	12.00
PAIR					
❏ PDL2-1102 [(2)]	All-Time Favorites	1986	3.00	6.00	12.00
VERVE					
❏ MV-5088	The Good Things in Life	1972	3.00	6.00	12.00
❏ MV-5094	Listen Easy	1973	3.00	6.00	12.00

BENNETT, TONY, AND COUNT BASIE

COLUMBIA

Number	Title (A Side/B Side)	Yr	VG	VG+	NM
❏ CL 1294 [M]	Tony Bennett In Person	1959	6.25	12.50	25.00
❏ CS 8104 [S]	Tony Bennett In Person	1959	10.00	20.00	40.00

ROULETTE

Number	Title (A Side/B Side)	Yr	VG	VG+	NM
❏ R 25072 [M]	Count Basie Swings/Tony Bennett Sings	1961	6.25	12.50	25.00
❏ SR 25072 [S]	Count Basie Swings/Tony Bennett Sings	1961	7.50	15.00	30.00
❏ R 25231 [M]	Bennett and Basie Strike Up the Band	1963	5.00	10.00	20.00
❏ SR 25231 [S]	Bennett and Basie Strike Up the Band	1963	6.25	12.50	25.00

BENNETT, TONY, AND BILL EVANS

DRG

Number	Title (A Side/B Side)	Yr	VG	VG+	NM
❏ MRS-901	Together Again	1985	2.00	4.00	8.00

FANTASY

| ❏ 9489 | The Tony Bennett/Bill Evans Album | 197? | 3.00 | 6.00 | 12.00 |

IMPROV

| ❏ 7117 | Together Again | 1978 | 3.00 | 6.00 | 12.00 |

MOBILE FIDELITY

| ❏ 1-117 | The Tony Bennett/Bill Evans Album | 1981 | 10.00 | 20.00 | 40.00 |
| —Audiophile vinyl | | | | | |

BENSON, GEORGE

A&M

Number	Title (A Side/B Side)	Yr	VG	VG+	NM
❏ SP-3014	Shape of Things to Come	1969	5.00	10.00	20.00
—Brown label					
❏ SP-3020	Tell It Like It Is	1969	5.00	10.00	20.00
—Brown label					
❏ SP-3028	The Other Side of Abbey Road	1970	6.25	12.50	25.00
—Brown label					

COLUMBIA

Number	Title (A Side/B Side)	Yr	VG	VG+	NM
❏ CL 2525 [M]	The Most Exciting New Guitarist on the Jazz Scene Today — It's Uptown	1966	5.00	10.00	20.00
❏ CL 2613 [M]	The George Benson Cook Book	1967	5.00	10.00	20.00
❏ CS 9325 [S]	The Most Exciting New Guitarist on the Jazz Scene Today — It's Uptown	1966	5.00	10.00	20.00
—Red "360 Sound" label					
❏ CS 9413 [S]	The George Benson Cook Book	1967	5.00	10.00	20.00
—Red "360 Sound" label					

MOBILE FIDELITY

| ❏ 1-011 | Breezin' | 1979 | 15.00 | 30.00 | 60.00 |
| —Audiophile vinyl | | | | | |

PRESTIGE

| ❏ PRLP-7310 [M] | The New Boss Guitar of George Benson | 1964 | 6.25 | 12.50 | 25.00 |
| ❏ PRST-7310 [S] | The New Boss Guitar of George Benson | 1964 | 7.50 | 15.00 | 30.00 |

VERVE

| ❏ V6-8749 | Giblet Gravy | 1968 | 5.00 | 10.00 | 20.00 |
| ❏ V6-8771 | Goodies | 1969 | 5.00 | 10.00 | 20.00 |

BENTON, BROOK

ALL PLATINUM

Number	Title (A Side/B Side)	Yr	VG	VG+	NM
❏ 3015	This Is Brook Benton	1976	3.00	6.00	12.00

ALLEGIANCE

| ❏ AV-5033 | Memories Are Made of This | 1986 | 2.50 | 5.00 | 10.00 |

COTILLION

❏ SD 9002	Do Your Own Thing	1969	3.00	6.00	12.00
❏ SD 9018	Brook Benton Today	1970	3.00	6.00	12.00
❏ SD 9028	Home Style	1970	3.00	6.00	12.00
❏ SD 9050	Story Teller	1971	3.00	6.00	12.00
❏ SD 9058	The Gospel Truth	1972	3.00	6.00	12.00

EPIC

| ❏ LN 3573 [M] | Brook Benton At His Best | 1959 | 12.50 | 25.00 | 50.00 |

HARMONY

| ❏ HL 7346 [M] | The Soul of Brook Benton | 196? | 3.00 | 6.00 | 12.00 |
| ❏ HS 11146 [R] | The Soul of Brook Benton | 196? | 3.00 | 6.00 | 12.00 |

HMC

| ❏ 830724 | Beautiful Memories of Christmas | 1983 | 3.00 | 6.00 | 12.00 |

MERCURY

❏ MG-20421 [M]	It's Just a Matter of Time	1959	10.00	20.00	40.00
❏ MG-20464 [M]	Endlessly	1959	7.50	15.00	30.00
❏ MG-20565 [M]	So Many Ways I Love You	1960	7.50	15.00	30.00
❏ MG-20602 [M]	Songs I Love to Sing	1960	7.50	15.00	30.00
❏ MG-20607 [M]	Golden Hits	1961	5.00	10.00	20.00
❏ MG-20619 [M]	If You Believe	1961	5.00	10.00	20.00
❏ MG-20641 [M]	The Boll Weevil Song and 11 Other Great Hits	1961	5.00	10.00	20.00
❏ MG-20673 [M]	There Goes That Song Again	1962	5.00	10.00	20.00
❏ MG-20740 [M]	Singing the Blues — Lie to Me	1962	5.00	10.00	20.00
❏ MG-20774 [M]	Golden Hits, Volume 2	1963	5.00	10.00	20.00
❏ MG-20830 [M]	Best Ballads of Broadway	1963	5.00	10.00	20.00
❏ MG-20886 [M]	Born to Sing the Blues	1964	5.00	10.00	20.00
❏ MG-20918 [M]	On the Country Side	1964	3.75	7.50	15.00
❏ MG-20934 [M]	This Bitter Earth	1964	3.75	7.50	15.00
❏ SR-60077 [S]	It's Just a Matter of Time	1959	12.50	25.00	50.00
❏ SR-60146 [S]	Endlessly	1959	10.00	20.00	40.00
❏ SR-60225 [S]	So Many Ways I Love You	1960	10.00	2.00	40.00
❏ SR-60602 [S]	Songs I Love to Sing	1960	10.00	20.00	40.00
❏ SR-60607 [S]	Golden Hits	1961	7.50	15.00	30.00
❏ SR-60619 [S]	If You Believe	1961	7.50	15.00	30.00
❏ SR-60641 [S]	The Boll Weevil Song and 11 Other Great Hits	1961	7.50	15.00	30.00
❏ SR-60673 [S]	There Goes That Song Again	1962	7.50	15.00	30.00
❏ SR-60740 [S]	Singing the Blues — Lie to Me	1962	7.50	15.00	30.00
❏ SR-60774 [S]	Golden Hits, Volume 2	1963	7.50	15.00	30.00
❏ SR-60830 [S]	Best Ballads of Broadway	1963	6.25	12.50	25.00
❏ SR-60886 [S]	Born to Sing the Blues	1964	6.25	12.50	25.00
❏ SR-60918 [S]	On the Country Side	1964	5.00	10.00	20.00
❏ SR-60934 [S]	This Bitter Earth	1964	5.00	10.00	20.00
❏ 822321-1	It's Just a Matter of Time: His Greatest Hits	1984	2.50	5.00	10.00

MGM

| ❏ SE-4874 | Something for Everyone | 1973 | 3.00 | 6.00 | 12.00 |

MUSICOR

| ❏ 4603 [(2)] | The Best of Brook Benton | 1977 | 3.00 | 6.00 | 12.00 |

PAIR

| ❏ PDL2-1100 [(2)] | Brook Benton's Best | 1986 | 3.00 | 6.00 | 12.00 |

RCA CAMDEN

| ❏ CAL-564 [M] | Brook Benton | 1960 | 3.75 | 7.50 | 15.00 |
| ❏ CAS-2431 | I Wanna Be with You | 1970 | 3.00 | 6.00 | 12.00 |

RCA VICTOR

❏ APL1-1044	Book Benton Sings a Love Story	1975	2.50	5.00	10.00
❏ LPM-3514 [M]	That Old Feeling	1966	3.75	7.50	15.00
❏ LSP-3514 [S]	That Old Feeling	1966	5.00	10.00	20.00
❏ LPM-3526 [M]	Mother Nature, Father Time	1965	3.75	7.50	15.00
❏ LSP-3526 [S]	Mother Nature, Father Time	1965	5.00	10.00	20.00
❏ LPM-3590 [M]	My Country	1966	3.75	7.50	15.00
❏ LSP-3590 [S]	My Country	1966	5.00	10.00	20.00

REPRISE

| ❏ R-6268 [M] | Laura (What's He Got That I Ain't Got) | 1967 | 5.00 | 10.00 | 20.00 |
| ❏ RS-6268 [S] | Laura (What's He Got That I Ain't Got) | 1967 | 3.75 | 7.50 | 15.00 |

RHINO

| ❏ RNFP 71497 [(2)] | The Brook Benton Anthology (1959-1970) | 1986 | 3.00 | 6.00 | 12.00 |

WING

| ❏ MGW-12314 [M] | Brook Benton | 1966 | 3.00 | 6.00 | 12.00 |
| ❏ SRW-16314 [S] | Brook Benton | 1966 | 3.00 | 6.00 | 12.00 |

BENTON, WALTER

JAZZLAND

| ❏ JLP-28 [M] | Out of This World | 1960 | 10.00 | 20.00 | 40.00 |
| ❏ JLP-928 [S] | Out of This World | 1960 | 10.00 | 20.00 | 40.00 |

B

Number	Title (A Side/B Side)	Yr	VG	VG+	NM
BERBERIAN, JOHN, WITH THE ROCK EAST ENSEMBLE					
MAINSTREAM					
❑ S-6123	Impressions East	1969	30.00	60.00	120.00
VERVE FORECAST					
❑ FTS-3073	Middle Eastern Rock	1969	12.50	25.00	50.00
BERG, GERTRUDE					
AMY					
❑ 8007 [M]	How to Be a Jewish Mother	1965	6.25	12.50	25.00
BERGEN, FRANCES					
COLUMBIA					
❑ CL 873 [M]	The Beguiling Miss Bergen	1956	7.50	15.00	30.00
BERGEN, POLLY					
COLUMBIA					
❑ CL 994 [M]	Bergen Sings Morgan	1957	7.50	15.00	30.00
❑ CL 1031 [M]	The Party's Over	1957	7.50	15.00	30.00
❑ CL 1138 [M]	Polly and Her Pop	1958	6.25	12.50	25.00
❑ CL 1218 [M]	My Heart Sings	1959	5.00	10.00	20.00
❑ CL 1300 [M]	All Alone by the Telephone	1959	5.00	10.00	20.00
❑ CL 1451 [M]	Four Seasons of Love	1960	5.00	10.00	20.00
❑ CL 1632 [M]	"Do Re Mi" and "Annie Get Your Gun"	1961	5.00	10.00	20.00
❑ CS 8018 [S]	My Heart Sings	1959	6.25	12.50	25.00
❑ CS 8100 [S]	All Alone by the Telephone	1959	6.25	12.50	25.00
❑ CS 8246 [S]	Four Seasons of Love	1960	6.25	12.50	25.00
❑ CS 8432 [S]	"Do Re Mi" and "Annie Get Your Gun"	1961	6.25	12.50	25.00
JUBILEE					
❑ JGL-14 [10]	Polly Bergen	1955	12.50	25.00	50.00
PHILIPS					
❑ PHM 200084 [M]	Act One — Sing, Too	1963	3.75	7.50	15.00
❑ PHS 600084 [S]	Act One — Sing, Too	1963	5.00	10.00	20.00
BERGER, KARL					
CMC					
❑ 00101 [(2)]	Peace Church	197?	5.00	10.00	20.00
ESP-DISK'					
❑ 1041 [M]	Karl Berger	1967	7.50	15.00	30.00
❑ S-1041 [S]	Karl Berger	1967	5.00	10.00	20.00
BERIGAN, BUNNY					
EPIC					
❑ LN 3109 [M]	Take It, Bunny!	1955	12.50	25.00	50.00
❑ LA 16004 [M]	Bunny Berigan and His Boys	196?	5.00	10.00	20.00
RCA CAMDEN					
❑ CAL-550 [M]	Bunny	195?	5.00	10.00	20.00
RCA VICTOR					
❑ LPT-10 [10]	Bunny Berigan 1937-38	1951	20.00	40.00	80.00
❑ LPV-550 [M]	Bunny	1966	5.00	10.00	20.00
❑ LPT-1003 [M]	Bunny Berigan Plays Again	1952	12.50	25.00	50.00
❑ LPM-2078 [M]	Great Dance Bands of the 30s and 40s	1959	10.00	20.00	40.00
BERIGAN, BUNNY, AND WINGY MANONE					
"X"					
❑ LVA-3034 [10]	Swing Session 1934	1954	20.00	40.00	80.00
BERLE, MILTON					
FORUM					
❑ F-9005 [M]	Songs My Mother Loved	1963	5.00	10.00	20.00
ROULETTE					
❑ R-25018 [M]	Songs My Mother Loved	1957	10.00	20.00	40.00
BERLIN					
ENIGMA					
❑ 3 [EP]	Pleasure Victim	1982	5.00	10.00	20.00
—Original issue					
GEFFEN					
❑ GHS 2036 [EP]	Pleasure Victim	1982	2.00	4.00	8.00
❑ GHS 4025	Love Life	1984	2.50	5.00	10.00
❑ GHS 24121	Count Three and Pray	1986	2.50	5.00	10.00
❑ GHS 24187	Best of Berlin 1979-1988	1988	2.50	5.00	10.00
❑ R 100731	Best of Berlin 1979-1988	1988	3.00	6.00	12.00
—BMG Direct Marketing edition					
❑ R 153624	Count Three and Pray	1986	3.00	6.00	12.00
—RCA Music Service edition					
BERMAN, SHELLEY					
METRO					
❑ M-546 [M]	Let Me Tell You a Funny Story	1965	3.75	7.50	15.00
❑ MS-546 [R]	Let Me Tell You a Funny Story	1965	3.00	6.00	12.00
VERVE					
❑ MGV-15003 [M]	Inside Shelley Berman	1959	6.25	12.50	25.00
❑ V-15003 [M]	Inside Shelley Berman	1962	3.75	7.50	15.00
❑ V6-15003 [R]	Inside Shelley Berman	196?	3.00	6.00	12.00
❑ MGV-15007 [M]	Outside Shelley Berman	1959	6.25	12.50	25.00
❑ V-15007 [M]	Outside Shelley Berman	1962	3.75	7.50	15.00
❑ V6-15007 [R]	Outside Shelley Berman	196?	3.00	6.00	12.00
❑ MGV-15008-2 [(2)M]	Inside and Outside Shelley Berman	1959	7.50	15.00	30.00
❑ V-15008-2 [(2)M]	Inside and Outside Shelley Berman	1962	5.00	10.00	20.00
❑ MGV-15013 [M]	The Edge of Shelley Berman	1960	6.25	12.50	25.00
❑ V-15013 [M]	The Edge of Shelley Berman	1962	3.75	7.50	15.00
❑ V6-15013 [R]	The Edge of Shelley Berman	196?	3.00	6.00	12.00
❑ MGV-15027 [M]	A Personal Appearance	1961	5.00	10.00	20.00
❑ V-15027 [M]	A Personal Appearance	1962	3.75	7.50	15.00
❑ V6-15027 [R]	A Personal Appearance	196?	3.00	6.00	12.00
❑ V-15036 [M]	New Sides	1962	3.75	7.50	15.00
❑ V6-15036 [R]	New Sides	196?	3.00	6.00	12.00
❑ V-15043 [M]	The Sex Life of the Primate (And Other Bits of Gossip)	1964	5.00	10.00	20.00
❑ V6-15043 [R]	The Sex Life of the Primate (And Other Bits of Gossip)	1964	3.75	7.50	15.00

Number	Title (A Side/B Side)	Yr	VG	VG+	NM
❑ V-15048 [M]	Great Moments in Comedy	1965	5.00	10.00	20.00
❑ V6-15048 [R]	Great Moments in Comedy	1965	3.75	7.50	15.00
BERMAN, SONNY					
ESOTERIC					
❑ ES-532 [M]	Sonny Berman 1946	1954	30.00	60.00	120.00
BERNARDI, HERSCHEL					
COLUMBIA					
❑ C 30004	Show Stopper	1970	5.00	10.00	20.00
COLUMBIA MASTERWORKS					
❑ OS 3010 [S]	Fiddler on the Roof	1966	6.25	12.50	25.00
❑ OL 6610 [M]	Fiddler on the Roof	1966	5.00	10.00	20.00
BERNE, TIM					
EMPIRE					
❑ EPC 24K	The Five Year Plan	1979	5.00	10.00	20.00
❑ EPC 36K	7X	1980	5.00	10.00	20.00
❑ EPC 48K	Spectres	1981	5.00	10.00	20.00
❑ EPC 60K-2 [(2)]	Songs and Rituals in Real Time	1982	6.25	12.50	25.00
BERNE, TIM, AND BILL FRISELL					
EMPIRE					
❑ EPC 72K	...Theoretically	1984	5.00	10.00	20.00
BERNHART, MILT					
DECCA					
❑ DL 9214 [M]	The Sounds of Bernhart	1959	7.50	15.00	30.00
❑ DL 79214 [S]	The Sounds of Bernhart	1959	10.00	20.00	40.00
RCA VICTOR					
❑ LPM-1123 [M]	Modern Brass	1955	12.50	25.00	50.00
BERRY, BILL					
DIRECTIONAL SOUND					
❑ 5002 [M]	Jazz and Swinging Percussion	1963	5.00	10.00	20.00
❑ S-5002 [S]	Jazz and Swinging Percussion	1963	6.25	12.50	25.00
PARADE					
❑ SP-353 [M]	Broadway Escapades	196?	5.00	10.00	20.00
REAL TIME					
❑ 101	For Duke	1980	6.25	12.50	25.00
—Direct-to-disc recording					
BERRY, BROOKS, AND SCRAPPER BLACKWELL					
BLUESVILLE					
❑ BVLP-1074 [M]	My Heart Struck Sorrow	1963	20.00	40.00	80.00
—Blue label, silver print					
❑ BVLP-1074 [M]	My Heart Struck Sorrow	1964	6.25	12.50	25.00
—Blue label with trident logo					
BERRY, CHU					
COMMODORE					
❑ FL-20024 [10]	Chu Berry Memorial	1952	62.50	125.00	250.00
❑ DL-30017 [M]	Chu Berry	1959	20.00	40.00	80.00
EPIC					
❑ LG 3124 [M]	Chu	1955	20.00	40.00	80.00
MAINSTREAM					
❑ 56038 [M]	Sittin' In	1965	7.50	15.00	30.00
BERRY, CHUCK					
ACCORD					
❑ SN-7171	Toronto Rock 'N' Roll Revival, Vol. 2	1982	2.50	5.00	10.00
❑ SN-7172	Toronto Rock 'N' Roll Revival, Vol. 3	1982	2.50	5.00	10.00
ARCHIVE OF FOLK AND JAZZ					
❑ 321	Chuck Berry's Greatest Hits	197?	2.50	5.00	10.00
ATCO					
❑ SD 38-118	Rockit	1979	3.00	6.00	12.00
CHESS					
❑ LP-1426 [M]	After School Session	1958	50.00	100.00	200.00
❑ LPS-1426 [R]	After School Session	196?	3.00	6.00	12.00
❑ LP-1432 [M]	One Dozen Berrys	1958	50.00	100.00	200.00
❑ LPS-1432 [R]	One Dozen Berrys	196?	3.00	6.00	12.00
❑ LP-1435 [M]	Chuck Berry Is On Top	1959	45.00	90.00	180.00
❑ LPS-1435 [R]	Chuck Berry Is On Top	196?	3.00	6.00	12.00
❑ LP-1448 [M]	Rockin' at the Hops	1960	45.00	90.00	180.00
❑ LP-1456 [M]	New Juke Box Hits	1961	45.00	90.00	180.00
❑ LP-1465 [M]	Chuck Berry Twist	1962	25.00	50.00	100.00
❑ LP-1465 [M]	More Chuck Berry	1963	30.00	60.00	120.00
—Retitled version of above					
❑ LPS-1465 [R]	More Chuck Berry	196?	3.00	6.00	12.00
❑ LP-1480 [M]	Chuck Berry On Stage	1963	30.00	60.00	120.00
❑ LPS-1480 [R]	Chuck Berry On Stage	196?	3.00	6.00	12.00
❑ LP-1485 [M]	Chuck Berry's Greatest Hits	1964	30.00	60.00	120.00
❑ LPS-1485 [R]	Chuck Berry's Greatest Hits	196?	3.00	6.00	12.00
❑ LP-1488 [M]	St. Louis to Liverpool	1964	15.00	30.00	60.00
❑ LPS-1488 [S]	St. Louis to Liverpool	1964	20.00	40.00	80.00
❑ LP-1495 [M]	Chuck Berry in London	1965	7.50	15.00	30.00
❑ LPS-1495 [S]	Chuck Berry in London	1965	10.00	20.00	40.00
❑ LP-1498 [M]	Fresh Berry's	1965	7.50	15.00	30.00
❑ LPS-1498 [S]	Fresh Berry's	1965	10.00	20.00	40.00
❑ 2CH-1514 [(2)R]	Chuck Berry's Golden Decade	1972	3.75	7.50	15.00
—New cover has a pink radio					
❑ LP-1514 [(2)M]	Chuck Berry's Golden Decade	1967	10.00	20.00	40.00
❑ LPS-1514 [(2)R]	Chuck Berry's Golden Decade	1967	5.00	10.00	20.00
—Old cover does not have a pink radio					
❑ LPS-1550	Back Home	1970	5.00	10.00	20.00
❑ CH-9171	New Juke Box Hits	1986	2.50	5.00	10.00
—Reissue of 1456					
❑ CH-9186	St. Louis to Liverpool	1988	2.50	5.00	10.00
—Reissue of 1488					
❑ CH-9190	More Rock 'n' Roll Rarities	1986	2.50	5.00	10.00
❑ CH-9256	Chuck Berry Is On Top	1987	2.50	5.00	10.00
—Reissue of 1435					

Number	Title (A Side/B Side)	Yr	VG	VG+	NM
❑ CH-9259	Rockin' at the Hop	1987	2.50	5.00	10.00
—Reissue of 1448					
❑ CH-9284	After School Session	1989	2.50	5.00	10.00
—Reissue of 1426					
❑ CH-9295	The London Chuck Berry Sessions	1989	2.50	5.00	10.00
—Reissue of 60020					
❑ CH-9318	Missing Berries: Rarities, Volume 3	1990	2.50	5.00	10.00
❑ CH-50008	San Fransisco Dues	1971	5.00	10.00	20.00
❑ CH-50043	Chuck Berry/Bio	1973	5.00	10.00	20.00
❑ CH-60020	The London Chuck Berry Sessions	1972	5.00	10.00	20.00
❑ 2CH-60023 [(2)]	Chuck Berry's Golden Decade, Vol. 2	1973	6.25	12.50	25.00
❑ 2CH-60028 [(2)]	Chuck Berry's Golden Decade, Vol. 3	1974	6.25	12.50	25.00
❑ CH6-80001 [(6)]	The Chess Box	1989	12.50	25.00	50.00
❑ CH2-92500 [(2)]	The Great Twenty-Eight	1983	3.00	6.00	12.00
❑ CH2-92521 [(2)]	Rock 'n' Roll Rarities	1986	3.75	7.50	15.00
GUSTO					
❑ 0004	The Best of the Best of Chuck Berry	198?	2.50	5.00	10.00
MERCURY					
❑ SRM-2-6501 [(2)]	St. Louis to Frisco to Memphis	1972	5.00	10.00	20.00
❑ MG-21103 [M]	Chuck Berry's Golden Hits	1967	3.75	7.50	15.00
❑ MG-21123 [M]	Chuck Berry in Memphis	1967	3.75	7.50	15.00
❑ MG-21138 [M]	Love at the Fillmore Auditorium	1967	5.00	10.00	20.00
❑ SR-61103 [S]	Chuck Berry's Golden Hits	1967	3.75	7.50	15.00
❑ SR-61123 [S]	Chuck Berry in Memphis	1967	3.75	7.50	15.00
❑ SR-61138 [S]	Love at the Fillmore Auditorium	1967	5.00	10.00	20.00
❑ SR-61176	From St. Louie to Frisco	1968	5.00	10.00	20.00
❑ SR-61223	Concerto in B Goode	1969	5.00	10.00	20.00
❑ 826256-1	Chuck Berry's Golden Hits	1985	2.00	4.00	8.00
—Reissue					
PICKWICK					
❑ PTP-2061 [(2)]	Flashback	1975	3.00	6.00	12.00
❑ SPC-3327	Johnny B. Goode	1973	2.50	5.00	10.00
❑ SPC-3345	Sweet Little Rock and Roller	1974	2.50	5.00	10.00
❑ SPC-3392	Wild Berrys	1974	2.50	5.00	10.00
QUICKSILVER					
❑ QS-1017	Live Hits	198?	2.50	5.00	10.00
SSS INTERNATIONAL					
❑ 36	Chuck Berry Live	1981	2.50	5.00	10.00

BERRY, KEN
BARNABY

Number	Title (A Side/B Side)	Yr	VG	VG+	NM
❑ Z 30014	R.F.D.	1970	6.25	12.50	25.00
❑ Z 30094	Ken Berry, R.F.D.	1970	7.50	15.00	30.00

BERRY, RICHARD
CROWN

Number	Title (A Side/B Side)	Yr	VG	VG+	NM
❑ CST-371 [R]	Richard Berry and the Dreamers	1963	7.50	15.00	30.00
❑ CLP-5371 [M]	Richard Berry and the Dreamers	1963	15.00	30.00	60.00
PAM					
❑ 1001	Live at the Century Restaurant	1968	10.00	20.00	40.00
❑ 1002	Wild Berry	196?	10.00	20.00	40.00

BERT, EDDIE
DISCOVERY

Number	Title (A Side/B Side)	Yr	VG	VG+	NM
❑ DL-3020 [M]	Eddie Bert Quintet	1953	25.00	50.00	100.00
JAZZTONE					
❑ J-1223 [M]	Modern Moods	1956	10.00	20.00	40.00
SAVOY					
❑ MG-12015 [M]	Musician of the Year	1955	15.00	30.00	60.00
❑ MG-12019 [M]	Encore	1955	15.00	30.00	60.00
SOMERSET					
❑ SF-5200 [M]	Like Cool	1958	10.00	20.00	40.00
—Reissue of Trans World LP					
TRANS WORLD					
❑ TWLP-208 [M]	Let's Dig Bert	1955	25.00	50.00	100.00

BERT, EDDIE/BILYL BYERS/JOE NEWMAN
JAZZTONE

Number	Title (A Side/B Side)	Yr	VG	VG+	NM
❑ J-1276 [M]	East Coast Sounds	1959	10.00	20.00	40.00

BEST, PETER (1)
PHOENIX

Number	Title (A Side/B Side)	Yr	VG	VG+	NM
❑ PHX-340	The Beatle That Time Forgot	1982	3.00	6.00	12.00
SAVAGE					
❑ BM-71	Best of the Beatles	1966	50.00	100.00	200.00

—Authentic copies have white circle around the word "Savage" and white circle around Pete Best's head on the album cover.

BETTERS, HAROLD
GATEWAY

Number	Title (A Side/B Side)	Yr	VG	VG+	NM
❑ GLP-7001 [M]	Harold Betters at the Encore	1964	5.00	10.00	20.00
❑ GLP-7004 [M]	Take Off	1964	5.00	10.00	20.00
❑ GLP-7008 [M]	Even Better	1966	5.00	10.00	20.00
❑ GLP-7009 [M]	Harold Betters Meets Slide Hampton	1966	5.00	10.00	20.00
❑ GLP-7014 [M]	Do Anything You Wanna	1966	5.00	10.00	20.00
❑ GLP-7015 [M]	Swingin' on the Railroad	1966	5.00	10.00	20.00
REPRISE					
❑ RS-6195 [S]	Ram-Bunk-Shush	1965	5.00	10.00	20.00
❑ RS-6208 [S]	Out of Sight and Sound	1966	5.00	10.00	20.00
❑ RS-6241 [S]	Funk City Express	1966	5.00	10.00	20.00

BEVERLY HILL BILLIES, THE
RAR-ARTS

Number	Title (A Side/B Side)	Yr	VG	VG+	NM
❑ 1000 [M]	Those Fabulous Beverly Hill Billies	1961	25.00	50.00	100.00
—Gold vinyl					

BIANCO
RCA/READER'S DIGEST

Number	Title (A Side/B Side)	Yr	VG	VG+	NM
❑ CSP-104 [S]	Joy to the World	1962	5.00	10.00	20.00

BIG BEATS, THE
LIBERTY

Number	Title (A Side/B Side)	Yr	VG	VG+	NM
❑ LRP-3407 [M]	The Big Beats Live	1965	7.50	15.00	30.00
❑ LST-7407 [S]	The Big Beats Live	1965	10.00	20.00	40.00

BIG BOPPER
MERCURY

Number	Title (A Side/B Side)	Yr	VG	VG+	NM
❑ MG-20402 [M]	Chantilly Lace	1959	125.00	250.00	500.00
—Black label					
❑ MG-20402 [M]	Chantilly Lace	196?	6.25	12.50	25.00
—Red label with twelve Mercury logos on label edge					
❑ MG-20402 [M]	Chantilly Lace	1964	50.00	100.00	200.00
—Red label with black or black & white Mercury logo at top					
❑ MG-20402 [M]	Chantilly Lace	1975	3.75	7.50	15.00
—Chicago skyline label					
❑ 832902-1 [M]	Chantilly Lace	1988	3.75	7.50	15.00
—New number, black label					
PICKWICK					
❑ SPC-3365	Chantilly Lace	1973	3.75	7.50	15.00
RHINO					
❑ R1-70164	Helloooo Baby! The Best of the Big Bopper 1954-1959	1989	3.00	6.00	12.00

BIG BOYS
ENIGMA

Number	Title (A Side/B Side)	Yr	VG	VG+	NM
❑ E-1128	Lullabies Help the Brain Grow	1984	3.75	7.50	15.00
—Reissue of Moment 002					
❑ 72028	No Matter How Long the Line Is at the Cafeteria, There's Always a Seat	1984	7.50	15.00	30.00
MOMENT					
❑ 001	Fun, Fun, Fun	1982	20.00	40.00	80.00
❑ 002	Lullabies Help the Brain Grow	1983	12.50	25.00	50.00
RAT RACE					
❑ RRR 80351	Recorded Live at Raul's	1980	20.00	40.00	80.00
—One side features the Big Boys; the other side, the Dicks					
UNSEEN HAND					
❑ UHT 727-3	Wreck Collection	1988	3.75	7.50	15.00
WASTED TALENT					
❑ JWP 3405	Where's My Towel/Industry Standard	1981	15.00	30.00	60.00

BIG BROTHER
ALL-AMERICAN

Number	Title (A Side/B Side)	Yr	VG	VG+	NM
❑ 5770	Big Brother	1970	37.50	75.00	150.00

BIG BROTHER AND THE HOLDING COMPANY
COLUMBIA

Number	Title (A Side/B Side)	Yr	VG	VG+	NM
❑ KCL 2900 [M]	Cheap Thrills	1968	75.00	150.00	300.00
—Red label stock copy has been confirmed					
❑ KCS 9700	Cheap Thrills	1970	3.00	6.00	12.00
—Orange label					
❑ KCS 9700 [M]	Cheap Thrills	1968	25.00	50.00	100.00
—White label "Special Mono Radio Station Copy" with stereo number					
❑ KCS 9700 [S]	Cheap Thrills	1968	6.25	12.50	25.00
—Red "360 Sound" label					
❑ PC 9700	Cheap Thrills	198?	2.00	4.00	8.00
—Reissue with new prefix					
❑ C 30222	Be a Brother	1970	5.00	10.00	20.00
❑ C 30631	Big Brother and the Holding Company	1971	5.00	10.00	20.00
—Reissue of Mainstream LP with two extra tracks					
❑ C 30738	How Hard It Is	1971	5.00	10.00	20.00
COLUMBIA SPECIAL PRODUCTS					
❑ P 13313	Big Brother and the Holding Company	197?	3.75	7.50	15.00
MAINSTREAM					
❑ S-6099 [S]	Big Brother and the Holding Company	1967	12.50	25.00	50.00
❑ 56099 [M]	Big Brother and the Holding Company	1967	25.00	50.00	100.00

BIG DADDY
REGENT

Number	Title (A Side/B Side)	Yr	VG	VG+	NM
❑ MG-6106 [M]	Twist Party	1962	17.50	35.00	70.00

BIG FOOT
WINRO

Number	Title (A Side/B Side)	Yr	VG	VG+	NM
❑ 1004	Big Foot	1969	7.50	15.00	30.00

BIG MAYBELLE
BRUNSWICK

Number	Title (A Side/B Side)	Yr	VG	VG+	NM
❑ BL 54107 [M]	What More Can a Woman Do	1962	12.50	25.00	50.00
❑ BL 754107 [S]	What More Can a Woman Do	1962	17.50	35.00	70.00
❑ BL 754142	The Gospel Soul of Big Maybelle	1968	10.00	20.00	40.00
EPIC					
❑ EE 22011 [M]	Gabbin' Blues	196?	7.50	15.00	30.00
—Reissue of Okeh recordings					
PARAMOUNT					
❑ PAS-1011 [(2)]	The Last of Big Maybelle	1973	6.25	12.50	25.00
ROJAC					
❑ RS 123	Saga of the Good Life and Hard Times	196?	10.00	20.00	40.00
❑ R 522 [M]	Got a Brand New Bag	1967	10.00	20.00	40.00
❑ RS 522 [S]	Got a Brand New Bag	1967	10.00	20.00	40.00
SAVOY					
❑ MG-14005 [M]	Big Maybelle Sings	1957	75.00	150.00	300.00
❑ MG-14011 [M]	Blues, Candy and Big Maybelle	1958	75.00	150.00	300.00
SAVOY JAZZ					
❑ SJL-1143	Roots of Rock 'n' Roll Vol. 13: Blues & Early Soul	1985	2.50	5.00	10.00
❑ SJL-1168	Blues, Candy and Big Maybelle	1986	2.50	5.00	10.00
—Reissue of 14011					
SCEPTER					
❑ S-522 [M]	The Soul of Big Maybelle	1964	10.00	20.00	40.00
❑ SS-522 [S]	The Soul of Big Maybelle	1964	12.50	25.00	50.00

Number	Title (A Side/B Side)	Yr	VG	VG+	NM

BIG STAR
ARDENT

Number	Title (A Side/B Side)	Yr	VG	VG+	NM
ADS-1501	Radio City	1974	7.50	15.00	30.00
ADS-2803	#1 Record	1972	6.25	12.50	25.00

PVC

Number	Title (A Side/B Side)	Yr	VG	VG+	NM
7903	Big Star's Third	1978	6.25	12.50	25.00
8933	Sister Lovers	1985	3.75	7.50	15.00

—Reissue of PVC 7903 with new title

BIG THREE, THE
FM

Number	Title (A Side/B Side)	Yr	VG	VG+	NM
307 [M]	The Big Three	1963	7.50	15.00	30.00
S-307 [S]	The Big Three	1963	10.00	20.00	40.00
311 [M]	Live at the Recording Studio	1964	7.50	15.00	30.00
S-311 [S]	Live at the Recording Studio	1964	10.00	20.00	40.00

ROULETTE

Number	Title (A Side/B Side)	Yr	VG	VG+	NM
R-42000 [M]	The Big Three Featuring Cass Elliot	1967	5.00	10.00	20.00
SR-42000 [S]	The Big Three Featuring Cass Elliot	1967	6.25	12.50	25.00

BIGARD, BARNEY
LIBERTY

Number	Title (A Side/B Side)	Yr	VG	VG+	NM
LRP-3072 [M]	Jazz Hall of Fame	1957	10.00	20.00	40.00

BIGARD, BARNEY/ALBERT NICHOLAS
RCA VICTOR

Number	Title (A Side/B Side)	Yr	VG	VG+	NM
LPV-566 [M]	Barney Bigard/Albert Nicholas	1966	5.00	10.00	20.00

BIGELOW, ARTHUR LYNDS
COLUMBIA

Number	Title (A Side/B Side)	Yr	VG	VG+	NM
CL 750 [M]	Christmas Carillon	1955	6.25	12.50	25.00

BIGGS, RICHARD KEYS
CAPITOL

Number	Title (A Side/B Side)	Yr	VG	VG+	NM
T 9013 [M]	Christmas Bells	1954	5.00	10.00	20.00

COLUMBIA

Number	Title (A Side/B Side)	Yr	VG	VG+	NM
CL 6076 [10]	An Organ Concert of Carols	1950	10.00	20.00	40.00

BILK, ACKER
ATCO

Number	Title (A Side/B Side)	Yr	VG	VG+	NM
33-129 [M]	Stranger on the Shore	1961	3.75	7.50	15.00
SD 33-129 [S]	Stranger on the Shore	1961	5.00	10.00	20.00
33-144 [M]	Above the Stars	1962	3.75	7.50	15.00
SD 33-144 [S]	Above the Stars	1962	5.00	10.00	20.00
33-150 [M]	Only You	1963	3.75	7.50	15.00
SD 33-150 [S]	Only You	1963	5.00	10.00	20.00
33-158 [M]	Call Me Mister	1963	3.75	7.50	15.00
SD 33-158 [S]	Call Me Mister	1963	5.00	10.00	20.00
33-168 [M]	A Touch of Latin	1964	3.00	6.00	12.00
SD 33-168 [S]	A Touch of Latin	1964	3.75	7.50	15.00
33-170 [M]	Great Themes from Great Foreign Films	1965	3.00	6.00	12.00
SD 33-170 [S]	Great Themes from Great Foreign Films	1965	3.75	7.50	15.00
33-181 [M]	Acker Bilk in Paris	1966	3.00	6.00	12.00
SD 33-181 [S]	Acker Bilk in Paris	1966	3.75	7.50	15.00
33-197 [M]	Mood for Love	1966	3.00	6.00	12.00
SD 33-197 [S]	Mood for Love	1966	3.75	7.50	15.00

GNP CRESCENDO

Number	Title (A Side/B Side)	Yr	VG	VG+	NM
GNPS-2116	The Best of Acker Bilk: His Clarinet and Strings	198?	2.50	5.00	10.00
GNPS-2171	The Best of Acker Bilk: His Clarinet and Strings, Volume 2	198?	2.50	5.00	10.00
GNPS-2191	Acker Bilk Plays Lennon and McCartney	1988	3.00	6.00	12.00

REPRISE

Number	Title (A Side/B Side)	Yr	VG	VG+	NM
R-6031 [M]	A Stranger No More	1962	5.00	10.00	20.00
RS-6031 [R]	A Stranger No More	1962	3.75	7.50	15.00

BILLION DOLLAR BABIES
POLYDOR

Number	Title (A Side/B Side)	Yr	VG	VG+	NM
PRO 022 [DJ]	Battle Axe	1977	5.00	10.00	20.00

—Promo-only sampler

Number	Title (A Side/B Side)	Yr	VG	VG+	NM
PD-1-6100	Battle Axe	1977	3.75	7.50	15.00

BILLY BOY
PRESTIGE

Number	Title (A Side/B Side)	Yr	VG	VG+	NM
PRLP-7389 [M]	Blues on the South Side	1965	7.50	15.00	30.00

—As "Billy Boy Arnold"

Number	Title (A Side/B Side)	Yr	VG	VG+	NM
PRST-7389 [S]	Blues on the South Side	1965	10.00	20.00	40.00

—As "Billy Boy Arnold"

BIRKIN, JANE, AND SERGE GAINSBOURG
FONTANA

Number	Title (A Side/B Side)	Yr	VG	VG+	NM
SRF-67610	Je T'aime	1970	5.00	10.00	20.00

BIRTH CONTROL
PROPHESY

Number	Title (A Side/B Side)	Yr	VG	VG+	NM
PRS-1002	Birth Control: A New German Rock Group	1970	7.50	15.00	30.00

BISHOP, ELVIN
ALLIGATOR

Number	Title (A Side/B Side)	Yr	VG	VG+	NM
AL-4767	Big Fun	1987	2.50	5.00	10.00

CAPRICORN

Number	Title (A Side/B Side)	Yr	VG	VG+	NM
CP 0134	Let It Flow	1974	3.00	6.00	12.00
CP 0151	Juke Joint Jump	1975	3.00	6.00	12.00
CP 0165	Struttin' My Stuff	1975	3.00	6.00	12.00
CPN-0165	Struttin' My Stuff	1980	2.50	5.00	10.00

—Reissue with revised prefix and Polygram distribution

Number	Title (A Side/B Side)	Yr	VG	VG+	NM
CP 0176	Hometown Boy Makes Good!	1976	3.00	6.00	12.00
2CP 0185 [(2)]	Live! Raisin' Hell	1977	3.75	7.50	15.00
CPN-0215	Hog Heaven	1978	3.00	6.00	12.00

EPIC

Number	Title (A Side/B Side)	Yr	VG	VG+	NM
KE 31563	Rock My Soul	1972	3.75	7.50	15.00
PE 33693	The Best of Elvin Bishop	1975	3.00	6.00	12.00

FILLMORE

Number	Title (A Side/B Side)	Yr	VG	VG+	NM
F 30001	Elvin Bishop Group	1969	5.00	10.00	20.00
Z 30239	Feel It	1970	5.00	10.00	20.00

BISHOP, JOEY
ABC

Number	Title (A Side/B Side)	Yr	VG	VG+	NM
ABCS-656	Joey Bishop Sings Country and Western	1968	7.50	15.00	30.00

BISHOP, WALTER, JR.
COTILLION

Number	Title (A Side/B Side)	Yr	VG	VG+	NM
SD 236	Walter Bishop	1969	5.00	10.00	20.00

JAZZTIME

Number	Title (A Side/B Side)	Yr	VG	VG+	NM
JS-002 [S]	Speak Low	1961	7.50	15.00	30.00
JT-002 [M]	Speak Low	1961	6.25	12.50	25.00

PRESTIGE

Number	Title (A Side/B Side)	Yr	VG	VG+	NM
PRST-7730	The Walter Bishop Trio 1965	1969	5.00	10.00	20.00

BIT 'A SWEET
ABC

Number	Title (A Side/B Side)	Yr	VG	VG+	NM
S-640	Hypnotic 1	1968	10.00	20.00	40.00

BIVONA, GUS
MERCURY

Number	Title (A Side/B Side)	Yr	VG	VG+	NM
MG-20157 [M]	Hey, Dig That Crazy Band	195?	7.50	15.00	30.00

BJOERLING, JUSSI
RCA VICTOR RED SEAL

Number	Title (A Side/B Side)	Yr	VG	VG+	NM
LSC-2570 [S]	The Incomparable Jussi Bjoerling	1962	5.00	10.00	20.00

—Original with "shaded dog" label

BLACK, BILL, 'S COMBO
COLUMBIA

Number	Title (A Side/B Side)	Yr	VG	VG+	NM
CS 1055	Basic Black	1970	3.00	6.00	12.00
CS 9848	Black with Sugar	1969	3.00	6.00	12.00
CS 9957	Raindrops Keep Fallin' on My Head	1970	3.00	6.00	12.00

HI

Number	Title (A Side/B Side)	Yr	VG	VG+	NM
6005	Award Winners	1978	2.50	5.00	10.00
8004	Memphis Tennessee	1977	2.50	5.00	10.00
HL-12001 [M]	Smokie	1960	10.00	20.00	40.00

—Orange and white label

Number	Title (A Side/B Side)	Yr	VG	VG+	NM
HL-12001 [M]	Smokie	1960	15.00	30.00	60.00

—Black label with red and silver logo

Number	Title (A Side/B Side)	Yr	VG	VG+	NM
HL-12002 [M]	Saxy Jazz	1960	10.00	20.00	40.00
HL-12003 [M]	Solid and Raunchy	1960	10.00	20.00	40.00
HL-12004 [M]	That Wonderful Feeling	1961	5.00	10.00	20.00
HL-12005 [M]	Movin'	1961	5.00	10.00	20.00
HL-12006 [M]	Let's Twist Her	1961	3.75	7.50	15.00

—Retitled version of above

Number	Title (A Side/B Side)	Yr	VG	VG+	NM
HL-12006 [M]	Bill Black's Record Hop	1961	6.25	12.50	25.00
HL-12009 [M]	The Untouchable Sound of Bill Black	1962	3.75	7.50	15.00
HL-12012 [M]	Bill Black's Greatest Hits	1963	3.75	7.50	15.00
HL-12013 [M]	Bill Black's Combo Goes West	1963	3.75	7.50	15.00
HL-12015 [M]	Bill Black Plays the Blues	1964	3.75	7.50	15.00
HL-12017 [M]	Bill Black Plays Tunes by Chuck Berry	1964	3.75	7.50	15.00
HL-12020 [M]	Bill Black's Combo Goes Big Band	1964	3.75	7.50	15.00
HL-12023 [M]	More Solid and Raunchy	1965	3.75	7.50	15.00
HL-12027 [M]	Mr. Beat	1965	3.75	7.50	15.00
HL-12032 [M]	All Timers	1966	3.00	6.00	12.00
HL-12033 [M]	Black Lace	1966	3.00	6.00	12.00
HL-12036 [M]	King of the Road	1966	3.00	6.00	12.00
HL-12041 [M]	The Beat Goes On	1967	3.75	7.50	15.00
HL-12044 [M]	Turn Your Lovelight On	1967	3.75	7.50	15.00
HL-12047 [M]	Soulin' the Blues	1968	3.75	7.50	15.00
SHL-32001 [R]	Smokie	1964	5.00	10.00	20.00
SHL-32002 [R]	Saxy Jazz	1964	5.00	10.00	20.00
SHL-32003 [R]	Solid and Raunchy	1964	5.00	10.00	20.00
SHL-32004 [S]	That Wonderful Feeling	1961	6.25	12.50	25.00
SHL-32005 [S]	Movin'	1961	6.25	12.50	25.00
SHL-32006 [S]	Let's Twist Her	1961	5.00	10.00	20.00

—Retitled version of above

Number	Title (A Side/B Side)	Yr	VG	VG+	NM
SHL-32006 [S]	Bill Black's Record Hop	1961	7.50	15.00	30.00
SHL-32009 [S]	The Untouchable Sound of Bill Black	1962	5.00	10.00	20.00
SHL-32012 [S]	Bill Black's Greatest Hits	1963	5.00	10.00	20.00
SHL-32013 [S]	Bill Black's Combo Goes West	1963	5.00	10.00	20.00
SHL-32015 [S]	Bill Black Plays the Blues	1964	5.00	10.00	20.00
SHL-32017 [S]	Bill Black Plays Tunes by Chuck Berry	1964	5.00	10.00	20.00
SHL-32020 [S]	Bill Black's Combo Goes Big Band	1964	5.00	10.00	20.00
SHL-32023 [S]	More Solid and Raunchy	1965	5.00	10.00	20.00
SHL-32027 [S]	Mr. Beat	1965	5.00	10.00	20.00
SHL-32032 [S]	All Timers	1966	3.75	7.50	15.00
SHL-32033 [S]	Black Lace	1966	3.75	7.50	15.00
SHL-32036 [S]	King of the Road	1966	3.75	7.50	15.00
SHL-32041 [S]	The Beat Goes On	1967	3.75	7.50	15.00
SHL-32044 [S]	Turn Your Lovelight On	1967	3.75	7.50	15.00
SHL-32047 [S]	Soulin' the Blues	1968	3.75	7.50	15.00
SHL-32052 [S]	Solid and Raunchy The 3rd	1969	3.75	7.50	15.00
SHL-32061 [S]	More Magic	1971	3.00	6.00	12.00
XSHL-32078	Bill Black's Greatest Hits, Vol. 2	1973	3.00	6.00	12.00
XSHL-32088	Solid and Country	1974	3.00	6.00	12.00
SHL-32093	The World's Greatest Honky Tonk Band	1975	3.00	6.00	12.00
SHL-32104	It's Honky Tonk Time	1976	3.00	6.00	12.00

MEGA

Number	Title (A Side/B Side)	Yr	VG	VG+	NM
MLPS-600	Bill Black Is Back	1973	3.00	6.00	12.00
31-1008	The Memphis Scene	1971	3.00	6.00	12.00
31-1014	Juke Box Favorites	1972	3.00	6.00	12.00
51-5008	Rock 'n' Roll Forever	1973	3.00	6.00	12.00

BLACK, CILLA
CAPITOL

Number	Title (A Side/B Side)	Yr	VG	VG+	NM
ST 2308 [S]	Is It Love?	1965	10.00	20.00	40.00
T 2308 [M]	Is It Love?	1965	6.25	12.50	25.00

BLACK, CLINT
RCA

Number	Title (A Side/B Side)	Yr	VG	VG+	NM
9668-1-R	Killin' Time	1989	3.75	7.50	15.00

B

Number	Title (A Side/B Side)	Yr	VG	VG+	NM
❑ R 124690	Put Yourself in My Place	1990	5.00	10.00	20.00
—Released on vinyl only through BMG Direct Marketing					

BLACK, JEANNE
CAPITOL

Number	Title (A Side/B Side)	Yr	VG	VG+	NM
❑ ST 1513 [S]	A Little Bit Lonely	1961	6.25	12.50	25.00
❑ T 1513 [M]	A Little Bit Lonely	1961	5.00	10.00	20.00

BLACK LIGHTNING
TOWER

Number	Title (A Side/B Side)	Yr	VG	VG+	NM
❑ ST 5129	Shades of Black Lightning	1968	5.00	10.00	20.00

BLACK MERDA
CHESS

Number	Title (A Side/B Side)	Yr	VG	VG+	NM
❑ LP-1551	Black Merda	1970	12.50	25.00	50.00

BLACK OAK ARKANSAS
ATCO

Number	Title (A Side/B Side)	Yr	VG	VG+	NM
❑ SD 36-101	Street Party	1974	3.00	6.00	12.00
❑ SD 36-111	Ain't Life Grand	1975	3.00	6.00	12.00
❑ SD 36-128	Live! Mutha	1976	3.00	6.00	12.00
❑ SD 36-150	The Best of Black Oak Arkansas	1976	3.00	6.00	12.00
❑ SD 33-354	Black Oak Arkansas	1971	3.75	7.50	15.00
❑ 33-381 [M]	Keep the Faith	1972	7.50	15.00	30.00
—White label promo, "DJ Copy Monaural" sticker on cover; no stock copies were issued in mono					
❑ SD 33-381 [S]	Keep the Faith	1972	3.75	7.50	15.00
❑ SD 7008	If An Angel Came to See You, Would You Make Her Feel at Home?	1972	3.75	7.50	15.00
❑ QD 7019 [Q]	Raunch 'n' Roll/Live	1974	5.00	10.00	20.00
❑ SD 7019	Raunch 'n' Roll/Live	1973	3.75	7.50	15.00
❑ SD 7035	High on the Hog	1973	3.75	7.50	15.00
CAPRICORN					
❑ CP 0191	Race with the Devil	1977	3.00	6.00	12.00
❑ CP 0207	I'd Rather Be Sailing	1978	3.00	6.00	12.00
MCA					
❑ 704	X-Rated	198?	2.00	4.00	8.00
—Budget-line reissue					
❑ 2155	X-Rated	1975	3.00	6.00	12.00
❑ 2199	Balls of Fire	1976	3.00	6.00	12.00
❑ 2224	10 Year Overnight Success	1977	3.00	6.00	12.00
STAX					
❑ STS-5504	Early Times	1974	3.75	7.50	15.00

BLACK PEARL
ATLANTIC

Number	Title (A Side/B Side)	Yr	VG	VG+	NM
❑ SD 8220	Black Pearl	1969	6.25	12.50	25.00
PROPHESY					
❑ PRS-1001	Black Pearl — Live!	1970	6.25	12.50	25.00

BLACK RANDY AND THE METROSQUAD
DANGERHOUSE

Number	Title (A Side/B Side)	Yr	VG	VG+	NM
❑ PCP 725	"Pass the Dust, I Think I'm Bowie"	1980	12.50	25.00	50.00

BLACK SABBATH
I.R.S.

Number	Title (A Side/B Side)	Yr	VG	VG+	NM
❑ 82002	Headless Cross	1989	2.50	5.00	10.00
WARNER BROS.					
❑ WS 1871	Black Sabbath	1970	3.75	7.50	15.00
—Green label					
❑ WS 1871	Black Sabbath	1973	2.50	5.00	10.00
—"Burbank" palm trees label					
❑ WS 1871	Black Sabbath	1979	2.00	4.00	8.00
—White or tan label					
❑ WS 1887	Paranoid	1971	3.75	7.50	15.00
—Green label					
❑ WS 1887	Paranoid	1973	2.50	5.00	10.00
—"Burbank" palm trees label					
❑ WS4 1887 [Q]	Paranoid	1974	7.50	15.00	30.00
—All quad copies have "Burbank" palm trees label					
❑ BS 2562	Master of Reality	1971	3.75	7.50	15.00
—Green label					
❑ BS 2562	Master of Reality Poster	1971	6.25	12.50	25.00
❑ BS 2562	Master of Reality	1973	2.50	5.00	10.00
—"Burbank" palm trees label					
❑ BS 2562	Master of Reality	1979	2.00	4.00	8.00
—White or tan label					
❑ BS 2602	Black Sabbath, Vol. 4	1972	3.75	7.50	15.00
—Green label					
❑ BS 2602	Black Sabbath, Vol. 4	1973	2.50	5.00	10.00
—"Burbank" palm trees label					
❑ BS 2602	Black Sabbath, Vol. 4	1979	2.00	4.00	8.00
—White or tan label					
❑ BS 2695	Sabbath Bloody Sabbath	1974	3.75	7.50	15.00
—"Burbank" palm trees label					
❑ BS 2695	Sabbath Bloody Sabbath	1979	2.00	4.00	8.00
—White or tan label					
❑ BS 2822	Sabotage	1975	3.75	7.50	15.00
—"Burbank" palm trees label					
❑ BS 2822	Sabotage	1979	2.00	4.00	8.00
—White or tan label					
❑ 2BS 2923 [(2)]	We Sold Our Souls for Rock 'N' Roll	1975	5.00	10.00	20.00
—"Burbank" palm trees label					
❑ 2BS 2923 [(2)]	We Sold Our Souls for Rock 'N' Roll	1979	2.50	5.00	10.00
—White or tan label					
❑ BS 2969	Technical Ecstasy	1976	3.75	7.50	15.00
—"Burbank" palm trees label					
❑ BS 2969	Technical Ecstasy	1979	2.00	4.00	8.00
—White or tan label					
❑ BSK 3104	Paranoid	1978	2.50	5.00	10.00
—Reissue; "Burbank" palm trees label					
❑ BSK 3104	Paranoid	1979	2.00	4.00	8.00
—Reissue; white or tan label					
❑ BSK 3186	Never Say Die!	1978	3.00	6.00	12.00
❑ BSK 3372	Heaven and Hell	1980	3.00	6.00	12.00
❑ BSK 3605	Mob Rules	1981	3.00	6.00	12.00
❑ 23742 [(2)]	Live Evil	1983	3.75	7.50	15.00
❑ 23978	Born Again	1983	2.50	5.00	10.00
❑ 25337	Seventh Star	1986	2.50	5.00	10.00
❑ 25548	The Eternal Idol	1987	2.50	5.00	10.00

BLACK SHEEP
CAPITOL

Number	Title (A Side/B Side)	Yr	VG	VG+	NM
❑ ST-11369	Black Sheep	1974	5.00	10.00	20.00
❑ ST-11447	Encouraging Words	1975	5.00	10.00	20.00

BLACK VELVET
OKEH

Number	Title (A Side/B Side)	Yr	VG	VG+	NM
❑ OKS 14130	Love City	1969	6.25	12.50	25.00

BLACKBYRDS, THE
FANTASY

Number	Title (A Side/B Side)	Yr	VG	VG+	NM
❑ FPM-4004 [Q]	Flying Start	1975	6.25	12.50	25.00
❑ F-9444	The Blackbyrds	1974	3.75	7.50	15.00
❑ F-9472	Flying Start	1974	3.75	7.50	15.00
❑ F-9490	City Life	1975	3.75	7.50	15.00
❑ F-9518	Unfinished Business	1976	3.75	7.50	15.00
❑ F-9535	Action	1977	3.00	6.00	12.00
❑ F-9570	Night Grooves	1978	3.00	6.00	12.00
❑ F-9602	Better Days	1980	3.00	6.00	12.00

BLACKFOOT, J.D.
FANTASY

Number	Title (A Side/B Side)	Yr	VG	VG+	NM
❑ F-9468	Song of Crazy Horse	1974	5.00	10.00	20.00
❑ F-9487	Southbound and Gone	1975	5.00	10.00	20.00
MERCURY					
❑ SR-61288	The Ultimate Prophecy	1970	15.00	30.00	60.00

BLACKHORSE
DSDA

Number	Title (A Side/B Side)	Yr	VG	VG+	NM
❑ 001	Blackhorse	1979	15.00	30.00	60.00

BLACKMAN, HONOR
LONDON

Number	Title (A Side/B Side)	Yr	VG	VG+	NM
❑ PS 408 [S]	Everything I've Got	1964	10.00	20.00	40.00
❑ LL 3408 [M]	Everything I've Got	1964	7.50	15.00	30.00

BLACKSMOKE
CHOCOLATE CITY

Number	Title (A Side/B Side)	Yr	VG	VG+	NM
❑ 2001	Blacksmoke	1976	5.00	10.00	20.00

BLACKWELL, OTIS
DAVIS

Number	Title (A Side/B Side)	Yr	VG	VG+	NM
❑ 109 [M]	Singin' the Blues	1956	125.00	250.00	500.00
INNER CITY					
❑ 1032	These Are My Songs	1977	5.00	10.00	20.00

BLACKWELL, SCRAPPER
BLUESVILLE

Number	Title (A Side/B Side)	Yr	VG	VG+	NM
❑ BVLP-1047	Mr. Scrapper's Blues	1962	45.00	90.00	180.00
—Blue label, silver print					
❑ BVLP-1047	Mr. Scrapper's Blues	1964	10.00	20.00	40.00
—Blue label with trident logo					

BLADES, JIMMY, AND CHARLES SMART
LONDON

Number	Title (A Side/B Side)	Yr	VG	VG+	NM
❑ LB 82 [10]	Christmas Chimes	195?	7.50	15.00	30.00
—Back cover with liner notes and other Christmas LPs mentioned					
❑ LB 82 [10]	Christmas Chimes	195?	10.00	20.00	40.00
—Back cover with liner notes and no reference to other LPs					

BLAINE, HAL
ABC DUNHILL

Number	Title (A Side/B Side)	Yr	VG	VG+	NM
❑ DS-50035	Have Fun!!! Play Drums!!!	1968	10.00	20.00	40.00
—Without instruction booklet					
❑ DS-50035	Have Fun!!! Play Drums!!!	1968	12.50	25.00	50.00
—With instruction booklet					
DUNHILL					
❑ D-50002 [M]	Drums! Drums! A-Go-Go	1966	7.50	15.00	30.00
❑ DS-50002 [S]	Drums! Drums! A-Go-Go	1966	10.00	20.00	40.00
❑ D-50019 [M]	Psychedelic Percussion	1967	10.00	20.00	40.00
❑ DS-50019 [S]	Psychedelic Percussion	1967	15.00	30.00	60.00
RCA VICTOR					
❑ LPM-2834 [M]	Deuces, "T's," Roadsters & Drums	1963	25.00	50.00	100.00
❑ LSP-2834 [S]	Deuces, "T's," Roadsters & Drums	1963	37.50	75.00	150.00

BLAIR, SALLIE
BETHLEHEM

Number	Title (A Side/B Side)	Yr	VG	VG+	NM
❑ BCP-6009 [M]	Squeeze Me	1957	20.00	40.00	80.00
MGM					
❑ E-3723 [M]	Hello, Tiger!	1959	10.00	20.00	40.00
❑ SE-3723 [S]	Hello, Tiger!	1959	12.50	25.00	50.00

BLAKE, BETTY
BETHLEHEM

Number	Title (A Side/B Side)	Yr	VG	VG+	NM
❑ BCP-6058 [M]	Betty Blake Sings in a Tender Mood	1962	10.00	20.00	40.00
❑ BCPS-6058 [S]	Betty Blake Sings in a Tender Mood	1962	12.50	25.00	50.00

BLAKE, EUBIE
COLUMBIA

Number	Title (A Side/B Side)	Yr	VG	VG+	NM
❑ C2S 847 [(2)]	The Eighty-Six Years of Eubie Blake	1969	5.00	10.00	20.00
—Red "360 Sound" labels					

BLAKE, RAN
ESP-DISK'

Number	Title (A Side/B Side)	Yr	VG	VG+	NM
❑ 1011 [M]	Ran Blake Plays Solo Piano	1965	5.00	10.00	20.00
❑ S-1011 [S]	Ran Blake Plays Solo Piano	1965	5.00	10.00	20.00

Number	Title (A Side/B Side)	Yr	VG	VG+	NM

BLAKE BABIES
CHEWBUD
❑ CBTW-001 [EP] Nicely, Nicely		1987	10.00	20.00	40.00

—1,000 copies pressed
MAMMOTH
❑ MR0016	Earwig	1989	3.00	6.00	12.00
❑ MR0022	Sunburn	1990	3.00	6.00	12.00
❑ MR0025 [EP]	Rosy Jack World	1991	2.50	5.00	10.00

—Red vinyl

BLAKEY, ART, AND THE JAZZ MESSENGERS
BETHLEHEM
❑ BCP-6023 [M]	Hard Drive	1957	20.00	40.00	80.00
❑ BCP-6027 [M]	Art Blakey's Big Band	1958	20.00	40.00	80.00
❑ BCPS-6027 [S]	Art Blakey's Big Band	1959	12.50	25.00	50.00

BLUE NOTE
❑ BLP-1507 [M]	At the Café Bohemia, Volume 1	1956	25.00	50.00	100.00

—Regular version, Lexington Ave. address on label
❑ BLP-1507 [M]	At the Café Bohemia, Volume 1	1956	37.50	75.00	150.00

—"Deep groove" version (deep indentation under label on both sides)
❑ BLP-1507 [M]	At the Café Bohemia, Volume 1	1957	12.50	25.00	50.00

—With W. 63rd St. address on label
❑ BLP-1507 [M]	At the Café Bohemia, Volume 1	1963	6.25	12.50	25.00

—With "New York, USA" address on label
❑ BLP-1508 [M]	At the Café Bohemia, Volume 2	1956	25.00	50.00	100.00

—Regular version, Lexington Ave. address on label
❑ BLP-1508 [M]	At the Café Bohemia, Volume 2	1956	37.50	75.00	150.00

—"Deep groove" version (deep indentation under label on both sides)
❑ BLP-1508 [M]	At the Café Bohemia, Volume 2	1957	12.50	25.00	50.00

—With W. 63rd St. address on label
❑ BLP-1508 [M]	At the Café Bohemia, Volume 2	1963	6.25	12.50	25.00

—With "New York, USA" address on label
❑ BLP-1521 [M]	A Night at Birdland, Volume 1	1956	25.00	50.00	100.00

—Regular version, Lexington Ave. address on label
❑ BLP-1521 [M]	A Night at Birdland, Volume 1	1956	50.00	100.00	200.00

—"Deep groove" version (deep indentation under label on both sides)
❑ BLP-1521 [M]	A Night at Birdland, Volume 1	1957	12.50	25.00	50.00

—With W. 63rd St. address on label
❑ BLP-1521 [M]	A Night at Birdland, Volume 1	1963	6.25	12.50	25.00

—With "New York, USA" address on label
❑ BLP-1522 [M]	A Night at Birdland, Volume 2	1956	25.00	50.00	100.00

—Regular version, Lexington Ave. address on label
❑ BLP-1522 [M]	A Night at Birdland, Volume 2	1956	50.00	100.00	200.00

—"Deep groove" version (deep indentation under label on both sides)
❑ BLP-1522 [M]	A Night at Birdland, Volume 2	1957	12.50	25.00	50.00

—With W. 63rd St. address on label
❑ BLP-1522 [M]	A Night at Birdland, Volume 2	1963	6.25	12.50	25.00

—With "New York, USA" address on label
❑ BLP-1554 [M]	Orgy in Rhythm, Volume 1	1957	25.00	50.00	100.00

—Regular version, with W. 63rd St. address on label
❑ BLP-1554 [M]	Orgy in Rhythm, Volume 1	1957	37.50	75.00	150.00

—"Deep groove" version (deep indentation under label on both sides)
❑ BLP-1554 [M]	Orgy in Rhythm, Volume 1	1963	6.25	12.50	25.00

—With "New York, USA" address on label
❑ BLP-1555 [M]	Orgy in Rhythm, Volume 2	1957	25.00	50.00	100.00

—Regular version, with W. 63rd St. address on label
❑ BLP-1555 [M]	Orgy in Rhythm, Volume 2	1957	37.50	75.00	150.00

—"Deep groove" version (deep indentation under label on both sides)
❑ BLP-1555 [M]	Orgy in Rhythm, Volume 2	1963	6.25	12.50	25.00

—With "New York, USA" address on label
❑ BLP-4003 [M]	Art Blakey and the Jazz Messengers	1958	25.00	50.00	100.00

—Regular version, with W. 63rd St. address on label
❑ BLP-4003 [M]	Art Blakey and the Jazz Messengers	1958	37.50	75.00	150.00

—"Deep groove" version (deep indentation under label on both sides)
❑ BLP-4003 [M]	Art Blakey and the Jazz Messengers	1963	6.25	12.50	25.00

—With "New York, USA" address on label
❑ BST-4003 [S]	Art Blakey and the Jazz Messengers	1959	25.00	50.00	100.00

—"Deep groove" version (deep indentation under label on both sides)
❑ BST-4003 [S]	Art Blakey and the Jazz Messengers	1959	20.00	40.00	80.00

—Regular version, with W. 63rd St. address on label
❑ BST-4003 [S]	Art Blakey and the Jazz Messengers	1963	5.00	10.00	20.00

—With "New York, USA" address on label
❑ BLP-4004 [M]	Holiday for Skins, Volume 1	1958	37.50	75.00	150.00

—Regular version, with W. 63rd St. address on label
❑ BLP-4004 [M]	Holiday for Skins, Volume 1	1958	50.00	100.00	200.00

—"Deep groove" version (deep indentation under label on both sides)
❑ BLP-4004 [M]	Holiday for Skins, Volume 1	1963	6.25	12.50	25.00

—With "New York, USA" address on label
❑ BST-4004 [S]	Holiday for Skins, Volume 1	1959	37.50	75.00	150.00

—"Deep groove" version (deep indentation under label on both sides)
❑ BST-4004 [S]	Holiday for Skins, Volume 1	1959	30.00	60.00	120.00

—Regular version, with W. 63rd St. address on label
❑ BST-4004 [S]	Holiday for Skins, Volume 1	1963	5.00	10.00	20.00

—With "New York, USA" address on label
❑ BLP-4005 [M]	Holiday for Skins, Volume 2	1958	37.50	75.00	150.00

—Regular version, with W. 63rd St. address on label
❑ BLP-4005 [M]	Holiday for Skins, Volume 2	1958	50.00	100.00	200.00

—"Deep groove" version (deep indentation under label on both sides)
❑ BLP-4005 [M]	Holiday for Skins, Volume 2	1963	6.25	12.50	25.00

—With "New York, USA" address on label
❑ BST-4005 [S]	Holiday for Skins, Volume 2	1959	37.50	75.00	150.00

—"Deep groove" version (deep indentation under label on both sides)
❑ BST-4005 [S]	Holiday for Skins, Volume 2	1959	30.00	60.00	120.00

—Regular version, with W. 63rd St. address on label
❑ BST-4005 [S]	Holiday for Skins, Volume 2	1963	5.00	10.00	20.00

—With "New York, USA" address on label
❑ BLP-4015 [M]	At the Jazz Corner of the World, Volume 1	1958	20.00	40.00	80.00

—Regular version, with W. 63rd St. address on label
❑ BLP-4015 [M]	At the Jazz Corner of the World, Volume 1	1958	30.00	60.00	120.00

—"Deep groove" version (deep indentation under label on both sides)
❑ BLP-4015 [M]	At the Jazz Corner of the World, Volume 1	1963	6.25	12.50	25.00

—With "New York, USA" address on label

Number	Title (A Side/B Side)	Yr	VG	VG+	NM
❑ BLP-4016 [M]	At the Jazz Corner of the World, Volume 2	1958	20.00	40.00	80.00

—Regular version, with W. 63rd St. address on label
❑ BLP-4016 [M]	At the Jazz Corner of the World, Volume 2	1958	30.00	60.00	120.00

—"Deep groove" version (deep indentation under label on both sides)
❑ BLP-4016 [M]	At the Jazz Corner of the World, Volume 2	1963	6.25	12.50	25.00

—With "New York, USA" address on label
❑ BLP-4029 [M]	The Big Beat	1960	20.00	40.00	80.00

—Regular version, with W. 63rd St. address on label
❑ BLP-4029 [M]	The Big Beat	1960	25.00	50.00	100.00

—"Deep groove" version (deep indentation under label on both sides)
❑ BLP-4029 [M]	The Big Beat	1963	6.25	12.50	25.00

—With "New York, USA" address on label
❑ BLP-4049 [M]	A Night in Tunisia	1960	20.00	40.00	80.00

—Regular version, with W. 63rd St. address on label
❑ BLP-4049 [M]	A Night in Tunisia	1960	25.00	50.00	100.00

—"Deep groove" version (deep indentation under label on both sides)
❑ BLP-4049 [M]	A Night in Tunisia	1963	6.25	12.50	25.00

—With "New York, USA" address on label
❑ BLP-4054 [M]	Meet You at the Jazz Corner of the World, Volume 1	1960	17.50	35.00	70.00

—With W. 63rd St. address on label
❑ BLP-4054 [M]	Meet You at the Jazz Corner of the World, Volume 1	1963	6.25	12.50	25.00

—With "New York, USA" address on label
❑ BLP-4055 [M]	Meet You at the Jazz Corner of the World, Volume 2	1960	17.50	35.00	70.00

—With W. 63rd St. address on label
❑ BLP-4055 [M]	Meet You at the Jazz Corner of the World, Volume 2	1963	6.25	12.50	25.00

—With "New York, USA" address on label
❑ BLP-4090 [M]	Mosaic	1961	20.00	40.00	80.00

—With 61st St. address on label
❑ BLP-4090 [M]	Mosaic	1963	6.25	12.50	25.00

—With "New York, USA" address on label
❑ BLP-4097 [M]	The African Beat	1961	20.00	40.00	80.00

—With 61st St. address on label
❑ BLP-4097 [M]	The African Beat	1963	6.25	12.50	25.00

—With "New York, USA" address on label
❑ BLP-4104 [M]	Buhaina's Delight	1962	7.50	15.00	30.00
❑ BLP-4156 [M]	The Freedom Rider	1964	7.50	15.00	30.00
❑ BLP-4170 [M]	Free for All	1965	7.50	15.00	30.00
❑ BLP-4193 [M]	Indestructible	1966	7.50	15.00	30.00
❑ BLP-4245 [M]	Like Someone in Love	1967	10.00	20.00	40.00
❑ BLP-5037 [10]	A Night at Birdland, Volume 1	1954	75.00	150.00	300.00
❑ BLP-5038 [10]	A Night at Birdland, Volume 2	1954	75.00	150.00	300.00
❑ BLP-5039 [10]	A Night at Birdland, Volume 3	1954	75.00	150.00	300.00
❑ BST-84015 [S]	At the Jazz Corner of the World, Volume 1	1963	5.00	10.00	20.00

—With "New York, USA" address on label
❑ BST-84015 [S]	At the Jazz Corner of the World, Volume 1	1959	15.00	30.00	60.00

—Regular version, with W. 63rd St. address on label
❑ BST-84016 [S]	At the Jazz Corner of the World, Volume 2	1959	20.00	40.00	80.00

—"Deep groove" version (deep indentation under label on both sides)
❑ BST-84016 [S]	At the Jazz Corner of the World, Volume 2	1959	15.00	30.00	60.00

—Regular version, with W. 63rd St. address on label
❑ BST-84016 [S]	At the Jazz Corner of the World, Volume 2	1963	5.00	10.00	20.00

—With "New York, USA" address on label
❑ BST-84029 [S]	The Big Beat	1960	15.00	30.00	60.00

—With W. 63rd St. address on label
❑ BST-84029 [S]	The Big Beat	1963	5.00	10.00	20.00

—With "New York, USA" address on label
❑ BST-84049 [S]	A Night in Tunisia	1960	15.00	30.00	60.00

—With W. 63rd St. address on label
❑ BST-84049 [S]	A Night in Tunisia	1963	5.00	10.00	20.00

—With "New York, USA" address on label
❑ BST-84054 [S]	Meet You at the Jazz Corner of the World, Volume 1	1960	15.00	30.00	60.00

—With W. 63rd St. address on label
❑ BST-84054 [S]	Meet You at the Jazz Corner of the World, Volume 1	1963	5.00	10.00	20.00

—With "New York, USA" address on label
❑ BST-84055 [S]	Meet You at the Jazz Corner of the World, Volume 2	1960	15.00	30.00	60.00

—With W. 63rd St. address on label
❑ BST-84055 [S]	Meet You at the Jazz Corner of the World, Volume 2	1963	5.00	10.00	20.00

—With "New York, USA" address on label
❑ BST-84090 [S]	Mosaic	1963	5.00	10.00	20.00

—With "New York, USA" address on label
❑ BST-84097 [S]	The African Beat	1961	15.00	30.00	60.00

—With 61st St. address on label
❑ BST-84097 [S]	The African Beat	1963	6.25	125.00	25.00

—With "New York, USA" address on label
❑ BST-84104 [S]	Buhaina's Delight	1962	10.00	20.00	40.00

—With "New York, USA" address on label
❑ BST-84156 [S]	The Freedom Rider	1964	10.00	20.00	40.00

—With "New York, USA" address on label
❑ BST-84170 [S]	Free for All	1965	10.00	20.00	40.00

—With "New York, USA" address on label
❑ BST-84193 [S]	Indestructible	1966	10.00	20.00	40.00

—With "New York, USA" address on label
❑ BST-84245 [S]	Like Someone in Love	1967	10.00	20.00	40.00

—With "New York, USA" address on label
❑ BST-84258 [S]	The Witch Doctor	1969	5.00	10.00	20.00

—With "A Division of Liberty Records" on label
CADET
❑ LP-4049 [M]	Tough!	1966	6.25	12.50	25.00
❑ LPS-4049 [S]	Tough!	1966	7.50	15.00	30.00

COLUMBIA
❑ CL 897 [M]	The Jazz Messengers	1956	20.00	40.00	80.00

—Red and black label with six "eye" logos
❑ CL 1002 [M]	Drum Suite	1957	12.50	25.00	50.00

—Red and black label with six "eye" logos

Number	Title (A Side/B Side)	Yr	VG	VG+	NM
❏ CL 1040 [M]	Hard Bop	1957	15.00	30.00	60.00
—Red and black label with six "eye" logos					
ELEKTRA					
❏ EKL-120 [M]	A Midnight Session with the Jazz Messengers	1957	20.00	40.00	80.00
EMARCY					
❏ MG-26030 [10]	Blakey	1954	62.50	125.00	250.00
EPIC					
❏ LA 16009 [M]	Paris Concert	1960	7.50	15.00	30.00
❏ LA 16017 [M]	Art Blakey in Paris	1961	7.50	15.00	30.00
❏ BA 17009 [S]	Paris Concert	1960	10.00	20.00	40.00
❏ BA 17017 [S]	Art Blakey in Paris	1961	10.00	20.00	40.00
IMPULSE!					
❏ A-7 [M]	Art Blakey!!!! Jazz Messengers!!!!	1961	7.50	15.00	30.00
❏ AS-7 [S]	Art Blakey!!!! Jazz Messengers!!!!	1961	10.00	20.00	40.00
❏ A-45 [M]	A Jazz Message	1963	7.50	15.00	30.00
❏ AS-45 [S]	A Jazz Message	1963	10.00	20.00	40.00
JOSIE					
❏ JOZ-3501 [M]	Cu-Bop	1962	10.00	20.00	40.00
—Reissue of Jubilee LP					
❏ JS-3501 [S]	Cu-Bop	1962	7.50	15.00	30.00
JUBILEE					
❏ JLP-1049 [M]	Cu-Bop	1958	20.00	40.00	80.00
LIMELIGHT					
❏ LM-82001 [M]	'S Make It	1965	5.00	10.00	20.00
❏ LM-82019 [M]	Soul Finger	1965	5.00	10.00	20.00
❏ LM-82034 [M]	Buttercorn Lady	1966	5.00	10.00	20.00
❏ LM-82038 [M]	Hold On, I'm Coming	1966	5.00	10.00	20.00
❏ LS-86001 [S]	'S Make It	1965	6.25	12.50	25.00
❏ LS-86019 [S]	Soul Finger	1965	6.25	12.50	25.00
❏ LS-86034 [S]	Buttercorn Lady	1966	6.25	12.50	25.00
❏ LS-86038 [S]	Hold On, I'm Coming	1966	6.25	12.50	25.00
MOSAIC					
❏ MR10-141 [(10)]	The Complete Blue Note Recordings of Art Blakey's 1960 Jazz Messengers	199?	37.50	75.00	150.00
PACIFIC JAZZ					
❏ PJ-15 [M]	Ritual	1961	10.00	20.00	40.00
—Reissue of 402					
❏ PJM-402 [M]	Ritual	1957	20.00	40.00	80.00
PRESTIGE					
❏ 10047	Child's Dance	197?	3.00	6.00	12.00
RCA VICTOR					
❏ LPM-2654 [M]	A Night in Tunisia	1963	10.00	20.00	40.00
—Reissue of Vik 1115					
❏ LSP-2654 [R]	A Night in Tunisia	1963	5.00	10.00	20.00
RIVERSIDE					
❏ RS-438 [M]	Caravan	1962	6.25	12.50	25.00
❏ RS-464 [M]	Ugetsu	1963	6.25	12.50	25.00
❏ RS-493 [M]	Kyoto	1966	5.00	10.00	20.00
❏ RS-9438 [S]	Caravan	1962	7.50	15.00	30.00
❏ RS-9464 [S]	Ugetsu	1963	7.50	15.00	30.00
❏ RS-9493 [S]	Kyoto	1966	6.25	12.50	25.00
SAVOY					
❏ MG-12171 [M]	Art Blakey and the Jazz Messengers	1960	7.50	15.00	30.00
UNITED ARTISTS					
❏ UAJ-14002 [M]	Three Blind Mice	1962	10.00	20.00	40.00
❏ UAJS-15002 [S]	Three Blind Mice	1962	12.50	25.00	50.00
VIK					
❏ LX-1103 [M]	Art Blakey and the Jazz Messengers Play Selections from Lerner and Loewe	1957	25.00	50.00	100.00
❏ LX-1115 [M]	A Night in Tunisia	1958	25.00	50.00	100.00

BLAKEY, ART, AND THE JAZZ MESSENGERS/ ELMO HOPE

PACIFIC JAZZ

Number	Title (A Side/B Side)	Yr	VG	VG+	NM
❏ PJ-33 [M]	The Jazz Messengers and Elmo Hope	1962	10.00	20.00	40.00

BLAKEY, ART, AND THE JAZZ MESSENGERS WITH THELONIOUS MONK

ATLANTIC

Number	Title (A Side/B Side)	Yr	VG	VG+	NM
❏ 1278 [M]	Art Blakey's Jazz Messengers with Thelonious Monk	1958	12.50	25.00	50.00
—Black label					
❏ 1278 [M]	Art Blakey's Jazz Messengers with Thelonious Monk	1960	5.00	10.00	20.00
—Multicolor label, white "fan" logo					
❏ SD 1278 [S]	Art Blakey's Jazz Messengers with Thelonious Monk	1959	10.00	20.00	40.00
—Green label					

BLANC, MEL

CAPITOL

Number	Title (A Side/B Side)	Yr	VG	VG+	NM
❏ H-436 [10]	Party Panic	1953	25.00	50.00	100.00

BLAND, BOBBY

ABC

Number	Title (A Side/B Side)	Yr	VG	VG+	NM
❏ D-895	Get On Down with Bobby Bland	1975	3.00	6.00	12.00
❏ AB-1018	Reflections in Blue	1977	2.50	5.00	10.00
❏ AA-1075	Come Fly with Me	1978	2.50	5.00	10.00
ABC DUKE					
❏ DLPS-74	Two Steps from the Blues	197?	3.00	6.00	12.00
❏ DLP-75	Here's the Man!!!	1974	3.00	6.00	12.00
❏ DLP-77	Call On Me/That's the Way Love Is	1974	3.00	6.00	12.00
❏ DLP-78	Ain't Nothing You Can Do	1974	3.00	6.00	12.00
❏ DLP-79	The Soul of the Man	1974	3.00	6.00	12.00
❏ DLP-84	The Best of Bobby Bland	1974	3.00	6.00	12.00
❏ DLP-86	The Best of Bobby Bland, Volume 2	1974	3.00	6.00	12.00
❏ DLP-88	A Touch of the Blues	1974	3.00	6.00	12.00
❏ DLP-89	Spotlighting the Man	1974	3.00	6.00	12.00
❏ DLP 92-2 [(2)]	Introspective of the Early Years	1974	5.00	10.00	20.00

Number	Title (A Side/B Side)	Yr	VG	VG+	NM
ABC DUNHILL					
❏ DSX-50163	His California Album	1973	3.75	7.50	15.00
❏ DSX-50169	Dreamer	1974	3.75	7.50	15.00
BLUESWAY					
❏ BLS-6065	Call On Me	197?	3.75	7.50	15.00
DUKE					
❏ DLP-74 [M]	Two Steps from the Blues	1961	62.50	125.00	250.00
—Purple and yellow label					
❏ DLP-74 [M]	Two Steps from the Blues	1962	25.00	50.00	100.00
—Orange label, black vinyl					
❏ DLP-74 [M]	Two Steps from the Blues	1962	62.50	125.00	250.00
—Orange label, red vinyl					
❏ DLPS-74 [R]	Two Steps from the Blues	196?	15.00	30.00	60.00
❏ DLP-75 [M]	Here's the Man!!!	1962	25.00	50.00	100.00
—Orange label					
❏ DLP-75 [M]	Here's the Man!!!	1962	50.00	100.00	200.00
—Purple and yellow label					
❏ DLPS-75 [S]	Here's the Man!!!	196?	25.00	50.00	100.00
—Without spoken intro to "36-22-36"					
❏ DLPS-75 [S]	Here's the Man!!!	1962	50.00	100.00	200.00
—With spoken intro to "36-22-36"					
❏ DLP-77 [M]	Call On Me/That's the Way Love Is	1963	25.00	50.00	100.00
❏ DLPS-77 [S]	Call On Me/That's the Way Love Is	1963	37.50	75.00	150.00
❏ DLP-78 [M]	Ain't Nothing You Can Do	1964	20.00	40.00	80.00
❏ DLPS-78 [S]	Ain't Nothing You Can Do	1964	30.00	60.00	120.00
❏ DLP-79 [M]	The Soul of the Man	1966	20.00	40.00	80.00
❏ DLPS-79 [S]	The Soul of the Man	1966	30.00	60.00	120.00
❏ DLP-84 [M]	The Best of Bobby Bland	1967	5.00	10.00	20.00
❏ DLPS-84 [P]	The Best of Bobby Bland	1967	6.25	12.50	25.00
❏ DLP-86 [M]	The Best of Bobby Bland, Volume 2	1968	6.25	12.50	25.00
❏ DLPS-86 [P]	The Best of Bobby Bland, Volume 2	1968	5.00	10.00	20.00
❏ DLP-88 [M]	A Touch of the Blues	1968	6.25	12.50	25.00
❏ DLPS-88 [S]	A Touch of the Blues	1968	5.00	10.00	20.00
❏ DLPS-89	Spotlighting the Man	1969	5.00	10.00	20.00
❏ DLPS-90	If Loving You Is Wrong	1970	5.00	10.00	20.00
MCA					
❏ 3157	I Feel Good, I Feel Fine	1979	2.50	5.00	10.00
❏ 4172 [(2)]	Introspective of the Early Years	198?	2.50	5.00	10.00
—Reissue of Duke 92					
❏ 5145	Sweet Vibrations	1980	2.50	5.00	10.00
❏ 5233	Try Me, I'm Real	1981	2.50	5.00	10.00
❏ 5297	Here We Go Again	1982	2.50	5.00	10.00
❏ 5425	Tell Mr. Bland	1983	2.50	5.00	10.00
❏ 5503	You've Got Me Loving You	1984	2.50	5.00	10.00
❏ 27013	The Best of Bobby Bland	198?	2.00	4.00	8.00
—Reissue of Duke 84					
❏ 27036	Two Steps from the Blues	198?	2.00	4.00	8.00
—Reissue of Duke 74					
❏ 27038	Here's the Man!!!	198?	2.00	4.00	8.00
—Reissue of Duke 75					
❏ 27040	Ain't Nothing You Can Do	198?	2.00	4.00	8.00
—Reissue of Duke 78					
❏ 27041	The Soul of the Man	1984	2.00	4.00	8.00
—Reissue of Duke 79					
❏ 27042	Call On Me/That's the Way Love Is	1984	2.00	4.00	8.00
—Reissue of Duke 77					
❏ 27043	Reflections in Blue	1984	2.00	4.00	8.00
—Reissue of ABC 1018					
❏ 27044	Come Fly with Me	1984	2.00	4.00	8.00
—Reissue of ABC 1075					
❏ 27045	The Best of Bobby Bland, Volume 2	1984	2.00	4.00	8.00
—Reissue of Duke 86					
❏ 27047	A Touch of the Blues	1984	2.00	4.00	8.00
—Reissue of Duke 88					
❏ 27048	Spotlighting the Man	1984	2.00	4.00	8.00
—Reissue of Duke 89					
❏ 27073	I Feel Good, I Feel Fine	1985	2.00	4.00	8.00
—Reissue of MCA 3157					
❏ 27076	Sweet Vibrations	198?	2.00	4.00	8.00
—Reissue of 5145					

BLAND, BOBBY, AND B.B. KING

ABC DUNHILL

Number	Title (A Side/B Side)	Yr	VG	VG+	NM
❏ DSY-50190 [(2)]	Together for the First Time...Live	1974	3.75	7.50	15.00
ABC IMPULSE!					
❏ 9317	Together Again...Live	1976	3.00	6.00	12.00
COMMAND					
❏ CQDY-40012 [(2)Q]	Together for the First Time...Live	1974	6.25	12.50	25.00
MCA					
❏ 4160 [(2)]	Together for the First Time...Live	198?	2.50	5.00	10.00
—Reissue of ABC Dunhill 50190					
❏ 27012	Together Again...Live	198?	2.00	4.00	8.00
—Reissue of ABC Impulse! 9317					

BLASSIE, FRED

RHINO

Number	Title (A Side/B Side)	Yr	VG	VG+	NM
❏ RNLP-813 [PD]	I Bite the Songs	1985	5.00	10.00	20.00

BLASTERS, THE

The group on Crown is not the same as the others.

CROWN

Number	Title (A Side/B Side)	Yr	VG	VG+	NM
❏ CST-392 [S]	Sounds of the Drags	1963	6.25	12.50	25.00
❏ CLP-5392 [M]	Sounds of the Drags	1963	5.00	10.00	20.00
ROLLIN' ROCK					
❏ 021	American Music	1980	12.50	25.00	50.00
SLASH					
❏ SR 109	The Blasters	1981	3.75	7.50	15.00
❏ BKS 3680	The Blasters	1982	2.50	5.00	10.00
—With blue labels; reissue of 109					
❏ 23735 [EP]	Over There: Live at the Venue, London	1982	2.50	5.00	10.00
❏ 23818	Non Fiction	1983	2.50	5.00	10.00

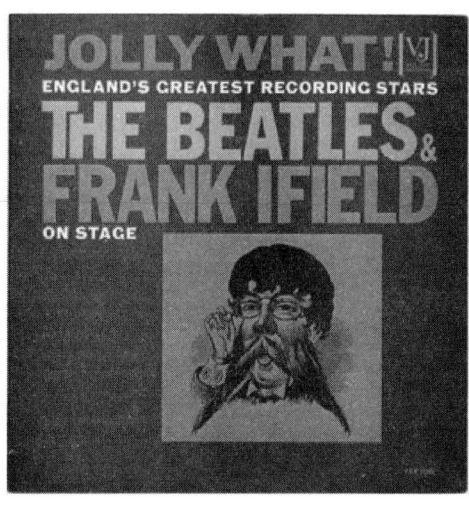

This outrageously rare album by Frank Ballard came out on the Phillips International label in 1962.

Jolly What! The Beatles and Frank Ifield On Stage was Vee Jay's first "milk the cash cow" Beatles compilation album. As such, it's not as rare as some of the others, but it has been counterfeited. Authentic covers are dark blue; counterfeits are black.

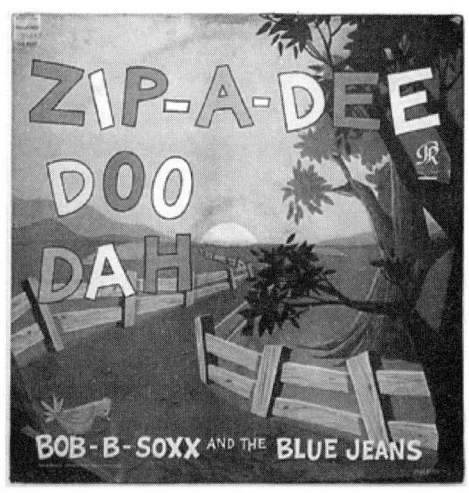

One of the rarest and most sought after of all the "late mono" American albums is Big Brother and the Holding Company's *Cheap Thrills.* Here's one of the mono labels.

Bob B. Soxx and the Blue Jeans had one hit, "Zip-a-Dee Do-Dah." Phil Spector put together this album as a result. As with all Philles LPs before 1965, it's quite rare.

The first album by David Bowie came out on the Deram label in 1968 and is among his top LP rarities. This stereo version is hard enough to find; the mono version is almost impossible.

This King "greatest hits" album was actually a reissue of *Try Me,* the second James Brown LP.

Number	Title (A Side/B Side)	Yr	VG	VG+	NM
❑ 25093	Hard Line	1985	2.50	5.00	10.00

WARNER BROS.

Number	Title (A Side/B Side)	Yr	VG	VG+	NM
❑ WBMS-130 [DJ]	Music and Interviews	1985	10.00	20.00	40.00

—Part of "The Warner Bros. Music Show" series; one side is The Blasters; the other side is The Smiths, which accounts for this piece's value

BLAZING REDHEADS
REFERENCE RECORDINGS

Number	Title (A Side/B Side)	Yr	VG	VG+	NM
❑ RR-26	Blazing Redheads	1988	5.00	10.00	20.00
❑ RR-41	Crazed Women	1991	5.00	10.00	20.00

BLESSED END
TNS

Number	Title (A Side/B Side)	Yr	VG	VG+	NM
❑ 248	Movin' On	1971	75.00	150.00	300.00

BLEY, CARLA
JCOA

Number	Title (A Side/B Side)	Yr	VG	VG+	NM
❑ 3-LP-EOTH [(3)]	Escalator Over the Hill	1971	6.25	12.50	25.00

BLEY, PAUL
DEBUT

Number	Title (A Side/B Side)	Yr	VG	VG+	NM
❑ DLP-7 [10]	Introducing Paul Bley	1954	75.00	150.00	300.00

EMARCY

Number	Title (A Side/B Side)	Yr	VG	VG+	NM
❑ MG-36092 [M]	Paul Bley	1955	25.00	50.00	100.00

ESP-DISK'

Number	Title (A Side/B Side)	Yr	VG	VG+	NM
❑ S-1008 [S]	Barrage	1965	5.00	10.00	20.00
❑ S-1021 [S]	Closer	1966	5.00	10.00	20.00

GENE NORMAN

Number	Title (A Side/B Side)	Yr	VG	VG+	NM
❑ GNP-31 [M]	Solemn Meditation	1957	6.25	12.50	25.00

LIMELIGHT

Number	Title (A Side/B Side)	Yr	VG	VG+	NM
❑ LM-82060 [M]	Mr. Joy	1967	5.00	10.00	20.00

SAVOY

Number	Title (A Side/B Side)	Yr	VG	VG+	NM
❑ MG-12182 [M]	Footloose!	1964	6.25	12.50	25.00

WING

Number	Title (A Side/B Side)	Yr	VG	VG+	NM
❑ MGW-60001 [M]	Paul Bley	1956	12.50	25.00	50.00

BLEYER, ARCHIE
CADENCE

Number	Title (A Side/B Side)	Yr	VG	VG+	NM
❑ CLP-3044 [M]	Moonlight Serenade	1962	5.00	10.00	20.00
❑ CLP-25044 [S]	Moonlight Serenade	1962	6.25	12.50	25.00

BLIND FAITH
Also see GINGER BAKER'S AIR FORCE; ERIC CLAPTON; STEVE WINWOOD.
ATCO

Number	Title (A Side/B Side)	Yr	VG	VG+	NM
❑ 33-304A [M]	Blind Faith	1969	50.00	100.00	200.00

—White label promo only

Number	Title (A Side/B Side)	Yr	VG	VG+	NM
❑ SD 33-304A [S]	Blind Faith	1969	6.25	12.50	25.00

—Cover with naked girl on Side 1 and same scene without girl on Side 2

Number	Title (A Side/B Side)	Yr	VG	VG+	NM
❑ SD 33-304B [S]	Blind Faith	1969	3.75	7.50	15.00

—Cover with band photo on Side 1 and song lyrics on Side 2
MOBILE FIDELITY

Number	Title (A Side/B Side)	Yr	VG	VG+	NM
❑ 1-186	Blind Faith	1985	10.00	20.00	40.00

—Audiophile vinyl
RSO

Number	Title (A Side/B Side)	Yr	VG	VG+	NM
❑ RS-1-3016	Blind Faith	1977	2.50	5.00	10.00

—Reissue with naked girl on one side and band photo on the other

Number	Title (A Side/B Side)	Yr	VG	VG+	NM
❑ 825094-1	Blind Faith	1986	2.00	4.00	8.00

BLOCKER, DAN
TREY

Number	Title (A Side/B Side)	Yr	VG	VG+	NM
❑ TLP-903 [M]	Tales for Young 'Uns	1961	12.50	25.00	50.00

BLOCKER, DAN, AND JOHN MITCHUM
Also see LORNE GREENE, MICHAEL LANDON AND DAN BLOCKER.
RCA VICTOR

Number	Title (A Side/B Side)	Yr	VG	VG+	NM
❑ LPM-2896 [M]	Our Land — Our Heritage	1964	7.50	15.00	30.00
❑ LSP-2896 [S]	Our Land — Our Heritage	1964	10.00	20.00	40.00

BLOND
FONTANA

Number	Title (A Side/B Side)	Yr	VG	VG+	NM
❑ SRF-67067	Blond	1969	5.00	10.00	20.00

BLONDE ON BLONDE
JANUS

Number	Title (A Side/B Side)	Yr	VG	VG+	NM
❑ JLP-3003	Contrasts	1969	6.25	12.50	25.00

BLONDIE
CHRYSALIS

Number	Title (A Side/B Side)	Yr	VG	VG+	NM
❑ CHS 24 PDJ [DJ]	At Home with Debbie Harry and Chris Stein	1981	12.50	25.00	50.00

—Open-end interview with script

Number	Title (A Side/B Side)	Yr	VG	VG+	NM
❑ CHR 1165	Blondie	1977	3.00	6.00	12.00

—Reissue of Private Stock album

Number	Title (A Side/B Side)	Yr	VG	VG+	NM
❑ CHR 1166	Plastic Letters	1977	3.00	6.00	12.00

—Blue and white label

Number	Title (A Side/B Side)	Yr	VG	VG+	NM
❑ CHR 1166	Plastic Letters	1977	5.00	10.00	20.00

—Green label

Number	Title (A Side/B Side)	Yr	VG	VG+	NM
❑ CHR 1192	Parallel Lines	1978	3.75	7.50	15.00

—First pressing, with 3:54 version of "Heart of Glass"

Number	Title (A Side/B Side)	Yr	VG	VG+	NM
❑ CHR 1192	Parallel Lines	1979	2.50	5.00	10.00

—Second pressing, with 5:50 version of "Heart of Glass (Disco Version)"

Number	Title (A Side/B Side)	Yr	VG	VG+	NM
❑ CHE 1225	Eat to the Beat	1979	2.50	5.00	10.00
❑ CHE 1290	Autoamerican	1980	2.50	5.00	10.00
❑ CHS 1337	The Best of Blondie	1981	2.50	5.00	10.00
❑ CHR 1384	The Hunter	1982	2.00	4.00	8.00
❑ CHP 5001 [PD]	Parallel Lines	1979	6.25	12.50	25.00

—Picture disc

Number	Title (A Side/B Side)	Yr	VG	VG+	NM
❑ F1 32748 [(2)]	The Remix Project: Remixed, Remade, Remodeled	1995	3.75	7.50	15.00
❑ PV 41165	Blondie	1983	2.00	4.00	8.00

—Reissue

Number	Title (A Side/B Side)	Yr	VG	VG+	NM
❑ PV 41166	Plastic Letters	1983	2.00	4.00	8.00

—Reissue

Number	Title (A Side/B Side)	Yr	VG	VG+	NM
❑ FV 41192	Parallel Lines	1983	2.00	4.00	8.00

—Reissue

Number	Title (A Side/B Side)	Yr	VG	VG+	NM
❑ PV 41192	Parallel Lines	1986	2.00	4.00	8.00

—Reissue

Number	Title (A Side/B Side)	Yr	VG	VG+	NM
❑ PV 41225	Eat to the Beat	1983	2.00	4.00	8.00

—Reissue

Number	Title (A Side/B Side)	Yr	VG	VG+	NM
❑ PV 41290	Autoamerican	1983	2.00	4.00	8.00

—Reissue

Number	Title (A Side/B Side)	Yr	VG	VG+	NM
❑ FV 41337	The Best of Blondie	1983	2.00	4.00	8.00

—Reissue

Number	Title (A Side/B Side)	Yr	VG	VG+	NM
❑ PV 41337	The Best of Blondie	1986	2.00	4.00	8.00

—Reissue

Number	Title (A Side/B Side)	Yr	VG	VG+	NM
❑ PV 41384	The Hunter	1983	2.00	4.00	8.00

—Reissue

Number	Title (A Side/B Side)	Yr	VG	VG+	NM
❑ V2X 41658 [(2)]	Once More into the Bleach	1988	3.75	7.50	15.00

—Remixes of Blondie and Debbie Harry tracks

Number	Title (A Side/B Side)	Yr	VG	VG+	NM
❑ R 200816 [(2)]	Once More into the Bleach	1988	4.50	9.00	18.00

—BMG Music Service edition
MOBILE FIDELITY

Number	Title (A Side/B Side)	Yr	VG	VG+	NM
❑ 1-050	Parallel Lines	1980	7.50	15.00	30.00

—Audiophile vinyl
PRIVATE STOCK

Number	Title (A Side/B Side)	Yr	VG	VG+	NM
❑ PS-2023	Blondie	1976	6.25	12.50	25.00

BLOOD, SWEAT AND TEARS
ABC

Number	Title (A Side/B Side)	Yr	VG	VG+	NM
❑ 1015	Brand New Day	1977	2.50	5.00	10.00

COLUMBIA

Number	Title (A Side/B Side)	Yr	VG	VG+	NM
❑ CS 9616	Child Is Father to the Man	1970	2.50	5.00	10.00

—Orange label

Number	Title (A Side/B Side)	Yr	VG	VG+	NM
❑ CS 9616 [M]	Child Is Father to the Man	1968	6.25	12.50	25.00

—White label promo only, "Special Mono Radio Station Copy" sticker on cover, with same number as stereo edition

Number	Title (A Side/B Side)	Yr	VG	VG+	NM
❑ CS 9616 [S]	Child Is Father to the Man	1968	3.75	7.50	15.00

—Red "360 Sound" label

Number	Title (A Side/B Side)	Yr	VG	VG+	NM
❑ PC 9619	Child Is Father to the Man	1980	2.00	4.00	8.00
❑ CS 9720	Blood, Sweat and Tears	1969	3.75	7.50	15.00

—Red "360 Sound" label

Number	Title (A Side/B Side)	Yr	VG	VG+	NM
❑ CS 9720	Blood, Sweat and Tears	1970	2.50	5.00	10.00

—Orange label

Number	Title (A Side/B Side)	Yr	VG	VG+	NM
❑ PC 9720	Blood, Sweat and Tears	1980	2.00	4.00	8.00
❑ KC 30090	Blood, Sweat and Tears 3	1970	2.50	5.00	10.00
❑ PC 30090	Blood, Sweat and Tears 3	1986	2.00	4.00	8.00
❑ KC 30590	BS&T; 4	1971	2.50	5.00	10.00
❑ CQ 30994 [Q]	Blood, Sweat and Tears	1972	5.00	10.00	20.00
❑ CQ 31170 [Q]	Blood, Sweat and Tears' Greatest Hits	1972	5.00	10.00	20.00
❑ KC 31170	Blood, Sweat and Tears' Greatest Hits	1972	2.50	5.00	10.00

—With the single versions of "You've Made Me So Very Happy," "Spinning Wheel," and "And When I Die" (all in mono)

Number	Title (A Side/B Side)	Yr	VG	VG+	NM
❑ PC 31170	Blood, Sweat and Tears' Greatest Hits	1980	2.00	4.00	8.00
❑ PCQ 31170 [Q]	Blood, Sweat and Tears' Greatest Hits	1976	4.50	9.00	18.00

—Reissue with new prefix

Number	Title (A Side/B Side)	Yr	VG	VG+	NM
❑ KC 31780	New Blood	1972	2.50	5.00	10.00
❑ KC 32180	No Sweat	1973	2.50	5.00	10.00
❑ CQ 32929 [Q]	Mirror Image	1974	5.00	10.00	20.00
❑ PC 32929	Mirror Image	1974	2.50	5.00	10.00
❑ PC 33484	New City	1975	2.50	5.00	10.00
❑ PC 34233	More Than Ever	1976	2.50	5.00	10.00
❑ HC 49619	Child Is Father to the Man	1981	12.50	25.00	50.00

—Half-speed mastered edition
DIRECT DISK

Number	Title (A Side/B Side)	Yr	VG	VG+	NM
❑ SD-16605	Blood, Sweat and Tears	1981	15.00	30.00	60.00

MCA

Number	Title (A Side/B Side)	Yr	VG	VG+	NM
❑ L33-1865 [DJ]	Nuclear Blues	1980	3.75	7.50	15.00

—Promo only on gold vinyl

Number	Title (A Side/B Side)	Yr	VG	VG+	NM
❑ 3061	Nuclear Blues	1980	2.50	5.00	10.00
❑ 3227	Blood, Sweat and Tears	1981	—	—	—

—Canceled?
MOBILE FIDELITY

Number	Title (A Side/B Side)	Yr	VG	VG+	NM
❑ 1-251	Blood, Sweat and Tears	1996	30.00	60.00	120.00

—Audiophile vinyl; fewer than 2,000 pressed

BLOODROCK
CAPITOL

Number	Title (A Side/B Side)	Yr	VG	VG+	NM
❑ ST-435	Bloodrock	1970	3.75	7.50	15.00
❑ ST-491	Bloodrock 2	1970	3.75	7.50	15.00
❑ SM-645	Bloodrock U.S.A.	197?	2.50	5.00	10.00

—Reissue with new prefix

Number	Title (A Side/B Side)	Yr	VG	VG+	NM
❑ SMAS-645	Bloodrock U.S.A.	1971	3.75	7.50	15.00
❑ SM-765	Bloodrock 3	197?	2.50	5.00	10.00

—Reissue with new prefix

Number	Title (A Side/B Side)	Yr	VG	VG+	NM
❑ ST-765	Bloodrock 3	1971	3.75	7.50	15.00
❑ SVBB-11038 [(2)]	Bloodrock Live	1972	5.00	10.00	20.00
❑ SW-11109	Bloodrock Passage	1972	3.75	7.50	15.00
❑ SMAS-11259	Whirlwind Tongues	1973	3.75	7.50	15.00
❑ SM-11417	Bloodrock 'N' Roll	1975	3.00	6.00	12.00

BLOODSTONE
LONDON

Number	Title (A Side/B Side)	Yr	VG	VG+	NM
❑ XPS 620	Natural High	1973	5.00	10.00	20.00
❑ XPS 634	Unreal	1973	5.00	10.00	20.00
❑ APS 647	I Need Time	1974	5.00	10.00	20.00
❑ PS 654	Riddle of the Sphinx	1975	3.75	7.50	15.00
❑ PS 671	Do a Thing?	1976	3.75	7.50	15.00

MOTOWN

Number	Title (A Side/B Side)	Yr	VG	VG+	NM
❑ M7-909	Don't Stop!	1978	3.00	6.00	12.00

T-NECK

Number	Title (A Side/B Side)	Yr	VG	VG+	NM
❑ FZ 38115	We Go a Long Way Back	1982	2.50	5.00	10.00
❑ FZ 39146	Bloodstone's Party	1984	2.50	5.00	10.00
❑ PZ 40016	Greatest Hits	1985	2.00	4.00	8.00
❑ PZ 40042	Lullaby of Broadway	1985	2.00	4.00	8.00

Number	Title (A Side/B Side)	Yr	VG	VG+	NM
BLOODY MARY					
FAMILY PRODUCTIONS					
❏ FPS-2707	Bloody Mary	1972	6.25	12.50	25.00
BLOOMFIELD, MIKE, AND AL KOOPER					
COLUMBIA					
❏ KGP 6 [(2)]	The Live Adventures of Mike Bloomfield & Al Kooper	1969	6.25	12.50	25.00
—Red "360 Sound" labels					
❏ PG 6 [(2)]	The Live Adventures of Mike Bloomfield & Al Kooper	197?	3.00	6.00	12.00
—Reissue with new prefix					
BLOOMFIELD, MIKE/AL KOOPER/STEVE STILLS					
COLUMBIA					
❏ CS 9701	Super Session	1968	5.00	10.00	20.00
—Red "360 Sound" label					
❏ CS 9701	Super Session	1970	2.50	5.00	10.00
—Orange label					
❏ PC 9701	Super Session	198?	2.00	4.00	8.00
—Reissue with new prefix					
❏ CQ 30991 [Q]	Super Session	1971	5.00	10.00	20.00
MOBILE FIDELITY					
❏ 1-178	Super Session	198?	10.00	20.00	40.00
—Audiophile vinyl					
BLUE, DAVID					
ASYLUM					
❏ 7E-1043	Com'n Back for More	1975	2.50	5.00	10.00
❏ 7E-1077	Cupid's Arrow	1976	2.50	5.00	10.00
❏ SD 5052	Stories	1972	3.00	6.00	12.00
❏ SD 5066	The Nice Baby and the Angel	1973	3.00	6.00	12.00
ELEKTRA					
❏ EKM-4003 [M]	David Blue	1966	5.00	10.00	20.00
❏ EKS-74003 [S]	David Blue	1966	5.00	10.00	20.00
REPRISE					
❏ RS 6296	These 23 Days in September	1968	3.75	7.50	15.00
BLUE ANGEL					
Features CYNDI LAUPER.					
POLYDOR					
❏ PD-1-6300	Blue Angel	1980	5.00	10.00	20.00
BLUE BARONS, THE					
PHILIPS					
❏ PHM 200017 [M]	Twist to the Great Blues Hits	1962	5.00	10.00	20.00
❏ PHS 600017 [S]	Twist to the Great Blues Hits	1962	6.25	12.50	25.00
BLUE BEATS, THE					
A.A.					
❏ 133 [M]	The Beatle Beat	1964	10.00	20.00	40.00
BLUE BOYS, THE					
RCA VICTOR					
❏ LPM-3331 [M]	We Remember Jim	1965	6.25	12.50	25.00
❏ LSP-3331 [S]	We Remember Jim	1965	7.50	15.00	30.00
❏ LPM-3529 [M]	Sounds of Jim Reeves	1966	5.00	10.00	20.00
❏ LSP-3529 [S]	Sounds of Jim Reeves	1966	6.25	12.50	25.00
❏ LPM-3696 [M]	The Blue Boys in Person	1967	5.00	10.00	20.00
❏ LSP-3696 [S]	The Blue Boys in Person	1967	6.25	12.50	25.00
❏ LPM-3794 [M]	Hit After Hit	1967	6.25	12.50	25.00
❏ LSP-3794 [S]	Hit After Hit	1967	5.00	10.00	20.00
BLUE CHEER					
MEGAFORCE					
❏ CAROL-1395-1	The Beast Is Back	198?	3.00	6.00	12.00
PHILIPS					
❏ PHM 200264 [M]	Vincebus Eruptum	1968	20.00	40.00	80.00
❏ PHS 600264 [S]	Vincebus Eruptum	1968	10.00	20.00	40.00
❏ PHS 600278	Outsideinside	1968	10.00	20.00	40.00
❏ PHS 600305	New! Improved! Blue Cheer	1969	10.00	20.00	40.00
❏ PHS 600333	Blue Cheer	1970	10.00	20.00	40.00
❏ PHS 600347	The Original Human Being	1970	10.00	20.00	40.00
❏ PHS 600350	Oh! Pleasant Hope	1971	10.00	20.00	40.00
RHINO					
❏ RNLP 70130	Louder Than God (The Best of Blue Cheer, 1968-1969)	1986	2.50	5.00	10.00
BLUE DIAMONDS, THE					
LONDON					
❏ LL 3235 [M]	Ramona1	1963	6.25	12.50	25.00
BLUE JAYS, THE (1)					
MILESTONE					
❏ 1001 [M]	The Blue Jays Meet Little Caesar and the Romans	1962	25.00	50.00	100.00
BLUE OYSTER CULT					
COLUMBIA					
❏ C 31063	Blue Oyster Cult	1972	3.00	6.00	12.00
❏ PC 31063	Blue Oyster Cult	197?	2.00	4.00	8.00
—Reissue with new prefix					
❏ CQ 32017 [Q]	Tyranny and Mutation	1973	7.50	15.00	30.00
❏ KC 32017	Tyranny and Mutation	1973	3.00	6.00	12.00
❏ PC 32017	Tyranny and Mutation	197?	2.00	4.00	8.00
—Reissue with new prefix					
❏ CQ 32858 [Q]	Secret Treaties	1974	7.50	15.00	30.00
❏ KC 32858	Secret Treaties	1974	3.00	6.00	12.00
❏ PC 32858	Secret Treaties	197?	2.00	4.00	8.00
—Reissue with new prefix					
❏ KG 33371 [(2)]	On Your Feet or On Your Knees	1975	3.75	7.50	15.00
❏ PC 34164	Agents of Fortune	1976	2.50	5.00	10.00
—Original gatefold with no bar code on cover					

Number	Title (A Side/B Side)	Yr	VG	VG+	NM
❏ PC 34164	Agents of Fortune	198?	2.00	4.00	8.00
—Budget-line reissue with bar code					
❏ JC 35019	Spectres	1977	2.50	5.00	10.00
❏ PC 35019	Spectres	198?	2.00	4.00	8.00
—Budget-line reissue					
❏ JC 35563	Some Enchanted Evening	1978	2.50	5.00	10.00
❏ PC 35563	Some Enchanted Evening	198?	2.00	4.00	8.00
—Budget-line reissue					
❏ JC 36009	Mirrors	1979	2.50	5.00	10.00
❏ PC 36009	Mirrors	198?	2.00	4.00	8.00
—Budget-line reissue					
❏ JC 36550	Cultosaurus Erectus	1980	2.50	5.00	10.00
❏ PC 36550	Cultosaurus Erectus	198?	2.00	4.00	8.00
—Budget-line reissue					
❏ FC 37389	Fire of Unknown Origin	1981	2.50	5.00	10.00
❏ PC 37389	Fire of Unknown Origin	1984	2.00	4.00	8.00
—Budget-line reissue					
❏ KG 37946 [(2)]	Extraterrestrial Live	1982	3.00	6.00	12.00
❏ FC 38947	The Revolution by Night	1983	2.50	5.00	10.00
❏ PC 38947	The Revolution by Night	1985	2.00	4.00	8.00
—Budget-line reissue					
❏ FC 39979	Club Ninja	1986	2.50	5.00	10.00
❏ FC 40618	Imaginos	1988	2.50	5.00	10.00
BLUE RIDGE MOUNTAIN BOYS, THE					
TIME					
❏ ST-2083 [S]	Hootenanny and Bluegrass	1963	5.00	10.00	20.00
❏ T-2083 [M]	Hootenanny and Bluegrass	1963	3.75	7.50	15.00
❏ ST-2103 [S]	Bluegrass Down Home	1963	5.00	10.00	20.00
❏ T-2103 [M]	Bluegrass Down Home	1963	3.75	7.50	15.00
BLUE SKY BOYS, THE					
CAPITOL					
❏ ST 2483 [S]	Presenting the Blue Sky Boys	1966	6.25	12.50	25.00
❏ T 2483 [M]	Presenting the Blue Sky Boys	1966	5.00	10.00	20.00
PINE MOUNTAIN					
❏ PMR 257	Together Again	198?	3.00	6.00	12.00
RCA CAMDEN					
❏ CAL-797 [M]	The Blue Sky Boys	1963	5.00	10.00	20.00
❏ CAS-797(e) [R]	The Blue Sky Boys	1963	3.75	7.50	15.00
ROUNDER					
❏ 0236	1964	198?	3.75	7.50	15.00
STARDAY					
❏ SLP-205 [M]	Rare Treasury of Old Song Gems	1962	10.00	20.00	40.00
❏ SLP-257 [M]	Together Again	1963	10.00	20.00	40.00
❏ SLP-269 [M]	The Blue Sky Boys	1964	10.00	20.00	40.00
BLUE STARS					
EMARCY					
❏ MG-36067 [M]	Lullaby of Birdland	1956	10.00	20.00	40.00
BLUE THINGS, THE					
RCA VICTOR					
❏ LPM-3603 [M]	The Blue Things	1966	30.00	60.00	120.00
❏ LSP-3603 [S]	The Blue Things	1966	45.00	90.00	180.00
BLUE VELVET BAND, THE					
WARNER BROS.					
❏ WS 1802	Sweet Moments	1969	7.50	15.00	30.00
BLUEGRASS HOPPERS, THE					
CUCA					
❏ 1160	The Country's Come to Town	196?	6.25	12.50	25.00
BLUES CLIMAX					
HORNE					
❏ JC-333	Blues Climax	1969	15.00	30.00	60.00
BLUES IMAGE					
ATCO					
❏ SD 33-300	Blues Image	1969	6.25	12.50	25.00
❏ SD 33-317	Open	1970	5.00	10.00	20.00
❏ SD 33-346	Red, White and Blues Image	1971	5.00	10.00	20.00
BLUES MAGOOS					
ABC					
❏ S-697	Never Goin' Back to Georgia	1969	5.00	10.00	20.00
❏ S-710	Gulf Coast Bound	1970	5.00	10.00	20.00
MERCURY					
❏ MG-21096 [M]	Psychedelic Lollipop	1966	10.00	20.00	40.00
—With "21096" in trail-off; this record is mono					
❏ MG-21096 [S]	Psychedelic Lollipop	1966	10.00	20.00	40.00
—With "2/61096" in trail-off; this record plays stereo, though labeled mono					
❏ 21104/61104	Electric Comic Book Comic Book	1967	3.75	7.50	15.00
❏ MG-21104 [M]	Electric Comic Book	1967	7.50	15.00	30.00
❏ SR-61096	Psychedelic Lollipop	197?	3.00	6.00	12.00
—Reissue on Chicago skyline label					
❏ SR-61096 [S]	Psychedelic Lollipop	1966	12.50	25.00	50.00
❏ SR-61104 [S]	Electric Comic Book	1967	10.00	20.00	40.00
❏ SR-61167	Basic Blues Magoos	1968	7.50	15.00	30.00
BLUES PROJECT, THE					
CAPITOL					
❏ ST-782	Lazarus	1971	3.00	6.00	12.00
❏ SMAS-11017	The Blues Project	1972	3.00	6.00	12.00
MCA					
❏ 8003 [(2)]	Reunion in Central Park	1975	3.75	7.50	15.00
—Reissue of Sounds of the South LP; black rainbow labels					
❏ 25984 [(2)]	Reunion in Central Park	1987	3.00	6.00	12.00
—Reissue of MCA 8003; blue rainbow labels					
MGM					
❏ GAS-118	The Blues Project	1970	3.00	6.00	12.00
❏ M3G-4953	Archetypes	1974	3.00	6.00	12.00

B

Number	Title (A Side/B Side)	Yr	VG	VG+	NM

RHINO

Number	Title (A Side/B Side)	Yr	VG	VG+	NM
❑ R1-70165	No Time Like the Right Time: The Best of the Blues Project	1989	3.00	6.00	12.00

SOUNDS OF THE SOUTH

❑ MCA2-8003 [(2)]	Reunion in Central Park	1973	5.00	10.00	20.00

—*Yellow labels*

VERVE

❑ 827918-1	Projections	1986	2.00	4.00	8.00

—*Reissue*

VERVE FOLKWAYS

❑ FT-3000 [M]	Live at the Café a Go Go	1966	5.00	10.00	20.00
❑ FTS-3000 [S]	Live at the Café a Go Go	1966	6.25	12.50	25.00
❑ FT-3008 [M]	Projections	1966	5.00	10.00	20.00
❑ FTS-3008 [S]	Projections	1966	6.25	12.50	25.00

VERVE FORECAST

❑ FT-3000 [M]	Live at the Café a Go Go	1967	3.75	7.50	15.00

—*Reissue of Verve Folkways 3000*

❑ FTS-3000 [S]	Live at the Café a Go Go	1967	5.00	10.00	20.00

—*Reissue of Verve Folkways 3000*

❑ FT-3008 [M]	Projections	1967	3.75	7.50	15.00

—*Reissue of Verve Folkways 3008*

❑ FTS-3008 [S]	Projections	1967	5.00	10.00	20.00

—*Reissue of Verve Folkways 3008*

❑ FT-3025 [M]	The Blues Project Live at Town Hall	1967	5.00	10.00	20.00
❑ FTS-3025 [S]	The Blues Project Live at Town Hall	1967	3.75	7.50	15.00
❑ FTS-3046	Planned Obsolescence	1968	3.75	7.50	15.00
❑ FTS-3069	Flanders/Kalb/Katz, Etc.	1969	3.75	7.50	15.00
❑ FTS-3077	Best of the Blues Project	1969	3.75	7.50	15.00

BLYTH, ANN
EVEREST

❑ SDBR-1113 [S]	Hail Mary	1960	10.00	20.00	40.00
❑ LPBR-5113 [M]	Hail Mary	1960	7.50	15.00	30.00

BLYTHE, JIMMY
RIVERSIDE

❑ RLP-1031 [10]	Chicago Stomps and the Dixie Four	1954	20.00	40.00	80.00
❑ RLP-1036 [10]	Jimmy Blythe's State Street Ramblers	1954	20.00	40.00	80.00

BLYTHE, STERLING
CROWN

❑ CLP-5179 [M]	Sterling Blythe Sings	1963	5.00	10.00	20.00

SAGE & SAND

❑ C-14 [M]	A Night at the Showboat	196?	6.25	12.50	25.00

—*Red vinyl; label print is multi-colored*

❑ C-14 [M]	A Night at the Showboat	1962	10.00	20.00	40.00

—*Red vinyl; label print is red and black*

BO GRUMPUS
ATCO

❑ 33-246 [M]	Bo Grumpus	1968	7.50	15.00	30.00
❑ SD 33-246 [S]	Bo Grumpus	1968	5.00	10.00	20.00

BOA
SNAKEFIELD

❑ SN-001	Wrong Road	1969	62.50	125.00	250.00

BOB AND EARL
CRESTVIEW

❑ CRS-3055	Bob & Earl	1969	6.25	12.50	25.00

TIP

❑ TLP-1011 [M]	Harlem Shuffle	1964	7.50	15.00	30.00
❑ TLS-9011 [S]	Harlem Shuffle	1964	12.50	25.00	50.00

BOB AND RAY
RCA VICTOR

❑ LPM-1773 [M]	Bob and Ray Throw a Stereo Spectacular	1958	7.50	15.00	30.00
❑ LSP-1773 [S]	Bob and Ray Throw a Stereo Spectacular	1958	20.00	40.00	80.00
❑ LSP-1773 [S]	Bob and Ray Throw a Stereo Spectacular	199?	7.50	15.00	30.00

—*Classic Records reissue*

❑ LPM-2131 [M]	Bob and Ray on a Platter	1960	7.50	15.00	30.00
❑ LSP-2131 [S]	Bob and Ray on a Platter	1960	12.50	25.00	50.00

UNICORN

❑ UN 1001 [10]	Write If You Get Work	1954	15.00	30.00	60.00

BOB B. SOXX AND THE BLUE JEANS
PHILLIES

❑ PHLP-4002 [M]	Zip-a-Dee Doo-Dah	1963	125.00	250.00	500.00

BOBO, WILLIE
ROULETTE

❑ R-52097 [M]	Bobo's Beat	1962	6.25	12.50	25.00
❑ SR-52097 [S]	Bobo's Beat	1962	7.50	15.00	30.00

TICO

❑ ST-1108 [S]	Do That Thing	1963	7.50	15.00	30.00
❑ T-1108 [M]	Do That Thing	1963	6.25	12.50	25.00

VERVE

❑ V6-8631 [S]	Spanish Grease	1965	5.00	10.00	20.00
❑ V6-8648 [S]	Uno, Dos, Tres	1966	5.00	10.00	20.00
❑ V6-8669 [S]	Feelin' So Good	1966	5.00	10.00	20.00
❑ V-8685 [M]	Juicy	1967	5.00	10.00	20.00
❑ V6-8685 [S]	Juicy	1967	5.00	10.00	20.00
❑ V-8699 [M]	Bobo Motion	1967	5.00	10.00	20.00
❑ V6-8699 [S]	Bobo Motion	1967	5.00	10.00	20.00
❑ V6-8736	Spanish Blues Band	1968	5.00	10.00	20.00

BOCAGE, PETER
RIVERSIDE

❑ RLP-379 [M]	Peter Bocage with His Creole Serenaders	1961	6.25	12.50	25.00
❑ RLP-9379 [S]	Peter Bocage with His Creole Serenaders	1961	7.50	15.00	30.00

BOETCHER, CURT
ELEKTRA

Number	Title (A Side/B Side)	Yr	VG	VG+	NM
❑ EKS-75037	There's an Innocent Face	1972	5.00	10.00	20.00

BOFFALONGO
UNITED ARTISTS

❑ UAS-6726	Boffalongo	1969	5.00	10.00	20.00
❑ UAS-6770	Beyond Your Head	1970	5.00	10.00	20.00

BOGARDE, DIRK
LONDON

❑ PS 210 [S]	Lyrics for Lovers	1960	7.50	15.00	30.00
❑ LL 3187 [M]	Lyrics for Lovers	1960	6.25	12.50	25.00

BOHANNON, GEORGE
WORKSHOP JAZZ

❑ WSJ-207 [M]	Boss Bossa Nova	1963	20.00	40.00	80.00

BOHEMIAN VENDETTA
MAINSTREAM

❑ S-6106 [S]	Bohemian Vendetta	1968	50.00	100.00	200.00
❑ 56106 [M]	Bohemian Vendetta	1968	30.00	60.00	120.00

BOLDER DAMN
HIT

❑ HRI-5061	Mourning	1971	250.00	500.00	1000.

BOLGER, RAY
DISNEYLAND

❑ ST-3930 [M]	The Story of the Scarecrow of Oz	1965	7.50	15.00	30.00

BOLIN, TOMMY
COLUMBIA

❑ PC 34329	Private Eyes	1976	3.00	6.00	12.00

—*Original with no bar code on cover*

❑ PC 34329	Private Eyes	198?	2.00	4.00	8.00

—*With bar code on cover*

GEFFEN

❑ 3GHS 24248 [(3)]	The Ultimate Tommy Bolin	1989	7.50	15.00	30.00

NEMPEROR

❑ NE 436	Teaser	1975	3.00	6.00	12.00
❑ PZ 37534	Teaser	1982	2.00	4.00	8.00

BOLLING, CLAUDE
BALLY

❑ BAL-12003 [M]	French Jazz	1956	10.00	20.00	40.00

CBS MASTERWORKS

❑ M3 36845 [(3)]	Bolling	1981	6.25	12.50	25.00

—*Combines 33233, 35128, and 35864 in one box*

OMEGA

❑ OKL-6 [M]	Rolling with Bolling	1960	6.25	12.50	25.00
❑ OSL-6 [S]	Rolling with Bolling	1960	7.50	15.00	30.00

PHILIPS

❑ PHS 600204 [S]	Two-Beat Mozart	1966	5.00	10.00	20.00

BOLTON, MICHAEL
COLUMBIA

❑ BFC 38357	Michael Bolton	1983	2.50	5.00	10.00
❑ PC 38357	Michael Bolton	1985	—	3.00	6.00

—*Reissue with new prefix*

❑ BFC 39328	Everybody's Crazy	1985	2.50	5.00	10.00
❑ FC 40473	The Hunger	1987	2.00	4.00	8.00
❑ OC 45012	Soul Provider	1989	2.50	5.00	10.00
❑ C 46771	Time, Love and Tenderness	1991	3.75	7.50	15.00

RCA VICTOR

❑ APL1-0992	Michael Bolotin	1975	5.00	10.00	20.00

—*As "Michael Bolotin"*

❑ APL1-1551	Every Day of My Life	1976	5.00	10.00	20.00

—*As "Michael Bolotin"*

BONADUCE, DANNY
LION

❑ LN-1015	Danny Bonaduce	1973	15.00	30.00	60.00

BONANO, SHARKEY
CAPITOL

❑ H 266 [10]	Sharkey's Southern Comfort	1951	12.50	25.00	50.00
❑ T 266 [M]	Kings of Dixieland	1954	10.00	20.00	40.00

CIRCLE

❑ LP-422 [10]	Sharkey Bonano	1951	12.50	25.00	50.00

ROULETTE

❑ R-25112 [M]	Dixieland at the Roundtable	1960	6.25	12.50	25.00

SOUTHLAND

❑ 205 [M]	New Orleans Jam Session	1961	7.50	15.00	30.00
❑ SLP-205 [10]	New Orleans Dixieland Session	1954	12.50	25.00	50.00
❑ 222 [M]	Kings of Dixieland	1959	7.50	15.00	30.00

BONANO, SHARKEY, AND LIZZIE MILES
CAPITOL

❑ H 367 [10]	Midnight on Bourbon Street	1952	12.50	25.00	50.00
❑ T 367 [M]	Midnight on Bourbon Street	1954	10.00	20.00	40.00
❑ T 792 [M]	A Night in Old New Orleans	1956	10.00	20.00	40.00

BOND, EDDIE
PHILLIPS INT'L.

❑ PLP-1980 [M]	The Greatest Country Gospel Hits	1961	100.00	200.00	400.00

BOND, GRAHAM
MERCURY

❑ SRM-1-612	We Put Our Magick on You	1971	5.00	10.00	20.00
❑ SR-61327	Holy Magick	1970	5.00	10.00	20.00

Number	Title (A Side/B Side)	Yr	VG	VG+	NM
PULSAR					
❑ 10604	Love Is the Law	1969	6.25	12.50	25.00
❑ 10606	Mighty Graham Bond	1969	6.25	12.50	25.00
WARNER BROS.					
❑ 2LS 2555 [(2)]	Solid Bond	1971	5.00	10.00	20.00
BOND, JAMES, SEXTETTE					
MIRWOOD					
❑ M-7001 [M]	The James Bond Songbook	1966	6.25	12.50	25.00
❑ S-7001 [S]	The James Bond Songbook	1966	7.50	15.00	30.00
BOND, JOHNNY					
CMH					
❑ 6212	The Singing Cowboy Again	1981	2.50	5.00	10.00
❑ 6213	The Return of the Singing Cowboy	1981	2.50	5.00	10.00
HARMONY					
❑ HL 7308 [M]	Johnny Bond's Best	1964	5.00	10.00	20.00
❑ HL 7353 [M]	Bottled in Bond	1965	5.00	10.00	20.00
NASHVILLE					
❑ 2054	Three Sheets to the Wind	196?	3.75	7.50	15.00
SHASTA					
❑ LP-516	Johnny Bond Rides Again	197?	3.75	7.50	15.00
STARDAY					
❑ SLP-147 [M]	That Wild, Wicked But Wonderful Wesy	1961	12.50	25.00	50.00
❑ SLP-227 [M]	Songs That Made Him Famous	1963	10.00	20.00	40.00
❑ SLP-298 [M]	Hot Rod Lincoln	1964	12.50	25.00	50.00
❑ SLP-333 [M]	Ten Little Bottles	1965	7.50	15.00	30.00
❑ SLP-354 [M]	Famous Hot Rodders I Have Known	1965	10.00	20.00	40.00
❑ SLP-368 [M]	The Man Who Comes Around	1966	6.25	12.50	25.00
❑ SLP-378 [M]	Bottles Up	1966	6.25	12.50	25.00
❑ SLP-388 [M]	The Branded Stock of Johnny Bond	1966	5.00	10.00	20.00
❑ SLP-402 [M]	Ten Nights in a Barroom	1967	5.00	10.00	20.00
❑ SLP-416	Drink Up and Go Home	1968	3.75	7.50	15.00
❑ SLP-444	The Best of Johnny Bond	1969	3.75	7.50	15.00
❑ SLP-456	Old, New, Patriotic and Blue	1970	3.75	7.50	15.00
❑ SLP-472	Here Come the Elephants	1971	3.75	7.50	15.00
❑ 954	The Best of Johnny Bond	1976	2.50	5.00	10.00
BONDS, GARY U.S.					
EMI AMERICA					
❑ SPRO-9666 [EP]	Dedication Sampler	1981	3.75	7.50	15.00
—Promo-only sampler with limited-edition number on pink sticker					
❑ SO-17051	Dedication	1981	2.50	5.00	10.00
❑ SO-17068	On the Line	1982	2.50	5.00	10.00
LEGRAND					
❑ LLP-3001 [M]	Dance 'Til Quarter to Three	1961	25.00	50.00	100.00
❑ LLP-3002 [M]	Twist Up Calypso	1962	17.50	35.00	70.00
❑ LLP-3003 [M]	Greatest Hits of Gary U.S. Bonds	1962	17.50	35.00	70.00
MCA					
❑ 905	The Best of Gary U.S. Bonds	1984	2.50	5.00	10.00
RHINO					
❑ RNLP-805	Certified Soul	1981	2.50	5.00	10.00
BONFA, LUIZ					
ATLANTIC					
❑ 8028 [M]	The Fabulous Guitar of Luiz Bonfa/Amor!	1959	10.00	20.00	40.00
—Black label					
❑ 8028 [M]	The Fabulous Guitar of Luiz Bonfa/Amor!	1960	7.50	15.00	30.00
—White "bullseye" label					
❑ 8028 [M]	The Fabulous Guitar of Luiz Bonfa/Amor!	1961	5.00	10.00	20.00
—Multicolor label, white "fan" logo at right					
❑ SD 8028 [S]	The Fabulous Guitar of Luiz Bonfa/Amor!	1959	12.50	25.00	50.00
—Green label					
❑ SD 8028 [S]	The Fabulous Guitar of Luiz Bonfa/Amor!	1960	10.00	20.00	40.00
—White "bullseye" label					
❑ SD 8028 [S]	The Fabulous Guitar of Luiz Bonfa/Amor!	1961	6.25	12.50	25.00
—Multicolor label, white "fan" logo at right					
❑ SD 8028 [S]	The Fabulous Guitar of Luiz Bonfa/Amor!	1963	5.00	10.00	20.00
—Multicolor label, black "fan" logo at right					
CAPITOL					
❑ T 10134 [M]	Brazilian Guitar	1958	10.00	20.00	40.00
—Turquoise label					
DOT					
❑ DLP-3804 [M]	Luiz Bonfa	1967	5.00	10.00	20.00
❑ DLP-25848	Black Orpheus Impressions	1969	3.75	7.50	15.00
EPIC					
❑ BN 26124 [S]	Softly	1964	5.00	10.00	20.00
PHILIPS					
❑ PHS 600087 [S]	Brazil's King of the Bossa Nova and Guitar	1963	5.00	10.00	20.00
RCA VICTOR					
❑ LSP-4376	The New Face of Bonfa	1970	3.75	7.50	15.00
VERVE					
❑ V6-8522 [S]	Luiz Bonfa Plays and Sings Bossa Nova	1963	5.00	10.00	20.00
BONFIRE, MARS					
COLUMBIA					
❑ CS 9834	Faster Than the Speed of Life	1969	3.75	7.50	15.00
UNI					
❑ 73027	Mars Bonfire	1968	5.00	10.00	20.00
BONNEMERE, EDDIE					
PRESTIGE					
❑ PRLP-7354 [M]	Jazz Oriented	1965	5.00	10.00	20.00
❑ PRST-7354 [S]	Jazz Oriented	1965	6.25	12.50	25.00
ROOST					
❑ RST-419 [10]	Piano Mambo with Bonnemere	1954	12.50	25.00	50.00
❑ RST-2236 [M]	Piano Bon Bons	1959	7.50	15.00	30.00
❑ SLP-2236 [S]	Piano Bon Bons	1959	10.00	20.00	40.00
❑ RST-2241 [M]	The Sound of Memory	1960	7.50	15.00	30.00

Number	Title (A Side/B Side)	Yr	VG	VG+	NM
❑ SLP-2241 [S]	The Sound of Memory	1960	10.00	20.00	40.00
BONNEVILLES, THE					
More than one group.					
DRUM BOY					
❑ DLM-1001 [M]	Meet the Bonnevilles	1963	25.00	50.00	100.00
❑ DLS-1001 [S]	Meet the Bonnevilles	1963	37.50	75.00	150.00
JUSTICE					
❑ JLP-146	Bringing It Home	196?	125.00	250.00	500.00
BONNIE LOU					
KING					
❑ 595 [M]	Bonnie Lou Sings	1958	35.00	70.00	140.00
BONNIWELL, T.S.					
CAPITOL					
❑ ST-377	Close	1969	12.50	25.00	50.00
BONZO DOG BAND, THE					
IMPERIAL					
❑ LP 9370 [M]	Gorilla	1968	5.00	10.00	20.00
—Without booklet					
❑ LP 9370 [M]	Gorilla	1968	7.50	15.00	30.00
—With booklet					
❑ LP 12370 [S]	Gorilla	1968	5.00	10.00	20.00
—Without booklet					
❑ LP 12370 [S]	Gorilla	1968	7.50	15.00	30.00
—With booklet					
❑ LP 12432	Urban Spaceman	1968	5.00	10.00	20.00
—Without booklet					
❑ LP 12432	Urban Spaceman	1968	7.50	15.00	30.00
—With booklet					
❑ LP 12445	Tadpoles	1969	5.00	10.00	20.00
❑ LP 12457	Keynsham	1969	5.00	10.00	20.00
LIBERTY					
❑ LN-10206	Some of the Best of the Bonzo Dog Band	1983	2.00	4.00	8.00
UNITED ARTISTS					
❑ UA-LA321-H2 [(2)]	The History of the Bonzos	1974	3.75	7.50	15.00
❑ UAS 5517	The Beast of the Bonzos	1971	3.75	7.50	15.00
❑ UAS 5584	Let's Make Up and Be Friendly	1972	3.75	7.50	15.00
BOOGIE KINGS, THE					
MONTEL					
❑ LP-104 [M]	The Boogie Kings	1966	6.25	12.50	25.00
❑ LP-109 [M]	Blue Eyed Soul	1967	6.25	12.50	25.00
BOOKER T. AND THE MG'S					
A&M					
❑ SP-4720	Try and Love Again	1978	2.50	5.00	10.00
—As "Booker T. Jones"					
❑ SP-4798	The Best of You	1979	2.50	5.00	10.00
—As "Booker T. Jones"					
❑ SP-4874	I Want You	1981	2.50	5.00	10.00
—As "Booker T. Jones"					
ASYLUM					
❑ 7E-1093	Universal Language	1977	2.50	5.00	10.00
ATLANTIC					
❑ 8202 [M]	The Best of Booker T. and the MG's	1968	12.50	25.00	50.00
—Mono is white label promo only					
❑ SD 8202 [S]	The Best of Booker T. and the MG's	1968	5.00	10.00	20.00
❑ 81285	The Best of Booker T. and the MG's	1985	2.00	4.00	8.00
EPIC					
❑ KE 33143	Evergreen	1974	3.00	6.00	12.00
MCA					
❑ 6282	The Runaway	1989	3.00	6.00	12.00
—As "Booker T. Jones"					
STAX					
❑ ST-701 [M]	Green Onions	1962	17.50	35.00	70.00
❑ STS-701 [R]	Green Onions	1966	12.50	25.00	50.00
❑ ST-705 [M]	Soul Dressing	1965	17.50	35.00	70.00
❑ STS-705 [R]	Soul Dressing	1966	12.50	25.00	50.00
❑ ST-711 [M]	And Now…Booker T. and the MG's	1966	12.50	25.00	50.00
❑ STS-711 [S]	And Now…Booker T. and the MG's	1966	20.00	40.00	80.00
❑ ST-713 [M]	In the Christmas Spirit	1966	100.00	200.00	400.00
—Fingers and piano keys cover					
❑ ST-713 [M]	In the Christmas Spirit	1967	50.00	100.00	200.00
—Same as above; Santa Claus cover					
❑ STS-713 [S]	In the Christmas Spirit	1966	100.00	200.00	400.00
—Fingers and piano keys cover					
❑ STS-713 [S]	In the Christmas Spirit	1967	50.00	100.00	200.00
—Santa Claus cover					
❑ ST-717 [M]	Hip Hug-Her	1967	10.00	20.00	40.00
❑ STS-717 [S]	Hip Hug-Her	1967	12.50	25.00	50.00
❑ STS-724	Doin' Our Thing	1968	12.50	25.00	50.00
❑ STS-2001	Soul Limbo	1968	6.25	12.50	25.00
❑ STS-2006	Uptight	1969	6.25	12.50	25.00
❑ STS-2009	The Booker T. Set	1969	6.25	12.50	25.00
❑ STS-2027	McLemore Avenue	1970	6.25	12.50	25.00
❑ STS-2033	Booker T. and the MG's Greatest Hits	1970	3.75	7.50	15.00
❑ STS-2035	Melting Pot	1971	3.75	7.50	15.00
❑ STX-4104	Free Ride	1978	2.50	5.00	10.00
❑ STX-4113	Soul Limbo	198?	2.50	5.00	10.00
—Reissue of 2001					
❑ MPS-8505	Booker T. and the MG's Greatest Hits	1981	2.50	5.00	10.00
❑ MPS-8521	Melting Pot	198?	2.50	5.00	10.00
—Reissue of 2035					
❑ MPS-8531	The Booker T. Set	1987	2.50	5.00	10.00
—Reissue of 2009					
❑ MPS-8552	McLemore Avenue	1990	3.00	6.00	12.00
—Reissue of 2027					

SUNDAZED

Number	Title (A Side/B Side)	Yr	VG	VG+	NM
LP 5042	Soul Dressing	2000	3.75	7.50	15.00
—Reissue on 180-gram vinyl					
LP 5043	And Now! Booker T. and the MG's	2000	3.75	7.50	15.00
—Reissue on 180-gram vinyl					
LP 5053	In the Christmas Spirit	2000	3.75	7.50	15.00
—Reissue on 180-gram vinyl					
LP 5079	Green Onions	2002	3.00	6.00	12.00
—Reissue on 180-gram vinyl					
LP 5080	Hip Hug-Her	2002	3.00	6.00	12.00
—Reissue on 180-gram vinyl					

BOOMERANG
RCA VICTOR

Number	Title (A Side/B Side)	Yr	VG	VG+	NM
LSP-4577	Boomerang	1971	5.00	10.00	20.00

BOONE, PAT
ABC

Number	Title (A Side/B Side)	Yr	VG	VG+	NM
4006	16 Great Performances	1975	2.50	5.00	10.00

BIBLE VOICE

Number	Title (A Side/B Side)	Yr	VG	VG+	NM
7076	The Solution to Crisis-America	1970	3.00	6.00	12.00

DOT

Number	Title (A Side/B Side)	Yr	VG	VG+	NM
DLP-3012 [M]	Pat Boone	1956	12.50	25.00	50.00
—Maroon label					
DLP-3012 [M]	Pat Boone	1957	6.25	12.50	25.00
—Black label					
DLP-3030 [M]	Howdy!	1956	12.50	25.00	50.00
—Maroon label					
DLP-3030 [M]	Howdy!	1957	6.25	12.50	25.00
—Black label					
DLP-3050 [M]	Pat	1957	6.25	12.50	25.00
DLP-3068 [M]	Hymns We Love	1957	6.25	12.50	25.00
DLP-3071 [M]	Pat's Great Hits	1957	6.25	12.50	25.00
DLP-3077 [M]	Pat Boone Sings Irving Berlin	1958	5.00	10.00	20.00
DLP-3118 [M]	Star Dust	1958	5.00	10.00	20.00
DLP-3121 [M]	Yes Indeed!	1958	5.00	10.00	20.00
DLP-3158 [M]	Pat Boone Sings	1959	5.00	10.00	20.00
DLP-3180 [M]	Tenderly	1959	5.00	10.00	20.00
DLP-3199 [M]	Side by Side	1959	5.00	10.00	20.00
DLP-3222 [M]	White Christmas	1959	6.25	12.50	25.00
DLP-3234 [M]	He Leadeth Me	1960	3.75	7.50	15.00
DLP-3261 [M]	Pat's Great Hits Volume 2	1960	3.75	7.50	15.00
DLP-3270 [M]	Moonglow	1960	3.75	7.50	15.00
DLP-3285 [M]	This and That	1960	3.75	7.50	15.00
DLP-3346 [M]	Great! Great! Great!	1961	3.75	7.50	15.00
DLP-3384 [M]	Moody River	1961	3.00	6.00	12.00
DLP-3386 [M]	My God and I	1961	3.00	6.00	12.00
DLP-3399 [M]	I'll See You in My Dreams	1961	3.00	6.00	12.00
DLP-3402 [M]	Pat Boone Reads from the Holy Bible	1962	3.75	7.50	15.00
DLP-3455 [M]	Pat Boone's Golden Hits	1962	3.00	6.00	12.00
DLP-3475 [M]	I Love You Truly	1962	3.00	6.00	12.00
DLP-3501 [M]	Pat Boone Sings Guess Who?	1963	12.50	25.00	50.00
DLP-3504 [M]	Pat Boone Sings "Days of Wine and Roses" and Other Great Movie Themes	1963	3.00	6.00	12.00
DLP-3513 [M]	Sing Along Without Pat Boone	1963	3.00	6.00	12.00
DLP-3520 [M]	The Star Spangled Banner	1963	3.00	6.00	12.00
DLP-3534 [M]	Tie Me Kangaroo Down, Sport	1963	3.00	6.00	12.00
DLP-3546 [M]	The Touch of Your Lips	1963	3.00	6.00	12.00
DLP-3582 [M]	The Lord's Prayer And Other Great Hymns	1964	3.00	6.00	12.00
DLP-3594 [M]	Boss Beat	1964	3.00	6.00	12.00
DLP-3601 [M]	Blest Be the Tie That Binds	1965	3.00	6.00	12.00
DLP-3606 [M]	Near You	1965	3.00	6.00	12.00
DLP-3626 [M]	The Golden Era of Country Hits	1965	3.00	6.00	12.00
DLP-3650 [M]	My 10th Anniversary with Dot Records	1965	3.00	6.00	12.00
DLP-3667 [M]	Winner of the Reader's Digest Poll	1965	3.00	6.00	12.00
DLP-3685 [M]	Great Hits of 1965	1965	3.00	6.00	12.00
DLP-3748 [M]	Memories	1966	3.00	6.00	12.00
DLP-3764 [M]	Wish You Were Here, Buddy	1966	3.00	6.00	12.00
DLP-3770 [M]	Christmas Is a-Comin'	1966	3.00	6.00	12.00
DLP-3798 [M]	How Great Thou Art	1967	3.75	7.50	15.00
DLP-3805 [M]	I Was Kaiser Bill's Batman	1967	3.75	7.50	15.00
DLP-3814 [M]	15 Hits of Pat Boone	1967	3.75	7.50	15.00
DLP-3876 [M]	Look Ahead	1968	3.75	7.50	15.00
DLP-25068 [S]	Hymns We Love	1959	7.50	15.00	30.00
DLP-25071 [P]	Pat's Great Hits	1959	7.50	15.00	30.00
DLP-25077 [S]	Pat Boone Sings Irving Berlin	1959	6.25	12.50	25.00
DLP-25118 [S]	Star Dust	1959	6.25	12.50	25.00
DLP-25121 [S]	Yes Indeed!	1959	6.25	12.50	25.00
DLP-25158 [S]	Pat Boone Sings	1959	6.25	12.50	25.00
DLP-25180 [S]	Tenderly	1959	6.25	12.50	25.00
DLP-25199 [S]	Side by Side	1959	6.25	12.50	25.00
DLP-25222 [S]	White Christmas	1959	7.50	15.00	30.00
DLP-25234 [S]	He Leadeth Me	1960	5.00	10.00	20.00
DLP-25261 [S]	Pat's Great Hits Volume 2	1960	5.00	10.00	20.00
DLP-25270 [S]	Moonglow	1960	5.00	10.00	20.00
—Black vinyl					
DLP-25270 [S]	Moonglow	1960	12.50	25.00	50.00
—Blue vinyl					
DLP-25285 [S]	This and That	1960	5.00	10.00	20.00
DLP-25346 [S]	Great! Great! Great!	1961	5.00	10.00	20.00
DLP-25384 [S]	Moody River	1961	3.75	7.50	15.00
DLP-25386 [S]	My God and I	1961	3.75	7.50	15.00
DLP-25399 [S]	I'll See You in My Dreams	1961	3.75	7.50	15.00
DLP-25455 [S]	Pat Boone's Golden Hits	1962	3.75	7.50	15.00
DLP-25475 [S]	I Love You Truly	1962	3.75	7.50	15.00
DLP-25501 [S]	Pat Boone Sings Guess Who?	1963	20.00	40.00	80.00
DLP-25504 [S]	Pat Boone Sings "Days of Wine and Roses" and Other Great Movie Themes	1963	3.75	7.50	15.00
DLP-25513 [S]	Sing Along Without Pat Boone	1963	3.75	7.50	15.00
DLP-25520 [S]	The Star Spangled Banner	1963	3.75	7.50	15.00
DLP-25534 [S]	Tie Me Kangaroo Down, Sport	1963	3.75	7.50	15.00
DLP-25546 [S]	The Touch of Your Lips	1963	3.75	7.50	15.00
DLP-25573 [R]	Pat Boone	1964	3.00	6.00	12.00
DLP-25582 [S]	The Lord's Prayer And Other Great Hymns	1964	3.75	7.50	15.00
DLP-25594 [S]	Boss Beat	1964	3.75	7.50	15.00
DLP-25601 [S]	Blest Be the Tie That Binds	1965	3.75	7.50	15.00
DLP-25606 [S]	Near You	1965	3.75	7.50	15.00
DLP-25626 [S]	The Golden Era of Country Hits	1965	3.75	7.50	15.00
DLP-25650 [S]	My 10th Anniversary with Dot Records	1965	3.75	7.50	15.00
DLP-25667 [S]	Winner of the Reader's Digest Poll	1965	3.75	7.50	15.00
DLP-25685 [S]	Great Hits of 1965	1965	3.75	7.50	15.00
DLP-25748 [S]	Memories	1966	3.75	7.50	15.00
DLP-25764 [S]	Wish You Were Here, Buddy	1966	3.75	7.50	15.00
DLP-25770 [S]	Christmas Is a-Comin'	1966	3.75	7.50	15.00
DLP-25798 [S]	How Great Thou Art	1967	3.00	6.00	12.00
DLP-25805 [S]	I Was Kaiser Bill's Batman	1967	3.00	6.00	12.00
DLP-25814 [S]	15 Hits of Pat Boone	1967	3.00	6.00	12.00
DLP-25876 [S]	Look Ahead	1968	3.00	6.00	12.00

HAMILTON

Number	Title (A Side/B Side)	Yr	VG	VG+	NM
HLP-118 [M]	12 Great Hits	196?	3.00	6.00	12.00
HLP-12118 [M]	12 Great Hits	196?	3.00	6.00	12.00

HITSVILLE

Number	Title (A Side/B Side)	Yr	VG	VG+	NM
H6-405	Texas Woman	1976	3.00	6.00	12.00

LAMB & LION

Number	Title (A Side/B Side)	Yr	VG	VG+	NM
1002	New Songs of the Jesus People	197?	3.00	6.00	12.00
1004	Pat Boone and the First Nashville Jesus Band	197?	3.00	6.00	12.00
1005	Christian People, Vol. 1	197?	2.50	5.00	10.00
1006	The Family Who Prays	197?	2.50	5.00	10.00
1007	Born Again	197?	2.50	5.00	10.00
1008	All in the Boone Family	1972	2.50	5.00	10.00
1013	S-A-V-E-D	197?	2.50	5.00	10.00
1016	Songs from the Inner Court	197?	2.50	5.00	10.00
5000	The Pat Boone Family in the Holy Land	197?	2.50	5.00	10.00

MCA

Number	Title (A Side/B Side)	Yr	VG	VG+	NM
658	16 Great Performances	1980	2.00	4.00	8.00
6020 [(2)]	The Best of Pat Boone	1980	3.00	6.00	12.00
15028 [S]	White Christmas	198?	2.50	5.00	10.00
—Reissue of Dot LP					

MELODYLAND

Number	Title (A Side/B Side)	Yr	VG	VG+	NM
6-501	The Country Side of Pat Boone	1975	3.00	6.00	12.00

MGM

Number	Title (A Side/B Side)	Yr	VG	VG+	NM
SE-4899	I Love You More and More Every Day	1973	2.50	5.00	10.00

PARAMOUNT

Number	Title (A Side/B Side)	Yr	VG	VG+	NM
1024 [(2)]	Pat Boone's Greatest Hymns	1974	3.75	7.50	15.00
1043 [(2)]	Pat Boone's Greatest Hits	1974	3.75	7.50	15.00

PICKWICK

Number	Title (A Side/B Side)	Yr	VG	VG+	NM
SPC-1024	White Christmas	1979	2.50	5.00	10.00
SPC-3079	True Love	196?	2.50	5.00	10.00
SPC-3107	Love Me Tender	196?	2.50	5.00	10.00
SPC-3123	Canadian Sunset	196?	2.50	5.00	10.00
SPC-3145	Favorite Hymns	197?	2.50	5.00	10.00
SPC-3219	You've Lost That Lovin' Feeling	197?	2.50	5.00	10.00
SPC-3568	The Old Rugged Cross	1978	2.00	4.00	8.00
SPC-3597	Great Hits	1978	2.00	4.00	8.00

SUPREME

Number	Title (A Side/B Side)	Yr	VG	VG+	NM
SS-2060	Rapture	1970	3.00	6.00	12.00

TETRAGRAMMATON

Number	Title (A Side/B Side)	Yr	VG	VG+	NM
T-118	Departure	1969	3.00	6.00	12.00

WORD

Number	Title (A Side/B Side)	Yr	VG	VG+	NM
WST-8536	The Pat Boone Family	1970	2.50	5.00	10.00
WST-8664	Hymns We Love	197?	2.50	5.00	10.00
WST-8711	He Leadeth Me	197?	2.50	5.00	10.00
WST-8725	The Star-Spangled Banner	197?	2.50	5.00	10.00
WST-8738	I Believe	198?	2.00	4.00	8.00

BOONE, RANDY
DECCA

Number	Title (A Side/B Side)	Yr	VG	VG+	NM
DL 4619 [M]	Singing Star of The Virginian	1965	6.25	12.50	25.00
DL 4663 [M]	Ramblin' Randy	1965	5.00	10.00	20.00
DL 74619 [S]	Singing Star of The Virginian	1965	8.75	17.50	35.00
DL 74663 [S]	Ramblin' Randy	1965	7.50	15.00	30.00

BOOT
AGAPE

Number	Title (A Side/B Side)	Yr	VG	VG+	NM
2601	Boot	1972	6.25	12.50	25.00

BORDERSONG
REAL GOOD

Number	Title (A Side/B Side)	Yr	VG	VG+	NM
1001	Morning	1975	17.50	35.00	70.00

BORODIN STRING QUARTET
MERCURY LIVING PRESENCE

Number	Title (A Side/B Side)	Yr	VG	VG+	NM
SR 90309 [S]	Shostakovich: String Quartets No. 4 and 8	196?	17.50	35.00	70.00
—Maroon label, no "Vendor: Mercury Record Corporation"					

BOSTIC, EARL
GRAND PRIX

Number	Title (A Side/B Side)	Yr	VG	VG+	NM
K-404 [M]	The Grand Prix Series	196?	3.75	7.50	15.00
KS-404 [R]	The Grand Prix Series	196?	3.00	6.00	12.00
K-416 [M]	Wild Man	196?	3.75	7.50	15.00
KS-416 [R]	Wild Man	196?	3.00	6.00	12.00

KING

Number	Title (A Side/B Side)	Yr	VG	VG+	NM
295-64 [10]	Earl Bostic and His Alto Sax	1951	50.00	100.00	200.00
—Black vinyl					
295-64 [10]	Earl Bostic and His Alto Sax	1951	100.00	200.00	400.00
—Red vinyl					
295-65 [10]	Earl Bostic and His Alto Sax	1951	50.00	100.00	200.00
—Black vinyl					
295-65 [10]	Earl Bostic and His Alto Sax	1951	100.00	200.00	400.00
—Red vinyl					
295-66 [10]	Earl Bostic and His Alto Sax	1951	50.00	100.00	200.00
—Black vinyl					

B

Number	Title (A Side/B Side)	Yr	VG	VG+	NM
❏ 295-66 [10]	Earl Bostic and His Alto Sax	1951	100.00	200.00	400.00
—Red vinyl					
❏ 295-72 [10]	Earl Bostic and His Alto Sax	1952	50.00	100.00	200.00
❏ 295-76 [10]	Earl Bostic and His Alto Sax	1952	50.00	100.00	200.00
❏ 295-77 [10]	Earl Bostic and His Alto Sax	1952	50.00	100.00	200.00
❏ 295-78 [10]	Earl Bostic and His Alto Sax	1952	50.00	100.00	200.00
❏ 295-79 [10]	Earl Bostic and His Alto Sax	1952	50.00	100.00	200.00
❏ 295-95 [10]	Earl Bostic Plays the Old Standards	1954	50.00	100.00	200.00
❏ 295-103 [10]	Earl Bostic and His Alto Sax	1954	50.00	100.00	200.00
❏ 395-500 [M]	Dance to the Best of Bostic	195?	20.00	40.00	80.00
—Second cover with girl in a swimsuit pictured					
❏ 395-500 [M]	Dance to the Best of Bostic	1956	25.00	50.00	100.00
—Original cover with Earl Bostic pictured					
❏ 395-503 [M]	Bostic for You	1956	25.00	50.00	100.00
❏ 395-515 [M]	Alto-Tude	1956	25.00	50.00	100.00
❏ 395-525 [M]	Dance Time	1956	20.00	40.00	80.00
❏ 395-529 [M]	Let's Dance with Earl Bostic	1956	20.00	40.00	80.00
❏ 395-547 [M]	Invitation to Dance	1956	20.00	40.00	80.00
❏ 558 [M]	C'mon and Dance with Earl Bostic	1956	20.00	40.00	80.00
❏ KS-558 [S]	C'mon and Dance with Earl Bostic	1959	37.50	75.00	150.00
❏ 571 [M]	Hits of the Swing Age	1957	20.00	40.00	80.00
❏ 583 [M]	Showcase of Swinging Dance Hits	1958	20.00	40.00	80.00
❏ 597 [M]	Alto Magic in Hi-Fi	1958	20.00	40.00	80.00
❏ KS-597 [S]	Alto Magic in Hi-Fi	1959	37.50	75.00	150.00
❏ 602 [M]	Sweet Tunes of the Fantastic Fifties	1959	12.50	25.00	50.00
❏ KSD-602 [S]	Sweet Tunes of the Fantastic Fifties	1959	25.00	50.00	100.00
❏ 613 [M]	Bostic Workshop	1959	12.50	25.00	50.00
❏ KS-613 [S]	Bostic Workshop	1959	25.00	50.00	100.00
❏ 620 [M]	Sweet Tunes from the Roaring Twenties	1959	12.50	25.00	50.00
❏ KS-620 [S]	Sweet Tunes from the Roaring Twenties	1959	25.00	50.00	100.00
❏ 632 [M]	Sweet Tunes of the Swinging Thirties	1959	12.50	25.00	50.00
❏ KS-632 [S]	Sweet Tunes of the Swinging Thirties	1959	25.00	50.00	100.00
❏ 640 [M]	Sweet Tunes of the Sentimental Forties	1960	12.50	25.00	50.00
❏ KS-640 [S]	Sweet Tunes of the Sentimental Forties	1960	20.00	40.00	80.00
❏ 662 [M]	Musical Pearls	1960	12.50	25.00	50.00
❏ KS-662 [S]	Musical Pearls	1960	20.00	40.00	80.00
❏ 705 [M]	Hit Tunes of Big Broadway Shows	1960	12.50	25.00	50.00
❏ KS-705 [S]	Hit Tunes of Big Broadway Shows	1960	20.00	40.00	80.00
❏ 786 [M]	By Popular Demand	1961	12.50	25.00	50.00
❏ 827 [M]	Earl Bostic Plays Bossa Nova	1963	12.50	25.00	50.00
❏ 838 [M]	Songs of the Fantastic Fifties, Volume 2	1963	12.50	25.00	50.00
❏ 846 [M]	Jazz As I Feel It	1963	12.50	25.00	50.00
❏ 881 [M]	The Best of Earl Bostic, Volume 2	1964	12.50	25.00	50.00
❏ 900 [M]	The New Sound	1964	12.50	25.00	50.00
❏ 921 [M]	The Great Hits of 1964	1964	12.50	25.00	50.00
❏ 947 [M]	24 Songs That Earl Loved the Most	1966	10.00	20.00	40.00
❏ KS-1048 [S]	Harlem Nocturne	1969	6.25	12.50	25.00
❏ K-5010X	14 Original Greatest Hits	1977	3.00	6.00	12.00
PHILIPS					
❏ PHM 200262 [M]	The Song Is Not Ended	1967	6.25	12.50	25.00
❏ PHS 600262 [S]	The Song Is Not Ended	1967	6.25	12.50	25.00

BOSTIC, EARL/JIMMY LUNCEFORD
ALLEGRO ELITE

Number	Title (A Side/B Side)	Yr	VG	VG+	NM
❏ 4053 [10]	Earl Bostic/Jimmy Lunceford Orchestras	195?	10.00	20.00	40.00

BOSTON
EPIC

Number	Title (A Side/B Side)	Yr	VG	VG+	NM
❏ E99 34188	Boston	1978	5.00	10.00	20.00
—Picture disc					
❏ HE 34188	Boston	1981	12.50	25.00	50.00
—First edition of the half-speed mastered edition					
❏ JE 34188	Boston	1977	2.00	4.00	8.00
—Second edition; orange label, different prefix					
❏ JE 34188	Boston	1979	—	3.00	6.00
—Third edition; dark blue label					
❏ PE 34188	Boston	1976	2.50	5.00	10.00
—Original edition; orange label					
❏ FE 35050	Don't Look Back	1978	2.50	5.00	10.00
—Original edition; orange label					
❏ FE 35050	Don't Look Back	1979	2.00	4.00	8.00
—Second edition; dark blue label					
❏ HE 44188	Boston	1982	10.00	20.00	40.00
—Second edition of the half-speed mastered edition					
❏ HE 45050	Don't Look Back	1982	12.50	25.00	50.00
—Half-speed mastered edition					
MCA					
❏ 6188	Third Stage	1986	2.00	4.00	8.00
❏ 10973	Walk On	1994	3.75	7.50	15.00
MOBILE FIDELITY					
❏ 1-249	Boston	1996	6.25	12.50	25.00
—Audiophile vinyl					

BOSTON POPS ORCHESTRA (ARTHUR FIEDLER, CONDUCTOR)

Perhaps the most popular orchestra and conductor in American history, Fiedler and the Pops released literally hundreds of albums, of which the below are merely a sample. Most of these are from the "golden age of stereo" and also exist in monaural, but the mono versions are in much less demand than the stereo editions.

RCA VICTOR RED SEAL

Number	Title (A Side/B Side)	Yr	VG	VG+	NM
❏ LSC-1817 [S]	Offenbach: Gaite Parisienne	1958	100.00	200.00	400.00
—Original with "shaded dog" label					
❏ LSC-1817 [S]	Offenbach: Gaite Parisienne	199?	7.50	15.00	30.00
—Classic Records reissue					
❏ LSC-1990 [S]	Offenbach: In America	1958	10.00	20.00	40.00
—Original with "shaded dog" label					
❏ LSC-1990 [S]	Offenbach: In America	1964	12.50	25.00	50.00
—Second pressing with "white dog" label; a rare case where the second edition is more desirable than the first					
❏ LSC-2028 [S]	Waltzes by the Strauss Family	1958	5.00	10.00	20.00
—Original with "shaded dog" label					
❏ LSC-2052 [S]	Tchaikovsky: The Nutcracker (selections)	1958	5.00	10.00	20.00
—Original with "shaded dog" label					

Number	Title (A Side/B Side)	Yr	VG	VG+	NM
❏ LSC-2084 [S]	Rossini-Respighi: La Boutique Fantasque	1958	30.00	60.00	120.00
—Original with "shaded dog" label					
❏ LSC-2100 [S]	Hi-Fi Fiedler	1958	6.25	12.50	25.00
—Original with "shaded dog" label					
❏ LSC-2125 [S]	Grieg: Music from Peer Gynt	1958	5.00	10.00	20.00
—Original with "shaded dog" label					
❏ LSC-2130 [S]	Strauss, Johann: Orchestral Music from Gypsy Baron and Die Fledermaus	1958	5.00	10.00	20.00
—Original with "shaded dog" label					
❏ LSC-2202 [S]	Pops Caviar	1959	5.00	10.00	20.00
—Original with "shaded dog" label					
❏ LSC-2213 [S]	Boston Tea Party	1959	5.00	10.00	20.00
—Original with "shaded dog" label					
❏ LSC-2229 [S]	Marches in Hi-Fi	1959	5.00	10.00	20.00
—Original with "shaded dog" label					
❏ LSC-2235 [S]	Good Music to Have Fun With	1959	6.25	12.50	25.00
—Original with "shaded dog" label					
❏ LSC-2240 [S]	Kay, Hershey: Stars and Stripes	1959	10.00	20.00	40.00
—Original with "shaded dog" label					
❏ LSC-2267 [S]	Offenbach: Gaite Parisienne; Khachatourian: Gayne Suite	1959	5.00	10.00	20.00
—Original with "shaded dog" label					
❏ LSC-2270 [S]	Pops Stoppers	1959	5.00	10.00	20.00
—Original with "shaded dog" label					
❏ LSC-2294 [S]	Rodgers: Slaughter on Tenth Avenue	1959	5.00	10.00	20.00
—Original with "shaded dog" label					
❏ LSC-2320 [S]	Song of India	1959	5.00	10.00	20.00
—Original with "shaded dog" label					
❏ LSC-2329 [S]	Pops Christmas Party	1959	10.00	20.00	40.00
—Original copies have "shaded dog" with small "RCA Victor" logo; large "Living Stereo" on front cover					
❏ LSC-2329 [S]	Pops Christmas Party	1964	10.00	20.00	40.00
—Second editions have "white dog" with large "RCA Victor" logo; small "Living Stereo" on front cover					
❏ LSC-2367 [S]	Gershwin: Rhapsody in Blue; An American in Paris	1960	5.00	10.00	20.00
—Earl Wild, piano; originals with "shaded dog" label					
❏ LSC-2380 [S]	Music from Million Dollar Movies	1960	5.00	10.00	20.00
—Original with "shaded dog" label					
❏ LSC-2439 [S]	All-Time Favorites	1960	5.00	10.00	20.00
—Original with "shaded dog" label					
❏ LSC-2442 [S]	The Music of Franz Liszt	1960	5.00	10.00	20.00
—Original with "shaded dog" label					
❏ LSC-2470 [S]	More Classical Music for People Who Hate Classical Music	1961	10.00	20.00	40.00
—Original with "shaded dog" label					
❏ LSC-2486 [S]	Music of Frank Loesser	1961	10.00	20.00	40.00
—Original with "shaded dog" label					
❏ LSC-2549 [S]	Family Fun	1961	10.00	20.00	40.00
—Original with "shaded dog" label					
❏ LSC-2586 [S]	Gershwin: Piano Concerto	1962	5.00	10.00	20.00
—Earl Wild, piano; originals with "shaded dog" label					
❏ LSC-2586 [S]	Gershwin: Piano Concerto	199?	6.25	12.50	25.00
—Earl Wild, piano; Classic Records reissue					
❏ LSC-2596 [S]	Saint-Saens: Carnival of the Animals; Britten: Young Person's Guide to the Orchestra	1962	15.00	30.00	60.00
—Original with "shaded dog" label					
❏ LSC-2621 [S]	Chopin: Les Sylphides; Prokofiev: Love for Three Oranges	1962	7.50	15.00	30.00
—Original with "shaded dog" label					
❏ LSC-2637 [S]	Rodgers: No Strings; State Fair	1962	5.00	10.00	20.00
—Original with "shaded dog" label					
❏ LSC-2702 [S]	Milhaud: A Frenchman in New York; Gershwin: An American in Paris	1963	6.25	12.50	25.00
—Original with "shaded dog" label					
❏ LSC-6082 [(2)S]	Everything But the Beer	1959	25.00	50.00	100.00
—Original with "shaded dog" label					

BOSTON SYMPHONY ORCHESTRA (AARON COPLAND, CONDUCTOR)
RCA VICTOR RED SEAL

Number	Title (A Side/B Side)	Yr	VG	VG+	NM
❏ LSC-2401 [S]	Copland: Appalachian Spring; The Tender Land Suite	1960	5.00	10.00	20.00
—Original with "shaded dog" label					

BOSTON SYMPHONY ORCHESTRA (ERICH LEINSDORF, CONDUCTOR)
RCA VICTOR RED SEAL

Number	Title (A Side/B Side)	Yr	VG	VG+	NM
❏ LSC-2707 [S]	Prokofiev: Symphony No. 5	1963	5.00	10.00	20.00
—Original with "shaded dog" label					

BOSTON SYMPHONY ORCHESTRA (PIERRE MONTEUX, CONDUCTOR)
RCA VICTOR RED SEAL

Number	Title (A Side/B Side)	Yr	VG	VG+	NM
❏ LSC-1901 [S]	Tchaikovsky: Symphony No. 6 "Pathetique"	1958	12.50	25.00	50.00
—Original with "shaded dog" label					
❏ LSC-1901 [S]	Tchaikovsky: Symphony No. 6 "Pathetique"	199?	7.50	15.00	30.00
—Classic Records reissue					
❏ LSC-2239 [S]	Tchaikovsky: Symphony No. 5	1959	6.25	12.50	25.00
—Original with "shaded dog" label					
❏ LSC-2239 [S]	Tchaikovsky: Symphony No. 5	1964	5.00	10.00	20.00
—Second edition with "white dog" label					
❏ LSC-2369 [S]	Tchaikovsky: Symphony No. 4	1959	12.50	25.00	50.00
—Original with "shaded dog" label					
❏ LSC-2369 [S]	Tchaikovsky: Symphony No. 4	199?	7.50	15.00	30.00
—Classic Records reissue					
❏ LSC-2376 [S]	Stravinsky: Petrouchka	1960	25.00	50.00	100.00
—Original with "shaded dog" label					
❏ LSC-2376 [S]	Stravinsky: Petrouchka	1964	12.50	25.00	50.00
—Second edition with "white dog" label					

Number	Title (A Side/B Side)	Yr	VG	VG+	NM
BOSTON SYMPHONY ORCHESTRA (CHARLES MUNCH, CONDUCTOR)					
RCA VICTOR RED SEAL					
❑ LSC-1893 [S]	Ravel: Daphnis and Chloe	1958	100.00	200.00	400.00
—Original with "shaded dog" label					
❑ LSC-1893 [S]	Ravel: Daphnis and Chloe	199?	7.50	15.00	30.00
—Classic Records reissue					
❑ LSC-1900 [S]	Berlioz: Symphonie Fantastique	1958	—	—	—
—No mention of Classic Records on cover. Unknown; "if a copy did exist it could fetch up to $25,000 or more," according to at least one audiophile source					
❑ LSC-1900 [S]	Berlioz: Symphonie Fantastique	199?	7.50	15.00	30.00
—Classic Records issue. This album is not known to have been issued in stereo before this.					
❑ LSC-1984 [S]	Ravel: Bolero; La Valse; Rapsodie Espagnole; Debussy: Prelude	1958	20.00	40.00	80.00
—Original with "shaded dog" label					
❑ LSC-2097 [S]	Brahms: Symphony No. 1	1958	37.50	75.00	150.00
—Original with "shaded dog" label					
❑ LSC-2105 [S]	Tchaikovsky: Serenade for Strings	1958	10.00	20.00	40.00
—Original with "shaded dog" label					
❑ LSC-2111 [S]	Debussy: La Mer	1958	12.50	25.00	50.00
—Original with "shaded dog" label					
❑ LSC-2131 [S]	Franck: Symphony in D	1958	5.00	10.00	20.00
—Original with "shaded dog" label					
❑ LSC-2221 [S]	Mendelssohn: Symphony No. 4 and No. 5	1959	5.00	10.00	20.00
—Original with "shaded dog" label					
❑ LSC-2228 [S]	Berlioz: Harold in Italy	1959	5.00	10.00	20.00
—Original with "shaded dog" label					
❑ LSC-2233 [S]	Beethoven: Symphony No. 3	1959	12.50	25.00	50.00
—Original with "shaded dog" label					
❑ LSC-2271 [S]	Ravel: Concerto in G; d'Indy: Symphony on a French Mountain Air	1959	25.00	50.00	100.00
—Original with "shaded dog" label					
❑ LSC-2271 [S]	Ravel: Concerto in G; d'Indy: Symphony on a French Mountain Air	199?	7.50	15.00	30.00
—Classic Records reissue					
❑ LM-2282 [M]	Debussy: Images	1959	5.00	10.00	20.00
❑ LSC-2282 [S]	Debussy: Images	1959	20.00	40.00	80.00
—Original with "shaded dog" label					
❑ LSC-2292 [S]	The French Touch	1959	50.00	100.00	200.00
—Original with "shaded dog" label					
❑ LSC-2297 [S]	Brahms: Symphony No. 4	1959	7.50	15.00	30.00
—Original with "shaded dog" label					
❑ LSC-2341 [S]	Saint-Saens: Symphony No. 3	1960	5.00	10.00	20.00
—Original with "shaded dog" label					
❑ LSC-2344 [S]	Schubert: Symphony No. 9	1960	10.00	20.00	40.00
—Original with "shaded dog" label					
❑ LSC-2344 [S]	Schubert: Symphony No. 9	1964	7.50	15.00	30.00
—Second edition with "white dog" label					
❑ LM-2352 [M]	Blackwood: Symphony No. 1; Haieff: Symphony No. 2	1960	5.00	10.00	20.00
❑ LSC-2352 [S]	Blackwood: Symphony No. 1; Haieff: Symphony No. 2	1960	15.00	30.00	60.00
—Original with "shaded dog" label					
❑ LSC-2371 [S]	Mahler: Songs of a Wayfarer	1960	6.25	12.50	25.00
—Original with "shaded dog" label					
❑ LSC-2438 [S]	Berlioz: Overtures	1960	17.50	35.00	70.00
—Original with "shaded dog" label					
❑ LSC-2474 [S]	Schumann: Symphony No. 1	1961	5.00	10.00	20.00
—Original with "shaded dog" label					
❑ LSC-2520 [S]	Mendelssohn: Symphony No. 3 "Scotch"; Scherzo from Octet in E-flat	1961	5.00	10.00	20.00
—Original with "shaded dog" label					
❑ LSC-2522 [S]	Schubert: Symphony No. 2; Beethoven: Prometheus Ballet Excerpts	1961	5.00	10.00	20.00
—Original with "shaded dog" label					
❑ LSC-2565 [S]	Tchaikovsky: Romeo and Juliet; Strauss, Richard: Till Eulenspiegel	1961	10.00	20.00	40.00
—Original with "shaded dog" label					
❑ LSC-2567 [S]	Poulenc: Organ Concerto; Stravinsky: Jeu de Cartes	1961	10.00	20.00	40.00
—Original with "shaded dog" label					
❑ LSC-2568 [S]	Ravel: Daphnis et Chloe	1961	5.00	10.00	20.00
—Original with "shaded dog" label					
❑ LSC-2608 [S]	Berlioz: Symphonie Fantastique	1962	6.25	12.50	25.00
—Original with "shaded dog" label					
❑ LDS-2625 [S]	Milhaud: La Creation du Monde; Suite Provencale	1962	50.00	100.00	200.00
—Original with "shaded dog" label					
❑ LSC-2625 [S]	Milhaude: La Creation Du Monde	1962	50.00	100.00	200.00
—With "shaded dog" or "white dog" label					
❑ LSC-2625 [S]	Milhaude: La Creation Du Monde	199?	7.50	15.00	30.00
—Classic Records reissue					
❑ LSC-2629 [S]	Dvorak: Symphony No. 4 (8) in G	1962	12.50	25.00	50.00
—Original with "shaded dog" label					
❑ LSC-2647 [S]	Chausson: Symphony in B-flat; Franck: Le Chasseur Maudit	1962	10.00	20.00	40.00
—Original with "shaded dog" label					
❑ LSC-2683 [S]	Tchaikovsky: Symphony No. 6	1962	5.00	10.00	20.00
—Original with "shaded dog" label					
❑ LSC-6140 [(3)S]	Bach: Brandenburg Concertos No. 1-6	196?	37.50	75.00	150.00
—Original with "shaded dog" label					
BOSTON TEA PARTY, THE					
FLICK DISC					
❑ 45000	The Boston Tea Party	1968	15.00	30.00	60.00
BOSWELL, CONNEE					
DECCA					
❑ DL 5390 [10]	Connee Boswell	1951	20.00	40.00	80.00
❑ DL 5445 [10]	Singing the Blues	1952	20.00	40.00	80.00
❑ DL 8356 [M]	Connee	1956	12.50	25.00	50.00

Number	Title (A Side/B Side)	Yr	VG	VG+	NM
RCA VICTOR					
❑ LPM-1426 [M]	Connee Boswell and the Original Memphis Five	1957	10.00	20.00	40.00
BOTHWELL, JOHNNY					
BRUNSWICK					
❑ BL 58033 [10]	Presenting Johnny Bothwell	1953	25.00	50.00	100.00
BOURBON STREET STOMPERS, THE					
TIME					
❑ S-2118 [S]	We Like Dixieland	196?	5.00	10.00	20.00
BOW STREET RUNNERS, THE					
B.T. PUPPY					
❑ BTPS-1026	The Bow Street Runners	1969	500.00	750.00	1000.
SUNDAZED					
❑ LP 5029	The Bow Street Runners	199?	2.50	5.00	10.00
—Reissue of B.T. Puppy LP					
BOW WOW WOW					
HARVEST					
❑ SK-12234	12 Original Recordings	1982	3.75	7.50	15.00
RCA VICTOR					
❑ AFL1-4147	See Jungle, See Jungle! Go Join Your Gang, Yeah! City All Over, Go Ape Crazy	1981	3.00	6.00	12.00
❑ DJL1-4193 [DJ]	RCA Special Radio Series	1981	7.50	15.00	30.00
❑ CPL1-4314 [EP]	The Last of the Mohicans	1982	2.50	5.00	10.00
❑ AFL1-4375	I Want Candy	1982	3.00	6.00	12.00
❑ AFL1-4570	When the Going Gets Tough, the Tough Get Going	1983	2.50	5.00	10.00
BOWEN, JIMMY					
DECCA					
❑ DL 4816 [M]	Margie Bowes Sings	1967	5.00	10.00	20.00
REPRISE					
❑ R-6210 [M]	Sunday Morning with the Comics	1966	7.50	15.00	30.00
❑ RS-6210 [S]	Sunday Morning with the Comics	1966	10.00	20.00	40.00
ROULETTE					
❑ R 25004 [M]	Jimmy Bowen	1957	75.00	150.00	300.00
—Black and silver label					
❑ R 25004 [M]	Jimmy Bowen	1958	37.50	75.00	150.00
—Red label					
❑ R 25004 [M]	Jimmy Bowen	198?	3.00	6.00	12.00
—Reissue for Publishers Central Bureau (it says so on the jacket)					
BOWES, MARGIE					
DECCA					
❑ DL 4816 [M]	Margie Bowes Sings	1967	5.00	10.00	20.00
❑ DL 74816 [S]	Margie Bowes Sings	1967	3.75	7.50	15.00
❑ DL 75023	Today's Country Sound	1968	3.75	7.50	15.00
BOWIE, DAVID					
COLUMBIA					
❑ C 86630	Heathen	2002	3.00	6.00	12.00
DERAM					
❑ DE 16003 [M]	David Bowie	1967	30.00	60.00	120.00
❑ DES 18003 [S]	David Bowie	1967	37.50	75.00	150.00
EMI AMERICA					
❑ SPRO 9960/1 [(2)DJ]	Let's Talk	1983	6.25	12.50	25.00
—Promo-only interview album					
❑ SO-17093	Let's Dance	1983	2.50	5.00	10.00
❑ SJ-17138	Tonight	1984	2.50	5.00	10.00
❑ PJ-17267	Never Let Me Down	1987	2.50	5.00	10.00
❑ SPRO-79112/3 [DJ]	Never Let Me Down: The Interview	1987	6.25	12.50	25.00
❑ R 153730	Let's Dance	1983	3.00	6.00	12.00
—RCA Music Service edition					
❑ R 174212	Never Let Me Down	1987	3.00	6.00	12.00
—BMG Direct Marketing edition					
LONDON					
❑ PS 628/9 [(2)]	Images 1966-1967	1973	12.50	25.00	50.00
—Original pressings have dark blue and silver labels. Later pressings, if any, are worth at least 50% less.					
❑ LC 50007	Starting Point	1977	3.00	6.00	12.00
MERCURY					
❑ SR 61246	Man of Words, Man of Music	1969	37.50	75.00	150.00
❑ SR 61325	The Man Who Sold the World	1970	10.00	20.00	40.00
—An often-counterfeited album; originals have matrix numbers stamped in the trail-off area					
MOBILE FIDELITY					
❑ 1-064	The Rise and Fall of Ziggy Stardust and the Spiders from Mars	1983	12.50	25.00	50.00
—Audiophile vinyl					
❑ 1-083	Let's Dance	1984	7.50	15.00	30.00
—Audiophile vinyl					
RCA RED SEAL					
❑ ARL1-2743	Peter and the Wolf	1978	5.00	10.00	20.00
—With the Philadelphia Orchestra conducted by Eugene Ormandy; black vinyl					
❑ ARL1-2743	Peter and the Wolf	1978	5.00	10.00	20.00
—With the Philadelphia Orchestra conducted by Eugene Ormandy; green vinyl					
RCA VICTOR					
❑ AFL1-0291	Pin Ups	1978	2.50	5.00	10.00
—Reissue					
❑ APL1-0291	Pin Ups	1973	5.00	10.00	20.00
❑ CPL1-0576	Diamond Dogs	1974	5.00	10.00	20.00
—Standard issue, with dog's genitals airbrushed					
❑ CPL1-0576	Diamond Dogs	1974	1000.	2000.	4000.
—Original copies have cover with dog's genitals clearly visible. Almost all were destroyed prior to release.					
❑ CPL2-0771 [(2)]	David Live	1974	5.00	10.00	20.00
—At time of release, available with either orange or tan labels					
❑ CPL2-0771 [(2)]	David Live	1976	3.00	6.00	12.00
—Reissue with black label, dog near top					

Number	Title (A Side/B Side)	Yr	VG	VG+	NM
❑ APL1-0998	Young Americans	1975	3.00	6.00	12.00
—At time of release, available with either orange or tan label					
❑ APL1-0998	Young Americans	1976	2.50	5.00	10.00
—Black label					
❑ AQK1-0998	Young Americans	1984	2.50	5.00	10.00
—Reissue					
❑ APL1-1327	Station to Station	1976	2.50	5.00	10.00
—Black label					
❑ APL1-1327	Station to Station	1976	3.00	6.00	12.00
—Originals have a brown label					
❑ AQK1-1327	Station to Station	1984	2.50	5.00	10.00
—Reissue					
❑ AFL1-1732	Changesonebowie	1978	2.50	5.00	10.00
—Reissue					
❑ APL1-1732	Changesonebowie	1976	2.50	5.00	10.00
❑ AQL1-1732	Changesonebowie	1984	2.50	5.00	10.00
—Reissue					
❑ APL1-2030	Low	1977	2.50	5.00	10.00
❑ AFL1-2522	"Heroes"	1977	2.50	5.00	10.00
❑ DJL1-2697 [DJ]	Bowie Now	1978	15.00	30.00	60.00
❑ CPL2-2913 [(2)]	Stage	1978	5.00	10.00	20.00
❑ DJL1-3016 [DJ]	An Evening with David Bowie	1978	12.50	25.00	50.00
—Music and interview for "Superstars Radio Network"					
❑ AQL1-3254	Lodger	1979	2.50	5.00	10.00
❑ DJL1-3545 [DJ]	1980 All Clear	1980	6.25	12.50	25.00
—Promo-only compilation					
❑ AQL1-3647	Scary Monsters	1980	2.50	5.00	10.00
❑ DJL1-3829 [DJ]	College Radio Series	1980	6.25	12.50	25.00
❑ DJL1-3829-A [DJ]	Special Radio Series	1980	6.25	12.50	25.00
—Same material as DJL1-3829					
❑ DJL1-3840 [DJ]	Scary Monsters Interview	1980	5.00	10.00	20.00
❑ AYL1-3843	The Rise and Fall of Ziggy Stardust and the Spiders from Mars	1980	2.00	4.00	8.00
—Reissue					
❑ AYL1-3844	Hunky Dory	1980	2.00	4.00	8.00
—Reissue					
❑ AYL1-3856	Low	1980	2.00	4.00	8.00
—Reissue					
❑ AYL1-3857	"Heroes"	1980	2.00	4.00	8.00
—Reissue					
❑ AYL1-3889	Diamond Dogs	1980	2.00	4.00	8.00
—Reissue					
❑ AYL1-3890	Aladdin Sane	1980	2.00	4.00	8.00
—Reissue					
❑ AFL1-4202	Changestwobowie	1981	2.50	5.00	10.00
❑ AYL1-4234	Lodger	1981	2.00	4.00	8.00
—Reissue					
❑ CPL1-4346 [EP]	David Bowie in Berthold Brecht's Baal	1982	2.50	5.00	10.00
❑ LSP-4623	Hunky Dory	1972	5.00	10.00	20.00
❑ AYL1-4653	Pin Ups	1982	2.00	4.00	8.00
—Reissue					
❑ AFL1-4702	The Rise and Fall of Ziggy Stardust and the Spiders from Mars	1977	2.50	5.00	10.00
—Reissue					
❑ LSP-4702	The Rise and Fall of Ziggy Stardust and the Spiders from Mars	1972	5.00	10.00	20.00
—Orange label					
❑ LSP-4702	The Rise and Fall of Ziggy Stardust and the Spiders from Mars	1975	3.00	6.00	12.00
—Tan label					
❑ AFL1-4792	Golden Years	1983	2.50	5.00	10.00
❑ LSP-4813	Space Oddity	1973	5.00	10.00	20.00
—Reissue of Mercury SR-61246; add 1/3 if bonus poster is enclosed					
❑ LSP-4816	The Man Who Sold the World	1973	5.00	10.00	20.00
—Reissue of Mercury SR-61325; add 1/3 if bonus poster is enclosed					
❑ AFL1-4852	Aladdin Sane	1977	2.50	5.00	10.00
—Reissue					
❑ LSP-4852	Aladdin Sane	1973	5.00	10.00	20.00
—Orange label is original (deduct 50% for tan labels)					
❑ CPL2-4862 [(2)]	Ziggy Stardust, The Motion Picture	1983	5.00	10.00	20.00
❑ CPL2-4862 [(2)DJ]	Ziggy Stardust, The Motion Picture	1983	12.50	25.00	50.00
—Promo version on clear vinyl					
❑ AFL1-4919	Fame and Fashion	1984	2.50	5.00	10.00
RYKO ANALOGUE					
❑ RALP 0120/1/2 [(6)]	Sound + Vision	1989	20.00	40.00	80.00
—Six-LP box set on clear vinyl with three gatefold cardboard inner sleeves					
❑ RALP 0131 [(2)]	Space Oddity	1990	5.00	10.00	20.00
—Clear vinyl with "Limited Edition" obi					
❑ RALP 0132 [(2)]	The Man Who Sold the World	1990	5.00	10.00	20.00
—Clear vinyl with "Limited Edition" obi					
❑ RALP 0133 [(2)]	Hunky Dory	1990	5.00	10.00	20.00
—Clear vinyl with "Limited Edition" obi					
❑ RALP 0134 [(2)]	The Rise and Fall of Ziggy Stardust and the Spiders from Mars	1990	5.00	10.00	20.00
—Clear vinyl with "Limited Edition" obi					
❑ RALP 0135 [(2)]	Aladdin Sane	1990	5.00	10.00	20.00
—Clear vinyl with "Limited Edition" obi					
❑ RALP 0136 [(2)]	Pin Ups	1990	5.00	10.00	20.00
—Clear vinyl with "Limited Edition" obi					
❑ RALP 0137 [(2)]	Diamond Dogs	1990	5.00	10.00	20.00
—Clear vinyl with "Limited Edition" obi; genitals on dog are restored					
❑ RALP 0138/9 [(2)]	David Live	1990	5.00	10.00	20.00
—Clear vinyl with "Limited Edition" obi					
❑ RALP 0171 [(2)]	Changesbowie	1990	5.00	10.00	20.00
—Clear vinyl with "Limited Edition" obi					
❑ LSD-4702 [DJ]	The Rise and Fall of Ziggy Stardust and the Spiders from Mars	1990	25.00	50.00	100.00
—Special promo-only package with both the LP and CD versions					

BOWIE, LESTER

Also see ART ENSEMBLE OF CHICAGO.

NESSA

| ❑ N-1 | Numbers 1 and 2 | 1968 | 6.25 | 12.50 | 25.00 |

Number	Title (A Side/B Side)	Yr	VG	VG+	NM
BOWIE, PAT					
PRESTIGE					
❑ PRLP-7385 [M]	Out of Sight	1965	7.50	15.00	30.00
❑ PRST-7385 [S]	Out of Sight	1965	7.50	15.00	30.00
❑ PRLP-7437 [M]	Feelin' Good	1967	7.50	15.00	30.00
❑ PRST-7437 [S]	Feelin' Good	1967	6.25	12.50	25.00
BOWMAN, DON					
LONE STAR					
❑ 4605	Still Fighting Mental Health	1979	3.75	7.50	15.00
RCA VICTOR					
❑ LPM-2831 [M]	Our Man in Trouble	1964	5.00	10.00	20.00
❑ LSP-2831 [S]	Our Man in Trouble	1964	6.25	12.50	25.00
❑ LPM-3345 [M]	Fresh from the Funny Farm	1965	5.00	10.00	20.00
❑ LSP-3345 [S]	Fresh from the Funny Farm	1965	6.25	12.50	25.00
❑ LPM-3495 [M]	Funny Way to Make an Album	1966	5.00	10.00	20.00
❑ LSP-3495 [S]	Funny Way to Make an Album	1966	6.25	12.50	25.00
❑ LPM-3646 [M]	Don Bowman Recorded Almost Live	1966	5.00	10.00	20.00
❑ LSP-3646 [S]	Don Bowman Recorded Almost Live	1966	6.25	12.50	25.00
❑ LPM-3795 [M]	From Mexico with Laughs Featuring the Tijuana Drum and Bugle Corps	1967	6.25	12.50	25.00
❑ LSP-3795 [S]	From Mexico with Laughs Featuring the Tijuana Drum and Bugle Corps	1967	5.00	10.00	20.00
❑ LPM-3920 [M]	Funny Folk Flops	1968	12.50	25.00	50.00
❑ LSP-3920 [S]	Funny Folk Flops	1968	5.00	10.00	20.00
BOWN, PATTI					
COLUMBIA					
❑ CL 1379 [M]	Patti Bown Plays Big Piano	1959	7.50	15.00	30.00
BOX TOPS, THE					
BELL					
❑ 6011 [M]	The Letter/Neon Rainbow	1967	6.25	12.50	25.00
❑ S-6011 [S]	The Letter/Neon Rainbow	1967	5.00	10.00	20.00
❑ 6017	Cry Like a Baby	1968	5.00	10.00	20.00
❑ 6023	Non-Stop	1968	5.00	10.00	20.00
❑ 6025	The Box Tops Super Hits	1968	5.00	10.00	20.00
❑ 6032	Dimensions	1969	5.00	10.00	20.00
RHINO					
❑ RNLP-161	The Greatest Hits	1982	3.00	6.00	12.00
BOXCAR WILLIE					
AHMC					
❑ AA 118	Marty Martin Sings Country Music	1976	12.50	25.00	50.00
—As "Marty Martin"; he changed his name to "Boxcar Willie" after one of his early songs					
MAIN STREET					
❑ 9309	... Not the Man I Used to Be	1984	2.50	5.00	10.00
❑ 73000	King of the Road	1981	3.00	6.00	12.00
❑ 73001	Last Train to Heaven	1982	3.00	6.00	12.00
❑ 73002	Best of Boxcar, Vol. 1	1982	3.00	6.00	12.00
BOYCE, TOMMY					
RCA CAMDEN					
❑ CAL-2202 [M]	Tommy Boyce	1967	5.00	10.00	20.00
❑ CAS-2202 [S]	Tommy Boyce	1967	6.25	12.50	25.00
BOYCE, TOMMY, AND BOBBY HART					
A&M					
❑ LP-126 [M]	Test Patterns	1967	5.00	10.00	20.00
❑ LP-143 [M]	I Wonder What She's Doing Tonite?	1968	7.50	15.00	30.00
❑ SP-4126 [S]	Test Patterns	1967	5.00	10.00	20.00
❑ SP-4143 [S]	I Wonder What She's Doing Tonite?	1968	5.00	10.00	20.00
❑ SP-4162	It's All Happening on the Inside	1968	5.00	10.00	20.00
BOYD, BILL, AND HIS COWBOY RAMBLERS					
BLUEBIRD					
❑ AXM2-5503 [(2)]	Bill Boyd and His Cowboy Ramblers	197?	5.00	10.00	20.00
BOYD, BILLY					
CROWN					
❑ CST-196 [R]	Twangy Guitars	196?	3.00	6.00	12.00
—Black vinyl					
❑ CST-196 [R]	Twangy Guitars	196?	12.50	25.00	50.00
—Red vinyl					
❑ CLP-5170 [M]	Twangy Guitars	1960	15.00	30.00	60.00
—Black label, silver print					
❑ CLP-5170 [M]	Twangy Guitars	1961	5.00	10.00	20.00
—Gray label					
BOYD, EDDIE					
EPIC					
❑ BN 26409	7936 South Rhodes	1968	7.50	15.00	30.00
LONDON					
❑ PS 554	I'll Dust My Broom	1969	7.50	15.00	30.00
BOYD, JIMMY					
COLUMBIA					
❑ CL 2543 [10]	I Saw Mommy Kissing Santa Claus	1955	10.00	20.00	40.00
—"House Party Series" reissue					
❑ CL 6270 [10]	Christmas with Jimmy Boyd	1953	25.00	50.00	100.00
BOYD, ROCKY					
JAZZTIME					
❑ JS-001 [S]	Ease It	1961	7.50	15.00	30.00
❑ JT-001 [M]	Ease It	1961	6.25	12.50	25.00
BOYER, CHARLES					
VALIANT					
❑ VLM-5001 [M]	Where Does Love Go?	1966	6.25	12.50	25.00
❑ VLS-25001 [S]	Where Does Love Go?	1966	7.50	15.00	30.00

Number	Title (A Side/B Side)	Yr	VG	VG+	NM

BOYZ II MEN
MOTOWN
- ❑ 31453 0323-1 [DJ]II | | 1994 | 6.25 | 12.50 | 25.00
—*Vinyl is promo only; in Motown company cover*
- ❑ 31453 0819-1 [(2)]Evolution | | 1997 | 3.00 | 6.00 | 12.00

BRACE, JANET
ABC-PARAMOUNT
- ❑ ABC-116 [M] | Special Delivery | 1956 | 12.50 | 25.00 | 50.00

BRADFORD, ALEX
CHECKER
- ❑ LP-10041 [M] | Alex Bradford | 196? | 6.25 | 12.50 | 25.00
SPECIALTY
- ❑ SP-2108 [M] | Too Close to Heaven | 1959 | 25.00 | 50.00 | 100.00
VEE JAY
- ❑ LP-5023 [M] | One Step | 1962 | 10.00 | 20.00 | 40.00
- ❑ LP-5056 [M] | The Soul of Alex Bradford | 1964 | 10.00 | 20.00 | 40.00

BRADFORD, BOBBY
Also see JOHN CARTER AND BOBBY BRADFORD.
EMANEM
- ❑ 3302 | Love's Dream | 1976 | 5.00 | 10.00 | 20.00

BRADFORD, CLEA
MAINSTREAM
- ❑ S-6042 [S] | Clea Bradford Now | 1965 | 7.50 | 15.00 | 30.00
- ❑ 56042 [M] | Clea Bradford Now | 1965 | 6.25 | 12.50 | 25.00
STATUS
- ❑ ST-8320 [M] | Clea Bradford with Clark Terry | 1965 | 10.00 | 20.00 | 40.00
TRU-SOUND
- ❑ TRU-15005 [M] | These Dues | 1962 | 12.50 | 25.00 | 50.00

BRADFORD, PERRY
CRISPUS ATTUCKS
- ❑ 101 [M] | The Perry Bradford Story | 1957 | 15.00 | 30.00 | 60.00

BRADFORD, SCOTT
PROBE
- ❑ 4509 | Rock Slides | 1969 | 5.00 | 10.00 | 20.00

BRADLEY, OWEN
CORAL
- ❑ CRL 56012 [10] | Christmas Time | 1950 | 20.00 | 40.00 | 80.00
- ❑ CRL 56022 [10] | Strauss Waltzes | 195? | 15.00 | 30.00 | 60.00
- ❑ CRL 56035 [10] | Lazy River | 195? | 15.00 | 30.00 | 60.00
- ❑ CRL 56047 [10] | Singin' in the Rain | 195? | 15.00 | 30.00 | 60.00
- ❑ CRL 56065 [10] | Cherished Hymns | 195? | 15.00 | 30.00 | 60.00
- ❑ CRL 57071 [M] | Organ and Chimes Played by Owen Bradley | 1956 | 7.50 | 15.00 | 30.00
DECCA
- ❑ DL 4078 [M] | Paradise Island | 1960 | 5.00 | 10.00 | 20.00
- ❑ DL 8652 [M] | Joyous Bells of Christmas | 1957 | 7.50 | 15.00 | 30.00
- ❑ DL 8724 [M] | Bandstand Hop | 1958 | 7.50 | 15.00 | 30.00
- ❑ DL 8868 [M] | Big Guitar | 1958 | 7.50 | 15.00 | 30.00
- ❑ DL 74078 [S] | Paradise Island | 1960 | 6.25 | 12.50 | 25.00
- ❑ DL 78868 [S] | Big Guitar | 1958 | 10.00 | 20.00 | 40.00

BRADLEY, WILL
EPIC
- ❑ LG 1005 [10] | Boogie Woogie | 1954 | 30.00 | 60.00 | 120.00
- ❑ LN 1127 [10] | The House of Bradley | 1954 | 30.00 | 60.00 | 120.00
- ❑ LN 3115 [M] | Boogie Woogie | 1955 | 12.50 | 25.00 | 50.00
- ❑ LN 3199 [M] | The House of Bradley | 1955 | 12.50 | 25.00 | 50.00
RCA VICTOR
- ❑ LPM-2098 [M] | Big Band Boogie | 1960 | 10.00 | 20.00 | 40.00
- ❑ LSP-2098 [S] | Big Band Boogie | 1960 | 12.50 | 25.00 | 50.00
WALDORF MUSIC HALL
- ❑ MH 33-122 [10] | Jazz Encounter | 195? | 10.00 | 20.00 | 40.00
- ❑ MH 33-132 [10] | Jazz — Dixieland and Chicago Style | 195? | 10.00 | 20.00 | 40.00

BRADSHAW, EVANS
RIVERSIDE
- ❑ RLP 12-263 [M] | Look Out for Evans Bradshaw | 1958 | 10.00 | 20.00 | 40.00
- ❑ RLP 12-296 [M] | Pieces of Eighty-Eight | 1959 | 10.00 | 20.00 | 40.00
- ❑ RLP-1136 [S] | Pieces of Eighty-Eight | 1959 | 7.50 | 15.00 | 30.00

BRADSHAW, TERRY
BENSON
- ❑ R-3702 | Until You | 1980 | 3.75 | 7.50 | 15.00
HEART WARMING
- ❑ 3735 | Here in My Heart | 1983 | 3.75 | 7.50 | 15.00
MERCURY
- ❑ SRM-1-1073 | I'm So Lonesome I Could Cry | 1976 | 5.00 | 10.00 | 20.00

BRADSHAW, TINY
KING
- ❑ 295-74 [10] | Off and On | 1955 | 250.00 | 500.00 | 1000.
- ❑ 395-501 [M] | Selections | 1956 | 175.00 | 350.00 | 700.00
- ❑ 653 [M] | Great Composer | 1960 | 75.00 | 150.00 | 300.00
- ❑ 953 [M] | 24 Great Songs | 1966 | 10.00 | 20.00 | 40.00

BRADY BUNCH, THE
PARAMOUNT
- ❑ PAS-5026 | Merry Christmas from the Brady Bunch | 1971 | 20.00 | 40.00 | 80.00
- ❑ PAS-6032 | Meet the Brady Bunch | 1972 | 12.50 | 25.00 | 50.00
- ❑ PAS-6037 | The Kids from the Brady Bunch | 1972 | 10.00 | 20.00 | 40.00
- ❑ PAS-6058 | The Brady Bunch Phonograph Record | 1973 | 20.00 | 40.00 | 80.00

BRAFF, RUBY
ABC-PARAMOUNT
- ❑ ABC-141 [M] | Ruby Braff Featuring Dave McKenna | 1956 | 10.00 | 20.00 | 40.00

AMERICAN RECORDING SOCIETY
- ❑ G-445 [M] | Hey, Ruby | 1957 | 10.00 | 20.00 | 40.00
BETHLEHEM
- ❑ BCP-5 [M] | Omnibus | 1955 | 12.50 | 25.00 | 50.00
- ❑ BCP-82 [M] | Handful of Cool Jazz | 1958 | 10.00 | 20.00 | 40.00
- ❑ BCP-1005 [10] | Ruby Braff Quartet | 1954 | 30.00 | 60.00 | 120.00
- ❑ BCP-1032 [10] | Holiday in Braff | 1955 | 25.00 | 50.00 | 100.00
- ❑ BCP-1034 [10] | Ball at Bethlehem | 1955 | 25.00 | 50.00 | 100.00
- ❑ BCP-6043 [M] | The Best of Braff | 1960 | 7.50 | 15.00 | 30.00
CONCERT HALL JAZZ
- ❑ 1210 [M] | Little Big Horn | 1955 | 12.50 | 25.00 | 50.00
EPIC
- ❑ LN 3377 [M] | Braff! | 1957 | 12.50 | 25.00 | 50.00
JAZZTONE
- ❑ J-1210 [M] | Little Big Horn | 1955 | 10.00 | 20.00 | 40.00
RCA VICTOR
- ❑ LPM-1008 [M] | To Fred Astaire with Love | 1955 | 12.50 | 25.00 | 50.00
- ❑ LPM-1332 [M] | The Magic Horn of Ruby Braff | 1956 | 10.00 | 20.00 | 40.00
- ❑ LPM-1510 [M] | Hi-Fi Salute to Bunny | 1957 | 10.00 | 20.00 | 40.00
- ❑ LPM-1966 [M] | Easy Now | 1959 | 7.50 | 15.00 | 30.00
- ❑ LSP-1966 [S] | Easy Now | 1959 | 10.00 | 20.00 | 40.00
STEREO-CRAFT
- ❑ RTN-507 [M] | You're Getting to Be a Habit with Me | 1959 | 7.50 | 15.00 | 30.00
- ❑ RTS-507 [S] | You're Getting to Be a Habit with Me | 1959 | 10.00 | 20.00 | 40.00
STORYVILLE
- ❑ STLP-320 [10] | Hustlin' and Bustlin' | 1955 | 20.00 | 40.00 | 80.00
- ❑ STLP-908 [M] | Hustlin' and Bustlin' | 1956 | 12.50 | 25.00 | 50.00
UNITED ARTISTS
- ❑ UAL-3045 [M] | Blowing Around the Around | 1959 | 7.50 | 15.00 | 30.00
- ❑ UAL-4093 [M] | Ruby Braff-Marshall Brown Sextet | 1960 | 7.50 | 15.00 | 30.00
- ❑ UAS-5093 [S] | Ruby Braff-Marshall Brown Sextet | 1960 | 10.00 | 20.00 | 40.00
- ❑ UAS-6045 [S] | Blowing Around the Around | 1959 | 10.00 | 20.00 | 40.00
VANGUARD
- ❑ VRS-8504 [M] | The Ruby Braff Special | 1955 | 10.00 | 20.00 | 40.00
WARNER BROS.
- ❑ W 1273 [M] | Ruby Braff Goes Girl Crazy | 1959 | 7.50 | 15.00 | 30.00
- ❑ WS 1273 [S] | Ruby Braff Goes Girl Crazy | 1959 | 10.00 | 20.00 | 40.00

BRAFF, RUBY, AND ELLIS LARKINS
VANGUARD
- ❑ VRS-8019 [10] | Inventions in Jazz — Volume 1 | 1955 | 20.00 | 40.00 | 80.00
- ❑ VRS-8020 [10] | Inventions in Jazz — Volume 2 | 1955 | 20.00 | 40.00 | 80.00
- ❑ VRS-8507 [M] | Two By Two | 1956 | 10.00 | 20.00 | 40.00
- ❑ VRS-8516 [M] | Pocketful of Dreams | 1957 | 10.00 | 20.00 | 40.00

BRAFF, RUBY; PEE WEE RUSSELL; BOBBY HENDERSON
VERVE
- ❑ MGV-8241 [M] | The Ruby Braff Octet with Pee Wee Russell and Bobby Henderson at Newport | 1958 | 12.50 | 25.00 | 50.00
- ❑ V-8241 [M] | The Ruby Braff Octet with Pee Wee Russell and Bobby Henderson at Newport | 1961 | 6.25 | 12.50 | 25.00

BRAITH, GEORGE
BLUE NOTE
- ❑ BLP-4148 [M] | Two Souls in One | 1963 | 10.00 | 20.00 | 40.00
—*With "New York, USA" on label*
- ❑ BLP-4161 [M] | Soul Dream | 1964 | 10.00 | 20.00 | 40.00
—*With "New York, USA" on label*
- ❑ BLP-4171 [M] | Extension | 1964 | 10.00 | 20.00 | 40.00
—*With "New York, USA" on label*
- ❑ BST-84148 [S] | Two Souls in One | 1963 | 12.50 | 25.00 | 50.00
—*With "New York, USA" on label*
- ❑ BST-84148 [S] | Two Souls in One | 1966 | 5.00 | 10.00 | 20.00
—*With "A Division of Liberty Records" on label*
- ❑ BST-84161 [S] | Soul Dream | 1964 | 12.50 | 25.00 | 50.00
—*With "New York, USA" on label*
- ❑ BST-84161 [S] | Soul Dream | 1966 | 5.00 | 10.00 | 20.00
—*With "A Division of Liberty Records" on label*
- ❑ BST-84171 [S] | Extension | 1964 | 12.50 | 25.00 | 50.00
—*With "New York, USA" on label*
- ❑ BST-84171 [S] | Extension | 1966 | 5.00 | 10.00 | 20.00
—*With "A Division of Liberty Records" on label*
PRESTIGE
- ❑ PRLP-7474 [M] | Laughing Soul | 1967 | 6.25 | 12.50 | 25.00
- ❑ PRST-7474 [S] | Laughing Soul | 1967 | 5.00 | 10.00 | 20.00
- ❑ PRLP-7515 [M] | Musart | 1967 | 6.25 | 12.50 | 25.00
- ❑ PRST-7515 [S] | Musart | 1967 | 5.00 | 10.00 | 20.00

BRAND, DOLLAR
See ABDULLAH IBRAHIM.

BRAND, OSCAR
ABC-PARAMOUNT
- ❑ ABC-388 [M] | Oscar Brand Sings for Adults | 1961 | 6.25 | 12.50 | 25.00
- ❑ ABCS-388 [S] | Oscar Brand Sings for Adults | 1961 | 7.50 | 15.00 | 30.00
AUDIO FIDELITY
- ❑ AFLP-1806 [M] | Bawdy Songs and Backroom Ballads, Vol. II | 195? | 6.25 | 12.50 | 25.00
- ❑ AFLP-1824 [M] | Bawdy Songs and Backroom Ballads, Vol. III | 195? | 6.25 | 12.50 | 25.00
- ❑ AFLP-1847 [M] | Bawdy Songs and Backroom Ballads, Vol. IV | 195? | 6.25 | 12.50 | 25.00
- ❑ AFLP-1884 [M] | Bawdy Sea Shanties (Vol. 5) | 1959 | 6.25 | 12.50 | 25.00
- ❑ AFLP-1906 [M] | Bawdy Songs and Backroom Ballads, Vol. I | 195? | 6.25 | 12.50 | 25.00
- ❑ AFLP-1920 [M] | Bawdy Western Songs (Vol. VI) | 1960 | 6.25 | 12.50 | 25.00
- ❑ AFLP-1952 [M] | Bawdy Songs Goes to College | 1961 | 6.25 | 12.50 | 25.00
- ❑ AFLP-1966 [M] | Rollicking Sea Shanties | 1962 | 6.25 | 12.50 | 25.00
- ❑ AFLP-1971 [M] | Sing Along Bawdy Songs and Backroom Ballads | 1962 | 6.25 | 12.50 | 25.00
- ❑ AFLP-2121 [M] | Bawdy Hootenanny | 1964 | 5.00 | 10.00 | 20.00
- ❑ AFSD-5824 [S] | Bawdy Songs and Backroom Ballads, Vol. III | 196? | 6.25 | 12.50 | 25.00
- ❑ AFSD-5847 [S] | Bawdy Songs and Backroom Ballads, Vol. IV | 195? | 6.25 | 12.50 | 25.00
- ❑ AFSD-5884 [S] | Bawdy Sea Shanties (Vol. 5) | 1959 | 7.50 | 15.00 | 30.00

Number	Title (A Side/B Side)	Yr	VG	VG+	NM
❏ AFSD-5920 [S]	Bawdy Western Songs (Vol. VI)	1960	7.50	15.00	30.00
❏ AFSD-5952 [S]	Bawdy Songs Goes to College	1961	7.50	15.00	30.00
❏ AFSD-5966 [S]	Rollicking Sea Shanties	1962	7.50	15.00	30.00
❏ AFSD-5971 [S]	Sing Along Bawdy Songs and Backroom Ballads	1962	7.50	15.00	30.00
❏ AFSD-6121 [S]	Bawdy Hootenanny	1964	6.25	12.50	25.00

CAEDMON

❏ TC 1658	Singing Is Believing: Songs of the Advent Season	1980	3.00	6.00	12.00

CHESTERFIELD

❏ CMS-101 [10]	Backroom Ballads	195?	12.50	25.00	50.00

DECCA

❏ DL 4275 [M]	Folk Songs for Fun	1962	5.00	10.00	20.00
❏ DL 74275 [S]	Folk Songs for Fun	1962	6.25	12.50	25.00

ELEKTRA

❏ EKL-168 [M]	The Wild Blue Yonder	1959	5.00	10.00	20.00
❏ EKL-169 [M]	Every Inch a Sailor	1960	5.00	10.00	20.00
❏ EKL-174 [M]	Tell It to the Marines	1960	5.00	10.00	20.00
❏ EKL-178 [M]	Out of the Blue: Songs of a Fighting Airforce	1960	5.00	10.00	20.00
❏ EKL-183 [M]	Boating Songs and All That Bilge	1960	5.00	10.00	20.00
❏ EKL-188 [M]	Sports Car Songs for Big Wheels	1960	6.25	12.50	25.00
❏ EKL-198 [M]	Up in the Air: Songs for the Madcap Airman	1961	5.00	10.00	20.00
❏ EKL-204 [M]	For Doctors Only	1961	5.00	10.00	20.00
❏ EKL-228 [M]	A Snow Job for Skiers	1963	5.00	10.00	20.00
❏ EKL-237 [M]	Songs Fore Golfers	1963	5.00	10.00	20.00
❏ EKL-242 [M]	Cough: Army Songs Out of the Barracks Bag	1963	5.00	10.00	20.00
❏ EKS-7168 [S]	The Wild Blue Yonder	1959	6.25	12.50	25.00
❏ EKS-7169 [S]	Every Inch a Sailor	1960	6.25	12.50	25.00
❏ EKS-7174 [S]	Tell It to the Marines	1960	6.25	12.50	25.00
❏ EKS-7178 [S]	Out of the Blue: Songs of a Fighting Airforce	1960	6.25	12.50	25.00
❏ EKS-7183 [S]	Boating Songs and All That Bilge	1960	6.25	12.50	25.00
❏ EKS-7188 [S]	Sports Car Songs for Big Wheels	1960	7.50	15.00	30.00
❏ EKS-7198 [S]	Up in the Air: Songs for the Madcap Airman	1961	6.25	12.50	25.00
❏ EKS-7204 [S]	For Doctors Only	1961	6.25	12.50	25.00
❏ EKS-7228 [S]	A Snow Job for Skiers	1963	6.25	12.50	25.00
❏ EKS-7237 [S]	Songs Fore Golfers	1963	6.25	12.50	25.00
❏ EKS-7242 [S]	Cough: Army Songs Out of the Barracks Bag	1963	6.25	12.50	25.00

FOLKWAYS

❏ FA 5280 [M]	Election Songs of the United States	1960	6.25	12.50	25.00

KAPP

❏ KS-3629	Oscar Brand "Live" On Campus	1970	3.75	7.50	15.00

RIVERSIDE

❏ RLP 12-630 [M]	American Drinking Songs	1956	7.50	15.00	30.00
❏ RLP 12-639 [M]	G.I. — American Army Songs	195?	7.50	15.00	30.00
❏ RLP 12-825 [M]	Absolute Nonsense	195?	7.50	15.00	30.00
❏ RLP 12-835 [M]	Songs Inane Only	1959	7.50	15.00	30.00
❏ RLP 12-844 [M]	Songs of the U.S. Army	1960	7.50	15.00	30.00
❏ RLP 1419	Everybody Sing, Vol. 2	196?	3.75	7.50	15.00
❏ RLP 1438	Oscar Brand's Children's Concert	196?	3.75	7.50	15.00

ROULETTE

❏ SR-42060	Brand X	1971	3.75	7.50	15.00

TRADITION

❏ RLP 1014 [M]	Laughing America	195?	7.50	15.00	30.00
❏ TLP 1022 [M]	Pie in the Sky	195?	7.50	15.00	30.00
❏ TLP 2053	The Best of Oscar Brand	1967	5.00	10.00	20.00

BRANDMEIER, JONATHON
BRANDMEIER

❏ BPI 2004	Almost Live	1984	5.00	10.00	20.00

BRASS ENSEMBLE OF THE JAZZ AND CLASSICAL MUSIC SOCIETY, THE
COLUMBIA

❏ CL 941 [M]	Music for Brass	1956	15.00	30.00	60.00

BRASS RING, THE
ABC DUNHILL

❏ DS-50034	Gazpacho	1968	3.00	6.00	12.00
❏ DS-50044	Only Love	1969	3.00	6.00	12.00
❏ DS-50051	The Best of the Brass Ring	1970	2.50	5.00	10.00

DUNHILL

❏ D 50008 [M]	Love Theme from The Flight of the Phoenix	1966	3.00	6.00	12.00
❏ DS 50008 [S]	Love Theme from The Flight of the Phoenix	1966	3.75	7.50	15.00
❏ D 50012 [M]	Lara's Theme	1966	3.00	6.00	12.00
❏ DS 50012 [S]	Lara's Theme	1966	3.75	7.50	15.00
❏ D 50015 [M]	Sunday Night at the Movies	1967	3.00	6.00	12.00
❏ DS 50015 [S]	Sunday Night at the Movies	1967	3.75	7.50	15.00
❏ D 50017 [M]	The Dis-Advantages of You	1967	3.00	6.00	12.00
❏ DS 50017 [S]	The Dis-Advantages of You	1967	3.75	7.50	15.00
❏ D 50023 [M]	The Now Sound	1967	3.00	6.00	12.00
❏ DS 50023 [S]	The Now Sound	1967	3.75	7.50	15.00
❏ ST-91039 [S]	Lara's Theme	1966	5.00	10.00	20.00

—Capitol Record Club edition

PROJECT 3

❏ 5067	The Brass Ring	1972	2.50	5.00	10.00

BRASSELLE, KEEFE
CORAL

❏ CRL 57295 [M]	Minstrel Man	1959	5.00	10.00	20.00
❏ CRL 757295 [S]	Minstrel Man	1959	6.25	12.50	25.00

BRAUN, BOB
DECCA

❏ DL 4339 [M]	Till Death Do Us Part	1962	5.00	10.00	20.00
❏ DL 74339 [S]	Till Death Do Us Part	1962	6.25	12.50	25.00

BRAUTIGAN, RICHARD
HARVEST

❏ ST-424	Listening to Richard Brautigan	1970	7.50	15.00	30.00

Number	Title (A Side/B Side)	Yr	VG	VG+	NM

BRAXTON, ANTHONY
ARISTA

❏ AL 5002 [(2)]	The Montreux/Berlin Concerts	1977	5.00	10.00	20.00

ARISTA FREEDOM

❏ AL 1902 [(2)]	The Complete Braxton 1971	1978	5.00	10.00	20.00

DELMARK

❏ DS-415	Three Compositions of New Jazz	1969	5.00	10.00	20.00
❏ DS-420/1 [(2)]	For Alto	1971	6.25	12.50	25.00
❏ DS-428	Together Alone	1973	5.00	10.00	20.00

—With Joseph Jarman

BRAXTON, TONI
LAFACE

❏ 26069 [(2)]	The Heat	2000	5.00	10.00	20.00

BRAZOS VALLEY BOYS, THE
WARNER BROS.

❏ W 1664 [M]	Where Is the Circus	1966	5.00	10.00	20.00
❏ WS 1664 [S]	Where Is the Circus	1966	6.25	12.50	25.00
❏ W 1679 [M]	The Countrypolitan Sound	1967	5.00	10.00	20.00
❏ WS 1679 [S]	The Countrypolitan Sound	1967	6.25	12.50	25.00
❏ W 1686 [M]	The Gold Standard Collection	1967	5.00	10.00	20.00
❏ WS 1686 [S]	The Gold Standard Collection	1967	6.25	12.50	25.00

BREAD
ELEKTRA

❏ BRD-1 [DJ]	Bread	1971	5.00	10.00	20.00

—In-store sampler; very similar to the future LP "The Best of Bread"

❏ 6E-108	The Best of Bread	1977	2.00	4.00	8.00

—Reissue of 75056

❏ 6E-110	The Best of Bread, Volume 2	1977	2.00	4.00	8.00

—Reissue of 7E-1005

❏ 7E-1005	The Best of Bread, Volume 2	1974	3.00	6.00	12.00
❏ 7E-1094	Lost Without Your Love	1976	2.50	5.00	10.00
❏ EQ-5015 [Q]	Baby I'm-a Want You	1974	5.00	10.00	20.00
❏ EQ-5056 [Q]	The Best of Bread	1973	5.00	10.00	20.00
❏ 60414	Anthology of Bread	1985	2.50	5.00	10.00
❏ EKS-74044	Bread	1969	3.75	7.50	15.00

—Red label with large stylized "E"

❏ EKS-74044	Bread	1971	2.50	5.00	10.00

—Butterfly label

❏ EKS-74076	On the Waters	1970	3.75	7.50	15.00

—Red label with large stylized "E"

❏ EKS-74076	On the Waters	1971	2.50	5.00	10.00

—Butterfly label

❏ EKS-74086	Manna	1971	3.00	6.00	12.00
❏ EKS-75015	Baby I'm-a Want You	197?	2.50	5.00	10.00

—Front photo is not raised

❏ EKS-75015	Baby I'm-a Want You	1971	3.75	7.50	15.00

—Gatefold with raised photo on front

❏ EKS-75047	Guitar Man	1972	3.00	6.00	12.00
❏ EKS-75056	The Best of Bread	1973	3.00	6.00	12.00

BREAD, LOVE AND DREAMS
LONDON

❏ PS 566	Bread, Love and Dreams	1969	7.50	15.00	30.00

BREAM, JULIAN
RCA VICTOR RED SEAL

❏ LSC-2448 [S]	The Art of Julian Bream	1960	7.50	15.00	30.00

—Original with "shaded dog" label

❏ LSC-2487 [S]	Giuliani: Guitar Concerto; Arnold: Guitar Concerto	1961	7.50	15.00	30.00

—Original with "shaded dog" label

❏ LDS-2560 [S]	The Golden Age of English Lute Music	1961	6.25	12.50	25.00

—Original with "shaded dog" label

❏ LSC-2606 [S]	Popular Classics for Spanish Guitar	1962	6.25	12.50	25.00

—Original with "shaded dog" label

❏ LDS-2656 [S]	An Evening of Elizabethan Music	1962	10.00	20.00	40.00

—Original with "shaded dog" label

BREEDLOVE, JIMMY
RCA CAMDEN

❏ CAL-430 [M]	Rock 'N' Roll Hits	1958	10.00	20.00	40.00

BREEN, BOBBY
LONDON

❏ LB 270 [10]	Songs at Yuletide	1953	12.50	25.00	50.00

BREGMAN, BUDDY
VERVE

❏ MGV-2042 [M]	Swingin' Kicks	1957	12.50	25.00	50.00
❏ V-2042 [M]	Swingin' Kicks	1961	5.00	10.00	20.00
❏ MGV-2064 [M]	Funny Face	1958	12.50	25.00	50.00
❏ V-2064 [M]	Funny Face	1961	5.00	10.00	20.00
❏ MGV-2093 [M]	The Gershwin Anniversary Album	1959	12.50	25.00	50.00
❏ V-2093 [M]	The Gershwin Anniversary Album	1961	5.00	10.00	20.00
❏ MGV-2094 [M]	Dig Buddy Bregman in Hi-Fi	1959	12.50	25.00	50.00
❏ V-2094 [M]	Dig Buddy Bregman in Hi-Fi	1961	5.00	10.00	20.00
❏ MGVS-6013 [S]	Swingin' Kicks	1960	10.00	20.00	40.00

WORLD PACIFIC

❏ ST-1024 [S]	Swingin' Standards	1959	7.50	15.00	30.00
❏ WP-1263 [M]	Swingin' Standards	1959	7.50	15.00	30.00

BRENDA AND THE TABULATIONS
CHOCOLATE CITY

❏ 2002	I Keep Coming Back for More	1977	2.50	5.00	10.00

DIONN

❏ LPM-2000 [M]	Dry Your Eyes	1967	10.00	20.00	40.00
❏ LPS-2000 [S]	Dry Your Eyes	1967	12.50	25.00	50.00

TOP & BOTTOM

❏ 100	Brenda and the Tabulations	1970	5.00	10.00	20.00

Number	Title (A Side/B Side)	Yr	VG	VG+	NM

BRENNAN, WALTER
DOT
| ❏ DLP-3309 [M] | Dutchman's Gold | 1960 | 6.25 | 12.50 | 25.00 |
| ❏ DLP-25309 [S] | Dutchman's Gold | 1960 | 7.50 | 15.00 | 30.00 |

EVEREST
❏ SDBR-1103 [S]	World of Miracles	1960	7.50	15.00	30.00
❏ SDBR-1123 [S]	The President: A Musical Biography of Our Chief Executive	1960	7.50	15.00	30.00
❏ LPBR-5103 [M]	World of Miracles	1960	6.25	12.50	25.00
❏ LPBR-5123 [M]	The President: A Musical Biography of Our Chief Executive	1960	6.25	12.50	25.00

HAMILTON
| ❏ HLP-159 [M] | Dutchman's Gold | 1965 | 3.00 | 6.00 | 12.00 |
| ❏ HLP-12159 [S] | Dutchman's Gold | 1965 | 3.00 | 6.00 | 12.00 |

LIBERTY
❏ LRP-3233 [M]	Old Rivers	1962	5.00	10.00	20.00
❏ LRP-3241 [M]	The President: A Musical Biography of Our Chief Executive	1962	3.75	7.50	15.00
—Reissue of Everest 5123					
❏ LRP-3244 [M]	World of Miracles	1962	3.75	7.50	15.00
—Reissue of Everest 5103					
❏ LRP-3257 [M]	'Twas the Night Before Christmas Back Home	1962	5.00	10.00	20.00
❏ LRP-3266 [M]	Mama Sang a Song	1963	5.00	10.00	20.00
❏ LRP-3317 [M]	Talkin' from the Heart	1964	5.00	10.00	20.00
❏ LRP-3372 [M]	Gunfight at the O.K. Corral	1964	5.00	10.00	20.00
❏ LST-7233 [S]	Old Rivers	1962	6.25	12.50	25.00
❏ LST-7241 [S]	The President: A Musical Biography of Our Chief Executive	1962	5.00	10.00	20.00
—Reissue of Everest 1123					
❏ LST-7244 [S]	World of Miracles	1962	5.00	10.00	20.00
—Reissue of Everest 1103					
❏ LST-7257 [S]	'Twas the Night Before Christmas Back Home	1962	6.25	12.50	25.00
❏ LST-7266 [S]	Mama Sang a Song	1963	6.25	12.50	25.00
❏ LST-7317 [S]	Talkin' from the Heart	1964	6.25	12.50	25.00
❏ LST-7372 [S]	Gunfight at the O.K. Corral	1964	6.25	12.50	25.00

LONDON
| ❏ PS 577 | Yesterday, When I Was Young | 1970 | 3.75 | 7.50 | 15.00 |

R.P.C.
| ❏ 108 [M] | By the Fireside | 1961 | 7.50 | 15.00 | 30.00 |
| ❏ 108S [S] | By the Fireside | 1961 | 10.00 | 20.00 | 40.00 |

SUNSET
❏ SUM-1100 [M]	Country Heart	1966	3.00	6.00	12.00
❏ SUS-5100 [S]	Country Heart	1966	3.00	6.00	12.00
❏ SUS-5269	God and Country	1970	2.50	5.00	10.00

UNITED ARTISTS
| ❏ UA-LA438-E | The Very Best of Walter Brennan | 1975 | 3.00 | 6.00 | 12.00 |

BREWER, TERESA
AMSTERDAM
❏ 12012	The Doo Dah Song	1973	2.50	5.00	10.00
❏ 12013	Music, Music, Music	1973	2.50	5.00	10.00
❏ 12015	Teresa Brewer In London	1974	2.50	5.00	10.00

COLUMBIA
❏ FC 37363	A Sophisticated Lady	1981	2.50	5.00	10.00
❏ PC 37363	A Sophisticated Lady	198?	2.00	4.00	8.00
—Budget-line reissue					

CORAL
❏ CXB 7 [(2)M]	The Best of Teresa Brewer	1965	5.00	10.00	20.00
❏ CXSB 7 [(2)P]	The Best of Teresa Brewer	1965	5.00	10.00	20.00
❏ CRL 56072 [10]	A Bouquet of Hits	1952	10.00	20.00	40.00
❏ CRL 56093 [10]	Till I Waltz Again with You	1953	10.00	20.00	40.00
❏ CRL 57027 [M]	Music, Music, Music	1955	7.50	15.00	30.00
❏ CRL 57053 [M]	Teresa	1956	7.50	15.00	30.00
❏ CRL 57135 [M]	For Teenagers in Love	1957	7.50	15.00	30.00
❏ CRL 57144 [M]	Teresa Brewer At Christmas Time	1957	7.50	15.00	30.00
❏ CRL 57179 [M]	Miss Music	1958	7.50	15.00	30.00
❏ CRL 57232 [M]	Time for Teresa	1958	7.50	15.00	30.00
❏ CRL 57245 [M]	Teresa Brewer and the Dixieland Band	1958	5.00	10.00	20.00
❏ 57297 [M]	Heavenly Lover	1959	5.00	10.00	20.00
❏ CRL 57297 [M]	When Your Lover Has Gone	1958	5.00	10.00	20.00
❏ CRL 57315 [M]	Ridin' High	1960	5.00	10.00	20.00
❏ CRL 57329 [M]	Naughty, Naughty, Naughty	1960	5.00	10.00	20.00
❏ CRL 57351 [M]	My Golden Favorites	1960	5.00	10.00	20.00
❏ CRL 57361 [M]	Songs Everybody Knows	1961	5.00	10.00	20.00
❏ CRL 57374 [M]	Aloha from Teresa	1961	5.00	10.00	20.00
❏ CRL 57414 [M]	Don't Mess with Tess	1962	5.00	10.00	20.00
❏ CRL 757245 [S]	Teresa Brewer and the Dixieland Band	1958	7.50	15.00	30.00
❏ CRL 757297 [S]	When Your Lover Has Gone	1959	7.50	15.00	30.00
❏ CRL 757315 [S]	Ridin' High	1960	6.25	12.50	25.00
❏ CRL 757329 [S]	Naughty, Naughty, Naughty	1960	6.25	12.50	25.00
❏ CRL 757351 [R]	My Golden Favorites	1960	5.00	10.00	20.00
❏ CRL 757361 [S]	Songs Everybody Knows	1961	6.25	12.50	25.00
❏ CRL 757374 [S]	Aloha from Teresa	1961	6.25	12.50	25.00
❏ CRL 757414 [S]	Don't Mess with Tess	1962	6.25	12.50	25.00

DOCTOR JAZZ
❏ ASLP 804	Good News	198?	2.50	5.00	10.00
❏ FW 38534	I Dig Big Band Singers	1983	2.50	5.00	10.00
❏ W2X 39521 [(2)]	Live at Carnegie Hall and Montreux, Switzerland	1984	3.00	6.00	12.00
❏ FW 40232	Midnight Café	1986	2.50	5.00	10.00
❏ FW 40951	Good News	198?	2.00	4.00	8.00

FLYING DUTCHMAN
| ❏ BSL1-0577 | Good News | 1974 | 3.00 | 6.00 | 12.00 |

LONDON
| ❏ APB-1006 [10] | Teresa Brewer | 1951 | 12.50 | 25.00 | 50.00 |

PHILIPS
| ❏ PHM 200062 [M] | Teresa Brewer's Greatest Hits | 1962 | 3.75 | 7.50 | 15.00 |
| ❏ PHM 200099 [M] | Terrific Teresa | 1963 | 3.75 | 7.50 | 15.00 |

❏ PHM 200119 [M]	Moments to Remember	1964	3.00	6.00	12.00
❏ PHM 200147 [M]	Golden Hits of 1964	1964	3.00	6.00	12.00
❏ PHM 200163 [M]	Dear Heart/Goldfinger	1965	3.00	6.00	12.00
❏ PHM 200200 [M]	Songs for Our Fighting Men	1966	3.00	6.00	12.00
❏ PHM 200216 [M]	Gold Country	1966	3.00	6.00	12.00
❏ PHM 200230 [M]	Texas Leather and Mexican Lace	1967	3.75	7.50	15.00
❏ PHS 600062 [S]	Teresa Brewer's Greatest Hits	1962	5.00	10.00	20.00
❏ PHS 600099 [S]	Terrific Teresa	1963	5.00	10.00	20.00
❏ PHS 600119 [S]	Moments to Remember	1964	3.75	7.50	15.00
❏ PHS 600147 [S]	Golden Hits of 1964	1964	3.75	7.50	15.00
❏ PHS 600163 [S]	Dear Heart/Goldfinger	1965	3.75	7.50	15.00
❏ PHS 600200 [S]	Songs for Our Fighting Men	1966	3.75	7.50	15.00
❏ PHS 600216 [S]	Gold Country	1966	3.75	7.50	15.00
❏ PHS 600230 [S]	Texas Leather and Mexican Lace	1967	3.00	6.00	12.00

PROJECT 3
| ❏ 5108 | Come Follow the Band | 1982 | 2.50 | 5.00 | 10.00 |

RCA VICTOR
| ❏ ANL1-1131 | The Best of Teresa Brewer | 1975 | 2.50 | 5.00 | 10.00 |

SIGNATURE
❏ FW 39421	Teresa Brewer In London	1984	2.00	4.00	8.00
—Reissue of Amsterdam 12015					
❏ PW 40113	Teresa Brewer At Christmas Time	1985	2.50	5.00	10.00
—Reissue of Coral 57144					

VOCALION
| ❏ VL 3693 [M] | Teresa Brewer | 1966 | 3.00 | 6.00 | 12.00 |
| ❏ VL 73847 [R] | Here's Teresa Brewer | 1969 | 2.50 | 5.00 | 10.00 |

BRIGADE, THE
BAND'N VOCAL
| ❏ 1066 | Last Laugh | 1970 | 1000. | 1500. | 2000. |

BRIGG
SUSQUEHANNA
| ❏ LP-301 | Brigg | 1973 | 45.00 | 90.00 | 180.00 |

BRIGGS, KAREN
VITAL
| ❏ VTL-009 | Karen | 1996 | 5.00 | 10.00 | 20.00 |

BRIGHT, RONNELL
REGENT
| ❏ MG-6041 [M] | Bright's Spot | 1957 | 10.00 | 20.00 | 40.00 |

SAVOY
| ❏ MG-12206 [M] | Bright's Spot | 196? | 7.50 | 15.00 | 30.00 |
| —Reissue of Regent LP | | | | | |

VANGUARD
| ❏ VRS-8512 [M] | Bright's Flight | 1957 | 10.00 | 20.00 | 40.00 |

BRIGMAN, GEORGE
SOLID
| ❏ SR-001 | Jungle Rot | 1975 | 30.00 | 60.00 | 120.00 |

BRILL, MARTY
MERCURY
| ❏ MG-20178 [M] | The Roving Balladeer | 1957 | 6.25 | 12.50 | 25.00 |

BRIMSTONE
BRIMSTONE
| ❏ (no #) | Paper Winged Dreams | 1968 | 50.00 | 100.00 | 200.00 |

BRINSLEY SCHWARZ
CAPITOL
❏ ST-589	Brinsley Schwarz	1970	5.00	10.00	20.00
❏ ST-744	Despite It All	1971	5.00	10.00	20.00
❏ SWBC-11869 [(2)]	Brinsley Schwarz	1978	3.75	7.50	15.00

LIBERTY
❏ LN 10145	Silver Pistol	1980	2.50	5.00	10.00
—10-track reissue					
❏ LN 10146	Nervous on the Road	1981	2.50	5.00	10.00
—10-track reissue					

UNITED ARTISTS
| ❏ UAS-5566 | Silver Pistol | 1972 | 3.75 | 7.50 | 15.00 |
| ❏ UAS-5647 | Nervous on the Road | 1972 | 3.75 | 7.50 | 15.00 |

BRITT, ELTON
Also see THE BEVERLY HILL BILLIES.
ABC-PARAMOUNT
❏ ABC-293 [M]	The Wandering Cowboy	1959	6.25	12.50	25.00
❏ ABCS-293 [S]	The Wandering Cowboy	1959	10.00	20.00	40.00
❏ ABC-322 [M]	Beyond the Sunset	1960	6.25	12.50	25.00
❏ ABCS-322 [S]	Beyond the Sunset	1960	10.00	20.00	40.00
❏ ABC-331 [M]	I Heard a Forest Praying	1960	6.25	12.50	25.00
❏ ABCS-331 [S]	I Heard a Forest Praying	1960	10.00	20.00	40.00
❏ ABC-521 [M]	The Singing Hills	1965	6.25	12.50	25.00
❏ ABCS-521 [S]	The Singing Hills	1965	10.00	20.00	40.00
❏ ABC-566 [M]	Somethin' for Everybody	1966	6.25	12.50	25.00
❏ ABCS-566 [S]	Somethin' for Everybody	1966	10.00	20.00	40.00

RCA VICTOR
❏ LPM-1288 [M]	Yodel Songs	1956	15.00	30.00	60.00
❏ LPM-2669 [M]	The Best of Elton Britt	1963	6.25	12.50	25.00
❏ LPM-3222 [10]	Yodel Songs	1954	30.00	60.00	120.00

BRITT, PAT
CRESTVIEW
| ❏ CR-3075 [M] | Jazz from San Francisco | 1967 | 5.00 | 10.00 | 20.00 |

BRITT, TINA
MINIT
| ❏ LP-24023 | Blue All the Way | 1968 | 5.00 | 10.00 | 20.00 |

B

Number	Title (A Side/B Side)	Yr	VG	VG+	NM
BROCAS HELM					
GARGOYLE					
❏ 138801	Black Death	1988	12.50	25.00	50.00
BROCK, B., AND THE SULTANS					
CROWN					
❏ CST-399 [S]	Do the Beetle	1964	12.50	25.00	50.00
❏ CLP-5399 [M]	Do the Beetle	1964	10.00	20.00	40.00
BROCK, HERBIE					
SAVOY					
❏ MG-12066 [M]	Herbie Brock Solo	1956	10.00	20.00	40.00
❏ MG-12069 [M]	Brock's Tops	1956	10.00	20.00	40.00
BROKENSHA, JACK					
SAVOY					
❏ MG-12180	And Then I Said	1962	7.50	15.00	30.00
BROLIN, JAMES					
ARTCO					
❏ LPC-1099	James Brolin Sings	1974	6.25	12.50	25.00
BROOKLYN BRIDGE, THE					
BUDDAH					
❏ BDS-5034	Brooklyn Bridge	1969	5.00	10.00	20.00
❏ BDS-5042	The Second Brooklyn Bridge	1969	5.00	10.00	20.00
❏ BDS-5065	The Brooklyn Bridge	1970	5.00	10.00	20.00
❏ BDS-5107	Bridge in Blue	1972	5.00	10.00	20.00
COLLECTABLES					
❏ COL-5015	The Greatest Hits	198?	3.00	6.00	12.00
—As "Johnny Maestro and the Brooklyn Bridge"					
BROOKMEYER, BOB					
ATLANTIC					
❏ 1320 [M]	Portrait of the Artist	1960	12.50	25.00	50.00
—Black label					
❏ 1320 [M]	Portrait of the Artist	1961	6.25	12.50	25.00
—Multicolor label, white "fan" logo at right					
❏ SD 1320 [S]	Portrait of the Artist	1960	12.50	25.00	50.00
—Green label					
❏ SD 1320 [S]	Portrait of the Artist	1961	5.00	10.00	20.00
—Multicolor label, white "fan" logo at right					
CLEF					
❏ MGC-644 [M]	Bob Brookmeyer Plays Bob Brookmeyer and Some Others	1955	25.00	50.00	100.00
❏ MGC-732 [M]	The Modernity of Bob Brookmeyer	1956	17.50	35.00	70.00
COLUMBIA					
❏ CS 9037 [S]	Bob Brookmeyer and Friends	1965	5.00	10.00	20.00
MERCURY					
❏ MG-20600 [M]	Jazz Is a Kick	1960	6.25	12.50	25.00
❏ SR-60600 [S]	Jazz Is a Kick	1960	7.50	15.00	30.00
NEW JAZZ					
❏ NJLP-8294 [M]	Revelation	1963	12.50	25.00	50.00
—Purple label					
❏ NJLP-8294 [M]	Revelation	1965	6.25	12.50	25.00
—Blue label, trident logo at right					
PACIFIC JAZZ					
❏ PJLP-16 [10]	Bob Brookmeyer Quartet	1954	37.50	75.00	150.00
PRESTIGE					
❏ PRLP-214 [10]	Bob Brookmeyer with Jimmy Raney	1955	37.50	75.00	150.00
❏ PRLP-7066 [M]	The Dual Role of Bob Brookmeyer	1956	20.00	40.00	80.00
STORYVILLE					
❏ STLP-305 [10]	Bob Brookmeyer Featuring Al Cohn	1954	75.00	150.00	300.00
TODAY'S JAZZ					
❏ J-1239 [M]	Bob Brookmeyer and Zoot Sims	196?	7.50	15.00	30.00
UNITED ARTISTS					
❏ UAL-4008 [M]	Kansas City Revisited	1959	12.50	25.00	50.00
❏ UAS-5008 [S]	Kansas City Revisited	1959	10.00	20.00	40.00
VERVE					
❏ MGV-8111 [M]	The Modernity of Bob Brookmeyer	1957	12.50	25.00	50.00
❏ V-8111 [M]	The Modernity of Bob Brookmeyer	1961	7.50	15.00	30.00
❏ MGV-8385 [M]	The Blues, Hot and Cold	1960	12.50	25.00	50.00
❏ V-8385 [M]	The Blues, Hot and Cold	1961	7.50	15.00	30.00
❏ V6-8385 [S]	The Blues, Hot and Cold	1961	6.25	12.50	25.00
❏ V-8413 [M]	7 X Wilder	1961	6.25	12.50	25.00
❏ V6-8413 [S]	7 X Wilder	1961	7.50	15.00	30.00
❏ V-8455 [M]	Gloomy Sunday and Other Bright Moments	1962	6.25	12.50	25.00
❏ V6-8455 [S]	Gloomy Sunday and Other Bright Moments	1962	7.50	15.00	30.00
❏ V-8498 [M]	Trombone Jazz Samba	1962	6.25	12.50	25.00
❏ V6-8498 [S]	Trombone Jazz Samba	1962	7.50	15.00	30.00
VIK					
❏ LX-1071 [M]	Brookmeyer	1957	12.50	25.00	50.00
WORLD PACIFIC					
❏ PJ-1233 [M]	Traditionalism Revisited	1958	20.00	40.00	80.00
BROOKMEYER, BOB, AND BILL EVANS					
UNITED ARTISTS					
❏ UAL-3044 [M]	The Ivory Hunters — Double Barreled Piano	1959	12.50	25.00	50.00
❏ UAS-6044 [S]	The Ivory Hunters — Double Barreled Piano	1959	10.00	20.00	40.00
BROOKMEYER, BOB; JIM HALL; JIMMY RANEY					
KIMBERLY					
❏ 2021 [M]	Brookmeyer and Guitars	1963	7.50	15.00	30.00
❏ 11021 [S]	Brookmeyer and Guitars	1963	5.00	10.00	20.00
WORLD PACIFIC					
❏ PJ-1239 [M]	The Street Swingers	1957	25.00	50.00	100.00
❏ WP-1239 [M]	The Street Swingers	1958	12.50	25.00	50.00
—Reissue with new prefix					

Number	Title (A Side/B Side)	Yr	VG	VG+	NM
BROOKMEYER, BOB, AND ZOOT SIMS					
JAZZTONE					
❏ J-1239 [M]	Bob Brookmeyer and Zoot Sims	1956	10.00	20.00	40.00
STORYVILLE					
❏ STLP-907 [M]	Tonight's Jazz Today	1956	20.00	40.00	80.00
❏ STLP-914 [M]	Whoo-eeee!	1956	20.00	40.00	80.00
BROOKS, DONNA					
DAWN					
❏ DLP-1105 [M]	I'll Take Romance	1956	30.00	60.00	120.00
BROOKS, DONNIE					
ERA					
❏ EL-105 [M]	The Happiest	1961	37.50	75.00	150.00
BROOKS, GARTH					
CAPITOL					
❏ 1P-8042	No Fences	1990	10.00	20.00	40.00
—Columbia House version; cover photo is the size of CD cover					
❏ C1-90897	Garth Brooks	1989	6.25	12.50	25.00
—Non-record club edition					
❏ C1-590897	Garth Brooks	1989	5.00	10.00	20.00
—Columbia House edition					
CAPITOL NASHVILLE					
❏ R 173266	No Fences	1990	12.50	25.00	50.00
—BMG Direct Marketing version has a large cover photo					
❏ C1-596330	Ropin' the Wind	1991	12.50	25.00	50.00
—Only released on U.S. vinyl by Columbia House					
BROOKS, HADDA					
CROWN					
❏ CLP-5010 [M]	Femme Fatale	1957	15.00	30.00	60.00
—Black label; reissue of Modern LP					
❏ CLP-5374 [M]	Hadda Brooks Sings and Swings	1963	6.25	12.50	25.00
—Gray label					
MODERN					
❏ MLP-1210 [M]	Femme Fatale	1956	50.00	100.00	200.00
BROOKS, HADDA / PETE JOHNSON					
CROWN					
❏ CLP-5058 [M]	Boogie	1958	12.50	25.00	50.00
BROOKS, JOHN BENSON					
DECCA					
❏ DL 5018 [M]	Avant Slant	1968	10.00	20.00	40.00
—White label promo only; in stereo cover with "Monaural" sticker on front					
❏ DL 75018 [S]	Avant Slant	1968	5.00	10.00	20.00
RIVERSIDE					
❏ RLP 12-276 [M]	The Alabama Concerto	1958	12.50	25.00	50.00
❏ RLP-1123 [S]	The Alabama Concerto	1959	10.00	20.00	40.00
VIK					
❏ LX-1083 [M]	Folk Jazz U.S.A.	1957	10.00	20.00	40.00
BROOKS, RANDY					
DECCA					
❏ DL 8201 [M]	Trumpet Moods	195?	7.50	15.00	30.00
BROOKS, ROY					
WORKSHOP JAZZ					
❏ WSJ-220 [M]	Roy Brooks Beat	1964	12.50	25.00	50.00
❏ WSJS-220 [S]	Roy Brooks Beat	1964	15.00	30.00	60.00
BROOKS, TINA					
BLUE NOTE					
❏ BLP-4041 [M]	True Blue	1960	125.00	250.00	500.00
❏ BLP-4052 [M]	Back to the Tracks	1960	—	—	—
—Canceled					
❏ B1-28975	True Blue	1994	5.00	10.00	20.00
❏ BST-84041 [S]	True Blue	1960	—	—	—
—Canceled					
❏ BST-84052 [S]	Back to the Tracks	1960	—	—	—
—Canceled					
❏ BST-84052 [S]	Back to the Tracks	199?	7.50	15.00	30.00
—Classic Records reissue; first U.S. vinyl issue					
MOSAIC					
❏ MR4-106 [(4)]	The Complete Blue Note Recordings of the Tina Brooks Quintets	1984	37.50	75.00	150.00
BROONZY, BIG BILL					
ARCHIVE OF FOLK AND JAZZ					
❏ 213	Big Bill Broonzy	1967	3.00	6.00	12.00
BIOGRAPH					
❏ C-15	Big Bill Broonzy 1932-1942	197?	2.50	5.00	10.00
CHESS					
❏ LP-1468 [M]	Big Bill Broonzy and Washboard Sam	1962	40.00	80.00	160.00
COLUMBIA					
❏ WL 111 [M]	Big Bill's Blues	1958	25.00	50.00	100.00
DIAL					
❏ LP-306 [10]	Blues Concert	1952	37.50	75.00	150.00
EMARCY					
❏ MG-26034 [10]	Folk Blues	1954	30.00	60.00	120.00
❏ MG-36137 [M]	Blues by Broonzy	1958	25.00	50.00	100.00
EPIC					
❏ EE 22017 [M]	Big Bill's Blues	196?	5.00	10.00	20.00
FOLKWAYS					
❏ FA-2315 [M]	Big Bill Broonzy	1957	12.50	25.00	50.00
❏ FA-2326 [M]	Country Blues	1957	12.50	25.00	50.00
❏ FG-3586 [M]	His Songs and Story	195?	12.50	25.00	50.00
❏ 31005 [R]	Big Bill Sings Country Blues	196?	3.75	7.50	15.00
GNP CRESCENDO					
❏ 10004	Feeling Low Down	1974	2.50	5.00	10.00

Number	Title (A Side/B Side)	Yr	VG	VG+	NM
❏ 10009	Lonesome Road Blues	1975	2.50	5.00	10.00

MERCURY

Number	Title (A Side/B Side)	Yr	VG	VG+	NM
❏ MG-20822 [M]	Big Bill Broonzy — Memorial	1963	7.50	15.00	30.00
❏ MG-20905 [M]	Remembering Big Bill Broonzy	1964	7.50	15.00	30.00
❏ SR-60822 [R]	Big Bill Broonzy — Memorial	1963	5.00	10.00	20.00
❏ SR-60905 [R]	Remembering Big Bill Broonzy	1964	5.00	10.00	20.00

PERIOD

Number	Title (A Side/B Side)	Yr	VG	VG+	NM
❏ SLP-1114 [M]	Big Bill Broonzy Sings (Blues)	1956	37.50	75.00	150.00
❏ SLP-1209 [M]	Big Bill Broonzy Sings and Josh White Comes a-Visiting	1958	17.50	35.00	70.00

PORTRAIT MASTERS

Number	Title (A Side/B Side)	Yr	VG	VG+	NM
❏ RJ 44089	Big Bill's Blues	1988	3.75	7.50	15.00

—*Reissue of Columbia 111*

SMITHSONIAN FOLKWAYS

Number	Title (A Side/B Side)	Yr	VG	VG+	NM
❏ SF-40023	Big Bill Broonzy Sings Folk Songs	1989	3.00	6.00	12.00

VERVE

Number	Title (A Side/B Side)	Yr	VG	VG+	NM
❏ MGV-3000-5 [(5)M]	The Big Bill Broonzy Story	1959	50.00	100.00	200.00
❏ MGV-3001 [M]	Last Session, Vol. 1	1959	12.50	25.00	50.00
❏ MGV-3002 [M]	Last Session, Vol. 2	1959	12.50	25.00	50.00
❏ MGV-3003 [M]	Last Session, Vol. 3	1959	12.50	25.00	50.00

YAZOO

Number	Title (A Side/B Side)	Yr	VG	VG+	NM
❏ L-1011	The Young Big Bill Broonzy	1969	3.75	7.50	15.00
❏ L-1035	Do That Guitar Rag	197?	3.75	7.50	15.00

BROTH

MERCURY

Number	Title (A Side/B Side)	Yr	VG	VG+	NM
❏ SR-61298	Broth	1970	5.00	10.00	20.00

BROTHER FOX AND TAR BABY

CAPITOL

Number	Title (A Side/B Side)	Yr	VG	VG+	NM
❏ ST-544	Brother Fox and Tar Baby	1970	7.50	15.00	30.00

ORACLE

Number	Title (A Side/B Side)	Yr	VG	VG+	NM
❏ 1001	Brother Fox and Tar Baby	1969	7.50	15.00	30.00

BROTHER MATTHEW

ABC-PARAMOUNT

Number	Title (A Side/B Side)	Yr	VG	VG+	NM
❏ ABC-121	Brother Matthew	1956	12.50	25.00	50.00

BROTHERS FOUR, THE

COLUMBIA

Number	Title (A Side/B Side)	Yr	VG	VG+	NM
❏ CL 1402 [M]	The Brothers Four	1960	3.00	6.00	12.00
❏ CL 1479 [M]	Rally 'Round the Brothers Four	1960	3.00	6.00	12.00
❏ CL 1578 [M]	B.M.O.C. (Best Music On/Off Campus)	1961	3.00	6.00	12.00
❏ CL 1625 [M]	Roamin'	1961	3.00	6.00	12.00
❏ CL 1697 [M]	The Brothers Four Song Book	1961	3.00	6.00	12.00
❏ CL 1803 [M]	The Brothers Four's Greatest Hits	1962	3.00	6.00	12.00
❏ CL 1828 [M]	The Brothers Four: In Person	1962	3.00	6.00	12.00
❏ CL 1946 [M]	Cross Country Concert	1963	3.00	6.00	12.00
❏ CL 2033 [M]	The Big Folk Hits	1963	3.00	6.00	12.00
❏ CL 2128 [M]	The Brothers Four Sing of Our Times	1964	3.00	6.00	12.00
❏ CL 2213 [M]	More Big Folk Hits	1964	3.00	6.00	12.00
❏ CL 2305 [M]	The Honey Wind Blows	1965	3.00	6.00	12.00
❏ CL 2379 [M]	Try to Remember	1965	3.00	6.00	12.00
❏ CL 2502 [M]	A Beatles' Songbook (The Brothers Four Sing Lennon/McCartney)	1966	3.75	7.50	15.00
❏ CL 2702 [M]	A New World's Record	1967	3.75	7.50	15.00

—*Corrected cover, with the guitarist using his right hand, as he does in real life*

Number	Title (A Side/B Side)	Yr	VG	VG+	NM
❏ CL 2702 [M]	A New World's Record	1967	6.25	12.50	25.00

—*Original cover has a flopped image on the front cover, which makes it appear as if the guitarist is left-handed*

Number	Title (A Side/B Side)	Yr	VG	VG+	NM
❏ CS 8197 [S]	The Brothers Four	1960	3.75	7.50	15.00
❏ CS 8270 [S]	Rally 'Round the Brothers Four	1960	3.75	7.50	15.00
❏ CS 8378 [S]	B.M.O.C. (Best Music On/Off Campus)	1961	3.75	7.50	15.00
❏ CS 8425 [S]	Roamin'	1961	3.75	7.50	15.00
❏ CS 8497 [S]	The Brothers Four Song Book	1961	3.75	7.50	15.00
❏ CS 8603	The Brothers Four's Greatest Hits	1970	2.50	5.00	10.00

—*Orange label*

Number	Title (A Side/B Side)	Yr	VG	VG+	NM
❏ CS 8603 [S]	The Brothers Four's Greatest Hits	1962	3.75	7.50	15.00

—*Red "360 Sound" label*

Number	Title (A Side/B Side)	Yr	VG	VG+	NM
❏ PC 8603	The Brothers Four's Greatest Hits	198?	2.00	4.00	8.00

—*Reissue with new prefix*

Number	Title (A Side/B Side)	Yr	VG	VG+	NM
❏ CS 8628 [S]	The Brothers Four: In Person	1962	3.75	7.50	15.00
❏ CS 8746 [S]	Cross Country Concert	1963	3.75	7.50	15.00
❏ CS 8833 [S]	The Big Folk Hits	1963	3.75	7.50	15.00
❏ CS 8928 [S]	The Brothers Four Sing of Our Times	1964	3.75	7.50	15.00
❏ CS 9013 [S]	More Big Folk Hits	1964	3.75	7.50	15.00
❏ CS 9105 [S]	The Honey Wind Blows	1965	3.75	7.50	15.00
❏ CS 9179 [S]	Try to Remember	1965	3.75	7.50	15.00
❏ CS 9302 [S]	A Beatles' Songbook (The Brothers Four Sing Lennon/McCartney)	1966	5.00	10.00	20.00
❏ CS 9502 [S]	A New World's Record	1967	3.00	6.00	12.00

—*Corrected cover, with the guitarist using his right hand, as he does in real life*

Number	Title (A Side/B Side)	Yr	VG	VG+	NM
❏ CS 9502 [S]	A New World's Record	1967	5.00	10.00	20.00

—*Original cover has a flopped image on the front cover, which makes it appear as if the guitarist is left-handed*

Number	Title (A Side/B Side)	Yr	VG	VG+	NM
❏ CS 9818	Let's Get Together	1969	3.00	6.00	12.00

FANTASY

Number	Title (A Side/B Side)	Yr	VG	VG+	NM
❏ 8400	The Brothers Four 1970	1970	2.50	5.00	10.00

FIRST AMERICAN

Number	Title (A Side/B Side)	Yr	VG	VG+	NM
❏ 7705	The Brothers Four Now	1978	2.50	5.00	10.00
❏ 7722 [(2)]	Greenfields and Other Gold	1980	3.00	6.00	12.00
❏ 7728	New Gold	1981	2.50	5.00	10.00

HARMONY

Number	Title (A Side/B Side)	Yr	VG	VG+	NM
❏ HS 11341	Four Strong Winds	1969	2.50	5.00	10.00
❏ H 31505	Great Songs of Our Times	1972	2.50	5.00	10.00

BROWN, AL

AMY

Number	Title (A Side/B Side)	Yr	VG	VG+	NM
❏ A-1 [M]	Madison Dance Party	1960	10.00	20.00	40.00
❏ AS-1 [S]	Madison Dance Party	1960	12.50	25.00	50.00

BROWN, ARTHUR, THE CRAZY WORLD OF

GULL

Number	Title (A Side/B Side)	Yr	VG	VG+	NM
❏ GU6-405	Dance	1975	3.00	6.00	12.00

PASSPORT

Number	Title (A Side/B Side)	Yr	VG	VG+	NM
❏ 98003	Journey	1974	3.00	6.00	12.00

TRACK

Number	Title (A Side/B Side)	Yr	VG	VG+	NM
❏ SD 8198	The Crazy World of Arthur Brown	1968	6.25	12.50	25.00

BROWN, BOBBY

DESTINY

Number	Title (A Side/B Side)	Yr	VG	VG+	NM
❏ 4001	Bobby Brown Live	1972	25.00	50.00	100.00
❏ 4002	The Enlightening Beam of Axonda	1972	30.00	60.00	120.00

BROWN, BOOTS / DAN DREW

GROOVE

Number	Title (A Side/B Side)	Yr	VG	VG+	NM
❏ LG-1000 [M]	Rock That Boat	1955	75.00	150.00	300.00

BROWN, BUSTER

COLLECTABLES

Number	Title (A Side/B Side)	Yr	VG	VG+	NM
❏ COL-5110	Golden Classics: The New King of the Blues	198?	2.50	5.00	10.00

FIRE

Number	Title (A Side/B Side)	Yr	VG	VG+	NM
❏ FLP-102 [M]	The New King of the Blues	1961	75.00	150.00	300.00

—*Red and black label, white cover*

Number	Title (A Side/B Side)	Yr	VG	VG+	NM
❏ FLP-102 [M]	The New King of the Blues	1961	100.00	200.00	400.00

—*Red and black label, purple cover*

Number	Title (A Side/B Side)	Yr	VG	VG+	NM
❏ FLP-102 [M]	The New King of the Blues	1961	175.00	350.00	700.00

—*White and red label*

SOUFFLE

Number	Title (A Side/B Side)	Yr	VG	VG+	NM
❏ 2014	Get Down	1973	3.00	6.00	12.00

BROWN, CHARLES

ALADDIN

Number	Title (A Side/B Side)	Yr	VG	VG+	NM
❏ LP-702 [10]	Mood Music	1953	1500.	2750.	4000.

—*Black vinyl*

Number	Title (A Side/B Side)	Yr	VG	VG+	NM
❏ LP-702 [10]	Mood Music	1953	3000.	5250.	7500.

—*Red vinyl*

Number	Title (A Side/B Side)	Yr	VG	VG+	NM
❏ LP-809 [M]	Mood Music	1956	—	—	—

—*Unreleased?*

ALLIGATOR

Number	Title (A Side/B Side)	Yr	VG	VG+	NM
❏ AL-4771	One More for the Road	1989	3.00	6.00	12.00

BIG TOWN

Number	Title (A Side/B Side)	Yr	VG	VG+	NM
❏ 1003	Merry Christmas Baby	1977	3.00	6.00	12.00
❏ 1005	Music Maestro Please	1978	2.50	5.00	10.00

BLUESWAY

Number	Title (A Side/B Side)	Yr	VG	VG+	NM
❏ BLS-6039	Charles Brown — Legend	1970	6.25	12.50	25.00

BULLSEYE BLUES

Number	Title (A Side/B Side)	Yr	VG	VG+	NM
❏ BB-9501	All My Life	1990	5.00	10.00	20.00

IMPERIAL

Number	Title (A Side/B Side)	Yr	VG	VG+	NM
❏ LP-9178 [M]	Charles Brown Sings Million Sellers	1961	100.00	200.00	400.00

JEWEL

Number	Title (A Side/B Side)	Yr	VG	VG+	NM
❏ 5006	Blues 'N' Brown	1972	3.00	6.00	12.00

KING

Number	Title (A Side/B Side)	Yr	VG	VG+	NM
❏ 775 [M]	Charles Brown Sings Christmas Songs	1961	37.50	75.00	150.00
❏ KS-775 [S]	Charles Brown Sings Christmas Songs	1963	75.00	150.00	300.00

—*Stereo copies (whether true stereo or rechanneled, we don't know) exist on blue labels with "King" in block letters (no crown)*

Number	Title (A Side/B Side)	Yr	VG	VG+	NM
❏ 878 [M]	The Great Charles Brown	1963	50.00	100.00	200.00

MAINSTREAM

Number	Title (A Side/B Side)	Yr	VG	VG+	NM
❏ S-6007 [S]	Boss of the Blues	1965	7.50	15.00	30.00
❏ S-6035 [S]	Ballads My Way	1965	7.50	15.00	30.00
❏ 56007 [M]	Boss of the Blues	1965	5.00	10.00	20.00
❏ 56035 [M]	Ballads My Way	1965	5.00	10.00	20.00

MOSAIC

Number	Title (A Side/B Side)	Yr	VG	VG+	NM
❏ MQ7-153 [(7)]	The Complete Aladdin Recordings of Charles Brown	199?	37.50	75.00	150.00

SCORE

Number	Title (A Side/B Side)	Yr	VG	VG+	NM
❏ SLP-4011 [M]	Driftin' Blues	1958	100.00	200.00	400.00
❏ SLP-4036 [M]	More Blues with Charles Brown	1959	—	—	—

—*Unreleased*

BROWN, CLIFFORD

BLUE NOTE

Number	Title (A Side/B Side)	Yr	VG	VG+	NM
❏ BLP-1526 [M]	Clifford Brown Memorial Album	1956	37.50	75.00	150.00

—*Regular edition, Lexington Ave. address on label*

Number	Title (A Side/B Side)	Yr	VG	VG+	NM
❏ BLP-1526 [M]	Clifford Brown Memorial Album	1956	50.00	100.00	200.00

—*"Deep groove" version (deep indentation under label on both sides)*

Number	Title (A Side/B Side)	Yr	VG	VG+	NM
❏ BLP-1526 [M]	Clifford Brown Memorial Album	196?	6.25	12.50	25.00

—*With "New York, USA" address on label*

Number	Title (A Side/B Side)	Yr	VG	VG+	NM
❏ BLP-1526 [M]	Clifford Brown Memorial Album	196?	12.50	25.00	50.00

—*With W. 63rd St. address on label*

Number	Title (A Side/B Side)	Yr	VG	VG+	NM
❏ BLP-5032 [10]	New Star on the Horizon	1953	125.00	250.00	500.00
❏ BLP-5047 [10]	Clifford Brown Quartet	1954	125.00	250.00	500.00

EMARCY

Number	Title (A Side/B Side)	Yr	VG	VG+	NM
❏ MG-36005 [M]	Clifford Brown with Strings	1955	30.00	60.00	120.00
❏ MG-36102 [M]	Clifford Brown All Stars	1956	30.00	60.00	120.00

JAZZTONE

Number	Title (A Side/B Side)	Yr	VG	VG+	NM
❏ J-1281 [M]	Jazz Messages	195?	10.00	20.00	40.00

LIMELIGHT

Number	Title (A Side/B Side)	Yr	VG	VG+	NM
❏ 2-8201 [(2)M]	The Immortal Clifford Brown	1965	10.00	20.00	40.00
❏ 2-8601 [(2)R]	The Immortal Clifford Brown	1965	6.25	12.50	25.00

MERCURY

Number	Title (A Side/B Side)	Yr	VG	VG+	NM
❏ MG-20827 [M]	Remember Clifford	1963	10.00	20.00	40.00
❏ SR-60827 [R]	Remember Clifford	1963	6.25	12.50	25.00

MOSAIC

Number	Title (A Side/B Side)	Yr	VG	VG+	NM
❏ MR5-104 [(5)]	The Complete Blue Note and Pacific Jazz Recordings of Clifford Brown	198?	20.00	40.00	80.00

PACIFIC JAZZ

Number	Title (A Side/B Side)	Yr	VG	VG+	NM
❏ PJ-3 [M]	Jazz Immortal	1956	37.50	75.00	150.00

Number	Title (A Side/B Side)	Yr	VG	VG+	NM
❑ PJLP-19 [10]	The Clifford Brown Ensemble	1955	75.00	150.00	300.00
PRESTIGE					
❑ PRLP-7055 [M]	Clifford Brown Memorial	1956	20.00	40.00	80.00
❑ PRLP-16008 [M]	Clifford Brown	1964	10.00	20.00	40.00

BROWN, CLIFFORD, AND ART FARMER
PRESTIGE

Number	Title (A Side/B Side)	Yr	VG	VG+	NM
❑ PRLP-167 [10]	Clifford Brown and Art Farmer with the Swedish All Stars	1953	75.00	150.00	300.00

BROWN, CLIFFORD, AND MAX ROACH
EMARCY

Number	Title (A Side/B Side)	Yr	VG	VG+	NM
❑ MG-26043 [10]	Clifford Brown and Max Roach	1954	100.00	200.00	400.00
❑ MG-36008 [M]	Brown and Roach Incorporated	1955	30.00	60.00	120.00
❑ MG-36036 [M]	Clifford Brown and Max Roach	1955	30.00	60.00	120.00
❑ MG-36037 [M]	A Study in Brown	1955	30.00	60.00	120.00
❑ MG-36070 [M]	Clifford Brown and Max Roach ar Basin Street	1956	30.00	60.00	120.00
GENE NORMAN					
❑ GNP-5 [10]	Clifford Brown and Max Roach, Vol. 1	1954	37.50	75.00	150.00
❑ GNP-7 [10]	Clifford Brown and Max Roach, Vol. 2	1954	37.50	75.00	150.00
❑ GNP-18 [M]	The Best of Max Roach and Clifford Brown In Concert	1955	30.00	60.00	120.00

BROWN, HYLO
CAPITOL

Number	Title (A Side/B Side)	Yr	VG	VG+	NM
❑ T 1168 [M]	Hylo Brown	1959	20.00	40.00	80.00
STARDAY					
❑ SLP-185 [M]	Bluegrass Balladeer	1962	10.00	20.00	40.00
❑ SLP-204 [M]	Bluegrass Goes to College	1962	10.00	20.00	40.00
❑ SLP-220 [M]	Hylo Brown Meets the Lonesome Pine Fiddlers	1963	10.00	20.00	40.00
❑ SLP-249 [M]	Sing Me a Bluegrass Song	1963	10.00	20.00	40.00

BROWN, JAMES
HRB

Number	Title (A Side/B Side)	Yr	VG	VG+	NM
❑ 1004 [(2)]	The Fabulous James Brown	1974	6.25	12.50	25.00
KING					
❑ 610 [M]	Please Please Please	1958	300.00	600.00	1200.
—"Woman's and man's legs" cover; "King" on label is two inches wide					
❑ 610 [M]	Please Please Please	1961	250.00	500.00	1000.
—"Woman's and man's legs" cover; "King" on label is three inches wide					
❑ 635 [M]	Try Me!	1959	225.00	450.00	900.00
—"Woman with cigarette and gun" cover; "King" on label is two inches wide					
❑ 635 [M]	Try Me!	1961	150.00	300.00	600.00
—"Woman with cigarette and gun" cover; "King" on label is three inches wide					
❑ 683 [M]	Think!	1960	225.00	450.00	900.00
—"Baby" cover; "King" on label is two inches wide					
❑ 683 [M]	Think!	1961	150.00	300.00	600.00
—"Baby" cover; "King" on label is three inches wide					
❑ 683 [M]	Think!	1963	25.00	50.00	100.00
—James Brown photo cover; "crownless" King label					
❑ 683 [M]	Think!	1966	12.50	25.00	50.00
—James Brown photo cover; "crown" King label					
❑ 743 [M]	The Amazing James Brown	1961	125.00	250.00	500.00
—"James Brown in suit" cover					
❑ 743 [M]	The Amazing James Brown	1963	37.50	75.00	150.00
—White title cover; "crownless" King label					
❑ 743 [M]	The Amazing James Brown	1966	125.00	250.00	500.00
—White title cover with "James Brown" in huge letters; "crown" King label					
❑ 771 [M]	Night Train	1961	75.00	150.00	300.00
—Original title					
❑ 771 [M]	Twist Around	1962	62.50	125.00	250.00
—Second title					
❑ 771 [M]	Jump Around	1963	50.00	100.00	200.00
—Third title					
❑ KS-771 [S]	Jump Around	1963	75.00	150.00	300.00
—Stereo copies of King 771 only exist with this title					
❑ 780 [M]	Good Good Twistin'	1962	50.00	100.00	200.00
—"Good Good Twistin' " on either label or cover, or both					
❑ 780 [M]	Shout and Shimmy	1962	62.50	125.00	250.00
—"Shout and Shimmy" on both cover and label					
❑ 780 [M]	Excitement	1963	37.50	75.00	150.00
—Third title; "crownless" King label					
❑ 780 [M]	Excitement	1966	12.50	25.00	50.00
—Third title; "crown" King label					
❑ 804 [M]	James Brown & His Famous Flames Tour the U.S.A.	1962	37.50	125.00	250.00
—"Crownless" King label					
❑ 804 [M]	James Brown & His Famous Flames Tour the U.S.A.	1966	12.50	25.00	50.00
—"Crown" King label					
❑ 826 [M]	Live at the Apollo	1963	37.50	75.00	150.00
—Other King albums on back cover; "crownless" King label					
❑ 826 [M]	Live at the Apollo	1963	50.00	100.00	200.00
—Custom back cover; "crownless" King label					
❑ 826 [M]	Live at the Apollo	1963	200.00	400.00	800.00
—White label promo, banded for airplay					
❑ 826 [M]	Live at the Apollo	1966	12.50	25.00	50.00
—"Crown" King label					
❑ KS-826 [S]	Live at the Apollo	1963	50.00	100.00	200.00
—Other King albums on back cover; "crownless" King label					
❑ KS-826 [S]	Live at the Apollo	1963	75.00	150.00	300.00
—Custom back cover; "crownless" King label					
❑ KS-826 [S]	Live at the Apollo	1966	17.50	35.00	70.00
—"Crown" King label					
❑ 851 [M]	Prisoner of Love	1963	25.00	50.00	100.00
—Other King albums on back cover; "crownless" King label					
❑ 851 [M]	Prisoner of Love	1963	50.00	100.00	200.00
—Custom back cover; "crownless" King label					
❑ 851 [M]	Prisoner of Love	1966	12.50	25.00	50.00
—"Crown" King label					
❑ 883 [M]	Pure Dynamite! Live at the Royal	1964	50.00	100.00	200.00
—"Crownless" King label					

Number	Title (A Side/B Side)	Yr	VG	VG+	NM
❑ 883 [M]	Pure Dynamite! Live at the Royal	1964	200.00	400.00	800.00
—White label promo; banded for airplay					
❑ 883 [M]	Pure Dynamite! Live at the Royal	1966	12.50	25.00	50.00
—"Crown" King label					
❑ 909 [M]	Please Please Please	1964	25.00	50.00	100.00
—Reissue of 610; "crownless" King label					
❑ 909 [M]	Please Please Please	1966	12.50	25.00	50.00
—"Crown" King label					
❑ 919 [M]	The Unbeatable James Brown — 16 Hits	1964	25.00	50.00	100.00
—Reissue of 635; "crownless" King label					
❑ 919 [M]	The Unbeatable James Brown — 16 Hits	1966	12.50	25.00	50.00
—"Crown" King label					
❑ 938 [M]	Papa's Got a Brand New Bag	1965	20.00	40.00	80.00
—Red cover; "crownless" King label					
❑ 938 [M]	Papa's Got a Brand New Bag	1966	10.00	20.00	40.00
—"Crown" King label					
❑ 938 [M]	Papa's Got a Brand New Bag	1966	12.50	25.00	50.00
—Green cover; "crownless" King label					
❑ LPS-938 [P]	Papa's Got a Brand New Bag	1965	25.00	50.00	100.00
—Red cover; "crownless" King label					
❑ LPS-938 [P]	Papa's Got a Brand New Bag	1966	12.50	25.00	50.00
—"Crown" King label					
❑ LPS-938 [P]	Papa's Got a Brand New Bag	1966	15.00	30.00	60.00
—Green cover; "crownless" King label					
❑ 946 [M]	I Got You (I Feel Good)	1966	10.00	20.00	40.00
—"Crown" King label					
❑ 946 [M]	I Got You (I Feel Good)	1966	25.00	50.00	100.00
—"Crownless" King label					
❑ LPS-946 [S]	I Got You (I Feel Good)	1966	12.50	25.00	50.00
—"Crown" King label					
❑ LPS-946 [S]	I Got You (I Feel Good)	1966	37.50	75.00	150.00
—"Crownless" King label					
❑ 961 [M]	Mighty Instrumentals	1966	25.00	50.00	100.00
❑ LPS-961 [S]	Mighty Instrumentals	1966	37.50	75.00	150.00
❑ 985 [M]	It's a Man's Man's Man's World	1966	12.50	25.00	50.00
❑ KS-985 [S]	It's a Man's Man's Man's World	1966	17.50	35.00	70.00
❑ 1010 [M]	Christmas Songs	1966	25.00	50.00	100.00
—Wreath on gray wall, no song titles on back					
❑ 1010 [M]	Christmas Songs	1967	20.00	40.00	80.00
—Wreath on white wall, song titles are on back					
❑ KS-1010 [S]	Christmas Songs	1966	37.50	75.00	150.00
—Wreath on gray wall, no song titles on back					
❑ KS-1010 [S]	Christmas Songs	1967	25.00	50.00	100.00
—Wreath on white wall, song titles are on back					
❑ 1016 [M]	Raw Soul	1967	12.50	25.00	50.00
❑ KS-1016 [P]	Raw Soul	1967	17.50	35.00	70.00
❑ 1018 [M]	Live at the Garden	1967	20.00	40.00	80.00
❑ 1018 [M]	Live at the Garden	1967	100.00	200.00	400.00
—Black label promo; banded for airplay					
❑ KS-1018 [S]	Live at the Garden	1967	25.00	50.00	100.00
❑ 1020 [M]	Cold Sweat	1967	12.50	25.00	50.00
❑ KS-1020 [S]	Cold Sweat	1967	17.50	35.00	70.00
❑ LPS-1022 [(2)]	Live at the Apollo, Volume II	1968	17.50	35.00	70.00
❑ LPS-1024	James Brown Presents His Show of Tomorrow	1968	12.50	25.00	50.00
—Various-artists album					
❑ LPS-1030	I Can't Stand Myself (When You Touch Me)	1968	12.50	25.00	50.00
❑ LPS-1031	I Got the Feelin'	1968	12.50	25.00	50.00
❑ LPS-1034	James Brown Plays Nothing But Soul	1968	12.50	25.00	50.00
❑ LPS-1038	Thinking About Little Willie John and a Few Nice Things	1968	12.50	25.00	50.00
❑ KS-1040	A Soulful Christmas	1968	20.00	40.00	80.00
❑ KS-1047	Say It Loud — I'm Black and I'm Proud	1969	12.50	25.00	50.00
❑ KS-1051	Gettin' Down To It	1969	12.50	25.00	50.00
❑ KSD-1055	James Brown Plays & Directs The Popcorn	1969	10.00	20.00	40.00
❑ KSD-1063	It's a Mother	1969	10.00	20.00	40.00
❑ KSD-1092	Ain't It Funky	1970	10.00	20.00	40.00
❑ KSD-1095	It's a New Day So Let a Man Come In	1970	10.00	20.00	40.00
❑ KSD-1100	Soul on Top	1970	10.00	20.00	40.00
❑ KSD-1110	Sho Is Funky Down Here	1971	10.00	20.00	40.00
❑ KSD-1115 [(2)]	Sex Machine	1970	12.50	25.00	50.00
❑ KSD-1124	Hey America!	1970	10.00	20.00	40.00
❑ KSD-1127	Super Bad	1971	10.00	20.00	40.00
POLYDOR					
❑ 25-3003 [(2)]	Revolution of the Mind — Live at the Apollo, Volume III	1971	15.00	30.00	60.00
❑ PD2-3004 [(2)]	Get On the Good Foot	1972	15.00	30.00	60.00
❑ PD2-3007 [(2)]	The Payback	1973	12.50	25.00	50.00
❑ 24-4054	Hot Pants	1971	10.00	20.00	40.00
❑ PD-5028	There It Is	1972	10.00	20.00	40.00
❑ SC-5401	James Brown Soul Classics	1972	6.25	12.50	25.00
❑ SC-5402	Soul Classics, Volume 2	1973	6.25	12.50	25.00
❑ PD-6014	Black Caesar	1973	12.50	25.00	50.00
❑ PD-6015	Slaughter's Big Rip-Off	1973	12.50	25.00	50.00
❑ PD-1-6039	Reality	1975	10.00	20.00	40.00
❑ PD-1-6042	Sex Machine Today	1975	10.00	20.00	40.00
❑ PD-1-6054	Everybody's Doin' the Hustle & Dead On the Double Bump	1975	10.00	20.00	40.00
❑ PD-1-6059	Hot	1976	10.00	20.00	40.00
❑ PD-1-6071	Get Up Offa That Thing	1976	10.00	20.00	40.00
❑ PD-1-6093	Bodyheat	1976	10.00	20.00	40.00
❑ PD-1-6111	Mutha's Nature	1977	10.00	20.00	40.00
❑ PD-1-6140	Jam/1980s	1978	10.00	20.00	40.00
❑ PD-1-6181	Take a Look at Those Cakes	1978	7.50	15.00	30.00
❑ PD-1-6212	The Original Disco Man	1979	7.50	15.00	30.00
❑ PD-1-6258	People	1980	7.50	15.00	30.00
❑ PD-2-6290 [(2)]	James Brown...Live/Hot on the One	1980	12.50	25.00	50.00
❑ PD-1-6318	Nonstop!	1981	7.50	15.00	30.00
❑ PD-1-6340	The Best of James Brown	1981	5.00	10.00	20.00
❑ PD-2-9001 [(2)]	Hell	1974	20.00	40.00	80.00
❑ PD-2-9004 [(2)]	Sex Machine Live	1976	12.50	25.00	50.00
❑ 821231-1	Ain't That a Groove: The James Brown Story 1966-1969	1984	3.75	7.50	15.00

Number	Title (A Side/B Side)	Yr	VG	VG+	NM
821232-1	Doing It to Death: The James Brown Story 1970-1973	1984	3.75	7.50	15.00
823275-1	The Best of James Brown	1984	3.00	6.00	12.00
—Reissue of 6340					
827439-1	Dead on the Heavy Funk: The James Brown Story 1974-1978	1985	3.75	7.50	15.00
829254-1 [(2)]	Solid Gold: 30 Golden Hits	1985	5.00	10.00	20.00
829417-1	James Brown's Funky People	1986	3.75	7.50	15.00
—Various-artists LP					
829624-1	In the Jungle Groove	1986	3.75	7.50	15.00
835857-1	James Brown's Funky People 2	1988	3.75	7.50	15.00
—Various-artists compilation					
837126-1	Motherlode	1988	3.75	7.50	15.00

RHINO

Number	Title (A Side/B Side)	Yr	VG	VG+	NM
RNLP-217	Live at the Apollo, Volume 2, Part 1	1985	3.75	7.50	15.00
RNLP-218	Live at the Apollo, Volume 2, Part 2	1985	3.75	7.50	15.00
RNLP-219	Greatest Hits (1964-1968)	1986	3.75	7.50	15.00
R1 70194	Santa's Got a Brand New Bag	1986	2.50	5.00	10.00
—Reissue of King material					
R1-70217	Live at the Apollo, Volume 2, Part 1	1988	3.00	6.00	12.00
—Reissue of 217					
R1-70218	Live at the Apollo, Volume 2, Part 2	1988	3.00	6.00	12.00
—Reissue of 218					
R1-70219	Greatest Hits (1964-1968)	1988	3.00	6.00	12.00
—Reissue of 219					

SCOTTI BROTHERS

Number	Title (A Side/B Side)	Yr	VG	VG+	NM
FZ 40380	Gravity	1986	3.00	6.00	12.00
FZ 44241	I'm Real	1988	3.00	6.00	12.00
FZ 45164	Soul Session Live	1989	3.75	7.50	15.00
75225-1	Love Overdue	1991	5.00	10.00	20.00

SMASH

Number	Title (A Side/B Side)	Yr	VG	VG+	NM
MGS-27054 [M]	Showtime	1964	7.50	15.00	30.00
MGS-27057 [M]	Grits & Soul	1965	7.50	15.00	30.00
MGS-27058 [M]	Out of Sight	1965	25.00	50.00	100.00
MGS-27072 [M]	James Brown Plays James Brown — Today & Yesterday	1965	7.50	15.00	30.00
MGS-27080 [M]	James Brown Plays New Breed	1966	7.50	15.00	30.00
MGS-27084 [M]	Handful of Soul	1966	7.50	15.00	30.00
MGS-27087 [M]	The James Brown Show	1967	7.50	15.00	30.00
—Various-artists LP					
MGS-27093 [M]	James Brown Plays the Real Thing	1967	7.50	15.00	30.00
SRS-67054 [S]	Showtime	1964	10.00	2.00	40.00
SRS-67057 [S]	Grits & Soul	1965	10.00	20.00	40.00
SRS-67058 [S]	Out of Sight	1965	37.50	75.00	150.00
SRS-67072 [S]	James Brown Plays James Brown — Today & Yesterday	1965	10.00	20.00	40.00
SRS-67080 [S]	James Brown Plays New Breed	1966	10.00	2.00	40.00
SRS-67084 [S]	Handful of Soul	1966	10.00	20.00	40.00
SRS-67087 [S]	The James Brown Show	1967	10.00	2.00	40.00
—Various-artists LP					
SRS-67093 [S]	James Brown Plays the Real Thing	1967	10.00	20.00	40.00
SRS-67109	James Brown Sings Out of Sight	1968	7.50	15.00	30.00
—Abridged reissue of 67058					

SOLID SMOKE

Number	Title (A Side/B Side)	Yr	VG	VG+	NM
SS-8006	Live and Lowdown at the Apollo, Vol. 1	1980	3.00	6.00	12.00
SS-8013	Can Your Heart Stand It	1981	3.00	6.00	12.00
SS-8023	The Federal Years, Part 1	198?	3.00	6.00	12.00
SS-8024	The Federal Years, Part 2	198?	3.00	6.00	12.00

T.K.

Number	Title (A Side/B Side)	Yr	VG	VG+	NM
615	Soul Syndrome	1980	7.50	15.00	30.00

BROWN, JIM ED
RCA CAMDEN

Number	Title (A Side/B Side)	Yr	VG	VG+	NM
ACL1-0197	Hey Good Lookin'	1973	2.50	5.00	10.00
ACL1-0618	The Three Bells	1974	2.50	5.00	10.00
CAS-2496	Gentle on My Mind	1971	2.50	5.00	10.00
CAS-2549	Country Cream	1972	2.50	5.00	10.00

RCA VICTOR

Number	Title (A Side/B Side)	Yr	VG	VG+	NM
APL1-0172	Bar-Rooms & Pop-A-Tops	1973	3.75	7.50	15.00
APL1-0324	Best of Jim Ed Brown	1973	3.75	7.50	15.00
APL1-0572	It's That Time of Night	1974	3.75	7.50	15.00
ANL1-1215	It's That Time of Night	1975	2.50	5.00	10.00
—Reissue of 0572					
LPM-3569 [M]	Alone with You	1966	5.00	10.00	20.00
LSP-3569 [S]	Alone with You	1966	6.25	12.50	25.00
LPM-3744 [M]	Just Jim	1967	6.25	12.50	25.00
LSP-3744 [S]	Just Jim	1967	5.00	10.00	20.00
LPM-3853 [M]	Gems by Jim	1967	6.25	12.50	25.00
LSP-3853 [S]	Gems by Jim	1967	5.00	10.00	20.00
LPM-3942 [M]	Bottle, Bottle	1968	10.00	20.00	40.00
LSP-3942 [S]	Bottle, Bottle	1968	5.00	10.00	20.00
LSP-4011	Country's Best on Record	1968	5.00	10.00	20.00
LSP-4130	This Is My Best!	1968	5.00	10.00	20.00
LSP-4175	Jim Ed Sings the Browns	1969	5.00	10.00	20.00
LSP-4262	Going Up the Country	1970	3.75	7.50	15.00
LSP-4366	Just for You	1970	3.75	7.50	15.00
LSP-4461	Morning	1971	3.75	7.50	15.00
LSP-4525	Angel's Sunday	1971	3.75	7.50	15.00
LSP-4614	She's Leavin'	1971	3.75	7.50	15.00
LSP-4713	Evening	1972	3.75	7.50	15.00
LSP-4755	Brown Is Blue	1972	3.75	7.50	15.00

BROWN, LAWRENCE
CLEF

Number	Title (A Side/B Side)	Yr	VG	VG+	NM
MGC-682 [M]	Slide Trombone	1955	30.00	60.00	120.00

IMPULSE!

Number	Title (A Side/B Side)	Yr	VG	VG+	NM
A-89 [M]	Inspired Abandon	1965	6.25	12.50	25.00
AS-89 [S]	Inspired Abandon	1965	7.50	15.00	30.00

VERVE

Number	Title (A Side/B Side)	Yr	VG	VG+	NM
MGV-8067 [M]	Slide Trombone	1957	12.50	25.00	50.00
V-8067 [M]	Slide Trombone	1961	5.00	10.00	20.00

BROWN, LES
CAPITOL

Number	Title (A Side/B Side)	Yr	VG	VG+	NM
T 657 [M]	College Classics	1955	7.50	15.00	30.00
—Turquoise or gray label					
T 659 [M]	The Les Brown All Stars	1955	7.50	15.00	30.00
—Turquoise or gray label					
T 746 [M]	Les Brown's in Town	1956	7.50	15.00	30.00
—Turquoise or gray label					
T 886 [M]	Composer's Holiday	1957	7.50	15.00	30.00
—Turquoise or gray label					
T 959 [M]	Concert Modern	1958	7.50	15.00	30.00
—Turquoise or gray label					
ST 1174 [S]	The Les Brown Story	1959	6.25	12.50	25.00
—Black colorband label, logo at left					
T 1174 [M]	The Les Brown Story	1959	6.25	12.50	25.00
—Black colorband label, logo at left					

COLUMBIA

Number	Title (A Side/B Side)	Yr	VG	VG+	NM
CL 539 [M]	Dance with Les Brown	1954	7.50	15.00	30.00
—Maroon label, gold print					
CL 649 [M]	Sentimental Journey	1955	6.25	12.50	25.00
—Red and black label with six "eye" logos					
CL 649 [M]	Sentimental Journey	1955	7.50	15.00	30.00
—Maroon label, gold print					
CL 2512 [10]	I've Got My Love to Keep Me Warm	1955	10.00	20.00	40.00
CL 2561 [10]	The Cool Classics	1955	10.00	20.00	40.00
CL 6060 [10]	Dance Parade	1949	10.00	20.00	40.00
CL 6123 [10]	Your Dance Date with Les Brown	1950	10.00	20.00	40.00
CL 6159 [10]	Classics in Rhythm	195?	10.00	20.00	40.00
CS 8288 [S]	Bandland	1960	5.00	10.00	20.00
—Red and black label with six "eye" logos					
CS 8394 [S]	The Lerner and Loewe Bandbook	1960	5.00	10.00	20.00
—Red and black label with six "eye" logos					
CS 8618 [S]	Revolution in Sound	1962	5.00	10.00	20.00
—Red and black label with six "eye" logos					
CS 8830 [S]	Explosive Sound	1964	5.00	10.00	20.00
—"360 Sound Stereo" in black on label					
CS 8919 [S]	The Young Beat	1964	5.00	10.00	20.00
—"360 Sound Stereo" in black on label					

CORAL

Number	Title (A Side/B Side)	Yr	VG	VG+	NM
CX-1 [(2)M]	Les Brown Concert at the Palladium	1953	15.00	30.00	60.00
CRL 56026 [10]	Over the Rainbow	1951	12.50	25.00	50.00
CRL 56030 [10]	The Sound of Renown	1951	12.50	25.00	50.00
CRL 56046 [10]	You're My Everything	1952	12.50	25.00	50.00
CRL 56077 [10]	Musical Weather Vane	1953	12.50	25.00	50.00
CRL 56094 [10]	Les Dance	1953	12.50	25.00	50.00
CRL 56108 [10]	Invitation	1954	12.50	25.00	50.00
CRL 56109 [10]	Time to Dance	1954	12.50	25.00	50.00
CRL 56116 [10]	Les Dream	1954	12.50	25.00	50.00
CRL 57000 [M]	Les Brown Concert at the Palladium, Part 1	1954	7.50	15.00	30.00
CRL 57001 [M]	Les Brown Concert at the Palladium, Part 1	1954	7.50	15.00	30.00
CRL 57030 [M]	The Sound of Renown	1955	6.25	12.50	25.00
CRL 57051 [M]	Open House	1956	6.25	12.50	25.00
CRL 57058 [M]	More from Les	1956	6.25	12.50	25.00
CRL 57165 [M]	Love Letters in the Sand	1957	6.25	12.50	25.00
CRL 57300 [M]	Swing Song Book	1959	6.25	12.50	25.00
CRL 57311 [M]	Jazz Song Book	1959	6.25	12.50	25.00
CRL 757300 [S]	Swing Song Book	1959	7.50	15.00	30.00
CRL 757311 [S]	Jazz Song Book	1959	7.50	15.00	30.00

DECCA

Number	Title (A Side/B Side)	Yr	VG	VG+	NM
DL 4965 [M]	The World of the Young	1968	5.00	10.00	20.00

GREAT AMERICAN

Number	Title (A Side/B Side)	Yr	VG	VG+	NM
1010	Les Brown Goes Direct to Disc	1981	5.00	10.00	20.00

BROWN, MARION
ESP-DISK'

Number	Title (A Side/B Side)	Yr	VG	VG+	NM
1022 [M]	Marion Brown Quartet	1966	5.00	10.00	20.00
1040 [M]	Why Not?	1967	5.00	10.00	20.00

IMPULSE!

Number	Title (A Side/B Side)	Yr	VG	VG+	NM
A-9139 [M]	Three for Shepp	1967	7.50	15.00	30.00
AS-9139 [S]	Three for Shepp	1967	5.00	10.00	20.00

BROWN, MAXINE
COLLECTABLES

Number	Title (A Side/B Side)	Yr	VG	VG+	NM
COL-5116	Golden Classics	198?	3.00	6.00	12.00

COMMONWEALTH UNITED

Number	Title (A Side/B Side)	Yr	VG	VG+	NM
CU-6001	We'll Cry Together	1969	5.00	10.00	20.00

GUEST STAR

Number	Title (A Side/B Side)	Yr	VG	VG+	NM
GS-1911 [M]	Maxine Brown	1964	3.00	6.00	12.00

WAND

Number	Title (A Side/B Side)	Yr	VG	VG+	NM
LP-656 [M]	The Fabulous Sound of Maxine Brown	1963	12.50	25.00	50.00
WDS-656 [S]	The Fabulous Sound of Maxine Brown	1963	15.00	30.00	60.00
WD-663 [M]	Spotlight on Maxine Brown	1965	7.50	15.00	30.00
WDS-663 [S]	Spotlight on Maxine Brown	1965	10.00	20.00	40.00
WD-684 [M]	Maxine Brown's Greatest Hits	1967	5.00	10.00	20.00
WDS-684 [S]	Maxine Brown's Greatest Hits	1967	6.25	12.50	25.00

BROWN, MAXINE
One of THE BROWNS, she is no relation to the above.
CHART

Number	Title (A Side/B Side)	Yr	VG	VG+	NM
1012	Sugar Cane Country	1969	5.00	10.00	20.00

BROWN, MEL
ABC IMPULSE!

Number	Title (A Side/B Side)	Yr	VG	VG+	NM
A-9152 [M]	Chicken Fat	1967	7.50	15.00	30.00
AS-9152 [S]	Chicken Fat	1967	5.00	10.00	20.00
A-9169 [M]	The Wizard	1968	10.00	20.00	40.00
AS-9169 [S]	The Wizard	1968	5.00	10.00	20.00
A-9180 [M]	Blues for We	1969	12.50	25.00	50.00
AS-9180 [S]	Blues for We	1969	5.00	10.00	20.00

Number	Title (A Side/B Side)	Yr	VG	VG+	NM
❑ AS-9186	I'd Rather Suck My Thumb	1970	5.00	10.00	20.00
❑ AS-9209	Fifth	1971	5.00	10.00	20.00

BROWN, NAPPY
BLACK TOP
❑ BT-1039	Something Gonna Jump Out the Bushes	1987	3.75	7.50	15.00

ICHIBAN
❑ ICH-1056	Apples and Lemons	1990	3.00	6.00	12.00

KING SNAKE/ICHIBAN
❑ ICH-9006	Aw! Shucks	1991	3.75	7.50	15.00

LANDSLIDE
❑ LD 1008	Tore Up	1984	3.75	7.50	15.00

MELTONE
❑ 1502	Deep Sea Diver	1989	3.75	7.50	15.00

SAVOY
❑ MG-14002 [M]	Nappy Brown Sings	1958	100.00	200.00	400.00
❑ MG-14025 [M]	The Right Time	1960	62.50	125.00	250.00
❑ 14427	Nappy Brown	1977	3.00	6.00	12.00

SAVOY JAZZ
❑ SJL-1149	Don't Be Angry	1984	2.50	5.00	10.00

BROWN, ODELL
CADET
❑ LPS-775 [S]	Raising the Roof	1966	5.00	10.00	20.00
❑ LP-788 [M]	Mellow Yellow	1967	5.00	10.00	20.00
❑ LP-800 [M]	Ducky	1967	5.00	10.00	20.00

BROWN, OSCAR, JR.
COLUMBIA
❑ CL 1577 [M]	Sin and Soul	1960	6.25	12.50	25.00
—Red and black label with six "eye" logos					
❑ CL 1774 [M]	Between Heaven and Hell	1962	6.25	12.50	25.00
—Red and black label with six "eye" logos					
❑ CL 1873 [M]	In a New Mood	1963	5.00	10.00	20.00
—Red label, "Guaranteed High Fidelity" in black					
❑ CL 2025 [M]	Oscar Brown Jr. Tells It Like It Is	1964	5.00	10.00	20.00
—Red label, "Guaranteed High Fidelity" in black					
❑ CS 8377 [S]	Sin and Soul	1960	7.50	15.00	30.00
—Red and black label with six "eye" logos					
❑ CS 8574 [S]	Between Heaven and Hell	1962	7.50	15.00	30.00
—Red and black label with six "eye" logos					
❑ CS 8673 [S]	In a New Mood	1963	6.25	12.50	25.00
—Red label, "360 Sound Stereo" in black					
❑ CS 8825 [S]	Oscar Brown Jr. Tells It Like It Is	1964	6.25	12.50	25.00
—Red label, "360 Sound Stereo" in black					

FONTANA
❑ SRF-67540 [S]	Mr. Oscar Brown Goes to Washington	1965	5.00	10.00	20.00
❑ SRF-67549 [S]	Finding a New Friend	1966	5.00	10.00	20.00

BROWN, PETE
BETHLEHEM
❑ BCP-1011 [10]	Peter the Great	1954	30.00	60.00	120.00

VERVE
❑ MGVS-6133 [S]	From the Heart	1960	10.00	20.00	40.00
❑ MGV-8365 [M]	From the Heart	1958	12.50	25.00	50.00
❑ V-8365 [M]	From the Heart	1962	5.00	10.00	20.00

BROWN, PETE/JONAH JONES
BETHLEHEM
❑ BCP-4 [M]	Jazz Kaleidoscope	1957	20.00	40.00	80.00

BROWN, RAY
VERVE
❑ MGV-8022 [M]	Bass Hit!	1957	12.50	25.00	50.00
❑ V-8022 [M]	Bass Hit!	1961	5.00	10.00	20.00
❑ MGV-8290 [M]	This Is Ray Brown	1958	12.50	25.00	50.00
❑ V-8290 [M]	This Is Ray Brown	1961	5.00	10.00	20.00
❑ MGV-8390 [M]	Jazz Cello	1960	12.50	25.00	50.00
❑ V-8390 [M]	Jazz Cello	1961	5.00	10.00	20.00
❑ V-8444 [M]	Ray Brown with the All Star Big Band Featuring Cannonball Adderley	1962	6.25	12.50	25.00
❑ V6-8444 [S]	Ray Brown with the All Star Big Band Featuring Cannonball Adderley	1962	7.50	15.00	30.00
❑ V-8580 [M]	Much in Common	1964	6.25	12.50	25.00
❑ V6-8580 [S]	Much in Common	1964	7.50	15.00	30.00
—With Milt Jackson					
❑ V-8615 [M]	Ray Brown/Milt Jackson	1965	6.25	12.50	25.00
❑ V6-8615 [S]	Ray Brown/Milt Jackson	1965	7.50	15.00	30.00

BROWN, RONNIE
PHILIPS
❑ PHS 600130 [S]	Jazz for Everyone	1964	5.00	10.00	20.00

BROWN, ROY
BLUESWAY
❑ BLS-6019	The Blues Are Brown	1968	6.25	12.50	25.00
❑ BLS-6056	Hard Times	1973	6.25	12.50	25.00

EPIC
❑ E 30473	Live at Monterey	1971	6.25	12.50	25.00

INTERMEDIA
❑ QS-5027	Good Rockin' Tonight	198?	2.50	5.00	10.00

KING
❑ 956 [M]	Roy Brown Sings 24 Hits	1966	12.50	25.00	50.00
❑ KS-956 [R]	Roy Brown Sings 24 Hits	1966	12.50	25.00	50.00
❑ KS-1130	Hard Luck Blues	1971	6.25	12.50	25.00

BROWN, ROY / WYNONIE HARRIS
KING
❑ 607 [M]	Battle of the Blues	1958	150.00	300.00	600.00
❑ 627 [M]	Battle of the Blues, Volume 2	1959	200.00	400.00	800.00

BROWN, ROY / WYNONIE HARRIS / EDDIE VINSON
KING
❑ 668 [M]	Battle of the Blues, Volume 4	1960	625.00	1250.	2500.

BROWN, RUTH
ATLANTIC
❑ 1308 [M]	Last Date with Ruth Brown	1959	50.00	100.00	200.00
—Black label					
❑ 1308 [M]	Last Date with Ruth Brown	1961	12.50	25.00	50.00
—Red and purple label, "fan" logo in white					
❑ SD 1308 [S]	Last Date with Ruth Brown	1959	75.00	150.00	300.00
—Green label					
❑ SD 1308 [S]	Last Date with Ruth Brown	1961	15.00	30.00	60.00
—Blue and green label, "fan" logo in white					
❑ 8004 [M]	Ruth Brown	1957	50.00	100.00	200.00
—Black label					
❑ 8004 [M]	Ruth Brown	1960	37.50	75.00	150.00
—White "bullseye" label					
❑ 8004 [M]	Ruth Brown	1961	12.50	25.00	50.00
—Red and purple label, "fan" logo in white					
❑ 8026 [M]	Miss Rhythm	1959	50.00	100.00	200.00
—Black label					
❑ 8026 [M]	Miss Rhythm	1960	37.50	75.00	150.00
—White "bullseye" label					
❑ 8026 [M]	Miss Rhythm	1961	12.50	25.00	50.00
—Red and purple label, "fan" logo in white					
❑ 8080 [M]	The Best of Ruth Brown	1963	10.00	20.00	40.00

DOBRE
❑ 1041	You Don't Know Me	1978	3.00	6.00	12.00

FANTASY
❑ F-9661	Have a Good Time	1988	3.00	6.00	12.00
❑ F-9662	Blues on Broadway	1989	3.00	6.00	12.00

ICHIBAN
❑ SPEG-4023	Brown, Black and Beautiful	198?	3.00	6.00	12.00

MAINSTREAM
❑ 369	Softly	1972	3.00	6.00	12.00
❑ S-6034 [S]	Ruth Brown '65	1965	7.50	15.00	30.00
❑ 56034 [M]	Ruth Brown '65	1965	6.25	12.50	25.00

PHILIPS
❑ PHM 200028 [M]	Along Comes Ruth	1962	10.00	20.00	40.00
❑ PHM 200055 [M]	Gospel Time	1962	7.50	15.00	30.00
❑ PHS 600028 [S]	Along Comes Ruth	1962	12.50	25.00	50.00
❑ PHS 600055 [S]	Gospel Time	1962	10.00	20.00	40.00

SKYE
❑ SK-13	Black Is Brown and Brown Is Beautiful	1970	3.75	7.50	15.00

BROWN, TED
VANGUARD
❑ VRS-8515 [M]	Free Wheeling	1956	125.00	250.00	500.00

BROWN SUGAR
CHELSEA
❑ BCL1-0368	Brown Sugar Featuring Clydie King	1973	5.00	10.00	20.00

BROWN'S FERRY FOUR, THE
KING
❑ 551 [M]	Sacred Songs	1957	20.00	40.00	80.00
❑ 590 [M]	Sacred Songs	1958	20.00	40.00	80.00
❑ 943	Wonderful Sacred Songs	1964	7.50	15.00	30.00

BROWNE, JACKSON
ASYLUM
❑ 6E-107	The Pretender	1977	2.50	5.00	10.00
—Reissue of 7E-1079					
❑ 6E-113	Running on Empty	1977	2.50	5.00	10.00
❑ 5E-511	Hold Out	1979	2.50	5.00	10.00
❑ 7E-1017	Late for the Sky	1974	3.00	6.00	12.00
❑ EQ-1017 [Q]	Late for the Sky	1974	7.50	15.00	30.00
❑ 7E-1079	The Pretender	1976	3.00	6.00	12.00
❑ SD 5051	Jackson Browne (Saturate Before Using)	1972	2.00	4.00	8.00
—Standard cover					
❑ SD 5051	Jackson Browne (Saturate Before Using)	1972	3.00	6.00	12.00
—Burlap cover; "clouds" label					
❑ SD 5051	Jackson Browne (Saturate Before Using)	1972	4.00	8.00	16.00
—Burlap cover, opens at right side; white label with "Asylum Records" logo in a circle at top					
❑ SD 5051	Jackson Browne (Saturate Before Using)	1972	5.00	10.00	20.00
—Burlap cover, opens at top; white label with "Asylum Records" logo in a circle at top					
❑ SD 5067	For Everyman	1973	3.00	6.00	12.00
❑ 60268	Lawyers in Love	1983	2.50	5.00	10.00
❑ 60457	Lives in the Balance	1986	2.50	5.00	10.00

ELEKTRA
❑ 60830	World in Motion	1989	2.50	5.00	10.00

MOBILE FIDELITY
❑ 1-055	The Pretender	1981	6.25	12.50	25.00
—Audiophile vinyl					

NINA MUSIC PUBLISHING
❑ (no #) [(2)]	Songs by Jackson Browne	1967	1000.	1500.	2000.
—Publisher's demo in plain cardboard jacket; three sides performed by Jackson Browne, one side by Steve Noonan					

BROWNS, THE
RCA CAMDEN
❑ CAL-885 [M]	I Heard the Bluebirds Sing	1965	3.00	6.00	12.00
❑ CAS-885 [S]	I Heard the Bluebirds Sing	1965	3.00	6.00	12.00
❑ CAL-2142 [M]	Big Ones from the Country	1967	3.00	6.00	12.00
❑ CAS-2142 [S]	Big Ones from the Country	1967	2.50	5.00	10.00
❑ CAS-2262	The Browns Sing a Harvest of Country Songs	1968	2.50	5.00	10.00

RCA VICTOR
❑ ANL1-1083	The Best of the Browns	1975	2.50	5.00	10.00
❑ LPM-1438 [M]	Jim Edward, Maxine and Bonnie Brown	1957	12.50	25.00	50.00
❑ LPM-2144 [M]	Sweet Sounds by the Browns	1959	7.50	15.00	30.00

Number	Title (A Side/B Side)	Yr	VG	VG+	NM
❑ LSP-2144 [S]	Sweet Sounds by the Browns	1959	10.00	20.00	40.00
❑ LPM-2174 [M]	Town and Country	1960	5.00	10.00	20.00
❑ LSP-2174 [S]	Town and Country	1960	6.25	12.50	25.00
❑ LPM-2260 [M]	The Browns Sing Their Hits	1960	5.00	10.00	20.00
❑ LSP-2260 [S]	The Browns Sing Their Hits	1960	6.25	12.50	25.00
❑ LPM-2333 [M]	Our Favorite Folk Songs	1961	5.00	10.00	20.00
❑ LSP-2333 [S]	Our Favorite Folk Songs	1961	6.25	12.50	25.00
❑ LPM-2345 [M]	The Little Brown Church Hymnal	1961	5.00	10.00	20.00
❑ LSP-2345 [S]	The Little Brown Church Hymnal	1961	6.25	12.50	25.00
❑ LPM-2784 [M]	Grand Ole Opry Favorites	1963	3.75	7.50	15.00
❑ LSP-2784 [S]	Grand Ole Opry Favorites	1963	5.00	10.00	20.00
❑ LPM-2860 [M]	This Young Land	1964	3.75	7.50	15.00
❑ LSP-2860 [S]	This Young Land	1964	5.00	10.00	20.00
❑ LPM-2987 [M]	Three Shades of Brown	1964	3.75	7.50	15.00
❑ LSP-2987 [S]	Three Shades of Brown	1964	5.00	10.00	20.00
❑ LPM-3423 [M]	When Love Is Gone	1965	3.75	7.50	15.00
❑ LSP-3423 [S]	When Love Is Gone	1965	5.00	10.00	20.00
❑ LPM-3561 [M]	The Best of the Browns	1966	3.75	7.50	15.00
❑ LSP-3561 [S]	The Best of the Browns	1966	5.00	10.00	20.00
❑ LPM-3668 [M]	Our Kind of Country	1966	3.75	7.50	15.00
❑ LSP-3668 [S]	Our Kind of Country	1966	5.00	10.00	20.00
❑ LPM-3798 [M]	The Old Country Church	1967	5.00	10.00	20.00
❑ LSP-3798 [S]	The Old Country Church	1967	3.75	7.50	15.00

BROWNSVILLE STATION

BIG TREE

Number	Title (A Side/B Side)	Yr	VG	VG+	NM
❑ BTS-2010	A Night on the Town	1972	3.00	6.00	12.00
❑ BTS-2102	Yeah!	1973	3.00	6.00	12.00
❑ BT 89500	School Punks	1974	3.00	6.00	12.00
❑ BT 89510	Motor City Connection	1975	3.00	6.00	12.00

EPIC

Number	Title (A Side/B Side)	Yr	VG	VG+	NM
❑ JE 35606	Air Special	1978	2.50	5.00	10.00
❑ JE 35606 [DJ]	Air Special	1978	5.00	10.00	20.00
—Orange vinyl promo					

PALLADIUM

Number	Title (A Side/B Side)	Yr	VG	VG+	NM
❑ P-1004	Brownsville Station	1970	7.50	15.00	30.00

PRIVATE STOCK

Number	Title (A Side/B Side)	Yr	VG	VG+	NM
❑ PS-2026	Brownsville Station	1977	2.50	5.00	10.00

WARNER BROS.

Number	Title (A Side/B Side)	Yr	VG	VG+	NM
❑ WS 1888	No B.S.	1970	3.75	7.50	15.00

BRUBECK, DAVE

COLUMBIA

Number	Title (A Side/B Side)	Yr	VG	VG+	NM
❑ C2L 26 [(2)M]	The Dave Brubeck Quartet at Carnegie Hall	1963	6.25	12.50	25.00
—Red "Guaranteed High Fidelity" label					
❑ CL 566 [M]	Jazz Goes to College	1954	20.00	40.00	80.00
—Dark red label, gold print; released at the same time as 6321 and 6322					
❑ CL 566 [M]	Jazz Goes to College	1955	12.50	25.00	50.00
—Red/black label with six "eye" logos					
❑ CL 566 [M]	Jazz Goes to College	1962	5.00	10.00	20.00
—Red "Guaranteed High Fidelity" label					
❑ CL 590 [M]	Dave Brubeck at Storyville: 1954	1954	20.00	40.00	80.00
—Dark red label, gold print; released at the same time as 6330 and 6331					
❑ CL 590 [M]	Dave Brubeck at Storyville: 1954	1955	12.50	25.00	50.00
—Red/black label with six "eye" logos					
❑ CL 590 [M]	Dave Brubeck at Storyville: 1954	1962	5.00	10.00	20.00
—Red "Guaranteed High Fidelity" label					
❑ CL 622 [M]	Brubeck Time	1955	15.00	30.00	60.00
—Red/black label with six "eye" logos					
❑ CL 622 [M]	Brubeck Time	1962	5.00	10.00	20.00
—Red "Guaranteed High Fidelity" label					
❑ CL 699 [M]	Jazz: Red Hot and Cool	1955	15.00	30.00	60.00
—Red/black label with six "eye" logos					
❑ CL 699 [M]	Jazz: Red Hot and Cool	1962	5.00	10.00	20.00
—Red "Guaranteed High Fidelity" label					
❑ C2S 826 [(2)S]	The Dave Brubeck Quartet at Carnegie Hall	1963	7.50	15.00	30.00
—Red label, "360 Sound" in black					
❑ C2S 826 [(2)S]	The Dave Brubeck Quartet at Carnegie Hall	1966	5.00	10.00	20.00
—Red label, "360 Sound" in white					
❑ CL 878 [M]	Brubeck Plays Brubeck	1956	15.00	30.00	60.00
—Red/black label with six "eye" logos					
❑ CL 878 [M]	Brubeck Plays Brubeck	1962	5.00	10.00	20.00
—Red "Guaranteed High Fidelity" label					
❑ CL 932 [M]	American Jazz Festival at Newport '56	1956	12.50	25.00	50.00
—Red/black label with six "eye" logos					
❑ CL 932 [M]	American Jazz Festival at Newport '56	1962	5.00	10.00	20.00
—Red "Guaranteed High Fidelity" label					
❑ CL 984 [M]	Jazz Impressions of the U.S.A.	1957	12.50	25.00	50.00
—Red/black label with six "eye" logos					
❑ CL 984 [M]	Jazz Impressions of the U.S.A.	1962	5.00	10.00	20.00
—Red "Guaranteed High Fidelity" label					
❑ CL 1034 [M]	Jazz Goes to Junior College	1957	10.00	20.00	40.00
—Red/black label with six "eye" logos					
❑ CL 1034 [M]	Jazz Goes to Junior College	1962	5.00	10.00	20.00
—Red "Guaranteed High Fidelity" label					
❑ CL 1059 [M]	Dave Digs Disney	1957	10.00	20.00	40.00
—Red/black label with six "eye" logos					
❑ CL 1059 [M]	Dave Digs Disney	1962	5.00	10.00	20.00
—Red "Guaranteed High Fidelity" label					
❑ CL 1168 [M]	The Dave Brubeck Quartet in Europe	1958	10.00	20.00	40.00
—Red/black label with six "eye" logos					
❑ CL 1168 [M]	The Dave Brubeck Quartet in Europe	1962	5.00	10.00	20.00
—Red "Guaranteed High Fidelity" label					
❑ CL 1249 [M]	Newport 1958	1958	10.00	20.00	40.00
—Red/black label with six "eye" logos					
❑ CL 1249 [M]	Newport 1958	1962	5.00	10.00	20.00
—Red "Guaranteed High Fidelity" label					
❑ CL 1251 [M]	Jazz Impressions of Eurasia	1958	10.00	20.00	40.00
—Red/black label with six "eye" logos					
❑ CL 1251 [M]	Jazz Impressions of Eurasia	1962	5.00	10.00	20.00
—Red "Guaranteed High Fidelity" label					

Number	Title (A Side/B Side)	Yr	VG	VG+	NM
❑ CL 1347 [M]	Gone with the Wind	1959	10.00	20.00	40.00
—Red/black label with six "eye" logos					
❑ CL 1347 [M]	Gone with the Wind	1962	5.00	10.00	20.00
—Red "Guaranteed High Fidelity" label					
❑ CL 1397 [M]	Time Out	1960	6.25	12.50	25.00
—Red/black label with six "eye" logos					
❑ CL 1439 [M]	Southern Scene	1960	6.25	12.50	25.00
—Red/black label with six "eye" logos					
❑ CL 1454 [M]	The Riddle	1960	6.25	12.50	25.00
—Red/black label with six "eye" logos					
❑ CL 1466 [M]	Bernstein Plays Brubeck Plays Bernstein	1960	6.25	12.50	25.00
—Red/black label with six "eye" logos					
❑ CL 1553 [M]	Brubeck and Rushing	1961	6.25	12.50	25.00
—Red/black label with six "eye" logos					
❑ CL 1609 [M]	Tonight Only!	1961	6.25	12.50	25.00
—Red/black label with six "eye" logos					
❑ CL 1690 [M]	Time Further Out	1961	6.25	12.50	25.00
—Red/black label with six "eye" logos					
❑ CL 1775 [M]	Countdown — Time in Outer Space	1962	7.50	15.00	30.00
—Red/black label with six "eye" logos					
❑ CL 1963 [M]	Brandenburg Gate Revisited	1963	5.00	10.00	20.00
—Red "Guaranteed High Fidelity" label					
❑ CL 1998 [M]	Bossa Nova U.S.A.	1963	5.00	10.00	20.00
—Red "Guaranteed High Fidelity" label					
❑ CL 2127 [M]	Time Changes	1964	5.00	10.00	20.00
—Red "Guaranteed High Fidelity" label					
❑ CL 2212 [M]	Jazz Impressions of Japan	1964	5.00	10.00	20.00
—Red "Guaranteed High Fidelity" label					
❑ CL 2275 [M]	Jazz Impressions of New York	1965	5.00	10.00	20.00
—Red "Guaranteed High Fidelity" label					
❑ CL 2316 [M]	Take Five	1965	5.00	10.00	20.00
—Red "Guaranteed High Fidelity" label					
❑ CL 2348 [M]	Angel Eyes	1965	5.00	10.00	20.00
—Red "Guaranteed High Fidelity" label					
❑ CL 2695 [M]	Bravo Brubeck!	1967	5.00	10.00	20.00
❑ CL 2712 [M]	Jackpot	1967	5.00	10.00	20.00
❑ CL 6321 [10]	Jazz Goes to College, Volume 1	1954	25.00	50.00	100.00
❑ CL 6322 [10]	Jazz Goes to College, Volume 2	1954	25.00	50.00	100.00
❑ CL 6330 [10]	Dave Brubeck at Storyville: 1954, Volume 1	1954	20.00	40.00	80.00
❑ CL 6331 [10]	Dave Brubeck at Storyville: 1954, Volume 2	1954	20.00	40.00	80.00
❑ CS 8058 [S]	Jazz Impressions of Eurasia	1959	12.50	25.00	50.00
—Red/black label with six "eye" logos					
❑ CS 8058 [S]	Jazz Impressions of Eurasia	1962	6.25	12.50	25.00
—Red label, "360 Sound" in black					
❑ CS 8082 [S]	Newport 1958	1959	12.50	25.00	50.00
—Red/black label with six "eye" logos					
❑ CS 8082 [S]	Newport 1958	1962	6.25	12.50	25.00
—Red label, "360 Sound" in black					
❑ CS 8090 [S]	Dave Digs Disney	1959	12.50	25.00	50.00
—Red/black label with six "eye" logos					
❑ CS 8090 [S]	Dave Digs Disney	1962	6.25	12.50	25.00
—Red label, "360 Sound" in black					
❑ CS 8156 [S]	Gone with the Wind	1959	12.50	25.00	50.00
—Red/black label with six "eye" logos					
❑ CS 8156 [S]	Gone with the Wind	1962	6.25	12.50	25.00
—Red label, "360 Sound" in black					
❑ CS 8192 [S]	Time Out	1995	7.50	15.00	30.00
—Audiophile vinyl, distributed by Classic Records					
❑ CS 8192 [S]	Time Out	1960	7.50	15.00	30.00
—Red/black label with six "eye" logos					
❑ CS 8192 [S]	Time Out Featuring "Take Five"	1962	5.00	10.00	20.00
—Red label, "360 Sound" in black; beginning with this issue, the cover was altered to emphasize the hit					
❑ CS 8235 [S]	Southern Scene	1960	7.50	15.00	30.00
—Red/black label with six "eye" logos					
❑ CS 8235 [S]	Southern Scene	1962	5.00	10.00	20.00
—Red label, "360 Sound" in black					
❑ CS 8248 [S]	The Riddle	1960	7.50	15.00	30.00
—Red/black label with six "eye" logos					
❑ CS 8248 [S]	The Riddle	1962	5.00	10.00	20.00
—Red label, "360 Sound" in black					
❑ CS 8257 [S]	Brubeck Plays Bernstein Plays Brubeck	1960	7.50	15.00	30.00
—Red/black label with six "eye" logos					
❑ CS 8257 [S]	Brubeck Plays Bernstein Plays Brubeck	1962	5.00	10.00	20.00
—Red label, "360 Sound" in black					
❑ CS 8353 [S]	Brubeck and Rushing	1961	7.50	15.00	30.00
—Red/black label with six "eye" logos					
❑ CS 8353 [S]	Brubeck and Rushing	1962	5.00	10.00	20.00
—Red label, "360 Sound" in black					
❑ CS 8409 [S]	Tonight Only!	1961	7.50	15.00	30.00
—Red/black label with six "eye" logos					
❑ CS 8409 [S]	Tonight Only!	1962	5.00	10.00	20.00
—Red label, "360 Sound" in black					
❑ CS 8490 [S]	Time Further Out	1961	7.50	15.00	30.00
—Red/black label with six "eye" logos					
❑ CS 8490 [S]	Time Further Out	1962	5.00	10.00	20.00
—Red label, "360 Sound" in black					
❑ CS 8575 [S]	Countdown — Time in Outer Space	1962	5.00	10.00	20.00
—Red label, "360 Sound" in black					
❑ CS 8575 [S]	Countdown — Time in Outer Space	1962	10.00	20.00	40.00
—Red/black label with six "eye" logos					
❑ CS 8763 [S]	Brandenburg Gate Revisited	1963	6.25	12.50	25.00
—Red label, "360 Sound" in black					
❑ CS 8798 [S]	Bossa Nova U.S.A.	1963	6.25	12.50	25.00
—Red label, "360 Sound" in black					
❑ CS 8927 [S]	Time Changes	1964	6.25	12.50	25.00
—Red label, "360 Sound" in black					
❑ CS 9012 [S]	Jazz Impressions of Japan	1964	6.25	12.50	25.00
—Red label, "360 Sound" in black					
❑ CS 9075 [S]	Jazz Impressions of New York	1965	6.25	12.50	25.00
—Red label, "360 Sound" in black					
❑ CS 9116 [S]	Take Five	1965	6.25	12.50	25.00
—Red label, "360 Sound" in black					

B

Number	Title (A Side/B Side)	Yr	VG	VG+	NM
❑ CS 9148 [S]	Angel Eyes	1965	6.25	12.50	25.00
—Red label, "360 Sound" in black					
❑ CS 9237 [S]	My Favorite Things	1966	5.00	10.00	20.00
—Red "360 Sound" label					
❑ CS 9284 [S]	Dave Brubeck's Greatest Hits	1966	5.00	10.00	20.00
—Red "360 Sound" label					
❑ CS 9312 [S]	Time In	1966	5.00	10.00	20.00
—Red "360 Sound" label					
❑ CS 9402 [S]	Anything Goes! Dave Brubeck Quartet Plays Cole Porter	1966	5.00	10.00	20.00
—Red "360 Sound" label					
DIRECT DISK					
❑ 106 [(2)]	A Cut Above	1979	6.25	12.50	25.00
FANTASY					
❑ 3-1 [10]	Dave Brubeck Trio	1951	37.50	75.00	150.00
❑ 3-2 [10]	Dave Brubeck Trio	1951	37.50	75.00	150.00
❑ 3-3 [10]	Dave Brubeck Octet	1951	37.50	75.00	150.00
❑ 3-4 [10]	Dave Brubeck Trio	1952	37.50	75.00	150.00
❑ 3-5 [10]	Dave Brubeck Quartet with Paul Desmond	1952	37.50	75.00	150.00
❑ 3-7 [10]	Dave Brubeck Quartet with Paul Desmond	1952	37.50	75.00	150.00
❑ 3-8 [10]	Jazz at Storyville	1953	37.50	75.00	150.00
❑ 3-10 [10]	Jazz at the Blackhawk	1953	37.50	75.00	150.00
❑ 3-11 [10]	Jazz at Oberlin	1953	37.50	75.00	150.00
❑ 3-13 [10]	Jazz at the College of the Pacific	1954	37.50	75.00	150.00
❑ 3-16 [10]	Old Sounds from San Francisco	1954	37.50	75.00	150.00
❑ 3-20 [10]	Paul and Dave's Jazz Interwoven	1955	37.50	75.00	150.00
❑ 3204 [M]	Dave Brubeck Trio	195?	15.00	30.00	60.00
—Black vinyl, red label, non-flexible vinyl					
❑ 3204 [M]	Dave Brubeck Trio	1956	25.00	50.00	100.00
—Dark red vinyl; reissue of 3-1					
❑ 3204 [M]	Dave Brubeck Trio	196?	10.00	20.00	40.00
—Black vinyl, red label, flexible vinyl					
❑ 3205 [M]	Dave Brubeck Trio: Distinctive Rhythm Instrumentals	195?	15.00	30.00	60.00
—Black vinyl, red label, non-flexible vinyl					
❑ 3205 [M]	Dave Brubeck Trio: Distinctive Rhythm Instrumentals	1956	25.00	50.00	100.00
—Dark red vinyl; reissue of 3-2					
❑ 3205 [M]	Dave Brubeck Trio: Distinctive Rhythm Instrumentals	196?	10.00	20.00	40.00
—Black vinyl, red label, flexible vinyl					
❑ 3210 [M]	Jazz at the Blackhawk	195?	15.00	30.00	60.00
—Black vinyl, red label, non-flexible vinyl					
❑ 3210 [M]	Jazz at the Blackhawk	1956	25.00	50.00	100.00
—Dark red vinyl; reissue of 3-10					
❑ 3210 [M]	Jazz at the Blackhawk	196?	10.00	20.00	40.00
—Black vinyl, red label, flexible vinyl					
❑ 3223 [M]	Jazz at the College of the Pacific	195?	15.00	30.00	60.00
—Black vinyl, red label, non-flexible vinyl					
❑ 3223 [M]	Jazz at the College of the Pacific	1956	25.00	50.00	100.00
—Dark red vinyl; reissue of 3-13					
❑ 3223 [M]	Jazz at the College of the Pacific	196?	10.00	20.00	40.00
—Black vinyl, red label, flexible vinyl					
❑ 3229 [M]	Brubeck-Desmond	195?	15.00	30.00	60.00
—Black vinyl, red label, non-flexible vinyl					
❑ 3229 [M]	Brubeck-Desmond	1956	25.00	50.00	100.00
—Dark red vinyl; reissue of 3-5					
❑ 3229 [M]	Brubeck-Desmond	196?	10.00	20.00	40.00
—Black vinyl, red label, flexible vinyl					
❑ 3230 [M]	Dave Brubeck Quartet	195?	15.00	30.00	60.00
—Black vinyl, red label, non-flexible vinyl					
❑ 3230 [M]	Dave Brubeck Quartet	1956	25.00	50.00	100.00
—Dark red vinyl; reissue of 3-7					
❑ 3230 [M]	Dave Brubeck Quartet	196?	10.00	20.00	40.00
—Black vinyl, red label, flexible vinyl					
❑ 3239 [M]	Dave Brubeck Octet	195?	15.00	30.00	60.00
—Black vinyl, red label, non-flexible vinyl					
❑ 3239 [M]	Dave Brubeck Octet	1956	25.00	50.00	100.00
—Dark red vinyl; reissue of 3-3					
❑ 3239 [M]	Dave Brubeck Octet	196?	10.00	20.00	40.00
—Black vinyl, red label, flexible vinyl					
❑ 3240 [M]	Brubeck Desmond: Jazz at Storyville	195?	15.00	30.00	60.00
—Black vinyl, red label, non-flexible vinyl					
❑ 3240 [M]	Brubeck Desmond: Jazz at Storyville	1957	25.00	50.00	100.00
—Dark red vinyl; reissue of 3-8					
❑ 3240 [M]	Brubeck Desmond: Jazz at Storyville	196?	10.00	20.00	40.00
—Black vinyl, red label, flexible vinyl					
❑ 3245 [M]	Jazz at Oberlin	195?	15.00	30.00	60.00
—Black vinyl, red label, non-flexible vinyl					
❑ 3245 [M]	Jazz at Oberlin	1957	25.00	50.00	100.00
—Dark red vinyl; reissue of 3-11					
❑ 3245 [M]	Jazz at Oberlin	196?	10.00	20.00	40.00
—Black vinyl, red label, flexible vinyl					
❑ 3249 [M]	Brubeck & Desmond at Wilshire-Ebell	195?	15.00	30.00	60.00
—Black vinyl, red label, non-flexible vinyl					
❑ 3249 [M]	Brubeck & Desmond at Wilshire-Ebell	1957	25.00	50.00	100.00
—Dark red vinyl					
❑ 3249 [M]	Brubeck & Desmond at Wilshire-Ebell	196?	10.00	20.00	40.00
—Black vinyl, red label, flexible vinyl					
❑ 3259 [M]	Dave Brubeck Plays and Plays and Plays and Plays and…	195?	10.00	20.00	40.00
—Black vinyl, red label, non-flexible vinyl					
❑ 3259 [M]	Dave Brubeck Plays and Plays and Plays and Plays and…	1958	15.00	30.00	60.00
—Red vinyl					
❑ 3259 [M]	Dave Brubeck Plays and Plays and Plays and Plays and…	196?	7.50	15.00	30.00
—Black vinyl, red label, flexible vinyl					
❑ 3268 [M]	Re-Union	195?	10.00	20.00	40.00
—Black vinyl, red label, non-flexible vinyl					
❑ 3268 [M]	Re-Union	1958	15.00	30.00	60.00
—Red vinyl					

Number	Title (A Side/B Side)	Yr	VG	VG+	NM
❑ 3268 [M]	Re-Union	196?	7.50	15.00	30.00
—Black vinyl, red label, flexible vinyl					
❑ 3298 [M]	Two Knights at the Black Hawk	1959	10.00	20.00	40.00
—Black vinyl, red label, non-flexible vinyl					
❑ 3298 [M]	Two Knights at the Black Hawk	1959	15.00	30.00	60.00
—Red vinyl					
❑ 3298 [M]	Two Knights at the Black Hawk	196?	7.50	15.00	30.00
—Black vinyl, red label, flexible vinyl					
❑ 3301 [M]	Brubeck A La Mode	196?	7.50	15.00	30.00
—Black vinyl, red label, flexible vinyl					
❑ 3301 [M]	Brubeck A La Mode	1960	10.00	20.00	40.00
—Black vinyl, red label, non-flexible vinyl					
❑ 3301 [M]	Brubeck A La Mode	1960	15.00	30.00	60.00
—Red vinyl					
❑ 3319 [M]	Near-Myth	196?	7.50	15.00	30.00
—Black vinyl, red label, flexible vinyl					
❑ 3319 [M]	Near-Myth	1961	10.00	20.00	40.00
—Black vinyl, red label, non-flexible vinyl					
❑ 3319 [M]	Near-Myth	1961	15.00	30.00	60.00
—Red vinyl					
❑ 3331 [M]	Dave Brubeck Trio Featuring Cal Tjader	196?	7.50	15.00	30.00
—Black vinyl, red label, flexible vinyl					
❑ 3331 [M]	Dave Brubeck Trio Featuring Cal Tjader	1962	10.00	20.00	40.00
—Black vinyl, red label, non-flexible vinyl					
❑ 3331 [M]	Dave Brubeck Trio Featuring Cal Tjader	1962	15.00	30.00	60.00
—Red vinyl					
❑ 3332 [M]	Brubeck Tjader	196?	7.50	15.00	30.00
—Black vinyl, red label, flexible vinyl					
❑ 3332 [M]	Brubeck Tjader	1962	10.00	20.00	40.00
—Black vinyl, red label, flexible vinyl					
❑ 3332 [M]	Brubeck Tjader	1962	15.00	30.00	60.00
—Red vinyl					
❑ 8007 [S]	Re-Union	196?	5.00	10.00	20.00
—Black vinyl, blue label, flexible vinyl					
❑ 8007 [S]	Re-Union	196?	7.50	15.00	30.00
—Black vinyl, blue label, non-flexible vinyl					
❑ 8007 [S]	Re-Union	1962	12.50	25.00	50.00
—Blue vinyl					
❑ 8047 [S]	Brubeck A La Mode	196?	5.00	10.00	20.00
—Black vinyl, blue label, flexible vinyl					
❑ 8047 [S]	Brubeck A La Mode	196?	7.50	15.00	30.00
—Black vinyl, blue label, non-flexible vinyl					
❑ 8047 [S]	Brubeck A La Mode	1962	12.50	25.00	50.00
—Blue vinyl					
❑ 8063 [S]	Near-Myth	196?	5.00	10.00	20.00
—Black vinyl, blue label, flexible vinyl					
❑ 8063 [S]	Near-Myth	196?	7.50	15.00	30.00
—Black vinyl, blue label, non-flexible vinyl					
❑ 8063 [S]	Near-Myth	1962	12.50	25.00	50.00
—Blue vinyl					
❑ 8069 [R]	Jazz at Oberlin	196?	5.00	10.00	20.00
—Black vinyl, blue label, non-flexible vinyl					
❑ 8069 [R]	Jazz at Oberlin	1962	10.00	20.00	40.00
—Blue vinyl					
❑ 8073 [R]	Dave Brubeck Trio Featuring Cal Tjader	1962	5.00	10.00	20.00
—Black vinyl, blue label, non-flexible vinyl					
❑ 8073 [R]	Dave Brubeck Trio Featuring Cal Tjader	1962	10.00	20.00	40.00
—Blue vinyl					
❑ 8074 [R]	Brubeck Tjader	1962	5.00	10.00	20.00
—Black vinyl, blue label, non-flexible vinyl					
❑ 8074 [R]	Brubeck Tjader	1962	10.00	20.00	40.00
—Blue vinyl					
❑ 8078 [R]	Jazz at the College of the Pacific	196?	5.00	10.00	20.00
—Black vinyl, blue label, non-flexible vinyl					
❑ 8078 [R]	Jazz at the College of the Pacific	1962	10.00	20.00	40.00
—Blue vinyl					
❑ 8080 [R]	Jazz at Storyville	1962	5.00	10.00	20.00
—Black vinyl, blue label, non-flexible vinyl					
❑ 8080 [R]	Jazz at Storyville	1962	10.00	20.00	40.00
—Blue vinyl					
❑ 8081 [R]	Two Knights at the Blackhawk	1962	5.00	10.00	20.00
—Black vinyl, blue label, non-flexible vinyl					
❑ 8081 [R]	Two Knights at the Blackhawk	1962	10.00	20.00	40.00
—Blue vinyl					
❑ 8092 [R]	Brubeck-Desmond	1962	5.00	10.00	20.00
—Black vinyl, blue label, non-flexible vinyl					
❑ 8092 [R]	Brubeck-Desmond	1962	10.00	20.00	40.00
—Blue vinyl					
❑ 8093 [R]	Dave Brubeck Quartet	1962	5.00	10.00	20.00
—Black vinyl, blue label, non-flexible vinyl					
❑ 8093 [R]	Dave Brubeck Quartet	1962	10.00	2.00	40.00
—Blue vinyl					
❑ 8094 [R]	Dave Brubeck Octet	1962	5.00	10.00	20.00
—Black vinyl, blue label, non-flexible vinyl					
❑ 8094 [R]	Dave Brubeck Octet	1962	10.00	20.00	40.00
—Blue vinyl					
❑ 8095 [S]	Brubeck and Desmond at Wilshire-Ebell	196?	5.00	10.00	20.00
—Black vinyl, blue label, flexible vinyl					
❑ 8095 [S]	Brubeck and Desmond at Wilshire-Ebell	1962	7.50	15.00	30.00
—Black vinyl, blue label, non-flexible vinyl					
❑ 8095 [S]	Brubeck and Desmond at Wilshire-Ebell	1962	12.50	25.00	50.00
—Blue vinyl					
JAZZTONE					
❑ J-1272 [M]	Best of Brubeck	195?	10.00	20.00	40.00
MOBILE FIDELITY					
❑ 1-216	We're All Together Again for the First Time	1994	15.00	30.00	60.00
—Audiophile vinyl					
MOON					
❑ 028	St. Louis Blues	1992	5.00	10.00	20.00

BRUCE, ED
EPIC

Number	Title (A Side/B Side)	Yr	VG	VG+	NM
❑ KE 35043	Tennesseean	1977	2.50	5.00	10.00

Number	Title (A Side/B Side)	Yr	VG	VG+	NM
❏ KE 35541	Cowboys and Dreamers	1978	2.50	5.00	10.00
MCA					
❏ 3242	Ed Bruce	1980	2.50	5.00	10.00
❏ 5188	One to One	1981	2.50	5.00	10.00
❏ 5323	I Write It Down	1982	2.50	5.00	10.00
❏ 5416	You're Not Leaving Here Tonight	1983	2.50	5.00	10.00
❏ 5511	Tell 'Em I've Gone Crazy	1984	2.50	5.00	10.00
❏ 5577	Greatest Hits	1985	2.50	5.00	10.00
❏ 27068	Ed Bruce	198?	2.00	4.00	8.00
—Reissue of 3242					
MONUMENT					
❏ SLP-18118	Shades	1969	5.00	10.00	20.00
RCA VICTOR					
❏ LPM-3948 [M]	If I Could Just Go Home	1968	12.50	25.00	50.00
❏ LSP-3948 [S]	If I Could Just Go Home	1968	6.25	12.50	25.00
❏ AHL1-5324	Homecoming	1985	2.50	5.00	10.00
❏ AHL1-5808	Night Things	1986	2.50	5.00	10.00
UNITED ARTISTS					
❏ UA-LA613-G	Ed Bruce	1976	3.00	6.00	12.00

BRUCE, LENNY

Number	Title (A Side/B Side)	Yr	VG	VG+	NM
BIZARRE					
❏ 2XS 6329 [(2)]	The Berkeley Concert	1969	6.25	12.50	25.00
DOUGLAS					
❏ 2	To Is a Preposition, Come Is a Verb	196?	5.00	10.00	20.00
❏ 788	The Essential Lenny Bruce Politics	1968	5.00	10.00	20.00
❏ Z 30872	What I Was Arrested For	1971	3.75	7.50	15.00
—Reissue of 2					
FANTASY					
❏ FP-1 [DJ]	The Promo Album	196?	50.00	100.00	200.00
—Promo-only compilation of material from albums 7001, 7003, 7007 and 7011					
❏ 7001 [M]	Interviews of Our Times	1959	10.00	20.00	40.00
—Non-flexible black vinyl; cover changed to blue tint					
❏ 7001 [M]	Interviews of Our Times	1959	25.00	50.00	100.00
—Opaque, non-flexible red vinyl; tan cover with Lenny Bruce's name blacked out throughout the back					
❏ 7001 [M]	Interviews of Our Times	1962	5.00	10.00	20.00
—Flexible black vinyl					
❏ 7001 [M]	Interviews of Our Times	1962	10.00	20.00	40.00
—Translucent, flexible red vinyl					
❏ 7003 [M]	The Sick Humor of Lenny Bruce	1959	10.00	20.00	40.00
—Non-flexible black vinyl					
❏ 7003 [M]	The Sick Humor of Lenny Bruce	1959	25.00	50.00	100.00
—Opaque, non-flexible red vinyl					
❏ 7003 [M]	The Sick Humor of Lenny Bruce	1962	5.00	10.00	20.00
—Flexible black vinyl					
❏ 7003 [M]	The Sick Humor of Lenny Bruce	1962	10.00	20.00	40.00
—Translucent, flexible red vinyl					
❏ 7007 [M]	I Am Not a Nut, Elect Me	1960	10.00	20.00	40.00
—Non-flexible black vinyl					
❏ 7007 [M]	I Am Not a Nut, Elect Me	1960	25.00	50.00	100.00
—Opaque, non-flexible red vinyl					
❏ 7007 [M]	I Am Not a Nut, Elect Me	1962	5.00	10.00	20.00
—Flexible black vinyl					
❏ 7007 [M]	I Am Not a Nut, Elect Me	1962	10.00	20.00	40.00
—Translucent, flexible red vinyl					
❏ 7011 [M]	Lenny Bruce, American	1961	10.00	20.00	40.00
—Non-flexible black vinyl					
❏ 7011 [M]	Lenny Bruce, American	1961	25.00	50.00	100.00
—Opaque, non-flexible red vinyl					
❏ 7011 [M]	Lenny Bruce, American	1962	5.00	10.00	20.00
—Flexible black vinyl					
❏ 7011 [M]	Lenny Bruce, American	1962	10.00	20.00	40.00
—Translucent, flexible red vinyl					
❏ 7012 [M]	The Best of Lenny Bruce	1962	5.00	10.00	20.00
—Black vinyl					
❏ 7012 [M]	The Best of Lenny Bruce	1962	12.50	25.00	50.00
—Red vinyl					
❏ 7017	Thank You Masked Man	1971	3.75	7.50	15.00
❏ 34201 [(3)]	Lenny Bruce at the Curran Theater	1971	10.00	20.00	40.00
❏ 79003 [(2)]	The Real Lenny Bruce	1975	5.00	10.00	20.00
LENNY BRUCE					
❏ LB-3001/2 [M]	Lenny Bruce Is Out Again	196?	75.00	150.00	300.00
—Privately pressed version with white labels and Lenny's address on cover					
❏ LB-9001/2 [10]	Warning: Sale of This Album...	1962	125.00	250.00	500.00
—Privately pressed LP with routines used as evidence in Lenny's obscenity trial					
PHILLIES					
❏ PHLP-4010 [M]	Lenny Bruce Is Out Again	1966	25.00	50.00	100.00
—Reissue of Lenny Bruce 3001/2					
UNITED ARTISTS					
❏ UAL 3580 [M]	The Midnight Concert	1967	6.25	12.50	25.00
❏ UAS 6580	The Midnight Concert	1967	5.00	10.00	20.00
❏ UAS 6794	The Midnight Concert	1972	3.75	7.50	15.00
—Reissue of 6580					
❏ UAS 9800 [(3)]	Lenny Bruce/Carnegie Hall	1972	6.25	12.50	25.00
WARNER/SPECTOR					
❏ SP 9101	The Law, the Language and Lenny Bruce	1975	3.75	7.50	15.00

BRUEL, MAX

Number	Title (A Side/B Side)	Yr	VG	VG+	NM
EMARCY					
❏ MG-36062 [M]	Cool Bruel	1955	15.00	30.00	60.00

BRUNIS, GEORG

Number	Title (A Side/B Side)	Yr	VG	VG+	NM
COMMODORE					
❏ FL-20008 [10]	King of the Tailgate Trombone	1950	20.00	40.00	80.00
❏ DL 30015 [M]	King of the Tailgate Trombone	1959	10.00	20.00	40.00
JOLLY ROGER					
❏ 5024 [10]	Georg Brunis and the New Orleans Rhythm Kings	1954	12.50	25.00	50.00

Number	Title (A Side/B Side)	Yr	VG	VG+	NM
RIVERSIDE					
❏ RLP-1024 [10]	Georg Brunis and the Original New Orleans Rhythm Kings	1954	20.00	40.00	80.00

BRUNSON, FRANKIE

Number	Title (A Side/B Side)	Yr	VG	VG+	NM
GEE					
❏ GLP-704 [M]	Big Daddy's Blues	1959	20.00	40.00	80.00
❏ SGLP-704 [S]	Big Daddy's Blues	1959	30.00	60.00	120.00

BRUTE FORCE

Number	Title (A Side/B Side)	Yr	VG	VG+	NM
B.T. PUPPY					
❏ BTPS-1015	Extemporaneous	1971	1000.	1500.	2000.
COLUMBIA					
❏ CL 2615 [M]	I, Brute Force — Confections of Love	1967	5.00	10.00	20.00
❏ CS 9415 [S]	I, Brute Force — Confections of Love	1967	5.00	10.00	20.00
EMBRYO					
❏ 522	Brute Force	1970	5.00	10.00	20.00

BRYAN, JOY

Number	Title (A Side/B Side)	Yr	VG	VG+	NM
CONTEMPORARY					
❏ M-3604 [M]	Make the Man Love Me	1961	10.00	20.00	40.00
❏ S-7604 [S]	Make the Man Love Me	1961	12.50	25.00	50.00
MODE					
❏ LP-108 [M]	Joy Bryan Sings	1957	20.00	40.00	80.00

BRYANT, ANITA

Number	Title (A Side/B Side)	Yr	VG	VG+	NM
CARLTON					
❏ LP-118 [M]	Anita Bryant	1959	5.00	10.00	20.00
❏ STLP-118 [S]	Anita Bryant	1959	7.50	15.00	30.00
❏ LP-127 [M]	Hear Anita Bryant in Your Home Tonight	1960	5.00	10.00	20.00
❏ STLP-127 [S]	Hear Anita Bryant in Your Home Tonight	1960	6.25	12.50	25.00
❏ LP-132 [M]	In My Little Corner of the World	1961	5.00	10.00	20.00
❏ STLP-132 [S]	In My Little Corner of the World	1961	6.25	12.50	25.00
COLUMBIA					
❏ CL 1719 [M]	Kisses Sweeter Than Wine	1961	3.75	7.50	15.00
❏ CL 1767 [M]	Abiding Love	1962	3.75	7.50	15.00
❏ CL 1885 [M]	In a Velvet Mood	1962	3.00	6.00	12.00
❏ CL 1956 [M]	Anita Bryant's Greatest Hits	1963	3.00	6.00	12.00
❏ CL 2035 [M]	As Long As He Needs Me	1963	3.00	6.00	12.00
❏ CL 2069 [M]	Country's Best	1964	3.00	6.00	12.00
❏ CL 2222 [M]	World of Lonely People	1964	3.00	6.00	12.00
❏ CL 2573 [M]	Mine Eyes Have Seen the Glory	1966	3.00	6.00	12.00
❏ CL 2706 [M]	I Believe	1967	3.75	7.50	15.00
❏ CL 2720 [M]	Do You Hear What I Hear?	1967	3.75	7.50	15.00
❏ CS 8519 [S]	Kisses Sweeter Than Wine	1961	5.00	10.00	20.00
❏ CS 8567 [S]	Abiding Love	1962	5.00	10.00	20.00
❏ CS 8685 [S]	In a Velvet Mood	1962	3.75	7.50	15.00
❏ CS 8756 [S]	Anita Bryant's Greatest Hits	1963	3.75	7.50	15.00
❏ CS 8835 [S]	As Long As He Needs Me	1963	3.75	7.50	15.00
❏ CS 8869 [S]	Country's Best	1964	3.75	7.50	15.00
❏ CS 9022 [S]	World of Lonely People	1964	3.75	7.50	15.00
❏ CS 9373 [S]	Mine Eyes Have Seen the Glory	1966	3.75	7.50	15.00
❏ CS 9506 [S]	I Believe	1967	3.00	6.00	12.00
❏ CS 9520 [S]	Do You Hear What I Hear?	1967	2.50	5.00	10.00
❏ CS 9607	In Remembrance of You (The Story of a Love Affair)	1968	3.00	6.00	12.00
❏ CS 9642	How Great Thou Art	1968	3.00	6.00	12.00
COLUMBIA SPECIAL PRODUCTS					
❏ CSS 900	The Sunshine Tree	1970	3.00	6.00	12.00
HARMONY					
❏ HL 9557 [M]	ABC Stories of Jesus	196?	3.00	6.00	12.00
❏ HS 11280	Anita Bryant	1968	2.50	5.00	10.00
❏ HS 11330	Little Things Mean a Lot	1969	2.50	5.00	10.00
❏ HS 11395	A World Without Love	1970	2.50	5.00	10.00
❏ H 31181	You'll Never Walk Alone	1972	2.50	5.00	10.00
MYRRH					
❏ MSB-6513	Naturally	197?	3.00	6.00	12.00
WORD					
❏ WST-8532	Abide with Me	1970	3.00	6.00	12.00
❏ WST-8540	Love Lifted Me	1971	3.00	6.00	12.00
❏ WST-8558	The Miracle of Christmas	197?	2.50	5.00	10.00
❏ WST-8571	Battle Hymn of the Republic	1972	3.00	6.00	12.00
❏ WST-8631	This Is My Story	1975	3.00	6.00	12.00
❏ WST-8652	Hymns	1976	3.00	6.00	12.00
❏ WST-8670	Old Fashioned Prayin'	1977	3.00	6.00	12.00
❏ 8785	Singing a New Song	198?	2.50	5.00	10.00

BRYANT, BOBBY

Number	Title (A Side/B Side)	Yr	VG	VG+	NM
CADET					
❏ LP-795 [M]	Ain't Doing Too B-A-D, Bad	1967	5.00	10.00	20.00
VEE JAY					
❏ VJS-3059	Big Band Blues	1974	5.00	10.00	20.00

BRYANT, BOUDLEAUX

Number	Title (A Side/B Side)	Yr	VG	VG+	NM
MONUMENT					
❏ MLP-8007 [M]	Boudleaux Bryant's Best Sellers	1963	5.00	10.00	20.00
❏ SLP-18007 [S]	Boudleaux Bryant's Best Sellers	1963	6.25	12.50	25.00

BRYANT, CLORA

Number	Title (A Side/B Side)	Yr	VG	VG+	NM
MODE					
❏ LP-106 [M]	Gal with a Horn	1957	25.00	50.00	100.00

BRYANT, JIMMY

Number	Title (A Side/B Side)	Yr	VG	VG+	NM
CAPITOL					
❏ ST 1314 [S]	Country Cabin Jazz	1960	25.00	50.00	100.00
❏ T 1314 [M]	Country Cabin Jazz	1960	20.00	40.00	80.00
DOLTON					
❏ BLP-16505 [M]	Play Country Guitar with Jimmy Bryant	196?	6.25	12.50	25.00
❏ BST-17505 [S]	Play Country Guitar with Jimmy Bryant	196?	7.50	15.00	30.00
IMPERIAL					
❏ LP-9310 [M]	Bryant's Back in Town	1966	5.00	10.00	20.00

Number	Title (A Side/B Side)	Yr	VG	VG+	NM
❑ LP-9315 [M]	Laughing Guitar, Crying Guitar	1966	5.00	10.00	20.00
❑ LP-9338 [M]	We Are Young	1967	5.00	10.00	20.00
❑ LP-9360 [M]	That Fastest Guitar in the Country	1967	6.25	12.50	25.00
❑ LP-12310 [S]	Bryant's Back in Town	1966	6.25	12.50	25.00
❑ LP-12315 [S]	Laughing Guitar, Crying Guitar	1966	6.25	12.50	25.00
❑ LP-12338 [S]	We Are Young	1967	6.25	12.50	25.00
❑ LP-12360 [S]	That Fastest Guitar in the Country	1967	5.00	10.00	20.00

BRYANT, PAUL
FANTASY

Number	Title (A Side/B Side)	Yr	VG	VG+	NM
❑ 3357 [M]	Something's Happening	1963	5.00	10.00	20.00
❑ 3363 [M]	Groove Time	1964	5.00	10.00	20.00
❑ 8357 [S]	Something's Happening	1963	6.25	12.50	25.00
❑ 8363 [S]	Groove Time	1964	6.25	12.50	25.00

PACIFIC JAZZ

Number	Title (A Side/B Side)	Yr	VG	VG+	NM
❑ PJ-12 [M]	Burnin'	1961	10.00	20.00	40.00

BRYANT, RAY
CADET

Number	Title (A Side/B Side)	Yr	VG	VG+	NM
❑ LPS-767 [S]	Gotta Travel On	1966	5.00	10.00	20.00
❑ LPS-778 [S]	Lonesome Traveler	1966	5.00	10.00	20.00
❑ LPS-781 [S]	Slow Freight	1967	5.00	10.00	20.00
❑ LP-793 [M]	The Ray Bryant Touch	1967	5.00	10.00	20.00
❑ LP-801 [S]	Take a Bryant Step	1967	5.00	10.00	20.00

COLUMBIA

Number	Title (A Side/B Side)	Yr	VG	VG+	NM
❑ CL 1449 [M]	Little Susie	1960	5.00	10.00	20.00
❑ CL 1476 [M]	The Madison Time	1960	6.25	12.50	25.00
❑ CL 1633 [M]	Con Alma	1961	5.00	10.00	20.00
❑ CL 1746 [M]	Dancing the Big Twist	1962	5.00	10.00	20.00
❑ CL 1867 [M]	Hollywood Jazz Beat	1962	5.00	10.00	20.00
❑ CS 8244 [S]	Little Susie	1960	6.25	12.50	25.00
❑ CS 8276 [S]	The Madison Time	1960	7.50	15.00	30.00
❑ CS 8433 [S]	Con Alma	1961	6.25	12.50	25.00
❑ CS 8546 [S]	Dancing the Big Twist	1962	6.25	12.50	25.00
❑ CS 8667 [S]	Hollywood Jazz Beat	1962	6.25	12.50	25.00

EPIC

Number	Title (A Side/B Side)	Yr	VG	VG+	NM
❑ LN 3279 [M]	Ray Bryant Trio	1956	17.50	35.00	70.00

NEW JAZZ

Number	Title (A Side/B Side)	Yr	VG	VG+	NM
❑ NJLP-8213 [M]	Alone with the Blues	1959	12.50	25.00	50.00
—Purple label					
❑ NJLP-8213 [M]	Alone with the Blues	1965	6.25	12.50	25.00
—Blue label with trident logo					
❑ NJLP-8227 [M]	Ray Bryant Trio	1959	12.50	25.00	50.00
—Purple label; reissue of Prestige 7098					
❑ NJLP-8227 [M]	Ray Bryant Trio	1965	6.25	12.50	25.00
—Blue label with trident logo					

PRESTIGE

Number	Title (A Side/B Side)	Yr	VG	VG+	NM
❑ PRLP-7098 [M]	Ray Bryant Trio	1957	17.50	35.00	70.00

SIGNATURE

Number	Title (A Side/B Side)	Yr	VG	VG+	NM
❑ SM-6008 [M]	Ray Bryant Plays	1960	50.00	100.00	200.00
❑ SS-6008 [S]	Ray Bryant Plays	1960	62.50	125.00	250.00

SUE

Number	Title (A Side/B Side)	Yr	VG	VG+	NM
❑ LP-1016 [M]	Groove House	1963	10.00	20.00	40.00
❑ LPS-1016 [S]	Groove House	1963	12.50	25.00	50.00
❑ LP-1019 [M]	Live at Basin Street	1964	10.00	20.00	40.00
❑ LPS-1019 [S]	Live at Basin Street	1964	12.50	25.00	50.00
❑ LP-1032 [M]	Cold Turkey	1964	10.00	20.00	40.00
❑ LPS-1032 [S]	Cold Turkey	1964	12.50	25.00	50.00
❑ LP-1036 [M]	Ray Bryant Soul	1965	10.00	20.00	40.00
❑ LPS-1036 [S]	Ray Bryant Soul	1965	12.50	25.00	50.00

BRYANT, RUSTY
DOT

Number	Title (A Side/B Side)	Yr	VG	VG+	NM
❑ DLP-3006 [M]	All Night Long	1956	10.00	20.00	40.00
—Maroon label					
❑ DLP-3079 [M]	Rusty Bryant Plays Jazz	1957	10.00	20.00	40.00
❑ DLP-25353 [S]	America's Greatest Jazz	1961	5.00	10.00	20.00

BRYNNER, YUL
VANGUARD

Number	Title (A Side/B Side)	Yr	VG	VG+	NM
❑ VRS-9256 [M]	The Gypsy and I	1967	7.50	15.00	30.00
❑ VSD-79256 [S]	The Gypsy and I	1967	10.00	20.00	40.00

BUA, GENE
HERITAGE

Number	Title (A Side/B Side)	Yr	VG	VG+	NM
❑ 35004	Love of Life	1973	5.00	10.00	20.00

BUBBLE GUM MACHINE, THE
SENATE

Number	Title (A Side/B Side)	Yr	VG	VG+	NM
❑ 21002 [M]	The Bubble Gum Machine	1968	6.25	12.50	25.00
❑ S-21002 [S]	The Bubble Gum Machine	1968	7.50	15.00	30.00

BUBBLE PUPPY, THE
INTERNATIONAL ARTISTS

Number	Title (A Side/B Side)	Yr	VG	VG+	NM
❑ 10	A Gathering of Promises	1969	25.00	50.00	100.00
—Original does not have "Masterfonics" in the dead wax					
❑ 10	A Gathering of Promises	1979	6.25	12.50	25.00
—Reissue has "Masterfonics" in the dead wax					

BUBBLES, JOHN W.
VEE JAY

Number	Title (A Side/B Side)	Yr	VG	VG+	NM
❑ VJ-1109 [M]	Bubbles, John W., That Is	1964	5.00	10.00	20.00

BUCCI, JOE
CAPITOL

Number	Title (A Side/B Side)	Yr	VG	VG+	NM
❑ ST 1840 [S]	Wild About Basie	1963	5.00	10.00	20.00

BUCHANAN, ROY
ALLIGATOR

Number	Title (A Side/B Side)	Yr	VG	VG+	NM
❑ AL-4741	When a Guitar Plays the Blues	1985	2.50	5.00	10.00
❑ AL-4747	Dancing on the Edge	1986	2.50	5.00	10.00
❑ AL-4756	Hot Wires	1988	2.50	5.00	10.00

ATLANTIC

Number	Title (A Side/B Side)	Yr	VG	VG+	NM
❑ SD 18170	A Street Called Straight	1976	3.00	6.00	12.00
❑ SD 18219	Loading Zone	1977	3.00	6.00	12.00
❑ SD 19138	Loading Zone	1978	2.00	4.00	8.00
—Reissue of 18219					
❑ SD 19170	You're Not Alone	1978	3.00	6.00	12.00

BIOYA

Number	Title (A Side/B Side)	Yr	VG	VG+	NM
❑ MM-519	Buch and the Snake Stretchers	1971	50.00	100.00	200.00

POLYDOR

Number	Title (A Side/B Side)	Yr	VG	VG+	NM
❑ PD-5033	Roy Buchanan	1972	3.75	7.50	15.00
❑ PD-5046	Second Album	1973	3.75	7.50	15.00
❑ PD-6020	That's What I Am Here For	1974	3.75	7.50	15.00
❑ PD-6035	In the Beginning	1974	3.75	7.50	15.00
❑ PD-6048	Live Stock	1975	3.75	7.50	15.00

WATERHOUSE

Number	Title (A Side/B Side)	Yr	VG	VG+	NM
❑ 12	My Babe	1981	2.50	5.00	10.00

BUCHANAN BROTHERS
EVENT

Number	Title (A Side/B Side)	Yr	VG	VG+	NM
❑ ES-101	Medicine Man	1969	6.25	12.50	25.00

BUCK, GARY
TOWER

Number	Title (A Side/B Side)	Yr	VG	VG+	NM
❑ DT 5054 [R]	Country Scene	1967	3.75	7.50	15.00
❑ T 5054 [M]	Country Scene	1967	5.00	10.00	20.00

BUCKAROOS, THE
CAPITOL

Number	Title (A Side/B Side)	Yr	VG	VG+	NM
❑ ST-194	Anywhere U.S.A.	1969	6.25	12.50	25.00
❑ ST-322	Roll Your Own with Buck Owens' Buckaroos	1969	6.25	12.50	25.00
❑ ST-440	Rompin' and Stompin'	1970	5.00	10.00	20.00
❑ ST-767	The Buckaroos Play the Hits	1971	5.00	10.00	20.00
❑ ST-860	The Buckaroos Play the Songs of Merle Haggard	1971	6.25	12.50	25.00
❑ ST 2436 [S]	The Buck Owens Song Book	1966	6.25	12.50	25.00
❑ T 2436 [M]	The Buck Owens Song Book	1966	5.00	10.00	20.00
❑ ST 2722 [S]	America's Most Wanted Band	1967	6.25	12.50	25.00
❑ T 2722 [M]	America's Most Wanted Band	1967	5.00	10.00	20.00
❑ ST 2828 [S]	The Buck Owens' Buckaroos Strike Again!	1968	6.25	12.50	25.00
❑ T 2828 [M]	The Buck Owens' Buckaroos Strike Again!	1968	10.00	20.00	40.00
❑ ST 2902	A Night on the Town with Buck Owens' Buckaroos	1968	6.25	12.50	25.00
❑ ST 2973	Meanwhile Back at the Ranch	1968	6.25	12.50	25.00

BUCKINGHAM NICKS
POLYDOR

Number	Title (A Side/B Side)	Yr	VG	VG+	NM
❑ PD-5058	Buckingham Nicks	1973	10.00	20.00	40.00
—Gatefold cover					
❑ PD-5058	Buckingham Nicks	1975	3.00	6.00	12.00
—Regular cover					

BUCKINGHAMS, THE (1)
COLUMBIA

Number	Title (A Side/B Side)	Yr	VG	VG+	NM
❑ CL 2669 [M]	Time & Charges	1967	6.25	12.50	25.00
❑ CL 2798 [M]	Portraits	1968	6.25	12.50	25.00
❑ CS 9469 [S]	Time & Charges	1967	5.00	10.00	20.00
❑ CS 9598 [S]	Portraits	1968	5.00	10.00	20.00
❑ CS 9703	In One Ear and Gone Tomorrow	1968	5.00	10.00	20.00
❑ CS 9812	The Buckinghams Greatest Hits	1969	5.00	10.00	20.00
—Red "360 Sound" label					
❑ CS 9812	The Buckinghams Greatest Hits	1970	3.00	6.00	12.00
—Orange label					
❑ PC 9812	The Buckinghams Greatest Hits	198?	2.00	4.00	8.00
—Reissue with new prefix					
❑ KG 33333 [(2)]	Made in Chicago	1975	5.00	10.00	20.00

U.S.A.

Number	Title (A Side/B Side)	Yr	VG	VG+	NM
❑ 107 [M]	Kind of a Drag	1967	7.50	15.00	30.00
—Without "I'm a Man"					
❑ 107 [M]	Kind of a Drag	1967	150.00	300.00	600.00
—With "I'm a Man"					
❑ 107 [S]	Kind of a Drag	1967	10.00	20.00	40.00
—No known stereo copy has "I'm a Man"					

BUCKLEY, LORD
CRESTVIEW

Number	Title (A Side/B Side)	Yr	VG	VG+	NM
❑ CRV-801 [M]	The Best of Lord Buckley	1963	12.50	25.00	50.00
❑ CRV7-801 [S]	The Best of Lord Buckley	1963	15.00	30.00	60.00

ELEKTRA

Number	Title (A Side/B Side)	Yr	VG	VG+	NM
❑ EKS-74047	The Best of Lord Buckley	1969	6.25	12.50	25.00
—Reissue of Crestview 7-801					

RCA VICTOR

Number	Title (A Side/B Side)	Yr	VG	VG+	NM
❑ LPM-3246 [10]	Hipsters, Flipsters and Finger Poppin' Daddies, Knock Me Your Lobes	1955	75.00	150.00	300.00

REPRISE

Number	Title (A Side/B Side)	Yr	VG	VG+	NM
❑ RS 6389	A Most Immaculately Hip Aristocrat	1970	6.25	12.50	25.00
—Reissue of Straight 1054					

STRAIGHT

Number	Title (A Side/B Side)	Yr	VG	VG+	NM
❑ STS-1054	A Most Immaculately Hip Aristocrat	1970	10.00	20.00	40.00

VAYA

Number	Title (A Side/B Side)	Yr	VG	VG+	NM
❑ 101/2 [M]	Euphoria, Volume 1	1955	37.50	75.00	150.00
❑ 107/8 [M]	Euphoria, Volume 2	1955	50.00	100.00	200.00
❑ 1715 [10]	Euphoria	195?	75.00	150.00	300.00
—Red vinyl					

WORLD PACIFIC

Number	Title (A Side/B Side)	Yr	VG	VG+	NM
❑ WP-1279 [M]	The Way Out Humor of Lord Buckley	1959	25.00	50.00	100.00
—With correct "Way Out Humor" on the back cover					
❑ WP-1279 [M]	The Way Out Humor of Lord Buckley	1959	30.00	60.00	120.00
—With "Far Out Humor" on the back cover					
❑ WP-1815 [M]	Lord Buckley in Concert	1964	12.50	25.00	50.00
—Reissue of 1279					
❑ WP-1849 [M]	Blowing His Mind (and Yours, Too)	1966	12.50	25.00	50.00

B

Number	Title (A Side/B Side)	Yr	VG	VG+	NM
❏ WPS-21879	Buckley's Best	1968	10.00	20.00	40.00
❏ WPS-21889	Bad Rapping of the Marquis de Sade	1969	7.50	15.00	30.00

BUCKLEY, TIM
DISCREET
❏ MS 2157	Sefronia	1973	3.75	7.50	15.00
❏ DS 2201	Look at the Fool	1974	3.75	7.50	15.00

ELEKTRA
❏ EKL-4004 [M]	Tim Buckley	1966	3.75	7.50	15.00
❏ EKL-4018 [M]	Goodbye and Hello	1967	6.25	12.50	25.00
❏ EKS-74004 [S]	Tim Buckley	1966	5.00	10.00	20.00
❏ EKS-74018 [S]	Goodbye and Hello	1967	5.00	10.00	20.00
—Brown labels					
❏ EKS-74018 [S]	Goodbye and Hello	1975	2.50	5.00	10.00
—Butterfly label with Warner Communications logo					
❏ EKS-74045	Happy Sad	1969	5.00	10.00	20.00
❏ EKS-74074	Lorca	1970	5.00	10.00	20.00

RHINO
❏ RNLP-112	The Best of Tim Buckley	1985	2.50	5.00	10.00

STRAIGHT
❏ STS-1060	Blue Afternoon	1969	7.50	15.00	30.00

WARNER BROS.
❏ WS 1842	Blue Afternoon	1970	3.75	7.50	15.00
❏ WS 1881	Starsailor	1970	3.75	7.50	15.00
❏ BS 2631	Greetings from L.A.	1972	3.75	7.50	15.00

BUCKNER, MILT
ARGO
❏ LPS-660 [S]	Mighty High	1960	5.00	10.00	20.00
❏ LPS-670 [S]	Please Mr. Organ Player	1960	5.00	10.00	20.00
❏ LPS-702 [S]	Midnight Mood	1962	5.00	10.00	20.00

BETHLEHEM
❏ BCP-6072 [M]	The New World of Milt Buckner	1963	7.50	15.00	30.00

CAPITOL
❏ T 642 [M]	Rockin' with Milt	1955	12.50	25.00	50.00
—Turquoise or gray label					
❏ T 722 [M]	Rockin' Hammond	1956	12.50	25.00	50.00
—Turquoise or gray label					
❏ T 938 [M]	Send Me Softly	1958	12.50	25.00	50.00
—Turquoise or gray label					

REGENT
❏ MG-6004 [M]	Organ — Sweet 'n' Swing	195?	7.50	15.00	30.00

SAVOY
❏ MG-15023 [10]	Milt Buckner Piano	1953	30.00	60.00	120.00

BUCKNER, TEDDY
DIXIELAND JUBILEE
❏ DJ-503 [M]	In Concert at the Dixieland Jubilee	195?	5.00	10.00	20.00
❏ DJ-504 [M]	Teddy Buckner and His Dixieland Band	195?	5.00	10.00	20.00
❏ DJ-505 [M]	A Salute to Louis Armstrong	1959	5.00	10.00	20.00
❏ DJ-507 [M]	Teddy Buckner and the All Stars	1959	5.00	10.00	20.00
❏ DJ-510 [M]	Teddy Buckner on the Sunset Strip	1960	5.00	10.00	20.00

GENE NORMAN
❏ GNP-(# unk) [10]	Dixieland Jubilee	195?	12.50	25.00	50.00
—Red vinyl					
❏ GNP-11 [M]	Teddy Buckner	1955	10.00	20.00	40.00

BUD AND TRAVIS
LIBERTY
❏ LRP-3125 [M]	Bud and Travis	1959	7.50	15.00	30.00
❏ LRP-3138 [M]	Spotlight On Bud and Travis	1960	5.00	10.00	20.00
❏ LRP-3222 [M]	Bud and Travis In Concert at the Santa Monica Civic Auditorium, Vol. 2	1961	5.00	10.00	20.00
❏ LRP-3295 [M]	Naturally	1963	5.00	10.00	20.00
❏ LRP-3341 [M]	Perspective on Bud and Travis	1964	5.00	10.00	20.00
❏ LRP-3386 [M]	Bud and Travis In Person (At the Cellar Door)	1964	5.00	10.00	20.00
❏ LRP-3398 [M]	The Latin Album	1965	5.00	10.00	20.00
❏ LST-7125 [S]	Bud and Travis	1959	10.00	20.00	40.00
❏ LST-7138 [S]	Spotlight On Bud and Travis	1960	6.25	12.50	25.00
❏ LST-7222 [S]	Bud and Travis In Concert at the Santa Monica Civic Auditorium, Vol. 2	1961	6.25	12.50	25.00
❏ LST-7295 [S]	Naturally	1963	6.25	12.50	25.00
❏ LST-7341 [S]	Perspective on Bud and Travis	1964	6.25	12.50	25.00
❏ LST-7386 [S]	Bud and Travis In Person (At the Cellar Door)	1964	6.25	12.50	25.00
❏ LST-7398 [S]	The Latin Album	1965	6.25	12.50	25.00
❏ LDM-11001 [(2)M]	Bud and Travis...In Concert	1960	6.25	12.50	25.00
❏ LDS-12001 [(2)S]	Bud and Travis...In Concert	1960	7.50	15.00	30.00

SUNSET
❏ SUM-1154 [M]	Bud and Travis	1967	3.00	6.00	12.00
❏ SUS-5154 [S]	Bud and Travis	1967	3.00	6.00	12.00

BUDDIES, THE
WING
❏ MGW-12293 [M]	The Buddies and the Compacts	1965	12.50	25.00	50.00
❏ MGW-12306 [M]	Go Go with the Buddies	1965	12.50	25.00	50.00
❏ SRW-16293 [S]	The Buddies and the Compacts	1965	20.00	40.00	80.00
❏ SRW-16306 [S]	Go Go with the Buddies	1965	20.00	40.00	80.00

BUDGIE
A&M
❏ SP-4593	If I Were Brittania I'd Waive the Rules	1976	3.75	7.50	15.00
❏ SP-4618	Bandolier	1977	3.75	7.50	15.00
❏ SP-4675	Impeckable	1978	3.75	7.50	15.00

KAPP
❏ KS-3656	Budgie	1971	7.50	15.00	30.00
❏ KS-3669	Squawk	1972	7.50	15.00	30.00

MCA
❏ 429	In for the Kill	1973	5.00	10.00	20.00

BUDIMIR, DENNIS
MAINSTREAM
❏ S-6059 [S]	Creeper	1966	6.25	12.50	25.00
❏ 56059 [M]	Creeper	1966	5.00	10.00	20.00

REVELATION
❏ REV-1 [S]	Alone Together	1967	5.00	10.00	20.00
❏ REV-M-1 [M]	Alone Together	1967	6.25	12.50	25.00
❏ REV-4	A Second Coming	1968	5.00	10.00	20.00
❏ REV-8	Sprung Free!	1969	5.00	10.00	20.00
❏ REV-14	Session with Albert	1971	5.00	10.00	20.00

BUFFALO NICKEL JUGBAND, THE
HAPPY TIGER
❏ 1018	The Buffalo Nickel Jugband	1971	6.25	12.50	25.00

BUFFALO SPRINGFIELD
ATCO
❏ SD 38-105 [S]	Retrospective/The Best of Buffalo Springfield	197?	2.00	4.00	8.00
—Reissue of 33-283					
❏ 33-200 [M]	Buffalo Springfield	1967	50.00	100.00	200.00
—With "Baby Don't Scold Me"					
❏ 33-200A [M]	Buffalo Springfield	1967	6.25	12.50	25.00
—With "For What It's Worth" replacing "Baby Don't Scold Me"					
❏ SD 33-200 [S]	Buffalo Springfield	1967	50.00	100.00	200.00
—With "Baby Don't Scold Me"					
❏ SD 33-200A [S]	Buffalo Springfield	1967	6.25	12.50	25.00
—With "For What It's Worth" replacing "Baby Don't Scold Me"; purple and brown label					
❏ SD 33-200A [S]	Buffalo Springfield	1969	3.75	7.50	15.00
—Reissue on yellow label					
❏ SD 33-200A [S]	Buffalo Springfield	197?	2.00	4.00	8.00
—Later white or gray label					
❏ 33-226 [M]	Buffalo Springfield Again	1967	20.00	40.00	80.00
❏ SD 33-226 [S]	Buffalo Springfield Again	1967	6.25	12.50	25.00
—Purple and brown label					
❏ SD 33-226 [S]	Buffalo Springfield Again	1969	3.75	7.50	15.00
—Reissue on yellow label					
❏ SD 33-226 [S]	Buffalo Springfield Again	197?	2.00	4.00	8.00
—Later white or gray label					
❏ 33-256 [M]	Last Time Around	1968	30.00	60.00	120.00
—White label promo only					
❏ SD 33-256 [S]	Last Time Around	1968	7.50	15.00	30.00
—Purple and brown label					
❏ SD 33-256 [S]	Last Time Around	1969	3.75	7.50	15.00
—Reissue on yellow label					
❏ SD 33-256 [S]	Last Time Around	197?	2.00	4.00	8.00
—Later white or gray label					
❏ 33-283 [M]	Retrospective/The Best of Buffalo Springfield	1969	25.00	50.00	100.00
—White label promo only					
❏ SD 33-283 [S]	Retrospective/The Best of Buffalo Springfield	1969	5.00	10.00	20.00
—Yellow label					
❏ SD 2-806 [(2)]	Buffalo Springfield	197?	3.00	6.00	12.00
—Later white or gray label					
❏ SD 2-806 [(2)]	Buffalo Springfield	1973	5.00	10.00	20.00
—Yellow label					

BUFFETT, JIMMY
ABC
❏ SPDJ-43 [DJ]	Special Jimmy Buffett Sampler	1978	5.00	10.00	20.00
❏ D-914	Havana Daydreamin'	1976	3.00	6.00	12.00
❏ AB-990	Changes in Latitudes, Changes in Attitudes	1977	3.00	6.00	12.00
❏ AK-1008 [(2)]	You Had to Be There	1978	3.75	7.50	15.00
❏ AA-1046	Son of a Son of a Sailor	1978	3.00	6.00	12.00

ABC DUNHILL
❏ DSD-50132	Living and Dying in 3/4 Time	1973	3.75	7.50	15.00
❏ DSX-50150	A White Sport Coat and a Pink Crustacean	1974	3.75	7.50	15.00
❏ DSD-50183	A1A	1975	3.75	7.50	15.00

BARNABY
❏ BR-6014	High Cumberland Jubilee	1975	10.00	20.00	40.00
❏ Z 30093	Down to Earth	1970	25.00	50.00	100.00

MCA
❏ 5102	Volcano	1979	2.50	5.00	10.00
❏ 5169	Coconut Telegraph	1981	2.50	5.00	10.00
❏ 5285	Somewhere Over China	1982	2.50	5.00	10.00
❏ 5447	One Particular Harbour	1983	2.50	5.00	10.00
❏ 5512	Riddles in the Sand	1984	2.50	5.00	10.00
❏ 5600	Last Mango in Paris	1985	2.50	5.00	10.00
❏ 5633	Songs You Know By Heart — Jimmy Buffett's Greatest Hit(s)	1985	2.50	5.00	10.00
❏ 5730	Floridays	1986	2.50	5.00	10.00
❏ 2-6005 [(2)]	You Had to Be There	1981	2.50	5.00	10.00
❏ 6314	Off to See the Lizard	1989	2.50	5.00	10.00
❏ 37023	Havana Daydreamin'	1981	2.00	4.00	8.00
❏ 37024	Son of a Son of a Sailor	1981	2.00	4.00	8.00
❏ 37025	Living and Dying in 3/4 Time	1981	2.00	4.00	8.00
❏ 37026	A White Sport Coat and a Pink Crustacean	1981	2.00	4.00	8.00
❏ 37027	A1A	1981	2.00	4.00	8.00
❏ 37150	Changes in Latitudes, Changes in Attitudes	1982	2.00	4.00	8.00
❏ 37156	Volcano	1982	2.00	4.00	8.00
❏ 37246	Somewhere Over China	1984	2.00	4.00	8.00
❏ 42093	Hot Water	1988	2.50	5.00	10.00

BUGALOOS, THE
CAPITOL
❏ SW-621	The Bugaloos	1970	7.50	15.00	30.00

BUGGS, THE
CORONET
❏ CX-212 [M]	The Beatle Beat	1964	5.00	10.00	20.00
❏ CXS-212 [R]	The Beatle Beat	1964	3.00	6.00	12.00

B

Number	Title (A Side/B Side)	Yr	VG	VG+	NM
BULLDOG					
BUDDAH					
❑ BDS-5600	Smasher	1974	3.75	7.50	15.00
DECCA					
❑ DL 75370	Bulldog	1972	5.00	10.00	20.00
BUNCH, THE					
A&M					
❑ SP-4354	The Bunch	1973	6.25	12.50	25.00
BUNKER, LARRY					
VAULT					
❑ LP-9005 [M]	Live at Shelly's Manne-Hole	1966	5.00	10.00	20.00
BUNKERS, THE					
RCA VICTOR					
❑ APL1-0102	Archie and Edith Side by Side	1973	5.00	10.00	20.00
BUOYS, THE					
SCEPTER					
❑ SPS-593	Timothy	1971	6.25	12.50	25.00
BURDON, ERIC					
CAPITOL					
❑ ST-11359	Sun Secrets	1974	3.00	6.00	12.00
❑ S?A?11426	Stop	1975	5.00	10.00	20.00
—Cover shaped like a hexagon					
❑ ST-11426	Stop	1975	3.00	6.00	12.00
—Regular square cover					
GNP CRESCENDO					
❑ GNPS-2194	Wicked Man	1988	2.50	5.00	10.00
LAX					
❑ PW 37110	Sun Secrets	1981	2.50	5.00	10.00
—Reissue of Capitol 11359					
STRIPED HORSE					
❑ SHL 2006	I Used to Be an Animal	1988	2.50	5.00	10.00
BURDON, ERIC, AND WAR					
ABC					
❑ D-988	Love Is All Around	1976	3.00	6.00	12.00
—As "War Featuring Eric Burdon"					
LAX					
❑ PW 37109	Spill the Wine	1981	2.50	5.00	10.00
—Reissue of MGM 4663 with new title					
MGM					
❑ SE-4663	Eric Burdon Declares "War"	1970	3.75	7.50	15.00
❑ SE-4710-2 [(2)]	The Black Man's Burdon	1970	5.00	10.00	20.00
—Add 50% if the package includes an "Official War Bond," entitling the bearer to $1 off any Eric Burdon and War concert before December 31, 1973					
BURGER, JACK					
HIFI					
❑ R-803 [M]	Let's Play Bongos!	1957	10.00	20.00	40.00
❑ R-804 [M]	The End on Bongos!	1957	10.00	20.00	40.00
❑ R-809 [M]	Let's Play Congas	1958	7.50	15.00	30.00
❑ RS-809 [S]	Let's Play Congas	1959	10.00	20.00	40.00
BURGESS, WILMA					
DECCA					
❑ DL 4788 [M]	Don't Touch Me	1966	3.75	7.50	15.00
❑ DL 4852 [M]	Wilma Burgess Sings Misty Blue	1967	3.75	7.50	15.00
❑ DL 4935 [M]	Tear Time	1967	6.25	12.50	25.00
❑ DL 74788 [S]	Don't Touch Me	1966	5.00	10.00	20.00
❑ DL 74852 [S]	Wilma Burgess Sings Misty Blue	1967	5.00	10.00	20.00
❑ DL 74935 [S]	Tear Time	1967	5.00	10.00	20.00
❑ DL 75024	The Tender Lovin' Country Sound	1968	5.00	10.00	20.00
❑ DL 75090	Parting Is Such Sweet Sorrow	1968	5.00	10.00	20.00
BURGHOFF, GARY					
SHALOM					
❑ 651	Gary Burghoff and His Mardi Gras Celebration Band	1983	10.00	20.00	40.00
BURKE, RAY					
SOUTHLAND					
❑ SLP-209 [10]	Contemporary New Orleans Jazz	1955	12.50	25.00	50.00
BURKE, SOLOMON					
ABC DUNHILL					
❑ DSX-50161	I Have a Dream	1974	3.00	6.00	12.00
AMHERST					
❑ AMH-1018	Please Don't You Say Goodbye to Me	1978	3.00	6.00	12.00
APOLLO					
❑ ALP-498 [M]	Solomon Burke	1962	125.00	250.00	500.00
ATLANTIC					
❑ 8067 [M]	Solomon Burke's Greatest Hits	1962	12.50	25.00	50.00
❑ SD 8067 [S]	Solomon Burke's Greatest Hits	1962	20.00	40.00	80.00
❑ 8085 [M]	If You Need Me	1963	12.50	25.00	50.00
❑ SD 8085 [S]	If You Need Me	1963	20.00	40.00	80.00
❑ 8096 [M]	Rock N' Soul	1964	12.50	25.00	50.00
❑ SD 8096 [S]	Rock N' Soul	1964	20.00	40.00	80.00
❑ 8109 [M]	The Best of Solomon Burke	1965	7.50	15.00	30.00
❑ SD 8109 [S]	The Best of Solomon Burke	1965	10.00	20.00	40.00
❑ 8158	King Solomon	1968	6.25	12.50	25.00
❑ SD 8185	I Wish I Knew	1968	6.25	12.50	25.00
BELL					
❑ 6033	Proud Mary	1969	5.00	10.00	20.00
CHESS					
❑ CH-19002	Back to My Roots	1976	3.00	6.00	12.00
❑ CH-60042	Music to Make Love By	1975	3.00	6.00	12.00
CLARION					
❑ 607 [M]	I Almost Lost My Mind	1966	5.00	10.00	20.00
❑ SD 607 [S]	I Almost Lost My Mind	1966	6.25	12.50	25.00
INFINITY					
❑ INF-9024	Sidewalks, Fences and Walls	1979	3.00	6.00	12.00
KENWOOD					
❑ LP-498 [M]	Solomon Burke	1964	50.00	100.00	200.00
—Reissue of Apollo 498					
MGM					
❑ SE-4767	Electronic Magnetism	1971	3.75	7.50	15.00
❑ SE-4830	King Heavy	1972	3.75	7.50	15.00
PRIDE					
❑ 0011	The History of Solomon Burke	1972	3.75	7.50	15.00
ROUNDER					
❑ 2042/3 [(2)]	Soul Alive!	1984	3.00	6.00	12.00
❑ 2053	A Change Is Gonna Come	1986	2.50	5.00	10.00
SAVOY					
❑ 14660	Solomon Burke	1981	2.50	5.00	10.00
❑ 14679	Into My Life	1982	2.50	5.00	10.00
❑ 14717	Take Me, Shake Me	1983	2.50	5.00	10.00
BURKE, VINNIE					
ABC-PARAMOUNT					
❑ ABC-139 [M]	The Vinnie Burke All Stars	1956	12.50	25.00	50.00
❑ ABC-170 [M]	The Vinnie Burke String Jazz Quartet	1957	12.50	25.00	50.00
BETHLEHEM					
❑ BCP-1010 [10]	East Coast Jazz 2	1954	30.00	60.00	120.00
BURNETT, CAROL					
DECCA					
❑ DL 4049 [M]	Carol Burnett Remembers How They Stopped the Show	1960	7.50	15.00	30.00
❑ DL 4437 [M]	Let Me Entertain You	1964	5.00	10.00	20.00
❑ DL 74049 [S]	Carol Burnett Remembers How They Stopped the Show	1960	10.00	20.00	40.00
❑ DL 74437 [S]	Let Me Entertain You	1964	6.25	12.50	25.00
RCA VICTOR					
❑ LPM-3839 [M]	Carol Burnett Sings	1967	5.00	10.00	20.00
❑ LSP-3839 [S]	Carol Burnett Sings	1967	5.00	10.00	20.00
BURNETT, J. HENRY					
See T-BONE BURNETT.					
BURNETT, T-BONE					
UNI					
❑ 73125	The B-52 Band and the Fabulous Skyhawks	1972	7.50	15.00	30.00
—As "J. Henry Burnett"					
BURNETTE, BILLY					
COLUMBIA					
❑ JC 36792	Billy Burnette	1980	2.50	5.00	10.00
❑ FC 37460	Gimme You	1981	2.50	5.00	10.00
ENTRANCE					
❑ Z 31228	Billy Burnette	1972	5.00	10.00	20.00
MCA CURB					
❑ 5604	Try Me	1985	2.50	5.00	10.00
POLYDOR					
❑ PD-1-6187	Billy Burnette	1979	2.50	5.00	10.00
BURNETTE, DORSEY					
CALLIOPE					
❑ CAL 7006	Things I Treasure	1977	3.00	6.00	12.00
CAPITOL					
❑ ST-11094	Here and Now	1972	3.75	7.50	15.00
❑ ST-11219	Dorsey Burnette	1973	3.75	7.50	15.00
DOT					
❑ DLP-3456 [M]	Dorsey Burnette Sings	1963	10.00	20.00	40.00
❑ DLP-25456 [S]	Dorsey Burnette Sings	1963	12.50	25.00	50.00
ERA					
❑ EL-102 [M]	Tall Oak Tree	1960	37.50	75.00	150.00
❑ ES-102 [S]	Tall Oak Tree	1960	75.00	150.00	300.00
❑ ES-800 [M]	Dorsey Burnette's Greatest Hits	1969	6.25	12.50	25.00
GUSTO					
❑ 0050	The Golden Hits of Dorsey Burnette	197?	3.00	6.00	12.00
BURNETTE, DORSEY AND JOHNNY					
SOLID SMOKE					
❑ SS-8005	Together Again	1978	3.75	7.50	15.00
BURNETTE, JOHNNY					
CORAL					
❑ CRL 57080 [M]	Johnny Burnette & the Rock 'N' Roll Trio	1956	2000.	4000.	6000.
—Originals have maroon labels, machine-stamped (not engraved) numbers in the dead wax, printing on jacket's spine and "Printed in U.S.A." in lower right of back cover					
LIBERTY					
❑ LRP-3179 [M]	Dreamin'	1960	10.00	20.00	40.00
❑ LRP-3183 [M]	Johnny Burnette	1961	10.00	20.00	40.00
❑ LRP-3190 [M]	Johnny Burnette Sings	1961	10.00	20.00	40.00
❑ LRP-3206 [M]	Johnny Burnette's Hits and Other Favorites	1962	10.00	20.00	40.00
❑ LRP-3255 [M]	Roses Are Red	1962	10.00	20.00	40.00
❑ LRP-3389 [M]	The Johnny Burnette Story	1964	10.00	20.00	40.00
❑ LST-7179 [S]	Dreamin'	1960	15.00	30.00	60.00
❑ LST-7183 [S]	Johnny Burnette	1961	15.00	30.00	60.00
❑ LST-7190 [S]	Johnny Burnette Sings	1961	15.00	30.00	60.00
❑ LST-7206 [S]	Johnny Burnette's Hits and Other Favorites	1962	12.50	25.00	50.00
❑ LST-7255 [S]	Roses Are Red	1962	12.50	25.00	50.00
❑ LST-7389 [S]	The Johnny Burnette Story	1964	12.50	25.00	50.00
MCA					
❑ 1513	Listen to Johnny Burnette and the Rock 'N' Roll Trio	1982	2.50	5.00	10.00

Number	Title (A Side/B Side)	Yr	VG	VG+	NM
SOLID SMOKE					
❑ SS-8001	Tear It Up	1978	3.75	7.50	15.00
—Black viinyl					
❑ SS-8001	Tear It Up	1978	7.50	15.00	30.00
—Blue vinyl					
SUNSET					
❑ SUM-1179 [M]	Dreamin'	1967	3.75	7.50	15.00
❑ SUS-5179 [S]	Dreamin'	1967	5.00	10.00	20.00
UNITED ARTISTS					
❑ UA-LA432-G	The Very Best of Johnny Burnette	1975	2.50	5.00	10.00
BURNETTE, SMILEY					
CRICKET					
❑ CR-11 [M]	Rodeo Songaree	1959	7.50	15.00	30.00
STARDAY					
❑ SLP-191 [M]	Ole Frog	1962	10.00	20.00	40.00
BURNS, GEORGE					
BUDDAH					
❑ BDS-5025	George Burns Sings	1969	3.75	7.50	15.00
❑ BDS-5127	A Musical Trip with George Burns	1972	3.00	6.00	12.00
—Reissue of 5027					
MERCURY					
❑ SRM-1-4061	Young at Heart	1982	2.50	5.00	10.00
❑ SRM-1-5025	I Wish I Was Eighteen Again	1980	2.50	5.00	10.00
❑ SRM-1-6001	George Burns in Nashville	1981	2.50	5.00	10.00
PRIDE					
❑ PRD-00 11 [(2)]	An Evening with George Burns	1974	5.00	10.00	20.00
BURNS, RALPH					
BETHLEHEM					
❑ BCP-68 [M]	Bijou	1957	12.50	25.00	50.00
CLEF					
❑ MGC-115 [10]	Free Forms	1953	50.00	100.00	200.00
DECCA					
❑ DL 8235 [M]	Jazz Studio 5	1956	20.00	40.00	80.00
❑ DL 8555 [M]	The Masters Revisited	1957	15.00	30.00	60.00
❑ DL 9068 [M]	New York's a Song	1959	10.00	20.00	40.00
❑ DL 9207 [M]	Very Warm for Jazz	1959	10.00	20.00	40.00
❑ DL 9215 [M]	Porgy and Bess	1959	7.50	15.00	30.00
❑ DL 79068 [S]	New York's a Song	1959	12.50	25.00	50.00
❑ DL 79207 [S]	Very Warm for Jazz	1959	12.50	25.00	50.00
❑ DL 79215 [S]	Porgy and Bess	1959	10.00	20.00	40.00
EPIC					
❑ LN 24015 [M]	Swingin' Down the Lane	1962	7.50	15.00	30.00
❑ BN 26015 [S]	Swingin' Down the Lane	1962	10.00	20.00	40.00
JAZZTONE					
❑ J-1228 [M]	Spring Sequence	1956	12.50	25.00	50.00
MERCURY					
❑ MGC-115 [10]	Free Forms	1952	62.50	125.00	250.00
MGM					
❑ E-3616 [M]	The Swinging Seasons	1958	12.50	25.00	50.00
❑ SE-3616 [M]	The Swinging Seasons	1959	10.00	20.00	40.00
NORGRAN					
❑ MGN-1028 [M]	Ralph Burns Among the JATP's	1955	30.00	60.00	120.00
PERIOD					
❑ SPL-1105 [10]	Spring Sequence	1955	30.00	60.00	120.00
❑ SPL-1109 [10]	Bijou	1955	30.00	60.00	120.00
VERVE					
❑ MGV-8121 [M]	Ralph Burns Among the JATP's	1957	12.50	25.00	50.00
❑ V-8121 [M]	Ralph Burns Among the JATP's	1961	5.00	10.00	20.00
WARWICK					
❑ W-5001 [M]	Where There's Burns There's Fire	1961	10.00	20.00	40.00
❑ W-5001 ST [S]	Where There's Burns There's Fire	1961	12.50	25.00	50.00
BURNS, RALPH/BILLIE HOLIDAY					
CLEF					
❑ MGC-718 [M]	The Free Forms of Ralph Burns/The Songs of Billie Holiday	1956	30.00	60.00	120.00
VERVE					
❑ MGV-8098 [M]	Jazz Recital	1957	12.50	25.00	50.00
❑ V-8098 [M]	Jazz Recital	1961	5.00	10.00	20.00
BURNS, RANDY					
ESP-DISK'					
❑ 1039	Songs of Love and War	1966	6.25	12.50	25.00
❑ 1089	Evening of the Magician	1968	6.25	12.50	25.00
❑ 2007	Song for an Uncertain Lady	1971	3.75	7.50	15.00
MERCURY					
❑ SR-61329	Randy Burns and the Skydog Band	1971	3.00	6.00	12.00
POLYDOR					
❑ PD-5030	I'm a Lover, Not a Fool	1972	3.00	6.00	12.00
❑ PD-5049	Still On Our Feet	1973	3.00	6.00	12.00
BURNS, RON					
ROULETTE					
❑ R-52095 [M]	Skin Burns	1963	5.00	10.00	20.00
❑ SR-52095 [S]	Skin Burns	1963	6.25	12.50	25.00
BURNT SUITE					
B.J.W.					
❑ 9	Burnt Suite	1967	50.00	100.00	200.00
BURRELL, DAVE					
DOUGLAS					
❑ SD 798	High	1969	5.00	10.00	20.00
HAT HUT					
❑ 05 [(2)]	Windward Passages	1979	5.00	10.00	20.00

Number	Title (A Side/B Side)	Yr	VG	VG+	NM
BURRELL, KENNY					
ARGO					
❑ LP-655 [M]	A Night at the Vanguard	1959	7.50	15.00	30.00
❑ LPS-655 [S]	A Night at the Vanguard	1959	10.00	20.00	40.00
BLUE NOTE					
❑ BLP-1523 [M]	Introducing Kenny Burrell	1956	37.50	75.00	150.00
—Regular version, Lexington Ave. address on label					
❑ BLP-1523 [M]	Introducing Kenny Burrell	1956	50.00	100.00	200.00
—"Deep groove" version (deep indentation under label on both sides)					
❑ BLP-1523 [M]	Introducing Kenny Burrell	1957	12.50	25.00	50.00
—W. 63rd St., NYC address on label					
❑ BLP-1523 [M]	Introducing Kenny Burrell	1963	6.25	12.50	25.00
—New York, USA address on label					
❑ BLP-1543 [M]	Kenny Burrell, Volume 2	1957	12.50	25.00	50.00
—W. 63rd St., NYC address on label					
❑ BLP-1543 [M]	Kenny Burrell, Volume 2	1957	37.50	75.00	150.00
—Regular version, Lexington Ave. address on label					
❑ BLP-1543 [M]	Kenny Burrell, Volume 2	1957	50.00	100.00	200.00
—"Deep groove" version (deep indentation under label on both sides)					
❑ BLP-1543 [M]	Kenny Burrell, Volume 2	1963	6.25	12.50	25.00
—New York, USA address on label					
❑ BLP-1596 [M]	Blue Lights, Volume 1	1958	17.50	35.00	70.00
—Regular version, W. 63rd St., NYC address on label					
❑ BLP-1596 [M]	Blue Lights, Volume 1	1958	25.00	50.00	100.00
—"Deep groove" version (deep indentation under label on both sides)					
❑ BLP-1596 [M]	Blue Lights, Volume 1	1963	6.25	12.50	25.00
—New York, USA address on label					
❑ BST-1596 [S]	Blue Lights, Volume 1	1959	17.50	35.00	70.00
—Regular version, W. 63rd St., NYC address on label					
❑ BST-1596 [S]	Blue Lights, Volume 1	1959	25.00	50.00	100.00
—"Deep groove" version (deep indentation under label on both sides)					
❑ BST-1596 [S]	Blue Lights, Volume 1	1963	6.25	12.50	25.00
—New York, USA address on label					
❑ BLP-1597 [M]	Blue Lights, Volume 2	1958	17.50	35.00	70.00
—Regular version, W. 63rd St., NYC address on label					
❑ BLP-1597 [M]	Blue Lights, Volume 2	1958	25.00	50.00	100.00
—"Deep groove" version (deep indentation under label on both sides)					
❑ BLP-1597 [M]	Blue Lights, Volume 2	1963	6.25	12.50	25.00
—New York, USA address on label					
❑ BST-1597 [S]	Blue Lights, Volume 2	1959	17.50	35.00	70.00
—Regular version, W. 63rd St., NYC address on label					
❑ BST-1597 [S]	Blue Lights, Volume 2	1959	25.00	50.00	100.00
—"Deep groove" version (deep indentation under label on both sides)					
❑ BST-1597 [S]	Blue Lights, Volume 2	1963	6.25	12.50	25.00
—New York, USA address on label					
❑ BLP-4021 [M]	On View at the Five Spot Café	1960	17.50	35.00	70.00
—Regular version, W. 63rd St., NYC address on label					
❑ BLP-4021 [M]	On View at the Five Spot Café	1960	25.00	50.00	100.00
—"Deep groove" version (deep indentation under label on both sides)					
❑ BLP-4021 [M]	On View at the Five Spot Café	1963	6.25	12.50	25.00
—New York, USA address on label					
❑ BLP-4123 [M]	Midnight Blue	1963	7.50	15.00	30.00
—New York, USA address on label					
❑ BST-84021 [S]	On View at the Five Spot Café	1960	15.00	30.00	60.00
—W. 63rd St., NYC address on label					
❑ BST-84021 [S]	On View at the Five Spot Café	1963	6.25	12.50	25.00
—New York, USA address on label					
❑ BST-84123 [S]	Midnight Blue	1963	10.00	20.00	40.00
—New York, USA address on label					
CADET					
❑ LPS-769 [S]	Men at Work	1965	5.00	10.00	20.00
—Reissue of Argo 655					
❑ LPS-772 [S]	The Tender Gender	1966	5.00	10.00	20.00
❑ LPS-779 [S]	Have Yourself a Soulful Little Christmas	1966	5.00	10.00	20.00
❑ LP-798 [M]	Ode to 52nd Street	1967	5.00	10.00	20.00
COLUMBIA					
❑ CL 1703 [M]	Weaver of Dreams	1961	5.00	10.00	20.00
❑ CS 8503 [S]	Weaver of Dreams	1961	6.25	12.50	25.00
KAPP					
❑ KL-1326 [M]	Lotta Bossa Nova	1962	5.00	10.00	20.00
❑ KS-3326 [S]	Lotta Bossa Nova	1962	6.25	12.50	25.00
MOODSVILLE					
❑ MVLP-29 [M]	Bluesy Burrell	1963	10.00	20.00	40.00
—Green label					
❑ MVLP-29 [M]	Bluesy Burrell	1965	5.00	10.00	20.00
—Blue label with trident logo					
❑ MVST-29 [S]	Bluesy Burrell	1963	10.00	20.00	40.00
—Green label					
❑ MVST-29 [S]	Bluesy Burrell	1965	6.25	12.50	25.00
—Blue label with trident logo					
PRESTIGE					
❑ PRLP-7073 [M]	All Night Long	1957	25.00	50.00	100.00
—Actually an all-star session; reissued as a Kenny Burrell album, thus it is listed here					
❑ PRLP-7081 [M]	All Day Long	1957	25.00	50.00	100.00
—Actually an all-star session; reissued as a Kenny Burrell album, thus it is listed here					
❑ PRLP-7088 [M]	Kenny Burrell	1957	20.00	40.00	80.00
❑ PRLP-7277 [M]	All Day Long	1963	12.50	25.00	50.00
—Reissue of 7081					
❑ PRST-7277 [R]	All Day Long	1963	5.00	10.00	20.00
❑ PRLP-7289 [M]	All Night Long	1964	12.50	25.00	50.00
—Reissue of 7073					
❑ PRST-7289 [R]	All Night Long	1964	5.00	10.00	20.00
❑ PRLP-7308 [M]	Blue Moods	1964	7.50	15.00	30.00
—Reissue of 7088					
❑ PRST-7308 [R]	Blue Moods	1964	5.00	10.00	20.00
❑ PRLP-7315 [M]	Soul Call	1964	6.25	12.50	25.00
❑ PRST-7315 [S]	Soul Call	1964	7.50	15.00	30.00
❑ PRLP-7347 [M]	Crash	1964	6.25	12.50	25.00
❑ PRST-7347 [S]	Crash	1964	7.50	15.00	30.00
❑ PRLP-7448 [M]	The Best of Kenny Burrell	1967	7.50	15.00	30.00
❑ PRST-7448 [S]	The Best of Kenny Burrell	1967	5.00	10.00	20.00

Number	Title (A Side/B Side)	Yr	VG	VG+	NM
VERVE					
❏ V-8553 [M]	Blue Bash!	1963	5.00	10.00	20.00
❏ V6-8553 [S]	Blue Bash!	1963	6.25	12.50	25.00
❏ V6-8612 [S]	Guitar Forms	1965	5.00	10.00	20.00
❏ V6-8656 [S]	A Generation Ago Today	1966	5.00	10.00	20.00
❏ V-8746 [M]	Blues— The Common Ground	1968	5.00	10.00	20.00

BURRELL, KENNY, AND JOHN COLTRANE
NEW JAZZ

Number	Title (A Side/B Side)	Yr	VG	VG+	NM
❏ NJLP-8217 [M]	The Cats	1959	20.00	40.00	80.00
—Purple label					
❏ NJLP-8217 [M]	The Cats	1965	6.25	12.50	25.00
—Blue label with trident logo					
❏ NJLP-8276 [M]	Kenny Burrell with John Coltrane	1962	15.00	30.00	60.00
—Purple label					
❏ NJLP-8276 [M]	Kenny Burrell with John Coltrane	1965	6.25	12.50	25.00
—Blue label with trident logo					
PRESTIGE					
❏ PRLP-7532 [M]	Kenny Burrell Quintet with John Coltrane	1967	7.50	15.00	30.00
❏ PRST-7532 [S]	Kenny Burrell Quintet with John Coltrane	1967	5.00	10.00	20.00

BURRELL, KENNY; TINY GRIMES; BILL JENNINGS
STATUS

Number	Title (A Side/B Side)	Yr	VG	VG+	NM
❏ ST-8318 [M]	Guitar Soul	1965	10.00	20.00	40.00

BURRELL, KENNY, AND JIMMY RANEY
PRESTIGE

Number	Title (A Side/B Side)	Yr	VG	VG+	NM
❏ PRLP-7119 [M]	Two Guitars	1957	20.00	40.00	80.00

BURRITO BROTHERS, THE
See THE FLYING BURRITO BROTHERS.

BURROUGHS, WILLIAM
ESP-DISK'

Number	Title (A Side/B Side)	Yr	VG	VG+	NM
❏ 1050 [M]	Call Me Burroughs	1967	25.00	50.00	100.00

BURROWS, ABE
COLUMBIA

Number	Title (A Side/B Side)	Yr	VG	VG+	NM
❏ CL 6128 [10]	Abe Burrows Sings?	1950	10.00	20.00	40.00
DECCA					
❏ DL 5288 [10]	The Girl with the 3 Blue Eyes	1951	10.00	20.00	40.00

BURTON, GARY
RCA VICTOR

Number	Title (A Side/B Side)	Yr	VG	VG+	NM
❏ LPM-2420 [M]	New Vibe Man in Town	1961	5.00	10.00	20.00
❏ LSP-2420 [S]	New Vibe Man in Town	1961	6.25	12.50	25.00
❏ LPM-2665 [M]	Who Is Gary Burton?	1963	5.00	10.00	20.00
❏ LSP-2665 [S]	Who Is Gary Burton?	1963	6.25	12.50	25.00
❏ LPM-2880 [M]	Something's Coming	1964	5.00	10.00	20.00
❏ LSP-2880 [S]	Something's Coming	1964	6.25	12.50	25.00
❏ LSP-3360 [S]	The Groovy Sound of Music	1965	5.00	10.00	20.00
❏ LSP-3642 [S]	The Time Machine	1966	5.00	10.00	20.00
❏ LSP-3719 [S]	Tennessee Firebird	1966	5.00	10.00	20.00
❏ LPM-3835 [M]	Duster	1967	5.00	10.00	20.00
❏ LPM-3901 [M]	Lofty Fake Anagram	1967	5.00	10.00	20.00
❏ LPM-3985 [M]	Gary Burton Quartet In Concert	1968	7.50	15.00	30.00

BURTON, GARY; SONNY ROLLINS; CLARK TERRY
RCA VICTOR

Number	Title (A Side/B Side)	Yr	VG	VG+	NM
❏ LSP-2725 [S]	Three in Jazz	1963	5.00	10.00	20.00

BURTON, JAMES
A&M

Number	Title (A Side/B Side)	Yr	VG	VG+	NM
❏ SP-4293	James Burton	1971	6.25	12.50	25.00

BURTON, JOE
CORAL

Number	Title (A Side/B Side)	Yr	VG	VG+	NM
❏ CRL 57098 [M]	Joe Burton Session	1957	10.00	20.00	40.00
❏ CRL 57175 [M]	Here I Am in Love Again	1958	10.00	20.00	40.00
❏ CRL 757175 [S]	Here I Am in Love Again	1959	7.50	15.00	30.00
JODAY					
❏ JS-1000 [S]	The Subtle Sound of Joe Burton	1963	5.00	10.00	20.00
REGENT					
❏ MG-6036 [M]	Jazz Pretty	1957	12.50	25.00	50.00

BUSH, JOHNNY
HILLTOP

Number	Title (A Side/B Side)	Yr	VG	VG+	NM
❏ JS-6081	You Ought to Hear Me Cry	197?	3.75	7.50	15.00
MILLION					
❏ 1001	The Best of Johnny Bush	1972	6.25	12.50	25.00
POWER PAK					
❏ PO-217	Bush Country	197?	3.00	6.00	12.00
RCA VICTOR					
❏ APL1-0216	Here Comes the World Again	1973	3.75	7.50	15.00
❏ APL1-0369	Texas Dance Hall Girl	1974	3.75	7.50	15.00
❏ LSP-10002	Whiskey River/There Stands the Glass	1973	3.75	7.50	15.00
STOP					
❏ 1028	The Greatest Hits of Johnny Bush	1972	5.00	10.00	20.00
❏ 10002	Sound of a Heartache	1968	6.25	12.50	25.00
❏ 10005	Undo the Night	1968	5.00	10.00	20.00
❏ 10008	You Gave Me a Mountain	1969	5.00	10.00	20.00
❏ 10014	Johnny Bush	1970	5.00	10.00	20.00
WHISKEY RIVER					
❏ 8024 [(2)]	Live at Dance Town USA	1979	3.75	7.50	15.00

BUSH, KATE
COLUMBIA

Number	Title (A Side/B Side)	Yr	VG	VG+	NM
❏ OC 44164	The Sensual World	1989	3.00	6.00	12.00
EMI AMERICA					
❏ SW-17003	The Kick Inside	1978	2.50	5.00	10.00
—Reissue of Harvest release					
❏ SMAS-17008	Lionheart	1978	3.75	7.50	15.00

Number	Title (A Side/B Side)	Yr	VG	VG+	NM
❏ ST-17084	The Dreaming	1982	2.50	5.00	10.00
❏ ST-17115	Never for Ever	1983	2.50	5.00	10.00
❏ ST-17171	Hounds of Love	1985	2.50	5.00	10.00
—Black vinyl					
❏ ST-17171	Hounds of Love	1985	7.50	15.00	30.00
—Marbled vinyl					
❏ PWAS-17242	The Whole Story	1986	3.75	7.50	15.00
❏ MLP-19004 [EP]	Kate Bush	1983	3.75	7.50	15.00
HARVEST					
❏ SW-11761	The Kick Inside	1978	6.25	12.50	25.00

BUSHKIN, JOE
ATLANTIC

Number	Title (A Side/B Side)	Yr	VG	VG+	NM
❏ ALR-108 [10]	I Love a Piano	1950	12.50	25.00	50.00
CAPITOL					
❏ T 711 [M]	Midnight Rhapsody	1956	7.50	15.00	30.00
—Turquoise or gray label					
❏ T 759 [M]	Skylight Rhapsody	1956	7.50	15.00	30.00
—Turquoise or gray label					
❏ T 832 [M]	A Fellow Needs a Girl	1957	7.50	15.00	30.00
—Turquoise or gray label					
❏ T 911 [M]	Bushkin Spotlights Berlin	1958	7.50	15.00	30.00
—Turquoise or gray label					
❏ ST 1094 [S]	Blue Angels	1959	7.50	15.00	30.00
—Black colorband label, logo at left					
❏ T 1094 [M]	Blue Angels	1959	5.00	10.00	20.00
—Black colorband label, logo at left					
COLUMBIA					
❏ CL 6152 [10]	Piano Moods	195?	12.50	25.00	50.00
❏ CL 6201 [10]	After Hours	195?	12.50	25.00	50.00
EPIC					
❏ LN 3345 [M]	Piano After Midnight	1956	7.50	15.00	30.00
REPRISE					
❏ RS-6119 [S]	In Concert, Town Hall	1964	5.00	10.00	20.00
ROYALE					
❏ 18118 [10]	Joe Bushkin	195?	12.50	25.00	50.00

BUSTA RHYMES
ELEKTRA

Number	Title (A Side/B Side)	Yr	VG	VG+	NM
❏ ED 6052 [(2)DJ]	When Disaster Strikes	1997	5.00	10.00	20.00
—Promo-only version					
❏ 61742 [(2)]	The Coming	1996	3.75	7.50	15.00
❏ 62064 [(2)]	When Disaster Strikes	1997	3.75	7.50	15.00
❏ 62211 [(2)]	E.L.E. (Extinction Level Event)	1998	3.75	7.50	15.00
❏ 62517 [(2)]	Anarchy	2000	3.75	7.50	15.00
J					
❏ 20009 [(2)]	Genesis	2001	5.00	10.00	20.00

BUTERA, SAM, AND THE WITNESSES
CAPITOL

Number	Title (A Side/B Side)	Yr	VG	VG+	NM
❏ ST 1098 [S]	The Big Horn	1959	10.00	20.00	40.00
❏ T 1098 [M]	The Big Horn	1958	7.50	15.00	30.00
❏ ST 1521 [S]	The Big Sax and the Big Voice	1960	7.50	15.00	30.00
❏ T 1521 [M]	The Big Sax and the Big Voice	1960	6.25	12.50	25.00
DOT					
❏ DLP-3272 [M]	The Wildest Clan	1960	5.00	10.00	20.00
❏ DLP-3381 [M]	Apache	1961	5.00	10.00	20.00
❏ DLP-25272 [S]	The Wildest Clan	1960	6.25	12.50	25.00
❏ DLP-25381 [S]	Apache	1961	6.25	12.50	25.00

BUTLER, ARTIE
A&M

Number	Title (A Side/B Side)	Yr	VG	VG+	NM
❏ SP-2007 [M]	Have You Met Miss Jones?	1968	12.50	25.00	50.00
—Mono appears to be promo only, in stereo cover with "Monaural" sticker					
❏ SP-3007 [S]	Have You Met Miss Jones?	1968	7.50	15.00	30.00

BUTLER, BILLY
PRESTIGE

Number	Title (A Side/B Side)	Yr	VG	VG+	NM
❏ PRST-7622	This Is Billy Butler	1968	6.25	12.50	25.00
❏ PRST-7734	Guitar Soul	1969	6.25	12.50	25.00
❏ PRST-7797	Yesterday, Today and Tomorrow	1970	6.25	12.50	25.00
❏ PRST-7854	Night Life	1971	6.25	12.50	25.00

BUTLER, CARL
COLUMBIA

Number	Title (A Side/B Side)	Yr	VG	VG+	NM
❏ CL 2002 [M]	Don't Let Me Cross Over	1963	5.00	10.00	20.00
❏ CS 8802 [S]	Don't Let Me Cross Over	1963	6.25	12.50	25.00
HARMONY					
❏ HL 7385 [M]	The Great Carl Butler Sings	1966	3.00	6.00	12.00
❏ HS 11185 [S]	The Great Carl Butler Sings	1966	3.75	7.50	15.00
❏ H 30674	For the First Time	1971	3.00	6.00	12.00

BUTLER, CARL, AND PEARL
CHART

Number	Title (A Side/B Side)	Yr	VG	VG+	NM
❏ 1051	Temptation Keeps Twistin' Her Arm	1972	3.75	7.50	15.00
COLUMBIA					
❏ CS 1039	Carl and Pearl Butler's Greatest Hits	1970	3.75	7.50	15.00
❏ CL 2125 [M]	Loving Arms	1964	5.00	10.00	20.00
❏ CL 2308 [M]	The Old and the New	1965	3.75	7.50	15.00
❏ CL 2640 [M]	Avenue of Prayer	1967	5.00	10.00	20.00
❏ CS 8925 [S]	Loving Arms	1964	6.25	12.50	25.00
❏ CS 9108 [S]	The Old and the New	1965	5.00	10.00	20.00
❏ CS 9440 [S]	Avenue of Prayer	1967	3.75	7.50	15.00
❏ CS 9651	Our Country World	1968	3.75	7.50	15.00
❏ CS 9769	Honky Tonkin'	1969	3.75	7.50	15.00
HARMONY					
❏ H 31182	Watch and Pray	1972	3.00	6.00	12.00

BUTLER, FREDDIE
KAPP

Number	Title (A Side/B Side)	Yr	VG	VG+	NM
❏ KS-3519	With a Dab of Soul	1968	7.50	15.00	30.00

BUTLER, JERRY

ABNER

Number	Title (A Side/B Side)	Yr	VG	VG+	NM
❑ R-2001 [M]	Jerry Butler, Esq.	1959	100.00	200.00	400.00

BUDDAH

Number	Title (A Side/B Side)	Yr	VG	VG+	NM
❑ BDS-4001	The Very Best of Jerry Butler	1969	3.75	7.50	15.00

FOUNTAIN

Number	Title (A Side/B Side)	Yr	VG	VG+	NM
❑ FR 2-82-1	Ice 'n Hot	1982	2.50	5.00	10.00

MERCURY

Number	Title (A Side/B Side)	Yr	VG	VG+	NM
❑ SRM-1-689	The Power of Love	1973	3.75	7.50	15.00
❑ SRM-1-1006	Sweet Sixteen	1974	3.75	7.50	15.00
❑ SRM-2-7502 [(2)]	The Spice of Life	1972	5.00	10.00	20.00
❑ MG-21005 [M]	The Soul Artistry of Jerry Butler	1967	5.00	10.00	20.00
❑ MG-21146 [M]	Mr. Dream Merchant	1967	5.00	10.00	20.00
❑ SR-61005 [S]	The Soul Artistry of Jerry Butler	1967	3.75	7.50	15.00
❑ SR-61146 [S]	Mr. Dream Merchant	1967	3.75	7.50	15.00
❑ SR-61151	Jerry Butler's Golden Hits Live	1968	3.75	7.50	15.00
❑ SR-61171	The Soul Goes On	1968	3.75	7.50	15.00
❑ SR-61198	The Ice Man Cometh	1968	3.75	7.50	15.00
❑ SR-61234	Ice On Ice	1969	3.75	7.50	15.00
❑ SR-61269	You & Me	1970	3.75	7.50	15.00
❑ SR-61281	The Best of Jerry Butler	1970	3.75	7.50	15.00
❑ SR-61320	Jerry Butler Sings Assorted Sounds	1971	3.75	7.50	15.00
❑ SR-61347	The Sagittarius Movement	1971	3.75	7.50	15.00
❑ 810369-1	The Best of Jerry Butler	1983	2.50	5.00	10.00
❑ 822212-1	Only the Strong Survive: The Great Philadelphia Hits	1984	2.50	5.00	10.00

MOTOWN

Number	Title (A Side/B Side)	Yr	VG	VG+	NM
❑ M6-850	Love's on the Menu	1976	3.00	6.00	12.00
❑ M6-878	Suite for the Single Girl	1977	2.50	5.00	10.00
❑ M6-892	It All Comes Out in My Songs	1977	2.50	5.00	10.00

PHILADELPHIA INT'L.

Number	Title (A Side/B Side)	Yr	VG	VG+	NM
❑ JZ 35510	Nothing Says I Love You Like I Love You	1978	2.50	5.00	10.00
❑ JZ 36413	The Best Love I Ever Had	1979	2.50	5.00	10.00

RHINO

Number	Title (A Side/B Side)	Yr	VG	VG+	NM
❑ RNLP-216	The Best of Jerry Butler (1958-1969)	1984	2.50	5.00	10.00

TRADITION

Number	Title (A Side/B Side)	Yr	VG	VG+	NM
❑ TLP-2068	Starring Jerry Butler	1969	3.75	7.50	15.00

TRIP

Number	Title (A Side/B Side)	Yr	VG	VG+	NM
❑ 8011 [(2)]	All Time Hits	1972	3.75	7.50	15.00

UNITED ARTISTS

Number	Title (A Side/B Side)	Yr	VG	VG+	NM
❑ UA-LA498-E	The Very Best of Jerry Butler	1975	2.50	5.00	10.00

VEE JAY

Number	Title (A Side/B Side)	Yr	VG	VG+	NM
❑ VJLP2-1003 [(2)]	Jerry Butler Gold	198?	3.75	7.50	15.00
❑ LP-1027 [M]	Jerry Butler, Esquire	1960	37.50	75.00	150.00
—Reissue of Abner 2001					
❑ LP-1029 [M]	He Will Break Your Heart	1960	20.00	40.00	80.00
❑ LP-1034 [M]	Love Me	1961	12.50	25.00	50.00
—Reissue of 1027					
❑ LP-1038 [M]	Aware of Love	1961	10.00	20.00	40.00
❑ SR-1038 [S]	Aware of Love	1961	12.50	25.00	50.00
❑ LP-1046 [M]	Moon River	1962	10.00	20.00	40.00
❑ SR-1046 [S]	Moon River	1962	12.50	25.00	50.00
❑ VJLP-1046	Moon River	1985	2.50	5.00	10.00
—Reissue of original 1046; has softer vinyl					
❑ LP-1048 [M]	The Best of Jerry Butler	1962	6.25	12.50	25.00
❑ SR-1048 [P]	The Best of Jerry Butler	1962	7.50	15.00	30.00
❑ VJLP-1048	The Best of Jerry Butler	1985	2.50	5.00	10.00
—Reissue of original 1048; has softer vinyl					
❑ LP-1057 [M]	Folk Songs	1963	6.25	12.50	25.00
❑ SR-1057 [S]	Folk Songs	1963	7.50	15.00	30.00
❑ LP-1075 [M]	For Your Precious Love	1963	6.25	12.50	25.00
❑ SR-1075 [S]	For Your Precious Love	1963	7.50	15.00	30.00
❑ LP-1076 [M]	Giving Up On Love/Need to Belong	1963	6.25	12.50	25.00
❑ VJS-1076 [S]	Giving Up On Love/Need to Belong	1963	7.50	15.00	30.00
❑ LP-1119 [M]	More of the Best of Jerry Butler	1965	6.25	12.50	25.00
❑ VJS-1119 [S]	More of the Best of Jerry Butler	1965	7.50	15.00	30.00
❑ D1-74807	He Will Break Your Heart	1989	3.00	6.00	12.00

BUTLER, LARRY

IMPERIAL

Number	Title (A Side/B Side)	Yr	VG	VG+	NM
❑ LP-9354 [M]	Take Me	1967	5.00	10.00	20.00
❑ LP-12354 [S]	Take Me	1967	3.75	7.50	15.00
❑ LP-12410	A Thing Called Love	1968	3.75	7.50	15.00

UNITED ARTISTS

Number	Title (A Side/B Side)	Yr	VG	VG+	NM
❑ UA-LA739-G	Larry Butler and Friends	1977	3.00	6.00	12.00

BUTTERFIELD, BILLY

CAPITOL

Number	Title (A Side/B Side)	Yr	VG	VG+	NM
❑ H 201 [10]	Stardusting	1950	12.50	25.00	50.00
❑ H 424 [10]	Classics in Jazz	195?	12.50	25.00	50.00

COLUMBIA

Number	Title (A Side/B Side)	Yr	VG	VG+	NM
❑ CL 1514 [M]	Billy Blows His Horn	1960	5.00	10.00	20.00
❑ CL 1673 [M]	The Golden Horn	1961	5.00	10.00	20.00
❑ CS 8314 [S]	Billy Blows His Horn	1960	6.25	12.50	25.00
❑ CS 8473 [S]	The Golden Horn	1961	6.25	12.50	25.00

EPIC

Number	Title (A Side/B Side)	Yr	VG	VG+	NM
❑ LA 16026 [M]	Billy Plays Bix	1962	7.50	15.00	30.00
❑ BA 17026 [S]	Billy Plays Bix	1962	10.00	20.00	40.00

ESSEX

Number	Title (A Side/B Side)	Yr	VG	VG+	NM
❑ ESLP-111 [10]	Far Away Places	195?	12.50	25.00	50.00
❑ 401 [M]	Billy Butterfield at Princeton	1955	10.00	20.00	40.00
❑ 402 [M]	Billy Butterfield Goes to NYU	1955	10.00	20.00	40.00
❑ 403 [M]	Billy Butterfield at Amherst	1955	10.00	20.00	40.00
❑ 404 [M]	Billy Butterfield at Rutgers	1955	10.00	20.00	40.00

RCA VICTOR

Number	Title (A Side/B Side)	Yr	VG	VG+	NM
❑ LPM-1212 [M]	New York Land Dixie	1956	10.00	20.00	40.00
❑ LPM-1441 [M]	They're Playing Our Song	1957	10.00	20.00	40.00
❑ LPM-1590 [M]	Thank You for a Lovely Evening	1958	7.50	15.00	30.00

WESTMINSTER

Number	Title (A Side/B Side)	Yr	VG	VG+	NM
❑ WL-3020 [10]	Billy Butterfield	1954	12.50	25.00	50.00
❑ WL-6006 [M]	Dancing for Two in Love	1955	10.00	20.00	40.00

BUTTERFIELD, ERSKINE

DAVIS

Number	Title (A Side/B Side)	Yr	VG	VG+	NM
❑ JD-104 [M]	Piano Cocktail	1951	10.00	20.00	40.00

BUTTERFIELD, PAUL

AMHERST

Number	Title (A Side/B Side)	Yr	VG	VG+	NM
❑ AMH-3305	The Legendary Paul Butterfield Rides Again	1986	3.00	6.00	12.00

BEARSVILLE

Number	Title (A Side/B Side)	Yr	VG	VG+	NM
❑ BR 2119	Paul Butterfield's Better Days	1973	3.00	6.00	12.00
❑ BR 2170	It All Comes Back	1973	3.00	6.00	12.00
❑ BR 6960	Put It In Your Ear	1976	3.00	6.00	12.00
❑ BRK 6995	North-South	1978	3.00	6.00	12.00

ELEKTRA

Number	Title (A Side/B Side)	Yr	VG	VG+	NM
❑ EKL-294 [M]	The Paul Butterfield Blues Band	1965	5.00	10.00	20.00
—Gold label with guitar player					
❑ EKL-294 [M]	The Paul Butterfield Blues Band	1966	3.75	7.50	15.00
—Brown label					
❑ EKL-315 [M]	East-West	1966	5.00	10.00	20.00
—Gold label with guitar player					
❑ EKL-315 [M]	East-West	1967	3.75	7.50	15.00
—Brown label					
❑ 7E-2001 [(2)]	The Butterfield Blues Band/Live	1970	6.25	12.50	25.00
❑ 7E-2005 [(2)]	Golden Butter/The Best of the Paul Butterfield Blues Band	1972	6.25	12.50	25.00
❑ EKL-4015 [M]	The Resurrection of Pigboy Crabshaw	1967	7.50	15.00	30.00
❑ EKS-7294 [S]	The Paul Butterfield Blues Band	1965	6.25	12.50	25.00
—Gold label with guitar player					
❑ EKS-7294 [S]	The Paul Butterfield Blues Band	1966	5.00	10.00	20.00
—Brown label					
❑ EKS-7294 [S]	The Paul Butterfield Blues Band	1969	3.75	7.50	15.00
—Red label with large stylized "E"					
❑ EKS-7294 [S]	The Paul Butterfield Blues Band	1971	3.00	6.00	12.00
—Butterfly label					
❑ EKS-7315 [S]	East-West	1966	6.25	12.50	25.00
—Gold label with guitar player					
❑ EKS-7315 [S]	East-West	1967	5.00	10.00	20.00
—Brown label					
❑ EKS-7315 [S]	East-West	1969	3.75	7.50	15.00
—Red label with large stylized "E"					
❑ EKS-7315 [S]	East-West	1971	3.00	6.00	12.00
—Butterfly label					
❑ EKS-74015 [S]	The Resurrection of Pigboy Crabshaw	1967	5.00	10.00	20.00
—Brown label					
❑ EKS-74015 [S]	The Resurrection of Pigboy Crabshaw	1969	3.75	7.50	15.00
—Red label with large stylized "E"					
❑ EKS-74015 [S]	The Resurrection of Pigboy Crabshaw	1971	3.00	6.00	12.00
—Butterfly label					
❑ EKS-74025	In My Own Dream	1968	5.00	10.00	20.00
—Brown label					
❑ EKS-74025	In My Own Dream	1969	3.75	7.50	15.00
—Red label with large stylized "E"					
❑ EKS-74025	In My Own Dream	1971	3.00	6.00	12.00
—Butterfly label					
❑ EKS-74053	Keep On Moving	1969	5.00	10.00	20.00
—Red label with large stylized "E"					
❑ EKS-74053	Keep On Moving	1971	3.00	6.00	12.00
—Butterfly label					
❑ EKS-75013	Sometimes I Just Feel Like Smilin'	1971	5.00	10.00	20.00

RHINO

Number	Title (A Side/B Side)	Yr	VG	VG+	NM
❑ RNLP-70877	Paul Butterfield's Better Days	1987	2.00	4.00	8.00
—Reissue of Bearsville 2119					
❑ RNLP-70878	It All Comes Back	1987	2.00	4.00	8.00
—Reissue of Bearsville 2170					
❑ RNLP-70879	Put It In Your Ear	1987	2.00	4.00	8.00
—Reissue of Bearsville 6960					
❑ RNLP-70880	North-South	1987	2.00	4.00	8.00
—Reissue of Bearsville 6995					

SUNDAZED

Number	Title (A Side/B Side)	Yr	VG	VG+	NM
❑ LP 5095 [S]	The Paul Butterfield Blues Band	2001	3.00	6.00	12.00
—Reissue on 180-gram vinyl					
❑ LP 5096	East-West	2001	3.00	6.00	12.00
—Reissue on 180-gram vinyl					

BUTTHOLE SURFERS

ALTERNATIVE TENTACLES

Number	Title (A Side/B Side)	Yr	VG	VG+	NM
❑ VIRUS 32 [EP]	Brown Reason to Live	198?	2.00	4.00	8.00
—Black vinyl					
❑ VIRUS 32 [EP]	Brown Reason to Live	1983	5.00	10.00	20.00
—Retitled version of debut EP with brown swirl vinyl					
❑ VIRUS 32 [EP]	Butthole Surfers	1983	6.25	12.50	25.00
—Original pressing of debut EP with no title					
❑ VIRUS 39 [EP]	Live PCPPEP	1984	2.00	4.00	8.00

CAPITOL

Number	Title (A Side/B Side)	Yr	VG	VG+	NM
❑ C1-29842 [(2)]	Electriclarryland	1996	3.75	7.50	15.00
❑ C1-98798	Independent Worm Saloon	1993	3.75	7.50	15.00

ROUGH TRADE

Number	Title (A Side/B Side)	Yr	VG	VG+	NM
❑ (# unknown)	Pioughd	1990	3.75	7.50	15.00

TOUCH & GO

Number	Title (A Side/B Side)	Yr	VG	VG+	NM
❑ 5	Psychic...Powerless...Another Man's Sac	1985	2.50	5.00	10.00
—Reissue on black vinyl					
❑ 5	Psychic...Powerless...Another Man's Sac	1985	5.00	10.00	20.00
—Original on clear vinyl					
❑ 8	Rembrandt Pussyhorse	1986	2.50	5.00	10.00
—Black vinyl					
❑ 8	Rembrandt Pussyhorse	1986	10.00	20.00	40.00
—Red vinyl; supposedly only 100 were pressed					
❑ 14 [EP]	Cream Corn from the Socket of Davis	1985	2.50	5.00	10.00
—Black vinyl					

Number	Title (A Side/B Side)	Yr	VG	VG+	NM
❑ 14 [EP]	Cream Corn from the Socket of Davis	1985	5.00	10.00	20.00
—Red vinyl					
❑ 14 [EP]	Cream Corn from the Socket of Davis	1985	6.25	12.50	25.00
—Yellow vinyl in green generic sleeve with sticker					
❑ 19	Locust Abortion Technician	1987	2.50	5.00	10.00
❑ 29	Hairway to Steven	1988	2.50	5.00	10.00
❑ 50	Widowermaker!	1989	2.50	5.00	10.00

BYARD, JAKI
MUSE
❑ 5007	There'll Be Some Changes Made	1974	5.00	10.00	20.00

NEW JAZZ
❑ NJLP-8256 [M]	Here's Jaki	1961	15.00	30.00	60.00
—Purple label					
❑ NJLP-8256 [M]	Here's Jaki	1965	7.50	15.00	30.00
—Blue label with trident logo at right					
❑ NJLP-8273 [M]	Hi-Fly	1962	15.00	30.00	60.00
—Purple label					
❑ NJLP-8273 [M]	Hi-Fly	1965	7.50	15.00	30.00
—Blue label with trident logo at right					

PRESTIGE
❑ PRLP-7397 [M]	Out Front	1965	7.50	15.00	30.00
—Blue label with trident logo at right					
❑ PRST-7397 [S]	Out Front	1965	10.00	20.00	40.00
—Blue label with trident logo at right					
❑ PRST-7397 [S]	Out Front	1968	6.25	12.50	25.00
—Blue label with trident logo in circle at top					
❑ PRLP-7419 [M]	Live!	1966	7.50	15.00	30.00
—Blue label with trident logo at right					
❑ PRST-7419 [S]	Live!	1966	10.00	20.00	40.00
—Blue label with trident logo at right					
❑ PRST-7419 [S]	Live!	1968	6.25	12.50	25.00
—Blue label with trident logo in circle at top					
❑ PRLP-7463 [M]	Freedom Together	1967	10.00	20.00	40.00
—Blue label with trident logo at right					
❑ PRST-7463 [S]	Freedom Together	1967	10.00	20.00	40.00
—Blue label with trident logo at right					
❑ PRST-7463 [S]	Freedom Together	1968	6.25	12.00	25.00
—Blue label with trident logo in circle at top					
❑ PRLP-7477 [M]	Live! Volume 2	1967	10.00	20.00	40.00
—Blue label with trident logo at right					
❑ PRST-7477 [S]	Live! Volume 2	1967	10.00	20.00	40.00
—Blue label with trident logo at right					
❑ PRST-7477 [S]	Live! Volume 2	1968	6.25	12.50	25.00
—Blue label with trident logo in circle at top					
❑ PRLP-7524 [M]	On the Spot	1967	12.50	25.00	50.00
—Blue label with trident logo at right					
❑ PRST-7524 [S]	On the Spot	1967	10.00	20.00	40.00
—Blue label with trident logo at right					
❑ PRST-7524 [S]	On the Spot	1968	6.25	12.50	25.00
—Blue label with trident logo in circle at top					
❑ PRST-7550	The Sunshine of My Soul	1968	6.25	12.50	25.00
❑ PRST-7573	Jaki Byard with Strings!	1968	6.25	12.50	25.00
❑ PRST-7615	The Jaki Byard Experience	1969	6.25	12.50	25.00
❑ PRST-7686	Solo Piano	1969	6.25	12.50	25.00
❑ 24086 [(2)]	Giant Steps	197?	5.00	10.00	20.00

BYAS, DON
ATLANTIC
❑ ALR-117 [10]	Don Byas Solos	1952	62.50	125.00	250.00

BATTLE
❑ B-6121 [M]	April in Paris	1963	7.50	15.00	30.00
❑ BS-6121 [S]	April in Paris	1963	10.00	20.00	40.00

DIAL
❑ LP-216 [10]	Tenor Saxophone Concerto	1951	75.00	150.00	300.00

DISCOVERY
❑ 3022 [10]	Don Byas with Beryl Booker	1954	37.50	75.00	150.00

EMARCY
❑ MG-26026 [10]	Don Byas Sax	1954	30.00	60.00	120.00

NORGRAN
❑ MGN-12 [10]	In France "Don Byas Et Ses Rhythmes"	1954	37.50	75.00	150.00

PRESTIGE
❑ PRST-7598	Don Byas In Paris	1969	5.00	10.00	20.00
❑ PRST-7692	Don Byas Meets Ben Webster	1969	5.00	10.00	20.00

REGENT
❑ MG-6044 [M]	Jazz Free and Easy	1957	20.00	40.00	80.00

SAVOY
❑ MG-9007 [10]	Don Byas Sax	1952	37.50	75.00	150.00
❑ MG-15043 [10]	Tenor Sax Solos	1955	30.00	60.00	120.00

SEECO
❑ SLP-35 [10]	Don Byas Favorites	1955	30.00	60.00	120.00

BYAS, DON/ BERNARD PEIFFER
VERVE
❑ MGV-8119 [M]	Jazz from Saint-Germain Des Pres	1957	12.50	25.00	50.00
❑ V-8119 [M]	Jazz from Saint-Germain Des Pres	1961	5.00	10.00	20.00

BYAS, DON/BUDDY TATE
ALLEGRO
❑ 1741	All Star Jazz	1956	10.00	20.00	40.00

BYERS, BILLY
CONCERT HALL JAZZ
❑ 1217 [M]	Byers' Guide	1955	12.50	25.00	50.00

RCA VICTOR
❑ LPM-1269 [M]	The Jazz Workshop	1956	15.00	30.00	60.00

BYERS, BRENDA
MTA
❑ 5013	The Auctioneer	1968	5.00	10.00	20.00
❑ 5016	Thank You for Loving Me	1969	5.00	10.00	20.00

BYRD, BILLY
REPRISE
Number	Title (A Side/B Side)	Yr	VG	VG+	NM
❑ R-6040 [M]	Lonesome Country Songs	1962	5.00	10.00	20.00
❑ R9-6040 [S]	Lonesome Country Songs	1962	6.25	12.50	25.00

WARNER BROS.
❑ W 1327 [M]	I Love a Guitar	1960	5.00	10.00	20.00
❑ WS 1327 [S]	I Love a Guitar	1960	6.25	12.50	25.00
❑ W 1576 [M]	The Golden Guitar of Billy Byrd	1964	5.00	10.00	20.00
❑ WS 1576 [S]	The Golden Guitar of Billy Byrd	1964	6.25	12.50	25.00

BYRD, BOBBY
KING
❑ KS-1118	I Need Help	1970	50.00	100.00	200.00

BYRD, CHARLIE
COLUMBIA
❑ CL 2592 [M]	Byrdland	1967	5.00	10.00	20.00
❑ CL 2652 [M]	Hollywood Byrd	1967	5.00	10.00	20.00
❑ CL 2692 [M]	More Brazilian Byrd	1967	5.00	10.00	20.00
❑ CS 9137 [S]	Brazilian Byrd	1965	5.00	10.00	20.00
—Red label, "360 Sound" in black					
❑ CS 9355 [S]	Christmas Carols for Solo Guitar	1966	5.00	10.00	20.00
❑ CS 9627 [M]	Hit Trip	1968	6.25	12.50	25.00
—"Special Mono Radio Station Copy" with white label					

CRYSTAL CLEAR
❑ 8002	Charlie Byrd	1979	7.50	15.00	30.00
—Direct-to-disc recording; plays at 45 rpm					

MOBILE FIDELITY
❑ 1-515	Byrd at the Gate	1982	10.00	20.00	40.00
—Audiophile vinyl					

OFFBEAT
❑ OJ-3001 [M]	Jazz at the Show Boat, Volume 1	1959	6.25	12.50	25.00
❑ OJ-3005 [M]	Jazz at the Show Boat, Volume 2	1959	6.25	12.50	25.00
❑ OJ-3006 [M]	Jazz at the Show Boat, Volume 3	1959	6.25	12.50	25.00
❑ OJ-3007 [M]	Charlie's Choice	1960	6.25	12.50	25.00
❑ OLP-3009 [M]	Blues Sonata	1960	6.25	12.50	25.00
❑ OS-93001 [S]	Jazz at the Show Boat, Volume 1	1959	7.50	15.00	30.00
❑ OS-93005 [S]	Jazz at the Show Boat, Volume 2	1959	7.50	15.00	30.00
❑ OS-93006 [S]	Jazz at the Show Boat, Volume 3	1959	7.50	15.00	30.00
❑ OS-93007 [S]	Charlie's Choice	1960	7.50	15.00	30.00
❑ OS-93009 [S]	Blues Sonata	1960	7.50	151.00	30.00

RIVERSIDE
❑ RM-427 [M]	Latin Impressions	1962	5.00	10.00	20.00
❑ RM-436 [M]	Bossa Nova Pelos Passaros	1962	5.00	10.00	20.00
❑ RM-448 [M]	Byrd's Word	1963	5.00	10.00	20.00
❑ RM-449 [M]	Byrd in the Wind	1963	5.00	10.00	20.00
❑ RM-450 [M]	Mr. Guitar	1963	5.00	10.00	20.00
❑ RM-451 [M]	The Guitar Artistry of Charlie Byrd	1963	5.00	10.00	20.00
❑ RM-452 [M]	Charlie Byrd at the Village Vanguard	1963	5.00	10.00	20.00
❑ RM-453 [M]	Blues Sonata	1963	5.00	10.00	20.00
❑ RM-454 [M]	Once More! Bossa Nova	1963	5.00	10.00	20.00
❑ RM-467 [M]	Byrd at the Gate	1964	5.00	10.00	20.00
❑ RM-498 [M]	Solo Flight	1967	5.00	10.00	20.00
❑ RS-9427 [S]	Latin Impressions	1962	6.25	12.50	25.00
❑ RS-9436 [S]	Bossa Nova Pelos Passaros	1962	6.25	12.50	25.00
❑ RS-9448 [S]	Byrd's Word	1963	6.25	12.50	25.00
❑ RS-9449 [S]	Byrd in the Wind	1963	6.25	12.50	25.00
❑ RS-9450 [S]	Mr. Guitar	1963	6.25	12.50	25.00
❑ RS-9451 [S]	The Guitar Artistry of Charlie Byrd	1963	6.25	12.50	25.00
❑ RS-9452 [S]	Charlie Byrd at the Village Vanguard	1963	6.25	12.50	25.00
❑ RS-9453 [S]	Blues Sonata	1963	6.25	12.50	25.00
❑ RS-9454 [S]	Once More! Bossa Nova	1963	6.25	12.50	25.00
❑ RS-9467 [S]	Byrd at the Gate	1964	6.25	12.50	25.00
❑ RS-9481 [S]	Byrd Song	1966	5.00	10.00	20.00

SAVOY
❑ MG-12099 [M]	Jazz Recital	1957	10.00	20.00	40.00
❑ MG-12116 [M]	Blues for Night People	1957	10.00	20.00	40.00

BYRD, CHARLIE, AND FATHER MALCOLM BOYD
COLUMBIA
❑ CS 9348 [S]	Are You Running With Me, Jesus?	1966	5.00	10.00	20.00

BYRD, CHARLIE, HERB ELLIS & BARNEY KESSEL
CONCORD JAZZ
❑ CJD-1002	Straight Tracks	1986	5.00	10.00	20.00
—Direct-to-disc recording					

BYRD, DONALD
AMERICAN RECORDING SOCIETY
❑ G-437 [M]	Modern Jazz	1957	10.00	20.00	40.00

BLUE NOTE
❑ BLP-4007 [M]	Off to the Races	1959	20.00	40.00	80.00
—W. 63rd St., NYC address on label					
❑ BLP-4007 [M]	Off to the Races	1959	30.00	60.00	120.00
—"Deep groove" version (deep indentation under label on both sides)					
❑ BLP-4007 [M]	Off to the Races	1963	6.25	12.50	25.00
—"New York, USA" address on label					
❑ BST-4007 [S]	Off to the Races	1959	15.00	30.00	60.00
—W. 63rd St., NYC address on label					
❑ BST-4007 [S]	Off to the Races	1959	20.00	40.00	80.00
—"Deep groove" version (deep indentation under label on both sides)					
❑ BST-4007 [S]	Off to the Races	1963	6.25	12.50	25.00
—"New York, USA" address on label					
❑ BLP-4019 [M]	Byrd in Hand	1959	20.00	40.00	80.00
—W. 63rd St., NYC address on label					
❑ BLP-4019 [M]	Byrd in Hand	1959	30.00	60.00	120.00
—"Deep groove" version (deep indentation under label on both sides)					
❑ BLP-4019 [M]	Byrd in Hand	1963	6.25	12.50	25.00
—"New York, USA" address on label					
❑ BLP-4026 [M]	Fuego	1960	20.00	40.00	80.00
—W. 63rd St., NYC address on label					

Number	Title (A Side/B Side)	Yr	VG	VG+	NM
❑ BLP-4026 [M]	Fuego	1960	30.00	60.00	120.00
—"Deep groove" version (deep indentation under label on both sides)					
❑ BLP-4026 [M]	Fuego	1963	6.25	12.50	25.00
—"New York, USA" address on label					
❑ BLP-4048 [M]	Byrd in Flight	1960	20.00	40.00	80.00
—W. 63rd St., NYC address on label					
❑ BLP-4048 [M]	Byrd in Flight	1960	30.00	60.00	120.00
—"Deep groove" version (deep indentation under label on both sides)					
❑ BLP-4048 [M]	Byrd in Flight	1963	6.25	12.50	25.00
—"New York, USA" address on label					
❑ BLP-4060 [M]	Donald Byrd at the Half Note Café, Volume 1	1961	20.00	40.00	80.00
—W. 63rd St., NYC address on label					
❑ BLP-4060 [M]	Donald Byrd at the Half Note Café, Volume 1	1963	6.25	12.50	25.00
—"New York, USA" address on label					
❑ BLP-4061 [M]	Donald Byrd at the Half Note Café, Volume 2	1961	20.00	40.00	80.00
—W. 63rd St., NYC address on label					
❑ BLP-4061 [M]	Donald Byrd at the Half Note Café, Volume 2	1963	6.25	12.50	25.00
—"New York, USA" address on label					
❑ BLP-4075 [M]	The Cat Walk	1961	20.00	40.00	80.00
—61st St, New York address on label					
❑ BLP-4075 [M]	The Cat Walk	1963	6.25	12.50	25.00
—"New York, USA" address on label					
❑ BLP-4101 [M]	Royal Flush	1962	5.00	10.00	20.00
❑ BLP-4118 [M]	Free Form	1963	5.00	10.00	20.00
❑ BLP-4124 [M]	A New Perspective	1964	5.00	10.00	20.00
❑ BLP-4188 [M]	I'm Tryin' to Get Home	1965	5.00	10.00	20.00
❑ BLP-4238 [M]	Mustang!	1966	5.00	10.00	20.00
❑ BLP-4259 [M]	Blackjack	1967	6.25	12.50	25.00
❑ BST-84019 [S]	Byrd in Hand	1959	15.00	30.00	60.00
—W. 63rd St., NYC address on label					
❑ BST-84019 [S]	Byrd in Hand	1963	6.25	12.50	25.00
—"New York, USA" address on label					
❑ BST-84026 [S]	Fuego	1959	15.00	30.00	60.00
—W. 63rd St., NYC address on label					
❑ BST-84026 [S]	Fuego	1963	6.25	12.50	25.00
—"New York, USA" address on label					
❑ BST-84048 [S]	Byrd in Flight	1960	15.00	30.00	60.00
—W. 63rd St., NYC address on label					
❑ BST-84048 [S]	Byrd in Flight	1963	6.25	12.50	25.00
—"New York, USA" address on label					
❑ BST-84060 [S]	Donald Byrd at the Half Note Café, Volume 1	1961	15.00	30.00	60.00
—W. 63rd St., NYC address on label					
❑ BST-84060 [S]	Donald Byrd at the Half Note Café, Volume 1	1963	6.25	12.50	25.00
—"New York, USA" address on label					
❑ BST-84061 [S]	Donald Byrd at the Half Note Café, Volume 2	1961	15.00	30.00	60.00
—W. 63rd St., NYC address on label					
❑ BST-84061 [S]	Donald Byrd at the Half Note Café, Volume 2	1963	6.25	12.50	25.00
—"New York, USA" address on label					
❑ BST-84075 [S]	The Cat Walk	1961	15.00	30.00	60.00
—61st St, New York address on label					
❑ BST-84075 [S]	The Cat Walk	1963	6.25	12.50	25.00
—"New York, USA" address on label					
❑ BST-84101 [S]	Royal Flush	1962	6.25	12.50	25.00
—"New York, USA" address on label					
❑ BST-84118 [S]	Free Form	1963	6.25	12.50	25.00
—"New York, USA" address on label					
❑ BST-84124 [S]	A New Perspective	1964	6.25	12.50	25.00
—"New York, USA" address on label					
❑ BST-84188 [S]	I'm Tryin' to Get Home	1965	6.25	12.50	25.00
—"New York, USA" address on label					
❑ BST-84238 [S]	Mustang!	1966	6.25	12.50	25.00
—"New York, USA" address on label					
❑ BST-84259 [S]	Blackjack	1967	5.00	10.00	20.00
❑ BST-84292	Slow Drag	1968	5.00	10.00	20.00
❑ BST-84319	Fancy Free	1969	5.00	10.00	20.00
❑ BST-84349	Electric	1970	5.00	10.00	20.00
❑ BST-84380	Ethiopian Nights	1972	5.00	10.00	20.00
SAVOY					
❑ MG-12032 [M]	Byrd's Word	1956	25.00	50.00	100.00
❑ MG-12064 [M]	The Jazz Message of Donald Byrd	1956	30.00	60.00	120.00
TRANSITION					
❑ TRLP-4 [M]	Byrd's Eye View	1956	150.00	300.00	600.00
❑ TRLP-5 [M]	Byrd Jazz	1956	150.00	300.00	600.00
❑ TRLP-17 [M]	Byrd Blows on Beacon Hill	1956	150.00	300.00	600.00
VERVE					
❑ V-8609 [M]	Up with Donald Byrd	1965	5.00	10.00	20.00
❑ V6-8609 [S]	Up with Donald Byrd	1965	6.25	12.50	25.00

BYRD, DONALD; HANY MOBLEY; KENNY BURRELL
STATUS

Number	Title (A Side/B Side)	Yr	VG	VG+	NM
❑ ST-8317 [M]	Donald Byrd, Hank Mobley & Kenny Burrell	1965	10.00	20.00	40.00

BYRD, JERRY
DECCA

Number	Title (A Side/B Side)	Yr	VG	VG+	NM
❑ DL 4078 [M]	Paradise Island	1961	5.00	10.00	20.00
❑ DL 8643 [M]	Hi-Fi Guitar	1958	10.00	20.00	40.00
❑ DL 74078 [S]	Paradise Island	1961	6.25	12.50	25.00
MERCURY					
❑ MG-20230 [M]	On the Shores of Waikiki	1960	7.50	15.00	30.00
❑ MG-20345 [M]	Steel Guitar Favorites	1961	7.50	15.00	30.00
❑ MG-20693 [M]	Hawaiian Golden Hits	1962	7.50	15.00	30.00
❑ MG-20856 [M]	Blue Hawaiian Steel Guitar	1963	7.50	15.00	30.00
❑ MG-20932 [M]	The Man of Steel	1964	5.00	10.00	20.00
❑ MG-25077 [10]	Nani Hawaii	1953	20.00	40.00	80.00
❑ MG-25134 [10]	Guitar Magic	1954	20.00	40.00	80.00
❑ MG-25169 [10]	Byrd's Expedition	1954	20.00	40.00	80.00
❑ SR-60230 [S]	On the Shores of Waikiki	1960	10.00	20.00	40.00
❑ SR-60345 [S]	Steel Guitar Favorites	1961	10.00	20.00	40.00
❑ SR-60693 [S]	Hawaiian Golden Hits	1962	10.00	20.00	40.00
❑ SR-60856 [S]	Blue Hawaiian Steel Guitar	1963	10.00	20.00	40.00
❑ SR-60932 [S]	The Man of Steel	1964	6.25	12.50	25.00

MONUMENT

Number	Title (A Side/B Side)	Yr	VG	VG+	NM
❑ MLP-4008 [M]	Memories of Maria	1962	5.00	10.00	20.00
❑ MLP-8009 [M]	Byrd of Paradise	1962	5.00	10.00	20.00
❑ MLP-8014 [M]	Admirable Byrd	1963	5.00	10.00	20.00
❑ SLP-14008 [S]	Memories of Maria	1962	6.25	12.50	25.00
❑ SLP-18009 [S]	Byrd of Paradise	1962	6.25	12.50	25.00
❑ SLP-18014 [S]	Admirable Byrd	1963	6.25	12.50	25.00

BYRD, JOE, AND THE FIELD HIPPIES
COLUMBIA MASTERWORKS

Number	Title (A Side/B Side)	Yr	VG	VG+	NM
❑ MS 7317	The American Metaphysical Circus	1969	10.00	20.00	40.00

BYRD, SENATOR ROBERT
COUNTY

Number	Title (A Side/B Side)	Yr	VG	VG+	NM
❑ 769	Mountain Fiddler	1978	6.25	12.50	25.00

BYRDS, THE
ASYLUM

Number	Title (A Side/B Side)	Yr	VG	VG+	NM
❑ 5058 [M]	Byrds	1973	10.00	20.00	40.00
—Mono is white label promo only; "dj copy monaural" sticker on stereo cover					
❑ SD 5058 [S]	Byrds	1973	3.00	6.00	12.00
COLUMBIA					
❑ CL 2372 [M]	Mr. Tambourine Man	1965	10.00	20.00	40.00
—"Guaranteed High Fidelity" on label					
❑ CL 2372 [M]	Mr. Tambourine Man	1966	7.50	15.00	30.00
—"360 Sound Mono" on label					
❑ CL 2454 [M]	Turn! Turn! Turn!	1965	7.50	15.00	30.00
❑ CL 2549 [M]	Fifth Dimension (5D)	1966	7.50	15.00	30.00
❑ CL 2642 [M]	Younger Than Yesterday	1967	7.50	15.00	30.00
❑ CL 2716 [M]	The Byrds' Greatest Hits	1967	7.50	15.00	30.00
❑ CL 2775 [M]	The Notorious Byrd Brothers	1968	12.50	25.00	50.00
❑ CS 9172 [S]	Mr. Tambourine Man	1965	10.00	20.00	40.00
—Red label, "360 Sound" in black					
❑ CS 9172 [S]	Mr. Tambourine Man	1966	6.25	12.50	25.00
—Red label, "360 Sound" in white					
❑ CS 9172 [S]	Mr. Tambourine Man	1971	2.50	5.00	10.00
—Orange label					
❑ PC 9172 [S]	Mr. Tambourine Man	198?	2.00	4.00	8.00
—Reissue with new prefix					
❑ CS 9254 [S]	Turn! Turn! Turn!	1965	6.25	12.50	25.00
—Red "360 Sound" label					
❑ CS 9254 [S]	Turn! Turn! Turn!	1971	2.50	5.00	10.00
—Orange label					
❑ PC 9254 [S]	Turn! Turn! Turn!	198?	2.00	4.00	8.00
—Reissue with new prefix					
❑ CS 9349 [S]	Fifth Dimension (5D)	1966	6.25	12.50	25.00
—Red "360 Sound" label					
❑ CS 9349 [S]	Fifth Dimension (5D)	1971	2.50	5.00	10.00
—Orange label					
❑ PC 9349 [S]	Fifth Dimension (5D)	198?	2.00	4.00	8.00
—Reissue with new prefix					
❑ CS 9442 [S]	Younger Than Yesterday	1967	6.25	12.50	25.00
—Red "360 Sound" label					
❑ CS 9442 [S]	Younger Than Yesterday	1971	2.50	5.00	10.00
—Orange label					
❑ PC 9442 [S]	Younger Than Yesterday	198?	2.00	4.00	8.00
—Reissue with new prefix					
❑ CS 9516 [S]	The Byrds' Greatest Hits	1967	5.00	10.00	20.00
—Red "360 Sound" label					
❑ KCS 9516 [S]	The Byrds' Greatest Hits	1971	2.50	5.00	10.00
—Orange label					
❑ PC 9516 [S]	The Byrds' Greatest Hits	197?	2.00	4.00	8.00
—Reissue with another new prefix					
❑ CS 9575 [S]	The Notorious Byrd Brothers	1968	5.00	10.00	20.00
—Red "360 Sound" label					
❑ CS 9575 [S]	The Notorious Byrd Brothers	1971	2.50	5.00	10.00
—Orange label					
❑ PC 9575 [S]	The Notorious Byrd Brothers	198?	2.00	4.00	8.00
—Reissue with new prefix					
❑ CS 9670 [S]	Sweetheart of the Rodeo	1968	25.00	50.00	100.00
—"Special Mono Radio Station Copy" with white label					
❑ CS 9670 [S]	Sweetheart of the Rodeo	1968	5.00	10.00	20.00
—Red "360 Sound" label					
❑ CS 9670 [S]	Sweetheart of the Rodeo	1971	2.50	5.00	10.00
—Orange label					
❑ PC 9670 [S]	Sweetheart of the Rodeo	198?	2.00	4.00	8.00
—Reissue with new prefix					
❑ CS 9755 [S]	Dr. Byrds and Mr. Hyde	1969	5.00	10.00	20.00
—Red "360 Sound" label					
❑ CS 9755 [S]	Dr. Byrds and Mr. Hyde	1971	2.50	5.00	10.00
—Orange label					
❑ PC 9755 [S]	Dr. Byrds and Mr. Hyde	198?	2.00	4.00	8.00
—Reissue with new prefix					
❑ CS 9942 [S]	Ballad of Easy Rider	1969	5.00	10.00	20.00
—Red "360 Sound" label					
❑ CS 9942 [S]	Ballad of Easy Rider	1971	2.50	5.00	10.00
—Orange label					
❑ PC 9942	Ballad of Easy Rider	1984	2.00	4.00	8.00
—Reissue with new prefix					
❑ G 30127 [(2)]	The Byrds (Untitled)	1970	3.75	7.50	15.00
—Without "Kathleen" listed on back cover					
❑ G 30127 [(2)]	The Byrds (Untitled)	1970	5.00	10.00	20.00
—With "Kathleen" listed on back cover (it is not on the set)					
❑ KC 30640	Byrdmaniax	1971	3.00	6.00	12.00
❑ C 31050	Farther Along	1971	3.00	6.00	12.00
❑ C 31795	The Best of the Byrds (Greatest Hits, Volume II)	197?	2.50	5.00	10.00
—Reissue with new prefix					
❑ KC 31795	The Best of the Byrds (Greatest Hits, Volume II)	1972	3.00	6.00	12.00
❑ PC 31795	The Best of the Byrds (Greatest Hits, Volume II)	198?	2.00	4.00	8.00
—Reissue with another new prefix					

Number	Title (A Side/B Side)	Yr	VG	VG+	NM
❑ C 32183	Preflyte	197?	2.50	5.00	10.00
—Reissue with new prefix					
❑ KC 32183	Preflyte	1973	3.00	6.00	12.00
—Reissue of Together LP					
❑ CG 33645 [(2)]	Mr. Tambourine Man/Turn! Turn! Turn!	1976	3.75	7.50	15.00
❑ PC 36293	The Byrds Play Dylan	1980	2.50	5.00	10.00
❑ FC 37335	The Original Singles Volume 1 (1965-1967)	1981	2.50	5.00	10.00
❑ PC 37335	The Original Singles Volume 1 (1965-1967)	1985	2.00	4.00	8.00
—Budget-line reissue					
PAIR					
❑ PDL2-1040 [(2)]	The Very Best of the Byrds	1986	3.00	6.00	12.00
RE-FLYTE					
❑ MH-70318	Never Before	1987	3.00	6.00	12.00
—Released by Muuray Hill Records via mail order					
RHINO					
❑ R1-70244	In the Beginning	1988	2.50	5.00	10.00
SUNDAZED					
❑ LP 5057	Mr. Tambourine Man	1999	3.75	7.50	15.00
—Reissue on 180-gram vinyl					
❑ LP 5058	Turn! Turn! Turn!	1999	3.75	7.50	15.00
—Reissue on 180-gram vinyl					
❑ LP 5059	Fifth Dimension	1999	3.75	7.50	15.00
—Reissue on 180-gram vinyl					
❑ LP 5060	Younger Than Yesterday	1999	3.75	7.50	15.00
—Reissue on 180-gram vinyl					
❑ LP 5061	Sanctuary	2000	3.00	6.00	12.00
❑ LP 5065	Sanctuary II	2000	3.00	6.00	12.00
❑ LP 5066	Sanctuary III	2001	3.00	6.00	12.00
❑ LP 5090	Sanctuary IV	2002	3.00	6.00	12.00
❑ LP 5114 [(2)]	The Preflyte Sessions	2001	3.75	7.50	15.00
TOGETHER					
❑ ST-T-1001	Preflyte	1969	6.25	12.50	25.00

BYRNE, BOBBY
COMMAND
❑ RS 928 SD	Sound in the 8th Dimension	1968	5.00	10.00	20.00
GRAND AWARD
❑ GA 206 SD [S]	Great Song Hits of the Tommy and Jimmy Dorsey Orchestras	1958	10.00	20.00	40.00
❑ GA 207 SD [S]	Great Song Hits of the Glenn Miller Orchestra	1958	10.00	20.00	40.00
❑ GA 225 SD [S]	Great Themes of America's Greatest Bands	1959	10.00	20.00	40.00
❑ GA 248 SD [S]	The Jazzbone's Connected to the Trombone	1959	10.00	20.00	40.00
❑ GA 33-381 [M]	Great Song Hits of the Glenn Miller Orchestra	1958	7.50	15.00	30.00
❑ GA 33-382 [M]	Great Song Hits of the Tommy and Jimmy Dorsey Orchestras	1958	7.50	15.00	30.00
❑ GA 33-392 [M]	Great Themes of America's Greatest Bands	1958	7.50	15.00	30.00
❑ GA 33-416 [M]	The Jazzbone's Connected to the Trombone	1959	7.50	15.00	30.00
WALDORF MUSIC HALL
❑ MH 33-121 [10]	Dixieland Jazz	195?	10.00	20.00	40.00

BYRNE, BOBBY; WILL BRADLEY; BUD FREEMAN
GRAND AWARD
❑ GA 33-313 [M]	Jazz, Dixieland-Chicago	1955	10.00	20.00	40.00

BYRNE, DAVID
VIRGIN
❑ PR 2204 [DJ]	The Making of The Last Emperor: An Interview with David Byrne and Ryuichi Sakamoto	1988	6.25	12.50	25.00

BYRNES, EDD
WARNER BROS.
❑ W 1309 [M]	Kookie	1959	25.00	50.00	100.00
❑ W/WS 1309	Kookie Bonus Photo	1959	12.50	25.00	50.00
❑ WS 1309 [S]	Kookie	1959	30.00	60.00	120.00

BYRON, GEORGE
ATLANTIC
❑ 1293 [M]	Premiere Performance	1958	10.00	20.00	40.00
—Blue label					
❑ SD 1293 [S]	Premiere Performance	1958	12.50	25.00	50.00
—Green label					

C

C.A. QUINTET, THE
CANDY FLOSS
❑ 7764	A Trip Through Hell	1969	500.00	1000.	1500.
SUNDAZED
❑ LP-5037 [(2)]	Trip Thru Hell	1997	3.75	7.50	15.00

C.C.S.
RAK
❑ Z 30559	Whole Lotta Love	1971	5.00	10.00	20.00
❑ KZ 31569	C.C.S.	1972	5.00	10.00	20.00

C.K. STRONG
EPIC
❑ BN 26473	C.K. Strong	1969	5.00	10.00	20.00

CABARET VOLTAIRE
CAROLINE
❑ CAROL 1331	The Covenant, the Sword, and the Arm of the Lord	1985	2.50	5.00	10.00
❑ CAROL 2451 [(2)EP]	Drinking Gasoline	1985	3.75	7.50	15.00
GIANT
❑ GR-16009	Eight Crepuscule Tracks	1988	3.75	7.50	15.00
MANHATTAN
❑ MLT-46999	Code	1987	3.75	7.50	15.00
RESTLESS
❑ 71475	Listen Up with Cabaret Voltaire	1990	2.50	5.00	10.00
❑ 71476	The Living Legends	1990	2.50	5.00	10.00
ROUGH TRADE
❑ ROUGH US-9	The Voice of America	1980	5.00	10.00	20.00
❑ TRADE US-12 [EP]	Three Crepuscule Tracks	1981	3.00	6.00	12.00
❑ ROUGH US-15	Red Mecca	1981	5.00	10.00	20.00
❑ ROUGH US-24	Hai! Live in Japan	1982	5.00	10.00	20.00

CABOT, SEBASTIAN
MGM
❑ E-4431 [M]	Sebastian Cabot, Actor; Bob Dylan, Poet: A Dramatic Reading with Music	1967	7.50	15.00	30.00
❑ SE-4431 [S]	Sebastian Cabot, Actor; Bob Dylan, Poet: A Dramatic Reading with Music	1967	10.00	20.00	40.00

CACTUS
ATCO
❑ SD 33-340	Cactus	1970	5.00	10.00	20.00
❑ SD 33-356	One Way...Or Another	1971	5.00	10.00	20.00
❑ SD 33-377	Restrictions	1971	5.00	10.00	20.00
❑ SD 7011	'Ot 'N' Sweaty	1972	5.00	10.00	20.00

CADETS, THE
CROWN
❑ CST-370 [R]	The Cadets	1963	25.00	50.00	100.00
❑ CLP-5015 [M]	Rockin' 'n' Reelin'	1957	62.50	125.00	250.00
—Black label					
❑ CLP-5370 [M]	The Cadets	1963	37.50	75.00	150.00
MODERN
❑ LPM-1215 [M]	Rockin' 'n' Reelin'	1956	—	—	—
—Canceled					
RELIC
❑ 5025	The Cadets' Greatest Hits	197?	3.00	6.00	12.00

CADILLACS, THE
HARLEM HIT PARADE
❑ 5009	Cruisin' with the Cadillacs	197?	2.50	5.00	10.00
JUBILEE
❑ JGM-1045 [M]	The Fabulous Cadillacs	1957	100.00	200.00	400.00
—Blue label					
❑ JGM-1045 [M]	The Fabulous Cadillacs	1959	62.50	125.00	250.00
—Flat black label					
❑ JGM-1045 [M]	The Fabulous Cadillacs	1960	25.00	50.00	100.00
—Glossy black label					
❑ JGM-1089 [M]	The Crazy Cadillacs	1959	75.00	150.00	300.00
—Flat black label					
❑ JGM-1089 [M]	The Crazy Cadillacs	1960	25.00	50.00	100.00
—Glossy black label					
❑ JGM-5009 [M]	Twisting with the Cadillacs	1962	50.00	100.00	200.00
MURRAY HILL
❑ 1195	The Very Best of the Cadillacs	198?	3.75	7.50	15.00
❑ 1285 [(5)]	The Cadillacs	198?	10.00	20.00	40.00
—Box set					

CADILLACS, THE/ THE ORIOLES
Also see each artist's individual listings.
JUBILEE
❑ JGM-1117 [M]	The Cadillacs Meet the Orioles	1961	50.00	100.00	200.00

CAGLE, BUDDY
IMPERIAL
❑ LP-9318 [M]	The Way You Like It	1966	5.00	10.00	20.00
❑ LP-9348 [M]	Mi Casa, Tu Casa	1967	5.00	10.00	20.00
❑ LP-9361 [M]	Longtime Traveling	1967	7.50	15.00	30.00
❑ LP-12318 [S]	The Way You Like It	1966	6.25	12.50	25.00
❑ LP-12348 [S]	Mi Casa, Tu Casa	1967	6.25	12.50	25.00
❑ LP-12361 [S]	Longtime Traveling	1967	6.25	12.50	25.00
❑ LP-12374	Through a Crack in a Boxcar Door	1968	6.25	12.50	25.00

CAIN
A.S.I.
❑ 204	A Pound of Flesh	1974	15.00	30.00	60.00
❑ 214	Stinger	1975	10.00	20.00	40.00

Number	Title (A Side/B Side)	Yr	VG	VG+	NM

CAIN, JACKIE, AND ROY KRAL
ABC-PARAMOUNT
❏ ABC-120 [M]	The Glory of Love	1956	12.50	25.00	50.00
❏ ABC-163 [M]	Bits and Pieces	1957	12.50	25.00	50.00
❏ ABC-207 [M]	Free and Easy	1958	12.50	25.00	50.00
❏ ABC-267 [M]	In the Spotlight	1959	10.00	20.00	40.00
❏ ABCS-267 [S]	In the Spotlight	1959	12.50	25.00	50.00

BRUNSWICK
❏ BL 54026 [M]	Jackie Cain and Roy Kral	1957	12.50	25.00	50.00

COLUMBIA
❏ CL 1469 [M]	Sweet and Low Down	1960	6.25	12.50	25.00
❏ CL 1704 [M]	Double Take	1961	6.25	12.50	25.00
❏ CL 1934 [M]	Like Sing	1963	5.00	10.00	20.00
❏ CS 8260 [S]	Sweet and Low Down	1960	7.50	15.00	30.00
❏ CS 8504 [S]	Double Take	1961	7.50	15.00	30.00
❏ CS 8734 [S]	Like Sing	1963	6.25	12.50	25.00

REGENT
❏ MG-6057 [M]	Jackie & Roy	1957	12.	25.00	50.00

ROULETTE
❏ R-25278 [M]	By Jupiter & Girl Crazy	1964	5.00	10.00	20.00
❏ SR-25278 [S]	By Jupiter & Girl Crazy	1964	6.25	12.50	25.00

SAVOY
❏ MG-12198 [M]	Jackie and Roy	196?	5.00	10.00	20.00

STORYVILLE
❏ STLP-322 [10]	Jackie & Roy	1955	30.00	60.00	120.00
❏ STLP-904 [M]	Storyville Presents Jackie & Roy	1955	15.00	30.00	60.00
❏ STLP-915 [M]	Sing Baby, Sing!	1956	15.00	30.00	60.00

VERVE
❏ V-8668 [M]	Changes	1966	5.00	10.00	20.00
❏ V6-8668 [S]	Changes	1966	6.25	12.50	25.00
❏ V-8688 [M]	Lovesick	1967	6.25	12.50	25.00
❏ V6-8688 [S]	Lovesick	1967	5.00	10.00	20.00

CAIOLA, AL
ATCO
❏ 33-117 [M]	Music for Space Squirrels	1960	6.25	12.50	25.00
❏ SD 33-117 [S]	Music for Space Squirrels	1960	7.50	15.00	30.00

AVALANCHE
❏ AV-LA058-F	The Magnificent Seven Ride '73	1973	2.50	5.00	10.00
❏ 9201	The Magnificent Seven	1972	3.00	6.00	12.00

AVCO EMBASSY
❏ 33019	Bonanza Guitars/50 Years of the Greatest Country Music	1971	2.50	5.00	10.00

BAINBRIDGE
❏ 1010	Soft Guitars	198?	2.00	4.00	8.00
❏ 1023	Italian Guitars	198?	2.00	4.00	8.00
❏ 1030	Guitar of Plenty	198?	2.00	4.00	8.00

CHANCELLOR
❏ CHL-5008 [M]	Great Pickin'	1960	6.25	12.50	25.00
❏ CHS-5008 [S]	Great Pickin'	1960	7.50	15.00	30.00

PICKWICK
❏ SPC-3034	Italian Style	196?	3.00	6.00	12.00

RCA CAMDEN
❏ CAL-710 [M]	The Guitar Style of Al Caiola	1962	3.00	6.00	12.00
❏ CAS-710 [S]	The Guitar Style of Al Caiola	1962	3.75	7.50	15.00
❏ CAS-2569	Music from "The Godfather"	1972	2.50	5.00	10.00

RCA VICTOR
❏ LPM-2031 [M]	High Strung	1959	6.25	12.50	25.00
❏ LSP-2031 [S]	High Strung	1959	7.50	15.00	30.00

ROULETTE
❏ R 25108 [M]	Salute Italia	1960	5.00	10.00	20.00
❏ SR 25108 [S]	Salute Italia	1960	6.25	12.50	25.00
❏ SR-42008	Roman Guitar	1968	2.50	5.00	10.00

SAVOY
❏ MG-12033 [M]	Deep in a Dream	1955	10.00	20.00	40.00
❏ MG-12057 [M]	Serenade in Blue	1956	10.00	20.00	40.00

SUNSET
❏ SUS-5292	Guitar in Love	1970	2.50	5.00	10.00

TIME
❏ S-2000 [S]	Percussion and Guitars	1960	6.25	12.50	25.00
❏ S-2006 [S]	Percussion Espanol	1960	6.25	12.50	25.00
❏ S-2026 [S]	Percussion Espanol, Vol. 2	1960	6.25	12.50	25.00
❏ S-2039 [S]	Spanish Guitars	1960	6.25	12.50	25.00
❏ S-2101 [S]	Gershwin and Guitars	1961	6.25	12.50	25.00
❏ 52000 [M]	Percussion and Guitars	1960	5.00	10.00	20.00
❏ 52006 [M]	Percussion Espanol	1960	5.00	10.00	20.00
❏ 52026 [M]	Percussion Espanol, Vol. 2	1960	5.00	10.00	20.00
❏ 52039 [M]	Spanish Guitars	1960	5.00	10.00	20.00
❏ 52101 [M]	Gershwin and Guitars	1961	5.00	10.00	20.00

UNITED ARTISTS
❏ UAL-3133 [M]	The Magnificent Seven	1960	5.00	10.00	20.00
❏ UAL-3142 [M]	Golden Instrumental Hits	1961	3.00	6.00	12.00
❏ UAL-3161 [M]	Hit Instrumentals from TV Westerns	1961	3.75	7.50	15.00
❏ UAL-3180 [M]	Solid Gold Guitar	1962	3.00	6.00	12.00
❏ UAL-3228 [M]	Midnight Dance Party	1962	3.00	6.00	12.00
❏ UAL-3240 [M]	Golden Guitar	1962	3.00	6.00	12.00
❏ UAL-3255 [M]	City Guy Goes Country	1963	3.00	6.00	12.00
❏ UAL-3256 [M]	Acapulco 1922 and The Lonely Bull	1963	3.00	6.00	12.00
❏ UAL-3263 [M]	Paradise Village	1963	3.00	6.00	12.00
❏ UAL-3276 [M]	Ciao	1963	3.00	6.00	12.00
❏ UAL-3280 [M]	Give Me the Simple Life	1963	3.00	6.00	12.00
❏ UAL-3299 [M]	Cleopatra and All That Jazz	1963	6.25	12.50	25.00
❏ UAL-3310 [M]	The Best of Al Caiola	1964	3.00	6.00	12.00
❏ UAL-3330 [M]	50 Fabulous Guitar Favorites	1964	3.00	6.00	12.00
❏ UAL-3354 [M]	50 Fabulous Italian Favorites	1964	3.00	6.00	12.00
❏ UAL-3362 [M]	On the Trail	1964	3.00	6.00	12.00
❏ UAL-3389 [M]	Tuff Guitar	1965	3.00	6.00	12.00

Number	Title (A Side/B Side)	Yr	VG	VG+	NM
❏ UAL-3403 [M]	Guitar for Lovers	1965	3.00	6.00	12.00
❏ UAL-3405 [M]	Have Guitar Will Travel	1965	3.00	6.00	12.00
❏ UAL-3418 [M]	Solid Gold Guitar Goes Hawaiian	1965	3.00	6.00	12.00
❏ UAL-3435 [M]	Sounds for Spies and Private Eyes	1965	3.75	7.50	15.00
❏ UAL-3454 [M]	Tuff Guitar English Style	1966	3.00	6.00	12.00
❏ UAS-6133 [S]	The Magnificent Seven	1960	6.25	12.50	25.00
❏ UAS-6142 [S]	Golden Instrumental Hits	1961	3.75	7.50	15.00
❏ UAS-6161 [S]	Hit Instrumentals from TV Westerns	1961	5.00	10.00	20.00
❏ UAS-6180 [S]	Solid Gold Guitar	1962	3.75	7.50	15.00
❏ UAS-6228 [S]	Midnight Dance Party	1962	3.75	7.50	15.00
❏ UAS-6240 [S]	Golden Guitar	1962	3.75	7.50	15.00
❏ UAS-6255 [S]	City Guy Goes Country	1963	3.75	7.50	15.00
❏ UAS-6256 [S]	Acapulco 1922 and The Lonely Bull	1963	3.75	7.50	15.00
❏ UAS-6263 [S]	Paradise Village	1963	3.75	7.50	15.00
❏ UAS-6276 [S]	Ciao	1963	3.75	7.50	15.00
❏ UAS-6280 [S]	Give Me the Simple Life	1963	3.75	7.50	15.00
❏ UAS-6299 [S]	Cleopatra and All That Jazz	1963	7.50	15.00	30.00
❏ UAS-6310 [S]	The Best of Al Caiola	1964	3.75	7.50	15.00
❏ UAS-6330 [S]	50 Fabulous Guitar Favorites	1964	3.75	7.50	15.00
❏ UAS-6354 [S]	50 Fabulous Italian Favorites	1964	3.75	7.50	15.00
❏ UAS-6362 [S]	On the Trail	1964	3.75	7.50	15.00
❏ UAS-6389 [S]	Tuff Guitar	1965	3.75	7.50	15.00
❏ UAS-6403 [S]	Guitar for Lovers	1965	3.75	7.50	15.00
❏ UAS-6405 [S]	Have Guitar Will Travel	1965	3.75	7.50	15.00
❏ UAS-6418 [S]	Solid Gold Guitar Goes Hawaiian	1965	3.75	7.50	15.00
❏ UAS-6435 [S]	Sounds for Spies and Private Eyes	1965	5.00	10.00	20.00
❏ UAS-6454 [S]	Tuff Guitar English Style	1966	3.75	7.50	15.00
❏ UAS-6712	Let the Sunshine In	1969	2.50	5.00	10.00

CAJUN PETE
MERCURY
❏ MG-20633 [M]	Tales of the Bayou	1961	5.00	10.00	20.00
❏ SR-60633 [S]	Tales of the Bayou	1961	6.25	12.50	25.00

CAKE, THE
DECCA
❏ DL 4927 [M]	The Cake	1967	5.00	10.00	20.00
❏ DL 74927 [S]	The Cake	1967	6.25	12.50	25.00
❏ DL 75039	A Slice of the Cake	1968	6.25	12.50	25.00

CALDWELL, LOUISE HARRISON
RECAR
❏ 2012 [M]	All About the Beatles	1965	37.50	75.00	150.00
—Without insert					
❏ 2012 [M]	All About the Beatles	1965	50.00	100.00	200.00
—With insert					

CALE, JOHN
Also see THE VELVET UNDERGROUND.
A&M
❏ SP-4849	Honi Soit	1981	2.50	5.00	10.00

ANTILLES
❏ AN-7063	Guts	198?	3.00	6.00	12.00
—Reissue of Island 9459					

COLUMBIA
❏ CS 1037	Vintage Violence	1970	6.25	12.50	25.00
—Red "360 Sound" label					
❏ CS 1037	Vintage Violence	1971	3.75	7.50	15.00
—Orange label					
❏ C 30131	Church of Anthrax	1971	3.75	7.50	15.00

ISLAND
❏ IXP-2 [DJ]	Hear Fear	1975	15.00	30.00	60.00
—Promo-only interview album					
❏ IT-8401	Caribbean Sunset	1984	2.50	5.00	10.00
❏ IT-8402	John Cale Comes Alive	1984	2.50	5.00	10.00
❏ ILPS 9301	Fear	1975	5.00	10.00	20.00
❏ ILPS 9317	Slow Dazzle	1975	3.75	7.50	15.00
❏ ILPS 9350	Helen of Troy	1975	5.00	10.00	20.00
❏ ILPS 9459	Guts	1977	5.00	10.00	20.00

OPAL/WARNER BROS.
❏ 26024	Words for the Dying	1989	3.00	6.00	12.00

PASSPORT
❏ PB 6019	Music for a New Society	1982	3.00	6.00	12.00

PVC
❏ 8947	Artificial Intelligence	1985	3.75	7.50	15.00

REPRISE
❏ MS 2079	The Academy in Peril	1972	6.25	12.50	25.00
❏ MS 2131	Paris, 1919	1973	6.25	12.50	25.00

SPY/I.R.S.
❏ SP-004	Sabotage/Live	1980	3.75	7.50	15.00

CALIFORNIA, RANDY
EPIC
❏ KE 31755	Kapt. Kopter & the Fabulous Twirly Birds	1972	6.25	12.50	25.00
—Yellow label					
❏ KE 31755	Kapt. Kopter & the Fabulous Twirly Birds	1973	3.00	6.00	12.00
—Orange label					

CALIFORNIA POPPY PICKERS, THE
ALSHIRE
❏ S-5153	Hair-Aquarius	1969	7.50	15.00	30.00
❏ S-5167	Honky Tonk Women	1970	10.00	20.00	40.00

CALIMAN, HADLEY
MAINSTREAM
❏ MRL-318	Hadley Caliman	1971	5.00	10.00	20.00
❏ MRL-342	Iapetus	1972	5.00	10.00	20.00

CALLENDER, BOBBY
MGM
❏ SE-4557	Rainbow	1968	37.50	75.00	150.00

Number	Title (A Side/B Side)	Yr	VG	VG+	NM
CALLENDER, RED					
CROWN					
☐ CLP-5012 [M]	Callender Speaks Low	1957	10.00	20.00	40.00
☐ CLP-5025 [M]	Swingin' Suite	1957	10.00	20.00	40.00
METROJAZZ					
☐ E-1007 [M]	The Lowest	1958	12.50	25.00	50.00
☐ SE-1007 [S]	The Lowest	1959	10.00	20.00	40.00
MODERN					
☐ MLP-1201 [M]	Swingin' Suite	1956	20.00	40.00	80.00
CALLIOPE					
BUDDAH					
☐ BDS-5023	Steamed	1968	5.00	10.00	20.00
CALLOWAY, CAB					
BRUNSWICK					
☐ BL 58101 [10]	Cab Calloway	1954	25.00	50.00	100.00
COLUMBIA					
☐ CG 32593 [(2)]	The Hi De Ho Man	1973	5.00	10.00	20.00
CORAL					
☐ CRL 57408 [M]	Blues Make Me Happy	1962	6.25	12.50	25.00
☐ CRL 757408 [S]	Blues Make Me Happy	1962	7.50	15.00	30.00
EPIC					
☐ LN 3265 [M]	Swing Showman	1957	12.50	25.00	50.00
GONE					
☐ LP-101 [M]	Cotton Club Revue '58	1958	20.00	40.00	80.00
RCA VICTOR					
☐ LPM-2021 [M]	Hi De Hi De Ho	1958	7.50	15.00	30.00
☐ LSP-2021 [S]	Hi De Hi De Ho	1958	10.00	20.00	40.00
CAMARATA					
BUENA VISTA					
☐ BV-3319 [M]	33 Great Walt Disney Motion Picture Melodies	1963	6.25	12.50	25.00
☐ STER-3319 [S]	33 Great Walt Disney Motion Picture Melodies	1963	7.50	15.00	30.00
☐ BV-3321 [M]	The Changing Seasons	1964	5.00	10.00	20.00
☐ STER-3321 [S]	The Changing Seasons	1964	7.50	15.00	30.00
☐ BV-3322 [M]	In the Still of the Night	1959	5.00	10.00	20.00
☐ STER-3322 [S]	In the Still of the Night	1960	7.50	15.00	30.00
☐ BV-3330 [M]	Tinpanorama	1965	5.00	10.00	20.00
☐ BV-4023 [M]	Camarata Conducts a Modern Interpretation of Snow White and the Seven Dwarfs	1963	7.50	15.00	30.00
—Gatefold cover					
☐ BV-4023 [M]	Camarata Conducts a Modern Interpretation of Snow White and the Seven Dwarfs	1967	5.00	10.00	20.00
—Regular cover					
☐ STER-4023 [S]	Camarata Conducts a Modern Interpretation of Snow White and the Seven Dwarfs	1963	10.00	20.00	40.00
—Gatefold cover					
☐ STER-4023 [S]	Camarata Conducts a Modern Interpretation of Snow White and the Seven Dwarfs	1967	6.25	12.50	25.00
—Regular cover					
☐ BV-4047	Camarata Featuring Tutti's Trumpets	1970	5.00	10.00	20.00
—Reissue of 3011					
☐ BV-4048	Camarata Featuring Tutti's Trombones	1970	5.00	10.00	20.00
DISNEYLAND					
☐ (# unknown) [(4)M]	Music of the Seasons	1959	10.00	20.00	40.00
—Box set with mono versions of 3021, 3026, 3027 and 3032					
☐ (# unknown) [(4)S]	Music of the Seasons	1959	20.00	40.00	80.00
—Box set with stereo versions of 3021, 3026, 3027 and 3032					
☐ DQ-1232 [M]	A Child's Introduction to Melody and Instruments of the Orchestra	1963	5.00	10.00	20.00
☐ STER-3011 [S]	Tutti's Trumpets	1959	7.50	15.00	30.00
☐ WDL-3011 [M]	Tutti's Trumpets	1957	5.00	10.00	20.00
☐ STER-3021 [S]	Autumn	1959	7.50	15.00	30.00
☐ WDL-3021 [M]	Autumn	1958	5.00	10.00	20.00
☐ STER-3026 [S]	Winter	1959	7.50	15.00	30.00
☐ WDL-3026 [M]	Winter	1958	5.00	10.00	20.00
☐ STER-3027 [S]	Summer	1959	6.25	12.50	25.00
☐ WDL-3027 [M]	Summer	1958	5.00	10.00	20.00
☐ STER-3032 [S]	Spring	1959	6.25	12.50	25.00
☐ WDL-3032 [M]	Spring	1958	5.00	10.00	20.00
☐ WDL-4009 [M]	Camarata Interprets Music from Cinderella and Bambi	1957	15.00	30.00	60.00
CAMBRIDGE, GODFREY					
EPIC					
☐ FLM 13101 [M]	Ready or Not…Here's Godfrey Cambridge	1964	5.00	10.00	20.00
☐ FLM 13102 [M]	Them Cotton Pickin' Days Is Over	1965	5.00	10.00	20.00
☐ FLM 13108 [M]	Godfrey Cambridge Toys with the World	1966	5.00	10.00	20.00
☐ FLM 13115 [M]	The Godfrey Cambridge Show Live at the Aladdin	1968	5.00	10.00	20.00
☐ FLS 15101 [S]	Ready or Not…Here's Godfrey Cambridge	1964	5.00	10.00	20.00
☐ FLS 15102 [S]	Them Cotton Pickin' Days Is Over	1965	5.00	10.00	20.00
☐ FLS 15108 [S]	Godfrey Cambridge Toys with the World	1966	5.00	10.00	20.00
☐ FLS 15115 [S]	The Godfrey Cambridge Show Live at the Aladdin	1968	5.00	10.00	20.00
CAMERON, JOHN					
DERAM					
☐ DES 18033	Off Centre	1969	5.00	10.00	20.00
CAMP, HAMILTON					
ELEKTRA					
☐ EKL-278 [M]	Paths of Victory	1965	6.25	12.50	25.00
☐ EKS-7278 [S]	Paths of Victory	1965	7.50	15.00	30.00
CAMP, RED					
COOK					
☐ LP-1087 [10]	Camp Inventions: Bold New Design for Jazz Piano	1955	12.50	25.00	50.00
☐ LP-1089 [10]	Red Camp	1955	12.50	25.00	50.00

Number	Title (A Side/B Side)	Yr	VG	VG+	NM
☐ LP-5005 [M]	Camp Has a Ball	1957	10.00	20.00	40.00
CAMPBELL, ALEX					
STARDAY					
☐ SLP-214 [M]	16 Radio Favorites	1963	6.25	12.50	25.00
☐ SLP-342 [M]	Travel On	1965	6.25	12.50	25.00
CAMPBELL, ARCHIE					
RCA VICTOR					
☐ LPM-3504 [M]	Have a Laugh on Me	1966	5.00	10.00	20.00
☐ LSP-3504 [S]	Have a Laugh on Me	1966	6.25	2.50	25.00
☐ LPM-3699 [M]	The Cockfight and Other Tall Tales	1967	5.00	10.00	20.00
☐ LSP-3699 [S]	The Cockfight and Other Tall Tales	1967	6.25	12.50	25.00
☐ LPM-3780 [M]	Kids I Love 'Em	1967	6.25	12.50	25.00
☐ LSP-3780 [S]	Kids I Love 'Em	1967	5.00	10.00	20.00
☐ LPM-3892 [M]	The Golden Years	1967	6.25	12.50	25.00
☐ LSP-3892 [S]	The Golden Years	1967	5.00	10.00	20.00
STARDAY					
☐ SLP-162 [M]	Make Friends with Archie Campbell	1962	7.50	15.00	30.00
☐ SLP-167 [M]	Bedtime Stories for Adults	1962	7.50	15.00	30.00
☐ SLP-223 [M]	The Joker Is Wild	1963	7.50	15.00	30.00
☐ SLP-377 [M]	The Grand Ole Opry's Good Humor Man	1966	6.25	12.50	25.00
CAMPBELL, ARCHIE, AND LORENE MANN					
RCA VICTOR					
☐ LSP-4086	Archie and Lorene Tell It Like It Is	1968	5.00	10.00	20.00
CAMPBELL, CECIL					
STARDAY					
☐ SLP-254 [M]	Steel Guitar Jamboree	1963	10.00	20.00	40.00
CAMPBELL, CHOKER					
MOTOWN					
☐ M-620 [M]	Hits of the Sixties	1964	25.00	50.00	100.00
☐ MS-620 [S]	Hits of the Sixties	1964	37.50	75.00	150.00
CAMPBELL, DICK					
MERCURY					
☐ MG-21060 [M]	Dick Campbell Sings Where It's At	1966	7.50	15.00	30.00
☐ SR-61060 [S]	Dick Campbell Sings Where It's At	1966	10.00	20.00	40.00
CAMPBELL, GLEN					
ATLANTIC AMERICA					
☐ 90016	Old Home Town	1983	2.00	4.00	8.00
☐ 90164	Letter to Home	1984	2.00	4.00	8.00
☐ 90483	It's Just a Matter of Time	1985	2.00	4.00	8.00
CAPITOL					
☐ SM-103	Wichita Lineman	1977	2.00	4.00	8.00
—Reissue with new prefix					
☐ ST-103	Wichita Lineman	1968	3.75	7.50	15.00
☐ ST-8-0103	Wichita Lineman	1968	5.00	10.00	20.00
—Capitol Record Club edition					
☐ ST-210	Galveston	1969	3.75	7.50	15.00
☐ STBO-268	Glen Campbell — "Live"	1969	5.00	10.00	20.00
☐ SM-389	Try a Little Kindness	1977	2.00	4.00	8.00
—Reissue with new prefix					
☐ SW-389	Try a Little Kindness	1970	3.00	6.00	12.00
☐ SW-443	Oh Happy Day	1970	3.00	6.00	12.00
☐ SW-493	The Glen Campbell Goodtime Album	1970	3.00	6.00	12.00
☐ SM-733	The Last Time I Saw Her	1977	2.00	4.00	8.00
—Reissue with new prefix					
☐ SW-733	The Last Time I Saw Her	1971	3.00	6.00	12.00
☐ SW-752	Glen Campbell's Greatest Hits	1971	3.00	6.00	12.00
☐ ST 1810 [S]	Big Bluegrass Special	1962	25.00	50.00	100.00
—As "The Green River Boys Featuring Glen Campbell"					
☐ T 1810 [M]	Big Bluegrass Special	1962	20.00	40.00	80.00
—As "The Green River Boys Featuring Glen Campbell"					
☐ ST 1881 [S]	Too Late to Worry, Too Blue to Cry	1963	6.25	12.50	25.00
☐ T 1881 [M]	Too Late to Worry, Too Blue to Cry	1963	5.00	10.00	20.00
☐ ST 2023 [S]	The Astounding 12-String Guitar of Glen Campbell	1964	5.00	10.00	20.00
☐ T 2023 [M]	The Astounding 12-String Guitar of Glen Campbell	1964	3.75	7.50	15.00
☐ ST 2392 [S]	The Big Bad Rock Guitar of Glen Campbell	1965	5.00	10.00	20.00
☐ T 2392 [M]	The Big Bad Rock Guitar of Glen Campbell	1965	3.75	7.50	15.00
☐ ST 2679 [S]	Burning Bridges	1967	3.75	7.50	15.00
☐ T 2679 [M]	Burning Bridges	1967	3.75	7.50	15.00
☐ ST 2809 [S]	Gentle on My Mind	1967	3.75	7.50	15.00
☐ T 2809 [M]	Gentle on My Mind	1967	3.75	7.50	15.00
☐ ST 2851 [S]	By the Time I Get to Phoenix	1967	3.75	7.50	15.00
☐ T 2851 [M]	By the Time I Get to Phoenix	1967	3.75	7.50	15.00
☐ ST 2878 [S]	Hey, Little One	1968	3.75	7.50	15.00
☐ T 2878 [M]	Hey, Little One	1968	6.25	12.50	25.00
☐ ST 2907	A New Place in the Sun	1968	3.75	7.50	15.00
☐ ST 2978	That Christmas Feeling	1968	3.75	7.50	15.00
☐ SW-11117	Glen Travis Campbell	1972	2.50	5.00	10.00
☐ SW-11185	I Knew Jesus (Before He Was a Star)	1973	2.50	5.00	10.00
☐ SW-11253	I Remember Hank Williams	1973	2.50	5.00	10.00
☐ SW-11293	Hosuton (I'm Comin' to See You)	1974	2.50	5.00	10.00
☐ SW-11336	Reunion (The Songs of Jimmy Webb)	1974	2.50	5.00	10.00
☐ SM-11407	Arkansas	1977	2.00	4.00	8.00
—Reissue with new prefix					
☐ SW-11407	Arkansas	1975	2.50	5.00	10.00
☐ SW-11430	Rhinestone Cowboy	1975	2.50	5.00	10.00
☐ SW-11516	Bloodline	1976	2.50	5.00	10.00
☐ ST-11577	The Best of Glen Campbell	1976	2.50	5.00	10.00
☐ SO-11601	Southern Nights	1977	2.50	5.00	10.00
☐ SWBC-11707 [(2)]	Live at the Royal Festival Hall	1977	3.00	6.00	12.00
☐ SW-11722	Basic	1978	2.50	5.00	10.00
☐ SM-11960	Gentle on My Mind	1979	2.00	4.00	8.00
—Reissue of 2809					
☐ SOO-12008	Highwayman	1979	2.50	5.00	10.00

Number	Title (A Side/B Side)	Yr	VG	VG+	NM
❏ SM-12040	By the Time I Get to Phoenix	1979	2.00	4.00	8.00
—Reissue of 2851					
❏ SOO-12075	Somethin' 'Bout You Baby I Like	1980	2.50	5.00	10.00
❏ SOO-12124	It's the World Gone Crazy	1981	2.50	5.00	10.00
❏ SN-16029	Rhinestone Cowboy	1980	—	3.00	6.00
—Budget-line reissue					
❏ SN-16030	Southern Nights	1980	—	3.00	6.00
—Budget-line reissue					
❏ SN-16031	Glen Travis Campbell	1980	—	3.00	6.00
—Budget-line reissue					
❏ SN-16160	Wichita Lineman	1981	—	3.00	6.00
—Budget-line reissue					
❏ SN-16258	Hey Little Girl	1982	—	3.00	6.00
—Budget-line reissue					
❏ SN-16259	Galveston	1982	—	3.00	6.00
—Budget-line reissue					
❏ SN-16297	Glen Campbell's Greatest Hits	1984	—	3.00	6.00
—Budget-line reissue					
❏ SN-16335	The Best of Glen Campbell	1984	—	3.00	6.00
—Budget-line reissue					
❏ SWAK-93157	Limited Collector's Edition	1970	5.00	10.00	20.00
—Capitol Record Club exclusive; includes tour program					
MCA					
❏ 42009	Still Within the Sound of My Voice	1987	2.00	4.00	8.00
❏ 42210	Light Years	1988	2.00	4.00	8.00
PAIR					
❏ PDL2-1089 [(2)]	All-Time Favorites	1986	3.00	6.00	12.00
PICKWICK					
❏ PTP-2048 [(2)]	Only the Lonely	197?	2.50	5.00	10.00
❏ PC-3052 [M]	The 12 String Guitar of Glen Campbell	196?	3.00	6.00	12.00
❏ SPC-3052 [S]	The 12 String Guitar of Glen Campbell	196?	2.50	5.00	10.00
❏ SPC-3134	A Satisfied Mind	197?	2.00	4.00	8.00
❏ SPC-3274	The Glen Campbell Album	197?	2.00	4.00	8.00
❏ SPC-3346	I'll Paint You a Song	197?	2.00	4.00	8.00
STARDAY					
❏ SLP-424	Country Soul	1968	3.75	7.50	15.00
❏ SLP-437	Country Music Star #1	1969	3.75	7.50	15.00
SURREY					
❏ S 1007 [M]	Country Shindig	196?	3.00	6.00	12.00

CAMPBELL, GLEN, AND BOBBIE GENTRY

CAPITOL

Number	Title (A Side/B Side)	Yr	VG	VG+	NM
❏ ST 2928	Bobbie Gentry & Glen Campbell	1968	3.75	7.50	15.00
❏ ST 8-2928	Bobbie Gentry & Glen Campbell	1968	5.00	10.00	20.00
—Capitol Record Club edition					

CAMPBELL, JO ANN

ABC-PARAMOUNT

Number	Title (A Side/B Side)	Yr	VG	VG+	NM
❏ 393 [M]	Twistin' and Listenin'	1962	20.00	40.00	80.00
❏ S-393 [S]	Twistin' and Listenin'	1962	25.00	50.00	100.00
CAMEO					
❏ C-1026 [M]	All the Hits of Jo Ann Campbell	1962	12.50	25.00	50.00
❏ SC-1026 [S]	All the Hits of Jo Ann Campbell	1962	25.00	50.00	100.00
CORONET					
❏ CX-199 [M]	Starring Jo Ann Campbell	196?	5.00	10.00	20.00
❏ CXS-199 [R]	Starring Jo Ann Campbell	196?	3.00	6.00	12.00
END					
❏ LP-306 [M]	I'm Nobody's Baby	1959	37.50	75.00	150.00

CAMPER VAN BEETHOVEN

INDEPENDENT PROJECT

Number	Title (A Side/B Side)	Yr	VG	VG+	NM
❏ 016	Telephone Free Landslide Victory	1985	6.25	12.50	25.00
—"Manufactured and Distributed within the United States of America by Rough Trade" on back cover; non-letterpress edition; several color schemes exist, all of equal value					
❏ 016	Telephone Free Landslide Victory	1985	12.50	25.00	50.00
—Letterpress cover, "Second Edition: 1175 cp./September 1985" on back (un-numbered promo)					
❏ 016	Telephone Free Landslide Victory	1985	15.00	30.00	60.00
—Letterpress cover, "Second Edition: 1175 cp./September 1985" on back (numbered edition from 1251-2425)					
❏ 016	Telephone Free Landslide Victory	1985	17.50	35.00	70.00
—Letterpress cover, "First Edition: June 1985" on back (un-numbered promo); the basic color scheme is red, black and flourescent orange on brown chipboard					
❏ 016	Telephone Free Landslide Victory	1985	20.00	40.00	80.00
—Letterpress cover, "First Edition: June 1985" on back (numbered edition from 1-1,250); the basic color scheme is white, black and flourescent orange on brown chipboard					
PITCH A TENT					
❏ 01	II & III	1985	3.75	7.50	15.00
❏ 02	Camper Van Beethoven	1986	3.75	7.50	15.00
❏ 05 [EP]	Vampire Can Mating Oven	1987	3.75	7.50	15.00
VIRGIN					
❏ 90918	Our Beloved Revolutionary Sweetheart	1988	2.50	5.00	10.00
❏ 91289	Key Lime Pie	1989	2.50	5.00	10.00

CAMPUS SINGERS, THE

ARGO

Number	Title (A Side/B Side)	Yr	VG	VG+	NM
❏ LP-4023 [M]	The Campus Singers at the Fickle Pickle	1963	5.00	10.00	20.00
❏ LPS-4023 [S]	The Campus Singers at the Fickle Pickle	1963	6.25	12.50	25.00
❏ LP-4033 [M]	Road of Blue	1964	5.00	10.00	20.00
❏ LPS-4033 [S]	Road of Blue	1964	6.25	12.50	25.00

CAN

MUTE

Number	Title (A Side/B Side)	Yr	VG	VG+	NM
❏ 9033-1 [(3)]	Sacrilege	1997	6.25	12.50	25.00
—Album of remixes					

CANADIAN BEADLES, THE

TIDE

Number	Title (A Side/B Side)	Yr	VG	VG+	NM
❏ 2005 [M]	Three Faces North	1964	12.50	25.00	50.00

CANADIAN SWEETHEARTS, THE

A&M

Number	Title (A Side/B Side)	Yr	VG	VG+	NM
❏ LP-106 [M]	Introducing the Canadian Sweethearts	1964	10.00	20.00	40.00
❏ SP-4106 [S]	Introducing the Canadian Sweethearts	1964	12.50	25.00	50.00

CANARIES, THE

B.T. PUPPY

Number	Title (A Side/B Side)	Yr	VG	VG+	NM
❏ BTS-1007	Flying High with the Canaries	1970	25.00	50.00	100.00

CANDIDO

ABC-PARAMOUNT

Number	Title (A Side/B Side)	Yr	VG	VG+	NM
❏ ABC-125 [M]	Candido Featuring Al Cohn	1956	12.50	25.00	50.00
❏ ABC-180 [M]	The Volcanic Candido	1957	12.50	25.00	50.00
❏ ABC-236 [M]	In Indigo	1958	12.50	25.00	50.00
❏ ABCS-236 [S]	In Indigo	1959	10.00	20.00	40.00
❏ ABC-286 [M]	Latin Fire	1959	10.00	20.00	40.00
❏ ABCS-286 [S]	Latin Fire	1959	12.50	25.00	50.00
❏ ABC-453 [M]	Candido's Comparsa	1963	5.00	10.00	20.00
❏ ABCS-453 [S]	Candido's Comparsa	1963	6.25	12.50	25.00
RCA VICTOR					
❏ LPM-2027 [M]	Beautiful	1959	7.50	15.00	30.00
❏ LSP-2027 [S]	Beautiful	1959	10.00	20.00	40.00
ROULETTE					
❏ R-52078 [M]	Conga Soul	1962	5.00	10.00	20.00
❏ SR-52078 [S]	Conga Soul	1962	6.25	12.50	25.00

CANDOLI, CONTE

ANDEX

Number	Title (A Side/B Side)	Yr	VG	VG+	NM
❏ A-3002 [M]	Mucho Calor	1958	12.50	25.00	50.00
❏ AS-3002 [S]	Mucho Calor	1959	10.00	20.00	40.00
BETHLEHEM					
❏ BCP-30 [M]	Toots Sweet	1956	20.00	40.00	80.00
❏ BCP-1016 [10]	Sincerely, Conte Candoli	1954	37.50	75.00	150.00
CROWN					
❏ CST-190 [R]	Little Band, Big Jazz	196?	6.25	12.50	25.00
—Red vinyl					
❏ CLP-5162 [M]	Little Band, Big Jazz	1960	5.00	10.00	20.00

CANDOLI, CONTE, AND STAN LEVEY

BETHLEHEM

Number	Title (A Side/B Side)	Yr	VG	VG+	NM
❏ BCP-9 [M]	West Coasting	1956	20.00	40.00	80.00

CANDOLI, PETE

DECCA

Number	Title (A Side/B Side)	Yr	VG	VG+	NM
❏ DL 74761 [S]	Moscow Mule (And Many More Kicks)	1966	5.00	10.00	20.00
KAPP					
❏ KL-1230 [M]	For Pete's Sake	1960	5.00	10.00	20.00
❏ KS-3230 [S]	For Pete's Sake	1960	6.25	12.50	25.00
SOMERSET					
❏ SF-17200 [M]	Blues, When Your Lover Has Gone	1963	5.00	10.00	20.00
❏ SFS-17200 [S]	Blues, When Your Lover Has Gone	1963	6.25	12.50	25.00

CANDOLI BROTHERS, THE

DOT

Number	Title (A Side/B Side)	Yr	VG	VG+	NM
❏ DLP-3062 [M]	The Brothers Candoli	1957	12.50	25.00	50.00
❏ DLP-3168 [M]	Bell, Book and Candoli	1959	7.50	15.00	30.00
❏ DLP-25168 [S]	Bell, Book and Candoli	1959	6.25	12.50	25.00
MERCURY					
❏ MG-20515 [M]	Two for the Money	1959	7.50	15.00	30.00
❏ SR-60191 [S]	Two for the Money	1959	6.25	12.50	25.00
WARNER BROS.					
❏ W 1462 [M]	The Brothers Candoli	1962	5.00	10.00	20.00
❏ WS 1462 [S]	The Brothers Candoli	1962	6.25	12.50	25.00

CANDY STORE, THE

DECCA

Number	Title (A Side/B Side)	Yr	VG	VG+	NM
❏ DL 75147	Turned-On Christmas	1969	6.25	12.50	25.00

CANDYMEN, THE

ABC

Number	Title (A Side/B Side)	Yr	VG	VG+	NM
❏ 616 [M]	The Candymen	1967	6.25	12.50	25.00
❏ S-616 [S]	The Candymen	1967	5.00	10.00	20.00
❏ S-633	The Candymen Bring You Candypower	1968	5.00	10.00	20.00

CANNED HEAT

ACCORD

Number	Title (A Side/B Side)	Yr	VG	VG+	NM
❏ SN-7144	Captured Live	1981	2.50	5.00	10.00
ATLANTIC					
❏ SD 7289	One More River to Cross	1973	3.75	7.50	15.00
DALI					
❏ DCLP-89022	Reheated	1990	3.75	7.50	15.00
JANUS					
❏ JLS-3009	Vintage — Canned Heat	1969	3.75	7.50	15.00
LIBERTY					
❏ LRP-3526 [M]	Canned Heat	1967	6.25	12.50	25.00
❏ LST-7526 [S]	Canned Heat	1967	5.00	10.00	20.00
❏ LST-7541	Boogie with Canned Heat	1968	5.00	10.00	20.00
❏ LST-7618	Hallelujah	1969	5.00	10.00	20.00
❏ LN-10105	Boogie with Canned Heat	1981	2.00	4.00	8.00
—Budget-line reissue					
❏ LN-10106	Canned Heat Cook Book (The Best of Canned Heat)	1981	2.00	4.00	8.00
—Budget-line reissue					
❏ LST-11000	Canned Heat Cook Book (The Best of Canned Heat)	1969	5.00	10.00	20.00
❏ LST-11002	Future Blues	1970	3.75	7.50	15.00
❏ LST-27200 [(2)]	Living the Blues	1968	6.25	12.50	25.00
PICKWICK					
❏ SPC-3364	Live at Topanga Canyon	197?	2.50	5.00	10.00
❏ SPC-3614	Boogie	1978	2.50	5.00	10.00
SCEPTER					
❏ CTN-18017	The Best of Canned Heat	1972	2.50	5.00	10.00

Number	Title (A Side/B Side)	Yr	VG	VG+	NM
SUNSET					
❏ SUS-5298	Collage	1971	2.50	5.00	10.00
TAKOMA					
❏ 7066	The Human Condition	1980	3.00	6.00	12.00
UNITED ARTISTS					
❏ UA-LA049-F	The New Age	1973	3.75	7.50	15.00
❏ LM-1015	Boogie with Canned Heat	1980	3.00	6.00	12.00
—Reissue of Liberty 7541					
❏ UAS-5509	Canned Heat Concert (Recorded Live in Europe)	1971	3.75	7.50	15.00
❏ UAS-5557	Historical Figures and Ancient Heads	1972	3.75	7.50	15.00
❏ UAS-9955 [(2)]	Living the Blues	1971	5.00	10.00	20.00
—Reissue of Liberty 27200					
WAND					
❏ WDS-693	Live at Topanga Canyon	1970	6.25	12.50	25.00

CANNED HEAT AND JOHN LEE HOOKER
See JOHN LEE HOOKER AND CANNED HEAT

CANNIBAL AND THE HEADHUNTERS

Number	Title (A Side/B Side)	Yr	VG	VG+	NM
DATE					
❏ TEM 3001 [M]	Land of 1000 Dances	1966	7.50	15.00	30.00
❏ TES 4001 [S]	Land of 1000 Dances	1966	10.00	20.00	40.00
RAMPART					
❏ RM-3302 [M]	Land of 1000 Dances	1965	12.50	25.00	50.00
❏ RS-3302 [S]	Land of 1000 Dances	1965	17.50	35.00	70.00

CANNON, ACE

Number	Title (A Side/B Side)	Yr	VG	VG+	NM
ALLEGIANCE					
❏ AV-5024	Ace in the Whole	1986	2.00	4.00	8.00
HI					
❏ 6006	After Hours	1978	2.50	5.00	10.00
❏ 8003	Sax Man	1977	2.50	5.00	10.00
❏ 8008	Cannon Country	1979	2.50	5.00	10.00
❏ HL-12007 [M]	Tuff Sax	1962	6.25	12.50	25.00
❏ HL-12008 [M]	Looking Back	1962	6.25	12.50	25.00
❏ HL-12014 [M]	The Moanin' Sax of Ace Cannon	1963	6.25	12.50	25.00
❏ HL-12016 [M]	Aces Hi	1964	5.00	10.00	20.00
❏ HL-12019 [M]	The Great Show Tunes	1964	5.00	10.00	20.00
❏ HL-12022 [M]	Christmas Cheer	1964	5.00	10.00	20.00
❏ HL-12025 [M]	Ace Cannon Live	1965	3.75	7.50	15.00
❏ HL-12028 [M]	Nashville Hits	1965	3.75	7.50	15.00
❏ HL-12030 [M]	Sweet and Tuff	1966	3.75	7.50	15.00
❏ HL-12035 [M]	The Misty Sax of Ace Cannon	1967	5.00	10.00	20.00
❏ HL-12040 [M]	Memphis Golden Hits	1967	5.00	10.00	20.00
❏ SHL-32007 [S]	Tuff Sax	1962	7.50	15.00	30.00
❏ SHL-32008 [S]	Looking Back	1962	7.50	15.00	30.00
❏ SHL-32014 [S]	The Moanin' Sax of Ace Cannon	1963	7.50	15.00	30.00
❏ SHL-32016 [S]	Aces Hi	1964	6.25	12.50	25.00
❏ SHL-32019 [S]	The Great Show Tunes	1964	6.25	12.50	25.00
❏ SHL-32022 [S]	Christmas Cheer	1964	6.25	12.50	25.00
❏ SHL-32025 [S]	Ace Cannon Live	1965	5.00	10.00	20.00
❏ SHL-32028 [S]	Nashville Hits	1965	5.00	10.00	20.00
❏ SHL-32030 [S]	Sweet and Tuff	1966	5.00	10.00	20.00
❏ SHL-32035 [S]	The Misty Sax of Ace Cannon	1967	3.75	7.50	15.00
❏ SHL-32040 [S]	Memphis Golden Hits	1967	3.75	7.50	15.00
❏ SHL-32043	The Incomparable Sax of Ace Cannon	1968	3.75	7.50	15.00
❏ SHL-32046	In the Spotlight	1968	3.75	7.50	15.00
❏ SHL-32051	The Ace of Sax	1969	3.75	7.50	15.00
❏ SHL-32057	The Happy and Mellow Sax of Ace Cannon	1970	3.00	6.00	12.00
❏ SHL-32060	Cool 'n Saxy	1971	3.00	6.00	12.00
❏ SHL-32067	Blowing Wild	1971	3.00	6.00	12.00
❏ SHL-32071	Cannon Country	1972	3.00	6.00	12.00
❏ SHL-32072/3 [(2)]	Aces Back to Back	1972	3.75	7.50	15.00
❏ SHL-32076	Baby Don't Get Hooked on Me	1973	2.50	5.00	10.00
❏ SHL-32080	Country Comfort	1974	2.50	5.00	10.00
❏ SHL-32086	That Music City Feeling	1974	2.50	5.00	10.00
❏ SHL-32090	Super Sax Country Style	1975	2.50	5.00	10.00
❏ SHL-32101	Peace in the Valley	1976	2.50	5.00	10.00

CANNON, FREDDY

Number	Title (A Side/B Side)	Yr	VG	VG+	NM
RHINO					
❏ RNLP-210	14 Booming Hits	1982	2.50	5.00	10.00
SWAN					
❏ LP-502 [M]	The Explosive! Freddy Cannon	1960	30.00	60.00	120.00
❏ LPS-502 [S]	The Explosive! Freddy Cannon	1960	75.00	150.00	300.00
❏ LP-504 [M]	Happy Shades of Blue	1960	37.50	75.00	150.00
❏ LP-505 [M]	Solid Gold Hits	1961	37.50	75.00	150.00
❏ LP-507 [M]	Freddy Cannon at Palisades Park	1962	37.50	75.00	150.00
❏ LP-511 [M]	Freddy Cannon Steps Out	1963	37.50	75.00	150.00
WARNER BROS.					
❏ W 1544 [M]	Freddie Cannon	1964	7.50	15.00	30.00
❏ WS 1544 [S]	Freddie Cannon	1964	10.00	20.00	40.00
❏ W 1612 [M]	Action!	1965	7.50	15.00	30.00
❏ WS 1612 [S]	Action!	1965	10.00	20.00	40.00
❏ W 1628 [M]	Freddy Cannon's Greatest Hits	1966	7.50	15.00	30.00
❏ WS 1628 [S]	Freddy Cannon's Greatest Hits	1966	10.00	20.00	40.00

CANNON, GUS

Number	Title (A Side/B Side)	Yr	VG	VG+	NM
STAX					
❏ ST-702 [M]	Walk Right In	1962	150.00	300.00	600.00

CANTELON, WILLARD

Number	Title (A Side/B Side)	Yr	VG	VG+	NM
SUPREME					
❏ M-113 [M]	L.S.D. Battle for the Mind	1966	7.50	15.00	30.00
❏ S-113 [S]	L.S.D. Battle for the Mind	1966	10.00	20.00	40.00

CANTOR, EDDIE

Number	Title (A Side/B Side)	Yr	VG	VG+	NM
VIK					
❏ LXA-1119 [M]	The Best of Eddie Cantor	1957	12.50	25.00	50.00

CAPITAL CITY ROCKETS

Number	Title (A Side/B Side)	Yr	VG	VG+	NM
ELEKTRA					
❏ EKS-75079	Capital City Rockets	1973	5.00	10.00	20.00

CAPITOLS, THE (1)

Number	Title (A Side/B Side)	Yr	VG	VG+	NM
ATCO					
❏ 33-190 [M]	Dance the Cool Jerk	1966	10.00	20.00	40.00
❏ SD 33-190 [S]	Dance the Cool Jerk	1966	12.50	25.00	50.00
❏ 33-201 [M]	We Got a Thing That's In the Groove	1966	10.00	20.00	40.00
❏ SD 33-201 [S]	We Got a Thing That's In the Groove	1966	12.50	25.00	50.00
COLLECTABLES					
❏ COL-5105	Golden Classics	1988	2.50	5.00	10.00
SOLID SMOKE					
❏ 8019	The Capitols: Their Greatest Hits	1983	3.00	6.00	12.00

CAPRARO, JOE

Number	Title (A Side/B Side)	Yr	VG	VG+	NM
SOUTHLAND					
❏ 220 [M]	Dixieland	1959	5.00	10.00	20.00

CAPTAIN BEEFHEART

Number	Title (A Side/B Side)	Yr	VG	VG+	NM
A&M					
❏ SP-12510 [EP]	The Legendary A&M Sessions	1984	2.50	5.00	10.00
BLUE THUMB					
❏ BTS-1	Strictly Personal	1968	12.50	25.00	50.00
—Black label, unbanded sides					
❏ BTS-1	Strictly Personal	1969	7.50	15.00	30.00
—White label, unbanded sides					
❏ BTS-1	Strictly Personal	197?	5.00	10.00	20.00
—White label, banded sides					
BUDDAH					
❏ 1001/5001	Safe As Milk "Baby Jesus" Bumper Sticker	1967	6.25	12.50	25.00
❏ BDM-1001 [M]	Safe As Milk	1967	25.00	50.00	100.00
❏ BDS-5001 [S]	Safe As Milk	1967	15.00	30.00	60.00
❏ BDS-5063	Safe As Milk	1969	6.25	12.50	25.00
❏ BDS-5077	Mirror Man	197?	6.25	12.50	25.00
—Regular cover					
❏ BDS-5077	Mirror Man	1971	12.50	25.00	50.00
—Die-cut gatefold cover					
MERCURY					
❏ SRM-1-709	Unconditionally Guaranteed	1974	3.75	7.50	15.00
❏ SRM-1-1018	Bluejeans and Moonbeams	1975	5.00	10.00	20.00
REPRISE					
❏ 2MS 2027 [(2)]	Trout Mask Replica	1970	7.50	15.00	30.00
—Stock copy with 2027 labels and 2027 jacket					
❏ MS 2050	The Spotlight Kid	1971	5.00	10.00	20.00
❏ MS 2115	Clear Spot	1972	5.00	10.00	20.00
❏ RS 6420	Lick My Decals Off, Baby	1970	5.00	10.00	20.00
STRAIGHT					
❏ 2 STS-1053 [(2)]	Trout Mask Replica	1969	62.50	125.00	250.00
—Stock copy with 1053 labels (this has been confirmed to exist)					
❏ 2 STS-1053 [(2)DJ]	Trout Mask Replica	1969	50.00	100.00	200.00
—White label promo with 1053 labels					
❏ 2MS 2027 [(2)]	Trout Mask Replica	1969	15.00	30.00	60.00
—Stock copy with 2027 labels inside 1053 jacket					
❏ 2MS 2027 [(2)DJ]	Trout Mask Replica	1969	37.50	75.00	150.00
—White label promo with 2027 labels inside 1053 jacket					
❏ RS 6420	Lick My Decals Off, Baby	1970	12.50	25.00	50.00
VERVE FORECAST					
❏ FTS-3054	Captain Beefheart and the Magic Band	1968	—	—	—
—Canceled					
VIRGIN					
❏ VA 13148	Doc at the Radar Station	1980	3.00	6.00	12.00
VIRGIN/EPIC					
❏ ARE 38274	Ice Cream for Crow	1982	3.00	6.00	12.00
WARNER BROS.					
❏ (no #)	Bat Chain Puller	1978	100.00	200.00	400.00
—Test pressing with different selections than stock version					
❏ BSK 3256	Shiny Beast (Bat Chain Puller)	1978	3.00	6.00	12.00

CAPTAIN BEYOND

Number	Title (A Side/B Side)	Yr	VG	VG+	NM
CAPRICORN					
❏ CP 0105	Captain Beyond	1972	3.75	7.50	15.00
—Later covers are normal					
❏ CP 0105	Captain Beyond	1972	7.50	15.00	30.00
—Original covers are 3-D					
❏ CP 0115	Sufficiently Breathless	1973	3.75	7.50	15.00
WARNER BROS.					
❏ BS 3047	Dawn Explosion	1977	2.50	5.00	10.00

CARAM, ANA

Number	Title (A Side/B Side)	Yr	VG	VG+	NM
CHESKY					
❏ JR-28	Rio After Dark	199?	6.25	12.50	25.00
—Audiophile vinyl					

CARAVAN

Number	Title (A Side/B Side)	Yr	VG	VG+	NM
ARISTA					
❏ AL 4088	Blind Dog	1976	2.50	5.00	10.00
BTM					
❏ 5000	Cunning Stunts	1975	2.50	5.00	10.00
LONDON					
❏ PS 582	If I Could Do It All Over Again…	1971	3.75	7.50	15.00
❏ PS 593	In the Land of the Grey & Pink	1971	3.75	7.50	15.00
❏ XPS 615	Waterloo Lily	1972	3.75	7.50	15.00
❏ XPS 637	For Girls Who Grow Plump in the Night	1973	3.75	7.50	15.00
❏ XPS 650	Caravan and the New Symphonia	1974	3.75	7.50	15.00
❏ LC 50011	The Best of Caravan	1978	2.50	5.00	10.00
VERVE FORECAST					
❏ FTS-3066	Caravan	1969	10.00	20.00	40.00

C

Number	Title (A Side/B Side)	Yr	VG	VG+	NM
CARAVAN, JIMMY					
TOWER					
❏ ST 5103 [S]	Look Into the Flower	1968	5.00	10.00	20.00
❏ T 5103 [M]	Look Into the Flower	1968	12.50	25.00	50.00
VAULT					
❏ 9007	Hey Jude	1969	5.00	10.00	20.00
CARAVELLES, THE (1)					
SMASH					
❏ MGS-27044 [M]	You Don't Have to Be a Baby to Cry	1963	15.00	30.00	60.00
❏ SRS-67044 [R]	You Don't Have to Be a Baby to Cry	1963	15.00	30.00	60.00
CARE PACKAGE					
LIBERTY					
❏ LST-7647	Keep On Keepin' On	1970	6.25	12.50	25.00
CAREFREES, THE					
LONDON					
❏ PS 379 [S]	From England! The Carefrees	1964	25.00	50.00	100.00
❏ LL 3379 [M]	From England! The Carefrees	1964	20.00	40.00	80.00
CAREY, DAVE					
LAURIE					
❏ LLP-1004 [M]	Bandwagon Plus 2	1959	6.25	12.50	25.00
CAREY, MARIAH					
COLUMBIA					
❏ C 45202	Mariah Carey	1990	5.00	10.00	20.00
❏ C 47980	Emotions	1991	3.75	7.50	15.00
❏ C 53205	Music Box	1993	3.75	7.50	15.00
❏ C2 63800 [(2)]	Rainbow	1999	3.75	7.50	15.00
❏ C2 69670 [(2)]	#1's	1998	5.00	10.00	20.00
VIRGIN					
❏ 10797 [(2)]	Glitter	2001	3.75	7.50	15.00
❏ SPRO-16452 [(2)DJ]	Glitter	2001	5.00	10.00	20.00
—Promo-only version					
CAREY, MUTT					
RIVERSIDE					
❏ RLP-1042 [10]	Mutt Carey Plays the Blues	1954	25.00	50.00	100.00
CAREY, MUTT, AND PUNCH MILLER					
SAVOY					
❏ MG-12038 [M]	Jazz — New Orleans	1955	12.50	25.00	50.00
❏ MG-12050 [M]	Jazz — New Orleans, Vol. 2	1955	12.50	25.00	50.00
CARGILL, HENSON					
ATLANTIC					
❏ SD 7279	This Is Henson Cargill Country	1973	3.00	6.00	12.00
HARMONY					
❏ KH 31397	Welcome to My World	1972	2.50	5.00	10.00
MEGA					
❏ 31-1016	On the Road	1972	3.75	7.50	15.00
MONUMENT					
❏ SLP-18094	Skip a Rope	1968	5.00	10.00	20.00
❏ SLP-18103	Coming On Strong	1968	5.00	10.00	20.00
❏ SLP-18117	None of My Business	1969	5.00	10.00	20.00
❏ SLP-18137	Uncomplicated	1970	5.00	10.00	20.00
CARISI, JOHN					
COLUMBIA					
❏ CS (# unk) [S]	The New Jazz Sound of "Show Boat"	1960	7.50	15.00	30.00
❏ CL 1419 [M]	The New Jazz Sound of "Show Boat"	1960	6.25	12.50	25.00
CARLIN, GEORGE					
ATLANTIC					
❏ SD 19326	A Place for My Stuff	1981	2.50	5.00	10.00
EARDRUM					
❏ 1001	Carlin On Campus	1984	2.50	5.00	10.00
❏ 90523	Playin' with Your Head	1986	2.50	5.00	10.00
❏ 90972	What Am I Doing in New Jersey?	1988	2.50	5.00	10.00
ERA					
❏ EL 103 [M]	George Carlin and Jack Burns At the Playboy Club Tonight	1960	6.25	12.50	25.00
❏ E 600	The Original George Carlin	1972	3.00	6.00	12.00
LAFF					
❏ A 219	Killer Carlin	197?	2.50	5.00	10.00
—Reissue of Era material					
LITTLE DAVID					
❏ LD 1004	Class Clown	1972	2.50	5.00	10.00
❏ LD 1005	Occupation: Foole	1973	2.50	5.00	10.00
❏ LD 1008	An Evening with Wally Londo	1975	2.50	5.00	10.00
❏ LD 1075	On the Road	1977	2.50	5.00	10.00
❏ LD 1076	Indecent Exposure (Some of the Best of George Carlin)	1978	2.50	5.00	10.00
❏ LD 3003	Toledo Window Box	1974	2.50	5.00	10.00
❏ LD 7214	FM & AM	1972	2.50	5.00	10.00
❏ 90129	Toledo Window Box	1983	2.00	4.00	8.00
—Reissue of 3003					
❏ 90241	The George Carlin Collection	1984	2.00	4.00	8.00
RCA CAMDEN					
❏ CAS-2566	Take-Offs and Put-Ons	1972	2.50	5.00	10.00
RCA VICTOR					
❏ LPM-3772 [M]	Take-Offs and Put-Ons	1967	5.00	10.00	20.00
❏ LSP-3772 [S]	Take-Offs and Put-Ons	1967	3.75	7.50	15.00
CARLISLE, BILL					
HICKORY					
❏ LPM-129 [M]	The Best of Bill Carlisle	1967	6.25	12.50	25.00
❏ LPS-129 [S]	The Best of Bill Carlisle	1967	6.25	12.50	25.00

Number	Title (A Side/B Side)	Yr	VG	VG+	NM
CARLISLE BROTHERS, THE					
KING					
❏ 643 [M]	Fresh from the Country	1959	12.50	25.00	50.00
MERCURY					
❏ MG-20359 [M]	On Stage with the Carlisles	1958	12.50	25.00	50.00
CARLOS, WALTER					
CBS MASTERWORKS					
❏ M 39340	Digital Moonscapes	1984	2.50	5.00	10.00
—As "Wendy Carlos"					
COLUMBIA					
❏ KG 31236 [(2)]	Sonic Seasonings	1972	3.75	7.50	15.00
❏ KC 31480	Walter Carlos' Clockwork Orange	1972	3.00	6.00	12.00
COLUMBIA MASTERWORKS					
❏ MS 7194	Switched-On Bach	1968	3.75	7.50	15.00
—"Standing Bach" cover; gray label with "360 Sound Stereo"					
❏ MS 7194	Switched-On Bach	1968	12.50	25.00	50.00
—"Sitting Bach" (sometimes called "Constipated Bach") cover that was quickly replaced; gray label with "360 Sound Stereo"					
❏ MS 7194	Switched-On Bach	1970	3.00	6.00	12.00
—Gray label with orange Columbia logos and no "360 Sound Stereo"					
❏ MS 7194	Switched-On Bach	198?	3.75	7.50	15.00
—Later reissue under the name "Wendy Carlos"; bar code on back cover					
❏ MS 7286	The Well-Tempered Synthesizer	1969	3.75	7.50	15.00
—Gray label with "360 Sound Stereo"					
❏ MS 7286	The Well-Tempered Synthesizer	1970	3.00	6.00	12.00
—Gray label with orange Columbia logos and no "360 Sound Stereo"					
❏ M 32088	Walter Carlos By Request	1973	3.00	6.00	12.00
❏ KM 32659	More Switched-On Bach	1974	3.00	6.00	12.00
❏ M2X 35895 [(2)]	Switched-On Brandenburgs	1979	3.75	7.50	15.00
❏ HM 45950	Switched-On Brandenburgs Vol. 1	1980	25.00	50.00	100.00
—Half-speed mastered edition					
❏ HM 47194	Switched-On Bach	198?	7.50	15.00	30.00
—Half-speed mastered edition					
CARLTON, LARRY					
UNI					
❏ 73036	With a Little Help from My Friends	1968	5.00	10.00	20.00
CARMEN					
EPIC					
❏ BN 26479	Carmen	1969	5.00	10.00	20.00
CARMICHAEL, HOAGY					
BOOK-OF-THE-MONTH					
❏ 61-5450 [(3)]	Hoagy Carmichael	1984	7.50	15.00	30.00
DECCA					
❏ DL 5068 [10]	Stardust Road	1950	20.00	40.00	80.00
❏ DL 8588 [M]	Stardust Road	1958	7.50	15.00	30.00
GOLDEN					
❏ LP-198-18 [M]	Havin' a Party	1958	7.50	15.00	30.00
JAZZTONE					
❏ J-1266 [M]	Hoagy Sings Carmichael	1957	7.50	15.00	30.00
KIMBERLY					
❏ 2023 [M]	The Legend of Hoagy Carmichael	1962	6.25	12.50	25.00
❏ 11023 [R]	The Legend of Hoagy Carmichael	196?	5.00	10.00	20.00
PACIFIC JAZZ					
❏ PJ-1223 [M]	Hoagy Sings Carmichael	1956	15.00	30.00	60.00
RCA VICTOR					
❏ LPT-3072 [10]	Old Rockin' Chair	1953	20.00	40.00	80.00
CARN, DOUG					
SAVOY					
❏ MG-12195	The Doug Carn Trio	1969	5.00	10.00	20.00
CARNES, KIM					
A&M					
❏ SP-3114	Sailin'	198?	2.00	4.00	8.00
—Budget-line reissue					
❏ SP-3204	The Best of Kim Carnes	1982	2.50	5.00	10.00
❏ SP-4548	Kim Carnes	1975	3.00	6.00	12.00
❏ SP-4606	Sailin'	1976	3.00	6.00	12.00
AMOS					
❏ AAS 7016	Rest on Me	1971	5.00	10.00	20.00
EMI AMERICA					
❏ SW-17004	St. Vincent's Court	1978	2.50	5.00	10.00
❏ SW-17030	Romance Dance	1980	2.50	5.00	10.00
❏ SO-17052	Mistaken Identity	1981	2.50	5.00	10.00
❏ SO-17078	Voyeur	1982	2.50	5.00	10.00
❏ SO-17107	Café Racers	1983	2.50	5.00	10.00
❏ SO-17159	Barking at Airplanes	1985	2.50	5.00	10.00
❏ ST-17198	Light House	1986	2.00	4.00	8.00
MCA					
❏ 914	The Early Years	1984	2.00	4.00	8.00
❏ 42200	View from the House	1988	2.00	4.00	8.00
MOBILE FIDELITY					
❏ 1-073	Mistaken Identity	1982	6.25	12.50	25.00
—Audiophile vinyl					
CARNEY, ART					
COLUMBIA					
❏ CL 2595 [10]	Doodle-Li-Boops and Rhinocelopes	1955	20.00	40.00	80.00
CARNEY, HARRY					
CLEF					
❏ MGC-640 [M]	Harry Carney with Strings	1955	20.00	40.00	80.00
VERVE					
❏ MGV-2028 [M]	Moods for Girl and Boy	1957	12.50	25.00	50.00
—Reissue of Clef 640					
❏ V-2028 [M]	Moods for Girl and Boy	1957	5.00	10.00	20.00

Number	Title (A Side/B Side)	Yr	VG	VG+	NM

CAROLEERS, THE
ALLEGRO ROYALE
| ❏ 1295 [M] | An Hour of Christmas Music | 195? | 5.00 | 10.00 | 20.00 |

—B-side by anonymous "Organ and Chimes"

CAROLINA SLIM
SHARP
| ❏ 2002 [M] | Blues from the Cotton Fields | 195? | 62.50 | 125.00 | 250.00 |

CARP
Actor Gary Busey was in this group.
EPIC
| ❏ E 30212 | Carp | 1970 | 6.25 | 12.50 | 25.00 |

CARPENTER, IKE
ALADDIN
| ❏ LP-811 [M] | Lights Out | 1957 | — | — | — |

—Unreleased
DISCOVERY
| ❏ DL 3003 [10] | Dancers in Love | 1949 | 75.00 | 150.00 | 300.00 |
INTRO
| ❏ 950 [10] | Lights Out | 1952 | 75.00 | 150.00 | 300.00 |
SCORE
| ❏ SLP-4010 [M] | Lights Out | 1957 | 37.50 | 75.00 | 150.00 |

CARPENTERS
A&M
| ❏ SP-3184 | Close to You | 1982 | 2.00 | 4.00 | 8.00 |

—Reissue of 4271
| ❏ SP-3197 | A Kind of Hush | 1982 | 2.00 | 4.00 | 8.00 |

—Reissue of 4581
| ❏ SP-3199 | Passage | 1982 | 2.00 | 4.00 | 8.00 |

—Reissue of 4703
| ❏ SP-3210 | Christmas Portrait | 198? | 2.00 | 4.00 | 8.00 |

—Reissue of SP-4726
❏ SP-3270	An Old-Fashioned Christmas	1984	2.50	5.00	10.00
❏ SP-3502	Carpenters	1971	3.00	6.00	12.00
❏ SP-3511	A Song for You	1972	3.00	6.00	12.00
❏ SP-3519	Now & Then	1973	3.00	6.00	12.00
❏ SP-3601	The Singles 1969-1973	1973	3.00	6.00	12.00
❏ SP-3723	Made in America	1981	3.00	6.00	12.00
❏ SP-4205	Offering	1969	20.00	40.00	80.00
❏ SP-4205	Ticket to Ride	1970	3.00	6.00	12.00

—Reissue of "Offering" with new title and cover
❏ SP-4271	Close to You	1970	3.00	6.00	12.00
❏ SP-4530	Horizon	1975	3.00	6.00	12.00
❏ SP-4581	A Kind of Hush	1976	3.00	6.00	12.00
❏ SP-4703	Passage	1977	3.00	6.00	12.00
❏ SP-4726	Christmas Portrait	1978	3.75	7.50	15.00
❏ SP-4954	Voice of the Heart	1983	3.00	6.00	12.00
❏ SP-5172	An Old Fashioned Christmas	1987	2.00	4.00	8.00

—Reissue of 3270 (record still says 3270 but cover is 5172)
❏ SP-6601 [(2)]	Yesterday Once More	1985	3.75	7.50	15.00
❏ QU-53502 [Q]	Carpenters	1974	5.00	10.00	20.00
❏ QU-53511 [Q]	A Song for You	1974	5.00	10.00	20.00
❏ QU-53519 [Q]	Now & Then	1974	5.00	10.00	20.00
❏ QU-53601 [Q]	The Singles 1969-1973	1974	5.00	10.00	20.00
❏ QU-54271 [Q]	Close to You	1974	5.00	10.00	20.00
❏ QU-54530 [Q]	Horizon	1975	5.00	10.00	20.00

CARR, CATHY
DOT
| ❏ DLP-3674 [M] | Ivory Tower | 1966 | 6.25 | 12.50 | 25.00 |
| ❏ DLP-25674 [S] | Ivory Tower | 1966 | 6.25 | 12.50 | 25.00 |
FRATERNITY
| ❏ 1005 [M] | Ivory Tower | 1957 | 30.00 | 60.00 | 120.00 |
ROULETTE
| ❏ R 25077 [M] | Shy | 1959 | 10.00 | 20.00 | 40.00 |
| ❏ SR 25077 [S] | Shy | 1959 | 12.50 | 25.00 | 50.00 |

CARR, GEORGIA
TOPS
| ❏ L-1617 [M] | Songs by a Moody Miss | 195? | 7.50 | 15.00 | 30.00 |
VEE JAY
| ❏ LP-1105 [M] | Rocks in My Bed | 1964 | 5.00 | 10.00 | 20.00 |
| ❏ VJS-1105 [S] | Rocks in My Bed | 1964 | 6.25 | 12.50 | 25.00 |

CARR, HELEN
BETHLEHEM
| ❏ BCP-45 [M] | Why Do I Love You | 1956 | 15.00 | 30.00 | 60.00 |
| ❏ BCP-1027 [10] | Down in the Depths on the 90th Floor | 1955 | 30.00 | 60.00 | 120.00 |

CARR, JAMES
GOLDWAX
| ❏ 3001S | You Got My Mind Messed Up | 1968 | 37.50 | 75.00 | 150.00 |
| ❏ 3002S | A Man Needs a Woman | 1968 | 37.50 | 75.00 | 150.00 |

CARR, JOE "FINGERS"
CAPITOL
❏ T 280 [M]	Bar Room Piano	1952	7.50	15.00	30.00
❏ T 345 [M]	Roughhouse Piano	1953	7.50	15.00	30.00
❏ T 443 [M]	Joe "Fingers" Carr and His Ragtime Band	1954	7.50	15.00	30.00
❏ T 527 [M]	Fireman's Ball	1954	7.50	15.00	30.00
❏ ST 1151 [S]	"Fingers" and the Flapper	1959	6.25	12.50	25.00
❏ T 1151 [M]	"Fingers" and the Flapper	1959	5.00	10.00	20.00
❏ ST 1217 [S]	Joe "Fingers" Carr and His Swingin' String Band	1959	6.25	12.50	25.00
❏ T 1217 [M]	Joe "Fingers" Carr and His Swingin' String Band	1959	5.00	10.00	20.00
WARNER BROS.
❏ W 1386 [M]	The World's Greatest Ragtime Piano Player	1960	3.75	7.50	15.00
❏ WS 1386 [S]	The World's Greatest Ragtime Piano Player	1960	5.00	10.00	20.00

CARR, LEROY
COLUMBIA
| ❏ CL 1911 [M] | Blues Before Sunrise | 1962 | 7.50 | 15.00 | 30.00 |
| ❏ CS 8511 [R] | Blues Before Sunrise | 1962 | 5.00 | 10.00 | 20.00 |

CARR, LODI
LAURIE
| ❏ LLP-1007 [M] | Lady Bird | 1960 | 6.25 | 12.50 | 25.00 |

CARR, VIKKI
COLUMBIA
❏ C 30662	Vikki Carr's Love Story	1971	2.50	5.00	10.00
❏ C 31040	Superstar	1971	2.50	5.00	10.00
❏ KC 31453	The First Time Ever (I Saw Your Face)	1972	2.50	5.00	10.00
❏ KC 31470	Canta En Espanol	1972	2.50	5.00	10.00
❏ KC 32251	Ms. America	1973	2.50	5.00	10.00
❏ KG 32656 [(2)]	Live at the Greek Theatre	1973	3.00	6.00	12.00
❏ KC 32860	One Hell of a Woman	1974	2.50	5.00	10.00
❏ PC 33340	Hoy (Today)	1975	2.50	5.00	10.00
❏ CG 33609 [(2)]	Love Story/The First Time Ever	1976	3.00	6.00	12.00
LIBERTY
❏ LRP-3314 [M]	Color Her Great	1963	3.75	7.50	15.00
❏ LRP-3354 [M]	Discovery!	1964	3.75	7.50	15.00
❏ LRP-3383 [M]	Discovery! Volume Two	1964	3.75	7.50	15.00
❏ LRP-3420 [M]	The Anatomy of Love	1965	3.75	7.50	15.00
❏ LRP-3456 [M]	The Way of Today	1966	3.75	7.50	15.00
❏ LRP-3506 [M]	Intimate Excitement	1967	5.00	10.00	20.00
❏ LRP-3533 [M]	It Must Be Him	1967	5.00	10.00	20.00
❏ LRP-3548 [M]	Vikki	1968	7.50	15.00	30.00

—Mono stock copy inside stereo cover with "Audition Mono LP Not for Sale" sticker
❏ LST-7314 [S]	Color Her Great	1963	5.00	10.00	20.00
❏ LST-7354 [S]	Discovery!	1964	5.00	10.00	20.00
❏ LST-7383 [S]	Discovery! Volume Two	1964	5.00	10.00	20.00
❏ LST-7420 [S]	The Anatomy of Love	1965	5.00	10.00	20.00
❏ LST-7456 [S]	The Way of Today	1966	5.00	10.00	20.00
❏ LST-7506 [S]	Intimate Excitement	1967	3.75	7.50	15.00
❏ LST-7533 [S]	It Must Be Him	1967	3.75	7.50	15.00
❏ LST-7548 [S]	Vikki	1968	3.75	7.50	15.00
❏ LST-7565	Don't Break My Pretty Balloon	1969	3.75	7.50	15.00
❏ LST-7604	For Once in My Life	1969	3.75	7.50	15.00
❏ LN-10108	The Best of Vikki Carr	1981	2.00	4.00	8.00
❏ LST-11001	Nashville by Carr	1970	3.75	7.50	15.00
PAIR
❏ PDL2-1082 [(2)]	From the Heart	1986	3.00	6.00	12.00
PICKWICK
❏ SPC-3587	Intimate	1978	2.00	4.00	8.00
❏ SPC-3613	Unforgettable	1978	2.00	4.00	8.00
SUNSET
❏ SUS-5228	That's All	1969	2.50	5.00	10.00
❏ SUS-5293	Unforgettable	1971	2.50	5.00	10.00
UNITED ARTISTS
❏ UA-LA089-G [(2)]	Vikki Carr's Golden Songbook/Superpak	1973	3.00	6.00	12.00
❏ UA-LA244-G	The Very Best of Vikki Carr	1974	2.50	5.00	10.00
❏ LM-1006	It Must Be Him	1980	2.50	5.00	10.00

—Abridged reissue of Liberty 7533
| ❏ UAS-5581 [(2)] | The Best of Vikki Carr | 1972 | 3.00 | 6.00 | 12.00 |
| ❏ UAS-6813 | The Ways to Love a Man | 1972 | 2.50 | 5.00 | 10.00 |

CARROLL, BAIKIDA
HAT HUT
| ❏ M/N [(2)] | The Spoken Word | 197? | 5.00 | 10.00 | 20.00 |

CARROLL, BARBARA
ATLANTIC
| ❏ ALR-132 [10] | Piano Panorama | 195? | 20.00 | 40.00 | 80.00 |
KAPP
| ❏ KS-(# unk) [S] | Flower Drum Song | 1958 | 6.25 | 12.50 | 25.00 |
| ❏ KL-1113 [M] | Flower Drum Song | 1958 | 6.25 | 12.50 | 25.00 |
LIVINGSTON
| ❏ 1081 [10] | Barbara Carroll Trio | 1953 | 20.00 | 40.00 | 80.00 |
RCA VICTOR
❏ LJM-1001 [M]	Barbara Carroll Trio	1954	12.50	25.00	50.00
❏ LJM-1023 [M]	Lullabies in Rhythm	1955	12.50	25.00	50.00
❏ LPM-1137 [M]	Have You Met Miss Carroll?	1956	12.50	25.00	50.00
❏ LPM-1296 [M]	We Just Couldn't Say Goodbye	1956	12.50	25.00	50.00
❏ LPM-1396 [M]	It's a Wonderful World	1957	12.50	25.00	50.00
SESAC
❏ N-3201 [M]	Why Not?	1959	7.50	15.00	30.00
❏ SN-3201 [S]	Why Not?	1959	10.00	20.00	40.00
UNITED ARTISTS
❏ UA-LA778-H	From the Beginning	1978	5.00	10.00	20.00
VERVE
❏ MGV-2063 [M]	Funny Face	1957	12.50	25.00	50.00

—Black label
| ❏ MGV-2063 [M] | Funny Face | 1957 | 15.00 | 30.00 | 60.00 |

—Orange label
❏ MGV-2092 [M]	The Best of George and Ira Gershwin	1958	10.00	20.00	40.00
❏ V-2092 [M]	The Best of George and Ira Gershwin	1961	5.00	10.00	20.00
❏ MGV-2095 [M]	Barbara	1958	10.00	20.00	40.00
❏ V-2095 [M]	Barbara	1961	5.00	10.00	20.00

CARROLL, BARBARA/MARY LOU WILLIAMS
ATLANTIC
| ❏ 1271 [M] | Ladies in Jazz | 1958 | 12.50 | 25.00 | 50.00 |

—Black label
| ❏ 1271 [M] | Ladies in Jazz | 1961 | 5.00 | 10.00 | 20.00 |

—Multi-color label, white "fan" logo

Number	Title (A Side/B Side)	Yr	VG	VG+	NM

CARROLL, DIAHANN
ATLANTIC
❑ 8048 [M]	Fun Life	1961	5.00	10.00	20.00
❑ SD 8048 [S]	Fun Life	1961	6.25	12.50	25.00

RCA VICTOR
❑ LPM-1467 [M]	Diahann Carroll Sings Harold Arlen	1957	10.00	20.00	40.00

UNITED ARTISTS
❑ UAL 3080 [M]	Diahann Carroll at the Persian Room	1960	5.00	10.00	20.00
❑ UAS 6080 [S]	Diahann Carroll at the Persian Room	1960	6.25	12.50	25.00

VIK
❑ LXA-1131 [M]	Best Beat Forward	1958	7.50	15.00	30.00

CARROLL, DIAHANN, AND ANDRE PREVIN
UNITED ARTISTS
❑ UAL 3069 [M]	Diahann Carroll and Andre Previn	1960	5.00	10.00	20.00
❑ UAL 4021 [M]	Porgy and Bess	1959	5.00	10.00	20.00
❑ UAS 5021 [S]	Porgy and Bess	1959	6.25	12.50	25.00
❑ UAS 6069 [S]	Diahann Carroll and Andre Previn	1960	6.25	12.50	25.00

CARROLL, JIM, BAND
ATCO
❑ SD 38-132	Catholic Boy	1980	3.00	6.00	12.00
❑ SD 38-145	Dry Dreams	1982	2.50	5.00	10.00

ATLANTIC
❑ 80123	I Write Your Name	1984	2.50	5.00	10.00

CARROLL, JOE
CHARLIE PARKER
❑ PLP-802 [M]	The Man with the Happy Sound	1962	7.50	15.00	30.00
❑ PLP-802S [S]	The Man with the Happy Sound	1962	7.50	15.00	30.00

EPIC
❑ LN 3272 [M]	Joe Carroll	1956	12.50	25.00	50.00

CARROLL BROTHERS, THE
CAMEO
❑ C-1015 [M]	College Twist Party	1962	6.25	12.50	25.00
❑ SC-1015 [S]	College Twist Party	1962	10.00	20.00	40.00

CARS, THE
DCC COMPACT CLASSICS
❑ LPZ-2056	The Cars Greatest Hits	1998	6.25	12.50	25.00
—Audiophile vinyl					

ELEKTRA
❑ R (# unk)	Candy-O	1979	3.00	6.00	12.00
—RCA Music Service edition has "The Cars Candy-O" printed on upper left front cover					
❑ 6E-135	The Cars	1978	2.50	5.00	10.00
❑ 5E-507	Candy-O	1979	2.50	5.00	10.00
—No title and artist listed on front cover (information was on a sticker on the shrink wrap)					
❑ 5E-514	Panorama	1980	2.50	5.00	10.00
❑ 5E-567	Shake It Up	1981	2.50	5.00	10.00
❑ 5E-567 [PD]	Shake It Up	1981	10.00	20.00	40.00
—Promo-only picture disc with blank back					
❑ 5E-567 [PD]	Shake It Up	1981	12.50	25.00	50.00
—Promo-only picture disc with "KMET-FM" imprinted on back					
❑ 60296	Heartbeat City	1984	2.00	4.00	8.00
❑ 60296 [DJ]	Heartbeat City	1984	3.75	7.50	15.00
—Promo-only audiophile pressing on Quiex II vinyl					
❑ 60464	Greatest Hits	1985	2.50	5.00	10.00
❑ 60747	Door to Door	1987	2.00	4.00	8.00
❑ R 143650	Heartbeat City	1984	2.50	5.00	10.00
—RCA Music Service edition					
❑ R 144033	The Cars	1978	3.00	6.00	12.00
—RCA Music Service edition					
❑ R 153702	Greatest Hits	1985	3.00	6.00	12.00
—RCA Music Service edition					
❑ R 161593	Door to Door	1987	2.50	5.00	10.00
—BMG Direct Marketing edition					

NAUTILUS
❑ NR-14	The Cars	1981	7.50	15.00	30.00
—Audiophile "Super Disc"					
❑ NR-49	Candy-O	1982	7.50	15.00	30.00
—Audiophile "Super Disc"					

CARSON, MARTHA
CAPITOL
❑ ST 1507 [S]	Satisfied	1960	7.50	15.00	30.00
❑ T 1507 [M]	Satisfied	1960	6.25	12.50	25.00
❑ ST 1607 [S]	A Talk with the Lord	1961	7.50	15.00	30.00
❑ T 1607 [M]	A Talk with the Lord	1961	6.25	12.50	25.00

RCA VICTOR
❑ LPM-1145 [M]	Journey to the Sky	1955	10.00	20.00	40.00
❑ LPM-1490 [M]	Rock-a My Soul	1957	12.50	25.00	50.00

SIMS
❑ LP-100 [M]	Martha Carson	196?	6.25	12.50	25.00

CARTER, ANITA
CAPITOL
❑ ST-11085	So Much Love	1972	3.75	7.50	15.00

MERCURY
❑ MG-20770 [M]	Folk Songs Old and New	1963	6.25	12.50	25.00
❑ MG-20847 [M]	Anita of the Carter Family	1964	6.25	12.50	25.00
❑ SR-60770 [S]	Folk Songs Old and New	1963	7.50	15.00	30.00
❑ SR-60847 [S]	Anita of the Carter Family	1964	7.50	15.00	30.00

CARTER, BENNY
ANALOGUE PRODUCTIONS
❑ AP-13	Jazz Giant	199?	7.50	15.00	30.00
—Audiophile reissue					

AUDIO LAB
❑ AL-1505 [M]	The Fabulous Benny Carter	1959	37.50	75.00	150.00

CLEF
❑ MGC-141 [10]	Cosmopolite	1953	50.00	100.00	200.00

CONTEMPORARY
❑ C-3555 [M]	Jazz Giant	1958	12.50	25.00	50.00
❑ M-3561 [M]	Swingin' the Twenties	1959	10.00	20.00	40.00
❑ S-7028 [S]	Jazz Giant	1960	7.50	15.00	30.00
—Reissue of Stereo Records 7028					
❑ S-7561 [S]	Swingin' the Twenties	1959	10.00	20.00	40.00

IMPULSE!
❑ A-12 [M]	Further Definitions	1962	6.25	12.50	25.00
❑ AS-12 [S]	Further Definitions	1962	7.50	15.00	30.00
❑ A-9116 [M]	Additions to Further Definitions	1966	7.50	15.00	30.00
❑ AS-9116 [S]	Additions to Further Definitions	1966	10.00	20.00	40.00

MOVIETONE
❑ 1020 [M]	Autumn Leaves	1967	5.00	10.00	20.00

NORGRAN
❑ MGN-10 [10]	The Urbane Mr. Carter	1954	37.50	75.00	150.00
❑ MGN-21 [10]	The Formidable Benny Carter	1954	37.50	75.00	150.00
❑ MGN-1015 [M]	Benny Carter Plays Pretty	1955	30.00	60.00	120.00
❑ MGN-1025 [M]	Benny Carter	1955	—	—	—
—Canceled					
❑ MGN-1044 [M]	New Jazz Sounds	1955	20.00	40.00	80.00
—With Dizzy Gillespie, Bill Harris					
❑ MGN-1058 [M]	Alone Together	1956	20.00	40.00	80.00
—With Oscar Peterson					
❑ MGN-1070 [M]	Cosmopolite	1956	20.00	40.00	80.00

STEREO RECORDS
❑ S-7028 [S]	Jazz Giant	1959	10.00	20.00	40.00

20TH CENTURY-FOX
❑ TFM-3134 [M]	Benny Carter in Paris	1963	5.00	10.00	20.00
❑ TFS-4134 [S]	Benny Carter in Paris	1963	6.25	12.50	25.00

UNITED ARTISTS
❑ UAL-3055 [M]	"Can Can" and "Anything Goes"	1959	7.50	15.00	30.00
❑ UAL-4017 [M]	Aspects	1960	7.50	15.00	30.00
❑ UAL-4073 [M]	"Can Can" and "Anything Goes"	1960	5.00	10.00	20.00
❑ UAL-4080 [M]	Jazz Calendar	1960	5.00	10.00	20.00
❑ UAL-4094 [M]	Sax A La Carter	1961	5.00	10.00	20.00
❑ UAS-5017 [S]	Aspects	1960	10.00	20.00	40.00
❑ UAS-5073 [S]	"Can Can" and "Anything Goes"	1960	6.25	12.50	25.00
❑ UAS-5080 [S]	Jazz Calendar	1960	6.25	12.50	25.00
❑ UAS-5094 [S]	Sax A La Carter	1961	6.25	12.50	25.00
❑ UAS-6055 [S]	"Can Can" and "Anything Goes"	1959	10.00	20.00	40.00

VERVE
❑ MGV-2025 [M]	Moonglow — Love Songs by Benny Carter	1957	15.00	30.00	60.00
—Reissue of Norgran 1015					
❑ V-2025 [M]	Moonglow — Love Songs by Benny Carter	1961	5.00	10.00	20.00
❑ MGV-8135 [M]	New Jazz Sounds	1957	15.00	30.00	60.00
—Reissue of Norgran 1044					
❑ V-8135 [M]	New Jazz Sounds	1961	5.00	10.00	20.00
❑ MGV-8148 [M]	Alone Together	1957	15.00	30.00	60.00
—Reissue of Norgran 1058					
❑ V-8148 [M]	Alone Together	1961	5.00	10.00	20.00
❑ MGV-8160 [M]	Cosmopolite	1957	15.00	30.00	60.00
—Reissue of Norgran 1070					
❑ V-8160 [M]	Cosmopolite	1961	5.00	10.00	20.00

CARTER, BENNY; BEN WEBSTER; BARNEY BIGARD
SWINGVILLE
❑ SVLP-2032 [M]	B.B.B. & Co.	1962	10.00	20.00	40.00
—Purple label					
❑ SVLP-2032 [M]	B.B.B. & Co.	1965	5.00	10.00	20.00
—Blue label, trident logo at right					
❑ SVST-2032 [S]	B.B.B. & Co.	1962	12.50	25.00	50.00
—Red label					
❑ SVST-2032 [S]	B.B.B. & Co.	1965	6.25	12.50	25.00
—Blue label, trident logo at right					

CARTER, BETTY
ABC IMPULSE!
❑ AS-9321 [(2)]	What a Little Moonlight	197?	5.00	10.00	20.00

ABC-PARAMOUNT
❑ ABC-363 [M]	The Modern Sound of Betty Carter	1960	15.00	30.00	60.00
❑ ABCS-363 [S]	The Modern Sound of Betty Carter	1960	20.00	40.00	80.00

ATCO
❑ 33-152 [M]	'Round Midnight	1963	12.50	25.00	50.00
❑ SD 33-152 [S]	'Round Midnight	1963	15.00	30.00	60.00

BET-CAR
❑ 1001	Betty Carter	1970	7.50	15.00	30.00
❑ 1002	The Betty Carter Album	197?	7.50	15.00	30.00
❑ MK 1003 [(2)]	The Audience with Betty Carter	1980	5.00	10.00	20.00

PEACOCK
❑ PLP-90 [M]	Out There with Betty Carter	1958	30.00	60.00	120.00

ROULETTE
❑ SR-5000	Finally	1969	6.25	12.50	25.00
❑ SR-5001	'Round Midnight	1975	5.00	10.00	20.00
❑ SR-5005	Now It's My Turn	1976	5.00	10.00	20.00

UNITED ARTISTS
❑ UAL 3379 [M]	Inside Betty Carter	1964	12.50	25.00	50.00
❑ UAS-5639	Inside Betty Carter	1971	5.00	10.00	20.00
—Reissue of 6379					
❑ UAS 6379 [S]	Inside Betty Carter	1964	15.00	30.00	60.00

CARTER, CALVIN
VEE JAY
❑ LP-1041 [M]	Twist with Calvin Carter	1962	25.00	50.00	100.00
❑ SR-1041 [S]	Twist with Calvin Carter	1962	37.50	75.00	150.00

CARTER, CLARENCE
ABC
❑ X-833	Real	1974	3.75	7.50	15.00

Number	Title (A Side/B Side)	Yr	VG	VG+	NM
❏ X-896	Loneliness & Temptation	1975	3.75	7.50	15.00
❏ X-943	A Heart Full of Song	1976	3.75	7.50	15.00
ATLANTIC					
❏ SD 8192	This Is Clarence Carter	1968	7.50	15.00	30.00
❏ SD 8199	The Dynamic Clarence Carter	1969	7.50	15.00	30.00
❏ SD 8238	Testifyin'	1969	7.50	15.00	30.00
❏ 8267 [M]	Patches	1970	15.00	30.00	60.00
—Mono is white label promo only; "d/j copy monaural" sticker on stereo cover					
❏ SD 8267 [S]	Patches	1970	7.50	15.00	30.00
❏ SD 8282	The Best of Clarence Carter	1971	5.00	10.00	20.00
FAME					
❏ FM-LA186-F	Sixty Minutes	1973	3.75	7.50	15.00
ICHIBAN					
❏ ICH-1001	Messin' with My Mind	1986	3.00	6.00	12.00
❏ ICH-1003	Dr. C.C.	1986	3.00	6.00	12.00
❏ ICH-1016	Hooked on Love	1987	3.00	6.00	12.00
❏ ICH-1032	Touch of Blues	1988	3.00	6.00	12.00
❏ ICH-1068	Between a Rock and a Hard Place	1989	3.00	6.00	12.00
❏ ICH-1116	The Best of Clarence Carter: The Dr.'s Greatest Presciptions	1991	3.00	6.00	12.00
VENTURE					
❏ VL 1005	Let's Burn	1980	2.50	5.00	10.00
❏ VL 1009	Mr. Clarence Carter In Person	1981	2.50	5.00	10.00
CARTER, JACK					
AAMCO					
❏ ALP-316 [M]	Broadway A La Carter	1958	6.25	12.50	25.00
CARTER, JOHN					
FLYING DUTCHMAN					
❏ FDS-109	John Carter	1969	5.00	10.00	20.00
CARTER, JOHN, AND BOBBY BRADFORD					
FLYING DUTCHMAN					
❏ FDS-108	Flight for Four	1969	5.00	10.00	20.00
❏ FDS-128	Self Determination Music	1970	5.00	10.00	20.00
CARTER, LYNDA					
EPIC					
❏ 35308 [PD]	Portrait	1978	15.00	30.00	60.00
—Picture disc version					
❏ JE 35308	Portrait	1978	3.75	7.50	15.00
CARTER, MEL					
AMOS					
❏ 7010	This Is My Life	1971	3.00	6.00	12.00
DERBY					
❏ LPM-702 [M]	When a Boy Falls in Love	1963	75.00	150.00	300.00
IMPERIAL					
❏ LP-9289 [M]	Hold Me, Thrill Me, Kiss Me	1965	3.75	7.50	15.00
❏ LP-9300 [M]	All of a Sudden My Heart Sings	1966	3.75	7.50	15.00
❏ LP-9319 [M]	Easy Listening	1966	3.75	7.50	15.00
❏ LP-12289 [S]	Hold Me, Thrill Me, Kiss Me	1965	5.00	10.00	20.00
❏ LP-12300 [S]	All of a Sudden My Heart Sings	1966	5.00	10.00	20.00
❏ LP-12319 [S]	Easy Listening	1966	5.00	10.00	20.00
SUNSET					
❏ SUS-5227	Mel Carter	1968	2.50	5.00	10.00
❏ SUS-5295	Easy Goin'	1970	2.50	5.00	10.00
CARTER, MOTHER MAYBELLE					
AMBASSADOR					
❏ 98069 [M]	Mother Maybelle Carter	195?	37.50	75.00	150.00
COLUMBIA					
❏ CL 2475 [M]	A Living Legend	1965	5.00	10.00	20.00
❏ CS 9275 [S]	A Living Legend	1965	6.25	12.50	25.00
❏ KG 32436 [(2)]	Mother Maybelle Carter	1973	6.25	12.50	25.00
KAPP					
❏ KL-1413 [M]	Queen of the Autoharp	1964	5.00	10.00	20.00
❏ KS-3413 [S]	Queen of the Autoharp	1964	6.25	12.50	25.00
SMASH					
❏ MGS-27025 [M]	Mother Maybelle Carter and Her Autoharp	1963	5.00	10.00	20.00
❏ MGS-27041 [M]	Pickin' and Singin'	1963	5.00	10.00	20.00
❏ SRS-67025 [S]	Mother Maybelle Carter and Her Autoharp	1963	6.25	12.50	25.00
❏ SRS-67041 [S]	Pickin' and Singin'	1963	6.25	12.50	25.00
CARTER, RON					
EMBRYO					
❏ 521	Uptown Conversation	1970	5.00	10.00	20.00
NEW JAZZ					
❏ NJLP-8265 [M]	Where?	1961	20.00	40.00	80.00
—With Eric Dolphy and Mal Waldron; purple label					
❏ NJLP-8265 [M]	Where?	1965	6.25	12.50	25.00
—With Eric Dolphy and Mal Waldron;; blue label, trident logo at right					
CARTER, WILF					
See MONTANA SLIM.					
CARTER FAMILY, THE					
ACME					
❏ LP-1 [M]	All Time Favorites	1960	50.00	100.00	200.00
❏ LP-2 [M]	In Memory of A.P. Carter	1960	50.00	100.00	200.00
COLUMBIA					
❏ CL 2319 [M]	The Best of the Carter Family	1965	3.75	7.50	15.00
❏ CL 2617 [M]	Country Album	1967	6.25	12.50	25.00
❏ CS 9119 [S]	The Best of the Carter Family	1965	5.00	10.00	20.00
❏ CS 9417 [S]	Country Album	1967	5.00	10.00	20.00
❏ KC 31454	Travelin' Minstrel Band	1972	5.00	10.00	20.00
❏ KC 33084	Three Generations	1974	5.00	10.00	20.00
❏ KC 34266	Country's First Family	1976	5.00	10.00	20.00
DECCA					
❏ DL 4404 [M]	A Collection of Favorites by the Carter Family	1963	7.50	15.00	30.00

Number	Title (A Side/B Side)	Yr	VG	VG+	NM
❏ DL 4557 [M]	More Favorites by the Carter Family	1964	7.50	15.00	30.00
LIBERTY					
❏ LRP-3230 [M]	The Carter Family Album	1962	7.50	15.00	30.00
❏ LST-7230 [S]	The Carter Family Album	1962	10.00	20.00	40.00
RCA VICTOR					
❏ LPM-2772 [M]	'Mid the Green Fields of Virginia	1963	10.00	20.00	40.00
❏ LSP-2772 [R]	'Mid the Green Fields of Virginia	1963	5.00	10.00	20.00
STARDAY					
❏ SLP-248 [M]	Echoes of the Carter Family	1963	10.00	20.00	40.00
CARTOONE					
ATLANTIC					
❏ SD 8219	Cartoone	1969	5.00	10.00	20.00
CARTWRIGHT, ANGELA					
STAR-BRIGHT					
❏ HLP-102 [M]	Angela Cartwright Sings	1959	12.50	25.00	50.00
CARVER, JOHNNY					
ABC					
❏ ABCX-792	Tie a Yellow Ribbon Around the Ole Oak Tree	1973	3.00	6.00	12.00
❏ ABCX-812	Double Exposure	1974	3.00	6.00	12.00
❏ ABCD-843	Please Don't Tell (That Sweet Ole Lady of Mine)	1974	3.00	6.00	12.00
❏ ABCD-864	Strings	1975	3.00	6.00	12.00
ABC DOT					
❏ DO-2042	Afternoon Delight	1976	3.00	6.00	12.00
❏ DO-2083	The Best of Johnny Carver	1977	3.00	6.00	12.00
HARMONY					
❏ KH 32476	I Start Thinking About You	1973	3.00	6.00	12.00
IMPERIAL					
❏ LP-9347 [M]	Really Country	1967	7.50	15.00	30.00
❏ LP-12347 [S]	Really Country	1967	5.00	10.00	20.00
❏ LP-12380	You're in Good Hands with Johnny Carver	1968	5.00	10.00	20.00
❏ LP-12412	Leaving Again	1968	5.00	10.00	20.00
CARY, DICK					
BELL					
❏ BLP-44 [M]	Hot and Cool	1961	7.50	15.00	30.00
GOLDEN CREST					
❏ GC-3024 [M]	Dixieland Goes Progressive	1958	12.50	25.00	50.00
STEREOCRAFT					
❏ RTN-106 [S]	Hot and Cool	196?	6.25	12.50	25.00
CASADESUS, JEAN					
RCA VICTOR RED SEAL					
❏ LSC-2415 [S]	Debussy: Preludes, Book 1	1960	10.00	20.00	40.00
—Original with "shaded dog" label					
CASCADES, THE					
UNI					
❏ 73069	Maybe the Rain Will Fall	1969	6.25	12.50	25.00
VALIANT					
❏ W 405 [M]	Rhythm of the Rain	1963	37.50	75.00	150.00
❏ WS 405 [S]	Rhythm of the Rain	1963	75.00	150.00	300.00
CASE, ALLEN					
COLUMBIA					
❏ CL 1406 [M]	"The Deputy" Sings	1960	5.00	10.00	20.00
❏ CS 8202 [S]	"The Deputy" Sings	1960	7.50	15.00	30.00
CASEY, AL					
STACY					
❏ STM-100 [M]	Surfin' Hootenanny	1963	75.00	150.00	300.00
❏ STS-100 [S]	Surfin' Hootenanny	1963	100.00	200.00	400.00
SUNDAZED					
❏ LP-5026	Surfin' Hootenanny	1996	2.50	5.00	10.00
CASEY, AL (2)					
MOODSVILLE					
❏ MVLP-12 [M]	The Al Casey Quartet	1960	12.50	25.00	50.00
—Green label					
❏ MVLP-12 [M]	The Al Casey Quartet	1965	6.25	12.50	25.00
—Blue label, trident logo at right					
SWINGVILLE					
❏ SVLP-2007 [M]	Buck Jumpin'	1960	12.50	25.00	50.00
—Purple label					
❏ SVLP-2007 [M]	Buck Jumpin'	1965	6.25	12.50	25.00
—Blue label, trident logo at right					
CASH, ALVIN					
MAR-V-LUS					
❏ 1827 [M]	Twine Time	1965	7.50	15.00	30.00
CASH, JOHNNY					
ACCORD					
❏ SN-7134	I Walk the Line	1983	2.50	5.00	10.00
❏ SN-7208	Years Gone By	1983	2.50	5.00	10.00
ALLEGIANCE					
❏ AV-5017	The First Years	1986	2.50	5.00	10.00
AMERICAN					
❏ 43097	Unchained	1996	3.00	6.00	12.00
❏ 45220	American Recordings	1994	3.00	6.00	12.00
❏ C 69691	American III: Solitary Man	2000	3.00	6.00	12.00
ARCHIVE OF FOLK MUSIC					
❏ 278	Johnny Cash	198?	3.00	6.00	12.00
CACHET					
❏ 9001	A Believer Sings the Truth	1979	3.75	7.50	15.00
COLUMBIA					
❏ GP 29 [(2)]	The World of Johnny Cash	1970	3.75	7.50	15.00
❏ C2L 38 [(2)M]	Ballads of the True West	1965	6.25	12.50	25.00

C

Number	Title (A Side/B Side)	Yr	VG	VG+	NM
❑ C2S 838 [(2)S]	Ballads of the True West	1965	6.25	12.50	25.00
❑ CL 1253 [M]	The Fabulous Johnny Cash	1958	5.00	10.00	20.00
❑ CL 1284 [M]	Hymns by Johnny Cash	1959	6.25	12.50	25.00
❑ CL 1339 [M]	Songs of Our Soil	1959	6.25	12.50	25.00
❑ CL 1463 [M]	Now, There Was a Song!	1960	6.25	12.50	25.00
❑ CL 1464 [M]	Ride This Train	1960	6.25	12.50	25.00
❑ CL 1622 [M]	The Lure of the Grand Canyon	1961	10.00	20.00	40.00
—Cash narrates; with Andre Kostelanetz and His Orchestra					
❑ CL 1722 [M]	Hymns from the Heart	1962	5.00	10.00	20.00
❑ CL 1802 [M]	The Sound of Johnny Cash	1962	5.00	10.00	20.00
❑ CL 1930 [M]	Blood, Sweat & Tears	1963	5.00	10.00	20.00
❑ CL 2052 [M]	Ring of Fire (The Best of Johnny Cash)	1963	5.00	10.00	20.00
❑ CL 2117 [M]	The Christmas Spirit	1963	6.25	12.50	25.00
❑ CL 2190 [M]	I Walk the Line	1964	3.75	7.50	15.00
❑ CL 2248 [M]	Bitter Tears (Ballads of the American Indian)	1964	3.75	7.50	15.00
❑ CL 2309 [M]	Orange Blossom Special	1965	3.75	7.50	15.00
❑ CL 2446 [M]	Mean as Hell	1965	3.75	7.50	15.00
❑ CL 2492 [M]	Everybody Loves a Nut	1966	3.75	7.50	15.00
❑ CL 2537 [M]	That's What You Get for Lovin' Me	1966	3.75	7.50	15.00
❑ CL 2647 [M]	From Sea to Shining Sea	1967	5.00	10.00	20.00
❑ CL 2678 [M]	Johnny Cash's Greatest Hits, Volume 1	1967	5.00	10.00	20.00
❑ CS 8122 [S]	The Fabulous Johnny Cash	1959	10.00	20.00	40.00
❑ CS 8125 [S]	Hymns by Johnny Cash	1959	10.00	20.00	40.00
❑ CS 8148 [S]	Songs of Our Soil	1959	10.00	20.00	40.00
❑ CS 8254 [S]	Now, There Was a Song!	1960	10.00	20.00	40.00
❑ CS 8255 [S]	Ride This Train	1960	10.00	20.00	40.00
❑ CS 8422 [S]	The Lure of the Grand Canyon	1961	12.50	25.00	50.00
—Cash narrates; with Andre Kostelanetz and His Orchestra					
❑ CS 8522 [S]	Hymns from the Heart	1962	7.50	15.00	30.00
❑ CS 8602 [S]	The Sound of Johnny Cash	1962	7.50	15.00	30.00
❑ CS 8730 [S]	Blood, Sweat & Tears	1963	6.25	12.50	25.00
❑ CS 8852 [S]	Ring of Fire (The Best of Johnny Cash)	1963	6.25	12.50	25.00
❑ CS 8917 [S]	The Christmas Spirit	1963	7.50	15.00	30.00
❑ CS 8990 [S]	I Walk the Line	1964	5.00	10.00	20.00
❑ CS 9048 [S]	Bitter Tears (Ballads of the American Indian)	1964	5.00	10.00	20.00
❑ CS 9109 [S]	Orange Blossom Special	1965	5.00	10.00	20.00
❑ CS 9246 [S]	Mean as Hell	1965	5.00	10.00	20.00
❑ CS 9292 [S]	Everybody Loves a Nut	1966	5.00	10.00	20.00
❑ CS 9337 [S]	That's What You Get for Lovin' Me	1966	5.00	10.00	20.00
❑ CS 9447 [S]	From Sea to Shining Sea	1967	5.00	10.00	20.00
❑ CS 9478 [S]	Johnny Cash's Greatest Hits, Volume 1	1967	5.00	10.00	20.00
❑ CS 9639 [M]	Johnny Cash at Folsom Prison	1968	12.50	25.00	50.00
—Mono is white label promo only with stereo number; "Special Mono Radio Station Copy" sticker on cover					
❑ CS 9639 [S]	Johnny Cash at Folsom Prison	1968	5.00	10.00	20.00
❑ KCS 9726	The Holy Land	1969	3.75	7.50	15.00
❑ CS 9827	Johnny Cash at San Quentin	1969	3.00	6.00	12.00
❑ KCS 9943	Hello, I'm Johnny Cash	1970	3.00	6.00	12.00
❑ C 30100	The Johnny Cash Show	1970	3.00	6.00	12.00
❑ S 30397	I Walk the Line	1970	3.00	6.00	12.00
—Soundtrack from movie					
❑ KC 30550	Man in Black	1971	3.00	6.00	12.00
❑ KC 30887	The Johnny Cash Collection (His Greatest Hits, Volume II)	1971	3.00	6.00	12.00
❑ CQ 30961 [Q]	Johnny Cash at San Quentin	1971	5.00	10.00	20.00
❑ KC 31256	Give My Love to Rose	1972	3.00	6.00	12.00
❑ KC 31332	A Thing Called Love	1972	3.00	6.00	12.00
❑ KC 31645	Johnny Cash: America (A 200-Year Salute in Story and Song)	1972	3.00	6.00	12.00
❑ KC 32091	Any Old Wind That Blows	1973	3.00	6.00	12.00
❑ C 32240	Sunday Morning Coming Down	1973	3.00	6.00	12.00
❑ C 32253	The Gospel Road	1973	3.00	6.00	12.00
❑ CG 32253 [(2)]	The Gospel Road	1973	6.25	12.50	25.00
❑ KC 32898	Children's Album	1974	3.00	6.00	12.00
❑ C 32917	The Ragged Old Flag	1974	3.00	6.00	12.00
❑ C 32951	Five Feet High and Rising	1974	3.00	6.00	12.00
❑ KC 33086	The Junkie and the Juicehead	1974	3.00	6.00	12.00
❑ C 33087	Johnny Cash Sings Precious Memories	1974	3.00	6.00	12.00
❑ KC 33370	John R. Cash	1975	3.00	6.00	12.00
❑ CG 33639 [(2)]	Johnny Cash at Folsom Prison/Johnny Cash at San Quentin	1974	3.75	7.50	15.00
❑ KC 33814	Look at Them Beans	1975	3.00	6.00	12.00
❑ KC 34088	Strawberry Cake	1976	3.00	6.00	12.00
❑ KC 34193	One Piece at a Time	1976	3.00	6.00	12.00
❑ JC 34314	The Last Gunfighter Ballad	1977	3.00	6.00	12.00
❑ JC 34833	The Rambler	1977	3.00	6.00	12.00
❑ KC 35313	I Would Like to See You Again	1978	2.50	5.00	10.00
❑ JC 35637	Johnny Cash's Greatest Hits, Volume 3	1978	3.00	6.00	12.00
❑ KC 35646	Gone Girl	1978	3.00	6.00	12.00
❑ JC 36086	Silver	1979	3.00	6.00	12.00
❑ JC 36779	Rockabilly Blues	1980	2.50	5.00	10.00
❑ JC 36866	Classic Christmas	1980	3.00	6.00	12.00
❑ FC 37179	The Baron	1981	2.50	5.00	10.00
❑ FC 37355	Encore	1981	2.50	5.00	10.00
❑ PC 38074	A Believer Sings the Truth	1985	2.00	4.00	8.00
—Reissue of Priority 38074					
❑ FC 38094	The Adventures of Johnny Cash	1982	2.50	5.00	10.00
❑ FC 38317	Johnny Cash's Biggest Hits	1982	2.50	5.00	10.00
❑ FC 38696	Johnny 99	1983	2.50	5.00	10.00
❑ PC 38696	Johnny 99	1986	2.00	4.00	8.00
—Budget-line reissue					
❑ FC 39951	Rainbow	1985	2.50	5.00	10.00
COLUMBIA SPECIAL PRODUCTS					
❑ 363	Legends and Love Songs	196?	5.00	10.00	20.00
❑ P 13832	Hello, I'm Johnny Cash	1977	3.00	6.00	12.00
DORAL/CSP					
❑ (# unknown)	Doral Presents Johnny Cash	1972	10.00	20.00	40.00
—Mail-order offer from Doral cigarettes					
EVEREST					
❑ 276	Johnny Cash	19??	3.00	6.00	12.00

Number	Title (A Side/B Side)	Yr	VG	VG+	NM
HARMONY					
❑ HS 11249	Golden Sounds of Country Music	1968	3.00	6.00	12.00
❑ HS 11342	Johnny Cash	1969	3.00	6.00	12.00
❑ KH 30138	The Walls of a Prison	1970	3.00	6.00	12.00
❑ KH 30916	Understand Your Man	1971	3.00	6.00	12.00
❑ KH 31602	The Johnny Cash Songbook	1972	3.00	6.00	12.00
❑ KH 32388	Ballads of the American Indian	1973	3.00	6.00	12.00
MERCURY					
❑ 832031-1	Johnny Cash Is Coming to Town	1987	2.50	5.00	10.00
❑ 834778-1	Water from the Wells of Home	1988	2.50	5.00	10.00
PAIR					
❑ PDL2-1107 [(2)]	Classic Cash	1986	3.75	7.50	15.00
POWER PAK					
❑ 246	Country Gold	198?	2.50	5.00	10.00
PRIORITY					
❑ UG 32253 [(2)]	The Gospel Road	1981	3.75	7.50	15.00
—Reissue of Columbia album of the same name					
❑ PU 33087	Johnny Cash Sings Precious Memories	1982	3.00	6.00	12.00
—Reissue of Columbia album of the same name					
❑ PU 38074	A Believer Sings the Truth	1982	3.00	6.00	12.00
—Reissue of Cachet album					
RHINO					
❑ RNLP 70229	The Vintage Years	1987	3.00	6.00	12.00
SHARE					
❑ 5000	I Walk the Line	197?	3.00	6.00	12.00
❑ 5001	Folsom Prison Blues	197?	3.00	6.00	12.00
❑ 5002	The Blue Train	197?	3.00	6.00	12.00
❑ 5003	Johnny Cash Sings the Greatest Hits	197?	3.00	6.00	12.00
SUN					
❑ LP-100	Original Golden Hits, Volume I	1969	3.00	6.00	12.00
❑ LP-101	Original Golden Hits, Volume II	1969	3.00	6.00	12.00
❑ LP-104	Story Songs of the Trains and Rivers	1969	3.00	6.00	12.00
❑ LP-105	Get Rhythm	1969	3.00	6.00	12.00
❑ LP-106	Showtime	1969	3.00	6.00	12.00
❑ LP-115	The Singing Story Teller	1970	3.00	6.00	12.00
❑ LP-118 [(2)]	Johnny Cash — The Legend	1970	5.00	10.00	20.00
❑ LP-122	The Rough Cut King of Country Music	1971	3.00	6.00	12.00
❑ LP-126 [(2)]	Johnny Cash: The Man, The World, His Music	1971	5.00	10.00	20.00
❑ LP-127	Original Golden Hits, Volume III	1972	3.00	6.00	12.00
❑ LP-139	I Walk the Line	1979	2.50	5.00	10.00
❑ LP-140	Folsom Prison Blues	1979	2.50	5.00	10.00
❑ LP-141	The Blue Train	1979	2.50	5.00	10.00
❑ LP-142	Johnny Cash Sings the Greatest Hits	1979	2.50	5.00	10.00
❑ 1002	Superbilly (1955-58)	198?	2.50	5.00	10.00
❑ 1006	The Original Johnny Cash	1980	2.50	5.00	10.00
❑ SLP-1220 [M]	Johnny Cash with His Hot and Blue Guitar	1956	25.00	50.00	100.00
❑ SLP-1220 [R]	Johnny Cash with His Hot and Blue Guitar	196?	5.00	10.00	20.00
—Reissue in rechanneled stereo; front cover says "STEREO"					
❑ SLP-1235 [M]	The Songs That Made Him Famous	1958	25.00	50.00	100.00
❑ SLP-1235 [R]	The Songs That Made Him Famous	196?	5.00	10.00	20.00
—Reissue in rechanneled stereo; front cover says "STEREO"					
❑ SLP-1240 [M]	Johnny Cash's Greatest!	1959	12.50	25.00	50.00
❑ SLP-1245 [M]	Johnny Cash Sings Hank Williams	1960	12.50	25.00	50.00
❑ SLP-1245 [R]	Johnny Cash Sings Hank Williams	196?	5.00	10.00	20.00
—Reissue in rechanneled stereo; front cover says "STEREO"					
❑ SLP-1255 [M]	Now Here's Johnny Cash	1961	12.50	25.00	50.00
❑ SLP-1255 [R]	Now Here's Johnny Cash	196?	5.00	10.00	20.00
—Reissue in rechanneled stereo; front cover says "STEREO"					
❑ SLP-1270 [M]	All Aboard the Blue Train	1963	12.50	25.00	50.00
❑ SLP-1275 [M]	The Original Sun Sound of Johnny Cash	1965	12.50	25.00	50.00
❑ DT-90668 [R]	The Songs That Made Him Famous	196?	6.25	12.50	25.00
—Capitol Record Club edition					
❑ DT-91458 [R]	All Aboard the Blue Train	196?	6.25	12.50	25.00
—Capitol Record Club edition					
❑ ST-92085	Original Golden Hits, Volume I	1969	5.00	10.00	20.00
—Capitol Record Club edition; uses older Sun label					
❑ ST-92086	Original Golden Hits, Volume II	1969	5.00	10.00	20.00
—Capitol Record Club edition; uses older Sun label					
WORD					
❑ WR-8333	Believe in Him	1986	3.00	6.00	12.00

CASH, JOHNNY, AND JUNE CARTER
COLUMBIA

Number	Title (A Side/B Side)	Yr	VG	VG+	NM
❑ CL 2728 [M]	Carryin' On with Johnny Cash and June Carter	1967	5.00	10.00	20.00
❑ CS 9528 [S]	Carryin' On with Johnny Cash and June Carter	1967	5.00	10.00	20.00
❑ KC 32443	Johnny Cash and His Woman	1973	3.75	7.50	15.00

CASH, ROSEANNE
COLUMBIA

Number	Title (A Side/B Side)	Yr	VG	VG+	NM
❑ AS 1527 [DJ]	Interview with Martha Hume	1982	7.50	15.00	30.00
—Generic cover with sticker					
❑ JC 36155	Right or Wrong	1980	2.50	5.00	10.00
❑ PC 36155	Right or Wrong	1984	2.00	4.00	8.00
—Budget-line reissue with new prefix and "02" added to bar code					
❑ JC 36965	Seven Year Ache	1981	2.50	5.00	10.00
❑ PC 36965	Seven Year Ache	1984	2.00	4.00	8.00
—Budget-line reissue with new prefix and "02" added to bar code					
❑ FC 37570	Somewhere in the Stars	1982	2.50	5.00	10.00
❑ PC 37570	Somewhere in the Stars	1984	2.00	4.00	8.00
—Budget-line reissue with new prefix and "02" added to bar code					
❑ FC 39463	Rhythm and Romance	1985	2.50	5.00	10.00
❑ FC 40777	King's Record Shop	1987	2.50	5.00	10.00
❑ OC 45054	Hits 1979-1989	1989	3.00	6.00	12.00
❑ HC 46965	Seven Year Ache	1981	12.50	25.00	50.00
—Half-speed mastered edition					

CASH, TOMMY
ELEKTRA

Number	Title (A Side/B Side)	Yr	VG	VG+	NM
❑ CM-5	Only a Stone	1975	3.75	7.50	15.00
EPIC					
❑ BN 26484	Your Lovin' Takes the Leavin' Out of Me	1969	5.00	10.00	20.00

Number	Title (A Side/B Side)	Yr	VG	VG+	NM
❏ BN 26535	Six White Horses	1970	3.75	7.50	15.00
❏ E 30107	Rise and Shine	1970	3.75	7.50	15.00
❏ E 30556	Cash Country	1971	3.75	7.50	15.00
❏ E 30860	American Way of Life	1971	3.75	7.50	15.00
❏ KE 31747	That Certain One	1972	3.75	7.50	15.00
❏ KE 31995	The Best of Tommy Cash, Volume I	1972	3.75	7.50	15.00

MONUMENT

❏ 7619	The New Spirit	1978	3.00	6.00	12.00

UNITED ARTISTS

❏ UAS-6628	Here Comes Tommy Cash	1968	5.00	10.00	20.00

CASHMAN, PISTILLI AND WEST
ABC

❏ ABCS-629	Bound to Happen	1968	5.00	10.00	20.00

CAPITOL

❏ ST-211	Cashman, Pistilli, and West	1969	3.75	7.50	15.00

CASINOS, THE (1)
FRATERNITY

❏ LP-1019 [M]	Then You Can Tell Me Goodbye	1967	10.00	20.00	40.00
❏ LPS-1019 [S]	Then You Can Tell Me Goodbye	1967	15.00	30.00	60.00

CASSELL, PETE
HILLTOP

❏ 6023	The Legend of Pete Cassell	1965	6.25	12.50	25.00

CASSIDY, DAVID
BELL

❏ 1109	Rock Me Baby	1972	5.00	10.00	20.00
❏ 1132	Dreams Are Nothing More Than Wishes	1973	5.00	10.00	20.00
❏ 1312	Cassidy Live	1974	6.25	12.50	25.00
❏ 1321	David Cassidy's Greatest Hits	1974	3.75	7.50	15.00
❏ 6070	Cherish	1972	5.00	10.00	20.00

RCA VICTOR

❏ APL1-1066	The Higher They Climb…	1975	3.75	7.50	15.00
—Black vinyl					
❏ APL1-1066	The Higher They Climb…	1975	25.00	50.00	100.00
—Blue vinyl					
❏ APL1-1309	Home Is Where the Heart Is	1976	3.75	7.50	15.00
❏ APL1-1852	Gettin' It in the Street	1976	10.00	20.00	40.00

CASTELLS, THE
ERA

❏ EL-109 [M]	So This Is Love	1962	30.00	60.00	120.00
❏ ES-109 [S]	So This Is Love	1962	100.00	200.00	400.00

CASTLE, LEE
CELEBRITY

❏ CEL-203 [M]	World Famous Dixieland Favorites	1952	10.00	20.00	40.00

DAVIS

❏ JD-105 [M]	Dixieland Heaven	1951	15.00	30.00	60.00

CASTOR, JIMMY, BUNCH
ATLANTIC

❏ SD 7305	The Everything Man	1974	2.50	5.00	10.00
❏ SD 18124	Butt Of Course	1975	2.50	5.00	10.00
❏ SD 18150	Supersound	1975	2.50	5.00	10.00
❏ SD 18186	E-Man Groovin'	1976	2.50	5.00	10.00
❏ SD 19111	Maximum Stimulation	1977	2.50	5.00	10.00

COTILLION

❏ SD 5215	The Jimmy Castor Bunch	1979	3.00	6.00	12.00

DRIVE

❏ 407	Let It Out	1978	3.00	6.00	12.00

LONG DISTANCE

❏ 1201	C	1980	3.00	6.00	12.00

RCA VICTOR

❏ APD1-0103 [Q]	Dimension III	1973	5.00	10.00	20.00
❏ APL1-0103	Dimension III	1973	3.75	7.50	15.00
❏ APL1-0313	The Everything Man	1974	3.75	7.50	15.00
❏ LSP-4640	It's Just Begun	1972	3.75	7.50	15.00
❏ LSP-4783	Phase Two	1972	3.75	7.50	15.00

SMASH

❏ MGS-27091 [M]	Hey Leroy!	1967	10.00	20.00	40.00
❏ SRS-67091 [S]	Hey Leroy!	1967	10.00	20.00	40.00

CASTRO, JOE
ATLANTIC

❏ 1264 [M]	Mood Jazz	1957	12.50	25.00	50.00
—Black label					
❏ 1264 [M]	Mood Jazz	1961	5.00	10.00	20.00
—Multicolor label with white "fan" logo					
❏ SD 1264 [S]	Mood Jazz	1959	10.00	20.00	40.00
—Green label					
❏ 1324 [M]	Groove Funk Soul	1960	10.00	20.00	40.00
—Black label					
❏ SD 1324 [S]	Groove Funk Soul	1960	12.50	25.00	50.00
—Green label					

CAT MOTHER AND THE ALL NIGHT NEWS BOYS
POLYDOR

❏ 24-4001	The Street Giveth…And the Street Taketh Away	1969	6.25	12.50	25.00
—Produced by Jimi Hendrix					
❏ 24-4023	Albion Doo-Wah	1970	3.75	7.50	15.00
❏ PD-5017	Cat Mother	1972	3.75	7.50	15.00
❏ PD-5042	Last Chance Dance	1972	3.75	7.50	15.00

CATALINAS, THE (1)
Studio band of Los Angeles session pros.
RIC

❏ M-1006 [M]	Fun, Fun, Fun	1964	25.00	50.00	100.00
❏ S-1006 [S]	Fun, Fun, Fun	1964	37.50	75.00	150.00

CATALYST
COBBLESTONE

❏ 9018	Catalyst	1972	5.00	10.00	20.00

CATANOOGA CATS, THE
FORWARD

❏ ST-F-1018	The Catanooga Cats	1969	10.00	20.00	40.00

CATAPILLA
VERTIGO

❏ 1006	Catapilla	1971	7.50	15.00	30.00

CATHCART, DICK
WARNER BROS.

❏ W 1275 [M]	Bix/MCMLIX	1959	6.25	12.50	25.00
❏ WS 1275 [S]	Bix/MCMLIX	1959	7.50	15.00	30.00

CATHY JEAN AND THE ROOMATES
VALMOR

❏ 78 [M]	Great Oldies	1962	200.00	400.00	800.00
—Reissue of 789 with titles on cover and no group shot					
❏ 789 [M]	At the Hop!	1961	225.00	450.00	900.00

CATINGUB, MATT
REFERENCE RECORDINGS

❏ RR-14	Your Friendly Neighborhood Big Band	1985	5.00	10.00	20.00
—Plays at 45 rpm					

CAUTHEN, STEVE
BAREBACK

❏ BB 3334	…And Steve Cauthen Sings Too!	1977	5.00	10.00	20.00

CAVANAUGH, PAGE
CAPITOL

❏ T 879 [M]	Fats Sent Me	1957	10.00	20.00	40.00
❏ T 1001 [M]	Swingin' Down the Road from Paris to Rome	1958	10.00	20.00	40.00

"X"

❏ LX-3027 [10]	Page Cavanaugh Trio	1954	12.50	25.00	50.00

CELESTIN, OSCAR
IMPERIAL

❏ LP-9125 [M]	Dixieland King	1961	5.00	10.00	20.00
❏ LP-9149 [M]	Birth of the Blues	1961	5.00	10.00	20.00
❏ LP-9199 [M]	Oscar "Papa" Celestin's New Orleans Jazz Band	1962	5.00	10.00	20.00

CELL BLOCK SEVEN
DIXIELAND JUBILEE

❏ DJ-506 [M]	A Dixieland Riot	195?	12.50	25.00	50.00

CENTAURUS
AZRA

❏ 61549	Centaurus	1978	12.50	25.00	50.00
—Issued on clear vinyl					

CENTIPEDE
RCA VICTOR

❏ CPL2-5042 [(2)]	Septober Energy	1974	12.50	25.00	50.00

CENTRAL NERVOUS SYSTEM
MUSIC FACTORY

❏ MF-12003 [M]	I Could Have Danced All Night	1968	7.50	15.00	30.00
—White label promo only (no stock copies were issued in mono)					
❏ MFS-12003 [S]	I Could Have Danced All Night	1968	5.00	10.00	20.00

CENTURIONS, THE
DEL-FI

❏ DFLP-1228 [M]	Surfer's Pajama Party	1963	25.00	50.00	100.00
❏ DFST-1228 [S]	Surfer's Pajama Party	1963	50.00	100.00	200.00
—Above has the same title and number, and almost the same cover, as the album of the same name by Bruce Johnston, but the contents are different					

CESANA
MODERN

❏ M-100 [M]	Tender Emotions	1964	5.00	10.00	20.00

CEYLEIB PEOPLE, THE
VAULT

❏ LP-117	Tanyet	1968	15.00	30.00	60.00

CHAD AND JEREMY
CAPITOL

❏ ST 2470 [P]	The Best of Chad and Jeremy	1966	3.00	6.00	12.00
—Black label with colorband					
❏ ST 2470 [P]	The Best of Chad and Jeremy	1967	2.50	5.00	10.00
—"Starline" label					
❏ T 2470 [M]	The Best of Chad and Jeremy	1966	2.50	5.00	10.00
—Black label with colorband					
❏ T 2470 [M]	The Best of Chad and Jeremy	1967	2.00	4.00	8.00
—"Starline" label					
❏ STT 2546 [P]	More Chad and Jeremy	1966	3.00	6.00	12.00
❏ TT 2546 [M]	More Chad and Jeremy	1966	2.50	5.00	10.00
❏ SN-16135 [P]	The Best of Chad and Jeremy	1980	2.00	4.00	8.00
—Budget-line reissue					

COLUMBIA

❏ CL 2374 [M]	Before and After	1965	5.00	10.00	20.00
❏ CL 2398 [M]	I Don't Want to Lose You Baby	1966	6.25	12.50	25.00
❏ CL 2564 [M]	Distant Shores	1966	5.00	10.00	20.00
❏ CL 2671 [M]	Of Cabbages and Kings	1967	5.00	10.00	20.00
❏ CL 2899 [M]	The Ark	1968	6.25	12.50	25.00
❏ CS 9174 [S]	Before and After	1965	7.50	15.00	30.00
❏ CS 9198 [S]	I Don't Want to Lose You Baby	1966	10.00	20.00	40.00
❏ CS 9364 [P]	Distant Shores	1966	6.25	12.50	25.00
—"Distant Shores" is rechanneled					
❏ CS 9471 [S]	Of Cabbages and Kings	1967	6.25	12.50	25.00

Number	Title (A Side/B Side)	Yr	VG	VG+	NM
❑ CS 9699 [S]	The Arc	1968	6.25	12.50	25.00

—Some copies spell the LP title this way on the cover

Number	Title (A Side/B Side)	Yr	VG	VG+	NM
❑ CS 9699 [S]	The Ark	1968	6.25	12.50	25.00

—Correct spelling of LP title on cover

FIDU

Number	Title (A Side/B Side)	Yr	VG	VG+	NM
❑ FM-101 [M]	5 + 10 = 15 Fabulous Hits	1966	2.50	5.00	10.00
❑ FS-101 [P]	5 + 10 = 15 Fabulous Hits	1966	3.00	6.00	12.00

HARMONY

❑ HS 11357 [S]	Chad and Jeremy	1973	2.00	4.00	8.00

ROCSHIRE

❑ XR-22018	Chad Stuart and Jeremy Clyde	1983	2.50	5.00	10.00

WORLD ARTISTS

❑ WAM-2002 [M]	Yesterday's Gone	1964	3.00	6.00	12.00
❑ WAM-2005 [M]	Chad and Jeremy Sing for You	1965	3.00	6.00	12.00
❑ WAS-3002 [P]	Yesterday's Gone	1964	3.75	7.50	15.00

—"Yesterday's Gone" is rechanneled.

❑ WAS-3005 [S]	Chad and Jeremy Sing for You	1965	3.75	7.50	15.00

CHAIRMEN OF THE BOARD

INVICTUS

Number	Title (A Side/B Side)	Yr	VG	VG+	NM
❑ ST-7300	Chairmen of the Board (Featuring "Give Me Just a Little More Time")	1970	10.00	20.00	40.00
❑ SKAO-7304	In Session	1970	10.00	20.00	40.00
❑ ST-9801	Bittersweet	1972	10.00	20.00	40.00
❑ KZ 32526	The Skin I'm In	1974	10.00	20.00	40.00

CHAKIRIS, GEORGE

CAPITOL

Number	Title (A Side/B Side)	Yr	VG	VG+	NM
❑ ST 1750 [S]	George Chakiris	1962	5.00	10.00	20.00
❑ T 1750 [M]	George Chakiris	1962	3.75	7.50	15.00
❑ ST 1813 [S]	Memories Are Made of These	1963	5.00	10.00	20.00
❑ T 1813 [M]	Memories Are Made of These	1963	3.75	7.50	15.00
❑ ST 2391 [S]	It's Been a Swingin' Summer	1965	3.75	7.50	15.00
❑ T 2391 [M]	It's Been a Swingin' Summer	1965	3.00	6.00	12.00

HORIZON

❑ ST-1610 [S]	The Gershwin Songbook	1962	5.00	10.00	20.00
❑ WP-1610 [M]	The Gershwin Songbook	1962	3.75	7.50	15.00

CHALKER, CURLY

COLUMBIA

❑ CL 2596 [M]	Big Hits on Big Steel	1965	5.00	10.00	20.00
❑ CS 9396 [S]	Big Hits on Big Steel	1965	7.50	15.00	30.00

CHALLENGERS, THE (1)

FANTASY

❑ F-9443	Where Were You in the Summer of '62	1973	3.00	6.00	12.00

GNP CRESCENDO

Number	Title (A Side/B Side)	Yr	VG	VG+	NM
❑ GNP-609 [(2)M]	25 Great Instrumental Hits	1967	6.25	12.50	25.00
❑ GNPS-609 [(2)S]	25 Great Instrumental Hits	1967	5.00	10.00	20.00
❑ GNP-2010 [M]	The Challengers at the Teenage Fair	1965	5.00	10.00	20.00
❑ GNPS-2010 [S]	The Challengers at the Teenage Fair	1965	6.25	12.50	25.00
❑ GNP-2018 [M]	The Man from U.N.C.L.E.	1965	5.00	10.00	20.00
❑ GNPS-2018 [S]	The Man from U.N.C.L.E.	1965	6.25	12.50	25.00
❑ GNP-2025 [M]	California Kicks	1966	5.00	10.00	20.00
❑ GNPS-2025 [S]	California Kicks	1966	6.25	12.50	25.00
❑ GNP-2030 [M]	Billy Strange and the Challengers	1966	5.00	10.00	20.00
❑ GNPS-2030 [S]	Billy Strange and the Challengers	1966	6.25	12.50	25.00
❑ GNP-2031 [M]	Wipe Out	1966	5.00	10.00	20.00
❑ GNPS-2031 [S]	Wipe Out	1966	6.25	12.50	25.00
❑ GNPS-2045	Light My Fire with Classical Gas	1968	5.00	10.00	20.00
❑ GNPS-2056	Vanilla Funk	1970	5.00	10.00	20.00
❑ GNPS-2093	Sidewalk Surfing	1975	3.00	6.00	12.00

RHINO

❑ RNLP-053	Best of the Challengers	1982	2.50	5.00	10.00

TRIUMPH

❑ TR-100 [M]	The Challengers Go Sidewalk Surfing	1965	5.00	10.00	20.00
❑ TRS-100 [S]	The Challengers Go Sidewalk Surfing	1965	6.25	12.50	25.00

VAULT

Number	Title (A Side/B Side)	Yr	VG	VG+	NM
❑ LP-100 [M]	Surfbeat	1963	12.50	25.00	50.00
❑ VS-100 [S]	Surfbeat	1963	20.00	40.00	80.00

—Black vinyl

❑ VS-100 [S]	Surfbeat	1963	62.50	12.50	250.00

—Orange vinyl

❑ VS-100 [S]	Surfbeat	1963	62.50	125.00	250.00

—Red vinyl

❑ VS-100 [S]	Surfbeat	1963	62.50	125.00	250.00

—Yellow vinyl

❑ LP-101 [M]	Surfin' with the Challengers	1963	12.50	25.00	50.00

—Altered title

❑ LP-101 [M]	Lloyd Thaxton Goes Surfin' with the Challengers	1963	15.00	30.00	60.00

—Original title

❑ VS-101 [S]	Surfin' with the Challengers	1963	20.00	40.00	80.00

—Altered title; black vinyl

❑ VS-101 [S]	Lloyd Thaxton Goes Surfin' with the Challengers	1963	25.00	50.00	100.00

—Original title; black vinyl

❑ VS-101 [S]	(Lloyd Thaxton Goes) Surfin' with the Challengers	1963	62.50	125.00	250.00

—Either title; blue vinyl

❑ VS-101 [S]	(Lloyd Thaxton Goes) Surfin' with the Challengers	1963	62.50	125.00	250.00

—Either title; orange vinyl

❑ VS-101 [S]	(Lloyd Thaxton Goes) Surfin' with the Challengers	1963	62.50	125.00	250.00

—Either title; red vinyl

❑ VS-101 [S]	(Lloyd Thaxton Goes) Surfin' with the Challengers	1963	62.50	125.00	250.00

—Either title; yellow vinyl

❑ LP-102 [M]	The Challengers On The Move	1963	10.00	20.00	40.00
❑ VS-102 [S]	The Challengers On The Move	1963	15.00	30.00	60.00

Number	Title (A Side/B Side)	Yr	VG	VG+	NM
❑ LP-107 [M]	K-39	1964	20.00	40.00	80.00
❑ LP-109 [M]	The Surf's Up	1965	10.00	20.00	40.00
❑ VS-109 [S]	The Surf's Up	1965	15.00	30.00	60.00
❑ LP-110 [M]	The Challengers A-Go-Go	1966	7.50	15.00	30.00
❑ VS-110 [S]	The Challengers A-Go-Go	1966	10.00	20.00	40.00
❑ LP-111 [M]	The Challengers' Greatest Hits	1967	6.25	12.50	25.00
❑ VS-111 [S]	The Challengers' Greatest Hits	1967	6.25	12.50	25.00

CHALOFF, SERGE

CAPITOL

❑ T 742 [M]	Blue Serge	1956	25.00	50.00	100.00

—Turquoise label

❑ T 742 [M]	Blue Serge	1959	15.00	30.00	60.00

—Black colorband label, logo at left

❑ T 6510 [M]	Boston Blow-Up	1955	25.00	50.00	100.00

MOSAIC

❑ MQ5-147 [(5)]	The Complete Serge Chaloff Sessions	1993	20.00	40.00	80.00

STORYVILLE

❑ STLP-317 [10]	The Fable of Mable	1954	50.00	100.00	200.00
❑ STLP-350 [10]	Serge & Boots	1955	50.00	100.00	200.00

CHALOFF, SERGE/OSCAR PETTIFORD

MERCER

❑ LP-1003 [10]	New Stars, New Sounds, Volume 2	1951	37.50	75.00	150.00

CHAMAELEON CHURCH

Chevy Chase was in this group.

MGM

❑ SE-4574	Chamaeleon Church	1968	5.00	10.00	20.00

CHAMBERLAIN, RICHARD

METRO

Number	Title (A Side/B Side)	Yr	VG	VG+	NM
❑ M-564 [M]	Richard Chamberlain Sings	1966	3.00	6.00	12.00
❑ MS-564 [S]	Richard Chamberlain Sings	1966	3.00	6.00	12.00

MGM

❑ E-4088 [M]	Richard Chamberlain Sings	1962	3.75	7.50	15.00
❑ SE-4088 [S]	Richard Chamberlain Sings	1962	5.00	10.00	20.00
❑ E-4185 [M]	Twilight of Honor	1963	3.75	7.50	15.00
❑ SE-4185 [S]	Twilight of Honor	1963	5.00	10.00	20.00
❑ E-4287 [M]	Joy in the Morning	1965	3.75	7.50	15.00
❑ SE-4287 [S]	Joy in the Morning	1965	5.00	10.00	20.00
❑ ST 90512 [S]	Richard Chamberlain Sings	1965	7.50	15.00	30.00

—Capitol Record Club edition

❑ T 90512 [M]	Richard Chamberlain Sings	1965	6.25	12.50	25.00

—Capitol Record Club edition

CHAMBERS, PAUL

BLUE NOTE

Number	Title (A Side/B Side)	Yr	VG	VG+	NM
❑ BLP-1534 [M]	Whims of Chambers	1956	25.00	50.00	100.00

—Regular version, Lexington Ave., NY address on label

❑ BLP-1534 [M]	Whims of Chambers	1956	75.00	150.00	300.00

—"Deep groove" version (deep indentation under label on both sides)

❑ BLP-1534 [M]	Whims of Chambers	1963	6.25	12.50	25.00

—"New York, USA" address on label

❑ BLP-1564 [M]	Paul Chambers Quintet	1957	20.00	40.00	80.00

—Regular version, W. 63rd St. address on label

❑ BLP-1564 [M]	Paul Chambers Quintet	1957	37.50	75.00	150.00

—"Deep groove" version (deep indentation under label on both sides)

❑ BLP-1564 [M]	Paul Chambers Quintet	1963	6.25	12.50	25.00

—"New York, USA" address on label

❑ BST-1564 [S]	Paul Chambers Quintet	1959	15.00	30.00	60.00

—Regular version, W. 63rd St. address on label

❑ BST-1564 [S]	Paul Chambers Quintet	1959	25.00	50.00	100.00

—"Deep groove" version (deep indentation under label on both sides)

❑ BST-1564 [S]	Paul Chambers Quintet	1963	5.00	10.00	20.00

—"New York, USA" address on label

❑ BLP-1569 [M]	Bass on Top	1957	20.00	40.00	80.00

—Regular version, W. 63rd St. address on label

❑ BLP-1569 [M]	Bass on Top	1957	37.50	75.00	150.00

—"Deep groove" version (deep indentation under label on both sides)

❑ BLP-1569 [M]	Bass on Top	1963	6.25	12.50	25.00

—"New York, USA" address on label

❑ BST-1569 [S]	Bass on Top	1959	15.00	30.00	60.00

—Regular version, W. 63rd St. address on label

❑ BST-1569 [S]	Bass on Top	1959	25.00	50.00	100.00

—"Deep groove" version (deep indentation under label on both sides)

❑ BST-1569 [S]	Bass on Top	1963	5.00	10.00	20.00

—"New York, USA" address on label

IMPERIAL

❑ LP-9182 [M]	A Jazz Delegation from the East: Chambers' Music	1961	10.00	20.00	40.00
❑ LP-12182 [S]	A Jazz Delegation from the East: Chambers' Music	1961	7.50	15.00	30.00

JAZZ WEST

❑ JWLP-7 [M]	A Jazz Delegation from the East: Chambers' Music	1956	150.00	300.00	600.00

SCORE

❑ SLP-4033 [M]	A Jazz Delegation from the East: Chambers' Music	1958	20.00	40.00	80.00

VEE JAY

❑ LP-1014 [M]	Go	1959	10.00	20.00	40.00
❑ SR-1014 [S]	Go	1959	12.50	25.00	50.00
❑ LP-3012 [M]	First Bassman	1960	7.50	15.00	30.00
❑ SR-3012 [S]	First Bassman	1960	10.00	20.00	40.00

CHAMBERS BROTHERS, THE

AVCO

❑ 11013	Unbonded	1974	3.00	6.00	12.00
❑ 69003	Night Move	1975	5.00	10.00	20.00

COLUMBIA

❑ KGP 20 [(2)]	Love, Peace and Happiness	1969	6.25	12.50	25.00
❑ CL 2722 [M]	The Time Has Come	1967	7.50	15.00	30.00

Number	Title (A Side/B Side)	Yr	VG	VG+	NM
❑ CS 9522	The Time Has Come	1971	3.00	6.00	12.00
—Orange label					
❑ CS 9522 [S]	The Time Has Come	1967	5.00	10.00	20.00
—Red "360 Sound" label					
❑ PC 9522	The Time Has Come	198?	2.00	4.00	8.00
—Reissue with new prefix					
❑ CS 9671	A New Time — A New Day	1968	5.00	10.00	20.00
❑ C 30032	New Generation	1970	3.75	7.50	15.00
❑ C 30871	The Chambers Brothers' Greatest Hits	1971	3.75	7.50	15.00
❑ PC 30871	The Chambers Brothers' Greatest Hits	198?	2.00	4.00	8.00
—Reissue with new prefix					
❑ KC 31158	Oh My God	1972	—	—	—
—Canceled					
❑ CG 33642 [(2)]	The Time Has Come/A New Time — A New Day	1975	3.75	7.50	15.00
FANTASY					
❑ 24718 [(2)]	The Best of the Chambers Brothers	1973	3.75	7.50	15.00
FOLKWAYS					
❑ 31008	Groovin' Time	1968	3.75	7.50	15.00
ROXBURY					
❑ RLX-106	Live In Concert on Mars	1976	7.50	15.00	30.00
VAULT					
❑ LP-115 [M]	The Chambers Brothers Now	1967	3.75	7.50	15.00
❑ VS-115 [S]	The Chambers Brothers Now	1967	3.75	7.50	15.00
❑ VS-120	The Chambers Brothers Shout	1968	3.75	7.50	15.00
❑ VS-128	Feelin' the Blues	1969	3.75	7.50	15.00
❑ VS-135 [(2)]	The Chambers Brothers Greatest Hits	1970	5.00	10.00	20.00
❑ LP-9003 [M]	People Get Ready	1966	5.00	10.00	20.00
❑ LPS-9003 [S]	People Get Ready	1966	6.25	12.50	25.00

CHAMBLEE, EDDIE

Number	Title (A Side/B Side)	Yr	VG	VG+	NM
EMARCY					
❑ MG-36124 [M]	Chamblee Music	1958	12.50	25.00	50.00
❑ MG-36131 [M]	Doodlin'	1958	12.50	25.00	50.00
❑ SR-80007 [S]	Doodlin'	1959	10.00	20.00	40.00
MERCURY					
❑ SR-60127 [S]	Chamblee Music	1960	6.25	12.50	25.00
PRESTIGE					
❑ PRLP-7321 [M]	The Rocking Tenor Sax of Eddie Chamblee	1964	6.25	12.50	25.00
—Yellow label					
❑ PRST-7321 [S]	The Rocking Tenor Sax of Eddie Chamblee	1964	7.50	15.00	30.00
—Silver label					

CHAMPS, THE

Number	Title (A Side/B Side)	Yr	VG	VG+	NM
CHALLENGE					
❑ CHL-601 [M]	Go Champs Go	1958	62.50	125.00	250.00
❑ CHL-601 [M]	Go Champs Go	1958	800.00	1600.	2400.
—Blue vinyl					
❑ CHL-605 [M]	Everybody's Rockin' with the Champs	1959	50.00	100.00	200.00
❑ CHL-613 [M]	Great Dance Hits	1962	30.00	60.00	120.00
❑ CHL-614 [M]	All American Music from the Champs	1962	30.00	60.00	120.00
❑ CHS-2500 [S]	Everybody's Rockin' with the Champs	1959	75.00	150.00	300.00
❑ CHS-2513 [S]	Great Dance Hits	1962	50.00	100.00	200.00
❑ CHS-2514 [S]	All American Music from the Champs	1962	50.00	100.00	200.00

CHANDLER, GENE

Number	Title (A Side/B Side)	Yr	VG	VG+	NM
BRUNSWICK					
❑ BL 54124 [M]	The Girl Don't Care	1967	6.25	12.50	25.00
❑ BL 754124 [S]	The Girl Don't Care	1967	5.00	10.00	20.00
❑ BL 754131	There Was a Time	1968	5.00	10.00	20.00
❑ BL 754149	The Two Sides of Gene Chandler	1969	5.00	10.00	20.00
CHECKER					
❑ LP-3003 [M]	The Duke of Soul	1967	12.50	25.00	50.00
❑ LPS-3003 [R]	The Duke of Soul	1967	7.50	15.00	30.00
CHI-SOUND					
❑ T-578	Get Down	1978	2.50	5.00	10.00
CONSTELLATION					
❑ LP 1421 [M]	Greatest Hits by Gene Chandler	1964	12.50	25.00	50.00
❑ LP 1423 [M]	Just Be True	1964	12.50	25.00	50.00
❑ LP 1425 [M]	Gene Chandler — Live On Stage in '65	1965	12.50	25.00	50.00
MERCURY					
❑ SR-61304	The Gene Chandler Situation	1970	3.75	7.50	15.00
SOLID SMOKE					
❑ SS-8027	Stroll On with the Duke	198?	2.50	5.00	10.00
20TH CENTURY					
❑ T-598	When You're #1	1979	2.50	5.00	10.00
❑ T-605	Gene Chandler '80	1980	2.50	5.00	10.00
❑ T-625	Ear Candy	1980	2.50	5.00	10.00
❑ T-629	Here's to Love	1981	2.50	5.00	10.00
VEE JAY					
❑ LP-1040 [M]	The Duke of Earl	1962	30.00	60.00	120.00
❑ SR-1040 [M]	The Duke of Earl	196?	12.50	25.00	50.00

—"Stereophonic" on front; no "Important Notice..." on back; record plays mono. Most labels are all-black with "VJ" in brackets. This was a semi-authorized reissue after ex-Vee Jay executives bought the company's remnants in bankruptcy court in 1966.

❑ SR-1040 [S]	The Duke of Earl	1962	62.50	125.00	250.00

—"Stereo" sticker on mono cover; "Stereo" on record labels

❑ SR-1040 [M]	The Duke of Earl	1962	200.00	400.00	800.00

—"Stereophonic" on front cover; top back cover contains note that begins: "Important Notice...This Is a Stereophonic Record"; "Stereo" on record labels

❑ VJLP-1040	The Duke of Earl	198?	2.50	5.00	10.00

—Mid-1980s authorized reissue

CHANDLER, JEFF

Number	Title (A Side/B Side)	Yr	VG	VG+	NM
LIBERTY					
❑ LRP-3067 [M]	Jeff Chandler Sings to You	1957	10.00	20.00	40.00
❑ LRP-3074 [M]	Warm and Easy	1958	10.00	20.00	40.00
SUNSET					
❑ SUS-5127	Sincerely Yours	1969	3.00	6.00	12.00

CHANNEL, BRUCE

Number	Title (A Side/B Side)	Yr	VG	VG+	NM
SMASH					
❑ MGS-27008 [M]	Hey! Baby (And 11 Other Songs About Your Baby)	1962	25.00	50.00	100.00
❑ SRS-67008 [R]	Hey! Baby (And 11 Other Songs About Your Baby)	1962	15.00	30.00	60.00

CHANNING, CAROL

Number	Title (A Side/B Side)	Yr	VG	VG+	NM
CAEDMON					
❑ TC 1303	The Year Without a Santa Claus and Other Stories for Christmas	1969	3.00	6.00	12.00
—Spoken-word recordings					
COMMAND					
❑ 880 SD [S]	Carol Channing Entertains	1966	5.00	10.00	20.00
❑ 33-880 [M]	Carol Channing Entertains	1966	3.75	7.50	15.00
PLANTATION					
❑ PLP-527	Carol Channing With the Original Country Cast	1978	5.00	10.00	20.00
VANGUARD					
❑ VSD-2041 [S]	Carol Channing	1959	10.00	20.00	40.00
❑ VRS-9056 [M]	Carol Channing	1959	7.50	15.00	30.00

CHANTAY'S

Number	Title (A Side/B Side)	Yr	VG	VG+	NM
DOT					
❑ DLP 3516 [M]	Pipeline	1963	12.50	25.00	50.00
❑ DLP 3771 [M]	Two Sides of the Chantays	1966	12.50	25.00	50.00
❑ DLP 25516 [S]	Pipeline	1963	20.00	40.00	80.00
❑ DLP 25771 [S]	Two Sides of the Chantays	1966	20.00	40.00	80.00
DOWNEY					
❑ DLP-1002 [M]	Pipeline	1963	55.00	110.00	220.00
❑ DLPS-1002 [S]	Pipeline	1963	87.50	175.00	350.00

CHANTELS, THE

Number	Title (A Side/B Side)	Yr	VG	VG+	NM
CARLTON					
❑ LP-144 [M]	The Chantels On Tour/Look in My Eyes	1962	50.00	100.00	200.00
❑ STLP-144 [P]	The Chantels On Tour/Look in My Eyes	1962	100.00	200.00	400.00
—Eight tracks are true stereo, two are mono, two are rechanneled					
END					
❑ LP-301 [M]	We Are the Chantels	1958	500.00	1000.	1500.
—Group photo on front cover; gray label with "11-17-58" in trail-off wax					
❑ LP-301 [M]	We Are the Chantels	1959	100.00	200.00	400.00
—Jukebox on front cover; gray label, "11-17-58" in trail-off wax					
❑ LP-301 [M]	We Are the Chantels	1962	50.00	100.00	200.00
—Jukebox on front cover; gray label, "1962" in trail-off wax					
❑ LP-301 [M]	We Are the Chantels	1965	20.00	40.00	80.00
—Jukebox on front cover; multicolor label, "8-65" in trail-off wax					
❑ LP-301 [M]	We Are the Chantels	1965	25.00	50.00	100.00
—Jukebox on front cover; gray label, "8-65" in trail-off wax					
❑ LP-312 [M]	There's Our Song Again	1962	30.00	60.00	120.00
FORUM					
❑ F-9104 [M]	The Chantels Sing Their Favorites	1964	12.50	25.00	50.00
❑ FS-9104 [R]	The Chantels Sing Their Favorites	1964	6.25	12.50	25.00

CHAPARRAL BROTHERS, THE

Number	Title (A Side/B Side)	Yr	VG	VG+	NM
CAPITOL					
❑ ST-551	Just for the Record	1970	3.75	7.50	15.00
❑ ST 2922	Introducing the Chaparral Brothers	1968	5.00	10.00	20.00

CHAPIN, JIM

Number	Title (A Side/B Side)	Yr	VG	VG+	NM
PRESTIGE					
❑ PRLP-213 [10]	Jim Chapin Sextet	1955	62.50	125.00	250.00

CHAPINS, THE

Number	Title (A Side/B Side)	Yr	VG	VG+	NM
ROCK-LAND					
❑ RR-66 [M]	Chapin Music	1966	7.50	15.00	30.00
—As "The Chapin Brothers"					

CHARIOT

Number	Title (A Side/B Side)	Yr	VG	VG+	NM
NATIONAL GENERAL					
❑ NG-2003	Chariot	1971	12.50	25.00	50.00

CHARIOTEERS, THE

Number	Title (A Side/B Side)	Yr	VG	VG+	NM
COLUMBIA					
❑ CL 6014 [10]	Sweet and Low	1949	75.00	150.00	300.00
HARMONY					
❑ HL 7089 [M]	The Charioteers with Billy Williams	1957	25.00	50.00	100.00

CHARISMA

Number	Title (A Side/B Side)	Yr	VG	VG+	NM
ROULETTE					
❑ SR-42037	Charisma	1970	5.00	10.00	20.00

CHARITY

Number	Title (A Side/B Side)	Yr	VG	VG+	NM
UNI					
❑ 73061	Charity Now	1969	6.25	12.50	25.00

CHARLATANS, THE

Number	Title (A Side/B Side)	Yr	VG	VG+	NM
PHILIPS					
❑ PHS 600309	The Charlatans	1969	25.00	50.00	100.00

CHARLENE

Number	Title (A Side/B Side)	Yr	VG	VG+	NM
MOTOWN					
❑ 6007 ML	Charlene	1981	2.50	5.00	10.00
❑ 6027 ML	Used to Be	1982	2.50	5.00	10.00
❑ 6090 ML	Hit and Run Lover	1985	2.50	5.00	10.00
PRODIGAL					
❑ P6-10015	Charlene	1976	5.00	10.00	20.00
❑ P6-10018	Songs of Love	1977	5.00	10.00	20.00

CHARLES, RAY

Number	Title (A Side/B Side)	Yr	VG	VG+	NM
ABC					
❑ S-335 [S]	The Genius Hits the Road	1967	3.00	6.00	12.00
❑ S-355 [S]	Dedicated to You	1967	3.00	6.00	12.00
❑ S-410 [S]	Modern Sounds in Country and Western Music	1967	3.00	6.00	12.00
❑ S-415 [S]	Ray Charles' Greatest Hits	1967	3.00	6.00	12.00

Number	Title (A Side/B Side)	Yr	VG	VG+	NM
❏ S-435 [S]	Modern Sounds in Country and Western Music (Volume Two)	1967	3.00	6.00	12.00
❏ S-465 [S]	Ingredients in a Recipe for Soul	1967	3.00	6.00	12.00
❏ S-480 [S]	Sweet & Sour Tears	1967	3.00	6.00	12.00
❏ S-495 [S]	Have a Smile with Me	1967	3.00	6.00	12.00
❏ S-500 [S]	Ray Charles Live in Concert	1967	3.00	6.00	12.00
❏ S-520 [S]	Together Again	1967	3.00	6.00	12.00
❏ S-544 [S]	Crying Time	1967	3.00	6.00	12.00
❏ S-550 [S]	Ray's Moods	1967	3.00	6.00	12.00
❏ 590X [(2)M]	A Man and His Soul	1967	3.75	7.50	15.00
❏ S-590X [(2)S]	A Man and His Soul	1967	5.00	10.00	20.00
❏ 595 [M]	Ray Charles Invites You to Listen	1967	5.00	10.00	20.00
❏ S-595 [S]	Ray Charles Invites You to Listen	1967	3.75	7.50	15.00
❏ S-625	A Portrait of Ray	1968	3.00	6.00	12.00
❏ S-675	I'm All Yours — Baby!	1969	3.00	6.00	12.00
❏ S-695	Doing His Thing	1969	3.00	6.00	12.00
❏ S-707	Love Country Style	1971	3.00	6.00	12.00
❏ S-726	Volcanic Action of My Soul	1971	3.00	6.00	12.00
❏ H-731 [(2)]	A 25th Anniversary in Show Business Salute to Ray Charles	1971	3.75	7.50	15.00
❏ X-755	A Message from the People	1972	3.00	6.00	12.00
❏ X-765	Through the Eyes of Love	1972	3.00	6.00	12.00
❏ X-781/2 [(2)]	All-Time Great Country & Western Hits	1973	3.75	7.50	15.00
❏ QBO-91036 [(2)M]	The Ray Charles Story	1967	7.50	15.00	30.00
—Capitol Record Club exclusive					
❏ SQBO-91036 [(2)S]	The Ray Charles Story	1967	6.25	12.50	25.00
—Capitol Record Club exclusive					
❏ ST-91233 [S]	Ray Charles Invites You to Listen	1967	3.75	7.50	15.00
—Capitol Record Club edition					

ABC IMPULSE!

Number	Title (A Side/B Side)	Yr	VG	VG+	NM
❏ AS-2 [S]	Genius + Soul = Jazz	1968	3.00	6.00	12.00

ABC-PARAMOUNT

Number	Title (A Side/B Side)	Yr	VG	VG+	NM
❏ 335 [M]	The Genius Hits the Road	1960	5.00	10.00	20.00
❏ S-335 [S]	The Genius Hits the Road	1960	7.50	15.00	30.00
❏ 355 [M]	Dedicated to You	1961	5.00	10.00	20.00
❏ S-355 [S]	Dedicated to You	1961	7.50	15.00	30.00
❏ 410 [M]	Modern Sounds in Country and Western Music	1962	6.25	12.50	25.00
❏ S-410 [S]	Modern Sounds in Country and Western Music	1962	7.50	15.00	30.00
❏ 415 [M]	Ray Charles' Greatest Hits	1962	5.00	10.00	20.00
❏ S-415 [S]	Ray Charles' Greatest Hits	1962	6.25	12.50	25.00
❏ 435 [M]	Modern Sounds in Country and Western Music (Volume Two)	1962	5.00	10.00	20.00
❏ S-435 [S]	Modern Sounds in Country and Western Music (Volume Two)	1962	6.25	12.50	25.00
❏ 465 [M]	Ingredients in a Recipe for Soul	1963	5.00	10.00	20.00
❏ S-465 [S]	Ingredients in a Recipe for Soul	1963	6.25	12.50	25.00
❏ 480 [M]	Sweet & Sour Tears	1964	5.00	10.00	20.00
❏ S-480 [S]	Sweet & Sour Tears	1964	6.25	12.50	25.00
❏ 495 [M]	Have a Smile with Me	1964	5.00	10.00	20.00
❏ S-495 [S]	Have a Smile with Me	1964	6.25	12.50	25.00
❏ 500 [M]	Ray Charles Live in Concert	1965	3.75	7.50	15.00
❏ S-500 [S]	Ray Charles Live in Concert	1965	5.00	10.00	20.00
❏ 520 [M]	Together Again	196?	3.75	7.50	15.00
—Retitled version of "Country and Western Meets Rhythm and Blues"					
❏ 520 [M]	Country & Western Meets Rhythm & Blues	1965	3.75	7.50	15.00
❏ S-520 [S]	Together Again	196?	5.00	10.00	20.00
—Retitled version of "Country and Western Meets Rhythm and Blues"					
❏ S-520 [S]	Country & Western Meets Rhythm & Blues	1965	5.00	10.00	20.00
❏ 544 [M]	Crying Time	1966	3.75	7.50	15.00
❏ S-544 [S]	Crying Time	1966	5.00	10.00	20.00
❏ 550 [M]	Ray's Moods	1966	3.75	7.50	15.00
❏ S-550 [S]	Ray's Moods	1966	5.00	10.00	20.00
❏ ST-90144 [S]	Ray Charles Live in Concert	1965	5.00	10.00	20.00
—Capitol Record Club edition					
❏ T-90144 [M]	Ray Charles Live in Concert	1965	5.00	10.00	20.00
—Capitol Record Club edition					
❏ ST-90625 [S]	Crying Time	1966	5.00	10.00	20.00
—Capitol Record Club edition					
❏ T-90625 [M]	Crying Time	1966	5.00	10.00	20.00
—Capitol Record Club edition					
❏ ST-90847 [S]	Together Again	196?	6.25	12.50	25.00
—Capitol Record Club edition					

ARCHIVE OF FOLK AND JAZZ

Number	Title (A Side/B Side)	Yr	VG	VG+	NM
❏ 244	Ray Charles	1970	3.00	6.00	12.00
❏ 292	Ray Charles, Vol. 2	197?	2.50	5.00	10.00
❏ 358	Rockin' with Ray	1979	2.50	5.00	10.00

ATLANTIC

Number	Title (A Side/B Side)	Yr	VG	VG+	NM
❏ SD 2-503 [(2)]	Ray Charles Live	1973	3.75	7.50	15.00
❏ 2-900 [(2)M]	The Ray Charles Story	1962	10.00	20.00	40.00
❏ 1259 [M]	The Great Ray Charles	1957	12.50	25.00	50.00
—Black label					
❏ 1259 [M]	The Great Ray Charles	1960	6.25	12.50	25.00
—Red and white label, white fan logo on right					
❏ 1259 [M]	The Great Ray Charles	1962	5.00	10.00	20.00
—Red and white label, black fan logo on right					
❏ SD 1259 [S]	The Great Ray Charles	1959	12.50	25.00	50.00
—Green label					
❏ SD 1259 [S]	The Great Ray Charles	1960	6.25	12.50	25.00
—Blue and green label, white fan logo on right					
❏ SD 1259 [S]	The Great Ray Charles	1962	5.00	10.00	20.00
—Blue and green label, black fan logo on right					
❏ 1289 [M]	Ray Charles at Newport	1958	12.50	25.00	50.00
—Black label					
❏ 1289 [M]	Ray Charles at Newport	1960	6.25	12.50	25.00
—Red and white label, white fan logo on right					
❏ 1289 [M]	Ray Charles at Newport	1962	5.00	10.00	20.00
—Red and white label, black fan logo on right					
❏ SD 1289 [S]	Ray Charles at Newport	1959	12.50	25.00	50.00
—Green label					
❏ SD 1289 [S]	Ray Charles at Newport	1960	6.25	12.50	25.00
—Blue and green label, white fan logo on right					

Number	Title (A Side/B Side)	Yr	VG	VG+	NM
❏ SD 1289 [S]	Ray Charles at Newport	1962	5.00	10.00	20.00
—Blue and green label, black fan logo on right					
❏ 1312 [M]	The Genius of Ray Charles	1960	6.25	12.50	25.00
—Red and white label, white fan logo on right					
❏ 1312 [M]	The Genius of Ray Charles	1960	10.00	20.00	40.00
—Black label					
❏ 1312 [M]	The Genius of Ray Charles	1960	10.00	20.00	40.00
—White "bullseye" label					
❏ 1312 [M]	The Genius of Ray Charles	1962	5.00	10.00	20.00
—Red and white label, black fan logo on right					
❏ SD 1312 [S]	The Genius of Ray Charles	1960	6.25	12.50	25.00
—Blue and green label, white fan logo on right					
❏ SD 1312 [S]	The Genius of Ray Charles	1960	12.50	25.00	50.00
—Green label					
❏ SD 1312 [S]	The Genius of Ray Charles	1960	12.50	25.00	50.00
—White "bullseye" label					
❏ SD 1312 [S]	The Genius of Ray Charles	1962	5.00	10.00	20.00
—Blue and green label, black fan logo on right					
❏ SD 1312 [S]	The Genius of Ray Charles	1968	5.00	10.00	20.00
—Brown and purple label					
❏ 1369 [M]	The Genius After Hours	1961	6.25	12.50	25.00
—Red and white label, white fan logo on right					
❏ 1369 [M]	The Genius After Hours	1962	5.00	10.00	20.00
—Red and white label, black fan logo on right					
❏ SD 1369 [S]	The Genius After Hours	1961	7.50	15.00	30.00
—Blue and green label, white fan logo on right					
❏ SD 1369 [S]	The Genius After Hours	1962	6.25	12.50	25.00
—Blue and green label, black fan logo on right					
❏ SD 1543	The Best of Ray Charles	1970	3.00	6.00	12.00
❏ 3700 [(6)]	Ray Charles: A Life in Music	198?	12.50	25.00	50.00
❏ SD 7101 [S]	The Great Hits of Ray Charles Recorded on 8-Track Stereo	1966	6.25	12.50	25.00
❏ 8006 [M]	Ray Charles (Rock and Roll)	1957	22.50	45.00	90.00
—Black label					
❏ 8006 [M]	Ray Charles (Rock and Roll)	1960	6.25	12.50	25.00
—Red and white label, white fan logo on right					
❏ 8006 [M]	Hallelujah! I Love Her So	1962	5.00	10.00	20.00
—Red and white label, black fan logo on right; retitled version					
❏ 8025 [M]	Yes, Indeed!	1958	12.50	25.00	50.00
—Black label; cover has screaming girls					
❏ 8025 [M]	Yes, Indeed!	1960	6.25	12.50	25.00
—Red and white label, white fan logo on right; cover has screaming girls					
❏ 8025 [M]	Yes, Indeed!	1962	5.00	10.00	20.00
—Red and white label, black fan logo on right; cover has Ray on it					
❏ 8029 [M]	What'd I Say	1959	12.50	25.00	50.00
—Black label					
❏ 8029 [M]	What'd I Say	1960	6.25	12.50	25.00
—Red and white label, white fan logo on right					
❏ 8029 [M]	What'd I Say	1960	10.00	20.00	40.00
—White "bullseye" label					
❏ 8029 [M]	What'd I Say	1962	5.00	10.00	20.00
—Red and white label, black fan logo on right					
❏ 8039 [M]	Ray Charles In Person	1960	6.25	12.50	25.00
—Red and white label, white fan logo on right					
❏ 8039 [M]	Ray Charles In Person	1960	10.00	20.00	40.00
—Black label					
❏ 8039 [M]	Ray Charles In Person	1962	5.00	10.00	20.00
—Red and white label, black fan logo on right					
❏ 8052 [M]	The Genius Sings the Blues	1961	6.25	12.50	25.00
—Red and white label, white fan logo on right					
❏ 8052 [M]	The Genius Sings the Blues	1962	5.00	10.00	20.00
—Red and white label, black fan logo on right					
❏ 8054 [M]	Do the Twist!	1961	6.25	12.50	25.00
—Red and white label, white fan logo on right					
❏ 8054 [M]	Do the Twist!	1962	5.00	10.00	20.00
—Red and white label, black fan logo on right					
❏ 8063 [M]	The Ray Charles Story, Volume 1	1962	5.00	10.00	20.00
❏ 8064 [M]	The Ray Charles Story, Volume 2	1962	5.00	10.00	20.00
❏ 8083 [M]	The Ray Charles Story, Volume 3	1963	5.00	10.00	20.00
❏ 8094 [M]	The Ray Charles Story, Volume 4	1964	5.00	10.00	20.00
❏ SD 8094 [S]	The Ray Charles Story, Volume 4	1964	6.25	12.50	25.00
❏ SD 19142	True to Life	1977	3.00	6.00	12.00
❏ SD 19199	Love and Peace	1978	3.00	6.00	12.00
❏ SD 19251	Ain't It So	1979	3.00	6.00	12.00
❏ SD 19281	Brother Ray Is At It Again	1980	3.00	6.00	12.00
❏ 90464	The Genius After Hours	1986	2.50	5.00	10.00
—Reissue					

BARONET

Number	Title (A Side/B Side)	Yr	VG	VG+	NM
❏ B-111 [M]	The Artistry of Ray Charles	196?	3.00	6.00	12.00
❏ BS-111 [R]	The Artistry of Ray Charles	196?	2.50	5.00	10.00
❏ B-117 [M]	The Great Ray Charles	196?	3.00	6.00	12.00
❏ BS-117 [R]	The Great Ray Charles	196?	2.50	5.00	10.00

BLUESWAY

Number	Title (A Side/B Side)	Yr	VG	VG+	NM
❏ 6053	The Genius Live	1973	3.00	6.00	12.00

COLUMBIA

Number	Title (A Side/B Side)	Yr	VG	VG+	NM
❏ AS 1920 [DJ]	Friendship Radio Show	1984	5.00	10.00	20.00
❏ FC 38293	Wish You Were Here Tonight	1983	2.50	5.00	10.00
❏ PC 38293	Wish You Were Here Tonight	1985	2.00	4.00	8.00
—Budget-line reissue					
❏ FC 38990	Do I Ever Cross Your Mind	1984	2.50	5.00	10.00
❏ FC 39415	Friendship	1985	2.50	5.00	10.00
❏ FC 40125	The Spirit of Christmas	1985	2.50	5.00	10.00
❏ FC 40338	From the Pages of My Mind	1986	2.50	5.00	10.00
❏ FC 45062	Seven Spanish Angels and Other Hits (1982-1986)	1989	3.00	6.00	12.00

CORONET

Number	Title (A Side/B Side)	Yr	VG	VG+	NM
❏ CX-173 [M]	Ray Charles	196?	3.00	6.00	12.00
❏ CXS-173 [R]	Ray Charles	196?	2.50	5.00	10.00

CROSSOVER

Number	Title (A Side/B Side)	Yr	VG	VG+	NM
❏ 9000	Come Live with Me	1974	3.00	6.00	12.00
❏ 9005	Renaissance	1975	3.00	6.00	12.00
❏ 9007	My Kind of Jazz, Part 3	1976	3.00	6.00	12.00

Number	Title (A Side/B Side)	Yr	VG	VG+	NM
DCC COMPACT CLASSICS					
❏ LPZ-2012	Greatest Country and Western Hits	1995	25.00	50.00	100.00
—Audiophile vinyl					
DUNHILL COMPACT CLASSICS					
❏ DZL-038	Genius + Soul = Jazz	1988	3.75	7.50	15.00
—Clear vinyl reissue					
HOLLYWOOD					
❏ 504 [M]	The Original Ray Charles	1959	37.50	75.00	150.00
❏ 505 [M]	The Fabuolus Ray Charles	1959	37.50	75.00	150.00
IMPULSE!					
❏ A-2 [M]	Genius + Soul = Jazz	1961	6.25	12.50	25.00
❏ AS-2 [S]	Genius + Soul = Jazz	1961	7.50	15.00	30.00
INTERMEDIA					
❏ QS-5013	Goin' Down Slow	198?	2.50	5.00	10.00
LONGINES SYMPHONETTE					
❏ 95647 [(5)]	The Greatest Hits of Ray Charles	1974	10.00	20.00	40.00
PAIR					
❏ PDL2-1139 [(2)]	The Real Ray Charles	1986	3.00	6.00	12.00
PREMIER					
❏ PM 2004 [M]	The Great Ray Charles	196?	3.00	6.00	12.00
❏ PS 2004 [R]	The Great Ray Charles	196?	2.50	5.00	10.00
❏ PS-6001 [R]	Fantastic Ray Charles	196?	2.50	5.00	10.00
RHINO					
❏ R1-70097	Greatest Hits, Volume 1	1988	2.50	5.00	10.00
❏ R1-70098	Greatest Hits, Volume 2	1988	2.50	5.00	10.00
❏ R1-70099	Modern Sounds in Country and Western Music	1988	2.50	5.00	10.00
TANGERINE					
❏ 1512	My Kind of Jazz	1970	3.00	6.00	12.00
❏ 1516	My Kind of Jazz No. II	1973	3.00	6.00	12.00
WARNER BROS.					
❏ 26343	Would You Believe?	1990	3.75	7.50	15.00

CHARLES, RAY / HARRY BELAFONTE

Number	Title (A Side/B Side)	Yr	VG	VG+	NM
CORONET					
❏ CX-203 [M]	The Greatest Ever	196?	3.00	6.00	12.00
❏ CXS-203 [R]	The Greatest Ever	196?	2.50	5.00	10.00

CHARLES, RAY, AND BETTY CARTER

Number	Title (A Side/B Side)	Yr	VG	VG+	NM
ABC					
❏ S-385 [S]	Ray Charles and Betty Carter	1967	5.00	10.00	20.00
—Reissue of ABC-Paramount ABCS-385					
ABC-PARAMOUNT					
❏ ABC-385 [M]	Ray Charles and Betty Carter	1961	10.00	20.00	40.00
❏ ABCS-385 [S]	Ray Charles and Betty Carter	1961	15.00	30.00	60.00
DCC COMPACT CLASSICS					
❏ LPZ-2005	Ray Charles and Betty Carter	1995	37.50	75.00	150.00
—Audiophile vinyl					
DUNHILL COMPACT CLASSICS					
❏ DZL-039	Ray Charles and Betty Carter	1988	3.75	7.50	15.00
—Clear vinyl reissue					

CHARLES, RAY/IVORY JOE HUNTER/JIMMY RUSHING

Number	Title (A Side/B Side)	Yr	VG	VG+	NM
DESIGN					
❏ DLP-909 [M]	Three of a Kind	196?	3.00	6.00	12.00
❏ DLS-909 [R]	Three of a Kind	196?	2.50	5.00	10.00

CHARLES, RAY, AND MILT JACKSON

Number	Title (A Side/B Side)	Yr	VG	VG+	NM
ATLANTIC					
❏ 1279 [M]	Soul Brothers	1958	12.50	25.00	50.00
—Black label					
❏ 1279 [M]	Soul Brothers	1960	6.25	12.50	25.00
—Red and white label, white fan logo on right					
❏ 1279 [M]	Soul Brothers	1962	5.00	10.00	20.00
—Red and white label, black fan logo on right					
❏ SD 1279 [S]	Soul Brothers	1959	12.50	25.00	50.00
—Green label					
❏ SD 1279 [S]	Soul Brothers	1960	6.25	12.50	25.00
—Blue and green label, white fan logo on right					
❏ SD 1279 [S]	Soul Brothers	1962	5.00	10.00	20.00
—Blue and green label, black fan logo on right					
❏ 1360 [M]	Soul Meeting	1961	6.25	12.50	25.00
—Red and white label, white fan logo on right					
❏ 1360 [M]	Soul Meeting	1962	5.00	10.00	20.00
—Red and white label, black fan logo on right					
❏ SD 1360 [S]	Soul Meeting	1961	7.50	15.00	30.00
—Blue and green label, white fan logo on right					
❏ SD 1360 [S]	Soul Meeting	1962	6.25	12.50	25.00
—Blue and green label, black fan logo on right					

CHARLES, RAY, AND CLEO LAINE

Number	Title (A Side/B Side)	Yr	VG	VG+	NM
RCA VICTOR					
❏ CPL2-1831 [(2)]	Porgy & Bess	1976	3.75	7.50	15.00
❏ DJL1-2163	Porgy & Bess	1976	5.00	10.00	20.00
—Promo-only excerpts from 2-record set					

CHARLES, TEDDY

Number	Title (A Side/B Side)	Yr	VG	VG+	NM
ATLANTIC					
❏ 1229 [M]	The Teddy Charles Tentet	1956	20.00	40.00	80.00
—Black label					
❏ 1229 [M]	The Teddy Charles Tentet	1961	7.50	15.00	30.00
—Multicolor label with white "fan" logo					
❏ 1274 [M]	Word from Bird	1956	20.00	40.00	80.00
—Black label					
❏ 1274 [M]	Word from Bird	1961	7.50	15.00	30.00
—Multicolor label with white "fan" logo					
BETHLEHEM					
❏ BCP-6032 [M]	Salute to Hamp	1959	12.50	25.00	50.00
❏ BCP-6044 [M]	On Campus — Ivy League Jazz Concert	1960	12.50	25.00	50.00
ELEKTRA					
❏ EKL-136 [M]	Vibe-Rant	1957	15.00	30.00	60.00

Number	Title (A Side/B Side)	Yr	VG	VG+	NM
JOSIE					
❏ JJS-3505 [S]	Teddy Charles Trio Plays Duke Ellington	1963	7.50	15.00	30.00
❏ JOZ-3505 [M]	Teddy Charles Trio Plays Duke Ellington	1963	7.50	15.00	30.00
JUBILEE					
❏ JGS-1047 [S]	Three for Duke	1959	10.00	20.00	40.00
❏ JLP-1047 [M]	Three for Duke	1957	12.50	25.00	50.00
NEW JAZZ					
❏ NJLP-1106 [10]	Teddy Charles New Directions Quartet	1955	75.00	150.00	300.00
PRESTIGE					
❏ PRLP-132 [10]	Teddy Charles and His Trio	1952	50.00	100.00	200.00
❏ PRLP-143 [10]	New Directions Vol. 1	1953	50.00	100.00	200.00
❏ PRLP-150 [10]	New Directions Vol. 2	1953	50.00	100.00	200.00
❏ PRLP-164 [10]	New Directions Vol. 3	1953	50.00	100.00	200.00
❏ PRLP-169 [10]	New Directions Vol. 4	1954	50.00	100.00	200.00
❏ PRLP-178 [10]	New Directions Vol. 5	1954	50.00	100.00	200.00
—With Bob Brookmeyer					
❏ PRLP-206 [10]	Teddy Charles New Directions Quartet	1955	50.00	100.00	200.00
—Reissue of New Jazz 1106					
❏ PRLP-7028 [M]	Collaboration: West	1956	25.00	50.00	100.00
—Yellow label					
❏ PRLP-7028 [M]	Collaboration: West	196?	7.50	15.00	30.00
—Blue label, trident logo on right					
❏ PRLP-7078 [M]	Evolution	1957	25.00	50.00	100.00
—Yellow label					
❏ PRLP-7078 [M]	Evolution	196?	7.50	15.00	30.00
—Blue label, trident logo on right					
SAVOY					
❏ MG-12174 [M]	The Vibe-Rant Quintet	1961	7.50	15.00	30.00
—Reissue of Elektra LP					
UNITED ARTISTS					
❏ UAL-3365 [M]	Russia Goes Jazz	1964	6.25	12.50	25.00
❏ UAS-6365 [S]	Russia Goes Jazz	1964	7.50	15.00	30.00
WARWICK					
❏ W-2033 [M]	Jazz in the Garden of the Museum of Modern Art	1960	12.50	25.00	50.00

CHARLES RIVER VALLEY BOYS, THE

Number	Title (A Side/B Side)	Yr	VG	VG+	NM
ELEKTRA					
❏ EKL-4006 [M]	Beatle Country	1967	5.00	10.00	20.00
❏ EKS-74006 [S]	Beatle Country	1967	6.25	12.50	25.00

CHARLESTON CITY ALL-STARS

Number	Title (A Side/B Side)	Yr	VG	VG+	NM
GRAND AWARD					
❏ GA 201 SD [S]	The Roaring 20's	1958	5.00	10.00	20.00
❏ GA 211 SD [S]	The Roaring 20's, Volume 2	1958	5.00	10.00	20.00
❏ GA 229 SD [S]	The Roaring 20's, Volume 3	1958	5.00	10.00	20.00

CHASE

Number	Title (A Side/B Side)	Yr	VG	VG+	NM
EPIC					
❏ E 30472	Chase	1971	3.00	6.00	12.00
❏ EQ 30472 [Q]	Chase	1973	5.00	10.00	20.00
❏ KE 31097	Ennea	1972	3.00	6.00	12.00
❏ EQ 32572 [Q]	Pure Music	1974	5.00	10.00	20.00
❏ KE 32572	Pure Music	1974	3.00	6.00	12.00
❏ EG 33737 [(2)]	Chase/Ennea	1976	3.75	7.50	15.00

CHASE, LINCOLN

Number	Title (A Side/B Side)	Yr	VG	VG+	NM
LIBERTY					
❏ LRP-3076 [M]	The Explosive Lincoln Chase	1958	12.50	25.00	50.00

CHEAP TRICK

Number	Title (A Side/B Side)	Yr	VG	VG+	NM
EPIC					
❏ AS 518 [DJ]	From Tokyo to You	1979	7.50	15.00	30.00
—Promo-only sampler from Cheap Trick at Budokan					
❏ PE 34400	Cheap Trick	1976	3.00	6.00	12.00
—Originals have orange labels					
❏ PE 34400	Cheap Trick	1979	2.00	4.00	8.00
—Later editions have dark blue labels; may or may not have bar code on back					
❏ JE 34884	In Color	1977	3.00	6.00	12.00
—Originals have orange labels					
❏ PE 34884	In Color	1979	2.00	4.00	8.00
—Later editions have dark blue labels; may or may not have bar code on back					
❏ JE 35312	Heaven Tonight	1978	3.00	6.00	12.00
—Originals have orange labels					
❏ PE 35312	Heaven Tonight	1979	2.00	4.00	8.00
—Later editions have dark blue labels; may or may not have bar code					
❏ FE 35773	Dream Police	1979	2.50	5.00	10.00
—Despite lower number, this came out after Epic 35795					
❏ PE 35773	Dream Police	1984	2.00	4.00	8.00
❏ FE 35795	Cheap Trick at Budokan	1979			
—Dark blue label; some copies came with gold-colored obi (add 100% if there) and all came with booklet (deduct 20% if missing)					
❏ FE 35795	Cheap Trick at Budokan	1979	3.00	6.00	12.00
—Orange label; came with gold-colored obi (add 5/6 if there) and booklet (deduct 1/6 if missing)					
❏ FE 35795 [DJ]	Cheap Trick at Budokan	1979	5.00	10.00	20.00
—White label promo					
❏ PE 35795	Cheap Trick at Budokan	1984	2.00	4.00	8.00
❏ FE 36498	All Shook Up	1980	2.50	5.00	10.00
❏ PE 36498	All Shook Up	1984	2.00	4.00	8.00
❏ FE 38021	One on One	1982	2.50	5.00	10.00
❏ PE 38021	One on One	1984	2.00	4.00	8.00
❏ PE 38541 [EP]	Found All the Parts	1983	2.00	4.00	8.00
—Six-song reissue of Epic/Nu-Disk release on 12-inch LP					
❏ FE 38794	Next Position Please	1983	2.50	5.00	10.00
❏ PE 38794	Next Position Please	1985	2.00	4.00	8.00
❏ FE 39592	Standing on the Edge	1985	2.50	5.00	10.00
❏ PE 39592	Standing on the Edge	1987	2.00	4.00	8.00
❏ FE 40405	The Doctor	1986	2.50	5.00	10.00
❏ PE 40405	The Doctor	1987	2.00	4.00	8.00
—Reissue with new prefix on cover					
❏ OE 40922	Lap of Luxury	1988	2.50	5.00	10.00
❏ E 46013	Busted	1990	3.00	6.00	12.00

Number	Title (A Side/B Side)	Yr	VG	VG+	NM

EPIC/NU-DISK

Number	Title (A Side/B Side)	Yr	VG	VG+	NM
❑ 4E 36453 [10]	Found All the Parts	1980	3.75	7.50	15.00

—10-inch, four-track EP with bonus 45, "Everything Works If You Let It" (AE7 1206)

CHECKER, CHUBBY
ABKCO

❑ 4219 [(2)]	Chubby Checker's Greatest Hits	1972	5.00	10.00	20.00

EVEREST

❑ 4111	Chubby Checker's Greatest Hits	1981	3.00	6.00	12.00

MCA

❑ 5291	The Change Has Come	1982	2.50	5.00	10.00

PARKWAY

❑ P 7001 [M]	Twist with Chubby Checker	1960	10.00	20.00	40.00

—All-orange label

❑ P 7001 [M]	Twist with Chubby Checker	1962	7.50	15.00	30.00

—Orange and yellow label

❑ P 7002 [M]	For Twisters Only	1960	10.00	20.00	40.00

—All-orange label

❑ P 7002 [M]	For Twisters Only	1962	7.50	15.00	30.00

—Orange and yellow label

❑ P 7003 [M]	It's Pony Time	1961	10.00	20.00	40.00

—All-orange label

❑ P 7003 [M]	It's Pony Time	1962	7.50	15.00	30.00

—Orange and yellow label

❑ P 7004 [M]	Let's Twist Again	1961	10.00	20.00	40.00

—All-orange label

❑ P 7004 [M]	Let's Twist Again	1962	7.50	15.00	30.00

—Orange and yellow label

❑ P 7007 [M]	Your Twist Party	1961	10.00	20.00	40.00

—All-orange label

❑ P 7007 [M]	Your Twist Party	1962	7.50	15.00	30.00

—Orange and yellow label

❑ P 7008 [M]	Twistin' Round the World	1962	7.50	15.00	30.00
❑ SP 7008 [B]	Twistin' Round the World	1962	10.00	20.00	40.00
❑ P 7009 [M]	For Teen Twisters Only	1962	7.50	15.00	30.00
❑ SP 7009 [S]	For Teen Twisters Only	1962	10.00	20.00	40.00
❑ P 7014 [M]	All the Hits (For Your Dancin' Party)	1962	7.50	15.00	30.00
❑ P 7020 [M]	Limbo Party	1962	7.50	15.00	30.00
❑ SP 7020 [S]	Limbo Party	1962	10.00	20.00	40.00
❑ P 7022 [M]	Chubby Checker's Biggest Hits	1962	7.50	15.00	30.00
❑ SP 7022 [R]	Chubby Checker's Biggest Hits	1962	7.50	15.00	30.00
❑ P 7026 [M]	Chubby Checker In Person	1963	7.50	15.00	30.00
❑ SP 7026 [S]	Chubby Checker In Person	1963	10.00	20.00	40.00

—The above record is labeled "Twist It Up"

❑ P 7027 [M]	Let's Limbo Some More	1963	7.50	15.00	30.00
❑ SP 7027 [S]	Let's Limbo Some More	1963	10.00	20.00	40.00
❑ P 7030 [M]	Beach Party	1963	7.50	15.00	30.00
❑ SP 7030 [S]	Beach Party	1963	10.00	20.00	40.00
❑ P 7036 [M]	Chubby Checker With Sy Oliver and His Orchestra	1964	7.50	15.00	30.00
❑ SP 7036 [S]	Chubby Checker With Sy Oliver and His Orchestra	1964	10.00	20.00	40.00
❑ P 7040 [M]	Folk Album	1964	7.50	15.00	30.00
❑ SP 7040 [S]	Folk Album	1964	10.00	20.00	40.00
❑ P 7045 [M]	Discotheque	1965	7.50	15.00	30.00
❑ SP 7045 [S]	Discotheque	1965	10.00	20.00	40.00
❑ P 7048 [M]	Chubby Checker's Eighteen Golden Hits	1966	7.50	15.00	30.00
❑ SP 7048 [P]	Chubby Checker's Eighteen Golden Hits	1966	10.00	20.00	40.00

CHECKMATES, THE
JUSTICE

❑ JLP-149	The Checkmates	1966	100.00	200.00	400.00

CHECKMATES LTD., THE
A&M

❑ SP-4183	Love Is All I Have to Give	1969	6.25	12.50	25.00

CAPITOL

❑ ST 2840 [S]	Live at Caesar's Palace	1968	5.00	10.00	20.00
❑ T 2840 [M]	Live at Caesar's Palace	1968	7.50	15.00	30.00

FANTASY

❑ 9541	We Got the Moves	1978	3.75	7.50	15.00

CHELSEA
Future Kiss member Peter Criss (as "Peter Cris") played drums on this LP.
DECCA

❑ DL 75262	The Chelsea Album	1972	37.50	75.00	150.00

CHER
ATCO

❑ 33-298 [M]	3614 Jackson Highway	1969	7.50	15.00	30.00

—White label promo only (no stock copies issued in mono)

❑ SD 33-298 [S]	3614 Jackson Highway	1969	5.00	10.00	20.00

CASABLANCA

❑ NBLP-7133	Take Me Home	1979	2.50	5.00	10.00
❑ NBPIX-7133 [PD]	Take Me Home	1979	12.50	25.00	50.00
❑ NBLP-7184	Prisoner	1980	2.50	5.00	10.00

COLUMBIA

❑ FC 38096	I Paralyze	1982	2.50	5.00	10.00

GEFFEN

❑ GHS 24164	Cher	1987	2.50	5.00	10.00
❑ GHS 24239	Heart of Stone	1989	2.50	5.00	10.00

—Later cover with larger picture of Cher and no rock

❑ GHS 24239	Heart of Stone	1989	3.75	7.50	15.00

—Original cover with Cher in heart-shaped pose next to "skeleton rock"

IMPERIAL

❑ LP-9292 [M]	All I Really Want to Do	1965	5.00	10.00	20.00
❑ LP-9301 [M]	The Sonny Side of Cher	1966	5.00	10.00	20.00
❑ LP-9320 [M]	Cher	1966	3.75	7.50	15.00
❑ LP-9358 [M]	With Love — Cher	1967	3.75	7.50	15.00
❑ LP-12292 [S]	All I Really Want to Do	1965	6.25	12.50	25.00
❑ LP-12301 [S]	The Sonny Side of Cher	1966	6.25	12.50	25.00
❑ LP-12320 [S]	Cher	1966	5.00	10.00	20.00
❑ LP-12358 [S]	With Love — Cher	1967	5.00	10.00	20.00
❑ LP-12373 [M]	Backstage	1968	10.00	20.00	40.00

—Stereo cover with designate mono sticker attached; label is stock

❑ LP-12373 [S]	Backstage	1968	5.00	10.00	20.00
❑ LP-12406	Cher's Golden Greats	1968	5.00	10.00	20.00

KAPP

❑ KS-3649	Gypsys, Tramps & Thieves	1971	3.75	7.50	15.00

—Retitled version of above LP

❑ KS-3649	Cher	1971	5.00	10.00	20.00

—Original title of LP (renamed "Gypsys, Tramps & Thieves")

❑ KRS-5514	Foxy Lady	1972	3.75	7.50	15.00

LIBERTY

❑ LN-10110	The Very Best of Cher, Vol. 1	1981	2.00	4.00	8.00
❑ LN-10111	The Very Best of Cher, Vol. 2	1981	2.00	4.00	8.00

MCA

❑ 624	Cher	197?	2.50	5.00	10.00
❑ 2101	Bittersweet White Light	1973	3.00	6.00	12.00
❑ 2104	Half-Breed	1973	3.00	6.00	12.00
❑ 2113	Dark Lady	1974	3.00	6.00	12.00
❑ 2127	Greatest Hits	1974	3.00	6.00	12.00
❑ 37028	Greatest Hits	1981	2.00	4.00	8.00

—Reissue of MCA 2127

SPRINGBOARD

❑ SPB-4028	Cher's Greatest Hits	197?	2.50	5.00	10.00
❑ SPB-4029	Cher Sings the Hits	197?	2.50	5.00	10.00

SUNSET

❑ SUS-5276	This Is Cher	1970	3.75	7.50	15.00

UNITED ARTISTS

❑ UXS-88 [(2)]	Cher Superpak	1971	5.00	10.00	20.00
❑ UXS-89 [(2)]	Cher Superpak, Vol. II	1972	5.00	10.00	20.00

—The above are reissues of Imperial recordings

❑ UA-LA237-G	The Very Best of Cher	1974	3.00	6.00	12.00
❑ UA-LA377-E	The Very Best of Cher	1975	2.50	5.00	10.00
❑ UA-LA435-E	The Very Best of Cher, Vol. 2	1975	3.00	6.00	12.00

WARNER BROS.

❑ BS 2850	Stars	1975	3.00	6.00	12.00
❑ BS 2898	I'd Rather Believe in You	1976	3.00	6.00	12.00
❑ BS 3046	Cherished	1977	3.00	6.00	12.00

CHEROKEE
ABC

❑ ABCS-719	Cherokee	1970	5.00	10.00	20.00

CHERRY, DON
COLUMBIA

❑ CL 893 [M]	Swingin' for Two	1956	6.25	12.50	25.00

MONUMENT

❑ MLP-8049 [M]	Don Cherry Smashes	1966	3.00	6.00	12.00
❑ MLP-8075 [M]	There Goes My Everything	1967	3.75	7.50	15.00
❑ 8601 [(2)]	The World of Don Cherry	197?	3.00	6.00	12.00

—Reissue of 32334

❑ SLP-18049 [S]	Don Cherry Smashes	1966	3.75	7.50	15.00
❑ SLP-18075 [S]	There Goes My Everything	1967	3.00	6.00	12.00
❑ SLP-18088	Let It Be Me	1968	3.00	6.00	12.00
❑ SLP-18109	Take a Message to Mary	1969	3.00	6.00	12.00
❑ SLP-18124	Don Cherry	1970	3.00	6.00	12.00
❑ KZG 32334 [(2)]	The World of Don Cherry	1972	3.75	7.50	15.00

CHERRY, DON (2)
Jazz trumpeter, also father of 1980s hitmaker Neneh Cherry and 1990s hitmaker Eagle-Eye Cherry.
BASF

❑ 20980	Eternal Rhythm	1972	5.00	10.00	20.00

BLUE NOTE

❑ BLP-4226 [M]	Complete Communion	1966	6.25	12.50	25.00
❑ BLP-4247 [M]	Symphony for Improvisers	1966	6.25	12.50	25.00
❑ BST-84226 [S]	Complete Communion	1966	7.50	15.00	30.00

—"New York, USA" address on label

❑ BST-84247 [S]	Symphony for Improvisers	1966	7.50	15.00	30.00

—"New York, USA" address on label

❑ BST-84311	Where Is Brooklyn?	1969	6.25	12.50	25.00

—"A Division of Liberty Records" on label

INNER CITY

❑ IC 1009	Togetherness	197?	5.00	10.00	20.00

JCOA

❑ 1006	Relativity Suite	1974	5.00	10.00	20.00

MOSAIC

❑ MQ3-145 [(3)]	The Complete Blue Note Recordings of Don Cherry	199?	15.00	30.00	60.00

CHERRY PEOPLE, THE
HERITAGE

❑ HT 35000 [M]	The Cherry People	1968	10.00	20.00	40.00

—Stereo cover with "Mono" and "DJ" stickers attached; all records appear to be white label promos

❑ HTS 35000 [S]	The Cherry People	1968	5.00	10.00	20.00

CHESS, TUBBY, AND HIS CANDY STRIPE TWISTERS
GRAND PRIX

❑ K-187 [M]	Do the Twist	1962	3.75	7.50	15.00
❑ KS-187 [S]	Do the Twist	1962	5.00	10.00	20.00

CHESTER, GARY
DCP

❑ DCL 3803 [M]	Yeah, Yeah, Yeah	1964	5.00	10.00	20.00
❑ DCS 6803 [S]	Yeah, Yeah, Yeah	1964	6.25	12.50	25.00

CHEVALIER, MAURICE
CAPITOL

❑ T 10360 [M]	The Young Chevalier	196?	5.00	10.00	20.00

Number	Title (A Side/B Side)	Yr	VG	VG+	NM
EPIC					
❏ FXS 15117	Maurice Chevalier at 80	1968	5.00	10.00	20.00
LONDON					
❏ GH 46001/4 [(4)M]	60 Years of Song	1966	10.00	20.00	40.00
❏ GHS 56001/4 [(4)S]	60 Years of Song	1966	12.50	25.00	50.00
MGM					
❏ 2E-5 [(2)M]	Yesterday…Today	1958	10.00	20.00	40.00
—Yellow label original; also released separately as 3702 and 3703					
❏ 2SE-5 [(2)S]	Yesterday…Today	1958	15.00	30.00	60.00
—Yellow label original; also released separately as 3702 and 3703					
❏ E-3702 [M]	Yesterday	1958	6.25	12.50	25.00
—Yellow label original					
❏ SE-3702 [S]	Yesterday	1958	7.50	15.00	30.00
—Yellow label original					
❏ E-3703 [M]	Today	1958	6.25	12.50	25.00
—Yellow label original					
❏ SE-3703 [S]	Today	1958	7.50	15.00	30.00
—Yellow label original					
❏ E-3738 [M]	Maurice Chevalier Sings Broadway	1959	6.25	12.50	25.00
—Yellow label original					
❏ SE-3738 [S]	Maurice Chevalier Sings Broadway	1959	7.50	15.00	30.00
—Yellow label original					
❏ E-3773 [M]	A Tribute to Al Jolson	1959	6.25	12.50	25.00
—Yellow label original					
❏ SE-3773 [S]	A Tribute to Al Jolson	1959	7.50	15.00	30.00
—Yellow label original					
❏ E-3801 [M]	Life Is Just a Bowl of Cherries	1960	5.00	10.00	20.00
❏ SE-3801 [S]	Life Is Just a Bowl of Cherries	1960	6.25	12.50	25.00
❏ E-3835 [M]	Thank Heaven for Little Girls	1960	5.00	10.00	20.00
❏ SE-3835 [S]	Thank Heaven for Little Girls	1960	6.25	12.50	25.00
❏ E-4015 [M]	Maurice Chevalier Sings Lerner, Loewe & Chevalier	1962	5.00	10.00	20.00
❏ SE-4015 [S]	Maurice Chevalier Sings Lerner, Loewe & Chevalier	1962	6.25	12.50	25.00
❏ E-4120 [M]	Paris to Broadway	1963	5.00	10.00	20.00
❏ SE-4120 [S]	Paris to Broadway	1963	6.25	12.50	25.00
❏ E-4205 [M]	The Very Best of Maurice Chevalier	1964	3.75	7.50	15.00
❏ SE-4205 [S]	The Very Best of Maurice Chevalier	1964	5.00	10.00	20.00
RCA VICTOR					
❏ LPM-2076 [M]	Thank Heaven for Maurice Chevalier	1960	6.25	12.50	25.00
❏ LSP-2076 [S]	Thank Heaven for Maurice Chevalier	1960	7.50	15.00	30.00
TIME					
❏ S-2072 [S]	Maurice Chevalier	1963	6.25	12.50	25.00
❏ 52072 [M]	Maurice Chevalier	1963	5.00	10.00	20.00

CHEVRONS, THE
TIME

Number	Title (A Side/B Side)	Yr	VG	VG+	NM
❏ T-10008 [M]	Sing-a-Long Rock & Roll	1961	20.00	40.00	80.00

CHI-LITES, THE
BRUNSWICK

Number	Title (A Side/B Side)	Yr	VG	VG+	NM
❏ BL 754152	Give It Away	1969	6.25	12.50	25.00
❏ BL 754165	I Like Your Lovin', Do You Like Mine?	1970	6.25	12.50	25.00
❏ BL 754170	(For God's Sake) Give More Power to the People	1971	6.25	12.50	25.00
❏ BL 754179	A Lonely Man	1972	6.25	12.50	25.00
❏ BL 754184	The Chi-Lites Greatest Hits	1972	6.25	12.50	25.00
❏ BL 754188	A Letter to Myself	1973	6.25	12.50	25.00
❏ BL 754197	Chi-Lites	1973	6.25	12.50	25.00
❏ BL 754200	Toby	1974	6.25	12.50	25.00
❏ BL 754204	Half a Love	1975	6.25	12.50	25.00
❏ BL 754208	The Chi-Lites Greatest Hits, Volume 2	1976	6.25	12.50	25.00
CHI-SOUND					
❏ T-619	Heavenly Body	1980	3.75	7.50	15.00
❏ T-635	Me and You	1982	3.75	7.50	15.00
EPIC					
❏ PE 38627	Greatest Hits	1983	2.50	5.00	10.00
ICHIBAN					
❏ ICH-1057	Just Say You Love Me	198?	2.50	5.00	10.00
LARC					
❏ 8103	Bottom's Up	1983	3.00	6.00	12.00
MERCURY					
❏ SRM-1-1118	Happy Being Lonely	1976	3.75	7.50	15.00
❏ SRM-1-1147	Fantastic	1977	3.75	7.50	15.00
PRIVATE I					
❏ FZ 39316	Steppin' Out	1984	2.50	5.00	10.00
❏ PZ 39316	Steppin' Out	1985	2.00	4.00	8.00
—Budget-line reissue					

CHICAGO
ACCORD

Number	Title (A Side/B Side)	Yr	VG	VG+	NM
❏ SN-7140	Toronto Rock 'n Roll Revival, Part I	1982	3.00	6.00	12.00
—Reissue of Magnum LP					
COLUMBIA					
❏ (no #) [(17)]	Chicago	1976	62.50	125.00	250.00
—Promo-only set: The first 10 Chicago LPs with gold stamps on covers, box, side panel and wraparound					
❏ GP 8 [(2)]	Chicago Transit Authority	1969	6.25	12.50	25.00
—Red labels with "360 Sound" at bottom					
❏ GP 8 [(2)]	Chicago Transit Authority	1970	5.00	10.00	20.00
—Orange labels; most copies add a Roman numeral "I" to the title on spine					
❏ KGP 24 [(2)]	Chicago II	1970	5.00	10.00	20.00
—Orange labels					
❏ KGP 24 [(2)]	Chicago II	1970	6.25	12.50	25.00
—Red labels with "360 Sound" at bottom; label and spine call the album "Chicago II"					
❏ KGP 24 [(2)]	Chicago	1970	10.00	20.00	40.00
—Red labels with "360 Sound" at bottom; label and spine call the album "Chicago"					
❏ C2 30110 [(2)]	Chicago III	1971	5.00	10.00	20.00
❏ C2Q 30110 [(2)Q]	Chicago III	1974	7.50	15.00	30.00

Number	Title (A Side/B Side)	Yr	VG	VG+	NM
❏ C2G 30863 [(2)]	Chicago at Carnegie Hall, Vol. 1 & 2	1971	5.00	10.00	20.00
—First half of the 4-LP box, possibly for Columbia Record Club only					
❏ C2G 30864 [(2)]	Chicago at Carnegie Hall, Vol. 3 & 4	1971	5.00	10.00	20.00
—Second half of the 4-LP box, possibly for Columbia Record Club only					
❏ C4Q 30865 [(4)Q]	Chicago at Carnegie Hall	1971	12.50	25.00	50.00
❏ C4X 30865 [(4)]	Chicago at Carnegie Hall	1971	10.00	20.00	40.00
—With box, 4 posters and program. Deduct for missing items.					
❏ CQ 31102 [Q]	Chicago V	1974	6.25	12.50	25.00
❏ KC 31102	Chicago V	1972	5.00	10.00	20.00
❏ CQ 32400 [Q]	Chicago VI	1974	6.25	12.50	25.00
❏ KC 32400	Chicago VI	1973	3.75	7.50	15.00
❏ C2 32810 [(2)]	Chicago VII	1974	5.00	10.00	20.00
❏ C2Q 32810 [(2)Q]	Chicago VII	1974	7.50	15.00	30.00
❏ PC 33100	Chicago VIII	1975	3.75	7.50	15.00
❏ PCQ 33100 [Q]	Chicago VIII	1975	6.25	12.50	25.00
❏ GQ 33255 [(2)Q]	Chicago Transit Authority	1975	6.25	12.50	25.00
❏ GQ 33258 [(2)Q]	Chicago II	1975	6.25	12.50	25.00
❏ PC 33900	Chicago IX — Chicago's Greatest Hits	1975	3.75	7.50	15.00
❏ PCQ 33900 [Q]	Chicago IX — Chicago's Greatest Hits	1975	6.25	12.50	25.00
❏ PC 34200	Chicago X	1976	3.75	7.50	15.00
❏ PCQ 34200 [Q]	Chicago X	1976	6.25	12.50	25.00
❏ JC 34860	Chicago XI	1977	3.75	7.50	15.00
❏ FC 35512	Hot Streets	1978	3.75	7.50	15.00
❏ FC 36105	Chicago 13	1979	3.75	7.50	15.00
❏ FC 36517	Chicago XIV	1980	3.75	7.50	15.00
❏ FC 37682	Chicago — Greatest Hits, Volume II	1981	3.75	7.50	15.00
❏ PC 38590	If You Leave Me Now	1982	3.00	6.00	12.00
❏ PC 39579	Take Me Back to Chicago	1983	3.00	6.00	12.00
❏ HC 43900	Chicago IX — Chicago's Greatest Hits	1982	7.50	15.00	30.00
—Half-speed mastered edition					
❏ HC 44200	Chicago X	1982	10.00	20.00	40.00
—Half-speed mastered edition					
FULL MOON					
❏ 23689	Chicago 16	1982	2.50	5.00	10.00
MAGNUM					
❏ MR 604	Chicago Transit Authority Live in Concert	1978	5.00	10.00	20.00
—Taken from their 1969 Toronto Rock 'n Roll Revival performance					
MOBILE FIDELITY					
❏ 2-128 [(2)]	Chicago Transit Authority	1983	20.00	40.00	80.00
—Audiophile vinyl					
REPRISE					
❏ 25714	Chicago 19	1988	2.50	5.00	10.00
❏ 26080	Greatest Hits 1982-1989	1989	2.50	5.00	10.00
❏ R 110533	Twenty 1	1991	5.00	10.00	20.00
—BMG Direct Marketing version					
WARNER BROS.					
❏ 25060	Chicago 17	1984	2.50	5.00	10.00
❏ 25060 [DJ]	Chicago 17	1984	5.00	10.00	20.00
—Promo pressing on Quiex II vinyl					
❏ 25509	Chicago 18	1986	2.50	5.00	10.00

CHICAGO SYMPHONY ORCHESTRA (PIERRE MONTEUX, CONDUCTOR)
RCA VICTOR RED SEAL

Number	Title (A Side/B Side)	Yr	VG	VG+	NM
❏ LSC-2514 [S]	Franck: Symphony in D	1961	5.00	10.00	20.00
—Original with "shaded dog" label					

CHICAGO SYMPHONY ORCHESTRA (FRITZ REINER, CONDUCTOR)
RCA VICTOR RED SEAL

Number	Title (A Side/B Side)	Yr	VG	VG+	NM
❏ LSC-1806 [S]	Strauss: Also Sprach Zarathustra	1958	75.00	150.00	300.00
—Original with "shaded dog" label					
❏ LSC-1806 [S]	Strauss: Also Sprach Zarathustra	199?	6.25	12.50	25.00
—Classic Records reissue					
❏ LSC-1934 [S]	Bartok: Concerto for Orchestra	1958	10.00	20.00	40.00
—Original with "shaded dog" label					
❏ LSC-1934 [S]	Bartok: Concerto for Orchestra	199?	6.25	12.50	25.00
—Classic Records reissue					
❏ LSC-1991 [S]	Beethoven: Symphony No. 7	1958	10.00	20.00	40.00
—Original with "shaded dog" label					
❏ LSC-2112 [S]	Vienna	1958	10.00	20.00	40.00
—Original with "shaded dog" label					
❏ LSC-2150 [S]	Prokofiev: Lieutenant Kije; Stravinsky: Song of the Nightingale	1958	10.00	20.00	40.00
—Original with "shaded dog" label					
❏ LSC-2150 [S]	Prokofiev: Lieutenant Kije; Stravinsky: Song of the Nightingale	1964	10.00	20.00	40.00
—Second edition with "white dog" label					
❏ LSC-2183 [S]	The Reiner Sound	1958	25.00	50.00	100.00
—Original with "shaded dog" label					
❏ LSC-2183 [S]	The Reiner Sound	199?	6.25	12.50	25.00
—Classic Records reissue					
❏ LSC-2201 [S]	Mussorgsky-Ravel: Pictures at an Exhibition	1959	12.50	25.00	50.00
—Original with "shaded dog" label					
❏ LSC-2201 [S]	Mussorgsky-Ravel: Pictures at an Exhibition	1964	10.00	20.00	40.00
—Second edition with "white dog" label					
❏ LSC-2209 [S]	Brahms: Symphony No. 3	1959	10.00	20.00	40.00
—Original with "shaded dog" label					
❏ LSC-2209 [S]	Brahms: Symphony No. 3	1964	5.00	10.00	20.00
—Second edition with "white dog" label					
❏ LSC-2214 [S]	Dvorak: Symphony No. 9 "From the New World"	1959	5.00	10.00	20.00
—Original with "shaded dog" label					
❏ LSC-2216 [S]	Tchaikovsky: Symphony No. 6 "Pathetique"	1959	5.00	10.00	20.00
—Original with "shaded dog" label					
❏ LSC-2222 [S]	Debussy: Iberia	1958	50.00	100.00	200.00
—Original with "shaded dog" label					
❏ LSC-2222 [S]	Debussy: Iberia	199?	6.25	12.50	25.00
—Classic Records reissue					
❏ LSC-2230 [S]	Spain	1958	25.00	50.00	100.00
—Original with "shaded dog" label					
❏ LSC-2230 [S]	Spain	1964	17.50	35.00	70.00
—Second issue with "white dog" label					

Number	Title (A Side/B Side)	Yr	VG	VG+	NM
❏ LSC-2230 [S]	Spain	199?	6.25	12.50	25.00
—Classic Records reissue					
❏ LSC-2241 [S]	Tchaikovsky: 1812 Overture	1958	125.00	250.00	500.00
—Original with "shaded dog" label					
❏ LSC-2241 [S]	Tchaikovsky: 1812 Overture	199?	6.25	12.50	25.00
—Classic Records reissue					
❏ LSC-2251 [S]	Hovhaness: Mysterious Mountain; Stravinsky: Divertimento	1959	12.50	25.00	50.00
—Original with "shaded dog" label					
❏ LSC-2251 [S]	Hovhaness: Mysterious Mountain; Stravinsky: Divertimento	1964	5.00	10.00	20.00
—Second edition with "white dog" label					
❏ LSC-2318 [S]	Rossini: Overtures	1959	7.50	15.00	30.00
—Original with "shaded dog" label					
❏ LSC-2328 [S]	Tchaikovsky: The Nutcracker	1959	12.50	25.00	50.00
—Original with "shaded dog" label					
❏ LSC-2343 [S]	Beethoven: Symphony No. 5	1960	5.00	10.00	20.00
—Original with "shaded dog" label					
❏ LSC-2364 [S]	Mahler: Symphony No. 4	1960	6.25	12.50	25.00
—Original with "shaded dog" label					
❏ LSC-2364 [S]	Mahler: Symphony No. 4	199?	6.25	12.50	25.00
—Classic Records reissue					
❏ LSC-2374 [S]	Bartok: Music for Strings, Percussion and Celesta	1959	10.00	20.00	40.00
—Original with "shaded dog" label					
❏ LSC-2374 [S]	Bartok: Music for Strings, Percussion and Celesta	199?	6.25	12.50	25.00
—Classic Records reissue					
❏ LDS-2384 [S]	Strauss, Richard: Don Quixote	1960	17.50	35.00	70.00
—Original with "shaded dog" label					
❏ LSS-2384 [S]	Strauss, Richard: Don Quixote	1960	30.00	60.00	120.00
—Original with "shaded dog" label; limited edition of 200 in box with booklet					
❏ LSC-2395 [S]	Prokofiev: Alexander Nevsky	1960	15.00	30.00	60.00
—Original with "shaded dog" label					
❏ LSC-2395 [S]	Prokofiev: Alexander Nevsky	1964	15.00	30.00	60.00
—Second edition with "white dog" label					
❏ LSC-2423 [S]	Festival	1960	37.50	75.00	150.00
—Original with "shaded dog" label					
❏ LSC-2423 [S]	Festival	199?	6.25	12.50	25.00
—Classic Records reissue					
❏ LSC-2436 [S]	Respighi: Pines of Rome; Fountains of Rome	1960	7.50	15.00	30.00
—Original with "shaded dog" label					
❏ LSC-2436 [S]	Respighi: Pines of Rome; Fountains of Rome	199?	6.25	12.50	25.00
—Classic Records reissue					
❏ LSC-2441 [S]	Reiner Conducts Wagner	1960	10.00	20.00	40.00
—Original with "shaded dog" label					
❏ LSC-2441 [S]	Reiner Conducts Wagner	1964	10.00	20.00	40.00
—Second edition with "white dog" label					
❏ LSC-2446 [S]	Rimsky-Korsakov: Scheherazade	1960	25.00	50.00	100.00
—Original with "shaded dog" label					
❏ LSC-2446 [S]	Rimsky-Korsakov: Scheherazade	1964	75.00	150.00	300.00
—Second edition with "white dog" label; a rare instance where a later edition is more desirable than the original					
❏ LSC-2446 [S]	Rimsky-Korsakov: Scheherazade	199?	6.25	12.50	25.00
—Classic Records reissue					
❏ LSC-2462 [S]	Debussy: La Mer; Strauss, Richard: Don Juan	1961	12.50	25.00	50.00
—Original with "shaded dog" label					
❏ LSC-2462 [S]	Debussy: La Mer; Strauss, Richard: Don Juan	1964	10.00	20.00	40.00
—Second edition with "white dog" label					
❏ LSC-2496 [S]	The Heart of the Symphony	1961	10.00	20.00	40.00
—Original with "shaded dog" label					
❏ LSC-2500 [S]	Strauss: Waltzes	1960	10.00	20.00	40.00
—Original with "shaded dog" label					
❏ LSC-2500 [S]	Strauss: Waltzes	1964	10.00	20.00	40.00
—Second edition with "white dog" label					
❏ LSC-2500 [S]	Strauss: Waltzes	199?	6.25	12.50	25.00
—Classic Records reissue					
❏ LSC-2516 [S]	Schubert: Symphonies No. 5 and 8	1961	5.00	10.00	20.00
—Original with "shaded dog" label					
❏ LSC-2609 [S]	Strauss, Richard: Also Sprach Zarathustra	1962	10.00	20.00	40.00
—Original with "shaded dog" label					
❏ LSC-2609 [S]	Strauss, Richard: Also Sprach Zarathustra	1964	5.00	10.00	20.00
—Second edition with "white dog" label					
❏ LMD-2614 [M]	Beethoven: Symphony No. 6 "Pastorale"	1962	10.00	20.00	40.00
—Gatefold with bound-in booklet					
❏ LSC-2614 [S]	Beethoven: Symphony No. 6 "Pastorale"	1962	5.00	10.00	20.00
—Original with "shaded dog" label; non-gatefold edition					
❏ LSCD-2614 [S]	Beethoven: Symphony No. 6 "Pastorale"	1962	25.00	50.00	100.00
—Gatefold with bound-in booklet					

CHICKEN SHACK

BLUE HORIZON

❏ BH 4809	Accept Chicken Shack	1970	6.25	12.50	25.00
❏ BH 7705	O.K. Ken?	1969	6.25	12.50	25.00
❏ BH 7706	100-Ton Chicken	1969	6.25	12.50	25.00

DERAM

❏ DES 18063	Imagination Lady	1972	5.00	10.00	20.00

EPIC

❏ LN 24414 [M]	Forty Blue Fingers, Freshly Packed and Ready to Serve	1968	25.00	50.00	100.00
❏ BN 26414 [M]	Forty Blue Fingers, Freshly Packed and Ready to Serve	1968	7.50	15.00	30.00

LONDON

❏ XPS 632	Unlucky Boy	1973	5.00	10.00	20.00

CHIFFONS, THE

B.T. PUPPY

❏ S-1011	My Secret Love	1970	100.00	200.00	400.00

COLLECTABLES

❏ COL-5042	Golden Classics	198?	3.00	6.00	12.00

LAURIE

❏ LLP-2018 [M]	He's So Fine	1963	30.00	60.00	120.00

Number	Title (A Side/B Side)	Yr	VG	VG+	NM
❏ LLP-2020 [M]	One Fine Day	1963	50.00	100.00	200.00
❏ LLP-2036 [M]	Sweet Talkin' Guy	1966	25.00	50.00	100.00
❏ SLP-2036 [S]	Sweet Talkin' Guy	1966	37.50	75.00	150.00
❏ 4001	Everything You Always Wanted to Hear by the Chiffons	1975	5.00	10.00	20.00
❏ DT-90075 [R]	He's So Fine	1965	50.00	100.00	200.00
—Capitol Record Club edition					
❏ ST-90779 [S]	Sweet Talkin' Guy	1966	50.00	100.00	200.00
—Capitol Record Club edition					

CHILDERS, BUDDY

LIBERTY

❏ LJH-6009 [M]	Sam Songs	1956	10.00	20.00	40.00
❏ LJH-6013 [M]	Buddy Childers Quartet	1957	10.00	20.00	40.00

CHILDRE, LEW

STARDAY

❏ SLP-153 [M]	Old Time Get Together	1961	6.25	12.50	25.00

CHILDREN, THE

ATCO

❏ SD 33-271	Rebirth	1968	6.25	12.50	25.00

CINEMA

❏ CLP-1	Rebirth	1968	37.50	75.00	150.00

CHILDS, SUE

STUDIO 4

❏ 200 [M]	Sue Childs	195?	12.50	25.00	50.00

CHILLIWACK

A&M

❏ SP-3509 [(2)]	Chilliwack	1971	6.25	12.50	25.00
❏ SP-4375	All Over You	1972	3.75	7.50	15.00

MILLENNIUM

❏ BXL1-7759	Wanna Be a Star	1981	2.50	5.00	10.00
❏ BXL1-7766	Opus X	1982	2.50	5.00	10.00

MUSHROOM

❏ MRS-5006	Dreams, Dreams, Dreams	1977	3.00	6.00	12.00
❏ MRS-5011	Lights from the Valley	1978	3.00	6.00	12.00
❏ MRS-5015	Breakdown in Paradise	1980	3.00	6.00	12.00

PARROT

❏ PAS 71040	Chilliwack	1970	5.00	10.00	20.00

SIRE

❏ SASD-7506	Chilliwack	1975	3.75	7.50	15.00
❏ SASD-7511	Rockerbox	1976	3.75	7.50	15.00

CHIPMUNKS, THE, DAVID SEVILLE AND

LIBERTY

❏ LM-1070	Christmas with the Chipmunks	1980	2.00	4.00	8.00
—Reissue with two tracks omitted					
❏ LRP-3132 [M]	Let's All Sing with the Chipmunks	1959	7.50	15.00	30.00
—Black vinyl; original cover features "realistic" chipmunks and no reference to "The Alvin Show"					
❏ LRP-3132 [M]	Let's All Sing with the Chipmunks	1959	15.00	30.00	60.00
—Red vinyl					
❏ LRP-3132 [M]	Let's All Sing with the Chipmunks	1961	5.00	10.00	20.00
—Second cover features the "cartoon" Chipmunks and a reference to "The Alvin Show"					
❏ LRP-3159 [M]	Sing Again with the Chipmunks	1960	10.00	20.00	40.00
—Original cover features "realistic" chipmunks					
❏ LRP-3159 [M]	Sing Again with the Chipmunks	1961	5.00	10.00	20.00
—Second cover features the "cartoon" Chipmunks					
❏ LRP-3170 [M]	Around the World with the Chipmunks	1960	10.00	20.00	40.00
—Original cover features "realistic" chipmunks on and near a plane					
❏ LRP-3170 [M]	Around the World with the Chipmunks	1961	5.00	10.00	20.00
—Second cover features the "cartoon" Chipmunks on and near a camel					
❏ LRP-3209 [M]	The Alvin Show	1961	6.25	12.50	25.00
❏ LRP-3229 [M]	The Chipmunks Songbook	1962	6.25	12.50	25.00
❏ LRP-3256 [M]	Christmas with the Chipmunks	1962	6.25	12.50	25.00
❏ LRP-3334 [M]	Christmas with the Chipmunks, Vol. 2	1963	6.25	12.50	25.00
❏ LRP-3388 [M]	The Chipmunks Sing the Beatles Hits	1964	7.50	15.00	30.00
❏ LRP-3405 [M]	The Chipmunks Sing with Children	1965	5.00	10.00	20.00
❏ LRP-3424 [M]	The Chipmunks A-Go-Go	1965	5.00	10.00	20.00
❏ LST-7132 [S]	Let's All Sing with the Chipmunks	1959	10.00	20.00	40.00
—Black vinyl; original cover features "realistic" chipmunks and no reference to "The Alvin Show"					
❏ LST-7132 [S]	Let's All Sing with the Chipmunks	1959	20.00	40.00	80.00
—Red vinyl					
❏ LST-7132 [S]	Let's All Sing with the Chipmunks	1961	6.25	12.50	25.00
—Second cover features the "cartoon" Chipmunks and a reference to "The Alvin Show"					
❏ LST-7159 [S]	Sing Again with the Chipmunks	1960	12.50	25.00	50.00
—Original cover features "realistic" chipmunks					
❏ LST-7159 [S]	Sing Again with the Chipmunks	1961	6.25	12.50	25.00
—Second cover features the "cartoon" Chipmunks					
❏ LST-7170 [S]	Around the World with the Chipmunks	1960	6.25	12.50	25.00
—Second cover features the "cartoon" Chipmunks on and near a camel					
❏ LST-7170 [S]	Around the World with the Chipmunks	1960	12.50	25.00	50.00
—Original covers have "realistic" chipmunks on and near a plane.					
❏ LST-7209 [S]	The Alvin Show	1961	7.50	15.00	30.00
❏ LST-7229 [S]	The Chipmunks Songbook	1962	7.50	15.00	30.00
❏ LST-7256 [S]	Christmas with the Chipmunks	1962	7.50	15.00	30.00
❏ LST-7334 [S]	Christmas with the Chipmunks, Vol. 2	1963	7.50	15.00	30.00
❏ LST-7388 [S]	The Chipmunks Sing the Beatles Hits	1964	10.00	20.00	40.00
❏ LST-7405 [S]	The Chipmunks Sing with Children	1965	6.25	12.50	25.00
❏ LST-7424 [S]	The Chipmunks A-Go-Go	1965	6.25	12.50	25.00

MISTLETOE

❏ MLP-1216	Christmas with the Chipmunks	197?	2.00	4.00	8.00
—Reissue of Liberty LST-7256					
❏ MLP-1217	Christmas with the Chipmunks, Vol. 2	197?	2.00	4.00	8.00
—Reissue of Liberty LST-7334					

PICKWICK

❏ SPC-1034	Christmas with the Chipmunks	1980	2.50	5.00	10.00
❏ SPC-1035	The Twelve Days of Christmas with The Chipmunks	1980	2.50	5.00	10.00
—Reissue of "Christmas with the Chipmunks, Vol. 2"					

Number	Title (A Side/B Side)	Yr	VG	VG+	NM
SUNSET					
❑ LST-7334 [S]	Christmas with the Chipmunks, Vol. 2	1968	5.00	10.00	20.00
—Budget-line reissue of Liberty LST-7334					
❑ LST-7424 [S]	The Chipmunks A-Go-Go	196?	3.75	7.50	15.00
—Same cover as Liberty 7424, but with "SUNSET" sticker at upper right					
UNITED ARTISTS					
❑ UA-LA352-E2 [(2)]	Christmas with the Chipmunks	1974	5.00	10.00	20.00
—Entire contents of both original Liberty LPs					

CHITTISON, HERMAN
COLUMBIA

Number	Title	Yr	VG	VG+	NM
❑ CL 6134 [10]	Herman Chittison	1950	12.50	25.00	50.00
❑ CL 6182 [10]	Herman Chittison Trio	1951	12.50	25.00	50.00
ROYALE					
❑ 1824 [10]	Cocktail Time	195?	10.00	20.00	40.00

CHOATES, HARRY
D

❑ 7000 [M]	Jole Blon	196?	10.00	20.00	40.00

CHOCO AND HIS MALIMBA DRUM RHYTHMS
AUDIO FIDELITY

❑ AFLP-2102 [M]	African Latin Voodoo Drums	1962	5.00	10.00	20.00
❑ AFSD-6102 [S]	African Latin Voodoo Drums	1962	7.50	15.00	30.00

CHOCOLATE WATCH BAND, THE
RHINO

❑ RNLP-108	The Best of the Chocolate Watch Band	1983	3.00	6.00	12.00
TOWER					
❑ ST 5096 [S]	No Way Out	1967	100.00	200.00	400.00
❑ T 5096 [M]	No Way Out	1967	75.00	150.00	300.00
❑ ST 5106 [S]	The Inner Mystique	1968	75.00	150.00	300.00
❑ T 5106 [M]	The Inner Mystique	1968	100.00	200.00	400.00
❑ ST 5153	One Step Beyond	1969	75.00	150.00	300.00

CHORDETTES, THE
BARNABY

❑ BR-4003	All the Very Best of the Chordettes	1976	3.00	6.00	12.00
CADENCE					
❑ CLP-1002 [10]	Close Harmony	1955	12.50	25.00	50.00
❑ CLP-3001 [M]	The Chordettes	1957	10.00	20.00	40.00
❑ CLP-3020 [M]	Barbershop Harmony	1958	10.00	20.00	40.00
❑ CLP-3056 [M]	Never on Sunday	1962	5.00	10.00	20.00
❑ CLP-25056 [S]	Never on Sunday	1962	7.50	15.00	30.00
COLUMBIA					
❑ CL 956 [M]	Listen	1955	12.50	25.00	50.00
❑ CL 2519 [10]	The Chordettes	1955	10.00	20.00	40.00
❑ CL 6111 [10]	Harmony Time	1950	12.50	25.00	50.00
❑ CL 6170 [10]	Harmony Time, Vol. 2	1951	12.50	25.00	50.00
❑ CL 6218 [10]	Harmony Encores	1952	12.50	25.00	50.00
❑ CL 6285 [10]	Your Requests	1953	12.50	25.00	50.00
HARMONY					
❑ HL 7164 [M]	The Chordettes	196?	3.75	7.50	15.00
RHINO					
❑ R1-70849	The Best of the Chordettes	1989	3.00	6.00	12.00

CHOSEN FEW, THE
MAPLE

❑ 6000	Takin' All the Love I Can	196?	5.00	10.00	20.00
RCA VICTOR					
❑ LSP-4242	The Chosen Few	1969	5.00	10.00	20.00

CHRISTIAN, CHARLIE
COLUMBIA

❑ G 30779 [(2)]	Solo Flight — The Genius of Charlie Christian	1972	5.00	10.00	20.00
COUNTERPOINT					
❑ 548 [M]	The Harlem Jazz Scene 1941	195?	15.00	30.00	60.00
ESOTERIC					
❑ ESJ-1 [10]	Jazz Immortal	1951	50.00	100.00	200.00
—Red vinyl					
❑ ES-548 [M]	The Harlem Jazz Scene 1941	1956	20.00	40.00	80.00

CHRISTIE, LOU
BUDDAH

❑ BDS-5052	I'm Gonna Make You Mine	1969	3.75	7.50	15.00
❑ BDS-5073	Paint America Love	1971	3.75	7.50	15.00
CO & CE					
❑ LP-1231 [M]	Lou Christie Strikes Back	1966	10.00	20.00	40.00
—The front cover and spine use this title, but the back cover and label use "Lou Christie Strikes Again"					
COLPIX					
❑ CP-4001 [M]	Lou Christie Strikes Again	1966	7.50	5.00	30.00
❑ SCP-4001 [S]	Lou Christie Strikes Again	1966	12.50	25.00	50.00
51 WEST					
❑ P 18260	Lou Christie Does Detroit	1983	3.75	7.50	15.00
MGM					
❑ E-4360 [M]	Lightnin' Strikes	1966	3.75	7.50	15.00
❑ SE-4360 [S]	Lightnin' Strikes	1966	5.00	10.00	20.00
❑ E-4394 [M]	Painter of Hits	1966	3.75	7.50	15.00
❑ SE-4394 [S]	Painter of Hits	1966	5.00	10.00	20.00
RHINO					
❑ R1-70246	EnLightnin'Ment: The Best of Lou Christie	1988	3.00	6.00	12.00
ROULETTE					
❑ R 25208 [M]	Lou Christie	1963	10.00	20.00	40.00
—White wall in background on front cover					
❑ R 25208 [M]	Lou Christie	1963	12.50	25.00	50.00
—Blue background on front cover					
❑ SR 25208 [S]	Lou Christie	1963	15.00	30.00	60.00
—White wall in background on front cover					

Number	Title (A Side/B Side)	Yr	VG	VG+	NM
❑ SR 25208 [S]	Lou Christie	1963	20.00	40.00	80.00
—Blue background on front cover					
❑ R 25332 [M]	Lou Christie Strikes Again	1966	6.25	12.50	25.00
❑ SR 25332 [S]	Lou Christie Strikes Again	1966	7.50	15.00	30.00
SPIN-O-RAMA					
❑ M-173 [M]	Starring Lou Christie and the Classics	1966	5.00	10.00	20.00
❑ S-173 [R]	Starring Lou Christie and the Classics	1966	3.00	6.00	12.00
—The above LP also includes other artists					
THREE BROTHERS					
❑ THB-2000	Lou Christie	1973	5.00	10.00	20.00

CHRISTOPHER (1)
BELL

❑ 1203	R.P.M.	1970	5.00	10.00	20.00

CHRISTOPHER (2)
CHRIS-TEE

❑ 12411	What'cha Gonna Do	1970	1500.	2250.	3000.
—100 copies were pressed					

CHRISTOPHER (3)
METROMEDIA

❑ 1024	Christopher	1970	75.00	150.00	300.00

CHRISTY, JUNE
CAPITOL

❑ H 516 [10]	Something Cool	1954	20.00	40.00	80.00
❑ ST 516 [S]	Something Cool	196?	3.75	7.50	15.00
—Re-recording of the original mono LP					
❑ T 516 [M]	Something Cool	1955	12.50	25.00	50.00
—Turquoise label					
❑ T 516 [M]	Something Cool	1959	6.25	12.50	25.00
—Black label with colorband, logo at left					
❑ T 516 [M]	Something Cool	196?	3.75	7.50	15.00
—Black label with colorband, logo at top					
❑ T 656 [M]	Duets	1955	10.00	20.00	40.00
—Turquoise label					
❑ T 725 [M]	The Misty Miss Christy	1956	10.00	20.00	40.00
—Turquoise label					
❑ T 833 [M]	June — Fair and Warmer!	1957	10.00	20.00	40.00
—Turquoise label					
❑ T 902 [M]	Gone for the Day	1957	10.00	20.00	40.00
—Turquoise label					
❑ T 1006 [M]	This Is June Christy!	1958	10.00	20.00	40.00
—Turquoise label					
❑ ST 1076 [S]	June's Got Rhythm	1958	10.00	20.00	40.00
—Black label with colorband, Capitol logo at left					
❑ T 1076 [M]	June's Got Rhythm	1958	7.50	15.00	30.00
—Black label with colorband, Capitol logo at left					
❑ ST 1114 [S]	The Song Is June!	1959	10.00	20.00	40.00
—Black label with colorband, Capitol logo at left					
❑ T 1114 [M]	The Song Is June!	1959	7.50	15.00	30.00
—Black label with colorband, Capitol logo at left					
❑ ST 1202 [S]	June Christy Recalls Those Kenton Days	1959	10.00	20.00	40.00
—Black label with colorband, Capitol logo at left					
❑ T 1202 [M]	June Christy Recalls Those Kenton Days	1959	7.50	15.00	30.00
—Black label with colorband, Capitol logo at left					
❑ ST 1308 [S]	Ballads for Night People	1959	10.00	20.00	40.00
—Black label with colorband, Capitol logo at left					
❑ T 1308 [M]	Ballads for Night People	1959	7.50	15.00	30.00
—Black label with colorband, Capitol logo at left					
❑ STBO 1327 [(2)S]	Road Show	1960	10.00	20.00	40.00
—Black label with colorband, Capitol logo at left					
❑ TBO 1327 [(2)M]	Road Show	1960	7.50	15.00	30.00
—Black label with colorband, Capitol logo at left					
❑ ST 1398 [S]	The Cool School	1960	10.00	20.00	40.00
—Black label with colorband, Capitol logo at left					
❑ T 1398 [M]	The Cool School	1960	7.50	15.00	30.00
—Black label with colorband, Capitol logo at left					
❑ ST 1498 [S]	Off Beat	1961	12.50	25.00	50.00
—Black label with colorband, Capitol logo at left					
❑ T 1498 [M]	Off Beat	1961	10.00	20.00	40.00
—Black label with colorband, Capitol logo at left					
❑ ST 1586 [S]	Do-Re-Mi	1961	12.50	25.00	50.00
—Black label with colorband, Capitol logo at left					
❑ T 1586 [M]	Do-Re-Mi	1961	10.00	20.00	40.00
—Black label with colorband, Capitol logo at left					
❑ ST 1605 [S]	That Time of Year	1961	12.50	25.00	50.00
—Black label with colorband, Capitol logo at left					
❑ T 1605 [M]	That Time of Year	1961	10.00	20.00	40.00
—Black label with colorband, Capitol logo at left					
❑ ST 1693 [S]	The Best of June Christy	1962	7.50	15.00	30.00
—Black logo with colorband					
❑ T 1693 [M]	The Best of June Christy	1962	6.25	12.50	25.00
—Black label with colorband					
❑ ST 1845 [S]	Big Band Specials	1962	6.25	12.50	25.00
❑ T 1845 [M]	Big Band Specials	1962	5.00	10.00	20.00
❑ ST 1953 [S]	The Intimate June Christy	1963	6.25	12.50	25.00
❑ T 1953 [M]	The Intimate June Christy	1963	5.00	10.00	20.00
❑ ST 2410 [S]	Something Broadway, Something Latin	1965	7.50	15.00	30.00
❑ T 2410 [M]	Something Broadway, Something Latin	1965	6.25	12.50	25.00

CHRYSALIS
MGM

❑ SE-4547	Definition	1968	7.50	15.00	30.00

CHURCH, THE
ARISTA

❑ AL 8521	Starfish	1988	2.50	5.00	10.00
❑ AL 8563	Of Skins and Heart	1988	2.50	5.00	10.00
—First U.S. issue of first Australian album					
❑ AL 8564	The Blurred Crusade	1988	2.50	5.00	10.00
—First U.S. issue of second Australian album					
❑ AL 8565	Seance	1988	2.50	5.00	10.00
—First U.S. issue of third Australian album					

Number	Title (A Side/B Side)	Yr	VG	VG+	NM
❑ AL 8566	Remote Luxury	1988	2.50	5.00	10.00
—Reissue of Warner Bros. 25152					
❑ AL 8567	Heyday	1988	2.50	5.00	10.00
—Reissue of Warner Bros. 25370					
❑ AL 8579	Gold Afternoon Fix	1990	2.50	5.00	10.00
❑ ADP 9713 [DJ]	Sum of the Parts	1988	10.00	20.00	40.00
—Interviews and live acoustic tracks					
❑ 18727-1 [(2)]	Sometime Anywhere	1994	3.75	7.50	15.00
❑ R 171667	Gold Afternoon Fix	1990	3.00	6.00	12.00
—BMG Direct Marketing edition					
❑ R 173703	Starfish	1988	3.00	6.00	12.00
—BMG Direct Marketing edition					
CAPITOL					
❑ ST-12193	The Church	1982	3.75	7.50	15.00
WARNER BROS.					
❑ 25152	Remote Luxury	1984	3.75	7.50	15.00
❑ 25370	Heyday	1985	3.75	7.50	15.00

CIRCLE
ECM

Number	Title (A Side/B Side)	Yr	VG	VG+	NM
❑ 1018/19 [(2)]	Paris Concert	197?	5.00	10.00	20.00

CIRCUS
METROMEDIA

Number	Title (A Side/B Side)	Yr	VG	VG+	NM
❑ 7401	Circus	1973	7.50	15.00	30.00

CIRCUS MAXIMUS
Group features JERRY JEFF WALKER.
VANGUARD

Number	Title (A Side/B Side)	Yr	VG	VG+	NM
❑ VRS-9260 [M]	Circus Maximus	1967	5.00	10.00	20.00
❑ VSD-79260 [S]	Circus Maximus	1967	6.25	12.50	25.00
❑ VSD-79274	Neverland Revisited	1968	6.25	12.50	25.00

CIRILLO, WALLY/BOBBY SCOTT
SAVOY

Number	Title (A Side/B Side)	Yr	VG	VG+	NM
❑ MG-15055 [10]	Cirillo and Scott	1955	20.00	40.00	80.00

CITY, THE
CAROLE KING was a member.
ODE

Number	Title (A Side/B Side)	Yr	VG	VG+	NM
❑ Z12 44012	Now That Everything's Been Said	1968	20.00	40.00	80.00
—Color front cover					
❑ Z12 44012	Now That Everything's Been Said	1971	3.00	6.00	12.00
—Black & white front cover					

CLANTON, JIMMY
ACE

Number	Title (A Side/B Side)	Yr	VG	VG+	NM
❑ DLP-100	Jimmy's Happy/Jimmy's Blue Poster	1960	20.00	40.00	80.00
❑ DLP-100 [M]	Jimmy's Happy/Jimmy's Blue	1960	37.50	75.00	150.00
—Black vinyl; also released as two separate albums, 1007 and 1008					
❑ DLP-100 [M]	Jimmy's Happy/Jimmy's Blue	1960	100.00	200.00	400.00
—The "Happy" album is red vinyl, the "Blue" album is blue					
❑ 1001 [M]	Just a Dream	1959	30.00	60.00	120.00
❑ 1007 [M]	Jimmy's Happy	1960	10.00	20.00	40.00
❑ 1008 [M]	Jimmy's Blue	1960	10.00	20.00	40.00
❑ 1011 [M]	My Best to You	1960	25.00	50.00	100.00
❑ 1014 [M]	Teenage Millionaire	1961	25.00	50.00	100.00
❑ 1026 [M]	Venus in Blue Jeans	1962	25.00	50.00	100.00
PHILIPS					
❑ PHM 200154 [M]	The Best of Jimmy Clanton	1964	6.25	12.50	25.00
❑ PHS 600154 [S]	The Best of Jimmy Clanton	1964	7.50	15.00	30.00

CLAP
NOVA SOL

Number	Title (A Side/B Side)	Yr	VG	VG+	NM
❑ 1001	Have You Reached Yet?	1970	250.00	500.00	1000.

CLAPTON, ERIC
ATCO

Number	Title (A Side/B Side)	Yr	VG	VG+	NM
❑ 33-329 [DJ]	Eric Clapton	1970	25.00	50.00	100.00
—Mono pressing is promo only					
❑ SD 33-329	Eric Clapton	1970	5.00	10.00	20.00
❑ SD 33-329	Eric Clapton	1970	50.00	100.00	200.00
—Odd pressing with alternate takes of "After Midnight" and "Blues Power" plus remixes of other tracks. Look for "CTH" in trail-off area.					
❑ SD 2-803 [(2)]	History of Eric Clapton	1972	5.00	10.00	20.00
—Contains tracks from the Yardbirds, John Mayall's Bluesbreakers, Cream, Blind Faith, and solo records					
DUCK					
❑ 23773	Money and Cigarettes	1983	2.50	5.00	10.00
❑ 25186	Behind the Sun	1985	2.50	5.00	10.00
❑ 25476	August	1986	2.50	5.00	10.00
MOBILE FIDELITY					
❑ 1-030	Slowhand	1980	17.50	35.00	70.00
—Audiophile vinyl					
❑ 1-220	Eric Clapton	1995	6.25	12.50	25.00
—Audiophile vinyl					
NAUTILUS					
❑ NR-32 [(2)]	Just One Night	1981	37.50	75.00	150.00
—Audiophile vinyl					
POLYDOR					
❑ PD 3503 [(2)]	Eric Clapton at His Best	1972	5.00	10.00	20.00
—Compiles tracks from his first solo album plus Derek and the Dominos					
❑ 24-5526	Clapton	1973	3.75	7.50	15.00
—Compiles tracks from his first solo album plus Derek and the Dominos					
❑ SKBO-94837 [(2)]	Eric Clapton at His Best	1972	7.50	15.00	30.00
—Capitol Record Club edition					
❑ 835261-1 [(6)]	Crossroads	1988	12.50	25.00	50.00
—Box set; contains material from all phases of his career					
REPRISE					
❑ 26074	Journeyman	1989	3.00	6.00	12.00
❑ W1-26420 [(2)]	24 Nights	1991	6.25	12.50	25.00
—Vinyl copies released only through Columbia House					

RSO

Number	Title (A Side/B Side)	Yr	VG	VG+	NM
❑ PRO 035 [DJ]	Slowhand	1977	10.00	20.00	40.00
—White vinyl promo sampler					
❑ SO 877	Eric Clapton's Rainbow Concert	1973	3.75	7.50	15.00
❑ RPO-1009 [DJ]	Limited Backless	1978	12.50	25.00	50.00
—White vinyl promo					
❑ RS-1-3004	No Reason to Cry	1976	3.00	6.00	12.00
❑ RS-1-3008	Eric Clapton	1977	3.00	6.00	12.00
—Reissue of Atco LP of the same name					
❑ RS-1-3023	461 Ocean Boulevard	1977	3.00	6.00	12.00
—Reissue of RSO 4801					
❑ RS-1-3030	Slowhand	1977	3.00	6.00	12.00
❑ RS-1-3039	Backless	1978	3.00	6.00	12.00
❑ RX-1-3095	Another Ticket	1981	2.50	5.00	10.00
❑ RS-1-3099	Time Pieces/The Best of Eric Clapton	1982	2.50	5.00	10.00
❑ RS-2-4202 [(2)]	Just One Night	1980	3.75	7.50	15.00
❑ QD 4801 [Q]	461 Ocean Boulevard	1974	6.25	12.50	25.00
❑ SO 4801	461 Ocean Boulevard	1974	3.00	6.00	12.00
—With "Better Make It Through the Day"					
❑ SO 4801	461 Ocean Boulevard	1974	3.75	7.50	15.00
—With "Give Me Strength"					
❑ QD 4806 [Q]	There's One in Every Crowd	1975	6.25	12.50	25.00
❑ SO 4806	There's One in Every Crowd	1975	3.00	6.00	12.00
❑ SO 4809	E.C. Was Here	1975	3.00	6.00	12.00
❑ 811697-1	461 Ocean Boulevard	198?	2.00	4.00	8.00
—Reissue of RSO 3023					
❑ 823276-1	Slowhand	1983	2.00	4.00	8.00
—Reissue of RSO 3030					
❑ 825093-1	Eric Clapton	1984	2.00	4.00	8.00
—Reissue of RSO 3008					
❑ 825382-1	Time Pieces/The Best of Eric Clapton	1984	2.00	4.00	8.00
—Reissue of RSO 3099					
❑ 825391-1 [(2)]	Just One Night	1984	2.50	5.00	10.00
—Reissue of RSO 4202					
❑ 827579-1	Another Ticket	1985	2.00	4.00	8.00
—Reissue of RSO 3095					

CLARK, ALICE
MAINSTREAM

Number	Title (A Side/B Side)	Yr	VG	VG+	NM
❑ MRL-362	Alice Clark	1972	5.00	10.00	20.00

CLARK, CHRIS
MOTOWN

Number	Title (A Side/B Side)	Yr	VG	VG+	NM
❑ M-664 [M]	Soul Sounds	1967	12.50	25.00	50.00
❑ MS-664 [S]	Soul Sounds	1967	15.00	30.00	60.00
WEED					
❑ 801	C.C. Rides Again	1969	20.00	40.00	80.00

CLARK, CLAUDINE
CHANCELLOR

Number	Title (A Side/B Side)	Yr	VG	VG+	NM
❑ CHL-5029 [M]	Party Lights	1962	62.50	125.00	250.00

CLARK, DAVE, FIVE
CORTLEIGH

Number	Title (A Side/B Side)	Yr	VG	VG+	NM
❑ C-1073 [M]	The Dave Clark Five with Ricky Astor	1964	7.50	15.00	30.00
—With two early DC5 tracks and assorted other stuff by other artists					
❑ CS-1073 [R]	The Dave Clark Five with Ricky Astor	1964	3.75	7.50	15.00
—With two early DC5 tracks and assorted other stuff by other artists					
CROWN					
❑ CST-400 [R]	The Dave Clark Five with the Playbacks	1964	3.75	7.50	15.00
—With two early DC5 tracks and assorted other stuff by other artists					
❑ CST-473 [R]	Chaquita/In Your Heart	1964	3.75	7.50	15.00
—With two early DC5 tracks and assorted other stuff by other artists					
❑ CLP-5400 [M]	The Dave Clark Five with the Playbacks	1964	7.50	15.00	30.00
—With two early DC5 tracks and assorted other stuff by other artists					
❑ CLP-5473 [M]	Chaquita/In Your Heart	1964	7.50	15.00	30.00
—With two early DC5 tracks and assorted other stuff by other artists					
EPIC					
❑ LN 24093 [M]	Glad All Over	1964	10.00	20.00	40.00
—Group photo with instruments					
❑ LN 24093 [M]	Glad All Over	1964	20.00	40.00	80.00
—Group photo, no instruments					
❑ LN 24104 [M]	The Dave Clark Five Return	1964	10.00	20.00	40.00
❑ LN 24117 [M]	American Tour	1964	10.00	20.00	40.00
❑ LN 24128 [M]	Coast to Coast	1965	10.00	20.00	40.00
❑ LN 24139 [M]	Weekend in London	1965	10.00	20.00	40.00
❑ LN 24162 [M]	Having a Wild Weekend	1965	10.00	20.00	40.00
❑ LN 24178 [M]	I Like It Like That	1965	10.00	20.00	40.00
❑ LN 24185 [M]	The Dave Clark Five's Greatest Hits	1966	6.25	12.50	25.00
❑ LN 24198 [M]	Try Too Hard	1966	7.50	15.00	30.00
❑ LN 24212 [M]	Satisfied with You	1966	7.50	15.00	30.00
❑ LN 24221 [M]	More Greatest Hits	1966	6.25	12.50	25.00
❑ LN 24236 [M]	5 by 5	1967	7.50	15.00	30.00
❑ LN 24312 [M]	You Got What It Takes	1967	7.50	15.00	30.00
❑ LN 24354 [M]	Everybody Knows	1968	7.50	15.00	30.00
❑ BN 26093 [R]	Glad All Over	1964	7.50	15.00	30.00
—Group photo with instruments					
❑ BN 26093 [R]	Glad All Over	1964	12.50	25.00	50.00
—Group photo, no instruments					
❑ BN 26104 [R]	The Dave Clark Five Return	1964	7.50	15.00	30.00
❑ BN 26117 [R]	American Tour	1964	7.50	15.00	30.00
❑ BN 26128 [R]	Coast to Coast	1965	7.50	15.00	30.00
❑ BN 26139 [R]	Weekend in London	1965	7.50	15.00	30.00
❑ BN 26162 [R]	Having a Wild Weekend	1965	7.50	15.00	30.00
❑ BN 26178 [R]	I Like It Like That	1965	7.50	15.00	30.00
❑ BN 26185 [R]	The Dave Clark Five's Greatest Hits	1966	5.00	10.00	20.00
—Yellow label					
❑ BN 26185 [R]	The Dave Clark Five's Greatest Hits	1973	10.00	20.00	40.00
—Orange label					
❑ BN 26198 [R]	Try Too Hard	1966	6.25	12.50	25.00
❑ BN 26212 [R]	Satisfied with You	1966	6.25	12.50	25.00
❑ BN 26221 [R]	More Greatest Hits	1966	5.00	10.00	20.00
❑ BN 26236 [S]	5 by 5	1967	10.00	20.00	40.00

Number	Title (A Side/B Side)	Yr	VG	VG+	NM
❏ BN 26312 [S]	You Got What It Takes	1967	10.00	20.00	40.00
❏ BN 26354 [S]	Everybody Knows	1968	10.00	20.00	40.00
❏ EG 30434 [(2)S]	The Dave Clark Five	1971	25.00	50.00	100.00
—Twenty hits and near-hits, all in true stereo! Yellow label.					
❏ EG 30434 [(2)S]	The Dave Clark Five	1973	20.00	40.00	80.00
—Twenty hits and near-hits, all in true stereo! Orange label.					
❏ KEG 33459 [(2)M]	Glad All Over Again	1975	12.50	25.00	50.00
❏ XEM 77238/9 [DJ]	The Dave Clark Five Interview	1964	150.00	300.00	600.00

CLARK, DEE
ABNER
Number	Title (A Side/B Side)	Yr	VG	VG+	NM
❏ LP-2000 [M]	Dee Clark	1959	30.00	60.00	120.00
❏ SR-2000 [S]	Dee Clark	1959	87.50	175.00	350.00
❏ LP-2002 [M]	How About That	1960	20.00	40.00	80.00
❏ SR-2002 [S]	How About That	1960	30.00	60.00	120.00
SOLID SMOKE					
❏ 8026	His Best Recordings	1983	2.50	5.00	10.00
SUNSET					
❏ SUS-5217	Wondering	1968	3.00	6.00	12.00
VEE JAY					
❏ LP-1019 [M]	You're Looking Good	1960	12.50	25.00	50.00
❏ LP-1037 [M]	Hold On, It's Dee Clark	1961	12.50	25.00	50.00
❏ SR-1037 [S]	Hold On, It's Dee Clark	1961	25.00	50.00	100.00
❏ LP-1047 [M]	The Best of Dee Clark	1964	12.50	25.00	50.00
❏ SR-1047 [S]	The Best of Dee Clark	1964	25.00	50.00	100.00
❏ VJLP-1047	The Best of Dee Clark	1986	3.00	6.00	12.00
—Authorized reissue					

CLARK, DICK
See VARIOUS ARTISTS COLLECTIONS.

CLARK, DOTTIE
MAINSTREAM
Number	Title (A Side/B Side)	Yr	VG	VG+	NM
❏ S-6006 [S]	I'm Lost	1966	6.25	12.50	25.00
❏ 56006 [M]	I'm Lost	1966	5.00	10.00	20.00

CLARK, DOUG, AND THE HOT NUTS
GROSS
Number	Title (A Side/B Side)	Yr	VG	VG+	NM
❏ 101	Nuts to You	196?	7.50	15.00	30.00
❏ 102	On Campus	196?	7.50	15.00	30.00
❏ 103	Homecoming	196?	7.50	15.00	30.00
❏ 104	Rush Week	1967	7.50	15.00	30.00
❏ 105	Panty Raid	196?	7.50	15.00	30.00
❏ 106	Summer Session	196?	7.50	15.00	30.00
❏ 107	Hell Night	196?	7.50	15.00	30.00
❏ 108	Freak Out	196?	7.50	15.00	30.00
❏ 109	With a Hat On	196?	7.50	15.00	30.00

CLARK, GENE
A&M
Number	Title (A Side/B Side)	Yr	VG	VG+	NM
❏ SP-4292	White Light	1971	3.75	7.50	15.00
ASYLUM					
❏ 7E-1016	No Other	1974	3.75	7.50	15.00
COLUMBIA					
❏ CL 2618 [M]	Gene Clark with the Gosdin Brothers	1967	7.50	15.00	30.00
❏ CS 9418 [S]	Gene Clark with the Gosdin Brothers	1967	12.50	25.00	50.00
❏ KC 31123	Early L.A. Sessions	1972	3.75	7.50	15.00
RSO					
❏ RS-1-3011	Two Sides to Every Story	1976	5.00	10.00	20.00
SUNDAZED					
❏ LP 5062	Gene Clark with the Gosdin Brothers	2000	3.75	7.50	15.00
—Reissue of Columbia LP					
TAKOMA					
❏ TAK-7112	Firebyrd	1984	2.50	5.00	10.00

CLARK, GUY
RCA VICTOR
Number	Title (A Side/B Side)	Yr	VG	VG+	NM
❏ AHL1-1303	Old No. 1	198?	2.50	5.00	10.00
—Reissue with new prefix					
❏ APL1-1303	Old No. 1	1976	5.00	10.00	20.00
❏ APL1-1944	Texas Cookin'	1976	5.00	10.00	20.00
SUGAR HILL					
❏ SH-1025	Old Friends	198?	3.00	6.00	12.00
WARNER BROS.					
❏ WBMS-105 [DJ]	On the Road, Live!	198?	15.00	30.00	60.00
—Part of "The Warner Bros. Music Show" series; promo only					
❏ BSK 3241	Guy Clark	1978	3.75	7.50	15.00
❏ BSK 3381	South Coast of Texas	1981	3.75	7.50	15.00
❏ 23880	Better Days	1983	3.00	6.00	12.00

CLARK, KEN, AND DON ANTHONY
STARDAY
Number	Title (A Side/B Side)	Yr	VG	VG+	NM
❏ SLP-114 [M]	Fiddlin' Country Style	1959	10.00	20.00	40.00

CLARK, PETULA
COCA-COLA
Number	Title (A Side/B Side)	Yr	VG	VG+	NM
❏ 103 [DJ]	Petula Clark Swings the Jingle	1966	37.50	75.00	150.00
GNP CRESCENDO					
❏ 2069	Live at the Royal Albert Hall	1972	2.50	5.00	10.00
❏ 2170	The Greatest Hits of Petula Clark	1984	2.00	4.00	8.00
IMPERIAL					
❏ LP-9079 [M]	Pet Clark	1959	12.50	25.00	50.00
❏ LP-9281 [M]	Uptown with Petula Clark	1965	5.00	10.00	20.00
—Reissue of Imperial 9079					
❏ LP-12027 [S]	Pet Clark	1959	20.00	40.00	80.00
❏ LP-12281 [S]	Uptown with Petula Clark	1965	6.25	12.50	25.00
—Reissue of Imperial 12079					
JANGO					
❏ 779	Give It a Try	1986	2.50	5.00	10.00
LAURIE					
❏ LLP-2032 [M]	In Love!	1965	3.75	7.50	15.00

Number	Title (A Side/B Side)	Yr	VG	VG+	NM
❏ SLP-2032 [S]	In Love!	1965	3.75	7.50	15.00
❏ ST-90497 [S]	In Love!	1965	5.00	10.00	20.00
—Capitol Record Club edition					
MGM					
❏ SE-4859	Pet Clark Now	1972	2.50	5.00	10.00
PREMIER					
❏ PM-9016 [M]	The English Sound Starring Petula Clark	1965	3.00	6.00	12.00
❏ PS-9016 [S]	The English Sound Starring Petula Clark	1965	3.75	7.50	15.00
ROULETTE					
❏ 1 [(3)]	Petula	1975	5.00	10.00	20.00
SUNSET					
❏ SUM-1101 [M]	This Is Petula Clark	1965	3.00	6.00	12.00
❏ SUS-5101 [S]	This Is Petula Clark	1965	3.75	7.50	15.00
WARNER BROS.					
❏ W 1590 [M]	Downtown	1965	3.75	7.50	15.00
—Originals have gray labels					
❏ W 1590 [M]	Downtown	1966	3.00	6.00	12.00
—Reissues have gold labels					
❏ WS 1590 [S]	Downtown	1965	5.00	10.00	20.00
—Originals have gray labels					
❏ W 1598 [M]	I Know a Place	1965	3.75	7.50	15.00
—Originals have gray labels					
❏ W 1598 [M]	I Know a Place	1966	3.00	6.00	12.00
—Reissues have gold labels					
❏ WS 1598 [S]	I Know a Place	1965	5.00	10.00	20.00
—Originals have gold labels					
❏ W 1608 [M]	The World's Greatest International Hits	1965	3.00	6.00	12.00
—Reissues have gold labels					
❏ W 1608 [M]	The World's Greatest International Hits	1965	3.75	7.50	15.00
—Originals have gray labels					
❏ WS 1608 [S]	The World's Greatest International Hits	1965	5.00	10.00	20.00
—Originals have gold labels					
❏ W 1630 [M]	My Love	1966	2.50	5.00	10.00
❏ WS 1630 [S]	My Love	1966	3.00	6.00	12.00
❏ W 1645 [M]	I Couldn't Live Without Your Love	1966	2.50	5.00	10.00
❏ WS 1645 [S]	I Couldn't Live Without Your Love	1966	3.00	6.00	12.00
❏ W 1673 [M]	Color My World/Who Am I	1967	2.50	5.00	10.00
❏ WS 1673 [S]	Color My World/Who Am I	1967	3.00	6.00	12.00
❏ W 1698 [M]	These Are My Songs	1967	2.50	5.00	10.00
❏ WS 1698 [S]	These Are My Songs	1967	3.00	6.00	12.00
❏ W 1719 [M]	The Other Man's Grass Is Always Greener	1968	3.00	6.00	12.00
❏ WS 1719 [P]	The Other Man's Grass Is Always Greener	1968	3.00	6.00	12.00
—"The Other Man's Grass Is Always Greener" is rechanneled.					
❏ W 1743 [M]	Petula	1968	3.00	6.00	12.00
❏ WS 1743 [S]	Petula	1968	3.00	6.00	12.00
❏ WS 1765	Greatest Hits, Volume I	1968	2.50	5.00	10.00
❏ WS 1789	Portrait of Petula	1969	2.50	5.00	10.00
❏ WS 1823	Just Pet	1969	2.50	5.00	10.00
❏ WS 1862	Memphis	1970	2.50	5.00	10.00
❏ WS 1865	Warm and Tender (The Song of My Life)	1971	2.50	5.00	10.00
❏ ST-91598	Greatest Hits, Volume I	1968	3.75	7.50	15.00
—Capitol Record Club edition					
❏ SQBO-93215 [(2)P]	Hits...My Way	1969	6.25	12.50	25.00
—Capitol Record Club exclusive; "The Other Man's Grass Is Always Greener" is rechanneled.					

CLARK, ROY
ABC
Number	Title (A Side/B Side)	Yr	VG	VG+	NM
❏ AB-1053	Labor of Love	1978	2.50	5.00	10.00
ABC DOT					
❏ DOSD-2001	Roy Clark/The Entertainer	1974	2.50	5.00	10.00
❏ DOSD-2005	Roy Clark, Family & Friends	1974	2.50	5.00	10.00
❏ DOSD-2010	Classic Clark	1974	2.50	5.00	10.00
❏ DOSD-2030	Roy Clark's Greatest Hits — Volume 1	1975	2.50	5.00	10.00
❏ DOSD-2041	Heart to Heart	1975	2.50	5.00	10.00
❏ DOSD-2054	Roy Clark In Concert	1976	2.50	5.00	10.00
❏ DO-2072 [(2)]	My Music and Me/Vocal & Instrumental	1977	3.00	6.00	12.00
❏ DO-2099	Hookin' It	1977	2.50	5.00	10.00
—Reissue of Record 2 of 2072					
CAPITOL					
❏ SKAO-369	The Greatest!	1969	3.00	6.00	12.00
❏ SM-369	The Greatest!	197?	2.50	5.00	10.00
—Reissue with new prefix					
❏ ST 1780 [S]	The Lightning Fingers of Roy Clark	1962	6.25	12.50	25.00
❏ T 1780 [M]	The Lightning Fingers of Roy Clark	1962	5.00	10.00	20.00
❏ ST 1972 [S]	The Tip of My Fingers	1963	6.25	12.50	25.00
❏ T 1972 [M]	The Tip of My Fingers	1963	5.00	10.00	20.00
❏ ST 2031 [S]	Happy to Be Unhappy	1964	6.25	12.50	25.00
❏ T 2031 [M]	Happy to Be Unhappy	1964	5.00	10.00	20.00
❏ SM-2425	The Roy Clark Guitar Spectacular	197?	2.50	5.00	10.00
—Reissue with new prefix					
❏ ST 2425 [S]	The Roy Clark Guitar Spectacular	1965	6.25	12.50	25.00
❏ T 2425 [M]	The Roy Clark Guitar Spectacular	1965	5.00	10.00	20.00
❏ ST 2452 [S]	Roy Clark Sings Lonesome Love Ballads	1966	6.25	12.50	25.00
❏ T 2452 [M]	Roy Clark Sings Lonesome Love Ballads	1966	5.00	10.00	20.00
❏ ST 2535 [S]	Stringing Along with the Blues	1966	6.25	12.50	25.00
❏ T 2535 [M]	Stringing Along with the Blues	1966	5.00	10.00	20.00
❏ SABB-11264 [(2)]	The Entertainer of the Year	1974	3.75	7.50	15.00
❏ SM-11412	So Much to Remember	1975	2.50	5.00	10.00
❏ SM-12032	The Tip of My Fingers	1980	2.00	4.00	8.00
❏ SN-16161	The Greatest!	198?	2.00	4.00	8.00
❏ SN-16227	The Lightning Fingers of Roy Clark	198?	2.00	4.00	8.00
CHURCHILL					
❏ 9421	The Roy Clark Show Live from Austin City Limits	1982	2.50	5.00	10.00
❏ 9425	Turned Loose	1982	2.50	5.00	10.00
DOT					
❏ DLP-25863	Urban, Suburban	1968	3.00	6.00	12.00
❏ DLP-25895	Do You Believe This Roy Clark	1968	3.00	6.00	12.00
❏ DLP-25953	Yesterday, When I Was Young	1969	3.00	6.00	12.00
❏ DLP-25972	The Everlovin' Soul of Roy Clark	1969	3.00	6.00	12.00

Number	Title (A Side/B Side)	Yr	VG	VG+	NM
❑ DLP-25977	The Other Side of Roy Clark	1970	3.00	6.00	12.00
❑ DLP-25980	I Never Picked Cotton	1970	3.00	6.00	12.00
❑ DLP-25986	The Best of Roy Clark	1971	3.00	6.00	12.00
❑ DLP-25990	The Incredible Roy Clark	1971	3.00	6.00	12.00
❑ DLP-25993	The Magnificent Sanctuary Band	1971	3.00	6.00	12.00
❑ DLP-25997	Roy Clark Country!	1972	3.00	6.00	12.00
❑ DOS-26005	Roy Clark Live!	1972	3.00	6.00	12.00
❑ DOS-26008	Roy Clark/Superpicker	1973	3.00	6.00	12.00
❑ DOS-26010	Come Live with Me	1973	3.00	6.00	12.00
❑ DOS-26018	Roy Clark's Family Album	1973	3.00	6.00	12.00
HILLTOP					
❑ 6046	Roy Clartk	196?	3.75	7.50	15.00
❑ 6080	Silver Threads and Golden Needles	1970	2.50	5.00	10.00
❑ 6094	He'll Have to Go	1970	2.50	5.00	10.00
❑ 6135	Take Me As I Am	197?	2.50	5.00	10.00
❑ 6154	Honky Tonk	197?	2.50	5.00	10.00
MCA					
❑ 675	Labor of Love	1980	2.00	4.00	8.00
❑ 676	Heart to Heart	1980	2.00	4.00	8.00
❑ 677	Hookin' It	1980	2.00	4.00	8.00
❑ 678	Yesterday, When I Was Young	198?	2.00	4.00	8.00
❑ 679	Roy Clark/Superpicker	198?	2.00	4.00	8.00
❑ 811	Back to the Country	198?	2.00	4.00	8.00
❑ 3161	Makin' Music	1980	2.50	5.00	10.00
—With Gatemouth Brown					
❑ 27015	The Best of Roy Clark	198?	2.00	4.00	8.00
❑ 27050	Roy Clark's Greatest Hits — Volume 1	198?	2.00	4.00	8.00
❑ 37130	Banjo Bandits	198?	2.00	4.00	8.00
—With Buck Trent					
❑ 37131	A Pair of Fives (Banjos, That Is)	198?	2.00	4.00	8.00
❑ 37132	Roy Clark In Concert	198?	2.00	4.00	8.00
❑ 37134	Roy Clark Live!	198?	2.00	4.00	8.00
❑ 37142	My Music	198?	2.00	4.00	8.00
PAIR					
❑ PDL2-1088 [(2)]	Country Standard Time	1986	3.00	6.00	12.00
PICKWICK					
❑ PTP-2043 [(2)]	Roy Clark	1973	3.00	6.00	12.00
SONGBIRD					
❑ 5260	The Last Word in Jesus Is Us	1981	2.50	5.00	10.00
TOWER					
❑ ST 5055 [S]	Roy Clark Live	1967	5.00	10.00	20.00
❑ T 5055 [M]	Roy Clark Live	1967	3.75	7.50	15.00
❑ DT 5118 [R]	In the Mood	1968	3.75	7.50	15.00
WORD					
❑ 8654	Roy Clark Sings Gospel	1975	3.00	6.00	12.00

CLARK, ROY, AND BUCK TRENT
ABC

Number	Title (A Side/B Side)	Yr	VG	VG+	NM
❑ AY-1084	Banjo Bandits	1978	2.50	5.00	10.00
ABC DOT					
❑ 2015	A Pair of Fives (Banjos, That Is)	1975	2.50	5.00	10.00

CLARK, SANFORD
LHI

Number	Title (A Side/B Side)	Yr	VG	VG+	NM
❑ 12003	Return of the Fool	1968	15.00	30.00	60.00

CLARK, SONNY
BLUE NOTE

Number	Title (A Side/B Side)	Yr	VG	VG+	NM
❑ BLP-1570 [M]	Dial "S" for Sonny	1957	20.00	40.00	80.00
—Regular version, W. 63rd St. address on label					
❑ BLP-1570 [M]	Dial "S" for Sonny	1957	37.50	75.00	150.00
—"Deep groove" version (deep indentation under label on both sides)					
❑ BLP-1570 [M]	Dial "S" for Sonny	1963	6.25	12.50	25.00
—"New York, USA" address on label					
❑ BST-1570 [S]	Dial "S" for Sonny	1959	15.00	30.00	60.00
—Regular version, W. 63rd St. address on label					
❑ BST-1570 [S]	Dial "S" for Sonny	1959	25.00	50.00	100.00
—"Deep groove" version (deep indentation under label on both sides)					
❑ BST-1570 [S]	Dial "S" for Sonny	1963	5.00	10.00	20.00
—"New York, USA" address on label					
❑ BLP-1576 [M]	Sonny's Crib	1957	20.00	40.00	80.00
—Regular version, W. 63rd St. address on label					
❑ BLP-1576 [M]	Sonny's Crib	1957	37.50	75.00	150.00
—"Deep groove" version (deep indentation under label on both sides)					
❑ BLP-1576 [M]	Sonny's Crib	1963	6.25	12.50	25.00
—"New York, USA" address on label					
❑ BST-1576 [S]	Sonny's Crib	1959	15.00	30.00	60.00
—Regular version, W. 63rd St. address on label					
❑ BST-1576 [S]	Sonny's Crib	1959	25.00	50.00	100.00
—"Deep groove" version (deep indentation under label on both sides)					
❑ BST-1576 [S]	Sonny's Crib	1963	5.00	10.00	20.00
—"New York, USA" address on label					
❑ BLP-1579 [M]	Sonny Clark Trio	1958	20.00	40.00	80.00
—Regular version, W. 63rd St. address on label					
❑ BLP-1579 [M]	Sonny Clark Trio	1958	37.50	75.00	150.00
—"Deep groove" version (deep indentation under label on both sides)					
❑ BLP-1579 [M]	Sonny Clark Trio	1963	6.25	12.50	25.00
—"New York, USA" address on label					
❑ BST-1579 [S]	Sonny Clark Trio	1959	15.00	30.00	60.00
—Regular version, W. 63rd St. address on label					
❑ BST-1579 [S]	Sonny Clark Trio	1959	25.00	50.00	100.00
—"Deep groove" version (deep indentation under label on both sides)					
❑ BST-1579 [S]	Sonny Clark Trio	1963	5.00	10.00	20.00
—"New York, USA" address on label					
❑ BLP-1588 [M]	Cool Struttin'	1958	20.00	40.00	80.00
—Regular version, W. 63rd St. address on label					
❑ BLP-1588 [M]	Cool Struttin'	1958	37.50	75.00	150.00
—"Deep groove" version (deep indentation under label on both sides)					
❑ BLP-1588 [M]	Cool Struttin'	1963	6.25	12.50	25.00
—"New York, USA" address on label					

Number	Title (A Side/B Side)	Yr	VG	VG+	NM
❑ BST-1588 [S]	Cool Struttin'	1959	15.00	30.00	60.00
—Regular version, W. 63rd St. address on label					
❑ BST-1588 [S]	Cool Struttin'	1959	25.00	50.00	100.00
—"Deep groove" version (deep indentation under label on both sides)					
❑ BST-1588 [S]	Cool Struttin'	1963	5.00	10.00	20.00
—"New York, USA" address on label					
❑ BLP-1592 [M]	Cool Struttin' — Volume 2	1959	—	—	—
—Canceled					
❑ BST-1592 [S]	Cool Struttin' — Volume 2	1959	—	—	—
—Canceled					
❑ BLP-4091 [M]	Leapin' and Lopin'	1961	15.00	30.00	60.00
—61st St. address on label					
❑ BLP-4091 [M]	Leapin' and Lopin'	1963	5.00	10.00	20.00
—"New York, USA" address on label					
❑ BST-84091 [S]	Leapin' and Lopin'	1961	20.00	40.00	80.00
—61st St. address on label					
❑ BST-84091 [S]	Leapin' and Lopin'	1963	6.25	12.50	25.00
—"New York, USA" address on label					
TIME					
❑ S-2101 [S]	Sonny Clark Trio	1962	7.50	15.00	30.00
❑ 52101 [M]	Sonny Clark Trio	1962	6.25	12.50	25.00
❑ ST-70010 [S]	Sonny Clark Trio	1960	12.50	25.00	50.00
❑ T-70010 [M]	Sonny Clark Trio	1960	10.00	20.00	40.00

CLARK, YODELING SLIM
CONTINENTAL

Number	Title (A Side/B Side)	Yr	VG	VG+	NM
❑ C-1505 [M]	Cowboy and Yodel Songs	1962	10.00	20.00	40.00
MASTERSEAL					
❑ MS-57 [M]	Cowboy Songs	1963	6.25	12.50	25.00
❑ MS-112 [M]	Songs by Yodeling Slim Clark	1964	6.25	12.50	25.00
❑ MS-135 [M]	Cowboy Songs Vol. 2	1964	6.25	12.50	25.00
PALOMINO					
❑ 300 [M]	Yodeling Slim Clark Sings the Legendary Jimmie Rodgers Songs	1966	15.00	30.00	60.00
❑ 301 [M]	Yodeling Slim Clark Sings and Yodels Favorite Montana Slim Songs of the Mountains and Plains, Vol. 1	1966	15.00	30.00	60.00
❑ 303 [M]	Yodeling Slim Clark Sings and Yodels Favorite Montana Slim Songs of the Mountains and Plains, Vol. 2	1966	10.00	20.00	40.00
❑ 306 [M]	I Feel a Trip Coming On	1966	10.00	20.00	40.00
❑ 307 [M]	Old Chestnuts	1967	10.00	20.00	40.00
❑ 310 [M]	Yodeling Slim Clark Happens Again	1967	10.00	20.00	40.00
❑ 311 [M]	The Ballad of Billy Venero	1968	10.00	20.00	40.00
❑ 314 [M]	Yodeling Slim Clark's 50th Anniversary Album	1968	12.50	25.00	50.00
—Gold vinyl					
PLAYHOUSE					
❑ 2017 [10]	Western Songs and Dances	1954	12.50	25.00	50.00

CLARK SISTERS, THE
CORAL

Number	Title (A Side/B Side)	Yr	VG	VG+	NM
❑ CRL 57290 [M]	Beauty Shop Beat	1960	5.00	10.00	20.00
❑ CRL 757290 [S]	Beauty Shop Beat	1960	6.25	12.50	25.00
DOT					
❑ DLP-3104 [M]	Sing, Sing, Sing	1957	7.50	15.00	30.00
❑ DLP-3137 [M]	The Clark Sisters Swing Again	1958	6.25	12.50	25.00
❑ DLP-25137 [S]	The Clark Sisters Swing Again	1958	7.50	15.00	30.00

CLARKE, BUCK
ARGO

Number	Title (A Side/B Side)	Yr	VG	VG+	NM
❑ LP-4007 [M]	Drum Sum	1961	6.25	12.50	25.00
❑ LPS-4007 [S]	Drum Sum	1961	7.50	15.00	30.00
❑ LP-4021 [M]	The Buck Clarke Sound	1963	6.25	12.50	25.00
❑ LPS-4021 [S]	The Buck Clarke Sound	1963	7.50	15.00	30.00
OFFBEAT					
❑ OLP-3003 [M]	Cool Hands	1960	7.50	15.00	30.00
❑ OS-93003 [S]	Cool Hands	1960	10.00	20.00	40.00

CLARKE, KEN
MGM

Number	Title (A Side/B Side)	Yr	VG	VG+	NM
❑ E-205 [10]	Jazz Piano	1953	12.50	25.00	50.00

CLARKE, KENNY
EPIC

Number	Title (A Side/B Side)	Yr	VG	VG+	NM
❑ LN 3376 [M]	Kenny Clarke Plays Andre Hodeir	1957	10.00	20.00	40.00
SAVOY					
❑ MG-12006 [M]	Telefunken Blues	1955	15.00	30.00	60.00
❑ MG-12017 [M]	Bohemia After Dark	1955	15.00	30.00	60.00
❑ MG-12065 [M]	Klook's Clique	1956	15.00	30.00	60.00
❑ MG-15051 [10]	Kenny Clarke, Vol. 1	195?	37.50	75.00	150.00
❑ MG-15053 [10]	Kenny Clarke, Vol. 2	195?	37.50	75.00	150.00

CLARKE, KENNY, AND ERNIE WILKINS
SAVOY

Number	Title (A Side/B Side)	Yr	VG	VG+	NM
❑ MG-12007 [M]	Plenty for Kenny	1955	15.00	30.00	60.00

CLARKE-BOLAND BIG BAND, THE
KENNY CLARKE and Francy Boland.
ATLANTIC

Number	Title (A Side/B Side)	Yr	VG	VG+	NM
❑ 1401 [M]	Jazz Is Universal	1963	7.50	15.00	30.00
❑ SD 1401 [S]	Jazz Is Universal	1963	10.00	20.00	40.00
❑ 1404 [M]	The Clarke-Boland Big Band	1963	7.50	15.00	30.00
❑ SD 1404 [S]	The Clarke-Boland Big Band	1963	10.00	20.00	40.00
BASF					
❑ 25102 [(2)]	The Big Band Sound	1971	5.00	10.00	20.00
BLUE NOTE					
❑ BLP-4092 [M]	The Golden Eight	1961	12.50	25.00	50.00
—61st St. address on label					
❑ BLP-4092 [M]	The Golden Eight	1963	6.25	12.50	25.00
—"New York, USA" address on label					

Number	Title (A Side/B Side)	Yr	VG	VG+	NM
❏ BST-84092 [S]	The Golden Eight	1961	12.50	25.00	50.00
—61st St. address on label					
❏ BST-84092 [S]	The Golden Eight	1963	5.00	10.00	20.00
—"New York, USA" address on label					
COLUMBIA					
❏ CS 9114 [S]	Now Hear Our Meanin'	1965	5.00	10.00	20.00

CLARY, ROBERT
ATLANTIC

Number	Title (A Side/B Side)	Yr	VG	VG+	NM
❏ 8053 [M]	Livin' It Up at the Playboy Club	1961	7.50	15.00	30.00
❏ SD 8053 [S]	Livin' It Up at the Playboy Club	1961	10.00	20.00	40.00
EPIC					
❏ LN 3171 [M]	Meet Robert Clary	1955	6.25	12.50	25.00
❏ LN 3281 [M]	Hooray for Love	1956	6.25	12.50	25.00
MERCURY					
❏ MG-20367 [M]	Gigi Sung by Robert Clary	1958	5.00	10.00	20.00
❏ SR-60042 [S]	Gigi Sung by Robert Clary	1958	7.50	15.00	30.00

CLASH, THE
EPIC

Number	Title (A Side/B Side)	Yr	VG	VG+	NM
❏ AS 913 [DJ]	Sandinista Now!	1981	7.50	15.00	30.00
—Promo-only sampler					
❏ AS 952 [DJ]	If Music Could Talk (Interchords)	1981	10.00	20.00	40.00
—Promo-only interview record					
❏ AS 99-1592 [PD]	Combat Rock	1982	10.00	20.00	40.00
—Promo-only picture disc					
❏ AS 1594 [DJ]	The World According to the Clash	1982	10.00	20.00	40.00
—Promo-only sampler					
❏ AS 99-1595 [DJ]	Combat Rock	1982	7.50	15.00	30.00
—Camouflage green vinyl promo					
❏ JE 35543	Give 'Em Enough Rope	1978	3.75	7.50	15.00
—Block letters on cover; orange label					
❏ JE 35543	Give 'Em Enough Rope	1978	3.75	7.50	15.00
—Script cover; orange label					
❏ JE 35543 [DJ]	Give 'Em Enough Rope	1978	7.50	15.00	30.00
—White label promo; timing strip; back cover has one incorrect song title					
❏ JE 36060	The Clash	1979	3.75	7.50	15.00
❏ PE 36060	The Clash	1979	2.00	4.00	8.00
—Budget-line reissue; no bonus single					
❏ E2 36238 [DJ]	London Calling	1980	6.25	12.50	25.00
—White label promo					
❏ E2 36329 [(2)]	London Calling	1979	3.75	7.50	15.00
❏ E3X 37037 [(3)]	Sandinista!	1981	5.00	10.00	20.00
❏ FE 37689	Combat Rock	1982	2.50	5.00	10.00
—Second and later pressings (with standard dark blue labels) delete commercial during "Inoculated City"					
❏ FE 37689	Combat Rock	1982	3.75	7.50	15.00
—First pressings (with custom labels) contain a commercial in the middle of the song "Inoculated City"					
❏ PE 38540	Black Market Clash	1982	2.50	5.00	10.00
—12-inch version of 10-inch record					
❏ FE 40017	Cut the Crap	1985	2.50	5.00	10.00
❏ E2 44025 [(2)]	The Story of the Clash, Vol. 1	1988	3.75	7.50	15.00
EPIC LEGACY					
❏ E3 53191 [(3)10]	Super Black Market Clash	1993	7.50	15.00	30.00
EPIC NU-DISK					
❏ 4E 36846 [10]	Black Market Clash	1980	3.75	7.50	15.00

CLASS-AIRES, THE
HONEY BEE

Number	Title (A Side/B Side)	Yr	VG	VG+	NM
❏ (# unknown)	Tears Start to Fall	195?	75.00	150.00	300.00

CLASSICS IV
ACCORD

Number	Title (A Side/B Side)	Yr	VG	VG+	NM
❏ SN-7107	Stormy	1981	2.50	5.00	10.00
IMPERIAL					
❏ LP-12371	Spooky	1968	5.00	10.00	20.00
❏ LP-12407	Mamas and Papas/Soul Train	1969	5.00	10.00	20.00
❏ LP-12429	Traces	1969	5.00	10.00	20.00
❏ LP-16000	Dennis Yost & the Classics IV/Golden Greats - Volume I	1969	5.00	10.00	20.00
LIBERTY					
❏ LN-10109	The Very Best of the Classics IV	198?	2.00	4.00	8.00
❏ LST-11003	Song	1970	3.75	7.50	15.00
MGM SOUTH					
❏ 702	Dennis Yost and the Classics IV	1973	3.75	7.50	15.00
UNITED ARTISTS					
❏ UA-LA446-E	The Very Best of the Classics IV	1975	3.00	6.00	12.00

CLAUSON, WILLIAM
CAPITOL

Number	Title (A Side/B Side)	Yr	VG	VG+	NM
❏ T 10158 [M]	Concert	195?	6.25	12.50	25.00
❏ T 10176 [M]	Scandinavia	195?	6.25	12.50	25.00
RCA VICTOR					
❏ LPM-1286 [M]	Folk Songs	1956	7.50	15.00	30.00

CLAY, CASSIUS
COLUMBIA

Number	Title (A Side/B Side)	Yr	VG	VG+	NM
❏ CL 2093 [M]	I Am the Greatest!	1963	10.00	20.00	40.00
❏ CS 8893 [S]	I Am the Greatest!	1963	12.50	25.00	50.00

CLAY, JAMES
RIVERSIDE

Number	Title (A Side/B Side)	Yr	VG	VG+	NM
❏ RLP-349 [M]	A Double Dose of Soul	1961	7.50	15.00	30.00
—Blue label					
❏ RS-9349 [S]	A Double Dose of Soul	1961	10.00	20.00	40.00
—Black label					

CLAY, JAMES, AND DAVID "FATHEAD" NEWMAN
RIVERSIDE

Number	Title (A Side/B Side)	Yr	VG	VG+	NM
❏ RLP 12-327 [M]	The Sound of the Wide Open Spaces!!!	1960	7.50	15.00	30.00
—Blue label					
❏ RLP-1178 [S]	The Sound of the Wide Open Spaces!!!	1960	10.00	20.00	40.00
—Black label					

CLAY, OTIS
HI

Number	Title (A Side/B Side)	Yr	VG	VG+	NM
❏ HLP 6003	I Can't Take It	1977	3.75	7.50	15.00
❏ SHL 32075	Trying to Live My Life Without You	1972	5.00	10.00	20.00
ROOSTER BLUES					
❏ R-7609 [(2)]	Soul Man: Live in Japan	1985	3.75	7.50	15.00

CLAYTON, BUCK
ALLEGRO ELITE

Number	Title (A Side/B Side)	Yr	VG	VG+	NM
❏ 4121 [10]	Buck Clayton All Stars	195?	10.00	20.00	40.00
COLUMBIA					
❏ CL 548 [M]	The Huckle-Buck and Robbins' Nest: A Jam Session	1954	12.50	25.00	50.00
—Maroon label, gold print					
❏ CL 548 [M]	The Huckle-Buck and Robbins' Nest: A Jam Session	1955	7.50	15.00	30.00
—Red and black label with six "eye" logos					
❏ CL 567 [M]	How Hi the Fi: A Jam Session	1954	12.50	25.00	50.00
—Maroon label, gold print					
❏ CL 567 [M]	How Hi the Fi: A Jam Session	1955	7.50	15.00	30.00
—Red and black label with six "eye" logos					
❏ CL 614 [M]	Buck Clayton Jams Benny Goodman	1955	7.50	15.00	30.00
—Red and black label with six "eye" logos					
❏ CL 614 [M]	Buck Clayton Jams Benny Goodman	1955	12.50	25.00	50.00
—Maroon label, gold print					
❏ CL 701 [M]	Jumpin' at the Woodside	1955	10.00	20.00	40.00
—Red and black label with six "eye" logos					
❏ CL 808 [M]	Jazz Spectacular	1956	10.00	20.00	40.00
—Red and black label with six "eye" logos					
❏ CL 882 [M]	All the Cats Join In	1956	10.00	20.00	40.00
—Red and black label with six "eye" logos					
❏ CL 1320 [M]	Songs for Swingers	1959	6.25	12.50	25.00
—Red and black label with six "eye" logos					
❏ CL 6325 [10]	Moten Swing — Sentimental Journey	1954	15.00	30.00	60.00
❏ CL 6326 [10]	How Hi the Fi: A Jam Session	1954	15.00	30.00	60.00
❏ CS 8123 [S]	Songs for Swingers	1959	7.50	15.00	30.00
—Red and black label with six "eye" logos					
JAZZTONE					
❏ J-1225 [M]	Meet Buck Clayton	1956	10.00	20.00	40.00

CLAYTON, BUCK; RUBY BRAFF; MEL POWELL
VANGUARD

Number	Title (A Side/B Side)	Yr	VG	VG+	NM
❏ VRS-8514 [M]	Buckin' the Blues	1957	10.00	20.00	40.00
❏ VRS-8517 [M]	Buck Meets Ruby and Mel	1957	10.00	20.00	40.00

CLAYTON, BUCK/WILD BILL DAVISON
JAZZTONE

Number	Title (A Side/B Side)	Yr	VG	VG+	NM
❏ J-1267 [M]	Singing Trumpets	1957	10.00	20.00	40.00

CLAYTON, BUCK, AND BUDDY TATE
SWINGVILLE

Number	Title (A Side/B Side)	Yr	VG	VG+	NM
❏ SVLP-2017 [M]	Buck and Buddy	1961	12.50	25.00	50.00
—Purple label					
❏ SVLP-2017 [M]	Buck and Buddy	1965	6.25	12.50	25.00
—Blue label, trident logo at right					
❏ SVLP-2030 [M]	Buck and Buddy Blow the Blues	1962	10.00	20.00	40.00
—Purple label					
❏ SVLP-2030 [M]	Buck and Buddy Blow the Blues	1965	5.00	10.00	20.00
—Blue label, trident logo at right					
❏ SVST-2030 [S]	Buck and Buddy Blow the Blues	1962	12.50	25.00	50.00
—Red label					
❏ SVST-2030 [S]	Buck and Buddy Blow the Blues	1965	6.25	12.50	25.00
—Blue label, trident logo at right					

CLAYTON, PAUL
ELEKTRA

Number	Title (A Side/B Side)	Yr	VG	VG+	NM
❏ EKL-147 [M]	Unholy Matrimony	1958	7.50	15.00	30.00
❏ EKL-155 [M]	Bobby Burns' Merry Muses	1958	7.50	15.00	30.00
FOLKWAYS					
❏ FA-2007 [M]	Cumberland Mountain Folksongs	1957	15.00	30.00	60.00
❏ FA-2106 [M]	Bay State Ballads	1956	15.00	30.00	60.00
❏ FA-2110 [M]	Folksongs and Ballads of Virginia	1956	15.00	30.00	60.00
❏ FA-2310 [M]	Folk Ballads of the English-Speaking World	1956	15.00	30.00	60.00
❏ FA-2429 [M]	Foc'sle Songs and Shanties	1959	7.50	15.00	30.00
❏ FW-8708 [M]	British Broadside Ballads in Popular Tradition	1957	10.00	20.00	40.00
MONUMENT					
❏ MLP-8017 [M]	Folk Singer	1965	5.00	10.00	20.00
❏ SLP-18017 [S]	Folk Singer	1965	6.25	12.50	25.00
RIVERSIDE					
❏ RLP 12-615 [M]	Bloody Ballads	1957	7.50	15.00	30.00
❏ RLP 12-640 [M]	Wanted for Murder — American Folksongs of Outlaws and Desperadoes	1958	7.50	15.00	30.00
❏ RLP 12-648 [M]	Timber-r-r! — Folk Songs and Ballads of the Lumberjack	1958	7.50	15.00	30.00
STINSON					
❏ SLP-69 [10]	Whaling Songs and Ballads	1958	10.00	20.00	40.00
❏ SLP-70 [10]	Waters of Tyme — English North Country Songs	1958	10.00	20.00	40.00
TRADITION					
❏ TLP-1005 [M]	Whaling and Sailing Songs from the Days of Moby Dick	1956	7.50	15.00	30.00

CLAYTON-THOMAS, DAVID
ABC

Number	Title (A Side/B Side)	Yr	VG	VG+	NM
❏ AA-1104	Clayton	1978	2.50	5.00	10.00
COLUMBIA					
❏ KC 31000	David Clayton-Thomas	1972	3.75	7.50	15.00
❏ KC 31700	Tequila Sunrise	1972	3.75	7.50	15.00

Number	Title (A Side/B Side)	Yr	VG	VG+	NM
DECCA					
❑ DL 75146	David Clayton-Thomas!	1969	5.00	10.00	20.00
RCA VICTOR					
❑ APD1-0173 [Q]	Harmony Junction	1973	5.00	10.00	20.00
❑ APL1-0173	Harmony Junction	1973	3.00	6.00	12.00

CLEANLINESS AND GODLINESS SKIFFLE BAND, THE
VANGUARD

Number	Title (A Side/B Side)	Yr	VG	VG+	NM
❑ VSD-79285	Greatest Hits	1968	6.25	12.50	25.00

CLEAR LIGHT
ELEKTRA

Number	Title (A Side/B Side)	Yr	VG	VG+	NM
❑ EKL-4011 [M]	Clear Light	1967	6.25	12.50	25.00
❑ EKS-74011 [S]	Clear Light	1967	6.25	12.50	25.00
SUNDAZED					
❑ LP 5125	Clear Light	2002	3.00	6.00	12.00
—Reissue on 180-gram vinyl					

CLEARY, DON
PALOMINO

Number	Title (A Side/B Side)	Yr	VG	VG+	NM
❑ 302 [M]	Don Cleary Sings Traditional Cowboy Songs	1966	12.50	25.00	50.00

CLEAVER, ELDRIDGE
MORE

Number	Title (A Side/B Side)	Yr	VG	VG+	NM
❑ 4000 [M]	Soul On Wax	1968	6.25	12.50	25.00

CLEFTONES, THE
GEE

Number	Title (A Side/B Side)	Yr	VG	VG+	NM
❑ GLP-705 [M]	Heart and Soul	1961	50.00	100.00	200.00
❑ SGLP-705 [S]	Heart and Soul	1961	125.00	250.00	500.00
❑ GLP-707 [M]	For Sentimental Reasons	1961	62.50	125.00	250.00
❑ SGLP-707 [S]	For Sentimental Reasons	1961	300.00	600.00	1200.

CLEVELAND, JIMMY
EMARCY

Number	Title (A Side/B Side)	Yr	VG	VG+	NM
❑ MG-26003 [M]	Rhythm Crazy	1964	6.25	12.50	25.00
❑ MG-36066 [M]	Introducing Jimmy Cleveland and His All Stars	1956	12.50	25.00	50.00
❑ MG-36126 [M]	Cleveland Style	1958	12.50	25.00	50.00
MERCURY					
❑ MG-20442 [M]	A Map of Jimmy Cleveland	1959	10.00	20.00	40.00
❑ MG-20553 [M]	Cleveland Style	1960	10.00	20.00	40.00
❑ SR-60117 [S]	A Map of Jimmy Cleveland	1959	7.50	15.00	30.00
❑ SR-60121 [S]	Cleveland Style	1959	7.50	15.00	30.00

CLIBURN, VAN
RCA VICTOR RED SEAL

Number	Title (A Side/B Side)	Yr	VG	VG+	NM
❑ LM-2252 [M]	Tchaikovsky: Piano Concerto No. 1	1958	5.00	10.00	20.00
❑ LSC-2252 [S]	Tchaikovsky: Piano Concerto No. 1	1958	6.25	12.50	25.00
—"Shaded dog" pressing ("Living Stereo" on label)					
❑ LSC-2252 [S]	Tchaikovsky: Piano Concerto No. 1	1965	3.75	7.50	15.00
—"White dog" pressing ("Stereo" on label)					
❑ LSC-2252 [S]	Tchaikovsky: Piano Concerto No. 1	1969	3.00	6.00	12.00
—"No dog" pressing ("RCA" sideways at left)					
❑ LSC-2252 [S]	Tchaikovsky: Piano Concerto No. 1	1976	2.00	4.00	8.00
—"Late dog" pressing (dog near top)					
❑ LM-2355 [M]	Rachmaninoff: Piano Concerto No. 3	1959	5.00	10.00	20.00
❑ LSC-2355 [S]	Rachmaninoff: Piano Concerto No. 3	1959	6.25	12.50	25.00
—"Shaded dog" pressing ("Living Stereo" on label)					
❑ LSC-2355 [S]	Rachmaninoff: Piano Concerto No. 3	1965	3.75	7.50	15.00
—"White dog" pressing ("Stereo" on label)					
❑ LSC-2355 [S]	Rachmaninoff: Piano Concerto No. 3	1969	3.00	6.00	12.00
—"No dog" pressing ("RCA" sideways at left)					
❑ LM-2455 [M]	Schumann: Piano Concerto in A Minor	1960	3.75	7.50	15.00
❑ LSC-2455 [S]	Schumann: Piano Concerto in A Minor	1960	5.00	10.00	20.00
—"Shaded dog" pressing ("Living Stereo" on label)					
❑ LSC-2455 [S]	Schumann: Piano Concerto in A Minor	1965	3.75	7.50	15.00
—"White dog" pressing ("Stereo" on label)					
❑ LSC-2455 [S]	Schumann: Piano Concerto in A Minor	1969	3.00	6.00	12.00
—"No dog" pressing ("RCA" sideways at left)					
❑ LM-2507 [M]	Prokofiev: Piano Concerto No. 3; MacDowell: Piano Concerto No. 2	1961	3.75	7.50	15.00
❑ LSC-2507 [S]	Prokofiev: Piano Concerto No. 3; MacDowell: Piano Concerto No. 2	1961	7.50	15.00	30.00
—"Shaded dog" pressing ("Living Stereo" on label)					
❑ LSC-2507 [S]	Prokofiev: Piano Concerto No. 3; MacDowell: Piano Concerto No. 2	1965	7.50	15.00	30.00
—"White dog" pressing ("Stereo" on label)					
❑ LSC-2507 [S]	Prokofiev: Piano Concerto No. 3; MacDowell: Piano Concerto No. 2	1969	3.00	6.00	12.00
—"No dog" pressing ("RCA" sideways at left)					
❑ LM-2562 [M]	Beethoven: Piano Concerto No. 5 (Emperor Concerto)	1961	3.75	7.50	15.00
❑ LSC-2562 [S]	Beethoven: Piano Concerto No. 5 (Emperor Concerto)	1961	5.00	10.00	20.00
—"Shaded dog" pressing ("Living Stereo" on label)					
❑ LSC-2562 [S]	Beethoven: Piano Concerto No. 5 (Emperor Concerto)	1964	5.00	10.00	20.00
—"White dog" pressing ("Stereo" on label)					
❑ LSC-2562 [S]	Beethoven: Piano Concerto No. 5 (Emperor Concerto)	1969	3.00	6.00	12.00
—"No dog" pressing ("RCA" sideways at left)					
❑ LM-2576 [M]	My Favorite Chopin	1962	3.75	7.50	15.00
❑ LSC-2576 [S]	My Favorite Chopin	1962	5.00	10.00	20.00
—"Shaded dog" pressing ("Living Stereo" on label)					
❑ LSC-2576 [S]	My Favorite Chopin	1965	3.75	7.50	15.00
—"White dog" pressing ("Stereo" on label)					
❑ LSC-2576 [S]	My Favorite Chopin	1969	3.00	6.00	12.00
—"No dog" pressing ("RCA" sideways at left)					
❑ LSC-2576 [S]	My Favorite Chopin	1976	2.00	4.00	8.00
—"Late dog" pressing (dog near top)					
❑ LM-2581 [M]	Brahms: Piano Concerto No. 2	1962	3.75	7.50	15.00
❑ LSC-2581 [S]	Brahms: Piano Concerto No. 2	1962	5.00	10.00	20.00
—"Shaded dog" pressing ("Living Stereo" on label)					

Number	Title (A Side/B Side)	Yr	VG	VG+	NM
❑ LSC-2581 [S]	Brahms: Piano Concerto No. 2	1965	3.75	7.50	15.00
—"White dog" pressing ("Stereo" on label)					
❑ LSC-2581 [S]	Brahms: Piano Concerto No. 2	1969	3.00	6.00	12.00
—"No dog" pressing ("RCA" sideways at left)					
❑ LSC-2581 [S]	Brahms: Piano Concerto No. 2	1976	2.00	4.00	8.00
—"Late dog" pressing (dog near top)					
❑ LM-2601 [M]	Rachmaninoff: Piano Concerto No. 2	1962	3.75	7.50	15.00
❑ LSC-2601 [S]	Rachmaninoff: Piano Concerto No. 2	1962	3.75	7.50	15.00
—"White dog" pressing ("Stereo" on label)					
❑ LSC-2601 [S]	Rachmaninoff: Piano Concerto No. 2	1962	5.00	10.00	20.00
—"Shaded dog" pressing ("Living Stereo" on label)					
❑ LSC-2601 [S]	Rachmaninoff: Piano Concerto No. 2	1969	3.00	6.00	12.00
—"No dog" pressing ("RCA" sideways at left)					
❑ LM-2680 [M]	Beethoven: Piano Concerto No. 4	1963	3.00	6.00	12.00
❑ LSC-2680 [S]	Beethoven: Piano Concerto No. 4	1963	3.75	7.50	15.00
—"Shaded dog" pressing ("Living Stereo" on label)					
❑ LSC-2680 [S]	Beethoven: Piano Concerto No. 4	1965	3.00	6.00	12.00
—"White dog" pressing ("Stereo" on label)					
❑ LSC-2680 [S]	Beethoven: Piano Concerto No. 4	1969	2.50	5.00	10.00
—"No dog" pressing ("RCA" sideways at left)					
❑ LSC-3323	The World's Favorite Piano Music	196?	3.00	6.00	12.00
❑ ARP1-4441	Tchaikovsky: Piano Concerto No. 1	198?	2.50	5.00	10.00
—Half-speed mastered reissue					

CLIFF, JIMMY
A&M

Number	Title (A Side/B Side)	Yr	VG	VG+	NM
❑ SP-3189	Wonderful World, Beautiful People	198?	2.00	4.00	8.00
—Reissue of 4251					
❑ SP-4251	Wonderful World, Beautiful People	1970	6.25	12.50	25.00
COLUMBIA					
❑ FC 38099	Special	1982	2.50	5.00	10.00
❑ PC 38099	Special	198?	2.00	4.00	8.00
—Budget-line reissue					
❑ FC 38986	The Power and the Glory	1983	2.50	5.00	10.00
❑ PC 38996	The Power and the Glory	1985	2.00	4.00	8.00
—Budget-line reissue					
❑ FC 40002	Cliff Hanger	1985	2.50	5.00	10.00
❑ FC 40845	Hanging Fire	1988	2.50	5.00	10.00
ISLAND					
❑ SW-9343	Struggling Man	1973	5.00	10.00	20.00
MANGO					
❑ ILPS 9235	Struggling Man	197?	3.00	6.00	12.00
—Reissue of Island SW-9343					
MCA					
❑ 813	I Am the Living	198?	2.00	4.00	8.00
—Reissue of 5153					
❑ 820	Give the People What They Want	198?	2.00	4.00	8.00
—Reissue of 5217					
❑ 5153	I Am the Living	1980	3.00	6.00	12.00
❑ 5217	Give the People What They Want	1981	3.00	6.00	12.00
REPRISE					
❑ MS 2147	Unlimited	1973	3.75	7.50	15.00
❑ MS 2188	Music Maker	1974	3.75	7.50	15.00
❑ MS 2218	Follow My Mind	1975	3.75	7.50	15.00
❑ MS 2256	In Concert: The Best of Jimmy Cliff	1976	3.75	7.50	15.00
VEEP					
❑ VPS-16536	Can't Get Enough of It	1969	10.00	20.00	40.00
WARNER BROS.					
❑ BSK 3240	Give Thankx	1978	3.00	6.00	12.00

CLIFFORD, BUZZ
COLUMBIA

Number	Title (A Side/B Side)	Yr	VG	VG+	NM
❑ CL 1616 [M]	Baby Sittin' with Buzz	1961	25.00	50.00	100.00
❑ CS 8416 [S]	Baby Sittin' with Buzz	1961	37.50	75.00	150.00
DOT					
❑ DLP-25965	See Your Way Clear	1969	7.50	15.00	30.00

CLIFFORD, MIKE
UNITED ARTISTS

Number	Title (A Side/B Side)	Yr	VG	VG+	NM
❑ UAL-3409 [M]	For the Love of Mike	1965	5.00	10.00	20.00
❑ UAS-6409 [S]	For the Love of Mike	1965	6.25	12.50	25.00

CLIFTON, BILL
COLUMBIA

Number	Title (A Side/B Side)	Yr	VG	VG+	NM
❑ CL 6166 [10]	Piano Moods	1951	12.50	25.00	50.00

CLIFTON, BILL, AND THE DIXIE MOUNTAIN BOYS
STARDAY

Number	Title (A Side/B Side)	Yr	VG	VG+	NM
❑ SLP-111 [M]	Mountain Folk Songs	1959	10.00	20.00	40.00
❑ SLP-146 [M]	The Carter Family Memorial Album	1961	7.50	15.00	30.00
❑ SLP-159 [M]	The Bluegrass Sound of Bill Clifton	1961	7.50	15.00	30.00
❑ SLP-213 [M]	Soldier, Sing Me a Song	1963	6.25	12.50	25.00
❑ SLP-271 [M]	Code of the Mountains	1965	6.25	12.50	25.00

CLINE, PATSY
ACCORD

Number	Title (A Side/B Side)	Yr	VG	VG+	NM
❑ SN-7153	Let the Teardrops Fall	1981	2.50	5.00	10.00
ALLEGIANCE					
❑ AV-5021	Stop, Look and Listen	198?	2.50	5.00	10.00
DECCA					
❑ DXB 176 [(2)M]	The Patsy Cline Story	1963	10.00	20.00	40.00
❑ DL 4202 [M]	Patsy Cline Showcase	1961	10.00	20.00	40.00
❑ DL 4282 [M]	Sentimentally Yours	1962	7.50	15.00	30.00
❑ DL 4508 [M]	A Portrait of Patsy Cline	1964	7.50	15.00	30.00
❑ DL 4586 [M]	That's How a Heartache Begins	1964	7.50	15.00	30.00
❑ DL 4854 [M]	Patsy Cline's Greatest Hits	1967	5.00	10.00	20.00
❑ DXSB 7176 [(2)S]	The Patsy Cline Story	1963	12.50	25.00	50.00
❑ DL 8611 [M]	Patsy Cline	1957	25.00	50.00	100.00
—Black label with silver print					
❑ DL 8611 [M]	Patsy Cline	1960	12.50	25.00	50.00
—Black label with color bars					

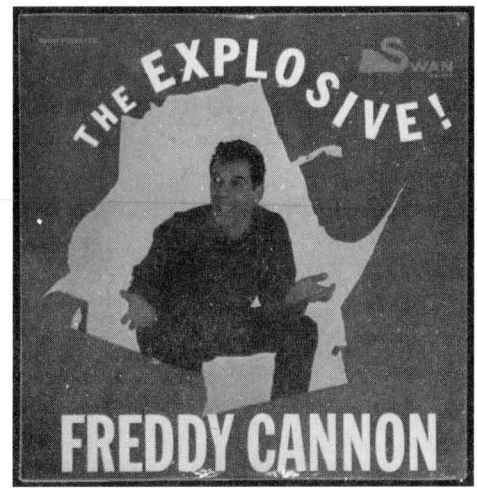

One of the more sought-after private-label psych records of the late 1960s is this one by the C.A. Quintet. Even with a vinyl reissue by Sundazed, the original retains high demand.

Freddy Cannon's Swan LPs are tough to find. This is the first of them, appropriately titled *The Explosive Freddy Cannon.*

The Carpenters' first album in 1969, *Offering,* featured this cover. Once they had a big hit single with "Close to You," the album was re-packaged and re-released under the name *Ticket to Ride.*

This was the debut full-length LP for David Seville and the Chipmunks. Note the more "realistic" chipmunks on this original cover. Also, some copies of this were issued on red vinyl.

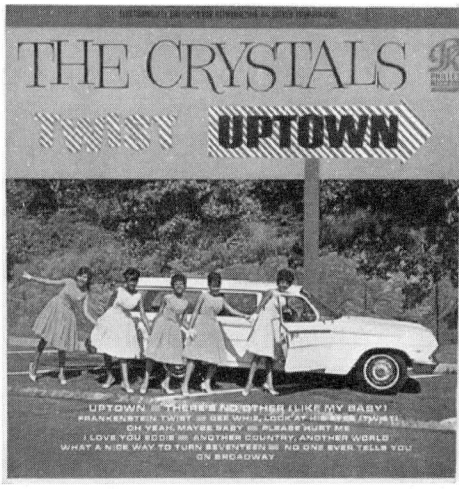

Alice Cooper's debut album, *Pretties for You,* was originally released on Frank Zappa's Straight label. Original copies are hard to find.

Here's an exception to the rule that rechanneled stereo albums go for less than the true mono counterpart. In 1965, the Capitol Record Club issued the Crystals' LP *Twist Uptown* in fake stereo, and it's so rare that near-mint copies can fetch over $1,000.

Number	Title (A Side/B Side)	Yr	VG	VG+	NM
❑ DL 74202 [S]	Patsy Cline Showcase	1961	12.50	25.00	50.00
❑ DL 74282 [S]	Sentimentally Yours	1962	10.00	20.00	40.00
❑ DL 74508 [S]	A Portrait of Patsy Cline	1964	10.00	20.00	40.00
❑ DL 74586 [S]	That's How a Heartache Begins	1964	10.00	20.00	40.00
❑ DL 74854 [S]	Patsy Cline's Greatest Hits	1967	6.25	12.50	25.00
EVEREST					
❑ 1200 [R]	Golden Hits	1962	3.00	6.00	12.00
❑ 1204 [R]	Encores	1962	3.00	6.00	12.00
❑ 1217 [R]	In Memoriam	1963	3.00	6.00	12.00
❑ 1229 [R]	Reflections	1964	3.00	6.00	12.00
❑ 5200 [M]	Golden Hits	1962	5.00	10.00	20.00
❑ 5204 [M]	Encores	1962	5.00	10.00	20.00
❑ 5217 [M]	In Memoriam	1963	5.00	10.00	20.00
❑ 5223 [M]	Legend	1963	5.00	10.00	20.00
❑ 5229 [M]	Reflections	1964	5.00	10.00	20.00
HILLTOP					
❑ 6001 [M]	Today, Tomorrow, Forever	1965	3.00	6.00	12.00
❑ S-6001 [R]	Today, Tomorrow, Forever	1965	2.50	5.00	10.00
❑ 6016 [M]	I Can't Forget You	1966	3.00	6.00	12.00
❑ S-6016 [R]	I Can't Forget You	1966	2.50	5.00	10.00
❑ S-6039	Stop the World	1968	2.50	5.00	10.00
❑ JS-6072	In Care of the Blues	1969	2.50	5.00	10.00
❑ 6148	Country Music Hall of Fame	197?	2.50	5.00	10.00
MCA					
❑ 12	Patsy Cline's Greatest Hits	1973	3.00	6.00	12.00
—Reissue of Decca 74854; black label with rainbow					
❑ 12	Patsy Cline's Greatest Hits	1977	2.50	5.00	10.00
—Tan label					
❑ 12	Patsy Cline's Greatest Hits	1980	2.00	4.00	8.00
—Blue label with rainbow					
❑ 87	Patsy Cline Showcase	1973	3.00	6.00	12.00
—Reissue of Decca 74202; black label with rainbow					
❑ 90	Sentimentally Yours	1973	3.00	6.00	12.00
—Reissue of Decca 74282; black label with rainbow					
❑ 224	A Portrait of Patsy Cline	1973	3.00	6.00	12.00
—Reissue of Decca 74508; black label with rainbow					
❑ 736	The Great Patsy Cline	198?	2.50	5.00	10.00
—Reissue of Vocalion 73872					
❑ 738	Here's Patsy Cline	198?	2.50	5.00	10.00
—Reissue of Vocalion 73753					
❑ 1440	Stop, Look and Listen	198?	2.00	4.00	8.00
❑ 1463	Today, Tomorrow and Forever	198?	2.00	4.00	8.00
❑ 3263	Always	1980	3.75	7.50	15.00
❑ 4038 [(2)]	The Patsy Cline Story	1974	3.75	7.50	15.00
—Reissue of Decca 7176;; black labels with rainbow					
❑ 6149	Sweet Dreams — The Life and Times of Patsy Cline	1985	2.50	5.00	10.00
❑ 27069	Always	198?	2.00	4.00	8.00
❑ 42142	Live at the Opry	1988	2.50	5.00	10.00
❑ 42284	Live Volume 2	1989	3.00	6.00	12.00
METRO					
❑ M-540 [M]	Gotta Lot of Rhythm in My Soul	1965	3.00	6.00	12.00
❑ MS-540 [R]	Gotta Lot of Rhythm in My Soul	1965	2.50	5.00	10.00
RHINO					
❑ R1-70048	Her First Recordings, Vol. 1: Walkin' Dreams	1989	3.00	6.00	12.00
❑ R1-70049	Her First Recordings, Vol. 2: Hungry for Love	1989	3.00	6.00	12.00
❑ R1-70050	Her First Recordings, Vol. 3: The Rockin' Side	1989	3.00	6.00	12.00
SEARS					
❑ SP-102 [M]	Walkin' After Midnight	196?	7.50	15.00	30.00
❑ SPS-102 [R]	Walkin' After Midnight	196?	5.00	10.00	20.00
❑ SPS-127	In Care of the Blues	1968	6.25	12.50	25.00
VOCALION					
❑ VL 3753 [M]	Here's Patsy Cline	1965	3.00	6.00	12.00
❑ VL 73753 [R]	Here's Patsy Cline	1965	2.50	5.00	10.00
❑ VL 73872	Country Great!	1969	2.50	5.00	10.00

CLINTON, GEORGE
ABC

Number	Title (A Side/B Side)	Yr	VG	VG+	NM
❑ D-831	The George Clinton Band Arrives	1974	3.75	7.50	15.00
CAPITOL					
❑ ST-12246	Computer Games	1982	2.50	5.00	10.00
❑ ST-12308	You Shouldn't-Nuf Bit Fish	1984	2.50	5.00	10.00
❑ ST-12417	Some of My Best Jokes Are Friends	1985	2.50	5.00	10.00
❑ ST-12481	R&B Skeletons in the Closet	1986	2.50	5.00	10.00
❑ MLP-15021 [EP]	The Mothership Connection Live from Houston, Texas	1986	3.75	7.50	15.00
❑ C1-33911 [(2)]	Greatest Funkin' Hits	1996	3.00	6.00	12.00
—Red vinyl					
❑ CJ-48424	The Best of George Clinton	1987	2.50	5.00	10.00
550 MUSIC					
❑ B2 67144 [(2)]	T.A.P.O.A.F.O.M. — The Awesome Power of a Fully Operational Mothership	1996	3.75	7.50	15.00
—Red vinyl					
INVICTUS					
❑ ST-9815	Black Vampire	1973	5.00	10.00	20.00
PAISLEY PARK					
❑ PRO-A-6537 [(2)DJ]	Hey Man... Smell My Finger	1993	6.25	12.50	25.00
—Promo-only vinyl issue					
❑ 25994	The Cinderella Theory	1989	3.00	6.00	12.00
WARNER BROS.					
❑ 25887	George Clinton Presents Our Gang Funky	1988	2.50	5.00	10.00
❑ 25991	Under a Nouveau Groove	1989	2.50	5.00	10.00

CLINTON, LARRY
EVEREST

Number	Title (A Side/B Side)	Yr	VG	VG+	NM
❑ SDBR-1096 [S]	My Million Sellers	196?	6.25	12.50	25.00
❑ LPBR-5096 [M]	My Million Sellers	196?	5.00	10.00	20.00

CLIQUE, THE (1)
WHITE WHALE

Number	Title (A Side/B Side)	Yr	VG	VG+	NM
❑ WWS-7126	The Clique	1969	5.00	10.00	20.00

CLOONEY, ROSEMARY
COLUMBIA

Number	Title (A Side/B Side)	Yr	VG	VG+	NM
❑ CL 585 [M]	Hollywood's Best	1955	12.50	25.00	50.00
❑ CL 872 [M]	Blue Rose	1956	10.00	20.00	40.00
❑ CL 969 [M]	Clooney Tunes	1957	20.00	40.00	80.00
❑ CL 1006 [M]	Ring Around the Rosie	1957	10.00	20.00	40.00
—With the Hi-Lo's					
❑ CL 1230 [M]	Rosie's Greatest Hits	1958	10.00	20.00	40.00
—Six "eye" logos on label					
❑ CL 1230 [M]	Rosie's Greatest Hits	1962	6.25	12.50	25.00
—"Guaranteed High Fidelity" on label					
❑ CL 1230 [M]	Rosie's Greatest Hits	1965	3.75	7.50	15.00
—"360 Sound Mono" on label					
❑ CL 2525 [10]	Tenderly	1955	12.50	25.00	50.00
❑ CL 2569 [10]	Children's Favorites	1955	12.50	25.00	50.00
❑ CL 2572 [10]	A Date with the King	1956	12.50	25.00	50.00
❑ CL 2581 [10]	On Stage	1956	12.50	25.00	50.00
❑ CL 2597 [10]	My Fair Lady	1956	12.50	25.00	50.00
❑ CL 6224 [10]	Hollywood's Best	1952	15.00	30.00	60.00
❑ CL 6297 [10]	Rosemary Clooney (While We're Young)	1954	15.00	30.00	60.00
❑ CL 6338 [10]	White Christmas	1954	15.00	30.00	60.00
COLUMBIA SPECIAL PRODUCTS					
❑ P 13083	Hollywood's Best	197?	3.00	6.00	12.00
❑ P 13085	Blue Rose	197?	3.00	6.00	12.00
❑ P 14382	Come On-a My House	197?	3.00	6.00	12.00
CONCORD JAZZ					
❑ CJ-47	Everything's Coming Up Rosie	1978	3.00	6.00	12.00
❑ CJ-60	Rosie Sings Bing	1979	3.00	6.00	12.00
❑ CJ-81	Here's to My Lady	1979	3.00	6.00	12.00
❑ CJ-112	Rosemary Clooney Sings Ira Gershwin	1980	3.00	6.00	12.00
❑ CJ-144	With Love	1981	3.00	6.00	12.00
❑ CJ-185	Rosemary Clooney Sings Cole Porter	1982	3.00	6.00	12.00
❑ CJ-210	Rosemary Clooney Sings Harold Arlen	1983	3.00	6.00	12.00
❑ CJ-226	My Buddy	1984	3.00	6.00	12.00
—With Woody Herman					
❑ CJ-255	Rosemary Clooney Sings the Music of Irving Berlin	1985	3.00	6.00	12.00
❑ CJ-282	Rosemary Clooney Sings Ballads	1985	3.00	6.00	12.00
❑ CJ-308	Rosemary Clooney Sings the Music of Jimmy Van Heusen	1987	3.00	6.00	12.00
❑ CJ-333	Rosemary Clooney Sings the Lyrics of Johnny Mercer	1988	3.00	6.00	12.00
❑ CJ-364	Show Tunes	1989	3.00	6.00	12.00
CORAL					
❑ CRL 57266 [M]	Swing Around Rosie	1959	7.50	15.00	30.00
❑ CRL 757266 [S]	Swing Around Rosie	1959	10.00	20.00	40.00
HARMONY					
❑ HL 7123 [M]	Rosemary Clooney in High Fidelity	195?	6.25	12.50	25.00
❑ HL 7213 [M]	Hollywood Hits	195?	6.25	12.50	25.00
❑ HL 7454 [M]	Mixed Emotions	1968	5.00	10.00	20.00
❑ HL 9501 [M]	Rosemary Clooney Sings for Children	196?	5.00	10.00	20.00
❑ HS 11254 [R]	Mixed Emotions	1968	3.00	6.00	12.00
HINDSIGHT					
❑ HSR-234	Rosemary Clooney 1951-1952	1988	2.50	5.00	10.00
HOLIDAY					
❑ 1946	Christmas with Rosemary Clooney	1981	2.50	5.00	10.00
MGM					
❑ E-3687 [M]	Oh, Captain!	1958	10.00	20.00	40.00
❑ E-3782 [M]	Hymns from the Heart	1959	7.50	15.00	30.00
❑ SE-3782 [S]	Hymns from the Heart	1959	10.00	20.00	40.00
❑ E-3834 [M]	Rosie Clooney Swings Softly	1960	7.50	15.00	30.00
❑ SE-3834 [S]	Rosie Clooney Swings Softly	1960	10.00	20.00	40.00
RCA VICTOR					
❑ LPM-2133 [M]	A Touch of Tabasco	1960	5.00	10.00	20.00
❑ LSP-2133 [S]	A Touch of Tabasco	1960	7.50	15.00	30.00
❑ LPM-2212 [M]	Clap Hands, Here Comes Rosie	1960	5.00	10.00	20.00
❑ LSP-2212 [S]	Clap Hands, Here Comes Rosie	1960	7.50	15.00	30.00
❑ LPM-2265 [M]	Rosie Solves the Swingin' Riddle	1961	5.00	10.00	20.00
❑ LSP-2265 [S]	Rosie Solves the Swingin' Riddle	1961	7.50	15.00	30.00
❑ LPM-2565 [M]	Country Hits from the Heart	1963	5.00	10.00	20.00
❑ LSP-2565 [S]	Country Hits from the Heart	1963	7.50	15.00	30.00
REPRISE					
❑ R-6088 [M]	Love	1963	7.50	15.00	30.00
❑ R9-6088 [S]	Love	1963	10.00	20.00	40.00
❑ R-6108 [M]	Thanks for Nothing	1964	7.50	15.00	30.00
❑ RS-6108 [S]	Thanks for Nothing	1964	10.00	20.00	40.00

CLOONEY, ROSEMARY, AND BING CROSBY
CAPITOL

Number	Title (A Side/B Side)	Yr	VG	VG+	NM
❑ ST 2300 [S]	That Travelin' Two-Beat	1965	7.50	15.00	30.00
❑ T 2300 [M]	That Travelin' Two-Beat	1965	5.00	10.00	20.00
RCA CAMDEN					
❑ CAS-2330	Rendezvous	1968	3.75	7.50	15.00
RCA VICTOR					
❑ LPM-1854 [M]	Fancy Meeting You Here	1958	5.00	10.00	20.00
❑ LSP-1854 [S]	Fancy Meeting You Here	1958	7.50	15.00	30.00

CLOONEY SISTERS, THE
Also see ROSEMARY CLOONEY.
EPIC

Number	Title (A Side/B Side)	Yr	VG	VG+	NM
❑ LN 3160 [M]	The Clooney Sisters with Tony Pastor	1956	15.00	30.00	60.00

CLOUD, BRUCE
CAPITOL

Number	Title (A Side/B Side)	Yr	VG	VG+	NM
❑ ST-343	California Soul	1969	5.00	10.00	20.00

Number	Title (A Side/B Side)	Yr	VG	VG+	NM
CLOVER					
FANTASY					
❑ 8395	Clover	1969	6.25	12.50	25.00
❑ 8405	Forty-Niner	1970	6.25	12.50	25.00
CLOVER, TIMOTHY					
TOWER					
❑ ST 5114	A Harvard Square Affair	1968	5.00	10.00	20.00
CLOVERS, THE					
ATCO					
❑ SD 33-374	Their Greatest Recordings/The Early Years	1971	3.00	6.00	12.00
ATLANTIC					
❑ 1248 [M]	The Clovers	1956	150.00	300.00	600.00
❑ 8009 [M]	The Clovers	1957	100.00	200.00	400.00
—Reissue of 1248 on the "pop" series; black label					
❑ 8009 [M]	The Clovers	1960	75.00	150.00	300.00
—White "bullseye" label					
❑ 8009 [M]	The Clovers	1961	50.00	100.00	200.00
—Red and white label					
❑ 8034 [M]	Dance Party	1959	100.00	200.00	400.00
—Black label					
❑ 8034 [M]	Dance Party	1960	75.00	150.00	300.00
—White "bullseye" label					
❑ 8034 [M]	Dance Party	1961	50.00	100.00	200.00
—Red and white label					
GRAND PRIX					
❑ K-428 [M]	The Original Love Potion Number Nine	1964	7.50	15.00	30.00
❑ KS-428 [R]	The Original Love Potion Number Nine	1964	3.00	6.00	12.00
POPLAR					
❑ 1001 [M]	The Clovers In Clover	1958	100.00	200.00	400.00
UNITED ARTISTS					
❑ UAL-3033 [M]	The Clovers In Clover	1959	75.00	150.00	300.00
❑ UAL-3099 [M]	Love Potion Number Nine	1959	62.50	125.00	250.00
❑ UAS-6033 [R]	The Clovers In Clover	196?	50.00	100.00	200.00
❑ UAS-6099 [S]	Love Potion Number Nine	1959	125.00	250.00	500.00
COASTERS, THE					
ATCO					
❑ 33-101 [M]	The Coasters	1958	75.00	150.00	300.00
—Yellow "harp" label					
❑ 33-101 [M]	The Coasters	196?	15.00	30.00	60.00
—Gold and dark blue label					
❑ 33-111 [M]	The Coasters' Greatest Hits	1959	37.50	75.00	150.00
—Yellow "harp" label					
❑ 33-111 [M]	The Coasters' Greatest Hits	196?	15.00	30.00	60.00
—Gold and gray label					
❑ 33-123 [M]	One By One	196?	15.00	30.00	60.00
—Gold and gray label					
❑ 33-123 [M]	One By One	1960	37.50	75.00	150.00
—Yellow "harp" label					
❑ SD 33-123 [S]	One By One	196?	37.50	75.00	150.00
—Purple and brown label					
❑ SD 33-123 [S]	One By One	1960	100.00	200.00	400.00
—Yellow "harp" label					
❑ 33-135 [M]	Coast Along with the Coasters	1962	25.00	50.00	100.00
—Gold and gray label					
❑ SD 33-135 [P]	Coast Along with the Coasters	1962	37.50	75.00	150.00
—Purple and brown label; "Wait a Minute" is rechanneled					
❑ SD 33-371	Their Greatest Recordings/The Early Years	1971	5.00	10.00	20.00
CLARION					
❑ 605 [M]	That Is Rock and Roll	1965	10.00	20.00	40.00
❑ SD 605 [S]	That Is Rock and Roll	1965	12.50	25.00	50.00
KING					
❑ KS-1146	The Coasters On Broadway	1971	6.25	12.50	25.00
POWER PAK					
❑ 310	Greatest Hits	198?	2.50	5.00	10.00
TRIP					
❑ 8028	It Ain't Sanitary	197?	3.00	6.00	12.00
COATES, JOHN, JR.					
SAVOY					
❑ MG-12082 [M]	Portrait	1956	10.00	20.00	40.00
COBB, ARNETT					
APOLLO					
❑ LAP-105 [10]	Swingin' with Arnett Cobb	1952	62.50	125.00	250.00
MOODSVILLE					
❑ MVLP-14 [M]	Ballads by Cobb	1961	12.50	25.00	50.00
—Green label					
❑ MVLP-14 [M]	Ballads by Cobb	1965	6.25	12.50	25.00
—Blue label, trident logo at right					
PRESTIGE					
❑ PRLP-7151 [M]	Blow, Arnett, Blow	1959	12.50	25.00	50.00
—Yellow label					
❑ PRLP-7151 [M]	Blow, Arnett, Blow	1963	6.25	12.50	25.00
—Blue label, trident logo at right					
❑ PRLP-7165 [M]	Party Time	1959	12.50	25.00	50.00
—Yellow label					
❑ PRLP-7165 [M]	Party Time	1963	6.25	12.50	25.00
—Blue label, trident logo at right					
❑ PRLP-7175 [M]	More Party Time	1960	12.50	25.00	50.00
—Yellow label					
❑ PRLP-7175 [M]	More Party Time	1963	6.25	12.50	25.00
—Blue label, trident logo at right					
❑ PRLP-7184 [M]	Smooth Sailing	1960	12.50	25.00	50.00
—Yellow label					
❑ PRLP-7184 [M]	Smooth Sailing	1963	6.25	12.50	25.00
—Blue label, trident logo at right					
❑ PRLP-7216 [M]	Movin' Right Along	1961	12.50	25.00	50.00
—Yellow label					
❑ PRLP-7216 [M]	Movin' Right Along	1963	6.25	12.50	25.00
—Blue label, trident logo at right					
❑ PRLP-7227 [M]	Sizzlin'	1962	10.00	20.00	40.00
—Yellow label					
❑ PRLP-7227 [M]	Sizzlin'	1963	5.00	10.00	20.00
—Blue label, trident logo at right					
❑ PRST-7227 [S]	Sizzlin'	1962	12.50	25.00	50.00
—Silver label					
❑ PRST-7227 [S]	Sizzlin'	1963	6.25	12.50	25.00
—Blue label, trident logo at right					
COCHRAN, EDDIE					
LIBERTY					
❑ LRP-3061 [M]	Singin' to My Baby	1957	200.00	400.00	800.00
—Green label					
❑ LRP-3061 [M]	Singin' to My Baby	1960	75.00	150.00	300.00
—Black label					
❑ LRP-3172 [M]	Eddie Cochran (12 of His Biggest Hits)	1960	30.00	60.00	120.00
❑ LRP-3220 [M]	Never to Be Forgotten	1962	25.00	50.00	100.00
❑ LN-10137	Singin' to My Baby	198?	3.00	6.00	12.00
—Budget-line reissue					
❑ LN-10204	Great Hits	198?	2.00	4.00	8.00
SUNSET					
❑ SUM-1123 [M]	Summertime Blues	1966	10.00	20.00	40.00
❑ SUS-5123 [R]	Summertime Blues	1966	6.25	12.50	25.00
UNITED ARTISTS					
❑ UA-LA428-E	The Very Best of Eddie Cochran	1975	3.00	6.00	12.00
❑ UAS-9959 [(2)]	Legendary Masters Series #4	1972	6.25	12.50	25.00
COCHRAN, HANK					
CAPITOL					
❑ ST-11807	With a Little Help from His Friends	1978	3.00	6.00	12.00
ELEKTRA					
❑ 6E-277	Make the World Go Away	1980	2.50	5.00	10.00
MONUMENT					
❑ SLP-18089	The Heart of Hank	1968	5.00	10.00	20.00
RCA VICTOR					
❑ LPM-3303 [M]	Hits from the Heart	1965	5.00	10.00	20.00
❑ LSP-3303 [S]	Hits from the Heart	1965	6.25	12.50	25.00
❑ LPM-3431 [M]	Going in Training	1965	5.00	10.00	20.00
❑ LSP-3431 [S]	Going in Training	1965	6.25	12.50	25.00
COCHRAN, TODD					
VITAL					
❑ VTL-001 [(2)]	Todd	1991	5.00	10.00	20.00
COCHRAN, WAYNE					
BETHLEHEM					
❑ 10002	High and Ridin'	1970	3.75	7.50	15.00
CHESS					
❑ LPS-1519	Wayne Cochran!	1968	10.00	20.00	40.00
EPIC					
❑ KE 30889	Cochran	1972	3.75	7.50	15.00
KING					
❑ KS-1116	Alive and Well	1970	5.00	10.00	20.00
COCKER, JOE					
A&M					
❑ SP-3106	With a Little Help from My Friends	1980	2.00	4.00	8.00
❑ SP-3175	I Can Stand a Little Rain	1980	2.00	4.00	8.00
❑ SP-3257	Joe Cocker's Greatest Hits	1982	2.00	4.00	8.00
❑ SP-3633	I Can Stand a Little Rain	1974	2.50	5.00	10.00
❑ SP-4182	With a Little Help from My Friends	1969	3.00	6.00	12.00
—Brown label					
❑ SP-4182	With a Little Help from My Friends	1974	2.50	5.00	10.00
—Silver label					
❑ SP-4224	Joe Cocker!	1969	3.00	6.00	12.00
—Brown label					
❑ SP-4224	Joe Cocker!	1974	2.50	5.00	10.00
—Silver label					
❑ SP-4368	Joe Cocker	1972	3.00	6.00	12.00
—Brown label					
❑ SP-4368	Joe Cocker	1974	2.50	5.00	10.00
—Silver label					
❑ SP-4529	Jamaica Say You Will	1975	2.50	5.00	10.00
❑ SP-4574	Stingray	1976	2.50	5.00	10.00
❑ SP-4670	Joe Cocker's Greatest Hits	1977	2.50	5.00	10.00
❑ SP-6002 [(2)]	Mad Dogs and Englishmen	1970	3.75	7.50	15.00
—Brown labels					
❑ SP-6002 [(2)]	Mad Dogs and Englishmen	1974	3.00	6.00	12.00
—Silver labels					
❑ QU-54182 [Q]	With a Little Help from My Friends	1974	5.00	10.00	20.00
❑ QU-54224 [Q]	Joe Cocker!	1974	5.00	10.00	20.00
ASYLUM					
❑ 6E-145	Luxury You Can Afford	1978	2.50	5.00	10.00
❑ DP-400 [PD]	Luxury You Can Afford	1978	3.75	7.50	15.00
CAPITOL					
❑ ST-12335	Civilized Man	1984	2.50	5.00	10.00
❑ ST-12394	Cocker	1986	2.50	5.00	10.00
❑ CLT-48285	Unchain My Heart	1988	2.50	5.00	10.00
❑ C1-92861	One Night of Sin	1989	3.00	6.00	12.00
ISLAND					
❑ IL 9750	Sheffield Steel	1982	2.50	5.00	10.00
❑ 90096	One More Time	1983	2.50	5.00	10.00
MOBILE FIDELITY					
❑ 1-223	Sheffield Steel	1995	10.00	20.00	40.00
—Audiophile vinyl					

Number	Title (A Side/B Side)	Yr	VG	VG+	NM

COCTEAU TWINS
CAPITOL
❑ SPRO 79066/7 [DJ]	Cocteau Twins	1991	12.50	25.00	50.00
—Promo-only 10-song collection					
❑ C1-90892	Blue Bell Knoll	1988	3.00	6.00	12.00
❑ C1-93669	Heaven Or Las Vegas	1990	3.75	7.50	15.00

RELATIVITY/4AD
❑ EMC 8040	The Pink Opaque	1986	3.00	6.00	12.00
❑ 88561-8141-1 [EP]	Love's Easy Tears	1986	3.00	6.00	12.00
❑ 88561-8143-1	The Moon and the Melodies	1987	3.00	6.00	12.00
—With Harold Budd					

COE, DAVID ALLAN
COLUMBIA
❑ KC 32942	Mysterious Rhinestone Cowboy	1974	3.00	6.00	12.00
❑ PC 32942	Mysterious Rhinestone Cowboy	197?	2.50	5.00	10.00
—Early reissue with new prefix and no bar code					
❑ KC 33085	Once Upon a Rhyme	1975	3.00	6.00	12.00
❑ PC 33085	Once Upon a Rhyme	197?	2.50	5.00	10.00
—Early reissue with new prefix and no bar code					
❑ PC 33916	Longhaired Redneck	1976	2.50	5.00	10.00
❑ PC 34310	David Allan Coe Rides Again	1977	2.50	5.00	10.00
❑ PC 34780	Tattoo	1977	2.50	5.00	10.00
❑ KC 35306	Family Album	1978	2.50	5.00	10.00
❑ KC 35535	Human Emotions — Happy Side/Su-I-Side	1978	2.50	5.00	10.00
❑ KC 35627	Greatest Hits	1978	2.50	5.00	10.00
❑ PC 35627	Greatest Hits	198?	2.00	4.00	8.00
—Budget-line reissue					
❑ KC 35789	Spectrum, VII	1979	2.50	5.00	10.00
❑ JC 36277	Compass Point	1980	2.50	5.00	10.00
❑ PC 36277	Compass Point	198?	2.00	4.00	8.00
—Budget-line reissue with new prefix					
❑ JC 36489	I've Got Something to Say	1980	2.50	5.00	10.00
❑ PC 36489	I've Got Something to Say	198?	2.00	4.00	8.00
—Budget-line reissue with new prefix					
❑ JC 36970	Invictus (Means) Unconquered	1981	2.50	5.00	10.00
❑ PC 36970	Invictus (Means) Unconquered	198?	2.00	4.00	8.00
—Budget-line reissue with new prefix					
❑ FC 37352	Encore	1981	2.50	5.00	10.00
❑ PC 37352	Encore	198?	2.00	4.00	8.00
—Budget-line reissue with new prefix					
❑ FC 37454	Tennessee Whiskey	1981	2.50	5.00	10.00
❑ PC 37454	Tennessee Whiskey	198?	2.00	4.00	8.00
—Budget-line reissue with new prefix					
❑ FC 37736	Rough Rider	1982	2.50	5.00	10.00
❑ PC 37736	Rough Rider	198?	2.00	4.00	8.00
—Budget-line reissue with new prefix					
❑ FC 38093	D.A.C.	1982	2.50	5.00	10.00
❑ FC 38318	Biggest Hits	1982	2.50	5.00	10.00
❑ FC 38535	Castles in the Sand	1983	2.50	5.00	10.00
❑ PC 38535	Castles in the Sand	1985	2.00	4.00	8.00
—Budget-line reissue with new prefix					
❑ FC 38926	Hello In There	1983	2.50	5.00	10.00
❑ FC 39269	Just Divorced	1984	2.50	5.00	10.00
❑ PC 39269	Just Divorced	1986	2.00	4.00	8.00
—Budget-line reissue with new prefix					
❑ KC2 39585 [(2)]	For the Record — The First 10 Years	1984	3.00	6.00	12.00
❑ FC 39617	Darlin', Darlin'	1985	2.50	5.00	10.00
❑ FC 40195	Unchained	1985	2.50	5.00	10.00
❑ FC 40346	Son of the South	1986	2.50	5.00	10.00
❑ FC 40571	A Matter of Life... And Death	1987	2.50	5.00	10.00
❑ FC 45057	Crazy Daddy	1989	2.50	5.00	10.00

PAIR
❑ PDL2-1075 [(2)]	Best of David Allan Coe	1986	3.00	6.00	12.00

PLANTATION
❑ 507	Texas Moon	197?	3.75	7.50	15.00

SSS INTERNATIONAL
❑ 9	Penitentiary Blues	1977	20.00	40.00	80.00

COHEN, LEONARD
COLUMBIA
❑ CL 2733 [M]	Leonard Cohen	1967	6.25	12.50	25.00
❑ CS 9533 [S]	Leonard Cohen	1967	3.00	6.00	12.00
—Red "360 Sound" label					
❑ CS 9533 [S]	Leonard Cohen	1970	2.50	5.00	10.00
—Orange label					
❑ PC 9533	Leonard Cohen	198?	2.00	4.00	8.00
—Reissue with new prefix					
❑ CS 9767	Songs From a Room	1969	3.00	6.00	12.00
—Red "360 Sound" label					
❑ CS 9767	Songs From a Room	1970	2.50	5.00	10.00
—Orange label					
❑ PC 9767	Songs From a Room	198?	2.00	4.00	8.00
—Reissue with new prefix					
❑ C 30103	Songs of Love and Hate	1971	3.00	6.00	12.00
❑ PC 30103	Songs of Love and Hate	198?	2.00	4.00	8.00
—Budget-line reissue					
❑ KC 31724	Leonard Cohen: Live Songs	1973	3.00	6.00	12.00
❑ KC 33167	New Skin for the Old Ceremony	1974	3.00	6.00	12.00
❑ PC 34077	The Best of Leonard Cohen	1975	2.50	5.00	10.00
—No bar code					
❑ PC 34077	The Best of Leonard Cohen	198?	2.00	4.00	8.00
—Reissue with bar code					
❑ JC 36264	Recent Songs	1979	2.50	5.00	10.00
❑ PC 36264	Recent Songs	198?	2.00	4.00	8.00
—Budget-line reissue					
❑ FC 44191	I'm Your Man	1988	2.50	5.00	10.00

PASSPORT
❑ PB-6045	Various Positions	1985	2.50	5.00	10.00

WARNER BROS.
❑ BSK 3125	Death of a Ladies' Man	1977	2.50	5.00	10.00

COHEN, MYRON
AUDIO FIDELITY
❑ 701 [M]	Myron Cohen	196?	5.00	10.00	20.00

RCA VICTOR
❑ LPM-3534 [M]	Everybody Gotta Be Someplace	1966	3.00	6.00	12.00
❑ LSP-3534 [S]	Everybody Gotta Be Someplace	1966	3.75	7.50	15.00
❑ LPM-3791 [M]	It's Not a Question	1967	3.00	6.00	12.00
❑ LSP-3791 [S]	It's Not a Question	1967	3.75	7.50	15.00
❑ VPS-6052 [(2)]	This Is Myron Cohen	1972	3.75	7.50	15.00

COHN, AL
CORAL
❑ CRL 57118 [M]	Al Cohn Quintet	1957	12.50	25.00	50.00

DAWN
❑ DLP-1110 [M]	Cohn on the Saxophone	1956	30.00	60.00	120.00

PROGRESSIVE
❑ PLP-3002 [10]	Al Cohn Quartet	1953	75.00	150.00	300.00
❑ PLP-3004 [10]	Al Cohn Quintet	1953	75.00	150.00	300.00

RCA VICTOR
❑ LJM-1024 [M]	Mr. Music	1955	20.00	40.00	80.00
❑ LPM-1116 [M]	The Natural Seven	1955	20.00	40.00	80.00
❑ LPM-1161 [M]	Four Brass, One Tenor	1956	20.00	40.00	80.00
❑ LPM-1207 [M]	That Old Feeling	1956	20.00	40.00	80.00
❑ LPM-2312 [M]	Son of Drum Suite	1960	10.00	20.00	40.00
❑ LSP-2312 [S]	Son of Drum Suite	1960	12.50	25.00	50.00

SAVOY
❑ MG-12048 [M]	Cohn's Tones	1956	20.00	40.00	80.00

COLDER, BEN
See SHEB WOOLEY.

COLE, BUDDY
COLUMBIA
❑ CL 1224 [M]	Pipes & Chimes of Christmas	1958	5.00	10.00	20.00
—Red label with six "eye" logos					
❑ CS 8032 [S]	Pipes & Chimes of Christmas	1958	6.25	12.50	25.00
—Red and black label with six "eye" logos					

COLE, COZY
AUDITION
❑ 33-5943 [M]	Cozy Cole	1955	12.50	25.00	50.00

BETHLEHEM
❑ BCP-21 [M]	Jazz at the Metropole Café	1955	12.50	25.00	50.00

CHARLIE PARKER
❑ PLP-403 [M]	A Cozy Conaption of Carmen	1962	5.00	10.00	20.00
❑ PLP-403S [S]	A Cozy Conaption of Carmen	1962	6.25	12.50	25.00

COLUMBIA
❑ CS 9353 [S]	It's a Rockin' Thing	1965	5.00	10.00	20.00

CORAL
❑ CRL 757423 [S]	Drum Beat Dancing Feet	1962	5.00	10.00	20.00
❑ CRL 757457 [S]	It's a Cozy World	1964	5.00	10.00	20.00

FELSTED
❑ 2002 [S]	Cozy's Caravan/Earl's Backroom	1958	10.00	20.00	40.00
❑ 7002 [M]	Cozy's Caravan/Earl's Backroom	1958	12.50	25.00	50.00

GRAND AWARD
❑ GA 33-334 [M]	After Hours	1956	10.00	20.00	40.00

KING
❑ 673 [M]	Cozy Cole	1959	15.00	30.00	60.00
❑ KS-673 [S]	Cozy Cole	1959	37.50	75.00	150.00

LOVE
❑ 500M [M]	Topsy	1959	25.00	50.00	100.00
❑ 500S [S]	Topsy	1959	50.00	100.00	200.00

PARIS
❑ 122 [M]	Cozy Cole and His All-Stars	1958	12.50	25.00	50.00

PLYMOUTH
❑ P 12-155 [M]	Cozy Cole and His All Stars	195?	7.50	15.00	30.00

SAVOY
❑ MG-12197 [M]	Concerto for Cozy	196?	5.00	10.00	20.00

COLE, COZY/JIMMY MCPARTLAND
WALDORF MUSIC HALL
❑ MH 33-162 [10]	After Hours	195?	12.50	25.00	50.00

COLE, IKE
DEE GEE
❑ 4001	Ike Cole's Tribute to His Brother Nat	1966	10.00	20.00	40.00

COLE, JERRY
BEAT ROCKET
❑ BR 117	Guitars A-Go-Go!	2000	3.00	6.00	12.00
❑ BR 118	Wild Strings!	2001	3.00	6.00	12.00

CAPITOL
❑ ST 2044 [S]	Outer Limits	1963	20.00	40.00	80.00
❑ T 2044 [M]	Outer Limits	1963	12.50	25.00	50.00
❑ (S)T 2061	Hot Rod Dance Party Bonus Photo	1964	6.25	12.50	25.00
❑ ST 2061 [S]	Hot Rod Dance Party	1964	25.00	50.00	100.00
❑ T 2061 [M]	Hot Rod Dance Party	1964	20.00	40.00	80.00
❑ ST 2112 [S]	Surf Age	1964	25.00	50.00	100.00
—With bonus single missing					
❑ ST 2112 [S]	Surf Age	1964	30.00	60.00	120.00
—With bonus single by Dick Dale, "Thunder Wave"/"Spanish Kiss"					
❑ T 2112 [M]	Surf Age	1964	20.00	40.00	80.00
—With bonus single missing					
❑ T 2112 [M]	Surf Age	1964	25.00	50.00	100.00
—With bonus single by Dick Dale, "Thunder Wave"/"Spanish Kiss"					

LIBERTY
❑ LRP-3362 [M]	Sounds of the Big Irons	1964	12.50	25.00	50.00
❑ LST-7362 [S]	Sounds of the Big Irons	1964	15.00	30.00	60.00

Number	Title (A Side/B Side)	Yr	VG	VG+	NM
COLE, MARIA					
KAPP					
❏ 102 [10]	Maria Cole	1954	12.50	25.00	50.00
COLE, NAT KING					
Includes reissues of material by the King Cole Trio.					
ARCHIVE OF FOLK AND JAZZ					
❏ 290	Nature Boy	197?	2.50	5.00	10.00
CAMAY					
❏ CA-3004	Nat King Cole	196?	3.00	6.00	12.00
CAPITOL					
❏ H 8 [10]	The King Cole Trio	1950	25.00	50.00	100.00
❏ H 29 [10]	The King Cole Trio, Volume 2	1950	25.00	50.00	100.00
❏ H 59 [10]	The King Cole Trio, Volume 3	1950	25.00	50.00	100.00
❏ H 156 [10]	Nat King Cole at the Piano	1950	25.00	50.00	100.00
❏ H 177 [10]	The King Cole Trio, Volume 4	1950	17.50	35.00	70.00
❏ H 213 [10]	Harvest of Hits	1950	17.50	35.00	70.00
❏ H 220 [10]	The Nat King Cole Trio	1950	15.00	30.00	60.00
❏ DWBB-252 [(2)]	Close-Up	1969	3.75	7.50	15.00
—Reissue of 680 and 1891					
❏ ST-310	There! I've Said It Again	1969	3.00	6.00	12.00
❏ H 332 [10]	Penthouse Serenade	1951	15.00	30.00	60.00
❏ T 332 [M]	Penthouse Serenade	1955	10.00	20.00	40.00
❏ DT 357 [R]	Unforgettable	1965	3.00	6.00	12.00
❏ H 357 [10]	Unforgettable	1952	15.00	30.00	60.00
❏ SM-357	Unforgettable	197?	2.00	4.00	8.00
—Reissue with new prefix					
❏ T 357 [M]	Unforgettable	1955	10.00	20.00	40.00
—Turquoise label					
❏ T 357 [M]	Unforgettable	1958	7.50	15.00	30.00
—Black label with colorband, "Capitol" at left					
❏ T 357 [M]	Unforgettable	1962	5.00	10.00	20.00
—Black label with colorband, "Capitol" at top					
❏ SKAO-373	Nat King Cole's Greatest	1969	3.00	6.00	12.00
❏ DT 420 [R]	Nat King Cole Sings for Two in Love	1963	3.75	7.50	15.00
❏ H 420 [10]	Nat King Cole Sings for Two in Love	1953	12.50	25.00	50.00
❏ T 420 [M]	Nat King Cole Sings for Two in Love	1955	10.00	20.00	40.00
—Turquoise label					
❏ T 420 [M]	Nat King Cole Sings for Two in Love	1958	7.50	15.00	30.00
—Black label with colorband, "Capitol" at left					
❏ T 420 [M]	Nat King Cole Sings for Two in Love	1962	5.00	10.00	20.00
—Black label with colorband, "Capitol" at top					
❏ STBB-503 [(2)]	Walkin' My Baby Back Home/A Blossom Fell	1970	3.75	7.50	15.00
❏ H 514 [10]	Tenth Anniversary Album	1954	12.50	25.00	50.00
❏ W 514 [M]	Tenth Anniversary Album	1955	10.00	20.00	40.00
❏ T 591 [M]	Vocal Classics	1955	10.00	20.00	40.00
❏ T 592 [M]	Instrumental Classics	1955	10.00	20.00	40.00
❏ DT 680 [R]	Ballads of the Day	1963	3.75	7.50	15.00
—Black label with colorband					
❏ T 680 [M]	Ballads of the Day	1956	10.00	20.00	40.00
—Turquoise label					
❏ T 680 [M]	Ballads of the Day	1958	7.50	15.00	30.00
—Black label with colorband, "Capitol" at left					
❏ T 680 [M]	Ballads of the Day	1962	5.00	10.00	20.00
—Black label with colorband, "Capitol" at top					
❏ W 689 [M]	The Piano Style of Nat King Cole	1956	10.00	20.00	40.00
—Turquoise label					
❏ W 689 [M]	The Piano Style of Nat King Cole	1958	7.50	15.00	30.00
—Black label with colorband, "Capitol" at left					
❏ W 689 [M]	The Piano Style of Nat King Cole	1962	5.00	10.00	20.00
—Black label with colorband, "Capitol" at top					
❏ W 782 [M]	After Midnight	1956	10.00	20.00	40.00
—Turquoise label					
❏ W 782 [M]	After Midnight	1958	7.50	15.00	30.00
—Black label with colorband, "Capitol" at left					
❏ W 782 [M]	After Midnight	1962	5.00	10.00	20.00
—Black label with colorband, "Capitol" at top					
❏ SM-824	Love Is the Thing	197?	2.00	4.00	8.00
—Reissue with new prefix					
❏ SW 824 [S]	Love Is the Thing	1959	7.50	15.00	30.00
—Black label with colorband, "Capitol" at left					
❏ SW 824 [S]	Love Is the Thing	1962	5.00	10.00	20.00
—Black label with colorband, "Capitol" at top					
❏ SW 824 [S]	Love Is the Thing	1969	3.00	6.00	12.00
—Lime green label					
❏ W 824 [M]	Love Is the Thing	1957	10.00	20.00	40.00
—Turquoise or gray label					
❏ W 824 [M]	Love Is the Thing	1958	7.50	15.00	30.00
—Black label with colorband, "Capitol" at left					
❏ W 824 [M]	Love Is the Thing	1962	5.00	10.00	20.00
—Black label with colorband, "Capitol" at top					
❏ DT 870 [R]	This Is Nat "King" Cole	1963	3.75	7.50	15.00
—Black label with colorband					
❏ T 870 [M]	This Is Nat "King" Cole	1957	10.00	20.00	40.00
—Turquoise or gray label					
❏ T 870 [M]	This Is Nat "King" Cole	1958	7.50	15.00	30.00
—Black label with colorband, "Capitol" at left					
❏ T 870 [M]	This Is Nat "King" Cole	1962	5.00	10.00	20.00
—Black label with colorband, "Capitol" at top					
❏ SW 903 [S]	Just One of Those Things	1959	7.50	15.00	30.00
—Black label with colorband, "Capitol" at left					
❏ SW 903 [S]	Just One of Those Things	1962	5.00	10.00	20.00
—Black label with colorband, "Capitol" at top					
❏ W 903 [M]	Just One of Those Things	1957	10.00	20.00	40.00
—Turquoise or gray label					
❏ W 903 [M]	Just One of Those Things	1958	7.50	15.00	30.00
—Black label with colorband, "Capitol" at left					
❏ W 903 [M]	Just One of Those Things	1962	5.00	10.00	20.00
—Black label with colorband, "Capitol" at top					
❏ SW 993 [S]	St. Louis Blues	1959	12.50	25.00	50.00
—Black label with colorband, "Capitol" at left					

Number	Title (A Side/B Side)	Yr	VG	VG+	NM
❏ W 993 [M]	St. Louis Blues	1958	12.50	25.00	50.00
—Turquoise or gray label					
❏ W 993 [M]	St. Louis Blues	1962	10.00	20.00	40.00
—Black label with colorband "Capitol" at left					
❏ DW 1031 [R]	Cole Espanol	196?	3.75	7.50	15.00
—Black label with colorband					
❏ SM-1031	Cole Espanol	197?	2.00	4.00	8.00
—Reissue with new prefix					
❏ W 1031 [M]	Cole Espanol	1958	7.50	15.00	30.00
—Black label with colorband, "Capitol" at left					
❏ W 1031 [M]	Cole Espanol	1962	5.00	10.00	20.00
—Black label with colorband, "Capitol" at top					
❏ SW 1084 [S]	The Very Thought of You	1959	7.50	15.00	30.00
—Black label with colorband, "Capitol" at left					
❏ SW 1084 [S]	The Very Thought of You	1962	5.00	10.00	20.00
—Black label with colorband, "Capitol" at top					
❏ W 1084 [M]	The Very Thought of You	1958	7.50	15.00	30.00
—Black label with colorband, "Capitol" at left					
❏ W 1084 [M]	The Very Thought of You	1962	5.00	10.00	20.00
—Black label with colorband, "Capitol" at top					
❏ SW 1120 [S]	Welcome to the Club	1959	10.00	20.00	40.00
—Black label with colorband, "Capitol" at left					
❏ W 1120 [M]	Welcome to the Club	1959	7.50	15.00	30.00
—Black label with colorband, "Capitol" at left					
❏ SW 1190 [S]	To Whom It May Concern	1959	10.00	20.00	40.00
—Black label with colorband, "Capitol" at left					
❏ W 1190 [M]	To Whom It May Concern	1959	7.50	15.00	30.00
—Black label with colorband, "Capitol" at left					
❏ SW 1220 [S]	A Mis Amigos	1959	10.00	20.00	40.00
—Black label with colorband, "Capitol" at left					
❏ SW 1220 [S]	A Mis Amigos	1962	6.25	12.50	25.00
—Black label with colorband, "Capitol" at top					
❏ W 1220 [M]	A Mis Amigos	1959	7.50	15.00	30.00
—Black label with colorband, "Capitol" at left					
❏ W 1220 [M]	A Mis Amigos	1962	5.00	10.00	20.00
—Black label with colorband, "Capitol" at top					
❏ SW 1249 [S]	Every Time I Feel the Spirit	1960	7.50	15.00	30.00
—Black label with colorband, "Capitol" at left					
❏ W 1249 [M]	Every Time I Feel the Spirit	1960	6.25	12.50	25.00
—Black label with colorband, "Capitol" at left					
❏ SW 1331 [S]	Tell Me About Yourself	1960	7.50	15.00	30.00
—Black label with colorband, "Capitol" at left					
❏ W 1331 [M]	Tell Me About Yourself	1960	6.25	12.50	25.00
—Black label with colorband, "Capitol" at left					
❏ SWAK 1392 [S]	Wild Is Love	1960	7.50	15.00	30.00
—Black label with colorband, "Capitol" at left					
❏ WAK 1392 [M]	Wild Is Love	1960	6.25	12.50	25.00
—Black label with colorband, "Capitol" at left					
❏ SW 1444 [S]	The Magic of Christmas	1960	5.00	10.00	20.00
❏ W 1444 [M]	The Magic of Christmas	1960	5.00	10.00	20.00
❏ SW 1574 [S]	The Touch of Your Lips	1961	6.25	12.50	25.00
—Black label with colorband, "Capitol" at left					
❏ SW 1574 [S]	The Touch of Your Lips	1962	5.00	10.00	20.00
—Black label with colorband, "Capitol" at top					
❏ W 1574 [M]	The Touch of Your Lips	1961	5.00	10.00	20.00
—Black label with colorband, "Capitol" at left					
❏ W 1574 [M]	The Touch of Your Lips	1962	3.75	7.50	15.00
—Black label with colorband, "Capitol" at top					
❏ SWCL 1613 [(3)S]	The Nat King Cole Story	1961	7.50	15.00	30.00
❏ WCL 1613 [(3)M]	The Nat King Cole Story	1961	6.25	12.50	25.00
❏ SM-1675	Nat King Cole Sings/George Shearing Plays	197?	2.00	4.00	8.00
—Reissue with new prefix					
❏ SW 1675 [S]	Nat King Cole Sings/George Shearing Plays	1962	7.50	15.00	30.00
—Black label with colorband, "Capitol" at left					
❏ SW 1675 [S]	Nat King Cole Sings/George Shearing Plays	1963	5.00	10.00	20.00
—Black label with colorband, "Capitol" at top					
❏ W 1675 [M]	Nat King Cole Sings/George Shearing Plays	1962	6.25	12.50	25.00
—Black label with colorband, "Capitol" at left					
❏ W 1675 [M]	Nat King Cole Sings/George Shearing Plays	1963	3.75	7.50	15.00
—Black label with colorband, "Capitol" at top					
❏ SW 1713 [S]	Nat King Cole Sings the Blues	1962	6.25	12.50	25.00
—Black label with colorband, "Capitol" at left					
❏ W 1713 [M]	Nat King Cole Sings the Blues	1962	5.00	10.00	20.00
—Black label with colorband, "Capitol" at left					
❏ SM-1749	More Cole Espanol	197?	2.00	4.00	8.00
—Reissue with new prefix					
❏ SW 1749 [S]	More Cole Espanol	1962	7.50	15.00	30.00
—Black label with colorband, "Capitol" at left					
❏ SW 1749 [S]	More Cole Espanol	1963	5.00	10.00	20.00
—Black label with colorband, "Capitol" at top					
❏ W 1749 [M]	More Cole Espanol	1962	6.25	12.50	25.00
—Black label with colorband, "Capitol" at left					
❏ W 1749 [M]	More Cole Espanol	1963	3.75	7.50	15.00
—Black label with colorband, "Capitol" at top					
❏ ST 1793 [S]	Ramblin' Rose	1962	5.00	10.00	20.00
❏ T 1793 [M]	Ramblin' Rose	1962	3.75	7.50	15.00
❏ ST 1838 [S]	Dear Lonely Hearts	1962	5.00	10.00	20.00
❏ T 1838 [M]	Dear Lonely Hearts	1962	3.75	7.50	15.00
❏ SW 1859 [S]	Where Did Everyone Go?	1963	5.00	10.00	20.00
❏ W 1859 [M]	Where Did Everyone Go?	1963	3.75	7.50	15.00
❏ DT 1891 [R]	Nat King Cole's Top Pops	1963	3.00	6.00	12.00
❏ T 1891 [M]	Nat King Cole's Top Pops	1963	3.75	7.50	15.00
❏ SW 1926 [S]	The Nat King Cole Story, Volume 1	1962	3.75	7.50	15.00
❏ W 1926 [M]	The Nat King Cole Story, Volume 1	1962	3.00	6.00	12.00
❏ SW 1927 [S]	The Nat King Cole Story, Volume 2	1963	3.75	7.50	15.00
❏ W 1927 [M]	The Nat King Cole Story, Volume 2	1963	3.00	6.00	12.00
❏ SW 1928 [S]	The Nat King Cole Story, Volume 3	1963	3.75	7.50	15.00
❏ W 1928 [M]	The Nat King Cole Story, Volume 3	1963	3.00	6.00	12.00
❏ SW 1929 [S]	Nat King Cole Sings the Blues, Volume 2	1963	5.00	10.00	20.00
❏ W 1929 [M]	Nat King Cole Sings the Blues, Volume 2	1963	3.75	7.50	15.00
❏ ST 1932 [S]	Those Lazy-Hazy-Crazy Days of Summer	1963	5.00	10.00	20.00
❏ T 1932 [M]	Those Lazy-Hazy-Crazy Days of Summer	1963	3.75	7.50	15.00

Number	Title (A Side/B Side)	Yr	VG	VG+	NM
SM-1967 [S]	The Christmas Song	197?	2.00	4.00	8.00
—Budget-line reissue					
SW 1967 [S]	The Christmas Song	1962	3.75	7.50	15.00
—Black label with colorband					
SW 1967 [S]	The Christmas Song	1969	3.00	6.00	12.00
—Lime-green label					
SW 1967 [S]	The Christmas Song	1971	3.00	6.00	12.00
—Red label					
SW 1967 [S]	The Christmas Song	1973	2.50	5.00	10.00
—Orange label, "Capitol" at bottom					
W 1967 [M]	The Christmas Song	1962	3.75	7.50	15.00
—Reissue of W 1444 with title song added and another deleted					
SW 2008 [S]	Let's Face the Music	1963	5.00	10.00	20.00
W 2008 [M]	Let's Face the Music	1963	3.75	7.50	15.00
SM-2117	My Fair Lady	197?	2.00	4.00	8.00
—Reissue with new prefix					
SW 2117 [S]	My Fair Lady	1964	5.00	10.00	20.00
—Black label with colorband					
SW 2117 [S]	My Fair Lady	1969	3.00	6.00	12.00
—Lime green label					
W 2117 [M]	My Fair Lady	1964	3.75	7.50	15.00
ST 2118 [S]	I Don't Want to Be Hurt Anymore	1964	5.00	10.00	20.00
T 2118 [M]	I Don't Want to Be Hurt Anymore	1964	3.75	7.50	15.00
ST 2195 [S]	L-O-V-E	1965	5.00	10.00	20.00
T 2195 [M]	L-O-V-E	1965	3.75	7.50	15.00
T 2311 [M]	The Nat King Cole Trio	1965	3.00	6.00	12.00
ST 2340 [S]	Songs from "Cat Ballou" and Other Motion Pictures	1965	3.75	7.50	15.00
T 2340 [M]	Songs from "Cat Ballou" and Other Motion Pictures	1965	3.00	6.00	12.00
DT 2348 [R]	Nature Boy	1965	3.00	6.00	12.00
T 2348 [M]	Nature Boy	1965	3.75	7.50	15.00
ST 2361 [S]	Looking Back	1965	3.75	7.50	15.00
T 2361 [M]	Looking Back	1965	3.00	6.00	12.00
MAS 2434 [M]	Nat King Cole at the Sands	1966	3.00	6.00	12.00
SM-2434	Nat King Cole at the Sands	197?	2.00	4.00	8.00
—Reissue with new prefix					
SMAS 2434 [S]	Nat King Cole at the Sands	1966	3.75	7.50	15.00
ST 2454 [S]	Hymns and Spirituals	1966	3.75	7.50	15.00
T 2454 [M]	Hymns and Spirituals	1966	3.00	6.00	12.00
T 2529 [M]	The Vintage Years	1966	3.00	6.00	12.00
ST 2558 [S]	The Great Songs!	1966	3.75	7.50	15.00
T 2558 [M]	The Great Songs!	1966	3.00	6.00	12.00
ST 2680 [S]	Sincerely, Nat King Cole	1967	3.00	6.00	12.00
T 2680 [M]	Sincerely, Nat King Cole	1967	3.75	7.50	15.00
ST 2759 [S]	Thank You Pretty Baby	1967	3.00	6.00	12.00
T 2759 [M]	Thank You Pretty Baby	1967	3.75	7.50	15.00
ST 2820 [S]	Beautiful Ballads	1967	3.00	6.00	12.00
T 2820 [M]	Beautiful Ballads	1967	3.75	7.50	15.00
STCL 2873 [(3)P]	The Nat King Cole Deluxe Set	1968	6.25	12.50	25.00
TCL 2873 [(3)M]	The Nat King Cole Deluxe Set	1968	7.50	15.00	30.00
SKAO 2944	The Best of Nat King Cole	1968	3.00	6.00	12.00
H 9110 [10]	Eight Top Pops	1954	12.50	25.00	50.00
M-11033 [M]	Trio Days	1972	3.75	7.50	15.00
SWAK-11355	Love Is Here to Stay	1974	3.00	6.00	12.00
SM-11796	After Midnight	1978	2.50	5.00	10.00
SM-11804	Songs from "Cat Ballou" and Other Motion Pictures	1978	2.50	5.00	10.00
SM-11882	Looking Back	1979	2.50	5.00	10.00
ST-12219	16 Grandes Exitos	1982	2.50	5.00	10.00
SN-16032	Ramblin' Rose	1980	2.00	4.00	8.00
SN-16033	The Nat King Cole Story, Volume 1	1980	2.00	4.00	8.00
SN-16034	The Nat King Cole Story, Volume 2	1980	2.00	4.00	8.00
SN-16035	The Nat King Cole Story, Volume 3	1980	2.00	4.00	8.00
SN-16036	The Best of Nat King Cole	1980	2.00	4.00	8.00
SN-16037	Wild Is Love	1980	2.00	4.00	8.00
SN-16136	A Mis Amigos	1980	2.00	4.00	8.00
SN-16137	St. Louis Blues	1980	2.00	4.00	8.00
SN-16162	Unforgettable	1981	2.00	4.00	8.00
SN-16163	Love Is the Thing	1981	2.00	4.00	8.00
DN-16164	Walkin' My Baby Back Home	1981	2.00	4.00	8.00
DN-16165	A Blossom Fell	1981	2.00	4.00	8.00
N-16166	Cole Espanol	1981	2.00	4.00	8.00
SN-16167	More Cole Espanol	1981	2.00	4.00	8.00
N-16260	The Best of the King Cole Trio — Volume 1	1982	2.00	4.00	8.00
N-16281	The Best of the King Cole Trio — Volume 2	1982	2.00	4.00	8.00
SQBO 90938 [(2)]	The Velvet Moods of Nat King Cole	1967	6.25	12.50	25.00
—Capitol Record Club exclusive					
SQBO 91278 [(2)]	The Swingin' Moods of Nat King Cole	1967	6.25	12.50	25.00
—Capitol Record Club exclusive					
SQBO-93741 [(2)]	The Man and His Music	197?	5.00	10.00	20.00
—Capitol Record Club exclusive; with booklet					

DCC COMPACT CLASSICS

Number	Title (A Side/B Side)	Yr	VG	VG+	NM
LPZ-2029	Love Is the Thing	1997	30.00	60.00	120.00
—Audiophile vinyl					
LPZ-2047	The Very Thought of You	1998	25.00	50.00	100.00
—Audiophile vinyl					
LPZ-2061 [(2)]	The Greatest Hits	1998	30.00	60.00	120.00
—Audiophile vinyl					

DECCA

Number	Title (A Side/B Side)	Yr	VG	VG+	NM
DL 8260 [M]	In the Beginning	1956	10.00	20.00	40.00
—Black label, silver print					
DL 8260 [M]	In the Beginning	1960	6.25	12.50	25.00
—Black label with color bars					

MARK 56

Number	Title (A Side/B Side)	Yr	VG	VG+	NM
739 [(2)]	Early 1940s	197?	3.75	7.50	15.00

MCA

Number	Title (A Side/B Side)	Yr	VG	VG+	NM
4020 [(2)]	From the Very Beginning	1973	3.00	6.00	12.00

MOBILE FIDELITY

Number	Title (A Side/B Side)	Yr	VG	VG+	NM
1-081	Nat King Cole Sings/George Shearing Plays	1981	10.00	20.00	40.00
—Audiophile vinyl					

MOSAIC

Number	Title (A Side/B Side)	Yr	VG	VG+	NM
MR27-138 [(27)]	The Complete Capitol Recordings of the Nat King Cole Trio	199?	150.00	300.00	600.00

PAIR

Number	Title (A Side/B Side)	Yr	VG	VG+	NM
PDL2-1025 [(2)]	Weaver of Dreams	1986	3.00	6.00	12.00
PDL2-1026 [(2)]	Love Moods	1986	3.00	6.00	12.00
PDL2-1128 [(2)]	Tenderly	1986	3.00	6.00	12.00

PICKWICK

Number	Title (A Side/B Side)	Yr	VG	VG+	NM
PTP-2058 [(2)]	Nature Boy	1973	3.00	6.00	12.00
SPC-3046	Love Is a Many Splendored Thing	196?	2.50	5.00	10.00
SPC-3071	When You're Smiling	196?	2.50	5.00	10.00
SPC-3105	Stay As Sweet As You Are	196?	2.50	5.00	10.00
SPC-3154	You're My Everything	197?	2.50	5.00	10.00
SPC-3249	Nature Boy	197?	2.50	5.00	10.00

SAVOY JAZZ

Number	Title (A Side/B Side)	Yr	VG	VG+	NM
SJL-1205	Nat King Cole & The King Cole Trio	1989	3.00	6.00	12.00

SCORE

Number	Title (A Side/B Side)	Yr	VG	VG+	NM
SLP-4019 [M]	The King Cole Trio and Lester Young	1957	20.00	40.00	80.00

TRIP

Number	Title (A Side/B Side)	Yr	VG	VG+	NM
7	The Nat "King" Cole Trio	197?	3.00	6.00	12.00

VERVE

Number	Title (A Side/B Side)	Yr	VG	VG+	NM
VSP-14 [M]	Nat Cole at JATP	1966	3.75	7.50	15.00
VSPS-14 [R]	Nat Cole at JATP	1966	3.00	6.00	12.00
VSP-25 [M]	Nat Cole at JATP 2	1966	3.75	7.50	15.00
VSPS-25 [R]	Nat Cole at JATP 2	1966	3.00	6.00	12.00

COLE, NATALIE

CAPITOL

Number	Title (A Side/B Side)	Yr	VG	VG+	NM
ST-11429	Inseparable	1975	2.50	5.00	10.00
ST-11517	Natalie	1976	2.50	5.00	10.00
SO-11600	Unpredictable	1977	2.50	5.00	10.00
SW-11708	Thankful	1978	2.50	5.00	10.00
SKBL-11709 [(2)]	Natalie..Live!	1978	3.00	6.00	12.00
SO-11928	I Love You So	1979	2.50	5.00	10.00
ST-12079	Don't Look Back	1980	2.50	5.00	10.00
ST-12165	Happy Love	1981	2.50	5.00	10.00
ST-12242	A Collection	1982	2.50	5.00	10.00
SN-16038	Inseparable	198?	2.00	4.00	8.00
—Budget-line reissue					
SN-16310	A Collection	1985	2.00	4.00	8.00
—Budget-line reissue					

ELEKTRA

Number	Title (A Side/B Side)	Yr	VG	VG+	NM
61049 [(2)]	Unforgettable	1991	5.00	10.00	20.00

EMI

Number	Title (A Side/B Side)	Yr	VG	VG+	NM
E1-48902	Good to Be Back	1989	2.50	5.00	10.00

EPIC

Number	Title (A Side/B Side)	Yr	VG	VG+	NM
FE 38280	I'm Ready	1983	2.50	5.00	10.00

MANHATTAN

Number	Title (A Side/B Side)	Yr	VG	VG+	NM
53051	Everlasting	1987	2.50	5.00	10.00

MOBILE FIDELITY

Number	Title (A Side/B Side)	Yr	VG	VG+	NM
1-032	Thankful	1980	5.00	10.00	20.00
—Audiophile vinyl					

MODERN

Number	Title (A Side/B Side)	Yr	VG	VG+	NM
90270	Dangerous	1985	2.50	5.00	10.00

COLE, RICHIE

ADELPHI

Number	Title (A Side/B Side)	Yr	VG	VG+	NM
AD 5001	Starburst	1976	5.00	10.00	20.00

COLEMAN, CY

BENIDA

Number	Title (A Side/B Side)	Yr	VG	VG+	NM
LP-1023A [10]	Cy Coleman	1955	12.50	25.00	50.00

CAPITOL

Number	Title (A Side/B Side)	Yr	VG	VG+	NM
ST 1952 [S]	Piano Witchcraft	1963	6.25	12.50	25.00
T 1952 [M]	Piano Witchcraft	1963	5.00	10.00	20.00
ST 2355 [S]	The Art of Love	1965	5.00	10.00	20.00

EVEREST

Number	Title (A Side/B Side)	Yr	VG	VG+	NM
SDBR-1092 [S]	Playboy's Penthouse	196?	7.50	15.00	30.00
LPBR-5092 [M]	Playboy's Penthouse	196?	6.25	12.50	25.00

MGM

Number	Title (A Side/B Side)	Yr	VG	VG+	NM
SE-4501	Ages of Rock	1968	6.25	12.50	25.00

WESTMINSTER

Number	Title (A Side/B Side)	Yr	VG	VG+	NM
WLP-15001 [M]	Cool Coleman	195?	10.00	20.00	40.00

COLEMAN, EARL

PRESTIGE

Number	Title (A Side/B Side)	Yr	VG	VG+	NM
PRLP-7045 [M]	Earl Coleman Returns	1956	12.50	25.00	50.00
—Yellow label					
PRLP-7045 [M]	Earl Coleman Returns	196?	6.25	12.50	25.00
—Blue label, trident logo at right					

COLEMAN, GLORIA

IMPULSE!

Number	Title (A Side/B Side)	Yr	VG	VG+	NM
A-47 [M]	Soul Sisters	1963	6.25	12.50	25.00
AS-47 [S]	Soul Sisters	1963	7.50	15.00	30.00

COLEMAN, ORNETTE

ABC IMPULSE!

Number	Title (A Side/B Side)	Yr	VG	VG+	NM
AS-9178	Ornette at 12	1968	6.25	12.50	25.00
AS-9187	Crisis	1969	6.25	12.50	25.00

ARISTA FREEDOM

Number	Title (A Side/B Side)	Yr	VG	VG+	NM
AL 1900 [(2)]	The Great London Concert	1978	5.00	10.00	20.00

ARTISTS HOUSE

Number	Title (A Side/B Side)	Yr	VG	VG+	NM
1	Body Meta	1977	5.00	10.00	20.00
6	Soapsuds	1978	5.00	10.00	20.00

ATLANTIC

Number	Title (A Side/B Side)	Yr	VG	VG+	NM
1317 [M]	The Shape of Jazz to Come	1959	10.00	20.00	40.00
—"Bullseye" label					

Number	Title (A Side/B Side)	Yr	VG	VG+	NM
❑ 1317 [M]	The Shape of Jazz to Come	1960	6.25	12.50	25.00
—Multicolor label, white "fan" logo					
❑ SD 1317 [S]	The Shape of Jazz to Come	1959	12.50	25.00	50.00
—"Bullseye" label					
❑ SD 1317 [S]	The Shape of Jazz to Come	1960	7.50	15.00	30.00
—Multicolor label, white "fan" logo					
❑ SD 1317 [S]	The Shape of Jazz to Come	1963	5.00	10.00	20.00
—Multicolor label, black "fan" logo					
❑ 1327 [M]	Change of the Century	1960	7.50	15.00	30.00
—Multicolor label, white "fan" logo					
❑ SD 1327 [S]	Change of the Century	1960	10.00	20.00	40.00
—Multicolor label, white "fan" logo					
❑ SD 1327 [S]	Change of the Century	1963	5.00	10.00	20.00
—Multicolor label, black "fan" logo					
❑ SD 1327 [S]	Change of the Century	1976	2.50	5.00	10.00
❑ 1353 [M]	This Is Our Music	1960	7.50	15.00	30.00
—Multicolor label, white "fan" logo					
❑ SD 1353 [S]	This Is Our Music	1960	10.00	20.00	40.00
—Multicolor label, white "fan" logo					
❑ SD 1353 [S]	This Is Our Music	1963	5.00	10.00	20.00
—Multicolor label, black "fan" logo					
❑ 1364 [M]	Free Jazz	1961	10.00	20.00	40.00
—Multicolor label, white "fan" logo					
❑ 1364 [M]	Free Jazz	1963	5.00	10.00	20.00
—Multicolor label, black "fan" logo					
❑ SD 1364 [S]	Free Jazz	1961	12.50	25.00	50.00
—Multicolor label, white "fan" logo					
❑ SD 1364 [S]	Free Jazz	1963	6.25	12.50	25.00
—Multicolor label, black "fan" logo					
❑ 1378 [M]	Ornette	1961	7.50	15.00	30.00
—Multicolor label, white "fan" logo					
❑ SD 1378 [S]	Ornette	1961	10.00	20.00	40.00
—Multicolor label, white "fan" logo					
❑ SD 1378 [S]	Ornette	1963	5.00	10.00	20.00
—Multicolor label, black "fan" logo					
❑ 1394 [M]	Ornette on Tenor	1962	5.00	10.00	20.00
—Multicolor label, white "fan" logo					
❑ SD 1394 [S]	Ornette on Tenor	1962	6.25	12.50	25.00
—Multicolor label, black "fan" logo					
BLUE NOTE					
❑ BLP-4224 [M]	Ornette Coleman at the Golden Circle, Stockholm, Volume 1	1965	7.50	15.00	30.00
❑ BLP-4225 [M]	Ornette Coleman at the Golden Circle, Stockholm, Volume 2	1965	7.50	15.00	30.00
❑ BLP-4246 [M]	The Empty Foxhole	1966	7.50	15.00	30.00
❑ BST-84224 [S]	Ornette Coleman at the Golden Circle, Stockholm, Volume 1	1965	10.00	20.00	40.00
—"New York, USA" on label					
❑ BST-84225 [S]	Ornette Coleman at the Golden Circle, Stockholm, Volume 2	1965	10.00	20.00	40.00
—"New York, USA" on label					
❑ BST-84246 [S]	The Empty Foxhole	1966	10.00	20.00	40.00
—"New York, USA" on label					
❑ BST-84246 [S]	The Empty Foxhole	1967	7.50	15.00	30.00
—"A Division of Liberty Records" on label					
❑ BST-84287	New York Is Now!	1968	6.25	12.50	25.00
❑ BST-84356	Love Call	1970	5.00	10.00	20.00
COLUMBIA					
❑ KC 31061	Science Fiction	1972	5.00	10.00	20.00
❑ KC 31562	Skies of America	1972	5.00	10.00	20.00
❑ CG 33669 [(2)]	Science Fiction/Skies of America	1976	5.00	10.00	20.00
CONTEMPORARY					
❑ C-3551 [M]	The Music of Ornette Coleman –– Something Else!	1958	30.00	60.00	120.00
❑ M-3569 [M]	Tomorrow Is the Question	1959	20.00	40.00	80.00
❑ S-7551 [S]	The Music of Ornette Coleman — Something Else!	1959	20.00	40.00	80.00
❑ S-7569 [S]	Tomorrow Is the Question	1959	15.00	30.00	60.00
ESP-DISK'					
❑ 1006 [M]	Town Hall Concert, December 1962	1965	5.00	10.00	20.00
❑ S-1006 [S]	Town Hall Concert, December 1962	1965	6.25	12.50	25.00
FLYING DUTCHMAN					
❑ 123	Friends and Neighbors	1970	5.00	10.00	20.00
IAI					
❑ 373852	Classics, Volume 1	197?	5.00	10.00	20.00
INNER CITY					
❑ 1001	Live at the Hillcrest Club 1958	197?	5.00	10.00	20.00
RCA VICTOR					
❑ LPM-2982 [M]	The Music of Ornette Coleman	1964	6.25	12.50	25.00
❑ LSP-2982 [S]	The Music of Ornette Coleman	1964	7.50	15.00	30.00

COLES, JOHNNY

BLUE NOTE					
❑ BLP-4144 [M]	Little Johnny C	1963	10.00	20.00	40.00
—"New York, USA" on label!					
❑ BST-84144 [S]	Little Johnny C	1963	12.50	25.00	50.00
—"New York, USA" on label					
EPIC					
❑ LA 16015 [M]	The Warm Sound	1961	30.00	60.00	120.00
❑ BA 17015 [S]	The Warm Sound	1961	37.50	75.00	150.00
MAINSTREAM					
❑ MRL-346	Katumbo (Dance)	1972	5.00	10.00	20.00

COLLAGE, THE

SMASH					
❑ SRS-67101	The Collage	1968	5.00	10.00	20.00

COLLECTORS, THE

WARNER BROS.					
❑ W 1746 [M]	The Collectors	1968	12.50	25.00	50.00
—May be white label promo only					

Number	Title (A Side/B Side)	Yr	VG	VG+	NM
❑ WS 1746 [S]	The Collectors	1968	6.25	12.50	25.00
❑ WS 1774	Grass and Wild Strawberries	1969	6.25	12.50	25.00

COLLEGIANS, THE (1)

LOST-NITE					
❑ LLP-5 [10]	The Best of the Collegians	1981	2.50	5.00	10.00
—Red vinyl					
WINLEY					
❑ LP-6004 [M]	Sing Along with the Collegians	195?	100.00	200.00	400.00

COLLETTE, BUDDY

ABC-PARAMOUNT					
❑ ABC-179 [M]	Calm, Cool and Collette	1957	15.00	30.00	60.00
CHALLENGE					
❑ CHL-603 [M]	Everybody's Buddy	1958	12.50	25.00	50.00
CONTEMPORARY					
❑ C-3522 [M]	Man of Many Parts	1956	12.50	25.00	50.00
❑ C-3531 [M]	Nice Day with Buddy Collette	1957	12.50	25.00	50.00
❑ S-7522 [S]	Man of Many Parts	1959	10.00	20.00	40.00
❑ S-7531 [S]	Nice Day with Buddy Collette	1959	10.00	20.00	40.00
CROWN					
❑ CLP-5019 [M]	Bongo Madness	195?	6.25	12.50	25.00
DIG					
❑ LP-101 [M]	Tanganyika	1956	25.00	50.00	100.00
DOOTO					
❑ DTL-245 [M]	Buddy's Best	1957	15.00	30.00	60.00
—Black vinyl					
❑ DTL-245 [M]	Buddy's Best	1957	25.00	50.00	100.00
—Red vinyl					
EMARCY					
❑ MG-36133 [M]	Swingin' Shepherds	1958	12.50	25.00	50.00
❑ SR-80005 [S]	Swingin' Shepherds	1959	10.00	20.00	40.00
INTERLUDE					
❑ MO-505 [M]	Modern Interpretations of Porgy & Bess	196?	7.50	15.00	30.00
❑ ST-1005 [S]	Modern Interpretations of Porgy & Bess	196?	10.00	20.00	40.00
MERCURY					
❑ MG-20447 [M]	At the Cinema	1959	10.00	20.00	40.00
❑ SR-60132 [S]	At the Cinema	1959	10.00	20.00	40.00
MUSIC & SOUND					
❑ 1001 [M]	Polynesia	196?	7.50	15.00	30.00
❑ S-1001 [S]	Polynesia	196?	10.00	20.00	40.00
SPECIALTY					
❑ SP-5002 [M]	Jazz Loves Paris	1960	12.50	25.00	50.00
SURREY					
❑ SS-1009 [S]	Buddy Collette on Broadway	1965	5.00	10.00	20.00
TAMPA					
❑ TP-34 [M]	Star Studded Cast	1959	20.00	40.00	80.00
WORLD PACIFIC					
❑ ST-1823 [S]	Warm Winds	1964	6.25	12.50	25.00
❑ WP-1823 [M]	Warm Winds	1964	5.00	10.00	20.00

COLLIER, MITTY

CHESS					
❑ LP-1492 [M]	Shades of a Genius	1965	10.00	20.00	40.00
❑ LPS-1492 [S]	Shades of a Genius	1965	15.00	30.00	60.00

COLLINS, AARON

CROWN					
❑ CLP-5028 [M]	Calypso U.S.A.	1958	150.00	300.00	600.00

COLLINS, AL "JAZZBO"

CORAL					
❑ CRL 57035 [M]	East Coast Jazz Scene	1956	20.00	40.00	80.00
EVEREST					
❑ SDBR-1097 [S]	Swingin' at the Opera	1960	10.00	20.00	40.00
❑ LPBR-5097 [M]	Swingin' at the Opera	1960	7.50	15.00	30.00
IMPULSE!					
❑ A-9150 [M]	A Lovely Bunch of Al "Jazzbo" Collins	1967	10.00	20.00	40.00
❑ AS-9150 [S]	A Lovely Bunch of Al "Jazzbo" Collins	1967	7.50	15.00	30.00
OLD TOWN					
❑ LP-2001 [M]	In the Purple Grotto	1961	7.50	15.00	30.00

COLLINS, ALBERT

ALLIGATOR					
❑ AL-4713	Ice Pickin'	1978	2.50	5.00	10.00
❑ AL-4719	Frostbite	1980	2.50	5.00	10.00
❑ AL-4725	Frozen Alive!	1981	2.50	5.00	10.00
❑ AL-4730	Don't Lose Your Cool	1983	2.50	5.00	10.00
❑ AL-4733	Live in Japan	1984	2.50	5.00	10.00
❑ AL-4743	Showdown!	1985	2.50	5.00	10.00
—With Robert Cray and Johnny Copeland					
❑ AL-4752	Cold Snap	1986	2.50	5.00	10.00
BLUE THUMB					
❑ BTS 8	Truckin' with Albert Collins	1969	6.25	12.50	25.00
—Reissue of TCF Hall LP					
IMPERIAL					
❑ LP-12428	Love Can Be Found Anywhere	1968	7.50	15.00	30.00
❑ LP-12438	Trash Talkin'	1969	7.50	15.00	30.00
❑ LP-12449	The Compleat Albert Collins	1970	7.50	15.00	30.00
MOBILE FIDELITY					
❑ 1-217	Showdown!	1995	7.50	15.00	30.00
—With Robert Cray and Johnny Copeland; audiophile vinyl					
❑ 1-226	Cold Snap	1995	5.00	10.00	20.00
—Audiophile vinyl					
TCF HALL					
❑ 8002 [M]	The Cool Sound of Albert Collins	1965	75.00	150.00	300.00
TUMBLEWEED					
❑ TWS-103	There's Gotta Be a Change	1971	3.75	7.50	15.00

Number	Title (A Side/B Side)	Yr	VG	VG+	NM

COLLINS, DICK
RCA VICTOR
❏ LJM-1019 [M]	Horn of Plenty	1955	15.00	30.00	60.00
❏ LJM-1027 [M]	King Richard the Swing Hearted	1955	15.00	30.00	60.00

COLLINS, DOROTHY
CORAL
❏ CRL 57105 [M]	Dorothy Collins at Home	1957	6.25	12.50	25.00
❏ CRL 57106 [M]	Songs by Dorothy Collins	1957	6.25	12.50	25.00
❏ CRL 57150 [M]	Picnic	1958	6.25	12.50	25.00
EVEREST
❏ SDBR-1026 [S]	Singing and Swinging	196?	6.25	12.50	25.00
❏ LPBR-5026 [M]	Singing and Swinging	196?	5.00	10.00	20.00
TOP RANK
❏ TM-340 [M]	A New Way to Travel	1959	6.25	12.50	25.00

COLLINS, JOYCE
JAZZLAND
❏ JLP-24 [M]	The Girl Here Plays Mean Piano	1960	6.25	12.50	25.00
❏ JLP-924 [S]	The Girl Here Plays Mean Piano	1960	7.50	15.00	30.00

COLLINS, JUDY
DCC COMPACT CLASSICS
❏ LPZ-2067	Colors of the Day/The Best of Judy Collins	1998	6.25	12.50	25.00
—Audiophile vinyl					
DIRECT DISK
❏ SD-16607	Judith	1980	10.00	20.00	40.00
—Audiophile vinyl					
ELEKTRA
❏ JC-1 [DJ]	Judy Collins	1967	3.75	7.50	15.00
—Promo-only compilation of six songs, each in mono on one side, stereo on the other					
❏ 6E-111	Judith	1977	2.00	4.00	8.00
—Reissue of 7E-1032					
❏ 6E-171	Hard Times for Lovers	1979	2.50	5.00	10.00
❏ EKL-209 [M]	Maid of Constant Sorrow	1961	10.00	20.00	40.00
—"Guitar player" label					
❏ EKL-209 [M]	Maid of Constant Sorrow	1966	5.00	10.00	20.00
—Gold/tan label					
❏ EKL-222 [M]	Golden Apples of the Sun	1962	7.50	15.00	30.00
—"Guitar player" label					
❏ EKL-222 [M]	Golden Apples of the Sun	1966	5.00	10.00	20.00
—Gold/tan label					
❏ EKL-243 [M]	Judy Collins #3	1963	7.50	15.00	30.00
—"Guitar player" label					
❏ EKL-243 [M]	Judy Collins #3	1966	5.00	10.00	20.00
—Gold/tan label					
❏ 6E-253	Running for My Life	1980	2.50	5.00	10.00
❏ EKL-280 [M]	Judy Collins' Concert	1964	7.50	15.00	30.00
—"Guitar player" label					
❏ EKL-280 [M]	Judy Collins' Concert	1966	5.00	10.00	20.00
—Gold/tan label					
❏ EKL-300 [M]	Judy Collins' Fifth Album	1965	7.50	15.00	30.00
—"Guitar player" label					
❏ EKL-300 [M]	Judy Collins' Fifth Album	1966	5.00	10.00	20.00
—Gold/tan label					
❏ EKL-320 [M]	In My Life	1966	5.00	10.00	20.00
❏ DS 500	Judy	1969	3.75	7.50	15.00
—Columbia Record Club exclusive; red label with large stylized "E"					
❏ 7E-1032	Judith	1975	3.00	6.00	12.00
❏ EQ-1032 [Q]	Judith	1975	5.00	10.00	20.00
❏ 7E-1076	Bread and Roses	1976	2.50	5.00	10.00
❏ EKL-4012 [M]	Wildflowers	1967	6.25	12.50	25.00
❏ EQ-5030 [Q]	Colors of the Day/The Best of Judy Collins	1973	5.00	10.00	20.00
❏ 8E-6002 [(2)]	So Early in the Spring: The First 15 Years	1977	3.00	6.00	12.00
❏ EKS-7209 [R]	Maid of Constant Sorrow	196?	3.00	6.00	12.00
—Gold/tan label or red label with large stylized "E"					
❏ EKS-7209 [R]	Maid of Constant Sorrow	1971	2.50	5.00	10.00
—Butterfly label, no Warner Communications logo					
❏ EKS-7209 [R]	Maid of Constant Sorrow	1975	2.00	4.00	8.00
—Any label with Warner Communications logo					
❏ EKS-7222 [R]	Golden Apples of the Sun	196?	3.00	6.00	12.00
—Gold/tan label or red label with large stylized "E"					
❏ EKS-7222 [R]	Golden Apples of the Sun	1971	2.50	5.00	10.00
—Butterfly label, no Warner Communications logo					
❏ EKS-7222 [R]	Golden Apples of the Sun	1975	2.00	4.00	8.00
—Any label with Warner Communications logo					
❏ EKS-7243 [S]	Judy Collins #3	1963	10.00	20.00	40.00
—"Guitar player" label					
❏ EKS-7243 [S]	Judy Collins #3	1966	6.25	12.50	25.00
—Gold/tan label					
❏ EKS-7243 [S]	Judy Collins #3	1969	3.75	7.50	15.00
—Red label with large stylized "E"					
❏ EKS-7243 [S]	Judy Collins #3	1971	2.50	5.00	10.00
—Butterfly label, no Warner Communications logo					
❏ EKS-7243 [S]	Judy Collins #3	1975	2.00	4.00	8.00
—Any label with Warner Communications logo					
❏ EKS-7280 [S]	Judy Collins' Concert	1964	10.00	20.00	40.00
—"Guitar player" label					
❏ EKS-7280 [S]	Judy Collins' Concert	1966	6.25	12.50	25.00
—Gold/tan label					
❏ EKS-7280 [S]	Judy Collins' Concert	1969	3.75	7.50	15.00
—Red label with large stylized "E"					
❏ EKS-7280 [S]	Judy Collins' Concert	1971	3.00	6.00	12.00
—Butterfly label, no Warner Communications logo					
❏ EKS-7280 [S]	Judy Collins' Concert	1975	2.00	4.00	8.00
—Any label with Warner Communications logo					
❏ EKS-7300 [S]	Judy Collins' Fifth Album	1965	10.00	20.00	40.00
—"Guitar player" label					
❏ EKS-7300 [S]	Judy Collins' Fifth Album	1966	6.25	12.50	25.00
—Gold/tan label					
❏ EKS-7300 [S]	Judy Collins' Fifth Album	1969	3.75	7.50	15.00
—Red label with large stylized "E"					

Number	Title (A Side/B Side)	Yr	VG	VG+	NM
❏ EKS-7300 [S]	Judy Collins' Fifth Album	1971	3.00	6.00	12.00
—Butterfly label, no Warner Communications logo					
❏ EKS-7300 [S]	Judy Collins' Fifth Album	1975	2.00	4.00	8.00
—Any label with Warner Communications logo					
❏ EKS-7320 [S]	In My Life	1966	6.25	12.50	25.00
❏ 60001	Times of Our Lives	1982	2.50	5.00	10.00
❏ 60304	Home Again	1985	2.50	5.00	10.00
❏ EKS-74012 [S]	Wildflowers	1967	5.00	10.00	20.00
—Gold/tan label					
❏ EKS-74012 [S]	Wildflowers	1969	3.75	7.50	15.00
—Red label with large stylized "E"					
❏ EKS-74012 [S]	Wildflowers	1971	3.00	6.00	12.00
—Butterfly label, no Warner Communications logo					
❏ EKS-74012 [S]	Wildflowers	1975	2.00	4.00	8.00
—Any label with Warner Communications logo					
❏ EKS-74027	In My Life	1968	5.00	10.00	20.00
—Reissue of 7320; gold/tan label					
❏ EKS-74027	In My Life	1969	3.75	7.50	15.00
—Red label with large stylized "E"					
❏ EKS-74027	In My Life	1971	3.00	6.00	12.00
—Butterfly label, no Warner Communications logo					
❏ EKS-74027	In My Life	1975	2.00	4.00	8.00
—Any label with Warner Communications logo					
❏ EKS-74033	Who Knows Where the Time Goes	1968	5.00	10.00	20.00
—Gold/tan label					
❏ EKS-74033	Who Knows Where the Time Goes	1969	3.75	7.50	15.00
—Red label with large stylized "E"					
❏ EKS-74033	Who Knows Where the Time Goes	1971	3.00	6.00	12.00
—Butterfly label, no Warner Communications logo					
❏ EKS-74033	Who Knows Where the Time Goes	1975	2.00	4.00	8.00
—Any label with Warner Communications logo					
❏ EKS-74055	Recollections	1969	3.75	7.50	15.00
—Red label with large stylized "E"					
❏ EKS-74055	Recollections	1971	3.00	6.00	12.00
—Butterfly label, no Warner Communications logo					
❏ EKS-74055	Recollections	1975	2.00	4.00	8.00
—Any label with Warner Communications logo					
❏ EKS-75010	Whales & Nightingales	1970	3.00	6.00	12.00
—Butterfly label, no Warner Communications logo					
❏ EKS-75010	Whales & Nightingales	1975	2.00	4.00	8.00
—Any label with Warner Communications logo					
❏ EKS-75014	Living	1971	3.00	6.00	12.00
—Butterfly label, no Warner Communications logo					
❏ EKS-75014	Living	1975	2.00	4.00	8.00
—Any label with Warner Communications logo					
❏ EKS-75030	Colors of the Day/The Best of Judy Collins	1972	3.00	6.00	12.00
—Butterfly label, no Warner Communications logo					
❏ EKS-75030	Colors of the Day/The Best of Judy Collins	1975	2.00	4.00	8.00
—Any label with Warner Communications logo					
❏ EKS-75053	True Stories and Other Dreams	1973	3.00	6.00	12.00
—Butterfly label					
❏ EKS-75053	True Stories and Other Dreams	1980	2.00	4.00	8.00
—Red or red/black label					
GOLD CASTLE
❏ D1-71302	Trust Your Heart	1989	3.00	6.00	12.00
—Reissue of 171002					
❏ D1-71318	Sanity and Grace	1989	3.00	6.00	12.00
❏ 171002	Trust Your Heart	1988	3.00	6.00	12.00
PAIR
❏ PDL2-1141 [(2)]	Her Finest Hour	1986	3.00	6.00	12.00
WARNER SPECIAL PRODUCTS
❏ 61-6462 [(4)]	Judy Collins	1981	20.00	40.00	80.00
—Book-of-the-Month Club exclusive					

COLLINS, LYN
PEOPLE
❏ PE-5602	Think (About It)	1972	15.00	30.00	60.00
❏ PE-6605	Check Me Out	1975	12.50	25.00	50.00

COLLINS, SHIRLEY AND DOROTHY
HARVEST
❏ SKAO-370	Anthems in Eden	1969	12.50	25.00	50.00

COLLINS, TOMMY
CAPITOL
❏ T 776 [M]	Words and Music Country Style	1957	25.00	50.00	100.00
❏ T 1125 [M]	Light of the Lord	1959	25.00	50.00	100.00
❏ T 1196 [M]	This Is Tommy Collins	1959	15.00	30.00	60.00
❏ ST 1436 [S]	Songs I Love to Sing	1961	15.00	30.00	60.00
❏ T 1436 [M]	Songs I Love to Sing	1961	12.50	25.00	50.00
COLUMBIA
❏ CL 2510 [M]	The Dynamic Tommy Collins	1966	7.50	15.00	30.00
❏ CL 2778 [M]	Tommy Collins On Tour — His Most Requested Songs	1968	15.00	30.00	60.00
❏ CS 9310 [S]	The Dynamic Tommy Collins	1966	10.00	20.00	40.00
❏ CS 9578 [S]	Tommy Collins On Tour — His Most Requested Songs	1968	7.50	15.00	30.00
STARDAY
❏ SLP-474	Tommy Collins Callin'	1972	5.00	10.00	20.00
TOWER
❏ DT 5021 [R]	Let's Live a Little	1966	5.00	10.00	20.00
❏ T 5021 [M]	Let's Live a Little	1966	7.50	15.00	30.00
❏ DT 5107 [R]	Shindig	1967	5.00	10.00	20.00
❏ T 5107 [M]	Shindig	1967	10.00	20.00	40.00

COLMAN, RONALD
DECCA
❏ DLP 8010 [M]	A Christmas Carol/Mr. Pickwick's Christmas	1949	5.00	10.00	20.00
—Side 2 read by Charles Laughton					
MCA
❏ 15010	A Christmas Carol/Mr. Pickwick's Christmas	1973	2.50	5.00	10.00
—Side 2 read by Charles Laughton; reissue of Decca LP					

Number	Title (A Side/B Side)	Yr	VG	VG+	NM
COLONNA, JERRY					
DECCA					
❏ DL 5540 [10]	Music? For Screaming!!!	1955	15.00	30.00	60.00
LIBERTY					
❏ LRP-3046 [M]	Let's All Sing with Jerry Colonna	1957	10.00	20.00	40.00
❏ SL-9004 [M]	Along the Dixieland Hi-Fi Way	1957	10.00	20.00	40.00
COLOSSEUM					
ABC DUNHILL					
❏ DS-50062	Those Who Are About to Die Salute You	1969	5.00	10.00	20.00
❏ DS-50079	The Grass Is Green	1970	5.00	10.00	20.00
❏ DSX-50101	Daughter of Time	1971	3.75	7.50	15.00
WARNER BROS.					
❏ PRO 500 [DJ]	Colosseum Live	1972	3.75	7.50	15.00
—Highlights for radio					
❏ 2WS 1942 [(2)]	Colosseum Live	1972	3.75	7.50	15.00
COLOURS					
DOT					
❏ DLP-3854 [M]	Colours	1968	12.50	25.00	50.00
—Record has a black label, resembling a stock copy, but it is in a stereo cover with "Monaural" and "Promotional Copy Not for Sale" stickers on front					
❏ DLP-25854 [S]	Colours	1968	6.25	12.50	25.00
❏ DLP-25935	Atmosphere	1969	6.25	12.50	25.00
COLTER, JESSI					
CAPITOL					
❏ ST-11363	I'm Jessi Colter	1975	2.50	5.00	10.00
❏ ST-11477	Jessi	1976	2.50	5.00	10.00
❏ ST-11543	Diamond in the Rough	1976	2.50	5.00	10.00
❏ ST-11583	Mirriam	1977	2.50	5.00	10.00
❏ ST-11863	That's the Way a Cowboy Rocks and Rolls	1978	2.50	5.00	10.00
❏ ST-12185	Ridin' Shotgun	1981	2.50	5.00	10.00
❏ ST-511863	That's the Way a Cowboy Rocks and Rolls	1978	3.00	6.00	12.00
—Columbia House edition					
RCA VICTOR					
❏ LSP-4333	Country Star	1970	5.00	10.00	20.00
COLTRANE, JOHN					
ABC IMPULSE!					
❏ AS-9148	Cosmic Music	1969	5.00	10.00	20.00
—Credited to "Alice and John Coltrane"; reissue of Coltrane LP					
❏ AS-9161	Selflessness	1969	5.00	10.00	20.00
❏ AS-9165	Transition	1969	5.00	10.00	20.00
❏ AS-9200 [(2)]	Greatest Years	1971	5.00	10.00	20.00
❏ AS-9202 [(2)]	Live in Seattle	1971	5.00	10.00	20.00
❏ AS-9211	Sun Ship	1971	5.00	10.00	20.00
ATLANTIC					
❏ 1311 [M]	Giant Steps	1959	12.50	25.00	50.00
—Black label					
❏ 1311 [M]	Giant Steps	1960	6.25	12.50	25.00
—Orange and purple label, white fan logo					
❏ SD 1311 [S]	Giant Steps	1959	15.00	30.00	60.00
—Green label					
❏ SD 1311 [S]	Giant Steps	1960	6.25	12.50	25.00
—Green and blue label, white fan logo					
❏ 1354 [M]	Coltrane Jazz	1960	7.50	15.00	30.00
—Orange and purple label, white fan logo					
❏ SD 1354 [S]	Coltrane Jazz	1960	7.50	15.00	30.00
—Green and blue label, white fan logo					
❏ 1361 [M]	My Favorite Things	1961	7.50	15.00	30.00
—Orange and purple label, white fan logo					
❏ SD 1361 [S]	My Favorite Things	1961	7.50	15.00	30.00
—Green and blue label, white fan logo					
❏ 1373 [M]	Ole' Coltrane	1961	7.50	15.00	30.00
—Orange and purple label, white fan logo					
❏ SD 1373 [S]	Ole' Coltrane	1961	7.50	15.00	30.00
—Green and blue label, white fan logo					
❏ 1382 [M]	Coltrane Plays the Blues	1962	7.50	15.00	30.00
❏ SD 1382 [S]	Coltrane Plays the Blues	1962	7.50	51.00	30.00
—Green and blue label, black fan logo					
❏ 1419 [M]	Coltrane's Sound	1964	6.25	12.50	25.00
❏ SD 1419 [S]	Coltrane's Sound	1964	6.25	12.50	25.00
—Green and blue label, black fan logo					
❏ 1451 [M]	The Avant Garde	1966	6.25	12.50	25.00
❏ SD 1451 [S]	The Avant Garde	1966	6.25	12.50	25.00
—Green and blue label, black fan logo					
ATLANTIC/RHINO					
❏ R1-71984 [(12)]	The Heavyweight Champion: The Complete Atlantic Recordings	1995	62.50	125.00	250.00
—Box set with liner notes; albums pressed on 150-gram vinyl					
❏ R1-71984 [(12)]	The Heavyweight Champion: The Complete Atlantic Recordings (Year 2000 Second Edition)	2000	50.00	100.00	200.00
—Limited edition of 1,500, un-numbered, on 180-gram vinyl; pressed in the U.S. for export					
❏ R1-71984 [(12)]	The Heavyweight Champion: The Complete Atlantic Recordings (Year 2000 Second Edition)	2000	50.00	100.00	200.00
—Limited, numbered edition of 1,500 copies on 180-gram vinyl					
BLUE NOTE					
❏ BLP-1577 [M]	Blue Train	1957	25.00	50.00	100.00
—Regular version, W. 63rd St., NYC address on label					
❏ BLP-1577 [M]	Blue Train	1957	37.50	75.00	150.00
—"Deep groove" version (deep indentation under label on both sides)					
❏ BLP-1577 [M]	Blue Train	196?	7.50	15.00	30.00
—New York, USA address on label					
❏ BST-1577 [S]	Blue Train	1959	20.00	40.00	80.00
—Regular version, W. 63rd St., NYC address on label					
❏ BST-1577 [S]	Blue Train	1959	30.00	60.00	120.00
—"Deep groove" version (deep indentation under label on both sides)					
❏ BST-1577 [S]	Blue Train	196?	6.25	12.50	25.00
—New York, USA address on label					

Number	Title (A Side/B Side)	Yr	VG	VG+	NM
COLTRANE					
❏ AU-4950	Cosmic Music	1966	75.00	150.00	300.00
❏ AU-5000	Cosmic Music	1966	50.00	100.00	200.00
DCC COMPACT CLASSICS					
❏ LPZ-2032	Lush Life	1997	15.00	30.00	60.00
—Audiophile vinyl					
IMPULSE!					
❏ A-6 [M]	Africa/Brass	1961	7.50	15.00	30.00
❏ AS-6 [S]	Africa/Brass	1961	10.00	20.00	40.00
❏ A-10 [M]	Live at the Village Vanguard	1962	7.50	15.00	30.00
❏ AS-10 [S]	Live at the Village Vanguard	1962	10.00	20.00	40.00
❏ A-21 [M]	Coltrane	1962	7.50	15.00	30.00
❏ AS-21 [S]	Coltrane	1962	10.00	20.00	40.00
❏ A-30 [M]	Duke Ellington and John Coltrane	1963	7.50	15.00	30.00
❏ AS-30 [S]	Duke Ellington and John Coltrane	1963	10.00	20.00	40.00
❏ A-32 [M]	Ballads	1963	7.50	15.00	30.00
❏ AS-32 [S]	Ballads	1963	10.00	20.00	40.00
❏ A-40 [M]	John Coltrane + Johnny Hartman	1963	10.00	20.00	40.00
❏ AS-40 [S]	John Coltrane + Johnny Hartman	1963	12.50	25.00	50.00
❏ A-42 [M]	Impressions	1963	6.25	12.50	25.00
❏ AS-42 [S]	Impressions	1963	7.50	15.00	30.00
❏ A-50 [M]	Coltrane Live at Birdland	1963	6.25	12.50	25.00
❏ AS-50 [S]	Coltrane Live at Birdland	1963	7.50	15.00	30.00
❏ A-66 [M]	Crescent	1964	6.25	12.50	25.00
❏ AS-66 [S]	Crescent	1964	7.50	15.00	30.00
❏ A-77 [M]	A Love Supreme	1965	7.50	15.00	30.00
❏ AS-77 [S]	A Love Supreme	1965	10.00	20.00	40.00
❏ A-85 [M]	The John Coltrane Quartet Plays	1965	6.25	12.50	25.00
❏ AS-85 [S]	The John Coltrane Quartet Plays	1965	7.50	15.00	30.00
❏ A-94 [M]	New Thing at Newport	1965	6.25	12.50	25.00
❏ AS-94 [S]	New Thing at Newport	1965	7.50	15.00	30.00
❏ A-95 [M]	Ascension	1965	20.00	40.00	80.00
—Without "Edition II" in dead wax					
❏ A-95 [M]	Ascension	1966	6.25	12.50	25.00
—With "Edition II" in dead wax					
❏ AS-95 [S]	Ascension	1965	25.00	50.00	100.00
—Without "Edition II" in dead wax					
❏ AS-95 [S]	Ascension	1966	7.50	15.00	30.00
—With "Edition II" in dead wax					
❏ A-9106 [M]	Kulu Se Mama	1966	6.25	12.50	25.00
❏ AS-9106 [S]	Kulu Se Mama	1966	7.50	15.00	30.00
❏ A-9110 [M]	Meditations	1966	6.25	12.50	25.00
❏ AS-9110 [S]	Meditations	1966	7.50	15.00	30.00
❏ A-9120 [M]	Expression	1967	7.50	15.00	30.00
❏ AS-9120 [S]	Expression	1967	6.25	12.50	25.00
❏ A-9124 [M]	Live at the Village Vanguard Again!	1967	7.50	15.00	30.00
❏ AS-9124 [S]	Live at the Village Vanguard Again!	1967	6.25	12.50	25.00
❏ A-9140 [M]	Om	1967	7.50	15.00	30.00
❏ AS-9140 [S]	Om	1967	6.25	12.50	25.00
PRESTIGE					
❏ PRLP-7105 [M]	Coltrane	1957	25.00	50.00	100.00
—Yellow label					
❏ PRLP-7105 [M]	Coltrane	1964	7.50	15.00	30.00
—Blue label with trident logo					
❏ PRLP-7123 [M]	John Coltrane and the Red Garland Trio	1957	25.00	50.00	100.00
—Yellow label					
❏ PRLP-7123 [M]	Traneing In	1964	7.50	15.00	30.00
—Blue label with trident logo; reissue with new title					
❏ PRLP-7142 [M]	Soultrane	1958	20.00	40.00	80.00
—Yellow label					
❏ PRLP-7142 [M]	Soultrane	1964	6.25	12.50	25.00
—Blue label with trident logo					
❏ PRLP-7158 [M]	Cattin' with Coltrane and Quinichette	1959	20.00	40.00	80.00
—Yellow label					
❏ PRLP-7158 [M]	Cattin' with Coltrane and Quinichette	1964	6.25	12.50	25.00
—Blue label with trident logo					
❏ PRLP-7188 [M]	Lush Life	1960	20.00	40.00	80.00
—Yellow label					
❏ PRLP-7188 [M]	Lush Life	1964	6.25	12.50	25.00
—Blue label with trident logo					
❏ PRLP-7213 [M]	Settin' the Pace	1961	20.00	40.00	80.00
—Yellow label					
❏ PRLP-7213 [M]	Settin' the Pace	1964	6.25	12.50	25.00
—Blue label with trident logo					
❏ PRLP-7243 [M]	Standard Coltrane	1962	10.00	20.00	40.00
—Yellow label					
❏ PRLP-7243 [M]	Standard Coltrane	1964	6.25	12.50	25.00
—Blue label with trident logo					
❏ PRST-7243 [S]	Standard Coltrane	1962	12.50	25.00	50.00
—Silver label					
❏ PRST-7243 [S]	Standard Coltrane	1964	6.25	12.50	25.00
—Blue label with trident logo					
❏ PRLP-7247 [M]	Mating Call	1962	10.00	20.00	40.00
—Yellow label					
❏ PRLP-7247 [M]	Mating Call	1964	6.25	12.50	25.00
—Blue label with trident logo					
❏ PRST-7247 [R]	Mating Call	196?	6.25	12.50	25.00
—Silver label					
❏ PRST-7247 [R]	Mating Call	1964	5.00	10.00	20.00
—Blue label with trident logo					
❏ PRLP-7249 [M]	Tenor Conclave	1962	10.00	20.00	40.00
—Yellow label					
❏ PRLP-7249 [M]	Tenor Conclave	1964	6.25	12.50	25.00
—Blue label with trident logo					
❏ PRST-7249 [R]	Tenor Conclave	196?	6.25	12.50	25.00
—Silver label					
❏ PRST-7249 [R]	Tenor Conclave	1964	5.00	10.00	20.00
—Blue label with trident logo					
❏ PRLP-7268 [M]	Stardust	1963	10.00	20.00	40.00
—Yellow label					
❏ PRLP-7268 [M]	Stardust	1964	6.25	12.50	25.00
—Blue label with trident logo					

Number	Title (A Side/B Side)	Yr	VG	VG+	NM
☐ PRST-7268 [S]	Stardust	1963	10.00	20.00	40.00
—Silver label					
☐ PRST-7268 [S]	Stardust	1964	6.25	12.50	25.00
—Blue label with trident logo					
☐ PRLP-7280 [M]	Dakar	1963	10.00	20.00	40.00
—Yellow label					
☐ PRLP-7280 [M]	Dakar	1964	6.25	12.50	25.00
—Blue label with trident logo					
☐ PRST-7280 [S]	Dakar	1963	10.00	20.00	40.00
—Silver label					
☐ PRST-7280 [S]	Dakar	1964	6.25	12.50	25.00
—Blue label with trident logo					
☐ PRLP-7292 [M]	The Believer	1964	6.25	12.50	25.00
—Blue label with trident logo					
☐ PRLP-7292 [M]	The Believer	1964	10.00	20.00	40.00
—Yellow label					
☐ PRST-7292 [S]	The Believer	1964	6.25	12.50	25.00
—Blue label with trident logo					
☐ PRST-7292 [S]	The Believer	1964	10.00	20.00	40.00
—Silver label					
☐ PRLP-7316 [M]	Black Pearls	1964	6.25	12.50	25.00
—Blue label with trident logo					
☐ PRLP-7316 [M]	Black Pearls	1964	10.00	20.00	40.00
—Yellow label					
☐ PRST-7316 [S]	Black Pearls	1964	6.25	12.50	25.00
—Blue label with trident logo					
☐ PRST-7316 [S]	Black Pearls	1964	10.00	20.00	40.00
—Silver label					
☐ PRLP-7353 [M]	Bahia	1965	6.25	12.50	25.00
☐ PRST-7353 [S]	Bahia	1965	6.25	12.50	25.00
☐ PRLP-7378 [M]	The Last Trane	1965	6.25	12.50	25.00
☐ PRST-7378 [S]	The Last Trane	1965	6.25	12.50	25.00
☐ PRLP-7426 [M]	John Coltrane Plays for Lovers	1966	6.25	12.50	25.00
☐ PRST-7426 [S]	John Coltrane Plays for Lovers	1966	6.25	12.50	25.00
☐ PRLP-7531 [M]	Soultrane	1967	6.25	12.50	25.00

SOLID STATE

Number	Title (A Side/B Side)	Yr	VG	VG+	NM
☐ SM-17025 [M]	Coltrane Time	1968	6.25	12.50	25.00

UNITED ARTISTS

Number	Title (A Side/B Side)	Yr	VG	VG+	NM
☐ UAJ-14001 [M]	Coltrane Time	1962	10.00	20.00	40.00
☐ UAJS-15001 [S]	Coltrane Time	1962	12.50	25.00	50.00

COLUMBIA CHOIR, THE
COLUMBIA

Number	Title (A Side/B Side)	Yr	VG	VG+	NM
☐ CL (# unk) [10]	The Christmas Mood	1954	12.50	25.00	50.00
—First appearance of the "Albert Burt Carols" on record					
☐ CL 1051 [M]	The Christmas Mood	1957	7.50	15.00	30.00
—Expanded version of 10-inch LP with B-side instrumentals					
☐ CL 2546 [10]	The Christmas Mood	1955	10.00	20.00	40.00
—"House Party Series" reissue					

COLUMBO, CHRIS
STRAND

Number	Title (A Side/B Side)	Yr	VG	VG+	NM
☐ SL-1044 [M]	Jazz Rediscovered	1962	7.50	15.00	30.00
☐ SLS-1044 [S]	Jazz Rediscovered	1962	10.00	20.00	40.00
☐ SL-1095 [M]	Summertime	1963	7.50	15.00	30.00
☐ SLS-1095 [S]	Summertime	1963	10.00	20.00	40.00

COLWELL-WINFIELD BLUES BAND, THE
VERVE FORECAST

Number	Title (A Side/B Side)	Yr	VG	VG+	NM
☐ FTS-3056	Cold Wind Blues	1968	5.00	10.00	20.00

ZA-ZOO

Number	Title (A Side/B Side)	Yr	VG	VG+	NM
☐ 1	Live Bust	1971	7.50	15.00	30.00

COLYER, KEN
LONDON

Number	Title (A Side/B Side)	Yr	VG	VG+	NM
☐ PB 904 [10]	New Orleans to London	1954	12.50	25.00	50.00
☐ LL 1340 [M]	Back to the Delta	1956	10.00	20.00	40.00
☐ LL 1618 [M]	Club Session with Colyer	1957	10.00	20.00	40.00

COMFORTABLE CHAIR, THE
ODE

Number	Title (A Side/B Side)	Yr	VG	VG+	NM
☐ Z12 44005	The Comfortable Chair	1968	5.00	10.00	20.00

COMMANDERS, THE
DECCA

Number	Title (A Side/B Side)	Yr	VG	VG+	NM
☐ DL 8117 [M]	Dance Party	1955	10.00	20.00	40.00
—Led by Eddie Grady					

COMMON PEOPLE, THE
CAPITOL

Number	Title (A Side/B Side)	Yr	VG	VG+	NM
☐ ST-266	Of the People/By the People/For the People/From the Common People	1969	25.00	50.00	100.00

COMO, PERRY
PAIR

Number	Title (A Side/B Side)	Yr	VG	VG+	NM
☐ PDL2-1001 [(2)]	Easy Listening	1986	3.00	6.00	12.00
☐ PDL2-1038 [(2)]	Love Moods	1986	3.00	6.00	12.00
☐ PDL2-1112 [(2)]	Blue Skies	1986	3.00	6.00	12.00

PICKWICK

Number	Title (A Side/B Side)	Yr	VG	VG+	NM
☐ CAS-660 [R]	Perry Como Sings Merry Christmas Music	1977	2.00	4.00	8.00
—Reissue of RCA Camden CAS-660 with another new cover					

RCA

Number	Title (A Side/B Side)	Yr	VG	VG+	NM
☐ 6368-1-R	Perry Como Today	1988	2.50	5.00	10.00

RCA CAMDEN

Number	Title (A Side/B Side)	Yr	VG	VG+	NM
☐ CAL-403 [M]	Dream Along with Me	1957	5.00	10.00	20.00
☐ CAS-403(e) [R]	Dream Along with Me	1962	2.50	5.00	10.00
☐ CAL-440 [M]	Perry Como Sings Just for You	1958	3.75	7.50	15.00
☐ CAS-440(e) [R]	Perry Como Sings Just for You	1962	2.50	5.00	10.00
☐ CAL-511 [M]	Como's Wednesday Night Music Hall	1959	5.00	10.00	20.00
☐ CAL-582 [M]	Dreamer's Holiday	1960	3.75	7.50	15.00
☐ CAL-660 [M]	Perry Como Sings Merry Christmas Music	1961	3.00	6.00	12.00
—Reissue of RCA Victor LPM-1243 with new cover					
☐ CAS-660(e) [R]	Perry Como Sings Merry Christmas Music	1961	2.50	5.00	10.00
☐ CAL-694 [M]	Make Someone Happy	1962	3.00	6.00	12.00
☐ CAL-742 [M]	An Evening with Perry Como	196?	3.75	7.50	15.00
☐ CAL-805 [M]	Love Makes the World Go 'Round	1964	3.00	6.00	12.00
☐ CAS-805 [S]	Love Makes the World Go 'Round	1964	2.50	5.00	10.00
☐ CAL-858 [M]	Somebody Loves Me	1965	3.00	6.00	12.00
☐ CAS-858 [S]	Somebody Loves Me	1965	2.50	5.00	10.00
☐ CAL-941 [M]	No Other Love	1966	3.00	6.00	12.00
☐ CAS-941 [S]	No Other Love	1966	2.50	5.00	10.00
☐ CAL-2122 [M]	Hello Young Lovers	1967	3.75	7.50	15.00
☐ CAS-2122 [R]	Hello Young Lovers	1967	2.50	5.00	10.00
☐ CAL-2201 [M]	You Are Never Far Away	1968	3.75	7.50	15.00
☐ CAS-2201 [S]	You Are Never Far Away	1968	2.50	5.00	10.00
☐ CAS-2299	The Lord's Prayer	1968	2.50	5.00	10.00
☐ CAS-2482	Door of Dreams	1971	2.50	5.00	10.00
☐ CAS-2547	The Shadow of Your Smile	1972	2.50	5.00	10.00
☐ CAS-2609	Dream On Little Dreamer	1972	2.50	5.00	10.00
☐ CXS-9002 [(2)]	Easy Listening	1972	3.00	6.00	12.00

RCA CUSTOM EDITION

Number	Title (A Side/B Side)	Yr	VG	VG+	NM
☐ DRL1-0010	Seattle	1973	3.00	6.00	12.00

RCA SPECIAL PRODUCTS

Number	Title (A Side/B Side)	Yr	VG	VG+	NM
☐ DPL1-0193	By Special Request	1974	3.00	6.00	12.00
—Sold only at Sylvania dealers					

RCA VICTOR

Number	Title (A Side/B Side)	Yr	VG	VG+	NM
☐ LPM-51 [10]	Merry Christmas	1951	10.00	20.00	40.00
☐ APD1-0100 [Q]	And I Love You So	1974	3.75	7.50	15.00
☐ APL1-0100	And I Love You So	1973	2.50	5.00	10.00
☐ ACL1-0444	The Sweetest Sounds	1974	2.50	5.00	10.00
☐ APD1-0585 [Q]	Perry	1974	3.75	7.50	15.00
☐ CPL1-0585	Perry	1974	2.50	5.00	10.00
☐ APD1-0863 [Q]	Just Out of Reach	1975	3.75	7.50	15.00
☐ APL1-0863	Just Out of Reach	1975	2.50	5.00	10.00
☐ ANL1-0972	Pure Gold	1975	2.50	5.00	10.00
☐ LSPX-1001	Perry Como at the International Hotel, Las Vegas	1970	3.75	7.50	15.00
☐ LOP-1004 [M]	Saturday Night with Mr. C.	1958	6.25	12.50	25.00
☐ LOP-1007 [M]	Como's Golden Records	1958	6.25	12.50	25.00
☐ LPM-1085 [M]	So Smooth	1955	7.50	15.00	30.00
☐ LPM-1172 [M]	I Believe	1956	7.50	15.00	30.00
☐ LSP-1172(e) [R]	I Believe	1962	3.00	6.00	12.00
☐ LPM-1176 [M]	Relaxing with Perry Como	1956	7.50	15.00	30.00
☐ LPM-1177 [M]	A Sentimental Date with Perry Como	1956	7.50	15.00	30.00
☐ LPM-1191 [M]	Hits from Broadway Shows	1956	7.50	15.00	30.00
☐ LPM-1243 [M]	Perry Como Sings Merry Christmas Music	1956	7.50	15.00	30.00
☐ LPM-1463 [M]	We Get Letters	1957	6.25	12.50	25.00
☐ CPL1-1752	A Legendary Performer	1976	2.50	5.00	10.00
☐ LPM-1885 [M]	When You Come to the End of the Day	1958	5.00	10.00	20.00
☐ LSP-1885 [S]	When You Come to the End of the Day	1958	7.50	15.00	30.00
☐ ANL1-1929	The Perry Como Christmas Album	1976	2.00	4.00	8.00
—Budget-line reissue of LSP-4016					
☐ LPM-1971 [M]	Saturday Night with Mr. C.	1959	5.00	10.00	20.00
—Reissue of LOP-1004					
☐ LSP-1971(e) [R]	Saturday Night with Mr. C.	1962	3.00	6.00	12.00
☐ AFL1-1981	Como's Golden Records	1977	2.50	5.00	10.00
—Reissue with new prefix					
☐ LPM-1981 [M]	Como's Golden Records	1959	5.00	10.00	20.00
—Reissue of LOP-1007					
☐ LSP-1981(e) [R]	Como's Golden Records	1962	3.00	6.00	12.00
☐ LPM-2010 [M]	Como Swings	1959	5.00	10.00	20.00
☐ LSP-2010 [S]	Como Swings	1959	6.25	12.50	25.00
☐ LPM-2066 [M]	Season's Greetings from Perry Como	1959	5.00	10.00	20.00
—Later front covers have "LPM-2066" in upper right, inside RCA Victor box					
☐ LPM-2066 [M]	Season's Greetings from Perry Como	1959	6.25	12.50	25.00
—Original front covers have "LPM-2066" in lower left corner					
☐ LSP-2066 [S]	Season's Greetings from Perry Como	1959	6.25	12.50	25.00
☐ LPM-2343 [M]	For the Young at Heart	1960	3.75	7.50	15.00
☐ LSP-2343 [S]	For the Young at Heart	1960	5.00	10.00	20.00
☐ LPM-2390 [M]	Sing to Me, Mr. C.	1961	3.75	7.50	15.00
☐ LSP-2390 [S]	Sing to Me, Mr. C.	1961	5.00	10.00	20.00
☐ ANL1-2485	Especially for You	1977	2.50	5.00	10.00
☐ LPM-2567 [M]	By Request	1962	3.75	7.50	15.00
☐ LSP-2567 [S]	By Request	1962	5.00	10.00	20.00
☐ LPM-2630 [M]	The Best of Irving Berlin's Songs from "Mr. President"	1962	3.75	7.50	15.00
☐ LSP-2630 [S]	The Best of Irving Berlin's Songs from "Mr. President"	1962	5.00	10.00	20.00
☐ AFL1-2641	Where You're Concerned	1978	2.50	5.00	10.00
☐ LPM-2708 [M]	The Songs I Love	1963	3.75	7.50	15.00
☐ LSP-2708 [S]	The Songs I Love	1963	5.00	10.00	20.00
☐ ANL1-2969(e)	Over the Rainbow	1976	2.50	5.00	10.00
☐ LPM-3013 [10]	TV Favorites	1952	10.00	20.00	40.00
☐ LPM-3035 [10]	A Sentimental Date with Perry Como	1952	10.00	20.00	40.00
☐ LPM-3044 [10]	Supper Club Favorites	1952	10.00	20.00	40.00
☐ LPM-3124 [10]	Hits from Broadway Shows	1953	10.00	20.00	40.00
☐ LPM-3133 [10]	Around the Christmas Tree	1953	10.00	20.00	40.00
☐ LPM-3188 [10]	I Believe	1954	10.00	20.00	40.00
☐ LPM-3224 [10]	Como's Golden Records	1954	10.00	20.00	40.00
☐ LPM-3396 [M]	The Scene Changes	1965	3.00	6.00	12.00
☐ LSP-3396 [S]	The Scene Changes	1965	3.75	7.50	15.00
☐ LPM-3552 [M]	Lightly Latin	1966	3.00	6.00	12.00
☐ LSP-3552 [S]	Lightly Latin	1966	3.75	7.50	15.00
☐ LPM-3608 [M]	Perry Como in Italy	1966	3.00	6.00	12.00
☐ LSP-3608 [S]	Perry Como in Italy	1966	3.75	7.50	15.00
☐ AFL1-3629	Perry Como	1980	2.50	5.00	10.00
☐ AYL1-3672	And I Love You So	1980	2.00	4.00	8.00
—Reissue					
☐ AYL1-3802	Como's Golden Records	1981	2.00	4.00	8.00
—Reissue					
☐ AYL1-3803	Where You're Concerned	1981	2.00	4.00	8.00
—Reissue					
☐ AYL1-3804	It's Impossible	1981	2.00	4.00	8.00
—Reissue					

Number	Title (A Side/B Side)	Yr	VG	VG+	NM
❏ LSP-4016	The Perry Como Christmas Album	1968	3.00	6.00	12.00
❏ LSP-4052	Look to Your Heart	1968	3.75	7.50	15.00
❏ LSP-4183	Seattle	1969	3.75	7.50	15.00
❏ AFL1-4272	So It Goes	1983	2.50	5.00	10.00
❏ AFL1-4473	It's Impossible	1977	2.50	5.00	10.00
—Reissue with new prefix					
❏ LSP-4473	It's Impossible	1970	3.75	7.50	15.00
❏ AYL1-4526	I Wish It Could Be Christmas Forever	1982	2.50	5.00	10.00
❏ AFL1-4539	I Think of You	1977	2.50	5.00	10.00
—Reissue with new prefix					
❏ LSP-4539	I Think of You	1971	3.75	7.50	15.00
❏ VPS-6026 [(2)]	This Is Perry Como	1970	3.75	7.50	15.00
❏ VPS-6067 [(2)]	This Is Perry Como, Volume 2	1972	3.75	7.50	15.00
READER'S DIGEST					
❏ RDA-144/D	Christmas with Perry Como	1983	2.50	5.00	10.00

COMPETITORS, THE
DOT

Number	Title (A Side/B Side)	Yr	VG	VG+	NM
❏ DLP-3542 [M]	Hits of the Street and Strip	1963	37.50	75.00	150.00
❏ DLP-25542 [S]	Hits of the Street and Strip	1963	50.00	100.00	200.00

COMPOSER'S WORKSHOP ENSEMBLE, THE
STRATA-EAST

Number	Title (A Side/B Side)	Yr	VG	VG+	NM
❏ 1972-3	The Composer's Workshop Ensemble	197?	7.50	15.00	30.00
❏ 7422	(We've Been) Around	1974	7.50	15.00	30.00

COMSTOCK, BOBBY
ASCOT

Number	Title (A Side/B Side)	Yr	VG	VG+	NM
❏ AM-13026 [M]	Out of Sight	1966	6.25	12.50	25.00
❏ AS-16026 [S]	Out of Sight	1966	7.50	15.00	30.00

CONCRETE BLONDE
I.R.S.

Number	Title (A Side/B Side)	Yr	VG	VG+	NM
❏ 5835	Concrete Blonde	1987	3.00	6.00	12.00
❏ X1-13037	Bloodletting	1990	6.25	12.50	25.00
—Stock copy; red vinyl					
❏ 82001	Free	1989	3.00	6.00	12.00
❏ 82037 [DJ]	Bloodletting	1990	7.50	15.00	30.00
—Promo only, sticker on generic cover, black vinyl					

CONDELLO
SCEPTER

Number	Title (A Side/B Side)	Yr	VG	VG+	NM
❏ SPS-542	Phase 1	1968	10.00	20.00	40.00

CONDON, EDDIE
COLUMBIA

Number	Title (A Side/B Side)	Yr	VG	VG+	NM
❏ CL 616 [M]	Jammin' at Condon's	1955	10.00	20.00	40.00
—Red and black label with six "eye" logos					
❏ CL 616 [M]	Jammin' at Condon's	1955	12.50	25.00	50.00
—Maroon label, gold print					
❏ CL 632 [M]	Chicago Style Jazz	1955	10.00	20.00	40.00
—Red and black label with six "eye" logos					
❏ CL 719 [M]	Bixieland	1955	10.00	20.00	40.00
—Red and black label with six "eye" logos					
❏ CL 881 [M]	Eddie Condon's Treasury of Jazz	1956	10.00	20.00	40.00
—Red and black label with six "eye" logos					
❏ CL 1089 [M]	The Roaring Twenties	1958	10.00	20.00	40.00
—Red and black label with six "eye" logos					
COMMODORE					
❏ FL 20022 [M]	Ballin' the Jack	195?	12.50	25.00	50.00
DECCA					
❏ DL 5137 [10]	George Gershwin Jazz Concert	1950	12.50	25.00	50.00
❏ DL 5195 [10]	Jazz Band Ball (Volume 1)	1951	12.50	25.00	50.00
❏ DL 5203 [10]	Jazz Concert at Eddie Condon's	1951	12.50	25.00	50.00
❏ DL 5218 [10]	Jazz Concert at Eddie Condon's	1950	12.50	25.00	50.00
❏ DL 5246 [10]	We Call It Music	1951	12.50	25.00	50.00
❏ DL 8282 [M]	Ivy League Jazz	195?	10.00	20.00	40.00
❏ DL 9234 [M]	Gershwin Program (1941-1945)	1968	6.25	12.50	25.00
DOT					
❏ DLP-3141 [M]	Dixieland Dance Party	1958	10.00	20.00	40.00
EPIC					
❏ BA 17024 [S]	Midnight in Moscow	1962	5.00	10.00	20.00
JAZZ PANORAMA					
❏ 1805 [10]	Eddie Condon	1951	10.00	20.00	40.00
JOLLY ROGER					
❏ 5018 [10]	Eddie Condon and His Orchestra Featuring Pee Wee Russell	1954	10.00	20.00	40.00
❏ 5025 [10]	Eddie Condon	1954	10.00	20.00	40.00
MAINSTREAM					
❏ 56024 [M]	Eddie Condon: A Legend	1965	6.25	12.50	25.00
MGM					
❏ E-3651 [M]	Eddie Condon Is Uptown Now	1960	6.25	12.50	25.00
❏ SE-3651 [S]	Eddie Condon Is Uptown Now	1960	7.50	15.00	30.00
MOSAIC					
❏ MQ7-152 [(7)]	The Complete CBS Recordings of Eddie Condon and His All-Stars	199?	30.00	60.00	120.00
SAVOY					
❏ MG-12055 [M]	Ringside at Condon's	1956	10.00	20.00	40.00
"X"					
❏ LX-3005 [M]	Eddie Condon's Hot Shots	1954	12.50	25.00	50.00

CONLEY, ARTHUR
ATCO

Number	Title (A Side/B Side)	Yr	VG	VG+	NM
❏ 33-215 [M]	Sweet Soul Music	1967	10.00	20.00	40.00
❏ SD 33-215 [S]	Sweet Soul Music	1967	7.50	15.00	30.00
❏ 33-220 [M]	Shake, Rattle & Roll	1967	10.00	20.00	40.00
❏ SD 33-220 [S]	Shake, Rattle & Roll	1967	7.50	15.00	30.00
❏ SD 33-243	Soul Directions	1968	7.50	15.00	30.00
❏ SD 33-276	More Sweet Soul	1969	7.50	15.00	30.00

CONNELLY, PEGGY
BETHLEHEM

Number	Title (A Side/B Side)	Yr	VG	VG+	NM
❏ BCP-53 [M]	That Old Black Magic	1957	30.00	60.00	120.00

CONNIFF, RAY
COLUMBIA

Number	Title (A Side/B Side)	Yr	VG	VG+	NM
❏ GP 3 [(2)]	Here We Come a-Caroling/Ray Conniff's World of Hits	1968	3.75	7.50	15.00
❏ CL 925 [M]	'S Wonderful!	1956	5.00	10.00	20.00
—Red and black label with six "eye" logos					
❏ CL 1004 [M]	Dance the Bop	1957	7.50	15.00	30.00
—Red and black label with six "eye" logos; includes instruction booklet					
❏ CS 1022	Bridge Over Troubled Water	1970	2.50	5.00	10.00
❏ CL 1074 [M]	'S Marvelous	1957	3.75	7.50	15.00
❏ CL 1137 [M]	'S Awful Nice	1958	3.75	7.50	15.00
❏ CL 1163 [M]	Concert in Rhythm	1958	3.75	7.50	15.00
❏ CL 1252 [M]	Broadway in Rhythm	1959	3.75	7.50	15.00
❏ CL 1310 [M]	Hollywood in Rhythm	1959	3.75	7.50	15.00
❏ CL 1334 [M]	It's the Talk of the Town	1959	3.00	6.00	12.00
❏ CL 1390 [M]	Christmas with Conniff	1959	3.75	7.50	15.00
❏ CL 1415 [M]	Concert in Rhythm — Volume II	1960	3.00	6.00	12.00
❏ CL 1489 [M]	Young at Heart	1960	3.00	6.00	12.00
❏ CL 1490 [M]	Say It With Music (A Touch of Latin)	1960	3.00	6.00	12.00
❏ CL 1574 [M]	Memories Are Made of This	1961	3.00	6.00	12.00
❏ CL 1642 [M]	Somebody Loves Me	1961	3.00	6.00	12.00
❏ CL 1720 [M]	So Much in Love	1962	3.00	6.00	12.00
❏ CL 1776 [M]	'S Continental	1962	3.00	6.00	12.00
❏ CL 1878 [M]	Rhapsody in Rhythm	1962	3.00	6.00	12.00
❏ CL 1892 [M]	We Wish You a Merry Christmas	1962	3.75	7.50	15.00
❏ CL 1949 [M]	The Happy Beat	1963	3.00	6.00	12.00
❏ CL 2022 [M]	Just Kiddin' Around	1963	3.00	6.00	12.00
❏ CL 2118 [M]	You Make Me Feel So Young	1964	3.00	6.00	12.00
❏ CL 2150 [M]	Speak to Me of Love	1964	2.50	5.00	10.00
❏ CL 2210 [M]	Friendly Persuasion	1964	2.50	5.00	10.00
❏ CL 2264 [M]	Invisible Tears	1964	2.50	5.00	10.00
❏ CL 2352 [M]	Love Affair	1965	2.50	5.00	10.00
❏ CL 2366 [M]	Music from Mary Poppins, The Sound of Music, My Fair Lady & Other Great Movie Themes	1965	2.50	5.00	10.00
❏ CL 2406 [M]	Here We Come a-Caroling	1965	3.00	6.00	12.00
❏ CL 2461 [M]	Happiness Is	1966	2.50	5.00	10.00
❏ CL 2500 [M]	Ray Conniff's World of Hits	1966	3.00	6.00	12.00
❏ CL 2519 [M]	Somewhere My Love	1966	3.00	6.00	12.00
❏ CL 2608 [M]	En Espanol	1967	3.00	6.00	12.00
❏ CL 2676 [M]	This Is My Song	1967	3.00	6.00	12.00
❏ CL 2747 [M]	Hawaiian Album	1967	3.00	6.00	12.00
❏ CL 2795 [M]	It Must Be Him	1968	3.75	7.50	15.00
❏ CS 8001 [S]	'S Awful Nice	1958	5.00	10.00	20.00
—Red and black label with six "eye" logos					
❏ CS 8022 [S]	Concert in Rhythm	1958	5.00	10.00	20.00
—Red and black label with six "eye" logos					
❏ PC 8022	Concert in Rhythm	1988	—	3.00	6.00
—Reissue with new prefix					
❏ CS 8037 [S]	'S Marvelous	1958	5.00	10.00	20.00
—Red and black label with six "eye" logos					
❏ CS 8064 [S]	Broadway in Rhythm	1959	5.00	10.00	20.00
—Red and black label with six "eye" logos					
❏ CS 8117 [S]	Hollywood in Rhythm	1959	5.00	10.00	20.00
—Red and black label with six "eye" logos					
❏ CS 8143 [S]	It's the Talk of the Town	1959	3.75	7.50	15.00
❏ CS 8155 [S]	Conniff Meets Butterfield	1959	6.25	12.50	25.00
—Red and black label with six "eye" logos					
❏ CS 8185 [S]	Christmas with Conniff	1959	3.00	6.00	12.00
❏ CS 8212 [S]	Concert in Rhythm — Volume II	1960	3.75	7.50	15.00
❏ CS 8281 [S]	Young at Heart	1960	3.75	7.50	15.00
❏ CS 8282 [S]	Say It With Music (A Touch of Latin)	1960	3.75	7.50	15.00
❏ CS 8374 [S]	Memories Are Made of This	1961	3.75	7.50	15.00
❏ CS 8442 [S]	Somebody Loves Me	1961	3.75	7.50	15.00
❏ CS 8520 [S]	So Much in Love	1962	3.75	7.50	15.00
❏ CS 8576 [S]	'S Continental	1962	3.75	7.50	15.00
❏ CS 8678 [S]	Rhapsody in Rhythm	1962	3.75	7.50	15.00
❏ CS 8692 [S]	We Wish You a Merry Christmas	1962	3.00	6.00	12.00
❏ CS 8749 [S]	The Happy Beat	1963	3.75	7.50	15.00
❏ CS 8822 [S]	Just Kiddin' Around	1963	3.75	7.50	15.00
❏ CS 8918 [S]	You Make Me Feel So Young	1964	3.75	7.50	15.00
❏ CS 8950 [S]	Speak to Me of Love	1964	3.00	6.00	12.00
❏ CS 9064 [S]	Invisible Tears	1964	3.00	6.00	12.00
❏ CS 9110 [S]	Friendly Persuasion	1964	3.00	6.00	12.00
❏ CS 9152 [S]	Love Affair	1965	3.00	6.00	12.00
❏ CS 9166 [S]	Music from Mary Poppins, The Sound of Music, My Fair Lady & Other Great Movie Themes	1965	3.00	6.00	12.00
❏ CS 9206 [S]	Here We Come a-Caroling	1965	2.50	5.00	10.00
❏ CS 9261 [S]	Happiness Is	1966	3.00	6.00	12.00
❏ CS 9300 [S]	Ray Conniff's World of Hits	1966	2.50	5.00	10.00
❏ CS 9319 [S]	Somewhere My Love	1966	2.50	5.00	10.00
❏ PC 9319	Somewhere My Love	198?	—	3.00	6.00
—Reissue with new prefix					
❏ CS 9408 [S]	En Espanol	1967	2.50	5.00	10.00
❏ CS 9476 [S]	This Is My Song	1967	2.50	5.00	10.00
❏ CS 9547 [S]	Hawaiian Album	1967	2.50	5.00	10.00
❏ PC 9547	Hawaiian Album	198?	—	3.00	6.00
—Reissue with new prefix					
❏ CS 9595 [S]	It Must Be Him	1968	2.50	5.00	10.00
❏ CS 9661	Honey	1968	2.50	5.00	10.00
❏ CS 9712	Turn Around Look at Me	1968	2.50	5.00	10.00
❏ CS 9777	I Love How You Love Me	1969	2.50	5.00	10.00
❏ CS 9839	Ray Conniff's Greatest Hits	1969	2.50	5.00	10.00
❏ PC 9839	Ray Conniff's Greatest Hits	198?	—	3.00	6.00
—Reissue with new prefix					
❏ CS 9920	Jean	1969	2.50	5.00	10.00
❏ G 30122 [(2)]	Concert in Stereo/Live at the Sahara/Tahoe	1970	3.75	7.50	15.00

Number	Title (A Side/B Side)	Yr	VG	VG+	NM
❑ C 30410	We've Only Just Begun	1970	2.50	5.00	10.00
❑ C 30498	Love Story	1971	2.50	5.00	10.00
❑ CQ 30498 [Q]	Love Story	1972	3.75	7.50	15.00
❑ C 30755	Great Contemporary Instrumental Hits	1971	2.50	5.00	10.00
❑ KC 31220	I'd Like to Teach the World to Sing	1972	2.50	5.00	10.00
❑ CQ 31473 [Q]	Love Theme from "The Godfather"	1972	3.75	7.50	15.00
❑ KC 31473	Love Theme from "The Godfather"	1972	2.50	5.00	10.00
❑ CQ 31629 [Q]	Alone Again (Naturally)	1972	3.75	7.50	15.00
❑ KC 31629	Alone Again (Naturally)	1972	2.50	5.00	10.00
❑ KC 32090	I Can See Clearly Now	1973	2.50	5.00	10.00
❑ KC 32376	You Are the Sunshine of My Life	1973	2.50	5.00	10.00
❑ C 32413	Charlotte's Web	1973	2.50	5.00	10.00
❑ CQ 32553 [Q]	Harmony	1973	3.75	7.50	15.00
❑ KC 32553	Harmony	1973	2.50	5.00	10.00
❑ CQ 32802 [Q]	The Way We Were	1974	3.75	7.50	15.00
❑ KC 32802	The Way We Were	1974	2.50	5.00	10.00
❑ CQ 33139 [Q]	The Happy Sound	1974	3.75	7.50	15.00
❑ KC 33139	The Happy Sound	1974	2.50	5.00	10.00
❑ CQ 33564 [Q]	Another Somebody Done Somebody Wrong Song	1975	3.75	7.50	15.00
❑ KC 33564	Another Somebody Done Somebody Wrong Song	1975	2.50	5.00	10.00
❑ CG 33603 [(2)]	Somewhere My Love/Bridge Over Troubled Water	1975	3.00	6.00	12.00
❑ CQ 33884 [Q]	Love Will Keep Us Together	1975	3.75	7.50	15.00
❑ KC 33884	Love Will Keep Us Together	1975	2.50	5.00	10.00
❑ CQ 34040 [Q]	I Write the Songs	1976	3.75	7.50	15.00
❑ KC 34040	I Write the Songs	1976	2.50	5.00	10.00
❑ CQ 34170 [Q]	Send In the Clowns	1976	3.75	7.50	15.00
❑ KC 34170	Send In the Clowns	1976	2.50	5.00	10.00
❑ CQ 34312 [Q]	S.W.A.T.	1976	3.75	7.50	15.00
❑ KC 34312	S.W.A.T.	1976	2.50	5.00	10.00
❑ PC 34477	After the Lovin'	1977	2.50	5.00	10.00
❑ JC 35659	Ray Conniff Plays the Bee Gees and Other Hits	1978	2.50	5.00	10.00
❑ PC 36255	I Will Survive	1979	2.50	5.00	10.00
❑ JC 36749	Perfect "10" Classics	1980	2.50	5.00	10.00
❑ FC 38072	The Nashville Connection	1981	2.50	5.00	10.00
❑ PC 38300	Christmas Album	1982	2.50	5.00	10.00
❑ PC 39470	Christmas Caroling	1984	2.50	5.00	10.00
❑ FC 40384	Say You, Say Me	1986	2.50	5.00	10.00
❑ FC 44152	Always in My Heart	1988	2.50	5.00	10.00

HARMONY

Number	Title (A Side/B Side)	Yr	VG	VG+	NM
❑ HS 11346	Love Is a Many-Splendored Thing	1969	2.50	5.00	10.00
❑ KH 30134	The Impossible Dream	1970	2.50	5.00	10.00

CONNOR, CHRIS
ABC

Number	Title (A Side/B Side)	Yr	VG	VG+	NM
❑ ABC-585 [M]	Chris Connor Now	1966	5.00	10.00	20.00
❑ ABCS-585 [S]	Chris Connor Now	1966	6.25	12.50	25.00

ABC-PARAMOUNT

| ❑ ABC-529 [M] | Gentle Bossa Nova | 1965 | 5.00 | 10.00 | 20.00 |
| ❑ ABCS-529 [S] | Gentle Bossa Nova | 1965 | 6.25 | 12.50 | 25.00 |

ATLANTIC

❑ 2-601 [(2)M]	Chris Connor Sings the George Gershwin Almanac of Song	1957	25.00	50.00	100.00
—Black label					
❑ 2-601 [(2)M]	Chris Connor Sings the George Gershwin Almanac of Song	196?	5.00	10.00	20.00
—Multi-color label, black "fan" logo					
❑ 2-601 [(2)M]	Chris Connor Sings the George Gershwin Almanac of Song	196?	10.00	20.00	40.00
—Multi-color label, white "fan" logo					
❑ 1228 [M]	Chris Connor	1956	12.50	25.00	50.00
—Black label					
❑ 1228 [M]	Chris Connor	196?	5.00	10.00	20.00
—Multi-color label, white "fan" logo					
❑ SD 1228 [S]	Chris Connor	1958	15.00	30.00	60.00
—Green label					
❑ SD 1228 [S]	Chris Connor	196?	6.25	12.50	25.00
—Multi-color label, white "fan" logo					
❑ 1240 [M]	He Loves Me, He Loves Me Not	1956	12.50	25.00	50.00
—Black label					
❑ 1240 [M]	He Loves Me, He Loves Me Not	196?	5.00	10.00	20.00
—Multi-color label, white "fan" logo					
❑ 1240 [M]	He Loves Me, He Loves Me Not	1960	10.00	20.00	40.00
—White "bullseye" label					
❑ SD 1240 [S]	He Loves Me, He Loves Me Not	1958	15.00	30.00	60.00
—Green label					
❑ SD 1240 [S]	He Loves Me, He Loves Me Not	196?	6.25	12.50	25.00
—Multi-color label, white "fan" logo					
❑ SD 1240 [S]	He Loves Me, He Loves Me Not	1960	12.50	25.00	50.00
—White "bullseye" label					
❑ 1286 [M]	A Jazz Date with Chris Connor	1958	12.50	25.00	50.00
—Black label					
❑ 1286 [M]	A Jazz Date with Chris Connor	196?	5.00	10.00	20.00
—Multi-color label, white "fan" logo					
❑ 1290 [M]	Chris Craft	1958	12.50	25.00	50.00
—Black label					
❑ 1290 [M]	Chris Craft	196?	5.00	10.00	20.00
—Multi-color label, white "fan" logo					
❑ 1307 [M]	Ballads of the Sad Café	1959	12.50	25.00	50.00
—Black label					
❑ 1307 [M]	Ballads of the Sad Café	196?	5.00	10.00	20.00
—Multi-color label, white "fan" logo					
❑ SD 1307 [S]	Ballads of the Sad Café	1959	15.00	30.00	60.00
—Green label					
❑ SD 1307 [S]	Ballads of the Sad Café	196?	6.25	12.50	25.00
—Multi-color label, white "fan" logo					
❑ 1309 [M]	Chris Connor Sings the George Gershwin Almanac of Song, Vol. 1	1959	10.00	20.00	40.00
—Black label					

Number	Title (A Side/B Side)	Yr	VG	VG+	NM
❑ 1309 [M]	Chris Connor Sings the George Gershwin Almanac of Song, Vol. 1	196?	5.00	10.00	20.00
—Multi-color label, white "fan" logo					
❑ 1310 [M]	Chris Connor Sings the George Gershwin Almanac of Song, Vol. 2	1959	10.00	20.00	40.00
—Black label					
❑ 1310 [M]	Chris Connor Sings the George Gershwin Almanac of Song, Vol. 2	196?	5.00	10.00	20.00
—Multi-color label, white "fan" logo					
❑ 8014 [M]	I Miss You So	1957	12.50	25.00	50.00
—Black label					
❑ 8014 [M]	I Miss You So	196?	5.00	10.00	20.00
—Multi-color label, white "fan" logo					
❑ 8014 [M]	I Miss You So	1960	10.00	20.00	40.00
—White "bullseye" label					
❑ 8032 [M]	Witchcraft	1959	12.50	25.00	50.00
—Black label					
❑ 8032 [M]	Witchcraft	196?	5.00	10.00	20.00
—Multi-color label, white "fan" logo					
❑ 8032 [M]	Witchcraft	1960	10.00	20.00	40.00
—White "bullseye" label					
❑ SD 8032 [S]	Witchcraft	1959	15.00	30.00	60.00
—Green label					
❑ SD 8032 [S]	Witchcraft	196?	6.25	12.50	25.00
—Multi-color label, white "fan" logo					
❑ 8040 [M]	Chris In Person	1959	12.50	25.00	50.00
—Black label					
❑ 8040 [M]	Chris In Person	196?	5.00	10.00	20.00
—Multi-color label, white "fan" logo					
❑ SD 8040 [S]	Chris In Person	1959	15.00	30.00	60.00
—Green label					
❑ SD 8040 [S]	Chris In Person	196?	6.25	12.50	25.00
—Multi-color label, white "fan" logo					
❑ 8046 [M]	A Portrait of Chris	1960	10.00	20.00	40.00
—Multi-color label, white "fan" logo					
❑ SD 8046 [S]	A Portrait of Chris	1960	12.50	25.00	50.00
—Multi-color label, white "fan" logo					
❑ 8061 [M]	Free Spirits	1962	7.50	15.00	30.00
—Multi-color label, black "fan" logo					
❑ SD 8061 [S]	Free Spirits	1962	10.00	20.00	40.00
—Multi-color label, black "fan" logo					

BETHLEHEM

❑ BCP-20 [M]	This Is Chris	1955	15.00	30.00	60.00
❑ BCP-56 [M]	Chris	1957	15.00	30.00	60.00
❑ BCP-1001 [10]	Chris Connor Sings Lullabys of Birdland	1954	20.00	40.00	80.00
❑ BCP-1002 [10]	Chris Connor Sings Lullabys for Lovers	1954	20.00	40.00	80.00
❑ BCP-6004 [M]	Chris Connor Sings Lullabys of Birdland	1955	12.50	25.00	50.00

FM

❑ 300 [M]	Chris Connor at the Village Gate	1963	12.50	25.00	50.00
❑ S-300 [S]	Chris Connor at the Village Gate	1963	15.00	30.00	60.00
❑ 312 [M]	A Weekend in Paris	1964	12.50	25.00	50.00
❑ S-312 [S]	A Weekend in Paris	1964	15.00	30.00	60.00

CONNOR, CHRIS, AND MAYNARD FERGUSON
ATLANTIC

Number	Title (A Side/B Side)	Yr	VG	VG+	NM
❑ 8049 [M]	Double Exposure	1961	7.50	15.00	30.00
—Multi-color label, white "fan" logo					
❑ SD 8049 [S]	Double Exposure	1961	10.00	20.00	40.00
—Multi-color label, white "fan" logo					

ROULETTE

❑ R 52068 [M]	Two's Company	1961	7.50	15.00	30.00
—White label with colored spokes					
❑ SR 52068 [S]	Two's Company	1961	10.00	20.00	40.00
—White label with colored spokes					

CONNY
CAPITOL

| ❑ T 10253 [M] | Germany's Greatest Record Star | 1960 | 7.50 | 15.00 | 30.00 |

CONSTANTINE, EDDIE
KAPP

| ❑ KL-1018 [M] | La Grande Sensation de la Paris | 1957 | 7.50 | 15.00 | 30.00 |

MERCURY

| ❑ MG-20339 [M] | The Rage of Paris | 1958 | 6.25 | 12.50 | 25.00 |

CONTEMPORARY JAZZ ENSEMBLE, THE
PRESTIGE

| ❑ PRLP-163 [10] | New Sounds from Rochester | 1953 | 25.00 | 50.00 | 100.00 |

CONTI, ROBERT
TREND

| ❑ TR-519 | Solo Guitar | 198? | 5.00 | 10.00 | 20.00 |
| —Direct-to-disc recording | | | | | |

CONTINENTAL OCTETTE, THE
CROWN

| ❑ CLP-5220 [M] | Modern Jazz Greats | 196? | 5.00 | 10.00 | 20.00 |

CONTOURS, THE
GORDY

| ❑ G 901 [M] | Do You Love Me? | 1962 | 125.00 | 250.00 | 500.00 |

MOTOWN

| ❑ M5-188V1 | Do You Love Me? | 1981 | 2.50 | 5.00 | 10.00 |

CONWAY, JULIE
HARMONY

| ❑ HL 7143 [M] | Good Housekeeping's Plan for Reducing Off-the-Record | 1960 | 5.00 | 10.00 | 20.00 |

COODER, RY
MOBILE FIDELITY

| ❑ 1-085 | Jazz | 198? | 100.00 | 200.00 | 400.00 |
| —Audiophile vinyl | | | | | |

Number	Title (A Side/B Side)	Yr	VG	VG+	NM
REPRISE					
❏ PRO 588 [DJ]	The Ry Cooder Radio Show	1976	25.00	50.00	100.00
❏ MS 2052	Into the Purple Valley	1972	3.00	6.00	12.00
❏ MS 2117	Boomer's Story	1973	3.00	6.00	12.00
❏ MS 2179	Paradise and Lunch	1974	3.00	6.00	12.00
❏ MS 2254	Chicken Skin Music	1976	3.00	6.00	12.00
❏ RS-6402	Ry Cooder	1969	3.75	7.50	15.00
—Two-tone orange label with "r:" and "W7" logos					
❏ RS-6402	Ry Cooder	1970	3.00	6.00	12.00
—No "W7" on label; one-tone orange (almost tan) label					
WARNER BROS.					
❏ BS 3059	Show Time	1977	2.50	5.00	10.00
❏ BSK 3197	Jazz	1978	2.50	5.00	10.00
❏ BSK 3358	Bop Till You Drop	1979	2.50	5.00	10.00
❏ HS 3448	The Long Riders	1980	2.50	5.00	10.00
❏ BSK 3489	Borderline	1980	2.50	5.00	10.00
❏ BSK 3651	The Slide Area	1982	2.50	5.00	10.00
❏ 25270	Paris, Texas	1984	2.50	5.00	10.00
❏ 25399	Crossroads	1986	2.50	5.00	10.00
❏ 25639	Get Rhythm	1987	2.50	5.00	10.00
❏ 25996	Johnny Handsome	1989	2.50	5.00	10.00
COOK, JUNIOR					
JAZZLAND					
❏ JLP-58 [M]	Junior's Cookin'	1961	10.00	20.00	40.00
❏ JLP-958 [S]	Junior's Cookin'	1961	12.50	25.00	50.00
COOKE, ALISTAIR					
COLUMBIA MASTERWORKS					
❏ ML 4970 [M]	An Evening with Alistair Cooke	1955	10.00	20.00	40.00
COOKE, SAM					
ABKCO					
❏ 1124-1	Sam Cooke's Night Beat	1995	3.00	6.00	12.00
—Reissue					
❏ 2970-1	Sam Cooke at the Copa	1988	3.00	6.00	12.00
—Reissue					
FAMOUS					
❏ 502	Sam's Songs	1969	10.00	20.00	40.00
❏ 505	Only Sixteen	1969	10.00	20.00	40.00
❏ 508	So Wonderful	1969	10.00	20.00	40.00
❏ 509	You Send Me	1969	10.00	20.00	40.00
❏ 512	Cha-Cha-Cha	1969	10.00	20.00	40.00
51 WEST					
❏ Q 16032	My Foolish Heart	198?	3.00	6.00	12.00
KEEN					
❏ A-2001 [M]	Sam Cooke	1958	50.00	100.00	200.00
❏ A-2003 [M]	Encore	1958	50.00	100.00	200.00
❏ A-2004 [M]	Tribute to the Lady	1959	37.50	75.00	150.00
❏ AS-2004 [S]	Tribute to the Lady	1959	50.00	100.00	200.00
❏ 86101 [M]	Hit Kit	1959	62.50	125.00	250.00
❏ 86103 [M]	I Thank God	1960	100.00	200.00	400.00
❏ 86106 [M]	The Wonderful World of Sam Cooke	1960	87.50	1175.	350.00
PAIR					
❏ PDL2-1006 [(2)]	You Send Me	1986	3.75	7.50	15.00
RCA CAMDEN					
❏ ACS1-0445	You Send Me	1974	3.00	6.00	12.00
❏ CAL-2264 [M]	The One and Only Sam Cooke	1967	5.00	10.00	20.00
❏ CAS-2264 [R]	The One and Only Sam Cooke	1967	3.00	6.00	12.00
❏ CAS-2433	Sam Cooke	1970	3.00	6.00	12.00
❏ CAS-2610	The Unforgettable Sam Cooke	1972	3.00	6.00	12.00
RCA VICTOR					
❏ LPM-2221 [M]	Cooke's Tour	1960	10.00	20.00	40.00
❏ LSP-2221 [S]	Cooke's Tour	1960	12.50	25.00	50.00
❏ LPM-2236 [M]	Hits of the 50's	1960	10.00	20.00	40.00
❏ LSP-2236 [S]	Hits of the 50's	1960	12.50	25.00	50.00
❏ LPM-2293 [M]	Swing Low	1960	10.00	20.00	40.00
❏ LSP-2293 [S]	Swing Low	1960	12.50	25.00	50.00
❏ LPM-2392 [M]	My Kind of Blues	1961	10.00	20.00	40.00
❏ LSP-2392 [S]	My Kind of Blues	1961	12.50	25.00	50.00
❏ LPM-2555 [M]	Twistin' the Night Away	1962	10.00	20.00	40.00
❏ LSP-2555 [S]	Twistin' the Night Away	1962	12.50	25.00	50.00
❏ AFL1-2625	The Best of Sam Cooke	1977	3.00	6.00	12.00
—Reissue with new prefix					
❏ LPM-2625 [M]	The Best of Sam Cooke	1962	7.50	15.00	30.00
❏ LSP-2625 [R]	The Best of Sam Cooke	1962	5.00	10.00	20.00
❏ ANL1-2658	Sam Cooke at the Copa	1977	3.00	6.00	12.00
—Reissue of LSP-2970					
❏ LPM-2673 [M]	Mr. Soul	1963	7.50	15.00	30.00
❏ LSP-2673 [S]	Mr. Soul	1963	10.00	20.00	40.00
❏ LPM-2709 [M]	Night Beat	1963	7.50	15.00	30.00
❏ LSP-2709 [S]	Night Beat	1963	10.00	20.00	40.00
❏ LPM-2899 [M]	Ain't That Good News	1964	7.50	15.00	30.00
❏ LSP-2899 [S]	Ain't That Good News	1964	10.00	20.00	40.00
❏ LPM-2970 [M]	Sam Cooke at the Copa	1964	7.50	15.00	30.00
❏ LSP-2970 [S]	Sam Cooke at the Copa	1964	10.00	20.00	40.00
❏ LPM-3367 [M]	Shake	1965	6.25	12.50	25.00
❏ LSP-3367 [S]	Shake	1965	7.50	15.00	30.00
❏ LPM-3373 [M]	The Best of Sam Cooke, Volume 2	1965	6.25	12.50	25.00
❏ LSP-3373 [S]	The Best of Sam Cooke, Volume 2	1965	7.50	15.00	30.00
❏ LPM-3435 [M]	Try a Little Love	1965	6.25	12.50	25.00
❏ LSP-3435 [S]	Try a Little Love	1965	7.50	15.00	30.00
❏ LPM-3517 [M]	The Unforgettable Sam Cooke	1966	5.00	10.00	20.00
❏ LSP-3517 [S]	The Unforgettable Sam Cooke	1966	6.25	12.50	25.00
❏ AYL1-3863	The Best of Sam Cooke	1981	2.00	4.00	8.00
—Budget-line reissue					
❏ LPM-3991 [M]	The Man Who Invented Soul	1968	12.50	25.00	50.00
❏ LSP-3991 [S]	The Man Who Invented Soul	1968	6.25	12.50	25.00
❏ AFL1-5181	Live at the Harlem Square Club, 1963	1985	3.00	6.00	12.00
❏ VPS-6027 [(2)]	This Is Sam Cooke	1970	5.00	10.00	20.00
❏ CPL2-7127 [(2)]	The Man and His Music	1986	3.75	7.50	15.00

Number	Title (A Side/B Side)	Yr	VG	VG+	NM
SPECIALTY					
❏ SPS-2106	Sam Cooke and the Soul Stirrers	1970	3.75	7.50	15.00
❏ SPS-2116	The Gospel Soul of Sam Cooke, Vol. 1	1970	3.75	7.50	15.00
❏ SPS-2119	Two Sides of Sam Cooke	1970	3.75	7.50	15.00
❏ SPS-2128	The Gospel Soul of Sam Cooke, Vol. 2	197?	3.75	7.50	15.00
❏ SPS-2146	That's Heaven to Me	197?	3.75	7.50	15.00
TRIP					
❏ 8030 [(2)]	The Golden Sound of Sam Cooke	1972	3.75	7.50	15.00
UPFRONT					
❏ 160	The Billie Holiday Story	1973	3.75	7.50	15.00
COOKIES, THE/LITTLE EVA/CAROLE KING					
DIMENSION					
❏ DLP-6001 [M]	The Dimension Dolls, Vol. 1	1964	62.50	125.00	250.00
COOL, CALVIN, AND THE SURF KNOBS					
CHARTER					
❏ CLP-103 [M]	The Surfer's Beat	1963	10.00	20.00	40.00
❏ CLS-103 [S]	The Surfer's Beat	1963	12.50	25.00	50.00
COOL BRITONS, THE					
BLUE NOTE					
❏ BLP-5052 [10]	New Sounds from Olde England	1954	75.00	150.00	300.00
COOLEY, SPADE					
COLUMBIA					
❏ CL 9007 [10]	Sagebrush Swing	1949	50.00	100.00	200.00
DECCA					
❏ DL 5563 [10]	Dance-O-Rama	1955	75.00	150.00	300.00
RAYNOTE					
❏ R-5007 [M]	Fidoolin'	1959	10.00	20.00	40.00
❏ RS-5007 [S]	Fidoolin'	1959	12.50	25.00	50.00
ROULETTE					
❏ R 25145 [M]	Fidoolin'	1961	7.50	15.00	30.00
❏ SR 25145 [S]	Fidoolin'	1961	10.00	20.00	40.00
COOLIDGE, RITA					
A&M					
❏ SP-3107	Rita Coolidge	198?	2.00	4.00	8.00
—Budget-line reissue					
❏ SP-3130	Nice Feelin'	198?	2.00	4.00	8.00
—Budget-line reissue					
❏ SP-3163	Anytime…Anywhere	198?	2.00	4.00	8.00
—Budget-line reissue					
❏ SP-3238	Greatest Hits	198?	2.00	4.00	8.00
—Budget-line reissue					
❏ SP-3627	Fall Into Spring	1974	2.50	5.00	10.00
❏ SP-3727	Heartbreak Radio	1981	2.50	5.00	10.00
❏ SP-4291	Rita Coolidge	1971	2.50	5.00	10.00
❏ SP-4325	Nice Feelin'	1971	2.50	5.00	10.00
❏ SP-4370	The Lady's Not for Sale	1972	2.50	5.00	10.00
❏ SP-4531	It's Only Love	1975	2.50	5.00	10.00
❏ SP-4616	Anytime…Anywhere	1977	2.50	5.00	10.00
❏ SP-4669	Love Me Again	1978	2.50	5.00	10.00
❏ SP-4781	Satisfied	1979	2.50	5.00	10.00
❏ SP-4836	Greatest Hits	1981	2.50	5.00	10.00
❏ SP-4914	Never Let You Go	1983	2.50	5.00	10.00
❏ SP-5003	Inside the Fire	1984	2.50	5.00	10.00
NAUTILUS					
❏ NR-16	Anytime…Anywhere	1981	6.25	12.50	25.00
—Audiophile vinyl					
COOPER, ALICE					
ACCORD					
❏ SN-7162	Toronto Rock 'n' Roll Revival 1969	1981	3.00	6.00	12.00
ATLANTIC					
❏ SD 18130	Welcome to My Nightmare	1975	2.50	5.00	10.00
❏ SD 19157	Welcome to My Nightmare	1978	2.00	4.00	8.00
—Reissue of 18130					
EPIC					
❏ OE 45137	Trash	1989	3.00	6.00	12.00
❏ E 46786	Hey Stoopid	1991	3.75	7.50	15.00
MCA					
❏ 5761	Constrictor	1986	2.00	4.00	8.00
❏ 42091	Raise Your Fist and Yell	1987	2.00	4.00	8.00
MOBILE FIDELITY					
❏ 1-063	Welcome to My Nightmare	1980	12.50	25.00	50.00
—Audiophile vinyl					
PAIR					
❏ PDL2-1163 [(2)]	A Man Called Alice	1987	3.75	7.50	15.00
STRAIGHT					
❏ STS-1051	Pretties for You	1969	37.50	75.00	150.00
—Yellow label stock copy					
❏ STS-1051 [DJ]	Pretties for You	1969	50.00	100.00	200.00
—White label promo					
❏ WS 1840	Pretties for You	1970	15.00	30.00	60.00
—Pink label stock copy					
❏ WS 1845	Easy Action	1970	7.50	15.00	30.00
—Pink label stock copy; "Alice Cooper" in white on cover					
❏ WS 1845	Easy Action	1970	12.50	25.00	50.00
—Pink label stock copy; "Alice Cooper" in black on cover					
❏ WS 1845 [DJ]	Easy Action	1970	25.00	50.00	100.00
—White label promo					
❏ WS 1883	Love It to Death	1971	12.50	25.00	50.00
—Pink label stock copy					
❏ WS 1883 [DJ]	Love It to Death	1971	25.00	50.00	100.00
—White label promo					
WARNER BROS.					
❏ PRO 789 [DJ]	The Alice Cooper Radio Show	1978	6.25	12.50	25.00

Number	Title (A Side/B Side)	Yr	VG	VG+	NM
❑ WS 1840	Pretties for You	1973	5.00	10.00	20.00

—"Burbank" palm trees label; comes in Straight cover

❑ WS 1883	Love It to Death	1971	3.00	6.00	12.00

—Version 4: Green "WB" label; with "I'm Eighteen" box and Alice's protruding thumb airbrushed off the cover

❑ WS 1883	Love It to Death	1971	5.00	10.00	20.00

—Version 2: Green "WB" label; same as above, but has a white box reading "Contains the Hit 'I'm Eighteen' "

❑ WS 1883	Love It to Death	1971	5.00	10.00	20.00

—Version 3: Green "WB" label; cover has large white areas at top and bottom with lower half of the photo cropped out

❑ WS 1883	Love It to Death	1971	7.50	15.00	30.00

—Version 1: Green "WB" label; cover has Alice's thumb sticking out in such a way that it appears to be another part of the body

❑ BS 2567	Killer	1971	7.50	15.00	30.00

—Early copies have an attached 1972 calendar/poster

❑ BS 2567	Killer	1972	3.00	6.00	12.00

—Later copies no longer have the calendar/poster

❑ BS 2623	School's Out	1972	3.00	6.00	12.00

—No panties, with song titles listed

❑ BS 2623	School's Out	1972	5.00	10.00	20.00

—Back cover does not list song titles, but panties are missing

❑ BS 2623	School's Out	1972	7.50	15.00	30.00

—With paper panties intact; back cover lists song titles

❑ BS 2623	School's Out	1972	10.00	20.00	40.00

—With paper panties intact; back cover does not list song titles

❑ BS 2685	Billion Dollar Babies	1973	3.00	6.00	12.00

—Green "WB" label

❑ BS4 2685 [Q]	Billion Dollar Babies	1974	6.25	12.50	25.00
❑ BS 2748	Muscle of Love	1973	2.50	5.00	10.00
❑ BS4 2748 [Q]	Muscle of Love	1974	6.25	12.50	25.00
❑ BS4 2803 [Q]	Alice Cooper's Greatest Hits	1974	6.25	12.50	25.00
❑ W 2803	Alice Cooper's Greatest Hits	1974	2.50	5.00	10.00
❑ BS 2896	Alice Cooper Goes to Hell	1976	2.50	5.00	10.00
❑ BSK 3027	Lace and Whiskey	1977	2.50	5.00	10.00
❑ BSK 3107	Alice Cooper's Greatest Hits	1977	2.00	4.00	8.00

—Reissue of BS 2803

❑ BSK 3138	The Alice Cooper Show	1977	2.50	5.00	10.00
❑ BSK 3263	From the Inside	1978	2.50	5.00	10.00
❑ BSK 3436	Flush the Fashion	1980	2.50	5.00	10.00
❑ BSK 3581	Special Forces	1981	2.50	5.00	10.00
❑ 23719	Zipper Catches Skin	1982	2.50	5.00	10.00
❑ 23969	Da Da	1983	2.50	5.00	10.00

COOPER, BOB
CAPITOL

❑ ST 1586 [S]	Do Re Mi	1961	7.50	15.00	30.00
❑ T 1586 [M]	Do Re Mi	1961	6.25	12.50	25.00
❑ H 6501 [10]	Bob Cooper	1954	20.00	40.00	80.00
❑ T 6501 [M]	Bob Cooper	1955	12.50	25.00	50.00
❑ H 6513 [10]	Shifting Winds	1955	15.00	30.00	60.00
❑ T 6513 [M]	Shifting Winds	1955	12.50	25.00	50.00

CONTEMPORARY

❑ C-3544 [M]	Coop!	1958	12.50	25.00	50.00
❑ S-7012 [S]	Coop!	1959	10.00	20.00	40.00

—Reissue of Stereo Records 7012

STEREO RECORDS

❑ S-7012 [S]	Coop!	1958	12.50	25.00	50.00

TREND

❑ TR-518	Tenor Sax Impressions	198?	5.00	10.00	20.00

—Direct-to-disc recording

WORLD PACIFIC

❑ WPM-411 [M]	Bob Cooper Swings TV	1958	12.50	25.00	50.00

COOPER, JACKIE
DOT

❑ DLP-3146 [M]	The Movies Swing!	1958	7.50	15.00	30.00

COOPER, LES, AND THE SOUL ROCKERS
EVERLAST

❑ ELP-202 [M]	Wiggle Wobble	1963	12.50	25.00	50.00

COOPER, WILMA LEE AND STONEY
DECCA

❑ DL 4784 [M]	Wilma Lee and Stoney Cooper Sing	1966	5.00	10.00	20.00
❑ DL 74784 [S]	Wilma Lee and Stoney Cooper Sing	1966	6.25	12.50	25.00

HARMONY

❑ HL 7233 [M]	Sacred Songs	1960	6.25	12.50	25.00

HICKORY

❑ LP-100 [M]	There's a Big Wheel	1960	12.50	25.00	50.00
❑ LP-106 [M]	Family Favorites	1962	10.00	20.00	40.00
❑ LP-112 [M]	New Songs of Inspiration	1962	10.00	20.00	40.00

COPAS, COWBOY
KING

❑ 553 [M]	Cowboy Copas Sings His All-Time Hits	1957	25.00	50.00	100.00
❑ 556 [M]	Favorite Sacred Songs	1957	20.00	40.00	80.00
❑ 619 [M]	Sacred Songs by Cowboy Copas	1959	20.00	40.00	80.00
❑ 714 [M]	Tragic Tales of Love and Life	1960	20.00	40.00	80.00
❑ 720 [M]	Broken Hearted Melodies	1960	20.00	40.00	80.00
❑ 817 [M]	Country Gentleman of Song	1963	10.00	20.00	40.00
❑ 824 [M]	As You Remember Cowboy Copas	1963	10.00	20.00	40.00
❑ 894 [M]	Cowboy Copas Hymns	1964	10.00	20.00	40.00

STARDAY

❑ SLP-118 [M]	All Time Country Music Great	1960	10.00	20.00	40.00
❑ SLP-133 [M]	Inspirational Songs	1961	10.00	20.00	40.00
❑ SLP-144 [M]	Cowboy Copas	1961	10.00	20.00	40.00
❑ SLP-157 [M]	Opry Star Spotlight on Cowboy Copas	1962	10.00	20.00	40.00
❑ SLP-175 [M]	Mister Country Music	1962	10.00	20.00	40.00
❑ SLP-184 [M]	Songs That Made Him Famous	1962	10.00	20.00	40.00
❑ SLP-208 [M]	Country Music Entertainer #1	1963	10.00	20.00	40.00
❑ SLP-212 [M]	Beyond the Sunset	1963	10.00	20.00	40.00

Number	Title (A Side/B Side)	Yr	VG	VG+	NM
❑ SLP-234 [M]	The Unforgettable Cowboy Copas	1963	10.00	20.00	40.00
❑ SLP-247 [M]	Star of the Grand Ole Opry	1963	10.00	20.00	40.00
❑ SLP-268 [M]	Cowboy Copas and His Friends	1964	10.00	20.00	40.00
❑ SLP-317 [M]	The Legend Lives On	1965	7.50	15.00	30.00
❑ SLP (9)-347 [(2)R]	The Cowboy Copas Story	1965	6.25	12.50	25.00
❑ SLP-347 [(2)M]	The Cowboy Copas Story	1965	7.50	15.00	30.00
❑ SLP-458	The Best of Cowboy Copas	1970	3.75	7.50	15.00

COPAS, COWBOY, AND HAWKSHAW HAWKINS
KING

❑ 835 [M]	In Memory	1963	10.00	20.00	40.00
❑ 850 [M]	The Legend of Cowboy Copas and Hawkshaw Hawkins	1964	10.00	20.00	40.00
❑ 984 [M]	24 Great Hits	1968	6.25	12.50	25.00

COPAS, COWBOY/HAWKSHAW HAWKINS/PATSY CLINE
STARDAY

❑ SLP-346 [M]	Gone But Not Forgotten	1965	7.50	15.00	30.00

COPPER PLATED INTEGRATED CIRCUIT, THE
COMMAND

❑ RS-945 SD	Plugged In Pop	1969	6.25	12.50	25.00

COPPERPENNY
RCA VICTOR

❑ LSP-4291	Copperpenny	1970	5.00	10.00	20.00

CORBIN, HAROLD
ROULETTE

❑ R-52079 [M]	Soul Brother	1961	6.25	12.50	25.00
❑ SR-52079 [S]	Soul Brother	1961	7.50	15.00	30.00

CORCORAN, CORKY
CELESTIAL

❑ Vol. 1 [M]	Sounds of Jazz	1958	30.00	60.00	120.00

—Black vinyl

❑ Vol. 1 [M]	Sounds of Jazz	1958	62.50	125.00	250.00

—Red vinyl

EPIC

❑ LN 3319 [M]	The Sound of Love	1956	20.00	40.00	80.00

CORDIALS, THE
CATAMOUNT

❑ 902	Blue Eyed Soul	1967	6.25	12.50	25.00

COREA, CHICK
BLUE NOTE

❑ BST-84353	Song of Singing	1970	5.00	10.00	20.00

GROOVE MERCHANT

❑ 2202	Sundance	1972	5.00	10.00	20.00

SOLID STATE

❑ SS-18039	Now He Sings, Now He Sobs	1969	5.00	10.00	20.00
❑ SS-18055	Chick Corea "Is"	1969	5.00	10.00	20.00

VORTEX

❑ 2004	Tones	1971	5.00	10.00	20.00

COREY, JILL
COLUMBIA

❑ CL 1095 [M]	Sometimes I'm Happy, Sometimes I'm Blue	1957	7.50	15.00	30.00

CORNELL, DON
ABC-PARAMOUNT

❑ ABC-537 [M]	Incomparable	1966	3.00	6.00	12.00
❑ ABCS-537 [S]	Incomparable	1966	3.75	7.50	15.00

CORAL

❑ CRL 57055 [M]	Don	1955	7.50	15.00	30.00
❑ CRL 57133 [M]	For Teenagers Only	1957	7.50	15.00	30.00

DOT

❑ DLP-3160 [M]	Don Cornell's Great Hits	1959	6.25	12.50	25.00
❑ DLP-25160 [S]	Don Cornell's Great Hits	1959	7.50	15.00	30.00

MOVIETONE

❑ 71013 [M]	I Wish You Love	1966	3.00	6.00	12.00
❑ S-72013 [S]	I Wish You Love	1966	3.75	7.50	15.00

SIGNATURE

❑ SM-1001 [M]	Don Cornell Sings Love Songs	1960	5.00	10.00	20.00
❑ SS-1001 [S]	Don Cornell Sings Love Songs	1960	6.25	12.50	25.00

VOCALION

❑ VL 3657 [M]	Don Cornell	196?	3.00	6.00	12.00

CORNELLS, THE
GAREX

❑ LPGA-100 [M]	Beach Bound	1963	125.00	250.00	500.00

SUNDAZED

❑ LP-5013	Surf Fever!	199?	2.50	5.00	10.00

CORPORATION, THE
AGE OF AQUARIUS

❑ 4150	Get On Our Swing	1968	7.50	15.00	30.00
❑ 4250	Hassles in My Mind	1969	7.50	15.00	30.00

CAPITOL

❑ ST-175	The Corporation	1969	12.50	25.00	50.00

CORPUS
ACORN

❑ 1001	Creation: A Child	1971	75.00	150.00	300.00

CORTEZ, DAVE "BABY"
CHESS

❑ LP-1473 [M]	Rinky Dink	1962	12.50	25.00	50.00

CLOCK

❑ C-331 [M]	Dave "Baby" Cortez	1960	10.00	20.00	40.00
❑ CS-331 [S]	Dave "Baby" Cortez	1960	12.50	25.00	50.00

Number	Title (A Side/B Side)	Yr	VG	VG+	NM
❏ MGC-20647 [M]	Dave "Baby" Cortez	1961	7.50	15.00	30.00
❏ SRC-60647 [S]	Dave "Baby" Cortez	1961	10.00	20.00	40.00
DESIGN					
❏ DLP-163 [R]	The Happy Organ	1962	3.00	6.00	12.00
METRO					
❏ M-550 [M]	The Fabulous Organ of Dave "Baby" Cortez	1965	3.75	7.50	15.00
❏ MS-550 [R]	The Fabulous Organ of Dave "Baby" Cortez	1965	3.00	6.00	12.00
RCA VICTOR					
❏ LPM-2099 [M]	The Happy Organ	1959	20.00	40.00	80.00
❏ LSP-2099 [S]	The Happy Organ	1959	25.00	50.00	100.00
ROULETTE					
❏ R-25298 [M]	Organ Shindig	1965	5.00	10.00	20.00
❏ SR-25298 [S]	Organ Shindig	1965	6.25	12.50	25.00
❏ R-25315 [M]	Tweety Pie	1966	5.00	10.00	20.00
❏ SR-25315 [S]	Tweety Pie	1966	6.25	12.50	25.00
❏ R-25328 [M]	In Orbit with Dave "Baby" Cortez	1966	5.00	10.00	20.00
❏ SR-25328 [S]	In Orbit with Dave "Baby" Cortez	1966	6.25	12.50	25.00
T-NECK					
❏ TNS-3005	The Isley Brothers Way	1970	5.00	10.00	20.00

CORWIN, BOB
RIVERSIDE

Number	Title (A Side/B Side)	Yr	VG	VG+	NM
❏ RLP 12-220 [M]	Bob Corwin Quartet with Don Elliott	1956	20.00	40.00	80.00

—White label, blue print

Number	Title	Yr	VG	VG+	NM
❏ RLP 12-220 [M]	Bob Corwin Quartet with Don Elliott	1957	10.00	20.00	40.00

—Blue label with microphone logo

CORYELL, LARRY
FLYING DUTCHMAN

Number	Title	Yr	VG	VG+	NM
❏ 51-1000	Fairyland	1971	5.00	10.00	20.00
VANGUARD					
❏ VSQ-40006 [Q]	Larry Coryell at the Village Gate	197?	5.00	10.00	20.00
❏ VSQ-40013 [Q]	Offering	197?	5.00	10.00	20.00
❏ VSQ-40023 [Q]	The Real Great Escape	197?	5.00	10.00	20.00
❏ VSQ-40036 [Q]	Introducing the Eleventh House	1974	5.00	10.00	20.00

COSBY, BILL
CAPITOL

Number	Title	Yr	VG	VG+	NM
❏ ST-11530	Bill Cosby Is Not Himself These Days, Rat Own, Rat Own, Rat Own	1976	2.50	5.00	10.00
❏ ST-11590	My Father Confused Me…What Must I Do? What Must I Do?	1977	2.50	5.00	10.00
❏ ST-11683	Let's Boogie (Disco Bill)	1977	2.50	5.00	10.00
❏ ST-11731	Bill's Best Friend	1978	2.50	5.00	10.00
GEFFEN					
❏ GHS 24104	Those of You With or Without Children, You'll Understand	1986	2.50	5.00	10.00
MCA					
❏ 169	When I Was a Kid	197?	2.00	4.00	8.00

—Reissue of Uni 73100

Number	Title	Yr	VG	VG+	NM
❏ 333	Fat Albert	1973	2.50	5.00	10.00
❏ 553	For Adults Only	197?	2.00	4.00	8.00

—Reissue of Uni 73112

Number	Title	Yr	VG	VG+	NM
❏ 554	Inside the Mind of Bill Cosby	197?	2.00	4.00	8.00

—Reissue of Uni 73139

Number	Title	Yr	VG	VG+	NM
❏ 8005 [(2)]	Bill	197?	3.00	6.00	12.00
MOTOWN					
❏ 6026 ML	Bill Cosby "Himself"	1982	2.50	5.00	10.00
TETRAGRAMMATON					
❏ T-5100 [(2)]	8:15 12:15	1969	5.00	10.00	20.00
UNI					
❏ 73066	Bill Cosby	1969	2.50	5.00	10.00
❏ 73082	"Live" Madison Square Garden Center	1970	2.50	5.00	10.00
❏ 73100	When I Was a Kid	1971	2.50	5.00	10.00
❏ 73101	Bill Cosby Talks to Kids About Drugs	1971	3.75	7.50	15.00
❏ 73112	For Adults Only	1971	2.50	5.00	10.00
❏ 73139	Inside the Mind of Bill Cosby	1972	2.50	5.00	10.00
WARNER BROS.					
❏ PRO 249 [DJ]	Radio Sampler Album—The Best of Bill Cosby	1969	5.00	10.00	20.00

—Promo LP with edits of 12 tracks for radio use

Number	Title	Yr	VG	VG+	NM
❏ W 1518 [M]	Bill Cosby Is a Very Funny Fellow Right!	1964	3.75	7.50	15.00
❏ W 1567 [M]	I Started Out as a Child	1964	3.75	7.50	15.00
❏ W 1606 [M]	Why Is There Air?	1965	3.75	7.50	15.00
❏ W 1634 [M]	Wonderfulness	1966	3.75	7.50	15.00
❏ WS 1634 [S]	Wonderfulness	1966	3.75	7.50	15.00

—Gold label

Number	Title	Yr	VG	VG+	NM
❏ W 1691 [M]	Revenge	1967	3.75	7.50	15.00
❏ W 1709 [M]	Bill Cosby Sings/Silver Throat	1967	3.75	7.50	15.00
❏ WS 1709 [S]	Bill Cosby Sings/Silver Throat	1967	3.00	6.00	12.00
❏ W 1728 [M]	Bill Cosby Sings/Hooray for the Salvation Army Band	1968	3.75	7.50	15.00
❏ WS 1728 [S]	Bill Cosby Sings/Hooray for the Salvation Army Band	1968	3.00	6.00	12.00
❏ W 1734 [M]	To Russell, My Brother, Whom I Slept With	1968	3.75	7.50	15.00
❏ WS 1734 [S]	To Russell, My Brother, Whom I Slept With	1968	3.00	6.00	12.00
❏ WS 1757	200 M.P.H.	1968	3.00	6.00	12.00
❏ WS 1770	It's True! It's True!	1969	3.00	6.00	12.00
❏ WS 1798	The Best of Bill Cosby	1969	3.00	6.00	12.00
❏ WS 1836	More of the Best of Bill Cosby	1970	3.00	6.00	12.00

COSMIC TWINS, THE
STRATA-EAST

Number	Title	Yr	VG	VG+	NM
❏ SES-7410	The Waterbearers	1974	7.50	15.00	30.00

COSTA, DON
ABC-PARAMOUNT

Number	Title	Yr	VG	VG+	NM
❏ ABC-107 [M]	Music to Break a Lease	1956	6.25	12.50	25.00
❏ ABC-212 [M]	Music to Break a Sub-Lease	1958	6.25	12.50	25.00
❏ ABC-362 [M]	Don Costa Conducts His 15 Hits	1961	6.25	12.50	25.00

Number	Title (A Side/B Side)	Yr	VG	VG+	NM
COLUMBIA					
❏ CL 1880 [M]	Hollywood Premiere	1962	3.75	7.50	15.00
❏ CL 2041 [M]	Hits! Hits! Hits!	1963	3.75	7.50	15.00
❏ CS 8680 [S]	Hollywood Premiere	1962	6.25	12.50	25.00
❏ CS 8841 [S]	Hits! Hits! Hits!	1963	6.25	12.50	25.00
DCP INTERNATIONAL					
❏ DCL 3802 [M]	The Golden Touch	1964	3.00	6.00	12.00
❏ DCL 3806 [M]	Don Costa Plays Music from Umbrellas of Cherbourg and Other Film Music	1965	3.00	6.00	12.00
❏ DCS 6802 [S]	The Golden Touch	1964	3.75	7.50	15.00
❏ DCS 6806 [S]	Don Costa Plays Music from Umbrellas of Cherbourg and Other Film Music	1965	3.75	7.50	15.00
HARMONY					
❏ HL 7347 [M]	Days of Wine and Roses and Other Great Hits	1965	3.00	6.00	12.00
❏ HS 11147 [S]	Days of Wine and Roses and Other Great Hits	1965	3.75	7.50	15.00
MERCURY					
❏ SR 61177	Instrumental Versions of Simon and Garfunkel	1968	5.00	10.00	20.00
❏ SR 61216	The Don Costa Concept	1969	5.00	10.00	20.00
UNITED ARTISTS					
❏ UAL 3119 [M]	The Unforgiven	1960	5.00	10.00	20.00
❏ UAL 3134 [M]	Magnificent Motion Picture Music	1960	3.75	7.50	15.00
❏ WW 3513 [M]	The Sound of the Million Sellers	1960	3.75	7.50	15.00
❏ UAS 6134 [S]	Magnificent Motion Picture Music	1960	5.00	10.00	20.00
❏ WW 7501 [M]	Echoing Voices and Trombones	1960	5.00	10.00	20.00
❏ WWS 8501 [S]	Echoing Voices and Trombones	1960	7.50	15.00	30.00
❏ WWS 8513 [S]	The Sound of the Million Sellers	1960	6.25	12.50	25.00
VERVE					
❏ V-8702 [M]	Modern Delights	1967	5.00	10.00	20.00
❏ V6-8702 [S]	Modern Delights	1967	3.75	7.50	15.00

COSTA, EDDIE
CORAL

Number	Title	Yr	VG	VG+	NM
❏ CRL 57230 [M]	Guys and Dolls Like Vibes	1958	12.50	25.00	50.00
DOT					
❏ DLP-3206 [M]	The House of Blue Lights	1959	10.00	20.00	40.00
❏ DLP-25206 [S]	The House of Blue Lights	1959	12.50	25.00	50.00
INTERLUDE					
❏ MO-508 [M]	Eddie Costa Quintet	1959	10.00	20.00	40.00

—Reissue of Mode 118

Number	Title	Yr	VG	VG+	NM
❏ ST-1008 [S]	Eddie Costa Quintet	1959	7.50	15.00	30.00
JOSIE					
❏ JSS-2509 [S]	Eddie Costa with the Burke Trio	1963	6.25	12.50	25.00
❏ JOZ-3509 [M]	Eddie Costa with the Burke Trio	1963	5.00	10.00	20.00
MODE					
❏ LP-118 [M]	Eddie Costa Quintet	1957	25.00	50.00	100.00

COSTA, EDDIE/MAT MATTHEWS AND DON ELLIOTT
VERVE

Number	Title	Yr	VG	VG+	NM
❏ MGV-8237 [M]	Eddie Costa with Rolf Kuhn and Dick Johnson/ Mat Matthews and Don Elliott at Newport	1958	10.00	20.00	40.00
❏ V-8237 [M]	Eddie Costa with Rolf Kuhn and Dick Johnson/ Mat Matthews and Don Elliott at Newport	1961	5.00	10.00	20.00

COSTA, JOHNNY
CORAL

Number	Title	Yr	VG	VG+	NM
❏ CRL 57117 [M]	The Most Beautiful Girl in the World	1957	7.50	15.00	30.00
SAVOY					
❏ MG-12052 [M]	The Amazing Johnny Costa	1956	12.50	25.00	50.00
❏ MG-15056 [10]	Johnny Costa	1955	20.00	40.00	80.00

COSTANZO, JACK
GENE NORMAN

Number	Title	Yr	VG	VG+	NM
❏ GNP-19 [M]	Mr. Bongo	1955	12.50	25.00	50.00
LIBERTY					
❏ LRP-3093 [M]	Latin Fever	1958	6.25	12.50	25.00
❏ LRP-3109 [M]	Bongo Fever	1959	6.25	12.50	25.00
❏ LRP-3137 [M]	Afro Can-Can	1960	6.25	12.50	25.00
❏ LRP-3177 [M]	Learn-Play Bongos	1960	6.25	12.50	25.00
❏ LRP-3195 [M]	Naked City	1961	6.25	12.50	25.00
❏ LST-7020 [S]	Latin Fever	1958	7.50	15.00	30.00
❏ LST-7109 [S]	Bongo Fever	1959	7.50	15.00	30.00
❏ LST-7137 [S]	Afro Can-Can	1960	7.50	15.00	30.00
❏ LST-7195 [S]	Naked City	1961	7.50	15.00	30.00
NORGRAN					
❏ MGN-32 [10]	Afro-Cubano	1954	37.50	75.00	150.00

COSTANZO, JACK/ANDRE'S CUBAN ALL STARS
NORGRAN

Number	Title	Yr	VG	VG+	NM
❏ MGN-1067 [M]	Afro-Cubano	1956	25.00	50.00	100.00

—Combined reissue of Norgran 32 (by the former) and Clef 515 (by the latter)
VERVE

Number	Title	Yr	VG	VG+	NM
❏ MGV-8157 [M]	Afro-Cubano	1957	12.50	25.00	50.00
❏ V-8157 [M]	Afro-Cubano	1961	6.25	12.50	25.00

COSTELLO, ELVIS
COLUMBIA

Number	Title	Yr	VG	VG+	NM
❏ (no #) [PD]	My Aim Is True/This Year's Model	1978	20.00	40.00	80.00

—Promo-only picture disc; contains six songs from one album and six from the other

Number	Title	Yr	VG	VG+	NM
❏ AS 529 [EP]	Live at Hollywood High	1978	5.00	10.00	20.00

—Promo-only 12-inch version of 7-inch single

Number	Title	Yr	VG	VG+	NM
❏ AS 958 [DJ]	The Elvis Costello Interview with Tom Snyder	1981	5.00	10.00	20.00
❏ AS 1318 [DJ]	Almost Blue: Elvis Introduces His Favorite Country Songs	1981	12.50	25.00	50.00

—Radio sampler with introductions by Elvis before each track

Number	Title	Yr	VG	VG+	NM
❏ JC 35037	My Aim Is True	1977	3.75	7.50	15.00

—First pressings have yellow back covers

Number	Title	Yr	VG	VG+	NM
❏ JC 35037	My Aim Is True	1978	2.50	5.00	10.00

—Second pressings have a white back cover and no bar code

Number	Title	Yr	VG	VG+	NM
❏ PC 35037	My Aim Is True	1984	2.00	4.00	8.00

—Budget-line reissue with new prefix

Number	Title (A Side/B Side)	Yr	VG	VG+	NM
❏ JC 35331	This Year's Model	1978	2.50	5.00	10.00
—With standard Columbia label					
❏ JC 35331	This Year's Model	1978	3.00	6.00	12.00
—With "Costello" replacing "Columbia" on labels					
❏ PC 35331	This Year's Model	1984	2.00	4.00	8.00
—Budget-line reissue with new prefix					
❏ JC 35709	Armed Forces	1979	2.50	5.00	10.00
—Stock copy; add 30 percent if bonus 7-inch single is there; add another 50 percent if the 7-inch's picture sleeve is there					
❏ JC 35709 [DJ]	Armed Forces	1979	3.75	7.50	15.00
—White label promo; add 20 percent if bonus 7-inch single is there; add another 33 percent if the 7-inch's picture sleeve is there					
❏ PC 35709	Armed Forces	1984	2.00	4.00	8.00
—Budget-line reissue with new prefix; not issued with bonus single					
❏ JC 36347	Get Happy!!	1980	2.50	5.00	10.00
❏ PC 36347	Get Happy!!	1984	2.00	4.00	8.00
—Budget-line reissue with new prefix					
❏ JC 36839	Taking Liberties	1980	2.00	4.00	8.00
❏ JC 36839	Taking Liberties	1980	2.50	5.00	10.00
—With custom old-style Columbia label					
❏ PC 36839	Taking Liberties	1984	2.00	4.00	8.00
—Budget-line reissue with new prefix					
❏ JC 37051	Trust	1981	2.50	5.00	10.00
❏ PC 37051	Trust	1984	2.00	4.00	8.00
—Budget-line reissue with new prefix					
❏ FC 37562	Almost Blue	1981	2.50	5.00	10.00
❏ PC 37562	Almost Blue	1984	2.00	4.00	8.00
—Budget-line reissue with new prefix					
❏ FC 38157	Imperial Bedroom	1982	2.50	5.00	10.00
❏ PC 38157	Imperial Bedroom	1984	2.00	4.00	8.00
—Budget-line reissue with new prefix					
❏ FC 38897	Punch the Clock	1983	2.50	5.00	10.00
❏ FC 39429	Goodbye Cruel World	1984	2.50	5.00	10.00
❏ PC 39429	Goodbye Cruel World	198?	2.00	4.00	8.00
—Budget-line reissue with new prefix					
❏ FC 40101	The Best of Elvis Costello	1985	3.00	6.00	12.00
❏ FC 40173	King of America	1986	2.50	5.00	10.00
—By "The Costello Show Featuring Elvis Costello"					
❏ PC 40173	King of America	198?	2.00	4.00	8.00
—By "The Costello Show Featuring Elvis Costello"; budget-line reissue with new prefix					
❏ FC 40518	Blood & Chocolate	1986	2.50	5.00	10.00
❏ HC 48157	Imperial Bedroom	1982	12.50	25.00	50.00
—Half-speed mastered edition					
COSTELLO					
❏ AS 847 [EP]	Taking Liberties	1980	3.75	7.50	15.00
—Promo-only four-song sampler' "Costello" is where "Columbia" would normally be on the 78-rpm-style label					
WARNER BROS.					
❏ PRO-A-3488 [(2)DJ]	The Elvis Costello Hour	1989	10.00	20.00	40.00
—Music and interview; generic gatefold sleeve with sticker on cover					
❏ 25848	Spike	1989	2.50	5.00	10.00
❏ 46198	All This Useless Beauty	1996	2.50	5.00	10.00
❏ R 100841	Spike	1989	3.00	6.00	12.00
—BMG Direct Marketing edition					

COTTON, JAMES
ALLIGATOR

Number	Title (A Side/B Side)	Yr	VG	VG+	NM
❏ AL-4737	High Compression	1984	2.50	5.00	10.00
❏ AL-4746	Live from Chicago	1986	2.50	5.00	10.00
ANTONE'S					
❏ ANT-0007	James Cotton Live	1988	3.00	6.00	12.00
BLIND PIG					
❏ BP-2587	Take Me Back	1987	2.50	5.00	10.00
BUDDAH					
❏ BDS-5620	100% Cotton	1974	3.00	6.00	12.00
❏ BDS-5650	High Energy	1975	3.00	6.00	12.00
❏ BDS-5661 [(2)]	Live & On the Move!	1976	3.75	7.50	15.00
CAPITOL					
❏ SM-814	Taking Care of Business	197?	2.50	5.00	10.00
—Reissue with new prefix					
❏ ST-814	Taking Care of Business	1971	3.75	7.50	15.00
INTERMEDIA					
❏ QS-5006	Dealing with the Devil	198?	2.50	5.00	10.00
❏ QS-5011	Two Sides of the Blues	198?	2.50	5.00	10.00
VANGUARD					
❏ VSD-79283	Cut You Loose!	1969	3.75	7.50	15.00
VERVE FORECAST					
❏ FT-3023 [M]	The James Cotton Blues Band	1967	6.25	12.50	25.00
❏ FTS-3023 [S]	The James Cotton Blues Band	1967	5.00	10.00	20.00
❏ FTS-3038	Pure Cotton	1968	5.00	10.00	20.00

COTTON PICKERS, THE
PHILIPS

Number	Title (A Side/B Side)	Yr	VG	VG+	NM
❏ PHM 200025 [M]	Country Guitar	1962	5.00	10.00	20.00
❏ PHS 600025 [S]	Country Guitar	1962	6.25	12.50	25.00

COTTRELL, LOUIS
RIVERSIDE

Number	Title (A Side/B Side)	Yr	VG	VG+	NM
❏ RLP-385 [M]	Bourbon Street	1961	5.00	10.00	20.00
❏ RS-9385 [S]	Bourbon Street	1961	6.25	12.50	25.00

COUCH, ORVILLE
VEE JAY

Number	Title (A Side/B Side)	Yr	VG	VG+	NM
❏ VJLP-1087 [M]	Hello Trouble	1964	5.00	10.00	20.00
❏ VJS-1087 [S]	Hello Trouble	1964	10.00	20.00	40.00

COULTER, CLIFF
ABC IMPULSE!

Number	Title (A Side/B Side)	Yr	VG	VG+	NM
❏ AS-9197	Eastside San Jose	1971	5.00	10.00	20.00
❏ AS-9216	Do It Now!	1972	5.00	10.00	20.00

COUNCE, CURTIS
CONTEMPORARY

Number	Title (A Side/B Side)	Yr	VG	VG+	NM
❏ C-3526 [M]	Curtis Counce Group	1957	20.00	40.00	80.00
❏ M-3539 [M]	You Get More Bounce with Curtis Counce	1957	20.00	40.00	80.00
❏ M-3574 [M]	Carl's Blues	1960	10.00	20.00	40.00
❏ S-7526 [S]	Curtis Counce Group	1959	15.00	30.00	60.00
❏ S-7526 [S]	Landslide	196?	7.50	15.00	30.00
—Retitled version of "Curtis Counce Group"					
❏ C-7539	Counceltation	197?	5.00	10.00	20.00
—Retitled version of "You Get More Bounce with Curtis Counce"					
❏ S-7539 [S]	You Get More Bounce with Curtis Counce	1959	15.00	30.00	60.00
❏ S-7574 [S]	Carl's Blues	1960	12.50	25.00	50.00
❏ C-7655	Sonority	198?	5.00	10.00	20.00
DOOTO					
❏ DTL-247 [M]	Exploring the Future	1958	12.50	25.00	50.00

COUNT FIVE, THE
DOUBLE SHOT

Number	Title (A Side/B Side)	Yr	VG	VG+	NM
❏ DSM-1001 [M]	Psychotic Reaction	1966	10.00	20.00	40.00
❏ DSS-5001 [R]	Psychotic Reaction	1966	6.25	12.50	25.00

COUNTRY ALL-STARS, THE
RCA VICTOR

Number	Title (A Side/B Side)	Yr	VG	VG+	NM
❏ LPM-3167 [10]	String Dustin'	1953	37.50	75.00	150.00

COUNTRY CUT-UPS, THE
TOWN HOUSE

Number	Title (A Side/B Side)	Yr	VG	VG+	NM
❏ 1000 [M]	The Country Cut-Ups Go to College	195?	20.00	40.00	80.00

COUNTRY GENTLEMEN, THE
CIMARRON

Number	Title (A Side/B Side)	Yr	VG	VG+	NM
❏ 2001 [M]	Songs of the Pioneers	1962	10.00	20.00	40.00
MERCURY					
❏ MG-20858 [M]	Folk Session Inside	1963	5.00	10.00	20.00
❏ SR-60858 [S]	Folk Session Inside	1963	6.25	12.50	25.00
STARDAY					
❏ SLP-109 [M]	Traveling Dobro Blues	1959	12.50	25.00	50.00
❏ SLP-174 [M]	Bluegrass at Carnegie Hall	1962	10.00	20.00	40.00
❏ SLP-311 [M]	Songs of the Pioneers	1965	6.25	12.50	25.00

COUNTRY GOSPELAIRES, THE
STARDAY

Number	Title (A Side/B Side)	Yr	VG	VG+	NM
❏ SLP-105 [M]	The Church Back Home	1959	7.50	15.00	30.00

COUNTRY JOE AND THE FISH
CUSTOM FIDELITY

Number	Title (A Side/B Side)	Yr	VG	VG+	NM
❏ CFS-2348	Joe McDonald	1968	500.00	750.00	1000.
—Recorded in 1964, 200 copies were pressed for Joe McDonald.					
FANTASY					
❏ 9495	Paradise with an Ocean View	1975	2.50	5.00	10.00
❏ 9511	Love Is a Fire	1976	2.50	5.00	10.00
❏ 9525	Goodbye Blues	1977	2.50	5.00	10.00
❏ 9530	Reunion	1977	3.00	6.00	12.00
❏ 9544	Rock and Roll Music From the Planet Earth	1978	2.50	5.00	10.00
❏ 9586	Leisure Suite	1980	2.50	5.00	10.00
FIRST AMERICAN					
❏ PIC-3309	The Early Years	1979	2.50	5.00	10.00
MOBLIE FIDELITY					
❏ 1-056	Paradise with an Ocean View	1981	7.50	15.00	30.00
—Audiophile vinyl					
VANGUARD					
❏ VSD-27/28 [(2)]	The Life and Times of Country Joe & the Fish From Haight-Ashbury to Woodstock	1971	5.00	10.00	20.00
❏ VSD-85/86 [(2)]	The Essential Country Joe	1977	3.00	6.00	12.00
❏ VSD-6545	Country Joe & The Fish/Greatest Hits	1969	5.00	10.00	20.00
❏ VSD-6546	Thinking of Woody	1969	3.75	7.50	15.00
❏ VSD-6555	C.J. Fish	1970	5.00	10.00	20.00
❏ VSD-6557	Tonight I'm Singing Just for You	1970	3.75	7.50	15.00
❏ VRS-9244 [M]	Electric Music for the Mind and Body	1967	5.00	10.00	20.00
—Gold label					
❏ VRS-9244 [M]	Electric Music for the Mind and Body	1967	25.00	50.00	100.00
—Black label					
❏ 9266/79266	I-Feel-Like-I'm-Fixin'-to-die "Fish Game" Poster	1967	2.50	5.00	10.00
❏ VRS-9266 [M]	I-Feel-Like-I'm-Fixin'-to-Die	1967	5.00	10.00	20.00
❏ VSQ-40004/5 [(2)Q]	The Life and Times of Country Joe & the Fish From Haight-Ashbury to Woodstock	197?	10.00	20.00	40.00
❏ VSD-79244 [S]	Electric Music for the Mind and Body	1967	5.00	10.00	20.00
—Gold label					
❏ VSD-79244 [S]	Electric Music for the Mind and Body	1967	12.50	25.00	50.00
—Black label					
❏ VSD-79266 [S]	I-Feel-Like-I'm-Fixin'-to-Die	1967	5.00	10.00	20.00
❏ VSD-79277	Together	1968	5.00	10.00	20.00
❏ VSD-79299	Here We Are Again	1969	5.00	10.00	20.00
❏ VSD-79304	Hold On It's Coming	1971	3.75	7.50	15.00
❏ VSD-79315	War, War, War	1971	3.75	7.50	15.00
❏ VSD-79316	Incredible! Live!	1972	3.00	6.00	12.00
❏ VSD-79328	Paris Sessions	1973	3.00	6.00	12.00
❏ VSD-79348	Country Joe	1974	3.00	6.00	12.00

COUNTS, THE (2)
Detroit-based funk group.
AWARE

Number	Title (A Side/B Side)	Yr	VG	VG+	NM
❏ 2002	Love Sign	1973	6.25	12.50	25.00
❏ 2006	Funk Pump	1975	5.00	10.00	20.00
WESTBOUND					
❏ 2011	What's Up Front That Counts	1972	7.50	15.00	30.00

COURTLAND, JEROME
JUBILEE

Number	Title (A Side/B Side)	Yr	VG	VG+	NM
❏ LP 22 [10]	Through a Long and Sleepless Night	1955	10.00	20.00	40.00

Number	Title (A Side/B Side)	Yr	VG	VG+	NM
COURTNEY, LOU					
EPIC					
❏ KE 33011	I'm in Need of Love	1974	3.00	6.00	12.00
RCA VICTOR					
❏ APL1-1969	Buffalo Smoke	1976	3.00	6.00	12.00
RIVERSIDE					
❏ 92000	Skate Now (Shing-a-Ling)	1967	6.25	12.50	25.00
COUSIN WILBUR					
C.W.					
❏ 100 [M]	The Cousin Wilbur Show	195?	12.50	25.00	50.00
COUSINS, THE (2)					
PARKWAY					
❏ P-7005 [M]	Music of the Strip	1961	5.00	10.00	20.00
❏ SP-7005 [S]	Music of the Strip	1961	6.25	12.50	25.00
COVAY, DON					
ATLANTIC					
❏ 8104 [M]	Mercy	1965	10.00	20.00	40.00
❏ SD 8104 [S]	Mercy	1965	12.50	25.00	50.00
❏ 8120 [M]	See Saw	1966	10.00	20.00	40.00
❏ SD 8120 [S]	See Saw	1966	12.50	25.00	50.00
❏ SD 8237	The House of Blue Lights	1969	6.25	12.50	25.00
JANUS					
❏ 3038	Different Strokes for Different Folks	1972	3.75	7.50	15.00
MERCURY					
❏ SRM-1-653	Super Dude I	1973	3.00	6.00	12.00
❏ SRM-1-1020	Hot Blood	1974	3.00	6.00	12.00
❏ 835030-1	Checkin' In with Don Covay	1988	2.50	5.00	10.00
PHILADELPHIA INT'L.					
❏ PZ 33958	Travelin' In Heavy Traffic	1977	2.50	5.00	10.00
COWARD, NOEL					
COLUMBIA MASTERWORKS					
❏ ML 5063 [M]	Noel Coward at Las Vegas	1955	7.50	15.00	30.00
COWARD, NOEL, AND GERTRUDE LAWRENCE					
RCA VICTOR					
❏ LPM-1156 [M]	Noel and Gertie	1955	7.50	15.00	30.00
COWBOY JUNKIES					
LATENT RECORDINGS					
❏ LATEX 4	Whites Off Earth Now!!	1986	7.50	15.00	30.00
—Canada-only release					
RCA					
❏ 8568-1-R	The Trinity Session	1988	3.75	7.50	15.00
❏ 8568-1-R	The Trinity Session	1997	10.00	20.00	40.00
—Classic Records reissue on audiophile vinyl					
COWELL, STANLEY					
ECM					
❏ 1026	Illusion Suite	1973	6.25	12.50	25.00
STRATA-EAST					
❏ SES-19743	Musa-Ancestral Streams	1974	5.00	10.00	20.00
❏ SES-19765	Regeneration	1976	5.00	10.00	20.00
COWSILLS, THE					
LONDON					
❏ PS 587	On My Side	1971	7.50	15.00	30.00
MGM					
❏ GAS-103	The Cowsills (Golden Archive Series)	1970	3.75	7.50	15.00
❏ E-4498 [M]	The Cowsills	1967	5.00	10.00	20.00
❏ SE-4498 [S]	The Cowsills	1967	3.75	7.50	15.00
❏ E-4534 [M]	We Can Fly	1968	7.50	15.00	30.00
—Appears to exist only as a yellow label promo					
❏ SE-4534 [S]	We Can Fly	1968	3.75	7.50	15.00
❏ E-4554 [M]	Captain Sad and His Ship of Fools	1968	10.00	20.00	40.00
—Mono appears to be yellow label promo only					
❏ SE-4554 [S]	Captain Sad and His Ship of Fools	1968	3.75	7.50	15.00
❏ SE-4597	The Best of the Cowsills	1968	3.75	7.50	15.00
❏ SE-4619	The Cowsills in Concert	1969	3.75	7.50	15.00
❏ SE-4639	II X II	1969	5.00	10.00	20.00
WING					
❏ SRW-16354	The Cowsills Plus the Lincoln Park Zoo	1968	3.00	6.00	12.00
COX, DANNY					
PIONEER					
❏ 2125	Sunny	196?	7.50	15.00	30.00
TOGETHER					
❏ 1011	Birth Announcement	1970	7.50	15.00	30.00
COX, IDA					
RIVERSIDE					
❏ RLP-374 [M]	Blues for Rampart Street	1961	7.50	15.00	30.00
❏ RS-9374 [S]	Blues for Rampart Street	1961	10.00	20.00	40.00
COX, KENNY, CONTEMPORARY JAZZ QUINTET					
BLUE NOTE					
❏ BST-84302	Introducing Kenny Cox	1969	5.00	10.00	20.00
❏ BST-84339	Multidirection	1970	5.00	10.00	20.00
COX, SONNY					
CADET					
❏ LPS-765 [S]	The Wailer	1966	5.00	10.00	20.00
COXON'S ARMY					
Also see PAT BENATAR.					
TRACE					
❏ (# unknown)	Coxon's Army	1975	100.00	200.00	400.00

Number	Title (A Side/B Side)	Yr	VG	VG+	NM
CRADDOCK, BILLY "CRASH"					
ABC					
❏ X-777	Two Sides of "Crash"	1973	3.75	7.50	15.00
—Retitled version of above					
❏ X-777	Afraid I'll Want to Love Her One More Time	1973	6.25	12.50	25.00
❏ X-788	Mr. Country Rock	1973	3.75	7.50	15.00
❏ X-817	Rub It In	1974	3.00	6.00	12.00
—Multicolor label					
❏ X-817	Rub It In	1974	3.75	7.50	15.00
—Black label					
❏ X-850	Greatest Hits — Volume One	1975	3.00	6.00	12.00
❏ ABCD-875	Still Thinkin' Bout You	1975	3.00	6.00	12.00
❏ AB-1078	Billy "Crash" Craddock Sings His Greatest Hits	1978	2.50	5.00	10.00
ABC DOT					
❏ DOSD-2040	Easy As Pie	1976	3.00	6.00	12.00
❏ 2063	Crash	1976	3.00	6.00	12.00
❏ 2082	Live!	1977	3.00	6.00	12.00
ATLANTIC					
❏ 82012	Back on Track	1989	3.00	6.00	12.00
CAPITOL					
❏ ST-11758	Billy "Crash" Craddock	1978	2.50	5.00	10.00
❏ SW-11853	Turning Up and Turning On	1978	2.50	5.00	10.00
❏ ST-11946	Laughing and Crying, Living and Dying	1979	2.50	5.00	10.00
❏ ST-12054	Changes	1980	2.50	5.00	10.00
❏ ST-12249	The New Will Never Wear Off	1981	2.50	5.00	10.00
❏ ST-12304	Greatest Hits	1983	2.50	5.00	10.00
CARTWHEEL					
❏ 193	Knock Three Times	1971	5.00	10.00	20.00
❏ 05001	You Better Move On	1972	5.00	10.00	20.00
CHART					
❏ 1053	The Best of Billy Crash Craddock	1973	3.75	7.50	15.00
HARMONY					
❏ KH 32186	Billy "Crash" Craddock	1973	3.00	6.00	12.00
KING					
❏ 912 [M]	I'm Tore Up	1964	25.00	50.00	100.00
MCA					
❏ 662	Greatest Hits — Volume One	1981	2.00	4.00	8.00
—Reissue of ABC 850					
❏ 663	Billy "Crash" Craddock Sings His Greatest Hits	1981	2.00	4.00	8.00
—Reissue of ABC 1078					
❏ 664	Easy As Pie	1981	2.00	4.00	8.00
—Reissue of ABC Dot 2040					
❏ 665	Live!	1981	2.00	4.00	8.00
—Reissue of ABC Dot 2082					
❏ 666	The First Time	1981	2.00	4.00	8.00
❏ 4165 [(2)]	The Best of Billy "Crash" Craddock	198?	3.00	6.00	12.00
MCA DOT					
❏ 39054	Crash Craddock	1986	2.50	5.00	10.00
STARDAY					
❏ 3005	16 Favorite Hits	1978	2.50	5.00	10.00
CRAMER, FLOYD					
MGM					
❏ E-3502 [M]	That Honky-Tonk Piano	1957	10.00	20.00	40.00
❏ E-4223 [M]	Floyd Cramer Goes Honky Tonkin'	1964	3.75	7.50	15.00
❏ SE-4223 [R]	Floyd Cramer Goes Honky Tonkin'	1964	3.00	6.00	12.00
❏ SE-4666	Floyd Cramer Goes Honky Tonkin'	1970	3.00	6.00	12.00
—Reissue of 4223					
PAIR					
❏ PDL2-1049 [(2)]	Country Classics	1986	3.00	6.00	12.00
RCA					
❏ 5621-1-R	Our Class Reunion	1987	2.50	5.00	10.00
RCA CAMDEN					
❏ ACL2-0128 [(2)]	Floyd Cramer Plays the Big Hits	1973	3.00	6.00	12.00
❏ ACL1-0563	Spotlight On Floyd Cramer	1974	2.50	5.00	10.00
❏ CAL-874 [M]	The Magic Touch	1965	3.00	6.00	12.00
❏ CAS-874(e) [P]	The Magic Touch	1965	3.00	6.00	12.00
—Even though this album is labeled "Stereo Electronically Reprocessed," nine of the 10 tracks are in true stereo					
❏ CAL-2104 [M]	Distinctive Piano Styling	196?	3.00	6.00	12.00
❏ CAS-2104 [S]	Distinctive Piano Styling	196?	3.00	6.00	12.00
❏ CAL-2152 [M]	Night Train	1967	3.00	6.00	12.00
❏ CAS-2152 [S]	Night Train	1967	3.00	6.00	12.00
❏ CAS-2508	Almost Persuaded	1971	3.00	6.00	12.00
❏ CXS-9016 [(2)]	A Date with Floyd Cramer	1972	3.75	7.50	15.00
RCA VICTOR					
❏ APD1-0155 [Q]	Super Country Hits	1973	3.75	7.50	15.00
❏ APL1-0155	Super Country Hits	1973	3.00	6.00	12.00
❏ APD1-0299 [Q]	Class of '73	1973	3.75	7.50	15.00
❏ APL1-0299	Class of '73	1973	3.00	6.00	12.00
❏ APD1-0469 [Q]	The Young and the Restless	1974	3.75	7.50	15.00
❏ APL1-0469	The Young and the Restless	1974	3.00	6.00	12.00
❏ APL1-0661	Floyd Cramer In Concert	1974	3.00	6.00	12.00
❏ APD1-0893 [Q]	Piano Masterpieces (1900-75)	1975	3.75	7.50	15.00
❏ APL1-0893	Piano Masterpieces (1900-75)	1975	2.50	5.00	10.00
❏ APD1-1191 [Q]	Class of '74 and '75	1975	3.75	7.50	15.00
❏ APL1-1191	Class of '74 and '75	1975	2.50	5.00	10.00
❏ APD1-1541 [Q]	Floyd Cramer Country	1976	3.75	7.50	15.00
❏ APL1-1541	Floyd Cramer Country	1976	2.50	5.00	10.00
❏ LPM-2151 [M]	Hello Blues	1960	3.75	7.50	15.00
❏ LSP-2151 [S]	Hello Blues	1960	5.00	10.00	20.00
❏ APL1-2278	Floyd Cramer & the Keyboard Kick Band	1977	2.50	5.00	10.00
❏ ANL1-2344	Hits from Country Hall	1977	2.50	5.00	10.00
❏ LPM-2350 [M]	Last Date	1961	5.00	10.00	20.00
❏ LSP-2350 [S]	Last Date	1961	6.25	12.50	25.00
❏ LPM-2359 [M]	On the Rebound	1961	3.75	7.50	15.00
❏ LSP-2359 [S]	On the Rebound	1961	5.00	10.00	20.00
❏ LPM-2428 [M]	Floyd Cramer Gets Organ-ized	1962	3.75	7.50	15.00

Number	Title (A Side/B Side)	Yr	VG	VG+	NM
❏ LSP-2428 [S]	Floyd Cramer Gets Organ-ized	1962	5.00	10.00	20.00
❏ LPM-2466 [M]	America's Biggest Selling Pianist	1962	3.75	7.50	15.00
❏ LSP-2466 [S]	America's Biggest Selling Pianist	1962	5.00	10.00	20.00
❏ LPM-2544 [M]	I Remember Hank Williams	1962	3.75	7.50	15.00
❏ LSP-2544 [S]	I Remember Hank Williams	1962	5.00	10.00	20.00
❏ LPM-2642 [M]	Swing Along	1963	3.75	7.50	15.00
❏ LSP-2642 [S]	Swing Along	1963	5.00	10.00	20.00
❏ AHL1-2644	Looking for Mr. Goodbar	1978	2.50	5.00	10.00
❏ LPM-2701 [M]	Comin' On	1963	3.75	7.50	15.00
❏ LSP-2701 [S]	Comin' On	1963	5.00	10.00	20.00
❏ LPM-2800 [M]	Country Piano — City Strings	1964	3.75	7.50	15.00
❏ LSP-2800 [S]	Country Piano — City Strings	1964	5.00	10.00	20.00
❏ LPM-2883 [M]	Cramer at the Console	1964	3.75	7.50	15.00
❏ LSP-2883 [S]	Cramer at the Console	1964	5.00	10.00	20.00
❏ LPM-2888 [M]	The Best of Floyd Cramer	1964	3.00	6.00	12.00
❏ LSP-2888 [S]	The Best of Floyd Cramer	1964	3.75	7.50	15.00
❏ AHL1-3209	Super Hits	1979	2.50	5.00	10.00
❏ LPM-3318 [M]	Hits from the Country Hall of Fame	1965	3.75	7.50	15.00
❏ LSP-3318 [S]	Hits from the Country Hall of Fame	1965	5.00	10.00	20.00
❏ LPM-3405 [M]	Class of '65	1965	3.00	6.00	12.00
❏ LSP-3405 [S]	Class of '65	1965	3.75	7.50	15.00
❏ ANL1-3469	Floyd Cramer In Concert	1979	2.00	4.00	8.00
❏ AHL1-3487	Last Date	1979	2.50	5.00	10.00
❏ LPM-3533 [M]	The Big Ones	1966	3.00	6.00	12.00
❏ LSP-3533 [S]	The Big Ones	1966	3.75	7.50	15.00
❏ AHL1-3613	Dallas	1980	2.50	5.00	10.00
❏ LPM-3650 [M]	Class of '66	1966	3.00	6.00	12.00
❏ LSP-3650 [S]	Class of '66	1966	3.75	7.50	15.00
❏ AYL1-3745	Piano Masterpieces (1900-75)	1980	2.00	4.00	8.00
❏ LPM-3746 [M]	Here's What's Happening!	1967	3.75	7.50	15.00
❏ LSP-3746 [S]	Here's What's Happening!	1967	3.75	7.50	15.00
❏ LPM-3811 [M]	Floyd Cramer Plays the Monkees	1967	3.75	7.50	15.00
❏ LSP-3811 [S]	Floyd Cramer Plays the Monkees	1967	3.75	7.50	15.00
❏ LPM-3827 [M]	Class of '67	1967	3.75	7.50	15.00
❏ LSP-3827 [S]	Class of '67	1967	3.75	7.50	15.00
❏ LPM-3828 [M]	We Wish You a Merry Christmas	1967	7.50	15.00	30.00
❏ LSP-3828 [S]	We Wish You a Merry Christmas	1967	3.00	6.00	12.00
❏ AYL1-3900	The Best of Floyd Cramer	1981	2.00	4.00	8.00
❏ LPM-3925 [M]	Floyd Cramer Plays Country Classics	1968	5.00	10.00	20.00
❏ LSP-3925 [S]	Floyd Cramer Plays Country Classics	1968	3.75	7.50	15.00
❏ AYL1-4008	Great Country Hits	1981	2.00	4.00	8.00
❏ LPM-4025 [M]	Class of '68	1968	—	—	—
—Canceled?					
❏ LSP-4025 [S]	Class of '68	1968	3.75	7.50	15.00
❏ LSP-4070	MacArthur Park	1968	3.75	7.50	15.00
❏ LSP-4091	The Best of Floyd Cramer, Volume 2	1969	3.75	7.50	15.00
❏ AHL1-4119	Best of the West	1982	2.50	5.00	10.00
❏ LSP-4162	Class of '69	1969	3.75	7.50	15.00
❏ LSP-4220	Floyd Cramer Plays More Country Classics	1969	3.75	7.50	15.00
❏ LSP-4312	The Big Ones, Volume II	1970	3.75	7.50	15.00
❏ LSP-4367	Floyd Cramer with the Music City Pops	1970	3.75	7.50	15.00
❏ LSP-4437	Class of '70	1970	3.75	7.50	15.00
❏ LSP-4500	Sounds of Sunday	1971	3.75	7.50	15.00
❏ LSP-4590	Class of '71	1971	3.75	7.50	15.00
❏ LSP-4676	Detours	1972	3.75	7.50	15.00
❏ LSP-4772	Class of '72	1972	3.75	7.50	15.00
❏ LSP-4821	Best of the Class of…	1973	3.75	7.50	15.00
❏ AHL1-5452	Collector's Series	1985	2.50	5.00	10.00
❏ VPS-6031 [(2)]	This Is Floyd Cramer	1970	5.00	10.00	20.00

CRAMPS, THE
ENIGMA
Number	Title (A Side/B Side)	Yr	VG	VG+	NM
❏ 21	Smell of Female	1983	3.75	7.50	15.00
❏ EPRO 268 [DJ]	Stay Sick!	1990	6.25	12.50	25.00
—Promo-only version					
❏ 73543	Stay Sick!	1990	3.75	7.50	15.00

EPITAPH
❏ 86449	Flamejob	199?	3.00	6.00	12.00
—Reissue of Medicine Label 24592					
❏ 86516	Big Beat from Badsville	1997	3.00	6.00	12.00

I.R.S.
❏ SP-007	Songs the Lord Taught Us	1980	5.00	10.00	20.00
❏ SP-501 [EP]	Gravest Hits	1979	6.25	12.50	25.00
❏ SP-70007	Songs the Lord Taught Us	198?	3.00	6.00	12.00
—Reissue of 007					
❏ SP-70016	Psychedelic Jungle	1981	5.00	10.00	20.00
❏ SP-70042	Bad Music for Bad People	1984	3.75	7.50	15.00
❏ SP-70501 [EP]	Gravest Hits	198?	2.50	5.00	10.00
—Reissue of 501					

MEDICINE LABEL
❏ 24592	Flamejob	1994	3.75	7.50	15.00

CRANE, BOB
EPIC
❏ LN 24224 [M]	The Funny Side of TV	1966	6.25	12.50	25.00
❏ BN 26224 [S]	The Funny Side of TV	1966	7.50	15.00	30.00

CRAWFORD, HANK
ATLANTIC
❏ 1356 [M]	More Soul	1960	5.00	10.00	20.00
—Purple and red label, white fan logo					
❏ SD 1356 [S]	More Soul	1960	6.25	12.50	25.00
—Green and blue label, white fan logo					
❏ 1372 [M]	The Soul Clinic	1961	5.00	10.00	20.00
—Purple and red label, white fan logo					
❏ SD 1372 [S]	The Soul Clinic	1961	6.25	12.50	25.00
—Green and blue label, white fan logo					
❏ SD 1387 [S]	From the Heart	1962	5.00	10.00	20.00
❏ SD 1405 [S]	Soul of the Ballad	1963	5.00	10.00	20.00
❏ SD 1423 [S]	True Blue	1964	5.00	10.00	20.00
❏ SD 1436 [S]	Dig These Blues	1965	5.00	10.00	20.00
❏ SD 1455 [S]	After Hours	1966	5.00	10.00	20.00

Number	Title (A Side/B Side)	Yr	VG	VG+	NM
❏ 1470 [M]	Mr. Blues	1967	5.00	10.00	20.00

MOBILE FIDELITY
❏ 1-224	Soul of the Ballad	1995	6.25	12.50	25.00
—Audiophile vinyl					

CRAWFORD, JOHNNY
DEL-FI
❏ DFLP-1220 [M]	The Captivating Johnny Crawford	1962	10.00	20.00	40.00
❏ DFLP-1223 [M]	A Young Man's Fancy	1962	7.50	15.00	30.00
❏ DFST-1223 [S]	A Young Man's Fancy	1962	10.00	20.00	40.00
❏ DFLP-1224 [M]	Rumors	1963	7.50	15.00	30.00
❏ DFST-1224 [S]	Rumors	1963	10.00	20.00	40.00
❏ DFLP-1229 [M]	His Greatest Hits	1963	7.50	15.00	30.00
❏ DFST-1229 [S]	His Greatest Hits	1963	10.00	20.00	40.00
❏ DFLP-1248 [M]	Greatest Hits, Volume 2	1964	5.00	10.00	20.00
❏ DFST-1248 [S]	Greatest Hits, Volume 2	1964	6.25	12.50	25.00

GUEST STAR
❏ GS-1470 [M]	Johnny Crawford	196?	5.00	10.00	20.00
❏ GSS-1470 [S]	Johnny Crawford	196?	6.25	12.50	25.00

RHINO
❏ RNDF-202	The Best of Johnny Crawford	1982	3.00	6.00	12.00

SUPREME
❏ M-110 [M]	Songs from "The Restless Ones"	1965	5.00	10.00	20.00
❏ MS-210 [S]	Songs from "The Restless Ones"	1965	6.25	12.50	25.00

CRAWFORD, RAY
CANDID
❏ CJM-8028 [M]	Smooth Groove	1963	6.25	12.50	25.00
❏ CJS-9028 [S]	Smooth Groove	1963	7.50	15.00	30.00

CRAYTON, PEE WEE
CROWN
❏ CLP-5175 [M]	Pee Wee Crayton	1959	25.00	50.00	100.00
—Black label					
❏ CLP-5175 [M]	Pee Wee Crayton	196?	5.00	10.00	20.00
—Gray label					

VANGUARD
❏ VSD-6566	The Things I Used to Do	1971	3.75	7.50	15.00

CRAZY ELEPHANT
BELL
❏ 6034	Crazy Elephant	1969	5.00	10.00	20.00

CRAZY OTTO
DECCA
❏ DL 4157 [M]	Have Piano, Will Travel	1961	3.75	7.50	15.00
❏ DL 8113 [M]	Crazy Otto	1955	5.00	10.00	20.00
—Black label, silver print					
❏ DL 8113 [M]	Crazy Otto	1960	3.00	6.00	12.00
—Black label with color bars					
❏ DL 8163 [M]	Crazy Otto Rides Again	1956	5.00	10.00	20.00
❏ DL 8627 [M]	Crazy Otto's Back in Town	1957	3.75	7.50	15.00
❏ DL 8737 [M]	Honky Tonk Piano	1958	3.75	7.50	15.00
❏ DL 8919 [M]	Golden Award Songs	1960	3.75	7.50	15.00
❏ DL 74157 [S]	Have Piano, Will Travel	1961	5.00	10.00	20.00
❏ DL 78919 [S]	Golden Award Songs	1960	5.00	10.00	20.00

MGM
❏ E-4150 [M]	Crazy Otto Plays Crazy Tunes	1963	3.00	6.00	12.00
❏ SE-4150 [S]	Crazy Otto Plays Crazy Tunes	1963	3.75	7.50	15.00

VOCALION
❏ VL 3663 [M]	Crazy Otto Goes Sentimental	196?	3.00	6.00	12.00

CREAM
ATCO
❏ 33-206 [M]	Fresh Cream	1967	12.50	25.00	50.00
❏ SD 33-206 [S]	Fresh Cream	1967	7.50	15.00	30.00
—Purple and brown labels					
❏ SD 33-206 [S]	Fresh Cream	1969	3.75	7.50	15.00
—Yellow labels					
❏ 33-232 [M]	Disraeli Gears	1967	12.50	25.00	50.00
❏ SD 33-232 [S]	Disraeli Gears	1967	7.50	15.00	30.00
—Purple and brown labels					
❏ SD 33-232 [S]	Disraeli Gears	1969	3.75	7.50	15.00
—Yellow labels					
❏ SD 33-291	Best of Cream	1969	6.25	12.50	25.00
❏ SD 33-328	Live Cream	1970	6.25	12.50	25.00
❏ 2-700 [(2)M]	Wheels of Fire	1968	50.00	100.00	200.00
—White label promo; no stock copies are mono					
❏ SD 2-700 [(2)S]	Wheels of Fire	1968	12.50	25.00	50.00
—Purple and brown labels; foil-like cover					
❏ SD 2-700 [(2)S]	Wheels of Fire	1969	5.00	10.00	20.00
—Yellow labels; dull gray cover					
❏ SD 7001	Goodbye	1969	3.75	7.50	15.00
—Yellow labels					
❏ SD 7001	Goodbye	1969	7.50	15.00	30.00
—Purple and brown labels; deduct 33% if poster is missing					
❏ SD 7005	Live Cream — Volume II	1972	6.25	12.50	25.00

DCC COMPACT CLASSICS
❏ LPZ-2015	Fresh Cream	1996	25.00	50.00	100.00
—Audiophile vinyl					

MOBILE FIDELITY
❏ 2-066 [(2)]	Wheels of Fire	1980	22.50	45.00	90.00
—Audiophile vinyl					
❏ 1-264	Goodbye	1996	—	—	—
—Audiophile vinyl; canceled					

POLYDOR
❏ 24-3502 [(2)]	Heavy Cream	1972	3.75	7.50	15.00
❏ 24-5529	Off the Top	1973	3.75	7.50	15.00

RSO
❏ 015 [(2)DJ]	Classic Cuts	1978	10.00	20.00	40.00
—Promo-only compilation					

Number	Title (A Side/B Side)	Yr	VG	VG+	NM
❑ RS-1-3009	Fresh Cream	1977	3.00	6.00	12.00
❑ RS-1-3010	Disraeli Gears	1977	3.00	6.00	12.00
❑ RS-1-3012	Best of Cream	1977	3.00	6.00	12.00
❑ RS-1-3013	Goodbye	1977	3.00	6.00	12.00
❑ RS-1-3014	Live Cream	1977	3.00	6.00	12.00
❑ RS-1-3015	Live Cream — Volume 2	1977	3.00	6.00	12.00
❑ RS-2-3802 [(2)]	Wheels of Fire	1977	3.75	7.50	15.00

SPRINGBOARD

Number	Title (A Side/B Side)	Yr	VG	VG+	NM
❑ SPB 4037	Early Cream	1972	3.75	7.50	15.00

CREATION OF SUNLIGHT
WINDI

Number	Title (A Side/B Side)	Yr	VG	VG+	NM
❑ 1001	Creation of Sunlight	1968	150.00	300.00	600.00

CREEDENCE CLEARWATER REVIVAL
ANALOGUE PRODUCTIONS

Number	Title (A Side/B Side)	Yr	VG	VG+	NM
❑ AAPP-8382	Creedence Clearwater Revival	2002	6.25	12.50	25.00
—Audiophile edition on heavy vinyl					
❑ AAPP-8387	Bayou Country	2002	6.25	12.50	25.00
—Audiophile edition on heavy vinyl					
❑ AAPP-8393	Green River	2002	6.25	12.50	25.00
—Audiophile edition on heavy vinyl					
❑ AAPP-8397	Willie and the Poor Boys	2002	6.25	12.50	25.00
—Audiophile edition on heavy vinyl					
❑ AAPP-8402	Cosmo's Factory	2002	6.25	12.50	25.00
—Audiophile edition on heavy vinyl					
❑ AAPP-9404	Mardi Gras	2002	6.25	12.50	25.00
—Audiophile edition on heavy vinyl					

DCC COMPACT CLASSICS

Number	Title (A Side/B Side)	Yr	VG	VG+	NM
❑ LPZ-2019	Willie and the Poor Boys	1996	12.50	25.00	50.00
—Audiophile vinyl					

FANTASY

Number	Title (A Side/B Side)	Yr	VG	VG+	NM
❑ CCR-1 [(2)]	Live in Europe	1973	3.00	6.00	12.00
❑ CCR-2 [(2)]	Chronicle (The 20 Greatest Hits)	1976	3.75	7.50	15.00
—Brown labels					
❑ CCR-2 [(2)]	Chronicle (The 20 Greatest Hits)	1979	3.00	6.00	12.00
—Whitish or light blue labels					
❑ CCR-3 [(2)]	Chronicle, Volume 2	1987	3.75	7.50	15.00
❑ CCR-68 [(2)]	Creedence Clearwater Revival 1968/69	1981	3.00	6.00	12.00
—Compilation of 8382 and 8387					
❑ CCR-69 [(2)]	Creedence Clearwater Revival 1969	1981	3.00	6.00	12.00
—Compilation of 8393 and 8397					
❑ CCR-70 [(2)]	Creedence Clearwater Revival 1970	1981	3.00	6.00	12.00
—Compilation of 8402 and 8410					
❑ FPM-4001 [Q]	Creedence Gold	197?	12.50	25.00	50.00
❑ MPF-4501	The Royal Albert Hall Concert	1980	3.75	7.50	15.00
—Album withdrawn and changed when it was discovered this didn't come from the Royal Albert Hall					
❑ MPF-4501	The Concert	1981	2.50	5.00	10.00
—Retitled version					
❑ MPF-4509	Creedence Country	1981	2.50	5.00	10.00
❑ ORC-4512	Creedence Clearwater Revival	1981	2.00	4.00	8.00
—Reissue of 8382					
❑ ORC-4513	Bayou Country	1981	2.00	4.00	8.00
—Reissue of 8387					
❑ ORC-4514	Green River	1981	2.00	4.00	8.00
—Reissue of 8393					
❑ ORC-4515	Willy and the Poor Boys	1981	2.00	4.00	8.00
—Reissue of 8397					
❑ ORC-4516	Cosmo's Factory	1981	2.00	4.00	8.00
—Reissue of 8402					
❑ ORC-4517	Pendulum	1981	2.00	4.00	8.00
—Reissue of 8410					
❑ ORC-4518	Mardi Gras	1981	2.00	4.00	8.00
—Reissue of 9404					
❑ MPF-4522	The Movie Album	1985	2.00	4.00	8.00
❑ ORC-4526 [(2)]	Live in Europe	1986	2.50	5.00	10.00
❑ F-8382	Creedence Clearwater Revival	1968	3.75	7.50	15.00
—With "Susie Q" mentioned on the front cover; dark blue label					
❑ F-8382	Creedence Clearwater Revival	1968	6.25	12.50	25.00
—With no reference to "Susie Q" on the front cover					
❑ F-8382	Creedence Clearwater Revival	1973	2.50	5.00	10.00
—Brown label					
❑ F-8382 [DJ]	Creedence Clearwater Revival	1968	20.00	40.00	80.00
—White label promo					
❑ F-8387	Bayou Country	1969	3.75	7.50	15.00
—Dark blue label					
❑ F-8387	Bayou Country	1973	2.50	5.00	10.00
—Brown label					
❑ F-8387 [DJ]	Bayou Country	1969	20.00	40.00	80.00
—White label promo					
❑ F-8393	Green River	1969	3.75	7.50	15.00
—Dark blue label					
❑ F-8393	Green River	1973	2.50	5.00	10.00
—Brown label					
❑ F-8393 [DJ]	Green River	1969	20.00	40.00	80.00
—White label promo					
❑ F-8397	Willy and the Poor Boys	1969	3.75	7.50	15.00
—Dark blue label					
❑ F-8397	Willy and the Poor Boys	1973	2.50	5.00	10.00
—Brown label					
❑ F-8397 [DJ]	Willy and the Poor Boys	1969	20.00	40.00	80.00
—White label promo					
❑ F-8402	Cosmo's Factory	1970	3.75	7.50	15.00
—Dark blue label					
❑ F-8402	Cosmo's Factory	1973	2.50	5.00	10.00
—Brown label					
❑ F-8402 [DJ]	Cosmo's Factory	1970	20.00	40.00	80.00
—White label promo					
❑ F-8410	Pendulum	1970	3.75	7.50	15.00
—Dark blue label					
❑ F-8410	Pendulum	1973	2.50	5.00	10.00
—Brown label					
❑ F-9404	Mardi Gras	1972	3.75	7.50	15.00
—Dark blue label					
❑ F-9404	Mardi Gras	1973	2.50	5.00	10.00
—Brown label					
❑ F-9418	Creedence Gold	1972	2.50	5.00	10.00
❑ F-9430	More Creedence Gold	1973	2.50	5.00	10.00
❑ F-9621	Chooglin'	1982	2.00	4.00	8.00

HEARTLAND

Number	Title (A Side/B Side)	Yr	VG	VG+	NM
❑ HR 2039 [(3)]	Creedence Clearwater Revival	1990	3.75	7.50	15.00

K-TEL

Number	Title (A Side/B Side)	Yr	VG	VG+	NM
❑ NU 9360	The Best of Creedence Clearwater Revival — 20 Super Hits	1978	3.75	7.50	15.00

MOBILE FIDELITY

Number	Title (A Side/B Side)	Yr	VG	VG+	NM
❑ 1-037	Cosmo's Factory	1979	17.50	35.00	70.00
—Audiophile vinyl					

TIME-LIFE

Number	Title (A Side/B Side)	Yr	VG	VG+	NM
❑ SCLR-18 [(2)]	Creedence Clearwater Revival	1989	3.75	7.50	15.00
—Part of Time-Life's "Classic Rock" series					

CREME SODA
TRINITY

Number	Title (A Side/B Side)	Yr	VG	VG+	NM
❑ CST-11	Tricky Zingers	197?	25.00	50.00	100.00
—With photo of group on cover					
❑ CST-11	Tricky Zingers	197?	10.00	20.00	40.00
—With white cover					

CRESCENDOS, THE (1)
GUEST STAR

Number	Title (A Side/B Side)	Yr	VG	VG+	NM
❑ G-1453 [M]	Oh Julie	1962	12.50	25.00	50.00
❑ GS-1453 [R]	Oh Julie	1962	5.00	10.00	20.00

CRESTS, THE
COED

Number	Title (A Side/B Side)	Yr	VG	VG+	NM
❑ LPC-901 [M]	The Crests Sing All Biggies	1960	50.00	100.00	200.00
—Red label					
❑ LPC-901 [M]	The Crests Sing All Biggies	1960	100.00	200.00	400.00
—Yellow label, black print					
❑ LPC-904 [M]	The Best of the Crests/16 Fabulous Hits	1961	100.00	200.00	400.00
—Label simply calls this "16 Fabulous Hits"					

COLLECTABLES

Number	Title (A Side/B Side)	Yr	VG	VG+	NM
❑ COL-5009	Greatest Hits	1982	3.00	6.00	12.00

POST

Number	Title (A Side/B Side)	Yr	VG	VG+	NM
❑ 3000	The Crests Sing	196?	10.00	20.00	40.00

RHINO

Number	Title (A Side/B Side)	Yr	VG	VG+	NM
❑ R1-70948	The Best of the Crests	1989	3.00	6.00	12.00

CREVELING, CAROLE
EUTERPE

Number	Title (A Side/B Side)	Yr	VG	VG+	NM
❑ ETP-101 [M]	Carole Creveling	1955	12.50	25.00	50.00

CREW CUTS, THE
CAMAY

Number	Title (A Side/B Side)	Yr	VG	VG+	NM
❑ CA-1002 [M]	The Great New Sound of the Crew Cuts	196?	5.00	10.00	20.00
❑ CA-3002 [S]	The Great New Sound of the Crew Cuts	196?	6.25	12.50	25.00

MERCURY

Number	Title (A Side/B Side)	Yr	VG	VG+	NM
❑ MG-20067 [M]	The Crew Cuts Go Longhair	1955	12.50	25.00	50.00
❑ MG-20140 [M]	The Crew Cuts On Campus	1956	12.50	25.00	50.00
❑ MG-20143 [M]	Crew Cut Capers	1956	12.50	25.00	50.00
❑ MG-20144 [M]	Rock and Roll Bash	1956	20.00	40.00	80.00
❑ MG-20199 [M]	Music A La Carte	1957	12.50	25.00	50.00
❑ MG-25200 [10]	The Crew Cuts On Campus	1956	20.00	40.00	80.00

PICADILLY

Number	Title (A Side/B Side)	Yr	VG	VG+	NM
❑ PIC-3560	The Wonderful Happy Crazy Innocent World	1980	2.50	5.00	10.00

RCA VICTOR

Number	Title (A Side/B Side)	Yr	VG	VG+	NM
❑ PR-102 [M]	The Crew Cuts Sing Out!	1960	6.25	12.50	25.00
❑ PR-129 [M]	The Crew Cuts Have a Ball	1960	6.25	12.50	25.00
—Produced for Ebonite bowling balls; Side 2 has "Bowling Tips by Top Stars"					
❑ LPM-1933 [M]	Surprise Package	1958	7.50	15.00	30.00
❑ LSP-1933 [S]	Surprise Package	1959	10.00	20.00	40.00
❑ LPM-2037 [M]	The Crew Cuts Sing	1959	7.50	15.00	30.00
❑ LSP-2037 [S]	The Crew Cuts Sing	1959	10.00	20.00	40.00
❑ LPM-2067 [M]	You Must Have Been a Beautiful Baby	1960	7.50	15.00	30.00
❑ LSP-2067 [S]	You Must Have Been a Beautiful Baby	1960	10.00	20.00	40.00

WING

Number	Title (A Side/B Side)	Yr	VG	VG+	NM
❑ MGW-12125 [M]	Rock and Roll Bash	196?	6.25	12.50	25.00
❑ MGW-12145 [M]	The Crew Cuts On Campus	196?	5.00	10.00	20.00
❑ MGW-12177 [M]	The Crew Cuts	196?	5.00	10.00	20.00
❑ MGW-12180 [M]	High School Favorites	196?	5.00	10.00	20.00
❑ MGW-12195 [M]	The Crew Cuts Sing the Masters	196?	5.00	10.00	20.00

CREWE, BOB
CGC

Number	Title (A Side/B Side)	Yr	VG	VG+	NM
❑ 1000	Let Me Touch You	1970	3.00	6.00	12.00

DYNO VOICE

Number	Title (A Side/B Side)	Yr	VG	VG+	NM
❑ DV-1902 [M]	Music to Watch Birds By	1967	3.75	7.50	15.00
❑ DV-1906 [M]	The Bob Crewe Generation In Classic Form	1968	3.75	7.50	15.00
❑ DV-9003 [M]	Music to Watch Girls By	1967	3.75	7.50	15.00
❑ DVS-9003 [S]	Music to Watch Girls By	1967	3.00	6.00	12.00
❑ DV-31902 [S]	Music to Watch Birds By	1967	3.00	6.00	12.00
❑ DV-31906 [S]	The Bob Crewe Generation In Classic Form	1968	3.00	6.00	12.00

ELEKTRA

Number	Title (A Side/B Side)	Yr	VG	VG+	NM
❑ 7E-1083	Street Talk	1976	3.00	6.00	12.00
❑ 7E-1103	Motivation	1977	3.00	6.00	12.00

PHILIPS

Number	Title (A Side/B Side)	Yr	VG	VG+	NM
❑ PHM 200150 [M]	All the Song Hits of the Four Seasons	1964	6.25	12.50	25.00
❑ PHM 200238 [M]	Bob Crewe Plays the Four Seasons' Hits	1967	5.00	10.00	20.00
❑ PHS 600150 [S]	All the Song Hits of the Four Seasons	1964	7.50	15.00	30.00
❑ PHS 600238 [S]	Bob Crewe Plays the Four Seasons' Hits	1967	3.75	7.50	15.00

WARWICK

Number	Title (A Side/B Side)	Yr	VG	VG+	NM
❑ W-2009 [M]	Kicks	1960	6.25	12.50	25.00

Number	Title (A Side/B Side)	Yr	VG	VG+	NM
❏ WST-2009 [S]	Kicks	1960	12.50	25.00	50.00
❏ W-2034 [M]	Crazy in the Heart	1961	6.25	12.50	25.00
❏ WST-2034 [S]	Crazy in the Heart	1961	12.50	25.00	50.00

CRICKETS, THE (1)
BARNABY

Number	Title (A Side/B Side)	Yr	VG	VG+	NM
❏ Z 30268	Rockin' 50's Rock 'N' Roll	1970	6.25	12.50	25.00

BRUNSWICK

Number	Title (A Side/B Side)	Yr	VG	VG+	NM
❏ BL 54038 [M]	The "Chirping" Crickets	1957	200.00	400.00	800.00
—Textured cover					
❏ BL 54038 [M]	The "Chirping" Crickets	1958	150.00	300.00	600.00
—Regular cover					

CORAL

Number	Title (A Side/B Side)	Yr	VG	VG+	NM
❏ CRL 57320 [M]	In Style with the Crickets	1960	50.00	100.00	200.00
❏ CRL 757320 [S]	In Style with the Crickets	1960	100.00	200.00	400.00

EPIC

Number	Title (A Side/B Side)	Yr	VG	VG+	NM
❏ FE 44446	T-Shirt	1988	3.75	7.50	15.00

LIBERTY

Number	Title (A Side/B Side)	Yr	VG	VG+	NM
❏ LRP-3272 [M]	Something Old, Something New, Something Blue, Somethin' Else	1962	37.50	75.00	150.00
❏ LRP-3351 [M]	California Sun/She Loves You	1964	25.00	50.00	100.00
❏ LST-7272 [S]	Something Old, Something New, Something Blue, Somethin' Else	1962	50.00	100.00	200.00
❏ LST-7351 [S]	California Sun/She Loves You	1964	37.50	75.00	150.00

VERTIGO

Number	Title (A Side/B Side)	Yr	VG	VG+	NM
❏ VEL-1020	Remnants	1973	5.00	10.00	20.00

CRISS, PETER
Also see CHELSEA; KISS.
CASABLANCA

Number	Title (A Side/B Side)	Yr	VG	VG+	NM
❏ NBLP-7122	Peter Criss	1978	5.00	10.00	20.00
❏ NBPIX-7122 [PD]	Peter Criss	1978	12.50	25.00	50.00
❏ NBLP-7240	Out of Control	1980	6.25	12.50	25.00

CRISS, SONNY
CLEF

Number	Title (A Side/B Side)	Yr	VG	VG+	NM
❏ MGC-122 [10]	Sonny Criss Collates	1953	62.50	125.00	250.00

IMPERIAL

Number	Title (A Side/B Side)	Yr	VG	VG+	NM
❏ LP-9006 [M]	Jazz U.S.A.	1956	50.00	100.00	200.00
❏ LP-9020 [M]	Go Man: It's Sonny Criss & Modern Jazz	1956	50.00	100.00	200.00
❏ LP-9024 [M]	Sonny Criss Plays Cole Porter	1956	50.00	100.00	200.00
❏ LP-9205 [M]	Criss Cross	1963	20.00	40.00	80.00
❏ LP-12205 [R]	Criss Cross	1963	5.00	10.00	20.00

MERCURY

Number	Title (A Side/B Side)	Yr	VG	VG+	NM
❏ MGC-122 [10]	Sonny Criss Collates	1953	—	—	—
—Cover exists, but all known copies contain Clef labels					

PEACOCK

Number	Title (A Side/B Side)	Yr	VG	VG+	NM
❏ PLP-91 [M]	At the Crossroads	1959	37.50	75.00	150.00

PRESTIGE

Number	Title (A Side/B Side)	Yr	VG	VG+	NM
❏ PRLP-7511 [M]	This Is Sonny Criss!	1966	6.25	12.50	25.00
❏ PRST-7511 [S]	This Is Sonny Criss!	1966	7.50	15.00	30.00
❏ PRLP-7526 [M]	Portrait of Sonny Criss	1967	7.50	15.00	30.00
❏ PRST-7526 [S]	Portrait of Sonny Criss	1967	6.25	12.50	25.00
❏ PRLP-7530 [M]	Up, Up and Away	1967	10.00	20.00	40.00
❏ PRST-7530 [S]	Up, Up and Away	1967	6.25	12.50	25.00
❏ PRST-7558	The Beat Goes On	1968	5.00	10.00	20.00
❏ PRST-7576	Sonny's Dream	1968	5.00	10.00	20.00
❏ PRST-7610	Rockin' in Rhythm	1969	5.00	10.00	20.00
❏ PRST-7628	I'll Catch the Sun	1969	5.00	10.00	20.00

CRISS, SONNY, AND KENNY DORHAM
ABC IMPULSE!

Number	Title (A Side/B Side)	Yr	VG	VG+	NM
❏ IA-9337 [(2)]	Bopmasters	197?	5.00	10.00	20.00

CRITTERS, THE
KAPP

Number	Title (A Side/B Side)	Yr	VG	VG+	NM
❏ KL-1485 [M]	Younger Girl	1966	7.50	15.00	30.00
❏ KS-3485 [S]	Younger Girl	1966	10.00	20.00	40.00

PROJECT 3

Number	Title (A Side/B Side)	Yr	VG	VG+	NM
❏ PR 4001SD	Touch 'n Go with the Critters	1968	7.50	15.00	30.00
❏ PR 4002SD	The Critters	1969	7.50	15.00	30.00

CRITTERS, THE /THE YOUNG RASCALS/LOU CHRISTIE
BOUTIQUE

Number	Title (A Side/B Side)	Yr	VG	VG+	NM
❏ CA-1079 [M]	A Taste of the Critters & The Young Rascals & Lou Christie	1966	10.00	20.00	40.00

CROCE, JIM
ABC

Number	Title (A Side/B Side)	Yr	VG	VG+	NM
❏ ABCX-756	You Don't Mess Around with Jim	1972	5.00	10.00	20.00
—Original covers have no green box advertising "Time in a Bottle"					
❏ ABCX-756	You Don't Mess Around with Jim	1973	3.75	7.50	15.00
—Posthumous covers have a green box advertising "Time in a Bottle"					
❏ ABCX-769	Life and Times	1973	3.75	7.50	15.00
❏ ABCX-797	I Got a Name	1973	3.75	7.50	15.00
❏ ABCD-835	Photographs & Memories/His Greatest Hits	1974	3.75	7.50	15.00

CAPITOL

Number	Title (A Side/B Side)	Yr	VG	VG+	NM
❏ SMAS-315	Jim and Ingrid Croce	1970	7.50	15.00	30.00

COMMAND

Number	Title (A Side/B Side)	Yr	VG	VG+	NM
❏ QD-40006 [Q]	You Don't Mess Around with Jim	1974	6.25	12.50	25.00
❏ QD-40007 [Q]	Life and Times	1974	6.25	12.50	25.00
❏ QD-40008 [Q]	I Got a Name	1974	6.25	12.50	25.00
❏ QD-40020 [Q]	Photographs & Memories/His Greatest Hits	1974	6.25	12.50	25.00

CROCE

Number	Title (A Side/B Side)	Yr	VG	VG+	NM
❏ 101	Facets	1966	75.00	150.00	300.00

DCC COMPACT CLASSICS

Number	Title (A Side/B Side)	Yr	VG	VG+	NM
❏ LPZ-2054	His Greatest Recordings	1998	10.00	20.00	40.00
—Audiophile vinyl					

LIFESONG

Number	Title (A Side/B Side)	Yr	VG	VG+	NM
❏ LS 900 [(2)]	The Faces I've Been	1975	3.75	7.50	15.00
❏ LS 6007	Time in a Bottle — Jim Croce's Greatest Love Songs	1976	3.00	6.00	12.00
❏ JZ 34993	You Don't Mess Around with Jim	1978	2.50	5.00	10.00
❏ JZ 35000	Time in a Bottle — Jim Croce's Greatest Love Songs	1978	2.50	5.00	10.00
❏ JZ 35008	Life and Times	1978	2.50	5.00	10.00
❏ JZ 35009	I Got a Name	1978	2.50	5.00	10.00
❏ JZ 35010	Photographs & Memories/His Greatest Hits	1978	2.50	5.00	10.00
❏ JZ 35571	Bad, Bad Leroy Brown: Jim Croce's Greatest Character Songs	1978	2.50	5.00	10.00

MOBILE FIDELITY

Number	Title (A Side/B Side)	Yr	VG	VG+	NM
❏ 1-079	You Don't Mess Around with Jim	1981	10.00	20.00	40.00
—Audiophile vinyl					

PICKWICK

Number	Title (A Side/B Side)	Yr	VG	VG+	NM
❏ SPC-3332	Another Day, Another Town	1973	2.50	5.00	10.00
—Reissue of Capitol LP					

21 RECORDS

Number	Title (A Side/B Side)	Yr	VG	VG+	NM
❏ 90467	Photographs & Memories/His Greatest Hits	1985	2.00	4.00	8.00
❏ 90468	Time in a Bottle — Jim Croce's Greatest Love Songs	1985	2.00	4.00	8.00
❏ 90469	Down the Highway	1985	2.50	5.00	10.00

CROME SYRCUS, THE
COMMAND

Number	Title (A Side/B Side)	Yr	VG	VG+	NM
❏ RS 925 SD	The Love Cycle	1968	10.00	20.00	40.00

CROSBY, BING
AMOS

Number	Title (A Side/B Side)	Yr	VG	VG+	NM
❏ AAS-7001	Hey Jude/Hey Bing!	1969	3.00	6.00	12.00

BIOGRAPH

Number	Title (A Side/B Side)	Yr	VG	VG+	NM
❏ M-1	When the Blue of the Night Meets the Gold of the Day	197?	2.50	5.00	10.00
❏ C-13	Bing Crosby 1929-33	1973	3.00	6.00	12.00

BRUNSWICK

Number	Title (A Side/B Side)	Yr	VG	VG+	NM
❏ BL 54005 [M]	The Voice of Bing in the 1930s	1957	6.25	12.50	25.00
❏ BL 58000 [10]	Bing Crosby, Volume 1	1950	12.50	25.00	50.00
❏ BL 58001 [10]	Bing Crosby, Volume 2	1950	12.50	25.00	50.00

CAPITOL

Number	Title (A Side/B Side)	Yr	VG	VG+	NM
❏ ST 2300 [S]	That Travelin' Two-Beat	1965	5.00	10.00	20.00
❏ T 2300 [M]	That Travelin' Two-Beat	1965	3.75	7.50	15.00
❏ ST 2346 [S]	Great Country Hits	1965	5.00	10.00	20.00
❏ T 2346 [M]	Great Country Hits	1965	3.75	7.50	15.00
❏ SM-11732	Bing Crosby's Christmas Classics	1977	2.50	5.00	10.00
—"A Capitol Re-Issue"; same recordings as on Warner Bros. 1484					
❏ SM-11736	That Travelin' Two-Beat	1977	2.50	5.00	10.00
❏ SM-11737	Great Country Hits	1977	2.50	5.00	10.00
❏ SM-11738	Bing Crosby Classics, Vol. 1	1977	2.50	5.00	10.00
❏ SM-11739	Bing Crosby Classics, Vol. 2	1977	2.50	5.00	10.00
❏ SM-11740	Bing Crosby Classics, Vol. 3	1977	2.50	5.00	10.00

COLUMBIA

Number	Title (A Side/B Side)	Yr	VG	VG+	NM
❏ C2L 43 [(2)]	Bing in Hollywood 1930-1934	196?	3.75	7.50	15.00
—Red "360 Sound" labels					
❏ C2L 43 [(2)]	Bing in Hollywood 1930-1934	1971	3.00	6.00	12.00
—Orange labels					
❏ CL 2502 [10]	Der Bingle	1955	10.00	20.00	40.00
❏ CL 6027 [10]	Crosby Classics	1949	12.50	25.00	50.00
❏ CL 6105 [10]	Crosby Classics, Volume 2	1950	12.50	25.00	50.00
❏ C 35093	Bing Crosby Collection, Vol. 1	1977	2.50	5.00	10.00
❏ C 35094	Bing Crosby Collection, Vol. 2	1977	2.50	5.00	10.00
❏ C4X 44229 [(4)]	The Crooner: The Columbia Years	1988	10.00	20.00	40.00

COLUMBIA SPECIAL PRODUCTS

Number	Title (A Side/B Side)	Yr	VG	VG+	NM
❏ P 14369	Bing	197?	2.50	5.00	10.00

DAYBREAK

Number	Title (A Side/B Side)	Yr	VG	VG+	NM
❏ 2006	A Time to Be Jolly	1971	3.00	6.00	12.00
❏ 2014	Bing and Basie	1972	3.00	6.00	12.00

DECCA

Number	Title (A Side/B Side)	Yr	VG	VG+	NM
❏ DX 151 [(5)M]	Bing: A Musical Autobiography	195?	37.50	75.00	150.00
❏ DX 152 [(2)M]	Old Masters	195?	37.50	75.00	150.00
❏ DXB 184 [(2)M]	The Best of Bing	1965	6.25	12.50	25.00
❏ DL 4086 [M]	My Golden Favorites	1961	6.25	12.50	25.00
❏ DL 4250 [M]	Bing's Hollywood: Easy to Remember	1962	6.25	12.50	25.00
❏ DL 4251 [M]	Bing's Hollywood: Pennies from Heaven	1962	6.25	12.50	25.00
❏ DL 4252 [M]	Bing's Hollywood: Pocket Full of Dreams	1962	6.25	12.50	25.00
❏ DL 4253 [M]	Bing's Hollywood: East Side of Heaven	1962	6.25	12.50	25.00
❏ DL 4254 [M]	Bing's Hollywood: The Road Begins	1962	6.25	12.50	25.00
❏ DL 4255 [M]	Bing's Hollywood: Only Forever	1962	6.25	12.50	25.00
❏ DL 4256 [M]	Bing's Hollywood: Holiday Inn	1962	6.25	12.50	25.00
❏ DL 4257 [M]	Bing's Hollywood: Swinging on a Star	1962	6.25	12.50	25.00
❏ DL 4258 [M]	Bing's Hollywood: Accentuate the Positive	1962	6.25	12.50	25.00
❏ DL 4259 [M]	Bing's Hollywood: Blue Skies	1962	6.25	12.50	25.00
❏ DL 4260 [M]	Bing's Hollywood: But Beautiful	1962	6.25	12.50	25.00
❏ DL 4261 [M]	Bing's Hollywood: Sunshine Cake	1962	6.25	12.50	25.00
❏ DL 4262 [M]	Bing's Hollywood: Cool of the Evening	1962	6.25	12.50	25.00
❏ DL 4263 [M]	Bing's Hollywood: Zing a Little Zong	1962	6.25	12.50	25.00
❏ DL 4264 [M]	Bing's Hollywood: Anything Goes	1962	6.25	12.50	25.00
❏ DL 4281 [M]	Holiday in Europe	1962	6.25	12.50	25.00
❏ DL 4283	Two Favorite Stories by Bing Crosby	1962	6.25	12.50	25.00
❏ DL 4415 [M]	Songs Everybody Knows	1964	6.25	12.50	25.00
❏ DLP 5000 [10]	Hits from Musical Comedies	1949	12.50	25.00	50.00
❏ DLP 5001 [10]	Jerome Kern Songs	1949	12.50	25.00	50.00
❏ DLP 5010 [10]	Stephen Foster Songs	1949	12.50	25.00	50.00
❏ DLP 5011 [10]	El Bingo	1949	12.50	25.00	50.00
❏ DLP 5019 [10]	Merry Christmas	1949	15.00	30.00	60.00
❏ DLP 5020 [10]	Christmas Greetings	1949	15.00	30.00	60.00
❏ DL 5028 [10]	Auld Lang Syne	1950	12.50	25.00	50.00
❏ DL 5037 [10]	St. Patrick's Day	1950	12.50	25.00	50.00
❏ DL 5039 [10]	St. Valentine's Day	1950	12.50	25.00	50.00
❏ DL 5042 [10]	Blue Skies	1950	12.50	25.00	50.00
❏ DL 5052 [10]	Going My Way/The Bells of St. Mary's	1950	15.00	30.00	60.00
❏ DL 5063 [10]	Don't Fence Me In	1950	12.50	25.00	50.00

Number	Title (A Side/B Side)	Yr	VG	VG+	NM
❏ DL 5064 [10]	Cole Porter Songs	1950	12.50	25.00	50.00
❏ DL 5081 [10]	Songs by Gershwin	1950	12.50	25.00	50.00
❏ DL 5102 [10]	Blue of the Night	1950	12.50	25.00	50.00
❏ DL 5107 [10]	Cowboy Songs	1950	12.50	25.00	50.00
❏ DL 5119 [10]	Drifting and Dreaming	1950	12.50	25.00	50.00
❏ DL 5122 [10]	Hawaiian Songs	1950	12.50	25.00	50.00
❏ DL 5126 [10]	Stardust	1950	12.50	25.00	50.00
❏ DL 5129 [10]	Cowboy Songs, Volume 2	1950	12.50	25.00	50.00
❏ DL 5220 [10]	Bing Sings Hits	1950	12.50	25.00	50.00
❏ DL 5272 [10]	Top o' the Morning/The Emperor Waltz	1950	12.50	25.00	50.00
❏ DL 5284 [10]	Mr. Music	1950	12.50	25.00	50.00
❏ DL 5298 [10]	Hits from Broadway Shows	1951	12.50	25.00	50.00
❏ DL 5299 [10]	Favorite Hawaiian Songs	1951	12.50	25.00	50.00
❏ DL 5302 [10]	Go West, Young Man	1951	12.50	25.00	50.00
❏ DL 5310 [10]	Way Back Home	1951	12.50	25.00	50.00
❏ DL 5323 [10]	Bing and the Dixieland Bands	1951	12.50	25.00	50.00
❏ DL 5326 [10]	Yours Is My Heart Alone	1951	12.50	25.00	50.00
❏ DL 5331 [10]	Country Style	1951	12.50	25.00	50.00
❏ DL 5340 [10]	Down Memory Lane	1951	12.50	25.00	50.00
❏ DL 5343 [10]	Down Memory Lane, Volume 2	1951	12.50	25.00	50.00
❏ DL 5351 [10]	Beloved Hymns	1951	12.50	25.00	50.00
❏ DL 5355 [10]	Bing Sings Victor Herbert	1951	12.50	25.00	50.00
❏ DL 5390 [10]	Bing and Connee	1953	12.50	25.00	50.00
—With Connee Boswell					
❏ DL 5403 [10]	When Irish Eyes Are Smiling	1952	12.50	25.00	50.00
❏ DL 5417 [10]	Just for You	1952	12.50	25.00	50.00
❏ DL 5444 [10]	The Road to Bali	1952	15.00	30.00	60.00
❏ DL 5499 [10]	Song Hits of Paris/Le Bing	1953	12.50	25.00	50.00
❏ DL 5508 [10]	Some Fine Old Chestnuts	1953	12.50	25.00	50.00
❏ DL 5520 [10]	Bing Sings the Hits	1954	12.50	25.00	50.00
❏ DL 5556 [10]	Country Girl/Little Boy Lost/Anything Goes	1954	12.50	25.00	50.00
❏ DL 6000 [10]	Two Favorite Stories by Bing Crosby	1950	15.00	30.00	60.00
❏ DL 6001 [10]	Ichabod/Rip Van Winkle	1950	12.50	25.00	50.00
❏ DL 6008 [10]	Collector's Classics: Mississippi/Here Is My Heart	1951	15.00	30.00	60.00
❏ DL 6009 [10]	Collector's Classics: Anything Goes/Two for Tonight	1951	15.00	30.00	60.00
❏ DL 6010 [10]	Collector's Classics: Rhythm on the Range/Pennies from Heaven	1951	15.00	30.00	60.00
❏ DL 6011 [10]	Collector's Classics: Waikiki Wedding	1951	15.00	30.00	60.00
❏ DL 6012 [10]	Collector's Classics: Paris Honeymoon	1951	15.00	30.00	60.00
❏ DL 6013 [10]	Collector's Classics: The Star Maker/Doctor Rhythm	1951	15.00	30.00	60.00
❏ DL 6014 [10]	Collector's Classics: Big Broadcast of 1936	1951	15.00	30.00	60.00
❏ DL 6015 [10]	Collector's Classics: The Road to Singapore/If I Had My Way	1951	15.00	30.00	60.00
❏ DXSB 7184 [(2)R]	The Best of Bing	1965	3.75	7.50	15.00
❏ DL 8020 [M]	The Man Without a Country/What So Proudly We Hail	1950	10.00	20.00	40.00
❏ DL 8110 [M]	Lullaby Time	1955	10.00	20.00	40.00
❏ DL 8128 [M]	Merry Christmas	1955	10.00	20.00	40.00
—Expanded version of 10-inch LP; all-black label					
❏ DL 8128 [M]	Merry Christmas	1960	6.25	12.50	25.00
—Reissue on black label with color bars					
❏ DL 8178 [M]	Merry Christmas	196?	15.00	30.00	60.00
—Black label with color bars; at least one copy is known to exist on red vinyl					
❏ DL 8207 [M]	Shillelaghs and Shamrocks	1956	10.00	20.00	40.00
❏ DL 8210 [M]	Home on the Range	1956	10.00	20.00	40.00
❏ DL 8262 [M]	When Irish Eyes Are Smiling	1956	10.00	20.00	40.00
❏ DL 8268 [M]	Drifting and Dreaming	1956	10.00	20.00	40.00
❏ DL 8269 [M]	Blue Hawaii	1956	10.00	20.00	40.00
❏ DL 8272 [M]	High Tor	1956	100.00	200.00	400.00
❏ DL 8318 [M]	Anything Goes	1956	12.50	25.00	50.00
❏ DL 8352 [M]	Song I Wish I Had Sung…The First Time Around	1956	10.00	20.00	40.00
❏ DL 8365 [M]	Twilight on the Trail	1957	10.00	20.00	40.00
❏ DL 8374 [M]	Some Fine Old Chestnuts	1957	10.00	20.00	40.00
❏ DL 8419 [M]	A Christmas Sing with Bing Around the World	1957	10.00	20.00	40.00
❏ DL 8493 [M]	Bing and the Dixieland Bands	1957	10.00	20.00	40.00
❏ DL 8575 [M]	New Tricks	1957	10.00	20.00	40.00
❏ DL 8687 [M]	Around the World	1958	10.00	20.00	40.00
❏ DL 8780 [M]	Bing in Paris	1958	10.00	20.00	40.00
❏ DL 8781 [M]	That Christmas Feeling	1958	7.50	15.00	30.00
—Expanded version of DL 5020; all-black label, textured cover					
❏ DL 8781 [M]	That Christmas Feeling	1960	5.00	10.00	20.00
—Reissue on black label with color bars, smooth cover					
❏ DL 8846 [M]	In a Little Spanish Town	1959	7.50	15.00	30.00
❏ DL 9054 [M]	Bing: A Musical Autobiography 1927-1934	1961	10.00	20.00	40.00
❏ DL 9064 [M]	Bing: A Musical Autobiography 1934-1941	1961	10.00	20.00	40.00
❏ DL 9067 [M]	Bing: A Musical Autobiography 1941-44	1961	10.00	20.00	40.00
❏ DL 9077 [M]	Bing: A Musical Autobiography 1944-47	1961	10.00	20.00	40.00
❏ DL 9078 [M]	Bing: A Musical Autobiography 1947-1953	1961	10.00	20.00	40.00
❏ DL 9106 [M]	Ichabod/Rip Van Winkle	1962	6.25	12.50	25.00
❏ DL 34522	Favorite Songs of Christmas	1968	3.75	7.50	15.00
—Decca Records Custom Division pressing					
❏ DL 74281 [R]	Holiday in Europe	1962	3.75	7.50	15.00
❏ DL 74283 [R]	The Small One	1962	2.50	5.00	10.00
❏ DL 74415 [R]	Songs Everybody Knows	1964	3.75	7.50	15.00
❏ DL 78128 [R]	Merry Christmas	196?	2.50	5.00	10.00
❏ DL 78207 [R]	Shillelaghs and Shamrocks	196?	2.50	5.00	10.00
❏ DL 78262 [R]	When Irish Eyes Are Smiling	196?	2.50	5.00	10.00
❏ DL 78352 [R]	Songs I Wish I Had Sung…The First Time Around	196?	2.50	5.00	10.00
❏ DL 78419 [R]	A Christmas Sing with Bing Around the World	196?	2.50	5.00	10.00
❏ DL 78781 [R]	That Christmas Feeling	196?	2.50	5.00	10.00
❏ DL 79106 [R]	Ichabod/Rip Van Winkle	1962	2.50	5.00	10.00
ENCORE					
❏ E2E-201 [(2)]	The Bing Crosby Story, Volume 1	1968	3.75	7.50	15.00
❏ E2E-202 [(2)]	The Bing Crosby Story, Volume 2	1968	3.75	7.50	15.00
FOX AMERICAN					
❏ SMF 210	Bing Crosby Sings Christmas	1978	2.50	5.00	10.00
—Side 1 from radio show Dec. 19, 1951; Side 2 from radio show Dec. 14, 1949					
GNP CRESCENDO					
❏ GNP-9044	The Radio Years, Vol. 1	1985	2.00	4.00	8.00
❏ GNP-9046	The Radio Years, Vol. 2	1986	2.00	4.00	8.00
❏ GNP-9047	The Radio Years, Vol. 3	1986	2.00	4.00	8.00
❏ GNP-9048	The Radio Years, Vol. 4	1986	2.00	4.00	8.00
GOLDEN					
❏ A298:20 [M]	Ali Baba and the 40 Thieves	1957	6.25	12.50	25.00
❏ A298:21 [M]	How Lovely Is Christmas/A Christmas Story	195?	6.25	12.50	25.00
HARMONY					
❏ HL 7094 [M]	Crosby Classics	1958	3.75	7.50	15.00
❏ HS 11313 [R]	Crosby Classics	196?	2.50	5.00	10.00
LONDON					
❏ PS 679	Feels Good	1977	3.00	6.00	12.00
MARK 56					
❏ 762	Original Radio Broadcasts	197?	2.50	5.00	10.00
MCA					
❏ 177	Shillelaghs and Shamrocks	1973	2.50	5.00	10.00
❏ 519	When Irish Eyes Are Smiling	197?	2.50	5.00	10.00
❏ 915	Hey Bing!	198?	2.50	5.00	10.00
❏ 1502	Rare 1930-31 Brunswick Recordings	198?	2.50	5.00	10.00
❏ 3031	Bing Crosby's Greatest Hits	1977	2.50	5.00	10.00
❏ 2-4045 [(2)]	The Best of Bing	197?	2.50	5.00	10.00
—Blue labels with rainbow; regular cover					
❏ 2-4045 [(2)]	The Best of Bing	197?	3.00	6.00	12.00
—Black labels with rainbow; gatefold cover					
❏ 15017	Two Favorite Stories by Bing Crosby	197?	2.50	5.00	10.00
—Reissue of Decca DL 4283					
❏ 15018 [R]	A Christmas Sing with Bing Around the World	197?	2.00	4.00	8.00
—Reissue of Decca DL7-8419					
❏ 15019 [R]	That Christmas Feeling	1973	2.00	4.00	8.00
—Reissue of Decca DL7-8781					
❏ 15024 [R]	Merry Christmas	197?	2.00	4.00	8.00
—Reissue of Decca DL7-8128					
❏ 37076	Bing Crosby's Greatest Hits	198?	2.00	4.00	8.00
METRO					
❏ M-523 [M]	Bing Crosby	1965	3.00	6.00	12.00
❏ MS-523 [S]	Bing Crosby	1965	3.75	7.50	15.00
MGM					
❏ E-3890 [M]	Senor Bing	1961	3.75	7.50	15.00
❏ SE-3890 [S]	Senor Bing	1961	5.00	10.00	20.00
❏ E-4129 [M]	The Great Standards	1963	3.75	7.50	15.00
❏ SE-4129 [S]	The Great Standards	1963	5.00	10.00	20.00
❏ E-4203 [M]	The Very Best of Bing Crosby	1964	3.75	7.50	15.00
❏ SE-4203 [S]	The Very Best of Bing Crosby	1964	5.00	10.00	20.00
MOBILE FIDELITY					
❏ 1-260	Bing Sings Whilst Bregman Swings	1996	5.00	10.00	20.00
—Audiophile vinyl					
MURRAY HILL					
❏ 894637 [(4)]	Bing Crosby and His Friends	197?	6.25	12.50	25.00
P.I.P.					
❏ 6802	Thoroughly Modern Bing	1971	3.00	6.00	12.00
PHILCO					
❏ LP 436 [10]	Crosby Classics	195?	10.00	20.00	40.00
—Custom item for Philco (front cover has "Philco: Famous for Quality the World Over")					
PICKWICK					
❏ SPC-3583	Thoroughly Modern Bing	1978	2.00	4.00	8.00
POLYDOR					
❏ PD-1-6128	Seasons: The Closing Chapter	1978	3.00	6.00	12.00
RCA VICTOR					
❏ LPM-1473 [M]	Bing with a Beat	1957	6.25	12.50	25.00
❏ AFL1-1854	Fancy Meeting You Here	1977	2.50	5.00	10.00
❏ LPM-1854 [M]	Fancy Meeting You Here	1958	5.00	10.00	20.00
❏ LSP-1854 [S]	Fancy Meeting You Here	1958	7.50	15.00	30.00
❏ LPM-2071 [M]	Young Bing Crosby	1959	5.00	10.00	20.00
❏ CPL1-2086(e)	A Legendary Performer	1976	2.50	5.00	10.00
READER'S DIGEST					
❏ RDA-175	Christmas with Bing	1980	2.50	5.00	10.00
—Repackage of Warner Bros. and Capitol recordings					
REPRISE					
❏ R-6106 [M]	Return to Paradise Islands	1964	3.75	7.50	15.00
❏ R9-6106 [S]	Return to Paradise Islands	1964	5.00	10.00	20.00
SPOKANE					
❏ 1	Bing Crosby On the Air, 1934 and 1938	197?	2.50	5.00	10.00
❏ 5	Der Bingle, Vol. 1	197?	2.50	5.00	10.00
❏ 10	Der Bingle, Vol. 2	197?	2.50	5.00	10.00
❏ 12	Bing in the 30's	197?	2.50	5.00	10.00
❏ 14	Bing in the 30s, Vol. 2	197?	2.50	5.00	10.00
❏ 15	Holiday Inn/The Bells of St. Mary's	197?	2.50	5.00	10.00
❏ 16	Kraft Music Hall Highlights	197?	2.50	5.00	10.00
❏ 19	Kraft Music Hall Highlights, Vol. 2	197?	2.50	5.00	10.00
❏ 20	Der Bingle, Vol. 3	197?	2.50	5.00	10.00
❏ 21	Bing Crosby & the Music Maids	197?	2.50	5.00	10.00
❏ 24	Bing in the 30s, Vol. 3	1986	2.00	4.00	8.00
❏ 25	Bing in the 30s, Vol. 4	1986	2.00	4.00	8.00
❏ 26	Bing in the 30s, Vol. 5	1986	2.00	4.00	8.00
❏ 27	Bing in the 30s, Vol. 6	1986	2.00	4.00	8.00
SUNBEAM					
❏ 502	Distinctively Bing, Vol. 1	197?	2.50	5.00	10.00
❏ 504	Distinctively Bing, Vol. 2	197?	2.50	5.00	10.00
20TH CENTURY					
❏ T-551	A Holiday Toast	1977	3.00	6.00	12.00
UNITED ARTISTS					
❏ UA-LA554-G	That's What Life Is All About	1976	3.00	6.00	12.00

Number	Title (A Side/B Side)	Yr	VG	VG+	NM

VERVE

❑ MGV 2020 [M]	Bing Sings Whilst Bregman Swings	1956	12.50	25.00	50.00
❑ V-2020 [M]	Bing Sings Whilst Bregman Swings	1961	6.25	12.50	25.00

VOCALION

❑ VL 3603 [M]	Bing Crosby Sings	195?	3.75	7.50	15.00
❑ VL 73603 [R]	Bing Crosby Sings	196?	2.50	5.00	10.00

WARNER BROS.

❑ W 1363 [M]	Join with Bing and Sing Along	1960	3.75	7.50	15.00
❑ WS 1363 [S]	Join with Bing and Sing Along	1960	5.00	10.00	20.00
❑ 2W 1401 [(2)M]	101 Gang Songs	1961	5.00	10.00	20.00
❑ 2WS 1401 [(2)S]	101 Gang Songs	1961	6.25	12.50	25.00
❑ W 1422 [M]	Join Bing in a Gang Song Sing-Along	1961	3.75	7.50	15.00
❑ WS 1422 [S]	Join Bing in a Gang Song Sing-Along	1961	5.00	10.00	20.00
❑ W 1435 [M]	Join Bing and Sing Along	1962	3.75	7.50	15.00
❑ WS 1435 [S]	Join Bing and Sing Along	1962	5.00	10.00	20.00
❑ W 1482 [M]	On the Happy Side	1962	3.75	7.50	15.00
❑ WS 1482 [S]	On the Happy Side	1962	5.00	10.00	20.00
❑ W 1484 [M]	I Wish You a Merry Christmas	1962	3.75	7.50	15.00
❑ WS 1484 [S]	I Wish You a Merry Christmas	1962	5.00	10.00	20.00

"X"

❑ XLVA-4250 [M]	Young Bing Crosby	1955	12.50	25.00	50.00

CROSBY, BING, AND LOUIS ARMSTRONG

CAPITOL

❑ SM-11735	Bing Crosby and Louis Armstrong	1977	2.50	5.00	10.00

MGM

❑ E-3882 [M]	Bing and Satchmo	1960	3.75	7.50	15.00
❑ SE-3882 [S]	Bing and Satchmo	1960	5.00	10.00	20.00

CROSBY, BOB

CAPITOL

❑ H 293 [10]	Bob Crosby and His Bobcats	1952	12.50	25.00	50.00
❑ T 293 [M]	Bob Crosby and His Bobcats	1955	10.00	20.00	40.00
❑ T 1556 [M]	The Hits of Bob Crosby's Bobcats	1961	5.00	10.00	20.00

COLUMBIA

❑ CL 766 [M]	The Bob Crosby Show	1956	7.50	15.00	30.00

CORAL

❑ CRL 56000 [10]	Swinging at the Sugar Bowl	1950	12.50	25.00	50.00
❑ CRL 56003 [10]	Dixieland Jazz 1	1950	12.50	25.00	50.00
❑ CRL 56018 [10]	Marches in Dixieland Style	1950	12.50	25.00	50.00
❑ CRL 56039 [10]	St. Louis Blues	1950	12.50	25.00	50.00
❑ CRL 57005 [M]	The Bobcats' Ball	1955	10.00	20.00	40.00
❑ CRL 57060 [M]	Bobcats' Blues	1956	10.00	20.00	40.00
❑ CRL 57061 [M]	Bobcats On Parade	1956	10.00	20.00	40.00
❑ CRL 57062 [M]	Bob Crosby in Hi-Fi	1956	10.00	20.00	40.00
❑ CRL 57089 [M]	Bob Crosby 1936-1956	1957	10.00	20.00	40.00
❑ CRL 57170 [M]	The Bobcats in Hi-Fi	1958	10.00	20.00	40.00

DECCA

❑ DL 4856 [M]	Bob Crosby's Bobcats — Their Greatest Hits	1967	5.00	10.00	20.00
❑ DL 8042 [M]	Five Feet of Swing	1954	10.00	20.00	40.00
❑ DL 8061 [M]	Bob Crosby's Bobcats	1954	10.00	20.00	40.00

DOT

❑ DLP-3136 [M]	South Pacific Blows Warm	1958	5.00	10.00	20.00
❑ DLP-3170 [M]	Petite Fleur	1959	5.00	10.00	20.00
❑ DLP-3278 [M]	Bob Crosby's Great Hits	196?	5.00	10.00	20.00
❑ DLP-3382 [M]	C'est Si Bon	196?	5.00	10.00	20.00
❑ DLP-25170 [S]	Petite Fleur	1959	6.25	12.50	25.00
❑ DLP-25278 [S]	Bob Crosby's Great Hits	196?	6.25	12.50	25.00
❑ DLP-25382 [S]	C'est Si Bon	196?	6.25	12.50	25.00

CROSBY, STILLS AND NASH

ATLANTIC

❑ SD 8229	Crosby, Stills & Nash	1969	5.00	10.00	20.00
❑ SD 8229	Crosby, Stills & Nash	2000	6.25	12.50	25.00
—Classic Records reissue on 180-gram vinyl					
❑ SD 16026	Replay	1980	3.00	6.00	12.00
—Also has solo cuts by Stephen Stills					
❑ SD 19104	CSN	1977	3.00	6.00	12.00
❑ SD 19117	Crosby, Stills & Nash	1977	2.50	5.00	10.00
—Reissue of 8229					
❑ SD 19360	Daylight Again	1982	3.00	6.00	12.00
❑ 80075	Allies	1983	3.00	6.00	12.00
❑ 82107	Live It Up	1990	3.75	7.50	15.00

NAUTILUS

❑ NR-48	Crosby, Stills and Nash	1982	37.50	75.00	150.00
—Audiophile vinyl					

CROSBY, STILLS, NASH & YOUNG

ATLANTIC

❑ PR 165 [M]	Celebration/CSNY Month	1974	25.00	50.00	100.00
—Promo-only LP in mono					
❑ PR 165 [S]	Celebration/CSNY Month	1974	12.50	25.00	50.00
—Promo-only LP in stereo					
❑ 2-902 [(2)M]	4 Way Street	1971	25.00	50.00	100.00
—White label promo; no stock copies are mono					
❑ SD 2-902 [(2)]	4 Way Street	1971	5.00	10.00	20.00
❑ SD 2-902 [(2)DJ]	4 Way Street	1971	12.50	25.00	50.00
—White label stereo promo					
❑ 7200 [M]	Deja Vu	1970	37.50	75.00	150.00
—White label promo; no stock copies are mono					
❑ SD 7200	Deja Vu	1970	3.75	7.50	15.00
—Pasted-on front cover photo must still be intact					
❑ SD 7200 [DJ]	Deja Vu	1970	15.00	30.00	60.00
—White label stereo promo					
❑ SD 18100	So Far	1974	3.00	6.00	12.00
❑ PR 18102 [DJ]	A Rap with C, S, N & Y	1974	12.50	25.00	50.00
—Promo-only interview album					
❑ SD 19118	Deja Vu	1977	2.50	5.00	10.00
—Reissue of 7200, this time with photo as part of the cover rather than as a paste-on					
❑ SD 19119	So Far	1977	2.50	5.00	10.00
—Reissue of 18100					

❑ 81888	American Dream	1988	2.50	5.00	10.00

MOBILE FIDELITY

❑ 1-088	Deja Vu	198?	50.00	100.00	200.00
—Audiophile vinyl					

CROSSFIRES, THE (3)

STRAND

❑ SL-1083 [M]	Limbo Rock	1963	5.00	10.00	20.00
❑ SLS-1083 [S]	Limbo Rock	1963	6.25	12.50	25.00

CROSTON, JILL

See LACY J. DALTON.

CROTHERS, SCATMAN

CRAFTSMAN

❑ 8036 [M]	Gone with the Scat Man	1960	7.50	15.00	30.00

DOOTO

❑ DTL 814 [M]	Comedy Sweepstakes	1961	6.25	12.50	25.00

MOTOWN

❑ M 777L	Big Ben Sings	1973	5.00	10.00	20.00

TOPS

❑ 1511 [M]	Rock and Roll with Scat Man	1956	20.00	40.00	80.00

CROW

AMARET

❑ ST-5002	Crow Music	1969	5.00	10.00	20.00
❑ ST-5006	Crow By Crow	1970	5.00	10.00	20.00
❑ ST-5009	Mosaic	1971	5.00	10.00	20.00
❑ AST-5012	Best of Crow	1972	3.75	7.50	15.00
❑ ST-5013	David Crow d/b/a Crow	1973	3.75	7.50	15.00

CROWELL, RODNEY

COLUMBIA

❑ CAS 2001 [DJ]	Dialog with T-Bone Burnett	1989	7.50	15.00	30.00
—Promo-only interview record					
❑ CAS 2456 [DJ]	Street Language Interchords	1986	7.50	15.00	30.00
—Promo-only interview record					
❑ FC 40116	Street Language	1986	2.00	4.00	8.00
❑ FC 44076	Diamonds and Dirt	1988	2.50	5.00	10.00
❑ FC 45242	Keys to the Highway	1989	3.00	6.00	12.00

WARNER BROS.

❑ BSK 3228	Ain't Living Long Like This	1978	3.75	7.50	15.00
❑ BSK 3407	But What Will the Neighbors Think	1980	2.50	5.00	10.00
❑ BSK 3587	Rodney Crowell	1981	2.50	5.00	10.00

CROWS, THE / THE HARPTONES

ROULETTE

❑ RE-114 [(2)]	Echoes of a Rock Era: The Groups	1973	5.00	10.00	20.00

CRUCIFIX

UNIVERSAL

❑ RON 2 [EP]	Crucifix	1982	10.00	20.00	40.00

CRUDUP, ARTHUR

COLLECTABLES

❑ COL-5130	Mean Ol' Frisco	1988	2.50	5.00	10.00

DELMARK

❑ DS-614	Look on Yonder's Wall	1969	10.00	20.00	40.00
❑ DS-621	Crudup's Mood	1969	10.00	20.00	40.00

FIRE

❑ 103 [M]	Mean Ol' Frisco	1960	300.00	600.00	900.00

RCA VICTOR

❑ LVP-573	Father of Rock and Roll	1971	5.00	10.00	20.00

TRIP

❑ 7501	Mean Ol' Frisco	1975	3.75	7.50	15.00

CRUM, SIMON

See FERLIN HUSKY.

CRUSADERS, THE (1)

APPLAUSE

❑ APBL-2313	Powerhouse	197?	3.00	6.00	12.00
—Reissue of Pacific Jazz 20136					

CRUSADERS

❑ 16000	Street Life	1982	6.25	12.50	25.00
—Audiophile vinyl					
❑ 16002	Ongaku-Kai: Live in Japan	1982	6.25	12.50	25.00
—Audiophile vinyl					

MOBILE FIDELITY

❑ 1-010	Chain Reaction	1979	5.00	10.00	20.00
—Audiophile vinyl					

PACIFIC JAZZ

❑ PJ-27 [M]	Freedom Sound	1961	6.25	12.50	25.00
❑ ST-27 [S]	Freedom Sound	1961	7.50	15.00	30.00
❑ PJ-43 [M]	Lookin' Ahead	1962	6.25	12.50	25.00
❑ ST-43 [S]	Lookin' Ahead	1962	7.50	15.00	30.00
—Black vinyl					
❑ ST-43 [S]	Lookin' Ahead	1962	15.00	30.00	60.00
—Yellow vinyl					
❑ PJ-57 [M]	The Jazz Crusaders at the Lighthouse	1962	6.25	12.50	25.00
❑ ST-57 [S]	The Jazz Crusaders at the Lighthouse	1962	7.50	15.00	30.00
❑ PJ-68 [M]	Tough Talk	1963	6.25	12.50	25.00
❑ ST-68 [S]	Tough Talk	1963	7.50	15.00	30.00
❑ PJ-76 [M]	Heat Wave	1963	6.25	12.50	25.00
❑ ST-76 [S]	Heat Wave	1963	7.50	15.00	30.00
❑ PJ-83 [M]	Stretchin' Out	1964	6.25	12.50	25.00
❑ ST-83 [S]	Stretchin' Out	1964	7.50	15.00	30.00
❑ PJ-87 [M]	The Thing	1964	6.25	12.50	25.00
❑ ST-87 [S]	The Thing	1964	7.50	15.00	30.00
❑ PJ-10092 [M]	Chili Con Soul	1965	5.00	10.00	20.00
❑ PJ-10098 [M]	Live at the Lighthouse '66	1966	5.00	10.00	20.00
❑ PJ-10106 [M]	Talk That Talk	1966	5.00	10.00	20.00

Number	Title (A Side/B Side)	Yr	VG	VG+	NM
☐ PJ-10115 [M]	The Festival Album	1967	6.25	12.50	25.00
☐ PJ-10124	Uh Huh	1967	6.25	12.50	25.00
☐ ST-20092 [S]	Chili Con Soul	1965	6.25	12.50	25.00
☐ ST-20098 [S]	Live at the Lighthouse '66	1966	6.25	12.50	25.00
☐ ST-20106 [S]	Talk That Talk	1966	6.25	12.50	25.00
☐ ST-20115 [S]	The Festival Album	1967	5.00	10.00	20.00
☐ ST-20124	Uh Huh	1967	5.00	10.00	20.00
☐ ST-20131	Lighthouse '68	1968	5.00	10.00	20.00
☐ ST-20136	Powerhouse	1968	5.00	10.00	20.00
☐ ST-20165	The Jazz Crusaders at the Lighthouse '69	1969	5.00	10.00	20.00
☐ ST-20175	The Best of the Jazz Crusaders	1969	5.00	10.00	20.00
☐ T-90598 [M]	Chili Con Soul	1965	6.25	12.50	25.00
—Capitol Record Club edition					

CRYAN' SHAMES, THE
COLUMBIA
Number	Title (A Side/B Side)	Yr	VG	VG+	NM
☐ CL 2589 [M]	Sugar & Spice	1967	5.00	10.00	20.00
☐ CL 2786 [M]	A Scratch in the Sky	1967	6.25	12.50	25.00
☐ CS 9389 [S]	Sugar & Spice	1967	6.25	12.50	25.00
☐ CS 9586 [S]	A Scratch in the Sky	1967	5.00	10.00	20.00
☐ CS 9719	Synthesis	1969	5.00	10.00	20.00

CRYSTAL MANSION, THE
CAPITOL
Number	Title (A Side/B Side)	Yr	VG	VG+	NM
☐ ST-227	The Crystal Mansion	1969	5.00	10.00	20.00

CRYSTALS, THE (1)
PHILLES
Number	Title (A Side/B Side)	Yr	VG	VG+	NM
☐ PHLP-4000 [M]	Twist Uptown	1962	150.00	300.00	600.00
☐ PHLP-4001 [M]	He's a Rebel	1963	150.00	300.00	600.00
☐ PHLP-4003 [M]	The Crystals Sing the Greatest Hits, Vol. 1	1963	150.00	300.00	600.00
☐ DT-90722 [R]	Twist Uptown	1965	300.00	600.00	1200.
—Capitol Record Club edition					
☐ T-90722 [M]	Twist Uptown	1965	150.00	300.00	600.00
—Capitol Record Club edition					

CUBY AND THE BLIZZARDS
PHILIPS
Number	Title (A Side/B Side)	Yr	VG	VG+	NM
☐ PHS 600307	Cuby and the Blizzards Live	1969	5.00	10.00	20.00
☐ PHS 600331	King of the World	1970	5.00	10.00	20.00

CUFF LINKS, THE (1)
DECCA
Number	Title (A Side/B Side)	Yr	VG	VG+	NM
☐ DL 75160	Tracy	1969	5.00	10.00	20.00
☐ DL 75235	The Cuff Links	1970	5.00	10.00	20.00

CUGAT, XAVIER
COLUMBIA
Number	Title (A Side/B Side)	Yr	VG	VG+	NM
☐ CL 515 [M]	Relaxing with Cugat (Quiet Music, Volume VI)	1953	10.00	20.00	40.00
—Second editions have maroon label, gold print and a "CL" prefix					
☐ GL 515 [M]	Relaxing with Cugat (Quiet Music, Volume VI)	1952	12.50	25.00	50.00
—Original copies have black label, silver print and a "GL" prefix					
☐ CL 537 [M]	Dance with Cugat	1953	10.00	20.00	40.00
—Maroon label, gold print					
☐ CL 537 [M]	Dance with Cugat	1955	6.25	12.50	25.00
—Red and black label with six "eye" logos					
☐ CL 579 [M]	Favorite Rhumbas	1954	10.00	20.00	40.00
—Maroon label, gold print					
☐ CL 579 [M]	Favorite Rhumbas	1955	6.25	12.50	25.00
—Red and black label with six "eye" logos					
☐ CL 579 [M]	Favorite Rhumbas	1962	3.75	7.50	15.00
—Red "Guaranteed High Fidelity" label					
☐ CL 579 [M]	Favorite Rhumbas	1965	3.00	6.00	12.00
—Red "Mono 360 Sound" label					
☐ CL 610 [M]	Ole	1955	6.25	12.50	25.00
—Red and black label with six "eye" logos					
☐ CL 610 [M]	Ole	1955	10.00	20.00	40.00
—Maroon label, gold print					
☐ CL 626 [M]	Mucho Mucho Mambo	1955	6.25	12.50	25.00
—Red and black label with six "eye" logos					
☐ CL 626 [M]	Mucho Mucho Mambo	1955	10.00	20.00	40.00
—Maroon label, gold print					
☐ CL 718 [M]	Cha Cha Cha	1956	7.50	15.00	30.00
—Red and black label with six "eye" logos					
☐ CL 732 [M]	Mambo at the Waldorf	1956	7.50	15.00	30.00
—Red and black label with six "eye" logos					
☐ CL 733 [M]	Merengue by Cugat	1956	7.50	15.00	30.00
—Red and black label with six "eye" logos					
☐ CL 733 [M]	Merengue by Cugat	1962	3.75	7.50	15.00
—Red "Guaranteed High Fidelity" label					
☐ CL 733 [M]	Merengue by Cugat	1965	3.00	6.00	12.00
—Red "Mono 360 Sound" label					
☐ CL 1064 [M]	Bread, Love and Cha Cha Cha	1957	6.25	12.50	25.00
—Red and black label with six "eye" logos					
☐ CL 1094 [M]	Cugar Cavalcade	1958	6.25	12.50	25.00
—Red and black label with six "eye" logos					
☐ CL 1143 [M]	Waltzes! But By Cugat	1959	6.25	12.50	25.00
—Red and black label with six "eye" logos					
☐ CL 2506 [10]	Mambo!	1955	12.50	25.00	50.00
☐ CL 6005 [10]	Cugat's Rhumba	1948	12.50	25.00	50.00
☐ CL 6021 [10]	Cugat's Favoprite Rhumbas	1949	12.50	25.00	50.00
☐ CL 6036 [10]	Rhumba with Cugat	1949	12.50	25.00	50.00
☐ CL 6077 [10]	Conga with Cugat	1949	12.50	25.00	50.00
☐ CL 6086 [10]	Tropical Bouquet	1950	12.50	25.00	50.00
☐ CL 6121 [10]	Dance Date	1950	12.50	25.00	50.00
☐ CL 6213 [10]	Mambo at the Waldorf	1951	12.50	25.00	50.00
☐ CL 6234 [10]	Tango with Cugat	1951	12.50	25.00	50.00
☐ CL 6236 [10]	Samba with Cugat	1951	12.50	25.00	50.00
☐ CS 8055 [S]	Cugar Cavalcade	1959	7.50	15.00	30.00
—Red and black label with six "eye" logos					
☐ CS 8059 [S]	Waltzes! But By Cugat	1959	7.50	15.00	30.00
—Red and black label with six "eye" logos					
☐ CS 8646 [R]	Merengue by Cugat	1963	3.00	6.00	12.00

DECCA
Number	Title (A Side/B Side)	Yr	VG	VG+	NM
☐ DL 4672 [M]	Feeling Good	1965	3.75	7.50	15.00
☐ DL 4740 [M]	Dance Party	1966	3.75	7.50	15.00
☐ DL 4799 [M]	Bang Bang	1966	3.75	7.50	15.00
☐ DL 4851 [M]	Xavier Cugat Today	1967	3.75	7.50	15.00
☐ DL 74672 [S]	Feeling Good	1965	5.00	10.00	20.00
☐ DL 74740 [S]	Dance Party	1966	5.00	10.00	20.00
☐ DL 74799 [S]	Bang Bang	1966	5.00	10.00	20.00
☐ DL 74851 [S]	Xavier Cugat Today	1967	5.00	10.00	20.00

MERCURY
Number	Title (A Side/B Side)	Yr	VG	VG+	NM
☐ PPS-2003 [M]	Viva Cugat!	1961	5.00	10.00	20.00
☐ PPS-2015 [M]	The Best of Cugat	1961	5.00	10.00	20.00
☐ PPS-2021 [M]	Cugat Plays Continental Favorites	1961	5.00	10.00	20.00
☐ PPS-6003 [S]	Viva Cugat!	1961	6.25	12.50	25.00
☐ PPS-6015 [S]	The Best of Cugat	1961	6.25	12.50	25.00
☐ PPS-6021 [S]	Cugat Plays Continental Favorites	1961	6.25	12.50	25.00
☐ MG 20065 [M]	Cugat's Favorites	1955	7.50	15.00	30.00
☐ MG 20108 [M]	Mambo!/Music for Latin Lovers	1957	7.50	15.00	30.00
☐ MG-20705 [M]	Twist with Cugat	1962	5.00	10.00	20.00
☐ MG-20745 [M]	The Most Popular Movie Themes As Styled by Cugat	1961	5.00	10.00	20.00
☐ MG-20798 [M]	Cugat's Golden Goodies	1963	5.00	10.00	20.00
☐ MG-20832 [M]	Cugi's Cocktails	1963	5.00	10.00	20.00
☐ MG-20868 [M]	Viva Cugat!	1964	3.75	7.50	15.00
—Reissue of 2003					
☐ MG-20870 [M]	The Best of Cugat	1964	3.75	7.50	15.00
—Reissue of 2015					
☐ MG-20888 [M]	Cugat Caricatures	1964	3.75	7.50	15.00
☐ MG 25120 [10]	Here's Cugat	195?	10.00	20.00	40.00
☐ MG 25149 [10]	Dance with Cugat/The Great Latin-American Rhythms of Xavier Cugat	195?	10.00	20.00	40.00
☐ MG 25168 [10]	Mambos by Cugat	195?	10.00	20.00	40.00
☐ SR-60705 [S]	Twist with Cugat	1962	6.25	12.50	25.00
☐ SR-60745 [S]	The Most Popular Movie Themes As Styled by Cugat	1961	6.25	12.50	25.00
☐ SR-60798 [S]	Cugat's Golden Goodies	1963	6.25	12.50	25.00
☐ SR-60832 [S]	Cugi's Cocktails	1963	6.25	12.50	25.00
☐ SR-60868 [S]	Viva Cugat!	1964	5.00	10.00	20.00
—Reissue of 6003					
☐ SR-60870 [S]	The Best of Cugat	1964	5.00	10.00	20.00
—Reissue of 6015					
☐ SR-60888 [S]	Cugat Caricatures	1964	5.00	10.00	20.00

RCA VICTOR
Number	Title (A Side/B Side)	Yr	VG	VG+	NM
☐ LPT-11 [10]	Tangos	195?	10.00	20.00	40.00
☐ ANL1-1310	Pure Gold	1976	2.00	4.00	8.00
☐ LPM-1882 [M]	The King Plays Some Aces	1958	5.00	10.00	20.00
☐ LSP-1882 [S]	The King Plays Some Aces	1958	6.25	12.50	25.00
☐ LPM-1894 [M]	Cugat in Spain	1959	5.00	10.00	20.00
☐ LSP-1894 [S]	Cugat in Spain	1959	6.25	12.50	25.00
☐ LPM-1987 [M]	Chili Con Cugie	1959	5.00	10.00	20.00
☐ LSP-1987 [S]	Chili Con Cugie	1959	6.25	12.50	25.00
☐ LPM-2173 [M]	Cugat in France, Spain and Italy	1960	5.00	10.00	20.00
☐ LSP-2173 [S]	Cugat in France, Spain and Italy	1960	6.25	12.50	25.00

CULLEY, FRANK "FLOORSHOW"
BATON
Number	Title (A Side/B Side)	Yr	VG	VG+	NM
☐ BL 1201 [M]	Rock 'n Roll: Instrumentals for Dancing the Lindy Hop	1955	150.00	300.00	600.00
—B-side tracks by Buddy Tate Orchestra					

CULT, THE
SIRE
Number	Title (A Side/B Side)	Yr	VG	VG+	NM
☐ 25259	Love	1985	2.50	5.00	10.00
☐ 25555	Electric	1987	2.50	5.00	10.00
☐ 25871	Sonic Temple	1989	2.50	5.00	10.00
☐ R 101015	Sonic Temple	1989	3.00	6.00	12.00
—BMG Direct Marketing edition					
☐ R 134608	Love	1985	3.00	6.00	12.00
—RCA Music Service edition					
☐ R 184083	Electric	1987	3.00	6.00	12.00
—RCA Music Service edition					

WARNER BROS.
Number	Title (A Side/B Side)	Yr	VG	VG+	NM
☐ WBMS-147 [DJ]	Electric Interview	1987	12.50	25.00	50.00
—Part of "The Warner Bros. Music Show" series					

CULTURE CLUB
VIRGIN/EPIC
Number	Title (A Side/B Side)	Yr	VG	VG+	NM
☐ ARE 38398	Kissing to Be Clever	1982	3.00	6.00	12.00
—First pressings have nine tracks and do not contain "Time (Clock of the Heart)"					
☐ FE 38398	Kissing to Be Clever	1983	2.50	5.00	10.00
—This version has 10 tracks with the addition of "Time (Clock of the Heart)" as the first song on side 2					
☐ QE 39107	Colour by Numbers	1983	2.50	5.00	10.00
☐ 9E9-39237 [PD]	Colour by Numbers	1983	6.25	12.50	25.00
—Picture disc in plastic sleeve					
☐ OE 39881	Waking Up with the House on Fire	1984	2.50	5.00	10.00
☐ 9E9-40005 [PD]	Waking Up with the House on Fire	1984	6.25	12.50	25.00
☐ OE 40345	From Luxury to Heartache	1986	2.50	5.00	10.00
☐ FE 40913	This Time: The First Four Years	1987	3.00	6.00	12.00

CUMBERLAND THREE, THE
ROULETTE
Number	Title (A Side/B Side)	Yr	VG	VG+	NM
☐ R 25121 [M]	Folk Scene U.S.A.	1960	5.00	10.00	20.00
☐ SR 25121 [S]	Folk Scene U.S.A.	1960	6.25	12.50	25.00
☐ R 25132 [M]	Civil War Almanac, Volume 1: The Yankees	1960	5.00	10.00	20.00
☐ SR 25132 [S]	Civil War Almanac, Volume 1: The Yankees	1960	6.25	12.50	25.00
☐ R 25133 [M]	Civil War Almanac, Volume 2: The Rebels	1960	5.00	10.00	20.00
☐ SR 25133 [S]	Civil War Almanac, Volume 2: The Rebels	1960	6.25	12.50	25.00

CUOZZO, MIKE
JUBILEE
Number	Title (A Side/B Side)	Yr	VG	VG+	NM
☐ JLP-1027 [M]	Mike Cuozzo	1957	10.00	20.00	40.00

C

Number	Title (A Side/B Side)	Yr	VG	VG+	NM

SAVOY
| ❏ MG-12051 [M] | Mighty Mike | 1956 | 10.00 | 20.00 | 40.00 |

CURE, THE
A&M
| ❏ SP-4902 | Pornography | 1982 | 3.75 | 7.50 | 15.00 |
| ❏ SP-6020 [(2)] | Happily Ever After | 1981 | 7.50 | 15.00 | 30.00 |

ELEKTRA
❏ 60435	The Head on the Door	1985	3.00	6.00	12.00
❏ 60477	Standing on a Beach — The Singles	1986	2.50	5.00	10.00
❏ 60737 [(2)]	Kiss Me, Kiss Me, Kiss Me	1987	3.75	7.50	15.00
❏ 60737 [(2)DJ]	Kiss Me, Kiss Me, Kiss Me	1987	7.50	15.00	30.00
—Promo-only audiophile pressing
❏ 60783	Faith	1988	2.50	5.00	10.00
—Reissue of first U.K. album
❏ 60784	Seventeen Seconds	1988	2.50	5.00	10.00
—Reissue of second U.K. album
❏ 60785	Pornography	1988	2.50	5.00	10.00
—Reissue of A&M SP-4902
❏ 60786	Boys Don't Cry	1988	2.50	5.00	10.00
—Reissue of PVC 7916
❏ 60855	Disintegration	1989	2.50	5.00	10.00
❏ 60978 [(2)]	Mixed Up	1990	5.00	10.00	20.00
—LP version has one extra track not on CD or cassette
❏ 61744 [(2)]	Wild Mood Swings	1996	3.00	6.00	12.00
❏ 62117 [(2)]	Galore: The Singles 1987-1997	1997	3.75	7.50	15.00
❏ 62236 [(2)]	Bloodflowers	2000	3.75	7.50	15.00
❏ R 101109	Disintegration	1989	3.00	6.00	12.00
—BMG Direct Marketing edition
❏ R 150024	Standing on a Beach — The Singles	1986	3.00	6.00	12.00
—BMG Direct Marketing edition
❏ R 242404	Kiss Me, Kiss Me, Kiss Me	1987	4.50	9.00	18.00
—BMG Direct Marketing edition
❏ R 274190	Mixed Up	1990	6.25	12.50	25.00
—BMG Direct Marketing edition

PVC
| ❏ 7916 | Boys Don't Cry | 1980 | 3.75 | 7.50 | 15.00 |

SIRE
❏ 23928 [EP]	The Walk	1983	3.00	6.00	12.00
❏ 25076	Japanese Whispers	1983	3.75	7.50	15.00
❏ 25086	The Top	1984	3.75	7.50	15.00

CURLESS, DICK
CAPITOL
❏ ST-552	Hard, Hard Travelin' Man	1970	5.00	10.00	20.00
❏ ST-689	Doggin' It	1971	5.00	10.00	20.00
❏ ST-792	Comin' On Country	1971	5.00	10.00	20.00
❏ ST-11011	Tombstone Every Mile	1972	3.75	7.50	15.00
—Reissue of Tower DT 5005
❏ ST-11087	Stonin' Around	1972	5.00	10.00	20.00
❏ ST-11119	Live at the Wheeling Truck Driver's Jamboree	1973	5.00	10.00	20.00
❏ ST-11211	The Last Blues Song	1973	5.00	10.00	20.00
—Second cover shows Dick Curless with no eye patch
❏ ST-11211	The Last Blues Song	1973	7.50	15.00	30.00
—First cover shows Dick Curless with an eye patch

TIFFANY
❏ 1016 [M]	Dick Curless Sings Songs of the Open Country	1958	25.00	50.00	100.00
❏ 1028 [M]	Singing Just for Fun	1959	25.00	50.00	100.00
❏ 1033 [M]	I Love to Tell a Story	1960	25.00	50.00	100.00

TOWER
❏ DT 5005 [R]	Tombstone Every Mile	1965	5.00	10.00	20.00
❏ T 5005 [M]	Tombstone Every Mile	1965	7.50	15.00	30.00
❏ DT 5012 [R]	Hymns	1965	5.00	10.00	20.00
❏ T 5012 [M]	Hymns	1965	7.50	15.00	30.00
❏ DT 5013 [R]	The Soul of Dick Curless	1966	5.00	10.00	20.00
❏ T 5013 [M]	The Soul of Dick Curless	1966	7.50	15.00	30.00
❏ DT 5015 [R]	Travelin' Man	1966	5.00	10.00	20.00
❏ T 5015 [M]	Travelin' Man	1966	7.50	15.00	30.00
❏ DT 5016 [R]	At Home with Dick Curless	1966	5.00	10.00	20.00
❏ T 5016 [M]	At Home with Dick Curless	1966	7.50	15.00	30.00
❏ ST 5066 [S]	All of Me Belongs to You	1967	7.50	15.00	30.00
❏ T 5066 [M]	All of Me Belongs to You	1967	7.50	15.00	30.00
❏ ST 5089 [S]	Ramblin' Country	1967	7.50	15.00	30.00
❏ T 5089 [M]	Ramblin' Country	1967	7.50	15.00	30.00
❏ ST 5108	The Long Lonesome Road	1968	7.50	15.00	30.00
❏ ST 5139	The Wild Side of Town	1969	7.50	15.00	30.00

CURLESS, DICK, AND KAY ADAMS
TOWER
| ❏ DT 5025 [R] | A Devil Like Me Needs an Angel Like You | 1966 | 5.00 | 10.00 | 20.00 |
| ❏ T 5025 [M] | A Devil Like Me Needs an Angel Like You | 1966 | 7.50 | 15.00 | 30.00 |

CURRAN, ED
SAVOY
| ❏ MG-12191 [M] | Elysa | 1967 | 5.00 | 10.00 | 20.00 |

CURRIE, CHERIE AND MARIE
CAPITOL
| ❏ ST-12022 | Messin' with the Boys | 1979 | 5.00 | 10.00 | 20.00 |

CURSON, TED
ATLANTIC
| ❏ 1441 [M] | The New Thing and the Blue Thing | 1965 | 5.00 | 10.00 | 20.00 |
| ❏ SD 1441 [S] | The New Thing and the Blue Thing | 1965 | 6.25 | 12.50 | 25.00 |

AUDIO FIDELITY
| ❏ AFLP-2123 [M] | Now Hear This | 1964 | 5.00 | 10.00 | 20.00 |
| ❏ AFSD-6123 [S] | Now Hear This | 1964 | 6.25 | 12.50 | 25.00 |

OLD TOWN
| ❏ LP-2003 [M] | Plenty of Horn | 1961 | 50.00 | 100.00 | 200.00 |

PRESTIGE
| ❏ PRLP-7263 [M] | Fire Down Below | 1965 | 5.00 | 10.00 | 20.00 |
| —Blue label with trident logo at right |
| ❏ PRLP-7263 [M] | Fire Down Below | 1963 | 7.50 | 15.00 | 30.00 |
| —Yellow label, Bergenfield, N.J. address |
| ❏ PRST-7263 [S] | Fire Down Below | 1963 | 10.00 | 20.00 | 40.00 |
| —Silver label, Bergenfield, N.J. address |
| ❏ PRST-7263 [S] | Fire Down Below | 1965 | 6.25 | 12.50 | 25.00 |
| —Blue label with trident logo at right |

CURTIS, KEN
CAPITOL
| ❏ ST 2418 [S] | Gunsmoke's Festus | 1965 | 10.00 | 20.00 | 40.00 |
| ❏ T 2418 [M] | Gunsmoke's Festus | 1965 | 7.50 | 15.00 | 30.00 |

DOT
| ❏ DLP-25859 | Gunsmoke's Festus Calls Out Ken Curtis | 1968 | 7.50 | 15.00 | 30.00 |

CURTIS, MAC
EPIC
| ❏ BN 26419 | The Sunshine Man | 1969 | 5.00 | 10.00 | 20.00 |

HMG/HIGHTONE
| ❏ HT 6601 | Rockabilly Uprising: The Best of Mac Curtis | 1997 | 2.50 | 5.00 | 10.00 |

ROLLIN' ROCK
| ❏ LP-002 | Ruffabilly | 197? | 2.50 | 5.00 | 10.00 |
| ❏ LP-007 | Good Rockin' Tomorrow | 197? | 2.50 | 5.00 | 10.00 |

CURTIS, SONNY
ELEKTRA
❏ 6E-227	Sonny Curtis	1979	2.50	5.00	10.00
❏ 6E-283	Love Is All Around	1980	2.50	5.00	10.00
❏ 6E-349	Rollin'	1981	2.50	5.00	10.00

IMPERIAL
| ❏ LP-9276 [M] | Beatle Hits Flamenco Style | 1964 | 10.00 | 20.00 | 40.00 |
| ❏ LP-12276 [S] | Beatle Hits Flamenco Style | 1964 | 12.50 | 25.00 | 50.00 |

VIVA
| ❏ V-36012 | The First of Sonny Curtis | 1968 | 6.25 | 12.50 | 25.00 |
| ❏ V-36021 | The Sonny Curtis Style | 1969 | 6.25 | 12.50 | 25.00 |

CYKLE, THE
LABEL
| ❏ 9-261 | The Cykle | 1969 | 125.00 | 250.00 | 500.00 |

CYMBAL, JOHNNY
KAPP
| ❏ KL-1324 [M] | Mr. Bass Man | 1963 | 12.50 | 25.00 | 50.00 |
| ❏ KS-3324 [S] | Mr. Bass Man | 1963 | 17.50 | 35.00 | 70.00 |

CYRILLE, ANDREW, AND MILFORD GRAVES
IPS
| ❏ 001 | Dialogue of the Drums | 1974 | 5.00 | 10.00 | 20.00 |

CYRKLE, THE
COLUMBIA
❏ CL 2544 [M]	Red Rubber Ball	1966	5.00	10.00	20.00
❏ CL 2632 [M]	Neon	1967	3.75	7.50	15.00
❏ CS 9344 [S]	Red Rubber Ball	1966	7.50	15.00	30.00
❏ CS 9432 [S]	Neon	1967	5.00	10.00	20.00

CYRUS, BILLY RAY
MERCURY
| ❏ 1P-8218 | Some Gave All | 1992 | 6.25 | 12.50 | 25.00 |
| —Only released on vinyl through Columbia House |

Number	Title (A Side/B Side)	Yr	VG	VG+	NM

D

D'AMICO, HANK
BETHLEHEM
❑ BCP-1006 [10]	Hank's Holiday	1954	30.00	60.00	120.00

DADDY COOL
REPRISE
❑ MS 2088	Teenage Heaven	1972	5.00	10.00	20.00
❑ RS 6471	Daddy Who? Daddy Cool!	1971	3.75	7.50	15.00

DADDY DEWDROP
SUNFLOWER
❑ SNF-5006	Daddy Dewdrop	1971	5.00	10.00	20.00

DAHLANDER, NILS-BERTIL "BERT"
VERVE
❑ MGV-8253 [M]	Skol	1958	12.50	25.00	50.00
❑ V-8253 [M]	Skol	1961	5.00	10.00	20.00

DAILEY, DON
CROWN
❑ CST-314 [R]	Surf Stompin'	1963	3.75	7.50	15.00
❑ CLP-5314 [M]	Surf Stompin'	1963	7.50	15.00	30.00

DAILY, PETE
CAPITOL
❑ H 183 [10]	Dixieland Band	1950	12.50	25.00	50.00
❑ T 183 [M]	Dixieland Band	1954	10.00	20.00	40.00
❑ H 385 [10]	Dixie by Daily	1953	12.50	25.00	50.00
❑ T 385 [M]	Dixie by Daily	1954	10.00	20.00	40.00

DAILY, PETE/PHIL NAPOLEON
DECCA
❑ DL 5261 [10]	Pete Daily/Phil Napoleon	195?	12.50	25.00	50.00

DAKUS, WES, AND THE REBELS
KAPP
❑ KL-1536 [M]	Wes Dakus' Rebels	1967	5.00	10.00	20.00
❑ KS-3536 [S]	Wes Dakus' Rebels	1967	6.25	12.50	25.00

DALE, DICK, AND THE DEL-TONES
CAPITOL
❑ ST 1930 [S]	King of the Surf Guitar	1963	25.00	50.00	100.00
❑ T 1930 [M]	King of the Surf Guitar	1963	15.00	30.00	60.00
❑ ST 2002 [S]	Checkered Flag	1963	20.00	40.00	80.00
❑ T 2002 [M]	Checkered Flag	1963	12.50	25.00	50.00
❑ ST 2053 [S]	Mr. Eliminator	1964	20.00	40.00	80.00
❑ T 2053 [M]	Mr. Eliminator	1964	12.50	25.00	50.00
❑ ST 2111 [S]	Summer Surf	1964	17.50	35.00	70.00
—Without bonus single					
❑ ST 2111 [S]	Summer Surf	1964	30.00	60.00	120.00
—With bonus single by Jerry Cole, "Racing Waves"/"Movin' Surf," in front cover pocket					
❑ T 2111 [M]	Summer Surf	1964	12.50	25.00	50.00
—Without bonus single					
❑ T 2111 [M]	Summer Surf	1964	25.00	50.00	100.00
—With bonus single by Jerry Cole, "Racing Waves"/"Movin' Surf," in front cover pocket					
❑ ST 2293 [S]	Rock Out — Live at Ciro's	1965	37.50	75.00	150.00
❑ T 2293 [M]	Rock Out — Live at Ciro's	1965	25.00	50.00	100.00
CLOISTER					
❑ CLP-6301 [M]	Silver Sounds of the Surf	1963	50.00	100.00	200.00
—With tracks by the Stompers					
DELTONE					
❑ LPM-1001 [M]	Surfer's Choice	1962	37.50	75.00	150.00
❑ DT 1886 [R]	Surfer's Choice	1962	10.00	20.00	40.00
❑ T 1886 [M]	Surfer's Choice	1962	15.00	30.00	60.00
DUB TONE					
❑ LP-1246 [M]	The Surf Family	1964	7.50	15.00	30.00
—With tracks by the Hollywood Surfers					
GNP CRESCENDO					
❑ GNPS-2095	Greatest Hits	1975	3.00	6.00	12.00
RHINO					
❑ RNLP-70074	King of the Surf Guitar: The Best of Dick Dale and the Del-Tones, 1961-1964	1986	3.00	6.00	12.00

DALE AND GRACE
MICHELLE
❑ 100 [M]	I'm Leaving It Up to You	1964	37.50	75.00	150.00
MONTEL					
❑ 100 [M]	I'm Leaving It Up to You	1964	37.50	75.00	150.00

DALEY, JOE
RCA VICTOR
❑ LPM-2763 [M]	Joe Daley at Newport '63	1963	5.00	10.00	20.00
❑ LSP-2763 [S]	Joe Daley at Newport '63	1963	6.25	12.50	25.00

DALLAS, DEAN, AND THE DOUGHBOYS
CUMBERLAND
❑ MGC-29516 [M]	Golden Country Hits	1965	5.00	10.00	20.00
❑ SRC-69516 [S]	Golden Country Hits	1965	6.25	12.50	25.00

DALLAS, MARIA
RCA VICTOR
❑ LPM-3950 [M]	Tumblin' Down	1968	10.00	20.00	40.00
❑ LSP-3950 [S]	Tumblin' Down	1968	5.00	10.00	20.00

DALTON, LACY J.
COLUMBIA
❑ JC 36322	Lacy J. Dalton	1980	2.50	5.00	10.00
❑ PC 36322	Lacy J. Dalton	198?	—	3.00	6.00
—Budget-line reissue with new prefix					
❑ JC 36763	Hard Times	1980	2.50	5.00	10.00

❑ PC 36763	Hard Times	1985	—	3.00	6.00
—Budget-line reissue with new prefix					
❑ FC 37327	Takin' It Easy	1981	2.00	4.00	8.00
❑ PC 37327	Takin' It Easy	1985	—	3.00	6.00
—Budget-line reissue with new prefix					
❑ FC 37975	16th Avenue	1982	2.00	4.00	8.00
❑ FC 38604	Dream Baby	1983	2.00	4.00	8.00
❑ FC 38883	Greatest Hits	1984	2.00	4.00	8.00
❑ FC 40028	Can't Run Away from Your Heart	1985	2.00	4.00	8.00
❑ FC 40393	Highway Diner	1986	2.00	4.00	8.00
❑ FC 40780	Blue Eyed Blues	1987	2.00	4.00	8.00
HARBOR					
❑ 001	Jill Croston	1978	6.25	12.50	25.00
—As "Jill Croston"					
UNIVERSAL					
❑ 42294	Survivor	1989	2.50	5.00	10.00

DAMERON, TADD
JAZZLAND
❑ JLP-50 [M]	Fats Navarro Featured with the Tadd Dameron Quintet	1962	12.50	25.00	50.00
❑ JLP-68 [M]	The Tadd Dameron Band	1962	12.50	25.00	50.00
PRESTIGE					
❑ PRLP-159 [10]	A Study in Dameronia	1953	50.00	100.00	200.00
❑ PRLP-7037 [M]	Fontainebleu	1956	25.00	50.00	100.00
❑ PRLP-7070 [M]	Mating Call	1956	25.00	50.00	100.00
—Reissued as 7247 and 7725 as a John Coltrane LP; see his listings					
❑ PRLP-16007 [M]	Dameronia	1964	10.00	20.00	40.00
RIVERSIDE					
❑ RLP-419 [M]	The Magic Touch of Tadd Dameron	1962	10.00	20.00	40.00
❑ RS-3019	Good Bait	1968	5.00	10.00	20.00
❑ RS-9419 [S]	The Magic Touch of Tadd Dameron	1962	12.50	25.00	50.00

DAMIN EIH, A.L.K. AND BROTHER CLARK
DEMELOT
❑ 7310	Never Mind	1973	37.50	75.00	150.00

DAMITA JO
ABC-PARAMOUNT
❑ 378 [M]	The Big Fifteen	1961	20.00	40.00	80.00
❑ S-378 [S]	The Big Fifteen	1961	25.00	50.00	100.00
EPIC					
❑ LN 24131 [M]	This Is Damita Jo	1965	3.75	7.50	15.00
❑ LN 24164 [M]	One More Time with Feeling	1965	3.75	7.50	15.00
❑ LN 24202 [M]	Midnight Session	1966	3.75	7.50	15.00
❑ LN 24244 [M]	If You Go Away	1967	5.00	10.00	20.00
❑ BN 26131 [S]	This Is Damita Jo	1965	5.00	10.00	20.00
❑ BN 26164 [S]	One More Time with Feeling	1965	5.00	10.00	20.00
❑ BN 26202 [S]	Midnight Session	1966	5.00	10.00	20.00
❑ BN 26244 [S]	If You Go Away	1967	3.75	7.50	15.00
MERCURY					
❑ MG-20642 [M]	I'll Save the Last Dance for You	1961	7.50	15.00	30.00
❑ MG-20703 [M]	Damita Jo Live at the Diplomat	1962	6.25	12.50	25.00
❑ MG-20734 [M]	Sing a Country Song	1962	6.25	12.50	25.00
❑ MG-20818 [M]	This One's for Me	1963	5.00	10.00	20.00
❑ SR-60642 [S]	I'll Save the Last Dance for You	1961	10.00	20.00	40.00
❑ SR-60703 [S]	Damita Jo Live at the Diplomat	1962	7.50	15.00	30.00
❑ SR-60734 [S]	Sing a Country Song	1962	7.50	15.00	30.00
❑ SR-60818 [S]	This One's for Me	1963	6.25	12.50	25.00
RANWOOD					
❑ RLP.8037	Miss Damita Jo	1968	3.75	7.50	15.00
RCA CAMDEN					
❑ CAL-900 [M]	Go Go with Damita Jo	196?	3.75	7.50	15.00
❑ CAS-900(e) [R]	Go Go with Damita Jo	196?	3.00	6.00	12.00
SUNSET					
❑ SUS-5198	The Irresistible Damita Jo	1968	3.00	6.00	12.00
VEE JAY					
❑ LP-1137 [M]	Damita Jo Sings	1965	6.25	12.50	25.00
❑ LPS-1137 [S]	Damita Jo Sings	1965	12.50	25.00	50.00
WING					
❑ WC-16333	This One's for Me	196?	3.00	6.00	12.00

DAMNATION OF ADAM BLESSING, THE
UNITED ARTISTS
❑ UAS-5533	Which Is the Justice, Which Is the Thief	1971	5.00	10.00	20.00
❑ UAS-6738	The Damnation of Adam Blessing	1970	5.00	10.00	20.00
❑ UAS-6773	The Second Damnation	1970	5.00	10.00	20.00

DAMON
ANKH
❑ 968	Song of a Gypsy	1970	500.00	1000.	1500.
—Regular cover					
❑ 968	Song of a Gypsy	1970	1500.	2250.	3000.
—Gatefold cover					

DAMONE, VIC
APPLAUSE
❑ 1018	Over the Rainbow	197?	2.50	5.00	10.00
CAPITOL					
❑ ST 1646 [S]	Linger Awhile with Vic Damone	1962	3.75	7.50	15.00
❑ T 1646 [M]	Linger Awhile with Vic Damone	1962	3.00	6.00	12.00
❑ ST 1691 [S]	Strange Enchantment	1962	3.75	7.50	15.00
❑ T 1691 [M]	Strange Enchantment	1962	3.00	6.00	12.00
❑ ST 1748 [S]	The Lively Ones	1962	3.75	7.50	15.00
❑ T 1748 [M]	The Lively Ones	1962	3.00	6.00	12.00
❑ ST 1811 [S]	My Baby Loves to Swing	1963	3.75	7.50	15.00
❑ T 1811 [M]	My Baby Loves to Swing	1963	3.00	6.00	12.00
❑ ST 1944 [S]	The Liveliest	1963	3.75	7.50	15.00
❑ T 1944 [M]	The Liveliest	1963	3.00	6.00	12.00
❑ ST 2123 [S]	On the Street Where You Live	1964	3.75	7.50	15.00
❑ T 2123 [M]	On the Street Where You Live	1964	3.00	6.00	12.00

Number	Title (A Side/B Side)	Yr	VG	VG+	NM
COLUMBIA					
❏ CL 900 [M]	That Towering Feeling!	1956	6.25	12.50	25.00
❏ CL 1088 [M]	Angela Mia	1957	5.00	10.00	20.00
❏ CL 1174 [M]	Closer Than a Kiss	195?	5.00	10.00	20.00
❏ CL 1368 [M]	This Game of Love	1960	3.75	7.50	15.00
❏ CL 1573 [M]	On the Swingin' Side	1961	3.75	7.50	15.00
❏ CS 8019 [S]	Closer Than a Kiss	1959	7.50	15.00	30.00
❏ CS 8046 [S]	Angela Mia	1959	7.50	15.00	30.00
❏ CS 8169 [S]	This Game of Love	1960	5.00	10.00	20.00
❏ CS 8373 [S]	On the Swingin' Side	1961	5.00	10.00	20.00
HARMONY					
❏ HL 7328 [M]	The Best of Vic Damone	196?	3.00	6.00	12.00
❏ HL 7431 [M]	Vic Damone Sings	196?	3.00	6.00	12.00
❏ HS 11128 [S]	The Best of Vic Damone	196?	3.00	6.00	12.00
❏ HS 11231 [S]	Vic Damone Sings	196?	3.00	6.00	12.00
HOLIDAY					
❏ HDY 1936	Christmas with Vic Damone	1981	2.50	5.00	10.00
MERCURY					
❏ MG-20163 [M]	Yours for a Song	1957	6.25	12.50	25.00
❏ MG-20193 [M]	My Favorites	1957	6.25	12.50	25.00
❏ MG-25028 [10]	Vic Damone	1950	10.00	20.00	40.00
❏ MG-25029 [10]	Vic Damone	1950	10.00	20.00	40.00
❏ MG-25045 [10]	Vic Damone	1950	10.00	20.00	40.00
❏ MG-25054 [10]	Song Hits	1950	10.00	20.00	40.00
❏ MG-25092 [10]	Christmas Favorites	1951	10.00	20.00	40.00
❏ MG-25120 [10]	Vic Damone and Others	1952	10.00	20.00	40.00
❏ MG-25131 [10]	The Night Has a Thousand Eyes	1952	10.00	20.00	40.00
❏ MG-25132 [10]	Vocals by Vic	1952	10.00	20.00	40.00
❏ MG-25133 [10]	April in Paris	1952	10.00	20.00	40.00
❏ MG-25156 [10]	Vic Damone	1952	10.00	20.00	40.00
RANWOOD					
❏ 8204	The Best of Vic Damone — Live	198?	2.50	5.00	10.00
RCA VICTOR					
❏ ANL1-2462	The Best of Vic Damone	1977	2.50	5.00	10.00
❏ LPM-3671 [M]	Stay with Me	1966	3.00	6.00	12.00
❏ LSP-3671 [S]	Stay with Me	1966	3.75	7.50	15.00
❏ LPM-3765 [M]	On the South Side of Chicago	1967	3.00	6.00	12.00
❏ LSP-3765 [S]	On the South Side of Chicago	1967	3.75	7.50	15.00
❏ LPM-3916 [M]	A Damone Type of Thing	1968	3.75	7.50	15.00
❏ LSP-3916 [S]	A Damone Type of Thing	1968	3.75	7.50	15.00
❏ LSP-3984	Why Can't I Walk Away	1968	3.75	7.50	15.00
REBECCA					
❏ 100 [(2)]	Let's Fall in Love Again	1981	3.00	6.00	12.00
❏ 1212	Feelings	1976	2.50	5.00	10.00
❏ 1213	Inspiration	19??	2.50	5.00	10.00
UNITED TALENT					
❏ 4501	Don't Let Me Go	1969	3.00	6.00	12.00
WARNER BROS.					
❏ W 1602 [M]	You Were Only Fooling	1965	3.00	6.00	12.00
❏ WS 1602 [S]	You Were Only Fooling	1965	3.75	7.50	15.00
❏ W 1607 [M]	Country Love Songs	1965	3.00	6.00	12.00
❏ WS 1607 [S]	Country Love Songs	1965	3.75	7.50	15.00
WING					
❏ MGW 12113 [M]	I'll Sing for You	196?	3.00	6.00	12.00
❏ MGW 12157 [M]	Tenderly	196?	3.00	6.00	12.00
❏ MGW 12182 [M]	Yours for a Song	196?	3.00	6.00	12.00
❏ SRW 16113 [R]	I'll Sing for You	196?	3.00	6.00	12.00
❏ SRW 16157 [R]	Tenderly	196?	3.00	6.00	12.00
❏ SRW 16182 [R]	Yours for a Song	196?	3.00	6.00	12.00

DAN AND DALE

Number	Title (A Side/B Side)	Yr	VG	VG+	NM
DIPLOMAT					
❏ D-2390 [M]	The Nearness of You	196?	2.50	5.00	10.00
❏ DS-2390 [S]	The Nearness of You	196?	3.00	6.00	12.00
TIFTON					
❏ M-8002 [M]	Batman and Robin	1966	7.50	15.00	30.00
❏ S-78002 [S]	Batman and Robin	1966	10.00	20.00	40.00

DANA, BILL
See JOSE JIMENEZ.

DANA, VIC

Number	Title (A Side/B Side)	Yr	VG	VG+	NM
DOLTON					
❏ BLP-2013 [M]	This Is Vic Dana	1961	5.00	10.00	20.00
❏ BLP-2015 [M]	Warm and Wild	1962	3.75	7.50	15.00
❏ BLP-2026 [M]	More	1963	3.75	7.50	15.00
❏ BLP-2028 [M]	Shangri-La	1964	3.75	7.50	15.00
❏ BLP-2032 [M]	Now	1964	3.75	7.50	15.00
❏ BLP-2034 [M]	Red Roses for a Blue Lady	1965	3.75	7.50	15.00
❏ BLP-2036 [M]	Moonlight and Roses	1965	3.75	7.50	15.00
❏ BLP-2041 [M]	Crystal Chandelier	1966	3.75	7.50	15.00
❏ BLP-2046 [M]	Town and Country	1966	3.75	7.50	15.00
❏ BLP-2048 [M]	Golden Greats	1966	3.75	7.50	15.00
❏ BLP-2049 [M]	Little Altar Boy and Other Christmas Songs	1966	3.75	7.50	15.00
❏ BST-8013 [S]	This Is Vic Dana	1961	7.50	15.00	30.00
❏ BST-8015 [S]	Warm and Wild	1962	5.00	10.00	20.00
❏ BST-8026 [S]	More	1963	5.00	10.00	20.00
❏ BST-8028 [S]	Shangri-La	1964	5.00	10.00	20.00
❏ BST-8032 [S]	Now	1964	5.00	10.00	20.00
❏ BST-8034 [S]	Red Roses for a Blue Lady	1965	5.00	10.00	20.00
❏ BST-8036 [S]	Moonlight and Roses	1965	5.00	10.00	20.00
❏ BST-8041 [S]	Crystal Chandelier	1966	5.00	10.00	20.00
❏ BST-8046 [S]	Town and Country	1966	5.00	10.00	20.00
❏ BST-8048 [S]	Golden Greats	1966	5.00	10.00	20.00
❏ BST-8049 [S]	Little Altar Boy and Other Christmas Songs	1966	5.00	10.00	20.00
LIBERTY					
❏ BST-8049 [S]	Little Altar Boy and Other Christmas Songs	1967	3.00	6.00	12.00
—Liberty record in Dolton cover					
❏ LST-8063	If I Never Knew Your Name	1969	3.00	6.00	12.00

Number	Title (A Side/B Side)	Yr	VG	VG+	NM
SUNSET					
❏ SUM-1130 [M]	Warm and Wonderful	196?	2.50	5.00	10.00
❏ SUM-1182 [M]	On the Country Side	1967	2.50	5.00	10.00
❏ SUS-5130 [S]	Warm and Wonderful	196?	3.00	6.00	12.00
❏ SUS-5182 [S]	On the Country Side	1967	3.00	6.00	12.00

DANE, BARBARA

Number	Title (A Side/B Side)	Yr	VG	VG+	NM
BARBARY COAST					
❏ 33014 [M]	Trouble in Mind	1959	10.00	20.00	40.00
—Reissue of San Francisco LP					
CAPITOL					
❏ ST 1758 [S]	On My Way	1962	10.00	20.00	40.00
❏ T 1758 [M]	On My Way	1962	7.50	15.00	30.00
DOT					
❏ DLP-3177 [M]	Living with the Blues	1959	7.50	15.00	30.00
❏ DLP-25177 [S]	Living with the Blues	1959	10.00	20.00	40.00
FOLKWAYS					
❏ FA-2468	Barbara Dane and the Chambers Brothers	1966	12.50	25.00	50.00
❏ FA-2471	Folk Songs	1966	7.50	15.00	30.00
HORIZON					
❏ WP-1602 [M]	When I Was a Young Girl	1962	7.50	15.00	30.00
❏ WPS-1602 [S]	When I Was a Young Girl	1962	10.00	20.00	40.00
—Black vinyl					
❏ WPS-1602 [S]	When I Was a Young Girl	1962	15.00	30.00	60.00
—Gold vinyl					
SAN FRANCISCO					
❏ 33014 [M]	Trouble in Mind	1957	15.00	30.00	60.00

DANIELS, CHARLIE, BAND

Number	Title (A Side/B Side)	Yr	VG	VG+	NM
CAPITOL					
❏ ST-790	Charlie Daniels	1971	6.25	12.50	25.00
❏ ST-11414	Charlie Daniels	1975	3.00	6.00	12.00
—Reissue of ST-790					
❏ SN-16039	Charlie Daniels	1979	2.00	4.00	8.00
—Budget-line reissue					
EPIC					
❏ AS 586 [DJ]	Interchords	1979	3.75	7.50	15.00
—Music and interviews; promo only					
❏ EAS 1780 [DJ]	The Charlie Daniels Story	1990	3.75	7.50	15.00
—Promo-only interview/radio show					
❏ PE 34150	Saddle Tramp	1976	2.50	5.00	10.00
—Orange label, no bar code on cover					
❏ PE 34150	Saddle Tramp	198?	2.00	4.00	8.00
—With bar code on cover					
❏ JE 34365	Fire on the Mountain	1976	2.50	5.00	10.00
—Reissue of Kama Sutra 2603 without bonus EP; orange label, no bar code on cover					
❏ PE 34365	Fire on the Mountain	198?	2.00	4.00	8.00
—Budget-line reissue					
❏ JE 34369	Uneasy Rider	1976	2.50	5.00	10.00
—Reissue of Kama Sutra 2071 with new name; orange label, no bar code on cover					
❏ PE 34369	Uneasy Rider	198?	2.00	4.00	8.00
—Budget-line reissue					
❏ JE 34377	High Lonesome	1976	2.50	5.00	10.00
—Orange label, no bar code on cover					
❏ PE 34377	High Lonesome	198?	2.00	4.00	8.00
—Budget-line reissue					
❏ JE 34402	Nightrider	1977	2.50	5.00	10.00
—Reissue of Kama Sutra 2607; orange label, no bar code on cover					
❏ PE 34402	Nightrider	198?	2.00	4.00	8.00
—Budget-line reissue					
❏ JE 34664	Whiskey	1977	2.50	5.00	10.00
—Reissue of Kama Sutra 2076 with new name; orange label, no bar code on cover					
❏ PE 34664	Whiskey	198?	2.00	4.00	8.00
—Budget-line reissue					
❏ JE 34665	Te John, Grease and Wolfman	1977	2.50	5.00	10.00
—Reissue of Kama Sutra 2060; orange label, no bar code on cover					
❏ PE 34665	Te John, Grease and Wolfman	198?	2.00	4.00	8.00
—Budget-line reissue					
❏ JE 34970	Midnight Wind	1977	2.50	5.00	10.00
—Orange label, no bar code on cover					
❏ PE 34970	Midnight Wind	198?	2.00	4.00	8.00
—Budget-line reissue					
❏ JE 35751	Million Mile Reflections	1979	2.50	5.00	10.00
❏ PE 35751	Million Mile Reflections	198?	2.00	4.00	8.00
—Budget-line reissue					
❏ FE 36571	Full Moon	1980	2.50	5.00	10.00
❏ PE 36571	Full Moon	198?	2.00	4.00	8.00
—Budget-line reissue					
❏ FE 37694	Windows	1982	2.50	5.00	10.00
❏ PE 37694	Windows	198?	2.00	4.00	8.00
—Budget-line reissue					
❏ FE 38795	A Decade of Hits	1983	2.50	5.00	10.00
❏ FE 39878	Me and the Boys	1985	2.50	5.00	10.00
❏ PE 39878	Me and the Boys	198?	2.00	4.00	8.00
—Budget-line reissue					
❏ FE 40760	Powder Keg	1987	2.00	4.00	8.00
❏ FE 44324	Homesick Man	1988	2.00	4.00	8.00
❏ HE 44365	Fire on the Mountain	1982	10.00	20.00	40.00
—Half-speed mastered edition					
❏ FE 45316	Simple Man	1989	3.00	6.00	12.00
❏ HE 45751	Million Mile Reflections	1982	10.00	20.00	40.00
—Half-speed mastered edition					
KAMA SUTRA					
❏ KSBS 2060	Te John, Grease and Wolfman	1972	3.75	7.50	15.00
❏ KSBS 2071	Honey in the Rock	1973	3.75	7.50	15.00
❏ KSBS 2076	Way Down Yonder	1974	3.75	7.50	15.00
❏ KSBS 2603	Fire on the Mountain	1974	3.75	7.50	15.00
—Includes bonus EP, "Volunteer Jam" (deduct 20% if missing)					
❏ KSBS 2607	Nightrider	1975	3.75	7.50	15.00

Number	Title (A Side/B Side)	Yr	VG	VG+	NM
MOBILE FIDELITY					
❏ 1-176	Million Mile Reflections	1984	7.50	15.00	30.00
—Audiophile vinyl					
DANIELS, EDDIE					
PRESTIGE					
❏ PRLP-7506 [M]	First Prize	1967	10.00	20.00	40.00
❏ PRST-7506 [S]	First Prize	1967	6.25	12.50	25.00
DANIELS, HALL					
JUMP					
❏ JL-9 [10]	Hall Daniels Septet	1955	20.00	40.00	80.00
—Issued on blue vinyl					
DANIELS, SLOPPY					
DOOTO					
❏ DTL-266 [M]	Sloppy's House Party	1959	6.25	12.50	25.00
DANKWORTH, JOHN					
FONTANA					
❏ SRF-67543 [S]	Zodiac Variations	1966	5.00	10.00	20.00
❏ SRF-67603	The Sophisticated Johnnie Dankworth	1969	5.00	10.00	20.00
ROULETTE					
❏ R-52040 [M]	England's Ambassador of Jazz	1960	5.00	10.00	20.00
❏ SR-52040 [S]	England's Ambassador of Jazz	1960	6.25	12.50	25.00
❏ R-52059 [M]	Collaboration	1961	5.00	10.00	20.00
❏ SR-52059 [S]	Collaboration	1961	6.25	12.50	25.00
❏ R-52096 [M]	Jazz from Abroad	1963	5.00	10.00	20.00
❏ SR-52096 [S]	Jazz from Abroad	1963	6.25	12.50	25.00
DANTE					
MADISON					
❏ MA-LP 1002 [M]	Dante and the Evergreens	1961	125.00	250.00	500.00
DANTE, RON					
HANDSHAKE					
❏ JW 37341	Street Angel	1981	3.00	6.00	12.00
KIRSHNER					
❏ KES-106	Ron Dante Brings You Up	1970	5.00	10.00	20.00
DARCEL, DENISE					
CAMEO					
❏ C-1002 [M]	Banned in Boston	1958	10.00	20.00	40.00
DARCH, BOB					
UNITED ARTISTS					
❏ UAL-3120 [M]	Ragtime Piano	1960	5.00	10.00	20.00
❏ UAS-6120 [S]	Ragtime Piano	1960	6.25	12.50	25.00
DARIN, BOBBY					
ATCO					
❏ 33-102 [M]	Bobby Darin	1958	25.00	50.00	100.00
—Yellow "harp" label					
❏ 33-102 [M]	Bobby Darin	1962	7.50	15.00	30.00
—Gold and dark blue label					
❏ 33-104 [M]	That's All	1959	10.00	20.00	40.00
—Yellow "harp" label					
❏ 33-104 [M]	That's All	1962	5.00	10.00	20.00
—Gold and dark blue label					
❏ SD 33-104 [S]	That's All	1959	25.00	50.00	100.00
—Yellow "harp" label					
❏ SD 33-104 [S]	That's All	1962	6.25	12.50	25.00
—Purple and brown label					
❏ 33-115 [M]	This Is Darin	1960	10.00	20.00	40.00
—Yellow "harp" label					
❏ 33-115 [M]	This Is Darin	1962	5.00	10.00	20.00
—Gold and dark blue label					
❏ SD 33-115 [S]	This Is Darin	1960	6.25	12.50	25.00
—Purple and brown label					
❏ SD 33-115 [S]	This Is Darin	1960	20.00	40.00	80.00
—Yellow "harp" label					
❏ 33-122 [M]	Darin at the Copa	1960	10.00	20.00	40.00
—Yellow "harp" label					
❏ 33-122 [M]	Darin at the Copa	1962	5.00	10.00	20.00
—Gold and dark blue label					
❏ SD 33-122 [S]	Darin at the Copa	1960	20.00	40.00	80.00
—Yellow "harp" label					
❏ SD 33-122 [S]	Darin at the Copa	1962	6.25	12.50	25.00
—Purple and brown label					
❏ 33-124 [M]	It's You or No One	1960	10.00	20.00	40.00
—Yellow "harp" label					
❏ 33-124 [M]	It's You or No One	1962	5.00	10.00	20.00
—Gold and dark blue label					
❏ SD 33-124 [S]	It's You or No One	1960	20.00	40.00	80.00
—Yellow "harp" label					
❏ SD 33-124 [S]	It's You or No One	1962	6.25	12.50	25.00
—Purple and brown label					
❏ 33-125 [M]	The 25th Day of December	1960	12.50	25.00	50.00
—Yellow "harp" label					
❏ 33-125 [M]	The 25th Day of December	1962	5.00	10.00	20.00
—Gold and dark blue label					
❏ SD 33-125 [S]	The 25th Day of December	1960	15.00	30.00	60.00
—Yellow "harp" label					
❏ SD 33-125 [S]	The 25th Day of December	1962	6.25	12.50	25.00
—Gold and dark blue label					
❏ 33-126 [M]	Two of a Kind	1961	10.00	20.00	40.00
—Yellow "harp" label					
❏ 33-126 [M]	Two of a Kind	1962	5.00	10.00	20.00
—Gold and dark blue label					
❏ SD 33-126 [S]	Two of a Kind	1961	12.50	25.00	50.00
—Yellow "harp" label					
❏ SD 33-126 [S]	Two of a Kind	1962	6.25	12.50	25.00
—Purple and brown label					

Number	Title (A Side/B Side)	Yr	VG	VG+	NM
❏ 33-131 [M]	The Bobby Darin Story	1961	10.00	20.00	40.00
—Yellow "harp" label; white cover					
❏ 33-131 [M]	The Bobby Darin Story	1962	5.00	10.00	20.00
—Gold and dark blue label; black cover					
❏ SD 33-131	The Bobby Darin Story	1969	3.00	6.00	12.00
—Yellow label, "Atco" on left					
❏ SD 33-131	The Bobby Darin Story	1978	2.00	4.00	8.00
—Any later Atco label					
❏ SD 33-131 [S]	The Bobby Darin Story	1961	12.50	25.00	50.00
—Yellow "harp" label; white cover					
❏ SD 33-131 [S]	The Bobby Darin Story	1962	6.25	12.50	25.00
—Purple and brown label; black cover					
❏ 33-134 [M]	Love Swings	1961	10.00	20.00	40.00
—Yellow "harp" label					
❏ 33-134 [M]	Love Swings	1962	5.00	10.00	20.00
—Gold and dark blue label					
❏ SD 33-134 [S]	Love Swings	1961	12.50	25.00	50.00
—Yellow "harp" label					
❏ SD 33-134 [S]	Love Swings	1962	6.25	12.50	25.00
—Purple and brown label					
❏ 33-138 [M]	Twist with Bobby Darin	1961	10.00	20.00	40.00
—Yellow "harp" label					
❏ 33-138 [M]	Twist with Bobby Darin	1962	5.00	10.00	20.00
—Gold and dark blue label					
❏ SD 33-138 [S]	Twist with Bobby Darin	1961	12.50	25.00	50.00
—Yellow "harp" label					
❏ SD 33-138 [S]	Twist with Bobby Darin	1962	6.25	12.50	25.00
—Purple and brown label					
❏ 33-140 [M]	Bobby Darin Sings Ray Charles	1962	6.25	12.50	25.00
❏ SD 33-140 [S]	Bobby Darin Sings Ray Charles	1962	7.50	15.00	30.00
❏ 33-146 [M]	Things & Other Things	1962	6.25	12.50	25.00
❏ SD 33-146 [S]	Things & Other Things	1962	7.50	15.00	30.00
❏ 33-167 [M]	Winners	1964	6.25	12.50	25.00
❏ SD 33-167 [S]	Winners	1964	7.50	15.00	30.00
❏ SP 1001 [M]	For Teenagers Only	1960	18.75	37.50	75.00
—With extras missing					
❏ SP 1001 [M]	For Teenagers Only	1960	37.50	75.00	150.00
—Gatefold with fold-open poster and paper insert					
❏ 90484	Two of a Kind	1986	2.50	5.00	10.00
ATLANTIC					
❏ 8121 [M]	The Shadow of Your Smile	1966	3.75	7.50	15.00
❏ SD 8121 [S]	The Shadow of Your Smile	1966	5.00	10.00	20.00
❏ 8126 [M]	In a Broadway Bag	1966	3.75	7.50	15.00
❏ SD 8126 [S]	In a Broadway Bag	1966	5.00	10.00	20.00
❏ 8135 [M]	If I Were a Carpenter	1967	3.75	7.50	15.00
❏ SD 8135 [S]	If I Were a Carpenter	1967	12.50	25.00	50.00
—Inexplicably rare in stereo					
❏ 8142 [M]	Inside Out	1967	3.75	7.50	15.00
❏ SD 8142 [S]	Inside Out	1967	7.50	15.00	30.00
❏ 8154 [M]	Bobby Darin Sings Doctor Dolittle	1967	3.75	7.50	15.00
❏ SD 8154 [S]	Bobby Darin Sings Doctor Dolittle	1967	3.75	7.50	15.00
BAINBRIDGE					
❏ 6220	Bobby Darin at the Copa	1981	2.50	5.00	10.00
CAPITOL					
❏ ST 1791 [S]	Oh! Look at Me Now	1962	5.00	10.00	20.00
❏ SW 1791 [S]	Oh! Look at Me Now	1962	6.25	12.50	25.00
❏ T 1791 [M]	Oh! Look at Me Now	1962	3.75	7.50	15.00
❏ W 1791 [M]	Oh! Look at Me Now	1962	5.00	10.00	20.00
❏ ST 1826 [S]	Earthy	1963	5.00	10.00	20.00
❏ T 1826 [M]	Earthy	1963	3.75	7.50	15.00
❏ ST 1866 [S]	You're the Reason I'm Living	1963	5.00	10.00	20.00
❏ T 1866 [M]	You're the Reason I'm Living	1963	3.75	7.50	15.00
❏ ST 1942 [S]	18 Yellow Roses	1963	5.00	10.00	20.00
❏ T 1942 [M]	18 Yellow Roses	1963	3.75	7.50	15.00
❏ ST 2007 [S]	Golden Folk Hits	1963	5.00	10.00	20.00
❏ T 2007 [M]	Golden Folk Hits	1963	3.75	7.50	15.00
❏ ST 2084 [S]	As Long As I'm Singing	1964	50.00	100.00	200.00
—Canceled; price is for an acetate, which is known to exist					
❏ T 2084 [M]	As Long As I'm Singing	1964	—	—	—
—Canceled					
❏ ST 2194 [S]	From Hello Dolly to Goodbye Charlie	1964	5.00	10.00	20.00
❏ T 2194 [M]	From Hello Dolly to Goodbye Charlie	1964	3.75	7.50	15.00
❏ ST 2322 [S]	Venice Blue	1965	5.00	10.00	20.00
❏ T 2322 [M]	Venice Blue	1965	3.75	7.50	15.00
❏ ST 2571 [S]	The Best of Bobby Darin	1966	3.75	7.50	15.00
❏ T 2571 [M]	The Best of Bobby Darin	1966	3.75	7.50	15.00
CLARION					
❏ 603 [M]	Clementine	1966	5.00	10.00	20.00
❏ SD 603 [S]	Clementine	1966	6.25	12.50	25.00
DIRECTION					
❏ 1936	Born Walden Robert Cassotto	1968	6.25	12.50	25.00
❏ 1937	Commitment	1969	6.25	12.50	25.00
MOTOWN					
❏ M5-185V1	Darin 1936-1973	1981	3.00	6.00	12.00
—Reissue					
❏ MS-739	Finally	1972	125.00	250.00	500.00
—Unreleased; value is for RCA test pressing					
❏ M 753L	Bobby Darin	1972	5.00	10.00	20.00
❏ M6-813L	Darin 1936-1973	1974	3.75	7.50	15.00
DARIUS					
CHARTMAKER					
❏ 1102	Darius	1969	62.50	125.00	250.00
DARNEL, BILL					
"X"					
❏ LVA-(# unk) [10]	Bill Darnel Sings	1955	10.00	20.00	40.00
DARR, ALICE					
CHARLIE PARKER					
❏ PLP-611 [M]	I Only Know How to Cry	1962	7.50	15.00	30.00
❏ PLP-611S [S]	I Only Know How to Cry	1962	10.00	20.00	40.00

Number	Title (A Side/B Side)	Yr	VG	VG+	NM

DARRELL, JOHNNY
CAPRICORN
| ❑ CP 0154 | Water Glass Full of Whiskey | 1975 | 2.50 | 5.00 | 10.00 |

SUNSET
| ❑ SUS-5232 | The Johnny Darrell Sound | 1969 | 2.50 | 5.00 | 10.00 |

UNITED ARTISTS
❑ UAL 3594 [M]	Ruby, Don't Take Your Love to Town	1967	6.25	12.50	25.00
❑ UAS 6594 [S]	Ruby, Don't Take Your Love to Town	1967	5.00	10.00	20.00
❑ UAS 6634	The Son of Hickory Holler's Tramp	1968	5.00	10.00	20.00
❑ UAS 6660	With Pen in Hand	1968	5.00	10.00	20.00
❑ UAS 6707	Why You Been Gone So Long	1969	5.00	10.00	20.00
❑ UAS 6752	California Stop-Over	1970	5.00	10.00	20.00
❑ UAS 6759	The Best of Johnny Darrell, Volume 1	1970	3.75	7.50	15.00

DARREN, JAMES
COLPIX
❑ CP-406 [M]	James Darren (Album No. 1)	1960	10.00	20.00	40.00
❑ CP-406 [M]	James Darren (Album No. 1)	1960	37.50	75.00	150.00
—Green vinyl					
❑ CP-418 [M]	Gidget Goes Hawaiian (James Darren Sings the Movies)	1961	7.50	15.00	30.00
❑ SCP-418 [S]	Gidget Goes Hawaiian (James Darren Sings the Movies)	1961	10.00	20.00	40.00
❑ CP-424 [M]	James Darren Sings for All Sizes	1962	7.50	15.00	30.00
❑ SCP-424 [S]	James Darren Sings for All Sizes	1962	10.00	20.00	40.00
❑ CP-428 [M]	Love Among the Young	1962	7.50	15.00	30.00
❑ SCP-428 [S]	Love Among the Young	1962	10.00	20.00	40.00

KIRSHNER
| ❑ KES-115 | Mammy Blue | 1971 | 3.75 | 7.50 | 15.00 |
| ❑ KES-116 | Love Songs from the Movies | 1972 | 3.75 | 7.50 | 15.00 |

WARNER BROS.
| ❑ W 1668 [M] | James Darren/All | 1967 | 3.75 | 7.50 | 15.00 |
| ❑ WS 1668 [S] | James Darren/All | 1967 | 5.00 | 10.00 | 20.00 |

DARREN, JAMES/ SHELLEY FABARES/PAUL PETERSEN
COLPIX
❑ CP-444 [M]	Teenage Triangle	1963	10.00	20.00	40.00
❑ SCP-444 [R]	Teenage Triangle	1963	10.00	20.00	40.00
❑ CP-468 [M]	More Teenage Triangle	1964	10.00	20.00	40.00
❑ SCP-468 [P]	More Teenage Triangle	1964	15.00	30.00	60.00

DARRIEU, DANIELLE
LONDON
| ❑ LB-616 [10] | Le Voix de France | 1954 | 12.50 | 25.00 | 50.00 |

DARRIEUX, DANIELLE
CAPITOL
| ❑ ST 10319 [S] | Incomparable Danielle Darrieux | 1963 | 7.50 | 15.00 | 30.00 |
| ❑ T 10319 [M] | Incomparable Danielle Darrieux | 1963 | 5.00 | 10.00 | 20.00 |

DARTELLS, THE
DOT
| ❑ DLP-3522 [M] | Hot Pastrami | 1963 | 7.50 | 15.00 | 30.00 |
| ❑ DLP-25522 [S] | Hot Pastrami | 1963 | 10.00 | 20.00 | 40.00 |

DARTMOUTH INDIAN CHIEFS
TRANSITION
| ❑ TRLP-23 [M] | Chiefly Jazz | 1956 | 30.00 | 60.00 | 120.00 |

DARTS, THE
DEL-FI
| ❑ DFLP-1244 [M] | Hollywood Drag | 1963 | 10.00 | 20.00 | 40.00 |
| ❑ DFST-1244 [S] | Hollywood Drag | 1963 | 12.50 | 25.00 | 50.00 |

DASH, JULIAN
MASTER JAZZ
| ❑ 8106 | Portrait | 1970 | 5.00 | 10.00 | 20.00 |

DASHIEL, BUD, AND THE KINSMEN
WARNER BROS.
❑ W 1429 [M]	Folk Music in a Contemporary Manner	1961	6.25	12.50	25.00
❑ WS 1429 [S]	Folk Music in a Contemporary Manner	1961	7.50	15.00	30.00
❑ W 1432 [M]	Live Concert Extraordinaire — Bud Dashiel and the Kinsmen Sing Everybody's Hits	1961	6.25	12.50	25.00
❑ WS 1432 [S]	Live Concert Extraordinaire — Bud Dashiel and the Kinsmen Sing Everybody's Hits	1961	7.50	15.00	30.00

DAUGHERTY, JACK
A&M
| ❑ SP-3038 | Jack Daugherty and the Class of '71 | 1971 | 5.00 | 10.00 | 20.00 |

DAUGHTERS OF ALBION, THE
FONTANA
| ❑ SRF-67586 | The Daughters of Albion | 1968 | 5.00 | 10.00 | 20.00 |

DAVE DEE, DOZY, BEAKY, MICK & TICH
FONTANA
❑ MGF-27567 [M]	Greatest Hits	1967	7.50	15.00	30.00
❑ SRF-67567 [P]	Greatest Hits	1967	10.00	20.00	40.00
—"Bend It" and "Hold Tight" are rechanneled.					

IMPERIAL
| ❑ LP-12402 [P] | Time to Take Off | 1968 | 10.00 | 20.00 | 40.00 |
| —"Zabadak" is rechanneled. | | | | | |

DAVEY AND THE BADMEN
GOTHIC
| ❑ KRW-054 | Wanted | 1963 | 50.00 | 100.00 | 200.00 |

DAVID, THE
V.M.C.
| ❑ 124 | Another Day, Another Lifetime | 1968 | 25.00 | 50.00 | 100.00 |

DAVID AND JONATHAN
CAPITOL
| ❑ ST 2473 [S] | Michelle | 1966 | 5.00 | 10.00 | 20.00 |
| ❑ T 2473 [M] | Michelle | 1966 | 3.75 | 7.50 | 15.00 |

DAVIDSON, LOWELL
ESP-DISK'
| ❑ S-1012 [S] | Lowell Davidson Trio | 1965 | 5.00 | 10.00 | 20.00 |

DAVIE, HUTCH
ATCO
| ❑ 33-105 [M] | Much Hutch | 1958 | 12.50 | 25.00 | 50.00 |

DAVIS, BOB
STEPHENY
| ❑ MF-4000 [M] | Jazz in Orbit | 1958 | 15.00 | 30.00 | 60.00 |
| ❑ MFS-8003 [S] | Jazz in Orbit | 1960 | 12.50 | 25.00 | 50.00 |

ZEPHYR
| ❑ 12001 [M] | Jazz from the North Coast | 1959 | 12.50 | 25.00 | 50.00 |

DAVIS, EDDIE "LOCKJAW"
BETHLEHEM
| ❑ BCP-6069 [M] | The Best of Eddie "Lockjaw" Davis | 1963 | 10.00 | 20.00 | 40.00 |
| ❑ BCPS-6069 [R] | The Best of Eddie "Lockjaw" Davis | 196? | 5.00 | 10.00 | 20.00 |

JAZZLAND
| ❑ JLP-97 [M] | Alma Alegre | 1962 | 6.25 | 12.50 | 25.00 |
| ❑ JLP-997 [S] | Alma Alegre | 1962 | 7.50 | 15.00 | 30.00 |

KING
❑ 395-506 [M]	Modern Jazz Expression	1956	25.00	50.00	100.00
❑ 395-526 [M]	Jazz with a Horn	1957	25.00	50.00	100.00
❑ 566 [M]	Jazz with a Beat	1957	25.00	50.00	100.00
❑ 599 [M]	Big Beat Jazz	1958	25.00	50.00	100.00
❑ 606 [M]	Uptown	1958	25.00	50.00	100.00
❑ 637 [M]	This and That	1959	25.00	50.00	100.00

PRESTIGE
❑ PRLP-7141 [M]	The Eddie "Lockjaw" Davis Cookbook	1958	20.00	40.00	80.00
—Cover photo features Davis with no hat					
❑ PRLP-7141 [M]	The Eddie "Lockjaw" Davis Cookbook	1959	12.50	25.00	50.00
—Cover photo features Davis with hat					
❑ PRLP-7161 [M]	The Eddie "Lockjaw" Davis Cookbook, Vol. 2	1959	12.50	25.00	50.00
❑ PRLP-7206 [M]	Trane Whistle	1961	12.50	25.00	50.00
❑ PRLP-7219 [M]	The Eddie "Lockjaw" Davis Cookbook, Vol. 3	1961	12.50	25.00	50.00
❑ PRST-7219 [S]	The Eddie "Lockjaw" Davis Cookbook, Vol. 3	1961	10.00	20.00	40.00
❑ PRLP-7242 [M]	Goin' to the Meeting	1962	10.00	20.00	40.00
❑ PRST-7242 [S]	Goin' to the Meeting	1962	12.50	25.00	50.00
❑ PRLP-7261 [M]	I Only Have Eyes for You	1963	10.00	20.00	40.00
❑ PRST-7261 [S]	I Only Have Eyes for You	1963	12.50	25.00	50.00
❑ PRLP-7271 [M]	Trackin'	1963	10.00	20.00	40.00
❑ PRST-7271 [S]	Trackin'	1963	12.50	25.00	50.00

RCA VICTOR
❑ LPM-3652 [M]	Lock the Fox	1966	5.00	10.00	20.00
❑ LSP-3652 [S]	Lock the Fox	1966	6.25	12.50	25.00
❑ LPM-3741 [M]	The Fox and the Hounds	1967	6.25	12.50	25.00
❑ LSP-3741 [S]	The Fox and the Hounds	1967	5.00	10.00	20.00
❑ LPM-3882 [M]	Love Calls	1967	6.25	12.50	25.00
❑ LSP-3882 [S]	Love Calls	1967	5.00	10.00	20.00

RIVERSIDE
❑ RLP-373 [M]	Afro-Jaws	1961	7.50	15.00	30.00
❑ RLP-430 [M]	Jawbreakers	1962	7.50	15.00	30.00
❑ RS-9373 [S]	Afro-Jaws	1961	10.00	20.00	40.00
❑ RS-9430 [S]	Jawbreakers	1962	10.00	20.00	40.00

ROOST
| ❑ LP-422 [10] | Goodies | 1954 | 37.50 | 75.00 | 150.00 |
| ❑ RST-2227 [M] | Eddie Davis Trio | 1957 | 25.00 | 50.00 | 100.00 |

ROULETTE
❑ R-52007 [M]	Count Basie Presents Eddie Davis	1958	15.00	30.00	60.00
—White label with color spokes					
❑ R-52007 [M]	Count Basie Presents Eddie Davis	1963	6.25	12.50	25.00
—Orange and yellow "roulette wheel" label					
❑ SR-52007 [S]	Count Basie Presents Eddie Davis	1959	12.50	25.00	50.00
—White label with color spokes					
❑ SR-52007 [S]	Count Basie Presents Eddie Davis	1963	5.00	10.00	20.00
—Orange and yellow "roulette wheel" label					
❑ R-52019 [M]	Eddie Davis Trio	1959	15.00	30.00	60.00
—White label with color spokes					
❑ R-52019 [M]	Eddie Davis Trio	1963	6.25	12.50	25.00
—Orange and yellow "roulette wheel" label					
❑ SR-52019 [S]	Eddie Davis Trio	1959	12.50	25.00	50.00
—White label with color spokes					
❑ SR-52019 [S]	Eddie Davis Trio	1963	5.00	10.00	20.00
—Orange and yellow "roulette wheel" label					

DAVIS, EDDIE "LOCKJAW", AND JOHNNY GRIFFIN
JAZZLAND
❑ JLP-31 [M]	Tough Tenors	1960	10.00	20.00	40.00
❑ JLP-39 [M]	Lookin' at Monk	1961	10.00	20.00	40.00
❑ JLP-42 [M]	Griff & Lock	1961	10.00	20.00	40.00
❑ JLP-60 [M]	Blues Up and Down	1961	10.00	20.00	40.00
❑ JLP-76 [M]	Tough Tenor Favorites	1962	10.00	20.00	40.00
❑ JLP-931 [S]	Tough Tenors	1960	12.50	25.00	50.00
❑ JLP-939 [S]	Lookin' at Monk	1961	12.50	25.00	50.00
❑ JLP-942 [S]	Griff & Lock	1961	12.50	25.00	50.00
❑ JLP-960 [S]	Blues Up and Down	1961	12.50	25.00	50.00
❑ JLP-976 [S]	Tough Tenor Favorites	1962	12.50	25.00	50.00

PRESTIGE
❑ PRLP-7191 [M]	The Tenor Scene	1961	12.50	25.00	50.00
❑ PRLP-7282 [M]	Battle Stations	1963	7.50	15.00	30.00
❑ PRST-7282 [S]	Battle Stations	1963	10.00	20.00	40.00
❑ PRLP-7309 [M]	The First Set — Recorded Live at Minton's	1964	7.50	15.00	30.00
❑ PRST-7309 [S]	The First Set — Recorded Live at Minton's	1964	10.00	20.00	40.00
❑ PRLP-7330 [M]	The Midnight Show at Minton's Playhouse	1964	6.25	12.50	25.00

Number	Title (A Side/B Side)	Yr	VG	VG+	NM
❏ PRST-7330 [S]	The Midnight Show at Minton's Playhouse	1964	7.50	15.00	30.00
❏ PRLP-7357 [M]	The Late Show — Recorded Live!	1965	6.25	12.50	25.00
❏ PRST-7357 [S]	The Late Show — Recorded Live!	1965	7.50	15.00	30.00
❏ PRLP-7407 [M]	The Breakfast Show	1965	7.50	15.00	30.00
—Reissue of 7191					
❏ PRST-7407 [S]	The Breakfast Show	1965	6.25	12.50	25.00

DAVIS, EDDIE "LOCKJAW", AND SHIRLEY SCOTT
MOODSVILLE

Number	Title (A Side/B Side)	Yr	VG	VG+	NM
❏ MVLP-4 [M]	Eddie "Lockjaw" Davis with Shirley Scott	1960	12.50	25.00	50.00
—Green label					
❏ MVLP-4 [M]	Eddie "Lockjaw" Davis with Shirley Scott	1965	6.25	12.50	25.00
—Blue label, trident logo on right					
❏ MVLP-30 [M]	Misty	1963	12.50	25.00	50.00
—Green label					
❏ MVLP-30 [M]	Misty	1965	6.25	12.50	25.00
—Blue label, trident logo on right					
❏ MVST-30 [S]	Misty	1963	12.50	25.00	50.00
—Green label					
❏ MVST-30 [S]	Misty	1965	6.25	12.50	25.00
—Blue label, trident logo on right					

PRESTIGE

Number	Title (A Side/B Side)	Yr	VG	VG+	NM
❏ PRLP-7154 [M]	Jaws	1959	12.50	25.00	50.00
❏ PRLP-7171 [M]	Jaws in Orbit	1959	12.50	25.00	50.00
❏ PRLP-7178 [M]	Bacalao	1960	12.50	25.00	50.00
❏ PRLP-7301 [M]	Smokin'	1964	10.00	20.00	40.00
❏ PRST-7301 [S]	Smokin'	1964	7.50	15.00	30.00

DAVIS, JACKIE
CAPITOL

Number	Title (A Side/B Side)	Yr	VG	VG+	NM
❏ T 815 [M]	Chasing Shadows	1957	10.00	20.00	40.00
—Turquoise or gray label					
❏ T 1180 [M]	Jackie Davis Meets the Trombones	1959	7.50	15.00	30.00
—Black colorband label, logo at left					

DAVIS, JIMMIE
DECCA

Number	Title (A Side/B Side)	Yr	VG	VG+	NM
❏ DL 4587 [M]	It's Christmas Time Again	1964	3.00	6.00	12.00
❏ DL 4868 [M]	Going Home for Christmas	1967	3.00	6.00	12.00
❏ DL 8174 [M]	Near the Cross	1955	6.25	12.50	25.00
❏ DL 8572 [M]	Hymn Time	1957	6.25	12.50	25.00
❏ DL 8729 [M]	The Door Is Always Open	1958	6.25	12.50	25.00
❏ DL 8786 [M]	Hail Him with a Song	1958	6.25	12.50	25.00
❏ DL 8896 [M]	You Are My Sunshine	1959	5.00	10.00	20.00
❏ DL 8953 [M]	Suppertime	1960	5.00	10.00	20.00
❏ DL 74587 [S]	It's Christmas Time Again	1964	3.75	7.50	15.00
❏ DL 74868 [S]	Going Home for Christmas	1967	3.00	6.00	12.00
❏ DL 78896 [S]	You Are My Sunshine	1959	6.25	12.50	25.00
❏ DL 78953 [S]	Suppertime	1960	6.25	12.50	25.00

DAVIS, JOHNNY "SCAT"
KING

Number	Title (A Side/B Side)	Yr	VG	VG+	NM
❏ 626 [M]	Here's Lookin' Atcha	1959	20.00	40.00	80.00

DAVIS, LINK
MERCURY

Number	Title (A Side/B Side)	Yr	VG	VG+	NM
❏ SR-61243	Cajun Crawdaddy	1969	5.00	10.00	20.00

DAVIS, MARTHA
Also see THE MOTELS.
CAPITOL

Number	Title (A Side/B Side)	Yr	VG	VG+	NM
❏ CLT-48054	Policy	1988	3.00	6.00	12.00
❏ CLT-79197/8 [DJ]	Policy (Radio Cue Card)	1987	6.25	12.50	25.00

DAVIS, MAXWELL
ALADDIN

Number	Title (A Side/B Side)	Yr	VG	VG+	NM
❏ LP-709 [10]	Maxwell Davis	1955	100.00	200.00	400.00
❏ LP-804 [M]	Maxwell Davis	1956	50.00	100.00	200.00
SCORE
| ❏ SLP-4106 [M] | Blue Tango | 1957 | 50.00 | 100.00 | 200.00 |

DAVIS, MEL
EPIC

Number	Title (A Side/B Side)	Yr	VG	VG+	NM
❏ LN 3268 [M]	Trumpet with a Soul	1956	10.00	20.00	40.00
TIME
❏ S-2087 [S]	Shoot the Trumpet Player	1962	6.25	12.50	25.00
❏ S-2117 [S]	We Like Broadway	1963	6.25	12.50	25.00
❏ 52087 [M]	Shoot the Trumpet Player	1962	5.00	10.00	20.00
❏ 52117 [M]	We Like Broadway	1963	5.00	10.00	20.00

DAVIS, MILES
BLUE NOTE

Number	Title (A Side/B Side)	Yr	VG	VG+	NM
❏ BLP-1501 [M]	Miles Davis, Volume 1	1955	37.50	75.00	150.00
—Regular version with Lexington Ave. address on label					
❏ BLP-1501 [M]	Miles Davis, Volume 1	1955	50.00	100.00	200.00
—"Deep groove" version (deep indentation under label on both sides)					
❏ BLP-1501 [M]	Miles Davis, Volume 1	1958	12.50	25.00	50.00
—Regular version with W. 63rd St. address on label					
❏ BLP-1501 [M]	Miles Davis, Volume 1	1963	6.25	12.50	25.00
—With New York, USA address on label					
❏ BLP-1502 [M]	Miles Davis, Volume 2	1955	37.50	75.00	150.00
—Regular version with Lexington Ave. address on label					
❏ BLP-1502 [M]	Miles Davis, Volume 2	1955	50.00	100.00	200.00
—"Deep groove" version (deep indentation under label on both sides)					
❏ BLP-1502 [M]	Miles Davis, Volume 2	1958	12.50	25.00	50.00
—Regular version with W. 63rd St. address on label					
❏ BLP-1502 [M]	Miles Davis, Volume 2	1963	6.25	12.50	25.00
—With New York, USA address on label					
❏ BLP-5013 [10]	Miles Davis (Young Man with a Horn)	1952	75.00	150.00	300.00
❏ BLP-5022 [10]	Miles Davis, Vol. 2	1953	75.00	150.00	300.00
❏ BLP-5040 [10]	Miles Davis, Vol. 3	1954	75.00	150.00	300.00
CAPITOL
| ❏ H 459 [10] | Jeru | 1954 | 62.50 | 125.00 | 250.00 |
| —First 33 1/3 rpm issue of some of the "Birth of the Cool" sessions | | | | | |

Number	Title (A Side/B Side)	Yr	VG	VG+	NM
❏ T 762 [M]	Birth of the Cool	1956	37.50	75.00	150.00
❏ T 1974 [M]	Birth of the Cool	1963	7.50	15.00	30.00
—Reissue of 762					

COLUMBIA

Number	Title (A Side/B Side)	Yr	VG	VG+	NM
❏ C2L 20 [(2)M]	Miles Davis in Person (Friday & Saturday Nights at the Blackhawk, San Francisco)	1961	12.50	25.00	50.00
—Six "eye" logos on label					
❏ C2L 20 [(2)M]	Miles Davis in Person (Friday & Saturday Nights at the Blackhawk, San Francisco)	1963	7.50	15.00	30.00
—"Guaranteed High Fidelity" on label					
❏ C2L 20 [(2)M]	Miles Davis in Person (Friday & Saturday Nights at the Blackhawk, San Francisco)	1965	6.25	12.50	25.00
—"Mono" on label					
❏ GP 26 [(2)]	Bitches Brew	1970	10.00	20.00	40.00
—"360 Sound Stereo" on red labels					
❏ C2S 820 [(2)S]	Miles Davis in Person (Friday & Saturday Nights at the Blackhawk, San Francisco)	1961	12.50	25.00	50.00
—Six "eye" logos on label					
❏ C2S 820 [(2)S]	Miles Davis in Person (Friday & Saturday Nights at the Blackhawk, San Francisco)	1963	7.50	15.00	30.00
—"360 Sound Stereo" in black on label					
❏ C2S 820 [(2)S]	Miles Davis in Person (Friday & Saturday Nights at the Blackhawk, San Francisco)	1965	6.25	12.50	25.00
—"360 Sound Stereo" in white on label					
❏ CL 949 [M]	'Round About Midnight	1957	12.50	25.00	50.00
—Six "eye" logos on label					
❏ CL 949 [M]	'Round About Midnight	1963	6.25	12.50	25.00
—"Guaranteed High Fidelity" on label					
❏ CL 949 [M]	'Round About Midnight	1965	5.00	10.00	20.00
—"Mono" on label					
❏ CL 1041 [M]	Miles Ahead	1957	12.50	25.00	50.00
—Six "eye" logos on label; cover has Miles Davis blowing his trumpet					
❏ CL 1041 [M]	Miles Ahead	1957	20.00	40.00	80.00
—Six "eye" logos on label; cover has a while woman and her child on a sailboat					
❏ CL 1041 [M]	Miles Ahead	1963	6.25	12.50	25.00
—"Guaranteed High Fidelity" on label					
❏ CL 1041 [M]	Miles Ahead	1965	5.00	10.00	20.00
—"Mono" on label					
❏ CL 1193 [M]	Milestones	1958	12.50	25.00	50.00
—Six "eye" logos on label					
❏ CL 1193 [M]	Milestones	1963	6.25	12.50	25.00
—"Guaranteed High Fidelity" on label					
❏ CL 1193 [M]	Milestones	1965	5.00	10.00	20.00
—"Mono" on label					
❏ CL 1268 [M]	Jazz Track	1958	12.50	25.00	50.00
—Six "eye" logos on label; with Miles and a woman on cover					
❏ CL 1268 [M]	Jazz Track	1958	20.00	40.00	80.00
—Six "eye" logos on label; with abstract drawing on cover					
❏ CL 1274 [M]	Porgy and Bess	1958	12.50	25.00	50.00
—Six "eye" logos on label					
❏ CL 1274 [M]	Porgy and Bess	1963	6.25	12.50	25.00
—"Guaranteed High Fidelity" on label					
❏ CL 1274 [M]	Porgy and Bess	1965	5.00	10.00	20.00
—"Mono" on label					
❏ CL 1355 [M]	Kind of Blue	1959	15.00	30.00	60.00
—Six "eye" logos on label					
❏ CL 1355 [M]	Kind of Blue	1963	6.25	12.50	25.00
—"Guaranteed High Fidelity" on label					
❏ CL 1355 [M]	Kind of Blue	1965	5.00	10.00	20.00
—"Mono" on label					
❏ CL 1480 [M]	Sketches of Spain	1960	12.50	25.00	50.00
—Six "eye" logos on label					
❏ CL 1480 [M]	Sketches of Spain	1963	6.25	12.50	25.00
—"Guaranteed High Fidelity" on label					
❏ CL 1480 [M]	Sketches of Spain	1965	5.00	10.00	20.00
—"Mono" on label					
❏ CL 1656 [M]	Someday My Prince Will Come	1961	10.00	20.00	40.00
—Six "eye" logos on label					
❏ CL 1656 [M]	Someday My Prince Will Come	1963	6.25	12.50	25.00
—"Guaranteed High Fidelity" on label					
❏ CL 1656 [M]	Someday My Prince Will Come	1965	5.00	10.00	20.00
—"Mono" on label					
❏ CL 1669 [M]	Miles Davis in Person, Vol. 1 (Friday Nights at the Blackhawk, San Francisco)	1961	7.50	15.00	30.00
—Six "eye" logos on label; later pressings may exist					
❏ CL 1670 [M]	Miles Davis in Person, Vol. 2 (Saturday Nights at the Blackhawk, San Francisco)	1961	7.50	15.00	30.00
—Six "eye" logos on label; later pressings may exist					
❏ CL 1812 [M]	Miles Davis at Carnegie Hall	1962	12.50	25.00	50.00
—Six "eye" logos on label					
❏ CL 1812 [M]	Miles Davis at Carnegie Hall	1963	6.25	12.50	25.00
—"Guaranteed High Fidelity" on label					
❏ CL 1812 [M]	Miles Davis at Carnegie Hall	1965	5.00	10.00	20.00
—"Mono" on label					
❏ CL 2051 [M]	Seven Steps to Heaven	1963	6.25	12.50	25.00
—"Guaranteed High Fidelity" on label					
❏ CL 2051 [M]	Seven Steps to Heaven	1965	5.00	10.00	20.00
—"Mono" on label					
❏ CL 2106 [M]	Quiet Nights	1964	6.25	12.50	25.00
—"Guaranteed High Fidelity" on label					
❏ CL 2106 [M]	Quiet Nights	1965	5.00	10.00	20.00
—"Mono" on label					
❏ CL 2183 [M]	Miles Davis in Europe	1964	6.25	12.50	25.00
—"Guaranteed High Fidelity" on label					
❏ CL 2183 [M]	Miles Davis in Europe	1965	5.00	10.00	20.00
—"Mono" on label					
❏ CL 2306 [M]	My Funny Valentine	1965	5.00	10.00	20.00
❏ CL 2306 [M]	My Funny Valentine	1965	6.25	12.50	25.00
—"Guaranteed High Fidelity" on label					
❏ CL 2350 [M]	E.S.P.	1965	5.00	10.00	20.00
—"Mono" on label					

Number	Title (A Side/B Side)	Yr	VG	VG+	NM
❏ CL 2350 [M]	E.S.P.	1965	6.25	12.50	25.00
—"Guaranteed High Fidelity" on label					
❏ CL 2453 [M]	"Four" & More — Recorded Live in Concert	1966	5.00	10.00	20.00
❏ CL 2601 [M]	Miles Smiles	1966	5.00	10.00	20.00
❏ CL 2628 [M]	Milestones	1967	7.50	15.00	30.00
—Reissue of 1193?					
❏ CL 2732 [M]	Sorcerer	1967	7.50	15.00	30.00
❏ CL 2794 [M]	Nefertiti	1968	12.50	25.00	50.00
❏ CL 2828 [M]	Miles in the Sky	1968	20.00	40.00	80.00
❏ CS 8021 [S]	Milestones	1959	12.50	25.00	50.00
—Six "eye" logos on label					
❏ CS 8021 [S]	Milestones	1963	6.25	12.50	25.00
—"360 Sound Stereo" in black on label					
❏ CS 8021 [S]	Milestones	1965	5.00	10.00	20.00
—"360 Sound Stereo" in white on label					
❏ CS 8085 [S]	Porgy and Bess	1959	12.50	25.00	50.00
—Six "eye" logos on label					
❏ CS 8085 [S]	Porgy and Bess	1963	6.25	12.50	25.00
—"360 Sound Stereo" in black on label					
❏ CS 8085 [S]	Porgy and Bess	1965	5.00	10.00	20.00
—"360 Sound Stereo" in white on label					
❏ CS 8163 [(2)]	Kind of Blue	1997	17.50	35.00	70.00
—Reissue; contains both the original Side 1, which was mastered slightly fast, and the "correct" Side 1 (as Side 3); distributed by Classic Records					
❏ CS 8163 [S]	Kind of Blue	1959	30.00	60.00	120.00
—Six "eye" logos on label					
❏ CS 8163 [S]	Kind of Blue	1963	6.25	12.50	25.00
—"360 Sound Stereo" in black on label					
❏ CS 8163 [S]	Kind of Blue	1965	5.00	10.00	20.00
—"360 Sound Stereo" in white on label					
❏ CS 8271 [S]	Sketches of Spain	1960	20.00	40.00	80.00
—Six "eye" logos on label					
❏ CS 8271 [S]	Sketches of Spain	1963	6.25	12.50	25.00
—"360 Sound Stereo" in black on label					
❏ CS 8271 [S]	Sketches of Spain	1965	5.00	10.00	20.00
—"360 Sound Stereo" in white on label					
❏ CS 8271 [S]	Sketckes of Spain	1999	6.25	12.50	25.00
—Audiophile reissue; distributed by Classic Records					
❏ CS 8456 [S]	Someday My Prince Will Come	1961	10.00	20.00	40.00
—Six "eye" logos on label					
❏ CS 8456 [S]	Someday My Prince Will Come	1963	6.25	12.50	25.00
—"360 Sound Stereo" in black on label					
❏ CS 8456 [S]	Someday My Prince Will Come	1965	5.00	10.00	20.00
—"360 Sound Stereo" in white on label					
❏ CS 8469 [S]	Miles Davis in Person, Vol. 1 (Friday Nights at the Blackhawk, San Francisco)	1961	7.50	15.00	30.00
—Six "eye" logos on label; later pressings may exist					
❏ CS 8470 [S]	Miles Davis in Person, Vol. 2 (Saturday Nights at the Blackhawk, San Francisco)	1961	7.50	15.00	30.00
—Six "eye" logos on label; later pressings may exist					
❏ CS 8612 [S]	Miles Davis at Carnegie Hall	1962	6.25	12.50	25.00
—"360 Sound Stereo" in black on label					
❏ CS 8612 [S]	Miles Davis at Carnegie Hall	1962	12.50	25.00	50.00
—Six "eye" logos on label					
❏ CS 8612 [S]	Miles Davis at Carnegie Hall	1965	5.00	10.00	20.00
—"360 Sound Stereo" in white on label					
❏ CS 8851 [S]	Seven Steps to Heaven	1963	6.25	12.50	25.00
—"360 Sound Stereo" in black on label					
❏ CS 8851 [S]	Seven Steps to Heaven	1965	5.00	10.00	20.00
—"360 Sound Stereo" in white on label					
❏ CS 8906 [S]	Quiet Nights	1964	6.25	12.50	25.00
—"360 Sound Stereo" in black on label					
❏ CS 8906 [S]	Quiet Nights	1965	5.00	10.00	20.00
—"360 Sound Stereo" in white on label					
❏ CS 8983 [S]	Miles Davis in Europe	1964	6.25	12.50	25.00
—"360 Sound Stereo" in black on label					
❏ CS 8983 [S]	Miles Davis in Europe	1965	5.00	10.00	20.00
—"360 Sound Stereo" in white on label					
❏ CS 9106 [S]	My Funny Valentine	1965	5.00	10.00	20.00
—"360 Sound Stereo" in white on label					
❏ CS 9106 [S]	My Funny Valentine	1965	6.25	12.50	25.00
—"360 Sound Stereo" in black on label					
❏ CS 9150 [S]	E.S.P.	1965	5.00	10.00	20.00
—"360 Sound Stereo" in white on label					
❏ CS 9150 [S]	E.S.P.	1965	6.25	12.50	25.00
—"360 Sound Stereo" in black on label					
❏ CS 9253 [S]	"Four" & More — Recorded Live in Concert	1966	5.00	10.00	20.00
—"360 Sound Stereo" on red label					
❏ CS 9401 [S]	Miles Smiles	1966	5.00	10.00	20.00
—"360 Sound Stereo" on red label					
❏ CS 9428 [S]	Milestones	1967	5.00	10.00	20.00
—"360 Sound Stereo" on red label; reissue of 8021?					
❏ CS 9532 [S]	Sorcerer	1967	5.00	10.00	20.00
—"360 Sound Stereo" on red label					
❏ CS 9594 [S]	Nefertiti	1968	5.00	10.00	20.00
—"360 Sound Stereo" on red label					
❏ CS 9628 [S]	Miles in the Sky	1968	5.00	10.00	20.00
—"360 Sound Stereo" on red label					
❏ CS 9750	Filles de Kilimanjaro	1969	5.00	10.00	20.00
—"360 Sound Stereo" on red label					
❏ CS 9808	Miles Davis' Greatest Hits	1969	5.00	10.00	20.00
—"360 Sound Stereo" on red label					
❏ CS 9875	In a Silent Way	1969	5.00	10.00	20.00
—"360 Sound Stereo" on red label					
❏ GQ 30954 [(2)Q]	Live-Evil	1973	7.50	15.00	30.00
❏ GQ 30997 [(2)Q]	Bitches Brew	1972	10.00	20.00	40.00
❏ C6X 36976 [(6)]	The Miles Davis Collection Vol. 1: 12 Sides of Miles	1980	12.50	25.00	50.00
❏ HC 46790	The Man with the Horn	1982	10.00	20.00	40.00
—Half-speed mastered edition					

DEBUT

Number	Title (A Side/B Side)	Yr	VG	VG+	NM
❏ DEB 120 [M]	Blue Moods	1955	62.50	125.00	250.00

FANTASY

Number	Title (A Side/B Side)	Yr	VG	VG+	NM
❏ 6001 [M]	Blue Moods	1962	12.50	25.00	50.00
—Reissue of Debut album; red vinyl					
❏ 6001 [M]	Blue Moods	1963	7.50	15.00	30.00
—Black vinyl, red label					
❏ 86001 [R]	Blue Moods	1962	7.50	15.00	30.00
—Blue vinyl					

MOBILE FIDELITY

Number	Title (A Side/B Side)	Yr	VG	VG+	NM
❏ 1-177	Someday My Prince Will Come	1985	20.00	40.00	80.00
—Audiophile vinyl					

MOSAIC

Number	Title (A Side/B Side)	Yr	VG	VG+	NM
❏ MQ10-158 [(10)]	The Complete Plugged Nickel Sessions	1995	50.00	100.00	200.00
❏ MQ11-164 [(11)]	Miles Davis & Gil Evans: The Complete Columbia Studio Recordings	1996	62.50	125.00	250.00
❏ MQ10-177 [(10)]	The Complete Studio Recordings of the Miles Davis Quintet 1965-June 1968	1998	37.50	75.00	150.00
❏ MQ6-183 [(6)]	The Complete Bitches Brew Sessions	1999	25.00	50.00	100.00
❏ MQ9-191 [(9)]	The Complete Columbia Recordings of Miles Davis with John Coltrane	2000	42.50	85.00	170.00
❏ MQ5-209 [(5)]	The Complete In a Silent Way Sessions (September 1968-February 1969)	2002	20.00	40.00	80.00

PRESTIGE

Number	Title (A Side/B Side)	Yr	VG	VG+	NM
❏ P-12 [(12)]	Chronicle: The Complete Prestige Recordings	1980	25.00	50.00	100.00
❏ PRLP-124 [10]	The New Sounds of Miles Davis	1952	62.50	125.00	250.00
❏ PRLP-140 [10]	Blue Period	1953	62.50	125.00	250.00
❏ PRLP-154 [10]	Miles Davis Plays Al Cohn Compositions	1953	62.50	125.00	250.00
❏ PRLP-161 [10]	Miles Davis Featuring Sonny Rollins	1953	62.50	125.00	250.00
❏ PRLP-182 [10]	Miles Davis Sextet	1954	62.50	125.00	250.00
❏ PRLP-185 [10]	Miles Davis Quintet	1954	62.50	125.00	250.00
❏ PRLP-187 [10]	Miles Davis Quintet Featuring Sonny Rollins	1954	62.50	125.00	250.00
❏ PRLP-196 [10]	Miles Davis All Stars, Volume 1	1955	62.50	125.00	250.00
❏ PRLP-200 [10]	Miles Davis All Stars, Volume 2	1955	62.50	125.00	250.00
❏ PRLP-7007 [M]	The Musings of Miles	1955	37.50	75.00	150.00
❏ PRLP-7012 [M]	Dig Miles Davis/Sonny Rollins	1956	37.50	75.00	150.00
—Gray cover					
❏ PRLP-7012 [M]	Dig Miles Davis/Sonny Rollins	1957	30.00	60.00	120.00
—Color cover					
❏ PRLP-7014 [M]	Miles — The New Miles Davis Quintet	1956	37.50	75.00	150.00
❏ PRLP-7025 [M]	Miles Davis and Horns	1956	37.50	75.00	150.00
❏ PRLP-7034 [M]	Miles Davis and the Milt Jackson Quintet/Sextet	1956	37.50	75.00	150.00
—With W. 50th St. address on yellow label					
❏ PRLP-7034 [M]	Miles Davis and the Milt Jackson Quintet/Sextet	196?	7.50	15.00	30.00
—With trident on blue label					
❏ PRLP-7044 [M]	Collectors' Item	1956	30.00	60.00	120.00
—With W. 50th St. address on yellow label					
❏ PRLP-7044 [M]	Collectors' Item	196?	7.50	15.00	30.00
—With trident on blue label					
❏ PRLP-7054 [M]	Blue Haze	1956	30.00	60.00	120.00
—With W. 50th St. address on yellow label					
❏ PRLP-7054 [M]	Blue Haze	196?	7.50	15.00	30.00
—With trident on blue label					
❏ PRLP-7076 [M]	All Stars	195?	17.50	35.00	70.00
—With Bergenfield, N.J. address on yellow label					
❏ PRLP-7076 [M]	All Stars	1957	25.00	50.00	100.00
—With W. 50th St. address on yellow label					
❏ PRLP-7076 [M]	All Stars	196?	7.50	15.00	30.00
—With trident on blue label					
❏ PRLP-7094 [M]	Cookin' with the Miles Davis Quintet	195?	15.00	30.00	60.00
—With Bergenfield, N.J. address on yellow label					
❏ PRLP-7094 [M]	Cookin' with the Miles Davis Quintet	1957	25.00	50.00	100.00
—With W. 50th St. address on yellow label					
❏ PRLP-7094 [M]	Cookin' with the Miles Davis Quintet	196?	7.50	15.00	30.00
—With trident on blue label					
❏ PRLP-7109 [M]	Bags Groove	1957	25.00	50.00	100.00
—With W. 50th St. address on yellow label					
❏ PRLP-7109 [M]	Bags Groove	196?	7.50	15.00	30.00
—With trident on blue label					
❏ PRLP-7129 [M]	Relaxin' with the Miles Davis Quintet	1957	15.00	30.00	60.00
—With Bergenfield, NJ address on yellow label					
❏ PRLP-7129 [M]	Relaxin' with the Miles Davis Quintet	1957	25.00	50.00	100.00
—With W. 50th St. address on yellow label					
❏ PRLP-7129 [M]	Relaxin' with the Miles Davis Quintet	196?	7.50	15.00	30.00
—With trident on blue label					
❏ PRLP-7150 [M]	Miles Davis and the Modern Jazz Giants	1958	20.00	40.00	80.00
—With Bergenfield, NJ address on yellow label					
❏ PRLP-7150 [M]	Miles Davis and the Modern Jazz Giants	196?	7.50	15.00	30.00
—With trident on blue label					
❏ PRLP-7166 [M]	Workin' with the Miles Davis Quintet	1959	20.00	40.00	80.00
—With Bergenfield, NJ address on yellow label					
❏ PRLP-7166 [M]	Workin' with the Miles Davis Quintet	196?	7.50	15.00	30.00
—With trident on blue label					
❏ PRLP-7168 [M]	Early Miles	1959	20.00	40.00	80.00
—Reissue of 7025; with Bergenfield, NJ address on yellow label					
❏ PRLP-7168 [M]	Early Miles	196?	7.50	15.00	30.00
—With trident on blue label					
❏ PRLP-7200 [M]	Steamin' with the Miles Davis Quintet	196?	7.50	15.00	30.00
—With trident on blue label					
❏ PRLP-7200 [M]	Steamin' with the Miles Davis Quintet	1961	20.00	40.00	80.00
—With Bergenfield, NJ address on yellow label					
❏ PRLP-7221 [M]	The Beginning	196?	7.50	15.00	30.00
—With trident on blue label					
❏ PRLP-7221 [M]	The Beginning	1962	12.50	25.00	50.00
—Reissue of 7007; with Bergenfield, NJ address on yellow label					
❏ PRLP-7254 [M]	The Original Quintet	196?	7.50	15.00	30.00
—With trident on blue label					
❏ PRLP-7254 [M]	The Original Quintet	1963	12.50	25.00	50.00
—Reissue of 7014; with Bergenfield, NJ address on yellow label					
❏ PRST-7254 [R]	The Original Quintet	1963	5.00	10.00	20.00
❏ PRLP-7281 [M]	Diggin'	196?	7.50	15.00	30.00
—With trident on blue label					

Number	Title (A Side/B Side)	Yr	VG	VG+	NM
❑ PRLP-7281 [M]	Diggin'	1963	12.50	25.00	50.00
—Reissue of 7012; with Bergenfield, NJ address on yellow label					
❑ PRST-7281 [R]	Diggin'	1963	5.00	10.00	20.00
❑ PRLP-7322 [M]	Miles Davis Plays Richard Rodgers	1964	7.50	15.00	30.00
❑ PRST-7322 [R]	Miles Davis Plays Richard Rodgers	1964	5.00	10.00	20.00
❑ PRLP-7352 [M]	Miles Davis Plays for Lovers	1965	7.50	15.00	30.00
❑ PRST-7352 [R]	Miles Davis Plays for Lovers	1965	5.00	10.00	20.00
❑ PRLP-7373 [M]	Jazz Classics	1965	7.50	15.00	30.00
❑ PRST-7373 [R]	Jazz Classics	1965	5.00	10.00	20.00
❑ PRLP-7457 [M]	Miles Davis' Greatest Hits	1967	5.00	10.00	20.00

DAVIS, MILES, AND JOHN COLTRANE
MOODSVILLE

Number	Title (A Side/B Side)	Yr	VG	VG+	NM
❑ MVLP-32 [M]	Miles Davis and John Coltrane Play Richard Rodgers	1963	12.50	25.00	50.00
—Green label					
❑ MVLP-32 [M]	Miles Davis and John Coltrane Play Richard Rodgers	1965	6.25	12.50	25.00
—Blue label, trident logo at right					

PRESTIGE

Number	Title (A Side/B Side)	Yr	VG	VG+	NM
❑ PRLP-7322 [M]	Miles Davis and John Coltrane Play Rodgers and Hart	1964	10.00	20.00	40.00
❑ PRST-7322 [R]	Miles Davis and John Coltrane Play Rodgers and Hart	1964	5.00	10.00	20.00

DAVIS, MILES, AND THELONIOUS MONK
COLUMBIA

Number	Title (A Side/B Side)	Yr	VG	VG+	NM
❑ CL 2178 [M]	Miles and Monk at Newport	1964	6.25	12.50	25.00
—"Guaranteed High Fidelity" on label					
❑ CL 2178 [M]	Miles and Monk at Newport	1965	5.00	10.00	20.00
—"Mono" on label					
❑ CS 8978 [S]	Miles and Monk at Newport	1964	6.25	12.50	25.00
—"360 Sound Stereo" in black on label					
❑ CS 8978 [S]	Miles and Monk at Newport	1965	5.00	10.00	20.00
—"360 Sound Stereo" in white on label					

DAVIS, PAUL
ARISTA

Number	Title (A Side/B Side)	Yr	VG	VG+	NM
❑ AL 8376	Cool Night	198?	2.00	4.00	8.00
—Reissue of 9578					
❑ AL 9578	Cool Night	1981	2.50	5.00	10.00

BANG

Number	Title (A Side/B Side)	Yr	VG	VG+	NM
❑ BLPS-223	A Little Bit of Paul Davis	1970	10.00	20.00	40.00
❑ 401	Ride 'Em Cowboy	1974	3.00	6.00	12.00
❑ 405	Southern Tracks and Fantasies	1976	3.00	6.00	12.00
❑ 410	Singer of Songs — Teller of Tales	1977	3.00	6.00	12.00
❑ JZ 36094	Paul Davis	1980	2.50	5.00	10.00
❑ PZ 37973	The Best of Paul Davis	1982	2.50	5.00	10.00

DAVIS, REVEREND GARY
BLUESVILLE

Number	Title (A Side/B Side)	Yr	VG	VG+	NM
❑ BVLP-1015 [M]	Harlem Street Singer	1961	25.00	50.00	100.00
—Blue label, silver print					
❑ BVLP-1015 [M]	Harlem Street Singer	1964	7.50	15.00	30.00
—Blue label with trident logo					
❑ BVLP-1032 [M]	A Little More Faith	1961	25.00	50.00	100.00
—Blue label, silver print					
❑ BVLP-1032 [M]	A Little More Faith	1964	7.50	15.00	30.00
—Blue label with trident logo					
❑ BVLP-1049 [M]	Say No to the Devil	1962	25.00	50.00	100.00
—Blue label, silver print					
❑ BVLP-1049 [M]	Say No to the Devil	1964	7.50	15.00	30.00
—Blue label with trident logo					

FOLKLORE

Number	Title (A Side/B Side)	Yr	VG	VG+	NM
❑ F-14028 [M]	Pure Religion	196?	10.00	20.00	40.00
❑ F-14033 [M]	Guitar and Banjo	196?	10.00	20.00	40.00

STINSON

Number	Title (A Side/B Side)	Yr	VG	VG+	NM
❑ SLP-56 [10]	The Singing Reverend	195?	25.00	50.00	100.00

DAVIS, SAMMY, JR.
DECCA

Number	Title (A Side/B Side)	Yr	VG	VG+	NM
❑ DXB 192 [(2)M]	The Best of Sammy Davis, Jr.	1966	3.75	7.50	15.00
❑ DL 4153 [M]	Mr. Entertainment	1961	3.75	7.50	15.00
❑ DL 4381 [M]	Forget-Me-Nots for First Nighters	1963	3.75	7.50	15.00
❑ DL 4582 [M]	Try a Little Tenderness	1965	3.00	6.00	12.00
❑ DXSB 7192 [(2)S]	The Best of Sammy Davis, Jr.	1966	5.00	10.00	20.00
❑ DL 8118 [M]	Starring Sammy Davis, Jr.	1955	7.50	15.00	30.00
❑ DL 8170 [M]	Just for Lovers	1955	7.50	15.00	30.00
❑ DL 8351 [M]	Here's Looking at You	1956	6.25	12.50	25.00
❑ DL 8486 [M]	Sammy Swings	1957	6.25	12.50	25.00
❑ DL 8641 [M]	It's All Over But the Swingin'	1957	6.25	12.50	25.00
❑ DL 8676 [M]	Mood to Be Wooed	1958	6.25	12.50	25.00
❑ DL 8779 [M]	All the Way And Then Some	1958	6.25	12.50	25.00
❑ DL 8841 [M]	Sammy Davis, Jr., at Town Hall	1959	5.00	10.00	20.00
❑ DL 8854 [M]	Porgy and Bess	1959	5.00	10.00	20.00
❑ DL 8921 [M]	The Sammy Awards	1960	5.00	10.00	20.00
❑ DL 8981 [M]	I Got a Right to Swing	1960	5.00	10.00	20.00
❑ DL 74153 [S]	Mr. Entertainment	1961	5.00	10.00	20.00
❑ DL 74381 [S]	Forget-Me-Nots for First Nighters	1963	5.00	10.00	20.00
❑ DL 74582 [S]	Try a Little Tenderness	1965	3.75	7.50	15.00
❑ DL 78841 [S]	Sammy Davis, Jr., at Town Hall	1959	6.25	12.50	25.00
❑ DL 78854 [S]	Porgy and Bess	1959	6.25	12.50	25.00
❑ DL 78921 [S]	The Sammy Awards	1960	6.25	12.50	25.00
❑ DL 78981 [S]	I Got a Right to Swing	1960	6.25	12.50	25.00

HARMONY

Number	Title (A Side/B Side)	Yr	VG	VG+	NM
❑ HS 11299	The Great Sammy Davis, Jr.	196?	3.00	6.00	12.00
❑ HS 11365	Let There Be Love	1970	2.50	5.00	10.00
❑ H 30568	What Kind of Fool Am I	1971	2.50	5.00	10.00

MCA

Number	Title (A Side/B Side)	Yr	VG	VG+	NM
❑ 4109 [(2)]	Sammy Davis Jr. At His Greatest	1975	3.00	6.00	12.00

MGM

Number	Title (A Side/B Side)	Yr	VG	VG+	NM
❑ SE-4832	Sammy Davis Jr. Now	1972	2.50	5.00	10.00

Number	Title (A Side/B Side)	Yr	VG	VG+	NM
❑ SE-4852	Portrait of Sammy Davis, Jr.	1972	2.50	5.00	10.00
❑ M3G-4965	That's Entertainment!	1974	2.50	5.00	10.00

MOTOWN

Number	Title (A Side/B Side)	Yr	VG	VG+	NM
❑ MS 710	Something for Everyone	1970	3.00	6.00	12.00
❑ 4519 ML	Hello Detroit!	1984	2.50	5.00	10.00

PICKWICK

Number	Title (A Side/B Side)	Yr	VG	VG+	NM
❑ SPC-3002	The Many Faces of Sammy Davis, Jr.	196?	2.50	5.00	10.00

REPRISE

Number	Title (A Side/B Side)	Yr	VG	VG+	NM
❑ R-2003 [M]	The Wham of Sam	1961	3.75	7.50	15.00
❑ R9-2003 [S]	The Wham of Sam	1961	5.00	10.00	20.00
❑ R-2010 [M]	Sammy Davis, Jr., Belts the Best of Broadway	1962	3.75	7.50	15.00
❑ R9-2010 [S]	Sammy Davis, Jr., Belts the Best of Broadway	1962	5.00	10.00	20.00
❑ R-6033 [M]	All Star Spectacular	1962	3.75	7.50	15.00
❑ R9-6033 [S]	All Star Spectacular	1962	5.00	10.00	20.00
❑ R-6051 [M]	What Kind of Fool Am I and Other Show-Stoppers	1962	3.75	7.50	15.00
❑ R9-6051 [S]	What Kind of Fool Am I and Other Show-Stoppers	1962	5.00	10.00	20.00
❑ R-6063 [(2)M]	Sammy Davis Jr. at the Cocoanut Grove	1963	5.00	10.00	20.00
❑ R9-6063 [(2)S]	Sammy Davis Jr. at the Cocoanut Grove	1963	6.25	12.50	25.00
❑ R-6082 [M]	As Long As She Needs Me	1963	3.75	7.50	15.00
❑ R9-6082 [S]	As Long As She Needs Me	1963	5.00	10.00	20.00
❑ R-6095 [M]	Sammy Davis Jr. Salutes the Stars of the London Palladium	1964	3.75	7.50	15.00
❑ RS-6095 [S]	Sammy Davis Jr. Salutes the Stars of the London Palladium	1964	5.00	10.00	20.00
❑ R-6096 [M]	Treasury of Golden Hits	1964	3.75	7.50	15.00
❑ RS-6096 [S]	Treasury of Golden Hits	1964	5.00	10.00	20.00
❑ R-6114 [M]	The Shelter of Your Arms	1964	3.75	7.50	15.00
❑ RS-6114 [S]	The Shelter of Your Arms	1964	5.00	10.00	20.00
❑ R-6126 [M]	California Suite	1964	3.75	7.50	15.00
❑ RS-6126 [S]	California Suite	1964	5.00	10.00	20.00
❑ R-6131 [M]	Sammy Davis Jr. Sings the Big Ones for Young Lovers	1964	3.00	6.00	12.00
❑ RS-6131 [S]	Sammy Davis Jr. Sings the Big Ones for Young Lovers	1964	3.75	7.50	15.00
❑ R-6144 [M]	When the Feeling Hits You	1965	3.00	6.00	12.00
❑ RS-6144 [S]	When the Feeling Hits You	1965	3.75	7.50	15.00
❑ R-6159 [M]	If I Ruled the World	1965	3.00	6.00	12.00
❑ RS-6159 [S]	If I Ruled the World	1965	3.75	7.50	15.00
❑ R-6164 [M]	The Nat Cole Song Book	1965	3.00	6.00	12.00
❑ RS-6164 [S]	The Nat Cole Song Book	1965	3.75	7.50	15.00
❑ R-6169 [M]	Sammy's Back on Broadway	1965	3.00	6.00	12.00
❑ RS-6169 [S]	Sammy's Back on Broadway	1965	3.75	7.50	15.00
❑ R-6188 [M]	The Sammy Davis, Jr., Show	1965	3.00	6.00	12.00
❑ RS-6188 [S]	The Sammy Davis, Jr., Show	1965	3.75	7.50	15.00
❑ R-6214 [M]	The Sounds of '66	1966	3.00	6.00	12.00
❑ RS-6214 [S]	The Sounds of '66	1966	3.75	7.50	15.00
❑ R-6236 [M]	Sammy Davis. Jr., Sings/Laurindo Almeida Plays	1966	3.00	6.00	12.00
❑ RS-6236 [S]	Sammy Davis. Jr., Sings/Laurindo Almeida Plays	1966	3.75	7.50	15.00
❑ R-6237 [(2)M]	That's All	1967	3.75	7.50	15.00
❑ RS-6237 [(2)S]	That's All	1967	5.00	10.00	20.00
❑ R-6264 [M]	Sammy Davis Jr. Sings the Complete Dr. Dolittle	1967	5.00	10.00	20.00
❑ RS-6264 [S]	Sammy Davis Jr. Sings the Complete Dr. Dolittle	1967	3.00	6.00	12.00
❑ RS-6291	Sammy Davis, Jr.'s Greatest Hits	1968	3.00	6.00	12.00
❑ RS-6308	Lonely Is the Name	1968	3.00	6.00	12.00
❑ RS-6324	I've Gotta Be Me	1969	3.00	6.00	12.00
❑ RS-6339	The Goin's Great	1969	3.00	6.00	12.00
❑ RS-6410	Sammy Davis, Jr., Steps Out	1970	3.00	6.00	12.00

WARNER BROS.

Number	Title (A Side/B Side)	Yr	VG	VG+	NM
❑ BSK 3128	Live Performance	1977	2.50	5.00	10.00

DAVIS, SAMMY, JR., AND CARMEN MCRAE
DECCA

Number	Title (A Side/B Side)	Yr	VG	VG+	NM
❑ DL 8490 [M]	Boy Meets Girl	1957	7.50	15.00	30.00

DAVIS, SKEETER
GUSTO

Number	Title (A Side/B Side)	Yr	VG	VG+	NM
❑ 0014	Best of the Best	1978	2.50	5.00	10.00

RCA CAMDEN

Number	Title (A Side/B Side)	Yr	VG	VG+	NM
❑ ACL1-0622	He Wakes Me with a Kiss	1974	2.50	5.00	10.00
❑ CAL-818 [M]	I Forgot More Than You'll Ever Know	196?	3.00	6.00	12.00
❑ CAS-818 [S]	I Forgot More Than You'll Ever Know	196?	3.75	7.50	15.00
❑ CAL-899 [M]	Blueberry Hill and Other Favorites	1965	3.00	6.00	12.00
❑ CAS-899 [S]	Blueberry Hill and Other Favorites	1965	3.75	7.50	15.00
❑ CAS-2367	Easy to Love	1970	3.00	6.00	12.00
❑ CAS-2517	Foggy Mountain Top	1971	3.00	6.00	12.00
❑ CAS-2607	The End of the World	1972	2.50	5.00	10.00

RCA VICTOR

Number	Title (A Side/B Side)	Yr	VG	VG+	NM
❑ APL1-0190	The Best of Skeeter Davis, Volume 2	1973	3.00	6.00	12.00
❑ APL1-0322	I Can't Believe That It's All Over	1974	3.00	6.00	12.00
❑ LPM-2197 [M]	I'll Sing You a Song and Harmonize, Too	1960	6.25	12.50	25.00
❑ LSP-2197 [S]	I'll Sing You a Song and Harmonize, Too	1960	7.50	15.00	30.00
❑ LPM-2327 [M]	Here's the Answer	1961	6.25	12.50	25.00
❑ LSP-2327 [S]	Here's the Answer	1961	7.50	15.00	30.00
❑ LPM-2699 [M]	The End of the World	1963	6.25	12.50	25.00
❑ LSP-2699 [S]	The End of the World	1963	7.50	15.00	30.00
❑ LPM-2736 [M]	Cloudy, With Occasional Tears	1963	6.25	12.50	25.00
❑ LSP-2736 [S]	Cloudy, With Occasional Tears	1963	7.50	15.00	30.00
❑ LPM-2980 [M]	Let Me Get Close to You	1964	5.00	10.00	20.00
❑ LSP-2980 [S]	Let Me Get Close to You	1964	6.25	12.50	25.00
❑ LPM-3374 [M]	The Best of Skeeter Davis	1965	5.00	10.00	20.00
❑ LSP-3374 [S]	The Best of Skeeter Davis	1965	6.25	12.50	25.00
❑ LPM-3382 [M]	Written by the Stars	1965	5.00	10.00	20.00
❑ LSP-3382 [S]	Written by the Stars	1965	6.25	12.50	25.00
❑ LPM-3463 [M]	Skeeter Sings Standards	1965	5.00	10.00	20.00
❑ LSP-3463 [S]	Skeeter Sings Standards	1965	6.25	12.50	25.00

Number	Title (A Side/B Side)	Yr	VG	VG+	NM
❑ LPM-3567 [M]	Singin' in the Summer Sun	1966	5.00	10.00	20.00
❑ LSP-3567 [S]	Singin' in the Summer Sun	1966	6.25	12.50	25.00
❑ LPM-3667 [M]	My Heart's in the Country	1966	5.00	10.00	20.00
❑ LSP-3667 [S]	My Heart's in the Country	1966	6.25	12.50	25.00
❑ LPM-3763 [M]	Hand in Hand with Jesus	1967	7.50	15.00	30.00
❑ LSP-3763 [S]	Hand in Hand with Jesus	1967	5.00	10.00	20.00
❑ LPM-3790 [M]	Skeeter Davis Sings Buddy Holly	1967	12.50	25.00	50.00
❑ LSP-3790 [S]	Skeeter Davis Sings Buddy Holly	1967	10.00	20.00	40.00
❑ LPM-3876 [M]	What Does It Take (To Keep a Man Like You Satisfied)	1967	7.50	15.00	30.00
❑ LSP-3876 [S]	What Does It Take (To Keep a Man Like You Satisfied)	1967	5.00	10.00	20.00
❑ LPM-3960 [M]	Why So Lonely?	1968	12.50	25.00	50.00
❑ LSP-3960 [S]	Why So Lonely?	1968	5.00	10.00	20.00
❑ LSP-4055	I Love Flatt & Scruggs	1968	5.00	10.00	20.00
❑ LSP-4124	The Closest Thing to Love	1969	5.00	10.00	20.00
❑ LSP-4200	Maryfrances	1969	5.00	10.00	20.00
❑ LSP-4310	A Place in the Country	1970	3.75	7.50	15.00
❑ LSP-4382	It's Hard to Be a Woman	1970	3.75	7.50	15.00
❑ LSP-4486	Skeeter	1971	3.75	7.50	15.00
❑ LSP-4557	Love Takes a Lot	1971	3.75	7.50	15.00
❑ LSP-4642	Bring It on Home	1972	3.75	7.50	15.00
❑ LSP-4732	Skeeter Sings Dolly	1972	3.75	7.50	15.00
❑ LSP-4818	Hillbilly Singer	1972	3.75	7.50	15.00

DAVIS, SPENCER, GROUP

ALLEGIANCE
❑ AV-442	Crossfire	1983	2.50	5.00	10.00

MEDIARTS
❑ 41-11	It's Been So Long	1971	3.00	6.00	12.00

RHINO
❑ RNLP 117	The Best of the Spencer Davis Group	1983	2.00	4.00	8.00
❑ RNLP 70172	The Best of the Spencer Davis Group (Golden Archive Series)	1987	3.00	6.00	12.00

UNITED ARTISTS
❑ UA-LA433-E	The Very Best of the Spencer Davis Group	1975	2.50	5.00	10.00
❑ UAL 3578 [M]	Gimme Some Lovin'	1967	12.50	25.00	50.00
❑ UAL 3589 [M]	I'm a Man	1967	10.00	20.00	40.00
❑ UAS 6578 [R]	Gimme Some Lovin'	1967	10.00	20.00	40.00
❑ UAS 6589 [P]	I'm a Man	1967	12.50	25.00	50.00
❑ UAS 6641 [P]	The Spencer Davis Group's Greatest Hits	1968	6.25	12.50	25.00
❑ UAS 6652	With Their New Face On	1968	5.00	10.00	20.00
❑ UAS 6691	Heavies	1969	5.00	10.00	20.00
❑ ST-91127 [R]	Gimme Some Lovin'	1967	12.50	25.00	50.00
—Capitol Record Club edition					

VERTIGO
❑ VEL-1015	Gluggo	1973	3.00	6.00	12.00
❑ VEL-1021	Living in a Back Street	1974	3.00	6.00	12.00

DAVIS, TYRONE

COLUMBIA
❑ PC 34268	Love and Touch	1976	3.00	6.00	12.00
❑ PC 34654	Let's Be Closer Together	1977	3.00	6.00	12.00
❑ JC 35305	I Can't Go On This Way	1978	3.00	6.00	12.00
❑ JC 35723	In the Mood with Tyrone Davis	1979	3.00	6.00	12.00
❑ JC 36230	Can't You Tell It's Me	1979	3.00	6.00	12.00
❑ JC 36598	I Just Can't Keep On Going	1980	3.00	6.00	12.00
❑ FC 37366	Everything in Place	1981	3.00	6.00	12.00
❑ PC 37979	The Best of Tyrone Davis	1982	2.50	5.00	10.00

DAKAR
❑ DK-9005	Can I Change My Mind	1969	7.50	15.00	30.00
❑ DK-9027	Turn Back the Hands of Time	1970	7.50	15.00	30.00
❑ DK-76901	I Had It All the Time	1972	7.50	15.00	30.00
❑ DK-76902	Tyrone Davis' Greatest Hits	1972	6.25	12.50	25.00
❑ DK-76904	Without You in My Life	1973	6.25	12.50	25.00
❑ DK-76909	It's All in the Game	1974	5.00	10.00	20.00
❑ DK-76915	Homewrecker	1975	5.00	10.00	20.00
❑ DK-76918	Turning Point	1976	5.00	10.00	20.00

EPIC
❑ PE 38626	Tyrone Davis' Greatest Hits	1983	2.00	4.00	8.00

HIGHRISE
❑ 103	Tyrone Davis	1982	2.50	5.00	10.00

ICHIBAN
❑ ICH 1103	I'll Always Love You	1991	3.00	6.00	12.00

DAVIS, WALTER, JR.

BLUE NOTE
❑ BLP-4018 [M]	Davis Cup	1959	20.00	40.00	80.00
—Regular version with W. 63rd St. address on label					
❑ BLP-4018 [M]	Davis Cup	1959	37.50	75.00	150.00
—"Deep groove" version (deep indentation under label on both sides)					
❑ BLP-4018 [M]	Davis Cup	1964	6.25	12.50	25.00
—With New York, USA address on label					
❑ BST-84018 [S]	Davis Cup	1959	15.00	30.00	60.00
—Regular version with W. 63rd St. address on label					
❑ BST-84018 [S]	Davis Cup	1964	5.00	10.00	20.00
—With New York, USA address on label					

DAVIS, WILD BILL

CORAL
❑ CRL 57417 [M]	One More Time	1962	5.00	10.00	20.00
❑ CRL 57427 [M]	Lover	1962	5.00	10.00	20.00
❑ CRL 757417 [S]	One More Time	1962	6.25	12.50	25.00
❑ CRL 757427 [S]	Lover	1962	6.25	12.50	25.00

EPIC
❑ LN 1004 [10]	Here's Wild Bill Davis	1954	25.00	50.00	100.00
❑ LN 1121 [M]	On the Loose	1955	15.00	30.00	60.00
❑ LN 3118 [M]	Wild Bill Davis at Birdland	1955	15.00	30.00	60.00
❑ LN 3308 [M]	Evening Concerto	1956	15.00	30.00	60.00

EVEREST
❑ SDBR-1014 [S]	My Fair Lady	1959	6.25	12.50	25.00

Number	Title (A Side/B Side)	Yr	VG	VG+	NM
❑ SDBR-1052 [S]	Flying High	1959	7.50	15.00	30.00
❑ SDBR-1094 [S]	Dance the Madison	1960	7.50	15.00	30.00
❑ SDBR-1116 [S]	Organ Grinder's Swing	1960	7.50	15.00	30.00
❑ SDBR-1125 [S]	Dis Heah	1961	7.50	15.00	30.00
❑ SDBR-1133 [S]	The Music from "Milk and Honey"	1961	7.50	15.00	30.00
❑ LPBR-5014 [M]	My Fair Lady	1958	7.50	15.00	30.00
❑ LPBR-5052 [M]	Flying High	1959	6.25	12.50	25.00
❑ LPBR-5094 [M]	Dance the Madison	1960	6.25	12.50	25.00
❑ LPBR-5116 [M]	Organ Grinder's Swing	1960	6.25	12.50	25.00
❑ LPBR-5125 [M]	Dis Heah	1961	6.25	12.50	25.00
❑ LPBR-5133 [M]	The Music from "Milk and Honey"	1961	6.25	12.50	25.00

IMPERIAL
❑ LP-9010 [M]	Wild Bill Davis on Broadway	1956	12.50	25.00	50.00
❑ LP-9015 [M]	Wild Bill Davis in Hollywood	1956	12.50	25.00	50.00
❑ LP-9201 [M]	Wild Wild Wild Wild Wild Wild Wild Wild Wild	1963	10.00	20.00	40.00
❑ LP-12201 [R]	Wild Wild Wild Wild Wild Wild Wild Wild Wild	1963	5.00	10.00	20.00

RCA VICTOR
❑ LSP-3314 [S]	Free, Frantic and Funky	1965	5.00	10.00	20.00
❑ LSP-3578 [S]	Live at Count Basie's	1966	5.00	10.00	20.00
❑ LPM-3799 [M]	Midnight to Dawn	1967	5.00	10.00	20.00

DAVISON, WILD BILL

CIRCLE
❑ LP-405 [10]	Showcase	1951	20.00	40.00	80.00

COLUMBIA
❑ CL 871 [M]	Pretty Wild: Wild Bill Davison with Strings	1956	10.00	20.00	40.00
❑ CL 983 [M]	Wild Bill Davison with Strings Attached	1957	10.00	20.00	40.00

COMMODORE
❑ FL-20000 [10]	Dixieland Jazz Jamboree	1950	25.00	50.00	100.00
❑ FL-30009 [M]	Mild and Wild	1959	15.00	30.00	60.00

DIXIELAND JUBILEE
❑ DJ-508 [M]	Greatest of the Greats	1958	6.25	12.50	25.00
❑ DJS-508 [S]	Greatest of the Greats	1958	5.00	10.00	20.00

JAZZOLOGY
❑ J-2 [M]	Wild Bill Davison's Jazzologists	1962	5.00	10.00	20.00
❑ J-14 [M]	Rompin' and Stompin'	196?	5.00	10.00	20.00

REGENT
❑ MG-6026 [M]	When the Saints Go Marching In	196?	5.00	10.00	20.00

RIVERSIDE
❑ RLP 12-211 [M]	Sweet and Hot	195?	7.50	15.00	30.00
—Blue label, microphone logo at top					
❑ RLP 12-211 [M]	Sweet and Hot	1956	15.00	30.00	60.00
—White label, blue print					

SAVOY
❑ MG-12035 [M]	Jazz at Storyville	1955	15.00	30.00	60.00
❑ MG-12055 [M]	Ringside at Condon's	1955	15.00	30.00	60.00
—Reissue of two 10-inch LPs (15029 and 15030) that are listed in the Various Artists Collection area					

DAWE, TIM

STRAIGHT
❑ STS-1058	Penrod	1969	7.50	15.00	30.00

WARNER BROS.
❑ WS 1841	Penrod	1970	3.75	7.50	15.00

DAWSON, SID

DELMAR
❑ DL-109 [10]	Sid Dawson's Riverboat Gamblers	195?	15.00	30.00	60.00

DAY, BOBBY

CLASS
❑ LP-5002 [M]	Rockin' with Robin	1959	100.00	200.00	400.00

COLLECTABLES
❑ COL-5074	Golden Classics	198?	2.50	5.00	10.00

RENDEZVOUS
❑ M-1312 [M]	Rockin' with Robin	196?	20.00	40.00	80.00

RHINO
❑ RNDF-208	The Best of Bobby Day	1984	3.00	6.00	12.00

DAY, CORA LEE

ROULETTE
❑ R-52048 [M]	My Crying Hour	1960	7.50	15.00	30.00
❑ SR-52048 [S]	My Crying Hour	1960	10.00	20.00	40.00

DAY, DENNIS

DESIGN
❑ DLPX-1 [M]	Dennis Day Sings "Christmas Is for the Family"	195?	5.00	10.00	20.00
—Cover features Jack Benny as Santa; he also appears briefly on the LP					

DAY, DORIS

COLUMBIA
❑ DD 1 [M]	Listen to Day	1960	5.00	10.00	20.00
❑ DDS 1 [S]	Listen to Day	1960	6.25	12.50	25.00
❑ C2L 5 [(2)M]	Hooray for Hollywood	1959	10.00	20.00	40.00
❑ CL 582 [M]	Young Man with a Horn	1954	10.00	20.00	40.00
—Reissue of 6106; red label, gold print					
❑ CL 624 [M]	Day Dreams	1955	10.00	20.00	40.00
—Red label, gold print					
❑ CL 624 [M]	Day Dreams	1956	6.25	12.50	25.00
—Six "eye" logos on label					
❑ CL 710 [M]	Love Me or Leave Me	1955	12.50	25.00	50.00
—Red label, gold print					
❑ CL 710 [M]	Love Me or Leave Me	1956	6.25	12.50	25.00
—Six "eye" logos on label					
❑ CL 710 [M]	Love Me or Leave Me	1962	3.75	7.50	15.00
—"Guaranteed High Fidelity" or "Mono" on label					
❑ CL 749 [M]	Day in Hollywood	1956	7.50	15.00	30.00
❑ C2S 805 [(2)S]	Hooray for Hollywood	1959	12.50	25.00	50.00
❑ CL 942 [M]	Day By Day	1957	7.50	15.00	30.00
❑ CL 1053 [M]	Day By Night	1958	5.00	10.00	20.00
❑ CL 1210 [M]	Doris Day's Greatest Hits	1958	7.50	15.00	30.00
—Six "eye" logos on label					

Number	Title (A Side/B Side)	Yr	VG	VG+	NM
☐ CL 1210 [M]	Doris Day's Greatest Hits	1962	3.00	6.00	12.00
—"Guaranteed High Fidelity" or "Mono" on label					
☐ CL 1232 [M]	Cuttin' Capers	1959	5.00	10.00	20.00
☐ CL 1366 [M]	Hooray for Hollywood, Volume 1	1959	5.00	10.00	20.00
☐ CL 1367 [M]	Hooray for Hollywood, Volume 2	1959	5.00	10.00	20.00
☐ CL 1438 [M]	What Every Girl Should Know	1960	5.00	10.00	20.00
☐ CL 1470 [M]	Show Time	1960	5.00	10.00	20.00
☐ CL 1614 [M]	Bright and Shiny	1960	5.00	10.00	20.00
☐ CL 1660 [M]	I Have Dreamed	1961	5.00	10.00	20.00
☐ CL 1752 [M]	Duet	1962	5.00	10.00	20.00
—With Andre Previn					
☐ CL 1904 [M]	You'll Never Walk Alone	1962	3.75	7.50	15.00
☐ CL 2131 [M]	Love Him!	1964	3.75	7.50	15.00
☐ CL 2226 [M]	The Doris Day Christmas Album	1964	3.00	6.00	12.00
☐ CL 2266 [M]	With a Smile and a Song	1965	3.00	6.00	12.00
☐ CL 2310 [M]	Latin for Lovers	1965	3.00	6.00	12.00
☐ CL 2360 [M]	Sentimental Journey	1965	3.00	6.00	12.00
☐ CL 2518 [10]	Lights, Camera, Action	1955	12.50	25.00	50.00
☐ CL 6071 [10]	You're My Thrill	1949	15.00	30.00	60.00
☐ CL 6106 [10]	Young Man with a Horn	1950	25.00	50.00	100.00
☐ CL 6149 [10]	Tea for Two	1950	15.00	30.00	60.00
☐ CL 6168 [10]	Lullaby of Broadway	1951	15.00	30.00	60.00
☐ CL 6186 [10]	On Moonlight Bay	1951	15.00	30.00	60.00
☐ CL 6198 [10]	I'll See You in My Dreams	1951	15.00	30.00	60.00
☐ CL 6248 [10]	By the Light of the Silvery Moon	1953	15.00	30.00	60.00
☐ CL 6273 [10]	Calamity Jane	1953	15.00	30.00	60.00
☐ CL 6339 [10]	Young at Heart	1954	15.00	30.00	60.00
—Six songs by Doris Day, two by Frank Sinatra					
☐ CS 8066 [S]	Hooray for Hollywood, Volume 1	1959	6.25	12.50	25.00
☐ CS 8067 [S]	Hooray for Hollywood, Volume 2	1959	6.25	12.50	25.00
☐ CS 8078 [S]	Cuttin' Capers	1959	6.25	12.50	25.00
☐ CS 8089 [S]	Day By Night	1959	6.25	12.50	25.00
☐ CS 8234 [S]	What Every Girl Should Know	1960	6.25	12.50	25.00
☐ CS 8261 [S]	Show Time	1960	5.00	10.00	20.00
☐ CS 8414 [S]	Bright and Shiny	1960	6.25	12.50	25.00
☐ CS 8460 [S]	I Have Dreamed	1961	6.25	12.50	25.00
☐ CS 8552 [S]	Duet	1962	6.25	12.50	25.00
—With Andre Previn					
☐ CS 8635 [P]	Doris Day's Greatest Hits	1962	3.75	7.50	15.00
—"360 Sound Stereo" in black at bottom					
☐ PC 8635	Doris Day's Greatest Hits	198?	2.00	4.00	8.00
—Budget-line reissue					
☐ CS 8704 [S]	You'll Never Walk Alone	1962	5.00	10.00	20.00
☐ CS 8773 [R]	Love Me or Leave Me	1963	3.00	6.00	12.00
☐ CS 8931 [S]	Love Him!	1964	5.00	10.00	20.00
☐ CS 9026 [S]	The Doris Day Christmas Album	1964	3.75	7.50	15.00
☐ CS 9066 [S]	With a Smile and a Song	1965	3.75	7.50	15.00
☐ CS 9110 [S]	Latin for Lovers	1965	3.75	7.50	15.00
☐ CS 9160 [S]	Sentimental Journey	1965	3.75	7.50	15.00
COLUMBIA SPECIAL PRODUCTS					
☐ C 10988	The Doris Day Christmas Album	197?	2.50	5.00	10.00
—Reissue of CS 9026					
☐ P2 13231 [(2)]	The Magic of Doris Day	1976	3.75	7.50	15.00
☐ P 13346	The Doris Day Christmas Album	197?	2.50	5.00	10.00
—Reissue of CS 9026					
☐ XTV 82021/2 [M]	Wonderful Day	1961	10.00	20.00	40.00
HARMONY					
☐ HL 7392 [M]	Great Movie Hits	1966	3.00	6.00	12.00
☐ HL 9559 [M]	Do Re Mi (And Other Children's Favorites)	196?	3.00	6.00	12.00
☐ HS 11192 [R]	Great Movie Hits	1966	3.00	6.00	12.00
☐ HS 11282	Whatever Will Be, Will Be (Que Sera, Sera)	1968	3.00	6.00	12.00
☐ HS 11382	It's Magic	1970	3.00	6.00	12.00
☐ HS 14559 [S]	Do Re Mi (And Other Children's Favorites)	196?	3.00	6.00	12.00
☐ KH 31498	Softly, As I Leave You	1972	2.50	5.00	10.00
HEARTLAND					
☐ HL 1102/3 [(2)]	The Best of Doris Day	1990	3.75	7.50	15.00
—Mail-order offer; alternate number is CBS Special Products P2 22031					
HINDSIGHT					
☐ HSR-200	Doris Day with Van Alexander's Orchestra	198?	2.50	5.00	10.00

DAY, JIMMY
PHILIPS

Number	Title (A Side/B Side)	Yr	VG	VG+	NM
☐ PHM 200016 [M]	Golden Steel Guitar Hits	1962	6.25	12.50	25.00
☐ PHM 200075 [M]	Steel and Strings	1963	6.25	12.50	25.00
☐ PHS 600016 [S]	Golden Steel Guitar Hits	1962	7.50	15.00	30.00
☐ PHS 600075 [S]	Steel and Strings	1963	7.50	15.00	30.00

DAY BLINDNESS
STUDIO 10

Number	Title (A Side/B Side)	Yr	VG	VG+	NM
☐ DBX-101	Day Blindness	1969	15.00	30.00	60.00

DE-FENDERS, THE
DEL-FI

Number	Title (A Side/B Side)	Yr	VG	VG+	NM
☐ DFLP-1242 [M]	Drag Beat	1963	12.50	25.00	50.00
☐ DFST-1242 [S]	Drag Beat	1963	15.00	30.00	60.00
WORLD PACIFIC					
☐ ST-1810 [S]	The De-Fenders Play the Big Ones	1963	17.50	35.00	70.00
—Black vinyl					
☐ ST-1810 [S]	The De-Fenders Play the Big Ones	1963	37.50	75.00	150.00
—Green vinyl					
☐ ST-1810 [S]	The De-Fenders Play the Big Ones	1963	37.50	75.00	150.00
—Red vinyl					
☐ WP-1810 [M]	The De-Fenders Play the Big Ones	1963	12.50	25.00	50.00

DE LA SOUL
TOMMY BOY

Number	Title (A Side/B Side)	Yr	VG	VG+	NM
☐ TB 1019	3 Feet High and Rising	1989	5.00	10.00	20.00
—Original edition					
☐ TB 1019 [(2)]	3 Feet High and Rising	2001	3.75	7.50	15.00
—Reissue, expanded to a two-disc set					
☐ TB 1029	De La Soul Is Dead	1991	5.00	10.00	20.00

Number	Title (A Side/B Side)	Yr	VG	VG+	NM
☐ TB 1041 [(2)DJ]	De La Soul Is Dead	1991	6.25	12.50	25.00
—Promo-only two-record set					
☐ TB 1063 [DJ]	Buhloone Mindstate	1993	6.25	12.50	25.00
—Vinyl appears to be promo only					
☐ TB 1093 [DJ]	Clear Lake Auditorium	1994	6.25	12.50	25.00
—Promo-only on clear vinyl (black vinyl editions are counterfeits)					
☐ TB 1149 [(2)]	Stakes Is High	1996	3.75	7.50	15.00
☐ TB 1175 [DJ]	Stakes Is High Sampler	1996	6.25	12.50	25.00
—Promo only; contains eight songs from the full-length edition					
☐ TB 1361 [(2)]	Art Official Intelligence: Mosaic Thump	2000	3.75	7.50	15.00
☐ TB 1362 [(2)]	AOI: Bionix	2001	3.75	7.50	15.00
☐ TB 1437 [(2)]	Art Official Intelligence: Mosaic Thump Instrumentals	2000	3.75	7.50	15.00
☐ TB 1443 [(2)DJ]	AOI: Bionix//Edited	2001	3.75	7.50	15.00
—Promo-only "clean" version					
☐ TB 1546 [(2)]	AOI: Bionix Instrumentals	2002	3.75	7.50	15.00

DEAD BOYS
BOMP!

Number	Title (A Side/B Side)	Yr	VG	VG+	NM
☐ 4017	Night of the Living Dead Boys	1981	3.75	7.50	15.00
SIRE					
☐ SR-6038	Young, Loud & Snotty	1977	6.25	12.50	25.00
☐ SRK-6054	We Have Come for Your Children	1978	6.25	12.50	25.00

DEAD KENNEDYS
ALTERNATIVE TENTACLES

Number	Title (A Side/B Side)	Yr	VG	VG+	NM
☐ VIRUS 1	Fresh Fruit for Rotting Vegetables	1988	3.00	6.00	12.00
—Reissue of I.R.S. album					
☐ VIRUS 5 [EP]	In God We Trust, Inc.	1981	3.00	6.00	12.00
☐ VIRUS 27	Plastic Surgery Disasters	1982	3.00	6.00	12.00
☐ VIRUS 45	Frankenchrist	1985	2.50	5.00	10.00
—Originals have a poster of H.R. Giger's painting Landscape #20, which was involved in an obscenity trial. The poster is still available, but only by mailing in a coupon inside the LP.					
☐ VIRUS 50	Bedtime for Democracy	1986	3.00	6.00	12.00
—Originals have a newspaper insert					
☐ VIRUS 57	Give Me Convenience or Give Me Death	1987	2.50	5.00	10.00
FAULTY					
☐ 70014	Fresh Fruit for Rotting Vegetables	1982	10.00	20.00	40.00
—With nursing home photo on back cover, no reference to I.R.S. on label or cover					
I.R.S./FAULTY PRODUCTS					
☐ SP-70014	Fresh Fruit for Rotting Vegetables	1980	3.75	7.50	15.00
—Reissues have a black front cover, same as imports; it was changed at the insistence of band member Jello Biafra					
☐ SP-70014	Fresh Fruit for Rotting Vegetables	1980	5.00	10.00	20.00
—Originals have an orange cover "to distinguish it from imports"					

DEADLY ONES, THE
VEE JAY

Number	Title (A Side/B Side)	Yr	VG	VG+	NM
☐ LP-1090 [M]	It's Monster Surfing Time	1964	25.00	50.00	100.00
☐ LPS-1090 [S]	It's Monster Surfing Time	1964	30.00	60.00	120.00

DEAL, BILL, AND THE RHONDELS
HERITAGE

Number	Title (A Side/B Side)	Yr	VG	VG+	NM
☐ HTS 35003	Vintage Rock	1969	7.50	15.00	30.00
☐ HTS 35006	The Best of Bill Deal and the Rhondels	1970	7.50	15.00	30.00
RHINO					
☐ RNLP-70129	The Best of Bill Deal and the Rhondels (1969-1970)	1986	2.50	5.00	10.00

DEAN, EDDIE
SAGE AND SAND

Number	Title (A Side/B Side)	Yr	VG	VG+	NM
☐ C-1 [M]	Greatest Westerns	1956	12.50	25.00	50.00
☐ C-5 [M]	Hi-Country	1957	12.50	25.00	50.00
☐ C-16 [M]	Hillbilly Heaven	1961	7.50	15.00	30.00
SOUND					
☐ LP-603 [M]	Greatest Westerns	1957	7.50	15.00	30.00

DEAN, JIMMY
COLUMBIA

Number	Title (A Side/B Side)	Yr	VG	VG+	NM
☐ CL 1025 [M]	Jimmy Dean's Hour of Prayer	1957	10.00	20.00	40.00
☐ CL 1735 [M]	Big Bad John and Other Fabulous Songs and Tales	1961	5.00	10.00	20.00
—It's possible that two different editions exist, one with the "hell of a man" lyrics of "Big Bad John" and the other with the "big, big man" lyrics, but this has not been confirmed.					
☐ CL 1894 [M]	Portrait of Jimmy Dean	1962	5.00	10.00	20.00
☐ CL 2027 [M]	Everybody's Favorite	1963	3.75	7.50	15.00
☐ CL 2188 [M]	Songs We All Love Best	1964	3.75	7.50	15.00
☐ CL 2401 [M]	The First Thing Every Morning	1965	3.75	7.50	15.00
☐ CL 2404 [M]	Jimmy Dean's Christmas Card	1965	3.75	7.50	15.00
☐ CL 2485 [M]	Jimmy Dean's Greatest Hits	1966	3.75	7.50	15.00
☐ CL 2538 [M]	The Big Ones	1966	3.75	7.50	15.00
☐ CS 8535 [S]	Big Bad John and Other Fabulous Songs and Tales	1961	6.25	12.50	25.00
—It's possible that two different editions exist, one with the "hell of a man" lyrics of "Big Bad John" and the other with the "big, big man" lyrics, but this has not been confirmed.					
☐ CS 8694 [S]	Portrait of Jimmy Dean	1962	6.25	12.50	25.00
☐ CS 8827 [S]	Everybody's Favorite	1963	5.00	10.00	20.00
☐ CS 8988 [S]	Songs We All Love Best	1964	5.00	10.00	20.00
☐ CS 9201 [S]	The First Thing Every Morning	1965	5.00	10.00	20.00
☐ CS 9204 [S]	Jimmy Dean's Christmas Card	1965	3.00	6.00	12.00
☐ CS 9285 [S]	Jimmy Dean's Greatest Hits	1966	3.75	7.50	15.00
☐ PC 9285	Jimmy Dean's Greatest Hits	198?	2.00	4.00	8.00
—Budget-line reissue					
☐ CS 9338 [S]	The Big Ones	1966	3.75	7.50	15.00
☐ CS 9424 [R]	Jimmy Dean's Hour of Prayer	1966	3.00	6.00	12.00
☐ CS 9677 [M]	Dean's List	1968	7.50	15.00	30.00
—White label promo; "Special Mono Radio Station Copy" sticker on cover					
☐ CS 9677 [S]	Dean's List	1968	3.75	7.50	15.00
CROWN					
☐ 291	Jimmy Dean and the Western Gentlemen	196?	3.00	6.00	12.00
GRT					
☐ 8014	I.O.U.	1977	2.50	5.00	10.00

Number	Title (A Side/B Side)	Yr	VG	VG+	NM
HARMONY					
❏ HL 7268 [M]	Hymns	1960	3.75	7.50	15.00
❏ HL 7408 [M]	Mr. Country Music	1967	3.00	6.00	12.00
❏ HS 11042 [R]	Hymns	1960	3.00	6.00	12.00
❏ HS 11208 [S]	Mr. Country Music	1967	3.00	6.00	12.00
❏ HS 11270	The Country's Favorite Son	1968	3.00	6.00	12.00
HILLTOP					
❏ 6004	Golden Favorites	196?	3.00	6.00	12.00
KING					
❏ 686 [M]	Favorites of Jimmy Dean	1961	15.00	30.00	60.00
MERCURY					
❏ MG-20319 [M]	Jimmy Dean Sings His Television Favorites	1957	10.00	20.00	40.00
RCA VICTOR					
❏ LPM-3727 [M]	Jimmy Dean Is Here	1967	3.75	7.50	15.00
❏ LSP-3727 [S]	Jimmy Dean Is Here	1967	3.75	7.50	15.00
❏ LPM-3824 [M]	Most Richly Blesed	1967	5.00	10.00	20.00
❏ LSP-3824 [S]	Most Richly Blesed	1967	3.75	7.50	15.00
❏ LPM-3890 [M]	The Jimmy Dean Show	1967	5.00	10.00	20.00
❏ LSP-3890 [S]	The Jimmy Dean Show	1967	3.75	7.50	15.00
❏ LPM-3999 [M]	A Thing Called Love	1968	7.50	15.00	30.00
❏ LSP-3999 [S]	A Thing Called Love	1968	3.75	7.50	15.00
❏ LSP-4035	Speaker of the House	1968	3.75	7.50	15.00
❏ LSP-4323	Dean of Country	1970	3.75	7.50	15.00
❏ LSP-4434	Country Boy and Country Girl	1970	3.75	7.50	15.00
❏ LSP-4511	Everybody Knows	1971	3.75	7.50	15.00
❏ LSP-4618	These Hands	1972	3.75	7.50	15.00
SEARS					
❏ 105	Jimmy Dean's Golden Favorites	196?	3.75	7.50	15.00
SPIN-O-RAMA					
❏ 108	Featuring the Coutnry Singing of Jimmy Dean	196?	3.00	6.00	12.00
❏ 137	Coutnry Round-Up Featuring Jimmy Dean	196?	3.00	6.00	12.00
WING					
❏ MGW-12292 [M]	Jimmy Dean Sings His Television Favorites	196?	3.75	7.50	15.00
❏ SRW-16292 [R]	Jimmy Dean Sings His Television Favorites	196?	3.00	6.00	12.00
WYNCOTE					
❏ 9032	Country Favorites	196?	3.00	6.00	12.00
DEAN, JIMMY / JOHNNY HORTON					
LA BREA					
❏ L 8014 [M]	Bummin' Around with Jimmy Dean and Johnny Horton	1961	20.00	40.00	80.00
STARDAY					
❏ SLP-325 [M]	Bummin' Around with Jimmy Dean and Johnny Horton	1965	7.50	15.00	30.00
DEARANGO, BILL					
EMARCY					
❏ MG-26020 [10]	Bill DeArango	1954	12.50	25.00	50.00
DEARIE, BLOSSOM					
CAPITOL					
❏ ST 2086 [S]	May I Come In	1964	5.00	10.00	20.00
DAFFODIL					
❏ BMD-103 [(2)]	My New Celebrity Is You	197?	5.00	10.00	20.00
❏ BMD-104 [(2)]	Winchester in Apple Blossom Time	197?	5.00	10.00	20.00
FONTANA					
❏ SRF-67562 [S]	Blossom Time	1966	5.00	10.00	20.00
VERVE					
❏ MGV-2037 [M]	Blossom Dearie	1957	15.00	30.00	60.00
❏ V-2037 [M]	Blossom Dearie	1961	5.00	10.00	20.00
❏ MGV-2081 [M]	Give Him the Ooh-La-La	1958	15.00	30.00	60.00
❏ V-2081 [M]	Give Him the Ooh-La-La	1961	5.00	10.00	20.00
❏ MGV-2109 [M]	Blossom Dearie Sings Comden & Green	1959	15.00	30.00	60.00
❏ V-2109 [M]	Blossom Dearie Sings Comden & Green	1961	5.00	10.00	20.00
❏ V6-2109 [S]	Blossom Dearie Sings Comden & Green	1961	6.25	12.50	25.00
❏ MGV-2111 [M]	Once Upon a Summertime	1958	15.00	30.00	60.00
❏ V-2111 [M]	Once Upon a Summertime	1961	5.00	10.00	20.00
❏ V6-2111 [S]	Once Upon a Summertime	1961	6.25	12.50	25.00
❏ MGV-2125 [M]	My Gentleman Friend	1959	15.00	30.00	60.00
❏ V-2125 [M]	My Gentleman Friend	1961	5.00	10.00	20.00
❏ V6-2125 [S]	My Gentleman Friend	1961	6.25	12.50	25.00
❏ MGV-2133 [M]	Broadway Song Hits	1960	12.50	25.00	50.00
❏ V-2133 [M]	Broadway Song Hits	1961	5.00	10.00	20.00
❏ V6-2133 [S]	Broadway Song Hits	1961	6.25	12.50	25.00
❏ MGVS-6020 [S]	Once Upon a Summertime	1960	12.50	25.00	50.00
❏ MGVS-6050 [S]	Blossom Dearie Sings Comden & Green	1960	12.50	25.00	50.00
❏ MGVS-6112 [S]	My Gentleman Friend	1960	12.50	25.00	50.00
❏ MGVS-6139 [S]	Broadway Song Hits	1960	15.00	30.00	60.00
DEAUVILLE, RONNIE					
ERA					
❏ 20002 [M]	Smoke Dreams	1957	10.00	20.00	40.00
IMPERIAL					
❏ LP-9060 [M]	Romance	1959	6.25	12.50	25.00
❏ LP-12009 [S]	Romance	1959	7.50	15.00	30.00
DEBRIS					
STATIC DISPOSAL					
❏ 0000	Debris	1976	20.00	40.00	80.00
DECARLO, YVONNE					
MASTERSEAL					
❏ 33-1869/70 [M]	Yvonne DeCarlo Sings	1957	20.00	40.00	80.00
DECASTRO SISTERS, THE					
ABBOTT					
❏ 5002 [M]	The DeCastro Sisters	1956	15.00	30.00	60.00
CAPITOL					
❏ ST 1402 [S]	The DeCastros Sing	1960	7.50	15.00	30.00
❏ T 1402 [M]	The DeCastros Sing	1960	6.25	12.50	25.00

Number	Title (A Side/B Side)	Yr	VG	VG+	NM
❏ ST 1501 [S]	The Rockin' Beat	1961	7.50	15.00	30.00
❏ T 1501 [M]	The Rockin' Beat	1961	6.25	12.50	25.00
DECEMBER'S CHILDREN					
MAINSTREAM					
❏ S-6128	December's Children	1970	12.50	25.00	50.00
DEDRICK, RUSTY					
COUNTERPOINT					
❏ 552 [M]	Salute to Bunny	1957	12.50	25.00	50.00
ESOTERIC					
❏ ESJ-9 [10]	Rhythm and Winds	1955	25.00	50.00	100.00
4 CORNERS OF THE WORLD					
❏ FCS-4207 [S]	The Big Band Sound	1964	5.00	10.00	20.00
KEYNOTE					
❏ 1103 [M]	Rusty Dedrick	1955	15.00	30.00	60.00
MONUMENT					
❏ SLP-16502 [S]	A Jazz Journey	1965	5.00	10.00	20.00
DEE, JOEY, AND THE STARLITERS					
FORUM					
❏ FC 9099 [M]	Joey Dee and the Starliters	1963	3.00	6.00	12.00
❏ FCS 9099 [S]	Joey Dee and the Starliters	1963	3.00	6.00	12.00
JUBILEE					
❏ JLP-8000 [M]	Hitsville	1966	5.00	10.00	20.00
❏ JLS-8000 [S]	Hitsville	1966	6.25	12.50	25.00
ROULETTE					
❏ R-25166 [M]	Doin' the Twist at the Peppermint Lounge	1961	10.00	20.00	40.00
❏ SR-25166 [S]	Doin' the Twist at the Peppermint Lounge	1961	12.50	25.00	50.00
❏ R-25171 [M]	All the World Is Twistin'	1962	7.50	15.00	30.00
❏ SR-25171 [S]	All the World Is Twistin'	1962	10.00	20.00	40.00
❏ R-25173 [M]	Back at the Peppermint Lounge — Twistin'	1962	7.50	15.00	30.00
❏ SR-25173 [S]	Back at the Peppermint Lounge — Twistin'	1962	10.00	20.00	40.00
❏ R-25197 [M]	Joey Dee	1963	6.25	12.50	25.00
❏ SR-25197 [S]	Joey Dee	1963	7.50	15.00	30.00
❏ R-25221 [M]	Dance, Dance, Dance	1963	6.25	12.50	25.00
❏ SR-25221 [S]	Dance, Dance, Dance	1963	7.50	15.00	30.00
SCEPTER					
❏ S 503 [M]	The Peppermint Twisters	1962	6.25	12.50	25.00
❏ SS 503 [S]	The Peppermint Twisters	1962	7.50	15.00	30.00
DEEP, THE					
PARKWAY					
❏ P 7051 [M]	Psychedelic Moods	1966	62.50	125.00	250.00
❏ SP 7051 [S]	Psychedelic Moods	1966	125.00	250.00	500.00
DEEP PURPLE					
DCC COMPACT CLASSICS					
❏ LPZ-2052 [(2)]	Made in Japan	1998	10.00	20.00	40.00
—Audiophile vinyl					
MERCURY					
❏ 824003-1	Perfect Strangers	1984	2.50	5.00	10.00
❏ 831318-1	The House of Blue Light	1987	2.00	4.00	8.00
❏ 835897-1	Nobody's Perfect	1988	2.50	5.00	10.00
RCA					
❏ 2421-1-R	Slaves and Masters	1990	3.75	7.50	15.00
SCEPTER					
❏ CTN-18010	The Best of Deep Purple	1972	2.50	5.00	10.00
TETRAGRAMMATON					
❏ T-102	Shades of Deep Purple	1968	7.50	15.00	30.00
❏ T-107	The Book of Taliesyn	1968	7.50	15.00	30.00
❏ T-119	Deep Purple	1969	7.50	15.00	30.00
❏ T-131	Concerto for Group and Orchestra	1970	75.00	150.00	300.00
WARNER BROS.					
❏ WS 1860	Concerto for Group and Orchestra	1970	3.00	6.00	12.00
❏ WS 1877	Deep Purple in Rock	1970	3.00	6.00	12.00
❏ BS 2564	Fireball	1971	3.00	6.00	12.00
❏ BS 2607	Machine Head	1972	3.00	6.00	12.00
—Original copies have green "WB" labels					
❏ BS 2607	Machine Head	1973	2.50	5.00	10.00
—"Burbank" labels					
❏ BS4 2607 [Q]	Machine Head	1974	6.25	12.50	25.00
❏ 2LS 2644 [(2)]	(Purple Passages)	1972	3.75	7.50	15.00
❏ BS 2678	Who Do We Think We Are!	1973	2.50	5.00	10.00
—"Burbank" labels					
❏ BS 2678	Who Do We Think We Are!	1973	3.00	6.00	12.00
—Original copies have green "WB" labels					
❏ 2WS 2701 [(2)]	Made in Japan	1973	3.75	7.50	15.00
❏ 2WS 2701 [(2)]	Made in Japan	1979	2.00	6.00	12.00
—White labels					
❏ W 2766	Burn	1974	2.50	5.00	10.00
❏ BSK 3100	Machine Head	1976	2.00	4.00	8.00
WARNER BROS./PURPLE					
❏ PR4 2832 [Q]	Stormbringer	1974	6.25	12.50	25.00
❏ PRK 2832	Stormbringer	1974	2.50	5.00	10.00
❏ PRK 2895	Come Taste the Band	1975	2.50	5.00	10.00
❏ PRK 2995	Made in Europe	1976	2.50	5.00	10.00
❏ PRK 3223	When We Rock, We Rock, and When We Roll, We Roll	1978	2.50	5.00	10.00
❏ PRK 3486	Deepest Purple: The Best of Deep Purple	1980	2.50	5.00	10.00
DEEP RIVER BOYS, THE					
QUE					
❏ FLS-104 [M]	Midnight Magic	1957	37.50	75.00	150.00
RCA CAMDEN					
❏ CAL-303 [M]	Presenting the Deep River Boys	1957	15.00	30.00	60.00
—Reissue of "X" album					
WALDORF MUSIC HALL					
❏ MH 33-108 [10]	The Deep River Boys Sing Songs of Jubilee	195?	37.50	75.00	150.00
—Cartoon on cover					

Number	Title (A Side/B Side)	Yr	VG	VG+	NM
❑ MH 33-108 [10]	The Deep River Boys Sing Songs of Jubilee	1954	75.00	150.00	300.00
—Photo of group on cover					
"X"					
❑ LXA-1019 [M]	Presenting the Deep River Boys	1956	30.00	60.00	120.00

DEEP SIX, THE
LIBERTY
Number	Title	Yr	VG	VG+	NM
❑ LRP-3475 [M]	The Deep Six	1966	3.75	7.50	15.00
❑ LST-7475 [S]	The Deep Six	1966	5.00	10.00	20.00

DEERFIELD
FLAT ROCK
❑ FRS-1	Nil Desperandum	1971	30.00	60.00	120.00

DEFRANCO, BUDDY
DECCA
❑ DL 4031 [M]	Pacific Standard Swingin' Time	1961	5.00	10.00	20.00
❑ DL 74031 [S]	Pacific Standard Swingin' Time	1961	6.25	12.50	25.00

DOT
❑ DLP-9006 [M]	Cross-Country Suite	1958	10.00	20.00	40.00

GENE NORMAN
❑ GNP-2 [10]	Buddy DeFranco Takes You to the Stars	1954	30.00	60.00	120.00

HAMILTON
❑ HL-133 [M]	Cross-Country Suite	1964	5.00	10.00	20.00

MGM
❑ E-177 [10]	King of the Clarinet	1952	30.00	60.00	120.00
❑ E-253 [10]	Buddy DeFranco with Strings	1954	25.00	50.00	100.00
❑ E-3396 [M]	Buddy DeFranco	1956	20.00	40.00	80.00

MOSAIC
❑ M5-117 [(5)]	The Complete Recordings of the Buddy DeFranco Quartet/Quintet with Sonny Clark	199?	25.00	50.00	100.00

NORGRAN
❑ MGN-3 [10]	The Buddy DeFranco Quartet	1954	37.50	75.00	150.00
❑ MGN-16 [10]	Pretty Moods by Buddy DeFranco	1954	37.50	75.00	150.00
❑ MGN-1006 [M]	The Progressive Mr. DeFranco	1954	30.00	60.00	120.00
❑ MGN-1012 [M]	Buddy DeFranco and His Clarinet	1954	25.00	50.00	100.00
❑ MGN-1016 [M]	Buddy DeFranco and Oscar Peterson Play George Gershwin	1955	25.00	50.00	100.00
❑ MGN-1026 [M]	Buddy DeFranco Quartet	1955	25.00	50.00	100.00
❑ MGN-1068 [M]	Jazz Tones	1956	20.00	40.00	80.00
❑ MGN-1069 [M]	Mr. Clarinet	1956	20.00	40.00	80.00
❑ MGN-1079 [M]	In a Mellow Mood	1956	20.00	40.00	80.00
❑ MGN-1085 [M]	The Buddy DeFranco Wailers	1956	20.00	40.00	80.00
❑ MGN-1094 [M]	Odalisque	1956	20.00	40.00	80.00
❑ MGN-1096 [M]	Autumn Leaves	1956	20.00	40.00	80.00

VERVE
❑ MGV-2022 [M]	The George Gershwin Songbook	1956	12.50	25.00	50.00
—Reissue of Norgran 1016					
❑ MGV-2033 [M]	Broadway Showcase	1957	12.50	25.00	50.00
❑ V-2033 [M]	Broadway Showcase	1961	5.00	10.00	20.00
❑ MGV-2089 [M]	Buddy DeFranco Plays Benny Goodman	1958	12.50	25.00	50.00
❑ V-2089 [M]	Buddy DeFranco Plays Benny Goodman	1961	5.00	10.00	20.00
❑ MGV-2090 [M]	Buddy DeFranco Plays Artie Shaw	1958	12.50	25.00	50.00
❑ V-2090 [M]	Buddy DeFranco Plays Artie Shaw	1961	5.00	10.00	20.00
❑ MGV-2108 [M]	I Hear Benny Goodman and Artie Shaw	1958	12.50	25.00	50.00
❑ V-2108 [M]	I Hear Benny Goodman and Artie Shaw	1961	5.00	10.00	20.00
❑ V6-2108 [S]	I Hear Benny Goodman and Artie Shaw	1961	5.00	10.00	20.00
❑ MGVS-6032 [S]	I Hear Benny Goodman and Artie Shaw	1960	10.00	20.00	40.00
❑ MGVS-6051 [S]	Bravura	1960	10.00	20.00	40.00
❑ MGVS-6132 [S]	Generalissimo	1960	10.00	20.00	40.00
❑ MGVS-6150 [S]	Wholly Cats	1960	10.00	20.00	40.00
❑ MGVS-6165 [S]	Closed Session	1960	10.00	20.00	40.00
❑ MGVS-6166 [S]	Live Date!	1960	10.00	20.00	40.00
❑ MGV-8158 [M]	Jazz Tones	1957	12.50	25.00	50.00
—Reissue of Norgran 1068					
❑ V-8158 [M]	Jazz Tones	1961	5.00	10.00	20.00
❑ MGV-8159 [M]	Mr. Clarinet	1957	12.50	25.00	50.00
—Reissue of Norgran 1069					
❑ V-8159 [M]	Mr. Clarinet	1961	5.00	10.00	20.00
❑ MGV-8169 [M]	In a Mellow Mood	1957	12.50	25.00	50.00
—Reissue of Norgran 1079					
❑ V-8169 [M]	In a Mellow Mood	1961	5.00	10.00	20.00
❑ MGV-8175 [M]	The Buddy DeFranco Wailers	1957	12.50	25.00	50.00
—Reissue of Norgran 1085					
❑ V-8175 [M]	The Buddy DeFranco Wailers	1961	5.00	10.00	20.00
❑ MGV-8182 [M]	Odalisque	1957	12.50	25.00	50.00
—Reissue of Norgran 1094					
❑ V-8182 [M]	Odalisque	1961	5.00	10.00	20.00
❑ MGV-8183 [M]	Autumn Leaves	1957	12.50	25.00	50.00
—Reissue of Norgran 1096					
❑ V-8183 [M]	Autumn Leaves	1961	5.00	10.00	20.00
❑ MGV-8210 [M]	Buddy DeFranco and the Oscar Peterson Quartet	1958	12.50	25.00	50.00
❑ V-8210 [M]	Buddy DeFranco and the Oscar Peterson Quartet	1961	5.00	10.00	20.00
❑ MGV-8221 [M]	Cooking the Blues	1958	20.00	40.00	80.00
❑ V-8221 [M]	Cooking the Blues	1961	5.00	10.00	20.00
❑ MGV-8224 [M]	Sweet and Lovely	1958	12.50	25.00	50.00
❑ V-8224 [M]	Sweet and Lovely	1961	5.00	10.00	20.00
❑ MGV-8315 [M]	Bravura	1959	12.50	25.00	50.00
❑ V-8315 [M]	Bravura	1961	5.00	10.00	20.00
❑ V6-8315 [S]	Bravura	1961	5.00	10.00	20.00
❑ MGV-8363 [M]	Generalissimo	1960	12.50	25.00	50.00
❑ V-8363 [M]	Generalissimo	1961	5.00	10.00	20.00
❑ V6-8363 [S]	Generalissimo	1961	5.00	10.00	20.00
❑ MGV-8375 [M]	Wholly Cats	1960	10.00	20.00	40.00
❑ V-8375 [M]	Wholly Cats	1961	5.00	10.00	20.00
❑ V6-8375 [S]	Wholly Cats	1961	5.00	10.00	20.00
❑ MGV-8382 [M]	Closed Session	1960	10.00	20.00	40.00
❑ V-8382 [M]	Closed Session	1961	5.00	10.00	20.00
❑ V6-8382 [S]	Closed Session	1961	5.00	10.00	20.00
❑ MGV-8383 [M]	Live Date!	1960	10.00	20.00	40.00
❑ V-8383 [M]	Live Date!	1961	5.00	10.00	20.00
❑ V6-8383 [S]	Live Date!	1961	5.00	10.00	20.00

DEFRANCO, BUDDY, AND TOMMY GUMINA
MERCURY
❑ MG-20685 [M]	Presenting the Buddy DeFranco-Tommy Gumina Quintet	1962	5.00	10.00	20.00
❑ MG-20743 [M]	Kaleidoscope	1962	5.00	10.00	20.00
❑ MG-20833 [M]	Polytones	1963	5.00	10.00	20.00
❑ MG-20900 [M]	The Girl from Ipanema	1964	5.00	10.00	20.00
❑ SR-60685 [S]	Presenting the Buddy DeFranco-Tommy Gumina Quintet	1962	6.25	12.50	25.00
❑ SR-60743 [S]	Kaleidoscope	1962	6.25	12.50	25.00
❑ SR-60833 [S]	Polytones	1963	6.25	12.50	25.00
❑ SR-60900 [S]	The Girl from Ipanema	1964	6.25	12.50	25.00

DEHAVEN, DOC
CUCA
❑ K-3000 [M]	Dixieland Treasure	1962	5.00	10.00	20.00
❑ K-3100 [M]	Doc DeHaven On Location	1963	5.00	10.00	20.00
❑ K-3200 [M]	Doc Swings a Little	1964	5.00	10.00	20.00
❑ K-3300 [M]	Just Off State Street	1966	5.00	10.00	20.00
❑ KS-3300 [S]	Just Off State Street	1966	6.25	12.50	25.00
❑ K-3400 [M]	Erle of Madison	1967	5.00	10.00	20.00

DEJOHN SISTERS, THE
EPIC
❑ LN 1116 [M]	The DeJohn Sisters	195?	7.50	15.00	30.00

UNITED ARTISTS
❑ UAL-3103 [M]	Yes Indeed	1960	5.00	10.00	20.00
❑ UAS-6103 [S]	Yes Indeed	1960	6.25	12.50	25.00

DEJOHNETTE, JACK
COLUMBIA
❑ C 31176	Compost (Take Off Your Body)	1971	5.00	10.00	20.00

MILESTONE
❑ MSP-9022	The DeJohnette Complex	1969	5.00	10.00	20.00

DEKKER, DESMOND, AND THE ACES
BULLDOG
❑ 1037	The Israelites	198?	2.50	5.00	10.00

UNI
❑ 73059	Israelites	1969	7.50	15.00	30.00

DEL SATINS
B.T. PUPPY
❑ BTS-1019	Out to Lunch	1972	75.00	150.00	300.00

DEL VIKINGS, THE
COLLECTABLES
❑ COL-5010	The Best of the Dell-Vikings	198?	3.00	6.00	12.00

DOT
❑ DLP-3685 [M]	Come Go with Me	1966	50.00	100.00	200.00
❑ DLP-25685 [R]	Come Go with Me	1966	37.50	75.00	150.00

LUNIVERSE
❑ LP-1000 [M]	Come Go with the Del Vikings	1957	125.00	250.00	500.00
—Eight tracks, cover is composed of slicks. Counterfeits have more tracks and a preprinted cover (not slicks)					

MERCURY
❑ MG-20314 [M]	They Sing — They Swing	1957	75.00	150.00	300.00
❑ MG-20353 [M]	A Swinging, Singing Record Session	1958	50.00	100.00	200.00

DEL VIKINGS, THE / THE SONNETS
CROWN
❑ CLP-5368 [M]	The Del Vikings and the Sonnets	1963	10.00	20.00	40.00

DELANEY, JACK
SOUTHLAND
❑ LP-201 [10]	Jack Delaney and George Girard in New Orleans	1954	12.50	25.00	50.00
❑ LP-214 [10]	Jack Delaney with Lee Collins	1954	12.50	25.00	50.00
❑ LP-214 [M]	Jack Delaney and the New Orleans Jazz Babies	195?	10.00	20.00	40.00

DELANEY AND BONNIE
ATCO
❑ SD 33-326	Delaney & Bonnie & Friends On Tour with Eric Clapton	197?	2.50	5.00	10.00
—Later pressings on other labels					
❑ SD 33-326	Delaney & Bonnie & Friends On Tour with Eric Clapton	1970	6.25	12.50	25.00
—Yellow label original					
❑ 33-341 [M]	To Bonnie from Delaney	1970	10.00	20.00	40.00
—White label promo; no stock copies were issued in mono					
❑ SD 33-341 [S]	To Bonnie from Delaney	1970	6.25	12.50	25.00
❑ SD 33-358	Motel Shot	1971	6.25	12.50	25.00
❑ SD 33-383	Country Life	1972	5.00	10.00	20.00
❑ SD 7014	The Best of Delaney and Bonnie	1972	5.00	10.00	20.00

COLUMBIA
❑ KC 31377	D&B Together	1972	5.00	10.00	20.00

ELEKTRA
❑ EKS-74039	Accept No Substitute — The Original Delaney & Bonnie & Friends	1969	7.50	15.00	30.00

GNP CRESCENDO
❑ GNPS-2054	Genesis	1970	5.00	10.00	20.00

STAX
❑ STS-2026	Home	1969	7.50	15.00	30.00

DELEGATES, THE (1)
MAINSTREAM
❑ 100	The Delegates	1973	5.00	10.00	20.00

Number	Title (A Side/B Side)	Yr	VG	VG+	NM

DELEGATES, THE (2)
See BILLY LARKIN.

DELFONICS, THE
ARISTA
| ❑ AL 8333 | The Best of the Delfonics | 198? | 2.50 | 5.00 | 10.00 |

COLLECTABLES
| ❑ COL-5109 | Golden Classics | 198? | 2.50 | 5.00 | 10.00 |

KORY
| ❑ 1002 | The Best of the Delfonics | 1977 | 3.00 | 6.00 | 12.00 |

PHILLY GROOVE
❑ 1150	La La Means I Love You	1968	20.00	40.00	80.00
❑ 1151	The Sexy Sound of Soul	1969	20.00	40.00	80.00
❑ 1152	The Delfonics Super Hits	1969	12.50	25.00	50.00
❑ 1153	The Delfonics	1970	12.50	25.00	50.00
❑ 1154	Tell Me This Is a Dream	1972	12.50	25.00	50.00
❑ 1501	Alive & Kicking	1974	12.50	25.00	50.00

POOGIE
| ❑ 121680 | The Delfonics Return | 1981 | 3.00 | 6.00 | 12.00 |

DELLER, ALFRED
VANGUARD
| ❑ VRS-479 [M] | The Three Ravens | 195? | 10.00 | 20.00 | 40.00 |
| ❑ VRS-499 [M] | The Holly and the Ivy — Christmas Songs of Old England | 1956 | 10.00 | 20.00 | 40.00 |

DELLS, THE
ABC
| ❑ AA-1100 | New Beginnings | 1978 | 3.00 | 6.00 | 12.00 |
| ❑ AA-1113 | Face to Face | 1978 | 3.00 | 6.00 | 12.00 |

BUDDAH
| ❑ BDS-5053 | The Dells | 1969 | 3.75 | 7.50 | 15.00 |

CADET
❑ LPS-804	There Is	1968	12.50	25.00	50.00
❑ LPS-822	The Dells Musical Menu/Always Together	1969	12.50	25.00	50.00
❑ LPS-824	The Dells Greatest Hits	1969	12.50	25.00	50.00
❑ LPS-829	Love Is Blue	1969	12.50	25.00	50.00
❑ LPS-837	Like It Is, Like It Was	1970	12.50	25.00	50.00
❑ 50004	Freedom Means	1971	6.25	12.50	25.00
❑ 50017	The Dells Sing Dionne Warwicke's Greatest Hits	1972	6.25	12.50	25.00
❑ 50021	Sweet As Funk Can Be	1972	6.25	12.50	25.00
❑ 50037	Give Your Baby a Standing Ovation	1973	6.25	12.50	25.00
❑ 50046	The Dells	1973	6.25	12.50	25.00
❑ 60030	The Mighty Mighty Dells	1974	6.25	12.50	25.00
❑ 60036	The Dells' Greatest Hits, Vol. 2	1975	5.00	10.00	20.00

CHESS
❑ CH-9103	The Dells	198?	2.50	5.00	10.00
—Reissue					
❑ CH-9288	There Is	1989	2.50	5.00	10.00
—Reissue of Cadet 804					

LOST-NITE
| ❑ LLP-21 [10] | The Dells | 1981 | 3.75 | 7.50 | 15.00 |
| —Red vinyl, generic red cover | | | | | |

MERCURY
❑ SRM-1-1059	We Got to Get Our Thing Together	1975	3.75	7.50	15.00
❑ SRM-1-1084	No Way Back	1976	3.75	7.50	15.00
❑ SRM-1-1145	They Said It Couldn't Be Done	1977	3.75	7.50	15.00
❑ SRM-1-3711	Love Connection	1977	3.75	7.50	15.00

PRIVATE I
| ❑ BFZ 39309 | One Step Closer | 1984 | 2.50 | 5.00 | 10.00 |

SOLID SMOKE
| ❑ 8029 | Breezy Ballads and Tender Tunes: The Best of the Early Years (1955-65) | 1984 | 2.50 | 5.00 | 10.00 |

20TH CENTURY
| ❑ T-618 | I Touched a Dream | 1980 | 3.00 | 6.00 | 12.00 |
| ❑ T-633 | Whatever Turns You On | 1981 | 3.00 | 6.00 | 12.00 |

UPFRONT
| ❑ UPF-105 | Stay In My Corner | 1968 | 3.75 | 7.50 | 15.00 |

URGENT
| ❑ URG-4108 | The Second Time | 1991 | 3.00 | 6.00 | 12.00 |

VEE JAY
❑ LP 1010 [M]	Oh What a Nite	1959	200.00	400.00	800.00
—Maroon label					
❑ LP 1010 [M]	Oh What a Nite	1961	75.00	150.00	300.00
—Black label with colorband					
❑ VJLP-1010	Oh What a Nite	198?	2.50	5.00	10.00
—Late-80s reissue on reactivated Vee Jay label. "Trade Mark Reg." on label.					
❑ LP 1141 [M]	It's Not Unusual	1965	25.00	50.00	100.00
❑ LPS 1141 [S]	It's Not Unusual	1965	37.50	75.00	150.00

VJ INTERNATIONAL
| ❑ 7305 | The Dells In Concert | 197? | 3.00 | 6.00 | 12.00 |

ZOO
| ❑ 11023 | I Salute You | 1992 | 3.75 | 7.50 | 15.00 |

DELLS, THE, AND THE DRAMATICS
CADET
| ❑ 60027 | The Dells Vs. the Dramatics | 1974 | 6.25 | 12.50 | 25.00 |

DELMORE BROTHERS, THE
KING
❑ 589 [M]	Songs by the Delmore Brothers	1958	37.50	75.00	150.00
❑ 785 [M]	30th Anniversary Album	1962	20.00	40.00	80.00
❑ 910 [M]	In Memory	1964	10.00	20.00	40.00
❑ 920 [M]	In Memory, Volume 2	1964	10.00	20.00	40.00
❑ 983 [M]	24 Great Country Songs	1966	7.50	15.00	30.00
❑ KS-983 [R]	24 Great Country Songs	1966	5.00	10.00	20.00

DEMANO, HANK
FREEWAY
| ❑ FLJP-1 [M] | Hank DeMano Quartet | 1955 | 12.50 | 25.00 | 50.00 |

DEMENSIONS, THE
CORAL
| ❑ CRL 57430 [M] | My Foolish Heart | 1963 | 37.50 | 75.00 | 150.00 |
| ❑ CRL 757430 [S] | My Foolish Heart | 1963 | 75.00 | 150.00 | 300.00 |

DEMIAN
ABC
| ❑ ABCS-718 | Demian | 1970 | 15.00 | 30.00 | 60.00 |

DENNIS, JOHN
DEBUT
| ❑ DEB-121 [M] | New Piano Expressions | 1955 | 30.00 | 60.00 | 120.00 |

DENNY, DOTTY
A440
| ❑ AJ-505 [M] | Tribute to Edgar Sampson | 1954 | 17.50 | 35.00 | 70.00 |
| ❑ AJ-506 [M] | Dotty Digs Duke | 1954 | 17.50 | 35.00 | 70.00 |

DENNY, MARTIN
FIRST AMERICAN
| ❑ 7743 | From Hawaii With Love | 1981 | 2.50 | 5.00 | 10.00 |

LIBERTY
❑ LM-1009	Exotica Vol. 1	1982	2.00	4.00	8.00
—Reissue of United Artists 1009					
❑ LRP-3034 [M]	Exotica	1957	10.00	20.00	40.00
—Turquoise label					
❑ LRP-3034 [M]	Exotica	1960	6.25	12.50	25.00
—Black rainbow label					
❑ LRP-3077 [M]	Exotica, Volume II	1957	7.50	15.00	30.00
—Turquoise label					
❑ LRP-3077 [M]	Exotica, Volume II	1960	5.00	10.00	20.00
—Black rainbow label					
❑ LRP-3081 [M]	Forbidden Island	1958	7.50	15.00	30.00
—Turquoise label; woman in jungle on cover					
❑ LRP-3081 [M]	Forbidden Island	1960	5.00	10.00	20.00
—Black rainbow label; white foil on cover					
❑ LRP-3087 [M]	Primitiva	1958	7.50	15.00	30.00
—Turquoise label					
❑ LRP-3087 [M]	Primitiva	1960	5.00	10.00	20.00
—Black rainbow label					
❑ LRP-3102 [M]	Hypnotique	1958	7.50	15.00	30.00
—Turquoise label					
❑ LRP-3102 [M]	Hypnotique	1960	5.00	10.00	20.00
—Black rainbow label					
❑ LRP-3111 [M]	Afro-Desia	1959	7.50	15.00	30.00
—Turquoise label					
❑ LRP-3111 [M]	Afro-Desia	1960	5.00	10.00	20.00
—Black rainbow label					
❑ LRP-3116 [M]	Exotica, Vol. III	1959	7.50	15.00	30.00
—Turquoise label					
❑ LRP-3116 [M]	Exotica, Vol. III	1960	5.00	10.00	20.00
—Black rainbow label					
❑ LRP-3122 [M]	Quiet Village	1959	7.50	15.00	30.00
—Turquoise label					
❑ LRP-3122 [M]	Quiet Village	1960	5.00	10.00	20.00
—Black rainbow label					
❑ LRP-3141 [M]	The Enchanted Sea	1959	7.50	15.00	30.00
—Turquoise label					
❑ LRP-3141 [M]	The Enchanted Sea	1960	5.00	10.00	20.00
—Black rainbow label					
❑ LRP-3158 [M]	Exotic Sounds from the Silver Screen	1960	5.00	10.00	20.00
❑ LRP-3163 [M]	Exotic Sounds Visit Broadway	1960	5.00	10.00	20.00
❑ LRP-3168 [M]	Exotic Percussion	1961	5.00	10.00	20.00
❑ LRP-3224 [M]	The Exotic Sounds of Martin Denny In Person	1962	3.75	7.50	15.00
❑ LRP-3237 [M]	A Taste of Honey	1962	3.75	7.50	15.00
❑ LRP-3277 [M]	Another Taste of Honey	1963	3.75	7.50	15.00
❑ LRP-3307 [M]	The Versatile Martin Denny	1963	3.75	7.50	15.00
❑ LRP-3328 [M]	A Taste of Hits	1964	3.00	6.00	12.00
❑ LRP-3378 [M]	Latin Village	1964	3.00	6.00	12.00
❑ LRP-3394 [M]	Hawaii Tattoo	1964	3.00	6.00	12.00
❑ LRP-3415 [M]	20 Golden Hawaiian Hits	1965	3.00	6.00	12.00
❑ LRP-3438 [M]	Martin Denny	1965	3.00	6.00	12.00
❑ LRP-3445 [M]	Hawaiian A-Go-Go	1966	3.00	6.00	12.00
❑ LRP-3467 [M]	Golden Greats	1966	3.00	6.00	12.00
❑ LRP-3488 [M]	Hawaii	1967	3.00	6.00	12.00
❑ LRP-3513 [M]	Exotica Classica	1967	3.00	6.00	12.00
❑ LST-7001 [S]	Forbidden Island	1958	10.00	20.00	40.00
—All-black label; woman in jungle on cover					
❑ LST-7001 [S]	Forbidden Island	1960	6.25	12.50	25.00
—Black rainbow label; white foil on cover					
❑ LST-7006 [S]	Exotica, Volume II	1958	10.00	20.00	40.00
—All-black label					
❑ LST-7006 [S]	Exotica, Volume II	1960	6.25	12.50	25.00
—Black rainbow label					
❑ LST-7023 [S]	Primitiva	1958	10.00	20.00	40.00
—All-black label					
❑ LST-7023 [S]	Primitiva	1960	6.25	12.50	25.00
—Black rainbow label					
❑ LST-7034 [R]	Exotica	1958	6.25	12.50	25.00
—All-black label					
❑ LST-7034 [R]	Exotica	1960	5.00	10.00	20.00
—Black rainbow label					
❑ LST-7102 [S]	Hypnotique	1958	10.00	20.00	40.00
—All-black label					
❑ LST-7102 [S]	Hypnotique	1960	6.25	12.50	25.00
—Black rainbow label					
❑ LST-7111 [S]	Afro-Desia	1959	10.00	20.00	40.00
—All-black label					
❑ LST-7111 [S]	Afro-Desia	1960	6.25	12.50	25.00
—Black rainbow label					

Number	Title (A Side/B Side)	Yr	VG	VG+	NM
❏ LST-7116 [S]	Exotica, Vol. III	1959	10.00	20.00	40.00
—All-black label					
❏ LST-7116 [S]	Exotica, Vol. III	1960	6.25	12.50	25.00
—Black rainbow label					
❏ LST-7122 [S]	Quiet Village	1959	10.00	20.00	40.00
—All-black label					
❏ LST-7122 [S]	Quiet Village	1960	6.25	12.50	25.00
—Black rainbow label					
❏ LST-7141 [S]	The Enchanted Sea	1959	10.00	20.00	40.00
—All-black label					
❏ LST-7141 [S]	The Enchanted Sea	1960	6.25	12.50	25.00
—Black rainbow label					
❏ LST-7158 [S]	Exotic Sounds from the Silver Screen	1960	6.25	12.50	25.00
❏ LST-7163 [S]	Exotic Sounds Visit Broadway	1960	6.25	12.50	25.00
❏ LST-7168 [S]	Exotic Percussion	1961	6.25	12.50	25.00
❏ LST-7224 [S]	The Exotic Sounds of Martin Denny In Person	1962	5.00	10.00	20.00
❏ LST-7237 [S]	A Taste of Honey	1962	5.00	10.00	20.00
❏ LST-7277 [S]	Another Taste of Honey	1963	5.00	10.00	20.00
❏ LST-7307 [S]	The Versatile Martin Denny	1963	5.00	10.00	20.00
❏ LST-7328 [S]	A Taste of Hits	1964	3.75	7.50	15.00
❏ LST-7378 [S]	Latin Village	1964	3.75	7.50	15.00
❏ LST-7394 [S]	Hawaii Tattoo	1964	3.75	7.50	15.00
❏ LST-7415 [S]	20 Golden Hawaiian Hits	1965	3.75	7.50	15.00
❏ LST-7438 [S]	Martin Denny	1965	3.75	7.50	15.00
❏ LST-7445 [S]	Hawaiian A-Go-Go	1966	3.75	7.50	15.00
❏ LST-7467 [S]	Golden Greats	1966	3.75	7.50	15.00
❏ LST-7488 [S]	Hawaii	1967	3.75	7.50	15.00
❏ LST-7513 [S]	Exotica Classica	1967	3.75	7.50	15.00
❏ LST-7621	Exotic Moog	1969	10.00	20.00	40.00
SUNSET					
❏ SUM-1102 [M]	Paradise Moods	196?	3.00	6.00	12.00
❏ SUM-1169 [M]	Sayonara	1967	3.00	6.00	12.00
❏ SUS-5102 [S]	Paradise Moods	196?	3.00	6.00	12.00
❏ SUS-5169 [S]	Sayonara	1967	3.00	6.00	12.00
❏ SUS-5199	Exotic Night	1969	3.00	6.00	12.00
UNITED ARTISTS					
❏ UA-LA234-G	The Very Best of Martin Denny	1974	2.50	5.00	10.00
❏ UA-LA383-E	The Very Best of Martin Denny	1975	2.50	5.00	10.00
❏ LM-1009	Exotica Vol. 1	1980	2.50	5.00	10.00
—Reissue of Liberty 7034					

DENNY, SANDY
A&M
| ❏ SP-4317 | The Northstar Grassman and the Ravens | 1971 | 3.75 | 7.50 | 15.00 |
| ❏ SP-4371 | Sandy | 1972 | 3.75 | 7.50 | 15.00 |
CARTHAGE
❏ CGLP-4423	Rendezvous	1985	2.50	5.00	10.00
—Reissue of Island 9433					
❏ CGLP-4425	Like an Old Fashioned Waltz	1985	2.50	5.00	10.00
—Reissue of Island 9340					
❏ CGLP-4429	The Northstar Grassman and the Ravens	1985	2.50	5.00	10.00
—Reissue of A&M 4317					
HANNIBAL
| ❏ HNBX-5301 [(3)] | Who Knows Where the Time Goes | 198? | 5.00 | 10.00 | 20.00 |
ISLAND
| ❏ SW-9340 | Like an Old Fashioned Waltz | 1974 | 3.75 | 7.50 | 15.00 |
| ❏ ILPS 9433 | Rendezvous | 1977 | 3.75 | 7.50 | 15.00 |

DENVER, JOHN
HJD
| ❏ 66 | John Denver Sings | 1966 | 125.00 | 250.00 | 500.00 |
| —Private issue of 300 or so, made by JD as Christmas gifts to friends. | | | | | |
MERCURY
❏ SRM-1-704	Beginnings	1972	5.00	10.00	20.00
—With illustration on cover					
❏ SRM-1-704	Beginnings	1974	3.00	6.00	12.00
—With mountain scene on cover					
RCA
❏ 7624-1-R	Back Home Again	1988	2.50	5.00	10.00
—Last vinyl reissue					
❏ 7631-1-R	Poems, Prayers and Promises	1988	2.50	5.00	10.00
—Last vinyl reissue					
❏ 7632-1-R	Rocky Mountain High	1988	2.50	5.00	10.00
—Last vinyl reissue					
RCA VICTOR
❏ DJL1-0075 [DJ]	The John Denver Radio Show	1973	7.50	15.00	30.00
❏ APL1-0101	Farewell Andromeda	1973	3.00	6.00	12.00
—Orange label					
❏ APL1-0101	Farewell Andromeda	1975	2.50	5.00	10.00
—Tan label or black label, dog near top					
❏ APL1-0374	John Denver's Greatest Hits	197?	2.00	4.00	8.00
—Reissue					
❏ AQL1-0374	John Denver's Greatest Hits	197?	2.00	4.00	8.00
—Later reissue					
❏ CPL1-0374	John Denver's Greatest Hits	1974	2.50	5.00	10.00
—Orange label					
❏ CPL1-0374	John Denver's Greatest Hits	1975	2.00	4.00	8.00
—Tan label or black label, dog near top					
❏ AFL1-0548	Back Home Again	197?	2.00	4.00	8.00
—Reissue					
❏ AQL1-0548	Back Home Again	197?	2.00	4.00	8.00
—Later reissue					
❏ CPL1-0548	Back Home Again	1974	2.50	5.00	10.00
—Orange or tan label					
❏ CPL1-0548	Back Home Again	1976	2.00	4.00	8.00
—Black label, dog near top					
❏ DJL1-0683 [DJ]	The Second John Denver Radio Show	1974	7.50	15.00	30.00
❏ CPL2-0764 [(2)]	An Evening with John Denver	1975	3.00	6.00	12.00
—Orange or tan labels					
❏ CPL2-0764 [(2)]	An Evening with John Denver	1976	2.50	5.00	10.00
—Black label, dog near top					

Number	Title (A Side/B Side)	Yr	VG	VG+	NM
❏ AFL1-1183	Windsong	197?	2.00	4.00	8.00
—Reissue					
❏ APL1-1183	Windsong	1975	2.50	5.00	10.00
—Tan label					
❏ APL1-1183	Windsong	1976	2.00	4.00	8.00
—Black label, dog near top					
❏ AQL1-1183	Windsong	197?	2.00	4.00	8.00
—Later reissue					
❏ AFL1-1201	Rocky Mountain Christmas	197?	2.00	4.00	8.00
—Reissue					
❏ APL1-1201	Rocky Mountain Christmas	1975	2.50	5.00	10.00
—Tan label					
❏ APL1-1201	Rocky Mountain Christmas	1976	2.00	4.00	8.00
—Black label, dog near top					
❏ APL2-1263 [(2)]	The John Denver Gift Pak	1974	7.50	15.00	30.00
—Contains "Rocky Mountain Christmas" and "Windsong" in a special Christmas sleeve.					
❏ AFL1-1694	Spirit	197?	2.00	4.00	8.00
—Reissue					
❏ APL1-1694	Spirit	1976	2.50	5.00	10.00
—Originals are black label, dog near top					
❏ AQL1-2195	John Denver's Greatest Hits, Volume 2	197?	2.00	4.00	8.00
—Reissue					
❏ CPL1-2195	John Denver's Greatest Hits, Volume 2	1977	2.50	5.00	10.00
❏ AFL1-2521	I Want to Live	1977	2.00	4.00	8.00
❏ AQL1-3075	John Denver	1979	2.00	4.00	8.00
❏ AQL1-3449	Autograph	1980	2.00	4.00	8.00
❏ AFL1-4055	Some Days Are Diamonds	1981	2.00	4.00	8.00
❏ LSP-4207	Rhymes & Reasons	1969	3.75	7.50	15.00
—Orange label, non-flexible vinyl					
❏ AFL1-4256	Seasons of the Heart	1982	2.00	4.00	8.00
❏ LSP-4278	Take Me to Tomorrow	1970	3.75	7.50	15.00
—Orange label, non-flexible vinyl					
❏ LSP-4414	Whose Garden Was This?	1970	3.75	7.50	15.00
—Orange label, non-flexible vinyl					
❏ AFL1-4499	Poems, Prayers and Promises	197?	2.00	4.00	8.00
—Reissue					
❏ LSP-4499	Poems, Prayers and Promises	1971	3.00	6.00	12.00
—Orange label					
❏ LSP-4499	Poems, Prayers and Promises	1975	2.50	5.00	10.00
—Tan label or black label, dog near top					
❏ AFL1-4607	Aerie	197?	2.00	4.00	8.00
—Reissue					
❏ LSP-4607	Aerie	1971	3.00	6.00	12.00
—Orange label					
❏ LSP-4607	Aerie	1975	2.50	5.00	10.00
—Tan label or black label, dog near top					
❏ AFL1-4683	It's About Time	1983	2.00	4.00	8.00
❏ AFL1-4731	Rocky Mountain High	197?	2.00	4.00	8.00
—Reissue					
❏ AQL1-4731	Rocky Mountain High	197?	2.00	4.00	8.00
—Later reissue					
❏ LSP-4731	Rocky Mountain High	1972	3.00	6.00	12.00
—Orange label					
❏ LSP-4731	Rocky Mountain High	1975	2.50	5.00	10.00
—Tan label or black label, dog near top					
❏ AYL1-5189	Poems, Prayers and Promises	198?	—	3.00	6.00
—"Best Buy Series" reissue					
❏ AYL1-5190	Rocky Mountain High	198?	—	3.00	6.00
—"Best Buy Series" reissue					
❏ AYL1-5191	Windsong	198?	—	3.00	6.00
—"Best Buy Series" reissue					
❏ AYL1-5192	I Want to Live	198?	—	3.00	6.00
—"Best Buy Series" reissue					
❏ AYL1-5193	Back Home Again	198?	—	3.00	6.00
—"Best Buy Series" reissue					
❏ AYL1-5194	Spirit	198?	—	3.00	6.00
—"Best Buy Series" reissue					
❏ AYL1-5195	Farewell Andromeda	198?	—	3.00	6.00
—"Best Buy Series" reissue					
❏ AJL1-5313	John Denver's Greatest Hits, Volume 3	1984	2.00	4.00	8.00
❏ DJL1-5398 [DJ]	The John Denver Holiday Radio Show	1984	5.00	10.00	20.00
❏ AFL1-5458	Dreamland Express	1985	2.00	4.00	8.00
❏ AFL1-5811	One World	1986	2.00	4.00	8.00

DEPARIS, SIDNEY
BLUE NOTE
| ❏ B-6501 | DeParis Dixie | 1969 | 5.00 | 10.00 | 20.00 |
| ❏ BLP-7016 [10] | Sidney DeParis' Blue Note Stompers | 1951 | 75.00 | 150.00 | 300.00 |

DEPARIS, SIDNEY/JAMES P. JOHNSON
BLUE NOTE
| ❏ B-6506 | Original Blue Note Jazz, Volume 3 | 1969 | 5.00 | 10.00 | 20.00 |

DEPARIS, WILBUR
A440
| ❏ AJ-503 [10] | New New Orleans Jazz | 1954 | 15.00 | 30.00 | 60.00 |
ATLANTIC
❏ ALS-141 [10]	Wilbur DeParis and His Rampart Street Ramblers	1952	25.00	50.00	100.00
❏ ALS-143 [10]	Wilbur DeParis, Volume 2	1953	25.00	50.00	100.00
❏ 1219 [M]	New New Orleans Jazz	1956	12.50	25.00	50.00
—Black label					
❏ 1219 [M]	New New Orleans Jazz	1961	5.00	10.00	20.00
—Multicolor label, white "fan" logo					
❏ SD 1219 [S]	New New Orleans Jazz	1958	10.00	20.00	40.00
—Green label					
❏ SD 1219 [S]	New New Orleans Jazz	1961	5.00	10.00	20.00
—Multicolor label, white "fan" logo					
❏ 1233 [M]	Marchin' and Swingin'	1956	12.50	25.00	50.00
—Black label					
❏ 1233 [M]	Marchin' and Swingin'	1961	5.00	10.00	20.00
—Multicolor label, white "fan" logo					
❏ SD 1233 [S]	Marchin' and Swingin'	1958	10.00	20.00	40.00
—Green label					

Number	Title (A Side/B Side)	Yr	VG	VG+	NM
❑ SD 1233 [S]	Marchin' and Swingin'	1961	5.00	10.00	20.00
—Multicolor label, white "fan" logo					
❑ 1253 [M]	Wilbur DeParis at Symphony Hall	1957	12.50	25.00	50.00
—Black label					
❑ 1253 [M]	Wilbur DeParis at Symphony Hall	1961	5.00	10.00	20.00
—Multicolor label, white "fan" logo					
❑ SD 1253 [S]	Wilbur DeParis at Symphony Hall	1958	10.00	20.00	40.00
—Green label					
❑ SD 1253 [S]	Wilbur DeParis at Symphony Hall	1961	5.00	10.00	20.00
—Multicolor label, white "fan" logo					
❑ 1288 [M]	Wilbur DeParis Plays Cole Porter	1958	12.50	25.00	50.00
—Black label					
❑ 1288 [M]	Wilbur DeParis Plays Cole Porter	1961	5.00	10.00	20.00
—Multicolor label, white "fan" logo					
❑ 1300 [M]	Something Old, New, Gay, Blue	1958	12.50	25.00	50.00
—Black label					
❑ 1300 [M]	Something Old, New, Gay, Blue	1961	5.00	10.00	20.00
—Multicolor label, white "fan" logo					
❑ SD 1300 [S]	Something Old, New, Gay, Blue	1958	10.00	20.00	40.00
—Green label					
❑ SD 1300 [S]	Something Old, New, Gay, Blue	1961	5.00	10.00	20.00
—Multicolor label, white "fan" logo					
❑ 1318 [M]	That's a-Plenty	1959	12.50	25.00	50.00
—Black label					
❑ 1318 [M]	That's a-Plenty	1961	5.00	10.00	20.00
—Multicolor label, white "fan" logo					
❑ SD 1318 [S]	That's a-Plenty	1959	10.00	20.00	40.00
—Green label					
❑ SD 1318 [S]	That's a-Plenty	1961	5.00	10.00	20.00
—Multicolor label, white "fan" logo					
❑ 1336 [M]	The Wild Jazz Age	1960	6.25	12.50	25.00
—Multicolor label, white "fan" logo					
❑ SD 1336 [S]	The Wild Jazz Age	1960	7.50	15.00	30.00
—Multicolor label, white "fan" logo					
❑ SD 1336 [S]	The Wild Jazz Age	1964	5.00	10.00	20.00
—Multicolor label, black "fan" logo					
❑ 1363 [M]	Wilbur DeParis on the Riviera	1961	6.25	12.50	25.00
—Multicolor label, white "fan" logo					
❑ SD 1363 [S]	Wilbur DeParis on the Riviera	1961	7.50	15.00	30.00
—Multicolor label, white "fan" logo					
❑ SD 1363 [S]	Wilbur DeParis on the Riviera	1964	5.00	10.00	20.00
—Multicolor label, black "fan" logo					
HERITAGE					
❑ SS-1207 [M]	Wilbur DeParis	1956	12.50	25.00	50.00

DEPARIS, WILBUR, AND JIMMY WITHERSPOON
ATLANTIC
Number	Title (A Side/B Side)	Yr	VG	VG+	NM
❑ 1266 [M]	New Orleans Blues	1957	17.50	35.00	70.00
—Black label					
❑ 1266 [M]	New Orleans Blues	1961	7.50	15.00	30.00
—Multicolor label, white "fan" logo					
❑ 1266 [M]	New Orleans Blues	1964	6.25	12.50	25.00
—Multicolor label, black "fan" logo					

DEPAUR CHORUS, THE
COLUMBIA
Number	Title (A Side/B Side)	Yr	VG	VG+	NM
❑ CL 725 [M]	The Spirit of Christmas/God Is With Us	1955	7.50	15.00	30.00
❑ CL 923 [M]	Calypso Christmas	1956	10.00	20.00	40.00
COLUMBIA MASTERWORKS					
❑ AL 45 [10]	Swing Low	1953	15.00	30.00	60.00
❑ ML 2119 [10]	Work Songs and Spirituals	195?	15.00	30.00	60.00
MERCURY LIVING PRESENCE					
❑ SR 90382 [S]	Songs of New Nations	196?	10.00	20.00	40.00
—Maroon label, with "Vendor: Mercury Record Corporation"					
❑ SR 90382 [S]	Songs of New Nations	196?	15.00	30.00	60.00
—Maroon label, no "Vendor: Mercury Record Corporation"					
❑ SR 90418 [S]	Danse Calinda! Creole Songs, Work Songs and Spirituals	196?	7.50	15.00	30.00
—Maroon label, with "Vendor: Mercury Record Corporation"					
❑ SR 90418 [S]	Danse Calinda! Creole Songs, Work Songs and Spirituals	196?	12.50	25.00	50.00
—Maroon label, no "Vendor: Mercury Record Corporation"					

DEPECHE MODE
MUTE
Number	Title (A Side/B Side)	Yr	VG	VG+	NM
❑ MUTEL 5 [(3)]	The Singles 86-98	1998	7.50	15.00	30.00
—Numbered, limited box set pressed in England with U.S. bar code sticker					
SIRE					
❑ SRK 3642	Speak & Spell	1981	3.75	7.50	15.00
❑ PRO-A-5192 [(2)DJ]	Selections from the Commercially Available Box Sets One and Two	1991	6.25	12.50	25.00
—Promo-only sampler					
❑ PRO-A-5242 [(2)DJ]	Selections from the Commercially Available Box Set Three	1991	10.00	20.00	40.00
❑ 23751	A Broken Frame	1982	3.00	6.00	12.00
❑ 23900	Construction Time Again	1983	3.00	6.00	12.00
❑ 25124	People Are People	1984	3.00	6.00	12.00
❑ 25194	Some Great Reward	1984	3.00	6.00	12.00
❑ 25346	Catching Up with Depeche Mode	1985	2.50	5.00	10.00
❑ 25429	Black Celebration	1986	2.50	5.00	10.00
❑ 25614	Music for the Masses	1987	2.50	5.00	10.00
❑ 25853 [(2)]	101	1989	3.75	7.50	15.00
❑ 26081	Violator	1990	3.75	7.50	15.00
❑ R 100560	Catching Up with Depeche Mode	1990	3.00	6.00	12.00
—BMG Direct Marketing edition; reissue					
❑ R 100598	Music for the Masses	1988	3.00	6.00	12.00
—BMG Direct Marketing edition					
❑ R 143674	Catching Up with Depeche Mode	1985	3.00	6.00	12.00
—RCA Music Service edition					
❑ R 173408	Violator	1990	3.75	7.50	15.00
—BMG Direct Marketing edition					

DEPENDABLES, THE
UNITED ARTISTS
Number	Title (A Side/B Side)	Yr	VG	VG+	NM
❑ UAS-6799	Klaatu Berrada Niktu	1971	5.00	10.00	20.00

DEPUTIES, THE
FARON YOUNG
| ❑ 002 [M] | Sounds of the Deputies | 1965 | 7.50 | 15.00 | 30.00 |

DEREK AND THE DOMINOS
Also see ERIC CLAPTON.
ATCO
Number	Title (A Side/B Side)	Yr	VG	VG+	NM
❑ 2-704 [(2)M]	Layla and Other Assorted Love Songs	1970	75.00	150.00	300.00
—White label promo only					
❑ SD 2-704 [(2)DJ]	Layla and Other Assorted Love Songs	1970	50.00	100.00	200.00
—White label promo					
❑ SD 2-704 [(2)S]	Layla and Other Assorted Love Songs	1970	7.50	15.00	30.00
DIRECT DISK					
❑ SD-16629 [(2)]	Layla and Other Assorted Love Songs	1981	37.50	75.00	150.00
—Audiophile vinyl					
MOBILE FIDELITY					
❑ 2-239 [(2)]	Derek and the Dominos in Concert	1996	12.50	25.00	50.00
—Audiophile vinyl					
POLYDOR					
❑ PD2-3501 [(2)]	Layla and Other Assorted Love Songs	1972	5.00	10.00	20.00
RSO					
❑ RS-2-3801 [(2)]	Layla and Other Assorted Love Songs	1977	3.75	7.50	15.00
❑ SO 2-8800 [(2)]	Derek and the Dominos in Concert	1973	5.00	10.00	20.00
❑ 823277-1 [(2)]	Layla and Other Assorted Love Songs	1985	3.00	6.00	12.00

DERISE, JOE
BETHLEHEM
Number	Title (A Side/B Side)	Yr	VG	VG+	NM
❑ BCP-51 [M]	Joe DeRise with the Australian Jazz Quintet	1956	12.50	25.00	50.00
❑ BCP-1039 [10]	Joe DeRise Sings	1955	25.00	50.00	100.00

DERRINGER, RICK
Also see THE McCOYS.
BLUE SKY
Number	Title (A Side/B Side)	Yr	VG	VG+	NM
❑ KZ 32481	All American Boy	1973	3.75	7.50	15.00
❑ PZ 32481	All American Boy	197?	2.00	4.00	8.00
—Reissue with new prefix					
❑ ZQ 32481 [Q]	All American Boy	1974	5.00	10.00	20.00
❑ PZ 33423	Spring Fever	1975	3.00	6.00	12.00
❑ PZ 34181	Derringer	1976	3.00	6.00	12.00
❑ PZ 34470	Sweet Evil	1977	3.00	6.00	12.00
❑ PZ 34848	Derringer Live	1977	3.00	6.00	12.00
—Without bar code					
❑ PZ 34848	Derringer Live	198?	2.00	4.00	8.00
—Reissue with bar code					
❑ JZ 35075	If I Weren't So Romantic I'd Shoot You	1978	2.50	5.00	10.00
❑ JZ 36092	Guitars and Women	1979	2.50	5.00	10.00
❑ JZ 36551	Face to Face	1980	2.50	5.00	10.00
PASSPORT					
❑ PB-6025	Good Dirty Fun	1983	2.50	5.00	10.00

DESANTO, SUGAR PIE
CHECKER
| ❑ LP-2979 [M] | Sugar Pie DeSanto | 1961 | 50.00 | 100.00 | 200.00 |

DESCENDANTS OF MIKE & PHOEBE, THE
STRATA-EAST
| ❑ SES-19744 | A Spirit Speaks | 1973 | 15.00 | 30.00 | 60.00 |

DESHANNON, JACKIE
AMHERST
Number	Title (A Side/B Side)	Yr	VG	VG+	NM
❑ AMX 1010	You're the Only Dancer	1977	3.00	6.00	12.00
❑ AMH 1016	Quick Touches	1978	3.00	6.00	12.00
ATLANTIC					
❑ SD 7231	Jackie	1972	3.00	6.00	12.00
❑ SD 7303	Your Baby Is a Lady	1974	3.00	6.00	12.00
CAPITOL					
❑ ST-772	Songs	1971	3.00	6.00	12.00
COLUMBIA					
❑ PC 33500	New Arrangement	1975	3.00	6.00	12.00
IMPERIAL					
❑ LP-9286 [M]	This Is Jackie DeShannon	1965	5.00	10.00	20.00
—Black and pink label					
❑ LP-9286 [M]	This Is Jackie DeShannon	1966	3.75	7.50	15.00
—Black and green label					
❑ LP-9294 [M]	You Won't Forget Me	1965	5.00	10.00	20.00
—Black and pink label					
❑ LP-9294 [M]	You Won't Forget Me	1966	3.75	7.50	15.00
—Black and green label					
❑ LP-9296 [M]	In the Wind	1965	5.00	10.00	20.00
—Black and pink label					
❑ LP-9296 [M]	In the Wind	1966	3.75	7.50	15.00
—Black and green label					
❑ LP-9328 [M]	Are You Ready for This?	1966	3.75	7.50	15.00
❑ LP-9344 [M]	New Image	1967	3.75	7.50	15.00
❑ LP-9352 [M]	For You	1967	3.75	7.50	15.00
❑ LP-12286 [S]	This Is Jackie DeShannon	1965	6.25	12.50	25.00
—Black and pink label					
❑ LP-12286 [S]	This Is Jackie DeShannon	1966	5.00	10.00	20.00
—Black and green label					
❑ LP-12294 [S]	You Won't Forget Me	1965	6.25	12.50	25.00
—Black and pink label					
❑ LP-12294 [S]	You Won't Forget Me	1966	5.00	10.00	20.00
—Black and green label					
❑ LP-12296 [S]	In the Wind	1965	6.25	12.50	25.00
—Black and pink label					
❑ LP-12296 [S]	In the Wind	1966	5.00	10.00	20.00
—Black and green label					
❑ LP-12328 [S]	Are You Ready for This?	1966	5.00	10.00	20.00

Number	Title (A Side/B Side)	Yr	VG	VG+	NM
❏ LP-12344 [S]	New Image	1967	5.00	10.00	20.00
❏ LP-12352 [S]	For You	1967	5.00	10.00	20.00
❏ LP-12386	Me About You	1968	3.75	7.50	15.00
❏ LP-12404	What the World Needs Now Is Love	1968	3.75	7.50	15.00
❏ LP-12415	Laurel Canyon	1969	3.75	7.50	15.00
❏ LP-12442	Put a Little Love in Your Heart	1969	3.75	7.50	15.00
❏ LP-12453	To Be Free	1970	3.75	7.50	15.00

LIBERTY

Number	Title (A Side/B Side)	Yr	VG	VG+	NM
❏ LRP-3320 [M]	Jackie DeShannon	1963	10.00	20.00	40.00
❏ LRP-3390 [M]	Breakin' It Up on the Beatles Tour!	1964	10.00	20.00	40.00
❏ LST-7320 [S]	Jackie DeShannon	1963	12.50	25.00	50.00
❏ LST-7390 [S]	Breakin' It Up on the Beatles Tour!	1964	12.50	25.00	50.00
❏ LN-10179	The Very Best of Jackie DeShannon	1983	2.00	4.00	8.00
—Reissue of United Artists 434					
❏ LN-10265	Jackie DeShannon	1985	2.00	4.00	8.00

SUNSET

Number	Title (A Side/B Side)	Yr	VG	VG+	NM
❏ SUS-5225	Lonely Girl	1968	3.00	6.00	12.00
❏ SUS-5322	Jackie DeShannon	1970	3.00	6.00	12.00

UNITED ARTISTS

Number	Title (A Side/B Side)	Yr	VG	VG+	NM
❏ UA-LA434-E	The Very Best of Jackie DeShannon	1975	3.00	6.00	12.00

DESMOND, JOHNNY
COLUMBIA

Number	Title (A Side/B Side)	Yr	VG	VG+	NM
❏ CL 1399 [M]	Once Upon a Time	1959	5.00	10.00	20.00
❏ CS 8194 [S]	Once Upon a Time	1959	6.25	12.50	25.00

MAYFAIR

Number	Title (A Side/B Side)	Yr	VG	VG+	NM
❏ 9635 [M]	Johnny Desmond Swings	196?	3.00	6.00	12.00
❏ 9635S [S]	Johnny Desmond Swings	196?	3.75	7.50	15.00
—Yellow vinyl					

MOVIETONE

Number	Title (A Side/B Side)	Yr	VG	VG+	NM
❏ 71011 [M]	Johnny Desmond On Location	1966	3.00	6.00	12.00
❏ S-72011 [S]	Johnny Desmond On Location	1966	3.75	7.50	15.00

VOCALION

Number	Title (A Side/B Side)	Yr	VG	VG+	NM
❏ VL 3773 [M]	Johnny Desmond	1966	3.00	6.00	12.00
❏ VL 73773 [R]	Johnny Desmond	1966	2.50	5.00	10.00

DESMOND, PAUL
FANTASY

Number	Title (A Side/B Side)	Yr	VG	VG+	NM
❏ 3-21 [10]	Paul Desmond	1955	25.00	50.00	100.00
❏ 3235 [M]	Paul Desmond Quartet Featuring Don Elliott	1956	20.00	40.00	80.00
—Red vinyl					
❏ 3235 [M]	Paul Desmond Quartet Featuring Don Elliott	1957	10.00	20.00	40.00
—Black vinyl, red label, non-flexible vinyl					
❏ 3235 [M]	Paul Desmond Quartet Featuring Don Elliott	1962	5.00	10.00	20.00
—Black vinyl, red label, flexible vinyl					

MOSAIC

Number	Title (A Side/B Side)	Yr	VG	VG+	NM
❏ M6-120 [(6)]	The Complete Recordings of the Paul Desmond Quartet with Jim Hall	199?	25.00	50.00	100.00

RCA VICTOR

Number	Title (A Side/B Side)	Yr	VG	VG+	NM
❏ LPM-2438 [M]	Desmond Blue	1961	7.50	15.00	30.00
❏ LSP-2438 [S]	Desmond Blue	1961	7.50	15.00	30.00
❏ LPM-2569 [M]	Take Ten	1962	6.25	12.50	25.00
❏ LSP-2569 [S]	Take Ten	1962	7.50	15.00	30.00
❏ LPM-2654 [M]	Two of a Mind	1963	6.25	12.50	25.00
❏ LSP-2654 [S]	Two of a Mind	1963	7.50	15.00	30.00
❏ LPM-3320 [M]	Boss Antigua	1965	5.00	10.00	20.00
❏ LSP-3320 [S]	Boss Antigua	1965	6.25	12.50	25.00
❏ LPM-3407 [M]	Glad to Be Unhappy	1965	5.00	10.00	20.00
❏ LSP-3407 [S]	Glad to Be Unhappy	1965	6.25	12.50	25.00
❏ LPM-3480 [M]	Easy Living	1965	5.00	10.00	20.00
❏ LSP-3480 [S]	Easy Living	1965	6.25	12.50	25.00

WARNER BROS.

Number	Title (A Side/B Side)	Yr	VG	VG+	NM
❏ W 1356 [M]	First Place Again	1960	7.50	15.00	30.00
❏ WS 1356 [S]	First Place Again	1960	7.50	15.00	30.00

DETERGENTS, THE
ROULETTE

Number	Title (A Side/B Side)	Yr	VG	VG+	NM
❏ R 25308 [M]	The Many Faces of the Detergents	1965	30.00	60.00	120.00
❏ SR 25308 [R]	The Many Faces of the Detergents	1965	25.00	50.00	100.00

DETROIT CITY LIMITS, THE
OKEH

Number	Title (A Side/B Side)	Yr	VG	VG+	NM
❏ OKS 14127	98c + Tax	1968	7.50	15.00	30.00

DETROIT EMERALDS
WESTBOUND

Number	Title (A Side/B Side)	Yr	VG	VG+	NM
❏ 302	Feel the Need	1977	3.75	7.50	15.00
❏ 2006	Do Me Right	1971	10.00	20.00	40.00
❏ 2013	You Want It, You Got It	1972	10.00	20.00	40.00
❏ 2018	I'm in Love with You	1973	10.00	20.00	40.00
❏ 6101	Let's Get Together	1978	3.75	7.50	15.00

DETROIT SYMPHONY ORCHESTRA (PAUL PARAY, CONDUCTOR)
MERCURY LIVING PRESENCE

Number	Title (A Side/B Side)	Yr	VG	VG+	NM
❏ SR 90001 [S]	Bizet: Carmen Suite	1959	12.50	25.00	50.00
—Maroon label, no "Vendor: Mercury Record Corporation"					
❏ SR 90005 [S]	Ravel: Bolero; Ma Mere L'Oye; Chabrier: Bourree Fantasque	1959	7.50	15.00	30.00
—Maroon label, no "Vendor: Mercury Record Corporation"					
❏ SR 90010 [S]	Debussy: La Mer; Iberia	1959	20.00	40.00	80.00
—Maroon label, no "Vendor: Mercury Record Corporation"					
❏ SR 90012 [S]	Saint-Saens: Symphony No. 3	1959	18.75	37.50	75.00
—Maroon label, no "Vendor: Mercury Record Corporation"					
❏ SR 90017 [S]	Chausson: Symphony in B-flat	1959	10.00	20.00	40.00
—Maroon label, no "Vendor: Mercury Record Corporation"					
❏ SR 90019 [S]	Rachmaninoff: Symphony No. 2	1959	10.00	20.00	40.00
—Maroon label, no "Vendor: Mercury Record Corporation"					
❏ SR 90102 [S]	Schumann: Symphony No. 2	196?	6.25	12.50	25.00
—Maroon label, with "Vendor: Mercury Record Corporation"					
❏ SR 90102 [S]	Schumann: Symphony No. 2	1960	10.00	20.00	40.00
—Maroon label, no "Vendor: Mercury Record Corporation"					

Number	Title (A Side/B Side)	Yr	VG	VG+	NM
❏ SR 90107 [S]	Wagner: Dawn & Sigfried's Rhine Journey, etc.	196?	5.00	10.00	20.00
—Maroon label, no "Vendor: Mercury Record Corporation"					
❏ SR 90128 [S]	Paray: Mass for Joan of Arc	1960	5.00	10.00	20.00
—Maroon label, no "Vendor: Mercury Record Corporation"					
❏ SR 90129 [S]	Haydn: Symphony No. 96; Mozart: Symphony No. 35	1960	10.00	20.00	40.00
—Maroon label, no "Vendor: Mercury Record Corporation"					
❏ SR 90133 [S]	Schumann: Symphony No. 3 "Rhenish"	1960	5.00	10.00	20.00
—Maroon label, no "Vendor: Mercury Record Corporation"					
❏ SR 90174 [S]	Mendelssohn: A Midsummer Night's Dream; Symphony No. 5	196?	6.25	12.50	25.00
—Maroon label, with "Vendor: Mercury Record Corporation"					
❏ SR 90174 [S]	Mendelssohn: A Midsummer Night's Dream; Symphony No. 5	196?	10.00	20.00	40.00
—Maroon label, no "Vendor: Mercury Record Corporation"					
❏ SR 90177 [S]	Schmitt: Tragedie de Salome; Strauss, Richard: Salome-Dance; Lalo: Namouna, Suite 1	196?	20.00	40.00	80.00
—Maroon label, no "Vendor: Mercury Record Corporation"					
❏ SR 90191 [S]	Ouvertures Francaises	196?	37.50	75.00	150.00
—Maroon label, no "Vendor: Mercury Record Corporation"					
❏ SR 90198 [S]	Schumann: Symphony No. 1; Manfred Overture	196?	6.25	12.50	25.00
—Maroon label, no "Vendor: Mercury Record Corporation"					
❏ SR 90203 [S]	Bouquet de Paray	196?	7.50	15.00	30.00
—Maroon label, with "Vendor: Mercury Record Corporation"					
❏ SR 90203 [S]	Bouquet de Paray	196?	15.00	30.00	60.00
—Maroon label, no "Vendor: Mercury Record Corporation"					
❏ SR 90204 [S]	Sibelius: Symphony No. 2	196?	5.00	10.00	20.00
—Third edition: Dark red (not maroon) label					
❏ SR 90204 [S]	Sibelius: Symphony No. 2	196?	12.50	25.00	50.00
—Maroon label, with "Vendor: Mercury Record Corporation"					
❏ S-90204 [S]	Sibelius: Symphony No. 2	196?	25.00	50.00	100.00
—Maroon label, no "Vendor: Mercury Record Corporation"					
❏ SR 90205 [S]	Beethoven: Symphonies No. 1 and 2	196?	30.00	60.00	120.00
—Maroon label, no "Vendor: Mercury Record Corporation"					
❏ SR 90211 [S]	Vive La Marche!	196?	7.50	15.00	30.00
—Maroon label, no "Vendor: Mercury Record Corporation"					
❏ SR 90212 [S]	Chabrier: Espana; Suite Pastorale; Fete Polonaise; Overture to "Gwendoline"; Danse Slave	196?	30.00	60.00	120.00
—Maroon label, no "Vendor: Mercury Record Corporation"					
❏ SR 90212 [S]	Chabrier: Espana; Suite Pastorale; Fete Polonaise; Overture to "Gwendoline"; Danse Slave	199?	6.25	12.50	25.00
—Classic Records reissue					
❏ SR 90213 [S]	Ravel: La Tombeau de Couperin; Valses Nobles et Sentimentales; Debussy: Petite Suite; Prelude	196?	50.00	100.00	200.00
—Maroon label, no "Vendor: Mercury Record Corporation"					
❏ SR 90215 [S]	Overtures	196?	15.00	30.00	60.00
—Maroon label, no "Vendor: Mercury Record Corporation"					
❏ SR 90232 [S]	Wagner: Rienzi Overture; Magic Fire Music; Flying Dutchman Overture; Meistersinger Excerpts	196?	7.50	15.00	30.00
—Maroon label, no "Vendor: Mercury Record Corporation"					
❏ SR 90247 [S]	French Overtures	196?	20.00	40.00	80.00
—Maroon label, no "Vendor: Mercury Record Corporation"					
❏ SR 90254 [S]	Berlioz: Symphonie Fantastique	196?	5.00	10.00	20.00
—Maroon label, with "Vendor: Mercury Record Corporation"					
❏ SR 90254 [S]	Berlioz: Symphonie Fantastique	196?	30.00	60.00	120.00
—Maroon label, no "Vendor: Mercury Record Corporation"					
❏ SR 90262 [S]	Dvorak: Symphony No. 9 "From the New World"	196?	37.50	75.00	150.00
—Maroon label, no "Vendor: Mercury Record Corporation"					
❏ SR 90269 [S]	Suppe: Overtures	196?	5.00	10.00	20.00
—Maroon label, with "Vendor: Mercury Record Corporation"					
❏ SR 90269 [S]	Suppe: Overtures	196?	7.50	15.00	30.00
—Maroon label, no "Vendor: Mercury Record Corporation"					
❏ SR 90281 [S]	Debussy: Nocturnes; Ravel: Daphnis et Chloe Suite 2	196?	75.00	150.00	300.00
—Maroon label, no "Vendor: Mercury Record Corporation"					
❏ SR 90285 [S]	Franck: Symphony in D	196?	5.00	10.00	20.00
—Maroon label, with "Vendor: Mercury Record Corporation"					
❏ SR 90285 [S]	Franck: Symphony in D	196?	12.50	25.00	50.00
—Maroon label, no "Vendor: Mercury Record Corporation"					
❏ SR 90313 [S]	Ravel: Rapsodie Espagnole; La Valse; Pavane; Alborada; Ibert: Escales	196?	125.00	250.00	500.00
—Maroon label, no "Vendor: Mercury Record Corporation"					
❏ SR 90318 [S]	Ballet Highlights from French Opera	196?	25.00	50.00	100.00
—Maroon label, with "Vendor: Mercury Record Corporation"					
❏ SR 90318 [S]	Ballet Highlights from French Opera	196?	37.50	75.00	150.00
—Maroon label, no "Vendor: Mercury Record Corporation"					
❏ SR 90330 [S]	Schumann: Symphonies No. 1 and 3	196?	6.25	12.50	25.00
—Maroon label, no "Vendor: Mercury Record Corporation"					
❏ SR 90330 [S]	Schumann: Symphonies No. 1 and 3	196?	6.25	12.50	25.00
—Maroon label, with "Vendor: Mercury Record Corporation"					
❏ SR 90331 [S]	Saint-Saens: Symphony No. 3; Chausson: Symphony in B-flat	196?	7.50	15.00	30.00
—Maroon label, no "Vendor: Mercury Record Corporation"					
❏ SR 90359 [S]	Curtain Up! Heroic Overtures	196?	7.50	15.00	30.00
—Maroon label, no "Vendor: Mercury Record Corporation"					
❏ SR 90372 [S]	Debussy: La Mer; Petite Suite; Iberia; Prelude	196?	10.00	20.00	40.00
—Maroon label, no "Vendor: Mercury Record Corporation"					
❏ SR 90373 [S]	Ravel: Ma Mere L'Oye; Pavane; Tombeau de Couperin; Valses Nobles et Sentimentales	196?	7.50	15.00	30.00
—Maroon label, no "Vendor: Mercury Record Corporation"					
❏ SR 90374 [S]	Bizet: Carmen Suite; L'Arlesienne Suites No. 1 and 2; Chabrier: Espana; Bourree; Marche	196?	5.00	10.00	20.00
—Maroon label, no "Vendor: Mercury Record Corporation"					
❏ SR 90375 [S]	Berlioz: Symphonie Fantastique; Le Corsair Overture; Royal Hunt and Storm	196?	12.50	25.00	50.00
—Maroon label, no "Vendor: Mercury Record Corporation"					

Number	Title (A Side/B Side)	Yr	VG	VG+	NM
❏ SR 90377 [S]	Overtures and Excerpts from French Opera	196?	10.00	20.00	40.00
—Maroon label, no "Vendor: Mercury Record Corporation"					

DEUCE COUPES, THE
May be two different groups.
CROWN

❏ CST-393 [S]	The Shut Downs	1963	6.25	12.50	25.00
❏ CLP-5393 [M]	The Shut Downs	1963	5.00	10.00	20.00

DEL-FI

❏ DFLP-1243 [M]	Hotrodder's Choice	1963	12.50	25.00	50.00
❏ DFST-1243 [S]	Hotrodder's Choice	1963	15.00	30.00	60.00

DEUCHAR, JIMMY
CONTEMPORARY

❏ C-3529 [M]	Pub Crawling	1957	12.50	25.00	50.00

DISCOVERY

❏ DL-2004 [10]	New Sounds from England	1953	20.00	40.00	80.00

DEVIANTS, THE
SIRE

❏ SES-97001	Ptoof!	1968	15.00	30.00	60.00
❏ SES-97005	Disposable	1969	15.00	30.00	60.00
❏ SES-97016	No. 3	1969	15.00	30.00	60.00

DEVIL'S ANVIL, THE
COLUMBIA

❏ CL 2664 [M]	Hard Rock from the Middle East	1967	6.25	12.50	25.00
❏ CS 9464 [S]	Hard Rock from the Middle East	1967	7.50	15.00	30.00

DEVILED HAM
SUPER K

❏ SKS-6003	I Had Too Much to Dream Last Night	1968	6.25	12.50	25.00

DEVO
DUTCH EAST INDIA

❏ DE-112008-1	Smooth Noodle Maps	1991	3.75	7.50	15.00
—Red vinyl, 1,000 copies pressed					

ENIGMA

❏ EPRO 326 [DJ]	Smooth Noodle Maps	1990	5.00	10.00	20.00
—Promo only, no picture cover					
❏ 73303	Total Devo	1988	2.50	5.00	10.00
❏ 73514	Now It Can Be Told!	1989	2.50	5.00	10.00

WARNER BROS.

❏ PRO-A-928 [EP]	Freedom of Choice/Whip It/Be Still/Gates of Steel	1980	2.50	5.00	10.00
—Promo version of "Dev-O Live"					
❏ BSK 3239	Q: Are We Not Men? A: We Are Devo!	1978	2.50	5.00	10.00
❏ BSK 3337	Duty Now for the Future	1979	2.50	5.00	10.00
❏ BSK 3435	Freedom of Choice	1980	2.50	5.00	10.00
❏ MINI 3548 [EP]	Dev-O Live	1981	2.50	5.00	10.00
—All copies came in plastic sleeve					
❏ BSK 3595	New Traditionalists	1981	3.75	7.50	15.00
—First pressings include bonus 45 (EP 3595) and poster; deduct 1/3 if missing					
❏ 23741	Oh No! It's Devo	1982	2.50	5.00	10.00
❏ W1-23741	Oh No! It's Devo	1982	3.00	6.00	12.00
—Columbia House version, no easel cutout on back cover					
❏ 25097	Shout	1984	2.50	5.00	10.00

DEVOL, FRANK
ABC-PARAMOUNT

❏ 513 [M]	Theme from "Peyton Place" and 11 Other Great Themes	1965	3.00	6.00	12.00
❏ S-513 [S]	Theme from "Peyton Place" and 11 Other Great Themes	1965	3.75	7.50	15.00
❏ 534 [M]	Italian Romance American Style	1966	3.00	6.00	12.00
❏ S-534 [S]	Italian Romance American Style	1966	3.75	7.50	15.00

COLUMBIA

❏ CS (# unk) [S]	Four Seasons of Love	1960	5.00	10.00	20.00
❏ C2L 12 [(2)M]	The Columbia Album of Irving Berlin	1958	7.50	15.00	30.00
❏ C2S 812 [(2)S]	The Columbia Album of Irving Berlin	1958	10.00	20.00	40.00
❏ CL 1108 [M]	Portraits	1957	3.75	7.50	15.00
❏ CL 1260 [M]	The Columbia Album of Irving Berlin, Volume 1	1958	3.75	7.50	15.00
❏ CL 1261 [M]	The Columbia Album of Irving Berlin, Volume 2	1958	3.75	7.50	15.00
❏ CL 1371 [M]	Fabulous Hollywood	1959	3.75	7.50	15.00
❏ CL 1413 [M]	The Old Sweet Songs	1960	3.75	7.50	15.00
❏ CL 1451 [M]	Four Seasons of Love	1960	3.75	7.50	15.00
❏ CL 1482 [M]	More Old Sweet Songs	1960	3.75	7.50	15.00
❏ CL 1543 [M]	The Old Sweet Songs of Christmas	1960	3.75	7.50	15.00
❏ CS 8172 [S]	Fabulous Hollywood	1959	5.00	10.00	20.00
❏ CS 8209 [S]	The Old Sweet Songs	1960	5.00	10.00	20.00
❏ CS 8273 [S]	More Old Sweet Songs	1960	5.00	10.00	20.00
❏ CS 8343 [S]	The Old Sweet Songs of Christmas	1960	3.75	7.50	15.00

COLUMBIA SPECIAL PRODUCTS

❏ EN2 16437 [(2)]	The Columbia Album of Irving Berlin	1983	3.00	6.00	12.00

HARMONY

❏ HL 7356 [M]	The Old Sweet Songs of Christmas	196?	3.00	6.00	12.00
❏ HS 11156 [S]	The Old Sweet Songs of Christmas	196?	3.75	7.50	15.00

DEVROE, BILLY, AND THE DEVILAIRES
TAMPA

❏ TP-31 [M]	Billy Devroe and the Devilaires, Vol. 1	1957	10.00	20.00	40.00
❏ TP-39 [M]	Billy Devroe and the Devilaires, Vol. 2	1958	10.00	20.00	40.00

DEWITT, GEORGE
EPIC

❏ BN 531 [S]	George DeWitt Sings That Tune	1959	7.50	15.00	30.00
❏ LN 3562 [M]	George DeWitt Sings That Tune	1959	5.00	10.00	20.00

DEXTER, AL
CAPITOL

❏ ST 1701 [S]	Al Dexter Sings and Plays His Greatest Hits	1962	10.00	20.00	40.00
❏ T 1701 [M]	Al Dexter Sings and Plays His Greatest Hits	1962	7.50	15.00	30.00

COLUMBIA

❏ CL 9005 [10]	Songs of the Southwest	195?	12.50	25.00	50.00

HARMONY

❏ HL 7293 [M]	Pistol Packin' Mama	1961	5.00	10.00	20.00

DIALOGUE
COLD

❏ (no #)	Dialogue	1968	25.00	50.00	100.00
—Orange cover with insert					
❏ (no #)	Dialogue	1968	75.00	150.00	300.00
—White cover with insert					

DIALS, THE
TIME

❏ S-2100 [S]	It's Monkey Time	1964	7.50	15.00	30.00
❏ 52100 [M]	It's Monkey Time	1964	6.25	12.50	25.00

DIAMOND, LEO
RCA VICTOR

❏ LPM-1165 [M]	Skin Diver Suite and Other Selections	1955	15.00	30.00	60.00

REPRISE

❏ R-6002 [M]	Exciting Sounds of the South Seas	1961	6.25	12.50	25.00
❏ R9-6002 [S]	Exciting Sounds of the South Seas	1961	7.50	15.00	30.00
❏ R-6009 [M]	Themes from Great Foreign Films	1961	6.25	12.50	25.00
❏ R9-6009 [S]	Themes from Great Foreign Films	1961	7.50	15.00	30.00
❏ R-6024 [M]	Off Shore	1962	6.25	12.50	25.00
❏ R9-6024 [S]	Off Shore	1962	7.50	15.00	30.00

DIAMOND, NEIL
BANG

❏ BLP 214 [M]	The Feel of Neil Diamond	1966	15.00	30.00	60.00
—All tracks play mono					
❏ BLP 214 [P]	The Feel of Neil Diamond	1966	20.00	40.00	80.00
—Album is labeled mono, but plays in stereo					
❏ BLPS 214	The Feel of Neil Diamond	1974	3.00	6.00	12.00
—Later pressing on blue "clouds" label					
❏ BLPS 214 [P]	The Feel of Neil Diamond	1966	25.00	50.00	100.00
—Album is labeled stereo and plays in stereo (except "Solitary Man," "Do It," "I'll Come Running" are rechanneled)					
❏ BLP 217 [M]	Just for You	1967	10.00	20.00	40.00
—With blurb for "Thank the Lord for the Night Time" on cover					
❏ BLPS 217	Just for You	1974	3.00	6.00	12.00
—Later pressing on blue "clouds" label					
❏ BLPS 217 [P]	Just for You	1967	12.50	25.00	50.00
—With blurb for "Thank the Lord for the Night Time" on cover					
❏ BLPS 217 [P]	Just for You	1968	10.00	20.00	40.00
—With blurb for "Shilo" pasted over "Thank the Lord for the Night Time" blurb					
❏ BLPS 217 [P]	Just for You	1970	5.00	10.00	20.00
—With blurb for "Shilo" imprinted on cover					
❏ BLPS 219	Neil Diamond's Greatest Hits	1974	3.00	6.00	12.00
—Later pressing on blue "clouds" label					
❏ BLPS 219 [P]	Neil Diamond's Greatest Hits	196?	5.00	10.00	20.00
—Later editions have an alternate take of "Solitary Man" in true stereo					
❏ BLPS 219 [P]	Neil Diamond's Greatest Hits	1968	10.00	20.00	40.00
—First editions have the single version of "Solitary Man" in rechanneled stereo					
❏ BLPS 221	Shilo	1974	3.00	6.00	12.00
—Later pressing on blue "clouds" label					
❏ BLPS 221 [S]	Shilo	1970	10.00	20.00	40.00
❏ BLPS 224	Do It!	1974	3.00	6.00	12.00
—Later pressing on blue "clouds" label					
❏ BLPS 224 [P]	Do It!	1971	7.50	15.00	30.00
❏ BLPS 227 [(2)]	Double Gold	1974	3.75	7.50	15.00
—Later pressing on blue "clouds" label					
❏ BLPS-227 [(2)S]	Double Gold	1973	10.00	20.00	40.00

CAPITOL

❏ SWAV-12120	The Jazz Singer	1980	2.50	5.00	10.00

COLUMBIA

❏ AS 99-1586 [DJ]	Heartlight	1982	6.25	12.50	25.00
—Promo-only picture disc					
❏ KS 32550	Jonathan Livingston Seagull	1973	3.00	6.00	12.00
—With booklet					
❏ PC 32919	Serenade	1974	3.00	6.00	12.00
❏ PCQ 32919 [Q]	Serenade	1974	6.25	12.50	25.00
❏ PC 33965	Beautiful Noise	1976	3.00	6.00	12.00
—Originals have no bar code					
❏ KC2 34404 [(2)]	Love at the Greek	1977	3.75	7.50	15.00
❏ JC 34990	I'm Glad You're Here with Me Tonight	1977	3.00	6.00	12.00
❏ FC 35625	You Don't Bring Me Flowers	1978	3.00	6.00	12.00
❏ FC 36121	September Morn	1979	3.00	6.00	12.00
❏ TC 37628	On the Way to the Sky	1981	2.50	5.00	10.00
❏ TC 38068	12 Greatest Hits, Vol. II	1982	2.50	5.00	10.00
❏ TC 38359	Heartlight	1982	2.50	5.00	10.00
❏ PC 38792	Classics — The Early Years	1983	2.50	5.00	10.00
—Possibly a reissue of Frog King 1					
❏ QC 39199	Primitive	1984	2.50	5.00	10.00
❏ 9C9 39915 [PD]	Primitive	1984	5.00	10.00	20.00
❏ OC 40368	Headed for the Future	1986	2.00	4.00	8.00
❏ CG2 40990 [(2)]	Hot August Night II	1987	3.00	6.00	12.00
❏ HC 42550	Jonathan Livingston Seagull	1982	12.50	25.00	50.00
—Half-speed mastered edition					
❏ OC 45025	The Best Years of Our Lives	1988	2.00	4.00	8.00
❏ HC 45625	You Don't Bring Me Flowers	1982	10.00	20.00	40.00
—Half-speed mastered edition					
❏ HC 47628	On the Way to the Sky	1982	7.50	15.00	30.00
—Half-speed mastered edition					
❏ HC 48068	12 Greatest Hits, Vol. II	1982	25.00	50.00	100.00
—Half-speed mastered edition					
❏ HC 48359	Heartlight	1982	10.00	20.00	40.00
—Half-speed mastered edition					
❏ C 48610	Lovescape	1991	3.75	7.50	15.00

Number	Title (A Side/B Side)	Yr	VG	VG+	NM
DIRECT DISK					
❏ SD 16612	His 12 Greatest Hits	1982	12.50	25.00	50.00
—Audiophile vinyl					
FROG KING					
❏ AAR-1	Early Classics	1972	10.00	20.00	40.00
—Compilation of Bang material for Columbia Record Club; includes songbook (deduct 25% if missing)					
MCA					
❏ 1489	Neil Diamond/His 12 Greatest Hits	1987	2.00	4.00	8.00
—Reissue of MCA 5219					
❏ 2005	Moods	1973	2.50	5.00	10.00
❏ 2006	Touching You Touching Me	1973	2.50	5.00	10.00
❏ 2007	Neil Diamond/Gold	1973	2.50	5.00	10.00
❏ 2008	Stones	1973	2.50	5.00	10.00
❏ 2011	Sweet Caroline (Brother Love's Travelling Salvation Show)	1973	2.50	5.00	10.00
❏ 2013	Tap Root Manuscript	1973	2.50	5.00	10.00
❏ 2103	Rainbow	1973	3.75	7.50	15.00
—Compilation of Uni tracks					
❏ 2106	Neil Diamond/His 12 Greatest Hits	1974	3.75	7.50	15.00
❏ 2227	And the Singer Sings His Song	1976	3.75	7.50	15.00
❏ 5219	Neil Diamond/His 12 Greatest Hits	1981	2.50	5.00	10.00
—Reissue of MCA 2106					
❏ 5239	Love Songs	1981	2.50	5.00	10.00
❏ 6896 [(2)]	Hot August Night	1980	3.00	6.00	12.00
—Reissue of MCA 2-8000					
❏ 8000 [(2)]	Hot August Night	1972	5.00	10.00	20.00
❏ 37056	Velvet Gloves and Spit	1980	2.00	4.00	8.00
❏ 37057	Sweet Caroline/Brother Love's Travelling Salvation Show	1980	2.00	4.00	8.00
❏ 37058	Touching You Touching Me	1980	2.00	4.00	8.00
❏ 37059	Rainbow	1980	2.00	4.00	8.00
❏ 37060	And the Singer Sings His Song	1980	2.00	4.00	8.00
❏ 37194	Moods	1981	2.00	4.00	8.00
❏ 37195	Stones	1981	2.00	4.00	8.00
❏ 37196	Tap Root Manuscript	1981	2.00	4.00	8.00
❏ 37209	Gold	1981	2.00	4.00	8.00
❏ 37252	Neil Diamond/His 12 Greatest Hits	198?	2.00	4.00	8.00
—Reissue of MCA 5219					
MOBILE FIDELITY					
❏ 2-024 [(2)]	Hot August Night	1979	10.00	20.00	40.00
—Audiophile vinyl					
❏ 1-071	The Jazz Singer	1981	7.50	15.00	30.00
—Audiophile vinyl					
SILVER EAGLE					
❏ MSM-35151 [(3)]	The Neil Diamond Collection	1988	6.25	12.50	25.00
—Mail-order offer; contains material from his Uni period					
UNI					
❏ ND-11 [DJ]	Neil Diamond DJ Sampler	1970	50.00	100.00	200.00
❏ 1913 [DJ]	Open-End Interview with Neil Diamond	1971	75.00	150.00	300.00
❏ 73030	Velvet Gloves and Spit	1968	7.50	15.00	30.00
—First editions do not include "Shilo"					
❏ 73030	Velvet Gloves and Spit	1970	5.00	10.00	20.00
—Later editions add a new recording of "Shilo"					
❏ 73047	Brother Love's Travelling Salvation Show	1969	5.00	10.00	20.00
—Later editions add "Sweet Caroline"					
❏ 73047	Brother Love's Travelling Salvation Show	1969	7.50	15.00	30.00
—First editions do not include "Sweet Caroline"					
❏ 73071	Touching You Touching Me	1969	5.00	10.00	20.00
❏ 73084	Neil Diamond/Gold	1970	5.00	10.00	20.00
❏ 73092	Tap Root Manuscript	1970	5.00	10.00	20.00
❏ 93106	Stones	1971	5.00	10.00	20.00
❏ 93136	Moods	1972	5.00	10.00	20.00
❏ ST-93501	Tap Root Manuscript	1970	6.25	12.50	25.00
—Capitol Record Club issue					
DIAMONDS, THE (1)					
MERCURY					
❏ MG-20213 [M]	Collection of Golden Hits	1956	30.00	60.00	120.00
❏ MG-20309 [M]	The Diamonds	1957	30.00	60.00	120.00
❏ MG-20368 [M]	The Diamonds Meet Pete Rugolo	1958	20.00	40.00	80.00
❏ MG-20480 [M]	Songs from the Old West	1959	20.00	40.00	80.00
❏ SR-60076 [S]	The Diamonds Meet Pete Rugolo	1959	30.00	60.00	120.00
❏ SR-60159 [S]	Songs from the Old West	1959	30.00	60.00	120.00
RHINO					
❏ RNDF-209	The Best of the Diamonds	1984	3.00	6.00	12.00
WING					
❏ MGW-12114 [M]	The Diamonds: America's Famous Song Stylists	1959	7.50	15.00	30.00
❏ MGW-12178 [M]	Pop Hits by the Diamonds	1962	7.50	15.00	30.00
DIAZ MENA, ANTONIO					
AUDIO FIDELITY					
❏ AFSD-6117 [S]	Eso Es En Latin Jazz Man	1963	5.00	10.00	20.00
DICK AND DEEDEE					
LIBERTY					
❏ LRP-3236 [M]	Tell Me/The Mountain's High	1962	12.50	25.00	50.00
❏ LST-7236 [R]	Tell Me/The Mountain's High	1962	10.00	20.00	40.00
WARNER BROS.					
❏ W 1500 [M]	Young and In Love	1963	6.25	12.50	25.00
❏ WS 1500 [S]	Young and In Love	1963	7.50	15.00	30.00
❏ W 1538 [M]	Turn Around	1964	6.25	12.50	25.00
❏ WS 1538 [S]	Turn Around	1964	7.50	15.00	30.00
❏ W 1586 [M]	Thou Shalt Not Steal	1965	6.25	12.50	25.00
❏ WS 1586 [S]	Thou Shalt Not Steal	1965	7.50	15.00	30.00
❏ W 1623 [M]	Song We've Sung on "Shindig"	1966	6.25	12.50	25.00
❏ WS 1623 [S]	Song We've Sung on "Shindig"	1966	7.50	15.00	30.00

Number	Title (A Side/B Side)	Yr	VG	VG+	NM
DICKENS, JIMMY					
COLUMBIA					
❏ CL 1047 [M]	Raisin' the Dickens	1957	20.00	40.00	80.00
❏ CL 1545 [M]	Big Songs by Little Jimmy Dickens	1960	7.50	15.00	30.00
❏ CL 1887 [M]	Little Jimmy Dickens Sings Out Behind the Barn	1962	7.50	15.00	30.00
❏ CL 2288 [M]	Handle with Care	1964	6.25	12.50	25.00
❏ CL 2442 [M]	May the Bird of Paradise Fly Up Your Nose	1965	6.25	12.50	25.00
❏ CL 2551 [M]	Little Jimmy Dickens' Greatest Hits	1966	6.25	12.50	25.00
❏ CS 8345 [S]	Big Songs by Little Jimmy Dickens	1960	10.00	20.00	40.00
❏ CS 8687 [S]	Little Jimmy Dickens Sings Out Behind the Barn	1962	10.00	20.00	40.00
❏ CL 9053 [10]	The Old Country Church	1954	30.00	60.00	120.00
❏ CS 9088 [S]	Handle with Care	1964	7.50	15.00	30.00
❏ CS 9242 [S]	May the Bird of Paradise Fly Up Your Nose	1965	7.50	15.00	30.00
❏ CS 9351 [S]	Little Jimmy Dickens' Greatest Hits	1966	7.50	15.00	30.00
DECCA					
❏ DL 4967 [M]	Jimmy Dickens Sings	1967	7.50	15.00	30.00
❏ DL 74967 [S]	Jimmy Dickens Sings	1967	5.00	10.00	20.00
❏ DL 75091	Jimmy Dickens Comes Callin'	1968	5.00	10.00	20.00
❏ DL 75133	Jimmy Dickens' Greatest Hits	1969	5.00	10.00	20.00
DICKENSON, VIC					
JAZZTONE					
❏ J-1259 [M]	Slidin' Swing	1956	10.00	20.00	40.00
STORYVILLE					
❏ STLP-920 [M]	Vic's Boston Story	1957	10.00	20.00	40.00
VANGUARD					
❏ VRS-8001 [10]	Vic Dickenson Septet, Volume 1	1953	12.50	25.00	50.00
❏ VRS-8002 [10]	Vic Dickenson Septet, Volume 2	1953	12.50	25.00	50.00
❏ VRS-8012 [10]	Vic Dickenson Septet, Volume 3	1954	12.50	25.00	50.00
❏ VRS-8013 [10]	Vic Dickenson Septet, Volume 4	1954	12.50	25.00	50.00
❏ VRS-8520 [M]	Vic Dickenson Showcase, Volume 1	1958	10.00	20.00	40.00
❏ VRS-8521 [M]	Vic Dickenson Showcase, Volume 2	1958	10.00	20.00	40.00
DICKENSON, VIC, AND JOE THOMAS					
ATLANTIC					
❏ 1303 [M]	Mainstream	1958	12.50	25.00	50.00
—Black label					
❏ 1303 [M]	Mainstream	1961	5.00	10.00	20.00
—Multicolor label, white "fan" logo					
❏ SD 1303 [S]	Mainstream	1958	10.00	20.00	40.00
—Green label					
❏ SD 1303 [S]	Mainstream	1961	5.00	10.00	20.00
—Multicolor label, white "fan" logo					
DICKERSON, WALT					
AUDIO FIDELITY					
❏ AFLP-2131 [M]	Unity	1963	5.00	10.00	20.00
❏ AFLP-2217 [M]	Vibes in Motion	1968	6.25	12.50	25.00
—Reissue of Dauntless 4313					
❏ AFSD-6131 [S]	Unity	1963	6.25	12.50	25.00
DAUNTLESS					
❏ DM-4313 [M]	Jazz Impressions of "Lawrence of Arabia"	1963	6.25	12.50	25.00
❏ DS-6313 [S]	Jazz Impressions of "Lawrence of Arabia"	1963	7.50	15.00	30.00
MGM					
❏ E-4358 [M]	Impressions of "A Patch of Blue"	1965	5.00	10.00	20.00
❏ SE-4358 [S]	Impressions of "A Patch of Blue"	1965	6.25	12.50	25.00
NEW JAZZ					
❏ NJLP-8254 [M]	This Is Walt Dickerson	1961	12.50	25.00	50.00
—Purple label					
❏ NJLP-8254 [M]	This Is Walt Dickerson	1965	6.25	12.50	25.00
—Blue label, trident logo at right					
❏ NJLP-8268 [M]	A Sense of Direction	1962	12.50	25.00	50.00
—Purple label					
❏ NJLP-8268 [M]	A Sense of Direction	1965	6.25	12.50	25.00
—Blue label, trident logo at right					
❏ NJLP-8275 [M]	Relativity	1962	12.50	25.00	50.00
—Purple label					
❏ NJLP-8275 [M]	Relativity	1965	6.25	12.50	25.00
—Blue label, trident logo at right					
❏ NJLP-8283 [M]	To My Queen	1962	12.50	25.00	50.00
—Purple label					
❏ NJLP-8283 [M]	To My Queen	1965	6.25	12.50	25.00
—Blue label, trident logo at right					
STEEPLECHASE					
❏ SCD-17002	Shades of Love	198?	6.25	12.50	25.00
—Direct-to-disc recording					
DICKIES, THE					
A&M					
❏ SP-4742	The Incredible Shrinking Dickies	1979	3.75	7.50	15.00
❏ SP-4742	The Incredible Shrinking Dickies	1979	5.00	10.00	20.00
—First pressing on yellow vinyl					
❏ SP-4796	Dawn of the Dickies	1979	3.75	7.50	15.00
ENIGMA					
❏ D1-73289	Second Coming	1989	2.00	4.00	8.00
❏ D1-73322 [EP]	Killer Klowns (From Outer Space)	1988	2.00	4.00	8.00
PVC					
❏ 6903	Stukas Over Disneyland	1983	3.00	6.00	12.00
TAANG!					
❏ 56	Locked and Loaded	1991	3.00	6.00	12.00
TRIPLE X					
❏ 51168	Idjit Savant	1994	2.50	5.00	10.00
DICKS, THE					
ALTERNATIVE TENTACLES					
❏ VIRUS 43	These People	1985	3.75	7.50	15.00

Number	Title (A Side/B Side)	Yr	VG	VG+	NM
RADICAL					
❏ RRR 80351	Recorded Live at Raul's	1980	15.00	30.00	60.00
—One side features the Big Boys; the other side, the Dicks					
SST					
❏ 017	Kill from the Heart	1983	6.25	12.50	25.00

DICKY DOO AND THE DON'TS
UNITED ARTISTS

Number	Title (A Side/B Side)	Yr	VG	VG+	NM
❏ UAL-3094 [M]	The Madison and Other Dances	1959	10.00	20.00	40.00
❏ UAL-3097 [M]	Teen Scene	1959	10.00	20.00	40.00
❏ UAS-6094 [S]	The Madison and Other Dances	1959	12.50	25.00	50.00
❏ UAS-6097 [S]	Teen Scene	1959	12.50	25.00	50.00

DIDDLEY, BO
ACCORD

Number	Title (A Side/B Side)	Yr	VG	VG+	NM
❏ SN-7182	Toronto Rock and Roll Revival, Vol. 5	1982	5.00	10.00	20.00
CHECKER					
❏ LP 1431 [M]	Bo Diddley	1958	37.50	75.00	150.00
❏ LP 1436 [M]	Go Bo Diddley	1959	37.50	75.00	150.00
❏ LP 2974 [M]	Have Guitar, Will Travel	1960	37.50	75.00	150.00
❏ LP 2976 [M]	Spotlight on Bo Diddley	1960	37.50	75.00	150.00
❏ LP 2977 [M]	Bo Diddley Is a Gunslinger	1961	37.50	75.00	150.00
❏ LP 2980 [M]	Bo Diddley Is a Lover	1961	37.50	75.00	150.00
❏ LP 2982 [M]	Bo Diddley's a Twister	1962	25.00	50.00	100.00
❏ LP 2982 [M]	Road Runner	1967	20.00	40.00	80.00
—Reissue of "Bo Diddley's a Twister"					
❏ LP 2984 [M]	Bo Diddley	1962	25.00	50.00	100.00
❏ LP 2985 [M]	Bo Diddley and Company	1963	40.00	80.00	120.00
❏ LP 2987 [M]	Surfin' with Bo Diddley	1964	40.00	80.00	120.00
❏ LPS 2987 [R]	Surfin' with Bo Diddley	1964	7.50	15.00	30.00
❏ LP 2988 [M]	Bo Diddley's Beach Party	1963	25.00	50.00	100.00
❏ LP 2989 [M]	16 All Time Greatest Hits	1964	12.50	25.00	50.00
❏ LPS 2989 [R]	16 All Time Greatest Hits	1964	7.50	15.00	30.00
❏ LP 2992 [M]	Hey! Good Lookin'	1965	15.00	30.00	60.00
❏ LPS 2992 [R]	Hey! Good Lookin'	1965	7.50	15.00	30.00
❏ LP 2996 [M]	500% More Man	1965	15.00	30.00	60.00
❏ LPS 2996 [R]	500% More Man	1965	7.50	15.00	30.00
❏ LP 3001 [M]	The Originator	1966	7.50	15.00	30.00
❏ LPS 3001 [S]	The Originator	1966	10.00	20.00	40.00
❏ LP 3006 [M]	Go Bo Diddley	1967	12.50	25.00	50.00
—Reissue of 1436					
❏ LPS 3006 [R]	Go Bo Diddley	1967	10.00	20.00	40.00
❏ LP 3007 [M]	Boss Man	1967	20.00	40.00	80.00
—Reissue of Chess 1431					
❏ LPS 3007 [R]	Boss Man	1967	12.50	25.00	50.00
❏ LPS 3013	The Black Gladiator	1968	7.50	15.00	30.00
CHESS					
❏ LP 1431 [M]	Bo Diddley	1958	50.00	100.00	200.00
❏ CH-9106	His Greatest Sides, Vol. 1	1984	2.50	5.00	10.00
❏ CH-9187	Have Guitar, Will Travel	1985	2.50	5.00	10.00
—Reissue of Checker 2974					
❏ CH-9194	Bo Diddley	1986	2.50	5.00	10.00
—Reissue of 1431					
❏ CH-9196	Go Bo Diddley	1986	2.50	5.00	10.00
—Reissue of Checker 1436					
❏ CH-9264	Spotlight on Bo Diddley	1987	2.50	5.00	10.00
—Reissue of Checker 2976					
❏ CH-9285	Bo Diddley Is a Gunslinger	1989	2.50	5.00	10.00
—Reissue of Checker 2977					
❏ CH-9296	The London Bo Diddley Sessions	1989	2.50	5.00	10.00
—Reissue of 50029					
❏ CH3-19502 [(3)]	The Chess Box	1990	10.00	20.00	40.00
❏ CH 50001	Another Dimension	1971	10.00	20.00	40.00
❏ CH 50016	Where It All Began	1972	10.00	20.00	40.00
❏ CH 50029	The London Bo Diddley Sessions	1973	6.25	12.50	25.00
❏ CH 50047	Big Bad Bo	1974	6.25	12.50	25.00
❏ 2CH 60005 [(2)]	Got My Own Bag of Tricks	1972	6.25	12.50	25.00
RCA VICTOR					
❏ APL1-1229	The 20th Anniversary of Rock and Roll	1976	5.00	10.00	20.00

DIDDLEY, BO/CHUCK BERRY
Also see each artist's individual listings.
CHECKER

Number	Title (A Side/B Side)	Yr	VG	VG+	NM
❏ LP 2991 [M]	Two Great Guitars	1964	15.00	30.00	60.00
❏ LPS 2991 [R]	Two Great Guitars	1964	10.00	20.00	40.00
CHESS					
❏ CH-9170	Two Great Guitars	1985	2.50	5.00	10.00
—Reissue of Checker 2991					

DIDDLEY, BO/MUDDY WATERS/HOWLIN' WOLF
Also see each artist's individual listings.
CHECKER

Number	Title (A Side/B Side)	Yr	VG	VG+	NM
❏ LP 3010 [M]	Super, Super Blues Band	1968	12.50	25.00	50.00
❏ LPS 3010 [S]	Super, Super Blues Band	1968	10.00	20.00	40.00
CHESS					
❏ CH-9169	Super, Super Blues Band	1985	2.50	5.00	10.00
—Reissue of Checker 3010					

DIDDLEY, BO/MUDDY WATERS/LITTLE WALTER
Also see each artist's individual listings.
CHECKER

Number	Title (A Side/B Side)	Yr	VG	VG+	NM
❏ LP 3008 [M]	Super Blues Band	1968	12.50	25.00	50.00
❏ LPS 3008 [S]	Super Blues Band	1968	10.00	20.00	40.00
CHESS					
❏ CH-9168	Super Blues Band	1985	2.50	5.00	10.00
—Reissue of Checker 3008					

DIETRICH, MARLENE
CAPITOL

Number	Title (A Side/B Side)	Yr	VG	VG+	NM
❏ STCR-300 [(3)]	The Magic of Marlene	1969	10.00	20.00	40.00
—All three of her Capitol LPs in one box					
❏ ST 10282 [S]	Wiedersehn Mit Marlene	1961	6.25	12.50	25.00
❏ T 10282 [M]	Wiedersehn Mit Marlene	1961	5.00	10.00	20.00
❏ ST 10397 [S]	Marlene (Songs in German by the Inimitable Dietrich)	1965	6.25	12.50	25.00
❏ T 10397 [M]	Marlene (Songs in German by the Inimitable Dietrich)	1965	5.00	10.00	20.00
❏ ST 10443 [S]	Marlene Dietrich's Berlin	1966	6.25	12.50	25.00
❏ T 10443 [M]	Marlene Dietrich's Berlin	1966	5.00	10.00	20.00
COLUMBIA					
❏ CL 105 [10]	Overseas — Songs for the O.S.S.	1953	25.00	50.00	100.00
❏ CL 1275 [M]	Lili Marlene	1959	12.50	25.00	50.00
❏ C 32245	The Best of Marlene Dietrich	1973	3.00	6.00	12.00
COLUMBIA MASTERWORKS					
❏ WL 164 [M]	Dietrich in Rio	195?	10.00	20.00	40.00
❏ WS 316 [S]	Dietrich in Rio	195?	12.50	25.00	50.00
❏ OS 2830 [S]	Dietrich in London	1966	7.50	15.00	30.00
❏ ML 4975 [M]	At the Café de Paris	1955	12.50	25.00	50.00
❏ OL 6430 [M]	Dietrich in London	1966	6.25	12.50	25.00
DECCA					
❏ DL 5100 [10]	Souvenir Album	1950	20.00	40.00	80.00
❏ DL 8465 [M]	Marlene Dietrich	1957	10.00	20.00	40.00
—Black label, silver print					
❏ DL 8465 [M]	Marlene Dietrich	196?	6.25	12.50	25.00
—Black label with color bars					
❏ DL 78465 [R]	Marlene Dietrich	196?	5.00	10.00	20.00
MURRAY HILL/CSP					
❏ P3 14689 [(3)]	The Legendary Marlene Dietrich	1978	7.50	15.00	30.00
VOX					
❏ VS-3040 [10]	Marlene Dietrich Sings	1950	20.00	40.00	80.00

DIGA RHYTHM BAND, THE
Also see THE GRATEFUL DEAD.
ROUND

Number	Title (A Side/B Side)	Yr	VG	VG+	NM
❏ RX-110	The Diga Rhythm Band	1976	6.25	12.50	25.00

DILL, DANNY
LIBERTY

Number	Title (A Side/B Side)	Yr	VG	VG+	NM
❏ LRP-3301 [M]	Folk Songs from the Country	1963	5.00	10.00	20.00
❏ LST-7301 [S]	Folk Songs from the Country	1963	6.25	12.50	25.00
MGM					
❏ E-3819 [M]	Folk Songs from the Wild West	1960	5.00	10.00	20.00
❏ SE-3819 [S]	Folk Songs from the Wild West	1960	6.25	12.50	25.00

DILLARD, DOUG
TOGETHER

Number	Title (A Side/B Side)	Yr	VG	VG+	NM
❏ STT-1003	The Banjo Album	1970	20.00	40.00	80.00

DILLARD AND CLARK
A&M

Number	Title (A Side/B Side)	Yr	VG	VG+	NM
❏ SP-4158	The Fantastic Expedition of Dillard and Clark	1968	5.00	10.00	20.00
—Brown label					

DILLARDS, THE
ANTHEM

Number	Title (A Side/B Side)	Yr	VG	VG+	NM
❏ ANS-5901	Roots and Branches	1972	3.75	7.50	15.00
CRYSTAL CLEAR					
❏ CCS-5007	Mountain Rock	1979	6.25	12.50	25.00
—Direct-to-disc recording					
ELEKTRA					
❏ EKL-232 [M]	Back Porch Bluegrass	1963	6.25	12.50	25.00
❏ EKL-265 [M]	The Dillards, Live!!! Almost!!!	1964	5.00	10.00	20.00
❏ EKL-285 [M]	Pickin' and Fiddlin'	1965	5.00	10.00	20.00
❏ EKS-7232 [S]	Back Porch Bluegrass	1963	7.50	5.00	30.00
—Mandolin-player label					
❏ EKS-7265 [S]	The Dillards, Live!!! Almost!!!	1964	6.25	12.50	25.00
—Mandolin-player label					
❏ EKS-7285 [S]	Pickin' and Fiddlin'	1965	6.25	12.50	25.00
—Mandolin-player label					
❏ EKS-74035	Wheatstraw Suite	1968	5.00	10.00	20.00
—Tan label with large stylized "E" on top					
❏ EKS-74035	Wheatstraw Suite	1969	3.75	7.50	15.00
—Red label with large stylized "E" on top					
❏ EKS-74054	Copperfields	1969	5.00	10.00	20.00
—Red label with large stylized "E" on top					
FLYING FISH					
❏ FF 040	The Dillards Vs. the Incredible L.A. Time Machine	1977	3.00	6.00	12.00
❏ FF 082	Decade Waltz	1979	3.00	6.00	12.00
❏ FF 215	Homecoming and Family Reunion	1979	3.00	6.00	12.00
POPPY					
❏ PP-LA175-F	Tribute to the American Duck	1973	3.75	7.50	15.00

DILLER, PHYLLIS
COLUMBIA

Number	Title (A Side/B Side)	Yr	VG	VG+	NM
❏ CS 9623	Born to Sing	1969	5.00	10.00	20.00

DIMENSIONS, THE
SAHARA

Number	Title (A Side/B Side)	Yr	VG	VG+	NM
❏ (# unknown)	From All Dimensions	1966	200.00	400.00	800.00

DIMEOLA, AL
COLUMBIA

Number	Title (A Side/B Side)	Yr	VG	VG+	NM
❏ HC 44461	Elegant Gypsy	198?	10.00	20.00	40.00
—Half-speed mastered edition					
❏ HC 46454	Electric Rendezvous	198?	12.50	25.00	50.00
—Half-speed mastered edition					
❏ HC 47152	Friday Night in San Francisco	198?	12.50	25.00	50.00
—Half-speed mastered edition					

DINNING, MARK
MGM

Number	Title (A Side/B Side)	Yr	VG	VG+	NM
❏ E-3828 [M]	Teen Angel	1960	20.00	40.00	80.00

Number	Title (A Side/B Side)	Yr	VG	VG+	NM
❏ SE-3828 [S]	Teen Angel	1960	37.50	75.00	150.00
❏ E-3855 [M]	Wanderin'	1960	20.00	40.00	80.00
❏ SE-3855 [S]	Wanderin'	1960	30.00	60.00	120.00

DINNING SISTERS, THE
CAPITOL
❏ H 318 [10]	The Dinning Sisters	195?	12.50	25.00	50.00

DINO, DESI AND BILLY
REPRISE
❏ R 6176 [M]	I'm a Fool	1965	5.00	10.00	20.00
❏ RS 6176 [S]	I'm a Fool	1965	6.25	12.50	25.00
❏ R 6194 [M]	Our Time's Coming	1966	5.00	10.00	20.00
❏ RS 6194 [S]	Our Time's Coming	1966	6.25	12.50	25.00
❏ R 6198 [M]	Memories Are Made of This	1966	5.00	10.00	20.00
❏ RS 6198 [S]	Memories Are Made of This	1966	6.25	12.50	25.00
❏ R 6224 [M]	Souvenir	1966	5.00	10.00	20.00
❏ R/RS 6224	Souvenir Bonus Photo Sheet	1966	—	2.50	5.00
❏ RS 6224 [S]	Souvenir	1966	6.25	12.50	25.00

DINOSAUR JR
HOMESTEAD
❏ 015-2	Dinosaur	1985	5.00	10.00	20.00

—Released under the name "Dinosaur"
SIRE
❏ 45108	Where You Been	1993	3.75	7.50	15.00
❏ 45719	Without a Sound	1994	2.50	5.00	10.00
SST
❏ 130	You're Living All Over Me	1987	2.50	5.00	10.00

—As "Dinosaur Jr"; black vinyl
❏ 130	You're Living All Over Me	1987	3.75	7.50	15.00

—As "Dinosaur Jr"; purple swirl vinyl
❏ 130	You're Living All Over Me	1987	5.00	10.00	20.00

—First released under the name "Dinosaur"
❏ 152 [EP]	Dinosaur Jr	1987	3.00	6.00	12.00

—Originals on purple swirl vinyl
❏ 216	Bug	1988	2.50	5.00	10.00
❏ 244 [EP]	Just Like Heaven	1989	2.00	4.00	8.00
❏ 275 [EP]	Fossils	1991	2.00	4.00	8.00
❏ 910 [10]	Dinosaur Jr	1987	—	3.00	6.00
❏ 914 [10]	Just Like Heaven	1989	—	3.00	6.00
❏ 925 [10]	Fossils	1991	—	3.00	6.00

DIO, RONNIE
JOVE
❏ J-108	Dio at Domino's	1963	50.00	100.00	200.00

DION
ARISTA
❏ AL 8549	Yo Frankie	1989	2.50	5.00	10.00
COLLECTABLES
❏ 5027	Runaround Sue	198?	2.50	5.00	10.00
COLUMBIA
❏ CL 2010 [M]	Ruby Baby	1963	7.50	15.00	30.00
❏ CL 2107 [M]	Donna the Prima Donna	1963	7.50	15.00	30.00
❏ CS 8810 [S]	Ruby Baby	1963	10.00	20.00	40.00
❏ CS 8907 [S]	Donna the Prima Donna	1963	10.00	20.00	40.00
❏ CS 9773	Wonder Where I'm Bound	1969	5.00	10.00	20.00
❏ KC 31942	Dion's Greatest Hits	1973	5.00	10.00	20.00
❏ PC 31942	Dion's Greatest Hits	198?	2.00	4.00	8.00

—Budget-line reissue
DAYSPRING
❏ DST-4022	Inside Job	1980	3.00	6.00	12.00
❏ DST-4027	Only Jesus	198?	3.00	6.00	12.00
❏ WR-8111	I Put Away My Idols	198?	3.00	6.00	12.00
❏ WR-8112	Seasons (The Best of Dion)	198?	3.00	6.00	12.00
LAURIE
❏ LLP 2004 [M]	Alone with Dion	1960	50.00	100.00	200.00

—With three wallet-size photos on inside strip (deduct 50% if missing)
❏ LLP 2009 [M]	Runaround Sue	1961	25.00	50.00	100.00

—Black vinyl
❏ LLP 2009 [M]	Runaround Sue	1961	200.00	400.00	800.00

—Colored vinyl (gold, green or blue)
❏ LLP 2009 [M]	Runaround Sue	1962	20.00	40.00	80.00

—Black vinyl; with sticker on front cover: "Includes the Hit Singles 'The Majestic'/'The Wanderer'"
❏ LLP 2012 [M]	Lovers Who Wander	1962	17.50	35.00	70.00
❏ LLP 2013 [M]	Dion Sings His Greatest Hits	1962	17.50	35.00	70.00
❏ SLP 2013 [R]	Dion Sings His Greatest Hits	196?	12.50	25.00	50.00
❏ LLP 2015 [M]	Love Came to Me	1963	17.50	35.00	70.00
❏ LLP 2017 [M]	Dion Sings to Sandy (And All His Other Girls)	1963	12.50	25.00	50.00
❏ LLP 2019 [M]	Dion Sings the 15 Million Sellers	1963	12.50	25.00	50.00
❏ SLP 2019 [R]	Dion Sings the 15 Million Sellers	196?	7.50	15.00	30.00
❏ LLP 2022 [M]	More of Dion's Greatest Hits	1964	12.50	25.00	50.00
❏ SLP 2022 [R]	More of Dion's Greatest Hits	196?	7.50	15.00	30.00
❏ SLP 2047	Dion	1968	5.00	10.00	20.00
❏ DT-90386 [R]	Dion Sings His Greatest Hits	1965	30.00	60.00	120.00

—Capitol Record Club edition
❏ T-90386 [M]	Dion Sings His Greatest Hits	1965	30.00	60.00	120.00

—Capitol Record Club edition
❏ DT-91027 [R]	Runaround Sue	196?	30.00	60.00	120.00

—Capitol Record Club edition
❏ T-91027 [M]	Runaround Sue	196?	30.00	60.00	120.00

—Capitol Record Club edition
❏ DT-91128 [R]	More of Dion's Greatest Hits	196?	30.00	60.00	120.00

—Capitol Record Club edition
❏ T-91128 [M]	More of Dion's Greatest Hits	196?	30.00	60.00	120.00

—Capitol Record Club edition
❏ ST-91577	Dion	1968	6.25	12.50	25.00

—Capitol Record Club edition
LIFESONG
❏ JZ 35356	Return of the Wanderer	1978	3.00	6.00	12.00

WARNER BROS.
Number	Title (A Side/B Side)	Yr	VG	VG+	NM
❏ WS 1826	Sit Down, Old Friend	1969	5.00	10.00	20.00
❏ WS 1872	You're Not Alone	1971	3.75	7.50	15.00
❏ WS 1945	Sanctuary	1971	3.75	7.50	15.00
❏ BS 2642	Suite for Late Summer	1972	3.75	7.50	15.00
❏ BS 2954	Streetheart	1976	3.75	7.50	15.00
WORD
❏ WR-8285	Kingdom in the Streets	1985	3.00	6.00	12.00

DION AND THE BELMONTS
ABC
❏ 599 [M]	Together Again	1967	7.50	15.00	30.00
❏ S-599 [S]	Together Again	1967	10.00	20.00	40.00
ARISTA
❏ A2L 8206 [(2)]	24 Original Classics	1984	3.00	6.00	12.00
COLLECTABLES
❏ 5025	Presenting Dion & The Belmonts	198?	2.50	5.00	10.00
❏ 5026	Wish Upon a Star	198?	2.50	5.00	10.00
❏ 5041	20 Golden Classics	198?	2.50	5.00	10.00
LAURIE
❏ LLP 1002 [M]	Presenting Dion & The Belmonts	1959	62.50	125.00	250.00
❏ LLP 2002 [M]	Presenting Dion & The Belmonts	1960	37.50	75.00	150.00
❏ SLP 2002 [R]	Presenting Dion & The Belmonts	196?	300.00	600.00	900.00

—Despite its rechanneled stereo sound, this record is collectible because of its utter rarity
❏ LLP 2006 [M]	Wish Upon a Star	1960	37.50	75.00	150.00
❏ LLP 2016 [M]	"Together" On Records — By Special Request	1963	12.50	25.00	50.00
❏ LES 4002	Everything You Always Wanted to Hear by Dion and the Belmonts	197?	3.75	7.50	15.00
❏ SLP 6000 [(3)]	60 Greatest Hits	197?	5.00	10.00	20.00

—In regular cover
❏ SLP 6000 [(3)]	60 Greatest Hits	197?	7.50	15.00	30.00

—In box
PAIR
❏ PDL2-1142 [(2)]	The Best of Dion and the Belmonts	1986	3.00	6.00	12.00
PICKWICK
❏ SPC-3521	Doo Wop	1975	2.50	5.00	10.00

—Reissue of ABC tracks
RHINO
❏ RNLP 70228	Reunion — Live at Madison Square Garden — 1972	1987	2.50	5.00	10.00

—Reissue of ABC tracks
WARNER BROS.
❏ BS 2664	Reunion — Live at Madison Square Garden — 1972	1973	3.75	7.50	15.00

DIRE STRAITS
WARNER BROS.
❏ WBMS-109 [DJ]	Dire Straits Live	1980	12.50	25.00	50.00

—"The Warner Bros. Music Show" promo
❏ BSK 3266	Dire Straits	1979	2.50	5.00	10.00
❏ HS 3330	Communique	1979	2.50	5.00	10.00
❏ BSK 3480	Making Movies	1980	2.50	5.00	10.00
❏ 23728	Love Over Gold	1982	2.50	5.00	10.00
❏ 23728 [DJ]	Love Over Gold	1982	12.50	25.00	50.00

—Promo on Quiex II vinyl; the times of the songs also are listed differently than on stock copies
❏ 25085 [(2)]	Dire Straits Live — Alchemy	1984	3.00	6.00	12.00
❏ 25085 [(2)]	Dire Straits Live — Alchemy	1984	12.50	25.00	50.00

—Promo on Quiex II vinyl
❏ 25264	Brothers in Arms	1985	2.50	5.00	10.00
❏ 25264 [DJ]	Brothers in Arms	1985	12.50	25.00	50.00

—Promo on Quiex II vinyl
❏ 25794	Money for Nothing	1989	3.00	6.00	12.00
❏ 26680	On Every Street	1991	3.75	7.50	15.00
❏ 29800 [EP]	Twisting by the Pool	1983	—	3.00	6.00

DIRECT FLIGHT
DIRECT DISC
❏ DD-104	Spectrum	1980	6.25	12.50	25.00

—Direct-to-disc recording

DIRKSEN, SENATOR EVERETT MCKINLEY
CAPITOL
❏ ST 2643 [S]	Gallant Men	1966	3.75	7.50	15.00
❏ T 2643 [M]	Gallant Men	1966	3.75	7.50	15.00
❏ ST 2754 [S]	Man Is Not Alone	1967	3.75	7.50	15.00
❏ T 2754 [M]	Man Is Not Alone	1967	5.00	10.00	20.00
❏ ST 2792 [S]	Everett McKinley Dirksen at Christmas Time	1967	5.00	10.00	20.00
❏ T 2792 [M]	Everett McKinley Dirksen at Christmas Time	1967	7.50	15.00	30.00

DIRT BAND, THE
See NITTY GRITTY DIRT BAND.

DIRTY BLUES BAND, THE
BLUESWAY
❏ BLS-6010	The Dirty Blues Band	1968	5.00	10.00	20.00
❏ BLS-6020	Stone Dirt	1968	5.00	10.00	20.00

DIVINYLS
CHRYSALIS
❏ F1-21627	Temperamental	1989	3.00	6.00	12.00
❏ BVW 41404	Desparate	1983	3.00	6.00	12.00
❏ BFV 41511	What a Life!	1985	3.00	6.00	12.00
❏ BFV 41627	Temperamental	1989	5.00	10.00	20.00

—Reissued as 21627

DIXIE CUPS, THE
ABC-PARAMOUNT
❏ 525 [M]	Riding High	1965	15.00	30.00	60.00
❏ S-525 [S]	Riding High	1965	20.00	40.00	80.00
RED BIRD
❏ RB 20-100 [M]	Chapel of Love	1964	15.00	30.00	60.00
❏ RBS 20-100 [S]	Chapel of Love	1964	20.00	40.00	80.00

Number	Title (A Side/B Side)	Yr	VG	VG+	NM
❑ RB 20-103 [M]	Iko Iko	1965	37.50	75.00	150.00

DIXIE DREGS, THE
DIRECT DISK
| ❑ SD-16620 | Dregs of the Earth | 1980 | 10.00 | 20.00 | 40.00 |
| —Audiophile vinyl | | | | | |

DIXIE SMALL FRY, THE
LIBERTY
| ❑ LRP-3057 [M] | The Dixie Small Fry in Hi-Fi | 1957 | 10.00 | 20.00 | 40.00 |
| ❑ LST-7010 [S] | The Dixie Small Fry in Hi-Fi | 1958 | 10.00 | 20.00 | 40.00 |

DIXIE STOMPERS, THE
DELMAR
❑ DL-112 [10]	The Dixie Stompers Play New Orleans Jazz	195?	20.00	40.00	80.00
❑ DL-113 [10]	Wake the Levee	195?	20.00	40.00	80.00
❑ DL-204 [M]	Jazz at Westminster College	195?	15.00	30.00	60.00
—Blue vinyl; label says "DL-201" though cover says "204"					
RCA VICTOR
❑ LPM-1212 [M]	New York Land Dixie	1956	20.00	40.00	80.00

DIXIEBELLES, THE
SOUND STAGE 7
| ❑ SSM-5000 [M] | Down at Papa Joe's | 1963 | 10.00 | 20.00 | 40.00 |
| ❑ SSS-15000 [R] | Down at Papa Joe's | 1963 | 7.50 | 15.00 | 30.00 |

DIXIELAND RHYTHM KINGS, THE
EMPIRICAL
| ❑ LP-102 [10] | The Dixieland Rhythm Kings | 1954 | 20.00 | 40.00 | 80.00 |
RIVERSIDE
❑ RLP 12-210 [M]	Dixieland in Hi-Fi	1956	15.00	30.00	60.00
—White label, blue print					
❑ RLP 12-210 [M]	Dixieland in Hi-Fi	1957	12.50	25.00	50.00
—Blue label, microphone logo					
❑ RLP 12-259 [M]	The Dixieland Rhythm Kings at the Hi-Fi Jazz Band Ball	1958	10.00	20.00	40.00
❑ RLP 12-289 [M]	Jazz in Retrospect	1959	10.00	20.00	40.00
❑ RLP-2505 [10]	New Orleans Jazz Party	1954	20.00	40.00	80.00

DIXON, BILL
CADENCE JAZZ
| ❑ CJ-1024/25 [(2)] | Collection | 1985 | 5.00 | 10.00 | 20.00 |
RCA VICTOR
| ❑ LPM-3844 [M] | Intents and Purposes | 1967 | 7.50 | 15.00 | 30.00 |
| ❑ LSP-3844 [S] | Intents and Purposes | 1967 | 5.00 | 10.00 | 20.00 |
SAVOY
| ❑ MG-12184 | The Bill Dixon 7-Tette | 1964 | 5.00 | 10.00 | 20.00 |

DIXON, WILLIE
BLUESVILLE
❑ BVLP-1003 [M]	Willie's Blues	1960	37.50	75.00	150.00
—Blue and silver label					
❑ BVLP-1003 [M]	Willie's Blues	1964	10.00	20.00	40.00
—Blue label, trident logo at right					
CHESS
❑ CH3-16500 [(3)]	The Chess Box: Willie Dixon	1988	7.50	15.00	30.00
COLUMBIA
❑ CS 9987	I Am the Blues	1970	6.25	12.50	25.00
—Red label, "360 Sound"					

DIXON, WILLIE, AND MEMPHIS SLIM
BATTLE
| ❑ BV-6122 [M] | In Paris | 1963 | 7.50 | 15.00 | 30.00 |
| ❑ BVS-6122 [S] | In Paris | 1963 | 10.00 | 20.00 | 40.00 |
VERVE
| ❑ MGV-3007 [M] | Blues Every Which Way | 1961 | 30.00 | 60.00 | 120.00 |

DOBKINS, CARL, JR.
DECCA
| ❑ DL 8938 [M] | Carl Dobkins, Jr. | 1959 | 25.00 | 50.00 | 100.00 |
| ❑ DL 78938 [S] | Carl Dobkins, Jr. | 1959 | 37.50 | 75.00 | 150.00 |

DOC HOLLIDAY
METROMEDIA
| ❑ 1017 | Doc Holliday | 1973 | 5.00 | 10.00 | 20.00 |

DR. FEELGOOD AND THE INTERNS
OKEH
| ❑ OKM 12101 [M] | Dr. Feelgood and the Interns | 1962 | 25.00 | 50.00 | 100.00 |
| ❑ OKS 14101 [S] | Dr. Feelgood and the Interns | 1962 | 50.00 | 100.00 | 200.00 |

DR. JOHN
ACCORD
| ❑ SN-7118 | Love Potion | 1982 | 2.50 | 5.00 | 10.00 |
ALLIGATOR
❑ AL-3901	Dr. John's Gumbo	1986	2.50	5.00	10.00
—Reissue of Atco 7006					
❑ AL-3904	Gris-Gris	1987	2.50	5.00	10.00
—Reissue of Atco 33-234					
ATCO
❑ SD 33-234	Gris-Gris	1968	3.75	7.50	15.00
—Yellow label					
❑ SD 33-234	Gris-Gris	1968	7.50	15.00	30.00
—Purple and brown label					
❑ SD 33-270	Babylon	1969	3.75	7.50	15.00
❑ SD 33-316	Remedies	1970	3.75	7.50	15.00
❑ SD 33-362	Dr. John, The Night Tripper (The Sun, Moon & Herbs)	1971	3.75	7.50	15.00
❑ SD 7006	Dr. John's Gumbo	1972	3.00	6.00	12.00
❑ SD 7018	In the Right Place	1973	3.00	6.00	12.00
❑ SD 7043	Desitively Bonaroo	1974	3.00	6.00	12.00
CLEAN CUTS
❑ 705	Dr. John Plays Mac Rebennack	1982	2.50	5.00	10.00

Number	Title (A Side/B Side)	Yr	VG	VG+	NM
❑ 707	The Brightest Smile in Town	1984	2.50	5.00	10.00

HORIZON
| ❑ SP-732 | City Lights | 1978 | 2.50 | 5.00 | 10.00 |
| ❑ SP-740 | Tango Palace | 1979 | 2.50 | 5.00 | 10.00 |
KARATE
| ❑ 5404 | One Night Late | 1978 | 2.50 | 5.00 | 10.00 |
TRIP
| ❑ TLX-350 [(2)] | Superpak | 1975 | 3.00 | 6.00 | 12.00 |
UNITED ARTISTS
| ❑ UA-LA552-G | Hollywood Be Thy Name | 1975 | 3.00 | 6.00 | 12.00 |
WARNER BROS.
| ❑ 25889 | In a Sentimental Mood | 1989 | 3.00 | 6.00 | 12.00 |

DOCTOR ROSS
FORTUNE
| ❑ F-3011 [M] | Doctor Ross, The Harmonica Boss | 1962 | 12.50 | 25.00 | 50.00 |
| ❑ FS-3011 [S] | Doctor Ross, The Harmonica Boss | 1962 | 25.00 | 50.00 | 100.00 |
TESTAMENT
| ❑ 2206 [M] | Doctor Ross | 196? | 5.00 | 10.00 | 20.00 |

DR. WEST'S MEDICINE SHOW AND JUG BAND
Also see NORMAN GREENBAUM.
GO GO
| ❑ 22-17-002 | The Eggplant That Ate Chicago | 1967 | 6.25 | 12.50 | 25.00 |
GREGAR
| ❑ GG-101 | Norman Greenbaum with Dr. West's Medicine Show and Jug Band | 1970 | 5.00 | 10.00 | 20.00 |

DODD, DICK
TOWER
| ❑ ST 5142 | The First Evolution of Dick Dodd | 1968 | 12.50 | 25.00 | 50.00 |

DODD, JIMMIE
DISNEYLAND
❑ WDL-1014 [M]	Jimmie Dodd Sings His Favorite Hymns	1959	6.25	12.50	25.00
—Reissue of 3014 with new number					
❑ DQ-1235 [M]	Sing Along with Jimmie Dodd	1963	7.50	15.00	30.00
❑ DQ-1302 [M]	Favorite Hymns for Family Singing	1967	3.75	7.50	15.00
—Reissue of 1014					
❑ WDL-3014 [M]	Jimmie Dodd Sings His Favorite Hymns	1958	6.25	12.50	25.00
IMPERIAL
❑ LP-9089 [M]	Lonely Guitar	1959	10.00	20.00	40.00
❑ LP-9121 [M]	Swing-A-Spell	1960	10.00	20.00	40.00
❑ LP-12058 [S]	Swing-A-Spell	1960	12.50	25.00	50.00

DODD, KEN
LIBERTY
| ❑ LRP-3442 [M] | Tears and The River | 1966 | 3.75 | 7.50 | 15.00 |
| ❑ LST-7442 [S] | Tears and The River | 1966 | 5.00 | 10.00 | 20.00 |

DODDS, BABY
AMERICAN MUSIC
❑ 1 [M]	Baby Dodds No. 1	1951	12.50	25.00	50.00
❑ 2 [M]	Baby Dodds No. 2	1951	12.50	25.00	50.00
❑ 3 [M]	Baby Dodds No. 3	1951	12.50	25.00	50.00
FOLKWAYS
❑ FP-30 [10]	Footnotes to Jazz, Vol. 1 — Baby Dodds' Drum Solos	1951	15.00	30.00	60.00

DODDS, JOHNNY
BRUNSWICK
| ❑ BL 58016 [10] | The King of New Orleans Clarinets | 1951 | 25.00 | 50.00 | 100.00 |
JOLLY ROGER
| ❑ 5012 [10] | Johnny Dodds | 1954 | 12.50 | 25.00 | 50.00 |
MILESTONE
| ❑ M-2002 [M] | The Immortal Johnny Dodds | 1967 | 5.00 | 10.00 | 20.00 |
| ❑ M-2011 | Chicago Mess Around | 1968 | 5.00 | 10.00 | 20.00 |
RCA VICTOR
| ❑ LPV-558 [M] | Sixteen Rare Recordings | 1965 | 6.25 | 12.50 | 25.00 |
RIVERSIDE
❑ RLP 12-104 [M]	Johnny Dodds' New Orleans Clarinet	195?	10.00	20.00	40.00
—Blue label with microphone logo					
❑ RLP 12-104 [M]	Johnny Dodds' New Orleans Clarinet	1956	15.00	30.00	60.00
—White label, blue print					
❑ RLP 12-135 [M]	In the Alley: Johnny Dodds, Volume 2	1961	10.00	20.00	40.00
❑ RLP-1002 [10]	Johnny Dodds, Volume 1	1953	20.00	40.00	80.00
❑ RLP-1015 [10]	Johnny Dodds, Volume 2	1953	20.00	40.00	80.00
"X"
| ❑ LX-3006 [10] | Johnny Dodds' Washboard Band | 1954 | 15.00 | 30.00 | 60.00 |

DODSON, MARGE
COLUMBIA
❑ CL 1309 [M]	In the Still of the Night	1959	7.50	15.00	30.00
❑ CL 1458 [M]	New Voice in Town	1960	7.50	15.00	30.00
❑ CS 8258 [S]	New Voice in Town	1960	10.00	20.00	40.00

DOGGETT, BILL
ABC-PARAMOUNT
| ❑ 507 [M] | Wow! | 1965 | 5.00 | 10.00 | 20.00 |
| ❑ S-507 [S] | Wow! | 1965 | 6.25 | 12.50 | 25.00 |
AFTER HOURS
| ❑ AFT-4112 | The Right Choice | 1991 | 3.75 | 7.50 | 15.00 |
COLUMBIA
❑ CL 1814 [M]	Oops!	1962	5.00	10.00	20.00
❑ CL 1942 [M]	Prelude to the Blues	1963	5.00	10.00	20.00
❑ CL 2082 [M]	Fingertips	1963	5.00	10.00	20.00
❑ CS 8614 [S]	Oops!	1962	6.25	12.50	25.00
❑ CS 8742 [S]	Prelude to the Blues	1963	6.25	12.50	25.00
❑ CS 8882 [S]	Fingertips	1963	6.25	12.50	25.00

Number	Title (A Side/B Side)	Yr	VG	VG+	NM
KING					
❏ 295-82 [10]	Bill Doggett — His Organ and Combo	1955	37.50	75.00	150.00
❏ 295-83 [10]	Bill Doggett — His Organ and Combo, Volume 2	1955	37.50	75.00	150.00
❏ 295-89 [10]	All-Time Christmas Favorites	1955	50.00	100.00	200.00
❏ 295-102 [10]	Sentimentally Yours	1956	37.50	75.00	150.00
❏ 395-502 [M]	Moondust	1957	15.00	30.00	60.00
❏ 395-514 [M]	Hot Doggett	1957	15.00	30.00	60.00
❏ 395-523 [M]	As You Desire	1957	15.00	30.00	60.00
❏ KLP-523 [M]	As You Desire	1987	2.50	5.00	10.00
—Reissue with "Highland Records" on label					
❏ 395-531 [M]	Everybody Dance to the Honky Tonk	1958	15.00	30.00	60.00
❏ 395-532 [M]	Dame Dreaming	1958	15.00	30.00	60.00
❏ KLP-532 [M]	Dame Dreaming	1987	2.50	5.00	10.00
—Reissue with "Highland Records" on label					
❏ 395-533 [M]	A Salute to Ellington	1958	15.00	30.00	60.00
❏ 395-557 [M]	The Doggett Beat for Dancing Feet	1958	15.00	30.00	60.00
❏ KLP-557 [M]	The Doggett Beat for Dancing Feet	1987	2.50	5.00	10.00
—Reissue with "Highland Records" on label					
❏ 395-563 [M]	Candle Glow	1958	15.00	30.00	60.00
❏ 395-582 [M]	Swingin' Easy	1959	15.00	30.00	60.00
❏ 395-585 [M]	Dance Awhile	1959	15.00	30.00	60.00
❏ KLP-585 [M]	Dance Awhile	1987	2.50	5.00	10.00
—Reissue with "Highland Records" on label					
❏ 395-600 [M]	A Bill Doggett Christmas	1959	10.00	20.00	40.00
❏ 395-609 [M]	Hold It	1959	15.00	30.00	60.00
❏ 633 [M]	High and Wide	1959	12.50	25.00	50.00
❏ 641 [M]	Big City Dance Party	1959	12.50	25.00	50.00
❏ 667 [M]	Bill Doggett On Tour	1959	12.50	25.00	50.00
❏ 706 [M]	For Reminiscent Lovers, Romantic Songs	1960	12.50	25.00	50.00
❏ 723 [M]	Back Again with More	1960	12.50	25.00	50.00
❏ 759 [M]	Bonanza of 24 Songs	1960	12.50	25.00	50.00
❏ 778 [M]	The Many Moods of Bill Doggett	1960	12.50	25.00	50.00
❏ KLP-778 [M]	The Many Moods of Bill Doggett	1987	2.50	5.00	10.00
—Reissue with "Highland Records" on label					
❏ 830 [M]	American Songs in the Bossa Nova Style	1963	10.00	20.00	40.00
❏ 868 [M]	Impressions	1964	10.00	20.00	40.00
❏ 908 [M]	The Best of Bill Doggett	1964	10.00	20.00	40.00
❏ 959 [M]	Bonanza of 24 Hit Songs	1966	7.50	15.00	30.00
❏ KS-1078	Honky Tonk Popcorn	1969	12.50	25.00	50.00
❏ KS-1097	The Nearness of You	1970	6.25	12.50	25.00
❏ KS-1101	Ram-Bunk-Shush	1970	6.25	12.50	25.00
❏ KS-1104	Sentimental Journey	1970	6.25	12.50	25.00
❏ KS-1108	Soft	1970	6.25	12.50	25.00
❏ K-5009	14 Original Greatest Hits	1977	2.50	5.00	10.00
POWER PAK					
❏ 269	Hold It!	197?	2.50	5.00	10.00
ROULETTE					
❏ R 25330 [M]	Honky Tonk A La Mod	1966	5.00	10.00	20.00
❏ SR 25330 [S]	Honky Tonk A La Mod	1966	6.25	12.50	25.00
STARDAY					
❏ 3023	16 Bandstand Favorites	197?	2.50	5.00	10.00
WARNER BROS.					
❏ W 1404 [M]	3,046 People Danced 'Til 4 AM	1960	5.00	10.00	20.00
❏ WS 1404 [S]	3,046 People Danced 'Til 4 AM	1960	6.25	12.50	25.00
❏ W 1421 [M]	The Band with the Beat	1961	5.00	10.00	20.00
❏ WS 1421 [S]	The Band with the Beat	1961	6.25	12.50	25.00
❏ W 1452 [M]	Bill Doggett Swings	1962	5.00	10.00	20.00
❏ WS 1452 [S]	Bill Doggett Swings	1962	6.25	12.50	25.00
WHO'S WHO IN JAZZ					
❏ 21002	Lionel Hampton Presents Bill Doggett	1977	3.00	6.00	12.00

DOJO

Number	Title (A Side/B Side)	Yr	VG	VG+	NM
ECLIPSE					
❏ ES-7309	Down for the Last Time	1971	6.25	12.50	25.00

DOLDINGER, KLAUS

Number	Title (A Side/B Side)	Yr	VG	VG+	NM
PHILIPS					
❏ PHM 200125 [M]	Dig Doldinger	1966	5.00	10.00	20.00
❏ PHS 600125 [S]	Dig Doldinger	1966	6.25	12.50	25.00
WORLD PACIFIC					
❏ WPS-20176	Blues Happening	1969	5.00	10.00	20.00

DOLLAR, JOHNNY

Number	Title (A Side/B Side)	Yr	VG	VG+	NM
DATE					
❏ TEM 3009 [M]	Johnny Dollar	1967	6.25	12.50	25.00
❏ TES 4009 [S]	Johnny Dollar	1967	5.00	10.00	20.00

DOLPHY, ERIC

Number	Title (A Side/B Side)	Yr	VG	VG+	NM
BLUE NOTE					
❏ BLP-4163 [M]	Out to Lunch!	1964	12.50	25.00	50.00
❏ BST-84163 [S]	Out to Lunch!	1964	20.00	40.00	80.00
—"New York, USA" on label					
❏ BT-85131	Other Aspects	1987	5.00	10.00	20.00
DOUGLAS					
❏ SD 785	Iron Man	1969	6.25	12.50	25.00
❏ KZ 30873	Iron Man	1971	5.00	10.00	20.00
EXODUS					
❏ EX-6005 [M]	The Memorial Album	1966	5.00	10.00	20.00
—Reissue of Vee Jay LP-2503					
❏ EXS-6005 [S]	The Memorial Album	1966	5.00	10.00	20.00
—Reissue of Vee Jay LPS-2503					
FM					
❏ 308 [M]	Conversations	1963	10.00	20.00	40.00
❏ S-308 [S]	Conversations	1963	12.50	25.00	50.00
LIMELIGHT					
❏ LM-82013 [M]	Last Date	1964	7.50	15.00	30.00
❏ LS-86013 [S]	Last Date	1964	10.00	20.00	40.00
NEW JAZZ					
❏ NJLP-8236 [M]	Outward Bound	1960	30.00	60.00	120.00

Number	Title (A Side/B Side)	Yr	VG	VG+	NM
❏ NJLP-8252 [M]	Out There	1960	30.00	60.00	120.00
—Purple label					
❏ NJLP-8252 [M]	Out There	1965	7.50	15.00	30.00
—Blue label, trident logo at right					
❏ NJLP-8260 [M]	Eric Dolphy at the Five Spot	1961	25.00	50.00	100.00
—Purple label					
❏ NJLP-8260 [M]	Eric Dolphy at the Five Spot	1965	7.50	15.00	30.00
—Blue label, trident logo at right					
❏ NJLP-8270 [M]	Far Cry	1962	25.00	50.00	100.00
—Purple label					
❏ NJLP-8270 [M]	Far Cry	1965	7.50	15.00	30.00
—Blue label, trident logo at right					
PRESTIGE					
❏ PRLP-7294 [M]	Eric Dolphy at the Five Spot, Volume 2	1964	10.00	20.00	40.00
—Yellow label					
❏ PRLP-7294 [M]	Eric Dolphy at the Five Spot, Volume 2	1965	5.00	10.00	20.00
—Blue label, trident logo at right					
❏ PRST-7294 [S]	Eric Dolphy at the Five Spot, Volume 2	1964	12.50	25.00	50.00
—Silver label					
❏ PRST-7294 [S]	Eric Dolphy at the Five Spot, Volume 2	1965	6.25	12.50	25.00
—Blue label, trident logo at right					
❏ PRLP-7304 [M]	Eric Dolphy in Europe, Volume 1	1964	10.00	20.00	40.00
—Yellow label					
❏ PRLP-7304 [M]	Eric Dolphy in Europe, Volume 1	1965	5.00	10.00	20.00
—Blue label, trident logo at right					
❏ PRST-7304 [S]	Eric Dolphy in Europe, Volume 1	1964	12.50	25.00	50.00
—Silver label					
❏ PRST-7304 [S]	Eric Dolphy in Europe, Volume 1	1965	6.25	12.50	25.00
—Blue label, trident logo at right					
❏ PRLP-7311 [M]	Outward Bound	1964	12.50	25.00	50.00
—Yellow label					
❏ PRLP-7311 [M]	Outward Bound	1965	6.25	12.50	25.00
—Blue label, trident logo at right					
❏ PRST-7311 [S]	Outward Bound	1964	10.00	20.00	40.00
—Silver label					
❏ PRST-7311 [S]	Outward Bound	1965	5.00	10.00	20.00
—Blue label, trident logo at right					
❏ PRLP-7334 [M]	Eric Dolphy Memorial Album	1964	5.00	10.00	20.00
❏ PRST-7334 [M]	Eric Dolphy Memorial Album	1964	6.25	12.50	25.00
❏ PRLP-7350 [M]	Eric Dolphy in Europe, Volume 2	1965	5.00	10.00	20.00
❏ PRST-7350 [S]	Eric Dolphy in Europe, Volume 2	1965	6.25	12.50	25.00
❏ PRLP-7366 [M]	Eric Dolphy in Europe, Volume 3	1965	5.00	10.00	20.00
❏ PRST-7366 [S]	Eric Dolphy in Europe, Volume 3	1965	6.25	12.50	25.00
❏ PRLP-7382 [M]	Here and There	1965	5.00	10.00	20.00
❏ PRST-7382 [S]	Here and There	1965	6.25	12.50	25.00
❏ 24008 [(2)]	Eric Dolphy	197?	5.00	10.00	20.00
❏ 24027 [(2)]	Copenhagen Concert	197?	5.00	10.00	20.00
❏ 34002 [(3)]	Great Concert	1974	6.25	12.50	25.00
VEE JAY					
❏ LP-2503 [M]	The Memorial Album	1964	7.50	15.00	30.00
❏ LPS-2503 [S]	The Memorial Album	1964	10.00	20.00	40.00

DOMINO, FATS

Number	Title (A Side/B Side)	Yr	VG	VG+	NM
ABC					
❏ S-455 [S]	Here Comes... Fats Domino	1967	3.75	7.50	15.00
❏ S-479 [S]	Fats on Fire	1967	3.75	7.50	15.00
❏ S-510 [S]	Get Away with Fats Domino	1967	3.75	7.50	15.00
❏ ST-90167 [S]	Get Away with Fats Domino	1969	6.25	12.50	25.00
—Capitol Record Club edition; reissue					
ABC-PARAMOUNT					
❏ 455 [M]	Here Comes... Fats Domino	1963	5.00	10.00	20.00
❏ S-455 [S]	Here Comes... Fats Domino	1963	6.25	12.50	25.00
❏ 479 [M]	Fats on Fire	1964	5.00	10.00	20.00
❏ S-479 [S]	Fats on Fire	1964	6.25	12.50	25.00
❏ 510 [M]	Get Away with Fats Domino	1965	5.00	10.00	20.00
❏ S-510 [S]	Get Away with Fats Domino	1965	6.25	12.50	25.00
❏ ST-90167 [S]	Get Away with Fats Domino	1965	7.50	15.00	30.00
—Capitol Record Club edition					
❏ T-90167 [M]	Get Away with Fats Domino	1965	6.25	12.50	25.00
—Capitol Record Club edition					
ARCHIVE OF FOLK AND JAZZ					
❏ 280	Fats Domino	1974	2.50	5.00	10.00
❏ 330	Fats Domino, Vol. II	1975	2.50	5.00	10.00
ATLANTIC					
❏ 81751	Live in Montreux	1987	3.00	6.00	12.00
COLUMBIA					
❏ C 35996	When I'm Walking	1979	2.50	5.00	10.00
—Reissue of Harmony LP					
❏ PC 35996	When I'm Walking	1986	2.00	4.00	8.00
—Budget-line reissue					
COLUMBIA SPECIAL PRODUCTS					
❏ P2 13197 [(2)]	The Legendary Music Man	1976	3.75	7.50	15.00
—Candelite Music TV offer					
GRAND AWARD					
❏ 267 [M]	Fats Domino	196?	5.00	10.00	20.00
❏ S-267 [R]	Fats Domino	196?	2.50	5.00	10.00
HARLEM HIT PARADE					
❏ 5005	Fats' Hits	197?	2.50	5.00	10.00
HARMONY					
❏ HS 11343	When I'm Walking	1969	3.00	6.00	12.00
IMPERIAL					
❏ LP-9004 [M]	Rock and Rollin' with Fats Domino	1956	37.50	75.00	150.00
—Maroon label					
❏ LP-9004 [M]	Rock and Rollin' with Fats Domino	1958	20.00	40.00	80.00
—Black label with stars on top					
❏ LP-9004 [M]	Rock and Rollin' with Fats Domino	1964	6.25	12.50	25.00
—Black and pink label					
❏ LP-9004 [M]	Rock and Rollin' with Fats Domino	1967	5.00	10.00	20.00
—Black and green label					

Number	Title (A Side/B Side)	Yr	VG	VG+	NM
❏ LP-9009 [M]	Fats Domino Rock and Rollin'	1956	37.50	75.00	150.00
—Maroon label					
❏ LP-9009 [M]	Fats Domino Rock and Rollin'	1958	20.00	40.00	80.00
—Black label with stars on top					
❏ LP-9009 [M]	Fats Domino Rock and Rollin'	1964	6.25	12.50	25.00
—Black and pink label					
❏ LP-9009 [M]	Fats Domino Rock and Rollin'	1967	5.00	10.00	20.00
—Black and green label					
❏ LP-9028 [M]	This Is Fats Domino!	1957	37.50	75.00	150.00
—Maroon label					
❏ LP-9028 [M]	This Is Fats Domino!	1958	20.00	40.00	80.00
—Black label with stars on top					
❏ LP-9028 [M]	This Is Fats Domino!	1964	6.25	12.50	25.00
—Black label with stars on top					
❏ LP-9028 [M]	This Is Fats Domino!	1967	5.00	10.00	20.00
—Black and green label					
❏ LP-9038 [M]	Here Stands Fats Domino	1957	37.50	75.00	150.00
—Maroon label					
❏ LP-9038 [M]	Here Stands Fats Domino	1958	20.00	40.00	80.00
—Black label with stars on top					
❏ LP-9038 [M]	Here Stands Fats Domino	1964	6.25	12.50	25.00
—Black and pink label					
❏ LP-9038 [M]	Here Stands Fats Domino	1967	5.00	10.00	20.00
—Black and green label					
❏ LP-9040 [M]	This Is Fats	1957	37.50	75.00	150.00
—Maroon label					
❏ LP-9040 [M]	This Is Fats	1958	20.00	40.00	80.00
—Black label with stars on top					
❏ LP-9040 [M]	This Is Fats	1964	6.25	12.50	25.00
—Black label with stars on top					
❏ LP-9040 [M]	This Is Fats	1967	5.00	10.00	20.00
—Black and green label					
❏ LP-9055 [M]	The Fabulous Mr. D.	1958	25.00	50.00	100.00
—Black label with stars on top					
❏ LP-9055 [M]	The Fabulous Mr. D.	1964	7.50	15.00	30.00
—Black and pink label					
❏ LP-9055 [M]	The Fabulous Mr. D.	1967	5.00	10.00	20.00
—Black and green label					
❏ LP-9062 [M]	Fats Domino Swings	1959	25.00	50.00	100.00
—Black label with stars on top					
❏ LP-9062 [M]	Fats Domino Swings	1964	7.50	15.00	30.00
—Black and pink label					
❏ LP-9062 [M]	Fats Domino Swings	1967	5.00	10.00	20.00
—Black and green label					
❏ LP-9065 [M]	Let's Play Fats Domino	1959	25.00	50.00	100.00
—Black label with stars on top					
❏ LP-9065 [M]	Let's Play Fats Domino	1964	7.50	15.00	30.00
—Black and pink label					
❏ LP-9065 [M]	Let's Play Fats Domino	1967	5.00	10.00	20.00
—Black and green label					
❏ LP-9103 [M]	Million Record Hits	1960	25.00	50.00	100.00
—Black label with stars on top					
❏ LP-9103 [M]	Million Record Hits	1964	7.50	15.00	30.00
—Black and pink label					
❏ LP-9103 [M]	Million Record Hits	1967	5.00	10.00	20.00
—Black and green label					
❏ LP-9127 [M]	A Lot of Dominos	1960	25.00	50.00	100.00
—Black label with stars on top					
❏ LP-9127 [M]	A Lot of Dominos	1964	7.50	15.00	30.00
—Black and pink label					
❏ LP-9127 [M]	A Lot of Dominos	1967	5.00	10.00	20.00
—Black and green label					
❏ LP-9138 [M]	I Miss You So	1961	25.00	50.00	100.00
—Black label with stars on top					
❏ LP-9138 [M]	I Miss You So	1964	7.50	15.00	30.00
—Black and pink label					
❏ LP-9138 [M]	I Miss You So	1967	5.00	10.00	20.00
—Black and green label					
❏ LP-9153 [M]	Let the Four Winds Blow	1961	25.00	50.00	100.00
—Black label with stars on top					
❏ LP-9153 [M]	Let the Four Winds Blow	1964	7.50	15.00	30.00
—Black and pink label					
❏ LP-9153 [M]	Let the Four Winds Blow	1967	5.00	10.00	20.00
—Black and green label					
❏ LP-9164 [M]	What a Party	1962	15.00	30.00	60.00
—Black label with stars on top					
❏ LP-9164 [M]	What a Party	1964	7.50	15.00	30.00
—Black and pink label					
❏ SR-9164 [M]	What a Party	1967	5.00	10.00	20.00
—Black and green label					
❏ LP-9170 [M]	Twistin' the Stomp	1962	15.00	30.00	60.00
—Black label with stars on top					
❏ LP-9170 [M]	Twistin' the Stomp	1964	7.50	15.00	30.00
—Black and pink label					
❏ QS-9170 [M]	Twistin' the Stomp	1967	5.00	10.00	20.00
—Black and green label					
❏ LP-9195 [M]	Million Sellers by Fats	1962	12.50	25.00	50.00
—Black label with stars on top					
❏ LP-9195 [M]	Million Sellers by Fats	1964	7.50	15.00	30.00
—Black and pink label					
❏ LP-9195 [M]	Million Sellers by Fats	1967	5.00	10.00	20.00
—Black and green label					
❏ LP-9208 [M]	Just Domino	1962	12.50	25.00	50.00
—Black label with stars on top					
❏ LP-9208 [M]	Just Domino	1964	7.50	15.00	30.00
—Black and pink label					
❏ LP-9208 [M]	Just Domino	1967	5.00	10.00	20.00
—Black and pink label					
❏ LP-9227 [M]	Walking to New Orleans	1963	12.50	25.00	50.00
—Black label with stars on top					
❏ LP-9227 [M]	Walking to New Orleans	1964	7.50	15.00	30.00
—Black and pink label					
❏ LP-9227 [M]	Walking to New Orleans	1967	5.00	10.00	20.00
—Black and green label					
❏ LP-9239 [M]	Let's Dance with Domino	1963	12.50	25.00	50.00
—Black label with stars on top					
❏ LP-9239 [M]	Let's Dance with Domino	1964	7.50	15.00	30.00
—Black and pink label					
❏ LP-9239 [M]	Let's Dance with Domino	1967	5.00	10.00	20.00
—Black and green label					
❏ LP-9248 [M]	Here He Comes Again	1963	12.50	25.00	50.00
—Black label with stars on top					
❏ LP-9248 [M]	Here He Comes Again	1964	7.50	15.00	30.00
—Black and pink label					
❏ LP-9248 [M]	Here He Comes Again	1967	5.00	10.00	20.00
—Black and green label					
❏ LP-12066 [S]	A Lot of Dominos	1961	37.50	75.00	150.00
—Black label with silver top					
❏ LP-12066 [S]	A Lot of Dominos	1964	10.00	20.00	40.00
—Black and pink label					
❏ LP-12066 [S]	A Lot of Dominos	1967	6.25	12.50	25.00
—Black and green label					
❏ LP-12073 [S]	Let the Four Winds Blow	1961	37.50	75.00	150.00
—Black label with silver top					
❏ LP-12073 [S]	Let the Four Winds Blow	1964	10.00	20.00	40.00
—Black and pink label					
❏ LP-12073 [S]	Let the Four Winds Blow	1967	6.25	12.50	25.00
—Black and green label					
❏ LP-12091 [R]	Fats Domino Swings	1964	5.00	10.00	20.00
—Black and pink label					
❏ LP-12091 [R]	Fats Domino Swings	1967	3.75	7.50	15.00
—Black and green label					
❏ LP-12103 [R]	Million Record Hits	1964	5.00	10.00	20.00
—Black and pink label					
❏ LP-12103 [R]	Million Record Hits	1967	3.75	7.50	15.00
—Black and green label					
❏ LP-12195 [R]	Million Sellers by Fats	1964	5.00	10.00	20.00
—Black and pink label					
❏ LP-12195 [R]	Million Sellers by Fats	1967	3.75	7.50	15.00
—Black and green label					
❏ LP-12227 [R]	Walking to New Orleans	1964	5.00	10.00	20.00
—Black and pink label					
❏ LP-12227 [R]	Walking to New Orleans	1967	3.75	7.50	15.00
—Black and green label					
❏ LP-12248 [R]	Here He Comes Again	1964	5.00	10.00	20.00
—Black and pink label					
❏ LP-12248 [R]	Here He Comes Again	1967	3.75	7.50	15.00
—Black and green label					
❏ LP-12387 [R]	Rock and Rollin' with Fats Domino	1968	3.00	6.00	12.00
—Rechanneled reissue of 9004					
❏ LP-12388 [R]	Fats Domino Rock and Rollin'	1968	3.00	6.00	12.00
—Rechanneled reissue of 9009					
❏ LP-12389 [R]	This Is Fats Domino!	1968	3.00	6.00	12.00
—Rechanneled reissue of 9028					
❏ LP-12390 [R]	Here Stands Fats Domino	1968	3.00	6.00	12.00
—Rechanneled reissue of 9038					
❏ LP-12391 [R]	This Is Fats	1968	3.00	6.00	12.00
—Rechanneled reissue of 9040					
❏ LP-12394 [R]	The Fabulous Mr. D.	1968	3.00	6.00	12.00
—Rechanneled reissue of 9055					
❏ LP-12395 [R]	Let's Play Fats Domino	1968	3.00	6.00	12.00
—Rechanneled reissue of 9065					
❏ LP-12398 [R]	I Miss You So	1968	3.00	6.00	12.00
—Rechanneled reissue of 9138					
LIBERTY					
❏ LWB-122 [(2)]	Cookin' with Fats (Superpak)	1981	3.00	6.00	12.00
—Budget-line reissue of UA 122					
❏ LM-1027	Million Sellers by Fats	1981	2.00	4.00	8.00
—Budget-line reissue of UA 1027					
❏ LWB-9958 [(2)]	Legendary Masters	1981	2.50	5.00	10.00
—Budget-line reissue of UA 9958					
❏ LN-10135	Let's Play Fats Domino	1981	2.00	4.00	8.00
—Budget-line reissue					
❏ LN-10136	The Fabulous Mr. D.	1981	2.00	4.00	8.00
—Budget-line reissue					
MCA/SILVER EAGLE					
❏ 6170	Greatest Hits	198?	2.50	5.00	10.00
MERCURY					
❏ MG-21039 [M]	Fats Domino '65	1965	6.25	12.50	25.00
❏ 21065/61065	Southland U.S.A.	1966	—	—	—
—Canceled					
❏ SR-61039 [S]	Fats Domino '65	1965	10.00	20.00	40.00
PICKWICK					
❏ SPC-3111	Blueberry Hill	197?	2.50	5.00	10.00
❏ SPC-3165	When My Dreamboat Comes Home	197?	2.50	5.00	10.00
❏ SPC-3295	My Blue Heaven	1971	2.50	5.00	10.00
QUICKSILVER					
❏ QS-1016	Live Hits	198?	2.50	5.00	10.00
REPRISE					
❏ RS 6304	Fats Is Back	1968	7.50	15.00	30.00
❏ RS 6439	Fats	1970	125.00	250.00	500.00
—Officially unreleased, test pressings and coverless stock copies are known to exist					
SEARS					
❏ SPS-473	Blueberry Hill!	1970	6.25	12.50	25.00
SUNSET					
❏ SUM-1103 [M]	Fats Domino	1966	3.00	6.00	12.00
❏ SUM-1158 [M]	Stompin' Fats Domino	1967	3.00	6.00	12.00
❏ SUS-5103 [R]	Fats Domino	1966	3.00	6.00	12.00
❏ SUS-5158 [R]	Stompin' Fats Domino	1967	3.00	6.00	12.00
❏ SUS-5200 [P]	Trouble in Mind	1968	5.00	10.00	20.00
❏ SUS-5299 [R]	Ain't That a Shame	1970	3.00	6.00	12.00
UNITED ARTISTS					
❏ UAMG-104 [DJ]	The Fats Domino Sound	1973	10.00	20.00	40.00
—Promo compilation of 30 excerpts of Fats hits					
❏ UA-LA122-F2 [(2)]	Cookin' with Fats (Superpak)	1974	7.50	15.00	30.00

Number	Title (A Side/B Side)	Yr	VG	VG+	NM
❑ UA-LA122-F2 [(2)DJ]	Cookin' with Fats (Superpak)	1974	75.00	150.00	300.00

—Promo with one black vinyl record and one colored vinyl record

Number	Title (A Side/B Side)	Yr	VG	VG+	NM
❑ UA-LA233-G	The Very Best of Fats Domino	1974	3.00	6.00	12.00
❑ LM-1027	Million Sellers by Fats	1980	2.50	5.00	10.00
❑ UAS-9958 [(2)]	Legendary Masters	1972	3.75	7.50	15.00

DOMINOES, THE
See BILLY WARD AND THE DOMINOES.

DOMNERUS, ARNE
PRESTIGE

Number	Title (A Side/B Side)	Yr	VG	VG+	NM
❑ PRLP-134 [10]	New Sounds from Sweden, Volume 4	1952	62.50	125.00	250.00

RCA VICTOR

❑ LPT-3032 [10]	Around the World in Jazz	1953	62.50	125.00	250.00

DOMNERUS, ARNE/LARS GULLIN
PRESTIGE

❑ PRLP-133 [10]	New Sounds from Sweden, Volume 3	1952	62.50	125.00	250.00

DON AND DEWEY
SPECIALTY

❑ SPS-2131	They're Rockin' Til Midnight, Rollin' Til Dawn	1970	7.50	15.00	30.00

—Original labels are black and gold

DON AND EDDIE
MODERN

❑ M 7014 [M]	Rock and Roll Party	1963	10.00	20.00	40.00

DON AND THE GOODTIMES
BEAT ROCKET

❑ BR-130	The Original Northwest Sound of Don and the Goodtimes	2000	3.00	6.00	12.00

BURDETTE

❑ 300 [M]	Don and the Goodtimes' Greatest Hits	1966	37.50	75.00	150.00
❑ 300S [R]	Don and the Goodtimes' Greatest Hits	1966	25.00	50.00	100.00

—LP plays rechanneled stereo

❑ 300S [S]	Don and the Goodtimes' Greatest Hits	1966	75.00	150.00	300.00

—LP plays true stereo
EPIC

❑ LN 24311 [M]	So Good	1967	5.00	10.00	20.00
❑ BN 26311 [S]	So Good	1967	5.00	10.00	20.00

PICCADILLY

❑ 3394	Goodtime Rock 'n' Roll	1980	6.25	12.50	25.00

WAND

❑ WDS-679	Where the Action Is	1969	7.50	15.00	30.00

DON, DICK & JIMMY
CROWN

❑ CLP-5005 [M]	Spring Fever	1958	10.00	20.00	40.00

DOT

❑ DLP-3152 [M]	Don, Dick & Jimmy	1959	7.50	15.00	30.00

MODERN

❑ MLP-1205 [M]	Spring Fever	1957	30.00	60.00	120.00

VERVE

❑ MGV-2084 [M]	Medium Rare	1958	10.00	20.00	40.00
❑ MGV-2107 [M]	Songs for the Hearth	1959	10.00	20.00	40.00

DONAHUE, SAM
CAPITOL

❑ H 613 [10]	For Young Moderns in Love	1955	15.00	30.00	60.00
❑ T 613 [M]	For Young Moderns in Love	1956	10.00	20.00	40.00
❑ H 626 [10]	Classics in Jazz	1955	12.50	25.00	50.00

DONALDSON, BOBBY
GOLDEN CREST

❑ GC-1003	Unlimited	196?	5.00	10.00	20.00

SAVOY

❑ MG-12128 [M]	Dixieland Jazz Party	1958	10.00	20.00	40.00
❑ SST-13003 [S]	Dixieland Jazz Party	1959	7.50	15.00	30.00

WORLD WIDE

❑ 20005	Bobby Donaldson and the 7th Avenue Stompers	196?	5.00	10.00	20.00

DONALDSON, LOU
ARGO

❑ LP-724 [M]	Signifyin'	1963	6.25	12.50	25.00
❑ LPS-724 [S]	Signifyin'	1963	6.25	12.50	25.00
❑ LP-734 [M]	Possum Head	1964	6.25	12.50	25.00
❑ LPS-734 [S]	Possum Head	1964	6.25	12.50	25.00
❑ LP-747 [M]	Cole Slaw	1965	6.25	12.50	25.00
❑ LPS-747 [S]	Cole Slaw	1965	6.25	12.50	25.00

BLUE NOTE

❑ BLP-1537 [M]	Lou Donaldson Quartet/Quintet/Sextet	1957	10.00	20.00	40.00

—Regular version with W. 63rd St. address on label

❑ BLP-1537 [M]	Lou Donaldson Quartet/Quintet/Sextet	1957	37.50	75.00	150.00

—Regular version with Lexington Ave. address on label

❑ BLP-1537 [M]	Lou Donaldson Quartet/Quintet/Sextet	1963	6.25	12.50	25.00

—With New York, USA address on label

❑ BLP-1545 [M]	Wailing with Lou	1957	20.00	40.00	80.00

—Regular version with W. 63rd St. address on label

❑ BLP-1545 [M]	Wailing with Lou	1957	30.00	60.00	120.00

—"Deep groove" version (deep indentation under label on both sides)

❑ BLP-1545 [M]	Wailing with Lou	1963	6.25	12.50	25.00

—With New York, USA address on label

❑ BLP-1566 [M]	Swing and Soul	1957	20.00	40.00	80.00

—Regular version with W. 63rd St. address on label

❑ BLP-1566 [M]	Swing and Soul	1957	30.00	60.00	120.00

—"Deep groove" version (deep indentation under label on both sides)

❑ BLP-1566 [M]	Swing and Soul	1963	6.25	12.50	25.00

—With New York, USA address on label

❑ BST-1566 [S]	Swing and Soul	1959	12.50	25.00	50.00

—Regular version with W. 63rd St. address on label

❑ BST-1566 [S]	Swing and Soul	1959	20.00	40.00	80.00

—"Deep groove" version (deep indentation under label on both sides)

❑ BST-1566 [S]	Swing and Soul	1963	5.00	10.00	20.00

—With New York, USA address on label

❑ BLP-1591 [M]	Lou Takes Off	1958	20.00	40.00	80.00

—Regular version with W. 63rd St. address on label

❑ BLP-1591 [M]	Lou Takes Off	1958	30.00	60.00	120.00

—"Deep groove" version (deep indentation under label on both sides)

❑ BLP-1591 [M]	Lou Takes Off	1963	6.25	12.50	25.00

—With New York, USA address on label

❑ BST-1591 [S]	Lou Takes Off	1959	12.50	25.00	50.00

—Regular version with W. 63rd St. address on label

❑ BST-1591 [S]	Lou Takes Off	1959	20.00	40.00	80.00

—"Deep groove" version (deep indentation under label on both sides)

❑ BST-1591 [S]	Lou Takes Off	1963	5.00	10.00	20.00

—With New York, USA address on label

❑ BLP-1593 [M]	Blues Walk	1958	20.00	40.00	80.00

—Regular version with W. 63rd St. address on label

❑ BLP-1593 [M]	Blues Walk	1958	30.00	60.00	120.00

—"Deep groove" version (deep indentation under label on both sides)

❑ BLP-1593 [M]	Blues Walk	1963	6.25	12.50	25.00

—With New York, USA address on label

❑ BST-1593 [S]	Blues Walk	1959	12.50	25.00	50.00

—Regular version with W. 63rd St. address on label

❑ BST-1593 [S]	Blues Walk	1959	20.00	40.00	80.00

—"Deep groove" version (deep indentation under label on both sides)

❑ BST-1593 [S]	Blues Walk	1963	5.00	10.00	20.00

—With New York, USA address on label

❑ BLP-4012 [M]	LD + 3	1959	20.00	40.00	80.00

—Regular version with W. 63rd St. address on label

❑ BLP-4012 [M]	LD + 3	1959	30.00	60.00	120.00

—"Deep groove" version (deep indentation under label on both sides)

❑ BLP-4012 [M]	LD + 3	1963	6.25	12.50	25.00

—With New York, USA address on label

❑ BST-4012 [S]	LD + 3	1960	12.50	25.00	50.00

—Regular version with W. 63rd St. address on label

❑ BST-4012 [S]	LD + 3	1960	20.00	40.00	80.00

—"Deep groove" version (deep indentation under label on both sides)

❑ BST-4012 [S]	LD + 3	1963	5.00	10.00	20.00

—With New York, USA address on label

❑ BLP-4025 [M]	The Time Is Right	1960	20.00	40.00	80.00

—Regular version with W. 63rd St. address on label

❑ BLP-4025 [M]	The Time Is Right	1960	30.00	60.00	120.00

—"Deep groove" version (deep indentation under label on both sides)

❑ BLP-4025 [M]	The Time Is Right	1963	6.25	12.50	25.00

—With New York, USA address on label

❑ BLP-4036 [M]	Sunny Side Up	1960	20.00	40.00	80.00

—Regular version with W. 63rd St. address on label

❑ BLP-4036 [M]	Sunny Side Up	1960	30.00	60.00	120.00

—"Deep groove" version (deep indentation under label on both sides)

❑ BLP-4036 [M]	Sunny Side Up	1963	6.25	12.50	25.00

—With New York, USA address on label

❑ BLP-4053 [M]	Light Foot	1960	20.00	40.00	80.00

—With W. 63rd St. address on label

❑ BLP-4053 [M]	Light Foot	1963	6.25	12.50	25.00

—With New York, USA address on label

❑ BLP-4066 [M]	Here 'Tis	1961	20.00	40.00	80.00

—With W. 63rd St. address on label

❑ BLP-4066 [M]	Here 'Tis	1963	6.25	12.50	25.00

—With New York, USA address on label

❑ BLP-4079 [M]	Gravy Train	1962	20.00	40.00	80.00

—With 61st St. address on label

❑ BLP-4079 [M]	Gravy Train	1963	6.25	12.50	25.00

—With New York, USA address on label

❑ BLP-4108 [M]	The Natural Soul	1963	6.25	12.50	25.00
❑ BLP-4125 [M]	Good Gracious	1963	6.25	12.50	25.00
❑ BLP-4263 [M]	Alligator Boogaloo	1967	7.50	15.00	30.00
❑ BLP-4271 [M]	Mr. Shing-a-Ling	1968	7.50	15.00	30.00
❑ BLP-5021 [10]	Lou Donaldson Quintet/Quartet	1953	50.00	100.00	200.00
❑ BLP-5030 [10]	Lou Donaldson-Clifford Brown	1954	50.00	100.00	200.00
❑ BLP-5055 [10]	Lou Donaldson Sextet, Volume 2	1955	50.00	100.00	200.00
❑ BST-84025 [S]	The Time Is Right	1960	12.50	25.00	50.00

—With W. 63rd St. address on label

❑ BST-84025 [S]	The Time Is Right	1963	5.00	10.00	20.00

—With New York, USA address on label

❑ BST-84036 [S]	Sunny Side Up	1960	12.50	25.00	50.00

—With W. 63rd St. address on label

❑ BST-84036 [S]	Sunny Side Up	1963	5.00	10.00	20.00

—With New York, USA address on label

❑ BST-84053 [S]	Light Foot	1960	12.50	25.00	50.00

—With W. 63rd St. address on label

❑ BST-84053 [S]	Light Foot	1963	5.00	10.00	20.00

—With New York, USA address on label

❑ BST-84066 [S]	Here 'Tis	1961	12.50	25.00	50.00

—With W. 63rd St. address on label

❑ BST-84066 [S]	Here 'Tis	1963	5.00	10.00	20.00

—With New York, USA address on label

❑ BST-84079 [S]	Gravy Train	1962	12.50	25.00	50.00

—With 61st St. address on label

❑ BST-84079 [S]	Gravy Train	1963	5.00	10.00	20.00

—With New York, USA address on label

❑ BST-84108 [S]	The Natural Soul	1963	6.25	12.50	25.00
❑ BST-84125 [S]	Good Gracious	1963	6.25	12.50	25.00
❑ BST-84263 [S]	Alligator Boogaloo	1967	5.00	10.00	20.00
❑ BST-84271 [S]	Mr. Shing-a-Ling	1968	5.00	10.00	20.00
❑ BST-84280	Midnight Creeper	1968	5.00	10.00	20.00
❑ BST-84299	Say It Loud!	1969	5.00	10.00	20.00
❑ BST-84318	Hot Dog	1969	5.00	10.00	20.00

CADET

❑ LP-724 [M]	Signifyin'	1966	5.00	10.00	20.00

—Reissue of Argo 724

❑ LP-734 [M]	Possum Head	1966	5.00	10.00	20.00

—Reissue of Argo 734

Number	Title (A Side/B Side)	Yr	VG	VG+	NM
❏ LP-747 [M]	Cole Slaw	1966	5.00	10.00	20.00
—Reissue of Argo 747					
❏ LP-759 [M]	Musty Rusty	1966	6.25	12.50	25.00
❏ LPS-759 [S]	Musty Rusty	1966	6.25	12.50	25.00
❏ LP-768 [M]	Rough House Blues	1966	6.25	12.50	25.00
❏ LPS-768 [S]	Rough House Blues	1966	6.25	12.50	25.00
❏ LP-789 [M]	Blowin' in the Wind	1967	6.25	12.50	25.00
❏ LPS-789 [S]	Blowin' in the Wind	1967	5.00	10.00	20.00
❏ LPS-815	Lou Donaldson At His Best	1969	5.00	10.00	20.00
❏ LPS-842	Fried Buzzard — Lou Donaldson Live	1970	5.00	10.00	20.00

DONATO, JOAO
BLUE THUMB
❏ BT-8821	A Bad Donato	1970	5.00	10.00	20.00
—Distributed by Capitol					

RCA VICTOR
❏ LSP-3473 [S]	The New Sound of Brazil	1966	5.00	10.00	20.00

DONEGAN, DOROTHY
CAPITOL
❏ ST 1135 [S]	Dorothy Donegan Live!	1959	10.00	20.00	40.00
❏ T 1135 [M]	Dorothy Donegan Live!	1959	7.50	15.00	30.00
❏ ST 1226 [S]	Donnybrook with Dorothy	1960	10.00	20.00	40.00
❏ T 1226 [M]	Donnybrook with Dorothy	1960	7.50	15.00	30.00

JUBILEE
❏ LP-11 [10]	Dorothy Donegan Trio	1955	20.00	40.00	80.00
❏ JLP-1013 [M]	September Song	1956	15.00	30.00	60.00

MGM
❏ E-278 [10]	Dorothy Donegan Piano	1954	20.00	40.00	80.00

ROULETTE
❏ R-25010 [M]	Dorothy Donegan at the Embers	1957	12.50	25.00	50.00
❏ R-25154 [M]	It Happened One Night	1961	7.50	15.00	30.00
❏ SR-25154 [S]	It Happened One Night	1961	10.00	20.00	40.00

DONEGAN, LONNIE
ABC-PARAMOUNT
❏ 433 [M]	Sing Hallelujah	1963	5.00	10.00	20.00
❏ S-433 [S]	Sing Hallelujah	1963	6.25	12.50	25.00

ATLANTIC
❏ 8038 [M]	Skiffle Folk Songs	1960	10.00	20.00	40.00
❏ SD 8038 [S]	Skiffle Folk Songs	1960	12.50	25.00	50.00

DOT
❏ DLP-3159 [M]	Lonnie Donegan	1959	10.00	20.00	40.00

MERCURY
❏ MG-20229 [M]	An Englishman Sings American Folk Songs	1957	12.50	25.00	50.00

UNITED ARTISTS
❏ UA-LA827-?	Puttin' On the Style	1977	2.50	5.00	10.00

DONNER, RAL
GONE
❏ LP-5012 [M]	Takin' Care of Business	1961	75.00	150.00	300.00

STARFIRE
❏ 1004	An Evening with Ral Donner	1982	3.75	7.50	15.00
—All copies on multi-color vinyl					

DONNER, RAL/RAY SMITH/BOBBY DALE
CROWN
❏ CST-335 [R]	Ral Donner, Ray Smith and Bobby Dale	1963	5.00	10.00	20.00
❏ CLP-5335 [M]	Ral Donner, Ray Smith and Bobby Dale	1963	10.00	20.00	40.00

DONNIE AND THE DELCHORDS
TAURUS
❏ 1000	Sing with Triple Stereo	1967	75.00	150.00	300.00

DONOVAN
ALLEGIANCE
❏ AV-437	Lady of the Stars	1983	2.50	5.00	10.00

ARISTA
❏ AB 4143	Donovan	1980	2.50	5.00	10.00

BELL
❏ 1135	Early Treasures	1973	2.50	5.00	10.00

EPIC
❏ B2N 171 [(2)S]	A Gift from a Flower to a Garden	1967	6.25	12.50	25.00
—Boxed set of two LPs with portfolio of lyrics and drawings. The two records also were issued separately as Epic 26349 and 26350.					
❏ E2 171 [(2)]	A Gift from a Flower to a Garden	1979	3.75	7.50	15.00
—Blue label					
❏ L2N 6071 [(2)M]	A Gift from a Flower to a Garden	1967	12.50	25.00	50.00
—Boxed set of two LPs with portfolio of lyrics and drawings. The two records also were issued separately as Epic 24349 and 24350.					
❏ LN 24217 [M]	Sunshine Superman	1966	7.50	15.00	30.00
—Contains the single version of "Sunshine Superman"					
❏ LN 24239 [M]	Mellow Yellow	1967	7.50	15.00	30.00
❏ LN 24349 [M]	Wear Your Love Like Heaven	1967	3.00	6.00	12.00
—Part of Epic 6071, issued simultaneously					
❏ LN 24350 [M]	For Little Ones	1967	3.00	6.00	12.00
—Part of Epic 6071, issued simultaneously					
❏ BN 26217 [R]	Sunshine Superman	1966	3.75	7.50	15.00
—Contains the single version of "Sunshine Superman" (rechanneled)					
❏ BN 26239 [R]	Mellow Yellow	1967	3.75	7.50	15.00
❏ BN 26349 [S]	Wear Your Love Like Heaven	1967	3.75	7.50	15.00
—Part of Epic 171, issued simultaneously					
❏ BN 26350 [S]	For Little Ones	1967	3.75	7.50	15.00
—Part of Epic 171, issued simultaneously					
❏ BN 26386	Donovan in Concert	1968	3.00	6.00	12.00
❏ BN 26420	Hurdy Gurdy Man	1968	3.00	6.00	12.00
❏ PE 26420	Hurdy Gurdy Man	1986	2.00	4.00	8.00
—Blue label, new prefix					
❏ BXN 26439 [P]	Donovan's Greatest Hits	1969	3.00	6.00	12.00
—Yellow label; "Mellow Yellow" is rechanneled; "Sunshine Superman" is the full-length version in stereo; "Catch the Wind" and "Colours" were re-recorded					
❏ BXN 26439 [P]	Donovan's Greatest Hits	1973	2.50	5.00	10.00
—Orange label					
❏ PE 26439	Donovan's Greatest Hits	1979	2.00	4.00	8.00
—Blue label					
❏ BN 26481	Barabajagal	1969	3.00	6.00	12.00
❏ PE 26481	Barabajagal	1987	2.00	4.00	8.00
—Blue label, new prefix					
❏ E 30125	Open Road	1970	3.00	6.00	12.00
❏ KEG 31210 [(2)]	The World of Donovan	1972	3.00	6.00	12.00
❏ KE 32156	Cosmic Wheels	1973	3.75	7.50	15.00
—With enclosed poster					
❏ KE 32800	Essence to Essence	1974	3.00	6.00	12.00
❏ PE 33245	7-Tease	1974	3.00	6.00	12.00
❏ EG 33731 [(2)]	Hurdy Gurdy Man/Barabajagal	1975	3.75	7.50	15.00
❏ EG 33734 [(2)]	Donovan in Concert/Sunshine Superman	1975	3.75	7.50	15.00
❏ PE 33945	Slow Down World	1976	3.00	6.00	12.00

HICKORY
❏ LPM-123 [M]	Catch the Wind	1965	6.25	12.50	25.00
—Most pressings have Donovan facing left, so he is correctly strumming his guitar with his right hand					
❏ LPM-123 [M]	Catch the Wind	1965	10.00	20.00	40.00
—First pressings have Donovan facing right, so it appears as if he's strumming his guitar with his left hand					
❏ LPS-123 [R]	Catch the Wind	1965	6.25	12.50	25.00
❏ LPM-127 [M]	Fairy Tale	1965	5.00	10.00	20.00
❏ LPS-127 [P]	Fairy Tale	1965	6.25	12.50	25.00
—"Colours" is rechanneled					
❏ LPM-135 [M]	The Real Donovan	1966	5.00	10.00	20.00
❏ LPS-135 [P]	The Real Donovan	1966	6.25	12.50	25.00
—Half stereo, including "Colours," the rest rechanneled.					
❏ LPS-143 [P]	Like It Is, Was and Evermore Shall Be	1968	5.00	10.00	20.00
❏ LPS-149 [P]	The Best of Donovan	1969	5.00	10.00	20.00

JANUS
❏ 3022	Donovan P. Leitch	1970	2.50	5.00	10.00
❏ 3025	Hear Me Now	1971	2.50	5.00	10.00

KORY
❏ 3012	Early Treasures	1977	2.00	4.00	8.00

PYE
❏ 502	Donovan	1975	2.50	5.00	10.00

DOOBIE BROTHERS, THE
CAPITOL
❏ C1-90371	Cycles	1989	3.00	6.00	12.00
❏ C1-594623	Brotherhood	1991	5.00	10.00	20.00
—U.S. vinyl version available only through Columbia House					

DCC COMPACT CLASSICS
❏ LPZ-2053	Best of the Doobies	1998	10.00	20.00	40.00
—Audiophile vinyl					

MOBILE FIDELITY
❏ 1-122	Takin' It to the Streets	1983	10.00	20.00	40.00
—Audiophile vinyl					

NAUTILUS
❏ NR-5	The Captain and Me	1980	10.00	20.00	40.00
—Audiophile vinyl					
❏ NR-18	Minute by Minute	1981	7.50	15.00	30.00
—Audiophile vinyl					

PICKWICK
❏ SPC-3721	Introducing the Doobie Brothers	1980	5.00	10.00	20.00
—Pre-Warner Bros. recordings; withdrawn shortly after release					

WARNER BROS.
❏ WS 1919	The Doobie Brothers	1971	3.75	7.50	15.00
—Green label original					
❏ WS 1919	The Doobie Brothers	1973	2.50	5.00	10.00
—"Burbank" label					
❏ BS 2634	Toulouse Street	1972	3.75	7.50	15.00
—Green label original					
❏ BS 2634	Toulouse Street	1973	2.50	5.00	10.00
—"Burbank" label					
❏ BS 2694	The Captain and Me	1973	3.00	6.00	12.00
—"Burbank" label					
❏ BS 2694	The Captain and Me	1973	5.00	10.00	20.00
—Green label					
❏ BS 2694	The Captain and Me	1979	2.00	4.00	8.00
—Cream label					
❏ BS4 2694 [Q]	The Captain and Me	1974	5.00	10.00	20.00
❏ W 2750	What Were Once Vices Are Now Habits	1974	2.50	5.00	10.00
—"Burbank" label					
❏ W 2750	What Were Once Vices Are Now Habits	1979	2.00	4.00	8.00
—Cream label					
❏ W4 2750 [Q]	What Were Once Vices Are Now Habits	1974	5.00	10.00	20.00
❏ BS 2835	Stampede	1975	2.50	5.00	10.00
—"Burbank" label					
❏ BS 2835	Stampede	1979	2.00	4.00	8.00
—Cream label					
❏ BS4 2835 [Q]	Stampede	1975	5.00	10.00	20.00
❏ BS 2899	Takin' It to the Streets	1976	2.50	5.00	10.00
—"Burbank" label					
❏ BS 2899	Takin' It to the Streets	1979	2.00	4.00	8.00
—Cream label					
❏ BS 2978	Best of the Doobies	1976	3.00	6.00	12.00
❏ BSK 3045	Livin' on the Fault Line	1977	2.00	4.00	8.00
—Cream label					
❏ BSK 3045	Livin' on the Fault Line	1977	2.50	5.00	10.00
—"Burbank" label					
❏ BSK 3112	Best of the Doobies	1978	2.50	5.00	10.00
—"Burbank" label					
❏ BSK 3112	Best of the Doobies	1979	2.00	4.00	8.00
—Cream label					
❏ BSK 3193	Minute by Minute	1978	2.50	5.00	10.00
❏ HS 3452	One Step Closer	1980	2.50	5.00	10.00
❏ BSK 3612	Best of the Doobies, Volume 2	1981	2.50	5.00	10.00
❏ 23772 [(2)]	Farewell Tour	1983	3.75	7.50	15.00

DOORS, THE

DCC COMPACT CLASSICS

Number	Title (A Side/B Side)	Yr	VG	VG+	NM
❑ LPZ-2045	Strange Days	1997	20.00	40.00	80.00
—Audiophile vinyl					
❑ LPZ-2046	The Doors	1997	37.50	75.00	150.00
—Audiophile vinyl					
❑ LPZ-2049	Waiting for the Sun	1998	30.00	60.00	120.00
—Audiophile vinyl					
❑ LPZ-2050	L.A. Woman	1998	37.50	75.00	150.00
—Audiophile vinyl					

ELEKTRA

Number	Title (A Side/B Side)	Yr	VG	VG+	NM
❑ 5E-502	An American Prayer	1978	3.00	6.00	12.00
—Butterfly labels					
❑ 5E-502	An American Prayer	1980	2.50	5.00	10.00
—Red labels with Warner Communications logo in lower right					
❑ 5E-502	An American Prayer	1983	2.00	4.00	8.00
—Red and black labels					
❑ 5E-515	Greatest Hits	1980	2.50	5.00	10.00
—Red labels with Warner Communications logo in lower right					
❑ 5E-515	Greatest Hits	1983	2.00	4.00	8.00
—Red and black labels					
❑ EKL-4007 [M]	The Doors	1967	50.00	100.00	200.00
❑ EKL-4014 [M]	Strange Days	1967	150.00	300.00	600.00
—Value assumes the record is mono. There are two different covers for this; some copies have mono numbers on the two covers and the stereo number on the spine, and others have the mono number on the spine and stereo number on front and back covers.					
❑ EKL-4024 [M]	Waiting for the Sun	1968	250.00	500.00	1000.
❑ EQ-5035 [Q]	Best of the Doors	1973	5.00	10.00	20.00
—Butterfly labels					
❑ EQ-5035 [Q]	Best of the Doors	1980	3.00	6.00	12.00
—Red labels with Warner Communications logo in lower right					
❑ EQ-5035 [Q]	Best of the Doors	1983	2.50	5.00	10.00
—Red and black labels					
❑ 8E-6001 [(2)]	Weird Scenes Inside the Gold Mine	1972	5.00	10.00	20.00
—Butterfly labels					
❑ 8E-6001 [(2)]	Weird Scenes Inside the Gold Mine	1980	3.00	6.00	12.00
—Red labels with Warner Communications logo in lower right					
❑ 8E-6001 [(2)]	Weird Scenes Inside the Gold Mine	1983	2.50	5.00	10.00
—Red and black labels					
❑ EKS-9002 [(2)]	Absolutely Live	1970	6.25	12.50	25.00
—Butterfly labels					
❑ EKS-9002 [(2)]	Absolutely Live	1980	3.75	7.50	15.00
—Red labels with Warner Communications logo in lower right					
❑ EKS-9002 [(2)]	Absolutely Live	1983	3.00	6.00	12.00
—Red and black labels					
❑ EKS-9002 [(2)DJ]	Absolutely Live	1970	20.00	40.00	80.00
—White label promo					
❑ 60269	Alive, She Cried	1984	3.00	6.00	12.00
❑ 60345 [(2)]	The Best of the Doors	1985	3.75	7.50	15.00
❑ 60345 [(2)]	The Best of the Doors	1985	10.00	20.00	40.00
—White label promo on audiophile vinyl					
❑ 60417	Classics	1986	3.00	6.00	12.00
❑ 60741 [EP]	Live at the Hollywood Bowl	1988	3.00	6.00	12.00
❑ E1-61047	The Doors	1991	5.00	10.00	20.00
—Soundtrack from the movie; only available on US vinyl from Columbia House					
❑ 61812	An American Prayer	1995		7.50	15.00
—Remastered and lengthened version of 5E-502					
❑ EKS-74007 [S]	The Doors	1967	12.50	25.00	50.00
—Brown labels					
❑ EKS-74007 [S]	The Doors	1969	3.75	7.50	15.00
—Red labels with large stylized "E"					
❑ EKS-74007 [S]	The Doors	1971	3.00	6.00	12.00
—Butterfly labels					
❑ EKS-74007 [S]	The Doors	1980	2.50	5.00	10.00
—Red labels with Warner Communications logo in lower right					
❑ EKS-74007 [S]	The Doors	1983	2.00	4.00	8.00
—Red and black labels					
❑ EKS-74014 [S]	Strange Days	1967	10.00	20.00	40.00
—Brown labels					
❑ EKS-74014 [S]	Strange Days	1969	3.75	7.50	15.00
—Red labels with large stylized "E"					
❑ EKS-74014 [S]	Strange Days	1971	3.00	6.00	12.00
—Butterfly labels					
❑ EKS-74014 [S]	Strange Days	1980	2.50	5.00	10.00
—Red labels with Warner Communications logo in lower right					
❑ EKS-74014 [S]	Strange Days	1983	2.00	4.00	8.00
—Red and black labels					
❑ EKS-74024 [S]	Waiting for the Sun	1968	7.50	15.00	30.00
—Brown labels					
❑ EKS-74024 [S]	Waiting for the Sun	1968	37.50	75.00	150.00
—White label promo					
❑ EKS-74024 [S]	Waiting for the Sun	1969	3.75	7.50	15.00
—Red labels with large stylized "E"					
❑ EKS-74024 [S]	Waiting for the Sun	1971	3.00	6.00	12.00
—Butterfly labels					
❑ EKS-74024 [S]	Waiting for the Sun	1980	2.50	5.00	10.00
—Red labels with Warner Communications logo in lower right					
❑ EKS-74024 [S]	Waiting for the Sun	1983	2.00	4.00	8.00
—Red and black labels					
❑ EKS-74079	13	1970	3.75	7.50	15.00
—Butterfly labels					
❑ EKS-74079	13	1980	2.50	5.00	10.00
—Red labels with Warner Communications logo in lower right					
❑ EKS-74079	13	1983	2.00	4.00	8.00
—Red and black labels					
❑ EKS-74079 [DJ]	13	1970	10.00	20.00	40.00
—White label promo					
❑ EKS-75005	The Soft Parade	1969	5.00	10.00	20.00
—Red labels with large stylized "E"					
❑ EKS-75005	The Soft Parade	1969	12.50	25.00	50.00
—Brown or tan labels					
❑ EKS-75005	The Soft Parade	1971	3.00	6.00	12.00
—Butterfly labels					
❑ EKS-75005	The Soft Parade	1980	2.50	5.00	10.00
—Red labels with Warner Communications logo in lower right					
❑ EKS-75005	The Soft Parade	1983	2.00	4.00	8.00
—Red and black labels					
❑ EKS-75007	Morrison Hotel	1970	6.25	12.50	25.00
—Red labels with large stylized "E"					
❑ EKS-75007	Morrison Hotel	1970	15.00	30.00	60.00
—Brown or tan labels					
❑ EKS-75007	Morrison Hotel	1971	3.00	6.00	12.00
—Butterfly labels					
❑ EKS-75007	Morrison Hotel	1980	2.50	5.00	10.00
—Red labels with Warner Communications logo in lower right					
❑ EKS-75007	Morrison Hotel	1983	2.00	4.00	8.00
—Red and black labels					
❑ EKS-75007 [DJ]	Morrison Hotel	1970	25.00	50.00	100.00
—White label promo					
❑ EKS-75011	L.A. Woman	197?	3.00	6.00	12.00
—Butterfly label, standard cover					
❑ EKS-75011	L.A. Woman	1971	12.50	25.00	50.00
—With see-through window on cover and yellow innersleeve with photo of Jim Morrison on a cross					
❑ EKS-75011	L.A. Woman	1980	2.50	5.00	10.00
—Red labels with Warner Communications logo in lower right					
❑ EKS-75011	L.A. Woman	1983	2.00	4.00	8.00
—Red and black labels					
❑ EKS-75011 [DJ]	L.A. Woman	1971	25.00	50.00	100.00
—White label promo					
❑ EKS-75017	Other Voices	1971	3.75	7.50	15.00
❑ EKS-75038	Full Circle	1972	3.75	7.50	15.00

MOBILE FIDELITY

Number	Title (A Side/B Side)	Yr	VG	VG+	NM
❑ 1-051	The Doors	1980	15.00	30.00	60.00
—Audiophile vinyl					

DORFMAN, ANIA

RCA VICTOR RED SEAL

Number	Title (A Side/B Side)	Yr	VG	VG+	NM
❑ LSC-2207 [S]	Schumann: Carnaval	1959	6.25	12.50	25.00
—Original with "shaded dog" label					

DORHAM, KENNY

ABC-PARAMOUNT

Number	Title (A Side/B Side)	Yr	VG	VG+	NM
❑ ABC-122 [M]	Kenny Dorham and the Jazz Prophets	1956	20.00	40.00	80.00

BLUE NOTE

Number	Title (A Side/B Side)	Yr	VG	VG+	NM
❑ BLP-1524 [M]	'Round About Midnight at the Café Bohemia	1956	37.50	75.00	150.00
—Regular version with Lexington Ave. address on label					
❑ BLP-1524 [M]	'Round About Midnight at the Café Bohemia	1956	50.00	100.00	200.00
—"Deep groove" version (deep indentation under label on both sides)					
❑ BLP-1524 [M]	'Round About Midnight at the Café Bohemia	1963	7.50	15.00	30.00
—"New York, USA" address on label					
❑ BLP-1535 [M]	Kenny Dorham Octet/Sextet	1956	37.50	75.00	150.00
—Regular version with Lexington Ave. address on label					
❑ BLP-1535 [M]	Kenny Dorham Octet/Sextet	1956	50.00	100.00	200.00
—"Deep groove" version (deep indentation under label on both sides)					
❑ BLP-1535 [M]	Kenny Dorham Octet/Sextet	1963	7.50	15.00	30.00
—"New York, USA" address on label					
❑ BLP-4063 [M]	Whistle Stop	1961	20.00	40.00	80.00
—W. 63rd St. address on label					
❑ BLP-4063 [M]	Whistle Stop	1963	7.50	15.00	30.00
—"New York, USA" address on label					
❑ BLP-4127 [M]	Una Mas	1963	7.50	15.00	30.00
—"New York, USA" address on label					
❑ BLP-4181 [M]	Trompeta Toccata	1964	7.50	15.00	30.00
—"New York, USA" address on label					
❑ BLP-5055 [10]	Afro-Cuban Holiday	1955	75.00	150.00	300.00
❑ BST-84063 [S]	Whistle Stop	1961	15.00	30.00	60.00
—W. 63rd St. address on label					
❑ BST-84063 [S]	Whistle Stop	1963	6.25	12.50	25.00
—"New York, USA" address on label					
❑ BST-84127 [S]	Una Mas	1963	10.00	20.00	40.00
—"New York, USA" address on label					
❑ BST-84181 [S]	Trompeta Toccata	1964	10.00	20.00	40.00
—"New York, USA" address on label					

DEBUT

Number	Title (A Side/B Side)	Yr	VG	VG+	NM
❑ DLP-9 [10]	Kenny Dorham Quintet	1954	75.00	150.00	300.00

JARO

Number	Title (A Side/B Side)	Yr	VG	VG+	NM
❑ JAM-5007 [M]	The Arrival of Kenny Dorham	1960	100.00	200.00	400.00
❑ JAS-8007 [S]	The Arrival of Kenny Dorham	1960	100.00	200.00	400.00

JAZZLAND

Number	Title (A Side/B Side)	Yr	VG	VG+	NM
❑ JLP-3 [M]	The Swingers	1960	10.00	20.00	40.00
❑ JLP-14 [M]	Kenny Dorham and Friends	1960	10.00	20.00	40.00
❑ JLP-82 [M]	Kenny Dorham and Friends	1962	5.00	10.00	20.00
❑ JLP-903 [S]	The Swingers	1960	12.50	25.00	50.00
❑ JLP-914 [S]	Kenny Dorham and Friends	1960	12.50	25.00	50.00
❑ JLP-982 [S]	Kenny Dorham and Friends	1962	6.25	12.50	25.00

NEW JAZZ

Number	Title (A Side/B Side)	Yr	VG	VG+	NM
❑ NJLP-8225 [M]	Quiet Kenny	1959	20.00	40.00	80.00
—Purple label					
❑ NJLP-8225 [M]	Quiet Kenny	1965	6.25	12.50	25.00
—Blue label, trident logo at right					

PACIFIC JAZZ

Number	Title (A Side/B Side)	Yr	VG	VG+	NM
❑ PJ-41 [M]	Inta Somethin' — Recorded Live at the Jazz Workshop	1962	7.50	15.00	30.00
❑ ST-41 [S]	Inta Somethin' — Recorded Live at the Jazz Workshop	1962	10.00	20.00	40.00

PRESTIGE

Number	Title (A Side/B Side)	Yr	VG	VG+	NM
❑ PRST-7754	Kenny Dorham 1959	1970	5.00	10.00	20.00

RIVERSIDE

Number	Title (A Side/B Side)	Yr	VG	VG+	NM
❑ RLP 12-239 [M]	Jazz Contrasts	1957	20.00	40.00	80.00
—White label, blue print					
❑ RLP 12-239 [M]	Jazz Contrasts	1959	10.00	20.00	40.00
—Blue label, microphone logo					
❑ RLP 12-255 [M]	2 Horns 2 Rhythm	1957	12.50	25.00	50.00
❑ RLP 12-275 [M]	This Is the Moment!	1958	12.50	25.00	50.00

Number	Title (A Side/B Side)	Yr	VG	VG+	NM
❏ RLP 12-297 [M]	Blue Spring	1959	12.50	25.00	50.00
❏ RLP-1105 [S]	Jazz Contrasts	1959	7.50	15.00	30.00
—Black label, microphone logo					
❏ RLP-1139 [S]	Blue Spring	1959	10.00	20.00	40.00
TIME					
❏ S-2004 [S]	Jazz Contemporary	1960	12.50	25.00	50.00
❏ S-2024 [S]	Show Boat	1960	12.50	25.00	50.00
❏ 52004 [M]	Jazz Contemporary	1960	10.00	20.00	40.00
❏ 52024 [M]	Show Boat	1960	10.00	20.00	40.00
UNITED ARTISTS					
❏ UAS-5051	Matador	1971	5.00	10.00	20.00
—Reissue of 15007					
❏ UAJ-14007 [M]	Matador	1962	7.50	15.00	30.00
❏ UAJS-15007 [S]	Matador	1962	10.00	20.00	40.00

DORHAM, KENNY/CLARK TERRY

Number	Title (A Side/B Side)	Yr	VG	VG+	NM
JAZZLAND					
❏ JLP-10 [M]	Top Trumpets	1960	10.00	20.00	40.00
❏ JLP-910 [S]	Top Trumpets	1960	12.50	25.00	50.00

DOROUGH, BOB

Number	Title (A Side/B Side)	Yr	VG	VG+	NM
BETHLEHEM					
❏ BCP-11 [M]	Devil May Care	1955	30.00	60.00	120.00
❏ BCP-6023	Yardbird Suite	197?	5.00	10.00	20.00
—Reissue of 11, distributed by RCA Victor					
FOCUS					
❏ FL-336 [M]	Better Than Anything	1967	6.25	12.50	25.00
❏ FS-336 [S]	Better Than Anything	1967	5.00	10.00	20.00
LAISSEZ-FAIRE					
❏ 02	Beginning to See the Light	1976	5.00	10.00	20.00
MUSIC MINUS ONE					
❏ 225 [M]	Oliver	1963	6.25	12.50	25.00

DORS, DIANA

Number	Title (A Side/B Side)	Yr	VG	VG+	NM
COLUMBIA					
❏ CL 1436 [M]	Swingin' Dors	1960	20.00	40.00	80.00
❏ CS 8232 [S]	Swingin' Dors	1960	25.00	50.00	100.00

DORSEY, JIMMY

Number	Title (A Side/B Side)	Yr	VG	VG+	NM
COLUMBIA					
❏ CL 608 [M]	Dixie by Dorsey	1955	7.50	15.00	30.00
—Red and black label with six "eye" logos					
❏ CL 608 [M]	Dixie by Dorsey	1955	10.00	20.00	40.00
—Maroon label with gold print					
❏ CL 6095 [10]	Dixie by Dorsey	1950	12.50	25.00	50.00
❏ CL 6114 [10]	Dorseyland Band	1950	12.50	25.00	50.00
CORAL					
❏ CRL 56004 [10]	Contrasting Music, Volume 1	1950	12.50	25.00	50.00
❏ CRL 56008 [10]	Contrasting Music, Volume 2	1950	12.50	25.00	50.00
❏ CRL 56033 [10]	Gershwin Music	1950	12.50	25.00	50.00
DECCA					
❏ DL 4853 [M]	Jimmy Dorsey's Greatest Hits	1967	5.00	10.00	20.00
❏ DL 5091 [10]	Latin American Favorites	1950	12.50	25.00	50.00
❏ DL 8153 [M]	Latin American Favorites	1955	7.50	15.00	30.00
—Black label, silver print					
❏ DL 8609 [M]	The Great Jimmy Dorsey	1957	6.25	12.50	25.00
—Black label, silver print					
DOT					
❏ DLP-3437 [M]	So Rare	1962	5.00	10.00	20.00
—Reissue of Fraternity LP					
FRATERNITY					
❏ F-1008 [M]	Fabulous Jimmy Dorsey	1957	7.50	15.00	30.00

DORSEY, LEE

Number	Title (A Side/B Side)	Yr	VG	VG+	NM
AMY					
❏ 8010 [M]	Ride Your Pony	1966	7.50	15.00	30.00
❏ 8010-S [S]	Ride Your Pony	1966	10.00	20.00	40.00
❏ 8011 [M]	The New Lee Dorsey/Working in the Coal Mine-Holy Cow	1966	6.25	12.50	25.00
❏ 8011-S [S]	The New Lee Dorsey/Working in the Coal Mine-Holy Cow	1966	7.50	15.00	30.00
ARISTA					
❏ AL 8387	Holy Cow! The Best of Lee Dorsey	1985	2.50	5.00	10.00
FURY					
❏ 1002 [M]	Ya Ya	1962	75.00	150.00	300.00
POLYDOR					
❏ 24-4024	Yes We Can	1970	3.00	6.00	12.00
SPHERE SOUND					
❏ SR-7003 [M]	Ya Ya	196?	25.00	50.00	100.00
—Reissue of Fury 1002					
❏ SSR-7003 [R]	Ya Ya	196?	12.50	25.00	50.00
—Rechanneled reissue of Fury 1002					

DORSEY, TOMMY

On albums with asterisks (*) after them, some of the tracks feature FRANK SINATRA as lead vocalist.

Number	Title (A Side/B Side)	Yr	VG	VG+	NM
DECCA					
❏ DL 5317 [10]	Tommy Dorsey Plays Howard Dietz	1951	12.50	25.00	50.00
❏ DL 5448 [10]	In a Sentimental Mood	1952	12.50	25.00	50.00
❏ DL 5449 [10]	Tenderly	1952	12.50	25.00	50.00
❏ DL 5452 [10]	Your Invitation to Dance	1952	12.50	25.00	50.00
RCA VICTOR					
❏ LPT-10 [M]	Getting Sentimental with Tommy Dorsey*	1951	20.00	40.00	80.00
❏ ALPT-15 [10]	All Time Hits*	1951	20.00	40.00	80.00
❏ LPM-22 [10]	Tommy Dorsey Plays Cole Porter for Dancing	1951	12.50	25.00	50.00
❏ LPM-1229 [M]	Yes Indeed*	1956	12.50	25.00	50.00
❏ LPM-1425 [M]	Tommy Dorsey Plays Cole Porter and Jerome Kern	1956	6.25	12.50	25.00
❏ LPM-1432 [M]	Tribute to Dorsey, Volume 1*	1956	10.00	20.00	40.00
❏ LPM-1433 [M]	Tribute to Dorsey, Volume 2*	1956	10.00	20.00	40.00
❏ LPM-1643 [M]	Having a Wonderful Time*	1958	10.00	20.00	40.00

Number	Title (A Side/B Side)	Yr	VG	VG+	NM
❏ LPT-3005 [M]	This Is Tommy Dorsey*	1952	20.00	40.00	80.00
❏ LPT-3018 [10]	This Is Tommy Dorsey	1952	12.50	25.00	50.00
❏ LPM-3674 [M]	The Best of Tommy Dorsey*	1966	5.00	10.00	20.00
❏ LPM-6003 [(2)M]	That Sentimental Gentleman*	1957	20.00	40.00	80.00
—Box set					
❏ VPM-6038 [(2)]	This Is Tommy Dorsey*	197?	6.25	12.50	25.00
❏ VPM-6064 [(2)]	This Is Tommy Dorsey, Volume 2*	197?	6.25	12.50	25.00
❏ VPM-6087 [(2)]	This Is Tommy Dorsey and His Clambake Seven	1973	5.00	10.00	20.00
—Orange labels					
❏ VPM-6087 [(2)]	This Is Tommy Dorsey and His Clambake Seven	1977	3.75	7.50	15.00
—Black labels, dog near top					
TIME-LIFE					
❏ STBB-02 [(2)]	Tommy Dorsey*	1983	5.00	10.00	20.00
20TH CENTURY FOX					
❏ TCF 101/102 [(2)M]	Tommy Dorsey's Greatest Band	1959	7.50	15.00	30.00
❏ TFM-3157 [M]	This Is Tommy Dorsey and His Greatest Band, Vol. 1	196?	5.00	10.00	20.00
❏ TFM-3158 [M]	This Is Tommy Dorsey and His Greatest Band, Vol. 2	196?	5.00	10.00	20.00

DORSEY, TOMMY, ORCHESTRA (WARREN COVINGTON, DIRECTOR)

Number	Title (A Side/B Side)	Yr	VG	VG+	NM
DECCA					
❏ DL 74120 [S]	Dance to the Songs Everybody Knows	1960	5.00	10.00	20.00
❏ DL 74130 [S]	Tricky Trombones	1961	5.00	10.00	20.00
❏ DL 78802 [S]	The Fabulous Arrangements of Tommy Dorsey	1958	5.00	10.00	20.00
❏ DL 78842 [S]	Tea for Two Cha Chas	1958	5.00	10.00	20.00
❏ DL 78904 [S]	Dance and Romance	1959	5.00	10.00	20.00
❏ DL 78943 [S]	More Tea for Two Cha Chas	1959	5.00	10.00	20.00
❏ DL 78980 [S]	It Takes Two to Cha-Cha…	1959	5.00	10.00	20.00
❏ DL 78996 [S]	It Takes Two to Bunny Hop..	1960	5.00	10.00	20.00

DORSEY BROTHERS, THE

Number	Title (A Side/B Side)	Yr	VG	VG+	NM
COLUMBIA					
❏ C2L 8 [(2)]	The Fabulous Dorseys in Hi-Fi	1958	10.00	20.00	40.00
—Red and black labels with six "eye" logos					
❏ CL 1240 [M]	Sentimental and Swinging	1958	6.25	12.50	25.00
—Red and black label with six "eye" logos					
DECCA					
❏ DL 8631 [M]	Dixieland Jazz	1958	6.25	12.50	25.00
—Black label, silver print					
❏ DL 8654 [M]	The Swinging Dorseys	1958	6.25	12.50	25.00
—Black label, silver print					
RIVERSIDE					
❏ RLP 12-811 [M]	A Backward Glance	1958	15.00	30.00	60.00
❏ RLP-1008 [10]	Jazz of the Roaring Twenties	1953	20.00	40.00	80.00
❏ RLP-1051 [10]	The Dorsey Brothers with the California Ramblers	1955	20.00	40.00	80.00

DOUBLE SIX OF PARIS, THE

Number	Title (A Side/B Side)	Yr	VG	VG+	NM
CAPITOL					
❏ ST 10259 [S]	The Double Six of Paris	1961	6.25	12.50	25.00
❏ T 10259 [M]	The Double Six of Paris	1961	5.00	10.00	20.00
PHILIPS					
❏ PHM 200026 [M]	Swingin' Singin'	1962	5.00	10.00	20.00
❏ PHM 200141 [M]	The Double Six of Paris Sings Ray Charles	1964	5.00	10.00	20.00
❏ PHS 600026 [S]	Swingin' Singin'	1962	6.25	12.50	25.00
❏ PHS 600141 [S]	The Double Six of Paris Sings Ray Charles	1964	6.25	12.50	25.00

DOUGLAS, GLENN

Number	Title (A Side/B Side)	Yr	VG	VG+	NM
DECCA					
❏ DL 8748 [M]	Heartbreak Alley	1958	12.50	25.00	50.00

DOUGLAS, K.C.

Number	Title (A Side/B Side)	Yr	VG	VG+	NM
BLUESVILLE					
❏ BVLP-1023 [M]	K.C.'s Blues	1961	20.00	40.00	80.00
—Blue label, silver print					
❏ BVLP-1023 [M]	K.C.'s Blues	1964	7.50	15.00	30.00
—Blue label, trident logo at right					
❏ BVLP-1050 [M]	Big Road Blues	1962	20.00	40.00	80.00
—Blue label, silver print					
❏ BVLP-1050 [M]	Big Road Blues	1964	7.50	15.00	30.00
—Blue label, trident logo at right					
COOK ROAD					
❏ 5002 [M]	A Dead Beat Guitar and the Mississippi Blues	1956	125.00	250.00	500.00

DOUGLAS, LEW

Number	Title (A Side/B Side)	Yr	VG	VG+	NM
CARLTON					
❏ LP 12-126 [M]	Themes from Motion Pictures and TV	1960	6.25	12.50	25.00

DOUGLAS, STEVE

Number	Title (A Side/B Side)	Yr	VG	VG+	NM
CROWN					
❏ CLP-5251 [M]	Twist with Steve Douglas and the Rebel Rousers	1962	5.00	10.00	20.00
MERCURY					
❏ SR-61217	Reflections in a Golden Horn	1969	6.25	12.50	25.00

DOUGLAS, TONY

Number	Title (A Side/B Side)	Yr	VG	VG+	NM
DOT					
❏ DLP-26009	Thank You for Touching My Life	1973	3.75	7.50	15.00
PAULA					
❏ LP 2198	Heart	1967	5.00	10.00	20.00

DOVAL, JIM, AND THE GAUCHOS

Number	Title (A Side/B Side)	Yr	VG	VG+	NM
ABC-PARAMOUNT					
❏ ABC-506 [M]	The Gauchos Featuring Jim Doval	1965	7.50	15.00	30.00
❏ ABCS-506 [S]	The Gauchos Featuring Jim Doval	1965	10.00	20.00	40.00

Number	Title (A Side/B Side)	Yr	VG	VG+	NM
DOVE, RONNIE					
DIAMOND					
❏ D 5002 [M]	Right or Wrong	1964	5.00	10.00	20.00
❏ DS 5002 [S]	Right or Wrong	1964	6.25	12.50	25.00
❏ D 5003 [M]	One Kiss for Old Times' Sake	1965	5.00	10.00	20.00
❏ DS 5003 [S]	One Kiss for Old Times' Sake	1965	6.25	12.50	25.00
❏ D 5004 [M]	I'll Make All Your Dreams Come True	1965	5.00	10.00	20.00
❏ DS 5004 [S]	I'll Make All Your Dreams Come True	1965	6.25	12.50	25.00
❏ D 5005 [M]	The Best of Ronnie Dove	1966	3.75	7.50	15.00
❏ DS 5005 [S]	The Best of Ronnie Dove	1966	5.00	10.00	20.00
❏ D 5006 [M]	Ronnie Dove Sings the Hits for You	1966	3.75	7.50	15.00
❏ DS 5006 [S]	Ronnie Dove Sings the Hits for You	1966	5.00	10.00	20.00
❏ D 5007 [M]	Cry	1967	3.75	7.50	15.00
❏ DS 5007 [S]	Cry	1967	5.00	10.00	20.00
❏ D-5008 [M]	The Best of Ronnie Dove — Vol. 2	1968	7.50	15.00	30.00
❏ SD-5008 [S]	The Best of Ronnie Dove — Vol. 2	1968	3.75	7.50	15.00
POWER PAK					
❏ 286	Greatest Hits	1975	3.00	6.00	12.00
DOVELLS, THE					
CAMEO					
❏ C-1082 [M]	Len Barry Sings with the Dovells	1965	7.50	15.00	30.00
❏ SC-1082 [S]	Len Barry Sings with the Dovells	1965	12.50	25.00	50.00
PARKWAY					
❏ P 7006 [M]	The Bristol Stomp	1961	20.00	40.00	80.00
—Light orange label					
❏ P 7006 [M]	The Bristol Stomp	1962	12.50	25.00	50.00
—Dark orange and yellow label					
❏ P 7010 [M]	All the Hits of the Teen Groups	1962	12.50	25.00	50.00
❏ P 7021 [M]	For Your Hully Gully Party	1962	12.50	25.00	50.00
❏ P 7025 [M]	You Can't Sit Down	1963	12.50	25.00	50.00
WYNCOTE					
❏ SW 9052 [R]	Discotheque	1965	3.75	7.50	15.00
❏ W 9052 [M]	Discotheque	1965	5.00	10.00	20.00
❏ SW 9114 [R]	The Dovells' Biggest Hits	1965	3.75	7.50	15.00
❏ W 9114 [M]	The Dovells' Biggest Hits	1965	5.00	10.00	20.00
DOWELL, JOE					
SMASH					
❏ MGS-27000 [M]	Wooden Heart	1961	10.00	20.00	40.00
❏ MGS-27011 [M]	German American Hits	1962	6.25	12.50	25.00
❏ SRS-67000 [S]	Wooden Heart	1961	12.50	25.00	50.00
❏ SRS-67011 [S]	German American Hits	1962	7.50	15.00	30.00
WING					
❏ MGW-12328 [M]	Wooden Heart	196?	5.00	10.00	20.00
❏ SRW-16328 [S]	Wooden Heart	196?	5.00	10.00	20.00
DOWLING, CHET, AND BILL MINKIN					
COLUMBIA					
❏ CL 2776 [M]	Senator Bobby's Christmas Party	1967	5.00	10.00	20.00
❏ CS 9576 [S]	Senator Bobby's Christmas Party	1967	5.00	10.00	20.00
DOWNS, HUGH					
EPIC					
❏ BN 541 [S]	An Evening with Hugh Downs	1961	7.50	15.00	30.00
❏ LN 3597 [M]	An Evening with Hugh Downs	1961	6.25	12.50	25.00
DOYLE, BOBBY, THREE					
KENNY ROGERS was in this group.					
COLUMBIA					
❏ CL 1858 [M]	In a Most Unusual Way	1962	10.00	20.00	40.00
❏ CS 8658 [S]	In a Most Unusual Way	1962	12.50	25.00	50.00
DOYLE, MIKE					
FLEETWOOD					
❏ FLP-3018 [M]	The Secrets of Surfing	1963	30.00	60.00	120.00
DOZIER, GENE, AND THE BROTHERHOOD					
MINIT					
❏ 24010 [S]	Blues Power	1967	6.25	12.50	25.00
❏ 40010 [M]	Blues Power	1967	6.25	12.50	25.00
DRAGONFLY					
MEGAPHONE					
❏ MS-1202	Dragonfly	1968	75.00	150.00	300.00
DRAGSTERS, THE					
WING					
❏ MGW-12269 [M]	Hey Little Cobra/Drag City	1964	20.00	40.00	80.00
❏ SRW-16269 [S]	Hey Little Cobra/Drag City	1964	25.00	50.00	100.00
DRAKE, DONNA					
LUXOR					
❏ LP-1 [M]	The Wynton Kelly Trio Introduces Donna Drake — Donna Sings Dinah	1968	7.50	15.00	30.00
❏ LPS-1 [S]	The Wynton Kelly Trio Introduces Donna Drake — Donna Sings Dinah	1968	5.00	10.00	20.00
DRAKE, GUY					
ROYAL AMERICAN					
❏ 1001	Welfare Cadillac	1970	6.25	12.50	25.00
DRAKE, NICK					
ANTILLES					
❏ AN-7010	Five Leaves Left	197?	3.75	7.50	15.00
—Released in England in 1969					
❏ AN-7028	Bryter Layter	1977	3.75	7.50	15.00
—Released in England in 1970					
HANNIBAL					
❏ NHBL-1318	Time of No Reply	198?	3.00	6.00	12.00
❏ HNBX-5302 [(3)]	Fruit Tree	198?	6.25	12.50	25.00
ISLAND					
❏ SMAS-9307	Nick Drake	1971	6.25	12.50	25.00
❏ SMAS-9318	Pink Moon	1972	6.25	12.50	25.00
DRAKE, PETE					
CANAAN					
❏ 4640 [M]	Steel Away	1967	3.75	7.50	15.00
❏ 9640 [S]	Steel Away	1967	5.00	10.00	20.00
CUMBERLAND					
❏ MGC-29053 [M]	Country Steel Guitar	1963	5.00	10.00	20.00
❏ SRC-69053 [S]	Country Steel Guitar	1963	6.25	12.50	25.00
HILLTOP					
❏ 6052 [M]	Are You Sincere	1967	3.00	6.00	12.00
❏ S-6052 [S]	Are You Sincere	1967	3.00	6.00	12.00
SMASH					
❏ MGS-27053 [M]	Forever	1964	3.75	7.50	15.00
❏ MGS-27060 [M]	Talking Steel Guitar	1965	3.75	7.50	15.00
❏ MGS-27064 [M]	Talking Steel and Singing Strings	1965	3.75	7.50	15.00
❏ SRS-67053 [S]	Forever	1964	5.00	10.00	20.00
❏ SRS-67060 [S]	Talking Steel Guitar	1965	5.00	10.00	20.00
❏ SRS-67064 [S]	Talking Steel and Singing Strings	1965	5.00	10.00	20.00
STARDAY					
❏ SLP-180 [M]	The Fabulous Steel Guitar of Pete Drake	1962	10.00	20.00	40.00
❏ SLP-319 [M]	The Amazing Incredible Pete Drake	1964	7.50	15.00	30.00
STOP					
❏ 1011	The Pete Drake Show	1970	3.00	6.00	12.00
DRAMATICS, THE					
ABC					
❏ D-867	The Dramatic Jackpot	1975	3.75	7.50	15.00
❏ D-916	Drama V	1975	3.75	7.50	15.00
❏ D-955	Joy Ride	1976	3.75	7.50	15.00
❏ AB-1010	Shake It Well	1977	3.75	7.50	15.00
❏ AA-1072	Do What You Wanna Do	1978	3.75	7.50	15.00
❏ AA-1125	Anytime, Anyplace	1979	3.75	7.50	15.00
CAPITOL					
❏ ST-12205	New Dimension	1982	2.50	5.00	10.00
FANTASY					
❏ 9642	Somewhere in Time: A Dramatic Reunion	1986	3.00	6.00	12.00
MCA					
❏ 761	Dramatic Way	198?	2.00	4.00	8.00
—Reissue of 5149					
❏ 762	10 1/2	198?	2.00	4.00	8.00
—Reissue of 3196					
❏ AA-1125	Anytime, Anyplace	1979	3.00	6.00	12.00
—Reissue of ABC 1125					
❏ 3196	10 1/2	1980	2.50	5.00	10.00
❏ 5149	Dramatic Way	1981	2.50	5.00	10.00
STAX					
❏ STX-4111	Whatcha See Is Whatcha Get	1978	3.00	6.00	12.00
—Reissue of Volt 6018					
❏ STX-4131	A Dramatic Experience	1979	3.00	6.00	12.00
—Reissue of Volt 6019					
❏ MPS-8523	Dramatically Yours	198?	2.00	4.00	8.00
—Reissue of Volt 9501					
❏ MPS-8526	The Best of the Dramatics	198?	2.50	5.00	10.00
❏ MPS-8545	The Dramatics Live	1988	2.50	5.00	10.00
VOLT					
❏ V-3402	Positive State of Mind	1989	2.50	5.00	10.00
❏ V-3407	Stone Cold	1990	2.50	5.00	10.00
❏ VOS-6018	Whatcha See Is Whatcha Get	1972	6.25	12.50	25.00
❏ VOS-6019	A Dramatic Experience	1973	6.25	12.50	25.00
❏ VOS-9501	Dramatically Yours	1974	6.25	12.50	25.00
DRAPER, RAY					
JOSIE					
❏ JLPS-3004 [S]	Tuba Jazz	1963	5.00	10.00	20.00
❏ JOZ-3004 [M]	Tuba Jazz	1963	6.25	12.50	25.00
JUBILEE					
❏ JLP-1090 [M]	Tuba Jazz	1959	12.50	25.00	50.00
NEW JAZZ					
❏ NJLP-8228 [M]	Ray Draper Quintet Featuring John Coltrane	1958	15.00	30.00	60.00
—Purple label					
❏ NJLP-8228 [M]	Ray Draper Quintet Featuring John Coltrane	1965	6.25	12.50	25.00
—Blue label, trident logo at right					
PRESTIGE					
❏ PRLP-7096 [M]	Tuba Sounds	1957	20.00	40.00	80.00
DRAPER, RUSTY					
GOLDEN CREST					
❏ 31029	The Rusty Draper Show	1973	3.00	6.00	12.00
❏ 31030	Tour the USA	1973	3.00	6.00	12.00
MERCURY					
❏ MG-20068 [M]	Music for a Rainy Night	1956	7.50	15.00	30.00
❏ MG-20117 [M]	Encores	1957	7.50	15.00	30.00
❏ MG-20118 [M]	Rusty Draper Sings	1957	7.50	15.00	30.00
❏ MG-20173 [M]	Rusty Meets Hoagy	1957	7.50	15.00	30.00
❏ MG-20499 [M]	Hits That Sold a Million	1960	7.50	15.00	30.00
❏ MG-20657 [M]	Country and Western Golden Greats	1961	7.50	15.00	30.00
❏ SR-60176 [S]	Hits That Sold a Million	1960	10.00	20.00	40.00
❏ SR-60657 [S]	Country and Western Golden Greats	1961	10.00	20.00	40.00
MONUMENT					
❏ 6638	Greatest Hits	1977	3.00	6.00	12.00
❏ MLP-8005 [M]	Greatest Hits	1964	3.75	7.50	15.00
❏ MLP-8018 [M]	Night Life	1964	3.75	7.50	15.00
❏ MLP-8026 [M]	Rusty Draper Plays Guitar	1965	3.75	7.50	15.00
❏ SLP-18005 [S]	Greatest Hits	1964	5.00	10.00	20.00
❏ SLP-18018 [S]	Night Life	1964	5.00	10.00	20.00
❏ SLP-18026 [S]	Rusty Draper Plays Guitar	1965	5.00	10.00	20.00
❏ SLP-18105	Something Old, Something New	1969	3.75	7.50	15.00

Number	Title (A Side/B Side)	Yr	VG	VG+	NM
❑ ZG 33870 [(2)]	Swingin' Country/Something Old, Something New	1976	3.75	7.50	15.00

WING

Number	Title (A Side/B Side)	Yr	VG	VG+	NM
❑ MGW-12243 [M]	Hits That Sold a Million	196?	3.75	7.50	15.00
❑ MGW-12274 [M]	Country Classics	196?	3.75	7.50	15.00
❑ SRW-16243 [S]	Hits That Sold a Million	196?	3.75	7.50	15.00
❑ SRW-16274 [S]	Country Classics	196?	3.75	7.50	15.00

DREAD ZEPPELIN
I.R.S.

Number	Title (A Side/B Side)	Yr	VG	VG+	NM
❑ X1-13048	Un-Led-Ed	1990	5.00	10.00	20.00

—All copies on gold vinyl

DREAM 6
With Johnette Napolitano, later of CONCRETE BLONDE.
HAPPY HERMIT

Number	Title (A Side/B Side)	Yr	VG	VG+	NM
❑ 1983 [EP]	Dream 6	1983	10.00	20.00	40.00

DREAM SYNDICATE, THE
A&M

Number	Title (A Side/B Side)	Yr	VG	VG+	NM
❑ SP-12511	This Is Not the New Dream Syndicate Album...Live	1984	3.00	6.00	12.00

BIG TIME

Number	Title (A Side/B Side)	Yr	VG	VG+	NM
❑ 10022	Out of the Grey	1985	2.50	5.00	10.00

DOWN THERE

Number	Title (A Side/B Side)	Yr	VG	VG+	NM
❑ 2 [EP]	Sure Thing + 3	1982	5.00	10.00	20.00

ENIGMA

Number	Title (A Side/B Side)	Yr	VG	VG+	NM
❑ 73341	Ghost Stories	1988	2.00	4.00	8.00

RUBY

Number	Title (A Side/B Side)	Yr	VG	VG+	NM
❑ 807	The Days of Wine and Roses	1982	5.00	10.00	20.00

SLASH

Number	Title (A Side/B Side)	Yr	VG	VG+	NM
❑ 23844	The Days of Wine and Roses	1982	3.75	7.50	15.00

DREAMLOVERS, THE
COLLECTABLES

Number	Title (A Side/B Side)	Yr	VG	VG+	NM
❑ COL-5004	The Best of the Dreamlovers	198?	3.00	6.00	12.00
❑ COL-5005	The Best of the Dreamlovers, Volume Two	198?	3.00	6.00	12.00

COLUMBIA

Number	Title (A Side/B Side)	Yr	VG	VG+	NM
❑ CL 2020 [M]	The Bird and Other Golden Dancing Grooves	1963	10.00	20.00	40.00
❑ CS 8820 [S]	The Bird and Other Golden Dancing Grooves	1963	12.50	25.00	50.00

DREAMS AND ILLUSIONS
VERVE FORECAST

Number	Title (A Side/B Side)	Yr	VG	VG+	NM
❑ FTS-3040	Dreams and Illusions	1968	5.00	10.00	20.00

DREW, DAN
See BOOTS BROWN.

DREW, DORIS
MODE

Number	Title (A Side/B Side)	Yr	VG	VG+	NM
❑ MOD-126 [M]	The Delightful Doris Drew	1957	20.00	40.00	80.00

DREW, KENNY
BLUE NOTE

Number	Title (A Side/B Side)	Yr	VG	VG+	NM
❑ BLP-4059 [M]	Undercurrent	1961	20.00	40.00	80.00

—"W. 63rd St." address on label

❑ BLP-4059 [M]	Undercurrent	1964	6.25	12.50	25.00

—"New York, USA" address on label

| ❑ BLP-5023 [10] | Introducing the Kenny Drew Trio | 1953 | 100.00 | 200.00 | 400.00 |
| ❑ BST-84059 [S] | Undercurrent | 1961 | 20.00 | 40.00 | 80.00 |

—"W. 63rd St." address on label

❑ BST-84059 [S]	Undercurrent	1964	6.25	12.50	25.00

—"New York, USA" address on label

JAZZ WEST

Number	Title (A Side/B Side)	Yr	VG	VG+	NM
❑ JWLP-4 [M]	Walkin' and Talkin' with the Kenny Drew Quartet	1955	75.00	150.00	300.00

JUDSON

Number	Title (A Side/B Side)	Yr	VG	VG+	NM
❑ L-3004 [M]	Harry Warren Showcase	1957	12.50	25.00	50.00
❑ L-3005 [M]	Harold Arlen Showcase	1957	12.50	25.00	50.00

NORGRAN

Number	Title (A Side/B Side)	Yr	VG	VG+	NM
❑ MGN-29 [10]	The Ideation of Kenny Drew	1954	62.50	125.00	250.00
❑ MGN-1002 [M]	Progressive Piano	1954	50.00	100.00	200.00
❑ MGN-1066 [M]	The Modernity of Kenny Drew	1956	37.50	75.00	150.00

RIVERSIDE

Number	Title (A Side/B Side)	Yr	VG	VG+	NM
❑ RLP 12-224 [M]	Kenny Drew Trio	195?	12.50	25.00	50.00

—Blue labe, microphone logo at top

❑ RLP 12-224 [M]	Kenny Drew Trio	1956	37.50	75.00	150.00

—White label, blue print

❑ RLP 12-236 [M]	This Is New	195?	12.50	25.00	50.00

—Blue labe, microphone logo at top

❑ RLP 12-236 [M]	This Is New	1957	37.50	75.00	150.00

—White label, blue print

❑ RLP 12-249 [M]	Pal Joey	1957	12.50	25.00	50.00
❑ RLP 12-811 [M]	I Love Jerome Kern	1956	37.50	75.00	150.00
❑ RLP-1112 [S]	Pal Joey	1959	10.00	20.00	40.00

DREW, KENNY; DONALD BYRD; HANK MOBLEY
JAZZLAND

Number	Title (A Side/B Side)	Yr	VG	VG+	NM
❑ JLP-6 [M]	Hard Bop	1960	12.50	25.00	50.00

—Reissue of Riverside 236

❑ JLP-906 [S]	Hard Bop	1960	10.00	20.00	40.00

DREW, KENNY; PAUL CHAMBERS; PHILLY JOE JONES
JAZZLAND

Number	Title (A Side/B Side)	Yr	VG	VG+	NM
❑ JLP-9 [M]	The Tough Piano Trio	1960	12.50	25.00	50.00

—Reissue of Riverside 224

❑ JLP-909 [S]	The Tough Piano Trio	1960	10.00	20.00	40.00

DREW, PATTI
CAPITOL

Number	Title (A Side/B Side)	Yr	VG	VG+	NM
❑ ST-156	I've Been Here All the Time	1969	5.00	10.00	20.00
❑ ST-408	Wild Is Love	1970	5.00	10.00	20.00

Number	Title (A Side/B Side)	Yr	VG	VG+	NM
❑ ST 2804 [S]	Tell Him	1968	7.50	15.00	30.00
❑ T 2804 [M]	Tell Him	1968	7.50	15.00	30.00

DRIFTERS, THE
ARISTA

Number	Title (A Side/B Side)	Yr	VG	VG+	NM
❑ AB 4140	Every Night Is Saturday Night	1976	3.00	6.00	12.00

ATCO

Number	Title (A Side/B Side)	Yr	VG	VG+	NM
❑ SD 33-375 [R]	Their Greatest Recordings — The Early Years	1971	3.00	6.00	12.00

ATLANTIC

Number	Title (A Side/B Side)	Yr	VG	VG+	NM
❑ 8003 [M]	Clyde McPhatter and the Drifters	1956	125.00	250.00	500.00

—Black label

❑ 8003 [M]	Clyde McPhatter and the Drifters	1959	15.00	30.00	60.00

—Red and purple label, white "fan" logo at right

❑ 8003 [M]	Clyde McPhatter and the Drifters	1963	10.00	20.00	40.00

—Red and purple label, black "fan" logo at right

❑ 8022 [M]	Rockin' and Driftin'	1958	125.00	250.00	500.00

—White "bullseye" label

❑ 8022 [M]	Rockin' and Driftin'	1958	150.00	300.00	600.00

—Black label

❑ 8022 [M]	Rockin' and Driftin'	1959	15.00	30.00	60.00

—Red and purple label, white "fan" logo at right

❑ 8022 [M]	Rockin' and Driftin'	1963	10.00	20.00	40.00

—Red and purple label, black "fan" logo at right

❑ 8041 [M]	The Drifters' Greatest Hits	1960	25.00	50.00	100.00

—Red and purple label, white "fan" logo at right

❑ 8041 [M]	The Drifters' Greatest Hits	1960	150.00	300.00	600.00

—Black label

❑ 8041 [M]	The Drifters' Greatest Hits	1963	12.50	25.00	50.00

—Red and purple label, black "fan" logo at right

❑ 8059 [M]	Save the Last Dance for Me	1962	30.00	60.00	120.00

—Red and purple label, white "fan" logo at right

❑ 8059 [M]	Save the Last Dance for Me	1963	15.00	30.00	60.00

—Red and purple label, black "fan" logo at right

❑ SD 8059 [S]	Save the Last Dance for Me	1962	50.00	100.00	200.00

—Green and blue label, white "fan" logo at right

❑ SD 8059 [S]	Save the Last Dance for Me	1963	25.00	50.00	100.00

—Green and blue label, black "fan" logo at right

❑ SD 8059 [S]	Save the Last Dance for Me	1969	6.25	12.50	25.00

—Red and green label, white horizontal stripe through center hole

❑ 8073 [M]	Up on the Roof — The Best of the Drifters	1963	25.00	50.00	100.00

—Red and purple label, black "fan" logo at right

❑ SD 8073 [S]	Up on the Roof — The Best of the Drifters	1963	37.50	75.00	150.00

—Green and blue label, black "fan" logo at right

❑ 8093 [M]	Our Biggest Hits	1964	15.00	30.00	60.00

—Red and purple label, white "fan" logo at right

❑ SD 8093 [S]	Our Biggest Hits	1964	20.00	40.00	80.00

—Mostly red label, black "fan" logo

❑ 8099 [M]	Under the Boardwalk	1964	12.50	25.00	50.00

—Color photo of group on cover

❑ 8099 [M]	Under the Boardwalk	1964	20.00	40.00	80.00

—Black and white photo of group on cover

❑ SD 8099 [S]	Under the Boardwalk	1964	15.00	30.00	60.00

—Color photo of group on cover

❑ SD 8099 [S]	Under the Boardwalk	1964	30.00	60.00	120.00

—Black and white photo of group on cover

❑ 8103 [M]	The Good Life with the Drifters	1965	10.00	20.00	40.00
❑ SD 8103 [S]	The Good Life with the Drifters	1965	12.50	25.00	50.00
❑ 8113 [M]	I'll Take You Where the Music's Playing	1965	10.00	20.00	40.00
❑ SD 8113 [S]	I'll Take You Where the Music's Playing	1965	12.50	25.00	50.00
❑ 8153 [M]	The Drifters' Golden Hits	1968	7.50	15.00	30.00
❑ SD 8153 [P]	The Drifters' Golden Hits	1968	7.50	15.00	30.00

—Green and blue label

❑ SD 8153 [P]	The Drifters' Golden Hits	1969	3.75	7.50	15.00

—Red and green label

| ❑ 81927 [(2)] | Let the Boogie-Woogie Roll: Greatest Hits 1953-1958 | 1989 | 3.75 | 7.50 | 15.00 |
| ❑ 81931 [(2)] | All-Time Greatest Hits and More: 1959-1965 | 1989 | 3.75 | 7.50 | 15.00 |

CLARION

Number	Title (A Side/B Side)	Yr	VG	VG+	NM
❑ 608 [M]	The Drifters	1964	5.00	10.00	20.00
❑ SD 608 [P]	The Drifters	1964	7.50	15.00	30.00

GUSTO

Number	Title (A Side/B Side)	Yr	VG	VG+	NM
❑ 0063	Greatest Hits — The Drifters	1980	2.50	5.00	10.00

TRIP

Number	Title (A Side/B Side)	Yr	VG	VG+	NM
❑ TOP-16-6	16 Greatest Hits — The Drifters	1976	2.50	5.00	10.00

DRIFTIN' SLIM
MILESTONE

Number	Title (A Side/B Side)	Yr	VG	VG+	NM
❑ MLS-93004 [(2)]	Driftin' Slim and His Blues Band	1968	6.25	12.50	25.00

DRIFTING COWBOYS, THE
MGM

Number	Title (A Side/B Side)	Yr	VG	VG+	NM
❑ SE-4626	We Remember Hank Williams	1968	5.00	10.00	20.00

DRIFTWOOD, JIMMIE
MONUMENT

Number	Title (A Side/B Side)	Yr	VG	VG+	NM
❑ MLP-8006 [M]	Voice of the People	1963	5.00	10.00	20.00
❑ MLP-8019 [M]	Down in the Arkansas	1965	5.00	10.00	20.00
❑ SLP-18006 [S]	Voice of the People	1963	6.25	12.50	25.00
❑ SLP-18019 [S]	Down in the Arkansas	1965	6.25	12.50	25.00

RCA VICTOR

Number	Title (A Side/B Side)	Yr	VG	VG+	NM
❑ LPM-1635 [M]	Newly Discovered Early American Folk Songs	1958	12.50	25.00	50.00
❑ LPM-1994 [M]	Jimmie Driftwood and the Wilderness Road	1959	7.50	15.00	30.00
❑ LSP-1994 [S]	Jimmie Driftwood and the Wilderness Road	1959	10.00	20.00	40.00
❑ LPM-2171 [M]	The Westward Movement	1960	7.50	15.00	30.00
❑ LSP-2171 [S]	The Westward Movement	1960	10.00	20.00	40.00
❑ LPM-2228 [M]	Tall Tales in Song	1960	7.50	15.00	30.00
❑ LSP-2228 [S]	Tall Tales in Song	1960	10.00	20.00	40.00
❑ LPM-2316 [M]	Songs of Billy Yank and Johnny Reb	1961	7.50	15.00	30.00
❑ LSP-2316 [S]	Songs of Billy Yank and Johnny Reb	1961	10.00	20.00	40.00
❑ LPM-2443 [M]	Driftwood at Sea	1962	7.50	15.00	30.00
❑ LSP-2443 [S]	Driftwood at Sea	1962	10.00	20.00	40.00

Number	Title (A Side/B Side)	Yr	VG	VG+	NM

DRUIDS OF STONEHENGE, THE
UNI

Number	Title (A Side/B Side)	Yr	VG	VG+	NM
☐ 3004 [M]	Creation	1967	15.00	30.00	60.00
☐ 73004 [S]	Creation	1967	20.00	40.00	80.00

DRUSKY, ROY
DECCA

☐ DL 4160 [M]	Anymore with Roy Drusky	1961	6.25	12.50	25.00
☐ DL 4340 [M]	It's My Way	1962	5.00	10.00	20.00
☐ DL 74160 [S]	Anymore with Roy Drusky	1961	7.50	15.00	30.00
☐ DL 74340 [S]	It's My Way	1962	6.25	12.50	25.00

MERCURY

☐ MG-20883 [M]	Songs of the Cities	1963	5.00	10.00	20.00
☐ MG-20919 [M]	Yesterday's Gone	1964	5.00	10.00	20.00
☐ MG-20973 [M]	The Pick of the Country	1964	5.00	10.00	20.00
☐ MG-21006 [M]	Country Music All Around the World	1965	5.00	10.00	20.00
☐ MG-21052 [M]	Roy Drusky's Greatest Hits	1965	5.00	10.00	20.00
☐ MG-21083 [M]	In a New Dimension	1966	5.00	10.00	20.00
☐ MG-21097 [M]	If the Whole World Stopped Lovin'	1966	5.00	10.00	20.00
☐ MG-21118 [M]	Now Is a Lonely Time	1967	6.25	12.50	25.00
☐ SR-60883 [S]	Songs of the Cities	1963	6.25	12.50	25.00
☐ SR-60919 [S]	Yesterday's Gone	1964	6.25	12.50	25.00
☐ SR-60973 [S]	The Pick of the Country	1964	6.25	12.50	25.00
☐ SR-61006 [S]	Country Music All Around the World	1965	6.25	12.50	25.00
☐ SR-61052 [S]	Roy Drusky's Greatest Hits	1965	6.25	12.50	25.00
☐ SR-61083 [S]	In a New Dimension	1966	6.25	12.50	25.00
☐ SR-61097 [S]	If the Whole World Stopped Lovin'	1966	6.25	12.50	25.00
☐ SR-61118 [S]	Now Is a Lonely Time	1967	5.00	10.00	20.00
☐ SR-61145	Roy Drusky's Greatest Hits Vol. 2	1968	5.00	10.00	20.00
☐ SR-61173	Jody and the Kid	1968	5.00	10.00	20.00
☐ SR-61206	Portrait of Roy Drusky	1969	5.00	10.00	20.00
☐ SR-61233	My Grass Is Green	1969	5.00	10.00	20.00
☐ SR-61260	I'll Make Amends	1970	5.00	10.00	20.00
☐ SR-61266	The Best of Roy Drusky	1970	5.00	10.00	20.00
☐ SR-61306	All My Hard Times	1970	5.00	10.00	20.00
☐ SR-61336	I Love the Way That You've Been Lovin' Me	1971	5.00	10.00	20.00

DRUSKY, ROY, AND PRISCILLA MITCHELL
MERCURY

☐ MG-21078 [M]	Together Again	1966	5.00	10.00	20.00
☐ SR-61078 [S]	Together Again	1966	6.25	12.50	25.00

DRY CITY SCAT BAND, THE
ELEKTRA

☐ EKL-292 [M]	The Dry City Scat Band	1965	6.25	12.50	25.00
☐ EKS-7292 [S]	The Dry City Scat Band	1965	7.50	15.00	30.00

DUALS, THE
SUE

☐ LP-2002 [M]	Stick Shift	1961	100.00	200.00	400.00
—Cartoon cover					
☐ LP-2002 [M]	Stick Shift	1964	50.00	100.00	200.00
—Photo cover					

DUBS, THE / THE SHELLS
Also see each artist's individual listings.
JOSIE

☐ JM-4001 [M]	The Dubs Meet the Shells	1962	75.00	150.00	300.00
☐ JSS-4001 [S]	The Dubs Meet the Shells	1962	150.00	300.00	600.00

DUDLEY, DAVE
GOLDEN RING

☐ GR 110 [M]	Dave Dudley Sings Six Days on the Road	1963	20.00	40.00	80.00

MERCURY

☐ SRM-1-669	Keep On Truckin'	1973	3.75	7.50	15.00
☐ MG-20899 [M]	Songs About the Working Man	1964	5.00	10.00	20.00
☐ MG-20927 [M]	Travelin' with Dave Dudley	1964	5.00	10.00	20.00
☐ MG-20970 [M]	Talk of the Town	1964	5.00	10.00	20.00
☐ MG-20999 [M]	Rural Route #1	1965	5.00	10.00	20.00
☐ MG-21028 [M]	Truck Drivin' Son-of-a-Gun	1965	5.00	10.00	20.00
☐ MG-21046 [M]	Dave Dudley's Greatest Hits	1965	5.00	10.00	20.00
☐ MG-21057 [M]	There's a Star Spangled Banner Waving Somewhere	1966	5.00	10.00	20.00
☐ MG-21074 [M]	Lonelyville	1966	5.00	10.00	20.00
☐ MG-21098 [M]	Free and Easy	1966	5.00	10.00	20.00
☐ MG-21133 [M]	Dave Dudley Country	1967	6.25	12.50	25.00
☐ MG-21144 [M]	Greatest Hits Vol. 2	1968	7.50	15.00	30.00
☐ SR-60899 [S]	Songs About the Working Man	1964	6.25	12.50	25.00
☐ SR-60927 [S]	Travelin' with Dave Dudley	1964	6.25	12.50	25.00
☐ SR-60970 [S]	Talk of the Town	1964	6.25	12.50	25.00
☐ SR-60999 [S]	Rural Route #1	1965	6.25	12.50	25.00
☐ SR-61028 [S]	Truck Drivin' Son-of-a-Gun	1965	6.25	12.50	25.00
☐ SR-61046 [S]	Dave Dudley's Greatest Hits	1965	6.25	12.50	25.00
☐ SR-61057 [S]	There's a Star Spangled Banner Waving Somewhere	1966	6.25	12.50	25.00
☐ SR-61074 [S]	Lonelyville	1966	6.25	12.50	25.00
☐ SR-61098 [S]	Free and Easy	1966	5.00	10.00	20.00
☐ SR-61133 [S]	Dave Dudley Country	1967	5.00	10.00	20.00
☐ SR-61144 [S]	Greatest Hits Vol. 2	1968	5.00	10.00	20.00
☐ SR-61172	Thanks for All the Miles	1968	5.00	10.00	20.00
☐ SR-61215	One More Mile	1969	5.00	10.00	20.00
☐ SR-61268	The Best of Dave Dudley	1970	3.75	7.50	15.00
☐ SR-61276	The Pool Shark	1970	3.75	7.50	15.00
☐ SR-61315	Dave Dudley Sings "Listen Betty, I'm Singing Your Song"	1971	3.75	7.50	15.00
☐ SR-61351	Will the Real Dave Dudley Please Sing	1971	3.75	7.50	15.00
☐ SR-61365	The Original Traveling Man	1972	3.75	7.50	15.00

UNITED ARTISTS

☐ UA-LA512-G	Uncommonly Good Country	1975	3.00	6.00	12.00

DUDZIAK, URSZULA
COLUMBIA

☐ KC 32902	Newborn Light	1972	5.00	10.00	20.00

DUKE, DOUGLAS
HERALD

☐ HLP-0102 [M]	Sounds Impossible	1956	12.50	25.00	50.00

REGENT

☐ MG-6013 [M]	Jazz Organist	196?	7.50	15.00	30.00

DUKE, KENO
STRATA-EAST

☐ SES-7416	Sense of Values	1974	6.25	12.50	25.00

TRIDENT

☐ 501	Crest of the Wave	197?	5.00	10.00	20.00

DUKE, PATTY
UNART

☐ 20005 [M]	TV's Teen Star	1967	3.00	6.00	12.00
☐ S 20005 [S]	TV's Teen Star	1967	3.75	7.50	15.00

UNITED ARTISTS

☐ UAL-3452 [M]	Don't Just Stand There	1965	5.00	10.00	20.00
☐ UAL-3492 [M]	Patty	1966	5.00	10.00	20.00
☐ UAL-3535 [M]	Patty Duke's Greatest Hits	1966	3.75	7.50	15.00
☐ UAS-6452 [S]	Don't Just Stand There	1965	7.50	15.00	30.00
☐ UAS-6492 [S]	Patty	1966	7.50	15.00	30.00
☐ UAS-6535 [S]	Patty Duke's Greatest Hits	1966	6.25	12.50	25.00
☐ UAS-6632	Songs from the Valley of the Dolls	1968	6.25	12.50	25.00

DUKE, PATTY, WITH NORMAN VINCENT PEALE
GUIDEPOSTS

☐ GP-101 [M]	Guideposts for Christmas	1963	20.00	40.00	80.00

DUKE, VERNON
ATLANTIC

☐ 407 [10]	Vernon Duke Plays Vernon Duke	1954	25.00	50.00	100.00

DUKE OF IRON, THE
PRESTIGE

☐ PRLP-13068 [M]	Limbo, Limbo, Limbo	1963	7.50	15.00	30.00

DUKE OF PADUCAH, THE
STARDAY

☐ SLP-148 [M]	Button Shoes, Belly Laughs and Monkey Business	1961	10.00	20.00	40.00

DUKE'S MEN, THE
EPIC

☐ LG 3108 [M]	The Duke's Men	1955	12.50	25.00	50.00
☐ LN 3237 [M]	Ellington's Sidekicks	1956	12.50	25.00	50.00

DUKES, JOE, AND JACK MCDUFF
PRESTIGE

☐ PRLP-7324 [M]	Soulful Drums	1964	6.25	12.50	25.00
☐ PRST-7324 [S]	Soulful Drums	1964	7.50	15.00	30.00

DUKES OF DIXIELAND, THE
AUDIO FIDELITY

☐ AFSD-5823 [S]	You Have to Hear It to Believe It — The Dukes of Dixieland, Vol. 1	196?	5.00	10.00	20.00
☐ AFSD-5840 [S]	You Have to Hear It to Believe It — The Dukes of Dixieland, Vol. 2	196?	5.00	10.00	20.00
☐ AFSD-5851 [S]	Marching Along with the Dukes of Dixieland, Vol. 3	1958	5.00	10.00	20.00
☐ AFSD-5860 [S]	The Dukes of Dixieland On Bourbon Street, Vol. 4	1958	5.00	10.00	20.00
☐ AFSD-5861 [S]	Minstrel Time with the Phenomenal Dukes of Dixieland, Volume 5	1958	5.00	10.00	20.00
☐ AFSD-5862 [S]	Mardi Gras Time	1958	5.00	10.00	20.00
☐ AFSD-5891 [S]	The Dukes of Dixieland On Campus	1959	5.00	10.00	20.00
☐ AFSD-5892 [S]	Up the Mississippi	1959	5.00	10.00	20.00

VIK

☐ LX-1025 [M]	The Dukes of Dixieland at the Jazz Band Ball	1956	7.50	15.00	30.00

DUNBAR, AYNSLEY
BLUE THUMB

☐ BTS-4	The Aynsley Dunbar Retaliation	1968	6.25	12.50	25.00
☐ BTS-6	Doctor Dunbar's Prescription	1969	6.25	12.50	25.00
☐ BTS-16	To Mum From Aynsley and the Boys	1970	6.25	12.50	25.00

DUNCAN, BILL
KING

☐ 825 [M]	A Scene Near My Country Home	1962	7.50	15.00	30.00

DUNCAN, DANNY
"X"

☐ LVA-3040 [10]	Ragtime Jamboree	1955	12.50	25.00	50.00

DUNCAN, JOHNNY
COLUMBIA

☐ CS 9824	Johnny One Time	1969	5.00	10.00	20.00
☐ C 30618	There's Something About a Lady	1971	3.75	7.50	15.00
☐ KC 32440	Sweet Country Woman	1973	3.75	7.50	15.00
☐ KC 34243	The Best of Johnny Duncan	1976	3.00	6.00	12.00
☐ PC 34442	Johnny Duncan	1977	3.00	6.00	12.00
☐ KC 35039	Come a Little Bit Closer	1977	3.00	6.00	12.00
☐ KC 35451	The Best Is Yet to Come	1978	3.00	6.00	12.00
☐ KC 35628	Greatest Hits	1978	3.00	6.00	12.00
☐ KC 35775	See You When the Sun Goes Down	1979	3.00	6.00	12.00
☐ JC 36260	Straight from Texas	1980	2.50	5.00	10.00
☐ JC 36508	In My Dreams	1980	2.50	5.00	10.00
☐ JC 36829	You're On My Mind	1981	2.50	5.00	10.00

Number	Title (A Side/B Side)	Yr	VG	VG+	NM
HARMONY					
❏ KH 32477	You're Gonna Need a Man	1973	3.00	6.00	12.00
DUNHAM, KATHERINE					
AUDIO FIDELITY					
❏ AFLP-1803 [M]	The Singing Gods-Drum Rhythms of Cuba, Haiti, Brazil	1957	10.00	20.00	40.00
DECCA					
❏ DL 5251 [10]	Afro-Caribbean Songs and Rhythms	1951	15.00	30.00	60.00
DUNN, HOLLY					
MTM					
❏ ST-71052	Holly Dunn	1986	3.00	6.00	12.00
❏ ST-71063	Cornerstone	1987	3.00	6.00	12.00
❏ ST-71070	Across the Rio Grande	1988	3.00	6.00	12.00
WARNER BROS.					
❏ PRO-A-3692 [DJ]	Blue Rose of Texas Radio Special	1989	7.50	15.00	30.00
—Promo-only interview record					
❏ 25939	The Blue Rose of Texas	1989	2.50	5.00	10.00
DUPRE, MARCEL					
MERCURY LIVING PRESENCE					
❏ SR 90168 [S]	Franck: Piece Heroique; 3 Chorales	196?	5.00	10.00	20.00
—Third edition: Dark red (not maroon) label					
❏ SR 90168 [S]	Franck: Piece Heroique; 3 Chorales	196?	6.25	12.50	25.00
—Maroon label, with "Vendor: Mercury Record Corporation"					
❏ SR 90168 [S]	Franck: Piece Heroique; 3 Chorales	196?	12.50	25.00	50.00
—Maroon label, no "Vendor: Mercury Record Corporation"					
❏ SR 90169 [S]	Organ Recital	196?	50.00	100.00	200.00
—Maroon label, no "Vendor: Mercury Record Corporation"					
❏ SR 90169 [S]	Organ Recital	196?	50.00	100.00	200.00
—Maroon label, with "Vendor: Mercury Record Corporation"					
❏ SR 90227 [S]	Dupre at Saint-Sulpice, Vol. 1	196?	10.00	20.00	40.00
—Maroon label, no "Vendor: Mercury Record Corporation"					
❏ SR 90228 [S]	Dupre at Saint-Sulpice, Vol. 3	196?	5.00	10.00	20.00
—Maroon label, with "Vendor: Mercury Record Corporation"					
❏ SR 90228 [S]	Dupre at Saint-Sulpice, Vol. 3	196?	10.00	20.00	40.00
—Maroon label, no "Vendor: Mercury Record Corporation"					
❏ SR 90229 [S]	Dupre at Saint-Sulpice, Vol. 2	196?	12.50	25.00	50.00
—Maroon label, with "Vendor: Mercury Record Corporation"					
❏ SR 90229 [S]	Dupre at Saint-Sulpice, Vol. 2	196?	20.00	40.00	80.00
—Maroon label, no "Vendor: Mercury Record Corporation"					
❏ SR 90230 [S]	Dupre at Saint-Sulpice, Vol. 4	196?	5.00	10.00	20.00
—Maroon label, with "Vendor: Mercury Record Corporation"					
❏ SR 90230 [S]	Dupre at Saint-Sulpice, Vol. 4	196?	20.00	40.00	80.00
—Maroon label, no "Vendor: Mercury Record Corporation"					
❏ SR 90231 [S]	Dupre at Saint-Sulpice, Vol. 5	196?	7.50	15.00	30.00
—Maroon label, with "Vendor: Mercury Record Corporation"					
❏ SR 90231 [S]	Dupre at Saint-Sulpice, Vol. 5	196?	15.00	30.00	60.00
—Maroon label, no "Vendor: Mercury Record Corporation"					
DUPREE, CHAMPION JACK					
ARCHIVE OF FOLK AND JAZZ					
❏ 217	Champion Jack Dupree	197?	2.50	5.00	10.00
ATLANTIC					
❏ 8019 [M]	Blues from the Gutter	1959	37.50	75.00	150.00
—Black label					
❏ 8019 [M]	Blues from the Gutter	1960	12.50	25.00	50.00
—White "fan' logo at right of label					
❏ 8019 [M]	Blues from the Gutter	1963	5.00	10.00	20.00
—Black "fan' logo at right of label					
❏ SD 8019 [S]	Blues from the Gutter	1959	50.00	100.00	200.00
—Green label					
❏ SD 8019 [S]	Blues from the Gutter	1960	15.00	30.00	60.00
—Green and blue label, white "fan' logo at right of label					
❏ SD 8019 [S]	Blues from the Gutter	1963	6.25	12.50	25.00
—Green and blue label, black "fan' logo at right of label					
❏ 8045 [M]	Natural and Soulful Blues	1961	12.50	25.00	50.00
—White "fan' logo at right of label					
❏ 8045 [M]	Natural and Soulful Blues	1963	5.00	10.00	20.00
—Black "fan' logo at right of label					
❏ SD 8045 [S]	Natural and Soulful Blues	1961	15.00	30.00	60.00
—Green and blue label, white "fan' logo at right of label					
❏ SD 8045 [S]	Natural and Soulful Blues	1963	6.25	12.50	25.00
—Green and blue label, black "fan' logo at right of label					
❏ 8056 [M]	Champion of the Blues	1961	12.50	25.00	50.00
—White "fan' logo at right of label					
❏ 8056 [M]	Champion of the Blues	1963	5.00	10.00	20.00
—Black "fan' logo at right of label					
❏ SD 8056 [R]	Champion of the Blues	196?	3.75	7.50	15.00
❏ SD 8255	Blues from the Gutter	1970	3.75	7.50	15.00
BLUE HORIZON					
❏ 7702	When You Feel the Feeling	1969	6.25	12.50	25.00
BULLSEYE					
❏ BB-9502	Back Home In New Orleans	1990	3.00	6.00	12.00
CONTINENTAL					
❏ CLP-16002 [M]	Low Down Blues	1961	62.50	125.00	250.00
FOLKWAYS					
❏ FS-3825 [M]	Women Blues of Champion Jack Dupree	1961	6.25	12.50	25.00
GNP CRESCENDO					
❏ GNPS-10001	Tricks	1974	3.00	6.00	12.00
❏ GNPS-10005	Happy to Be Free	1974	3.00	6.00	12.00
❏ GNPS-10013	Legacy of Blues 3	197?	3.00	6.00	12.00
JAZZ MAN					
❏ BLZ-5501	Champion Jack Dupree	1982	2.50	5.00	10.00
KING					
❏ 735 [M]	Champion Jack Dupree Sings the Blues	1961	75.00	150.00	300.00
❏ KS-1084	Walking the Blues	1970	3.75	7.50	15.00
LONDON					
❏ PS 553	From New Orleans to Chicago	1969	5.00	10.00	20.00

Number	Title (A Side/B Side)	Yr	VG	VG+	NM
OKEH					
❏ OKM 12103 [M]	Cabbage Greens	1963	7.50	15.00	30.00
STORYVILLE					
❏ 4010	Best of the Blues	1982	2.50	5.00	10.00
❏ 4040	I'm Growing Older Every Day	198?	2.50	5.00	10.00
DUPREE, CHAMPION JACK, AND MICKEY BAKER					
Also see each artist's individual listings.					
SIRE					
❏ SES-97010	In Heavy Blues	1969	7.50	15.00	30.00
DUPREE, CHAMPION JACK, AND JIMMY RUSHING					
AUDIO LAB					
❏ AL-1512 [M]	Two Shades of Blue	1958	50.00	100.00	200.00
DUPREE, SIMON, AND THE BIG SOUND					
TOWER					
❏ ST-5097 [S]	Without Reservations	1968	10.00	20.00	40.00
❏ T-5097 [M]	Without Reservations	1968	25.00	50.00	100.00
DUPREES, THE					
COED					
❏ LPC-905 [M]	You Belong to Me	1962	75.00	150.00	300.00
❏ LPC-906 [M]	Have You Heard	1963	50.00	100.00	200.00
COLLECTABLES					
❏ COL-5008	The Best of the Duprees	198?	3.00	6.00	12.00
COLOSSUS					
❏ 5000	Duprees Gold	1970	7.50	15.00	30.00
—As "The Italian Asphalt & Pavement Co."					
HERITAGE					
❏ HT-35002 [M]	Total Recall	1968	20.00	40.00	80.00
—Mono is promo only; in stereo cover with "DJ Monaural" sticker on front					
❏ HTS-35002 [S]	Total Recall	1968	7.50	15.00	30.00
POST					
❏ 1000	The Duprees Sing	196?	7.50	15.00	30.00
DURAN, EDDIE					
FANTASY					
❏ 3247 [M]	Jazz Guitarist	195?	10.00	20.00	40.00
—Black vinyl					
❏ 3247 [M]	Jazz Guitarist	1957	20.00	40.00	80.00
—Red vinyl					
DURAN DURAN					
CAPITOL					
❏ ST-12158	Duran Duran	1983	2.50	5.00	10.00
—Reissue, with new cover and "Is There Something I Should Know"					
❏ ST-12211	Rio	1983	2.50	5.00	10.00
—Version 3: Capitol logo replaces Harvest logo on back cover					
❏ ST-12310	Seven and the Ragged Tiger	1983	2.50	5.00	10.00
❏ SWAV-12374	Arena	1984	2.50	5.00	10.00
—With booklet (deduct 25% if cut out)					
❏ PJ-12540	Notorious	1986	2.50	5.00	10.00
❏ SPRO-79097/8 [EP]	Duran Goes Dutch	1987	12.50	25.00	50.00
—Promo-only five-song EP recorded live in Rotterdam					
❏ C1-90958	Big Thing	1988	2.50	5.00	10.00
❏ C1-93178	Decade	1989	2.50	5.00	10.00
❏ C1-94292	Liberty	1990	3.00	6.00	12.00
❏ R 100682	Big Thing	1988	3.00	6.00	12.00
—BMG Direct Marketing edition					
❏ R 114794	Notorious	1987	3.00	6.00	12.00
—RCA Music Service edition					
❏ R 134452	Duran Duran	1983	3.00	6.00	12.00
—RCA Music Service edition; with "Is There Something I Should Know?"					
❏ R 140395	Arena	1984	3.00	6.00	12.00
—RCA Music Service edition					
❏ R 163452	Rio	1983	3.00	6.00	12.00
—RCA Music Service edition					
❏ R 163458	Liberty	1990	3.00	6.00	12.00
—BMG Direct Marketing edition					
❏ R 173573	Decade	1989	3.00	6.00	12.00
—BMG Direct Marketing edition					
HARVEST					
❏ ST-12158	Duran Duran	1981	3.75	7.50	15.00
❏ ST-12211	Rio	1982	3.00	6.00	12.00
—Version 2: Harvest logo on lower back cover, with remixes by David Kershenbaum					
❏ ST-12211	Rio	1982	3.75	7.50	15.00
—Version 1: Harvest logo on lower back cover, no mention of remixes by David Kershenbaum					
❏ MLP-15006 [EP]	Carnival	1982	6.25	12.50	25.00
—Imports of this are relatively common and worth much less.					
MOBILE FIDELITY					
❏ 1-182	Seven and the Ragged Tiger	1985	5.00	10.00	20.00
—Audiophile vinyl					
DURANTE, JIMMY					
DECCA					
❏ DL 5116 [10]	Jimmy Durante	195?	12.50	25.00	50.00
❏ DL 8884 [M]	Jimmy Durante at the Piano	1959	3.75	7.50	15.00
❏ DL 9049 [M]	Club Durant	195?	6.25	12.50	25.00
❏ DL 78884 [S]	Jimmy Durante at the Piano	1959	5.00	10.00	20.00
LION					
❏ L-70053 [M]	Jimmy Durante in Person	195?	7.50	15.00	30.00
MGM					
❏ E-3242 [M]	Jimmy Durante in Person	1955	7.50	15.00	30.00
❏ E-4207 [M]	The Very Best of Jimmy Durante	1964	3.00	6.00	12.00
❏ SE-4207 [S]	The Very Best of Jimmy Durante	1964	3.75	7.50	15.00
ROULETTE					
❏ R-25123 [M]	Jimmy Durante at the Copacabana	1961	5.00	10.00	20.00
❏ SR-25123 [S]	Jimmy Durante at the Copacabana	1961	6.25	12.50	25.00
WARNER BROS.					
❏ W 1506 [M]	September Song	1963	3.75	7.50	15.00

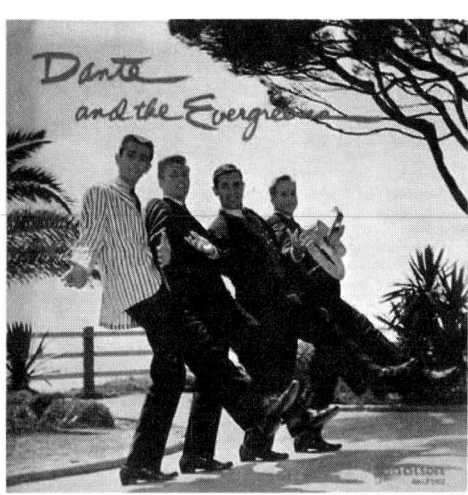

Dante and the Evergreens were best known for their cover of the Hollywood Argyles' hit "Alley Oop." This album was issued in 1961 and is very rare.

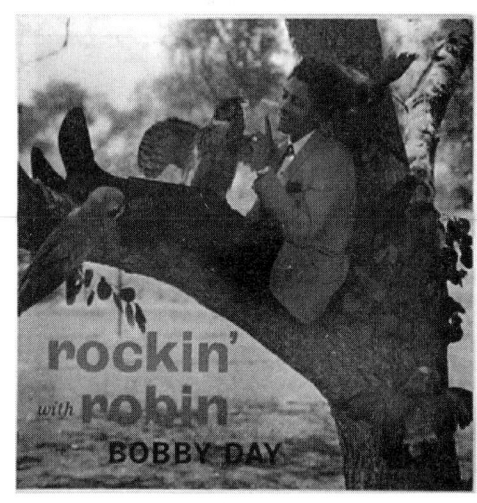

Bobby Day's *Rockin' with Robin* was one of the very few LPs issued by the Class label.

The only album ever on Buchanan and Goodman's Luniverse label was this rarity by the Dell Vikings.

Ral Donner was regarded as the best of the Elvis Presley sound-alikes by Elvis fans. This was his only album during his early-1960s heyday.

You have to start somewhere, and Bob Dylan started with an acoustic album, mostly of new versions of folk standards. It didn't sell well initially, so original pressings with the red and black Columbia "6 eye" label are highly sought-after.

The El Dorados' Vee Jay album, *Crazy Little Mama,* didn't come out until three years after the song with this line, "At My Front Door," was a hit.

Number	Title (A Side/B Side)	Yr	VG	VG+	NM
❏ WS 1506 [S]	September Song	1963	5.00	10.00	20.00
❏ W 1531 [M]	Hello Young Lovers	1964	3.75	7.50	15.00
❏ WS 1531 [S]	Hello Young Lovers	1964	5.00	10.00	20.00
❏ W 1577 [M]	Jimmy Durante's Way of Life	1965	3.75	7.50	15.00
❏ WS 1577 [S]	Jimmy Durante's Way of Life	1965	5.00	10.00	20.00
❏ W 1655 [M]	One of Those Songs	1966	3.75	7.50	15.00
❏ WS 1655 [S]	One of Those Songs	1966	5.00	10.00	20.00
❏ W 1713 [M]	Songs for Sunday	1967	3.75	7.50	15.00
❏ WS 1713 [S]	Songs for Sunday	1967	5.00	10.00	20.00

DURBIN, DEANNA
DECCA
Number	Title (A Side/B Side)	Yr	VG	VG+	NM
❏ DL 8785 [M]	Deanna Durbin	1958	12.50	25.00	50.00

DUSHON, JEAN
ARGO
Number	Title (A Side/B Side)	Yr	VG	VG+	NM
❏ LP-4039 [M]	Make Way for Jean DuShon	1964	6.25	12.50	25.00
❏ LPS-4039 [S]	Make Way for Jean DuShon	1964	7.50	15.00	30.00

DUST
KAMA SUTRA
Number	Title (A Side/B Side)	Yr	VG	VG+	NM
❏ KSBS-2041	Dust	1971	6.25	12.50	25.00
—Pink label					
❏ KSBS-2059	Hard Attack	1972	6.25	12.50	25.00
—Pink label					

DUTCH SWING COLLEGE BAND, THE
EPIC
Number	Title (A Side/B Side)	Yr	VG	VG+	NM
❏ LN 3211 [M]	Dixieland Goes Dutch	1955	10.00	20.00	40.00
PHILIPS
Number	Title (A Side/B Side)	Yr	VG	VG+	NM
❏ PHS 600010 [S]	Dixie Goes Dutch	1962	5.00	10.00	20.00

DUVAL, DENISE / GEORGES PRETRE
RCA VICTOR RED SEAL
Number	Title (A Side/B Side)	Yr	VG	VG+	NM
❏ LDS-2385 [S]	Poulenc: La Voix Humana	1960	15.00	30.00	60.00
—Original with "shaded dog" label; also includes booklet					

DWARVES
SUB POP
Number	Title (A Side/B Side)	Yr	VG	VG+	NM
❏ 67	Blood, Guts and Pussy	1990	2.50	5.00	10.00
❏ 67	Blood, Guts and Pussy	1990	5.00	10.00	20.00
—First 1,000 on red vinyl					
❏ 126	Thank Heaven for Little Girls	1991	2.50	5.00	10.00
❏ 197	Sugar Fix	1993	2.50	5.00	10.00

DYANI, JOHNNY; OKAY TEMIZ; MONGEZI FEZA
ANTILLES
Number	Title (A Side/B Side)	Yr	VG	VG+	NM
❏ AN-7035	Music for Xaba	197?	7.50	15.00	30.00

DYKE AND THE BLAZERS
ORIGINAL SOUND
Number	Title (A Side/B Side)	Yr	VG	VG+	NM
❏ LP 8876 [M]	The Funky Broadway	1967	12.50	25.00	50.00
❏ LPS 8876 [S]	The Funky Broadway	1967	18.75	37.50	75.00
❏ LPS 8877	Dyke's Greatest Hits	1968	18.75	37.50	75.00

DYLAN, BOB
ASYLUM
Number	Title (A Side/B Side)	Yr	VG	VG+	NM
❏ AB-201 [(2)]	Before the Flood	1974	5.00	10.00	20.00
❏ AB-201 [(2)DJ]	Before the Flood	1974	12.50	25.00	50.00
—White label promo					
❏ 7E-1003	Planet Waves	1974	3.75	7.50	15.00
—Without wraparound (olive green) second cover					
❏ 7E-1003	Planet Waves	1974	5.00	10.00	20.00
—With wraparound (olive green) second cover					
❏ 7E-1003 [DJ]	Planet Waves	1974	12.50	25.00	50.00
—White label promo					
❏ 7E-1003 [DJ]	Ceremonies of the Horsemen	1974	1500.	2250.	3000.
—Original title of "Planet Waves"; no records were pressed with this title, but never-glued covers exist, of which 3 or 4 are known. Value is for one of these covers.					
❏ EQ-1003 [Q]	Planet Waves	1974	12.50	25.00	50.00
COLUMBIA
Number	Title (A Side/B Side)	Yr	VG	VG+	NM
❏ C2L 41 [(2)M]	Blonde on Blonde	1966	25.00	50.00	100.00
—"Female photos" inner gatefold with two women pictured					
❏ C2L 41 [(2)M]	Blonde on Blonde	1966	250.00	500.00	1000.
—White label promo					
❏ C2L 41 [(2)M]	Blonde on Blonde	1968	75.00	150.00	300.00
—No photos of women inside gatefold					
❏ AS 422 [DJ]	Renaldo and Clara	1976	12.50	25.00	50.00
—Promo-only sampler from the movie. Authentic copies have a sticker on a white cover; counterfeits have the title printed on the cover					
❏ AS 798 [DJ]	Saved	1980	6.25	12.50	25.00
—Promo sampler from LP					
❏ C2S 841 [(2)S]	Blonde on Blonde	1966	15.00	30.00	60.00
—"Female photos" inner gatefold with two women pictured					
❏ C2S 841 [(2)S]	Blonde on Blonde	1968	7.50	15.00	30.00
—No photos of women inside gatefold; "360 Sound Stereo" on label					
❏ C2S 841 [(2)S]	Blonde on Blonde	1970	3.75	7.50	15.00
—Orange label					
❏ CG 841 [(2)S]	Blonde on Blonde	198?	3.00	6.00	12.00
❏ AS 1259 [DJ]	The Dylan London Interview, July 1981	1981	6.25	12.50	25.00
❏ AS 1471 [DJ]	Electric Lunch	1982	6.25	12.50	25.00
—Promo-only sampler					
❏ AS 1770 [DJ]	Infidels	1983	5.00	10.00	20.00
—Promo-only sampler					
❏ CL 1779 [M]	Bob Dylan	1962	62.50	125.00	250.00
—Black and red (not orange) label with six white "eye" logos, three at 9 o'clock, three at 3 o'clock; stock copy					
❏ CL 1779 [M]	Bob Dylan	1962	125.00	250.00	500.00
—Six "eye" logos on label; "A New Star on Columbia" sticker on cover and promo stamp on label					
❏ CL 1779 [M]	Bob Dylan	1963	10.00	20.00	40.00
—"Guaranteed High Fidelity" on label					
❏ CL 1779 [M]	Bob Dylan	1966	7.50	15.00	30.00
—"Mono" on label					

Number	Title (A Side/B Side)	Yr	VG	VG+	NM
❏ CL 1986 [M]	The Freewheelin' Bob Dylan	1963	10.00	20.00	40.00
—"Guaranteed High Fidelity" on label; corrected version (record plays what label says)					
❏ CL 1986 [M]	The Freewheelin' Bob Dylan	1963	125.00	250.00	500.00
—White label promo; label AND timing strip list, and record plays, "correct" tracks					
❏ CL 1986 [M]	The Freewheelin' Bob Dylan	1963	200.00	400.00	800.00
—White label promo; timing strip lists deleted tracks; label lists, and record plays, "correct" tracks					
❏ CL 1986 [M]	The Freewheelin' Bob Dylan	1963	500.00	1000.	2000.
—White label promo; label lists deleted tracks; timing strip lists, and record plays, "correct" tracks					
❏ CL 1986 [M]	The Freewheelin' Bob Dylan	1963	1000.	2000.	3000.
—White label promo; label and timing strip list the deleted tracks but record plays the "correct" tracks					
❏ CL 1986 [M]	The Freewheelin' Bob Dylan	1963	4000.	8000.	12000.
—"Guaranteed High Fidelity" on label; plays "Let Me Die in My Footsteps," "Rocks and Gravel," "Talkin' John Birch Blues" and "Gamblin' Willie's Dead Man's Hand." Label does NOT list these. In dead wax, matrix number ends in "--1" followed by a letter					
❏ CL 1986 [M]	The Freewheelin' Bob Dylan	1966	7.50	15.00	30.00
—"Mono" on label					
❏ CL 2105 [M]	The Times They Are a-Changin'	1964	10.00	20.00	40.00
—"Guaranteed High Fidelity" on label					
❏ CL 2105 [M]	The Times They Are a-Changin'	1964	100.00	200.00	400.00
—White label promo					
❏ CL 2105 [M]	The Times They Are a-Changin'	1965	7.50	15.00	30.00
—"Mono" on label					
❏ CL 2193 [M]	Another Side of Bob Dylan	1964	10.00	20.00	40.00
—"Guaranteed High Fidelity" on label					
❏ CL 2193 [M]	Another Side of Bob Dylan	1964	100.00	200.00	400.00
—White label promo					
❏ CL 2193 [M]	Another Side of Bob Dylan	1965	7.50	15.00	30.00
—"Mono" on label					
❏ CAS 2222 [DJ]	Time Passes Slowly	1985	6.25	12.50	25.00
—Promo-only sampler from Biograph box set					
❏ CL 2302/CS 9102	Bob Dylan In Concert	1965	2000.	3000.	4000.
—Never pressed; value is for a cover slick, some of which were printed					
❏ CL 2328 [M]	Bringing It All Back Home	1965	7.50	15.00	30.00
—"Mono" on label					
❏ CL 2328 [M]	Bringing It All Back Home	1965	12.50	25.00	50.00
—"Guaranteed High Fidelity" on label					
❏ CL 2328 [M]	Bringing It All Back Home	1965	75.00	150.00	300.00
—White label promo					
❏ CL 2389 [M]	Highway 61 Revisited	1965	20.00	40.00	80.00
❏ CL 2389 [M]	Highway 61 Revisited	1965	100.00	200.00	400.00
—White label promo					
❏ 2663/9463	Bob Dylan's Greatest Hits Poster	1967	—	2.00	4.00
—Almost every copy into the late 1970s came with a poster					
❏ KCL 2663 [M]	Bob Dylan's Greatest Hits	1967	12.50	25.00	50.00
❏ CL 2804 [M]	John Wesley Harding	1968	37.50	75.00	150.00
❏ CS 8579 [S]	Bob Dylan	1962			
—Red and black label with six white "eye" logos, three together at the left, three together at the right; stock copy					
❏ CS 8579 [S]	Bob Dylan	1962	150.00	300.00	600.00
—Six "eye" logos on label; "A New Star on Columbia" sticker on cover and promo stamp on label					
❏ CS 8579 [S]	Bob Dylan	1963	10.00	20.00	40.00
—"360 Sound Stereo" in black on label					
❏ CS 8579 [S]	Bob Dylan	1965	6.25	12.50	25.00
—"360 Sound Stereo" in white on label					
❏ CS 8579 [S]	Bob Dylan	1970	3.00	6.00	12.00
—Orange label					
❏ JC 8579 [S]	Bob Dylan	197?	2.00	4.00	8.00
—Some copies of this pressing of the above album may have the song "You're No Good" listed on the label as "She's No Good." No extra premium has been attached to this error as yet.					
❏ KCS 8579 [S]	Bob Dylan	197?	2.50	5.00	10.00
❏ PC 8579 [S]	Bob Dylan	198?	2.00	4.00	8.00
—Budget-line reissue					
❏ PC 8579 [S]	Bob Dylan	2001	3.00	6.00	12.00
—Reissue on 180-gram vinyl (sealed copies have a sticker indicating this)					
❏ CS 8786 [S]	The Freewheelin' Bob Dylan	1963	12.50	25.00	50.00
—"360 Sound Stereo" in black on label (no arrows)					
❏ CS 8786 [S]	The Freewheelin' Bob Dylan	1963	100.00	200.00	400.00
—Canadian pressing with the deleted tracks listed on the front cover. The label lists, and the record plays, the "correct" tracks.					
❏ CS 8786 [S]	The Freewheelin' Bob Dylan	1963	15000.	22500.	30000.
—"360 Sound Stereo" in black on label (no arrows); record plays, and label lists, "Let Me Die in My Footsteps," "Rocks and Gravel," "Talkin' John Birch Blues" and "Gamblin' Willie's Dead Man's Hand." No known stereo copies play these without listing them, but just in case, check the trail-off for the numbers "XSM-58719-1A" and "XSM-58720-1A." If the number after the dash is "2" or higher, it's the standard version.					
❏ CS 8786 [S]	The Freewheelin' Bob Dylan	1964	10.00	20.00	40.00
—"360 Sound Stereo" in black on label (with arrows)					
❏ CS 8786 [S]	The Freewheelin' Bob Dylan	1965	6.25	12.50	25.00
—"360 Sound Stereo" in white on label					
❏ CS 8786 [S]	The Freewheelin' Bob Dylan	197?	250.00	500.00	1000.
—Orange label; unauthorized red vinyl pressing					
❏ CS 8786 [S]	The Freewheelin' Bob Dylan	1970	3.00	6.00	12.00
—Orange label					
❏ KCS 8786 [S]	The Freewheelin' Bob Dylan	197?	2.50	5.00	10.00
❏ PC 8786 [S]	The Freewheelin' Bob Dylan	198?	2.00	4.00	8.00
—Budget-line reissue					
❏ PC 8786 [S]	The Freewheelin' Bob Dylan	2001	3.00	6.00	12.00
—Reissue on 180-gram vinyl (sealed copies have a sticker indicating this)					
❏ CS 8905 [S]	The Times They Are a-Changin'	1964	10.00	20.00	40.00
—"360 Sound Stereo" in black on label					
❏ CS 8905 [S]	The Times They Are a-Changin'	1965	6.25	12.50	25.00
—"360 Sound Stereo" in white on label					
❏ CS 8905 [S]	The Times They Are a-Changin'	1970	3.00	6.00	12.00
—Orange label					
❏ KCS 8905 [S]	The Times They Are a-Changin'	197?	2.50	5.00	10.00
❏ PC 8905 [S]	The Times They Are a-Changin'	198?	2.00	4.00	8.00
—Budget-line reissue					
❏ PC 8905 [S]	The Times They Are a-Changin'	2001	3.00	6.00	12.00
—Reissue on 180-gram vinyl (sealed copies have a sticker indicating this)					
❏ CS 8993 [S]	Another Side of Bob Dylan	1964	10.00	20.00	40.00
—"360 Sound Stereo" in black on label					
❏ CS 8993 [S]	Another Side of Bob Dylan	1965	6.25	12.50	25.00
—"360 Sound Stereo" in white on label					

Number	Title (A Side/B Side)	Yr	VG	VG+	NM
❑ CS 8993 [S]	Another Side of Bob Dylan	1970	3.00	6.00	12.00
—Orange label					
❑ KCS 8993 [S]	Another Side of Bob Dylan	197?	2.50	5.00	10.00
❑ PC 8993 [S]	Another Side of Bob Dylan	198?	2.00	4.00	8.00
—Budget-line reissue					
❑ PC 8993 [S]	Another Side of Bob Dylan	2001	3.00	6.00	12.00
—Reissue on 180-gram vinyl (sealed copies have a sticker indicating this)					
❑ CS 9128 [S]	Bringing It All Back Home	1965	6.25	12.50	25.00
—"360 Sound Stereo" in white on label					
❑ CS 9128 [S]	Bringing It All Back Home	1965	10.00	20.00	40.00
—"360 Sound Stereo" in black on label					
❑ CS 9128 [S]	Bringing It All Back Home	1970	3.00	6.00	12.00
—Orange label					
❑ JC 9128 [S]	Bringing It All Back Home	197?	2.50	5.00	10.00
❑ KCS 9128 [S]	Bringing It All Back Home	197?	2.50	5.00	10.00
❑ PC 9128 [S]	Bringing It All Back Home	198?	2.00	4.00	8.00
—Budget-line reissue					
❑ PC 9128 [S]	Bringing It All Back Home	2001	3.00	6.00	12.00
—Reissue on 180-gram vinyl (sealed copies have a sticker indicating this)					
❑ CS 9189 [S]	Highway 61 Revisited	1965	7.50	15.00	30.00
—With "regular" take of "From a Buick 6." Matrix number on Side 1 will end in "--2" or higher, plus a					
letter; "360 Sound Stereo" on label					
❑ CS 9189 [S]	Highway 61 Revisited	1965	62.50	125.00	250.00
—With alternate take of "From a Buick 6." Matrix number on Side 1 will end in "--1" plus a letter					
❑ CS 9189 [S]	Highway 61 Revisited	1970	3.00	6.00	12.00
—Orange label					
❑ JC 9189 [S]	Highway 61 Revisited	197?	2.50	5.00	10.00
❑ KCS 9189 [S]	Highway 61 Revisited	197?	2.50	5.00	10.00
❑ PC 9189 [S]	Highway 61 Revisited	198?	2.00	4.00	8.00
—Budget-line reissue					
❑ PC 9189 [S]	Highway 61 Revisited	2001	3.00	6.00	12.00
—Reissue on 180-gram vinyl (sealed copies have a sticker indicating this)					
❑ JC 9463 [S]	Bob Dylan's Greatest Hits	197?	2.50	5.00	10.00
❑ JC 9463 [S]	Bob Dylan's Greatest Hits	2001	3.00	6.00	12.00
—Reissue on 180-gram vinyl (sealed copies have a sticker indicating this)					
❑ KCS 9463 [S]	Bob Dylan's Greatest Hits	1967	3.75	7.50	15.00
—"360 Sound Stereo" label					
❑ KCS 9463 [S]	Bob Dylan's Greatest Hits	1970	3.00	6.00	12.00
—Orange label					
❑ CS 9604 [S]	John Wesley Harding	1968	5.00	10.00	20.00
—"360 Sound Stereo" label					
❑ CS 9604 [S]	John Wesley Harding	1970	3.00	6.00	12.00
—Orange label					
❑ JC 9604 [S]	John Wesley Harding	197?	2.50	5.00	10.00
❑ KCS 9604 [S]	John Wesley Harding	197?	2.50	5.00	10.00
❑ PC 9604 [S]	John Wesley Harding	198?	2.00	4.00	8.00
—Budget-line reissue					
❑ PC 9604 [S]	John Wesley Harding	2001	3.00	6.00	12.00
—Reissue on 180-gram vinyl (sealed copies have a sticker indicating this)					
❑ JC 9825	Nashville Skyline	197?	2.50	5.00	10.00
❑ KCS 9825	Nashville Skyline	1969	7.50	15.00	30.00
—"360 Sound Stereo" label					
❑ KCS 9825	Nashville Skyline	1970	3.00	6.00	12.00
—Orange label					
❑ PC 9825	Nashville Skyline	198?	2.00	4.00	8.00
—Budget-line reissue					
❑ C2X 30050 [(2)]	Self Portrait	1970	5.00	10.00	20.00
—Orange labels					
❑ C2X 30050 [(2)]	Self Portrait	1970	37.50	75.00	150.00
—"360 Sound Stereo" labels					
❑ CG 30050 [(2)]	Self Portrait	198?	3.00	6.00	12.00
❑ P2X 30050 [(2)]	Self Portrait	197?	3.75	7.50	15.00
❑ KC 30290	New Morning	1970	3.75	7.50	15.00
❑ PC 30290	New Morning	197?	2.00	4.00	8.00
❑ PC 30290	New Morning	2001	3.00	6.00	12.00
—Reissue on 180-gram vinyl (sealed copies have a sticker indicating this)					
❑ CG 31120 [(2)]	Bob Dylan's Greatest Hits, Vol. II	198?	2.50	5.00	10.00
❑ KG 31120 [(2)]	Bob Dylan's Greatest Hits, Vol. II	1971	3.75	7.50	15.00
❑ PG 31120 [(2)]	Bob Dylan's Greatest Hits, Vol. II	197?	3.00	6.00	12.00
❑ KC 32460	Pat Garrett and Billy the Kid	1973	3.75	7.50	15.00
❑ PC 32460	Pat Garrett and Billy the Kid	197?	2.00	4.00	8.00
❑ PC 32747	Dylan	1973	3.75	7.50	15.00
—No bar code on cover					
❑ PC 32747	Dylan	1979	2.00	4.00	8.00
—With bar code on back cover					
❑ KCQ 32825 [Q]	Nashville Skyline	1973	7.50	15.00	30.00
❑ PC 33235	Blood on the Tracks	1975	3.00	6.00	12.00
—With liner notes on back cover. Original pressings have them, then they were deleted, then restored					
after they won a Grammy Award! No bar code on cover.					
❑ PC 33235	Blood on the Tracks	1975	3.75	7.50	15.00
—With drawing on back cover and no liner notes. Actually a second pressing, but available only for					
a short time					
❑ PC 33235	Blood on the Tracks	1979	2.00	4.00	8.00
—With bar code on back cover					
❑ PC 33235	Blood on the Tracks	2001	3.00	6.00	12.00
—Reissue on 180-gram vinyl (sealed copies have a sticker indicating this)					
❑ PC 33235 [DJ]	Blood on the Tracks	1975	7.50	15.00	30.00
—Regular white label promo					
❑ PC 33235 [DJ]	Blood on the Tracks	1975	2500.	3750.	5000.
—Test pressing with radically different versions of five songs including "Idiot Wind" and "Tangled Up					
in Blue"					
❑ CG 33682 [(2)]	The Basement Tapes	198?	3.00	6.00	12.00
❑ PC2 33682 [(2)]	The Basement Tapes	1975	5.00	10.00	20.00
❑ PC2 33682 [(2)DJ]	The Basement Tapes	1975	10.00	20.00	40.00
—White label promo					
❑ JC 33893	Desire	1977	2.50	5.00	10.00
—No bar code on back cover					
❑ JC 33893	Desire	1979	2.00	4.00	8.00
—With bar code on back cover					
❑ PC 33893	Desire	1976	3.00	6.00	12.00
❑ PC 33893 [DJ]	Desire	1976	7.50	15.00	30.00
—White label promo					
❑ PCQ 33893 [Q]	Desire	1976	7.50	15.00	30.00

Number	Title (A Side/B Side)	Yr	VG	VG+	NM
❑ JC 34349	Hard Rain	1977	2.50	5.00	10.00
❑ PC 34349	Hard Rain	1976	3.00	6.00	12.00
—No bar code on back cover					
❑ PC 34349	Hard Rain	198?	2.00	4.00	8.00
—With bar code on back cover					
❑ PC 34349 [DJ]	Hard Rain	1976	7.50	15.00	30.00
—White label promo					
❑ JC 35453	Street Legal	1978	3.00	6.00	12.00
❑ JC 35453 [DJ]	Street Legal	1978	6.25	12.50	25.00
—White label promo					
❑ PC 35453	Street Legal	198?	2.00	4.00	8.00
❑ CG 36067 [(2)]	Bob Dylan at Budokan	198?	3.00	6.00	12.00
❑ PC2 36067 [(2)]	Bob Dylan at Budokan	1979	3.75	7.50	15.00
❑ PC2 36067 [(2)DJ]	Bob Dylan at Budokan	1979	7.50	15.00	30.00
—White label promo					
❑ FC 36120	Slow Train Coming	1979	2.50	5.00	10.00
❑ FC 36120 [DJ]	Slow Train Coming	1979	6.25	12.50	25.00
—White label promo					
❑ PC 36120	Slow Train Coming	198?	2.00	4.00	8.00
—Budget-line reissue					
❑ FC 36553	Saved	1980	2.50	5.00	10.00
❑ PC 36553	Saved	198?	2.00	4.00	8.00
—Budget-line reissue with new cover					
❑ PC 37496	Shot of Love	198?	2.00	4.00	8.00
—Budget-line reissue					
❑ TC 37496	Shot of Love	1981	2.50	5.00	10.00
❑ PC 37637	Planet Waves	1981	2.50	5.00	10.00
—Reissue of Asylum 7E-1003					
❑ CG 37661 [(2)]	Before the Flood	1983	3.00	6.00	12.00
—Reissue of Asylum AB-201					
❑ PC 38819	Infidels	1986	2.00	4.00	8.00
—Budget-line reissue					
❑ QC 38819	Infidels	1983	2.50	5.00	10.00
❑ C5X 38830 [(5)]	Biograph	1985	7.50	15.00	30.00
❑ FC 39944	Real Live	1984	2.50	5.00	10.00
❑ FC 40110	Empire Burlesque	1985	2.50	5.00	10.00
❑ OC 40439	Knocked Out Loaded	1986	2.50	5.00	10.00
❑ OC 40957	Down in the Groove	1988	2.50	5.00	10.00
❑ HC 43235	Blood on the Tracks	198?	12.50	25.00	50.00
—Half-speed mastered edition					
❑ OC 45056	Dylan and the Dead	1989	3.00	6.00	12.00
—With backing by The Grateful Dead					
❑ OC 45281	Oh Mercy	1989	3.00	6.00	12.00
❑ C 46794	Under the Red Sky	1990	3.00	6.00	12.00
❑ HC 49825	Nashville Skyline	198?	15.00	30.00	60.00
—Half-speed mastered edition					
❑ C 53200	Good As I Been to You	1992	5.00	10.00	20.00
❑ CK2-65759-1 [(2)]	The Bootleg Series Vol. 4: Bob Dylan Live				
	1966, The "Royal Albert Hall" Concert	1999	25.00	50.00	100.00
—Classic Records box set with 12x12 booklet and two records individually packaged in cardboard					
jackets and sleeves					
❑ C2 67000 [(2)]	MTV Unplugged	1995	3.75	7.50	15.00
❑ C2 68556 [(2)]	Time Out of Mind	1998	3.75	7.50	15.00
❑ C2 85975 [(2)]	Love and Theft	2001	3.75	7.50	15.00
❑ 474000 [(3)]	Bob Dylan — The 30th Anniversary Concert				
	Celebration	1993	7.50	15.00	30.00
—Albums pressed in US for export to Europe; some stayed here					

ISLAND

Number	Title (A Side/B Side)	Yr	VG	VG+	NM
❑ AB-201 [(2)]	Before the Flood	1974	10.00	20.00	40.00
—Error pressing with wrong labels (should be Asylum)					

MOBILE FIDELITY

❑ 1-114	The Times They Are a-Changin'	1982	12.50	25.00	50.00
—Audiophile vinyl					

SUNDAZED

❑ LP 5070	Bringing It All Back Home	2001	3.75	7.50	15.00
—180-gram reissue of the original mono mix					
❑ LP 5071	Highway 61 Revisited	2001	3.75	7.50	15.00
—180-gram reissue of the original mono mix					
❑ LP 5108	The Times They Are a-Changin'	2001	3.75	7.50	15.00
—180-gram reissue of the original mono mix					
❑ LP 5110 [(2)]	Blonde on Blonde	2002	6.25	12.50	25.00
—180-gram reissue of the original mono mix					
❑ LP 5115	The Freewheelin' Bob Dylan	2001	3.75	7.50	15.00
—180-gram reissue of the original mono mix					
❑ LP 5121	Another Side of Bob Dylan	2002	3.75	7.50	15.00
—180-gram reissue of the original mono mix					
❑ LP 5156	Bob Dylan's Greatest Hits	2003	3.75	7.50	15.00
—180-gram reissue of the original mono mix					

WARNER BROS./7 ARTS MUSIC

❑ XTV 221567 [DJ]	Bob Dylan	1969	375.00	750.00	1500.
—One-sided publisher's demo with 8 Dylan performances of then-unreleased songs from the					
"Basement Tapes" era					

DYLAN, BOB, AND ALAN J. WEBERMAN
FOLKWAYS

❑ FB-5322 [M]	Bob Dylan Vs. A.J. Weberman	1977	75.00	150.00	300.00
—A tape-recorded phone conversation; quickly withdrawn from the market					

DYNAMICS, THE (2)
BOLO

❑ BLP-8001 [M]	The Dynamics with Jimmy Hanna	1964	12.50	25.00	50.00

DYNATONES, THE
HANNA-BARBERA

❑ HLP-8509 [M]	The Fife Piper	1966	5.00	10.00	20.00
❑ HST-8509 [S]	The Fife Piper	1966	6.25	12.50	25.00

E

EAGER, ALLAN

Number	Title (A Side/B Side)	Yr	VG	VG+	NM
SAVOY					
❑ MG-9015 [10]	New Trends in Modern Music, Volume 2	1952	62.50	125.00	250.00
❑ MG-15044 [10]	Tenor Sax	1954	50.00	100.00	200.00

EAGLE

Number	Title (A Side/B Side)	Yr	VG	VG+	NM
JANUS					
❑ JLS-3011	Come Under Nancy's Tent	1970	5.00	10.00	20.00

EAGLES

Number	Title (A Side/B Side)	Yr	VG	VG+	NM
ASYLUM					
❑ 6E-103	Hotel California	1977	2.00	4.00	8.00
❑ 6E-105	Eagles — Their Greatest Hits 1971-1975	1977	2.00	4.00	8.00
❑ 5E-508	The Long Run	1979	2.00	4.00	8.00
❑ BB-705 [(2)]	Eagles Live	1980	3.00	6.00	12.00
❑ 7E-1004	On the Border	1974	3.00	6.00	12.00
—Clouds label					
❑ EQ 1004 [Q]	On the Border	1974	5.00	10.00	20.00
❑ 7E-1039	One of These Nights	1975	2.50	5.00	10.00
—Clouds label					
❑ EQ 1039 [Q]	One of These Nights	1975	5.00	10.00	20.00
❑ 7E-1052	Eagles — Their Greatest Hits 1971-1975	1976	2.50	5.00	10.00
❑ 7E-1084	Hotel California	1976	2.50	5.00	10.00
❑ SD 5054	Eagles	1972	3.75	7.50	15.00
—Gatefold cover; white label with door-in-a-circle logo at top					
❑ SD 5054	Eagles	1973	3.00	6.00	12.00
—Regular cover; clouds label					
❑ SD 5068	Desperado	1973	3.00	6.00	12.00
—Clouds label					
❑ 60205	Eagles Greatest Hits, Volume 2	1982	2.50	5.00	10.00
DCC COMPACT CLASSICS					
❑ LPZ-2043	Hotel California	1997	30.00	60.00	120.00
—Audiophile vinyl					
❑ LPZ-2051	Eagles — Their Greatest Hits 1971-1975	1998	25.00	50.00	100.00
—Audiophile vinyl					
ELEKTRA					
❑ 60422	Anthology of the Eagles	1985	—	—	—
—Canceled					
MOBILE FIDELITY					
❑ 1-126	Hotel California	1984	25.00	50.00	100.00
—Audiophile vinyl					

EAGLIN, SNOOKS

Number	Title (A Side/B Side)	Yr	VG	VG+	NM
ARHOOLIE					
❑ 2014	Possum Up a Simmon Tree	198?	2.50	5.00	10.00
BLACK TOP					
❑ BT-1037	Baby, You Can Get Your Gun	1987	2.50	5.00	10.00
❑ BT-1046	Out of Nowhere	198?	2.50	5.00	10.00
BLUESVILLE					
❑ BVLP-1046 [M]	That's All Right	1962	15.00	30.00	60.00
—Blue label, silver print					
❑ BVLP-1046 [M]	That's All Right	1964	6.25	12.50	25.00
—Blue label, trident logo at right					
FOLKWAYS					
❑ FA-2476 [M]	New Orleans Street Singer	1959	10.00	20.00	40.00
GNP CRECENDO					
❑ 10023	Down Yonder	1979	2.50	5.00	10.00

EARDLEY, JON

Number	Title (A Side/B Side)	Yr	VG	VG+	NM
NEW JAZZ					
❑ NJLP-1105 [10]	Jon Eardley in Hollywood	1954	50.00	100.00	200.00
PRESTIGE					
❑ PRLP-205 [10]	Jon Eardley in Hollywood	1955	37.50	75.00	150.00
❑ PRLP-207 [10]	Hey There	1955	37.50	75.00	150.00
❑ PRLP-7033 [M]	Jon Eardley Seven	1956	25.00	50.00	100.00

EARLAND, CHARLES

Number	Title (A Side/B Side)	Yr	VG	VG+	NM
PRESTIGE					
❑ PRST-7758	Black Talk!	1970	5.00	10.00	20.00

EARLS, THE (1)

Number	Title (A Side/B Side)	Yr	VG	VG+	NM
CHANCE					
❑ 1001	The Earls Today	1983	3.00	6.00	12.00
OLD TOWN					
❑ LP-104 [M]	Remember Me Baby	1963	125.00	250.00	500.00
—Counterfeit identification: Counterfeits have more than 1-inch trailoffs or as little as 1/2 inch trailoffs; legitimate copies have 5/8- to 3/4-inch trailoff					
WOODBURY					
❑ 104	Remember Me Baby	1976	3.75	7.50	15.00

EARTH ISLAND

Number	Title (A Side/B Side)	Yr	VG	VG+	NM
PHILPS					
❑ PHS 600340	We Must Survive	1970	6.25	12.50	25.00

EARTH OPERA

Number	Title (A Side/B Side)	Yr	VG	VG+	NM
ELEKTRA					
❑ EKS-74016	Earth Opera	1968	5.00	10.00	20.00
❑ EKS-74038	The Great American Eagle Tragedy	1969	5.00	10.00	20.00

EARTH, WIND, AND FIRE

Number	Title (A Side/B Side)	Yr	VG	VG+	NM
ARC					
❑ FC 35647	The Best of Earth, Wind & Fire, Vol. 1	1978	2.50	5.00	10.00
❑ FC 35730	I Am	1979	2.50	5.00	10.00
❑ PC 35730	I Am	1984	2.00	4.00	8.00
—Budget-line reissue					
❑ KC2 36795 [(2)]	Faces	1980	3.00	6.00	12.00
❑ PC 37548	Raise!	1984	2.00	4.00	8.00
—Budget-line reissue					
❑ TC 37548	Raise!	1981	2.50	5.00	10.00
❑ HC 45647	The Best of Earth, Wind & Fire, Vol. 1	1981	7.50	15.00	30.00
—Half-speed mastered edition					
❑ HC 45730	I Am	1981	7.50	15.00	30.00
—Half-speed mastered edition					
❑ HC 47548	Raise!	1982	7.50	15.00	30.00
—Half-speed mastered edition					
COLUMBIA					
❑ KC 31702	Last Days and Time	1972	3.75	7.50	15.00
❑ PC 31702	Last Days and Time	197?	2.00	4.00	8.00
—Reissue					
❑ CQ 32194 [Q]	Head to the Sky	1973	5.00	10.00	20.00
❑ KC 32194	Head to the Sky	1973	3.00	6.00	12.00
❑ PC 32194	Head to the Sky	197?	2.00	4.00	8.00
—Reissue					
❑ CQ 32712 [Q]	Open Our Eyes	1974	5.00	10.00	20.00
❑ KC 32712	Open Our Eyes	1974	3.00	6.00	12.00
❑ PC 32712	Open Our Eyes	197?	2.00	4.00	8.00
—Reissue					
❑ PC 33280	That's the Way of the World	1975	3.00	6.00	12.00
—No bar code					
❑ PC 33280	That's the Way of the World	198?	2.00	4.00	8.00
—Budget-line reissue with bar code					
❑ PG 33694 [(2)]	Gratitude	1975	3.75	7.50	15.00
—No bar code					
❑ PG 33694 [(2)]	Gratitude	198?	2.50	5.00	10.00
—Budget-line reissue with bar code					
❑ PC 34241	Spirit	1976	3.00	6.00	12.00
—No bar code					
❑ PC 34241	Spirit	198?	2.00	4.00	8.00
—Budget-line reissue with bar code					
❑ PCQ 34241 [Q]	Spirit	1976	6.25	12.50	25.00
❑ JC 34905	All 'N All	1977	3.00	6.00	12.00
❑ PC 34905	All 'N All	198?	2.00	4.00	8.00
—Budget-line reissue					
❑ PC 38367	Powerlight	1984	2.00	4.00	8.00
—Budget-line reissue					
❑ TC 38367	Powerlight	1983	2.50	5.00	10.00
❑ QC 38980	Electric Universe	1983	2.50	5.00	10.00
❑ FC 40596	Touch the World	1987	2.50	5.00	10.00
❑ OC 45013	The Best of Earth, Wind & Fire, Vol. II	1988	2.50	5.00	10.00
❑ C 45268	Heritage	1990	3.75	7.50	15.00
❑ HC 48367	Powerlight	1983	10.00	20.00	40.00
—Half-speed mastered edition					
MOBILE FIDELITY					
❑ 1-159	That's the Way of the World	198?	7.50	15.00	30.00
—Audiophile vinyl					
PAIR					
❑ PDL2-1064 [(2)]	Beat It to Life	1986	3.00	6.00	12.00
WARNER BROS.					
❑ WS 1905	Earth, Wind, and Fire	1971	5.00	10.00	20.00
—Green label					
❑ WS 1958	The Need of Love	1971	5.00	10.00	20.00
—Green label					
❑ 2WS 2798 [(2)]	Another Time	1974	5.00	10.00	20.00
—"Burbank" palm trees labels					

EAST

Number	Title (A Side/B Side)	Yr	VG	VG+	NM
CAPITOL					
❑ ST-11083	East	1972	6.25	12.50	25.00

EAST OF EDEN

Number	Title (A Side/B Side)	Yr	VG	VG+	NM
DERAM					
❑ DES 18023	Mercator Projected	1969	5.00	10.00	20.00
❑ DES 18043	Snafu	1970	5.00	10.00	20.00
HARVEST					
❑ SW-806	East of Eden	1971	5.00	10.00	20.00

EAST SIDE KIDS, THE

Number	Title (A Side/B Side)	Yr	VG	VG+	NM
UNI					
❑ 73032	The Tiger and the Lamb	1968	6.25	12.50	25.00

EASTMAN-ROCHESTER ORCHESTRA (HOWARD HANSON, CONDUCTOR)

Number	Title (A Side/B Side)	Yr	VG	VG+	NM
MERCURY LIVING PRESENCE					
❑ SR 90018 [S]	Chadwick: Symphonic Sketches	1959	7.50	15.00	30.00
—Maroon label, no "Vendor: Mercury Record Corporation"					
❑ SR 90049 [S]	Grofe: Grand Canyon Suite; Mississippi Suite	1959	7.50	15.00	30.00
—Maroon label, no "Vendor: Mercury Record Corporation"					
❑ SR 90053 [S]	Music for Quiet Listening	1959	15.00	30.00	60.00
—Maroon label, no "Vendor: Mercury Record Corporation"					
❑ SR 90053 [S]	Music for Quiet Listening	196?	12.50	25.00	50.00
—Maroon label, with "Vendor: Mercury Record Corporation"					
❑ SR 90103 [S]	McPhee: Tabuh-Tauhan; Sessions: The Black Maskers	196?	62.50	125.00	250.00
—Maroon label, no "Vendor: Mercury Record Corporation"					
❑ SR 90134 [S]	Fiesta in Hi-Fi	1960	25.00	50.00	100.00
—Maroon label, no "Vendor: Mercury Record Corporation"					
❑ SR 90136 [S]	Carpenter: Adventures in a Perambulator; Phillips: Selections from McGuffey's Readers	1960	25.00	50.00	100.00
—Maroon label, no "Vendor: Mercury Record Corporation"					
❑ SR 90147 [S]	Kennan: Three Pieces; Rogers: Once Upon a Time; Bergama: Gold and the Senor Commandante	196?	50.00	100.00	200.00
—Maroon label, no "Vendor: Mercury Record Corporation"					
❑ SR 90149 [S]	Ives: Three Places in New England; Symphony No. 3	196?	5.00	10.00	20.00
—Maroon label, with "Vendor: Mercury Record Corporation"					
❑ SR 90149 [S]	Ives: Three Places in New England; Symphony No. 3	196?	10.00	20.00	40.00
—Maroon label, no "Vendor: Mercury Record Corporation"					
❑ SR 90150 [S]	Hanson: Elegy in Memory of Koussevitzky; Song of Democracy; Lane: 4 Songs	196?	12.50	25.00	50.00
—Maroon label, with "Vendor: Mercury Record Corporation"					

Number	Title (A Side/B Side)	Yr	VG	VG+	NM
❏ SR 90150 [S]	Hanson: Elegy in Memory of Koussevitzky; Song of Democracy; Lane: 4 Songs	196?	25.00	50.00	100.00
—Maroon label, no "Vendor: Mercury Record Corporation"					
❏ SR 90163 [S]	Herbert: Cello Concerto; Peter: Sinfonia in G	196?	10.00	20.00	40.00
—Maroon label, no "Vendor: Mercury Record Corporation"					
❏ SR 90165 [S]	Hanson: Symphony No. 1 "Nordic"; Fantasy Variations on a Theme of Youth	196?	5.00	10.00	20.00
—Maroon label, with "Vendor: Mercury Record Corporation"					
❏ SR 90165 [S]	Hanson: Symphony No. 1 "Nordic"; Fantasy Variations on a Theme of Youth	196?	10.00	20.00	40.00
—Maroon label, no "Vendor: Mercury Record Corporation"					
❏ SR 90175 [S]	The Composer and His Orchestra	196?	5.00	10.00	20.00
—Maroon label, with "Vendor: Mercury Record Corporation"					
❏ SR 90175 [S]	The Composer and His Orchestra	196?	6.25	12.50	25.00
—Maroon label, no "Vendor: Mercury Record Corporation"					
❏ SR 90192 [S]	Hanson: Symphony No. 2 "Romantic"; Lament for Beowulf	196?	5.00	10.00	20.00
—Maroon label, with "Vendor: Mercury Record Corporation"					
❏ SR 90192 [S]	Hanson: Symphony No. 2 "Romantic"; Lament for Beowulf	196?	7.50	15.00	30.00
—Maroon label, no "Vendor: Mercury Record Corporation"					
❏ SR 90206 [S]	Piston: The Incredible Flutist; Moore: Pageant of P.T. Barnum	196?	5.00	10.00	20.00
—Maroon label, with "Vendor: Mercury Record Corporation"					
❏ SR 90206 [S]	Piston: The Incredible Flutist; Moore: Pageant of P.T. Barnum	196?	10.00	20.00	40.00
—Maroon label, no "Vendor: Mercury Record Corporation"					
❏ SR 90223 [S]	Bloch: Concerti Grossi No. 1 and 2	196?	5.00	10.00	20.00
—Third edition: Dark red (not maroon) label					
❏ SR 90223 [S]	Bloch: Concerti Grossi No. 1 and 2	196?	7.50	15.00	30.00
—Maroon label, no "Vendor: Mercury Record Corporation"					
❏ SR 90223 [S]	Bloch: Concerti Grossi No. 1 and 2	196?	10.00	20.00	40.00
—Maroon label, with "Vendor: Mercury Record Corporation"; a rare instance where the second edition is more sought-after than the first					
❏ SR 90224 [S]	Barber: Medea; Capricorn Concerto	196?	5.00	10.00	20.00
—Maroon label, no "Vendor: Mercury Record Corporation"					
❏ SR 90257 [S]	Ginastera: Overture to a Creole "Faust"; Guarnieri: Three Dances; Still: Sahdji Ballet	196?	50.00	100.00	200.00
—Maroon label, no "Vendor: Mercury Record Corporation"					
❏ SR 90263 [S]	Gould, Morton: Fall River Legend; Spirituals	196?	5.00	10.00	20.00
—Maroon label, with "Vendor: Mercury Record Corporation"					
❏ SR 90263 [S]	Gould, Morton: Fall River Legend; Spirituals	196?	10.00	20.00	40.00
—Maroon label, no "Vendor: Mercury Record Corporation"					
❏ SR 90267 [S]	The Composer and His Orchestra, Volume 2	196?	5.00	10.00	20.00
—Maroon label, with "Vendor: Mercury Record Corporation"					
❏ SR 90267 [S]	The Composer and His Orchestra, Volume 2	196?	6.25	12.50	25.00
—Maroon label, no "Vendor: Mercury Record Corporation"					
❏ SR 90277 [S]	Loeffler: Deux Rapsodies; Barlow: Night Song; McCauley: Five Miniatures	196?	50.00	100.00	200.00
—Maroon label, no "Vendor: Mercury Record Corporation"					
❏ SR 90286 [S]	Bloch: Schelomo; Herbert: Cello Concerto No. 2	196?	12.50	25.00	50.00
—Maroon label, no "Vendor: Mercury Record Corporation"					
❏ SR 90379 [S]	Schuman: New England Tripytch; Mennin: Symphony No. 5; Griffes: Poem for Flute and Orchestra	196?	5.00	10.00	20.00
—Maroon label, with "Vendor: Mercury Record Corporation"					
❏ SR 90379 [S]	Schuman: New England Tripytch; Mennin: Symphony No. 5; Griffes: Poem for Flute and Orchestra	196?	12.50	25.00	50.00
—Maroon label, no "Vendor: Mercury Record Corporation"					
❏ SR 90429 [S]	Thomson: Symphony on a Hymn Tune; The Feast of Love; Hanson: Four Psalms	196?	5.00	10.00	20.00
—Maroon label, with "Vendor: Mercury Record Corporation"					
❏ SR 90429 [S]	Thomson: Symphony on a Hymn Tune; The Feast of Love; Hanson: Four Psalms	196?	5.00	10.00	20.00
—Third edition: Dark red (not maroon) label					
❏ SR 90429 [S]	Thomson: Symphony on a Hymn Tune; The Feast of Love; Hanson: Four Psalms	196?	10.00	20.00	40.00
—Maroon label, no "Vendor: Mercury Record Corporation"					
❏ SR 90430 [S]	Hanson: Piano Concerto; Mosaics; LaMontaine: Birds of Paradise	196?	5.00	10.00	20.00
—Maroon label, with "Vendor: Mercury Record Corporation"					
❏ SR 90430 [S]	Hanson: Piano Concerto; Mosaics; LaMontaine: Birds of Paradise	1965	5.00	10.00	20.00
—Maroon label, no "Vendor: Mercury Record Corporation"					
❏ SR 90449 [S]	Hanson: Symphony No. 3; MacDowell: Symphony No. 1	1965	10.00	20.00	40.00
—Maroon label, no "Vendor: Mercury Record Corporation"					

EASTMAN-ROCHESTER PHILHARMONIA (HOWARD HANSON, CONDUCTOR)
MERCURY LIVING PRESENCE

Number	Title (A Side/B Side)	Yr	VG	VG+	NM
❏ SR 90299 [S]	Musical Diplomats USA	196?	6.25	12.50	25.00
—Maroon label, no "Vendor: Mercury Record Corporation"					
❏ SR 90357 [S]	The Composer and His Orchestra, Volume 3	196?	5.00	10.00	20.00
—Maroon label, no "Vendor: Mercury Record Corporation"					

EASTMAN-ROCHESTER "POPS" ORCHESTRA (FREDERICK FENNELL, CONDUCTOR)
MERCURY LIVING PRESENCE

Number	Title (A Side/B Side)	Yr	VG	VG+	NM
❏ SR 90043 [S]	Music of Leroy Anderson, Vol. 2	1959	6.25	12.50	25.00
—Maroon label, no "Vendor: Mercury Record Corporation"					
❏ SR 90043 [S]	Music of Leroy Anderson, Vol. 2	196?	5.00	10.00	20.00
—Maroon label, with "Vendor: Mercury Record Corporation"					
❏ SR 90144 [S]	Hi-Fi A La Espanola	196?	250.00	500.00	1000.
—Maroon label, no "Vendor: Mercury Record Corporation"					
❏ SR 90144 [S]	Hi-Fi A La Espanola	199?	6.25	12.50	25.00
—Classic Records reissue					
❏ SR 90219 [S]	Grainger: Country Gardens	196?	12.50	25.00	50.00
—Maroon label, no "Vendor: Mercury Record Corporation"					
❏ SR 90222 [S]	Popovers	196?	5.00	10.00	20.00
—Maroon label, no "Vendor: Mercury Record Corporation"					

Number	Title (A Side/B Side)	Yr	VG	VG+	NM
❏ SR 90271 [S]	Marches for Orchestra	196?	6.25	12.50	25.00
—Maroon label, with "Vendor: Mercury Record Corporation"					
❏ SR 90271 [S]	Marches for Orchestra	196?	10.00	20.00	40.00
—Maroon label, no "Vendor: Mercury Record Corporation"					
❏ SR 90400 [S]	Music of Leroy Anderson, Volume 3	196?	12.50	25.00	50.00
—Maroon label, with "Vendor: Mercury Record Corporation"					
❏ SR 90400 [S]	Music of Leroy Anderson, Volume 3	196?	20.00	40.00	80.00
—Maroon label, no "Vendor: Mercury Record Corporation"					

EASTMAN-ROCHESTER WIND ENSEMBLE (FREDERICK FENNELL, CONDUCTOR)
MERCURY LIVING PRESENCE

Number	Title (A Side/B Side)	Yr	VG	VG+	NM
❏ SR 90105 [S]	Marching Along	196?	10.00	20.00	40.00
—Maroon label, with "Vendor: Mercury Record Corporation"; a rare instance where the second edition is more sought-after than the first					
❏ SR 90105 [S]	Marching Along	1960	5.00	10.00	20.00
—Maroon label, no "Vendor: Mercury Record Corporation"					
❏ SR 90111 [S]	Spirit of '76: Music for Fifes and Drums	1960	10.00	20.00	40.00
—Maroon label, no "Vendor: Mercury Record Corporation"					
❏ SR 90112 [S]	Ruffles and Flourishes	1960	6.25	12.50	25.00
—Maroon label, no "Vendor: Mercury Record Corporation"					
❏ SR 90143 [S]	Hindemith: Symphony in B-flat; Schoenberg: Theme and Variations; Stravinsky: Symphony of Wind Instru	196?	7.50	15.00	30.00
—Maroon label, no "Vendor: Mercury Record Corporation"					
❏ SR 90143 [S]	Hindemith: Symphony in B-flat; Schoenberg: Theme and Variations; Stravinsky: Symphony of Wind Instru	196?	15.00	30.00	60.00
—Maroon label, no "Vendor: Mercury Record Corporation"					
❏ SR 90170 [S]	March Time	196?	5.00	10.00	20.00
—Maroon label, no "Vendor: Mercury Record Corporation"					
❏ SR 90173 [S]	Winds in Hi-Fi	196?	5.00	10.00	20.00
—Third edition: Dark red (not maroon) label					
❏ SR 90173 [S]	Winds in Hi-Fi	196?	12.50	25.00	50.00
—Maroon label, with "Vendor: Mercury Record Corporation"					
❏ SR 90173 [S]	Winds in Hi-Fi	196?	20.00	40.00	80.00
—Maroon label, no "Vendor: Mercury Record Corporation"					
❏ SR 90176 [S]	Mozart: Serenade No. 10 in E-flat	196?	6.25	12.50	25.00
—Maroon label, with "Vendor: Mercury Record Corporation"					
❏ SR 90176 [S]	Mozart: Serenade No. 10 in E-flat	196?	12.50	25.00	50.00
—Maroon label, no "Vendor: Mercury Record Corporation"					
❏ SR 90197 [S]	British Band Classics, Vol. 2	196?	5.00	10.00	20.00
—Third edition: Dark red (not maroon) label					
❏ SR 90197 [S]	British Band Classics, Vol. 2	196?	10.00	20.00	40.00
—Maroon label, with "Vendor: Mercury Record Corporation"					
❏ SR 90197 [S]	British Band Classics, Vol. 2	196?	37.50	75.00	150.00
—Maroon label, no "Vendor: Mercury Record Corporation"					
❏ SR 90207 [S]	Hands Across the Sea	196?	12.50	25.00	50.00
—Maroon label, no "Vendor: Mercury Record Corporation"					
❏ SR 90220 [S]	Gould: West Point Symphony; Bennett: Songs; Williams: Fanfare and Allegro; Work: Autumn Walk	196?	12.50	25.00	50.00
—Maroon label, with "Vendor: Mercury Record Corporation"					
❏ SR 90220 [S]	Gould: West Point Symphony; Bennett: Songs; Williams: Fanfare and Allegro; Work: Autumn Walk	196?	17.50	35.00	70.00
—Maroon label, no "Vendor: Mercury Record Corporation"					
❏ SR 90221 [S]	Diverse Winds	196?	30.00	60.00	120.00
—Maroon label, no "Vendor: Mercury Record Corporation"					
❏ SR 90245 [S]	Gabrieli Music for Wind Instruments	196?	5.00	10.00	20.00
—Maroon label, no "Vendor: Mercury Record Corporation"					
❏ SR 90256 [S]	Ballet for Band	196?	20.00	40.00	80.00
—Maroon label, with "Vendor: Mercury Record Corporation"					
❏ SR 90256 [S]	Ballet for Band	196?	45.00	90.00	180.00
—Maroon label, no "Vendor: Mercury Record Corporation"					
❏ SR 90264 [S]	Sousa Sound Off	196?	6.25	12.50	25.00
—Maroon label, no "Vendor: Mercury Record Corporation"					
❏ SR 90276 [S]	Wagner for Band	196?	10.00	20.00	40.00
—Third edition: Dark red (not maroon) label					
❏ SR 90276 [S]	Wagner for Band	196?	12.50	25.00	50.00
—Maroon label, with "Vendor: Mercury Record Corporation" (second edition is more sought after than the first)					
❏ SR 90276 [S]	Wagner for Band	196?	17.50	35.00	70.00
—Maroon label, no "Vendor: Mercury Record Corporation"					
❏ SR 90284 [S]	Sousa on Review	196?	7.50	15.00	30.00
—Maroon label, no "Vendor: Mercury Record Corporation"					
❏ SR 90284 [S]	Sousa on Review	196?	20.00	40.00	80.00
—Maroon label, with "Vendor: Mercury Record Corporation"; a rare instance where the second edition is more sought-after than the first					
❏ SR 90314 [S]	Screamers (Circus Marches)	196?	6.25	12.50	25.00
—Maroon label, with "Vendor: Mercury Record Corporation"					
❏ SR 90314 [S]	Screamers (Circus Marches)	196?	10.00	20.00	40.00
—Maroon label, no "Vendor: Mercury Record Corporation"					
❏ SR 90390 [S]	Broadway Marches	196?	5.00	10.00	20.00
—Maroon label, no "Vendor: Mercury Record Corporation"					

EASTMAN-ROCHESTER WIND ENSEMBLE (A. CLYDE ROLLER, CONDUCTOR)
MERCURY LIVING PRESENCE

Number	Title (A Side/B Side)	Yr	VG	VG+	NM
❏ SR 90366 [S]	Hovhaness: Symphony No. 4; Giannini: Symphony No. 3	196?	5.00	10.00	20.00
—Third edition: Dark red (not maroon) label					
❏ SR 90366 [S]	Hovhaness: Symphony No. 4; Giannini: Symphony No. 3	196?	10.00	20.00	40.00
—Maroon label, with "Vendor: Mercury Record Corporation"					
❏ SR 90366 [S]	Hovhaness: Symphony No. 4; Giannini: Symphony No. 3	196?	20.00	40.00	80.00
—Maroon label, no "Vendor: Mercury Record Corporation"					

EASTWOOD, CLINT
CAMEO

Number	Title (A Side/B Side)	Yr	VG	VG+	NM
❏ C-1056 [M]	Clint Eastwood Sings Cowboy Favorites	1963	25.00	50.00	100.00
❏ SC-1056 [S]	Clint Eastwood Sings Cowboy Favorites	1963	37.50	75.00	150.00

E

Number	Title (A Side/B Side)	Yr	VG	VG+	NM

EASY RIDERS, THE
See TERRY GILKYSON.

EASY RIDERS JAZZ BAND, THE
JAZZ CRUSADE
| ❏ 1002 | My Life Will Be Sweeter Someday | 1963 | 10.00 | 20.00 | 40.00 |

EASYBEATS, THE
RARE EARTH
| ❏ 517 | Easy Ridin' | 1970 | — | — | — |

—Canceled
RHINO
| ❏ RNLP-124 | The Best of the Easybeats | 1985 | 2.00 | 4.00 | 8.00 |

UNITED ARTISTS
| ❏ UAL 3588 [M] | Friday on My Mind | 1967 | 10.00 | 20.00 | 40.00 |
| ❏ UAS 6588 [P] | Friday on My Mind | 1967 | 12.50 | 25.00 | 50.00 |

—"Make You Feel Alright" is rechanneled.
| ❏ UAS 6667 [P] | Falling Off the Edge of the World | 1968 | 10.00 | 20.00 | 40.00 |

—"Women" is rechanneled.

EATON, CLEVELAND
OVATION
| ❏ OV-1703 | Instant Hip | 1974 | 5.00 | 10.00 | 20.00 |

EATON, JOHNNY
COLUMBIA
| ❏ CL 737 [M] | College Jazz: Modern | 1956 | 10.00 | 20.00 | 40.00 |
| ❏ CL 996 [M] | Far Out, Far In | 1957 | 10.00 | 20.00 | 40.00 |

EAVES, HUBERT
INNER CITY
| ❏ IC-6012 | Esteric Funk | 1976 | 5.00 | 10.00 | 20.00 |

EBON-KNIGHTS, THE
STEPHENY
| ❏ 4001 [M] | First Date | 1959 | 375.00 | 750.00 | 1500. |

EBONYS, THE
BUDDAH
| ❏ BDS 5679 | Sing About Life | 1976 | 10.00 | 20.00 | 40.00 |

EBSEN, BUDDY
REPRISE
| ❏ R-6174 [M] | Buddy Ebsen Sings Howdy! | 1965 | 7.50 | 15.00 | 30.00 |
| ❏ RS-6174 [S] | Buddy Ebsen Sings Howdy! | 1965 | 10.00 | 20.00 | 40.00 |

ECHOES OF HARLEM
ROYALE
| ❏ LP-18128 [10] | Echoes of Harlem | 195? | 20.00 | 40.00 | 80.00 |

ECKSTINE, BILLY
AUDIO LAB
| ❏ AL-1549 [M] | Mr. B | 1960 | 30.00 | 60.00 | 120.00 |

DELUXE
| ❏ FA-2010 [M] | Billy Eckstine and His Orchestra | 195? | 20.00 | 40.00 | 80.00 |

EMARCY
❏ MG-26025 [10]	Blues for Sale	1954	30.00	60.00	120.00
❏ MG-26027 [10]	The Love Songs of Mr. B	1954	30.00	60.00	120.00
❏ MG-36010 [M]	I Surrender, Dear	1955	20.00	40.00	80.00
❏ MG-36029 [M]	Blues for Sale	1955	20.00	40.00	80.00
❏ MG-36030 [M]	The Love Songs of Mr. B	1955	20.00	40.00	80.00
❏ MG-36129 [M]	Billy Eckstine's Imagination	1958	15.00	30.00	60.00

KING
| ❏ 295-12 [10] | The Great Mr. B | 1953 | 75.00 | 150.00 | 300.00 |

LION
| ❏ L-70057 [M] | The Best of Billy Eckstine | 1958 | 6.25 | 12.50 | 25.00 |

MERCURY
❏ MG-20333 [M]	Billy's Best	1958	10.00	20.00	40.00
❏ MG-20637 [M]	Broadway, Bongos and Mr. B	1961	6.25	12.50	25.00
❏ MG-20674 [M]	Billy Eckstine and Quincy Jones at Basin St. East	1962	6.25	12.50	25.00
❏ MG-20736 [M]	Don't Worry 'Bout Me	1962	6.25	12.50	25.00
❏ SR-60086 [S]	Billy's Best	1958	12.50	25.00	50.00
❏ SR-60637 [S]	Broadway, Bongos and Mr. B	1961	7.50	15.00	30.00
❏ SR-60674 [S]	Billy Eckstine and Quincy Jones at Basin St. East	1962	7.50	15.00	30.00
❏ SR-60736 [S]	Don't Worry 'Bout Me	1962	7.50	15.00	30.00
❏ SR-60796 [S]	The Golden Hits of Billy Eckstine	1963	5.00	10.00	20.00

MGM
❏ E-153 [10]	Billy Eckstine Sings Rodgers & Hammerstein	1952	37.50	75.00	150.00
❏ E-219 [10]	Tenderly	1953	37.50	75.00	150.00
❏ E-257 [10]	I Let a Song Go Out of My Heart	1954	37.50	75.00	150.00
❏ E-523 [10]	Songs by Billy Eckstine	1951	40.00	80.00	160.00
❏ E-548 [10]	Favorites	1951	40.00	80.00	160.00
❏ E-3176 [M]	Mr. B with a Beat	1955	12.50	25.00	50.00
❏ E-3209 [M]	Rendezvous	1955	12.50	25.00	50.00
❏ E-3275 [M]	That Old Feeling	1956	12.50	25.00	50.00

MOTOWN
❏ M 632 [M]	Prime of My Life	1965	5.00	10.00	20.00
❏ MS 632 [S]	Prime of My Life	1965	6.25	12.50	25.00
❏ M 646 [M]	My Way	1966	5.00	10.00	20.00
❏ MS 646 [S]	My Way	1966	6.25	12.50	25.00
❏ MS 677	For Love of Ivy	1969	6.25	12.50	25.00

NATIONAL
| ❏ NLP-2001 [10] | Billy Eckstine Sings | 1949 | 50.00 | 100.00 | 200.00 |

REGENT
❏ MG-6052 [M]	Prisoner of Love	1957	12.50	25.00	50.00
❏ MG-6053 [M]	The Duke, the Blues and Me	1957	12.50	25.00	50.00
❏ MG-6054 [M]	My Deep Blue Dream	1957	12.50	25.00	50.00
❏ MG-6058 [M]	You Call It Madness	1957	12.50	25.00	50.00

ROULETTE
❏ R-25052 [M]	No Cover, No Minimum	1961	6.25	12.50	25.00
❏ SR-25052 [S]	No Cover, No Minimum	1961	7.50	15.00	30.00
❏ R-25104 [M]	Once More with Feeling	1962	6.25	12.50	25.00
❏ SR-25104 [S]	Once More with Feeling	1962	7.50	15.00	30.00

EDDIE AND BETTY
WARNER BROS.
| ❏ W 1350 [M] | Nightlife for Daydreamers | 1959 | 6.25 | 12.50 | 25.00 |
| ❏ WS 1350 [S] | Nightlife for Daydreamers | 1959 | 7.50 | 15.00 | 30.00 |

EDDIE AND THE SUBTITLES
(NO LABEL)
| ❏ (no #) | Skeletons in the Closet | 1981 | 10.00 | 20.00 | 40.00 |

13TH STORY
| ❏ MR 3301 | Dead Drunks Don't Dance | 1983 | 6.25 | 12.50 | 25.00 |

EDDY, DUANE
CAPITOL
| ❏ ST-12567 | Duane Eddy | 1987 | 3.00 | 6.00 | 12.00 |

COLPIX
❏ CP-490 [M]	Duane A-Go-Go	1965	7.50	15.00	30.00
❏ CPS-490 [S]	Duane A-Go-Go	1965	10.00	20.00	40.00
❏ CPL-494 [M]	Duane Eddy Does Bob Dylan	1965	7.50	15.00	30.00
❏ CPS-494 [S]	Duane Eddy Does Bob Dylan	1965	10.00	20.00	40.00

JAMIE
| ❏ JLP-3000 [M] | Have "Twangy" Guitar — Will Travel | 1958 | 30.00 | 60.00 | 120.00 |
—Duane sitting with guitar case, title on cover in white (1st)
| ❏ JLP-3000 [M] | Have "Twangy" Guitar — Will Travel | 1959 | 12.50 | 25.00 | 50.00 |
—Duane standing with guitar (3rd)
| ❏ JLP-3000 [M] | Have "Twangy" Guitar — Will Travel | 1959 | 25.00 | 50.00 | 100.00 |
—Duane sitting with guitar case, title on cover in green and red (2nd)
| ❏ JLPS-3000 [R] | Have "Twangy" Guitar — Will Travel | 196? | 12.50 | 25.00 | 50.00 |
—Duane standing with guitar (3rd), album plays fake stereo
| ❏ JLPS-3000 [S] | Have "Twangy" Guitar — Will Travel | 1958 | 100.00 | 200.00 | 400.00 |
—Duane sitting with guitar case, title on cover in white (1st)
| ❏ JLPS-3000 [S] | Have "Twangy" Guitar — Will Travel | 1959 | 25.00 | 50.00 | 100.00 |
—Duane standing with guitar (3rd), album plays true stereo
| ❏ JLPS-3000 [S] | Have "Twangy" Guitar — Will Travel | 1959 | 75.00 | 150.00 | 300.00 |
—Duane sitting with guitar case, title on cover in green and red (2nd)
❏ JLPM-3006 [M]	Especially for You…	1959	10.00	20.00	40.00
❏ JLPS-3006 [S]	Especially for You…	1959	15.00	30.00	60.00
❏ JLPM-3009 [M]	The "Twangs" The "Thang"	1959	10.00	20.00	40.00
❏ JLPS-3009 [S]	The "Twangs" The "Thang"	1959	15.00	30.00	60.00
❏ JLPM-3011 [M]	Songs of Our Heritage	196?	7.50	15.00	30.00
—Regular cover
| ❏ JLPM-3011 [M] | Songs of Our Heritage | 1960 | 20.00 | 40.00 | 80.00 |
—Gatefold cover
| ❏ JLPS-3011 [S] | Songs of Our Heritage | 196? | 10.00 | 20.00 | 40.00 |
—Regular cover
| ❏ JLPS-3011 [S] | Songs of Our Heritage | 1960 | 25.00 | 50.00 | 100.00 |
—Gatefold cover
| ❏ JLPS-3011 [S] | Songs of Our Heritage | 1960 | 125.00 | 250.00 | 500.00 |
—Gatefold cover, blue vinyl
| ❏ JLPS-3011 [S] | Songs of Our Heritage | 1960 | 125.00 | 250.00 | 500.00 |
—Gatefold cover, red vinyl
| ❏ JLPM-3014 [M] | $1,000,000.00 Worth of Twang | 1960 | 10.00 | 20.00 | 40.00 |
| ❏ JLPS-3014 [S] | $1,000,000.00 Worth of Twang | 1960 | 17.50 | 35.00 | 70.00 |
—All but one song -- "Up and Down" -- is in true stereo
❏ JLPM-3019 [M]	Girls! Girls! Girls!	1961	10.00	20.00	40.00
❏ JLPS-3019 [R]	Girls! Girls! Girls!	1961	7.50	15.00	30.00
❏ JLPM-3021 [M]	$1,000,000.00 Worth of Twang, Volume 2	1962	10.00	20.00	40.00
❏ JLPS-3021 [R]	$1,000,000.00 Worth of Twang, Volume 2	1962	7.50	15.00	30.00
❏ JLPM-3022 [M]	Twistin' with Duane Eddy	1962	10.00	20.00	40.00
❏ JLPS-3022 [P]	Twistin' with Duane Eddy	1962	10.00	20.00	40.00
❏ JLPM-3024 [M]	Surfin'	1963	12.50	25.00	50.00
❏ JLPS-3024 [S]	Surfin'	1963	20.00	40.00	80.00
❏ JLPM-3025 [M]	Duane Eddy & The Rebels — In Person	1963	7.50	15.00	30.00
❏ JLPS-3025 [S]	Duane Eddy & The Rebels — In Person	1963	10.00	20.00	40.00
❏ JLPM-3026 [M]	16 Greatest Hits	1964	10.00	20.00	40.00
❏ JLPS-3026 [R]	16 Greatest Hits	1964	7.50	15.00	30.00
❏ ST-90663 [S]	Duane Eddy & The Rebels — In Person	1965	12.50	25.00	50.00
—Capitol Record Club edition
| ❏ T-90663 [M] | Duane Eddy & The Rebels — In Person | 1965 | 10.00 | 20.00 | 40.00 |
—Capitol Record Club edition
| ❏ ST-90682 [S] | Have "Twangy" Guitar — Will Travel | 1965 | 20.00 | 40.00 | 80.00 |
—Capitol Record Club edition
| ❏ T-90682 [M] | Have "Twangy" Guitar — Will Travel | 1965 | 15.00 | 30.00 | 60.00 |
—Capitol Record Club edition
| ❏ ST-91301 [S] | The "Twangs" The "Thang" | 1966 | 15.00 | 30.00 | 60.00 |
—Capitol Record Club edition
| ❏ T-91301 [M] | The "Twangs" The "Thang" | 1966 | 15.00 | 30.00 | 60.00 |
—Capitol Record Club edition

RCA VICTOR
❏ LPM-2525 [M]	Twistin' 'N' Twangin'	1962	6.25	12.50	25.00
❏ LSP-2525 [S]	Twistin' 'N' Twangin'	1962	10.00	20.00	40.00
❏ LPM-2576 [M]	Twangy Guitar — Silky Strings	1962	6.25	12.50	25.00
❏ LSP-2576 [S]	Twangy Guitar — Silky Strings	1962	10.00	20.00	40.00
❏ LPM-2648 [M]	Dance with the Guitar Man	1962	6.25	12.50	25.00
❏ LSP-2648 [S]	Dance with the Guitar Man	1962	10.00	20.00	40.00
❏ ANL1-2671	Pure Gold	1978	2.50	5.00	10.00
❏ LPM-2681 [M]	Twang a Country Song	1963	6.25	12.50	25.00
❏ LSP-2681 [S]	Twang a Country Song	1963	10.00	20.00	40.00
❏ LPM-2700 [M]	"Twangin' " Up a Storm!	1963	6.25	12.50	25.00
❏ LSP-2700 [S]	"Twangin' " Up a Storm!	1963	10.00	20.00	40.00
❏ LPM-2798 [M]	Lonely Guitar	1964	5.00	10.00	20.00
❏ LSP-2798 [S]	Lonely Guitar	1964	7.50	15.00	30.00
❏ LPM-2918 [M]	Water Skiing	1964	5.00	10.00	20.00
❏ LSP-2918 [S]	Water Skiing	1964	7.50	15.00	30.00
❏ LPM-2993 [M]	Twangin' the Golden Hits	1965	5.00	10.00	20.00
❏ LSP-2993 [S]	Twangin' the Golden Hits	1965	7.50	15.00	30.00
❏ LPM-3432 [M]	Twangsville	1965	5.00	10.00	20.00

Number	Title (A Side/B Side)	Yr	VG	VG+	NM
❑ LSP-3432 [S]	Twangsville	1965	7.50	15.00	30.00
❑ LPM-3477 [M]	The Best of Duane Eddy	1965	5.00	10.00	20.00
❑ LSP-3477 [P]	The Best of Duane Eddy	1965	6.25	12.50	25.00
—Black "Stereo" label					
❑ LSP-3477 [P]	The Best of Duane Eddy	1969	3.75	7.50	15.00
—Orange label					
REPRISE					
❑ R-6218 [M]	The Biggest Twang of Them All	1966	7.50	15.00	30.00
❑ RS-6218 [S]	The Biggest Twang of Them All	1966	10.00	20.00	40.00
❑ R-6240 [M]	The Roaring Twangies	1967	7.50	15.00	30.00
❑ RS-6240 [S]	The Roaring Twangies	1967	10.00	20.00	40.00
SIRE					
❑ SASH-3707-2 [(2)]	The Vintage Years	1975	6.25	12.50	25.00

EDDY, NELSON
HARMONY

Number	Title (A Side/B Side)	Yr	VG	VG+	NM
❑ HL 7201 [M]	Nelson Eddy Sings the Best Loved Carols of Christmas	195?	5.00	10.00	20.00

EDEN, BARBARA
DOT

Number	Title (A Side/B Side)	Yr	VG	VG+	NM
❑ DLP-3795 [M]	Miss Barbara Eden	1967	10.00	20.00	40.00
❑ DLP-25795 [S]	Miss Barbara Eden	1967	12.50	25.00	50.00

EDEN'S CHILDREN
ABC

Number	Title (A Side/B Side)	Yr	VG	VG+	NM
❑ 624 [M]	Eden's Children	1968	10.00	20.00	40.00
❑ S-624 [S]	Eden's Children	1968	6.25	12.50	25.00
❑ S-652	Sure Looks Real	1968	5.00	10.00	20.00

EDGE, THE
NOSE

Number	Title (A Side/B Side)	Yr	VG	VG+	NM
❑ NRS-48003	The Edge	1970	10.00	20.00	40.00

EDISON, HARRY "SWEETS"
AMERICAN RECORDING SOCIETY

Number	Title (A Side/B Side)	Yr	VG	VG+	NM
❑ G-430 [M]	Sweets	1957	10.00	20.00	40.00
CLEF					
❑ MGC-717 [M]	Sweets	1956	20.00	40.00	80.00
LIBERTY					
❑ LRP-3484 [M]	When Lights Are Low	1966	5.00	10.00	20.00
❑ LST-7484 [S]	When Lights Are Low	1966	6.25	12.50	25.00
PACIFIC JAZZ					
❑ PJLP-4 [10]	Harry Edison Quartet	1953	37.50	75.00	150.00
❑ PJ-11 [M]	The Inventive Harry Edison	1960	125.00	25.00	50.00
ROULETTE					
❑ R-52023 [M]	Sweetenings	1960	10.00	20.00	40.00
❑ SR-52023 [S]	Sweetenings	1960	10.00	20.00	40.00
❑ R-52041 [M]	Patented by Edison	1960	7.50	15.00	30.00
❑ SR-52041 [S]	Patented by Edison	1960	10.00	20.00	40.00
SUE					
❑ LP-1030 [M]	Sweets for the Sweet	1964	10.00	20.00	40.00
❑ STLP-1030 [S]	Sweets for the Sweet	1964	12.50	25.00	50.00
VEE JAY					
❑ LP-1104 [M]	For the Sweet Taste of Love	1964	7.50	15.00	30.00
❑ LPS-1104 [S]	For the Sweet Taste of Love	1964	10.00	20.00	40.00
❑ VJS-3065	Home with Sweets	1975	5.00	10.00	20.00
VERVE					
❑ MGVS-6016 [S]	Harry Edison Swings Buck Clayton, And Vice Versa	1959	10.00	20.00	40.00
❑ MGVS-6037 [S]	The Swinger	1960	10.00	20.00	40.00
❑ MGVS-6118 [S]	Mr. Swing	1960	10.00	20.00	40.00
❑ MGV-8097 [M]	Sweets	1957	12.50	25.00	50.00
❑ V-8097 [M]	Sweets	1961	5.00	10.00	20.00
❑ MGV-8211 [M]	Gee Baby, Ain't I Good to You?	1958	12.50	25.00	50.00
❑ V-8211 [M]	Gee Baby, Ain't I Good to You?	1961	5.00	10.00	20.00
❑ MGV-8293 [M]	Harry Edison Swings Buck Clayton, And Vice Versa	1958	12.50	25.00	50.00
❑ V-8293 [M]	Harry Edison Swings Buck Clayton, And Vice Versa	1961	5.00	10.00	20.00
❑ V6-8293 [S]	Harry Edison Swings Buck Clayton, And Vice Versa	1961	5.00	10.00	20.00
❑ MGV-8295 [M]	The Swinger	1959	12.50	25.00	50.00
❑ V-8295 [M]	The Swinger	1961	5.00	10.00	20.00
❑ V6-8295 [S]	The Swinger	1961	5.00	10.00	20.00
❑ MGV-8353 [M]	Mr. Swing	1959	12.50	25.00	50.00
❑ V-8353 [M]	Mr. Swing	1961	5.00	10.00	20.00
❑ V6-8358 [S]	Mr. Swing	1961	5.00	10.00	20.00

EDMONSON, TRAVIS
Also see BUD AND TRAVIS.
HORIZON

Number	Title (A Side/B Side)	Yr	VG	VG+	NM
❑ WP-1606 [M]	Travis On Cue	1962	5.00	10.00	20.00
❑ WPS-1606 [S]	Travis On Cue	1962	6.25	12.50	25.00
REPRISE					
❑ R-6035 [M]	Travis On His Own	1962	6.25	12.50	25.00
❑ R9-6035 [S]	Travis On His Own	1962	7.50	15.00	30.00

EDMUNDS, DAVE
ATLANTIC

Number	Title (A Side/B Side)	Yr	VG	VG+	NM
❑ PR 320 [DJ]	College Network	1978	12.50	25.00	50.00
—Promo-only interview album					
CAPITOL					
❑ C1-90372	Closer to the Flame	1990	3.75	7.50	15.00
COLUMBIA					
❑ FC 37930	D.E. 7th	1982	3.00	6.00	12.00
❑ PC 37930	D.E. 7th	198?	2.00	4.00	8.00
—Budget-line reissue ("02" added to bar code on back cover)					
❑ FC 38651	Information	1983	3.00	6.00	12.00
❑ PC 38651	Information	198?	2.00	4.00	8.00
—Budget-line reissue ("02" added to bar code on back cover)					
❑ FC 39273	Riff Raff	1984	2.50	5.00	10.00
❑ FC 40603	I Hear You Rockin'	1987	2.50	5.00	10.00
❑ PC 40603	I Hear You Rockin'	198?	2.00	4.00	8.00
—Budget-line reissue ("02" added to bar code on back cover)					
MAM					
❑ 3	Rockpile	1972	10.00	20.00	40.00
RCA VICTOR					
❑ AYL1-4238	Subtle as a Flying Mallet	1982	2.50	5.00	10.00
—Reissue (black label, dog near top)					
❑ LPL1-5003	Subtle as a Flying Mallet	1975	3.00	6.00	12.00
SWAN SONG					
❑ SS 8418	Get It	1977	3.75	7.50	15.00
❑ SS 8505	Trax on Wax 4	1978	3.75	7.50	15.00
❑ SS 8507	Repeat When Necessary	1979	3.75	7.50	15.00
❑ SS 8510	The Best of Dave Edmunds	1981	3.00	6.00	12.00
❑ SD 16034	Twangin'	1981	3.00	6.00	12.00

EDWARDS, EDDIE
COMMODORE

Number	Title (A Side/B Side)	Yr	VG	VG+	NM
❑ FL-20003 [10]	Eddie Edwards' Original Dixieland Jazz Band	1950	15.00	30.00	60.00

EDWARDS, JONATHAN AND DARLENE
Actually JO STAFFORD and PAUL WESTON as a comedy team.
COLUMBIA

Number	Title (A Side/B Side)	Yr	VG	VG+	NM
❑ CL 1024 [M]	The Piano Artistry of Jonathan Edwards	1955	12.50	25.00	50.00
❑ CL 1513 [M]	Jonathan and Darlene Edwards In Paris	1960	6.25	12.50	25.00
❑ CS 8313 [S]	Jonathan and Darlene Edwards In Paris	1960	7.50	15.00	30.00
CORINTHIAN					
❑ 103	Jonathan and Darlene Edwards In Paris	198?	2.50	5.00	10.00
❑ 104	The Original Piano Artistry of Jonathan Edwards	198?	2.50	5.00	10.00
❑ 120	Sing Along with Jonathan and Darlene	198?	2.50	5.00	10.00
❑ 122	Songs for Sheiks and Flappers	1986	2.50	5.00	10.00
DOT					
❑ DLP-3792 [M]	Songs for Sheiks and Flappers	1967	3.75	7.50	15.00
❑ DLP-25792 [S]	Songs for Sheiks and Flappers	1967	5.00	10.00	20.00
RCA VICTOR					
❑ LPM-2495 [M]	Sing Along with Jonathan and Darlene	1962	5.00	10.00	20.00
❑ LSP-2495 [S]	Sing Along with Jonathan and Darlene	1962	6.25	12.50	25.00

EDWARDS, STONEY
CAPITOL

Number	Title (A Side/B Side)	Yr	VG	VG+	NM
❑ ST-741	Country Singer	1970	6.25	12.50	25.00
❑ ST-834	Down Home in the Country	1971	5.00	10.00	20.00
❑ ST-11090	Stoney Edwards	1972	5.00	10.00	20.00
❑ ST-11173	She's My Rock	1973	5.00	10.00	20.00
❑ ST-11401	Mississippi on My Mind	1975	5.00	10.00	20.00
❑ ST-11499	Blackbird	1976	5.00	10.00	20.00

EDWARDS, TEDDY
CONTEMPORARY

Number	Title (A Side/B Side)	Yr	VG	VG+	NM
❑ M-3583 [M]	Teddy's Ready	1960	6.25	12.50	25.00
❑ M-3588 [M]	Together Again	1961	7.50	15.00	30.00
❑ M-3592 [M]	Good Gravy	1961	6.25	12.50	25.00
❑ M-3606 [M]	Heart and Soul	1962	6.25	12.50	25.00
❑ S-7583 [S]	Teddy's Ready	1960	7.50	15.00	30.00
❑ S-7588 [S]	Together Again	1961	10.00	20.00	40.00
❑ S-7592 [S]	Good Gravy	1961	7.50	15.00	30.00
❑ S-7606 [S]	Heart and Soul	1962	7.50	15.00	30.00
PACIFIC JAZZ					
❑ PJ-6 [M]	It's About Time	1960	10.00	20.00	40.00
❑ ST-6 [S]	It's About Time	1960	10.00	20.00	40.00
❑ PJ-14 [M]	Sunset Eyes	1961	10.00	20.00	40.00
PRESTIGE					
❑ PRLP-7518 [M]	Nothin' But the Truth	1967	7.50	15.00	30.00
❑ PRST-7518 [S]	Nothin' But the Truth	1967	6.25	12.50	25.00
❑ PRLP-7522 [M]	It's Alright	1967	7.50	15.00	30.00
❑ PRST-7522 [S]	It's Alright	1967	6.25	12.50	25.00

EDWARDS, TOMMY
LION

Number	Title (A Side/B Side)	Yr	VG	VG+	NM
❑ L-70120 [M]	Tommy Edwards	1959	7.50	15.00	30.00
METRO					
❑ M-511 [M]	Tommy Edwards	1965	3.00	6.00	12.00
❑ MS-511 [S]	Tommy Edwards	1965	3.75	7.50	15.00
MGM					
❑ E-3732 [M]	It's All in the Game	1958	7.50	15.00	30.00
—Yellow label					
❑ E-3732 [M]	It's All in the Game	1960	5.00	10.00	20.00
—Black label					
❑ SE-3732 [S]	It's All in the Game	1959	10.00	20.00	40.00
—Yellow label					
❑ SE-3732 [S]	It's All in the Game	1960	6.25	12.50	25.00
—Black label					
❑ E-3760 [M]	For Young Lovers	1959	7.50	15.00	30.00
—Yellow label					
❑ E-3760 [M]	For Young Lovers	1960	5.00	10.00	20.00
—Black label					
❑ SE-3760 [S]	For Young Lovers	1959	10.00	20.00	40.00
—Yellow label					
❑ SE-3760 [S]	For Young Lovers	1960	6.25	12.50	25.00
—Black label					
❑ E-3805 [M]	You Started Me Dreaming	1960	5.00	10.00	20.00
❑ SE-3805 [S]	You Started Me Dreaming	1960	6.25	12.50	25.00
❑ E-3822 [M]	Step Out Singing	1960	5.00	10.00	20.00
❑ SE-3822 [S]	Step Out Singing	1960	6.25	12.50	25.00
❑ E-3838 [M]	Tommy Edwards in Hawaii	1960	5.00	10.00	20.00
❑ SE-3838 [S]	Tommy Edwards in Hawaii	1960	6.25	12.50	25.00
❑ E-3884 [M]	Tommy Edwards' Greatest Hits	1961	5.00	10.00	20.00
❑ SE-3884 [S]	Tommy Edwards' Greatest Hits	1961	6.25	12.50	25.00
❑ E-3959 [M]	Golden Coutnry Hits	1961	5.00	10.00	20.00

E

Number	Title (A Side/B Side)	Yr	VG	VG+	NM
❏ SE-3959 [S]	Golden Coutnry Hits	1961	6.25	12.50	25.00
❏ E-4020 [M]	Stardust	1962	5.00	10.00	20.00
❏ SE-4020 [S]	Stardust	1962	6.25	12.50	25.00
❏ E-4060 [M]	Soft Strings and Two Guitars	1962	5.00	10.00	20.00
❏ SE-4060 [S]	Soft Strings and Two Guitars	1962	6.25	12.50	25.00
❏ E-4141 [M]	The Very Best of Tommy Edwards	1963	3.75	7.50	15.00
❏ SE-4141 [S]	The Very Best of Tommy Edwards	1963	5.00	10.00	20.00

REGENT

Number	Title (A Side/B Side)	Yr	VG	VG+	NM
❏ MG-6096 [M]	Tommy Edwards Sings	1958	15.00	30.00	60.00

EDWARDS, VINCENT
DECCA

Number	Title (A Side/B Side)	Yr	VG	VG+	NM
❏ DL 4311 [M]	Vincent Edwards Sings	1962	5.00	10.00	20.00
❏ DL 4336 [M]	Sometimes I'm Happy…Sometimes I'm Blue	1962	5.00	10.00	20.00
❏ DL 4399 [M]	In Person at the Riviera	1963	5.00	10.00	20.00
❏ DL 74311 [S]	Vincent Edwards Sings	1962	6.25	12.50	25.00
❏ DL 74336 [S]	Sometimes I'm Happy…Sometimes I'm Blue	1962	6.25	12.50	25.00
❏ DL 74399 [S]	In Person at the Riviera	1963	6.25	12.50	25.00

VOCALION

Number	Title (A Side/B Side)	Yr	VG	VG+	NM
❏ VL 3852 [M]	Here's Vincent Edwards	1967	3.00	6.00	12.00
❏ VL 73852 [S]	Here's Vincent Edwards	1967	3.00	6.00	12.00

EIRE APPARENT, THE
BUDDAH

Number	Title (A Side/B Side)	Yr	VG	VG+	NM
❏ BDS-5031	Sunrise	1969	10.00	20.00	40.00

EL CAMPO JADES, THE
GOLDEN EAGLE

Number	Title (A Side/B Side)	Yr	VG	VG+	NM
❏ LP-101 [M]	The El Campo Jades	1966	12.50	25.00	50.00

EL DORADOS
LOST-NITE

Number	Title (A Side/B Side)	Yr	VG	VG+	NM
❏ LLP-20 [10]	The El Dorados	1981	3.00	6.00	12.00
—Red vinyl					

SOLID SMOKE

Number	Title (A Side/B Side)	Yr	VG	VG+	NM
❏ 8025	Low Mileage/High Octane	1984	2.50	5.00	10.00

VEE JAY

Number	Title (A Side/B Side)	Yr	VG	VG+	NM
❏ LP-1001 [M]	Crazy Little Mama	1959	200.00	400.00	800.00
—Maroon label, thick silver band					
❏ LP-1001 [M]	Crazy Little Mama	1960	100.00	200.00	400.00
—Maroon label, thin silver band					
❏ LP-1001 [M]	Crazy Little Mama	1962	62.50	125.00	250.00
—Black label with colorband					
❏ VJLP-1001 [M]	Crazy Little Mama	198?	2.50	5.00	10.00
—Authorized reissue					

ELBERT, DONNIE
ALL PLATINUM

Number	Title (A Side/B Side)	Yr	VG	VG+	NM
❏ 3007	Where Did Our Love Go	1971	6.25	12.50	25.00
❏ 3019	Dancin' the Night Away	1977	6.25	12.50	25.00

DELUXE

Number	Title (A Side/B Side)	Yr	VG	VG+	NM
❏ 12003	Have I Sinned	1971	6.25	12.50	25.00

KING

Number	Title (A Side/B Side)	Yr	VG	VG+	NM
❏ 629 [M]	The Sensational Donnie Elbert Sings	1959	100.00	200.00	400.00

SUGAR HILL

Number	Title (A Side/B Side)	Yr	VG	VG+	NM
❏ 256	From the Git Go	1981	3.00	6.00	12.00

TRIP

Number	Title (A Side/B Side)	Yr	VG	VG+	NM
❏ 9514	Donnie Elbert Sings	197?	3.75	7.50	15.00
❏ 9524	Stop in the Name of Love	197?	3.75	7.50	15.00

ELDRIDGE, ROY
AMERICAN RECORDING SOCIETY

Number	Title (A Side/B Side)	Yr	VG	VG+	NM
❏ G-420 [M]	Swing Goes Dixie	1956	10.00	20.00	40.00

CLEF

Number	Title (A Side/B Side)	Yr	VG	VG+	NM
❏ MGC-113 [10]	Roy Eldridge Collates	1953	37.50	75.00	150.00
❏ MGC-150 [10]	The Roy Eldridge Quintet	1954	37.50	75.00	150.00
❏ MGC-162 [10]	The Strolling Mr. Eldridge	1954	37.50	75.00	150.00
❏ MGC-683 [M]	Little Jazz	1956	25.00	50.00	100.00
❏ MGC-704 [M]	Rockin' Chair	1956	25.00	50.00	100.00
❏ MGC-705 [M]	Dale's Wail	1956	25.00	50.00	100.00

DIAL

Number	Title (A Side/B Side)	Yr	VG	VG+	NM
❏ LP-304 [10]	Little Jazz Four: Trumpet Fantasy	1953	100.00	200.00	400.00

DISCOVERY

Number	Title (A Side/B Side)	Yr	VG	VG+	NM
❏ DL-2009 [10]	Roy Eldridge with Zoot Sims	1954	30.00	60.00	120.00

EMARCY

Number	Title (A Side/B Side)	Yr	VG	VG+	NM
❏ MG-36084 [M]	Roy's Got Rhythm	1956	20.00	40.00	80.00

LONDON

Number	Title (A Side/B Side)	Yr	VG	VG+	NM
❏ PB 375 [10]	Roy Eldridge Quartet	1954	30.00	60.00	120.00

MASTER JAZZ

Number	Title (A Side/B Side)	Yr	VG	VG+	NM
❏ 8110	The Nifty Cat	1970	5.00	10.00	20.00
❏ 8121	The Nifty Cat Strikes West	197?	5.00	10.00	20.00

MERCURY

Number	Title (A Side/B Side)	Yr	VG	VG+	NM
❏ MGC-113 [10]	Roy Eldridge Collates	1952	50.00	100.00	200.00

PRESTIGE

Number	Title (A Side/B Side)	Yr	VG	VG+	NM
❏ PRLP-114 [10]	Roy Eldridge in Sweden	1951	62.50	125.00	250.00

VERVE

Number	Title (A Side/B Side)	Yr	VG	VG+	NM
❏ MGV-1010 [M]	Swing Goes Dixie	1957	12.50	25.00	50.00
❏ V-1010 [M]	Swing Goes Dixie	1961	5.00	10.00	20.00
❏ MGV-8068 [M]	Little Jazz	1957	12.50	25.00	50.00
—Reissue of Clef 683					
❏ V-8068 [M]	Little Jazz	1961	5.00	10.00	20.00
❏ MGV-8088 [M]	Rockin' Chair	1957	12.50	25.00	50.00
—Reissue of Clef 704					
❏ V-8088 [M]	Rockin' Chair	1961	5.00	10.00	20.00
❏ MGV-8089 [M]	Dale's Wail	1957	12.50	25.00	50.00
—Reissue of Clef 705					
❏ V-8089 [M]	Dale's Wail	1961	5.00	10.00	20.00
❏ MGV-8389 [M]	Swingin' on the Town	1960	12.50	25.00	50.00
❏ V-8389 [M]	Swingin' on the Town	1961	5.00	10.00	20.00

Number	Title (A Side/B Side)	Yr	VG	VG+	NM

ELDRIDGE, ROY, AND BENNY CARTER
AMERICAN RECORDING SOCIETY

Number	Title (A Side/B Side)	Yr	VG	VG+	NM
❏ G-413 [M]	The Urbane Jazz of Roy Eldridge and Benny Carter	1957	10.00	20.00	40.00

VERVE

Number	Title (A Side/B Side)	Yr	VG	VG+	NM
❏ MGV-8202 [M]	The Urbane Jazz of Roy Eldridge and Benny Carter	1957	12.50	25.00	50.00
❏ V-8202 [M]	The Urbane Jazz of Roy Eldridge and Benny Carter	1961	5.00	10.00	20.00

ELDRIDGE, ROY, AND DIZZY GILLESPIE
CLEF

Number	Title (A Side/B Side)	Yr	VG	VG+	NM
❏ MGC-641 [M]	Roy and Diz	1955	37.50	75.00	150.00
❏ MGC-671 [M]	Roy and Diz, Volume 2	1955	37.50	75.00	150.00
❏ MGC-730 [M]	Trumpet Battle	1956	25.00	50.00	100.00
❏ MGC-731 [M]	The Trumpet Kings	1956	25.00	50.00	100.00

VERVE

Number	Title (A Side/B Side)	Yr	VG	VG+	NM
❏ MGV-8109 [M]	Trumpet Battle	1957	12.50	25.00	50.00
❏ V-8109 [M]	Trumpet Battle	1961	5.00	10.00	20.00
❏ MGV-8110 [M]	The Trumpet Kings	1957	12.50	25.00	50.00
❏ V-8110 [M]	The Trumpet Kings	1961	5.00	10.00	20.00

ELDRIDGE, ROY; DIZZY GILLESPIE; HARRY "SWEETS" EDISON
VERVE

Number	Title (A Side/B Side)	Yr	VG	VG+	NM
❏ MGV-8212 [M]	Tour de Force	1958	12.50	25.00	50.00
❏ V-8212 [M]	Tour de Force	1961	5.00	10.00	20.00

ELDRIDGE, ROY/SAMMY PRICE
BRUNSWICK

Number	Title (A Side/B Side)	Yr	VG	VG+	NM
❏ BL 58045 [10]	Battle of Jazz, Volume 7	1953	15.00	30.00	60.00

ELECTRIC LIGHT ORCHESTRA
CBS ASSOCIATED

Number	Title (A Side/B Side)	Yr	VG	VG+	NM
❏ FZ 40048	Balance of Power	1986	2.50	5.00	10.00

JET

Number	Title (A Side/B Side)	Yr	VG	VG+	NM
❏ JT-LA823-L2 [(2)]	Out of the Blue	1977	3.75	7.50	15.00
—Originals include poster and die-cut cardboard "spaceship"					
❏ JT-LA823-L2 [(2)DJ]	Out of the Blue	1977	6.25	12.50	25.00
—Promo only on blue vinyl					
❏ JZ 35524	No Answer	1978	2.50	5.00	10.00
❏ PZ 35524	No Answer	1981	2.00	4.00	8.00
❏ JZ 35525	On the Third Day	1978	2.50	5.00	10.00
❏ PZ 35525	On the Third Day	1981	2.00	4.00	8.00
❏ JZ 35526	Eldorado	1978	2.50	5.00	10.00
❏ PZ 35526	Eldorado	198?	2.00	4.00	8.00
❏ JZ 35527	Face the Music	1978	2.50	5.00	10.00
❏ PZ 35527	Face the Music	1981	2.00	4.00	8.00
❏ JZ 35528	Ole Elo	1978	2.50	5.00	10.00
❏ PZ 35528	Ole Elo	1981	2.00	4.00	8.00
❏ JZ 35529	A New World Record	1978	2.50	5.00	10.00
❏ PZ 35529	A New World Record	1981	2.00	4.00	8.00
❏ KZ2 35530 [(2)]	Out of the Blue	1978	3.00	6.00	12.00
❏ JZ 35533	Electric Light Orchestra II	1978	2.50	5.00	10.00
❏ PZ 35533	Electric Light Orchestra II	1981	2.00	4.00	8.00
❏ FZ 35769	Discovery	1979	2.50	5.00	10.00
❏ PZ 35769	Discovery	1987	2.00	4.00	8.00
❏ FZ 36310	ELO's Greatest Hits	1979	2.50	5.00	10.00
❏ HZ 36310	ELO's Greatest Hits	1981	10.00	20.00	40.00
—Half-speed mastered edition					
❏ PZ 36310	ELO's Greatest Hits	1987	2.00	4.00	8.00
❏ Z4X 36966 [(4)]	A Box of Their Best	1980	6.25	12.50	25.00
❏ FZ 37371	Time	1981	2.50	5.00	10.00
❏ PZ 37371	Time	1987	2.00	4.00	8.00
❏ PZ 38490	Secret Messages	1987	2.00	4.00	8.00
❏ QZ 38490	Secret Messages	1983	2.50	5.00	10.00
❏ HZ 45789	Discovery	1980	6.25	12.50	25.00
—Half-speed mastered edition					
❏ HZ 47371	Time	1982	6.25	12.50	25.00
—Half-speed mastered edition					
❏ HZ 48490	Secret Messages	1983	7.50	15.00	30.00
—Half-speed mastered edition					

UNITED ARTISTS

Number	Title (A Side/B Side)	Yr	VG	VG+	NM
❏ UA-LA040-F	Electric Light Orchestra II	1973	3.75	7.50	15.00
—Tan label					
❏ UA-LA040-F	Electric Light Orchestra II	1978	2.50	5.00	10.00
—Sunrise label					
❏ SP-123 [DJ]	Ole Elo	1976	12.50	25.00	50.00
—Gold vinyl promo with generic cover					
❏ SP-123 [DJ]	Ole Elo	1976	20.00	40.00	80.00
—Red, blue or white vinyl promos with generic cover					
❏ SP-123 [DJ]	Ole Elo	1976	25.00	50.00	100.00
—Gold vinyl, cover similar to the released version except for the single line "Ole Elo" (no "Electric Light Orchestra" underneath) at the top of the front cover					
❏ UA-LA188-F	On the Third Day	1973	3.75	7.50	15.00
—Tan label					
❏ UA-LA188-F	On the Third Day	1978	2.50	5.00	10.00
—Sunrise label					
❏ UA-LA318-F	The Night the Light Went On in Long Beach	1974	—	—	—
—Canceled					
❏ UA-LA339-G	Eldorado	1974	3.00	6.00	12.00
—Tan label					
❏ UA-LA339-G	Eldorado	1977	2.50	5.00	10.00
—Sunrise label					
❏ UA-LA546-DJ [DJ]	Face the Music	1975	6.25	12.50	25.00
—Promo only, banded for airplay					
❏ UA-LA546-G	Face the Music	1975	3.00	6.00	12.00
—Tan label					
❏ UA-LA546-G	Face the Music	1978	2.50	5.00	10.00
—Sunrise label					
❏ UA-LA630-G	Ole Elo	1976	3.00	6.00	12.00
—Tan label					

Number	Title (A Side/B Side)	Yr	VG	VG+	NM
❑ UA-LA630-G	Ole Elo	1978	2.50	5.00	10.00
—Sunrise label					
❑ UA-LA679-G	A New World Record	1976	3.00	6.00	12.00
—All copies have custom labels					
❑ UAS-5573	No Answer	1972	3.75	7.50	15.00
—Tan label					
❑ UAS-5573	No Answer	1978	2.50	5.00	10.00
—Sunrise label					

ELECTRIC PRUNES, THE
REPRISE
❑ R-6248 [M]	The Electric Prunes	1967	12.50	25.00	50.00
❑ RS-6248 [S]	The Electric Prunes	1967	10.00	20.00	40.00
❑ R-6262 [M]	Underground	1967	12.50	25.00	50.00
❑ RS-6262 [S]	Underground	1967	10.00	20.00	40.00
❑ R-6275 [M]	Mass in F Minor	1967	10.00	20.00	40.00
❑ RS-6275 [S]	Mass in F Minor	1967	7.50	15.00	30.00
❑ RS-6316	Release of an Oath	1968	7.50	15.00	30.00
❑ RS-6342	Just Good Rock 'n Roll	1969	7.50	15.00	30.00

ELECTRIC TOILET, THE
NASCO
❑ 9004	In the Hands of Karma	1970	50.00	100.00	200.00

ELECTRIC UNDERGROUND, THE
PREMIER
❑ P-9060 [M]	Guitar Explosion	1967	12.50	25.00	50.00
❑ PS-9060 [S]	Guitar Explosion	1967	12.50	25.00	50.00

ELECTROSONICS, THE
PHILIPS
❑ PHM 200047 [M]	Electronic Music	1962	17.50	35.00	70.00
❑ PHS 600047 [S]	Electronic Music	1962	22.50	45.00	90.00

ELEPHANTS MEMORY
APPLE
❑ SMAS-3389	Elephants Memory	1972	6.25	12.50	25.00
### BUDDAH					
❑ BDS-5033	Elephants Memory	1969	3.75	7.50	15.00
❑ BDS-5038	Songs from Midnight Cowboy	1970	3.75	7.50	15.00
### METROMEDIA					
❑ MD-1035	Take It to the Streets	1970	5.00	10.00	20.00
### RCA VICTOR					
❑ APL1-0569	Angela Forever	1974	3.75	7.50	15.00

ELEVENTH HOUSE, THE
See LARRY CORYELL.

ELF
EPIC
❑ KE 31789	Elf	1972	7.50	15.00	30.00
—Yellow label					
❑ KE 31789	Elf	1973	5.00	10.00	20.00
—Orange label					
### MGM					
❑ M3G 4974	L.A. 59	1974	5.00	10.00	20.00
❑ M3G 4994	Trying to Burn the Sun	1975	5.00	10.00	20.00

ELGART, BILL
MARK LEVINSON
❑ 3	A Life	1980	6.25	12.50	25.00

ELGART, LARRY
BRUNSWICK
❑ BL 58054 [10]	Impressions of Outer Space	1954	15.00	30.00	60.00
### DECCA					
❑ DL 5526 [10]	The Larry Elgart Band with Strings	1954	25.00	50.00	100.00
❑ DL 8034 [M]	Music for Barefoot Ballerinas	1955	10.00	20.00	40.00
### MGM					
❑ SE-3891 [S]	Sophisticated Sixties	1960	5.00	10.00	20.00
❑ SE-3896 [S]	The Shape of Sounds to Come	1961	5.00	10.00	20.00
❑ SE-3961 [S]	Visions	1961	5.00	10.00	20.00
❑ SE-4007 [S]	The City	1961	5.00	10.00	20.00
❑ SE-4028 [S]	Music in Motion!	1962	5.00	10.00	20.00
❑ SE-4080 [S]	More Music in Motion!	1962	5.00	10.00	20.00
### RCA VICTOR					
❑ LSP-1961 [S]	Larry Elgart and His Orchestra	1959	5.00	10.00	20.00
❑ LSP-2045 [S]	New Sounds at the Roosevelt	1959	5.00	10.00	20.00
❑ LSP-2166 [S]	Saratoga	1960	5.00	10.00	20.00

ELGART, LES
COLUMBIA
❑ CL 536 [M]	Sophisticated Swing	1953	7.50	15.00	30.00
—Maroon label, gold print					
❑ CL 594 [M]	Just One More Dance	1954	7.50	15.00	30.00
—Maroon label, gold print					
❑ CL 594 [M]	Just One More Dance	1955	5.00	10.00	20.00
—Red and black label with six "eye" logos					
❑ CL 619 [M]	The Band of the Year	1955	10.00	20.00	40.00
—Maroon label, gold print; first LP appearance of "Bandstand Boogie"					
❑ CL 684 [M]	The Dancing Sound	1955	7.50	15.00	30.00
❑ CL 803 [M]	For Dancers Only	1956	7.50	15.00	30.00
❑ CL 875 [M]	The Elgart Touch	1956	7.50	15.00	30.00
—Red and black label, six "eye" logos					
❑ CL 1008 [M]	For Dancers Also	1957	6.25	12.50	25.00
❑ CL 1052 [M]	Les and Larry Elgart and Their Orchestra	1957	5.00	10.00	20.00
❑ CL 1291 [M]	Les Elgart On Tour	1959	5.00	10.00	20.00
❑ CL 1350 [M]	The Great Sound of Les Elgart	1959	5.00	10.00	20.00
❑ CL 1450 [M]	The Band with That Sound	1960	5.00	10.00	20.00
❑ CL 1500 [M]	Designs for Dancing	1960	5.00	10.00	20.00
❑ CL 1567 [M]	Half Satin - Half Latin	1961	5.00	10.00	20.00
❑ CL 1659 [M]	It's De-Lovely	1961	5.00	10.00	20.00
❑ CL 1785 [M]	The Twist Goes to College	1962	5.00	10.00	20.00
❑ CL 1890 [M]	Best Band on Campus	1963	5.00	10.00	20.00
❑ CL 2503 [10]	Prom Date	1954	10.00	20.00	40.00
❑ CL 2578 [10]	Campus Hop	1955	10.00	20.00	40.00
❑ CL 2590 [10]	More of Les	1955	10.00	20.00	40.00
❑ CL 6287 [10]	Just One More Dance	195?	10.00	20.00	40.00
❑ CS 8002 [S]	Sound Ideas	1958	6.25	12.50	25.00
❑ CS 8092 [S]	Les and Larry Elgart and Their Orchestra	1959	6.25	12.50	25.00
❑ CS 8103 [S]	Les Elgart On Tour	1959	6.25	12.50	25.00
❑ CS 8159 [S]	The Great Sound of Les Elgart	1959	6.25	12.50	25.00
❑ CS 8245 [S]	The Band with That Sound	1960	6.25	12.50	25.00
❑ CS 8291 [S]	Designs for Dancing	1960	6.25	12.50	25.00
❑ CS 8367 [S]	Half Satin - Half Latin	1961	6.25	12.50	25.00
❑ CS 8459 [S]	It's De-Lovely	1961	6.25	12.50	25.00
❑ CS 8585 [S]	The Twist Goes to College	1962	6.25	12.50	25.00
❑ CS 8690 [S]	Best Band on Campus	1963	6.25	12.50	25.00

ELGART, LES AND LARRY
COLUMBIA
❑ CL 1123 [M]	Sound Ideas	1958	5.00	10.00	20.00
❑ CL 2633 [M]	Girl Watchers	1967	5.00	10.00	20.00
❑ CL 2780 [M]	The Wonderful World of Today's Hits	1968	6.25	12.50	25.00
❑ CS 8912 [S]	Big Band Hootenanny	1963	5.00	10.00	20.00
❑ CS 9021 [S]	Command Performance! Les & Larry Elgart Play the Great Dance Hits	1964	5.00	10.00	20.00
❑ CS 9101 [S]	The New Elgart Touch	1965	5.00	10.00	20.00
❑ CS 9155 [S]	Elgart Au-Go-Go	1965	5.00	10.00	20.00
❑ CS 9311 [S]	Sound of the Times	1966	5.00	10.00	20.00
❑ CS 9391 [S]	Warm and Sensuous	1966	5.00	10.00	20.00

ELGINS, THE (1)
V.I.P.
❑ 400 [M]	Darling Baby	1966	17.50	35.00	70.00
❑ S-400 [S]	Darling Baby	1966	25.00	50.00	100.00

ELIAS, ROSALIND, AND GIORGIO TOZZI
RCA VICTOR RED SEAL
❑ LSC-2350 [S]	A Yuletide Song Fest	1959	10.00	20.00	40.00
—Original with "shaded dog" label					

ELIGIBLES, THE
CAPITOL
❑ ST 1310 [S]	Along the Trail	1960	7.50	15.00	30.00
❑ T 1310 [M]	Along the Trail	1960	6.25	12.50	25.00
❑ ST 1411 [S]	Love Is a Gamble	1960	7.50	15.00	30.00
❑ T 1411 [M]	Love Is a Gamble	1960	6.25	12.50	25.00

ELIMINATORS, THE
LIBERTY
❑ LRP-3365 [M]	Liverpool! Dragsters! Cycles! Surfing!	1964	20.00	40.00	80.00
❑ LST-7365 [S]	Liverpool! Dragsters! Cycles! Surfing!	1964	25.00	50.00	100.00

ELIZABETH
VANGUARD
❑ VSD-6501	Elizabeth	1968	15.00	30.00	60.00

ELLIE POP
MAINSTREAM
❑ S-6115	Ellie Pop	1968	10.00	20.00	40.00

ELLINGTON, DUKE
AAMCO
❑ ALP-301 [M]	The Royal Concert of Duke Ellington, Vol. 1	196?	7.50	15.00	30.00
—Reissue of Bethlehem material					
❑ ALP-313 [M]	The Royal Concert of Duke Ellington, Vol. 2	196?	7.50	15.00	30.00
—Reissue of Bethlehem material					
### ALLEGRO					
❑ 1591 [M]	Duke Ellington and His Orchestra Play	1955	12.50	25.00	50.00
❑ 3082 [M]	Duke Ellington	1953	12.50	25.00	50.00
❑ 4014 [10]	Duke Ellington and His Orchestra Play	1954	25.00	50.00	100.00
❑ 4038 [10]	Duke Ellington and His Orchestra Play	1954	25.00	50.00	100.00
### ATLANTIC					
❑ QD 1580 [Q]	New Orleans Suite	1974	6.25	12.50	25.00
### BETHLEHEM					
❑ BCP-60 [M]	Historically Speaking, The Duke	1956	15.00	30.00	60.00
❑ BCP-6005 [M]	Duke Ellington Presents	1956	15.00	30.00	60.00
### BLUEBIRD					
❑ 5659-1-RB [(4)]	Duke Ellington: The Blanton-Webster Band	1986	6.25	12.50	25.00
❑ 6641-1-RB [(4)]	Black, Brown and Beige	1988	6.25	12.50	25.00
### BRUNSWICK					
❑ BL 54007 [M]	Early Ellington	1954	12.50	25.00	50.00
❑ BL 58002 [10]	Ellingtonia, Volume 1	1950	25.00	50.00	100.00
❑ BL 58012 [10]	Ellingtonia, Volume 2	1950	25.00	50.00	100.00
### CAPITOL					
❑ H 440 [10]	Premiered by Ellington	1953	25.00	50.00	100.00
❑ H 477 [10]	The Duke Plays Ellington	1954	25.00	50.00	100.00
❑ T 477 [M]	The Duke Plays Ellington	1954	10.00	20.00	40.00
—Turquoise label					
❑ T 477 [M]	The Duke Plays Ellington	1958	5.00	10.00	20.00
—Black label with colorband, logo at left					
❑ T 521 [M]	Ellington '55	1955	10.00	20.00	40.00
—Turquoise label					
❑ T 521 [M]	Ellington '55	1958	5.00	10.00	20.00
—Black label with colorband, logo at left					
❑ T 637 [M]	Dance to the Duke	1955	10.00	20.00	40.00
—Turquoise label					
❑ T 637 [M]	Dance to the Duke	1958	5.00	10.00	20.00
—Black label with colorband, logo at left					
❑ T 679 [M]	Ellington Showcase	1956	10.00	20.00	40.00
—Turquoise label					
❑ T 679 [M]	Ellington Showcase	1958	5.00	10.00	20.00
—Black label with colorband, logo at left					
❑ T 1602 [M]	The Best of Duke Ellington	1961	5.00	10.00	20.00

E

Number	Title (A Side/B Side)	Yr	VG	VG+	NM
COLUMBIA					
❑ C3L 27 [(3)M]	The Ellington Era, Vol. 1	1963	10.00	20.00	40.00
❑ C3L 39 [(3)M]	The Ellington Era, Vol. 2	1964	10.00	20.00	40.00
❑ CL 558 [M]	The Music of Duke Ellington	1954	12.50	25.00	50.00
—Maroon label with gold print					
❑ CL 558 [M]	The Music of Duke Ellington	1956	10.00	20.00	40.00
—Red and black label with six "eye" logos					
❑ CL 663 [M]	Blue Light	1955	10.00	20.00	40.00
❑ CL 825 [M]	Masterpieces by Ellington	1956	10.00	20.00	40.00
—Reissue of Columbia Masterworks 4418					
❑ CL 830 [M]	Hi-Fi Ellington Uptown	1956	10.00	20.00	40.00
❑ CL 848 [M]	Liberian Suite	1956	10.00	20.00	40.00
—Reissue of Columbia 6073					
❑ CL 934 [M]	Ellington at Newport '56	1957	10.00	20.00	40.00
—Red and black label with six "eye" logos					
❑ CL 951 [M]	A Drum Is a Woman	1957	10.00	20.00	40.00
❑ CL 1033 [M]	Such Sweet Thunder	1957	10.00	20.00	40.00
❑ CL 1085 [M]	Ellington Indigos	1958	6.25	12.50	25.00
❑ CL 1162 [M]	Brown, Black and Beige	1958	6.25	12.50	25.00
❑ CL 1198 [M]	The Cosmic Scene	1959	20.00	40.00	80.00
❑ CL 1245 [M]	Newport 1958	1959	6.25	12.50	25.00
❑ CL 1282 [M]	Duke Ellington at the Bal Masque	1959	6.25	12.50	25.00
❑ CL 1323 [M]	Duke Ellington Jazz Party	1959	6.25	12.50	25.00
❑ CL 1400 [M]	Festival Session	1960	6.25	12.50	25.00
❑ CL 1445 [M]	Blues in Orbit	1960	6.25	12.50	25.00
❑ CL 1541 [M]	The Nutcracker Suite	1960	7.50	15.00	30.00
❑ CL 1546 [M]	Piano in the Background	1960	7.50	15.00	30.00
❑ CL 1597 [M]	Peer Gynt Suite/Suite Thursday	1961	6.25	12.50	25.00
❑ CL 1715 [M]	First Time	1962	6.25	12.50	25.00
❑ CL 1790 [M]	All American	1962	5.00	10.00	20.00
❑ CL 1907 [M]	Midnight in Paris	1963	5.00	10.00	20.00
❑ CL 2522 [10]	Duke's Mixture	1955	20.00	40.00	80.00
❑ CL 2562 [10]	Here's the Duke	1955	20.00	40.00	80.00
❑ CL 2593 [10]	Al Hibbler with the Duke	1956	20.00	40.00	80.00
❑ CL 6024 [10]	Mood Ellington	1949	25.00	50.00	100.00
❑ CL 6073 [10]	Liberian Suite	1949	25.00	50.00	100.00
❑ CS 8015 [S]	Brown, Black and Beige	1958	7.50	15.00	30.00
❑ CS 8053 [S]	Ellington Indigos	1958	7.50	15.00	30.00
❑ CS 8072 [S]	Newport 1958	1959	7.50	15.00	30.00
❑ CS 8098 [S]	Duke Ellington at the Bal Masque	1959	7.50	15.00	30.00
❑ CS 8127 [S]	Duke Ellington Jazz Party	1959	7.50	15.00	30.00
❑ CS 8241 [S]	Blues in Orbit	1960	7.50	15.00	30.00
❑ CS 8341 [S]	The Nutcracker Suite	1960	10.00	20.00	40.00
❑ CS 8346 [S]	Piano in the Background	1960	10.00	20.00	40.00
❑ CS 8397 [S]	Peer Gynt Suite/Suite Thursday	1961	7.50	15.00	30.00
❑ CS 8515 [S]	First Time	1962	7.50	15.00	30.00
❑ CS 8590 [S]	All American	1962	6.25	12.50	25.00
❑ CS 8829 [S]	Midnight in Paris	1963	6.25	12.50	25.00
COLUMBIA MASTERWORKS					
❑ ML 4418 [M]	Masterpieces by Ellington	1951	25.00	50.00	100.00
❑ ML 4639 [M]	Ellington Uptown	195?	12.50	25.00	50.00
—Oddly, this exists as a reissue on the red and black "6 eye" label					
❑ ML 4639 [M]	Ellington Uptown	1951	25.00	50.00	100.00
—Blue or green label, gold print					
DECCA					
❑ DL 9224 [M]	Duke Ellington, Volume 1 — In the Beginning	1958	10.00	20.00	40.00
—Black label, silver print					
❑ DL 9241 [M]	Duke Ellington, Volume 2 — Hot in Harlem	1959	10.00	20.00	40.00
—Black label, silver print					
❑ DL 9247 [M]	Duke Ellington, Volume 3 — Rockin' in Rhythm	1959	10.00	20.00	40.00
—Black label, silver print					
❑ DL 79224 [R]	Duke Ellington, Volume 1 — In the Beginning	1958	6.25	12.50	25.00
—Black label, silver print					
❑ DL 79241 [R]	Duke Ellington, Volume 2 — Hot in Harlem	1959	6.25	12.50	25.00
—Black label, silver print					
❑ DL 79247 [R]	Duke Ellington, Volume 3 — Rockin' in Rhythm	1959	6.25	12.50	25.00
—Black label, silver print					
HALL OF FAME					
❑ 625/6/7 [(3)]	The Immortal Duke Ellington	197?	5.00	10.00	20.00
JAZZ PANORAMA					
❑ 1802 [10]	Duke Ellington — Vol. 1	1951	25.00	50.00	100.00
❑ 1811 [10]	Duke Ellington — Vol. 2	1951	25.00	50.00	100.00
❑ 1816 [10]	Duke Ellington — Vol. 3	1951	25.00	50.00	100.00
LONDON					
❑ AL-3551 [10]	The Duke — 1926	195?	25.00	50.00	100.00
MOBILE FIDELITY					
❑ 1-214	Anatomy of a Murder	1995	10.00	20.00	40.00
—Audiophile vinyl					
MOSAIC					
❑ MQ8-160 [(8)]	The Complete Capitol Recordings of Duke Ellington	199?	37.50	75.00	150.00
PRESTIGE					
❑ 34003 [(3)]	The Carnegie Hall Concerts: January 1943	197?	5.00	10.00	20.00
RCA CAMDEN					
❑ CAL-394 [M]	Duke Ellington at Tanglewood	1958	5.00	10.00	20.00
❑ CAL-459 [M]	Duke Ellington at the Cotton Club	1959	5.00	10.00	20.00
RCA VICTOR					
❑ WPT-11 [10]	Duke Ellington	1951	25.00	50.00	100.00
❑ SP-33-394 [M]	The Duke at Tanglewood	1966	6.25	12.50	25.00
—"Special Interview Recording for Radio Station Programming"					
❑ LPV-506 [M]	Daybreak Express	1964	5.00	10.00	20.00
❑ LPV-517 [M]	Jumpin' Punkins	1965	5.00	10.00	20.00
❑ LPV-541 [M]	Johnny Come Lately	1967	5.00	10.00	20.00
❑ LPV-553 [M]	Pretty Woman	1968	5.00	10.00	20.00
❑ LPV-568 [M]	Flaming Youth	1969	5.00	10.00	20.00
❑ LJM-1002 [M]	Seattle Concert	1954	12.50	25.00	50.00
❑ LPT-1004 [M]	Ellington's Greatest	1954	10.00	20.00	40.00
❑ LPM-1092 [M]	Duke and His Men	1955	10.00	20.00	40.00
❑ LPM-1364 [M]	In a Mellotone	1957	10.00	20.00	40.00
—Black label, dog at top, "Long Play" at bottom					

Number	Title (A Side/B Side)	Yr	VG	VG+	NM
❑ LPM-1364 [M]	In a Mellotone	196?	6.25	12.50	25.00
—Black label, dog at top, "Mono" at bottom					
❑ LPM-1364 [M]	In a Mellotone	1969	5.00	10.00	20.00
—Orange label					
❑ LPM-1715 [M]	Duke Ellington at His Very Best	1958	10.00	20.00	40.00
❑ LPT-3017 [10]	This Is Duke Ellington and His Orchestra	1952	25.00	50.00	100.00
❑ LPT-3067 [10]	Duke Ellington Plays the Blues	1952	25.00	50.00	100.00
❑ LSP-3576 [S]	The Popular Duke Ellington	1966	5.00	10.00	20.00
❑ LSP-3582 [S]	Concert of Sacred Music	1966	5.00	10.00	20.00
❑ LPM-3782 [M]	Far East Suite	1967	6.25	12.50	25.00
❑ LPM-3906 [M]	And His Mother Called Him Bill	1968	12.50	25.00	50.00
❑ LPM-6009 [(2)M]	The Indispensible Duke Ellington	1961	12.50	25.00	50.00
RCA VICTOR RED SEAL					
❑ LSC-2857 [S]	The Duke at Tanglewood	1966	5.00	10.00	20.00
REPRISE					
❑ R-6069 [M]	Afro-Bossa	1962	5.00	10.00	20.00
❑ R9-6069 [S]	Afro-Bossa	1962	5.00	10.00	20.00
❑ R-6097 [M]	The Symphonic Ellington	1963	5.00	10.00	20.00
❑ R9-6097 [S]	The Symphonic Ellington	1963	5.00	10.00	20.00
❑ R-6122 [M]	Ellington '65: Hits of the '60s/This Time by Ellington	1964	5.00	10.00	20.00
❑ RS-6122 [S]	Ellington '65: Hits of the '60s/This Time by Ellington	1964	5.00	10.00	20.00
❑ R-6141 [M]	Mary Poppins	1964	5.00	10.00	20.00
❑ RS-6141 [S]	Mary Poppins	1964	5.00	10.00	20.00
❑ R-6154 [M]	Ellington '66	1965	5.00	10.00	20.00
❑ R-6168 [M]	Will Big Bands Ever Come Back?	1965	5.00	10.00	20.00
❑ R-6185 [M]	Concert in the Virgin Islands	1965	5.00	10.00	20.00
❑ R-6234 [M]	Duke Ellington's Greatest Hits	1967	5.00	10.00	20.00
RIVERSIDE					
❑ RLP 12-129 [M]	Birth of Big Band Jazz	195?	7.50	15.00	30.00
—Blue label with mike logo					
❑ RLP 12-129 [M]	Birth of Big Band Jazz	1956	15.00	30.00	60.00
—White label, blue print					
❑ RLP-475 [M]	Great Times!	1963	6.25	12.50	25.00
❑ RS-9475 [S]	Great Times!	1963	6.25	12.50	25.00
RONDO-LETTE					
❑ A-7 [M]	Duke Ellington and Orchestra	1958	7.50	15.00	30.00
ROYALE					
❑ 18143 [10]	Duke Ellington and His Orchestra	195?	12.50	25.00	50.00
❑ 18152 [10]	Duke Ellington Plays Ellington	195?	12.50	25.00	50.00
SOLID STATE					
❑ SS-19000 [(2)]	75th Birthday	1970	5.00	10.00	20.00
TREND					
❑ 529	The Symphonic Ellington	1982	5.00	10.00	20.00
UNITED ARTISTS					
❑ UAJ-14017 [M]	Money Jungle	1962	10.00	20.00	40.00
❑ UAJS-15017 [S]	Money Jungle	1962	10.00	20.00	40.00
"X"					
❑ LVA-3037 [10]	Duke Ellington Plays	1955	25.00	50.00	100.00
ELLINGTON, HARVEY					
STEPHENY					
❑ MF-4010 [M]	I Can't Hide the Blues	1959	20.00	40.00	80.00
ELLINGTON, MERCER					
CORAL					
❑ CRL (# unk) [M]	Black and Tan Fantasy	1958	7.50	15.00	30.00
❑ CRL (# unk) [S]	Black and Tan Fantasy	1958	10.00	20.00	40.00
❑ CRL 57225 [M]	Stepping Into Swing Society	1958	7.50	15.00	30.00
❑ CRL 57293 [M]	Colors in Rhythm	1959	7.50	15.00	30.00
❑ CRL 757225 [S]	Stepping Into Swing Society	1958	10.00	20.00	40.00
❑ CRL 757293 [S]	Colors in Rhythm	1959	10.00	20.00	40.00
ELLINGTONIANS, THE					
MERCER					
❑ LP-1004 [10]	The Ellingtonians with Al Hibbler	1951	30.00	60.00	120.00
ELLIOT, CASS					
Also see THE BIG THREE; THE MAMAS AND THE PAPAS; DAVE MASON; THE MUGWUMPS.					
ABC DUNHILL					
❑ DS-50040	Dream a Little Dream	1968	5.00	10.00	20.00
❑ DS-50055	Bubble Gum, Lemonade &...Something for Mama	1969	5.00	10.00	20.00
❑ DS-50071	Make Your Own Kind of Music	1969	3.75	7.50	15.00
—Reissue of 50055 with new title and one added song					
❑ DS-50093	Mama's Big Ones	1970	3.75	7.50	15.00
MCA					
❑ 719	Mama's Big Ones	1980	2.00	4.00	8.00
RCA VICTOR					
❑ APL1-0303	Don't Call Me Mama Anymore	1973	3.75	7.50	15.00
❑ LSP-4619	Cass Elliot	1971	3.75	7.50	15.00
❑ LSP-4753	The Road Is No Place for a Lady	1972	3.75	7.50	15.00
ELLIOTT, DEAN					
CAPITOL					
❑ ST 1834 [S]	Zounds! What Sounds!	1962	12.50	25.00	50.00
❑ T 1834 [M]	Zounds! What Sounds!	1962	10.00	20.00	40.00
❑ ST 1864 [S]	Heartstrings	1962	6.25	12.50	25.00
❑ T 1864 [M]	Heartstrings	1962	5.00	10.00	20.00
ELLIOTT, DON					
ABC-PARAMOUNT					
❑ ABC-106 [M]	Musical Offering	1956	10.00	20.00	40.00
❑ ABC-142 [M]	Don Elliott at the Modern Jazz Room	1956	10.00	20.00	40.00
❑ ABC-190 [M]	The Voices of Don Elliott	1957	12.50	25.00	50.00
❑ ABC-228 [M]	Jamaica Jazz	1958	10.00	20.00	40.00
❑ ABCS-228 [S]	Jamaica Jazz	1959	7.50	15.00	30.00
BETHLEHEM					
❑ BCP-12 [M]	Mellophone	1955	12.50	25.00	50.00
❑ BCP-15 [M]	Don Elliott Sings	1955	12.50	25.00	50.00

Number	Title (A Side/B Side)	Yr	VG	VG+	NM
DECCA					
☐ DL 9208 [M]	The Mello Sound	1958	10.00	20.00	40.00
☐ DL 79208 [S]	The Mello Sound	1958	12.50	25.00	50.00
HALLMARK					
☐ 317 [M]	Pal Joey	1957	12.50	25.00	50.00
JAZZLAND					
☐ JLP-15 [M]	Double Trumpet Doings	1960	10.00	20.00	40.00
☐ JLP-915 [S]	Double Trumpet Doings	1960	7.50	15.00	30.00
RCA VICTOR					
☐ LJM-1007 [M]	Don Elliott Quintet	1954	15.00	30.00	60.00
RIVERSIDE					
☐ RLP 12-218 [M]	Counterpoint for Six Valves	195?	10.00	20.00	40.00
—Blue label, microphone logo					
☐ RLP 12-218 [M]	Counterpoint for Six Valves	1956	25.00	50.00	100.00
—White label, blue print					
☐ RLP-2517 [10]	Six Valves	1955	30.00	60.00	120.00
SAVOY					
☐ MG-9033 [10]	The Versatile Don Elliott	1953	30.00	60.00	120.00
VANGUARD					
☐ VRS-8016 [10]	Doubles in Brass	1954	25.00	50.00	100.00

ELLIOTT, DON/SAM MOST

Number	Title (A Side/B Side)	Yr	VG	VG+	NM
JAZZTONE					
☐ J-1256 [M]	Doubles in Jazz	1957	10.00	20.00	40.00
VANGUARD					
☐ VRS-8522 [M]	Doubles in Jazz	1957	15.00	30.00	60.00
—Partial reissue of 8016 and 8014					

ELLIOTT, RAMBLIN' JACK

Number	Title (A Side/B Side)	Yr	VG	VG+	NM
FOLKLORE					
☐ FL 14011 [M]	The Songs of Woody Guthrie	1964	5.00	10.00	20.00
☐ FL 14014 [M]	Ramblin'	1964	5.00	10.00	20.00
☐ FL 14019 [M]	Hootenanny with Jack Elliott	1964	5.00	10.00	20.00
☐ FL 14029 [M]	Country Style	1964	5.00	10.00	20.00
MONITOR					
☐ MF-379 [M]	Ramblin' Cowboy	1962	6.25	12.50	25.00
☐ MF-380 [M]	Jack Elliott Sings Woody Guthrie and Jimmie Rodgers	1962	6.25	12.50	25.00
☐ MS-380 [S]	Jack Elliott Sings Woody Guthrie and Jimmie Rodgers	1962	7.50	15.00	30.00
PRESTIGE					
☐ PRLP-13016 [M]	The Songs of Woody Guthrie	1961	7.50	15.00	30.00
☐ PRLP-13033 [M]	Ramblin'	1961	7.50	15.00	30.00
☐ PRLP-13045 [M]	Country Style	1962	7.50	15.00	30.00
☐ PRLP-13065 [M]	Jack Elliott at the Second Fret	1962	7.50	15.00	30.00
TOPIC					
☐ T-15 [10]	Jack Takes the Floor	195?	10.00	20.00	40.00
VANGUARD					
☐ VRS-9151 [M]	Jack Elliott	1964	5.00	10.00	20.00
☐ VSD-79151 [S]	Jack Elliott	1964	6.25	12.50	25.00

ELLIOTT, WALTER & BENNETT

Number	Title (A Side/B Side)	Yr	VG	VG+	NM
JAM					
☐ (# unknown)	Save a Piece of the World	1975	12.50	25.00	50.00
—As "Elliott and Walter"					
☐ 104/105 [(2)]	Elliott, Walter & Bennett	197?	5.00	10.00	20.00
☐ 106	Zeti Reticuli	197?	20.00	40.00	80.00

ELLIS, ANITA

Number	Title (A Side/B Side)	Yr	VG	VG+	NM
ELEKTRA					
☐ EKL-179 [M]	The World in My Arms	1959	10.00	20.00	40.00
EPIC					
☐ LN 3280 [M]	I Wonder What Became of Me	1956	10.00	20.00	40.00
☐ LN 3419 [M]	Him	1958	10.00	20.00	40.00

ELLIS, DON

Number	Title (A Side/B Side)	Yr	VG	VG+	NM
CANDID					
☐ CJM-8004 [M]	How Time Passes	1961	12.50	25.00	50.00
☐ CJS-9004 [S]	How Time Passes	1961	15.00	30.00	60.00
COLUMBIA					
☐ CL 2785 [M]	Electric Bath	1968	7.50	15.00	30.00
☐ CS 9889	The New Don Ellis Band Goes Underground	1969	5.00	10.00	20.00
☐ G 30243 [(2)]	Don Ellis at the Fillmore	1970	5.00	10.00	20.00
☐ G 30927 [(2)]	Tears of Joy	1971	5.00	10.00	20.00
NEW JAZZ					
☐ NJLP-8257 [M]	New Ideas	1961	12.50	25.00	50.00
—Purple label					
☐ NJLP-8257 [M]	New Ideas	1965	6.25	12.50	25.00
—Blue label, trident logo at right					
PACIFIC JAZZ					
☐ PJ-55 [M]	Essence	1962	7.50	15.00	30.00
☐ ST-55 [S]	Essence	1962	10.00	20.00	40.00
☐ PJ-10112 [M]	Don Ellis "Live" At Monterey	1967	5.00	10.00	20.00
☐ PJ-10123 [M]	Live in 3/2 3/4 Time	1967	5.00	10.00	20.00

ELLIS, HERB

Number	Title (A Side/B Side)	Yr	VG	VG+	NM
COLUMBIA					
☐ CS 9130 [S]	Herb Ellis Guitar	1965	5.00	10.00	20.00
DOT					
☐ DLP-25678 [S]	The Man with the Guitar	1965	5.00	10.00	20.00
EPIC					
☐ LA 16034 [M]	The Midnight Roll	1962	6.25	12.50	25.00
☐ LA 16036 [M]	Three Guitars in Bossa Nova Time	1963	5.00	10.00	20.00
☐ LA 16039 [M]	Herb Ellis and "Stuff" Smith Together	1963	5.00	10.00	20.00
☐ BA 17034 [S]	The Midnight Roll	1962	7.50	15.00	30.00
☐ BA 17036 [S]	Three Guitars in Bossa Nova Time	1963	6.25	12.50	25.00
☐ BA 17039 [S]	Herb Ellis and "Stuff" Smith Together	1963	6.25	12.50	25.00
NORGRAN					
☐ MGN-1081 [M]	Ellis in Wonderland	1956	25.00	50.00	100.00

Number	Title (A Side/B Side)	Yr	VG	VG+	NM
VERVE					
☐ MGVS-6045 [S]	Herb Ellis Meets Jimmy Giuffre	1960	10.00	20.00	40.00
☐ MGVS-6164 [S]	Thank You, Charlie Christian	1960	10.00	20.00	40.00
☐ MGV-8171 [M]	Ellis in Wonderland	1957	12.50	25.00	50.00
—Reissue of Norgran 1081					
☐ V-8171 [M]	Ellis in Wonderland	1961	5.00	10.00	20.00
☐ MGV-8252 [M]	Nothing But the Blues	1958	12.50	25.00	50.00
☐ V-8252 [M]	Nothing But the Blues	1961	5.00	10.00	20.00
☐ MGV-8311 [M]	Herb Ellis Meets Jimmy Giuffre	1959	12.50	25.00	50.00
☐ V-8311 [M]	Herb Ellis Meets Jimmy Giuffre	1961	5.00	10.00	20.00
☐ V6-8311 [S]	Herb Ellis Meets Jimmy Giuffre	1961	5.00	10.00	20.00
☐ MGV-8381 [M]	Thank You, Charlie Christian	1960	12.50	25.00	50.00
☐ V-8381 [M]	Thank You, Charlie Christian	1961	5.00	10.00	20.00
☐ V6-8381 [S]	Thank You, Charlie Christian	1961	5.00	10.00	20.00
☐ V-8448 [M]	Softly…But With That Feeling	1962	5.00	10.00	20.00
☐ V6-8448 [S]	Softly…But With That Feeling	1962	6.25	12.50	25.00

ELLIS, JIMMY

Number	Title (A Side/B Side)	Yr	VG	VG+	NM
BOBLO					
☐ 78-829	By Request Jimmy Sings Elvis	1978	25.00	50.00	100.00

ELLIS, LLOYD

Number	Title (A Side/B Side)	Yr	VG	VG+	NM
CARLTON					
☐ LP 12-104 [M]	Fastest Guitar in the World	1958	12.50	25.00	50.00
TREY					
☐ T-902 [M]	So Tall, So Cool	1960	7.50	15.00	30.00

ELLIS, PEE WEE

Number	Title (A Side/B Side)	Yr	VG	VG+	NM
SAVOY					
☐ SJL-3301	Home in the Country	1976	5.00	10.00	20.00

ELLIS, RED

Number	Title (A Side/B Side)	Yr	VG	VG+	NM
STARDAY					
☐ SLP-168 [M]	Holy Cry from the Cross	1962	6.25	12.50	25.00
☐ SLP-203 [M]	The Sacred Sound of Bluegrass Music	1962	6.25	12.50	25.00
☐ SLP-273 [M]	Old Time Religion Bluegrass Style	1963	6.25	12.50	25.00

ELLIS, SHIRLEY

Number	Title (A Side/B Side)	Yr	VG	VG+	NM
COLUMBIA					
☐ CL 2679 [M]	Sugar, Let's Shing-a-Ling	1967	5.00	10.00	20.00
☐ CS 9479 [S]	Sugar, Let's Shing-a-Ling	1967	6.25	12.50	25.00
CONGRESS					
☐ CGL-3002 [M]	Shirley Ellis In Action	1964	6.25	12.50	25.00
☐ CGS-3002 [S]	Shirley Ellis In Action	1964	7.50	15.00	30.00
☐ CGL-3003 [M]	The Name Game	1965	6.25	12.50	25.00
☐ CGS-3003 [S]	The Name Game	1965	7.50	15.00	30.00

ELLIS, STEVE, AND THE STARFIRES

Number	Title (A Side/B Side)	Yr	VG	VG+	NM
I.G.L.					
☐ 105	The Steve Ellis Songbook	1967	125.00	250.00	500.00

ELMAN, ZIGGY

Number	Title (A Side/B Side)	Yr	VG	VG+	NM
MGM					
☐ E-163 [10]	Dancing with Zig	1952	12.50	25.00	50.00
☐ E-535 [10]	Ziggy Elman and His Orchestra	195?	12.50	25.00	50.00
☐ E-3389 [M]	Sentimental Trumpet	1956	10.00	20.00	40.00

ELMER GANTRY'S VELVET OPERA

Number	Title (A Side/B Side)	Yr	VG	VG+	NM
EPIC					
☐ BN 26415	Elmer Gantry's Velvet Opera	1968	12.50	25.00	50.00

ELMORE, ROBERT

Number	Title (A Side/B Side)	Yr	VG	VG+	NM
MERCURY LIVING PRESENCE					
☐ SR 90109 [S]	Boardwalk Pipes	196?	25.00	50.00	100.00
—Maroon label, no "Vendor: Mercury Record Corporation"					
☐ SR 90127 [S]	Bach on the Biggest	1960	7.50	15.00	30.00
—Maroon label, no "Vendor: Mercury Record Corporation"					

ELSTAK, NEDLEY

Number	Title (A Side/B Side)	Yr	VG	VG+	NM
ESP-DISK'					
☐ 1076	The Machine	1969	5.00	10.00	20.00

EMANUELE, VITTORIO

Number	Title (A Side/B Side)	Yr	VG	VG+	NM
RCA VICTOR RED SEAL					
☐ LSC-2424 [S]	Vivaldi: The Four Seasons	1960	5.00	10.00	20.00
—With the Societa Corelli; original with "shaded dog" label					

EMBERS, THE

Number	Title (A Side/B Side)	Yr	VG	VG+	NM
JCP					
☐ 2006 [M]	The Embers Roll Eleven	1965	50.00	100.00	200.00
☐ 2009 [M]	Just for the Birds	1966	37.50	75.00	150.00

EMERSON, KEITH

Number	Title (A Side/B Side)	Yr	VG	VG+	NM
EMERSON					
☐ KEITH LP-1	The Christmas Album	1993	5.00	10.00	20.00
—British import only					

EMERSON, LAKE AND PALMER

Number	Title (A Side/B Side)	Yr	VG	VG+	NM
ATLANTIC					
☐ PR 277 [DJ]	Works Volume 1	1977	3.75	7.50	15.00
—Promo-only sampler					
☐ PR 281 [DJ]	On Tour with Emerson, Lake and Palmer	1977	10.00	20.00	40.00
☐ SD 7000 [(2)]	Works Volume 1	1977	3.75	7.50	15.00
☐ SD 19120	Emerson, Lake and Palmer	1977	2.00	4.00	8.00
☐ SD 19121	Tarkus	1977	2.00	4.00	8.00
☐ SD 19122	Pictures at an Exhibition	1977	2.00	4.00	8.00
☐ SD 19123	Trilogy	1977	2.00	4.00	8.00
☐ SD 19124	Brain Salad Surgery	1977	2.00	4.00	8.00
☐ SD 19147	Works Volume 2	1977	2.50	5.00	10.00
☐ SD 19211	Love Beach	1978	2.50	5.00	10.00
☐ SD 19255	Emerson, Lake and Palmer In Concert	1979	2.50	5.00	10.00
☐ SD 19283	The Best of Emerson, Lake and Palmer	1980	2.50	5.00	10.00
COTILLION					
☐ SD 9040	Emerson, Lake and Palmer	1971	3.00	6.00	12.00
☐ SD 9900	Tarkus	1971	3.00	6.00	12.00

E

Number	Title (A Side/B Side)	Yr	VG	VG+	NM
❑ SD 9903	Trilogy	1972	3.00	6.00	12.00
❑ ELP 66666	Pictures at an Exhibition	1971	3.00	6.00	12.00
❑ SMAS-94773	Trilogy	1972	3.75	7.50	15.00
—Capitol Record Club edition					
MANTICORE					
❑ SD 3-200 [(3)]	Welcome Back, My Friends, to the Show That Never Ends, Ladies and Gentlemen	1974	5.00	10.00	20.00
❑ ELP 66669	Brain Salad Surgery	1973	3.00	6.00	12.00
MOBILE FIDELITY					
❑ 1-031	Pictures at an Exhibition	1980	7.50	15.00	30.00
—Audiophile vinyl					
❑ 1-203	Tarkus	1994	6.25	12.50	25.00
—Audiophile vinyl					
❑ 1-218	Trilogy	1994	10.00	20.00	40.00
—Audiophile vinyl					

EMERSON'S OLD-TIMEY CUSTARD-SUCKIN' BAND
ESP-DISK'

Number	Title (A Side/B Side)	Yr	VG	VG+	NM
❑ 2006	Emerson's Old-Timey Custard-Suckin' Band	1970	7.50	15.00	30.00

EMMONS, BOBBY
HI

❑ HL-32024 [M]	Blues with a Beat	1965	6.25	12.50	25.00
❑ SHL-32024 [S]	Blues with a Beat	1965	7.50	15.00	30.00

EMMONS, BUDDY
MERCURY

❑ MG-20843 [M]	Steel Guitar Jazz	1963	20.00	40.00	80.00
❑ SR-60843 [S]	Steel Guitar Jazz	1963	25.00	50.00	100.00

EMMONS, BUDDY, AND SHOT JACKSON
STARDAY

❑ SLP-230 [M]	Singing Strings of Steel and Dobro	196?	10.00	20.00	40.00

EMOTIONS, THE (1)
ARC

❑ JC 36149	Come Into Our World	1979	2.50	5.00	10.00
❑ FC 37456	New Affair	1981	2.50	5.00	10.00
COLUMBIA					
❑ PC 34163	Flowers	1976	2.50	5.00	10.00
—No bar code on cover					
❑ PC 34163	Flowers	198?	2.00	4.00	8.00
—With bar code on cover					
❑ PC 34762	Rejoice	1977	2.50	5.00	10.00
—No bar code on cover					
❑ PC 34762	Rejoice	198?	2.00	4.00	8.00
—With bar code on cover					
❑ JC 35385	Sunbeam	1978	2.50	5.00	10.00
MOTOWN					
❑ 6136 ML	If I Only Knew	1985	2.00	4.00	8.00
RED LABEL					
❑ 001	Sincerely	1984	2.50	5.00	10.00
STAX					
❑ STX-4100	Sunshine	1977	2.50	5.00	10.00
❑ STX-4110	So I Can Love You	1978	2.50	5.00	10.00
—Reissue of Volt 6008					
❑ STX-4112	Untouched	1978	2.50	5.00	10.00
—Reissue of Volt 6015					
❑ STX-4121	Chronicle	1979	2.50	5.00	10.00
VOLT					
❑ VOS-6008	So I Can Love You	1971	6.25	12.50	25.00
❑ VOS-6015	Untouched	1972	6.25	12.50	25.00

END, THE
LONDON

❑ PS 560	Introspection	1969	12.50	25.00	50.00

ENESCU, GEORGE
CONTINENTAL

❑ CLP 104 [(3)M]	Bach: Six Sonatas and Partitas for Unaccompanied Violin	1949	2500.	5000.	10000.
—In original box					
❑ CLP 106 [M]	Bach: Sonatas 5 and 6	1949	1000.	2000.	4000.

ENEVOLDSEN, BOB
LIBERTY

❑ LJH-6008 [M]	Smorgasboard	1956	12.50	25.00	50.00
NOCTURNE					
❑ NLP-6 [M]	Bob Enevoldsen Quintet	1954	37.50	75.00	150.00
TAMPA					
❑ TP-14 [M]	Reflections in Jazz	1957	25.00	50.00	100.00
—Colored vinyl					
❑ TP-14 [M]	Reflections in Jazz	1958	12.50	25.00	50.00
—Black vinyl					

ENGEL, SCOTT, AND JOHN STEWART
See THE WALKER BROTHERS.

ENNIS, ETHEL
CAPITOL

❑ T 941	Change of Scenery	1957	10.00	20.00	40.00
❑ T 1078 [M]	Have You Forgotten?	1959	10.00	20.00	40.00
JUBILEE					
❑ JLP-1021 [M]	Lullabies for Losers	1956	12.50	25.00	50.00
❑ JLP-5024 [M]	Ethel Ennis Sings	1963	5.00	10.00	20.00
❑ SJLP-5024 [S]	Ethel Ennis Sings	1963	6.25	12.50	25.00
RCA VICTOR					
❑ LPM-2786 [M]	This Is Ethel Ennis	1964	5.00	10.00	20.00
❑ LSP-2786 [S]	This Is Ethel Ennis	1964	6.25	12.50	25.00
❑ LPM-2984 [M]	Eyes for You	1964	5.00	10.00	20.00
❑ LSP-2984 [S]	Eyes for You	1964	6.25	12.50	25.00

ENO, BRIAN
ANTILLES

Number	Title (A Side/B Side)	Yr	VG	VG+	NM
❑ AN-7001	No Pussyfooting	1973	3.75	7.50	15.00
—By Robert Fripp and Eno					
❑ AN-7018	Evening Star	1975	3.00	6.00	12.00
—By Robert Fripp and Eno					
❑ AN-7030	Discreet Music	1975	3.00	6.00	12.00
❑ AN-7070	Music for Films	1978	3.75	7.50	15.00
EDITIONS EG					
❑ ENO-1	Here Come the Warm Jets	1982	2.50	5.00	10.00
—Reissue					
❑ EGBS-2 [(11)]	Working Backwards: 1983-1973	1984	15.00	30.00	60.00
—Boxed set of nine albums plus Music For Films II and Rarities 12"					
❑ ENO-2	Taking Tiger Mountain (By Strategy)	1982	2.50	5.00	10.00
—Reissue					
❑ ENO-3	Another Green World	1982	2.50	5.00	10.00
—Reissue					
❑ ENO-4	Before and After Science	1982	2.50	5.00	10.00
—Reissue					
❑ ENO-5	Apollo: Atmospheres and Soundtracks	1983	2.50	5.00	10.00
❑ EGED-20	Ambient 4 — On Land	1982	2.50	5.00	10.00
❑ EGED-37	The Pearl	1984	3.00	6.00	12.00
—By Harold Budd and Brian Eno					
❑ EGS-102	No Pussyfooting	1982	2.50	5.00	10.00
—By Robert Fripp and Eno; reissue					
❑ EGS-103	Evening Star	1982	2.50	5.00	10.00
—By Robert Fripp and Eno; reissue					
❑ EGS-105	Music for Films	1982	2.50	5.00	10.00
—Reissue					
❑ EGS-107	Fourth World Volume 1: Possible Musics	1980	3.00	6.00	12.00
—With Jon Hassell					
❑ EGS-201	Ambient #1 — Music for Airports	1982	3.00	6.00	12.00
—Reissue					
❑ EGS-202	Ambient 2 — The Plateaux of Mirrors	1982	3.00	6.00	12.00
—By Harold Budd and Brian Eno					
❑ EGS-301	Pavilion of Dreams	1982	3.00	6.00	12.00
—By Harold Budd and Brian Eno					
❑ EGS-303	Discreet Music	1983	3.00	6.00	12.00
—Reissue					
ISLAND					
❑ ILPS 9268	Here Come the Warm Jets	1973	3.00	6.00	12.00
❑ ILPS 9309	Taking Tiger Mountain (By Strategy)	1974	3.00	6.00	12.00
❑ ILPS 9351	Another Green World	1975	3.00	6.00	12.00
❑ ILPS 9478	Before and After Science	1977	3.00	6.00	12.00
—Double the value if four lithographs are included with the package.					
JEM					
❑ ENO DJ [DJ]	Music for Airplay	1981	12.50	25.00	50.00
—Promo-only 10-track sampler					
OPAL/WARNER BROS.					
❑ 25769	Music for Films, Vol. III	1988	2.50	5.00	10.00
❑ 26421	Wrong Way Up	1990	2.50	5.00	10.00
—With John Cale					
PVC					
❑ 7908	Ambient #1 — Music for Airports	1979	3.00	6.00	12.00

ENSEMBLE AL-SALAAM, THE
STRATA-EAST

❑ SES-7418	The Sojourner	1974	10.00	20.00	40.00

ENTWISTLE, JOHN
ATCO

❑ SD 38-142	Too Late the Hero	1981	2.50	5.00	10.00
DECCA					
❑ DL 79183	Smash Your Head Against the Wall	1971	6.25	12.50	25.00
MCA					
❑ 2024	Smash Your Head Against the Wall	1973	3.00	6.00	12.00
—Reissue of Decca 79183					
TRACK					
❑ MCA-321	Rigor Mortis Sets In	1973	3.75	7.50	15.00
❑ L33-1926 [DJ]	Who's Ox	1975	12.50	25.00	50.00
—Promo-only sampler					
❑ MCA-2129	Mad Dog	1975	3.75	7.50	15.00
❑ DL 79190	Whistle Rymes	1972	6.25	12.50	25.00

EPIC CHOIR, THE
EPIC

❑ LC 3144 [M]	The Story of Christmas	1954	6.25	12.50	25.00
—Gatefold cover with bound-in booklet					

EPPS, PRESTON
ORIGINAL SOUND

❑ LPM-5002 [M]	Bongo, Bongo, Bongo	1960	12.50	25.00	50.00
❑ LPM-5009 [M]	Surfin' Bongos	1963	10.00	20.00	40.00
❑ LPS-8851 [S]	Bongo, Bongo, Bongo	1960	20.00	40.00	80.00
❑ LPS-8872 [S]	Surfin' Bongos	1963	12.50	25.00	50.00
TOP RANK					
❑ RM-349 [M]	Bongola	1961	10.00	20.00	40.00
❑ RS-349 [S]	Bongola	1961	12.50	25.00	50.00

EQUALS, THE
LAURIE

❑ LLP-2045 [M]	Unequalled	1967	6.25	12.50	25.00
❑ SLP-2045 [S]	Unequalled	1967	7.50	15.00	30.00
PRESIDENT					
❑ PTL-1015	Equal Sensation	1968	6.25	12.50	25.00
❑ PTL-1020	The Sensational Equals	1968	6.25	12.50	25.00
❑ PTL-1025	Equals Supreme	1968	6.25	12.50	25.00
❑ PTL-1030	Strikeback	1969	6.25	12.50	25.00
RCA VICTOR					
❑ LSP-4078	Baby Come Back	1968	6.25	12.50	25.00

Number	Title (A Side/B Side)	Yr	VG	VG+	NM
ERASURE					
MUTE/ELEKTRA					
❑ 5621 [DJ]	Abba-esque (Remixes)	1992	6.25	12.50	25.00
—Promo-only vinyl; remixes of 4-song EP; no special jacket					
SIRE					
❑ 25354	Wonderland	1987	3.00	6.00	12.00
❑ 25554	The Circus	1987	3.00	6.00	12.00
❑ 25667 [(2)]	The Two Ring Circus	1988	3.75	7.50	15.00
❑ 25730	The Innocents	1988	2.50	5.00	10.00
❑ 25904 [EP]	Crackers International	1989	2.00	4.00	8.00
❑ 26026	Wild!	1989	2.50	5.00	10.00
❑ R 101009	The Innocents	1988	3.00	6.00	12.00
—BMG Music Service edition					
ERICA					
ESP-DISK'					
❑ 1099	You Used to Think	1968	15.00	30.00	60.00
ERICSON, ROLF					
EMARCY					
❑ MG-36106 [M]	Rolf Ericson and His All American Stars	1957	12.50	25.00	50.00
ERIK					
VANGUARD					
❑ VRS-9267 [M]	Look Where I Am	1967	5.00	10.00	20.00
❑ VSD-79267 [S]	Look Where I Am	1967	5.00	10.00	20.00
ERIK AND THE VIKINGS					
KARATE					
❑ KLP-1401 [M]	Sing A-Long Rock 'n Roll	1965	50.00	100.00	200.00
ERVIN, BOOKER					
BETHLEHEM					
❑ BCP-6048 [M]	The Book Cooks	1961	10.00	20.00	40.00
BLUE NOTE					
❑ BN-LA488-H2 [(2)]	Back from the Gig	1975	5.00	10.00	20.00
❑ BST-84283	The In Between	1969	7.50	15.00	30.00
CANDID					
❑ CJM-8014 [M]	That's It!	1961	10.00	20.00	40.00
❑ CJS-9014 [S]	That's It!	1961	12.50	25.00	50.00
PACIFIC JAZZ					
❑ PJ-10199 [M]	Structurally Sound	1968	10.00	20.00	40.00
❑ ST-20199 [S]	Structurally Sound	1968	5.00	10.00	20.00
PRESTIGE					
❑ PRLP-7293 [M]	Exultation!	1964	6.25	12.50	25.00
❑ PRST-7293 [S]	Exultation!	1964	7.50	15.00	30.00
❑ PRLP-7295 [M]	The Freedom Book	1964	6.25	12.50	25.00
❑ PRST-7295 [S]	The Freedom Book	1964	7.50	15.00	30.00
❑ PRLP-7318 [M]	The Song Book	1964	6.25	12.50	25.00
❑ PRST-7318 [S]	The Song Book	1964	7.50	15.00	30.00
❑ PRLP-7340 [M]	The Blues Book	1965	6.25	12.50	25.00
❑ PRST-7340 [S]	The Blues Book	1965	7.50	15.00	30.00
❑ PRLP-7386 [M]	The Space Book	1965	6.25	12.50	25.00
❑ PRST-7386 [S]	The Space Book	1965	7.50	15.00	30.00
❑ PRLP-7417 [M]	Groovin' High	1966	5.00	10.00	20.00
❑ PRST-7417 [S]	Groovin' High	1966	6.25	12.50	25.00
❑ PRLP-7435 [M]	Settin' the Pace	1967	6.25	12.50	25.00
❑ PRST-7435 [S]	Settin' the Pace	1967	5.00	10.00	20.00
❑ PRLP-7462 [M]	The Trance	1967	6.25	12.50	25.00
❑ PRST-7462 [S]	The Trance	1967	5.00	10.00	20.00
❑ PRLP-7499 [M]	Heavy!	1968	7.50	15.00	30.00
❑ PRST-7499 [S]	Heavy!	1968	5.00	10.00	20.00
SAVOY					
❑ MG-12154 [M]	Cookin'	1960	12.50	25.00	50.00
ERVIN, SENATOR SAM					
COLUMBIA					
❑ KC 32756	Senator Sam at Home	1973	6.25	12.50	25.00
ERWIN, PEE WEE					
BRUNSWICK					
❑ BL 54011 [M]	The Land of Dixie	1956	10.00	20.00	40.00
CADENCE					
❑ CLP-1011 [M]	Dixieland at Grandview Inn	1956	10.00	20.00	40.00
STRAND					
❑ SL-1001 [M]	Peter Meets the Wolf in Dixieland	1959	12.50	25.00	50.00
❑ SLS-1001 [S]	Peter Meets the Wolf in Dixieland	1959	15.00	30.00	60.00
URANIA					
❑ UJLP-1202 [M]	Accent on Dixieland	1955	10.00	20.00	40.00
ESCORTS, THE (4)					
TEO					
❑ LPM-5000 [M]	The Escorts Bring Down the House	1966	30.00	60.00	120.00
ESP					
DREAM					
❑ DRE 187301	The Future Is Now	1986	12.50	25.00	50.00
ESQUERITA					
CAPITOL					
❑ T 1186 [M]	Esquerita	1959	250.00	500.00	1000.
ESQUIRES, THE (1)					
BUNKY					
❑ 300	Get On Up and Get Away	1968	8.75	17.50	35.00
ESQUIVEL					
BAR NONE					
❑ LP-043	Space Age Bachelor Pad Music	1994	3.00	6.00	12.00
❑ LP-056	Music for a Sparkling Planet	1995	3.00	6.00	12.00
RCA VICTOR					
❑ LPM-1345 [M]	To Love Again	1957	12.50	25.00	50.00
❑ LPM-1749 [M]	Four Corners of the World	1958	6.25	12.50	25.00
❑ LSP-1749 [S]	Four Corners of the World	1958	12.50	25.00	50.00
❑ LPM-1753 [M]	Other Worlds, Other Sounds	1959	6.25	12.50	25.00
❑ LSP-1753 [S]	Other Worlds, Other Sounds	1959	12.50	25.00	50.00
❑ LPM-1978 [M]	Exploring New Sounds in Hi-Fi	1959	7.50	15.00	30.00
❑ LSP-1978 [S]	Exploring New Sounds in Hi-Fi	1959	15.00	30.00	60.00
❑ LPM-1988 [M]	Strings Aflame	1959	6.25	12.50	25.00
❑ LSP-1988 [S]	Strings Aflame	1959	12.50	25.00	50.00
❑ LPM-2225 [M]	Infinity in Sound	1960	7.50	15.00	30.00
❑ LSP-2225 [S]	Infinity in Sound	1960	15.00	30.00	60.00
❑ LPM-2296 [M]	Infinity in Sound, Vol. 2	1961	7.50	15.00	30.00
❑ LSP-2296 [S]	Infinity in Sound, Vol. 2	1961	15.00	30.00	60.00
❑ LPM-2418 [M]	Latin-esque	1962	5.00	10.00	20.00
❑ LSP-2418 [S]	Latin-esque	1962	10.00	20.00	40.00
—Standard cover					
❑ LSP-2418 [S]	Latin-esque	1962	15.00	30.00	60.00
—Die-cut cover that reveals inner sleeve					
❑ LPM-3502 [M]	The Best of Esquivel	1966	5.00	10.00	20.00
❑ LSP-3502 [S]	The Best of Esquivel	1966	7.50	15.00	30.00
❑ LPM-3697 [M]	The Genius of Esquivel	1967	5.00	10.00	20.00
❑ LSP-3697 [S]	The Genius of Esquivel	1967	7.50	15.00	30.00
REPRISE					
❑ P9-6046 [S]	More of Other World, Other Sounds	1962	7.50	15.00	30.00
❑ R-6046 [M]	More of Other World, Other Sounds	1962	6.25	12.50	25.00
ESSEX, DAVID					
COLUMBIA					
❑ CQ 32560 [Q]	Rock On	1974	7.50	15.00	30.00
❑ KC 32560	Rock On	1974	5.00	10.00	20.00
❑ KC 33289	David Essex	1974	3.75	7.50	15.00
❑ PC 33813	All the Fun of the Fair	1975	3.75	7.50	15.00
MERCURY					
❑ 812936-1	David Essex	1983	3.75	7.50	15.00
ESSEX, THE					
ROULETTE					
❑ R-25234 [M]	Easier Said Than Done	1963	10.00	20.00	40.00
❑ SR-25234 [S]	Easier Said Than Done	1963	12.50	25.00	50.00
❑ R-25235 [M]	A Walkin' Miracle	1963	10.00	20.00	40.00
❑ SR-25235 [S]	A Walkin' Miracle	1963	12.50	25.00	50.00
❑ R-25246 [M]	Young and Lively	1964	10.00	20.00	40.00
❑ SR-25246 [S]	Young and Lively	1964	12.50	25.00	50.00
ETC.					
WINDI					
❑ WLPS-1011	Etc. Is the Name of the Band!	1976	6.25	12.50	25.00
ETERNITY'S CHILDREN					
TOWER					
❑ ST-5123	Eternity's Children	1968	6.25	12.50	25.00
❑ ST-5144	Timeless	1969	7.50	15.00	30.00
EUPHONIOUS WAIL					
KAPP					
❑ KS-3668	Euphonious Wail	1973	10.00	20.00	40.00
EUPHORIA (2)					
HERITAGE					
❑ HTS 35005	Euphoria	1971	7.50	15.00	30.00
EUPHORIA (3)					
CAPITOL					
❑ SKAO-363	A Gift from Euphoria	1969	30.00	60.00	120.00
EUPHORIA (4)					
RAINBOW					
❑ 1003	Lost in a Trance	1973	75.00	150.00	300.00
EUREKA BRASS BAND, THE					
ATLANTIC					
❑ SD 1408 [S]	The Eureka Brass Band	1963	5.00	10.00	20.00
—Multicolor label with black "fan" logo at right					
FOLKWAYS					
❑ FA-2642 [M]	Music of New Orleans	195?	12.50	25.00	50.00
PAX					
❑ LP-9001 [10]	New Orleans Parade	1954	15.00	30.00	60.00
EUROPEAN JAZZ QUARTET, THE					
PULSE					
❑ 3001 [M]	New Jazz from the Old World	1957	12.50	25.00	50.00
EURYTHMICS					
ARISTA					
❑ AL 8606	We Too Are One	1989	3.00	6.00	12.00
RCA					
❑ AFL1-4681	Sweet Dreams (Are Made of This)	1983	3.00	6.00	12.00
❑ AFL1-4917	Touch	1984	3.00	6.00	12.00
❑ ABL1-5371	1984 (For the Love of Big Brother)	1984	3.00	6.00	12.00
❑ AJL1-5429	Be Yourself Tonight	1985	3.00	6.00	12.00
❑ AJL1-5827	Revenge	1986	3.00	6.00	12.00
❑ 6794-1-R	Savage	1987	3.00	6.00	12.00
RCA VICTOR					
❑ CPL1-5086 [EP]	Touch Dance	1983	3.00	6.00	12.00
❑ DJL1-5707 [DJ]	Rough and Tough — Live at the Roxy	1986	7.50	15.00	30.00
—Promo-only 4-song live album					
EVANS, BILL (1)					
MOSAIC					
❑ MQ10-171 [(10)]	The Final Village Vanguard Sessions — June 1980	1996	50.00	100.00	200.00
RIVERSIDE					
❑ R-018 [(18)]	The Complete Riverside Recordings	1985	50.00	100.00	200.00

E

Number	Title (A Side/B Side)	Yr	VG	VG+	NM
❑ RLP 12-223 [M]	New Jazz Conceptions	1956	125.00	250.00	500.00
—Photo on cover, label is white with blue print					
❑ RLP 12-223 [M]	New Jazz Conceptions	1958	7.50	15.00	30.00
—New cover, label is blue with microphone logo at top					
❑ RLP 12-291 [M]	Everybody Digs Bill Evans	1958	10.00	20.00	40.00
❑ RLP 12-315 [M]	Portrait in Jazz	1959	10.00	20.00	40.00
❑ RLP-351 [M]	Explorations	1960	7.50	15.00	30.00
❑ RLP-376 [M]	Sunday at the Village Vanguard	1961	6.25	12.50	25.00
❑ RLP-399 [M]	Waltz for Debby	1961	6.25	12.50	25.00
❑ RLP-428 [M]	Moonbeams	1962	6.25	12.50	25.00
❑ RLP-445 [M]	Interplay	1963	6.25	12.50	25.00
❑ RLP-473 [M]	How My Heart Sings!	1964	6.25	12.50	25.00
❑ RLP-487 [M]	Bill Evans at Shelly's Manne-Hole, Hollywood, California	1965	5.00	10.00	20.00
❑ RLP 1129 [S]	Everybody Digs Bill Evans	1959	7.50	15.00	30.00
❑ RLP 1162 [S]	Portrait in Jazz	1959	7.50	15.00	30.00
❑ RS-9351 [S]	Explorations	1960	7.50	15.00	30.00
❑ RS-9376 [S]	Sunday at the Village Vanguard	1961	7.50	15.00	30.00
❑ RS9399 [S]	Waltz for Debby	1961	7.50	15.00	30.00
❑ RS-9428 [S]	Moonbeams	1962	7.50	15.00	30.00
❑ RS-9445 [S]	Interplay	1963	7.50	15.00	30.00
❑ RS-9473 [S]	How My Heart Sings!	1964	7.50	15.00	30.00
❑ RS-9487 [S]	Bill Evans at Shelly's Manne-Hole, Hollywood, California	1965	6.25	12.50	25.00
VERVE					
❑ V-8497 [M]	Empathy	1962	6.25	12.50	25.00
❑ V6-8497 [S]	Empathy	1962	7.50	15.00	30.00
❑ V-8526 [M]	Conversations with Myself	1963	5.00	10.00	20.00
❑ V6-8526 [S]	Conversations with Myself	1963	6.25	12.50	25.00
❑ V6-8578 [S]	Bill Evans Trio '64	1964	5.00	10.00	20.00
❑ V6-8613 [S]	Bill Evans Trio '65	1965	5.00	10.00	20.00
❑ V6-8640 [S]	Bill Evans Trio with Symphony Orchestra	1965	5.00	10.00	20.00
❑ V6-8655 [S]	Intermodulation	1966	5.00	10.00	20.00
❑ V6-8675 [S]	A Simple Matter of Conviction	1966	5.00	10.00	20.00
❑ V6-8683 [S]	Bill Evans at Town Hall	1966	5.00	10.00	20.00
❑ V-8727 [M]	Further Conversations with Myself	1967	5.00	10.00	20.00
❑ V-8747 [M]	The Best of Bill Evans	1967	5.00	10.00	20.00
❑ V6-8762	Bill Evans at the Montreux Jazz Festival	199?	6.25	12.50	25.00
—Classic Records reissue on audiophile vinyl					
❑ V3HB-8841 [(3)]	Return Engagement	1973	5.00	10.00	20.00

EVANS, BILL (1), AND JIM HALL
SOLID STATE

Number	Title (A Side/B Side)	Yr	VG	VG+	NM
❑ SS-18018	Undercurrent	1968	5.00	10.00	20.00
UNITED ARTISTS					
❑ UAJ-14003 [M]	Undercurrent	1962	10.00	20.00	40.00
❑ UAJS-15003 [S]	Undercurrent	1962	12.50	25.00	50.00

EVANS, DALE
ALLEGRO ELITE

Number	Title (A Side/B Side)	Yr	VG	VG+	NM
❑ 4116 [10]	Dale Evans Sings	195?	10.00	20.00	40.00
CAPITOL					
❑ ST-399	Get to Know the Lord	1970	3.75	7.50	15.00
❑ ST 2772 [S]	It's Real	1967	6.25	12.50	25.00
❑ T 2772 [M]	It's Real	1967	6.25	12.50	25.00
EVON					
❑ 336 [M]	Dale Evans Sings Western Favorites/Johnny 'O Calls Western Dances	195?	7.50	15.00	30.00
—Only Side 1 is by Dale Evans					
MANNA					
❑ MS-2075	Reflections of Life	1981	3.00	6.00	12.00
SACRED					
❑ LPS-4507	Favorite Gospel Songs	197?	3.00	6.00	12.00
—Reissue of Word WST-8546					
WORD					
❑ WST-8546	It's Real	1971	3.75	7.50	15.00
❑ WST-8566	Faith, Hope and Charity	1972	3.75	7.50	15.00
❑ WST-8658	Heart of the Country	1975	3.75	7.50	15.00
❑ WST-8661	Country Dale	1976	3.00	6.00	12.00
❑ WST-8803	Totally Free	1979	3.00	6.00	12.00

EVANS, DOC
AUDIOPHILE

Number	Title (A Side/B Side)	Yr	VG	VG+	NM
❑ AP-11 [M]	Doc Evans and His Band, Volume 1	195?	10.00	20.00	40.00
❑ AP-12 [M]	Doc Evans and His Band, Volume 2	195?	10.00	20.00	40.00
❑ AP-29 [M]	Dixieland Session	195?	10.00	20.00	40.00
❑ AP-31 [M]	The Cornet Artistry of Doc Evans	195?	10.00	20.00	40.00
❑ AP-33 [M]	Traditional Jazz	195?	10.00	20.00	40.00
—Red vinyl					
❑ AP-34 [M]	Traditional Jazz	195?	10.00	20.00	40.00
—Red vinyl					
❑ AP-44 [M]	Traditional Jazz	195?	10.00	20.00	40.00
—Red vinyl					
❑ AP-45 [M]	Traditional Jazz	195?	10.00	20.00	40.00
—Red vinyl					
❑ AP-50 [M]	Classics of the 20's	195?	10.00	20.00	40.00
—Red vinyl					
❑ AP-95 [M]	Doc Evans at the Gas Light	196?	5.00	10.00	20.00
❑ AS-95 [S]	Doc Evans at the Gas Light	196?	6.25	12.50	25.00
❑ XL-328 [M]	Traditional Jazz	195?	10.00	20.00	40.00
❑ XL-329 [M]	Traditional Jazz	195?	10.00	20.00	40.00
❑ APS-5968	Reminiscing in Dixieland	196?	6.25	12.50	25.00
—Red vinyl					
CONCERT DISC					
❑ CS-48	Muskrat Ramble	196?	6.25	12.50	25.00
FOLKWAYS					
❑ FA-2855	Doc Evans and His Dixieland Jazz Band	195?	5.00	10.00	20.00
SOMA					
❑ MG-100 [M]	Dixieland Concert	1953	12.50	25.00	50.00
❑ MG-101 [10]	Dixieland Concert	1953	12.50	25.00	50.00
❑ MG-1201 [M]	Classic Jazz at Carleton	1954	10.00	20.00	40.00

EVANS, GIL
ATLANTIC

Number	Title (A Side/B Side)	Yr	VG	VG+	NM
❑ QD 1643 [Q]	Svengali	1973	5.00	10.00	20.00
IMPULSE!					
❑ A-4 [M]	Out of the Cool	1961	6.25	12.50	25.00
❑ AS-4 [S]	Out of the Cool	1961	7.50	15.00	30.00
❑ A-9 [M]	Into the Hot	1962	6.25	12.50	25.00
❑ AS-9 [S]	Into the Hot	1962	7.50	15.00	30.00
NEW JAZZ					
❑ NJLP-8215 [M]	Big Stuff	1959	12.50	25.00	50.00
—Purple label					
❑ NJLP-8215 [M]	Big Stuff	1965	6.25	12.50	25.00
—Blue label, trident logo at right					
PACIFIC JAZZ					
❑ PJ-28 [M]	America's #1 Arranger	1961	7.50	15.00	30.00
❑ PJ-40 [M]	Cannonball Adderley/Gil Evans	1962	6.25	12.50	25.00
❑ ST-40 [S]	Cannonball Adderley/Gil Evans	1962	7.50	15.00	30.00
PRESTIGE					
❑ PRLP-7120 [M]	Gil Evans Plus Ten	1957	20.00	40.00	80.00
RCA VICTOR					
❑ CPL1-0667	Gil Evans Plays Jimi Hendrix	1974	5.00	10.00	20.00
❑ LPM-1057 [M]	There Comes a Time	1955	20.00	40.00	80.00
VERVE					
❑ V-8555 [M]	The Individualism of Gil Evans	1963	5.00	10.00	20.00
❑ V6-8555 [S]	The Individualism of Gil Evans	1963	6.25	12.50	25.00
WORLD PACIFIC					
❑ ST-1011 [S]	New Bottle, Old Wine	1959	10.00	20.00	40.00
❑ ST-1027 [S]	Great Jazz Standards	1959	10.00	20.00	40.00
❑ WP-1246 [M]	New Bottle, Old Wine	1958	12.50	25.00	50.00
❑ WP-1270 [M]	Great Jazz Standards	1959	12.50	25.00	50.00

EVANS, JOHN
OMEGA

Number	Title (A Side/B Side)	Yr	VG	VG+	NM
❑ OL-49 [M]	Mainstream Jazz Piano	1960	5.00	10.00	20.00
❑ OSL-49 [S]	Mainstream Jazz Piano	1960	5.00	10.00	20.00

EVANS, LEE
CAPITOL

Number	Title (A Side/B Side)	Yr	VG	VG+	NM
❑ ST 1625 [S]	Big Piano/Big Band/Big Sound	1962	5.00	10.00	20.00
❑ ST 1847 [S]	The Lee Evans Trio	1963	5.00	10.00	20.00

EVANS, PAUL
CARLTON

Number	Title (A Side/B Side)	Yr	VG	VG+	NM
❑ STLP-129 [S]	Hear Paul Evans in Your Home Tonight	1961	15.00	30.00	60.00
❑ TLP-129 [M]	Hear Paul Evans in Your Home Tonight	1961	10.00	20.00	40.00
❑ STLP-130 [S]	Folk Songs of Many Lands	1961	15.00	30.00	60.00
❑ TLP-130 [M]	Folk Songs of Many Lands	1961	10.00	20.00	40.00
GUARANTEED					
❑ GUL-1000 [M]	Fabulous Teens	1960	17.50	35.00	70.00
❑ GUS-1000 [S]	Fabulous Teens	1960	20.00	40.00	80.00
KAPP					
❑ KL-1346 [M]	21 Years in a Tennessee Jail	1964	6.25	12.50	25.00
❑ KL-1475 [M]	Another Town, Another Jail	1966	6.25	12.50	25.00
❑ KS-3346 [S]	21 Years in a Tennessee Jail	1964	10.00	20.00	40.00
❑ KS-3475 [S]	Another Town, Another Jail	1966	7.50	15.00	30.00

EVANS, RICHARD
ARGO

Number	Title (A Side/B Side)	Yr	VG	VG+	NM
❑ LP-658 [M]	Richard's Almanac	1960	7.50	15.00	30.00
❑ LPS-658 [S]	Richard's Almanac	1960	10.00	20.00	40.00
❑ LP-675 [M]	Home Cookin'	1961	6.25	12.50	25.00
❑ LPS-675 [S]	Home Cookin'	1961	7.50	15.00	30.00

EVEN DOZEN JUG BAND, THE
Among the members of the group were John Sebastian and Maria D'Amato (later Muldaur).
ELEKTRA

Number	Title (A Side/B Side)	Yr	VG	VG+	NM
❑ EKL-246 [M]	The Even Dozen Jug Band	1964	7.50	15.00	30.00
❑ EKS-7246 [S]	The Even Dozen Jug Band	1964	12.50	25.00	50.00

EVERETT, BETTY
FANTASY

Number	Title (A Side/B Side)	Yr	VG	VG+	NM
❑ 9447	Love Rhymes	1974	3.00	6.00	12.00
❑ 9480	Happy Endings	1975	3.00	6.00	12.00
SUNSET					
❑ SUS-5220	I Need You So	1968	3.75	7.50	15.00
UNI					
❑ 73048	There'll Come a Time	1969	6.25	12.50	25.00
VEE JAY					
❑ LP 1077 [M]	It's In His Kiss	1964	7.50	15.00	30.00
❑ LP 1077 [M]	You're No Good	1964	10.00	20.00	40.00
❑ SR 1077 [S]	It's In His Kiss	1964	12.50	25.00	50.00
❑ SR 1077 [S]	You're No Good	1964	17.50	35.00	70.00
❑ LP 1122 [M]	The Very Best of Betty Everett	1965	10.00	20.00	40.00
❑ VJLP 1122	The Very Best of Betty Everett	198?	2.50	5.00	10.00
—Authorized reissue					
❑ VJS 1122 [S]	The Very Best of Betty Everett	1965	12.50	25.00	50.00

EVERETT, BETTY, AND JERRY BUTLER
BUDDAH

Number	Title (A Side/B Side)	Yr	VG	VG+	NM
❑ BDS-7505	Together	1969	3.75	7.50	15.00
TRADITION					
❑ 2073	Starring Betty Everett with Jerry Butler	197?	3.00	6.00	12.00
VEE JAY					
❑ LP 1099 [M]	Delicious Together	1964	5.00	10.00	20.00
❑ LP-1099 [M]	Delicious Together	1964	5.00	10.00	20.00
❑ VJLP 1099	Delicious Together	198?	3.00	6.00	12.00
—Authorized reissue					
❑ VJLP-1099	Delicious Together	198?	2.50	5.00	10.00
—Reissue of original 1099; has softer vinyl					
❑ VJS 1099 [S]	Delicious Together	1964	6.25	12.50	25.00

Number	Title (A Side/B Side)	Yr	VG	VG+	NM
❑ VJS-1099 [S]	Delicious Together	1964	6.25	12.50	25.00

EVERETTE, LEON
MERCURY
❑ 824309-1	Where's the Fire	1985	2.00	4.00	8.00

ORLANDO
❑ 1101	I Don't Want to Lose	1980	3.00	6.00	12.00

RCA VICTOR
❑ AHL1-3916	If I Keep On Going Crazy	1981	2.50	5.00	10.00
❑ AHL1-4152	Hurricane	1981	2.50	5.00	10.00
❑ MHL1-8513 [EP]	Doin' What I Feel	1984	2.00	4.00	8.00
❑ MHL1-8600 [EP]	Leon Everette	1983	2.00	4.00	8.00

TRUE
❑ 1002	Goodbye King of Rock and Roll	1977	6.25	12.50	25.00
—Deduct 40% if poster of Elvis Presley is missing					

EVERGREEN BLUES, THE
ABC
❑ S-669	Comin' On	1969	3.75	7.50	15.00

MERCURY
❑ SR-61157	7 Do 11	1968	5.00	10.00	20.00

EVERLY BROTHERS, THE
ARISTA
❑ AL9-8207 [(2)]	24 Original Classics	1985	3.75	7.50	15.00

BARNABY
❑ BGP-350 [(2)]	The Everly Brothers' Original Golden Hits	1970	5.00	10.00	20.00
❑ 4004	Greatest Hits, Vol. 1	1977	2.50	5.00	10.00
❑ 4005	Greatest Hits, Vol. 2	1977	2.50	5.00	10.00
❑ 4006	Greatest Hits, Vol. 3	1977	2.50	5.00	10.00
❑ BR-6006 [(2)]	The Everly Brothers' Greatest Hits	1974	3.75	7.50	15.00
❑ BR-15008 [(2)]	History of the Everly Brothers	1973	3.75	7.50	15.00
❑ ZG 30260 [(2)]	End of an Era	1971	3.75	7.50	15.00

CADENCE
❑ CLP-3003 [M]	The Everly Brothers	1958	25.00	50.00	100.00
—Maroon label with metronome logo					
❑ CLP-3003 [M]	The Everly Brothers	1962	15.00	30.00	60.00
—Red label with black border					
❑ CLP-3016 [M]	Songs Our Daddy Taught Us	1958	25.00	50.00	100.00
—Maroon label with metronome logo					
❑ CLP-3016 [M]	Songs Our Daddy Taught Us	1962	15.00	30.00	60.00
—Red label with black border					
❑ CLP-3025 [M]	The Everly Brothers' Best	1959	22.50	45.00	90.00
—Maroon label with metronome logo					
❑ CLP-3025 [M]	The Everly Brothers' Best	1962	15.00	30.00	60.00
—Red label with black border					
❑ CLP-3040 [M]	The Fabulous Style of the Everly Brothers	1960	20.00	40.00	80.00
—Maroon label with metronome logo					
❑ CLP-3040 [M]	The Fabulous Style of the Everly Brothers	1962	12.50	25.00	50.00
—Red label with black border					
❑ CLP-3059 [M]	Folk Songs of the Everly Brothers	1963	12.50	25.00	50.00
—Reissue of 3016					
❑ CLP-3062 [M]	15 Everly Hits 15	1963	10.00	20.00	40.00
❑ CLP-25040 [P]	The Fabulous Style of the Everly Brothers	1960	30.00	60.00	120.00
—Maroon label with metronome logo					
❑ CLP-25040 [P]	The Fabulous Style of the Everly Brothers	1962	15.00	30.00	60.00
—Red label with black border					
❑ CLP-25059 [R]	Folk Songs of the Everly Brothers	1963	10.00	20.00	40.00
❑ CLP-25062 [P]	15 Everly Hits 15	1963	12.50	25.00	50.00

HARMONY
❑ HS 11304	Wake Up Little Susie	1969	3.00	6.00	12.00
❑ HS 11350	Christmas with the Everly Brothers and the Boys Town Choir	1969	5.00	10.00	20.00
❑ KH 11388	Chained to a Memory	1970	3.00	6.00	12.00

MERCURY
❑ 822431-1	EB 84	1984	2.50	5.00	10.00
❑ 826142-1	Born Yesterday	1986	2.50	5.00	10.00
❑ 832520-1	Some Hearts	1989	3.00	6.00	12.00

PAIR
❑ PDL1-1063 [(2)]	Living Legends	1986	3.00	6.00	12.00

PASSPORT
❑ 11001 [(2)]	The Everly Brothers Reunion Concert	1984	3.75	7.50	15.00

RCA VICTOR
❑ LSP-4620	Stories We Could Tell	1972	3.75	7.50	15.00
❑ LSP-4781	Pass the Chicken and Listen	1972	3.75	7.50	15.00
❑ AFL1-5401	Home Again	1985	2.50	5.00	10.00

RHINO
❑ RNLP-211	The Everly Brothers	1985	2.50	5.00	10.00
❑ RNLP-212	Songs Our Daddy Taught Us	1985	2.50	5.00	10.00
❑ RNLP-213	The Fabulous Style of the Everly Brothers	1985	2.50	5.00	10.00
❑ RNLP-214	All They Had to Do Was Dream	1985	2.50	5.00	10.00
❑ RNDF-258 [PD]	Heartaches and Harmonies	1985	5.00	10.00	20.00
❑ RNLP-70173	The Best of the Everly Brothers (Golden Archive Series)	1987	2.50	5.00	10.00

TIME-LIFE
❑ SRNR-09 [(2)]	The Everly Brothers: 1957-1962	1986	5.00	10.00	20.00
—Part of "The Rock 'n' Roll Era" series; box set with insert					

WARNER BROS.
❑ PRO 134 [10]	It's Everly Time!	1960	150.00	300.00	600.00
—Promo "souvenir sampler" from their debut on WB					
❑ W 1381 [M]	It's Everly Time!	1960	7.50	15.00	30.00
❑ WS 1381 [S]	It's Everly Time!	1960	10.00	20.00	40.00
❑ W 1395 [M]	A Date with the Everly Brothers	1960	10.00	20.00	40.00
—Gatefold edition without poster or photos					
❑ W 1395 [M]	A Date with the Everly Brothers	1960	12.50	25.00	50.00
—Gatefold edition with poster and wallet-size photos					
❑ W 1395 [M]	A Date with the Everly Brothers	1961	7.50	15.00	30.00
—Regular edition					
❑ WS 1395 [S]	A Date with the Everly Brothers	1960	12.50	25.00	50.00
—Gatefold edition without poster or photos					

Number	Title (A Side/B Side)	Yr	VG	VG+	NM
❑ WS 1395 [S]	A Date with the Everly Brothers	1960	18.75	37.50	75.00
—Gatefold edition with poster and wallet-size photos					
❑ WS 1395 [S]	A Date with the Everly Brothers	1961	10.00	20.00	40.00
—Regular edition					
❑ W 1418 [M]	Both Sides of an Evening	1961	7.50	15.00	30.00
❑ WS 1418 [S]	Both Sides of an Evening	1961	10.00	20.00	40.00
❑ W 1430 [M]	Instant Party!	1962	7.50	15.00	30.00
❑ WS 1430 [S]	Instant Party!	1962	10.00	20.00	40.00
❑ W 1471 [M]	The Golden Hits of the Everly Brothers	1962	7.50	15.00	30.00
❑ WS 1471	The Golden Hits of the Everly Brothers	1967	5.00	10.00	20.00
—Green "W7" label					
❑ WS 1471	The Golden Hits of the Everly Brothers	1970	3.75	7.50	15.00
—Green "WB" label					
❑ WS 1471	The Golden Hits of the Everly Brothers	1973	3.00	6.00	12.00
—"Burbank" palm-tree label					
❑ WS 1471	The Golden Hits of the Everly Brothers	1979	2.50	5.00	10.00
—White or tan label					
❑ WS 1471 [S]	The Golden Hits of the Everly Brothers	1962	10.00	20.00	40.00
—Gold label					
❑ W 1483 [M]	Christmas with the Everly Brothers and the Boys Town Choir	1962	10.00	20.00	40.00
❑ WS 1483 [S]	Christmas with the Everly Brothers and the Boys Town Choir	1962	12.50	25.00	50.00
❑ W 1513 [M]	Great Country Hits	1963	10.00	20.00	40.00
❑ WS 1513 [S]	Great Country Hits	1963	12.50	25.00	50.00
❑ W 1554 [M]	The Very Best of the Everly Brothers	1964	7.50	15.00	30.00
—Originals have yellow covers					
❑ W 1554 [M]	The Very Best of the Everly Brothers	1965	5.00	10.00	20.00
—Later pressings have white covers					
❑ WS 1554	The Very Best of the Everly Brothers	1967	5.00	10.00	20.00
—Green "W7" label					
❑ WS 1554	The Very Best of the Everly Brothers	1970	3.75	7.50	15.00
—Green "WB" label					
❑ WS 1554	The Very Best of the Everly Brothers	1973	3.00	6.00	12.00
—"Burbank" palm-tree label					
❑ WS 1554	The Very Best of the Everly Brothers	1979	2.50	5.00	10.00
—White or tan label					
❑ WS 1554 [S]	The Very Best of the Everly Brothers	1964	10.00	20.00	40.00
—Originals have yellow covers					
❑ WS 1554 [S]	The Very Best of the Everly Brothers	1965	6.25	12.50	25.00
—White cover; gold label					
❑ W 1578 [M]	Rock & Soul	1964	10.00	20.00	40.00
❑ WS 1578 [S]	Rock & Soul	1964	12.50	25.00	50.00
❑ W 1585 [M]	Gone, Gone, Gone	1965	10.00	20.00	40.00
❑ WS 1585 [S]	Gone, Gone, Gone	1965	12.50	25.00	50.00
❑ W 1605 [M]	Beat & Soul	1965	10.00	20.00	40.00
❑ WS 1605 [S]	Beat & Soul	1965	12.50	25.00	50.00
❑ W 1620 [M]	In Our Image	1966	10.00	20.00	40.00
❑ WS 1620 [S]	In Our Image	1966	12.50	25.00	50.00
❑ W 1646 [M]	Two Yanks in London	1966	10.00	20.00	40.00
❑ WS 1646 [S]	Two Yanks in London	1966	12.50	25.00	50.00
❑ W 1676 [M]	The Hit Sound of the Everly Brothers	1967	12.50	25.00	50.00
❑ WS 1676 [S]	The Hit Sound of the Everly Brothers	1967	10.00	20.00	40.00
❑ W 1708 [M]	The Everly Brothers Sing	1967	12.50	25.00	50.00
❑ WS 1708 [S]	The Everly Brothers Sing	1967	10.00	20.00	40.00
❑ WS 1752	Roots	1968	10.00	20.00	40.00
❑ WS 1858	The Everly Brothers Show	1970	7.50	15.00	30.00
❑ ST-91343 [S]	The Very Best of the Everly Brothers	1967	10.00	20.00	40.00
—Capitol Record Club edition					
❑ ST-91601	Roots	1968	12.50	25.00	50.00
—Capitol Record Club edition					
❑ STAO-93286	The Everly Brothers Show	1970	10.00	20.00	40.00
—Capitol Record Club edition					

EVERPRESENT FULLNESS, THE
WHITE WHALE
❑ 7132	The Everpresent Fullness	1970	6.25	12.50	25.00

EVERY MOTHERS' SON
MGM
❑ E-4471 [M]	Every Mothers' Son	1967	5.00	10.00	20.00
❑ SE-4471 [S]	Every Mothers' Son	1967	5.00	10.00	20.00
❑ E-4504 [M]	Every Mothers' Son's Back	1967	5.00	10.00	20.00
❑ SE-4504 [S]	Every Mothers' Son's Back	1967	5.00	10.00	20.00

EVERYTHING IS EVERYTHING
VANGUARD
❑ VSD-6512	Everything Is Everything	1969	6.25	12.50	25.00

EWELL, DON
ANALOGUE PRODUCTIONS
❑ APJ-19	Yellow Dog Blues	199?	6.25	12.50	25.00
—Audiophile reissue on red vinyl					

AUDIOPHILE
❑ APS-5966	Yellow Dog Blues	196?	5.00	10.00	20.00

GHB
❑ 30	Don Ewell in New Orleans	196?	5.00	10.00	20.00

GOOD TIME JAZZ
❑ S-10043 [S]	The Man Here Plays Fine Piano	1960	6.25	12.50	25.00
❑ S-10046 [S]	Free 'N Easy	1960	6.25	12.50	25.00
❑ L-12021 [M]	Music to Listen to Don Ewell By	1955	10.00	20.00	40.00
❑ L-12043 [M]	The Man Here Plays Fine Piano	1956	10.00	20.00	40.00
❑ L-12046 [M]	Free 'N Easy	1956	10.00	20.00	40.00

WINDIN' BALL
❑ LP-101 [10]	Don Ewell	1953	12.50	25.00	50.00
❑ LP-102 [10]	Don Ewell and Mama Yancey	1953	12.50	25.00	50.00
❑ LP-103 [10]	Don Ewell Plays Tunes Played by the King Oliver Band	1953	12.50	25.00	50.00
❑ LP-103 [M]	Don Ewell Plays Tunes Played by the King Oliver Band	195?	7.50	15.00	30.00

E

Number	Title (A Side/B Side)	Yr	VG	VG+	NM

EXCITERS, THE
RCA VICTOR
| ❑ LSP-4211 | Caviar and Chitlins | 1969 | 7.50 | 15.00 | 30.00 |

ROULETTE
| ❑ R 25326 [M] | The Exciters | 1966 | 7.50 | 15.00 | 30.00 |
| ❑ SR 25326 [S] | The Exciters | 1966 | 10.00 | 20.00 | 40.00 |

TODAY
| ❑ 1001 | Black Beauty | 1971 | 5.00 | 10.00 | 20.00 |

UNITED ARTISTS
| ❑ UAL-3264 [M] | Tell Him | 1963 | 17.50 | 35.00 | 70.00 |
| ❑ UAS-6264 [S] | Tell Him | 1963 | 37.50 | 75.00 | 150.00 |

EYES OF BLUE
MERCURY
| ❑ SR-61184 | Crossroads of Time | 1968 | 7.50 | 15.00 | 30.00 |
| ❑ SR-61220 | In Fields of Ardath | 1969 | 7.50 | 15.00 | 30.00 |

EZELL, WILLIAM
RIVERSIDE
| ❑ RLP-1043 [10] | Gin Mill Jazz | 1954 | 20.00 | 40.00 | 80.00 |

F

FABARES, SHELLEY
COLPIX
❑ CP-426 [M]	Shelley!	1962	37.50	75.00	150.00
❑ SCP-426 [S]	Shelley!	1962	150.00	300.00	600.00
❑ CP-431 [M]	The Things We Did Last Summer	1962	25.00	50.00	100.00
❑ SCP-431 [S]	The Things We Did Last Summer	1962	100.00	200.00	400.00

FABIAN
ABC
| ❑ X-806 | 16 Greatest Hits | 1973 | 3.00 | 6.00 | 12.00 |

CHANCELLOR
❑ CHL-5003 [M]	Hold That Tiger!	1959	12.50	25.00	50.00
—Black label					
❑ CHL-5003 [M]	Hold That Tiger!	1959	25.00	50.00	100.00
—Pink label					
❑ CHLS-5003 [S]	Hold That Tiger!	1959	18.75	37.50	75.00
—Black label					
❑ CHLS-5003 [S]	Hold That Tiger!	1959	37.50	75.00	150.00
—Pink label					
❑ CHL-5005 [M]	Fabulous Fabian	1959	12.50	25.00	50.00
❑ CHLS-5005 [S]	Fabulous Fabian	1959	18.75	37.50	75.00
❑ CHL-5012 [M]	The Good Old Summertime	1960	12.50	25.00	50.00
❑ CHLS-5012 [S]	The Good Old Summertime	1960	18.75	37.50	75.00
❑ CHL-5019 [M]	Rockin' Hot	1961	18.75	37.50	75.00
❑ CHL-5024 [M]	Fabian's 16 Fabulous Hits	1962	18.75	37.50	75.00
❑ CHL-69802 [M]	The Fabian Facade: Young and Wonderful	1960	20.00	40.00	80.00
—Felt gatefold cover with die-cut window					

MCA
| ❑ 27095 | The Best of Fabian | 1985 | 2.00 | 4.00 | 8.00 |

UNITED ARTISTS
| ❑ UA-LA449-E | The Very Best of Fabian | 1975 | 3.00 | 6.00 | 12.00 |

FABIAN / FRANKIE AVALON
CHANCELLOR
| ❑ CHL-5009 [M] | The Hit Makers | 1960 | 25.00 | 50.00 | 100.00 |

FABRIC, BENT
ATCO
| ❑ SD 33-148 [S] | Alley Cat | 1962 | 5.00 | 10.00 | 20.00 |

FABULOUS COUNTS, THE
COTILLION
❑ SD 9011	Jan Jan	1969	25.00	50.00	100.00
❑ SD 9011	Jan Jan	199?	3.00	6.00	12.00
—Reissue; superficially almost identical to original					

FABULOUS FLIPPERS, THE
VERITAS
| ❑ VS-2570 | Something Tangible | 1970 | 6.25 | 12.50 | 25.00 |

FABULOUS JOKERS, THE
MONUMENT
| ❑ MLP-8059 [M] | Guitars Extraordinaire | 1966 | 25.00 | 50.00 | 100.00 |
| ❑ SLP-18059 [S] | Guitars Extraordinaire | 1966 | 37.50 | 75.00 | 150.00 |

FABULOUS POODLES
EPIC
| ❑ JE 35666 [DJ] | Mirror Stars | 1978 | 5.00 | 10.00 | 20.00 |
| —White label promo on pink vinyl | | | | | |

FACENDA, JOHN (NARRATOR)
MANUSCRIPT
| ❑ MLP-571 [M] | The Nativity | 1957 | 10.00 | 20.00 | 40.00 |
| —Original Philadelphia-area issue; gatefold with 12-page booklet | | | | | |
RCA VICTOR
| ❑ LOP-1504 [M] | The Nativity | 1958 | 7.50 | 15.00 | 30.00 |
| —National reissue of Manuscript LP; very similar to original issue | | | | | |

FACES
Also see SMALL FACES; ROD STEWART; RONNIE WOOD.
WARNER BROS.
❑ WS 1851	First Step	197?	3.00	6.00	12.00
—Later pressings have "faces." on front cover					
❑ WS 1851	First Step	1970	5.00	10.00	20.00
—First pressings have "small faces." on front cover					
❑ WS 1892	Long Player	1971	3.75	7.50	15.00

❑ BS 2574	A Nod Is As Good As a Wink...To a Blind Horse	1971	3.75	7.50	15.00
—Green label					
❑ BS 2574	A Nod Is As Good As a Wink...To a Blind Horse	1973	3.00	6.00	12.00
—"Burbank" palm trees label					
❑ BS 2665	Ooh La La	1973	3.00	6.00	12.00
—"Burbank" palm trees label					
❑ BS 2665	Ooh La La	1973	3.75	7.50	15.00
—Green label					
❑ BS 2897	Snakes and Ladders: The Best of Faces	1976	3.00	6.00	12.00

FAGEN, DONALD
MOBILE FIDELITY
| ❑ 1-120 | The Nightfly | 1982 | 10.00 | 20.00 | 40.00 |
| —Audiophile vinyl | | | | | |
WARNER BROS.
| ❑ 23696 | The Nightfly | 1982 | 2.00 | 4.00 | 8.00 |

FAGERQUIST, DON
MODE
| ❑ LP-124 [M] | Music to Fill a Void | 1957 | 25.00 | 50.00 | 100.00 |

FAHEY, JOHN
REPRISE
| ❑ MS 2089 | Of Rivers and Religions | 1972 | 5.00 | 10.00 | 20.00 |
| ❑ MS 2145 | After the Ball | 1973 | 5.00 | 10.00 | 20.00 |
RIVERBOAT
| ❑ 1 [M] | The Transfiguration of Blind Joe Death | 1965 | 25.00 | 50.00 | 100.00 |
| —With booklet | | | | | |
SHANACHIE
| ❑ 97006 | God, Time and Causality | 1990 | 3.75 | 7.50 | 15.00 |
TABLE OF THE ELEMENTS
| ❑ 38 [(2)] | Georgia Stomps, Atlanta Struts, and Other Contemporary Dance Favorites | 1999 | 5.00 | 10.00 | 20.00 |
TAKOMA
❑ C-1002	Blind Joe Death	196?	10.00	20.00	40.00
❑ C-1003	Death Chants, Breakdowns and Military Waltzes	196?	10.00	20.00	40.00
❑ C-1004	Dance of Death and Other Plantation Favorites	196?	10.00	20.00	40.00
❑ C-1008	The Great San Bernardino Birthday Party	196?	7.50	15.00	30.00
❑ C-1014	Days Have Gone By	196?	7.50	15.00	30.00
❑ C-1019	The Voice of the Turtle	197?	3.75	7.50	15.00
—Later pressings with no gatefold					
❑ C-1019	The Voice of the Turtle	1971	7.50	15.00	30.00
—With gatefold jacket and booklet					
❑ C-1020	The New Possibility: John Fahey's Guitar Soli Christmas Album	1968	6.25	12.50	25.00
—Originals with back cover liner notes					
❑ C-1020	The New Possibility: John Fahey's Guitar Soli Christmas Album	197?	3.75	7.50	15.00
—Later pressings with no liner notes					
❑ C-1030	America	197?	3.75	7.50	15.00
—Later pressings with no gatefold					
❑ C-1030	America	1972	6.25	12.50	25.00
—With gatefold jacket and booklet					
❑ C-1035	Fare Forward Voyagers	1973	5.00	10.00	20.00
❑ C-1043	Old Fashioned Love	1975	3.75	7.50	15.00
❑ C-1045	Christmas with John Fahey, Vol. 2	1975	3.75	7.50	15.00
❑ C-1058	The Best of John Fahey 1959-1977	1977	3.75	7.50	15.00
❑ TAK-7003	Blind Joe Death	1979	3.00	6.00	12.00
—Reissue of 1002					
❑ TAK-7003	Death Chants, Breakdowns and Military Waltzes	198?	3.00	6.00	12.00
—Reissue of 1003					
❑ TAK-7004	Dance of Death and Other Plantation Favorites	198?	3.00	6.00	12.00
—Reissue of 1004					
❑ TAK-7020	The New Possibility: John Fahey's Guitar Soli Christmas Album	198?	3.00	6.00	12.00
—Reissue of 1020					
❑ TAK-7035	Fare Forward Voyagers	198?	3.00	6.00	12.00
—Reissue of 1035					
❑ TAK-7043	Old Fashioned Love	198?	3.00	6.00	12.00
—Reissue of 1043					
❑ TAK-7045	Christmas with John Fahey, Vol. 2	198?	3.00	6.00	12.00
—Reissue of 1045					
❑ TAK-7058	The Best of John Fahey 1959-1977	198?	3.00	6.00	12.00
—Reissue of 1058					
❑ TAK-7069	John Fahey Visits Washington, D.C.	1979	3.00	6.00	12.00
❑ TAK-7085	Yes! Jesus Loves Me	1980	3.00	6.00	12.00
❑ TAK-7089	Live in Tasmania	198?	3.00	6.00	12.00
❑ TAK-7102	Railroads I	1981	3.00	6.00	12.00
TERRA
| ❑ T-2 | Requia | 1985 | 2.50 | 5.00 | 10.00 |
| —Reissue of Vanguard 79259 | | | | | |
VANGUARD
❑ VSD 55/56 [(2)]	Essential John Fahey	1974	5.00	10.00	20.00
❑ VRS-9259 [M]	Requia	1968	6.25	12.50	25.00
❑ VSD-79259 [S]	Requia	1968	5.00	10.00	20.00
❑ VSD-79293	The Yellow Princess	1969	5.00	10.00	20.00
VARRICK
❑ VR-002	John Fahey Christmas Guitar, Volume 1	1982	3.75	7.50	15.00
❑ VR-008	Let Go	1983	3.75	7.50	15.00
❑ VR-012	Popular Songs of Christmas and New Year's	1983	3.75	7.50	15.00
❑ VR-019	Rain Forests, Oceans & Other Themes	1985	3.00	6.00	12.00
❑ VR-028	I Remember Blind Joe Death	1987	3.00	6.00	12.00

FAIR, YVONNE
MOTOWN
| ❑ M6-832S1 | The Bitch Is Black | 1975 | 7.50 | 15.00 | 30.00 |

FAIRPORT CONVENTION
A&M
| ❑ SP-3530 [(2)] | The Fairport Chronicles | 1976 | 3.75 | 7.50 | 15.00 |

Number	Title (A Side/B Side)	Yr	VG	VG+	NM
❏ SP-3603	Fairport Nine	1974	3.00	6.00	12.00
—Early reissue of 4407					
❏ SP-4185	Fairport Convention	1969	3.75	7.50	15.00
—Not a reissue of Cotillion LP, but the US issue of the second UK LP "What We Did On Our Holidays"					
❏ SP-4206	Unhalfbricking	1969	3.75	7.50	15.00
❏ SP-4257	Liege and Lief	1970	3.75	7.50	15.00
❏ SP-4265	Full House	1970	3.75	7.50	15.00
❏ SP-4316	Angel Delight	1971	3.75	7.50	15.00
❏ SP-4333	"Babbacombe" Lee	1972	3.75	7.50	15.00
❏ SP-4383	Rosie	1973	3.75	7.50	15.00
❏ SP-4407	Fairport Nine	1973	3.75	7.50	15.00
❏ SP-6016 [(2)]	The Fairport Chronicles	198?	3.00	6.00	12.00
—Reissue of 3530					
ANTILLES					
❏ 7054	Gottle O' Geer	1976	3.00	6.00	12.00
CARTHAGE					
❏ CGLP-4417	Full House	198?	2.50	5.00	10.00
—Reissue of A&M 4265					
❏ CGLP-4418	Unhalfbricking	198?	2.50	5.00	10.00
—Reissue of A&M 4206					
❏ CGLP-4430	What We Did on Our Holidays	198?	2.50	5.00	10.00
—Reissue of A&M 4185 with UK title restored					
COTILLION					
❏ 9024 [M]	Fairport Convention	1968	20.00	40.00	80.00
—Mono is white label promo only; "DJ Copy Monaural" sticker on front cover					
❏ SD 9024 [S]	Fairport Convention	1968	7.50	15.00	30.00
HANNIBAL					
❏ HNBL-1319	House Full	1986	2.50	5.00	10.00
❏ HNBL-1329	Heyday	1987	2.50	5.00	10.00
ISLAND					
❏ ILPS-9285	Fairport Live/A Movable Feast	1974	3.00	6.00	12.00
❏ ILPS-9313	Rising for the Moon	1975	3.00	6.00	12.00
❏ 90678	In Real Time — Live '87	1987	2.50	5.00	10.00
VARRICK					
❏ VR-023	Gladys' Leap	1986	2.50	5.00	10.00
❏ VR-029	Expletive Delighted!	1987	2.50	5.00	10.00

FAITH, ADAM
AMY

Number	Title (A Side/B Side)	Yr	VG	VG+	NM
❏ 8005 [M]	Adam Faith	1965	6.25	12.50	25.00
❏ S-8005 [S]	Adam Faith	1965	0.50	15.00	30.00
MGM					
❏ E-3951 [M]	England's Top Singer	1961	10.00	20.00	40.00
❏ SE-3951 [S]	England's Top Singer	1961	12.50	25.00	50.00

FAITH, PERCY
COLUMBIA

Number	Title (A Side/B Side)	Yr	VG	VG+	NM
❏ GP 1 [(2)]	Forever Young	1968	3.75	7.50	15.00
❏ C2L 15 [(2)M]	The Columbia Album of Christmas Music	1958	7.50	15.00	30.00
—Combines CL 588 and CL 1187 into one gatefold package					
❏ CL 525 [M]	Continental Music	1955	5.00	10.00	20.00
❏ CL 550 [M]	Kismet	1955	5.00	10.00	20.00
❏ CL 577 [M]	Music from Hollywood	1955	5.00	10.00	20.00
❏ CL 588 [M]	Music of Christmas	1955	6.25	12.50	25.00
❏ CL 640 [M]	House of Flowers	1956	5.00	10.00	20.00
❏ CL 681 [M]	Delicado	1956	5.00	10.00	20.00
❏ CL 705 [M]	Music for Her	1956	5.00	10.00	20.00
❏ CL 880 [M]	Passport to Romance	1956	5.00	10.00	20.00
❏ CL 895 [M]	My Fair Lady	1957	5.00	10.00	20.00
❏ CL 955 [M]	L'il Abner	1957	5.00	10.00	20.00
❏ CL 1010 [M]	Adventure in the Sun	1957	5.00	10.00	20.00
❏ CS 1019	Held Over! Today's Great Movie Themes	1970	3.00	6.00	12.00
❏ CL 1075 [M]	Viva!	1957	5.00	10.00	20.00
❏ CL 1105 [M]	South Pacific	1957	3.75	7.50	15.00
❏ CL 1182 [M]	Touchdown!	1957	5.00	10.00	20.00
❏ CL 1187 [M]	Hallelujah!	1957	5.00	10.00	20.00
❏ CL 1188 [M]	Jubilation!	1957	5.00	10.00	20.00
❏ CL 1267 [M]	Malaguena	1958	5.00	10.00	20.00
❏ CL 1298 [M]	Porgy and Bess	1958	3.75	7.50	15.00
❏ CL 1302 [M]	A Night with Sigmund Romberg	1959	3.75	7.50	15.00
❏ CL 1322 [M]	Bouquet	1959	3.75	7.50	15.00
❏ CL 1381 [M]	Music of Christmas	1959	5.00	10.00	20.00
—Re-recorded version of CL 588 with same track order					
❏ CL 1386 [M]	A Night with Jerome Kern	1959	3.75	7.50	15.00
❏ CL 1417 [M]	Bon Voyage!	1960	3.75	7.50	15.00
❏ CL 1418 [M]	The Sound of Music	1960	3.75	7.50	15.00
❏ CL 1493 [M]	Percy Faith's Greatest Hits	1960	3.75	7.50	15.00
❏ CL 1501 [M]	Jealousy	1960	3.00	6.00	12.00
❏ CL 1570 [M]	Camelot	1960	3.00	6.00	12.00
❏ CL 1627 [M]	Tara's Theme from "Gone with the Wind" and Other Themes	1961	3.00	6.00	12.00
❏ CL 1639 [M]	Mucho Gusto! More Music of Brazil	1961	3.00	6.00	12.00
❏ CL 1681 [M]	Bouquet of Love	1962	3.00	6.00	12.00
❏ CL 1783 [M]	Hollywood's Great Themes	1962	3.00	6.00	12.00
❏ CL 1822 [M]	The Music of Brazil!	1962	3.00	6.00	12.00
❏ CL 1902 [M]	Exotic Strings	1963	3.00	6.00	12.00
❏ CL 1957 [M]	American Serenade	1963	3.00	6.00	12.00
❏ CL 2023 [M]	Themes for Young Lovers	1963	3.00	6.00	12.00
❏ CL 2024 [M]	Shangri-La!	1963	3.00	6.00	12.00
❏ CL 2108 [M]	Great Folk Themes	1964	3.00	6.00	12.00
❏ CL 2167 [M]	More Themes for Young Lovers	1964	3.00	6.00	12.00
❏ CL 2209 [M]	Love Goddess	1966	3.00	6.00	12.00
❏ CL 2279 [M]	Latin Themes for Young Lovers	1966	3.00	6.00	12.00
❏ CL 2317 [M]	Do I Hear a Waltz	1965	3.00	6.00	12.00
❏ CL 2356 [M]	Broadway Bouquet	1965	3.00	6.00	12.00
❏ CL 2405 [M]	Music of Christmas, Volume 2	1965	3.00	6.00	12.00
❏ CL 2441 [M]	Themes for the "In" Crowd	1966	3.00	6.00	12.00
❏ CL 2529 [M]	Bim Bam Boom	1966	3.00	6.00	12.00
❏ CL 2577 [M]	Christmas Is…	1966	3.00	6.00	12.00
❏ CL 2650 [M]	The Academy Award Winner and Other Great Movie Themes	1967	3.75	7.50	15.00

Number	Title (A Side/B Side)	Yr	VG	VG+	NM
❏ CL 2704 [M]	Today's Themes for Young Lovers	1967	3.75	7.50	15.00
❏ CL 2810 [M]	For Those in Love	1968	5.00	10.00	20.00
❏ CL 2906 [M]	Angel of the Morning (Hit Themes for Young Lovers)	1968	5.00	10.00	20.00
❏ CS 8033 [S]	South Pacific	1958	6.25	12.50	25.00
❏ CS 8033 [S]	Hallelujah!	1958	6.25	12.50	25.00
❏ CS 8038 [S]	Viva!	1958	6.25	12.50	25.00
❏ CS 8081 [S]	Malaguena	1958	6.25	12.50	25.00
❏ CS 8105 [S]	Porgy and Bess	1959	5.00	10.00	20.00
❏ CS 8108 [S]	A Night with Sigmund Romberg	1959	5.00	10.00	20.00
❏ CS 8124 [S]	Bouquet	1959	3.75	7.50	15.00
❏ CS 8176 [S]	Music of Christmas	1959	3.75	7.50	15.00
❏ CS 8181 [S]	A Night with Jerome Kern	1959	5.00	10.00	20.00
❏ CS 8214 [S]	Bon Voyage!	1960	3.75	7.50	15.00
❏ CS 8215 [S]	The Sound of Music	1960	3.75	7.50	15.00
❏ CS 8292 [S]	Jealousy	1960	3.75	7.50	15.00
❏ CS 8370 [S]	Camelot	1960	3.75	7.50	15.00
❏ CS 8427 [S]	Tara's Theme from "Gone with the Wind" and Other Themes	1961	3.75	7.50	15.00
❏ CS 8439 [S]	Mucho Gusto! More Music of Brazil	1961	3.75	7.50	15.00
❏ CS 8481 [S]	Bouquet of Love	1962	3.75	7.50	15.00
❏ CS 8583 [S]	Hollywood's Great Themes	1962	3.75	7.50	15.00
❏ CS 8622 [S]	The Music of Brazil!	1962	3.75	7.50	15.00
❏ CS 8637 [R]	Percy Faith's Greatest Hits	1963	2.50	5.00	10.00
❏ PC 8637 [R]	Percy Faith's Greatest Hits	198?	2.00	4.00	8.00
—Budget-line reissue					
❏ CS 8642 [R]	Kismet	1963	2.50	5.00	10.00
❏ CS 8702 [S]	Exotic Strings	1963	3.00	6.00	12.00
❏ CS 8757 [S]	American Serenade	1963	3.00	6.00	12.00
❏ CS 8823 [S]	Themes for Young Lovers	1963	3.00	6.00	12.00
❏ CS 8824 [S]	Shangri-La!	1963	3.00	6.00	12.00
❏ CS 8908 [S]	Great Folk Themes	1964	3.00	6.00	12.00
❏ CS 8967 [S]	More Themes for Young Lovers	1964	3.00	6.00	12.00
❏ CS 9004 [R]	My Fair Lady	1964	3.00	6.00	12.00
❏ CS 9009 [S]	Love Goddess	1964	3.00	6.00	12.00
❏ CS 9079 [S]	Latin Themes for Young Lovers	1965	3.00	6.00	12.00
❏ CS 9117 [S]	Do I Hear a Waltz	1965	3.00	6.00	12.00
❏ CS 9156 [S]	Broadway Bouquet	1965	3.00	6.00	12.00
❏ CS 9205 [S]	Music of Christmas, Volume 2	1965	3.00	6.00	12.00
❏ CS 9241 [S]	Themes for the "In" Crowd	1966	3.00	6.00	12.00
❏ CS 9329 [S]	Bim Bam Boom	1966	3.00	6.00	12.00
❏ 3C 9377	Christmas Is…	198?	2.00	4.00	8.00
—Budget-line reissue					
❏ CS 9377 [S]	Christmas Is…	1966	3.00	6.00	12.00
❏ CS 9450 [S]	The Academy Award Winner and Other Great Movie Themes	1967	3.00	6.00	12.00
❏ CS 9504 [S]	Today's Themes for Young Lovers	1967	3.00	6.00	12.00
❏ CS 9610 [S]	For Those in Love	1968	3.00	6.00	12.00
❏ CS 9706 [S]	Angel of the Morning (Hit Themes for Young Lovers)	1968	3.00	6.00	12.00
❏ CS 9762	Those Were the Days	1969	3.00	6.00	12.00
❏ CS 9835	Windmills of Your Mind	1969	3.00	6.00	12.00
❏ CS 9906	Love Theme from "Romeo & Juliet"	1969	3.00	6.00	12.00
❏ CS 9983	Leaving on a Jet Plane	1970	3.00	6.00	12.00
❏ C 30097	The Beatles Album	1970	3.00	6.00	12.00
❏ G 30330 [(2)]	A Time for Love	1971	3.75	7.50	15.00
❏ C 30502	I Think I Love You	1971	2.50	5.00	10.00
❏ C 30800	Black Magic Woman	1971	2.50	5.00	10.00
❏ CQ 31004 [Q]	Love Theme from "Romeo & Juliet"	1971	3.75	7.50	15.00
❏ C 31042	Jesus Christ Superstar	1971	2.50	5.00	10.00
❏ C 31301	Joy	1972	2.50	5.00	10.00
❏ KG 31588 [(2)]	All-Time Greatest Hits	1972	3.00	6.00	12.00
❏ PG 31588 [(2)]	All-Time Greatest Hits	198?	2.50	5.00	10.00
—Budget-line reissue					
❏ KC 31627	Day By Day	1972	2.50	5.00	10.00
❏ CQ 32164 [Q]	Clair	1973	3.75	7.50	15.00
❏ KC 32164	Clair	1973	2.50	5.00	10.00
❏ KC 32380	My Love	1973	2.50	5.00	10.00
❏ C 32585	Remembering the Hits of the 60's	1973	2.50	5.00	10.00
❏ KC 32714	Corazon	1974	2.50	5.00	10.00
❏ KC 32803	A New Thing	1974	2.50	5.00	10.00
❏ KC 33142	Country Bouquet	1975	2.50	5.00	10.00
❏ CQ 33244 [Q]	Chinatown (Featuring "The Entertainer")	1974	3.75	7.50	15.00
❏ KC 33244	Chinatown (Featuring "The Entertainer")	1974	2.50	5.00	10.00
❏ KC 33549	Disco Party	1975	2.50	5.00	10.00
❏ CG 33606 [(2)]	Viva!/Mucho Gusto!	1975	3.00	6.00	12.00
❏ CG 33895 [(2)]	Great Moments of Percy Faith	1976	3.00	6.00	12.00
❏ KC 33915	Summer of '76	1976	2.50	5.00	10.00
❏ PC 38302	Music of Christmas	1983	2.00	4.00	8.00
❏ PC 39471	Christmas Melodies	1984	2.00	4.00	8.00
—Repackage of previously released material					
COLUMBIA LIMITED EDITION					
❏ LE 10082	Music of Christmas	197?	2.50	5.00	10.00
—Brown label "Limited Edition" series; same contents as CS 8176					
COLUMBIA SPECIAL PRODUCTS					
❏ P 13091	Broadway Bouquet	197?	2.00	4.00	8.00
❏ P2 13719 [(2)]	The Columbia Album of George Gershwin	197?	3.00	6.00	12.00
❏ P 13827	American Serenade	197?	2.00	4.00	8.00
HARMONY					
❏ HS 11348	Sounds of Music	1969	2.50	5.00	10.00
❏ H 30020	Younger Than Springtime	1970	2.50	5.00	10.00
❏ KH 30607	A Summer Place	1971	2.50	5.00	10.00
❏ KH 30977	Raindrops Keep Fallin'	1971	2.50	5.00	10.00
❏ KH 31777	Every Night at the Movies	1972	2.50	5.00	10.00
VOCALION					
❏ VL 3600 [M]	North and South of the Border	1958	3.75	7.50	15.00

FAITH BAND
MERCURY

Number	Title (A Side/B Side)	Yr	VG	VG+	NM
❏ SRM-1-3759	Rock'n Romance	1978	3.00	6.00	12.00
❏ SRM-1-3770	Face to Face	1979	3.00	6.00	12.00

F

Number	Title (A Side/B Side)	Yr	VG	VG+	NM
❏ SRM-1-3807	Vital Signs	1979	2.50	5.00	10.00
VILLAGE					
❏ VR 7703	Excuse Me ... I Just Cut an Album	1977	5.00	10.00	20.00
❏ VR 7805	Rock'n Romance	1978	5.00	10.00	20.00

FAITH NO MORE
MORDAM

Number	Title (A Side/B Side)	Yr	VG	VG+	NM
❏ FNM 1	We Care a Lot	1985	5.00	10.00	20.00
SLASH					
❏ 25559	Introduce Yourself	1987	2.50	5.00	10.00
❏ 25878	The Real Thing	1989	5.00	10.00	20.00
❏ 45723 [(2)]	King for a Day/Fool for a Lifetime	1995	3.00	6.00	12.00

FAITHFULL, MARIANNE
ABKCO

Number	Title (A Side/B Side)	Yr	VG	VG+	NM
❏ 75471	Greatest Hits	1988	2.50	5.00	10.00
—Reissue of London PS 547					
ISLAND					
❏ PRO 794 [EP]	Blazing Away Sampler	1990	5.00	10.00	20.00
—Promo-only sampler for radio					
❏ ILPS 9570	Broken English	1979	2.50	5.00	10.00
❏ ILPS 9648	Dangerous Acquaintances	1981	2.50	5.00	10.00
❏ 90039	Broken English	1983	2.00	4.00	8.00
—Reissue					
❏ 90066	A Child's Adventure	1983	2.50	5.00	10.00
❏ 90066 [DJ]	A Child's Adventure	1983	3.75	7.50	15.00
—Promo-only Quiex II audiophile pressing					
❏ 90613	Strange Weather	1987	2.50	5.00	10.00
LONDON					
❏ PS 423 [R]	Marianne Faithfull	1965	3.75	7.50	15.00
❏ PS 452 [S]	Go Away from My World	1965	5.00	10.00	20.00
❏ PS 482 [S]	Faithfull Forever	1966	5.00	10.00	20.00
❏ PS 547	Greatest Hits	1969	3.75	7.50	15.00
❏ LL 3423 [M]	Marianne Faithfull	1965	5.00	10.00	20.00
❏ LL 3452 [M]	Go Away from My World	1965	3.75	7.50	15.00
❏ LL 3482 [M]	Faithfull Forever	1966	3.75	7.50	15.00
MOBILE FIDELITY					
❏ 1-235	Broken English	1995	6.25	12.50	25.00
—Audiophile vinyl					

FALL, THE
BEGGARS BANQUET

Number	Title (A Side/B Side)	Yr	VG	VG+	NM
❏ 2430-1-H	458489	1990	2.50	5.00	10.00
❏ 6897-1-H	The Frenz Experiment	1988	2.50	5.00	10.00
❏ 9582-1-H	I Am Kurious Oranj	1988	2.50	5.00	10.00
❏ 9807-1-H	Seminal Live	1989	2.50	5.00	10.00
I.R.S.					
❏ SP-003	Live at the Witch Trials	1979	5.00	10.00	20.00
I.R.S./FAULTY					
❏ COPE-2	Early Years 77-79	1981	3.75	7.50	15.00
MATADOR					
❏ OLE 55-1	The Infotainment Scan	1993	2.50	5.00	10.00
❏ OLE 95-1	Middle Class Revolt	1994	2.50	5.00	10.00
PVC					
❏ 8932	The Wonderful and Frightening World of The Fall	1984	4.00	8.00	16.00
❏ 8940	This Nation's Saving Grace	1985	3.75	7.50	15.00
ROUGH TRADE					
❏ TRADE 3/10 [10]	Slates	1981	3.00	6.00	12.00
—10-inch EP					
❏ ROUGH US-8	Grotesque (After the Gramme)	1981	3.75	7.50	15.00

FALLEN ANGELS, THE
ROULETTE

Number	Title (A Side/B Side)	Yr	VG	VG+	NM
❏ R 25358 [M]	The Fallen Angels	1967	7.50	15.00	30.00
❏ SR 25358 [S]	The Fallen Angels	1967	10.00	20.00	40.00
❏ SR 42011	It's a Long Way Down	1968	25.00	50.00	100.00

FAME, GEORGIE
EPIC

Number	Title (A Side/B Side)	Yr	VG	VG+	NM
❏ BN 26368	The Ballad of Bonnie and Clyde	1968	6.25	12.50	25.00
IMPERIAL					
❏ LP-9282 [M]	Yeh, Yeh	1965	6.25	12.50	25.00
❏ LP-9331 [M]	Get Away	1966	6.25	12.50	25.00
❏ LP-12282 [P]	Yeh, Yeh	1965	7.50	15.00	30.00
—Entire album is stereo except "Yeh, Yeh" (rechanneled)					
❏ LP-12331 [R]	Get Away	1966	5.00	10.00	20.00
ISLAND					
❏ ILPS 9293	Georgie Fame	1975	2.50	5.00	10.00

FAME GANG, THE
FAME

Number	Title (A Side/B Side)	Yr	VG	VG+	NM
❏ SKAO-4200	Solid Gold from Muscle Shoals	1969	6.25	12.50	25.00

FAMILY
REPRISE

Number	Title (A Side/B Side)	Yr	VG	VG+	NM
❏ RS-6313	Music in a Doll's House	1968	5.00	10.00	20.00
❏ RS-6340	Family Entertainment	1969	3.75	7.50	15.00
❏ RS-6384	A Song for Me	1970	3.75	7.50	15.00
UNITED ARTISTS					
❏ UA-LA181-F	It's Only a Movie	1974	3.00	6.00	12.00
❏ UAS-5527	Anyway	1971	3.75	7.50	15.00
❏ UAS-5562	Fearless	1972	3.75	7.50	15.00
❏ UAS-5644	Bandstand	1972	3.75	7.50	15.00

FAMILY DOGG
BUDDAH

Number	Title (A Side/B Side)	Yr	VG	VG+	NM
❏ BDS-5100	The View from Rowland's Head	1972	6.25	12.50	25.00

FAMOUS CASTLE JAZZ BAND, THE
GOOD TIME JAZZ

Number	Title (A Side/B Side)	Yr	VG	VG+	NM
❏ S-7021 [S]	The Famous Castle Jazz Band in Stereo	1959	7.50	15.00	30.00

Number	Title (A Side/B Side)	Yr	VG	VG+	NM
❏ S-10037 [S]	The Famous Castle Jazz Band Plays the Five Pennies	1959	7.50	15.00	30.00
❏ L-12030 [M]	The Famous Castle Jazz Band in Hi-Fi	1957	10.00	20.00	40.00
❏ L-12037 [M]	The Famous Castle Jazz Band Plays the Five Pennies	1959	10.00	20.00	40.00
STEREO RECORDS					
❏ S-7021 [S]	The Famous Castle Jazz Band in Stereo	1958	10.00	20.00	40.00

FANKHAUSER, MERRILL
Also see FAPARDOKLY.
MAUI

Number	Title (A Side/B Side)	Yr	VG	VG+	NM
❏ 101	Merrill Fankhauser	1976	12.50	25.00	50.00
SHAMLEY					
❏ SS-701	Things Going Round in My Mind	1968	20.00	40.00	80.00

FANTASTIC BAGGYS, THE
IMPERIAL

Number	Title (A Side/B Side)	Yr	VG	VG+	NM
❏ LP-9270 [M]	Tell 'Em I'm Surfin'	1964	37.50	75.00	150.00
❏ LP-12270 [S]	Tell 'Em I'm Surfin'	1964	75.00	150.00	300.00
LIBERTY					
❏ LN-10192	Tell 'Em I'm Surfin'	1982	2.50	5.00	10.00

FANTASTIC DEE JAYS, THE
STONE

Number	Title (A Side/B Side)	Yr	VG	VG+	NM
❏ SLP-4003	The Fantastic Dee Jays	1966	250.00	500.00	1000.

FANTASTIC FOUR, THE
SOUL

Number	Title (A Side/B Side)	Yr	VG	VG+	NM
❏ SS-717	The Best of the Fantastic Four	1969	10.00	20.00	40.00
❏ SS-722	How Sweet He Is	1970	—	—	—
—Canceled					
WESTBOUND					
❏ W 201	Alvin Stone (The Birth and Death of a Gangster)	1975	3.75	7.50	15.00
❏ W 226	Night People	1976	3.75	7.50	15.00
❏ WT 306	Got to Have Your Love	1977	3.75	7.50	15.00
❏ WT 6108	BYOF (Bring Your Own Funk)	1978	3.75	7.50	15.00

FANTASTIC JOHNNY C, THE
PHIL-LA OF SOUL

Number	Title (A Side/B Side)	Yr	VG	VG+	NM
❏ 4000	Boogaloo Down Broadway	1968	20.00	40.00	80.00

FANTASY
LIBERTY

Number	Title (A Side/B Side)	Yr	VG	VG+	NM
❏ LSP-7643	Fantasy	1970	5.00	10.00	20.00

FAPARDOKLY
Also see MERRILL FANKHAUSER.
U.I.P.

Number	Title (A Side/B Side)	Yr	VG	VG+	NM
❏ 2250	Fapardokly	1967	250.00	500.00	1000.

FAR CRY
VANGUARD

Number	Title (A Side/B Side)	Yr	VG	VG+	NM
❏ VSD-6510	Far Cry	1969	6.25	12.50	25.00

FARDON, DON
DECCA

Number	Title (A Side/B Side)	Yr	VG	VG+	NM
❏ DL 75225	I've Paid My Dues	1970	3.75	7.50	15.00
GNP CRESCENDO					
❏ GNPS-2044	Indian Reservation	1968	5.00	10.00	20.00

FARLOW, TAL
AMERICAN RECORDING SOCIETY

Number	Title (A Side/B Side)	Yr	VG	VG+	NM
❏ G-418 [M]	The Swinging Guitar of Tal Farlow	1957	10.00	20.00	40.00
BLUE NOTE					
❏ BLP-5042 [10]	Tal Farlow Quartet	1954	75.00	150.00	300.00
NORGRAN					
❏ MGN-19 [10]	The Tal Farlow Album	1954	37.50	75.00	150.00
❏ MGN-1014 [M]	The Artistry of Tal Farlow	1955	30.00	60.00	120.00
❏ MGN-1027 [M]	The Interpretations of Tal Farlow	1955	30.00	60.00	120.00
❏ MGN-1030 [M]	A Recital by Tal Farlow	1955	25.00	50.00	100.00
❏ MGN-1047 [M]	The Tal Farlow Album	1955	25.00	50.00	100.00
❏ MGN-1097 [M]	Autumn in New York	1956	25.00	50.00	100.00
❏ MGN-1101 [M]	Fascinating Rhythm	1956	25.00	50.00	100.00
❏ MGN-1102 [M]	Tal	1956	25.00	50.00	100.00
PRESTIGE					
❏ PRST-7732	The Return of Tal Farlow/1969	1969	5.00	10.00	20.00
❏ 24042 [(2)]	Guitar Player	197?	5.00	10.00	20.00
VERVE					
❏ MGVS-6143 [S]	The Guitar Artistry of Tal Farlow	1960	10.00	20.00	40.00
❏ MGV-8011 [M]	The Interpretations of Tal Farlow	1957	12.50	25.00	50.00
—Reissue of Norgran 1027					
❏ V-8011 [M]	The Interpretations of Tal Farlow	1961	5.00	10.00	20.00
❏ MGV-8021 [M]	Tal	1957	12.50	25.00	50.00
—Reissue of Norgran 1102					
❏ V-8021 [M]	Tal	1961	5.00	10.00	20.00
❏ MGV-8123 [M]	A Recital by Tal Farlow	1957	12.50	25.00	50.00
—Reissue of Norgran 1030					
❏ V-8123 [M]	A Recital by Tal Farlow	1961	5.00	10.00	20.00
❏ MGV-8138 [M]	The Tal Farlow Album	1957	12.50	25.00	50.00
—Reissue of Norgran 1047					
❏ V-8138 [M]	The Tal Farlow Album	1961	5.00	10.00	20.00
❏ MGV-8184 [M]	Autumn in New York	1957	12.50	25.00	50.00
—Reissue of Norgran 1097					
❏ V-8184 [M]	Autumn in New York	1961	5.00	10.00	20.00
❏ MGV-8201 [M]	The Swinging Guitar of Tal Farlow	1957	12.50	25.00	50.00
❏ V-8201 [M]	The Swinging Guitar of Tal Farlow	1961	5.00	10.00	20.00
❏ MGV-8289 [M]	This Is Tal Farlow	1958	12.50	25.00	50.00
❏ V-8289 [M]	This Is Tal Farlow	1961	5.00	10.00	20.00
❏ MGV-8370 [M]	The Guitar Artistry of Tal Farlow	1960	12.50	25.00	50.00
❏ V-8370 [M]	The Guitar Artistry of Tal Farlow	1961	5.00	10.00	20.00
❏ MGV-8371 [M]	Tal Farlow Plays the Music of Harold Arlen	1960	12.50	25.00	50.00

Number	Title (A Side/B Side)	Yr	VG	VG+	NM
❑ V-8371 [M]	Tal Farlow Plays the Music of Harold Arlen	1961	5.00	10.00	20.00

FARLOWE, CHRIS
COLUMBIA
❑ CL 2593 [M]	The Fabulous Chris Farlowe	1966	10.00	20.00	40.00
❑ CS 9393 [R]	The Fabulous Chris Farlowe	1966	6.25	12.50	25.00

IMMEDIATE
❑ Z12 52010	Paint It Farlowe	1968	5.00	10.00	20.00

POLYDOR
❑ 24-4041	From Here to Mama Rosa with the Hill	1970	3.00	6.00	12.00

FARM BAND, THE
MANTRA
❑ 777 [(2)]	The Farm Band	1972	7.50	15.00	30.00
—With poster					

FARMER, ART
ABC-PARAMOUNT
❑ ABC-200 [M]	Last Night When We Were Young	1958	15.00	30.00	60.00

ARGO
❑ LP-678 [M]	Art	1961	6.25	12.50	25.00
❑ LPS-678 [S]	Art	1961	7.50	15.00	30.00
❑ LP-738 [M]	Perception	1964	6.25	12.50	25.00
❑ LPS-738 [S]	Perception	1964	7.50	15.00	30.00

ATLANTIC
❑ 1412 [M]	Interaction	1963	6.25	12.50	25.00
❑ SD 1412 [S]	Interaction	1963	7.50	15.00	30.00
❑ 1421 [M]	Live at the Half Note	1964	6.25	12.50	25.00
❑ SD 1421 [S]	Live at the Half Note	1964	7.50	15.00	30.00
❑ 1430 [M]	To Sweden with Love	1964	5.00	10.00	20.00
❑ SD 1430 [S]	To Sweden with Love	1964	6.25	12.50	25.00
❑ 1442 [M]	Sing Me Softly of the Blues	1965	5.00	10.00	20.00
❑ SD 1442 [S]	Sing Me Softly of the Blues	1965	6.25	12.50	25.00

COLUMBIA
❑ CL 2588 [M]	Baroque Sketches	1966	5.00	10.00	20.00
❑ CL 2649 [M]	The Time and the Place	1967	6.25	12.50	25.00
❑ CL 2746 [M]	Art Farmer Plays the Great Jazz Hits	1967	7.50	15.00	30.00
❑ CS 9388 [S]	Baroque Sketches	1966	5.00	10.00	20.00
❑ CS 9449 [S]	The Time and the Place	1967	5.00	10.00	20.00
❑ CS 9546 [S]	Art Farmer Plays the Great Jazz Hits	1967	5.00	10.00	20.00

CONTEMPORARY
❑ C-3554 [M]	Portrait of Art Farmer	1958	12.50	25.00	50.00
❑ S-7027 [S]	Portrait of Art Farmer	1959	7.50	15.00	30.00

MAINSTREAM
❑ MRL-332	Homecoming	1971	5.00	10.00	20.00
❑ MRL-371	Gentle Eyes	1972	5.00	10.00	20.00

MERCURY
❑ MG-20786 [M]	Listen to Art Farmer and the Orchestra	1963	5.00	10.00	20.00
❑ SR-60786 [S]	Listen to Art Farmer and the Orchestra	1963	6.25	12.50	25.00

NEW JAZZ
❑ NJLP-8203 [M]	Farmer's Market	1958	12.50	25.00	50.00
—Purple label					
❑ NJLP-8203 [M]	Farmer's Market	1958	25.00	50.00	100.00
—Yellow label					
❑ NJLP-8203 [M]	Farmer's Market	1965	6.25	12.50	25.00
—Blue label, trident logo at right					
❑ NJLP-8258 [M]	Early Art	1961	10.00	20.00	40.00
—Purple label					
❑ NJLP-8258 [M]	Early Art	1965	6.25	12.50	25.00
—Blue label, trident logo at right					
❑ NJLP-8278 [M]	Work of Art	1962	10.00	20.00	40.00
—Purple label					
❑ NJLP-8278 [M]	Work of Art	1965	6.25	12.50	25.00
—Blue label, trident logo at right					
❑ NJLP-8289 [M]	Evening in Casablanca	1962	10.00	20.00	40.00
—Purple label					
❑ NJLP-8289 [M]	Evening in Casablanca	1965	6.25	12.50	25.00
—Blue label, trident logo at right					

PRESTIGE
❑ PRLP-162 [10]	Art Farmer Septet	1953	50.00	100.00	200.00
❑ PRLP-177 [10]	Art Farmer Quintet Featuring Sonny Rollins	1954	50.00	100.00	200.00
❑ PRLP-181 [10]	Art Farmer Quintet	1954	50.00	100.00	200.00
❑ PRLP-193 [10]	Art Farmer Quartet	1954	50.00	100.00	200.00
❑ PRLP-209 [10]	Art Farmer Quintet	1955	50.00	100.00	200.00
❑ PRLP-7017 [M]	Art Farmer Quintet Featuring Gigi Gryce	1956	25.00	50.00	100.00
❑ PRLP-7031 [M]	Art Farmer Septet	1956	25.00	50.00	100.00
❑ PRLP-7062 [M]	Two Trumpets	1956	25.00	50.00	100.00
❑ PRLP-7085 [M]	When Farmer Met Gryce	1957	25.00	50.00	100.00
❑ PRLP-7092 [M]	Three Trumpets	1957	25.00	50.00	100.00
❑ PRLP-7344 [(2)M]	Trumpets All Out	1964	12.50	25.00	50.00
❑ PRST-7344 [(2)R]	Trumpets All Out	1964	7.50	15.00	30.00

SCEPTER
❑ S-521 [M]	The Many Faces of Art Farmer	1964	5.00	10.00	20.00
❑ SS-521 [S]	The Many Faces of Art Farmer	1964	6.25	12.50	25.00

STEREO RECORDS
❑ S-7027 [S]	Portrait of Art Farmer	1958	10.00	20.00	40.00

UNITED ARTISTS
❑ UAL-4007 [M]	Modern Art	1958	12.50	25.00	50.00
❑ UAL-4047 [M]	Brass Shout	1959	12.50	25.00	50.00
❑ UAL-4062 [M]	Aztec Suite	1959	12.50	25.00	50.00
❑ UAS-5007 [S]	Modern Art	1959	10.00	20.00	40.00
❑ UAS-5047 [S]	Brass Shout	1959	10.00	20.00	40.00
❑ UAS-5062 [S]	Aztec Suite	1959	10.00	20.00	40.00

FARMER, ART/ART TAYLOR
PRESTIGE
❑ PRLP-7342 [(2)M]	Hard Cookin'	1964	12.50	25.00	50.00
❑ PRST-7342 [(2)R]	Hard Cookin'	1964	7.50	15.00	30.00

FARNER, MARK, AND DON BREWER
QUADICO
❑ 7401	Monumental Funk	1977	2.50	5.00	10.00
❑ 7401 [PD]	Monumental Funk	1977	5.00	10.00	20.00
—Picture disc					

FARRAH, SHAMEK
STRATA-EAST
❑ SES-7412	First Impressions	1974	10.00	20.00	40.00

FARRELL, JOE
CTI
❑ 6003	Joe Farrell Quartet	1970	5.00	10.00	20.00
❑ 6014	Outback	1971	5.00	10.00	20.00
❑ 6023	Moon Germs	1972	5.00	10.00	20.00

FARRELL, JOE; FLORA PURIM; AIRTO MOREIRA
REFERENCE RECORDINGS
❑ RR-24	Three-Way Mirror	1989	5.00	10.00	20.00

FARRELL, RICHARD
MERCURY LIVING PRESENCE
❑ SR 90126 [S]	Liszt: Piano Concerto No. 1; Grieg: Piano Concerto in A	1960	6.25	12.50	25.00
—Maroon label, no "Vendor: Mercury Record Corporation"					

FAT CITY
ABC PROBE
❑ 4508	Reincarnation	1969	5.00	10.00	20.00

PARAMOUNT
❑ PAS-6028	Welcome to Fat City	1972	3.75	7.50	15.00

FAT MATTRESS
ATCO
❑ 33-309 [M]	Fat Mattress	1969	10.00	20.00	40.00
—White label promo only; "DJ Copy Monaural" sticker on cover					
❑ SD 33-309 [S]	Fat Mattress	1969	5.00	10.00	20.00
❑ SD 33-347	Fat Mattress II	1970	3.75	7.50	15.00

FATHER M.C.
UPTOWN
❑ 10061	Father's Day	1990	3.75	7.50	15.00
❑ 10542	Close to You	1992	5.00	10.00	20.00
❑ 10937	Sex Is Law	1993	5.00	10.00	20.00
—As "Father"					

FATHER YOD AND THE SPIRIT OF '76
See YA HO WA 13.

FAUN
GREGAR
❑ 7000	Faun	1969	12.50	25.00	50.00

FAY, FRANK
BALLY
❑ BAL-10215 [M]	Be Frank with Fay	1957	10.00	20.00	40.00

FAYE, FRANCES
BETHLEHEM
❑ BCP-23 [M]	I'm Wild Again	1955	12.50	25.00	50.00
❑ BCP-62 [M]	Relaxin' with Frances Faye	1957	10.00	20.00	40.00
❑ BCP-6017 [M]	Frances Faye Sings Folk Songs	1957	10.00	20.00	40.00

CAPITOL
❑ H 512 [10]	No Reservations	1954	20.00	40.00	80.00
❑ T 512 [M]	No Reservations	1955	12.50	25.00	50.00
—Turquoise or gray label					
❑ T 512 [M]	No Reservations	1958	7.50	15.00	30.00
—Black label with colorband, logo at left					

GENE NORMAN
❑ GNP-41 [M]	Caught in the Act	1958	10.00	20.00	40.00
❑ GNP-92 [M]	Caught in the Act, Volume 2	1959	10.00	20.00	40.00

IMPERIAL
❑ LP-9059 [M]	Frances Faye Swings Fats Domino	1958	10.00	20.00	40.00
❑ LP-9158 [M]	Frances Faye Sings the Blues	1961	10.00	20.00	40.00
❑ LP-12007 [S]	Frances Faye Swings Fats Domino	1959	12.50	25.00	50.00

REGINA
❑ R-315 [M]	You Gotta Go! Go! Go!	1964	6.25	12.50	25.00
❑ RS-315 [S]	You Gotta Go! Go! Go!	1964	7.50	15.00	30.00

VERVE
❑ MGV-2147 [M]	Frances Faye in Frenzy	1961	10.00	20.00	40.00
❑ V-2147 [M]	Frances Faye in Frenzy	1961	5.00	10.00	20.00
❑ V-8434 [M]	Swinging All the Way with Frances Faye	1962	5.00	10.00	20.00
❑ V6-8434 [S]	Swinging All the Way with Frances Faye	1962	6.25	12.50	25.00

FAZOLA, IRVING
MERCURY
❑ MG-25016 [10]	Irving Fazola and His Dixielanders	1950	12.50	25.00	50.00

FAZOLA, IRVING/GEORGE HARTMANN
EMARCY
❑ MG-36022 [M]	New Orleans Express	1954	10.00	20.00	40.00

FEAR
RESTLESS
❑ 72039	More Beer	1985	3.75	7.50	15.00

SLASH
❑ SR 111	The Record	1982	5.00	10.00	20.00
❑ 23933	The Record	1982	2.50	5.00	10.00

FEAR ITSELF
DOT
❑ DLP-25942	Fear Itself	1969	5.00	10.00	20.00

F

Number	Title (A Side/B Side)	Yr	VG	VG+	NM

FEATHER, LEONARD

ABC-PARAMOUNT
❏ ABC-110 [M]	Swingin' on the Vibories	1956	15.00	30.00	60.00

INTERLUDE
❏ MO-511 [M]	Leonard Feather Presents 52nd Street	1959	10.00	20.00	40.00
❏ ST-1011 [S]	Leonard Feather Presents 52nd Street	1959	7.50	15.00	30.00

MAINSTREAM
❏ MRL-348	Night Blooming Jazzmen	1972	5.00	10.00	20.00
❏ MRL-388	Freedom Jazz Dance	1974	5.00	10.00	20.00

MGM
❏ E-270 [10]	Winter Sequence	1954	30.00	60.00	120.00
❏ E-3494 [M]	Hi-Fi Suite	1957	12.50	25.00	50.00
❏ E-3650 [M]	Oh, Captain!	1958	12.50	25.00	50.00

MODE
❏ LP-127 [M]	Leonard Feather Presents Bop	1957	15.00	30.00	60.00

FEDERAL DUCK

MUSICOR
❏ MS-3162	Federal Duck	1968	5.00	10.00	20.00

FEELIES, THE

A&M
❏ SP-5214	Only Life	1988	3.00	6.00	12.00
❏ 75021 5344-1	Time for a Witness	1991	3.00	6.00	12.00
❏ 75021 7403-1 [DJ]	Paint It Black + 5	1990	3.75	7.50	15.00
—Promo-only 6-song sampler					

COYOTE/TWINTONE
❏ TTC 8673	The Good Earth	1986	3.00	6.00	12.00

STIFF
❏ USE-4	Crazy Rhythms	1980	7.50	15.00	30.00
—Price is for an actual U.S. pressing. Most copies sold in U.S. were U.K. copies with stickers.					

FELDMAN, VICTOR

AVA
❏ A-19 [M]	Soviet Jazz Themes	1963	6.25	12.00	25.00
❏ AS-19 [S]	Soviet Jazz Themes	1963	6.25	12.00	25.00

CONTEMPORARY
❏ C-3541 [M]	Suite Sixteen	1957	10.00	20.00	40.00
❏ C-3549 [M]	The Arrival of Victor Feldman	1958	10.00	20.00	40.00
❏ M-5005 [M]	Latinsville	1960	37.50	75.00	150.00
❏ S-7541 [S]	Suite Sixteen	1959	7.50	15.00	30.00
❏ S-7549 [S]	The Arrival of Victor Feldman	1959	7.50	15.00	30.00
❏ S-9005 [S]	Latinsville	1960	25.00	50.00	100.00

INTERLUDE
❏ MO-510 [M]	With Mallets Aforethought	1959	10.00	20.00	40.00
—Reissue of Mode LP					

MODE
❏ LP-120 [M]	Victor Feldman on Vibes	1957	15.00	30.00	60.00

NAUTILUS
❏ NR-50	The Secret of the Andes	1982	5.00	10.00	20.00
—Audiophile vinyl					

PACIFIC JAZZ
❏ PJ-10121 [M]	Victor Feldman Plays Everything in Sight	196?	5.00	10.00	20.00
❏ ST-20121 [S]	Victor Feldman Plays Everything in Sight	196?	6.25	12.50	25.00
❏ PJ-20128 [M]	Venezuela Joropo	196?	6.25	12.50	25.00
❏ ST-20128 [S]	Venezuela Joropo	196?	6.25	12.50	25.00

RIVERSIDE
❏ RLP-366 [M]	Merry Ole Soul	1961	6.25	12.00	25.00
❏ RS-9366 [S]	Merry Ole Soul	1961	6.25	12.00	25.00

VEE JAY
❏ LP-1096 [M]	Love Me with All Your Heart	1964	7.50	15.00	30.00
❏ LP-2507 [M]	It's a Wonderful World	1965	5.00	10.00	20.00

WORLD PACIFIC
❏ ST-1807 [S]	Stop the World, I Want to Get Off	1962	5.00	10.00	20.00
—Black vinyl					
❏ ST-1807 [S]	Stop the World, I Want to Get Off	1962	12.50	25.00	50.00
—Yellow vinyl					
❏ WP-1807 [M]	Stop the World, I Want to Get Off	1962	7.50	5.00	30.00

FELICE, DEE

BETHLEHEM
❏ B-10000	In Heat	1969	12.50	25.00	50.00
—Produced by JAMES BROWN.					

FELICE, ERNICE

CAPITOL
❏ H 192 [10]	Ernice Felice Quartet	1950	15.00	30.00	60.00

FELICIANO, JOSE

MOTOWN
❏ M8-953	Jose Feliciano	1981	2.50	5.00	10.00
❏ 6018 ML	Escenas de Amor	1982	2.50	5.00	10.00
❏ 6035 ML	Romance in the Night	1983	2.50	5.00	10.00

PAIR
❏ PDL2-1091 [(2)]	His Hits and Other Classics	1986	3.00	6.00	12.00

PRIVATE STOCK
❏ PS-2010	Angela	1976	2.50	5.00	10.00
❏ PS-2022	Sweet Soul	1977	2.50	5.00	10.00

RCA CAMDEN
❏ CAS-2563	Jose Feliciano Sings	1972	2.50	5.00	10.00

RCA VICTOR
❏ APD1-0141 [Q]	Compartments	1973	3.75	7.50	15.00
❏ APL1-0141	Compartments	1973	2.50	5.00	10.00
❏ FSP-253	Fantastico	1970	4.50	9.00	18.00
❏ AFL1-0266	For My Love...Mother Music	1977	2.00	4.00	8.00
—Reissue with new prefix					
❏ APL1-0266	For My Love...Mother Music	1974	2.50	5.00	10.00
❏ FSP-277	En Mi Soldead	1971	4.50	9.00	18.00

Number	Title (A Side/B Side)	Yr	VG	VG+	NM
❏ AFL1-0407	And the Feeling's Good	1977	2.00	4.00	8.00
—Reissue with new prefix					
❏ CPL1-0407	And the Feeling's Good	1974	2.50	5.00	10.00
❏ AFL1-1005	Just Wanna Rock 'n' Roll	1977	2.00	4.00	8.00
—Reissue with new prefix					
❏ APL1-1005	Just Wanna Rock 'n' Roll	1975	2.50	5.00	10.00
❏ LSPX-1005	Encore! Jose Feliciano's Finest Performances	1971	3.00	6.00	12.00
❏ AFL1-2824	Encore! Jose Feliciano's Finest Performances	1978	2.50	5.00	10.00
—Reissue of LSPX-1005					
❏ LPM-3358 [M]	The Voice and Guitar of Jose Feliciano	1965	3.75	7.50	15.00
❏ LSP-3358 [S]	The Voice and Guitar of Jose Feliciano	1965	5.00	10.00	20.00
❏ LPM-3503 [M]	Bag Full of Soul (Folk, Rock and Blues)	1966	3.75	7.50	15.00
❏ LSP-3503 [S]	Bag Full of Soul (Folk, Rock and Blues)	1966	5.00	10.00	20.00
❏ LPM-3581 [M]	Fantastic Feliciano	1966	3.75	7.50	15.00
❏ LSP-3581 [S]	Fantastic Feliciano	1966	5.00	10.00	20.00
❏ AFL1-3957	Feliciano!	1977	2.00	4.00	8.00
—Reissue with new prefix					
❏ LPM-3957 [M]	Feliciano!	1968	6.25	12.50	25.00
❏ LSP-3957 [S]	Feliciano!	1968	3.75	7.50	15.00
❏ LSP-4045	Souled	1968	3.75	7.50	15.00
❏ AFL1-4185	Feliciano/10 to 23	1977	2.00	4.00	8.00
—Reissue with new prefix					
❏ LSP-4185	Feliciano/10 to 23	1969	3.75	7.50	15.00
❏ AFL1-4370	Fireworks	1977	2.00	4.00	8.00
—Reissue with new prefix					
❏ LSP-4370	Fireworks	1970	3.00	6.00	12.00
❏ LSP-4421	Jose Feliciano	1970	3.75	7.50	15.00
❏ LSP-4573	That the Spirit Needs	1971	3.00	6.00	12.00
❏ LSP-4656	Memphis Menu	1972	3.00	6.00	12.00
❏ LSP-6021 [(2)]	Alive Alive-O!	1969	3.75	7.50	15.00

FELT

NASCO
❏ 9006	Felt	1971	50.00	100.00	200.00

FEMININE COMPLEX, THE

ATHENA
❏ 600	The Feminine Complex	1969	7.50	15.00	30.00

FENDERMEN, THE

BEAT ROCKET
❏ BR 116	Mule Skinner Blues	199?	3.00	6.00	12.00

SOMA
❏ MG-1240 [M]	Mule Skinner Blues	1960	300.00	600.00	1200.
—Black vinyl					
❏ MG-1240 [M]	Mule Skinner Blues	1960	2000.	3000.	4000.
—Blue vinyl					

FERGUSON, ALLYN

AVA
❏ A-32 [M]	Pictures at an Exhibition Framed in Jazz	1963	6.25	12.50	25.00
❏ AS-32 [S]	Pictures at an Exhibition Framed in Jazz	1963	7.50	15.00	30.00

FERGUSON, MAYNARD

CAMEO
❏ C-1046 [M]	The New Sounds of Maynard Ferguson	1963	5.00	10.00	20.00
❏ SC-1046 [S]	The New Sounds of Maynard Ferguson	1963	6.25	12.50	25.00
❏ C-1066 [M]	Come Blow Your Horn	1964	5.00	10.00	20.00
❏ SC-1066 [S]	Come Blow Your Horn	1964	6.25	12.50	25.00

COLUMBIA
❏ PCQ 34457 [Q]	Conquistador	1977	5.00	10.00	20.00
❏ HC 44457	Conquistador	1982	12.50	25.00	50.00
—Half-speed mastered edition					

EMARCY
❏ MG-26017 [10]	Maynard Ferguson's Hollywood Party	1954	25.00	50.00	100.00
❏ MG-26024 [10]	Dimensions	1954	25.00	50.00	100.00
❏ MG-36009 [M]	Jam Session Featuring Maynard Ferguson	1955	12.50	25.00	50.00
❏ MG-36021 [M]	Maynard Ferguson Octet	1955	15.00	30.00	60.00
❏ MG-36044 [M]	Dimensions	1956	12.50	25.00	50.00
❏ MG-36046 [M]	Maynard Ferguson's Hollywood Party	1956	12.50	25.00	50.00
❏ MG-36076 [M]	Around the Horn with Maynard Ferguson	1956	12.50	25.00	50.00
❏ MG-36114 [M]	Boy with Lots of Brass	1957	12.50	25.00	50.00

EMUS
❏ ES-12024 [S]	Maynard	197?	2.50	5.00	10.00
—Reissue of Roulette material					

MAINSTREAM
❏ S-6031 [S]	Color Him Wild	1965	5.00	10.00	20.00
❏ S-6045 [S]	The Blues Roar	1965	5.00	10.00	20.00
❏ S-6060 [S]	Maynard Ferguson Sextet	1966	5.00	10.00	20.00

MERCURY
❏ MG-20556 [M]	Boy with Lots of Brass	1960	7.50	15.00	30.00
❏ SR-60124 [S]	Boy with Lots of Brass	1960	7.50	15.00	30.00

MOSAIC
❏ MQ14-156 [(14)]	The Complete Roulette Recordings of the Maynard Ferguson Orchestra	199?	62.50	125.00	250.00

NAUTILUS
❏ NR-57	Storm	1983	10.00	20.00	40.00
—Audiophile vinyl					

ROULETTE
❏ R 52012 [M]	A Message from Newport	1958	6.25	12.50	25.00
❏ SR 52012 [S]	A Message from Newport	1958	6.25	12.50	25.00
❏ R 52027 [M]	A Message from Birdland	1959	6.25	12.50	25.00
❏ SR 52027 [S]	A Message from Birdland	1959	6.25	12.50	25.00
❏ R 52038 [M]	Maynard Ferguson Plays Jazz for Dancing	1959	6.25	12.50	25.00
❏ SR 52038 [S]	Maynard Ferguson Plays Jazz for Dancing	1959	6.25	12.50	25.00
❏ R 52047 [M]	Newport Suite	1960	6.25	12.50	25.00
❏ SR 52047 [S]	Newport Suite	1960	6.25	12.50	25.00
❏ R 52055 [M]	Let's Face the Music and Dance	1960	6.25	12.50	25.00
❏ SR 52055 [S]	Let's Face the Music and Dance	1960	6.25	12.50	25.00
❏ R 52058 [M]	Swingin' My Way Through College	1960	6.25	12.50	25.00
❏ SR 52058 [S]	Swingin' My Way Through College	1960	6.25	12.50	25.00

Number	Title (A Side/B Side)	Yr	VG	VG+	NM
❏ R 52064 [M]	Maynard '61	1961	6.25	12.50	25.00
❏ SR 52064 [S]	Maynard '61	1961	6.25	12.50	25.00
❏ SR 52083 [S]	Maynard '62	1962	5.00	10.00	20.00
❏ SR 52084 [S]	Si! Si! M.F.	1962	5.00	10.00	20.00
❏ SR 52097 [S]	Maynard '63	1963	5.00	10.00	20.00
❏ SR 52107 [S]	Maynard '64	1964	5.00	10.00	20.00
❏ SR 52110 [S]	The World of Maynard Ferguson	1964	5.00	10.00	20.00

FERKO STRING BAND
ABC-PARAMOUNT

Number	Title (A Side/B Side)	Yr	VG	VG+	NM
❏ ABC 440 [M]	The World Renowned Ferko String Band	1963	3.00	6.00	12.00
❏ ABC 440 [S]	The World Renowned Ferko String Band	1963	3.75	7.50	15.00

ESSEX
| ❏ ESLP-209 [M] | Happy Days Are Here Again! | 1956 | 5.00 | 10.00 | 20.00 |
FERKO
| ❏ LP 3301 [10] | Favorites | 195? | 5.00 | 10.00 | 20.00 |
REGENT
| ❏ MG-6007 [M] | Ferko String Band | 195? | 3.75 | 7.50 | 15.00 |
| ❏ MG-6008 [M] | Ferko String Band, Vol. 2 | 195? | 3.75 | 7.50 | 15.00 |
SOMERSET
| ❏ P 3700 [M] | The Happiest Music in the World | 196? | 2.50 | 5.00 | 10.00 |
| ❏ P 12700 [M] | Happy Days Are Here Again! | 196? | 2.50 | 5.00 | 10.00 |
STEREO-FIDELITY
| ❏ SF 12700 [S] | Happy Days Are Here Again! | 196? | 3.00 | 6.00 | 12.00 |
SURE
❏ SM-7 [M]	The World Renowned Ferko String Band	1963	3.75	7.50	15.00
❏ Vol. 8	Ferko String Band On Broadway	196?	2.50	5.00	10.00
❏ Vol. 42	Before the Parade Passes By	197?	2.50	5.00	10.00

FERLINGHETTI, LAWRENCE
FANTASY
❏ 7004 [M]	The Impeachment of Eisenhower	1958	25.00	50.00	100.00
—Black vinyl					
❏ 7004 [M]	The Impeachment of Eisenhower	1958	50.00	100.00	200.00
—Red vinyl					

FERRANTE AND TEICHER
ABC
❏ 553 [M]	World's Greatest Semi-Classical Favorites	1966	2.50	5.00	10.00
❏ S-553 [S]	World's Greatest Semi-Classical Favorites	1966	3.00	6.00	12.00
❏ 554 [M]	Memories	1966	2.50	5.00	10.00
❏ S-554 [S]	Memories	1966	3.00	6.00	12.00
❏ 555 [M]	Heaven Sounds	1966	2.50	5.00	10.00
❏ S-555 [S]	Heaven Sounds	1966	3.00	6.00	12.00
❏ 556 [M]	We've Got Rhythm	1966	2.50	5.00	10.00
❏ S-556 [S]	We've Got Rhythm	1966	3.00	6.00	12.00
❏ 557 [M]	Twin Piano Magic, Vol. 1	1966	2.50	5.00	10.00
❏ S-557 [S]	Twin Piano Magic, Vol. 1	1966	3.00	6.00	12.00
❏ 558 [M]	Autumn Leaves	1966	2.50	5.00	10.00
❏ S-558 [S]	Autumn Leaves	1966	3.00	6.00	12.00
❏ 559 [M]	Twin Piano Magic, Vol. 2	1966	2.50	5.00	10.00
❏ S-559 [S]	Twin Piano Magic, Vol. 2	1966	3.00	6.00	12.00
❏ 560 [M]	Bolero	1966	2.50	5.00	10.00
❏ S-560 [S]	Bolero	1966	3.00	6.00	12.00
❏ 561 [M]	Temptation	1966	2.50	5.00	10.00
❏ S-561 [S]	Temptation	1966	3.00	6.00	12.00
ABC-PARAMOUNT
❏ 221 [M]	Heavenly Sounds in Hi-Fi	1958	3.75	7.50	15.00
❏ S-221 [S]	Heavenly Sounds in Hi-Fi	1958	5.00	10.00	20.00
❏ 248 [M]	Ferrante and Teicher with Percussion	1958	3.75	7.50	15.00
❏ S-248 [S]	Ferrante and Teicher with Percussion	1958	5.00	10.00	20.00
❏ 285 [M]	Ferrante and Teicher Blast Off	1959	3.75	7.50	15.00
❏ S-285 [S]	Ferrante and Teicher Blast Off	1959	5.00	10.00	20.00
❏ 313 [M]	Ferrante and Teicher Play Light Classics	1960	3.75	7.50	15.00
❏ S-313 [S]	Ferrante and Teicher Play Light Classics	1960	5.00	10.00	20.00
❏ 336 [M]	Themes from Broadway Shows	1960	3.75	7.50	15.00
❏ S-336 [S]	Themes from Broadway Shows	1960	5.00	10.00	20.00
❏ 430 [M]	Postcards from Paris	1962	3.00	6.00	12.00
❏ S-430 [S]	Postcards from Paris	1962	3.75	7.50	15.00
❏ 437 [M]	Popular Classics	1962	3.00	6.00	12.00
❏ S-437 [S]	Popular Classics	1962	3.75	7.50	15.00
❏ 454 [M]	The Artistry of Ferrante and Teicher	1963	3.00	6.00	12.00
❏ S-454 [S]	The Artistry of Ferrante and Teicher	1963	3.75	7.50	15.00
BAINBRIDGE
| ❏ BT-6263 | A Few of Our Favorites on Stage | 1986 | 2.50 | 5.00 | 10.00 |
| ❏ BT-6266 | American Fantasy | 1987 | 2.50 | 5.00 | 10.00 |
COLUMBIA
| ❏ CL 573 [M] | Hi-Fire Works | 1955 | 6.25 | 12.50 | 25.00 |
GRAND AWARD
| ❏ GA-263 | Themes from Broadway Shows | 1962 | 3.00 | 6.00 | 12.00 |
HARMONY
❏ HL 7325 [M]	Twin Piano Magic	1965	3.00	6.00	12.00
❏ HL 7427 [M]	Fireworks	1967	3.00	6.00	12.00
❏ HS 11125 [R]	Twin Piano Magic	1965	2.50	5.00	10.00
❏ HS 11227 [R]	Fireworks	1967	2.50	5.00	10.00
❏ HS 11411	Encore	1970	2.50	5.00	10.00
LIBERTY
❏ LWB-70 [(2)]	10th Anniversary — Golden Piano Hits	198?	2.50	5.00	10.00
—Reissue of United Artists 70					
❏ LWB-73 [(2)]	The Best of Ferrante and Teicher	198?	2.50	5.00	10.00
—Reissue of United Artists 73					
❏ LW-662	Feelings	198?	2.00	4.00	8.00
—Reissue of United Artists 662					
❏ LT-782	Rocky and Other Knockouts	198?	2.00	4.00	8.00
—Reissue of United Artists 782					
❏ LKDL-831 [(4)]	For You with Love	198?	4.50	9.00	18.00
—Reissue of United Artists 831					
❏ LT-908	You Light Up My Life	198?	2.00	4.00	8.00
—Reissue of United Artists 908					

Number	Title (A Side/B Side)	Yr	VG	VG+	NM
❏ LT-980	Classical Disco	198?	2.00	4.00	8.00
—Reissue of United Artists 980					
❏ LM-1016	Midnight Cowboy	1981	2.00	4.00	8.00
—Reissue of United Artists 1016					
❏ LN-10112	Supermen	198?	2.00	4.00	8.00
—Reissue of United Artists 941					
❏ LN-10113	Star Wars	198?	2.00	4.00	8.00
—Reissue of United Artists 855					
❏ LN-10141	The People's Choice	1981	2.00	4.00	8.00
—Budget-line reissue of United Artists 6385					
❏ LN-10142	Snowbound	1981	2.00	4.00	8.00
—Budget-line reissue of United Artists 6233					
❏ LN-10158	Concert for Lovers	1981	2.00	4.00	8.00
—Budget-line reissue of United Artists 6315					
❏ LN-10175	Showstoppers	1983	2.00	4.00	8.00
❏ LN-10176	The Movie Theme Team	1983	2.00	4.00	8.00
❏ LN-10198	Classic Lites	1983	2.00	4.00	8.00
❏ LN-10210	The Movie Theme Team II	1984	2.00	4.00	8.00
❏ LN-10242 [(2)]	Ferrante and Teicher Superpak	1984	2.50	5.00	10.00
PICKWICK
❏ PC-3003 [M]	Excitement	196?	2.50	5.00	10.00
❏ SPC-3003 [S]	Excitement	196?	2.50	5.00	10.00
❏ PC-3077 [M]	In Love	196?	2.50	5.00	10.00
❏ SPC-3077 [S]	In Love	196?	2.50	5.00	10.00
❏ SPC-3397	How High the Moon	197?	2.00	4.00	8.00
❏ SPC-3586	Getting Together	1978	2.00	4.00	8.00
❏ SPC-3612	Fabulous Favorites	197?	2.00	4.00	8.00
SUNSET
❏ SUS-5235	Incomparable Piano	1969	2.00	4.00	8.00
❏ SUS-5277	Midnight Memories	1970	2.00	4.00	8.00
❏ SUS-5313	Love Is a Rainbow	1971	2.00	4.00	8.00
UNITED ARTISTS
❏ UA-LA018-F	Hear & Now	1972	2.50	5.00	10.00
❏ UXS-70 [(2)]	10th Anniversary — Golden Piano Hits	1969	3.00	6.00	12.00
❏ UA-LA072-G	The Roaring 20's	1973	2.50	5.00	10.00
❏ UXS-73 [(2)]	The Best of Ferrante and Teicher	1971	3.00	6.00	12.00
❏ UXS-77 [(2)]	Ferrante and Teicher Superpak	1972	3.00	6.00	12.00
❏ UA-LA101-G2 [(2)]	Greatest Love Themes of the Twentieth Century	1973	3.00	6.00	12.00
❏ UA-LA118-G	Killing Me Softly	1973	2.50	5.00	10.00
❏ UA-LA195-G	Dial M for Music	1974	2.50	5.00	10.00
❏ UA-LA227-G	In a Soulful Mood	1974	2.50	5.00	10.00
❏ UA-LA236-G	The Very Best of Ferrante and Teicher	1974	2.50	5.00	10.00
❏ UA-LA490-G	The Carpenters Songbook	1975	2.50	5.00	10.00
❏ UA-LA573-G	Spirit of 1976	1975	2.50	5.00	10.00
❏ UA-LA585-G	Piano Portraits	1976	2.50	5.00	10.00
❏ UA-LA662-G	Feelings	1976	2.50	5.00	10.00
❏ UA-LA681-G	Around	1977	2.50	5.00	10.00
❏ UA-LA782-G	Rocky and Other Knockouts	1977	2.50	5.00	10.00
❏ UA-LA831-P [(4)]	For You with Love	1978	5.00	10.00	20.00
❏ UA-LA855-G	Star Wars	1978	3.00	6.00	12.00
❏ UA-LA908-H	You Light Up My Life	1978	2.50	5.00	10.00
❏ UA-LA941-H	Supermen	1979	2.50	5.00	10.00
❏ LT-980	Classical Disco	1979	2.50	5.00	10.00
❏ LM-1016	Midnight Cowboy	1980	2.00	4.00	8.00
—Reissue of 6725					
❏ UAL 3121 [M]	The World's Greatest Themes	1960	3.00	6.00	12.00
❏ UAL 3135 [M]	Latin Pianos	1960	3.00	6.00	12.00
❏ UAL 3166 [M]	West Side Story & Other Motion Picture & Broadway Hits	1961	3.00	6.00	12.00
❏ UAL 3171 [M]	Tonight	1962	3.00	6.00	12.00
❏ UAL 3210 [M]	Golden Themes from Motion Pictures	1962	3.00	6.00	12.00
❏ UAL 3211 [M]	The Many Moods of Ferrante & Teicher	1962	3.00	6.00	12.00
❏ UAL 3230 [M]	Pianos in Paradise	1962	3.00	6.00	12.00
❏ UAL 3233 [M]	Snowbound	1962	3.00	6.00	12.00
❏ UAL 3247 [M]	Keys to Her Apartment	1963	3.00	6.00	12.00
❏ UAL 3269 [M]	Golden Piano Hits	1963	2.50	5.00	10.00
—Reissue of 7505					
❏ UAL 3282 [M]	Love Themes	1963	2.50	5.00	10.00
—Reissue of 7514					
❏ UAL 3284 [M]	Keyboard Kapers	1963	2.50	5.00	10.00
❏ UAL 3290 [M]	Love Themes from Cleopatra	1963	3.00	6.00	12.00
❏ UAL 3298 [M]	Holiday for Pianos	1963	2.50	5.00	10.00
❏ UAL 3315 [M]	Concert for Lovers	1964	3.00	6.00	12.00
❏ UAL 3340 [M]	Exotic Love Themes	1964	3.00	6.00	12.00
❏ UAL 3343 [M]	50 Fabulous Piano Favorites	1964	3.00	6.00	12.00
❏ UAL 3361 [M]	My Fair Lady	1964	2.50	5.00	10.00
❏ UAL 3375 [M]	The Enchanted World of Ferrante and Teicher	1964	3.00	6.00	12.00
❏ UAL 3385 [M]	The People's Choice	1964	2.50	5.00	10.00
❏ UAL 3406 [M]	Springtime	1965	2.50	5.00	10.00
❏ UAL 3416 [M]	By Popular Demand	1965	2.50	5.00	10.00
❏ UAL 3434 [M]	Only the Best	1965	2.50	5.00	10.00
❏ UAL 3444 [M]	The Ferrante and Teicher Concert	1965	2.50	5.00	10.00
❏ UAL 3475 [M]	The Ferrante and Teicher Concert, Part 2	1966	2.50	5.00	10.00
❏ UAL 3483 [M]	For Lovers of All Ages	1966	2.50	5.00	10.00
❏ UAL 3526 [M]	You Asked For It!	1966	2.50	5.00	10.00
❏ UAL 3536 [M]	We Wish You a Merry Christmas	1966	3.75	7.50	15.00
❏ UAL 3556 [M]	Our Golden Favorites	1967	3.00	6.00	12.00
❏ UAL 3572 [M]	A Man and a Woman & Other Motion Picture Themes	1967	2.50	5.00	10.00
❏ UAS 5501	Getting Together	1970	2.50	5.00	10.00
❏ UAS 5531	It's Too Late	1971	2.50	5.00	10.00
❏ UAS 5552	Fiddler on the Roof	1971	2.50	5.00	10.00
❏ UAS 5588	Ferrante and Teicher Play Hit Themes	1972	2.50	5.00	10.00
❏ UAS 5645	Ferrante and Teicher Salute Nashville	1972	2.50	5.00	10.00
❏ UAS 6121 [S]	The World's Greatest Themes	1960	3.75	7.50	15.00
❏ UAS 6135 [S]	Latin Pianos	1960	3.75	7.50	15.00
❏ UAS 6166 [S]	West Side Story & Other Motion Picture & Broadway Hits	1961	3.75	7.50	15.00
❏ UAS 6171 [S]	Tonight	1962	3.75	7.50	15.00
❏ UAS 6210 [S]	Golden Themes from Motion Pictures	1962	3.75	7.50	15.00

F

Number	Title (A Side/B Side)	Yr	VG	VG+	NM
❑ UAS 6211 [S]	The Many Moods of Ferrante & Teicher	1962	3.75	7.50	15.00
❑ UAS 6230 [S]	Pianos in Paradise	1962	3.75	7.50	15.00
❑ UAS 6233 [S]	Snowbound	1962	3.75	7.50	15.00
❑ UAS 6247 [S]	Keys to Her Apartment	1963	3.75	7.50	15.00
❑ UAS 6269 [S]	Golden Piano Hits	1963	3.00	6.00	12.00
—Reissue of 8505					
❑ UAS 6282 [S]	Love Themes	1963	3.00	6.00	12.00
—Reissue of 8514					
❑ UAS 6284 [S]	Keyboard Kapers	1963	3.00	6.00	12.00
❑ UAS 6290 [S]	Love Themes from Cleopatra	1963	3.75	7.50	15.00
❑ UAS 6298 [S]	Holiday for Pianos	1963	3.00	6.00	12.00
❑ UAS 6315 [S]	Concert for Lovers	1964	3.75	7.50	15.00
❑ UAS 6340 [S]	Exotic Love Themes	1964	3.75	7.50	15.00
❑ UAS 6343 [S]	50 Fabulous Piano Favorites	1964	3.75	7.50	15.00
❑ UAS 6361 [S]	My Fair Lady	1964	3.00	6.00	12.00
❑ UAS 6375 [S]	The Enchanted World of Ferrante and Teicher	1964	3.75	7.50	15.00
❑ UAS 6385 [S]	The People's Choice	1964	3.00	6.00	12.00
❑ UAS 6406 [S]	Springtime	1965	3.00	6.00	12.00
❑ UAS 6416 [S]	By Popular Demand	1965	3.00	6.00	12.00
❑ UAS 6434 [S]	Only the Best	1965	3.00	6.00	12.00
❑ UAS 6444 [S]	The Ferrante and Teicher Concert	1965	3.00	6.00	12.00
❑ UAS 6475 [S]	The Ferrante and Teicher Concert, Part 2	1966	3.00	6.00	12.00
❑ UAS 6483 [S]	For Lovers of All Ages	1966	3.00	6.00	12.00
❑ UAS 6526 [S]	You Asked For It!	1966	3.00	6.00	12.00
❑ UAS 6536 [S]	We Wish You a Merry Christmas	1966	3.00	6.00	12.00
❑ UAS 6536 [S]	We Wish You a Merry Christmas	1972	2.00	4.00	8.00
—Tan label (may also exist on late-1960s UA labels)					
❑ UAS 6556 [S]	Our Golden Favorites	1967	2.50	5.00	10.00
❑ UAS 6572 [S]	A Man and a Woman & Other Motion Picture Themes	1967	3.00	6.00	12.00
❑ UAS 6659	A Bouquet of Hits	1968	2.50	5.00	10.00
❑ UAS 6701	Listen to the Movies	1969	2.50	5.00	10.00
❑ UAS 6725	Midnight Cowboy	1969	2.50	5.00	10.00
❑ UAS 6771	Love Is a Soft Touch	1970	2.50	5.00	10.00
❑ UAS 6792	The Music Lovers	1971	2.50	5.00	10.00
❑ WW 7504 [M]	Dynamic Twin Pianos	1961	3.00	6.00	12.00
❑ WW 7505 [M]	Golden Piano Hits	1961	3.00	6.00	12.00
❑ WW 7514 [M]	Love Themes	1961	3.00	6.00	12.00
❑ WWS 8505 [S]	Golden Piano Hits	1961	3.75	7.50	15.00
❑ WWS 8514 [S]	Love Themes	1961	3.75	7.50	15.00
URANIA					
❑ 8011	Rhapsody	196?	3.00	6.00	12.00
WESTMINSTER					
❑ SW 1045 [S]	Soundproof	195?	6.25	12.50	25.00
❑ SW 1048 [S]	Latin American Adventure	195?	6.25	12.50	25.00
❑ WL 3044 [M]	Christmas Hi-Fi Favorites	195?	5.00	10.00	20.00
❑ WP 6001 [M]	Postcards from Paris	195?	5.00	10.00	20.00
❑ WP 6021 [M]	Adventure in Carols	195?	5.00	10.00	20.00

FERRE, BOULOU
4 CORNERS OF THE WORLD

Number	Title (A Side/B Side)	Yr	VG	VG+	NM
❑ FCL-4211 [M]	Boulou with the Paris All Stars	1966	5.00	10.00	20.00
❑ FCS-4211 [S]	Boulou with the Paris All Stars	1966	6.25	12.50	25.00
❑ FCL-4234 [M]	Jazz/Left Bank	1967	6.25	12.50	25.00
❑ FCS-4234 [S]	Jazz/Left Bank	1967	5.00	10.00	20.00
—As "Boulou with the Paris All Stars"					

FESTIVAL CHAMBER ORCHESTRA (ANTAL DORATI, CONDUCTOR)
MERCURY LIVING PRESENCE

Number	Title (A Side/B Side)	Yr	VG	VG+	NM
❑ SR 90436 [S]	Haydn: Symphonies No. 59 and 81	1965	5.00	10.00	20.00
—Maroon label, with "Vendor: Mercury Record Corporation"					
❑ SR 90438 [S]	Mozart: Marches; Lucio Silva Overture; Menuet; German Dances	1965	7.50	15.00	30.00
—Maroon label, with "Vendor: Mercury Record Corporation"					

FESTIVAL QUARTET
RCA VICTOR RED SEAL

Number	Title (A Side/B Side)	Yr	VG	VG+	NM
❑ LSC-2147 [S]	Schubert: Trout Quintet	1958	45.00	90.00	180.00
—Original with "shaded dog" label					
❑ LSC-2147 [S]	Schubert: Trout Quintet	1964	30.00	60.00	120.00
—Second edition with "white dog" label					
❑ LSC-2330 [S]	Brahms: Piano Quartet in C	1959	50.00	100.00	200.00
—Original with "shaded dog" label					
❑ LM-2473 [M]	Brahms: Piano Quartet in G	1961	5.00	10.00	20.00
—Originals with "shaded dog" label; a rare instance when even the mono version is sought after					
❑ LSC-2473 [S]	Brahms: Piano Quartet in G	1961	30.00	60.00	120.00
—Originals with "shaded dog" label					
❑ LSC-2517 [S]	Brahms: Piano Quartet in A	1961	50.00	100.00	200.00
—Originals with "shaded dog" label					
❑ LSC-2735 [S]	Faure: Piano Quartet in G	1963	15.00	30.00	60.00
—Original with "shaded dog" label					

FEVER TREE
AMPEX

Number	Title (A Side/B Side)	Yr	VG	VG+	NM
❑ A-10113	For Sale	1970	6.25	12.50	25.00
MCA					
❑ 551	Fever Tree	197?	2.50	5.00	10.00
UNI					
❑ 73024	Fever Tree	1968	6.25	12.50	25.00
❑ 73040	Another Time, Another Place	1968	6.25	12.50	25.00
❑ 73067	Creation	1970	6.25	12.50	25.00

FIELD, SALLY
COLGEMS

Number	Title (A Side/B Side)	Yr	VG	VG+	NM
❑ COM-106 [M]	The Flying Nun	1967	7.50	15.00	30.00
❑ COS-106 [S]	The Flying Nun	1967	6.25	12.50	25.00

FIELDING, JANE
JAZZ WEST

Number	Title (A Side/B Side)	Yr	VG	VG+	NM
❑ LP-3 [M]	Jazz Trio for Voice, Piano and Bass	1955	75.00	150.00	300.00
❑ LP-5 [M]	Embers Glow	1956	75.00	150.00	300.00

FIELDING, JERRY
ABC-PARAMOUNT

Number	Title (A Side/B Side)	Yr	VG	VG+	NM
❑ ABCS-542 [S]	Hollywood Brass	1966	5.00	10.00	20.00
COMMAND					
❑ RS 33-921 [M]	Near East Brass	1967	7.50	15.00	30.00
DECCA					
❑ DL 8100 [M]	Sweet with a Beat	1955	7.50	15.00	30.00
❑ DL 8371 [M]	Swingin' in Hi-Fi	1956	7.50	15.00	30.00
❑ DL 8450 [M]	Fielding's Formula	1957	7.50	15.00	30.00
❑ DL 8669 [M]	Hollywood Wind Jazztet	1958	7.50	15.00	30.00
KAPP					
❑ KL-1026 [M]	Dance Concert	1956	12.50	25.00	50.00
SIGNATURE					
❑ SM-1028 [M]	Favorite Christmas Music	1960	5.00	10.00	20.00
❑ SS-1028 [S]	Favorite Christmas Music	1960	6.25	12.50	25.00
TIME					
❑ S-2042 [S]	Magnificence in Brass	196?	5.00	10.00	20.00
❑ S-2059 [S]	A Bit of Ireland	196?	5.00	10.00	20.00
❑ S-2119 [S]	We Like Brass	196?	5.00	10.00	20.00
TREND					
❑ TL-1000 [10]	Jerry Fielding and His Great New Orchestra	1953	30.00	60.00	120.00
❑ TL-1004 [10]	Jerry Fielding Plays a Dance Concert	1954	25.00	50.00	100.00

FIELDS, ERNIE
RENDEZVOUS

Number	Title (A Side/B Side)	Yr	VG	VG+	NM
❑ 1309 [M]	In the Mood	1960	15.00	30.00	60.00

FIELDS, GRACIE
LIBERTY

Number	Title (A Side/B Side)	Yr	VG	VG+	NM
❑ LRP-3059 [M]	Our Gracie	1957	10.00	20.00	40.00

FIELDS, HERBIE
DECCA

Number	Title (A Side/B Side)	Yr	VG	VG+	NM
❑ DL 8130 [M]	Blow Hot — Blow Cool	1956	10.00	20.00	40.00
FRATERNITY					
❑ F-1011 [M]	Fields in Clover	1959	15.00	30.00	60.00
RKO UNIQUE					
❑ ULP-146 [M]	A Night at Kitty's	1957	12.50	25.00	50.00

FIELDS, IRVING
ABC-PARAMOUNT

Number	Title (A Side/B Side)	Yr	VG	VG+	NM
❑ ABC-187 [M]	Irving Fields at the St. Moritz	1956	7.50	15.00	30.00
DECCA					
❑ DL 4114 [M]	More Bagels and Bongos	1961	5.00	10.00	20.00
❑ DL 4174 [M]	Pizzas and Bongos	1961	5.00	10.00	20.00
❑ DL 4238 [M]	Champagne and Bongos	1962	5.00	10.00	20.00
❑ DL 4323 [M]	Bikinis and Bongos	1962	5.00	10.00	20.00
❑ DL 8856 [M]	Bagels and Bongos	1959	5.00	10.00	20.00
❑ DL 8901 [M]	At the Emerald Room, Hotel Astor	1959	5.00	10.00	20.00
❑ DL 74114 [S]	More Bagels and Bongos	1961	6.25	12.50	25.00
❑ DL 74174 [S]	Pizzas and Bongos	1961	6.25	12.50	25.00
❑ DL 74238 [S]	Champagne and Bongos	1962	6.25	12.00	25.00
❑ DL 74323 [S]	Bikinis and Bongos	1962	6.25	12.00	25.00
❑ DL 78856 [S]	Bagels and Bongos	1959	7.50	15.00	30.00
❑ DL 78901 [S]	At the Emerald Room, Hotel Astor	1959	7.50	15.00	30.00
EVEREST					
❑ SDBR-1134 [S]	Twisting	1962	6.25	12.50	25.00
❑ LPBR-5134 [M]	Twisting	1962	5.00	10.00	20.00
FIESTA					
❑ FLP-1228 [M]	Fabulous Fingers	195?	7.50	15.00	30.00
GONE					
❑ LP-5003 [M]	Fabulous Touch	1959	6.25	12.50	25.00
KING					
❑ 703 [M]	Irving Fields Favorites	1960	7.50	15.00	30.00
❑ 709 [M]	Live It Up	1960	7.50	15.00	30.00
❑ 724 [M]	Classics Go Latin	1960	5.00	10.00	20.00
❑ 724-S [S]	Classics Go Latin	1960	7.50	15.00	30.00
❑ 742 [M]	Lox, Latin and Bongos	1960	5.00	10.00	20.00
❑ 742-S [S]	Lox, Latin and Bongos	1960	7.50	15.00	30.00
RCA VICTOR					
❑ LPT-38 [10]	Fields Favorites	195?	12.50	25.00	50.00
TOPS					
❑ L-1562 [M]	Irving Fields Plays Irving Berlin	1957	7.50	15.00	30.00

FIELDS, SHEP
DOT

Number	Title (A Side/B Side)	Yr	VG	VG+	NM
❑ DLP-25348 [S]	The Rippling Rhythm of Shep Fields	1960	5.00	10.00	20.00
GOLDEN CREST					
❑ 3037 [M]	Rippling Rhythms	196?	5.00	10.00	20.00
❑ 3061 [M]	Shep Fields at the Shamrock Hilton	196?	5.00	10.00	20.00
JUBILEE					
❑ JLP-1056 [M]	Cocktails, Dinner and Dancing	1958	5.00	10.00	20.00

FIFTH DIMENSION, THE
ABC

Number	Title (A Side/B Side)	Yr	VG	VG+	NM
❑ D-897	Earthbound	1975	2.50	5.00	10.00
ARISTA					
❑ ABM-1106	Greatest Hits on Earth	1975	2.00	4.00	8.00
—Reissue of Bell 1106					
❑ AL 8335	Greatest Hits on Earth	198?	2.00	4.00	8.00
—Reissue of Arista 1106					
BELL					
❑ 1106	Greatest Hits on Earth	1972	2.50	5.00	10.00
❑ 1116	Living Together, Growing Together	1973	2.50	5.00	10.00
❑ 1315	Soul and Inspiration	1974	2.50	5.00	10.00
❑ 6045	Portrait	1970	3.00	6.00	12.00
❑ 6060	Love's Lines, Angles and Rhymes	1971	3.00	6.00	12.00
❑ 6065	Reflections	1971	2.50	5.00	10.00

Number	Title (A Side/B Side)	Yr	VG	VG+	NM
❏ 6073	Individually & Collectively	1972	2.50	5.00	10.00
❏ 9000 [(2)]	The 5th Dimension/Live!!	1971	3.00	6.00	12.00
MOTOWN					
❏ M7-896	Star	1978	2.50	5.00	10.00
PAIR					
❏ PDL2-1108 [(2)]	The Glory Days	1986	3.00	6.00	12.00
RHINO					
❏ RNDA-71104 [(2)]	The 5th Dimension Anthology	1986	3.00	6.00	12.00
SOUL CITY					
❏ SCS-33900	The 5th Dimension/Greatest Hits	1970	3.00	6.00	12.00
❏ SCS-33901	The July 5th Album	1970	3.00	6.00	12.00
❏ SCM-91000 [M]	Up, Up and Away	1967	5.00	10.00	20.00
❏ SCM-91001 [M]	The Magic Garden	1967	5.00	10.00	20.00
❏ SCS-92000 [S]	Up, Up and Away	1967	3.75	7.50	15.00
❏ SCS-92001 [S]	The Magic Garden	1967	3.75	7.50	15.00
❏ SCS-92002	Stoned Soul Picnic	1968	3.75	7.50	15.00
❏ SCS-92005	The Age of Aquarius	1969	3.75	7.50	15.00

FIFTH ESTATE, THE
JUBILEE

Number	Title (A Side/B Side)	Yr	VG	VG+	NM
❏ JGM-8005 [M]	Ding Dong! The Witch Is Dead	1967	6.25	12.50	25.00
❏ JGS-8005 [S]	Ding Dong! The Witch Is Dead	1967	7.50	15.00	30.00

FIFTY FOOT HOSE
LIMELIGHT

| ❏ 86062 | Cauldron | 1968 | 25.00 | 50.00 | 100.00 |

FILETS OF SOUL
SQUID

| ❏ 4857 | Freedom | 1968 | 25.00 | 50.00 | 100.00 |

FINCHLEY BOYS, THE
GOLDEN THROAT

| ❏ 200-19 | Everlasting Tribute | 1971 | 50.00 | 100.00 | 200.00 |

FINE, MILO
HAT HUT

| ❏ S/T [(2)] | MFG in Minnesota | 1978 | 5.00 | 10.00 | 20.00 |

FINNEY, ALBERT
MOTOWN

| ❏ M6-889 | The Albert Finney Album | 1977 | 5.00 | 10.00 | 20.00 |

FIRE
ABC

| ❏ ABCS-661 | Fire | 1969 | 5.00 | 10.00 | 20.00 |

FIRE & ICE LTD.
CAPITOL

| ❏ ST 2577 [S] | The Happening | 1966 | 10.00 | 20.00 | 40.00 |
| ❏ T 2577 [M] | The Happening | 1966 | 7.50 | 15.00 | 30.00 |

FIRE ESCAPE, THE
GNP CRESCENDO

| ❏ GNP-2034 [M] | Psychotic Reaction | 1967 | 10.00 | 20.00 | 40.00 |
| ❏ GNPS-2034 [S] | Psychotic Reaction | 1967 | 7.50 | 15.00 | 30.00 |

FIREBALLS, THE
ATCO

❏ 33-239 [M]	Bottle of Wine	1968	10.00	20.00	40.00
❏ SD 33-239 [S]	Bottle of Wine	1968	6.25	12.50	25.00
❏ SD 33-275	Come On, React!	1969	6.25	12.50	25.00
CROWN					
❏ CST-376 [R]	Jimmy Gilmer and the Fireballs & The Sugar Shackers	1963	6.25	12.50	25.00
❏ CST-387 [R]	The Sensational Jimmy Gilmer & The Fireballs	1964	6.25	12.50	25.00
❏ CLP-5376 [M]	Jimmy Gilmer and the Fireballs & The Sugar Shackers	1963	6.25	12.50	25.00
❏ CLP-5387 [M]	The Sensational Jimmy Gilmer & The Fireballs	1964	6.25	12.50	25.00
DOT					
❏ DLP-3512 [M]	Torquay	1963	12.50	25.00	50.00
❏ DLP-3545 [M]	Sugar Shack	1963	10.00	20.00	40.00
—Jimmy Gilmer and the Fireballs					
❏ DLP-3577 [M]	Buddy's Buddy	1964	12.50	25.00	50.00
—Jimmy Gilmer and the Fireballs					
❏ DLP-3643 [M]	Lucky 'Leven	1965	7.50	15.00	30.00
❏ DLP-3668 [M]	Folkbeat	1965	7.50	15.00	30.00
❏ DLP-3709 [M]	Campusology	1966	7.50	15.00	30.00
❏ DLP-3856 [M]	Firewater	1968	12.50	25.00	50.00
—Stereo cover with "Monaural" and "Promotional Copy Not for Sale" stickers, but the record is stock mono					
❏ DLP-25512 [S]	Torquay	1963	20.00	40.00	80.00
❏ DLP-25545 [S]	Sugar Shack	1963	15.00	30.00	60.00
—Jimmy Gilmer and the Fireballs					
❏ DLP-25577 [S]	Buddy's Buddy	1964	20.00	40.00	80.00
—Jimmy Gilmer and the Fireballs					
❏ DLP-25643 [S]	Lucky 'Leven	1965	10.00	20.00	40.00
❏ DLP-25668 [S]	Folkbeat	1965	10.00	20.00	40.00
❏ DLP-25709 [S]	Campusology	1966	10.00	20.00	40.00
❏ DLP-25856 [S]	Firewater	1968	6.25	12.50	25.00
SUNDAZED					
❏ LP-5016	The Fireballs	1995	2.50	5.00	10.00
❏ LP-5017	Torquay	1995	2.50	5.00	10.00
❏ LP-5018	Gunshot!	1995	2.50	5.00	10.00
TOP RANK					
❏ RM-324 [M]	The Fireballs	1960	37.50	75.00	150.00
❏ RM-343 [M]	Vaquero	1960	37.50	75.00	150.00
❏ RS-643 [S]	Vaquero	1960	50.00	100.00	200.00
WARWICK					
❏ W-2042 [M]	Here Are the Fireballs	1961	37.50	75.00	150.00
❏ WST-2042 [S]	Here Are the Fireballs	1961	62.50	125.00	250.00

FIREBIRDS, THE
CROWN

Number	Title (A Side/B Side)	Yr	VG	VG+	NM
❏ CST-589	Light My Fire	1968	17.50	35.00	70.00

FIREFLIES, THE
TAURUS

| ❏ 1002 [M] | You Were Mine | 196? | 25.00 | 50.00 | 100.00 |
| ❏ S-1002 [S] | You Were Mine | 196? | 75.00 | 150.00 | 300.00 |

FIREHOUSE FIVE PLUS TWO, THE
GOOD TIME JAZZ

❏ L-1 [10]	The Firehouse Five Plus Two, Volume 1	1953	12.50	25.00	50.00
❏ L-2 [10]	The Firehouse Five Plus Two, Volume 2	1953	12.50	25.00	50.00
❏ L-6 [10]	The Firehouse Five Plus Two, Volume 3	1953	12.50	25.00	50.00
❏ L-16 [10]	The Firehouse Five Plus Two, Volume 4	1953	12.50	25.00	50.00
❏ L-23 [10]	The Firehouse Five Plus Two Goes South!, Volume 5	1954	15.00	30.00	60.00
❏ S-10028 [S]	The Firehouse Five Plus Two Goes to Sea	1960	6.25	12.50	25.00
❏ S-10038 [S]	The Firehouse Five Plus Two Crashes a Party	1960	6.25	12.50	25.00
❏ S-10040 [S]	Dixieland Favorites	1960	6.25	12.50	25.00
❏ S-10044 [S]	Around the World	1960	6.25	12.50	25.00
❏ S-10049 [S]	The Firehouse Five Plus Two at Disneyland	1960	6.25	12.50	25.00
❏ S-10052 [S]	The Firehouse Five Plus Two Goes to a Fire	1960	6.25	12.50	25.00
❏ S-10054 [S]	Twenty Years Later	1960	6.25	12.50	25.00
❏ L-12010 [M]	The Firehouse Five Story, Volume 1	1955	7.50	15.00	30.00
❏ L-12011 [M]	The Firehouse Five Story, Volume 2	1955	7.50	15.00	30.00
❏ L-12012 [M]	The Firehouse Five Story, Volume 3	1955	7.50	15.00	30.00
❏ L-12014 [M]	The Firehouse Five Plus Two Plays for Lovers	1955	7.50	15.00	30.00
❏ L-12018 [M]	The Firehouse Five Plus Two Goes South!	1955	7.50	15.00	30.00
❏ L-12028 [M]	The Firehouse Five Plus Two Goes to Sea	1956	7.50	15.00	30.00
❏ L-12038 [M]	The Firehouse Five Plus Two Crashes a Party	1957	7.50	15.00	30.00
❏ L-12040 [M]	Dixieland Favorites	1957	7.50	15.00	30.00
❏ L-12044 [M]	Around the World	1958	7.50	15.00	30.00
❏ L-12049 [M]	The Firehouse Five Plus Two at Disneyland	1958	7.50	15.00	30.00
❏ L-12052 [M]	The Firehouse Five Plus Two Goes to a Fire	1959	6.25	12.50	25.00
❏ L-12054 [M]	Twenty Years Later	1959	6.25	12.50	25.00
STEREO RECORDS					
❏ S-7005 [S]	The Firehouse Five Plus Two Goes to Sea	1959	10.00	20.00	40.00

FIRESIGN THEATRE, THE
BUTTERFLY

❏ 001	Jost Folks...A Firesign Chat	1977	2.50	5.00	10.00
COLUMBIA					
❏ CL 2718 [M]	Waiting for the Electrician or Someone Like Him	1968	6.25	12.50	25.00
❏ CS 9518 [S]	Waiting for the Electrician or Someone Like Him	1968	3.75	7.50	15.00
—"360 Sound" label					
❏ CS 9884	How Can You Be in Two Places at Once When You're Not Anywhere at All	1969	3.75	7.50	15.00
—"360 Sound" label					
❏ C 30102	Don't Crush That Dwarf, Hand Me the Pliers	1970	3.75	7.50	15.00
❏ C 30737	I Think We're All Bozos on This Bus	1971	3.75	7.50	15.00
❏ CQ 30737 [Q]	I Think We're All Bozos on This Bus	1972	5.00	10.00	20.00
❏ KG 31099 [(2)]	Dear Friends	1972	5.00	10.00	20.00
❏ KC 31585	Not Insane or Anything You Want To	1972	3.75	7.50	15.00
❏ KC 32411	David Ossman's How Time Flys	1973	3.00	6.00	12.00
❏ KC 32730	The Tale of the Giant Rat of Sumatra	1974	3.00	6.00	12.00
❏ CQ 33141 [Q]	Everything You Know Is Wrong	1974	5.00	10.00	20.00
❏ KC 33141	Everything You Know Is Wrong	1974	3.00	6.00	12.00
❏ PC 33475	In the Next World You're On Your Own	1975	3.00	6.00	12.00
❏ PG 34391 [(2)]	Forward Into the Past (An Anthology)	1977	3.75	7.50	15.00
MERCURY					
❏ 826452-1	Eat or Be Eaten	1985	2.50	5.00	10.00
RHINO					
❏ RNLP-018	Fighting Clowns	1979	3.00	6.00	12.00
❏ RNEP-506 [EP]	Nick Danger, Third Eye	1983	2.50	5.00	10.00
❏ RNLP-806	Lawyer's Hospital	1981	3.00	6.00	12.00
❏ RNLP-807	Shakespeare's Lost Comedie	1982	3.00	6.00	12.00
❏ RNLP-812	Nick Danger In: The Three Faces of Al	1984	3.00	6.00	12.00
❏ RNLP-904	Reagan/Carter	1980	3.00	6.00	12.00

FIRM, THE
ATLANTIC

| ❏ PR 883 [DJ] | Talks Business | 1985 | 5.00 | 10.00 | 20.00 |
| *—Promo-only music and interview album* | | | | | |

FIRST EDITION, THE
JOLLY ROGERS

❏ 5001	Backroads	1973	3.75	7.50	15.00
❏ 5003	Rollin'	1974	3.75	7.50	15.00
❏ 5004	Monumental	1974	3.75	7.50	15.00
—All the above as "Kenny Rogers and the First Edition"					
MCA					
❏ 912	Love Songs	1984	2.00	4.00	8.00
❏ 913	Country Songs	1984	2.00	4.00	8.00
❏ 942	Hits and Pieces	1985	2.00	4.00	8.00
❏ 943	The 60's Revisited	1985	2.00	4.00	8.00
❏ 944	Pieces of Calico Silver	1985	2.00	4.00	8.00
❏ 1460	Greatest Hits	1985	2.00	4.00	8.00
—Reissue of Reprise 6437					
REPRISE					
❏ MS 2039	Transition	1971	5.00	10.00	20.00
—As "Kenny Rogers and the First Edition"					
❏ R-6276 [M]	The First Edition	1967	7.50	15.00	30.00
❏ RS-6276 [S]	The First Edition	1967	6.25	12.50	25.00
❏ RS-6302	The First Edition's Second	1968	6.25	12.50	25.00
❏ RS-6328	The First Edition '69	1969	6.25	12.50	25.00
❏ RS-6352	Ruby, Don't Take Your Love to Town	1969	5.00	10.00	20.00
—Starting above, as "Kenny Rogers and the First Edition"					
❏ RS-6385	Something's Burning	1970	5.00	10.00	20.00

F

Number	Title (A Side/B Side)	Yr	VG	VG+	NM
❏ RS-6412	Tell It All Brother	1970	5.00	10.00	20.00
❏ RS-6437	Greatest Hits	1971	5.00	10.00	20.00
❏ 2XS 6476 [(2)]	The Ballad of Calico	1972	6.25	12.50	25.00
❏ ST-92060	Ruby, Don't Take Your Love to Town	1969	6.25	12.50	25.00

—Capitol Record Club edition

WARNER SPECIAL PRODUCTS

Number	Title (A Side/B Side)	Yr	VG	VG+	NM
❏ OP-2514 [(2)]	Kenny Rogers and the First Edition	1979	3.75	7.50	15.00

—Manufactured for Lakeshore Music

FIRST JAZZ PIANO QUARTET, THE
WARNER BROS.

Number	Title (A Side/B Side)	Yr	VG	VG+	NM
❏ W 1274 [M]	The First Jazz Piano Quartet	1959	6.25	12.50	25.00
❏ WS 1274 [S]	The First Jazz Piano Quartet	1959	7.50	15.00	30.00

FISCHER, CLARE
COLUMBIA

Number	Title (A Side/B Side)	Yr	VG	VG+	NM
❏ CL 2691 [M]	Songs for Rainy Day Lovers	1967	6.25	12.50	25.00

PACIFIC JAZZ

Number	Title (A Side/B Side)	Yr	VG	VG+	NM
❏ PJ-52 [M]	First Time Out	1962	6.25	12.50	25.00
❏ ST-52 [S]	First Time Out	1962	7.50	15.00	30.00
❏ PJ-67 [M]	Surging Ahead	1963	6.25	12.50	25.00
❏ ST-67 [S]	Surging Ahead	1963	7.50	15.00	30.00
❏ PJ-77 [M]	Extension	1963	6.25	12.50	25.00
❏ ST-77 [S]	Extension	1963	7.50	15.00	30.00
❏ ST-20096 [S]	Manteca	1966	5.00	10.00	20.00

WORLD PACIFIC

Number	Title (A Side/B Side)	Yr	VG	VG+	NM
❏ WP-1830 [M]	So Danco Samba	1964	5.00	10.00	20.00
❏ ST-21830 [S]	So Danco Samba	1964	6.25	12.50	25.00

FISCHER, WILD MAN
REPRISE

Number	Title (A Side/B Side)	Yr	VG	VG+	NM
❏ 2XS 6332 [(2)]	An Evening with Wild Man Fischer	1969	12.50	25.00	50.00

RHINO

Number	Title (A Side/B Side)	Yr	VG	VG+	NM
❏ RNLP-001	Wildmania	1978	3.75	7.50	15.00
❏ RNLP-021	Pronounced Normal	1981	2.50	5.00	10.00
❏ RNLP-022	Nothing Scary	1981	2.50	5.00	10.00

FISCHOFF, GEORGE
MMG

Number	Title (A Side/B Side)	Yr	VG	VG+	NM
❏ 1140	Pretty Kitty: The Piano Magic of George Fischoff	1982	5.00	10.00	20.00

FISELE, JERRY
DELMAR

Number	Title (A Side/B Side)	Yr	VG	VG+	NM
❏ DL-101 [10]	Jerry Fisele and the Fabulous Windy City Six	1954	12.50	25.00	50.00

FISHER, AL, AND LOU MARKS
CAMEO

Number	Title (A Side/B Side)	Yr	VG	VG+	NM
❏ C-1081 [M]	Rome on the Range	1964	5.00	10.00	20.00

SWAN

Number	Title (A Side/B Side)	Yr	VG	VG+	NM
❏ SLP-514 [M]	It's a Beatle (Coo-Coo) World	1964	10.00	20.00	40.00

FISHER, CHIP
RCA VICTOR

Number	Title (A Side/B Side)	Yr	VG	VG+	NM
❏ LPM-1797 [M]	Chipper at the Sugar Bowl	1958	10.00	20.00	40.00
❏ LSP-1797 [S]	Chipper at the Sugar Bowl	1958	12.50	25.00	50.00

FISHER, EDDIE
DOT

Number	Title (A Side/B Side)	Yr	VG	VG+	NM
❏ DLP-3631 [M]	Eddie Fisher Today!	1965	3.00	6.00	12.00
❏ DLP-3648 [M]	When I Was Young	1965	3.00	6.00	12.00
❏ DLP-3658 [M]	Mary Christmas	1965	3.75	7.50	15.00
❏ DLP-3670 [M]	Young and Foolish	1966	3.00	6.00	12.00
❏ DLP-3785 [M]	His Greatest Hits	1967	3.00	6.00	12.00
❏ DLP-25361 [S]	Eddie Fisher Today!	1965	3.75	7.50	15.00
❏ DLP-25648 [S]	When I Was Young	1965	3.75	7.50	15.00
❏ DLP-25658 [S]	Mary Christmas	1965	5.00	10.00	20.00
❏ DLP-25670 [S]	Young and Foolish	1966	3.75	7.50	15.00
❏ DLP-25785 [S]	His Greatest Hits	1967	3.75	7.50	15.00

MCA

Number	Title (A Side/B Side)	Yr	VG	VG+	NM
❏ 1549	The Best of Eddie Fisher	1983	2.00	4.00	8.00

PICKWICK

Number	Title (A Side/B Side)	Yr	VG	VG+	NM
❏ SPC-3141	Oh My Papa	196?	3.00	6.00	12.00

RAMROD

Number	Title (A Side/B Side)	Yr	VG	VG+	NM
❏ RR-1 [(2)M]	Eddie Fisher at the Winter Garden	1963	3.75	7.50	15.00
❏ RRS-1 [(2)S]	Eddie Fisher at the Winter Garden	1963	5.00	10.00	20.00

RCA CAMDEN

Number	Title (A Side/B Side)	Yr	VG	VG+	NM
❏ CAL-789 [M]	Bring Back the Thrill	196?	3.00	6.00	12.00
❏ CAS-789 [R]	Bring Back the Thrill	196?	2.50	5.00	10.00

RCA VICTOR

Number	Title (A Side/B Side)	Yr	VG	VG+	NM
❏ LOC-1024 [M]	Academy Award Winners	1955	10.00	20.00	40.00
❏ LPM-1097 [M]	I Love You	1955	7.50	15.00	30.00
❏ ANL1-1138	Eddie Fisher's Greatest Hits	1975	2.00	4.00	8.00
❏ LPM-1180 [M]	I'm in the Mood for Love	1955	7.50	15.00	30.00
❏ LPM-1181 [M]	May I Sing to You?	1955	7.50	15.00	30.00
❏ LPM-1399 [M]	Bundle of Joy	1957	7.50	15.00	30.00
❏ LPM-1548 [M]	Thinking of You	1957	7.50	15.00	30.00
❏ LPM-1647 [M]	As Long As There's Music	1958	7.50	15.00	30.00
❏ LSP-1647 [S]	As Long As There's Music	1958	12.50	25.00	50.00
❏ LPM-2504 [M]	Eddie Fisher's Greatest Hits	1962	3.75	7.50	15.00
❏ LSP-2504 [S]	Eddie Fisher's Greatest Hits	1962	5.00	10.00	20.00
❏ LPM-3025 [10]	Fisher Sings	1952	12.50	25.00	50.00
❏ LPM-3058 [10]	I'm in the Mood for Love	1952	12.50	25.00	50.00
❏ LPM-3065 [10]	Christmas with Fisher	1952	12.50	25.00	50.00
❏ LPM-3122 [10]	Irving Berlin Favorites	1953	12.50	25.00	50.00
❏ LPM-3185 [10]	May I Sing to You?	1953	12.50	25.00	50.00
❏ LPM-3375 [M]	The Best of Eddie Fisher	1965	3.75	7.50	15.00
❏ LSP-3375 [R]	The Best of Eddie Fisher	1965	3.00	6.00	12.00
❏ LPM-3726 [M]	Games That Lovers Play	1966	3.75	7.50	15.00
❏ LSP-3726 [S]	Games That Lovers Play	1966	3.75	7.50	15.00
❏ LPM-3820 [M]	People Like You	1967	5.00	10.00	20.00
❏ LSP-3820 [S]	People Like You	1967	3.00	6.00	12.00
❏ LSP-3914	You Ain't Heard Nothin' Yet	1968	3.00	6.00	12.00

FISHER, TONI
SIGNET

Number	Title (A Side/B Side)	Yr	VG	VG+	NM
❏ WP-509 [S]	The Big Hurt	1960	12.50	25.00	50.00

—Issued in "Stereomonic"

FITCH, MAL
EMARCY

Number	Title (A Side/B Side)	Yr	VG	VG+	NM
❏ MG-36041 [M]	Mal Fitch	1956	12.50	25.00	50.00

FITZGERALD, ELLA
CAPITOL

Number	Title (A Side/B Side)	Yr	VG	VG+	NM
❏ T 2685 [M]	Brighten the Corner	1967	5.00	10.00	20.00
❏ T 2805 [M]	Ella Fitzgerald's Christmas	1967	5.00	10.00	20.00

DECCA

Number	Title (A Side/B Side)	Yr	VG	VG+	NM
❏ DXB 156 [(2)M]	The Best of Ella	1959	10.00	20.00	40.00

—Black labels, silver print

Number	Title (A Side/B Side)	Yr	VG	VG+	NM
❏ DXB 156 [(2)M]	The Best of Ella	1961	6.25	12.50	25.00

—Black labels with color bars

Number	Title (A Side/B Side)	Yr	VG	VG+	NM
❏ DL 4129 [M]	Golden Favorites	1961	5.00	10.00	20.00
❏ DL 5084 [10]	Souvenir Album	1950	30.00	60.00	120.00
❏ DL 5300 [10]	Ella Fitzgerald Sings Gershwin Songs	1951	30.00	60.00	120.00
❏ DXSB 7156 [(2)R]	The Best of Ella	196?	5.00	10.00	20.00
❏ DL 8068 [M]	Songs in a Mellow Mood	1954	12.50	25.00	50.00
❏ DL 8149 [M]	Lullabies of Birdland	1955	12.50	25.00	50.00
❏ DL 8155 [M]	Sweet and Hot	1955	12.50	25.00	50.00
❏ DL 8378 [M]	Ella Sings Gershwin	1957	10.00	20.00	40.00
❏ DL 8477 [M]	Ella and Her Fellas	1957	10.00	20.00	40.00
❏ DL 8695 [M]	The First Lady of Song	1958	10.00	20.00	40.00
❏ DL 8696 [M]	Miss Ella Fitzgerald and Mr. Nelson Riddle Invite You to Listen and Relax	1958	10.00	20.00	40.00
❏ DL 8832 [M]	For Sentimental Reasons	1958	10.00	20.00	40.00

VERVE

Number	Title (A Side/B Side)	Yr	VG	VG+	NM
❏ V-10-4 [(4)M]	Ella Fitzgerald Sings the Duke Ellington Song Book	196?	12.50	25.00	50.00
❏ V-29-5 [(5)M]	Ella Fitzgerald Sings the George and Ira Gershwin Song Book	196?	25.00	50.00	100.00

—Reissue of MGV-4029

Number	Title (A Side/B Side)	Yr	VG	VG+	NM
❏ V6-29-5 [(5)S]	Ella Fitzgerald Sings the George and Ira Gershwin Song Book	196?	25.00	50.00	100.00

—Reissue of MGVS-6082

Number	Title (A Side/B Side)	Yr	VG	VG+	NM
❏ MGV-4001-2 [(2)M]	Ella Fitzgerald Sings the Cole Porter Song Book	1956	20.00	40.00	80.00
❏ V-4001-2 [(2)M]	Ella Fitzgerald Sings the Cole Porter Song Book	1961	6.25	12.50	25.00
❏ MGV-4002-2 [(2)M]	Ella Fitzgerald Sings the Rodgers & Hart Song Book	1956	20.00	40.00	80.00
❏ V-4002-2 [(2)M]	Ella Fitzgerald Sings the Rodgers and Hart Song Book	1961	6.25	12.50	25.00
❏ MGV-4004 [M]	Like Someone in Love	1957	12.50	25.00	50.00
❏ V-4004 [M]	Like Someone in Love	1961	5.00	10.00	20.00
❏ V6-4004 [S]	Like Someone in Love	1961	5.00	10.00	20.00
❏ MGV-4008-2 [(2)M]	Ella Fitzgerald Sings the Duke Ellington Song Book, Vol. 1	1957	20.00	40.00	80.00
❏ V-4008-2 [(2)M]	Ella Fitzgerald Sings the Duke Ellington Song Book, Vol. 1	1961	6.25	12.50	25.00
❏ MGV-4009-2 [(2)M]	Ella Fitzgerald Sings the Duke Ellington Song Book, Vol. 2	1957	20.00	40.00	80.00
❏ V-4009-2 [(2)M]	Ella Fitzgerald Sings the Duke Ellington Song Book, Vol. 2	1961	6.25	12.50	25.00
❏ MGV-4010-4 [(4)M]	Ella Fitzgerald Sings the Duke Ellington Song Book	1957	37.50	75.00	150.00

—Combines 4008 and 4009 into one package

Number	Title (A Side/B Side)	Yr	VG	VG+	NM
❏ MGV-4013 [M]	Ella Fitzgerald Sings the Gershwin Song Book	1957	12.50	25.00	50.00
❏ MGV-4019-2 [(2)M]	Ella Fitzgerald Sings the Irving Berlin Song Book	1958	20.00	40.00	80.00
❏ V-4019-2 [(2)M]	Ella Fitzgerald Sings the Irving Berlin Song Book	1961	6.25	12.50	25.00
❏ V6-4019-2 [(2)S]	Ella Fitzgerald Sings the Irving Berlin Song Book	1961	6.25	12.50	25.00
❏ MGV-4021 [M]	Ella Swings Lightly	1958	12.50	25.00	50.00
❏ V-4021 [M]	Ella Swings Lightly	1961	5.00	10.00	20.00
❏ V6-4021 [S]	Ella Swings Lightly	1961	5.00	10.00	20.00
❏ MGV-4022 [M]	Ella Fitzgerald Sings the Rodgers & Hart Song Book, Vol. 1	1959	12.50	25.00	50.00
❏ V-4022 [M]	Ella Fitzgerald Sings the Rodgers & Hart Song Book, Vol. 1	1961	5.00	10.00	20.00
❏ V6-4022 [S]	Ella Fitzgerald Sings the Rodgers & Hart Song Book, Vol. 1	1961	5.00	10.00	20.00
❏ MGV-4023 [M]	Ella Fitzgerald Sings the Rodgers & Hart Song Book, Vol. 2	1959	12.50	25.00	50.00
❏ V-4023 [M]	Ella Fitzgerald Sings the Rodgers & Hart Song Book, Vol. 2	1961	5.00	10.00	20.00
❏ V6-4023 [S]	Ella Fitzgerald Sings the Rodgers & Hart Song Book, Vol. 2	1961	5.00	10.00	20.00
❏ MGV-4024 [M]	Ella Fitzgerald Sings the George and Ira Gershwin Song Book, Vol. 1	1959	12.50	25.00	50.00
❏ V-4024 [M]	Ella Fitzgerald Sings the George and Ira Gershwin Song Book, Vol. 1	1961	5.00	10.00	20.00
❏ V6-4024 [S]	Ella Fitzgerald Sings the George and Ira Gershwin Song Book, Vol. 1	1961	5.00	10.00	20.00
❏ MGV-4025 [M]	Ella Fitzgerald Sings the George and Ira Gershwin Song Book, Vol. 2	1959	12.50	25.00	50.00
❏ V-4025 [M]	Ella Fitzgerald Sings the George and Ira Gershwin Song Book, Vol. 2	1961	5.00	10.00	20.00
❏ V6-4025 [S]	Ella Fitzgerald Sings the George and Ira Gershwin Song Book, Vol. 2	1961	5.00	10.00	20.00
❏ MGV-4026 [M]	Ella Fitzgerald Sings the George and Ira Gershwin Song Book, Vol. 3	1959	12.50	25.00	50.00
❏ V-4026 [M]	Ella Fitzgerald Sings the George and Ira Gershwin Song Book, Vol. 3	1961	5.00	10.00	20.00

Number	Title (A Side/B Side)	Yr	VG	VG+	NM
V6-4026 [S]	Ella Fitzgerald Sings the George and Ira Gershwin Song Book, Vol. 3	1961	5.00	10.00	20.00
MGV-4027 [M]	Ella Fitzgerald Sings the George and Ira Gershwin Song Book, Vol. 4	1959	12.50	25.00	50.00
V-4027 [M]	Ella Fitzgerald Sings the George and Ira Gershwin Song Book, Vol. 4	1961	5.00	10.00	20.00
V6-4027 [S]	Ella Fitzgerald Sings the George and Ira Gershwin Song Book, Vol. 4	1961	5.00	10.00	20.00
MGV-4028 [M]	Ella Fitzgerald Sings the George and Ira Gershwin Song Book, Vol. 5	1959	12.50	25.00	50.00
V-4028 [M]	Ella Fitzgerald Sings the George and Ira Gershwin Song Book, Vol. 5	1961	5.00	10.00	20.00
V6-4028 [S]	Ella Fitzgerald Sings the George and Ira Gershwin Song Book, Vol. 5	1961	5.00	10.00	20.00
MGV-4029-5 [(5)M]	Ella Fitzgerald Sings the George and Ira Gershwin Song Book	1959	62.50	125.00	250.00
—Box set with 4024 through 4028 plus bonus 10-inch LP					
MGV-4029-5 [(5)M]	Ella Fitzgerald Sings the George and Ira Gershwin Song Book	1959	125.00	250.00	500.00
—Box set with 4024 through 4028 plus bonus 10-inch LP, all in walnut box with leather pockets					
MGV-4030 [M]	Ella Fitzgerald Sings the Irving Berlin Song Book, Vol. 1	1959	12.50	25.00	50.00
V-4030 [M]	Ella Fitzgerald Sings the Irving Berlin Song Book, Vol. 1	1961	5.00	10.00	20.00
V6-4030 [S]	Ella Fitzgerald Sings the Irving Berlin Song Book, Vol. 1	1961	5.00	10.00	20.00
MGV-4031 [M]	Ella Fitzgerald Sings the Irving Berlin Song Book, Vol. 2	1959	12.50	25.00	50.00
V-4031 [M]	Ella Fitzgerald Sings the Irving Berlin Song Book, Vol. 2	1961	5.00	10.00	20.00
V6-4031 [S]	Ella Fitzgerald Sings the Irving Berlin Song Book, Vol. 2	1961	5.00	10.00	20.00
MGV-4032 [M]	Sweet Songs for Swingers	1959	12.50	25.00	50.00
V-4032 [M]	Sweet Songs for Swingers	1961	5.00	10.00	20.00
V6-4032 [S]	Sweet Songs for Swingers	1961	5.00	10.00	20.00
MGV-4034 [M]	Hello, Love	1959	12.50	25.00	50.00
V-4034 [M]	Hello, Love	1961	5.00	10.00	20.00
V6-4034 [S]	Hello, Love	1961	5.00	10.00	20.00
MGV-4036 [M]	Get Happy!	1960	10.00	20.00	40.00
V-4036 [M]	Get Happy!	1961	5.00	10.00	20.00
V6-4036 [S]	Get Happy!	1961	5.00	10.00	20.00
MGV-4041 [M]	Mack the Knife — Ella in Berlin	1960	10.00	20.00	40.00
V-4041 [M]	Mack the Knife — Ella in Berlin	1961	5.00	10.00	20.00
V6-4041 [S]	Mack the Knife — Ella in Berlin	1961	5.00	10.00	20.00
MGV-4042 [M]	Ella Wishes You a Swinging Christmas	1960	12.50	25.00	50.00
V-4042 [M]	Ella Wishes You a Swinging Christmas	1961	10.00	20.00	40.00
V6-4042 [S]	Ella Wishes You a Swinging Christmas	1961	12.50	25.00	50.00
MGV-4043 [M]	Let No Man Write My Epitaph	1961	10.00	20.00	40.00
V-4043 [M]	Let No Man Write My Epitaph	1961	5.00	10.00	20.00
V6-4043 [S]	Let No Man Write My Epitaph	1961	5.00	10.00	20.00
MGV-4046-2 [(2)M]	Ella Fitzgerald Sings the Harold Arlen Song Book	1961	15.00	30.00	60.00
MGV-4049 [M]	Ella Fitzgerald Sings Cole Porter	1961	10.00	20.00	40.00
V-4049 [M]	Ella Fitzgerald Sings Cole Porter	1961	5.00	10.00	20.00
MGV-4050 [M]	Ella Fitzgerald Sings More Cole Porter	1961	10.00	20.00	40.00
V-4050 [M]	Ella Fitzgerald Sings More Cole Porter	1961	5.00	10.00	20.00
MGV-4052 [M]	Ella in Hollywood	1961	10.00	20.00	40.00
V-4052 [M]	Ella in Hollywood	1961	5.00	10.00	20.00
V-4053 [M]	Clap Hands, Here Comes Charley	1962	10.00	20.00	40.00
V6-4053 [S]	Clap Hands, Here Comes Charley	1962	37.50	75.00	150.00
V-4054 [M]	Ella Swings Brightly with Nelson	1962	7.50	15.00	30.00
V6-4054 [S]	Ella Swings Brightly with Nelson	1962	7.50	15.00	30.00
V-4055 [M]	Ella Swings Gently with Nelson	1962	7.50	15.00	30.00
V6-4055 [S]	Ella Swings Gently with Nelson	1962	7.50	15.00	30.00
V-4056 [M]	Rhythm Is My Business	1962	7.50	15.00	30.00
V6-4056 [S]	Rhythm Is My Business	1962	7.50	15.00	30.00
V-4057 [M]	Ella Fitzgerald Sings the Harold Arlen Song Book, Vol. 1	1962	7.50	15.00	30.00
V6-4057 [S]	Ella Fitzgerald Sings the Harold Arlen Song Book, Vol. 1	1962	7.50	15.00	30.00
V-4058 [M]	Ella Fitzgerald Sings the Harold Arlen Song Book, Vol. 2	1962	7.50	15.00	30.00
V6-4058 [S]	Ella Fitzgerald Sings the Harold Arlen Song Book, Vol. 2	1962	7.50	15.00	30.00
V-4059 [M]	Ella Sings Broadway	1963	6.25	12.50	25.00
V6-4059 [S]	Ella Sings Broadway	1963	6.25	12.50	25.00
V-4060 [M]	Ella Fitzgerald Sings the Jerome Kern Song Book	1963	6.25	12.50	25.00
V6-4060 [S]	Ella Fitzgerald Sings the Jerome Kern Song Book	1963	6.25	12.50	25.00
V-4061 [M]	Ella and Basie!	1963	6.25	12.50	25.00
V6-4061 [S]	Ella and Basie!	1963	6.25	12.50	25.00
V-4062 [M]	These Are the Blues	1963	6.25	12.50	25.00
V6-4062 [S]	These Are the Blues	1963	6.25	12.50	25.00
V-4064 [M]	Hello, Dolly!	1964	6.25	12.50	25.00
V6-4064 [S]	Hello, Dolly!	1964	6.25	12.50	25.00
V-4065 [M]	Ella at Juan Les Pins	1964	6.25	12.50	25.00
V6-4065 [S]	Ella at Juan Les Pins	1964	6.25	12.50	25.00
V-4066 [M]	A Tribute to Cole Porter	1964	6.25	12.50	25.00
V6-4066 [S]	A Tribute to Cole Porter	1964	6.25	12.50	25.00
V-4067 [M]	Ella Fitzgerald Sings the Johnny Mercer Song Book	1965	5.00	10.00	20.00
V6-4067 [S]	Ella Fitzgerald Sings the Johnny Mercer Song Book	1965	5.00	10.00	20.00
V-4068 [M]	Porgy & Bess	1965	5.00	10.00	20.00
V6-4068 [S]	Porgy & Bess	1965	5.00	10.00	20.00
V-4069 [M]	Ella in Hamburg	1966	5.00	10.00	20.00
V6-4069 [S]	Ella in Hamburg	1966	5.00	10.00	20.00
V-4070 [M]	Ella at Duke's Place	1966	5.00	10.00	20.00
V6-4070 [S]	Ella at Duke's Place	1966	5.00	10.00	20.00
V-4071 [M]	Whisper Not	1966	5.00	10.00	20.00
V6-4071 [S]	Whisper Not	1966	5.00	10.00	20.00
V-4072 [M]	Ella & Duke at Cote d'Azur	1967	6.25	12.50	25.00

Number	Title (A Side/B Side)	Yr	VG	VG+	NM
MGVS-6000 [S]	Like Someone in Love	1960	10.00	20.00	40.00
MGVS-6005-2 [(2)S]	Ella Fitzgerald Sings the Irving Berlin Song Book	1960	15.00	30.00	60.00
MGVS-6009 [S]	Ella Fitzgerald Sings the Rodgers & Hart Song Book, Vol. 1	1960	10.00	20.00	40.00
MGVS-6010 [S]	Ella Fitzgerald Sings the Rodgers & Hart Song Book, Vol. 2	1960	10.00	20.00	40.00
MGVS-6019 [S]	Ella Swings Lightly	1960	10.00	20.00	40.00
MGVS-6026 [S]	Ella Fitzgerald at the Opera House	1960	10.00	20.00	40.00
MGVS-6052 [S]	Ella Fitzgerald Sings the Irving Berlin Song Book, Vol. 1	1960	10.00	20.00	40.00
MGVS-6053 [S]	Ella Fitzgerald Sings the Irving Berlin Song Book, Vol. 2	1960	10.00	20.00	40.00
MGVS-6072 [S]	Sweet Songs for Swingers	1960	10.00	20.00	40.00
MGVS-6077 [S]	Ella Fitzgerald Sings the George and Ira Gershwin Song Book, Vol. 1	1960	10.00	20.00	40.00
MGVS-6078 [S]	Ella Fitzgerald Sings the George and Ira Gershwin Song Book, Vol. 2	1960	10.00	20.00	40.00
MGVS-6079 [S]	Ella Fitzgerald Sings the George and Ira Gershwin Song Book, Vol. 3	1960	10.00	20.00	40.00
MGVS-6080 [S]	Ella Fitzgerald Sings the George and Ira Gershwin Song Book, Vol. 4	1960	10.00	20.00	40.00
MGVS-6081 [S]	Ella Fitzgerald Sings the George and Ira Gershwin Song Book, Vol. 5	1960	10.00	20.00	40.00
MGVS-6082-5 [(5)S]	Ella Fitzgerald Sings the George and Ira Gershwin Song Book	1960	50.00	100.00	200.00
—Box set with 6077 through 6081 plus bonus 10-inch LP					
MGVS-6100 [S]	Hello, Love	1960	10.00	20.00	40.00
MGVS-6102 [S]	Get Happy!	1960	10.00	20.00	40.00
MGVS-6163 [S]	Mack the Knife — Ella in Berlin	1960	10.00	20.00	40.00
MGVS-7000 [S]	Ella Fitzgerald Sings the Gershwin Song Book	1959	12.50	25.00	50.00
MGV-8264 [M]	Ella Fitzgerald at the Opera House	1958	12.50	25.00	50.00
V-8264 [M]	Ella Fitzgerald at the Opera House	1961	5.00	10.00	20.00
V6-8264 [S]	Ella Fitzgerald at the Opera House	1961	5.00	10.00	20.00
MGV-8288 [M]	One O'Clock Jump	1958	12.50	25.00	50.00
V-8288 [M]	One O'Clock Jump	1961	5.00	10.00	20.00
V-8745 [M]	Ella "Live"	1968	7.50	15.00	30.00
MGVS-64042 [S]	Ella Wishes You a Swinging Christmas	1960	15.00	30.00	60.00
ST-90028 [S]	Ella and Basie!	1964	7.50	15.00	30.00
—Capitol Record Club edition					
T-90028 [M]	Ella and Basie!	1964	7.50	15.00	30.00
—Capitol Record Club edition					
825024-1 [(5)]	The George and Ira Gershwin Songbook (Complete)	198?	6.25	12.50	25.00

FITZGERALD, ELLA, AND LOUIS ARMSTRONG
Also see each artist's individual listings.
MOBILE FIDELITY

Number	Title (A Side/B Side)	Yr	VG	VG+	NM
2-248 [(2)]	Ella and Louis Again	1996	37.50	75.00	150.00
—Audiophile vinyl					

VERVE

Number	Title (A Side/B Side)	Yr	VG	VG+	NM
MGV-4003 [M]	Ella and Louis	1956	12.50	25.00	50.00
V-4003 [M]	Ella and Louis	1961	5.00	10.00	20.00
MGV-4006-2 [(2)M]	Ella and Louis Again	1956	20.00	40.00	80.00
V-4006-2 [(2)M]	Ella and Louis Again	1961	6.25	12.50	25.00
MGV-4011-2 [(2)M]	Porgy and Bess	1957	20.00	40.00	80.00
V-4011-2 [(2)M]	Porgy and Bess	1961	6.25	12.50	25.00
V6-4011-2 [(2)S]	Porgy and Bess	1961	6.25	12.50	25.00
MGV-4017 [M]	Ella and Louis Again, Vol. 1	1958	12.50	25.00	50.00
V-4017 [M]	Ella and Louis Again, Vol. 1	1961	5.00	10.00	20.00
MGV-4018 [M]	Ella and Louis Again, Vol. 2	1958	12.50	25.00	50.00
V-4018 [M]	Ella and Louis Again, Vol. 2	1961	5.00	10.00	20.00
MGVS-6040-2 [(2)S]	Porgy and Bess	1960	15.00	30.00	60.00

FITZGERALD, ELLA, AND BILLIE HOLIDAY
Also see each artist's individual listings.
AMERICAN RECORDING SOCIETY

Number	Title (A Side/B Side)	Yr	VG	VG+	NM
G-433 [M]	Ella Fitzgerald and Billie Holiday at Newport	1957	10.00	20.00	40.00

VERVE

Number	Title (A Side/B Side)	Yr	VG	VG+	NM
MGVS-6022 [S]	Ella Fitzgerald and Billie Holiday at Newport	1960	10.00	20.00	40.00
MGV-8234 [M]	Ella Fitzgerald and Billie Holiday at Newport	1958	12.50	25.00	50.00
V-8234 [M]	Ella Fitzgerald and Billie Holiday at Newport	1961	5.00	10.00	20.00
V6-8234 [S]	Ella Fitzgerald and Billie Holiday at Newport	1961	5.00	10.00	20.00

FIVE, THE
RCA VICTOR

Number	Title (A Side/B Side)	Yr	VG	VG+	NM
LPM-1121 [M]	The Five	1955	20.00	40.00	80.00

FIVE AMERICANS, THE
ABNAK

Number	Title (A Side/B Side)	Yr	VG	VG+	NM
AB-1967 [M]	Western Union/Sound of Love	1967	5.00	10.00	20.00
AB-1969 [M]	Progressions	1967	5.00	10.00	20.00
ABST-2067 [S]	Western Union/Sound of Love	1967	7.50	15.00	30.00
ABST-2069 [S]	Progressions	1967	7.50	15.00	30.00
ABST-2071 [(2)]	Now and Then	1968	6.25	12.50	25.00

HANNA-BARBERA

Number	Title (A Side/B Side)	Yr	VG	VG+	NM
HLP-8503 [M]	I See the Light	1966	10.00	20.00	40.00
HST-9503 [S]	I See the Light	1966	15.00	30.00	60.00

FIVE BROTHERS
TAMPA

Number	Title (A Side/B Side)	Yr	VG	VG+	NM
TP-25 [M]	Five Brothers	1957	37.50	75.00	150.00
—Colored vinyl					
TP-25 [M]	Five Brothers	1958	20.00	40.00	80.00
—Black vinyl					

FIVE BY FIVE
PAULA

Number	Title (A Side/B Side)	Yr	VG	VG+	NM
LPS-2202	Next Exit	1969	6.25	12.50	25.00

FIVE DISCS, THE
CRYSTAL BALL

Number	Title (A Side/B Side)	Yr	VG	VG+	NM
119	Unchained	1978	3.75	7.50	15.00

F

Number	Title (A Side/B Side)	Yr	VG	VG+	NM

MAGIC CARPET

| ❏ 1002 | The Five Discs Sing Again | 1991 | 5.00 | 10.00 | 20.00 |

—*Dark blue cover*

FIVE EMPREES, THE
FREEPORT

| ❏ 3001 [M] | The Five Emprees | 1965 | 12.50 | 25.00 | 50.00 |
| ❏ 3001 [M] | Little Miss Sad | 1966 | 7.50 | 15.00 | 30.00 |

—*Same LP, new title*

| ❏ 4001 [S] | The Five Emprees | 1965 | 15.00 | 30.00 | 60.00 |
| ❏ 4001 [S] | Little Miss Sad | 1966 | 10.00 | 20.00 | 40.00 |

—*Same LP, new title*

FIVE KEYS, THE
ALADDIN

| ❏ LP-806 [M] | The Best of the Five Keys | 1956 | 1000. | 1500. | 2000. |

—*Copies of Aladdin 806 entitled "On the Town" are bootlegs.*
CAPITOL

| ❏ T 828 [M] | The Five Keys On Stage! | 1957 | 75.00 | 150.00 | 300.00 |

—*On cover, the far left singer has his thumb sticking out (inadvertently?) in a phallic way*

| ❏ T 828 [M] | The Five Keys On Stage! | 1957 | 125.00 | 250.00 | 500.00 |

—*On cover, the far left singer's "offending" thumb is airbrushed out*

| ❏ M-1769 | The Fantastic Five Keys | 1977 | 5.00 | 10.00 | 20.00 |

—*Reissue with new prefix*

| ❏ T 1769 [M] | The Fantastic Five Keys | 1962 | 75.00 | 150.00 | 300.00 |

HARLEM HIT PARADE

| ❏ 5004 | The Five Keys | 1972 | 3.75 | 7.50 | 15.00 |

KING

❏ 688 [M]	The Five Keys	1960	200.00	400.00	800.00
❏ 692 [M]	Rhythm and Blues Hits, Past and Present	1960	150.00	300.00	600.00
❏ 5013	14 Hits	1978	3.00	6.00	12.00

SCORE

| ❏ LP-4003 [M] | The Five Keys On the Town | 1957 | 200.00 | 400.00 | 800.00 |

—*Reissue of Aladdin 806.*

FIVE MAN ELECTRICAL BAND
CAPITOL

| ❏ ST-165 | Five Man Electrical Band | 1969 | 5.00 | 10.00 | 20.00 |

LION

| ❏ LN-1009 | Sweet Paradise | 1973 | 5.00 | 10.00 | 20.00 |

LIONEL

| ❏ LRS-1100 | Good-Byes & Butterflies | 1970 | 7.50 | 15.00 | 30.00 |
| ❏ LRS-1101 | Coming of Age | 1971 | 5.00 | 10.00 | 20.00 |

MGM

| ❏ SE-4725 | Good-Byes & Butterflies | 1970 | 12.50 | 25.00 | 50.00 |

PICKWICK

| ❏ SPC-3289 | Five Man Electrical Band | 1973 | 2.50 | 5.00 | 10.00 |

—*Reissue of Capitol material*

FIVE ROYALES, THE
APOLLO

| ❏ LP-488 [M] | The Rockin' 5 Royales | 1956 | 250.00 | 500.00 | 1000. |

—*Yellow label*

| ❏ LP-488 [M] | The Rockin' 5 Royales | 1956 | 1000. | 1500. | 2000. |

—*Green label*

| ❏ LP-488 [M] | The Rockin' 5 Royales | 1956 | 2000. | 3000. | 4000. |

—*Purple label*
KING

❏ 580 [M]	Dedicated to You	1957	125.00	250.00	500.00
❏ 616 [M]	The 5 Royales Sing for You	1959	100.00	200.00	400.00
❏ 678 [M]	The Five Royales	1960	62.50	125.00	250.00
❏ 955 [M]	24 All Time Hits	1966	25.00	50.00	100.00
❏ 5014	17 Hits	197?	3.00	6.00	12.00

FIVE SATINS, THE
BUDDAH

| ❏ BDS-5654 | Black Satin | 1976 | 3.75 | 7.50 | 15.00 |

—*As "Black Satin"*
CELEBRITY SHOWCASE

| ❏ JB-7671 | The Best of the Five Satins | 1970 | 5.00 | 10.00 | 20.00 |

COLLECTABLES

| ❏ COL-5017 | The Five Satins Sing Their Greatest Hits | 198? | 2.50 | 5.00 | 10.00 |

EMBER

| ❏ ELP-100 [M] | The Five Satins Sing | 1957 | 150.00 | 300.00 | 600.00 |

—*Red label; group pictured on front cover; black vinyl*

| ❏ ELP-100 [M] | The Five Satins Sing | 1957 | 1000. | 1500. | 2000. |

—*Red label; group pictured on front cover; blue vinyl*

| ❏ ELP-100 [M] | The Five Satins Sing | 1959 | 50.00 | 100.00 | 200.00 |

—*Mostly white "logs" label; no picture on cover*

| ❏ ELP-100 [M] | The Five Satins Sing | 1959 | 75.00 | 150.00 | 300.00 |

—*Mostly white "logs" label; group pictured on front cover*

| ❏ ELP-100 [M] | The Five Satins Sing | 1961 | 25.00 | 50.00 | 100.00 |

—*Black label; no picture on cover*

| ❏ ELP-401 [M] | The Five Satins Encore | 1960 | 50.00 | 100.00 | 200.00 |

—*Mostly white "logs" label*

| ❏ ELP-401 [M] | The Five Satins Encore | 1961 | 25.00 | 50.00 | 100.00 |

—*Black label*
LOST-NITE

| ❏ LLP-8 [10] | The Five Satins | 1981 | 2.50 | 5.00 | 10.00 |

—*Red vinyl*

| ❏ LLP-9 [10] | The Five Satins | 1981 | 2.50 | 5.00 | 10.00 |

—*Red vinyl*
MOUNT VERNON

| ❏ 108 | The Five Satins Sing | 196? | 7.50 | 15.00 | 30.00 |

RELIC

❏ 5008	The Five Satins' Greatest Hits (1956-1959), Volume 1	198?	2.50	5.00	10.00
❏ 5013	The Five Satins' Greatest Hits (1956-1959), Volume 2	198?	2.50	5.00	10.00
❏ 5024	The Five Satins' Greatest Hits (1956-1959), Volume 3	198?	2.50	5.00	10.00

FIVE SPECIAL
ELEKTRA

| ❏ 5E-553 | Trak'n | 1981 | 5.00 | 10.00 | 20.00 |

FIVE STAIRSTEPS, THE
BUDDAH

| ❏ BDS-5008 | Our Family Portrait | 1967 | 5.00 | 10.00 | 20.00 |
| ❏ BDS-5061 | Stairsteps | 1970 | 3.75 | 7.50 | 15.00 |

—*As "Stairsteps"*

| ❏ BDS-5068 | Step by Step by Step | 1970 | 3.75 | 7.50 | 15.00 |

—*As "Stairsteps"*
COLLECTABLES

| ❏ COL-5023 | Greatest Hits | 1985 | 2.50 | 5.00 | 10.00 |

CURTOM

| ❏ 8002 | Love's Happening | 1969 | 5.00 | 10.00 | 20.00 |

WINDY C

| ❏ 6000 [M] | The Five Stairsteps | 1967 | 6.25 | 12.50 | 25.00 |
| ❏ S-6000 [S] | The Five Stairsteps | 1967 | 6.25 | 12.50 | 25.00 |

FLACK, ROBERTA
ATLANTIC

❏ SD 1569	Chapter Two	1970	2.50	5.00	10.00
❏ SD 1594	Quiet Fire	1971	2.50	5.00	10.00
❏ QD 7271 [Q]	Killing Me Softly	1973	3.75	7.50	15.00
❏ SD 7271	Killing Me Softly	1973	2.50	5.00	10.00
❏ SD 8230	First Take	1969	2.50	5.00	10.00

—*Red and green label (second edition)*

| ❏ SD 8230 | First Take | 1969 | 5.00 | 10.00 | 20.00 |

—*Brown and purple label (first edition)*

| ❏ SD 16013 | Roberta Flack Featuring Donny Hathaway | 1980 | 2.50 | 5.00 | 10.00 |

—*Only two tracks feature Mr. Hathaway*

❏ SD 18131	Feel Like Makin' Love	1974	2.50	5.00	10.00
❏ SD 19149	Blue Lights in the Basement	1977	2.50	5.00	10.00
❏ SD 19154	Killing Me Softly	1978	2.00	4.00	8.00

—*Reissue of 7271*

❏ SD 19186	Roberta Flack	1978	2.50	5.00	10.00
❏ SD 19317	The Best of Roberta Flack	1981	2.50	5.00	10.00
❏ SD 19354	I'm the One	1982	2.50	5.00	10.00
❏ 81916	Oasis	1988	2.50	5.00	10.00
❏ SW-94346	First Take	1972	3.75	7.50	15.00

—*Capitol Record Club edition*

FLAGG, FANNIE
RCA VICTOR

| ❏ LPM-3856 [M] | Rally 'Round the Flagg | 1967 | 5.00 | 10.00 | 20.00 |
| ❏ LSP-3856 [S] | Rally 'Round the Flagg | 1967 | 3.75 | 7.50 | 15.00 |

FLAIRS, THE (1)
CROWN

| ❏ CLP-5356 [M] | The Flairs | 1963 | 20.00 | 40.00 | 80.00 |

FLAME, THE
BROTHER

| ❏ BR-2500 | The Flame | 1970 | 7.50 | 15.00 | 30.00 |

—*Deduct 1/3 if poster is missing*

FLAMIN' GROOVIES, THE
BUDDAH

| ❏ BDS-5683 | Shill Shakin' | 1977 | 3.75 | 7.50 | 15.00 |

EPIC

| ❏ BN 26487 | Supersnazz | 1969 | 12.50 | 25.00 | 50.00 |

KAMA SUTRA

| ❏ KSBS-2021 | Flamingo | 1970 | 7.50 | 15.00 | 30.00 |

—*Pink label*

| ❏ KSBS-2021 | Flamingo | 1972 | 3.75 | 7.50 | 15.00 |

—*Blue label*

| ❏ KSBS-2031 | Teenage Head | 1971 | 7.50 | 15.00 | 30.00 |

—*Pink label*

| ❏ KSBS-2031 | Teenage Head | 1972 | 3.75 | 7.50 | 15.00 |

—*Blue label*
SIRE

| ❏ SRK 6059 | The Flamin' Groovies Now | 1978 | 3.00 | 6.00 | 12.00 |

—*Reissues have 14 tracks*

| ❏ SRK 6059 | The Flamin' Groovies Now | 1978 | 3.75 | 7.50 | 15.00 |

—*Originals have 12 tracks*

| ❏ SRK 6067 | Jumpin' in the Night | 1979 | 3.00 | 6.00 | 12.00 |
| ❏ SASD-7521 | Shake Some Action | 1976 | 3.75 | 7.50 | 15.00 |

SNAZZ

| ❏ R-2371 [10] | Sneekers | 1969 | 25.00 | 50.00 | 100.00 |

—*This album has been counterfeited*

FLAMING LIPS, THE
ATAVISTIC

| ❏ ALP-04 [EP] | Unconsciously Screamin' | 1991 | 6.25 | 12.50 | 25.00 |

LOVELY SORTS OF DEATH

| ❏ (# unknown) [EP] | The Flaming Lips (Bag Full of Thoughts) | 1984 | 20.00 | 40.00 | 80.00 |

—*Red vinyl; black background on jacket*

| ❏ (# unknown) [EP] | The Flaming Lips (Bag Full of Thoughts) | 1984 | 30.00 | 60.00 | 120.00 |

—*Green vinyl; dark brown background on jacket*
PINK DUST

| ❏ 72173 | Hear It Is | 1986 | 10.00 | 20.00 | 40.00 |

—*Originals on white vinyl*

| ❏ 72188 [EP] | The Flaming Lips | 1985 | 10.00 | 20.00 | 40.00 |

—*Originals on lavender vinyl; reissue of Lovely Sorts of Death EP*
RESTLESS

| ❏ 72207 | Oh My Gawd, The Flaming Lips | 1987 | 10.00 | 20.00 | 40.00 |

—*Clear vinyl*

| ❏ 72350 | Telepathic Surgery | 1989 | 6.25 | 12.50 | 25.00 |
| ❏ 72359 | In a Priest Driven Ambulance | 1990 | 6.25 | 12.50 | 25.00 |

—*Pink vinyl*
WARNER BROS.

| ❏ 45334 | Transmissions from the Satellite Heart | 1993 | 5.00 | 10.00 | 20.00 |

Number	Title (A Side/B Side)	Yr	VG	VG+	NM
❑ 45911	Clouds Taste Metallic	1995	3.75	7.50	15.00
❑ 48141	Yoshimi Battles the Pink Robots	2002	5.00	10.00	20.00

FLAMING YOUTH
Phil Collins was in this group.
UNI

❑ 73075	Ark 2	1969	10.00	20.00	40.00

FLAMINGO, JOHNNY
DIADON

❑ 201 [M]	Johnny Flamingo Sings In the Wee Small Hours	1961	25.00	50.00	100.00

FLAMINGOS, THE
CHECKER

❑ LP-1433 [M]	The Flamingos	1959	100.00	200.00	400.00
—Black label					
❑ LP-1433 [M]	The Flamingos	196?	37.50	75.00	150.00
—Blue label					
❑ LPS-3005 [R]	The Flamingos	1966	6.25	12.50	25.00
—Rechanneled reissue of 1433					

CONSTELLATION

❑ CS-3 [M]	Collectors Showcase: The Flamingos	1964	12.50	25.00	50.00
—With more restrained pink lettering on cover					
❑ CS-3 [M]	Collectors Showcase: The Flamingos	1964	25.00	50.00	100.00
—With hot pink lettering on cover					

END

❑ LP-304 [M]	Flamingo Serenade	1959	50.00	100.00	200.00
—Gray label with dog					
❑ LP-304 [M]	Flamingo Serenade	1959	100.00	200.00	400.00
—Black label with shadow print logo					
❑ LPS-304 [S]	Flamingo Serenade	1959	125.00	250.00	500.00
—Cover says "Stereo"					
❑ LPS-304 [S]	Flamingo Serenade	196?	50.00	100.00	200.00
—Cover says "Rechanneled Stereo" (only one track is)					
❑ LP-307 [M]	Flamingo Favorites	1960	25.00	50.00	100.00
❑ LPS-307 [R]	Flamingo Favorites	1960	17.50	35.00	70.00
❑ LP-308 [M]	Requestfully Yours	1960	25.00	50.00	100.00
❑ LPS-308 [R]	Requestfully Yours	1960	17.50	35.00	70.00
❑ LP-316 [M]	The Sound of the Flamingos	1962	25.00	50.00	100.00
❑ LPS-316 [R]	The Sound of the Flamingos	1962	17.50	35.00	70.00
❑ LPS-316 [S]	The Sound of the Flamingos	1962	50.00	100.00	200.00
—"Stereo" at upper right corner of front cover					

LOST-NITE

❑ LLP-7 [10]	The Flamingos	1981	2.50	5.00	10.00
—Red vinyl					

PHILIPS

❑ PHM 200206 [M]	Their Hits — Then and Now	1966	6.25	12.50	25.00
❑ PHS 600206 [S]	Their Hits — Then and Now	1966	7.50	15.00	30.00

RONZE

❑ RLP-1001	The Flamingos Today	1972	3.75	7.50	15.00

SOLID SMOKE

❑ 8018	Golden Teardrops	198?	2.50	5.00	10.00

FLAMINGOS, THE, AND THE MOONGLOWS
VEE JAY

❑ LP-1052 [M]	The Flamingos Meet the Moonglows on the Dusty Road of Hits	1962	37.50	75.00	150.00
❑ VJLP-1052 [M]	The Flamingos Meet the Moonglows on the Dusty Road of Hits	198?	3.00	6.00	12.00
—Authorized reissue					

FLANAGAN, TOMMY
MOODSVILLE

❑ MVLP-9 [M]	The Tommy Flanagan Trio	1960	12.50	25.00	50.00
—Green label					
❑ MVLP-9 [M]	The Tommy Flanagan Trio	1965	6.25	12.50	25.00
—Blue label, trident logo at right					

PRESTIGE

❑ PRLP-7134 [M]	Overseas	1958	37.50	75.00	150.00

REGENT

❑ MG-6055 [M]	Jazz... It's Magic	1958	20.00	40.00	80.00

FLANDERS, TOMMY
VERVE FORECAST

❑ FTS-3075	Moonstone	1969	5.00	10.00	20.00

FLANDERS AND SWANN
ANGEL

❑ 35797 [M]	At the Drop of a Hat	196?	5.00	10.00	20.00
❑ S 35797 [S]	At the Drop of a Hat	196?	6.25	12.50	25.00
❑ 36112 [M]	The Bestiary of Flanders and Swann	196?	5.00	10.00	20.00
❑ S 36112 [S]	The Bestiary of Flanders and Swann	196?	6.25	12.50	25.00
❑ 36388 [M]	At the Drop of Another Hat	1966	5.00	10.00	20.00
❑ S 36388 [S]	At the Drop of Another Hat	1966	6.25	12.50	25.00
❑ 65042 [M]	At the Drop of a Hat	1959	6.25	12.50	25.00
—Original issue					

FLARES, THE
PRESS

❑ PR 73001 [M]	Encore of Foot Stompin' Hits	196?	20.00	40.00	80.00
❑ PRS 83001 [S]	Encore of Foot Stompin' Hits	196?	30.00	60.00	120.00

FLAT EARTH SOCIETY, THE
FLEETWOOD

❑ 3027	Waleeco	1968	75.00	150.00	300.00

FLATT, LESTER
COLUMBIA

❑ CS 1006	Flatt Out	1970	5.00	10.00	20.00

NUGGET

❑ 104	The One and Only	1971	5.00	10.00	20.00

RCA VICTOR

❑ APL1-0131	Country Boy	1973	3.75	7.50	15.00
❑ LSP-4495	Lester Flatt on Victor	1971	5.00	10.00	20.00
❑ LSP-4633	Kentucky Ridgerunner	1972	5.00	10.00	20.00
❑ LSP-4789	Foggy Mountain Breakdown	1972	5.00	10.00	20.00

FLATT, LESTER, AND MAC WISEMAN
RCA VICTOR

❑ LSP-4547	Lester 'n' Mac	1971	5.00	10.00	20.00
❑ LSP-4688	On the South Bound	1972	5.00	10.00	20.00

FLATT AND SCRUGGS
ARCHIVE OF FOLK AND JAZZ

❑ 259	Lester Flatt & Earl Scruggs	197?	2.50	5.00	10.00

COLUMBIA

❑ GP 30 [(2)]	20 All-Time Great Recordings	1970	5.00	10.00	20.00
❑ CL 1019 [M]	Foggy Mountain Jamboree	1957	12.50	25.00	50.00
❑ CL 1424 [M]	Songs of Glory	1960	5.00	10.00	20.00
❑ CL 1564 [M]	Foggy Mountain Banjo	1961	5.00	10.00	20.00
❑ CL 1664 [M]	Songs of the Famous Carter Family	1961	5.00	10.00	20.00
❑ CL 1830 [M]	Folk Songs of Our Land	1962	5.00	10.00	20.00
❑ CL 1951 [M]	Hard Travelin' Featuring The Ballad of Jed Clampett	1963	5.00	10.00	20.00
❑ CL 2045 [M]	Flatt and Scruggs at Carnegie Hall	1963	5.00	10.00	20.00
❑ CL 2134 [M]	Recorded Live at Vanderbilt University	1964	5.00	10.00	20.00
❑ CL 2255 [M]	The Fabulous Sound of Flatt & Scruggs	1964	5.00	10.00	20.00
❑ CL 2354 [M]	Pickin' Strummin' and Singin'	1965	3.75	7.50	15.00
❑ CL 2443 [M]	Town and Country	1966	3.75	7.50	15.00
❑ CL 2513 [M]	When the Saints Go Marching In	1966	3.75	7.50	15.00
❑ CL 2570 [M]	Flatt and Scruggs' Greatest Hits	1966	3.75	7.50	15.00
❑ CL 2643 [M]	Strictly Instrumental	1967	5.00	10.00	20.00
❑ CL 2686 [M]	Hear the Whistle Blow	1967	5.00	10.00	20.00
❑ CS 8221 [S]	Songs of Glory	1960	6.25	12.50	25.00
❑ CS 8364 [S]	Foggy Mountain Banjo	1961	6.25	12.50	25.00
❑ CS 8464 [S]	Songs of the Famous Carter Family	1961	6.25	12.50	25.00
❑ CS 8630 [S]	Folk Songs of Our Land	1962	6.25	12.50	25.00
❑ CS 8751 [S]	Hard Travelin' Featuring The Ballad of Jed Clampett	1963	6.25	12.50	25.00
❑ CS 8845 [S]	Flatt and Scruggs at Carnegie Hall	1963	6.25	12.50	25.00
❑ PC 8845	Flatt and Scruggs at Carnegie Hall	198?	2.00	4.00	8.00
—Budget-line reissue					
❑ CS 8934 [S]	Recorded Live at Vanderbilt University	1964	6.25	12.50	25.00
❑ CS 9055 [S]	The Fabulous Sound of Flatt & Scruggs	1964	6.25	12.50	25.00
❑ CS 9154 [S]	Pickin' Strummin' and Singin'	1965	5.00	10.00	20.00
❑ CS 9243 [S]	Town and Country	1966	5.00	10.00	20.00
❑ CS 9313 [S]	When the Saints Go Marching In	1966	5.00	10.00	20.00
❑ CS 9370 [S]	Flatt and Scruggs' Greatest Hits	1966	5.00	10.00	20.00
❑ PC 9370	Flatt and Scruggs' Greatest Hits	198?	2.00	4.00	8.00
—Budget-line reissue					
❑ CS 9443 [S]	Strictly Instrumental	1967	5.00	10.00	20.00
❑ CS 9486 [S]	Hear the Whistle Blow	1967	5.00	10.00	20.00
❑ CS 9596	Changin' Times Featuring Foggy Mountain Breakdown	1968	5.00	10.00	20.00
—Red "360 Sound" label					
❑ CS 9596	Changin' Times Featuring Foggy Mountain Breakdown	1970	3.00	6.00	12.00
—Orange label with six "Columbia"s along edge					
❑ CS 9649	The Story of Bonnie & Clyde	1968	5.00	10.00	20.00
❑ CS 9741	Nashville Airplane	1969	5.00	10.00	20.00
❑ CS 9945	Final Fling	1970	3.75	7.50	15.00
❑ C 30347	Breaking Out	1971	3.00	6.00	12.00
❑ CG 31964 [(2)]	The World of Flatt and Scruggs	1972	3.75	7.50	15.00
❑ C 32244	A Boy Named Sue	1973	3.00	6.00	12.00
❑ FC 37469	Lester Flatt & Earl Scruggs	1981	2.50	5.00	10.00

COLUMBIA LIMITED EDITION

❑ LE 10149	Breaking Out	197?	2.50	5.00	10.00
—Brown label "Limited Edition"					

COLUMBIA MUSICAL TREASURY

❑ DS 493	Detroit City	1969	3.75	7.50	15.00

COUNTY

❑ CCS-111	You Can Feel It in Your Soul	1988	2.50	5.00	10.00

HARMONY

❑ HL 7250 [M]	Lester Flatt & Earl Scruggs	1960	3.75	7.50	15.00
❑ HL 7340 [M]	Great Original Recordings	1965	3.75	7.50	15.00
❑ HL 7402 [M]	Sacred Songs	1967	3.75	7.50	15.00
❑ HL 7465 [M]	Songs to Cherish	1968	3.75	7.50	15.00
❑ HS 11202 [S]	Sacred Songs	1967	3.00	6.00	12.00
❑ HS 11265 [S]	Songs to Cherish	1968	3.00	6.00	12.00
❑ HS 11401	Foggy Mountain Chimes	1970	3.00	6.00	12.00
❑ H 30932	Wabash Cannonball	197?	2.50	5.00	10.00

MERCURY

❑ MG-20358 [M]	Country Music	1958	10.00	20.00	40.00
❑ MG-20542 [M]	Lester Flatt & Earl Scruggs	1959	10.00	20.00	40.00
❑ MG-20773 [M]	The Original Sound of Flatt & Scruggs	1963	6.25	12.50	25.00
❑ SR-60773 [R]	The Original Sound of Flatt & Scruggs	1963	3.75	7.50	15.00
❑ SR-61162	Original Theme from Bonnie & Clyde	1968	5.00	10.00	20.00

NASHVILLE

❑ 2087	The Best of Flatt and Scruggs	1970	3.00	6.00	12.00

PICKWICK

❑ 6093	Foggy Mountain Breakdown	197?	3.00	6.00	12.00
❑ 6140	Blue Grass Banjos	197?	2.50	5.00	10.00

POWER PAK

❑ 297	Golden Hits	197?	2.50	5.00	10.00

ROUNDER

❑ SS-05	The Golden Era	198?	2.50	5.00	10.00
❑ SS-08	Don't Get Above Your Raisin'	198?	2.50	5.00	10.00
❑ SS-18	The Mercury Sessions, Volume 1	1985	2.50	5.00	10.00
❑ SS-19	The Mercury Sessions, Volume 2	1985	2.50	5.00	10.00

F

Number	Title (A Side/B Side)	Yr	VG	VG+	NM
STARDAY					
❏ SLP-365 [M]	Stars of the Grand Ol' Opry	1966	6.25	12.50	25.00
—With Jim and Jesse					
WING					
❏ SRW-16376	The Original Foggy Mountain Breakdown	1968	3.00	6.00	12.00
FLAVOR					
JU-PAR					
❏ JP6-1002S1	In Good Taste	1976	5.00	10.00	20.00
FLEETWOOD MAC					
Also see BUCKINGHAM NICKS; PETER GREEN; STEVIE NICKS.					
BLUE HORIZON					
❏ BH-3801 [(2)]	Fleetwood Mac in Chicago	1970	7.50	15.00	30.00
❏ BH-4802	Blues Jam in Chicago, Vol. 1	1970	3.75	7.50	15.00
❏ BH-4803	Blues Jam in Chicago, Vol. 2	1970	3.75	7.50	15.00
EPIC					
❏ LN 24402 [M]	Fleetwood Mac	1968	25.00	50.00	100.00
—White label promo only					
❏ LN 24446 [M]	English Rose	1969	25.00	50.00	100.00
—White label promo only					
❏ BN 26402 [S]	Fleetwood Mac	1968	7.50	15.00	30.00
❏ BN 26446 [S]	English Rose	1969	7.50	15.00	30.00
❏ KE 30632 [(2)]	Black Magic Woman	1971	5.00	10.00	20.00
❏ KE 33740 [(2)]	Fleetwood Mac/English Rose	1974	3.75	7.50	15.00
MOBILE FIDELITY					
❏ 1-012	Fleetwood Mac	1980	10.00	20.00	40.00
—Audiophile vinyl					
❏ 1-119	Mirage	1984	10.00	20.00	40.00
—Audiophile vinyl					
NAUTILUS					
❏ NR-8	Rumours	1980	10.00	20.00	40.00
—Audiophile vinyl					
REPRISE					
❏ MS 2080	Bare Trees	197?	3.75	7.50	15.00
—Without brown line on front cover; uncommon with the MS 2080 number					
❏ MS 2080	Bare Trees	1972	3.00	6.00	12.00
—With brown line near all four edges of the front cover					
❏ MS 2138	Penguin	1973	3.75	7.50	15.00
❏ MS 2158	Mystery to Me	1973	3.00	6.00	12.00
—With "For Your Love" listed correctly on the back cover					
❏ MS 2158	Mystery to Me	1973	5.00	10.00	20.00
—With "Good Things (Come to Those Who Wait)" listed on the album cover; it was replaced at the last minute by "For Your Love"					
❏ MS 2196	Heroes Are Hard to Find	1974	3.00	6.00	12.00
❏ MS 2225	Fleetwood Mac	1975	2.50	5.00	10.00
❏ MSK 2278	Bare Trees	1977	2.00	4.00	8.00
—Reissue; no brown line on the front cover					
❏ MSK 2279	Mystery to Me	1977	2.00	4.00	8.00
❏ MSK 2281	Fleetwood Mac	1977	2.00	4.00	8.00
❏ RS 6368	Then Play On	1970	3.75	7.50	15.00
—Later pressings replace above two tracks with "Oh Well (Parts 1 and 2)."					
❏ RS 6368	Then Play On	1969	6.25	12.50	25.00
—First pressings include "When You Say" and "My Dream"					
❏ RS 6408	Kiln House	1970	3.75	7.50	15.00
❏ RS 6465	Future Games	1971	6.25	12.50	25.00
—Originals have a pale yellow cover					
❏ RS 6465	Future Games	1972	3.75	7.50	15.00
—Later pressings have a pale green cover					
SIRE					
❏ SASH-3706 [(2)]	Vintage Years	1975	3.75	7.50	15.00
❏ SASH-3715 [(2)]	Fleetwood Mac in Chicago	1975	3.75	7.50	15.00
—Reissue of Blue Horizon 3801					
❏ 2XS-6006 [(2)]	Vintage Years	1977	3.00	6.00	12.00
❏ 2XS-6009 [(2)]	Fleetwood Mac in Chicago	1977	3.00	6.00	12.00
❏ 2XS-6045 [(2)]	The Original Fleetwood Mac	1977	3.00	6.00	12.00
VARRICK					
❏ VR-020	Jumping at Shadows	1985	3.00	6.00	12.00
WARNER BROS.					
❏ PRO-A-866 [DJ]	Tusk Remix	1979	5.00	10.00	20.00
—Promo-only EP					
❏ BSK 3010	Rumours	1977	2.00	4.00	8.00
—With long version (2:16) of "Never Going Back Again"; we do not yet know how to identify these without playing them					
❏ BSK 3010	Rumours	1977	2.50	5.00	10.00
—With short version (2:02) of "Never Going Back Again"; we do not yet know how to identify these without playing them					
❏ 2HS 3350 [(2)]	Tusk	1979	3.75	7.50	15.00
❏ 2WB 3500 [(2)]	Fleetwood Mac Live	1980	3.00	6.00	12.00
❏ 23607	Mirage	1982	2.50	5.00	10.00
❏ 23607 [DJ]	Mirage	1982	5.00	10.00	20.00
—Promo on Quiex II vinyl					
❏ 25471	Tango in the Night	1987	2.50	5.00	10.00
❏ 25801	Greatest Hits	1989	2.50	5.00	10.00
❏ 26111	Behind the Mask	1990	3.75	7.50	15.00
FLEETWOODS, THE					
DOLTON					
❏ BLP-2001 [M]	Mr. Blue	1959	20.00	40.00	80.00
—Pale blue label with dolphins on top					
❏ BLP-2001 [M]	Mr. Blue	1963	5.00	10.00	20.00
—Dark label, logo on left					
❏ BLP-2002 [M]	The Fleetwoods	1960	12.50	25.00	50.00
—Pale blue label with dolphins on top					
❏ BLP-2002 [M]	The Fleetwoods	1963	5.00	10.00	20.00
—Dark label, logo on left					
❏ BLP-2005 [M]	Softly	1961	12.50	25.00	50.00
—Pale blue label with dolphins on top					
❏ BLP-2005 [M]	Softly	1963	5.00	10.00	20.00
—Dark label, logo on left					
❏ BLP-2007 [M]	Deep in a Dream	1961	10.00	20.00	40.00
—Pale blue label with dolphins on top					

Number	Title (A Side/B Side)	Yr	VG	VG+	NM
❏ BLP-2007 [M]	Deep in a Dream	1963	5.00	10.00	20.00
—Dark label, logo on left					
❏ BLP-2011 [M]	The Best of the Oldies	1962	10.00	20.00	40.00
—Pale blue label with dolphins on top					
❏ BLP-2011 [M]	The Best of the Oldies	1963	5.00	10.00	20.00
—Dark label, logo on left					
❏ BLP-2018 [M]	The Fleetwoods' Greatest Hits	1962	6.25	12.50	25.00
❏ BLP-2020 [M]	The Fleetwoods Sings for Lovers by Night	1963	7.50	15.00	30.00
❏ BLP-2025 [M]	Goodnight My Love	1963	7.50	15.00	30.00
❏ BLP-2030 [M]	Before and After	1965	7.50	15.00	30.00
❏ BLP-2039 [M]	Folk Rock	1965	7.50	15.00	30.00
❏ BST-8001 [S]	Mr. Blue	1959	25.00	50.00	100.00
—Pale blue label with dolphins on top					
❏ BST-8001 [S]	Mr. Blue	1963	6.25	12.50	25.00
—Dark label, logo on left					
❏ BST-8002 [S]	The Fleetwoods	1960	17.50	35.00	70.00
—Pale blue label with dolphins on top					
❏ BST-8002 [S]	The Fleetwoods	1963	6.25	12.50	25.00
—Dark label, logo on left					
❏ BST-8005 [S]	Softly	1961	17.50	35.00	70.00
—Pale blue label with dolphins on top					
❏ BST-8005 [S]	Softly	1963	6.25	12.50	25.00
—Dark label, logo on left					
❏ BST-8007 [S]	Deep in a Dream	1961	12.50	25.00	50.00
—Pale blue label with dolphins on top					
❏ BST-8007 [S]	Deep in a Dream	1963	6.25	12.50	25.00
—Dark label, logo on left					
❏ BST-8011 [S]	The Best of the Oldies	1962	12.50	25.00	50.00
—Pale blue label with dolphins on top					
❏ BST-8011 [S]	The Best of the Oldies	1963	6.25	12.50	25.00
—Dark label, logo on left					
❏ BST-8018 [S]	The Fleetwoods' Greatest Hits	1962	7.50	15.00	30.00
❏ BST-8020 [S]	The Fleetwoods Sings for Lovers by Night	1963	10.00	20.00	40.00
❏ BST-8025 [S]	Goodnight My Love	1963	10.00	20.00	40.00
❏ BST-8030 [S]	Before and After	1965	10.00	20.00	40.00
❏ BST-8039 [S]	Folk Rock	1965	10.00	20.00	40.00
LIBERTY					
❏ LN-10159	The Fleetwoods' Greatest Hits	1982	2.00	4.00	8.00
❏ LN-10160	The Best Goodies of the Oldies	1982	2.00	4.00	8.00
❏ LN-10199	Buried Treasure	1983	2.00	4.00	8.00
SUNSET					
❏ SUM-1131 [M]	In a Mellow Mood	1966	3.00	6.00	12.00
❏ SUS-5131 [S]	In a Mellow Mood	1966	3.75	7.50	15.00
UNITED ARTISTS					
❏ UA-LA334-E	The Very Best of the Fleetwoods	1975	3.00	6.00	12.00
FLEMING, KING					
ARGO					
❏ LP-4004 [M]	Misty Night	1961	6.25	12.50	25.00
❏ LPS-4004 [S]	Misty Night	1961	7.50	15.00	30.00
❏ LP-4019 [M]	Stand By!	1962	6.25	12.50	25.00
❏ LPS-4019 [S]	Stand By!	1962	7.50	15.00	30.00
CADET					
❏ LPS-4053 [S]	Weary Traveler	1966	5.00	10.00	20.00
FLEMING, RHONDA					
COLUMBIA					
❏ CL 1080 [M]	Rhonda	1958	15.00	30.00	60.00
FLEMONS, WADE					
VEE JAY					
❏ LP-1011 [M]	Wade Flemons	1959	37.50	75.00	150.00
—Maroon label					
❏ LP-1011 [M]	Wade Flemons	196?	20.00	40.00	80.00
—Black label					
FLESH FOR LULU					
CAPITOL					
❏ C1-48217	Long Live the New Flesh	1987	3.00	6.00	12.00
❏ SPRO 79992 [DJ]	Final Vinyl (Every Little Word + 7 Live)	1989	5.00	10.00	20.00
—Red vinyl; sticker on generic cover					
❏ C1-90232	Plastic Fantastic	1989	3.00	6.00	12.00
FLESHEATERS					
HOMESTEAD					
❏ (# unknown)	Prehistoric Hits Vol. 1	198?	3.00	6.00	12.00
❏ 124-1	Live	1988	2.50	5.00	10.00
RUBY					
❏ JRR-101	A Minute to Pray, a Second to Die	1981	5.00	10.00	20.00
❏ JRR 805	Forever Came Today	1982	5.00	10.00	20.00
SST					
❏ 094	Greatest Hits	1986	3.00	6.00	12.00
❏ 094	Destroyed by Fire/Greatest Hits	1991	2.50	5.00	10.00
—Reissue with new name					
❏ 264	Prehistoric Fits	1990	3.00	6.00	12.00
❏ 273 [(2)]	Dragstrip Riot	1991	3.00	6.00	12.00
UPSETTER					
❏ UPCJ-34	No Questions Asked	1980	10.00	20.00	40.00
❏ UP 56	A Hard Road to Follow	1983	7.50	15.00	30.00
FLETCHER, SAM					
VAULT					
❏ LP-116 [M]	The Look of Love, the Sound of Soul	1967	7.50	15.00	30.00
❏ VS-116 [S]	The Look of Love, the Sound of Soul	1967	7.50	15.00	30.00
VEE JAY					
❏ LP-1094 [M]	Sam Fletcher Sings	1964	10.00	20.00	40.00
FLINT, SHELBY					
MAD SATYR					
❏ MSR-101	You've Been On My Mind	1982	6.25	12.50	25.00
VALIANT					
❏ LP-401 [M]	Shelby Flint — The Quiet Girl	1961	10.00	20.00	40.00

Whether on blue or black vinyl, the original Soma issue of the Fendermen's *Mule Skinner Blues* album is a big-ticket item.

Flamingo Serenade is the album that came out in the wake of the Flamingos' biggest pop hit, "I Only Have Eyes for You."

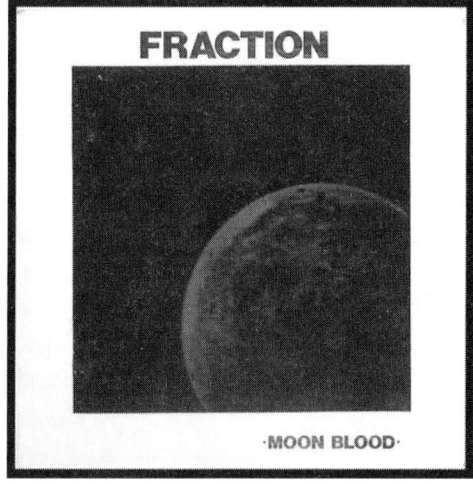

One of the most highly desirable private-label psych records is this one, *Moon Blood* by Fraction.

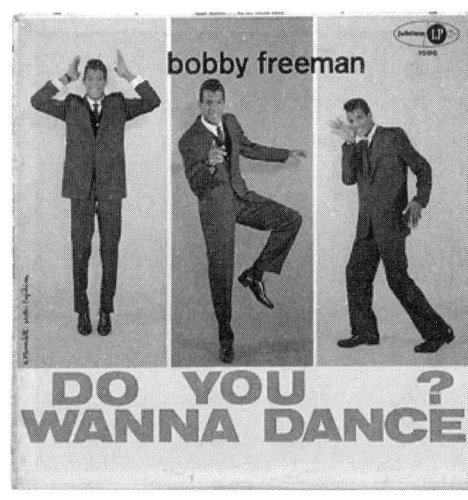

This is the album that the Jubilee label released in the wake of Bobby Freeman's top-10 success with "Do You Wanna Dance?"

Here's *The Fugs First Album,* which is a reissue on ESP-Disk' of their debut. That album was originally issued on the Broadside label.

The second of two albums on the Mustang label for the Bobby Fuller Four spotlighted their biggest hit, "I Fought the Law."

Number	Title (A Side/B Side)	Yr	VG	VG+	NM
❑ LP-403 [M]	Shelby Flint Sings Folk	1962	10.00	20.00	40.00
❑ LPS-403 [S]	Shelby Flint Sings Folk	1962	12.50	25.00	50.00
❑ VL-5003 [M]	Cast Your Fate to the Wind	1966	6.25	12.50	25.00
❑ VLS-25003 [S]	Cast Your Fate to the Wind	1966	7.50	15.00	30.00

FLIRTATIONS, THE (1)
DERAM
❑ DES-18028	Nothing But a Heartache	1969	5.00	10.00	20.00

FLO AND EDDIE
COLUMBIA
❑ PC 33554	Illegal, Immoral and Fattening	1975	3.00	6.00	12.00
❑ PC 34262	Moving Targets	1976	3.00	6.00	12.00

EPIPHANY
❑ ELP-4010	Rock Steady with Flo & Eddie	1981	2.50	5.00	10.00

REPRISE
❑ MS 2099	The Phlorescent Leech and Eddie	1972	5.00	10.00	20.00
❑ MS 2141	Flo and Eddie	1973	5.00	10.00	20.00

RHINO
❑ RNTA-1999 [(3)]	History of Flo & Eddie	198?	5.00	10.00	20.00

FLOATERS, THE
ABC
❑ AB-1030	Floaters	1977	2.50	5.00	10.00
❑ AA-1047	Magic	1978	2.50	5.00	10.00

FEE
❑ WW-711	Get Ready for the Floaters and Shu-Ga	1981	7.50	15.00	30.00

FLOATING BRIDGE, THE
VAULT
❑ VS-124	The Floating Bridge	1969	7.50	15.00	30.00

FLOCK, THE
COLUMBIA
❑ CS 9911	The Flock	1969	5.00	10.00	20.00
—"360 Sound" label					
❑ CS 9911	The Flock	1970	3.75	7.50	15.00
—Orange label					
❑ C 30007	Dinosaur Swamps	1970	3.75	7.50	15.00
—Orange label					
❑ C 30007	Dinosaur Swamps	1970	5.00	10.00	20.00
—"360 Sound" label					

MERCURY
❑ SRM-1-1035	Inside Out	1975	3.75	7.50	15.00

FLORENCE, BOB
CARLTON
❑ LP 12-115 [M]	Name Band: 1959	1959	10.00	20.00	40.00
❑ STLP 12-115 [S]	Name Band: 1959	1959	15.00	30.00	60.00

ERA
❑ EL-20003 [M]	Bob Florence and Trio	1956	25.00	50.00	100.00

WORLD PACIFIC
❑ WP-1860 [M]	Pet Project: The Bob Florence Big Band Plays Petula Clark Hits	196?	5.00	10.00	20.00
❑ WPS-21860 [S]	Pet Project: The Bob Florence Big Band Plays Petula Clark Hits	196?	6.25	12.50	25.00

FLORY, MED
JOSIE
❑ JJS-3506 [S]	Med Flory Big Band	1963	5.00	10.00	20.00
❑ JOZ-3506 [M]	Med Flory Big Band	1963	6.25	12.50	25.00

JUBILEE
❑ JLP-1066 [M]	Jazzwave	1958	12.50	25.00	50.00
❑ SDJLP-1066 [S]	Jazzwave	1959	10.00	20.00	40.00

FLOW
CTI
❑ 1003	Flow	1970	5.00	10.00	20.00

FLOWERS, PHIL
GUEST STAR
❑ G-1456 [M]	I Am the Greatest	1964	7.50	15.00	30.00
❑ GS-1456 [S]	I Am the Greatest	1964	10.00	20.00	40.00
❑ G-1457 [M]	Phil Flowers Sings a Tribute	1964	7.50	15.00	30.00
❑ GS-1457 [S]	Phil Flowers Sings a Tribute	1964	10.00	20.00	40.00

MOUNT VERNON
❑ 154 [M]	Rhythm and Blues	196?	6.25	12.50	25.00

FLOYD, EDDIE
MALACO
❑ 6352	Experience	1977	3.00	6.00	12.00

STAX
❑ 714 [M]	Knock on Wood	1967	17.50	35.00	70.00
❑ ST 714 [S]	Knock on Wood	1967	17.50	35.00	70.00
❑ STS-2002	I've Never Found a Girl	1968	7.50	15.00	30.00
❑ STS-2011	Rare Stamps	1969	6.25	12.50	25.00
❑ STS-2017	You've Got to Have Eddie	1969	6.25	12.50	25.00
❑ STS-2029	California Girl	1970	6.25	12.50	25.00
❑ STS-2041	Down to Earth	1971	6.25	12.50	25.00
❑ STS-3016	Baby Lay Your Head Down	1973	6.25	12.50	25.00
❑ STX-4122	Chronicle	1979	3.00	6.00	12.00
❑ STS-5512	Soul Street	1974	6.25	12.50	25.00
❑ MPS-8527	Soul Street	198?	2.50	5.00	10.00

FLOYD, KING
CHIMNEYVILLE
❑ SD 9047	King Floyd	1971	3.75	7.50	15.00

PULSAR
❑ 10602	A Man in Love	1969	5.00	10.00	20.00

V.I.P.
❑ 407	The Heart of the Matter	1970	10.00	20.00	40.00

FLYING BURRITO BROTHERS, THE
A&M
❑ SP-3122	The Gilded Palace of Sin	198?	2.00	4.00	8.00
—Budget-line reissue					
❑ SP-3631 [(2)]	Close Up the Honky-Tonks	1974	3.75	7.50	15.00
❑ SP-4175	The Gilded Palace of Sin	1969	5.00	10.00	20.00
—Brown label					
❑ SP-4175	The Gilded Palace of Sin	1974	3.00	6.00	12.00
—Silvery label					
❑ SP-4258	Burrito Deluxe	1970	3.75	7.50	15.00
—Brown label					
❑ SP-4258	Burrito Deluxe	1974	3.00	6.00	12.00
—Silvery label					
❑ SP-4295	The Flying Burrito Bros.	1971	3.75	7.50	15.00
—Brown label					
❑ SP-4295	The Flying Burrito Bros.	1974	3.00	6.00	12.00
—Silvery label					
❑ SP-4343	Last of the Red Hot Burritos	1972	3.75	7.50	15.00
—Brown label					
❑ SP-4343	Last of the Red Hot Burritos	1974	3.00	6.00	12.00
—Silvery label					
❑ SP-4578	Sleepless Nights	1976	3.00	6.00	12.00
—As "Gram Parsons/The Flying Burrito Bros."					
❑ SP-6510 [(2)]	Close Up the Honky-Tonks	198?	3.00	6.00	12.00
—Reissue of 3631					
❑ SP-8070 [DJ]	Hot Burrito	1975	10.00	20.00	40.00
—Promo-only issue with poster					

COLUMBIA
❑ PC 33817	Flying Again	1975	3.00	6.00	12.00
❑ PC 34222	Airborne	1976	3.00	6.00	12.00

CURB
❑ JZ 37004	Hearts on the Line	1981	2.50	5.00	10.00
—As "Burrito Brothers"					
❑ FZ 37705	Sunset Sundown	1982	2.50	5.00	10.00
—As "Burrito Brothers"					

REGENCY
❑ REG-79001	Live from Tokyo	1980	2.50	5.00	10.00

FOCUS
ATCO
❑ SD 36-100	Hamburger Concerto	1974	3.00	6.00	12.00
❑ SD 36-117	Mother Focus	1975	3.00	6.00	12.00

HARVEST
❑ ST-11721	Focus Con Proby	1978	3.00	6.00	12.00
—With P.J. Proby					

MERCURY
❑ 824524-1	Focus: Jan Akkerman and Thijs Van Leer	1986	3.00	6.00	12.00

SIRE
❑ SAS-3901 [(2)]	Focus 3	1973	3.75	7.50	15.00
❑ SAS-7401	Moving Waves	1972	3.00	6.00	12.00
❑ SAS-7404	In and Out of Focus	1973	3.00	6.00	12.00
—Reissue of 97027					
❑ SAS-7408	Live at the Rainbow	1973	3.00	6.00	12.00
❑ SASD-7505	Dutch Masters — A Selection of Their Finest Recordings 1969-1973	1975	3.00	6.00	12.00
❑ SASD-7531	Ship of Memories	1977	3.00	6.00	12.00
❑ SES-97027	In and Out of Focus	1970	5.00	10.00	20.00
—Original issue					

FOGELBERG, DAN
COLUMBIA
❑ KC 31751	Home Free	1972	3.00	6.00	12.00
❑ PC 31751	Home Free	197?	2.00	4.00	8.00
—Reissue with new prefix					

FULL MOON/EPIC
❑ AS 1284 [DJ]	The Innocent Age Sampler	1982	3.00	6.00	12.00
—Promo only; 6 songs					
❑ A2S 1335 [(2)DJ]	Interchords	1982	6.25	12.50	25.00
—Promo-only release					
❑ KE 33137	Souvenirs	1974	3.00	6.00	12.00
—First pressings have orange Epic label with small Full Moon logo					
❑ KE 33137	Souvenirs	1975	2.50	5.00	10.00
—Second pressings have dark blue/black Full Moon label					
❑ PE 33137	Souvenirs	197?	2.00	4.00	8.00
—Reissue with new prefix					
❑ PE 33499	Captured Angel	1975	2.50	5.00	10.00
—No bar code on cover					
❑ PE 33499	Captured Angel	198?	2.00	4.00	8.00
—With bar code on cover					
❑ PEQ 33499 [Q]	Captured Angel	1975	5.00	10.00	20.00
❑ PE 34185	Nether Lands	1977	2.50	5.00	10.00
—No bar code on cover					
❑ PE 34185	Nether Lands	198?	2.00	4.00	8.00
—With bar code on cover					
❑ PE 35364	Phoenix	198?	2.00	4.00	8.00
—Budget-line reissue					
❑ FE 35634	Phoenix	1979	2.50	5.00	10.00
❑ KE2 37393 [(2)]	The Innocent Age	1981	3.00	6.00	12.00
❑ QE 38308	Dan Fogelberg/Greatest Hits	1982	2.50	5.00	10.00
❑ QE 39004	Windows and Walls	1984	2.50	5.00	10.00
❑ FE 39616	High Country Snows	1985	2.50	5.00	10.00
❑ OE 40271	Exiles	1987	2.50	5.00	10.00
❑ HE 45634	Phoenix	1981	7.50	15.00	30.00
—Half-speed mastered edition					
❑ HE 48308	Dan Fogelberg/Greatest Hits	1983	7.50	15.00	30.00
—Half-speed mastered edition					

FOGELBERG, DAN, AND TIM WEISBERG
FULL MOON/EPIC
❑ JE 35339	Twin Sons of Different Mothers	1978	2.50	5.00	10.00

Number	Title (A Side/B Side)	Yr	VG	VG+	NM
❑ PE 35339	Twin Sons of Different Mothers	198?	2.00	4.00	8.00
—Budget-line reissue					
❑ HE 45339	Twin Sons of Different Mothers	198?	7.50	15.00	30.00
—Half-speed mastered edition					

FOGERTY, JOHN
Includes records as "The Blue Ridge Rangers." Also see CREEDENCE CLEARWATER REVIVAL; THE GOLLIWOGS.
ASYLUM

Number	Title	Yr	VG	VG+	NM
❑ 7E-1046	John Fogerty	1975	3.00	6.00	12.00
❑ 7E-1081	Hoodoo	1976	—	—	—
—Canceled; poor quality bootleg cassettes exist					

FANTASY

❑ MPF-4502	John Fogerty: The Blue Ridge Rangers	1981	2.50	5.00	10.00
—Reissues prominently place John Fogerty's name on the cover					
❑ F-9415	The Blue Ridge Rangers	1973	3.75	7.50	15.00
—As "The Blue Ridge Rangers"					

WARNER BROS.

❑ 25203	Centerfield	1985	3.75	7.50	15.00
—Originals have the last song on side 2 as "Zanz Kant Danz"					
❑ 25203	Centerfield	1986	2.50	5.00	10.00
—Later editions have the last song on side 2 re-recorded and listed as "Vanz Kant Danz"					
❑ 25203 [DJ]	Centerfield	1985	7.50	15.00	30.00
—Promo versions on Quiex II audiophile vinyl					
❑ 25449	Eye of the Zombie	1986	2.50	5.00	10.00

FOLDS, BEN, FIVE
Includes Ben Folds solo.
EPIC

❑ E2 61610 [(2)]	Rockin' the Suburbs	2001	3.75	7.50	15.00

550 MUSIC

❑ B 67762	Whatever and Ever, Amen	1997	3.75	7.50	15.00
❑ B 68809	Fear of Pop Volume 1	1998	3.75	7.50	15.00
—By Ben Folds with numerous guests					

SUNDAZED

❑ LP 5164 [(2)]	Ben Folds Live	2003	5.00	10.00	20.00

FOLEY, LORD ADRIAN
MGM

❑ E-3358 [M]	Lord Adrian Foley at the Piano	1955	10.00	20.00	40.00

FOLEY, RED
DECCA

❑ DXB 177 [(2)M]	The Red Foley Story	1964	6.25	12.50	25.00
❑ DL 4107 [M]	Red Foley's Golden Favorites	1961	5.00	10.00	20.00
❑ DL 4140 [M]	Company's Comin'	1961	5.00	10.00	20.00
❑ DL 4198 [M]	Songs of Devotion	1961	5.00	10.00	20.00
❑ DL 4290 [M]	Dear Hearts and Gentle People	1962	5.00	10.00	20.00
❑ DL 4341 [M]	The Red Foley Show	1963	5.00	10.00	20.00
❑ DL 4603 [M]	Songs Everybody Knows	1965	5.00	10.00	20.00
❑ DL 4849 [M]	Songs for the Soul	1967	6.25	12.50	25.00
❑ DL 5003 [M]	Red Foley's Greatest Hits	1968	12.50	25.00	50.00
—White label promo; mono copies may only exist as promos					
❑ DL 5303 [10]	Red Foley Souvenir Album	1951	20.00	40.00	80.00
❑ DL 5338 [10]	Lift Up Your Voice	1952	20.00	40.00	80.00
❑ DXSB 7177 [(2)S]	The Red Foley Story	1964	7.50	15.00	30.00
❑ DL 8294 [M]	Red Foley Souvenir Album	1956	12.50	25.00	50.00
❑ DL 8296 [M]	Beyond the Sunset	1956	12.50	25.00	50.00
❑ DL 8767 [M]	He Walks with Thee	1958	12.50	25.00	50.00
❑ DL 8806 [M]	My Keepsake Album	1958	12.50	25.00	50.00
❑ DL 8847 [M]	Let's All Sing with Red Foley	1959	10.00	20.00	40.00
❑ DL 8903 [M]	Let's All Sing to Him	1959	10.00	20.00	40.00
❑ DL 38068 [M]	Gratefully	1958	25.00	50.00	100.00
—Special-products issue for Dickies clothing					
❑ DL 74107 [S]	Red Foley's Golden Favorites	1961	6.25	12.50	25.00
❑ DL 74140 [S]	Company's Comin'	1961	6.25	12.50	25.00
❑ DL 74198 [S]	Songs of Devotion	1961	6.25	12.50	25.00
❑ DL 74290 [S]	Dear Hearts and Gentle People	1962	6.25	12.50	25.00
❑ DL 74341 [S]	The Red Foley Show	1963	6.25	12.50	25.00
❑ DL 74603 [S]	Songs Everybody Knows	1965	6.25	12.50	25.00
❑ DL 74849 [S]	Songs for the Soul	1967	5.00	10.00	20.00
❑ DL 75003 [S]	Red Foley's Greatest Hits	1968	3.75	7.50	15.00
❑ DL 78847 [S]	Let's All Sing with Red Foley	1959	12.50	25.00	50.00
❑ DL 78903 [S]	Let's All Sing to Him	1959	12.50	25.00	50.00

FOLK SINGERS, THE
ELEKTRA

❑ EKL-157 [M]	The Folk Singers	1958	7.50	15.00	30.00

FOLKNIKS, THE
HIFI-LIFE SERIES

❑ L-1017 [M]	The Sound of Twelve-String Guitar and Banjo	1964	5.00	10.00	20.00
❑ SL-1017 [S]	The Sound of Twelve-String Guitar and Banjo	1964	6.25	12.50	25.00

FOLKSWINGERS, THE
WORLD PACIFIC

❑ ST-1812 [S]	12 String Guitar!	1963	7.50	15.00	30.00
—Black vinyl					
❑ ST-1812 [S]	12 String Guitar!	1963	15.00	30.00	60.00
—Red vinyl					
❑ WP-1812 [M]	12 String Guitar!	1963	6.25	12.50	25.00
❑ ST-1814 [S]	12 String Guitar, Volume 2	1963	7.50	15.00	30.00
❑ WP-1814 [M]	12 String Guitar, Volume 2	1963	6.25	12.50	25.00
❑ ST-1846 [S]	Raga Rock	1966	7.50	15.00	30.00
❑ WP-1846 [M]	Raga Rock	1966	6.25	12.50	25.00

FONDA, HENRY
CORAL

❑ CRL 57308 [M]	Voices of the 20th Century	1958	15.00	30.00	60.00

FONTAINE, FRANK
ABC-PARAMOUNT

❑ 442 [M]	Songs I Sing on the Jackie Gleason Show	1963	3.75	7.50	15.00

Number	Title (A Side/B Side)	Yr	VG	VG+	NM
❑ S-442 [S]	Songs I Sing on the Jackie Gleason Show	1963	5.00	10.00	20.00
❑ 460 [M]	Sings Like Crazy	1963	3.75	7.50	15.00
❑ S-460 [S]	Sings Like Crazy	1963	5.00	10.00	20.00
❑ 470 [M]	How Sweet It Is	1964	3.75	7.50	15.00
❑ S-470 [S]	How Sweet It Is	1964	5.00	10.00	20.00
❑ 490 [M]	More Songs I Sing on the Jackie Gleason Show	1964	3.75	7.50	15.00
❑ S-490 [S]	More Songs I Sing on the Jackie Gleason Show	1964	5.00	10.00	20.00
❑ 514 [M]	I'm Counting on You	1965	3.75	7.50	15.00
❑ S-514 [S]	I'm Counting on You	1965	5.00	10.00	20.00
❑ 541 [M]	All Time Great Hits	1966	3.75	7.50	15.00
❑ S-541 [S]	All Time Great Hits	1966	5.00	10.00	20.00

MGM

❑ E-4470 [M]	Frank Fontaine's Ireland	1967	3.00	6.00	12.00
❑ SE-4470 [S]	Frank Fontaine's Ireland	1967	3.75	7.50	15.00

FONTANA, WAYNE
Also see WAYNE FONTANA AND THE MINDBENDERS.
MGM

❑ E-4459 [M]	Wayne Fontana	1967	5.00	10.00	20.00
❑ SE-4459 [S]	Wayne Fontana	1967	6.25	12.50	25.00

FONTANA, WAYNE, AND THE MINDBENDERS
Also see WAYNE FONTANA; THE MINDBENDERS.
FONTANA

❑ MGF-27542 [M]	The Game of Love	1965	7.50	15.00	30.00
❑ SRF-67542 [R]	The Game of Love	1965	6.25	12.50	25.00

FONTANE SISTERS, THE
DOT

❑ DLP-104 [10]	The Fontane Sisters	1955	12.50	25.00	50.00
❑ DLP-3004 [M]	The Fontanes Sing	1956	10.00	20.00	40.00
—Maroon label					
❑ DLP-3004 [M]	The Fontanes Sing	1957	6.25	12.50	25.00
—Black label					
❑ DLP-3042 [M]	A Visit with the Fontane Sisters	1957	7.50	15.00	30.00
❑ DLP-3531 [M]	The Tips of My Fingers	1963	3.75	7.50	15.00
❑ DLP-25531 [S]	The Tips of My Fingers	1963	5.00	10.00	20.00

FOO FIGHTERS
RCA

❑ 68008 [(2)10]	One By One	2002	3.75	7.50	15.00

ROSWELL/CAPITOL

❑ 55832 [(2)]	The Colour and the Shape	1997	7.50	15.00	30.00

FOOD
CAPITOL

❑ ST-304	Forever Is a Dream	1969	15.00	30.00	60.00

FOOL, THE
MERCURY

❑ SR-61178	The Fool	1968	7.50	15.00	30.00

FOOLS, THE
EMI AMERICA

❑ SPRO-9393/4 [DJ]	The First Annual Official Unofficial April Fools Day Live Bootleg...	1980	5.00	10.00	20.00
❑ SW-17024	Sold Out	1980	3.00	6.00	12.00
❑ SW-17046	Heavy Mental	1981	3.00	6.00	12.00

PVC

❑ 4908	World Dance Party//Do Wah Diddy/Psycho Chicken	1985	3.00	6.00	12.00
—Also known as 'The 12" Fools'					
❑ 8930	World Dance Party	1985	3.75	7.50	15.00

FORBES, GRAHAM
PHILLIPS INTERNATIONAL

❑ PLP-1955 [M]	The Martini Set	1959	200.00	400.00	800.00

FORD, FRANKIE
ACE

❑ LP 1005 [M]	Let's Take a Sea Cruise	1959	75.00	150.00	300.00

BRIARMEADE

❑ BR-5002	Frankie Ford	1976	3.00	6.00	12.00

FORD, LITA
Also see THE RUNAWAYS.
MERCURY

❑ 810331-1	Out for Blood	1984	2.00	4.00	8.00
—Reissue cover has a different photo of Lita holding a non-bloody guitar					
❑ 810331-1	Out for Blood	1984	6.25	12.50	25.00
—Original cover has Lita holding a bloody, gored guitar					
❑ 818864-1	Dancin' on the Edge	1984	2.50	5.00	10.00

RCA

❑ 2090-1-R	Stiletto	1990	2.50	5.00	10.00
❑ 6397-1-R	Lita	1988	2.00	4.00	8.00

FORD, MARY
Also see LES PAUL AND MARY FORD.
CHALLENGE

❑ CHL-623 [M]	A Brand New Ford	1966	6.25	12.50	25.00
❑ CHS-2623 [S]	A Brand New Ford	1966	7.50	15.00	30.00

FORD, NEAL, AND THE FANATICS
HICKORY

❑ LPS-141	Neal Ford and the Fanatics	1968	6.25	12.50	25.00

FORD, RITA
COLUMBIA

❑ CL 1698 [M]	A Music Box Christmas	1961	5.00	10.00	20.00
—Black and red label with six "eye" logos					

Number	Title (A Side/B Side)	Yr	VG	VG+	NM

FORD, ROCKY BILLY

EPIC
❑ LN 24022 [M]	Music Box Wonderland Christmas with Rita Ford's Music Boxes	1962	5.00	10.00	20.00

FORD, ROCKY BILLY
AUDIO LAB
❑ AL-1561 [M]	A New Singing Star	1960	37.50	75.00	150.00

FORD, TENNESSEE ERNIE
ARCHIVE OF FOLK AND JAZZ
❑ 279	Tennessee Ernie Ford	197?	2.50	5.00	10.00

CAPITOL
❑ ST-127	Songs I Like to Sing	1969	3.00	6.00	12.00
❑ ST-334	Holy, Holy, Holy	1969	3.00	6.00	12.00
❑ SM-412	America the Beautiful	197?	2.00	4.00	8.00
—Reissue with new prefix					
❑ STAO-412	America the Beautiful	1970	3.00	6.00	12.00
❑ STBB-485 [(2)]	Christmas Special	1970	3.75	7.50	15.00
❑ STBB-506 [(2)]	Sweet Hour of Prayer/Let Me Walk with Thee	1971	3.75	7.50	15.00
❑ SF-8-0507	Sweet Hour of Prayer	1970	3.75	7.50	15.00
—Capitol Record Club edition					
❑ SF-8-0508	Let Me Walk with Thee	1970	3.75	7.50	15.00
—Capitol Record Club edition					
❑ ST-583	Everything Is Beautiful	1971	3.00	6.00	12.00
❑ DT 700 [R]	This Lusty Land!	196?	3.00	6.00	12.00
❑ T 700 [M]	This Lusty Land	1956	6.25	12.50	25.00
—Turquoise label					
❑ T 700 [M]	This Lusty Land	1959	5.00	10.00	20.00
—Black label with colorband, logo at left					
❑ T 700 [M]	This Lusty Land!	1963	3.75	7.50	15.00
—Black label with colorband, logo at top					
❑ ST-730	Abide with Me	1971	3.00	6.00	12.00
❑ ST 756 [S]	Hymns	1962	3.75	7.50	15.00
—Re-recording of the original mono LP					
❑ T 756 [M]	Hymns	1956	6.25	12.50	25.00
—Turquoise label					
❑ T 756 [M]	Hymns	1959	5.00	10.00	20.00
—Black label with colorband, logo at left					
❑ T 756 [M]	Hymns	1962	3.75	7.50	15.00
—Black label with colorband, logo at top					
❑ ST 818 [S]	Spirituals	1962	3.75	7.50	15.00
—Re-recording of the original mono LP					
❑ T 818 [M]	Spirituals	1957	6.25	12.50	25.00
—Turquoise label					
❑ T 818 [M]	Spirituals	1959	5.00	10.00	20.00
—Black label with colorband, logo at left					
❑ T 818 [M]	Spirituals	1962	3.75	7.50	15.00
—Black label with colorband, logo at top					
❑ ST-831 [S]	C-H-R-I-S-T-M-A-S	1971	3.00	6.00	12.00
❑ ST-833	The Folk Album	1971	3.00	6.00	12.00
❑ DT 841 [R]	Tennessee Ernie Ford Favorites	196?	3.00	6.00	12.00
❑ T 841 [M]	Tennessee Ernie Ford Favorites	1957	7.50	15.00	30.00
—Turquoise label					
❑ T 841 [M]	Tennessee Ernie Ford Favorites	1958	5.00	10.00	20.00
—Black label with colorband, logo at left					
❑ T 841 [M]	Tennessee Ernie Ford Favorites	1962	3.75	7.50	15.00
—Black label with colorband, logo at top					
❑ T 888 [M]	Ol' Rockin' Ern	1957	12.50	25.00	50.00
—Turquoise or gray label					
❑ ST 1005 [S]	Nearer the Cross	1959	6.25	12.50	25.00
—Black label with colorband, logo at left					
❑ ST 1005 [S]	Nearer the Cross	1962	5.00	10.00	20.00
—Black label with colorband, logo at top					
❑ T 1005 [M]	Nearer the Cross	1958	5.00	10.00	20.00
—Black label with colorband, logo at left					
❑ T 1005 [M]	Nearer the Cross	1962	3.75	7.50	15.00
—Black label with colorband, logo at top					
❑ ST 1071 [S]	The Star Carol	1958	7.50	15.00	30.00
—Black labels with colorband, Capitol logo on left					
❑ ST 1071 [S]	The Star Carol	1962	5.00	10.00	20.00
—Black label with colorband, "Capitol" logo on top. This was also reissued on later Capitol labels into the 1970s with values no more than half the above.					
❑ T 1071 [M]	The Star Carol	1958	6.25	12.50	25.00
—Black labels with colorband, "Capitol" logo on left					
❑ T 1071 [M]	The Star Carol	1962	3.75	7.50	15.00
—Black label with colorband, logo on top					
❑ ST 1227 [S]	Gather 'Round	1959	5.00	10.00	20.00
❑ T 1227 [M]	Gather 'Round	1959	3.75	7.50	15.00
❑ ST 1272 [S]	A Friend We Have	1959	5.00	10.00	20.00
❑ T 1272 [M]	A Friend We Have	1959	3.75	7.50	15.00
❑ STAO 1332 [S]	Sing a Hymn with Me	1960	6.25	12.50	25.00
—With hymnal					
❑ TAO 1332 [M]	Sing a Hymn with Me	1960	5.00	10.00	20.00
—With hymnal					
❑ DT 1380 [R]	Sixteen Tons	196?	3.00	6.00	12.00
❑ T 1380 [M]	Sixteen Tons	1960	3.75	7.50	15.00
❑ ST 1539 [S]	Civil War Songs of the North	1961	5.00	10.00	20.00
❑ T 1539 [M]	Civil War Songs of the North	1961	3.75	7.50	15.00
❑ ST 1540 [S]	Civil War Songs of the South	1961	5.00	10.00	20.00
❑ T 1540 [M]	Civil War Songs of the South	1961	3.75	7.50	15.00
❑ ST 1679 [S]	Sing a Hymn with Me	1962	3.75	7.50	15.00
—Reissue of 1332 with standard cover?					
❑ T 1679 [M]	Sing a Hymn with Me	1962	3.00	6.00	12.00
—Reissue of 1332 with standard cover?					
❑ ST 1680 [S]	Sing a Spiritual with Me	1962	3.75	7.50	15.00
❑ T 1680 [M]	Sing a Spiritual with Me	1962	3.00	6.00	12.00
❑ ST 1684 [S]	Here Comes the Mississippi Showboat	1962	3.75	7.50	15.00
❑ T 1684 [M]	Here Comes the Mississippi Showboat	1962	3.00	6.00	12.00
❑ ST 1694 [S]	Hymns at Home	1962	3.75	7.50	15.00
❑ T 1694 [M]	Hymns at Home	1962	3.00	6.00	12.00
❑ ST 1751 [S]	I Love to Tell the Story	1962	3.75	7.50	15.00
❑ T 1751 [M]	I Love to Tell the Story	1962	3.00	6.00	12.00
❑ ST 1794 [S]	Book of Favorite Hymns	1962	5.00	10.00	20.00
❑ T 1794 [M]	Book of Favorite Hymns	1962	3.75	7.50	15.00
❑ ST 1875 [S]	Long Long Ago	1963	3.75	7.50	15.00
❑ T 1875 [M]	Long Long Ago	1963	3.00	6.00	12.00
❑ ST 1937 [S]	We Gather Together	1963	3.75	7.50	15.00
❑ T 1937 [M]	We Gather Together	1963	3.00	6.00	12.00
❑ ST 1994 [S]	The Story of Christmas	1963	5.00	10.00	20.00
❑ T 1994 [M]	The Story of Christmas	1963	3.75	7.50	15.00
—With the Roger Wagner Chorale					
❑ SM-2026	Great Gospel Songs	197?	2.00	4.00	8.00
—Reissue with new prefix					
❑ ST 2026 [S]	Great Gospel Songs	1964	3.75	7.50	15.00
❑ T 2026 [M]	Great Gospel Songs	1964	3.00	6.00	12.00
❑ SM-2097	Country Hits…Feelin' Blue	197?	2.00	4.00	8.00
—Reissue with new prefix					
❑ ST 2097 [S]	Country Hits…Feelin' Blue	1964	3.75	7.50	15.00
❑ T 2097 [M]	Country Hits…Feelin' Blue	1964	3.00	6.00	12.00
❑ STBL 2183 [(2)S]	The World's Best Loved Hymns	1964	6.25	12.50	25.00
❑ TBL 2183 [(2)M]	The World's Best Loved Hymns	1964	5.00	10.00	20.00
❑ ST 2296 [S]	Let Me Walk with Thee	1965	3.75	7.50	15.00
❑ T 2296 [M]	Let Me Walk with Thee	1965	3.00	6.00	12.00
❑ ST 2394 [S]	Sing We Now of Christmas	1965	3.75	7.50	15.00
—Same as above, but in stereo					
❑ T 2394 [M]	Sing We Now of Christmas	1965	3.00	6.00	12.00
❑ ST 2444 [S]	My Favorite Things	1966	3.75	7.50	15.00
❑ T 2444 [M]	My Favorite Things	1966	3.00	6.00	12.00
❑ ST 2557 [S]	Wonderful Peace	1966	3.75	7.50	15.00
❑ T 2557 [M]	Wonderful Peace	1966	3.00	6.00	12.00
❑ ST 2618 [S]	God Lives	1966	3.75	7.50	15.00
❑ T 2618 [M]	God Lives	1966	3.00	6.00	12.00
❑ ST 2681 [S]	Aloha from Tennessee Ernie Ford	1967	3.00	6.00	12.00
❑ T 2681 [M]	Aloha from Tennessee Ernie Ford	1967	3.75	7.50	15.00
❑ SM-2761	Faith of Our Fathers	197?	2.00	4.00	8.00
—Reissue with new prefix					
❑ ST 2761 [S]	Faith of Our Fathers	1967	3.00	6.00	12.00
❑ T 2761 [M]	Faith of Our Fathers	1967	3.75	7.50	15.00
❑ ST 2845 [S]	Our Garden of Hymns	1968	3.00	6.00	12.00
❑ T 2845 [M]	Our Garden of Hymns	1968	5.00	10.00	20.00
❑ ST 2896	The World of Pop and Country Hits	1968	3.00	6.00	12.00
❑ STCL 2942 [(3)]	The Tennessee Ernie Ford Deluxe Set	1968	5.00	10.00	20.00
❑ SKAO 2949	Best Hymns	1968	3.00	6.00	12.00
❑ ST 2968	O Come All Ye Faithful	1968	3.00	6.00	12.00
❑ ST-11001	Mr. Words and Music	1972	2.50	5.00	10.00
❑ ST-11092	It's Tennessee Ernie Ford	1973	2.50	5.00	10.00
❑ ST-11232	Tennessee Ernie Ford Sings About Jesus	1973	2.50	5.00	10.00
❑ ST-11290	Make a Joyful Noise	1974	2.50	5.00	10.00
❑ SVBB-11325 [(2)]	25th Anniversary/Yesterday and Today	1974	3.00	6.00	12.00
❑ SVBB-11326 [(2)]	25th Anniversary/Hymns & Gospel	1974	3.00	6.00	12.00
❑ SVBB-11382 [(2)]	Precious Memories	1975	3.00	6.00	12.00
❑ ST-11495	Tennessee Ernie Ford Sings His Great Love Songs	1975	2.50	5.00	10.00
❑ SM-12033	Book of Favorite Hymns	1980	2.50	5.00	10.00
❑ SN-16040	Yesterday	1981	2.00	4.00	8.00
❑ SN-16042	Gospel	1981	2.00	4.00	8.00
❑ SN-16043	Hymns	1981	2.00	4.00	8.00
❑ SN-16173	Hymns	1981	2.00	4.00	8.00
❑ SN-16174	Spirituals	1981	2.00	4.00	8.00
❑ SN-16289	The Star Carol	1982	2.00	4.00	8.00
—Budget-line reissue					

PICKWICK
❑ PTP-2016 [(2)]	Tennessee Ernie Ford	197?	3.00	6.00	12.00
❑ PTP-2050 [(2)]	Hymns	197?	3.00	6.00	12.00
❑ SPC-3047	Bless Your Pea-Pickin' Heart	196?	3.00	6.00	12.00
❑ SPC-3066	I Love You So Much	196?	3.00	6.00	12.00
❑ SPC-3222	The Need for Prayer	197?	2.50	5.00	10.00
❑ SPC-3268	Sixteen Tons	197?	2.50	5.00	10.00
❑ SPC-3273	Jesus Loves Me	197?	2.50	5.00	10.00
❑ SPC-3308	Amazing Grace	197?	2.50	5.00	10.00
❑ SPC-3353	Rock of Ages	197?	2.50	5.00	10.00

RANWOOD
❑ RLP-7026 [(2)]	Tennessee Ernie Ford Sings 22 Favorite Hymns	198?	3.00	6.00	12.00

WORD
❑ 8764	He Touched Me	1978	2.50	5.00	10.00
❑ 8798	Swing Wide Your Golden Gate	198?	2.50	5.00	10.00
❑ 8841	Tell Me the Old Story	1979	2.50	5.00	10.00
❑ 8841	Tell Me the Old Story	198?	2.50	5.00	10.00
❑ 8858	There's a Song in My Heart	198?	2.50	5.00	10.00

FORD THEATRE, THE
ABC
❑ S-658	Trilogy	1968	6.25	12.50	25.00
❑ S-681	Time Changes	1969	5.00	10.00	20.00

FOREFRONT, THE
AFI
❑ 21557	Incantation	197?	5.00	10.00	20.00

FOREIGNER
ATLANTIC
❑ SD 16999	4	1981	2.50	5.00	10.00
—First pressings have a hologram sticker on the upper back cover					
❑ SD 16999	4	1982	2.00	4.00	8.00
—No hologram sticker on back cover					
❑ SD 18215	Foreigner	1977	2.50	5.00	10.00
❑ SD 19109	Foreigner	1977	2.00	4.00	8.00
—Reissue of 18215					
❑ SD 19999	Double Vision	1978	2.50	5.00	10.00
—Second cover has a blue tint with the words "Double Vision" right under the band name					
❑ SD 19999	Double Vision	1978	3.00	6.00	12.00
—Original cover is mostly brown with the words "Double Vision" barely visible along the bottom edge of front cover					

Number	Title (A Side/B Side)	Yr	VG	VG+	NM
❏ SD 19999	Double Vision	1979	2.00	4.00	8.00

—*Third cover is the same as the second cover, but has a red tint*

Number	Title (A Side/B Side)	Yr	VG	VG+	NM
❏ SD 29999	Head Games	1979	2.50	5.00	10.00
❏ 80999	Records	1982	2.50	5.00	10.00
❏ 81808	Inside Information	1988	2.50	5.00	10.00
❏ 81999	Agent Provocateur	1984	2.50	5.00	10.00
❏ A1-82299	Unusual Heat	1990	6.25	12.50	25.00

—*U.S. vinyl available only through Columbia House*

MOBILE FIDELITY

Number	Title (A Side/B Side)	Yr	VG	VG+	NM
❏ 1-052	Double Vision	1981	7.50	15.00	30.00

—*Audiophile vinyl*

FOREST
HARVEST

❏ SKAO-419	Forest	1970	12.50	25.00	50.00

FORGOTTEN CHILD
BLUE LAMPION

❏ BLM 10001	Forgotten Child	1986	15.00	30.00	60.00

FORMULA V
BURLINGUEN

❏ (# unknown)	Formula V	197?	6.25	12.50	25.00

MIAMI

❏ 6076	Formula V	197?	6.25	12.50	25.00

FORREST, EUGENE "FLIP"
SAVOY

❏ MG-14392	I Heard It on the Radio	197?	5.00	10.00	20.00

FORREST, HELEN
AUDIOPHILE

❏ AP-47	On the Sunny Side of the Street	1958	10.00	20.00	40.00

CAPITOL

❏ T 704 [M]	Voice of the Name Bands	1956	12.50	25.00	50.00

FORREST, JIMMY
NEW JAZZ

❏ NJLP-8250 [M]	Forrest Fire	1960	15.00	30.00	60.00

—*Purple label*

❏ NJLP-8250 [M]	Forrest Fire	1965	7.50	15.00	30.00

—*Blue label with trident logo at right*

❏ NJLP-8293 [M]	Soul Street	1962	15.00	30.00	60.00

—*Purple label*

❏ NJLP-8293 [M]	Soul Street	1965	7.50	15.00	30.00

—*Blue label with trident logo at right*

PRESTIGE

❏ PRLP-7202 [M]	Out of the Forrest	1961	10.00	20.00	40.00

—*Yellow label*

❏ PRLP-7202 [M]	Out of the Forrest	1965	5.00	10.00	20.00

—*Blue label with trident logo at right*

❏ PRLP-7218 [M]	Most Much!	1961	10.00	20.00	40.00

—*Yellow label*

❏ PRLP-7218 [M]	Most Much!	1965	5.00	10.00	20.00

—*Blue label with trident logo at right*

❏ PRLP-7235 [M]	Sit Down and Relax with Jimmy Forrest	1962	10.00	20.00	40.00

—*Yellow label*

❏ PRLP-7235 [M]	Sit Down and Relax with Jimmy Forrest	1965	5.00	10.00	20.00

—*Blue label with trident logo at right*

❏ PRST-7235 [S]	Sit Down and Relax with Jimmy Forrest	1962	15.00	30.00	60.00

—*Silver label*

❏ PRST-7235 [S]	Sit Down and Relax with Jimmy Forrest	1965	6.25	12.50	25.00

—*Blue label with trident logo at right*

UNITED

❏ 002 [10]	Night Train	1955	30.00	60.00	120.00

FORRESTER, HOWDY
CUB

❏ 8008 [M]	Fancy Fiddlin' Country Style	1960	10.00	20.00	40.00

MGM

❏ E-4035 [M]	Fancy Fiddlin' Country Style	1962	7.50	15.00	30.00

—*Reissue of Cub LP*

UNITED ARTISTS

❏ UAL-3295 [M]	Fiddlin' Country Style	1963	5.00	10.00	20.00
❏ UAS-6295 [S]	Fiddlin' Country Style	1963	6.25	12.50	25.00

FORRESTER, MAUREEN
RCA VICTOR RED SEAL

❏ LSC-2275 [S]	Brahms, Schumann: Lieder	1959	5.00	10.00	20.00

—*Original with "shaded dog" label*

FORT MUDGE MEMORIAL DUMP, THE
MERCURY

❏ SR-61256	The Fort Mudge Memorial Dump	1970	7.50	15.00	30.00

FORTUNE, JOHNNY
PARK AVENUE

❏ S-401 [S]	Soul Surfer	1963	75.00	150.00	300.00
❏ P-1301 [M]	Soul Surfer	1963	50.00	100.00	200.00

FORTUNE, SONNY
STRATA-EAST

❏ SES-7423	Long Before Our Mothers Cried	1974	5.00	10.00	20.00

FORTUNES, THE (1)
CAPITOL

❏ ST-647	Freedom	1971	—	—	—

—*Canceled*

❏ ST-809	Here Comes That Rainy Day Feeling Again	1971	5.00	10.00	20.00
❏ ST-11041	Storm in a Teacup	1972	3.75	7.50	15.00

—*Contains the canceled "Freedom" LP with one track deleted, plus the title song added*

COCA-COLA

❏ (no #) [DJ]	It's the Real Thing	1969	15.00	30.00	60.00

PRESS

Number	Title (A Side/B Side)	Yr	VG	VG+	NM
❏ PR 73002 [M]	The Fortunes	1965	8.75	17.50	35.00
❏ PRS 83002 [S]	The Fortunes	1965	12.50	25.00	50.00

WORLD PACIFIC

❏ WPS-21904	That Same Old Feeling	1970	3.75	7.50	15.00

49TH PARALLEL, THE
MAVERICK

❏ MAS-7001	The 49th Parallel	1969	62.50	125.00	250.00

FORUM, THE
MIRA

❏ MLP-301 [M]	The River Is Wide	1967	3.75	7.50	15.00
❏ MLPS-301 [S]	The River Is Wide	1967	5.00	10.00	20.00

FOSTER, CHUCK
PHILLIPS INTERNATIONAL

❏ PLP-1965 [M]	Chuck Foster at the Hotel Peabody	1961	50.00	100.00	200.00

FOSTER, DAVID
MOBILE FIDELITY

❏ 1-123	The Best of Me	1982	5.00	10.00	20.00

—*Audiophile vinyl*

FOSTER, FRANK
ARGO

❏ LP-717 [M]	Basie Is Our Boss	1963	6.25	12.50	25.00
❏ LPS-717 [S]	Basie Is Our Boss	1963	7.50	15.00	30.00

BLUE NOTE

❏ BLP-5043 [10]	Frank Foster Quintet	1954	100.00	200.00	400.00
❏ BST-84278	Manhattan Fever	1968	6.25	12.50	25.00

MAINSTREAM

❏ MRL-349	The Loud Minority	1972	5.00	10.00	20.00

PRESTIGE

❏ PRLP-7461 [M]	Fearless	1966	6.25	12.50	25.00
❏ PRST-7461 [S]	Fearless	1966	7.50	15.00	30.00
❏ PRLP-7479 [M]	Soul Outing!	1967	7.50	15.00	30.00
❏ PRST-7479 [S]	Soul Outing!	1967	6.25	12.50	25.00

FOSTER, GARY
REVELATION

❏ REV-5	Subconsciously	1968	5.00	10.00	20.00
❏ REV-19	Grand Clu Classe	197?	5.00	10.00	20.00

FOSTER, HERMAN
ARGO

❏ LP-727 [M]	Ready and Willing	1964	5.00	10.00	20.00
❏ LPS-727 [S]	Ready and Willing	1964	6.25	12.50	25.00

EPIC

❏ LA 16010 [M]	Have You Heard?	1960	5.00	10.00	20.00
❏ LA 16016 [M]	The Explosive Piano of Herman Foster	1961	5.00	10.00	20.00
❏ BA 17010 [S]	Have You Heard?	1960	6.25	12.50	25.00
❏ BA 17016 [S]	The Explosive Piano of Herman Foster	1961	6.25	12.50	25.00

FOSTER, PAT
COUNTERPOINT

❏ CPT-560 [M]	Documentary Talking Blues	195?	10.00	20.00	40.00

RIVERSIDE

❏ RLP-12-654 [M]	Gold Rush Songs	195?	10.00	20.00	40.00

FOSTER, RONNIE
BLUE NOTE

❏ BST-84382	Two Headed Freap	1972	5.00	10.00	20.00

FOUL DOGS, THE
RHYTHM SOUND

❏ GA-481	No. 1	1968	75.00	150.00	300.00

FOUNDATIONS, THE
UNI

❏ 73016	Baby Now That I've Found You	1968	7.50	15.00	30.00
❏ 73043	Build Me Up Buttercup	1969	7.50	15.00	30.00
❏ 73058	Digging the Foundations	1969	7.50	15.00	30.00

FOUNTAIN, PETE
CORAL

❏ CRL 57200 [M]	Lawrence Welk Presents Pete Fountain	1958	5.00	10.00	20.00
❏ CRL 757282 [S]	Pete Fountain's New Orleans	1959	5.00	10.00	20.00
❏ CRL 757284 [S]	The Blues	1959	5.00	10.00	20.00
❏ CRL 757313 [S]	Pete Fountain Day	1960	5.00	10.00	20.00
❏ CRL 757314 [S]	Pete Fountain at the Bateau Lounge	1960	5.00	10.00	20.00
❏ CRL 757333 [S]	Pete Fountain Salutes the Great Clarinetists	1960	5.00	10.00	20.00
❏ CRL 757357 [S]	Pete Fountain On Tour	1961	5.00	10.00	20.00
❏ CRL 757359 [S]	Pete Fountain's French Quarter	1961	5.00	10.00	20.00
❏ CRL 757378 [S]	I Love Paris	1961	5.00	10.00	20.00
❏ CRL 757394 [S]	Swing Low Sweet Chariot	1962	5.00	10.00	20.00
❏ CRL 757401 [S]	Pete Fountain's Music from Dixie	1962	5.00	10.00	20.00
❏ CRL 757419 [S]	New Orleans Scene	1963	5.00	10.00	20.00

RCA VICTOR

❏ LSP-2097 [S]	Pete Fountain at the Jazz Band Ball	1960	5.00	10.00	20.00

FOUNTAIN, PETE, AND AL HIRT
CORAL

❏ CRL 757389 [S]	Bourbon Street	1962	5.00	10.00	20.00

FOUNTAIN, PETE, AND "BIG" TINY LITTLE
CORAL

❏ CRL 757334 [S]	Mr. New Orleans Meets Mr. Honky Tonk	1961	5.00	10.00	20.00

FOUR ACES
DECCA

❏ DL 4013 [M]	The Golden Hits of the Four Aces	1960	5.00	10.00	20.00
❏ DL 5429 [10]	The Four Aces	1952	20.00	40.00	80.00

F

Number	Title (A Side/B Side)	Yr	VG	VG+	NM
DL 8122 [M]	The Mood for Love	1955	12.50	25.00	50.00
—All-black label, silver print					
DL 8122 [M]	The Mood for Love	196?	5.00	10.00	20.00
—Black label with color bars					
DL 8191 [M]	Merry Christmas	1956	12.50	25.00	50.00
DL 8227 [M]	Sentimental Souvenirs	1956	12.50	25.00	50.00
—All-black label, silver print					
DL 8227 [M]	Sentimental Souvenirs	196?	5.00	10.00	20.00
—Black label with color bars					
DL 8228 [M]	Heart and Soul	1956	12.50	25.00	50.00
—All-black label, silver print					
DL 8228 [M]	Heart and Soul	196?	5.00	10.00	20.00
—Black label with color bars					
DL 8312 [M]	She Sees All the Hollywood Hits	1957	12.50	25.00	50.00
DL 8567 [M]	Shuffling Along	1957	12.50	25.00	50.00
—All-black label, silver print					
DL 8567 [M]	Shuffling Along	196?	5.00	10.00	20.00
—Black label with color bars					
DL 8693 [M]	Hits from Hollywood	1958	12.50	25.00	50.00
—All-black label, silver print					
DL 8693 [M]	Hits from Hollywood	196?	5.00	10.00	20.00
—Black label with color bars					
DL 8766 [M]	The Swingin' Aces	1958	10.00	20.00	40.00
—All-black label, silver print					
DL 8766 [M]	The Swingin' Aces	196?	5.00	10.00	20.00
—Black label with color bars					
DL 8855 [M]	Hits from Broadway	1959	10.00	20.00	40.00
—All-black label, silver print					
DL 8855 [M]	Hits from Broadway	196?	5.00	10.00	20.00
—Black label with color bars					
DL 8944 [M]	Beyond the Blue Horizon	1959	10.00	20.00	40.00
—All-black label, silver print					
DL 8944 [M]	Beyond the Blue Horizon	196?	5.00	10.00	20.00
—Black label with color bars					
DL 74013 [S]	The Golden Hits of the Four Aces	1960	6.25	12.50	25.00
DL 78766 [S]	The Swingin' Aces	1958	12.50	25.00	50.00
—All-black label, silver print					
DL 78766 [S]	The Swingin' Aces	196?	6.25	12.50	25.00
—Black label with color bars					
DL 78855 [S]	Hits from Broadway	1959	12.50	25.00	50.00
—All-black label, silver print					
DL 78855 [S]	Hits from Broadway	196?	6.25	12.50	25.00
—Black label with color bars					
DL 78944 [S]	Beyond the Blue Horizon	1959	12.50	25.00	50.00
—All-black label, silver print					
DL 78944 [S]	Beyond the Blue Horizon	196?	6.25	12.50	25.00
—Black label with color bars					

MCA

4033 [(2)]	The Best of the Four Aces	197?	3.75	7.50	15.00

PICKWICK

SPC-3527	Love Is a Many-Splendored Thing	197?	2.50	5.00	10.00

UNITED ARTISTS

UAL-3337 [M]	Record Oldies	1963	5.00	10.00	20.00
UAS-6337 [S]	Record Oldies	1963	6.25	12.50	25.00

VOCALION

VL 3604 [M]	The Four Aces Sing	196?	3.75	7.50	15.00
VL 73881	There Goes My Heart	1969	3.00	6.00	12.00
VL 73902	Written on the Wind	1970	3.00	6.00	12.00

FOUR BROTHERS, THE
VIK

LX-1096 [M]	The Four Brothers — Together Again	1957	20.00	40.00	80.00

FOUR COINS, THE
EPIC

LN 1104 [M]	The Four Coins	1955	12.50	25.00	50.00
LN 3445 [M]	The Four Coins in Shangri-La	1958	7.50	15.00	30.00

MGM

E-3944 [M]	Greek Songs	1961	3.75	7.50	15.00
SE-3944 [S]	Greek Songs	1961	5.00	10.00	20.00

ROULETTE

R-25288 [M]	Greek Songs Mama Never Taught Me	1965	3.75	7.50	15.00
SR-25288 [S]	Greek Songs Mama Never Taught Me	1965	5.00	10.00	20.00

FOUR FRESHMEN, THE
CAPITOL

H 522 [10]	Voices in Modern	1955	12.50	25.00	50.00
T 522 [M]	Voices in Modern	1955	10.00	20.00	40.00
T 683 [M]	Four Freshmen and Five Trombones	1956	10.00	20.00	40.00
DT 743 [R]	Freshmen Favorites	196?	3.00	6.00	12.00
SM-743	Freshmen Favorites	197?	2.50	5.00	10.00
T 743 [M]	Freshmen Favorites	1956	10.00	20.00	40.00
T 763 [M]	4 Freshmen and 5 Trumpets	1957	10.00	20.00	40.00
T 844 [M]	Four Freshmen and Five Saxes	1957	10.00	20.00	40.00
T 992 [M]	Voices in Latin	1958	7.50	15.00	30.00
ST 1008 [S]	The Four Freshmen In Person	1958	10.00	20.00	40.00
T 1008 [M]	The Four Freshmen In Person	1958	7.50	15.00	30.00
ST 1074 [S]	Voices in Love	1958	7.50	15.00	30.00
T 1074 [M]	Voices in Love	1958	5.00	10.00	20.00
ST 1103 [S]	Freshmen Favorites, Vol. 2	1959	7.50	15.00	30.00
T 1103 [M]	Freshmen Favorites, Vol. 2	1959	5.00	10.00	20.00
ST 1189 [S]	Love Lost	1959	7.50	15.00	30.00
T 1189 [M]	Love Lost	1959	5.00	10.00	20.00
ST 1255 [S]	The Four Freshmen and Five Guitars	1959	7.50	15.00	30.00
T 1255 [M]	The Four Freshmen and Five Guitars	1959	5.00	10.00	20.00
ST 1295 [S]	Voices and Brass	1960	7.50	15.00	30.00
T 1295 [M]	Voices and Brass	1960	5.00	10.00	20.00
ST 1378 [S]	First Affair	1960	7.50	15.00	30.00
T 1378 [M]	First Affair	1960	5.00	10.00	20.00
ST 1485 [S]	Freshmen Year	1961	6.25	12.50	25.00
T 1485 [M]	Freshmen Year	1961	5.00	10.00	20.00
ST 1543 [S]	Voices in Fun	1961	6.25	12.50	25.00
T 1543 [M]	Voices in Fun	1961	5.00	10.00	20.00
ST 1640 [S]	The Best of the Four Freshmen	1962	6.25	12.50	25.00
T 1640 [M]	The Best of the Four Freshmen	1962	5.00	10.00	20.00
ST 1682 [S]	Stars in Our Eyes	1962	6.25	12.50	25.00
T 1682 [M]	Stars in Our Eyes	1962	5.00	10.00	20.00
ST 1753 [S]	Swingers	1963	5.00	10.00	20.00
T 1753 [M]	Swingers	1963	3.75	7.50	15.00
ST 1860 [S]	The Four Freshmen In Person, Volume 2	1963	5.00	10.00	20.00
T 1860 [M]	The Four Freshmen In Person, Volume 2	1963	3.75	7.50	15.00
ST 1950 [S]	Got That Feelin'	1963	5.00	10.00	20.00
T 1950 [M]	Got That Feelin'	1963	3.75	7.50	15.00
ST 2067 [S]	Funny How Time Slips Away	1964	5.00	10.00	20.00
T 2067 [M]	Funny How Time Slips Away	1964	3.75	7.50	15.00
ST 2168 [S]	More Four Freshmen and Five Trombones	1964	5.00	10.00	20.00
T 2168 [M]	More Four Freshmen and Five Trombones	1964	3.75	7.50	15.00
SM-11639	Four Freshmen and Five Trombones	1977	2.50	5.00	10.00
SM-11965	Best of the Four Freshmen	1978	2.50	5.00	10.00

CREATIVE WORLD

ST-1059 [(2)]	Stan Kenton and the Four Freshmen at Butler University	1972	5.00	10.00	20.00

LIBERTY

LST-7563	Today Is Tomorrow	1968	3.75	7.50	15.00
LST-7590	In a Class By Themselves	1969	3.75	7.50	15.00
LST-7630	Different Strokes	1969	3.75	7.50	15.00
LN-10181	In a Class By Themselves	198?	2.00	4.00	8.00

PAUSA

PR-7193	Fresh!	1986	2.50	5.00	10.00
PR-9029	The Four Freshmen and Five Guitars	198?	2.50	5.00	10.00
PR-9040	4 Freshmen and 5 Trumpets	1985	2.50	5.00	10.00

PICKWICK

SPC-3080	The Fabulous Four Freshmen	196?	3.00	6.00	12.00
SPC-3563	A Taste of Honey	1977	2.50	5.00	10.00

SUNSET

SUS-5289	My Special Angel	1970	3.00	6.00	12.00

FOUR GIRLS, THE
CORAL

CRL 57158 [M]	Make a Joyful Noise Unto the Lord	1957	15.00	30.00	60.00

FOUR JACKS AND A JILL (1)
RCA VICTOR

LPM-4019 [M]	Master Jack	1968	7.50	15.00	30.00
LSP-4019 [S]	Master Jack	1968	3.75	7.50	15.00
LSP-4103	Fables	1968	3.75	7.50	15.00

FOUR KNIGHTS, THE
CAPITOL

H 346 [10]	Spotlight Songs	1953	50.00	100.00	200.00
T 346 [M]	Spotlight Songs	1956	37.50	75.00	150.00

CORAL

CRL 57221 [M]	The Four Knights	1959	25.00	50.00	100.00
CRL 57309 [M]	Million Dollar Baby	1960	15.00	30.00	60.00
CRL 757309 [S]	Million Dollar Baby	1960	20.00	40.00	80.00

FOUR LADS, THE
COLUMBIA

CL 861 [M]	The Four Lads with Frankie Laine	1956	10.00	20.00	40.00
CL 912 [M]	On the Sunny Side	1956	10.00	20.00	40.00
CL 1045 [M]	The Four Lads Sing Frank Loesser	1957	10.00	20.00	40.00
CL 1111 [M]	Four on the Aisle	1958	6.25	12.50	25.00
CL 1223 [M]	Breezin' Along	1958	6.25	12.50	25.00
CL 1235 [M]	The Four Lads' Greatest Hits	1958	6.25	12.50	25.00
CL 1299 [M]	The Four Lads Swing Along	1959	6.25	12.50	25.00
CL 1407 [M]	High Spirits!	1959	6.25	12.50	25.00
CL 1502 [M]	Love Affair	1960	3.75	7.50	15.00
CL 1550 [M]	Everything Goes	1960	3.75	7.50	15.00
CL 2545 [10]	The Four Lads Sing Frank Loesser	1956	12.50	25.00	50.00
CL 2577 [10]	Stage Show	1956	12.50	25.00	50.00
CL 6329 [10]	Stage Show	1954	12.50	25.00	50.00
CS 8035 [S]	Breezin' Along	1958	7.50	15.00	30.00
CS 8047 [S]	Four on the Aisle	1958	7.50	15.00	30.00
CS 8106 [S]	The Four Lads Swing Along	1959	7.50	15.00	30.00
CS 8203 [S]	High Spirits!	1959	7.50	15.00	30.00
CS 8293 [S]	Love Affair	1960	5.00	10.00	20.00
CS 8350 [S]	Everything Goes	1960	5.00	10.00	20.00

DOT

DLP-3438 [M]	Hits of the 60's	1962	3.75	7.50	15.00
DLP-3533 [M]	Oh Happy Day	1963	3.75	7.50	15.00
DLP-25438 [S]	Hits of the 60's	1962	5.00	10.00	20.00
DLP-25533 [S]	Oh Happy Day	1963	5.00	10.00	20.00

HARMONY

HS 11369	Moments to Remember	1970	3.00	6.00	12.00

KAPP

KL-1224 [M]	Twelve Hits	1961	3.75	7.50	15.00
KL-1254 [M]	Dixieland Doin's	1961	3.75	7.50	15.00
KS-3224 [S]	Twelve Hits	1961	5.00	10.00	20.00
KS-3254 [S]	Dixieland Doin's	1961	5.00	10.00	20.00

UNITED ARTISTS

UAL-3356 [M]	This Year's Top Movie Hits	1964	3.75	7.50	15.00
UAL-3399 [M]	Songs of World War I	1964	3.75	7.50	15.00
UAS-6356 [S]	This Year's Top Movie Hits	1964	5.00	10.00	20.00
UAS-6399 [S]	Songs of World War I	1964	5.00	10.00	20.00

FOUR LOVERS, THE
RCA VICTOR

LPM-1317 [M]	Joyride	1956	175.00	350.00	700.00

FOUR MOST, THE
DAWN

DLP-1111 [M]	The Four Most	1956	20.00	40.00	80.00

Number	Title (A Side/B Side)	Yr	VG	VG+	NM

FOUR PREPS, THE
CAPITOL
Number	Title (A Side/B Side)	Yr	VG	VG+	NM
❑ T 994 [M]	The Four Preps	1958	7.50	15.00	30.00
❑ T 1090 [M]	The Things We Did Last Summer	1958	6.25	12.50	25.00
❑ ST 1216 [S]	Dancing and Dreaming	1959	6.25	12.50	25.00
❑ T 1216 [M]	Dancing and Dreaming	1959	5.00	10.00	20.00
❑ DT 1291 [R]	Early in the Morning	1960	3.00	6.00	12.00
❑ T 1291 [M]	Early in the Morning	1960	6.25	12.50	25.00
❑ ST 1566 [S]	The Four Preps on Campus	1961	6.25	12.50	25.00
❑ T 1566 [M]	The Four Preps on Campus	1961	5.00	10.00	20.00
❑ ST 1647 [S]	Campus Encore	1962	6.25	12.50	25.00
❑ T 1647 [M]	Campus Encore	1962	5.00	10.00	20.00
❑ ST 1814 [S]	Campus Confidential	1963	5.00	10.00	20.00
❑ T 1814 [M]	Campus Confidential	1963	3.75	7.50	15.00
❑ ST 1976 [S]	Songs for a Campus Party	1963	5.00	10.00	20.00
❑ T 1976 [M]	Songs for a Campus Party	1963	3.75	7.50	15.00
❑ ST 2169 [S]	How to Succeed in Love	1964	5.00	10.00	20.00
❑ T 2169 [M]	How to Succeed in Love	1964	3.75	7.50	15.00
❑ ST 2708 [S]	The Best of the Four Preps	1967	3.00	6.00	12.00
❑ T 2708 [M]	The Best of the Four Preps	1967	3.75	7.50	15.00

FOUR SEASONS, THE
MCA/CURB
Number	Title (A Side/B Side)	Yr	VG	VG+	NM
❑ 5632	Starfighter	1985	2.50	5.00	10.00

MOTOWN
| ❑ 788 | Inside Out | 1973 | — | — | — |
| | | | | | |

—*Canceled*

MOWEST
| ❑ MW 108L | Chameleon | 1972 | 3.00 | 6.00 | 12.00 |

PHILIPS
| ❑ PHS-2-6501 [(2)] | Edizione d'Oro | 1968 | 6.25 | 12.50 | 25.00 |

—*Number "4" on cover is red on gold foil*

| ❑ PHS-2-6501 [(2)] | Edizione d'Oro | 1968 | 7.50 | 15.00 | 30.00 |

—*Number "4" on cover is white on gold foil*

| ❑ PHS-2-6501 [(2)] | Edizione d'Oro | 1969 | 6.25 | 12.50 | 25.00 |

—*Number "4" on cover is white on gold board*

❑ PHM 200124 [M]	Dawn (Go Away) and 11 Other Great Songs	1964	5.00	10.00	20.00
❑ PHM 200129 [M]	Born to Wander	1964	5.00	10.00	20.00
❑ PHM 200146 [M]	Rag Doll	1964	5.00	10.00	20.00

—*With yellow seal noting presence of "Save It For Me"*

| ❑ PHM 200146 [M] | Rag Doll | 1964 | 5.00 | 10.00 | 20.00 |

—*Without yellow seal noting presence of "Save It For Me"*

| ❑ PHM 200150 [M] | All the Song Hits of the Four Seasons | 1964 | 5.00 | 10.00 | 20.00 |
| ❑ PHM 200164 [M] | The 4 Seasons Entertain You | 1965 | 3.75 | 7.50 | 15.00 |

—*With blue seal noting presence of "Bye Bye Baby" and "Toy Soldier"*

| ❑ PHM 200164 [M] | The 4 Seasons Entertain You | 1965 | 5.00 | 10.00 | 20.00 |

—*With orange seal noting presence of "Bye Bye Baby" and "Toy Soldier"*

| ❑ PHM 200164 [M] | The 4 Seasons Entertain You | 1965 | 5.00 | 10.00 | 20.00 |

—*With orange seal noting presence of "Bye Bye Baby"*

| ❑ PHM 200193 [M] | Big Hits by Burt Bacharach...Hal David...Bob Dylan | 1965 | 5.00 | 10.00 | 20.00 |

—*"Open book" cover*

| ❑ PHM 200193 [M] | Big Hits by Burt Bacharach...Hal David...Bob Dylan | 1966 | 7.50 | 15.00 | 30.00 |

—*Group photos on cover*

| ❑ PHM 200196 [M] | The 4 Seasons' Gold Vault of Hits | 196? | 3.00 | 6.00 | 12.00 |

—*Title in all-black print*

| ❑ PHM 200196 [M] | The 4 Seasons' Gold Vault of Hits | 1965 | 3.75 | 7.50 | 15.00 |

—*Title in red print with black border*

| ❑ PHM 200196 [M] | The 4 Seasons' Gold Vault of Hits | 1965 | 5.00 | 10.00 | 20.00 |

—*Title in red print with no border*

❑ PHM 200201 [M]	Working My Way Back to You	1966	5.00	10.00	20.00
❑ PHM 200221 [M]	2nd Vault of Golden Hits	1966	3.75	7.50	15.00
❑ PHM 200222 [M]	Lookin' Back	1966	5.00	10.00	20.00
❑ PHM 200223 [M]	The Four Seasons' Christmas Album	1966	6.25	12.50	25.00

—*Reissue of Vee Jay album (same contents and order) with new cover*

❑ PHM 200243 [M]	New Gold Hits	1967	5.00	10.00	20.00
❑ PHS 600124 [S]	Dawn (Go Away) and 11 Other Great Songs	1964	6.25	12.50	25.00
❑ PHS 600129 [S]	Born to Wander	1964	6.25	12.50	25.00
❑ PHS 600146 [S]	Rag Doll	1964	6.25	12.50	25.00

—*With yellow seal noting presence of "Save It For Me"*

| ❑ PHS 600146 [S] | Rag Doll | 1964 | 6.25 | 12.50 | 25.00 |

—*Without yellow seal noting presence of "Save It For Me"*

| ❑ PHS 600150 [S] | All the Song Hits of the Four Seasons | 1964 | 6.25 | 12.50 | 25.00 |
| ❑ PHS 600164 [S] | The 4 Seasons Entertain You | 1965 | 5.00 | 10.00 | 20.00 |

—*With blue seal noting presence of "Bye Bye Baby" and "Toy Soldier"*

| ❑ PHS 600164 [S] | The 4 Seasons Entertain You | 1965 | 6.25 | 12.50 | 25.00 |

—*With orange seal noting presence of "Bye Bye Baby" and "Toy Soldier"*

| ❑ PHS 600164 [S] | The 4 Seasons Entertain You | 1965 | 6.25 | 12.50 | 25.00 |

—*With orange seal noting presence of "Bye Bye Baby"*

| ❑ PHS 600193 [S] | Big Hits by Burt Bacharach...Hal David...Bob Dylan | 1965 | 6.25 | 12.50 | 25.00 |

—*"Open book" cover*

| ❑ PHS 600193 [S] | Big Hits by Burt Bacharach...Hal David...Bob Dylan | 1966 | 10.00 | 20.00 | 40.00 |

—*Group photos on cover*

| ❑ PHS 600196 [S] | The 4 Seasons' Gold Vault of Hits | 196? | 3.75 | 7.50 | 15.00 |

—*Title in all-black print*

| ❑ PHS 600196 [S] | The 4 Seasons' Gold Vault of Hits | 1965 | 5.00 | 10.00 | 20.00 |

—*Title in red print with black border*

| ❑ PHS 600196 [S] | The 4 Seasons' Gold Vault of Hits | 1965 | 6.25 | 12.50 | 25.00 |

—*Title in red print with no border*

❑ PHS 600201 [S]	Working My Way Back to You	1966	6.25	12.50	25.00
❑ PHS 600221 [S]	2nd Vault of Golden Hits	1966	5.00	10.00	20.00
❑ PHS 600222 [S]	Lookin' Back	1966	6.25	12.50	25.00
❑ PHS 600223 [S]	The Four Seasons' Christmas Album	1966	7.50	15.00	30.00
❑ PHS 600243 [S]	New Gold Hits	1967	6.25	12.50	25.00
❑ PHS 600290	The Genuine Imitation Life Gazette	1969	3.75	7.50	15.00

—*White newspaper*

| ❑ PHS 600290 | The Genuine Imitation Life Gazette | 1969 | 6.25 | 12.50 | 25.00 |

—*Yellow newspaper*

| ❑ PHS 600341 | Half & Half | 1970 | 5.00 | 10.00 | 20.00 |

PICKWICK
Number	Title (A Side/B Side)	Yr	VG	VG+	NM
❑ SPC-3223	Brotherhood of Man	1970	3.00	6.00	12.00

—*Mass-market version of Sears 609*

PRIVATE STOCK
| ❑ PS-7000 [(2)] | The Four Seasons Story | 1975 | 3.75 | 7.50 | 15.00 |

RHINO
| ❑ RNLP 70234 | The Four Seasons' Christmas Album | 1987 | 3.00 | 6.00 | 12.00 |

—*Reissue of Philips album (same contents and order)*

| ❑ R1-70247 | Working My Way Back to You | 1988 | 2.50 | 5.00 | 10.00 |

—*Reissue of Philips 600-201*

| ❑ R1-70249 | The Genuine Imitation Life Gazette | 1988 | 2.50 | 5.00 | 10.00 |

—*Reissue of Philips 600-290*

| ❑ R1-71248 | Big Hits by Burt Bacharach...Hal David...Bob Dylan | 1988 | 2.50 | 5.00 | 10.00 |

—*Reissue of Philips 600-193*

| ❑ R1-71490 [(2)] | Anthology | 1988 | 3.00 | 6.00 | 12.00 |
| ❑ RNRP-72998 [(4)] | 25th Anniversary Collection | 1987 | 6.25 | 12.50 | 25.00 |

SEARS
| ❑ SPS-609 | Brotherhood of Man | 1970 | 6.25 | 12.50 | 25.00 |

VEE JAY
❑ LP-1053 [M]	Sherry & 11 Others	1962	10.00	20.00	40.00
❑ SR-1053 [S]	Sherry & 11 Others	1962	15.00	30.00	60.00
❑ LP 1055 [M]	The Four Seasons Greetings	1962	7.50	15.00	30.00
❑ SR 1055 [S]	The Four Seasons Greetings	1962	10.00	20.00	40.00
❑ LP-1056 [M]	Big Girls Don't Cry and Twelve Others	1963	7.50	15.00	30.00
❑ SR-1056 [S]	Big Girls Don't Cry and Twelve Others	1963	10.00	20.00	40.00
❑ LP-1059 [M]	Ain't That a Shame and 11 Others	1963	7.50	15.00	30.00
❑ SR-1059 [S]	Ain't That a Shame and 11 Others	1963	10.00	20.00	40.00
❑ LP-1065 [M]	Golden Hits of the Four Seasons	1963	7.50	15.00	30.00
❑ SR-1065 [S]	Golden Hits of the Four Seasons	1963	10.00	20.00	40.00
❑ LP-1082 [M]	Stay & Other Great Hits	1964	6.25	12.50	25.00

—*Retitled version of Folk-Nanny*

| ❑ LP-1082 [M] | Folk-Nanny | 1964 | 7.50 | 15.00 | 30.00 |
| ❑ SR-1082 [S] | Stay & Other Great Hits | 1964 | 7.50 | 15.00 | 30.00 |

—*Retitled version of Folk-Nanny*

| ❑ SR-1082 [S] | Folk-Nanny | 1964 | 10.00 | 20.00 | 40.00 |
| ❑ LP-1088 [M] | More Golden Hits by the Four Seasons | 1964 | 5.00 | 10.00 | 20.00 |

—*With "Apple of My Eye" on record*

| ❑ LP-1088 [M] | More Golden Hits by the Four Seasons | 1964 | 7.50 | 15.00 | 30.00 |

—*With "Long Lonely Nights" on record*

| ❑ SR-1088 [S] | More Golden Hits by the Four Seasons | 1964 | 6.25 | 12.50 | 25.00 |

—*With "Apple of My Eye" on record*

| ❑ SR-1088 [S] | More Golden Hits by the Four Seasons | 1964 | 10.00 | 20.00 | 40.00 |

—*With "Long Lonely Nights" on record*

❑ LP-1121 [M]	We Love Girls	1965	7.50	15.00	30.00
❑ LPS-1121 [S]	We Love Girls	1965	10.00	20.00	40.00
❑ LP-1154 [M]	Recorded Live on Stage	1965	7.50	15.00	30.00
❑ LPS-1154 [S]	Recorded Live on Stage	1965	10.00	20.00	40.00

WARNER BROS.
❑ BS 2900	Who Loves You	1975	3.00	6.00	12.00
❑ BS 3016	Helicon	1977	3.00	6.00	12.00
❑ 2WB 3497 [(2)]	Reunited Live	1980	3.75	7.50	15.00

FOUR TOPS, THE
ABC
Number	Title (A Side/B Side)	Yr	VG	VG+	NM
❑ D-862	Night Lights Harmony	1975	3.00	6.00	12.00
❑ D-968	Catfish	1976	3.00	6.00	12.00
❑ D-1014	The Show Must Go On	1977	3.00	6.00	12.00
❑ AA-1092	At the Top	1978	3.00	6.00	12.00

ABC DUNHILL
❑ DSX-50129	Keeper of the Castle	1972	3.00	6.00	12.00
❑ DSX-50144	Main Street People	1973	3.00	6.00	12.00
❑ DSX-50166	Meeting of the Minds	1974	3.00	6.00	12.00
❑ DSX-50188	Live & In Concert	1974	3.00	6.00	12.00

ARISTA
| ❑ AL-8492 | Indestructible | 1988 | 2.00 | 4.00 | 8.00 |

CASABLANCA
| ❑ NBLP 7258 | Tonight! | 1981 | 2.50 | 5.00 | 10.00 |
| ❑ NBLP 7266 | One More Mountain | 1982 | 2.50 | 5.00 | 10.00 |

COMMAND
| ❑ CQD-40011 [Q] | Keeper of the Castle | 1974 | 5.00 | 10.00 | 20.00 |
| ❑ CQD-40012 [Q] | Main Street People | 1974 | 5.00 | 10.00 | 20.00 |

MCA
| ❑ 27019 | Greatest Hits | 198? | 2.50 | 5.00 | 10.00 |

MOTOWN
| ❑ M5-114V1 | Superstar Series, Vol. 14 | 1981 | 2.50 | 5.00 | 10.00 |
| ❑ M5-122V1 | Four Tops | 1981 | 2.00 | 4.00 | 8.00 |

—*Reissue of 622*

| ❑ M5-149V1 | Four Tops Reach Out | 1981 | 2.00 | 4.00 | 8.00 |

—*Reissue of 660*

| ❑ M5-209V1 | The Four Tops' Greatest Hits | 1981 | 2.00 | 4.00 | 8.00 |

—*Reissue of 662*

❑ 622 [M]	Four Tops	1964	7.50	15.00	30.00
❑ MS-622 [S]	Four Tops	1964	10.00	20.00	40.00
❑ 634 [M]	Four Tops Second Album	1965	6.25	12.50	25.00
❑ MS-634 [S]	Four Tops Second Album	1965	7.50	15.00	30.00
❑ 647 [M]	4 Tops On Top	1966	6.25	12.50	25.00
❑ MS-647 [S]	4 Tops On Top	1966	7.50	15.00	30.00
❑ 654 [M]	Four Tops Live!	1966	6.25	12.50	25.00
❑ MS-654 [S]	Four Tops Live!	1966	7.50	15.00	30.00
❑ 657 [M]	4 Tops on Broadway	1967	6.25	12.50	25.00
❑ MS-657 [S]	4 Tops on Broadway	1967	7.50	15.00	30.00
❑ 660 [M]	Four Tops Reach Out	1967	7.50	15.00	30.00
❑ MS-660 [S]	Four Tops Reach Out	1967	6.25	12.50	25.00
❑ 662 [M]	The Four Tops Greatest Hits	1967	7.50	15.00	30.00
❑ MS-662 [S]	The Four Tops Greatest Hits	1967	5.00	10.00	20.00
❑ 669 [M]	Yesterday's Dreams	1968	7.50	15.00	30.00
❑ MS-669 [S]	Yesterday's Dreams	1968	5.00	10.00	20.00
❑ MS-675	Four Tops Now!	1969	5.00	10.00	20.00
❑ MS-695	Soul Spin	1969	5.00	10.00	20.00

F

Number	Title (A Side/B Side)	Yr	VG	VG+	NM
❑ MS-704	Still Waters Run Deep	1970	5.00	10.00	20.00
❑ MS-721	Changing Times	1970	5.00	10.00	20.00
❑ M-740L	Four Tops Greatest Hits, Vol. 2	1971	5.00	10.00	20.00
❑ M-748L	Nature Planned It	1972	5.00	10.00	20.00
❑ M-764D [(2)]	The Best of the 4 Tops	1973	3.75	7.50	15.00
❑ M9-809A3 [(3)]	Anthology	1974	5.00	10.00	20.00
❑ 5224 ML	Still Waters Run Deep	1982	2.00	4.00	8.00
—Reissue of 704					
❑ 5258 ML	Four Tops Live!	1983	2.00	4.00	8.00
—Reissue of 654					
❑ 5314 ML	Great Songs	1983	2.50	5.00	10.00
❑ 6066 ML	Back Where I Belong	1983	2.50	5.00	10.00
❑ 6130 ML	Magic	1985	2.50	5.00	10.00
WORKSHOP JAZZ					
❑ 217 [M]	Breakin' Through	1962	—	—	—
—This album is pictured on some early Motown inner sleeves, but is not known to exist					

FOUR TUNES, THE
JUBILEE

Number	Title (A Side/B Side)	Yr	VG	VG+	NM
❑ LP-1039 [M]	12 x 4	1957	62.50	125.00	250.00

FOURTH CEKCION, THE
SOLAR

Number	Title (A Side/B Side)	Yr	VG	VG+	NM
❑ 110	The Fourth Cekcion	1970	15.00	30.00	60.00

FOURTH WAY, THE
CAPITOL

Number	Title (A Side/B Side)	Yr	VG	VG+	NM
❑ ST-317	The Fourth Way	1969	6.25	12.50	25.00
HARVEST					
❑ SKAO-423	The Sun and Moon Have Come Together	1970	5.00	10.00	20.00
❑ ST-666	Werewolf	1971	5.00	10.00	20.00

FOWLER, WALLY
DECCA

Number	Title (A Side/B Side)	Yr	VG	VG+	NM
❑ DL 8560 [M]	Call of the Cross	1958	10.00	20.00	40.00
DOVE					
❑ 1000	A Tribute to Elvis Presley	1977	5.00	10.00	20.00
KING					
❑ 702 [M]	Gospel Song Festival	1960	25.00	50.00	100.00
STARDAY					
❑ SLP-112 [M]	All Nite Singing Gospel Concert	1960	10.00	20.00	40.00
❑ SLP-301 [M]	All Nite Singing Concert	1964	7.50	15.00	30.00

FOWLEY, KIM
ANTILLES

Number	Title (A Side/B Side)	Yr	VG	VG+	NM
❑ AN-7075	Snake Document Masquerade	1979	3.00	6.00	12.00
CAPITOL					
❑ ST-11075	I'm Bad	1972	5.00	10.00	20.00
❑ ST-11159	International Heroes	1973	5.00	10.00	20.00
❑ ST-11248	Automatic	1974	5.00	10.00	20.00
GNP CRESCENDO					
❑ GNPS-2132	Hollywood Confidential	197?	3.00	6.00	12.00
IMPERIAL					
❑ LP-12413	Born to Be Wild	1968	10.00	20.00	40.00
❑ LP-12423	Outrageous	1969	10.00	20.00	40.00
❑ LP-12443	Good Clean Fun	1969	10.00	20.00	40.00
PVC					
❑ 7906	Sunset Boulevard	1978	3.00	6.00	12.00
TOWER					
❑ ST 5080 [S]	Love Is Alive and Well	1967	10.00	20.00	40.00
❑ T 5080 [M]	Love Is Alive and Well	1967	7.50	15.00	30.00

FOX, CURLY
HARMONY

Number	Title (A Side/B Side)	Yr	VG	VG+	NM
❑ HL 7302 [M]	Traveling Blues	1963	5.00	10.00	20.00
STARDAY					
❑ SLP-235 [M]	Curly Fox and Texas Ruby	1963	7.50	15.00	30.00

FOXX, INEZ (AND CHARLIE)
DYNAMO

Number	Title (A Side/B Side)	Yr	VG	VG+	NM
❑ DM-7000 [M]	Come By Here	1967	7.50	15.00	30.00
❑ DM-7002 [M]	Inez and Charlie Foxx's Greatest Hits	1967	7.50	15.00	30.00
❑ DS-8000 [S]	Come By Here	1967	10.00	20.00	40.00
❑ DS-8002 [S]	Inez and Charlie Foxx's Greatest Hits	1967	10.00	20.00	40.00
❑ DS-8003	Swingin' Mockin' Band	1968	7.50	15.00	30.00
SUE					
❑ LP-1027 [M]	Mockingbird	1966	25.00	50.00	100.00
SYMBOL					
❑ SYM-4400 [M]	Mockingbird	1963	37.50	75.00	150.00
VOLT					
❑ VOS-6022	Inez Foxx at Memphis	1973	3.75	7.50	15.00

FRACTION
ANGELUS

Number	Title (A Side/B Side)	Yr	VG	VG+	NM
❑ 571	Moon Blood	1971	1000.	1500.	2000.

FRAGER, MALCOLM
RCA VICTOR RED SEAL

Number	Title (A Side/B Side)	Yr	VG	VG+	NM
❑ LSC-2465 [S]	Prokofiev: Piano Concerto No. 2	1961	25.00	50.00	100.00
—Originals with "shaded dog" label					

FRAMPTON, PETER
A&M

Number	Title (A Side/B Side)	Yr	VG	VG+	NM
❑ SP-3133	Wind of Change	198?	2.00	4.00	8.00
—Budget-line reissue					
❑ SP-3619	Somethin's Happening	1974	3.00	6.00	12.00
❑ PR-3703	Frampton Comes Alive!	1976	5.00	10.00	20.00
—Single-record picture disc of highlights					
❑ SP-3703 [(2)]	Frampton Comes Alive!	1976	3.00	6.00	12.00
❑ SP-3710	Where I Should Be	1979	2.50	5.00	10.00
❑ SP-3722	Breaking All the Rules	1981	2.50	5.00	10.00

Number	Title (A Side/B Side)	Yr	VG	VG+	NM
❑ SP-4348	Wind of Change	1972	3.00	6.00	12.00
—Brown label					
❑ SP-4348	Wind of Change	1974	2.50	5.00	10.00
—Silvery label					
❑ SP-4389	Frampton's Camel	1973	3.00	6.00	12.00
—Brown label					
❑ SP-4389	Frampton's Camel	1974	2.50	5.00	10.00
—Silvery label					
❑ SP-4512	Frampton	1975	2.50	5.00	10.00
❑ SP-4704	I'm In You	1977	2.50	5.00	10.00
❑ SP-4704 [DJ]	I'm In You	1977	10.00	20.00	40.00
—Promo-only picture disc					
❑ SP-4905	The Art of Control	1982	2.50	5.00	10.00
❑ SP-6505 [(2)]	Frampton Comes Alive!	198?	2.50	5.00	10.00
—Budget-line reissue					
❑ SP-17100 [DJ]	Peter Frampton Radio Special	1979	5.00	10.00	20.00
—Promo-only interview record					
ATLANTIC					
❑ PR 848 [DJ]	Frampton Is Alive!	1986	5.00	10.00	20.00
—Promo-only interview record					
❑ PR 3093 [DJ]	Perfect Fit: A Candid Interview	1989	5.00	10.00	20.00
—Promo-only album					
❑ 81290	Premonition	1986	2.00	4.00	8.00
❑ 82030	Where All the Pieces Fit	1989	2.00	4.00	8.00
MOBILE FIDELITY					
❑ 2-262 [(2)]	Frampton Comes Alive!	1996	10.00	20.00	40.00
—Audiophile vinyl					
SWEET THUNDER					
❑ 6 [(2)]	Frampton Comes Alive!	198?	25.00	50.00	100.00
—Audiophile edition					

FRANCIS, CONNIE
LEO

Number	Title (A Side/B Side)	Yr	VG	VG+	NM
❑ LE-903 [M]	Connie Francis and the Kids Next Door	1967	12.50	25.00	50.00
❑ LES-903 [S]	Connie Francis and the Kids Next Door	1967	15.00	30.00	60.00
MATI-MOR					
❑ 8002 [M]	Sing Along wth Connie Francis	1961	10.00	20.00	40.00
—Made for Brylcreem					
METRO					
❑ M-519 [M]	Connie Francis	1964	5.00	10.00	20.00
❑ MS-519 [S]	Connie Francis	1964	6.25	12.50	25.00
❑ M-538 [M]	Folk Favorites	1965	5.00	10.00	20.00
❑ MS-538 [S]	Folk Favorites	1965	6.25	12.50	25.00
❑ M-571 [M]	Songs of Love	1966	5.00	10.00	20.00
❑ MS-571 [S]	Songs of Love	1966	6.25	12.50	25.00
❑ M-603 [M]	The Incomparable Connie Francis	1967	5.00	10.00	20.00
❑ MS-603 [S]	The Incomparable Connie Francis	1967	6.25	12.50	25.00
MGM					
❑ GAS-109	Greatest Golden Groovie Goodies (Golden Archive Series)	1970	6.25	12.50	25.00
❑ E-3686 [M]	Who's Sorry Now?	1958	25.00	50.00	100.00
—Yellow label					
❑ E-3686 [M]	Who's Sorry Now?	1960	10.00	20.00	40.00
—Black label					
❑ E-3761 [M]	The Exciting Connie Francis	1959	7.50	15.00	30.00
—Black label					
❑ E-3761 [M]	The Exciting Connie Francis	1959	20.00	40.00	80.00
—Yellow label					
❑ SE-3761 [S]	The Exciting Connie Francis	1959	10.00	20.00	40.00
—Black label					
❑ SE-3761 [S]	The Exciting Connie Francis	1959	25.00	50.00	100.00
—Yellow label					
❑ E-3776 [M]	My Thanks to You	1959	7.50	15.00	30.00
❑ SE-3776 [S]	My Thanks to You	1959	10.00	20.00	40.00
❑ E-3791 [M]	Italian Favorites	1959	7.50	15.00	30.00
❑ SE-3791 [S]	Italian Favorites	1959	10.00	20.00	40.00
❑ E-3792 [M]	Christmas in My Heart	1959	7.50	15.00	30.00
❑ SE-3792 [S]	Christmas in My Heart	1959	10.00	20.00	40.00
—Same as above, but in stereo					
❑ E-3793 [M]	Connie's Greatest Hits	1960	7.50	15.00	30.00
❑ E-3794 [M]	Rock 'N' Roll Million Sellers	1960	7.50	15.00	30.00
❑ SE-3794 [S]	Rock 'N' Roll Million Sellers	1960	10.00	20.00	40.00
❑ E-3795 [M]	Country and Western Golden Hits	1960	7.50	15.00	30.00
❑ SE-3795 [S]	Country and Western Golden Hits	1960	10.00	20.00	40.00
❑ E-3853 [M]	Spanish and Latin American Favorites	1960	7.50	15.00	30.00
❑ SE-3853 [S]	Spanish and Latin American Favorites	1960	10.00	20.00	40.00
❑ E-3869 [M]	Jewish Favorites	1961	7.50	15.00	30.00
❑ SE-3869 [S]	Jewish Favorites	1961	10.00	20.00	40.00
❑ E-3871 [M]	More Italian Favorites	1960	7.50	15.00	30.00
❑ SE-3871 [S]	More Italian Favorites	1960	10.00	20.00	40.00
❑ E-3893 [M]	Songs to a Swinging Band	1961	7.50	15.00	30.00
❑ SE-3893 [S]	Songs to a Swinging Band	1961	10.00	20.00	40.00
❑ E-3913 [M]	Connie Francis at the Copa	1961	7.50	15.00	30.00
❑ SE-3913 [S]	Connie Francis at the Copa	1961	10.00	20.00	40.00
❑ E-3942 [M]	More Greatest Hits	1961	7.50	15.00	30.00
❑ SE-3942 [S]	More Greatest Hits	1961	10.00	20.00	40.00
❑ E-3965 [M]	Never on Sunday and Other Title Songs from Motion Pictures	1961	7.50	15.00	30.00
❑ SE-3965 [S]	Never on Sunday and Other Title Songs from Motion Pictures	1961	10.00	20.00	40.00
❑ E-3969 [M]	Folk Song Favorites	1961	7.50	15.00	30.00
❑ SE-3969 [S]	Folk Song Favorites	1961	10.00	20.00	40.00
❑ E-4013 [M]	Irish Favorites	1962	7.50	15.00	30.00
❑ SE-4013 [S]	Irish Favorites	1962	10.00	20.00	40.00
❑ E-4022 [M]	Dance Party	196?	6.25	12.50	25.00
—Retitled version of "Do the Twist"					
❑ E-4022 [M]	Do the Twist	1962	7.50	15.00	30.00
❑ SE-4022 [S]	Dance Party	196?	7.50	15.00	30.00
—Retitled version of "Do the Twist"					
❑ SE-4022 [S]	Do the Twist	1962	10.00	20.00	40.00
❑ E-4023 [M]	Fun Songs for Children	1962	12.50	25.00	50.00

Number	Title (A Side/B Side)	Yr	VG	VG+	NM
❏ E-4048 [M]	Award Winning Motion Picture Hits	1963	6.25	12.50	25.00
❏ SE-4048 [S]	Award Winning Motion Picture Hits	1963	7.50	15.00	30.00
❏ E-4049 [M]	Connie Francis Sings Second Hand Love and Other Hits	1962	6.25	12.50	25.00
❏ SE-4049 [S]	Connie Francis Sings Second Hand Love and Other Hits	1962	7.50	15.00	30.00
❏ E-4079 [M]	Country Music Connie Style	1962	6.25	12.50	25.00
❏ SE-4079 [S]	Country Music Connie Style	1962	7.50	15.00	30.00
❏ E-4102 [M]	Modern Italian Hits	1963	6.25	12.50	25.00
❏ SE-4102 [S]	Modern Italian Hits	1963	7.50	15.00	30.00
❏ E-4123 [M]	Follow the Boys	1963	6.25	12.50	25.00
❏ SE-4123 [S]	Follow the Boys	1963	7.50	15.00	30.00
❏ E-4124 [M]	German Favorites	1963	6.25	12.50	25.00
❏ SE-4124 [S]	German Favorites	1963	7.50	15.00	30.00
❏ E-4145 [M]	Greatest American Waltzes	1963	6.25	12.50	25.00
❏ SE-4145 [S]	Greatest American Waltzes	1963	7.50	15.00	30.00
❏ E-4161 [M]	Mala Femmena & Connie's Big Hits from Italy	1963	6.25	12.50	25.00
❏ SE-4161 [S]	Mala Femmena & Connie's Big Hits from Italy	1963	7.50	15.00	30.00
❏ E-4167 [M]	The Very Best of Connie Francis	1963	6.25	12.50	25.00
❏ SE-4167 [S]	The Very Best of Connie Francis	1963	7.50	15.00	30.00
❏ E-4210 [M]	In the Summer of His Years	1964	6.25	12.50	25.00
❏ SE-4210 [S]	In the Summer of His Years	1964	7.50	15.00	30.00
❏ E-4229 [M]	Looking for Love	1964	6.25	12.50	25.00
❏ SE-4229 [S]	Looking for Love	1964	7.50	15.00	30.00
❏ E-4253 [M]	A New Kind of Connie	1964	6.25	12.50	25.00
❏ SE-4253 [S]	A New Kind of Connie	1964	7.50	15.00	30.00
❏ E-4294 [M]	Connie Francis Sings For Mama	1965	6.25	12.50	25.00
❏ SE-4294 [S]	Connie Francis Sings For Mama	1965	7.50	15.00	30.00
❏ E-4298 [M]	All Time International Hits	1965	6.25	12.50	25.00
❏ SE-4298 [S]	All Time International Hits	1965	7.50	15.00	30.00
❏ E-4355 [M]	Jealous Heart	1966	6.25	12.50	25.00
❏ SE-4355 [S]	Jealous Heart	1966	7.50	15.00	30.00
❏ E-4382 [M]	Movie Greats of the 60's	1966	6.25	12.50	25.00
❏ SE-4382 [S]	Movie Greats of the 60's	1966	7.50	15.00	30.00
❏ E-4399 [M]	Connie's Christmas	1966	6.25	12.50	25.00
❏ SE-4399 [S]	Connie's Christmas	1966	7.50	15.00	30.00
❏ E-4411 [M]	Live at the Sahara in Las Vegas	1967	6.25	12.50	25.00
❏ SE-4411 [S]	Live at the Sahara in Las Vegas	1967	7.50	15.00	30.00
❏ E-4448 [M]	Love, Italian Style	1967	6.25	12.50	25.00
❏ SE-4448 [S]	Love, Italian Style	1967	7.50	15.00	30.00
❏ E-4472 [M]	Connie Francis On Broadway Today	1967	6.25	12.50	25.00
❏ SE-4472 [S]	Connie Francis On Broadway Today	1967	7.50	15.00	30.00
❏ E-4474 [M]	Grandes Exitos del Cine de los Anos 60	1967	6.25	12.50	25.00
❏ SE-4474 [S]	Grandes Exitos del Cine de los Anos 60	1967	7.50	15.00	30.00
❏ E-4487 [M]	My Heart Cries for You	1967	7.50	15.00	30.00
❏ SE-4487 [S]	My Heart Cries for You	1967	6.25	12.50	25.00
❏ E-4522 [M]	Hawaii: Connie	1968	25.00	50.00	100.00
❏ SE-4522 [S]	Hawaii: Connie	1968	6.25	12.50	25.00
❏ SE-4573	Connie & Clyde	1968	6.25	12.50	25.00
❏ SE-4585	Connie Francis Sings Bacharach & David	1968	6.25	12.50	25.00
❏ SE-4637	The Wedding Cake	1969	6.25	12.50	25.00
❏ SE-4655	The Songs of Les Reed	1969	6.25	12.50	25.00
❏ MG-1-5406	I'm Me Again	198?	3.00	6.00	12.00
❏ MG-1-5410	Greatest Hits	198?	3.00	6.00	12.00
❏ MG-1-5411	Greatest Jewish Hits	198?	3.00	6.00	12.00
❏ T-90027 [M]	Award Winning Motion Picture Hits	196?	7.50	15.00	30.00
—Capitol Record Club edition					
❏ ST-90068 [S]	A New Kind of Connie	1964	8.75	17.50	35.00
—Capitol Record Club issue					
❏ T-90068 [M]	A New Kind of Connie	1964	7.50	15.00	30.00
—Capitol Record Club issue					
❏ ST 90510 [S]	The Very Best of Connie Francis	1965	10.00	20.00	40.00
—Capitol Record Club edition					
❏ T 90510 [M]	The Very Best of Connie Francis	1965	10.00	20.00	40.00
—Capitol Record Club edition					
❏ ST-91145	My Best to You	1968	7.50	15.00	30.00
—Capitol Record Club					

POLYDOR

Number	Title (A Side/B Side)	Yr	VG	VG+	NM
❏ 827569-1	The Very Best of Connie Francis	1985	2.50	5.00	10.00
❏ 827582-1	Greatest Hits	1985	2.50	5.00	10.00
❏ 827584-1	Greatest Jewish Hits	1985	2.50	5.00	10.00
❏ 839922-1	Lo Mejor De Su Repertorio	198?	2.50	5.00	10.00
❏ 839923-1	12 Exitos De Connie Francis	198?	2.50	5.00	10.00

FRANCIS, CONNIE, AND HANK WILLIAMS, JR.

Also see each artist's individual listings.

MGM

Number	Title (A Side/B Side)	Yr	VG	VG+	NM
❏ E-4251 [M]	Connie Francis & Hank Williams, Jr. Sing Great Country Favorites	1964	7.50	15.00	30.00
❏ SE-4251 [S]	Connie Francis & Hank Williams, Jr. Sing Great Country Favorites	1964	10.00	20.00	40.00

FRANCIS, PANAMA

EPIC

Number	Title (A Side/B Side)	Yr	VG	VG+	NM
❏ BN 629 [S]	Exploding Drums	1959	7.50	15.00	30.00
❏ LN 3839 [M]	Exploding Drums	1959	7.50	15.00	30.00

20TH CENTURY FOX

Number	Title (A Side/B Side)	Yr	VG	VG+	NM
❏ TFM-6101 [M]	Tough Talk	196?	6.25	12.50	25.00
❏ TFS-6101 [S]	Tough Talk	196?	7.50	15.00	30.00

FRANKE AND THE KNOCKOUTS

MILLENNIUM

Number	Title (A Side/B Side)	Yr	VG	VG+	NM
❏ DJL1-4015 [DJ]	Special Radio Series Volume X	1981	5.00	10.00	20.00
—Promo-only music and interview disc					
❏ DJL1-7764 [EP]	Below the Belt Sampler	1982	5.00	10.00	20.00
—Promo-only three-song sampler; contains live version of "I Need Love (The Knockout Shuffle)" that was not issued on LP					

FRANKLIN, ALAN, EXPLOSION

ALADDIN

Number	Title (A Side/B Side)	Yr	VG	VG+	NM
❏ 104049	Come Home Baby	1969	20.00	40.00	80.00

HORNE

Number	Title (A Side/B Side)	Yr	VG	VG+	NM
❏ JC-888	The Blues Climax	1970	20.00	40.00	80.00

FRANKLIN, ARETHA

ARISTA

Number	Title (A Side/B Side)	Yr	VG	VG+	NM
❏ AL8-8019	Get It Right	1983	2.50	5.00	10.00
❏ AL8-8286	Who's Zoomin' Who	1985	2.50	5.00	10.00
❏ AL-8344	Jump To It	1985	2.00	4.00	8.00
—Budget-line reissue					
❏ AL-8368	Love All the Hurt Away	1985	2.00	4.00	8.00
—Budget-line reissue					
❏ AL-8442	Aretha	1986	2.50	5.00	10.00
—Different album than 9538					
❏ A2L-8497 [(2)]	One Lord, One Faith, One Baptism	1987	5.00	10.00	20.00
❏ AL-8572	Through the Storm	1989	2.50	5.00	10.00
❏ AL-9538	Aretha	1980	2.50	5.00	10.00
❏ AL-9552	Love All the Hurt Away	1981	2.50	5.00	10.00
❏ AL-9602	Jump To It	1982	2.50	5.00	10.00

ATLANTIC

Number	Title (A Side/B Side)	Yr	VG	VG+	NM
❏ SD 2-906 [(2)]	Amazing Grace	1972	5.00	10.00	20.00
❏ SD 7205	Aretha Live at Fillmore West	1971	3.75	7.50	15.00
❏ SD 7213	Yoing, Gifted & Black	1972	3.75	7.50	15.00
❏ SD 7265	Hey Now Hey (The Other Side of the Sky)	1973	3.00	6.00	12.00
❏ SD 7292	Let Me in Your Life	1974	3.00	6.00	12.00
❏ 8139 [M]	I Never Loved a Man the Way I Love You	1967	6.25	12.50	25.00
❏ SD 8139	I Never Loved a Man the Way I Love You	1969	3.00	6.00	12.00
—Green and red label					
❏ SD 8139 [S]	I Never Loved a Man the Way I Love You	1967	5.00	10.00	20.00
—Green and blue label					
❏ 8150 [M]	Aretha Arrives	1967	6.25	12.50	25.00
❏ SD 8150	Aretha Arrives	1969	3.00	6.00	12.00
—Green and red label					
❏ SD 8150 [S]	Aretha Arrives	1967	5.00	10.00	20.00
—Green and blue label					
❏ 8176 [M]	Aretha: Lady Soul	1968	7.50	15.00	30.00
❏ SD 8176	Aretha: Lady Soul	1969	3.00	6.00	12.00
—Green and red label					
❏ SD 8176 [S]	Aretha: Lady Soul	1968	5.00	10.00	20.00
—Green and blue label					
❏ SD 8186	Aretha Now	1968	5.00	10.00	20.00
—Green and blue label					
❏ SD 8186	Aretha Now	1969	3.00	6.00	12.00
—Green and red label					
❏ SD 8207	Aretha in Paris	1968	3.75	7.50	15.00
❏ 8212 [M]	Aretha Franklin: Soul '69	1969	12.50	25.00	50.00
—White label promo; no stock copies in mono					
❏ SD 8212	Aretha Franklin: Soul '69	1969	3.75	7.50	15.00
❏ SD 8227	Aretha's Gold	1969	3.75	7.50	15.00
❏ SD 8248	This Girl's in Love with You	1970	3.75	7.50	15.00
❏ SD 8265	Spirit in the Dark	1970	3.75	7.50	15.00
❏ SD 8295	Aretha's Greatest Hits	1971	3.75	7.50	15.00
❏ QD 8305 [Q]	The Best of Aretha Franklin	1974	5.00	10.00	20.00
❏ SD 18116	With Everything I Feel in Me	1974	3.00	6.00	12.00
❏ SD 18151	You	1975	3.00	6.00	12.00
❏ SD 18176	Sparkle	1976	3.00	6.00	12.00
❏ SD 18204	Ten Years of Gold	1976	3.00	6.00	12.00
❏ SD 19102	Sweet Passion	1977	3.00	6.00	12.00
❏ SD 19161	Almighty Fire	1978	3.00	6.00	12.00
❏ SD 19248	La Diva	1979	3.00	6.00	12.00
❏ 81230	Aretha's Jazz	1984	2.50	5.00	10.00
❏ 81280	The Best of Aretha Franklin	1985	2.50	5.00	10.00
❏ 81668 [(2)]	30 Greatest Hits	1986	3.75	7.50	15.00
❏ STAO-95151	Hey Now Hey (The Other Side of the Sky)	1973	3.75	7.50	15.00
—Capitol Record Club edition					

CHECKER

Number	Title (A Side/B Side)	Yr	VG	VG+	NM
❏ 10009 [M]	Songs of Faith	1965	125.00	250.00	500.00
—Original issue of this album; cover has Aretha sitting at a piano					
❏ 10009 [M]	Gospel Soul	1967	5.00	10.00	20.00
—Reissue with new title and cover					

COLUMBIA

Number	Title (A Side/B Side)	Yr	VG	VG+	NM
❏ GP 4 [(2)]	Two All-Time Great Albums in One Great Package	196?	6.25	12.50	25.00
—Contains CS 9081 and CS 9429					
❏ CL 1612 [M]	Aretha	1961	12.50	25.00	50.00
—Red and black label with six "eye" logos					
❏ CL 1612 [M]	Aretha	1963	5.00	10.00	20.00
—"Guaranteed High Fidelity" on label					
❏ CL 1612 [M]	Aretha	1965	3.75	7.50	15.00
—"360 Sound Mono" on label					
❏ CL 1761 [M]	The Electrifying Aretha Franklin	1962	10.00	20.00	40.00
—Red and black label with six "eye" logos					
❏ CL 1761 [M]	The Electrifying Aretha Franklin	1963	5.00	10.00	20.00
—"Guaranteed High Fidelity" on label					
❏ CL 1761 [M]	The Electrifying Aretha Franklin	1965	3.75	7.50	15.00
—"360 Sound Mono" on label					
❏ CL 1876 [M]	The Tender, The Moving, The Swinging Aretha Franklin	1962	10.00	20.00	40.00
—Red and black label with six "eye" logos					
❏ CL 1876 [M]	The Tender, The Moving, The Swinging Aretha Franklin	1963	5.00	10.00	20.00
—"Guaranteed High Fidelity" on label					
❏ CL 1876 [M]	The Tender, The Moving, The Swinging Aretha Franklin	1965	3.75	7.50	15.00
—"360 Sound Mono" on label					
❏ CL 2079 [M]	Laughing on the Outside	1963	5.00	10.00	20.00
—"Guaranteed High Fidelity" on label					
❏ CL 2079 [M]	Laughing on the Outside	1965	3.75	7.50	15.00
—"360 Sound Mono" on label					
❏ CL 2163 [M]	Unforgettable	1964	5.00	10.00	20.00
—"Guaranteed High Fidelity" on label					
❏ CL 2163 [M]	Unforgettable	1965	3.75	7.50	15.00
—"360 Sound Mono" on label					

Number	Title (A Side/B Side)	Yr	VG	VG+	NM
❑ CL 2281 [M]	Runnin' Out of Fools	1964	5.00	10.00	20.00
—"Guaranteed High Fidelity" on label					
❑ CL 2281 [M]	Runnin' Out of Fools	1965	3.75	7.50	15.00
—"360 Sound Mono" on label					
❑ CL 2351 [M]	Yeah!!!	1965	5.00	10.00	20.00
—"Guaranteed High Fidelity" on label					
❑ CL 2351 [M]	Yeah!!!	1966	3.75	7.50	15.00
—"360 Sound Mono" on label					
❑ CL 2521 [M]	Soul Sister	1966	5.00	10.00	20.00
❑ CL 2629 [M]	Take It Like You Give It	1967	6.25	12.50	25.00
❑ CL 2673 [M]	Aretha Franklin's Greatest Hits	1967	6.25	12.50	25.00
❑ CL 2754 [M]	Take a Look	1967	7.50	15.00	30.00
❑ CS 8412 [S]	Aretha	1961	20.00	40.00	80.00
—Red and black label with six "eye" logos					
❑ CS 8412 [S]	Aretha	1963	6.25	12.50	25.00
—"360 Sound Stereo" on label					
❑ CS 8561 [S]	The Electrifying Aretha Franklin	1962	12.50	25.00	50.00
—Red and black label with six "eye" logos					
❑ CS 8561 [S]	The Electrifying Aretha Franklin	1963	6.25	12.50	25.00
—"360 Sound Stereo" on label					
❑ CS 8676 [S]	The Tender, The Moving, The Swinging Aretha Franklin	1962	12.50	25.00	50.00
—Red and black label with six "eye" logos					
❑ CS 8676 [S]	The Tender, The Moving, The Swinging Aretha Franklin	1963	6.25	12.50	25.00
—"360 Sound Stereo" on label					
❑ CS 8879 [S]	Laughing on the Outside	1963	6.25	12.50	25.00
—"360 Sound Stereo" on label					
❑ CS 8963 [S]	Unforgettable	1964	6.25	12.50	25.00
—"360 Sound Stereo" on label					
❑ CS 9081 [S]	Runnin' Out of Fools	1964	6.25	12.50	25.00
—"360 Sound Stereo" on label					
❑ CS 9151 [S]	Yeah!!!	1965	6.25	12.50	25.00
—"360 Sound Stereo" on label					
❑ CS 9321 [S]	Soul Sister	1966	6.25	12.50	25.00
—"360 Sound Stereo" on label					
❑ CS 9429 [S]	Take It Like You Give It	1967	5.00	10.00	20.00
—"360 Sound Stereo" on label					
❑ CS 9473 [S]	Aretha Franklin's Greatest Hits	1967	5.00	10.00	20.00
—"360 Sound Stereo" on label					
❑ CS 9554 [S]	Take a Look	1967	5.00	10.00	20.00
—"360 Sound Stereo" on label					
❑ CS 9601	Aretha Franklin's Greatest Hits, Volume 2	1968	5.00	10.00	20.00
—"360 Sound Stereo" on label					
❑ CS 9776	Soft and Beautiful	1969	5.00	10.00	20.00
—"360 Sound Stereo" on label					
❑ CS 9956	Today I Sing the Blues	1970	3.75	7.50	15.00
—"360 Sound Stereo" on label					
❑ KG 31355 [(2)]	In the Beginning/The World of Aretha Franklin 1960-1967	1972	5.00	10.00	20.00
❑ KC 31953	The First 12 Sides	1973	3.00	6.00	12.00
❑ C2 37377 [(2)]	The Legendary Queen of Soul	1981	3.00	6.00	12.00
❑ PC 38042	Sweet Bitter Love	1982	2.50	5.00	10.00
❑ FC 40105	Aretha Franklin Sings the Blues	1985	2.50	5.00	10.00
❑ FC 40708	Aretha After Hours	1987	2.50	5.00	10.00
COLUMBIA SPECIAL PRODUCTS					
❑ C 10589	Take a Look	1971	3.00	6.00	12.00
HARMONY					
❑ HS 11349	Once in a Lifetime	1969	3.00	6.00	12.00
❑ HS 11418	Two Sides of Love	1970	3.00	6.00	12.00
❑ KH 30606	Greatest Hits 1960-1965	1971	3.00	6.00	12.00
❑ KH 30606	Greatest Hits 1960-1966	1972	3.00	6.00	12.00

FRANKLIN, CAROLYN
RCA VICTOR

Number	Title (A Side/B Side)	Yr	VG	VG+	NM
❑ LSP-4160	Baby Dynamite	1969	5.00	10.00	20.00
❑ LSP-4317	Chain Reaction	1970	5.00	10.00	20.00
❑ LSP-4411	I'd Rather Be Lonely	1973	5.00	10.00	20.00

FRANKLIN, ERMA
BRUNSWICK

Number	Title (A Side/B Side)	Yr	VG	VG+	NM
❑ BL 754147	Soul Sister	1969	5.00	10.00	20.00
EPIC					
❑ BN 619 [S]	Her Name Is Erma	1962	10.00	20.00	40.00
❑ LN 3824 [M]	Her Name Is Erma	1962	7.50	15.00	30.00

FRANKLIN, HENRY
BLACK JAZZ

Number	Title (A Side/B Side)	Yr	VG	VG+	NM
❑ QD-7	The Skipper	1972	5.00	10.00	20.00
❑ QD-17	The Skipper At Home	1974	5.00	10.00	20.00

FRANKS, MICHAEL
BRUT

Number	Title (A Side/B Side)	Yr	VG	VG+	NM
❑ 6005	Michael Franks	1973	5.00	10.00	20.00
DIRECT DISK					
❑ SD-16611	Tiger in the Rain	1980	7.50	15.00	30.00
—Audiophile vinyl					

FRANTIC
LIZARD

Number	Title (A Side/B Side)	Yr	VG	VG+	NM
❑ 20103	Conception	1971	6.25	12.50	25.00

FRATERNITY OF MAN, THE
ABC

Number	Title (A Side/B Side)	Yr	VG	VG+	NM
❑ S-647	The Fraternity of Man	1968	7.50	15.00	30.00
DOT					
❑ DLP-25955	Get It On	1969	6.25	12.50	25.00

FRAWLEY, WILLIAM
DOT

Number	Title (A Side/B Side)	Yr	VG	VG+	NM
❑ DLP-3061 [M]	William Frawley Sings the Old Ones	1958	10.00	20.00	40.00

FRAZIER, CAESAR
Some of these may spell his first name "Ceasar."
EASTBOUND

Number	Title (A Side/B Side)	Yr	VG	VG+	NM
❑ 9002	Hail Caesar!	1973	12.50	25.00	50.00
❑ 9009	Caesar Frazier '74	1974	10.00	20.00	40.00
WESTBOUND					
❑ 206	Caesar Frazier '75	1975	7.50	15.00	30.00
❑ WT 6103	Another Life	1978	7.50	15.00	30.00

FRAZIER, DALLAS
CAPITOL

Number	Title (A Side/B Side)	Yr	VG	VG+	NM
❑ ST 2552 [S]	Elvira	1966	6.25	12.50	25.00
❑ T 2552 [M]	Elvira	1966	5.00	10.00	20.00
❑ ST 2764 [S]	Tell It Like It Is	1967	5.00	10.00	20.00
❑ T 2764 [M]	Tell It Like It Is	1967	6.25	12.50	25.00

FREAK SCENE, THE
COLUMBIA

Number	Title (A Side/B Side)	Yr	VG	VG+	NM
❑ CL 2656 [M]	Psychedelic Psoul	1967	17.50	35.00	70.00
❑ CS 9456 [S]	Psychedelic Psoul	1967	25.00	50.00	100.00

FREBERG, STAN
CAPITOL

Number	Title (A Side/B Side)	Yr	VG	VG+	NM
❑ T 777 [M]	A Child's Garden of Freberg	1957	12.50	25.00	50.00
—Turquoise label					
❑ WBO 1035 [(2)M]	The Best of the Stan Freberg Shows	1958	15.00	30.00	60.00
❑ SM-1242 [R]	Stan Freberg with the Original Cast	197?	2.50	5.00	10.00
❑ T 1242 [M]	Stan Freberg with the Original Cast	1959	7.50	15.00	30.00
❑ SW 1573 [S]	Stan Freberg Presents the United States of America	1961	7.50	15.00	30.00
❑ W 1573 [M]	Stan Freberg Presents the United States of America	1961	6.25	12.50	25.00
❑ T 1694 [M]	Face the Funnies	1962	6.25	12.50	25.00
❑ T 1816 [M]	Madison Ave. Werewolf	1962	6.25	12.50	25.00
❑ SM-2020 [R]	The Best of Stan Freberg	197?	2.50	5.00	10.00
❑ T 2020 [M]	The Best of Stan Freberg	1964	6.25	12.50	25.00
❑ SM-2551 [R]	The Stan Freberg Underground Show #1	197?	2.50	5.00	10.00
❑ ST 2551 [S]	The Stan Freberg Underground Show #1	1966	6.25	12.50	25.00
❑ T 2551 [M]	The Stan Freberg Underground Show #1	1966	5.00	10.00	20.00
❑ SM-11765	The Best of the Stan Freberg Shows	197?	3.00	6.00	12.00

FRED, JOHN, AND HIS PLAYBOY BAND
JIN

Number	Title (A Side/B Side)	Yr	VG	VG+	NM
❑ 9027	The Best of John Fred and His Playboys	198?	2.50	5.00	10.00
PAULA					
❑ LP-2191 [M]	John Fred and His Playboys	1966	5.00	10.00	20.00
❑ LPS-2191 [S]	John Fred and His Playboys	1966	6.25	12.50	25.00
❑ LP-2193 [M]	34:40 of John Fred and His Playboys	1967	5.00	10.00	20.00
❑ LPS-2193 [S]	34:40 of John Fred and His Playboys	1967	6.25	12.50	25.00
❑ LP-2197 [M]	Agnes English	1967	6.25	12.50	25.00
❑ LPS-2197 [S]	Agnes English	1967	5.00	10.00	20.00
❑ LPS-2197 [S]	Judy in Disguise with Glasses	1968	5.00	10.00	20.00
—Retitled version of "Agnes English"					
❑ LPS-2201	Permanently Stated	1969	5.00	10.00	20.00
UNI					
❑ 73077	Love in My Soul	1970	10.00	20.00	40.00

FREDDIE AND THE DREAMERS
CAPITOL

Number	Title (A Side/B Side)	Yr	VG	VG+	NM
❑ SM-11896 [B]	The Best of Freddie and the Dreamers	1976	2.50	5.00	10.00
—"I'm Telling You Now," "You Were Made for Me," "I Just Don't Understand," "A Little You" and "Over You" are in stereo, the rest are mono.					
MERCURY					
❑ MG-21017 [M]	Freddie and the Dreamers	1965	6.25	12.50	25.00
❑ MG-21026 [M]	Do the Freddie	1965	5.00	10.00	20.00
❑ MG-21031 [M]	Seaside Swingers	1965	5.00	10.00	20.00
❑ MG-21053 [M]	Frantic Freddie	1965	3.75	7.50	15.00
❑ MG-21061 [M]	Fun Lovin' Freddie	1966	3.75	7.50	15.00
❑ SR-61017 [R]	Freddie and the Dreamers	1965	5.00	10.00	20.00
❑ SR-61026 [S]	Do the Freddie	1965	6.25	12.50	25.00
❑ SR-61031 [S]	Seaside Swingers	1965	6.25	12.50	25.00
❑ SR-61053 [S]	Frantic Freddie	1965	5.00	10.00	20.00
❑ SR-61061 [S]	Fun Lovin' Freddie	1966	5.00	10.00	20.00
TOWER					
❑ DT 5003 [R]	I'm Telling You Now	1965	5.00	10.00	20.00
—Contains only two Freddie and the Dreamers songs, but the group's picture is on the cover. Also includes Four Just Men (2), Heinz (2), Linda Laine and the Sinners (2), Mike Rabin and the Demons (2) and The Toggery Five (2)					
❑ T 5003 [M]	I'm Telling You Now	1965	6.25	12.50	25.00
—Contains only two Freddie and the Dreamers songs, but the group's picture is on the cover. Also includes Four Just Men (2), Heinz (2), Linda Laine and the Sinners (2), Mike Rabin and the Demons (2) and The Toggery Five (2)					

FREDRIC
FORTE

Number	Title (A Side/B Side)	Yr	VG	VG+	NM
❑ 80461	Phases and Faces	1968	200.00	400.00	800.00

FREE BAND, THE
VANGUARD

Number	Title (A Side/B Side)	Yr	VG	VG+	NM
❑ VSD-6507	The Free Band	1969	5.00	10.00	20.00

FREE DESIGN, THE
AMBROTYPE

Number	Title (A Side/B Side)	Yr	VG	VG+	NM
❑ 1016	There Is a Song	1972	12.50	25.00	50.00
PROJECT 3					
❑ PR 4006 SD	The Free Design Sing for Very Important People	1970	6.25	12.50	25.00
❑ PR-5019 SD	Kites Are Fun	1967	6.25	12.50	25.00
❑ PR-5031 SD	You Could Be Born Again	1968	6.25	12.50	25.00
❑ PR-5037 SD	Heaven/Earth	1969	6.25	12.50	25.00
❑ PR-5045 SD	Stars/Times/Bubbles/Love	1971	6.25	12.50	25.00
❑ PR-5061 SD	One By One	1971	6.25	12.50	25.00

Number	Title (A Side/B Side)	Yr	VG	VG+	NM
FREE MUSIC QUARTET, THE					
ESP-DISK'					
❑ 1083	Free Music One and Two	1969	5.00	10.00	20.00
FREEBORNE					
MONITOR					
❑ MPS-607	Peak Impressions	1967	25.00	50.00	100.00
FREED, ALAN					
BRUNSWICK					
❑ BL 54043 [M]	The Alan Freed Rock 'n' Roll Show	1959	37.50	75.00	150.00
CORAL					
❑ CRL 57063 [M]	Alan Freed's Rock 'n' Roll Dance Party, Vol. 1	1956	37.50	75.00	150.00
❑ CRL 57115 [M]	Alan Freed's Rock 'n' Roll Dance Party, Vol. 2	1957	37.50	75.00	150.00
❑ CRL 57177 [M]	Go Go Go — Alan Freed's TV Record Hop	1957	37.50	75.00	150.00
❑ CRL 57213 [M]	Rock Around the Block	1958	37.50	75.00	150.00
❑ CRL 57216 [M]	Alan Freed Presents the King's Henchmen	1958	37.50	75.00	150.00
MGM					
❑ E-293 [10]	The Big Beat	195?	50.00	100.00	200.00
FREEDMAN, BOB					
COBBLESTONE					
❑ 9009	Journeys of Odysseus	1972	5.00	10.00	20.00
SAVOY					
❑ MG-15040 [10]	Piano Moods	1954	12.50	25.00	50.00
FREEMAN, BOBBY					
AUTUMN					
❑ LP 102 [M]	C'mon and S-W-I-M	1964	12.50	25.00	50.00
JOSIE					
❑ JM-4007 [M]	Get In the Swim with Bobby Freeman	1965	7.50	15.00	30.00
❑ JS-4007 [R]	Get In the Swim with Bobby Freeman	1965	6.25	12.50	25.00
JUBILEE					
❑ JLP-1086 [M]	Do You Wanna Dance?	1959	35.00	70.00	140.00
❑ JLPS-1086 [S]	Do You Wanna Dance?	1959	50.00	100.00	200.00
❑ JGM-5010 [M]	Twist with Bobby Freeman	1962	25.00	50.00	100.00
KING					
❑ 930 [M]	The Lovable Style of Bobby Freeman	1965	62.50	125.00	250.00
FREEMAN, BUD					
BETHLEHEM					
❑ BCP-29 [M]	Newport News	1955	20.00	40.00	80.00
CAPITOL					
❑ H 625 [10]	Classics in Jazz	1955	20.00	40.00	80.00
❑ T 625 [M]	Classics in Jazz	1955	12.50	25.00	50.00
COLUMBIA					
❑ CL 2558 [10]	Jazz — Chicago Style	1955	20.00	40.00	80.00
❑ CL 6107 [10]	Comes Jazz	1950	25.00	50.00	100.00
DECCA					
❑ DL 5213 [10]	Wolverine Jazz	1950	25.00	50.00	100.00
DOT					
❑ DLP-3166 [M]	Bud Freeman and His Summa Cum Laude Trio	1959	10.00	20.00	40.00
❑ DLP-3254 [M]	Midnight Session	1960	7.50	15.00	30.00
❑ DLP-25166 [S]	Bud Freeman and His Summa Cum Laude Trio	1959	7.50	15.00	30.00
❑ DLP-25254 [S]	Midnight Session	1960	10.00	20.00	40.00
EMARCY					
❑ MG-36013 [M]	Midnight at Eddie Condon's	1955	15.00	30.00	60.00
HARMONY					
❑ HL 7046 [M]	Bud Freeman and His All-Star Jazz	1957	6.25	12.50	25.00
MONMOUTH-EVERGREEN					
❑ 7022	The Compleat Bud Freeman	1970	5.00	10.00	20.00
PARAMOUNT					
❑ CJS-105 [10]	Bud Freeman and the Chicagoans	195?	20.00	40.00	80.00
RCA VICTOR					
❑ LPM-1508 [M]	Chicago Austin High School Jazz in Hi-Fi	1957	12.50	25.00	50.00
SWINGVILLE					
❑ SVLP-2012 [M]	Bud Freeman All Stars	1960	12.50	25.00	50.00
—Purple label					
❑ SVLP-2012 [M]	Bud Freeman All Stars	1965	6.25	12.50	25.00
—Blue label with trident logo at right					
UNITED ARTISTS					
❑ UAJ-14033 [M]	Something Tender — Bud Freeman and Two Guitars	1963	10.00	20.00	40.00
❑ UAJS-15033 [S]	Something Tender — Bud Freeman and Two Guitars	1963	12.50	25.00	50.00
FREEMAN, ERNIE					
DUNHILL					
❑ D 50026 [M]	Hitmaker	1967	3.00	6.00	12.00
❑ DS 50026 [S]	Hitmaker	1967	3.75	7.50	15.00
IMPERIAL					
❑ LP-9022 [M]	Ernie Freeman Plays Irving Berlin	1957	12.50	25.00	50.00
❑ LP-9030 [M]	Jivin' Around	1957	12.50	25.00	50.00
❑ LP-9057 [M]	Ernie Freeman	1958	12.50	25.00	50.00
❑ LP-9133 [M]	Dark at the Top of the Stairs	1959	7.50	15.00	30.00
❑ LP-9148 [M]	Raunchy	1960	12.50	25.00	50.00
❑ LP-9157 [M]	Twistin' Time	1961	7.50	15.00	30.00
❑ LP-9193 [M]	The Stripper	1962	5.00	10.00	20.00
❑ LP-12067 [S]	Dark at the Top of the Stairs	1959	10.00	20.00	40.00
❑ LP-12081 [S]	Twistin' Time	1961	10.00	20.00	40.00
❑ LP-12193 [S]	The Stripper	1962	6.25	12.50	25.00
LIBERTY					
❑ LRP-3264 [M]	Ernie Freeman's Soulful Sounds of Country Classics	1962	5.00	10.00	20.00
❑ LRP-3283 [M]	Limbo Dance Party	1962	5.00	10.00	20.00
❑ LRP-3331 [M]	Comin' Home Baby	1963	5.00	10.00	20.00
❑ LST-7264 [S]	Ernie Freeman's Soulful Sounds of Country Classics	1962	6.25	12.50	25.00
❑ LST-7283 [S]	Limbo Dance Party	1962	6.25	12.50	25.00
❑ LST-7331 [S]	Comin' Home Baby	1963	6.25	12.50	25.00
FREEMAN, EVELYN					
IMPERIAL					
❑ LP-9101 [M]	Sky High	1960	5.00	10.00	20.00
❑ LP-12043 [S]	Sky High	1960	7.50	15.00	30.00
UNITED ARTISTS					
❑ UAL-3178 [M]	Didn't It Rain	1962	5.00	10.00	20.00
❑ UAS-6178 [S]	Didn't It Rain	1962	6.25	12.50	25.00
FREEMAN, RUSS					
PACIFIC JAZZ					
❑ PJLP-8 [10]	The Russ Freeman Trio	1953	30.00	60.00	120.00
❑ PJ-1212 [M]	Trio: Russ Freeman/Richard Twardzik	1956	25.00	50.00	100.00
❑ PJ-1232 [M]	Quartet: Russ Freeman/Chet Baker	1957	25.00	50.00	100.00
—Label says Pacific Jazz, but cover is on World Pacific					
WORLD PACIFIC					
❑ WP-1212 [M]	Trio: Russ Freeman/Richard Twardzik	1958	12.50	25.00	50.00
❑ WP-1232 [M]	Quartet: Russ Freeman/Chet Baker	1958	12.50	25.00	50.00
—Both label and cover are on World Pacific					
FREEMAN, STAN					
COLUMBIA					
❑ CL 1120 [M]	Stan Freeman Swings "The Music Man"	1958	7.50	15.00	30.00
❑ CL 6158 [10]	Piano Moods	1951	12.50	25.00	50.00
❑ CL 6193 [10]	Come On-a Stan's House	1951	15.00	30.00	60.00
HARMONY					
❑ HL 7067 [M]	Stan Freeman Plays 30 All-Time Hits	195?	5.00	10.00	20.00
FREEPORT					
MAINSTREAM					
❑ S-6130	Freeport	1970	12.50	25.00	50.00
FREES, PAUL					
MGM					
❑ SE-4735	Paul Frees and the Poster People	1969	6.25	12.50	25.00
FREHLEY, ACE					
Also see KISS.					
CASABLANCA					
❑ NBLP-7121	Ace Frehley	1978	5.00	10.00	20.00
❑ NBPIX-7121 [PD]	Ace Frehley	1978	12.50	25.00	50.00
MEGAFORCE/ATLANTIC					
❑ 81749	Frehley's Comet	1987	2.00	4.00	8.00
❑ 81826	Live + 1	1988	2.00	4.00	8.00
❑ 81862	Second Sighting	1988	2.00	4.00	8.00
❑ 82042	Trouble Walkin'	1989	2.50	5.00	10.00
FRENCH, ALBERT "PAPA"					
NOBILITY					
❑ LP-702 [M]	A Night at Dixieland Hall	195?	10.00	20.00	40.00
FRESH, DOUG E., AND THE GET FRESH CREW					
GEE STREET					
❑ 444069-1	Play	1993	3.75	7.50	15.00
REALITY					
❑ 9649	Oh, My God!	1986	10.00	20.00	40.00
❑ 9658	The World's Greatest Entertainer	1988	7.50	15.00	30.00
FRIAR TUCK					
MERCURY					
❑ MG-21111 [M]	Friar Tuck and His Psychedelic Guitar	1967	10.00	20.00	40.00
❑ SR-61111 [S]	Friar Tuck and His Psychedelic Guitar	1967	12.50	25.00	50.00
FRICKE, JANIE					
COLUMBIA					
❑ AS99 1535 [DJ]	Janie Fricke On Tour	1982	15.00	30.00	60.00
—Promo-only picture disc					
❑ KC 35315	Singer of Songs	1978	3.00	6.00	12.00
❑ PC 35315	Singer of Songs	198?	2.00	4.00	8.00
—Budget-line reissue with new prefix					
❑ KC 35774	Love Notes	1979	3.00	6.00	12.00
❑ PC 35774	Love Notes	198?	2.00	4.00	8.00
—Budget-line reissue with new prefix					
❑ JC 36268	From the Heart	1980	3.00	6.00	12.00
❑ JC 36820	I'll Need Someone to Hold Me When I Cry	1980	2.50	5.00	10.00
❑ PC 36820	I'll Need Someone to Hold Me When I Cry	198?	2.00	4.00	8.00
—Budget-line reissue with new prefix					
❑ FC 37535	Sleeping with Your Memory	1981	2.50	5.00	10.00
❑ PC 37535	Sleeping with Your Memory	198?	2.00	4.00	8.00
—Budget-line reissue with new prefix					
❑ FC 38214	It Ain't Easy	1982	2.50	5.00	10.00
❑ FC 38310	Greatest Hits	1982	2.50	5.00	10.00
❑ FC 38730	Love Lies	1983	2.50	5.00	10.00
❑ PC 38730	Love Lies	1985	2.00	4.00	8.00
—Budget-line reissue with new prefix					
❑ FC 39338	The First Word in Memory	1984	2.50	5.00	10.00
❑ FC 39975	Somebody Else's Fire	1985	2.50	5.00	10.00
❑ FC 40165	The Very Best of Janie	1985	2.50	5.00	10.00
❑ FC 40383	Black & White	1986	2.50	5.00	10.00
❑ FC 40666	After Midnight	1987	2.50	5.00	10.00
❑ C2 40684 [(2)]	Celebration	1987	3.00	6.00	12.00
❑ FC 44143	Saddle the Wind	1988	2.50	5.00	10.00
❑ FC 45087	Labor of Love	1989	3.00	6.00	12.00
FRIEDMAN, DON					
PRESTIGE					
❑ PRLP-7488 [M]	Metamorphosis	1966	6.25	12.50	25.00
❑ PRST-7488 [S]	Metamorphosis	1966	7.50	15.00	30.00
RIVERSIDE					
❑ RLP-384 [M]	A Day in the City	1961	10.00	20.00	40.00
❑ RLP-431 [M]	Circle Waltz	1962	7.50	15.00	30.00
❑ RLP-463 [M]	Flashback	1963	7.50	15.00	30.00

F

Number	Title (A Side/B Side)	Yr	VG	VG+	NM
❑ RLP-485 [M]	Dreams and Explorations	1965	5.00	10.00	20.00
❑ RS-9384 [S]	A Day in the City	1961	12.50	25.00	50.00
❑ RS-9431 [S]	Circle Waltz	1962	10.00	20.00	40.00
❑ RS-9463 [S]	Flashback	1963	10.00	20.00	40.00
❑ RS-9485 [S]	Dreams and Explorations	1965	6.25	12.50	25.00

FRIEDMAN, ERICK
RCA VICTOR RED SEAL

Number	Title (A Side/B Side)	Yr	VG	VG+	NM
❑ LSC-2610 [S]	Paganini: Violin Concerto No. 1; Saint-Saens: Intro and Rondo Capriccioso	1962	10.00	20.00	40.00
—Original with "shaded dog" label					
❑ LSC-2610 [S]	Paganini: Violin Concerto No. 1; Saint-Saens: Intro and Rondo Capriccioso	1964	5.00	10.00	20.00
—Second edition with "white dog" label					

FRIEND AND LOVER
VERVE FORECAST

Number	Title (A Side/B Side)	Yr	VG	VG+	NM
❑ FTS-3055	Reach Out of the Darkness	1968	5.00	10.00	20.00

FRIENDS
OBLIVION

Number	Title (A Side/B Side)	Yr	VG	VG+	NM
❑ OD-3	Friends	1974	5.00	10.00	20.00
—Jazz-rock band with John Abercrombie and Marc Cohen					

FRIENDS OF DISTINCTION, THE
RCA VICTOR

Number	Title (A Side/B Side)	Yr	VG	VG+	NM
❑ APD1-0276	Greatest Hits	1973	5.00	10.00	20.00
❑ LSP-4149	Grazin'	1969	3.75	7.50	15.00
❑ LSP-4212	Highly Distinct	1969	3.75	7.50	15.00
❑ LSP-4313	Real Friends	1970	3.75	7.50	15.00
❑ LSP-4408	Whatever	1970	3.75	7.50	15.00
❑ LSP-4492	Friends & People	1971	3.75	7.50	15.00
❑ LSP-4819	Greatest Hits	1972	3.00	6.00	12.00
❑ LSP-4829	Love Can Make It Easier	1973	3.00	6.00	12.00

FRIGO, JOHNNY
MERCURY

Number	Title (A Side/B Side)	Yr	VG	VG+	NM
❑ MG-20285 [M]	I Love Johnny Frigo, He Swings	1957	7.50	15.00	30.00

FRIJID PINK
FANTASY

Number	Title (A Side/B Side)	Yr	VG	VG+	NM
❑ 9464	All Pink Inside	1974	3.75	7.50	15.00

LION

Number	Title (A Side/B Side)	Yr	VG	VG+	NM
❑ LN-1004	Earth Omen	1972	5.00	10.00	20.00

PARROT

Number	Title (A Side/B Side)	Yr	VG	VG+	NM
❑ PAS 71033	Frijid Pink	1970	6.25	12.50	25.00
❑ PAS 71041	Defrosted	1970	6.25	12.50	25.00

FRIZZELL, LEFTY
ABC

Number	Title (A Side/B Side)	Yr	VG	VG+	NM
❑ ABCX-799	The Legendary Lefty Frizzell	1974	5.00	10.00	20.00
—Revised title					
❑ ABCX-799	Lefty	1974	7.50	15.00	30.00
—Original title					
❑ AC-30035	The ABC Collection	1976	5.00	10.00	20.00

COLUMBIA

Number	Title (A Side/B Side)	Yr	VG	VG+	NM
❑ CL 1342 [M]	The One and Only Lefty Frizzell	1959	30.00	60.00	120.00
❑ CL 2169 [M]	Saginaw, Michigan	1964	7.50	15.00	30.00
❑ CL 2386 [M]	The Sad Side of Love	1965	7.50	15.00	30.00
❑ CL 2488 [M]	Lefty Frizzell's Greatest Hits	1966	7.50	15.00	30.00
❑ CL 2772 [M]	Puttin' On	1967	12.50	25.00	50.00
❑ CS 8969 [S]	Saginaw, Michigan	1964	10.00	20.00	40.00
❑ CL 9019 [10]	Lefty Frizzell Sings the Songs of Jimmie Rodgers	1951	62.50	125.00	250.00
❑ CL 9021 [10]	Listen to Lefty	1952	62.50	125.00	250.00
❑ CS 9186 [S]	The Sad Side of Love	1965	10.00	20.00	40.00
❑ CS 9288 [S]	Lefty Frizzell's Greatest Hits	1966	10.00	20.00	40.00
—Red label, "360 Sound Stereo" at bottom					
❑ CS 9572 [S]	Puttin' On	1967	10.00	20.00	40.00
❑ C 32249	Lefty Frizzell Sings the Songs of Jimmie Rodgers	1973	5.00	10.00	20.00
❑ PC 33882	Remembering…The Greatest Hits of Lefty Frizzell	1975	5.00	10.00	20.00

HARMONY

Number	Title (A Side/B Side)	Yr	VG	VG+	NM
❑ HL 7241 [M]	Lefty Frizzell Sings the Songs of Jimmie Rodgers	1960	7.50	15.00	30.00

FROEBA, FRANK
DECCA

Number	Title (A Side/B Side)	Yr	VG	VG+	NM
❑ DL 5043 [10]	Back Room Piano	1950	12.50	25.00	50.00
❑ DL 5048 [10]	Old Time Piano	1950	12.50	25.00	50.00

ROYALE

Number	Title (A Side/B Side)	Yr	VG	VG+	NM
❑ 1818 [10]	Old Time Piano	1954	10.00	20.00	40.00

VARSITY

Number	Title (A Side/B Side)	Yr	VG	VG+	NM
❑ 6031 [10]	Boys in the Backroom	1950	12.50	25.00	50.00

FROGGIE BEAVER
FROGGIE BEAVER

Number	Title (A Side/B Side)	Yr	VG	VG+	NM
❑ 7301	From the Pond	1973	12.50	25.00	50.00

FROLK HEAVEN
LRS

Number	Title (A Side/B Side)	Yr	VG	VG+	NM
❑ RF-6023	At the Apex of High	197?	100.00	200.00	400.00

FROMAN, JANE
CAPITOL

Number	Title (A Side/B Side)	Yr	VG	VG+	NM
❑ H 354 [10]	Yours Alone	1952	10.00	20.00	40.00
❑ T 726 [M]	Faith	1956	6.25	12.50	25.00
❑ T 889 [M]	Songs at Sunset	1957	6.25	12.50	25.00

DECCA

Number	Title (A Side/B Side)	Yr	VG	VG+	NM
❑ DL 6021 [10]	Souvenirs	1952	10.00	20.00	40.00

RCA VICTOR

Number	Title (A Side/B Side)	Yr	VG	VG+	NM
❑ LPT-3055 [10]	Gems from Gershwin	1952	10.00	20.00	40.00

FRONTIERE, DOMINIC
COLUMBIA

Number	Title (A Side/B Side)	Yr	VG	VG+	NM
❑ CL 1273 [M]	Pagan Festival	1958	10.00	20.00	40.00
❑ CL 1427 [M]	Love Eyes: The Moods of Romance	1960	7.50	15.00	30.00
❑ CS 8224 [S]	Love Eyes: The Moods of Romance	1960	10.00	20.00	40.00

LIBERTY

Number	Title (A Side/B Side)	Yr	VG	VG+	NM
❑ LRP-3015 [M]	Fabulous!	1956	10.00	20.00	40.00
❑ LRP-3032 [M]	Dom Frontiere Plays the Classics	1957	10.00	20.00	40.00
❑ LJH-6002 [M]	The Dom Frontiere Sextet	1956	12.50	25.00	50.00
❑ LST-7008 [S]	Mr. Accordion	1958	10.00	20.00	40.00
—Evidently not issued in mono					

FROST, FRANK
EARWIG

Number	Title (A Side/B Side)	Yr	VG	VG+	NM
❑ 4901	Rockin' the Juke Joint Down	1986	2.50	5.00	10.00
❑ 4914	Midnight Prowler	1990	2.50	5.00	10.00

JEWEL

Number	Title (A Side/B Side)	Yr	VG	VG+	NM
❑ LPS-5013	Frank Frost	1973	3.75	7.50	15.00

PHILLIPS INTERNATIONAL

Number	Title (A Side/B Side)	Yr	VG	VG+	NM
❑ PLP-1975 [M]	Hey Boss Man!	1961	1500.	2250.	3000.

FROST, MAX, AND THE TROOPERS
TOWER

Number	Title (A Side/B Side)	Yr	VG	VG+	NM
❑ ST-5147	Shape of Things to Come	1968	12.50	25.00	50.00

FROST, THE
VANGUARD

Number	Title (A Side/B Side)	Yr	VG	VG+	NM
❑ VSD-6520	Frost Music	1969	5.00	10.00	20.00
❑ VSD-6541	Rock and Roll Music	1969	5.00	10.00	20.00
❑ VSD-6556	Through the Eyes of Love	1970	5.00	10.00	20.00
❑ VSD-79392	Early Frost	1978	3.75	7.50	15.00

FRUSCELLA, TONY
ATLANTIC

Number	Title (A Side/B Side)	Yr	VG	VG+	NM
❑ 1220 [M]	Tony Fruscella	1955	20.00	40.00	80.00

FRUT
TRASH

Number	Title (A Side/B Side)	Yr	VG	VG+	NM
❑ (# unknown)	Keep On Truckin'	1971	20.00	40.00	80.00
—Originals on yellow vinyl					

WESTBOUND

Number	Title (A Side/B Side)	Yr	VG	VG+	NM
❑ WB-2005	Keep On Truckin'	1971	7.50	15.00	30.00
—Reissue of Trash LP					
❑ WB-2008	Spoiled Rotten	1972	7.50	15.00	30.00

FUGITIVES, THE
HIDEOUT

Number	Title (A Side/B Side)	Yr	VG	VG+	NM
❑ 1001 [M]	The Fugitives at Dave's Hideout	1965	300.00	600.00	1200.

JUSTICE

Number	Title (A Side/B Side)	Yr	VG	VG+	NM
❑ JLP-141	The Fugitives On the Run	1967	75.00	150.00	300.00

FUGITIVES, THE, AND OTHERS
WESTCHESTER

Number	Title (A Side/B Side)	Yr	VG	VG+	NM
❑ 1005 [M]	Friday at the Cage A-Go-Go	1965	375.00	750.00	1500.

FUGS, THE
BROADSIDE

Number	Title (A Side/B Side)	Yr	VG	VG+	NM
❑ 304 [M]	The Village Fugs Sing Ballads of Contemporary Protest, Point of View, and General Dissatisfaction	1965	100.00	200.00	400.00
—Without insert					
❑ 304 [M]	The Village Fugs Sing Ballads of Contemporary Protest, Point of View, and General Dissatisfaction	1965	125.00	250.00	500.00
—With insert					

ESP-DISK

Number	Title (A Side/B Side)	Yr	VG	VG+	NM
❑ 1018 [M]	The Fugs First Album	1966	10.00	20.00	40.00
—"Reissue of Broadside 304" on cover					
❑ 1018 [M]	The Fugs First Album	1966	37.50	75.00	150.00
—Turquoise and black cover, different from all other versions					
❑ 1018 [M]	The Fugs First Album	1967	7.50	15.00	30.00
—No reference to reissue on cover					
❑ 1028 [S]	The Fugs	1966	7.50	5.00	30.00
—Black and white cover, back cover photos aligned					
❑ 1028 [S]	The Fugs	1966	12.50	25.00	50.00
—Black and white cover, back cover photos staggered					
❑ 1028 [S]	The Fugs	1966	20.00	40.00	80.00
—Psychedelic color shield on cover					
❑ 1038 [S]	Virgin Fugs	1967	7.50	15.00	30.00
—"For Adult Minds" printed on cover					
❑ 1038 [S]	Virgin Fugs	1967	12.50	25.00	50.00
—"For Adult Minds" stamped on cover					
❑ 1038 [S]	Virgin Fugs	1967	12.50	25.00	50.00
—"For Adult Minds" sticker, no inserts					
❑ 1038 [S]	Virgin Fugs	1967	25.00	50.00	100.00
—"For Adult Minds" sticker on cover; with poster, book and stickers					
❑ 2018	Fugs 4, Rounders Score	196?	20.00	40.00	80.00

PVC

Number	Title (A Side/B Side)	Yr	VG	VG+	NM
❑ 8914	Proto Punk: The Fugs Greatest Hits, Vol. 1	1982	3.75	7.50	15.00

REPRISE

Number	Title (A Side/B Side)	Yr	VG	VG+	NM
❑ R-6280 [M]	Tenderness Junction	1968	10.00	20.00	40.00
❑ RS-6280 [S]	Tenderness Junction	1968	7.50	15.00	30.00
❑ RS-6305	It Crawled Into My Hand, Honest	1968	6.25	12.50	25.00
❑ RS-6359	Belle of Avenue A	1969	6.25	12.50	25.00
❑ RS-6396	Golden Fifth	1970	6.25	12.50	25.00

FULLER, BOBBY, FOUR
MUSTANG

Number	Title (A Side/B Side)	Yr	VG	VG+	NM
❑ M-900 [M]	KRLA King of the Wheels	1965	37.50	75.00	150.00
❑ MS-900 [S]	KRLA King of the Wheels	1965	50.00	100.00	200.00
❑ M-901 [M]	I Fought the Law	1966	20.00	40.00	80.00
❑ MS-901 [S]	I Fought the Law	1966	37.50	75.00	150.00

Number	Title (A Side/B Side)	Yr	VG	VG+	NM
RHINO					
❑ RNLP-057	The Bobby Fuller Tapes, Vol. 1	1983	2.50	5.00	10.00
❑ RNDF-201	The Best of the Bobby Fuller Four	1981	3.00	6.00	12.00
❑ RNLP 70174	The Best of the Bobby Fuller Four (Golden Archive Series)	1987	2.50	5.00	10.00
VOXX					
❑ VXS 200028	The Bobby Fuller Tapes, Vol. 2	1984	2.50	5.00	10.00

FULLER, CURTIS
BLUE NOTE

Number	Title (A Side/B Side)	Yr	VG	VG+	NM
❑ BLP-1567 [M]	The Opener	1957	20.00	40.00	80.00
—Regular version with W. 63rd St. address on label					
❑ BLP-1567 [M]	The Opener	1957	30.00	60.00	120.00
—"Deep groove" version (deep indentation under label on both sides)					
❑ BLP-1567 [M]	The Opener	1963	6.25	12.50	25.00
—"New York, USA" address on label					
❑ BST-1567 [S]	The Opener	1959	12.50	25.00	50.00
—Regular version with W. 63rd St. address on label					
❑ BST-1567 [S]	The Opener	1959	20.00	40.00	80.00
—"Deep groove" version (deep indentation under label on both sides)					
❑ BST-1567 [S]	The Opener	1963	5.00	10.00	20.00
—"New York, USA" address on label					
❑ BLP-1572 [M]	Bone and Bari	1957	20.00	40.00	80.00
—Regular version with W. 63rd St. address on label					
❑ BLP-1572 [M]	Bone and Bari	1957	30.00	60.00	120.00
—"Deep groove" version (deep indentation under label on both sides)					
❑ BLP-1572 [M]	Bone and Bari	1963	6.25	12.50	25.00
—"New York, USA" address on label					
❑ BST-1572 [S]	Bone and Bari	1959	12.50	25.00	50.00
—Regular version with W. 63rd St. address on label					
❑ BST-1572 [S]	Bone and Bari	1959	20.00	40.00	80.00
—"Deep groove" version (deep indentation under label on both sides)					
❑ BST-1572 [S]	Bone and Bari	1963	5.00	10.00	20.00
—"New York, USA" address on label					
❑ BLP-1583 [M]	Curtis Fuller, Volume 3	1958	20.00	40.00	80.00
—Regular version with W. 63rd St. address on label					
❑ BLP-1583 [M]	Curtis Fuller, Volume 3	1958	30.00	60.00	120.00
—"Deep groove" version (deep indentation under label on both sides)					
❑ BLP-1583 [M]	Curtis Fuller, Volume 3	1963	6.25	12.50	25.00
—"New York, USA" address on label					
❑ BST-1583 [S]	Curtis Fuller, Volume 3	1959	12.50	25.00	50.00
—Regular version with W. 63rd St. address on label					
❑ BST-1583 [S]	Curtis Fuller, Volume 3	1959	20.00	40.00	80.00
—"Deep groove" version (deep indentation under label on both sides)					
❑ BST-1583 [S]	Curtis Fuller, Volume 3	1963	5.00	10.00	20.00
—"New York, USA" address on label					
EPIC					
❑ LA 16013 [M]	The Magnificent Trombone	1961	7.50	15.00	30.00
❑ LA 16020 [M]	South American Cookin'	1961	10.00	20.00	40.00
❑ BA 17013 [S]	The Magnificent Trombone	1961	10.00	20.00	40.00
❑ BA 17020 [S]	South American Cookin'	1961	12.50	25.00	50.00
IMPULSE!					
❑ A-13 [M]	Soul Trombone	1962	6.25	12.50	25.00
❑ AS-13 [S]	Soul Trombone	1962	7.50	15.00	30.00
❑ A-22 [M]	Cabin in the Sky	1962	6.25	12.50	25.00
❑ AS-22 [S]	Cabin in the Sky	1962	7.50	15.00	30.00
MAINSTREAM					
❑ MRL-333	Crankin'	1971	5.00	10.00	20.00
❑ MRL-370	Smokin'	1972	5.00	10.00	20.00
NEW JAZZ					
❑ NJLP-8277 [M]	Curtis Fuller with Red Garland	1962	12.50	25.00	50.00
—Purple label					
❑ NJLP-8277 [M]	Curtis Fuller with Red Garland	1965	6.25	12.50	25.00
—Blue label, trident logo at right					
PRESTIGE					
❑ PRLP-7107 [M]	New Trombone	1957	25.00	50.00	100.00
REGENT					
❑ MG-6055 [M]	Jazz...It's Magic	1957	20.00	40.00	80.00
SAVOY					
❑ MG-12141 [M]	Blues-Ette	1959	12.50	25.00	50.00
❑ MG-12143 [M]	The Curtis Fuller Jazztet with Benny Golson	1959	10.00	20.00	40.00
❑ MG-12144 [M]	Imagination	1959	10.00	20.00	40.00
❑ MG-12151 [M]	Curtis Fuller	1960	10.00	20.00	40.00
❑ MG-12164 [M]	Images of Curts Fuller	1960	10.00	20.00	40.00
❑ MG-12209 [M]	Jazz...It's Magic	196?	5.00	10.00	20.00
❑ ST-13006 [S]	Blues-Ette	1959	10.00	20.00	40.00
SMASH					
❑ MGS-27034 [M]	Jazz Conference Abroad	1962	6.25	12.50	25.00
❑ SRS-67034 [S]	Jazz Conference Abroad	1962	7.50	15.00	30.00
STATUS					
❑ ST-8305 [M]	Curtis Fuller and Hampton Hawes with French Horns	1965	10.00	20.00	40.00
UNITED ARTISTS					
❑ UAL-4051 [M]	Sliding Easy	1959	12.50	25.00	50.00
❑ UAS-5051 [S]	Sliding Easy	1959	10.00	20.00	40.00
WARWICK					
❑ W-2038 [M]	Boss of the Soul Stream Trombone	1961	7.50	15.00	30.00
❑ W-2038ST [S]	Boss of the Soul Stream Trombone	1961	12.50	25.00	50.00

FULLER, GIL
PACIFIC JAZZ

Number	Title (A Side/B Side)	Yr	VG	VG+	NM
❑ PJ-93 [M]	Gil Fuller and the Monterey Jazz Orchestra with Dizzy Gillespie	1965	6.25	12.50	25.00
❑ ST-93 [S]	Gil Fuller and the Monterey Jazz Orchestra with Dizzy Gillespie	1965	7.50	15.00	30.00
❑ PJ-10101 [M]	Night Flight	1966	5.00	10.00	20.00
❑ ST-20101 [S]	Night Flight	1966	6.25	12.50	25.00

FULLER, JERRY
Country-pop singer.
LIN

Number	Title (A Side/B Side)	Yr	VG	VG+	NM
❑ 100 [M]	Teenage Love	1960	62.50	125.00	250.00

FULLER, JERRY (2)
Jazz clarinetist.
ANDEX

Number	Title (A Side/B Side)	Yr	VG	VG+	NM
❑ A-3008 [M]	Clarinet Portrait	1958	10.00	20.00	40.00
❑ AS-3008 [S]	Clarinet Portrait	1959	7.50	15.00	30.00

FULSON, LOWELL
ARHOOLIE

Number	Title (A Side/B Side)	Yr	VG	VG+	NM
❑ R-2003	Early Recordings	1962	7.50	15.00	30.00
BIG TOWN					
❑ 1008	Lovemaker	1978	3.00	6.00	12.00
CHESS					
❑ 408	Hung Down Head	197?	3.75	7.50	15.00
GRANITE					
❑ 1006	Ol' Blues Singer	1976	3.75	7.50	15.00
JEWEL					
❑ LPS-5003	In a Heavy Bag	1970	3.75	7.50	15.00
❑ LPS-5009	I've Got the Blues	1973	3.75	7.50	15.00
KENT					
❑ KST-516 [S]	Lowell Fulsom	1965	10.00	20.00	40.00
❑ KST-520 [S]	Tramp	1967	10.00	20.00	40.00
❑ KST-531	Lowell Fulsom Now	1969	7.50	15.00	30.00
❑ KLP-5016 [M]	Lowell Fulsom	1965	7.50	15.00	30.00
❑ KLP-5020 [M]	Tramp	1967	7.50	15.00	30.00
ROUNDER					
❑ 2088	It's a Good Day	198?	3.00	6.00	12.00

FUN AND GAMES
UNI

Number	Title (A Side/B Side)	Yr	VG	VG+	NM
❑ 73042	Elephant Candy	1968	6.25	12.50	25.00

FUNKADELIC
Also see PARLIAMENT.
SCARFACE/PRIORITY

Number	Title (A Side/B Side)	Yr	VG	VG+	NM
❑ 53872	One Nation Under a Groove	1993	3.75	7.50	15.00
—Limited-edition reissue of Warner Bros. 3209					
❑ 53873	Hardcore Jollies	1993	3.75	7.50	15.00
—Limited-edition reissue of Warner Bros. 2973					
❑ 53874	The Electric Spanking of War Babies	1993	3.75	7.50	15.00
—Limited-edition reissue of Warner Bros. 3482					
❑ 53875	Uncle Jam Wants You	1993	3.75	7.50	15.00
—Limited-edition reissue of Warner Bros. 3371					
WARNER BROS.					
❑ BS 2973	Hardcore Jollies	1976	6.25	12.50	25.00
❑ BS 3209	One Nation Under a Groove	1978	6.25	12.50	25.00
—Includes bonus 7-inch single with small hole (deduct 20% if missing)					
❑ BSK 3371	Uncle Jam Wants You	1979	6.25	12.50	25.00
❑ BSK 3482	The Electric Spanking of War Babies	1981	6.25	12.50	25.00
WESTBOUND					
❑ 208	Standing on the Verge of Getting It On	1975	6.25	12.50	25.00
—Reissue of Westbound 1001					
❑ 215	Let's Take It to the Stage	1975	12.50	25.00	50.00
❑ 215	Let's Take It to the Stage	1992	3.75	7.50	15.00
—Reissue with bar code					
❑ 216	Funkadelic	1975	7.50	15.00	30.00
—Reissue of Westbound 2000					
❑ 217	Free Your Mind...And Your Ass Will Follow	1975	6.25	12.50	25.00
—Reissue of Westbound 2001					
❑ 218	Maggot Brain	1975	6.25	12.50	25.00
—Reissue of Westbound 2007					
❑ 221 [(2)]	America Eats Its Young	1976	6.25	12.50	25.00
—Reissue of Westbound 2020					
❑ 223	Cosmic Slop	1976	6.25	12.50	25.00
—Reissue of Westbound 2022					
❑ 227	Tales of Kidd Funkadelic	1976	12.50	25.00	50.00
❑ 227	Tales of Kidd Funkadelic	1992	3.75	7.50	15.00
—Reissue with bar code					
❑ 303	Best of the Early Years	197?	10.00	20.00	40.00
❑ 1001	Standing on the Verge of Getting It On	1974	12.50	25.00	50.00
❑ 1001	Standing on the Verge of Getting It On	1991	3.75	7.50	15.00
—Reissue with bar code					
❑ 1004	Funkadelic's Greatest Hits	1975	12.50	25.00	50.00
❑ 2000	Funkadelic	1970	12.50	25.00	50.00
❑ 2000	Funkadelic	1990	3.75	7.50	15.00
—Reissue with bar code					
❑ 2001	Free Your Mind...And Your Ass Will Follow	1970	12.50	25.00	50.00
❑ 2001	Free Your Mind...And Your Ass Will Follow	1990	3.75	7.50	15.00
—Reissue with bar code					
❑ 2007	Maggot Brain	1971	12.50	25.00	50.00
❑ 2007	Maggot Brain	1990	3.75	7.50	15.00
—Reissue with bar code					
❑ 2020 [(2)]	America Eats Its Young	1972	15.00	30.00	60.00
❑ 2020 [(2)]	America Eats Its Young	1991	5.00	10.00	20.00
—Reissue with bar code					
❑ 2022	Cosmic Slop	1973	12.50	25.00	50.00
❑ 2022	Cosmic Slop	1991	3.75	7.50	15.00
—Reissue with bar code					

FURAY, RICHIE
MYRRH

Number	Title (A Side/B Side)	Yr	VG	VG+	NM
❑ MSB-6672	I've Got a Reason	1981	5.00	10.00	20.00
—Christian-market reissue of Asylum 7E-1067					
❑ MSB-6695	Seasons of Change	1982	2.50	5.00	10.00

Number	Title (A Side/B Side)	Yr	VG	VG+	NM

FUSE
EPIC
| ❏ BN 26502 | Fuse | 1970 | 20.00 | 40.00 | 80.00 |

FUTURE, THE
SHAMLEY
| ❏ 703 | Down the Country Road | 1969 | 5.00 | 10.00 | 20.00 |

G

G.T.O.'S, THE (2)
REPRISE
| ❏ RS 6390 | Permanent Damage | 1970 | 12.50 | 25.00 | 50.00 |
—Without booklet
| ❏ RS 6390 | Permanent Damage | 1970 | 17.50 | 35.00 | 70.00 |
—With booklet
STRAIGHT
| ❏ STS-1059 | Permanent Damage | 1969 | 20.00 | 40.00 | 80.00 |
—Without booklet
| ❏ STS-1059 | Permanent Damage | 1969 | 25.00 | 50.00 | 100.00 |
—With booklet

GABRIEL, PETER
Also see GENESIS.
ATCO
| ❏ SD 36-147 | Peter Gabriel | 1977 | 3.75 | 7.50 | 15.00 |
—(The "Solsbury Hill" album) -- Original pressing has yellow labels
| ❏ SD 36-147 | Peter Gabriel | 1980 | 2.50 | 5.00 | 10.00 |
—(The "Solsbury Hill" album) -- Other than yellow labels
ATLANTIC
| ❏ SD-19181 | Peter Gabriel | 1978 | 3.75 | 7.50 | 15.00 |
—(The "D.I.Y." album)
DIRECT DISK
| ❏ SD-16615 | Peter Gabriel | 1980 | 20.00 | 40.00 | 80.00 |
—The "Solsbury Hill" album; contains a long version of "Slowburn" not available elsewhere
GEFFEN
| ❏ GHS 2011 | Peter Gabriel (Security) | 1982 | 2.50 | 5.00 | 10.00 |
| ❏ GHS 2011 [DJ] | Peter Gabriel (Security) | 1982 | 3.75 | 7.50 | 15.00 |
—Promo-only Quiex II audiophile pressing
| ❏ GHSP 2035 | Peter Gabriel | 1983 | 2.50 | 5.00 | 10.00 |
—Reissue of Mercury album
❏ 2GHS 4012 [(2)]	Plays Live	1983	3.75	7.50	15.00
❏ GHS 24070	Birdy (Soundtrack)	1985	2.50	5.00	10.00
❏ GHS 24088	So	1986	2.50	5.00	10.00
❏ GHS 24206	Passion: Music for "The Last Temptation of Christ"	1989	3.75	7.50	15.00
❏ R 114764	So	1986	3.00	6.00	12.00
—BMG Direct Marketing edition
| ❏ R 153801 | Peter Gabriel (Security) | 1982 | 3.00 | 6.00 | 12.00 |
—RCA Music Service edition
| ❏ R 243372 [(2)] | Plays Live | 1983 | 4.50 | 9.00 | 18.00 |
—RCA Music Service edition
MERCURY
| ❏ SRM-1-3848 | Peter Gabriel | 1980 | 3.00 | 6.00 | 12.00 |
—(The "Games Without Frontiers" album)
REAL WORLD
| ❏ PGDLP-1 | Peter Gabriel | 2002 | 6.25 | 12.50 | 25.00 |
—(The "Solsbury Hill" album) -- Classic Records audiophile issue
| ❏ PGDLP-2 | Peter Gabriel | 2002 | 6.25 | 12.50 | 25.00 |
—(The "D.I.Y." album) -- Classic Records audiophile issue
| ❏ PGDLP-3 | Peter Gabriel | 2003 | 6.25 | 12.50 | 25.00 |
—(The "Games Without Frontiers" album) -- Classic Records audiophile issue
| ❏ PGDLP 11 [(2)] | Up | 2002 | 10.00 | 20.00 | 40.00 |
—Classic Records audiophile issue; includes bonus 45 in picture sleeve

GABRIEL BONDAGE
DHARMA
| ❏ D-804 | Angel Dust | 1975 | 12.50 | 25.00 | 50.00 |
| ❏ D-808 | Another Trip to Earth | 1977 | 5.00 | 10.00 | 20.00 |
—Exists on white, red, or blue vinyl; each of similar value

GAILLARD, SLIM
ALLEGRO ELITE
| ❏ 4050 [10] | Slim Gaillard Plays | 195? | 7.50 | 15.00 | 30.00 |
CLEF
| ❏ MGC-126 [10] | Mish Mash | 1953 | 25.00 | 50.00 | 100.00 |
| ❏ MGC-138 [10] | Slim Cavorts | 1953 | 25.00 | 50.00 | 100.00 |
DISC
| ❏ DLP-505 [10] | Opera in Vout | 195? | 50.00 | 100.00 | 200.00 |
DOT
| ❏ DLP-3190 [M] | Slim Gaillard Rides Again | 1959 | 7.50 | 15.00 | 30.00 |
| ❏ DLP-25190 [S] | Slim Gaillard Rides Again | 1959 | 10.00 | 20.00 | 40.00 |
KING
| ❏ 295-80 [10] | Slim Gaillard/Boogie | 195? | 25.00 | 50.00 | 100.00 |
NORGRAN
| ❏ MGN-13 [10] | Slim Gaillard and His Musical Aggregation Wherever They May Be | 1954 | 25.00 | 50.00 | 100.00 |
VERVE
| ❏ MGV-2013 [M] | Smorgasbord, Help Yourself | 1956 | 12.50 | 25.00 | 50.00 |
| ❏ V-2013 [M] | Smorgasbord, Help Yourself | 1961 | 5.00 | 10.00 | 20.00 |

GAILLARD, SLIM/DIZZY GILLESPIE
ULTRAPHONIC
| ❏ ULP-50273 [M] | Gaillard and Gillespie | 1958 | 10.00 | 20.00 | 40.00 |

GAILLARD, SLIM/MEADE LUX LEWIS
CLEF
| ❏ MGC-506 [10] | Boogie Woogie at the Philharmonic | 1954 | 25.00 | 50.00 | 100.00 |
MERCURY
| ❏ MGC-506 [10] | Boogie Woogie at the Philharmonic | 1951 | 37.50 | 75.00 | 150.00 |

GALAHADS, THE
LIBERTY
| ❏ LRP-3371 [M] | Hello, Galahads | 1964 | 5.00 | 10.00 | 20.00 |
| ❏ LST-7371 [S] | Hello, Galahads | 1964 | 6.25 | 12.50 | 25.00 |

GALBRAITH, BARRY
DECCA
| ❏ DL 9200 [M] | Guitar and the Wind | 1958 | 12.50 | 25.00 | 50.00 |
| ❏ DL 79200 [S] | Guitar and the Wind | 1959 | 10.00 | 20.00 | 40.00 |

GALE, EDDIE
BLUE NOTE
| ❏ BST-84294 | Eddie Gale's Ghetto Music | 1968 | 6.25 | 12.50 | 25.00 |
| ❏ BST-84320 | Black Rhythm Happening | 1969 | 6.25 | 12.50 | 25.00 |

GALE, SUNNY
CANADIAN AMERICAN
| ❏ CALP-1015 [M] | Goldies by the Girls | 1964 | 6.25 | 12.50 | 25.00 |
RCA VICTOR
| ❏ LPM-1277 [M] | Sunny and Blue | 1956 | 10.00 | 20.00 | 40.00 |
WARWICK
| ❏ W-2018 [M] | Sunny | 1960 | 7.50 | 15.00 | 30.00 |

GALLODORO, AL
ARCO
| ❏ AL-3 [10] | Al Gallodoro Concert | 1950 | 12.50 | 25.00 | 50.00 |
COLUMBIA
| ❏ CL 6188 [10] | Al Gallodoro | 1951 | 12.50 | 25.00 | 50.00 |

GALLOP, FRANK
MUSICOR
| ❏ MM-2110 [M] | Frank Gallop Sings | 1966 | 3.75 | 7.50 | 15.00 |
| ❏ MS-3110 [S] | Frank Gallop Sings | 1966 | 5.00 | 10.00 | 20.00 |

GALPER, HAL
MAINSTREAM
❏ MRL-337	The Guerrilla Band	1971	5.00	10.00	20.00
❏ MRL-354	Wild Bird	1972	5.00	10.00	20.00
❏ MRL-398	Inner Journey	1974	5.00	10.00	20.00

GALS & PALS
FONTANA
❏ MGF-27538 [M]	Gals & Pals (The Exciting Vocal Sounds of Europe's Newest "In" Group)	1965	3.75	7.50	15.00
❏ MGF-27557 [M]	Gals & Pals Sing Something for Everybody	1966	3.75	7.50	15.00
❏ SRF-67538 [S]	Gals & Pals (The Exciting Vocal Sounds of Europe's Newest "In" Group)	1965	5.00	10.00	20.00
❏ SRF-67557 [S]	Gals & Pals Sing Something for Everybody	1966	5.00	10.00	20.00

GAMBRELL, FREDDIE
WORLD PACIFIC
| ❏ WP-1256 [M] | Freddie Gambrell | 1959 | 12.50 | 25.00 | 50.00 |

GAMBRELL, FREDDIE, AND PAUL HORN
WORLD PACIFIC
| ❏ ST-1023 [S] | Mikado | 1959 | 7.50 | 15.00 | 30.00 |
| ❏ WP-1262 [M] | Mikado | 1959 | 10.00 | 20.00 | 40.00 |

GAME
EVOLUTION
| ❏ 2021 | Game | 1970 | 3.00 | 6.00 | 12.00 |
| ❏ 3008 | Long Hot Summer | 1971 | 3.00 | 6.00 | 12.00 |
FAITHFUL VIRTUE
| ❏ 2003 | Game | 1969 | 5.00 | 10.00 | 20.00 |

GANDALF
CAPITOL
| ❏ ST-121 | Gandalf | 1969 | 50.00 | 100.00 | 200.00 |

GANDALF THE GREY
G.W.R.
| ❏ 7 | The Grey Wizard Am I | 1972 | 75.00 | 150.00 | 300.00 |

GANG STARR
VIRGIN
| ❏ 47279 [(4)] | Full Clip — A Decade of Gang Starr | 1999 | 5.00 | 10.00 | 20.00 |

GANT, CECIL
KING
| ❏ 671 [M] | Cecil Gant | 1960 | 20.00 | 40.00 | 80.00 |
RED MILL
| ❏ (no #) [M] | Cecil Gant | 1956 | 125.00 | 250.00 | 500.00 |
—Red vinyl
SOUND
| ❏ 601 [M] | The Incomparable Cecil Gant | 1958 | 25.00 | 50.00 | 100.00 |

GANTS, THE
LIBERTY
❏ LRP-3432 [M]	Road Runner	1965	7.50	15.00	30.00
❏ LRP-3455 [M]	The Gants Galore	1966	7.50	15.00	30.00
❏ LRP-3473 [M]	The Gants Again	1966	7.50	15.00	30.00
❏ LST-7432 [S]	Road Runner	1965	10.00	20.00	40.00
❏ LST-7455 [S]	The Gants Galore	1966	10.00	20.00	40.00
❏ LST-7473 [S]	The Gants Again	1966	10.00	20.00	40.00

GARAGIOLA, JOE
UNITED ARTISTS
| ❏ UAL-3032 [M] | That Holler Guy! | 1959 | 10.00 | 20.00 | 40.00 |

Number	Title (A Side/B Side)	Yr	VG	VG+	NM
❑ UAS-6032 [S]	That Holler Guy!	1959	12.50	25.00	50.00

GARBAREK, JAN
FLYING DUTCHMAN
Number	Title (A Side/B Side)	Yr	VG	VG+	NM
❑ FD-10125	The Esoteric Circle	1971	5.00	10.00	20.00

GARBER, JAN
DECCA
Number	Title (A Side/B Side)	Yr	VG	VG+	NM
❑ DL 8482 [M]	Dance at Home	195?	5.00	10.00	20.00
—Black label, silver print					
❑ DL 8483 [M]	In a Dancing Mood	195?	5.00	10.00	20.00
—Black label, silver print					
❑ DL 8484 [M]	Designed for Dancing	195?	5.00	10.00	20.00
—Black label, silver print					
❑ DL 78793 [S]	Music from the Blue Room, Roosevelt Hotel, New Orleans	195?	5.00	10.00	20.00
—Black label, silver print					
❑ DL 78824 [S]	Waltzes	195?	5.00	10.00	20.00
—Black label, silver print					
❑ DL 78867 [S]	Jan Garber in Danceland	195?	5.00	10.00	20.00
—Black label, silver print					
❑ DL 78932 [S]	Christmas Dance Party	1959	5.00	10.00	20.00
—Black label, silver print					

GARBO, GRETA
MGM
Number	Title (A Side/B Side)	Yr	VG	VG+	NM
❑ E-4201 [M]	Garbo	1964	10.00	20.00	40.00

GARCIA, DICK
DAWN
Number	Title (A Side/B Side)	Yr	VG	VG+	NM
❑ DLP-1106 [M]	A Message from Dick Garcia	1956	12.50	25.00	50.00
SEECO
| ❑ SLP-428 [M] | A Message from Dick Garcia | 1958 | 10.00 | 20.00 | 40.00 |

GARCIA, JERRY
ARISTA
Number	Title (A Side/B Side)	Yr	VG	VG+	NM
❑ AB 4160	Cats Under the Stars	1978	3.00	6.00	12.00
❑ AL 8364	Run for the Roses	198?	2.00	4.00	8.00
—Reissue of 9603					
❑ AL 9603	Run for the Roses	1982	3.00	6.00	12.00
ROUND
❑ RX-102	Garcia	1974	6.25	12.50	25.00
❑ RX-107	Reflections	1975	7.50	15.00	30.00
❑ RN-LA565-G	Reflections	1976	5.00	10.00	20.00
—Reissue of Round 107 with United Artists distribution					
WARNER BROS.
| ❑ BS 2582 | Garcia | 1972 | 10.00 | 20.00 | 40.00 |
| —Green label with "WB" logo | | | | | |

GARCIA, RUSS
ABC-PARAMOUNT
Number	Title (A Side/B Side)	Yr	VG	VG+	NM
❑ ABC-147 [M]	The Johnny Evergreens	1956	12.50	25.00	50.00
BETHLEHEM
| ❑ BCP-46 [M] | Four Horns and a Lush Life | 1956 | 12.50 | 25.00 | 50.00 |
| ❑ BCP-1040 [10] | Wigville | 1955 | 50.00 | 100.00 | 200.00 |
KAPP
| ❑ KL-1050 [M] | Listen to the Music of Russell Garcia | 1957 | 12.50 | 25.00 | 50.00 |
LIBERTY
❑ LRP-3062 [M]	Enchantment (The Music of Joe Greene)	1958	6.25	12.50	25.00
❑ LRP-3084 [M]	Fantastica	1958	7.50	15.00	30.00
❑ LST-7005 [S]	Fantastica	1958	10.00	20.00	40.00
VERVE
| ❑ MGV-2088 [M] | The Warm Feeling | 1957 | 12.50 | 25.00 | 50.00 |
| ❑ V-2088 [M] | The Warm Feeling | 1961 | 5.00 | 10.00 | 20.00 |

GARCIA, RUSS, AND MARTY PAICH
BETHLEHEM
Number	Title (A Side/B Side)	Yr	VG	VG+	NM
❑ BCP-6039 [M]	Jazz Music for Birds and Hep Cats	1960	12.50	25.00	50.00
❑ SBCP-6039 [S]	Jazz Music for Birds and Hep Cats	1960	12.50	25.00	50.00

GARDNER, BROTHER DAVE
CAPITOL
Number	Title (A Side/B Side)	Yr	VG	VG+	NM
❑ ST 1867 [S]	It Don't Make No Difference	1963	6.25	12.50	25.00
❑ T 1867 [M]	It Don't Make No Difference	1963	5.00	10.00	20.00
❑ ST 2055 [S]	It's All in How You Look at It	1964	6.25	12.50	25.00
❑ T 2055 [M]	It's All in How You Look at It	1964	5.00	10.00	20.00
4 STAR
| ❑ 4S 75003 | Brother Dave Gardner's New Comedy Album | 1976 | 5.00 | 10.00 | 20.00 |
RCA VICTOR
❑ LPM-2083 [M]	Rejoice, Dear Hearts!	1960	5.00	10.00	20.00
❑ LSP-2083(e) [S]	Rejoice, Dear Hearts!	196?	6.25	12.50	25.00
❑ LPM-2239 [M]	Kick Thy Own Self	1960	5.00	10.00	20.00
❑ LSP-2239(e) [S]	Kick Thy Own Self	196?	6.25	12.50	25.00
❑ LPM-2335 [M]	Ain't That Weird?	1961	5.00	10.00	20.00
❑ LSP-2335 [S]	Ain't That Weird?	1961	6.25	12.50	25.00
❑ LPM-2498 [M]	Did You Ever?	1962	5.00	10.00	20.00
❑ LSP-2498 [S]	Did You Ever?	1962	6.25	12.50	25.00
❑ LPM-2628 [M]	All Seriousness Aside	1963	5.00	10.00	20.00
❑ LSP-2628 [S]	All Seriousness Aside	1963	6.25	12.50	25.00
❑ LPM-2761 [M]	It's Bigger Than Both of Us	1963	5.00	10.00	20.00
❑ LSP-2761 [S]	It's Bigger Than Both of Us	1963	6.25	12.50	25.00
❑ LPM-2852 [M]	Best of Dave Gardner	1964	5.00	10.00	20.00
❑ LSP-2852 [S]	Best of Dave Gardner	1964	6.25	12.50	25.00
TONKA
| ❑ TLP 713 | Out Front | 1969 | 5.00 | 10.00 | 20.00 |
TOWER
❑ ST 5050 [S]	Hip-ocracy	1966	5.00	10.00	20.00
❑ T 5050 [M]	Hip-ocracy	1966	3.75	7.50	15.00
❑ ST 5075 [S]	It Don't Make No Difference	1967	5.00	10.00	20.00
❑ T 5075 [M]	It Don't Make No Difference	1967	3.75	7.50	15.00

GARDNER, DON, AND DEE DEE FORD
COLLECTABLES
Number	Title (A Side/B Side)	Yr	VG	VG+	NM
❑ COL-5155	Golden Classics: Need Your Lovin'	198?			
FIRE
| ❑ LP-105 [M] | Need Your Lovin' | 1962 | | | |
SUE
| ❑ LP-1044 [M] | Don Gardner and Dee Dee Ford In Sweden | 1965 | | | 120.00 |

GARDNER, FREDDY
COLUMBIA
Number	Title (A Side/B Side)	Yr	VG	VG+	NM
❑ CL 6187 [10]	Freddy Gardner	195?	12.50	25.00	50.00

GARDNER, FREDDY, AND AL GALLODORO
COLUMBIA
Number	Title (A Side/B Side)	Yr	VG	VG+	NM
❑ CL 623 [M]	The Immortal Freddy Gardner and Al Gallodoro	1954	10.00	20.00	40.00
—Maroon label, gold print					

GARDNERS, THE
PRESTIGE INT'L.
Number	Title (A Side/B Side)	Yr	VG	VG+	NM
❑ PRLP-13062 [M]	Folk Songs Far and Near	1962	7.50	15.00	30.00

GARFUNKEL, ART
COLUMBIA
Number	Title (A Side/B Side)	Yr	VG	VG+	NM
❑ CQ 31474 [Q]	Angel Clare	1973	5.00	10.00	20.00
❑ KC 31474	Angel Clare	1973	3.00	6.00	12.00
❑ PC 31474	Angel Clare	197?	2.00	4.00	8.00
—Reissue					
❑ PC 33700	Breakaway	197?	2.00	4.00	8.00
—With bar code on cover					
❑ PC 33700	Breakaway	1975	3.00	6.00	12.00
—Originals have no bar code					
❑ PCQ 33700 [Q]	Breakaway	1975	5.00	10.00	20.00
❑ JC 34975	Watermark	1978	3.00	6.00	12.00
—Stock copy with "(What a) Wonderful World" on side 2					
❑ JC 34975	Watermark	1978	25.00	50.00	100.00
—Stock copy with "Fingerpaint" on side 2					
❑ JC 34975 [DJ]	Watermark	1978	15.00	30.00	60.00
—Test pressing or white label promo with "Fingerpaint" on side 2					
❑ PC 34975	Watermark	198?	2.00	4.00	8.00
—Reissue					
❑ JC 35780	Fate for Breakfast	1979	3.00	6.00	12.00
—With six different covers, each illustrating Art Garfunkel at a different stage of eating breakfast. No difference in value.					
❑ FC 37392	Scissors Cut	1981	2.50	5.00	10.00
❑ FC 40212	The Animals' Christmas By Jimmy Webb	1986	2.50	5.00	10.00
—With Amy Grant					
❑ FC 40942	Lefty	1988	2.00	4.00	8.00
❑ OC 45008	Garfunkel	1989	2.50	5.00	10.00

GARI, RALPH
EMARCY
Number	Title (A Side/B Side)	Yr	VG	VG+	NM
❑ MG-36019 [M]	Ralph Gari	1955	12.50	25.00	50.00

GARLAND, HANK
COLUMBIA
Number	Title (A Side/B Side)	Yr	VG	VG+	NM
❑ CL 1572 [M]	Jazz Winds from a New Direction	1961	7.50	15.00	30.00
❑ CL 1913 [M]	The Unforgettable Guitar of Hank Garland	1962	7.50	15.00	30.00
❑ CS 8372 [S]	Jazz Winds from a New Direction	1961	10.00	20.00	40.00
❑ CS 8713 [S]	The Unforgettable Guitar of Hank Garland	1962	10.00	20.00	40.00
HARMONY
| ❑ HL 7231 [M] | Velvet Guitar | 196? | 5.00 | 10.00 | 20.00 |
| ❑ HS 11028 [S] | Velvet Guitar | 196? | 6.25 | 12.50 | 25.00 |
SESAC
| ❑ SN-2301/2 [M] | Subtle Swing | 196? | 25.00 | 50.00 | 100.00 |

GARLAND, JUDY
A.E.I.
Number	Title (A Side/B Side)	Yr	VG	VG+	NM
❑ 2108	Judy Garland Vol. 1: Born in a Trunk	198?	2.50	5.00	10.00
❑ 2109	Judy Garland Vol. 2: 1940-45	198?	2.50	5.00	10.00
❑ 2110	Judy Garland Vol. 3: Superstar 1945-50	198?	2.50	5.00	10.00
ABC
❑ 620 [M]	Judy Garland At Home at the Palace — Opening Night	1967	5.00	10.00	20.00
❑ S-620 [S]	Judy Garland At Home at the Palace — Opening Night	1967	6.25	12.50	25.00
❑ AC-30007	The ABC Collection	1976	3.75	7.50	15.00
CAPITOL
❑ DW 676 [R]	Miss Show Business	1963	3.00	6.00	12.00
❑ W 676 [M]	Miss Show Business	1955	10.00	20.00	40.00
❑ DT 734 [R]	Judy	1963	3.75	7.50	15.00
❑ T 734 [M]	Judy	1956	10.00	20.00	40.00
❑ DT 835 [R]	Alone	1963	3.75	7.50	15.00
❑ T 835 [M]	Alone	1957	10.00	20.00	40.00
❑ ST 1036 [S]	Judy in Love	1959	10.00	20.00	40.00
❑ T 1036 [M]	Judy in Love	1958	6.25	12.50	25.00
❑ ST 1118 [S]	Garland at the Grove	1959	10.00	20.00	40.00
❑ T 1118 [M]	Garland at the Grove	1959	6.25	12.50	25.00
❑ ST 1188 [S]	The Letter	1959	10.00	20.00	40.00
—Add 80% if letter is on cover					
❑ T 1188 [M]	The Letter	1959	6.25	12.50	25.00
—Add 80% if letter is on cover					
❑ ST 1467 [S]	Judy — That's Entertainment	196?	5.00	10.00	20.00
—Black rainbow label, Capitol logo at top					
❑ ST 1467 [S]	Judy — That's Entertainment	1960	10.00	20.00	40.00
—Black rainbow label, Capitol logo at left					
❑ T 1467 [M]	Judy — That's Entertainment	196?	3.75	7.50	15.00
—Black rainbow label, Capitol logo at top					
❑ T 1467 [M]	Judy — That's Entertainment	1960	6.25	12.50	25.00
—Black rainbow label, Capitol logo at left					
❑ SWBO 1569 [(2)S]	Judy at Carnegie Hall	1961	12.50	25.00	50.00
❑ WBO 1569 [(2)M]	Judy at Carnegie Hall	1961	10.00	20.00	40.00

G

Number	Title (A Side/B Side)	Yr	VG	VG+	NM
SW 1710 [S]	The Garland Touch	1962	7.50	15.00	30.00
W 1710 [M]	The Garland Touch	1962	5.00	10.00	20.00
SW 1861 [P]	I Could Go On Singing	1963	15.00	30.00	60.00
—"I Am the Monarch of the Sea" and "It Never Was You" are rechanneled					
W 1861 [M]	I Could Go On Singing	1963	10.00	20.00	40.00
ST 1941 [S]	Our Love Letter	1963	7.50	15.00	30.00
—Reissue of ST 1188					
T 1941 [M]	Our Love Letter	1963	5.00	10.00	20.00
—Reissue of T 1188					
SM-1999	The Hits of Judy Garland	197?	2.50	5.00	10.00
—Reissue					
ST 1999 [P]	The Hits of Judy Garland	1964	7.50	15.00	30.00
—"Over the Rainbow," "Come Rain or Come Shine" and "April Showers" are rechanneled					
T 1999 [M]	The Hits of Judy Garland	1964	5.00	10.00	20.00
DW 2062 [R]	Just for Openers	1964	3.75	7.50	15.00
W 2062 [M]	Just for Openers	1964	5.00	10.00	20.00
STCL 2988 [(3)]	The Judy Garland Deluxe Set	1968	10.00	20.00	40.00
DNFR-7632 [(6)]	The Magic of Judy Garland	196?	10.00	20.00	40.00
—Box set with 4-page insert; 20 of the 60 tracks are rechanneled					
SM-11763	Alone	1978	2.50	5.00	10.00
—Edited reissue of 835					
SM-11876	Judy — That's Entertainment	1978	2.50	5.00	10.00
—Edited reissue					
M-12034	Just for Openers	1979	2.50	5.00	10.00
—Edited reissue					
SN-16175	The Hits of Judy Garland	198?	2.00	4.00	8.00
—Budget-line reissue					

DECCA

Number	Title (A Side/B Side)	Yr	VG	VG+	NM
DXB 172 [(2)M]	The Best of Judy Garland	1963	5.00	10.00	20.00
DL 4199 [M]	The Magic of Judy Garland	1961	7.50	15.00	30.00
DL 6020 [10]	Judy at the Palace	1952	25.00	50.00	100.00
DXSB 7172 [(2)R]	The Best of Judy Garland	1963	5.00	10.00	20.00
DL 8190 [M]	Judy Garland's Greatest Performances	1955	10.00	20.00	40.00
—Black label, silver print					
DL 8190 [M]	Judy Garland's Greatest Performances	196?	6.25	12.50	25.00
—Black label with color bars					
DL 75150 [R]	Judy Garland's Greatest Hits	1969	3.00	6.00	12.00

DRG

Number	Title (A Side/B Side)	Yr	VG	VG+	NM
SL 5179	The Wit and the Wonder of Judy Garland	1977	3.75	7.50	15.00
SL-5187	The Beginning	1979	3.75	7.50	15.00

LONGINES SYMPHONETTE

Number	Title (A Side/B Side)	Yr	VG	VG+	NM
SY 5217 [(5)]	The Magic of Judy Garland	197?	7.50	15.00	30.00

MARK 56

Number	Title (A Side/B Side)	Yr	VG	VG+	NM
632 [PD]	In Concert: San Francisco	1978	15.00	30.00	60.00

MCA

Number	Title (A Side/B Side)	Yr	VG	VG+	NM
907	From the Decca Vaults	1984	2.50	5.00	10.00
4003 [(2)]	The Best of Judy Garland	1973	3.75	7.50	15.00
—Black label with rainbow					
4003 [(2)]	The Best of Judy Garland	1980	2.50	5.00	10.00
—Blue label with rainbow					
4046 [(2)]	Collector's Items (1936-45)	197?	3.00	6.00	12.00
25165	The Best of Judy Garland from MGM Classic Films	1988	3.00	6.00	12.00

METRO

Number	Title (A Side/B Side)	Yr	VG	VG+	NM
M-505 [M]	Judy Garland	1965	3.75	7.50	15.00
MS-505 [S]	Judy Garland	1965	5.00	10.00	20.00
M-581 [M]	Judy Garland in Song	1966	3.75	7.50	15.00
MS-581 [S]	Judy Garland in Song	1966	5.00	10.00	20.00

MGM

Number	Title (A Side/B Side)	Yr	VG	VG+	NM
SDP-1 [(2)]	Golden Years at MGM	1969	7.50	15.00	30.00
E-82 [10]	Judy Garland Sings	1951	25.00	50.00	100.00
PX 102	Forever Judy	1969	6.25	12.50	25.00
—White label "Limited Edition" with poster					
E-3149 [M]	If You Feel Like Singing, Sing	1955	15.00	30.00	60.00
E-3989 [M]	The Judy Garland Story Vol. 1: The Star Years	1961	7.50	15.00	30.00
E-4005 [M]	The Judy Garland Story Vol. 2: The Hollywood Years	1962	7.50	15.00	30.00
E-4204 [M]	The Very Best of Judy Garland	1964	7.50	15.00	30.00
SE-4204 [R]	The Very Best of Judy Garland	1964	2.50	5.00	10.00
—Blue and gold label					
SE-4204 [R]	The Very Best of Judy Garland	1964	3.75	7.50	15.00
—Black label					

MINERVA

Number	Title (A Side/B Side)	Yr	VG	VG+	NM
LP-6JG-FNJ	Judy Garland and Friends	1982	2.50	5.00	10.00
LP-6JG-FST	The Judy Garland Show: Mutual Admiration Society	1982	2.50	5.00	10.00

PAIR

Number	Title (A Side/B Side)	Yr	VG	VG+	NM
PDL2-1030 [(2)]	Golden Memories	1986	3.00	6.00	12.00
PDL2-1127 [(2)]	The Legendary Judy Garland	1986	3.00	6.00	12.00

PICKWICK

Number	Title (A Side/B Side)	Yr	VG	VG+	NM
PTP-2010 [(2)]	Her Greatest Hits	197?	3.00	6.00	12.00
SPC-3053	I Feel a Song Coming On	197?	3.00	6.00	12.00

SPRINGBOARD

Number	Title (A Side/B Side)	Yr	VG	VG+	NM
SPB-4054	Over the Rainbow	197?	2.00	4.00	8.00

STANYAN

Number	Title (A Side/B Side)	Yr	VG	VG+	NM
POW-3001	More Than a Memory	198?	2.50	5.00	10.00
—Reissue of 10095					
10095	More Than a Memory	1974	2.50	5.00	10.00

TROPHY

Number	Title (A Side/B Side)	Yr	VG	VG+	NM
TR-7-2145 [(2)]	Judy Garland Concert	1974	3.75	7.50	15.00

GARLAND, JUDY, AND LIZA MINNELLI
CAPITOL

Number	Title (A Side/B Side)	Yr	VG	VG+	NM
SWBO 2295 [(2)S]	"Live" at the London Palladium	1965	7.50	15.00	30.00
WBO 2295 [(2)M]	"Live" at the London Palladium	1965	6.25	12.50	25.00
ST-11191	"Live" at the London Palladium	1973	3.00	6.00	12.00
—Condensation of above 2-record set					

MOBILE FIDELITY

Number	Title (A Side/B Side)	Yr	VG	VG+	NM
1-048	"Live" at the London Palladium	1981	6.25	12.50	25.00
—Audiophile vinyl					

GARLAND, RED
JAZZLAND

Number	Title (A Side/B Side)	Yr	VG	VG+	NM
JLP-48 [M]	Bright and Breezy	1961	7.50	15.00	30.00
JLP-62 [M]	The Nearness of You — Ballads Played by Red Garland	1962	7.50	15.00	30.00
JLP-73 [M]	Solar	1962	7.50	15.00	30.00
JLP-87 [M]	Red's Good Groove!	1963	7.50	15.00	30.00
JLP-948 [S]	Bright and Breezy	1961	10.00	20.00	40.00
JLP-962 [S]	The Nearness of You — Ballads Played by Red Garland	1962	10.00	20.00	40.00
JLP-973 [S]	Solar	1962	10.00	20.00	40.00
JLP-987 [S]	Red's Good Groove!	1963	10.00	20.00	40.00

MOODSVILLE

Number	Title (A Side/B Side)	Yr	VG	VG+	NM
MVLP-1 [M]	Red Garland & Eddie "Lockjaw' Davis	1960	12.50	25.00	50.00
—Green label					
MVLP-1 [M]	Red Garland & Eddie "Lockjaw' Davis	1965	6.25	12.50	25.00
—Blue label, trident logo at right					
MVLP-3 [M]	Red Alone — Vol. 3	1960	12.50	25.00	50.00
—Green label					
MVLP-3 [M]	Red Alone — Vol. 3	1965	6.25	12.50	25.00
—Blue label, trident logo at right					
MVLP-6 [M]	The Red Garland Trio	1960	12.50	25.00	50.00
—Green label					
MVLP-6 [M]	The Red Garland Trio	1965	6.25	12.50	25.00
—Blue label, trident logo at right					
MVLP-10 [M]	Alone with the Blues	1960	12.50	25.00	50.00
—Green label					
MVLP-10 [M]	Alone with the Blues	1965	6.25	12.50	25.00
—Blue label, trident logo at right					

PRESTIGE

Number	Title (A Side/B Side)	Yr	VG	VG+	NM
PRLP-7064 [M]	A Garland of Red	1956	20.00	40.00	80.00
—W. 50th St., New York address on label					
PRLP-7064 [M]	A Garland of Red	1958	15.00	30.00	60.00
—Yellow label with Bergenfield, N.J. address					
PRLP-7086 [M]	Red Garland's Piano	1957	20.00	40.00	80.00
—W. 50th St., New York address on label					
PRLP-7086 [M]	Red Garland's Piano	1958	15.00	30.00	60.00
—Yellow label with Bergenfield, N.J. address					
PRLP-7113 [M]	Groovy	1957	20.00	40.00	80.00
—W. 50th St., New York address on label					
PRLP-7113 [M]	Groovy	1958	15.00	30.00	60.00
—Yellow label with Bergenfield, N.J. address					
PRLP-7130 [M]	All Morning Long	1958	15.00	30.00	60.00
—Yellow label with Bergenfield, N.J. address					
PRLP-7130 [M]	All Morning Long	1958	20.00	40.00	80.00
—W. 50th St., New York address on label					
PRLP-7139 [M]	Manteca	1958	12.50	25.00	50.00
—Yellow label with Bergenfield, N.J. address					
PRLP-7148 [M]	All Kinds of Weather	1958	12.50	25.00	50.00
—Yellow label with Bergenfield, N.J. address					
PRLP-7157 [M]	Red in Bluesville	1959	12.50	25.00	50.00
—Yellow label with Bergenfield, N.J. address					
PRLP-7170 [M]	Red Garland at the Prelude	1959	12.50	25.00	50.00
—Yellow label with Bergenfield, N.J. address					
PRLP-7181 [M]	Soul Junction	1960	12.50	25.00	50.00
—Yellow label with Bergenfield, N.J. address					
PRLP-7193 [M]	Rojo	1961	10.00	20.00	40.00
—Yellow label with Bergenfield, N.J. address					
PRLP-7209 [M]	High Pressure	1961	12.50	25.00	50.00
—Yellow label with Bergenfield, N.J. address					
PRLP-7229 [M]	Dig It!	1962	10.00	20.00	40.00
PRST-7229 [S]	Dig It!	1962	12.50	25.00	50.00
PRLP-7258 [M]	When There Are Grey Skies	1963	7.50	15.00	30.00
PRST-7258 [S]	When There Are Grey Skies	1963	10.00	20.00	40.00
PRLP-7276 [M]	Can't See for Lookin'	1963	7.50	15.00	30.00
PRST-7276 [S]	Can't See for Lookin'	1963	10.00	20.00	40.00
PRLP-7288 [M]	Halleloo-Y'all	1964	7.50	15.00	30.00
PRST-7288 [S]	Halleloo-Y'all	1964	10.00	20.00	40.00
PRLP-7307 [M]	Soul Burnin'	1964	6.25	12.50	25.00
PRST-7307 [S]	Soul Burnin'	1964	7.50	15.00	30.00

STATUS

Number	Title (A Side/B Side)	Yr	VG	VG+	NM
ST-8314 [M]	Li'l Darlin'	1965	7.50	15.00	30.00
ST-8325 [M]	High Pressure	1965	7.50	15.00	30.00
ST-8326 [M]	Red Garland Live!	1965	7.50	15.00	30.00

GARNER, ERROLL
ABC-PARAMOUNT

Number	Title (A Side/B Side)	Yr	VG	VG+	NM
365 [M]	Dreamstreet	1961	5.00	10.00	20.00
S-365 [S]	Dreamstreet	1961	6.25	12.50	25.00
395 [M]	Closeup in Swing	1961	5.00	10.00	20.00
S-395 [S]	Closeup in Swing	1961	6.25	12.50	25.00

ATLANTIC

Number	Title (A Side/B Side)	Yr	VG	VG+	NM
ALR-109 [10]	Rhapsody	1950	20.00	40.00	80.00
ALR-112 [10]	Erroll Garner at the Piano	1951	20.00	40.00	80.00
ALR-128 [10]	Passport to Fame	1952	25.00	50.00	100.00
ALR-135 [10]	Piano Solos, Volume 2	1952	20.00	40.00	80.00
1227 [M]	The Greatest Garner	1956	10.00	20.00	40.00
—Black label					
1315 [M]	Perpetual Motion	1959	10.00	20.00	40.00
—Black label					

BLUE NOTE

Number	Title (A Side/B Side)	Yr	VG	VG+	NM
BLP-5007 [10]	Overture to Dawn, Volume 1	1952	50.00	100.00	200.00
BLP-5008 [10]	Overture to Dawn, Volume 2	1952	50.00	100.00	200.00
BLP-5014 [10]	Overture to Dawn, Volume 3	1953	50.00	100.00	200.00
BLP-5015 [10]	Overture to Dawn, Volume 4	1953	50.00	100.00	200.00
BLP-5016 [10]	Overture to Dawn, Volume 5	1953	50.00	100.00	200.00

Number	Title (A Side/B Side)	Yr	VG	VG+	NM
COLUMBIA					
❏ C2L 9 [(2)M]	Paris Impressions	1958	10.00	20.00	40.00
❏ CL 535 [M]	Erroll Garner	1953	15.00	30.00	60.00
—Red label with gold print					
❏ CL 535 [M]	Erroll Garner	1956	7.50	15.00	30.00
—Red and black label with six "eye" logos					
❏ CL 583 [M]	Gems	1954	15.00	30.00	60.00
—Red label with gold print					
❏ CL 583 [M]	Gems	1956	7.50	15.00	30.00
—Red and black label with six "eye" logos					
❏ CL 617 [M]	Gone Garner Gonest	1955	15.00	30.00	60.00
—Red label with gold print					
❏ CL 617 [M]	Gone Garner Gonest	1956	7.50	15.00	30.00
—Red and black label with six "eye" logos					
❏ CL 667 [M]	Erroll Garner Plays for Dancing	1956	7.50	15.00	30.00
❏ CL 883 [M]	Concert by the Sea	1956	7.50	15.00	30.00
❏ CL 939 [M]	The Most Happy Piano	1957	7.50	15.00	30.00
❏ CL 1014 [M]	Other Voices	1957	7.50	15.00	30.00
❏ CL 1060 [M]	Soliloquy	1957	7.50	15.00	30.00
❏ CL 1141 [M]	Encores in Hi-Fi	1958	7.50	15.00	30.00
❏ CL 1216 [M]	Paris Impressions, Volume 1	1958	5.00	10.00	20.00
❏ CL 1217 [M]	Paris Impressions, Volume 2	1958	5.00	10.00	20.00
❏ CL 1452 [M]	The One and Only Erroll Garner	1960	5.00	10.00	20.00
❏ CL 1512 [M]	Swinging Solos	1960	5.00	10.00	20.00
❏ CL 1587 [M]	The Provocative Erroll Garner	1961	5.00	10.00	20.00
❏ CL 2540 [10]	Garnerland	1955	15.00	30.00	60.00
❏ CL 2606 [10]	He's Here! He's Gone! He's Garner!	1956	15.00	30.00	60.00
❏ CL 6139 [10]	Piano Moods	1950	20.00	40.00	80.00
❏ CL 6173 [10]	Gems	1951	20.00	40.00	80.00
❏ CL 6209 [10]	Solo Flight	1952	20.00	40.00	80.00
❏ CL 6259 [10]	Erroll Garner Plays for Dancing	1953	20.00	40.00	80.00
❏ CS 8252 [S]	The One and Only Erroll Garner	1960	6.25	12.50	25.00
❏ CS 8312 [S]	Swinging Solos	1960	6.25	12.50	25.00
❏ CS 8387 [S]	The Provocative Erroll Garner	1961	6.25	12.50	25.00
DIAL					
❏ LP-205 [10]	Erroll Garner, Volume 1	1950	50.00	100.00	200.00
❏ LP-902 [M]	Free Piano Improvisations Recorded by Baron Timme Rosenkranz at One of His Famous Gaslight Jazz Sessions	1949	75.00	150.00	300.00
EMARCY					
❏ MG-26016 [10]	Garnering	1954	20.00	40.00	80.00
❏ MG-26042 [10]	Gone with Garner	1954	20.00	40.00	80.00
❏ MG-36001 [M]	Contrasts	1955	7.50	15.00	30.00
❏ MG-36026 [M]	Garnering	1955	7.50	15.00	30.00
❏ MG-36069 [M]	Erroll!	1956	7.50	15.00	30.00
JAZZTONE					
❏ J-1269 [M]	Early Erroll	1957	10.00	20.00	40.00
KING					
❏ 295-17 [10]	Piano Stylist	1952	20.00	40.00	80.00
❏ 395-540 [M]	Piano Variations	1958	12.50	25.00	50.00
MERCURY					
❏ MG-20009 [M]	Erroll Garner at the Piano	1953	12.50	25.00	50.00
❏ MG-20055 [M]	Mambo Moves Garner	1954	12.50	25.00	50.00
❏ MG-20063 [M]	Solitaire	1954	12.50	25.00	50.00
❏ MG-20090 [M]	Afternoon of an Elf	1955	12.50	25.00	50.00
❏ MG-25117 [10]	Erroll Garner at the Piano	1951	20.00	40.00	80.00
❏ MG-25157 [10]	Gone with Garner	1951	20.00	40.00	80.00
❏ SR-60662 [S]	Erroll Garner Plays Misty	1962	5.00	10.00	20.00
—Black label, all-silver print					
❏ SR-60803 [S]	The Best of Erroll Garner	1963	5.00	10.00	20.00
❏ SR-60859 [S]	New Kind of Love	1963	5.00	10.00	20.00
❏ SR-61308 [S]	Feeling Is Believing	1964	5.00	10.00	20.00
REPRISE					
❏ R 6080 [DJ]	One World Concert	1963	10.00	20.00	40.00
—Six-song sampler -- three on each side -- on a 12-inch record that plays at 45 rpm. This comes in a different cover than the stock copy; this is clearly marked "Special 45 RPM Preview Record" on the top front.					
❏ R 6080 [M]	One World Concert	1963	5.00	10.00	20.00
❏ RS 6080 [S]	One World Concert	1963	6.25	12.50	25.00
RONDO-LETTE					
❏ A-15 [M]	Erroll Garner	1958	6.25	12.50	25.00
SAVOY					
❏ MG-12002 [M]	Penthouse Serenade	1955	7.50	15.00	30.00
❏ MG-12003 [M]	Serenade to "Laura"	1955	7.50	15.00	30.00
❏ MG-15000 [10]	Erroll Garner Plays Piano Solos	1950	20.00	40.00	80.00
❏ MG-15001 [10]	Erroll Garner Plays Piano Solos, Volume 2	1950	20.00	40.00	80.00
❏ MG-15002 [10]	Erroll Garner Plays Piano Solos, Volume 3	1950	20.00	40.00	80.00
❏ MG-15003 [10]	Erroll Garner Plays Piano Solos, Volume 4	1950	20.00	40.00	80.00
❏ MG-15026 [10]	Erroll Garner at the Piano	1953	20.00	40.00	80.00

GARNER, ERROLL/PETE JOHNSON
GRAND AWARD

Number	Title (A Side/B Side)	Yr	VG	VG+	NM
❏ GA 33-321 [M]	Jazz Piano	1956	6.25	12.50	25.00
—Without removable cover					
❏ GA 33-321 [M]	Jazz Piano	1956	20.00	40.00	80.00
—With removable David Stone Martin cover still attached					

GARNER, ERROLL/BILLY TAYLOR
SAVOY

Number	Title (A Side/B Side)	Yr	VG	VG+	NM
❏ MG-12008 [M]	Erroll Garner/Billy Taylor	1955	12.50	25.00	50.00

GARNER, MORRIS
THUNDERBIRD

Number	Title (A Side/B Side)	Yr	VG	VG+	NM
❏ TH-1958 [M]	The Worst of Morris Garner	196?	6.25	12.50	25.00

GARNETT, CARLOS
MUSE

Number	Title (A Side/B Side)	Yr	VG	VG+	NM
❏ MR-5057	Journey to Enlightenment	1974	5.00	10.00	20.00
❏ MR-5079	Let the Melody Ring On	1975	7.50	15.00	30.00
❏ MR-5104	Cosmos Nucleus	1976	10.00	20.00	40.00
❏ MR-5133	New Love	1977	10.00	20.00	40.00

G

GARNETT, GALE
COLUMBIA

Number	Title (A Side/B Side)	Yr	VG	VG+	NM
❏ CL 2825 [M]	An Audience with the King of Wands	1968	5.00	10.00	20.00
❏ CS 9625 [S]	An Audience with the King of Wands	1968	3.75	7.50	15.00
❏ CS 9760	Sausalito Heliport	1969	3.75	7.50	15.00
RCA VICTOR					
❏ LPM-2833 [M]	My Kind of Folk Songs	1964	10.00	20.00	40.00
—Black and white/blueish cover					
❏ LPM-2833 [M]	My Kind of Folk Songs	1965	3.75	7.50	15.00
—Color photo on cover					
❏ LSP-2833 [S]	My Kind of Folk Songs	1964	12.50	25.00	50.00
—Black and white/blueish cover					
❏ LSP-2833 [S]	My Kind of Folk Songs	1965	5.00	10.00	20.00
—Color photo on cover					
❏ LPM-3305 [M]	Lovin' Place	1965	3.75	7.50	15.00
❏ LSP-3305 [S]	Lovin' Place	1965	5.00	10.00	20.00
❏ LPM-3325 [M]	The Many Faces of Gale Garnett	1965	3.75	7.50	15.00
❏ LSP-3325 [S]	The Many Faces of Gale Garnett	1965	5.00	10.00	20.00
❏ LPM-3493 [M]	Variety Is the Spice of Gale Garnett	1966	3.75	7.50	15.00
❏ LSP-3493 [S]	Variety Is the Spice of Gale Garnett	1966	5.00	10.00	20.00
❏ LPM-3586 [M]	New Adventures	1966	3.75	7.50	15.00
❏ LSP-3586 [S]	New Adventures	1966	5.00	10.00	20.00
❏ LPM-3747 [M]	Gale Garnett Sings About Flying & Rainbows & Love & Other Groovy Things	1967	6.25	12.50	25.00
❏ LSP-3747 [S]	Gale Garnett Sings About Flying & Rainbows & Love & Other Groovy Things	1967	5.00	10.00	20.00

GARROWAY, DAVE
CAMEO

Number	Title (A Side/B Side)	Yr	VG	VG+	NM
❏ C-1001 [M]	An Adventure in Hi-Fi Music	1958	10.00	20.00	40.00
—Black label, brown print, cameo figure at top					

GARSON, GREER
LION

Number	Title (A Side/B Side)	Yr	VG	VG+	NM
❏ L-70102 [M]	Greer Garson Babysits with Stories and Songs	1958	7.50	15.00	30.00

GARSON, MIKE
REFERENCE RECORDINGS

Number	Title (A Side/B Side)	Yr	VG	VG+	NM
❏ RR-37	The Oxnard Sessions	1991	5.00	10.00	20.00
❏ RR-53 [(2)]	The Oxnard Sessions, Volume Two	1993	6.25	12.50	25.00

GARVIN, REX, AND THE MIGHTY CRAVERS
TOWER

Number	Title (A Side/B Side)	Yr	VG	VG+	NM
❏ ST 5130	Raw Funky Earth	1968	7.50	15.00	30.00

GARY, JOHN
CHURCHILL

Number	Title (A Side/B Side)	Yr	VG	VG+	NM
❏ 67236	In a Class By Himself	1977	2.50	5.00	10.00
LA BREA					
❏ 8010 [M]	John Gary	1961	6.25	12.50	25.00
❏ S-8010 [S]	John Gary	1961	7.50	15.00	30.00
METRO					
❏ M-522 [M]	John Gary	1966	2.50	5.00	10.00
❏ MS-522 [S]	John Gary	1966	3.00	6.00	12.00
PICKWICK					
❏ SPC-3025	John Gary	197?	2.50	5.00	10.00
RCA CAMDEN					
❏ CAL-983 [M]	The One and Only John Gary	1966	2.50	5.00	10.00
❏ CAS-983 [S]	The One and Only John Gary	1966	3.00	6.00	12.00
RCA VICTOR					
❏ LOC-1139 [M]	The John Gary Carnegie Hall Concert	1967	5.00	10.00	20.00
❏ LSO-1139 [S]	The John Gary Carnegie Hall Concert	1967	3.00	6.00	12.00
❏ ANL1-2342	Pure Gold	1977	2.50	5.00	10.00
❏ ANL1-2672	A Little Bit of Heaven	1978	2.50	5.00	10.00
—Reissue of LSP-2994					
❏ LPM-2745 [M]	Catch a Rising Star	1963	3.75	7.50	15.00
❏ LSP-2745 [S]	Catch a Rising Star	1963	5.00	10.00	20.00
❏ LPM-2804 [M]	Encore	1964	3.75	7.50	15.00
❏ LSP-2804 [S]	Encore	1964	5.00	10.00	20.00
❏ LPM-2922 [M]	So Tenderly	1964	3.75	7.50	15.00
❏ LSP-2922 [S]	So Tenderly	1964	5.00	10.00	20.00
❏ LPM-2940 [M]	The John Gary Christmas Album	1964	3.75	7.50	15.00
❏ LSP-2940 [S]	The John Gary Christmas Album	1964	5.00	10.00	20.00
❏ LPM-2994 [M]	A Little Bit of Heaven	1965	3.00	6.00	12.00
❏ LSP-2994 [S]	A Little Bit of Heaven	1965	3.75	7.50	15.00
❏ LPM-3349 [M]	The Nearness of You	1965	3.00	6.00	12.00
❏ LSP-3349 [S]	The Nearness of You	1965	3.75	7.50	15.00
❏ LPM-3411 [M]	Your All-Time Favorite Songs	1965	3.00	6.00	12.00
❏ LSP-3411 [S]	Your All-Time Favorite Songs	1965	3.75	7.50	15.00
❏ LPM-3501 [M]	Choice	1966	3.00	6.00	12.00
❏ LSP-3501 [S]	Choice	1966	3.75	7.50	15.00
❏ LPM-3570 [M]	Your All-Time Country Favorites	1966	3.00	6.00	12.00
❏ LSP-3570 [S]	Your All-Time Country Favorites	1966	3.75	7.50	15.00
❏ LPM-3666 [M]	A Heart Filled with Song	1966	3.00	6.00	12.00
❏ LSP-3666 [S]	A Heart Filled with Song	1966	3.75	7.50	15.00
❏ LPM-3695 [M]	Especially for You	1967	3.75	7.50	15.00
❏ LSP-3695 [S]	Especially for You	1967	3.00	6.00	12.00
❏ LPM-3730 [M]	The Best of John Gary	1967	3.75	7.50	15.00
❏ LSP-3730 [S]	The Best of John Gary	1967	3.00	6.00	12.00
❏ LPM-3785 [M]	Spanish Moonlight	1967	3.75	7.50	15.00
❏ LSP-3785 [S]	Spanish Moonlight	1967	3.00	6.00	12.00
❏ LPM-3928 [M]	John Gary On Broadway	1968	5.00	10.00	20.00
❏ LSP-3928 [S]	John Gary On Broadway	1968	3.00	6.00	12.00
❏ LPM-3992 [M]	John Gary Sings/John Gary Swings	1968	5.00	10.00	20.00
❏ LSP-3992 [S]	John Gary Sings/John Gary Swings	1968	3.00	6.00	12.00
❏ LSP-4075	Holding Your Mind	1968	3.00	6.00	12.00
❏ LSP-4134	Love of a Gentle Woman	1969	3.00	6.00	12.00
❏ VPS-6041 [(2)]	This Is John Gary	1971	3.75	7.50	15.00

Number	Title (A Side/B Side)	Yr	VG	VG+	NM

	Title (A Side/B Side)	Yr	VG	VG+	NM
	and Work Songs	1958	7.50	15.00	30.00
		1970	5.00	10.00	20.00

GASKIN, LEONARD
SWINGVILLE
| ❑ SVLP-2031 [M] | At the Jazz Band Ball | 1962 | 10.00 | 20.00 | 40.00 |

—Purple label
| ❑ SVLP-2031 [M] | At the Jazz Band Ball | 1965 | 5.00 | 10.00 | 20.00 |

—Blue label, trident logo at right
| ❑ SVST-2031 [S] | At the Jazz Band Ball | 1962 | 12.50 | 25.00 | 50.00 |

—Red label
| ❑ SVST-2031 [S] | At the Jazz Band Ball | 1965 | 6.25 | 12.50 | 25.00 |

—Blue label, trident logo at right
| ❑ SVLP-2033 [M] | At the Darktown Strutters' Ball | 1962 | 10.00 | 20.00 | 40.00 |

—Purple label
| ❑ SVLP-2033 [M] | At the Darktown Strutters' Ball | 1965 | 5.00 | 10.00 | 20.00 |

—Blue label, trident logo at right
| ❑ SVST-2033 [S] | At the Darktown Strutters' Ball | 1962 | 12.50 | 25.00 | 50.00 |

—Red label
| ❑ SVST-2033 [S] | At the Darktown Strutters' Ball | 1965 | 6.25 | 12.50 | 25.00 |

—Blue label, trident logo at right

GATES, DAVID
ARISTA
| ❑ AL 9563 | Take Me Now | 1981 | 2.50 | 5.00 | 10.00 |
ELEKTRA
❑ 6E-148	Goodbye Girl	1978	3.00	6.00	12.00
❑ 6E-251	Falling in Love Again	1980	2.50	5.00	10.00
❑ 7E-1028	Never Let Her Go	1975	3.00	6.00	12.00
❑ EQ-5066 [Q]	First	1973	5.00	10.00	20.00
❑ EKS-75066	First	1973	3.00	6.00	12.00

GATES, HEN
MASTERSEAL
| ❑ MLP-700 [M] | Let's All Dance to Rock and Roll | 1956 | 25.00 | 50.00 | 100.00 |
PALACE
| ❑ P-700 [M] | Let's All Dance to Rock and Roll | 1958 | 15.00 | 30.00 | 60.00 |

—Reissue of Masterseal 700
| ❑ PST-700 [S] | Let's All Dance to Rock and Roll | 1958 | 20.00 | 40.00 | 80.00 |

—Labeled stereo, but plays in mono
PARIS
| ❑ 101 [M] | Rock and Roll Festival | 1957 | 15.00 | 30.00 | 60.00 |
PLYMOUTH
| ❑ R12-144 [M] | Rock and Roll | 1956 | 15.00 | 30.00 | 60.00 |
| ❑ R12-149 [M] | Rock and Roll, No. 2 | 1957 | 15.00 | 30.00 | 60.00 |

GATEWAY SINGERS, THE
DECCA
❑ DL 8413 [M]	Puttin' On the Style	1956	10.00	20.00	40.00
❑ DL 8671 [M]	The Gateway Singers at the Hungry I	1958	7.50	15.00	30.00
❑ DL 8742 [M]	The Gateway Singers in Hi-Fi	1958	7.50	15.00	30.00
MGM
❑ E-3905 [M]	Down in the Valley	1961	5.00	10.00	20.00
❑ SE-3905 [S]	Down in the Valley	1961	6.25	12.50	25.00
❑ E-4154 [M]	Hootenanny	1963	5.00	10.00	20.00
❑ SE-4154 [S]	Hootenanny	1963	6.25	12.50	25.00
WARNER BROS.
❑ W 1295 [M]	The Gateway Singers on the Lot	1959	6.25	12.50	25.00
❑ WS 1295 [S]	The Gateway Singers on the Lot	1959	7.50	15.00	30.00
❑ W 1334 [M]	Wagons West	1960	6.25	12.50	25.00
❑ WS 1334 [S]	Wagons West	1960	7.50	15.00	30.00

GATEWAY TRIO, THE
CAPITOL
❑ ST 1868 [S]	The Mad, Mad, Mad Gateway Trio	1963	5.00	10.00	20.00
❑ T 1868 [M]	The Mad, Mad, Mad Gateway Trio	1963	3.75	7.50	15.00
❑ ST 2184 [S]	The Gateway Trio	1964	5.00	10.00	20.00
❑ T 2184 [M]	The Gateway Trio	1964	3.75	7.50	15.00

GATLIN, LARRY, AND THE GATLIN BROTHERS BAND
COLUMBIA
| ❑ JC 36250 | Straight Ahead | 1979 | 2.50 | 5.00 | 10.00 |
| ❑ JC 36488 | Larry Gatlin's Greatest Hits, Volume 1 | 1980 | 2.00 | 4.00 | 8.00 |

—Reissue of Monument 7628
| ❑ PC 36541 | The Pilgrim | 1980 | 2.00 | 4.00 | 8.00 |

—Reissue of Monument 6632
| ❑ JC 36582 | Help Yourself | 1980 | 2.50 | 5.00 | 10.00 |
| ❑ PC 36582 | Help Yourself | 198? | 2.00 | 4.00 | 8.00 |

—Budget-line reissue
| ❑ FC 37464 | Not Guilty | 1981 | 2.50 | 5.00 | 10.00 |
| ❑ PC 37464 | Not Guilty | 198? | 2.00 | 4.00 | 8.00 |

—Budget-line reissue
| ❑ FC 38135 | Sure Feels Like Love | 1982 | 2.50 | 5.00 | 10.00 |
| ❑ PC 38135 | Sure Feels Like Love | 198? | 2.00 | 4.00 | 8.00 |

—Budget-line reissue
| ❑ FC 38183 | A Gatlin Family Christmas | 1982 | 3.00 | 6.00 | 12.00 |
| ❑ PC 38183 | A Gatlin Family Christmas | 198? | 2.00 | 4.00 | 8.00 |

—Budget-line reissue
| ❑ PC 38336 | Love Is Just a Game | 1982 | 2.00 | 4.00 | 8.00 |

—Reissue of Monument 7616
| ❑ PC 38337 | Larry Gatlin with Family and Friends | 1982 | 2.00 | 4.00 | 8.00 |

—Reissue of Monument 6634
| ❑ PC 38338 | High Time | 1982 | 2.00 | 4.00 | 8.00 |

—Reissue of Monument 6644
| ❑ PC 38339 | Rain-Rainbow | 1982 | 2.00 | 4.00 | 8.00 |

—Reissue of Monumnet 6633

| ❑ PC 38340 | Oh! Brother | 1982 | 2.00 | 4.00 | 8.00 |

—Reissue of Monumnet 7626
❑ FC 38923	Larry Gatlin's Greatest Hits, Volume 2	1983	2.50	5.00	10.00
❑ FC 39291	Houston to Denver	1984	2.50	5.00	10.00
❑ FC 40068	Smile!	1985	2.50	5.00	10.00
❑ FC 40431	Partners	1986	2.50	5.00	10.00
❑ FC 40905	Alive and Well…Living in the Land of Dreams	1988	2.50	5.00	10.00
❑ FC 44471	The Gatlin Brothers' Biggest Hits (1984-88)	1989	2.50	5.00	10.00
❑ HC 48135	Sure Feels Like Love	1982	62.50	125.00	250.00

—Half-speed mastered edition
MONUMENT
| ❑ 6632 | The Pilgrim | 1976 | 3.00 | 6.00 | 12.00 |

—Reissue of KZ 32571
| ❑ 6633 | Rain-Rainbow | 1976 | 3.00 | 6.00 | 12.00 |

—Reissue of KZ 33069
| ❑ 6634 | Larry Gatlin with Family and Friends | 1976 | 3.00 | 6.00 | 12.00 |

—Reissue of KZ 34042
❑ 6644	High Time	1977	3.00	6.00	12.00
❑ MG 7616	Love Is Just a Game	1978	3.00	6.00	12.00
❑ MG 7626	Oh! Brother	1978	3.00	6.00	12.00
❑ MG 7628	Larry Gatlin's Greatest Hits	1978	3.00	6.00	12.00
❑ KZ 32571	The Pilgrim	1974	3.75	7.50	15.00
❑ KZ 33069	Rain-Rainbow	1974	3.75	7.50	15.00
❑ KZ 34042	Larry Gatlin with Family & Friends	1975	3.75	7.50	15.00
SWORD & SHIELD
❑ 9009 [M]	The Old Country Church	1961	25.00	50.00	100.00

—As "The Gatlin Quartet" (with sister La Donna joining Larry, Rudy and Steve)

GAUCHOS, THE
See JIM DOVAL AND THE GAUCHOS.

GAVIN, KEVIN
CHARLIE PARKER
| ❑ PLP-810 [M] | Hey! This Is Kevin Gavin | 1962 | 7.50 | 15.00 | 30.00 |
| ❑ PLP-810S [S] | Hey! This Is Kevin Gavin | 1962 | 10.00 | 20.00 | 40.00 |

GAYE, MARVIN
COLUMBIA
| ❑ FC 38197 | Midnight Love | 1982 | 2.50 | 5.00 | 10.00 |
| ❑ PC 38197 | Midnight Love | 1986 | 2.00 | 4.00 | 8.00 |

—Budget-line reissue
❑ FC 39916	Dream of a Lifetime	1985	2.50	5.00	10.00
❑ 9C9 40133 [PD]	Dream of a Lifetime	1985	5.00	10.00	20.00
❑ FC 40208	Romantically Yours	1986	2.50	5.00	10.00
❑ HC 48197	Midnight Love	1984	10.00	20.00	40.00

—Half-speed mastered edition
MOTOWN
| ❑ M5-115V1 | Motown Superstar Series, Vol. 15 | 1981 | 2.50 | 5.00 | 10.00 |
| ❑ M5-125V1 | M.P.G. | 1981 | 2.50 | 5.00 | 10.00 |

—Reissue of Tamla 292
| ❑ M5-181V1 | Marvin Gaye Live! | 1981 | 2.50 | 5.00 | 10.00 |

—Reissue of Tamla 333
| ❑ M5-191V1 | Marvin Gaye's Greatest Hits | 1981 | 2.50 | 5.00 | 10.00 |

—Reissue of Tamla 348
| ❑ M5-192V1 | Let's Get It On | 1981 | 2.50 | 5.00 | 10.00 |

—Reissue of Tamla 329
| ❑ M5-216V1 | A Tribute to the Great Nat King Cole | 1981 | 2.50 | 5.00 | 10.00 |

—Reissue of Tamla 261
| ❑ M5-218V1 | That Stubborn Kinda' Fellow | 1981 | 2.50 | 5.00 | 10.00 |

—Reissue of Tamla 239
| ❑ M9-791A3 [(3)] | Anthology | 1974 | 5.00 | 10.00 | 20.00 |
| ❑ 37463 1296-1 [DJ] | The Master 1961-1984 | 1995 | 5.00 | 10.00 | 20.00 |

—Vinyl is promo only; 8-song sampler from box set
| ❑ 5259 ML [(2)] | Marvin Gaye Live at the London Palladium | 1983 | 3.00 | 6.00 | 12.00 |

—Reissue of Tamla 352
| ❑ 5306 ML | Super Hits | 198? | 2.50 | 5.00 | 10.00 |
| ❑ 5339 ML | What's Going On | 198? | 2.50 | 5.00 | 10.00 |

—Reissue of Tamla 322
| ❑ 6058 ML | Every Great Motown Hit of Marvin Gaye | 1983 | 2.50 | 5.00 | 10.00 |
| ❑ 6255 ML [(2)] | A Musical Testament 1964-1984 | 1988 | 3.00 | 6.00 | 12.00 |
NATURAL RESOURCES
| ❑ NR 4007T1 | The Soulful Moods of Marvin Gaye | 1978 | 3.00 | 6.00 | 12.00 |

—Reissue of Tamla 221
TAMLA
❑ TM 221 [M]	The Soulful Moods of Marvin Gaye	1961	250.00	500.00	1000.
❑ T 239 [M]	That Stubborn Kinda' Fella	1963	150.00	300.00	600.00
❑ T 242 [M]	Recorded Live — Marvin Gaye on Stage	1963	75.00	150.00	300.00
❑ T 251 [M]	When I'm Alone I Cry	1964	62.50	125.00	250.00
❑ T 252 [M]	Marvin Gaye/Greatest Hits	1964	7.50	15.00	30.00
❑ TS 252 [S]	Marvin Gaye/Greatest Hits	1964	10.00	20.00	40.00
❑ T 258 [M]	How Sweet It Is to Be Loved by You	1965	10.00	20.00	40.00
❑ TS 258 [S]	How Sweet It Is to Be Loved by You	1965	12.50	25.00	50.00
❑ T 259 [M]	Hello Broadway, This Is Marvin	1965	10.00	20.00	40.00
❑ TS 259 [S]	Hello Broadway, This Is Marvin	1965	12.50	25.00	50.00
❑ T 261 [M]	A Tribute to the Great Nat King Cole	1965	10.00	20.00	40.00
❑ TS 261 [S]	A Tribute to the Great Nat King Cole	1965	12.50	25.00	50.00
❑ T 266 [M]	Moods of Marvin Gaye	1966	10.00	20.00	40.00
❑ TS 266 [S]	Moods of Marvin Gaye	1966	12.50	25.00	50.00
❑ T 278 [M]	Marvin Gaye/Greatest Hits, Vol. 2	1967	6.25	12.50	25.00
❑ TS 278 [S]	Marvin Gaye/Greatest Hits, Vol. 2	1967	5.00	10.00	20.00
❑ T 285 [M]	In the Groove	1968	12.50	25.00	50.00
❑ TS 285 [S]	In the Groove	1968	6.25	12.50	25.00
❑ TS 285 [S]	I Heard It Through the Grapevine	1969	5.00	10.00	20.00

—Retitled version of "In the Groove"
| ❑ TS 292 | M.P.G. | 1969 | 5.00 | 10.00 | 20.00 |
| ❑ TS 293 | Marvin Gaye and His Girls | 1969 | 5.00 | 10.00 | 20.00 |

—Includes duets with Tammi Terrell, Mary Wells, Kim Weston
❑ TS 299	That's the Way Love Is	1969	5.00	10.00	20.00
❑ TS 300	Marvin Gaye Super Hits	1970	5.00	10.00	20.00
❑ T5-310	What's Going On	1971	3.75	7.50	15.00
❑ T5-322	Trouble Man	1972	3.75	7.50	15.00
❑ T6-329	Let's Get It On	1973	3.75	7.50	15.00

Number	Title (A Side/B Side)	Yr	VG	VG+	NM
❑ T6-333	Marvin Gaye Live!	1974	3.75	7.50	15.00
❑ T6-342	I Want You	1976	3.75	7.50	15.00
❑ T6-348	Marvin Gaye's Greatest Hits	1976	3.75	7.50	15.00
❑ T7-352 [(2)]	Marvin Gaye Live at the London Palladium	1977	3.75	7.50	15.00
❑ T13-364 [(2)]	Here, My Dear	1978	3.75	7.50	15.00
❑ T8-374	In Our Lifetime	1981	2.50	5.00	10.00
❑ 6172 TL	Motown Remembers Marvin Gaye	1986	2.50	5.00	10.00

GAYE, MARVIN, AND TAMMI TERRELL
MOTOWN

Number	Title (A Side/B Side)	Yr	VG	VG+	NM
❑ M5-102V1	Motown Superstar Series, Vol. 2	1981	2.50	5.00	10.00
❑ M5-142V1	You're All I Need	1981	2.50	5.00	10.00
—Reissue of Tamla 284					
❑ M5-200V1	United	1981	2.50	5.00	10.00
—Reissue of Tamla 277					

TAMLA

Number	Title (A Side/B Side)	Yr	VG	VG+	NM
❑ T 277 [M]	United	1967	7.50	15.00	30.00
❑ TS 277 [S]	United	1967	6.25	12.50	25.00
❑ T 284 [M]	You're All I Need	1968	12.50	25.00	50.00
❑ TS 284 [S]	You're All I Need	1968	5.00	10.00	20.00
❑ TS 294	Easy	1969	5.00	10.00	20.00
❑ TS 302	Marvin Gaye & Tammi Terrell/Greatest Hits	1970	5.00	10.00	20.00

GAYE, MARVIN, AND MARY WELLS
MOTOWN

Number	Title (A Side/B Side)	Yr	VG	VG+	NM
❑ M 613 [M]	Together	1964	12.50	25.00	50.00
❑ 5260 ML	Together	1982	2.50	5.00	10.00

GAYE, MARVIN, AND KIM WESTON
TAMLA

Number	Title (A Side/B Side)	Yr	VG	VG+	NM
❑ T/TS 260	Side by Side	1965	—	—	—
—Canceled					
❑ T 270 [M]	Take Two	1966	7.50	15.00	30.00
❑ TS 270 [S]	Take Two	1966	10.00	20.00	40.00

GAYLE, CRYSTAL
COLUMBIA

Number	Title (A Side/B Side)	Yr	VG	VG+	NM
❑ JC 36203	Miss the Mississippi	1979	2.50	5.00	10.00
❑ PC 36203	Miss the Mississippi	198?	2.00	4.00	8.00
—Budget-line reissue					
❑ JC 36512	These Days	1980	2.50	5.00	10.00
❑ PC 36512	These Days	198?	2.00	4.00	8.00
—Budget-line reissue					
❑ FC 37438	Hollywood, Tennessee	1981	2.50	5.00	10.00
❑ PC 37438	Hollywood, Tennessee	198?	2.00	4.00	8.00
—Budget-line reissue					
❑ FC 38803	Crystal Gayle's Greatest Hits	1983	2.50	5.00	10.00

ELEKTRA

Number	Title (A Side/B Side)	Yr	VG	VG+	NM
❑ 60200	True Love	1982	2.50	5.00	10.00

LIBERTY

Number	Title (A Side/B Side)	Yr	VG	VG+	NM
❑ LMAS-858	When I Dream	1981	2.00	4.00	8.00
—Reissue of UA 858					
❑ LOO-1034	Favorites	1981	2.00	4.00	8.00
—Reissue of UA 1034					
❑ LOO-1080	A Woman's Heart	1981	2.50	5.00	10.00
❑ LN-10002	Crystal Gayle	1981	2.00	4.00	8.00
❑ LN-10003	Somebody Loves You	1981	2.00	4.00	8.00
—Budget-line reissue of UA 543					
❑ LN-10004	Crystal	1981	2.00	4.00	8.00
—Budget-line reissue of UA 614					
❑ LN-10005	We Must Believe in Magic	1981	2.00	4.00	8.00
—Budget-line reissue of UA 771					
❑ LN-10006	We Should Be Together	1980	2.00	4.00	8.00
—Budget-line reissue					
❑ LN-10150	Classic Crystal	1982	2.00	4.00	8.00
—Budget-line reissue of UA 982					
❑ LN-10227	When I Dream	1984	2.00	4.00	8.00
—Budget-line reissue					
❑ LN-10229	Favorites	1984	2.00	4.00	8.00
—Budget-line reissue					

MCA

Number	Title (A Side/B Side)	Yr	VG	VG+	NM
❑ 2334	I've Cried the Blue Right Out of My Eyes	1977	2.50	5.00	10.00
—Reissue of Decca material					
❑ 37077	I've Cried the Blue Right Out of My Eyes	198?	2.00	4.00	8.00
—Budget-line reissue					

MOBILE FIDELITY

Number	Title (A Side/B Side)	Yr	VG	VG+	NM
❑ 1-043	We Must Believe in Magic	1981	5.00	10.00	20.00
—Audiophile vinyl					

NAUTILUS

Number	Title (A Side/B Side)	Yr	VG	VG+	NM
❑ NR-36	When I Dream	198?	7.50	15.00	30.00
—Audiophile vinyl					

PAIR

Number	Title (A Side/B Side)	Yr	VG	VG+	NM
❑ PDL2-1083 [(2)]	Country Pure	1986	3.00	6.00	12.00
❑ PDL2-1126 [(2)]	Musical Jewels	1986	3.00	6.00	12.00

UNITED ARTISTS

Number	Title (A Side/B Side)	Yr	VG	VG+	NM
❑ UA-LA543-G	Somebody Loves You	1975	3.00	6.00	12.00
❑ UA-LA614-G	Crystal	1976	3.00	6.00	12.00
❑ UA-LA771-G	We Must Believe in Magic	1977	2.50	5.00	10.00
❑ UA-LA858-H	When I Dream	1978	2.50	5.00	10.00
❑ UA-LA969-H	We Should Be Together	1979	2.50	5.00	10.00
❑ LOO-982	Classic Crystal	1979	2.50	5.00	10.00
❑ LOO-1034	Favorites	1980	2.50	5.00	10.00

WARNER BROS.

Number	Title (A Side/B Side)	Yr	VG	VG+	NM
❑ 23958	Cage the Songbird	1983	2.50	5.00	10.00
❑ 25154	Nobody Wants to Be Alone	1984	2.50	5.00	10.00
❑ 25405	Straight to the Heart	1986	2.50	5.00	10.00
❑ 25508	A Crystal Christmas	1986	3.75	7.50	15.00
—Original cover has decorated Christmas tree on front					
❑ 25508	A Crystal Christmas	1987	2.50	5.00	10.00
—Reissue cover has photo of Crystal Gayle on front					
❑ 25622	The Best of Crystal Gayle	1987	2.50	5.00	10.00

Number	Title (A Side/B Side)	Yr	VG	VG+	NM
❑ 25706	Nobody's Angel	1988	2.50	5.00	10.00
❑ 60200	True Love	1983	2.00	4.00	8.00
—Reissue of Elektra 60200					

GAYLE, ROZELLE
MERCURY

Number	Title (A Side/B Side)	Yr	VG	VG+	NM
❑ MG-20374 [M]	Like, Be My Guest	1958	10.00	20.00	40.00

GAYLORDS, THE
MERCURY

Number	Title (A Side/B Side)	Yr	VG	VG+	NM
❑ MG-20186 [M]	Italia	1957	7.50	15.00	30.00
❑ MG-20213 [M]	Collection of Golden Hits	1957	7.50	15.00	30.00
❑ MG-20356 [M]	Let's Have a Pizza Party	1958	5.00	10.00	20.00
❑ MG-20430 [M]	That's Amore	1959	5.00	10.00	20.00
❑ MG-20620 [M]	American Hits in Italian	1961	5.00	10.00	20.00
❑ MG-20695 [M]	The Gaylords at the Shamrock	1962	5.00	10.00	20.00
❑ MG-20742 [M]	Party Style	1963	5.00	10.00	20.00
❑ MG-25198 [10]	By Request	1955	12.50	25.00	50.00
❑ SR-60075 [S]	Let's Have a Pizza Party	1959	7.50	15.00	30.00
❑ SR-60102 [S]	That's Amore	1959	7.50	15.00	30.00
❑ SR-60620 [S]	American Hits in Italian	1961	7.50	15.00	30.00
❑ SR-60695 [S]	The Gaylords at the Shamrock	1962	6.25	12.50	25.00
❑ SR-60742 [S]	Party Style	1963	6.25	12.50	25.00

TIME

Number	Title (A Side/B Side)	Yr	VG	VG+	NM
❑ S-2109 [S]	Live at Lake Tahoe	196?	5.00	10.00	20.00
❑ S-2127 [S]	Bella Italia	196?	5.00	10.00	20.00
❑ 52109 [M]	Live at Lake Tahoe	196?	3.75	7.50	15.00
❑ 52127 [M]	Bella Italia	196?	3.75	7.50	15.00

WING

Number	Title (A Side/B Side)	Yr	VG	VG+	NM
❑ MGW-12139 [M]	Italiano Favorites	196?	3.00	6.00	12.00
❑ MGW-12278 [M]	Let's Have a Pizza Party	196?	3.00	6.00	12.00
❑ SRW-16139 [S]	Italiano Favorites	196?	3.00	6.00	12.00
❑ SRW-16278 [S]	Let's Have a Pizza Party	196?	3.00	6.00	12.00

GAYNOR, MITZI
VERVE

Number	Title (A Side/B Side)	Yr	VG	VG+	NM
❑ MGV-2110 [M]	Mitzi	1959	7.50	15.00	30.00
❑ MGV-2115 [M]	Mitzi Gaynor Sings the Lyrics of Ira Gershwin	1959	7.50	15.00	30.00
❑ MGVS-6014 [S]	Mitzi	1959	10.00	20.00	40.00
❑ MGVS-6049 [S]	Mitzi Gaynor Sings the Lyrics of Ira Gershwin	1959	10.00	20.00	40.00

GEARS, THE
PLAYGEMS

Number	Title (A Side/B Side)	Yr	VG	VG+	NM
❑ GS 6471	Rockin' at Ground Zero	1980	7.50	15.00	30.00

GEE, MATTHEW
RIVERSIDE

Number	Title (A Side/B Side)	Yr	VG	VG+	NM
❑ RLP 12-221 [M]	Jazz by Gee!	1956	20.00	40.00	80.00
—White label, blue print					
❑ RLP 12-221 [M]	Jazz by Gee!	1958	10.00	20.00	40.00
—Blue label, microphone logo at top					

GEEZINSLAW BROTHERS, THE
CAPITOL

Number	Title (A Side/B Side)	Yr	VG	VG+	NM
❑ ST-130	The Geezinslaw Brothers Are Alive	1969	5.00	10.00	20.00
❑ ST 2570 [S]	Can You Believe...The Geezinslaw Brothers!	1966	6.25	12.50	25.00
❑ T 2570 [M]	Can You Believe...The Geezinslaw Brothers!	1966	5.00	10.00	20.00
❑ ST 2771 [S]	My Dirty, Lowdown, Rotten, Cotton-Pickin' Little Darlin'	1967	6.25	12.50	25.00
❑ T 2771 [M]	My Dirty, Lowdown, Rotten, Cotton-Pickin' Little Darlin'	1967	5.00	10.00	20.00
❑ ST 2885	The Geezinslaw Brothers & "Chubby"	1968	6.25	12.50	25.00

COLUMBIA

Number	Title (A Side/B Side)	Yr	VG	VG+	NM
❑ CL 2100 [M]	The Kooky World of the Geezinslaw Brothers	1963	6.25	12.50	25.00
❑ CS 8900 [S]	The Kooky World of the Geezinslaw Brothers	1963	7.50	15.00	30.00

GEILS, J., BAND
ATLANTIC

Number	Title (A Side/B Side)	Yr	VG	VG+	NM
❑ SD 2-507 [(2)]	Live — Blow Your Face Out	1976	3.75	7.50	15.00
❑ SD 7241	"Live" — Full House	1972	3.00	6.00	12.00
❑ QD 7260 [Q]	Bloodshot	1973	5.00	10.00	20.00
❑ SD 7260	Bloodshot	1973	3.00	6.00	12.00
—Black vinyl					
❑ SD 7260	Bloodshot	1973	5.00	10.00	20.00
—Red vinyl					
❑ QD 7286 [Q]	Ladies Invited	1973	5.00	10.00	20.00
❑ SD 7286	Ladies Invited	1973	3.00	6.00	12.00
❑ 8275 [M]	The J. Geils Band	1970	10.00	20.00	40.00
—Mono is white label promo only; stereo cover with "dj copy monaural" sticker					
❑ SD 8275 [S]	The J. Geils Band	1970	3.75	7.50	15.00
❑ SD 8297	The Morning After	1971	3.00	6.00	12.00
❑ QD 18107 [Q]	Nightmares and Other Tales from the Vinyl Jungle	1974	5.00	10.00	20.00
❑ SD 18107	Nightmares and Other Tales from the Vinyl Jungle	1974	3.00	6.00	12.00
❑ SD 18147	Hotline	1975	3.00	6.00	12.00
❑ SD 19103	Monkey Island	1977	3.00	6.00	12.00
—As "Geils"					
❑ SD 19234	Best of the J. Geils Band	1979	2.50	5.00	10.00
❑ SD 19284	Best of the J. Geils Band — 2	1980	2.50	5.00	10.00

EMI AMERICA

Number	Title (A Side/B Side)	Yr	VG	VG+	NM
❑ SN-16316	Sanctuary	1985	2.00	4.00	8.00
—Reissue					
❑ SN-16373	Showtime!	1986	2.00	4.00	8.00
—Reissue					
❑ SN-16374	Freeze-Frame	1986	2.00	4.00	8.00
—Reissue					
❑ SN-16375	Love Stinks	1986	2.00	4.00	8.00
—Reissue					
❑ SO-17006	Sanctuary	1978	2.50	5.00	10.00
❑ SOO-17016	Love Stinks	1980	2.50	5.00	10.00
❑ SOO-17062	Freeze-Frame	1981	2.50	5.00	10.00
❑ SO-17087	Showtime!	1982	2.50	5.00	10.00

G

Number	Title (A Side/B Side)	Yr	VG	VG+	NM
❑ SJ-17137	You're Gettin' Even While I'm Gettin' Odd	1984	2.00	4.00	8.00
❑ ST-17174	Flashback — The Best of the J. Geils Band	1985	2.00	4.00	8.00

NAUTILUS

Number	Title (A Side/B Side)	Yr	VG	VG+	NM
❑ NR-25	Love Stinks	1982	5.00	10.00	20.00

—*Audiophile vinyl*

GELLER, HERB
ATCO

Number	Title (A Side/B Side)	Yr	VG	VG+	NM
❑ 33-109 [M]	Gypsy	1959	10.00	20.00	40.00

EMARCY

Number	Title (A Side/B Side)	Yr	VG	VG+	NM
❑ MG-26045 [10]	Herb Geller Plays	1954	30.00	60.00	120.00
❑ MG-36024 [M]	The Gellers	1955	25.00	50.00	100.00
❑ MG-36040 [M]	The Herb Geller Sextette	1955	20.00	40.00	80.00
❑ MG-36045 [M]	Herb Geller Plays	1955	20.00	40.00	80.00

JOSIE

Number	Title (A Side/B Side)	Yr	VG	VG+	NM
❑ JLPS-3502 [S]	Alto Saxophone	1962	5.00	10.00	20.00
❑ JOZ-3502 [M]	Alto Saxophone	1962	6.25	12.50	25.00

JUBILEE

Number	Title (A Side/B Side)	Yr	VG	VG+	NM
❑ JLP-1044 [M]	Fire in the West	1957	12.50	25.00	50.00
❑ SDJLP-1044 [S]	Fire in the West	1959	10.00	20.00	40.00
❑ JG-1044 [M]	Stax of Sax	1959	12.50	25.00	50.00

GELLER, LORRAINE
DOT

Number	Title (A Side/B Side)	Yr	VG	VG+	NM
❑ DLP-3174 [M]	Lorraine Geller at the Piano	1959	125.00	250.00	500.00

GENE AND DEBBE
TRX

Number	Title (A Side/B Side)	Yr	VG	VG+	NM
❑ 1001	Here and Now	1968	6.25	12.50	25.00

GENE LOVES JEZEBEL
GEFFEN

Number	Title (A Side/B Side)	Yr	VG	VG+	NM
❑ 141 [DJ]	Discover Interview	1986	6.25	12.50	25.00
❑ 4192 [EP]	Remix Sampler	1990	5.00	10.00	20.00

—*Promo-only collection*

Number	Title (A Side/B Side)	Yr	VG	VG+	NM
❑ GHS 24118	Discover	1986	2.50	5.00	10.00
❑ GHS 24165	Promise	1988	2.50	5.00	10.00

—*First American issue of 1983 U.K. debut*

Number	Title (A Side/B Side)	Yr	VG	VG+	NM
❑ GHS 24171	The House of Dolls	1988	2.50	5.00	10.00
❑ GHS 24260	Kiss of Life	1990	3.00	6.00	12.00

RELATIVITY

Number	Title (A Side/B Side)	Yr	VG	VG+	NM
❑ EMC 8036	Immigrant	1985	2.50	5.00	10.00
❑ 8075 [EP]	Desire	1985	2.00	4.00	8.00

GENERATION BAND, THE
NAUTILUS

Number	Title (A Side/B Side)	Yr	VG	VG+	NM
❑ NR-62	Soft Shoulder	198?	10.00	20.00	40.00

—*Audiophile vinyl*

GENESIS
Also see PHIL COLLINS; PETER GABRIEL.
ABC

Number	Title (A Side/B Side)	Yr	VG	VG+	NM
❑ X-816	Trespass	1971	3.00	6.00	12.00

—*Reissue of Impulse album*

ABC IMPULSE!

Number	Title (A Side/B Side)	Yr	VG	VG+	NM
❑ ASD-9205	Trespass	1971	7.50	15.00	30.00

ATCO

Number	Title (A Side/B Side)	Yr	VG	VG+	NM
❑ SD 38-100	Wind & Wuthering	1978	2.50	5.00	10.00
❑ SD 38-101	A Trick of the Tail	1978	2.50	5.00	10.00
❑ SD 36-129	A Trick of the Tail	1976	3.00	6.00	12.00
❑ SD 36-144	Wind & Wuthering	1977	3.00	6.00	12.00
❑ SD 2-401 [(2)]	The Lamb Lies Down on Broadway	1974	3.75	7.50	15.00

—*Originals have yellow labels (other labels worth less)*

ATLANTIC

Number	Title (A Side/B Side)	Yr	VG	VG+	NM
❑ SD 2-2000 [(2)]	Three Sides Live	1982	3.00	6.00	12.00
❑ SD 2-9002 [(2)]	Seconds Out	1977	3.00	6.00	12.00
❑ SD 16014	Duke	1980	2.50	5.00	10.00
❑ SD 19173	…And Then There Were Three	1978	2.50	5.00	10.00
❑ SD 19277	Selling England by the Pound	1981	2.00	4.00	8.00

—*Reissue of Charisma LP of same name*

Number	Title (A Side/B Side)	Yr	VG	VG+	NM
❑ SD 19313	Abacab	1981	2.50	5.00	10.00

—*Released with four different covers, lettered "A" through "D" on spine; no difference in value*

Number	Title (A Side/B Side)	Yr	VG	VG+	NM
❑ 80030	Nursery Cryme	1982	2.00	4.00	8.00

—*Reissue of Charisma LP of same name*

Number	Title (A Side/B Side)	Yr	VG	VG+	NM
❑ 80116	Genesis	1983	2.00	4.00	8.00
❑ 81641	Invisible Touch	1986	2.00	4.00	8.00
❑ 81848	Foxtrot	1988	2.50	5.00	10.00

—*Reissue of Charisma LP of the same name*

Number	Title (A Side/B Side)	Yr	VG	VG+	NM
❑ 81855	Genesis Live	1988	2.50	5.00	10.00

—*Reissue of Charisma LP of the same name*

BUDDAH

Number	Title (A Side/B Side)	Yr	VG	VG+	NM
❑ BDS-5659	The Best of Genesis	1976	3.75	7.50	15.00

CHARISMA

Number	Title (A Side/B Side)	Yr	VG	VG+	NM
❑ CAS-1052	Nursery Cryme	1971	3.75	7.50	15.00
❑ CAS-1052	Nursery Cryme	2000	6.25	12.50	25.00

—*Classic Records reissue on 180-gram vinyl*

Number	Title (A Side/B Side)	Yr	VG	VG+	NM
❑ CAS-1058	Foxtrot	1972	3.75	7.50	15.00
❑ CAS-1058	Foxtrot	2001	6.25	12.50	25.00

—*Classic Records reissue on 180-gram vinyl*

Number	Title (A Side/B Side)	Yr	VG	VG+	NM
❑ CAS-1666	Genesis Live	1974	3.75	7.50	15.00
❑ CAS-1666	Genesis Live	2001	6.25	12.50	25.00

—*Classic Records reissue on 180-gram vinyl*

Number	Title (A Side/B Side)	Yr	VG	VG+	NM
❑ CA-2701 [(2)]	Nursery Cryme/Foxtrot	1976	3.75	7.50	15.00

—*Repackage of the individual albums of these names*

Number	Title (A Side/B Side)	Yr	VG	VG+	NM
❑ CAS-6060	Selling England by the Pound	1973	3.75	7.50	15.00
❑ FC-6060	Selling England by the Pound	2001	6.25	12.50	25.00

—*Classic Records reissue on 180-gram vinyl*

LONDON

Number	Title (A Side/B Side)	Yr	VG	VG+	NM
❑ PS 643	From Genesis to Revelation	1974	5.00	10.00	20.00

—*First US release of debut album*

Number	Title (A Side/B Side)	Yr	VG	VG+	NM
❑ LC-50006	In the Beginning	1977	3.00	6.00	12.00

Number	Title (A Side/B Side)	Yr	VG	VG+	NM
❑ 820322-1	In the Beginning	198?	2.00	4.00	8.00

—*Reissue of London 50006*

MCA

Number	Title (A Side/B Side)	Yr	VG	VG+	NM
❑ 816	Trespass	1979	2.50	5.00	10.00

—*Reissue of ABC album*

Number	Title (A Side/B Side)	Yr	VG	VG+	NM
❑ 37151	Trespass	198?	2.00	4.00	8.00

—*Reissue of MCA 816*

MOBILE FIDELITY

Number	Title (A Side/B Side)	Yr	VG	VG+	NM
❑ 1-062	A Trick of the Tail	1981	12.50	25.00	50.00

—*Audiophile vinyl*

GENTLE SOUL
EPIC

Number	Title (A Side/B Side)	Yr	VG	VG+	NM
❑ BN 26374	Gentle Soul	1969	25.00	50.00	100.00

GENTRY, BOBBIE
CAPITOL

Number	Title (A Side/B Side)	Yr	VG	VG+	NM
❑ ST-155	Touch 'Em with Love	1969	3.75	7.50	15.00
❑ SKAO-381	Bobbie Gentry's Greatest!	1969	3.75	7.50	15.00
❑ SM-381	Bobbie Gentry's Greatest!	197?	2.00	4.00	8.00
❑ ST-428	Fancy	1970	3.75	7.50	15.00
❑ ST-494	Patchwork	1970	3.75	7.50	15.00
❑ STBB-704 [(2)]	Sittin' Pretty/Tobacco Road	1971	3.75	7.50	15.00
❑ SM-2830	Ode to Billie Joe	197?	2.00	4.00	8.00
❑ ST 2830 [S]	Ode to Billie Joe	1967	3.75	7.50	15.00
❑ T 2830 [M]	Ode to Billie Joe	1967	5.00	10.00	20.00
❑ ST 2842 [S]	The Delta Sweete	1968	3.75	7.50	15.00
❑ T 2842 [M]	The Delta Sweete	1968	6.25	12.50	25.00
❑ ST 2964	The Local Gentry	1968	3.75	7.50	15.00

GENTRYS, THE
MGM

Number	Title (A Side/B Side)	Yr	VG	VG+	NM
❑ GAS-127	The Gentrys (Golden Archive Series)	1970	5.00	10.00	20.00
❑ E-4336 [M]	Keep On Dancing	1965	6.25	12.50	25.00
❑ SE-4336 [P]	Keep On Dancing	1965	7.50	15.00	30.00
❑ E-4346 [M]	Gentry Time	1966	5.00	10.00	20.00
❑ SE-4346 [S]	Gentry Time	1966	6.25	12.50	25.00

SUN

Number	Title (A Side/B Side)	Yr	VG	VG+	NM
❑ LP-117	The Gentrys	1970	7.50	15.00	30.00

GEORDIE
MGM

Number	Title (A Side/B Side)	Yr	VG	VG+	NM
❑ SE-4903	Hope You Like It	1973	7.50	15.00	30.00

GEORGE, BARBARA
A.F.O.

Number	Title (A Side/B Side)	Yr	VG	VG+	NM
❑ LP 5001 [M]	I Know (You Don't Love Me No More)	1962	62.50	125.00	250.00

GERHARD, RAMONA
SOMA

Number	Title (A Side/B Side)	Yr	VG	VG+	NM
❑ MG 1202	Christmas in Hi-Fi with Ramona Gerhard	195?	5.00	10.00	20.00

—*Red vinyl*

GERMS, THE
MOHAWK

Number	Title (A Side/B Side)	Yr	VG	VG+	NM
❑ SCALP-001	Recorded Live at the Whiskey, June, 1977	1981	5.00	10.00	20.00

—*Second edition: Un-numbered edition, with sticker*

Number	Title (A Side/B Side)	Yr	VG	VG+	NM
❑ SCALP-001	Recorded Live at the Whiskey, June, 1977	1981	12.50	25.00	50.00

—*First edition: Numbered edition, with sticker*

SLASH

Number	Title (A Side/B Side)	Yr	VG	VG+	NM
❑ SR-103	(GI)	1981	3.75	7.50	15.00
❑ SREP 108	What We Do Is Secret	1981	3.75	7.50	15.00
❑ 23932	(GI)	1983	3.00	6.00	12.00

—*Reissue*

GERONIMO BLACK
UNI

Number	Title (A Side/B Side)	Yr	VG	VG+	NM
❑ 73132	Geronimo Black	1972	6.25	12.50	25.00

GERRY AND THE PACEMAKERS
CAPITOL

Number	Title (A Side/B Side)	Yr	VG	VG+	NM
❑ SM-11898 [B]	The Best of Gerry and the Pacemakers	1979	2.00	4.00	8.00

—*All stereo except "I Like It," "Away from You" and "I'm the One," which are mono.*

LAURIE

Number	Title (A Side/B Side)	Yr	VG	VG+	NM
❑ LLP-2024 [M]	Don't Let the Sun Catch You Crying	1964	7.50	15.00	30.00
❑ SLP-2024 [R]	Don't Let the Sun Catch You Crying	1964	6.25	12.50	25.00
❑ LLP-2027 [M]	Gerry and the Pacemakers' Second Album	1964	7.50	15.00	30.00
❑ SLP-2027 [R]	Gerry and the Pacemakers' Second Album	1964	6.25	12.50	25.00
❑ LLP-2030 [M]	I'll Be There	1964	7.50	15.00	30.00
❑ SLP-2030 [R]	I'll Be There	1964	6.25	12.50	25.00
❑ LLP-2031 [M]	Greatest Hits	1965	6.25	12.50	25.00
❑ SLP-2031 [R]	Greatest Hits	1965	3.75	7.50	15.00
❑ LLP-2037 [M]	Girl on a Swing	1966	6.25	12.50	25.00
❑ SLP-2037 [S]	Girl on a Swing	1966	5.00	10.00	20.00
❑ DT 90384 [R]	Greatest Hits	1965	6.25	12.50	25.00

—*Capitol Record Club edition*

Number	Title (A Side/B Side)	Yr	VG	VG+	NM
❑ T 90384 [M]	Greatest Hits	1965	6.25	12.50	25.00

—*Capitol Record Club edition*

Number	Title (A Side/B Side)	Yr	VG	VG+	NM
❑ DT 90555 [R]	Don't Let the Sun Catch You Crying	1964	7.50	15.00	30.00

—*Capitol Record Club edition*

Number	Title (A Side/B Side)	Yr	VG	VG+	NM
❑ T 90555 [M]	Don't Let the Sun Catch You Crying	1964	10.00	20.00	40.00

—*Capitol Record Club edition*

UNITED ARTISTS

Number	Title (A Side/B Side)	Yr	VG	VG+	NM
❑ UAL 3387 [M]	Ferry Cross the Mersey	1965	6.25	12.50	25.00

—*Also contains incidental music by George Martin*

Number	Title (A Side/B Side)	Yr	VG	VG+	NM
❑ UAS 6387 [S]	Ferry Cross the Mersey	1965	10.00	20.00	40.00
❑ ST 90812 [S]	Ferry Cross the Mersey	1965	12.50	25.00	50.00

—*Capitol Record Club edition*

Number	Title (A Side/B Side)	Yr	VG	VG+	NM
❑ T 90812 [M]	Ferry Cross the Mersey	1965	10.00	20.00	40.00

—*Capitol Record Club edition*

Number	Title (A Side/B Side)	Yr	VG	VG+	NM

GETZ, EDDIE
MGM

Number	Title (A Side/B Side)	Yr	VG	VG+	NM
❏ E-3462 [M]	The Eddie Getz Quintette	1957	12.50	25.00	50.00

GETZ, STAN
AMERICAN RECORDING SOCIETY

Number	Title (A Side/B Side)	Yr	VG	VG+	NM
❏ G-407 [M]	Cool Jazz of Stan Getz	1956	10.00	20.00	40.00
❏ G-428 [M]	Intimate Portrait	1957	10.00	20.00	40.00
❏ G-443 [M]	Stan Getz '57	1957	10.00	20.00	40.00

BLUE RIBBON

❏ BR-8012 [M]	Rhythms	1961	5.00	10.00	20.00

CLEF

❏ MGC-137 [10]	Stan Getz Plays	1953	50.00	100.00	200.00
❏ MGC-143 [10]	The Artistry of Stan Getz	1953	50.00	100.00	200.00

CROWN

❏ CLP-5002 [M]	Groovin' High	1957	10.00	20.00	40.00

—Reissue of Modern 1202

❏ CLP-5284 [M]	Groovin' High	196?	5.00	10.00	20.00

—Reissue of 5002

DALE

❏ 21 [10]	In Retrospect	1951	75.00	150.00	300.00

JAZZTONE

❏ J-1230 [M]	Stan Getz	1956	10.00	20.00	40.00
❏ J-1240 [M]	Stan Getz '57	1957	10.00	20.00	40.00

METRONOME

❏ BLP-6 [M]	The Sound	1956	12.50	25.00	50.00

MODERN

❏ MLP-1202 [M]	Groovin' High	1956	37.50	75.00	150.00

MOSAIC

❏ M4-131 [(4)]	The Complete Recordings of the Stan Getz Quintet with Jimmy Raney	199?	15.00	30.00	60.00

NEW JAZZ

❏ NJLP-8214 [M]	Long Island Sound	1959	15.00	30.00	60.00

—Reissue of Prestige 7002; purple label

❏ NJLP-8214 [M]	Long Island Sound	1965	6.25	12.50	25.00

—Blue label with trident logo on right

NORGRAN

❏ MGN-1000 [M]	Interpretations by the Stan Getz Quintet	1954	30.00	60.00	120.00
❏ MGN-1008 [M]	Interpretations by the Stan Getz Quintet #2	1954	30.00	60.00	120.00
❏ MGN-1029 [M]	Interpretations by the Stan Getz Quintet #3	1955	37.50	75.00	150.00
❏ MGN-1032 [M]	West Coast Jazz	1955	37.50	75.00	150.00
❏ MGN-1042 [M]	Stan Getz Plays	1955	25.00	50.00	100.00

—Reissue of Clef 137 and 143 on one 12-inch LP

❏ MGN-1087 [M]	Stan Getz '56	1956	25.00	50.00	100.00
❏ MGN-1088 [M]	More West Coast Jazz with Stan Getz	1956	25.00	50.00	100.00
❏ MGN-2000-2 [(2)M]	Stan Getz at the Shrine	1955	50.00	100.00	200.00

—Boxed set with booklet

PRESTIGE

❏ PRLP-102 [10]	Stan Getz and the Tenor Sax Stars	1951	50.00	100.00	200.00
❏ PRLP-104 [10]	Stan Getz, Volume 2	1951	50.00	100.00	200.00
❏ PRLP-108 [10]	Stan Getz-Lee Konitz	1951	50.00	100.00	200.00
❏ PRLP-7002 [M]	Stan Getz Quartets	1955	25.00	50.00	100.00
❏ PRLP-7255 [M]	Early Stan	1963	10.00	20.00	40.00
❏ PRST-7255 [R]	Early Stan	1963	5.00	10.00	20.00
❏ PRLP-7256 [M]	Stan Getz' Greatest Hits	1963	10.00	20.00	40.00
❏ PRST-7256 [R]	Stan Getz' Greatest Hits	1963	5.00	10.00	20.00
❏ PRLP-7337 [M]	Stan Getz' Greatest Hits	1967	6.25	12.50	25.00

—Reissue of PRLP 7256

❏ PRLP-7434 [M]	Getz Plays Jazz Classics	1967	6.25	12.50	25.00

—Reissue of PRLP 7255

❏ PRLP-7516 [M]	Preservation	1967	6.25	12.50	25.00

ROOST

❏ RK-103 [(2)M]	The Stan Getz Years	1964	10.00	20.00	40.00
❏ SRK-103 [(2)R]	The Stan Getz Years	1964	6.25	12.50	25.00
❏ R-402 [10]	Stan Getz	1950	50.00	100.00	200.00
❏ R-404 [10]	Stan Getz and the Swedish All Stars	1951	50.00	100.00	200.00
❏ R-407 [10]	Jazz at Storyville	1952	37.50	75.00	150.00
❏ R-411 [10]	Jazz at Storyville, Volume 2	1952	37.50	75.00	150.00
❏ R-417 [10]	Chamber Music	1953	37.50	75.00	150.00
❏ R-420 [10]	Jazz at Storyville, Volume 3	1954	37.50	75.00	150.00
❏ R-423 [10]	Split Kick	1954	37.50	75.00	150.00
❏ LP-2207 [M]	The Sounds of Stan Getz	1956	20.00	40.00	80.00

—Reissue of R-402

❏ LP-2209 [M]	Storyville	1956	20.00	40.00	80.00

—Reissue of R-407 and half of R-411

❏ LP-2225 [M]	Storyville, Volume 2	1957	20.00	40.00	80.00

—Reissue of R-423 and the other half of R-411

❏ LP-2249 [M]	The Greatest of Stan Getz	1963	7.50	15.00	30.00
❏ LP-2251 [M]	Moonlight in Vermont	1963	7.50	15.00	30.00
❏ LP-2255 [M]	Modern World	1963	7.50	15.00	30.00
❏ LP-2258 [M]	Getz Age	1963	7.50	15.00	30.00

SAVOY

❏ MG-9004 [10]	New Sounds in Modern Music	1951	75.00	150.00	300.00

VERVE

❏ MGV-8028 [M]	West Coast Jazz	1957	12.50	25.00	50.00

—Reissue of Norgran 1032

❏ V-8028 [M]	West Coast Jazz	1961	5.00	10.00	20.00
❏ MGV-8029 [M]	Stan Getz '57	1957	12.50	25.00	50.00

—Reissue of Norgran 1087 with revised title

❏ V-8029 [M]	Stan Getz '57	1961	5.00	10.00	20.00

—Reissue of MGV-8029

❏ MGV-8122 [M]	Interpretations by the Stan Getz Quintet #3	1957	12.50	25.00	50.00

—Reissue of Norgran 1029

❏ V-8122 [M]	Interpretations by the Stan Getz Quintet #3	1961	5.00	10.00	20.00

—Reissue of MGV-8122

❏ MGV-8133 [M]	Stan Getz Plays	1957	12.50	25.00	50.00

—Reissue of Norgran 1042

❏ V-8133 [M]	Stan Getz Plays	1961	5.00	10.00	20.00
❏ MGV-8177 [M]	More West Coast Jazz with Stan Getz	1957	12.50	25.00	50.00

—Reissue of Norgran 1088

❏ V-8177 [M]	More West Coast Jazz with Stan Getz	1961	5.00	10.00	20.00

—Reissue of MGV-8177

❏ MGV-8188-2 [M]	Stan Getz at the Shrine	1957	25.00	50.00	100.00

—Reissue of Norgran 2000-2

❏ V-8188-2 [(2)M]	Stan Getz at the Shrine	1961	6.25	12.50	25.00

—Reissue of MGV-8188-2

❏ MGV-8200 [M]	Stan Getz and the Cool Sounds	1957	12.50	25.00	50.00

—Reissue of American Recording Society 407 with new name

❏ V-8200 [M]	Stan Getz and the Cool Sounds	1961	5.00	10.00	20.00

—Reissue of MGV-8200

❏ MGV-8213 [M]	Stan Getz in Stockholm	1958	12.50	25.00	50.00

—Reissue of American Recording Society 428 with new name

❏ V-8213 [M]	Stan Getz in Stockholm	1961	5.00	10.00	20.00
❏ MGV-8263 [M]	Stan Meets Chet	1958	15.00	30.00	60.00

—With Chet Baker

❏ V-8263 [M]	Stan Meets Chet	1961	5.00	10.00	20.00

—Reissue of MGV-8263

❏ MGV-8294 [M]	The Steamer	1959	12.50	25.00	50.00
❏ V-8294 [M]	The Steamer	1961	5.00	10.00	20.00

—Reissue of MGV-8294

❏ MGV-8296 [M]	Award Winner	1959	12.50	25.00	50.00
❏ V-8296 [M]	Award Winner	1961	5.00	10.00	20.00

—Reissue of MGV-8296

❏ MGV-8321 [M]	The Soft Swing	1959	12.50	25.00	50.00
❏ V-8321 [M]	The Soft Swing	1961	5.00	10.00	20.00

—Reissue of MGV-8321

❏ MGV-8331 [M]	Imported from Europe	1959	12.50	25.00	50.00
❏ V-8331 [M]	Imported from Europe	1961	5.00	10.00	20.00

—Reissue of MGV-8331

❏ MGV-8379 [M]	Cool Velvet — Stan Getz and Strings	1960	12.50	25.00	50.00
❏ V-8379 [M]	Cool Velvet — Stan Getz and Strings	1961	5.00	10.00	20.00

—Reissue of MGV-8379

❏ V6-8379 [S]	Cool Velvet — Stan Getz and Strings	1961	5.00	10.00	20.00
❏ MGV-8393-2 [(2)M]	Stan Getz At Large	1960	15.00	30.00	60.00
❏ V-8393-2 [(2)M]	Stan Getz At Large	1961	6.25	12.50	25.00

—Reissue of MGV-8393-2

❏ V-8412 [M]	Focus	1961	6.25	12.50	25.00
❏ V6-8412 [S]	Focus	1961	5.00	10.00	20.00
❏ V-8494 [M]	Big Band Bossa Nova	1962	5.00	10.00	20.00
❏ V6-8494 [S]	Big Band Bossa Nova	1962	6.25	12.50	25.00
❏ V-8523 [M]	Jazz Samba Encore!	1963	5.00	10.00	20.00

—With Luiz Bonfa

❏ V6-8523 [S]	Jazz Samba Encore!	1963	6.25	12.50	25.00

—With Luiz Bonfa

❏ V6-8554 [S]	Reflections	1964	5.00	10.00	20.00
❏ V6-8600 [S]	Getz Au Go Go	1964	5.00	10.00	20.00
❏ V-8693 [M]	Sweet Rain	1967	6.25	12.50	25.00
❏ V-8707 [M]	Voices	1967	6.25	12.50	25.00
❏ V-8719 [M]	The Best of Stan Getz	1967	6.25	12.50	25.00
❏ V-8752 [M]	What the World Needs Now — Stan Getz Plays Bacharach and David	1968	7.50	15.00	30.00
❏ V6-8802-2 [(2)]	Dynasty	1971	5.00	10.00	20.00
❏ 823611-1 [(5)]	The Girl from Ipanema: The Bossa Nova Years	1984	12.50	25.00	50.00

GETZ, STAN, AND LAURINDO ALMEIDA
VERVE

❏ V6-8665 [S]	Stan Getz with Guest Artist Laurindo Almeida	1965	5.00	10.00	20.00

GETZ, STAN, AND BOB BROOKMEYER
VERVE

❏ V-8418 [M]	Stan Getz and Bob Brookmeyer (Recorded Fall 1961)	1961	5.00	10.00	20.00
❏ V6-8418 [S]	Stan Getz and Bob Brookmeyer (Recorded Fall 1961)	1961	5.00	10.00	20.00

GETZ, STAN, AND CHARLIE BYRD
DCC COMPACT CLASSICS

❏ LPZ-2011	Jazz Samba	1995	6.25	12.50	25.00

—Audiophile vinyl

VERVE

❏ V-8432 [M]	Jazz Samba	1962	5.00	10.00	20.00
❏ V6-8432 [S]	Jazz Samba	1962	6.25	12.50	25.00

—With "MGM Records" on label print

❏ V6-8432 [S]	Jazz Samba	1976	3.00	6.00	12.00

—"Manufactured and Marketed by Polydor Incorporated" on label

GETZ, STAN, AND JOAO GILBERTO
MOBILE FIDELITY

❏ 1-208	Getz/Gilberto	1994	12.50	25.00	50.00

—Audiophile vinyl

VERVE

❏ V6-8545 [S]	Getz/Gilberto	1964	5.00	10.00	20.00
❏ V6-8623 [S]	Getz/Gilberto #2	1965	5.00	10.00	20.00

GETZ, STAN; DIZZY GILLESPIE; SONNY STITT
VERVE

❏ MGV-8198 [M]	For Musicians Only	1958	20.00	40.00	80.00
❏ V-8198 [M]	For Musicians Only	1961	6.25	12.50	25.00

GETZ, STAN, AND WARDELL GRAY
DAWN

❏ DLP-1126 [M]	Tenors Anyone?	1958	20.00	40.00	80.00

SEECO

❏ SLP-7 [10]	Highlights in Modern Jazz	1954	50.00	100.00	200.00

G

Number	Title (A Side/B Side)	Yr	VG	VG+	NM

GETZ, STAN, AND J.J. JOHNSON
VERVE
Number	Title (A Side/B Side)	Yr	VG	VG+	NM
❑ MGVS-6027 [S]	Stan Getz and J.J. Johnson at the Opera House	1960	10.00	20.00	40.00
❑ MGV-8265 [M]	Stan Getz and J.J. Johnson at the Opera House	1958	12.50	25.00	50.00
❑ V-8265 [M]	Stan Getz and J.J. Johnson at the Opera House	1961	5.00	10.00	20.00
❑ V-8490 [M]	Stan Getz and J.J. Johnson at the Opera House	1962	3.75	7.50	15.00

GETZ, STAN, AND OSCAR PETERSON
VERVE
Number	Title (A Side/B Side)	Yr	VG	VG+	NM
❑ MGV-8251 [M]	Stan Getz and the Oscar Peterson Trio	1958	12.50	25.00	50.00
❑ V-8251 [M]	Stan Getz and the Oscar Peterson Trio	1961	5.00	10.00	20.00
—Reissue of MGV-8251					
❑ MGV-8348 [M]	Stan Getz with Gerry Mulligan and the Oscar Peterson Trio	1959	12.50	25.00	50.00
❑ V-8348 [M]	Stan Getz with Gerry Mulligan and the Oscar Peterson Trio	1961	5.00	10.00	20.00
—Reissue of MGV-8348					

GETZ, STAN, AND ZOOT SIMS
PRESTIGE
Number	Title (A Side/B Side)	Yr	VG	VG+	NM
❑ PRLP-7022 [M]	The Brothers	1956	37.50	75.00	150.00
❑ PRLP-7252 [M]	The Brothers	1963	12.50	25.00	50.00

GHOULS, THE
CAPITOL
Number	Title (A Side/B Side)	Yr	VG	VG+	NM
❑ ST 2215 [S]	Dracula's Deuce	1965	37.50	75.00	150.00
❑ T 2215 [M]	Dracula's Deuce	1965	30.00	60.00	120.00

GIANT CRAB, THE
UNI
Number	Title (A Side/B Side)	Yr	VG	VG+	NM
❑ 73037	A Giant Crab Comes Forth	1968	6.25	12.50	25.00
❑ 73057	Cool It, Helios	1969	6.25	12.50	25.00

GIBB, ROBIN
ATCO
Number	Title (A Side/B Side)	Yr	VG	VG+	NM
❑ SD 33-323	Robin's Reign	1969	5.00	10.00	20.00
MIRAGE
| ❑ 90170 | Secret Agent | 1984 | 2.00 | 4.00 | 8.00 |
POLYDOR
| ❑ 810896-1 | How Old Are You? | 1983 | 2.50 | 5.00 | 10.00 |

GIBBS, GEORGIA
BELL
Number	Title (A Side/B Side)	Yr	VG	VG+	NM
❑ 6000 [M]	Call Me Georgia Gibbs	1966	3.75	7.50	15.00
❑ 6000S [S]	Call Me Georgia Gibbs	1966	5.00	10.00	20.00
CORAL
| ❑ CRL 56037 [10] | Ballin' the Jack | 1951 | 12.50 | 25.00 | 50.00 |
| ❑ CRL 57183 [M] | Her Nibs | 1957 | 10.00 | 20.00 | 40.00 |
EMARCY
| ❑ MG-36103 [M] | Swingin' with Gibbs | 1957 | 7.50 | 15.00 | 30.00 |
EPIC
| ❑ LN 24059 [M] | Georgia Gibbs' Greatest Hits | 1963 | 3.75 | 7.50 | 15.00 |
| ❑ BN 26059 [S] | Georgia Gibbs' Greatest Hits | 1963 | 5.00 | 10.00 | 20.00 |
IMPERIAL
| ❑ LP-9107 [M] | Something's Gotta Give | 1960 | 5.00 | 10.00 | 20.00 |
| ❑ LP-12064 [S] | Something's Gotta Give | 1960 | 6.25 | 12.50 | 25.00 |
MERCURY
❑ MG-20071 [M]	Music and Memories	1955	10.00	20.00	40.00
❑ MG-20114 [M]	Song Favorites	1956	10.00	20.00	40.00
❑ MG-20170 [M]	Swingin' with Her Nibs	1956	10.00	20.00	40.00
❑ MG-25175 [10]	Georgia Gibbs Sings Oldies	1953	12.50	25.00	50.00
❑ MG-25199 [10]	The Man That Got Away	1954	12.50	25.00	50.00
ROYALE
| ❑ 18126 [10] | Georgia Gibbs and Orchestra | 195? | 10.00 | 20.00 | 40.00 |
SUNSET
| ❑ SUM-1113 [M] | Her Nibs, Miss Georgia Gibbs | 196? | 3.75 | 7.50 | 15.00 |
| ❑ SUS-5113 [S] | Her Nibs, Miss Georgia Gibbs | 196? | 3.75 | 7.50 | 15.00 |

GIBBS, MICHAEL
DERAM
Number	Title (A Side/B Side)	Yr	VG	VG+	NM
❑ DES 18048	Michael Gibbs	1970	5.00	10.00	20.00

GIBBS, TERRY
BRUNSWICK
Number	Title (A Side/B Side)	Yr	VG	VG+	NM
❑ BL 54009 [M]	Terry	1955	12.50	25.00	50.00
❑ BL 56055 [10]	Terry Gibbs Quartet	1954	25.00	50.00	100.00
DOT
| ❑ DLP-25726 [S] | Reza | 1966 | 5.00 | 10.00 | 20.00 |
EMARCY
❑ MG-36047 [M]	Terry Gibbs	1956	12.50	25.00	50.00
❑ MG-36064 [M]	Vibes on Velvet	1956	12.50	25.00	50.00
❑ MG-36075 [M]	Mallets A-Plenty	1956	12.50	25.00	50.00
❑ MG-36103 [M]	Swingin' Terry Gibbs	1957	12.50	25.00	50.00
❑ MG-36128 [M]	Terry Plays the Duke	1958	12.50	25.00	50.00
❑ MG-36138 [M]	Steve Allen's All Stars	1958	12.50	25.00	50.00
❑ MG-36148 [M]	More Vibes on Velvet	1959	12.50	25.00	50.00
❑ SR-80004 [S]	Steve Allen's All Stars	1959	10.00	20.00	40.00
IMPULSE!
| ❑ A-58 [M] | Take It from Me | 1964 | 6.25 | 12.50 | 25.00 |
| ❑ AS-58 [S] | Take It from Me | 1964 | 7.50 | 15.00 | 30.00 |
INTERLUDE
| ❑ MO-506 [M] | Vibrations | 1959 | 10.00 | 20.00 | 40.00 |
| ❑ ST-1006 [S] | Vibrations | 1959 | 7.50 | 15.00 | 30.00 |
LIMELIGHT
| ❑ LM-82005 [M] | El Nutto | 1964 | 5.00 | 10.00 | 20.00 |
| ❑ LS-86005 [S] | El Nutto | 1964 | 6.25 | 12.50 | 25.00 |

MAINSTREAM
Number	Title (A Side/B Side)	Yr	VG	VG+	NM
❑ S-6048 [S]	It's Time We Met	1965	5.00	10.00	20.00
MERCURY
❑ MG-20440 [M]	Launching a New Sound in Music	1959	10.00	20.00	40.00
❑ MG-20518 [M]	Steve Allen's All Stars	1960	7.50	15.00	30.00
❑ SR-60112 [S]	Launching a New Sound in Music	1959	7.50	15.00	30.00
❑ SR-60195 [S]	Steve Allen's All Stars	1960	6.25	12.50	25.00
❑ SR-60704 [S]	Explosion!	1962	5.00	10.00	20.00
❑ SR-60812 [S]	Jewish Melodies in Jazztime	1963	5.00	10.00	20.00
MODE
| ❑ LP-123 [M] | A Jazz Band Ball | 1957 | 20.00 | 40.00 | 80.00 |
ROOST
| ❑ RS-2260 [S] | Latino | 1965 | 5.00 | 10.00 | 20.00 |
TIME
❑ S-2105 [S]	Hootenanny My Way	1963	7.50	15.00	30.00
❑ S-2120 [S]	Terry Gibbs with Sal Nistico	196?	6.25	12.50	25.00
❑ 52105 [M]	Hootenanny My Way	1963	6.25	12.50	25.00
❑ 52120 [M]	Terry Gibbs with Sal Nistico	196?	5.00	10.00	20.00
VERVE
❑ MGV-2134 [M]	Swing Is Here!	1960	10.00	20.00	40.00
❑ V-2134 [M]	Swing Is Here!	1961	5.00	10.00	20.00
❑ V6-2134 [S]	Swing Is Here!	1961	5.00	10.00	20.00
❑ MGV-2136 [M]	Music from Cole Porter's "Can-Can"	1960	10.00	20.00	40.00
❑ V-2136 [M]	Music from Cole Porter's "Can-Can"	1961	5.00	10.00	20.00
❑ V6-2136 [S]	Music from Cole Porter's "Can-Can"	1961	5.00	10.00	20.00
❑ MGV-2151 [M]	The Exciting Terry Gibbs Big Band	1960	10.00	20.00	40.00
❑ V-2151 [M]	The Exciting Terry Gibbs Big Band	1961	5.00	10.00	20.00
❑ V6-2151 [S]	The Exciting Terry Gibbs Big Band	1961	6.25	12.50	25.00
❑ MGVS-6140 [S]	Swing Is Here!	1960	10.00	20.00	40.00
❑ MGVS-6145 [S]	Music from Cole Porter's "Can-Can"	1960	10.00	20.00	40.00
❑ V-8447 [M]	That Swing Thing	1962	5.00	10.00	20.00
❑ V6-8447 [S]	That Swing Thing	1962	6.25	12.50	25.00
❑ V-8496 [M]	Straight Ahead	1962	5.00	10.00	20.00
❑ V6-8496 [S]	Straight Ahead	1962	6.25	12.50	25.00

GIBBS, TERRY, AND BILL HARRIS
MODE
Number	Title (A Side/B Side)	Yr	VG	VG+	NM
❑ LP-129 [M]	The Ex-Hermanites	1957	20.00	40.00	80.00

GIBSON, ALTHEA
DOT
Number	Title (A Side/B Side)	Yr	VG	VG+	NM
❑ DLP-3105 [M]	Althea Gibson Sings	1959	10.00	20.00	40.00
❑ DLP-25105 [S]	Althea Gibson Sings	1959	12.50	25.00	50.00

GIBSON, BOB
ELEKTRA
Number	Title (A Side/B Side)	Yr	VG	VG+	NM
❑ EKL-177 [M]	Ski Songs	1959	6.25	12.50	25.00
❑ EKL-197 [M]	Yes I See	1961	5.00	10.00	20.00
❑ EKL-239 [M]	Where I'm Bound	1964	5.00	10.00	20.00
❑ EKS-7177 [S]	Ski Songs	1959	7.50	15.00	30.00
❑ EKS-7197 [S]	Yes I See	1961	6.25	12.50	25.00
❑ EKS-7239 [S]	Where I'm Bound	1964	6.25	12.50	25.00
RIVERSIDE
❑ RLP 12-802 [M]	Offbeat Folk Songs	1956	10.00	20.00	40.00
❑ RLP 12-806 [M]	I Come For to Sing	1957	10.00	20.00	40.00
❑ RLP 12-816 [M]	Carnegie Concert	1958	10.00	20.00	40.00
❑ RLP 12-830 [M]	There's a Meetin' Here Tonight	1958	10.00	20.00	40.00
❑ RLP-1111 [S]	There's a Meetin' Here Tonight	1959	12.50	25.00	50.00
❑ RM 7542 [M]	Hootenanny at Carnegie	1963	5.00	10.00	20.00
—Reissue of 12-816 with slightly altered lineup					
STINSON
| ❑ SLP-76 [10] | Folksongs of Ohio | 1954 | 12.50 | 25.00 | 50.00 |

GIBSON, BOB, AND BOB CAMP
ELEKTRA
Number	Title (A Side/B Side)	Yr	VG	VG+	NM
❑ EKL-207 [M]	Gibson and Camp at the Gate of Horn	1961	5.00	10.00	20.00
❑ EKS-7207 [S]	Gibson and Camp at the Gate of Horn	1961	6.25	12.50	25.00

GIBSON, DON
ABC HICKORY
Number	Title (A Side/B Side)	Yr	VG	VG+	NM
❑ AH-44001	I'm All Wrapped Up in You	1976	3.00	6.00	12.00
❑ AH-44007	If You Ever	1977	3.00	6.00	12.00
❑ AH-44010	Starting All Over	1978	3.00	6.00	12.00
❑ AH-44014	Look Who's Blue	1978	3.00	6.00	12.00
HARMONY
❑ HL 7358 [M]	The Fabulous Don Gibson Sings	196?	3.75	7.50	15.00
❑ HS 11158 [R]	The Fabulous Don Gibson Sings	196?	3.00	6.00	12.00
❑ KH 31765	Sample Kisses	1972	2.50	5.00	10.00
HICKORY
❑ LPS-153	Hits, The Don Gibson Way	1970	3.75	7.50	15.00
❑ LPS-155	Perfect Mountain	1971	3.75	7.50	15.00
❑ LPS-157	Don Gibson Sings Hank Williams	1971	3.75	7.50	15.00
❑ LPS-160	Country Green	1971	3.75	7.50	15.00
❑ LPS-166	Woman (Sensuous Woman)	1972	3.75	7.50	15.00
❑ ST-94817	Woman (Sensuous Woman)	1972	5.00	10.00	20.00
—Capitol Record Club edition					
HICKORY/MGM
❑ HR-4501	Touch the Morning/That's What I'll Do	1973	3.75	7.50	15.00
❑ H3G-4502	The Very Best of Don Gibson	1974	3.75	7.50	15.00
❑ H3F-4509	Snap Your Fingers	1974	3.75	7.50	15.00
❑ H3G-4516	Bring Back Your Love to Me	1974	3.00	6.00	12.00
❑ H3G-4519	I'm the Loneliest Man	1975	3.00	6.00	12.00
LION
| ❑ L-70069 [M] | Songs by Don Gibson | 1958 | 20.00 | 40.00 | 80.00 |
METRO
| ❑ M-529 [M] | Don Gibson | 1965 | 3.00 | 6.00 | 12.00 |
| ❑ MS-529 [R] | Don Gibson | 1965 | 2.50 | 5.00 | 10.00 |
MGM
| ❑ GAS-138 | Don Gibson (Golden Archive Series) | 1970 | 3.75 | 7.50 | 15.00 |

Number	Title (A Side/B Side)	Yr	VG	VG+	NM
RCA CAMDEN					
❏ ACL1-0328	Just Call Me Lonesome	1973	2.50	5.00	10.00
❏ ACL1-0758	Just One Time	1974	2.50	5.00	10.00
❏ CAL-852 [M]	A Blue Million Tears	196?	3.00	6.00	12.00
❏ CAS-852 [P]	A Blue Million Tears	196?	3.00	6.00	12.00
—All tracks are rechanneled except "I Let Her Get Lonely" and "I May Never Get to Heaven," which are true stereo					
❏ CAL-2101 [M]	Hurtin' Inside	1966	3.00	6.00	12.00
❏ CAS-2101 [S]	Hurtin' Inside	1966	3.75	7.50	15.00
❏ CAS-2246	I Love You So Much	1968	3.00	6.00	12.00
❏ CAS-2317	My God Is Real	1969	3.00	6.00	12.00
❏ CAS-2392	Lovin' Lies	1970	3.00	6.00	12.00
❏ CAS-2502	I Walk Alone	1971	3.00	6.00	12.00
❏ CAS-2592	Am I That Easy to Forget	1972	3.00	6.00	12.00
RCA VICTOR					
❏ LPM-1743 [M]	Oh Lonesome Me	1958	12.50	25.00	50.00
❏ LPM-1918 [M]	No One Stands Alone	1959	7.50	15.00	30.00
❏ LSP-1918 [S]	No One Stands Alone	1959	10.00	20.00	40.00
❏ LPM-2038 [M]	That Gibson Boy	1959	7.50	15.00	30.00
❏ LSP-2038 [S]	That Gibson Boy	1959	10.00	20.00	40.00
❏ LPM-2184 [M]	Look Who's Blue	1960	7.50	15.00	30.00
❏ LSP-2184 [S]	Look Who's Blue	1960	10.00	20.00	40.00
❏ LPM-2269 [M]	Sweet Dreams	1960	7.50	15.00	30.00
❏ LSP-2269 [S]	Sweet Dreams	1960	10.00	20.00	40.00
❏ LPM-2361 [M]	Girls, Guitars and Gibson	1961	7.50	15.00	30.00
❏ LSP-2361 [S]	Girls, Guitars and Gibson	1961	10.00	20.00	40.00
❏ LPM-2448 [M]	Some Favorites of Mine	1962	7.50	15.00	30.00
❏ LSP-2448 [S]	Some Favorites of Mine	1962	10.00	20.00	40.00
❏ LPM-2702 [M]	I Wrote a Song	1963	7.50	15.00	30.00
❏ LSP-2702 [S]	I Wrote a Song	1963	10.00	20.00	40.00
❏ LPM-2878 [M]	God Walks These Hills	1964	5.00	10.00	20.00
❏ LSP-2878 [S]	God Walks These Hills	1964	6.25	12.50	25.00
❏ LPM-3376 [M]	The Best of Don Gibson	1965	5.00	10.00	20.00
❏ LSP-3376 [S]	The Best of Don Gibson	1965	6.25	12.50	25.00
❏ LPM-3470 [M]	Too Much Hurt	1965	5.00	10.00	20.00
❏ LSP-3470 [S]	Too Much Hurt	1965	6.25	12.50	25.00
❏ LPM-3594 [M]	Don Gibson with Spanish Guitars	1966	5.00	10.00	20.00
❏ LSP-3594 [S]	Don Gibson with Spanish Guitars	1966	6.25	12.50	25.00
❏ LPM-3680 [M]	Great Country Songs	1966	5.00	10.00	20.00
❏ LSP-3680 [S]	Great Country Songs	1966	6.25	12.50	25.00
❏ LPM-3843 [M]	All My Love	1967	5.00	10.00	20.00
❏ LSP-3843 [S]	All My Love	1967	6.25	12.50	25.00
❏ LPM-3974 [M]	The King of Country Soul	1968	12.50	25.00	50.00
❏ LSP-3974 [S]	The King of Country Soul	1968	5.00	10.00	20.00
❏ LSP-4053	More Country Soul	1968	5.00	10.00	20.00
❏ LSP-4169	All-Time Country Gold	1969	3.75	7.50	15.00
❏ LSP-4281	The Best of Don Gibson, Vol. 2	1970	3.75	7.50	15.00
❏ CPL1-7052	Collector's Series	1985	2.50	5.00	10.00
GIBSON, STEVE, AND THE RED CAPS					
MERCURY					
❏ MG-25115 [10]	You're Driving Me Crazy (Harmony Time)	1952	100.00	200.00	400.00
❏ MG-25116 [10]	Blueberry Hill (Singing & Swinging)	1952	100.00	200.00	400.00
GIFFORD, KATHIE LEE					
HEARTLAND					
❏ HL-3046 [(2)]	Christmas with Kathie Lee Gifford	1993	5.00	10.00	20.00
GILBERT, ANN					
GROOVE					
❏ LG-1004 [M]	The Many Moods of Ann	1956	12.50	25.00	50.00
GILBERT, RONNIE					
Also see THE WEAVERS.					
MERCURY					
❏ MG-20917 [M]	Alone with Ronnie Gilbert	1964	5.00	10.00	20.00
❏ SR-60917 [S]	Alone with Ronnie Gilbert	1964	6.25	12.50	25.00
RCA VICTOR					
❏ LPM-1591 [M]	In Hi-Fi, The Legend of Bessie Smith	1958	10.00	20.00	40.00
GILBERT & SULLIVAN JAZZ WORKSHOP, THE					
ANDEX					
❏ A-27101 [M]	The Coolest Mikado	1961	5.00	10.00	20.00
❏ AS-27101 [S]	The Coolest Mikado	1961	6.25	12.50	25.00
GILBERTO, JOAO					
ATLANTIC					
❏ SD 8070 [S]	The Boss of the Bossa Nova	1963	5.00	10.00	20.00
❏ SD 8076 [S]	The Warm World of Joao Gilberto	1964	5.00	10.00	20.00
CAPITOL					
❏ ST 2160 [S]	Joao Gilberto and Antonio Carlos Jobim	1964	5.00	10.00	20.00
❏ ST 2160 [S]	Joao Gilberto and Antonio Carlos Jobim	1978	2.50	5.00	10.00
—Purple label, large Capitol logo					
❏ ST 10280 [S]	Pops in Portuguese	196?	6.25	12.50	25.00
❏ T 10280 [M]	Pops in Portuguese	196?	5.00	10.00	20.00
GILELS, EMIL					
RCA VICTOR RED SEAL					
❏ LSC-2219 [S]	Brahms: Piano Concerto No. 2	1959	20.00	40.00	80.00
—With Fritz Reiner/Chicago Symphony Orchestra; original with "shaded dog" label					
❏ LSC-2493 [S]	Schubert: Piano Sonata, op. 53	1961	12.50	25.00	50.00
—Original with "shaded dog" label					
GILES, GILES & FRIPP					
DERAM					
❏ DES 18019	The Cheerful Insanity of Giles, Giles & Fripp	1968	15.00	30.00	60.00
GILKYSON, TERRY					
COLUMBIA					
❏ CL 990 [M]	Marianne and Other Songs	1957	12.50	25.00	50.00
❏ CL 1302 [M]	Wanderin' Folk Songs	1959	7.50	15.00	30.00
DECCA					
❏ DL 5263 [10]	Folk Songs	1950	12.50	25.00	50.00

Number	Title (A Side/B Side)	Yr	VG	VG	
❏ DL 5457 [10]	Golden Minutes of Folk Music	1952	12.50	25.	
KAPP					
❏ KL 1196 [M]	Rollin'	1960	3.75	7.50	15.00
❏ KL 1327 [M]	The Cry of the Wild Goose	1963	3.75	7.50	15.00
❏ KS 3196 [S]	Rollin'	1960	5.00	10.00	20.00
❏ KS 3327 [S]	The Cry of the Wild Goose	1963	5.00	10.00	20.00
GILL, VINCE					
MCA					
❏ 42321	When I Call Your Name	1989	5.00	10.00	20.00
❏ R 173599	Pocket Full of Gold	1991	5.00	10.00	20.00
—Only released on vinyl through BMG Direct Marketing					
RCA					
❏ 5923-1-R	The Way Back Home	1987	3.75	7.50	15.00
RCA VICTOR					
❏ CPL1-5348	The Things That Matter	1985	3.75	7.50	15.00
❏ MHL1-8517 [EP]	Turn Me Loose	1984	2.50	5.00	10.00
GILLESPIE, DANA					
LONDON					
❏ PS 540	Foolish Seasons	1968	5.00	10.00	20.00
GILLESPIE, DARLENE					
DISNEYLAND					
❏ WDL-1010 [M]	Top Tunes of the '50's — Darlene Gillespie Sings TV Favorites	1959	10.00	20.00	40.00
—Reissue of 3010					
❏ DQ-1228 [M]	Sleeping Beauty	1962	5.00	10.00	20.00
—Cover is black and white; later pressings, which go for less, are shaded blue on the back					
❏ WDL-3010 [M]	Darlene of the Teens	1957	20.00	40.00	80.00
❏ WDL-3010 [M]	Top Tunes of the '50's — Darlene Gillespie Sings TV Favorites	1958	12.50	25.00	50.00
—Reissue with new title and cover					
MICKEY MOUSE CLUB					
❏ MM-32 [M]	Sleeping Beauty	1959	10.00	20.00	40.00
GILLESPIE, DIZZY					
ALLEGRO					
❏ 3017 [M]	Dizzy Gillespie Plays	195?	30.00	60.00	120.00
❏ 3083 [M]	Dizzy Gillespie	195?	30.00	60.00	120.00
❏ 4023 [10]	Dizzy Gillespie	195?	50.00	100.00	200.00
❏ 4108 [10]	Dizzy Gillespie Plays	195?	50.00	100.00	200.00
AMERICAN RECORDING SOCIETY					
❏ G-405 [M]	Jazz Creations/Dizzy Gillespie	1955	25.00	50.00	100.00
❏ G-423 [M]	Big Band Jazz	1955	25.00	50.00	100.00
ATLANTIC					
❏ ALR-138 [10]	Dizzy Gillespie	1952	100.00	200.00	400.00
❏ ALR-142 [10]	Dizzy Gillespie, Vol. 2	1952	100.00	200.00	400.00
❏ 1257 [M]	Dizzy at Home and Abroad	1957	25.00	50.00	100.00
—Black label					
❏ 1257 [M]	Dizzy at Home and Abroad	1961	7.50	15.00	30.00
—Multi-color label with white "fan" logo					
BARONET					
❏ 105 [M]	A Handful of Modern Jazz	1961	10.00	20.00	40.00
BLUE NOTE					
❏ BLP-5017 [10]	Horn of Plenty	1953	75.00	150.00	300.00
CLEF					
❏ MGC-136 [10]	Dizzy Gillespie with Strings	1953	50.00	100.00	200.00
CONTEMPORARY					
❏ C-2504 [10]	Dizzy in Paris	1953	50.00	100.00	200.00
DEE GEE					
❏ LP-1000 [10]	Dizzy Gillespie	1950	75.00	150.00	300.00
DIAL					
❏ 212 [10]	Modern Trumpets	1952	100.00	200.00	400.00
DISCOVERY					
❏ DL-3013 [10]	Dizzy Gillespie Plays, Johnny Richards Conducts	1950	75.00	150.00	300.00
GENE NORMAN					
❏ GNP-4 [10]	Dizzy Gillespie with His Original Big Band	195?	50.00	100.00	200.00
❏ GNP-23 [M]	Dizzy Gillespie and His Big Band	1957	20.00	40.00	80.00
GNP CRESCENDO					
❏ GNP-23 [M]	Dizzy Gillespie and His Big Band	196?	5.00	10.00	20.00
IMPULSE!					
❏ AS-9149	Swing Low, Sweet Cadillac!	1967	5.00	10.00	20.00
LIMELIGHT					
❏ LM-82007 [M]	Jambo Caribe	1964	5.00	10.00	20.00
❏ LM-82022 [M]	The New Continent	1965	5.00	10.00	20.00
❏ LM-82042 [M]	The Melody Lingers On	1967	5.00	10.00	20.00
❏ LS-86007 [S]	Jambo Caribe	1964	6.25	12.50	25.00
❏ LS-86022 [S]	The New Continent	1965	6.25	12.50	25.00
❏ LS-86042 [S]	The Melody Lingers On	1967	6.25	12.50	25.00
NORGRAN					
❏ MGN-1003 [M]	Afro Dizzy	1954	30.00	60.00	120.00
❏ MGN-1023 [M]	Dizzy and Strings	1955	30.00	60.00	120.00
❏ MGN-1083 [M]	Jazz Recital	1956	30.00	60.00	120.00
❏ MGN-1084 [M]	World Statesman	1956	30.00	60.00	120.00
❏ MGN-1090 [M]	Diz Big Band	1956	30.00	60.00	120.00
PHILIPS					
❏ PHM 200048 [M]	Dizzy at the French Riviera	1962	5.00	10.00	20.00
❏ PHM 200070 [M]	New Wave!	1962	5.00	10.00	20.00
❏ PHM 200091 [M]	Something Old, Something New	1963	5.00	10.00	20.00
❏ PHM 200106 [M]	Dizzy Gillespie and the Double Six of Paris	1963	5.00	10.00	20.00
❏ PHM 200123 [M]	Dizzy Gillespie Goes Hollywood	1964	5.00	10.00	20.00
❏ PHS 600048 [S]	Dizzy at the French Riviera	1962	6.25	12.50	25.00
❏ PHS 600070 [S]	New Wave!	1962	6.25	12.50	25.00
❏ PHS 600091 [S]	Something Old, Something New	1963	6.25	12.50	25.00
❏ PHS 600106 [S]	Dizzy Gillespie and the Double Six of Paris	1963	6.25	12.50	25.00
❏ PHS 600123 [S]	Dizzy Gillespie Goes Hollywood	1964	6.25	12.50	25.00

G

Number	Title (A Side/B Side)	Yr	VG	VG+	NM
RCA VICTOR					
❑ LPV-530 [M]	Dizzy Gillespie	1966	6.25	12.50	25.00
❑ LJM-1009 [M]	Dizzier and Dizzier	1954	30.00	60.00	120.00
❑ LPM-2398 [M]	The Greatest of Dizzy Gillespie	1961	12.50	25.00	50.00
—"Long Play" on label					
REGENT					
❑ MG-6043 [M]	School Days	1957	25.00	50.00	100.00
REPRISE					
❑ R-6072 [M]	Dateline: Europe	1963	5.00	10.00	20.00
❑ R9-6072 [S]	Dateline: Europe	1963	6.25	12.50	25.00
RONDO-LETTE					
❑ A-11 [M]	Dizzy Gillespie	195?	7.50	15.00	30.00
ROOST					
❑ R-414 [10]	Dizzy Over Paris	1953	62.50	125.00	250.00
❑ LP-2214 [M]	Concert in Paris	1957	30.00	60.00	120.00
SAVOY					
❑ MG-12020 [M]	Groovin' High	1955	15.00	30.00	60.00
❑ MG-12047 [M]	The Champ	1956	15.00	30.00	60.00
❑ MG-12110 [M]	The Dizzy Gillespie Story	1957	15.00	30.00	60.00
SOLID STATE					
❑ SS-18034	Live at the Village Vanguard	1968	5.00	10.00	20.00
❑ SS-18054	My Way	1969	5.00	10.00	20.00
❑ SS-18061	Cornucopia	1969	5.00	10.00	20.00
VERVE					
❑ MGVS-6023 [S]	Dizzy Gillespie at Newport	1960	15.00	30.00	60.00
❑ MGVS-6047 [S]	Have Trumpet, Will Excite	1960	15.00	30.00	60.00
❑ MGVS-6068 [S]	The Ebullient Mr. Gillespie	1960	15.00	30.00	60.00
❑ MGVS-6117 [S]	Greatest Trumpet of Them All	1960	15.00	30.00	60.00
❑ MGV-8017 [M]	Dizzy in Greece	1957	15.00	30.00	60.00
❑ V-8017 [M]	Dizzy in Greece	1961	6.25	12.50	25.00
❑ MGV-8173 [M]	Jazz Recital	1957	15.00	30.00	60.00
❑ V-8173 [M]	Jazz Recital	1961	6.25	12.50	25.00
❑ MGV-8174 [M]	World Statesman	1957	15.00	30.00	60.00
❑ V-8174 [M]	World Statesman	1961	6.25	12.50	25.00
❑ MGV-8178 [M]	Diz Big Band	1957	17.50	35.00	70.00
❑ V-8178 [M]	Diz Big Band	1961	6.25	12.50	25.00
❑ MGV-8191 [M]	Afro Dizzy	1957	15.00	30.00	60.00
❑ MGV-8208 [M]	Manteca	1958	15.00	30.00	60.00
❑ V-8208 [M]	Manteca	1961	6.25	12.50	25.00
❑ MGV-8214 [M]	Dizzy Gillespie and Stuff Smith	1958	15.00	30.00	60.00
❑ V-8214 [M]	Dizzy Gillespie and Stuff Smith	1961	6.25	12.50	25.00
❑ MGV-8242 [M]	Dizzy Gillespie at Newport	1958	15.00	30.00	60.00
❑ V-8242 [M]	Dizzy Gillespie at Newport	1961	6.25	12.50	25.00
❑ V6-8242 [S]	Dizzy Gillespie at Newport	1961	6.25	12.50	25.00
❑ MGV-8260 [M]	Duets	1958	15.00	30.00	60.00
—With Sonny Rollins and Sonny Stitt					
❑ MGV-8313 [M]	Have Trumpet, Will Excite	1959	15.00	30.00	60.00
❑ V-8313 [M]	Have Trumpet, Will Excite	1961	6.25	12.50	25.00
❑ V6-8313 [S]	Have Trumpet, Will Excite	1961	6.25	12.50	25.00
❑ MGV-8328 [M]	The Ebullient Mr. Gillespie	1959	15.00	30.00	60.00
❑ V-8328 [M]	The Ebullient Mr. Gillespie	1961	6.25	12.50	25.00
❑ V6-8328 [S]	The Ebullient Mr. Gillespie	1961	6.25	12.50	25.00
❑ MGV-8352 [M]	Greatest Trumpet of Them All	1959	15.00	30.00	60.00
❑ V-8352 [M]	Greatest Trumpet of Them All	1961	6.25	12.50	25.00
❑ V6-8352 [S]	Greatest Trumpet of Them All	1961	6.25	12.50	25.00
❑ MGV-8386 [M]	Portrait of Duke	1960	15.00	30.00	60.00
❑ V-8386 [M]	Portrait of Duke	1961	6.25	12.50	25.00
❑ MGV-8394 [M]	Gillespiana	1960	15.00	30.00	60.00
❑ V-8394 [M]	Gillespiana	1961	6.25	12.50	25.00
❑ V6-8394 [S]	Gillespiana	1961	6.25	12.50	25.00
❑ V-8401 [M]	An Electrifying Evening with the Dizzy Gillespie Quintet	1961	5.00	10.00	20.00
❑ V6-8401 [S]	An Electrifying Evening with the Dizzy Gillespie Quintet	1961	6.25	12.50	25.00
❑ V-8411 [M]	Perceptions	1961	5.00	10.00	20.00
❑ V6-8411 [S]	Perceptions	1961	6.25	12.50	25.00
❑ V-8423 [M]	Carnegie Hall Concert	1962	5.00	10.00	20.00
❑ V6-8423 [S]	Carnegie Hall Concert	1962	6.25	12.50	25.00
❑ V-8477 [M]	Dizzy, Rollins & Stitt	1962	5.00	10.00	20.00
—Reissue of MGV-8260					
❑ V6-8477 [S]	Dizzy, Rollins & Stitt	1962	6.25	12.50	25.00
❑ V-8560 [M]	Dizzy at Newport	1964	5.00	10.00	20.00
❑ V6-8560 [S]	Dizzy at Newport	1964	6.25	12.50	25.00
❑ V-8566 [M]	The Essential Dizzy Gillespie	1964	5.00	10.00	20.00
❑ V6-8566 [S]	The Essential Dizzy Gillespie	1964	6.25	12.50	25.00

GILLESPIE, DIZZY, AND STAN GETZ

Number	Title (A Side/B Side)	Yr	VG	VG+	NM
NORGRAN					
❑ MGN-2 [10]	The Dizzy Gillespie-Stan Getz Sextet #1	1954	75.00	150.00	300.00
❑ MGN-18 [10]	The Dizzy Gillespie-Stan Getz Sextet #2	1954	75.00	150.00	300.00
❑ MGN-1050 [M]	Diz and Getz	1956	30.00	60.00	120.00
VERVE					
❑ MGV-8141 [M]	Diz and Getz	1957	20.00	40.00	80.00
—Reissue of Norgran 1050					

GILLESPIE, DIZZY/JIMMY MCPARTLAND

Number	Title (A Side/B Side)	Yr	VG	VG+	NM
MGM					
❑ E-3286 [M]	Hot vs. Cool	1955	20.00	40.00	80.00

GILLESPIE, DIZZY, AND CHARLIE PARKER

Number	Title (A Side/B Side)	Yr	VG	VG+	NM
ROOST					
❑ SK-106 [(2)M]	The Beginning: Diz and Bird	1960	25.00	50.00	100.00
❑ LP-2234 [M]	Diz 'n' Bird In Concert	1959	20.00	40.00	80.00

GILLESPIE, DIZZY, AND DJANGO REINHARDT

Number	Title (A Side/B Side)	Yr	VG	VG+	NM
VERVE					
❑ MGV-8015 [M]	Jazz from Paris	1957	15.00	30.00	60.00
❑ V-8015 [M]	Jazz from Paris	1961	6.25	12.50	25.00

GILLEY, MICKEY

Number	Title (A Side/B Side)	Yr	VG	VG+	NM
ACCORD					
❑ SN-7151	Suburban Cowboy	1981	2.50	5.00	10.00
ASTRO					
❑ 101 [M]	Lonely Wine	1964	75.00	150.00	300.00
COLUMBIA SPECIAL PRODUCTS					
❑ P 16198	All My Best	1982	2.50	5.00	10.00
EPIC					
❑ PE 34736	Room Full of Roses	198?	2.00	4.00	8.00
—Budget-line reissue					
❑ PE 34749	Smokin'	198?	2.00	4.00	8.00
—Budget-line reissue					
❑ PE 34776	First Class	198?	2.00	4.00	8.00
—Budget-line reissue					
❑ KE 35174	Songs We Made Love To	1979	2.50	5.00	10.00
❑ JE 36201	Mickey Gilley	1980	2.50	5.00	10.00
❑ JE 36492	That's All That Matters to Me	1980	2.50	5.00	10.00
❑ PE 36492	That's All That Matters to Me	198?	2.00	4.00	8.00
—Budget-line reissue					
❑ JE 36851	Encore	1981	2.50	5.00	10.00
❑ FE 37416	You Don't Know Me	1981	2.50	5.00	10.00
❑ PE 37416	You Don't Know Me	198?	2.00	4.00	8.00
—Budget-line reissue					
❑ PE 37595	Christmas at Gilley's	1981	2.50	5.00	10.00
—Some labels have "FE" prefix					
❑ FE 38082	Put Your Dreams Away	1982	2.50	5.00	10.00
❑ PE 38082	Put Your Dreams Away	198?	2.00	4.00	8.00
—Budget-line reissue					
❑ FE 38320	Mickey Gilley's Biggest Hits	1982	2.50	5.00	10.00
❑ FE 38583	Fool for Your Love	1983	2.50	5.00	10.00
❑ PE 38583	Fool for Your Love	1985	2.00	4.00	8.00
—Budget-line reissue					
❑ FE 39000	You've Really Got a Hold on Me	1983	2.50	5.00	10.00
❑ FE 39324	Too Good to Stop Now	1983	2.50	5.00	10.00
❑ KE2 39867 [(2)]	Ten Years of Hits	1984	3.00	6.00	12.00
❑ FE 39900	Live at Gilley's	1984	2.50	5.00	10.00
❑ FE 40115	I Feel Good (About Lovin' You)	1985	2.50	5.00	10.00
❑ FE 40353	The One and Only	1986	2.50	5.00	10.00
INTERMEDIA					
❑ QS-5024	With Love from Pasadena, Texas	198?	2.50	5.00	10.00
J.M.					
❑ 8127	Norwegian Wood	1981	3.00	6.00	12.00
PAIR					
❑ PDL2-1072 [(2)]	The Best of Mickey Gilley	1986	3.00	6.00	12.00
PAULA					
❑ LP-2195 [M]	Down the Line	1967	10.00	20.00	40.00
❑ LPS-2195 [S]	Down the Line	1967	10.00	20.00	40.00
❑ LPS-2224	Mickey Gilley at His Best	1974	3.75	7.50	15.00
❑ LPS-2234	Mickey Gilley	1978	3.00	6.00	12.00
PICKWICK					
❑ SPC-6180	Wild Side of Life	1975	2.50	5.00	10.00
PLAYBOY					
❑ PB-128	Room Full of Roses	1974	5.00	10.00	20.00
❑ PB-403	City Lights	1974	5.00	10.00	20.00
❑ PB-405	Mickey's Movin' On	1975	3.75	7.50	15.00
❑ PB-408	Overnight Sensation	1976	3.75	7.50	15.00
❑ PB-409	Gilley's Greatest Hits Vol. 1	1976	3.75	7.50	15.00
❑ PB-415	Gilley's Smokin'	1976	3.75	7.50	15.00
❑ PZ 34736	Room Full of Roses	1977	2.50	5.00	10.00
—Reissue of 128					
❑ PZ 34742	Overnight Sensation	1977	2.50	5.00	10.00
—Reissue of 408					
❑ PZ 34743	Gilley's Greatest Hits Vol. 1	1977	2.50	5.00	10.00
—Reissue of 409					
❑ PZ 34749	Gilley's Smokin'	1977	3.00	6.00	12.00
—Reissue of 415					
❑ PZ 34776	First Class	1977	3.00	6.00	12.00
❑ KZ 34881	Gilley's Greatest Hits, Vol. 2	1977	3.00	6.00	12.00
❑ KZ 35099	Flyin' High	1978	3.00	6.00	12.00

GILMER, JIMMY, AND THE FIREBALLS

See THE FIREBALLS.

GILMER, JULIA ANN

Number	Title (A Side/B Side)	Yr	VG	VG+	NM
ABC-PARAMOUNT					
❑ ABC-168 [M]	Cads, Blackguards and False True-Loves	1956	7.50	15.00	30.00

GIN BLOSSOMS

Number	Title (A Side/B Side)	Yr	VG	VG+	NM
A&M					
❑ 75021 5369 1 [EP]	Up and Crumbling	1991	3.75	7.50	15.00
SAN JACINTO					
❑ DRAM 019	Dusted	1989	5.00	10.00	20.00
—With picture insert and biographical material					

GINNY AND THE GALLIONS

Number	Title (A Side/B Side)	Yr	VG	VG+	NM
DOWNEY					
❑ D-1003 [M]	Two Sides of Ginny and the Gallions	1964	7.50	15.00	30.00
❑ DS-1003 [S]	Two Sides of Ginny and the Gallions	1964	10.00	20.00	40.00

GINSBERG, ALLEN

Number	Title (A Side/B Side)	Yr	VG	VG+	NM
ATLANTIC					
❑ 4001 [M]	Allen Ginsburg Reads Kaddish	1966	7.50	15.00	30.00
FANTASY					
❑ F-7006 [M]	Howl and Other Poems	1959	50.00	100.00	200.00
—Black non-flexible vinyl					
❑ F-7006 [M]	Howl and Other Poems	1959	100.00	200.00	400.00
—Red vinyl					

GIRARD, GEORGE

Number	Title (A Side/B Side)	Yr	VG	VG+	NM
VIK					
❑ LX-1058 [M]	Jam Session on Bourbon Street	1957	10.00	20.00	40.00

Number	Title (A Side/B Side)	Yr	VG	VG+	NM
❑ LX-1063 [M]	Stompin' at the Famous Door	1957	10.00	20.00	40.00

GITS, THE
BROKEN REKIDS

Number	Title (A Side/B Side)	Yr	VG	VG+	NM
❑ SKIP 44	Kings & Queens	1995	3.00	6.00	12.00
❑ SKIP 87	Seafish Louisville	2000	3.00	6.00	12.00

C/Z
❑ 051	Frenching the Bully	1992	6.25	12.50	25.00

—Originals on red vinyl

GIUFFRE, JIMMY
ATLANTIC

Number	Title (A Side/B Side)	Yr	VG	VG+	NM
❑ 1238 [M]	The Jimmy Giuffre Clarinet	1956	12.50	25.00	50.00

—Black label

❑ 1238 [M]	The Jimmy Giuffre Clarinet	1960	5.00	10.00	20.00

—Multicolor label, white "fan" logo at right

❑ 1254 [M]	The Jimmy Giuffre Three	1957	12.50	25.00	50.00

—Black label

❑ 1254 [M]	The Jimmy Giuffre Three	1960	5.00	10.00	20.00

—Multicolor label, white "fan" logo at right

❑ 1276 [M]	Music Man	1958	12.50	25.00	50.00

—Black label

❑ 1276 [M]	Music Man	1960	5.00	10.00	20.00

—Multicolor label, white "fan" logo at right

❑ SD 1276 [S]	Music Man	1959	12.50	25.00	50.00

—Green label

❑ SD 1276 [S]	Music Man	1960	5.00	10.00	20.00

—Multicolor label, white "fan" logo at right

❑ 1282 [M]	Trav'lin' Light	1958	12.50	25.00	50.00

—Black label

❑ 1282 [M]	Trav'lin' Light	1960	5.00	10.00	20.00

—Multicolor label, white "fan" logo at right

❑ SD 1282 [S]	Trav'lin' Light	1959	12.50	25.00	50.00

—Green label

❑ SD 1282 [S]	Trav'lin' Light	1960	5.00	10.00	20.00

—Multicolor label, white "fan" logo at right

❑ 1295 [M]	Four Brothers Sound	1959	12.50	25.00	50.00

—Black label

❑ 1295 [M]	Four Brothers Sound	1960	5.00	10.00	20.00

—Multicolor label, white "fan" logo at right

❑ SD 1295 [S]	Four Brothers Sound	1959	12.50	25.00	50.00

—Green label

❑ SD 1295 [S]	Four Brothers Sound	1960	5.00	10.00	20.00

—Multicolor label, white "fan" logo at right

❑ 1330 [M]	Western Suite	1960	6.25	12.50	25.00

—Multicolor label, white "fan" logo at right

❑ SD 1330 [S]	Western Suite	1960	7.50	15.00	30.00

—Multicolor label, white "fan" logo at right

CAPITOL
❑ H 549 [10]	Jimmy Giuffre	1954	37.50	75.00	150.00
❑ T 549 [M]	Jimmy Giuffre	1955	20.00	40.00	80.00
❑ T 634 [M]	Tangents in Jazz	1955	20.00	40.00	80.00

COLUMBIA
❑ CS 8764 [S]	Free Fall	1963	5.00	10.00	20.00

VERVE
❑ MGVS-6039 [S]	Seven Pieces	1960	7.50	15.00	30.00
❑ MGVS-6095 [S]	The Easy Way	1960	7.50	15.00	30.00
❑ MGVS-6130 [S]	Ad Lib	1960	7.50	15.00	30.00
❑ MGV-8307 [M]	Seven Pieces	1959	10.00	20.00	40.00
❑ V-8307 [M]	Seven Pieces	1961	5.00	10.00	20.00
❑ MGV-8337 [M]	The Easy Way	1960	10.00	20.00	40.00
❑ V-8337 [M]	The Easy Way	1961	5.00	10.00	20.00
❑ MGV-8361 [M]	Ad Lib	1960	10.00	20.00	40.00
❑ V-8361 [M]	Ad Lib	1961	5.00	10.00	20.00
❑ MGV-8387 [M]	The Jimmy Giuffre Quartet In Person	1961	10.00	20.00	40.00
❑ V-8387 [M]	The Jimmy Giuffre Quartet In Person	1961	5.00	10.00	20.00
❑ V6-8387 [S]	The Jimmy Giuffre Quartet In Person	1961	6.25	12.50	25.00
❑ MGV-8395 [M]	Piece for Clarinet and String Orchestra	1961	10.00	20.00	40.00
❑ V-8395 [M]	Piece for Clarinet and String Orchestra	1961	5.00	10.00	20.00
❑ V6-8395 [S]	Piece for Clarinet and String Orchestra	1961	6.25	12.50	25.00
❑ MGV-8397 [M]	Fusion	1961	10.00	20.00	40.00
❑ V-8397 [M]	Fusion	1961	5.00	10.00	20.00
❑ V6-8397 [S]	Fusion	1961	6.25	12.50	25.00
❑ MGV-8402 [M]	Thesis	1961	10.00	20.00	40.00
❑ V-8402 [M]	Thesis	1961	5.00	10.00	20.00
❑ V6-8402 [S]	Thesis	1961	6.25	12.50	25.00

GLACIERS, THE
MERCURY
❑ MG-20895 [M]	From Sea to Ski	1964	12.50	25.00	50.00
❑ SR-60895 [S]	From Sea to Ski	1964	15.00	30.00	60.00

GLAD, THE
ABC
❑ S-655	Feelin' Glad	1969	6.25	12.50	25.00

GLASEL, JOHN
ABC-PARAMOUNT
❑ ABC-165 [M]	Jazz Session	1957	12.50	25.00	50.00

GOLDEN CREST
❑ 1002 [M]	Jazz Unlimited	1960	7.50	15.00	30.00

GLASER, JIM
MCA
❑ 5612	Past the Point of No Return	1985	2.00	4.00	8.00
❑ 5723	Everybody Knows I'm Yours	1986	2.00	4.00	8.00

NOBLE VISION
❑ 2001	The Man in the Mirror	1983	2.50	5.00	10.00

STARDAY
❑ SLP-149 [M]	Old Time Christmas Singing	1960	17.50	35.00	70.00
❑ SLP-158 [M]	Just Looking for a Home	1961	15.00	30.00	60.00

GLASS HARP
DECCA

Number	Title (A Side/B Side)	Yr	VG	VG+	NM
❑ DL 75261	Glass Harp	1971	6.25	12.50	25.00
❑ DL 75306	Synergy	1971	6.25	12.50	25.00
❑ DL 75358	It Makes Me Glad	1972	6.25	12.50	25.00

MCA
❑ 293	Glass Harp	1974	2.50	5.00	10.00

—Reissue of Decca 75261

GLAZER, TOM
UNITED ARTISTS
❑ UAL 3540 [M]	Tom Glazer Sings the Ballad of Namu the Killer Whale and Other Ballads of Adventure	1966	6.25	12.50	25.00
❑ UAS 6540 [S]	Tom Glazer Sings the Ballad of Namu the Killer Whale and Other Ballads of Adventure	1966	7.50	15.00	30.00

WASHINGTON
❑ WC-301 [M]	The Tom Glazer Concert For and With Children	1959	6.25	12.50	25.00

GLEASON, JACKIE
CAPITOL

❑ SW-106	Irving Berlin's Music	1968	3.00	6.00	12.00
❑ SKAO-146	The Best of Jackie Gleason (Vol. 2)	1968	3.00	6.00	12.00
❑ SWBB-256 [(2)]	Close-Up	1969	3.75	7.50	15.00

—Reissue of Capitol DW 352 and DW 509 in one package

❑ STBB-346 [(2)]	All I Want for Christmas	1969	3.75	7.50	15.00
❑ DW 352 [R]	Music for Lovers Only	196?	2.50	5.00	10.00
❑ H 352 [10]	Music for Lovers Only	1952	7.50	15.00	30.00
❑ SM-352	Music for Lovers Only	197?	2.50	5.00	10.00

—Reissue

❑ W 352 [M]	Music for Lovers Only	1953	6.25	12.50	25.00
❑ H 366 [10]	Lover's Rhapsody	1953	7.50	15.00	30.00
❑ ST-398	Romeo and Juliet	1970	3.00	6.00	12.00
❑ DW 455 [R]	Music to Make You Misty	196?	2.50	5.00	10.00
❑ H 455 [10]	Music to Make You Misty	1954	7.50	15.00	30.00
❑ SM-455	Music to Make You Misty	197?	2.50	5.00	10.00

—Reissue

❑ W 455 [M]	Music to Make You Misty	1954	6.25	12.50	25.00
❑ L 471 [10]	Tawny	1954	7.50	15.00	30.00
❑ W 471 [M]	Tawny	1954	6.25	12.50	25.00
❑ WAO 475 [(2)M]	Music for Lovers Only/Music to Make You Misty	1954	10.00	20.00	40.00
❑ ST-480	Come Saturday Morning	1970	3.00	6.00	12.00
❑ DW 509 [R]	Music, Martini and Memories	196?	2.50	5.00	10.00
❑ SM-509	Music, Martini and Memories	197?	2.50	5.00	10.00

—Reissue

❑ W 509 [M]	Music, Martini and Memories	1954	6.25	12.50	25.00
❑ STBB-510 [(2)]	Tenderly/Laura	1971	3.75	7.50	15.00
❑ H 511 [10]	And Awaaay We Go!	1954	20.00	40.00	80.00
❑ W 511 [M]	And Awaaay We Go!	1955	10.00	20.00	40.00
❑ W 568 [M]	Romantic Jazz	1955	6.25	12.50	25.00
❑ DW 570 [R]	Music to Remember Her	196?	2.50	5.00	10.00
❑ W 570 [M]	Music to Remember Her	1955	6.25	12.50	25.00
❑ DW 627 [R]	Lonesome Echo	196?	2.50	5.00	10.00
❑ H 627 [10]	Lonesome Echo	1955	7.50	15.00	30.00
❑ W 627 [M]	Lonesome Echo	1955	6.25	12.50	25.00
❑ DW 632 [R]	Music to Change Her Mind	196?	2.50	5.00	10.00
❑ W 632 [M]	Music to Change Her Mind	1956	6.25	12.50	25.00
❑ ST-693	Words of Love	1971	3.00	6.00	12.00
❑ DW 717 [R]	Night Winds	196?	2.50	5.00	10.00
❑ W 717 [M]	Night Winds	1956	6.25	12.50	25.00
❑ DW 758 [R]	Merry Christmas	196?	2.50	5.00	10.00
❑ W 758 [M]	Merry Christmas	1956	6.25	12.50	25.00
❑ DW 816 [R]	Music for the Love Hours	196?	2.50	5.00	10.00
❑ W 816 [M]	Music for the Love Hours	1957	6.25	12.50	25.00
❑ SM-859	Velvet Brass	197?	2.50	5.00	10.00

—Reissue

❑ SW 859 [S]	Velvet Brass	1959	6.25	12.50	25.00

—We haven't confirmed if this is in true stereo or not.

❑ W 859 [M]	Velvet Brass	1957	6.25	12.50	25.00
❑ SW 905 [S]	Jackie Gleason Presents "Oooo!"	1959	6.25	12.50	25.00

—We haven't confirmed if this is in true stereo or not.

❑ W 905 [M]	Jackie Gleason Presents "Oooo!"	1957	6.25	12.50	25.00
❑ SW 961 [S]	The Torch with Blue Flame	1959	6.25	12.50	25.00
❑ W 961 [M]	The Torch with Blue Flame	1958	5.00	10.00	20.00
❑ SW 1020 [S]	Riff Jazz	1959	6.25	12.50	25.00
❑ W 1020 [M]	Riff Jazz	1958	5.00	10.00	20.00
❑ SW 1075 [S]	Rebound	1959	6.25	12.50	25.00
❑ W 1075 [M]	Rebound	1959	5.00	10.00	20.00
❑ SW 1147 [S]	That Moment	1959	6.25	12.50	25.00
❑ W 1147 [M]	That Moment	1959	5.00	10.00	20.00
❑ SW 1250 [S]	Aphrodisia	1960	6.25	12.50	25.00
❑ W 1250 [M]	Aphrodisia	1960	5.00	10.00	20.00
❑ SW 1315 [S]	Opiate D'Amour	1960	5.00	10.00	20.00
❑ W 1315 [M]	Opiate D'Amour	1960	3.75	7.50	15.00
❑ SW 1439 [S]	Lazy Lively Love	1961	6.25	12.50	25.00
❑ W 1439 [M]	Lazy Lively Love	1961	5.00	10.00	20.00
❑ SW 1519 [S]	The Gentle Touch	1961	6.25	12.50	25.00
❑ W 1519 [M]	The Gentle Touch	1961	5.00	10.00	20.00
❑ SWBO 1619 [(2)S]	A Lover's Portfolio	1962	6.25	12.50	25.00
❑ WBO 1619 [(2)M]	A Lover's Portfolio	1962	5.00	10.00	20.00
❑ SW 1689 [S]	Love, Embers and Flame	1962	5.00	10.00	20.00
❑ W 1689 [M]	Love, Embers and Flame	1962	3.75	7.50	15.00
❑ SW 1830 [S]	Champagne, Candlelight & Kisses	1963	3.75	7.50	15.00
❑ W 1830 [M]	Champagne, Candlelight & Kisses	1963	3.00	6.00	12.00
❑ SW 1877 [S]	Movie Themes — For Lovers Only	1963	3.75	7.50	15.00
❑ W 1877 [M]	Movie Themes — For Lovers Only	1963	3.00	6.00	12.00
❑ SW 1978 [S]	Today's Romantic Hits/For Lovers Only	1963	3.75	7.50	15.00
❑ W 1978 [M]	Today's Romantic Hits/For Lovers Only	1963	3.00	6.00	12.00
❑ SW 1979 [S]	A Lover's Portfolio, Vol. 1 (Music for Sippin' and Dancin')	1963	3.75	7.50	15.00

Number	Title (A Side/B Side)	Yr	VG	VG+	NM
❑ W 1979 [M]	A Lover's Portfolio, Vol. 1 (Music for Sippin' and Dancin')	1963	3.00	6.00	12.00
❑ SW 1980 [S]	A Lover's Portfolio, Vol. 2 (Music for Listenin' and Lovin')	1963	3.75	7.50	15.00
❑ W 1980 [M]	A Lover's Portfolio, Vol. 2 (Music for Listenin' and Lovin')	1963	3.00	6.00	12.00
❑ SW 2056 [S]	Today's Romantic Hits/For Lovers Only, Vol. 2	1964	3.75	7.50	15.00
❑ W 2056 [M]	Today's Romantic Hits/For Lovers Only, Vol. 2	1964	3.00	6.00	12.00
❑ SW 2144 [S]	Last Dance For Lovers Only	1964	3.75	7.50	15.00
❑ W 2144 [M]	Last Dance For Lovers Only	1964	3.00	6.00	12.00
❑ SW 2409 [S]	Silk 'N' Brass	1966	3.75	7.50	15.00
❑ W 2409 [M]	Silk 'N' Brass	1966	3.00	6.00	12.00
❑ SW 2471 [S]	Music Around the World — For Lovers Only	1966	3.75	7.50	15.00
❑ W 2471 [M]	Music Around the World — For Lovers Only	1966	3.00	6.00	12.00
❑ SW 2582 [S]	How Sweet It Is For Lovers	1966	3.75	7.50	15.00
❑ W 2582 [M]	How Sweet It Is For Lovers	1966	3.00	6.00	12.00
❑ SW 2684 [S]	A Taste of Brass For Lovers Only	1967	3.75	7.50	15.00
❑ W 2684 [M]	A Taste of Brass For Lovers Only	1967	3.00	6.00	12.00
❑ ST 2791 [S]	'Tis the Season	1967	3.75	7.50	15.00
❑ T 2791 [M]	'Tis the Season	1967	5.00	10.00	20.00
❑ SM-2796	The Best of Jackie Gleason	197?	2.50	5.00	10.00
—Reissue					
❑ SW 2796 [S]	The Best of Jackie Gleason	1967	3.75	7.50	15.00
❑ W 2796 [M]	The Best of Jackie Gleason	1967	3.75	7.50	15.00
❑ STCL 2816 [(3)S]	The Jackie Gleason Deluxe Set	1968	6.25	12.50	25.00
—Reissue of three complete LPs (titles unknown)					
❑ TCL 2816 [(3)M]	The Jackie Gleason Deluxe Set	1968	6.25	12.50	25.00
PAIR					
❑ PDL2-1069 [(2)]	Lush Moods	1986	3.00	6.00	12.00
PICKWICK					
❑ SPC-1008	White Christmas	197?	2.50	5.00	10.00
—Abridged version of Capitol ST 2791					
❑ SPC-2004	Romantic Moods	197?	2.50	5.00	10.00
❑ SPC-2029	The More I See You	197?	2.50	5.00	10.00
❑ SPC-3064	Plays Pretty for the People	196?	2.50	5.00	10.00
❑ SPC-3218	Shangri-La	197?	2.50	5.00	10.00

GLENN, DARRELL
NRC
Number	Title (A Side/B Side)	Yr	VG	VG+	NM
❑ LPA-5 [M]	Crying in the Chapel	1959	6.25	12.50	25.00
❑ SLPA-5 [S]	Crying in the Chapel	1959	7.50	15.00	30.00

GLENN, LLOYD
ALADDIN
Number	Title (A Side/B Side)	Yr	VG	VG+	NM
❑ LP-808 [M]	Chica-Boo	1956	250.00	500.00	1000.
—Black vinyl					
❑ LP-808 [M]	Chica-Boo	1956	1000.	1500.	2000.
—Red vinyl					
BLACK & BLUE					
❑ 33077	Old Time Shuffle	1977	3.00	6.00	12.00
IMPERIAL					
❑ LP-9174 [M]	Chica-Boo	1962	37.50	75.00	150.00
❑ LP-9175 [M]	After Hours	1962	37.50	75.00	150.00
❑ LP-12174 [S]	Chica-Boo	1962	50.00	100.00	200.00
❑ LP-12175 [S]	After Hours	1962	50.00	100.00	200.00
SCORE					
❑ SLP-4006 [M]	Lloyd Glenn	1957	250.00	500.00	1000.
❑ SLP-4020 [M]	After Hours	1958	250.00	500.00	1000.
SWING TIME					
❑ 1901 [10]	Lloyd Glenn Presents All Time Favorites	1954	1500.	2250.	3000.

GLENN, TYREE
ROULETTE
Number	Title (A Side/B Side)	Yr	VG	VG+	NM
❑ R-25009 [M]	Tyree Glenn at the Embers	1957	10.00	20.00	40.00
❑ R-25050 [M]	Tyree Glenn at the Roundtable	1959	10.00	20.00	40.00
❑ SR-25050 [S]	Tyree Glenn at the Roundtable	1959	7.50	15.00	30.00
❑ R-25075 [M]	Try a Little Tenderness	1959	10.00	20.00	40.00
❑ SR-25075 [S]	Try a Little Tenderness	1959	7.50	15.00	30.00
❑ R-25115 [M]	Let's Have a Ball	1960	6.25	12.50	25.00
❑ SR-25115 [S]	Let's Have a Ball	1960	7.50	15.00	30.00
❑ R-25138 [M]	Tyree Glenn at London House in Chicago	1961	5.00	10.00	20.00
❑ SR-25138 [S]	Tyree Glenn at London House in Chicago	1961	6.25	12.50	25.00
❑ R-25184 [M]	The Trombone Artistry of Tyree Glenn	1962	5.00	10.00	20.00
❑ SR-25184 [S]	The Trombone Artistry of Tyree Glenn	1962	6.25	12.50	25.00

GLITTERHOUSE
DYNOVOICE
Number	Title (A Side/B Side)	Yr	VG	VG+	NM
❑ 31905	Color Bland	1968	5.00	10.00	20.00

GLOBETROTTERS, THE
KIRSHNER
Number	Title (A Side/B Side)	Yr	VG	VG+	NM
❑ KES-108	The Globetrotters	1970	5.00	10.00	20.00

GLORY (2)
TEXAS REVOLUTION
Number	Title (A Side/B Side)	Yr	VG	VG+	NM
❑ CFS-2531	A Meat Music Sampler	1969	25.00	50.00	100.00

GO-GO'S, THE
RCA VICTOR
Number	Title (A Side/B Side)	Yr	VG	VG+	NM
❑ LPM-2930 [M]	Swim with the Go-Go's	1964	6.25	12.50	25.00
❑ LSP-2930 [S]	Swim with the Go-Go's	1964	7.50	15.00	30.00

GODCHAUX, KEITH AND DONNA
See KEITH AND DONNA.

GODZ, THE
ESP-DISK'
Number	Title (A Side/B Side)	Yr	VG	VG+	NM
❑ 1037 [M]	Contact High with the Godz	1967	15.00	30.00	60.00
❑ S-1037 [S]	Contact High with the Godz	1967	12.50	25.00	50.00
❑ 1047	Godz 2	1968	12.50	25.00	50.00
❑ 1077	Third Testament	1969	12.50	25.00	50.00
❑ 2017	Godzundheit	1970	12.50	25.00	50.00

GOLD, SANFORD
PRESTIGE
Number	Title (A Side/B Side)	Yr	VG	VG+	NM
❑ PRLP-7019 [M]	Piano d'Or	1956	15.00	30.00	60.00

GOLDBERG, BARRY
ATCO
Number	Title (A Side/B Side)	Yr	VG	VG+	NM
❑ SD 7040	Barry Goldberg	1974	3.00	6.00	12.00
BUDDAH					
❑ BDM-1012 [M]	The Barry Goldberg Reunion	1968	12.50	25.00	50.00
—White-label promo in stereo cover with "mono" sticker					
❑ BDS-5012 [S]	The Barry Goldberg Reunion	1968	6.25	12.50	25.00
❑ BDS-5029	Two Jews Blues	1969	6.25	12.50	25.00
❑ BDS-5051	Street Man	1970	3.75	7.50	15.00
❑ BDS-5081	Blast from My Past	1974	3.75	7.50	15.00
EPIC					
❑ LN 24199 [M]	Blowing My Mind	1966	7.50	15.00	30.00
❑ BN 26199 [S]	Blowing My Mind	1966	10.00	20.00	40.00
RECORD MAN					
❑ CR 5015	Barry Goldberg and Friends	1972	3.75	7.50	15.00

GOLDEBRIARS, THE
EPIC
Number	Title (A Side/B Side)	Yr	VG	VG+	NM
❑ LN 24087 [M]	The Goldebriars	1964	3.75	7.50	15.00
❑ LN 24114 [M]	Straight Ahead	1964	3.75	7.50	15.00
❑ BN 26087 [S]	The Goldebriars	1964	5.00	10.00	20.00
❑ BN 26114 [S]	Straight Ahead	1964	5.00	10.00	20.00

GOLDEN DAWN
INTERNATIONAL ARTISTS
Number	Title (A Side/B Side)	Yr	VG	VG+	NM
❑ 4	Power Plant	1968	25.00	50.00	100.00
❑ 4	Power Plant	1979	3.75	7.50	15.00
—Reissue with "Masterfonics" in trail-off wax					

GOLDEN EARRING
ATLANTIC
Number	Title (A Side/B Side)	Yr	VG	VG+	NM
❑ SD 8244	Eight Miles High	1970	6.25	12.50	25.00
CAPITOL					
❑ ST-164	Miracle Mirror	1969	10.00	20.00	40.00
❑ ST 2823 [S]	Winter Harvest	1967	6.25	12.50	25.00
❑ T 2823 [M]	Winter Harvest	1967	12.50	25.00	50.00
❑ ST-11315	The Golden Earring	1974	3.00	6.00	12.00
DWARF					
❑ 2000	Golden Earring	1971	6.25	12.50	25.00
MCA					
❑ 703	Grab It For a Second	198?	2.00	4.00	8.00
—Reissue of 3057					
❑ 827	Switch	198?	2.00	4.00	8.00
—Reissue of 2139					
❑ 2139	Switch	197?	2.50	5.00	10.00
—Reissue of Track 2139					
❑ 2183	To the Hilt	1976	3.00	6.00	12.00
❑ 2254	Mad Love	1977	3.00	6.00	12.00
❑ 2352	Moontan	1978	2.50	5.00	10.00
—Reissue of Track 396					
❑ 3057	Grab It For a Second	1978	3.00	6.00	12.00
❑ 6004 [(2)]	Golden Earring Live!	198?	2.50	5.00	10.00
—Reissue of 8009					
❑ 8009 [(2)]	Golden Earring Live!	1977	3.75	7.50	15.00
❑ 37172	Moontan	198?	2.00	4.00	8.00
—Reissue of 2352					
POLYDOR					
❑ PD-1-6223	No Promises...No Debts	1979	3.00	6.00	12.00
❑ PD-1-6303	Long Blond Animal	1980	3.00	6.00	12.00
TRACK					
❑ 396	Moontan	1974	3.75	7.50	15.00
—Reissue cover with close-up of earring in ear					
❑ 396	Moontan	1974	6.25	12.50	25.00
—Original cover with nude dancer					
❑ 2139	Switch	1975	3.75	7.50	15.00
21 RECORDS					
❑ T1-1-9004	Cut	1982	2.50	5.00	10.00
❑ T1-1-9008	N.E.W.S.	1984	2.50	5.00	10.00
❑ 90514	The Hole	1986	2.50	5.00	10.00
❑ 817585-1	Cut	1985	2.00	4.00	8.00
—Reissue					
❑ 823717-1	Something Heavy Going Down — Live from the Twilight Zone	1984	2.50	5.00	10.00

GOLDEN GATE QUARTET, THE
COLUMBIA
Number	Title (A Side/B Side)	Yr	VG	VG+	NM
❑ CL 6102 [10]	Golden Gate Spirituals	1950	37.50	75.00	150.00
HARMONY					
❑ HL 7018 [M]	The Golden Chariot	195?	6.25	12.50	25.00
—Second pressing has black labels					
❑ HL 7018 [M]	The Golden Chariot	1957	20.00	40.00	80.00
—Original pressing has maroon labels					
MERCURY					
❑ MG-25063 [10]	Spirituals	1951	37.50	75.00	150.00
RCA CAMDEN					
❑ CAL-308 [M]	The Golden Gate Quartet	1956	20.00	40.00	80.00

GOLDEN GATE STRINGS, THE
EPIC
Number	Title (A Side/B Side)	Yr	VG	VG+	NM
❑ LN 24158 [M]	The Bob Dylan Song Book	1965	3.00	6.00	12.00
❑ LN 24160 [M]	A String of Hits	1965	3.00	6.00	12.00
❑ LN 24248 [M]	The Monkees Song Book	1967	3.00	6.00	12.00
❑ BN 26158 [S]	The Bob Dylan Song Book	1965	3.75	7.50	15.00
❑ BN 26160 [S]	A String of Hits	1965	3.75	7.50	15.00
❑ BN 26248 [S]	The Monkees Song Book	1967	3.75	7.50	15.00

Number	Title (A Side/B Side)	Yr	VG	VG+	NM

GOLDENROD
CHARTMAKER
| ❏ CSG-1101 | Goldenrod | 1968 | 50.00 | 100.00 | 200.00 |

GOLDIE, DON
ARGO
❏ LP-708 [M]	Trumpet Caliente	1963	6.25	12.50	25.00
❏ LPS-708 [S]	Trumpet Caliente	1963	7.50	15.00	30.00
❏ LP-4010 [M]	Brilliant!	1961	6.25	12.50	25.00
❏ LPS-4010 [S]	Brilliant!	1961	7.50	15.00	30.00
VERVE
❏ V-8475 [M]	Trumpet Exodus	1962	6.25	12.50	25.00
❏ V6-8475 [S]	Trumpet Exodus	1962	7.50	15.00	30.00

GOLDKETTE, JEAN
"X"
| ❏ LVA-3017 [10] | Jean Goldkette and His Orchestra Featuring Bix Beiderbecke | 1954 | 15.00 | 30.00 | 60.00 |

GOLDSBORO, BOBBY
CURB
| ❏ JZ 36822 | Bobby Goldsboro | 1980 | 3.00 | 6.00 | 12.00 |
| ❏ FZ 37734 | Round-Up Saloon | 1982 | 2.50 | 5.00 | 10.00 |
EPIC
| ❏ PE 34703 | Goldsboro | 1977 | 3.00 | 6.00 | 12.00 |
LIBERTY
❏ LMAS-5502	Bobby Goldsboro's Greatest Hits	1981	2.00	4.00	8.00
—Reissue of United Artists 5502					
❏ LN-10007	Bobby Goldsboro's 10th Anniversary Album, Volume 1	1981	2.00	4.00	8.00
❏ LN-10047	Bobby Goldsboro's 10th Anniversary Album, Volume 2	1981	2.00	4.00	8.00
❏ LN-10114	The Best of Bobby Goldsboro	1981	2.00	4.00	8.00
SUNSET
❏ SUS-5236	This Is Bobby Goldsboro	1969	3.00	6.00	12.00
❏ SUS-5284	Pledge of Love	1970	3.00	6.00	12.00
❏ SUS-5313	Autumn of My Life	1971	3.00	6.00	12.00
UNITED ARTISTS
❏ UA-LA019-F	Brand New Kind of Love	1972	3.75	7.50	15.00
❏ SP-58 [DJ]	The Bobby Goldsboro Family Album	1971	12.50	25.00	50.00
—Promo-only compilation					
❏ UA-LA124-F	Summer (The First Time)	1973	3.75	7.50	15.00
❏ UA-LA311-H2 [(2)]	Bobby Goldsboro's 10th Anniversary Album	1974	5.00	10.00	20.00
❏ UA-LA424-G	Through the Eyes of a Man	1975	3.00	6.00	12.00
❏ UA-LA639-G	Butterfly for Bucky	1976	3.00	6.00	12.00
❏ UAL 3358 [M]	The Bobby Goldsboro Album	1964	5.00	10.00	20.00
❏ UAL 3381 [M]	I Can't Stop Loving You	1964	5.00	10.00	20.00
❏ UAL 3425 [M]	Little Things	1965	5.00	10.00	20.00
❏ UAL 3471 [M]	Broomstick Cowboy	1966	5.00	10.00	20.00
❏ UAL 3486 [M]	It's Too Late	1966	5.00	10.00	20.00
❏ UAL 3552 [M]	Blue Autumn	1967	5.00	10.00	20.00
❏ UAL 3561 [M]	Solid Goldsboro/Bobby Goldsboro's Greatest Hits	1967	5.00	10.00	20.00
❏ UAL 3599 [M]	Romantic, Soulful, Wacky	1967	5.00	10.00	20.00
❏ UAS 5502	Bobby Goldsboro's Greatest Hits	1970	5.00	10.00	20.00
❏ UAS 5516	Come Back Home	1971	3.75	7.50	15.00
❏ UAS 5578	California Wine	1972	3.75	7.50	15.00
❏ UAS 6358 [S]	I Can't Stop Loving You	1964	6.25	12.50	25.00
❏ UAS 6358 [S]	The Bobby Goldsbob Album	1964	6.25	12.50	25.00
❏ UAS 6425 [S]	Little Things	1965	6.25	12.50	25.00
❏ UAS 6471 [S]	Broomstick Cowboy	1966	6.25	12.50	25.00
❏ UAS 6486 [S]	It's Too Late	1966	6.25	12.50	25.00
❏ UAS 6552 [S]	Blue Autumn	1967	6.25	12.50	25.00
❏ UAS 6561 [S]	Solid Goldsboro/Bobby Goldsboro's Greatest Hits	1967	5.00	10.00	20.00
❏ UAS 6599 [S]	Romantic, Soulful, Wacky	1967	5.00	10.00	20.00
❏ UAS 6642	Honey	1968	5.00	10.00	20.00
❏ UAS 6657	Word Pictures Featuring Autumn of My Life	1968	5.00	10.00	20.00
❏ UAS 6704	Today	1969	5.00	10.00	20.00
❏ UAS 6735	Muddy Mississippi Line	1969	5.00	10.00	20.00
❏ UAS 6777	We Gotta Start Lovin'	1970	5.00	10.00	20.00
❏ UAS 6777	Watching Scotty Grow	1971	3.75	7.50	15.00
—Retitled version of above					
❏ SKAO-91543	Word Pictures Featuring Autumn of My Life	1968	6.25	12.50	25.00
—Capitol Record Club edition					

GOLDTONES, THE
LABREA
| ❏ L-8011 [M] | The Goldtones | 1961 | 10.00 | 20.00 | 40.00 |
| ❏ LS-8011 [S] | The Goldtones | 1961 | 12.50 | 25.00 | 50.00 |

GOLIA, VINNY
NINE WINDS
| ❏ NW 0110 [(3)] | Compositions for Large Ensemble | 1984 | 5.00 | 10.00 | 20.00 |

GOLLIWOGS, THE
Early CREEDENCE CLEARWATER REVIVAL.
FANTASY
| ❏ F-9474 | Pre-Creedence | 1975 | 7.50 | 15.00 | 30.00 |
| —Reissue of Fantasy and Scorpio sides | | | | | |

GOLSON, BENNY
ARGO
❏ LP-681 [M]	Take a Number from 1 to 10	1961	7.50	15.00	30.00
❏ LPS-681 [S]	Take a Number from 1 to 10	1961	10.00	20.00	40.00
❏ LP-716 [M]	Free	1963	7.50	15.00	30.00
❏ LPS-716 [S]	Free	1963	10.00	20.00	40.00
AUDIO FIDELITY
❏ AFSD-5978 [S]	Pop + Jazz = Swing	1962	5.00	10.00	20.00
❏ AFSD-6150 [S]	Just Jazz	1966	5.00	10.00	20.00
CONTEMPORARY
❏ C-3552 [M]	Benny Golson's New York Scene	1958	12.50	25.00	50.00
JAZZLAND
❏ JLP-85 [M]	Reunion	1962	10.00	20.00	40.00
❏ JLP-985 [S]	Reunion	1962	7.50	15.00	30.00
MERCURY
❏ SR-60801 [S]	Turning Point	1963	5.00	10.00	20.00
NEW JAZZ
❏ NJLP-8220 [M]	Groovin' with Golson	1959	12.50	25.00	50.00
—Purple label					
❏ NJLP-8220 [M]	Groovin' with Golson	1965	6.25	12.50	25.00
—Blue label, trident logo at right					
❏ NJLP-8235 [M]	Gone with Golson	1960	12.50	25.00	50.00
—Purple label					
❏ NJLP-8235 [M]	Gone with Golson	1965	6.25	12.50	25.00
—Blue label, trident logo at right					
❏ NJLP-8248 [M]	Gettin' With It	1960	12.50	25.00	50.00
—Purple label					
❏ NJLP-8248 [M]	Gettin' With It	1965	6.25	12.50	25.00
—Blue label, trident logo at right					
PRESTIGE
❏ PRLP-7361 [M]	Stockholm Sojourn	1965	5.00	10.00	20.00
❏ PRST-7361 [S]	Stockholm Sojourn	1965	6.25	12.50	25.00
RIVERSIDE
❏ RLP 12-256 [M]	The Modern Touch of Benny Golson	1957	15.00	30.00	60.00
❏ RLP 12-290 [M]	The Other Side of Benny Golson	1958	15.00	30.00	60.00
UNITED ARTISTS
❏ UAL-4020 [M]	Benny Golson and the Philadelphians	1959	12.50	25.00	50.00
❏ UAS-5020 [S]	Benny Golson and the Philadelphians	1959	10.00	20.00	40.00
VERVE
❏ V-8710 [M]	Turn In, Turn On	1967	5.00	10.00	20.00

GOMEZ, VICENTE
DECCA
❏ DL 4088 [M]	Concerto Flamenco	1960	3.75	7.50	15.00
❏ DL 4156 [M]	Rio Flamenco	1961	3.75	7.50	15.00
❏ DL 4312 [M]	Guitar Extraordinary	1962	3.75	7.50	15.00
❏ DL 8017 [M]	Spanish Guitar Recital	195?	7.50	15.00	30.00
—Black label, silver print					
❏ DL 8439 [M]	Romantic Guitar	1957	6.25	12.50	25.00
—Black label, silver print					
❏ DL 8918 [M]	Vicente Gomez	1959	5.00	10.00	20.00
—Black label, silver print					
❏ DL 8965 [M]	The Artistry of Vicente Gomez	1959	5.00	10.00	20.00
—Black label, silver print					
❏ DL 74088 [S]	Concerto Flamenco	1960	5.00	10.00	20.00
❏ DL 74156 [S]	Rio Flamenco	1961	5.00	10.00	20.00
❏ DL 74312 [S]	Guitar Extraordinary	1962	5.00	10.00	20.00
❏ DL 78918 [S]	Vicente Gomez	1959	6.25	12.50	25.00
—Maroon or black label					
❏ DL 78965 [S]	The Artistry of Vicente Gomez	1959	6.25	12.50	25.00
—Maroon or black label					

GONSALVES, PAUL
ARGO
| ❏ LP-626 [M] | Cookin' | 1958 | 12.50 | 25.00 | 50.00 |
| ❏ LPS-626 [S] | Cookin' | 1959 | 10.00 | 20.00 | 40.00 |
IMPULSE!
❏ A-41 [M]	Cleopatra Feelin' Jazzy	1963	6.25	12.50	25.00
❏ AS-41 [S]	Cleopatra Feelin' Jazzy	1963	7.50	15.00	30.00
❏ A-52 [M]	Salt and Pepper	1963	6.25	12.50	25.00
❏ AS-52 [S]	Salt and Pepper	1963	7.50	15.00	30.00
❏ A-55 [M]	Tell It the Way It Is	1963	6.25	12.50	25.00
❏ AS-55 [S]	Tell It the Way It Is	1963	7.50	15.00	30.00
JAZZLAND
❏ JLP-36 [M]	Gettin' Together	1961	7.50	15.00	30.00
❏ JLP-936 [S]	Gettin' Together	1961	10.00	20.00	40.00

GONSALVES, VIRGIL
LIBERTY
| ❏ LJH-6010 [M] | Jazz San Francisco Style | 1956 | 12.50 | 25.00 | 50.00 |
NOCTURNE
| ❏ NLP-8 [10] | Virgil Gonsalves | 1954 | 20.00 | 40.00 | 80.00 |
OMEGA
| ❏ OML-1047 [M] | Jazz at Monterey | 1959 | 10.00 | 20.00 | 40.00 |

GONZALES, BABS
DAUNTLESS
| ❏ DM-4311 [M] | Sunday Afternoon at Small's Paradise | 1963 | 10.00 | 20.00 | 40.00 |
| ❏ DS-6311 [S] | Sunday Afternoon at Small's Paradise | 1963 | 12.50 | 25.00 | 50.00 |
HOPE
| ❏ 001 [M] | Voila! | 1958 | 37.50 | 75.00 | 150.00 |
JARO
| ❏ JAM-5000 [M] | Cool Philosophy | 1959 | 20.00 | 40.00 | 80.00 |
| ❏ JAS-8000 [S] | Cool Philosophy | 1959 | 25.00 | 50.00 | 100.00 |

GOO GOO DOLLS
ENIGMA
| ❏ 7 73406-1 | JED | 1989 | 5.00 | 10.00 | 20.00 |
MERCENARY
| ❏ MER-2102 | Goo Goo Dolls | 1987 | 7.50 | 15.00 | 30.00 |

GOOD AND PLENTY
SENATE
| ❏ LP-21001 [M] | The World of Good and Plenty | 1967 | 7.50 | 15.00 | 30.00 |
| ❏ LPS-21001 [S] | The World of Good and Plenty | 1967 | 7.50 | 15.00 | 30.00 |

GOOD GUYS, THE
GNP CRESCENDO
| ❏ GNP-2001 [M] | Sidewalk Surfing | 1964 | 7.50 | 15.00 | 30.00 |

G

Number	Title (A Side/B Side)	Yr	VG	VG+	NM
☐ GNPS-2001 [S]	Sidewalk Surfing	1964	10.00	20.00	40.00

UNITED ARTISTS

Number	Title (A Side/B Side)	Yr	VG	VG+	NM
☐ UAL-3370 [M]	The Good Guys Sing	1964	3.75	7.50	15.00
☐ UAS-6370 [S]	The Good Guys Sing	1964	5.00	10.00	20.00

GOOD RATS, THE
KAPP

Number	Title (A Side/B Side)	Yr	VG	VG+	NM
☐ KS-3580	The Good Rats	1969	10.00	20.00	40.00

PASSPORT

Number	Title (A Side/B Side)	Yr	VG	VG+	NM
☐ SP-20 [DJ]	Rats the Way You Like It (Live)	1978	15.00	30.00	60.00
☐ PB-9825	From Rats to Riches	1978	3.00	6.00	12.00
☐ PB-9830	Birth Comes to Us All	1978	3.00	6.00	12.00

RAT CITY

Number	Title (A Side/B Side)	Yr	VG	VG+	NM
☐ 998 [(2)]	Live at Last	1979	3.75	7.50	15.00
☐ RCR-8001	Rat City in Blue	1975	5.00	10.00	20.00
☐ RCR-8002	Tasty	1978	3.00	6.00	12.00
☐ RCR-8003	Great American Music	1981	3.00	6.00	12.00

WARNER BROS.

Number	Title (A Side/B Side)	Yr	VG	VG+	NM
☐ BS 2813	Tasty	1974	7.50	15.00	30.00

GOOD TIMES, THE
KAMA SUTRA

Number	Title (A Side/B Side)	Yr	VG	VG+	NM
☐ KLP-8052 [M]	The Good Times	1966	3.75	7.50	15.00
☐ KSLP-8052 [S]	The Good Times	1966	5.00	10.00	20.00

GOODEES, THE
HIP

Number	Title (A Side/B Side)	Yr	VG	VG+	NM
☐ HIS-7002	Candy Coated Goodees	1969	6.25	12.50	25.00

GOODMAN, BENNY
BRUNSWICK

Number	Title (A Side/B Side)	Yr	VG	VG+	NM
☐ BL 54010 [M]	Benny Goodman 1927-34	1954	7.50	15.00	30.00
☐ BL 58015 [10]	Chicago Jazz Classics	1950	12.50	25.00	50.00

CAPITOL

Number	Title (A Side/B Side)	Yr	VG	VG+	NM
☐ H 202 [10]	Session for Six	1950	12.50	25.00	50.00
☐ H 295 [10]	Easy Does It	1952	12.50	25.00	50.00
☐ H 343 [10]	The Benny Goodman Trio	1952	12.50	25.00	50.00
☐ T 395 [M]	Session for Six	1953	10.00	20.00	40.00
—Turquoise label					
☐ T 395 [M]	Session for Six	1958	5.00	10.00	20.00
—Black label with colorband, Capitol logo on left					
☐ H 409 [10]	The Benny Goodman Band	1953	12.50	25.00	50.00
☐ T 409 [M]	The Benny Goodman Band	1953	10.00	20.00	40.00
—Turquoise label					
☐ T 409 [M]	The Benny Goodman Band	1958	5.00	10.00	20.00
—Black label with colorband, Capitol logo on left					
☐ H 441 [10]	The Goodman Touch	1953	12.50	25.00	50.00
☐ T 441 [M]	The Goodman Touch	1953	10.00	20.00	40.00
—Turquoise label					
☐ T 441 [M]	The Goodman Touch	1958	5.00	10.00	20.00
—Black label with colorband, Capitol logo on left					
☐ H 479 [10]	Small Combo 1947	1954	12.50	25.00	50.00
☐ H1-565 [10]	B.G. in Hi-Fi (Volume 1)	1955	7.50	15.00	30.00
☐ H2-565 [10]	B.G. in Hi-Fi (Volume 2)	1955	7.50	15.00	30.00
☐ W 565 [M]	B.G. in Hi-Fi	1955	10.00	20.00	40.00
—Gray label					
☐ W 565 [M]	B.G. in Hi-Fi	1958	5.00	10.00	20.00
—Black label with colorband, Capitol logo on left					
☐ T 668 [M]	Mostly Sextets	1956	7.50	15.00	30.00
—Turquoise label					
☐ T 668 [M]	Mostly Sextets	1958	5.00	10.00	20.00
—Black label with colorband, Capitol logo on left					
☐ T 669 [M]	Benny Goodman Combos	1956	7.50	15.00	30.00
—Turquoise label					
☐ T 669 [M]	Benny Goodman Combos	1958	5.00	10.00	20.00
—Black label with colorband, Capitol logo on left					
☐ S 706 [M]	Selections Featured in "The Benny Goodman Story"	1956	7.50	15.00	30.00
—Turquoise label					
☐ S 706 [M]	Selections Featured in "The Benny Goodman Story"	1958	5.00	10.00	20.00
—Black label with colorband, Capitol logo on left					
☐ T 1514 [M]	The Hits of Benny Goodman	1961	5.00	10.00	20.00
—Black label with colorband, Capitol logo on left					

CENTURY

Number	Title (A Side/B Side)	Yr	VG	VG+	NM
☐ 1150	The King of Swing Direct to Disc	1979	7.50	15.00	30.00
—Direct-to-disc audiophile recording					

CHESS

Number	Title (A Side/B Side)	Yr	VG	VG+	NM
☐ LP-1440 [DJ]	Benny Rides Again	1960	25.00	50.00	100.00
—Multi-color swirl vinyl					
☐ LP-1440	Benny Rides Again	1960	12.50	25.00	50.00
☐ LPS-1440 [S]	Benny Rides Again	1960	7.50	15.00	30.00

CLASSICS RECORD LIBRARY

Number	Title (A Side/B Side)	Yr	VG	VG+	NM
☐ RL-7673 [(3)M]	An Album of Swing Classics	1967	12.50	25.00	50.00
☐ SRL-7673 [(3)S]	An Album of Swing Classics	1967	10.00	20.00	40.00
—Above two were compiled for Book-of-the-Month Club					

COLUMBIA

Number	Title (A Side/B Side)	Yr	VG	VG+	NM
☐ C2L 16 [(2)M]	Benny in Brussels	195?	10.00	20.00	40.00
—Red and black label with six white "eye" logos					
☐ GL 102 [10]	Let's Hear the Melody	1950	15.00	30.00	60.00
☐ CL 500 [M]	Combos	1952	10.00	20.00	40.00
—Maroon label with gold print					
☐ CL 500 [M]	Combos	1955	7.50	15.00	30.00
—Red and black label with six "eye" logos					
☐ GL 500 [M]	Combos	1951	12.50	25.00	50.00
—Black label, silver print					
☐ CL 501 [M]	The Golden Era Series Presents Benny Goodman and His Orchestra	1952	10.00	20.00	40.00
—Maroon label with gold print					

Number	Title (A Side/B Side)	Yr	VG	VG+	NM
☐ CL 501 [M]	The Golden Era Series Presents Benny Goodman and His Orchestra	1955	7.50	15.00	30.00
—Red and black label with six "eye" logos					
☐ GL 501 [M]	The Golden Era Series Presents Benny Goodman and His Orchestra	1951	12.50	25.00	50.00
—Black label, silver print					
☐ CL 516 [M]	The Benny Goodman Trio Plays for the Fletcher Henderson Fund	1953	10.00	20.00	40.00
—Maroon label with gold print					
☐ CL 516 [M]	The Benny Goodman Trio Plays for the Fletcher Henderson Fund	1955	7.50	15.00	30.00
—Red and black label with six "eye" logos					
☐ GL 516 [M]	The Benny Goodman Trio Plays for the Fletcher Henderson Fund	1952	12.50	25.00	50.00
—Reissue of Martin Block 1000; black label, silver print					
☐ CL 523 [M]	Benny Goodman Presents Eddie Sauter Arrangements	1953	10.00	20.00	40.00
—Maroon label with gold print					
☐ CL 523 [M]	Benny Goodman Presents Eddie Sauter Arrangements	1955	7.50	15.00	30.00
—Red and black label with six "eye" logos					
☐ GL 523 [M]	Benny Goodman Presents Eddie Sauter Arrangements	1953	12.50	25.00	50.00
—Black label, silver print					
☐ CL 524 [M]	Benny Goodman Presents Fletcher Henderson Arrangements	1953	7.50	15.00	30.00
—Red and black label with six "eye" logos					
☐ CL 524 [M]	Benny Goodman Presents Fletcher Henderson Arrangements	1954	10.00	20.00	40.00
—Maroon label with gold print					
☐ GL 524 [M]	Benny Goodman Presents Fletcher Henderson Arrangements	1953	12.50	25.00	50.00
—Black label, silver print					
☐ CL 534 [M]	Benny Goodman and His Orchestra	1953	10.00	20.00	40.00
—Maroon label with gold print					
☐ CL 534 [M]	Benny Goodman and His Orchestra	1955	7.50	15.00	30.00
—Red and black label with six "eye" logos					
☐ CL 552 [M]	The New Benny Goodman Sextet	1954	10.00	20.00	40.00
—Maroon label with gold print					
☐ CL 552 [M]	The New Benny Goodman Sextet	1955	7.50	15.00	30.00
—Red and black label with six "eye" logos					
☐ CL 652 [M]	The Benny Goodman Sextet and Orchestra with Charlie Christian	1955	7.50	15.00	30.00
—Red and black label with six "eye" logos					
☐ CL 652 [M]	The Benny Goodman Sextet and Orchestra with Charlie Christian	1963	5.00	10.00	20.00
—Red label with "Guaranteed High Fidelity" or "Mono" at bottom					
☐ CL 814 [M]	Carnegie Hall Jazz Concert, Volume 1	1956	7.50	15.00	30.00
—Red and black label with six "eye" logos					
☐ CL 814 [M]	Carnegie Hall Jazz Concert, Volume 1	1963	5.00	10.00	20.00
—Red label with "Guaranteed High Fidelity" or "Mono" at bottom					
☐ CL 815 [M]	Carnegie Hall Jazz Concert, Volume 2	1956	7.50	15.00	30.00
—Red and black label with six "eye" logos					
☐ CL 815 [M]	Carnegie Hall Jazz Concert, Volume 2	1963	5.00	10.00	20.00
—Red label with "Guaranteed High Fidelity" or "Mono" at bottom					
☐ CL 815 [M]	Carnegie Hall Jazz Concert, Volume 2	197?	3.00	6.00	12.00
—Orange label with "Mono" under "CL 815" at left					
☐ CL 816 [M]	Carnegie Hall Jazz Concert, Volume 3	1956	7.50	15.00	30.00
—Red and black label with six "eye" logos					
☐ CL 816 [M]	Carnegie Hall Jazz Concert, Volume 3	1963	5.00	10.00	20.00
—Red label with "Guaranteed High Fidelity" or "Mono" at bottom					
☐ CL 817 [M]	The King of Swing, Volume 1	1956	7.50	15.00	30.00
☐ CL 818 [M]	The King of Swing, Volume 2	1956	7.50	15.00	30.00
☐ CL 819 [M]	The King of Swing, Volume 3	1956	7.50	15.00	30.00
☐ CL 820 [M]	The Great Benny Goodman	1956	7.50	15.00	30.00
—Red and black label with six "eye" logos					
☐ CL 820 [M]	The Great Benny Goodman	1963	5.00	10.00	20.00
—Red label with "Guaranteed High Fidelity" or "Mono" at bottom					
☐ CL 821 [M]	Vintage Goodman	1956	7.50	15.00	30.00
☐ CL 1247 [M]	Benny in Brussels, Vol. I	1958	7.50	15.00	30.00
☐ CL 1248 [M]	Benny in Brussels, Vol. II	1958	7.50	15.00	30.00
☐ CL 1324 [M]	The Happy Session	1959	7.50	15.00	30.00
☐ CL 1579 [M]	Benny Goodman Swings Again	1960	7.50	15.00	30.00
☐ CL 2533 [10]	Benny at the Ballroom	1955	10.00	20.00	40.00
—Retitled reissue of 6100					
☐ CL 2564 [10]	The B.G. Six	1955	10.00	20.00	40.00
—Retitled reissue of 6052					
☐ CL 6033 [10]	Benny Goodman and Peggy Lee	1949	20.00	40.00	80.00
☐ CL 6048 [10]	Dance Parade	1949	12.50	25.00	50.00
☐ CL 6052 [10]	Goodman Sextet Session	1949	12.50	25.00	50.00
☐ CL 6100 [10]	Dance Parade, Volume 2	1950	12.50	25.00	50.00
☐ CL 6302 [10]	Let's Hear the Melody	1951	12.50	25.00	50.00
—Reissue of GL 102					
☐ CS 8075 [S]	Benny in Brussels, Vol. I	1959	10.00	20.00	40.00
☐ CS 8076 [S]	Benny in Brussels, Vol. II	1959	10.00	20.00	40.00
☐ CS 8129 [S]	The Happy Session	1959	6.25	12.50	25.00
☐ CS 8379 [S]	Benny Goodman Swings Again	1960	6.25	12.50	25.00
☐ XTV 28995/6 [M]	Swing Into Spring	1959	5.00	10.00	20.00
—Special item made for Texaco service stations					

COLUMBIA MASTERWORKS

Number	Title (A Side/B Side)	Yr	VG	VG+	NM
☐ OSL 160 [(2)M]	The Famous 1938 Carnegie Hall Jazz Concert	1956	18.75	37.50	75.00
—Gray and black labels with six "eye" logos					
☐ OSL 160 [(2)M]	The Famous 1938 Carnegie Hall Jazz Concert	1963	10.00	20.00	40.00
—Gray labels with "Columbia" at top					
☐ OSL 160 [(2)M]	The Famous 1938 Carnegie Hall Jazz Concert	1970	5.00	10.00	20.00
—Olive labels with "Columbia" circling edge					
☐ SL 160 [(2)M]	The Famous 1938 Carnegie Hall Jazz Concert	1950	25.00	50.00	100.00
—Green labels					
☐ SL 176 [(6)M]	King of Swing	1950	37.50	75.00	150.00
☐ OSL 180 [(2)M]	The King of Swing	1956	18.75	37.50	75.00
—Gray and black labels with six "eye" logos					
☐ OSL 180 [(2)M]	The King of Swing	1963	10.00	20.00	40.00
—Gray labels with "Columbia" at top					

Number	Title (A Side/B Side)	Yr	VG	VG+	NM
❑ SL 180 [(2)M]	1937-38 Jazz Concert No. 2	1950	18.75	37.50	75.00
❑ ML 4358 [M]	Carnegie Hall Jazz Concert, Volume 1	1950	10.00	20.00	40.00
❑ ML 4359 [M]	Carnegie Hall Jazz Concert, Volume 2	1950	10.00	20.00	40.00
❑ ML 4590 [M]	1937-38 Jazz Concert No. 2, Volume 1	1950	10.00	20.00	40.00
❑ ML 4591 [M]	1937-38 Jazz Concert No. 2, Volume 2	1950	10.00	20.00	40.00
❑ ML 4613 [M]	King of Swing, Volume 1	1950	10.00	20.00	40.00
❑ ML 4614 [M]	King of Swing, Volume 2	1950	10.00	20.00	40.00
❑ MS 6805 [S]	Meeting at the Summit	1961	5.00	10.00	20.00
—With the Columbia Jazz Combo and the Columbia Orchestra					

COLUMBIA MUSICAL TREASURY

Number	Title (A Side/B Side)	Yr	VG	VG+	NM
❑ P4M 5678 [(4)]	The Best of Benny Goodman	197?	7.50	15.00	30.00
—Issued by Columbia House					

DECCA

Number	Title (A Side/B Side)	Yr	VG	VG+	NM
❑ DXB 188 [(2)M]	The Benny Goodman Story	1956	15.00	30.00	60.00
—Black label, silver print					
❑ DXB 188 [(2)M]	The Benny Goodman Story	1961	10.00	20.00	40.00
—Black label with color bars					
❑ DL 8252 [M]	The Benny Goodman Story, Volume 1	1956	7.50	15.00	30.00
—Black label, silver print					
❑ DL 8252 [M]	The Benny Goodman Story, Volume 1	1961	5.00	10.00	20.00
—Black label with color bars					
❑ DL 8253 [M]	The Benny Goodman Story, Volume 2	1956	7.50	15.00	30.00
—Black label, silver print					
❑ DL 8253 [M]	The Benny Goodman Story, Volume 2	1961	5.00	10.00	20.00
—Black label with color bars					

HARMONY

Number	Title (A Side/B Side)	Yr	VG	VG+	NM
❑ HL 7005 [M]	Peggy Lee Sings with Benny Goodman	1957	5.00	10.00	20.00

MARTIN BLOCK

Number	Title (A Side/B Side)	Yr	VG	VG+	NM
❑ MB-1000 [M]	The Benny Goodman Trio Plays for the Fletcher Henderson Fund	1951	15.00	30.00	60.00

MGM

Number	Title (A Side/B Side)	Yr	VG	VG+	NM
❑ 3E-9 [(3)M]	The Benny Goodman Treasure Chest	1959	37.50	75.00	150.00
❑ E-3788 [M]	Performance Recordings, Volume 1	1959	6.25	12.50	25.00
❑ E-3789 [M]	Performance Recordings, Volume 2	1959	6.25	12.50	25.00
❑ E-3790 [M]	Performance Recordings, Volume 3	1959	6.25	12.50	25.00
❑ E-3810 [M]	The Sound of Music	1960	5.00	10.00	20.00
❑ SE-3810 [S]	The Sound of Music	1960	6.25	12.50	25.00

MOSAIC

Number	Title (A Side/B Side)	Yr	VG	VG+	NM
❑ MQ6-148 [(6)]	The Complete Capitol Small Group Recordings of Benny Goodman 1944-1955	199?	25.00	50.00	100.00

RCA VICTOR

Number	Title (A Side/B Side)	Yr	VG	VG+	NM
❑ WPT 12 [10]	Benny Goodman	1951	12.50	25.00	50.00
❑ LPT-17 [10]	A Treasury of Immortal Performances	1951	12.50	25.00	50.00
❑ WPT 26 [10]	Immortal Performances	1952	12.50	25.00	50.00
❑ LPT-1005 [M]	Benny Goodman	1954	10.00	20.00	40.00
❑ LPM-1099 [M]	The Golden Age of Benny Goodman	1956	10.00	20.00	40.00
❑ LPM-1226 [M]	The Benny Goodman Trio/Quartet/Quintet	1956	10.00	20.00	40.00
❑ LPM-1239 [M]	This Is Benny Goodman	1956	10.00	20.00	40.00
❑ LPM-2247 [M]	The Kingdom of Swing	1960	5.00	10.00	20.00
❑ LSP-2247 [S]	The Kingdom of Swing	1960	6.25	12.50	25.00
❑ LSP-2698 [S]	Together Again	1964	5.00	10.00	20.00
❑ LPT-3004 [10]	Benny Goodman Quartet	1952	12.50	25.00	50.00
❑ LPT-3056 [10]	This Is Benny Goodman and His Orchestra	1954	12.50	25.00	50.00
❑ LOC-6008 [(2)M]	Benny Goodman in Moscow	1962	5.00	10.00	20.00
❑ LSO-6008 [(2)S]	Benny Goodman in Moscow	1962	6.25	12.50	25.00
❑ LPT-6703 [(5)M]	The Golden Age of Swing	1956	150.00	300.00	600.00
—Five-record set in white vinyl binder with bound-in booklet					

SUNBEAM

Number	Title (A Side/B Side)	Yr	VG	VG+	NM
❑ 116/27 [(12)]	Manhattan Room 1937	197?	15.00	30.00	60.00
❑ 128/32 [(5)]	From the Congress Hotel, Chicago, 1935-36	197?	6.25	12.50	25.00

WESTINGHOUSE

Number	Title (A Side/B Side)	Yr	VG	VG+	NM
❑ (no #) [M]	Benny Goodman Plays World Favorites in High Fidelity	1958	7.50	15.00	30.00
❑ (no #) [(5)M]	Benny in Brussels	1958	25.00	50.00	100.00

GOODMAN, DICKIE

CASH

Number	Title (A Side/B Side)	Yr	VG	VG+	NM
❑ CR 6000	Mr. Jaws and Other Fables	1975	6.25	12.50	25.00

COMET

Number	Title (A Side/B Side)	Yr	VG	VG+	NM
❑ 69	My Son, the Joke	1963	10.00	20.00	40.00

IX CHAINS

Number	Title (A Side/B Side)	Yr	VG	VG+	NM
❑ NCS 9000	The Original Flying Saucers	1973	10.00	20.00	40.00

RHINO

Number	Title (A Side/B Side)	Yr	VG	VG+	NM
❑ RNLP-811	Dickie Goodman's Greatest Hits	1983	3.75	7.50	15.00

RORI

Number	Title (A Side/B Side)	Yr	VG	VG+	NM
❑ 3301	The Many Heads of Dickie Goodman	1962	20.00	40.00	80.00

GOODMAN, DODY

CORAL

Number	Title (A Side/B Side)	Yr	VG	VG+	NM
❑ CRL 57196 [M]	Dody Goodman Sings?	1958	7.50	15.00	30.00

GORDIAN KNOT, THE

VERVE

Number	Title (A Side/B Side)	Yr	VG	VG+	NM
❑ V-5062 [M]	Tones	1968	7.50	15.00	30.00
—White label promo only (no stock copies were issued in mono)					
❑ V6-5062 [S]	Tones	1968	3.75	7.50	15.00

GORDON, BOB

PACIFIC JAZZ

Number	Title (A Side/B Side)	Yr	VG	VG+	NM
❑ PJLP-12 [10]	Meet Mr. Gordon	1954	30.00	60.00	120.00

TAMPA

Number	Title (A Side/B Side)	Yr	VG	VG+	NM
❑ TP-26 [M]	Jazz Impressions	1957	25.00	50.00	100.00
—Colored vinyl					
❑ TP-26 [M]	Jazz Impressions	1958	12.50	25.00	50.00
—Black vinyl					

GORDON, BOB/CLIFFORD BROWN

PACIFIC JAZZ

Number	Title (A Side/B Side)	Yr	VG	VG+	NM
❑ PJ-3 [M]	Jazz Immortal	1960	12.50	25.00	50.00

Number	Title (A Side/B Side)	Yr	VG	VG+	NM
❑ PJ-1214 [M]	The Bob Gordon Quintet/The Clifford Brown Ensemble	1956	25.00	50.00	100.00

GORDON, DEXTER

BETHLEHEM

Number	Title (A Side/B Side)	Yr	VG	VG+	NM
❑ BCP-36 [M]	Daddy Plays the Horn	1956	30.00	60.00	120.00

BLUE NOTE

Number	Title (A Side/B Side)	Yr	VG	VG+	NM
❑ BLP-4077 [M]	Doin' Allright	1961	37.50	75.00	150.00
—With W. 63rd St. addresss on label					
❑ BLP-4077 [M]	Doin' Allright	1963	6.25	12.50	25.00
—With "New York, USA" address on label					
❑ BLP-4083 [M]	Dexter Calling	1961	15.00	30.00	60.00
—With 61st. St. address on label					
❑ BLP-4083 [M]	Dexter Calling	1963	6.25	12.50	25.00
—With "New York, USA" address on label					
❑ BLP-4112 [M]	Go	1962	7.50	15.00	30.00
—With "New York, USA" address on label					
❑ BLP-4133 [M]	A Swingin' Affair	1963	7.50	15.00	30.00
—With "New York, USA" address on label					
❑ BLP-4146 [M]	Our Man in Paris	1963	7.50	15.00	30.00
—With "New York, USA" address on label					
❑ BLP-4176 [M]	One Flight Up	1964	7.50	15.00	30.00
—With "New York, USA" address on label					
❑ BLP-4204 [M]	Gettin' Around	1965	7.50	15.00	30.00
—With "New York, USA" address on label					
❑ BST-84077 [S]	Doin' Allright	1961	50.00	100.00	200.00
—With W. 63rd St. addresss on label					
❑ BST-84077 [S]	Doin' Allright	1963	7.50	15.00	30.00
—With "New York, USA" address on label					
❑ BST-84083 [S]	Dexter Calling	1961	20.00	40.00	80.00
—With 61st. St. address on label					
❑ BST-84083 [S]	Dexter Calling	1963	7.50	15.00	30.00
—With "New York, USA" address on label					
❑ BST-84112 [S]	Go	1962	10.00	20.00	40.00
—With "New York, USA" address on label					
❑ BST-84133	A Swingin' Affair	199?	7.50	15.00	30.00
—Classic Records 180-gram audiophile reissue					
❑ BST-84133 [S]	A Swingin' Affair	1963	10.00	20.00	40.00
—With "New York, USA" address on label					
❑ BST-84146 [S]	Our Man in Paris	1963	10.00	20.00	40.00
—With "New York, USA" address on label					
❑ BST-84176 [S]	One Flight Up	1964	10.00	20.00	40.00
—With "New York, USA" address on label					
❑ BST-84204 [S]	Gettin' Around	1965	10.00	20.00	40.00
—With "New York, USA" address on label					

DIAL

Number	Title (A Side/B Side)	Yr	VG	VG+	NM
❑ LP-204 [10]	Dexter Gordon Quintet	1950	100.00	200.00	400.00

DOOTO

Number	Title (A Side/B Side)	Yr	VG	VG+	NM
❑ DL-207 [M]	Dexter Blows Hot and Cool	196?	12.50	25.00	50.00

DOOTONE

Number	Title (A Side/B Side)	Yr	VG	VG+	NM
❑ DL-207 [M]	Dexter Blows Hot and Cool	1956	62.50	125.00	250.00
—Red vinyl					
❑ DL-207 [M]	Dexter Blows Hot and Cool	1957	30.00	60.00	120.00
—Black vinyl					

JAZZLAND

Number	Title (A Side/B Side)	Yr	VG	VG+	NM
❑ JLP-29 [M]	The Resurgence of Dexter Gordon	1960	12.50	25.00	50.00
❑ JLP-929 [S]	The Resurgence of Dexter Gordon	1960	15.00	30.00	60.00

PRESTIGE

Number	Title (A Side/B Side)	Yr	VG	VG+	NM
❑ PRST-7623	The Tower of Power	1969	5.00	10.00	20.00
❑ PRST-7680	More Power	1969	5.00	10.00	20.00
❑ PRST-7763	A Day in Copenhagen	1970	5.00	10.00	20.00
❑ PRST-7829	Panther!	1971	5.00	10.00	20.00

SAVOY

Number	Title (A Side/B Side)	Yr	VG	VG+	NM
❑ MG-9003 [10]	All Star Series — Dexter Gordon	1951	62.50	125.00	250.00
❑ MG-9016 [10]	New Trends in Modern Jazz, Volume 3	1952	62.50	125.00	250.00
❑ MG-12130 [M]	Dexter Rides Again	1958	25.00	50.00	100.00

GORDON, DEXTER/HOWARD MCGHEE

JAZZTONE

Number	Title (A Side/B Side)	Yr	VG	VG+	NM
❑ J-1235 [M]	The Chase	1956	10.00	20.00	40.00

GORDON, HONI

PRESTIGE

Number	Title (A Side/B Side)	Yr	VG	VG+	NM
❑ PRLP-7230 [M]	Honi Gordon Sings	1962	10.00	20.00	40.00
❑ PRST-7230 [S]	Honi Gordon Sings	1962	12.50	25.00	50.00

GORDON, JOE

CONTEMPORARY

Number	Title (A Side/B Side)	Yr	VG	VG+	NM
❑ M-3597 [M]	Lookin' Good	1961	7.50	15.00	30.00
❑ S-7597 [S]	Lookin' Good	1961	10.00	20.00	40.00

EMARCY

Number	Title (A Side/B Side)	Yr	VG	VG+	NM
❑ MG-26046 [10]	Introducing Joe Gordon	1954	37.50	75.00	150.00
❑ MG-36025 [M]	Introducing Joe Gordon	1955	25.00	50.00	100.00

GORDON, JOHN

STRATA-EAST

Number	Title (A Side/B Side)	Yr	VG	VG+	NM
❑ SES-19760	Step by Step	197?	5.00	10.00	20.00

GORDON, JUSTIN

DOT

Number	Title (A Side/B Side)	Yr	VG	VG+	NM
❑ DLP-3214 [M]	Justin Gordon Swings	1959	10.00	20.00	40.00

GORDON, KELLY

CAPITOL

Number	Title (A Side/B Side)	Yr	VG	VG+	NM
❑ ST-201	Defunked	1969	5.00	10.00	20.00

GORDON, ROBERT

PRIVATE STOCK

Number	Title (A Side/B Side)	Yr	VG	VG+	NM
❑ PS-2030	Robert Gordon with Link Wray	1977	4.00	8.00	16.00
—Formerly with Tuff Darts					
❑ PS-7008	Fresh Fish Special	1978	4.00	8.00	16.00

Number	Title (A Side/B Side)	Yr	VG	VG+	NM
RCA VICTOR					
❏ AFL1-3294	Rock Billy Boogie	1979	3.00	6.00	12.00
❏ AFL1-3294	Rock Billy Boogie	1979	5.00	10.00	20.00
—Original pressing on white vinyl					
❏ AFL1-3296	Robert Gordon with Link Wray	1979	3.00	6.00	12.00
—Reissue					
❏ AFL1-3299	Fresh Fish Special	1979	3.00	6.00	12.00
—Reissue					
❏ DJL1-3411 [DJ]	Essential Robert Gordon	1979	7.50	15.00	30.00
—Promo-only live album with tracks from Tuff Darts					
❏ AFL1-3523	Bad Boy	1980	3.00	6.00	12.00
❏ AFL1-3773	Are You Gonna Be the One	1981	3.00	6.00	12.00
❏ AFL1-4380	Too Fast to Live, Too Young to Die	1982	3.00	6.00	12.00

GORDON 'N ROGERS' INTER-URBAN ELECTRIC A&E PIT CREW & RHYTHM BAND

Number	Title (A Side/B Side)	Yr	VG	VG+	NM
CAPITOL					
❏ STAO-276	Bug In!	1969	5.00	10.00	20.00

GORE, CHARLIE

Number	Title (A Side/B Side)	Yr	VG	VG+	NM
AUDIO LAB					
❏ AL-1526 [M]	The Country Gentleman	1959	50.00	100.00	200.00

GORE, LESLEY

Number	Title (A Side/B Side)	Yr	VG	VG+	NM
A&M					
❏ SP-4564	Love Me by Name	1975	3.75	7.50	15.00
MERCURY					
❏ ML-8016	I'll Cry If I Want To	1980	2.50	5.00	10.00
—Reissue of 60805					
❏ MG 20805 [M]	I'll Cry If I Want To	1963	7.50	15.00	30.00
—With no blurb for "It's My Party"					
❏ MG 20805 [M]	I'll Cry If I Want To	1964	5.00	10.00	20.00
—With blurb for "It's My Party"					
❏ MG 20849 [M]	Lesley Gore Sings of Mixed-Up Hearts	1963	7.50	15.00	30.00
❏ MG 20901 [M]	Boys, Boys, Boys	1964	7.50	15.00	30.00
❏ MG 20943 [M]	Girl Talk	1964	7.50	15.00	30.00
❏ MG 21024 [M]	The Golden Hits of Lesley Gore	1965	7.50	15.00	30.00
❏ MG 21042 [M]	My Town, My Guy & Me	1965	7.50	15.00	30.00
❏ MG 21066 [M]	All About Love	1966	7.50	15.00	30.00
❏ MG 21120 [M]	California Nights	1967	7.50	15.00	30.00
❏ SR 60805 [S]	I'll Cry If I Want To	1963	10.00	20.00	40.00
—With no blurb for "It's My Party"					
❏ SR 60805 [S]	I'll Cry If I Want To	1964	7.50	15.00	30.00
—With blurb for "It's My Party"					
❏ SR 60849 [S]	Lesley Gore Sings of Mixed-Up Hearts	1963	10.00	20.00	40.00
❏ SR 60901 [S]	Boys, Boys, Boys	1964	10.00	20.00	40.00
❏ SR 60943 [S]	Girl Talk	1964	10.00	20.00	40.00
❏ SR 61024 [S]	The Golden Hits of Lesley Gore	196?	3.75	7.50	15.00
—Reissues have 10 tracks					
❏ SR 61024 [S]	The Golden Hits of Lesley Gore	1965	10.00	20.00	40.00
—Originals have 12 tracks					
❏ SR 61042 [S]	My Town, My Guy & Me	1965	10.00	20.00	40.00
❏ SR 61066 [S]	All About Love	1966	10.00	20.00	40.00
—Stereo version has a different cover and liner notes than the mono version					
❏ SR 61120 [S]	California Nights	1967	10.00	20.00	40.00
❏ SR 61185	Golden Hits Vol. 2	1968	10.00	20.00	40.00
❏ 810370-1	The Golden Hits of Lesley Gore	1983	2.50	5.00	10.00
—Reissue of 61024					
MOWEST					
❏ MW 117L	Someplace Else Now	1972	3.75	7.50	15.00
RHINO					
❏ RNFP-71496 [(2)]	The Lesley Gore Anthology (1963-1968)	1986	3.75	7.50	15.00
WING					
❏ PRW-2-119 [(2)]	The Sound of Young Love	1969	5.00	10.00	20.00
❏ SRW-16350	Girl Talk	1968	3.75	7.50	15.00
❏ SRW-16382	Love, Love, Love	1968	3.75	7.50	15.00

GORME, EYDIE

Number	Title (A Side/B Side)	Yr	VG	VG+	NM
ABC-PARAMOUNT					
❏ 150 [M]	Eydie Gorme	1957	7.50	15.00	30.00
❏ 192 [M]	Eydie Swings the Blues	1957	7.50	15.00	30.00
❏ 218 [M]	Eydie Gorme Vamps the Roaring 20's	1958	7.50	15.00	30.00
❏ S-218 [S]	Eydie Gorme Vamps the Roaring 20's	196?	3.00	6.00	12.00
❏ 246 [M]	Eydie in Love	1958	7.50	15.00	30.00
❏ S-246 [S]	Eydie in Love	196?	3.00	6.00	12.00
❏ 254 [M]	Show Stoppers	1959	6.25	12.50	25.00
❏ S-254 [S]	Show Stoppers	1959	7.50	15.00	30.00
❏ 273 [M]	Love Is a Season	1959	6.25	12.50	25.00
❏ S-273 [S]	Love Is a Season	1959	7.50	15.00	30.00
❏ 307 [M]	On Stage	1959	6.25	12.50	25.00
❏ S-307 [S]	On Stage	1959	7.50	15.00	30.00
❏ 343 [M]	Eydie in Dixieland	1960	6.25	12.50	25.00
❏ S-343 [S]	Eydie in Dixieland	1960	7.50	15.00	30.00
❏ 512 [M]	The Best of Romance, Ballads, Blues, Dixieland, Roaring 20's, Showstoppers	1965	3.75	7.50	15.00
❏ S-512 [S]	The Best of Romance, Ballads, Blues, Dixieland, Roaring 20's, Showstoppers	1965	5.00	10.00	20.00
COLUMBIA					
❏ CL 2012 [M]	Blame It on the Bossa Nova	1963	3.75	7.50	15.00
❏ CL 2065 [M]	Let the Good Times Roll	1963	3.75	7.50	15.00
❏ CL 2120 [M]	Gorme Country Style	1964	3.75	7.50	15.00
❏ CL 2203 [M]	Amor	1964	3.75	7.50	15.00
❏ CL 2300 [M]	The Sound of Music (And Other Broadway Hits)	1965	3.75	7.50	15.00
❏ CL 2376 [M]	More Amor	1965	3.75	7.50	15.00
❏ CL 2476 [M]	Don't Go to Strangers	1966	3.75	7.50	15.00
❏ CL 2557 [M]	Navidad Means Christmas	1966	3.75	7.50	15.00
—With Trio Los Panchos					
❏ CL 2594 [M]	Softly, As I Leave You	1967	3.75	7.50	15.00
❏ CL 2764 [M]	Eydie Gorme's Greatest Hits	1967	5.00	10.00	20.00
❏ CS 8812 [S]	Blame It on the Bossa Nova	1963	5.00	10.00	20.00

Number	Title (A Side/B Side)	Yr	VG	VG+	NM
❏ CS 8865 [S]	Let the Good Times Roll	1963	5.00	10.00	20.00
❏ CS 8920 [S]	Gorme Country Style	1964	5.00	10.00	20.00
❏ CS 9003 [S]	Amor	1964	5.00	10.00	20.00
❏ PC 9003	Amor	198?	2.00	4.00	8.00
—Budget-line reissue					
❏ CS 9100 [S]	The Sound of Music (And Other Broadway Hits)	1965	5.00	10.00	20.00
❏ CS 9176 [S]	More Amor	1965	5.00	10.00	20.00
❏ CS 9276 [S]	Don't Go to Strangers	1966	5.00	10.00	20.00
❏ CS 9357 [S]	Navidad Means Christmas	1966	5.00	10.00	20.00
—With Trio Los Panchos					
❏ CS 9394 [S]	Softly, As I Leave You	1967	5.00	10.00	20.00
❏ CS 9564 [S]	Eydie Gorme's Greatest Hits	1967	3.75	7.50	15.00
❏ PC 9564	Eydie Gorme's Greatest Hits	198?	2.00	4.00	8.00
—Budget-line reissue					
❏ CS 9652 [M]	The Look of Love	1968	7.50	15.00	30.00
—White label promo; "Special Mono Radio Station Copy" sticker on front of stereo jacket					
❏ CS 9652 [S]	The Look of Love	1968	3.75	7.50	15.00
CORAL					
❏ CRL 57109 [M]	Delight	1957	10.00	20.00	40.00
HARMONY					
❏ HS 11361	Yes Indeed!	1970	2.50	5.00	10.00
❏ KH 30319	If He Walked Into My Life	1971	2.50	5.00	10.00
MGM					
❏ SE-4780	It Was a Good Time	1971	3.00	6.00	12.00
RCA VICTOR					
❏ LSP-4093	Eydie	1968	3.00	6.00	12.00
❏ LSP-4303	Tonight I'll Say a Prayer	1970	3.00	6.00	12.00
UNITED ARTISTS					
❏ UAL 3143 [M]	Come Sing with Me	1961	5.00	10.00	20.00
❏ UAL 3152 [M]	I Feel So Spanish	1961	5.00	10.00	20.00
❏ UAL 3189 [M]	The Very Best of Eydie	1962	5.00	10.00	20.00
❏ UAS 6143 [S]	Come Sing with Me	1961	6.25	12.50	25.00
❏ UAS 6152 [S]	I Feel So Spanish	1961	6.25	12.50	25.00
❏ UAS 6189 [S]	The Very Best of Eydie	1962	6.25	12.50	25.00
VOCALION					
❏ VL 3708 [M]	Here's Eydie Gorme	196?	3.75	7.50	15.00
❏ VL 73708 [R]	Here's Eydie Gorme	196?	3.00	6.00	12.00

GOSDIN, VERN

Number	Title (A Side/B Side)	Yr	VG	VG+	NM
AMI					
❏ 1502	Today My World Slipped Away	1983	3.00	6.00	12.00
COLUMBIA					
❏ 1P 8037	10 Years of Greatest Hits — Newly Recorded	1990	5.00	10.00	20.00
—Columbia House vinyl edition (only U.S. version)					
❏ FC 40982	Chiseled in Stone	1988	2.00	4.00	8.00
❏ FC 45104	Alone	1989	3.00	6.00	12.00
COMPLEAT					
❏ 1004	If You're Gonna Do Me Wrong (Do It Right)	1983	2.50	5.00	10.00
❏ 1008	There Is a Season	1984	2.50	5.00	10.00
❏ 671012	Time Stood Still	1984	2.50	5.00	10.00
❏ 671022	Greatest Hits	1986	2.50	5.00	10.00
ELEKTRA					
❏ 6E-124	Never My Love	1978	2.50	5.00	10.00
❏ 6E-180	You've Got Somebody	1979	2.50	5.00	10.00
❏ 6E-228	The Best of Vern Gosdin	1979	2.50	5.00	10.00
❏ 7E-1112	Till the End	1977	2.50	5.00	10.00

GOSDIN BROTHERS, THE

Also see GENE CLARK.

Number	Title (A Side/B Side)	Yr	VG	VG+	NM
CAPITOL					
❏ ST 2852	Sounds of Goodbye	1968	5.00	10.00	20.00

GOSPEL STARS, THE

Number	Title (A Side/B Side)	Yr	VG	VG+	NM
TAMLA					
❏ TM-222 [M]	The Great Gospel Stars	1961	1000.	2000.	3000.

GOSSETT, LOU

Number	Title (A Side/B Side)	Yr	VG	VG+	NM
B.T. PUPPY					
❏ BTS-1013	From Me to You	1970	10.00	20.00	40.00

GOSSEZ, PIERRE

Number	Title (A Side/B Side)	Yr	VG	VG+	NM
VANGUARD CARDINAL					
❏ C-10061	Bach Takes a Trip	1969	5.00	10.00	20.00

GOULD, CHUCK

Number	Title (A Side/B Side)	Yr	VG	VG+	NM
VIK					
❏ LX-1123 [M]	Chuck Gould Plays A La Fletcher Henderson	1957	12.50	25.00	50.00

GOULD, MORTON

Number	Title (A Side/B Side)	Yr	VG	VG+	NM
COLUMBIA MASTERWORKS					
❏ ML 2065 [10]	Christmas Music for Orchestra	1949	10.00	20.00	40.00
RCA VICTOR RED SEAL					
❏ LSC-1994 [S]	Jungle Drums	1958	7.50	15.00	30.00
—Original with "shaded dog" label					
❏ LSC-2080 [S]	Brass and Percussion	1958	5.00	10.00	20.00
—Original with "shaded dog" label					
❏ LSC-2104 [S]	Blues in the Night	1958	7.50	15.00	30.00
—Original with "shaded dog" label					
❏ LSC-2195 [S]	Copland: Billy the Kid; Rodeo	1959	10.00	20.00	40.00
—Original with "shaded dog" label					
❏ LSC-2195 [S]	Copland: Billy the Kid; Rodeo	1964	7.50	15.00	30.00
—Second edition with "white dog" label					
❏ LSC-2217 [S]	Baton and Bows	1959	6.25	12.50	25.00
—Original with "shaded dog" label					
❏ LSC-2224 [S]	Where's the Melody?	1959	5.00	10.00	20.00
—Original with "shaded dog" label					
❏ LSC-2232 [S]	Moon, Wind and Stars	1959	5.00	10.00	20.00
—Original with "shaded dog" label					
❏ LSC-2308 [S]	Doubling in Brass	1959	12.50	25.00	50.00
—Original with "shaded dog" label					

Number	Title (A Side/B Side)	Yr	VG	VG+	NM
LSC-2317 [S]	Living Strings	1959	6.25	12.50	25.00
—Original with "shaded dog" label					
LSC-2345 [S]	Tchaikovsky: 1812 Overture; Ravel: Bolero	1960	5.00	10.00	20.00
—Original with "shaded dog" label					
LSC-2437 [S]	Bizet: Carmen for Orchestra	1960	10.00	20.00	40.00
—Original with "shaded dog" label					
LSC-2532 [S]	Fall River Legend	1961	6.25	12.50	25.00
—Original with "shaded dog" label					
LSC-2559 [S]	Jerome Kern and Cole Porter Favorites	1961	5.00	10.00	20.00
—Original with "shaded dog" label					
LSC-2579 [S]	Piano Favorites	1962	12.50	25.00	50.00
—Original with "shaded dog" label					
LSC-2686 [S]	Spirituals for Strings	1962	7.50	15.00	30.00
—Original with "shaded dog" label					

GOULDMAN, GRAHAM
RCA VICTOR
LPM-3954 [M]	The Graham Gouldman Thing	1968	12.50	25.00	50.00
LSP-3954 [S]	The Graham Gouldman Thing	1968	12.50	25.00	50.00

GOWANS, BRAD
RCA VICTOR
LJM-3000 [10]	Brad Gowans' New York Nine	1954	12.50	25.00	50.00

GOZZO, CONRAD
RCA VICTOR
LPM-1124 [M]	Goz the Great	1955	12.50	25.00	50.00

GRAAS, JOHN
ANDEX
A-3003 [M]	Premiere in Jazz	1958	12.50	25.00	50.00
AS-3003 [S]	Premiere in Jazz	1959	10.00	20.00	40.00

DECCA
DL 8079 [M]	Jazz Studio 2	1954	12.50	25.00	50.00
DL 8104 [M]	Jazz Studio 3	1955	12.50	25.00	50.00
DL 8343 [M]	Jazz Lab 1	1956	12.50	25.00	50.00
DL 8478 [M]	Jazz Lab 2	1957	12.50	25.00	50.00
DL 8677 [M]	Jazzmantics	1958	12.50	25.00	50.00

EMARCY
MG-36117 [M]	Coup de Graas	1958	12.50	25.00	50.00

KAPP
KL-1046 [M]	French Horn Jazz	1957	12.50	25.00	50.00

MERCURY
SR-80020 [S]	Coup de Graas	1959	10.00	20.00	40.00

TREND
TL-1005 [10]	French Horn Jazz	1954	30.00	60.00	120.00

GRACEN, THELMA
EMARCY
MG-36096 [M]	Thelma Gracen	1956	50.00	100.00	200.00

WING
MGW-60005 [M]	Thelma Gracen	1956	37.50	75.00	150.00

GRACIOUS
PAUL DAVIS was in this group.
CAPITOL
ST-602	Gracious	1970	10.00	20.00	40.00

GRAFFITI
ABC
S-663	Graffiti	1968	15.00	30.00	60.00

GRAFFMAN, GARY
RCA VICTOR RED SEAL
LSC-2274 [S]	Brahms: Piano Concerto No. 1	1959	6.25	12.50	25.00
—With Charles Munch/Boston Symphony Orchestra; original with "shaded dog" label					
LSC-2304 [S]	Chopin: Ballades	1959	5.00	10.00	20.00
—Original with "shaded dog" label					
LSC-2396 [S]	Beethoven: Piano Concerto No. 3	1960	75.00	150.00	300.00
—Original with "shaded dog" label					
LSC-2468 [S]	Chopin: Concerto No. 1; Mendelssohn: Capriccio Brilliant	1961	25.00	50.00	100.00
—Original with "shaded dog" label					

GRAHAM, ED
M&K REALTIME
106	Hot Stix	1980	10.00	20.00	40.00
—Direct-to-disc recording; plays at 45 rpm					

GRAMERCY SIX, THE
EDISON INTERNATIONAL
P-502 [M]	Great Swinging Sounds Vol. 1	1959	7.50	15.00	30.00

GRAMMER, BILLY
DECCA
DL 4212 [M]	Gospel Guitar	1962	3.75	7.50	15.00
DL 4460 [M]	Golden Gospel Favorites	1964	3.00	6.00	12.00
DL 4542 [M]	Gotta Travel On	1965	3.00	6.00	12.00
DL 4642 [M]	Country Guitar	1965	3.00	6.00	12.00
DL 74212 [S]	Gospel Guitar	1962	5.00	10.00	20.00
DL 74460 [S]	Golden Gospel Favorites	1964	3.75	7.50	15.00
DL 74542 [S]	Gotta Travel On	1965	3.75	7.50	15.00
DL 74642 [S]	Country Guitar	1965	3.75	7.50	15.00

EPIC
LN 24233 [M]	Sunday Guitar	1967	3.75	7.50	15.00
BN 26233 [S]	Sunday Guitar	1967	3.75	7.50	15.00

MONUMENT
MLP-4000 [M]	Travelin' On	1959	10.00	20.00	40.00
MLP-8039 [M]	Travelin' On	1965	6.25	12.50	25.00
SLP-18039 [P]	Travelin' On	1965	7.50	15.00	30.00

VOCALION
VL 73826	Favorites	1968	3.00	6.00	12.00

GRANATA, ROCCO
LAURIE
Number	Title (A Side/B Side)	Yr	VG	VG+	NM
LLP-2003 [M]	Marina and Other Italian Favorites	1960	6.25	12.50	25.00

GRAND FUNK RAILROAD
CAPITOL
ST-307	On Time	1969	3.75	7.50	15.00
SKAO-406	Grand Funk	1970	3.75	7.50	15.00
SKAO-471	Closer to Home	1970	3.75	7.50	15.00
SWBB-633 [(2)]	Live Album	1970	3.75	7.50	15.00
—Includes poster					
SW-764	Survival	1971	3.75	7.50	15.00
SW-853	E Pluribus Funk	1971	3.75	7.50	15.00
—Round cover designed like a coin					
SABB-11042 [(2)]	Mark, Don and Mel 1969-71	1972	3.75	7.50	15.00
SMAS-11099	Phoenix	1972	3.00	6.00	12.00
SMAS-11207	We're An American Band	1973	2.50	5.00	10.00
—Black vinyl					
SMAS-11207	We're An American Band	1973	5.00	10.00	20.00
—Gold vinyl without sheet of four stickers					
SMAS-11207	We're An American Band	1973	7.50	15.00	30.00
—Gold vinyl with sheet of four stickers					
SWAE-11278	Shinin' On	1974	2.00	4.00	8.00
—With 3-D glasses missing and no poster					
SWAE-11278	Shinin' On	1974	3.00	6.00	12.00
—With 3-D glasses attached to cover and with 3-D poster					
SO-11356	All the Girls in the World Beware!!!	1974	3.75	7.50	15.00
—With poster (deduct 33% if missing)					
SABB-11445	Caught in the Act	1975	2.50	5.00	10.00
ST-11482	Born to Die	1976	2.50	5.00	10.00
ST-11579	Grand Funk Hits	1976	2.50	5.00	10.00
SN-16138	Grand Funk Hits	1981	2.00	4.00	8.00
SN-16176	Closer to Home	1981	2.00	4.00	8.00
SN-16177	Grand Funk	1981	2.00	4.00	8.00
SN-16178	On Time	1981	2.00	4.00	8.00
21692	We're An American Band	1999	6.25	12.50	25.00
—Limited-edition reissue on 180-gram gold vinyl with original 1973 packaging					

FULL MOON
HS 3625	Grand Funk Lives	1981	2.50	5.00	10.00
23750	What's Funk	1983	2.50	5.00	10.00

MCA
2216	Good Singin' Good Playin'	1976	3.00	6.00	12.00
—Produced by Frank Zappa					

GRANDMA'S ROCKERS
FREDLO
6727	Homemade Apple Pie	1967	500.00	1000.	1500.

GRANDMASTER FLASH
ELEKTRA
60389	They Said It Couldn't Be Done	1985	3.00	6.00	12.00
60723	Ba-Dop-Boom-Bang	1987	2.50	5.00	10.00
60769	On the Strength	1988	3.00	6.00	12.00

SUGAR HILL
SH 268	The Message	1982	5.00	10.00	20.00
—Note: This album has been reissued to look like the original					
SH 9121	Greatest Messages	1984	5.00	10.00	20.00

GRANT, AMY
A&M
SP-3900	The Collection	1986	2.00	4.00	8.00
—Issued simultaneously with Myrrh 684306					
SP-5051	Amy Grant	1985	2.00	4.00	8.00
—Reissue of Myrrh 6586 with new cover					
SP-5052	My Father's Eyes	1985	2.00	4.00	8.00
—Reissue of Myrrh 6625					
SP-5053	Never Alone	1985	2.00	4.00	8.00
—Reissue of Myrrh 6645					
SP-5054	Amy Grant In Concert	1985	2.00	4.00	8.00
—Reissue of Myrrh 6668					
SP-5055	Amy Grant In Concert, Volume Two	1985	2.00	4.00	8.00
—Reissue of Myrrh 6677					
SP-5056	Age to Age	1985	2.00	4.00	8.00
—Reissue of Myrrh 6697					
SP-5057	A Christmas Album	1985	2.50	5.00	10.00
—Reissue of Myrrh 6768					
SP-5058	Straight Ahead	1985	2.00	4.00	8.00
—Reissue of Myrrh 675706					
SP-5060	Unguarded	1985	2.00	4.00	8.00
—Issued simultaneously with Myrrh 680606, and with four different covers; "D" on spine					
SP-5060	Unguarded	1985	2.00	4.00	8.00
—Issued simultaneously with Myrrh 680606, and with four different covers; "O" on spine					
SP-5060	Unguarded	1985	2.00	4.00	8.00
—Issued simultaneously with Myrrh 680606, and with four different covers; "R" on spine					
SP-5060	Unguarded	1985	2.00	4.00	8.00
—Issued simultaneously with Myrrh 680606, and with four different covers; "W" on spine					
SP-5199	Lead Me On	1988	2.00	4.00	8.00
—Issued simultaneously with Myrrh 687106					
75021 5321 1	Heart in Motion	1991	3.75	7.50	15.00

MYRRH
MSB-6586	Amy Grant	1977	3.75	7.50	15.00
—With colorized "ugly cover" of Amy's head and shoulders; "Amy Grant" at upper left					
MSB-6586	Amy Grant	198?	2.50	5.00	10.00
—With new cover of Amy in natural color; "Amy Grant" at upper right					
MSB-6625	My Father's Eyes	1979	3.00	6.00	12.00
MSB-6645	Never Alone	1980	3.00	6.00	12.00
MSB-6668	Amy Grant In Concert	1981	3.00	6.00	12.00
MSB-6677	Amy Grant In Concert, Volume Two	1981	3.00	6.00	12.00
MSB-6697	Age to Age	1982	3.00	6.00	12.00
MSB-6768	A Christmas Album	1983	3.00	6.00	12.00
MSB-6768 [PD]	A Christmas Album	1983	20.00	40.00	80.00
—Promo-only picture disc					

G

Number	Title (A Side/B Side)	Yr	VG	VG+	NM
❑ 701-675706-4	Straight Ahead	1984	2.50	5.00	10.00
❑ 701-680606-5	Unguarded	1985	2.50	5.00	10.00

—Issued simultaneously with A&M 5060, and with four different covers; "D" on spine

❑ 701-680606-5	Unguarded	1985	2.50	5.00	10.00

—Issued simultaneously with A&M 5060, and with four different covers; "O" on spine

❑ 701-680606-5	Unguarded	1985	2.50	5.00	10.00

—Issued simultaneously with A&M 5060, and with four different covers; "R" on spine

❑ 701-680606-5	Unguarded	1985	2.50	5.00	10.00

—Issued simultaneously with A&M 5060, and with four different covers; "W" on spine

❑ 701-684306-8	The Collection	1986	2.50	5.00	10.00

—Issued simultaneously with A&M 3900

❑ 701-687106-1	Lead Me On	1988	2.50	5.00	10.00

—Issued simultaneously with A&M 5199

GRANT, EARL
DECCA

Number	Title (A Side/B Side)	Yr	VG	VG+	NM
❑ DL 4044 [M]	The Magic of Earl Grant	1960	3.00	6.00	12.00
❑ DL 4165 [M]	Ebb Tide	1961	3.00	6.00	12.00
❑ DL 4188 [M]	Earl After Dark	1961	3.00	6.00	12.00
❑ DL 4231 [M]	Beyond the Reef	1962	3.00	6.00	12.00
❑ DL 4299 [M]	Earl Grant at Basin Street East	1962	3.00	6.00	12.00
❑ DL 4338 [M]	Midnight Sun	1963	3.00	6.00	12.00
❑ DL 4405 [M]	Yes Sirree	1963	3.00	6.00	12.00
❑ DL 4454 [M]	Fly Me to the Moon	1963	3.00	6.00	12.00
❑ DL 4506 [M]	Just for a Thrill	1964	3.00	6.00	12.00
❑ DL 4576 [M]	Just One More Time	1964	3.00	6.00	12.00
❑ DL 4623 [M]	Trade Winds	1965	3.00	6.00	12.00
❑ DL 4624 [M]	Spotlight on Earl Grant	1965	3.00	6.00	12.00
❑ DL 4677 [M]	Winter Wonderland	1965	3.00	6.00	12.00
❑ DL 4729 [M]	Songs Made Famous by Nat Cole	1966	3.00	6.00	12.00
❑ DL 4738 [M]	Stand By Me	1966	3.00	6.00	12.00
❑ DL 4806 [M]	Bali Ha'i	1967	3.00	6.00	12.00
❑ DL 4811 [M]	Just a Closer Walk with Thee	1967	3.75	7.50	15.00
❑ DL 4813 [M]	Earl Grant's Greatest Hits	1967	3.75	7.50	15.00
❑ DL 4937 [M]	Gently Swingin'	1968	5.00	10.00	20.00
❑ DL 4974 [M]	Spanish Eyes	1968	6.25	12.50	25.00
❑ DXS 7204 [(2)]	The Best of Earl Grant	1969	5.00	10.00	20.00
❑ DL 8672 [M]	The Versatile Earl Grant	1958	5.00	10.00	20.00
❑ DL 8830 [M]	The End	1959	3.75	7.50	15.00
❑ DL 8905 [M]	Grant Takes Rhythm	1959	3.75	7.50	15.00
❑ DL 8916 [M]	Nothing But the Blues	1960	3.75	7.50	15.00
❑ DL 8935 [M]	Paris Is My Beat	1960	3.75	7.50	15.00
❑ DL 74044 [S]	The Magic of Earl Grant	1960	3.75	7.50	15.00
❑ DL 74165 [S]	Ebb Tide	1961	3.75	7.50	15.00
❑ DL 74188 [S]	Earl After Dark	1961	3.75	7.50	15.00
❑ DL 74231 [S]	Beyond the Reef	1962	3.75	7.50	15.00
❑ DL 74299 [S]	Earl Grant at Basin Street East	1962	3.75	7.50	15.00
❑ DL 74338 [S]	Midnight Sun	1963	3.75	7.50	15.00
❑ DL 74405 [S]	Yes Sirree	1963	3.75	7.50	15.00
❑ DL 74454 [S]	Fly Me to the Moon	1963	3.75	7.50	15.00
❑ DL 74506 [S]	Just for a Thrill	1964	3.75	7.50	15.00
❑ DL 74576 [S]	Just One More Time	1964	3.75	7.50	15.00
❑ DL 74623 [S]	Trade Winds	1965	3.75	7.50	15.00
❑ DL 74624 [S]	Spotlight on Earl Grant	1965	3.75	7.50	15.00
❑ DL 74677 [S]	Winter Wonderland	1965	3.75	7.50	15.00
❑ DL 74729 [S]	Songs Made Famous by Nat Cole	1966	3.75	7.50	15.00
❑ DL 74738 [S]	Stand By Me	1966	3.75	7.50	15.00
❑ DL 74806 [S]	Bali Ha'i	1967	3.75	7.50	15.00
❑ DL 74811 [S]	Just a Closer Walk with Thee	1967	3.75	7.50	15.00
❑ DL 74813 [S]	Earl Grant's Greatest Hits	1967	3.75	7.50	15.00
❑ DL 74937 [S]	Gently Swingin'	1968	3.75	7.50	15.00
❑ DL 74974 [S]	Spanish Eyes	1968	3.75	7.50	15.00
❑ DL 75052	In Motion	1969	3.75	7.50	15.00
❑ DL 75108	This Magic Moment	1970	3.75	7.50	15.00
❑ DL 75158	A Time for Us	1970	3.00	6.00	12.00
❑ DL 75223	Earl Grant	1970	3.00	6.00	12.00
❑ DL 78830 [S]	The End	1959	5.00	10.00	20.00
❑ DL 78905 [S]	Grant Takes Rhythm	1959	5.00	10.00	20.00
❑ DL 78916 [S]	Nothing But the Blues	1960	5.00	10.00	20.00
❑ DL 78935 [S]	Paris Is My Beat	1960	5.00	10.00	20.00

VOCALION

Number	Title (A Side/B Side)	Yr	VG	VG+	NM
❑ VL 3793 [M]	It's So Good	1967	3.00	6.00	12.00
❑ VL 73793 [S]	It's So Good	1967	3.00	6.00	12.00
❑ VL 73860	Send for Me	1969	3.00	6.00	12.00
❑ VL 73893	One for My Baby	1969	3.00	6.00	12.00

GRANT, GOGI
ERA

Number	Title (A Side/B Side)	Yr	VG	VG+	NM
❑ EL-106 [M]	The Wayward Wind	196?	6.25	12.50	25.00
❑ 20001 [M]	Suddenly There's Gogi Grant	1956	15.00	30.00	60.00

—Black vinyl

❑ 20001 [M]	Suddenly There's Gogi Grant	1956	25.00	50.00	100.00

—Red vinyl

LIBERTY

Number	Title (A Side/B Side)	Yr	VG	VG+	NM
❑ LRP-3144 [M]	If You Want to Get to Heaven, Shout	1960	7.50	15.00	30.00
❑ LST-7144 [S]	If You Want to Get to Heaven, Shout	1960	10.00	20.00	40.00

PETE

Number	Title (A Side/B Side)	Yr	VG	VG+	NM
❑ S-1101	Gogi Grant	1968	3.75	7.50	15.00
❑ S-1111	The Way a Woman Feels	1970	3.75	7.50	15.00

RCA VICTOR

Number	Title (A Side/B Side)	Yr	VG	VG+	NM
❑ LOC-1030 [M]	The Helen Morgan Story	1957	15.00	30.00	60.00
❑ LPM-1717 [M]	Welcome to My Heart	1958	10.00	20.00	40.00
❑ LPM-1940 [M]	Torch Time	1959	7.50	15.00	30.00
❑ LSP-1940 [S]	Torch Time	1959	10.00	20.00	40.00
❑ LPM-2000 [M]	Granted… It's Gogi	1960	7.50	15.00	30.00
❑ LSP-2000 [S]	Granted… It's Gogi	1960	10.00	20.00	40.00

GRAPEFRUIT
ABC DUNHILL

Number	Title (A Side/B Side)	Yr	VG	VG+	NM
❑ DS-50050	Around Grapefruit	1968	5.00	10.00	20.00

RCA VICTOR

Number	Title (A Side/B Side)	Yr	VG	VG+	NM
❑ LSP-4215	Deep Water	1969	3.75	7.50	15.00

GRAPPELLI, STEPHANE
ATLANTIC

Number	Title (A Side/B Side)	Yr	VG	VG+	NM
❑ SD 1391 [S]	Feeling + Finesse = Jazz	1962	5.00	10.00	20.00

BARCLAY

❑ 820007	Music to Pass the Time	196?	5.00	10.00	20.00

BLACK LION

❑ 047 [(2)]	I Got Rhythm	1974	5.00	10.00	20.00

CLASSIC JAZZ

❑ 23 [(2)]	Homage to Django	197?	5.00	10.00	20.00

EMARCY

❑ MG-36120 [M]	Improvisations	1957	15.00	30.00	60.00

GRAPPELLI, STEPHANE, AND BARNEY KESSEL
MOBILE FIDELITY

Number	Title (A Side/B Side)	Yr	VG	VG+	NM
❑ 1-111	I Remember Django	1984	12.50	25.00	50.00

—Audiophile vinyl

GRASS ROOTS, THE
ABC

Number	Title (A Side/B Side)	Yr	VG	VG+	NM
❑ AC-30003	The ABC Collection	1976	3.75	7.50	15.00

ABC DUNHILL

❑ DS-50027	Feelings	1968	3.75	7.50	15.00

—Reissue with ABC logo

❑ DS-50047	Golden Grass	1968	5.00	10.00	20.00
❑ DS-50052	Lovin' Things	1969	5.00	10.00	20.00
❑ DS-50067	Leaving It All Behind	1969	5.00	10.00	20.00
❑ DS-50087	More Golden Grass	1970	5.00	10.00	20.00
❑ DSX-50107	Their 16 Greatest Hits	1971	5.00	10.00	20.00
❑ DSX-50112	Move Along	1972	3.75	7.50	15.00
❑ DSX-50137	A Lotta Mileage	1973	3.75	7.50	15.00

COMMAND

❑ QD-40013 [Q]	Their 16 Greatest Hits	1974	7.50	15.00	30.00

DUNHILL

❑ D-50011 [M]	Where Were You When I Needed You	1966	37.50	75.00	150.00
❑ DS-50011 [S]	Where Were You When I Needed You	1966	25.00	50.00	100.00
❑ D-50020 [M]	Let's Live for Today	1967	6.25	12.50	25.00
❑ DS-50020 [S]	Let's Live for Today	1967	7.50	15.00	30.00
❑ D-50027 [M]	Feelings	1968	7.50	15.00	30.00
❑ DS-50027 [S]	Feelings	1968	5.00	10.00	20.00

HAVEN

❑ ST-9204	The Grass Roots	1975	3.75	7.50	15.00

MCA

❑ 5331	Powers of the Night	1982	3.00	6.00	12.00
❑ 37154	Their 16 Greatest Hits	198?	2.00	4.00	8.00

—Budget-line reissue of ABC Dunhill 50107

GRATEFUL DEAD, THE
Also see JERRY GARCIA; MICKEY HART; KEITH AND DONNA; BOB WEIR.
ARISTA

Number	Title (A Side/B Side)	Yr	VG	VG+	NM
❑ SP-35 [DJ]	Grateful Dead Sampler	1978	7.50	15.00	30.00
❑ AB 4198	Shakedown Street	1978	3.00	6.00	12.00
❑ AL 7001	Terrapin Station	1977	3.75	7.50	15.00
❑ AL 7001 [DJ]	Terrapin Station	1977	12.50	25.00	50.00

—Radio station promos are banded for airplay

❑ AL 8112 [(2)]	Dead Set	198?	2.50	5.00	10.00

—Budget-line reissue of 8606

❑ AL 8321	Shakedown Street	198?	2.00	4.00	8.00

—Budget-line reissue of 4198

❑ AL 8329	Terrapin Station	198?	2.00	4.00	8.00

—Budget-line reissue of 7001

❑ AL 8332	Go to Heaven	198?	2.00	4.00	8.00

—Budget-line reissue of 9508

❑ AL 8452	In the Dark	1987	2.50	5.00	10.00
❑ AL 8575	Built to Last	1989	2.50	5.00	10.00
❑ A2L 8604 [(2)]	Reckoning	1981	3.75	7.50	15.00
❑ A2L 8606 [(2)]	Dead Set	1981	3.75	7.50	15.00
❑ AL3 8634 [(3)]	Without a Net	1990	6.25	12.50	25.00
❑ AL 9508	Go to Heaven	1980	3.00	6.00	12.00

DIRECT DISK

❑ SD-16619	Terrapin Station	1980	25.00	50.00	100.00

—Audiophile vinyl

GRATEFUL DEAD

❑ GD-01	Wake of the Flood	1973	5.00	10.00	20.00

—With no contributing artists on back cover

❑ GD-01	Wake of the Flood	1975	3.75	7.50	15.00

—With contributing artists on back cover and United Artists distribution

❑ GD-01 [DJ]	Wake of the Flood	1973	100.00	200.00	400.00

—Green vinyl meant for fan-club members; ironically, most copies were damaged in a flood before distribution

❑ GD-102	Grateful Dead from the Mars Hotel	1974	5.00	10.00	20.00

—Without United Artists distribution

❑ GD-102	Grateful Dead from the Mars Hotel	1975	3.75	7.50	15.00

—With United Artists distribution

❑ GD-LA494-G	Blues for Allah	1975	5.00	10.00	20.00
❑ GD-LA620-J2 [(2)]	Steal Your Face	1976	6.25	12.50	25.00

MOBILE FIDELITY

❑ 1-014	American Beauty	1980	12.50	25.00	50.00

—Audiophile vinyl

❑ 1-172	Grateful Dead from the Mars Hotel	1984	10.00	20.00	40.00

—Audiophile vinyl

PAIR

❑ PDL2-1053 [(2)]	For the Faithful...	1986	3.00	6.00	12.00

SUNFLOWER

❑ SUN-5001	Vintage Dead	1970	10.00	20.00	40.00

—Album has been counterfeited, but bogus covers are 1/4" shorter than normal LP cover

❑ SNF-5004	Historic Dead	1971	10.00	20.00	40.00

Number	Title (A Side/B Side)	Yr	VG	VG+	NM
WARNER BROS.					
❏ W 1689 [M]	The Grateful Dead	1967	50.00	100.00	200.00
❏ WS 1689 [S]	The Grateful Dead	1967	20.00	40.00	80.00
—Gold label					
❏ WS 1689 [S]	The Grateful Dead	1968	6.25	12.50	25.00
—Green label with "W7" logo					
❏ WS 1689 [S]	The Grateful Dead	1970	3.75	7.50	15.00
—Green label with "WB" logo					
❏ WS 1689 [S]	The Grateful Dead	1973	3.00	6.00	12.00
—"Burbank" palm-trees label					
❏ WS 1689 [S]	The Grateful Dead	1979	2.00	4.00	8.00
—White or tan label					
❏ WS 1749	Anthem of the Sun	1968	7.50	15.00	30.00
—Green label with "W7" logo					
❏ WS 1749	Anthem of the Sun	197?	12.50	25.00	50.00
—Green label with "WB" logo, white background on cover with radically remixed version of LP					
❏ WS 1749	Anthem of the Sun	1970	3.75	7.50	15.00
—Green label with "WB" logo, purple cover					
❏ WS 1749	Anthem of the Sun	1973	3.00	6.00	12.00
—"Burbank" palm-trees label					
❏ WS 1749	Anthem of the Sun	1979	2.00	4.00	8.00
—White or tan label					
❏ WS 1790	Aoxomoxoa	1969	7.50	15.00	30.00
—Green label with "W7" logo					
❏ WS 1790	Aoxomoxoa	1970	3.75	7.50	15.00
—Green label with "WB" logo					
❏ WS 1790	Aoxomoxoa	1973	3.00	6.00	12.00
—"Burbank" palm-trees label					
❏ WS 1790	Aoxomoxoa	1979	2.00	4.00	8.00
—White or tan label					
❏ 2WS 1830 [(2)]	Live/Dead	1969	10.00	20.00	40.00
—Green labels with "W7" logo					
❏ 2WS 1830 [(2)]	Live/Dead	1970	5.00	10.00	20.00
—Green labels with "WB" logo					
❏ 2WS 1830 [(2)]	Live/Dead	1973	3.75	7.50	15.00
—"Burbank" palm-trees labels					
❏ 2WS 1830 [(2)]	Live/Dead	1979	2.50	5.00	10.00
—White or tan labels					
❏ WS 1869	Workingman's Dead	1970	6.25	12.50	25.00
—Green label with "WB" logo; textured cover with back cover slick upside down					
❏ WS 1869	Workingman's Dead	1973	3.00	6.00	12.00
—"Burbank" palm-trees label; standard cover with back cover right side up					
❏ WS 1869	Workingman's Dead	1979	2.00	4.00	8.00
—White or tan label					
❏ WS 1893	American Beauty	1970	6.25	12.50	25.00
—Green label with "WB" logo					
❏ WS 1893	American Beauty	1973	3.00	6.00	12.00
—"Burbank" palm-trees label					
❏ WS 1893	American Beauty	1979	2.00	4.00	8.00
—White or tan label					
❏ 2WS 1935 [(2)]	Grateful Dead	1971	7.50	15.00	30.00
—Green labels with "WB" logo					
❏ 2WS 1935 [(2)]	Grateful Dead	1973	3.75	7.50	15.00
—"Burbank" palm-trees labels					
❏ 2WS 1935 [(2)]	Grateful Dead	1979	2.50	5.00	10.00
—White or tan labels					
❏ 3WX 2668 [(3)]	Europe '72	1972	10.00	20.00	40.00
—Green labels with "WB" logo					
❏ 3WX 2668 [(3)]	Europe '72	1973	5.00	10.00	20.00
—"Burbank" palm-trees labels					
❏ 3WX 2668 [(3)]	Europe '72	1979	3.00	6.00	12.00
—White or tan labels					
❏ BS 2721	History of the Grateful Dead, Vol. 1 (Bear's Choice)	1973	2.00	4.00	8.00
—"Burbank" palm-trees labels					
❏ BS 2721	History of the Grateful Dead, Vol. 1 (Bear's Choice)	1973	5.00	10.00	20.00
—"Burbank" palm-trees labels					
❏ W 2764	The Best of/Skeletons from the Closet	1974	5.00	10.00	20.00
—"Burbank" palm-trees labels					
❏ W 2764	The Best of/Skeletons from the Closet	1979	2.00	4.00	8.00
—White or tan labels					
❏ 2WS 3091 [(2)]	What a Long Strange Trip It's Been: The Best of the Grateful Dead	1977	5.00	10.00	20.00
—"Burbank" palm-trees labels					
❏ 2WS 3091 [(2)]	What a Long Strange Trip It's Been: The Best of the Grateful Dead	1979	2.50	5.00	10.00
—White or tan labels					
❏ ST-93416	American Beauty	1970	12.50	25.00	50.00
—Capitol Record Club edition; green label with "W7" logo					
GRAVES, CONLEY					
DECCA					
❏ DL 8220 [M]	Genius at Work	1956	10.00	20.00	40.00
❏ DL 8412 [M]	Piano Dynamics	1957	10.00	20.00	40.00
❏ DL 8475 [M]	Rendezvous in Paris	1957	10.00	20.00	40.00
LIBERTY					
❏ LRP-3007 [M]	V.I.P. (Very Important Pianist)	1956	10.00	20.00	40.00
NOCTURNE					
❏ NLP-4 [10]	Piano Artistry	1954	25.00	50.00	100.00
GRAVES, JOE					
CAPITOL					
❏ ST 1977 [S]	The Great New Swingers	1963	7.50	15.00	30.00
❏ T 1977 [M]	The Great New Swingers	1963	6.25	12.50	25.00
GRAVES, MILFORD					
ESP-DISK'					
❏ 1015 [M]	Milford Graves Percussion Ensemble	1966	5.00	10.00	20.00
❏ S-1015 [S]	Milford Graves Percussion Ensemble	1966	6.25	12.50	25.00

Number	Title (A Side/B Side)	Yr	VG	VG+	NM
GRAVES, TERESA					
KIRSHNER					
❏ KOS-104	Teresa Graves	1970	6.25	12.50	25.00
GRAVITY ADJUSTERS EXPANSION BAND					
NOCTURNE					
❏ NRS-302	One	1973	75.00	150.00	300.00
GRAY, BILLY					
DECCA					
❏ DL 5567 [10]	Dance-O-Rama	1956	50.00	100.00	200.00
GRAY, CLAUDE					
DECCA					
❏ DL 4882 [M]	Claude Gray Sings	1967	6.25	12.50	25.00
❏ DL 74882 [S]	Claude Gray Sings	1967	5.00	10.00	20.00
❏ DL 74963	The Easy Way of Claude Gray	1968	5.00	10.00	20.00
HILLTOP					
❏ JM-6051 [M]	Treasure of Love	1967	3.75	7.50	15.00
❏ JS-6051 [S]	Treasure of Love	1967	3.00	6.00	12.00
MERCURY					
❏ MG-20658 [M]	Songs of Broken Love Affairs	1962	5.00	10.00	20.00
❏ MG-20718 [M]	Country Goes to Town	1962	5.00	10.00	20.00
❏ SR-60658 [S]	Songs of Broken Love Affairs	1962	6.25	12.50	25.00
❏ SR-60718 [S]	Country Goes to Town	1962	6.25	12.50	25.00
GRAY, DOBIE					
CAPITOL					
❏ ST-12489	From Where I Stand	1986	2.50	5.00	10.00
CAPRICORN					
❏ CP 0163	New Ray of Sunshine	1976	2.50	5.00	10.00
CHARGER					
❏ CHR-M-2002 [M]	Dobie Gray Sings for "In" Crowders That Go "Go Go"	1965	10.00	20.00	40.00
❏ CHR-S-2002 [S]	Dobie Gray Sings for "In" Crowders That Go "Go Go"	1965	30.00	60.00	120.00
DECCA					
❏ DL 75397	Drift Away	1973	3.00	6.00	12.00
INFINITY					
❏ INF-9001	Midnight Diamond	1979	2.50	5.00	10.00
MCA					
❏ 371	Loving Arms	1973	2.50	5.00	10.00
❏ 449	Hey Dixie	1974	2.50	5.00	10.00
❏ 515	Drift Away	1974	2.50	5.00	10.00
—Reissue of Decca 75397					
ROBOX					
❏ RBX 8102	Welcome Home	1981	2.50	5.00	10.00
STRIPE					
❏ LPM 2001 [M]	Look — Dobie Gray	1963	25.00	50.00	100.00
GRAY, DOLORES					
CAPITOL					
❏ T 897 [M]	Warm Brandy	1957	7.50	15.00	30.00
GRAY, GLEN					
CAPITOL					
❏ W 747 [M]	Casa Loma in Hi-Fi!	1956	6.25	12.50	25.00
CORAL					
❏ CRL 56006 [10]	Hoagy Carmichael Songs	1950	12.50	25.00	50.00
❏ CRL 56009 [10]	Glen Gray Souvenirs	1950	12.50	25.00	50.00
DECCA					
❏ DL 5089 [10]	Musical Smoke Rings	1950	12.50	25.00	50.00
❏ DL 5397 [10]	No-Name Jive	1953	12.50	25.00	50.00
❏ DL 8570 [M]	Smoke Rings	1957	5.00	10.00	20.00
HARMONY					
❏ HL 7045 [M]	The Great Recordings of Glen Gray	1957	5.00	10.00	20.00
GRAY, JERRY					
CRAFTSMAN					
❏ 8035 [M]	More Miller Hits	195?	5.00	10.00	20.00
DECCA					
❏ DL 5266 [10]	Dance to the Music of Gray	1950	12.50	25.00	50.00
❏ DL 5375 [10]	A Tribute to Glenn Miller	1951	12.50	25.00	50.00
❏ DL 5478 [10]	Dance Time	1952	12.50	25.00	50.00
❏ DL 8101 [M]	Jerry Gray and His Orchestra	1955	10.00	20.00	40.00
LIBERTY					
❏ LRP-3038 [M]	Hi-Fi Shades of Gray	1956	10.00	20.00	40.00
❏ LRP-3089 [M]	Jerry Gray at the Hollywood Palladium	1958	10.00	20.00	40.00
❏ LST-7002 [S]	Hi-Fi Shades of Gray	1958	10.00	20.00	40.00
❏ LST-7013 [S]	Jerry Gray at the Hollywood Palladium	1958	10.00	20.00	40.00
TOPS					
❏ L-1627 [M]	A Salute to Glenn Miller	1958	5.00	10.00	20.00
❏ L-1640 [M]	Glenn Miller Greats	1958	5.00	10.00	20.00
VOCALION					
❏ VL 3602 [M]	A Tribute to Glenn Miller	196?	5.00	10.00	20.00
WARNER BROS.					
❏ W 1446 [M]	Singin' and Swingin'	1962	5.00	10.00	20.00
❏ WS 1446 [S]	Singin' and Swingin'	1962	6.25	12.50	25.00
GRAY, WARDELL					
CROWN					
❏ CLP-5004 [M]	Way Out Wardell	1957	10.00	20.00	40.00
—Original have black label with the word "crown" in small letters at top					
MODERN					
❏ MLP-1204 [M]	Way Out Wardell	1956	37.50	75.00	150.00
PRESTIGE					
❏ PRLP-115 [10]	Wardell Gray Tenor Sax	1951	62.50	125.00	250.00
❏ PRLP-128 [10]	Jazz Concert	1952	62.50	125.00	250.00
❏ PRLP-147 [10]	Wardell Gray's Los Angeles Stars	1953	62.50	125.00	250.00

G

Number	Title (A Side/B Side)	Yr	VG	VG+	NM
❏ PRLP-7008 [M]	Wardell Gray Memorial, Volume 1	1955	25.00	50.00	100.00
❏ PRLP-7009 [M]	Wardell Gray Memorial, Volume 2	1955	25.00	50.00	100.00
❏ PRLP-7343 [(2)M]	Wardell Gray Memorial Album	1964	10.00	20.00	40.00
❏ PRST-7343 [(2)R]	Wardell Gray Memorial Album	1964	5.00	10.00	20.00

GRAY, WARDELL, AND DEXTER GORDON
DECCA

Number	Title (A Side/B Side)	Yr	VG	VG+	NM
❏ DL 7025 [10]	The Chase and the Steeple Chase	1952	62.50	125.00	250.00

JAZZTONE

Number	Title (A Side/B Side)	Yr	VG	VG+	NM
❏ J-1235 [M]	The Chase and the Steeple Chase	1956	12.50	25.00	50.00

GREAT JAZZ TRIO, THE
EAST WIND

Number	Title (A Side/B Side)	Yr	VG	VG+	NM
❏ 10005	Direct from L.A.	1978	6.25	12.50	25.00

—Direct-to-disc recording

GREAT SOCIETY, THE
COLUMBIA

Number	Title (A Side/B Side)	Yr	VG	VG+	NM
❏ CS 9627 [M]	Conspicuous Only In Its Absence	1968	12.50	25.00	50.00

—White label promo only; "Special Mono Radio Station Copy" sticker on front; same number as stereo version`

Number	Title (A Side/B Side)	Yr	VG	VG+	NM
❏ CS 9627 [S]	Conspicuous Only In Its Absence	1968	6.25	12.50	25.00

—Red label, "360 Sound Stereo"

Number	Title (A Side/B Side)	Yr	VG	VG+	NM
❏ CS 9702	How It Was	1968	6.25	12.50	25.00

—Red label, "360 Sound Stereo"

Number	Title (A Side/B Side)	Yr	VG	VG+	NM
❏ G 30459 [(2)]	The Great Society Collectors Item	1971	3.75	7.50	15.00

HARMONY

Number	Title (A Side/B Side)	Yr	VG	VG+	NM
❏ KH 30391	Somebody to Love	1970	3.00	6.00	12.00

GREAT SPECKLED BIRD
AMPEX

Number	Title (A Side/B Side)	Yr	VG	VG+	NM
❏ A-10103	Great Speckled Bird	1970	5.00	10.00	20.00

GREAVES, R.B.
ATCO

Number	Title (A Side/B Side)	Yr	VG	VG+	NM
❏ SD 33-311	R.B. Greaves	1969	5.00	10.00	20.00

INTERMEDIA

Number	Title (A Side/B Side)	Yr	VG	VG+	NM
❏ QS-5032	Rock and Roll	198?	2.50	5.00	10.00

GRECO, BUDDY
CORAL

Number	Title (A Side/B Side)	Yr	VG	VG+	NM
❏ CRL 57022 [M]	Buddy Greco at Mister Kelly's	1956	6.25	12.50	25.00

GRECO, JULIETTE
COLUMBIA

Number	Title (A Side/B Side)	Yr	VG	VG+	NM
❏ CL 569 [M]	St. Germain-des-Pres	1954	7.50	15.00	30.00

—Maroon label, gold print

GREEK FOUNTAIN RIVER FRONT BAND, THE
MONTEL

Number	Title (A Side/B Side)	Yr	VG	VG+	NM
❏ 110 [M]	The Greek Fountain River Band Takes Requests	1965	30.00	60.00	120.00

GREELEY, GEORGE
CAPITOL

Number	Title (A Side/B Side)	Yr	VG	VG+	NM
❏ H 438 [10]	Piano Demitasse	1954	7.50	15.00	30.00

REPRISE

Number	Title (A Side/B Side)	Yr	VG	VG+	NM
❏ R 6092 [M]	Piano Rhapsodies of Love	1964	2.50	5.00	10.00
❏ RS 6092 [S]	Piano Rhapsodies of Love	1964	3.00	6.00	12.00

WARNER BROS.

Number	Title (A Side/B Side)	Yr	VG	VG+	NM
❏ W 1249 [M]	The World's Greatest Popular Piano Concertos	1958	3.75	7.50	15.00
❏ WS 1249 [S]	The World's Greatest Popular Piano Concertos	1959	5.00	10.00	20.00
❏ W 1291 [M]	World Renowned Popular Piano Concertos	1959	3.75	7.50	15.00
❏ WS 1291 [S]	World Renowned Popular Piano Concertos	1959	5.00	10.00	20.00
❏ W 1319 [M]	The Greatest Motion Picture Piano Concertos	1959	3.75	7.50	15.00
❏ WS 1319 [S]	The Greatest Motion Picture Piano Concertos	1959	5.00	10.00	20.00
❏ WS 1338 [S]	22 Best Loved Christmas Piano Concertos	1959	5.00	10.00	20.00
❏ W 1366 [M]	The Most Beautiful Music of Hawaii	1960	3.00	6.00	12.00
❏ WS 1366 [S]	The Most Beautiful Music of Hawaii	1960	3.75	7.50	15.00
❏ W 1387 [M]	The World's Greatest Love Themes	1960	3.00	6.00	12.00
❏ WS 1387 [S]	The World's Greatest Love Themes	1960	3.75	7.50	15.00
❏ W 1402 [M]	Piano Italiano	1961	3.00	6.00	12.00
❏ WS 1402 [S]	Piano Italiano	1961	3.75	7.50	15.00
❏ W 1410 [M]	The Best of the Popular Piano Concertos	1961	3.00	6.00	12.00
❏ WS 1410 [S]	The Best of the Popular Piano Concertos	1961	3.75	7.50	15.00
❏ W 1415 [M]	Great Broadway Musicals	1961	3.00	6.00	12.00
❏ WS 1415 [S]	Great Broadway Musicals	1961	3.75	7.50	15.00
❏ W 1427 [M]	Famous Film Themes	1961	3.00	6.00	12.00
❏ WS 1427 [S]	Famous Film Themes	1961	3.75	7.50	15.00
❏ W 1451 [M]	George Greeley Plays George Gershwin	1962	3.00	6.00	12.00
❏ WS 1451 [S]	George Greeley Plays George Gershwin	1962	3.75	7.50	15.00
❏ W 1476 [M]	Themes from Mutiny on the Bounty and Other Great Films	1962	3.00	6.00	12.00
❏ WS 1476 [S]	Themes from Mutiny on the Bounty and Other Great Films	1962	3.75	7.50	15.00
❏ W 1503 [M]	A Classic Affair	1963	3.00	6.00	12.00
❏ WS 1503 [S]	A Classic Affair	1963	3.75	7.50	15.00
❏ W 1560 [M]	Best Loved Christmas Piano Concertos	1965	3.00	6.00	12.00
❏ WS 1560 [S]	Best Loved Christmas Piano Concertos	1965	3.75	7.50	15.00

GREEN, AL
A&M

Number	Title (A Side/B Side)	Yr	VG	VG+	NM
❏ SP-5150	Soul Survivor	1987	2.50	5.00	10.00
❏ SP-5228	I Get Joy	1989	2.50	5.00	10.00

BELL

Number	Title (A Side/B Side)	Yr	VG	VG+	NM
❏ 6076	Al Green	1972	5.00	10.00	20.00

—Reissue of Hot Line LP

DCC COMPACT CLASSICS

Number	Title (A Side/B Side)	Yr	VG	VG+	NM
❏ LPZ-2058	Greatest Hits	1998	7.50	15.00	30.00

—Audiophile vinyl

HI

Number	Title (A Side/B Side)	Yr	VG	VG+	NM
❏ 6004	The Belle Album	1977	3.00	6.00	12.00
❏ 6009	Truth 'N' Time	1978	3.00	6.00	12.00
❏ 8000	Tired of Being Alone	1977	3.00	6.00	12.00
❏ 8001	Al Green Gets Next to You	1977	3.00	6.00	12.00
❏ 8007	Let's Stay Together	1977	3.00	6.00	12.00
❏ SHL-32055	Green Is Blues	1969	3.75	7.50	15.00
❏ SHL-32062	Al Green Gets Next to You	1971	3.75	7.50	15.00
❏ SHL-32070	Let's Stay Together	1972	3.75	7.50	15.00
❏ SHL-32074	I'm Still in Love with You	1972	3.75	7.50	15.00
❏ SHL-32077	Call Me	1973	3.75	7.50	15.00
❏ SHL-32082	Livin' for You	1973	3.75	7.50	15.00
❏ SHL-32087	Al Green Explores Your Mind	1974	3.75	7.50	15.00
❏ SHL-32089	Al Green/Greatest Hits	1975	3.75	7.50	15.00
❏ SHL-32092	Al Green Is Love	1975	3.75	7.50	15.00
❏ SHL-32097	Full of Fire	1976	3.75	7.50	15.00
❏ SHL-32103	Have a Good Time	1976	3.75	7.50	15.00
❏ SHL-32105	Al Green's Greatest Hits, Volume II	1977	3.75	7.50	15.00

HOT LINE

Number	Title (A Side/B Side)	Yr	VG	VG+	NM
❏ 1500 [M]	Back Up Train	1967	12.50	25.00	50.00

—As "Al Greene"

Number	Title (A Side/B Side)	Yr	VG	VG+	NM
❏ S-1500 [S]	Back Up Train	1967	20.00	40.00	80.00

—As "Al Greene"

KORY

Number	Title (A Side/B Side)	Yr	VG	VG+	NM
❏ 1005	Al Green	1977	2.50	5.00	10.00

—Reissue of Bell LP

MCA

Number	Title (A Side/B Side)	Yr	VG	VG+	NM
❏ 42308	Love Ritual	1988	2.50	5.00	10.00

MOTOWN

Number	Title (A Side/B Side)	Yr	VG	VG+	NM
❏ 5283 ML	Al Green/Greatest Hits	198?	2.50	5.00	10.00

—Reissue of Hi 32089

Number	Title (A Side/B Side)	Yr	VG	VG+	NM
❏ 5284 ML	I'm Still in Love with You	198?	2.50	5.00	10.00

—Reissue of Hi 32074

Number	Title (A Side/B Side)	Yr	VG	VG+	NM
❏ 5290 ML	Let's Stay Together	198?	2.50	5.00	10.00

—Reissue of Hi 32070

Number	Title (A Side/B Side)	Yr	VG	VG+	NM
❏ 5291 ML	Al Green's Greatest Hits, Volume II	198?	2.50	5.00	10.00

—Reissue of Hi 32105

Number	Title (A Side/B Side)	Yr	VG	VG+	NM
❏ 5317 ML	Truth N' Time	198?	2.50	5.00	10.00

MYRRH

Number	Title (A Side/B Side)	Yr	VG	VG+	NM
❏ MSB-6661	The Lord Will Make a Way	1980	2.50	5.00	10.00
❏ MSB-6671	Higher Plane	1981	2.50	5.00	10.00
❏ MSB-6702	Precious Lord	1981	2.50	5.00	10.00
❏ MSB-6747	I'll Rise Again	1982	2.50	5.00	10.00
❏ MSB-6774	Al Green and the Full Gospel Tabernacle Choir	1984	2.50	5.00	10.00
❏ WR-8113	The Lord Will Make a Way	1985	2.00	4.00	8.00

—Reissue with new number and A&M logo

Number	Title (A Side/B Side)	Yr	VG	VG+	NM
❏ WR-8114	Higher Plane	1985	2.00	4.00	8.00

—Reissue with new number and A&M logo

Number	Title (A Side/B Side)	Yr	VG	VG+	NM
❏ WR-8115	Precious Lord	1985	2.00	4.00	8.00

—Reissue with new number and A&M logo

Number	Title (A Side/B Side)	Yr	VG	VG+	NM
❏ WR-8116	I'll Rise Again	1985	2.00	4.00	8.00

—Reissue with new number and A&M logo

Number	Title (A Side/B Side)	Yr	VG	VG+	NM
❏ WR-8117	White Christmas	1985	2.50	5.00	10.00

—Reissue with new number and A&M logo

Number	Title (A Side/B Side)	Yr	VG	VG+	NM
❏ WR-8118	Trust in God	1985	2.00	4.00	8.00

—Reissue with new number and A&M logo

Number	Title (A Side/B Side)	Yr	VG	VG+	NM
❏ WR-8209	Al Green and the Full Gospel Tabernacle Choir	1986	2.00	4.00	8.00

—Reissue with new number and A&M logo

Number	Title (A Side/B Side)	Yr	VG	VG+	NM
❏ 7-01-678006-6	White Christmas	1984	3.00	6.00	12.00
❏ 7-01-678306-?	Trust in God	1984	2.50	5.00	10.00

THE RIGHT STUFF

Number	Title (A Side/B Side)	Yr	VG	VG+	NM
❏ T1-27121	Let's Stay Together	1995	3.75	7.50	15.00

—Green vinyl reissue

Number	Title (A Side/B Side)	Yr	VG	VG+	NM
❏ T1-27627	I'm Still in Love with You	1995	3.75	7.50	15.00

—Green vinyl reissue

WORD

Number	Title (A Side/B Side)	Yr	VG	VG+	NM
❏ E 77000	One in a Million	1991	3.00	6.00	12.00

GREEN, BENNIE
BARBARY

Number	Title (A Side/B Side)	Yr	VG	VG+	NM
❏ M 33015 [M]	Play More Than You Can Stand	196?	6.25	12.50	25.00

BETHLEHEM

Number	Title (A Side/B Side)	Yr	VG	VG+	NM
❏ BCP-4019 [M]	Hornful of Soul	196?	5.00	10.00	20.00

—Reissue of 6054

Number	Title (A Side/B Side)	Yr	VG	VG+	NM
❏ BCP-6054 [M]	Hornful of Soul	1961	7.50	15.00	30.00

BLUE NOTE

Number	Title (A Side/B Side)	Yr	VG	VG+	NM
❏ BLP-1587 [M]	Back on the Scene	1958	20.00	40.00	80.00

—Regular version with W. 63rd St. addresss on label

Number	Title (A Side/B Side)	Yr	VG	VG+	NM
❏ BLP-1587 [M]	Back on the Scene	1958	30.00	60.00	120.00

—"Deep groove" version (deep indentation under label on both sides)

Number	Title (A Side/B Side)	Yr	VG	VG+	NM
❏ BLP-1587 [M]	Back on the Scene	1963	6.25	12.50	25.00

—With "New York, USA" address on label

Number	Title (A Side/B Side)	Yr	VG	VG+	NM
❏ BST-1587 [S]	Back on the Scene	1959	15.00	30.00	60.00

—Regular version with W. 63rd St. addresss on label

Number	Title (A Side/B Side)	Yr	VG	VG+	NM
❏ BST-1587 [S]	Back on the Scene	1959	20.00	40.00	80.00

—"Deep groove" version (deep indentation under label on both sides)

Number	Title (A Side/B Side)	Yr	VG	VG+	NM
❏ BLP-1599 [M]	Soul Stirrin'	1958	20.00	40.00	80.00

—Regular version with W. 63rd St. addresss on label

Number	Title (A Side/B Side)	Yr	VG	VG+	NM
❏ BLP-1599 [M]	Soul Stirrin'	1958	30.00	60.00	120.00

—"Deep groove" version (deep indentation under label on both sides)

Number	Title (A Side/B Side)	Yr	VG	VG+	NM
❏ BLP-1599 [M]	Soul Stirrin'	1963	6.25	12.50	25.00

—With "New York, USA" address on label

Number	Title (A Side/B Side)	Yr	VG	VG+	NM
❏ BST-1599 [S]	Soul Stirrin'	1959	15.00	30.00	60.00

—Regular version with W. 63rd St. addresss on label

Number	Title (A Side/B Side)	Yr	VG	VG+	NM
❏ BST-1599 [S]	Soul Stirrin'	1959	20.00	40.00	80.00

—"Deep groove" version (deep indentation under label on both sides)

Number	Title (A Side/B Side)	Yr	VG	VG+	NM
❏ BLP-4010 [M]	Walkin' and Talkin'	1959	20.00	40.00	80.00

—Regular version with W. 63rd St. addresss on label

Number	Title (A Side/B Side)	Yr	VG	VG+	NM
❏ BLP-4010 [M]	Walkin' and Talkin'	1959	30.00	60.00	120.00

—"Deep groove" version (deep indentation under label on both sides)

Number	Title (A Side/B Side)	Yr	VG	VG+	NM
❑ BLP-4010 [M]	Walkin' and Talkin'	1963	6.25	12.50	25.00
—With "New York, USA" address on label					
❑ BST-4010 [S]	Walkin' and Talkin'	1959	15.00	30.00	60.00
—Regular version with W. 63rd St. addresss on label					
❑ BST-4010 [S]	Walkin' and Talkin'	1959	20.00	40.00	80.00
—"Deep groove" version (deep indentation under label on both sides)					
❑ BST-81587 [S]	Back on the Scene	1963	5.00	10.00	20.00
—With "New York, USA" address on label					
❑ BST-81599 [S]	Soul Stirrin'	1963	5.00	10.00	20.00
—With "New York, USA" address on label					
❑ BST-84010 [S]	Walkin' and Talkin'	1963	5.00	10.00	20.00
—With "New York, USA" address on label					
ENRICA					
❑ 2002 [M]	Bennie Green Swings the Blues	1960	7.50	15.00	30.00
❑ S-2002 [S]	Bennie Green Swings the Blues	1960	10.00	20.00	40.00
JAZZLAND					
❑ JLP-43 [M]	Glidin' Along	1961	6.25	12.50	25.00
❑ JLP-943 [S]	Glidin' Along	1961	7.50	15.00	30.00
PRESTIGE					
❑ PRLP-210 [10]	Bennie Blows His Horn	1955	37.50	75.00	150.00
❑ PRLP-7041 [M]	Bennie Green and Art Farmer	1956	25.00	50.00	100.00
❑ PRLP-7049 [M]	Walking Down	1956	25.00	50.00	100.00
❑ PRLP-7052 [M]	Bennie Green Blows His Horn	1956	25.00	50.00	100.00
❑ PRLP-7160 [M]	Bennie Green Blows His Horn	1959	20.00	40.00	80.00
RCA VICTOR					
❑ LPM-2376 [M]	Futura	1961	6.25	12.50	25.00
❑ LSP-2376 [S]	Futura	1961	7.50	15.00	30.00
TIME					
❑ S-2021 [S]	Bennie Green	1960	12.50	25.00	50.00
❑ 52021 [M]	Bennie Green	1960	10.00	20.00	40.00
VEE JAY					
❑ LP-1005 [M]	The Swingin'est	1959	12.50	25.00	50.00
❑ SR-1005 [S]	The Swingin'est	1959	12.50	25.00	50.00
—This LP was reissued as "Juggin' Around" by GENE AMMONS on Vee Jay 3024					

GREEN, BENNIE/PAUL QUINICHETTE
DECCA

Number	Title (A Side/B Side)	Yr	VG	VG+	NM
❑ DL 8176 [M]	Blow Your Horn	1955	12.50	25.00	50.00

GREEN, BERNIE, WITH THE STEREO MAD-MEN
RCA VICTOR

Number	Title (A Side/B Side)	Yr	VG	VG+	NM
❑ LPM-1929 [M]	Musically Mad	1959	15.00	30.00	60.00
❑ LSP-1929 [S]	Musically Mad	1959	30.00	60.00	120.00

GREEN, BUNKY
ARGO

Number	Title (A Side/B Side)	Yr	VG	VG+	NM
❑ LP-753 [M]	Testifyin' Time	1965	6.25	12.50	25.00
❑ LPS-753 [S]	Testifyin' Time	1965	7.50	15.00	30.00
CADET					
❑ LPS-753 [S]	Testifyin' Time	1966	5.00	10.00	20.00
❑ LP-766 [M]	Playin' for Keeps	1966	6.25	12.50	25.00
❑ LPS-766 [S]	Playin' for Keeps	1966	7.50	15.00	30.00
❑ LP-780 [M]	The Latinization of Bunky Green	1967	7.50	15.00	30.00
❑ LPS-780 [S]	The Latinization of Bunky Green	1967	6.25	12.50	25.00

GREEN, BYRDIE
PRESTIGE

Number	Title (A Side/B Side)	Yr	VG	VG+	NM
❑ PRLP-7503 [M]	The Golden Thrush Speaks	1967	5.00	10.00	20.00
❑ PRLP-7509 [M]	I Got It Bad	1967	5.00	10.00	20.00

GREEN, FREDDIE
RCA VICTOR

Number	Title (A Side/B Side)	Yr	VG	VG+	NM
❑ LPM-1210 [M]	Mr. Rhythm	1956	12.50	25.00	50.00

GREEN, GARLAND
RCA VICTOR

Number	Title (A Side/B Side)	Yr	VG	VG+	NM
❑ APL1-2351	Love Is What We Came Here For	1977	3.00	6.00	12.00
UNI					
❑ 73073	Jealous Kind of Fellow	1969	5.00	10.00	20.00

GREEN, GRANT
BLUE NOTE

Number	Title (A Side/B Side)	Yr	VG	VG+	NM
❑ BN-LA037-G [(2)]	Live at the Lighthouse	1973	5.00	10.00	20.00
❑ BLP-4064 [M]	Grant's First Stand	1961	20.00	40.00	80.00
—With W. 63rd St. addresss on label					
❑ BLP-4064 [M]	Grant's First Stand	1963	6.25	12.50	25.00
—With New York, USA address on label					
❑ BLP-4071 [M]	Green Street	1961	15.00	30.00	60.00
—With W. 63rd St. addresss on label					
❑ BLP-4071 [M]	Green Street	1963	6.25	12.50	25.00
—With New York, USA address on label					
❑ BLP-4086 [M]	Grant Stand	1962	15.00	30.00	60.00
—With 61st St. address on label					
❑ BLP-4086 [M]	Grant Stand	1963	6.25	12.50	25.00
—With New York, USA address on label					
❑ BLP-4099 [M]	Sunday Mornin'	1962	15.00	30.00	60.00
—With 61st St. address on label					
❑ BLP-4099 [M]	Sunday Mornin'	1963	6.25	12.50	25.00
—With New York, USA address on label					
❑ BLP-4111 [M]	The Latin Bit	1962	10.00	20.00	40.00
❑ BLP-4132 [M]	Feelin' the Spirit	1963	10.00	20.00	40.00
❑ BLP-4139 [M]	Am I Blue	1963	10.00	20.00	40.00
❑ BLP-4154 [M]	Idle Moments	1964	10.00	20.00	40.00
❑ BLP-4183 [M]	Talkin' About!	1964	10.00	20.00	40.00
❑ BLP-4202 [M]	I Want to Hold Your Hand	1964	10.00	20.00	40.00
❑ BLP-4253 [M]	Street of Dreams	1967	12.50	25.00	50.00
❑ BLP-84064 [S]	Grant's First Stand	1961	15.00	30.00	60.00
—With W. 63rd St. addresss on label					
❑ BLP-84064 [S]	Grant's First Stand	1963	5.00	10.00	20.00
—With New York, USA address on label					
❑ BLP-84071 [S]	Green Street	1961	12.50	25.00	50.00
—With W. 63rd St. addresss on label					

Number	Title (A Side/B Side)	Yr	VG	VG+	NM
❑ BLP-84071 [S]	Green Street	1963	5.00	10.00	20.00
—With New York, USA address on label					
❑ BLP-84086 [S]	Grant Stand	1962	12.50	25.00	50.00
—With 61st St. address on label					
❑ BLP-84086 [S]	Grant Stand	1963	5.00	10.00	20.00
—With New York, USA address on label					
❑ BLP-84099 [S]	Sunday Mornin'	1962	12.50	25.00	50.00
—With 61st St. address on label					
❑ BLP-84099 [S]	Sunday Mornin'	1963	5.00	10.00	20.00
—With New York, USA address on label					
❑ BLP-84111 [S]	The Latin Bit	1962	10.00	20.00	40.00
—With New York, USA address on label					
❑ BLP-84132 [S]	Feelin' the Spirit	1963	10.00	20.00	40.00
—With New York, USA address on label					
❑ BLP-84139 [S]	Am I Blue	1963	10.00	20.00	40.00
—With New York, USA address on label					
❑ BLP-84154 [S]	Idle Moments	1964	10.00	20.00	40.00
—With New York, USA address on label					
❑ BLP-84183 [S]	Talkin' About!	1964	10.00	20.00	40.00
—With New York, USA address on label					
❑ BLP-84202 [S]	I Want to Hold Your Hand	1964	10.00	20.00	40.00
—With New York, USA address on label					
❑ BLP-84253 [S]	Street of Dreams	1967	10.00	20.00	40.00
❑ BLP-84310	Goin' West	1969	10.00	20.00	40.00
❑ BLP-84327	Carryin' On	1969	10.00	20.00	40.00
❑ BLP-84340	Green Is Beautiful	1970	6.25	12.50	25.00
❑ BLP-84360	Alive!	1970	6.25	12.50	25.00
❑ BLP-84373	Visions	1971	5.00	10.00	20.00
❑ BLP-84413	Shades of Green	1972	5.00	10.00	20.00
DELMARK					
❑ DL-404 [M]	All the Gin Is Gone	1966	6.25	12.50	25.00
❑ DS-404 [S]	All the Gin Is Gone	1966	6.25	12.50	25.00
❑ DL-427 [M]	Black Forrest	1966	6.25	12.50	25.00
❑ DS-427 [S]	Black Forrest	1966	6.25	12.50	25.00
MOSAIC					
❑ M5-133 [(5)]	The Complete Blue Note Recordings of Grant Green with Sonny Clark	199?	20.00	40.00	80.00
VERVE					
❑ V-8627 [M]	His Majesty, King Funk	1965	7.50	15.00	30.00
❑ V6-8627 [S]	His Majesty, King Funk	1965	7.50	15.00	30.00

GREEN, LLOYD
CHART

Number	Title (A Side/B Side)	Yr	VG	VG+	NM
❑ CHM-1006 [M]	Mr. Nashville Sound	1968	12.50	25.00	50.00
❑ CHS-1006 [S]	Mr. Nashville Sound	1968	6.25	12.50	25.00
❑ CHS-1010	Cool Steel Man	1969	6.25	12.50	25.00
❑ 1024	Moody River	1970	6.25	12.50	25.00
GRT					
❑ 8018	Feelings	1977	3.00	6.00	12.00
LITTLE DARLIN'					
❑ LD-4002	Day for Decision	196?	6.25	12.50	25.00
❑ LD 4005	The Hit Sounds of Lloyd Green	196?	6.25	12.50	25.00
MONUMENT					
❑ KZ 32532	Shades of Steel	1973	3.75	7.50	15.00
❑ KZ 33368	Steel Rides	1975	3.75	7.50	15.00
TIME					
❑ ST-2152 [S]	Big Steel Guitar	1964	10.00	20.00	40.00
❑ T-2152 [M]	Big Steel Guitar	1964	7.50	15.00	30.00

GREEN, PETER
Also see FLEETWOOD MAC.
REPRISE

Number	Title (A Side/B Side)	Yr	VG	VG+	NM
❑ RS 6436	The End of the Game	1970	5.00	10.00	20.00
SAIL					
❑ 0110	In the Skies	1979	2.50	5.00	10.00
❑ 0112	Little Dreamer	1980	2.50	5.00	10.00

GREEN, PHIL
LONDON

Number	Title (A Side/B Side)	Yr	VG	VG+	NM
❑ LPB-17 [10]	Rhythm on Reeds	1950	12.50	25.00	50.00

GREEN, URBIE
ABC-PARAMOUNT

Number	Title (A Side/B Side)	Yr	VG	VG+	NM
❑ ABC-101 [M]	Blues and Other Shades of Green	1955	15.00	30.00	60.00
❑ ABC-137 [M]	All About Urbie Green	1956	12.50	25.00	50.00
BETHLEHEM					
❑ BCP-14 [M]	East Coast Jazz, Volume 6	1955	20.00	40.00	80.00
BLUE NOTE					
❑ BLP-5036 [10]	Urbie Green Septet	1954	62.50	125.00	250.00
RCA VICTOR					
❑ LPM-1667 [M]	Let's Face the Music and Dance	1958	10.00	20.00	40.00
❑ LSP-1667 [S]	Let's Face the Music and Dance	1958	10.00	20.00	40.00
❑ LPM-1741 [M]	Jimmy McHugh in Hi-Fi	1958	12.50	25.00	50.00
❑ LSP-1741 [S]	Jimmy McHugh in Hi-Fi	1958	15.00	30.00	60.00
❑ LPM-1969 [M]	Best of the New Broadway Show Hits	1959	10.00	20.00	40.00
❑ LSP-1969 [S]	Best of the New Broadway Show Hits	1959	10.00	20.00	40.00
VANGUARD					
❑ VRS-8010 [10]	Urbie Green and His Band	1954	30.00	60.00	120.00
"X"					
❑ LXA-3026 [10]	A Cool Yuletide	1954	30.00	60.00	120.00

GREEN, URBIE/VIC DICKENSON
JAZZTONE

Number	Title (A Side/B Side)	Yr	VG	VG+	NM
❑ J-1259 [M]	Urbie Green Octet/Slidin' Swing	1957	10.00	20.00	40.00

GREEN, WILLIAM
EVEREST

Number	Title (A Side/B Side)	Yr	VG	VG+	NM
❑ SDBR-1213 [S]	Shades of Green	1963	5.00	10.00	20.00

G

Number	Title (A Side/B Side)	Yr	VG	VG+	NM

GREEN BULLFROG
DECCA
| ❏ DL 75269 | Green Bullfrog | 1971 | 6.25 | 12.50 | 25.00 |

GREEN DAY
ADELINE
| ❏ 012-1 | Warning: | 2000 | 3.00 | 6.00 | 12.00 |
LOOKOUT
| ❏ 22 | 39/Smooth | 1990 | 2.50 | 5.00 | 10.00 |
| ❏ 46 | Kerplunk | 1992 | 2.50 | 5.00 | 10.00 |
REPRISE
❏ 45529	Dookie	1994	3.75	7.50	15.00
—Original stock issue on black vinyl					
❏ 45529	Dookie	1995	2.50	5.00	10.00
—Reissue on pink vinyl					
❏ 45529 [DJ]	Dookie	1994	7.50	15.00	30.00
—Promo version on milky pale-green vinyl					
❏ 45529 [DJ]	Dookie	1994	8.75	17.50	35.00
—Promo version on clear green vinyl in plain white cover					
❏ 46046	Insomniac	1995	2.50	5.00	10.00

GREEN RIVER
Members of this band later joined MOTHER LOVE BONE, MUDHONEY and PEARL JAM.
HOMESTEAD
| ❏ 031 | Come On Down | 198? | 3.00 | 6.00 | 12.00 |
| —Originals do not have a UPC code (deduct 25% if UPC is there) | | | | | |
SUB POP
❏ 11 [EP]	Dry as a Bone	1987	8.75	17.50	35.00
—Later copies have pink inserts					
❏ 11 [EP]	Dry as a Bone	1987	12.50	25.00	50.00
—First 2,000 copies have yellow inserts					
❏ 15 [EP]	Rehab Doll	1988	6.25	12.50	25.00
❏ 15 [EP]	Rehab Doll	1988	8.75	17.50	35.00
—First 1,000 copies on green vinyl					

GREENBAUM, NORMAN
Also see DR. WEST'S MEDICINE SHOW AND JUG BAND.
REPRISE
❏ MS 2048	Petaluma	1972	3.75	7.50	15.00
❏ RS 6365	Spirit in the Sky	1969	5.00	10.00	20.00
❏ RS 6422	Back Home Again	1970	3.75	7.50	15.00

GREENBRIAR BOYS, THE
ELEKTRA
| ❏ EKL-233 [M] | Dian and the Greenbriar Boys | 1963 | 6.25 | 12.50 | 25.00 |
| ❏ EKS-7233 [S] | Dian and the Greenbriar Boys | 1963 | 7.50 | 15.00 | 30.00 |
VANGUARD
❏ VRS-9104 [M]	The Greenbriar Boys	1962	6.25	12.50	25.00
❏ VRS-9159 [M]	Ragged But Right	1964	5.00	10.00	20.00
❏ VRS-9233 [M]	Better Late Than Never	1966	5.00	10.00	20.00
❏ VSD-79159 [S]	Ragged But Right	1964	6.25	12.50	25.00
❏ VSD-79233 [S]	Better Late Than Never	1966	6.25	12.50	25.00

GREENE, BURTON
ESP-DISK'
❏ 1024 [M]	Burton Greene	1966	6.25	12.50	25.00
❏ S-1024 [S]	Burton Greene	1966	5.00	10.00	20.00
❏ S-1074	Burton Greene Concert Tour	1968	6.25	12.50	25.00

GREENE, DODO
BLUE NOTE
❏ BLP-9001 [M]	My Hour of Need	1962	12.50	25.00	50.00
—With W. 63rd St. addresss on label					
❏ BLP-9001 [M]	My Hour of Need	1963	6.25	12.50	25.00
—With "New York, USA" address on label					
❏ BST-89001 [S]	My Hour of Need	1967	5.00	10.00	20.00
—With "A Division of Liberty Records" on label					

GREENE, JACK
DECCA
❏ DL 4845 [M]	There Goes My Everything	1967	5.00	10.00	20.00
❏ DL 4904 [M]	All the Time	1967	5.00	10.00	20.00
❏ DL 4939 [M]	What Locks the Door	1968	6.25	12.50	25.00
❏ DL 4979 [M]	You Are My Treasure	1968	7.50	15.00	30.00
❏ DL 74845 [S]	There Goes My Everything	1967	3.75	7.50	15.00
❏ DL 74904 [S]	All the Time	1967	3.75	7.50	15.00
❏ DL 74939 [S]	What Locks the Door	1968	3.75	7.50	15.00
❏ DL 74979 [S]	You Are My Treasure	1968	3.75	7.50	15.00
❏ DL 75080	I Am Not Alone	1969	3.75	7.50	15.00
❏ DL 75124	Statue of a Fool	1969	3.75	7.50	15.00
❏ DL 75188	Lord Is That Me	1970	3.75	7.50	15.00
❏ DL 75208	Greatest Hits	1970	3.75	7.50	15.00
❏ DL 75283	There's a Whole Lot About a Woman	1971	3.75	7.50	15.00
❏ DL 75308	Greene Country	1972	3.75	7.50	15.00
❏ ST-91433 [S]	What Locks the Door	1968	5.00	10.00	20.00
—Capitol Record Club edition					
❏ T-91433 [M]	What Locks the Door	1968	10.00	20.00	40.00
—Capitol Record Club edition					
MCA
❏ 291	Greatest Hits	1973	3.00	6.00	12.00
—Reissue of Decca 75208					
❏ 295	Greene Country	1973	3.00	6.00	12.00
—Reissue of Decca 75308					
PICKWICK
| ❏ SPC-6173 | I Never Had It So Good | 197? | 2.50 | 5.00 | 10.00 |

GREENE, LORNE
RCA CAMDEN
| ❏ CAS-2391 | Five Card Stud | 1970 | 6.25 | 12.50 | 25.00 |
RCA VICTOR
| ❏ SP-33-327 [DJ] | Palaver with The Man | 1965 | 12.50 | 25.00 | 50.00 |
| —Promo-only interview record with script | | | | | |

Number	Title (A Side/B Side)	Yr	VG	VG+	NM
❏ LPM-2661 [M]	Young at Heart	1963	6.25	12.50	25.00
❏ LSP-2661 [S]	Young at Heart	1963	7.50	15.00	30.00
❏ LPM-2843 [M]	Welcome to the Ponderosa	1964	6.25	12.50	25.00
❏ LSP-2843 [S]	Welcome to the Ponderosa	1964	7.50	15.00	30.00
❏ LPM-3302 [M]	The Man	1965	6.25	12.50	25.00
❏ LSP-3302 [S]	The Man	1965	7.50	15.00	30.00
❏ LPM-3409 [M]	Lorne Greene's American West	1965	6.25	12.50	25.00
❏ LSP-3409 [S]	Lorne Greene's American West	1965	7.50	15.00	30.00
❏ LPM-3410 [M]	Have a Happy Holiday	1965	6.25	12.50	25.00
❏ LSP-3410 [S]	Have a Happy Holiday	1965	7.50	15.00	30.00
❏ LPM-3678 [M]	Portrait of the West	1966	6.25	12.50	25.00
❏ LSP-3678 [S]	Portrait of the West	1966	7.50	15.00	30.00
RCA VICTOR RED SEAL
❏ LM-2783 [M]	Peter and the Wolf	1964	6.25	12.50	25.00
❏ LSC-2783 [S]	Peter and the Wolf	1964	7.50	15.00	30.00
—Above with the London Symphony Orchestra					

GREENE, LORNE; MICHAEL LANDON; DAN BLOCKER
RCA VICTOR
❏ LPM-2583 [M]	Bonanza — Ponderosa Party Time!	1962	7.50	15.00	30.00
❏ LSP-2583 [S]	Bonanza — Ponderosa Party Time!	1962	10.00	20.00	40.00
❏ LPM-2757 [M]	Christmas on the Ponderosa	1963	6.25	12.50	25.00
❏ LSP-2757 [S]	Christmas on the Ponderosa	1963	7.50	15.00	30.00

GREENSLEEVES, EDDIE
CAMEO
| ❏ C-1031 [M] | Humorous Folk Songs | 1963 | 5.00 | 10.00 | 20.00 |
| ❏ SC-1031 [S] | Humorous Folk Songs | 1963 | 6.25 | 12.50 | 25.00 |

GREENWICH, ELLIE
Also see THE RAINDROPS.
UNITED ARTISTS
| ❏ UAS-6648 | Ellie Greenwich Composes, Produces and Sings | 1968 | 12.50 | 25.00 | 50.00 |
VERVE
| ❏ V6-5091 | Let It Be Written, Let It Be Sung | 1973 | 6.25 | 12.50 | 25.00 |

GREER, PAULA
WORKSHOP JAZZ
| ❏ WSJ 203 [M] | Introducing Miss Paula Greer | 1963 | 62.50 | 125.00 | 250.00 |

GREGG, BOBBY
EPIC
| ❏ LN 24051 [M] | Let's Stomp and Wild Weekend | 1963 | 7.50 | 15.00 | 30.00 |
| ❏ BN 26051 [S] | Let's Stomp and Wild Weekend | 1963 | 10.00 | 20.00 | 40.00 |

GREGORY, DICK
COLPIX
❏ CP 417 [M]	In Living Black and White	1961	6.25	12.50	25.00
❏ CP 420 [M]	East and West	1961	6.25	12.50	25.00
❏ CP 480 [M]	We All Have Problems	1964	6.25	12.50	25.00
GATEWAY
| ❏ GLP 9007 [M] | My Brother's Keeper | 1963 | 10.00 | 20.00 | 40.00 |
POPPY
❏ PP-LA176-G2 [(2)]	Caught in the Act	1973	3.75	7.50	15.00
❏ PYS 40008	Dick Gregory On...	1970	3.75	7.50	15.00
❏ PYS 40011	Dick Gregory at the Village Gate	1972	3.75	7.50	15.00
❏ PYS 60003 [(2)]	The Light Side: The Dark Side	1969	5.00	10.00	20.00
❏ PYS 60004 [(2)]	Frankenstein	1970	3.75	7.50	15.00
❏ PYS 60005 [(2)]	Dick Gregory at Kent State	1971	3.75	7.50	15.00
TOMATO
| ❏ 9001 [(3)] | The Best of Dick Gregory | 1978 | 5.00 | 10.00 | 20.00 |
VEE JAY
❏ LP 1093 [M]	Running for President	1964	6.25	12.50	25.00
❏ LP 4001 [M]	Dick Gregory Talks Turkey	1962	6.25	12.50	25.00
❏ LP 4005 [M]	Two Sides of Dick Gregory	1963	6.25	12.50	25.00

GRENFELL, JOYCE
ELEKTRA
| ❏ EKL-184 [M] | Presenting Joyce Grenfell | 1960 | 7.50 | 15.00 | 30.00 |

GREY, AL
ARGO
❏ LP-653 [M]	The Last of the Big Plungers	1960	6.25	12.50	25.00
❏ LPS-653 [S]	The Last of the Big Plungers	1960	6.25	12.50	25.00
❏ LP-677 [M]	The Thinking Man's Trombone	1961	5.00	10.00	20.00
❏ LPS-677 [S]	The Thinking Man's Trombone	1961	6.25	12.50	25.00
❏ LP-689 [M]	Al Grey and the Billy Mitchell Sextet	1962	5.00	10.00	20.00
❏ LPS-689 [S]	Al Grey and the Billy Mitchell Sextet	1962	6.25	12.50	25.00
❏ LP-700 [M]	Snap Your Fingers	1962	5.00	10.00	20.00
❏ LPS-700 [S]	Snap Your Fingers	1962	6.25	12.50	25.00
❏ LP-711 [M]	Night Song	1963	5.00	10.00	20.00
❏ LPS-711 [S]	Night Song	1963	6.25	12.50	25.00
❏ LP-718 [M]	Having a Ball	1963	5.00	10.00	20.00
❏ LPS-718 [S]	Having a Ball	1963	6.25	12.50	25.00
❏ LP-731 [M]	Boss Bones	1964	5.00	10.00	20.00
❏ LPS-731 [S]	Boss Bones	1964	6.25	12.50	25.00
TANGERINE
| ❏ TRCS-1504 [S] | Shades of Grey | 1965 | 5.00 | 10.00 | 20.00 |

GRIER, ROOSEVELT
RIC
| ❏ M-1008 [M] | Soul City | 1964 | 5.00 | 10.00 | 20.00 |
| ❏ S-1008 [S] | Soul City | 1964 | 6.25 | 12.50 | 25.00 |
WORD
| ❏ WR-8342 | Committed | 1986 | 3.00 | 6.00 | 12.00 |

GRIFF, RAY
ABC DOT
| ❏ DOSD-2011 | Expressions | 1974 | 3.00 | 6.00 | 12.00 |
CAPITOL
| ❏ ST-11486 | Ray Griff | 1976 | 2.50 | 5.00 | 10.00 |

Number	Title (A Side/B Side)	Yr	VG	VG+	NM
❑ ST-11566	The Last of the Winfield Amateurs	1976	2.50	5.00	10.00
❑ ST-11718	Raymond's Place	1977	2.50	5.00	10.00
DOT					
❑ DLP-25868	A Ray of Sunshine	1968	5.00	10.00	20.00
❑ DOS-26013	Songs for Everyone	1973	3.75	7.50	15.00
ROYAL AMERICAN					
❑ RAS 1007	Ray Griff Sings	1972	3.75	7.50	15.00

GRIFFIN, DICK
STRATA-EAST

Number	Title (A Side/B Side)	Yr	VG	VG+	NM
❑ SES-19747	The Eighth Wonder	1975	5.00	10.00	20.00

GRIFFIN, JIMMY
POLYDOR

Number	Title (A Side/B Side)	Yr	VG	VG+	NM
❑ PD 6018	James Griffin and Co.	1973	3.75	7.50	15.00
REPRISE					
❑ R-6091 [M]	Summer Holiday	1963	12.50	25.00	50.00
❑ R9-6091 [S]	Summer Holiday	1963	15.00	30.00	60.00

GRIFFIN, JOHNNY
ARGO

Number	Title (A Side/B Side)	Yr	VG	VG+	NM
❑ LP-624 [M]	Johnny Griffin Quartet	1958	12.50	25.00	50.00
BLUE NOTE					
❑ BLP-1533 [M]	Introducing Johnny Griffin	1956	37.50	75.00	150.00
—Regular version, Lexington Ave. address on label					
❑ BLP-1533 [M]	Introducing Johnny Griffin	1956	50.00	100.00	200.00
—"Deep groove" version (deep indentation under label on both sides)					
❑ BLP-1533 [M]	Introducing Johnny Griffin	1957	15.00	30.00	60.00
—With "W. 63rd St." address on label					
❑ BLP-1533 [M]	Introducing Johnny Griffin	1963	6.25	12.50	25.00
—With "New York, USA" address on label					
❑ BLP-1559 [M]	A Blowing Session	1957	25.00	50.00	100.00
—Regular version, "W. 63rd St." address on label					
❑ BLP-1559 [M]	A Blowing Session	1957	37.50	75.00	150.00
—"Deep groove" version (deep indentation under label on both sides)					
❑ BLP-1559 [M]	A Blowing Session	1963	6.25	12.50	25.00
—With "New York, USA" address on label					
❑ BLP-1580 [M]	The Congregation	1958	20.00	40.00	80.00
—Regular version, "W. 63rd St." address on label					
❑ BLP-1580 [M]	The Congregation	1958	30.00	60.00	120.00
—"Deep groove" version (deep indentation under label on both sides)					
❑ BLP-1580 [M]	The Congregation	1963	6.25	12.50	25.00
—With "New York, USA" address on label					
❑ BST-1580 [S]	The Congregation	1959	15.00	30.00	60.00
—Regular version, "W. 63rd St." address on label					
❑ BST-1580 [S]	The Congregation	1959	20.00	40.00	80.00
—"Deep groove" version (deep indentation under label on both sides)					
❑ BST-1580 [S]	The Congregation	1963	5.00	10.00	20.00
—With "New York, USA" address on label					
EMARCY					
❑ MG-26001 [M]	Night Lady	1967	10.00	20.00	40.00
❑ SR-66001 [S]	Night Lady	1967	6.25	12.50	25.00
INNER CITY					
❑ IC-6042 [(2)]	Live Tokyo	197?	5.00	10.00	20.00
JAZZLAND					
❑ JLP-93 [M]	The Little Giant	1961	10.00	20.00	40.00
❑ JLP-993 [S]	The Little Giant	1961	7.50	15.00	30.00
MILESTONE					
❑ 47014 [(2)]	Big Soul	197?	5.00	10.00	20.00
RIVERSIDE					
❑ RLP 12-264 [M]	Johnny Griffin Sextet	1958	12.50	25.00	50.00
❑ RLP 12-274 [M]	Way Out!	1958	12.50	25.00	50.00
❑ RLP 12-304 [M]	The Little Giant	1959	12.50	25.00	50.00
❑ RLP 12-331 [M]	The Big Soul-Band	1960	10.00	20.00	40.00
❑ RLP-338 [M]	Studio Jazz Party	1960	10.00	20.00	40.00
❑ RLP-368 [M]	Change of Pace	1961	7.50	15.00	30.00
❑ RLP-387 [M]	White Gardenia	1961	7.50	15.00	30.00
❑ RLP-420 [M]	The Kerry Dancers	1962	6.25	12.50	25.00
❑ RLP-437 [M]	Grab This!	1962	6.25	12.50	25.00
❑ RLP-462 [M]	Do Nothing 'Til You Hear from Me	1963	6.25	12.50	25.00
❑ RLP-479 [M]	Wade in the Water	1964	5.00	10.00	20.00
❑ RLP-1149 [S]	The Little Giant	1959	10.00	20.00	40.00
❑ RLP-1171 [S]	The Big Soul-Band	1960	7.50	15.00	30.00
❑ RS-9338 [S]	Studio Jazz Party	1960	7.50	15.00	30.00
❑ RS-9368 [S]	Change of Pace	1961	7.50	15.00	30.00
❑ RS-9387 [S]	White Gardenia	1961	7.50	15.00	30.00
❑ RS-9420 [S]	The Kerry Dancers	1962	7.50	15.00	30.00
❑ RS-9437 [S]	Grab This!	1962	7.50	15.00	30.00
❑ RS-9462 [S]	Do Nothing 'Til You Hear from Me	1963	7.50	15.00	30.00
❑ RS-9479 [S]	Wade in the Water	1964	6.25	12.50	25.00

GRIFFIN, JOHNNY, AND MATTHEW GEE
ATLANTIC

Number	Title (A Side/B Side)	Yr	VG	VG+	NM
❑ 1431 [M]	Soul Groove	1965	5.00	10.00	20.00
❑ SD 1431 [S]	Soul Groove	1965	6.25	12.50	25.00

GRIFFIN, KEN
COLUMBIA

Number	Title (A Side/B Side)	Yr	VG	VG+	NM
❑ CL 692 [M]	The Organ Plays at Christmas	1955	6.25	12.50	25.00
—Red and black label with six "eye" logos					
❑ CL 6130 [10]	Christmas Carols by Ken Griffin	1950	7.50	15.00	30.00

GRIFFIN, MERV
CAMEO

Number	Title (A Side/B Side)	Yr	VG	VG+	NM
❑ C-1060 [M]	My Favorite Songs	1964	5.00	10.00	20.00
❑ SC-1060 [S]	My Favorite Songs	1964	6.25	12.50	25.00
CARLTON					
❑ LP-12-134 [M]	Merv Griffin's Dance Party	1961	7.50	15.00	30.00
❑ STLP-12-134 [S]	Merv Griffin's Dance Party	1961	10.00	20.00	40.00

GRIFFITH, ANDY
CAPITOL

Number	Title (A Side/B Side)	Yr	VG	VG+	NM
❑ T 962 [M]	Just for Laughs				
❑ ST 1105 [S]	Andy Griffith Shouts the Blues and Old Songs				
❑ T 1105 [M]	Andy Griffith Shouts the Blues and Old Songs				
❑ ST 1215 [S]	This Here Andy Griffith				
❑ T 1215 [M]	This Here Andy Griffith				
❑ ST 1611 [S]	Songs, Themes and Laughs from The Griffith Show				
❑ T 1611 [M]	Songs, Themes and Laughs from The Griffith Show				
❑ ST 2066 [S]	Andy and Cleopatra	1964	6.25	12.50	25.00
❑ T 2066 [M]	Andy and Cleopatra	1964	5.00	10.00	20.00

GRIFFITH, JOHNNY, TRIO
WORKSHOP JAZZ

Number	Title (A Side/B Side)	Yr	VG	VG+	NM
❑ WSJ 205 [M]	Jazz	1963	50.00	100.00	200.00

GRIFFITH, NANCI
B.F. DEAL

Number	Title (A Side/B Side)	Yr	VG	VG+	NM
❑ BFD 9	There's a Light Beyond These Woods	1978	12.50	25.00	50.00
ELEKTRA					
❑ 62015	Blue Roses from the Moons	1997	3.00	6.00	12.00
FEATHERBED					
❑ FB 902	Poet in My Window	1982	5.00	10.00	20.00
❑ FB 903	There's a Light Beyond These Woods	1982	5.00	10.00	20.00
MCA					
❑ 5927	Lone Star State of Mind	1987	2.00	4.00	8.00
❑ 6319	Storms	1989	2.50	5.00	10.00
❑ 42102	Little Love Affairs	1988	2.00	4.00	8.00
❑ 42255	One Fair Summer Evening	1988	2.00	4.00	8.00
PHILO					
❑ PH-1096	Once in a Very Blue Moon	1984	3.00	6.00	12.00
❑ PH-1097	There's a Light Beyond These Woods	1986	3.00	6.00	12.00
❑ PH-1098	Poet in My Window	1986	3.00	6.00	12.00
❑ PH-1109	Last of the True Believers	1986	3.00	6.00	12.00

GRIFFITH, SHIRLEY
BLUESVILLE

Number	Title (A Side/B Side)	Yr	VG	VG+	NM
❑ BVLP-1087 [M]	The Blues of Shirley Griffith	1964	6.25	12.50	25.00
—Blue label, trident logo at right					
❑ BVLP-1087 [M]	The Blues of Shirley Griffith	1964	12.50	25.00	50.00
—Blue label, silver print					

GRIMES, GARY
DIRECT DISK

Number	Title (A Side/B Side)	Yr	VG	VG+	NM
❑ SD-16630	Starhand Visions	198?	7.50	15.00	30.00
—Audiophile vinyl					

GRIMES, HENRY
ESP-DISK'

Number	Title (A Side/B Side)	Yr	VG	VG+	NM
❑ 1027 [M]	Henry Grimes Trio	1966	5.00	10.00	20.00
❑ S-1027 [S]	Henry Grimes Trio	1966	6.25	12.50	25.00

GRIMES, TINY
PRESTIGE

Number	Title (A Side/B Side)	Yr	VG	VG+	NM
❑ PRLP-7138 [M]	Blues Grooves	1958	25.00	50.00	100.00
❑ PRLP-7144 [M]	Callin' the Blues	1958	25.00	50.00	100.00
SWINGVILLE					
❑ SVLP-2002 [M]	Tiny in Swingville	1960	12.50	25.00	50.00
—Purple label					
❑ SVLP-2002 [M]	Tiny in Swingville	1965	6.25	12.50	25.00
—Blue label, trident logo at right					
❑ SVLP-2004 [M]	Callin' the Blues	1960	12.50	25.00	50.00
—Purple label					
❑ SVLP-2004 [M]	Callin' the Blues	1965	6.25	12.50	25.00
—Blue label, trident logo at right					
UNITED ARTISTS					
❑ UAL-3232 [M]	Big Time Guitar	1962	6.25	12.50	25.00
❑ UAS-6232 [S]	Big Time Guitar	1962	7.50	15.00	30.00

GRISMAN, DAVID
KALEIDOSCOPE

Number	Title (A Side/B Side)	Yr	VG	VG+	NM
❑ 5	David Grisman Quintet	1977	5.00	10.00	20.00

GRISSOM, JIMMY
ARGO

Number	Title (A Side/B Side)	Yr	VG	VG+	NM
❑ LP-729 [M]	World of Trouble	1963	6.25	12.50	25.00
❑ LPS-729 [S]	World of Trouble	1963	7.50	15.00	30.00

GRODECK WHIPPERJENNY
PEOPLE

Number	Title (A Side/B Side)	Yr	VG	VG+	NM
❑ 3000	Grodeck Whipperjenny	1969	50.00	100.00	200.00

GROOV-U
GATEWAY

Number	Title (A Side/B Side)	Yr	VG	VG+	NM
❑ GLP-3010	Groov-U On Campus	196?	10.00	20.00	40.00

GROOVE COLLECTIVE, THE
REPRISE

Number	Title (A Side/B Side)	Yr	VG	VG+	NM
❑ 45541 [(2)]	The Groove Collective	1994	5.00	10.00	20.00

GROOVIE GOOLIES, THE
RCA VICTOR

Number	Title (A Side/B Side)	Yr	VG	VG+	NM
❑ LSP-4420	The Groovie Goolies	1970	6.25	12.50	25.00

GROSZ, MARTY
RIVERSIDE

Number	Title (A Side/B Side)	Yr	VG	VG+	NM
❑ RLP 12-268 [M]	Hurrah for Bix	1958	10.00	20.00	40.00
❑ RLP-1109 [S]	Hurrah for Bix	1959	7.50	15.00	30.00

Number	Title (A Side/B Side)	Yr	VG	VG+	NM

GROUNDHOGS, THE

Number	Title (A Side/B Side)	Yr	VG	VG+	NM
□ ...671	The Groundhogs with John Lee Hooker and John Mayall	196?	25.00	50.00	100.00
IMPERIAL					
□ LP-12452	Blues Obituary	1969	10.00	20.00	40.00
LIBERTY					
□ LST-7644	Thank Christ for the Bomb	1970	7.50	15.00	30.00
UNITED ARTISTS					
□ UA-LA008-F	Hogwash	1973	5.00	10.00	20.00
□ UA-LA603-G	Crosscut Saw	1976	5.00	10.00	20.00
□ UA-LA680-G	Black Diamond	1976	5.00	10.00	20.00
□ UAS-5513	The Groundhogs Split	1971	5.00	10.00	20.00
□ UAS-5570	Who Will Save the World	1972	5.00	10.00	20.00
WORLD PACIFIC					
□ WPS-21892	Scratching the Surface	1968	10.00	20.00	40.00

GROUP, THE

Number	Title (A Side/B Side)	Yr	VG	VG+	NM
BELL					
□ 6038	The Group	1970	5.00	10.00	20.00
RCA VICTOR					
□ LPM-2663 [M]	The Group	1963	5.00	10.00	20.00
□ LSP-2663 [S]	The Group	1963	6.25	12.50	25.00

GROUP IMAGE, THE

Number	Title (A Side/B Side)	Yr	VG	VG+	NM
COMMUNITY					
□ A-101	A Mouth in the Clouds	1968	7.50	15.00	30.00

GROUP ONE

Number	Title (A Side/B Side)	Yr	VG	VG+	NM
RCA VICTOR					
□ LPM-3524 [M]	Brothers Go to Mothers and Others	1966	3.75	7.50	15.00
□ LSP-3524 [S]	Brothers Go to Mothers and Others	1966	5.00	10.00	20.00

GROUP THERAPY

Number	Title (A Side/B Side)	Yr	VG	VG+	NM
PHILIPS					
□ PHS 600303	37 Minutes of Group Therapy	1969	3.75	7.50	15.00
RCA VICTOR					
□ LPM-3976 [M]	People Get Ready for Group Therapy	1968	10.00	20.00	40.00
□ LSP-3976 [S]	People Get Ready for Group Therapy	1968	5.00	10.00	20.00

GROVE, BOBBY

Number	Title (A Side/B Side)	Yr	VG	VG+	NM
KING					
□ 831 [M]	It Was for You	1963	10.00	20.00	40.00

GROVE, DICK

Number	Title (A Side/B Side)	Yr	VG	VG+	NM
PACIFIC JAZZ					
□ PJ-74 [M]	Little Bird Suite	1963	5.00	10.00	20.00
□ ST-74 [S]	Little Bird Suite	1963	6.25	12.50	25.00

GROWING CONCERN, THE

Number	Title (A Side/B Side)	Yr	VG	VG+	NM
MAINSTREAM					
□ S-6108 [S]	The Growing Concern	1968	30.00	60.00	120.00
□ 56108 [M]	The Growing Concern	1968	20.00	40.00	80.00

GROWL

Number	Title (A Side/B Side)	Yr	VG	VG+	NM
DISCREET					
□ DS 2209	Growl	1974	5.00	10.00	20.00

GRUNTZ, GEORGE

Number	Title (A Side/B Side)	Yr	VG	VG+	NM
PHILIPS					
□ PHS 600162 [S]	Bach Humbug	1964	5.00	10.00	20.00

GRUSIN, DAVE

Number	Title (A Side/B Side)	Yr	VG	VG+	NM
COLUMBIA					
□ CL 2344 [M]	Kaleidoscope	1965	5.00	10.00	20.00
□ CS 9144 [S]	Kaleidoscope	1965	6.25	12.50	25.00
EPIC					
□ BN 622 [S]	Subways Are for Sleeping	1962	6.25	12.50	25.00
□ LN 3829 [M]	Subways Are for Sleeping	1962	5.00	10.00	20.00
□ LN 24023 [M]	Piano Strings and Moonlight	1962	6.25	12.50	25.00
□ BN 26023 [S]	Piano Strings and Moonlight	1962	7.50	15.00	30.00
SHEFFIELD LABS					
□ 5	Discovered Again!	1976	6.25	12.50	25.00
—Direct-to-disc recording					
SHEFFIELD TREASURY					
□ ST-500	Discovered Again!	198?	5.00	10.00	20.00
—Reissue of Sheffield Labs 5					

GRYCE, GIGI

Number	Title (A Side/B Side)	Yr	VG	VG+	NM
BLUE NOTE					
□ BLP-5049 [10]	Gigi Gryce's Jazztime Paris	1954	75.00	150.00	300.00
□ BLP-5050 [10]	Gigi Gryce and His Little Band, Volume 2	1954	75.00	150.00	300.00
□ BLP-5051 [10]	Gigi Gryce Quintet/Sextet, Volume 3	1954	75.00	150.00	300.00
MERCURY					
□ MG-20628 [M]	Reminiscin'	1961	7.50	15.00	30.00
□ SR-60628 [S]	Reminiscin'	1961	10.00	20.00	40.00
METROJAZZ					
□ E-1006 [M]	Gigi Gryce	1958	20.00	40.00	80.00
□ SE-1006 [S]	Gigi Gryce	1959	15.00	30.00	60.00
NEW JAZZ					
□ NJLP-8230 [M]	Sayin' Somethin'!	1959	12.50	25.00	50.00
—Purple label					
□ NJLP-8230 [M]	Sayin' Somethin'!	1965	6.25	12.50	25.00
—Blue label, trident logo at right					
□ NJLP-8246 [M]	The Hap'nin's	1960	12.50	25.00	50.00
—Purple label					
□ NJLP-8246 [M]	The Hap'nin's	1965	6.25	12.50	25.00
—Blue label, trident logo at right					
□ NJLP-8262 [M]	The Rat Race Blues	1961	12.50	25.00	50.00
—Purple label					
□ NJLP-8262 [M]	The Rat Race Blues	1965	6.25	12.50	25.00
—Blue label, trident logo at right					
SAVOY					
□ MG-12137 [M]	Nica's Tempo	1958	20.00	40.00	80.00
SIGNAL					
□ S-1201 [M]	Gigi Gryce Quartet	1955	75.00	150.00	300.00

GRYCE, GIGI, AND CLIFFORD BROWN

Number	Title (A Side/B Side)	Yr	VG	VG+	NM
BLUE NOTE					
□ BLP-5048 [10]	Gigi Gryce-Clifford Brown Sextet	1954	100.00	200.00	400.00

GRYPHON

Number	Title (A Side/B Side)	Yr	VG	VG+	NM
(NO LABEL)					
□ 12497	Gryphon	197?	20.00	40.00	80.00
BELL					
□ 1316	Red Queen to Gryphon Three	1974	3.75	7.50	15.00

GUADALCANAL DIARY

Number	Title (A Side/B Side)	Yr	VG	VG+	NM
DB					
□ 73	Walking in the Shadow of the Big Man	1984	5.00	10.00	20.00
ELEKTRA					
□ 60429	Walking in the Shadow of the Big Man	1985	2.50	5.00	10.00
□ 60478	Jamboree	1986	2.50	5.00	10.00
□ 60752	2X4	1987	2.50	5.00	10.00
□ 60848	Flip-Flop	1989	2.00	4.00	8.00
□ 60848 [DJ]	Flip-Flop	1989	2.50	5.00	10.00
—Promo-only white label audiophile vinyl					
ENTERTAINMENT ON DISC					
□ EOD 102 [EP]	Watusi Rodeo	1983	5.00	10.00	20.00

GUARALDI, VINCE

Number	Title (A Side/B Side)	Yr	VG	VG+	NM
FANTASY					
□ 3213 [M]	Modern Music from San Francisco	195?	6.25	12.50	25.00
—Black vinyl, red label, non-flexible vinyl					
□ 3213 [M]	Modern Music from San Francisco	1956	12.50	25.00	50.00
—Red vinyl					
□ 3225 [M]	Vince Guaraldi Trio	195?	6.25	12.50	25.00
—Black vinyl, red label, non-flexible vinyl					
□ 3225 [M]	Vince Guaraldi Trio	1956	12.50	25.00	50.00
—Red vinyl					
□ 3257 [M]	A Flower Is a Lovesome Thing	195?	6.25	12.50	25.00
—Black vinyl, red label, non-flexible vinyl					
□ 3257 [M]	A Flower Is a Lovesome Thing	1958	10.00	20.00	40.00
—Red vinyl					
□ 3337 [M]	Jazz Impressions of Black Orpheus (Cast Your Fate to the Wind)	1962	6.25	12.50	25.00
—Black vinyl, red label, non-flexible vinyl					
□ 3337 [M]	Jazz Impressions of Black Orpheus (Cast Your Fate to the Wind)	1962	10.00	20.00	40.00
—Red vinyl					
□ 3352 [M]	Vince Guaraldi in Person	1963	6.25	12.50	25.00
□ 3356 [M]	Vince Guaraldi and Bola Sete and Friends	1964	6.25	12.50	25.00
□ 3358 [M]	Tour de Force	1964	6.25	12.50	25.00
□ 3359 [M]	Jazz Impressions	1965	6.25	12.50	25.00
□ 3360 [M]	The Latin Side of Vince Guaraldi	1965	6.25	12.50	25.00
□ 3362 [M]	From All Sides	1966	5.00	10.00	20.00
□ 3367 [M]	Vince Guaraldi at Grace Cathedral	1967	5.00	10.00	20.00
□ 3371 [M]	Live at the El Matador	1967	5.00	10.00	20.00
□ 5019 [M]	A Charlie Brown Christmas	1964	7.50	15.00	30.00
□ 8089 [S]	Jazz Impressions of Black Orpheus (Cast Your Fate to the Wind)	1962	6.25	12.50	25.00
—Black vinyl, blue label, non-flexible vinyl					
□ 8089 [S]	Jazz Impressions of Black Orpheus (Cast Your Fate to the Wind)	1962	10.00	20.00	40.00
—Blue vinyl					
□ 8356 [S]	Vince Guaraldi and Bola Sete and Friends	1964	6.25	12.50	25.00
□ 8358 [S]	Tour de Force	1964	6.25	12.50	25.00
□ 8359 [S]	Jazz Impressions	1965	6.25	12.50	25.00
□ 8360 [S]	The Latin Side of Vince Guaraldi	1965	6.25	12.50	25.00
□ 8362 [S]	From All Sides	1966	5.00	10.00	20.00
□ 8367 [S]	Vince Guaraldi at Grace Cathedral	1967	5.00	10.00	20.00
□ 8371 [S]	Live at the El Matador	1967	5.00	10.00	20.00
□ 8377	Live-Live-Live	1968	5.00	10.00	20.00
□ 8430	A Boy Named Charlie Brown — Jazz Impressions	1971	5.00	10.00	20.00
—Reissue of 85017					
□ 8431	A Charlie Brown Christmas	1971	6.25	12.50	25.00
—Reissue of 85019; dark blue label					
□ 85017	A Boy Named Charlie Brown — Jazz Impressions	196?	6.25	12.50	25.00
□ 85019 [S]	A Charlie Brown Christmas	1964	10.00	20.00	40.00
MOBILE FIDELITY					
□ 1-112	Jazz Impressions of Black Orpheus (Cast Your Fate to the Wind)	1983	12.50	25.00	50.00
—Audiophile vinyl					
WARNER BROS.					
□ WS 1747	Oh Good Grief!	1968	5.00	10.00	20.00

GUARD, DAVE, AND THE WHISKEYHILL SINGERS

Number	Title (A Side/B Side)	Yr	VG	VG+	NM
CAPITOL					
□ ST 1728 [S]	Dave Guard and the Whiskeyhill Singers	1962	6.25	12.50	25.00
□ T 1728 [M]	Dave Guard and the Whiskeyhill Singers	1962	5.00	10.00	20.00

GUARNIERI, JOHNNY

Number	Title (A Side/B Side)	Yr	VG	VG+	NM
CORAL					
□ CRL 57085 [M]	Songs of Hudson and DeLange	1957	10.00	20.00	40.00
□ CRL 57086 [M]	The Duke Again	1957	10.00	20.00	40.00
GOLDEN CREST					
□ GC-3020 [M]	Johnny Guarnieri Plays Johnny Guarnieri	1958	10.00	20.00	40.00
ROYALE					
□ 1296 [M]	An Hour of Modern Music	1952	10.00	20.00	40.00

The works of J.R.R. Tolkien were a strong influence on psych and prog music. Gandalf took it one step further than most by actually naming itself after a character from *The Lord of the Rings*. This is their self-titled LP on Capitol from 1969.

Years before he started having country hits, Mickey Gilley released this rare album on the Astro label in 1964.

G

The Grateful Dead's first album was in print on vinyl for over two decades, but only the original 1967 editions have gold labels.

Ronnie Hawkins was lead singer of The Hawks, which later became The Band. His first album for Roulette was in print for a few years, but is most collectible on the white label with colored spokes – and even better, on red vinyl.

The Hollywood Argyles, a studio group concocted by Gary Paxton, had a huge hit in 1960 with "Alley Oop." This album came out after the hit, and it disappeared as quickly as the group did.

Husker Du's first album, *Everything Falls Apart,* was on the Reflex label. The label was unusual because it "numbered" its records with letters!

Number	Title (A Side/B Side)	Yr	VG	VG+	NM
❑ VLP 6047 [10]	Johnny Guarnieri/Tony Mottola/Bob Haggart/ Cozy Cole	195?	12.50	25.00	50.00

SAVOY

Number	Title (A Side/B Side)	Yr	VG	VG+	NM
❑ MG-15007 [10]	Hot Piano	1951	20.00	40.00	80.00

GUESS WHO, THE
COMPLEAT

Number	Title (A Side/B Side)	Yr	VG	VG+	NM
❑ 672012-1 [(2)]	The Best of the Gues Who, Live	1986	5.00	10.00	20.00

HILLTAK

Number	Title (A Side/B Side)	Yr	VG	VG+	NM
❑ SD 19227	All This for a Song	1979	3.00	6.00	12.00

MGM

Number	Title (A Side/B Side)	Yr	VG	VG+	NM
❑ SE-4645	The Guess Who	1969	3.75	7.50	15.00

—Compilation of pre-RCA Victor recordings

P.I.P.

Number	Title (A Side/B Side)	Yr	VG	VG+	NM
❑ 6806	The Guess Who Play Pure Guess Who	197?	3.00	6.00	12.00

PICKWICK

Number	Title (A Side/B Side)	Yr	VG	VG+	NM
❑ SPC-3246	The Guess Who	1970	2.50	5.00	10.00

PRIDE

Number	Title (A Side/B Side)	Yr	VG	VG+	NM
❑ PRD 0012	The History of the Guess Who	197?	3.00	6.00	12.00

RCA

Number	Title (A Side/B Side)	Yr	VG	VG+	NM
❑ 7622-1-R	The Greatest of the Guess Who	1987	2.50	5.00	10.00

—Late reissue

RCA VICTOR

Number	Title (A Side/B Side)	Yr	VG	VG+	NM
❑ APD1-0130 [Q]	#10	1974	6.25	12.50	25.00
❑ APL1-0130	#10	1973	3.75	7.50	15.00
❑ AFL1-0269	The Best of the Guess Who, Volume II	1977	2.50	5.00	10.00
—Reissue with new prefix					
❑ APD1-0269 [Q]	The Best of the Guess Who, Volume II	1974	6.25	12.50	25.00
❑ APL1-0269	The Best of the Guess Who, Volume II	1973	3.75	7.50	15.00
❑ APD1-0405 [Q]	Road Food	1974	6.25	12.50	25.00
❑ APL1-0405	Road Food	1974	3.75	7.50	15.00
❑ CPD1-0636 [Q]	Flavours	1975	6.25	12.50	25.00
❑ CPL1-0636	Flavours	1975	3.75	7.50	15.00
❑ ANL1-0983	Canned Wheat Packed By the Guess Who	1975	2.50	5.00	10.00
—Reissue of LSP-4157					
❑ APL1-0995	Power in the Music	1975	3.75	7.50	15.00
❑ LSPX-1004	The Best of the Guess Who	1971	3.75	7.50	15.00
❑ ANL1-1117	Wheatfield Soul	1975	2.50	5.00	10.00
—Reissue of LSP-4141					
❑ APL1-1778	The Way They Were	1976	3.75	7.50	15.00
❑ APL1-2253	The Greatest of the Guess Who	1977	3.75	7.50	15.00
❑ AFL1-2594	The Best of the Guess Who	1978	2.50	5.00	10.00
❑ AYL1-3662	The Best of the Guess Who	1979	2.00	4.00	8.00
—"Best Buy Series" reissue					
❑ AYL1-3673	American Woman	1979	2.00	4.00	8.00
—"Best Buy Series" reissue					
❑ AYL1-3746	The Greatest of the Guess Who	1980	2.00	4.00	8.00
—"Best Buy Series" reissue					
❑ LSP-4141	Wheatfield Soul	1969	5.00	10.00	20.00
—Orange label, non-flexible vinyl					
❑ LSP-4141	Wheatfield Soul	1971	3.00	6.00	12.00
—Orange label, flexible vinyl					
❑ LSP-4157	Canned Wheat Packed By the Guess Who	1969	5.00	10.00	20.00
—Orange label, non-flexible vinyl					
❑ LSP-4157	Canned Wheat Packed By the Guess Who	1971	3.00	6.00	12.00
—Orange label, flexible vinyl					
❑ AFL1-4266	American Woman	1977	2.50	5.00	10.00
—Reissue with new prefix					
❑ LSP-4266	American Woman	1970	5.00	10.00	20.00
—Orange label, non-flexible vinyl					
❑ LSP-4266	American Woman	1971	3.00	6.00	12.00
—Orange label, flexible vinyl					
❑ LSP-4359	Share the Land	1970	5.00	10.00	20.00
—Orange label, non-flexible vinyl					
❑ LSP-4359	Share the Land	1971	3.00	6.00	12.00
—Orange label, flexible vinyl					
❑ LSP-4574	So Long, Bannatyne	1971	3.75	7.50	15.00
❑ LSP-4602	Rockin'	1972	3.75	7.50	15.00
❑ LSP-4779	Live at the Paramount (Seattle)	1972	6.25	12.50	25.00
❑ LSP-4830	Artificial Paradise	1973	3.75	7.50	15.00
—Add 1/3 if paper bag is with package					

SCEPTER

Number	Title (A Side/B Side)	Yr	VG	VG+	NM
❑ SP-533 [M]	Shakin' All Over	1966	10.00	20.00	40.00
❑ SPS-533 [P]	Shakin' All Over	1966	6.25	12.50	25.00
—The above lists the artist as "The Guess Who's Chad Allan & The Expressions" on the cover					

SPRINGBOARD

Number	Title (A Side/B Side)	Yr	VG	VG+	NM
❑ SPB-4022	Shakin' All Over	1972	2.50	5.00	10.00

SUNDAZED

Number	Title (A Side/B Side)	Yr	VG	VG+	NM
❑ LP 5113 [(2)]	Shakin' All Over	2001	3.75	7.50	15.00

WAND

Number	Title (A Side/B Side)	Yr	VG	VG+	NM
❑ WDS-691 [P]	Born in Canada	1969	3.75	7.50	15.00
—Reissue of Scepter LP; three tracks are rechanneled					

GUIDED BY VOICES
E RECORDS

Number	Title (A Side/B Side)	Yr	VG	VG+	NM
❑ GBV 0001	Devil Between My Toes	1987	30.00	60.00	120.00

HALO

Number	Title (A Side/B Side)	Yr	VG	VG+	NM
❑ 1	Sandbox	1987	10.00	20.00	40.00
❑ 2	Self Inflicted Aerial Nostalgia	1989	10.00	20.00	40.00

I WANNA

Number	Title (A Side/B Side)	Yr	VG	VG+	NM
❑ (no #) [EP]	Forever Since Breakfast	1986	25.00	50.00	100.00

MATADOR

Number	Title (A Side/B Side)	Yr	VG	VG+	NM
❑ OLE-123	Alien Lanes	1995	2.50	5.00	10.00
❑ OLE-161 [(2)]	Under the Bushes, Under the Stars	1996	3.00	6.00	12.00
—One side of Record 2 is blank					
❑ OLE-185 [EP]	Sunfish Holy Breakfast	1996	2.50	5.00	10.00
❑ OLE-241	Mag Earwhig!	1997	2.50	5.00	10.00

ROCKATHON

Number	Title (A Side/B Side)	Yr	VG	VG+	NM
❑ (no #)	Propeller	1992	12.50	25.00	50.00
—Hand-colored cover with nature-book paste-on					
❑ 02	Tonics & Twisted Chasers	1997	3.00	6.00	12.00
—1,000 copies were pressed on various colors of vinyl					

ROCKATHON/FADING CAPTAIN SERIES

Number	Title (A Side/B Side)	Yr	VG	VG+	NM
❑ 7	Suitcase Abridged: Drinks and Deliveries	2000	3.00	6.00	12.00
—500 copies were pressed					
❑ 10	Daredevil Stamp Collector: Do the Collapse B-Sides	2001	3.00	6.00	12.00
—1,000 copies were pressed					

ROCKET #9

Number	Title (A Side/B Side)	Yr	VG	VG+	NM
❑ (no #)	Same Place the Fly Got Smashed	1990	10.00	20.00	40.00

SCAT

Number	Title (A Side/B Side)	Yr	VG	VG+	NM
❑ 31	Vampire on Titus	1993	3.75	7.50	15.00
❑ 35	Bee Thousand	1994	3.00	6.00	12.00
❑ 40 [(6)]	Box	1994	15.00	30.00	60.00

TVT

Number	Title (A Side/B Side)	Yr	VG	VG+	NM
❑ 1980	Do the Collapse	1999	2.50	5.00	10.00
❑ 2160	Isolation Drills	2001	2.50	5.00	10.00

GUITAR, BONNIE
DOT

Number	Title (A Side/B Side)	Yr	VG	VG+	NM
❑ DLP-3069 [M]	Moonlight and Shadows	1957	12.50	25.00	50.00
❑ DLP-3151 [M]	Whispering Hope	1958	10.00	20.00	40.00
❑ DLP-3335 [M]	Dark Moon	1961	6.25	12.50	25.00
❑ DLP-3696 [M]	Two Worlds	1966	5.00	10.00	20.00
❑ DLP-3737 [M]	Miss Bonnie Guitar	1966	5.00	10.00	20.00
❑ DLP-3746 [M]	Merry Christmas from Bonnie Guitar	1966	5.00	10.00	20.00
❑ DLP-3793 [M]	Award Winner	1967	5.00	10.00	20.00
❑ DLP-25069 [R]	Moonlight and Shadows	196?	3.75	7.50	15.00
❑ DLP-25151 [S]	Whispering Hope	1958	12.50	25.00	50.00
❑ DLP-25335 [R]	Dark Moon	196?	3.75	7.50	15.00
❑ DLP-25696 [S]	Two Worlds	1966	6.25	12.50	25.00
❑ DLP-25737 [S]	Miss Bonnie Guitar	1966	6.25	12.50	25.00
❑ DLP-25746 [S]	Merry Christmas from Bonnie Guitar	1966	6.25	12.50	25.00
❑ DLP-25793 [S]	Award Winner	1967	5.00	10.00	20.00
❑ DLP-25840	Bonnie Guitar	1968	5.00	10.00	20.00
❑ DLP-25892	Leaves Are the Tears of Autumn	1968	5.00	10.00	20.00
❑ DLP-25947	Affair!	1969	5.00	10.00	20.00

PARAMOUNT

Number	Title (A Side/B Side)	Yr	VG	VG+	NM
❑ PAS-5018	Allegheny	1970	3.75	7.50	15.00

PICKWICK

Number	Title (A Side/B Side)	Yr	VG	VG+	NM
❑ SPC-3086	Favorite Lady of Song	196?	3.00	6.00	12.00

RCA CAMDEN

Number	Title (A Side/B Side)	Yr	VG	VG+	NM
❑ CAS-2339	Night Train to Memphis	1969	3.75	7.50	15.00

GUITAR RAMBLERS, THE
COLUMBIA

Number	Title (A Side/B Side)	Yr	VG	VG+	NM
❑ CL 2067 [M]	The Happy, Youthful New Sounds of the Guitar Ramblers	1964	6.25	12.50	25.00
❑ CS 8867 [S]	The Happy, Youthful New Sounds of the Guitar Ramblers	1964	7.50	15.00	30.00

GUITAR SLIM
ATLANTIC

Number	Title (A Side/B Side)	Yr	VG	VG+	NM
❑ 81760	The Atco Sessions	1987	2.50	5.00	10.00

SPECIALTY

Number	Title (A Side/B Side)	Yr	VG	VG+	NM
❑ SP-2130	Things That I Used to Do	1969	5.00	10.00	20.00

GULDA, FRIEDRICH
RCA VICTOR

Number	Title (A Side/B Side)	Yr	VG	VG+	NM
❑ LPM-1355 [M]	Friedrich Gulda at Birdland	1957	12.50	25.00	50.00

GULLIN, LARS
ATLANTIC

Number	Title (A Side/B Side)	Yr	VG	VG+	NM
❑ 1246 [M]	Baritone Sax	1956	30.00	60.00	120.00
—Black label					
❑ 1246 [M]	Baritone Sax	1960	12.50	25.00	50.00
—Multicolor label, white "fan" logo at right					

CONTEMPORARY

Number	Title (A Side/B Side)	Yr	VG	VG+	NM
❑ C-2505 [10]	Modern Sounds	1953	62.50	125.00	250.00

EASTWEST

Number	Title (A Side/B Side)	Yr	VG	VG+	NM
❑ 4003 [M]	Lars Gullin Swings	196?	10.00	20.00	40.00

EMARCY

Number	Title (A Side/B Side)	Yr	VG	VG+	NM
❑ MG-26041 [10]	Lars Gullin Quartet	1954	50.00	100.00	200.00
❑ MG-26044 [10]	Gullin's Garden	1954	50.00	100.00	200.00
❑ MG-36012 [M]	Lars Gullin	1955	30.00	60.00	120.00
❑ MG-36059 [M]	Lars Gullin with the Moretone Singers	1955	30.00	60.00	120.00

PRESTIGE

Number	Title (A Side/B Side)	Yr	VG	VG+	NM
❑ PRLP-144 [10]	New Sounds from Sweden, Volume 5	1953	50.00	100.00	200.00
❑ PRLP-151 [10]	New Sounds from Sweden, Volume 7	1953	50.00	100.00	200.00

GULLIVER
With Daryl Hall. John Oates joined later, but is not on these records.

ELEKTRA

Number	Title (A Side/B Side)	Yr	VG	VG+	NM
❑ EKS-74070	Gulliver	1970	5.00	10.00	20.00

GUN
EPIC

Number	Title (A Side/B Side)	Yr	VG	VG+	NM
❑ BN 26468	Gun	1969	5.00	10.00	20.00
❑ BN 26551	Gunsight	1970	6.25	12.50	25.00

GUNS N' ROSES
GEFFEN

Number	Title (A Side/B Side)	Yr	VG	VG+	NM
❑ GHS 24148	Appetite for Destruction	1988	2.50	5.00	10.00
❑ XXXG 24148	Appetite for Destruction	1988	12.50	25.00	50.00
—Original "rape cover"; the XXXG prefix is on the cover only; all copies of the record use the GHS prefix					
❑ GHS 24198	G N' R Lies	1988	2.50	5.00	10.00
❑ GEF 24415 [(2)]	Use Your Illusion I	1991	5.00	10.00	20.00

Number	Title (A Side/B Side)	Yr	VG	VG+	NM
❏ GEF 24420 [(2)]	Use Your Illusion II	1991	5.00	10.00	20.00
❏ GEF 24617	The Spaghetti Incident?	1993	3.75	7.50	15.00
—Orange vinyl					
❏ R 100805	G N' R Lies	1988	3.00	6.00	12.00
—BMG Direct Marketing edition					
❏ R 170348	Appetite for Destruction	1987	3.00	6.00	12.00
—BMG Direct Marketing edition					
❏ 490514-1 [(4)]	Live Era '87-'93	1999	6.25	12.50	25.00

UZI SUICIDE

Number	Title (A Side/B Side)	Yr	VG	VG+	NM
❏ USR 001 [EP]	Live ?!*@ Like a Suicide	1986	30.00	60.00	120.00

GUNTER, ARTHUR
EXCELLO

Number	Title (A Side/B Side)	Yr	VG	VG+	NM
❏ LPS-8017	Black and Blues	1971	6.25	12.50	25.00

GURU
CHRYSALIS

Number	Title (A Side/B Side)	Yr	VG	VG+	NM
❏ F1-21998	Jazzmatazz Vol. 1	1993	5.00	10.00	20.00
❏ F1-34290 [(2)]	Jazzmatazz Vol. 2: The New Reality	1995	3.75	7.50	15.00

VIRGIN

Number	Title (A Side/B Side)	Yr	VG	VG+	NM
❏ 50188 [(2)]	Jazzmatazz Vol. 3: Streetsoul	2000	3.75	7.50	15.00

GUTHRIE, ARLO
REPRISE

Number	Title (A Side/B Side)	Yr	VG	VG+	NM
❏ MS 2060	Hobo's Lullabye	1972	3.00	6.00	12.00
❏ MS 2142	Last of the Brooklyn Cowboys	1973	3.00	6.00	12.00
❏ MS4 2142 [Q]	Last of the Brooklyn Cowboys	1973	5.00	10.00	20.00
❏ MS 2183	Arlo Guthrie	1974	3.00	6.00	12.00
❏ MS 2239	Amigo	1976	3.00	6.00	12.00
❏ R 6267 [M]	Alice's Restaurant	1967	5.00	10.00	20.00
❏ RS 6267 [S]	Alice's Restaurant	1967	3.75	7.50	15.00
—Pink, green and gold label					
❏ RS 6267 [S]	Alice's Restaurant	1968	3.00	6.00	12.00
—With "W7" and "r:" logos on two-tone orange label					
❏ RS 6267 [S]	Alice's Restaurant	1970	2.50	5.00	10.00
—With only "r:" logo on all-orange (tan) label					
❏ RS 6299	Arlo	1968	3.75	7.50	15.00
—With "W7" and "r:" logos on two-tone orange label					
❏ RS 6299	Arlo	1970	2.50	5.00	10.00
—With only "r:" logo on all-orange (tan) label					
❏ RS 6346	Running Down the Road	1969	3.75	7.50	15.00
—With "W7" and "r:" logos on two-tone orange label					
❏ RS 6346	Running Down the Road	1970	2.50	5.00	10.00
—With only "r:" logo on all-orange (tan) label					
❏ RS 6411	Washington County	1970	3.00	6.00	12.00

WARNER BROS.

Number	Title (A Side/B Side)	Yr	VG	VG+	NM
❏ BSK 3117	The Best of Arlo Guthrie	1977	2.50	5.00	10.00
—"Burbank" palm trees label					
❏ BSK 3117	The Best of Arlo Guthrie	1979	2.00	4.00	8.00
—White or tan label					
❏ BSK 3232	One Night	1978	2.50	5.00	10.00
❏ BSK 3336	Outlasting the Blues	1979	2.50	5.00	10.00
❏ BSK 3558	Power of Love	1981	2.50	5.00	10.00

GUTHRIE, JACK
CAPITOL

Number	Title (A Side/B Side)	Yr	VG	VG+	NM
❏ T 2456 [M]	Jack Guthrie's Greatest Songs	1966	6.25	12.50	25.00

GUTHRIE, WOODY
ARCHIVE OF FOLK AND JAZZ

Number	Title (A Side/B Side)	Yr	VG	VG+	NM
❏ 204	Woody Guthrie	1966	3.00	6.00	12.00

COLLECTABLES

Number	Title (A Side/B Side)	Yr	VG	VG+	NM
❏ COL-5095	Golden Classics Vol. 1: Worried Man Blues	198?	3.00	6.00	12.00
❏ COL-5098	Golden Classics Vol. 2: Immortal	198?	3.00	6.00	12.00

ELEKTRA

Number	Title (A Side/B Side)	Yr	VG	VG+	NM
❏ EKL-271/2 [(3)M]	The Library of Congress Recordings	1964	10.00	20.00	40.00
—Original pressing has "guitar player" labels					

FOLKWAYS

Number	Title (A Side/B Side)	Yr	VG	VG+	NM
❏ FP-11 [10]	Dust Bowl Ballads	1950	150.00	300.00	600.00
❏ FP-715 [10]	Songs to Grow On For Mother and Child	195?	150.00	30.00	600.00
❏ FA-2011 [10]	Dust Bowl Ballads	195?	125.00	250.00	500.00
—Reissue of FP-11					
❏ FA-2481 [M]	Bound for Glory: Songs and Stories of Woody Guthrie	1956	37.50	75.00	150.00
❏ FA-2483 [M]	Woody Guthrie Sings Folk Songs	1964	12.50	25.00	50.00
❏ FA-2484 [M]	Woody Guthrie Sings Folk Songs, Vol. 2	1964	12.50	25.00	50.00
❏ FA-2485 [M]	Struggle	1964	12.50	25.00	50.00
❏ FH-5212 [M]	Dust Bowl Ballads	1964	7.50	15.00	30.00
❏ FH-5485 [M]	Ballds of Sacco and Vanzetti	196?	7.50	15.00	30.00
❏ FC-7005 [10]	Songs to Grow On	1950	125.00	250.00	500.00
❏ FC-7015 [10]	Songs to Grow On For Mother and Child	1953	125.00	250.00	500.00
—Reissue of FP-715					
❏ FC-7027 [10]	Songs to Grow On Vol. 3	1951	125.00	250.00	500.00
❏ 31001 [R]	This Land Is Your Land	196?	3.00	6.00	12.00

RCA VICTOR

Number	Title (A Side/B Side)	Yr	VG	VG+	NM
❏ LPV-502 [M]	Dust Bowl Ballads	1964	6.25	12.50	25.00

ROUNDER

Number	Title (A Side/B Side)	Yr	VG	VG+	NM
❏ 1036	Columbia River Collection	1987	2.50	5.00	10.00
❏ 1040	Dust Bowl Ballads	1988	2.50	5.00	10.00
❏ 1041/2/3 [(3)]	The Library of Congress Recordings	1988	5.00	10.00	20.00

SMITHSONIAN FOLKWAYS

Number	Title (A Side/B Side)	Yr	VG	VG+	NM
❏ SF-40007	Woody Guthrie Sings Folk Songs	1989	3.00	6.00	12.00
❏ SF-40025	Struggle	1989	3.00	6.00	12.00

VERVE FOLKWAYS

Number	Title (A Side/B Side)	Yr	VG	VG+	NM
❏ FV-9007 [M]	Bed on the Floor	1965	7.50	15.00	30.00
❏ FVS-9007 [R]	Bed on the Floor	1965	5.00	10.00	20.00
❏ FV-9036 [M]	Bonneville Dam & Other Columbia River Songs	1965	7.50	15.00	30.00
❏ FVS-9036 [R]	Bonneville Dam & Other Columbia River Songs	1965	5.00	10.00	20.00

GUTHRIE, WOODY, AND CISCO HOUSTON
STINSON

Number	Title (A Side/B Side)	Yr	VG	VG+	NM
❏ SLP-32 [10]	Cowboy Songs	195?	50.00	100.00	
❏ SLP-44 [10]	Folk Songs, Vol. 1	195?	50.00	100.00	200.00
❏ SLP-53 [10]	More Songs	195?	50.00	100.00	200.00

GUTHRIE, WOODY; SONNY TERRY; ALEX STEWART
STINSON

Number	Title (A Side/B Side)	Yr	VG	VG+	NM
❏ SLP-7 [10]	Chain Gang, Vol. 1	195?	50.00	100.00	200.00
❏ SLP-8 [10]	Chain Gang, Vol. 2	195?	50.00	100.00	200.00

GUY, BUDDY
BLUE THUMB

Number	Title (A Side/B Side)	Yr	VG	VG+	NM
❏ BTS 20	Buddy and the Juniors	1970	6.25	12.50	25.00

CHESS

Number	Title (A Side/B Side)	Yr	VG	VG+	NM
❏ LP-409	I Was Walking Through the Woods	1970	5.00	10.00	20.00
❏ LP-1527 [M]	I Left My Blues in San Francisco	1968	7.50	15.00	30.00
❏ CH-9115	Buddy Guy	1984	2.00	4.00	8.00

MCA

Number	Title (A Side/B Side)	Yr	VG	VG+	NM
❏ 11165	I Was Walking Through the Woods	1995	6.25	12.50	25.00
—"Heavy Vinyl" audiophile reissue					

VANGUARD

Number	Title (A Side/B Side)	Yr	VG	VG+	NM
❏ VSD-79272	A Man and the Blues	1968	6.25	12.50	25.00
❏ VSD-79290	This Is Buddy Guy	1969	6.25	12.50	25.00
❏ VSD-79323	Hold That Plane!	1972	5.00	10.00	20.00

GUY, CHARLES
CAPITOL

Number	Title (A Side/B Side)	Yr	VG	VG+	NM
❏ ST 1920 [S]	Prisoner's Dream	1963	6.25	12.50	25.00
❏ T 1920 [M]	Prisoner's Dream	1963	5.00	10.00	20.00

GWALTNEY, TOMMY
RIVERSIDE

Number	Title (A Side/B Side)	Yr	VG	VG+	NM
❏ RLP-353 [M]	Goin' to Kansas City	1960	7.50	15.00	30.00
❏ RS-9353 [S]	Goin' to Kansas City	1960	10.00	20.00	40.00

GYPSY
METROMEDIA

Number	Title (A Side/B Side)	Yr	VG	VG+	NM
❏ MD-1031 [(2)]	Gypsy	1970	5.00	10.00	20.00
❏ MD 1044	In the Garden	1971	3.75	7.50	15.00

RCA VICTOR

Number	Title (A Side/B Side)	Yr	VG	VG+	NM
❏ APL1-0093	Unlock the Gates	1973	3.75	7.50	15.00
❏ LSP-4775	Antithesis	1972	3.75	7.50	15.00

H

H.P. LOVECRAFT
MERCURY

Number	Title (A Side/B Side)	Yr	VG	VG+	NM
❏ SRM-1-1041	We Love You	1975	3.75	7.50	15.00

PHILIPS

Number	Title (A Side/B Side)	Yr	VG	VG+	NM
❏ PHM 200252 [M]	H.P. Lovecraft	1967	5.00	10.00	20.00
❏ PHS 600252 [S]	H.P. Lovecraft	1967	6.25	12.50	25.00
❏ PHS 600279	Lovecraft II	1968	6.25	12.50	25.00

REPRISE

Number	Title (A Side/B Side)	Yr	VG	VG+	NM
❏ RS 6419	Valley of the Moon	1970	5.00	10.00	20.00

SUNDAZED

Number	Title (A Side/B Side)	Yr	VG	VG+	NM
❏ LP-5004	Live May 11, 1968	199?	2.50	5.00	10.00

H.Y. SLEDGE
SSS INTERNATIONAL

Number	Title (A Side/B Side)	Yr	VG	VG+	NM
❏ 22	Bootleg Music	1971	5.00	10.00	20.00

HA'PENNYS, THE
FERSCH

Number	Title (A Side/B Side)	Yr	VG	VG+	NM
❏ FL-1110	Love Is Not the Same	1968	50.00	100.00	200.00

HACKETT, BOBBY
BRUNSWICK

Number	Title (A Side/B Side)	Yr	VG	VG+	NM
❏ BL 56014 [10]	Trumpet Solos	1950	12.50	25.00	50.00

CAPITOL

Number	Title (A Side/B Side)	Yr	VG	VG+	NM
❏ H 458 [10]	Soft Lights	1954	12.50	25.00	50.00
❏ T 458 [M]	Soft Lights	1955	6.25	12.50	25.00
—Black colorband label, logo at left					
❏ T 458 [M]	Soft Lights	1955	10.00	20.00	40.00
—Turquoise or gray label					
❏ T 575 [M]	In a Mellow Mood	1955	6.25	12.50	25.00
—Black colorband label, logo at left					
❏ T 575 [M]	In a Mellow Mood	1955	10.00	20.00	40.00
—Turquoise or gray label					
❏ T 692 [M]	Coast Concert	1956	6.25	12.50	25.00
—Black colorband label, logo at left					
❏ T 692 [M]	Coast Concert	1956	10.00	20.00	40.00
—Turquoise or gray label					
❏ T 719 [M]	Rendezvous	1956	6.25	12.50	25.00
—Black colorband label, logo at left					
❏ T 719 [M]	Rendezvous	1956	10.00	20.00	40.00
—Turquoise or gray label					
❏ T 857 [M]	Gotham Jazz Scene	1957	6.25	12.50	25.00
—Black colorband label, logo at left					
❏ T 857 [M]	Gotham Jazz Scene	1957	10.00	20.00	40.00
—Turquoise or gray label					
❏ ST 933 [S]	Jazz Ultimate	1959	7.50	15.00	30.00
—Black colorband label, logo at left					
❏ T 933 [M]	Jazz Ultimate	1958	6.25	12.50	25.00
—Black colorband label, logo at left					
❏ T 933 [M]	Jazz Ultimate	1958	10.00	20.00	40.00
—Turquoise or gray label					

Number	Title (A Side/B Side)	Yr	VG	VG+	NM
❏ T 1002 [M]	Don't Take Your Love from Me	1958	6.25	12.50	25.00
—Black colorband label, logo at left					
❏ T 1002 [M]	Don't Take Your Love from Me	1958	10.00	20.00	40.00
—Turquoise or gray label					
❏ ST 1077 [S]	Bobby Hackett at the Embers	1958	7.50	15.00	30.00
—Black colorband label, logo at left					
❏ ST 1077 [S]	Bobby Hackett at the Embers	1962	5.00	10.00	20.00
—Black colorband label, logo at top					
❏ T 1077 [M]	Bobby Hackett at the Embers	1958	6.25	12.50	25.00
—Black colorband label, logo at left					
❏ T 1077 [M]	Bobby Hackett at the Embers	1962	3.75	7.50	15.00
—Black colorband label, logo at top					
❏ ST 1172 [S]	Blues with a Kick	1959	7.50	15.00	30.00
❏ T 1172 [M]	Blues with a Kick	1959	6.25	12.50	25.00
❏ ST 1235 [S]	Bobby Hackett Quartet	1959	7.50	15.00	30.00
❏ T 1235 [M]	Bobby Hackett Quartet	1959	6.25	12.50	25.00
❏ ST 1413 [S]	Easy Beat	1960	6.25	12.50	25.00
❏ T 1413 [M]	Easy Beat	1960	5.00	10.00	20.00
COLUMBIA					
❏ CL 1602 [M]	Dream Awhile	1961	5.00	10.00	20.00
❏ CL 1729 [M]	The Most Beautiful Horn in the World	1962	5.00	10.00	20.00
❏ CL 2566 [10]	The Bobby Hackett Horn	1955	12.50	25.00	50.00
❏ CL 6156 [10]	Jazz Session	1951	12.50	25.00	50.00
❏ CS 8402 [S]	Dream Awhile	1961	6.25	12.50	25.00
❏ CS 8529 [S]	The Most Beautiful Horn in the World	1962	6.25	12.50	25.00
❏ CS 8695 [S]	Night Love	1962	5.00	10.00	20.00
COMMODORE					
❏ FL-20016 [10]	Horn A Plenty	1951	12.50	25.00	50.00
EPIC					
❏ LN 3106 [M]	The Hackett Horn	1956	10.00	20.00	40.00
❏ FLS 15107 [S]	The Swingin'est Gals in Town	196?	5.00	10.00	20.00
SESAC					
❏ N-4101 [M]	The Spirit Swings Me	1960	6.25	12.50	25.00
❏ SN-4101 [S]	The Spirit Swings Me	1960	7.50	15.00	30.00
❏ N-4105 [M]	Candlelight and Romance	1960	6.25	12.50	25.00
❏ SN-4105 [S]	Candlelight and Romance	1960	7.50	15.00	30.00

HACKETT, BOBBY/MAX KAMINSKY
BRUNSWICK

Number	Title (A Side/B Side)	Yr	VG	VG+	NM
❏ BL 58043 [10]	Battle of Jazz, Vol. 5	1953	12.50	25.00	50.00

HADEN, CHARLIE
ABC IMPULSE!

Number	Title (A Side/B Side)	Yr	VG	VG+	NM
❏ AS-9183	Liberation Music Orchestra	1973	10.00	20.00	40.00

HAGAR, ERNIE
SAGE AND SAND

Number	Title (A Side/B Side)	Yr	VG	VG+	NM
❏ C-42 [M]	Swinging Steel Guitar	1965	7.50	15.00	30.00

HAGGARD, MERLE
CAPITOL

Number	Title (A Side/B Side)	Yr	VG	VG+	NM
❏ SKAO-168	Pride In What I Am	1969	6.25	12.50	25.00
❏ SM-168	Pride In What I Am	197?	2.50	5.00	10.00
—Reissue with new prefix					
❏ SWBB-223 [(2)]	Same Train, A Different Time	1969	7.50	15.00	30.00
❏ SWBB-259 [(2)]	Close-Up	1969	7.50	15.00	30.00
—Reissue in one package of "Strangers" and "Swinging Doors"					
❏ ST-319	A Portrait of Merle Haggard	1969	5.00	10.00	20.00
❏ ST-384	Okie from Muskogee	1970	5.00	10.00	20.00
❏ ST-451	The Fightin' Side of Me	1970	5.00	10.00	20.00
❏ ST-638	A Tribute to the Best Damn Fiddle Player in the World (Or, My Salute to Bob Wills)	1970	6.25	12.50	25.00
❏ STBB-707 [(2)]	Sing a Sad Song/High on a Hilltop	1971	7.50	15.00	30.00
❏ ST-735	Hag	1971	3.75	7.50	15.00
❏ SWBO-803 [(2)]	The Land of Many Churches	1971	15.00	30.00	60.00
❏ ST-823	Truly the Best of Merle Haggard	1971	10.00	20.00	40.00
❏ ST-835	Someday We'll Look Back	1971	5.00	10.00	20.00
❏ ST-882	Let Me Tell You About a Song	1972	5.00	10.00	20.00
❏ ST 2373 [S]	Strangers	1965	7.50	15.00	30.00
❏ T 2373 [M]	Strangers	1965	6.25	12.50	25.00
❏ SM-2585	Swinging Doors	197?	2.50	5.00	10.00
—Reissue with new prefix					
❏ ST 2585 [S]	Swinging Doors	1966	7.50	15.00	30.00
❏ T 2585 [M]	Swinging Doors	1966	6.25	12.50	25.00
❏ SM-2702	I'm a Lonesome Fugitive	197?	2.50	5.00	10.00
—Reissue with new prefix					
❏ ST 2702 [S]	I'm a Lonesome Fugitive	1967	7.50	15.00	30.00
❏ T 2702 [M]	I'm a Lonesome Fugitive	1967	6.25	12.50	25.00
❏ ST 2789 [S]	Branded Man	1967	7.50	15.00	30.00
❏ T 2789 [M]	Branded Man	1967	6.25	12.50	25.00
❏ ST 2848 [S]	Sing Me Back Home	1968	6.25	12.50	25.00
❏ T 2848 [M]	Sing Me Back Home	1968	7.50	15.00	30.00
❏ ST 2912	The Legend of Bonnie and Clyde	1968	6.25	12.50	25.00
❏ SKAO 2951	The Best of Merle Haggard	1968	6.25	12.50	25.00
❏ ST 2972	Mama Tried	1968	6.25	12.50	25.00
❏ ST-11082	The Best of the Best of Merle Haggard	1972	3.75	7.50	15.00
❏ ST-11127	It's Not Love	1972	3.00	6.00	12.00
❏ ST-11141	Totally Instrumental with One Exception	1973	3.75	7.50	15.00
❏ ST-11200	I Love Dixie Blues...So I Recorded "Live" in New Orleans	1973	3.00	6.00	12.00
❏ ST-11230	Merle Haggard's Christmas Present (Something Old, Something New)	1973	3.00	6.00	12.00
❏ ST-11276	If We Make It Through December	1974	3.00	6.00	12.00
❏ ST-11331	Merle Haggard Presents His 30th Album	1974	3.00	6.00	12.00
❏ ST-11365	Keep Movin' On	1975	3.00	6.00	12.00
❏ ST-11483	It's All in the Movies	1975	3.00	6.00	12.00
❏ SABB-11531 [(2)]	Songs I'll Always Sing	1976	3.75	7.50	15.00
❏ ST-11544	My Love Affair with Trains	1976	3.00	6.00	12.00
❏ ST-11586	The Roots of My Raising	1976	3.00	6.00	12.00
❏ ST-11693	A Working Man Can't Get Nowhere Today	1977	3.00	6.00	12.00
❏ ST-11745	Eleven Winners	1977	3.00	6.00	12.00

Number	Title (A Side/B Side)	Yr	VG	VG+	NM
❏ SM-11823	My Love Affair with Trains	1978	2.50	5.00	10.00
—Reissue					
❏ SW-11839	The Way It Was	1978	3.00	6.00	12.00
❏ SM-12036	It's All in the Movies	1979	2.50	5.00	10.00
—Reissue					
❏ SN-16052	Sing a Sad Song	1979	2.00	4.00	8.00
—Budget-line reissue					
❏ SN-16053	High on a Hilltop	1979	2.00	4.00	8.00
—Budget-line reissue					
❏ SN-16054	The Best of Merle Haggard	1979	2.00	4.00	8.00
—Budget-line reissue					
❏ SN-16277	Okie from Muskogee	1982	2.00	4.00	8.00
—Budget-line reissue					
❏ SN-16278	The Fightin' Side of Me	1982	2.00	4.00	8.00
—Budget-line reissue					
❏ SN-16279	A Tribute to the Best Damn Fiddle Player in the World (Or, My Salute to Bob Wills)	1982	2.00	4.00	8.00
—Budget-line reissue					
❏ SN-16303	Eleven Winners	1984	2.00	4.00	8.00
—Budget-line reissue					
CAPITOL SPECIAL MARKETS					
❏ SL-8086 [(2)]	Songs I'll Always Sing	1977	5.00	10.00	20.00
❏ SLB-8137 [(2)]	Merle Haggard Salutes the Greats	1980	3.75	7.50	15.00
EPIC					
❏ FE 37593	Big City	1981	2.50	5.00	10.00
❏ PE 37593	Big City	1985	2.00	4.00	8.00
—Budget-line reissue					
❏ FE 38092	Going Where the Lonely Go	1982	2.50	5.00	10.00
❏ PE 38092	Going Where the Lonely Go	1985	2.00	4.00	8.00
—Budget-line reissue					
❏ PE 38307	Goin' Home for Christmas	1982	2.50	5.00	10.00
❏ FE 38815	That's the Way Love Goes	1983	2.50	5.00	10.00
❏ FE 39159	The Epic Collection	1983	2.50	5.00	10.00
❏ PE 39159	The Epic Collection	1985	2.00	4.00	8.00
—Budget-line reissue					
❏ FE 39364	It's All in the Game	1984	2.50	5.00	10.00
❏ FE 39545	His Epic Hits: The First 11	1985	2.50	5.00	10.00
❏ FE 39602	Kern River	1985	2.50	5.00	10.00
❏ FE 40107	Out Among the Stars	1986	2.50	5.00	10.00
❏ PE 40107	Out Among the Stars	1986	2.00	4.00	8.00
—Budget-line reissue					
❏ FE 40224	Amber Waves of Grain	1985	2.50	5.00	10.00
❏ FE 40286	A Friend in California	1986	2.50	5.00	10.00
❏ FE 40986	Chill Factor	1988	2.50	5.00	10.00
❏ FE 44283	5:01 Blues	1989	2.50	5.00	10.00
MCA					
❏ 2267	Ramblin' Fever	1977	3.00	6.00	12.00
❏ 2314	My Farewell to Elvis	1977	3.75	7.50	15.00
❏ 2375	I'm Always on a Mountain	1978	3.00	6.00	12.00
❏ 3089	Serving 190 Proof	1979	3.00	6.00	12.00
❏ 3229	The Way I Am	1980	3.00	6.00	12.00
❏ 5139	Back to the Barrooms	1980	3.00	6.00	12.00
❏ 5250	Songs for the Mamma	1981	3.00	6.00	12.00
❏ 5386	Greatest Hits	1982	3.00	6.00	12.00
❏ 5573	His Best	1985	2.50	5.00	10.00
❏ 37138	Ramblin' Fever	1980	2.00	4.00	8.00
—Budget-line reissue					
❏ 37139	My Farewell to Elvis	1980	2.00	4.00	8.00
—Budget-line reissue					
❏ 37140	I'm Always on a Mountain	1980	2.00	4.00	8.00
—Budget-line reissue					
❏ 37141	Serving 190 Proof	1980	2.00	4.00	8.00
—Budget-line reissue					
❏ 37207	The Way I Am	1982	2.00	4.00	8.00
—Budget-line reissue					

HAGGARD, MERLE, AND BONNIE OWENS
CAPITOL

Number	Title (A Side/B Side)	Yr	VG	VG+	NM
❏ ST 2453 [S]	Just Between the Two of Us	1966	7.50	15.00	30.00
❏ T 2453 [M]	Just Between the Two of Us	1966	6.25	12.50	25.00

HAHN, JERRY
CHANGES

Number	Title (A Side/B Side)	Yr	VG	VG+	NM
❏ LP-7001	Arabein	1968	5.00	10.00	20.00

HAIG, AL
COUNTERPOINT

Number	Title (A Side/B Side)	Yr	VG	VG+	NM
❏ C-551 [M]	Jazz Will o' the Wisp	1957	25.00	50.00	100.00
ESOTERIC					
❏ ESJ-7 [10]	Al Haig Trio	1954	50.00	100.00	200.00
MINT					
❏ AL-711 [M]	Al Haig Today	1964	37.50	75.00	150.00
PACIFIC JAZZ					
❏ PJLP-18 [10]	Al Haig Trio	1955	37.50	75.00	150.00
PERIOD					
❏ SPL-1104 [10]	Al Haig Quartet	1954	37.50	75.00	150.00
SEECO					
❏ SLP-7 [10]	Highlights in Modern Jazz	195?	30.00	60.00	120.00

HAIG, AL/MARY LOU WILLIAMS
PRESTIGE

Number	Title (A Side/B Side)	Yr	VG	VG+	NM
❏ PRLP-175 [10]	Piano Moderns	1953	50.00	100.00	200.00

HAINES, CONNIE
CORAL

Number	Title (A Side/B Side)	Yr	VG	VG+	NM
❏ CRL 56055 [10]	Connie Haines Sings	1955	30.00	60.00	120.00
RCA VICTOR					
❏ LPM-2264 [M]	Faith, Hope and Charity	1961	5.00	10.00	20.00
❏ LSP-2264 [S]	Faith, Hope and Charity	1961	7.50	15.00	30.00
TOPS					
❏ L-1606 [M]	Connie Haines Sings Helen Morgan	1959	7.50	15.00	30.00

Number	Title (A Side/B Side)	Yr	VG	VG+	NM

HALE, CORKY
GENE NORMAN
❑ GNP-17 [M]	Corky Hale	1956	12.50	25.00	50.00

HALEN, CARL
EMPIRICAL
❑ LP-101 [10]	Gin Bottle Seven	1957	12.50	25.00	50.00

RIVERSIDE
❑ RLP 12-231 [M]	Gin Bottle Jazz	1958	15.00	30.00	60.00
—White label, blue print					
❑ RLP 12-231 [M]	Gin Bottle Jazz	1959	7.50	15.00	30.00
—Blue label, microphone logo at top					
❑ RLP 12-261 [M]	Whoopee Makers' Jazz	1958	10.00	20.00	40.00
❑ RLP-1103 [S]	Whoopee Makers' Jazz	1958	7.50	15.00	30.00

HALEY, BILL, AND HIS COMETS
ACCORD
❑ SN-7125	Rockin' and Rollin'	1981	2.50	5.00	10.00

DECCA
❑ DL 5560 [10]	Shake, Rattle and Roll	1955	200.00	400.00	800.00
❑ DXSE-7211 [(2)]	Bill Haley's Golden Hits	1972	3.75	7.50	15.00
❑ DL 8225 [M]	Rock Around the Clock	1955	37.50	75.00	150.00
—All-black label with silver print					
❑ DL 8225 [M]	Rock Around the Clock	1960	12.50	25.00	50.00
—Black label with colorband, no mention of MCA on label					
❑ DL 8225 [M]	Rock Around the Clock	1967	7.50	15.00	30.00
—Black label with colorband, "A Division of MCA" on label					
❑ DL 8315 [M]	Music for the Boyfriend	1956	37.50	75.00	150.00
❑ DL 8345 [M]	Rock 'n Roll Stage Show	1956	37.50	75.00	150.00
❑ DL 8569 [M]	Rockin' the Oldies	1957	37.50	75.00	150.00
❑ DL 8692 [M]	Rockin' Around the World	1958	37.50	75.00	150.00
❑ DL 8775 [M]	Rockin' the Joint	1958	37.50	75.00	150.00
❑ DL 8821 [M]	Bill Haley's Chicks	1959	25.00	50.00	100.00
❑ DL 8964 [M]	Strictly Instrumental	1960	25.00	50.00	100.00
❑ DL 75027	Bill Haley's Greatest Hits	1968	3.75	7.50	15.00
❑ DL 78225 [R]	Rock Around the Clock	1959	18.75	37.50	75.00
—All-black label with silver print					
❑ DL 78225 [R]	Rock Around the Clock	1960	6.25	12.50	25.00
—Black label with colorband, no mention of MCA on label					
❑ DL 78225 [R]	Rock Around the Clock	1967	3.75	7.50	15.00
—Black label with colorband, "A Division of MCA" on label					
❑ DL 78821 [S]	Bill Haley's Chicks	1959	37.50	75.00	150.00
❑ DL 78964 [S]	Strictly Instrumental	1960	37.50	75.00	150.00

ESSEX
❑ LP 202 [M]	Rock with Bill Haley and the Comets	1955	125.00	250.00	500.00

51 WEST
❑ Q 16120	Live in New York/Greatest Hits	1981	2.50	5.00	10.00
—"All selections under license from Buddah Records"					

GNP CRESCENDO
❑ GNPS-2077	Rock 'N' Roll	1973	3.00	6.00	12.00
❑ GNPS-2097	Rock Around the Country	1976	3.00	6.00	12.00

GREAT NORTHWEST
❑ GNW 4015	Interviewed by Red Robinson	1981	3.00	6.00	12.00

JANUS
❑ 3035	Travelin' Band	1972	6.25	12.50	25.00
❑ 7003 [(2)]	Razzle-Dazzle	1972	3.75	7.50	15.00

KAMA SUTRA
❑ KLPS-2014	Scrapbook	1970	7.50	15.00	30.00

MCA
❑ 161	Bill Haley's Greatest Hits	1973	2.50	5.00	10.00
—Reissue of Decca 75027					
❑ 4010 [(2)]	Bill Haley's Golden Hits	1973	3.00	6.00	12.00
—Reissue of Decca 7211					
❑ 5539 [(2)]	From the Original Master Tapes	1987	3.00	6.00	12.00

PAIR
❑ MSM2-35069 [(2)]	Rock and Roll Giant	1986	3.00	6.00	12.00

PICCADILLY
❑ PIC-3408	Greatest Hits	1980	2.50	5.00	10.00

PICKWICK
❑ PTP-2077 [(2)]	Rock 'N' Roll	197?	3.00	6.00	12.00
❑ SPC-3256	Bill Haley and the Comets	1970	2.50	5.00	10.00
❑ SPC-3280	Rock 'N' Roll Revival	197?	2.50	5.00	10.00

ROULETTE
❑ R 25174 [M]	Twistin' Knights at the Roundtable	1962	20.00	40.00	80.00
❑ SR 25174 [S]	Twistin' Knights at the Roundtable	1962	25.00	50.00	100.00

SOMERSET
❑ P-4600 [M]	Rock with Bill Haley and the Comets	1958	37.50	75.00	150.00

TRANS WORLD
❑ LP 202 [M]	Rock with Bill Haley and the Comets	1956	75.00	150.00	300.00

VOCALION
❑ VL 3696 [M]	Bill Haley and the Comets	1963	6.25	12.50	25.00

WARNER BROS.
❑ W 1378 [M]	Bill Haley and His Comets	1959	12.50	25.00	50.00
❑ WS 1378 [S]	Bill Haley and His Comets	1959	17.50	35.00	70.00
❑ W 1391 [M]	Bill Haley's Jukebox	1960	12.50	25.00	50.00
❑ WS 1391 [S]	Bill Haley's Jukebox	1960	17.50	35.00	70.00
❑ WS 1831	Rock 'N' Roll Revival	1970	3.75	7.50	15.00
❑ ST-93103	Rock 'N' Roll Revival	1970	6.25	12.50	25.00
—Capitol Record Club edition					

HALFNELSON
See SPARKS.

HALL, ADELAIDE
MONMOUTH-EVERGREEN
❑ 7080	That Wonderful...	1970	5.00	10.00	20.00

HALL, BECKY
AAMCO
❑ ALP-324 [M]	A Tribute to Bessie Smith	1958	7.50	15.00	30.00

HALL, CONNIE
DECCA
❑ DL 4217 [M]	Connie Hall	1962	6.25	12.50	25.00
❑ DL 74217 [S]	Connie Hall	1962	7.50	15.00	30.00

VOCALION
❑ VL 3752 [M]	Country Songs	1965	5.00	10.00	20.00
❑ VL 3801 [M]	Country Style	1968	5.00	10.00	20.00
❑ VL 73752 [S]	Country Songs	1965	6.25	12.50	25.00
❑ VL 73801 [S]	Country Style	1968	5.00	10.00	20.00

HALL, DARYL, AND JOHN OATES
ALLEGIANCE
❑ AV-5014	Nucleus	198?	2.00	4.00	8.00

ARISTA
❑ AL-8539	Ooh Yeah!	1988	2.50	5.00	10.00
❑ AL-8614	Change of Season	1989	3.00	6.00	12.00

ATLANTIC
❑ SD 7242	Whole Oats	1972	3.00	6.00	12.00
❑ SD 7269	Abandoned Luncheonette	1973	3.00	6.00	12.00
❑ SD 18109	War Babies	1974	3.00	6.00	12.00
❑ SD 18213	No Goodbyes	1977	2.50	5.00	10.00
❑ SD 19139	Abandoned Luncheonette	1977	2.00	4.00	8.00

CHELSEA
❑ CHL-547	Past Times Behind	1976	3.00	6.00	12.00

INTERMEDIA
❑ QS-5040	The Early Years	198?	2.00	4.00	8.00

JEM
❑ 55002	Early Years	198?	2.00	4.00	8.00

MOBILE FIDELITY
❑ 1-069	Abandoned Luncheonette	1982	5.00	10.00	20.00
—Audiophile vinyl					

RCA VICTOR
❑ APL1-1144	Daryl Hall & John Oates	1976	2.50	5.00	10.00
❑ APL1-1467	Bigger Than Both of Us	1976	2.50	5.00	10.00
❑ AFL1-2300	Beauty on a Back Street	1977	2.50	5.00	10.00
❑ AFL1-2802	Livetime!	1978	2.50	5.00	10.00
❑ AFL1-2804	Along the Red Ledge	1978	2.50	5.00	10.00
❑ AFL1-2804	Along the Red Ledge	1978	3.75	7.50	15.00
—Red vinyl					
❑ ANL1-3463	Daryl Hall & John Oates	1979	2.00	4.00	8.00
❑ AFL1-3494	X-Static	1979	2.50	5.00	10.00
❑ DJL1-3512 [DJ]	Post Static	1979	5.00	10.00	20.00
—Promo-only one-sided 4-song sampler					
❑ AQL1-3646	Voices	1980	2.00	4.00	8.00
—"RE 4" on back cover: Color photo of Hall and Oates on each side					
❑ AQL1-3646	Voices	1980	2.50	5.00	10.00
—"RE 2" on back cover: Cover not embossed; Hall's head 3 inches-plus below "Voices" on front cover					
❑ AQL1-3646	Voices	1980	3.00	6.00	12.00
—No "RE" of any type on back cover: Embossed lettering and sound waves, Hall's head almost touches the word "Voices" on front					
❑ AQL1-3646	Voices	1980	3.00	6.00	12.00
—"RE 3" on back cover: Cover lettering in black					
❑ AQL1-3646	Voices	1980	3.00	6.00	12.00
—"RE" on back cover: Variation unknown					
❑ AQL1-3646	Voices	1981	2.00	4.00	8.00
—"RE 5" on back cover: Variation unknown					
❑ AQL1-3646	Voices	1981	2.00	4.00	8.00
—"RE 6" on back cover: Bar code on upper left back cover					
❑ DJL1-3832	RCA Radio Special Interview Series	1980	3.75	7.50	15.00
❑ AYL1-3836	Daryl Hall & John Oates	1980	2.00	4.00	8.00
❑ AYL1-3866	Bigger Than Both of Us	1980	2.00	4.00	8.00
❑ AFL1-4028	Private Eyes	1981	2.50	5.00	10.00
❑ DJL1-4179	Special Radio Series	1981	3.75	7.50	15.00
❑ AYL1-4230	Beauty on a Back Street	1981	2.00	4.00	8.00
❑ AYL1-4231	Along the Red Ledge	1981	2.00	4.00	8.00
❑ AYL1-4303	X-Static	1982	2.00	4.00	8.00
❑ AFL1-4383	H2O	1982	2.50	5.00	10.00
❑ AYL1-4722	Livetime!	1983	2.00	4.00	8.00
❑ CPL1-4858	Rock 'n Soul Part 1	1983	2.00	4.00	8.00
—"RE 2" on lower left back: Variation unknown					
❑ CPL1-4858	Rock 'n Soul Part 1	1983	2.50	5.00	10.00
—"RE" on lower left back: back cover says "Plus Two New Songs (Recorded September 1983)," then mentions "Say It Isn't So" and "Adult Education"					
❑ CPL1-4858	Rock 'n Soul Part 1	1983	3.00	6.00	12.00
—Original cover: back cover says "Plus Two New Songs (Recorded September 1983)" WITHOUT mentioning what the songs are					
❑ AFL1-5309	Big Bam Boom	1984	3.00	6.00	12.00
❑ AJL1-5336	Big Bam Boom	1984	2.50	5.00	10.00
❑ AFL1-7035	Live at the Apollo	1985	2.50	5.00	10.00

HALL, DICKSON
EPIC
❑ LN 3427 [M]	25 All-Time Country and Western Hits	1958	6.25	12.50	25.00

KAPP
❑ KL-1067 [M]	Fabulous Country Hits Way Out West	1957	7.50	15.00	30.00
❑ KL-1464 [M]	24 Fabulous Country Hits	1966	5.00	10.00	20.00
❑ KS-3464 [S]	24 Fabulous Country Hits	1966	6.25	12.50	25.00

MGM
❑ E-329 [10]	Outlaws of the Old West	1954	15.00	30.00	60.00
❑ E-3263 [M]	Outlaws of the Old West	1956	10.00	20.00	40.00

PERFECT
❑ P-14016 [M]	Country & Western Million Sellers	1960	5.00	10.00	20.00
❑ PS-14016 [S]	Country & Western Million Sellers	1960	6.25	12.50	25.00

Number	Title (A Side/B Side)	Yr	VG	VG+	NM
HALL, EDMOND					
BLUE NOTE					
❏ B-6505 [M]	Celestial Express	1969	5.00	10.00	20.00
MOSAIC					
❏ M6-109 [(6)]	The Complete Edmond Hall/James P. Johnson/Sidney De Paris/Vic Dickenson Blue Note Sessions	199?	25.00	50.00	100.00
UNITED ARTISTS					
❏ UAL-4028 [M]	Petite Fleur	1959	10.00	20.00	40.00
❏ UAS-5028 [S]	Petite Fleur	1959	7.50	15.00	30.00
HALL, EDMOND/SIDNEY DEPARIS					
BLUE NOTE					
❏ BLP-7007 [10]	Jamming in Jazz Hall	1951	50.00	100.00	200.00
HALL, EDMOND/ART HODES					
BLUE NOTE					
❏ B-6504 [M]	Original Blue Note Jazz, Volume 1	1969	5.00	10.00	20.00
HALL, JIM					
PACIFIC JAZZ					
❏ PJ-10 [M]	Good Friday Blues	1960	10.00	20.00	40.00
❏ PJ-79 [M]	Jazz Guitar	1963	7.50	15.00	30.00
❏ ST-79 [S]	Jazz Guitar	1963	6.25	12.50	25.00
❏ PJ-1227 [M]	Jazz Guitar	1957	20.00	40.00	80.00
WORLD PACIFIC					
❏ WP-1227 [M]	Jazz Guitar	1958	12.50	25.00	50.00
HALL, JOANIE					
SAGE AND SAND					
❏ C-34 [M]	Western Meets Country	1962	6.25	12.50	25.00
HALL, JUANITA					
COUNTERPOINT					
❏ 558 [S]	Juanita Hall Sings the Blues	1959	37.50	75.00	150.00
HALL, LARRY					
STRAND					
❏ SL-1005 [M]	Sandy	1960	37.50	75.00	150.00
❏ SLS-1005 [S]	Sandy	1960	50.00	100.00	200.00
HALL, TOM T.					
MERCURY					
❏ SRM-1-500	Songs of Fox Hollow	1975	3.00	6.00	12.00
❏ SRM-1-668	The Rhymer and Other Five and Dimers	1973	3.00	6.00	12.00
❏ SRM-1-687	For the People in the Last Hard Town	1974	3.00	6.00	12.00
❏ SRM-1-1009	Country Is	1974	3.00	6.00	12.00
❏ SRM-1-1033	I Wrote	1975	3.00	6.00	12.00
❏ SRM-1-1044	Greatest Hits, Volume 2	1975	3.00	6.00	12.00
❏ SRM-1-1076	Faster Horses	1976	3.00	6.00	12.00
❏ SRM-1-1111	Magnificent Music	1977	3.00	6.00	12.00
❏ SRM-1-1139	About Love	1977	3.00	6.00	12.00
❏ SRM-1-5008	Greatest Hits, Volume 3	1978	3.00	6.00	12.00
❏ SR-61211	Ballad of Forty Dollars and His Other Great Songs	1969	5.00	10.00	20.00
❏ SR-61247	Homecoming	1969	5.00	10.00	20.00
❏ SR-61277	Witness Life	1970	5.00	10.00	20.00
❏ SR-61307	100 Children	1970	5.00	10.00	20.00
❏ SR-61350	In Search of a Song	1971	3.75	7.50	15.00
❏ SR-61362	We All Got Together And…	1972	3.75	7.50	15.00
❏ SR-61369	Greatest Hits	1972	3.75	7.50	15.00
❏ 814025-1	Jesus to Jack Daniels	1983	2.00	4.00	8.00
❏ 822425-1	Natural Dreams	1984	2.00	4.00	8.00
❏ 822500-1	In Search of a Song	1987	2.00	4.00	8.00
❏ 824143-1	Greatest Hits	1985	2.00	4.00	8.00
—Reissue					
❏ 824144-1	Greatest Hits, Volume 2	1985	2.00	4.00	8.00
—Reissue					
❏ 824145-1	Greatest Hits, Volume 3	1985	2.00	4.00	8.00
—Reissue					
❏ 824508-1	Song in a Seashell	1985	2.00	4.00	8.00
❏ 832350-1	Songs of Fox Hollow	1987	2.00	4.00	8.00
—Reissue					
❏ 834779-1	Country Songs for Children	1988	2.00	4.00	8.00
—Reissue					
PICCADILLY					
❏ 3558	I Like Beer	198?	2.00	4.00	8.00
RCA VICTOR					
❏ AHL1-2622	New Train	1978	2.50	5.00	10.00
❏ AHL1-3018	Places I've Been	1979	2.50	5.00	10.00
❏ AHL1-3495	T's in Town	1979	2.50	5.00	10.00
❏ AHL1-3685	Soldier of Fortune	1980	2.50	5.00	10.00
❏ AHL1-4749	In Concert: Recorded Live at the Grand Ole Opry	1983	2.50	5.00	10.00
❏ AYL1-5432	In Concert: Recorded Live at the Grand Ole Opry	1985	2.00	4.00	8.00
—"Best Buy Series" reissue					
HALLBERG, BENGT					
EPIC					
❏ LN 3375 [M]	Bengt Hallberg	1957	25.00	50.00	100.00
PRESTIGE					
❏ PRLP-176 [10]	Bengt Hallberg's Swedish All-Stars	1953	45.00	90.00	180.00
HALLBERG, BENGT/ARNE DOMNERUS					
PRESTIGE					
❏ PRLP-145 [10]	New Sounds from Sweden, Volume 6	1953	50.00	100.00	200.00
HALLBERG, BENGT/LARS GULLIN					
PRESTIGE					
❏ PRLP-121 [10]	New Sounds from Sweden, Volume 2	1952	50.00	100.00	200.00

Number	Title (A Side/B Side)	Yr	VG	VG+	NM
HALLE ORCHESTRA (JOHN BARBIROLLI, CONDUCTOR)					
MERCURY LIVING PRESENCE					
❏ SR 90115 [S]	Williams, Vaughan: Symphony No. 8; Bax: Garden of Fand; Butterworth: Shropshire Lad	1960	6.25	12.50	25.00
—Maroon label, no "Vendor: Mercury Record Corporation"					
❏ SR 90124 [S]	Viennese Night at the Proms	1960	7.50	15.00	30.00
—Maroon label, no "Vendor: Mercury Record Corporation"					
❏ SR 90125 [S]	Elgar: Enigma Variations; Purcell: Suite for Strings	1960	5.00	10.00	20.00
—Maroon label, no "Vendor: Mercury Record Corporation"					
❏ SR 90160 [S]	Suppe: Overtures	196?	12.50	25.00	50.00
—Maroon label, no "Vendor: Mercury Record Corporation"					
❏ SR 90161 [S]	Encore Please, Sir John!	196?	50.00	100.00	200.00
—Maroon label, no "Vendor: Mercury Record Corporation"					
❏ SR 90164 [S]	Grieg: Peer Gynt Suite; Symphonic Dances; Elegiac Melodies	196?	20.00	40.00	80.00
—Maroon label, no "Vendor: Mercury Record Corporation"					
HALLE ORCHESTRA (GEORGE WELDON, CONDUCTOR)					
MERCURY LIVING PRESENCE					
❏ SR 90137 [S]	Khachaturian: Gayne Ballet Suite; Mussorgsky: Night on Bare Mountain	196?	7.50	15.00	30.00
—Maroon label, no "Vendor: Mercury Record Corporation"					
HALLYDAY, JOHNNY					
PHILIPS					
❏ PHM 200019 [M]	America's Rockin' Hits	1962	20.00	40.00	80.00
❏ PHS 600019 [S]	America's Rockin' Hits	1962	25.00	50.00	100.00
HALOS, THE					
WARWICK					
❏ W-2046 [M]	The Halos	1962	100.00	200.00	400.00
HAMBLEN, STUART					
COLUMBIA					
❏ CL 1588 [M]	The Spell of the Yukon	1961	5.00	10.00	20.00
❏ CL 1769 [M]	Of God I Sing	1962	5.00	10.00	20.00
❏ CS 8388 [S]	The Spell of the Yukon	1961	6.25	12.50	25.00
❏ CS 8569 [S]	Of God I Sing	1962	6.25	12.50	25.00
CORAL					
❏ CRL 57254 [M]	Remember Me	1960	6.25	12.50	25.00
HARMONY					
❏ HL 7009 [M]	Hymns	1957	6.25	12.50	25.00
RCA CAMDEN					
❏ CAL-537 [M]	Beyond the Sun	1959	6.25	12.50	25.00
RCA VICTOR					
❏ LPM-1253 [M]	It Is No Secret	1956	10.00	20.00	40.00
❏ LPM-1436 [M]	Grand Old Hymns	1957	10.00	20.00	40.00
❏ LPM-3265 [10]	It Is No Secret	1954	15.00	30.00	60.00
HAMBRO, LENNY					
COLUMBIA					
❏ CL 757 [M]	Message from Hambro	1956	10.00	20.00	40.00
EPIC					
❏ LN 3361 [M]	The Nature of Things	1956	10.00	20.00	40.00
SAVOY					
❏ MG-15031 [10]	Mambo Hambro	1954	12.50	25.00	50.00
HAMILTON, CHICO					
ABC IMPULSE!					
❏ AS-9213 [(2)]	His Great Hits	1971	5.00	10.00	20.00
COLUMBIA					
❏ CL 1590 [M]	Selections from "Bye Bye Birdie"	1961	5.00	10.00	20.00
❏ CL 1619 [M]	Chico Hamilton Special	1961	5.00	10.00	20.00
❏ CL 1807 [M]	Drumfusion	1962	5.00	10.00	20.00
❏ CS 8390 [S]	Selections from "Bye Bye Birdie"	1961	6.25	12.50	25.00
❏ CS 8419 [S]	Chico Hamilton Special	1961	6.25	12.50	25.00
❏ CS 8607 [S]	Drumfusion	1962	6.25	12.50	25.00
DECCA					
❏ DL 8614 [M]	Jazz from the Sweet Smell of Success	1957	12.50	25.00	50.00
IMPULSE!					
❏ A-29 [M]	Passin' Thru	1963	6.25	12.50	25.00
❏ AS-29 [S]	Passin' Thru	1963	7.50	15.00	30.00
❏ A-59 [M]	Man from Two Worlds	1964	6.25	12.50	25.00
❏ AS-59 [S]	Man from Two Worlds	1964	7.50	15.00	30.00
❏ A-82 [M]	Chi Chi Chico	1965	5.00	10.00	20.00
❏ AS-82 [S]	Chi Chi Chico	1965	6.25	12.50	25.00
❏ A-9102 [M]	El Chico	1965	5.00	10.00	20.00
❏ AS-9102 [S]	El Chico	1965	6.25	12.50	25.00
❏ A-9114 [M]	The Further Adventures of El Chico	1966	5.00	10.00	20.00
❏ AS-9114 [S]	The Further Adventures of El Chico	1966	6.25	12.50	25.00
❏ A-9130 [M]	The Dealer	1966	5.00	10.00	20.00
❏ AS-9130 [S]	The Dealer	1966	6.25	12.50	25.00
JAZZTONE					
❏ J-1264 [M]	Delightfully Modern	1957	10.00	20.00	40.00
NAUTILUS					
❏ NR-13	Reaching for the Top	1981	7.50	15.00	30.00
—Audiophile vinyl					
PACIFIC JAZZ					
❏ PJLP-17 [10]	Chico Hamilton Trio	1955	25.00	50.00	100.00
❏ PJ-39 [M]	Spectacular	1962	6.25	12.50	25.00
—Reissue of 1209					
❏ PJ-1209 [M]	Chico Hamilton Quintet	1955	18.75	37.50	75.00
❏ PJ-1216 [M]	Chico Hamilton Quintet In Hi-Fi	1956	18.75	37.50	75.00
❏ PJ-1220 [M]	Chico Hamilton Trio	1956	18.75	37.50	75.00
❏ PJ-1225 [M]	Chico Hamilton Quintet	1957	18.75	37.50	75.00
❏ PJ-1231 [M]	Chico Hamilton Plays the Music of Fred Katz	1957	18.75	37.50	75.00
REPRISE					
❏ R-6078 [M]	A Different Journey	1963	7.50	15.00	30.00
❏ R9-6078 [S]	A Different Journey	1963	10.00	20.00	40.00

Number	Title (A Side/B Side)	Yr	VG	VG+	NM
WARNER BROS.					
❑ W 1245 [M]	Chico Hamilton Quintet with Strings Attached	1958	12.50	25.00	50.00
❑ WS 1245 [S]	Chico Hamilton Quintet with Strings Attached	1958	15.00	30.00	60.00
❑ W 1271 [M]	Gongs East	1958	12.50	25.00	50.00
❑ WS 1271 [S]	Gongs East	1958	15.00	30.00	60.00
❑ W 1344 [M]	The Three Faces of Chico	1959	12.50	25.00	50.00
❑ WS 1344 [S]	The Three Faces of Chico	1959	15.00	30.00	60.00
WORLD PACIFIC					
❑ ST-1003 [S]	South Pacific in Hi-Fi	1958	10.00	20.00	40.00
❑ ST-1005 [S]	Chico Hamilton Quintet	1958	10.00	20.00	40.00
❑ ST-1008 [S]	The Chico Hamilton Trio Featuring Freddie Gambrell	1959	10.00	20.00	40.00
❑ ST-1016 [S]	Ellington Suite	1959	10.00	20.00	40.00
❑ WP-1216 [M]	Chico Hamilton Quintet In Hi-Fi	1958	12.50	25.00	50.00
❑ WP-1225 [M]	Chico Hamilton Quintet	1958	12.50	25.00	50.00
❑ WP-1231 [M]	Chico Hamilton Plays the Music of Fred Katz	1958	12.50	25.00	50.00
❑ PJ-1238 [M]	South Pacific in Hi-Fi	1957	12.50	25.00	50.00
❑ WP-1238 [M]	South Pacific in Hi-Fi	1958	10.00	20.00	40.00
❑ PJ-1242 [M]	The Chico Hamilton Trio Featuring Freddie Gambrell	1957	12.50	25.00	50.00
❑ WP-1242 [M]	The Chico Hamilton Trio Featuring Freddie Gambrell	1958	10.00	20.00	40.00
❑ WP-1258 [M]	Ellington Suite	1959	12.50	25.00	50.00
❑ WP-1287 [M]	The Original Hamilton Quintet	1960	12.50	25.00	50.00

HAMILTON, DAVE

Number	Title (A Side/B Side)	Yr	VG	VG+	NM
WORKSHOP JAZZ					
❑ WSJ-206 [M]	Blue Vibrations	1963	20.00	40.00	80.00

HAMILTON, GEORGE

Number	Title (A Side/B Side)	Yr	VG	VG+	NM
ABC-PARAMOUNT					
❑ 535 [M]	By George	1966	5.00	10.00	20.00
❑ S-535 [S]	By George	1966	6.25	12.50	25.00

HAMILTON, GEORGE, IV

Number	Title (A Side/B Side)	Yr	VG	VG+	NM
ABC					
❑ X-750	16 Greatest Hits	1972	2.50	5.00	10.00
❑ AC-30032	The ABC Collection	1975	3.00	6.00	12.00
ABC-PARAMOUNT					
❑ 220 [M]	On Campus	1958	10.00	20.00	40.00
❑ S-220 [S]	On Campus	1958	12.50	25.00	50.00
❑ 251 [M]	Sing Me a Sad Song (A Tribute to Hank Williams)	1958	10.00	20.00	40.00
❑ S-251 [S]	Sing Me a Sad Song (A Tribute to Hank Williams)	1958	12.50	25.00	50.00
❑ 461 [M]	George Hamilton IV's Big 15	1963	7.50	15.00	30.00
❑ S-461 [P]	George Hamilton IV's Big 15	1963	10.00	20.00	40.00
ABC/DOT					
❑ DO-2081	Fine Lace	1977	2.50	5.00	10.00
DOT					
❑ 39033	George Hamilton IV	1985	2.50	5.00	10.00
HARMONY					
❑ HS 11379	Your Cheatin' Heart	1970	2.50	5.00	10.00
LAMB AND LION					
❑ 1015	Bluegrass Gospel	1974	3.00	6.00	12.00
MCA					
❑ 705	Forever Young	198?	2.00	4.00	8.00
—Reissue of 3206					
❑ 3206	Forever Young	1980	2.50	5.00	10.00
RCA CAMDEN					
❑ ACL1-0242	Singin' on the Mountains	1973	2.50	5.00	10.00
❑ CAL-2200 [M]	A Rose and a Baby Ruth	1967	3.75	7.50	15.00
❑ CAS-2200 [S]	A Rose and a Baby Ruth	1967	2.50	5.00	10.00
❑ CAS-2468	Early Morning Rain	1971	2.50	5.00	10.00
RCA VICTOR					
❑ APL1-0455	Greatest Hits	1974	3.00	6.00	12.00
❑ LPM-2373 [M]	To You and Yours from Me and Mine	1961	6.25	12.50	25.00
❑ LSP-2373 [S]	To You and Yours from Me and Mine	1961	7.50	15.00	30.00
❑ LPM-2778 [M]	Abilene	1963	6.25	12.50	25.00
❑ LSP-2778 [S]	Abilene	1963	7.50	15.00	30.00
❑ LPM-2972 [M]	Fort Worth, Dallas or Houston	1964	6.25	12.50	25.00
❑ LSP-2972 [S]	Fort Worth, Dallas or Houston	1964	7.50	15.00	30.00
❑ LPM-3371 [M]	Mister Sincerity... A Tribute to Ernest Tubb	1965	6.25	12.50	25.00
❑ LSP-3371 [S]	Mister Sincerity... A Tribute to Ernest Tubb	1965	7.50	15.00	30.00
❑ LPM-3510 [M]	Coast Country	1966	6.25	12.50	25.00
❑ LSP-3510 [S]	Coast Country	1966	7.50	15.00	30.00
❑ LPM-3601 [M]	Steel Rail Blues	1966	5.00	10.00	20.00
❑ LSP-3601 [S]	Steel Rail Blues	1966	5.00	10.00	20.00
❑ LPM-3752 [M]	Folk Country Classics	1967	6.25	12.50	25.00
❑ LSP-3752 [S]	Folk Country Classics	1967	5.00	10.00	20.00
❑ LPM-3854 [M]	Folksy	1967	6.25	12.50	25.00
❑ LSP-3854 [S]	Folksy	1967	5.00	10.00	20.00
❑ LPM-3962 [M]	The Gentle Country Sound of George Hamilton IV	1968	10.00	20.00	40.00
❑ LSP-3962 [S]	The Gentle Country Sound of George Hamilton IV	1968	5.00	10.00	20.00
❑ LSP-4066	In the 4th Dimension	1968	5.00	10.00	20.00
❑ LSP-4164	Canadian Pacific	1969	3.75	7.50	15.00
❑ LSP-4265	The Best of George Hamilton IV	1970	3.75	7.50	15.00
❑ LSP-4342	Back Where It's At	1970	3.75	7.50	15.00
❑ LSP-4435	Down Home in the Country	1971	3.75	7.50	15.00
❑ LSP-4517	North Country	1971	3.75	7.50	15.00
❑ LSP-4609	West Texas Highway	1971	3.75	7.50	15.00
❑ LSP-4700	Country Music in My Soul	1972	3.00	6.00	12.00
❑ LSP-4772	Travelin' Light	1972	3.00	6.00	12.00
❑ LSP-4826	International Ambassador	1973	3.00	6.00	12.00

HAMILTON, JIMMY

Number	Title (A Side/B Side)	Yr	VG	VG+	NM
EVEREST					
❑ SDBR-1100 [S]	Swing Low, Sweet Chariot	1960	7.50	15.00	30.00
❑ LPBR-5100 [M]	Swing Low, Sweet Chariot	1960	6.25	12.50	25.00

Number	Title (A Side/B Side)	Yr	VG	VG+	NM
SWINGVILLE					
❑ SVLP-2022 [M]	It's About Time	1961	12.50	25.00	50.00
—Purple label					
❑ SVLP-2022 [M]	It's About Time	1965	6.25	12.50	25.00
—Blue label, trident logo at right					
❑ SVLP-2028 [M]	Can't Help Swingin'	1961	12.50	25.00	50.00
—Purple label					
❑ SVLP-2028 [M]	Can't Help Swingin'	1965	6.25	12.50	25.00
—Blue label, trident logo at right					
URANIA					
❑ UJLP-1003 [10]	Clarinet in Hi-Fi	1954	30.00	60.00	120.00
❑ UJLP-1204 [M]	Accent on Clarinet	1955	12.50	25.00	50.00
❑ UJLP-1208 [M]	Clarinet in Hi-Fi	1955	12.50	25.00	50.00

HAMILTON, ROY

Number	Title (A Side/B Side)	Yr	VG	VG+	NM
EPIC					
❑ BN 518 [S]	With All My Love	1958	10.00	20.00	40.00
❑ BN 525 [S]	Why Fight The Feeling?	1959	7.50	15.00	30.00
❑ BN 530 [S]	Come Out Swingin'	1959	7.50	15.00	30.00
❑ BN 535 [S]	Have Blues, Must Travel	1959	7.50	15.00	30.00
❑ BN 551 [S]	Spirituals	1960	7.50	15.00	30.00
❑ BN 578 [S]	Soft 'n Warm	1960	7.50	15.00	30.00
❑ BN 595 [S]	You Can Have Her	1961	10.00	20.00	40.00
❑ BN 610 [S]	Only You	1961	7.50	15.00	30.00
❑ BN 632 [R]	You'll Never Walk Alone	1962	5.00	10.00	20.00
❑ LN 1023 [10]	You'll Never Walk Alone	1954	50.00	100.00	200.00
❑ LN 1103 [10]	The Voice of Roy Hamilton	1954	50.00	100.00	200.00
❑ LN 3176 [M]	Roy Hamilton	1955	15.00	30.00	60.00
❑ LN 3294 [M]	You'll Never Walk Alone	1956	17.50	35.00	70.00
❑ LN 3364 [M]	Golden Boy	1957	12.50	25.00	50.00
❑ LN 3519 [M]	With All My Love	1958	7.50	15.00	30.00
❑ LN 3545 [M]	Why Fight The Feeling?	1959	6.25	12.50	25.00
❑ LN 3561 [M]	Come Out Swingin'	1959	6.25	12.50	25.00
❑ LN 3580 [M]	Have Blues, Must Travel	1959	6.25	12.50	25.00
❑ LN 3628 [M]	Roy Hamilton At His Best	1960	10.00	20.00	40.00
❑ LN 3654 [M]	Spirituals	1960	6.25	12.50	25.00
❑ LN 3717 [M]	Soft 'n Warm	1960	6.25	12.50	25.00
❑ LN 3775 [M]	You Can Have Her	1961	7.50	15.00	30.00
❑ LN 3807 [M]	Only You	1961	6.25	12.50	25.00
❑ LN 24000 [M]	Mr. Rock and Soul	1962	6.25	12.50	25.00
❑ LN 24009 [M]	Roy Hamilton's Greatest Hits	1962	5.00	10.00	20.00
❑ LN 24316 [M]	Roy Hamilton's Greatest Hits, Vol. 2	1967	5.00	10.00	20.00
❑ BN 26000 [S]	Mr. Rock and Soul	1962	7.50	15.00	30.00
❑ BN 26009 [S]	Roy Hamilton's Greatest Hits	1962	6.25	12.50	25.00
❑ BN 26316 [S]	Roy Hamilton's Greatest Hits, Vol. 2	1967	6.25	12.50	25.00
MGM					
❑ E-4139 [M]	Warm and Soul	1963	3.75	7.50	15.00
❑ SE-4139 [S]	Warm and Soul	1963	5.00	10.00	20.00
❑ E-4233 [M]	Sentimental, Lonely & Blue	1964	3.75	7.50	15.00
❑ SE-4233 [S]	Sentimental, Lonely & Blue	1964	5.00	10.00	20.00
RCA VICTOR					
❑ LPM-3552 [M]	The Impossible Dream	1966	3.75	7.50	15.00
❑ LSP-3552 [S]	The Impossible Dream	1966	5.00	10.00	20.00

HAMILTON, RUSS

Number	Title (A Side/B Side)	Yr	VG	VG+	NM
KAPP					
❑ KL-1076 [M]	Rainbow	1957	20.00	40.00	80.00

HAMILTON, SCOTT

Number	Title (A Side/B Side)	Yr	VG	VG+	NM
FAMOUS DOOR					
❑ 119	The Swinging Young Scott	197?	5.00	10.00	20.00

HAMILTON STREETCAR

Number	Title (A Side/B Side)	Yr	VG	VG+	NM
DOT					
❑ DLP-25939	Hamilton Streetcar	1969	6.25	12.50	25.00

HAMLIN, JOHNNY

Number	Title (A Side/B Side)	Yr	VG	VG+	NM
ARGO					
❑ LP-4001 [M]	Johnny Hamiln Quintet	1961	6.25	12.50	25.00
❑ LPS-4001 [S]	Johnny Hamiln Quintet	1961	7.50	15.00	30.00

HAMMACK, BOBBY

Number	Title (A Side/B Side)	Yr	VG	VG+	NM
LIBERTY					
❑ LRP-3016 [M]	Power House	1956	10.00	20.00	40.00

HAMMER

Number	Title (A Side/B Side)	Yr	VG	VG+	NM
SAN FRANCISCO					
❑ SD 203	Hammer	1970	5.00	10.00	20.00

HAMMER, BOB

Number	Title (A Side/B Side)	Yr	VG	VG+	NM
ABC-PARAMOUNT					
❑ ABC-497 [M]	Beatle Jazz	1964	7.50	15.00	30.00
❑ ABCS-497 [S]	Beatle Jazz	1964	10.00	20.00	40.00

HAMMER, JACK

Number	Title (A Side/B Side)	Yr	VG	VG+	NM
WARWICK					
❑ W-2014 [M]	Rebellion: Jack Hammer Sings and Reads Songs and Poems of the Beat Generation	1960	20.00	40.00	80.00

HAMMER, MC

Number	Title (A Side/B Side)	Yr	VG	VG+	NM
BUSTIN'					
❑ BR-LP-001	Feel My Power	1987	6.25	12.50	25.00
CAPITOL					
❑ SPRO-79080 [EP]	A Bit Legit	1991	2.00	4.00	8.00
—Promo-only three-track sampler					
❑ C1-90924	Let's Get It Started	1988	2.50	5.00	10.00
❑ C1-92857	Please Hammer Don't Hurt 'Em	1990	3.75	7.50	15.00
❑ C1-98151 [(2)]	Too Legit to Quit	1991	3.75	7.50	15.00
GIANT					
❑ PRO-A-6798 [(2)DJ]	The Funky Headhunter	1994	3.75	7.50	15.00
—Vinyl version is promo only					

Number	Title (A Side/B Side)	Yr	VG	VG+	NM

HAMMOND, JOHN

ATLANTIC
Number	Title (A Side/B Side)	Yr	VG	VG+	NM
❏ 8152 [M]	I Can Tell	1967	7.50	15.00	30.00
❏ SD 8152 [S]	I Can Tell	1967	7.50	15.00	30.00
❏ SD 8206	Sooner or Later	1968	3.75	7.50	15.00
❏ SD 8251	Southern Fried	1969	3.75	7.50	15.00

CAPRICORN
❏ CP 0153	Can't Beat the Kid	1975	3.00	6.00	12.00

COLUMBIA
❏ C 30458	Source Point	1971	3.00	6.00	12.00
❏ KC 31318	I'm Satisfied	1972	3.00	6.00	12.00

FLYING FISH
❏ FF-502	Nobody But You	1988	2.50	5.00	10.00

ROUNDER
❏ 3042	Mileage	1980	2.50	5.00	10.00
❏ 3060	Frogs for Snakes	1982	2.50	5.00	10.00
❏ 3074	John Hammond Live	1984	2.50	5.00	10.00

VANGUARD
❏ VSD 11/12 [(2)]	The Best of John Hammond	1970	3.75	7.50	15.00
❏ VSD-2148 [S]	John Hammond	1964	10.00	20.00	40.00
❏ VRS-9132 [M]	John Hammond	1964	7.50	15.00	30.00
❏ VRS-9153 [M]	Big City Blues	1964	7.50	15.00	30.00
❏ VRS-9178 [M]	So Many Roads	1965	7.50	15.00	30.00
❏ VRS-9198 [M]	Country Blues	1966	7.50	15.00	30.00
❏ VRS-9245 [M]	Mirrors	1967	7.50	15.00	30.00
❏ VSD-79153 [S]	Big City Blues	1964	10.00	20.00	40.00
❏ VSD-79178 [S]	So Many Roads	1965	10.00	20.00	40.00
❏ VSD-79198 [S]	Country Blues	1966	10.00	20.00	40.00
❏ VSD-79245 [S]	Mirrors	1967	7.50	15.00	30.00
❏ VSD-79380	Solo	1976	2.50	5.00	10.00
❏ VSD-79400	Footwork	1978	2.50	5.00	10.00
❏ VSD-79424	Hot Tracks	1979	2.50	5.00	10.00

HAMMOND, JOHNNY

NEW JAZZ
❏ NJLP-8221 [M]	All Soul	1959	12.50	25.00	50.00
—Purple label					
❏ NJLP-8221 [M]	All Soul	1965	6.25	12.50	25.00
—Blue label with trident logo					
❏ NJLP-8229 [M]	That Good Feelin'	1959	12.50	25.00	50.00
—Purple label					
❏ NJLP-8229 [M]	That Good Feelin'	1965	6.25	12.50	25.00
—Blue label with trident logo					
❏ NJLP-8241 [M]	Talk That Talk	1960	12.50	25.00	50.00
—Purple label					
❏ NJLP-8241 [M]	Talk That Talk	1965	6.25	12.50	25.00
—Blue label with trident logo					
❏ NJLP-8288 [M]	Look Out!	1962	12.50	25.00	50.00
—Purple label					
❏ NJLP-8288 [M]	Look Out!	1965	6.25	12.50	25.00
—Blue label with trident logo					

PRESTIGE
❏ PRLP-7203 [M]	Stimulation	1961	10.00	20.00	40.00
—Yellow label					
❏ PRLP-7203 [M]	Stimulation	1965	6.25	12.50	25.00
—Blue label with trident logo					
❏ PRLP-7217 [M]	Gettin' the Message	1961	10.00	20.00	40.00
—Yellow label					
❏ PRLP-7217 [M]	Gettin' the Message	1965	6.25	12.50	25.00
—Blue label with trident logo					
❏ PRLP-7408 [M]	The Stinger	1965	5.00	10.00	20.00
❏ PRST-7408 [S]	The Stinger	1965	6.25	12.50	25.00
❏ PRLP-7420 [M]	Opus de Funk	1966	5.00	10.00	20.00
❏ PRST-7420 [S]	Opus de Funk	1966	6.25	12.50	25.00
❏ PRLP-7464 [M]	The Stinger Meets the Golden Thrush	1966	5.00	10.00	20.00
❏ PRST-7464 [S]	The Stinger Meets the Golden Thrush	1966	6.25	12.50	25.00
❏ PRLP-7482 [M]	Love Potion #9	1967	6.25	12.50	25.00
❏ PRST-7482 [S]	Love Potion #9	1967	5.00	10.00	20.00
❏ PRLP-7494 [M]	Ebb Tide	1967	6.25	12.50	25.00
❏ PRST-7494 [S]	Ebb Tide	1967	5.00	10.00	20.00
❏ PRST-7549	Soul Flowers	1968	5.00	10.00	20.00
❏ PRST-7564	Dirty Grape	1968	5.00	10.00	20.00
❏ PRST-7588	Nasty	1968	5.00	10.00	20.00
❏ PRST-7681	Soul Talk	1969	5.00	10.00	20.00

RIVERSIDE
❏ RLP-442 [M]	Black Coffee	1963	6.25	12.50	25.00
❏ RLP-466 [M]	Mr. Wonderful	1963	6.25	12.50	25.00
❏ RLP-482 [M]	Open House!	1965	5.00	10.00	20.00
❏ RLP-496 [M]	A Little Taste	1965	5.00	10.00	20.00
❏ RS-9442 [S]	Black Coffee	1963	7.50	15.00	30.00
❏ RS-9466 [S]	Mr. Wonderful	1963	7.50	15.00	30.00
❏ RS-9482 [S]	Open House!	1965	6.25	12.50	25.00
❏ RS-9496 [S]	A Little Taste	1965	6.25	12.50	25.00

SALVATION
❏ 702	A Gambler's Life	1974	3.00	6.00	12.00

HAMPEL, GUNTER

BIRTH
❏ 001	The 8th of July, 1969	1969	10.00	20.00	40.00
❏ 002	Dances	1970	7.50	15.00	30.00
❏ 003	Symphony No. 5 and 6	1970	7.50	15.00	30.00
❏ 005	People Symphony	1970	7.50	15.00	30.00
❏ 007	Spirits	1971	5.00	10.00	20.00
❏ 008	Familie	1972	5.00	10.00	20.00
❏ 009	Angel	1972	5.00	10.00	20.00
❏ 0010	Waltz for 3 Universes in a Corridor	1972	5.00	10.00	20.00
❏ 0011	Broadway/Folksong	1972	5.00	10.00	20.00
❏ 0012	I Love Being with You	1972	5.00	10.00	20.00
❏ 0013	Unity Dance	1973	5.00	10.00	20.00
❏ 0016	Out from Under	1974	5.00	10.00	20.00
❏ 0017	Journey to the Song Within	1974	5.00	10.00	20.00
❏ 0021/0022 [(2)]	Celebrations	1974	7.50	15.00	30.00
❏ 0023	Ruomi	1975	5.00	10.00	20.00
❏ 0024	Cosmic Dancer	1975	5.00	10.00	20.00
❏ 0025	Enfant Terrible	1976	5.00	10.00	20.00
❏ 0026	Transformation	1976	5.00	10.00	20.00
❏ 0027	That Came Down on Me	1978	5.00	10.00	20.00
❏ 0028	All Is Real	1978	5.00	10.00	20.00
❏ 0029	Vogelfrei	1978	5.00	10.00	20.00
❏ 0030	Freedom of the Universe	1978	5.00	10.00	20.00
❏ 0031	All the Things You Could Be If Charles Mingus Was Your Daddy	1980	5.00	10.00	20.00
❏ 0032	A Place to Be with Us	1981	5.00	10.00	20.00
❏ 0033	Life on This Planet 1981	1981	5.00	10.00	20.00
❏ 0034	Cavana	1982	5.00	10.00	20.00
❏ 0035	Generator	1982	5.00	10.00	20.00
❏ 0036	Companion	1983	5.00	10.00	20.00
❏ 0038	Jubilation	1984	5.00	10.00	20.00
❏ 0039	Fresh Heat	1985	5.00	10.00	20.00

ESP-DISK'
❏ 1042 [M]	Music from Europe	1967	6.25	12.50	25.00
❏ S-1042 [S]	Music from Europe	1967	5.00	10.00	20.00

FLYING DUTCHMAN
❏ 126	The 8th of July, 1969	1970	10.00	20.00	40.00
❏ FD-10126	The 8th of July, 1969	1971	5.00	10.00	20.00

HORO
❏ 33/34 [(2)]	Oasis	1978	7.50	15.00	30.00

HAMPEL, GUNTER, AND BOULOU FERRE

BIRTH
❏ 006	Espace	1970	6.25	12.50	25.00

HAMPTON, LIONEL

AMERICAN RECORDING SOCIETY
❏ G-403 [M]	The Swinging Jazz of Lionel Hampton	1956	10.00	20.00	40.00

AUDIO FIDELITY
❏ AFLP-1849 [M]	Lionel	1957	7.50	15.00	30.00
❏ AFLP-1913 [M]	Hamp's Big Band	1958	7.50	15.00	30.00
❏ AFSD-5849 [S]	Lionel	1958	10.00	20.00	40.00
❏ AFSD-5913 [S]	Hamp's Big Band	1958	10.00	20.00	40.00

BLUE NOTE
❏ BLP-5046 [10]	Rockin' and Groovin'	1954	75.00	150.00	300.00

BLUEBIRD
❏ AXM6-5536 [(6)]	The Complete Lionel Hampton 1937-1941	1976	12.50	25.00	50.00

CLEF
❏ MGC-142 [10]	The Lionel Hampton Quartet	1953	30.00	60.00	120.00
❏ MGC-611 [M]	The Lionel Hampton Quartet	1954	20.00	40.00	80.00
❏ MGC-628 [M]	The Lionel Hampton Quintet	1954	20.00	40.00	80.00
❏ MGC-642 [M]	The Lionel Hampton Quintet, Volume 2	1955	25.00	50.00	100.00
❏ MGC-667 [M]	The Lionel Hampton Quartet and Quintet	1955	25.00	50.00	100.00
❏ MGC-670 [M]	Lionel Hampton Big Band	1955	25.00	50.00	100.00
❏ MGC-673 [M]	The Lionel Hampton Quartet	1955	20.00	40.00	80.00
❏ MGC-714 [M]	Lionel Hampton Plays Love Songs	1956	17.50	35.00	70.00
❏ MGC-726 [M]	King of the Vibes	1956	17.50	35.00	70.00
❏ MGC-727 [M]	Air Mail Special	1956	17.50	35.00	70.00
❏ MGC-735 [M]	Flying Home	1956	17.50	35.00	70.00
❏ MGC-736 [M]	Swingin' with Hamp	1956	17.50	35.00	70.00
❏ MGC-738 [M]	Hamp!	1956	17.50	35.00	70.00
❏ MGC-744 [M]	Hamp's Big Four	1956	17.50	35.00	70.00

COLUMBIA
❏ CL 711 [M]	Wailin' at the Trianon	1956	10.00	20.00	40.00
❏ CL 1304 [M]	Golden Vibes	1959	6.25	12.50	25.00
❏ CL 1486 [M]	Silver Vibes	1960	6.25	12.50	25.00
❏ CL 1661 [M]	Soft Vibes	1961	5.00	10.00	20.00
❏ CS 8110 [S]	Golden Vibes	1959	5.00	10.00	20.00
❏ CS 8277 [S]	Silver Vibes	1960	5.00	10.00	20.00
❏ CS 8461 [S]	Soft Vibes	1961	5.00	10.00	20.00

CONTEMPORARY
❏ C-3502 [M]	Hampton in Paris	1955	12.50	25.00	50.00

DECCA
❏ DL 5230 [10]	Boogie Woogie	1950	20.00	40.00	80.00
❏ DL 5297 [10]	Moonglow	1951	20.00	40.00	80.00
❏ DL 7013 [10]	Just Jazz	1962	20.00	40.00	80.00
❏ DL 8088 [M]	All American Award Concert at Carnegie Hall	1955	12.50	25.00	50.00
—Black label, silver print					
❏ DL 8088 [M]	All American Award Concert at Carnegie Hall	196?	5.00	10.00	20.00
—Black label with color bars					
❏ DL 8230 [M]	Moonglow	1956	12.50	25.00	50.00
—Black label, silver print					
❏ DL 8230 [S]	Moonglow	196?	5.00	10.00	20.00
—Black label with color bars					
❏ DL 9055 [M]	Just Jazz	1958	12.50	25.00	50.00
❏ DL 74194 [S]	The Original Star Dust	1962	5.00	10.00	20.00
❏ DL 74296 [S]	Hamp's Golden Favorites	1962	5.00	10.00	20.00

EMARCY
❏ MG-27537 [10]	Hamp in Paris	1954	25.00	50.00	100.00
❏ MG-27538 [10]	Crazy Hamp	1954	25.00	50.00	100.00
❏ MG-36032 [M]	Hamp in Paris	1955	12.50	25.00	50.00
❏ MG-36034 [M]	Crazy Rhythm	1955	12.50	25.00	50.00
❏ MG-36035 [M]	Jam Session in Paris	1955	12.50	25.00	50.00

EPIC
❏ LN 3190 [M]	Apollo Hall Concert 1954	1955	12.50	25.00	50.00
❏ LA 16027 [M]	Many Splendored Vibes	1962	5.00	10.00	20.00
❏ BA 17027 [S]	Many Splendored Vibes	1962	6.25	12.50	25.00

GENE NORMAN
❏ GNP-15 [M]	Lionel Hampton with the Just Jazz All-Stars	1956	12.50	25.00	50.00

GLAD HAMP
❏ GH-1001 [M]	The Many Sides of Lionel Hampton	1961	6.25	12.50	25.00
❏ GHS-1001 [S]	The Many Sides of Lionel Hampton	1961	7.50	15.00	25.00

Number	Title (A Side/B Side)	Yr	VG	VG+	NM
❑ GH-1003 [M]	The Exciting Hamp in Europe	1962	6.25	12.50	25.00
❑ GHS-1003 [S]	The Exciting Hamp in Europe	1962	7.50	15.00	30.00
❑ GH-1004 [M]	Bossa Nova Jazz	1963	6.25	12.50	25.00
❑ GHS-1004 [S]	Bossa Nova Jazz	1963	7.50	15.00	30.00
❑ GH-1005 [M]	Lionel Hampton on Tour	1963	6.25	12.50	25.00
❑ GHS-1005 [S]	Lionel Hampton on Tour	1963	7.50	15.00	30.00
❑ GH-1006 [M]	Hamp in Japan	1964	6.25	12.50	25.00
❑ GHS-1006 [S]	Hamp in Japan	1964	7.50	15.00	30.00
❑ GH-1007 [M]	East Meets West	1965	6.25	12.50	25.00
❑ GHS-1007 [S]	East Meets West	1965	7.50	15.00	30.00
❑ GH-1009 [M]	A Taste of Hamp	1965	6.25	12.50	25.00
❑ GHS-1009 [S]	A Taste of Hamp	1965	7.50	15.00	30.00
❑ GH-3050 [M]	All That Twistin' Jazz	1962	6.25	12.50	25.00
❑ GHS-3050 [M]	All That Twistin' Jazz	1962	7.50	15.00	30.00

GNP CRESCENDO

Number	Title (A Side/B Side)	Yr	VG	VG+	NM
❑ GNP-15 [M]	Lionel Hampton with the Just Jazz All-Stars	196?	5.00	10.00	20.00

HARMONY

Number	Title (A Side/B Side)	Yr	VG	VG+	NM
❑ HL 7115 [M]	Hamp in Hi-Fi	1958	5.00	10.00	20.00
❑ HL 7281 [M]	The One and Only Lionel Hampton	1961	5.00	10.00	20.00

IMPULSE!

Number	Title (A Side/B Side)	Yr	VG	VG+	NM
❑ A-78 [M]	You Better Know It	1965	6.25	12.50	25.00
❑ AS-78 [S]	You Better Know It	1965	7.50	15.00	30.00

JAZZTONE

Number	Title (A Side/B Side)	Yr	VG	VG+	NM
❑ J-1040 [10]	Visit on a Skyscraper	195?	12.50	25.00	50.00
❑ J-1238 [M]	The Fabulous Lionel Hampton and His All-Stars	1957	10.00	20.00	40.00
❑ J-1246 [M]	Lionel Hampton's All Star Groups	1957	10.00	20.00	40.00

LION

Number	Title (A Side/B Side)	Yr	VG	VG+	NM
❑ L-70064 [M]	Lionel Hampton and His Orchestra	1958	5.00	10.00	20.00

MGM

Number	Title (A Side/B Side)	Yr	VG	VG+	NM
❑ E-285 [10]	Oh, Rock	1954	30.00	60.00	120.00
❑ E-3386 [M]	Oh, Rock	1956	12.50	25.00	50.00

NORGRAN

Number	Title (A Side/B Side)	Yr	VG	VG+	NM
❑ MGN-1080 [M]	Lionel Hampton and His Giants	1956	25.00	50.00	100.00

PERFECT

Number	Title (A Side/B Side)	Yr	VG	VG+	NM
❑ 12002 [M]	Lionel Hampton Swings	1959	7.50	15.00	30.00
❑ 14002 [S]	Lionel Hampton Swings	1959	10.00	20.00	40.00

RCA CAMDEN

Number	Title (A Side/B Side)	Yr	VG	VG+	NM
❑ CAL-317 [M]	Open House	1957	5.00	10.00	20.00
❑ CAL-402 [M]	Jivin' the Vibes	1958	5.00	10.00	20.00

RCA VICTOR

Number	Title (A Side/B Side)	Yr	VG	VG+	NM
❑ LPT-18 [10]	A Treasury of Immortal Performances	1951	25.00	50.00	100.00
❑ LJM-1000 [M]	Hot Mallets	1954	12.50	25.00	50.00
❑ LPM-1422 [M]	Jazz Flamenco	1957	12.50	25.00	50.00
❑ LPM-2318 [M]	Swing Classics	1961	6.25	12.50	25.00
❑ LPM-3917 [M]	Lionel Hampton Plays Bert Kaempfert	1968	6.25	12.50	25.00

VERVE

Number	Title (A Side/B Side)	Yr	VG	VG+	NM
❑ MGV-2018 [M]	Lionel Hampton Plays Love Songs	1957	12.50	25.00	50.00
❑ V-2018 [M]	Lionel Hampton Plays Love Songs	1961	5.00	10.00	20.00
❑ MGV-8019 [M]	Travelin' Band	1957	12.50	25.00	50.00
❑ V-8019 [M]	Travelin' Band	1961	5.00	10.00	20.00
❑ MGV-8105 [M]	King of the Vibes	1957	12.50	25.00	50.00
❑ V-8105 [M]	King of the Vibes	1961	5.00	10.00	20.00
❑ MGV-8106 [M]	Air Mail Special	1957	12.50	25.00	50.00
❑ V-8106 [M]	Air Mail Special	1961	5.00	10.00	20.00
❑ MGV-8112 [M]	Flying Home	1957	12.50	25.00	50.00
❑ V-8112 [M]	Flying Home	1961	5.00	10.00	20.00
❑ MGV-8113 [M]	Swingin' with Hamp	1957	12.50	25.00	50.00
❑ V-8113 [M]	Swingin' with Hamp	1961	5.00	10.00	20.00
❑ MGV-8114 [M]	Hamp!	1957	12.50	25.00	50.00
❑ V-8114 [M]	Hamp!	1961	5.00	10.00	20.00
❑ MGV-8117 [M]	Hamp's Big Four	1957	12.50	25.00	50.00
❑ V-8117 [M]	Hamp's Big Four	1961	5.00	10.00	20.00
❑ MGV-8170 [M]	Lionel Hampton and His Giants	1957	12.50	25.00	50.00
❑ V-8170 [M]	Lionel Hampton and His Giants	1961	5.00	10.00	20.00
❑ MGV-8215 [M]	The Genius of Lionel Hampton	1958	12.50	25.00	50.00
❑ V-8215 [M]	The Genius of Lionel Hampton	1961	5.00	10.00	20.00
❑ MGV-8223 [M]	Lionel Hampton '58	1958	12.50	25.00	50.00
❑ V-8223 [M]	Lionel Hampton '58	1961	5.00	10.00	20.00
❑ MGV-8226 [M]	Hallelujah Hamp	1958	12.50	25.00	50.00
❑ V-8226 [M]	Hallelujah Hamp	1961	5.00	10.00	20.00
❑ MGV-8228 [M]	The High and the Mighty	1958	12.50	25.00	50.00
❑ V-8228 [M]	The High and the Mighty	1961	5.00	10.00	20.00

HAMPTON, LIONEL, AND STAN GETZ
NORGRAN

Number	Title (A Side/B Side)	Yr	VG	VG+	NM
❑ MGN-1037 [M]	Hamp and Getz	1955	25.00	50.00	100.00

VERVE

Number	Title (A Side/B Side)	Yr	VG	VG+	NM
❑ MGV-8128 [M]	Hamp and Getz	1957	12.50	25.00	50.00
❑ V-8128 [M]	Hamp and Getz	1961	5.00	10.00	20.00

HAMPTON, LIONEL; ART TATUM; BUDDY RICH
CLEF

Number	Title (A Side/B Side)	Yr	VG	VG+	NM
❑ MGC-709 [M]	The Hampton-Tatum-Rich Trio	1956	20.00	40.00	80.00

VERVE

Number	Title (A Side/B Side)	Yr	VG	VG+	NM
❑ MGV-8093 [M]	The Hampton-Tatum-Rich Trio	1957	12.50	25.00	50.00
❑ V-8093 [M]	The Hampton-Tatum-Rich Trio	1961	5.00	10.00	20.00

HAMPTON, LIONEL, AND CHARLIE TEAGARDEN
CORAL

Number	Title (A Side/B Side)	Yr	VG	VG+	NM
❑ CRL 57438 [M]	The Great Hamp and Little T.	1963	5.00	10.00	20.00
❑ CRL 757438 [S]	The Great Hamp and Little T.	1963	6.25	12.50	25.00

HAMPTON, SLIDE
ATLANTIC

Number	Title (A Side/B Side)	Yr	VG	VG+	NM
❑ 1339 [M]	Sister Salvation	1960	7.50	15.00	30.00
—Multicolor label, white "fan" logo at right					
❑ SD 1339 [S]	Sister Salvation	1960	10.00	20.00	40.00
—Multicolor label, white "fan" logo at right					

Number	Title (A Side/B Side)	Yr	VG	VG+	NM
❑ 1362 [M]	Somethin' Sanctified	1961	7.50	15.00	30.00
—Multicolor label, white "fan" logo at right					
❑ SD 1362 [S]	Somethin' Sanctified	1961	10.00	20.00	40.00
—Multicolor label, white "fan" logo at right					
❑ 1379 [M]	Jazz with a Twist	1962	6.25	12.50	25.00
❑ SD 1379 [S]	Jazz with a Twist	1962	7.50	15.00	30.00
❑ 1396 [M]	Explosion!	1962	5.00	10.00	20.00
❑ SD 1396 [S]	Explosion!	1962	6.25	12.50	25.00

CHARLIE PARKER

Number	Title (A Side/B Side)	Yr	VG	VG+	NM
❑ PLP-803 [M]	Two Sides of Slide	1962	6.25	12.50	25.00
❑ PLP-803S [S]	Two Sides of Slide	1962	6.25	12.50	25.00

EPIC

Number	Title (A Side/B Side)	Yr	VG	VG+	NM
❑ LA 16030 [M]	Drum Suite	1963	5.00	10.00	20.00
❑ BA 17030 [S]	Drum Suite	1963	6.25	12.50	25.00

STRAND

Number	Title (A Side/B Side)	Yr	VG	VG+	NM
❑ SL-1006 [M]	Slide Hampton and His Horn of Plenty	1959	10.00	20.00	40.00
❑ SLS-1006 [S]	Slide Hampton and His Horn of Plenty	1959	10.00	20.00	40.00

HANCOCK, HERBIE
BLUE NOTE

Number	Title (A Side/B Side)	Yr	VG	VG+	NM
❑ BLP-4109 [M]	Takin' Off	1962	12.50	25.00	50.00
❑ BLP-4126 [M]	My Point of View	1963	8.75	17.50	35.00
❑ BLP-4147 [M]	Inventions and Dimensions	1963	8.75	17.50	35.00
❑ BLP-4175 [M]	Empyrean Isles	1964	8.75	17.50	35.00
❑ BLP-4195 [M]	Maiden Voyage	1965	8.75	17.50	35.00
❑ B1-46339	Maiden Voyage	1997	5.00	10.00	20.00
—Audiophile reissue					
❑ BST-84109 [S]	Takin' Off	1962	10.00	20.00	40.00
—With New York, USA address on label					
❑ BST-84126 [S]	My Point of View	1963	8.75	17.50	35.00
—With New York, USA address on label					
❑ BST-84147 [S]	Inventions and Dimensions	1963	8.75	17.50	35.00
—With New York, USA address on label					
❑ BST-84175 [S]	Empyrean Isles	1964	8.75	17.50	35.00
—With New York, USA address on label					
❑ BST-84195 [S]	Maiden Voyage	1965	8.75	17.50	35.00
—With New York, USA address on label					

COLUMBIA

Number	Title (A Side/B Side)	Yr	VG	VG+	NM
❑ CQ 32371 [Q]	Head Hunters	1973	6.25	12.50	25.00
❑ PCQ 32965 [Q]	Thrust	1974	6.25	12.50	25.00
❑ PCQ 34280 [Q]	Secrets	1976	6.25	12.50	25.00

MGM

Number	Title (A Side/B Side)	Yr	VG	VG+	NM
❑ E-4447 [M]	Blow-Up	1967	8.75	17.50	35.00
❑ SE-4447 [S]	Blow-Up	1967	10.00	20.00	40.00
—Also includes one track by the Yardbirds					

HANDY, CAP'N JOHN
RCA VICTOR

Number	Title (A Side/B Side)	Yr	VG	VG+	NM
❑ LPM-3762 [M]	Introducing Cap'n John Handy	1967	6.25	12.50	25.00

HANDY, GEORGE
"X"

Number	Title (A Side/B Side)	Yr	VG	VG+	NM
❑ LXA-1004 [M]	Handyland, U.S.A.	1954	15.00	30.00	60.00
❑ LXA-1032 [M]	By George! Handy, Of Course	1954	15.00	30.00	60.00

HANDY, JOHN
ROULETTE

Number	Title (A Side/B Side)	Yr	VG	VG+	NM
❑ R 52042 [M]	In the Ver-nac'-u-lar	1960	5.00	10.00	20.00
❑ SR 52042 [S]	In the Ver-nac'-u-lar	1960	6.25	12.50	25.00
❑ R 52088 [M]	No Coast Jazz	1962	5.00	10.00	20.00
❑ SR 52088 [S]	No Coast Jazz	1962	6.25	12.50	25.00
❑ SR 52121 [S]	John Handy Jazz	1964	5.00	10.00	20.00
❑ SR 52124 [S]	Quote, Unquote	1964	5.00	10.00	20.00

HANDY, W.C.
HERITAGE

Number	Title (A Side/B Side)	Yr	VG	VG+	NM
❑ 0052 [10]	Blues Revisited	195?	30.00	60.00	120.00

HANGMEN, THE
MONUMENT

Number	Title (A Side/B Side)	Yr	VG	VG+	NM
❑ MLP-8077 [M]	Bitter Sweet	1967	7.50	15.00	30.00
❑ SLP-18077 [S]	Bitter Sweet	1967	10.00	20.00	40.00

HANKINS, ESCO
AUDIO LAB

Number	Title (A Side/B Side)	Yr	VG	VG+	NM
❑ AL-1547 [M]	Country Style	1961	50.00	100.00	200.00

HANNA, KEN
CAPITOL

Number	Title (A Side/B Side)	Yr	VG	VG+	NM
❑ T 6512 [M]	Jazz for Dancers	1955	10.00	20.00	40.00

HANNA, ROLAND
ATCO

Number	Title (A Side/B Side)	Yr	VG	VG+	NM
❑ 33-108 [M]	Destry Rides Again	1959	10.00	20.00	40.00
❑ SD 33-108 [S]	Destry Rides Again	1959	10.00	20.00	40.00
❑ 33-121 [M]	Easy to Love	1960	7.50	15.00	30.00
❑ SD 33-121 [S]	Easy to Love	1960	10.00	20.00	40.00

BASF

Number	Title (A Side/B Side)	Yr	VG	VG+	NM
❑ 20875	Child of Gemini	1972	6.25	12.50	25.00

HANRAHAN, KIP
PANGAEA

Number	Title (A Side/B Side)	Yr	VG	VG+	NM
❑ 42137	Days & Nights of Blue Luck Inverted	1988	5.00	10.00	20.00

HAPPENINGS, THE
B.T. PUPPY

Number	Title (A Side/B Side)	Yr	VG	VG+	NM
❑ BTP-1001 [M]	The Happenings (Bye-Bye, So Long, Farewell…See You in September)	1966	6.25	12.50	25.00
❑ BTS-1001 [S]	The Happenings (Bye-Bye, So Long, Farewell…See You in September)	1966	7.50	15.00	30.00
❑ BT-1003 [M]	Psycle	1967	6.25	12.50	25.00
❑ BTS-1003 [S]	Psycle	1967	7.50	15.00	30.00
❑ BTS-1004	The Happenings Golden Hits!	1968	10.00	20.00	40.00

Number	Title (A Side/B Side)	Yr	VG	VG+	NM

JUBILEE

❑ JGS-8028	Piece of Mind	1969	6.25	12.50	25.00
❑ JGS-8030	The Happenings' Greatest Hits	1969	6.25	12.50	25.00

HAPPY CHIPMUNKS, THE
HOLIDAY

❑ HDY-1950	Merry Christmas from the Happy Chipmunks	1982	6.25	12.50	25.00

—Record quickly pulled from market because of unauthorized use of the name "Chipmunks"

HAPPY DRAGON BAND, THE
FIDDLER'S MUSIC

❑ 1157	The Happy Dragon Band	1977	20.00	40.00	80.00

HAPSHASH AND THE COLOURED COAT
IMPERIAL

❑ LP-9377 [M]	Hapshash and the Coloured Coat	1968	12.50	25.00	50.00
❑ LP-12377 [S]	Hapshash and the Coloured Coat	1968	10.00	20.00	40.00
❑ LP-12430	Western Flyer	1969	10.00	20.00	40.00

HARD TIMES, THE
WORLD PACIFIC

❑ WP-1867 [M]	Blew Mind	1968	6.25	12.50	25.00
❑ WPS-21867 [S]	Blew Mind	1968	7.50	15.00	30.00

HARDAWAY, BOB
BETHLEHEM

❑ BCP-1028 [10]	Bob Hardaway	1955	30.00	60.00	120.00

HARDEN, ARLENE
COLUMBIA

❑ CL 2833 [M]	Sing Me Back Home	1967	7.50	15.00	30.00
❑ CS 9633 [S]	Sing Me Back Home	1967	5.00	10.00	20.00
❑ CS 9674	What Can I Say	1968	5.00	10.00	20.00

HARDEN, WILBUR
SAVOY

❑ MG-12127 [M]	Mainstream 1958/The East Coast Jazz Scene Featuring John Coltrane	1958	15.00	30.00	60.00
❑ MG-12131 [M]	Jazz Way Out	1958	12.50	25.00	50.00
❑ MG-12134 [M]	The King and I	1958	12.50	25.00	50.00
❑ MG-12136 [M]	Tanganyika Suite	1958	12.50	25.00	50.00
❑ SST-13002 [S]	The King and I	1959	10.00	20.00	40.00
❑ SST-13004 [S]	Jazz Way Out	1959	10.00	20.00	40.00
❑ SST-13005 [S]	Tanganyika Suite	1959	10.00	20.00	40.00

HARDEN TRIO, THE
COLUMBIA

❑ CL 2506 [M]	Tippy Toeing	1966	5.00	10.00	20.00
❑ CS 9306 [S]	Tippy Toeing	1966	6.25	12.50	25.00

HARDIN, TIM
ANTILLES

❑ 7023	Nine	1974	3.75	7.50	15.00

ATCO

❑ 33-210 [M]	This Is Tim Hardin	1967	6.25	12.50	25.00
❑ SD 33-210 [R]	This Is Tim Hardin	1967	3.75	7.50	15.00

COLUMBIA

❑ CS 9787	Suite for Susan Moore and Damion — We Are — One, One, All in One	1969	6.25	12.50	25.00

—"360 Sound" label

❑ C 30551	Bird on a Wire	1971	5.00	10.00	20.00
❑ KC 31764	Painted Head	1972	5.00	10.00	20.00
❑ PC 37164	The Shock of Grace	1981	3.00	6.00	12.00

MGM

❑ GAS-104	Tim Hardin (Golden Archive Series)	1970	5.00	10.00	20.00
❑ M3G-4952	Archetypes	1974	3.75	7.50	15.00

POLYDOR

❑ PD-1-6333	Memorial Album	1981	3.00	6.00	12.00

VERVE FOLKWAYS

❑ FT-3004 [M]	Tim Hardin/1	1966	6.25	12.50	25.00
❑ FTS-3004 [S]	Tim Hardin/1	1966	7.50	15.00	30.00

VERVE FORECAST

❑ FT-3004 [M]	Tim Hardin/1	1967	3.75	7.50	15.00
❑ FTS-3004 [S]	Tim Hardin/1	1967	5.00	10.00	20.00
❑ FTS-3022	Tim Hardin/2	1967	6.25	12.50	25.00
❑ FTS-3049	Tim Hardin/3 — Live in Concert	1968	6.25	12.50	25.00
❑ FTS-3064	Tim Hardin/4	1969	6.25	12.50	25.00
❑ FTS-3078	The Best of Tim Hardin	1970	5.00	10.00	20.00

HARDMAN, BILL
SAVOY

❑ MG-12170 [M]	Bill Hardman Quintet	1961	15.00	30.00	60.00

HARDWATER
CAPITOL

❑ ST-2954	Hardwater	1968	10.00	20.00	40.00

HARDY, FRANCOISE
4 CORNERS OF THE WORLD

❑ FCL-4208 [M]	The "Yeh Yeh" Girl from Paris!	196?	5.00	10.00	20.00
❑ FCS-4208 [S]	The "Yeh Yeh" Girl from Paris!	196?	6.25	12.50	25.00
❑ FCL-4219 [M]	Maid in Paris	196?	5.00	10.00	20.00
❑ FCS-4219 [S]	Maid in Paris	196?	6.25	12.50	25.00
❑ FCL-4231 [M]	Francoise...	196?	5.00	10.00	20.00
❑ FCS-4231 [S]	Francoise...	196?	6.25	12.50	25.00
❑ FCL-4238 [M]	Je Vous Aime	196?	5.00	10.00	20.00
❑ FCS-4238 [S]	Je Vous Aime	196?	6.25	12.50	25.00

REPRISE

❑ RS 6290	Francoise Hardy	1968	6.25	12.50	25.00
❑ RS 6318	Loving	1969	5.00	10.00	20.00
❑ RS 6345	Mon Amour, Adieu	1969	5.00	10.00	20.00

HARDY BOYS, THE
RCA VICTOR

❑ LSP-4217	Here Come the Hardy Boys	1969	5.00	10.00	20.00
❑ LSP-4315	Wheels	1970	5.00	10.00	20.00

HARIAN, KENT
CARAVAN

❑ LP-15611 [M]	Echoes of Joy	1956	62.50	125.00	250.00

HARLEY, RUFUS
ATLANTIC

❑ 3001 [M]	Bagpipe Blues	1967	6.25	12.50	25.00

HARMONAIRES MALE QUINTET, THE
VARSITY

❑ 6915 [10]	Spirituals	195?	20.00	40.00	80.00

HARMONY BLAZERS, THE
HARMONY

❑ HL 7103 [M]	Ten Big Hits	1959	10.00	20.00	40.00
❑ HL 7126 [M]	Rock & Roll Vol. II	1959	10.00	20.00	40.00
❑ HL 7200 [M]	The Big Ten	1959	10.00	20.00	40.00

HARNELL, JOE
CAPITOL

❑ ST-11657	Harnell	1977	3.00	6.00	12.00

COLUMBIA

❑ CL 2466 [M]	Golden Piano Hits	1966	3.00	6.00	12.00
❑ CL 2699 [M]	Bossa Now	1967	3.75	7.50	15.00
❑ CS 9266 [S]	Golden Piano Hits	1966	3.75	7.50	15.00
❑ CS 9499 [S]	Bossa Now	1967	3.00	6.00	12.00

EPIC

❑ LN (# unknown) [M]	I Want to Be Happy	1960	3.75	7.50	15.00
❑ BN 573 [S]	I Want to Be Happy	1960	5.00	10.00	20.00

JUBILEE

❑ JLP-1015 [M]	Piano Inventions of Jo Harnell	1956	12.50	25.00	50.00
❑ JGM-5020 [M]	Joe Harnell and His Trio	1963	3.75	7.50	15.00

—Reissue of 1015

KAPP

❑ KL 1318 [M]	Fly Me to the Moon and the Bossa Nova Pops	1962	3.75	7.50	15.00
❑ KL 1325 [M]	More Joe Harnell, More Bossa Nova Pops	1963	3.75	7.50	15.00
❑ KL 1339 [M]	Joe Harnell	1963	3.75	7.50	15.00
❑ KL 1416 [M]	The Rhythm and the Fire	1965	3.00	6.00	12.00
❑ KL 1480 [M]	The Best of Joe Harnell	1966	3.00	6.00	12.00
❑ KS 3318 [S]	Fly Me to the Moon and the Bossa Nova Pops	1962	5.00	10.00	20.00
❑ KS 3325 [S]	More Joe Harnell, More Bossa Nova Pops	1963	5.00	10.00	20.00
❑ KS 3339 [S]	Joe Harnell	1963	5.00	10.00	20.00
❑ KS 3416 [S]	The Rhythm and the Fire	1965	3.75	7.50	15.00
❑ KS 3480 [S]	The Best of Joe Harnell	1966	3.75	7.50	15.00

MOTOWN

❑ MS-698	Moving On!!	1969	10.00	20.00	40.00

HARPER, BILLY
STRATA-EAST

❑ SES-19739	Capra Black	1973	10.00	20.00	40.00

HARPER, HERBIE
BETHLEHEM

❑ BCP-1025 [10]	Herbie Harper	1955	30.00	60.00	120.00

LIBERTY

❑ LRP-6003 [M]	Herbie Harper	1956	20.00	40.00	80.00

MODE

❑ LP-100 [M]	Herbie Harper Sextet	1957	25.00	50.00	100.00

NOCTURNE

❑ NLP-1 [10]	Herbie Harper Quintet	1954	37.50	75.00	150.00
❑ NLP-7 [10]	Herbie Harper	1954	37.50	75.00	150.00

TAMPA

❑ TP-11 [M]	Herbie Harper Quintet	1957	25.00	50.00	100.00

—Red vinyl

❑ TP-11 [M]	Herbie Harper Quintet	1958	12.50	25.00	50.00

—Black vinyl

HARPER, JANICE
CAPITOL

❑ ST 1337 [S]	Embers of Love	1960	6.25	12.50	25.00
❑ T 1337 [M]	Embers of Love	1960	5.00	10.00	20.00

HARPER, ROY
CHRYSALIS

❑ PRO-620 [DJ]	Introduction to Roy Harper	1976	7.50	15.00	30.00
❑ CHR 1105	When An Old Cricketer Leaves the Crease	1976	3.75	7.50	15.00
❑ CHR 1139	One of Those Days in England	1977	3.75	7.50	15.00
❑ CHR 1160	Flat Baroque and Berserk	1978	3.00	6.00	12.00

—Reissue of Harvest LP

❑ CHR 1161	Stormcock	1978	3.00	6.00	12.00

—Released in the UK in 1971

❑ CHR 1162	Lifemask	1978	3.00	6.00	12.00

—Released in the UK in 1973

❑ CHR 1163	Valentine	1978	3.00	6.00	12.00

—Released in the UK in 1974

❑ CH2 1164 [(2)]	Flashes from the Archives of Oblivion	1978	3.75	7.50	15.00

—Released in the UK in 1974

HARVEST

❑ SKAO-418	Flat Baroque and Berserk	1970	5.00	10.00	20.00

PVC

❑ 8937	Whatever Happened to Jugula	198?	3.00	6.00	12.00

WORLD PACIFIC

❑ WPS-21888	Folkjokeopus	1969	6.25	12.50	25.00

Number	Title (A Side/B Side)	Yr	VG	VG+	NM
HARPER, TONI					
RCA VICTOR					
❏ LPM-2092 [M]	Lady Lonely	1960	6.25	12.50	25.00
❏ LSP-2092 [S]	Lady Lonely	1960	7.50	15.00	30.00
❏ LPM-2253 [M]	Night Mood	1960	6.25	12.50	25.00
❏ LSP-2253 [S]	Night Mood	1960	7.50	15.00	30.00
VERVE					
❏ MGV-2001 [M]	Toni Harper Sings	1956	20.00	40.00	80.00
❏ V-2001 [M]	Toni Harper Sings	1961	7.50	15.00	30.00
HARPER, WALT					
GATEWAY					
❏ 7016 [M]	On the Road	1966	5.00	10.00	20.00
HARPERS BIZARRE					
FOREST BAY					
❏ 7545	As Time Goes By	1976	3.75	7.50	15.00
WARNER BROS.					
❏ W 1693 [M]	Feelin' Groovy	1967	6.25	12.50	25.00
❏ WS 1693 [S]	Feelin' Groovy	1967	5.00	10.00	20.00
—Gold label					
❏ WS 1693 [S]	Feelin' Groovy	1968	3.75	7.50	15.00
—Green "W7" label					
❏ WS 1716	Anything Goes	1967	5.00	10.00	20.00
❏ WS 1739	The Secret Life of Harpers Bizarre	1968	5.00	10.00	20.00
❏ WS 1784	Harpers Bizarre Four	1969	5.00	10.00	20.00
❏ ST-91351	Anything Goes	1968	6.25	12.50	25.00
—Capitol Record Club edition					
HARPO, SLIM					
EXCELLO					
❏ LP-8003 [M]	Raining in My Heart	1961	62.50	125.00	250.00
—Orange and blue label					
❏ LPS-8003 [M]	Raining in My Heart	196?	25.00	50.00	100.00
—All-blue label					
❏ LP-8005 [M]	Baby Scratch My Back	1966	50.00	100.00	200.00
—Orange and blue label					
❏ LPS-8005 [M]	Baby Scratch My Back	196?	25.00	50.00	100.00
—All-blue label					
❏ LPS-8008 [M]	Tip On In	1968	12.50	25.00	50.00
❏ LPS-8010 [M]	The Best of Slim Harpo	1969	12.50	25.00	50.00
❏ LPS-8013 [M]	Slim Harpo Knew the Blues	1970	12.50	25.00	50.00
RHINO					
❏ RNLP-106	The Best of Slim Harpo	198?	3.75	7.50	15.00
❏ R1-70169	Scratch My Back: The Best of Slim Harpo	1989	3.00	6.00	12.00
HARRIOTT, JOE					
CAPITOL					
❏ T 10351 [M]	Abstract	1962	5.00	10.00	20.00
JAZZLAND					
❏ JLP-37 [M]	Southern Horizons	1961	6.25	12.50	25.00
❏ JLP-49 [M]	Free Form	1961	6.25	12.50	25.00
❏ JLP-937 [S]	Southern Horizons	1961	7.50	15.00	30.00
❏ JLP-949 [S]	Free Form	1961	7.50	15.00	30.00
HARRIS, ART					
KAPP					
❏ KL-1015 [M]	Jazz Goes to Post-Graduate School	1956	10.00	20.00	40.00
HARRIS, ART, AND MITCH LEIGH					
EPIC					
❏ LG 1010 [10]	Modern Woodwind Expressions	1954	12.50	25.00	50.00
❏ LN 3200 [M]	New Jazz in Hi-Fi	1956	10.00	20.00	40.00
KAPP					
❏ KL-1011 [M]	Baroque Band and Brass Choir — Jazz 1775	1956	10.00	20.00	40.00
HARRIS, BARRY					
ARGO					
❏ LP-644 [M]	Breakin' It Up	1959	10.00	20.00	40.00
❏ LPS-644 [S]	Breakin' It Up	1959	7.50	15.00	30.00
CADET					
❏ LP-644 [M]	Breakin' It Up	1966	5.00	10.00	20.00
PRESTIGE					
❏ PRLP-7498 [M]	Luminescence	1967	7.50	15.00	30.00
❏ PRST-7498 [S]	Luminescence	1967	5.00	10.00	20.00
❏ PRST-7600	Bull's Eye	1969	5.00	10.00	20.00
❏ PRST-7733	Magnificent!	1970	5.00	10.00	20.00
RIVERSIDE					
❏ RLP 12-326 [M]	Barry Harris at the Jazz Workshop	1960	7.50	15.00	30.00
❏ RLP-354 [M]	Preminado	1961	7.50	15.00	30.00
❏ RLP-392 [M]	Listen to Barry Harris	1961	7.50	15.00	30.00
❏ RLP-413 [M]	Newer Than New	1962	6.25	12.50	25.00
❏ RLP-435 [M]	Chasin' the Bird	1962	6.25	12.50	25.00
❏ RLP-1177 [S]	Barry Harris at the Jazz Workshop	1960	10.00	20.00	40.00
❏ RS-9354 [S]	Preminado	1961	10.00	20.00	40.00
❏ RS-9392 [S]	Listen to Barry Harris	1961	10.00	20.00	40.00
❏ RS-9413 [S]	Newer Than New	1962	7.50	15.00	30.00
❏ RS-9435 [S]	Chasin' the Bird	1962	7.50	15.00	30.00
HARRIS, BILL (1)					
CLEF					
❏ MGC-125 [10]	Bill Harris Collates	1953	37.50	75.00	150.00
FANTASY					
❏ 3263 [M]	Bill Harris and Friends	1958	10.00	20.00	40.00
—Red vinyl					
❏ 3263 [M]	Bill Harris and Friends	1959	6.25	12.50	25.00
—Black vinyl					
NORGRAN					
❏ MGN-1062 [M]	The Bill Harris Herd	1956	30.00	60.00	120.00
HARRIS, BILL (2)					
EMARCY					
❏ MG-36097 [M]	Bill Harris	1956	10.00	20.00	40.00
❏ MG-36113 [M]	The Harris Touch	1957	10.00	20.00	40.00
MERCURY					
❏ MG-20552 [M]	The Harris Touch	1960	7.50	15.00	30.00
❏ SR-60552 [S]	The Harris Touch	1960	6.25	12.50	25.00
WING					
❏ MGW-12220 [M]	Great Guitar Sounds	1963	5.00	10.00	20.00
HARRIS, EDDIE					
ATLANTIC					
❏ 1545 [M]	The Best of Eddie Harris	1970	6.25	12.50	25.00
—Promo-only white label mono pressing					
COLUMBIA					
❏ CS 8968 [S]	Cool Sax, Warm Heart	1964	5.00	10.00	20.00
❏ CS 9095 [S]	Cool Sax from Hollywood to Broadway	1965	5.00	10.00	20.00
❏ CS 9681 [S]	Here Comes the Judge	1968	6.25	12.50	25.00
—Mono copies are promo only					
VEE JAY					
❏ VJLPS 1081 [S]	The Theme from Exodus and Other Film Spectaculars	1964	5.00	10.00	20.00
❏ LP 3016 [M]	Exodus to Jazz	1961	7.50	15.00	30.00
❏ SR 3016 [S]	Exodus to Jazz	1961	10.00	20.00	40.00
❏ LP 3025 [M]	Mighty Like a Rose	1961	7.50	15.00	30.00
❏ SR 3025 [S]	Mighty Like a Rose	1961	10.00	20.00	40.00
❏ LP 3027 [M]	Jazz for "Breakfast at Tiffany's"	1961	7.50	15.00	30.00
❏ SR 3027 [S]	Jazz for "Breakfast at Tiffany's"	1961	10.00	20.00	40.00
❏ LP 3028 [M]	A Study in Jazz	1962	5.00	10.00	20.00
❏ SR 3028 [S]	A Study in Jazz	1962	7.50	15.00	30.00
❏ LP 3031 [M]	Eddie Harris Goes to the Movies	1962	5.00	10.00	20.00
❏ SR 3031 [S]	Eddie Harris Goes to the Movies	1962	7.50	15.00	30.00
❏ LP 3034 [M]	Bossa Nova	1963	5.00	10.00	20.00
❏ SR 3034 [S]	Bossa Nova	1963	7.50	15.00	30.00
❏ LP 3037 [M]	Half and Half	1963	6.25	12.50	25.00
❏ SR 3037 [S]	Half and Half	1963	7.50	15.00	30.00
HARRIS, EMMYLOU					
JUBILEE					
❏ JGS-8031	Gliding Bird	1969	30.00	60.00	120.00
—Originals have color covers; counterfeit covers are black and white					
MOBILE FIDELITY					
❏ 1-015	Quarter Moon in a Ten Cent Town	1979	10.00	20.00	40.00
—Audiophile vinyl					
REPRISE					
❏ MS 2213	Pieces of the Sky	1975	2.50	5.00	10.00
❏ MS 2236	Elite Hotel	1976	2.50	5.00	10.00
❏ MSK 2284	Pieces of the Sky	1977	2.00	4.00	8.00
—Reissue of 2213					
❏ MSK 2286	Elite Hotel	1977	2.00	4.00	8.00
—Reissue of 2236					
❏ 25776	Bluebird	1989	3.00	6.00	12.00
WARNER BROS.					
❏ BS 2998	Luxury Liner	1977	3.00	6.00	12.00
❏ BSK 3115	Luxury Liner	1977	2.50	5.00	10.00
—Reissue of 2998					
❏ BSK 3141	Quarter Moon in a Ten Cent Town	1978	2.50	5.00	10.00
❏ BSK 3258	Profile/Best of Emmylou Harris	1978	2.50	5.00	10.00
❏ BSK 3318	Blue Kentucky Girl	1979	2.50	5.00	10.00
❏ BSK 3422	Roses in the Snow	1980	2.50	5.00	10.00
❏ BSK 3484	Light of the Stable: The Christmas Album	1980	2.50	5.00	10.00
❏ BSK 3508	Evangeline	1981	2.50	5.00	10.00
❏ BSK 3603	Cimarron	1981	2.50	5.00	10.00
❏ 23740	Last Date	1982	2.50	5.00	10.00
❏ 23961	White Shoes	1983	2.50	5.00	10.00
❏ 25161	Profile II — The Best of Emmylou Harris	1984	2.50	5.00	10.00
❏ 25205	The Ballad of Sally Rose	1985	2.50	5.00	10.00
❏ 25352	Thirteen	1986	2.50	5.00	10.00
❏ 25585	Angel Band	1987	2.50	5.00	10.00
HARRIS, GENE					
BLUE NOTE					
❏ BN-LA141-G [(2)]	Yesterday, Today and Tomorrow	1973	6.25	12.50	25.00
❏ BN-LA313-G	Astral Signal	1974	5.00	10.00	20.00
❏ BST-84378	The Three Sounds	1971	5.00	10.00	20.00
❏ BST-84423	Gene Harris of the Three Sounds	1972	5.00	10.00	20.00
JUBILEE					
❏ JLP-1005 [M]	Our Love Is Here to Stay	1955	12.50	25.00	50.00
❏ JGM-1115 [M]	Genie in My Soul	1959	10.00	20.00	40.00
HARRIS, HAROLD					
VEE JAY					
❏ LP-3018 [M]	Here's Harold	1962	6.25	12.50	25.00
❏ SR-3018 [S]	Here's Harold	1962	7.50	15.00	30.00
❏ LP-3036 [M]	Harold Harris at the Playboy Club	1963	6.25	12.50	25.00
❏ SR-3036 [S]	Harold Harris at the Playboy Club	1963	7.50	15.00	30.00
HARRIS, PEPPERMINT					
TIME					
❏ 5 [M]	Peppermint Harris	1962	50.00	100.00	200.00
HARRIS, PHIL					
RCA CAMDEN					
❏ CAL-456 [M]	That's What I Like About the South	1963	3.75	7.50	15.00
RCA VICTOR					
❏ LPM-1985 [M]	The South Shall Rise Again	1959	6.25	12.50	25.00
❏ LPM-3037 [10]	Phil Harris On the Record	1952	10.00	20.00	40.00
HARRIS, RICHARD					
ABC DUNHILL					
❏ DS-50032	A Tramp Shining	1968	3.75	7.50	15.00

Number	Title (A Side/B Side)	Yr	VG	VG+	NM
☐ DS-50042	The Yard Went On Forever	1968	3.75	7.50	15.00
☐ DS-50074	The Love Album	1970	3.75	7.50	15.00
☐ DSX-50116	My Boy	1971	3.00	6.00	12.00
☐ DSX-50133	Slides	1972	3.00	6.00	12.00
☐ DSX-50139	The Great Performances	1973	3.00	6.00	12.00
☐ DSX-50159	I, In the Membership	1974	3.00	6.00	12.00
☐ DSX-50160	Jonathan Livingston Seagull	1973	3.00	6.00	12.00
—Spoken-word recording					
ATLANTIC					
☐ QD 18120 [Q]	The Prophet by Kahlil Gibran	1974	5.00	10.00	20.00
—Spoken-word recording					
☐ SD 18120	The Prophet by Kahlil Gibran	1974	3.00	6.00	12.00
—Spoken-word recording					
MCA					
☐ 27016	A Tramp Shining	198?	2.00	4.00	8.00
—Budget-line reissue					

HARRIS, ROLF
EPIC

Number	Title (A Side/B Side)	Yr	VG	VG+	NM
☐ LN 24053 [M]	Tie Me Kangaroo Down, Sport & Sun Arise	1963	5.00	10.00	20.00
☐ LN 24110 [M]	Join Rolf Harris Singing The Count of King Caractacus (And Other Fun Songs)	1964	5.00	10.00	20.00
☐ BN 26053 [S]	Tie Me Kangaroo Down, Sport & Sun Arise	1963	6.25	12.50	25.00
☐ BN 26110 [S]	Join Rolf Harris Singing The Count of King Caractacus (And Other Fun Songs)	1964	6.25	12.50	25.00

HARRIS, SHAUN
Also see THE WEST COAST POP ART EXPERIMENTAL BAND.
CAPITOL

Number	Title (A Side/B Side)	Yr	VG	VG+	NM
☐ ST-11168	Shaun Harris	1973	7.50	15.00	30.00

HARRIS, WYNONIE
KING

Number	Title (A Side/B Side)	Yr	VG	VG+	NM
☐ KS-1086	Good Rockin' Blues	1970	6.25	12.50	25.00

HARRISON, CASS
MGM

Number	Title (A Side/B Side)	Yr	VG	VG+	NM
☐ E-3388 [M]	The Duke and I	1956	10.00	20.00	40.00
☐ E-3495 [M]	Wrappin' It Up	1957	10.00	20.00	40.00

HARRISON, GEORGE
Also see THE BEATLES; TRAVELING WILBURYS.
APPLE

Number	Title (A Side/B Side)	Yr	VG	VG+	NM
☐ STCH-639 [(3)]	All Things Must Pass	1970	10.00	20.00	40.00
—Apple labels on first two records and "Apple Jam" labels on third; includes poster and lyric innersleeves					
☐ ST-3350	Wonderwall Music Bonus Photo	1968	—	2.50	5.00
☐ ST-3350	Wonderwall Music	1968	6.25	12.50	25.00
—With "Mfd. by Apple" on label					
☐ ST-3350	Wonderwall Music	1968	37.50	75.00	150.00
—With Capitol logo on Side 2 bottom					
☐ SMAS-3410	Living in the Material World	1973	3.75	7.50	15.00
☐ SMAS-3418	Dark Horse	1974	3.75	7.50	15.00
☐ SW-3420	Extra Texture (Read All About It)	1975	3.75	7.50	15.00
CAPITOL					
☐ STCH-639 [(3)]	All Things Must Pass	1976	7.50	15.00	30.00
—Orange labels with poster and lyric innersleeves					
☐ STCH-639 [(3)]	All Things Must Pass	1978	6.25	12.50	25.00
—Purple labels with poster and lyric innersleeves					
☐ STCH-639 [(3)]	All Things Must Pass	1983	25.00	50.00	100.00
—Black labels, print in colorband, with poster and lyric innersleeves					
☐ ST-11578	The Best of George Harrison	1976	3.75	7.50	15.00
—Custom label, no bar code on back					
☐ ST-11578	The Best of George Harrison	1976	45.00	90.00	180.00
—Orange label					
☐ ST-11578	The Best of George Harrison	1978	2.50	5.00	10.00
—Purple label, large Capitol logo					
☐ ST-11578	The Best of George Harrison	1983	6.25	12.50	25.00
—Black label, print in colorband					
☐ ST-11578	The Best of George Harrison	1988	6.25	12.50	25.00
—Odd reissue with custom label; large stand-alone "S" in trail-off area; bar code on cover					
☐ ST-11578	The Best of George Harrison	1989	20.00	40.00	80.00
—Purple label, small Capitol logo					
☐ SN-16055	Dark Horse	1980	3.75	7.50	15.00
—Budget-line reissue; reverses front and back covers					
☐ SN-16216	Living in the Material World	1980	5.00	10.00	20.00
—Budget-line reissue					
☐ SN-16217	Extra Texture (Read All About It)	1980	6.25	12.50	25.00
—Budget-line reissue					
CAPITOL/APPLE					
☐ STCH-639 [(3)]	All Things Must Pass	1988	20.00	40.00	80.00
—Odd pressing with Apple labels and Capitol cover (look for stand-alone "S" in trail-off wax); with large sticker on back cover					
DARK HORSE					
☐ (no #) [DJ]	Dark Horse Radio Special	1974	100.00	200.00	400.00
—Promo-only; George Harrison introduces his new record label and artists					
☐ PRO 649 [DJ]	A Personal Music Dialogue at Thirty Three and 1/3	1976	12.50	25.00	50.00
☐ DH 3005	Thirty Three and 1/3	1976	2.50	5.00	10.00
—Deduct 30% for cut-outs					
☐ DHK 3255	George Harrison	1979	2.50	5.00	10.00
—Deduct 30% for cut-outs					
☐ DHK 3255	George Harrison	1979	10.00	20.00	40.00
—Columbia House edition (back cover says "Manufactured by Columbia House Under License")					
☐ DHK 3492	Somewhere in England	1981	2.50	5.00	10.00
—Deduct 30% for cut-outs					
☐ 23724	Gone Troppo	1982	2.50	5.00	10.00
—Deduct 30% for cut-outs					
☐ 23724 [DJ]	Gone Troppo	1982	6.25	12.50	25.00
—Promo on Quiex II vinyl					
☐ 25643	Cloud Nine	1987	2.50	5.00	10.00
☐ W1-25643	Cloud Nine	1987	3.00	6.00	12.00
—Columbia House edition					

Number	Title (A Side/B Side)	Yr	VG	VG+	NM
☐ 25726	Best of Dark Horse 1976-1989	1989	6.25	12.50	25.00
☐ W1-25726	Best of Dark Horse 1976-1989	1989	3.75	7.50	15.00
—Columbia House edition					
☐ R 174328	Cloud Nine	1987	3.75	7.50	15.00
—BMG Direct Marketing edition					
☐ R 180307	Best of Dark Horse 1976-1989	1989	3.75	7.50	15.00
—BMG Direct Marketing edition					
ZAPPLE					
☐ ST-3358	Electronic Sound	1969	10.00	20.00	40.00

HARRISON, GEORGE, AND FRIENDS
The "Friends" include BADFINGER; ERIC CLAPTON; BOB DYLAN; BILLY PRESTON; LEON RUSSELL; RAVI SHANKAR; RINGO STARR.
APPLE

Number	Title (A Side/B Side)	Yr	VG	VG+	NM
☐ STCX-3385 [(3)]	The Concert for Bangla Desh	1971	10.00	20.00	40.00
—With 64-page booklet and custom innersleeves					
☐ STCX-3385 [(3)]	The Concert for Bangla Desh	1975	12.50	25.00	50.00
—As above, but with "All Rights Reserved" on labels					
CAPITOL					
☐ SABB-12248 [(2)]	The Concert for Bangla Desh	1982	75.00	150.00	300.00
—Scheduled reissue that was never officially released, though a few copies got out by mistake					

HARRISON, NOEL
LONDON

Number	Title (A Side/B Side)	Yr	VG	VG+	NM
☐ PS 459 [S]	Noel Harrison	1966	6.25	12.50	25.00
☐ LL 3459 [M]	Noel Harrison	1966	5.00	10.00	20.00
REPRISE					
☐ R-6263 [M]	Collage	1967	3.75	7.50	15.00
☐ RS-6263 [S]	Collage	1967	5.00	10.00	20.00
☐ RS-6295	Santa Monica Pier	1968	3.75	7.50	15.00
☐ RS-6321	The Great Electric Experiment Is Over	1969	3.75	7.50	15.00

HARRISON, WENDELL
TRIBE

Number	Title (A Side/B Side)	Yr	VG	VG+	NM
☐ PRSD-2212	Evening with the Devil	197?	25.00	50.00	100.00
☐ PRSD-4002	Message from the Tribe, Vol. 3	197?	25.00	50.00	100.00
WENHA					
☐ 015	Dreams of a Love Supreme	198?	12.50	25.00	50.00
☐ 016	Organic Dream	198?	10.00	20.00	40.00
☐ 2212	Evening with the Devil	198?	5.00	10.00	20.00
—Reissue of Tribe 2212					
☐ 4002	Message from the Tribe	198?	5.00	10.00	20.00
—Reissue of Tribe 4002					

HARRISON, WES
PHILIPS

Number	Title (A Side/B Side)	Yr	VG	VG+	NM
☐ PHM 200103 [M]	You Won't Believe Your Ears	1963	5.00	10.00	20.00
☐ PHS 600103 [S]	You Won't Believe Your Ears	1963	6.25	12.50	25.00

HARRISON, WILBERT
BUDDAH

Number	Title (A Side/B Side)	Yr	VG	VG+	NM
☐ BDS-5002	Wilbert Harrison	1971	7.50	15.00	30.00
CHELSEA					
☐ CH 523	Wilbert Harrison	1977	5.00	10.00	20.00
JUGGERNAUT					
☐ ST-8803	Shoot You Full of Love	1971	12.50	25.00	50.00
SAVOY JAZZ					
☐ SJL-1182	Listen to My Song	1987	3.00	6.00	12.00
SPHERE SOUND					
☐ SSR-7000 [M]	Kansas City	1965	62.50	125.00	250.00
☐ SSSR-7000 [R]	Kansas City	1965	50.00	100.00	200.00
SUE					
☐ SSLP-8801	Let's Work Together	1970	12.50	25.00	50.00
WET SOUL					
☐ 1001	Anything You Want	197?	12.50	25.00	50.00

HARROW, NANCY
ATLANTIC

Number	Title (A Side/B Side)	Yr	VG	VG+	NM
☐ 8075 [M]	You Never Know	1963	6.25	12.50	25.00
☐ SD 8075 [S]	You Never Know	1963	7.50	15.00	30.00
CANDID					
☐ CD-8008 [M]	Wild Women Don't Have the Blues	1962	7.50	15.00	30.00
☐ CD-9008 [S]	Wild Women Don't Have the Blues	1962	10.00	20.00	40.00

HART, FREDDIE
CAPITOL

Number	Title (A Side/B Side)	Yr	VG	VG+	NM
☐ ST-469	New Sounds	1970	3.00	6.00	12.00
☐ ST-593	California Grapevine	1970	3.00	6.00	12.00
☐ ST-838	Easy Loving	1971	3.00	6.00	12.00
☐ ST-11014	My Hang-Up Is You	1972	3.00	6.00	12.00
☐ ST-11073	Bless Your Heart	1972	3.00	6.00	12.00
☐ ST-11107	Got the All-Overs	1972	3.00	6.00	12.00
☐ ST-11156	Super Kind of Woman	1973	3.00	6.00	12.00
☐ ST-11197	Trip to Heaven	1973	3.00	6.00	12.00
☐ ST-11252	If You Can't Feel It	1974	3.00	6.00	12.00
☐ ST-11296	Hang In There Girl	1974	3.00	6.00	12.00
☐ ST-11353	Country Heart 'N' Soul	1975	3.00	6.00	12.00
☐ ST-11374	Greatest Hits	1975	3.00	6.00	12.00
☐ ST-11449	The First Time	1975	2.50	5.00	10.00
☐ ST-11504	People Put to Music	1976	2.50	5.00	10.00
☐ ST-11568	That Look in Her Eyes	1976	2.50	5.00	10.00
☐ ST-11626	The Pleasure's Been All Mine	1977	2.50	5.00	10.00
☐ ST-11724	Only You	1978	2.50	5.00	10.00
COLUMBIA					
☐ CL 1792 [M]	The Spirited Freddie Hart	1962	10.00	20.00	40.00
☐ G 31550 [(2)]	The World of Freddie Hart	1972	3.75	7.50	15.00
HARMONY					
☐ HL 7412 [M]	The Best of Freddie Hart	1967	3.00	6.00	12.00
☐ HS 11212 [S]	The Best of Freddie Hart	1967	3.00	6.00	12.00
☐ KH 31165	Lonesome Love	1972	2.50	5.00	10.00
☐ KH 32467	You Are My World	1973	2.50	5.00	10.00

Number	Title (A Side/B Side)	Yr	VG	VG+	NM
HILLTOP					
❑ 6117	From Canada to Tennessee	1972	2.50	5.00	10.00
KAPP					
❑ KL-1456 [M]	The Hart of Country Music	1966	3.75	7.50	15.00
❑ KL-1492 [M]	Straight from the Heart	1966	3.75	7.50	15.00
❑ KL-1513 [M]	Hurtin' Man	1967	5.00	10.00	20.00
❑ KL-1539 [M]	The Neon and the Rain	1967	5.00	10.00	20.00
❑ KS-3456 [S]	The Hart of Country Music	1966	5.00	10.00	20.00
❑ KS-3492 [S]	Straight from the Heart	1966	5.00	10.00	20.00
❑ KS-3513 [S]	Hurtin' Man	1967	5.00	10.00	20.00
❑ KS-3539 [S]	The Neon and the Rain	1967	5.00	10.00	20.00
❑ KS-3546	Togetherness	1968	5.00	10.00	20.00
❑ KS-3568	Born a Fool	1968	5.00	10.00	20.00
❑ KS-3592	Greatest Hits	1969	3.75	7.50	15.00
MCA					
❑ 4088 [(2)]	The Best of Freddie Hart	1975	3.75	7.50	15.00
SUNBIRD					
❑ ST-50100	Sure Thing	1980	3.00	6.00	12.00

HART, MICKEY
Also see THE GRATEFUL DEAD.

Number	Title (A Side/B Side)	Yr	VG	VG+	NM
RELIX					
❑ 2026	Rolling Thunder	1987	3.00	6.00	12.00
WARNER BROS.					
❑ BS 2635	Rolling Thunder	1972	7.50	15.00	30.00

HARTFORD, JOHN

Number	Title (A Side/B Side)	Yr	VG	VG+	NM
FLYING FISH					
❑ FF-020	Mark Twang	1976	2.50	5.00	10.00
❑ FF-028	Nobody Knows What You Do	1977	2.50	5.00	10.00
❑ FF-044	All in the Name of Love	1983	2.50	5.00	10.00
❑ FF-063	Headin' Down Into the Mystery Below	1978	2.50	5.00	10.00
❑ FF-095	Slumberin' on the Cumberland	1979	2.50	5.00	10.00

—With Pat Burton and Benny Martin

Number	Title (A Side/B Side)	Yr	VG	VG+	NM
❑ FF-228	You and Me at Home	1980	2.50	5.00	10.00
❑ FF-259	Catalogue	1982	2.50	5.00	10.00
❑ FF-289	Gum Tree Canoe	1984	2.50	5.00	10.00
❑ FF-440	Me Oh My, How Time Flies	1987	2.50	5.00	10.00
MCA					
❑ 5861	Annual Waltz	1987	2.00	4.00	8.00
RCA VICTOR					
❑ LPM-3687 [M]	John Hartford Looks at Life	1966	5.00	10.00	20.00
❑ LSP-3687 [S]	John Hartford Looks at Life	1966	3.75	7.50	15.00
❑ LPM-3796 [M]	Earthwords and Music	1967	6.25	12.50	25.00
❑ LSP-3796 [S]	Earthwords and Music	1967	3.75	7.50	15.00
❑ LPM-3884 [M]	The Love Album	1967	6.25	12.50	25.00
❑ LSP-3884 [S]	The Love Album	1967	3.75	7.50	15.00
❑ LPM-3998 [M]	Housing Project	1968	12.50	25.00	50.00
❑ LSP-3998 [S]	Housing Project	1968	3.75	7.50	15.00
❑ LSP-4068	Gentle on My Mind and Other Originals	1968	3.75	7.50	15.00
❑ LSP-4156	John Hartford	1969	3.75	7.50	15.00
❑ LSP-4337	Iron Mountain Depot	1970	3.75	7.50	15.00
WARNER BROS.					
❑ WS 1916	Aereo-Plain	1971	3.00	6.00	12.00
❑ BS 2651	Morning Bugle	1972	3.00	6.00	12.00

HARTMAN, JOHNNY

Number	Title (A Side/B Side)	Yr	VG	VG+	NM
ABC-PARAMOUNT					
❑ ABC-574 [M]	The Unforgettable Johnny Hartman	1966	7.50	15.00	30.00
❑ ABCS-574 [S]	The Unforgettable Johnny Hartman	1966	10.00	20.00	40.00
BETHLEHEM					
❑ BCP-43 [M]	Songs from the Heart	1956	20.00	40.00	80.00
❑ BCP-6014 [M]	All of Me: The Debonair Mr. Hartman	1957	20.00	40.00	80.00
IMPULSE!					
❑ A-57 [M]	I Just Dropped By to Say Hello	1964	7.50	15.00	30.00
❑ AS-57 [S]	I Just Dropped By to Say Hello	1964	10.00	20.00	40.00
❑ A-74 [M]	The Voice That Is	1965	7.50	15.00	30.00
❑ AS-74 [S]	The Voice That Is	1965	10.00	20.00	40.00
REGENT					
❑ MG-6014 [M]	Just You, Just Me	1956	20.00	40.00	80.00

HARTMAN, LISA

Number	Title (A Side/B Side)	Yr	VG	VG+	NM
KIRSHNER					
❑ PZ 34109	Lisa Hartman	1976	10.00	20.00	40.00
❑ JZ 35609	Hold On	1978	5.00	10.00	20.00

HARUMI

Number	Title (A Side/B Side)	Yr	VG	VG+	NM
VERVE FORECAST					
❑ FTS-3030	Harumi	1968	6.25	12.50	25.00

HARVEY, LAURENCE

Number	Title (A Side/B Side)	Yr	VG	VG+	NM
ATLANTIC					
❑ 1367 [M]	This Is My Beloved	1962	10.00	20.00	40.00
❑ SD 1367 [S]	This Is My Beloved	1962	12.50	25.00	50.00

HASKELL, JACK

Number	Title (A Side/B Side)	Yr	VG	VG+	NM
STRAND					
❑ SL-1020 [M]	Jack Haskell Swings for Jack Paar	1961	5.00	10.00	20.00
❑ SLS-1020 [S]	Jack Haskell Swings for Jack Paar	1961	7.50	15.00	30.00

HASKELL, JIMMIE

Number	Title (A Side/B Side)	Yr	VG	VG+	NM
IMPERIAL					
❑ LP-9068 [M]	Countdown	1959	7.50	15.00	30.00
❑ LP-12015 [S]	Countdown	1959	12.50	25.00	50.00

HASKILL, CLARA

Number	Title (A Side/B Side)	Yr	VG	VG+	NM
MERCURY LIVING PRESENCE					
❑ SR 90413 [S]	Mozart: Piano Concertos No. 20 and 23; Rondo in A	196?	7.50	15.00	30.00

—Maroon label, no "Vendor: Mercury Record Corporation"

Number	Title (A Side/B Side)	Yr	VG	VG+	NM
❑ SR 90413 [S]	Mozart: Piano Concertos No. 20 and 23; Rondo in A	196?	20.00	40.00	80.00

—Maroon label, with "Vendor: Mercury Record Corporation" (second edition is more sought after than the first)

HASSLES, THE
BILLY JOEL was in this group.

Number	Title (A Side/B Side)	Yr	VG	VG+	NM
LIBERTY					
❑ LN-10138	The Hassles	1981	3.00	6.00	12.00
❑ LN-10139	Hour of the Wolf	1981	3.00	6.00	12.00
UNITED ARTISTS					
❑ UAS-6631	The Hassles	1968	6.25	12.50	25.00
❑ UAS-6699	Hour of the Wolf	1969	6.25	12.50	25.00

HATZA, GREG

Number	Title (A Side/B Side)	Yr	VG	VG+	NM
CORAL					
❑ CRL 757495 [S]	Organized Jazz	1963	5.00	10.00	20.00

HAVENS, RICHIE

Number	Title (A Side/B Side)	Yr	VG	VG+	NM
A&M					
❑ SP-4598	The End of the Beginning	1976	2.50	5.00	10.00
❑ SP-4641	Mirage	1977	2.50	5.00	10.00
DOUGLAS					
❑ D-779 [M]	Richie Havens' Record	1966	3.75	7.50	15.00
❑ SD-779 [S]	Richie Havens' Record	1966	5.00	10.00	20.00
❑ D-780 [M]	Electric Havens	1966	6.25	12.50	25.00
❑ SD-780 [S]	Electric Havens	1966	5.00	10.00	20.00
ELEKTRA					
❑ 6E-242	Connections	1980	2.50	5.00	10.00
MGM					
❑ SE-4698	Mixed Bag	1970	3.75	7.50	15.00

—Reissue of Verve Forecast 3006

Number	Title (A Side/B Side)	Yr	VG	VG+	NM
❑ SE-4699	Something Else Again	1970	3.75	7.50	15.00

—Reissue of Verve Forecast 3034

Number	Title (A Side/B Side)	Yr	VG	VG+	NM
❑ SE-4700 [(2)]	Richard P. Havens, 1983	1970	5.00	10.00	20.00

—Reissue of Verve Forecast 3047

Number	Title (A Side/B Side)	Yr	VG	VG+	NM
RBI					
❑ 400	Simple Things	1987	2.50	5.00	10.00
STORMY FOREST					
❑ SFS-6001	Stonehenge	1969	3.75	7.50	15.00
❑ SFS-6005	Alarm Clock	1970	3.00	6.00	12.00
❑ SFS-6010	The Great Blind Degree	1971	3.00	6.00	12.00
❑ SFS-6012 [(2)]	Richie Havens On Stage	1972	3.75	7.50	15.00
❑ SFS-6013	Portfolio	1973	3.00	6.00	12.00
❑ SFS-6201	Mixed Bag II	1974	3.00	6.00	12.00
VERVE FOLKWAYS					
❑ FT-3006 [M]	Mixed Bag	1967	6.25	12.50	25.00
❑ FTS-3006 [S]	Mixed Bag	1967	5.00	10.00	20.00
VERVE FORECAST					
❑ FTS-3006	Mixed Bag	1968	3.75	7.50	15.00
❑ FT-3034 [M]	Something Else Again	1968	10.00	20.00	40.00
❑ FTS-3034 [S]	Something Else Again	1968	5.00	10.00	20.00
❑ FTS-3047 [(2)]	Richard P. Havens, 1983	1968	6.25	12.50	25.00
❑ FTS-3061	Richie Havens	1969	—	—	—

—Canceled

HAWES, HAMPTON

Number	Title (A Side/B Side)	Yr	VG	VG+	NM
CONTEMPORARY					
❑ C-3505 [M]	Hampton Hawes	1955	12.50	25.00	50.00
❑ C-3515 [M]	This Is Hampton Hawes	1956	12.50	25.00	50.00
❑ C-3523 [M]	Everybody Likes Hampton Hawes	1956	12.50	25.00	50.00
❑ C-3545 [M]	All Night Session! Volume 1	1958	12.50	25.00	50.00
❑ C-3546 [M]	All Night Session! Volume 2	1958	12.50	25.00	50.00
❑ C-3547 [M]	All Night Session! Volume 3	1958	12.50	25.00	50.00
❑ C-3553 [M]	Four! Hampton Hawes!!!	1958	12.50	25.00	50.00
❑ M-3589 [M]	For Real!	1959	10.00	20.00	40.00
❑ M-3614 [M]	The Green Leaves of Summer	1964	7.50	15.00	30.00
❑ M-3616 [M]	Here and Now	1965	5.00	10.00	20.00
❑ M-3621 [M]	The Seance	1966	5.00	10.00	20.00
❑ M-3631 [M]	I'm All Smiles	1967	6.25	12.50	25.00
❑ S-7545 [S]	All Night Session! Volume 1	1960	10.00	20.00	40.00
❑ S-7546 [S]	All Night Session! Volume 2	1960	10.00	20.00	40.00
❑ S-7547 [S]	All Night Session! Volume 3	1960	10.00	20.00	40.00
❑ S-7553 [S]	Four! Hampton Hawes!!!	1960	10.00	20.00	40.00
❑ S-7589 [S]	For Real!	1959	7.50	15.00	30.00
❑ S-7614 [S]	The Green Leaves of Summer	1964	10.00	20.00	40.00
❑ S-7616 [S]	Here and Now	1965	6.25	12.50	25.00
❑ S-7621 [S]	The Seance	1966	6.25	12.50	25.00
❑ S-7631 [S]	I'm All Smiles	1967	5.00	10.00	20.00
PRESTIGE					
❑ PRLP-212 [10]	Hampton Hawes Quartet	1955	25.00	50.00	100.00
STEREO RECORDS					
❑ S-7026 [S]	Four! Hampton Hawes!!!	1959	12.50	25.00	50.00
VANTAGE					
❑ VLP-1 [10]	Hamp Hawes	1954	37.50	75.00	150.00
VAULT					
❑ LPS-9009	Hampton Hawes Plays Movie Musicals	1969	5.00	10.00	20.00
❑ LPS-9010	High in the Sky	1970	5.00	10.00	20.00

HAWKINS, COLEMAN

Number	Title (A Side/B Side)	Yr	VG	VG+	NM
ADVANCE					
❑ LSP-9 [10]	Coleman Hawkins Favorites	1951	75.00	150.00	300.00
AMERICAN RECORDING SOCIETY					
❑ G-316 [M]	Coleman Hawkins and His Orchestra	1956	12.50	25.00	50.00
APOLLO					
❑ LAP-101 [10]	Coleman Hawkins All Stars	1951	75.00	150.00	300.00
BRUNSWICK					
❑ BL 58030 [10]	Tenor Sax	1952	50.00	100.00	200.00

Number	Title (A Side/B Side)	Yr	VG	VG+	NM
CAPITOL					
❏ H 327 [10]	Classics in Jazz	1952	62.50	125.00	250.00
❏ T 819 [M]	Gilded Hawk	1957	20.00	40.00	80.00
COMMODORE					
❏ FL-20025 [10]	King of the Tenor Sax	1952	75.00	150.00	300.00
CONCERT HALL JAZZ					
❏ J-1201 [M]	Improvisations Unlimited	1955	15.00	30.00	60.00
CONTINENTAL					
❏ 16006 [M]	On the Bean	1962	6.25	12.50	25.00
❏ S-16006 [S]	On the Bean	1962	7.50	15.00	30.00
CROWN					
❏ CLP-5181 [M]	Coleman Hawkins and His Orchestra	1960	5.00	10.00	20.00
❏ CLP-5207 [M]	The Hawk Swing	1961	5.00	10.00	20.00
DECCA					
❏ DL 4081 [M]	The Hawk Blows at Midnight	1961	7.50	15.00	30.00
❏ DL 8127 [M]	The Hawk Talks	1955	20.00	40.00	80.00
❏ DL 74081 [S]	The Hawk Blows at Midnight	1961	10.00	20.00	40.00
EMARCY					
❏ MG-26013 [10]	The Bean	1954	50.00	100.00	200.00
FELSTED					
❏ SJA-2005 [S]	The High and Mighty Hawk	1959	20.00	40.00	80.00
❏ FAJ-7005 [M]	The High and Mighty Hawk	1959	15.00	30.00	60.00
IMPULSE!					
❏ A-26 [M]	Duke Ellington Meets Coleman Hawkins	1962	6.25	12.00	25.00
❏ AS-26 [S]	Duke Ellington Meets Coleman Hawkins	1962	7.50	15.00	30.00
❏ A-28 [M]	Desafinado	1963	6.25	12.50	25.00
❏ AS-28 [S]	Desafinado	1963	7.50	15.00	30.00
❏ A-34 [M]	Today and Now	1963	6.25	12.50	25.00
❏ AS-34 [S]	Today and Now	1963	7.50	15.00	30.00
❏ A-87 [M]	Wrapped Tight	1965	6.25	12.50	25.00
❏ AS-87 [S]	Wrapped Tight	1965	7.50	15.00	30.00
JAZZTONE					
❏ J-1201 [M]	Timeless Jazz	1955	12.50	25.00	50.00
—Reissue of Concert Hall Jazz 1201					
MAINSTREAM					
❏ 56037 [M]	Meditations	1965	6.25	12.50	25.00
MOODSVILLE					
❏ MVLP-7 [M]	At Ease with Coleman Hawkins	1960	12.50	25.00	50.00
—Green label					
❏ MVLP-7 [M]	At Ease with Coleman Hawkins	1965	6.25	12.50	25.00
—Blue label, trident logo at right					
❏ MVLP-15 [M]	The Hawk Relaxes	1961	12.50	25.00	50.00
—Green label					
❏ MVLP-15 [M]	The Hawk Relaxes	1965	6.25	12.50	25.00
—Blue label, trident logo at right					
❏ MVLP-23 [M]	Good Old Broadway	1962	10.00	20.00	40.00
—Gren label					
❏ MVLP-23 [M]	Good Old Broadway	1965	5.00	10.00	20.00
—Blue label, trident logo at right					
❏ MVST-23 [S]	Good Old Broadway	1962	12.50	25.00	50.00
—Green label					
❏ MVST-23 [S]	Good Old Broadway	1965	6.25	12.50	25.00
—Blue label, trident logo at right					
❏ MVLP-25 [M]	The Jazz Version of No Strings	1962	10.00	20.00	40.00
—Green label					
❏ MVLP-25 [M]	The Jazz Version of No Strings	1965	5.00	10.00	20.00
—Blue label, trident logo at right					
❏ MVST-25 [S]	The Jazz Version of No Strings	1962	12.50	25.00	50.00
—Green label					
❏ MVST-25 [S]	The Jazz Version of No Strings	1965	6.25	12.50	25.00
—Blue label, trident logo at right					
❏ MVLP-31 [M]	Make Someone Happy	1963	10.00	20.00	40.00
—Green label					
❏ MVLP-31 [M]	Make Someone Happy	1965	5.00	10.00	20.00
—Blue label, trident logo at right					
❏ MVST-31 [S]	Make Someone Happy	1963	12.50	25.00	50.00
—Green label					
❏ MVST-31 [S]	Make Someone Happy	1965	6.25	12.50	25.00
—Blue label, trident logo at right					
PHILIPS					
❏ PHM 200022 [M]	Jazz at the Metropole	1962	5.00	10.00	20.00
❏ PHS 600022 [S]	Jazz at the Metropole	1962	6.25	12.00	25.00
PRESTIGE					
❏ PRLP-7149 [M]	Soul	1958	20.00	40.00	80.00
❏ PRLP-7156 [M]	Hawk Eyes	1958	20.00	40.00	80.00
RCA VICTOR					
❏ LPV-501 [M]	Body and Soul	1965	5.00	10.00	20.00
❏ LJM-1017 [M]	Hawk In Flight	1955	20.00	40.00	80.00
❏ LPM-1281 [M]	Hawk in Hi-Fi	1956	20.00	40.00	80.00
RIVERSIDE					
❏ RLP 12-117/8 [(2)M]	Coleman Hawkins: A Documentary	1956	50.00	100.00	200.00
❏ RLP 12-233 [M]	The Hawk Flies High	1957	25.00	50.00	100.00
—White label, blue print					
❏ RLP 12-233 [M]	The Hawk Flies High	1959	12.50	25.00	50.00
—Blue label, microphone logo at top					
SAVOY					
❏ MG-12013 [M]	The Hawk Returns	1955	30.00	60.00	120.00
❏ MG-15039 [10]	The Hawk Talks	1954	50.00	100.00	200.00
STINSON					
❏ SLP-22 [10]	Originals with Hawkins	1950	75.00	150.00	300.00
❏ SLP-22 [S]	Originals with Hawkins	195?	10.00	20.00	40.00
SWINGVILLE					
❏ SVLP-2001 [M]	Coleman Hawkins Plus the Red Garland Trio	1960	12.50	25.00	50.00
—Purple label					
❏ SVLP-2001 [M]	Coleman Hawkins Plus the Red Garland Trio	1965	6.25	12.50	25.00
—Blue label, trident logo at right					
❏ SVLP-2005 [M]	The Coleman Hawkins All Stars	1960	12.50	25.00	50.00
—Purple label					

Number	Title (A Side/B Side)	Yr	VG	VG+	NM
❏ SVLP-2005 [M]	The Coleman Hawkins All Stars	1965	6.25	12.50	25.00
—Blue label, trident logo at right					
❏ SVLP-2016 [M]	Night Hawk	1961	12.50	25.00	50.00
—Purple label					
❏ SVLP-2016 [M]	Night Hawk	1965	6.25	12.50	25.00
—Blue label, trident logo at right					
❏ SVLP-2024 [M]	Things Ain't What They Used to Be	1961	10.00	20.00	40.00
—Purple label					
❏ SVLP-2024 [M]	Things Ain't What They Used to Be	1965	5.00	10.00	20.00
—Blue label, trident logo at right					
❏ SVST-2024 [S]	Things Ain't What They Used to Be	1961	12.50	25.00	50.00
—Red label					
❏ SVST-2024 [S]	Things Ain't What They Used to Be	1965	6.25	12.50	25.00
—Blue label, trident logo at right					
❏ SVLP-2025 [M]	Years Ago	1961	10.00	20.00	40.00
—Purple label					
❏ SVLP-2025 [M]	Years Ago	1965	5.00	10.00	20.00
—Blue label, trident logo at right					
❏ SVST-2025 [S]	Years Ago	1961	12.50	25.00	50.00
—Red label					
❏ SVST-2025 [S]	Years Ago	1965	6.25	12.50	25.00
—Blue label, trident logo at right					
❏ SVLP-2035 [M]	Blues Groove	1962	12.50	25.00	50.00
—Purple label					
❏ SVLP-2035 [M]	Blues Groove	1965	6.25	12.50	25.00
—Blue label, trident logo at right					
❏ SVST-2035 [S]	Blues Groove	1962	10.00	20.00	40.00
—Red label					
❏ SVST-2035 [S]	Blues Groove	1965	5.00	10.00	20.00
—Blue label, trident logo at right					
❏ SVLP-2038 [M]	Soul	1962	12.50	25.00	50.00
—Purple label					
❏ SVLP-2038 [M]	Soul	1965	6.25	12.50	25.00
—Blue label, trident logo at right					
❏ SVST-2038 [S]	Soul	1962	10.00	20.00	40.00
—Red label					
❏ SVST-2038 [S]	Soul	1965	5.00	10.00	20.00
—Blue label, trident logo at right					
❏ SVLP-2039 [M]	Hawk Eyes	1962	12.50	25.00	50.00
—Purple label					
❏ SVLP-2039 [M]	Hawk Eyes	1965	6.25	12.50	25.00
—Blue label, trident logo at right					
❏ SVST-2039 [S]	Hawk Eyes	1962	10.00	20.00	40.00
—Red label					
❏ SVST-2039 [S]	Hawk Eyes	1965	5.00	10.00	20.00
—Blue label, trident logo at right					
URANIA					
❏ UJLP-1201 [M]	Accent on Tenor Sax	1955	25.00	50.00	100.00
❏ UJLP-41201 [R]	Accent on Tenor Sax	196?	5.00	10.00	20.00
VERVE					
❏ MGVS-6033 [S]	The Genius of Coleman Hawkins	1960	10.00	20.00	40.00
❏ MGVS-6066 [S]	Coleman Hawkins Encounters Ben Webster	1960	10.00	20.00	40.00
❏ MGVS-6066 [S]	Coleman Hawkins Encounters Ben Webster	199?	6.25	12.50	25.00
—Classic Records reissue on audiophile vinyl					
❏ MGVS-6110 [S]	Coleman Hawkins and His Confreres with the Oscar Peterson Trio	1960	10.00	20.00	40.00
❏ MGV-8261 [M]	The Genius of Coleman Hawkins	1958	12.50	25.00	50.00
❏ V-8261 [M]	The Genius of Coleman Hawkins	1961	6.25	12.50	25.00
❏ V6-8261 [S]	The Genius of Coleman Hawkins	1961	5.00	10.00	20.00
❏ MGV-8327 [M]	Coleman Hawkins Encounters Ben Webster	1959	12.50	25.00	50.00
❏ V-8327 [M]	Coleman Hawkins Encounters Ben Webster	1961	6.25	12.50	25.00
❏ V6-8327 [S]	Coleman Hawkins Encounters Ben Webster	1961	5.00	10.00	20.00
❏ MGV-8346 [M]	Coleman Hawkins and His Confreres with the Oscar Peterson Trio	1959	12.50	25.00	50.00
❏ V-8346 [M]	Coleman Hawkins and His Confreres with the Oscar Peterson Trio	1961	6.25	12.50	25.00
❏ V6-8346 [S]	Coleman Hawkins and His Confreres with the Oscar Peterson Trio	1961	5.00	10.00	20.00
❏ V-8509 [M]	Hawkins! Alive! At the Village Gate	1963	6.25	12.50	25.00
❏ V6-8509 [S]	Hawkins! Alive! At the Village Gate	1963	7.50	15.00	30.00
❏ V-8568 [M]	The Essential Coleman Hawkins	1964	5.00	10.00	20.00
❏ V6-8568 [S]	The Essential Coleman Hawkins	1964	6.25	12.50	25.00
VIK					
❏ LX-1059 [M]	The Hawk in Paris	1957	20.00	40.00	80.00
WORLD WIDE					
❏ MGS-20001 [S]	Coleman Hawkins with the Basie Saxophone Section	1958	12.50	25.00	50.00

HAWKINS, COLEMAN/GEORGIE AULD

GRAND AWARD

Number	Title (A Side/B Side)	Yr	VG	VG+	NM
❏ GA 33-316 [M]	Jazz Concert	1955	12.50	25.00	50.00
—Without wrap-around cover					
❏ GA 33-316 [M]	Jazz Concert	1955	25.00	50.00	100.00
—With wrap-around cover intact					

HAWKINS, COLEMAN, AND ROY ELDREDGE

VERVE

Number	Title (A Side/B Side)	Yr	VG	VG+	NM
❏ MGVS-6028 [S]	At the Opera House	1960	10.00	20.00	40.00
❏ MGV-8266 [M]	At the Opera House	1958	12.50	25.00	50.00
❏ V-8266 [M]	At the Opera House	1961	6.25	12.50	25.00
❏ V6-8266 [S]	At the Opera House	1961	5.00	10.00	20.00

HAWKINS, COLEMAN; ROY ELDREDGE; PETE BROWN; JO JONES

VERVE

Number	Title (A Side/B Side)	Yr	VG	VG+	NM
❏ MGV-8240 [M]	All Stars at Newport	1958	12.50	25.00	50.00
❏ V-8240 [M]	All Stars at Newport	1961	5.00	10.00	20.00

HAWKINS, COLEMAN; ROY ELDREDGE; JOHNNY HODGES

VERVE

Number	Title (A Side/B Side)	Yr	VG	VG+	NM
❏ V-8509 [M]	Alive at the Village Gate	1963	5.00	10.00	20.00
❏ V6-8509 [S]	Alive at the Village Gate	1963	6.25	12.50	25.00
❏ V6-8509 [S]	Alive at the Village Gate	199?	6.25	12.50	25.00
—Classic Records reissue on audiophile vinyl					

Number	Title (A Side/B Side)	Yr	VG	VG+	NM

HAWKINS, COLEMAN, AND FRANK HUNTER
MIRA
| ❏ M-3003 [M] | The Hawk and the Hunter | 1965 | 5.00 | 10.00 | 20.00 |
| ❏ MS-3003 [S] | The Hawk and the Hunter | 1965 | 6.25 | 12.50 | 25.00 |

HAWKINS, COLEMAN, AND PEE WEE RUSSELL
CANDID
| ❏ CD-8020 [M] | Jazz Reunion | 1960 | 10.00 | 20.00 | 40.00 |
| ❏ CS-9020 [S] | Jazz Reunion | 1960 | 10.00 | 20.00 | 40.00 |

HAWKINS, COLEMAN, AND CLARK TERRY
COLUMBIA
❏ CS 8791 [S]	Back in Bean's Bag	1963	5.00	10.00	20.00
❏ CS 8791 [S]	Back in Bean's Bag	1999	6.25	12.50	25.00
—Classic Records reissue on audiophile vinyl					

HAWKINS, COLEMAN/BEN WEBSTER
BRUNSWICK
| ❏ BL 54016 [M] | The Big Sounds of Coleman Hawkins and Ben Webster | 1956 | 20.00 | 40.00 | 80.00 |

HAWKINS, DALE
BELL
| ❏ 6036 | L.A., Memphis and Tyler, Texas | 1969 | 10.00 | 20.00 | 40.00 |
CHESS
| ❏ ACRR-706 | Dale Hawkins | 1976 | 3.75 | 7.50 | 15.00 |
| ❏ LP-1429 [M] | Oh! Susie-Q | 1958 | 500.00 | 1000. | 1500. |
ROULETTE
| ❏ R 25175 [M] | Let's All Twist at the Miami Beach Peppermint Lounge | 1962 | 50.00 | 100.00 | 200.00 |
| ❏ SR 25175 [S] | Let's All Twist at the Miami Beach Peppermint Lounge | 1962 | 75.00 | 150.00 | 300.00 |

HAWKINS, DOLORES
EPIC
| ❏ LN 1119 [M] | Meet Dolores Hawkins | 1955 | 10.00 | 20.00 | 40.00 |
| ❏ LN 3250 [M] | Dolores | 1957 | 10.00 | 20.00 | 40.00 |

HAWKINS, ERSKINE
CORAL
| ❏ CRL 56051 [10] | After Hours | 1954 | 30.00 | 60.00 | 120.00 |
DECCA
| ❏ DL 4081 [M] | The Hawk Blows at Midnight | 1960 | 7.50 | 15.00 | 30.00 |
| ❏ DL 74081 [S] | The Hawk Blows at Midnight | 1960 | 10.00 | 20.00 | 40.00 |
IMPERIAL
❏ LP-9191 [M]	25 Golden Years of Jazz, Volume 1	1962	6.25	12.50	25.00
❏ LP-9197 [M]	25 Golden Years of Jazz, Volume 2	1962	6.25	12.50	25.00
❏ LP-12191 [S]	25 Golden Years of Jazz, Volume 1	1962	7.50	15.00	30.00
❏ LP-12197 [S]	25 Golden Years of Jazz, Volume 2	1962	7.50	15.00	30.00
RCA VICTOR
❏ LPM-2227 [M]	After Hours	1960	10.00	20.00	40.00

HAWKINS, HAWKSHAW
GLADWYNNE
| ❏ G-2006 [M] | Country Western Cavalcade with Hawkshaw Hawkins | 195? | 30.00 | 60.00 | 120.00 |
HARMONY
| ❏ HL 7301 [M] | The Great Hawkshaw Hawkins | 1963 | 5.00 | 10.00 | 20.00 |
| ❏ HS 11044 [R] | The Great Hawkshaw Hawkins | 1963 | 3.75 | 7.50 | 15.00 |
KING
❏ 587 [M]	Hawkshaw Hawkins	1958	25.00	50.00	100.00
❏ 592 [M]	Grand Ole Opry Favorites	1958	25.00	50.00	100.00
❏ 599 [M]	Hawkshaw Hawkins	1959	25.00	50.00	100.00
❏ 808 [M]	The All New Hawkshaw Hawkins	1963	20.00	40.00	80.00
❏ KS-808 [S]	The All New Hawkshaw Hawkins	1963	25.00	50.00	100.00
❏ 858 [M]	Taken From Our Vaults, Volume 1	1963	10.00	20.00	40.00
❏ 870 [M]	Taken From Our Vaults, Volume 2	1963	10.00	20.00	40.00
❏ 873 [M]	Taken From Our Vaults, Volume 3	1964	10.00	20.00	40.00
LABREA
❏ 8020 [M]	Hawkshaw Hawkins	195?	25.00	50.00	100.00
RCA CAMDEN
❏ CAL-808 [M]	Hawkshaw Hawkins Sings	1964	5.00	10.00	20.00
❏ CAS-808 [R]	Hawkshaw Hawkins Sings	1964	3.75	7.50	15.00
❏ CAL-931 [M]	The Country Gentleman	1966	5.00	10.00	20.00
❏ CAS-931 [R]	The Country Gentleman	1966	3.75	7.50	15.00

HAWKINS, JENNELL
AMAZON
| ❏ 1001 [M] | The Many Moods of Jenny | 1961 | 37.50 | 75.00 | 150.00 |
| ❏ 1002 [M] | Moments to Remember | 1962 | 37.50 | 75.00 | 150.00 |

HAWKINS, RONNIE
ACCORD
| ❏ SN-7213 | Premonition | 1983 | 2.50 | 5.00 | 10.00 |
COTILLION
| ❏ SD 9019 | Ronnie Hawkins | 1970 | 3.75 | 7.50 | 15.00 |
| ❏ SD 9039 | The Hawk | 1971 | 3.75 | 7.50 | 15.00 |
MONUMENT
❏ KZ 31330	Rock and Roll Resurrection	1972	3.00	6.00	12.00
❏ KZ 32940	The Giant of Rock 'n' Roll	1974	3.00	6.00	12.00
❏ ZG 33855 [(2)]	Rock and Roll Resurrection/The Ghost of Rock and Roll	1976	3.75	7.50	15.00
ROULETTE
❏ R 25078 [M]	Ronnie Hawkins	1959	37.50	75.00	150.00
—White label with spokes					
❏ R 25078 [M]	Ronnie Hawkins	1964	12.50	25.00	50.00
—Orange/yellow label					
❏ SR 25078 [S]	Ronnie Hawkins	1959	50.00	100.00	200.00
—White label with spokes; black vinyl					
❏ SR 25078 [S]	Ronnie Hawkins	1959	150.00	300.00	600.00
—White label with spokes; red vinyl					

❏ SR 25078 [S]	Ronnie Hawkins	1964	15.00	30.00	60.00
—Orange/yellow label					
❏ R 25102 [M]	Mr. Dynamo	1960	37.50	75.00	150.00
❏ SR 25102 [S]	Mr. Dynamo	1960	50.00	100.00	200.00
—Black vinyl					
❏ SR 25102 [S]	Mr. Dynamo	1960	150.00	300.00	600.00
—Red vinyl					
❏ R 25120 [M]	The Folk Ballads of Ronnie Hawkins	1960	25.00	50.00	100.00
❏ SR 25120 [S]	The Folk Ballads of Ronnie Hawkins	1960	37.50	75.00	150.00
❏ R 25137 [M]	Ronnie Hawkins Sings the Songs of Hank Williams	1960	25.00	50.00	100.00
❏ SR 25137 [S]	Ronnie Hawkins Sings the Songs of Hank Williams	1960	37.50	75.00	150.00
❏ SR 42045	The Best of Ronnie Hawkins and His Band	1970	6.25	12.50	25.00
UNITED ARTISTS
❏ UA-LA968-H	The Hawk	1979	2.50	5.00	10.00

HAWKINS, SCREAMIN' JAY
EPIC
❏ LN 3448 [M]	At Home with Screamin' Jay Hawkins	1958	300.00	600.00	1200.
❏ LN 3457 [M]	I Put a Spell on You	1958	125.00	250.00	500.00
❏ BN 26457 [R]	I Put a Spell on You	1969	15.00	30.00	60.00
PHILIPS
❏ PHS 600319	What That Is	1969	10.00	20.00	40.00
❏ PHS 600336	Screamin' Jay Hawkins	1970	10.00	20.00	40.00
SOUNDS OF HAWAII
❏ 5015	A Night at Forbidden City	196?	12.50	25.00	50.00

HAWKS, BILLY
PRESTIGE
❏ PRLP-7501 [M]	New Genius of the Blues	1967	6.25	12.50	25.00
❏ PRST-7501 [S]	New Genius of the Blues	1967	5.00	10.00	20.00
❏ PRST-7556	More Heavy Soul	1968	5.00	10.00	20.00

HAWKWIND
ATCO
| ❏ SD 36-115 | Warrior on the Edge of Time | 1975 | 3.75 | 7.50 | 15.00 |
GWR
| ❏ 1237 [(2)] | Live Chronicles | 1986 | 3.00 | 6.00 | 12.00 |
LIBERTY
❏ LWB-120 [(2)]	Space Ritual/Alive in Liverpool and London	1981	3.00	6.00	12.00
—Reissue of United Artists 120					
❏ LW-5567	In Search of Space	1981	2.00	4.00	8.00
—Reissue of United Artists 5567					
SIRE
❏ SRK 6047	Quark Strangeness and Charm	1978	3.00	6.00	12.00
UNITED ARTISTS
❏ UA-LA001-F	Doremi Fasol Latido	1973	3.75	7.50	15.00
❏ UA-LA120-H [(2)]	Space Ritual/Alive in Liverpool and London	1973	5.00	10.00	20.00
❏ UA-LA328-G	Hall of the Mountain Grill	1974	3.75	7.50	15.00
❏ UAS-5519	Hawkwind	1971	3.75	7.50	15.00
❏ UAS-5567	In Search of Space	1972	3.75	7.50	15.00

HAWN, GOLDIE
REPRISE
| ❏ MS 2061 | Goldie | 1972 | 6.25 | 12.50 | 25.00 |

HAYDEN, WILLIE
DOOTO
❏ DTL-293 [M]	Blame It on the Blues	196?	50.00	100.00	200.00
—Multi-color label					
❏ DTL-293 [M]	Blame It on the Blues	1960	125.00	250.00	500.00
—Maroon label					

HAYES, BILL
ABC-PARAMOUNT
| ❏ 194 [M] | Bill Hayes Sings the Best of Disney | 1957 | 10.00 | 20.00 | 40.00 |
DAYBREAK
| ❏ DR-2020 | The Look of Love | 1972 | 6.25 | 12.50 | 25.00 |
KAPP
| ❏ KL-1106 [M] | Jimmy Crack Corn | 1958 | 6.25 | 12.50 | 25.00 |

HAYES, CLANCY
DELMARK
| ❏ DE-210 [M] | Oh By Jingo | 1965 | 5.00 | 10.00 | 20.00 |
| ❏ DS-9210 [S] | Oh By Jingo | 1965 | 6.25 | 12.50 | 25.00 |
DOWN HOME
| ❏ MGD-3 [M] | Clancy Hayes Sings | 1956 | 15.00 | 30.00 | 60.00 |
GOOD TIME JAZZ
| ❏ S-10050 [S] | Swingin' Minstrel | 1963 | 6.25 | 12.50 | 25.00 |
| ❏ L-12050 [M] | Swingin' Minstrel | 1963 | 5.00 | 10.00 | 20.00 |
VERVE
| ❏ MGV-1003 [M] | Clancy Hayes Sings | 1957 | 10.00 | 20.00 | 40.00 |

HAYES, ISAAC
ABC/HBS
❏ D-874	Chocolate Chip	1975	3.75	7.50	15.00
❏ D-923	Disco Connection	1975	3.00	6.00	12.00
❏ D-925	Groove-a-Thon	1976	3.00	6.00	12.00
❏ D-953	Juicy Fruit (Disco Freak)	1976	3.00	6.00	12.00
ATLANTIC
❏ SD 1599	In the Beginning	1972	3.75	7.50	15.00
—Reissue of Enterprise 100					
COLUMBIA
❏ FC 40316	U-Turn	1986	2.50	5.00	10.00
❏ FC 40941	Love Attack	1988	2.50	5.00	10.00
ENTERPRISE
❏ E-100 [M]	Presenting Isaac Hayes	1968	10.00	20.00	40.00
❏ ES-100 [S]	Presenting Isaac Hayes	1968	7.50	15.00	30.00
❏ ENS-1001	Hot Buttered Soul	1969	5.00	10.00	20.00

Number	Title (A Side/B Side)	Yr	VG	VG+	NM
❑ ENS-1010	The Isaac Hayes Movement	1970	5.00	10.00	20.00
❑ ENS-1014	To Be Continued	1970	5.00	10.00	20.00
❑ ENS-5002 [(2)]	Shaft	1971	5.00	10.00	20.00
❑ ENS-5003 [(2)]	Black Moses	1971	5.00	10.00	20.00
❑ ENS-5005 [(2)]	Live at the Sahara Tahoe	1973	3.75	7.50	15.00
❑ ENS-5007	Joy	1973		6.00	12.00
❑ ENS-7504	Tough Guys	1974	3.00	6.00	12.00
❑ ENS-7507 [(2)]	Truck Turner	1974	3.75	7.50	15.00
❑ ENS-7510	The Best of Isaac Hayes	1975	3.00	6.00	12.00
POINTBLANK					
❑ SPRO-12787 [DJ]	Funky Junky	1995	3.75	7.50	15.00
—Vinyl is promo only					
POLYDOR					
❑ PD-1-6120	New Horizon	1977	2.50	5.00	10.00
❑ PD-1-6164	For the Sake of Love	1978	2.50	5.00	10.00
❑ PD-1-6224	Don't Let Go	1979	2.50	5.00	10.00
❑ PD-1-6269	And Once Again	1980	2.50	5.00	10.00
STAX					
❑ STX-4102	Hotbed	197?	2.50	5.00	10.00
❑ STX-4114	Hot Buttered Soul	1978	2.50	5.00	10.00
—Reissue of Enterprise 1001					
❑ STX-4129	The Isaac Hayes Movement	197?	2.50	5.00	10.00
—Reissue of Enterprise 1010					
❑ STX-4133	To Be Continued	197?	2.50	5.00	10.00
—Reissue of Enterprise 1014					
❑ MPS-8509	Excerpts from Black Moses	1981	2.50	5.00	10.00
❑ MPS-8515	His Greatest Hit Singles	1982	2.50	5.00	10.00
❑ MPS-8530	Joy	1984	2.50	5.00	10.00
—Reissue of Enterprise 5007					
❑ STX-88002 [(2)]	Shaft	1979	3.00	6.00	12.00
—Reissue of Enterprise 5002					
❑ STX-88003 [(2)]	Enterprise: His Greatest Hits	1980	3.00	6.00	12.00
❑ STX-88004 [(2)]	Live at the Sahara Tahoe	198?	3.00	6.00	12.00
—Reissue of Enterprise 5005					

HAYES, LOUIS
VEE JAY

Number	Title (A Side/B Side)	Yr	VG	VG+	NM
❑ LP-3010 [M]	Louis Hayes	1960	10.00	20.00	40.00
❑ SR-3010 [S]	Louis Hayes	1960	12.50	25.00	50.00

HAYES, MARTHA
JUBILEE

❑ JLP-1023 [M]	A Hayes Named Martha	1956	12.50	25.00	50.00

HAYES, ROLAND
VANGUARD

❑ VRS-462 [M]	The Life of Christ in Folk Song	1954	7.50	15.00	30.00
❑ VRS-494 [M]	My Songs, Aframerican Religious Folk Songs	1955	7.50	15.00	30.00
❑ VRS-7016 [10]	Christmas Carols of the Nations	195?	12.50	25.00	50.00

HAYES, TUBBY
EPIC

❑ LA 16019 [M]	Introducing Tubby	1961	10.00	20.00	40.00
❑ LA 16023 [M]	Tubby the Tenor	1962	10.00	20.00	40.00
❑ BA 17019 [S]	Introducing Tubby	1961	12.50	25.00	50.00
❑ BA 17023 [S]	Tubby the Tenor	1962	12.50	25.00	50.00
❑ BA 17023 [S]	Tubby the Tenor	199?	6.25	12.50	25.00
—Classic Records reissue on audiophile vinyl					

IMPERIAL

❑ LP-9046 [M]	Little Giant of Jazz	1957	20.00	40.00	80.00

SMASH

❑ MGS-27026 [M]	Tubby's Back in Town	1963	10.00	20.00	40.00
❑ SRS-67026 [S]	Tubby's Back in Town	1963	12.50	25.00	50.00

HAYMARKET SQUARE
CHAPARRAL

❑ 201	Magic Lantern	1968	375.00	750.00	1500.

HAYMES, DICK
CAPITOL

❑ T 713 [M]	Rain or Shine	1956	7.50	15.00	30.00
❑ T 787 [M]	Moondreams	1956	7.50	15.00	30.00

DECCA

❑ DL 5012 [10]	Souvenir Album	1949	12.50	25.00	50.00
❑ DL 5022 [10]	Christmas Songs	1949	12.50	25.00	50.00
❑ DL 5023 [10]	Dick Haymes Sings Irving Berlin	1949	12.50	25.00	50.00
❑ DL 5038 [10]	Little Shamrocks	1950	12.50	25.00	50.00
❑ DL 5243 [10]	Dick Haymes Sings with Helen Forrest, Volume 1	195?	12.50	25.00	50.00
❑ DL 8773 [M]	Little White Lies	1959	10.00	20.00	40.00

WARWICK

❑ W-2023 [M]	Richard the Lion-Hearted	1960	7.50	15.00	30.00

HAYNES, ROY
EMARCY

❑ MG-26048 [10]	Bushman's Holiday	1954	37.50	75.00	150.00

IMPULSE!

❑ A-23 [M]	Out of the Afternoon	1962	7.50	15.00	30.00
❑ AS-23 [S]	Out of the Afternoon	1962	10.00	20.00	40.00

MAINSTREAM

❑ MRL-313	Hip Ensemble	1971	5.00	10.00	20.00
❑ MRL-351	Senyah	1972	5.00	10.00	20.00

NEW JAZZ

❑ NJLP-8245 [M]	Just Us	1960	20.00	40.00	80.00
—Purple label					
❑ NJLP-8245 [M]	Just Us	1965	6.25	12.50	25.00
—Blue label, trident logo at right					
❑ NJLP-8286 [M]	Cracklin'	1962	20.00	40.00	80.00
—Purple label					
❑ NJLP-8286 [M]	Cracklin'	1965	6.25	12.50	25.00
—Blue label, trident logo at right					

Number	Title (A Side/B Side)	Yr	VG	VG+	NM
❑ NJLP-8287 [M]	Cymbalism	1962	20.00	40.00	80.00
—Purple label					
❑ NJLP-8287 [M]	Cymbalism	1965	6.25	12.50	25.00
—Blue label, trident logo at right					
PACIFIC JAZZ					
❑ PJ-82 [M]	People	1964	7.50	15.00	30.00
❑ ST-82 [S]	People	1964	10.00	20.00	40.00

HAYNES, ROY/QUINCY JONES
EMARCY

❑ MG-36083 [M]	Jazz Abroad	1956	20.00	40.00	80.00

HAYNES, ROY; PHINEAS NEWBORN; PAUL CHAMBERS
NEW JAZZ

❑ NJLP-8210 [M]	We Three	1958	25.00	50.00	100.00

HAYWARD, JUSTIN, AND JOHN LODGE
Also see THE MOODY BLUES.
THRESHOLD

❑ THS 14	Blue Jays	1975	3.75	7.50	15.00
❑ THSX 101 [DJ]	Blue Jays	1975	12.50	25.00	50.00
—Open-end interview with script; used to promote the LP of the same name					

HAYWOOD, LEON
COLUMBIA

❑ PC 34363	Intimate	1976	2.50	5.00	10.00

DECCA

❑ DL 74949	It's Got to Be Mellow	1969	5.00	10.00	20.00

FAT FISH

❑ LP 2525	Soul Cargo	1966	15.00	30.00	60.00

GALAXY

❑ 8206	Mellow, Mellow	196?	5.00	10.00	20.00

MCA

❑ 2322	Double My Pleasure	1978	2.50	5.00	10.00
❑ 3090	Energy	1979	2.50	5.00	10.00

20TH CENTURY

❑ T-411	Back to Stay	1973	3.00	6.00	12.00
❑ T-440	Keep It in the Family	1974	3.00	6.00	12.00
❑ T-476	Come and Get Yourself Some	1975	2.50	5.00	10.00
❑ T-613	Naturally	1980	2.50	5.00	10.00

HAZEL, EDDIE
Member of PARLIAMENT/FUNKADELIC.
WARNER BROS.

❑ BSK 3058	Games, Dames and Guitar Thangs	1977	10.00	20.00	40.00

HAZEL, MONK
SOUTHLAND

❑ SLP-217 [M]	Monk Hazel	1956	10.00	20.00	40.00

HAZLEWOOD, LEE
MERCURY

❑ MG-20860 [M]	Trouble Is a Lonesome Town	1964	5.00	10.00	20.00
❑ SR-60860 [S]	Trouble Is a Lonesome Town	1964	6.25	12.50	25.00

MGM

❑ E-4362 [M]	The World of Lee Hazlewood	1966	3.75	7.50	15.00
❑ SE-4362 [S]	The World of Lee Hazlewood	1966	5.00	10.00	20.00
❑ E-4403 [M]	Lee Hazlewoodism - Its Cause and Cure	1966	3.75	7.50	15.00
❑ SE-4403 [S]	Lee Hazlewoodism - Its Cause and Cure	1966	5.00	10.00	20.00

HEAD
BUDDAH

❑ BDS-5062	Head	1970	7.50	15.00	30.00
—With coloring book (deduct 1/3 if missing)					

HEAD, JIM, AND HIS DEL RAYS
HP

❑ 22893 [M]	Jim Head and His Del Rays	1963	75.00	150.00	300.00

HEAD, ROY
ABC

❑ AB-1054	Tonight's the Night	1978	2.50	5.00	10.00

ABC DOT

❑ DO-2051	Head First	1976	3.00	6.00	12.00
❑ DO-2066	A Head of His Time	1977	3.00	6.00	12.00

ABC DUNHILL

❑ DS-50080	Same People	1970	5.00	10.00	20.00

ELEKTRA

❑ 6E-234	In Our Room	1979	2.50	5.00	10.00
❑ 6E-298	The Many Sides of Roy Head	1980	2.50	5.00	10.00

MCA

❑ 796	Tonight's the Night	1980	2.00	4.00	8.00
—Reissue of ABC album					

SCEPTER

❑ S-532 [M]	Treat Me Right	1965	7.50	15.00	30.00
❑ SS-532 [S]	Treat Me Right	1965	10.00	20.00	40.00

TMI

❑ 1000	Dismal Prisoner	1972	3.75	7.50	15.00

TNT

❑ 101 [M]	Roy Head and the Traits	1965	37.50	75.00	150.00
—Counterfeit alert: Authentics do NOT contain the hit "Treat Her Right."					

HEAD OVER HEELS
CAPITOL

❑ ST-797	Head Over Heels	1971	7.50	15.00	30.00

HEAD SHOP, THE
EPIC

❑ BN 26476	The Head Shop	1969	15.00	30.00	60.00

Number	Title (A Side/B Side)	Yr	VG	VG+	NM
HEADS, THE					
LIBERTY					
❑ LST-7581	Heads Up	1968	6.25	12.50	25.00
HEADS, HANDS AND FEET					
ATCO					
❑ SD 7025	Old Soldiers Never Die	1973	5.00	10.00	20.00
CAPITOL					
❑ SVBB-680 [(2)]	Heads, Hands and Feet	1971	6.25	12.50	25.00
❑ ST-11051	Tracks	1972	5.00	10.00	20.00
HEADSTONE					
STARR					
❑ (# unknown)	Still Looking	1974	37.50	75.00	150.00
HEALY, PAT					
WORLD PACIFIC					
❑ WP-409 [M]	Just Before Dawn	1958	20.00	40.00	80.00
HEARD, J.C.					
ARGO					
❑ LP-633 [M]	This Is Me, J.C.	1958	10.00	20.00	40.00
❑ LPS-633 [S]	This Is Me, J.C.	1959	7.50	15.00	30.00
HEART					
CAPITOL					
❑ ST-12410	Heart	1985	2.50	5.00	10.00
—With remix of "Never." Side one trail-off wax has an "RE-1"					
❑ ST-12410	Heart	1985	3.75	7.50	15.00
—With original mix of "Never"					
❑ SQ-12500	Dreamboat Annie	1986	2.00	4.00	8.00
❑ SQ-12501	Magazine	1986	2.00	4.00	8.00
❑ PJ-12546	Bad Animals	1987	2.50	5.00	10.00
❑ C1-91820	Brigade	1990	3.00	6.00	12.00
❑ ST-512410	Heart	1985	3.75	7.50	15.00
—Columbia House edition; has original mix of "Never"					
EPIC					
❑ AS 884 [DJ]	Heart	1980	5.00	10.00	20.00
—Promo-only sampler from "Greatest Hits/Live"					
❑ FE 36371	Bebe Le Strange	1980	2.50	5.00	10.00
❑ KE2 36888 [(2)]	Greatest Hits/Live	1980	3.00	6.00	12.00
❑ FE 38049	Private Audition	1982	2.50	5.00	10.00
❑ PE 38049	Private Audition	1985	2.00	4.00	8.00
❑ PE 38800	Passionworks	1985	2.00	4.00	8.00
❑ QE 38800	Passionworks	1983	2.50	5.00	10.00
MUSHROOM					
❑ MRS-1-SP [PD]	Magazine	1978	5.00	10.00	20.00
❑ MRS-2-SP [PD]	Dreamboat Annie	1978	6.25	12.50	25.00
❑ MRS-5005	Dreamboat Annie	1976	2.50	5.00	10.00
❑ MRS-5008	Magazine	1977	15.00	30.00	60.00
—Side 2, Track 3 is "Blues Medley (Mother Earth) (You Shook Me Babe)." Also, at the bottom of the back cover is a lengthy statement beginning "Mushroom Records regrets that a contractural dispute..."					
❑ MRS-5008	Magazine	1978	2.50	5.00	10.00
—Side 2, Track 3 is "Mother Earth Blues."					
NAUTILUS					
❑ NR-3	Dreamboat Annie	1980	10.00	20.00	40.00
—Audiophile pressing					
PORTRAIT					
❑ JR 34799	Little Queen	1977	2.50	5.00	10.00
❑ PR 34799	Little Queen	1984	2.00	4.00	8.00
❑ FR 35555	Dog and Butterfly	1978	2.50	5.00	10.00
❑ PR 35555	Dog and Butterfly	1981	2.00	4.00	8.00
❑ HR 44799	Little Queen	1981	12.50	25.00	50.00
—Half-speed mastered edition					
HEARTBEATS, THE					
EMUS					
❑ ES-12033	A Thousand Miles Away	1979	6.25	12.50	25.00
ROULETTE					
❑ R 25107 [M]	A Thousand Miles Away	1960	100.00	200.00	400.00
HEARTS, THE					
ZELLA					
❑ 337 [M]	I Feel Good	1963	100.00	200.00	400.00
HEARTS AND FLOWERS					
CAPITOL					
❑ ST 2762 [S]	Now Is the Time for Hearts and Flowers	1967	10.00	20.00	40.00
❑ T 2762 [M]	Now Is the Time for Hearts and Flowers	1967	10.00	20.00	40.00
❑ ST 2868	Of Horses, Kids and Forgotten Women	1968	12.50	25.00	50.00
HEARTS OF STONE					
V.I.P.					
❑ VIPS-404	Stop the World... We Wanna Get On	1970	10.00	20.00	40.00
HEATH, ALBERT					
MUSE					
❑ MR-5031	Kwanza (The First)	1974	5.00	10.00	20.00
O'BE					
❑ LP-301	Kawaida	1969	10.00	20.00	40.00
TRIP					
❑ 5032	Kawaida	1974	6.25	12.50	25.00
—As "Kuumba Toudie Heath"					
HEATH, JIMMY					
RIVERSIDE					
❑ RLP 12-314 [M]	The Thumper	1960	10.00	20.00	40.00
❑ RLP 12-333 [M]	Really Big	1960	7.50	15.00	30.00
❑ RLP-372 [M]	The Quota	1961	7.50	15.00	30.00
❑ RLP-400 [M]	Triple Threat	1962	7.50	15.00	30.00
❑ RLP-465 [M]	Swamp Soul	1963	7.50	15.00	30.00
❑ RLP-486 [M]	On the Trail	1965	5.00	10.00	20.00

Number	Title (A Side/B Side)	Yr	VG	VG+	NM
❑ RLP-1160 [S]	The Thumper	1960	10.00	20.00	40.00
❑ RLP-1188 [S]	Really Big	1960	10.00	20.00	40.00
❑ RS-9372 [S]	The Quota	1961	10.00	20.00	40.00
❑ RS-9400 [S]	Triple Threat	1962	10.00	20.00	40.00
❑ RS-9465 [S]	Swamp Soul	1963	10.00	20.00	40.00
❑ RS-9486 [S]	On the Trail	1965	6.25	12.50	25.00
HEATH, TED					
LONDON					
❑ PS 116 [S]	Hits I Missed	1958	6.25	12.50	25.00
❑ PS 117 [S]	All Time Top Twelve	1958	6.25	12.50	25.00
❑ PS 138 [S]	Swing Session	1958	6.25	12.50	25.00
—New stereo recordings of the same material as appears on LL 802					
❑ PS 140 [S]	Ted Heath Swings in High Stereo	1958	6.25	12.50	25.00
❑ PS 148 [S]	Shall We Dance	1959	6.25	12.50	25.00
❑ PS 159 [S]	Great Film Hits	1959	6.25	12.50	25.00
❑ PS 171 [S]	Pop Hits from the Classics	1959	6.25	12.50	25.00
❑ PS 172 [S]	Big Band Blues	1959	6.25	12.50	25.00
❑ PS 174 [S]	My Very Good Friends The Bandleaders	1959	6.25	12.50	25.00
❑ PS 175 [S]	The Hits of the Twenties	1960	5.00	10.00	20.00
❑ PS 184 [S]	The Big Band Dixie Sound	1960	5.00	10.00	20.00
❑ PS 187 [S]	Ted Heath in Concert	1960	5.00	10.00	20.00
❑ PS 190 [S]	Songs for the Young at Heart	1960	5.00	10.00	20.00
❑ PS 216 [S]	The Hits of the Thirties	1961	5.00	10.00	20.00
❑ PS 219 [S]	Latin Swingers	1961	5.00	10.00	20.00
❑ LPB-340 [10]	Tempo for Dancing	195?	10.00	20.00	40.00
❑ LPB-374 [10]	Ted Heath and His Orchestra	195?	10.00	20.00	40.00
❑ LB-511 [10]	Listen to My Music	195?	10.00	20.00	40.00
❑ LB-732 [10]	Black and White Magic	195?	10.00	20.00	40.00
❑ LL 750 [M]	Ted Heath Strikes Up the Band	1953	5.00	10.00	20.00
❑ LL 802 [M]	Ted Heath at the London Palladium	1953	5.00	10.00	20.00
❑ LL 978 [M]	Ted Heath Plays the Music of Fats Waller	1954	5.00	10.00	20.00
❑ LL 1000 [M]	The 100th London Palladium Concert	1955	5.00	10.00	20.00
❑ LL 1211 [M]	Jazz Concert at the London Palladium, Vol. 3	1955	5.00	10.00	20.00
❑ LL 1217 [M]	Gershwin for Moderns	1956	5.00	10.00	20.00
❑ LL 1279 [M]	Kern for Moderns	1956	5.00	10.00	20.00
❑ LL 1379 [M]	Jazz Concert at the London Palladium, Vol. 4	1956	5.00	10.00	20.00
❑ AS 1475 [M]	Ted Heath Swings in Hi-Fi	1956	5.00	10.00	20.00
❑ LL 1500 [M]	Rodgers for Moderns	1956	5.00	10.00	20.00
❑ LL 1564 [M]	Ted Heath's First American Tour	1956	5.00	10.00	20.00
❑ LL 1566 [M]	Ted Heath at Carnegie Hall	1956	5.00	10.00	20.00
❑ LL 1676 [M]	A Yank in Europe	1956	5.00	10.00	20.00
❑ LL 1716 [M]	All Time Top Twelve	1957	5.00	10.00	20.00
❑ LL 1721 [M]	Spotlight on Sidemen	1957	5.00	10.00	20.00
❑ LL 1737 [M]	Showcase	1957	5.00	10.00	20.00
❑ LL 1743 [M]	Tribute to the Fabulous Dorseys	1957	5.00	10.00	20.00
❑ LL 1749 [M]	Rhapsody in Blue	1957	5.00	10.00	20.00
❑ LL 3047 [M]	Things to Come	1958	5.00	10.00	20.00
❑ LL 3057 [M]	Hits I Missed	1958	5.00	10.00	20.00
❑ LL 3058 [M]	Old English	1958	5.00	10.00	20.00
❑ LL 3062 [M]	Shall We Dance	1959	5.00	10.00	20.00
❑ LL 3106 [M]	Great Film Hits	1959	5.00	10.00	20.00
❑ LL 3124 [M]	Pop Hits from the Classics	1959	5.00	10.00	20.00
❑ LL 3125 [M]	Big Band Blues	1959	5.00	10.00	20.00
❑ LL 3127 [M]	My Very Good Friends The Bandleaders	1959	5.00	10.00	20.00
HEATH BROTHERS, THE					
STRATA-EAST					
❑ SES-19766	Marchin' On	1975	6.25	12.50	25.00
HEATHER BLACK					
AMERICAN PLAYBOY					
❑ 1001	Heather Black Live	197?	15.00	30.00	60.00
❑ 1001 [(2)]	Heather Black Live	197?	37.50	75.00	150.00
—Evidently, some copies of this were 2-record sets					
DOUBLE BAYOU					
❑ 2000	Heather Black	197?	7.50	15.00	30.00
HEATS, THE					
ALBATROSS					
❑ 1001	The Heats	1980	6.25	12.50	25.00
HEAVY BALLOON, THE					
ELEPHANT					
❑ EVS-104	32,000 Lbs.	1969	17.50	35.00	70.00
HEBB, BOBBY					
EPIC					
❑ BN 26523	Love Games	1970	3.00	6.00	12.00
PHILIPS					
❑ PHM 200212 [M] Sunny		1966	6.25	12.50	25.00
—With "200-212" in trail-off; this record is mono					
❑ PHM 200212 [S] Sunny		1966	6.25	12.50	25.00
—With "2/600-212" in trail-off; this record plays stereo, though labeled mono					
❑ PHS 600212 [S] Sunny		1966	7.50	15.00	30.00
HECKMAN, DON					
ICTUS					
❑ 101	Summerlin Improvisational Jazz Workshop	1967	15.00	30.00	60.00
HEFTI, NEAL					
COLUMBIA					
❑ CL 1516 [M]	Light and Right	1960	5.00	10.00	20.00
❑ CS 8316 [S]	Light and Right	1960	6.25	12.50	25.00
CORAL					
❑ 7CX 2 [(2)S]	Hollywood Song Book	1959	15.00	30.00	60.00
❑ CX 2 [(2)M]	Hollywood Song Book	1959	10.00	20.00	40.00
❑ CRL 56083 [10]	Swingin' on a Coral Reef	1953	12.50	25.00	50.00
❑ CRL 57241 [M]	Hollywood Song Book, Volume 1	1958	5.00	10.00	20.00
❑ CRL 57242 [M]	Hollywood Song Book, Volume 2	1958	5.00	10.00	20.00
❑ CRL 57256 [M]	Music U.S.A.	1959	5.00	10.00	20.00
❑ CRL 757241 [S]	Hollywood Song Book, Volume 1	1959	7.50	15.00	30.00
❑ CRL 757242 [S]	Hollywood Song Book, Volume 2	1959	7.50	15.00	30.00
❑ CRL 757256 [S]	Music U.S.A.	1959	7.50	15.00	30.00

Number	Title (A Side/B Side)	Yr	VG	VG+	NM
EPIC					
❏ LN 3113 [M]	Singing Instrumentals	1956	12.50	25.00	50.00
❏ LN 3440 [M]	Singing Instrumentals	1958	7.50	15.00	30.00
❏ LN 3481 [M]	Pardon My Do-Wah	1958	7.50	15.00	30.00
RCA VICTOR					
❏ LPM-3573 [M]	Batman Theme (and 11 Other Bat-Songs)	1966	12.50	25.00	50.00
❏ LSP-3573 [S]	Batman Theme (and 11 Other Bat-Songs)	1966	15.00	30.00	60.00
❏ LPM-3621 [M]	Hefti in Gotham City	1966	12.50	25.00	50.00
❏ LSP-3621 [S]	Hefti in Gotham City	1966	15.00	30.00	60.00
REPRISE					
❏ R-6018 [M]	Themes from TV's Top 12	1962	6.25	12.50	25.00
❏ R9-6018 [S]	Themes from TV's Top 12	1962	7.50	15.00	30.00
❏ R-6039 [M]	Jazz Pops	1962	5.00	10.00	20.00
❏ R9-6039 [S]	Jazz Pops	1962	6.25	12.50	25.00
"X"					
❏ LXA-3021 [10]	Music of Rudolf Frimi	1954	12.50	25.00	50.00

HEIFETZ, JASCHA
RCA VICTOR RED SEAL

Number	Title (A Side/B Side)	Yr	VG	VG+	NM
❏ LSC-1903 [S]	Brahms: Violin Concerto	1958	12.50	25.00	50.00
—With Fritz Reiner/Chicago Symphony Orchestra; original with "shaded dog" label					
❏ LSC-1992 [S]	Beethoven: Violin Concerto in D	1958	12.50	25.00	50.00
—With Charles Munch/Boston Symphony Orchestra					
❏ LSC-2129 [S]	Tchaikovsky: Violin Concerto	1958	10.00	20.00	40.00
—With Fritz Reiner/Chicago Symphony Orchestra; original with "shaded dog" label					
❏ LSC-2129 [S]	Tchaikovsky: Violin Concerto	1999	6.25	12.50	25.00
—Classic Records reissue					
❏ LSC-2314 [S]	Mendelssohn: Violin Concerto in E; Prokofiev: Violin Concerton in G	1959	7.50	15.00	30.00
—With Charles Munch/Boston Symphony Orchestra					
❏ LSC-2435 [S]	Sibelius: Violin Concerto	1960	10.00	20.00	40.00
—Originals with "shaded dog" label					
❏ LSC-2577 [S]	Bach: Concerto for Two Violins; Beethoven: Kreutzer Sonata	1962	17.50	35.00	70.00
—Original with "shaded dog" label					
❏ LSC-2603 [S]	Bruch: Scottish Fantasy; Vieuxtemps; Violin Concerto No. 5	1962	12.50	25.00	50.00
—Original with "shaded dog" label					
❏ LSC-2652 [S]	Bruch: Violin Concerto No. 1 in G; Mozart: Violin Concerto No. 4 in D	1962	15.00	30.00	60.00
—Original with "shaded dog" label					
❏ LSC-2734 [S]	Glazunov: Violin Concerto; Mozart: Sinfonia Concertante	1963	25.00	50.00	100.00
—Original with "shaded dog" label					

HEIFETZ, JASCHA, AND GREGOR PIATIGORSKI
RCA VICTOR RED SEAL

Number	Title (A Side/B Side)	Yr	VG	VG+	NM
❏ LDS-2513 [S]	Brahms: Double Concerto	1961	10.00	20.00	40.00
—Originals with "shaded dog" label					

HEIFETZ, JASCHA; WILLIAM PRIMROSE; GREGOR PIATIGORSKI
RCA VICTOR RED SEAL

Number	Title (A Side/B Side)	Yr	VG	VG+	NM
❏ LSC-2550 [S]	Beethoven: Serenade, op. 8; Kodaly: Duo	1961	10.00	20.00	40.00
—Originals with "shaded dog" label					
❏ LSC-2563 [S]	Beethoven: Trio in D; Bach: Three Sinfonias; Schubert: Trio No. 2	1961	10.00	20.00	40.00
—Original with "shaded dog" label					

HEINDORF, RAY
DCC COMPACT CLASSICS

Number	Title (A Side/B Side)	Yr	VG	VG+	NM
❏ LPZ-2023	For Whom the Bell Tolls	1996	6.25	12.50	25.00
—Audiophile vinyl					
WARNER BROS.					
❏ B 1201 [M]	For Whom the Bell Tolls	1958	7.50	15.00	30.00
—Re-recording of 1943 movie score; the first LP on Warner Bros. Records					
❏ BS 1201 [S]	For Whom the Bell Tolls	1959	10.00	20.00	40.00
—Gold label					
❏ W 1213 [M]	Spellbound	1958	7.50	15.00	30.00
—Re-recording of 1945 movie score					
❏ WS 1213 [S]	Spellbound	1959	10.00	20.00	40.00
—Gold label					

HELL, RICHARD, AND THE VOIDOIDS
RED STAR

Number	Title (A Side/B Side)	Yr	VG	VG+	NM
❏ RED 801	Destiny Street	1982	3.75	7.50	15.00
—Richard Hell solo					
SIRE					
❏ SRK 6037	Blank Generation	1977	6.25	12.50	25.00

HELLBORG, JONAS
DAY EIGHT

Number	Title (A Side/B Side)	Yr	VG	VG+	NM
❏ DEM 001	The Bassic Thing	1982	5.00	10.00	20.00

HELLERS, THE
COMMAND

Number	Title (A Side/B Side)	Yr	VG	VG+	NM
❏ RS 934 SD	Singers, Talkers, Players, Swingers and Doers	1968	10.00	20.00	40.00

HELM, BOB
RIVERSIDE

Number	Title (A Side/B Side)	Yr	VG	VG+	NM
❏ RLP-2510 [10]	Bob Helm	1954	20.00	40.00	80.00

HELM, BOB/LU WATTERS
RIVERSIDE

Number	Title (A Side/B Side)	Yr	VG	VG+	NM
❏ RLP 12-213 [M]	San Francisco Style	1956	15.00	30.00	60.00

HELMS, BOBBY
COLUMBIA

Number	Title (A Side/B Side)	Yr	VG	VG+	NM
❏ CL 2060 [M]	The Best of Bobby Helms	1963	6.25	12.50	25.00
❏ CS 8860 [S]	The Best of Bobby Helms	1963	7.50	15.00	30.00
DECCA					
❏ DL 8638 [M]	Bobby Helms Sings to My Special Angel	1957	30.00	60.00	120.00
HARMONY					
❏ HL 7409 [M]	Fraulein	1967	3.00	6.00	12.00
❏ HS 11209 [S]	Fraulein	1967	3.00	6.00	12.00

Number	Title (A Side/B Side)	Yr	VG	VG+	NM
KAPP					
❏ KL 1463 [M]	I'm the Man	1966	3.75	7.50	15.00
❏ KL 1505 [M]	Sorry My Name Isn't Fred	1966	3.75	7.50	15.00
❏ KS 3463 [S]	I'm the Man	1966	5.00	10.00	20.00
❏ KS 3505 [S]	Sorry My Name Isn't Fred	1966	5.00	10.00	20.00
LITTLE DARLIN'					
❏ 8088	All New Just for You	1968	6.25	12.50	25.00
MISTLETOE					
❏ MLP-1206	Jingle Bell Rock	197?	3.00	6.00	12.00
POWER PAK					
❏ 283	Greatest Hits	197?	2.50	5.00	10.00
VOCALION					
❏ VL 3743 [M]	Someone Already There	1965	3.75	7.50	15.00
❏ VL 73743 [R]	Someone Already There	1965	3.00	6.00	12.00
❏ VL 73874	My Special Angel	1969	3.00	6.00	12.00

HELMS, DON
SMASH

Number	Title (A Side/B Side)	Yr	VG	VG+	NM
❏ MGS-27001 [M]	The Steel Guitar Sounds of Hank Williams	1962	5.00	10.00	20.00
❏ MGS-27019 [M]	Don Helms' Steel Guitar	1962	5.00	10.00	20.00
❏ SRS-67001 [S]	The Steel Guitar Sounds of Hank Williams	1962	6.25	12.50	25.00
❏ SRS-67019 [S]	Don Helms' Steel Guitar	1962	6.25	12.50	25.00

HELP
DECCA

Number	Title (A Side/B Side)	Yr	VG	VG+	NM
❏ DL 75257	Help	1970	7.50	15.00	30.00
❏ DL 75304	Second Coming	1971	7.50	15.00	30.00

HEMPHILL, JULIUS
ARISTA FREEDOM

Number	Title (A Side/B Side)	Yr	VG	VG+	NM
❏ AL 1012	'Coon Bid'ness	1975	5.00	10.00	20.00
❏ AL 1028	Dogon A.D.	1976	6.25	12.50	25.00
MBARI					
❏ (# unknown)	'Coon Bid'ness	1974	10.00	20.00	40.00
❏ (# unknown) [(2)]	Blue Boye	1977	15.00	30.00	60.00
❏ 5001	Dogon A.D.	1972	12.50	25.00	50.00

HENDERSON, BILL
MGM

Number	Title (A Side/B Side)	Yr	VG	VG+	NM
❏ E-4128 [M]	Bill Henderson with the Oscar Peterson Trio	1963	6.25	12.50	25.00
❏ SE-4128 [S]	Bill Henderson with the Oscar Peterson Trio	1963	7.50	15.00	30.00
VEE JAY					
❏ LP-1015 [M]	Bill Henderson Sings	1959	6.25	12.50	25.00
❏ SR-1015 [S]	Bill Henderson Sings	1959	10.00	20.00	40.00
❏ LP-1031 [M]	Bill Henderson	1961	6.25	12.50	25.00
❏ SR-1031 [S]	Bill Henderson	1961	10.00	20.00	40.00
VERVE					
❏ V-8619 [M]	When My Dreamboat Comes Home	1965	5.00	10.00	20.00
❏ V6-8619 [S]	When My Dreamboat Comes Home	1965	6.25	12.50	25.00

HENDERSON, BOBBY
HALCYON

Number	Title (A Side/B Side)	Yr	VG	VG+	NM
❏ 102	Home in the Clouds	1970	5.00	10.00	20.00
VANGUARD					
❏ VRS-8511 [M]	Handful of Keys	1955	10.00	20.00	40.00

HENDERSON, BUGS
ARMADILLO

Number	Title (A Side/B Side)	Yr	VG	VG+	NM
❏ LP-78-1	The Bugs Henderson Group At Last	1978	10.00	20.00	40.00

HENDERSON, EDDIE
BLUE NOTE

Number	Title (A Side/B Side)	Yr	VG	VG+	NM
❏ BN-LA464-G	Sunburst	1975	5.00	10.00	20.00
❏ BN-LA636-G	Heritage	1976	5.00	10.00	20.00

HENDERSON, FLETCHER
COLUMBIA

Number	Title (A Side/B Side)	Yr	VG	VG+	NM
❏ C4L 19 [(4)M]	The Fletcher Henderson Story	1961	25.00	50.00	100.00
—Box set with booklet; red and black labels with six "eye" logos					
❏ C4L 19 [(4)M]	The Fletcher Henderson Story	1963	12.50	25.00	50.00
—Red "Guaranteed High Fidelity" labels					
❏ C4L 19 [(4)M]	The Fletcher Henderson Story	1966	7.50	15.00	30.00
—Red "360 Sound Mono" labels					
DECCA					
❏ DL 6025 [10]	Fletcher Henderson Memorial Album	1952	37.50	75.00	150.00
❏ DL 9227 [M]	Fletcher Henderson: First Impression (Vol. 1 1924-1931)	1958	12.50	25.00	50.00
—Black label, silver print					
❏ DL 9227 [M]	Fletcher Henderson: First Impression (Vol. 1 1924-1931)	1961	7.50	15.00	30.00
—Black label with color bars					
❏ DL 9228 [M]	Fletcher Henderson: The Swing's the Thing (Vol. 2 1931-1934)	1958	12.50	25.00	50.00
—Black label, silver print					
❏ DL 9228 [M]	Fletcher Henderson: The Swing's the Thing (Vol. 2 1931-1934)	1961	7.50	15.00	30.00
—Black label with color bars					
HISTORICAL					
❏ 13	Fletcher Henderson 1923-24	1967	5.00	10.00	20.00
❏ 18	Fletcher Henderson Volume 2: 1923-25	1967	5.00	10.00	20.00
JAZZTONE					
❏ J-1285 [M]	The Big Reunion	1958	7.50	15.00	30.00
MILESTONE					
❏ M-2005	The Immortal Fletcher Henderson	196?	6.25	12.50	25.00
RIVERSIDE					
❏ RLP-1055 [10]	Fletcher Henderson	1954	37.50	75.00	150.00
SUTTON					
❏ SSL-286 [M]	Fletcher Henderson with Slam Stewart	195?	6.25	12.50	25.00
"X"					
❏ LVA-3013 [10]	Fletcher Henderson and His Connie's Inn Orchestra	1954	37.50	75.00	150.00

Number	Title (A Side/B Side)	Yr	VG	VG+	NM

HENDERSON, JOE
BLUE NOTE
❑ BLP-4140 [M]	Page One	1963	6.25	12.50	25.00
❑ BLP-4152 [M]	Our Thing	1963	6.25	12.50	25.00
❑ BLP-4166 [M]	In 'n Out	1964	6.25	12.50	25.00
❑ BLP-4189 [M]	Inner Urge	1965	6.25	12.50	25.00
❑ BLP-4227 [M]	Mode for Joe	1966	6.25	12.50	25.00
❑ BST-84140 [S]	Page One	1963	7.50	15.00	30.00
—"New York, USA" address on label					
❑ BST-84152 [S]	Our Thing	1963	7.50	15.00	30.00
—"New York, USA" address on label					
❑ BST-84166 [S]	In 'n Out	1964	7.50	15.00	30.00
—"New York, USA" address on label					
❑ BST-84189 [S]	Inner Urge	1965	7.50	15.00	30.00
—"New York, USA" address on label					
❑ BST-84227 [S]	Mode for Joe	1966	7.50	15.00	30.00
—"New York, USA" address on label					

FONTANA
❑ SRF-67590	Hits, Hits, Hits!	1969	7.50	15.00	30.00

MILESTONE
❑ M-9008	The Kicker	1968	5.00	10.00	20.00
❑ M-9017	Tetragon	1969	5.00	10.00	20.00
❑ M-9024	Power to the People	1970	5.00	10.00	20.00
❑ M-9028	If You're Not Part	1970	5.00	10.00	20.00
❑ M-9034	In Pursuit of Blackness	1971	5.00	10.00	20.00
❑ M-9040	Black Is the Color	1972	5.00	10.00	20.00
❑ M-9047	Joe Henderson In Japan	1972	5.00	10.00	20.00

TODD
❑ MT-2701 [M]	Snap Your Fingers	1962	12.50	25.00	50.00
❑ ST-2701 [S]	Snap Your Fingers	1962	17.50	35.00	70.00

HENDERSON, SKITCH
CAPITOL
❑ H 110 [10]	Keyboard Sketches	1950	12.50	25.00	50.00

HENDRICKS, JON
COLUMBIA
❑ CL 1583 [M]	Evolution of the Blues	1961	7.50	15.00	30.00
❑ CL 1805 [M]	Fast Livin' Blues	1962	7.50	15.00	30.00
❑ CS 8383 [S]	Evolution of the Blues	1961	10.00	20.00	40.00
❑ CS 8605 [S]	Fast Livin' Blues	1962	10.00	20.00	40.00

REPRISE
❑ R-6089 [M]	Salud!	1964	6.25	12.50	25.00
❑ R9-6089 [S]	Salud!	1964	7.50	15.00	30.00

SMASH
❑ MGS-27069 [M]	Recorded In Person at the Trident	1963	6.25	12.50	25.00
❑ SRS-67069 [S]	Recorded In Person at the Trident	1963	7.50	15.00	30.00

WORLD PACIFIC
❑ WP-1283 [M]	A Good Git-Together	1959	20.00	40.00	80.00

HENDRIX, JIMI
ACCORD
❑ SN-7101	Kaleidoscope	1981	2.50	5.00	10.00
❑ SN-7112	Before London	1981	2.50	5.00	10.00
❑ SN-7139	Cosmic Feeling	1981	2.50	5.00	10.00

CAPITOL
❑ STAO-472	Band of Gypsys	1970	5.00	10.00	20.00
❑ SWBB-659 [(2)]	Get That Feeling/Flashing	1971	6.25	12.50	25.00
❑ ST 2856 [S]	Get That Feeling	1967	10.00	20.00	40.00
❑ T 2856 [M]	Get That Feeling	1967	20.00	40.00	80.00
❑ ST 2894 [S]	Flashing	1968	10.00	20.00	40.00
❑ T 2894 [M]	Flashing	1968	25.00	50.00	100.00
❑ SJ-12416	Band of Gypsys 2	1986	2.50	5.00	10.00
—Side 2 lists, and plays, three songs					
❑ SJ-12416	Band of Gypsys 2	1986	37.50	75.00	150.00
—Side 2 lists three songs, but plays four completely different songs. Four bands are visible on the record.					
❑ MLP-15022 [EP]	Johnny B. Goode	1986	2.00	4.00	8.00
❑ SN-16319	Band of Gypsys	1985	2.50	5.00	10.00
—Budget-line reissue					
❑ C1-96414	Band of Gypsys	1995	3.75	7.50	15.00
—Numbered reissue					

EXPERIENCE HENDRIX
❑ RTH 2006 [(2)]	Blues	2002	10.00	20.00	40.00
—Limited edition on 200-gram blue vinyl					

EXPERIENCE HENDRIX/CAPITOL
❑ ST-472	Band of Gypsys	1997	6.25	12.50	25.00
—Limited edition on "heavy vinyl" with booklet; distributed by Classic Records					

EXPERIENCE HENDRIX/MCA
❑ 11599 [(2)]	First Rays of the New Rising Sun	1997	12.50	25.00	50.00
—Limited edition on "heavy vinyl" with booklet					
❑ 11600 [(2)]	Electric Ladyland	1997	10.00	20.00	40.00
—Limited edition on "heavy vinyl" with booklet					
❑ 11601	Axis: Bold As Love	1997	12.50	25.00	50.00
—Limited edition on "heavy vinyl" with booklet					
❑ 11602 [(2)]	Are You Experienced?	1997	12.50	25.00	50.00
—Limited edition on "heavy vinyl" with booklet					
❑ 11607	Band of Gypsys	1997	6.25	12.50	25.00
—Limited edition on "heavy vinyl" with booklet; pressed in U.S. for export to Europe					
❑ 11608	Are You Experienced?	1997	10.00	20.00	40.00
—Limited edition on "heavy vinyl" with booklet; pressed in U.S. for export to Europe; has different cover than US version					
❑ 11671 [(2)]	Experience Hendrix: The Best of Jimi Hendrix	1998	6.25	12.50	25.00
—Despite lower number, was released after South Saturn Delta					
❑ 11684 [(2)]	South Saturn Delta	1997	6.25	12.50	25.00
—Numbered, limited edition on "heavy vinyl"					
❑ 11742 [(3)]	BBC Sessions	1998	7.50	15.00	30.00
❑ 11931 [(3)]	Live at the Fillmore East	1999	7.50	15.00	30.00
❑ 11987 [(3)]	Live at Woodstock	1999	7.50	15.00	30.00

❑ 112316 [(8)]	The Jimi Hendrix Experience	2000	17.50	35.00	70.00
—Limited edition of 5,000 in purple felt box					
❑ 112984	Smash Hits	2002	3.75	7.50	15.00
—Limited edition on "heavy vinyl"					

NUTMEG
❑ 1001	High, Live 'N' Dirty	1978	6.25	12.50	25.00
—Black vinyl					
❑ 1001	High, Live 'N' Dirty	1978	6.25	12.50	25.00
—Red vinyl					
❑ 1002	Cosmic Turnaround	1981	3.00	6.00	12.00

PICKWICK
❑ SPC-3528	Jimi	197?	2.50	5.00	10.00

REPRISE
❑ MS 2025	Smash Hits	1969	10.00	20.00	40.00
—With "W7" and "r:" logos on two-tone orange label					
❑ MS 2025	Smash Hits Bonus Poster	1969	10.00	20.00	40.00
❑ MS 2025	Smash Hits	1970	3.00	6.00	12.00
—With only "r:" logo on all-orange (tan) label					
❑ MS 2025	Smash Hits	198?	2.00	4.00	8.00
—Red and black label or gold and light blue label					
❑ MS 2029	Historic Performances As Recorded at the Monterey International Pop Festival	1970	5.00	10.00	20.00
—Side 1: Jimi Hendrix; Side 2: Otis Redding					
❑ MS 2034	The Cry of Love	1971	3.75	7.50	15.00
❑ MS 2034	The Cry of Love	1971	125.00	250.00	500.00
—With "W7" and "r:" logos on two-tone orange label					
❑ MS 2040	Rainbow Bridge	1971	5.00	10.00	20.00
❑ MS 2049	Hendrix in the West	1972	5.00	10.00	20.00
❑ MS 2103	War Heroes	1972	5.00	10.00	20.00
❑ MS 2204	Crash Landing	1975	3.75	7.50	15.00
❑ MS 2229	Midnight Lightning	1975	3.75	7.50	15.00
❑ 2RS 2245 [(2)]	The Essential Jimi Hendrix	1978	5.00	10.00	20.00
❑ MSK 2276	Smash Hits	1977	2.50	5.00	10.00
—Reissue					
❑ HS 2293	The Essential Jimi Hendrix Volume Two	1979	3.75	7.50	15.00
—Add 100% if bonus single of "Gloria" with picture sleeve is enclosed					
❑ HS 2299	Nine to the Universe	1980	2.50	5.00	10.00
❑ R 6261 [M]	Are You Experienced?	1967	50.00	100.00	200.00
❑ RS 6261 [S]	Are You Experienced?	1967	12.50	25.00	50.00
—Pink, gold and green label					
❑ RS 6261 [S]	Are You Experienced?	1968	6.25	12.50	25.00
—With "W7" and "r:" logos on two-tone orange label					
❑ RS 6261 [S]	Are You Experienced?	1970	3.00	6.00	12.00
—With only "r:" logo on all-orange (tan) label					
❑ RS 6261 [S]	Are You Experienced?	198?	2.00	4.00	8.00
—Red and black label or gold and light blue label					
❑ R 6281 [M]	Axis: Bold As Love	1968	625.00	1250.	2500.
❑ RS 6281 [S]	Axis: Bold As Love	1968	6.25	12.50	25.00
—With "W7" and "r:" logos on two-tone orange label					
❑ RS 6281 [S]	Axis: Bold As Love	1968	20.00	40.00	80.00
—Pink, gold and green label					
❑ RS 6281 [S]	Axis: Bold As Love	1970	3.00	6.00	12.00
—With only "r:" logo on all-orange (tan) label					
❑ RS 6281 [S]	Axis: Bold As Love	198?	2.00	4.00	8.00
—Red and black label or gold and light blue label					
❑ 2R 6307 [(2)M]	Electric Ladyland	1968	2000.	3000.	4000.
—Mono is promo only					
❑ 2RS 6307 [(2)S]	Electric Ladyland	1968	25.00	50.00	100.00
—With "W7" and "r:" logos on two-tone orange label					
❑ 2RS 6307 [(2)S]	Electric Ladyland	1970	3.75	7.50	15.00
—With only "r:" logo on all-orange (tan) label					
❑ 2RS 6307 [(2)S]	Electric Ladyland	198?	3.00	6.00	12.00
—Red and black label or gold and light blue label					
❑ 2RS 6481 [(2)]	Soundtrack Recordings from the Film Jimi Hendrix	1973	6.25	12.50	25.00
❑ 22306 [(2)]	The Jimi Hendrix Concerts	1982	3.00	6.00	12.00
❑ 25119	Kiss the Sky	1984	2.50	5.00	10.00
❑ 25358	Jimi Plays Monterey	1986	2.50	5.00	10.00
❑ SKAO-91441	Axis: Bold As Love	1968	10.00	20.00	40.00
—Capitol Record Club edition; two-tone orange label with "W7" and "r:" at top					
❑ STBO-91568 [(2)]	Electric Ladyland	1968	37.50	75.00	150.00
—Capitol Record Club edition					
❑ SMAS-93467	The Cry of Love	1971	15.00	30.00	60.00
—Capitol Record Club edition					
❑ SMAS-93972	Rainbow Bridge	1971	12.50	25.00	50.00
—Capitol Record Club edition					

RHINO
❑ RNDF-254 [PD]	The Jimi Hendrix Interview	1982	6.25	12.50	25.00

RYKO ANALOGUE
❑ RALP-0038 [(2)]	Live at Winterland	1988	3.75	7.50	15.00
❑ RALP-0078 [(2)]	Radio One	1988	3.75	7.50	15.00
—Clear vinyl					

TRACK
❑ 612003 [M]	Axis: Bold As Love	2000	6.25	12.50	25.00
—Classic Records issue of the original U.K. mono mix, on a reproduction of the original British label					

TRIP
❑ 3509 [(2)]	Superpak	197?	3.75	7.50	15.00
❑ TLP-9500	Rare Hendrix	1972	3.75	7.50	15.00
❑ TLP-9501	Roots of Hendrix	1972	3.00	6.00	12.00
❑ TLP-9512	Moods	1973	3.00	6.00	12.00
❑ TLP-9523	The Genius of Jimi Hendrix	1973	3.00	6.00	12.00

UNITED ARTISTS
❑ UA-LA505-E	The Very Best of Jimi Hendrix	1975	3.00	6.00	12.00

WARNER BROS.
❑ HS 2299	Nine to the Universe	1980	3.00	6.00	12.00
—Reprise cover, Warner Bros. tan "pinstripe" label; possibly Columbia House edition?					

HENDRIX, JIMI, AND LONNIE YOUNGBLOOD
MAPLE
❑ 6004	Two Great Experiences Together	1971	12.50	25.00	50.00

Number	Title (A Side/B Side)	Yr	VG	VG+	NM

HENKE, MEL

CONTEMPORARY
❏ C-5001 [M]	Dig Mel Henke	1955	12.50	25.00	50.00
❏ C-5003 [M]	Now Spin This	1956	12.50	25.00	50.00

WARNER BROS.
❏ W 1472 [M]	La Dolce Henke	1962	10.00	20.00	40.00
❏ WS 1472 [S]	La Dolce Henke	1962	12.50	25.00	50.00

HENRIQUE, LUIZ

FONTANA
❏ MGF-27553 [M]	Listen to Me	1966	5.00	10.00	20.00
❏ SRF-67553 [S]	Listen to Me	1966	6.25	12.50	25.00

VERVE
❏ V-8697 [M]	Barra Limpa	1967	7.50	15.00	30.00
❏ V6-8697 [S]	Barra Limpa	1967	5.00	10.00	20.00

HENRY, CLARENCE

ARGO
❏ LP-4009 [M]	You Always Hurt the One You Love	1961	75.00	125.00	250.00

CADET
❏ LP-4009 [M]	You Always Hurt the One You Love	1966	12.50	25.00	50.00

—Includes copies of Cadet LP in Argo sleeves

ROULETTE
❏ SR 42039	Alive and Well and Living in New Orleans	1969	6.25	12.50	25.00

HENRY, ERNIE

RIVERSIDE
❏ RLP 12-222 [M]	Presenting Ernie Henry	1956	30.00	60.00	120.00

HENRY TREE

MAINSTREAM
❏ S-6129	Electric Holy Man	1968	7.50	15.00	30.00

HENSKE, JUDY

ELEKTRA
❏ EKL-231 [M]	Judy Henske	1963	5.00	10.00	20.00
❏ EKL-241 [M]	High Flying Bird	1964	5.00	10.00	20.00
❏ EKS-7231 [S]	Judy Henske	1963	6.25	12.50	25.00
❏ EKL-7241 [S]	High Flying Bird	1964	6.25	12.50	25.00

MERCURY
❏ MG-21010 [M]	Little Bit of Sunshine…Little Bit of Rain	1965	5.00	10.00	20.00
❏ SR-61010 [S]	Little Bit of Sunshine…Little Bit of Rain	1965	6.25	12.50	25.00

REPRISE
❏ R-6203 [M]	The Death Defying Judy Henske: The First Concert Album	1966	5.00	10.00	20.00
❏ RS-6203 [S]	The Death Defying Judy Henske: The First Concert Album	1966	6.25	12.50	25.00

HENSKE, JUDY, AND JERRY YESTER

REPRISE
❏ RS-6388	Farewell Aldebaran	1969	5.00	10.00	20.00

STRAIGHT
❏ STS-1052	Farewell Aldebaran	1968	7.50	15.00	30.00

HENSLEY, WALTER

CAPITOL
❏ ST 2149 [S]	The Five-String Banjo Today	1964	5.00	10.00	20.00
❏ T 2149 [M]	The Five-String Banjo Today	1964	3.75	7.50	15.00

HERBERT, MORT

SAVOY
❏ MG-12073 [M]	Night People	1956	10.00	20.00	40.00

HERD, THE

FONTANA
❏ SRF-67579	Lookin' Thru You	1968	6.25	12.50	25.00

HERDSMEN, THE

FANTASY
❏ 3201 [M]	The Herdsmen Play Paris	1955	10.00	20.00	40.00
—Black vinyl					
❏ 3201 [M]	The Herdsmen Play Paris	1955	20.00	40.00	80.00
—Green vinyl					

HERMAN, JERRY

UNITED ARTISTS
❏ UAL-3432 [M]	Hello, Jerry!	1965	5.00	10.00	20.00
❏ UAS-6432 [S]	Hello, Jerry!	1965	6.25	12.50	25.00

HERMAN, WOODY

AMERICAN RECORDING SOCIETY
❏ G-410 [M]	The Progressive Big Band Sound	1956	10.00	20.00	40.00

ATLANTIC
❏ 1328 [M]	Woody Herman at the Monterey Jazz Festival	1960	10.00	20.00	40.00
❏ SD 1328 [S]	Woody Herman at the Monterey Jazz Festival	1960	7.50	15.00	30.00

BRUNSWICK
❏ BL 54024 [M]	The Swinging Herman Herd	1957	10.00	20.00	40.00

CAPITOL
❏ H 324 [10]	Classics in Jazz	1952	17.50	35.00	70.00
❏ T 324 [M]	Classics in Jazz	1955	10.00	20.00	40.00
❏ T 560 [M]	The Woody Herman Band	1955	10.00	20.00	40.00
❏ T 658 [M]	Road Band	1955	10.00	20.00	40.00
❏ T 748 [M]	Jackpot!	1956	10.00	20.00	40.00
❏ T 784 [M]	Blues Groove	1956	10.00	20.00	40.00
❏ T 1554 [M]	The Hits of Woody Herman	1961	5.00	10.00	20.00

CENTURY
❏ CRDD-1080	Road Father	1979	6.25	12.50	25.00
—Direct-to-disc recording					

CLEF
❏ MGC-745 [M]	Jazz, the Utmost!	1956	20.00	40.00	80.00

COLUMBIA
❏ C3L 25 [(3)M]	The Thundering Herds	1963	12.50	25.00	50.00
❏ CL 592 [M]	The Three Herds	1955	12.50	25.00	50.00
—Maroon label with gold print					
❏ CL 592 [M]	The Three Herds	1956	7.50	15.00	30.00
—Red and black label with six "eye" logos					
❏ CL 651 [M]	Music for Tired Lovers	1955	10.00	20.00	40.00
❏ CL 683 [M]	Twelve Shades of Blue	1956	7.50	15.00	30.00
❏ CL 2509 [10]	Ridin' Herd	1955	15.00	30.00	60.00
❏ CL 2563 [10]	Woody!	1955	15.00	30.00	60.00
❏ CL 6026 [10]	Sequence in Jazz	1949	17.50	35.00	70.00
❏ CL 6049 [10]	Dance Parade	1949	17.50	35.00	70.00
❏ CL 6092 [10]	Woody Herman and His Woodchoppers	1950	17.50	35.00	70.00

CORAL
❏ CRL 56005 [10]	Blue Prelude	1950	17.50	35.00	70.00
❏ CRL 56010 [10]	Woody Herman Souvenirs	1950	17.50	35.00	70.00
❏ CRL 56090 [10]	Woody's Best	1953	17.50	35.00	70.00

CROWN
❏ CLP 5180 [M]	The New Swingin' Herman Band	1960	5.00	10.00	20.00

DECCA
❏ DL 8133 [M]	Woodchopper's Ball	1955	10.00	20.00	40.00

DIAL
❏ LP-210 [10]	Swinging with the Woodchoppers	1950	37.50	75.00	150.00

EVEREST
❏ SDBR-1003 [S]	The Herd Rides Again…In Stereo	1958	10.00	20.00	40.00
❏ SDBR-1032 [S]	Moody Woody	1958	10.00	20.00	40.00
❏ LPBR-5003 [M]	The Herd Rides Again	1958	7.50	15.00	30.00
❏ LPBR-5032 [M]	Moody Woody	1958	7.50	15.00	30.00

FANTASY
❏ FPM-4003 [Q]	Children of Lima	1975	5.00	10.00	20.00

FORUM
❏ F-9016 [M]	Woody Herman Sextet at the Round Table	196?	5.00	10.00	20.00
❏ FS-9016 [S]	Woody Herman Sextet at the Round Table	196?	6.25	12.50	25.00

HARMONY
❏ HL 7013 [M]	Bijou	1957	5.00	10.00	20.00
❏ HL 7093 [M]	Summer Sequence	1957	5.00	10.00	20.00

JAZZLAND
❏ JLP-17 [M]	The Fourth Herd	1960	6.25	12.50	25.00
❏ JLP-917 [S]	The Fourth Herd	1960	6.25	12.50	25.00

LION
❏ L-70059 [M]	The Herman Herd at Carnegie Hall	1958	6.25	12.50	25.00

MARS
❏ MRX-1 [10]	Dance Date on Mars	1952	37.50	75.00	150.00
❏ MRX-2 [10]	Woody Herman Goes Native	1953	37.50	75.00	150.00

MGM
❏ E-158 [10]	Woody Herman at Carnegie Hall, 1946, Vol. 1	1952	17.50	35.00	70.00
❏ E-159 [10]	Woody Herman at Carnegie Hall, 1946, Vol. 2	1952	17.50	35.00	70.00
❏ E-192 [10]	The Third Herd	1953	17.50	35.00	70.00
❏ E-284 [10]	Blue Flame	1955	17.50	35.00	70.00
❏ E-3043 [M]	Carnegie Hall 1946	1953	12.50	25.00	50.00
—Compiles 158 and 159 on one 12-inch LP					
❏ E-3385 [M]	Hi-Fi-ing Herd	1956	10.00	20.00	40.00

MOBILE FIDELITY
❏ 1-219	The Fourth Herd	1994	7.50	15.00	30.00
—Audiophile vinyl					

PHILIPS
❏ PHS 600065 [S]	Woody Herman 1963	1963	5.00	10.00	20.00
❏ PHS 600092 [S]	Encore: Woody Herman 1963	1963	5.00	10.00	20.00
❏ PHS 600118 [S]	Woody Herman: 1964	1964	5.00	10.00	20.00
❏ PHS 600131 [S]	The Swinging Herman Herd Recorded Live	1964	5.00	10.00	20.00
❏ PHS 600171 [S]	Woody's Big Band Goodies	1965	5.00	10.00	20.00

ROULETTE
❏ R 25067 [M]	Woody Herman Sextet at the Round Table	1959	7.50	15.00	30.00
❏ SR 25067 [S]	Woody Herman Sextet at the Round Table	1959	10.00	20.00	40.00

VERVE
❏ MGV-2030 [M]	Early Autumn	1957	10.00	20.00	40.00
❏ MGV-2069 [M]	Songs for Hip Lovers	1957	10.00	20.00	40.00
❏ MGV-2096 [M]	Love Is the Sweetest Thing — Sometimes	1958	10.00	20.00	40.00
❏ MGV-8014 [M]	Jazz, the Utmost!	1957	10.00	20.00	40.00
—Reissue of Clef LP					
❏ MGV-8216 [M]	Men from Mars	1958	10.00	20.00	40.00
❏ MGV-8255 [M]	Woody Herman '58	1958	10.00	20.00	40.00
❏ V-8558 [M]	Hey! Heard the Herd?	1963	5.00	10.00	20.00
—Reissue of Verve 8216					
❏ V6-8764	Concerto for Herd	1968	5.00	10.00	20.00

HERMAN, WOODY/TITO PUENTE

EVEREST
❏ SDBR-1010 [S]	Herman's Beat of Puente	1958	10.00	20.00	40.00
❏ LPBR-5010 [M]	Herman's Beat of Puente	1958	10.00	20.00	40.00

HERMAN'S HERMITS

ABKCO
❏ 4227-1	Their Greatest Hits	1988	2.00	4.00	8.00
—Abridged version of AB 4227					
❏ AB-4227 [(2)]	XX (Greatest Hits)	1973	3.00	6.00	12.00

MGM
❏ E-4282 [M]	Introducing Herman's Hermits	1965	3.75	7.50	15.00
—Version 3: With "Including 'Mrs. Brown You've Got a Lovely Daughter'" on front cover					
❏ E-4282 [M]	Introducing Herman's Hermits	1965	5.00	10.00	20.00
—Version 2: Same as above, but with a sticker that says "Featuring "Mrs. Brown You Have a Lovely Daughter'."					
❏ E-4282 [M]	Introducing Herman's Hermits	1965	6.25	12.50	25.00
—Version 1: With "Including Their Hit Single 'I'm Into Something Good'" on front cover					
❏ SE-4282 [R]	Introducing Herman's Hermits	1965	2.50	5.00	10.00
—Version 3: With "Including 'Mrs. Brown You've Got a Lovely Daughter'" on front cover					

Number	Title (A Side/B Side)	Yr	VG	VG+	NM
❑ SE-4282 [R]	Introducing Herman's Hermits	1965	3.75	7.50	15.00

—Version 2: Same as above, but with a sticker that says "Featuring "Mrs. Brown You Have a Lovely Daughter"."

Number	Title (A Side/B Side)	Yr	VG	VG+	NM
❑ SE-4282 [R]	Introducing Herman's Hermits	1965	5.00	10.00	20.00

—Version 1: With "Including Their Hit Single 'I'm Into Something Good'" on front cover

Number	Title (A Side/B Side)	Yr	VG	VG+	NM
❑ E-4295 [M]	Herman's Hermits On Tour	1965	3.00	6.00	12.00
❑ SE-4295 [R]	Herman's Hermits On Tour	1965	2.50	5.00	10.00
❑ E-4315 [M]	The Best of Herman's Hermits	1965	3.00	6.00	12.00
❑ SE-4315 [R]	The Best of Herman's Hermits	1965	2.50	5.00	10.00
❑ E-4342 [M]	Hold On!	1966	2.50	5.00	10.00
❑ SE-4342 [P]	Hold On!	1966	3.00	6.00	12.00
❑ E-4386 [M]	Both Sides of Herman's Hermits	1966	2.50	5.00	10.00
❑ SE-4386 [R]	Both Sides of Herman's Hermits	1966	2.00	4.00	8.00
❑ E-4416 [M]	The Best of Herman's Hermits, Volume 2	1966	3.00	6.00	12.00

—Add 50% if bonus photo of Herman is included

Number	Title (A Side/B Side)	Yr	VG	VG+	NM
❑ SE-4416 [P]	The Best of Herman's Hermits, Volume 2	1966	2.50	5.00	10.00

—Add 50% if bonus photo of Herman is included. "Hold On" and "Leaning on the Lamp Post" are in true stereo.

Number	Title (A Side/B Side)	Yr	VG	VG+	NM
❑ E-4438 [M]	There's a Kind of Hush All Over the World	1967	2.50	5.00	10.00
❑ SE-4438 [R]	There's a Kind of Hush All Over the World	1967	2.00	4.00	8.00
❑ E-4478 [M]	Blaze	1967	2.50	5.00	10.00
❑ SE-4478 [S]	Blaze	1967	2.50	5.00	10.00
❑ E-4505 [M]	The Best of Herman's Hermits, Volume 3	1967	2.50	5.00	10.00
❑ SE-4505 [P]	The Best of Herman's Hermits, Volume 3	1967	2.50	5.00	10.00

—"Don't Go Out Into the Rain," "Museum," "Last Bus Home" and "Mum and Dad" are in true stereo.

Number	Title (A Side/B Side)	Yr	VG	VG+	NM
❑ SE-4548 [P]	Mrs. Brown You've Got a Lovely Daughter	1968	2.50	5.00	10.00

—"Mrs. Brown You've Got a Lovely Daughter" and "There's a Kind of Hush" are rechanneled

Number	Title (A Side/B Side)	Yr	VG	VG+	NM
❑ ST-90416 [S]	Introducing Herman's Hermits	1965	5.00	10.00	20.00

—Capitol Record Club edition

Number	Title (A Side/B Side)	Yr	VG	VG+	NM
❑ T-90416 [M]	Introducing Herman's Hermits	1965	6.25	12.50	25.00

—Capitol Record Club edition

Number	Title (A Side/B Side)	Yr	VG	VG+	NM
❑ ST-90421 [R]	Herman's Hermits On Tour	1965	5.00	10.00	20.00

—Capitol Record Club edition

Number	Title (A Side/B Side)	Yr	VG	VG+	NM
❑ T-90421 [M]	Herman's Hermits On Tour	1965	6.25	12.50	25.00

—Capitol Record Club edition

Number	Title (A Side/B Side)	Yr	VG	VG+	NM
❑ KAO-90613 [M]	The Best of Herman's Hermits	1966	3.75	7.50	15.00

—Capitol Record Club edition

Number	Title (A Side/B Side)	Yr	VG	VG+	NM
❑ ST-90646 [R]	Hold On!	1966	5.00	10.00	20.00

—Capitol Record Club edition

Number	Title (A Side/B Side)	Yr	VG	VG+	NM
❑ T-90646 [M]	Hold On!	1966	6.25	12.50	25.00

—Capitol Record Club edition

Number	Title (A Side/B Side)	Yr	VG	VG+	NM
❑ ST-91286 [S]	Blaze	1967	5.00	10.00	20.00

—Capitol Record Club edition

Number	Title (A Side/B Side)	Yr	VG	VG+	NM
❑ T-91286 [M]	Blaze	1967	7.50	15.00	30.00

—Capitol Record Club edition

HERON, MIKE
ELEKTRA

Number	Title (A Side/B Side)	Yr	VG	VG+	NM
❑ EKS-74093	Smiling Men with Bad Reputations	1971	5.00	10.00	20.00

HERRMANN, BERNARD
MOBILE FIDELITY

Number	Title (A Side/B Side)	Yr	VG	VG+	NM
❑ 1-240	The Fantasy Film World of Bernard Herrmann	1996	5.00	10.00	20.00

—Audiophile vinyl

Number	Title (A Side/B Side)	Yr	VG	VG+	NM
❑ 1-255	The Four Faces of Jazz	1996	5.00	10.00	20.00

—Audiophile vinyl

HERSCH, FRED
CHESKY

Number	Title (A Side/B Side)	Yr	VG	VG+	NM
❑ 90	Dancing in the Dark	1993	5.00	10.00	20.00

HESITATIONS, THE
KAPP

Number	Title (A Side/B Side)	Yr	VG	VG+	NM
❑ KL-1525 [M]	Soul Superman	1967	7.50	15.00	30.00
❑ KS-3525 [S]	Soul Superman	1967	6.25	12.50	25.00
❑ KS-3548	The New Born Free	1968	6.25	12.50	25.00
❑ KS-3561	Where We're At	1968	6.25	12.50	25.00
❑ KS-3574	Solid Gold	1969	6.25	12.50	25.00

HESS, CHUCK
STRAND

Number	Title (A Side/B Side)	Yr	VG	VG+	NM
❑ SL-1084 [M]	Country & Western Favorites	1960	5.00	10.00	20.00
❑ SLS-1084 [S]	Country & Western Favorites	1960	6.25	12.50	25.00

HESTER, CAROLYN
COLUMBIA

Number	Title (A Side/B Side)	Yr	VG	VG+	NM
❑ CL 1796 [M]	Carolyn Hester	1962	15.00	30.00	60.00

—With Bob Dylan on harmonica on three tracks; black and red label with six "eye" logos

Number	Title (A Side/B Side)	Yr	VG	VG+	NM
❑ CL 1796 [M]	Carolyn Hester	1963	5.00	10.00	20.00

—Red label with "Guaranteed High Fidelity"

Number	Title (A Side/B Side)	Yr	VG	VG+	NM
❑ CL 2032 [M]	This Life I'm Living	1963	5.00	10.00	20.00
❑ CS 8596 [S]	Carolyn Hester	1962	20.00	40.00	80.00

—With Bob Dylan on harmonica on three tracks; black and red label with six "eye" logos

Number	Title (A Side/B Side)	Yr	VG	VG+	NM
❑ CS 8596 [S]	Carolyn Hester	1963	6.25	12.50	25.00

—Red label, "360 Sound Stereo" in black

Number	Title (A Side/B Side)	Yr	VG	VG+	NM
❑ CS 8832 [S]	This Life I'm Living	1963	6.25	12.50	25.00

CORAL

Number	Title (A Side/B Side)	Yr	VG	VG+	NM
❑ CRL 57143 [M]	Scarlet Ribbons	1957	12.50	25.00	50.00

DOT

Number	Title (A Side/B Side)	Yr	VG	VG+	NM
❑ DLP-3604 [M]	That's My Song	1964	3.75	7.50	15.00
❑ DLP-3638 [M]	Carolyn Hester at Town Hall One	1965	3.75	7.50	15.00
❑ DLP-3649 [M]	Carolyn Hester at Town Hall Two	1965	3.75	7.50	15.00
❑ DLP-25604 [S]	That's My Song	1964	5.00	10.00	20.00
❑ DLP-25638 [S]	Carolyn Hester at Town Hall One	1965	5.00	10.00	20.00
❑ DLP-25649 [S]	Carolyn Hester at Town Hall Two	1965	5.00	10.00	20.00

FOLK ODYSSEY

Number	Title (A Side/B Side)	Yr	VG	VG+	NM
❑ 32160264	Simply Carolyn Hester	196?	5.00	10.00	20.00

METROMEDIA

Number	Title (A Side/B Side)	Yr	VG	VG+	NM
❑ MD-1001	The Carolyn Hester Coalition	1969	5.00	10.00	20.00
❑ MD-1022	Magazine	1970	15.00	30.00	60.00

RCA VICTOR

Number	Title (A Side/B Side)	Yr	VG	VG+	NM
❑ APD1-0086 [Q]	Carolyn Hester	1973	5.00	10.00	20.00

—Only released in quadraphonic

TRADITION

Number	Title (A Side/B Side)	Yr	VG	VG+	NM
❑ TLP-1043 [M]	Carolyn Hester	1961	10.00	20.00	40.00

HEYWOOD, EDDIE
BRUNSWICK

Number	Title (A Side/B Side)	Yr	VG	VG+	NM
❑ BL 58036 [10]	Eddie Heywood '45	1953	12.50	25.00	50.00

COLUMBIA

Number	Title (A Side/B Side)	Yr	VG	VG+	NM
❑ CL 6157 [10]	Piano Moods	1951	12.50	25.00	50.00

COMMODORE

Number	Title (A Side/B Side)	Yr	VG	VG+	NM
❑ FL-20007 [10]	Eight Selections	1950	18.75	37.50	75.00

CORAL

Number	Title (A Side/B Side)	Yr	VG	VG+	NM
❑ CRL 57095 [M]	Featuring Eddie Heywood	1957	10.00	20.00	40.00

DECCA

Number	Title (A Side/B Side)	Yr	VG	VG+	NM
❑ DL 8202 [M]	Lightly and Politely	1956	7.50	15.00	30.00
❑ DL 8270 [M]	Swing Low Sweet Heywood	1956	7.50	15.00	30.00

EMARCY

Number	Title (A Side/B Side)	Yr	VG	VG+	NM
❑ MG-36042 [M]	Eddie Heywood	1955	10.00	20.00	40.00

EPIC

Number	Title (A Side/B Side)	Yr	VG	VG+	NM
❑ LN 3327 [M]	Eddie Heywood at Twilight	1956	7.50	15.00	30.00

MERCURY

Number	Title (A Side/B Side)	Yr	VG	VG+	NM
❑ MG-20445 [M]	Breezin' Along with the Breeze	1959	5.00	10.00	20.00
❑ MG-20590 [M]	Eddie Heywood at the Piano	1960	5.00	10.00	20.00
❑ MG-20632 [M]	One for My Baby	1960	5.00	10.00	20.00
❑ SR-60115 [S]	Breezin' Along with the Breeze	1959	6.25	12.50	25.00
❑ SR-60248 [S]	Eddie Heywood at the Piano	1960	6.25	12.50	25.00
❑ SR-60632 [S]	One for My Baby	1960	6.25	12.50	25.00

MGM

Number	Title (A Side/B Side)	Yr	VG	VG+	NM
❑ E-135 [10]	It's Easy to Remember	1952	12.50	25.00	50.00
❑ E-3093 [M]	Pianorama	1955	10.00	20.00	40.00
❑ E-3260 [M]	Eddie Heywood	1956	10.00	20.00	40.00

RCA VICTOR

Number	Title (A Side/B Side)	Yr	VG	VG+	NM
❑ LPM-1466 [M]	The Touch of Eddie Heywood	1957	7.50	15.00	30.00
❑ LPM-1529 [M]	Canadian Sunset	1957	7.50	15.00	30.00
❑ LSP-1529 [S]	Canadian Sunset	1958	10.00	20.00	40.00
❑ LPM-1900 [M]	The Keys and I	1958	7.50	15.00	30.00

HI-LITES, THE (2)
DANDEE

Number	Title (A Side/B Side)	Yr	VG	VG+	NM
❑ DLP-206 [M]	For Your Precious Love	1958	500.00	1000.	2000.

HI-LO'S, THE
COLUMBIA

Number	Title (A Side/B Side)	Yr	VG	VG+	NM
❑ CL 952 [M]	Suddenly It's the Hi-Lo's	1957	7.50	15.00	30.00
❑ CL 1023 [M]	Now Hear This	1957	7.50	15.00	30.00
❑ CL 1259 [M]	The Hi-Lo's and All That Jazz	1958	7.50	15.00	30.00
❑ CL 1416 [M]	Broadway Playbill	1959	7.50	15.00	30.00
❑ CL 1509 [M]	All Over the Place	1960	6.25	12.50	25.00
❑ CL 1723 [M]	This Time It's Love	1962	6.25	12.50	25.00
❑ CS 8057 [S]	Love Nest	1958	10.00	20.00	40.00
❑ CS 8077 [S]	The Hi-Lo's and All That Jazz	1958	10.00	20.00	40.00
❑ CS 8213 [S]	Broadway Playbill	1959	10.00	20.00	40.00
❑ CS 8300 [S]	All Over the Place	1960	7.50	15.00	30.00
❑ CS 8523 [S]	This Time It's Love	1962	7.50	15.00	30.00

KAPP

Number	Title (A Side/B Side)	Yr	VG	VG+	NM
❑ KL 1027 [M]	The Hi-Lo's and the Jerry Fielding Band	1956	7.50	15.00	30.00
❑ KL 1184 [M]	Under Glass	1959	6.25	12.50	25.00

—Reissue of Starlite 7005

Number	Title (A Side/B Side)	Yr	VG	VG+	NM
❑ KL 1194 [M]	On Hand	1960	6.25	12.50	25.00

—Reissue of Starlite 7008

OMEGA

Number	Title (A Side/B Side)	Yr	VG	VG+	NM
❑ OSL-11 [S]	The Hi-Lo's in Stereo	195?	7.50	15.00	30.00

REPRISE

Number	Title (A Side/B Side)	Yr	VG	VG+	NM
❑ R-6066 [M]	The Hi-Lo's Happen to Bossa Nova	1963	5.00	10.00	20.00
❑ R9-6066 [S]	The Hi-Lo's Happen to Bossa Nova	1963	6.25	12.50	25.00

STARLITE

Number	Title (A Side/B Side)	Yr	VG	VG+	NM
❑ 6004 [10]	Listen!	1955	15.00	30.00	60.00
❑ 6005 [10]	The Hi-Lo's, I Presume	1955	15.00	30.00	60.00
❑ 7005 [M]	Under Glass	1956	10.00	20.00	40.00
❑ 7006 [M]	Listen!	1956	10.00	20.00	40.00

—Reissue of 6004

Number	Title (A Side/B Side)	Yr	VG	VG+	NM
❑ 7007 [M]	The Hi-Lo's. I Presume	1956	10.00	20.00	40.00

—Reissue of 6005

Number	Title (A Side/B Side)	Yr	VG	VG+	NM
❑ 7008 [M]	On Hand	1956	10.00	20.00	40.00

HI-TONES, THE
HI

Number	Title (A Side/B Side)	Yr	VG	VG+	NM
❑ HL-31011 [M]	Raunchy Sounds	1963	5.00	10.00	20.00
❑ SHL-32011 [S]	Raunchy Sounds	1963	6.25	12.50	25.00

L&M

Number	Title (A Side/B Side)	Yr	VG	VG+	NM
❑ 223	I'm So Sorry	196?	50.00	100.00	200.00

HIATT, JOHN
A&M

Number	Title (A Side/B Side)	Yr	VG	VG+	NM
❑ SP-5158	Bring the Family	1987	2.50	5.00	10.00
❑ SP-5206	Slow Turning	1988	2.50	5.00	10.00
❑ 75021 5310 1	Stolen Moments	1990	3.00	6.00	12.00

EPIC

Number	Title (A Side/B Side)	Yr	VG	VG+	NM
❑ KE 32688	Hangin' Around the Observatory	1974	3.75	7.50	15.00
❑ KE 33190	Overcoats	1975	3.75	7.50	15.00
❑ PE 33190	Overcoats	198?	2.00	4.00	8.00

—Budget-line reissue

GEFFEN

Number	Title (A Side/B Side)	Yr	VG	VG+	NM
❑ GHS 2009	All of a Sudden	1982	3.00	6.00	12.00
❑ GHS 4017	Riding with the King	1983	3.00	6.00	12.00
❑ GHS 24055	Warming Up to the Ice Age	1984	3.00	6.00	12.00

MCA

Number	Title (A Side/B Side)	Yr	VG	VG+	NM
❑ 741	Two-Bit Monster	198?	2.00	4.00	8.00

—Reissue

Number	Title (A Side/B Side)	Yr	VG	VG+	NM
❑ 747	Slug Line	198?	2.00	4.00	8.00

—Reissue

Number	Title (A Side/B Side)	Yr	VG	VG+	NM
❏ 3088	Slug Line	1979	3.00	6.00	12.00
❏ 5123	Two-Bit Monster	1980	3.00	6.00	12.00
MOBILE FIDELITY					
❏ 1-210	Bring the Family	1994	12.50	25.00	50.00
—Audiophile vinyl					

HIBBLER, AL
ARGO

Number	Title (A Side/B Side)	Yr	VG	VG+	NM
❏ LP-601 [M]	Melodies by Al Hibbler	1956	10.00	20.00	40.00
—Reissue of Marterry LP					
ATLANTIC					
❏ 1251 [M]	After the Lights Go Down Low	1957	12.50	25.00	50.00
—Black label					
❏ 1251 [M]	After the Lights Go Down Low	1961	6.25	12.50	25.00
—Mostly red label, white fan logo					
❏ 1251 [M]	After the Lights Go Down Low	1963	5.00	10.00	20.00
—Mostly red label, black fan logo					
BRUNSWICK					
❏ BL 54036 [M]	Al Hibbler with the Ellingtonians	1957	12.50	25.00	50.00
DECCA					
❏ DL 8328 [M]	Starring Al Hibbler	1956	7.50	15.00	30.00
❏ DL 8420 [M]	Here's Hibbler	1957	7.50	15.00	30.00
❏ DL 8697 [M]	Torchy and Blue	1958	7.50	15.00	30.00
❏ DL 8757 [M]	Hits by Hibbler	1958	7.50	15.00	30.00
❏ DL 8862 [M]	Al Hibbler Remembers the Big Songs of the Big Bands	1959	7.50	15.00	30.00
❏ DL 78862 [S]	Al Hibbler Remembers the Big Songs of the Big Bands	1959	10.00	20.00	40.00
DISCOVERY					
❏ 842	It's Monday Every Day	198?	3.00	6.00	12.00
—Reissue of Reprise LP					
LMI					
❏ 10001 [M]	Early One Morning	1964	7.50	15.00	30.00
MARTERRY					
❏ LP-601 [M]	Melodies by Al Hibbler	1956	20.00	40.00	80.00
MCA					
❏ 4098 [(2)]	The Best of Al Hibbler	197?	3.75	7.50	15.00
NORGRAN					
❏ MGN-4 [10]	Al Hibbler Favorites	1954	37.50	75.00	150.00
❏ MGN-15 [10]	Al Hibbler Sings Duke Ellington	1954	37.50	75.00	150.00
OPEN SKY					
❏ OSR-3126	For Sentimental Reasons	1986	3.00	6.00	12.00
REPRISE					
❏ R-2005 [M]	It's Monday Every Day	1961	7.50	15.00	30.00
❏ R9-2005 [S]	It's Monday Every Day	1961	10.00	20.00	40.00
SCORE					
❏ SLP-4013 [M]	I Surrender, Dear	1957	25.00	50.00	100.00
VERVE					
❏ MGV-4000 [M]	Al Hibbler Sings Love Songs	1956	15.00	30.00	60.00
❏ V-4000 [M]	Al Hibbler Sings Love Songs	1961	5.00	10.00	20.00

HICKEY, ERSEL
BACK-TRAC

Number	Title (A Side/B Side)	Yr	VG	VG+	NM
❏ P 18750	The Rockin' Bluebird	1985	15.00	30.00	60.00
—Allegedly, only 200 copies of this were pressed					

HICKMAN, DWAYNE
CAPITOL

Number	Title (A Side/B Side)	Yr	VG	VG+	NM
❏ ST 1441 [S]	Dobie!	1960	12.50	25.00	50.00
❏ T 1441 [M]	Dobie!	1960	10.00	20.00	40.00

HIGGINS, CHUCK
COMBO

Number	Title (A Side/B Side)	Yr	VG	VG+	NM
❏ LP-300 [M]	Pachuko Hop	195?	100.00	200.00	40.00
—Chuck Higgins on cover, fully clothed					
❏ LP-300 [M]	Pachuko Hop	195?	200.00	400.00	800.00
—"Naked woman" cover (well, she's wearing a scarf)					

HIGGINS, EDDIE
ATLANTIC

Number	Title (A Side/B Side)	Yr	VG	VG+	NM
❏ SD 1446 [S]	Soulero	1966	5.00	10.00	20.00
VEE JAY					
❏ LP-3017 [M]	Eddie Higgins	1961	7.50	15.00	30.00
❏ SR-3017 [S]	Eddie Higgins	1961	10.00	20.00	40.00

HIGH TIDE
LIBERTY

Number	Title (A Side/B Side)	Yr	VG	VG+	NM
❏ LST-7638	Sea Shanties	1969	6.25	12.50	25.00

HIGH TREASON
ABBOTT

Number	Title (A Side/B Side)	Yr	VG	VG+	NM
❏ ABS-1209	High Treason	1968	15.00	30.00	60.00

HIGHTOWER, DEAN
ABC-PARAMOUNT

Number	Title (A Side/B Side)	Yr	VG	VG+	NM
❏ ABC-312 [M]	Twangy Guitar with a Beat	1959	6.25	12.50	25.00
❏ ABCS-312 [S]	Twangy Guitar with a Beat	1959	7.50	15.00	30.00

HIGHTOWER, DONNA
CAPITOL

Number	Title (A Side/B Side)	Yr	VG	VG+	NM
❏ ST 1133 [S]	Take One	1959	12.50	25.00	50.00
❏ T 1133 [M]	Take One	1959	10.00	20.00	40.00
❏ ST 1273 [S]	Gee Baby…Ain't I Good to You	1959	12.50	25.00	50.00
❏ T 1273 [M]	Gee Baby…Ain't I Good to You	1959	10.00	20.00	40.00

HIGHWAYMEN, THE
ABC-PARAMOUNT

Number	Title (A Side/B Side)	Yr	VG	VG+	NM
❏ 522 [M]	On a New Road	1965	3.00	6.00	12.00
❏ S-522 [S]	On a New Road	1965	3.75	7.50	15.00
UNITED ARTISTS					
❏ UAL 3125 [M]	The Highwaymen	1961	3.75	7.50	15.00

Number	Title (A Side/B Side)	Yr	VG	VG+	NM
❏ UAL 3168 [M]	Standing Room Only!	1962	3.75	7.50	15.00
❏ UAL 3225 [M]	Encore!	1962	3.75	7.50	15.00
❏ UAL 3245 [M]	March On, Brothers	1963	3.75	7.50	15.00
❏ UAL 3294 [M]	Hootenanny with the Highwaymen	1963	3.75	7.50	15.00
❏ UAL 3323 [M]	One More Time	1964	3.75	7.50	15.00
❏ UAL 3348 [M]	Homecoming	1964	3.75	7.50	15.00
❏ UAS 6125 [S]	The Highwaymen	1961	5.00	10.00	20.00
❏ UAS 6168 [S]	Standing Room Only!	1962	5.00	10.00	20.00
❏ UAS 6225 [S]	Encore!	1962	5.00	10.00	20.00
❏ UAS 6245 [S]	March On, Brothers	1963	5.00	10.00	20.00
❏ UAS 6294 [S]	Hootenanny with the Highwaymen	1963	5.00	10.00	20.00
❏ UAS 6323 [S]	One More Time	1964	5.00	10.00	20.00
❏ UAS 6348 [S]	Homecoming	1964	5.00	10.00	20.00

HILDEGARDE
DECCA

Number	Title (A Side/B Side)	Yr	VG	VG+	NM
❏ DL 8656 [M]	Souvenir Album	1958	7.50	15.00	30.00
—Black label, silver print					

HILDINGER, DAVE
BATON

Number	Title (A Side/B Side)	Yr	VG	VG+	NM
❏ 1204 [M]	The Young Moderns	1957	10.00	20.00	40.00

HILL, ANDREW
BLUE NOTE

Number	Title (A Side/B Side)	Yr	VG	VG+	NM
❏ BN-LA459-H2 [(2)]	One for One	1975	5.00	10.00	20.00
❏ BLP-4151 [M]	Black Fire	1963	7.50	15.00	30.00
❏ BLP-4159 [M]	Judgment!	1964	7.50	15.00	30.00
❏ BLP-4160 [M]	Smoke Stack	1964	7.50	15.00	30.00
❏ BLP-4167 [M]	Point of Departure	1964	7.50	15.00	30.00
❏ BLP-4217 [M]	Compulsion	1965	6.25	12.50	25.00
❏ BST-84151 [S]	Black Fire	1963	10.00	20.00	40.00
—With "New York, USA" address on label					
❏ BST-84159 [S]	Judgment!	1964	10.00	20.00	40.00
—With "New York, USA" address on label					
❏ BST-84160 [S]	Smoke Stack	1964	10.00	20.00	40.00
—With "New York, USA" address on label					
❏ BST-84167 [S]	Point of Departure	1964	10.00	20.00	40.00
—With "New York, USA" address on label					
❏ BST-84203 [S]	Andrew!!! — The Music of Andrew Hill	1967	6.25	12.50	25.00
—With "A Division of Liberty Records" on label; version with "New York, USA" on label not known to exist					
❏ BST-84217 [S]	Compulsion	1965	7.50	15.00	30.00
—With "New York, USA" address on label					
❏ BST-84303	Grass Roots	1968	5.00	10.00	20.00
❏ BST-84330	Lift Every Voice	1969	5.00	10.00	20.00
MOSAIC					
❏ MQ10-161 [(10)]	The Complete Andrew Hill Blue Note Sessions	199?	45.00	90.00	180.00
WARWICK					
❏ W-2002 [M]	So in Love	1960	15.00	30.00	60.00
❏ W-2002ST [S]	So in Love	1960	20.00	40.00	80.00

HILL, GOLDIE
DECCA

Number	Title (A Side/B Side)	Yr	VG	VG+	NM
❏ DL 4034 [M]	Goldie Hill	1960	6.25	12.50	25.00
❏ DL 4148 [M]	Lonely Heartaches	1961	5.00	10.00	20.00
❏ DL 4219 [M]	According to My Heart	1962	5.00	10.00	20.00
❏ DL 4492 [M]	Country Hit Parade	1964	5.00	10.00	20.00
❏ DL 74034 [S]	Goldie Hill	1960	7.50	15.00	30.00
❏ DL 74148 [S]	Lonely Heartaches	1961	6.25	12.50	25.00
❏ DL 74219 [S]	According to My Heart	1962	6.25	12.50	25.00
❏ DL 74492 [S]	Country Hit Parade	1964	6.25	12.50	25.00
VOCALION					
❏ VL 73800	Country Songs	196?	3.00	6.00	12.00

HILL, TINY
MERCURY

Number	Title (A Side/B Side)	Yr	VG	VG+	NM
❏ MG-20630 [M]	Dancin' and Singin' with Tiny Hill	195?	6.25	12.50	25.00
❏ MG-20631 [M]	Golden Hits	195?	6.25	12.50	25.00
❏ MG-25126 [10]	Tiny Hill	1952	12.50	25.00	50.00
❏ SR-60631 [R]	Golden Hits	196?	3.75	7.50	15.00

HILL, VINCE
TOWER

Number	Title (A Side/B Side)	Yr	VG	VG+	NM
❏ T 5064 [M]	At the Club	1966	6.25	12.50	25.00

HILL, VINSON
SAVOY

Number	Title (A Side/B Side)	Yr	VG	VG+	NM
❏ MG-12187 [M]	The Vinson Hill Trio	1966	7.50	15.00	30.00

HILLMEN, THE
TOGETHER

Number	Title (A Side/B Side)	Yr	VG	VG+	NM
❏ STT-1012	The Hillmen	1970	20.00	40.00	80.00

HILLOW HAMMET
HOUSE OF FOX

Number	Title (A Side/B Side)	Yr	VG	VG+	NM
❏ 2	Hammer	1968	37.50	75.00	150.00

HILLTOPPERS, THE
DOT

Number	Title (A Side/B Side)	Yr	VG	VG+	NM
❏ DLP-105 [10]	The Hilltoppers	1954	15.00	30.00	60.00
❏ DLP-106 [10]	The Hilltoppers	1954	15.00	30.00	60.00
❏ DLP-3003 [M]	The Hilltoppers Present Tops in Pops	1955	12.50	25.00	50.00
—Cartoon of female fan on cover					
❏ DLP-3003 [M]	The Hilltoppers Present Tops in Pops	1956	7.50	15.00	30.00
—Four caps with "W" on them on cover					
❏ DLP-3029 [M]	The Towering Hilltoppers	1957	7.50	15.00	30.00
❏ DLP-3073 [M]	Love in Bloom	1958	7.50	15.00	30.00

HINES, EARL "FATHA"
ADVANCE

Number	Title (A Side/B Side)	Yr	VG	VG+	NM
❏ 4 [10]	Fats Waller Memorial Set	1951	37.50	75.00	150.00
ATLANTIC					
❏ ALS-120 [10]	Earl Hines: QRS Solos	1952	50.00	100.00	200.00

Number	Title (A Side/B Side)	Yr	VG	VG+	NM
BRUNSWICK					
❑ BL 58035 [10]	Earl Hines Plays Fats Waller	1953	30.00	60.00	120.00
CAPITOL					
❑ ST 1971 [S]	Earl "Fatha" Hines	1963	7.50	15.00	30.00
❑ T 1971 [M]	Earl "Fatha" Hines	1963	6.25	12.50	25.00
CHIAROSCURO					
❑ 116 [(2)]	An Evening with Hines	1972	5.00	10.00	20.00
COLUMBIA					
❑ CL 2320 [M]	The New Earl Hines Trio	1965	5.00	10.00	20.00
❑ CL 6171 [10]	Piano Moods	1951	30.00	60.00	120.00
❑ CS 9120 [S]	The New Earl Hines Trio	1965	6.25	12.50	25.00
CONTACT					
❑ 2 [M]	Spontaneous Explorations	1964	6.25	12.50	25.00
❑ S-2 [S]	Spontaneous Explorations	1964	7.50	15.00	30.00
CRAFTSMEN					
❑ 8041 [M]	Swingin' and Singin'	1960	6.25	12.50	25.00
DECCA					
❑ DL 9221 [M]	Southside Swing (1934-35)	1967	6.25	12.50	25.00
❑ DL 9235 [M]	Earl Hines at the Apex Club	1968	6.25	12.50	25.00
DIAL					
❑ LP-303 [10]	Earl Hines Trio	1952	62.50	125.00	250.00
❑ LP-306 [10]	Earl Hines All Stars	1953	62.50	125.00	250.00
ENSIGN					
❑ 22021	Earl Hines Rhythm	1969	5.00	10.00	20.00
EPIC					
❑ LN 3223 [M]	Oh, Fatha!	1956	12.50	25.00	50.00
❑ LN 3501 [M]	Earl "Fatha" Hines	1958	12.50	25.00	50.00
FANTASY					
❑ 3217 [M]	"Fatha" Plays "Fats"	195?	12.50	25.00	50.00
—Black vinyl					
❑ 3217 [M]	"Fatha" Plays "Fats"	1956	25.00	50.00	100.00
—Red vinyl					
❑ 3238 [M]	Earl "Fatha" Hines Solo	195?	12.50	25.00	50.00
—Black vinyl					
❑ 3238 [M]	Earl "Fatha" Hines Solo	1956	25.00	50.00	100.00
—Red vinyl					
FOCUS					
❑ FM-335 [M]	The Real Earl Hines In Concert	1965	6.25	12.50	25.00
❑ FS-335 [S]	The Real Earl Hines In Concert	1965	7.50	15.00	30.00
HALCYON					
❑ 101	The Quintessential Recording Session	196?	5.00	10.00	20.00
IMPULSE!					
❑ A-9108 [M]	Once Upon a Time	1966	6.25	12.50	25.00
❑ AS-9108 [S]	Once Upon a Time	1966	7.50	15.00	30.00
JAZZ PANORAMA					
❑ 7 [M]	All Stars	1961	10.00	20.00	40.00
M&K					
❑ 105	"Fatha"	1979	6.25	12.50	25.00
—Direct-to-disc recording					
MASTER JAZZ					
❑ 8126 [(2)]	Earl Hines Plays Duke Ellington, Volumes 2 and 3	1973	5.00	10.00	20.00
MERCURY					
❑ MG-25018 [10]	Earl Hines and the All Stars	1950	62.50	125.00	250.00
MGM					
❑ E-3832 [M]	Earl's Pearls	1960	6.25	12.50	25.00
❑ SE-3832 [S]	Earl's Pearls	1960	7.50	15.00	30.00
NOCTURNE					
❑ NLP-5 [10]	Earl "Fatha" Hines	1954	37.50	75.00	150.00
RCA VICTOR					
❑ LPT-20 [10]	Earl Hines with Billy Eckstine	1953	30.00	60.00	120.00
❑ LPV-512 [M]	The Grand Terrace Band	1965	6.25	12.50	25.00
❑ LPM-3380 [M]	Up to Date	1965	5.00	10.00	20.00
❑ LSP-3380 [S]	Up to Date	1965	6.25	12.50	25.00
RIVERSIDE					
❑ RLP-398 [M]	A Monday Date	1961	7.50	15.00	30.00
❑ RS-9398 [R]	A Monday Date	196?	5.00	10.00	20.00
ROYALE					
❑ 18166 [10]	Eal "Fatha" Hines — Great Piano Solos	195?	30.00	60.00	120.00
TIARA					
❑ TMT-7524 [M]	Earl "Fatha" Hines with Buck Clayton	195?	5.00	10.00	20.00
TOPS					
❑ L-1599 [M]	"Fatha"	195?	7.50	15.00	30.00
VERVE					
❑ VSP-35 [M]	Life with Fatha	1966	5.00	10.00	20.00
"X"					
❑ LVA-3023 [10]	Piano Solos	1954	30.00	60.00	120.00

HINES, EARL "FATHA," AND ROY ELDRIDGE

Number	Title (A Side/B Side)	Yr	VG	VG+	NM
LIMELIGHT					
❑ LM-82028 [M]	The Grand Reunion, Volume 2	1965	5.00	10.00	20.00
❑ LS-86028 [S]	The Grand Reunion, Volume 2	1965	6.25	12.50	25.00

HINES, EARL "FATHA," AND COLEMAN HAWKINS

Number	Title (A Side/B Side)	Yr	VG	VG+	NM
LIMELIGHT					
❑ LM-82020 [M]	The Grand Reunion	1965	5.00	10.00	20.00
❑ LS-86020 [S]	The Grand Reunion	1965	6.25	12.50	25.00

HINES, ERNIE

Number	Title (A Side/B Side)	Yr	VG	VG+	NM
WE PRODUCE					
❑ 1902	Electrified	1972	12.50	25.00	50.00

HINES, MIMI

Number	Title (A Side/B Side)	Yr	VG	VG+	NM
DECCA					
❑ DL 4709 [M]	Mimi Hines Sings	1966	5.00	10.00	20.00
❑ DL 4834 [M]	Mimi Hines Is a Happening	1967	6.25	12.50	25.00
❑ DL 74709 [S]	Mimi Hines Sings	1966	6.25	12.50	25.00
❑ DL 74834 [S]	Mimi Hines Is a Happening	1967	5.00	10.00	20.00

HINES, HINES & DAD

Number	Title (A Side/B Side)	Yr	VG	VG+	NM
COLUMBIA					
❑ CS 9679	Pandemonium	1968	5.00	10.00	20.00

HINSON, DON, AND THE RIGAMORTICIANS

Number	Title (A Side/B Side)	Yr	VG	VG+	NM
CAPITOL					
❑ ST 2219 [S]	Monster Dance Party	1964	10.00	20.00	40.00
❑ T 2219 [M]	Monster Dance Party	1964	7.50	15.00	30.00

HINTON, JOE

Number	Title (A Side/B Side)	Yr	VG	VG+	NM
BACK BEAT					
❑ B-60 [M]	Funny (How Time Slips Away)	1965	12.50	25.00	50.00
❑ BS-60 [S]	Funny (How Time Slips Away)	1965	17.50	35.00	70.00
DUKE					
❑ DLPS-91	Duke-Peacock Remembers Joe Hinton	1969	5.00	10.00	20.00

HINTON, MILT

Number	Title (A Side/B Side)	Yr	VG	VG+	NM
BETHLEHEM					
❑ BCP-10 [M]	East Coast Jazz Series #5	1957	12.50	25.00	50.00
❑ BCP-1020 [10]	Milt Hinton Quartet	1955	20.00	40.00	80.00
EPIC					
❑ LN 3271 [M]	The Rhythm Section	1956	12.50	25.00	50.00

HINTON, MILT; WENDELL MARSHALL; BULL RUTHER

Number	Title (A Side/B Side)	Yr	VG	VG+	NM
RCA VICTOR					
❑ LPM-1107 [M]	Basses Loaded!	1955	20.00	40.00	80.00

HINTON, SAM

Number	Title (A Side/B Side)	Yr	VG	VG+	NM
DECCA					
❑ DL 8108 [M]	Singing Across the Land	1955	10.00	20.00	40.00
❑ DL 8418 [M]	A Family Tree of Folk Songs	1957	7.50	15.00	30.00

HIPP, JUTTA

Number	Title (A Side/B Side)	Yr	VG	VG+	NM
BLUE NOTE					
❑ BLP-1515 [M]	Jutta Hipp at the Hickory House, Volume 1	1956	50.00	100.00	200.00
—Regular version, Lexington Ave. address on label					
❑ BLP-1515 [M]	Jutta Hipp at the Hickory House, Volume 1	1956	62.50	125.00	250.00
—"Deep groove" version (deep indentation under label on both sides)					
❑ BLP-1515 [M]	Jutta Hipp at the Hickory House, Volume 1	1963	7.50	15.00	30.00
—With "New York, USA" address on label					
❑ BLP-1516 [M]	Jutta Hipp at the Hickory House, Volume 2	1956	50.00	100.00	200.00
—Regular version, Lexington Ave. address on label					
❑ BLP-1516 [M]	Jutta Hipp at the Hickory House, Volume 2	1956	62.50	125.00	250.00
—"Deep groove" version (deep indentation under label on both sides)					
❑ BLP-1516 [M]	Jutta Hipp at the Hickory House, Volume 2	1963	7.50	15.00	30.00
—With "New York, USA" address on label					
❑ BLP-1530 [M]	Jutta Hipp with Zoot Sims	1956	50.00	100.00	200.00
—Regular version, Lexington Ave. address on label					
❑ BLP-1530 [M]	Jutta Hipp with Zoot Sims	1956	62.50	125.00	250.00
—"Deep groove" version (deep indentation under label on both sides)					
❑ BLP-1530 [M]	Jutta Hipp with Zoot Sims	1963	7.50	15.00	30.00
—With "New York, USA" address on label					
❑ BLP-5056 [10]	New Faces-New Sounds from Germany	1955	75.00	150.00	300.00
MGM					
❑ E-3157 [M]	Cool Europe	1955	37.50	75.00	150.00

HIRT, AL

Number	Title (A Side/B Side)	Yr	VG	VG+	NM
AUDIO FIDELITY					
❑ AFSD-5877 [S]	Swingin' Dixie (At Dan's Pier 600 in New Orleans)	1959	5.00	10.00	20.00
❑ AFSD-5878 [S]	Swingin' Dixie	1959	5.00	10.00	20.00
❑ AFSD-5926 [S]	Swingin' Dixie (Vol. 3)	1961	5.00	10.00	20.00
❑ AFSD-5927 [S]	Swingin' Dixie (Vol. 4)	1961	5.00	10.00	20.00
RCA VICTOR					
❑ LSC-2729 [S]	"Pops" Goes the Trumpet	1964	5.00	10.00	20.00
—With the Boston Pops Orchestra conducted by Arthur Fiedler					
❑ LPM-3917 [M]	Al Hirt Plays Bert Kaempfert	1968	5.00	10.00	20.00
❑ LPM-3979 [M]	Unforgettable	1968	6.25	12.50	25.00
VERVE					
❑ MGV-1012 [M]	Swinging Dixie from Dan's Pier 600	1957	12.50	25.00	50.00
❑ MGV-1027 [M]	Blockbustin' Dixie!	195?	10.00	20.00	40.00
❑ V-1027 [M]	Blockbustin' Dixie!	1961	5.00	10.00	20.00

HIRT, AL, AND ANN-MARGRET

Number	Title (A Side/B Side)	Yr	VG	VG+	NM
RCA VICTOR					
❑ LPM-2690 [M]	Beauty and the Beard	1964	6.25	12.50	25.00
❑ LSP-2690 [S]	Beauty and the Beard	1964	7.50	15.00	30.00

HITCHCOCK, STAN

Number	Title (A Side/B Side)	Yr	VG	VG+	NM
AUDIOGRAPH					
❑ 6004	Stan Hitchcock	1982	2.50	5.00	10.00
CINNAMON					
❑ CIN 5001	Stan Hitchcock Country	1973	3.75	7.50	15.00
EPIC					
❑ LN 24138 [M]	Just Call Me Lonesome	1965	5.00	10.00	20.00
❑ BN 26138 [S]	Just Call Me Lonesome	1965	6.25	12.50	25.00
❑ BN 26408 [M]	I'm Easy to Love	1968	10.00	20.00	40.00
—White label promo with stereo number; "Epic Mono" sticker on front cover					
❑ BN 26408 [S]	I'm Easy to Love	1968	5.00	10.00	20.00
❑ BN 26438	Softly and Tenderly	1969	5.00	10.00	20.00
❑ BN 26530	Honey, I'm Home	1969	3.75	7.50	15.00
GRT					
❑ 20001	Dixie Belle	1970	3.75	7.50	15.00

HOBBITS, THE

Number	Title (A Side/B Side)	Yr	VG	VG+	NM
DECCA					
❑ DL 4920 [M]	Down to Middle-Earth	1967	10.00	20.00	40.00
❑ DL 5009 [M]	Men and Doors	1968	20.00	40.00	80.00
❑ DL 74920 [S]	Down to Middle-Earth	1967	12.50	25.00	50.00
❑ DL 75009 [S]	Men and Doors	1968	7.50	15.00	30.00

Number	Title (A Side/B Side)	Yr	VG	VG+	NM

HODEIR, ANDRE
PHILIPS
| ❑ PHM 200073 [M] | Jazz Et Al | 1963 | 6.25 | 12.50 | 25.00 |
| ❑ PHS 600073 [S] | Jazz Et Al | 1963 | 7.50 | 15.00 | 30.00 |
SAVOY
| ❑ MG-12104 [M] | American Jazzmen Play Andre Hodeir | 1957 | 10.00 | 20.00 | 40.00 |
| ❑ MG-12113 [M] | Andre Hodeir Presents the Paris Scene | 1957 | 10.00 | 20.00 | 40.00 |

HODES, ART
BLUE NOTE
❑ B-6502 [M]	The Funky Side of Art Hodes	1969	5.00	10.00	20.00
❑ B-6508 [M]	Sittin' In	1969	5.00	10.00	20.00
❑ BLP-7004 [10]	The Best in Two-Beat	1950	62.50	125.00	250.00
❑ BLP-7005 [10]	Art Hodes' Hot Five	1950	62.50	125.00	250.00
❑ BLP-7006 [10]	Dixieland Jubilee	1950	62.50	125.00	250.00
❑ BLP-7015 [10]	Dixieland Clambake	1951	62.50	125.00	250.00
❑ BLP-7021 [10]	Out of the Backroom	1952	62.50	125.00	250.00
DOTTED EIGHTH
| ❑ 1000 [M] | Art for Art's Sake | 195? | 12.50 | 25.00 | 50.00 |
EMARCY
| ❑ MG-26104 [10] | Jazz Chicago Style | 1954 | 20.00 | 40.00 | 80.00 |
JAZZOLOGY
| ❑ J-46 [M] | For Art's Sake | 196? | 5.00 | 10.00 | 20.00 |
MERCURY
| ❑ MG-20185 [M] | Chicago Style Jazz | 1957 | 12.50 | 25.00 | 50.00 |
MOSAIC
| ❑ M5-114 [(5)] | The Complete Art Hodes Blue Note Sessions | 199? | 20.00 | 40.00 | 80.00 |
PARAMOUNT
| ❑ LP-113 [M] | The Trios | 1955 | 20.00 | 40.00 | 80.00 |
RIVERSIDE
| ❑ RLP-1012 [10] | Chicago Rhythm Kings | 1953 | 20.00 | 40.00 | 80.00 |

HODES, JOHNNY
AMERICAN RECORDING SOCIETY
| ❑ G-421 [M] | Johnny Hodges and the Ellington All-Stars | 195? | 10.00 | 20.00 | 40.00 |
CLEF
| ❑ MGC-111 [10] | Johnny Hodges Collates | 1953 | 37.50 | 75.00 | 150.00 |
| ❑ MGC-128 [10] | Johnny Hodges Collates #2 | 1953 | 50.00 | 100.00 | 200.00 |
EPIC
| ❑ LN 3105 [M] | Hodge Podge | 1955 | 15.00 | 30.00 | 60.00 |
FLYING DUTCHMAN
| ❑ 120 | Three Shades of Blue | 1971 | 5.00 | 10.00 | 20.00 |
IMPULSE!
| ❑ A-61 [M] | Everybody Knows | 1964 | 6.25 | 12.50 | 25.00 |
| ❑ AS-61 [S] | Everybody Knows | 1964 | 7.50 | 15.00 | 30.00 |
JAZZ PANORAMA
| ❑ 1806 [10] | Johnny Hodges | 1951 | 37.50 | 75.00 | 150.00 |
MERCER
| ❑ LP-1000 [10] | Johnny Hodges, Vol. 1 | 1951 | 37.50 | 75.00 | 150.00 |
| ❑ LP-1006 [10] | Johnny Hodges, Vol. 2 | 1951 | 37.50 | 75.00 | 150.00 |
MERCURY
| ❑ MGC-111 [10] | Johnny Hodges Collates | 1952 | 62.50 | 125.00 | 250.00 |
MOSAIC
| ❑ M6-126 [(6)] | The Complete Johnny Hodges Recordings 1951-1956 | 199? | 25.00 | 50.00 | 100.00 |
NORGRAN
❑ MGN-1 [10]	Swing with Johnny Hodges	1954	50.00	100.00	200.00
❑ MGN-1004 [M]	Memories of Ellington	1954	37.50	75.00	150.00
❑ MGN-1009 [M]	More of Johnny Hodges	1954	37.50	75.00	150.00
❑ MGN-1024 [M]	Johnny Hodges Dance Bash	1955	37.50	75.00	150.00
❑ MGN-1045 [M]	Creamy	1955	37.50	75.00	150.00
❑ MGN-1048 [M]	Castle Rock	1955	30.00	60.00	120.00
❑ MGN-1055 [M]	Ellingtonia '56	1956	25.00	50.00	100.00
❑ MGN-1059 [M]	In a Tender Mood	1956	25.00	50.00	100.00
❑ MGN-1060 [M]	Used to Be Duke	1956	25.00	50.00	100.00
❑ MGN-1061 [M]	The Blues	1956	25.00	50.00	100.00
❑ MGN-1091 [M]	Perdido	1956	25.00	50.00	100.00
❑ MGN-1092 [M]	In a Mellow Tone	1956	25.00	50.00	100.00
RCA VICTOR
❑ LPV-533 [M]	Things Ain't What They Used to Be	1966	5.00	10.00	20.00
❑ LPT-3000 [10]	Alto Sax	1952	37.50	75.00	150.00
❑ LPM-3867 [M]	Triple Play	1967	7.50	15.00	30.00
❑ LSP-3867 [S]	Triple Play	1967	5.00	10.00	20.00
VERVE
❑ MGVS-6017 [S]	The Big Sound	1960	10.00	20.00	40.00
❑ MGVS-6048 [S]	The Prettiest Gershwin	1960	10.00	20.00	40.00
❑ MGVS-6055 [S]	Back to Back — Duke Ellington and Johnny Hodges Play the Blues	1960	10.00	20.00	40.00
❑ MGVS-6109 [S]	Side by Side	1960	10.00	20.00	40.00
❑ MGVS-6109 [S]	Side by Side	199?	6.25	12.50	25.00
—Classic Records reissue on audiophile vinyl					
❑ MGV-8136 [M]	Creamy	1957	12.50	25.00	50.00
—Reissue of Norgran 1045					
❑ V-8136 [M]	Creamy	1961	5.00	10.00	20.00
❑ MGV-8139 [M]	Castle Rock	1957	12.50	25.00	50.00
—Reissue of Norgran 1048					
❑ V-8139 [M]	Castle Rock	1961	5.00	10.00	20.00
❑ MGV-8145 [M]	Ellingtonia '56	1957	12.50	25.00	50.00
—Reissue of Norgran 1055					
❑ V-8145 [M]	Ellingtonia '56	1961	5.00	10.00	20.00
❑ MGV-8149 [M]	In a Tender Mood	1957	12.50	25.00	50.00
—Reissue of Norgran 1059					
❑ V-8149 [M]	In a Tender Mood	1961	5.00	10.00	20.00
❑ MGV-8150 [M]	Used to Be Duke	1957	12.50	25.00	50.00
—Reissue of Norgran 1060					
❑ V-8150 [M]	Used to Be Duke	1961	5.00	10.00	20.00

Number	Title (A Side/B Side)	Yr	VG	VG+	NM
❑ MGV-8151 [M]	The Blues	1957	12.50	25.00	50.00
—Reissue of Norgran 1061					
❑ V-8151 [M]	The Blues	1961	5.00	10.00	20.00
❑ MGV-8179 [M]	Perdido	1957	12.50	25.00	50.00
—Reissue of Norgran 1091					
❑ V-8179 [M]	Perdido	1961	5.00	10.00	20.00
❑ MGV-8180 [M]	In a Mellow Tone	1957	12.50	25.00	50.00
—Reissue of Norgran 1092					
❑ V-8180 [M]	In a Mellow Tone	1961	5.00	10.00	20.00
❑ MGV-8203 [M]	Duke's in Bed	1957	12.50	25.00	50.00
❑ V-8203 [M]	Duke's in Bed	1961	5.00	10.00	20.00
❑ MGV-8271 [M]	The Big Sound	1958	12.50	25.00	50.00
❑ V-8271 [M]	The Big Sound	1961	5.00	10.00	20.00
❑ V6-8271 [S]	The Big Sound	1961	5.00	10.00	20.00
❑ MGV-8314 [M]	The Prettiest Gershwin	1959	12.50	25.00	50.00
❑ V-8314 [M]	The Prettiest Gershwin	1961	5.00	10.00	20.00
❑ V6-8314 [S]	The Prettiest Gershwin	1961	5.00	10.00	20.00
❑ MGV-8317 [M]	Back to Back — Duke Ellington and Johnny Hodges Play the Blues	1959	12.50	25.00	50.00
❑ V-8317 [M]	Back to Back — Duke Ellington and Johnny Hodges Play the Blues	1961	5.00	10.00	20.00
❑ V6-8317 [S]	Back to Back — Duke Ellington and Johnny Hodges Play the Blues	1961	5.00	10.00	20.00
❑ MGV-8345 [M]	Side by Side	1959	12.50	25.00	50.00
❑ V-8345 [M]	Side by Side	1961	5.00	10.00	20.00
❑ V6-8345 [S]	Side by Side	1961	5.00	10.00	20.00
❑ MGV-8355 [M]	Not So Dukish	1960	12.50	25.00	50.00
❑ V-8355 [M]	Not So Dukish	1961	5.00	10.00	20.00
❑ MGV-8358 [M]	Blues-a-Plenty	1960	12.50	25.00	50.00
❑ V-8358 [M]	Blues-a-Plenty	1961	5.00	10.00	20.00
❑ V6-8358 [S]	Blues-a-Plenty	1961	5.00	10.00	20.00
❑ V6-8358 [S]	Blues-a-Plenty	199?	6.25	12.50	25.00
—Classic Records reissue on audiophile vinyl					
❑ V-8452 [M]	Johnny Hodges with Billy Strayhorn	1962	6.25	12.50	25.00
❑ V6-8452 [S]	Johnny Hodges with Billy Strayhorn	1962	7.50	15.00	30.00
❑ V-8492 [M]	The Eleventh Hour	1962	6.25	12.50	25.00
❑ V6-8492 [S]	The Eleventh Hour	1962	7.50	15.00	30.00
❑ V-8561 [M]	Sandy's Gone	1963	6.25	12.50	25.00
❑ V6-8561 [S]	Sandy's Gone	1963	7.50	15.00	30.00
❑ V6-8680 [S]	Blue Notes	1966	5.00	10.00	20.00
❑ V-8726 [M]	Don't Sleep in the Subway	1967	5.00	10.00	20.00

HODGES, JOHNNY, AND WILD BILL DAVIS
RCA VICTOR
❑ LPM-3393 [M]	Con-Soul and Sax	1965	5.00	10.00	20.00
❑ LSP-3393 [S]	Con-Soul and Sax	1965	6.25	12.50	25.00
❑ LSP-3706 [S]	Eddie Hodges and Wild Bill Davis In Atlantic City	1966	5.00	10.00	20.00
VERVE
❑ V-8406 [M]	Blue Hodges	1961	5.00	10.00	20.00
❑ V6-8406 [S]	Blue Hodges	1961	6.25	12.50	25.00
❑ V-8570 [M]	A Mess of Blues	1964	5.00	10.00	20.00
❑ V6-8570 [S]	A Mess of Blues	1964	6.25	12.50	25.00
❑ V-8599 [M]	Blue Rabbit	1964	5.00	10.00	20.00
❑ V6-8599 [S]	Blue Rabbit	1964	6.25	12.50	25.00
❑ V-8617 [M]	Joe's Blues	1965	5.00	10.00	20.00
❑ V6-8617 [S]	Joe's Blues	1965	6.25	12.50	25.00
❑ V-8630 [M]	Wings and Things	1965	5.00	10.00	20.00
❑ V6-8630 [S]	Wings and Things	1965	6.25	12.50	25.00
❑ V-8635 [M]	Blue Pyramid	1965	5.00	10.00	20.00
❑ V6-8635 [S]	Blue Pyramid	1965	6.25	12.50	25.00

HODGES, JOHNNY, AND EARL "FATHA" HINES
VERVE
❑ V-8647 [M]	Stride Right	1966	5.00	10.00	20.00
❑ V6-8647 [S]	Stride Right	1966	6.25	12.50	25.00
❑ V-8732 [M]	Swing's Our Thing	1967	6.25	12.50	25.00

HOFFMAN, ABBIE
BIG TOE
| ❑ 1 | Wake Up, America! | 196? | 7.50 | 15.00 | 30.00 |

HOFNER, ADOLPH
COLUMBIA
| ❑ CL 9017 [10] | Dude Ranch Dances | 1951 | 50.00 | 100.00 | 200.00 |
DECCA
| ❑ DL 5564 [10] | Dance-O-Rama | 1955 | 100.00 | 200.00 | 400.00 |

HOG HEAVEN
The Shondells after Tommy James went solo.
ROULETTE
| ❑ SR 42057 | Hog Heaven | 1971 | 5.00 | 10.00 | 20.00 |

HOGAN, CLAIRE
MGM
| ❑ E-4501 [M] | Boozers and Losers | 1967 | 5.00 | 10.00 | 20.00 |
| ❑ SE-4501 [S] | Boozers and Losers | 1967 | 6.25 | 12.50 | 25.00 |

HOGAN, SILAS
EXCELLO
| ❑ LPS-8019 | Trouble at Home | 1972 | 5.00 | 10.00 | 20.00 |

HOGG, SMOKEY
CROWN
| ❑ CLP-5226 [M] | Smokey Hogg Sings the Blues | 1962 | 12.50 | 25.00 | 50.00 |
TIME
| ❑ 6 [M] | Smokey Hogg | 1962 | 20.00 | 40.00 | 80.00 |
UNITED
| ❑ US-7745 | Smokey Hogg | 1970 | 3.00 | 6.00 | 12.00 |

HOLDEN, RANDY
HOBBIT
| ❑ 5002 | Population II | 1968 | 50.00 | 100.00 | 200.00 |

Number	Title (A Side/B Side)	Yr	VG	VG+	NM

HOLDEN, RON

DONNA

Number	Title (A Side/B Side)	Yr	VG	VG+	NM
❏ DLP-2111 [M]	I Love You So	1960	62.50	125.00	250.00
❏ DLPS-2111 [M]	I Love You So	1960	75.00	150.00	300.00

—*Stereo records not known to exist; this is for a mono record in a stereo cover*

HOLIDAY, BILLIE

AMERICAN RECORDING SOCIETY

❏ G-409 [M]	Billie Holiday Sings	1956	15.00	30.00	60.00

—*Reissue of Clef 713*

❏ G-431 [M]	Lady Sings the Blues	1957	15.00	30.00	60.00

—*Reissue of Clef 721*

CLEF

❏ MGC-118 [10]	Billie Holiday Sings	1953	45.00	90.00	180.00
❏ MGC-144 [10]	An Evening with Billie Holiday	1954	45.00	90.00	180.00
❏ MGC-161 [10]	Billie Holiday Favorites	1954	45.00	90.00	180.00
❏ MGC-169 [10]	Billie Holiday at Jazz at the Philharmonic	1955	45.00	90.00	180.00
❏ MGC-669 [M]	Music for Torching	1955	25.00	50.00	100.00
❏ MGC-686 [M]	A Recital by Billie Holiday	1956	30.00	60.00	120.00

—*Reissue of 144 and 161 as one 12-inch LP*

❏ MGC-690 [M]	Solitude — Songs by Billie Holiday	1956	30.00	60.00	120.00

—*Reissue of 118*

❏ MGC-713 [M]	Velvet Moods	1956	30.00	60.00	120.00
❏ MGC-721 [M]	Lady Sings the Blues	1956	30.00	60.00	120.00

COLUMBIA

❏ C3L 21 [(3)M]	The Golden Years	1962	12.50	25.00	50.00

—*Red and black label with six "eye" logos*

❏ C3L 21 [(3)M]	The Golden Years	1963	6.25	12.50	25.00

—*Red "Guaranteed High Fidelity" or "360 Sound" label*

❏ C3L 40 [(3)M]	The Golden Years, Volume 2	1966	7.50	15.00	30.00

—*Red label, "Mono" at bottom*

❏ C3L 40 [(3)M]	The Golden Years, Volume 2	197?	5.00	10.00	20.00

—*Orange labels*

❏ CL 637 [M]	Lady Day	1954	17.50	35.00	70.00

—*Maroon label, gold print*

❏ CL 637 [M]	Lady Day	1956	10.00	20.00	40.00

—*Red and black label with six "eye" logos*

❏ CL 1157 [M]	Lady in Satin	1958	10.00	20.00	40.00

—*Red and black label with six "eye" logos*

❏ CL 6129 [10]	Billie Holiday Sings	1950	50.00	100.00	200.00
❏ CL 6163 [10]	Billie Holiday Favorites	1951	50.00	100.00	200.00
❏ CS 8048 [S]	Lady in Satin	1958	10.00	20.00	40.00

—*Red and black label with six "eye" logos*

❏ CS 8048 [S]	Lady in Satin	1999	6.25	12.50	25.00

—*Classic Records reissue on audiophile vinyl*

❏ G 30782 [(2)]	God Bless the Child	1972	5.00	10.00	20.00

COLUMBIA MUSICAL TREASURY

❏ P3M 5869 [(3)]	The Golden Years	197?	5.00	10.00	20.00

COMMODORE

❏ FL-20005 [10]	Billie Holiday, Volume 1	1950	62.50	125.00	250.00
❏ FL-20006 [10]	Billie Holiday, Volume 2	1950	62.50	125.00	250.00
❏ DL-30008 [M]	Billie Holiday	1959	12.50	25.00	50.00

—*Reissue of 20006*

❏ DL-30011 [M]	Billie Holiday with Eddie Heywood and His Orchestra	1959	12.50	25.00	50.00

—*Reissue of 20005*

CROWN

❏ CLP-5380 [M]	Billie Holiday & Vivian Fears	196?	5.00	10.00	20.00

DECCA

❏ DXB-161 [(2)M]	The Billie Holiday Story	1959	5.00	10.00	20.00
❏ DL 5345 [10]	Lover Man	1951	50.00	100.00	200.00
❏ DL 8215 [M]	The Lady Sings	1956	15.00	30.00	60.00
❏ DL 8701 [M]	The Blues Are Brewin'	1958	15.00	30.00	60.00
❏ DL 8702 [M]	Lover Man	1958	15.00	30.00	60.00

JAZZTONE

❏ J-1209 [M]	Billie Holiday Sings	1955	12.50	25.00	50.00

—*Reissue of Commodore 20005*

JOLLY ROGER

❏ 5020 [10]	Billie Holiday, Volume 1	1954	25.00	50.00	100.00
❏ 5021 [10]	Billie Holiday, Volume 2	1954	25.00	50.00	100.00
❏ 5022 [10]	Billie Holiday, Volume 3	1954	25.00	50.00	100.00

MAINSTREAM

❏ 56000 [M]	The Commodore Recordings	1965	6.25	12.50	25.00
❏ 56022 [M]	Once Upon a Time	1965	6.25	12.50	25.00

MGM

❏ E-3764 [M]	Billie Holiday	1959	10.00	20.00	40.00
❏ SE-3764 [S]	Billie Holiday	1959	12.50	25.00	50.00

MOBILE FIDELITY

❏ 1-247	Body and Soul	1996	30.00	60.00	120.00

—*Audiophile vinyl*

RIC

❏ R-2001 [M]	Rare Live Recordings	1964	6.25	12.50	25.00

SCORE

❏ SLP-4014 [M]	Billie Holiday Sings the Blues	1957	30.00	60.00	120.00

UNITED ARTISTS

❏ UAJ-14014 [M]	Lady Love	1962	10.00	20.00	40.00
❏ UAJS-15014 [S]	Lady Love	1962	12.50	25.00	50.00

VERVE

❏ MGVS-6021 [S]	Songs for Distingue Lovers	1960	15.00	30.00	60.00
❏ MGVS-6021 [S]	Songs for Distingue Lovers	199?	6.25	12.50	25.00

—*Classic Records reissue on audiophile vinyl*

❏ MGVS-6021-45 [(2)S]	Songs for Distingue Lovers	1999	5.00	10.00	20.00

—*Classic Records reissue on two 12-inch 45-rpm records*

❏ MGV-8026 [M]	Music for Torching	1957	10.00	20.00	40.00

—*Reissue of Clef 669*

❏ V-8026 [M]	Music for Torching	1961	5.00	10.00	20.00
❏ MGV-8027 [M]	A Recital by Billie Holiday	1957	10.00	20.00	40.00

—*Reissue of Clef 686*

❏ V-8027 [M]	A Recital by Billie Holiday	1961	5.00	10.00	20.00

❏ MGV-8074 [M]	Solitude — Songs by Billie Holiday	1957	10.00	20.00	40.00

—*Reissue of Clef 690*

❏ V-8074 [M]	Solitude — Songs by Billie Holiday	1961	5.00	10.00	20.00
❏ MGV-8096 [M]	Velvet Moods	1957	10.00	20.00	40.00

—*Reissue of Clef 713*

❏ V-8096 [M]	Velvet Moods	1961	5.00	10.00	20.00
❏ MGV-8099 [M]	Lady Sings the Blues	1957	10.00	20.00	40.00

—*Reissue of Clef 721*

❏ V-8099 [M]	Lady Sings the Blues	1957	5.00	10.00	20.00
❏ MGV-8197 [M]	Body and Soul	1957	15.00	30.00	60.00
❏ V-8197 [M]	Body and Soul	1961	5.00	10.00	20.00
❏ MGV-8257 [M]	Songs for Distingue Lovers	1958	15.00	30.00	60.00
❏ V-8257 [M]	Songs for Distingue Lovers	1961	5.00	10.00	20.00
❏ V6-8257 [S]	Songs for Distingue Lovers	1961	6.25	12.50	25.00
❏ MGV-8302 [M]	Stay with Me	1959	12.50	25.00	50.00
❏ V-8302 [M]	Stay with Me	1961	5.00	10.00	20.00
❏ MGV-8329 [M]	All or Nothing at All	1959	12.50	25.00	50.00
❏ V-8329 [M]	All or Nothing at All	1959	5.00	10.00	20.00
❏ MGV-8338-2 [(2)M]	The Unforgettable Lady Day	1959	20.00	40.00	80.00
❏ V-8338-2 [(2)M]	The Unforgettable Lady Day	1961	6.25	12.50	25.00
❏ V-8410 [M]	The Essential Billie Holiday	1961	5.00	10.00	20.00
❏ V-8505 [M]	The Essential Jazz Vocals	1963	5.00	10.00	20.00

HOLIDAY, BILLIE, AND STAN GETZ

DALE

❏ 25 [10]	Billie and Stan	1951	100.00	200.00	400.00

HOLIDAY, BILLIE/AL HIBBLER

IMPERIAL

❏ LP-9185 [M]	Billie Holiday, Al Hibbler and the Blues	1962	12.50	25.00	50.00
❏ LP-12185 [R]	Billie Holiday, Al Hibbler and the Blues	196?	7.50	15.00	30.00

HOLIDAY, JIMMY

MINIT

❏ LP-24005 [M]	Turning Point	1966	7.50	15.00	30.00
❏ LP-40005 [S]	Turning Point	1966	10.00	20.00	40.00

HOLIDAY, JOE

DECCA

❏ DL 8487 [M]	Holiday for Jazz	1957	15.00	30.00	60.00

PRESTIGE

❏ PRLP-131 [10]	Joe Holiday	1952	50.00	100.00	200.00

HOLIDAY, JOE/BILLY TAYLOR

PRESTIGE

❏ PRLP-171 [10]	Mambo Jazz	1953	37.50	75.00	150.00

HOLLAND, EDDIE

MOTOWN

❏ 604 [M]	Eddie Holland	1963	100.00	200.00	400.00

HOLLIDAY, JUDY

COLUMBIA

❏ CL 1153 [M]	Trouble Is a Man	1958	7.50	15.00	30.00
❏ CS 8041 [S]	Trouble Is a Man	1959	10.00	20.00	40.00

HOLLIES, THE

ATLANTIC

❏ 80076	What Goes Around	1983	2.50	5.00	10.00

CAPITOL

❏ N-16056	Hollies' Greatest	1980	2.00	4.00	8.00

COLUMBIA LIMITED EDITION

❏ LE 10178	He Ain't Heavy, He's My Brother	1976	3.00	6.00	12.00

EMI AMERICA

❏ SN-16397	More Great Hits (1963-1968)	1986	2.00	4.00	8.00

EPIC

❏ AS 138 [DJ]	Everything You Always Wanted to Hear by the Hollies But Were Afraid to Ask For	1976	5.00	10.00	20.00

—*Promo-only sampler album*

❏ LN 24315 [M]	Evolution	1967	7.50	15.00	30.00
❏ LN 24344 [M]	Dear Eloise/King Midas in Reverse	1967	7.50	15.00	30.00
❏ BN 26315 [S]	Evolution	1967	6.25	12.50	25.00
❏ BN 26344 [S]	Dear Eloise/King Midas in Reverse	1967	6.25	12.50	25.00
❏ BN 26447	Words and Music by Bob Dylan	1969	3.75	7.50	15.00

—*Yellow label*

❏ BN 26447	Words and Music by Bob Dylan	1973	2.50	5.00	10.00

—*Orange label*

❏ BN 26538	He Ain't Heavy, He's My Brother	1970	5.00	10.00	20.00
❏ E 30255	Moving Finger	1971	5.00	10.00	20.00
❏ KE 30958	Distant Light	1972	3.75	7.50	15.00

—*Yellow label*

❏ KE 30958	Distant Light	1974	2.50	5.00	10.00

—*Orange label*

❏ PE 30958	Distant Light	1986	2.00	4.00	8.00

—*Blue label*

❏ KE 31992	Romany	1972	3.00	6.00	12.00

—*Yellow label*

❏ KE 31992	Romany	1974	2.50	5.00	10.00

—*Orange label*

❏ KE 32061	The Hollies' Greatest Hits	1973	3.00	6.00	12.00

—*Yellow label*

❏ KE 32061	The Hollies' Greatest Hits	1974	2.50	5.00	10.00

—*Orange label*

❏ PE 32061	The Hollies' Greatest Hits	1979	2.00	4.00	8.00

—*Blue label*

❏ KE 32574	Hollies	1974	2.50	5.00	10.00
❏ PE 33387	Another Night	1975	2.50	5.00	10.00
❏ PE 34714	Clarke, Hicks, Sylvester, Calvert & Elliot	1977	2.50	5.00	10.00
❏ JE 35334	A Crazy Steal	1978	2.50	5.00	10.00

IMPERIAL

❏ LP-9265 [M]	Here I Go Again	1964	12.50	25.00	50.00

—*Black and pink label*

Number	Title (A Side/B Side)	Yr	VG	VG+	NM
❏ LP-9265 [M]	Here I Go Again	1964	37.50	75.00	150.00
—Black label with stars					
❏ LP-9299 [M]	Hear! Here!	1965	12.50	25.00	50.00
❏ LP-9312 [M]	The Hollies — Beat Group	1966	7.50	15.00	30.00
❏ LP-9330 [M]	Bus Stop	1966	6.25	12.50	25.00
—Black and green label					
❏ LP-9330 [M]	Bus Stop	1966	7.50	15.00	30.00
—Black and pink label					
❏ LP-9339 [M]	Stop! Stop! Stop!	1966	6.25	12.50	25.00
❏ LP-9350 [M]	The Hollies' Greatest Hits	1967	5.00	10.00	20.00
❏ LP-12265 [R]	Here I Go Again	1964	7.50	15.00	30.00
—Black and pink label					
❏ LP-12265 [R]	Here I Go Again	1964	25.00	50.00	100.00
—Black label with silver print					
❏ LP-12299 [R]	Hear! Here!	1965	7.50	15.00	30.00
❏ LP-12312 [S]	The Hollies — Beat Group	1966	10.00	20.00	40.00
❏ LP-12330 [R]	Bus Stop	1966	5.00	10.00	20.00
—Black and green label					
❏ LP-12330 [R]	Bus Stop	1966	6.25	12.50	25.00
—Black and pink label					
❏ LP-12339 [S]	Stop! Stop! Stop!	1966	7.50	15.00	30.00
❏ LP-12350 [P]	The Hollies' Greatest Hits	1967	6.25	12.50	25.00
LIBERTY					
❏ LN-10216	Pay You Back with Interest	1982	2.00	4.00	8.00
PAIR					
❏ PDL2-1041 [(2)]	Hottest Hits	1986	3.75	7.50	15.00
REALM					
❏ 2V-8026 [(2)]	The Hollies, Volume 1	1976	3.75	7.50	15.00
—Two-record TV package					
❏ 1V-8027	The Hollies, Volume 2	1976	3.00	6.00	12.00
—TV package sold with Realm 8026					
UNITED ARTISTS					
❏ UA-LA329-E	The Very Best of the Hollies	1975	2.50	5.00	10.00

HOLLOWAY, BRENDA
MOTOWN

Number	Title (A Side/B Side)	Yr	VG	VG+	NM
❏ 5242 ML	Every Little Bit Hurts	1982	3.00	6.00	12.00
TAMLA					
❏ T 257 [M]	Every Little Bit Hurts	1964	50.00	100.00	200.00
❏ TS 257 [R]	Every Little Bit Hurts	1964	37.50	75.00	150.00

HOLLOWAY, LOLEATTA
GOLD MIND

Number	Title (A Side/B Side)	Yr	VG	VG+	NM
❏ 7500	Loleatta	1977	5.00	10.00	20.00
❏ A-9501	Queen of the Night	1978	5.00	10.00	20.00
❏ GA-9506	Love Sensation	1979	5.00	10.00	20.00

HOLLOWAY, RED
PRESTIGE

Number	Title (A Side/B Side)	Yr	VG	VG+	NM
❏ PRLP-7299 [M]	Burner	1964	12.50	25.00	50.00
—Yellow label, Bergenfield, N.J. address					
❏ PRLP-7299 [M]	Burner	1965	6.25	12.50	25.00
—Blue label, trident logo at right					
❏ PRST-7299 [S]	Burner	1964	12.50	25.00	50.00
—Yellow label, Bergenfield, N.J. address					
❏ PRST-7299 [S]	Burner	1965	6.25	12.50	25.00
—Blue label, trident logo at right					
❏ PRLP-7325 [M]	Cookin' Together	1964	7.50	15.00	30.00
❏ PRST-7325 [S]	Cookin' Together	1964	10.00	20.00	40.00
❏ PRLP-7390 [M]	Sax, Strings and Soul	1965	5.00	10.00	20.00
❏ PRST-7390 [S]	Sax, Strings and Soul	1965	6.25	12.50	25.00
❏ PRLP-7473 [M]	Red Soul	1966	5.00	10.00	20.00
❏ PRST-7473 [S]	Red Soul	1966	6.25	12.50	25.00

HOLLY, BUDDY
CORAL

Number	Title (A Side/B Side)	Yr	VG	VG+	NM
❏ CXB 8 [(2)M]	The Best of Buddy Holly	1966	20.00	40.00	80.00
❏ CXSB 8 [(2)R]	The Best of Buddy Holly	1966	12.50	25.00	50.00
❏ CRL 57210 [M]	Buddy Holly	1958	100.00	200.00	400.00
—Maroon label					
❏ CRL 57210 [M]	Buddy Holly	1964	25.00	50.00	100.00
—Black label with color bars					
❏ CRL 57279 [M]	The Buddy Holly Story	1959	37.50	75.00	150.00
—Maroon label; back color print in all black					
❏ CRL 57279 [M]	The Buddy Holly Story	1959	75.00	150.00	300.00
—Maroon label; back color print in black and red					
❏ CRL 57279 [M]	The Buddy Holly Story	1963	20.00	40.00	80.00
—Black label with color bars					
❏ CRL 57326 [M]	The Buddy Holly Story, Vol. 2	1959	50.00	100.00	200.00
—Maroon label					
❏ CRL 57326 [M]	The Buddy Holly Story, Vol. 2	1963	20.00	40.00	80.00
—Black label with color bars					
❏ CRL 57405 [M]	Buddy Holly and the Crickets	1962	37.50	75.00	150.00
—Reissue of the Crickets LP on Brunswick 54038					
❏ CRL 57426 [M]	Reminiscing	1963	50.00	100.00	200.00
—Maroon label					
❏ CRL 57426 [M]	Reminiscing	1964	20.00	40.00	80.00
—Black label with color bars					
❏ CRL 57450 [M]	Buddy Holly Showcase	1964	25.00	50.00	100.00
❏ CRL 57463 [M]	Holly in the Hills	1965	30.00	60.00	120.00
❏ CRL 57492 [M]	Buddy Holly's Greatest Hits	1967	20.00	40.00	80.00
❏ CRL 757279 [R]	The Buddy Holly Story	1963	10.00	20.00	40.00
❏ CRL 757326 [R]	The Buddy Holly Story, Vol. 2	1963	10.00	20.00	40.00
❏ CRL 757405 [R]	Buddy Holly and the Crickets	1963	10.00	20.00	40.00
❏ CRL 757426 [R]	Reminiscing	1964	10.00	20.00	40.00
❏ CRL 757450 [R]	Buddy Holly Showcase	1964	20.00	40.00	80.00
❏ CRL 757463 [R]	Holly in the Hills	1965	25.00	50.00	100.00
❏ CRL 757492 [P]	Buddy Holly's Greatest Hits	1967	12.50	25.00	50.00
❏ CRL 757504 [S]	Giant	1969	12.50	25.00	50.00
CRICKET					
❏ C001000	Buddy Holly Live — Volume 1	197?	5.00	10.00	20.00
❏ C001001	Buddy Holly Live — Volume 1	197?	5.00	10.00	20.00

Number	Title (A Side/B Side)	Yr	VG	VG+	NM
DECCA					
❏ DXSE 7207 [(2)]	A Rock 'n' Roll Collection	1972	10.00	20.00	40.00
❏ DL 8707 [M]	That'll Be the Day	1958	375.00	750.00	1500.
—Black label with silver print					
❏ DL 8707 [M]	That'll Be the Day	1961	75.00	150.00	300.00
—Black label with color bars					
GREAT NORTHWEST					
❏ GNW-4014	Visions of Buddy	197?	2.50	5.00	10.00
—Interview album					
MCA					
❏ 737	The Great Buddy Holly	197?	2.50	5.00	10.00
—Reissue of MCA Coral LP					
❏ 1484	Buddy Holly/The Crickets 20 Golden Greats	198?	2.00	4.00	8.00
—Reissue of 3040					
❏ 3040	Buddy Holly/The Crickets 20 Golden Greats	1978	3.75	7.50	15.00
❏ 4009 [(2)]	A Rock 'n' Roll Collection	1973	5.00	10.00	20.00
—Black labels with rainbow					
❏ 4009 [(2)]	A Rock 'n' Roll Collection	1978	3.00	6.00	12.00
—Later pressings on tan or blue/rainbow labels					
❏ 4184 [(2)]	Legend	1985	5.00	10.00	20.00
❏ 5540 [(2)]	From the Original Master Tapes	1986	6.25	12.50	25.00
❏ 11161	Buddy Holly	1995	10.00	20.00	40.00
—Audiophile "Heavy Vinyl" reissue with gatefold cover					
❏ 25239	Buddy Holly	1989	3.00	6.00	12.00
—Reissue of Coral 57210					
❏ 27059	For the First Time Anywhere	1983	2.50	5.00	10.00
❏ 80000 [(6)]	The Complete Buddy Holly	1981	12.50	25.00	50.00
—Box set with booklet and custom innersleeves					
MCA CORAL					
❏ CD-20101	The Great Buddy Holly	1973	3.00	6.00	12.00
VOCALION					
❏ VL 3811 [M]	The Great Buddy Holly	1967	20.00	40.00	80.00
❏ VL 73811 [R]	The Great Buddy Holly	1967	12.50	25.00	50.00
❏ VL 73923	Good Rockin'	1971	30.00	60.00	120.00

HOLLYRIDGE STRINGS, THE
CAPITOL

Number	Title (A Side/B Side)	Yr	VG	VG+	NM
❏ ST-883	Hits of the 70's	1971	3.00	6.00	12.00
❏ SM-2116	The Beatles Song Book	197?	2.50	5.00	10.00
❏ ST 2116 [S]	The Beatles Song Book	1964	5.00	10.00	20.00
❏ T 2116 [M]	The Beatles Song Book	1964	3.75	7.50	15.00
❏ SM-2156	The Beach Boys Song Book	197?	2.50	5.00	10.00
❏ ST 2156 [S]	The Beach Boys Song Book	1964	5.00	10.00	20.00
❏ T 2156 [M]	The Beach Boys Song Book	1964	3.75	7.50	15.00
❏ ST 2199 [S]	Hits Made Famous by the Four Seasons	1965	5.00	10.00	20.00
❏ T 2199 [M]	Hits Made Famous by the Four Seasons	1965	3.75	7.50	15.00
❏ ST 2202 [S]	The Beatles Song Book, Vol. 2	1965	5.00	10.00	20.00
❏ T 2202 [M]	The Beatles Song Book, Vol. 2	1965	3.75	7.50	15.00
❏ ST 2221 [S]	Hits Made Famous by Elvis Presley	1965	5.00	10.00	20.00
❏ T 2221 [M]	Hits Made Famous by Elvis Presley	1965	3.75	7.50	15.00
❏ ST 2310 [S]	The Nat King Cole Song Book	1965	5.00	10.00	20.00
❏ T 2310 [M]	The Nat King Cole Song Book	1965	3.75	7.50	15.00
❏ ST 2404 [S]	Christmas Favorites by the Hollyridge Strings	1965	3.75	7.50	15.00
❏ T 2404 [M]	Christmas Favorites by the Hollyridge Strings	1965	3.00	6.00	12.00
❏ SM-2429	The New Beatles Song Book	197?	2.50	5.00	10.00
❏ ST 2429 [S]	The New Beatles Song Book	1966	5.00	10.00	20.00
❏ T 2429 [M]	The New Beatles Song Book	1966	3.75	7.50	15.00
❏ ST 2564 [S]	Oldies But Goldies	1966	5.00	10.00	20.00
❏ T 2564 [M]	Oldies But Goldies	1966	3.75	7.50	15.00
❏ ST 2611 [S]	Skyscraper	1966	5.00	10.00	20.00
❏ T 2611 [M]	Skyscraper	1966	3.75	7.50	15.00
❏ ST 2656 [S]	The Beatles Song Book, Vol. 4	1967	3.75	7.50	15.00
❏ T 2656 [M]	The Beatles Song Book, Vol. 4	1967	5.00	10.00	20.00
❏ ST 2749 [S]	The Beach Boys Song Book, Vol. 2	1967	3.75	7.50	15.00
❏ T 2749 [M]	The Beach Boys Song Book, Vol. 2	1967	5.00	10.00	20.00
❏ ST 2998	Hits Made Famous by Simon and Garfunkel	1968	3.75	7.50	15.00
❏ SM-11830	Christmas Favorites by the Hollyridge Strings	1978	2.50	5.00	10.00
—Abridged reissue of ST 2404					

HOLLYWOOD ARGYLES, THE
LUTE

Number	Title (A Side/B Side)	Yr	VG	VG+	NM
❏ L-9001 [M]	The Hollywood Argyles (Alley Oop)	1960	175.00	350.00	700.00

HOLLYWOOD PERSUADERS, THE
ORIGINAL SOUND

Number	Title (A Side/B Side)	Yr	VG	VG+	NM
❏ LPM-5013 [M]	Drums a-Go-Go	1965	12.50	25.00	50.00
❏ LPS-8874 [S]	Drums a-Go-Go	1965	15.00	30.00	60.00

HOLLYWOOD SAXOPHONE QUARTET, THE
LIBERTY

Number	Title (A Side/B Side)	Yr	VG	VG+	NM
❏ LRP-3047 [M]	Gold Rush Suite	1957	10.00	20.00	40.00
❏ LRP-3080 [M]	Sax Appeal	1958	7.50	15.00	30.00
❏ LRP-6005 [M]	The Hollywood Saxophone Quartet	1955	10.00	20.00	40.00

HOLMAN, BILL
ANDEX

Number	Title (A Side/B Side)	Yr	VG	VG+	NM
❏ A-3004 [M]	In a Jazz Orbit	1958	10.00	20.00	40.00
❏ AS-3004 [S]	In a Jazz Orbit	1959	7.50	15.00	30.00
❏ A-3005 [M]	Jive for Five	1958	10.00	20.00	40.00
❏ AS-3005 [S]	Jive for Five	1959	7.50	15.00	30.00
CAPITOL					
❏ ST 1464 [S]	Great Big Band	1960	7.50	15.00	30.00
❏ T 1464 [M]	Great Big Band	1960	6.25	12.50	25.00
❏ H 6500 [10]	The Bill Holman Octet	1954	30.00	60.00	120.00
CORAL					
❏ CRL 57188 [M]	The Fabulous Bill Holman	1958	20.00	40.00	80.00

HOLMAN, EDDIE
ABC

Number	Title (A Side/B Side)	Yr	VG	VG+	NM
❏ S-701	I Love You	1970	7.50	15.00	30.00
SALSOUL					
❏ 5511	A Night to Remember	1977	2.50	5.00	10.00

Number	Title (A Side/B Side)	Yr	VG	VG+	NM
HOLMBERG, JIM					
ESP-DISK'					
❑ 1098	MIJ	196?	5.00	10.00	20.00
HOLMES, JAKE					
COLUMBIA					
❑ C 30996	Jake Holmes	1972	3.00	6.00	12.00
POLYDOR					
❑ 24-4007	Jake Holmes	1969	3.00	6.00	12.00
❑ 24-4034	So Close, So Very Far to Go	1970	3.00	6.00	12.00
TOWER					
❑ DT 5079 [R]	Above Ground	1967	3.75	7.50	15.00
❑ T 5079 [M]	Above Ground	1967	5.00	10.00	20.00
❑ ST 5127	Letter to Katherine December	1968	3.75	7.50	15.00
HOLMES, MARVIN					
BROWN DOOR					
❑ MH-6573	Summer of '73	1973	6.25	12.50	25.00
❑ MH-6581	Honor Thy Father	1975	6.25	12.50	25.00
UNI					
❑ 73046	Ooh, Ooh, The Dragon And Other Monsters	1969	7.50	15.00	30.00
HOLMES, RICHARD "GROOVE"					
PACIFIC JAZZ					
❑ PJ-23 [M]	Richard "Groove" Holmes	1961	6.25	12.50	25.00
❑ ST-23 [S]	Richard "Groove" Holmes	1961	7.50	15.00	30.00
❑ PJ-32 [M]	Groovin' with Jug	1961	7.50	15.00	30.00
❑ ST-32 [S]	Groovin' with Jug	1961	10.00	20.00	40.00
❑ PJ-51 [M]	Somethin' Special	1962	5.00	10.00	20.00
❑ ST-51 [S]	Somethin' Special	1962	6.25	12.50	25.00
❑ PJ-59 [M]	After Hours	1962	5.00	10.00	20.00
❑ ST-59 [S]	After Hours	1962	6.25	12.50	25.00
❑ ST-20105 [S]	Tell It Like It Tis	1966	5.00	10.00	20.00
PRESTIGE					
❑ PRST-7435 [S]	Soul Message	1966	5.00	10.00	20.00
❑ PRST-7468 [S]	Living Soul	1966	5.00	10.00	20.00
❑ PRST-7485 [S]	Misty	1966	5.00	10.00	20.00
❑ PRLP-7493 [M]	Spicy	1967	5.00	10.00	20.00
❑ PRLP-7497 [M]	Super Cool	1967	5.00	10.00	20.00
❑ PRLP-7514 [M]	Get Up and Get It	1967	5.00	10.00	20.00
WARNER BROS.					
❑ W 1553 [M]	Book of the Blues	1964	5.00	10.00	20.00
❑ WS 1553 [S]	Book of the Blues	1964	6.25	12.50	25.00
WORLD PACIFIC					
❑ ST-20147	Welcome Home	1968	5.00	10.00	20.00
HOLT, RED					
ARGO					
❑ LP-696 [M]	Look Out! Look Out!	1962	5.00	10.00	20.00
❑ LPS-696 [S]	Look Out! Look Out!	1962	6.25	12.50	25.00
HOLY MACKEREL, THE					
REPRISE					
❑ RS-6311	The Holy Mackerel	1968	6.25	12.50	25.00
HOLY MODAL ROUNDERS, THE					
ADELPHIA					
❑ 1030	Last Round	198?	2.50	5.00	10.00
ELEKTRA					
❑ EKS-74026	The Moray Eels Eat the Holy Modal Rounders	1968	7.50	15.00	30.00
ESP-DISK'					
❑ 1068 [M]	Indian War Whoop	1967	10.00	20.00	40.00
❑ 1068-S [S]	Indian War Whoop	1967	10.00	20.00	40.00
FANTASY					
❑ F-24711	Stampfel and Weber	1972	5.00	10.00	20.00
FOLKLORE					
❑ FRLP-14031 [M]	The Holy Modal Rounders	1964	20.00	40.00	80.00
METROMEDIA					
❑ MD-1039	Good Taste Is Timeless	1970	7.50	15.00	30.00
PRESTIGE					
❑ PRLP-7410 [M]	The Holy Modal Rounders 2	1965	10.00	20.00	40.00
❑ PRLP-7451 [M]	The Holy Modal Rounders	1966	10.00	20.00	40.00
—Reissue of Folklore LP					
❑ PR-7720	The Holy Modal Rounders	1969	6.25	12.50	25.00
ROUNDER					
❑ 3004	Alleged in Their Own Time	198?	2.50	5.00	10.00
SUNDAZED					
❑ LP 5126	The Moray Eels Eat the Holy Modal Rounders	2002	3.00	6.00	12.00
—Reissue on 180-gram vinyl					
HOMBRES, THE					
VERVE FORECAST					
❑ FT-3036 [M]	Let It Out (Let It All Hang Out)	1967	7.50	15.00	30.00
❑ FTS-3036 [S]	Let It Out (Let It All Hang Out)	1967	6.25	12.50	25.00
❑ FTS-3068	The Hombres	1968	—	—	—
—Canceled					
HOMER					
UNITED					
❑ HS-101	Grown in U.S.A.	1970	62.50	125.00	250.00
HOMER AND JETHRO					
AUDIO LAB					
❑ AL-1513 [M]	Musical Madness	1958	25.00	50.00	100.00
KING					
❑ 639 [M]	They Sure Are Corny	1959	25.00	50.00	100.00
❑ 848 [M]	Cornier Than Corn	1963	17.50	35.00	70.00
❑ KS-1005	24 Great Songs in the Homer & Jethro Style	1967	5.00	10.00	20.00
RCA VICTOR					
❑ LPM-1412 [M]	Barefoot Ballads	1957	12.50	25.00	50.00

Number	Title (A Side/B Side)	Yr	VG	VG+	NM
❑ LPM-1560 [M]	The Worst of Homer & Jethro	1958	12.50	25.00	50.00
❑ LPM-1880 [M]	Life Can Be Miserable	1958	7.50	15.00	30.00
❑ LSP-1880 [S]	Life Can Be Miserable	1958	12.50	25.00	50.00
❑ LPM-2181 [M]	Homer and Jethro at the Country Club	1960	6.25	12.50	25.00
❑ LSP-2181 [S]	Homer and Jethro at the Country Club	1960	10.00	20.00	40.00
❑ LPM-2286 [M]	Songs My Mother Never Sang	1961	6.25	12.50	25.00
❑ LSP-2286 [S]	Songs My Mother Never Sang	1961	7.50	15.00	30.00
❑ LPM-2455 [M]	Zany Songs of the '30s	1962	6.25	12.50	25.00
❑ LSP-2455 [S]	Zany Songs of the '30s	1962	7.50	15.00	30.00
❑ LPM-2459 [M]	Playing It Straight	1962	6.25	12.50	25.00
❑ LSP-2459 [S]	Playing It Straight	1962	7.50	15.00	30.00
❑ LPM-2492 [M]	Homer and Jethro at the Convention	1962	6.25	12.50	25.00
❑ LSP-2492 [S]	Homer and Jethro at the Convention	1962	7.50	15.00	30.00
❑ LPM-2674 [M]	Homer and Jethro Go West	1963	6.25	12.50	25.00
❑ LSP-2674 [S]	Homer and Jethro Go West	1963	7.50	15.00	30.00
❑ LPM-2743 [M]	Ooh, That's Corny	1963	6.25	12.50	25.00
❑ LSP-2743 [S]	Ooh, That's Corny	1963	7.50	15.00	30.00
❑ LPM-2928 [M]	Cornfucius Say	1964	6.25	12.50	25.00
❑ LSP-2928 [S]	Cornfucius Say	1964	7.50	15.00	30.00
❑ LPM-2954 [M]	Fractured Folk Songs	1964	6.25	12.50	25.00
❑ LSP-2954 [S]	Fractured Folk Songs	1964	7.50	15.00	30.00
❑ LPM-3112 [10]	Homer & Jethro Fracture Frank Loesser	1953	37.50	75.00	150.00
❑ LPM-3357 [M]	Homer and Jethro Sing Tenderly	1965	6.25	12.50	25.00
❑ LSP-3357 [S]	Homer and Jethro Sing Tenderly	1965	7.50	15.00	30.00
❑ LPM-3462 [M]	The Old Crusty Minstrels	1965	6.25	12.50	25.00
❑ LSP-3462 [S]	The Old Crusty Minstrels	1965	7.50	15.00	30.00
❑ LPM-3474 [M]	The Best of Homer and Jethro	1966	6.25	12.50	25.00
❑ LSP-3474 [S]	The Best of Homer and Jethro	1966	7.50	15.00	30.00
❑ LPM-3538 [M]	Any News from Nashville?	1966	6.25	12.50	25.00
❑ LSP-3538 [S]	Any News from Nashville?	1966	7.50	15.00	30.00
❑ LPM-3673 [M]	Wanted for Murder	1966	6.25	12.50	25.00
❑ LSP-3673 [S]	Wanted for Murder	1966	7.50	15.00	30.00
❑ LPM-3701 [M]	It Ain't Necessarily Square	1967	7.50	15.00	30.00
❑ LSP-3701 [S]	It Ain't Necessarily Square	1967	6.25	12.50	25.00
❑ LPM-3822 [M]	Nashville Cats	1967	10.00	20.00	40.00
❑ LSP-3822 [S]	Nashville Cats	1967	6.25	12.50	25.00
❑ LPM-3877 [M]	Somethin' Stupid	1967	12.50	25.00	50.00
❑ LSP-3877 [S]	Somethin' Stupid	1967	6.25	12.50	25.00
❑ LPM-3973 [M]	There's Nothing Like an Old Hippie	1968	25.00	50.00	100.00
❑ LSP-3973 [S]	There's Nothing Like an Old Hippie	1968	6.25	12.50	25.00
❑ LSP-4001	Cool, Crazy Christmas	1968	5.00	10.00	20.00
❑ LSP-4024	Homer and Jethro at Vanderbilt U.	1969	5.00	10.00	20.00
❑ LSP-4148	Homer and Jethro's Next Album	1969	5.00	10.00	20.00
HOMESICK JAMES					
PRESTIGE					
❑ PRLP-7388 [M]	Homesick James	1965	7.50	15.00	30.00
HONDELLS, THE					
MERCURY					
❑ MG-20940 [M]	Go Little Honda	1964	10.00	20.00	40.00
❑ MG-20982 [M]	The Hondells	1965	12.50	25.00	50.00
❑ SR-60940 [S]	Go Little Honda	1964	15.00	30.00	60.00
❑ SR-60982 [S]	The Hondells	1965	20.00	40.00	80.00
HONEY AND THE BEES					
JOSIE					
❑ JOS-4013	Love	1970	5.00	10.00	20.00
HONEY DREAMERS, THE					
FANTASY					
❑ 3207 [M]	The Honey Dreamers Sing Gershwin	195?	10.00	20.00	40.00
—Black vinyl					
❑ 3207 [M]	The Honey Dreamers Sing Gershwin	1956	20.00	40.00	80.00
—Red vinyl					
HONEYCOMBS, THE					
INTERPHON					
❑ IN-88001 [M]	Here Are the Honeycombs	1964	10.00	20.00	40.00
❑ IN-88001 [R]	Here Are the Honeycombs	1964	7.50	15.00	30.00
VEE JAY					
❑ IN-88001 [M]	Here Are the Honeycombs	1964	12.50	25.00	50.00
❑ IN-88001 [R]	Here Are the Honeycombs	1964	10.00	20.00	40.00
HOODOO RHYTHM DEVILS, THE					
CAPITOL					
❑ ST-842	The Hoodoo Rhythm Devils	1971	5.00	10.00	20.00
HOOK, THE					
UNI					
❑ 73023	The Hook Will Grab You	1968	6.25	12.50	25.00
❑ 73038	Hooked	1969	6.25	12.50	25.00
HOOKER, EARL					
ARHOOLIE					
❑ LP 1044	2 Bugs and a Roach	1968	6.25	12.50	25.00
❑ LP 1051	Hooker and Steve	1969	6.25	12.50	25.00
❑ LP 1066	His First and Last Recordings	1970	6.25	12.50	25.00
BLUE THUMB					
❑ BTS 12	Sweet Black Angel	1969	7.50	15.00	30.00
BLUES ON BLUES					
❑ 10002	The Last of the Great Earl Hooker	197?	5.00	10.00	20.00
BLUESWAY					
❑ BLS-6032	Don't Have to Worry	1969	6.25	12.50	25.00
❑ BLS-6038	If You Miss Him	1970	6.25	12.50	25.00
❑ BLS-6072	Do You Remember the Great Earl Hooker	1973	3.75	7.50	15.00
CUCA					
❑ 3400 [M]	The Genius of Earl Hooker	1965	62.50	125.00	250.00
HOOKER, JOHN LEE					
ABC					
❑ S-720 [(2)]	Endless Boogie	1971	5.00	10.00	20.00
❑ X-736	Never Get Out of These Blues Alive	1972	5.00	10.00	20.00

Number	Title (A Side/B Side)	Yr	VG	VG+	NM
❑ XQ-736 [Q]	Never Get Out of These Blues Alive	1974	6.25	12.50	25.00
❑ X-761	Live at Soledad Prison	1972	5.00	10.00	20.00
❑ XQ-761 [Q]	Live at Soledad Prison	1974	6.25	12.50	25.00
❑ X-768	Born in Mississippi, Raised Up in Tennessee	1973	5.00	10.00	20.00
❑ XQ-768 [Q]	Born in Mississippi, Raised Up in Tennessee	1974	6.25	12.50	25.00
❑ X-838	Free Beer and Chicken	1974	3.75	7.50	15.00
❑ XQ-838 [Q]	Free Beer and Chicken	1974	6.25	12.50	25.00

ARCHIVE OF FOLK AND JAZZ

Number	Title (A Side/B Side)	Yr	VG	VG+	NM
❑ 222	John Lee Hooker	1968	3.00	6.00	12.00
❑ 347	Hooked On Blues	1980	3.00	6.00	12.00

ATCO

❑ 33-151 [M]	Don't Turn Me From Your Door	1963	25.00	50.00	100.00
❑ SD 33-151 [R]	Don't Turn Me From Your Door	1967	12.50	25.00	50.00

ATLANTIC

❑ SD 7228	Detroit Special	1972	5.00	10.00	20.00

BATTLE

❑ BLP-6113 [M]	John Lee Hooker	196?	37.50	75.00	150.00
❑ BLP-6114 [M]	How Long Blues	196?	37.50	75.00	150.00

BLUESWAY

❑ BL-6002 [M]	Live at Café A-Go-Go	1967	6.25	12.50	25.00
❑ BLS-6002 [S]	Live at Café A-Go-Go	1967	5.00	10.00	20.00
❑ BL-6012 [M]	Urban Blues	1967	6.25	12.50	25.00
❑ BLS-6012 [S]	Urban Blues	1967	5.00	10.00	20.00
❑ BLS-6023	Simply the Truth	1968	5.00	10.00	20.00
❑ BLS-6038	If You Miss 'Em	1969	5.00	10.00	20.00
❑ BLQ-6052 [Q]	Live at Kabuki-Wuki	1974	6.25	12.50	25.00
❑ BLS-6052	Live at Kabuki-Wuki	1973	3.75	7.50	15.00

BUDDAH

❑ BDS-4002	The Very Best of John Lee Hooker	1970	3.75	7.50	15.00
❑ BDS-7506	Big Band Blues	1970	3.75	7.50	15.00

CHAMELEON

❑ D1-74794	The Hook	1989	2.50	5.00	10.00
❑ D1-74808	The Healer	1989	2.50	5.00	10.00

CHESS

❑ LP-1438 [M]	House of the Blues	1960	75.00	150.00	300.00
—Black label					
❑ LP-1438 [M]	House of the Blues	1966	12.50	25.00	50.00
—Blue and white label					
❑ LP-1454 [M]	John Lee Hooker Plays and Sings the Blues	1961	75.00	150.00	300.00
—Black label					
❑ LP-1454 [M]	John Lee Hooker Plays and Sings the Blues	1966	12.50	25.00	50.00
—Blue and white label					
❑ LP-1508 [M]	Real Folk Blues	1966	12.50	25.00	50.00
❑ LPS-1508 [R]	Real Folk Blues	1966	7.50	15.00	30.00
❑ CH-9199	John Lee Hooker Plays and Sings the Blues	1986	2.00	4.00	8.00
—Reissue					
❑ CH-9258	House of the Blues	1987	2.00	4.00	8.00
❑ CH-9271	The Real Folk Blues	1988	2.00	4.00	8.00
❑ 60011 [(2)]	Mad Man Blues	1973	5.00	10.00	20.00
❑ CH2-92507 [(2)]	Mad Man Blues	198?	3.00	6.00	12.00

COLLECTABLES

❑ COL-5151	Golden Classics	198?	3.00	6.00	12.00

CROWN

❑ CLP-5157 [M]	The Blues	196?	3.00	6.00	12.00
—Black label with multi-color "Crown"					
❑ CLP-5157 [M]	The Blues	1960	25.00	50.00	100.00
—Black label with silver "Crown"					
❑ CLP-5157 [M]	The Blues	1962	7.50	15.00	30.00
—Gray label					
❑ CLP-5232 [M]	John Lee Hooker Sings the Blues	196?	3.00	6.00	12.00
—Black label with multi-color "Crown"					
❑ CLP-5232 [M]	John Lee Hooker Sings the Blues	1962	7.50	15.00	30.00
—Gray label					
❑ CLP-5232 [M]	John Lee Hooker Sings the Blues	1962	25.00	50.00	100.00
—Black label with silver "Crown"					
❑ CLP-5295 [M]	Folk Blues	1962	3.00	6.00	12.00
—Black label with multi-color "Crown"					
❑ CLP-5295 [M]	Folk Blues	1962	7.50	15.00	30.00
—Gray label					
❑ CLP-5353 [M]	The Great John Lee Hooker	1963	3.00	6.00	12.00
—Black label with multi-color "Crown"					
❑ CLP-5353 [M]	The Great John Lee Hooker	1963	7.50	15.00	30.00
—Gray label					

EXODUS

❑ 325 [M]	Is He the World's Greatest Blues Singer?	1966	6.25	12.50	25.00

FANTASY

❑ 24706 [(2)]	Boogie Chillun	1972	3.75	7.50	15.00
❑ 24722 [(2)]	Black Snake	197?	3.75	7.50	15.00

GALAXY

❑ 8201 [M]	I'm John Lee Hooker	1962	62.50	125.00	250.00
❑ 8205 [M]	Live at Sugar Hill	196?	62.50	125.00	250.00

GNP CRESCENDO

❑ GNPS-10007 [(2)]	The Best of John Lee Hooker	1974	3.75	7.50	15.00

GREENE BOTTLE

❑ 3130 [(2)]	Johnny Lee	1972	3.75	7.50	15.00

IMPULSE!

❑ A-9103 [M]	It Serves You Right to Suffer	1966	7.50	15.00	30.00
❑ AS-9103 [S]	It Serves You Right to Suffer	1966	10.00	20.00	40.00

JEWEL

❑ 5005	I Feel Good	1971	3.75	7.50	15.00

KING

❑ 727 [M]	John Lee Hooker Sings the Blues	1960	125.00	250.00	500.00
❑ KLP-727	John Lee Hooker Sings the Blues	1988	2.00	4.00	8.00
—Reissue of earlier 727					
❑ KS-1085	Moanin' and Stompin' Blues	1970	6.25	12.50	25.00

LABOR

❑ 4	Alone	1982	2.50	5.00	10.00

MUSE

Number	Title (A Side/B Side)	Yr	VG	VG+	NM
❑ 5205	Sittin' Here Thinkin'	1980	3.00	6.00	12.00

PAUSA

❑ PR-7197	Jealous	1986	2.50	5.00	10.00

RIVERSIDE

❑ RLP 12-321 [M]	That's My Story	1960	25.00	50.00	100.00
❑ RLP 12-838 [M]	The Country Blues of John Lee Hooker	1959	25.00	50.00	100.00

SPECIALTY

❑ SPS-2125	Alone	1970	7.50	15.00	30.00
❑ SPS-2127	Going Down Highway 51	1970	7.50	15.00	30.00

STAX

❑ STS-2013	That's Where It's At	1970	3.75	7.50	15.00
❑ STX-4134	That's Where It's At	1979	2.50	5.00	10.00
—Reissue of 2013					

TOMATO

❑ 7009 [(2)]	The Cream	1978	3.75	7.50	15.00

TRADITION

❑ 2089	Real Blues	1970	3.75	7.50	15.00

UNITED ARTISTS

❑ UA-LA127-J [(3)]	John Lee Hooker's Detroit	1974	6.25	12.50	25.00
❑ UAS-5512	Coast to Coast Blues Band	1971	3.75	7.50	15.00

VEE JAY

❑ LP-1007 [M]	I'm John Lee Hooker	1959	75.00	150.00	300.00
—Maroon label					
❑ LP-1007 [M]	I'm John Lee Hooker	1960	20.00	40.00	80.00
—Black label with colorband					
❑ VJLP-1007	I'm John Lee Hooker	1986	2.00	4.00	8.00
—Reissue of original on flimsier vinyl					
❑ LP-1023 [M]	Travelin'	1960	20.00	40.00	80.00
❑ LP-1033 [M]	The Folk Lore of John Lee Hooker	1961	12.50	25.00	50.00
❑ SR-1033 [S]	The Folk Lore of John Lee Hooker	1961	20.00	40.00	80.00
❑ LP-1043 [M]	Burnin'	1962	12.50	25.00	50.00
❑ SR-1043 [S]	Burnin'	1962	37.50	75.00	150.00
❑ LP-1049 [M]	The Best of John Lee Hooker	1962	12.50	25.00	50.00
❑ SR-1049 [P]	The Best of John Lee Hooker	1962	20.00	40.00	80.00
❑ VJLP-1049	The Best of John Lee Hooker	1986	2.00	4.00	8.00
—Reissue of original on flimsier vinyl					
❑ LP-1058 [M]	The Big Soul of John Lee Hooker	1963	12.50	25.00	50.00
❑ SR-1058 [S]	The Big Soul of John Lee Hooker	1963	37.50	75.00	150.00
❑ VJLP-1058	The Big Soul of John Lee Hooker	1986	2.00	4.00	8.00
—Reissue of original on flimsier vinyl					
❑ LP-1066 [M]	John Lee Hooker On Campus	1963	12.50	25.00	50.00
❑ SR-1066 [S]	John Lee Hooker On Campus	1963	37.50	75.00	150.00
❑ LP-1078 [M]	John Lee Hooker at Newport	1964	12.50	25.00	50.00
❑ SR-1078 [S]	John Lee Hooker at Newport	1964	37.50	751.00	150.00
❑ VJLP-1078	John Lee Hooker at Newport	1986	2.00	4.00	8.00
—Reissue of original on flimsier vinyl					
❑ DY-7301	John Lee Hooker In Person	198?	2.00	4.00	8.00
❑ LP-8502 [M]	Is He the World's Greatest Blues Singer?	1965	10.00	20.00	40.00
—This is the title on the cover; the label calls it "Is He Really the World's Greatest Blues Singer?"					
❑ VJLP-8502	Is He the World's Greatest Blues Singer?	1986	2.00	4.00	8.00
—Reissue of original on flimsier vinyl; this is the title on the cover; the label calls it "Is He Really the World's Greatest Blues Singer?"					

VERVE FOLKWAYS

❑ FT-3003 [M]	John Lee Hooker and Seven Nights	1965	6.25	12.50	25.00
❑ FTS-3003 [S]	John Lee Hooker and Seven Nights	1965	10.00	20.00	40.00

WAND

❑ WDS-689	On the Waterfront	1972	3.75	7.50	15.00

HOOKER, JOHN LEE, AND CANNED HEAT

LIBERTY

❑ 35002	Hooker 'n' Heat	1971	5.00	10.00	20.00

RHINO

❑ RNLP-801	Recorded Live at the Fox Venice Theatre	1985	3.00	6.00	12.00
❑ RNDA-71105	Infinite Boogie	1987	3.00	6.00	12.00

HOOTCH

PROGRESS

❑ PRS-4844	Hootch	1974	150.00	300.00	600.00

HOOTERS

ANTENNA

❑ HOO 83	Amore	1983	5.00	10.00	20.00

COLUMBIA

❑ BFC 39912	Nervous Night	1985	3.00	6.00	12.00
❑ FC 39912	Nervous Night	1985	2.50	5.00	10.00
—Reissue with new prefix					
❑ OC 40659	One Way Home	1987	2.50	5.00	10.00
❑ C 45058	Zig Zag	1989	2.50	5.00	10.00

HOPE, BOB

DECCA

❑ DL 4396 [M]	Hope in Russia and One Other Place	1963	5.00	10.00	20.00
❑ DL 74396 [S]	Hope in Russia and One Other Place	1963	6.25	12.50	25.00

HOPE, ELMO

AUDIO FIDELITY

❑ AFLP-2119 [M]	Sounds from Riker's Island	1963	7.50	15.00	30.00
❑ AFSD-6119 [S]	Sounds from Riker's Island	1963	10.00	20.00	40.00

BEACON

❑ B-401 [M]	High Hopes	1961	7.50	15.00	30.00
❑ BS-401 [S]	High Hopes	1961	10.00	20.00	40.00

BLUE NOTE

❑ BLP-5029 [10]	Elmo Hope Trio	1953	75.00	150.00	300.00
❑ BLP-5044 [10]	Elmo Hope Quintet	1954	75.00	150.00	300.00

CELEBRITY

❑ 209 [M]	Elmo Hope Trio	1962	6.25	12.50	25.00
❑ S-209 [S]	Elmo Hope Trio	1962	7.50	15.00	30.00

Number	Title (A Side/B Side)	Yr	VG	VG+	NM
CONTEMPORARY					
❏ M-3620 [M]	The Elmo Hope Trio	1966	6.25	12.50	25.00
❏ S-7620 [S]	The Elmo Hope Trio	1966	7.50	15.00	30.00
HIFI					
❏ J-616 [M]	Elmo Hope	1960	10.00	20.00	40.00
❏ JS-616 [S]	Elmo Hope	1960	12.50	25.00	50.00
PRESTIGE					
❏ PRLP-7010 [M]	Meditations	1956	30.00	60.00	120.00
❏ PRLP-7021 [M]	Hope Meets Foster	1956	30.00	60.00	120.00
❏ PRLP-7021 [M]	Wail, Frank, Wail	1957	20.00	40.00	80.00
—Retitled reissue of above album					
❏ PRLP-7043 [M]	Informal Jazz	1956	30.00	60.00	120.00
RIVERSIDE					
❏ RLP-381 [M]	Homecoming!	1961	10.00	20.00	40.00
❏ RLP-408 [M]	Hope-Full	1962	6.25	12.50	25.00
❏ RS-9381 [S]	Homecoming!	1961	12.50	25.00	50.00
❏ RS-9408 [S]	Hope-Full	1962	7.50	15.00	30.00
HOPE, LYNN					
ALADDIN					
❏ LP-707 [10]	Lynn Hope and His Tenor Sax	1953	150.00	300.00	600.00
❏ LP-805 [M]	Lynn Hope and His Tenor Sax	1955	125.00	250.00	500.00
IMPERIAL					
❏ LP-9177-A [M]	Tenderly	1962	10.00	20.00	40.00
❏ LP-12177-A [S]	Tenderly	1962	15.00	30.00	60.00
KING					
❏ 717 [M]	Maharajah of the Saxophone	1961	30.00	60.00	120.00
SCORE					
❏ SLP-4015 [M]	Tenderly	1957	50.00	100.00	200.00
HOPKIN, MARY					
APPLE					
❏ ST-3351	Post Card	1969	6.25	12.50	25.00
❏ ST-5-3351	Post Card	1969	7.50	15.00	30.00
—Capitol Record Club edition					
❏ SMAS-3381	Earth Song/Ocean Song	1970	6.25	12.50	25.00
❏ SW-3395	Those Were the Days	1972	10.00	20.00	40.00
HOPKINS, CLAUDE					
DESIGN					
❏ DLP-30 [M]	Golden Era of Dixieland Jazz 1887-1937	1957	6.25	12.50	25.00
SWINGVILLE					
❏ SVLP-2009 [M]	Yes Indeed	1960	12.50	25.00	50.00
—Purple label					
❏ SVLP-2009 [M]	Yes Indeed	1965	6.25	12.50	25.00
—Blue label, trident logo at right					
❏ SVLP-2020 [M]	Let's Jam	1961	12.50	25.00	50.00
—Purple label					
❏ SVLP-2020 [M]	Let's Jam	1965	6.25	12.50	25.00
—Blue label, trident logo at right					
❏ SVLP-2041 [M]	Swing Time	1962	12.50	25.00	50.00
—Purple label					
❏ SVLP-2041 [M]	Swing Time	1965	6.25	12.50	25.00
—Blue label, trident logo at right					
HOPKINS, KENYON					
VERVE					
❏ V-8694 [M]	Dream Songs	1967	5.00	10.00	20.00
HOPKINS, LIGHTNIN'					
ANALOGUE PRODUCTIONS					
❏ AAPB-014	Goin' Away	199?	10.00	20.00	40.00
—Audiophile reissue					
ARCHIVE OF FOLK AND JAZZ					
❏ 241	Lightnin' Hopkins	1969	3.75	7.50	15.00
❏ 313	Lightnin' Hopkins, Vol. 2	197?	3.75	7.50	15.00
❏ 342	Autobiography in Blues	1979	3.00	6.00	12.00
ARHOOLIE					
❏ 1011	Lightnin' Hopkins and His Guitar	196?	5.00	10.00	20.00
❏ 1022	Lightnin' Hopkins, His Brother and Barbara Dane	196?	5.00	10.00	20.00
❏ 1030	Blues Festival	196?	3.75	7.50	15.00
❏ 1034	Texas Blues Man	1968	3.75	7.50	15.00
❏ 1063	Lightnin' Hopkins in Berkeley	1969	3.75	7.50	15.00
❏ 1087	Poor Lightnin'	1970	3.75	7.50	15.00
❏ 2007	Early Recordings	197?	3.75	7.50	15.00
❏ 2010	Early Recordings Volume 2	197?	3.75	7.50	15.00
BARNABY					
❏ Z 30247	Lightnin' Hopkins in New York	1970	3.75	7.50	15.00
BLUES CLASSICS					
❏ 30	Historic Recordings 1952-1953	1986	3.00	6.00	12.00
BLUESVILLE					
❏ BVLP-1019 [M]	Lightnin'	1961	25.00	50.00	100.00
—Blue label, silver print					
❏ BVLP-1019 [M]	Lightnin'	1964	7.50	15.00	30.00
—Blue label, trident logo on right					
❏ BVLP-1029 [M]	Last Night Blues	1961	25.00	50.00	100.00
—Blue label, silver print					
❏ BVLP-1045 [M]	Blues in My Bottle	1962	25.00	50.00	100.00
—Blue label, silver print					
❏ BVLP-1045 [M]	Blues in My Bottle	1964	7.50	15.00	30.00
—Blue label, trident logo on right					
❏ BVLP-1057 [M]	Walkin' This Street	1962	25.00	50.00	100.00
—Blue label, silver print					
❏ BVLP-1057 [M]	Walkin' This Street	1964	7.50	15.00	30.00
—Blue label, trident logo on right					
❏ BVLP-1061 [M]	Lightnin' & Co.	1963	25.00	50.00	100.00
—Blue label, silver print					
❏ BVLP-1061 [M]	Lightnin' & Co.	1964	7.50	15.00	30.00
—Blue label, trident logo on right					

Number	Title (A Side/B Side)	Yr	VG	VG+	NM
❏ BVLP-1070 [M]	Smokes Like Lightnin'	1963	25.00	50.00	100.00
—Blue label, silver print					
❏ BVLP-1070 [M]	Smokes Like Lightnin'	1964	7.50	15.00	30.00
—Blue label, trident logo on right					
❏ BVLP-1073 [M]	Goin' Away	1963	25.00	50.00	100.00
—Blue label, silver print					
❏ BVLP-1073 [M]	Goin' Away	1964	7.50	15.00	30.00
—Blue label, trident logo on right					
❏ BVLP-1081 [M]	Gotta Move Your Baby	1964	7.50	15.00	30.00
—Blue label, trident logo on right					
❏ BVLP-1084 [M]	Lightnin' Hopkins' Greatest Hits	1964	10.00	20.00	40.00
❏ BVLP-1086 [M]	Down Home Blues	1964	6.25	12.50	25.00
BLUESWAY					
❏ S-6039	If You Miss 'Im	1969	5.00	10.00	20.00
BULLDOG					
❏ 1010	The Texas Bluesman	1965	3.75	7.50	15.00
CANDID					
❏ CM-8010 [M]	Lightnin' in New York	1961	30.00	60.00	120.00
❏ CS-9010 [S]	Lightnin' in New York	1961	37.50	75.00	150.00
COLLECTABLES					
❏ COL-5111	Golden Classics — Mojo Hand	198?	2.50	5.00	10.00
❏ COL-5121	The Herald Recordings/1954.	198?	2.50	5.00	10.00
❏ COL-5143	Golden Classics, Part 1: Drinkin' the Blues.	198?	2.50	5.00	10.00
❏ COL-5144	Golden Classics, Part 2: Prison Blues.	198?	2.50	5.00	10.00
❏ COL-5145	Golden Classics, Part 3: Mama and Papa Hopkins.	198?	2.50	5.00	10.00
❏ COL-5146	Golden Classics, Part 4: Nothin' But the Blues.	198?	2.50	5.00	10.00
❏ COL-5203	The Lost Texas Tapes, Vol. 1.	198?	2.50	5.00	10.00
❏ COL-5204	The Lost Texas Tapes, Vol. 2.	198?	2.50	5.00	10.00
❏ COL-5205	The Lost Texas Tapes, Vol. 3.	198?	2.50	5.00	10.00
❏ COL-5206	The Lost Texas Tapes, Vol. 4.	198?	2.50	5.00	10.00
❏ COL-5207	The Lost Texas Tapes, Vol. 5.	198?	2.50	5.00	10.00
CROWN					
❏ CLP-5224 [M]	Lightnin' Hopkins Sings the Blues	196?	6.25	12.50	25.00
—Black label, multi-color logo					
❏ CLP-5224 [M]	Lightnin' Hopkins Sings the Blues	1962	12.50	25.00	50.00
—Gray label					
❏ CLP-5224 [M]	Lightnin' Hopkins Sings the Blues	1962	25.00	50.00	100.00
—Black label, silver "Crown"					
DART					
❏ D-8000 [M]	Blues Underground	196?	50.00	100.00	200.00
—Retitled version of above					
❏ D-8000 [M]	Lightning Strikes Again	1960	100.00	200.00	400.00
DCC COMPACT CLASSICS					
❏ LPZ-2007	Blues Hoot	1996	7.50	15.00	30.00
—Audiophile vinyl					
FANTASY					
❏ OBC-506	Blues in My Bottle	198?	3.00	6.00	12.00
❏ OBC-522	Goin' Away	1988	3.00	6.00	12.00
❏ OBC-532	Lightnin'	1990	3.00	6.00	12.00
❏ 24702 [(2)]	Double Blues	1972	5.00	10.00	20.00
❏ 24725 [(2)]	How Many More Years	1981	3.75	7.50	15.00
FIRE					
❏ FLP 104 [M]	Mojo Hand	1960	375.00	750.00	1500.
FOLKLORE					
❏ FRLP-14021 [M]	Hootin' the Blues	1964	15.00	30.00	60.00
❏ FRST-14021 [S]	Hootin' the Blues	1964	17.50	35.00	70.00
FOLKWAYS					
❏ FS-3822 [M]	Lightnin' Hopkins	1962	10.00	20.00	40.00
❏ 31011	Roots	196?	3.75	7.50	15.00
GNP CRESCENDO					
❏ 10022	Legacy of the Blues, Volume 12	1978	3.00	6.00	12.00
GUEST STAR					
❏ G-1459 [M]	"Live" at the Bird Lounge, Houston, Texas	1964	7.50	15.00	30.00
❏ GS-1459 [R]	"Live" at the Bird Lounge, Houston, Texas	1964	5.00	10.00	20.00
HERALD					
❏ LP 1012 [M]	Lightnin' and the Blues	1959	200.00	400.00	800.00
—Yellow label					
❏ LP 1012 [M]	Lightnin' and the Blues	1959	750.00	1125.	1500.
—Black label					
❏ LP 1012 [M]	Lightnin' and the Blues	196?	125.00	250.00	500.00
—Multi-color label					
IMPERIAL					
❏ LP-9180 [M]	Lightnin' Hopkins On Stage	1962	75.00	150.00	300.00
❏ LP-9186 [M]	Lightnin' Hopkins Sings the Blues	1962	75.00	150.00	300.00
❏ LP-9211 [M]	Lightnin' Hopkins and the Blues	1963	50.00	100.00	200.00
❏ LP-12211 [R]	Lightnin' Hopkins and the Blues	1963	25.00	50.00	100.00
INTERNATIONAL ARTISTS					
❏ IA-6	Free Form Patterns	1968	12.50	25.00	50.00
—With psychedelic art on cover					
❏ IA-6	Free Form Patterns	1968	50.00	100.00	200.00
—With photo on cover					
JAZZ MAN					
❏ BLZ-5502	Lightnin' in New York	1982	2.50	5.00	10.00
JEWEL					
❏ 5000	Blue Lightnin'	1967	3.75	7.50	15.00
❏ 5001	Talkin' Some Sense	1968	3.75	7.50	15.00
❏ 5015	Great Electric Show and Dance	1970	3.75	7.50	15.00
KING					
❏ KS-1085	Moanin' Blues	1969	3.75	7.50	15.00
MAINSTREAM					
❏ 311	The Blues	1971	3.75	7.50	15.00
❏ 326	Dirty Blues	197?	3.75	7.50	15.00
❏ 405	Low Down Dirty Blues	1974	3.75	7.50	15.00
❏ S-6040 [S]	Blues	196?	7.50	15.00	30.00
❏ 56040 [M]	Blues	196?	6.25	12.50	25.00
MOUNT VERNON					
❏ 104 [M]	Nothin' But the Blues	196?	6.25	12.50	25.00

Number	Title (A Side/B Side)	Yr	VG	VG+	NM
OLYMPIC GOLD MEDAL					
❏ 7110	Blues Giant	1974	3.00	6.00	12.00
POPPY					
❏ 60002 [(2)]	Lightnin'!	1969	6.25	12.50	25.00
PRESTIGE					
❏ PRLPT-7370 [(2)M]My Life with the Blues		1965	15.00	30.00	60.00
❏ PRST-7370 [(2)S]My Life with the Blues		1965	17.50	35.00	70.00
❏ PRLP-7377 [M]	Soul Blues	1966	12.50	25.00	50.00
❏ PRST-7377 [S]	Soul Blues	1966	15.00	30.00	60.00
❏ PRST-7592	Lightnin' Hopkins' Greatest Hits	1969	3.75	7.50	15.00
❏ PRST-7714	The Best of Lightnin' Hopkins & His Texas Blues Band	1969	3.75	7.50	15.00
❏ PRST-7806	Hootin' the Blues	1969	3.75	7.50	15.00
❏ PRST-7811	The Blues of Lightnin' Hopkins	1969	3.75	7.50	15.00
❏ PRST-7831	Gotta Move Your Baby	1970	3.75	7.50	15.00
RHINO					
❏ RNLP 103	Los Angeles Blues	1982	2.50	5.00	10.00
SCORE					
❏ SLP-4022 [M]	Lightnin' Hopkins Strums the Blues	1958	300.00	600.00	1200.
SMITHSONIAN FOLKWAYS					
❏ SF-40019	Lightnin' Hopkins	1990	3.00	6.00	12.00
SPHERE SOUND					
❏ SSR-7001 [M]	Lightnin' Hopkins	1964	100.00	200.00	400.00
❏ SSSR-7001 [R]	Lightnin' Hopkins	1964	75.00	150.00	300.00
TIME					
❏ 1 [M]	Blues/Folk	1960	30.00	60.00	120.00
❏ 2 [M]	Blues/Folk Volume 2	1960	30.00	60.00	120.00
❏ ST-70004 [S]	Last of the Great Blues Singers	1962	30.00	60.00	120.00
❏ T-70004 [M]	Last of the Great Blues Singers	1962	30.00	60.00	120.00
TOMATO					
❏ 7004 [(2)]	Lightnin'!	1977	3.75	7.50	15.00
TRADITION					
❏ TLP-1035 [M]	Country Blues	1960	7.50	15.00	30.00
❏ TLP-1040 [M]	Autobiography in Blues	1961	7.50	15.00	30.00
❏ TLP-2056 [S]	The Best of Lightnin' Hopkins	1967	5.00	10.00	20.00
❏ TLP-2103 [M]	Lightnin' Strikes	1972	3.75	7.50	15.00
TRIP					
❏ TLP-8015	Lightnin' Hopkins	1971	3.00	6.00	12.00
UNITED					
❏ US-7713	Lightnin' Hopkins Sings the Blues	196?	3.75	7.50	15.00
❏ US-7744	Original Folk Blues	196?	3.75	7.50	15.00
❏ US-7785	A Legend in His Time	196?	3.75	7.50	15.00
UNITED ARTISTS					
❏ UAS-5512	Coast to Coast Blues Band	197?	3.75	7.50	15.00
UP FRONT					
❏ 158	Lightnin' Blues	1973	3.00	6.00	12.00
VAULT					
❏ 129	California Mudslide	1969	6.25	12.50	25.00
VEE JAY					
❏ LP 1044 [M]	Lightnin' Strikes	1962	12.50	25.00	50.00
VERVE					
❏ V-8453 [M]	Fast Life Woman	1962	10.00	20.00	40.00
VERVE FOLKWAYS					
❏ FV-9000 [M]	The Roots of Lightnin' Hopkins	1965	6.25	12.50	25.00
❏ FVS-9000 [S]	The Roots of Lightnin' Hopkins	1965	7.50	15.00	30.00
❏ FV-9022 [M]	Lightnin' Strikes	1965	6.25	12.50	25.00
❏ FVS-9022 [S]	Lightnin' Strikes	1965	7.50	15.00	30.00
VERVE FORECAST					
❏ FT-3013 [M]	Something Blue	1967	5.00	10.00	20.00
❏ FTS-3013 [S]	Something Blue	1967	6.25	12.50	25.00
❏ FTS-3031	Lightnin' Strikes	1968	5.00	10.00	20.00
WORLD PACIFIC					
❏ ST-1817 [S]	First Meetin'	1963	10.00	20.00	40.00
—Black vinyl					
❏ ST-1817 [S]	First Meetin'	1963	20.00	40.00	80.00
—Red vinyl					
❏ WP-1817 [M]	First Meetin'	1963	7.50	15.00	30.00

HOPKINS, NICKY

COLUMBIA

Number	Title (A Side/B Side)	Yr	VG	VG+	NM
❏ KC 32074	The Tin Man Was a Dreamer	1973	5.00	10.00	20.00

HOPNEY

ILLUSION

Number	Title (A Side/B Side)	Yr	VG	VG+	NM
❏ CM-1032	End and Means	197?	62.50	125.00	250.00
❏ CM-1033	Perils of Love	197?	62.50	125.00	250.00
❏ CM-1034	Cosmic Rockout	197?	125.00	250.00	500.00

HORN, PAUL

COLUMBIA

Number	Title (A Side/B Side)	Yr	VG	VG+	NM
❏ CL 1677 [M]	The Sound of Paul Horn	1961	6.25	12.50	25.00
❏ CS 8477 [S]	The Sound of Paul Horn	1961	7.50	15.00	30.00
❏ CS 8722 [S]	Profile of a Jazz Musician	1962	5.00	10.00	20.00
❏ CS 8850 [S]	Impressions of "Cleopatra"	1963	5.00	10.00	20.00
DOT					
❏ DLP-3091 [M]	House of Horn	1957	12.50	25.00	50.00
❏ DLP-9002 [M]	Plenty of Horn	1958	12.50	25.00	50.00
❏ DLP-29002 [S]	Plenty of Horn	1959	10.00	20.00	40.00
HIFI					
❏ J-615 [M]	Something Blue	1960	7.50	15.00	30.00
❏ JS-615 [S]	Something Blue	1960	10.00	20.00	40.00
ISLAND					
❏ ILSD 6 [(2)]	Special Edition	197?	5.00	10.00	20.00
KUCKUCK					
❏ KU-060/061 [(2)]	Inside the Great Pyramid	198?	5.00	10.00	20.00
RCA VICTOR					
❏ LSP-3386 [S]	Cycle	1965	5.00	10.00	20.00

Number	Title (A Side/B Side)	Yr	VG	VG+	NM
❏ LSP-3414 [S]	Jazz Suite on the Mass Texts	1965	5.00	10.00	20.00
❏ LSP-3519 [S]	Here's That Rainy Day	1966	5.00	10.00	20.00
❏ LSP-3613 [S]	Monday, Monday	1966	5.00	10.00	20.00
WORLD PACIFIC					
❏ WP-1266 [M]	Impressions	1959	12.50	25.00	50.00

HORN, SHIRLEY

ABC-PARAMOUNT

Number	Title (A Side/B Side)	Yr	VG	VG+	NM
❏ ABC-538 [M]	Travelin' Light	1965	10.00	20.00	40.00
❏ ABCS-538 [S]	Travelin' Light	1965	12.50	25.00	50.00
MERCURY					
❏ MG-20761 [M]	Loads of Love	1963	12.50	25.00	50.00
❏ MG-20835 [M]	Shirley Horn with Horns	1963	12.50	25.00	50.00
❏ SR-60761 [S]	Loads of Love	1963	15.00	30.00	60.00
❏ SR-60835 [S]	Shirley Horn with Horns	1963	15.00	30.00	60.00
❏ SR-60835 [S]	Shirley Horn with Horns	199?	6.25	12.50	25.00
—Classic Records reissue on audiophile vinyl					
STEREO-CRAFT					
❏ RTN-16 [M]	Embers and Ashes	1961	15.00	30.00	60.00
❏ RTS-16 [S]	Embers and Ashes	1961	20.00	40.00	80.00

HORNE, LENA

CHARTER

Number	Title (A Side/B Side)	Yr	VG	VG+	NM
❏ CLS-101 [S]	Lena Sings Your Requests	1963	5.00	10.00	20.00
❏ CLS-106 [S]	Like Latin	1964	5.00	10.00	20.00
JAZZTONE					
❏ J-1262 [M]	Lena and Ivie	1957	12.50	25.00	50.00
LION					
❏ L-70050 [M]	I Feel So Smoochie	1959	5.00	10.00	20.00
MGM					
❏ E-545 [10]	Lena Horne Sings	1952	12.50	25.00	50.00
MOBILE FIDELITY					
❏ 2-094 [(2)]	Lena Horne: The Lady and Her Music	1982	10.00	20.00	40.00
—Audiophile vinyl					
MOVIETONE					
❏ MTS 72005 [S]	Once in a Lifetime	196?	5.00	10.00	20.00
RCA VICTOR					
❏ LOC-1028 [M]	Lena Horne at the Waldorf Astoria	1957	7.50	15.00	30.00
❏ LSO-1028 [S]	Lena Horne at the Waldorf Astoria	1957	10.00	20.00	40.00
❏ LPM-1148 [M]	It's Love	1955	12.50	25.00	50.00
❏ LPM-1375 [M]	Stormy Weather	1956	12.50	25.00	50.00
❏ LPM-1879 [M]	Give the Lady What She Wants	1958	7.50	15.00	30.00
❏ LSP-1879 [S]	Give the Lady What She Wants	1958	10.00	20.00	40.00
❏ LPM-1895 [M]	Songs of Burke and Van Heusen	1959	7.50	15.00	30.00
❏ LSP-1895 [S]	Songs of Burke and Van Heusen	1959	10.00	20.00	40.00
❏ LPM-2364 [M]	Lena Horne at the Sands	1961	6.25	12.50	25.00
❏ LSP-2364 [S]	Lena Horne at the Sands	1961	7.50	15.00	30.00
❏ LPM-2465 [M]	Lena on the Blue Side	1962	6.25	12.50	25.00
❏ LSP-2465 [S]	Lena on the Blue Side	1962	7.50	15.00	30.00
❏ LPM-2587 [M]	Lena…Lovely and Alive	1963	6.25	12.50	25.00
❏ LSP-2587 [S]	Lena…Lovely and Alive	1963	7.50	15.00	30.00
❏ LPT-3061 [10]	This Is Lena Horne	1952	12.50	25.00	50.00
TOPS					
❏ L-910 [10]	Moanin' Low	195?	10.00	20.00	40.00
❏ L-931 [10]	Lena Horne Sings	195?	10.00	20.00	40.00
❏ L-1502 [M]	Lena Horne	1958	5.00	10.00	20.00
20TH CENTURY FOX					
❏ TFS-4115 [S]	Here's Lena Now	1964	5.00	10.00	20.00
UNITED ARTISTS					
❏ UAS 6433 [S]	Feelin' Good	1965	5.00	10.00	20.00
❏ UAS 6470 [S]	Lena in Hollywood	1966	5.00	10.00	20.00
❏ UAS 6496 [S]	Soul	1966	5.00	10.00	20.00

HORNE, LENA, AND HARRY BELAFONTE

RCA VICTOR

Number	Title (A Side/B Side)	Yr	VG	VG+	NM
❏ LOC-1507 [M]	Porgy and Bess	1959	6.25	12.50	25.00
❏ LSO-1507 [S]	Porgy and Bess	1959	10.00	20.00	40.00

HORNETS, THE

LIBERTY

Number	Title (A Side/B Side)	Yr	VG	VG+	NM
❏ LRP-3348 [M]	Motorcycles U.S.A.	1963	10.00	20.00	40.00
❏ LRP-3364 [M]	Big Drag Boats U.S.A.	1964	12.50	25.00	50.00
❏ LST-7348 [S]	Motorcycles U.S.A.	1963	12.50	25.00	50.00
❏ LST-7364 [S]	Big Drag Boats U.S.A.	1964	15.00	30.00	60.00

HOROWITZ, VLADIMIR

RCA VICTOR RED SEAL

Number	Title (A Side/B Side)	Yr	VG	VG+	NM
❏ LSC-2366 [S]	Beethoven: Piano Sonata in D "Appassionata"	1960	5.00	10.00	20.00
—Originals with "shaded dog" label					

HORSES

Don Johnson of "Miami Vice" and "Nash Bridges" fame was in this band.

WHITE WHALE

Number	Title (A Side/B Side)	Yr	VG	VG+	NM
❏ WWS-7121	Horses	1970	10.00	20.00	40.00

HORTON, JOHNNY

BRIAR

Number	Title (A Side/B Side)	Yr	VG	VG+	NM
❏ 104 [M]	Done Rovin'	196?	37.50	75.00	150.00
COLUMBIA					
❏ CL 1362 [M]	The Spectacular Johnny Horton	1959	7.50	15.00	30.00
❏ CL 1478 [M]	Johnny Horton Makes History	1960	7.50	15.00	30.00
❏ 1596/8396	Johnny Horton's Greatest Hits Bonus Photo	1961	2.50	5.00	10.00
❏ CL 1596 [M]	Johnny Horton's Greatest Hits	1961	6.25	12.50	25.00
❏ CL 1721 [M]	Honky-Tonk Man	1962	7.50	15.00	30.00
❏ CL 2299 [M]	I Can't Forget You	1965	6.25	12.50	25.00
❏ CL 2566 [M]	Johnny Horton on Stage at the Louisiana Hayride	1966	5.00	10.00	20.00
❏ CS 8167 [S]	The Spectacular Johnny Horton	1959	10.00	20.00	40.00
❏ CS 8269 [S]	Johnny Horton Makes History	1960	10.00	20.00	40.00
❏ CS 8396 [S]	Johnny Horton's Greatest Hits	1961	7.50	15.00	30.00

Number	Title (A Side/B Side)	Yr	VG	VG+	NM
❑ PC 8396	Johnny Horton's Greatest Hits	198?	2.00	4.00	8.00
—Budget-line reissue					
❑ CS 8779 [R]	Honky-Tonk Man	1962	3.75	7.50	15.00
❑ CS 9099 [R]	I Can't Forget You	1965	3.75	7.50	15.00
❑ CS 9366 [S]	Johnny Horton on Stage at the Louisiana Hayride	1966	6.25	12.50	25.00
❑ CS 9940	Johnny Horton On the Road	1969	3.75	7.50	15.00
❑ G 30884 [(2)]	The World of Johnny Horton	1971	3.75	7.50	15.00
DOT					
❑ DLP 3221 [M]	Johnny Horton	1962	7.50	15.00	30.00
❑ DLP 25221 [R]	Johnny Horton	1962	3.75	7.50	15.00
HARMONY					
❑ HS 11291 [R]	The Unforgettable Johnny Horton	196?	3.00	6.00	12.00
❑ HS 11384	The Legendary Johnny Horton	1970	3.00	6.00	12.00
❑ KH 30394	The Battle of New Orleans	1971	3.00	6.00	12.00
HILLTOP					
❑ 6012	The Voice of Johnny Horton	196?	3.00	6.00	12.00
❑ 6060	All for the Love of a Girl	196?	3.00	6.00	12.00
MERCURY					
❑ MG-20478 [M]	The Fantastic Johnny Horton	1959	12.50	25.00	50.00
SESAC					
❑ 1201 [M]	Free and Easy Songs	1959	37.50	75.00	150.00

HORTON, ROBERT
COLUMBIA

Number	Title (A Side/B Side)	Yr	VG	VG+	NM
❑ CL 2202 [M]	The Very Thought of You	1964	6.25	12.50	25.00
❑ CL 2408 [M]	A Man Called Shenandoah	1966	6.25	12.50	25.00
❑ CS 9002 [S]	The Very Thought of You	1964	7.50	15.00	30.00
❑ CS 9208 [S]	A Man Called Shenandoah	1966	7.50	15.00	30.00

HORTON, WALTER "SHAKEY"
ARGO

Number	Title (A Side/B Side)	Yr	VG	VG+	NM
❑ LP-4037 [M]	The Soul of Blues Harmonica	1964	37.50	75.00	150.00
❑ LPS-4037 [S]	The Soul of Blues Harmonica	1964	62.50	125.00	250.00

HOT BUTTER
MUSICOR

Number	Title (A Side/B Side)	Yr	VG	VG+	NM
❑ MS-3242	Popcorn	1972	3.00	6.00	12.00
—Regular cover					
❑ MS-3242	Popcorn	1972	5.00	10.00	20.00
—Die-cut cover					

HOT DOGGERS, THE
EPIC

Number	Title (A Side/B Side)	Yr	VG	VG+	NM
❑ LN 24054 [M]	Surfin' U.S.A.	1963	37.50	75.00	150.00
❑ BN 26054 [S]	Surfin' U.S.A.	1963	50.00	100.00	200.00

HOT POOP
HOT POOP

Number	Title (A Side/B Side)	Yr	VG	VG+	NM
❑ 3072	Hot Poop Does Their Own Thing	1971	75.00	150.00	300.00

HOT RODDERS, THE
CROWN

Number	Title (A Side/B Side)	Yr	VG	VG+	NM
❑ CST-378 [S]	Big Hot Rod	1963	6.25	12.50	25.00
❑ CLP-5378 [M]	Big Hot Rod	1963	5.00	10.00	20.00

HOT TUNA
Offshoot of JEFFERSON AIRPLANE.
GRUNT

Number	Title (A Side/B Side)	Yr	VG	VG+	NM
❑ BFL1-0348	The Phosphorescent Rat	1974	3.75	7.50	15.00
❑ BFD1-0820 [Q]	America's Choice	1975	6.25	12.50	25.00
❑ BFL1-0820	America's Choice	1975	3.75	7.50	15.00
❑ FTR-1004	Burgers	1972	3.75	7.50	15.00
❑ BFD1-1238 [Q]	Yellow Fever	1975	6.25	12.50	25.00
❑ BFL1-1238	Yellow Fever	1975	3.75	7.50	15.00
❑ BFL1-1920	Hoppkorv	1976	3.75	7.50	15.00
❑ CYL2-2545 [(2)]	Double Dose	1978	5.00	10.00	20.00
❑ BXL1-2591	Burgers	1978	3.00	6.00	12.00
—Reissue of 1004					
❑ DJL1-2852 [DJ]	The Last Interview? A Live Hot Tuna Radio Classic	1978	7.50	15.00	30.00
❑ BXL1-3357	Final Vinyl	1979	3.00	6.00	12.00
RCA VICTOR					
❑ AYL1-3864	Hot Tuna	1981	2.00	4.00	8.00
—"Best Buy Series" reissue					
❑ AYL1-3865	First Pull Up Then Pull Down	1981	2.00	4.00	8.00
—"Best Buy Series" reissue					
❑ AYL1-3951	Burgers	1981	2.00	4.00	8.00
—"Best Buy Series" reissue					
❑ LSP-4353	Hot Tuna	1970	3.75	7.50	15.00
❑ LSP-4550	First Pull Up Then Pull Down	1971	3.75	7.50	15.00

HOTHOUSE FLOWERS
LONDON

Number	Title (A Side/B Side)	Yr	VG	VG+	NM
❑ 085 [DJ]	Conversation and Music with Hothouse Flowers	1988	3.75	7.50	15.00
❑ PRO 884-1 [DJ]	Live	1990	6.25	12.50	25.00
—Six-song promo-only live EP					
❑ 828101-1	People	1988	3.00	6.00	12.00

HOTLEGS
Early incarnation of 10CC. Also see GRAHAM GOULDMAN.
CAPITOL

Number	Title (A Side/B Side)	Yr	VG	VG+	NM
❑ ST-587	Hotlegs Thinks: School Stinks	1970	6.25	12.50	25.00

HOUK, RALPH
CARLTON

Number	Title (A Side/B Side)	Yr	VG	VG+	NM
❑ HH-16 [M]	Hear How to Play Better Baseball	1961	10.00	20.00	40.00

HOUR GLASS, THE
LIBERTY

Number	Title (A Side/B Side)	Yr	VG	VG+	NM
❑ LRP-3536 [M]	The Hour Glass	1967	6.25	12.50	25.00
❑ LST-7536 [S]	The Hour Glass	1967	7.50	15.00	30.00
❑ LST-7555	The Power of Love	1968	7.50	15.00	30.00

SPRINGBOARD

Number	Title (A Side/B Side)	Yr	VG	VG+	NM
❑ SPB-4016	Duane and Gregg Allman with the Hour Glass	1976	2.50	5.00	10.00
UNITED ARTISTS					
❑ UA-LA013-G2 [(2)]	The Hour Glass	1973	3.75	7.50	15.00

HOUSE, SON
COLUMBIA

Number	Title (A Side/B Side)	Yr	VG	VG+	NM
❑ CL 2417 [M]	Father of the Folk Blues	1965	5.00	10.00	20.00
❑ CS 9217 [S]	Father of the Folk Blues	1965	6.25	12.50	25.00
—Red "360 Sound" label					

HOUSE, SON, AND J.D. SHORT
VERVE FOLKWAYS

Number	Title (A Side/B Side)	Yr	VG	VG+	NM
❑ FV-9035 [M]	Blues from the Mississippi Delta	1966	10.00	20.00	40.00
❑ FVS-9035 [R]	Blues from the Mississippi Delta	1966	5.00	10.00	20.00

HOUSTON, DAVID
EPIC

Number	Title (A Side/B Side)	Yr	VG	VG+	NM
❑ EGP 502 [(2)]	The World of David Houston	1970	5.00	10.00	20.00
❑ LN 24112 [M]	New Voice from Nashville	1964	3.75	7.50	15.00
❑ LN 24156 [M]	12 Great Country Hits	1965	3.75	7.50	15.00
❑ LN 24213 [M]	Almost Persuaded	1966	3.75	7.50	15.00
❑ LN 24303 [M]	A Loser's Cathedral	1967	5.00	10.00	20.00
❑ LN 24320 [M]	Golden Hymns	1967	5.00	10.00	20.00
❑ LN 24338 [M]	You Mean the World to Me	1967	5.00	10.00	20.00
❑ LN 24342 [M]	David Houston's Greatest Hits	1968	7.50	15.00	30.00
❑ BN 26112 [S]	New Voice from Nashville	1964	5.00	10.00	20.00
❑ BN 26156 [S]	12 Great Country Hits	1965	5.00	10.00	20.00
❑ BN 26213 [S]	Almost Persuaded	1966	5.00	10.00	20.00
❑ BN 26303 [S]	A Loser's Cathedral	1967	3.75	7.50	15.00
❑ BN 26320 [S]	Golden Hymns	1967	3.75	7.50	15.00
❑ BN 26338 [S]	You Mean the World to Me	1967	3.75	7.50	15.00
❑ BN 26342 [S]	David Houston's Greatest Hits	1968	3.75	7.50	15.00
❑ BN 26391	Already It's Heaven	1968	3.75	7.50	15.00
❑ BN 26432	Where Love Used to Live	1969	3.75	7.50	15.00
❑ BN 26482	David	1969	3.75	7.50	15.00
❑ BN 26539	Baby, Baby	1970	3.75	7.50	15.00
❑ E 30108	Wonders of the Wine	1970	3.75	7.50	15.00
❑ E 30437	Sweet Lovin'	1971	3.75	7.50	15.00
❑ E 30602	David Houston's Greatest Hits, Volume 2	1971	3.75	7.50	15.00
❑ E 30657	A Woman Always Knows	1971	3.75	7.50	15.00
❑ KE 31385	The Day Love Walked In	1972	3.00	6.00	12.00
❑ KE 32189	Good Things	1973	3.00	6.00	12.00
❑ KE 33350	A Man Needs Love	1975	3.00	6.00	12.00
❑ KE 33948	What a Night	1976	3.00	6.00	12.00
GUSTO					
❑ 0012	The Best of David Houston	1978	2.50	5.00	10.00
HARMONY					
❑ HS 11412	David Houston	1970	2.50	5.00	10.00
❑ KH 31778	The Many Sides of David Houston	1972	2.50	5.00	10.00
❑ KH 32287	Old Time Religion	1973	2.50	5.00	10.00
RCA CAMDEN					
❑ CAL-2126 [M]	David Houston Sings	1966	3.75	7.50	15.00
❑ CAS-2126 [R]	David Houston Sings	1966	2.50	5.00	10.00
STARDAY					
❑ 990	David Houston	1978	2.50	5.00	10.00

HOUSTON, DAVID, AND TAMMY WYNETTE
EPIC

Number	Title (A Side/B Side)	Yr	VG	VG+	NM
❑ LN 24325 [M]	My Elusive Dreams	1967	5.00	10.00	20.00
❑ BN 26325 [S]	My Elusive Dreams	1967	3.75	7.50	15.00

HOUSTON, JOE
COMBO

Number	Title (A Side/B Side)	Yr	VG	VG+	NM
❑ LP-100 [M]	Joe Houston	195?	100.00	200.00	400.00
—Color photo of Joe Houston on cover					
❑ LP-100 [M]	Joe Houston	195?	100.00	200.00	400.00
—Silver cover with "J" in the shape of a saxophone					
❑ LP-400 [M]	Rockin' at the Drive In	195?	50.00	100.00	200.00
—Blue ink on front and back covers					
❑ LP-400 [M]	Rockin' at the Drive In	195?	75.00	150.00	300.00
—Black ink on front and back covers					
CROWN					
❑ CST-313 [R]	Surf Rockin'	1963	7.50	15.00	30.00
❑ CST-319 [R]	Limbo	1963	7.50	15.00	30.00
❑ CLP-5006 [M]	Joe Houston Rock and Rolls All Night Long	195?	25.00	50.00	100.00
—Black label, gold print					
❑ CLP-5006 [M]	Joe Houston Rock and Rolls All Night Long	196?	10.00	20.00	40.00
—Gray label, black print					
❑ CLP-5203 [M]	Wild Man of the Tenor Sax	1962	10.00	20.00	40.00
❑ CLP-5246 [M]	Doin' the Twist	1962	10.00	20.00	40.00
❑ CLP-5313 [M]	Surf Rockin'	1963	10.00	20.00	40.00
❑ CLP-5319 [M]	Limbo	1963	10.00	20.00	40.00
MODERN					
❑ LMP-1206 [M]	Joe Houston Blows All Night Long	1956	75.00	150.00	300.00
TOPS					
❑ L-1518 [M]	Rock and Roll	195?	20.00	40.00	80.00

HOUSTON, THELMA
ABC DUNHILL

Number	Title (A Side/B Side)	Yr	VG	VG+	NM
❑ DS-50054	Sun Shower	1969	6.25	12.50	25.00
MCA					
❑ 5395	Thelma Houston	1983	2.50	5.00	10.00
❑ 5527	Qualifying Heat	1984	2.50	5.00	10.00
MOTOWN					
❑ M5-120V1	Superstar Series, Vol. 20	1981	2.50	5.00	10.00
❑ M5-127V1	Sunshower	1981	2.00	4.00	8.00
❑ M5-226V1	Any Way You Like It	1982	2.50	5.00	10.00
MOWEST					
❑ MW-102	Thelma Houston	1972	5.00	10.00	20.00

Number	Title (A Side/B Side)	Yr	VG	VG+	NM

RCA VICTOR
| ❑ AFL1-3500 | Breakwater Cat | 1980 | 2.50 | 5.00 | 10.00 |
| ❑ AFL1-3842 | Never Gonna Be Another One | 1981 | 2.50 | 5.00 | 10.00 |

REPRISE
| ❑ 26234 | Throw You Down | 1990 | 3.75 | 7.50 | 15.00 |

SHEFFIELD LABS
| ❑ 2 | I've Got the Music In Me | 1975 | 10.00 | 20.00 | 40.00 |

SHEFFIELD TREASURY
| ❑ ST-200 | I've Got the Music In Me | 1983 | 5.00 | 10.00 | 20.00 |
| —Reissue of Sheffield Labs 2 | | | | | |

TAMLA
❑ T6-345R1	Any Way You Like It	1976	3.00	6.00	12.00
❑ T7-358R1	The Devil in Me	1977	2.50	5.00	10.00
❑ T7-361R1	Ready to Roll	1978	2.50	5.00	10.00

HOUSTON, WHITNEY
ARISTA
❑ AL 8212	Whitney Houston	1985	2.00	4.00	8.00
❑ AL 8405	Whitney	1987	2.00	4.00	8.00
❑ 14652 [(4)]	The Unreleased Mixes	2000	5.00	10.00	20.00
—Box set of 12-inch single remixes					
❑ AL 18616	I'm Your Baby Tonight	1990	2.50	5.00	10.00
❑ 19037 [(2)]	My Love Is Your Love	1998	3.00	6.00	12.00

HOUSTON FEARLESS
IMPERIAL
| ❑ LP-12421 | Houston Fearless | 1969 | 5.00 | 10.00 | 20.00 |

HOWARD, DAVE
CHOREO
| ❑ C-5 [M] | I Love Everybody | 1961 | 6.25 | 12.50 | 25.00 |
| ❑ CS-5 [S] | I Love Everybody | 1961 | 7.50 | 15.00 | 30.00 |

HOWARD, EDDY
CIRCLE
| ❑ 29 | Eddy Howard 1949-1952 | 198? | 2.50 | 5.00 | 10.00 |
| ❑ 79 | Eddy Howard 1949-1953 | 1985 | 2.50 | 5.00 | 10.00 |

COLUMBIA
| ❑ CL 6067 [10] | Eddy Howard | 1949 | 15.00 | 30.00 | 60.00 |

HINDSIGHT
❑ HSR-119	Eddy Howard 1946-1951	198?	2.50	5.00	10.00
❑ HSR-156	Eddy Howard 1945-1948	198?	2.50	5.00	10.00
❑ HSR-405 [(2)]	Eddy Howard and His Orchestra Play 22 Original Big Band Favorites	198?	3.00	6.00	12.00

INSIGHT
| ❑ 205 | Eddy Howard and His Orchestra 1945-1951 | 198? | 2.50 | 5.00 | 10.00 |

MERCURY
❑ MG-20112 [M]	Singing in the Rain	195?	6.25	12.50	25.00
❑ MG-20312 [M]	Paradise Isle	195?	6.25	12.50	25.00
❑ MG-20432 [M]	Great for Dancing	1958	5.00	10.00	20.00
❑ MG-20562 [M]	Eddy Howard's Golden Hits	1961	3.75	7.50	15.00
❑ MG-20593 [M]	More Eddy Howard's Golden Hits	1962	3.75	7.50	15.00
❑ MG-20665 [M]	Eddy Howard Sings and Plays the Great Old Waltzes	1962	3.75	7.50	15.00
❑ MG-20817 [M]	Eddy Howard Sings and Plays the Great Band Hits	196?	3.75	7.50	15.00
❑ MG-20910 [M]	Intimately Yours	1965	3.75	7.50	15.00
❑ MG-21014 [M]	Softly and Sincerely	196?	3.75	7.50	15.00
❑ SR-60104 [S]	Great for Dancing	1959	6.25	12.50	25.00
❑ SR-60562 [S]	Eddy Howard's Golden Hits	1961	5.00	10.00	20.00
❑ SR-60593 [S]	More Eddy Howard's Golden Hits	1962	5.00	10.00	20.00
❑ SR-60665 [S]	Eddy Howard Sings and Plays the Great Old Waltzes	1962	5.00	10.00	20.00
❑ SR-60817 [S]	Eddy Howard Sings and Plays the Great Band Hits	196?	5.00	10.00	20.00
❑ SR-60910 [S]	Intimately Yours	1965	5.00	10.00	20.00
❑ SR-61014 [S]	Softly and Sincerely	196?	5.00	10.00	20.00

WING
❑ MGW-12104 [M]	Saturday Night Dance Date	196?	3.00	6.00	12.00
❑ MGW-12171 [M]	Eddy Howard Sings Words of Love	196?	3.00	6.00	12.00
❑ MGW-12171 [M]	Words of Love	196?	3.00	6.00	12.00
❑ MGW-12194 [M]	Sleepy Serenade	196?	3.00	6.00	12.00
❑ MGW-12249 [M]	The Velvet Voice	196?	3.00	6.00	12.00
❑ SRW-16104 [S]	Saturday Night Dance Date	196?	3.00	6.00	12.00
❑ SRW-16171 [S]	Eddy Howard Sings Words of Love	196?	3.00	6.00	12.00
❑ SRW-16171 [S]	Words of Love	196?	3.00	6.00	12.00
❑ SRW-16194 [S]	Sleepy Serenade	196?	3.00	6.00	12.00
❑ SRW-16249 [S]	The Velvet Voice	196?	3.00	6.00	12.00

HOWARD, HARLAN
CAPITOL
| ❑ ST 1631 [S] | Harlan Howard Sings Harlan Howard | 1961 | 10.00 | 20.00 | 40.00 |
| ❑ T 1631 [M] | Harlan Howard Sings Harlan Howard | 1961 | 7.50 | 15.00 | 30.00 |

MONUMENT
| ❑ MLP-8038 [M] | All-Time Favorite Country Songwriter | 1965 | 6.25 | 12.50 | 25.00 |
| ❑ SLP-18038 [S] | All-Time Favorite Country Songwriter | 1965 | 7.50 | 15.00 | 30.00 |

RCA VICTOR
❑ LPM-3729	Mr. Songwriter	1967	6.25	12.50	25.00
❑ LSP-3729	Mr. Songwriter	1967	5.00	10.00	20.00
❑ LPM-3886	Down to Earth	1968	12.50	25.00	50.00
❑ LSP-3886	Down to Earth	1968	5.00	10.00	20.00

HOWARD, JAN
CAPITOL
| ❑ ST 1779 [S] | Sweet and Sentimental | 1962 | 6.25 | 12.50 | 25.00 |
| ❑ T 1779 [M] | Sweet and Sentimental | 1962 | 5.00 | 10.00 | 20.00 |

DECCA
❑ DL 4793 [M]	Jan Howard Sings Evil on Your Mind	1966	3.75	7.50	15.00
❑ DL 4832 [M]	Bad Seed	1966	3.75	7.50	15.00
❑ DL 4931 [M]	This Is Jan Howard Country	1967	6.25	12.50	25.00
❑ DL 5012 [M]	Count Your Blessings, Woman	1968	10.00	20.00	40.00
—White label promo only					
❑ DL 74793 [S]	Jan Howard Sings Evil on Your Mind	1966	5.00	10.00	20.00
❑ DL 74832 [S]	Bad Seed	1966	5.00	10.00	20.00
❑ DL 74931 [S]	This Is Jan Howard Country	1967	5.00	10.00	20.00
❑ DL 75012 [S]	Count Your Blessings, Woman	1968	5.00	10.00	20.00
❑ DL 75130	Jan Howard	1969	5.00	10.00	20.00
❑ DL 75166	For God and Country	1969	6.25	12.50	25.00
❑ DL 75207	Rock Me Back to Little Rock	1970	5.00	10.00	20.00
❑ DL 75293	Love Is Like a Spinning Wheel	1972	5.00	10.00	20.00

TOWER
❑ ST 5068 [S]	Lonely Country	1967	5.00	10.00	20.00
❑ T 5068 [S]	Lonely Country	1967	5.00	10.00	20.00
❑ DT 5119 [R]	The Real Me	1968	3.75	7.50	15.00

WRANGLER
| ❑ 1005 [M] | Jan Howard | 1962 | 6.25 | 12.50 | 25.00 |
| ❑ S-1005 [S] | Jan Howard | 1962 | 7.50 | 15.00 | 30.00 |

HOWARD, JOE
KING
| ❑ 661 [M] | The Golden Sound | 1959 | 12.50 | 25.00 | 50.00 |

SUNSET
| ❑ SU-3001 [M] | Patterns for Trombone | 1955 | 10.00 | 20.00 | 40.00 |

HOWARD, NOAH
ESP-DISK'
❑ 1031 [M]	Noah Howard Quartet	1966	5.00	10.00	20.00
❑ S-1031 [S]	Noah Howard Quartet	1966	6.25	12.50	25.00
❑ S-1064 [S]	Live at Judson Hall	1969	5.00	10.00	20.00

HOWL THE GOOD
RARE EARTH
| ❑ RS-537 | Howl the Good | 1972 | 5.00 | 10.00 | 20.00 |

HOWLIN' WOLF
CADET
| ❑ LPS-319 | This Is Howlin' Wolf's New Album | 1969 | 6.25 | 12.50 | 25.00 |

CHESS
❑ 201 [(2)]	Howlin' Wolf	1976	3.75	7.50	15.00
❑ LP-1434 [M]	Moanin' in the Moonlight	1958	150.00	300.00	600.00
❑ LP-1469 [M]	Howlin' Wolf	1962	150.00	300.00	600.00
❑ LP-1502 [M]	The Real Folk Blues	1966	12.50	25.00	50.00
❑ LP-1512 [M]	More Real Folk Blues	1966	12.50	25.00	50.00
❑ LP-1540	Evil	1969	6.25	12.50	25.00
❑ CH-9107	His Greatest Sides, Vol. 1	1985	2.50	5.00	10.00
❑ CH-9182	Chicago — 26 Golden Years	1985	2.50	5.00	10.00
❑ CH-9195	Moanin' in the Moonlight	1986	2.00	4.00	8.00
—Reissue of 1434					
❑ CH-9273	The Real Folk Blues	1988	2.50	5.00	10.00
—Reissue of 1502					
❑ CH-9279	More Real Folk Blues	1988	2.50	5.00	10.00
—Reissue of 1512					
❑ CH-9297	The London Howlin' Wolf Sessions	1989	2.50	5.00	10.00
—Reissue of 60008					
❑ CH5-9332 [(5)]	The Chess Box	1991	10.00	20.00	40.00
❑ CH-50002	Message to the Young	1971	5.00	10.00	20.00
❑ CH-50015	Live and Cookin'	1972	5.00	10.00	20.00
❑ CH-50045	Back Door Wolf	1974	5.00	10.00	20.00
❑ CH-60008	The London Howlin' Wolf Sessions	1971	5.00	10.00	20.00
❑ CH-60016 [(2)]	Howlin' Wolk, AKA Chester Burnett	1972	6.25	12.50	25.00
❑ CH-93001	Change My Way	198?	2.50	5.00	10.00

CROWN
| ❑ CLP-5240 [M] | Howlin' Wolf Sings the Blues | 1962 | 6.25 | 12.50 | 25.00 |

CUSTOM
| ❑ CM-2055 [M] | Big City Blues | 196? | 10.00 | 20.00 | 40.00 |
| ❑ CS-2055 [R] | Big City Blues | 196? | 5.00 | 10.00 | 20.00 |

KENT
❑ KLP-526 [M]	Original Folk Blues	1967	3.75	7.50	15.00
❑ KST-526 [R]	Original Folk Blues	1967	3.00	6.00	12.00
❑ KST-527	Howlin' Wolf's 20 Greatest R&B Hits	1968	3.00	6.00	12.00
❑ KST-535	Underground Blues	1968	3.00	6.00	12.00

ROUNDER
| ❑ SS-28 | Cadillac Daddy: Memphis Recordings, 1952 | 1989 | 3.00 | 6.00 | 12.00 |

HUBBARD, FREDDIE
ATLANTIC
| ❑ 1477 [M] | Backlash | 1967 | 6.25 | 12.50 | 25.00 |

BLUE NOTE
❑ BLP-4040 [M]	Open Sesame	1960	20.00	40.00	80.00
—Regular version with W. 63rd St. address on label					
❑ BLP-4040 [M]	Open Sesame	1960	30.00	60.00	120.00
—"Deep groove" version (deep indentation under label on both sides)					
❑ BLP-4040 [M]	Open Sesame	1963	5.00	10.00	20.00
—With New York, USA address on label					
❑ BLP-4056 [M]	Goin' Up	1960	20.00	40.00	80.00
—With W. 63rd St. address on label					
❑ BLP-4056 [M]	Goin' Up	1963	5.00	10.00	20.00
—With New York, USA address on label					
❑ BLP-4073 [M]	Hub Cap	1961	20.00	40.00	80.00
—With W. 63rd St. address on label					
❑ BLP-4073 [M]	Hub Cap	1963	5.00	10.00	20.00
—With New York, USA address on label					
❑ BLP-4085 [M]	Ready for Freddie	1961	20.00	40.00	80.00
—With 61st St. address on label					
❑ BLP-4085 [M]	Ready for Freddie	1963	5.00	10.00	20.00
—With New York, USA address on label					
❑ BLP-4115 [M]	Hub Tones	1962	6.25	12.50	25.00
❑ BLP-4172 [M]	Breaking Point	1964	6.25	12.50	25.00
❑ BLP-4196 [M]	Blue Spirits	1965	6.25	12.50	25.00
❑ BLP-4207 [M]	The Night of the Cookers — Live at Club Le Marchal, Vol. 1	1965	6.25	12.50	25.00

Number	Title (A Side/B Side)	Yr	VG	VG+	NM
❏ BLP-4208 [M]	The Night of the Cookers — Live at Club Le Marchal, Vol. 2	1965	6.25	12.50	25.00
❏ BST-84040 [S]	Open Sesame	1960	15.00	30.00	60.00
—With W. 63rd St. addresss on label					
❏ BST-84040 [S]	Open Sesame	1963	6.25	12.50	25.00
—With New York, USA address on label					
❏ BST-84040 [S]	Open Sesame	199?	6.25	12.50	25.00
—Classic Records reissue on audiophile vinyl					
❏ BST-84056 [S]	Goin' Up	1960	15.00	30.00	60.00
—With W. 63rd St. address on label					
❏ BST-84056 [S]	Goin' Up	1963	6.25	12.50	25.00
—With New York, USA address on label					
❏ BST-84073 [S]	Hub Cap	1961	15.00	30.00	60.00
—With W. 63rd St. address on label					
❏ BST-84073 [S]	Hub Cap	1963	6.25	12.50	25.00
—With New York, USA address on label					
❏ BST-84085 [S]	Ready for Freddie	1961	15.00	30.00	60.00
—With 61st St. address on label					
❏ BST-84085 [S]	Ready for Freddie	1963	6.25	12.50	25.00
—With New York, USA address on label					
❏ BST-84115 [S]	Hub-Tones	1962	7.50	15.00	30.00
—With New York, USA address on label					
❏ BST-84172 [S]	Breaking Point	1964	7.50	15.00	30.00
—With New York, USA address on label					
❏ BST-84196 [S]	Blue Spirits	1965	7.50	15.00	30.00
—With New York, USA address on label					
❏ BST-84207 [S]	The Night of the Cookers — Live at Club Le Marchal, Vol. 1	1965	7.50	15.00	30.00
❏ BST-84208 [S]	The Night of the Cookers — Live at Club Le Marchal, Vol. 2	1965	7.50	15.00	30.00
—With New York, USA address on label					
IMPULSE!					
❏ A-27 [M]	The Artistry of Freddie Hubbard	1962	6.25	12.50	25.00
❏ AS-27 [S]	The Artistry of Freddie Hubbard	1962	7.50	15.00	30.00
❏ A-38 [M]	The Body and Soul of Freddie Hubbard	1963	6.25	12.50	25.00
❏ AS-38 [S]	The Body and Soul of Freddie Hubbard	1963	7.50	15.00	30.00

HUCKO, PEANUTS
GRAND AWARD

Number	Title (A Side/B Side)	Yr	VG	VG+	NM
❏ GA 33-331 [M]	Tribute to Benny Goodman	1956	10.00	20.00	40.00
JAZZTONE					
❏ J-1250 [M]	In the Style of Benny Goodman	1957	7.50	15.00	30.00
WALDORF MUSIC HALL					
❏ MH 33-153 [10]	A Tribute to Benny Goodman	1956	7.50	15.00	30.00

HUCKO, PEANUTS/RAY MCKINLEY
GRAND AWARD

Number	Title (A Side/B Side)	Yr	VG	VG+	NM
❏ GA 33-333 [M]	The Swingin' 30s	1956	10.00	20.00	40.00

HUDSON, ROCK
STANYAN

Number	Title (A Side/B Side)	Yr	VG	VG+	NM
❏ SR-10014	Rock Gently	1971	6.25	12.50	25.00

HUDSON AND LANDRY
DORE

Number	Title (A Side/B Side)	Yr	VG	VG+	NM
❏ 324	Hanging In There	1971	5.00	10.00	20.00
❏ 326	Losing Their Heads	1971	5.00	10.00	20.00
❏ 329	Right-Off!	1972	5.00	10.00	20.00
❏ 331	Weird Kingdom	1973	5.00	10.00	20.00
❏ 333	The Best of Hudson and Landry	1974	3.75	7.50	15.00
❏ 334	The Best of Hudson and Landry 2	1975	3.75	7.50	15.00

HUG, ARMAND
CIRCLE

Number	Title (A Side/B Side)	Yr	VG	VG+	NM
❏ L-411 [10]	New Orleans 88	1951	12.50	25.00	50.00
PARAMOUNT					
❏ LP-114 [10]	Armand Hug Plays Armand Piron	1954	12.50	25.00	50.00

HUGHES, FREDDIE
WAND

Number	Title (A Side/B Side)	Yr	VG	VG+	NM
❏ WDS-664	Send My Baby Back	1968	6.25	12.50	25.00
—The numbering system suggests this would have been issued in 1965, but the singles from this LP were issued in 1968, thus we use the later date.					

HUGHES, JIMMY
ATCO

Number	Title (A Side/B Side)	Yr	VG	VG+	NM
❏ 33-209 [M]	Why Not Tonight	1967	5.00	10.00	20.00
❏ SD 33-209 [S]	Why Not Tonight	1967	5.00	10.00	20.00
VEE JAY					
❏ VJ-1102 [M]	Steal Away	1965	6.25	12.50	25.00
❏ VJS-1102 [R]	Steal Away	1965	6.25	12.50	25.00
VOLT					
❏ VOS-6003	Something Special	1969	5.00	10.00	20.00

HUGHES, LANGSTON
FOLKWAYS

Number	Title (A Side/B Side)	Yr	VG	VG+	NM
❏ FA-7312 [10]	The Story of Jazz for Children	1954	12.50	25.00	50.00
—With booklet					
MGM					
❏ E-3697 [M]	The Weary Blues	1958	12.50	25.00	50.00
—Yellow label					
VERVE					
❏ VSP-36 [M]	The Weary Blues	1966	5.00	10.00	20.00
❏ VSPS-36 [R]	The Weary Blues	1966	3.00	6.00	12.00

HUGHES, RHETA
COLUMBIA

Number	Title (A Side/B Side)	Yr	VG	VG+	NM
❏ CL 2385 [M]	Introducing An Electrifying New Star	1965	7.50	15.00	30.00
❏ CS 9185 [S]	Introducing An Electrifying New Star	1965	10.00	20.00	40.00

HUGO AND LUIGI
RCA VICTOR

Number	Title (A Side/B Side)	Yr	VG	VG+	NM
❏ LPM-2254 [M]	The Sound of Children at Christmas	1960	3.75	7.50	15.00
❏ LSP-2254 [S]	The Sound of Children at Christmas	1960	5.00	10.00	20.00
❏ LPM-2641 [M]	The Cascading Voices of the Hugo & Luigi Chorus	1963	2.50	5.00	10.00
❏ LSP-2641 [S]	The Cascading Voices of the Hugo & Luigi Chorus	1963	3.00	6.00	12.00
❏ LPM-2717 [M]	Let's Fall in Love	1963	2.50	5.00	10.00
❏ LSP-2717 [S]	Let's Fall in Love	1963	3.00	6.00	12.00
❏ LPM-2789 [M]	The Cascading Voices of the Hugo & Luigi Chorus — With Brass	1964	2.50	5.00	10.00
❏ LSP-2789 [S]	The Cascading Voices of the Hugo & Luigi Chorus — With Brass	1964	3.00	6.00	12.00
❏ LPM-2863 [M]	The Cascading Voices of the Hugo & Luigi Chorus — With Strings	1964	2.50	5.00	10.00
❏ LSP-2863 [S]	The Cascading Voices of the Hugo & Luigi Chorus — With Strings	1964	3.00	6.00	12.00
❏ LSP-4083	Maggie Flynn	1968	2.50	5.00	10.00
ROULETTE					
❏ R-25044 [M]	When Good Fellows Get Together	1959	5.00	10.00	20.00
❏ R-25283 [M]	Cascading Voices	1965	3.00	6.00	12.00
❏ SR-25283 [S]	Cascading Voices	1965	3.75	7.50	15.00
WING					
❏ MGW 12207 [M]	Sing Along by the Fireside	195?	3.00	6.00	12.00

HULLABALLOOS, THE
ROULETTE

Number	Title (A Side/B Side)	Yr	VG	VG+	NM
❏ R-25297 [M]	England's Newest Singing Sensations	1965	12.50	25.00	50.00
❏ SR-25297 [P]	England's Newest Singing Sensations	1965	18.75	37.50	75.00
❏ R-25310 [M]	The Hullabaloos on Hullabaloo	1965	12.50	25.00	50.00
❏ SR-25310 [P]	The Hullabaloos on Hullabaloo	1965	18.75	37.50	75.00

HULLABALOO SINGERS AND ORCHESTRA, THE
COLUMBIA

Number	Title (A Side/B Side)	Yr	VG	VG+	NM
❏ CL 2410 [M]	The Hullabaloo Show	1965	5.00	10.00	20.00
❏ CS 9210 [S]	The Hullabaloo Show	1965	6.25	12.50	25.00

HUMAN BEINZ, THE
CAPITOL

Number	Title (A Side/B Side)	Yr	VG	VG+	NM
❏ ST 2906	Nobody But Me	1968	7.50	15.00	30.00
❏ ST 2926	Evolutions	1968	10.00	20.00	40.00
GATEWAY					
❏ GLP-3012	Nobody But Me	1968	10.00	20.00	40.00
—With added tracks by The Mammals					

HUMBLE PIE
A&M

Number	Title (A Side/B Side)	Yr	VG	VG+	NM
❏ SP-3127	Humble Pie	1981	2.00	4.00	8.00
—Budget-line reissue					
❏ SP-3132	Smokin'	1981	2.00	4.00	8.00
—Budget-line reissue					
❏ SP-3208	The Best of Humble Pie	1982	2.50	5.00	10.00
❏ SP-3506 [(2)]	Performance — Rockin' the Fillmore	1971	3.75	7.50	15.00
❏ SP-3513 [(2)]	Lost and Found	1972	3.75	7.50	15.00
❏ SP-3611	Thunderbox	1974	3.00	6.00	12.00
❏ SP-3701 [(2)]	Eat It	1973	3.75	7.50	15.00
❏ SP-4270	Humble Pie	1970	3.00	6.00	12.00
❏ SP-4301	Rock On	1971	3.00	6.00	12.00
❏ SP-4342	Smokin'	1972	3.00	6.00	12.00
❏ SP-4514	Street Rats	1975	3.00	6.00	12.00
❏ SP-6008 [(2)]	Performance — Rockin' the Fillmore	1981	2.50	5.00	10.00
—Budget-line reissue					
❏ SP-6009 [(2)]	Lost and Found	1981	2.50	5.00	10.00
—Budget-line reissue					
❏ SP-6503 [(2)]	Eat It	1981	2.50	5.00	10.00
—Budget-line reissue					
ACCORD					
❏ SN-7192	Recaptured	1981	2.50	5.00	10.00
ATCO					
❏ SD 38-122	On to Victory	1980	2.50	5.00	10.00
❏ SD 38-131	Go for the Throat	1981	2.50	5.00	10.00
COMPLEAT					
❏ 672009-1 [(2)]	A Slice of Humble Pie	1985	3.00	6.00	12.00
IMMEDIATE					
❏ IMOCS-101	As Safe As Yesterday Is	1969	6.25	12.50	25.00

HUMBLEBUMS, THE
GERRY RAFFERTY was in this group.
LIBERTY

Number	Title (A Side/B Side)	Yr	VG	VG+	NM
❏ LST-7636	The Humblebums	1969	7.50	15.00	30.00
❏ LST-7656	Open Up the Door	1970	7.50	15.00	30.00

HUMES, ANITA
See THE ESSEX.

HUMES, HELEN
CONTEMPORARY

Number	Title (A Side/B Side)	Yr	VG	VG+	NM
❏ M-3571 [M]	'Tain't Nobody's Biz-Ness If I Do	1960	10.00	20.00	40.00
❏ M-3582 [M]	Songs I Like to Sing	1960	10.00	20.00	40.00
❏ M-3598 [M]	Swingin' with Humes	1961	7.50	15.00	30.00
❏ S-7571 [S]	'Tain't Nobody's Biz-Ness If I Do	1960	10.00	20.00	40.00
❏ S-7582 [S]	Songs I Like to Sing	1960	10.00	20.00	40.00
❏ S-7598 [S]	Swingin' with Humes	1961	10.00	20.00	40.00

HUMPERDINCK, ENGELBERT
EPIC

Number	Title (A Side/B Side)	Yr	VG	VG+	NM
❏ (no #) [PD]	Last of the Romantics	1978	6.25	12.50	25.00
❏ PE 34381	After the Lovin'	1976	2.50	5.00	10.00
—Orange label					
❏ PE 34381	After the Lovin'	1979	2.00	4.00	8.00
—Dark blue label; back cover does not yet have bar code					

Number	Title (A Side/B Side)	Yr	VG	VG+	NM
❑ PE 34381	After the Lovin'	198?	—	3.00	6.00
—Dark blue label; back cover has bar code					
❑ E 34436	The Ultimate	1977	2.50	5.00	10.00
—Orange label					
❑ PE 34436	The Ultimate	198?	2.00	4.00	8.00
—Reissue with bar code; dark blue label					
❑ E 34719	Golden Love Songs	1977	2.50	5.00	10.00
—Orange label					
❑ PE 34719	Golden Love Songs	198?	2.00	4.00	8.00
—Reissue with bar code; dark blue label					
❑ PE 34730	Miracles	1977	2.50	5.00	10.00
—Orange label					
❑ PE 34730	Miracles	198?	2.00	4.00	8.00
—Reissue with bar code; dark blue label					
❑ JE 35020	Last of the Romantics	1978	2.50	5.00	10.00
—Orange label					
❑ PE 35020	Last of the Romantics	198?	2.00	4.00	8.00
—Reissue with bar code; dark blue label					
❑ PE 35031	Christmas Tyme	1977	3.00	6.00	12.00
❑ JE 35791	This Moment in Time	1979	2.50	5.00	10.00
❑ PE 35791	This Moment in Time	198?	2.00	4.00	8.00
—Budget-line reissue					
❑ JE 36431	Love's Only Love	1980	2.50	5.00	10.00
❑ PE 36765	A Merry Christmas with Engelbert				
	Humperdinck	1980	2.50	5.00	10.00
—Some copies of the record have a "JE" prefix					
❑ E2X 36782 [(2)]	All of Me/Live in Concert	1980	3.00	6.00	12.00
❑ FE 37128	Don't You Love Me Anymore	1981	2.50	5.00	10.00
❑ PE 37128	Don't You Love Me Anymore	1983	2.00	4.00	8.00
—Budget-line reissue					
❑ FE 38087	You and Your Lover	1983	2.50	5.00	10.00
❑ PE 39469	White Christmas	1984	2.50	5.00	10.00
LONDON					
❑ BP 688/9 [(2)]	Engelbert Humperdinck Sings for You	1977	3.75	7.50	15.00
❑ PS 709	Love Letters	1978	2.50	5.00	10.00
PARROT					
❑ PA 61012 [M]	Release Me	1967	5.00	10.00	20.00
❑ PA 61015 [M]	The Last Waltz	1967	5.00	10.00	20.00
❑ PAS 71012 [S]	Release Me	1967	3.75	7.50	15.00
❑ PAS 71015 [S]	The Last Waltz	1967	3.75	7.50	15.00
❑ PAS 71022	A Man Without Love	1968	3.75	7.50	15.00
❑ PAS 71026	Engelbert	1969	3.75	7.50	15.00
❑ XPAS 71030	Engelbert Humperdinck	1969	3.75	7.50	15.00
❑ XPAS 71038	We Made It Happen	1970	3.75	7.50	15.00
❑ XPAS 71043	Sweetheart	1971	3.75	7.50	15.00
❑ XPAS 71048	Another Time, Another Place	1971	3.75	7.50	15.00
❑ XPAS 71051	Live at the Riviera, Las Vegas	1971	3.75	7.50	15.00
❑ XPAS 71056	In Time	1972	3.75	7.50	15.00
❑ XPAS 71061	King of Hearts	1973	3.75	7.50	15.00
❑ APAS 71065	My Love	1974	3.75	7.50	15.00
❑ PAS 71067	His Greatest Hits	1974	3.75	7.50	15.00
❑ SW-93216	We Made It Happen	1970	5.00	10.00	20.00
—Capitol Record Club edition					
SILVER EAGLE					
❑ SE 1034 [(2)]	A Lovely Way to Spend an Evening	1985	3.75	7.50	15.00
—Mail-order offer					

HUMPHREY, PERCY
RIVERSIDE

Number	Title (A Side/B Side)	Yr	VG	VG+	NM
❑ RLP-378 [M]	Percy Humphrey's Crescent City Joymakers	1961	7.50	15.00	30.00

HUNGER
PUBLIC

❑ 1006	Strictly from Hunger	1969	150.00	300.00	600.00

HUNT, PEE WEE
ALLEGRO

❑ 1633 [M]	Dixieland	1956	6.25	12.50	25.00
CAPITOL					
❑ H 203 [10]	Straight from Dixie	1950	10.00	20.00	40.00
❑ H 312 [10]	Dixieland Detour	1952	10.00	20.00	40.00
❑ H 492 [10]	Swingin' Around	1954	10.00	20.00	40.00
❑ T 573 [M]	Dixieland Classics	1955	7.50	15.00	30.00
❑ T 783 [M]	Pee Wee and Fingers	1956	7.50	15.00	30.00
❑ T 984 [M]	Cole Porter Ala Dixie	1957	7.50	15.00	30.00
—Turquoise label					
❑ T 1362 [M]	Pee Wee Hunt's Dance Party	1960	3.75	7.50	15.00
ROYALE					
❑ 18153 [10]	Pee Wee Hunt and His Dixieland Band	195?	10.00	20.00	40.00
SOLITAIRE					
❑ 507 [10]	Dixieland Capers	195?	7.50	15.00	30.00

HUNT, PEE WEE/PEE WEE RUSSELL
RONDO-LETTE

❑ A 2 [M]	Dixieland: Pee Wee Hunt and Pee Wee				
	Russell	195?	6.25	12.50	25.00

HUNT, TOMMY
DYNAMO

❑ D-7001 [M]	Tommy Hunt's Greatest Hits	1967	5.00	10.00	20.00
❑ DS-8001 [S]	Tommy Hunt's Greatest Hits	1967	6.25	12.50	25.00
SCEPTER					
❑ 506 [M]	I Just Don't Know What to Do with Myself	1962	12.50	25.00	50.00
❑ SS-506 [S]	I Just Don't Know What to Do with Myself	1962	15.00	30.00	60.00

HUNTER, ALBERTA
RIVERSIDE

❑ RLP-418 [M]	Alberta Hunter with Lovie Austin's Blues				
	Serenaders	1962	7.50	15.00	30.00

HUNTER, FRANK
JUBILEE

Number	Title (A Side/B Side)	Yr	VG	VG+	NM
❑ JLP-1020 [M]	Sounds of Hunter	1956	12.50	25.00	50.00

HUNTER, IVORY JOE
ARCHIVE OF FOLK AND JAZZ

❑ 289	Ivory Joe Hunter	1974	3.00	6.00	12.00
ATLANTIC					
❑ 8008 [M]	Ivory Joe Hunter	1957	50.00	100.00	200.00
—Black label					
❑ 8008 [M]	Ivory Joe Hunter	1960	25.00	50.00	100.00
—Purple and red label					
❑ 8015 [M]	The Old and the New	1958	50.00	100.00	200.00
—Black label					
❑ 8015 [M]	The Old and the New	1960	25.00	50.00	100.00
—Purple and red label					
DOT					
❑ DLP-3569 [M]	This Is Ivory Joe Hunter	1964	10.00	20.00	40.00
❑ DLP-25569 [S]	This Is Ivory Joe Hunter	1964	12.50	25.00	50.00
EPIC					
❑ E 30348	The Return of Ivory Joe Hunter	1971	5.00	10.00	20.00
GOLDISC					
❑ 403 [M]	The Fabulous Ivory Joe Hunter	1961	15.00	30.00	60.00
HOME COOKING					
❑ 112	I'm Coming Down with the Blues	1989	3.00	6.00	12.00
KING					
❑ 605 [M]	16 of His Greatest Hits	1958	100.00	200.00	400.00
LION					
❑ L-70068 [M]	I Need You So	1959	15.00	30.00	60.00
MGM					
❑ E-3488 [M]	I Get That Lonesome Feeling	1957	75.00	150.00	300.00
PARAMOUNT					
❑ PAS-6080	I've Always Been Country	1974	3.00	6.00	12.00
POLYDOR					
❑ 830897-1	Since I Met You Baby	1987	3.00	6.00	12.00
SMASH					
❑ MGS-27037 [M]	Ivory Joe Hunter's Golden Hits	1963	10.00	20.00	40.00
❑ SRS-67037 [S]	Ivory Joe Hunter's Golden Hits	1963	12.50	25.00	50.00
SOUND					
❑ M-603 [M]	Ivory Joe Hunter	1959	37.50	75.00	150.00
STRAND					
❑ SL-1123 [M]	The Artistry of Ivory Joe Hunter	196?	10.00	20.00	40.00
❑ SLS-1123 [S]	The Artistry of Ivory Joe Hunter	196?	12.50	25.00	50.00

HUNTER, LURLEAN
ATLANTIC

❑ 1344 [M]	Blue and Sentimental	1960	12.50	25.00	50.00
❑ SD 1344 [S]	Blue and Sentimental	1960	15.00	30.00	60.00
RCA VICTOR					
❑ LPM-1151 [M]	Lonesome Gal	1955	25.00	50.00	100.00
VIK					
❑ LX-1061 [M]	Night Life	1956	20.00	40.00	80.00
❑ LX-1116 [M]	Stepping Out	1957	20.00	40.00	80.00

HUNTER, ROBERT
RELIX

❑ 2002 [PD]	Promontory Rider	1982	5.00	10.00	20.00
—Limited edition of 1,000 picture discs					
ROUND					
❑ RX-101	Tales of the Great Rum Runners	1974	10.00	20.00	40.00
❑ RX-105	Tiger Rose	1975	10.00	20.00	40.00

HUNTER, STAN, AND SONNY FORTUNE
PRESTIGE

❑ PRLP-7458 [M]	Trip on the Strip	1967	7.50	15.00	30.00
❑ PRST-7458 [S]	Trip on the Strip	1967	5.00	10.00	20.00

HUNTER, TAB
DOT

❑ DLP-3370 [M]	Young Love	1961	7.50	15.00	30.00
❑ DLP-25370 [S]	Young Love	1961	7.50	15.00	30.00
WARNER BROS.					
❑ W 1221 [M]	Tab Hunter	1958	7.50	15.00	30.00
❑ WS 1221 [S]	Tab Hunter	1958	10.00	20.00	40.00
❑ W 1292 [M]	When I Fall in Love	1959	7.50	15.00	30.00
❑ WS 1292 [S]	When I Fall in Love	1959	10.00	20.00	40.00
❑ W 1367 [M]	R.F.D. Tab Hunter	1960	7.50	15.00	30.00
❑ WS 1367 [S]	R.F.D. Tab Hunter	1960	10.00	20.00	40.00

HUNTER MUSKETT
BRADLEY

❑ 1003	Hunter Muskett	1973	20.00	40.00	80.00

HURT, MISSISSIPPI JOHN
BIOGRAPH

❑ C-4 [M]	1928: His First Recordings	1972	6.25	12.50	25.00
PIEDMONT					
❑ PLP-13157 [M]	Folk Songs and Blues	1963	20.00	40.00	80.00
❑ PLP-13181 [M]	Worried Blues	1964	20.00	40.00	80.00
VANGUARD					
❑ VSD-19/20 [(2)]	The Best of Mississippi John Hurt	197?	6.25	12.50	25.00
❑ VRS-9145 [M]	Blues at Newport	1965	6.25	12.50	25.00
❑ VRS-9220 [M]	Mississippi John Hurt/Today	1966	6.25	12.50	25.00
❑ VRS-9248 [M]	The Immortal Mississippi John Hurt	1967	6.25	12.50	25.00
❑ VSD-79145 [S]	Blues at Newport	1965	7.50	15.00	30.00
❑ VSD-79220 [S]	Mississippi John Hurt/Today	1966	7.50	15.00	30.00
❑ VSD-79248 [S]	The Immortal Mississippi John Hurt	1967	7.50	15.00	30.00
❑ VSD-79327	The Last Session	1972	5.00	10.00	20.00

Number	Title (A Side/B Side)	Yr	VG	VG+	NM

HURVITZ, SANDY
VERVE
| ❑ V6-5064 | Sandy's Album Is Here at Last | 1968 | 7.50 | 15.00 | 30.00 |

—Produced by FRANK ZAPPA

HUSKER DU
NEW ALLIANCE
| ❑ 007 | Land Speed Record | 1982 | 3.00 | 6.00 | 12.00 |

—Second pressing, "Marketed by SST" on cover

| ❑ 007 | Land Speed Record | 1982 | 6.25 | 12.50 | 25.00 |

—No reference to SST on cover

REFLEX
| ❑ #D | Everything Falls Apart | 1982 | 10.00 | 20.00 | 40.00 |

SST
❑ 020 [EP]	Metal Circus	1983	2.00	4.00	8.00
❑ 027 [(2)]	Zen Arcade	1984	3.75	7.50	15.00
❑ PSST E-27 [DJ]	Eight Miles High/6 from Zen Arcade	1984	7.50	15.00	30.00

—Promo sampler, etched design on side 1, sticker cover

❑ 031	New Day Rising	1985	2.50	5.00	10.00
❑ 055	Flip Your Wig	1985	2.50	5.00	10.00
❑ 195	Land Speed Record	198?	2.50	5.00	10.00

—Reissue of New Alliance 007

| ❑ 908 [10] | Metal Circus | 199? | 2.00 | 4.00 | 8.00 |
| ❑ 915 [10] | Eight Miles High/Makes No Sense at All | 199? | 2.00 | 4.00 | 8.00 |

WARNER BROS.
| ❑ WBMS-145 [DJ] | The Warehouse Interview | 1987 | 6.25 | 12.50 | 25.00 |

—Promo only, part of the Warner Bros. Music Show series

| ❑ PRO-A-2719 [DJ] | Warehouse: Songs and Stories | 1987 | 2.00 | 4.00 | 8.00 |

—Promo-only four-song sampler

| ❑ 25385 | Candy Apple Grey | 1986 | 3.00 | 6.00 | 12.00 |
| ❑ 25544 [(2)] | Warehouse: Songs and Stories | 1987 | 3.00 | 6.00 | 12.00 |

HUSKY, FERLIN
ABC
❑ X-776	True True Lovin'	1973	3.00	6.00	12.00
❑ X-803	Sweet Honky Tonk	1974	3.00	6.00	12.00
❑ X-818	Freckles and Polliwog Days	1974	3.00	6.00	12.00
❑ X-849	Champagne Ladies and Blue Ribbon Babies	1974	3.00	6.00	12.00
❑ X-884	The Foster-Rice Songbook	1975	3.00	6.00	12.00

CAPITOL
❑ ST-115	White Fences and Evergreen Trees	1968	3.75	7.50	15.00
❑ SKAO-143	The Best of Ferlin Husky	1969	3.75	7.50	15.00
❑ SM-143	The Best of Ferlin Husky	197?	2.50	5.00	10.00

—Reissue with new prefix

❑ ST-239	That's Why I Love You So Much	1969	3.75	7.50	15.00
❑ ST-433	Your Love Is Heavenly Sunshine	1970	3.75	7.50	15.00
❑ ST-591	Your Sweet Love Lifted Me	1970	3.75	7.50	15.00
❑ T 718 [M]	Songs of the Home and Heart	1956	15.00	30.00	60.00

—Turquoise label

| ❑ T 718 [M] | Songs of the Home and Heart | 1959 | 10.00 | 20.00 | 40.00 |

—Black colorband label, Capitol logo at left

| ❑ T 718 [M] | Songs of the Home and Heart | 1962 | 6.25 | 12.50 | 25.00 |

—Black colorband label, Capitol logo at top

| ❑ ST-768 | One More Time | 1971 | 3.75 | 7.50 | 15.00 |
| ❑ T 880 [M] | Boulevard of Broken Dreams | 1957 | 15.00 | 30.00 | 60.00 |

—Turquoise label

| ❑ T 880 [M] | Boulevard of Broken Dreams | 1958 | 10.00 | 20.00 | 40.00 |

—Black colorband label, Capitol logo at left

| ❑ T 976 [M] | Sittin' On a Rainbow | 1958 | 15.00 | 30.00 | 60.00 |

—Turquoise label

| ❑ T 1204 [M] | Born to Lose | 1959 | 10.00 | 20.00 | 40.00 |

—Black colorband label, Capitol logo at left

| ❑ T 1204 [M] | Born to Lose | 1962 | 6.25 | 12.50 | 25.00 |

—Black colorband label, Capitol logo at top

| ❑ T 1280 [M] | Ferlin's Favorites | 1960 | 10.00 | 20.00 | 40.00 |

—Black colorband label, Capitol logo at left

| ❑ T 1280 [M] | Ferlin's Favorites | 1962 | 6.25 | 12.50 | 25.00 |

—Black colorband label, Capitol logo at top

| ❑ DT 1383 [R] | Gone | 196? | 3.00 | 6.00 | 12.00 |
| ❑ T 1383 [M] | Gone | 196? | 5.00 | 10.00 | 20.00 |

—Gold "The Star Line" label; "The Star Line" logo on cover

| ❑ T 1383 [M] | Gone | 1960 | 10.00 | 20.00 | 40.00 |

—Black colorband label, Capitol logo at left

| ❑ T 1383 [M] | Gone | 1962 | 6.25 | 12.50 | 25.00 |

—Black colorband label, Capitol logo at top

| ❑ ST 1546 [S] | Walkin' and Hummin' | 1961 | 7.50 | 15.00 | 30.00 |

—Black colorband label, Capitol logo at left

| ❑ ST 1546 [S] | Walkin' and Hummin' | 1962 | 5.00 | 10.00 | 20.00 |

—Black colorband label, Capitol logo at top

| ❑ T 1546 [M] | Walkin' and Hummin' | 1961 | 6.25 | 12.50 | 25.00 |

—Black colorband label, Capitol logo at left

| ❑ T 1546 [M] | Walkin' and Hummin' | 1962 | 3.75 | 7.50 | 15.00 |

—Black colorband label, Capitol logo at top

| ❑ ST 1633 [S] | Memories of Home | 1961 | 7.50 | 15.00 | 30.00 |

—Black colorband label, Capitol logo at left

| ❑ ST 1633 [S] | Memories of Home | 1962 | 5.00 | 10.00 | 20.00 |

—Black colorband label, Capitol logo at top

| ❑ T 1633 [M] | Memories of Home | 1961 | 6.25 | 12.50 | 25.00 |

—Black colorband label, Capitol logo at left

| ❑ T 1633 [M] | Memories of Home | 1962 | 3.75 | 7.50 | 15.00 |

—Black colorband label, Capitol logo at top

❑ ST 1720 [S]	Some of My Favorites	1962	5.00	10.00	20.00
❑ T 1720 [M]	Some of My Favorites	1962	3.75	7.50	15.00
❑ ST 1885 [S]	The Heart and Soul of Ferlin Husky	1963	5.00	10.00	20.00
❑ T 1885 [M]	The Heart and Soul of Ferlin Husky	1963	3.75	7.50	15.00
❑ DT 1991 [R]	The Hits of Ferlin Husky	1963	3.00	6.00	12.00
❑ T 1991 [M]	The Hits of Ferlin Husky	1963	3.75	7.50	15.00
❑ ST 2101 [S]	By Request	1964	5.00	10.00	20.00
❑ T 2101 [M]	By Request	1964	3.75	7.50	15.00
❑ ST 2305 [S]	True, True Lovin'	1965	5.00	10.00	20.00
❑ T 2305 [M]	True, True Lovin'	1965	3.75	7.50	15.00

❑ ST 2439 [S]	Ferlin Husky Sings the Songs of Music City, U.S.A.	1966	5.00	10.00	20.00
❑ T 2439 [M]	Ferlin Husky Sings the Songs of Music City, U.S.A.	1966	3.75	7.50	15.00
❑ ST 2548 [S]	I Could Sing All Night	1966	5.00	10.00	20.00
❑ T 2548 [M]	I Could Sing All Night	1966	3.75	7.50	15.00
❑ ST 2705 [S]	What Am I Gonna Do Now?	1967	3.75	7.50	15.00
❑ T 2705 [M]	What Am I Gonna Do Now?	1967	5.00	10.00	20.00
❑ ST 2793 [S]	Christmas All Year Long	1967	3.75	7.50	15.00
❑ T 2793 [M]	Christmas All Year Long	1967	3.75	7.50	15.00
❑ ST 2870 [S]	Just for You	1968	3.75	7.50	15.00
❑ T 2870 [M]	Just for You	1968	7.50	15.00	30.00
❑ ST 2913	Where No One Stands Alone	1968	3.75	7.50	15.00
❑ ST-11069	Just Plain Lonely	1972	3.75	7.50	15.00

HILLTOP
❑ 6005	Ole Opry Favorites	196?	3.00	6.00	12.00
❑ 6086	Green, Green Grass of Home	1970	3.00	6.00	12.00
❑ 6099	Wings of a Dove	197?	3.00	6.00	12.00

KING
| ❑ 647 [M] | Country Tunes Sung from the Heart | 1959 | 17.50 | 35.00 | 70.00 |
| ❑ 728 [M] | Easy Livin' | 1960 | 17.50 | 35.00 | 70.00 |

STARDAY
| ❑ 3018 | Greatest Hits | 197? | 3.00 | 6.00 | 12.00 |

HUTCHERSON, BOBBY
BLUE NOTE
❑ BLP-4198 [M]	Dialogue	1965	6.25	12.50	25.00
❑ BLP-4213 [M]	Components	1966	6.25	12.50	25.00
❑ BLP-4231 [M]	Happenings	1967	7.50	15.00	30.00
❑ BST-84198 [S]	Dialogue	1965	7.50	15.00	30.00

—With "New York, USA" address on label

| ❑ BST-84213 [S] | Components | 1966 | 7.50 | 15.00 | 30.00 |

—With "New York, USA" address on label

| ❑ BST-84231 [S] | Happenings | 1967 | 6.25 | 12.50 | 25.00 |

—With "New York, USA" address on label

| ❑ BST-84244 [S] | Stick-Up! | 1968 | 5.00 | 10.00 | 20.00 |

—With "A Division of Liberty Records" on label

| ❑ BST-84291 | Total Eclipse | 1969 | 5.00 | 10.00 | 20.00 |

—With "A Division of Liberty Records" on label

| ❑ BST-84333 | Bobby Hutcherson Now | 1969 | 5.00 | 10.00 | 20.00 |

—With "A Division of Liberty Records" on label

| ❑ BST-84362 | San Francisco | 1970 | 5.00 | 10.00 | 20.00 |

HUTTON, BETTY
CAPITOL
| ❑ H 256 [10] | Square in the Social Circle | 1950 | 15.00 | 30.00 | 60.00 |

WARNER BROS.
| ❑ W 1267 [M] | Betty Hutton at the Saints and Sinners Ball | 1959 | 5.00 | 10.00 | 20.00 |
| ❑ WS 1267 [S] | Betty Hutton at the Saints and Sinners Ball | 1959 | 6.25 | 12.50 | 25.00 |

HUTTON, DANNY
Also see THREE DOG NIGHT.
MGM
| ❑ SE-4664 | Pre-Dog Night | 1970 | 7.50 | 15.00 | 30.00 |

HYLAND, BRIAN
ABC-PARAMOUNT
❑ 400 [M]	Let Me Belong to You	1961	7.50	15.00	30.00
❑ S-400 [S]	Let Me Belong to You	1961	10.00	20.00	40.00
❑ 431 [M]	Sealed with a Kiss	1962	7.50	15.00	30.00
❑ S-431 [S]	Sealed with a Kiss	1962	10.00	20.00	40.00
❑ 463 [M]	Country Meets Folk	1964	7.50	15.00	30.00
❑ S-463 [S]	Country Meets Folk	1964	10.00	20.00	40.00

DOT
| ❑ DLP 25926 | Tragedy/A Million to One | 1969 | 3.75 | 7.50 | 15.00 |
| ❑ DLP 25954 | Stay and Love Me All Summer | 1969 | 3.75 | 7.50 | 15.00 |

KAPP
| ❑ KL 1202 [M] | The Bashful Blonde | 1960 | 12.50 | 25.00 | 50.00 |
| ❑ KS 3202 [S] | The Bashful Blonde | 1960 | 20.00 | 40.00 | 80.00 |

PHILIPS
❑ PHM 200136 [M]	Here's to Our Love	1964	5.00	10.00	20.00
❑ PHM 200158 [M]	Rockin' Folk	1965	5.00	10.00	20.00
❑ PHM 200217 [M]	Run, Run, Look and See/The Joker Went Wild	1966	5.00	10.00	20.00

—With "200-217" in trail-off; this record plays mono

| ❑ PHM 200217 [S] | Run, Run, Look and See/The Joker Went Wild | 1966 | 5.00 | 10.00 | 20.00 |

—With "2/600-217" in trail-off; this record plays stereo, though labeled mono

❑ PHS 600136 [S]	Here's to Our Love	1964	6.25	12.50	25.00
❑ PHS 600158 [S]	Rockin' Folk	1965	6.25	12.50	25.00
❑ PHS 600217 [S]	Run, Run, Look and See/The Joker Went Wild	1966	6.25	12.50	25.00

PICKWICK
| ❑ SPC-3261 | Young Years | 197? | 2.50 | 5.00 | 10.00 |

PRIVATE STOCK
| ❑ PS-7003 | In a State of Bayou | 1977 | 3.00 | 6.00 | 12.00 |

RHINO
| ❑ RNLP-70226 | Greatest Hits | 1987 | 2.50 | 5.00 | 10.00 |

UNI
| ❑ 73097 | Brian Hyland | 1970 | 3.75 | 7.50 | 15.00 |

—The album is listed as "stereo," but "Gypsy Woman" is rechanneled

WING
| ❑ MGW-12341 [M] | Here's to Our Love | 1967 | 3.00 | 6.00 | 12.00 |
| ❑ SRW-16341 [S] | Here's to Our Love | 1967 | 3.00 | 6.00 | 12.00 |

HYMAN, DICK
COMMAND
❑ RS 811 SD [S]	Provocative Piano	1960	5.00	10.00	20.00
❑ RS 824 SD [S]	Provocative Piano Volume 2	1961	5.00	10.00	20.00
❑ RS 832 SD [S]	The Dick Hyman Trio	1961	5.00	10.00	20.00
❑ RS 856 SD [S]	Electrodynamics	1963	5.00	10.00	20.00
❑ RS 862 SD [S]	Fabulous	1963	5.00	10.00	20.00
❑ RS 875 SD [S]	Keyboard Kaleidoscope	1964	5.00	10.00	20.00

Number	Title (A Side/B Side)	Yr	VG	VG+	NM
❏ RS 891 SD [S]	The Man from O.R.G.A.N.	1965	6.25	12.50	25.00
❏ RS 33-891 [M]	The Man from O.R.G.A.N.	1965	5.00	10.00	20.00
❏ RS 899 SD [S]	Happening!	1966	5.00	10.00	20.00
❏ RS 911 SD [S]	Brazilian Impressions	1966	5.00	10.00	20.00
❏ RS 924 SD	Mirrors	1967	5.00	10.00	20.00
❏ RS 938 SD	Moog — The Electric Eclectics of Dick Hyman	1968	7.50	15.00	30.00
❏ RS 946 SD	The Age of Electronicus	1969	7.50	15.00	30.00
❏ RS 951 SD	Concerto Electro	1970	7.50	15.00	30.00

MGM

Number	Title (A Side/B Side)	Yr	VG	VG+	NM
❏ E-3280 [M]	The Dick Hyman Trio Swings	1954	6.25	12.50	25.00
—Yellow label					
❏ E-3329 [M]	The "Unforgettable" Sound of the Dick Hyman Trio	1955	6.25	12.50	25.00
—Yellow label					
❏ E-3379 [M]	Behind a Shady Nook	1956	6.25	12.50	25.00
—Yellow label					
❏ E-3483 [M]	Red Sails in the Sunset	1957	6.25	12.50	25.00
—Yellow label					
❏ E-3494 [M]	Hi-Fi Suite	1957	6.25	12.50	25.00
—Yellow label					
❏ E-3535 [M]	60 Great All-Time Songs, Vol. 1	1957	5.00	10.00	20.00
—Yellow label					
❏ E-3536 [M]	60 Great All-Time Songs, Vol. 2	1957	5.00	10.00	20.00
—Yellow label					
❏ E-3537 [M]	60 Great All-Time Songs, Vol. 3	1957	5.00	10.00	20.00
—Yellow label					
❏ E-3553 [M]	Rockin' Sax and Rollin' Organ	1958	6.25	12.50	25.00
—Yellow label					
❏ E-3586 [M]	60 Great All-Time Songs, Vol. 4	1958	5.00	10.00	20.00
—Yellow label					
❏ E-3587 [M]	60 Great All-Time Songs, Vol. 5	1958	5.00	10.00	20.00
—Yellow label					
❏ E-3588 [M]	60 Great All-Time Songs, Vol. 6	1958	5.00	10.00	20.00
—Yellow label					
❏ E-3606 [M]	Dick Hyman and Harpsichord in Hi-Fi	1958	5.00	10.00	20.00
—Yellow label					
❏ E-3642 [M]	Gigi	1958	5.00	10.00	20.00
—Yellow label					
❏ E-3724 [M]	60 Great Songs That Say "I Love You"	1959	5.00	10.00	20.00
—Yellow label					
❏ E-3725 [M]	60 Great Songs from Broadway Musicals	1959	5.00	10.00	20.00
—Yellow label					
❏ E-3747 [M]	Whoop-Up!	1959	5.00	10.00	20.00
—Yellow label					
❏ E-3808 [M]	Strictly Organic	1960	5.00	10.00	20.00
❏ E-4119 [M]	Moon Gas	1963	5.00	10.00	20.00
❏ SE-4119 [S]	Moon Gas	1963	7.50	15.00	30.00

REFERENCE RECORDINGS

Number	Title (A Side/B Side)	Yr	VG	VG+	NM
❏ RR-33	Dick Hyman Plays Fats Waller	1991	6.25	12.50	25.00

I

IAN, JANIS

ANALOGUE PRODUCTIONS

Number	Title (A Side/B Side)	Yr	VG	VG+	NM
❏ AAP 027	Breaking Silence	1995	6.25	12.50	25.00
—Audiophile vinyl					

CAPITOL

Number	Title (A Side/B Side)	Yr	VG	VG+	NM
❏ SKAO-683	Present Company	1971	3.75	7.50	15.00
❏ SN-683	Present Company	1975	2.50	5.00	10.00

COLUMBIA

Number	Title (A Side/B Side)	Yr	VG	VG+	NM
❏ KC 32857	Stars	1974	2.50	5.00	10.00
❏ PC 32857	Stars	197?	2.00	4.00	8.00
❏ PC 33394	Between the Lines	1975	2.50	5.00	10.00
—No bar code on cover					
❏ PC 33394	Between the Lines	1979	2.00	4.00	8.00
—With bar code on cover					
❏ PCQ 33394 [Q]	Between the Lines	1975	3.75	7.50	15.00
❏ PC 33919	Aftertones	1976	2.50	5.00	10.00
—No bar code on cover					
❏ PC 33919	Aftertones	1979	2.00	4.00	8.00
—With bar code on cover					
❏ PCQ 33919 [Q]	Aftertones	1976	3.75	7.50	15.00
❏ JC 34440	Miracle Row	1977	2.50	5.00	10.00
❏ JC 35325	Janis Ian	1978	2.50	5.00	10.00
❏ JC 36139	Night Rains	1979	2.50	5.00	10.00
❏ PC 36139	Night Rains	198?	2.00	4.00	8.00
❏ FC 37360	Restless Eyes	1981	2.50	5.00	10.00

MGM

Number	Title (A Side/B Side)	Yr	VG	VG+	NM
❏ GAS-121	Janis Ian (Golden Archive Series)	1970	6.25	12.50	25.00

POLYDOR

Number	Title (A Side/B Side)	Yr	VG	VG+	NM
❏ PD-6058	Janis Ian	1976	2.50	5.00	10.00

VERVE

Number	Title (A Side/B Side)	Yr	VG	VG+	NM
❏ V/VS-5027	Janis Ian	1967	—	—	—
—Scheduled, possibly not released; same LP is Verve Forecast 3017					

VERVE FORECAST

Number	Title (A Side/B Side)	Yr	VG	VG+	NM
❏ FT-3017 [M]	Janis Ian	1967	5.00	10.00	20.00
❏ FTS-3017 [S]	Janis Ian	1967	3.75	7.50	15.00
❏ FT-3024 [M]	For All the Seasons of Your Mind	1967	5.00	10.00	20.00
❏ FTS-3024 [S]	For All the Seasons of Your Mind	1967	3.75	7.50	15.00
❏ FTS-3048	The Secret Life of J. Eddy Fink	1968	3.75	7.50	15.00
❏ FTS-3063	Who Really Cares?	1969	3.75	7.50	15.00

IAN AND SYLVIA

AMPEX

Number	Title (A Side/B Side)	Yr	VG	VG+	NM
❏ A-10103	Great Speckled Bird	1970	5.00	10.00	20.00

COLUMBIA

Number	Title (A Side/B Side)	Yr	VG	VG+	NM
❏ C 30736	Ian and Sylvia	1971	3.00	6.00	12.00
❏ KC 31337	You Were On My Mind	1972	3.00	6.00	12.00
❏ G 32516 [(2)]	The Best of Ian and Sylvia	1973	3.75	7.50	15.00

MGM

Number	Title (A Side/B Side)	Yr	VG	VG+	NM
❏ GAS-115	Ian and Sylvia (Golden Archive Series)	1970	3.75	7.50	15.00
❏ E-4388 [M]	Lovin' Sound	1967	5.00	10.00	20.00
❏ SE-4388 [S]	Lovin' Sound	1967	3.75	7.50	15.00
❏ SE-4550	Full Circle	1968	5.00	10.00	20.00

VANGUARD

Number	Title (A Side/B Side)	Yr	VG	VG+	NM
❏ VSD-5/6 [(2)]	Ian and Sylvia's Greatest Hits	1969	3.75	7.50	15.00
❏ VSD-23/24 [(2)]	Ian and Sylvia's Greatest Hits, Vol. 2	1970	3.75	7.50	15.00
❏ VSD-2113 [S]	Ian and Sylvia	1963	7.50	15.00	30.00
❏ VSD-2149 [S]	Four Strong Winds	1963	6.25	12.50	25.00
❏ VRS-9109 [M]	Ian and Sylvia	1963	6.25	12.50	25.00
❏ VRS-9133 [M]	Four Strong Winds	1963	5.00	10.00	20.00
❏ VRS-9154 [M]	Northern Journey	1964	5.00	10.00	20.00
❏ VRS-9175 [M]	Early Morning Rain	1965	5.00	10.00	20.00
❏ VRS-9215 [M]	Play One More	1966	5.00	10.00	20.00
❏ VRS-9241 [M]	So Much for Dreaming	1967	5.00	10.00	20.00
❏ VSD-73114	Greatest Hits	1985	2.50	5.00	10.00
❏ VSD-79154 [S]	Northern Journey	1964	6.25	12.50	25.00
❏ VSD-79175 [S]	Early Morning Rain	1965	6.25	12.50	25.00
❏ VSD-79215 [S]	Play One More	1966	6.25	12.50	25.00
❏ VSD-79241 [S]	So Much for Dreaming	1967	6.25	12.50	25.00
❏ VSD-79269	The Best of Ian & Sylvia	1968	3.75	7.50	15.00
❏ VSD-79284	Nashville	1968	3.75	7.50	15.00

IAN AND THE ZODIACS

PHILIPS

Number	Title (A Side/B Side)	Yr	VG	VG+	NM
❏ PHM 200176 [M]	Ian and the Zodiacs	1965	10.00	20.00	40.00
❏ PHS 600176 [S]	Ian and the Zodiacs	1965	12.50	25.00	50.00

IBRAHIM, ABDULLAH

Originally recorded as "Dollar Brand," which is the name on these records.

REPRISE

Number	Title (A Side/B Side)	Yr	VG	VG+	NM
❏ R-6111 [M]	Duke Ellington Presents the Dollar Brand Trio	1965	5.00	10.00	20.00
❏ RS-6111 [S]	Duke Ellington Presents the Dollar Brand Trio	1965	6.25	12.50	25.00

ICE-T

ATOMIC POP

Number	Title (A Side/B Side)	Yr	VG	VG+	NM
❏ AP 0011 [(2)]	Greatest Hits: The Evidence	2000	5.00	10.00	20.00

RHYME SYNDICATE

Number	Title (A Side/B Side)	Yr	VG	VG+	NM
❏ 53858	Home Invasion	1993	2.50	5.00	10.00

SIRE

Number	Title (A Side/B Side)	Yr	VG	VG+	NM
❏ PRO-A-4959 [(2)DJ]	O.G. Original Gangster	1991	6.25	12.50	25.00
—Promo-only radio-ready version of album otherwise unavailable on U.S. vinyl					
❏ 25602	Rhyme Pays	1987	2.50	5.00	10.00
❏ 25765	Power	1988	3.00	6.00	12.00
❏ 26028	The Iceberg/Freedom of Speech...Just Watch What You Say	1989	3.00	6.00	12.00

ID, THE

Two different groups.

AURA

Number	Title (A Side/B Side)	Yr	VG	VG+	NM
❏ 1000	Where Are We Going?	1976	12.50	25.00	50.00

RCA VICTOR

Number	Title (A Side/B Side)	Yr	VG	VG+	NM
❏ LPM-3805 [M]	The Inner Sounds of the Id	1967	10.00	20.00	40.00
❏ LSP-3805 [S]	The Inner Sounds of the Id	1967	10.00	20.00	40.00

IDES OF MARCH, THE

RCA VICTOR

Number	Title (A Side/B Side)	Yr	VG	VG+	NM
❏ APL1-0143	Midnight Oil	1973	3.75	7.50	15.00
❏ LSP-4812	World Woven	1972	3.75	7.50	15.00

SUNDAZED

Number	Title (A Side/B Side)	Yr	VG	VG+	NM
❏ LP-5032	Ideology	199?	3.00	6.00	12.00

WARNER BROS.

Number	Title (A Side/B Side)	Yr	VG	VG+	NM
❏ WS 1863	Vehicle	1970	3.75	7.50	15.00
—Green "WB" label					
❏ WS 1863	Vehicle	1970	5.00	10.00	20.00
—Green "W7" label					
❏ WS 1896	Common Bond	1971	3.75	7.50	15.00

IDLE RACE, THE

Jeff Lynne, later of THE MOVE and ELECTRIC LIGHT ORCHESTRA, was in this group.

LIBERTY

Number	Title (A Side/B Side)	Yr	VG	VG+	NM
❏ LST-7603	Birthday Party	1969	12.50	25.00	50.00

IF

CAPITOL

Number	Title (A Side/B Side)	Yr	VG	VG+	NM
❏ ST-539	If	1970	5.00	10.00	20.00
❏ SW-676	If2	1971	5.00	10.00	20.00
❏ SMAS-820	If3	1971	5.00	10.00	20.00
❏ ST-11299	Not Just Another Bunch of Pretty Faces	1974	3.00	6.00	12.00
❏ ST-11344	Tea Break Over — Back On Your 'Eads!	1974	3.00	6.00	12.00

METROMEDIA

Number	Title (A Side/B Side)	Yr	VG	VG+	NM
❏ BML1-0174	Double Diamond	1973	3.00	6.00	12.00
❏ KMD-1057	Waterfall	1972	3.00	6.00	12.00

IFIELD, FRANK

CAPITOL

Number	Title (A Side/B Side)	Yr	VG	VG+	NM
❏ ST 10356 [S]	I'm Confessin'	1963	6.25	12.50	25.00
❏ T 10356 [M]	I'm Confessin'	1963	5.00	10.00	20.00

HICKORY

Number	Title (A Side/B Side)	Yr	VG	VG+	NM
❏ LPM-132 [M]	The Best of Frank Ifield	1966	5.00	10.00	20.00
❏ LPS-132 [P]	The Best of Frank Ifield	1966	5.00	10.00	20.00
❏ LPM-136 [M]	Tale of Two Cities	1967	3.75	7.50	15.00
❏ LPS-136 [S]	Tale of Two Cities	1967	5.00	10.00	20.00
❏ ST-90753 [S]	The Best of Frank Ifield	1966	6.25	12.50	25.00
—Capitol Record Club edition					

Number	Title (A Side/B Side)	Yr	VG	VG+	NM
❏ T-90753 [M]	The Best of Frank Ifield	1966	6.25	12.50	25.00
—Capitol Record Club edition					
VEE JAY					
❏ LP 1054 [M]	I Remember You	1962	7.50	15.00	30.00
❏ SR 1054 [S]	I Remember You	1962	12.50	25.00	50.00

IGGY AND THE STOOGES
Includes records as "The Stooges." Also see IGGY POP.
BOMP!

❏ 1018	Kill City	1978	2.00	4.00	8.00
—By "Iggy Pop and James Williamson"					
COLUMBIA					
❏ KC 32111	Raw Power	1973	12.50	25.00	50.00
ELEKTRA					
❏ EKS 74051	The Stooges	1969	12.50	25.00	50.00
—By "The Stooges"; red label with large stylized "E" (butterfly label, deduct 60%)					
❏ EKS 74101	Fun House	1970	12.50	25.00	50.00
—By "The Stooges"; red label with large stylized "E" (butterfly label, deduct 60%)					
IMPORT/BOMP!					
❏ 1015	Metallic K.O.	1977	4.50	9.00	18.00
❏ 1018	Kill City	1978	3.00	6.00	12.00
—By "Iggy Pop and James Williamson"; original issue on green vinyl					
SUNDAZED					
❏ LP 5149	The Stooges	2002	3.75	7.50	15.00
—By "The Stooges"; reissue on 180-gram vinyl					
❏ LP 5150	Fun House	2002	3.75	7.50	15.00
—By "The Stooges"; reissue on 180-gram vinyl					

IGGY POP
Also see IGGY AND THE STOOGES.
A&M

❏ SP-5145	Blah Blah Blah	1986	2.50	5.00	10.00
❏ SP-5198	Instinct	1988	2.50	5.00	10.00
❏ SP-17641 [DJ]	Live at the Channel 7/19/88	1988	10.00	20.00	40.00
—Numbered, rubber-stamped promo-only edition					
❏ R 134099	Blah Blah Blah	1986	3.00	6.00	12.00
—RCA Music Service edition					
ANIMAL					
❏ 6000	Zombie Birdhouse	1982	3.00	6.00	12.00
❏ FV 41399	Zombie Birdhouse	1983	2.00	4.00	8.00
—Reissue					
ARISTA					
❏ SP-115 [EP]	Special Rock Club Versions	1981	4.50	9.00	18.00
—Promo-only remixes of 4 songs from the "Party" LP					
❏ AL 4237	New Values	1979	3.75	7.50	15.00
❏ AB 4259	Soldier	1980	3.00	6.00	12.00
❏ AL5-8172	Soldier	198?	2.00	4.00	8.00
—Reissue					
❏ AL5-8189	Party	198?	2.00	4.00	8.00
—Reissue					
❏ AL 9572	Party	1981	3.00	6.00	12.00
PAIR					
❏ PDL2-1051 [(2)]	Iggy Pop	1986	3.00	6.00	12.00
—Compilation of RCA Victor material					
RCA VICTOR					
❏ APL1-2275	The Idiot	1977	4.50	9.00	18.00
❏ AFL1-2488	Lust for Life	1977	4.50	9.00	18.00
❏ AFL1-2796	TV Eye — 1977 Live	1978	3.00	6.00	12.00
❏ AFL1-4957	Choice Cuts	1984	3.75	7.50	15.00
SUNDAZED					
❏ LP 5039	New Values	200?	3.00	6.00	12.00
—Reissue on 180-gram vinyl					
❏ LP 5041	Soldier	200?	3.00	6.00	12.00
—Reissue on 180-gram vinyl					
VIRGIN					
❏ 91381	Brick by Brick	1990	2.50	5.00	10.00

IKETTES, THE
MODERN

❏ M-102 [M]	Soul Hits	1965	7.50	15.00	30.00
❏ MST-102 [S]	Soul Hits	1965	10.00	20.00	40.00
UNITED ARTISTS					
❏ UA-LA190-F	(G)Old and New	1973	3.00	6.00	12.00

ILL WIND, THE
ABC

❏ S-641	Flashes	1968	25.00	50.00	100.00

ILLUSION, THE
STEED

❏ ST-37003	The Illusion	1969	5.00	10.00	20.00
❏ ST-37005	Together (As a Way of Life)	1969	3.75	7.50	15.00
❏ ST-37006	If It's So	1970	3.75	7.50	15.00

ILLUSTRATION
JANUS

❏ JLP-3010	Illustration	1969	6.25	12.50	25.00

ILMO SMOKEHOUSE
BEAUTIFUL SOUND

❏ 3002	Ilmo Smokehouse	1971	10.00	20.00	40.00
ROULETTE					
❏ RS-3002	Ilmo Smokehouse	1971	5.00	10.00	20.00

ILORI, SOLOMON
BLUE NOTE

❏ BLP-4136 [M]	African High Life	1963	15.00	30.00	60.00
❏ BST-84136 [S]	African High Life	1963	20.00	40.00	80.00
—With "New York, USA" address on label					
❏ BST-84136 [S]	African High Life	1967	6.25	12.50	25.00
—With "A Division of Liberty Records" on label					

IMPACS, THE
KING

❏ 886 [M]	Impact!	1964	50.00	100.00	200.00
❏ KS-886 [S]	Impact!	1964	75.00	150.00	300.00
❏ 916 [M]	A Weekend with the Impacs	1964	50.00	100.00	200.00
❏ KS-916 [S]	A Weekend with the Impacs	1964	75.00	150.00	300.00

IMPACTS, THE
DEL-FI

❏ DFLP-1234 [M]	Wipe Out	1963	15.00	30.00	60.00
❏ DFS-1234 [S]	Wipe Out	1963	20.00	40.00	80.00
❏ DLF-1234	Wipe Out	199?	3.00	6.00	12.00
—Reissue with bar code					

IMPALA SYNDROME, THE
PARALLAX

❏ 4002	The Impala Syndrome	1970	25.00	50.00	100.00

IMPALAS, THE
CUB

❏ 8003 [M]	Sorry (I Ran All the Way Home)	1959	100.00	200.00	400.00
❏ S-8003 [S]	Sorry (I Ran All the Way Home)	1959	150.00	300.00	600.00

IMPRESSIONS, THE
Also see JERRY BUTLER; CURTIS MAYFIELD.
ABC

❏ 606 [M]	The Fabulous Impressions	1967	6.25	12.50	25.00
❏ S-606 [S]	The Fabulous Impressions	1967	5.00	10.00	20.00
❏ S-635	We're a Winner	1968	3.75	7.50	15.00
❏ S-654	The Best of the Impressions	1968	3.75	7.50	15.00
❏ S-668	The Versatile Impressions	1969	3.75	7.50	15.00
❏ S-727	16 Greatest Hits	1971	3.00	6.00	12.00
❏ D-780 [(2)]	Curtis Mayfield/His Early Years with the Impressions	1973	5.00	10.00	20.00
❏ ST-91540	The Best of the Impressions	1968	5.00	10.00	20.00
—Capitol Record Club edition					
ABC-PARAMOUNT					
❏ 450 [M]	The Impressions	1963	7.50	15.00	30.00
❏ S-450 [S]	The Impressions	1963	10.00	20.00	40.00
❏ 468 [M]	The Never Ending Impressions	1964	7.50	15.00	30.00
❏ S-468 [S]	The Never Ending Impressions	1964	10.00	20.00	40.00
❏ 493 [M]	Keep On Pushing	1964	7.50	15.00	30.00
❏ S-493 [S]	Keep On Pushing	1964	10.00	20.00	40.00
❏ 505 [M]	People Get Ready	1965	7.50	15.00	30.00
❏ S-505 [S]	People Get Ready	1965	10.00	20.00	40.00
❏ 515 [M]	The Impressions' Greatest Hits	1965	5.00	10.00	20.00
❏ S-515 [S]	The Impressions' Greatest Hits	1965	6.25	12.50	25.00
❏ 523 [M]	One By One	1965	5.00	10.00	20.00
❏ S-523 [S]	One By One	1965	6.25	12.50	25.00
❏ 545 [M]	Ridin' High	1966	5.00	10.00	20.00
❏ S-545 [S]	Ridin' High	1966	6.25	12.50	25.00
❏ ST-90106 [S]	Keep On Pushing	1965	12.50	25.00	50.00
—Capitol Record Club edition					
❏ T-90472 [M]	The Impressions	1965	10.00	20.00	40.00
—Capitol Record Club edition					
❏ ST-90520 [S]	One By One	1965	7.50	15.00	30.00
—Capitol Record Club edition					
❏ T-90520 [M]	One By One	1965	6.25	12.50	25.00
—Capitol Record Club edition					
CHI-SOUND					
❏ T-596	Come to My Party	1979	2.50	5.00	10.00
❏ T-624	Fan the Fire	1981	2.50	5.00	10.00
COTILLION					
❏ SD 9912	It's About Time	1976	3.00	6.00	12.00
CURTOM					
❏ CUR-2006	Lasting Impressions	198?	2.50	5.00	10.00
❏ CU 5003	First Impressions	1975	3.00	6.00	12.00
❏ CU 5009	Loving Power	1976	3.00	6.00	12.00
❏ CRS-8001	This Is My Country	1968	3.75	7.50	15.00
❏ CRS-8003	The Young Mods' Forgotten Story	1969	3.75	7.50	15.00
❏ CRS-8004	Best Impressions — Curtis, Sam, Dave	1969	3.75	7.50	15.00
❏ CRS-8006	Check Out Your Mind	1970	3.75	7.50	15.00
❏ CRS-8012	Times Have Changed	1972	3.75	7.50	15.00
❏ CRS-8016	Preacher Man	1973	3.75	7.50	15.00
❏ CRS-8019	Finally Got Myself Together	1974	3.75	7.50	15.00
LOST-NITE					
❏ LLP-22 [10]	Jerry Butler and the Impressions	1981	3.75	7.50	15.00
—Red vinyl					
MCA					
❏ 1500	The Impressions Greatest Hits	1982	2.00	4.00	8.00
❏ 5373	In the Heat of the Night	1982	2.50	5.00	10.00
PICKWICK					
❏ SPC-3602	The Impressions	1978	2.00	4.00	8.00
SCEPTER CITATION					
❏ CTN-18018	The Best of Curtis Mayfield and the Impressions	1972	2.50	5.00	10.00
SIRE					
❏ SASH-3717 [(2)]	The Vintage Years	1977	3.75	7.50	15.00
—Includes solo hits by Jerry Butler and Curtis Mayfield					

IMPROVISATION CHAMBER ENSEMBLE
RCA VICTOR RED SEAL

❏ LSC-2558 [S]	Studies in Improvisation	1961	7.50	15.00	30.00
—Original with "shaded dog" label					

IMUS, DON
BANG

❏ 407	This Honky's Nuts	1974	6.25	12.50	25.00
RCA VICTOR					
❏ LSP-4699	1200 Hamburgers to Go	1972	6.25	12.50	25.00
—As "Imus in the Morning"					
❏ LSP-4819	One Sacred Chicken to Go	1973	6.25	12.50	25.00

I

Number	Title (A Side/B Side)	Yr	VG	VG+	NM

IN GROUP, THE
IN
❏ I-1002 [M]	Swinging 12 String	1964	5.00	10.00	20.00
❏ IS-1002 [S]	Swinging 12 String	1964	6.25	12.50	25.00

IN-SECT, THE
RCA CAMDEN
❏ CAL-909 [M]	Introducing the In-Sect Direct from England	1964	10.00	20.00	40.00
❏ CAS-909 [S]	Introducing the In-Sect Direct from England	1964	12.50	25.00	50.00

INCREDIBLE STRING BAND, THE
CARTHAGE
❏ CGLP-4421	The Hangman's Beautiful Daughter	198?	3.00	6.00	12.00

ELEKTRA
❏ EKM-322 [M]	The Incredible String Band	1967	7.50	15.00	30.00
❏ 7E-2002 [(2)]	'U'	1971	6.25	12.50	25.00
—Butterfly label					
❏ 7E-2004 [(2)]	Relics of the Incredible String Band	1971	5.00	10.00	20.00
—Butterfly label					
❏ EKM-4010 [M]	The 5,000 Spirits	1967	7.50	15.00	30.00
❏ EKS-7322	The Incredible String Band	1969	3.75	7.50	15.00
—Red label, large stylized "E"					
❏ EKS-7322	The Incredible String Band	1971	3.00	6.00	12.00
—Butterfly label					
❏ EKS-7322 [S]	The Incredible String Band	1967	5.00	10.00	20.00
—Brown label					
❏ EKS-74010	The 5,000 Spirits	1969	3.75	7.50	15.00
—Red label, large stylized "E"					
❏ EKS-74010	The 5,000 Spirits	1971	3.00	6.00	12.00
—Butterfly label					
❏ EKS-74010 [S]	The 5,000 Spirits	1967	5.00	10.00	20.00
—Brown label					
❏ EKS-74021	The Hangman's Beautiful Daughter	1968	5.00	10.00	20.00
—Brown label					
❏ EKS-74021	The Hangman's Beautiful Daughter	1969	3.75	7.50	15.00
—Red label, large stylized "E"					
❏ EKS-74021	The Hangman's Beautiful Daughter	1971	3.00	6.00	12.00
—Butterfly label					
❏ EKS-74036	Wee Tam	1969	3.75	7.50	15.00
—Red label, large stylized "E"					
❏ EKS-74036	Wee Tam	1969	5.00	10.00	20.00
—Brown label					
❏ EKS-74036	Wee Tam	1971	3.00	6.00	12.00
—Butterfly label					
❏ EKS-74037	The Big Huge	1969	3.75	7.50	15.00
—Red label, large stylized "E"					
❏ EKS-74037	The Big Huge	1969	5.00	10.00	20.00
—Brown label					
❏ EKS-74037	The Big Huge	1971	3.00	6.00	12.00
—Butterfly label					
❏ EKS-74057	Changing Horses	1969	3.75	7.50	15.00
—Red label, large stylized "E"					
❏ EKS-74057	Changing Horses	1971	3.00	6.00	12.00
—Butterfly label					
❏ EKS-74061	I Looked Up	1970	3.75	7.50	15.00
—Red label, large stylized "E"					
❏ EKS-74061	I Looked Up	1971	3.00	6.00	12.00
—Butterfly label					
❏ EKS-74112	Liquid Acrobat As Regards the Air	1972	3.75	7.50	15.00
—Butterfly label					

REPRISE
❏ MS 2122	Earthspan	1973	3.00	6.00	12.00
❏ MS 2139	No Ruinous Feud	1973	3.00	6.00	12.00
❏ MS 2198	Hard Rope and Silver Twine	1974	3.00	6.00	12.00

INCREDIBLES, THE
AUDIO ARTS
❏ AAS-7000	Heart and Soul	1970	5.00	10.00	20.00

IND, PETER
WAVE
❏ W-1 [M]	Looking Out	1961	6.25	12.50	25.00
❏ WS-1 [S]	Looking Out	1961	7.50	15.00	30.00

INDEPENDENTS, THE
WAND
❏ WDS-694	The First Time We Met	1973	6.25	12.50	25.00
❏ WDS-696	The Independents	1973	6.25	12.50	25.00
❏ WDS-699	Discs of Gold	1974	6.25	12.50	25.00

INDEX
DC
❏ 71	The Index	1968	1500.	2250.	3000.
—Black label; issued with black and white jacket; number is from dead wax					
❏ 4736	The Index	1968	1000.	1500.	2000.
—Red label; issued with generic white jacket, though sometimes found in first LP's jacket; number in dead wax					

INDIAN SUMMER
RCA/NEON
❏ NE-3	Indian Summer	1971	5.00	10.00	20.00

INDIGO GIRLS
DRAGON PATH
❏ LMM-I [EP]	Indigo Girls	1986	37.50	75.00	150.00
—Black vinyl					
❏ LMM-I [EP]	Indigo Girls	1986	50.00	100.00	200.00
—Blue or clear vinyl (each of equal value)					

EPIC
❏ EAS 1481 [EP]	Kid Fears/Closer to Fine/Center Stage/Prince of Darkness	1989	7.50	15.00	30.00
—Promo-only with tour-dates sticker on white cardboard cover					
❏ EAS 1861 [DJ]	Land of Canaan Plus Five Live	1989	10.00	20.00	40.00
—Promo-only item with five live tracks on B-side					
❏ EAS 2201 [DJ]	Shades of Indigo: An Interview by Shawn Colvin	1990	10.00	20.00	40.00
❏ EAS 4020 [DJ]	Indigo Girls Live	1991	10.00	20.00	40.00
—Promo-only version of "Back on the Bus Y'All"					
❏ FE 45044	Indigo Girls	1989	5.00	10.00	20.00
❏ FE 45427	Strange Fire	1989	5.00	10.00	20.00
—Reissue of Indigo release					
❏ E 46820	Nomads*Indians*Saints	1990	5.00	10.00	20.00
❏ E 57621	Swamp Ophelia	1994	7.50	15.00	30.00
—Black vinyl; all copies autographed on the label by the Indigo Girls					
❏ E 57621	Swamp Ophelia	1994	10.00	20.00	40.00
—Green vinyl; all copies autographed on the label by the Indigo Girls					

INDIGO
❏ LMM-II	Strange Fire	1987	37.50	75.00	150.00
—Black vinyl					
❏ LMM-II	Strange Fire	1987	50.00	100.00	200.00
—Blue, clear or red vinyl (each of equal value)					

INFLUENCE
ABC
❏ ABCS-630	Influence	1968	7.50	15.00	30.00

INGMANN, JORGEN
ATCO
❏ 33-130 [M]	Apache	1961	10.00	20.00	40.00
❏ 33-139 [M]	The Many Guitars of Jorgen Ingmann	1962	10.00	20.00	40.00

MERCURY
❏ MG-20200 [M]	Swinging Guitar	1956	15.00	30.00	60.00
❏ MG-20292 [M]	Swing Softly	1956	15.00	30.00	60.00

UNITED ARTISTS
❏ UAS-6785	El Condor Pasa	1970	5.00	10.00	20.00

INK SPOTS
ARCHIVE OF FOLK AND JAZZ
❏ 350	The Ink Spots in London	197?	2.50	5.00	10.00

COLORTONE
❏ 4901 [M]	The Ink Spots	1958	15.00	30.00	60.00
❏ 4947 [M]	The Ink Spots, Vol. 2	1959	15.00	30.00	60.00

CROWN
❏ CST-144 [S]	The Ink Spots' Greatest Hits	1959	6.25	12.50	25.00
—Black vinyl					
❏ CST-144 [S]	The Ink Spots' Greatest Hits	1959	12.50	25.00	50.00
—Red vinyl					
❏ CST-175 [S]	The Ink Spots	1961	6.25	12.50	25.00
—Black vinyl					
❏ CST-175 [S]	The Ink Spots	1961	12.50	25.00	50.00
—Red vinyl					
❏ CST-217 [S]	The Sensational Ink Spots	1962	6.25	12.50	25.00
—Black vinyl					
❏ CST-217 [S]	The Sensational Ink Spots	1962	12.50	25.00	50.00
—Red vinyl					
❏ CLP-5112 [M]	The Ink Spots' Greatest Hits	1959	5.00	10.00	20.00
❏ CLP-5142 [M]	The Ink Spots	1961	5.00	10.00	20.00
❏ CLP-5187 [M]	The Sensational Ink Spots	1962	5.00	10.00	20.00
❏ CLP 5221 [M]	More Ink Spots	196?	3.75	7.50	15.00

DECCA
❏ DXB 182 [(2)M]	The Best of the Ink Spots	1965	7.50	15.00	30.00
❏ DL 4297 [M]	Our Golden Favorites	1962	6.25	12.50	25.00
❏ DL 5056 [10]	The Ink Spots	1950	12.50	25.00	50.00
❏ DL 5071 [10]	The Ink Spots, Vol. 2	1950	12.50	25.00	50.00
❏ DL 5333 [10]	Precious Memories	1951	12.50	25.00	50.00
❏ DL 5541 [10]	Street of Dreams	1954	12.50	25.00	50.00
❏ DXSB 7182 [(2)P]	The Best of the Ink Spots	1965	5.00	10.00	20.00
❏ DL 8154 [M]	The Best of the Ink Spots	1955	10.00	20.00	40.00
—Black label, silver print					
❏ DL 8232 [M]	Time Our for Tears	1956	10.00	20.00	40.00
—Black label, silver print					
❏ DL 8768 [M]	Torch Time	1958	10.00	20.00	40.00
—Black label, silver print					
❏ DL 74297 [S]	Our Golden Favorites	1962	5.00	10.00	20.00

GRAND AWARD
❏ GA 232 SD [S]	The Ink Spots' Greatest, Volume 3	1959	10.00	20.00	40.00
❏ GA 33-328 [M]	The Ink Spots' Greatest, Volume 1	1958	6.25	12.50	25.00
❏ GA 33-354 [M]	The Ink Spots' Greatest, Volume 2	1958	6.25	12.50	25.00
❏ GA 33-396 [M]	The Ink Spots' Greatest, Volume 3	1959	6.25	12.50	25.00

KING
❏ 535 [M]	Something Old, Something New	1956	100.00	200.00	400.00
❏ 642 [M]	Songs That Will Live Forever	1959	75.00	150.00	300.00
—Reissue of 535					
❏ 5001	18 Hits by the Ink Spots	197?	2.50	5.00	10.00

LONGINES SYMPHONETTE
❏ SYS 5830	10 of the Best Ink Spots Hits	197?	2.50	5.00	10.00
—Label calls this "The Best of the Ink Spots"; also on label is "New Premiun for Mills Bros. V&R Offer"					

MCA
❏ 4005 [(2)]	The Best of the Ink Spots	197?	3.00	6.00	12.00

OPEN SKY
❏ 3125	Just Like Old Times	198?	2.50	5.00	10.00

PAULA
❏ 2212	The Ink Spots Sing Country	1972	2.50	5.00	10.00

TOPS
❏ L-1561 [M]	The Ink Spots	1957	10.00	20.00	40.00
❏ L-1668 [M]	The Ink Spots, Vol. 2	1959	10.00	20.00	40.00

VERVE
❏ MGV-2124 [M]	The Ink Spots' Favorites	1959	6.25	12.50	25.00
❏ MGVS-6096 [S]	The Ink Spots' Favorites	1959	10.00	20.00	40.00

VOCALION
❏ VL 3606 [M]	Sincerely Yours	196?	3.00	6.00	12.00
❏ VL 3725 [M]	Lost in a Dream	1965	3.00	6.00	12.00
❏ VL 73606 [R]	Sincerely Yours	196?	2.50	5.00	10.00
❏ VL 73725 [R]	Lost in a Dream	1965	2.50	5.00	10.00

Number	Title (A Side/B Side)	Yr	VG	VG+	NM
WALDORF MUSIC HALL					
❑ MH 33-144 [10]	Songs of the South Seas	195?	20.00	40.00	80.00
❑ MH 33-152 [10]	The Ink Spots Quartet	195?	20.00	40.00	80.00
INMAN, AUTRY					
EPIC					
❑ BN 26428	Ballad of Two Brothers	1968	5.00	10.00	20.00
JUBILEE					
❑ JGM-2055 [M]	Riscotheque Saturday Night	1964	5.00	10.00	20.00
❑ JGS-2055 [S]	Riscotheque Saturday Night	1964	6.25	12.50	25.00
❑ JGM-2056 [M]	New Year's Eve with Autry Inman	1964	5.00	10.00	20.00
❑ JGS-2056 [S]	New Year's Eve with Autry Inman	1964	6.25	12.50	25.00
MOUNTAIN DEW					
❑ 7022 [M]	Autry Inman	1963	5.00	10.00	20.00
❑ S-7022 [S]	Autry Inman	1963	6.25	12.50	25.00
SIMS					
❑ 107 [M]	Autry Inman at the Frontier Club	1964	5.00	10.00	20.00
❑ S-107 [S]	Autry Inman at the Frontier Club	1964	6.25	12.50	25.00
INMAN, JERRY					
COLUMBIA					
❑ CL 2793 [M]	Lennon-McCartney Country Style R.F.D.	1967	7.50	15.00	30.00
❑ CS 9593 [S]	Lennon-McCartney Country Style R.F.D.	1967	5.00	10.00	20.00
ELEKTRA					
❑ 7E-1068	You Betchum!	1976	3.00	6.00	12.00
INNOCENCE, THE					
KAMA SUTRA					
❑ KLP-8059 [M]	The Innocence	1967	5.00	10.00	20.00
❑ KLPS-8059 [S]	The Innocence	1967	7.50	15.00	30.00
INNOCENT, THE					
With Trent Reznor, pre-NINE INCH NAILS.					
RED LABEL					
❑ 7300	Livin' in the Street	1985	15.00	30.00	60.00
INNOCENTS, THE					
INDIGO					
❑ 503 [M]	Inocently Yours	1961	20.00	40.00	80.00
❑ 503 [M]	Inocently Yours	1961	125.00	250.00	500.00
—Plain white cover; promo only					
INSECT TRUST, THE					
ATCO					
❑ SD 33-313	Hoboken Saturday Night	1970	10.00	20.00	40.00
CAPITOL					
❑ SKAO-109	The Insect Trust	1968	10.00	20.00	40.00
INSIDE OUT					
FREDLO					
❑ 6834	Bringing It All Back	1968	50.00	100.00	200.00
INSTANT COMPOSERS POOL (ICP ORCHESTRA)					
ICP					
❑ 020	Tetterettet	1977	6.25	12.50	25.00
❑ 022	Live Soncino	1980	6.25	12.50	25.00
INTERNATIONAL SUBMARINE BAND, THE					
With Gram Parsons, later of THE BYRDS and THE FLYING BURRITO BROTHERS.					
LHI					
❑ 12001	Safe at Home	1968	25.00	50.00	100.00
—Counterfeits have white labels, legitimate copies have multi-color labels					
SUNDAZED					
❑ LP 5112	Safe at Home	2001	3.00	6.00	12.00
—Reissue on 180-gram vinyl					
INTERPRETERS, THE					
CADET					
❑ LP-762 [M]	The Knack	1966	3.75	7.50	15.00
❑ LPS-762 [S]	The Knack	1966	5.00	10.00	20.00
INTRIGUES, THE					
YEW					
❑ YS-777	In a Moment	1970	7.50	15.00	30.00
INTRUDERS, THE (1)					
GAMBLE					
❑ G-5001 [M]	The Intruders Are Together	1967	10.00	20.00	40.00
❑ GS-5001 [S]	The Intruders Are Together	1967	12.50	25.00	50.00
❑ GS-5004	Cowboys to Girls	1968	12.50	25.00	50.00
❑ GS-5005	The Intruders Greatest Hits	1969	10.00	20.00	40.00
❑ GS-5008	When We Get Married	1970	12.50	25.00	50.00
❑ KZ 31991	Save the Children	1973	5.00	10.00	20.00
❑ KZ 32131	Super Hits	1973	5.00	10.00	20.00
PHILADELPHIA INT'L.					
❑ PZ 32131	Super Hits	198?	2.00	4.00	8.00
—Reissue of Gamble 32131					
TSOP					
❑ KZ 33149	Energy of Love	1974	3.75	7.50	15.00
INVADERS, THE					
JUSTICE					
❑ JLP-125	On the Right Track	196?	75.00	150.00	300.00
INVICTAS, THE					
INVICTAS					
❑ M80P-5816/7 [M]The Invictas		196?	62.50	125.00	250.00
SAHARA					
❑ 101 [M]	The Invictas A-Go-Go	1965	30.00	60.00	120.00
20TH CENTURY FOX					
❑ TCF-3152 [M]	The Invictas	1964	10.00	20.00	40.00
INVISIBLE MAN'S BAND, THE					
Successor to THE FIVE STAIRSTEPS.					
BOARDWALK					
❑ NB1-33238	Really Wanna See Ya	1981	5.00	10.00	20.00
INXS					
ATCO					
❑ 90072	Shabooh Shoobah	1983	3.00	6.00	12.00
❑ 90115 [EP]	Dekadance	1983	3.75	7.50	15.00
❑ 90160	The Swing	1984	3.00	6.00	12.00
❑ 90184	INXS	1984	3.00	6.00	12.00
—U.S. issue of 1980 Australian album					
❑ 90185	Underneath the Colours	1984	3.00	6.00	12.00
—U.S. issue of 1981 Australian album					
ATLANTIC					
❑ 81277	Listen Like Thieves	1985	2.50	5.00	10.00
❑ 81796	Kick	1987	2.50	5.00	10.00
❑ 82140	X	1990	2.50	5.00	10.00
❑ A1-82294 [(2)]	Live Baby Live	1991	5.00	10.00	20.00
—Columbia House version (only U.S. vinyl pressing)					
❑ R 114468	Listen Like Thieves	1985	3.00	6.00	12.00
—RCA Music Service edition					
❑ R 153606	Kick	1987	3.00	6.00	12.00
—BMG Direct Marketing edition					
❑ R 164378	X	1990	3.00	6.00	12.00
—BMG Direct Marketing edition					
IRISH ROVERS, THE					
DECCA					
❑ DL 4835 [M]	First	1967	5.00	10.00	20.00
❑ DL 4951 [M]	The Unicorn	1968	6.25	12.50	25.00
❑ DL 74835 [S]	First	1967	3.75	7.50	15.00
❑ DL 74951 [S]	The Unicorn	1968	3.75	7.50	15.00
❑ DL 75037	All Hung Up	1968	3.75	7.50	15.00
❑ DL 75081	Tales to Warm Your Mind	1969	3.75	7.50	15.00
❑ DL 75157	Life of the Rover	1969	3.75	7.50	15.00
❑ DL 75302	On the Shores of Americay	1971	3.75	7.50	15.00
MCA					
❑ 15	The Unicorn	1973	2.50	5.00	10.00
—Reissue of Decca 74951					
❑ 175	On the Shores of Americay	1973	2.50	5.00	10.00
—Reissue of Decca 75302					
❑ 249	First	1973	2.50	5.00	10.00
—Reissue of Decca 74835					
❑ 284	Life of the Rover	1973	2.50	5.00	10.00
—Reissue of Decca 75157					
❑ 4066 [(2)]	Greatest Hits	1976	3.75	7.50	15.00
IRON BUTTERFLY					
ATCO					
❑ 33-227 [M]	Heavy	1967	7.50	15.00	30.00
❑ SD 33-227 [S]	Heavy	1967	6.25	12.50	25.00
—Brown and purple label					
❑ SD 33-227 [S]	Heavy	1969	3.75	7.50	15.00
—Yellow label					
❑ 33-250 [M]	In-A-Gadda-Da-Vida	1968	12.50	25.00	50.00
❑ SD 33-250 [S]	In-A-Gadda-Da-Vida	1968	6.25	12.50	25.00
—Brown and purple label					
❑ SD 33-250 [S]	In-A-Gadda-Da-Vida	1969	3.75	7.50	15.00
—Yellow label					
❑ SD 33-250 [S]	In-A-Gadda-Da-Vida	197?	2.50	5.00	10.00
—Any later Atco label; LP was in print into the late 1980s					
❑ SD 33-280	Ball	1969	3.75	7.50	15.00
❑ SD 33-318	Iron Butterfly Live	197?	2.50	5.00	10.00
—Any later Atco label; LP was in print into the late 1980s					
❑ SD 33-318	Iron Butterfly Live	1970	3.75	7.50	15.00
—Yellow label					
❑ SD 33-339	Metamorphosis	1970	3.75	7.50	15.00
❑ SD 33-369	The Best of Iron Butterfly/Evolution	1971	3.75	7.50	15.00
MCA					
❑ 465	Scorching Beauty	1975	3.00	6.00	12.00
❑ 2164	Sun and Steel	1976	3.00	6.00	12.00
PAIR					
❑ PDL2-1065 [(2)]	Rare Flight	1986	3.75	7.50	15.00
IRON MAIDEN					
CAPITOL					
❑ ST-12094	Iron Maiden	198?	2.00	4.00	8.00
—Reissue of Harvest 12094					
❑ ST-12141	Killers	198?	2.00	4.00	8.00
—Reissue of Harvest 12141					
❑ ST-12202	The Number of the Beast	1982	2.00	4.00	8.00
❑ SEAX-12219 [PD]	The Number of the Beast	1982	12.50	25.00	50.00
❑ ST-12274	Piece of Mind	1983	2.00	4.00	8.00
❑ SEAX-12306 [PD]Piece of Mind		1983	15.00	30.00	60.00
❑ SJ-12321	Powerslave	1984	2.00	4.00	8.00
❑ SABB-12441 [(2)]Live After Death		1985	2.50	5.00	10.00
❑ SJ-12524	Somewhere in Time	1986	2.00	4.00	8.00
❑ SQ-15017 [EP]	Maiden Japan	198?	—	3.00	6.00
—Reissue of Harvest 15000					
❑ 53185 [(4)]	Best of the Beast	1996	20.00	40.00	80.00
—Box set with booklet; probably a UK pressing stickered with US bar code					
❑ C1-90258	Seventh Son of a Seventh Son	1988	2.50	5.00	10.00
EPIC					
❑ E 46905	No Prayer for the Dying	1990	6.25	12.50	25.00
—Red vinyl					
HARVEST					
❑ ST-12094	Iron Maiden	1980	3.00	6.00	12.00
❑ ST-12141	Killers	1981	3.00	6.00	12.00
❑ MLP-15000 [EP]	Maiden Japan	1981	2.00	4.00	8.00

Number	Title (A Side/B Side)	Yr	VG	VG+	NM
IRVINE, WELDON					
NODLEW					
❑ 1001	Liberated Brother	1972	25.00	50.00	100.00
❑ 1002	Time Capsule	1973	25.00	50.00	100.00
RCA VICTOR					
❑ APL1-0703	Cosmic Vortex	1974	20.00	40.00	80.00
❑ APL1-0909	Spirit Man	1975	20.00	40.00	80.00
❑ APL1-1363	Sinbad	1976	20.00	40.00	80.00
STRATA-EAST					
❑ SES-19479	In Harmony	1974	10.00	20.00	40.00
ISLEY BROTHERS, THE					
BUDDAH					
❑ BDS-5652 [(2)]	The Best of the Isley Brothers	1976	3.75	7.50	15.00
COLLECTABLES					
❑ COL-5103	Shout!	198?	2.50	5.00	10.00
ISLAND					
❑ 7243 [(2)DJ]	Mission to Please	1996	5.00	10.00	20.00
—Promo-only vinyl in generic cover					
MOTOWN					
❑ M5-106V1	Motown Superstar Series, Volume 6	1981	2.00	4.00	8.00
❑ M5-128V1	This Old Heart of Mine	1981	2.00	4.00	8.00
—Reissue of Tamla 269					
❑ M5-143V1	Doin' Their Thing (Best of the Isley Brothers)	1981	2.00	4.00	8.00
—Reissue of Tamla 287					
PICKWICK					
❑ SPC-3331	Soul Shout!	197?	2.50	5.00	10.00
RCA CAMDEN					
❑ ACL1-0126	Rock On Brother	1973	3.00	6.00	12.00
❑ ACL1-0861	Rock Around the Clock	1975	3.00	6.00	12.00
RCA VICTOR					
❑ LPM-2156 [M]	Shout!	1959	30.00	60.00	120.00
—"Long Play" label					
❑ LSP-2156 [S]	Shout!	1959	50.00	100.00	200.00
—"Living Stereo" label					
SCEPTER					
❑ SC-552 [M]	Take Some Time Out for the Isley Brothers	1966	7.50	15.00	30.00
❑ SCS-552 [S]	Take Some Time Out for the Isley Brothers	1966	10.00	20.00	40.00
SUNSET					
❑ SUS-5257	The Isley Brothers Do Their Thing	1969	3.75	7.50	15.00
T-NECK					
❑ ASZ 137 [DJ]	Everything You Always Wanted to Hear by the Isley Brothers But Were Afraid to Ask For	1976	5.00	10.00	20.00
—Promo-only compilation					
❑ TNS-3001	It's Our Thing	1969	5.00	10.00	20.00
❑ TNS-3002	The Brothers: Isley	1969	5.00	10.00	20.00
❑ TNS-3006	Get Into Something	1970	3.75	7.50	15.00
❑ TNS-3007	In the Beginning (With Jimi Hendrix)	1970	5.00	10.00	20.00
❑ TNS-3008	Givin' It Back	1971	3.75	7.50	15.00
❑ TNS-3009	Brother, Brother, Brother	1972	3.75	7.50	15.00
❑ TNS-3010 [(2)]	The Isleys Live	1973	5.00	10.00	20.00
❑ TNS-3011	Isleys' Greatest Hits	1973	3.75	7.50	15.00
❑ KZ 32453	3 + 3	1973	3.00	6.00	12.00
❑ PZ 32453	3 + 3	197?	2.00	4.00	8.00
—Reissue with new prefix					
❑ ZQ 32453 [Q]	3 + 3	1974	5.00	10.00	20.00
❑ PZ 33070	Live It Up	1974	3.00	6.00	12.00
—No bar code on cover					
❑ PZQ 33070 [Q]	Live It Up	1974	5.00	10.00	20.00
❑ PZ 33536	The Heat Is On	1975	3.00	6.00	12.00
—No bar code on cover					
❑ PZ 33536	The Heat Is On	198?	2.00	4.00	8.00
—Budget-line reissue with bar code					
❑ PZ 33809	Harvest for the World	1976	3.00	6.00	12.00
—No bar code on cover					
❑ PZQ 33809 [Q]	Harvest for the World	1976	5.00	10.00	20.00
❑ PZ 34432	Go for Your Guns	1977	3.00	6.00	12.00
—No bar code on cover					
❑ PZ 34432	Go for Your Guns	198?	2.00	4.00	8.00
—Budget-line reissue with bar code					
❑ PZQ 34432 [Q]	Go for Your Guns	1977	5.00	10.00	20.00
❑ PZ 34452	Forever Gold	1977	2.50	5.00	10.00
❑ JZ 34930	Showdown	1978	2.50	5.00	10.00
❑ PZ 34930	Showdown	198?	2.00	4.00	8.00
—Budget-line reissue					
❑ KZ2 35650 [(2)]	Timeless	1978	3.00	6.00	12.00
❑ PZ2 36077 [(2)]	Winner Takes All	1979	3.00	6.00	12.00
❑ FZ 36305	Go All the Way	1980	2.50	5.00	10.00
❑ PZ 36305	Go All the Way	198?	2.00	4.00	8.00
—Budget-line reissue					
❑ FZ 37080	Grand Slam	1981	2.50	5.00	10.00
❑ PZ 37080	Grand Slam	198?	2.00	4.00	8.00
—Budget-line reissue					
❑ FZ 37533	Inside You	1981	2.50	5.00	10.00
❑ FZ 38047	The Real Deal	1982	2.50	5.00	10.00
❑ FZ 38674	Between the Sheets	1983	2.50	5.00	10.00
❑ PZ 38674	Between the Sheets	1985	2.00	4.00	8.00
—Budget-line reissue					
❑ FZ 39240	Greatest Hits, Vol. 1	1984	2.50	5.00	10.00
❑ PZ 39240	Greatest Hits, Vol. 1	1985	2.00	4.00	8.00
—Budget-line reissue					
TAMLA					
❑ T-269 [M]	This Old Heart of Mine	1966	6.25	12.50	25.00
❑ TS-269 [S]	This Old Heart of Mine	1966	7.50	15.00	30.00
❑ T-275 [M]	Soul on the Rocks	1967	6.25	12.50	25.00
❑ TS-275 [S]	Soul on the Rocks	1967	7.50	15.00	30.00
❑ TS-287	Doin' Their Thing (Best of the Isley Brothers)	1969	5.00	10.00	20.00
UNITED ARTISTS					
❑ UA-LA500-E	The Very Best of the Isley Brothers	1975	2.50	5.00	10.00
❑ UAL-3313 [M]	The Famous Isley Brothers	1963	12.50	25.00	50.00
❑ UAS-6313 [S]	The Famous Isley Brothers	1963	15.00	30.00	60.00
WAND					
❑ WD-653 [M]	Twist & Shout	1962	20.00	40.00	80.00
❑ WDS-653 [S]	Twist & Shout	1962	25.00	50.00	100.00
WARNER BROS.					
❑ 25347	Masterpiece	1985	2.50	5.00	10.00
❑ 25586	Smooth Sailin'	1987	2.50	5.00	10.00
❑ 25940	Spend the Night	1989	2.50	5.00	10.00
IT'S A BEAUTIFUL DAY					
COLUMBIA					
❑ CS 1058	Marrying Maiden	1970	3.75	7.50	15.00
—Orange label					
❑ CS 1058	Marrying Maiden	1970	7.50	15.00	30.00
—Red "360 Sound" label					
❑ CS 9768	It's A Beautiful Day	1969	7.50	15.00	30.00
—Red "360 Sound" label					
❑ CS 9768	It's A Beautiful Day	1970	5.00	10.00	20.00
—Orange label					
❑ C 30734	Choice Quality Stuff/Anytime	1971	3.75	7.50	15.00
❑ KC 31338	It's a Beautiful Day at Carnegie Hall	1972	3.75	7.50	15.00
❑ KC 32181	It's a Beautiful Day...Today	1973	3.75	7.50	15.00
❑ KC 32660 [DJ]	A Thousand and One Nights	1973	12.50	25.00	50.00
—Canceled before commercial release?					
SAN FRANCISCO SOUND					
❑ 11790	It's A Beautiful Day	1985	6.25	12.50	25.00
—Limited reissue					
IVERS, PETER					
EPIC					
❑ BN 26500	Knight of the Blue Communion	1970	10.00	20.00	40.00
WARNER BROS.					
❑ BS 2804	Terminal Love	1974	3.00	6.00	12.00
❑ BS 2930	Peter Ivers	1976	3.00	6.00	12.00
IVES, BURL					
ARCHIVE OF FOLK AND JAZZ					
❑ 340	Burl Ives Live	1978	2.50	5.00	10.00
BELL					
❑ 6055	Time	1971	2.50	5.00	10.00
COLUMBIA					
❑ CL 628 [M]	The Wayfaring Stranger	1955	7.50	15.00	30.00
❑ CL 980 [M]	Burl Ives Sings Songs for All Ages	1956	7.50	15.00	30.00
❑ CL 1459 [M]	Return of the Wayfaring Stranger	1960	7.50	15.00	30.00
❑ CL 2570 [10]	Children's Favorites	1955	10.00	20.00	40.00
—"House Party Series" issue					
❑ CL 6058 [10]	The Return of the Wayfaring Stranger	1949	12.50	25.00	50.00
❑ CL 6109 [10]	The Wayfaring Stranger	1950	12.50	25.00	50.00
❑ CL 6144 [10]	More Folk Songs	1950	12.50	25.00	50.00
❑ CS 9041 [R]	The Wayfaring Stranger	1964	3.00	6.00	12.00
❑ CS 9675	The Times They Are a-Changin'	1969	3.00	6.00	12.00
❑ CS 9728	Burl Ives Christmas Album	1968	3.00	6.00	12.00
❑ CS 9925	Softly and Tenderly	1969	3.00	6.00	12.00
DECCA					
❑ DXB 167 [(2)M]	The Best of Burl Ives	1961	6.25	12.50	25.00
❑ DL 4152 [M]	The Versatile Burl Ives	1961	3.75	7.50	15.00
❑ DL 4179 [M]	Songs of the West	1961	3.75	7.50	15.00
❑ DL 4279 [M]	It's Just My Funny Way of Laughin'	1962	3.75	7.50	15.00
❑ DL 4304 [M]	Sing Out, Sweet Land	1962	3.75	7.50	15.00
❑ DL 4320 [M]	Sunshine in My Soul	1962	3.75	7.50	15.00
❑ DL 4361 [M]	Burl	1963	3.75	7.50	15.00
❑ DL 4390 [M]	The Best of Burl's for Boys and Girls	1963	3.75	7.50	15.00
❑ DL 4433 [M]	Singin' Easy	1964	3.75	7.50	15.00
❑ DL 4533 [M]	True Love	1964	3.75	7.50	15.00
❑ DL 4578 [M]	Pearly Shells	1964	3.75	7.50	15.00
❑ DL 4606 [M]	My Gal Sal	1965	3.00	6.00	12.00
❑ DL 4668 [M]	On the Beach at Waikiki	1965	3.00	6.00	12.00
❑ DL 4689 [M]	Have a Holly Jolly Christmas	1965	3.00	6.00	12.00
❑ DL 4734 [M]	Burl's Choice	1966	3.00	6.00	12.00
❑ DL 4789 [M]	Something Special	1966	3.00	6.00	12.00
❑ DL 4850 [M]	Burl Ives' Greatest Hits	1967	3.75	7.50	15.00
❑ DL 4876 [M]	Broadway	1967	3.75	7.50	15.00
❑ DL 4972 [M]	Big Country Hits	1968	3.75	7.50	15.00
❑ DL 5013 [10]	Ballads and Folk Songs, Volume II	1949	12.50	25.00	50.00
❑ DL 5080 [10]	A Collection of Ballads and Folk Songs, Volume One	1949	12.50	25.00	50.00
❑ DL 5093 [10]	Ballads, Folk and Country Songs	1949	12.50	25.00	50.00
❑ DL 5428 [10]	Christmas Day in the Morning	1952	12.50	25.00	50.00
❑ DL 5467 [10]	Folk Songs Dramatic and Dangerous	1953	12.50	25.00	50.00
❑ DL 5490 [10]	Women: Folk Songs About the Fair Sex	1954	12.50	25.00	50.00
❑ DXSB 7167 [(2)S]	The Best of Burl Ives	1961	7.50	15.00	30.00
❑ DL 8080 [M]	Coronation Concert	1953	10.00	20.00	40.00
❑ DL 8107 [M]	The Wild Side of Life	1955	6.25	12.50	25.00
❑ DL 8125 [M]	Men	1956	6.25	12.50	25.00
❑ DL 8245 [M]	Down to the Sea in Ships	1956	6.25	12.50	25.00
❑ DL 8246 [M]	Women	1956	6.25	12.50	25.00
❑ DL 8247 [M]	In the Quiet of Night	1956	6.25	12.50	25.00
❑ DL 8248 [M]	Burl Ives Sings for Fun	1956	6.25	12.50	25.00
❑ DL 8391 [M]	Christmas Eve	1957	6.25	12.50	25.00
❑ DL 8444 [M]	Songs of Ireland	1958	6.25	12.50	25.00
❑ DL 8587 [M]	Captain Burl Ives' Ark	1958	6.25	12.50	25.00
❑ DL 8637 [M]	Old Time Varieties	1958	6.25	12.50	25.00
❑ DL 8749 [M]	Australian Folk Songs	1959	6.25	12.50	25.00
❑ DL 8886 [M]	Cheers	1959	6.25	12.50	25.00
❑ DL 74152 [S]	The Versatile Burl Ives	1961	5.00	10.00	20.00
❑ DL 74179 [S]	Songs of the West	1961	5.00	10.00	20.00
❑ DL 74279 [S]	It's Just My Funny Way of Laughin'	1962	5.00	10.00	20.00
❑ DL 74304 [S]	Sing Out, Sweet Land	1962	5.00	10.00	20.00
❑ DL 74320 [S]	Sunshine in My Soul	1962	5.00	10.00	20.00
❑ DL 74361 [S]	Burl	1963	5.00	10.00	20.00

Index was a Detroit-area band that recorded two albums' worth of material and had it pressed privately. As so often happens, their LPs ended up in the hands of collectors, who raved about the music and created a huge demand. This is the first of their records.

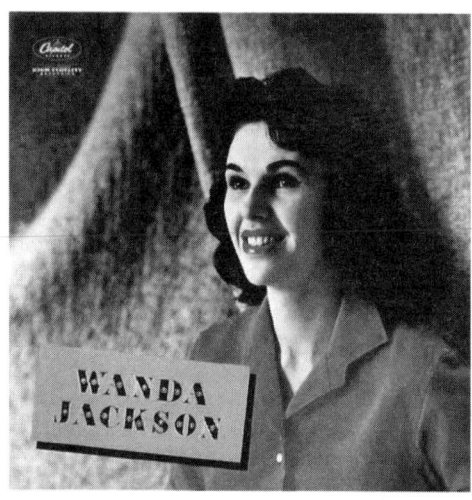

Wanda Jackson, often considered the greatest female rockabilly artist, later became a popular country singer. But before she did, she put out sought-after albums such as this one, her first for Capitol.

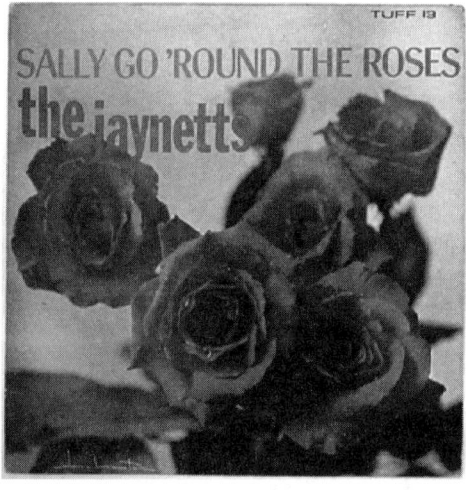

The Jaynetts were another one-hit wonder ("Sally Go 'Round the Roses") that managed to end up with an LP released in addition to their hit single. As is so often the case, the single is fairly easy to find, but the LP is almost impossible.

This album helped introduce Robert Johnson to a wider audience when Columbia issued it in 1961. It was in print for decades; original copies of this LP on the "6-eye" label are quite scarce today.

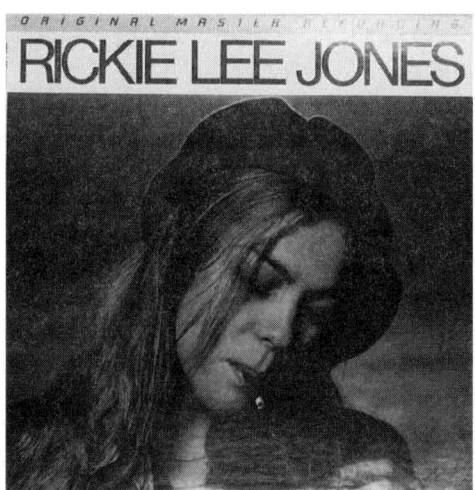

One of the crown jewels of the Mobile Fidelity LP catalog was the debut album by Rickie Lee Jones. It's one of the most expensive MoFi albums today.

The only album by the group July, released in 1969 on Epic, is highly collectible.

Number	Title (A Side/B Side)	Yr	VG	VG+	NM
❏ DL 74390 [S]	The Best of Burl's for Boys and Girls	1963	5.00	10.00	20.00
❏ DL 74433 [S]	Singin' Easy	1964	5.00	10.00	20.00
❏ DL 74533 [S]	True Love	1964	5.00	10.00	20.00
❏ DL 74578 [S]	Pearly Shells	1964	5.00	10.00	20.00
❏ DL 74606 [S]	My Gal Sal	1965	3.75	7.50	15.00
❏ DL 74668 [S]	On the Beach at Waikiki	1965	3.75	7.50	15.00
❏ DL 74689 [S]	Have a Holly Jolly Christmas	1965	3.75	7.50	15.00
❏ DL 74734 [S]	Burl's Choice	1966	3.75	7.50	15.00
❏ DL 74789 [S]	Something Special	1966	3.75	7.50	15.00
❏ DL 74850 [S]	Burl Ives' Greatest Hits	1967	3.00	6.00	12.00
❏ DL 74876 [S]	Broadway	1967	3.00	6.00	12.00
❏ DL 74972 [S]	Big Country Hits	1968	3.00	6.00	12.00
❏ DL 78391 [R]	Christmas Eve	196?	2.50	5.00	10.00
❏ DL 78886 [S]	Cheers	1959	7.50	15.00	30.00
DISNEYLAND					
❏ ST-3927 [M]	Chim Chim Chiree and Other Children's Choices	1964	3.75	7.50	15.00
❏ STER-3927 [S]	Chim Chim Chiree and Other Children's Choices	1964	5.00	10.00	20.00
HARMONY					
❏ HL 9507 [M]	The Little White Duck	196?	3.75	7.50	15.00
❏ HL 9551 [M]	The Lollipop Tree	196?	3.75	7.50	15.00
❏ HS 11275	Got the World by the Tail	196?	2.50	5.00	10.00
MCA					
❏ 114	Burl Ives' Greatest Hits	1973	2.50	5.00	10.00
—Reissue of Decca 74850					
❏ 318	Paying My Dues Again	1973	2.50	5.00	10.00
❏ 4034 [(2)]	The Best of Burl Ives	197?	3.00	6.00	12.00
❏ 4089 [(2)]	The Best of Burl Ives Volume 2	197?	3.00	6.00	12.00
❏ 15002	Have a Holly Jolly Christmas	1973	3.00	6.00	12.00
—Reissue of Decca 74689; black label with rainbow					
❏ 15002	Have a Holly Jolly Christmas	1980	2.00	4.00	8.00
—Blue label with rainbow					
❏ 15030	Santa Claus Is Coming to Town	198?	2.50	5.00	10.00
NATIONAL GEOGRAPHIC					
❏ 07806	We Americans	1978	3.00	6.00	12.00
PICKWICK					
❏ SPC-1018	Twelve Days of Christmas	197?	2.50	5.00	10.00
STINSON					
❏ SLP-1 [10]	The Wayfaring Stranger	1949	15.00	30.00	60.00
SUNSET					
❏ SUS-5280	Favorites	1970	2.50	5.00	10.00
UNITED ARTISTS					
❏ UAL 3060 [M]	Ballads	1959	3.75	7.50	15.00
❏ UAS 6060 [S]	Ballads	1959	5.00	10.00	20.00
WORD					
❏ 3259 [M]	Faith and Joy	196?	3.75	7.50	15.00
❏ 3339 [M]	Shall We Gather at the River	1966	3.00	6.00	12.00
❏ 3391 [M]	I Do Believe	1967	3.00	6.00	12.00
❏ 8140 [S]	Faith and Joy	196?	5.00	10.00	20.00
❏ 8339 [S]	Shall We Gather at the River	1966	3.75	7.50	15.00
❏ 8391 [S]	I Do Believe	1967	3.75	7.50	15.00
❏ 8537	How Great Thou Art	1971	3.00	6.00	12.00

IVEYS, THE
See BADFINGER.

IVORY
PLAYBOY

Number	Title (A Side/B Side)	Yr	VG	VG+	NM
❏ 115	Ivory	1973	3.00	6.00	12.00
TETRAGRAMMATON					
❏ T-104	Ivory	1968	5.00	10.00	20.00

IVORY, JACKIE
ATCO

Number	Title (A Side/B Side)	Yr	VG	VG+	NM
❏ 33-178 [M]	Soul Discovery	1965	5.00	10.00	20.00
❏ SD 33-178 [S]	Soul Discovery	1965	6.25	12.50	25.00

IVY LEAGUE, THE
CAMEO

Number	Title (A Side/B Side)	Yr	VG	VG+	NM
❏ C 2000 [M]	Tossing and Turning	1965	7.50	15.00	30.00
❏ CS 2000 [R]	Tossing and Turning	1965	7.50	15.00	30.00

J

J.B.'S, THE
See FRED WESLEY.

J.F.K. QUINTET, THE
RIVERSIDE

Number	Title (A Side/B Side)	Yr	VG	VG+	NM
❏ RLP-396 [M]	New Frontiers from Washington	1961	7.50	15.00	30.00
❏ RLP-424 [M]	Young Ideas	1962	7.50	15.00	30.00
❏ RS-9396 [S]	New Frontiers from Washington	1961	10.00	20.00	40.00
❏ RS-9424 [S]	Young Ideas	1962	10.00	20.00	40.00

J.K. AND COMPANY
BEAT ROCKET

Number	Title (A Side/B Side)	Yr	VG	VG+	NM
❏ BR-126	Suddenly One Summer	2000	3.00	6.00	12.00
—Reissue on 180-gram vinyl					
WHITE WHALE					
❏ WWS-7117	Suddenly One Summer	1969	6.25	12.50	25.00

JACINTHA
GROOVE NOTE

Number	Title (A Side/B Side)	Yr	VG	VG+	NM
❏ 2001	Here's to Ben	1999	6.25	12.50	25.00
—Audiophile vinyl					

JACKIE AND ROY
See JACKIE CAIN AND ROY KRAL.

JACKS, THE
CROWN

Number	Title (A Side/B Side)	Yr	VG	VG+	NM
❏ CST-372 [R]	Jumpin' with the Jacks	1962	12.50	25.00	50.00
❏ CLP-5021 [M]	Jumpin' with the Jacks	1960	50.00	100.00	200.00
❏ CLP-5372 [M]	Jumpin' with the Jacks	1962	25.00	50.00	100.00
RELIC					
❏ 5023	The Jacks' Greatest Hits	198?	2.50	5.00	10.00
RPM					
❏ LRP-3006 [M]	Jumpin' with the Jacks	1956	1000.	1500.	2000.
UNITED					
❏ US-7797	Rock 'n' Roll Hits of the 50's	197?	3.75	7.50	15.00

JACKSON, ALAN
ARISTA

Number	Title (A Side/B Side)	Yr	VG	VG+	NM
❏ AL 8623	Here in the Real World	1990	5.00	10.00	20.00
❏ AL 8681	Don't Rock the Jukebox	1991	6.25	12.50	25.00
—Columbia House vinyl edition					
❏ R 143877	Don't Rock the Jukebox	1991	6.25	12.50	25.00
—BMG Direct Marketing vinyl version					

JACKSON, BULL MOOSE
AUDIO LAB

Number	Title (A Side/B Side)	Yr	VG	VG+	NM
❏ AL-1524 [M]	Bull Moose Jackson	1959	150.00	300.00	600.00
BOGUS					
❏ 6-0214851	Moosemania!	1985	2.50	5.00	10.00

JACKSON, CALVIN
COLUMBIA

Number	Title (A Side/B Side)	Yr	VG	VG+	NM
❏ CL 756 [M]	Calvin Jackson and the All Stars Quartet	1956	12.50	25.00	50.00
❏ CL 824 [M]	Rave Notice	1956	12.50	25.00	50.00
LIBERTY					
❏ LRP-3071 [M]	Jazz Variations	1957	10.00	20.00	40.00
"X"					
❏ LXA-1005 [M]	Calvin Jackson at the Plaza	1954	12.50	25.00	50.00

JACKSON, CHUBBY
ARGO

Number	Title (A Side/B Side)	Yr	VG	VG+	NM
❏ LP-614 [M]	Chubby's Back	1957	12.50	25.00	50.00
❏ LPS-614 [S]	Chubby's Back	1959	10.00	20.00	40.00
❏ LP-625 [M]	I'm Entitled to You	1958	12.50	25.00	50.00
EVEREST					
❏ SDBR-1009 [S]	Chubby Takes Over	1959	10.00	20.00	40.00
❏ SDBR-1029 [S]	The Big Three	1959	10.00	20.00	40.00
❏ SDBR-1041 [S]	Jazz Then Till Now	1960	10.00	20.00	40.00
❏ LPBR-5009 [M]	Chubby Takes Over	1959	7.50	15.00	30.00
❏ LPBR-5029 [M]	The Big Three	1959	7.50	15.00	30.00
❏ LPBR-5041 [M]	Jazz Then Till Now	1960	7.50	15.00	30.00
LAURIE					
❏ LLP-2011 [M]	Twist Calling	1962	6.25	12.50	25.00
NEW JAZZ					
❏ NJLP-105 [10]	Chubby Jackson and His All Star Band	1950	100.00	200.00	400.00
—Either an original or erroneous pressing of Prestige 105					
PRESTIGE					
❏ PRLP-105 [10]	Chubby Jackson and His All Star Band	1951	75.00	150.00	300.00
❏ PRST-7641	Chubby Jackson Sextet and Big Band	1969	5.00	10.00	20.00
RAINBOW					
❏ 708 [10]	Chubby Jackson	1951	50.00	100.00	200.00
STEREO-CRAFT					
❏ RTN-108 [M]	The Big Three	195?	12.50	25.00	50.00
❏ RTS-108 [S]	The Big Three	195?	12.50	25.00	50.00

JACKSON, CHUBBY, AND BILL HARRIS
EMARCY

Number	Title (A Side/B Side)	Yr	VG	VG+	NM
❏ MG-26003 [10]	The Small Herd	1954	25.00	50.00	100.00
❏ MG-26012 [M]	Out of the Herd	1965	5.00	10.00	20.00
MERCURY					
❏ MG-25076 [10]	Jazz Journey	1950	75.00	150.00	300.00

JACKSON, CHUCK
ABC

Number	Title (A Side/B Side)	Yr	VG	VG+	NM
❏ X-798	Through All Times	1973	3.75	7.50	15.00
ALL PLATINUM					
❏ 3014	Needing You, Wanting You	1976	3.75	7.50	15.00
COLLECTABLES					
❏ COL-5115	Golden Classics	198?	2.50	5.00	10.00
EMI AMERICA					
❏ SW-17031	I Wanna Give You Some Love	1980	2.50	5.00	10.00
GUEST STAR					
❏ GS-1912 [M]	Chuck Jackson	196?	5.00	10.00	20.00
❏ GSS-1912 [R]	Chuck Jackson	196?	3.00	6.00	12.00
MOTOWN					
❏ M-667 [M]	Chuck Jackson Arrives!	1967	10.00	20.00	40.00
❏ MS-667 [S]	Chuck Jackson Arrives!	1967	6.25	12.50	25.00
❏ MS-687	Goin' Back to Chuck Jackson	1969	6.25	12.50	25.00
SCEPTER					
❏ 5100	A Tribute to Burt Bacharach	1972	3.75	7.50	15.00
SPIN-O-RAMA					
❏ 123 [M]	Starring Chuck Jackson	196?	5.00	10.00	20.00
❏ S-123 [R]	Starring Chuck Jackson	196?	3.00	6.00	12.00
STRAND					
❏ SL-1125 [M]	The Great Chuck Jackson	196?	6.25	12.50	25.00
❏ SLS-1125 [S]	The Great Chuck Jackson	196?	7.50	15.00	30.00
UNITED ARTISTS					
❏ UA-LA499-E	The Very Best of Chuck Jackson	1974	2.50	5.00	10.00

Number	Title (A Side/B Side)	Yr	VG	VG+	NM

V.I.P.
❑ 403	Teardrops Keep Fallin' on My Heart	1970	10.00	20.00	40.00

WAND
❑ LP-650 [M]	I Don't Want to Cry	1961	10.00	20.00	40.00
❑ LP-654 [M]	Any Day Now	1962	10.00	20.00	40.00
❑ WD-655 [M]	Encore	1963	10.00	20.00	40.00
❑ WD-658 [M]	Chuck Jackson On Tour	1964	10.00	20.00	40.00
❑ WDM-667 [M]	Mr. Everything	1965	7.50	15.00	30.00
❑ WDS-667 [S]	Mr. Everything	1965	10.00	20.00	40.00
❑ WD-673 [M]	A Tribute to Rhythm and Blues	1966	7.50	15.00	30.00
❑ WDS-673 [S]	A Tribute to Rhythm and Blues	1966	10.00	20.00	40.00
❑ WD-676 [M]	A Tribute to Rhythm and Blues, Volume 2	1966	7.50	15.00	30.00
❑ WDS-676 [S]	A Tribute to Rhythm and Blues, Volume 2	1966	10.00	20.00	40.00
❑ WD-680 [M]	Dedicated to the King!!	1966	10.00	20.00	40.00
❑ WDS-680 [S]	Dedicated to the King!!	1966	12.50	25.00	50.00
❑ WD-683 [M]	Chuck Jackson's Greatest Hits	1967	5.00	10.00	20.00
❑ WDS-683 [S]	Chuck Jackson's Greatest Hits	1967	6.25	12.50	25.00

JACKSON, CHUCK, AND MAXINE BROWN
Also see each artist's individual listings.
WAND
❑ WD-669 [M]	Say Something	1965	7.50	15.00	30.00
❑ WDS-669 [S]	Say Something	1965	10.00	20.00	40.00
❑ WD-678 [M]	Hold On, We're Coming	1966	7.50	15.00	30.00
❑ WDS-678 [S]	Hold On, We're Coming	1966	10.00	20.00	40.00

JACKSON, CHUCK, AND TAMMI TERRELL
Also see each artist's individual listings.
WAND
❑ WD-682 [M]	The Early Show	1967	7.50	15.00	30.00
❑ WDS-682 [S]	The Early Show	1967	7.50	15.00	30.00

JACKSON, DEON
ATCO
❑ 33-188 [M]	Love Makes the World Go Round	1966	7.50	15.00	30.00
❑ SD 33-188 [S]	Love Makes the World Go Round	1966	10.00	20.00	40.00
COLLECTABLES
❑ COL-5106	Golden Classics	198?	2.50	5.00	10.00

JACKSON, FRANZ
PINNACLE
❑ 102 [M]	No Saints	1961	5.00	10.00	20.00
❑ S-104 [S]	Night at Red Arrow	196?	5.00	10.00	20.00
❑ 109 [M]	Franz Jackson	1966	5.00	10.00	20.00
RIVERSIDE
❑ RLP-406 [M]	Franz Jackson and the Original Jass All-Stars	1962	7.50	15.00	30.00

JACKSON, FRED
BLUE NOTE
❑ BLP-4094 [M]	Hootin' 'N Tootin'	1962	15.00	30.00	60.00
—With 61st St. address on label					
❑ BLP-4094 [M]	Hootin' 'N Tootin'	1963	6.25	12.50	25.00
—With "New York, USA" address on label					
❑ BST-84094 [S]	Hootin' 'N Tootin'	1962	20.00	40.00	80.00
—With 61st St. address on label					
❑ BST-84094 [S]	Hootin' 'N Tootin'	1963	7.50	15.00	30.00
—With "New York, USA" address on label					
❑ BST-84094 [S]	Hootin' 'N Tootin'	1967	5.00	10.00	20.00
—With "A Division of Liberty Records" on label					

JACKSON, J.J.
CALLA
❑ C-1101 [M]	But It's Alright/I Dig Girls	1967	5.00	10.00	20.00
❑ CS-1101 [S]	But It's Alright/I Dig Girls	1967	6.25	12.50	25.00
CONGRESS
❑ CS-7000	The Greatest Little Soul Band in the World	1968	6.25	12.50	25.00
PERCEPTION
❑ 3	J.J. Jackson's Dilemma	1970	3.75	7.50	15.00
WARNER BROS.
❑ WS 1797	The Great J.J. Jackson	1969	5.00	10.00	20.00

JACKSON, JOE
A&M
❑ SP-3187	Look Sharp!	198?	2.00	4.00	8.00
—Reissue of SP-4743					
❑ SP-3221	I'm the Man	198?	2.00	4.00	8.00
—Reissue of SP-4794					
❑ SP-3241	Beat Crazy	198?	2.00	4.00	8.00
—Reissue of SP-4837					
❑ SP-3271	Joe Jackson's Jumpin' Jive	198?	2.00	4.00	8.00
—Reissue of SP-4871					
❑ SP-3286	Body and Soul	1986	2.00	4.00	8.00
—Reissue of SP-5000					
❑ SP-3666 [(2)]	Look Sharp!	1979	5.00	10.00	20.00
—Two 10-inch records in gatefold sleeve with button					
❑ SP-3908	Will Power	1987	3.00	6.00	12.00
❑ SP-4743	Look Sharp!	1979	3.00	6.00	12.00
❑ SP-4794	I'm the Man	1979	2.50	5.00	10.00
❑ SP-4837	Beat Crazy	1980	2.50	5.00	10.00
❑ SP-4871	Joe Jackson's Jumpin' Jive	1981	2.50	5.00	10.00
❑ SP-4906	Night and Day	1982	2.50	5.00	10.00
❑ SP-4931	Mike's Murder [Soundtrack]	1983	3.00	6.00	12.00
❑ SP-5000	Body and Soul	1984	2.50	5.00	10.00
❑ SP-5249	Blaze of Glory	1989	2.50	5.00	10.00
❑ SP-6021 [(2)]	Big World	1986	3.75	7.50	15.00
❑ SP-6706 [(2)]	Live: 1980-1986	1988	3.75	7.50	15.00
❑ R 101141	Blaze of Glory	1989	3.00	6.00	12.00
—BMG Direct Marketing edition					
❑ R 209597 [(2)]	Live 1980-1986	1987	4.50	9.00	18.00
—BMG Direct Marketing edition					
❑ R 244331 [(2)]	Big World	1986	4.50	9.00	18.00
—RCA Music Service edition					

MOBILE FIDELITY
❑ 1-080	Night and Day	1982	7.50	15.00	30.00
—Audiophile vinyl					

JACKSON, LIL' SON
ARHOOLIE
❑ 1004 [M]	Lil' Son Jackson	1960	6.25	12.50	25.00
IMPERIAL
❑ LP-9142 [M]	Rockin' and Rollin'	1961	100.00	200.00	400.00

JACKSON, MAHALIA
APOLLO
❑ 201/202 [M]	Spirituals	1954	7.50	15.00	30.00
❑ 482 [M]	No Matter How You Pray	1959	6.25	12.50	25.00
❑ 499 [M]	Mahalia Jackson	1962	6.25	12.50	25.00
❑ 1001/2 [M]	Command Performance	1961	6.25	12.50	25.00
COLUMBIA
❑ CL 644 [M]	Mahalia Jackson	1955	10.00	20.00	40.00
❑ CL 702 [M]	Sweet Little Jesus Boy	1955	10.00	20.00	40.00
❑ CL 899 [M]	Bless This House	1956	7.50	15.00	30.00
❑ CL 1244 [M]	Newport 1958	1959	5.00	10.00	20.00
❑ CL 1343 [M]	That Great Gettin' Up Morning	1959	5.00	10.00	20.00
❑ CL 1428 [M]	Come On Children, Let's Sing	1960	5.00	10.00	20.00
❑ CL 1473 [M]	The Power and the Glory	1960	5.00	10.00	20.00
❑ CL 1549 [M]	I Believe	1960	3.75	7.50	15.00
❑ CL 1643 [M]	Every Time I Feel the Spirit	1961	3.75	7.50	15.00
❑ CL 1726 [M]	Recorded in Europe During Her Latest Concert Tour	1962	3.75	7.50	15.00
❑ CL 1824 [M]	Great Songs of Love and Faith	1962	3.75	7.50	15.00
❑ CL 1903 [M]	Silent Night	1962	3.75	7.50	15.00
❑ CL 1936 [M]	Make a Joyful Noise Unto the Lord	1962	3.75	7.50	15.00
❑ CL 2004 [M]	Mahalia Jackson's Greatest Hits	1963	3.00	6.00	12.00
❑ CL 2130 [M]	Let's Pray Together	1964	3.00	6.00	12.00
❑ CL 2452 [M]	Mahalia Sings	1966	3.00	6.00	12.00
❑ CL 2546 [M]	Garden of Prayer	1967	3.75	7.50	15.00
❑ CL 2552 [10]	You'll Never Walk Alone	1955	12.50	25.00	50.00
❑ CL 2605 [M]	My Faith	1967	3.75	7.50	15.00
❑ CL 2690 [M]	Mahalia Jackson In Concert, Easter Sunday 1967	1967	3.75	7.50	15.00
❑ CS 8071 [S]	Newport 1958	1959	7.50	15.00	30.00
❑ CS 8153 [S]	That Great Gettin' Up Morning	1959	6.25	12.50	25.00
❑ CS 8225 [S]	Come On Children, Let's Sing	1960	6.25	12.50	25.00
❑ CS 8264 [S]	The Power and the Glory	1960	6.25	12.50	25.00
❑ CS 8349 [S]	I Believe	1960	5.00	10.00	20.00
❑ CS 8443 [S]	Every Time I Feel the Spirit	1961	5.00	10.00	20.00
❑ CS 8526 [S]	Recorded in Europe During Her Latest Concert Tour	1962	5.00	10.00	20.00
❑ CS 8624 [S]	Great Songs of Love and Faith	1962	5.00	10.00	20.00
❑ CS 8703 [S]	Silent Night	1962	5.00	10.00	20.00
❑ CS 8736 [S]	Make a Joyful Noise Unto the Lord	1962	5.00	10.00	20.00
❑ CS 8759 [R]	Mahalia Jackson	1963	3.00	6.00	12.00
❑ CS 8761 [R]	Bless This House	1963	3.00	6.00	12.00
❑ PC 8761	Bless This House	198?	2.00	4.00	8.00
—Budget-line reissue					
❑ CS 8804 [S]	Mahalia Jackson's Greatest Hits	1963	3.75	7.50	15.00
❑ CS 8930 [S]	Let's Pray Together	1964	3.75	7.50	15.00
❑ CS 9252 [S]	Mahalia Sings	1966	3.75	7.50	15.00
❑ CS 9346 [S]	Garden of Prayer	1967	3.00	6.00	12.00
❑ CS 9405 [S]	My Faith	1967	3.00	6.00	12.00
❑ CS 9490 [S]	Mahalia Jackson In Concert, Easter Sunday 1967	1967	3.00	6.00	12.00
❑ CS 9659	A Mighty Fortress	1968	3.00	6.00	12.00
❑ CS 9686	The Best-Loved Hymns of Dr. Martin Luther King Jr.	1968	3.75	7.50	15.00
❑ PC 9686	The Best-Loved Hymns of Dr. Martin Luther King Jr.	198?	2.00	4.00	8.00
—Budget-line reissue					
❑ CS 9727	Christmas with Mahalia	1968	3.00	6.00	12.00
❑ CS 9813	Right Out of the Church	1969	3.00	6.00	12.00
❑ CS 9950	What the World Needs Now	1970	3.00	6.00	12.00
❑ CG 30744 [(2)]	America's Favorite Hymns	1971	3.75	7.50	15.00
❑ KG 31379 [(2)]	The Great Mahalia Jackson	1972	3.75	7.50	15.00
❑ KC 34073	How I Got Over	1976	2.50	5.00	10.00
❑ PC 37710	Mahalia Jackson's Greatest Hits	198?	2.00	4.00	8.00
❑ 3C 38304	Silent Night	1982	2.00	4.00	8.00
—Reissue					
COLUMBIA SPECIAL PRODUCTS
❑ P2 13200 [(2)]	(HRB Music Proudly Presents) The Best of Mahalia Jackson: Hymns, Spirituals & Songs of Inspiration	1976	3.75	7.50	15.00
FOLKWAYS
❑ 31101	I Sing Because I'm Happy, Volume 1	198?	2.50	5.00	10.00
❑ 31102	I Sing Because I'm Happy, Volume 2	198?	2.50	5.00	10.00
GRAND AWARD
❑ GA 265 SD	I Believe	1966	3.75	7.50	15.00
—Reissue of 326					
❑ GA 33-326 [M]	Mahalia Jackson	1955	7.50	15.00	30.00
❑ GA 33-390 [M]	Mahalia Jackson	195?	7.50	15.00	30.00
HARMONY
❑ HS 11279	You'll Never Walk Alone	196?	2.50	5.00	10.00
❑ HS 11372	Abide with Me	1970	2.50	5.00	10.00
❑ H 30019	Sunrise, Sunset	1970	2.50	5.00	10.00
❑ KH 31111	Lord Don't Let Me Fall	1972	2.50	5.00	10.00
KENWOOD
❑ 474	In the Upper Room	196?	3.75	7.50	15.00
❑ 479	Just As I Am	196?	3.75	7.50	15.00
❑ 482	No Matter How You Pray	196?	3.75	7.50	15.00
❑ 486	Mahalia	196?	3.75	7.50	15.00
❑ 489	Mahalia Jackson With the Greatest Spiritual Singers	196?	3.75	7.50	15.00

Number	Title (A Side/B Side)	Yr	VG	VG+	NM
500	The Best of Mahalia Jackson	196?	3.75	7.50	15.00
501	I Lift My Voice	196?	3.75	7.50	15.00
502	Sing Out	196?	3.75	7.50	15.00
1001/2 [(2)]	Command Performance	196?	5.00	10.00	20.00

PICKWICK

Number	Title (A Side/B Side)	Yr	VG	VG+	NM
SPC-3510	I Believe	197?	2.50	5.00	10.00

PRIORITY

Number	Title (A Side/B Side)	Yr	VG	VG+	NM
PU 37710	Mahalia Jackson's Greatest Hits	1981	2.50	5.00	10.00

JACKSON, MARY ANNE
HANOVER

Number	Title (A Side/B Side)	Yr	VG	VG+	NM
HM-8009 [M]	The Wild Piano of Mary Anne Jackson	1959	20.00	40.00	80.00

JACKSON, MICHAEL
Also see THE JACKSONS.
EPIC

Number	Title (A Side/B Side)	Yr	VG	VG+	NM
FE 35745	Off the Wall	1979	2.00	4.00	8.00
QE 38112	Thriller	1982	2.00	4.00	8.00
8E8 38867 [PD]	Thriller	1983	5.00	10.00	20.00
OE 40600	Bad	1987	2.00	4.00	8.00
9E9 44043 [PD]	Bad	1987	3.00	6.00	12.00
E2 45400 [(2)]	Dangerous	1991	3.75	7.50	15.00
HE 47545	Off the Wall	1982	10.00	20.00	40.00
—Half-speed mastered edition					
HE 48112	Thriller	1982	10.00	20.00	40.00
—Half-speed mastered edition					
E3 59000 [(3)]	HIStory: Past, Present and Future — Book I	1995	5.00	10.00	20.00
—Box set with 12x12 booklet					
E2 68000 [(2)]	Blood on the Dance Floor: HIStory in the Mix	1997	3.75	7.50	15.00
E2 69400 [(2)]	Invincible	2001	3.75	7.50	15.00

MOTOWN

Number	Title (A Side/B Side)	Yr	VG	VG+	NM
M5-107V1	Motown Superstar Series, Vol. 7	1981	2.00	4.00	8.00
M5-130V1	Got to Be There	1981	2.50	5.00	10.00
—Reissue of Motown 747					
M5-153V1	Ben	1981	2.50	5.00	10.00
—Reissue of Motown 755					
M5-194V1	The Best of Michael Jackson	1981	2.50	5.00	10.00
—Reissue of Motown 851					
M 747	Got to Be There	1972	3.75	7.50	15.00
M 755	Ben	1972	3.75	7.50	15.00
—With only Michael Jackson on front cover					
M 755	Ben	1972	15.00	30.00	60.00
—With Michael Jackson on top half of cover, rats on the bottom half					
M 767	Music and Me	1973	3.75	7.50	15.00
M6-825S	Forever, Michael	1975	3.00	6.00	12.00
M6-851S	The Best of Michael Jackson	1975	3.00	6.00	12.00
M8-956M1	One Day in Your Life	1981	2.50	5.00	10.00
6099 ML	Michael Jackson and The Jackson 5 — 14 Greatest Hits	1984	2.50	5.00	10.00
—Picture disc packaged with one glove					
6101 ML	Farewell My Summer Love 1984	1984	2.50	5.00	10.00

JACKSON, MICHAEL GREGORY
BIJA

Number	Title (A Side/B Side)	Yr	VG	VG+	NM
1000	Clarity	1976	6.25	12.50	25.00

IAI

Number	Title (A Side/B Side)	Yr	VG	VG+	NM
373857	Karmonic Suite	1978	5.00	10.00	20.00

JACKSON, MILT
ABC IMPULSE!

Number	Title (A Side/B Side)	Yr	VG	VG+	NM
AS-9189	That's the Way It Is	1969	5.00	10.00	20.00
AS-9193	Memphis Jackson	1969	5.00	10.00	20.00

ATLANTIC

Number	Title (A Side/B Side)	Yr	VG	VG+	NM
1242 [M]	Ballads and Blues	1956	10.00	20.00	40.00
—Black label					
1242 [M]	Ballads and Blues	1961	5.00	10.00	20.00
—Multicolor label, white "fan" logo at right					
1269 [M]	Plenty, Plenty Soul	1957	10.00	20.00	40.00
—Black label					
1269 [M]	Plenty, Plenty Soul	1961	5.00	10.00	20.00
—Multicolor label, white "fan" logo at right					
SD 1269 [S]	Plenty, Plenty Soul	1959	10.00	20.00	40.00
—Green label					
SD 1269 [S]	Plenty, Plenty Soul	1961	5.00	10.00	20.00
—Multicolor label, white "fan" logo at right					
1294 [M]	Bags & Flutes	1958	10.00	20.00	40.00
—Black label					
1294 [M]	Bags & Flutes	1961	5.00	10.00	20.00
—Multicolor label, white "fan" logo at right					
SD 1294 [S]	Bags & Flutes	1959	10.00	20.00	40.00
—Green label					
SD 1294 [S]	Bags & Flutes	1961	5.00	10.00	20.00
—Multicolor label, white "fan" logo at right					
1316 [M]	Bean Bags	1959	10.00	20.00	40.00
—Black label					
1316 [M]	Bean Bags	1961	5.00	10.00	20.00
—Multicolor label, white "fan" logo at right					
SD 1316 [S]	Bean Bags	1959	10.00	20.00	40.00
—Green label					
SD 1316 [S]	Bean Bags	1961	5.00	10.00	20.00
—Multicolor label, white "fan" logo at right					
1342 [M]	Ballad Artistry	1960	5.00	10.00	20.00
—Multicolor label, white "fan" logo at right					
SD 1342 [S]	Ballad Artistry	1960	6.25	12.50	25.00
—Multicolor label, white "fan" logo at right					
SD 1417 [S]	Vibrations	1964	5.00	10.00	20.00

BLUE NOTE

Number	Title (A Side/B Side)	Yr	VG	VG+	NM
BLP-1509 [M]	Milt Jackson	1956	25.00	50.00	100.00
—Regular version with Lexington Ave. address on label					
BLP-1509 [M]	Milt Jackson	1956	37.50	75.00	150.00
—"Deep groove" version (deep indentation under label on both sides)					
BLP-1509 [M]	Milt Jackson	1963	6.25	12.50	25.00
—With "New York, USA" address on label					
BLP-5011 [10]	Wizard of the Vibes	1952	75.00	150.00	300.00

DEE GEE

Number	Title (A Side/B Side)	Yr	VG	VG+	NM
1002 [10]	Milt Jackson	1952	75.00	150.00	300.00

IMPULSE!

Number	Title (A Side/B Side)	Yr	VG	VG+	NM
A-14 [M]	Statements	1962	6.25	12.50	25.00
AS-14 [S]	Statements	1962	7.50	15.00	30.00
A-70 [M]	Jazz n' Samba	1964	6.25	12.50	25.00
AS-70 [S]	Jazz n' Samba	1964	7.50	15.00	30.00

LIMELIGHT

Number	Title (A Side/B Side)	Yr	VG	VG+	NM
LM-82006 [M]	In a New Setting	1964	5.00	10.00	20.00
LM-82024 [M]	At the Museum of Modern Art	1965	5.00	10.00	20.00
LM-82045 [M]	Born Free	1966	5.00	10.00	20.00
LS-86006 [S]	In a New Setting	1964	6.25	12.50	25.00
LS-86024 [S]	At the Museum of Modern Art	1965	6.25	12.50	25.00
LS-86045 [S]	Born Free	1966	6.25	12.50	25.00

PRESTIGE

Number	Title (A Side/B Side)	Yr	VG	VG+	NM
PRLP-183 [10]	Milt Jackson Quintet	1954	50.00	100.00	200.00
PRLP-7003 [M]	Milt Jackson	1955	30.00	60.00	120.00
PRLP-7224 [M]	Soul Pioneers	1962	10.00	20.00	40.00

RIVERSIDE

Number	Title (A Side/B Side)	Yr	VG	VG+	NM
RLP-429 [M]	Big Bags	1962	5.00	10.00	20.00
RLP-446 [M]	Invitation	1963	5.00	10.00	20.00
RLP-478 [M]	For Someone I Love	1966	5.00	10.00	20.00
RLP-495 [M]	"Live" at the Village Gate	1967	6.25	12.50	25.00
RS-9429 [S]	Big Bags	1962	6.25	12.50	25.00
RS-9446 [S]	Invitation	1963	6.25	12.50	25.00
RS-9478 [S]	For Someone I Love	1966	6.25	12.50	25.00
RS-9495 [S]	"Live" at the Village Gate	1967	5.00	10.00	20.00

SAVOY

Number	Title (A Side/B Side)	Yr	VG	VG+	NM
MG-12042 [M]	Roll 'Em Bags	1955	12.50	25.00	50.00
MG-12046 [M]	Milt Jackson Quartette	1955	12.50	25.00	50.00
MG-12061 [M]	Meet Milt	1956	12.50	25.00	50.00
MG-12070 [M]	Jazz Skyline	1956	12.50	25.00	50.00
MG-12080 [M]	Jackson's Ville	1956	12.50	25.00	50.00
MG-15058 [10]	Milt Jackson	1954	37.50	75.00	150.00

UNITED ARTISTS

Number	Title (A Side/B Side)	Yr	VG	VG+	NM
UAL-4022 [M]	Bags' Opus	1959	10.00	20.00	40.00
UAS-5022 [S]	Bags' Opus	1959	7.50	15.00	30.00

JACKSON, MILT, AND JOHN COLTRANE
Also see each artist's individual listings.
ATLANTIC

Number	Title (A Side/B Side)	Yr	VG	VG+	NM
1368 [M]	Bags and Trane	1961	7.50	15.00	30.00
—Multicolor label, white "fan" logo at right					
1368 [M]	Bags and Trane	1963	5.00	10.00	20.00
—Multicolor label, black "fan" logo at right					
SD 1368 [S]	Bags and Trane	1961	10.00	20.00	40.00
—Multicolor label, white "fan" logo at right					
SD 1368 [S]	Bags and Trane	1963	6.25	12.50	25.00
—Multicolor label, black "fan" logo at right					

JACKSON, MILT, AND WES MONTGOMERY
Also see each artist's individual listings.
RIVERSIDE

Number	Title (A Side/B Side)	Yr	VG	VG+	NM
RLP-407 [M]	Bags Meets Wes	1962	5.00	10.00	20.00
RS-9407 [S]	Bags Meets Wes	1962	6.25	12.50	25.00

JACKSON, RONALD SHANNON
ABOUT TIME

Number	Title (A Side/B Side)	Yr	VG	VG+	NM
AT-1003	Eye on You	1980	5.00	10.00	20.00

MOERS

Number	Title (A Side/B Side)	Yr	VG	VG+	NM
01081	Street Priest	1981	5.00	10.00	20.00
01086	Nasty	1981	5.00	10.00	20.00

JACKSON, SAMMY
ARVEE

Number	Title (A Side/B Side)	Yr	VG	VG+	NM
A-434 [M]	Ladies Man	1962	12.50	25.00	50.00
SA-434 [S]	Ladies Man	1962	15.00	30.00	60.00

JACKSON, SHOT
CUMBERLAND

Number	Title (A Side/B Side)	Yr	VG	VG+	NM
MGC-29513 [M]	Bluegrass Dobro	1965	5.00	10.00	20.00
SRC-69513 [S]	Bluegrass Dobro	1965	6.25	12.00	25.00

STARDAY

Number	Title (A Side/B Side)	Yr	VG	VG+	NM
SLP-230 [M]	The Singing Strings of Steel Guitar and Dobro	1962	7.50	15.00	30.00

JACKSON, STONEWALL
COLUMBIA

Number	Title (A Side/B Side)	Yr	VG	VG+	NM
CL 1391 [M]	The Dynamic Stonewall Jackson	1959	6.25	12.50	25.00
CL 1770 [M]	Sadness in a Song	1962	5.00	10.00	20.00
CL 2059 [M]	I Love a Song	1963	5.00	10.00	20.00
CL 2278 [M]	Trouble & Me	1964	3.75	7.50	15.00
CL 2377 [M]	Stonewall Jackson's Greatest Hits	1965	3.75	7.50	15.00
CL 2509 [M]	All's Fair in Love 'n' War	1966	3.75	7.50	15.00
CL 2674 [M]	Help Stamp Out Loneliness	1967	6.25	12.50	25.00
CL 2762 [M]	Stonewall Jackson Country	1967	6.25	12.50	25.00
CS 8186 [S]	The Dynamic Stonewall Jackson	1959	7.50	15.00	30.00
CS 8570 [S]	Sadness in a Song	1962	6.25	12.50	25.00
CS 8859 [S]	I Love a Song	1963	6.25	12.50	25.00
CS 9078 [S]	Trouble & Me	1964	5.00	10.00	20.00
CS 9177 [S]	Stonewall Jackson's Greatest Hits	1965	5.00	10.00	20.00
CS 9309 [S]	All's Fair in Love 'n' War	1966	5.00	10.00	20.00
CS 9474 [S]	Help Stamp Out Loneliness	1967	5.00	10.00	20.00
CS 9562 [S]	Stonewall Jackson Country	1967	5.00	10.00	20.00
CS 9669	Nothing Takes the Place of Loving You	1968	5.00	10.00	20.00
CS 9708	The Great Old Songs	1968	5.00	10.00	20.00
CS 9754	The Old Country Church	1969	6.25	12.50	25.00
CS 9880	Tribute to Hank Williams	1969	5.00	10.00	20.00

Number	Title (A Side/B Side)	Yr	VG	VG+	NM
HARMONY					
❏ HS 11187	The Exciting Stonewall Jackson	196?	3.00	6.00	12.00
JACKSON, TOMMY					
DECCA					
❏ DL 8950 [M]	Square Dances Without Calls	1959	5.00	10.00	20.00
❏ DL 78950 [S]	Square Dances Without Calls	1959	6.25	12.50	25.00
DOT					
❏ DLP-3015 [M]	Popular Square Dance Music	1957	7.50	15.00	30.00
❏ DLP-3085 [M]	Square Dance Tonight!	1958	6.25	12.50	25.00
❏ DLP-3163 [M]	Do-Si-Do	1959	5.00	10.00	20.00
❏ DLP-3330 [M]	Square Dance Festival, Vol. 1	1960	5.00	10.00	20.00
❏ DLP-3331 [M]	Square Dance Festival, Vol. 2	1960	5.00	10.00	20.00
❏ DLP-3454 [M]	Swing Your Partner	1962	3.75	7.50	15.00
❏ DLP-3471 [M]	Greatest Bluegrass Hits	1962	5.00	10.00	20.00
❏ DLP-3532 [M]	Square Dance Festival, Vol. 3	1961	5.00	10.00	20.00
❏ DLP-3580 [M]	Square Dances	1963	3.75	7.50	15.00
❏ DLP-25380 [S]	Square Dances	1963	5.00	10.00	20.00
❏ DLP-25454 [S]	Swing Your Partner	1962	5.00	10.00	20.00
❏ DLP-25471 [S]	Greatest Bluegrass Hits	1962	6.25	12.50	25.00
MERCURY					
❏ MG-20346 [M]	Square Dance Fiddle Favorites	1958	6.25	12.50	25.00
JACKSON, WALTER					
CHI-SOUND					
❏ CS-LA656-G	Feeling Good	1976	3.00	6.00	12.00
❏ CS-LA733-G	I Want to Come Back As A Song	1977	3.00	6.00	12.00
❏ CS-LA844-G	Good to See You	1978	3.00	6.00	12.00
COLUMBIA					
❏ FC 37132	Tell Me Where It Hurts	1981	2.50	5.00	10.00
EPIC					
❏ E 34657	Greatest Hits	1977	2.50	5.00	10.00
❏ PE 40434	Greatest Hits	1987	2.00	4.00	8.00
OKEH					
❏ OKM 12107 [M]	It's All Over	1965	6.25	12.50	25.00
❏ OKM 12108 [M]	Welcome Home	1966	6.25	12.50	25.00
❏ OKM 12120 [M]	Speak Her Name	1967	6.25	12.50	25.00
❏ OKS 14107 [S]	It's All Over	1965	7.50	15.00	30.00
❏ OKS 14108 [S]	Welcome Home	1966	7.50	15.00	30.00
❏ OKS 14120 [S]	Speak Her Name	1967	7.50	15.00	30.00
❏ OKS 14128	Walter Jackson's Greatest Hits	1969	3.75	7.50	15.00
JACKSON, WANDA					
CAPITOL					
❏ ST-129	The Many Moods of Wanda Jackson	1969	3.75	7.50	15.00
❏ ST-238	The Happy Side of Wanda Jackson	1969	3.75	7.50	15.00
❏ ST 8-0345	Wanda Jackson In Person	1970	5.00	10.00	20.00
—Capitol Record Club edition					
❏ ST-345	Wanda Jackson In Person	1970	3.75	7.50	15.00
❏ ST-434	Wanda Jackson Country!	1970	3.75	7.50	15.00
❏ ST-554	A Woman Lives for Love	1970	3.75	7.50	15.00
❏ ST-669	I've Gotta Sing!	1971	3.75	7.50	15.00
❏ T 1041 [M]	Wanda Jackson	1958	75.00	150.00	300.00
—Black colorband label, Capitol logo at left					
❏ T 1041 [M]	Wanda Jackson	1962	25.00	50.00	100.00
—Black colorband label, Capitol logo at top					
❏ T 1384 [M]	Rockin' with Wanda	1960	100.00	200.00	400.00
—Black colorband label, Capitol logo at left					
❏ T 1384 [M]	Rockin' with Wanda	1962	62.50	125.00	250.00
—Gold "Star Line" label					
❏ T 1384 [M]	Rockin' with Wanda	1963	37.50	75.00	150.00
—Black "Star Line" label					
❏ ST 1511 [S]	There's a Party Goin' On	1961	100.00	200.00	400.00
—Black colorband label, Capitol logo at left					
❏ T 1511 [M]	There's a Party Goin' On	1961	62.50	125.00	250.00
—Black colorband label, Capitol logo at left					
❏ ST 1596 [S]	Right or Wrong	1961	12.50	25.00	50.00
—Black colorband label, Capitol logo at left					
❏ ST 1596 [S]	Right or Wrong	1962	6.25	12.50	25.00
—Black colorband label, Capitol logo at top					
❏ T 1596 [M]	Right or Wrong	1961	10.00	20.00	40.00
—Black colorband label, Capitol logo at left					
❏ T 1596 [M]	Right or Wrong	1962	5.00	10.00	20.00
—Black colorband label, Capitol logo at top					
❏ ST 1776 [S]	Wonderful Wanda	1962	7.50	15.00	30.00
❏ T 1776 [M]	Wonderful Wanda	1962	6.25	12.50	25.00
❏ ST 1911 [S]	Love Me Forever	1963	7.50	15.00	30.00
❏ T 1911 [M]	Love Me Forever	1963	6.25	12.50	25.00
❏ ST 2030 [S]	Two Sides of Wanda	1964	7.50	15.00	30.00
❏ T 2030 [M]	Two Sides of Wanda	1964	6.25	12.50	25.00
❏ ST 2306 [S]	Blues in My Heart	1965	7.50	15.00	30.00
❏ T 2306 [M]	Blues in My Heart	1965	6.25	12.50	25.00
❏ ST 2438 [S]	Wanda Jackson Sings Country Songs	1965	7.50	15.00	30.00
❏ T 2438 [M]	Wanda Jackson Sings Country Songs	1965	6.25	12.50	25.00
❏ ST 2606 [S]	Wanda Jackson Salutes the Country Music Hall of Fame	1966	5.00	10.00	20.00
❏ T 2606 [M]	Wanda Jackson Salutes the Country Music Hall of Fame	1966	3.75	7.50	15.00
❏ ST 2704 [S]	Reckless Love Affair	1967	3.75	7.50	15.00
❏ T 2704 [M]	Reckless Love Affair	1967	5.00	10.00	20.00
❏ ST 2812 [S]	You'll Always Have My Love	1967	3.75	7.50	15.00
❏ T 2812 [M]	You'll Always Have My Love	1967	5.00	10.00	20.00
❏ ST 2883 [S]	The Best of Wanda Jackson	1968	3.75	7.50	15.00
❏ T 2883 [M]	The Best of Wanda Jackson	1968	10.00	20.00	40.00
—Red and white "Starline" label					
❏ ST 2976	Cream of the Crop	1968	3.75	7.50	15.00
❏ ST-11023	Praise the Lord	1972	3.75	7.50	15.00
❏ ST-11096	I Wouldn't Want You Any Other Way	1972	3.75	7.50	15.00
❏ ST-11161	Country Keepsakes	1973	3.75	7.50	15.00
DECCA					
❏ DL 4224 [M]	Lovin' Country Style	1962	12.50	25.00	50.00

Number	Title (A Side/B Side)	Yr	VG	VG+	NM
HILLTOP					
❏ 6058	Please Help Me I'm Falling	197?	2.50	5.00	10.00
❏ 6074	Leave My Baby Alone	197?	3.00	6.00	12.00
❏ 6116	We'll Sing in the Sunshine	197?	3.00	6.00	12.00
❏ 6123	Phoenix	197?	2.50	5.00	10.00
❏ 6182	Tears at the Grand Ole Opry	197?	2.50	5.00	10.00
MYRRH					
❏ 6533	Now I Have Everything	197?	3.00	6.00	12.00
❏ 6556	Make Me Like a Child Again	197?	3.00	6.00	12.00
PICKWICK					
❏ PTP-2053 [(2)]	Wanda Jackson	197?	3.00	6.00	12.00
VARRICK					
❏ VR-025	Rock 'n' Roll Away Your Blues	1987	3.00	6.00	12.00
WORD					
❏ WST-8614	Country Gospel	197?	3.00	6.00	12.00
❏ WST-8781	Closer to Jesus	197?	3.00	6.00	12.00
JACKSON, WILLIS					
CADET					
❏ LPS-763 [S]	Smoking with Willis	1966	5.00	10.00	20.00
MOODSVILLE					
❏ MVLP-17 [M]	In My Solitude	1961	12.50	25.00	50.00
—Green label					
❏ MVLP-17 [M]	In My Solitude	1965	6.25	12.50	25.00
—Blue label, trident logo at right					
PRESTIGE					
❏ PRLP-7162 [M]	Please, Mr. Jackson	1959	12.50	25.00	50.00
❏ PRLP-7172 [M]	Cool Gator	1959	12.50	25.00	50.00
❏ PRLP-7183 [M]	Blue Gator	1960	12.50	25.00	50.00
❏ PRLP-7196 [M]	Really Groovin'	1961	12.50	25.00	50.00
❏ PRLP-7211 [M]	Cookin' Sherry	1961	7.50	15.00	30.00
❏ PRST-7211 [S]	Cookin' Sherry	1961	10.00	20.00	40.00
❏ PRLP-7232 [M]	Thunderbird	1962	7.50	15.00	30.00
❏ PRST-7232 [S]	Thunderbird	1962	10.00	20.00	40.00
❏ PRLP-7260 [M]	Bossa Nova Plus	1962	7.50	15.00	30.00
❏ PRST-7260 [S]	Bossa Nova Plus	1962	10.00	20.00	40.00
❏ PRLP-7264 [M]	Neapolitan Nights	1963	7.50	15.00	30.00
❏ PRST-7264 [S]	Neapolitan Nights	1963	10.00	20.00	40.00
❏ PRLP-7273 [M]	Loose...	1963	7.50	15.00	30.00
❏ PRST-7273 [S]	Loose...	1963	10.00	20.00	40.00
❏ PRLP-7285 [M]	Grease 'n' Gravy	1963	7.50	15.00	30.00
❏ PRST-7285 [S]	Grease 'n' Gravy	1963	10.00	20.00	40.00
❏ PRLP-7296 [M]	The Good Life	1964	7.50	15.00	30.00
❏ PRST-7296 [S]	The Good Life	1964	10.00	20.00	40.00
❏ PRLP-7317 [M]	More Gravy	1964	7.50	15.00	30.00
❏ PRST-7317 [S]	More Gravy	1964	10.00	20.00	40.00
❏ PRLP-7329 [M]	Boss Shoutin'	1964	6.25	12.50	25.00
❏ PRST-7329 [S]	Boss Shoutin'	1964	7.50	15.00	30.00
❏ PRLP-7348 [M]	Live! Jackson's Action	1965	6.25	12.50	25.00
❏ PRST-7348 [S]	Live! Jackson's Action	1965	7.50	15.00	30.00
❏ PRLP-7364 [M]	Together Again	1965	6.25	12.50	25.00
❏ PRST-7364 [S]	Together Again	1965	7.50	15.00	30.00
❏ PRLP-7380 [M]	Live! Action	1965	6.25	12.50	25.00
❏ PRST-7380 [S]	Live! Action	1965	7.50	15.00	30.00
❏ PRLP-7396 [M]	Soul Night — Live!	1965	6.25	12.50	25.00
❏ PRST-7396 [S]	Soul Night — Live!	1965	7.50	15.00	30.00
❏ PRLP-7412 [M]	Tell It...	1966	5.00	10.00	20.00
❏ PRST-7412 [S]	Tell It...	1966	6.25	12.50	25.00
❏ PRLP-7428 [M]	Together Again...Again	1966	5.00	10.00	20.00
❏ PRST-7428 [S]	Together Again...Again	1966	6.25	12.50	25.00
❏ PRST-7551	Soul Grabber	1968	5.00	10.00	20.00
❏ PRST-7571	Star Bag	1968	5.00	10.00	20.00
❏ PRST-7602	Swivel Hips	1969	5.00	10.00	20.00
❏ PRST-7648	Gator's Groove	1969	5.00	10.00	20.00
❏ PRST-7783	Please Mr. Jackson	1970	5.00	10.00	20.00
❏ PRST-7830	Keep On a-Blowing	1971	5.00	10.00	20.00
VERVE					
❏ V6-8589 [S]	'Gator Tails	1964	5.00	10.00	20.00
JACKSON HEIGHTS					
MERCURY					
❏ SR-61331	King Progress	1970	6.25	12.00	25.00
VERVE					
❏ V6-5089	Jackson Heights	1973	5.00	10.00	20.00
JACKSONS, THE					
Includes records as "The Jackson Five." Also see MICHAEL JACKSON.					
EPIC					
❏ PE 34229	The Jacksons	1976	2.50	5.00	10.00
—Orange label					
❏ PE 34229	The Jacksons	198?	—	3.00	6.00
—Budget-line reissue with bar code and dark blue label					
❏ JE 34835	Goin' Places	1977	2.50	5.00	10.00
—Orange label					
❏ PE 34835	Goin' Places	198?	—	3.00	6.00
—Budget-line reissue					
❏ JE 35552	Destiny	1978	2.50	5.00	10.00
—Orange label					
❏ JE 35552	Destiny	1979	2.00	4.00	8.00
—Dark blue label					
❏ FE 36424	Triumph	1980	2.00	4.00	8.00
❏ KE2 37545 [(2)]	Jacksons Live	1981	3.00	6.00	12.00
❏ QE 38946	Victory	1984	2.00	4.00	8.00
❏ 8E8 39576 [PD]	Victory	1984	3.75	7.50	15.00
❏ OE 40911	2300 Jackson Street	1989	2.00	4.00	8.00
❏ HE 46424	Triumph	1982	15.00	30.00	60.00
—Half-speed mastered edition					
MOTOWN					
❏ M5-112V1	Motown Superstar Series, Vol. 12	1981	2.50	5.00	10.00
❏ M5-129V1	Diana Ross Presents the Jackson Five	1981	2.00	4.00	8.00
❏ M5-152V1	ABC	1981	2.00	4.00	8.00

J

Number	Title (A Side/B Side)	Yr	VG	VG+	NM
❑ M5-157V1	Third Album	1981	2.00	4.00	8.00
❑ M5-201V1	Jackson 5 Greatest Hits	1981	2.00	4.00	8.00
❑ MS 700	Diana Ross Presents the Jackson 5	1969	6.25	12.50	25.00
❑ MS 709	ABC	1970	6.25	12.50	25.00
❑ MS 713	Christmas Album	1970	6.25	12.50	25.00
❑ MS 718	Third Album	1970	3.75	7.50	15.00
❑ M-735	Maybe Tomorrow	1971	3.75	7.50	15.00
❑ M-741	Jackson 5 Greatest Hits	1971	3.75	7.50	15.00
❑ M-742	Goin' Back to Indiana	1971	3.75	7.50	15.00
❑ M-750	Lookin' Through the Windows	1972	3.75	7.50	15.00
❑ M-761	Skywriter	1973	3.00	6.00	12.00
❑ M6-780	Dancing Machine	1974	3.00	6.00	12.00
❑ M6-783	Get It Together	1973	3.00	6.00	12.00
❑ M6-829	Moving Violation	1975	3.00	6.00	12.00
❑ M6-865	Joyful Jukebox Music	1976	3.00	6.00	12.00
❑ M7-868 [(3)]	Anthology	1976	5.00	10.00	20.00
❑ 37463 1294-1 [DJ]	Soulsation!	1995	5.00	10.00	20.00
—Vinyl is promo only; 4-song sampler from box set					
❑ 5228 ML	Maybe Tomorrow	1982	2.00	4.00	8.00
❑ 5250 ML	Christmas Album	1982	2.00	4.00	8.00
—Reissue of Motown 713					

JACOBI, LOU
CAPITOL

Number	Title (A Side/B Side)	Yr	VG	VG+	NM
❑ ST 2596 [S]	Al Tijuana and His Jewish Brass	1966	5.00	10.00	20.00
❑ T 2596 [M]	Al Tijuana and His Jewish Brass	1966	3.75	7.50	15.00

JACOBS, DICK
CORAL

Number	Title (A Side/B Side)	Yr	VG	VG+	NM
❑ CRL 57381 [M]	The Electro-Sonic Orchestra Presenting a New Concept in Sound	1958	5.00	10.00	20.00
❑ CRL 757381 [S]	The Electro-Sonic Orchestra Presenting a New Concept in Sound	1958	7.50	15.00	30.00

JACOBS, FREDDIE
WESTMINSTER

Number	Title (A Side/B Side)	Yr	VG	VG+	NM
❑ WP-6087 [M]	Swingin' Folk Tunes	195?	7.50	15.00	30.00

JACOBS, HANK
SUE

Number	Title (A Side/B Side)	Yr	VG	VG+	NM
❑ LP-1023 [M]	So Far Away	1964	20.00	40.00	80.00

JACOBY, DON
DECCA

Number	Title (A Side/B Side)	Yr	VG	VG+	NM
❑ DL 74241 [S]	The Swinging Big Sound	1963	5.00	10.00	20.00

JACQUET, ILLINOIS
ALADDIN

Number	Title (A Side/B Side)	Yr	VG	VG+	NM
❑ LP-708 [10]	Illinois Jacquet and His Tenor Sax	1954	62.50	125.00	250.00
❑ LP-803 [M]	Illinois Jacquet and His Tenor Sax	1956	20.00	40.00	80.00

APOLLO

| ❑ LP-104 [10] | Illinois Jacquet Jam Session | 1951 | 75.00 | 150.00 | 300.00 |

ARGO

❑ LP-722 [M]	Message	1963	6.25	12.50	25.00
❑ LPS-722 [S]	Message	1963	7.50	15.00	30.00
❑ LP-735 [M]	Desert Winds	1964	6.25	12.50	25.00
❑ LPS-735 [S]	Desert Winds	1964	7.50	15.00	30.00
❑ LP-746 [M]	Illinois Jacquet Plays Cole Porter	1964	6.25	12.50	25.00
❑ LPS-746 [S]	Illinois Jacquet Plays Cole Porter	1964	7.50	15.00	30.00

CADET

❑ LPS-722 [S]	Message	1966	5.00	10.00	20.00
❑ LPS-735 [S]	Desert Winds	1966	5.00	10.00	20.00
❑ LPS-746 [S]	Bosses of the Ballad	1966	5.00	10.00	20.00
❑ LP-754 [M]	Spectrum	1965	5.00	10.00	20.00
❑ LPS-754 [S]	Spectrum	1965	6.25	12.50	25.00
❑ LP-773 [M]	Go Power!	1966	5.00	10.00	20.00
❑ LPS-773 [S]	Go Power!	1966	6.25	12.50	25.00

CLEF

❑ MGC-112 [10]	Illinois Jacquet Collates	1953	37.50	75.00	150.00
❑ MGC-129 [10]	Illinois Jacquet Collates #2	1953	37.50	75.00	150.00
❑ MGC-167 [10]	Jazz by Jacquet	1954	37.50	75.00	150.00
❑ MGC-622 [M]	Jazz Moods	1955	30.00	60.00	120.00
❑ MGC-676 [M]	Illinois Jacquet Septet	1955	30.00	60.00	120.00
❑ MGC-700 [M]	Jazz Moods by Illinois Jacquet	1956	25.00	50.00	100.00
❑ MGC-701 [M]	Port of Rico	1956	25.00	50.00	100.00
❑ MGC-702 [M]	Groovin' with Jacquet	1956	30.00	60.00	120.00
❑ MGC-750 [M]	Swing's the Thing	1956	25.00	50.00	100.00

EPIC

❑ LA 16033 [M]	Illinois Jacquet	1963	7.50	15.00	30.00
❑ BA 17033 [S]	Illinois Jacquet	1963	10.00	20.00	40.00
❑ BA 17033 [S]	Illinois Jacquet	199?	6.25	12.50	25.00
—Classic Records reissue on audiophile vinyl					

GROOVE NOTE

| ❑ 2003 [(2)] | Birthday Party | 1999 | 7.50 | 15.00 | 30.00 |
| —Audiophile vinyl; one record has the entire album, the other has two tracks at 45 rpm | | | | | |

IMPERIAL

| ❑ LP-9184 [M] | Flying Home | 1962 | 7.50 | 15.00 | 30.00 |
| ❑ LP-12184 [S] | Flying Home | 1962 | 10.00 | 20.00 | 40.00 |

MERCURY

| ❑ MGC-112 [10] | Illinois Jacquet Collates | 1952 | 62.50 | 125.00 | 250.00 |

MOSAIC

| ❑ MQ6-165 [(6)] | The Complete Illinois Jacquet Sessions 1945-50 | 199? | 25.00 | 50.00 | 100.00 |

PRESTIGE

❑ PRST-7575	Bottoms Up!	1968	6.25	12.50	25.00
❑ PRST-7597	The King!	1968	6.25	12.50	25.00
❑ PRST-7629	The Soul Explosion	1969	6.25	12.50	25.00
❑ PRST-7731	The Blues — That's Me	1969	6.25	12.50	25.00

RCA VICTOR

| ❑ LPM-3236 [10] | Black Velvet | 1954 | 62.50 | 125.00 | 250.00 |

ROULETTE

Number	Title (A Side/B Side)	Yr	VG	VG+	NM
❑ R-52035 [M]	Illinois Jacquet Flies Again	1959	12.50	25.00	50.00
❑ SR-52035 [S]	Illinois Jacquet Flies Again	1959	10.00	20.00	40.00

SAVOY

| ❑ MG-15024 [10] | Tenor Sax | 1953 | 50.00 | 100.00 | 200.00 |

VERVE

❑ MGV-8023 [M]	Swing's the Thing	1957	12.50	25.00	50.00
—Reissue of Clef 750					
❑ V-8023 [M]	Swing's the Thing	1961	6.25	12.50	25.00
❑ MGV-8061 [M]	Illinois Jacquet and His Orchestra	1957	12.50	25.00	50.00
—Reissue of Clef 676					
❑ V-8061 [M]	Illinois Jacquet and His Orchestra	1961	6.25	12.50	25.00
❑ MGV-8084 [M]	Jazz Moods by Illinois Jacquet	1957	12.50	25.00	50.00
—Reissue of Clef 700					
❑ V-8084 [M]	Jazz Moods by Illinois Jacquet	1961	6.25	12.50	25.00
❑ MGV-8085 [M]	Port of Rico	1957	12.50	25.00	50.00
—Reissue of Clef 701					
❑ V-8085 [M]	Port of Rico	1961	6.25	12.50	25.00
❑ MGV-8086 [M]	Groovin' with Jacquet	1957	12.50	25.00	50.00
—Reissue of Clef 702					
❑ V-8086 [M]	Groovin' with Jacquet	1961	6.25	12.50	25.00

JACQUET, ILLINOIS, AND BEN WEBSTER
CLEF

| ❑ MGC-680 [M] | "The Kid" and "The Brute" | 1955 | 30.00 | 60.00 | 120.00 |

VERVE

❑ MGV-8065 [M]	"The Kid" and "The Brute"	1957	12.50	25.00	50.00
—Reissue of Clef 680					
❑ V-8065 [M]	"The Kid" and "The Brute"	1961	5.00	10.00	20.00

JACQUET, RUSSELL
KING

| ❑ 295-81 [10] | Russell Jacquet and His All Stars | 1954 | 62.50 | 125.00 | 250.00 |

JADE
GENERAL AMERICAN

| ❑ 11311 | The Faces of Jade | 1968 | 20.00 | 40.00 | 80.00 |

JADE, FAINE
RSVP

| ❑ 8002 | Introspection: A Faine Jade Recital | 1968 | 100.00 | 200.00 | 400.00 |

JADES, THE
JARRETT

| ❑ 21517 [M] | Live at the Disco a-Go-Go | 1965 | 30.00 | 60.00 | 120.00 |

JAG PANZER
AZRA IRON WORKS

| ❑ 1001 [PD] | Ample Destruction | 1985 | 6.25 | 12.00 | 25.00 |
| —Allegedly, 250 were pressed as picture discs | | | | | |

JAGGERZ, THE
GAMBLE

| ❑ GS-5006 | Introducing the Jaggerz | 1969 | 5.00 | 10.00 | 20.00 |

KAMA SUTRA

| ❑ KSBS-2017 | We Went to Different Schools Together | 1970 | 3.75 | 7.50 | 15.00 |

WOODEN NICKEL

| ❑ BWL1-0772 | Come Again | 1975 | 3.00 | 6.00 | 12.00 |

JAIM
ETHEREAL

| ❑ 1001 | Prophecy Fulfilled | 1970 | 12.50 | 25.00 | 50.00 |

JALOPY FIVE, THE
MODERN SOUND

| ❑ M-561 [M] | I Love That West Coast Sound | 1965 | 12.50 | 25.00 | 50.00 |
| ❑ MS-561 [S] | I Love That West Coast Sound | 1965 | 12.50 | 25.00 | 50.00 |

JAM, THE
POLYDOR

❑ PX1-503 [EP]	The Jam	1982	3.00	6.00	12.00
❑ PX1-506 [EP]	The Bitterest Pill	1982	3.00	6.00	12.00
❑ PD1-6110	In the City	1977	6.25	12.50	25.00
❑ PD1-6129	This Is the Modern World	1978	5.00	10.00	20.00
❑ PD1-6188	All Mod Cons	1979	3.75	7.50	15.00
❑ PD1-6249	Setting Sons	1980	3.75	7.50	15.00
❑ PD1-6315	Sound Affects	1981	3.75	7.50	15.00
❑ PD1-6349	The Gift	1982	3.00	6.00	12.00
❑ PD1-6365	Dig the New Breed	1982	2.50	5.00	10.00
❑ 810751-1 [EP]	Beat Surrender	1982	2.50	5.00	10.00
❑ 815537-1 [(2)]	Snap!	1983	3.75	7.50	15.00
❑ 817124-1	In the City	198?	2.50	5.00	10.00
—Reissue					
❑ 823281-1	This Is the Modern World	198?	2.50	5.00	10.00
—Reissue					

JAMAL, AHMAD
ARGO

❑ LP-602 [M]	Chamber Music of New Jazz	1956	7.50	15.00	30.00
—Reissue of Creative 602					
❑ LP-610 [M]	Count 'Em 88	1957	7.50	15.00	30.00
❑ LP-628 [M]	But Not for Me/Ahmad Jamal at the Pershing	1958	7.50	15.00	30.00
❑ LPS-628 [S]	But Not for Me/Ahmad Jamal at the Pershing	1958	10.00	20.00	40.00
❑ LP-636 [M]	Ahmad Jamal, Volume IV	1958	7.50	15.00	30.00
❑ LPS-636 [S]	Ahmad Jamal, Volume IV	1958	10.00	20.00	40.00
❑ LP-638 [(2)M]	Portfolio of Ahmad Jamal	1959	10.00	20.00	40.00
❑ LPS-638 [(2)S]	Portfolio of Ahmad Jamal	1959	12.50	25.00	50.00
❑ LP-646 [M]	Jamal at the Penthouse	1959	7.50	15.00	30.00
❑ LPS-646 [S]	Jamal at the Penthouse	1959	10.00	20.00	40.00
❑ LP-662 [M]	Happy Moods	1960	5.00	10.00	20.00
❑ LPS-662 [S]	Happy Moods	1960	6.25	12.50	25.00
❑ LP-667 [M]	Ahmad Jamal at the Pershing Volume 2	1961	5.00	10.00	20.00
❑ LPS-667 [S]	Ahmad Jamal at the Pershing Volume 2	1961	6.25	12.50	25.00

Number	Title (A Side/B Side)	Yr	VG	VG+	NM
❏ LP-673 [M]	Listen to Ahmad Jamal	1961	5.00	10.00	20.00
❏ LPS-673 [S]	Listen to Ahmad Jamal	1961	6.25	12.50	25.00
❏ LP-685 [M]	Alhambra	1961	5.00	10.00	20.00
❏ LPS-685 [S]	Alhambra	1961	6.25	12.50	25.00
❏ LP-691 [M]	All of You	1962	5.00	10.00	20.00
❏ LPS-691 [S]	All of You	1962	6.25	12.50	25.00
❏ LP-703 [M]	Ahmad Jamal at the Blackhawk	1962	5.00	10.00	20.00
❏ LPS-703 [S]	Ahmad Jamal at the Blackhawk	1962	6.25	12.50	25.00
❏ LP-712 [M]	Macanudo	1963	5.00	10.00	20.00
❏ LPS-712 [S]	Macanudo	1963	6.25	12.50	25.00
❏ LP-719 [M]	Poin'-ci-an'a	1963	5.00	10.00	20.00
❏ LPS-719 [S]	Poin'-ci-an'a	1963	6.25	12.50	25.00
❏ LP-733 [M]	"Naked City" Theme	1964	5.00	10.00	20.00
❏ LPS-733 [S]	"Naked City" Theme	1964	6.25	12.50	25.00
❏ LP-751 [M]	The Roar of the Greasepaint	1965	5.00	10.00	20.00
❏ LPS-751 [S]	The Roar of the Greasepaint	1965	6.25	12.50	25.00
❏ LP-758 [M]	Extensions	1965	5.00	10.00	20.00
❏ LPS-758 [S]	Extensions	1965	6.25	12.50	25.00
CADET					
❏ LPS-638 [(2)S]	Portfolio of Ahmad Jamal	1966	5.00	10.00	20.00
❏ LPS-764 [S]	Rhapsody	1966	5.00	10.00	20.00
❏ LPS-777 [S]	Heat Wave	1966	5.00	10.00	20.00
❏ LPS-786 [S]	Standard Eyes	1967	5.00	10.00	20.00
❏ LP-792 [M]	Cry Young	1967	5.00	10.00	20.00
CREATIVE					
❏ LP-602 [M]	Chamber Music of New Jazz	1956	12.50	25.00	50.00
EPIC					
❏ BN 627 [R]	Ahmad Jamal Trio	196?	5.00	10.00	20.00
❏ BN 634 [S]	The Piano Scene of Ahmad Jamal	1959	5.00	10.00	20.00
❏ LN 3212 [M]	Ahmad Jamal Trio	1956	12.50	25.00	50.00
—Yellow label with lines around rim					
❏ LN 3212 [M]	Ahmad Jamal Trio	1963	6.25	12.50	25.00
—Yellow label, no lines around rim					
❏ LN 3631 [M]	The Piano Scene of Ahmad Jamal	1959	7.50	15.00	30.00
PARROT					
❏ 55-245/6 [M]	Ahmad Jamal Plays	1955	500.00	1000.	1500.

JAMES, BOB
ESP-DISK'

❏ 1009 [M]	Explosions	1965	5.00	10.00	20.00
❏ S-1009 [S]	Explosions	1965	6.25	12.50	25.00
MERCURY					
❏ MG-20768 [M]	Bold Conceptions	1963	5.00	10.00	20.00
❏ SR-60768 [S]	Bold Conceptions	1963	6.25	12.50	25.00
TAPPAN ZEE					
❏ HC 45594	Touchdown	1982	7.50	15.00	30.00
—Half-speed mastered edition					
❏ HC 47495	Sign of the Times	1982	7.50	15.00	30.00
—Half-speed mastered edition					

JAMES, BOB, AND EARL KLUGH
MOBILE FIDELITY

❏ 1-124	Two of a Kind	1984	10.00	20.00	40.00
—Audiophile vinyl					
TAPPAN ZEE					
❏ HC 46241	One on One	198?	7.50	15.00	30.00
—Half-speed mastered edition					

JAMES, DENNIS
KAPP

❏ KL-1009 [M]	Let's All Sing a Song for Christmas	1955	7.50	15.00	30.00

JAMES, ELMORE
BELL

❏ 6037	Elmore James	1969	6.25	12.50	25.00
CHESS					
❏ LP-1537	Whose Muddy Shoes	1969	6.25	12.50	25.00
COLLECTABLES					
❏ COL-5112	Golden Classics	198?	3.00	6.00	12.00
❏ COL-5184	The Complete Fire and Enjoy Sessions, Part 1	198?	2.50	5.00	10.00
❏ COL-5185	The Complete Fire and Enjoy Sessions, Part 2	198?	2.50	5.00	10.00
❏ COL-5186	The Complete Fire and Enjoy Sessions, Part 3	198?	2.50	5.00	10.00
❏ COL-5187	The Complete Fire and Enjoy Sessions, Part 4	198?	2.50	5.00	10.00
CROWN					
❏ CLP-5168 [M]	Blues After Hours	1961	62.50	125.00	250.00
—Black label, silver "Crown"					
❏ CLP-5168 [M]	Blues After Hours	1962	12.50	25.00	50.00
—Gray label					
INTERMEDIA					
❏ QS-5034	Red Hot Blues	198?	2.50	5.00	10.00
KENT					
❏ KST-522 [R]	Original Folk Blues	1964	6.25	12.50	25.00
❏ KLP-5022 [M]	Original Folk Blues	1964	10.00	20.00	40.00
❏ KLP-9001	Anthology of the Blues Legend	196?	6.25	12.50	25.00
❏ KLP-9010	The Resurrection of Elmore James	196?	6.25	12.50	25.00
SPHERE SOUND					
❏ SR-7002 [M]	The Sky Is Crying	1965	45.00	90.00	180.00
❏ SSR-7002 [R]	The Sky Is Crying	1965	30.00	60.00	120.00
❏ SR-7008 [M]	I Need You	1966	37.50	75.00	150.00
❏ SSR-7008 [R]	I Need You	1966	30.00	60.00	120.00
UP FRONT					
❏ UP-122	The Great Elmore James	1970	3.00	6.00	12.00

JAMES, ETTA
ARGO

❏ LP-4003 [M]	At Last!	1961	10.00	20.00	40.00
❏ LPS-4003 [S]	At Last!	1961	15.00	30.00	60.00
❏ LP-4011 [M]	The Second Time Around	1961	7.50	15.00	30.00
❏ LPS-4011 [S]	The Second Time Around	1961	10.00	20.00	40.00
❏ LP-4013 [M]	Etta James	1962	7.50	15.00	30.00

Number	Title (A Side/B Side)	Yr	VG	VG+	NM
❏ LPS-4013 [P]	Etta James	1962	10.00	20.00	40.00
—Two duets with Harvey Fuqua are rechanneled					
❏ LP-4018 [M]	Etta James Sings for Lovers	1962	7.50	15.00	30.00
❏ LPS-4018 [S]	Etta James Sings for Lovers	1962	10.00	20.00	40.00
❏ LP-4025 [M]	Etta James Top Ten	1963	7.50	15.00	30.00
❏ LPS-4025 [S]	Etta James Top Ten	1963	10.00	20.00	40.00
❏ LP-4032 [M]	Etta James Rocks the House	1964	25.00	50.00	100.00
❏ LPS-4032 [S]	Etta James Rocks the House	1964	37.50	75.00	150.00
❏ LP-4040 [M]	The Queen of Soul	1965	7.50	15.00	30.00
❏ LPS-4040 [S]	The Queen of Soul	1965	10.00	20.00	40.00
CADET					
❏ LP-802 [M]	Tell Mama	1968	6.25	12.50	25.00
❏ LPS-802 [S]	Tell Mama	1968	5.00	10.00	20.00
❏ LPS-832	Etta James Sings Funk	1969	5.00	10.00	20.00
❏ LPS-847	Losers Weepers	1970	3.75	7.50	15.00
❏ LP-4003 [M]	At Last!	1966	3.00	6.00	12.00
❏ LPS-4003 [S]	At Last!	1966	3.75	7.50	15.00
❏ LP-4011 [M]	The Second Time Around	1966	3.00	6.00	12.00
❏ LPS-4011 [S]	The Second Time Around	1966	3.75	7.50	15.00
❏ LP-4013 [M]	Etta James	1966	3.00	6.00	12.00
❏ LPS-4013 [S]	Etta James	1966	3.75	7.50	15.00
❏ LP-4018 [M]	Etta James Sings for Lovers	1966	3.00	6.00	12.00
❏ LPS-4018 [S]	Etta James Sings for Lovers	1966	3.75	7.50	15.00
❏ LP-4025 [M]	Etta James Top Ten	1966	3.00	6.00	12.00
❏ LPS-4025 [S]	Etta James Top Ten	1966	3.75	7.50	15.00
❏ LP-4040 [M]	The Queen of Soul	1966	3.00	6.00	12.00
❏ LPS-4040 [S]	The Queen of Soul	1966	3.75	7.50	15.00
❏ LP-4055 [M]	Call My Name	1967	3.75	7.50	15.00
❏ LPS-4055 [S]	Call My Name	1967	5.00	10.00	20.00
CHESS					
❏ CH2-6028 [(2)]	The Sweetest Peaches	1989	3.00	6.00	12.00
❏ CH-9110	Her Greatest Sides, Vol. 1	1984	2.50	5.00	10.00
❏ CH-9184	Etta James Rocks the House	1986	2.00	4.00	8.00
—Reissue					
❏ CH-9266	At Last!	1987	2.00	4.00	8.00
—Reissue					
❏ CH-9269	Tell Mama	1987	2.00	4.00	8.00
—Reissue					
❏ CH-9287	The Second Time Around	1989	2.00	4.00	8.00
—Reissue					
❏ ACH-19003	Etta Is Betta Than Evvah!	1976	3.75	7.50	15.00
❏ CH-50042	Etta James	1973	3.75	7.50	15.00
❏ 2CH-60004 [(2)]	Peaches	1971	5.00	10.00	20.00
❏ CH-60029	Come a Little Closer	1974	3.75	7.50	15.00
❏ CH-91509	Come a Little Closer	198?	2.00	4.00	8.00
—Reissue					
CROWN					
❏ CST-360 [R]	Etta James	1963	5.00	10.00	20.00
—With Etta smiling on cover					
❏ CST-360 [R]	Etta James	1963	5.00	10.00	20.00
—With Etta somber on cover					
❏ CLP-5209 [M]	Miss Etta James	1961	25.00	50.00	100.00
—First edition, with framed picture on cover					
❏ CLP-5209 [M]	Miss Etta James	1962	15.00	30.00	60.00
—Second edition, all-white cover with "Miss Etta James"					
❏ CLP-5234 [M]	The Best of Etta James	1962	15.00	30.00	60.00
—Black label					
❏ CLP-5234 [M]	The Best of Etta James	1963	7.50	15.00	30.00
—Gray label					
❏ CLP-5250 [M]	Twist with Etta James	1962	15.00	30.00	60.00
—Black label					
❏ CLP-5250 [M]	Twist with Etta James	1963	7.50	15.00	30.00
—Gray label					
❏ CLP-5360 [M]	Etta James	1963	7.50	15.00	30.00
—With Etta smiling on cover					
❏ CLP-5360 [M]	Etta James	1963	7.50	15.00	30.00
—With Etta somber on cover					
INTERMEDIA					
❏ QS-5014	Etta, Red Hot 'N' Live!	198?	2.50	5.00	10.00
ISLAND					
❏ 91018	Seven Year Itch	1988	2.50	5.00	10.00
❏ 842926-1	Sticking to My Guns	1990	3.00	6.00	12.00
KENT					
❏ KST-500 [R]	Miss Etta James	1964	6.25	12.50	25.00
—Black vinyl					
❏ KST-500 [R]	Miss Etta James	1964	20.00	40.00	80.00
—Red vinyl					
❏ KLP-5000 [M]	Miss Etta James	1964	7.50	15.00	30.00
UNITED					
❏ US 7712	Etta James Sings	197?	2.50	5.00	10.00
WARNER BROS.					
❏ BSK 3156	Deep in the Night	1978	3.00	6.00	12.00

JAMES, HARRY
On items with asterisks (*), at least one track has FRANK SINATRA as lead vocalist.

CAPITOL

❏ W 654 [M]	Harry James in Hi-Fi	1955	7.50	15.00	30.00
❏ W 712 [M]	More Harry James in Hi-Fi	1956	7.50	15.00	30.00
❏ T 874 [M]	Wild About Harry	1957	7.50	15.00	30.00
❏ T 1037 [M]	The New James	1958	7.50	15.00	30.00
❏ T 1093 [M]	Harry's Choice	1958	7.50	15.00	30.00
❏ T 1515 [M]	The Hits of Harry James	1961	5.00	10.00	20.00
—Black colorband label, logo at left					
COLUMBIA					
❏ CL 522 [M]	One Night Stand	1953	10.00	20.00	40.00
—Maroon label, gold print					
❏ GL 522 [M]	One Night Stand	1953	12.50	25.00	50.00
—Black label, silver print					
❏ CL 553 [M]	Trumpet After Midnight	1954	10.00	20.00	40.00
—Maroon label, gold print					

Number	Title (A Side/B Side)	Yr	VG	VG+	NM
CL 562 [M]	Dancing in Person with Harry James at the Hollywood Palladium	1954	10.00	20.00	40.00
—Maroon label, gold print					
CL 581 [M]	Soft Lights, Sweet Trumpet	1954	10.00	20.00	40.00
—Maroon label, gold print					
CL 615 [M]	Juke Box Jamboree	1955	10.00	20.00	40.00
—Maroon label, gold print					
CL 655 [M]	*All Time Favorites	1955	10.00	20.00	40.00
—Maroon label, gold print					
CL 669 [M]	Jazz Session	1955	10.00	20.00	40.00
CL 2527 [10]	The Man with the Horn	1955	12.50	25.00	50.00
CL 2630 [M]	*Harry James' Greatest Hits	1967	5.00	10.00	20.00
CL 6009 [10]	*All Time Favorites	1949	12.50	25.00	50.00
CL 6044 [10]	Trumpet Time	1950	12.50	25.00	50.00
CL 6088 [10]	Dance Parade	1950	12.50	25.00	50.00
CL 6138 [10]	Your Dance Date	1951	12.50	25.00	50.00
CL 6207 [10]	Soft Lights, Sweet Trumpet	1952	12.50	25.00	50.00

LONGINES SYMPHONETTE

Number	Title (A Side/B Side)	Yr	VG	VG+	NM
LS-217 [(5)]	Harry James Dance Band Spectacular	196?	7.50	15.00	30.00

MGM

Number	Title (A Side/B Side)	Yr	VG	VG+	NM
E-3778 [M]	Harry James and His New Swingin' Band	1959	5.00	10.00	20.00
SE-3778 [S]	Harry James and His New Swingin' Band	1959	6.25	12.50	25.00
E-3848 [M]	Harry James Today	1960	5.00	10.00	20.00
SE-3848 [S]	Harry James Today	1960	6.25	12.50	25.00
E-4003 [M]	Requests on the Road	1961	5.00	10.00	20.00
SE-4003 [S]	Requests on the Road	1961	6.25	12.50	25.00
SE-4058 [S]	The Solid Gold Trumpet	1962	5.00	10.00	20.00
SE-4137 [S]	Double Dixie	1963	5.00	10.00	20.00

JAMES, JIMMY, AND THE VAGABONDS

ATCO

Number	Title (A Side/B Side)	Yr	VG	VG+	NM
33-222 [M]	The New Religion	1967	5.00	10.00	20.00
SD 33-222 [S]	The New Religion	1967	5.00	10.00	20.00

PYE

Number	Title (A Side/B Side)	Yr	VG	VG+	NM
12111	You Don't Stand a Chance If You Can't Dance	1975	2.50	5.00	10.00

JAMES, JONI

MGM

Number	Title (A Side/B Side)	Yr	VG	VG+	NM
E-222 [10]	Let There Be Love	1953	50.00	100.00	200.00
E-234 [10]	Award Winning Album	1954	50.00	100.00	200.00
E-272 [10]	Little Girl Blue	1955	50.00	100.00	200.00
E-3240 [M]	When I Fall in Love	1955	20.00	40.00	80.00
—Yellow label					
E-3240 [M]	When I Fall in Love	1960	10.00	20.00	40.00
—Black label					
E-3328 [M]	In the Still of the Night	1956	20.00	40.00	80.00
—Yellow label					
E-3328 [M]	In the Still of the Night	1960	10.00	20.00	40.00
—Black label					
E-3346 [M]	Award Winning Album	1956	20.00	40.00	80.00
—Yellow label					
E-3346 [M]	Award Winning Album	1960	10.00	20.00	40.00
—Black label					
E-3347 [M]	Little Girl Blue	1956	20.00	40.00	80.00
—Yellow label					
E-3347 [M]	Little Girl Blue	1960	10.00	20.00	40.00
—Black label					
E-3348 [M]	Let There Be Love	1956	20.00	40.00	80.00
—Yellow label					
E-3348 [M]	Let There Be Love	1960	10.00	20.00	40.00
—Black label					
E-3449 [M]	Songs by Victor Young and Frank Loesser	1956	20.00	40.00	80.00
—Yellow label					
E-3449 [M]	Songs by Victor Young and Frank Loesser	1960	10.00	20.00	40.00
—Black label					
E-3468 [M]	Merry Christmas from Joni	1956	30.00	60.00	120.00
—Yellow label original					
E-3468 [M]	Merry Christmas from Joni	1960	15.00	30.00	60.00
—Black label reissue					
E-3528 [M]	Give Us This Day	1957	20.00	40.00	80.00
—Yellow label					
E-3528 [M]	Give Us This Day	1960	10.00	20.00	40.00
—Black label					
E-3533 [M]	Songs by Jerome Kern and Harry Warren	1957	20.00	40.00	80.00
—Yellow label					
E-3533 [M]	Songs by Jerome Kern and Harry Warren	1960	10.00	20.00	40.00
—Black label					
E-3602 [M]	Among My Souvenirs	1958	20.00	40.00	80.00
—Yellow label					
E-3602 [M]	Among My Souvenirs	1960	10.00	20.00	40.00
—Black label					
E-3623 [M]	Ti Voglio Bene	1958	20.00	40.00	80.00
—Yellow label					
E-3623 [M]	Ti Voglio Bene	1960	10.00	20.00	40.00
—Black label					
E-3706 [M]	Award Winning Album, Volume 2	1958	20.00	40.00	80.00
—Yellow label					
E-3706 [M]	Award Winning Album, Volume 2	1960	10.00	20.00	40.00
—Black label					
E-3718 [M]	Je T'aime (I Love You)	1958	20.00	40.00	80.00
—Yellow label					
E-3718 [M]	Je T'aime (I Love You)	1960	10.00	20.00	40.00
—Black label					
SE-3718 [S]	Je T'aime (I Love You)	1958	30.00	60.00	120.00
—Yellow label					
SE-3718 [S]	Je T'aime (I Love You)	1960	12.50	25.00	50.00
—Black label					
E-3739 [M]	Songs of Hank Williams	1959	20.00	40.00	80.00
—Yellow label					
E-3739 [M]	Songs of Hank Williams	1960	10.00	20.00	40.00
—Black label					
SE-3739 [S]	Songs of Hank Williams	1959	30.00	60.00	120.00
—Yellow label					
SE-3739 [S]	Songs of Hank Williams	1960	12.50	25.00	50.00
—Black label					
E-3749 [M]	Irish Favorites	1959	20.00	40.00	80.00
—Yellow label					
E-3749 [M]	Irish Favorites	1960	10.00	20.00	40.00
—Black label					
SE-3749 [S]	Irish Favorites	1959	30.00	60.00	120.00
—Yellow label					
SE-3749 [S]	Irish Favorites	1960	12.50	25.00	50.00
—Black label					
E-3755 [M]	100 Strings and Joni	1959	20.00	40.00	80.00
—Yellow label					
E-3755 [M]	100 Strings and Joni	1960	10.00	20.00	40.00
—Black label					
SE-3755 [S]	100 Strings and Joni	1959	30.00	60.00	120.00
—Yellow label					
SE-3755 [S]	100 Strings and Joni	1960	12.50	25.00	50.00
—Black label					
E-3772 [M]	Joni James Swings Sweet	1959	15.00	30.00	60.00
SE-3772 [S]	Joni James Swings Sweet	1959	20.00	40.00	80.00
E-3800 [M]	Joni James at Carnegie Hall	1959	15.00	30.00	60.00
SE-3800 [S]	Joni James at Carnegie Hall	1959	20.00	40.00	80.00
E-3837 [M]	I'm in the Mood for Love	1960	15.00	30.00	60.00
SE-3837 [S]	I'm in the Mood for Love	1960	20.00	40.00	80.00
E-3839 [M]	100 Strings and Joni On Broadway	1960	15.00	30.00	60.00
SE-3839 [S]	100 Strings and Joni On Broadway	1960	17.50	35.00	70.00
E-3840 [M]	100 Strings and Joni In Hollywood	1960	15.00	30.00	60.00
SE-3840 [S]	100 Strings and Joni In Hollywood	1960	17.50	35.00	70.00
E-3885 [M]	More Joni Hits	1960	12.50	25.00	50.00
SE-3885 [S]	More Joni Hits	1960	15.00	30.00	60.00
E-3892 [M]	100 Voices, 100 Strings	1960	12.50	25.00	50.00
SE-3892 [S]	100 Voices, 100 Strings	1960	15.00	30.00	60.00
E-3958 [M]	Folk Songs by Joni James	1961	12.50	25.00	50.00
SE-3958 [S]	Folk Songs by Joni James	1961	15.00	30.00	60.00
E-3987 [M]	The Mood Is Swinging	1961	12.50	25.00	50.00
SE-3987 [S]	The Mood Is Swinging	1961	15.00	30.00	60.00
E-3990 [M]	The Mood Is Romance	1961	12.50	25.00	50.00
SE-3990 [S]	The Mood Is Romance	1961	15.00	30.00	60.00
E-3991 [M]	The Mood Is Blue	1961	12.50	25.00	50.00
SE-3991 [S]	The Mood Is Blue	1961	15.00	30.00	60.00
E-4008 [M]	After Hours	1962	12.50	25.00	50.00
SE-4008 [S]	After Hours	1962	15.00	30.00	60.00
E-4053 [M]	I Feel a Song Comin' On	1962	12.50	25.00	50.00
SE-4053 [S]	I Feel a Song Comin' On	1962	15.00	30.00	60.00
E-4054 [M]	I'm Your Girl	1962	12.50	25.00	50.00
SE-4054 [S]	I'm Your Girl	1962	15.00	30.00	60.00
E-4101 [M]	Country Girl Style	1962	12.50	25.00	50.00
SE-4101 [S]	Country Girl Style	1962	15.00	30.00	60.00
E-4151 [M]	The Very Best of Joni James	1963	10.00	20.00	40.00
SE-4151 [S]	The Very Best of Joni James	1963	12.50	25.00	50.00
E-4158 [M]	Something for the Boys	1963	10.00	20.00	40.00
SE-4158 [S]	Something for the Boys	1963	12.50	25.00	50.00
E-4182 [M]	Three O'Clock in the Morning	1963	10.00	20.00	40.00
SE-4182 [S]	Three O'Clock in the Morning	1963	12.50	25.00	50.00
E-4200 [M]	My Favorite Things	1963	10.00	20.00	40.00
SE-4200 [S]	My Favorite Things	1963	12.50	25.00	50.00
E-4208 [M]	Italianissime!	1963	10.00	20.00	40.00
SE-4208 [S]	Italianissime!	1963	12.50	25.00	50.00
E-4248 [M]	Put On a Happy Face	1964	10.00	20.00	40.00
SE-4248 [S]	Put On a Happy Face	1964	12.50	25.00	50.00
E-4255 [M]	Joni James Sings the Gershwins	1964	10.00	20.00	40.00
SE-4255 [S]	Joni James Sings the Gershwins	1964	12.50	25.00	50.00
E-4263 [M]	Beyond the Reef	1964	10.00	20.00	40.00
SE-4263 [S]	Beyond the Reef	1964	12.50	25.00	50.00
E-4286 [M]	Bossa Nova Style	1965	10.00	20.00	40.00
SE-4286 [S]	Bossa Nova Style	1965	12.50	25.00	50.00

JAMES, LEONARD

DECCA

Number	Title (A Side/B Side)	Yr	VG	VG+	NM
DL 8772 [M]	Boppin' and a-Strollin'	1958	12.50	25.00	50.00

JAMES, SKIP

VANGUARD

Number	Title (A Side/B Side)	Yr	VG	VG+	NM
VRS-9219 [M]	Skip James Today!	1966	7.50	15.00	30.00
VSD-79219 [S]	Skip James Today!	1966	6.25	12.50	25.00
VSD-79273	Devil Got My Woman	1968	6.25	12.50	25.00

JAMES, SONNY

ABC

Number	Title (A Side/B Side)	Yr	VG	VG+	NM
AC-30027	The ABC Collection	1976	3.00	6.00	12.00

CAPITOL

Number	Title (A Side/B Side)	Yr	VG	VG+	NM
ST-111	Born to Be with You	1968	3.75	7.50	15.00
SKAO-144	The Best of Sonny James Vol. 2	1969	3.75	7.50	15.00
ST 8-0193	Only the Lonely	1969	5.00	10.00	20.00
—Capitol Record Club edition					
ST-193	Only the Lonely	1969	3.75	7.50	15.00
SWBB-258 [(2)]	Close-Up	1969	5.00	10.00	20.00
—Combines ST 2500 and ST 2788 in one package					
ST-320	The Astrodome Presents In Person Sonny James	1969	3.75	7.50	15.00
ST 8-0432	It's Just a Matter of Time	1970	5.00	10.00	20.00
—Capitol Record Club edition					
ST-432	It's Just a Matter of Time	1970	3.75	7.50	15.00
ST-478	My Love/Don't Keep Me Hangin' On	1970	3.75	7.50	15.00
STBB-535 [(2)]	You're the Only World I Know/I'll Never Find Another You	1970	5.00	10.00	20.00
—Combines the two listed albums in one package					
ST-629	#1	1970	3.75	7.50	15.00
ST-734	Empty Arms	1971	3.75	7.50	15.00
T 779 [M]	The Southern Gentleman	1957	12.50	25.00	50.00
—Turquoise label					

Number	Title (A Side/B Side)	Yr	VG	VG+	NM
❏ T 779 [M]	The Southern Gentleman	1964	5.00	10.00	20.00
—Black label with colorband, logo on top					
❏ ST-804	The Sensational Sonny James	1971	3.75	7.50	15.00
❏ ST-849	Here Comes Honey Again	1971	3.75	7.50	15.00
❏ T 867 [M]	Sonny	1957	12.50	25.00	50.00
—Turquoise label					
❏ T 867 [M]	Sonny	1964	5.00	10.00	20.00
—Black label with colorband, logo on top					
❏ T 988 [M]	Honey	1958	12.50	25.00	50.00
—Turquoise label					
❏ T 988 [M]	Honey	1964	5.00	10.00	20.00
—Black label with colorband, logo on top					
❏ T 1178 [M]	This Is Sonny James	1959	10.00	20.00	40.00
—Black label with colorband, logo at left					
❏ T 1178 [M]	This Is Sonny James	1964	5.00	10.00	20.00
—Black label with colorband, logo on top					
❏ ST 2017 [S]	The Minute You're Gone	1964	6.25	12.50	25.00
❏ T 2017 [M]	The Minute You're Gone	1964	5.00	10.00	20.00
❏ ST 2209 [S]	You're the Only World I Know	1965	6.25	12.50	25.00
❏ T 2209 [M]	You're the Only World I Know	1965	5.00	10.00	20.00
❏ ST 2317 [S]	I'll Keep Holding On	1965	6.25	12.50	25.00
❏ T 2317 [M]	I'll Keep Holding On	1965	5.00	10.00	20.00
❏ ST 2415 [S]	Behind the Tear	1965	6.25	12.50	25.00
❏ T 2415 [M]	Behind the Tear	1965	5.00	10.00	20.00
❏ ST 2500 [S]	True Love's a Blessing	1966	6.25	12.50	25.00
❏ T 2500 [M]	True Love's a Blessing	1966	5.00	10.00	20.00
❏ ST 2561 [S]	Till the Last Leaf Shall Fall	1966	6.25	12.50	25.00
❏ T 2561 [M]	Till the Last Leaf Shall Fall	1966	5.00	10.00	20.00
❏ ST 2589 [S]	My Christmas Dream	1966	6.25	12.50	25.00
❏ T 2589 [M]	My Christmas Dream	1966	5.00	10.00	20.00
❏ SM-2615	The Best of Sonny James	197?	2.50	5.00	10.00
❏ ST 2615 [S]	The Best of Sonny James	1966	5.00	10.00	20.00
—Black Starline label					
❏ T 2615 [M]	The Best of Sonny James	1966	3.75	7.50	15.00
❏ ST 2703 [S]	Need You	1967	3.75	7.50	15.00
❏ T 2703 [M]	Need You	1967	5.00	10.00	20.00
❏ ST 2788 [S]	I'll Never Find Another You	1967	3.75	7.50	15.00
❏ T 2788 [M]	I'll Never Find Another You	1967	5.00	10.00	20.00
❏ ST 2884 [S]	A World of Our Own	1968	3.75	7.50	15.00
❏ T 2884 [M]	A World of Our Own	1968	6.25	12.50	25.00
❏ ST 2937	Heaven Says Hello	1968	3.75	7.50	15.00
❏ SM-11013	The Biggest Hits of Sonny James	197?	2.50	5.00	10.00
❏ ST-11013	The Biggest Hits of Sonny James	1972	3.75	7.50	15.00
❏ ST-11067	That's Why I Love You Like I Do	1972	3.75	7.50	15.00
❏ ST-11108	Traces	1972	3.00	6.00	12.00
❏ ST-11144	The Gentleman from the South	1973	3.00	6.00	12.00
❏ ST-11196	Young Love	1973	3.00	6.00	12.00
❏ SQBO-91357 [(2)]	That Special Country Feeling	196?	7.50	15.00	30.00
—Capitol Record Club exclusive					
COLUMBIA					
❏ KC 31646	When the Snow Is On the Roses	1972	3.00	6.00	12.00
❏ KC 32028	Sonny James Sings the Greatest Country Hits of '72	1973	3.00	6.00	12.00
❏ KC 32291	If She Just Helps Me Get Over You	1973	3.00	6.00	12.00
❏ KC 32805	Is It Wrong	1974	3.00	6.00	12.00
❏ KC 33056	A Mi Esposa Con Amor (To My Wife with Love)	1974	3.00	6.00	12.00
❏ KC 33428	A Little Bit South of Saskatoon/Little Band of Gold	1975	3.00	6.00	12.00
❏ KC 33477	The Guitars of Sonny James	1975	3.00	6.00	12.00
❏ CG 33627 [(2)]	When the Snow Is On the Roses/If She Just Helps Me Get Over You	1975	3.75	7.50	15.00
❏ PC 33846	Country Male Artist of the Decade	1975	3.00	6.00	12.00
❏ PC 34035	200 Years of Country Music	1976	3.00	6.00	12.00
❏ PC 34309	When Something Is Wrong with My Baby	1976	3.00	6.00	12.00
❏ PC 34472	You're Free to Go	1977	3.00	6.00	12.00
❏ PC 34706	Sonny James In Prison, In Person	1977	3.00	6.00	12.00
❏ KC 35379	This Is the Love	1978	3.00	6.00	12.00
❏ KC 35626	Sonny James' Greatest Hits	1978	3.00	6.00	12.00
DOT					
❏ DLP 3462 [M]	Young Love	1962	10.00	20.00	40.00
❏ DLP 25462 [S]	Young Love	1962	12.50	25.00	50.00
DOT/MCA					
❏ 39087	Sonny James	198?	2.50	5.00	10.00
HILLTOP					
❏ 6067	Invisible Tears	1969	2.50	5.00	10.00
❏ 6079	Timberline	1969	2.50	5.00	10.00
PICKWICK					
❏ SPC-3594	Young Love	1977	2.00	4.00	8.00
RCA CAMDEN					
❏ CAL-2140 [M]	Young Love	1967	3.75	7.50	15.00
❏ CAS-2140 [S]	Young Love	1967	3.00	6.00	12.00

JAMES, TOMMY, AND THE SHONDELLS

Number	Title (A Side/B Side)	Yr	VG	VG+	NM
RHINO					
❏ R1-70920 [(2)]	Anthology	1989	3.75	7.50	15.00
ROULETTE					
❏ R 25336 [M]	Hanky Panky	1966	5.00	10.00	20.00
❏ SR 25336 [P]	Hanky Panky	1966	6.25	12.50	25.00
—"Hanky Panky" is rechanneled					
❏ R 25344 [M]	It's Only Love	1967	7.50	15.00	30.00
❏ SR 25344 [S]	It's Only Love	1967	6.25	12.50	25.00
❏ R 25353 [M]	I Think We're Alone Now	1967	7.50	15.00	30.00
❏ SR 25353 [P]	I Think We're Alone Now	1967	3.75	7.50	15.00
—Photo cover					
❏ SR 25353 [P]	I Think We're Alone Now	1967	6.25	12.50	25.00
—Footprints cover; "I Think We're Alone Now" is rechanneled					
❏ R 25355 [M]	Something Special! The Best of Tommy James & The Shondells	1968	12.50	25.00	50.00
❏ SR 25355 [S]	Something Special! The Best of Tommy James & The Shondells	1968	6.25	12.50	25.00
❏ R 25357 [M]	Gettin' Together	1968	10.00	20.00	40.00

Number	Title (A Side/B Side)	Yr	VG	VG+	NM
❏ SR 25357 [S]	Gettin' Together	1968	6.25	12.50	25.00
❏ SR 42005	Something Special! The Best of Tommy James & The Shondells	1968	3.75	7.50	15.00
❏ SR 42012	Mony Mony	1968	5.00	10.00	20.00
❏ SR 42023	Crimson and Clover	1969	5.00	10.00	20.00
❏ SR 42030	Cellophane Symphony	1969	5.00	10.00	20.00
❏ SR 42040	The Best of Tommy James & The Shondells	1969	5.00	10.00	20.00
—Original versions are in a Unipak (gatefold must be opened to remove record)					
❏ SR 42040	The Best of Tommy James & The Shondells	197?	3.75	7.50	15.00
—Later versions have gatefold covers, but record can be removed without opening it					
❏ SR 42044	Travelin'	1970	3.75	7.50	15.00

JAMES GANG, THE (1)

Number	Title (A Side/B Side)	Yr	VG	VG+	NM
ABC					
❏ S-688	Yer' Album	1970	3.00	6.00	12.00
❏ S-711	James Gang Rides Again	1970	3.00	6.00	12.00
—Standard pressing without "Bolero" as part of "The Bomber"; "RE-1" in trail-off wax					
❏ S-711	James Gang Rides Again	1970	6.25	12.50	25.00
—First pressing with a short version of Ravel's "Bolero" as part of the song "The Bomber"; exists on both promos and early stock copies; no "RE-1" in trail-off wax					
❏ X-721	Thirds	1971	3.00	6.00	12.00
❏ X-733	James Gang Live in Concert	1971	3.00	6.00	12.00
❏ X-741	Straight Shooter	1972	3.00	6.00	12.00
❏ X-760	Passin' Thru	1972	3.00	6.00	12.00
❏ ABCX-774	The Best of the James Gang Featuring Joe Walsh	1973	3.00	6.00	12.00
—Most copies of this LP contain the edited version of "The Bomber." The full title of the LP is on the spine, and the record's trail-off wax has the number "ABCX-774-A-RE-1".					
❏ ABCX-774	The Best of the James Gang Featuring Joe Walsh	1973	5.00	10.00	20.00
—A few copies of this LP contain the full version of "The Bomber" with the "Bolero" excerpt. The words "The Best Of" do NOT appear on the spine, and the record's trail-off wax has the number "ABCX-774-A".					
❏ X-801 [(2)]	16 Greatest Hits	1973	3.75	7.50	15.00
ATCO					
❏ SD 36-102	Miami	1974	2.50	5.00	10.00
❏ SD 36-112	Newborn	1975	2.50	5.00	10.00
❏ SD 36-141	Jesse Come Home	1976	2.50	5.00	10.00
❏ SD 7037	Bang	1973	2.50	5.00	10.00
BLUESWAY					
❏ BLS-6034	Yer' Album	1969	3.75	7.50	15.00
MCA					
❏ 6012 [(2)]	16 Greatest Hits	1980	2.50	5.00	10.00
—Reissue					
❏ 37111	James Gang Rides Again	1980	2.00	4.00	8.00
—Reissue					
❏ 37112	The Best of the James Gang Featuring Joe Walsh	1980	2.00	4.00	8.00
—Reissue					

JAMME

Number	Title (A Side/B Side)	Yr	VG	VG+	NM
ABC DUNHILL					
❏ DS-50072	Jamme	1970	5.00	10.00	20.00

JAN AND DEAN

Number	Title (A Side/B Side)	Yr	VG	VG+	NM
COLUMBIA					
❏ CL 2661 [M]	Save for a Rainy Day	1967	—	—	—
—Canceled					
❏ CS 9461 [S]	Save for a Rainy Day	1967	2000.	3000.	4000.
—LP not known to exist, but an acetate does, and possibly an import on this label and number					
DEADMAN'S CURVE					
❏ (no #)	Live at the Keystone Berkeley	1981	6.25	12.50	25.00
—With front and back covers pasted on					
❏ (no #)	Live at the Keystone Berkeley	1981	12.50	25.00	50.00
—Plain jacket with front and back cover inserts					
DORE					
❏ LP-101	Jan and Dean Bonus Photo	1960	30.00	60.00	120.00
❏ LP-101	Jan and Dean	197?	3.75	7.50	15.00
—Reissue with black label					
❏ LP-101 [M]	Jan and Dean	1960	100.00	200.00	400.00
—Original with blue label					
J&D					
❏ 101 [M]	Save for a Rainy Day	1967	75.00	150.00	300.00
—Private pressing by Dean Torrence of unreleased Columbia album					
LIBERTY					
❏ LRP-3248 [M]	Jan and Dean's Golden Hits	1962	7.50	15.00	30.00
❏ LRP-3294 [M]	Jan and Dean Take Linda Surfin'	1963	12.50	25.00	50.00
❏ LRP-3314 [M]	Surf City and Other Swingin' Cities	1963	10.00	20.00	40.00
❏ LRP-3339 [M]	Drag City	1963	10.00	20.00	40.00
❏ LRP-3361 [M]	The New Girl in School/Dead Man's Curve	1964	5.00	10.00	20.00
—Reissue with reversed title					
❏ LRP-3361 [M]	Dead Man's Curve/The New Girl in School	1964	7.50	15.00	30.00
—Full-color cover					
❏ LRP-3361 [M]	Dead Man's Curve/The New Girl in School	1964	10.00	20.00	40.00
—Black and white cover with pink tint					
❏ LRP-3368 [M]	Ride the Wild Surf	1964	7.50	15.00	30.00
❏ LRP-3377 [M]	The Little Old Lady from Pasadena	1964	7.50	15.00	30.00
❏ LRP-3403 [M]	Command Performance/Live in Person	1965	7.50	15.00	30.00
❏ LRP-3417 [M]	Jan and Dean's Golden Hits, Volume 2	1965	6.25	12.50	25.00
❏ LRP-3431 [M]	Folk 'N' Roll	1965	7.50	15.00	30.00
❏ LRP-3441 [M]	Filet of Soul	1966	7.50	15.00	30.00
❏ LRP-3444 [M]	Jan and Dean Meet Batman	1966	12.50	25.00	50.00
❏ LRP-3458 [M]	Popsicle	1966	7.50	15.00	30.00
❏ LRP-3460 [M]	Jan and Dean's Golden Hits, Volume 3	1966	6.25	12.50	25.00
❏ LST-7248 [S]	Jan and Dean's Golden Hits	1962	10.00	20.00	40.00
❏ LST-7294 [S]	Jan and Dean Take Linda Surfin'	1963	20.00	40.00	80.00
❏ LST-7314 [S]	Surf City and Other Swingin' Cities	1963	12.50	25.00	50.00
❏ LST-7339 [S]	Drag City	1963	12.50	25.00	50.00
❏ LST-7361 [S]	The New Girl in School/Dead Man's Curve	1964	7.50	15.00	30.00
—Reissue with reversed title					
❏ LST-7361 [S]	Dead Man's Curve/The New Girl in School	1964	10.00	2.00	40.00
—Full-color cover					

J

Number	Title (A Side/B Side)	Yr	VG	VG+	NM
❏ LST-7361 [S]	Dead Man's Curve/The New Girl in School	1964	12.50	25.00	50.00
—Black and white cover with pink tint					
❏ LST-7368 [S]	Ride the Wild Surf	1964	10.00	20.00	40.00
❏ LST-7377 [S]	The Little Old Lady from Pasadena	1964	10.00	20.00	40.00
❏ LST-7403 [S]	Command Performance/Live in Person	1965	10.00	20.00	40.00
❏ LST-7417 [S]	Jan and Dean's Golden Hits, Volume 2	1965	7.50	15.00	30.00
❏ LST-7431 [S]	Folk 'N' Roll	1965	10.00	20.00	40.00
❏ LST-7441 [S]	Filet of Soul	1966	10.00	20.00	40.00
❏ LST-7444 [S]	Jan and Dean Meet Batman	1966	17.50	35.00	70.00
❏ LST-7458 [S]	Popsicle	1966	10.00	20.00	40.00
❏ LST-7460 [S]	Jan and Dean's Golden Hits, Volume 3	1966	7.50	15.00	30.00
❏ LN-10011	Dead Man's Curve	1980	2.00	4.00	8.00
—Budget-line reissue					
❏ LN-10115	The Best of Jan and Dean	1981	2.00	4.00	8.00
❏ LN-10151	The Little Old Lady from Pasadena	1982	2.00	4.00	8.00
—Budget-line reissue					
PAIR					
❏ PDL2-1071 [(2)]	California Gold	1986	3.00	6.00	12.00
RHINO					
❏ RNDA 1498 [(2)]	One Summer Night — Live	1982	5.00	10.00	20.00
SUNDAZED					
❏ LP 5022 [(2)]	Save for a Rainy Day	1996	3.75	7.50	15.00
—First release to the general public; colored vinyl					
❏ LP 5040	Jan and Dean (The Dore Album)	1996	2.50	5.00	10.00
—Reissue of Dore LP on colored vinyl with extra tracks and poster					
SUNSET					
❏ SUM-1156 [M]	Jan and Dean	1967	3.75	7.50	15.00
❏ SUS-5156 [S]	Jan and Dean	1967	3.75	7.50	15.00
UNITED ARTISTS					
❏ UA-LA341-H2 [(2)]	Gotta Take That One Last Ride	1974	3.75	7.50	15.00
❏ UA-LA443-E	The Very Best of Jan and Dean	1975	2.50	5.00	10.00
❏ UA-LA515-E	The Very Best of Jan and Dean, Volume 2	1975	2.50	5.00	10.00
❏ UAS-9961 [(2)]	Anthology (Legendary Masters Series, Vol. 3)	1971	6.25	12.50	25.00

JAN AND KJELD
KAPP

Number	Title (A Side/B Side)	Yr	VG	VG+	NM
❏ KL-1190 [M]	Banjo Boy	1960	7.50	15.00	30.00

JAN AND LORRAINE
ABC

Number	Title (A Side/B Side)	Yr	VG	VG+	NM
❏ S-691	Gypsy People	1969	6.25	12.50	25.00

JANE'S ADDICTION
TRIPLE X

Number	Title (A Side/B Side)	Yr	VG	VG+	NM
❏ 51004	Jane's Addiction	1987	3.75	7.50	15.00
WARNER BROS.					
❏ PRO-A-3369 [DJ]	Words and Music	1988	10.00	20.00	40.00
—Promo-only interview album					
❏ 25727	Nothing's Shocking	1988	3.00	6.00	12.00
❏ 25993	Ritual de lo Habitual	1990	3.00	6.00	12.00
—First cover, with drawing					
❏ 26223	Ritual de lo Habitual	1990	2.50	5.00	10.00
—Second cover, all white with text of First Amendment					

JANIGRO, ANTONIO
RCA VICTOR RED SEAL

Number	Title (A Side/B Side)	Yr	VG	VG+	NM
❏ LSC-2365 [S]	Cello Concertos	1960	7.50	15.00	30.00
—Original with "shaded dog" label					
❏ LSC-2460 [S]	Bach: Suite No. 2 in B; Brandenburg Concerto No. 5	1961	5.00	10.00	20.00
—Original with "shaded dog" label					
❏ LSC-2653 [S]	Music for Strings	1962	10.00	20.00	40.00
—Original with "shaded dog" label					

JANIS, BYRON
MERCURY LIVING PRSENSCE

Number	Title (A Side/B Side)	Yr	VG	VG+	NM
❏ SR 90260 [S]	Rachmaninoff: Piano Concerto No. 2; Preludes in C# and E-flat	196?	6.25	12.50	25.00
—With Antal Dorati/Minneapolis Symphony Orchestra; maroon label, with "Vendor: Mercury Record Corporation"					
❏ SR 90260 [S]	Rachmaninoff: Piano Concerto No. 2; Preludes in C# and E-flat	196?	15.00	30.00	60.00
—With Antal Dorati/Minneapolis Symphony Orchestra; maroon label, no "Vendor: Mercury Record Corporation"					
❏ SR 90266 [S]	Tchaikovsky: Piano Concerto No. 1	196?	6.25	12.50	25.00
—With Herbert Menges/London Symphony Orchestra; maroon label, with "Vendor: Mercury Record Corporation"					
❏ SR 90266 [S]	Tchaikovsky: Piano Concerto No. 1	196?	12.50	25.00	50.00
—With Herbert Menges/London Symphony Orchestra; maroon label, no "Vendor: Mercury Record Corporation"					
❏ SR 90283 [S]	Rachmaninoff: Piano Concerto No. 3	196?	10.00	20.00	40.00
—With Antal Dorati/London Symphony Orchestra; maroon label, with "Vendor: Mercury Record Corporation"					
❏ SR 90283 [S]	Rachmaninoff: Piano Concerto No. 3	196?	25.00	50.00	100.00
—With Antal Dorati/London Symphony Orchestra; maroon label, no "Vendor: Mercury Record Corporation"					
❏ SR 90300 [S]	Prokofiev: Piano Concerto No. 2; Rachmaninoff: Piano Concerto No. 1	196?	5.00	10.00	20.00
—Third edition: Dark red (not maroon) label					
❏ SR 90300 [S]	Prokofiev: Piano Concerto No. 2; Rachmaninoff: Piano Concerto No. 1	196?	6.25	12.50	25.00
—Maroon label, with "Vendor: Mercury Record Corporation"					
❏ SR 90300 [S]	Prokofiev: Piano Concerto No. 2; Rachmaninoff: Piano Concerto No. 1	196?	10.00	20.00	40.00
—Maroon label, no "Vendor: Mercury Record Corporation"					
❏ SR 90305 [S]	Encore	196?	37.50	75.00	150.00
—Maroon label, no "Vendor: Mercury Record Corporation"					
❏ SR 90329 [S]	Liszt: Piano Concertos No. 1 and 2	196?	12.50	25.00	50.00
—Maroon label, no "Vendor: Mercury Record Corporation"					
❏ SR 90383 [S]	Schumann: Piano Concerto; Arabesque; Wieck Variations	196?	7.50	15.00	30.00
—With Stanislaw Skrowaczewski/London Symphony Orchestra; maroon label, no "Vendor: Mercury Record Corporation"					

RCA VICTOR RED SEAL

Number	Title (A Side/B Side)	Yr	VG	VG+	NM
❏ LSC-2237 [S]	Rachmaninoff: Piano Concerto No. 3	1959	50.00	100.00	200.00
—With Charles Munch/Boston Symphony Orchestra; original with "shaded dog" label					
❏ LSC-2541 [S]	Liszt: Todtentanz; Rachmaninoff: Piano Concerto No. 1	1961	6.25	12.50	25.00
—With Fritz Reiner/Chicago Symphony Orch.; Classic Records reissue					
❏ LSC-2541 [S]	Liszt: Todtentanz; Rachmaninoff: Piano Concerto No. 1	1961	25.00	50.00	100.00
—With Fritz Reiner/Chicago Symphony Orch.; originals with "shaded dog" label					

JANIS, CONRAD
CIRCLE

Number	Title (A Side/B Side)	Yr	VG	VG+	NM
❏ L-404 [10]	Conrad Janis' Tailgate Jazz Band	1951	12.50	25.00	50.00
JUBILEE					
❏ JLP-7 [10]	Conrad Janis and His Tailgaters	1954	12.50	25.00	50.00
❏ JLP-1010 [M]	Conrad Janis and His Tailgate Five	1955	10.00	20.00	40.00
RIVERSIDE					
❏ RLP 12-215 [M]	Dixieland Jam Session	1956	12.50	25.00	50.00
—White label, blue print					
❏ RLP 12-215 [M]	Dixieland Jam Session	1959	7.50	15.00	30.00
—Blue label, microphone label at top					

JANIS, JOHNNY
ABC-PARAMOUNT

Number	Title (A Side/B Side)	Yr	VG	VG+	NM
❏ ABC-140 [M]	For the First Time	1956	15.00	30.00	60.00
COLUMBIA					
❏ CL 1674 [M]	The Start of Something Big	1961	6.25	12.50	25.00
❏ CS 8474 [S]	The Start of Something Big	1961	7.50	15.00	30.00
MONUMENT					
❏ MLP-8036 [M]	Once in a Blue Moon	1965	3.75	7.50	15.00
❏ SLP-18036 [S]	Once in a Blue Moon	1965	5.00	10.00	20.00

JANSSEN, DAVID
EPIC

Number	Title (A Side/B Side)	Yr	VG	VG+	NM
❏ LN 24150 [M]	Hidden Island	1965	5.00	10.00	20.00
❏ BN 26150 [S]	Hidden Island	1965	6.25	12.50	25.00

JARMAN, JOSEPH
DELMARK

Number	Title (A Side/B Side)	Yr	VG	VG+	NM
❏ DS-410	Song for	1968	5.00	10.00	20.00
❏ DS-417	As If It Were the Seasons	1969	5.00	10.00	20.00

JARMAN, JOSEPH, AND DON MOYEE
INDIA NAVIGATION

Number	Title (A Side/B Side)	Yr	VG	VG+	NM
❏ IN-1033 [(2)]	Egwu-Anwu	1978	5.00	10.00	20.00

JARRE, JEAN-MICHEL
MOBILE FIDELITY

Number	Title (A Side/B Side)	Yr	VG	VG+	NM
❏ 1-212	Oxygene	1995	5.00	10.00	20.00
—Audiophile vinyl					
❏ 1-227	Equinoxe	1995	5.00	10.00	20.00
—Audiophile vinyl					

JARREAU, AL
MOBILE FIDELITY

Number	Title (A Side/B Side)	Yr	VG	VG+	NM
❏ 1-019	All Fly Home	1980	5.00	10.00	20.00
—Audiophile vinyl					

JARRETT, KEITH
ECM

Number	Title (A Side/B Side)	Yr	VG	VG+	NM
❏ 1035/6/7 [(3)]	Solo Concerts	1974	5.00	10.00	20.00
❏ 1100 [(10)]	The Sun Bear Concerts	1977	20.00	40.00	80.00
❏ 1227 [(3)]	Concerts	1982	5.00	10.00	20.00
VORTEX					
❏ 2006	Life Between the Exit Signs	1969	5.00	10.00	20.00
❏ 2008	Restoration Ruin	1969	5.00	10.00	20.00
❏ 2012	Somewhere Before	1970	5.00	10.00	20.00

JARVIS, JOHN
CRYSTAL CLEAR

Number	Title (A Side/B Side)	Yr	VG	VG+	NM
❏ 8004	Evolutions	1980	5.00	10.00	20.00
—Direct-to-disc recording					

JASPAR, BOBBY
EMARCY

Number	Title (A Side/B Side)	Yr	VG	VG+	NM
❏ MG-36105 [M]	Bobby Jaspar and His All Stars	1957	20.00	40.00	80.00
RIVERSIDE					
❏ RLP 12-240 [M]	Bobby Jaspar	1957	20.00	40.00	80.00
—White label, blue print					
❏ RLP 12-240 [M]	Bobby Jaspar	1959	10.00	20.00	40.00
—Blue label, microphone label at top					

JASPER WRATH
SUNFLOWER

Number	Title (A Side/B Side)	Yr	VG	VG+	NM
❏ SNF-5003	Jasper Wrath	1971	10.00	20.00	40.00

JAUME, ANDRE
HAT HUT

Number	Title (A Side/B Side)	Yr	VG	VG+	NM
❏ 1989/90 [(2)]	Musique Pour 8: L'oc	1981	5.00	10.00	20.00

JAUME, ANDRE, AND JOE MCPHEE
HAT HUT

Number	Title (A Side/B Side)	Yr	VG	VG+	NM
❏ 12 [(2)]	Tales and Prophecies	1980	5.00	10.00	20.00

JAY AND THE AMERICANS
LIBERTY

Number	Title (A Side/B Side)	Yr	VG	VG+	NM
❏ LM-1010	Jay and the Americans Greatest Hits	1981	2.00	4.00	8.00
—Another reissue					
RHINO					
❏ RNLP 70224	All-Time Greatest Hits	1986	3.00	6.00	12.00
SUNSET					
❏ SUS-5252	Jay and the Americans!!	1968	3.00	6.00	12.00
❏ SUS-5278	Early American Hits	1969	3.75	7.50	15.00

Number	Title (A Side/B Side)	Yr	VG	VG+	NM
UNART					
❏ M-20018 [M]	Jay and the Americans!!	196?	3.00	6.00	12.00
❏ MS-21018 [S]	Jay and the Americans!!	196?	3.00	6.00	12.00
UNITED ARTISTS					
❏ UA-LA357-E	The Very Best of Jay and the Americans	1975	3.00	6.00	12.00
❏ LM-1010	Jay and the Americans Greatest Hits	1980	2.50	5.00	10.00
—Reissue					
❏ UAL-3222 [M]	She Cried	1962	12.50	25.00	50.00
❏ UAL-3300 [M]	At the Café Wha?	1963	12.50	25.00	50.00
❏ UAL-3407 [M]	Come a Little Bit Closer	1964	6.25	12.50	25.00
❏ UAL-3417 [M]	Blockbusters	1965	6.25	12.50	25.00
❏ UAL-3453 [M]	Jay and the Americans Greatest Hits	1965	5.00	10.00	20.00
❏ UAL-3474 [M]	Sunday and Me	1966	5.00	10.00	20.00
❏ UAL-3534 [M]	Livin' Above Your Head	1966	5.00	10.00	20.00
❏ UAL-3555 [M]	Jay and the Americans Greatest Hits, Volume 2	1966	5.00	10.00	20.00
❏ UAL-3562 [M]	Try Some of This!	1967	5.00	10.00	20.00
❏ UAS-6222 [S]	She Cried	1962	25.00	50.00	100.00
❏ UAS-6300 [S]	At the Café Wha?	1963	25.00	50.00	100.00
❏ UAS-6407 [S]	Come a Little Bit Closer	1964	7.50	15.00	30.00
❏ UAS-6417 [S]	Blockbusters	1965	7.50	15.00	30.00
❏ UAS-6453 [S]	Jay and the Americans Greatest Hits	1965	6.25	12.50	25.00
❏ UAS-6474 [S]	Sunday and Me	1966	6.25	12.50	25.00
❏ UAS-6534 [S]	Livin' Above Your Head	1966	6.25	12.50	25.00
❏ UAS-6555 [S]	Jay and the Americans Greatest Hits, Volume 2	1966	5.00	10.00	20.00
❏ UAS-6562 [S]	Try Some of This!	1967	5.00	10.00	20.00
❏ UAS-6671	Sands of Time	1969	5.00	10.00	20.00
❏ UAS-6719	Wax Museum	1970	5.00	10.00	20.00
❏ UAS-6751	Wax Museum, Volume 2	1970	5.00	10.00	20.00
❏ UAS-6762	Capture the Moment	1970	5.00	10.00	20.00
❏ ST-90814 [S]	Jay and the Americans Greatest Hits	1966	7.50	15.00	30.00
—Capitol Record Club edition					
❏ ST-90815 [S]	Jay and the Americans Greatest Hits, Volume 2	1966	7.50	15.00	30.00
—Capitol Record Club edition					
JAY AND THE TECHNIQUES					
SMASH					
❏ MGS-27095 [M]	Apples, Peaches, Pumpkin Pie	1967	7.50	15.00	30.00
❏ SRS-67095 [S]	Apples, Peaches, Pumpkin Pie	1967	7.50	15.00	30.00
—First cover with "live" photo of the band					
❏ SRS-67095 [S]	Apples, Peaches, Pumpkin Pie	1968	5.00	10.00	20.00
—Second cover with "posed" photo of the band					
❏ SRS-67102	Love Lost and Found	1968	7.50	15.00	30.00
JAYE, JERRY					
HI					
❏ HL-12038 [M]	My Girl Josephine	1967	5.00	10.00	20.00
❏ SHL-32038 [S]	My Girl Josephine	1967	5.00	10.00	20.00
❏ SHL-32102	Honky Tonk Women Love Redneck Men	1976	3.00	6.00	12.00
JAYHAWKS, THE					
This is the alt-country group, not the 1950s vocal group.					
AMERICAN					
❏ 43006	Tomorrow the Green Grass	1995	2.50	5.00	10.00
❏ 43114	Sound of Lies	1997	3.00	6.00	12.00
BUNKHOUSE					
❏ 7001	The Jayhawks	1986	20.00	40.00	80.00
TWIN/TONE					
❏ TTR 89151	Blue Earth	1989	3.75	7.50	15.00
JAYNETTS, THE					
TUFF					
❏ LP 13 [M]	Sally Go 'Round the Roses	1963	75.00	150.00	300.00
JAZZ ARTISTS GUILD, THE					
CANDID					
❏ CD-8022 [M]	Newport Rebels	1960	10.00	20.00	40.00
❏ CS-9022 [S]	Newport Rebels	1960	12.50	25.00	50.00
JAZZ BROTHERS, THE					
RIVERSIDE					
❏ RLP-335 [M]	Jazz Brothers	1960	6.25	12.50	25.00
❏ RLP-371 [M]	Hey, Baby!	1961	6.25	12.50	25.00
❏ RLP-405 [M]	Spring Fever	1962	6.25	12.50	25.00
❏ RS-9335 [S]	Jazz Brothers	1960	7.50	15.00	30.00
❏ RS-9371 [S]	Hey, Baby!	1961	7.50	15.00	30.00
❏ RS-9405 [S]	Spring Fever	1962	7.50	15.00	30.00
JAZZ CITY					
RAHMP					
❏ 2	Jazz City	197?	5.00	10.00	20.00
JAZZ CITY ALL-STARS, THE					
BETHLEHEM					
❏ BCP-79 [M]	Jazz City Presents the Jazz City All-Stars	1957	12.50	25.00	50.00
JAZZ COMPOSERS ORCHESTRA					
JCOA					
❏ LP-1001/2 [(2)]	Jazz Composers Orchestra	1968	15.00	30.00	60.00
JAZZ CORPS, THE					
PACIFIC JAZZ					
❏ PJ-10116 [M]	The Jazz Corps Under the Direction of Tommy Peltier	1967	6.25	12.50	25.00
JAZZ COURIERS, THE					
CARLTON					
❏ LP 12-116 [M]	The Couriers of Jazz	1959	12.50	25.00	50.00
❏ ST 12-116 [S]	The Couriers of Jazz	1959	10.00	20.00	40.00
JAZZLAND					
❏ JLP-34 [M]	Message from Britain	1961	6.25	12.50	25.00
❏ JLP-934 [S]	Message from Britain	1961	7.50	15.00	30.00

Number	Title (A Side/B Side)	Yr	VG	VG+	NM
WHIPPET					
❏ WLP-700 [M]	The Jazz Couriers	1956	30.00	60.00	120.00
JAZZ CRUSADERS, THE					
See THE CRUSADERS.					
JAZZ EXPONENTS, THE					
ARGO					
❏ LP-622 [M]	The Jazz Exponents	1958	10.00	20.00	40.00
JAZZ FIVE, THE					
RIVERSIDE					
❏ RLP-361 [M]	The Hooter	1961	6.25	12.50	25.00
❏ RS-9361 [S]	The Hooter	1961	7.50	15.00	30.00
JAZZ INTERACTIONS ORCHESTRA, THE					
VERVE					
❏ V-8731 [M]	Jazzhattan Suite	1967	5.00	10.00	20.00
JAZZ LAB, THE					
COLUMBIA					
❏ CL 998 [M]	Jazz Lab	1957	20.00	40.00	80.00
❏ CL 1058 [M]	Modern Jazz Perspective/Jazz Lab, Volume 2	1957	20.00	40.00	80.00
JAZZLAND					
❏ JLP-1 [M]	Jazz Lab	1960	7.50	15.00	30.00
❏ JLP-901 [S]	Jazz Lab	1960	10.00	20.00	40.00
JOSIE					
❏ JOZ-3500 [M]	Gigi Gryce and Donald Byrd	1962	10.00	20.00	40.00
—Reissue of Jubilee album					
❏ JS-3500 [R]	Gigi Gryce and Donald Byrd	196?	5.00	10.00	20.00
JUBILEE					
❏ JLP-1059 [M]	Jazz Lab	1958	25.00	50.00	100.00
RIVERSIDE					
❏ RLP 12-229 [M]	Gigi Gryce and the Jazz Lab Quintet	1957	25.00	50.00	100.00
—White label, blue print					
❏ RLP 12-229 [M]	Gigi Gryce and the Jazz Lab Quintet	1959	12.50	25.00	50.00
—Blue label, microphone logo at top					
❏ RLP-1110 [S]	Gigi Gryce and the Jazz Lab Quintet	1959	12.50	25.00	50.00
JAZZ MESSENGERS, THE					
See ART BLAKEY.					
JAZZ SYMPHONICS					
RENFRO					
❏ LP-12369	The Beginning	1968	15.00	30.00	60.00
JAZZPICKERS, THE					
EMARCY					
❏ MG-36111 [M]	The Jazzpickers	1957	12.50	25.00	50.00
❏ MG-36123 [M]	Command Performance	1958	12.50	25.00	50.00
MERCURY					
❏ SR-80013 [S]	For Moderns Only	1959	10.00	20.00	40.00
JAZZTET, THE					
ARGO					
❏ LP-664 [M]	Meet the Jazztet	1960	7.50	15.00	30.00
❏ LPS-664 [S]	Meet the Jazztet	1960	10.00	20.00	40.00
❏ LP-672 [M]	Big City Sounds	1961	6.25	12.50	25.00
❏ LPS-672 [S]	Big City Sounds	1961	7.50	15.00	30.00
❏ LP-684 [M]	The Jazztet and John Lewis	1961	6.25	12.50	25.00
❏ LPS-684 [S]	The Jazztet and John Lewis	1961	7.50	15.00	30.00
❏ LP-688 [M]	The Jazztet at Birdhouse	1961	6.25	12.50	25.00
❏ LPS-688 [S]	The Jazztet at Birdhouse	1961	7.50	15.00	30.00
CADET					
❏ LPS-664 [S]	Meet the Jazztet	1966	5.00	10.00	20.00
MERCURY					
❏ MG-20698 [M]	Here and Now	1962	6.25	12.50	25.00
❏ MG-20737 [M]	Another Git-Together	1962	6.25	12.50	25.00
❏ SR-60698 [S]	Here and Now	1962	7.50	15.00	30.00
❏ SR-60737 [S]	Another Git-Together	1962	7.50	15.00	30.00
JAZZY JEFF AND FRESH PRINCE					
JIVE					
❏ 1026-1-J	Rock the House	1986	2.50	5.00	10.00
—Reissued in 1989 with same catalog number and one new track					
❏ 1091-1-J [(2)]	He's the D.J., I'm the Rapper	1988	3.00	6.00	12.00
—Without "Nightmare on My Street" disclaimer on cover					
❏ 1091-1-J RE [(2)]	He's the D.J., I'm the Rapper	1988	4.00	8.00	16.00
—With "Nightmare on My Street" disclaimer on cover (much scarcer than original)					
❏ 1188-1-J	And in This Corner...	1989	2.50	5.00	10.00
❏ 1392-1-J	Homebase	1991	3.00	6.00	12.00
❏ JL6-8399	On Fire	1985	3.00	6.00	12.00
❏ 41489-1	Code Red	1993	3.00	6.00	12.00
—LP in generic black cover with center hole and sticker					
WORD UP					
❏ WDLP-0001	Rock the House	1985	6.25	12.50	25.00
JEFFERSON					
JANUS					
❏ JLS-3006	Jefferson	1969	6.25	12.50	25.00
JEFFERSON, BLIND LEMON					
MILESTONE					
❏ MLP-2004 [M]	The Immortal Blind Lemon Jefferson	1968	6.25	12.50	25.00
❏ MLP-2007 [M]	The Immortal Blind Lemon Jefferson, Vol. 2	1969	6.25	12.50	25.00
❏ MLP-2013 [M]	Black Snake Moan	1970	6.25	12.50	25.00
RIVERSIDE					
❏ RLP 12-125 [M]	Blind Lemon Jefferson — Classic Folk Blues	1957	30.00	60.00	120.00
❏ RLP 12-136 [M]	Blind Lemon Jefferson, Volume 2	1958	30.00	60.00	120.00
❏ 1014 [10]	The Folk Blues of Blind Lemon Jefferson	1953	62.50	125.00	250.00
❏ 1053 [10]	Penitentiary Blues	1955	62.50	125.00	250.00

Number	Title (A Side/B Side)	Yr	VG	VG+	NM

JEFFERSON, EDDIE
PRESTIGE
Number	Title (A Side/B Side)	Yr	VG	VG+	NM
❏ PRST-7619	Body and Soul	1969	5.00	10.00	20.00
❏ PRST-7698	Come Along with Me	1969	5.00	10.00	20.00

RIVERSIDE
| ❏ RLP-411 [M] | Letter from Home | 1962 | 7.50 | 15.00 | 30.00 |
| ❏ RS-9411 [S] | Letter from Home | 1962 | 10.00 | 20.00 | 40.00 |

JEFFERSON, RON
PACIFIC JAZZ
| ❏ PJ-36 [M] | Love Lifted Me | 1962 | 7.50 | 15.00 | 30.00 |
| ❏ ST-36 [S] | Love Lifted Me | 1962 | 10.00 | 20.00 | 40.00 |

JEFFERSON AIRPLANE
Also see MARTY BALIN; HOT TUNA; JEFFERSON STARSHIP; PAUL KANTNER; GRACE SLICK.
DCC COMPACT CLASSICS
| ❏ LPZ-2033 | Surrealistic Pillow | 1997 | 6.25 | 12.50 | 25.00 |
—Audiophile vinyl
EPIC
| ❏ OE 45271 | Jefferson Airplane | 1989 | 3.75 | 7.50 | 15.00 |
GRUNT
❏ BFL1-0147	Thirty Seconds Over Winterland	1973	3.00	6.00	12.00
❏ APL1-0437	Early Flight	1974	3.00	6.00	12.00
❏ FTR-1001	Bark	1971	2.50	5.00	10.00
—Without brown paper bag
| ❏ FTR-1001 | Bark | 1971 | 3.75 | 7.50 | 15.00 |
—With brown paper bag
❏ FTR-1007	Long John Silver	1972	3.00	6.00	12.00
❏ CYL2-1255 [(2)]	Flight Log 1966-1976	1977	3.00	6.00	12.00
❏ AYL1-4386	Bark	1981	2.00	4.00	8.00
❏ AYL1-4391	Thirty Seconds Over Winterland	1981	2.00	4.00	8.00
MOBILE FIDELITY
| ❏ 1-148 | Crown of Creation | 1984 | 5.00 | 10.00 | 20.00 |
—Audiophile vinyl
PAIR
| ❏ PDL2-1090 [(2)] | Time Machine | 1986 | 3.00 | 6.00 | 12.00 |
RCA
| ❏ 5724-1-R [(2)] | 2400 Fulton Street: An Anthology | 1987 | 3.75 | 7.50 | 15.00 |
RCA VICTOR
| ❏ APD1-0320 [Q] | Volunteers | 1973 | 20.00 | 40.00 | 80.00 |
—Yellow/orange label
| ❏ APD1-0320 [Q] | Volunteers | 1975 | 12.50 | 25.00 | 50.00 |
—Tan label
| ❏ LOP-1511 [M] | After Bathing at Baxter's | 1967 | 12.50 | 25.00 | 50.00 |
| ❏ LSO-1511 [S] | After Bathing at Baxter's | 1967 | 5.00 | 10.00 | 20.00 |
—Black label, dog on top
| ❏ LSO-1511 [S] | After Bathing at Baxter's | 1969 | 3.00 | 6.00 | 12.00 |
—Orange label
| ❏ LSO-1511 [S] | After Bathing at Baxter's | 1975 | 2.50 | 5.00 | 10.00 |
—Tan label
| ❏ LPM-3584 [M] | Jefferson Airplane Takes Off! | 1966 | 6.25 | 12.50 | 25.00 |
—Version 3: No "Runnin' 'Round This World", altered lyrics to "Let Me In" ("Don't tell me it's so funny") and "Run Around ("That sway as you stay here by me"). All later versions confirm to Version 3.
| ❏ LPM-3584 [M] | Jefferson Airplane Takes Off! | 1966 | 250.00 | 500.00 | 1000. |
—Version 2: No "Runnin' 'Round This World", but "questionable" lyrics remain in "Let Me In" ("Don't tell me you want money") and "Run Around" ("That sway as you lay under me"). Until the exact matrix numbers are known, it must be heard to confirm.
| ❏ LPM-3584 [M] | Jefferson Airplane Takes Off! | 1966 | 1500. | 2250. | 3000. |
—Version 1: With "Runnin' 'Round This World" as last song on side 1. Count the number of bands on Side 1 of the record; don't rely on the cover listing, as some jackets list the title when it's not on the record
| ❏ LSP-3584 [S] | Jefferson Airplane Takes Off! | 1966 | 6.25 | 12.50 | 25.00 |
—Version 3: See Version 3 note under mono version
| ❏ LSP-3584 [S] | Jefferson Airplane Takes Off! | 1966 | 450.00 | 900.00 | 1800. |
—Version 2: See Version 2 note under mono version
| ❏ LSP-3584 [S] | Jefferson Airplane Takes Off! | 1966 | 2000. | 3500. | 5000. |
—Version 1: See Version 1 note under mono version
| ❏ LSP-3584 [S] | Jefferson Airplane Takes Off! | 1969 | 3.00 | 6.00 | 12.00 |
—Orange label
| ❏ LSP-3584 [S] | Jefferson Airplane Takes Off! | 1975 | 2.50 | 5.00 | 10.00 |
—Tan label
❏ AYL1-3661	The Worst of Jefferson Airplane	1980	2.00	4.00	8.00
❏ AYL1-3738	Surrealistic Pillow	1980	2.00	4.00	8.00
❏ AYL1-3739	Jefferson Airplane Takes Off!	1980	2.00	4.00	8.00
❏ LPM-3766 [M]	Surrealistic Pillow	1967	15.00	30.00	60.00
❏ LSP-3766 [S]	Surrealistic Pillow	1967	7.50	15.00	30.00
—Black label, dog on top
| ❏ LSP-3766 [S] | Surrealistic Pillow | 1969 | 3.00 | 6.00 | 12.00 |
—Orange label
| ❏ LSP-3766 [S] | Surrealistic Pillow | 1975 | 2.50 | 5.00 | 10.00 |
—Tan label
❏ AYL1-3797	Crown of Creation	1980	2.00	4.00	8.00
❏ AYL1-3798	Bless Its Pointed Little Head	1980	2.00	4.00	8.00
❏ AYL1-3867	Volunteers	1980	2.00	4.00	8.00
❏ LSP-4058	Crown of Creation	1968	7.50	15.00	30.00
—Black label, dog on top
| ❏ LSP-4058 | Crown of Creation | 1969 | 3.00 | 6.00 | 12.00 |
—Orange label
| ❏ LSP-4058 | Crown of Creation | 1975 | 2.50 | 5.00 | 10.00 |
—Tan label
| ❏ LSP-4133 | Bless Its Pointed Little Head | 1969 | 3.00 | 6.00 | 12.00 |
—Orange label
| ❏ LSP-4133 | Bless Its Pointed Little Head | 1975 | 2.50 | 5.00 | 10.00 |
—Tan label
| ❏ LSP-4238 | Volunteers | 1969 | 3.00 | 6.00 | 12.00 |
—Orange label
| ❏ LSP-4238 | Volunteers | 1975 | 2.50 | 5.00 | 10.00 |
—Tan label
❏ LSP-4459	The Worst of Jefferson Airplane	1970	3.00	6.00	12.00
❏ AFL1-4545	After Bathing at Baxter's	1981	2.00	4.00	8.00
❏ AYL1-4718	After Bathing at Baxter's	1983	2.00	4.00	8.00

JEFFERSON STARSHIP
See cross-references under JEFFERSON AIRPLANE.
DCC COMPACT CLASSICS
Number	Title (A Side/B Side)	Yr	VG	VG+	NM
❏ LPZ-2036	Red Octopus	1997	6.25	12.50	25.00
—Audiophile vinyl
GRUNT
❏ BFD1-0717 [Q]	Dragon Fly	1974	3.75	7.50	15.00
❏ BFL1-0717	Dragon Fly	1974	2.50	5.00	10.00
❏ BFD1-0999 [Q]	Red Octopus	1975	3.75	7.50	15.00
❏ BFL1-0999	Red Octopus	1975	2.50	5.00	10.00
❏ BFD1-1557 [Q]	Spitfire	1976	3.75	7.50	15.00
❏ BFL1-1557	Spitfire	1976	2.50	5.00	10.00
❏ BXL1-2515	Earth	1978	2.50	5.00	10.00
❏ BZL1-3247	Gold	1978	2.50	5.00	10.00
❏ DJL1-3363 [PD]	Gold	1978	3.75	7.50	15.00
—Promo-only picture disc
❏ BZL1-3452	Freedom at Point Zero	1979	2.50	5.00	10.00
❏ AYL1-3660	Red Octopus	1980	2.00	4.00	8.00
❏ AYL1-3796	Dragon Fly	1980	2.00	4.00	8.00
❏ BZL1-3848	Modern Times	1981	2.50	5.00	10.00
❏ AYL1-3953	Spitfire	1981	2.00	4.00	8.00
❏ AYL1-4172	Earth	1981	2.00	4.00	8.00
❏ BXL1-4372	Winds of Change	1982	2.50	5.00	10.00
❏ BXL1-4921	Nuclear Furniture	1984	2.50	5.00	10.00
❏ AYL1-5161	Freedom at Point Zero	1984	2.00	4.00	8.00

JEFFREY, JOE, GROUP
WAND
| ❏ WDS-686 | My Pledge of Love | 1969 | 7.50 | 15.00 | 30.00 |

JEFFREY, PAUL
SAVOY
| ❏ MG-12192 [M] | Electrifying Sounds | 1968 | 5.00 | 10.00 | 20.00 |

JEFFRIES, FRAN
WARWICK
| ❏ W-2020 [M] | Fran Can Really Hang You Up the Most | 1960 | 5.00 | 10.00 | 20.00 |

JEFFRIES, HERB
BETHLEHEM
| ❏ BCP-72 [M] | Say It Isn't So | 1957 | 15.00 | 30.00 | 60.00 |
CORAL
| ❏ CRL 56044 [10] | Time on My Hands | 1951 | 25.00 | 50.00 | 100.00 |
MERCURY
| ❏ MG-25089 [10] | Magenta Moods | 1950 | 25.00 | 50.00 | 100.00 |
| ❏ MG-25091 [10] | Just Jeffries | 1950 | 25.00 | 50.00 | 100.00 |

JELLY BEAN BANDITS, THE
MAINSTREAM
| ❏ S-6103 [S] | The Jelly Bean Bandits | 1967 | 37.50 | 75.00 | 150.00 |
| ❏ 56103 [M] | The Jelly Bean Bandits | 1967 | 25.00 | 50.00 | 100.00 |

JELLYBREAD
BLUE HORIZON
| ❏ BH-4801 | First Slice | 1970 | 7.50 | 15.00 | 30.00 |

JELVING, AKE
CAPITOL
| ❏ T 10079 [M] | Christmas in Sweden | 195? | 5.00 | 10.00 | 20.00 |
—Black label with colorband, logo on left
| ❏ T 10079 [M] | Christmas in Sweden | 1957 | 7.50 | 15.00 | 30.00 |
—Turquoise label

JENKINS, FLORENCE FOSTER
One of the world's worst singers ever to be recorded — and unlike MRS. MILLER, Jenkins sang arias!
RCA VICTOR
| ❏ LM-2597 [M] | The Glory (????) of the Human Voice | 1961 | 5.00 | 10.00 | 20.00 |
| ❏ LRT-7001 [10] | A Florence! Foster!! Jenkins!!! Recital!!!! | 195? | 12.50 | 25.00 | 50.00 |

JENKINS, GORDON
CAPITOL
| ❏ T 766 [M] | The Complete Manhattan Tower | 1956 | 7.50 | 15.00 | 30.00 |
—Turquoise or gray label
DECCA
| ❏ DL 8011 [M] | Manhattan Tower/California (The Golden State) | 1951 | 7.50 | 15.00 | 30.00 |
—Black label, gold print

JENKINS, JOHN
BLUE NOTE
| ❏ BLP-1573 [M] | John Jenkins with Kenny Burrell | 1958 | 20.00 | 40.00 | 80.00 |
—Regular version with W. 63rd St., New York address on label
| ❏ BLP-1573 [M] | John Jenkins with Kenny Burrell | 1958 | 30.00 | 60.00 | 120.00 |
—"Deep groove" version (deep indentation under label on both sides)
| ❏ BLP-1573 [M] | John Jenkins with Kenny Burrell | 1963 | 6.25 | 12.50 | 25.00 |
—With "New York, USA" address on label
| ❏ BST-1573 [S] | John Jenkins with Kenny Burrell | 1959 | 12.50 | 25.00 | 50.00 |
—Regular version with W. 63rd St., New York address on label
| ❏ BST-1573 [S] | John Jenkins with Kenny Burrell | 1959 | 20.00 | 40.00 | 80.00 |
—"Deep groove" version (deep indentation under label on both sides)
| ❏ BST-1573 [S] | John Jenkins with Kenny Burrell | 1963 | 5.00 | 10.00 | 20.00 |
—With "New York, USA" address on label
REGENT
| ❏ MG-6056 [M] | Jazz Eyes | 1957 | 25.00 | 50.00 | 100.00 |
SAVOY
| ❏ MG-12201 [M] | Jazz Eyes | 196? | 5.00 | 10.00 | 20.00 |

JENKINS, JOHN; CLIFF JORDAN; BOBBY TIMMONS
NEW JAZZ
| ❏ NJLP-8232 [M] | Jenkins, Jordan and Timmons | 1960 | 15.00 | 30.00 | 60.00 |
| ❏ NJLP-8232 [M] | Jenkins, Jordan and Timmons | 1965 | 6.25 | 12.50 | 25.00 |

Number	Title (A Side/B Side)	Yr	VG	VG+	NM

JENKINS, MARV
OROVOX
| ❑ 1001 [M] | Marv Jenkins Arrives | 196? | 10.00 | 20.00 | 40.00 |
| ❑ S-1001 [S] | Marv Jenkins Arrives | 196? | 10.00 | 20.00 | 40.00 |

REPRISE
| ❑ R-6077 [M] | Good Little Man at the Rubaiyat Room | 1963 | 5.00 | 10.00 | 20.00 |
| ❑ R9-6077 [S] | Good Little Man at the Rubaiyat Room | 1963 | 6.25 | 12.50 | 25.00 |

JENNEY, JACK
COLUMBIA
| ❑ GL 100 [10] | The Golden Era | 1949 | 12.50 | 25.00 | 50.00 |

COLUMBIA MASTERWORKS
| ❑ ML 4803 [M] | Jack Jenney | 195? | 20.00 | 40.00 | 80.00 |

JENNIFER
See JENNIFER WARNES.

JENNINGS, BILL
AUDIO LAB
| ❑ AL-1514 [M] | Guitar/Vibes | 1959 | 25.00 | 50.00 | 100.00 |

KING
❑ 295-105 [10]	Jazz Interlude	195?	62.50	125.00	250.00
❑ 295-106 [10]	The Fabulous Guitar of Bill Jennings	195?	62.50	125.00	250.00
❑ 398-508 [M]	Mood Indigo	1955	25.00	50.00	100.00
❑ 398-527 [M]	Billy in the Lion's Den	1956	25.00	50.00	100.00

PRESTIGE
| ❑ PRLP-7164 [M] | Enough Said! | 1959 | 12.50 | 25.00 | 50.00 |
| ❑ PRLP-7177 [M] | Glide On | 1960 | 12.50 | 25.00 | 50.00 |

JENNINGS, WAYLON
A&M
| ❑ SP-4238 | Don't Think Twice | 1969 | 10.00 | 20.00 | 40.00 |

BAT
| ❑ 1001 [M] | Waylon Jennings at JD's | 1964 | 175.00 | 350.00 | 700.00 |
—Approximately 500 copies pressed

MCA
| ❑ 731 | Waylon Jennings | 198? | 3.00 | 6.00 | 12.00 |
—Reissue of Vocalion LP
❑ 5688	Will the Wolf Survive	1986	2.50	5.00	10.00
❑ 5911	Hangin' Tough	1987	2.50	5.00	10.00
❑ 42038	A Man Called Hoss	1987	2.50	5.00	10.00
❑ 42038 [DJ]	A Man Called Hoss	1987	15.00	30.00	60.00
—Promo-only edition with letter and 48-page book
| ❑ 42222 | Full Circle | 1988 | 2.50 | 5.00 | 10.00 |
| ❑ 42287 | New Classic Waylon | 1989 | 2.50 | 5.00 | 10.00 |

PAIR
❑ PDL1-1005 [(2)]	Waylon!	1986	3.00	6.00	12.00
❑ PDL1-1033 [(2)]	A Couple More Years	1986	3.00	6.00	12.00
❑ PDL1-1110 [(2)]	Honly Tonk Hero	1986	3.00	6.00	12.00

PICKWICK
| ❑ ACL-0306 | Only Daddy That'll Walk the Line | 197? | 2.00 | 4.00 | 8.00 |
—Reissue of RCA Camden LP

RCA
| ❑ 5620-1-RB | The Best of Waylon | 1987 | 2.50 | 5.00 | 10.00 |
| ❑ 9561-1-R | The Early Years (1965-1969) | 1989 | 2.50 | 5.00 | 10.00 |

RCA CAMDEN
❑ ACL1-0306	Only Daddy That'll Walk the Line	1973	2.50	5.00	10.00
❑ CAL-2183 [M]	The One and Only Waylon Jennings	1967	3.75	7.50	15.00
❑ CAS-2183 [S]	The One and Only Waylon Jennings	1967	3.00	6.00	12.00
❑ CAS-2556	Heartaches by the Number	1972	3.00	6.00	12.00
❑ CAS-2608	Ruby, Don't Take Your Love to Town	1972	3.00	6.00	12.00

RCA VICTOR
❑ APL1-0240	Honky Tonk Heroes	1973	3.75	7.50	15.00
❑ APL1-0539	This Time	1974	3.00	6.00	12.00
❑ APL1-0734	The Ramblin' Man	1974	3.00	6.00	12.00
❑ APL1-1062	Dreaming My Dreams	1975	2.50	5.00	10.00
❑ APL1-1108	Waylon Live	1976	2.50	5.00	10.00
❑ APL1-1816	Are You Ready for the Country	1976	2.50	5.00	10.00
❑ AAL1-2317	Ol' Waylon	198?	2.00	4.00	8.00
—Reissue
❑ APL1-2317	Ol' Waylon	1977	2.50	5.00	10.00
❑ AFL1-2979	I've Always Been Crazy	1978	2.50	5.00	10.00
❑ AHL1-3378	Greatest Hits	1979	2.50	5.00	10.00
❑ AHL1-3493	What Goes Around Comes Around	1979	2.50	5.00	10.00
❑ LPM-3523 [M]	Folk-Country	1966	7.50	15.00	30.00
❑ LSP-3523 [S]	Folk-Country	1966	10.00	20.00	40.00
❑ AHL1-3602	Music Man	1980	2.50	5.00	10.00
❑ LPM-3620 [M]	Leavin' Town	1966	7.50	15.00	30.00
❑ LSP-3620 [S]	Leavin' Town	1966	10.00	20.00	40.00
❑ LPM-3660 [M]	Waylon Sings Ol' Harlan	1967	7.50	15.00	30.00
❑ LSP-3660 [S]	Waylon Sings Ol' Harlan	1967	10.00	20.00	40.00
❑ AYL1-3663	Are You Ready for the Country	1980	2.00	4.00	8.00
—Budget-line reissue
❑ LPM-3736 [M]	Nashville Rebel	1967	10.00	20.00	40.00
❑ LSP-3736 [S]	Nashville Rebel	1967	12.50	25.00	50.00
❑ LPM-3825 [M]	Love of the Common People	1967	7.50	15.00	30.00
❑ LSP-3825 [S]	Love of the Common People	1967	6.25	12.50	25.00
❑ AYL1-3897	Honky Tonk Heroes	1980	2.00	4.00	8.00
—Budget-line reissue
❑ LPM-3918 [M]	Hangin' On	1968	25.00	50.00	100.00
❑ LSP-3918 [S]	Hangin' On	1968	6.25	12.50	25.00
❑ LPM-4023 [M]	Only the Greatest	1968	—	—	—
—Canceled?
| ❑ LSP-4023 [S] | Only the Greatest | 1968 | 6.25 | 12.50 | 25.00 |
| ❑ AYL1-4072 | Dreaming My Dreams | 1981 | 2.00 | 4.00 | 8.00 |
—Budget-line reissue
| ❑ AYL1-4073 | The Ramblin' Man | 1981 | 2.00 | 4.00 | 8.00 |
—Budget-line reissue
| ❑ LSP-4085 | Jewels | 1968 | 6.25 | 12.50 | 25.00 |
| ❑ LSP-4137 | Just to Satisfy You | 1969 | 6.25 | 12.50 | 25.00 |

| ❑ AYL1-4163 | Waylon Live | 1981 | 2.00 | 4.00 | 8.00 |
—Budget-line reissue
| ❑ AYL1-4164 | I've Always Been Crazy | 1981 | 2.00 | 4.00 | 8.00 |
—Budget-line reissue
❑ LSP-4180	Country-Folk	1969	6.25	12.50	25.00
❑ AHL1-4247	Black On Black	1982	2.50	5.00	10.00
❑ AYL1-4250	Music Man	1982	2.00	4.00	8.00
—Budget-line reissue
❑ LSP-4260	Waylon	1970	5.00	10.00	20.00
❑ LSP-4341	The Best of Waylon Jennings	1970	5.00	10.00	20.00
❑ LSP-4418	Singer of Sad Songs	1970	5.00	10.00	20.00
❑ LSP-4487	The Taker/Tulsa	1971	5.00	10.00	20.00
❑ LSP-4567	Cedartown, Georgia	1971	5.00	10.00	20.00
❑ LSP-4647	Good Hearted Woman	1972	5.00	10.00	20.00
❑ AFL1-4673	It's Only Rock & Roll	1983	2.50	5.00	10.00
❑ LSP-4751	Ladies Love Outlaws	1972	5.00	10.00	20.00
❑ AHL1-4826	Waylon and Company	1983	2.50	5.00	10.00
❑ AYL1-4828	The Best of Waylon Jennings	1983	2.00	4.00	8.00
—Budget-line reissue
❑ LSP-4854	Lonesome, On'ry and Mean	1973	3.75	7.50	15.00
❑ AHL1-5017	Never Could Toe the Mark	1984	2.50	5.00	10.00
❑ AYL1-5126	Ol' Waylon	1984	2.00	4.00	8.00
—Budget-line reissue
❑ AHL1-5325	Waylon's Greatest Hits, Vol. 2	1984	2.50	5.00	10.00
❑ AHL1-5428	Turn the Page	1985	2.50	5.00	10.00
❑ AYL1-5433	Waylon and Company	1985	2.00	4.00	8.00
—Budget-line reissue
| ❑ AHL1-5473 | Collector's Series | 1985 | 2.50 | 5.00 | 10.00 |
| ❑ AYL1-7046 | Never Could Toe the Mark | 1985 | 2.00 | 4.00 | 8.00 |
—Budget-line reissue
| ❑ AHL1-7184 | Sweet Mother Texas | 1986 | 2.50 | 5.00 | 10.00 |

SOUNDS
| ❑ 1001 [M] | Waylon Jennings at JD's | 1964 | 125.00 | 250.00 | 500.00 |
—Approximately 500 copies pressed; reissue of Bat 1001

VOCALION
| ❑ DL 73873 | Waylon Jennings | 1969 | 6.25 | 12.50 | 25.00 |

JENSEN, KRIS
HICKORY
| ❑ LP 110 [M] | Torture | 1963 | 20.00 | 40.00 | 80.00 |

JENSEN, KURT
HOLLYWOOD
| ❑ LPH-137 [M] | An Evening with Jayne | 195? | 15.00 | 30.00 | 60.00 |
—Collectible for its "cheesecake" cover of Jayne Mansfield

JEREMY AND THE SATYRS
REPRISE
| ❑ R-6282 [M] | Jeremy and the Satyrs | 1968 | 10.00 | 20.00 | 40.00 |
—Mono is white label promo only
| ❑ RS-6282 [S] | Jeremy and the Satyrs | 1968 | 5.00 | 10.00 | 20.00 |

JEREMY'S FRIENDS
WARWICK
| ❑ W-2019 [M] | Jeremy's Friends | 1960 | 12.50 | 25.00 | 50.00 |

JERICHO
AMPEX
| ❑ A-10112 | Jericho | 1971 | 6.25 | 12.50 | 25.00 |

JESSE J. AND THE BANDITS
RECAR
| ❑ 2011 [M] | Top Teen Hits | 1965 | 25.00 | 50.00 | 100.00 |

JESUS JONES
SBK
| ❑ 05348 [DJ] | A Conversation with Jesus | 1990 | 5.00 | 10.00 | 20.00 |
—Generic cover with sticker

JETHRO TULL
CHRYSALIS
| ❑ PRO 623 [DJ] | The Jethro Tull Radio Show | 1975 | 12.50 | 25.00 | 50.00 |
| ❑ CHR 1003 | Thick as a Brick | 1973 | 3.00 | 6.00 | 12.00 |
—Green label, "3300 Warner Blvd." address
| ❑ CHR 1003 | Thick as a Brick | 1977 | 2.50 | 5.00 | 10.00 |
—Blue label, New York address
| ❑ 2CH 1035 [(2)] | Living in the Past | 1972 | 5.00 | 10.00 | 20.00 |
—Two-record set with booklet; green labels
| ❑ CHR 1035 [(2)] | Living in the Past | 1977 | 3.75 | 7.50 | 15.00 |
—Blue label, New York address
| ❑ CHR 1040 | A Passion Play | 1973 | 3.00 | 6.00 | 12.00 |
—Green label, "3300 Warner Blvd." address
| ❑ CHR 1040 | A Passion Play | 1977 | 2.50 | 5.00 | 10.00 |
—Blue label, New York address
| ❑ CHR 1041 | This Was | 1973 | 3.00 | 6.00 | 12.00 |
—Green label, "3300 Warner Blvd." address
| ❑ CHR 1041 | This Was | 1977 | 2.50 | 5.00 | 10.00 |
—Blue label, New York address
| ❑ CHR 1042 | Stand Up | 1973 | 3.00 | 6.00 | 12.00 |
—Green label, "3300 Warner Blvd." address
| ❑ CHR 1042 | Stand Up | 1977 | 2.50 | 5.00 | 10.00 |
—Blue label, New York address
| ❑ CHR 1043 | Benefit | 1973 | 3.00 | 6.00 | 12.00 |
—Green label, "3300 Warner Blvd." address
| ❑ CHR 1043 | Benefit | 1977 | 2.50 | 5.00 | 10.00 |
—Blue label, New York address
| ❑ CH4 1044 [Q] | Aqualung | 1974 | 10.00 | 20.00 | 40.00 |
| ❑ CHR 1044 | Aqualung | 1973 | 3.00 | 6.00 | 12.00 |
—Green label, "3300 Warner Blvd." address
| ❑ CHR 1044 | Aqualung | 1977 | 2.50 | 5.00 | 10.00 |
—Blue label, New York address
| ❑ CH4 1067 [Q] | War Child | 1974 | 10.00 | 20.00 | 40.00 |
| ❑ CHR 1067 | War Child | 1974 | 2.50 | 5.00 | 10.00 |
—Blue label, New York address

Number	Title (A Side/B Side)	Yr	VG	VG+	NM
❑ CHR 1067	War Child	1974	3.00	6.00	12.00
—Green label, "3300 Warner Blvd." address					
❑ CHR 1078	M.U. — The Best of Jethro Tull	1975	3.00	6.00	12.00
—Green label, "3300 Warner Blvd." address					
❑ CHR 1078	M.U. — The Best of Jethro Tull	1977	2.50	5.00	10.00
—Blue label, New York address					
❑ CHR 1082	Minstrel in the Gallery	1975	3.00	6.00	12.00
—Green label, "3300 Warner Blvd." address					
❑ CHR 1082	Minstrel in the Gallery	1977	2.50	5.00	10.00
—Blue label, New York address					
❑ CHR 1111	Too Old to Rock 'N' Roll; Too Young to Die!	1976	3.00	6.00	12.00
—Green label, "3300 Warner Blvd." address					
❑ CHR 1111	Too Old to Rock 'N' Roll; Too Young to Die!	1977	2.50	5.00	10.00
—Blue label, New York address					
❑ CHR 1132	Songs from the Wood	1977	2.50	5.00	10.00
❑ CHR 1135	Repeat — The Best of Jethro Tull, Vol. II	1977	2.50	5.00	10.00
❑ CHR 1175	Heavy Horses	1978	2.50	5.00	10.00
❑ CHR2 1201 [(2)]	Jethro Tull Live — Bursting Out	1978	3.00	6.00	12.00
❑ CHR 1238	Stormwatch	1979	2.50	5.00	10.00
❑ CHR 1301	"A"	1980	2.50	5.00	10.00
❑ CHR 1380	The Broadsword and the Beast	1982	2.50	5.00	10.00
❑ F1-21708	Rock Island	1989	2.50	5.00	10.00
❑ FV 41003	Thick as a Brick	1983	2.00	4.00	8.00
❑ PV 41003	Thick as a Brick	1986	2.00	4.00	8.00
❑ KV2 41035 [(2)]	Living in the Past	1983	3.00	6.00	12.00
❑ PV 41040	A Passion Play	1983	2.00	4.00	8.00
❑ PV 41041	This Was	1983	2.00	4.00	8.00
❑ PV 41042	Stand Up	1983	2.00	4.00	8.00
❑ PV 41043	Benefit	1983	2.00	4.00	8.00
❑ FV 41044	Aqualung	1983	2.00	4.00	8.00
❑ PV 41067	War Child	1983	2.00	4.00	8.00
❑ FV 41078	M.U. — The Best of Jethro Tull	1983	2.00	4.00	8.00
❑ PV 41082	Minstrel in the Gallery	1983	2.00	4.00	8.00
❑ PV 41111	Too Old to Rock 'N' Roll; Too Young to Die!	1983	2.00	4.00	8.00
❑ PV 41132	Songs from the Wood	1983	2.00	4.00	8.00
❑ FV 41135	Repeat — The Best of Jethro Tull, Vol. II	1983	2.00	4.00	8.00
❑ PV 41135	Repeat — The Best of Jethro Tull, Vol. II	1986	2.00	4.00	8.00
❑ PV 41175	Heavy Horses	1983	2.00	4.00	8.00
❑ V2X 41201 [(2)]	Jethro Tull Live — Bursting Out	1983	3.00	6.00	12.00
❑ PV 41238	Stormwatch	1983	2.00	4.00	8.00
❑ PV 41301	"A"	1983	2.00	4.00	8.00
❑ FV 41380	The Broadsword and the Beast	1983	2.00	4.00	8.00
❑ PV 41380	The Broadsword and the Beast	1986	2.00	4.00	8.00
❑ FV 41461	Under Wraps	1984	2.50	5.00	10.00
❑ PV 41461	Under Wraps	1986	2.00	4.00	8.00
❑ FV 41515	Original Masters	1985	2.50	5.00	10.00
❑ FV 41590	Crest of a Knave	1987	2.50	5.00	10.00
❑ V5X 41653 [(5)]	20 Years of Jethro Tull	1988	20.00	40.00	80.00
❑ VX2 41655 [(2)]	20 Years of Jethro Tull	1989	6.25	12.50	25.00
—Abridged version of Chrysalis 41653					
DCC COMPACT CLASSICS					
❑ LPZ 2033	Aqualung	1997	25.00	50.00	100.00
—Audiophile vinyl					
❑ LPZ-2059	Original Masters	1998	10.00	20.00	40.00
—Audiophile vinyl					
MOBILE FIDELITY					
❑ 1-061	Aqualung	1980	17.50	35.00	70.00
—Audiophile vinyl					
❑ 1-092	The Broadsword and the Beast	1982	10.00	20.00	40.00
—Audiophile vinyl					
❑ 1-187	Thick as a Brick	1985	7.50	15.00	30.00
—Audiophile vinyl					
REPRISE					
❑ MS 2035	Aqualung	1971	3.75	7.50	15.00
❑ MS 2072	Thick as a Brick	1972	3.75	7.50	15.00
❑ 2MS 2106 [(2)]	Living in the Past	1972	6.25	12.50	25.00
—Two-record set with booklet; original edition, rather than using cardboard outer sleeve for the records, has record sleeves attached to enclosed booklet, and thus is difficult to find intact					
❑ RS 6336	This Was	1969	5.00	10.00	20.00
—Two-tone orange label with "r:" and "W7" logos on label					
❑ RS 6336	This Was	1970	3.75	7.50	15.00
—All-one-color (orange/brown) label with no "W7" on label					
❑ RS 6360	Stand Up	1969	5.00	10.00	20.00
—Two-tone orange label with "r:" and "W7" logos on label; band "stands up" when gatefold is opened					
❑ RS 6360	Stand Up	1970	3.75	7.50	15.00
—All-one-color (orange/brown) label with no "W7" on label					
❑ RS 6400	Benefit	1970	3.75	7.50	15.00
—All-one-color (orange/brown) label with no "W7" on label					
❑ RS 6400	Benefit	1970	5.00	10.00	20.00
—Two-tone orange label with "r:" and "W7" logos on label					
JETT, JOAN, AND THE BLACKHEARTS					
BLACKHEART					
❑ JJ 707	Joan Jett	1980	12.50	25.00	50.00
❑ BFZ 40544	Good Music	1986	3.00	6.00	12.00
❑ FZ 44146	Up Your Alley	1988	2.50	5.00	10.00
❑ Z 45473	The Hit List	1990	3.00	6.00	12.00
❑ Z 47488	Notorious	1991	3.00	6.00	12.00
BOARDWALK					
❑ NB1-33243	I Love Rock-n-Roll	1982	2.50	5.00	10.00
—First pressing contains "Little Drummer Boy," which was replaced on second pressings					
❑ NB1-33243	I Love Rock-n-Roll	1982	3.00	6.00	12.00
—Second pressing, with "Oh Woe Is Me"					
❑ NB1-33251	Bad Reputation	1982	2.50	5.00	10.00
—Reissue of FW 37065					
❑ FW 37065	Bad Reputation	1981	3.00	6.00	12.00
—Essentially a reissue of Blackheart JJ 707					
MCA					
❑ 5437	Album	1983	3.00	6.00	12.00
❑ 5476	Glorious Results of a Misspent Youth	1984	3.00	6.00	12.00
❑ R 163731	Glorious Results of a Misspent Youth	1984	4.00	8.00	16.00
—RCA Music Service edition					

Number	Title (A Side/B Side)	Yr	VG	VG+	NM
REPRISE					
❑ 45567	Pure and Simple	1994	3.00	6.00	12.00
JIM & JESSE					
EPIC					
❑ LN 24031 [M]	Bluegrass Special	1963	5.00	10.00	20.00
❑ LN 24074 [M]	Bluegrass Classics	1963	5.00	10.00	20.00
❑ LN 24107 [M]	The Old Country Church	1964	5.00	10.00	20.00
❑ LN 24144 [M]	Y'All Come	1964	5.00	10.00	20.00
❑ LN 24176 [M]	Berry Pickin' the Country	1965	5.00	10.00	20.00
❑ LN 24204 [M]	Sing Unto Him	1966	5.00	10.00	20.00
❑ LN 24314 [M]	Diesel on My Tail	1967	5.00	10.00	20.00
❑ BN 26031 [S]	Bluegrass Special	1963	6.25	12.50	25.00
❑ BN 26074 [S]	Bluegrass Classics	1963	6.25	12.50	25.00
❑ BN 26107 [S]	The Old Country Church	1964	6.25	12.50	25.00
❑ BN 26144 [S]	Y'All Come	1964	6.25	12.50	25.00
❑ BN 26176 [S]	Berry Pickin' the Country	1965	6.25	12.50	25.00
❑ BN 26204 [S]	Sing Unto Him	1966	6.25	12.50	25.00
❑ BN 26314 [S]	Diesel on My Tail	1967	6.25	12.50	25.00
❑ BN 26394	All-Time Great Country Instrumentals	1968	5.00	10.00	20.00
❑ BN 26465	Saluting the Louvin Brothers	1969	5.00	10.00	20.00
JIMENEZ, JOSE					
A&M					
❑ SP-4144	Mashuganishi Yogi	1968	3.75	7.50	15.00
CAPITOL					
❑ ST-464	Hoo Ha! Direct from Nashville	1970	3.75	7.50	15.00
KAPP					
❑ KL 1215 [M]	More Jose Jimenez	1961	5.00	10.00	20.00
❑ KL 1215 [M]	Jose Jimenez the Submarine Officer	1961	6.25	12.50	25.00
—Original title					
❑ KL 1238 [M]	Jose Jimenez at the Hungry I	196?	3.75	7.50	15.00
—Reissue with new title					
❑ KL 1238 [M]	Jose Jimenez — The Astronaut (The First Man in Space)	1961	5.00	10.00	20.00
❑ KL-1257 [M]	Jose Jimenez in Orbit — Bill Dana on Earth	1961	5.00	10.00	20.00
❑ KL-1304 [M]	Jose Jimenez Talks to Teenagers of All Ages	1962	5.00	10.00	20.00
❑ KL-1320 [M]	Jose Jimenez — Our Secret Weapon	1963	5.00	10.00	20.00
❑ KL-1332 [M]	Jose Jimenez in Jollywood	1963	5.00	10.00	20.00
❑ KL-1402 [M]	Bill Dana in Las Vegas	1964	5.00	10.00	20.00
❑ KS 3238 [S]	Jose Jimenez at the Hungry I	196?	3.75	7.50	15.00
❑ KS-3332 [S]	Jose Jimenez in Jollywood	1963	6.25	12.50	25.00
ROULETTE					
❑ R 25161 [M]	My Name…Jose Jimenez	1961	5.00	10.00	20.00
—Reissue of Signature LP					
SIGNATURE					
❑ SM 1013 [M]	My Name…Jose Jimenez	1960	6.25	12.50	25.00
JIVE FIVE, THE					
AMBIENT SOUND					
❑ FZ 37717	Here We Are	1982	3.75	7.50	15.00
AMBIENT SOUND/ROUNDER					
❑ ASR-801	Way Back	1985	3.00	6.00	12.00
COLLECTABLES					
❑ COL-5022	Greatest Hits	198?	2.50	5.00	10.00
RELIC					
❑ 5020	The Jive Five's Greatest Hits (1961-1963)	198?	2.50	5.00	10.00
UNITED ARTISTS					
❑ UAL-3455 [M]	The Jive Five	1965	12.50	25.00	50.00
❑ UAS-6455 [S]	The Jive Five	1965	18.75	37.50	75.00
JOBIM, ANTONIO CARLOS					
WARNER BROS.					
❑ WS 1611 [S]	The Wonderful World of Antonio Carlos Jobim	1966	5.00	10.00	20.00
❑ WS 1636 [S]	Love, Strings	1966	5.00	10.00	20.00
—Gold label					
JOE & EDDIE					
GNP CRESCENDO					
❑ GNP-75 [M]	Joe & Eddie	1963	5.00	10.00	20.00
❑ GNP-86 [M]	There's a Meetin' Here Tonite.	1963	5.00	10.00	20.00
❑ GNP-96 [M]	Coast to Coast.	1964	5.00	10.00	20.00
❑ GNPS-96 [S]	Coast to Coast.	1964	6.25	12.50	25.00
❑ GNP-99 [M]	Joe & Eddie, Volume 4.	1964	5.00	10.00	20.00
❑ GNPS-99 [S]	Joe & Eddie, Volume 4.	1964	6.25	12.50	25.00
❑ GNP-2005 [M]	Tear Down the Walls.	1965	3.75	7.50	15.00
❑ GNPS-2005 [S]	Tear Down the Walls.	1965	5.00	10.00	20.00
❑ GNP-2007 [M]	Joe & Eddie Live in Hollywood.	1965	3.75	7.50	15.00
❑ GNPS-2007 [S]	Joe & Eddie Live in Hollywood.	1965	5.00	10.00	20.00
❑ GNP-2014 [M]	Walkin' Down the Line.	1965	3.75	7.50	15.00
❑ GNPS-2014 [S]	Walkin' Down the Line.	1965	5.00	10.00	20.00
❑ GNP-2021 [M]	The Magic of Their Singing.	1966	3.75	7.50	15.00
❑ GNPS-2021 [S]	The Magic of Their Singing.	1966	5.00	10.00	20.00
❑ GNP-2032 [M]	The Best of Joe & Eddie.	1966	3.75	7.50	15.00
❑ GNPS-2032 [S]	The Best of Joe & Eddie.	1966	5.00	10.00	20.00
JOEL, BILLY					
COLUMBIA					
❑ AS 326 [DJ]	Souvenir	1976	7.50	15.00	30.00
—Promo-only LP with one side live, one side a compilation of studio tracks					
❑ AS 402 [DJ]	Inter Chords/Billy Joel Interview	1977	6.25	12.50	25.00
—Promo-only interview album					
❑ AS 1343 [DJ]	Billy Joel Interview	1982	6.25	12.50	25.00
❑ CQ 32544 [Q]	Piano Man	1974	5.00	10.00	20.00
❑ KC 32544	Piano Man	1973	3.00	6.00	12.00
—Some copies have the first song spelled "Travelin' Prayer," others have it "Travellin' Prayer." No difference in value.					
❑ PC 32544	Piano Man	1976	2.50	5.00	10.00
—No bar code on back cover					
❑ PC 32544	Piano Man	1979	2.00	4.00	8.00
—With bar code on back cover					

Number	Title (A Side/B Side)	Yr	VG	VG+	NM
❏ PC 33146	Streetlife Serenade	1975	2.50	5.00	10.00
—No bar code on back cover					
❏ PC 33146	Streetlife Serenade	1979	2.00	4.00	8.00
—With bar code on back cover					
❏ PCQ 33146 [Q]	Streetlife Serenade	1975	5.00	10.00	20.00
❏ PC 33848	Turnstiles	1976	2.00	4.00	8.00
—With bar code on back cover					
❏ PC 33848	Turnstiles	1976	2.50	5.00	10.00
—No bar code on back cover					
❏ PCQ 33848 [Q]	Turnstiles	1976	5.00	10.00	20.00
❏ HC 34987	The Stranger	1981	7.50	15.00	30.00
—Original pressing of half-speed mastered edition					
❏ JC 34987	The Stranger	1977	2.50	5.00	10.00
❏ PC 34987	The Stranger	1979	2.00	4.00	8.00
❏ FC 35609	52nd Street	1978	2.50	5.00	10.00
❏ PC 35609	52nd Street	1985	2.00	4.00	8.00
❏ FC 36384	Glass Houses	1980	2.50	5.00	10.00
❏ PC 36384	Glass Houses	1986	2.00	4.00	8.00
❏ PC 37461	Songs in the Attic	1984	2.00	4.00	8.00
❏ TC 37461	Songs in the Attic	1981	2.50	5.00	10.00
❏ QC 38200	The Nylon Curtain	1982	2.50	5.00	10.00
❏ QC 38837	An Innocent Man	1983	2.50	5.00	10.00
❏ PC 38984	Cold Spring Harbor	1983	2.00	4.00	8.00
—Remixed, remastered version of Family Productions album					
❏ C2 40121 [(2)]	Greatest Hits, Volumes 1 and 2	1985	3.00	6.00	12.00
❏ OC 40402	The Bridge	1986	2.50	5.00	10.00
❏ C2 40996 [(2)]	KOHUEPT	1987	3.75	7.50	15.00
❏ OC 44366	Storm Front	1989	3.00	6.00	12.00
❏ HC 44987	The Stranger	1982	6.25	12.50	25.00
—Half-speed mastered edition (reissue)					
❏ HC 45609	52nd Street	1982	6.25	12.50	25.00
—Half-speed mastered edition					
❏ HC 47461	Songs in the Attic	1982	17.50	35.00	70.00
—Half-speed mastered edition					
❏ HC 48837	An Innocent Man	1983	7.50	15.00	30.00
—Half-speed mastered edition					

FAMILY PRODUCTIONS

Number	Title (A Side/B Side)	Yr	VG	VG+	NM
❏ FPS-2700	Cold Spring Harbor	1971	10.00	20.00	40.00

—Authentic copies have mostly dark blue labels; when reissued on Columbia, the entire LP was remixed and remastered, and "You Can Make Me Free" was shortened by three minutes

JOHANSEN, DAVID
Also see NEW YORK DOLLS.

BLUE SKY

Number	Title (A Side/B Side)	Yr	VG	VG+	NM
❏ AS 519 [DJ]	The David Johansen Group Live	1978	7.50	15.00	30.00
❏ AS 1281 [DJ]	Live and Sampler	1981	3.00	6.00	12.00
—Promo-only four-song sampler					
❏ JZ 34926	David Johansen	1978	2.50	5.00	10.00
❏ JZ 36082	In Style.	1979	2.50	5.00	10.00
❏ FZ 36589	Here Comes the Night.	1981	2.50	5.00	10.00
❏ ARZ 38004	Live It Up.	1982	2.50	5.00	10.00

PASSPORT

Number	Title (A Side/B Side)	Yr	VG	VG+	NM
❏ PB-6043	Sweet Revenge	1984	2.50	5.00	10.00

JOHANSSON, JAN

DOT

Number	Title (A Side/B Side)	Yr	VG	VG+	NM
❏ DLP-3416 [M]	Sweden Non-Stop	1962	5.00	10.00	20.00
❏ DLP-25416 [S]	Sweden Non-Stop	1962	6.25	12.50	25.00

JOHN, ELTON

COLUMBIA SPECIAL PRODUCTS

Number	Title (A Side/B Side)	Yr	VG	VG+	NM
❏ P 16196	The Best of Elton John, Volume One	1981	3.00	6.00	12.00
❏ P 16197	The Best of Elton John, Volume Two	1981	3.00	6.00	12.00
—Both of the above "Distributed Exclusively by Scott Distributing Corp."					

DCC COMPACT CLASSICS

Number	Title (A Side/B Side)	Yr	VG	VG+	NM
❏ LPZ-2004	Madman Across the Water	1994	30.00	60.00	120.00
—Audiophile vinyl					
❏ LPZ-2013	Elton John's Greatest Hits	1995	25.00	50.00	100.00
—Audiophile vinyl					
❏ LPZ-2020	Elton John's Greatest Hits, Volume 2	1996	—	—	—
—Canceled					

DIRECT DISC

Number	Title (A Side/B Side)	Yr	VG	VG+	NM
❏ SD-16614 [(2)]	Goodbye Yellow Brick Road	1980	12.50	25.00	50.00
—Audiophile vinyl					

GEFFEN

Number	Title (A Side/B Side)	Yr	VG	VG+	NM
❏ GHS 2002	The Fox	1981	2.50	5.00	10.00
❏ GHS 2013	Jump Up!	1982	2.50	5.00	10.00
❏ GHS 4006	Too Low for Zero	1983	2.50	5.00	10.00
❏ GHS 24031	Breaking Hearts	1984	2.50	5.00	10.00
❏ GHS 24031 [DJ]	Breaking Hearts	1984	5.00	10.00	20.00
—Promo pressing on Quiex II vinyl					
❏ GHS 24077	Ice on Fire	1985	2.50	5.00	10.00
❏ GHS 24114	Leather Jackets	1986	2.50	5.00	10.00
❏ GHS 24153	Elton John's Greatest Hits, Vol. 3, 1979-1987	1987	2.50	5.00	10.00

MCA

Number	Title (A Side/B Side)	Yr	VG	VG+	NM
❏ 619	11-17-70	1979	2.00	4.00	8.00
❏ 620	Empty Sky	1979	2.00	4.00	8.00
❏ 621	Rock of the Westies	1979	2.00	4.00	8.00
❏ 622	Here and There	1979	2.00	4.00	8.00
❏ 771	Victim of Love	1981	2.00	4.00	8.00
❏ 772	21 at 33	1981	2.00	4.00	8.00
❏ L33-1173/4 [DJ]	Get Up and Dance	1977	25.00	50.00	100.00
—Promo-only sampler from "Blue Moves" LP; blue vinyl					
❏ 1689	Elton John's Greatest Hits	198?	2.00	4.00	8.00
❏ 4L33-1848 [(4)DJ]	Victim of Love	1979	25.00	50.00	100.00
—Promo-only collection of the entire album as four 12-inch singles					
❏ L33-1995 [PD]	A Single Man	1978	10.00	20.00	40.00
—Promo picture disc					
❏ 2012	Elton John	1973	2.50	5.00	10.00
❏ 2014	Tumbleweed Connection	1973	2.50	5.00	10.00
—With booklet					
❏ 2015	11-17-70	1973	2.50	5.00	10.00

Number	Title (A Side/B Side)	Yr	VG	VG+	NM
❏ 2016	Madman Across the Water	1973	2.50	5.00	10.00
—With booklet					
❏ 2017	Honky Chateau	1973	2.50	5.00	10.00
❏ 2100	Don't Shoot Me, I'm Only the Piano Player	1973	2.50	5.00	10.00
—With black rainbow label and booklet					
❏ 2100	Don't Shoot Me, I'm Only the Piano Player	1973	5.00	10.00	20.00
—With all-black label (no rainbow) and booklet					
❏ 2116	Caribou	1974	2.50	5.00	10.00
❏ 2128	Elton John's Greatest Hits	1974	2.50	5.00	10.00
❏ 2130	Empty Sky	1975	2.50	5.00	10.00
—First American issue of his 1969 debut					
❏ 2142	Captain Fantastic and the Brown Dirt Cowboy	1975	3.00	6.00	12.00
—With custom label, two booklets and poster					
❏ 2142 [DJ]	Captain Fantastic and the Brown Dirt Cowboy	1975	75.00	150.00	300.00
—Brown vinyl promo, autographed by Elton John and Bernie Taupin					
❏ 2163	Rock of the Westies	1975	2.50	5.00	10.00
❏ 2197	Here and There	1976	2.50	5.00	10.00
❏ 3001	Tumbleweed Connection	1977	2.00	4.00	8.00
❏ 3003	Madman Across the Water	1977	2.00	4.00	8.00
❏ 3027	Elton John's Greatest Hits, Volume 2	1977	2.50	5.00	10.00
❏ 3065	A Single Man	1978	2.50	5.00	10.00
❏ 5104	Victim of Love	1979	2.50	5.00	10.00
❏ 5121	21 at 33	1980	2.50	5.00	10.00
—Originals have custom labels					
❏ 5224	Elton John's Greatest Hits	1981	2.00	4.00	8.00
❏ 5225	Elton John's Greatest Hits, Volume 2	1981	2.00	4.00	8.00
❏ 6011 [(2)]	Blue Moves	1979	2.50	5.00	10.00
❏ 6240	Reg Strikes Back	1988	2.50	5.00	10.00
❏ 6321	Sleeping with the Past	1989	2.50	5.00	10.00
❏ 6894 [(2)]	Goodbye Yellow Brick Road	1980	2.50	5.00	10.00
❏ 8022 [(2)]	Live in Australia with the Melbourne Symphony Orchestra	1987	3.75	7.50	15.00
❏ 2-10003 [(2)]	Goodbye Yellow Brick Road	1973	3.75	7.50	15.00
❏ 13921 [EP]	The Thom Bell Sessions	1979	2.00	4.00	8.00
❏ 14951 [PD]	A Single Man	1978	5.00	10.00	20.00
—Stock picture disc					
❏ 37064	Honky Chateau	1979	2.00	4.00	8.00
❏ 37065	Caribou	1979	2.00	4.00	8.00
❏ 37066	Captain Fantastic and the Brown Dirt Cowboy	1979	2.00	4.00	8.00
❏ 37067	Elton John	1979	2.00	4.00	8.00
❏ 37068	A Single Man	1979	2.00	4.00	8.00
❏ 37113	Don't Shoot Me, I'm Only the Piano Player	1979	2.00	4.00	8.00
❏ 37199	Tumbleweed Connection	1982	2.00	4.00	8.00
❏ 37200	Madman Across the Water	1982	2.00	4.00	8.00
❏ 37215	Elton John's Greatest Hits	1983	2.00	4.00	8.00
❏ 37216	Elton John's Greatest Hits	1983	2.00	4.00	8.00
❏ 37266	Your Songs	1986	2.50	5.00	10.00
❏ 39115	The Complete Thom Bell Sessions	1989	3.75	7.50	15.00

MOBILE FIDELITY

Number	Title (A Side/B Side)	Yr	VG	VG+	NM
❏ 2-160 [(2)]	Goodbye Yellow Brick Road	1984	10.00	20.00	40.00
—Audiophile vinyl					

NAUTILUS

Number	Title (A Side/B Side)	Yr	VG	VG+	NM
❏ NR-42	Elton John's Greatest Hits	198?	25.00	50.00	100.00
—Audiophile vinyl					

PARAMOUNT

Number	Title (A Side/B Side)	Yr	VG	VG+	NM
❏ PAS 6004	Friends (Soundtrack)	1971	5.00	10.00	20.00
—Whitish gray label original					
❏ PAS 6004	Friends (Soundtrack)	1975	6.25	12.50	25.00
—Dark blue label with "Paramount" logo at top and ABC Records reference along edge; much rarer than the original					

ROCKET

Number	Title (A Side/B Side)	Yr	VG	VG+	NM
❏ 2-11004 [(2)]	Blue Moves	1976	3.75	7.50	15.00
—Originals have light blue labels with a train at the top of the label					
❏ 526915-1	Made in England	1995	5.00	10.00	20.00
—U.S. version is on 180-gram vinyl, distributed by Classic Records					

UNI

Number	Title (A Side/B Side)	Yr	VG	VG+	NM
❏ 73090	Elton John	1970	3.75	7.50	15.00
❏ 73096	Tumbleweed Connection	1971	3.75	7.50	15.00
—With booklet					
❏ 93090	Elton John	1971	3.00	6.00	12.00
❏ 93096	Tumbleweed Connection	1971	3.00	6.00	12.00
—With booklet					
❏ 93105	11-17-70	1971	3.75	7.50	15.00
❏ 93120	Madman Across the Water	1971	3.75	7.50	15.00
—With booklet					
❏ 93135	Honky Chateau	1972	3.75	7.50	15.00

JOHN, LITTLE WILLIE

BLUESWAY

Number	Title (A Side/B Side)	Yr	VG	VG+	NM
❏ BLS-6069	Free at Last	1973	6.25	12.50	25.00

KING

Number	Title (A Side/B Side)	Yr	VG	VG+	NM
❏ 564 [M]	Fever	1957	150.00	300.00	600.00
—White cover with "Fever" in large colorful letters					
❏ 395-564 [M]	Fever	1956	250.00	500.00	1000.
—"Nurse with thermometer" cover					
❏ 596 [M]	Talk to Me	1958	75.00	150.00	300.00
❏ 603 [M]	Mister Little Willie John	1958	62.50	125.00	250.00
❏ 691 [M]	Little Willie John In Action	1960	62.50	125.00	250.00
❏ 739 [M]	Sure Things	1961	37.50	75.00	150.00
❏ 767 [M]	The Sweet, the Hot, the Teenage Beat	1961	37.50	75.00	150.00
❏ 802 [M]	Come On and Join Little Willie John	1962	30.00	60.00	120.00
❏ 895 [M]	These Are My Favorite Songs	1964	25.00	50.00	100.00
❏ 949 [M]	Little Willie Sings All Originals	1966	25.00	50.00	100.00
❏ KS-949 [S]	Little Willie Sings All Originals	1966	37.50	75.00	150.00
❏ KS-1081	Free at Last	1970	10.00	20.00	40.00

JOHN, ROBERT

COLUMBIA

Number	Title (A Side/B Side)	Yr	VG	VG+	NM
❏ CS 9687	If You Don't Want My Love	1968	5.00	10.00	20.00

EMI AMERICA

Number	Title (A Side/B Side)	Yr	VG	VG+	NM
❏ SW-17007	Robert John	1979	2.50	5.00	10.00
❏ SW-17027	Back on the Street	1980	2.50	5.00	10.00

Number	Title (A Side/B Side)	Yr	VG	VG+	NM
HARMONY					
❏ KH 31353	On the Way Up	1972	3.00	6.00	12.00
JOHN'S CHILDREN					
WHITE WHALE					
❏ WWS 7128	Orgasm	1970	50.00	100.00	200.00
JOHNNIE AND JACK					
DECCA					
❏ DL 4308 [M]	Smiles and Tears	1962	5.00	10.00	20.00
❏ DL 74308 [S]	Smiles and Tears	1962	6.25	12.50	25.00
RCA CAMDEN					
❏ CAL-747 [M]	Johnny & Jack Sing "Poison Love" and Other Country Favorites	1963	6.25	12.50	25.00
❏ CAS-747 [R]	Johnny & Jack Sing "Poison Love" and Other Country Favorites	1963	3.00	6.00	12.00
❏ CAL-822 [M]	Sincerely	1964	6.25	12.50	25.00
❏ CAS-822 [R]	Sincerely	1964	3.00	6.00	12.00
RCA VICTOR					
❏ LPM-1587 [M]	The Tennessee Mountain Boys	1957	10.00	20.00	40.00
❏ LPM-2017 [M]	Hits by Johnnie & Jack	1959	7.50	15.00	30.00
❏ LSP-2017 [R]	Hits by Johnnie & Jack	1959	5.00	10.00	20.00
❏ VPM-6022 [(2)]	All the Best of Johnnie & Jack	1970	6.25	12.50	25.00
JOHNNY AND THE BLUE BEATS					
WINSOR					
❏ 1001	Smile	196?	10.00	20.00	40.00
JOHNNY AND THE HURRICANES					
ATILA					
❏ 1030 [M]	Live at the Star-Club	1964	75.00	150.00	300.00
BIG TOP					
❏ 13-1302 [M]	The Big Sound of Johnny and the Hurricanes	1960	62.50	125.00	250.00
❏ ST 13-1302 [S]	The Big Sound of Johnny and the Hurricanes	1960	75.00	150.00	300.00
WARWICK					
❏ W-2007 [M]	Johnny and the Hurricanes	1959	37.50	75.00	150.00
❏ W-2007ST [S]	Johnny and the Hurricanes	1959	75.00	150.00	300.00
❏ W-2010 [M]	Stormsville	1960	37.50	75.00	150.00
❏ W-2010ST [S]	Stormsville	1960	62.50	125.00	250.00
JOHNSON, BETTY					
ATLANTIC					
❏ 8017 [M]	Betty Johnson	1958	12.50	25.00	50.00
❏ 8027 [M]	The Song You Heard When You Fell in Love	1959	12.50	25.00	50.00
—Black label					
❏ 8027 [M]	The Song You Heard When You Fell in Love	1960	5.00	10.00	20.00
—White "fan" logo on right					
❏ SD 8027 [S]	The Song You Heard When You Fell in Love	1959	20.00	40.00	80.00
—Green label					
❏ SD 8027 [S]	The Song You Heard When You Fell in Love	1960	6.25	12.50	25.00
—White "fan" logo on right					
JOHNSON, BLIND WILLIE					
FOLKWAYS					
❏ FG-3585 [M]	Blind Willie Johnson: His Story	1957	25.00	50.00	100.00
RBF					
❏ 10 [M]	Blind Willie Johnson 1927-1930	1965	17.50	35.00	70.00
JOHNSON, BOB, AND THE LONESOME TRAVELERS					
PARKWAY					
❏ P-7017 [M]	12 Shades of Bluegrass	1962	12.50	25.00	50.00
JOHNSON, BUBBER					
KING					
❏ 569 [M]	Come Home	1957	50.00	100.00	200.00
❏ 624 [M]	Bubber Johnson Sings Sweet Love Songs	1959	37.50	75.00	150.00
JOHNSON, BUDD					
ARGO					
❏ LP-721 [M]	French Cookin'	1963	6.25	12.50	25.00
❏ LPS-721 [S]	French Cookin'	1963	7.50	15.00	30.00
❏ LP-736 [M]	Ya! Ya!	1964	6.25	12.50	25.00
❏ LPS-736 [S]	Ya! Ya!	1964	7.50	15.00	30.00
❏ LP-748 [M]	Off the Wall	1965	6.25	12.50	25.00
❏ LPS-748 [S]	Off the Wall	1965	7.50	15.00	30.00
FELSTED					
❏ SJA-2007 [S]	Blues A La Mode	1959	20.00	40.00	80.00
❏ FAJ-7007 [M]	Blues A La Mode	1959	15.00	30.00	60.00
RIVERSIDE					
❏ RLP-343 [M]	Budd Johnson and the Four Brass Giants	1960	10.00	20.00	40.00
❏ RS-9343 [S]	Budd Johnson and the Four Brass Giants	1960	12.50	25.00	50.00
SWINGVILLE					
❏ SVLP-2015 [M]	Let's Swing	1961	12.50	25.00	50.00
—Purple label					
❏ SVLP-2015 [M]	Let's Swing	1965	6.25	12.50	25.00
—Blue label, trident logo at right					
JOHNSON, BUDDY					
MERCURY					
❏ MG-20209 [M]	Rock 'N' Roll	195?	20.00	40.00	80.00
❏ MG-20322 [M]	Walkin'	195?	20.00	40.00	80.00
❏ MG-20330 [M]	Buddy Johnson Wails	195?	20.00	40.00	80.00
❏ MG-20347 [M]	Swing Me	195?	20.00	40.00	80.00
❏ SR-60072 [S]	Buddy Johnson Wails	195?	25.00	50.00	100.00
WING					
❏ MGW-12005 [M]	Rock 'N' Roll	1956	37.50	75.00	150.00
❏ MGW-12111 [M]	Rock 'n' Roll Stage Show	1963	10.00	20.00	40.00
JOHNSON, BUDDY & ELLA					
MERCURY					
❏ MG-20347 [M]	Swing Me	195?	20.00	40.00	80.00

Number	Title (A Side/B Side)	Yr	VG	VG+	NM
ROULETTE					
❏ R 25085 [M]	Go Ahead and Rock and Roll	1959	20.00	40.00	80.00
❏ SR 25085 [S]	Go Ahead and Rock and Roll	1959	30.00	60.00	120.00
JOHNSON, BUNK					
AMERICAN MUSIC					
❏ 638 [10]	Bunk Plays the Blues — The Spirituals	1951	15.00	30.00	60.00
❏ 644 [10]	Bunk Johnson Talking	1952	15.00	30.00	60.00
COLUMBIA					
❏ CL 520 [M]	Bunk Johnson and His Band	1953	12.50	25.00	50.00
—Maroon label, gold print					
❏ CL 520 [M]	Bunk Johnson and His Band	1955	10.00	20.00	40.00
—Red and black label with six "eye" logos					
❏ GL 520 [M]	Bunk Johnson and His Band	1952	15.00	30.00	60.00
—Black label, silver print					
❏ CL 829 [M]	Bunk Johnson	1955	10.00	20.00	40.00
—Red and black label with six "eye" logos					
COLUMBIA MASTERWORKS					
❏ ML 4802 [M]	The Last Testament of a Great New Orleans Jazzman	1950	20.00	40.00	80.00
COMMODORE					
❏ DL-30007 [M]	The Bunk Johnson Band	1952	12.50	25.00	50.00
GOOD TIME JAZZ					
❏ L-17 [10]	Bunk Johnson and the Yerba Buena Jazz Band	1953	12.50	25.00	50.00
❏ L-12048 [M]	Bunk Johnson and His Superior Jazz Band	1962	7.50	15.00	30.00
MAINSTREAM					
❏ 56039 [M]	Bunk Johnson — A Legend	1965	5.00	10.00	20.00
JOHNSON, BUNK, AND LU WATTERS					
GOOD TIME JAZZ					
❏ L-12024 [M]	Bunk and Lu	195?	10.00	20.00	40.00
JOHNSON, CANDY					
CANJO					
❏ LP-1001 [M]	The Candy Johnson Show	1964	10.00	20.00	40.00
❏ LP-1002 [M]	Bikini Beach	1964	10.00	20.00	40.00
JOHNSON, CHARLIE					
"X"					
❏ LVA-3026 [10]	Harlem in the Twenties, Vol. 2	1954	15.00	30.00	60.00
JOHNSON, DICK					
EMARCY					
❏ MG-36081 [M]	Music for Swinging Moderns	1956	20.00	40.00	80.00
RIVERSIDE					
❏ RLP 12-253 [M]	Most Likely...	1957	12.50	25.00	50.00
JOHNSON, J.J.					
BLUE NOTE					
❏ BLP-1505 [M]	The Eminent Jay Jay Johnson, Volume 1	1955	25.00	50.00	100.00
—Regular version, Lexington Ave. address on label					
❏ BLP-1505 [M]	The Eminent Jay Jay Johnson, Volume 1	1955	37.50	75.00	150.00
—"Deep groove" version (deep indentation under label on both sides)					
❏ BLP-1505 [M]	The Eminent Jay Jay Johnson, Volume 1	1963	6.25	12.50	25.00
—"New York, USA" address on label					
❏ BLP-1506 [M]	The Eminent Jay Jay Johnson, Volume 2	1955	25.00	50.00	100.00
—Regular version, Lexington Ave. address on label					
❏ BLP-1506 [M]	The Eminent Jay Jay Johnson, Volume 2	1955	37.50	75.00	150.00
—"Deep groove" version (deep indentation under label on both sides)					
❏ BLP-1506 [M]	The Eminent Jay Jay Johnson, Volume 2	1963	6.25	12.50	25.00
—"New York, USA" address on label					
❏ BLP-5028 [10]	Jay Jay Johnson All Stars	1953	75.00	150.00	300.00
❏ BLP-5057 [10]	Jay Jay Johnson, Volume 2	1955	75.00	150.00	300.00
❏ BLP-5070 [10]	Jay Jay Johnson, Volume 3	1955	75.00	150.00	300.00
COLUMBIA					
❏ CL 935 [M]	"J" Is for Jazz	1956	12.50	25.00	50.00
—Red and black label with six "eye" logos					
❏ CL 1030 [M]	First Place	1957	12.50	25.00	50.00
—Red and black label with six "eye" logos					
❏ CL 1084 [M]	Dial J.J. 5	1957	12.50	25.00	50.00
—Red and black label with six "eye" logos					
❏ CL 1161 [M]	J.J. In Person	1958	12.50	25.00	50.00
—Red and black label with six "eye" logos					
❏ CL 1303 [M]	Blue Trombone	1959	10.00	20.00	40.00
—Red and black label with six "eye" logos					
❏ CL 1383 [M]	Really Livin'	1959	10.00	20.00	40.00
—Red and black label with six "eye" logos					
❏ CL 1547 [M]	Trombones and Voices	1960	7.50	15.00	30.00
—Red and black label with six "eye" logos					
❏ CL 1606 [M]	J.J. Inc	1961	7.50	15.00	30.00
—Red and black label with six "eye" logos					
❏ CL 1737 [M]	A Touch of Satin	1962	10.00	20.00	40.00
—Red and black label with six "eye" logos					
❏ CS 8009 [S]	J.J. In Person	1959	10.00	20.00	40.00
—Red and black label with six "eye" logos					
❏ CS 8109 [S]	Blue Trombone	1959	12.50	25.00	50.00
—Red and black label with six "eye" logos					
❏ CS 8178 [S]	Really Livin'	1959	12.50	25.00	50.00
—Red and black label with six "eye" logos					
❏ CS 8347 [S]	Trombones and Voices	1960	10.00	20.00	40.00
—Red and black label with six "eye" logos					
❏ CS 8406 [S]	J.J. Inc	1961	10.00	20.00	40.00
—Red and black label with six "eye" logos					
❏ CS 8537 [S]	A Touch of Satin	1962	12.50	25.00	50.00
—Red and black label with six "eye" logos					
❏ CS 8537 [S]	A Touch of Satin	1963	5.00	10.00	20.00
—Red label with "360 Sound Stereo" in black or white at bottom					
IMPULSE!					
❏ A-68 [M]	Proof Positive	1965	6.25	12.50	25.00
❏ AS-68 [S]	Proof Positive	1965	7.50	15.00	30.00

Number	Title (A Side/B Side)	Yr	VG	VG+	NM
MOSAIC					
❑ MQ11-169 [(11)]	The Complete Columbia J.J. Johnson Small Group Sessions	199?	50.00	100.00	200.00
RCA VICTOR					
❑ LPM-3350 [M]	J.J.!	1965	5.00	10.00	20.00
❑ LSP-3350 [S]	J.J.!	1965	6.25	12.50	25.00
❑ LPM-3458 [M]	Goodies	1965	5.00	10.00	20.00
❑ LSP-3458 [S]	Goodies	1965	6.25	12.50	25.00
❑ LPM-3544 [M]	Broadway Express	1966	5.00	10.00	20.00
❑ LSP-3544 [S]	Broadway Express	1966	6.25	12.50	25.00
❑ LPM-3833 [M]	The Total J.J. Johnson	1967	7.50	15.00	30.00
❑ LSP-3833 [S]	The Total J.J. Johnson	1967	5.00	10.00	20.00
REGENT					
❑ MG-6001 [M]	Jazz South Pacific	1956	12.50	25.00	50.00
VERVE					
❑ V-8530 [M]	J.J.'s Broadway	1963	5.00	10.00	20.00
❑ V6-8530 [S]	J.J.'s Broadway	1963	6.25	12.50	25.00

JOHNSON, J.J./BENNIE GREEN

Number	Title (A Side/B Side)	Yr	VG	VG+	NM
PRESTIGE					
❑ PRLP-123 [10]	Modern Jazz Trombones, Volume 2	1952	50.00	100.00	200.00

JOHNSON, J.J., AND KAI WINDING

Number	Title (A Side/B Side)	Yr	VG	VG+	NM
A&M					
❑ SP-3008	Israel	1968	5.00	10.00	20.00
❑ SP-3016	Betwixt and Between	1969	5.00	10.00	20.00
BETHLEHEM					
❑ BCP-6001 [M]	K + J.J. (East Coast Jazz/7)	1955	12.50	25.00	50.00
—Some copies of this album have the number "BCP 13" on the upper right corner of the front cover, with "BCP 6001" stickers on the back cover. As far as we can tell, this record was not issued with "BCP 13" on the label.					
COLUMBIA					
❑ CL 742 [M]	Trombone for Two	1956	12.50	25.00	50.00
—Red label with "360 Sound Stereo" in black or white at bottom					
❑ CL 742 [M]	Trombone for Two	1963	5.00	10.00	20.00
—Red label with "Guaranteed High Fidelity" or "360 Sound Mono" at bottom					
❑ CL 892 [M]	J.J. Johnson, Kai Winding + 6	1963	5.00	10.00	20.00
—Red label with "Guaranteed High Fidelity" or "360 Sound Mono" at bottom					
❑ CL 892 [M]	J.J. Johnson, Kai Winding + 6	1956	12.50	25.00	50.00
—Red and black "6-eye" label					
❑ CL 973 [M]	Jay and Kai	1957	12.50	25.00	50.00
—Red and black label with six "eye" logos					
❑ CL 973 [M]	Jay and Kai	1963	5.00	10.00	20.00
—Red label with "Guaranteed High Fidelity" or "360 Sound Mono" at bottom					
❑ CL 2573 [10]	Kai + J.J.	1955	20.00	40.00	80.00
IMPULSE!					
❑ A-1 [M]	The Great Kai & J.J.	1961	7.50	15.00	30.00
❑ AS-1 [S]	The Great Kai & J.J.	1961	10.00	20.00	40.00
PRESTIGE					
❑ PRLP-109 [10]	Modern Jazz Trombones	1951	50.00	100.00	200.00
❑ PRLP-195 [10]	Jay and Kai	1954	50.00	100.00	200.00
❑ PRLP-7253 [M]	Looking Back	1963	12.50	25.00	50.00
❑ PRST-7253 [R]	Looking Back	1963	7.50	15.00	30.00
SAVOY					
❑ MG-12010 [M]	Jay and Kai	1955	20.00	40.00	80.00
❑ MG-12106 [M]	J.J. Johnson's Jazz Quintets	1957	20.00	40.00	80.00
❑ MG-15038 [10]	Jay and Kai	1954	30.00	60.00	120.00
❑ MG-15048 [10]	Jay and Kai, Volume 2	1955	25.00	50.00	100.00
❑ MG-15049 [10]	Jay and Kai, Volume 3	1955	25.00	50.00	100.00
VIK					
❑ LXA-1040 [M]	An Afternoon at Birdland	1956	20.00	40.00	80.00

JOHNSON, J.J.; KAI WINDING; BENNIE GREEN

Number	Title (A Side/B Side)	Yr	VG	VG+	NM
DEBUT					
❑ DLP-5 [10]	Jazz Workshop, Volume 1	1953	50.00	100.00	200.00
❑ DLP-14 [10]	Jazz Workshop, Volume 2	1955	50.00	100.00	200.00
❑ DEB-126 [M]	Four Trombones	1958	25.00	50.00	100.00
FANTASY					
❑ 6005 [M]	Four Trombones	1963	7.50	15.00	30.00
—Black vinyl					
❑ 6005 [M]	Four Trombones	1963	12.50	25.00	50.00
—Red vinyl					
❑ 86005 [R]	Four Trombones	1963	5.00	10.00	20.00
—Black vinyl					
❑ 86005 [R]	Four Trombones	1963	10.00	20.00	40.00
—Blue vinyl					
PRESTIGE					
❑ PRLP-7023 [M]	Trombones by Three	1956	20.00	40.00	80.00
❑ PRLP-7030 [M]	J.J. Johnson, Kai Winding, Bennie Green	1956	20.00	40.00	80.00

JOHNSON, JAMES P.

Number	Title (A Side/B Side)	Yr	VG	VG+	NM
BLUE NOTE					
❑ BLP-7011 [10]	Stomps, Rags and Blues	1951	75.00	150.00	300.00
❑ BLP-7012 [10]	Jazz Band Ball	1951	75.00	150.00	300.00
COLUMBIA					
❑ CL 1780 [M]	Father of the Stride Piano	1961	6.25	12.50	25.00
—Red and black label with six "eye" logos					
DECCA					
❑ DL 5190 [10]	The Daddy of the Piano	1950	25.00	50.00	100.00
❑ DL 5228 [10]	James P. Johnson Plays Fats Waller Favorites	1951	25.00	50.00	100.00
FOLKWAYS					
❑ FJ-2816	Striding in Dixieland	196?	5.00	10.00	20.00
❑ FJ-2842 [M]	Yamekraw	1962	5.00	10.00	20.00
❑ FJ-2850	The Original James P. Johnson	196?	5.00	10.00	20.00
RIVERSIDE					
❑ RLP 12-105 [M]	Rediscovered Early Solos	1955	15.00	30.00	60.00
—White label, blue print					
❑ RLP 12-105 [M]	Rediscovered Early Solos	1959	10.00	20.00	40.00
—Blue label, microphone logo at top					

Number	Title (A Side/B Side)	Yr	VG	VG+	NM
❑ RLP 12-151 [M]	Backwater Blues	1955	15.00	30.00	60.00
—White label, blue print					
❑ RLP 12-151 [M]	Backwater Blues	1959	10.00	20.00	40.00
—Blue label, microphone logo at top					
❑ RLP-1011 [10]	Rent Party	1953	30.00	60.00	120.00
❑ RLP-1046 [10]	Early Harlem Piano, Vol. 2	1954	30.00	60.00	120.00
❑ RLP-1056 [10]	Harlem Rent Party	1955	25.00	50.00	100.00
STINSON					
❑ SLP-21 [10]	New York Jazz	1950	30.00	60.00	120.00
❑ SLP-21 [M]	New York Jazz	195?	12.50	25.00	50.00

JOHNSON, KEITH

Number	Title (A Side/B Side)	Yr	VG	VG+	NM
REFERENCE RECORDINGS					
❑ RR-7	Prof. Johnson's Astounding Sound Show	198?	5.00	10.00	20.00
—Plays at 45 rpm					

JOHNSON, LAURIE

Number	Title (A Side/B Side)	Yr	VG	VG+	NM
COLPIX					
❑ CP 471 [M]	England's New Big Band	1964	5.00	10.00	20.00

JOHNSON, LONNIE

Number	Title (A Side/B Side)	Yr	VG	VG+	NM
BLUESVILLE					
❑ BVLP-1007 [M]	Blues by Lonnie	1960	50.00	100.00	200.00
—Blue label, silver print					
❑ BVLP-1007 [M]	Blues by Lonnie	1964	15.00	30.00	60.00
—Blue label with trident logo at right					
❑ BVLP-1011 [M]	Blues and Ballads	1960	50.00	100.00	200.00
—Blue label, silver print					
❑ BVLP-1011 [M]	Blues and Ballads	1964	15.00	30.00	60.00
—Blue label with trident logo at right					
❑ BVLP-1024 [M]	Losing Game	1961	50.00	100.00	200.00
—Blue label, silver print					
❑ BVLP-1024 [M]	Losing Game	1964	15.00	30.00	60.00
—Blue label with trident logo at right					
❑ BVLP-1062 [M]	Another Night to Cry	1963	50.00	100.00	200.00
—Blue label, silver print					
❑ BVLP-1062 [M]	Another Night to Cry	1964	15.00	30.00	60.00
—Blue label with trident logo at right					
COLUMBIA					
❑ C 46221	Steppin' On the Blues	1990	5.00	10.00	20.00
FANTASY					
❑ OBC-502	Blues by Lonnie	198?	3.00	6.00	12.00
❑ OBC-531	Blues and Ballads	1990	3.00	6.00	12.00
KING					
❑ 395-520 [M]	Lonesome Road	1958	750.00	1375.	2000.
❑ 958 [M]	Lonnie Johnson 24 Twelve-Bar Blues	1966	15.00	30.00	60.00
❑ KS-958 [R]	Lonnie Johnson 24 Twelve-Bar Blues	1966	15.00	30.00	60.00
❑ KS-1083	Tomorrow Night	1970	6.25	12.50	25.00
PRESTIGE					
❑ PRST-7724	The Blues of Lonnie Johnson	1970	5.00	10.00	20.00

JOHNSON, LONNIE, AND VICTORIA SPIVEY

Number	Title (A Side/B Side)	Yr	VG	VG+	NM
BLUESVILLE					
❑ BVLP-1044 [M]	Idle Hours	1962	37.50	75.00	150.00
—Blue label, silver print					
❑ BVLP-1044 [M]	Idle Hours	1964	12.50	25.00	50.00
—Blue label with trident logo at right					
❑ BVLP-1054 [M]	Woman Blues	1962	37.50	75.00	150.00
—Blue label, silver print					
❑ BVLP-1054 [M]	Woman Blues	1964	12.50	25.00	50.00
—Blue label with trident logo at right					
FANTASY					
❑ OBC-518	Idle Hours	198?	3.00	6.00	12.00

JOHNSON, MARV

Number	Title (A Side/B Side)	Yr	VG	VG+	NM
UNITED ARTISTS					
❑ UAL 3081 [M]	Marvelous Marv Johnson	1960	37.50	75.00	150.00
❑ UAL 3118 [M]	More Marv Johnson	1961	37.50	75.00	150.00
❑ UAL 3187 [M]	I Believe	1962	37.50	75.00	150.00
❑ UAS 6081 [S]	Marvelous Marv Johnson	1960	50.00	100.00	200.00
❑ UAS 6118 [S]	More Marv Johnson	1961	50.00	100.00	200.00
❑ UAS 6187 [S]	I Believe	1962	50.00	100.00	200.00

JOHNSON, OSIE

Number	Title (A Side/B Side)	Yr	VG	VG+	NM
BETHLEHEM					
❑ BCP-66 [M]	The Happy Jazz of Osie Johnson	1957	12.50	25.00	50.00
PERIOD					
❑ SPL-1108 [10]	Osie's Oasis	1955	20.00	40.00	80.00
❑ SPL-1112 [10]	Johnson's Whacks	1955	20.00	40.00	80.00
RCA VICTOR					
❑ LPM-1369 [M]	A Bit of the Blues	1957	10.00	20.00	40.00

JOHNSON, PETE

Number	Title (A Side/B Side)	Yr	VG	VG+	NM
BLUE NOTE					
❑ BLP-7019 [10]	Boogie Woogie Blues and Skiffle	1952	75.00	150.00	300.00
BRUNSWICK					
❑ BL 58041 [10]	Boogie Woogie Mood	1953	20.00	40.00	80.00
MOSAIC					
❑ M-119	The Pete Johnson/Earl Hines/Teddy Bunn Blue Note Sessions	199?	5.00	10.00	20.00
RIVERSIDE					
❑ RLP-1056 [10]	Jumpin' with Pete Johnson	1955	20.00	40.00	80.00
SAVOY					
❑ MG-14018 [M]	Pete's Blues	1958	30.00	60.00	120.00

JOHNSON, PETE/HADDA BROOKS

Number	Title (A Side/B Side)	Yr	VG	VG+	NM
CROWN					
❑ CLP-5058 [M]	Boogie	195?	5.00	10.00	20.00

JOHNSON, PLAS

Number	Title (A Side/B Side)	Yr	VG	VG+	NM
CAPITOL					
❑ ST 1281 [S]	This Must Be the Plas!	1960	7.50	15.00	30.00

Number	Title (A Side/B Side)	Yr	VG	VG+	NM
❑ T 1281 [M]	This Must Be the Plas!	1960	6.25	12.50	25.00
❑ ST 1503 [S]	Mood for the Blues	1961	7.50	15.00	30.00
❑ T 1503 [M]	Mood for the Blues	1961	6.25	12.50	25.00

TAMPA

❑ TP-24 [M]	Bop Me, Daddy	1957	25.00	50.00	100.00
—Colored vinyl					
❑ TP-24 [M]	Bop Me, Daddy	1958	12.50	25.00	50.00
—Black vinyl					

JOHNSON, ROBERT
COLUMBIA

❑ CL 1654 [M]	King of the Delta Blues Singers	1961	125.00	250.00	500.00
—Red and black label with six "eye" logos					
❑ CL 1654 [M]	King of the Delta Blues Singers	1963	12.50	25.00	50.00
—"Guaranteed High Fidelity" label					
❑ CL 1654 [M]	King of the Delta Blues Singers	1965	6.25	12.50	25.00
—"360 Sound Mono" label					
❑ CL 1654 [M]	King of the Delta Blues Singers	1970	3.00	6.00	12.00
—Orange label with "Columbia" circling the edge					
❑ CL 1654 [M]	King of the Delta Blues Singers	1998	2.50	5.00	10.00
—Red label, "Columbia" in white at top, "Sony Music" under side numbers					
❑ CL 1654 [M]	King of the Delta Blues Singers	2001	3.75	7.50	15.00
—Reissue on 180-gram vinyl (sealed copies have a sticker indicating this)					
❑ C 30034 [M]	King of the Delta Blues Singers, Volume 2	1970	5.00	10.00	20.00
❑ PC 30034 [M]	King of the Delta Blues Singers, Volume 2	1979	2.50	5.00	10.00
❑ C3 46222 [(3)]	Robert Johnson — The Complete Recordings	1990	12.50	25.00	50.00

JOHNSON, RUDOLPH
BLACK JAZZ

❑ 4	Spring Rain	1971	6.25	12.50	25.00
❑ 11	Second Coming	1972	6.25	12.50	25.00

JOHNSON, SYL
TWINIGHT

❑ LPS-1002	Is It Because I'm Black?	1968	7.50	15.00	30.00

JOHNSON FAMILY SINGERS, THE
RCA VICTOR

❑ LPM-1128 [M]	Old Time Religion	1955	6.25	12.50	25.00

JOHNSTON, BRUCE
COLUMBIA

❑ CL 2057 [M]	Surfin' 'Round the World	1963	37.50	75.00	150.00
❑ CS 8857 [S]	Surfin' 'Round the World	1963	75.00	150.00	300.00
❑ PC 34459	Going Public	1976	3.75	7.50	15.00

DEL-FI

❑ DFLP-1228 [M]	Surfers' Pajama Party	1963	25.00	50.00	100.00
❑ DFST-1228 [S]	Surfers' Pajama Party	1963	50.00	100.00	200.00

JOHNSTON, COLONEL JUBILATION B., AND THE MYSTIC KNIGHTS BAND AND STREET SINGERS
COLUMBIA

❑ CL 2532 [M]	Moldy Goldies	1966	6.25	12.50	25.00
❑ CS 9332 [S]	Moldy Goldies	1966	7.50	15.00	30.00

JOLLY, PETE
AVA

❑ A-22 [M]	Little Bird	1963	5.00	10.00	20.00
❑ AS-22 [S]	Little Bird	1963	6.25	12.50	25.00
❑ A-39 [M]	Sweet September	1963	5.00	10.00	20.00
❑ AS-39 [S]	Sweet September	1963	6.25	12.50	25.00
❑ A-51 [M]	Hello Jolly	1964	5.00	10.00	20.00
❑ AS-51 [S]	Hello Jolly	1964	6.25	12.50	25.00

CHARLIE PARKER

❑ PLP-825 [M]	Pete Jolly Gasses Everybody	1962	5.00	10.00	20.00
❑ PLP-825S [S]	Pete Jolly Gasses Everybody	1962	6.25	12.50	25.00

COLUMBIA

❑ CL 2397 [M]	Too Much, Baby	1965	5.00	10.00	20.00
❑ CS 9197 [S]	Too Much, Baby	1965	6.25	12.50	25.00

METROJAZZ

❑ E-1014 [M]	Impossible	1958	8.75	17.50	35.00
❑ SE-1014 [S]	Impossible	1958	8.75	17.50	35.00

MGM

❑ E-4127 [M]	5 O'Clock Shadows	1963	5.00	10.00	20.00
❑ SE-4127 [S]	5 O'Clock Shadows	1963	6.25	12.50	25.00

RCA VICTOR

❑ LPM-1105 [M]	Jolly Jumps In	1955	12.50	25.00	50.00
❑ LPM-1125 [M]	Duo, Trio, Quartet	1955	12.50	25.00	50.00
❑ LPM-1367 [M]	When Lights Are Low	1957	12.50	25.00	50.00

STEREO FIDELITY

❑ SFS-11000 [S]	Continental Jazz	1960	6.25	12.50	25.00

JOLSON, AL
DECCA

❑ DXA 169 [(2)M]	The Best of Jolson	196?	6.25	12.50	25.00
❑ DLP 5006 [10]	Jolson Sings Again	1949	7.50	15.00	30.00
❑ DLP 5026 [10]	Al Jolson In Songs He Made Famous	1949	7.50	15.00	30.00
❑ DLP 5029 [10]	Souvenir Album, Vol. II	1949	7.50	15.00	30.00
❑ DLP 5030 [10]	Al Jolson, Vol. III	1949	7.50	15.00	30.00
❑ DLP 5031 [10]	Souvenir Album, Vol. IV	1949	7.50	15.00	30.00
❑ DL 5308 [10]	Stephen Foster Songs	1950	25.00	50.00	100.00
❑ DL 5314 [10]	Souvenir Album, Vol. V	1951	7.50	15.00	30.00
❑ DL 5315 [10]	Souvenir Album, Vol. VI	1951	7.50	15.00	30.00
❑ DXSA 7169 [(2)R]	The Best of Jolson	196?	3.75	7.50	15.00
❑ DL 9034 [M]	You Made Me Love You	1957	6.25	12.50	25.00
—Black label, silver print					
❑ DL 9034 [M]	You Made Me Love You	196?	3.75	7.50	15.00
—Black label with color bars					
❑ DL 9035 [M]	Rock-a-Bye Your Baby	1957	6.25	12.50	25.00
—Black label, silver print					
❑ DL 9035 [M]	Rock-a-Bye Your Baby	196?	3.75	7.50	15.00
—Black label with color bars					

Number	Title (A Side/B Side)	Yr	VG	VG+	NM
❑ DL 9036 [M]	Rainbow 'Round My Shoulder	1957	6.25	12.50	25.00
—Black label, silver print					
❑ DL 9036 [M]	Rainbow 'Round My Shoulder	196?	3.75	7.50	15.00
—Black label with color bars					
❑ DL 9037 [M]	You Ain't Heard Nothin' Yet!	1957	3.75	7.50	15.00
—Black label with color bars					
❑ DL 9037 [M]	You Ain't Heard Nothin' Yet!	1957	6.25	12.50	25.00
—Black label, silver print					
❑ DL 9038 [M]	Memories	1957	3.75	7.50	15.00
—Black label with color bars					
❑ DL 9038 [M]	Memories	1957	6.25	12.50	25.00
—Black label, silver print					
❑ DL 9050 [M]	Among My Souvenirs	1957	6.25	12.50	25.00
—Black label, silver print					
❑ DL 9050 [M]	Among My Souvenirs	196?	3.75	7.50	15.00
—Black label with color bars					
❑ DL 9063 [M]	The Immortal Al Jolson	1958	6.25	12.50	25.00
—Maroon label, silver print					
❑ DL 9063 [M]	The Immortal Al Jolson	196?	3.75	7.50	15.00
—Black label with color bars					
❑ DL 9070 [M]	Overseas	1959	7.50	15.00	30.00
—Black label, silver print					
❑ DL 9070 [M]	Overseas	196?	3.75	7.50	15.00
—Black label with color bars					
❑ DL 9074 [M]	The World's Greatest Entertainer	1959	6.25	12.50	25.00
—Black label, silver print					
❑ DL 9074 [M]	The World's Greatest Entertainer	196?	3.75	7.50	15.00
—Black label with color bars					
❑ DL 9095 [M]	Al Jolson with Oscar Levant at the Piano	1961	7.50	15.00	30.00
❑ DL 9099 [M]	Jolie	196?	6.25	12.50	25.00
—Black label, silver print					
❑ DL 79034 [R]	You Made Me Love You	196?	3.00	6.00	12.00
❑ DL 79035 [R]	Rock-a-Bye Your Baby	196?	3.00	6.00	12.00
❑ DL 79036 [R]	Rainbow 'Round My Shoulder	196?	3.00	6.00	12.00
❑ DL 79037 [R]	You Ain't Heard Nothin' Yet!	196?	3.00	6.00	12.00
❑ DL 79038 [R]	Memories	196?	3.00	6.00	12.00
❑ DL 79050 [R]	Among My Souvenirs	196?	3.00	6.00	12.00
❑ DL 79070 [R]	Overseas	196?	3.00	6.00	12.00
❑ DL 79074 [R]	The World's Greatest Entertainer	196?	3.00	6.00	12.00
❑ DL 79095 [R]	Al Jolson with Oscar Levant at the Piano	196?	3.00	6.00	12.00

MCA

❑ 2057	You Made Me Love You	197?	2.50	5.00	10.00
❑ 2058	Rock-a-Bye Your Baby	197?	2.50	5.00	10.00
❑ 2059	Rainbow 'Round My Shoulder	197?	2.50	5.00	10.00
❑ 2060	You Ain't Heard Nothin' Yet!	197?	2.50	5.00	10.00
❑ 2061	Memories	197?	2.50	5.00	10.00
❑ 2064	Among My Souvenirs	197?	2.50	5.00	10.00
❑ 2066	The Immortal Al Jolson	197?	2.50	5.00	10.00
❑ 2067	The World's Greatest Entertainer	197?	2.50	5.00	10.00
❑ 10002 [(2)]	The Best of Jolson	1973	3.00	6.00	12.00
❑ 27051	You Made Me Love You	198?	2.00	4.00	8.00
❑ 27052	Rock-a-Bye Your Baby	198?	2.00	4.00	8.00
❑ 27053	Rainbow 'Round My Shoulder	198?	2.00	4.00	8.00
❑ 27054	You Ain't Heard Nothin' Yet!	198?	2.00	4.00	8.00
❑ 27055	Memories	198?	2.00	4.00	8.00
❑ 27057	The Immortal Al Jolson	198?	2.00	4.00	8.00
❑ 27058	The World's Greatest Entertainer	198?	2.00	4.00	8.00

SUNBEAM

❑ 503	Steppin' Out	197?	2.50	5.00	10.00
❑ 505	California, Here I Come	197?	2.50	5.00	10.00

TOTEM

❑ 1006	Al Jolson On the Air, Volume 1	197?	2.50	5.00	10.00
❑ 1012	Al Jolson On the Air, Volume 2	197?	2.50	5.00	10.00
❑ 1019	Al Jolson On the Air, Volume 3	197?	2.50	5.00	10.00
❑ 1030	Al Jolson On the Air, Volume 4	197?	2.50	5.00	10.00
❑ 1040	Al Jolson On the Air, Volume 5	197?	2.50	5.00	10.00

JON AND ROBIN AND THE IN CROWD
ABNAK

❑ ABM-2068 [M]	Soul of a Boy and Girl	1967	5.00	10.00	20.00
❑ ABST-2068 [S]	Soul of a Boy and Girl	1967	5.00	10.00	20.00
❑ ABST-2070	Elastic Event	1968	5.00	10.00	20.00

JONES, ANN, AND HER AMERICAN SWEETHEARTS
AUDIO LAB

❑ AL-1521 [M]	Ann Jones and Her American Sweethearts	1959	37.50	75.00	150.00
❑ AL-1556 [M]	Hit and Run	1960	37.50	75.00	150.00

JONES, BOOGALOO JOE
PRESTIGE

❑ PRST-7557	Mind Bender	1968	5.00	10.00	20.00
❑ PRST-7617	My Fire! More of the Psychedelic Soul Jazz Guitar of Joe Jones	1968	5.00	10.00	20.00
❑ PRST-7697	Boogaloo Joe	1969	5.00	10.00	20.00
❑ PRST-7766	Right On Brother!	1970	5.00	10.00	20.00
❑ 10004	No Way!	1971	6.25	12.50	25.00
❑ 10035	What It Is	1971	7.50	15.00	30.00
❑ 10056	Snake Rhythm Rock	1972	7.50	15.00	30.00
❑ 10072	Black Whip	1973	7.50	15.00	30.00

JONES, BRIAN
ROLLING STONES

❑ COC 49100	Brian Jones Presents the Pipes of Pan at Joujouka	1971	15.00	30.00	60.00

JONES, CARMELL
PACIFIC JAZZ

❑ PJ-29 [M]	The Remarkable Carmell Jones	1961	10.00	20.00	40.00
❑ ST-29 [S]	The Remarkable Carmell Jones	1961	12.50	25.00	50.00
❑ PJ-53 [M]	Business Meetin'	1962	10.00	20.00	40.00
❑ ST-53 [S]	Business Meetin'	1962	12.50	25.00	50.00
—Black vinyl					

Number	Title (A Side/B Side)	Yr	VG	VG+	NM
❑ ST-53 [S]	Business Meetin'	1962	20.00	40.00	80.00
—Colored vinyl					
PRESTIGE					
❑ PRLP-7401 [M]	Jay Hawk Talk	1965	7.50	15.00	30.00
❑ PRST-7401 [S]	Jay Hawk Talk	1965	10.00	20.00	40.00
❑ PRST-7669	Carmell Jones in Europe	1969	5.00	10.00	20.00

JONES, CURTIS
BLUESVILLE

Number	Title (A Side/B Side)	Yr	VG	VG+	NM
❑ BVLP-1022 [M]	Trouble Blues	1961	20.00	40.00	80.00
—Blue label, silver print					
❑ BVLP-1022 [M]	Trouble Blues	1964	6.25	12.50	25.00
—Blue label, trident logo at right					
DELMARK					
❑ DL-605 [M]	Lonesome Bedroom Blues	1963	10.00	20.00	40.00

JONES, DAVY
Also see THE MONKEES.
BELL

Number	Title (A Side/B Side)	Yr	VG	VG+	NM
❑ 6067	Davy Jones	1971	5.00	10.00	20.00
COLPIX					
❑ CP 493 [M]	David Jones	1965	6.25	12.50	25.00
❑ CPS 493 [S]	David Jones	1965	10.00	20.00	40.00
—This album charted in 1967 thanks to the singer's membership in The Monkees					

JONES, DEAN
VALIANT

Number	Title (A Side/B Side)	Yr	VG	VG+	NM
❑ VLM-407 [M]	Introducing Dean Jones	196?	5.00	10.00	20.00
❑ VLS-407 [S]	Introducing Dean Jones	196?	5.00	10.00	20.00

JONES, ELVIN
ABC IMPULSE!

Number	Title (A Side/B Side)	Yr	VG	VG+	NM
❑ AS-9160	Heavy Sounds	1968	5.00	10.00	20.00
ATLANTIC					
❑ 1443 [M]	And Then Again	1965	5.00	10.00	20.00
❑ SD 1443 [S]	And Then Again	1965	6.25	12.50	25.00
❑ 1485 [M]	Midnight Walk	1967	5.00	10.00	20.00
❑ SD 1485 [S]	Midnight Walk	1967	6.25	12.50	25.00
BLUE NOTE					
❑ BN-LA015-G [(2)]	Live at the Lighthouse	1973	5.00	10.00	20.00
❑ BN-LA506-H2 [(2)]	Prime Element	1976	5.00	10.00	20.00
❑ BST-84282	Puttin' It Together	1968	6.25	12.50	25.00
❑ BST-84305	The Ultimate Elvin Jones	1969	6.25	12.50	25.00
❑ BST-84331	Poly-Currents	1969	6.25	12.50	25.00
❑ BST-84361	Coalition	1970	6.25	12.50	25.00
❑ BST-84369	Genesis	1971	5.00	10.00	20.00
❑ BST-84414	Elvin Jones	1972	5.00	10.00	20.00
IMPULSE!					
❑ A-88 [M]	Dear John C.	1965	6.25	12.50	25.00
❑ AS-88 [S]	Dear John C.	1965	7.50	15.00	30.00
RIVERSIDE					
❑ RLP-409 [M]	Elvin!	1962	6.25	12.50	25.00
❑ RS-9409 [S]	Elvin!	1962	7.50	15.00	30.00

JONES, ELVIN, AND THE JIMMY GARRISON SEXTETTE
IMPULSE!

Number	Title (A Side/B Side)	Yr	VG	VG+	NM
❑ A-49 [M]	Illumination	1963	6.25	12.50	25.00
❑ AS-49 [S]	Illumination	1963	7.50	15.00	30.00

JONES, ETTA
KING

Number	Title (A Side/B Side)	Yr	VG	VG+	NM
❑ 544 [M]	The Jones Girl...Etta	1956	25.00	50.00	100.00
❑ 707 [M]	Etta Jones Sings	1960	12.50	25.00	50.00
PRESTIGE					
❑ PRLP-7186 [M]	Don't Go to Strangers	1960	10.00	20.00	40.00
—Yellow label					
❑ PRLP-7186 [M]	Don't Go to Strangers	1964	5.00	10.00	20.00
—Blue label, trident logo at right					
❑ PRST-7186 [S]	Don't Go to Strangers	1960	12.50	25.00	50.00
—Silver label					
❑ PRST-7186 [S]	Don't Go to Strangers	1964	6.25	12.50	25.00
—Blue label, trident logo at right					
❑ PRLP-7194 [M]	Something Nice	1961	12.50	25.00	50.00
—Yellow label					
❑ PRLP-7194 [M]	Something Nice	1964	6.25	12.50	25.00
—Blue label, trident logo at right					
❑ PRLP-7204 [M]	So Warm — Etta Jones and Strings	1961	10.00	20.00	40.00
—Yellow label					
❑ PRLP-7204 [M]	So Warm — Etta Jones and Strings	1964	5.00	10.00	20.00
—Blue label, trident logo at right					
❑ PRST-7204 [S]	So Warm — Etta Jones and Strings	1961	12.50	25.00	50.00
—Silver label					
❑ PRST-7204 [S]	So Warm — Etta Jones and Strings	1964	6.25	12.50	25.00
—Blue label, trident logo at right					
❑ PRLP-7214 [M]	From the Heart	1961	10.00	20.00	40.00
—Yellow label					
❑ PRLP-7214 [M]	From the Heart	1964	5.00	10.00	20.00
—Blue label, trident logo at right					
❑ PRST-7214 [S]	From the Heart	1961	12.50	25.00	50.00
—Silver label					
❑ PRST-7214 [S]	From the Heart	1964	6.25	12.50	25.00
—Blue label, trident logo at right					
❑ PRLP-7241 [M]	Lonely and Blue	1962	10.00	20.00	40.00
—Yellow label					
❑ PRLP-7241 [M]	Lonely and Blue	1964	5.00	10.00	20.00
—Blue label, trident logo at right					
❑ PRST-7241 [S]	Lonely and Blue	1962	12.50	25.00	50.00
—Silver label					
❑ PRST-7241 [S]	Lonely and Blue	1964	6.25	12.50	25.00
—Blue label, trident logo at right					
❑ PRLP-7272 [M]	Love Shout	1963	10.00	20.00	40.00
—Yellow label					

Number	Title (A Side/B Side)	Yr	VG	VG+	NM
❑ PRLP-7272 [M]	Love Shout	1964	5.00	10.00	20.00
—Blue label, trident logo at right					
❑ PRST-7272 [S]	Love Shout	1963	12.50	25.00	50.00
—Silver label					
❑ PRST-7272 [S]	Love Shout	1964	6.25	12.50	25.00
—Blue label, trident logo at right					
❑ PRLP-7284 [M]	Holler!	1963	10.00	20.00	40.00
—Yellow label					
❑ PRLP-7284 [M]	Holler!	1964	5.00	10.00	20.00
—Blue label, trident logo at right					
❑ PRST-7284 [S]	Holler!	1963	12.50	25.00	50.00
—Silver label					
❑ PRST-7284 [S]	Holler!	1964	6.25	12.50	25.00
—Blue label, trident logo at right					
❑ PRLP-7443 [M]	Etta Jones' Greatest Hits	1967	6.25	12.50	25.00
❑ PRST-7443 [S]	Etta Jones' Greatest Hits	1967	5.00	10.00	20.00
ROULETTE					
❑ R-25329 [M]	Etta Jones Sings	1965	5.00	10.00	20.00
❑ SR-25329 [S]	Etta Jones Sings	1965	6.25	12.50	25.00
WESTBOUND					
❑ 203	Etta Jones '75	1975	5.00	10.00	20.00

JONES, GEORGE
ACCORD

Number	Title (A Side/B Side)	Yr	VG	VG+	NM
❑ SN-7201	Tender Years	1982	2.50	5.00	10.00
ALLEGIANCE					
❑ AV-5015	Cold Cold Heart	198?	2.50	5.00	10.00
ARCHIVE OF FOLK AND JAZZ					
❑ 353	George Jones Sings Country Hits	198?	2.50	5.00	10.00
BULLDOG					
❑ BDL-2009	20 Golden Pieces of George Jones	198?	2.50	5.00	10.00
EPIC					
❑ KE 31321	George Jones	1972	3.75	7.50	15.00
—Yellow label					
❑ KE 31321	George Jones	1973	3.00	6.00	12.00
—Orange label					
❑ KE 31718	A Picture of Me (Without You)	1972	3.75	7.50	15.00
—Yellow label					
❑ KE 31718	A Picture of Me (Without You)	1973	3.00	6.00	12.00
—Orange label					
❑ KE 32412	Nothing Ever Hurt Me (Half As Bad As Losing You)	1973	3.75	7.50	15.00
❑ KE 32563	In a Gospel Way	1974	3.75	7.50	15.00
❑ KE 33083	The Grand Tour	1974	3.75	7.50	15.00
❑ KE 33352	The Best of George Jones	1975	3.75	7.50	15.00
❑ PE 33352	The Best of George Jones	198?	2.00	4.00	8.00
—Budget-line reissue					
❑ KE 33547	Memories of Us	1975	3.75	7.50	15.00
❑ BG 33749 [(2)]	George Jones/A Picture of Me (Without You)	1976	3.75	7.50	15.00
❑ KE 34034	The Battle	1976	3.00	6.00	12.00
❑ KE 34290	Alone Again	1976	3.00	6.00	12.00
❑ PE 34692	All-Time Greatest Hits Volume 1	1977	3.00	6.00	12.00
—Orange label					
❑ PE 34692	All-Time Greatest Hits Volume 1	198?	2.00	4.00	8.00
—Dark blue label					
❑ PE 34717	I Wanta Sing	1977	3.00	6.00	12.00
—Orange label					
❑ PE 34717	I Wanta Sing	198?	2.00	4.00	8.00
—Dark blue label					
❑ KE 35414	Bartender's Blues	1978	3.00	6.00	12.00
❑ PE 35414	Bartender's Blues	198?	2.00	4.00	8.00
—Budget-line reissue					
❑ JE 35544	My Very Special Guests	1979	3.00	6.00	12.00
❑ PE 35544	My Very Special Guests	198?	2.00	4.00	8.00
—Budget-line reissue					
❑ JE 36586	I Am What I Am	1980	3.00	6.00	12.00
❑ FE 37106	Still the Same Old Me	1981	2.50	5.00	10.00
❑ PE 37106	Still the Same Ole Me	198?	2.00	4.00	8.00
—Budget-line reissue					
❑ FE 37346	Encore	1981	2.50	5.00	10.00
❑ KE2 38323 [(2)]	Anniversary — 10 Years of Hits	1982	3.00	6.00	12.00
❑ FE 38406	Shine On	1983	2.50	5.00	10.00
❑ PE 38406	Shine On	198?	2.00	4.00	8.00
—Budget-line reissue					
❑ FE 38978	Jones Country	1983	2.50	5.00	10.00
❑ PE 38978	Jones Country	1985	2.00	4.00	8.00
—Budget-line reissue					
❑ FE 39002	You've Still Got a Place in My Heart	1984	2.50	5.00	10.00
❑ FE 39272	Ladies' Choice	1984	2.50	5.00	10.00
❑ FE 39546	By Request	1984	2.50	5.00	10.00
❑ FE 39598	Who's Gonna Fill Their Shoes	1985	2.50	5.00	10.00
❑ FE 39899	First Time Live!	1985	2.50	5.00	10.00
❑ FE 40413	Wine Colored Roses	1986	2.50	5.00	10.00
❑ FE 40776	Super Hits	1987	2.50	5.00	10.00
❑ FE 40781	Too Wild Too Long	1988	2.50	5.00	10.00
❑ FE 44078	One Woman Man	1989	2.50	5.00	10.00
HILLTOP					
❑ 6048	You're In My Heart	1968	3.75	7.50	15.00
❑ 6092	Heartaches by the Number	1969	3.75	7.50	15.00
❑ 6133	Oh Lonesome Me	1970	3.75	7.50	15.00
INTERMEDIA					
❑ QS-5044	I Can't Change Overnight	198?	2.50	5.00	10.00
❑ QS-5061	How I Love These Old Songs	198?	2.50	5.00	10.00
LIBERTY					
❑ LN-10167	Trouble in Mind	1981	2.00	4.00	8.00
❑ LN-10168	I Get Lonely in a Hurry	1981	2.00	4.00	8.00
MCA					
❑ 10398	And Along Came Jones	1991	5.00	10.00	20.00
—Vinyl issued only through Columbia House					

Number	Title (A Side/B Side)	Yr	VG	VG+	NM
MERCURY					
❑ ML-8014	Greatest Hits	1980	3.00	6.00	12.00
❑ MG-20282 [M]	Hillbilly Hit Parade, Volume 1	1957	37.50	75.00	150.00
—Five tracks by George Jones, one by George Jones with Benny Barnes, and four by other artists					
❑ MG-20306 [M]	14 Country Favorites	1957	37.50	75.00	150.00
❑ MG-20462 [M]	Country Church Time	1959	50.00	100.00	200.00
❑ MG-20477 [M]	George Jones Sings White Lightning and Other Favorites	1959	37.50	75.00	150.00
❑ MG-20596 [M]	George Jones Salutes Hank Williams	1960	20.00	40.00	80.00
❑ MG-20621 [M]	George Jones' Greatest Hits	1961	10.00	20.00	40.00
❑ MG-20624 [M]	Country and Western Hits	1961	10.00	20.00	40.00
❑ MG-20694 [M]	George Jones Sings From the Heart	1962	10.00	20.00	40.00
❑ MG-20793 [M]	The Novelty Side of George Jones	1963	20.00	40.00	80.00
❑ MG-20836 [M]	The Ballad Side of George Jones	1963	10.00	20.00	40.00
❑ MG-20906 [M]	Blue and Lonesome	1964	6.25	12.50	25.00
❑ MG-20937 [M]	Country and Western No. 1 Male Singer	1964	6.25	12.50	25.00
❑ MG-20990 [M]	Heartaches and Tears	1965	6.25	12.50	25.00
❑ MG-21029 [M]	Singing the Blues	1965	6.25	12.50	25.00
❑ MG-21048 [M]	George Jones' Greatest Hits Volume 2	1965	6.25	12.50	25.00
❑ SR-60257 [S]	George Jones Salutes Hank Williams	1960	25.00	50.00	100.00
❑ SR-60621 [P]	George Jones' Greatest Hits	1961	12.50	25.00	50.00
❑ SR-60624 [P]	Country and Western Hits	1961	12.50	25.00	50.00
❑ SR-60694 [S]	George Jones Sings From the Heart	1962	12.50	25.00	50.00
❑ SR-60793 [S]	The Novelty Side of George Jones	1963	25.00	50.00	100.00
❑ SR-60836 [S]	The Ballad Side of George Jones	1963	12.50	25.00	50.00
❑ SR-60906 [S]	Blue and Lonesome	1964	7.50	15.00	30.00
❑ SR-60937 [S]	Country and Western No. 1 Male Singer	1964	7.50	15.00	30.00
❑ SR-60990 [S]	Heartaches and Tears	1965	7.50	15.00	30.00
❑ SR-61029 [S]	Singing the Blues	1965	7.50	15.00	30.00
❑ SR-61048 [S]	George Jones' Greatest Hits Volume 2	1965	7.50	15.00	30.00
❑ 822646-1	George Jones Salutes Hank Williams	1985	2.50	5.00	10.00
❑ 826095-1	Rockin' the Country	1985	2.50	5.00	10.00
❑ 826248-1	Greatest Hits	1986	2.50	5.00	10.00
MUSICOR					
❑ MM-2046 [M]	Mr. Country and Western Music	1965	7.50	15.00	30.00
❑ MM-2060 [M]	New Country Hits	1965	7.50	15.00	30.00
❑ MM-2061 [M]	Old Brush Arbors	1966	7.50	15.00	30.00
❑ MM-2088 [M]	Love Bug	1966	7.50	15.00	30.00
❑ MM-2099 [M]	I'm a People	1966	6.25	12.50	25.00
❑ MM-2106 [M]	We Found Heaven Right Here on Earth	1966	6.25	12.50	25.00
❑ MM-2116 [M]	George Jones' Greatest Hits	1967	6.25	12.50	25.00
❑ MM-2119 [M]	Walk Through This World with Me	1967	7.50	15.00	30.00
❑ MM-2124 [M]	Cup of Loneliness	1967	7.50	15.00	30.00
❑ MM-2128 [M]	Hits by George	1967	7.50	15.00	30.00
❑ MS-3046 [S]	Mr. Country and Western Music	1965	10.00	20.00	40.00
❑ MS-3060 [S]	New Country Hits	1965	10.00	20.00	40.00
❑ MS-3061 [S]	Old Brush Arbors	1966	10.00	20.00	40.00
❑ MS-3088 [S]	Love Bug	1966	10.00	20.00	40.00
❑ MS-3099 [S]	I'm a People	1966	7.50	15.00	30.00
❑ MS-3106 [S]	We Found Heaven Right Here on Earth	1966	7.50	15.00	30.00
❑ MS-3116 [S]	George Jones' Greatest Hits	1967	6.25	12.50	25.00
❑ MS-3119 [S]	Walk Through This World with Me	1967	5.00	10.00	20.00
❑ MS-3124 [S]	Cup of Loneliness	1967	5.00	10.00	20.00
❑ MS-3128 [S]	Hits by George	1967	5.00	10.00	20.00
❑ MS-3149	The Songs of Dallas Frazier	1968	5.00	10.00	20.00
❑ MS-3158	If My Heart Had Windows	1968	5.00	10.00	20.00
❑ M2S-3159 [(2)]	The George Jones Story: The Musical Loves, Life and Sorrows of America's Great Country Star	1968	7.50	15.00	30.00
❑ M2S-3169 [(2)]	My Country	1969	7.50	15.00	30.00
❑ MS-3177	I'll Share My World with You	1969	5.00	10.00	20.00
❑ MS-3181	Where Grass Won't Grow	1969	5.00	10.00	20.00
❑ MS-3188	Will You Visit Me on Sunday?	1970	5.00	10.00	20.00
❑ MS-3191	The Best of George Jones	1970	5.00	10.00	20.00
❑ MS-3194	George Jones With Love	1971	5.00	10.00	20.00
❑ MS-3203	The Best of Sacred Music	1971	5.00	10.00	20.00
❑ MS-3204	The Great Songs of Leon Payne	1971	5.00	10.00	20.00
NASHVILLE					
❑ 2076	Seasons of My Heart	1970	3.75	7.50	15.00
PAIR					
❑ PDL2-1074 [(2)]	The Best of George Jones	1986	3.00	6.00	12.00
❑ PDL2-1080 [(2)]	Country, By George!	1986	3.00	6.00	12.00
POWER PAK					
❑ 271	The Crown Prince of Country Music	197?	2.50	5.00	10.00
QUICKSILVER					
❑ QS-1011	Frozen in Time	198?	2.50	5.00	10.00
❑ QS-1012	If My Heart Had Windows	198?	2.50	5.00	10.00
RCA CAMDEN					
❑ ACL1-0377	The Race Is On	1973	3.00	6.00	12.00
❑ CAS-2591	Flowers for Mama	1973	3.00	6.00	12.00
RCA VICTOR					
❑ APL1-0316	Best of George Jones Vol. II	1973	3.75	7.50	15.00
❑ APL1-0486	You Gotta Be My Baby	1974	3.75	7.50	15.00
❑ APL1-0612	His Songs	1974	3.75	7.50	15.00
❑ APL1-0815	I Can Love You Enough	1974	3.75	7.50	15.00
❑ APL1-1113	The Best of the Best	1975	3.75	7.50	15.00
❑ LSP-4672	First in the Hearts of Country Music Lovers	1972	3.75	7.50	15.00
❑ LSP-4716	Best of George Jones Vol. I	1972	3.75	7.50	15.00
❑ LSP-4725	Poor Man's Riches	1972	3.75	7.50	15.00
❑ LSP-4726	I Made Leaving (Easy for You)	1972	3.75	7.50	15.00
❑ LSP-4727	Country Singer	1972	3.75	7.50	15.00
❑ LSP-4733	George Jones And Friends	1972	3.75	7.50	15.00
❑ LSP-4785	Four-O Thirty-Three	1972	3.75	7.50	15.00
❑ LSP-4786	Tender Years	1972	3.75	7.50	15.00
❑ LSP-4787	Take Me	1972	3.75	7.50	15.00
❑ LSP-4801	Wrapped Around Her Finger	1973	3.75	7.50	15.00
❑ LSP-4847	I Can Still See Him	1973	3.75	7.50	15.00
ROUNDER					
❑ SS-15	Burn the Honky Tonk Down	198?	2.50	5.00	10.00
❑ SS-17	Heartaches & Hangovers	198?	2.50	5.00	10.00

Number	Title (A Side/B Side)	Yr	VG	VG+	NM
SEARS					
❑ SPS-125	Maybe, Little Baby	196?	5.00	10.00	20.00
STARDAY					
❑ SLP 101 [M]	The Grand Ole Opry's New Star	1958	300.00	600.00	1200.
❑ SLP 125 [M]	The Crown Prince of Country Music	1960	40.00	80.00	160.00
❑ SLP 150 [M]	George Jones Sings His Greatest Hits	1962	12.50	25.00	50.00
❑ SLP 151 [M]	The Fabulous Country Music Sound of George Jones	1962	12.50	25.00	50.00
❑ SLP 335 [M]	George Jones	1965	10.00	20.00	40.00
❑ SLP 344 [M]	Long Live King George	1965	10.00	20.00	40.00
❑ SLP 366	The George Jones Story Bonus Photo	1966	5.00	10.00	20.00
❑ SLP 366 [(2)M]	The George Jones Story	1966	7.50	15.00	30.00
❑ SLP 401	The George Jones Song Book & Picture Album	1967	12.50	25.00	50.00
—With book					
❑ SLP 401 [M]	The George Jones Song Book & Picture Album	1967	7.50	15.00	30.00
—Without book					
❑ SLP 440 [M]	The Golden Country Hits of George Jones	1969	7.50	15.00	30.00
❑ 3021	16 Greatest Hits	197?	2.50	5.00	10.00
❑ DT-90080 [R]	George Jones Sings His Greatest Hits	1964	20.00	40.00	80.00
—Capitol Record Club edition					
UNITED ARTISTS					
❑ UXS-85 [(2)]	George Jones Superpak	1972	5.00	10.00	20.00
❑ UAL-3193 [M]	The New Favorites of George Jones	1962	7.50	15.00	30.00
❑ UAL-3218 [M]	George Jones Sings the Hits of His Country Cousins	1962	7.50	15.00	30.00
❑ UAL-3219 [M]	Homecoming in Heaven	1962	7.50	15.00	30.00
❑ UAL-3220 [M]	My Favorites of Hank Williams	1962	7.50	15.00	30.00
❑ UAL-3221 [M]	George Jones Sings Bob Wills	1962	10.00	20.00	40.00
❑ UAL-3270 [M]	I Wish the Night Would Never End	1963	6.25	12.50	25.00
❑ UAL-3291 [M]	The Best of George Jones	1963	6.25	12.50	25.00
❑ UAL-3338 [M]	More New Favorites	1964	6.25	12.50	25.00
❑ UAL-3364 [M]	George Jones Sings Like the Dickens	1964	10.00	20.00	40.00
❑ UAL-3388 [M]	I Get Lonely in a Hurry	1964	7.50	15.00	30.00
❑ UAL-3408 [M]	Trouble in Mind	1965	7.50	15.00	30.00
❑ UAL-3422 [M]	The Race Is On	1965	5.00	10.00	20.00
—With cartoon on front					
❑ UAL-3422 [M]	The Race Is On	1965	7.50	15.00	30.00
—With photo of George Jones on front					
❑ UAL-3442 [M]	King of Broken Hearts	1965	7.50	15.00	30.00
❑ UAL-3457 [M]	The Great George Jones	1966	7.50	15.00	30.00
❑ UAL-3532 [M]	George Jones' Golden Hits, Volume 1	1966	5.00	10.00	20.00
❑ UAL-3558 [M]	The Young George Jones	1967	7.50	15.00	30.00
❑ UAL-3566 [M]	George Jones' Golden Hits, Volume 2	1967	7.50	15.00	30.00
❑ UAS-6193 [S]	The New Favorites of George Jones	1962	10.00	20.00	40.00
❑ UAS-6218 [S]	George Jones Sings the Hits of His Country Cousins	1962	10.00	20.00	40.00
❑ UAS-6219 [S]	Homecoming in Heaven	1962	10.00	20.00	40.00
❑ UAS-6220 [S]	My Favorites of Hank Williams	1962	10.00	20.00	40.00
❑ UAS-6221 [S]	George Jones Sings Bob Wills	1962	12.50	25.00	50.00
❑ UAS-6270 [S]	I Wish the Night Would Never End	1963	7.50	15.00	30.00
❑ UAS-6291 [S]	The Best of George Jones	1963	7.50	15.00	30.00
❑ UAS-6328 [S]	More New Favorites	1964	7.50	15.00	30.00
❑ UAS-6364 [S]	George Jones Sings Like the Dickens	1964	12.50	25.00	50.00
❑ UAS-6388 [S]	I Get Lonely in a Hurry	1964	10.00	20.00	40.00
❑ UAS-6408 [S]	Trouble in Mind	1965	10.00	20.00	40.00
❑ UAS-6422 [S]	The Race Is On	1965	6.25	12.50	25.00
—With cartoon on front					
❑ UAS-6422 [S]	The Race Is On	1965	10.00	20.00	40.00
—With photo of George Jones on front					
❑ UAS-6442 [S]	King of Broken Hearts	1965	10.00	20.00	40.00
❑ UAS-6457 [S]	The Great George Jones	1966	10.00	20.00	40.00
❑ UAS-6532 [S]	George Jones' Golden Hits, Volume 1	1966	6.25	12.50	25.00
❑ UAS-6558 [S]	The Young George Jones	1967	5.00	10.00	20.00
❑ UAS-6566 [S]	George Jones' Golden Hits, Volume 2	1967	5.00	10.00	20.00
❑ UAS-6696 [S]	George Jones' Golden Hits, Volume 3	1968	5.00	10.00	20.00
WING					
❑ MGW-12266 [M]	The Great George Jones	196?	3.75	7.50	15.00
❑ SRW-16266 [S]	The Great George Jones	196?	3.75	7.50	15.00

JONES, GEORGE, AND MELBA MONTGOMERY

Number	Title (A Side/B Side)	Yr	VG	VG+	NM
GUEST STAR					
❑ GS 1465 [M]	George Jones and Melba Montgomery	196?	3.00	6.00	12.00
—Contains two solo records by each artist (no duets!) and assorted stuff by others					
LIBERTY					
❑ LN-10169	Singing What's In Our Hearts	1981	2.00	4.00	8.00
MUSICOR					
❑ MM-2127 [M]	Close Together (As You and Me)	1966	5.00	10.00	20.00
❑ MM-2127 [M]	Let's Get Together/Boy Meets Girl	1967	7.50	15.00	30.00
❑ MM-2127 [M]	Party Pickin'	1967	7.50	15.00	30.00
—Alternate title					
❑ MS-3109 [S]	Close Together (As You and Me)	1966	6.25	12.50	25.00
❑ MS-3127 [S]	Let's Get Together/Boy Meets Girl	1967	5.00	10.00	20.00
❑ MS-3127 [S]	Party Pickin'	1967	5.00	10.00	20.00
—Alternate title					
UNITED ARTISTS					
❑ UAL-3301 [M]	Singing What's In Our Hearts	1963	6.25	12.50	25.00
❑ UAL-3352 [M]	Bluegrass Hootenanny	1964	6.25	12.50	25.00
❑ UAL-3472 [M]	Blue Moon of Kentucky	1966	5.00	10.00	20.00
❑ UAS-6301 [S]	Singing What's In Our Hearts	1963	7.50	15.00	30.00
❑ UAS-6352 [S]	Bluegrass Hootenanny	1964	7.50	15.00	30.00
❑ UAS-6472 [S]	Blue Moon of Kentucky	1966	6.25	12.50	25.00
❑ T-90832 [M]	Blue Moon of Kentucky	1966	6.25	12.50	25.00
—Capitol Record Club edition					

JONES, GEORGE; MELBA MONTGOMERY; JUDY LYNN

Number	Title (A Side/B Side)	Yr	VG	VG+	NM
UNITED ARTISTS					
❑ UAL-3367 [M]	A King and Two Queens	1964	5.00	10.00	20.00
❑ UAS-6367 [S]	A King and Two Queens	1964	6.25	12.50	25.00

Number	Title (A Side/B Side)	Yr	VG	VG+	NM

JONES, GEORGE; MELBA MONTGOMERY; GENE PITNEY
MUSICOR
| ❏ MM-2079 [M] | Famous Country Duets | 1965 | 5.00 | 10.00 | 20.00 |
| ❏ MS-3079 [S] | Famous Country Duets | 1965 | 6.25 | 12.50 | 25.00 |

JONES, GEORGE, AND MARGIE SINGLETON
MERCURY
| ❏ MG-20747 [M] | Duets Country Style | 1962 | 7.50 | 15.00 | 30.00 |
| ❏ SR-60747 [S] | Duets Country Style | 1962 | 10.00 | 20.00 | 40.00 |

JONES, GRANDPA
DECCA
| ❏ DL 4364 [M] | An Evening with Grandpa Jones | 1963 | 6.25 | 12.50 | 25.00 |
| ❏ DL 74364 [S] | An Evening with Grandpa Jones | 1963 | 7.50 | 15.00 | 30.00 |
KING
❏ 554 [M]	Grandpa Jones Sings His Biggest Hits	1958	25.00	50.00	100.00
❏ 625 [M]	Strictly Country Tunes	1959	25.00	50.00	100.00
❏ 809 [M]	Rollin' Along with Grandpa Jones	1963	15.00	30.00	60.00
❏ 822 [M]	16 Sacred Gospel Songs	1963	15.00	30.00	60.00
❏ 845 [M]	Do You Remember?	1963	15.00	30.00	60.00
❏ 888 [M]	The Other Side of Grandpa Jones	1964	15.00	30.00	60.00
❏ KS-1042	The Living Legend of Country Music	1969	5.00	10.00	20.00
MONUMENT
❏ MLP-4006 [M]	Grandpa Jones Makes the Rafters Ring	1962	6.25	12.50	25.00
❏ MLP-8001 [M]	Yodeling Hits	1963	5.00	10.00	20.00
❏ MLP-8021 [M]	Real Folk Songs	1964	5.00	10.00	20.00
❏ MLP-8041 [M]	Grandpa Jones Remembers the Brown's Ferry Four	1966	6.25	12.50	25.00
❏ SLP-14006 [S]	Grandpa Jones Makes the Rafters Ring	1962	7.50	15.00	30.00
❏ SLP-18001 [S]	Yodeling Hits	1963	6.25	12.50	25.00
❏ SLP-18021 [S]	Real Folk Songs	1964	6.25	12.50	25.00
❏ SLP-18041 [S]	Grandpa Jones Remembers the Brown's Ferry Four	1966	7.50	15.00	30.00
❏ SLP-18083	Everybody's Grandpa	1968	5.00	10.00	20.00
❏ SLP-18131	Grandpa Jones Sings Hits from Hee Haw	1969	5.00	10.00	20.00

JONES, HANK
ABC-PARAMOUNT
| ❏ ABC-496 [M] | This Is Ragtime Now | 1964 | 5.00 | 10.00 | 20.00 |
| ❏ ABCS-496 [S] | This Is Ragtime Now | 1964 | 6.25 | 12.50 | 25.00 |
ARGO
| ❏ LP-728 [M] | Here's Love | 1963 | 5.00 | 10.00 | 20.00 |
| ❏ LPS-728 [S] | Here's Love | 1963 | 6.25 | 12.50 | 25.00 |
CAPITOL
❏ ST 1044 [S]	The Talented Touch of Hank Jones	1958	7.50	15.00	30.00
❏ T 1044 [M]	The Talented Touch of Hank Jones	1958	10.00	20.00	40.00
❏ ST 1175 [S]	Porgy and Bess	1959	7.50	15.00	30.00
❏ T 1175 [M]	Porgy and Bess	1959	10.00	20.00	40.00
CLEF
| ❏ MGC-100 [10] | Hank Jones Piano | 1953 | 30.00 | 60.00 | 120.00 |
| ❏ MGC-707 [M] | Urbanity — Piano Solos by Hank Jones | 1956 | 25.00 | 50.00 | 100.00 |
GOLDEN CREST
❏ GC-3042 [M]	Hank Jones Swings "Gigi"	1958	12.50	25.00	50.00
❏ GCS-3042 [S]	Hank Jones Swings "Gigi"	196?	5.00	10.00	20.00
❏ GC-5002 [S]	Hank Jones Swings "Gigi"	1959	10.00	20.00	40.00
MERCURY
❏ MGC-100 [10]	Hank Jones Piano	195?	37.50	75.00	150.00
❏ MG-25022 [10]	Hank Jones Piano	1950	50.00	100.00	200.00
❏ MG-35014 [10]	Hank Jones Piano	1950	50.00	100.00	200.00
RCA VICTOR
| ❏ LPM-2570 [M] | Arrival Time | 1962 | 6.25 | 12.50 | 25.00 |
| ❏ LSP-2570 [S] | Arrival Time | 1962 | 7.50 | 15.00 | 30.00 |
SAVOY
❏ MG-12037 [M]	Hank Jones Quartet-Quintet	1955	20.00	40.00	80.00
❏ MG-12053 [M]	The Trio	1956	20.00	40.00	80.00
❏ MG-12084 [M]	Have You Met Hank Jones	1956	20.00	40.00	80.00
❏ MG-12087 [M]	Hank Jones Trio	1956	20.00	40.00	80.00
VERVE
| ❏ MGV-8091 [M] | Urbanity — Piano Solos by Hank Jones | 1957 | 20.00 | 40.00 | 80.00 |
| ❏ V-8091 [M] | Urbanity — Piano Solos by Hank Jones | 1961 | 6.25 | 12.50 | 25.00 |

JONES, ISHAM
RCA VICTOR
| ❏ LPV-504 [M] | The Great Isham Jones and His Orchestra | 1966 | 5.00 | 10.00 | 20.00 |

JONES, JACK
CAPITOL
❏ ST 1274 [S]	This Love of Mine	1959	7.50	15.00	30.00
❏ T 1274 [M]	This Love of Mine	1959	6.25	12.50	25.00
❏ ST 2100 [S]	In Love	1964	5.00	10.00	20.00
—Reissue of 1274					
❏ T 2100 [M]	In Love	1964	3.75	7.50	15.00
KAPP
❏ KL-1228 [M]	Shall We Dance	1961	3.00	6.00	12.00
❏ KL-1259 [M]	This Was My Love	1962	3.00	6.00	12.00
❏ KL-1265 [M]	I've Got a Lot of Livin' to Do	1962	3.00	6.00	12.00
❏ KL-1328 [M]	Call Me Irresponsible	1963	3.00	6.00	12.00
❏ KL-1337 [M]	She Loves Me	1963	3.00	6.00	12.00
❏ KL-1352 [M]	Wives and Lovers	1963	3.00	6.00	12.00
❏ KL-1365 [M]	Bewitched	1964	3.00	6.00	12.00
❏ KL-1396 [M]	Where Love Has Gone	1964	3.00	6.00	12.00
❏ KL 1399 [M]	Jack Jones' Christmas Album	1964	3.00	6.00	12.00
❏ KL-1415 [M]	Dear Heart	1964	3.00	6.00	12.00
❏ KL-1433 [M]	My Kind of Town	1965	3.00	6.00	12.00
❏ KL-1435 [M]	There's Love & There's Love & There's Love	1965	3.00	6.00	12.00
❏ KL-1465 [M]	For the "In" Crowd	1966	3.00	6.00	12.00
❏ KL-1486 [M]	The Impossible Dream	1966	3.00	6.00	12.00
❏ KL-1500 [M]	Jack Jones Sings	1966	3.00	6.00	12.00
❏ KL-1511 [M]	Lady	1967	3.75	7.50	15.00
❏ KL-1531 [M]	Our Song	1967	3.75	7.50	15.00

❏ KL-1551 [M]	What the World Needs Now Is Love!	1968	5.00	10.00	20.00
—May only exist as a white label promo; covers are stereo with "Mono" sticker					
❏ KL-1559 [M]	Greatest Hits	1968	5.00	10.00	20.00
—May only exist as a white label promo; covers are stereo with a "Mono" sticker					
❏ KS-3228 [S]	Shall We Dance	1961	3.75	7.50	15.00
❏ KS-3259 [S]	This Was My Love	1962	3.75	7.50	15.00
❏ KS-3265 [S]	I've Got a Lot of Livin' to Do	1962	3.75	7.50	15.00
❏ KS-3328 [S]	Call Me Irresponsible	1963	3.75	7.50	15.00
❏ KS-3337 [S]	She Loves Me	1963	3.75	7.50	15.00
❏ KS-3352 [S]	Wives and Lovers	1963	3.75	7.50	15.00
❏ KS-3365 [S]	Bewitched	1964	3.75	7.50	15.00
❏ KS-3396 [S]	Where Love Has Gone	1964	3.75	7.50	15.00
❏ KS 3399 [S]	Jack Jones' Christmas Album	1964	3.75	7.50	15.00
❏ KS-3415 [S]	Dear Heart	1964	3.75	7.50	15.00
❏ KS-3433 [S]	My Kind of Town	1965	3.75	7.50	15.00
❏ KS-3435 [S]	There's Love & There's Love & There's Love	1965	3.75	7.50	15.00
❏ KS-3465 [S]	For the "In" Crowd	1966	3.75	7.50	15.00
❏ KS-3486 [S]	The Impossible Dream	1966	3.75	7.50	15.00
❏ KS-3500 [S]	Jack Jones Sings	1966	3.75	7.50	15.00
❏ KS-3511 [S]	Lady	1967	3.00	6.00	12.00
❏ KS-3531 [S]	Our Song	1967	3.00	6.00	12.00
❏ KS-3551 [S]	What the World Needs Now Is Love!	1968	3.00	6.00	12.00
❏ KS-3559	Greatest Hits	1968	3.00	6.00	12.00
❏ KS-3566	Curtain Time	1968	3.00	6.00	12.00
❏ KS-3602	Greatest Hits Vol. 2	1970	3.00	6.00	12.00
❏ KXS-5009 [(2)]	The Best of Jack Jones	196?	3.75	7.50	15.00
MCA
❏ 4115 [(2)]	The Best of Jack Jones	197?	3.00	6.00	12.00
—Reissue of Kapp KXS-5009					
❏ 15014	Jack Jones' Christmas Album	197?	2.50	5.00	10.00
—Reissue					
❏ 15036	White Christmas	198?	2.00	4.00	8.00
MGM
| ❏ MG-1-5023 | Nobody Does It Better | 1979 | 2.50 | 5.00 | 10.00 |
| ❏ MG-1-5024 | Don't Stop Now | 1980 | 2.50 | 5.00 | 10.00 |
PICKWICK
❏ PC-3001 [M]	This Love of Mine	196?	3.00	6.00	12.00
❏ SPC-3001 [S]	This Love of Mine	196?	3.00	6.00	12.00
❏ SPC-3041	A Very Precious Love	196?	2.50	5.00	10.00
RCA VICTOR
❏ APL1-0139	Together	1973	2.50	5.00	10.00
❏ APL1-0408	Harbour	1974	2.50	5.00	10.00
❏ APL1-0773	Write Me a Letter	1975	2.50	5.00	10.00
❏ ANL1-1081	Jack Jones Sings Michel Legrand	1975	2.00	4.00	8.00
—Reissue					
❏ APL1-1111	What I Did for Love	1975	2.50	5.00	10.00
❏ APL1-2067	A Full Life	1976	2.50	5.00	10.00
❏ APL1-2361	With One More	1977	2.50	5.00	10.00
❏ LPM-3911 [M]	Without Her	1967	5.00	10.00	20.00
❏ LSP-3911 [S]	Without Her	1967	3.00	6.00	12.00
❏ LPM-3969 [M]	If You Ever Leave Me	1968	5.00	10.00	20.00
❏ LSP-3969 [S]	If You Ever Leave Me	1968	3.00	6.00	12.00
❏ LSP-4048	Where Is Love	1968	3.00	6.00	12.00
❏ LSP-4108	L.A. Break Down	1969	3.00	6.00	12.00
❏ LSP-4209	A Time for Us	1969	3.00	6.00	12.00
❏ LSP-4234	Christmas	1969	3.00	6.00	12.00
❏ LSP-4413	In Person at the Sands, Las Vegas	1970	3.00	6.00	12.00
❏ LSP-4480	Jack Jones Sings Michel Legrand	1970	3.00	6.00	12.00
❏ LSP-4613	A Song for You	1971	3.00	6.00	12.00
❏ LSP-4692	Bread Winners	1972	2.50	5.00	10.00
VOCALION
| ❏ VL 73913 | Jack Jones Showcase | 1970 | 2.50 | 5.00 | 10.00 |

JONES, JIMMY
JEN JILLUS
| ❏ 1001 | The Handy Man's Back in Town | 1977 | 3.00 | 6.00 | 12.00 |
MGM
| ❏ E-3847 [M] | Good Timin' | 1960 | 30.00 | 60.00 | 120.00 |
| ❏ SE-3847 [S] | Good Timin' | 1960 | 40.00 | 80.00 | 160.00 |

JONES, JO
EVEREST
❏ SDBR-1023 [S]	Jo Jones Trio	1959	7.50	15.00	30.00
❏ SDBR-1099 [S]	Vamp Till Ready	1960	7.50	15.00	30.00
❏ SDBR-1110 [S]	Percussion and Bass	1960	7.50	15.00	30.00
❏ LPBR-5023 [M]	Jo Jones Trio	1959	6.25	12.50	25.00
❏ LPBR-5099 [M]	Vamp Till Ready	1960	6.25	12.50	25.00
❏ LPBR-5110 [M]	Percussion and Bass	1960	6.25	12.50	25.00
JAZZTONE
| ❏ J-1242 [M] | Jo Jones Special | 1956 | 12.50 | 25.00 | 50.00 |
VANGUARD
❏ VSD-2031 [S]	Jo Jones Plus Two	1959	7.50	15.00	30.00
❏ VRS-8503 [M]	Jo Jones Special	1955	15.00	30.00	60.00
❏ VRS-8525 [M]	Jo Jones Plus Two	1959	10.00	20.00	40.00

JONES, JOE
ROULETTE
| ❏ R 25143 [M] | You Talk Too Much | 1961 | 37.50 | 75.00 | 150.00 |
| ❏ SR 25143 [R] | You Talk Too Much | 1961 | 25.00 | 50.00 | 100.00 |

JONES, JOHN PAUL
Also see LED ZEPPELIN
COLUMBIA
| ❏ KC 32047 | John Paul Jones | 1973 | 5.00 | 10.00 | 20.00 |

JONES, JONAH
ANGEL
| ❏ ANG.60005 [10] | Jonah Wails — 1st Blast | 1954 | 18.75 | 37.50 | 75.00 |
| ❏ ANG.60006 [10] | Jonah Wails — 2nd Blast | 1954 | 18.75 | 37.50 | 75.00 |
BETHLEHEM
| ❏ BCP-1014 [10] | Jonah Jones Sextet | 1954 | 20.00 | 40.00 | 80.00 |

Number	Title (A Side/B Side)	Yr	VG	VG+	NM

CAPITOL

Number	Title (A Side/B Side)	Yr	VG	VG+	NM
❑ T 839 [M]	Muted Jazz	1957	10.00	20.00	40.00
❑ T 963 [M]	Swingin' On Broadway	1958	10.00	20.00	40.00
❑ ST 1039 [S]	Jumpin' with Jonah	1958	7.50	15.00	30.00
❑ T 1039 [M]	Jumpin' with Jonah	1958	6.25	12.50	25.00
❑ ST 1083 [S]	Swingin' at the Cinema	1958	7.50	15.00	30.00
❑ T 1083 [M]	Swingin' at the Cinema	1958	6.25	12.50	25.00
❑ ST 1115 [S]	Jonah Jumps Again	1959	7.50	15.00	30.00
❑ T 1115 [M]	Jonah Jumps Again	1959	6.25	12.50	25.00
❑ ST 1193 [S]	I Dig Chicks	1959	6.25	12.50	25.00
❑ T 1193 [M]	I Dig Chicks	1959	5.00	10.00	20.00
❑ ST 1237 [S]	Swingin' 'Round the World	1959	6.25	12.50	25.00
❑ T 1237 [M]	Swingin' 'Round the World	1959	5.00	10.00	20.00
❑ ST 1375 [S]	Hit Me Again!	1960	6.25	12.50	25.00
❑ T 1375 [M]	Hit Me Again!	1960	5.00	10.00	20.00
❑ ST 1404 [S]	Jumpin' with a Shuffle	1960	6.25	12.50	25.00
❑ T 1404 [M]	Jumpin' with a Shuffle	1960	5.00	10.00	20.00
❑ ST 1405 [S]	A Touch of Blue	1960	6.25	12.50	25.00
❑ T 1405 [M]	A Touch of Blue	1960	5.00	10.00	20.00
❑ ST 1532 [S]	The Unsinkable Molly Brown	1961	6.25	12.50	25.00
❑ T 1532 [M]	The Unsinkable Molly Brown	1961	5.00	10.00	20.00
❑ ST 1557 [S]	Great Instrumental Hits Styled by Jonah Jones	1961	6.25	12.50	25.00
❑ T 1557 [M]	Great Instrumental Hits Styled by Jonah Jones	1961	5.00	10.00	20.00
❑ ST 1641 [S]	Broadway Swings Again	1961	6.25	12.50	25.00
❑ T 1641 [M]	Broadway Swings Again	1961	5.00	10.00	20.00
❑ ST 1660 [S]	Jonah Jones/Glenn Gray	1961	6.25	12.50	25.00
❑ T 1660 [M]	Jonah Jones/Glenn Gray	1961	5.00	10.00	20.00
❑ ST 1773 [S]	Jazz Bonus	1962	5.00	10.00	20.00
❑ ST 1948 [S]	And Now, In Person — Jonah Jones	1963	5.00	10.00	20.00
❑ ST 2087 [S]	Blowin' Up a Storm	1964	5.00	10.00	20.00

GROOVE

Number	Title (A Side/B Side)	Yr	VG	VG+	NM
❑ LG-1001 [M]	Jonah Jones at the Embers	1956	12.50	25.00	50.00

MOTOWN

Number	Title (A Side/B Side)	Yr	VG	VG+	NM
❑ M-683	Along Came Jonah	1969	10.00	20.00	40.00
❑ M-690	Little Dis, Little Dat	1970	10.00	20.00	40.00

RCA VICTOR

Number	Title (A Side/B Side)	Yr	VG	VG+	NM
❑ LPM-2004 [M]	Jonah Jones at the Embers	1959	10.00	20.00	40.00
—Reissue of Groove and Vik LP					

VIK

Number	Title (A Side/B Side)	Yr	VG	VG+	NM
❑ LXA-1135 [M]	Jonah Jones at the Embers	1958	10.00	20.00	40.00
—Reissue of Groove LP					

JONES, JONAH/CHARLIE SHAVERS

BETHLEHEM

Number	Title (A Side/B Side)	Yr	VG	VG+	NM
❑ BCP-6034 [M]	Sounds of the Trumpets	1959	10.00	20.00	40.00

JONES, LINDA

LOMA

Number	Title (A Side/B Side)	Yr	VG	VG+	NM
❑ 5907	Hypnotized	1967	7.50	15.00	30.00

TURBO

Number	Title (A Side/B Side)	Yr	VG	VG+	NM
❑ 7007	Your Precious Love	1972	5.00	10.00	20.00

JONES, NORAH

CLASSICRECORDS.COM

Number	Title (A Side/B Side)	Yr	VG	VG+	NM
❑ JP-5004	Come Away with Me	2002	6.25	12.50	25.00
—Audiophile pressing					

JONES, PAUL

Original lead singer for MANFRED MANN.

CAPITOL

Number	Title (A Side/B Side)	Yr	VG	VG+	NM
❑ ST 2795 [S]	Paul Jones Sings Songs from the Film "Privilege" and Others	1967	7.50	15.00	30.00
❑ T 2795 [M]	Paul Jones Sings Songs from the Film "Privilege" and Others	1967	7.50	15.00	30.00

LONDON

Number	Title (A Side/B Side)	Yr	VG	VG+	NM
❑ XPS 605	Crucifix in a Horseshoe	1971	3.00	6.00	12.00

JONES, PHILLY JOE

ATLANTIC

Number	Title (A Side/B Side)	Yr	VG	VG+	NM
❑ 1340 [M]	Philly Joe's Beat	1960	6.25	12.50	25.00
—Multicolor label, white "fan" logo on right					
❑ SD 1340 [S]	Philly Joe's Beat	1960	7.50	15.00	30.00
—Multicolor label, white "fan" logo on right					

RIVERSIDE

Number	Title (A Side/B Side)	Yr	VG	VG+	NM
❑ RLP 12-282 [M]	Blues for Dracula	1958	12.50	25.00	50.00
❑ RLP 12-302 [M]	Drums Around the World	1959	12.50	25.00	50.00
❑ RLP 12-313 [M]	Showcase	1959	12.50	25.00	50.00
❑ RLP-1147 [S]	Drums Around the World	1959	10.00	20.00	40.00
❑ RLP-1159 [S]	Showcase	1959	10.00	20.00	40.00

JONES, PHILLY JOE, AND ELVIN JONES

ATLANTIC

Number	Title (A Side/B Side)	Yr	VG	VG+	NM
❑ 1428 [M]	Together	1964	6.25	12.50	25.00
❑ SD 1428 [S]	Together	1964	7.50	15.00	30.00

JONES, QUINCY

A&M

Number	Title (A Side/B Side)	Yr	VG	VG+	NM
❑ QU-53041 [Q]	You've Got It Bad Girl	1974	5.00	10.00	20.00
❑ QU-53617 [Q]	Body Heat	1974	5.00	10.00	20.00
❑ QU-54526 [Q]	Mellow Madness	1975	5.00	10.00	20.00

ABC-PARAMOUNT

Number	Title (A Side/B Side)	Yr	VG	VG+	NM
❑ 149 [M]	This Is How I Feel About Jazz	1956	25.00	50.00	100.00
❑ 186 [M]	Go West, Man!	1957	25.00	50.00	100.00

COLGEMS

Number	Title (A Side/B Side)	Yr	VG	VG+	NM
❑ COM-107 [M]	In Cold Blood	1967	5.00	10.00	20.00
❑ COS-107 [S]	In Cold Blood	1967	6.25	12.50	25.00

EMARCY

Number	Title (A Side/B Side)	Yr	VG	VG+	NM
❑ MG-36083 [M]	Jazz Abroad	1956	25.00	50.00	100.00

IMPULSE!

Number	Title (A Side/B Side)	Yr	VG	VG+	NM
❑ A-11 [M]	The Quintessence	1962	7.50	15.00	30.00
❑ AS-11 [S]	The Quintessence	1962	10.00	20.00	40.00

LIBERTY

Number	Title (A Side/B Side)	Yr	VG	VG+	NM
❑ LOM-16004 [M]	Enter Laughing	1967	6.25	12.50	25.00
❑ LOS-17004 [S]	Enter Laughing	1967	7.50	15.00	30.00

MERCURY

Number	Title (A Side/B Side)	Yr	VG	VG+	NM
❑ PPS-2014 [M]	Around the World	1961	7.50	15.00	30.00
❑ PPS-6014 [S]	Around the World	1961	10.00	20.00	40.00
❑ MG-20444 [M]	Birth of a Band	1959	12.50	25.00	50.00
❑ MG-20561 [M]	The Great, Wide World of Quincy Jones	1960	12.50	25.00	50.00
❑ MG-20612 [M]	I Dig Dancers	1960	10.00	20.00	40.00
❑ MG-20653 [M]	Quincy Jones at Newport '61	1961	7.50	15.00	30.00
❑ MG-20751 [M]	Big Band Bossa Nova	1962	7.50	15.00	30.00
❑ MG-20799 [M]	Quincy Jones Plays Hip Hits	1963	7.50	15.00	30.00
❑ MG-20863 [M]	Quincy Jones Explores the Music of Henry Mancini	1964	5.00	10.00	20.00
❑ MG-20938 [M]	Golden Boy	1964	5.00	10.00	20.00
❑ MG-21011 [M]	The Pawnbroker	1964	5.00	10.00	20.00
❑ MG-21025 [M]	Mirage	1965	5.00	10.00	20.00
❑ MG-21050 [M]	Quincy Jones Plays for Pussycats	1965	5.00	10.00	20.00
❑ MG-21063 [M]	Quincy's Got a Brand New Bag	1965	5.00	10.00	20.00
❑ MG-21070 [M]	Slender Thread	1966	5.00	10.00	20.00
❑ SR-60129 [S]	Birth of a Band	1959	15.00	30.00	60.00
❑ SR-60221 [S]	The Great, Wide World of Quincy Jones	1960	15.00	30.00	60.00
❑ SR-60612 [S]	I Dig Dancers	1960	12.50	25.00	50.00
❑ SR-60653 [S]	Quincy Jones at Newport '61	1961	10.00	20.00	40.00
❑ SR-60751 [S]	Big Band Bossa Nova	1962	10.00	20.00	40.00
❑ SR-60799 [S]	Quincy Jones Plays Hip Hits	1963	10.00	20.00	40.00
❑ SR-60863 [S]	Quincy Jones Explores the Music of Henry Mancini	1964	6.25	12.50	25.00
❑ SR-60938 [S]	Golden Boy	1964	6.25	12.50	25.00
❑ SR-61011 [S]	The Pawnbroker	1964	6.25	12.50	25.00
❑ SR-61025 [S]	Mirage	1965	6.25	12.50	25.00
❑ SR-61050 [S]	Quincy Jones Plays for Pussycats	1965	6.25	12.50	25.00
❑ SR-61063 [S]	Quincy's Got a Brand New Bag	1965	6.25	12.50	25.00
❑ SR-61070 [S]	Slender Thread	1966	6.25	12.50	25.00

MOBILE FIDELITY

Number	Title (A Side/B Side)	Yr	VG	VG+	NM
❑ 1-078	You've Got It Bad Girl	1981	6.25	12.50	25.00
—Audiophile vinyl					

NAUTILUS

Number	Title (A Side/B Side)	Yr	VG	VG+	NM
❑ NR-52	The Dude	198?	10.00	20.00	40.00
—Audiophile vinyl					

PRESTIGE

Number	Title (A Side/B Side)	Yr	VG	VG+	NM
❑ PRLP-172 [10]	Quincy Jones with the Swedish-American All Stars	1953	50.00	100.00	200.00

QWEST

Number	Title (A Side/B Side)	Yr	VG	VG+	NM
❑ 25356 [(2)]	The Color Purple	1985	5.00	10.00	20.00
—Boxed set on purple vinyl					

UNITED ARTISTS

Number	Title (A Side/B Side)	Yr	VG	VG+	NM
❑ UAS-5214	They Call Me Mister Tibbs	1970	6.25	12.50	25.00

JONES, RICHARD

PAX

Number	Title (A Side/B Side)	Yr	VG	VG+	NM
❑ 6010 [10]	New Orleans Style	1954	20.00	40.00	80.00

RIVERSIDE

Number	Title (A Side/B Side)	Yr	VG	VG+	NM
❑ RLP-1017 [10]	Richard P. Jones and Clarence Williams	1953	20.00	40.00	80.00

JONES, RICKIE LEE

GEFFEN

Number	Title (A Side/B Side)	Yr	VG	VG+	NM
❑ GHS 24246	Flying Cowboys	1989	2.50	5.00	10.00

MOBILE FIDELITY

Number	Title (A Side/B Side)	Yr	VG	VG+	NM
❑ 1-089	Rickie Lee Jones	1982	50.00	100.00	200.00
—Audiophile vinyl.					

WARNER BROS.

Number	Title (A Side/B Side)	Yr	VG	VG+	NM
❑ BSK 3296	Rickie Lee Jones	1979	2.00	4.00	8.00
❑ BSK 3432	Pirates	1981	2.00	4.00	8.00
❑ 23805 [10]	Girl at Her Volcano	1983	2.00	4.00	8.00
❑ 23805 [10]	Girl at Her Volcano	1983	3.75	7.50	15.00
—Promo-only version on Quiex II vinyl					
❑ 25117	The Magazine	1984	2.00	4.00	8.00

JONES, RUFUS

CAMEO

Number	Title (A Side/B Side)	Yr	VG	VG+	NM
❑ C-1076 [M]	Five on Eight	1964	6.25	12.50	25.00
❑ SC-1076 [S]	Five on Eight	1964	7.50	15.00	30.00

JONES, SAM

RIVERSIDE

Number	Title (A Side/B Side)	Yr	VG	VG+	NM
❑ RLP 12-324 [M]	The Soul Society	1960	10.00	20.00	40.00
❑ RLP-358 [M]	The Chant!	1961	7.50	15.00	30.00
❑ RLP-432 [M]	Down Home	1962	7.50	15.00	30.00
❑ RLP-1172 [S]	The Soul Society	1960	10.00	20.00	40.00
❑ RS-9358 [S]	The Chant!	1961	10.00	20.00	40.00
❑ RS-9432 [S]	Down Home	1962	10.00	20.00	40.00

JONES, SPIKE, AND THE CITY SLICKERS

CORNOGRAPHIC

Number	Title (A Side/B Side)	Yr	VG	VG+	NM
❑ 1001	King of Corn	197?	2.50	5.00	10.00

GOLDBERG & O'REILY

Number	Title (A Side/B Side)	Yr	VG	VG+	NM
❑ MF 205/4 [(3)]	The Craziest Show on Earth	1977	5.00	10.00	20.00
—Collection of radio show performances					

HINDSIGHT

Number	Title (A Side/B Side)	Yr	VG	VG+	NM
❑ HSR-185	The Uncollected Spike Jones 1946	198?	2.50	5.00	10.00

LIBERTY

Number	Title (A Side/B Side)	Yr	VG	VG+	NM
❑ LRP-3140 [M]	Omnibust	1959	12.50	25.00	50.00
❑ LRP-3154 [M]	60 Years of Music America Hates Best	1960	12.50	25.00	50.00
❑ LRP-3338 [M]	Washington Square	1963	5.00	10.00	20.00
❑ LRP-3349 [M]	Spike Jones' New Band	1964	7.50	15.00	30.00
❑ LRP-3370 [M]	My Man	1964	5.00	10.00	20.00
❑ LRP-3401 [M]	Spike Jones Plays Hank Williams Hits	1965	5.00	10.00	20.00
❑ LST-7140 [S]	Omnibust	1959	18.75	37.50	75.00
—Black vinyl					

Number	Title (A Side/B Side)	Yr	VG	VG+	NM
❏ LST-7140 [S]	Omnibust	1959	37.50	75.00	150.00
—Red vinyl					
❏ LST-7154 [S]	60 Years of Music America Hates Best	1960	18.75	37.50	75.00
❏ LST-7338 [S]	Washington Square	1963	6.25	12.50	25.00
❏ LST-7349 [S]	Spike Jones' New Band	1964	10.00	20.00	40.00
❏ LST-7370 [S]	My Man	1964	6.25	12.50	25.00
❏ LST-7401 [S]	Spike Jones Plays Hank Williams Hits	1965	6.25	12.50	25.00

RCA GOLD SEAL

Number	Title	Yr	VG	VG+	NM
❏ AGL1-4142	Spike Jones Is Murdering the Classics!	1982	2.00	4.00	8.00
—Reissue					

RCA RED SEAL

❏ LSC-3235 [R]	Spike Jones Is Murdering the Classics!	1971	5.00	10.00	20.00

RCA VICTOR

❏ LPT-18 [10]	Spike Jones Plays the Charleston	1952	50.00	100.00	200.00
❏ ANL1-1035	The Best of Spike Jones	1975	2.50	5.00	10.00
—Reissue					
❏ LPM-2224 [M]	Thank You Music Lovers	1960	12.50	25.00	50.00
❏ ANL1-2312	The Best of Spike Jones, Volume 2	1977	2.50	5.00	10.00
—Reissue					
❏ LPM-3054 [10]	Bottoms Up	1952	50.00	100.00	200.00
❏ LPM-3128 [10]	Spike Jones Murders Carmen and Kids the Classics	1953	50.00	100.00	200.00
❏ AYL1-3748	The Best of Spike Jones, Volume 1	1980	2.00	4.00	8.00
—"Best Buy Series" reissue					
❏ LPM-3849 [M]	The Best of Spike Jones	1967	6.25	12.50	25.00
❏ LSP-3849 [R]	The Best of Spike Jones	1967	5.00	10.00	20.00
❏ AYL1-3870	The Best of Spike Jones, Volume 2	1981	2.00	4.00	8.00
—"Best Buy Series" reissue					

RHINO

❏ R1 70196	It's a Spike Jones Christmas	1988	3.00	6.00	12.00
❏ R1 70261	Dinner Music…For People Who Aren't Very Hungry	1988	3.00	6.00	12.00

UNITED ARTISTS

❏ UA-LA439-E	The Very Best of Spike Jones	1975	3.00	6.00	12.00

VERVE

❏ MGV-2021 [M]	Let's Sing a Song for Christmas	1956	12.50	25.00	50.00
❏ V-2021 [M]	Let's Sing a Song for Christmas	1961	7.50	15.00	30.00
❏ MGV-4005 [M]	Dinner Music…For People Who Aren't Very Hungry	1957	12.50	25.00	50.00
❏ V-4005 [M]	Dinner Music…For People Who Aren't Very Hungry	1961	6.25	12.50	25.00

WARNER BROS.

❏ W 1332 [M]	Spike Jones in Hi-Fi	1959	10.00	20.00	40.00
❏ WS 1332 [S]	Spike Jones in Stereo	1959	12.50	25.00	50.00

JONES, STAN

BUENA VISTA

❏ BV-3306 [M]	Ghost Riders in the Sky	1961	6.25	12.50	25.00
—Reissue of Disneyland WDL-3015					

DISNEYLAND

❏ WDL-1005 [M]	Songs of the National Parks	1958	10.00	20.00	40.00
—Sold only at national parks					
❏ WDL-3015 [M]	Creakin' Leather	1958	10.00	20.00	40.00
❏ WDL-3033 [M]	This Was the West — The Story and the Songs	1958	10.00	20.00	40.00

JONES, TAMIKO

A&M

❏ SP-3011	I'll Be Anything for You	1969	5.00	10.00	20.00

DECEMBER

❏ 8500	Tamiko	1970	5.00	10.00	20.00

METROMEDIA

❏ MD 1030	Tamiko Jones in Muscle Shoals	1970	5.00	10.00	20.00

JONES, THAD

BLUE NOTE

❏ BLP-1513 [M]	Detroit-New York Junction	1956	37.50	75.00	150.00
—Regular version, Lexington Ave. address on label					
❏ BLP-1513 [M]	Detroit-New York Junction	1956	50.00	100.00	200.00
—"Deep groove" version (deep indentation under label on both sides)					
❏ BLP-1513 [M]	Detroit-New York Junction	1963	6.25	12.50	25.00
—With "New York, USA" address on label					
❏ BLP-1527 [M]	The Magnificent Thad Jones	1956	37.50	75.00	150.00
—Regular version, Lexington Ave. address on label					
❏ BLP-1527 [M]	The Magnificent Thad Jones	1956	50.00	100.00	200.00
—"Deep groove" version (deep indentation under label on both sides)					
❏ BLP-1527 [M]	The Magnificent Thad Jones	1963	6.25	12.50	25.00
—With "New York, USA" address on label					
❏ BLP-1546 [M]	The Magnificent Thad Jones, Volume 3	1957	30.00	60.00	120.00
—Regular version, W. 63rd St., NY address on label					
❏ BLP-1546 [M]	The Magnificent Thad Jones, Volume 3	1957	37.50	75.00	150.00
—"Deep groove" version (deep indentation under label on both sides)					
❏ BLP-1546 [M]	The Magnificent Thad Jones, Volume 3	1963	6.25	12.50	25.00
—With "New York, USA" address on label					

DEBUT

❏ DLP-12 [10]	The Fabulous Thad Jones	1954	75.00	150.00	300.00
❏ DLP-17 [10]	Jazz Collaborations	1954	75.00	150.00	300.00
❏ DEB-127 [M]	Thad Jones	1958	50.00	100.00	200.00

FANTASY

❏ 6004 [M]	The Fabulous Thad Jones	1962	6.25	12.50	25.00
—Black vinyl					
❏ 6004 [M]	The Fabulous Thad Jones	1962	12.50	25.00	50.00
—Red vinyl					
❏ 86004 [R]	The Fabulous Thad Jones	1962	7.50	15.00	30.00
—Blue vinyl					

MOSAIC

❏ MQ5-172 [(5)]	The Complete Blue Note/UA/Roulette Recordings of Thad Jones	199?	25.00	50.00	100.00

PERIOD

❏ SPL-1208 [M]	Mad Thad	1956	37.50	75.00	150.00

Number	Title (A Side/B Side)	Yr	VG	VG+	NM
PRESTIGE					
❏ PRLP-7118 [M]	After Hours	1957	20.00	40.00	80.00
UNITED ARTISTS					
❏ UAL-4025 [M]	Motor City Scene	1959	20.00	40.00	80.00
❏ UAS-5025 [S]	Motor City Scene	1959	15.00	30.00	60.00

JONES, THAD, AND PEPPER ADAMS

MILESTONE

❏ MLP-1001 [M]	Mean What You Say	1966	5.00	10.00	20.00
❏ MSP-9001 [S]	Mean What You Say	1966	6.25	12.50	25.00

JONES, THAD, AND MEL LEWIS

BLUE NOTE

❏ BST-84346	Consummation	1970	5.00	10.00	20.00
❏ BST-89905 [(2)]	The Jazz Wave Ltd. On Tour (Volume 1)	1970	6.25	12.50	25.00

MOSAIC

❏ MQ7-151 [(7)]	The Complete Solid State Recordings of the Thad Jones-Mel Lewis Orchestra	199?	37.50	75.00	150.00

SOLID STATE

❏ SM-17003 [M]	Presenting Thad Jones, Mel Lewis and the Jazz Orchestra	1966	5.00	10.00	20.00
❏ SM-17016 [M]	Live at the Village Vanguard	1967	6.25	12.50	25.00
❏ SS-18003 [S]	Presenting Thad Jones, Mel Lewis and the Jazz Orchestra	1966	5.00	10.00	20.00

JONES, TOM

EPIC

❏ PE 34383	Classic Tom Jones	1976	3.00	6.00	12.00
❏ PE 34468	Say You'll Stay Until Tomorrow	1977	3.00	6.00	12.00
❏ PE 34720	Tom Is Love	1977	2.50	5.00	10.00
❏ JE 35023	What a Night	1978	2.50	5.00	10.00

JIVE

❏ 1214-1-J	Move Closer	1989	3.00	6.00	12.00

LONDON

❏ PS 717	The Country Side of Tom Jones	1978	2.50	5.00	10.00
❏ LC-50002	Tom Jones' Greatest Hits	1977	3.00	6.00	12.00
❏ 820234-1	This Is Tom Jones	1985	2.00	4.00	8.00
❏ 820319-1	Tom Jones' Greatest Hits	1985	2.50	5.00	10.00

MCA

❏ 3182	Tom Jones	1979	2.50	5.00	10.00
❏ 37114	Rescue Me	1980	2.00	4.00	8.00

MERCURY

❏ SRM-1-4010	Darlin'	1981	2.50	5.00	10.00
❏ SRM-1-4062	Tom Jones Country	1982	2.50	5.00	10.00
❏ 814448-1	Don't Let Our Dreams Die Young	1983	2.50	5.00	10.00
❏ 822701-1	Love Is on the Radio	1984	2.50	5.00	10.00
❏ 826140-1	Tender Loving Care	1985	2.50	5.00	10.00
❏ 830409-1	Things That Matter Most to Me	1987	2.50	5.00	10.00

PARROT

❏ XPAS-1 [DJ]	Special Tom Jones Interview	1970	25.00	50.00	100.00
—Promo-only open-end interview with gatefold cover and script					
❏ PA 61004 [M]	It's Not Unusual	1965	3.75	7.50	15.00
❏ PA 61006 [M]	What's New Pussycat?	1965	3.75	7.50	15.00
❏ PA 61007 [M]	A-Tom-Ic Jones	1966	3.75	7.50	15.00
❏ PA 61009 [M]	Green, Green Grass of Home	1967	3.75	7.50	15.00
❏ PA 61011 [M]	Funny Familiar Forgotten Feelings	1967	3.75	7.50	15.00
❏ PA 61014 [M]	Tom Jones Live	1967	3.75	7.50	15.00
❏ PAS 71004 [S]	It's Not Unusual	1965	3.75	7.50	15.00
❏ PAS 71006 [S]	What's New Pussycat?	1965	3.75	7.50	15.00
❏ PAS 71007 [S]	A-Tom-Ic Jones	1966	3.75	7.50	15.00
❏ PAS 71009 [S]	Green, Green Grass of Home	1967	3.75	7.50	15.00
❏ PAS 71011 [S]	Funny Familiar Forgotten Feelings	1967	3.75	7.50	15.00
❏ PAS 71014 [S]	Tom Jones Live	1967	3.75	7.50	15.00
❏ PAS 71019	The Tom Jones Fever Zone	1968	3.00	6.00	12.00
❏ PAS 71025	Help Yourself	1969	3.00	6.00	12.00
❏ PAS 71028	This Is Tom Jones	1969	3.00	6.00	12.00
❏ PAS 71031	Live in Las Vegas	1969	3.00	6.00	12.00
❏ PAS 71037	Tom	1970	3.00	6.00	12.00
❏ PAS 71039	I (Who Have Nothing)	1970	3.00	6.00	12.00
❏ PAS 71046	She's a Lady	1971	3.00	6.00	12.00
❏ PAS 71049	Live at Caesar's Palace	1971	3.00	6.00	12.00
❏ XPAS 71055	Close Up	1972	3.00	6.00	12.00
❏ XPAS 71060	The Body and Soul of Tom Jones	197?	3.00	6.00	12.00
❏ XPAS 71062	Tom Jones' Greatest Hits	1973	3.00	6.00	12.00
❏ PAS 71066	Somethin' 'Bout You Baby I Like	1974	3.00	6.00	12.00
❏ PAS 71068	Memories Don't Leave Like People Do	197?	3.00	6.00	12.00

JONES BOYS, THE

MUSICOR

❏ MM-2017 [M]	Country and Western Songbook	1964	6.25	12.50	25.00
❏ MS-3017 [S]	Country and Western Songbook	1964	7.50	15.00	30.00
❏ MS-3182	My Boys, the Jones Boys	1970	5.00	10.00	20.00

JONES BOYS, THE (2)

All-star jazz group of musicians with the last name of Jones, none of whom were related.

PERIOD

❏ SPL-1210 [M]	The Jones Bash	1954	20.00	40.00	80.00

JONES BROTHERS, THE

METROJAZZ

❏ E-1003 [M]	Keepin' Up with the Joneses	1958	20.00	40.00	80.00
❏ SE-1003 [S]	Keepin' Up with the Joneses	1958	15.00	30.00	60.00

JOPLIN, JANIS

Also see BIG BROTHER AND THE HOLDING COMPANY.

COLUMBIA

❏ AS 1377 [DJ]	A Collection	1982	5.00	10.00	20.00
❏ KCS 9913	I Got Dem Ol' Kozmik Blues Again Mama!	1969	5.00	10.00	20.00
—"360 Sound Stereo" on label					
❏ KCS 9913	I Got Dem Ol' Kozmik Blues Again Mama!	1970	3.00	6.00	12.00
—Orange label					

J

Number	Title (A Side/B Side)	Yr	VG	VG+	NM
❏ PC 9913	I Got Dem Ol' Kozmik Blues Again Mama!	198?	2.00	4.00	8.00
—Budget-line reissue					
❏ CQ 30322 [Q]	Pearl	1974	5.00	10.00	20.00
❏ KC 30322	Pearl	1971	3.75	7.50	15.00
❏ PC 30322	Pearl	1975	3.00	6.00	12.00
—Reissue without bar code					
❏ PC 30322	Pearl	198?	2.00	4.00	8.00
—Reissue with bar code					
❏ C2X 31160 [(2)]	Joplin in Concert	1972	5.00	10.00	20.00
❏ CG 31160	Joplin in Concert	198?	3.00	6.00	12.00
❏ KC 32168	Janis Joplin's Greatest Hits	1973	3.75	7.50	15.00
❏ PC 32168	Janis Joplin's Greatest Hits	197?	2.00	4.00	8.00
❏ CG 33345 [(2)]	Janis	198?	3.00	6.00	12.00
❏ PG 33345 [(2)]	Janis	1975	3.75	7.50	15.00
❏ PC 37569	Farewell Song	1982	2.50	5.00	10.00

COLUMBIA SPECIAL PRODUCTS

Number	Title (A Side/B Side)	Yr	VG	VG+	NM
❏ 2P 13792 [(2)]	The Greatest Hits of Janis Joplin	1977	5.00	10.00	20.00

JORDAN, CLIFFORD
ATLANTIC

Number	Title (A Side/B Side)	Yr	VG	VG+	NM
❏ 1444 [M]	These Are My Roots	1965	6.25	12.50	25.00
❏ SD 1444 [S]	These Are My Roots	1965	7.50	15.00	30.00
BLUE NOTE					
❏ BLP-1549 [M]	Blowing In from Chicago	1957	20.00	40.00	80.00
—Regular version, W. 63rd St., NY address on label					
❏ BLP-1549 [M]	Blowing In from Chicago	1957	30.00	60.00	120.00
—"Deep groove" version (deep indentation under label on both sides)					
❏ BLP-1549 [M]	Blowing In from Chicago	1963	6.25	12.50	25.00
—With "New York, USA" address on label					
❏ BLP-1565 [M]	Clifford Jordan	1957	20.00	40.00	80.00
—Regular version, W. 63rd St., NY address on label					
❏ BLP-1565 [M]	Clifford Jordan	1957	30.00	60.00	120.00
—"Deep groove" version (deep indentation under label on both sides)					
❏ BLP-1565 [M]	Clifford Jordan	1963	6.25	12.50	25.00
—With "New York, USA" address on label					
❏ BST-1565 [S]	Clifford Jordan	1959	15.00	30.00	60.00
—Regular version, W. 63rd St., NY address on label					
❏ BST-1565 [S]	Clifford Jordan	1959	20.00	40.00	80.00
—"Deep groove" version (deep indentation under label on both sides)					
❏ BST-1565 [S]	Clifford Jordan	1963	5.00	10.00	20.00
—With "New York, USA" address on label					
❏ BLP-1582 [M]	Cliff Craft	1958	20.00	40.00	80.00
—Regular version, W. 63rd St., NY address on label					
❏ BLP-1582 [M]	Cliff Craft	1958	30.00	60.00	120.00
—"Deep groove" version (deep indentation under label on both sides)					
❏ BLP-1582 [M]	Cliff Craft	1963	6.25	12.50	25.00
—With "New York, USA" address on label					
❏ BST-1582 [S]	Cliff Craft	1959	15.00	30.00	60.00
—Regular version, W. 63rd St., NY address on label					
❏ BST-1582 [S]	Cliff Craft	1959	20.00	40.00	80.00
—"Deep groove" version (deep indentation under label on both sides)					
❏ BST-1582 [S]	Cliff Craft	1963	5.00	10.00	20.00
—With "New York, USA" address on label					
❏ BST-81582 [S]	Cliff Craft	199?	6.25	12.50	25.00
—Classic Records reissue on audiophile vinyl					
JAZZLAND					
❏ JLP-40 [M]	A Story Tale	1961	7.50	15.00	30.00
❏ JLP-52 [M]	Starting Time	1961	7.50	15.00	30.00
❏ JLP-69 [M]	Bearcat	1962	7.50	15.00	30.00
❏ JLP-940 [S]	A Story Tale	1961	10.00	20.00	40.00
❏ JLP-952 [S]	Starting Time	1961	10.00	20.00	40.00
❏ JLP-969 [S]	Bearcat	1962	10.00	20.00	40.00
RIVERSIDE					
❏ RLP-340 [M]	Spellbound	1960	10.00	20.00	40.00
❏ RS-9340 [S]	Spellbound	1960	7.50	15.00	30.00
STRATA-EAST					
❏ SES 1972-1	In the World	1972	5.00	10.00	20.00
❏ SES 19737/8 [(2)]	Glass Bead Games	1974	6.25	12.50	25.00
VORTEX					
❏ 2010	Soul Fountain	1970	5.00	10.00	20.00

JORDAN, DUKE
BLUE NOTE

Number	Title (A Side/B Side)	Yr	VG	VG+	NM
❏ BLP-4046 [M]	Flight to Jordan	1960	20.00	40.00	80.00
—With W. 63rd St., NY address on label					
❏ BLP-4046 [M]	Flight to Jordan	1963	6.25	12.50	25.00
—With "New York, USA" address on label					
❏ BST-84046 [S]	Flight to Jordan	1960	15.00	30.00	60.00
—With W. 63rd St., NY address on label					
❏ BST-84046 [S]	Flight to Jordan	1963	5.00	10.00	20.00
—With "New York, USA" address on label					
CHARLIE PARKER					
❏ PLP-805 [M]	East and West of Jazz	1962	6.25	12.50	25.00
❏ PLP-805S [S]	East and West of Jazz	1962	7.50	15.00	30.00
NEW JAZZ					
❏ NJ-810 [10]	Jordu	195?	50.00	100.00	200.00
SAVOY					
❏ MG-12149 [M]	Duke Jordan	1959	20.00	40.00	80.00
SIGNAL					
❏ S-1202 [M]	Duke Jordan	1955	62.50	125.00	250.00

JORDAN, DUKE/HALL OVERTON
SAVOY

Number	Title (A Side/B Side)	Yr	VG	VG+	NM
❏ MG-12145 [M]	Do It Yourself Jazz	1959	25.00	50.00	100.00
❏ MG-12146 [M]	Jazz Laboratory Series	1959	25.00	50.00	100.00
SIGNAL					
❏ S-101/2 [M]	Jazz Laboratory Series	1955	62.50	125.00	250.00
—Deduct 20 percent if book is missing					

JORDAN, KING
CORAL

Number	Title (A Side/B Side)	Yr	VG	VG+	NM
❏ CRL 57372 [M]	Phantom Guitar	1962	5.00	10.00	20.00
❏ CRL 757372 [S]	Phantom Guitar	1962	6.25	12.50	25.00

JORDAN, LOUIS
DECCA

Number	Title (A Side/B Side)	Yr	VG	VG+	NM
❏ DL 5035 [M]	Greatest Hits	1968	7.50	15.00	30.00
❏ DL 8551 [M]	Let the Good Times Roll	1958	25.00	50.00	100.00
—Black label, silver print					
MERCURY					
❏ MG-20242 [M]	Somebody Up There Digs Me	1957	30.00	60.00	120.00
❏ MG-20331 [M]	Man, We're Wailin'	1958	30.00	60.00	120.00
SCORE					
❏ SLP-4007 [M]	Go Blow Your Horn	1957	50.00	100.00	200.00
TANGERINE					
❏ 1503 [M]	Hallelujah	1964	5.00	10.00	20.00
❏ S-1503 [S]	Hallelujah	1964	6.25	12.50	25.00
WING					
❏ MGW-12126 [M]	Somebody Up There Digs Me	1962	6.25	12.50	25.00

JORDAN, SHEILA
BLUE NOTE

Number	Title (A Side/B Side)	Yr	VG	VG+	NM
❏ BLP-9002 [M]	Portrait of Sheila Jordan	1962	37.50	75.00	150.00
—With W. 63rd St., NY address on label					
❏ BLP-9002 [M]	Portrait of Sheila Jordan	1963	6.25	12.50	25.00
—With "New York, USA" address on label					
WAVE					
❏ W-1 [M]	Looking Out	1961	15.00	30.00	60.00
❏ WS-1 [S]	Looking Out	1961	20.00	40.00	80.00

JORDAN, TAFT
MERCURY

Number	Title (A Side/B Side)	Yr	VG	VG+	NM
❏ MG-20429 [M]	The Moods of Taft Jordan	1959	10.00	20.00	40.00
❏ SR-60101 [S]	The Moods of Taft Jordan	1959	10.00	20.00	40.00
MOODSVILLE					
❏ MVLP-21 [M]	Mood Indigo — Taft Jordan Plays Duke Ellington	1961	12.50	25.00	50.00
—Green label					
❏ MVLP-21 [M]	Mood Indigo — Taft Jordan Plays Duke Ellington	1965	6.25	12.50	25.00
—Blue label, trident logo at right					

JORDANAIRES, THE
CAPITOL

Number	Title (A Side/B Side)	Yr	VG	VG+	NM
❏ T 1011 [M]	Heavenly Spirit	1958	10.00	20.00	40.00
❏ T 1167 [M]	Gloryland	1959	10.00	20.00	40.00
❏ ST 1311 [S]	Land of Jordan	1960	10.00	20.00	40.00
❏ T 1311 [M]	Land of Jordan	1960	7.50	15.00	30.00
❏ ST 1559 [S]	To God Be the Glory	1961	6.25	12.50	25.00
❏ T 1559 [M]	To God Be the Glory	1961	5.00	10.00	20.00
❏ ST 1742 [S]	Spotlight on the Jordanaires	1962	7.50	15.00	30.00
❏ T 1742 [M]	Spotlight on the Jordanaires	1962	6.25	12.50	25.00
CLASSIC					
❏ CCR 1935	Christmas to Elvis from the Jordanaires	1978	3.00	6.00	12.00
COLUMBIA					
❏ CL 2214 [M]	This Land	1964	5.00	10.00	20.00
❏ CL 2458 [M]	The Big Country Hits	1966	5.00	10.00	20.00
❏ CS 9014 [S]	This Land	1964	6.25	12.50	25.00
❏ CS 9258 [S]	The Big Country Hits	1966	6.25	12.50	25.00
DECCA					
❏ DL 8681 [M]	Peace in the Valley	1957	12.50	25.00	50.00
RCA VICTOR					
❏ LPM-3081 [10]	Beautiful City	1953	25.00	50.00	100.00
SESAC					
❏ 1401/2 [M]	Of Rivers and Plains	195?	20.00	40.00	80.00

JORGENSON, CHRISTINE
J RECORDS

Number	Title (A Side/B Side)	Yr	VG	VG+	NM
❏ J-1 [M]	Christine Jorgenson Reveals	1958	12.50	25.00	50.00

JOSEFUS
HOOKAH

Number	Title (A Side/B Side)	Yr	VG	VG+	NM
❏ 330	Dead Man	1969	75.00	150.00	300.00
MAINSTREAM					
❏ S-6127	Josefus	1970	25.00	50.00	100.00

JOSEPH
SCEPTER

Number	Title (A Side/B Side)	Yr	VG	VG+	NM
❏ SRS-674	Stoned Age Man	1970	20.00	40.00	80.00

JOSEPH, MARGIE
ATLANTIC

Number	Title (A Side/B Side)	Yr	VG	VG+	NM
❏ SD 7248	Margie Joseph	1973	3.00	6.00	12.00
❏ SD 7277	Sweet Surrender	1974	3.00	6.00	12.00
❏ SD 18126	Margie	1975	3.00	6.00	12.00
❏ SD 19182	Feeling My Way	1978	2.50	5.00	10.00
COTILLION					
❏ SD 9906	Hear the Words, Feel the Feeling	1976	3.00	6.00	12.00
H.C.R.C.					
❏ 20009	Knockout	1983	2.50	5.00	10.00
VOLT					
❏ VOS-6012	Margie Joseph Makes a New Impression	1971	7.50	15.00	30.00
❏ VOS-6016	Phase II	1971	7.50	15.00	30.00

JOSHUA FOX
TETRAGRAMMATON

Number	Title (A Side/B Side)	Yr	VG	VG+	NM
❏ T-125	Joshua Fox	1969	7.50	15.00	30.00

Number	Title (A Side/B Side)	Yr	VG	VG+	NM

JOSIE AND THE PUSSYCATS
CAPITOL
❏ ST-665   Josie and the Pussycats   1970   50.00   100.00   200.00

JOURNEY
COLUMBIA
❏ AS 914 [DJ]   Journey   1975   3.75   7.50   15.00
—Promo-only sampler
❏ AS 1606 [DJ]   A Candid Conversation with Journey   197?   3.75   7.50   15.00
—Promo-only interview and songs LP
❏ PC 33388   Journey   1975   2.50   5.00   10.00
—No bar code on cover
❏ PC 33388   Journey   198?   —   3.00   6.00
—With bar code on cover
❏ PC 33904   Look Into the Future   1976   2.50   5.00   10.00
—No bar code on cover
❏ PC 33904   Look Into the Future   198?   —   3.00   6.00
—With bar code on cover
❏ PCQ 33904 [Q]   Look Into the Future   1976   3.75   7.50   15.00
❏ PC 34311   Next   1977   2.50   5.00   10.00
—No bar code on cover
❏ PC 34311   Next   198?   —   3.00   6.00
—With bar code on cover
❏ JC 34912   Infinity   1978   2.50   5.00   10.00
—No bar code on cover
❏ JC 34912   Infinity   1979   —   3.00   6.00
—With bar code on cover
❏ FC 35797   Evolution   1979   2.00   4.00   8.00
❏ PC 35797   Evolution   1985   —   3.00   6.00
—Budget-line reissue
❏ C2 36324 [(2)]   In the Beginning   1979   2.50   5.00   10.00
❏ FC 36339   Departure   1980   2.00   4.00   8.00
❏ KC2 37016 [(2)]   Captured   1981   2.50   5.00   10.00
❏ TC 37408   Escape   1981   2.00   4.00   8.00
❏ FC 37998   Dream After Dream   1982   3.00   6.00   12.00
❏ PC 37998   Dream After Dream   1986   2.00   4.00   8.00
—Budget-line reissue
❏ QC 38504   Frontiers   1983   2.00   4.00   8.00
❏ OC 39936   Raised on Radio   1986   2.00   4.00   8.00
❏ OC 44493   Greatest Hits   1988   2.50   5.00   10.00
❏ HC 44912   Infinity   1982   7.50   15.00   30.00
—Half-speed mastered edition
❏ HC 46339   Departure   1980   5.00   10.00   20.00
—Half-speed mastered edition
❏ HC 47408   Escape   1982   5.00   10.00   20.00
—Half-speed mastered edition
❏ HC 47998   Dream After Dream   1982   7.50   15.00   30.00
—Half-speed mastered edition
❏ HC 48504   Frontiers   1983   7.50   15.00   30.00
—Half-speed mastered edition
MOBILE FIDELITY
❏ 1-144   Escape   1984   50.00   100.00   200.00
—Audiophile vinyl

JOURNEYMEN, THE (1)
CAPITOL
❏ ST 1629 [S]   The Journeymen   1961   7.50   15.00   30.00
❏ T 1629 [M]   The Journeymen   1961   6.25   12.50   25.00
❏ ST 1770 [S]   Coming Attraction — Live!   1962   7.50   51.00   30.00
❏ T 1770 [M]   Coming Attraction — Live!   1962   6.25   12.50   25.00
❏ ST 1951 [S]   New Directions in Folk Music   1963   7.50   15.00   30.00
❏ T 1951 [M]   New Directions in Folk Music   1963   6.25   12.50   25.00

JOY DIVISION
FACTORY
❏ FACT US 1   Unknown Pleasures   1979   5.00   10.00   20.00
❏ FACT US 6   Closer   1980   6.25   12.50   25.00
—Red tint vinyl
❏ FACT US 6   Closer   1980   12.50   25.00   50.00
—Purple tint vinyl
WARNER BROS.
❏ 25747   Substance   1988   2.50   5.00   10.00
❏ 25840   Unknown Pleasures   1989   2.50   5.00   10.00
—Reissue of FACT US 1
❏ 25841   Closer   1989   2.50   5.00   10.00
—Reissue of FACT US 6

JOY STRINGS, THE
EPIC
❏ LN 24321 [M]   Well Seasoned   1967   5.00   10.00   20.00
❏ BN 26321 [S]   Well Seasoned   1967   5.00   10.00   20.00

JOY UNLIMITED
BASF
❏ 21090   Butterflies   1972   6.25   12.50   25.00
MERCURY
❏ SR-61283   Joy Unlimited   1970   6.25   12.50   25.00

JOYCE, JIMMY
WARNER BROS.
❏ WS 1237 [S]   A Christmas to Remember   1959   5.00   10.00   20.00
❏ WS 1566 [S]   This Is Christmas: A Complete Collection of the Alfred S. Burt Carols   1964   5.00   10.00   20.00

JOYOUS NOISE
CAPITOL
❏ SMAS-844   Joyous Noise   1971   5.00   10.00   20.00

JUDAS PRIEST
COLUMBIA
❏ AS99 1543 [DJ]   Screaming for Vengeance   1982   5.00   10.00   20.00
—Promo-only "world tour" picture disc; plays the correct LP

❏ AS99 1543 [DJ]   Screaming for Vengeance   1982   7.50   15.00   30.00
—Promo-only "world tour" picture disc; plays Neil Diamond's "Heartlight" LP in error
❏ PC 34787   Sin After Sin   1977   3.00   6.00   12.00
—Originals have no bar code on back cover
❏ PC 34787   Sin After Sin   198?   —   3.00   6.00
—Reissue; bar code on back cover
❏ JC 35296   Stained Class   1978   2.00   4.00   8.00
❏ PC 35296   Stained Class   198?   —   3.00   6.00
—Budget-line reissue
❏ JC 35706   Hell Bent for Leather   1979   2.00   4.00   8.00
❏ JC 36179   Unleashed in the East (Live in Japan)   1979   2.00   4.00   8.00
❏ PC 36179   Unleashed in the East (Live in Japan)   1985   —   3.00   6.00
—Budget-line reissue with new prefix
❏ JC 36443   British Steel   1980   2.00   4.00   8.00
❏ FC 37052   Point of Entry   1981   2.00   4.00   8.00
❏ FC 38160   Screaming for Vengeance   1982   2.00   4.00   8.00
❏ FC 38219   Defenders of the Faith   1984   2.00   4.00   8.00
❏ 9C9 39926 [PD]   Great Vinyl and Concert Hits   1984   15.00   30.00   60.00
❏ OC 40158   Turbo   1986   2.00   4.00   8.00
❏ C2 40794 [(2)]   Priest ... Live!   1987   2.50   5.00   10.00
❏ FC 44244   Ram It Down   1988   2.00   4.00   8.00
GULL
❏ GU6-403S1   Rocka-Rolla   1975   —   —   —
—Canceled
JANUS
❏ JXS-7019   Sad Wings of Destiny   1976   6.25   12.50   25.00
❏ JXS-7019 [DJ]   Sad Wings of Destiny   1976   7.50   15.00   30.00
—Promo version, with "Specially faded for easier programming" sticker on cover
OVATION
❏ OV-1751   Sad Wings of Destiny   1980   3.75   7.50   15.00
RCA VICTOR
❏ AYL1-4747   Sad Wings of Destiny   1983   2.50   5.00   10.00
—Reissue of Ovation LP
❏ AYL1-4933   The Best of Judas Priest   1984   2.00   4.00   8.00
❏ AYL1-5041   Rocka-Rolla   1984   2.50   5.00   10.00
—Reissue of Visa 7001 with new cover
❏ CYL1-5399 [(2)]   Hero, Hero   1985   3.00   6.00   12.00
VISA
❏ IMP-7001   Rocka Rolla   1979   3.75   7.50   15.00
—First U.S. issue of unreleased Gull LP; front cover has a bottle-cap motif

JUDD, WYNONNA
MCA
❏ 1P-8201   Wynonna   1992   6.25   12.50   25.00
—Only released on vinyl through Columbia House; label misspells her name as "Wyonna"!

JUDDS, THE
HEARTLAND
❏ HL-2041 [(2)]   Classic Gold   1992   5.00   10.00   20.00
RCA
❏ 5916-1-R   Heartland   1987   2.50   5.00   10.00
❏ 6422-1-R   Christmas Time with the Judds   1987   2.50   5.00   10.00
❏ 8318-1-R   Greatest Hits   1988   2.50   5.00   10.00
❏ 9595-1-R   River of Time   1989   3.00   6.00   12.00
RCA VICTOR
❏ AHL1-5319   Why Not Me   1984   2.50   5.00   10.00
❏ AHL1-7042   Rockin' with the Rhythm   1985   2.50   5.00   10.00
❏ MHL1-8515 [EP]   The Judds   1984   2.00   4.00   8.00

JULIAN'S TREATMENT
DECCA
❏ DL 75224   A Time Before This   1970   5.00   10.00   20.00

JULLIARD STRING QUARTET
RCA VICTOR RED SEAL
❏ LSC-2378 [S]   Schubert: String Quartet No. 14 "Death and the Maiden"   1960   20.00   40.00   80.00
—Original with "shaded dog" label
❏ LSC-2413 [S]   Debussy: String Quartet in G; Ravel: String Quartet in F   1960   37.50   75.00   150.00
—Original with "shaded dog" label
❏ LSC-2481 [S]   Carter: String Quartet No. 2; Schuman: String Quartet No. 3   1961   10.00   20.00   40.00
—Original with "shaded dog" label
❏ LSC-2524 [S]   Dvorak: String Quartet in C; Wolf: Italian Serenade   1961   6.25   12.50   25.00
—Originals with "shaded dog" label
❏ LSC-2531 [S]   Berg: Lyric Suite; Webern: 5 Pieces; Six Bagatelles   1961   12.50   25.00   50.00
—Originals with "shaded dog" label
❏ LSC-2626 [S]   Beethoven: String Quartet in C# Minor   1962   7.50   15.00   30.00
—Original with "shaded dog" label
❏ LSC-2626 [S]   Beethoven: String Quartet in C# Minor   1964   12.50   25.00   50.00
—Second edition with "white dog" label; a rare instance where the later pressing is more sought after than the original
❏ LSC-2632 [S]   Beethoven: String Quartet in F, Op. 95; String Quartet in F, Op. 135   1962   15.00   30.00   60.00
—Original with "shaded dog" label

JULY
EPIC
❏ BN 26416   July   1969   50.00   100.00   200.00

JUNIOR'S EYES
A&M
❏ SP-4189   Junior's Eyes   1970   5.00   10.00   20.00

JUST IV
LIBERTY
❏ LRP-3340 [M]   First Twelve Sides   1964   5.00   10.00   20.00
❏ LST-7340 [S]   First Twelve Sides   1964   6.25   12.50   25.00

Number	Title (A Side/B Side)	Yr	VG	VG+	NM

JUST US
KAPP
❏ KL-1502 [M]	I Can't Grow Peaches on a Cherry Tree	1966	5.00	10.00	20.00
❏ KS-3502 [S]	I Can't Grow Peaches on a Cherry Tree	1966	6.25	12.50	25.00

JUSTICE, JIMMY
KAPP
❏ KL-1308 [M]	Justice for All	1963	6.25	12.50	25.00
❏ KS-3308 [S]	Justice for All	1963	10.00	20.00	40.00

JUSTIS, BILL
HARMONY
❏ KH 31189	Enchanted Sea	1972	3.00	6.00	12.00

MONUMENT
❏ MLP 8078 [M]	The Eternal Sea	1967	3.75	7.50	15.00
❏ SLP 18078 [S]	The Eternal Sea	1967	3.75	7.50	15.00

PHILLIPS INTERNATIONAL
❏ PLP-1950 [M]	Cloud Nine	1959	100.00	200.00	400.00

SMASH
❏ MGS-27021 [M]	Bill Justis Plays 12 Big Instrumental Hits (Alley Cat/Green Onions)	1962	3.75	7.50	15.00
❏ MGS-27030 [M]	Bill Justis Plays 12 More Big Instrumental Hits (Telstar/The Lonely Bull)	1963	3.75	7.50	15.00
❏ MGS-27031 [M]	Bill Justis Plays 12 Smash Instrumental Hits	1963	3.75	7.50	15.00
❏ MGS-27036 [M]	Bill Justis Plays 12 Top Tunes	1963	3.75	7.50	15.00
❏ MGS-27043 [M]	Bill Justis Plays 12 Other Instrumental Hits	1964	3.75	7.50	15.00
❏ MGS-27047 [M]	Dixieland Folk Style	1964	3.75	7.50	15.00
❏ MGS-27065 [M]	More Instrumental Hits	1965	3.75	7.50	15.00
❏ MGS-27077 [M]	Taste of Honey/The "In" Crowd	1966	3.75	7.50	15.00
❏ SRS-67021 [S]	Bill Justis Plays 12 Big Instrumental Hits (Alley Cat/Green Onions)	1962	5.00	10.00	20.00
❏ SRS-67030 [S]	Bill Justis Plays 12 More Big Instrumental Hits (Telstar/The Lonely Bull)	1963	5.00	10.00	20.00
❏ SRS-67031 [S]	Bill Justis Plays 12 Smash Instrumental Hits	1963	5.00	10.00	20.00
❏ SRS-67036 [S]	Bill Justis Plays 12 Top Tunes	1963	5.00	10.00	20.00
❏ SRS-67043 [S]	Bill Justis Plays 12 Other Instrumental Hits	1964	5.00	10.00	20.00
❏ SRS-67047 [S]	Dixieland Folk Style	1964	5.00	10.00	20.00
❏ SRS-67065 [S]	More Instrumental Hits	1965	5.00	10.00	20.00
❏ SRS-67077 [S]	Taste of Honey/The "In" Crowd	1966	5.00	10.00	20.00
❏ 830898-1	Raunchy	1987	2.50	5.00	10.00

SUN
❏ LP-109	Raunchy	1969	3.00	6.00	12.00

K

K-DOE, ERNIE
JANUS
❏ JLS-3030	Ernie K-Doe	1971	6.25	12.50	25.00

MINIT
❏ LP-0002 [M]	Mother-in-Law	1961	50.00	100.00	200.00
—Orange label					
❏ LP-24002 [R]	Mother-in-Law	196?	37.50	75.00	150.00
—Black label, not issued until after Imperial bought Minit					

KAEMPFERT, BERT
DECCA
❏ DL 4101 [M]	Wonderland by Night	1960	3.75	7.50	15.00
❏ DL 4117 [M]	The Wonderland of Bert Kaempfert	1961	3.75	7.50	15.00
❏ DL 4161 [M]	Dancing in Wonderland	1961	3.75	7.50	15.00
❏ DL 4228 [M]	With a "Sound" in My Heart	1962	3.00	6.00	12.00
❏ DL 4265 [M]	Lights Out, Sweet Dreams	1963	3.00	6.00	12.00
❏ DL 4273 [M]	Afrikaan Beat and Other Favorites	1962	3.00	6.00	12.00
❏ DL 4305 [M]	That Happy Feeling	1962	3.00	6.00	12.00
❏ DL 4374 [M]	Living It Up!	1963	3.00	6.00	12.00
❏ DL 4441 [M]	Christmas Wonderland	1963	3.75	7.50	15.00
❏ DL 4490 [M]	That Latin Feeling	1964	3.00	6.00	12.00
❏ DL 4569 [M]	Blue Midnight	1965	3.00	6.00	12.00
❏ DL 4616 [M]	The Magic Music of Far Away Places	1965	3.00	6.00	12.00
❏ DL 4670 [M]	Three O'Clock in the Morning	1965	3.00	6.00	12.00
❏ DL 4693 [M]	Bye Bye Blues	1966	3.00	6.00	12.00
❏ DL 4795 [M]	Strangers in the Night	1966	3.00	6.00	12.00
❏ DL 4810 [M]	Bert Kaempfert's Greatest Hits	1966	3.00	6.00	12.00
❏ DL 4860 [M]	Hold Me	1967	3.00	6.00	12.00
❏ DL 4925 [M]	The World We Knew	1967	5.00	10.00	20.00
❏ DL 4986 [M]	Love That	1968	5.00	10.00	20.00
❏ DXS 7200 [(2)]	The Best of Bert Kaempfert	197?	5.00	10.00	20.00
❏ DL 8881 [M]	April in Portugal	1959	3.75	7.50	15.00
❏ DL 34485	The Best of Bert Kaempfert	197?	5.00	10.00	20.00
—Special Decca Custom Division edition					
❏ DL 74101 [S]	Wonderland by Night	1960	5.00	10.00	20.00
❏ DL 74117 [S]	The Wonderland of Bert Kaempfert	1961	5.00	10.00	20.00
❏ DL 74161 [S]	Dancing in Wonderland	1961	5.00	10.00	20.00
❏ DL 74228 [S]	With a "Sound" in My Heart	1962	3.75	7.50	15.00
❏ DL 74265 [S]	Lights Out, Sweet Dreams	1963	3.75	7.50	15.00
❏ DL 74273 [S]	Afrikaan Beat and Other Favorites	1962	3.75	7.50	15.00
❏ DL 74305 [S]	That Happy Feeling	1962	3.75	7.50	15.00
❏ DL 74374 [S]	Living It Up!	1963	3.75	7.50	15.00
❏ DL 74441 [S]	Christmas Wonderland	1963	4.00	8.00	16.00
—Same as above, but in stereo					
❏ DL 74490 [S]	That Latin Feeling	1964	3.75	7.50	15.00
❏ DL 74569 [S]	Blue Midnight	1965	3.75	7.50	15.00
❏ DL 74616 [S]	The Magic Music of Far Away Places	1965	3.75	7.50	15.00
❏ DL 74670 [S]	Three O'Clock in the Morning	1965	3.75	7.50	15.00
❏ DL 74693 [S]	Bye Bye Blues	1966	3.75	7.50	15.00
❏ DL 74795 [S]	Strangers in the Night	1966	3.75	7.50	15.00
❏ DL 74810 [S]	Bert Kaempfert's Greatest Hits	1966	3.75	7.50	15.00
❏ DL 74860 [S]	Hold Me	1967	3.75	7.50	15.00
❏ DL 74925 [S]	The World We Knew	1967	3.75	7.50	15.00
❏ DL 74986 [S]	Love That	1968	3.75	7.50	15.00
❏ DL 75059	My Way of Life	1968	3.75	7.50	15.00
❏ DL 75089	Warm and Wonderful	1969	3.75	7.50	15.00
❏ DL 75140	Traces of Love	1969	3.75	7.50	15.00
❏ DL 75175	The Kaempfert Touch	1970	3.75	7.50	15.00
❏ DL 75234	Free and Easy	1970	3.75	7.50	15.00
❏ DL 75256	Orange Colored Sky	1971	3.75	7.50	15.00
❏ DL 75305	Bert Kaempfert Now!	1971	3.75	7.50	15.00
❏ DL 75322	Six Plus Six	1972	3.75	7.50	15.00
❏ DL 78881 [S]	April in Portugal	1959	5.00	10.00	20.00

MCA
❏ 11	Bert Kaempfert's Greatest Hits	1973	2.50	5.00	10.00
—Reissue of Decca 74810					
❏ 314	The Fabulous Fifties	1973	3.00	6.00	12.00
❏ 447	Gallery	1974	3.00	6.00	12.00

KAK
EPIC
❏ BN 26429	Kak	1969	62.50	125.00	250.00
—Beware -- a reissue that looks almost identical to the original and sells for around $12 appeared in stores in 2000-2001					

KALABASH CORP., THE
UNCLE BILL
❏ KB-3114	The Kalabash Corp.	1970	20.00	40.00	80.00

KALEIDOSCOPE, THE
EPIC
❏ LN 24304 [M]	Side Trips	1967	7.50	15.00	30.00
❏ LN 24333 [M]	Beacon from Mars	1967	15.00	30.00	60.00
❏ BN 26304 [S]	Side Trips	1967	10.00	20.00	40.00
❏ BN 26333 [S]	Beacon from Mars	1967	25.00	50.00	100.00
❏ BN 26467	Incredible Kaleidoscope	1969	7.50	15.00	30.00
❏ BN 26508	Bernice	1970	7.50	15.00	30.00

PACIFIC ARTS
❏ 102	When Scopes Collide	1978	3.00	6.00	12.00

KALIN TWINS, THE
DECCA
❏ DL 8812 [M]	The Kalin Twins	1959	25.00	50.00	100.00

VOCALION
❏ VL 3771 [M]	When	1966	3.75	7.50	15.00
❏ VL 73771 [R]	When	1966	3.00	6.00	12.00

KALLAO, ALEX
BATON
❏ BL-1205 [M]	Alex Kallao in Concert, University of Ottawa	1957	15.00	30.00	60.00

RCA VICTOR
❏ LJM-1011 [M]	Evening at the Embers	1954	12.50	25.00	50.00

KALLEN, KITTY
COLUMBIA
❏ CL 1404 [M]	If I Give My Heart to You	1960	5.00	10.00	20.00
❏ CL 1662 [M]	Honky Tonk Angel	1961	5.00	10.00	20.00
❏ CS 8204 [S]	If I Give My Heart to You	1960	6.25	12.50	25.00
❏ CS 8462 [S]	Honky Tonk Angel	1961	6.25	12.50	25.00

DECCA
❏ DL 8397 [M]	It's a Lonesome Old Town	1958	10.00	20.00	40.00

MERCURY
❏ MG 25206 [10]	Pretty Kitty Kallen Sings	1955	12.50	25.00	50.00

MOVIETONE
❏ 71026 [M]	Delightfully	1967	3.75	7.50	15.00
❏ S-72026 [S]	Delightfully	1967	3.75	7.50	15.00

RCA VICTOR
❏ LPM-2640 [M]	My Coloring Book	1963	5.00	10.00	20.00
❏ LSP-2640 [S]	My Coloring Book	1963	6.25	12.50	25.00

VOCALION
❏ VL 3679 [M]	Little Things Mean a Lot	1959	6.25	12.50	25.00

WING
❏ MGW-12241 [M]	Kitty Kallen Sings	196?	3.75	7.50	15.00
❏ SRW-16241 [R]	Kitty Kallen Sings	196?	3.00	6.00	12.00

KALLMAN, DICK
RCA VICTOR
❏ LPM-3485 [M]	Dick Kallman Drops In as Hank	1966	5.00	10.00	20.00
❏ LSP-3485 [S]	Dick Kallman Drops In as Hank	1966	6.25	12.50	25.00

KAMINSKY, MAX
COMMODORE
❏ FL-20019 [10]	Max Kaminsky	1952	12.50	25.00	50.00

CONCERT HALL JAZZ
❏ 1009 [10]	Windy City Jazz	1955	12.50	25.00	50.00

JAZZTONE
❏ J-1208 [M]	Chicago Style	1955	10.00	20.00	40.00

MGM
❏ E-261 [10]	When the Saints Go Marching In	1954	12.50	25.00	50.00

RCA VICTOR
❏ LJM-3003 [10]	Jazz on the Campus, Ltd.	1954	12.50	25.00	50.00

UNITED ARTISTS
❏ UAL-3174 [M]	Max Goes East	1961	5.00	10.00	20.00
❏ UAS-6174 [S]	Max Goes East	1961	6.25	12.50	25.00

KAMUCA, RICHIE
HIFI
❏ R-604 [M]	Jazz Erotica	1957	15.00	30.00	60.00
❏ J-609 [M]	West Coast Jazz in Hi-Fi	1959	7.50	15.00	30.00
❏ JS-609 [S]	West Coast Jazz in Hi-Fi	1959	10.00	20.00	40.00

MODE
❏ LP-102 [M]	Richie Kamuka Quartet	1957	20.00	40.00	80.00

Number	Title (A Side/B Side)	Yr	VG	VG+	NM

KANE, BIG DADDY
COLD CHILLIN'

Number	Title (A Side/B Side)	Yr	VG	VG+	NM
❏ PRO-A-5205 [(2)DJ]	Prince of Darkness	1991	7.50	15.00	30.00
—Vinyl is promo only					
❏ 25731	Long Live the Kane	1988	10.00	20.00	40.00
❏ 25941	It's a Big Daddy Thing	1989	7.50	15.00	30.00
❏ 26303	Taste of Chocolate	1990	5.00	10.00	20.00

KANE'S COUSINS
SHOVE LOVE

❏ 9827	Undergum Bubbleground	1969	10.00	20.00	40.00

KANGAROO
MGM

❏ SE-4586	Kangaroo	1968	6.25	12.50	25.00

KANNIBAL KOMIX
COLOSSUS

❏ 1004	Kannibal Komix	1970	5.00	10.00	20.00

KANSAS
CBS ASSOCIATED

❏ QZ 38733	Drastic Measures	1983	2.00	4.00	8.00
❏ QZ 39283	The Best of Kansas	1984	2.00	4.00	8.00

KIRSHNER

❏ AS 555 [DJ]	Two for the Show (Sampler)	1978	5.00	10.00	20.00
—Promo-only single disc of selections from 35660					
❏ KZ 32817	Kansas	1974	3.00	6.00	12.00
❏ PZ 32817	Kansas	197?	2.00	4.00	8.00
—Reissue					
❏ PZ 33385	Song for America	1975	3.00	6.00	12.00
—Without bar code on cover					
❏ PZ 33385	Song for America	198?	2.00	4.00	8.00
—With bar code on cover					
❏ PZ 33806	Masque	1975	3.00	6.00	12.00
—Without bar code on cover					
❏ PZ 33806	Masque	198?	2.00	4.00	8.00
—With bar code on cover					
❏ JZ 34224	Leftoverture	1976	2.50	5.00	10.00
❏ PZ 34224	Leftoverture	198?	2.00	4.00	8.00
—Budget-line reissue					
❏ JZ 34929	Point of Know Return	1977	2.50	5.00	10.00
❏ PZ2 35660 [(2)]	Two for the Show	1978	3.75	7.50	15.00
❏ FZ 36008	Monolith	1979	2.50	5.00	10.00
❏ PZ 36008	Monolith	198?	2.00	4.00	8.00
—Budget-line reissue					
❏ FZ 36588	Audio-Visions	1980	2.50	5.00	10.00
❏ PZ 36588	Audio-Visions	198?	2.00	4.00	8.00
—Budget-line reissue					
❏ FZ 38002	Vinyl Confessions	1982	2.50	5.00	10.00
❏ PZ 38002	Vinyl Confessions	198?	2.00	4.00	8.00
—Budget-line reissue					
❏ HZ 44224	Leftoverture	1982	10.00	20.00	40.00
—Half-speed mastered edition					
❏ HZ 44929	Point of Know Return	1982	10.00	20.00	40.00
—Half-speed mastered edition					
❏ HZ 46008	Monolith	1982	12.50	25.00	50.00
—Half-speed mastered edition					
❏ HZ 48002	Vinyl Confessions	1982	25.00	50.00	100.00
—Half-speed mastered edition					

MCA

❏ 5838	Power	1986	2.00	4.00	8.00
❏ 6254	In the Spirit of Things	1988	2.00	4.00	8.00

KANTNER, PAUL/JEFFERSON STARSHIP
RCA VICTOR

❏ AYL1-3868	Blows Against the Empire	1981	2.00	4.00	8.00
—Budget-line reissue					
❏ AFL1-4448	Blows Against the Empire	1977	2.50	5.00	10.00
—Reissue of LSP-4448					
❏ LSP-4448	Blows Against the Empire	1970	3.75	7.50	15.00
❏ LSP-4448 [DJ]	Blows Against the Empire	1970	37.50	75.00	150.00
—Clear vinyl promo					

KAPLAN, ARTIE
HOPI

❏ VHS 901	Confessions of a Male Chauvinist Pig	1971	6.25	12.50	25.00

KARLOFF, BORIS
CAEDMON

❏ TC-1038 [M]	Just So Stories and Other Tales	195?	6.25	12.50	25.00
❏ TC-1074 [M]	The Reluctant Dragon	196?	6.25	12.50	25.00
❏ TC-1075 [M]	The Pied Piper; The Hunting of the Snarks	196?	6.25	12.50	25.00
❏ TC-1088 [M]	More of Kipling's Just So Stories	196?	6.25	12.50	25.00
❏ TC-1100 [M]	Kipling's Jungle Books: How Fear Came	196?	6.25	12.50	25.00
❏ TC-1109 [M]	The Ugly Duckling and Other Tales	196?	6.25	12.50	25.00
❏ TC-1117 [M]	The Little Match Girl and Other Tales	196?	6.25	12.50	25.00
❏ TC-1129 [M]	The Three Bears, Henny Penny and Other Fairy Tales	1962	6.25	12.50	25.00
❏ TC-1139 [M]	The Cat That Walked By Herself	196?	6.25	12.50	25.00
❏ TC-1176 [M]	Kipling's Jungle Books: Toomai of the Elephants	196?	6.25	12.50	25.00
❏ TC-1221 [M]	Aesop's Fables	1967	5.00	10.00	20.00

DECCA

❏ DL 4833 [M]	An Evening with Boris Karloff and His Friends	1967	5.00	10.00	20.00
❏ DL 74833 [S]	An Evening with Boris Karloff and His Friends	1967	6.25	12.50	25.00

MERCURY

❏ MG-20815 [M]	Tales of the Frightened, Volume 1	1963	10.00	20.00	40.00
❏ MG-20816 [M]	Tales of the Frightened, Volume 2	1963	10.00	20.00	40.00
❏ SR-60815 [S]	Tales of the Frightened, Volume 1	1963	12.50	25.00	50.00
❏ SR-60816 [S]	Tales of the Frightened, Volume 2	1963	12.50	25.00	50.00

KASSEL, ART
KAPP

❏ KL-1248 [M]	Dance to the Music of Art Kassel	1962	5.00	10.00	20.00
❏ KS-3248 [S]	Dance to the Music of Art Kassel	1962	6.25	12.50	25.00

KATMANDU
MAINSTREAM

❏ S-6131	Katmandu	1971	10.00	20.00	40.00

KATZ, DICK
ATLANTIC

❏ 1314 [M]	Piano and Pin	1959	10.00	20.00	40.00
—Black label					
❏ 1314 [M]	Piano and Pin	1961	6.25	12.50	25.00
—Multicolor label, white "fan" logo at right					
❏ SD 1314 [S]	Piano and Pin	1959	10.00	20.00	40.00
—Green label					
❏ SD 1314 [S]	Piano and Pin	1961	5.00	10.00	20.00
—Multicolor label, white "fan" logo at right					

KATZ, DICK; DEREK SMITH; RENE URTREGER
ATLANTIC

❏ 1287 [M]	John Lewis Presents Jazz Piano International	1958	10.00	20.00	40.00
—Black label					
❏ 1287 [M]	John Lewis Presents Jazz Piano International	1961	6.25	12.50	25.00
—Multicolor label, white "fan" logo at right					

KATZ, FRED
DECCA

❏ DL 9202 [M]	Soulo Cello	1958	10.00	20.00	40.00
❏ DL 9213 [M]	4-5-6 Trio	1958	10.00	20.00	40.00
❏ DL 9217 [M]	Fred Katz and Jammers	1958	10.00	20.00	40.00
❏ DL 79202 [S]	Soulo Cello	1958	7.50	15.00	30.00
❏ DL 79213 [S]	4-5-6 Trio	1958	7.50	15.00	30.00
❏ DL 79217 [S]	Fred Katz and Jammers	1958	7.50	15.00	30.00

WARNER BROS.

❏ W 1277 [M]	Folk Songs for Far Out Folks	1959	6.25	12.50	25.00
❏ WS 1277 [S]	Folk Songs for Far Out Folks	1959	7.50	15.00	30.00

KATZ, MICKEY
CAPITOL

❏ H 298 [10]	Mickey Katz: The Star of Broadway's Borschtcapades	195?	10.00	20.00	40.00
❏ T 298 [M]	The Very Best of Mickey Katz	195?	7.50	15.00	30.00
—Turquoise or gray label					
❏ H 457 [10]	The Family Danced	195?	10.00	20.00	40.00
❏ T 799 [M]	Mish Mosh	1957	7.50	15.00	30.00
—Turquoise or gray label					
❏ T 934 [M]	Katz Puts On the Dog	1958	7.50	15.00	30.00
—Turquoise or gray label					
❏ T 1021 [M]	Katz Plays Music for Weddings, Bar Mitzvahs and Brisses	1958	7.50	15.00	30.00
—Turquoise or gray label					
❏ T 1102 [M]	The Most Mishige	1959	6.25	12.50	25.00
—Black colorband label, logo at left					
❏ W 1257 [M]	Katz Pajamas	1959	6.25	12.50	25.00
—Black colorband label, logo at left					
❏ W 1307 [M]	Comin' Round the Katzkills	1959	6.25	12.50	25.00
—Black colorband label, logo at left					
❏ ST 1445 [S]	The Borscht Jester	1960	6.25	12.50	25.00
—Black colorband label, logo at left					
❏ T 1445 [M]	The Borscht Jester	1960	5.00	10.00	20.00
—Black colorband label, logo at left					
❏ ST 1603 [S]	At the U.N.	1961	6.25	12.50	25.00
—Black colorband label, logo at left					
❏ T 1603 [M]	At the U.N.	1961	5.00	10.00	20.00
—Black colorband label, logo at left					
❏ ST 1744 [S]	Sing Along with Mickele	1962	6.25	12.50	25.00
❏ T 1744 [M]	Sing Along with Mickele	1962	5.00	10.00	20.00

RCA VICTOR

❏ LPM-3193 [10]	Borscht	1954	10.00	20.00	40.00

KAUFMANN, BOB
LHI

❏ 12002	Trip Through a Blown Mind	1967	15.00	30.00	60.00

KAY, JOHN, AND SPARROW
See SPARROW.

KAY, JOHN, AND STEPPENWOLF
See STEPPENWOLF.

KAYAK
HARVEST

❏ ST-11305	See See the Sun	1973	3.75	7.50	15.00

JANUS

❏ (no #) [PD]	Phantom of the Night	1979	6.25	12.50	25.00
—Numbered limited edition of 3,000					
❏ NXS-7023	Royal Bed Bouncer	1975	2.50	5.00	10.00
❏ NXS-7034	Starlight Dancer	1978	2.50	5.00	10.00
❏ NXS-7039	Phantom of the Night	1979	2.50	5.00	10.00

MERCURY

❏ SRM-1-3824	Periscope Life	1980	2.50	5.00	10.00

KAYE, DANNY
CAPITOL

❏ T 937 [M]	Mommy Gimme a Drinka Water	1958	10.00	20.00	40.00

COLUMBIA

❏ CL 6023 [10]	Danny Kaye	1949	12.50	25.00	50.00
❏ CL 6249 [10]	Danny Kaye Entertains	195?	12.50	25.00	50.00

DECCA

❏ DSXB 175 [(2)R]	The Best of Danny Kaye	1965	3.75	7.50	15.00
❏ DXB 175 [(2)M]	The Best of Danny Kaye	1965	6.25	12.50	25.00

Number	Title (A Side/B Side)	Yr	VG	VG+	NM
❏ DLP 5033 [10]	Danny Kaye	1950	12.50	25.00	50.00
❏ DL 5094 [10]	Gilbert and Sullivan and Danny Kaye	1950	12.50	25.00	50.00
❏ DL 8212 [M]	The Court Jester	1955	12.50	25.00	50.00
—Black label, silver print					
❏ DL 8461 [M]	Danny at the Palace	1957	12.50	25.00	50.00
—Black label, silver print					
❏ DL 8461 [M]	Danny at the Palace	1960	6.25	12.50	25.00
—Black label with color bars					
❏ DL 8726 [M]	Danny Kaye for Children	1959	7.50	15.00	30.00
—Black label, silver print					
❏ DL 8726 [M]	Danny Kaye for Children	1960	6.25	12.50	25.00
—Black label with color bars					

KAYE, MARY, TRIO
COLUMBIA

Number	Title (A Side/B Side)	Yr	VG	VG+	NM
❏ CL 1910 [M]	Our Hawaii	1962	3.75	7.50	15.00
❏ CS 8710 [S]	Our Hawaii	1962	5.00	10.00	20.00

DECCA

❏ DL 8238 [M]	The Mary Kaye Trio	1956	7.50	15.00	30.00
❏ DL 8434 [M]	Music on a Silver Platter	1957	7.50	15.00	30.00
❏ DL 8650 [M]	You Don't Know What Love Is	1958	7.50	15.00	30.00

MOVIETONE

❏ 71027 [M]	Just Us	1967	3.00	6.00	12.00
❏ S 72027 [S]	Just Us	1967	3.00	6.00	12.00

20TH CENTURY FOX

❏ TFM-3117 [M]	Night Life	1964	3.00	6.00	12.00
❏ TFS-4117 [S]	Night Life	1964	3.75	7.50	15.00

VERVE

❏ MGV-2142 [M]	Up Front!	1960	10.00	20.00	40.00
❏ V-8446 [M]	For the Record	1962	5.00	10.00	20.00
❏ V6-8446 [S]	For the Record	1962	6.25	12.50	25.00

WARNER BROS.

❏ B 1222 [M]	Too Much!	1958	5.00	10.00	20.00
❏ W 1263 [M]	Jackpot	1959	5.00	10.00	20.00
❏ WS 1263 [S]	Jackpot	1959	6.25	12.50	25.00
❏ W 1342 [M]	The Mary Kaye Trio on the Sunset Strip	1959	5.00	10.00	20.00
❏ WS 1342 [S]	The Mary Kaye Trio on the Sunset Strip	1959	6.25	12.50	25.00

KAYE, SAMMY
COLUMBIA

❏ CL 561 [M]	Swing and Sway with Sammy Kaye	195?	7.50	15.00	30.00
❏ CL 668 [M]	Music, Maestro, Please!	195?	7.50	15.00	30.00
❏ CL 885 [M]	My Fair Lady (For Dancing)	1956	5.00	10.00	20.00
❏ CL 891 [M]	What Makes Sammy Swing and Sway	1956	5.00	10.00	20.00
❏ CL 964 [M]	Sunday Serenade	1957	5.00	10.00	20.00
❏ CL 1018 [M]	Popular American Waltzes	1957	5.00	10.00	20.00
❏ CL 2541 [10]	Christmas Serenade	1955	10.00	20.00	40.00
—"House Party Series" issue					
❏ CL 6155 [10]	Sunday Serenade	1953	10.00	20.00	40.00

RCA CAMDEN

❏ CAL-355 [M]	Swing and Sway with Sammy Kaye	1957	5.00	10.00	20.00

RCA VICTOR

❏ LPM 15 [10]	Sammy Kaye Plays Irving Berlin for Dancing	1950	12.50	25.00	50.00
❏ LPM-3966 [M]	The Best of Sammy Kaye	1967	5.00	10.00	20.00

KAZ, FRED
ATLANTIC

❏ 1335 [M]	Eastern Exposure	1960	6.25	12.50	25.00
—Multicolor label, white "fan" logo at right					
❏ SD 1335 [S]	Eastern Exposure	1960	7.50	15.00	30.00
—Multicolor label, white "fan" logo at right					

KAZAN, LAINIE
MGM

❏ E-4340 [M]	Right Now	1966	5.00	10.00	20.00
❏ SE-4340 [S]	Right Now	1966	6.25	12.50	25.00
❏ E-4385 [M]	Lainie Kazan	1966	5.00	10.00	20.00
❏ SE-4385 [S]	Lainie Kazan	1966	6.25	12.50	25.00
❏ E-4451 [M]	The Love Album	1967	6.25	12.50	25.00
❏ SE-4451 [S]	The Love Album	1967	5.00	10.00	20.00
❏ SE-4496	Love Is	1968	5.00	10.00	20.00
❏ SE-4631	The Best of Lainie Kazan	1969	5.00	10.00	20.00

KEATING, JOHNNY
BALLY

❏ BAL-12001 [M]	English Jazz	1956	12.50	25.00	50.00

DOT

❏ DLP-3066 [M]	Swinging Scots	1957	10.00	20.00	40.00

KEENE, BOB
ANDEX

❏ S-4001 [M]	Solo for 7	1958	12.50	25.00	50.00

DEL-FI

❏ DFLP-1202 [M]	Unforgettable Love Songs of the 50's	1959	10.00	20.00	40.00
❏ DFLP-1222 [M]	Twist to Radio KRLA	1962	7.50	15.00	30.00

GENE NORMAN

❏ GNP-149 [10]	Bob Keene	1954	12.50	25.00	50.00

KEITH
MERCURY

❏ MG-21102 [M]	98.6/Ain't Gonna Lie	1967	3.75	7.50	15.00
❏ MG-21129 [M]	Out of Crank	1967	3.75	7.50	15.00
❏ SR-61102 [S]	98.6/Ain't Gonna Lie	1967	5.00	10.00	20.00
❏ SR-61129 [S]	Out of Crank	1967	5.00	10.00	20.00

RCA VICTOR

❏ LSP-4143	The Adventures of Keith	1969	5.00	10.00	20.00

KEITH AND DONNA
Also see THE GRATEFUL DEAD.
ROUND

❏ RX-104	Keith and Donna	1975	7.50	15.00	30.00

KELLAWAY, ROGER
DISCWASHER

Number	Title (A Side/B Side)	Yr	VG	VG+	NM
❏ 003	Nostalgia Suite	1979	5.00	10.00	20.00

PACIFIC JAZZ

❏ PJ-10122 [M]	Spirit Feel	196?	5.00	10.00	20.00

PRESTIGE

❏ PRLP-7399 [M]	The Roger Kellaway Trio	1965	6.25	12.50	25.00
❏ PRST-7399 [S]	The Roger Kellaway Trio	1965	7.50	15.00	30.00

REGINA

❏ R-298 [M]	Portraits	1964	5.00	10.00	20.00
❏ RS-298 [S]	Portraits	1964	6.25	12.50	25.00

WORLD PACIFIC

❏ WP-21861 [M]	Stride	1967	5.00	10.00	20.00

KELLER, ALLEN
CHARLIE PARKER

❏ PLP-817 [M]	A New Look at the World	1962	6.25	12.50	25.00
❏ PLP-817S [S]	A New Look at the World	1962	7.50	15.00	30.00

KELLER, HAL
SAND

❏ 7 [M]	Hal Keller Debut	1957	12.50	25.00	50.00

SOUND

❏ 602 [M]	Hal Keller Debut	1959	10.00	20.00	40.00

KELLER, JERRY
KAPP

❏ KL-1178 [M]	Here Comes Jerry Keller	1959	10.00	20.00	40.00
❏ KS-3178 [S]	Here Comes Jerry Keller	1959	12.50	25.00	50.00

KELLERMAN, SALLY
DECCA

❏ DL 75359	Roll with the Feelin'	1972	5.00	10.00	20.00

KELLIN, MIKE
VERVE FORECAST

❏ FT-3028 [M]	Mike Kellin	1967	6.25	12.50	25.00
❏ FTS-3028 [S]	Mike Kellin	1967	6.25	12.50	25.00

KELLY, BEVERLY
AUDIO FIDELITY

❏ AFLP-1874 [M]	Beverly Kelly Sings	1958	7.50	15.00	30.00
❏ AFSD-5874 [S]	Beverly Kelly Sings	1958	10.00	20.00	40.00

RIVERSIDE

❏ RLP-328 [M]	Love Locked Out	1960	6.25	12.50	25.00
❏ RLP-345 [M]	Bev Kelly In Person	1960	6.25	12.50	25.00
❏ RS-9328 [S]	Love Locked Out	1960	7.50	15.00	30.00
❏ RS-9345 [S]	Bev Kelly In Person	1960	7.50	15.00	30.00

KELLY, EMMETT
ROULETTE

❏ R-25130 [M]	Sing Along with Emmett Kelly	1962	6.25	12.50	25.00
❏ SR-25130 [S]	Sing Along with Emmett Kelly	1962	7.50	15.00	30.00

KELLY, JACK
JUBILEE

❏ JLP-21 [10]	Jack Kelly's Badinage	1955	12.50	25.00	50.00

KELLY, MONTY
ALSHIRE

❏ SAS 610	Passport to Romance	196?	2.50	5.00	10.00

CARLTON

❏ LP 12-111 [M]	Porgy and Bess	1959	5.00	10.00	20.00
❏ STLP 12-111 [S]	Porgy and Bess	1959	6.25	12.50	25.00
❏ LP 12-123 [M]	Summer Set	1960	5.00	10.00	20.00
❏ STLP 12-123 [S]	Summer Set	1960	6.25	12.50	25.00

ESSEX

❏ ESLP-106 [10]	I Love	1954	7.50	15.00	30.00
❏ ESLP-108 [10]	Monty Kelly Takes Me to Far Away Places	1954	7.50	15.00	30.00
❏ ESLP-203 [M]	Tropicana	1955	6.25	12.50	25.00

SOMERSET

❏ P 7300 [M]	Tropicana	196?	2.50	5.00	10.00
—Reissue of Trans World 203					

TRANS WORLD

❏ TWLP-203 [M]	Tropicana	1956	5.00	10.00	20.00
—Reissue of Essex 203					

KELLY, WYNTON
BLUE NOTE

❏ BLP-5025 [10]	Piano Interpretations by Wynton Kelly	1953	75.00	150.00	300.00

JAZZLAND

❏ JLP-83 [M]	Whisper Not	1962	7.50	15.00	30.00
❏ JLP-983 [S]	Whisper Not	1962	6.25	12.50	25.00

RIVERSIDE

❏ RLP 12-254 [M]	Wynton Kelly Piano	1957	12.50	25.00	50.00
❏ RLP 12-298 [M]	Kelly Blue	1959	12.50	25.00	50.00
❏ RLP-1142 [S]	Kelly Blue	1959	10.00	20.00	40.00

VEE JAY

❏ LP-1016 [M]	Kelly Great	1960	7.50	15.00	30.00
❏ SR-1016 [S]	Kelly Great	1960	10.00	20.00	40.00
❏ VJ-1086 [M]	Best of Wynton Kelly	1964	5.00	10.00	20.00
❏ VJS-1086 [S]	Best of Wynton Kelly	1964	6.25	12.50	25.00
❏ LP-3004 [M]	Kelly Great	1960	6.25	12.50	25.00
—Reissue of LP-1016					
❏ SR-3004 [S]	Kelly Great	1960	7.50	15.00	30.00
—Reissue of SR-1016					
❏ LP-3011 [M]	Kelly at Midnight	1960	6.25	12.50	25.00
❏ SR-3011 [S]	Kelly at Midnight	1960	7.50	15.00	30.00
❏ LP-3022 [M]	Wynton Kelly	1961	6.25	12.50	25.00
❏ SR-3022 [S]	Wynton Kelly	1961	7.50	15.00	30.00
❏ VJS-3072-2 [(2)]	Final Notes	1977	5.00	10.00	20.00

Number	Title (A Side/B Side)	Yr	VG	VG+	NM
VERVE					
❏ V6-8576 [S]	Comin' In the Back Door	1964	5.00	10.00	20.00
❏ V6-8588 [S]	It's All Right	1964	5.00	10.00	20.00
❏ V6-8622 [S]	Undiluted	1965	5.00	10.00	20.00
❏ V6-8633 [S]	Smokin' at the Half Note	1965	5.00	10.00	20.00

KELLY BROTHERS, THE

Number	Title (A Side/B Side)	Yr	VG	VG+	NM
EXCELLO					
❏ LPS-8007	Sweet Soul	1968	12.50	25.00	50.00
KING					
❏ 810 [M]	The Kelly Brothers Sing a Page of Songs from the Good Book	1962	25.00	50.00	100.00

KENDALLS, THE

Number	Title (A Side/B Side)	Yr	VG	VG+	NM
DOT					
❏ DLP-26001	Two Divided by Love	1972	3.75	7.50	15.00
EPIC					
❏ E2 45249 [(2)]	20 Favorites	1989	3.75	7.50	15.00
GUSTO					
❏ GT 0001	1978 Grammy Award Winners — Best Country Duo	1978	2.50	5.00	10.00
MCA					
❏ 27021	Never Ending Song of Love	198?	2.50	5.00	10.00
MCA CURB					
❏ 5724	Fire at First Sight	1986	2.00	4.00	8.00
MERCURY					
❏ SRM-1-4046	Stickin' Together	1982	2.50	5.00	10.00
❏ SRM-1-6005	Lettin' You In on a Feelin'	1981	2.50	5.00	10.00
❏ 812779-1	Movin' Train	1983	2.00	4.00	8.00
❏ 824250-1	Two Heart Harmony	1985	2.00	4.00	8.00
❏ 826307-1	Thank God for the Radio... And All the Hits	1986	2.00	4.00	8.00
OVATION					
❏ 1719	Heaven's Just a Sin Away	1977	3.00	6.00	12.00
❏ 1733	Old Fashioned Love	1978	3.00	6.00	12.00
❏ 1739	Just Like Real People	1979	3.00	6.00	12.00
❏ 1746	Heart of the Matter	1979	3.00	6.00	12.00
❏ 1756	The Best of the Kendalls	1980	3.00	6.00	12.00
POWER PAK					
❏ PO-216	Leavin' on a Jet Plane	197?	2.50	5.00	10.00
STEP ONE					
❏ 0023	Break the Routine	1987	2.50	5.00	10.00
STOP					
❏ 1020	Meet the Kendalls	1970	5.00	10.00	20.00

KENNEDY, DAVE

Number	Title (A Side/B Side)	Yr	VG	VG+	NM
COULEE					
❏ 1001 [M]	Breaking Up Is Hard to Do	1964	12.50	25.00	50.00

KENNEDY, JERRY

Also see TOM AND JERRY (2).

Number	Title (A Side/B Side)	Yr	VG	VG+	NM
SMASH					
❏ MGS-27004 [M]	Dancing Guitars Rock Elvis' Hits	1962	7.50	15.00	30.00
❏ MGS-27024 [M]	Jerry Kennedy's Guitars and Strings Play the Golden Standards	1963	5.00	10.00	20.00
❏ MGS-27066 [M]	From Nashville to Soulville	1965	5.00	10.00	20.00
❏ SRS-67004 [S]	Dancing Guitars Rock Elvis' Hits	1962	10.00	20.00	40.00
❏ SRS-67024 [S]	Jerry Kennedy's Guitars and Strings Play the Golden Standards	1963	6.25	12.50	25.00
❏ SRS-67066 [S]	From Nashville to Soulville	1965	6.25	12.50	25.00

KENNEDY, JOHN FITZGERALD

Various tribute records, most of which were released in the immediate aftermath of his assassination in 1963.

Number	Title (A Side/B Side)	Yr	VG	VG+	NM
CAEDMON					
❏ TC-2021 [(2)]	Self-Portrait	196?	5.00	10.00	20.00
CAPITOL					
❏ ST 2486 [S]	Years of Lightning, Day of Drums	1966	7.50	15.00	30.00
❏ T 2486 [M]	Years of Lightning, Day of Drums	1966	5.00	10.00	20.00
—Narrated by Gregory Peck; U.S. Information Agency movie soundtrack					
COLPIX					
❏ CP 2500 [M]	Four Days That Shocked the World	1964	12.50	25.00	50.00
—Narrated by Reid Collins; covers Nov. 22-25, 1963					
DECCA					
❏ DL 9116 [M]	That Was The Week That Was	1963	5.00	10.00	20.00
—BBC show's tribute to JFK, broadcast Nov. 23, 1963					
DIPLOMAT					
❏ 10000 [M]	John F. Kennedy — A Memorial Album	1963	3.75	7.50	15.00
DOCUMENTARIES UNLIMITED					
❏ (no #) [M]	JFK The Man, The President	1963	5.00	10.00	20.00
—Narrated by Barry Gray					
HARMONICA					
❏ HLP-3005 [M]	Kennedy Speaks	1963	5.00	10.00	20.00
LEGACY					
❏ L2L 1017 [(2)M]	John Fitzgerald Kennedy...As We Remember Him	1965	6.25	12.50	25.00
—Narrated by Charles Kuralt; with 240-page book					
PICKWICK					
❏ 169 [M]	The Presidential Years (1960-1963)	1963	3.75	7.50	15.00
PREMIER					
❏ 2099 [M]	A Memorial Album	1963	5.00	10.00	20.00
—From WMCA Radio, New York, Nov. 22, 1963					
RCA VICTOR					
❏ VDM-101 [M]	The Kennedy Wit	1964	3.75	7.50	15.00
—Narrated by David Brinkley with introduction by Adlai E. Stevenson					
SOMERSET					
❏ 16100 [M]	Actual Speeches of Franklin D. Roosevelt and John F. Kennedy	1963	3.75	7.50	15.00
—One side has FDR speeches, the other, JFK speeches					

Number	Title (A Side/B Side)	Yr	VG	VG+	NM
20TH CENTURY					
❏ TCF 3127 [M]	The Presidential Years 1960-1963	1963	5.00	10.00	20.00
—Narrated by David Teig					

KENNEDY, MIKE

Also see LOS BRAVOS.

Number	Title (A Side/B Side)	Yr	VG	VG+	NM
ABC					
❏ ABCX-754	Louisianna	1972	5.00	10.00	20.00

KENNEDY, ROBERT FRANCIS

Tribute album released shortly after his death.

Number	Title (A Side/B Side)	Yr	VG	VG+	NM
COLUMBIA					
❏ C2S 792 [(2)]	A Memorial	1968	5.00	10.00	20.00

KENNER, CHRIS

Number	Title (A Side/B Side)	Yr	VG	VG+	NM
ATLANTIC					
❏ 8117 [M]	Land of 1,000 Dances	1965	20.00	40.00	80.00
COLLECTABLES					
❏ COL-5116	Golden Classics: I Like It Like That	198?	3.00	6.00	12.00

KENNEY, BEVERLY

Number	Title (A Side/B Side)	Yr	VG	VG+	NM
DECCA					
❏ DL 8743 [M]	Beverly Kenney Sings for Playboys	1958	50.00	100.00	200.00
❏ DL 8850 [M]	Born to Be Blue	1959	50.00	100.00	200.00
❏ DL 8948 [M]	Like Yesterday	1960	37.50	75.00	150.00
❏ DL 78948 [S]	Like Yesterday	1960	50.00	100.00	200.00
ROOST					
❏ RST-2206 [M]	Beverly Kenney Sings for Johnny Smith	1956	37.50	75.00	150.00
❏ RST-2212 [M]	Come Swing with Me	1956	37.50	75.00	150.00
❏ RST-2218 [M]	Beverly Kenney with Jimmy Jones and the Basie-ites	1957	37.50	75.00	150.00

KENNY, BILL

Number	Title (A Side/B Side)	Yr	VG	VG+	NM
WARWICK					
❏ W-2021 [M]	Mr. Ink Spot	1960	6.25	12.50	25.00

KENNY AND THE KASUALS

Number	Title (A Side/B Side)	Yr	VG	VG+	NM
MARK					
❏ 5000 [M]	The Impact Sound of Kenny and the Kasuals Live at the Studio Club	1966	250.00	500.00	1000.
❏ 5000 [M]	The Impact Sound of Kenny and the Kasuals Live at the Studio Club	1977	6.25	12.50	25.00
—"Reissue, 1977" appears on cover					
❏ 6000 [M]	Teen Dreams	1978	62.50	125.00	250.00
—Red vinyl; numbered, signed limited edition					
❏ 7000 [S]	Garage Kings	1979	6.25	12.50	25.00

KENSINGTON MARKET

Number	Title (A Side/B Side)	Yr	VG	VG+	NM
WARNER BROS.					
❏ WS 1754	Avenue Road	1968	5.00	10.00	20.00
❏ WS 1780	Aardvark	1969	5.00	10.00	20.00

KENT, GEORGE

Number	Title (A Side/B Side)	Yr	VG	VG+	NM
SHANNON					
❏ 1003	George Kent	1974	5.00	10.00	20.00

KENTON, STAN

Number	Title (A Side/B Side)	Yr	VG	VG+	NM
CAPITOL					
❏ H 155 [10]	Encores	1950	15.00	30.00	60.00
❏ T 155 [M]	Encores	195?	10.00	20.00	40.00
—Turquoise label					
❏ H 167 [10]	Artistry in Rhythm	1950	15.00	30.00	60.00
❏ T 167 [M]	Artistry in Rhythm	195?	10.00	20.00	40.00
—Turquoise label					
❏ H 172 [10]	A Presentation of Progressive Jazz	1950	15.00	30.00	60.00
❏ T 172 [M]	A Presentation of Progressive Jazz	195?	10.00	20.00	40.00
❏ P 189 [10]	Innovations in Modern Music	1950	15.00	30.00	60.00
❏ H 190 [10]	Milestones	1950	15.00	30.00	60.00
❏ T 190 [M]	Milestones	195?	10.00	20.00	40.00
—Turquoise label					
❏ T 190 [M]	Milestones	196?	6.25	12.50	25.00
—Black colorband label, logo at left					
❏ PRO-206/7 [DJ]	The Kenton Era (Excerpts)	1955	10.00	20.00	40.00
❏ L 248 [10]	Stan Kenton Presents	1951	15.00	30.00	60.00
❏ T 248 [M]	Stan Kenton Presents	195?	10.00	20.00	40.00
—Turquoise label					
❏ T 248 [M]	Stan Kenton Presents	196?	3.75	7.50	15.00
—Black colorband label, logo at top					
❏ T 248 [M]	Stan Kenton Presents	196?	6.25	12.50	25.00
—Black colorband label, logo at left					
❏ H 353 [10]	City of Glass	1952	15.00	30.00	60.00
❏ H 358 [10]	Classics	1952	15.00	30.00	60.00
❏ T 358 [M]	Classics	195?	10.00	20.00	40.00
—Turquoise label					
❏ H 383 [10]	New Concepts of Artistry in Rhythm	1953	15.00	30.00	60.00
❏ T 383 [M]	New Concepts of Artistry in Rhythm	195?	10.00	20.00	40.00
—Turquoise label					
❏ H 386 [10]	Prologue: This Is an Orchestra	1953	15.00	30.00	60.00
❏ H 421 [10]	Popular Favorites	1953	15.00	30.00	60.00
❏ T 421 [M]	Popular Favorites	195?	10.00	20.00	40.00
—Turquoise label					
❏ H 426 [10]	Sketches on Standards	1953	15.00	30.00	60.00
❏ T 426 [M]	Sketches on Standards	195?	10.00	20.00	40.00
—Turquoise label					
❏ H 460 [10]	This Modern World	1953	15.00	30.00	60.00
❏ H 462 [10]	Portraits on Standards	1953	15.00	30.00	60.00
❏ T 462 [M]	Portraits on Standards	195?	10.00	20.00	40.00
—Turquoise label					
❏ T 462 [M]	Portraits on Standards	196?	6.25	12.50	25.00
—Black colorband label, logo at left					
❏ W 524 [M]	Kenton Showcase	1954	10.00	20.00	40.00
❏ H 525 [10]	Kenton Showcase — The Music of Bill Russo	1954	15.00	30.00	60.00
❏ H 526 [10]	Kenton Showcase — The Music of Bill Holman	1954	15.00	30.00	60.00

Number	Title (A Side/B Side)	Yr	VG	VG+	NM
❑ TDB 569 [(4)M]	The Kenton Era	1955	25.00	50.00	100.00
—Box set with 44-page book					
❑ WDX 569 [(4)M]	The Kenton Era	196?	17.50	35.00	70.00
—Box set with 44-page book; limited edition reissue with black label, Capitol logo at left					
❑ STCL-575 [(3)]	Stan Kenton	1970	5.00	10.00	20.00
❑ T 666 [M]	Duet	1955	10.00	20.00	40.00
—With June Christy; turquoise label					
❑ T 666 [M]	Contemporary Concepts	1955	10.00	20.00	40.00
—Turquoise label					
❑ SW 724 [S]	Kenton in Hi-Fi	1959	12.50	25.00	50.00
—Black label with colorband, logo at left; one fewer track than mono version					
❑ SW 724 [S]	Kenton in Hi-Fi	1962	7.50	15.00	30.00
—Black label with colorband, logo at top; one fewer track than mono version					
❑ W 724 [M]	Kenton in Hi-Fi	1956	10.00	20.00	40.00
—Gray label					
❑ W 724 [M]	Kenton in Hi-Fi	1959	5.00	10.00	20.00
—Black label with colorband, logo at left					
❑ T 731 [M]	Cuban Fire!	1956	10.00	20.00	40.00
—Turquoise label					
❑ T 731 [M]	Cuban Fire!	1959	5.00	10.00	20.00
—Black label with colorband, Capitol logo at left					
❑ T 736 [M]	City of Glass/This Modern World	1956	10.00	20.00	40.00
—Combination of 353 and 460 onto one 12-inch LP, turquoise label					
❑ T 810 [M]	Kenton with Voices	1957	10.00	20.00	40.00
—Turquoise label					
❑ T 932 [M]	Rendezvous with Kenton	1957	10.00	20.00	40.00
—Turquoise label					
❑ T 995 [M]	Back to Balboa	1958	10.00	20.00	40.00
—Turquoise label					
❑ ST 1068 [S]	The Ballad Style of Stan Kenton	1959	5.00	10.00	20.00
—Black label with colorband, Capitol logo at left					
❑ T 1068 [M]	The Ballad Style of Stan Kenton	1959	6.25	12.50	25.00
—Black label with colorband, Capitol logo at left					
❑ ST 1130 [S]	Lush Interlude	1959	5.00	10.00	20.00
—Black label with colorband, Capitol logo at left					
❑ T 1130 [M]	Lush Interlude	1959	6.25	12.50	25.00
—Black label with colorband, Capitol logo at left					
❑ ST 1166 [S]	The Stage Door Swings	1959	5.00	10.00	20.00
—Black label with colorband, Capitol logo at left					
❑ T 1166 [M]	The Stage Door Swings	1959	6.25	12.50	25.00
—Black label with colorband, Capitol logo at left					
❑ ST 1276 [S]	The Kenton Touch	1960	5.00	10.00	20.00
—Black label with colorband, Capitol logo at left					
❑ T 1276 [M]	The Kenton Touch	1960	6.25	12.50	25.00
—Black label with colorband, Capitol logo at left					
❑ SW 1305 [S]	Viva Kenton!	1960	5.00	10.00	20.00
—Black label with colorband, Capitol logo at left					
❑ W 1305 [M]	Viva Kenton!	1960	6.25	12.50	25.00
—Black label with colorband, Capitol logo at left					
❑ STBO 1327 [(2)S]	Road Show	1960	7.50	15.00	30.00
—Black label with colorband, Capitol logo at left					
❑ TBO 1327 [(2)M]	Road Show	1960	10.00	20.00	40.00
—Black label with colorband, Capitol logo at left					
❑ TBO 1327 [(2)M]	Road Show	1962	5.00	10.00	20.00
—Black label with colorband, Capitol logo at top					
❑ ST 1394 [S]	Standards in Silhouette	1960	5.00	10.00	20.00
—Black label with colorband, Capitol logo at left					
❑ T 1394 [M]	Standards in Silhouette	1960	6.25	12.50	25.00
—Black label with colorband, Capitol logo at left					
❑ ST 1460 [S]	Kenton at the Las Vegas Tropicana	1961	5.00	10.00	20.00
—Black label with colorband, Capitol logo at left					
❑ T 1460 [M]	Kenton at the Las Vegas Tropicana	1961	6.25	12.50	25.00
—Black label with colorband, Capitol logo at left					
❑ ST 1533 [S]	The Romantic Approach	1961	5.00	10.00	20.00
—Black label with colorband, Capitol logo at left					
❑ T 1533 [M]	The Romantic Approach	1961	6.25	12.50	25.00
—Black label with colorband, Capitol logo at left					
❑ ST 1609 [S]	Kenton's West Side Story	1961	3.00	6.00	12.00
—Black label with colorband, Capitol logo at top					
❑ ST 1609 [S]	Kenton's West Side Story	1961	5.00	10.00	20.00
—Black label with colorband, Capitol logo at left					
❑ T 1609 [M]	Kenton's West Side Story	1961	6.25	12.50	25.00
—Black label with colorband, Capitol logo at left					
❑ STCL 2989 [(3)]	The Stan Kenton Deluxe Set	1968	5.00	10.00	20.00

CREATIVE WORLD

Number	Title (A Side/B Side)	Yr	VG	VG+	NM
❑ ST 1030 [(4)R]	The Kenton Era	197?	5.00	10.00	20.00
—Reissue of Capitol TDB 569					
❑ ST 1058 [(2)Q]	Live at Butler University	1972	5.00	10.00	20.00
❑ ST 1059 [(2)Q]	Stan Kenton with the Four Freshmen at Butler University	1972	5.00	10.00	20.00
❑ ST 1060 [(2)Q]	National Anthems of the World	1972	5.00	10.00	20.00

DECCA

Number	Title (A Side/B Side)	Yr	VG	VG+	NM
❑ DL 8259 [M]	Stan Kenton — Formative Years	195?	6.25	12.50	25.00
—All-black label with silver print					

LONDON PHASE 4

Number	Title (A Side/B Side)	Yr	VG	VG+	NM
❑ BP 44179/80 [(2)]	Stan Kenton Today	1972	10.00	20.00	40.00

MOBILE FIDELITY

Number	Title (A Side/B Side)	Yr	VG	VG+	NM
❑ 1-091	Kenton Plays Wagner	1982	6.25	12.50	25.00
—Audiophile vinyl					

MOSAIC

Number	Title (A Side/B Side)	Yr	VG	VG+	NM
❑ M6-136 [(6)]	The Complete Capitol Recordings of the Holman and Russo Charts	199?	30.00	60.00	120.00
❑ MQ10-163 [(10)]	The Complete Capitol Studio Recordings of Stan Kenton 1943-47	199?	50.00	100.00	200.00

KENTON, STAN, AND TEX RITTER

Also see each artist's individual listings.

CAPITOL

Number	Title (A Side/B Side)	Yr	VG	VG+	NM
❑ ST 1757 [S]	Stan Kenton/Tex Ritter	1962	20.00	40.00	80.00
❑ T 1757 [M]	Stan Kenton/Tex Ritter	1962	15.00	30.00	60.00

KENTUCKY COLONELS, THE

BRIAR

Number	Title (A Side/B Side)	Yr	VG	VG+	NM
❑ 109	The New Sounds of Bluegrass America	1976	10.00	20.00	40.00
❑ BT-7202	Livin' in the Past	1975	7.50	15.00	30.00

WORLD PACIFIC

Number	Title (A Side/B Side)	Yr	VG	VG+	NM
❑ ST 1821 [S]	Appalachian Swing	1964	15.00	30.00	60.00
❑ T 1821 [M]	Appalachian Swing	1964	12.50	25.00	50.00

KENYATTA, ROBIN

ATLANTIC

Number	Title (A Side/B Side)	Yr	VG	VG+	NM
❑ SD 1633	Gypsy Man	1972	5.00	10.00	20.00

ECM

Number	Title (A Side/B Side)	Yr	VG	VG+	NM
❑ 1008	The Girl from Martinique	197?	5.00	10.00	20.00

VORTEX

Number	Title (A Side/B Side)	Yr	VG	VG+	NM
❑ 2005	Until	1969	5.00	10.00	20.00

KEROUAC, JACK

DOT

Number	Title (A Side/B Side)	Yr	VG	VG+	NM
❑ DLP-3154 [M]	Poetry for the Beat Generation	1959	5000.	7500.	10000.
—Acknowledged to be extremely rare; fewer than 1,000 copies were distributed and only a small handful are known to exist today; the same performance is on Hanover 5000					

HANOVER

Number	Title (A Side/B Side)	Yr	VG	VG+	NM
❑ HML-5000 [M]	Poetry for the Beat Generation	1959	62.50	125.00	250.00
❑ HML-5006 [M]	Blues and Haikus	1959	62.50	125.00	250.00
—STEVE ALLEN plays piano behind Kerouac on this album					

RHINO

Number	Title (A Side/B Side)	Yr	VG	VG+	NM
❑ R1-70939 [(4)]	The Jack Kerouac Collection	1990	15.00	30.00	60.00
—Box set compiling the Hanover and Verve LPs plus an LP of unreleased material					

VERVE

Number	Title (A Side/B Side)	Yr	VG	VG+	NM
❑ MGV-15005 [M]	Readings on the Beat Generation	1960	62.50	125.00	250.00

KERR, ANITA, SINGERS

AMPEX

Number	Title (A Side/B Side)	Yr	VG	VG+	NM
❑ A-10136	Grow to Know Me	1971	2.50	5.00	10.00
❑ A-10142	A Christmas Story	1971	3.00	6.00	12.00
—With the Royal Philharmonic Orchestra					

BAINBRIDGE

Number	Title (A Side/B Side)	Yr	VG	VG+	NM
❑ 6224	Slightly Baroque	1981	2.50	5.00	10.00
❑ 6226	I Sang with Jim Reeves	1981	2.50	5.00	10.00
❑ 6227	The Simon and Garfunkel Songbook	1981	2.50	5.00	10.00
❑ 6228	'Round Midnight	1981	2.50	5.00	10.00

CENTURY

Number	Title (A Side/B Side)	Yr	VG	VG+	NM
❑ 1160	Anita Kerr Performs Wonder's	1979	2.50	5.00	10.00

DECCA

Number	Title (A Side/B Side)	Yr	VG	VG+	NM
❑ DL 4061 [M]	For You, For Me, Forevermore	1960	3.75	7.50	15.00
❑ DL 8647 [M]	Quartet Voices in Hi-Fi	1958	3.75	7.50	15.00
❑ DL 74061 [S]	For You, For Me, Forevermore	1960	5.00	10.00	20.00
❑ DL 75159	Till the End of Time	1970	2.50	5.00	10.00

DOT

Number	Title (A Side/B Side)	Yr	VG	VG+	NM
❑ DLP 25906	The Anita Kerr Singers Reflect on the Hits of Burt Bacharach & Hal David	1969	2.50	5.00	10.00
❑ DLP 25944	Precious Teresa	1969	2.50	5.00	10.00
❑ DLP 25961	Velvet Voices and Bold Brass	1969	2.50	5.00	10.00
❑ DLP 25970	Touchlove	1970	2.50	5.00	10.00

RCA CAMDEN

Number	Title (A Side/B Side)	Yr	VG	VG+	NM
❑ CAS-2209	Georgia on My Mind	1968	2.50	5.00	10.00

RCA VICTOR

Number	Title (A Side/B Side)	Yr	VG	VG+	NM
❑ APL1-1166	The Anita Kerr Singers	1975	2.50	5.00	10.00
❑ APL1-2298	Anite Kerr and the French Connection	1977	2.50	5.00	10.00
❑ LPM-2480 [M]	From Nashville…The Hit Sound	1962	3.00	6.00	12.00
❑ LSP-2480 [S]	From Nashville…The Hit Sound	1962	3.75	7.50	15.00
❑ LPM-2581 [M]	"The Genius" In Harmony	1962	3.00	6.00	12.00
❑ LSP-2581 [S]	"The Genius" In Harmony	1962	3.75	7.50	15.00
❑ LPM-2679 [M]	Tender Words	1963	3.00	6.00	12.00
❑ LSP-2679 [S]	Tender Words	1963	3.75	7.50	15.00
❑ LPM-3322 [M]	Mellow Moods of Love	1965	3.00	6.00	12.00
❑ LSP-3322 [S]	Mellow Moods of Love	1965	3.75	7.50	15.00
❑ LPM-3428 [M]	We Dig Mancini	1965	3.00	6.00	12.00
❑ LSP-3428 [S]	We Dig Mancini	1965	3.75	7.50	15.00
❑ LPM-3485 [M]	Sunday Serenade	1966	3.00	6.00	12.00
❑ LSP-3485 [S]	Sunday Serenade	1966	3.75	7.50	15.00

VOCALION

Number	Title (A Side/B Side)	Yr	VG	VG+	NM
❑ VL 73899	For You	1969	2.50	5.00	10.00

WARNER BROS.

Number	Title (A Side/B Side)	Yr	VG	VG+	NM
❑ W 1665 [M]	Slightly Baroque	1966	3.00	6.00	12.00
❑ WS 1665 [S]	Slightly Baroque	1966	3.75	7.50	15.00
❑ W 1707 [M]	Bert Kaempfert Turns Us On!	1967	3.75	7.50	15.00
❑ WS 1707 [S]	Bert Kaempfert Turns Us On!	1967	3.00	6.00	12.00
❑ W 1724 [M]	All You Need Is Love	1967	3.75	7.50	15.00
❑ WS 1724 [S]	All You Need Is Love	1967	3.00	6.00	12.00

WORD

Number	Title (A Side/B Side)	Yr	VG	VG+	NM
❑ 8647	Hallelujah Brass	197?	2.50	5.00	10.00
❑ 8692	Hymns	197?	2.50	5.00	10.00
—With Kurt Kaiser					
❑ 8696	Walk a Little Slower	197?	2.50	5.00	10.00
❑ 8706	Precious Memories	197?	2.50	5.00	10.00
❑ 8707	Hallelujah Guitars	197?	2.50	5.00	10.00
❑ 8741	Hallelujah Woodwinds	197?	2.50	5.00	10.00
❑ 8808	Hallelujah Voices	197?	2.50	5.00	10.00

KERSHAW, DOUG

SCOTTI BROTHERS

Number	Title (A Side/B Side)	Yr	VG	VG+	NM
❑ SB 7115	Instant Hero	1981	3.00	6.00	12.00
❑ FZ 37428	Instant Hero	1981	2.50	5.00	10.00

WARNER BROS.

Number	Title (A Side/B Side)	Yr	VG	VG+	NM
❑ WS 1820	Cajun Way	1969	5.00	10.00	20.00
—Green label, "W7" box logo at top					
❑ WS 1820	Cajun Way	1970	3.75	7.50	15.00
—Green label, "WB" shield logo at top					

Number	Title (A Side/B Side)	Yr	VG	VG+	NM
❏ WS 1861	Spanish Moss	1970	3.75	7.50	15.00
—Green label					
❏ WS 1906	Doug Kershaw	1971	3.75	7.50	15.00
—Green label					
❏ BS 2581	Swamp Grass	1972	3.75	7.50	15.00
—Green label					
❏ BS 2649	Devil's Elbow	1973	3.75	7.50	15.00
❏ BS 2725	Douglas James Kershaw	1973	3.75	7.50	15.00
❏ BS 2793	Mama Kershaw's Boy	1974	3.75	7.50	15.00
❏ BS 2851	Alive & Pickin'	1975	3.00	6.00	12.00
❏ BS 2910	Ragin' Cajun	1976	3.00	6.00	12.00
❏ BS 3025	Flip, Flop & Fly	1977	3.00	6.00	12.00
❏ BSK 3166	Louisiana Man	1978	3.00	6.00	12.00

KERSHAW, RUSTY AND DOUG
HICKORY
❏ LPM-103 [M]	Rusty and Doug Sing Louisiana Man	1960	30.00	60.00	120.00

HICKORY/MGM
❏ H3G-4506	Louisiana Man	1974	5.00	10.00	20.00

KESEY, KEN
SOUND CITY
❏ 27690 [M]	The Acid Test	1967	75.00	150.00	300.00
—THE GRATEFUL DEAD appear on this LP					

KESNER, DICK
BRUNSWICK
❏ BL 54044 [M]	Lawrence Welk Presents Dick Kesner	1958	5.00	10.00	20.00
❏ BL 54051 [M]	Dick Kesner and His Magic Stradivarius	1959	3.75	7.50	15.00
❏ BL 54054 [M]	Intermezzo	1960	3.75	7.50	15.00
❏ BL 754044 [S]	Lawrence Welk Presents Dick Kesner	1959	6.25	12.50	25.00
❏ BL 754051 [S]	Dick Kesner and His Magic Stradivarius	1959	5.00	10.00	20.00
❏ BL 754054 [S]	Intermezzo	1960	5.00	10.00	20.00

CORAL
❏ CRL 57352 [M]	Music of Hawaii	1960	3.00	6.00	12.00
❏ CRL 57360 [M]	A "New" Old Refrain	1961	3.00	6.00	12.00
❏ CRL 57376 [M]	The Sound of Gypsy Music	1961	3.00	6.00	12.00
❏ CRL 57393 [M]	Amor Latino	1962	3.00	6.00	12.00
❏ CRL 57435 [M]	Golden Favorites	1964	3.00	6.00	12.00
❏ CRL 757352 [S]	Music of Hawaii	1960	3.75	7.50	15.00
❏ CRL 757360 [S]	A "New" Old Refrain	1961	3.75	7.50	15.00
❏ CRL 757376 [S]	The Sound of Gypsy Music	1961	3.75	7.50	15.00
❏ CRL 757393 [S]	Amor Latino	1962	3.75	7.50	15.00
❏ CRL 757435 [S]	Golden Favorites	1964	3.75	7.50	15.00

VOCALION
❏ VL 3777 [M]	Latin Favorites	196?	3.00	6.00	12.00
❏ VL 73777 [S]	Latin Favorites	196?	3.75	7.50	15.00

KESSEL, BARNEY
CONTEMPORARY
❏ C-2508 [10]	Barney Kessel, Volume 1	1953	30.00	60.00	120.00
❏ C-2514 [10]	Barney Kessel, Volume 2	1954	30.00	60.00	120.00
❏ C-3511 [M]	Easy Like	1956	20.00	40.00	80.00
❏ C-3512 [M]	Kessel Plays Standards	1956	20.00	40.00	80.00
❏ C-3513 [M]	To Swing or Not to Swing	1956	20.00	40.00	80.00
❏ C-3521 [M]	Music to Listen to Barney Kessel By	1956	15.00	30.00	60.00
❏ M-3563 [M]	Barney Kessel Plays "Carmen"	1959	10.00	20.00	40.00
❏ M-3565 [M]	Some Like It Hot	1959	10.00	20.00	40.00
❏ M-3585 [M]	Workin' Out!	1960	10.00	20.00	40.00
❏ M-3603 [M]	Let's Cook!	1962	6.25	12.50	25.00
❏ M-3613 [M]	Swingin' Party	1963	5.00	10.00	20.00
❏ M-3618 [M]	Feeling Free	1965	5.00	10.00	20.00
❏ S-7521 [S]	Music to Listen to Barney Kessel By	1959	10.00	20.00	40.00
❏ S-7563 [S]	Barney Kessel Plays "Carmen"	1959	7.50	15.00	30.00
❏ S-7565 [S]	Some Like It Hot	1959	7.50	15.00	30.00
❏ S-7585 [S]	Workin' Out!	1960	7.50	15.00	30.00
❏ S-7603 [S]	Let's Cook!	1962	6.25	12.50	25.00
❏ S-7613 [S]	Swingin' Party	1963	6.25	12.50	25.00
❏ S-7618 [S]	Feeling Free	1965	6.25	12.50	25.00

EMERALD
❏ 2401 [S]	On Fire	1965	5.00	10.00	20.00

REPRISE
❏ R9-6019 [S]	Breakfast at Tiffany's	1961	5.00	10.00	20.00
❏ R9-6049 [S]	Bossa Nova	1962	5.00	10.00	20.00
❏ R9-6073 [S]	Kessel/Jazz	1963	5.00	10.00	20.00

STEREO RECORDS
❏ S-7001 [S]	Music to Listen to Barney Kessel By	1958	12.50	25.00	50.00

KEYMEN, THE
ABC-PARAMOUNT
❏ 258 [M]	Dance with Dick Clark	1958	7.50	15.00	30.00
❏ S-258 [S]	Dance with Dick Clark	1958	12.50	25.00	50.00
❏ 288 [M]	Dance with Dick Clark, Volume 2	1959	7.50	15.00	30.00
❏ S-288 [S]	Dance with Dick Clark, Volume 2	1959	12.50	25.00	50.00

CORAL
❏ CRL 57112 [M]	Vocal Sounds of the Keymen	1957	7.50	15.00	30.00

GOLDUST
❏ LPS-153 [M]	The Keymen Live	196?	12.50	25.00	50.00

KEYS, CALVIN
BLACK JAZZ
❏ 5	Shawn-neeq	1972	5.00	10.00	20.00

KHAZAD DOOM
LPL
❏ 892	Level 6 1/2	1970	250.00	500.00	1000.

KICKSTANDS, THE
CAPITOL
❏ ST 2078 [S]	Black Boots and Bikes	1964	37.50	75.00	150.00
❏ T 2078 [M]	Black Boots and Bikes	1964	30.00	60.00	120.00
❏ T/ST 2078	Black Boots and Bikes Bonus Fold-Out	1964	12.50	25.00	50.00

KID ROCK
ATLANTIC
❏ 83482 [(2)]	Cocky	2001	5.00	10.00	20.00

JIVE
❏ 1409-1-J [(2)]	Grits Sandwiches for Breakfast	1990	6.25	12.50	25.00

KID THOMAS
AMERICAN MUSIC
❏ 642 [10]	Kid Thomas	1952	12.50	25.00	50.00

GHB
❏ GHB-24 [M]	Kid Thomas + The Hall Brothers Jazz Band	196?	5.00	10.00	20.00

RIVERSIDE
❏ RLP-365 [M]	Kid Thomas and His Algiers Stompers	1961	7.50	15.00	30.00
❏ RLP-386 [M]	Kid Thomas and His Algiers Stompers	1961	7.50	15.00	30.00
❏ RS-9365 [R]	Kid Thomas and His Algiers Stompers	1961	5.00	10.00	20.00
❏ RS-9386 [R]	Kid Thomas and His Algiers Stompers	1961	5.00	10.00	20.00

KILGORE, MERLE
STARDAY
❏ SLP-251 [M]	There's Gold in Them Thar Hills	1963	7.50	15.00	30.00

WING
❏ MGW-12316 [M]	Tall Texan	196?	3.75	7.50	15.00
❏ SRW-16316 [S]	Tall Texan	196?	3.00	6.00	12.00

KILLING FLOOR
SIRE
❏ SES-97019	Killing Floor	1970	12.50	25.00	50.00

KINCAID, BRADLEY
VARSITY
❏ 34 [M]	Bradley Kincaid Sings American Ballads and Folk Songs	1957	10.00	20.00	40.00
❏ 6988 [10]	American Ballads	1955	15.00	30.00	60.00

KINCAIDE, DEAN
WEATHERS
❏ 5610 [M]	Arranged for You	1954	12.50	25.00	50.00

KINES, TOM
ELEKTRA
❏ EKL-137 [M]	Of Maids and Mistresses	1958	7.50	15.00	30.00

KING, ALBERT
ATLANTIC
❏ SD 8213	King of the Blues Guitar	1969	6.25	12.50	25.00

FANTASY
❏ 9627	San Francisco '83	1983	2.50	5.00	10.00
❏ 9633	I'm in a Phone Booth, Baby	1984	2.50	5.00	10.00

KING
❏ 852 [M]	Big Blues	1963	125.00	250.00	500.00
❏ KS-1060	Travelin' to California	1969	6.25	12.50	25.00

MODERN BLUES
❏ MBLP-723	Let's Have a Natural Ball	198?	2.50	5.00	10.00

STAX
❏ ST-723 [M]	Born Under a Bad Sign	1967	20.00	40.00	80.00
❏ STS-723 [S]	Born Under a Bad Sign	1967	30.00	60.00	120.00
❏ STS-2003	Live Wire/Blues Power	1968	12.50	25.00	50.00
❏ STS-2010	Years Gone By	1969	6.25	12.50	25.00
❏ STS-2015	King Does the King's Thing	1969	6.25	12.50	25.00
❏ STS-2040	Lovejoy	1971	5.00	10.00	20.00
❏ STS-3009	I'll Play the Blues for You	1972	5.00	10.00	20.00
❏ STX-4101	The Pinch	1977	3.00	6.00	12.00
❏ STX-4128	Live Wire/Blues Power	1979	2.50	5.00	10.00
—Reissue of 2003					
❏ STX-4132	Montreux Festival	1980	2.50	5.00	10.00
—Retitled reissue of 5520					
❏ STS-5505	I Wanna Get Funky	1974	3.75	7.50	15.00
❏ STS-5520	Montreux Festival	1975	3.75	7.50	15.00
❏ MPS-8504	Blues for Elvis	1981	2.50	5.00	10.00
—Retitled reissue of 2015					
❏ MPS-8513	I'll Play the Blues for You	1981	2.50	5.00	10.00
—Reissue of 3309					
❏ MPS-8517	Lovejoy	1981	2.50	5.00	10.00
—Reissue of 2040					
❏ MPS-8522	Years Gone By	1982	2.50	5.00	10.00
—Reissue of 2010					
❏ MPS-8534	The Lost Session	1986	2.50	5.00	10.00
❏ MPS-8536	I Wanna Get Funky	1987	2.50	5.00	10.00
—Reissue of 5505					
❏ MPS-8546	Blues at Sunrise	1988	2.50	5.00	10.00
❏ MPS-8556	Wednesday Night in San Francisco	1990	2.50	5.00	10.00
❏ MPS-8557	Tuesday Night in San Francisco	1990	2.50	5.00	10.00

SUNDAZED
❏ LP 5031	Born Under a Bad Sign	1999	3.75	7.50	15.00
—Reissue on 180-gram vinyl					

TOMATO
❏ TOM-6002	King Albert	1978	3.00	6.00	12.00
❏ TOM-7022	New Orleans Heat	1979	3.00	6.00	12.00

UTOPIA
❏ BUL1-1387	Truckload of Lovin'	1976	3.00	6.00	12.00
❏ BUL1-1731	Albert	1976	3.00	6.00	12.00
❏ CUL2-2205 [(2)]	Albert Live	1977	3.75	7.50	15.00

KING, ALBERT/STEVE CROPPER/POP STAPLES
STAX
❏ STS-2020	Jammed Together	1969	6.25	12.50	25.00
❏ MPS-8544	Jammed Together	1988	2.50	5.00	10.00
—Reissue					

Number	Title (A Side/B Side)	Yr	VG	VG+	NM

KING, ALBERT/OTIS RUSH
CHESS
Number	Title (A Side/B Side)	Yr	VG	VG+	NM
❑ LPS 1538	Door to Door	1969	6.25	12.50	25.00
❑ CH-9322	Door to Door	1990	2.50	5.00	10.00
—Reissue					

KING, ANNA
SMASH
| ❑ MGS-27059 [M] | Back to Soul | 1964 | 25.00 | 50.00 | 100.00 |
| ❑ SRS-67059 [S] | Back to Soul | 1964 | 30.00 | 60.00 | 120.00 |

KING, B.B.
ABC
❑ D-704	Blues Is King	1970	3.00	6.00	12.00
—Reissue of BluesWay 6001					
❑ D-709	Blues on Top of Blues	1970	3.00	6.00	12.00
—Reissue of BluesWay 6011					
❑ D-712	Lucille	1970	3.00	6.00	12.00
—Reissue of BluesWay 6016					
❑ D-713	Indianola Mississippi Seeds	1970	3.00	6.00	12.00
❑ D-723	Live in Cook County Jail	1971	3.00	6.00	12.00
❑ D-724	Live at the Regal	1971	3.00	6.00	12.00
—Reissue of ABC-Paramount 509					
❑ D-730	B.B. King in London	1971	3.00	6.00	12.00
❑ D-743	L.A. Midnight	1972	3.00	6.00	12.00
❑ X-759	Guess Who	1972	3.00	6.00	12.00
❑ X-767	The Best of B.B. King	1973	3.00	6.00	12.00
❑ X-794	To Know You Is to Love You	1973	3.00	6.00	12.00
❑ D-813	His Best/The Electric B.B. King	1974	3.00	6.00	12.00
—Reissue of BluesWay 6022					
❑ D-819	Live and Well	1974	3.00	6.00	12.00
—Reissue of BluesWay 6031					
❑ D-825	Friends	1974	3.00	6.00	12.00
❑ D-868	Completely Well	1975	3.00	6.00	12.00
—Reissue of BluesWay 6037					
❑ D-878	Back in the Alley	1975	3.00	6.00	12.00
—Reissue of BluesWay 6050					
❑ D-898	Lucille Talks Back	1975	3.00	6.00	12.00
❑ AB-977	King Size	1977	3.00	6.00	12.00
❑ AA-1061	Midnight Believer	1978	3.00	6.00	12.00
ABC-PARAMOUNT
❑ 456 [M]	Mr. Blues	1963	7.50	15.00	30.00
❑ S-456 [S]	Mr. Blues	1963	10.00	20.00	40.00
❑ 509 [M]	Live at the Regal	1965	10.00	20.00	40.00
❑ S-509 [S]	Live at the Regal	1965	12.50	25.00	50.00
❑ 528 [M]	Confessin' the Blues	1965	7.50	15.00	30.00
❑ S-528 [S]	Confessin' the Blues	1965	10.00	20.00	40.00
BLUESWAY
❑ BL-6001 [M]	Blues Is King	1967	10.00	20.00	40.00
❑ BLS-6001 [S]	Blues Is King	1967	6.25	12.50	25.00
❑ BLS-6011	Blues On to Top of Blues	1968	6.25	12.50	25.00
❑ BLS-6016	Lucille	1968	6.25	12.50	25.00
❑ BLS-6022	His Best/The Electric B.B. King	1969	5.00	10.00	20.00
❑ BLS-6031	Live and Well	1969	5.00	10.00	20.00
❑ BLS-6037	Completely Well	1969	5.00	10.00	20.00
❑ BLS-6050	Back in the Alley	1970	5.00	10.00	20.00
CROWN
❑ CST-147 [R]	B.B. King Wails	1960	3.00	6.00	12.00
—Black vinyl					
❑ CST-147 [R]	B.B. King Wails	1960	25.00	50.00	100.00
—Red vinyl					
❑ CST-152 [R]	B.B. King Sings Spirituals	1960	3.00	6.00	12.00
—Black vinyl					
❑ CST-152 [R]	B.B. King Sings Spirituals	1960	25.00	50.00	100.00
—Red vinyl					
❑ CST-195 [S]	King of the Blues	1961	5.00	10.00	20.00
—Black vinyl; this album is in true stereo, contrary to prior reports					
❑ CST-195 [S]	King of the Blues	1961	30.00	60.00	120.00
—Red vinyl; this album is in true stereo, contrary to prior reports					
❑ CST-309 [R]	Blues in My Heart	1963	3.00	6.00	12.00
❑ CST-359 [P]	B.B. King	1963	3.00	6.00	12.00
—Half of the album is in stereo, half is rechanneled					
❑ CLP-5020 [M]	Singin' the Blues	1957	25.00	50.00	100.00
—Black label, silver "Crown"					
❑ CLP-5020 [M]	Singin' the Blues	196?	3.00	6.00	12.00
—Black label, multi-color "Crown"					
❑ CLP-5020 [M]	Singin' the Blues	1963	5.00	10.00	20.00
—Gray label, black "Crown"					
❑ CLP-5063 [M]	The Blues	1958	20.00	40.00	80.00
—Black label, silver "Crown"					
❑ CLP-5063 [M]	The Blues	196?	3.00	6.00	12.00
—Black label, multi-color "Crown"					
❑ CLP-5063 [M]	The Blues	1963	5.00	10.00	20.00
—Gray label, black "Crown"					
❑ CLP-5115 [M]	B.B. King Wails	1959	20.00	40.00	80.00
—Black label, silver "Crown"					
❑ CLP-5115 [M]	B.B. King Wails	196?	3.00	6.00	12.00
—Black label, multi-color "Crown"					
❑ CLP-5115 [M]	B.B. King Wails	1963	5.00	10.00	20.00
—Gray label, black "Crown"					
❑ CLP-5119 [M]	B.B. King Sings Spirituals	196?	3.00	6.00	12.00
—Black label, multi-color "Crown"					
❑ CLP-5119 [M]	B.B. King Sings Spirituals	1960	15.00	30.00	60.00
—Gray label, black "Crown"					
❑ CLP-5143 [M]	The Great B.B. King	196?	3.00	6.00	12.00
—Black label, multi-color "Crown"					
❑ CLP-5143 [M]	The Great B.B. King	1961	15.00	30.00	60.00
—Gray label, black "Crown"					
❑ CLP-5167 [M]	King of the Blues	196?	3.00	6.00	12.00
—Black label, multi-color "Crown"					
❑ CLP-5167 [M]	King of the Blues	1961	15.00	30.00	60.00
—Gray label, black "Crown"					

Number	Title (A Side/B Side)	Yr	VG	VG+	NM
❑ CLP-5188 [M]	My Kind of Blues	196?	3.00	6.00	12.00
—Black label, multi-color "Crown"					
❑ CLP-5188 [M]	My Kind of Blues	1961	15.00	30.00	60.00
—Gray label, black "Crown"					
❑ CLP-5230 [M]	More B.B. King	196?	3.00	6.00	12.00
—Black label, multi-color "Crown"					
❑ CLP-5230 [M]	More B.B. King	1962	15.00	30.00	60.00
—Gray label, black "Crown"					
❑ CLP-5248 [M]	Twist with B.B. King	196?	3.00	6.00	12.00
—Black label, multi-color "Crown"					
❑ CLP-5248 [M]	Twist with B.B. King	1962	15.00	30.00	60.00
—Gray label, black "Crown"					
❑ CLP-5286 [M]	Easy Listening Blues	196?	3.00	6.00	12.00
—Black label, multi-color "Crown"					
❑ CLP-5286 [M]	Easy Listening Blues	1962	15.00	30.00	60.00
—Gray label, black "Crown"					
❑ CLP-5309 [M]	Blues in My Heart	196?	3.00	6.00	12.00
—Black label, multi-color "Crown"					
❑ CLP-5309 [M]	Blues in My Heart	1963	10.00	20.00	40.00
—Gray label, black "Crown"					
❑ CLP-5359 [M]	B.B. King	196?	3.00	6.00	12.00
—Black label, multi-color "Crown"					
❑ CLP-5359 [M]	B.B. King	1963	10.00	20.00	40.00
—Gray label, black "Crown"					
CRUSADERS
| ❑ 16013 | Live in London | 1982 | 6.25 | 12.50 | 25.00 |
| —Part of MCA's "Audiophile Series" | | | | | |
CUSTOM
❑ CM-2046 [M]	Blues for Me	196?	3.00	6.00	12.00
❑ CM-2049 [M]	I Love You So	196?	3.00	6.00	12.00
❑ CM-2052 [M]	The Soul of B.B. King	196?	3.00	6.00	12.00
DIRECT DISK
| ❑ SD-16616 | Midnight Believer | 1980 | 12.50 | 25.00 | 50.00 |
| —Audiophile vinyl | | | | | |
GALAXY
| ❑ 202 [M] | 16 Greatest Hits | 1963 | 15.00 | 30.00 | 60.00 |
| ❑ 8202 [S] | 16 Greatest Hits | 1963 | 20.00 | 40.00 | 80.00 |
GRP
| ❑ GR-9637 | Live at the Apollo | 1991 | 3.75 | 7.50 | 15.00 |
KENT
❑ KST-512 [R]	Rock Me Baby	1964	3.75	7.50	15.00
❑ KST-513 [R]	Let Me Love You.	1965	3.75	7.50	15.00
❑ KST-515 [R]	B.B. King Live on Stage.	1965	3.75	7.50	15.00
❑ KST-516 [R]	The Soul of B.B. King.	1966	3.75	7.50	15.00
❑ KST-517 [R]	Pure Soul.	1966	3.75	7.50	15.00
❑ KST-521 [R]	The Jungle.	1967	3.75	7.50	15.00
❑ KST-529 [R]	Boss of the Blues.	1968	3.75	7.50	15.00
❑ KST-533 [(2)]	From the Beginning.	1969	5.00	10.00	20.00
❑ KST-535	Underground Blues.	1969	3.75	7.50	15.00
❑ KST-539	The Incredible Soul of B.B. King.	1970	3.75	7.50	15.00
❑ KST-548	Turn On to B.B. King.	1970	3.75	7.50	15.00
❑ KST-552	Greatest Hits, Volume 1.	1971	3.75	7.50	15.00
❑ KST-561	Better Than Ever.	1971	3.75	7.50	15.00
❑ KST-563	Doing My Thing, Lord.	1971	3.75	7.50	15.00
❑ KST-565	B.B. King Live.	1972	3.75	7.50	15.00
❑ KST-568	The Original Sweet Sixteen.	1972	3.75	7.50	15.00
❑ KLP-2008	Incredible Soul of B.B. King.	1987	3.00	6.00	12.00
❑ KLP-5012 [M]	Rock Me Baby.	1964	5.00	10.00	20.00
❑ KLP-5013 [M]	Let Me Love You.	1965	5.00	10.00	20.00
❑ KLP-5015 [M]	B.B. King Live on Stage.	1965	5.00	10.00	20.00
❑ KLP-5016 [M]	The Soul of B.B. King.	1966	5.00	10.00	20.00
❑ KLP-5017 [M]	Pure Soul.	1966	5.00	10.00	20.00
❑ KLP-5021 [M]	The Jungle.	1967	5.00	10.00	20.00
❑ KLP-5029 [M]	Boss of the Blues.	1968	5.00	10.00	20.00
MCA
❑ 3151	Take It Home	1979	2.50	5.00	10.00
❑ 5162	There Must Be a Better World Somewhere	1981	2.50	5.00	10.00
❑ 5307	Love Me Tender	1982	2.50	5.00	10.00
❑ 5413	Blues 'N' Jazz	1983	2.50	5.00	10.00
❑ 5616	Six Silver Strings	1985	2.50	5.00	10.00
❑ 6455	Live at San Quentin	1990	3.00	6.00	12.00
❑ 2-8016 [(2)]	"Now Appearing" at Ole Miss	1980	3.00	6.00	12.00
❑ 27005	Live in Cook County Jail	1980	2.00	4.00	8.00
—Reissue of ABC 723					
❑ 27006	Live at the Regal	1980	2.00	4.00	8.00
—Reissue of ABC 724					
❑ 27007	His Best/The Electric B.B. King	1980	2.00	4.00	8.00
—Reissue of ABC 813					
❑ 27008	Live and Well	1980	2.00	4.00	8.00
—Reissue of ABC 819					
❑ 27009	Completely Well	1980	2.00	4.00	8.00
—Reissue of ABC 868					
❑ 27010	Back in the Alley	1980	2.00	4.00	8.00
—Reissue of ABC 878					
❑ 27011	Midnight Believer	1980	2.00	4.00	8.00
—Reissue of ABC 1061					
❑ 27028	Take It Home	1981	2.00	4.00	8.00
—Reissue of MCA 3151					
❑ 27034	There Must Be a Better World Somewhere	1983	2.00	4.00	8.00
—Reissue of MCA 5162					
❑ 27074	The Best of B.B. King	1984	2.00	4.00	8.00
—Reissue of ABC 767					
❑ 42183	The King of the Blues: 1989	1989	2.50	5.00	10.00
MCA IMPULSE!
| ❑ MCA2-4124 [(2)] | Great Moments with B.B. King | 1981 | 3.00 | 6.00 | 12.00 |
MOBILE FIDELITY
| ❑ 1-235 | Lucille | 1995 | 6.25 | 12.50 | 25.00 |
| —Audiophile vinyl | | | | | |
PICKWICK
| ❑ SPC-3593 | Live at the Regal | 197? | 2.00 | 4.00 | 8.00 |
| ❑ SPC-3654 | Live in Cook County Jail | 197? | 2.00 | 4.00 | 8.00 |

Number	Title (A Side/B Side)	Yr	VG	VG+	NM
STAX					
❑ ORS-4508	16 Original Big Hits	198?	2.00	4.00	8.00
UNITED					
❑ US-7703	Heart Full of Blues	197?	2.00	4.00	8.00
❑ US-7705	Easy Listening Blues	197?	2.00	4.00	8.00
—Reissue of Crown 5286					
❑ US-7708	Blues for Me	197?	2.00	4.00	8.00
—Reissue of Custom 2046					
❑ US-7711	I Love You So	197?	2.00	4.00	8.00
—Reissue of Custom 2049					
❑ US-7714	The Soul of B.B. King	197?	2.00	4.00	8.00
—Reissue of Custom 2052					
❑ US-7721	Swing Low	197?	2.00	4.00	8.00
❑ US-7724	My Kind of Blues	197?	2.00	4.00	8.00
—Reissue of Crown 5188					
❑ US-7726	Singin' the Blues	197?	2.00	4.00	8.00
—Reissue of Crown 5020					
❑ US-7728	The Great B.B. King	197?	2.00	4.00	8.00
—Reissue of Crown 5143					
❑ US-7732	The Blues	197?	2.00	4.00	8.00
—Reissue of Crown 5063					
❑ US-7733	Rock Me, Baby	197?	2.00	4.00	8.00
—Reissue of Kent 5012					
❑ US-7734	Let Me Love You	197?	2.00	4.00	8.00
—Reissue of Kent 513					
❑ US-7736	B.B. King Live on Stage	197?	2.00	4.00	8.00
—Reissue of Kent 515					
❑ US-7742	The Jungle	197?	2.00	4.00	8.00
—Reissue of Kent 521					
❑ US-7750	Boss of the Blues	197?	2.00	4.00	8.00
—Reissue of Kent 529					
❑ US-7756	The Incredible Soul of B.B. King	197?	2.00	4.00	8.00
—Reissue of Kent 539					
❑ US-7763	Turn On with B.B. King	197?	2.00	4.00	8.00
—Reissue of Kent 548					
❑ US-7766	Greatest Hits, Volume 1	197?	2.00	4.00	8.00
—Reissue of Kent 552					
❑ US-7773	The Original Sweet Sixteen	197?	2.00	4.00	8.00
—Reissue of Kent 568					
❑ US-7788	9 x 9	197?	2.00	4.00	8.00

KING, BEN E.
Also see AVERAGE WHITE BAND; THE DRIFTERS.

Number	Title (A Side/B Side)	Yr	VG	VG+	NM
ATCO					
❑ 33-133 [M]	Spanish Harlem	1961	25.00	50.00	100.00
—Yellow label with harp					
❑ 33-133 [M]	Spanish Harlem	1962	10.00	20.00	40.00
—Gold and gray label					
❑ SD 33-133 [S]	Spanish Harlem	1961	37.50	75.00	150.00
—Yellow label with harp					
❑ SD 33-133 [S]	Spanish Harlem	1962	12.50	25.00	50.00
—Purple and brown label					
❑ 33-137 [M]	Ben E. King Sings for Soulful Lovers	1962	10.00	20.00	40.00
❑ SD 33-137 [S]	Ben E. King Sings for Soulful Lovers	1962	15.00	30.00	60.00
❑ 33-142 [M]	Don't Play That Song	1962	10.00	20.00	40.00
❑ SD 33-142 [S]	Don't Play That Song	1962	15.00	30.00	60.00
❑ 33-165 [M]	Ben E. King's Greatest Hits	1964	7.50	15.00	30.00
❑ SD 33-165 [S]	Ben E. King's Greatest Hits	1964	10.00	20.00	40.00
—Purple and brown label					
❑ SD 33-165 [S]	Ben E. King's Greatest Hits	1969	3.00	6.00	12.00
—Yellow label					
❑ SD 33-165 [S]	Ben E. King's Greatest Hits	197?	2.00	4.00	8.00
—Any other color label					
❑ 33-174 [M]	Seven Letters	1965	10.00	20.00	40.00
❑ SD 33-174 [S]	Seven Letters	1965	12.50	25.00	50.00
ATLANTIC					
❑ SD 18132	Supernatural	1975	3.00	6.00	12.00
❑ SD 18169	I Have a Love	1976	3.00	6.00	12.00
❑ SD 18191	Rhapsody	1976	3.00	6.00	12.00
❑ SD 19200	Let Me Live in Your Life	1978	3.00	6.00	12.00
❑ SD 19269	Music Trance	1980	2.50	5.00	10.00
❑ SD 19300	Street Tough	1981	2.50	5.00	10.00
❑ 81716	Stand By Me: The Best of Ben E. King	1987	2.00	4.00	8.00
—Includes seven Ben E. King tracks and three by the Drifters					
CLARION					
❑ 606 [M]	Young Boy Blues	1966	6.25	12.50	25.00
❑ SD 606 [S]	Young Boy Blues	1966	7.50	15.00	30.00
MANDALA					
❑ MLP 3007	The Beginning of It All for Ben E. King	1972	5.00	10.00	20.00
❑ MLP-3008 [DJ]	Audio Biography	1972	7.50	15.00	30.00
—Promo-only interview by Richard Robinson					
MAXWELL					
❑ ML-88001	Rough Edges	1969	5.00	10.00	20.00

KING, CAROLE

Number	Title (A Side/B Side)	Yr	VG	VG+	NM
ATLANTIC					
❑ SD 19344	One to One	1982	2.50	5.00	10.00
❑ 80118	Speeding Time	1983	2.50	5.00	10.00
CAPITOL					
❑ SPRO-9103/4 [EP]	Touch the Sky Sampler	1979	3.75	7.50	15.00
—Promo-only four-song excerpt from "Touch the Sky"					
❑ SMAS-11667	Simple Things	1977	2.50	5.00	10.00
❑ SW-11785	Welcome Home	1978	2.50	5.00	10.00
❑ SW-11785	Welcome Home	1978	2.50	5.00	10.00
❑ ST-11953	Touch the Sky	1979	2.50	5.00	10.00
❑ SWAK-11963	Touch the Sky	1979	2.50	5.00	10.00
❑ SOO-12073	Pearls — Songs of Goffin and King	1980	2.50	5.00	10.00
❑ SN-16057	Simple Things	1980	2.00	4.00	8.00
—Budget-line reissue					
❑ SN-16058	Welcome Home	1980	2.00	4.00	8.00
—Budget-line reissue					

Number	Title (A Side/B Side)	Yr	VG	VG+	NM
❑ SN-16059	Touch the Sky	1980	2.00	4.00	8.00
—Budget-line reissue					
❑ C1-90885	City Streets	1989	3.00	6.00	12.00
ODE					
❑ PE 34944	Carole King: Writer	1977	2.50	5.00	10.00
—Reissue of 77006					
❑ FE 34946	Tapestry	1979	2.50	5.00	10.00
—Reissue with new prefix					
❑ PE 34946	Tapestry	1977	2.50	5.00	10.00
—Reissue of 77009					
❑ PE 34949	Music	1977	2.50	5.00	10.00
—Reissue of 77013					
❑ PE 34950	Rhymes and Reasons	1977	2.50	5.00	10.00
—Reissue of 77016					
❑ PE 34953	Wrap Around Joy	1977	2.50	5.00	10.00
—Reissue of 77024					
❑ PE 34955	Really Rosie	1977	2.50	5.00	10.00
—Reissue of 77027					
❑ PE 34962	Fantasy	1977	2.50	5.00	10.00
—Reissue of 77018					
❑ PE 34963	Thoroughbred	1977	2.50	5.00	10.00
—Reissue of 77034					
❑ JE 34967	Her Greatest Hits	1978	2.50	5.00	10.00
❑ HE 44946	Tapestry	1980	12.50	25.00	50.00
—Half-speed mastered edition					
❑ SP-77006	Writer: Carole King	1970	3.00	6.00	12.00
❑ SP-77009	Tapestry	1971	3.00	6.00	12.00
❑ SP-77013	Music	1971	3.00	6.00	12.00
❑ SP-77016	Rhymes and Reasons	1972	3.00	6.00	12.00
❑ SP-77018	Fantasy	1973	3.00	6.00	12.00
❑ SP-77024	Wrap Around Joy	1974	3.00	6.00	12.00
❑ SP-77027	Really Rosie	1975	3.00	6.00	12.00
❑ SP-77034	Thoroughbred	1976	3.00	6.00	12.00
❑ SQ-88013 [Q]	Music	1974	5.00	10.00	20.00

KING, CLAUDE

Number	Title (A Side/B Side)	Yr	VG	VG+	NM
COLUMBIA					
❑ CS 1024	Friend, Lover, Woman, Wife	1970	3.75	7.50	15.00
❑ CL 1810 [M]	Meet Claude King	1962	6.25	12.50	25.00
—Six "eye" logos on label					
❑ CL 1810 [M]	Meet Claude King	1963	3.75	7.50	15.00
—"Guaranteed High Fidelity" or "Mono" on red label					
❑ CL 2415 [M]	Tiger Woman	1965	5.00	10.00	20.00
❑ CS 8610 [S]	Meet Claude King	1962	10.00	20.00	40.00
—Six "eye" logos on label					
❑ CS 8610 [S]	Meet Claude King	1963	5.00	10.00	20.00
—"360 Sound Stereo" on red label					
❑ CS 9215 [S]	Tiger Woman	1965	6.25	12.50	25.00
—"360 Sound Stereo" on red label					
❑ CS 9789	I Remember Johnny Horton	1968	3.75	7.50	15.00
—"360 Sound Stereo" on red label					
❑ C 30804	Chip 'n' Dale's Place	1971	3.75	7.50	15.00
HARMONY					
❑ HS 11300	The Best of Claude King	1969	3.00	6.00	12.00

KING, FREDDIE

Number	Title (A Side/B Side)	Yr	VG	VG+	NM
COTILLION					
❑ SD 9004	Freddie King Is a Blues Master	1969	6.25	12.50	25.00
❑ SD 9016	My Feeling for the Blues	1970	6.25	12.50	25.00
KING					
❑ 762 [M]	Freddie King Sings the Blues	1961	62.50	125.00	250.00
❑ 773 [M]	Let's Hide Away and Dance Away	1961	62.50	125.00	250.00
❑ 821 [M]	Bossa Nova and Blues	1962	37.50	75.00	150.00
❑ 856 [M]	Freddie King Goes Surfin'	1963	20.00	40.00	80.00
❑ KS-856 [S]	Freddie King Goes Surfin'	1963	30.00	60.00	120.00
❑ 928 [M]	A Bonanza of Instrumentals	1965	12.50	25.00	50.00
❑ KS-928 [S]	A Bonanza of Instrumentals	1965	15.00	30.00	60.00
❑ 964 [M]	24 Vocals and Instrumentals	1966	6.25	12.50	25.00
❑ KS-1059	Hide Away	1969	3.75	7.50	15.00
MCA					
❑ 690	The Best of Freddie King	1979	2.00	4.00	8.00
—Reissue of Shelter 52021					
MODERN BLUES					
❑ MB2LP-721 [(2)]	Just Pickin'	198?	3.75	7.50	15.00
❑ MBLP-722	Freddie King Sings	198?	2.50	5.00	10.00
RSO					
❑ RS-1-3025	Freddie King 1934-1976	1977	3.00	6.00	12.00
❑ SD 4803	Burglar	1974	3.00	6.00	12.00
❑ SD 4811	Larger Than Life	1975	3.00	6.00	12.00
SHELTER					
❑ 2140	The Best of Freddie King	1975	3.75	7.50	15.00
—Original with MCA distribution					
❑ SW-8905	Getting Ready	1971	3.75	7.50	15.00
❑ SW-8913	Texas Cannonball	1972	3.75	7.50	15.00
❑ SW-8919	Woman Across the River	1973	3.75	7.50	15.00
❑ SRL 52021	The Best of Freddie King	1977	3.00	6.00	12.00
—Second edition with ABC distribution					
STARDAY/GUSTO					
❑ 5012	17 Original Hits	1977	2.50	5.00	10.00
❑ 5033	Hide Away	1978	2.50	5.00	10.00

KING, FREDDIE/LULA REED/BOBBY THOMPSON

Number	Title (A Side/B Side)	Yr	VG	VG+	NM
KING					
❑ 777 [M]	Boy-Girl-Boy	1962	62.50	125.00	250.00

KING, JEAN

Number	Title (A Side/B Side)	Yr	VG	VG+	NM
HANNA-BARBERA					
❑ HLP-8505 [M]	Jean King Sings for the In Crowd	1966	5.00	10.00	20.00

KING, JONATHAN

Number	Title (A Side/B Side)	Yr	VG	VG+	NM
PARROT					
❑ PA 61013 [M]	Jonathan King Or Then Again....	1967	10.00	20.00	40.00

Number	Title (A Side/B Side)	Yr	VG	VG+	NM
❏ PAS 71013 [P]	Jonathan King Or Then Again....	1967	12.50	25.00	50.00
—Only "Where the Sun Has Never Shown" is rechanneled.					

U.K.

❏ 53101	Bubble Rock Is Here to Stay	1972	6.25	12.50	25.00
❏ 53104	Pandora's Box	1973	6.25	12.50	25.00

KING, MORGANA

ASCOT

❏ AM 13014 [M]	The Winter of My Discontent	1964	6.25	12.50	25.00
❏ AM 13019 [M]	The End of a Love Affair	1965	6.25	12.50	25.00
—Reissue of United Artists 30020					
❏ AM 13020 [M]	Everybody Loves Saturday Night	1965	6.25	12.50	25.00
❏ AM 13025 [M]	More Morgana	1965	6.25	12.50	25.00
❏ AS 16014 [S]	The Winter of My Discontent	1964	7.50	15.00	30.00
❏ AS 16019 [S]	The End of a Love Affair	1965	7.50	15.00	30.00
—Reissue of United Artists 40020					
❏ AS 16020 [S]	Everybody Loves Saturday Night	1965	7.50	15.00	30.00
❏ AS 16025 [S]	More Morgana	1965	7.50	15.00	30.00

EMARCY

❏ MG-36079 [M]	For You, For Me, Forever More	1956	20.00	40.00	80.00

MAINSTREAM

❏ S-6015 [S]	With a Taste of Honey	1964	6.25	12.50	25.00
❏ S-6052 [S]	Miss Morgana King	1965	6.25	12.50	25.00
❏ 56015 [M]	With a Taste of Honey	1964	5.00	10.00	20.00
❏ 56052 [M]	Miss Morgana King	1965	5.00	10.00	20.00

MERCURY

❏ MG-20231 [M]	Morgana King Sings the Blues	1958	20.00	40.00	80.00

RCA CAMDEN

❏ CAL-543 [M]	The Greatest Songs Ever Swung	1959	5.00	10.00	20.00
❏ CAS-543 [S]	The Greatest Songs Ever Swung	1959	7.50	15.00	30.00

REPRISE

❏ R 6192 [M]	It's a Quiet Thing	1966	5.00	10.00	20.00
❏ RS 6192 [S]	It's a Quiet Thing	1966	6.25	12.50	25.00
❏ R 6205 [M]	Wild Is Love	1966	5.00	10.00	20.00
❏ RS 6205 [S]	Wild Is Love	1966	6.25	12.50	25.00
❏ R 6257 [M]	Gemini Changes	1967	5.00	10.00	20.00
❏ RS 6257 [S]	Gemini Changes	1967	6.25	12.50	25.00

UNITED ARTISTS

❏ UAL 3028 [M]	Folk Songs A La King	1960	10.00	20.00	40.00
❏ UAS 6028 [S]	Folk Songs A La King	1960	12.50	25.00	50.00
❏ UAL 30020 [M]	Let Me Love You	1960	12.50	25.00	50.00
❏ UAS 40020 [S]	Let Me Love You	1960	15.00	30.00	60.00

VERVE

❏ V-5061 [M]	I Know How It Feels	1968	6.25	12.50	25.00
❏ V6-5061 [S]	I Know How It Feels	1968	6.25	12.50	25.00

WING

❏ SRW-16307 [S]	More Morgana King	1965	5.00	10.00	20.00

KING, PEE WEE

BRIAR

❏ 102	Golden Olde Tyme Dances	1975	15.00	30.00	60.00

LONGHORN

❏ 1236 [M]	The Legendary Pee Wee King	1967	6.25	12.50	25.00

RCA CAMDEN

❏ CAL-876 [M]	Country Barn Dance	1965	5.00	10.00	20.00
❏ CAS-876 [R]	Country Barn Dance	1965	3.00	6.00	12.00

RCA VICTOR

❏ LPM-1237 [M]	Swing West	1956	10.00	20.00	40.00
❏ LPM-3028 [10]	Pee Wee King	195?	20.00	40.00	80.00
❏ LPM-3071 [10]	Western Hits	195?	20.00	40.00	80.00
❏ LPM-3109 [10]	Waltzes	195?	20.00	40.00	80.00
❏ LPM-3280 [10]	Swing West	195?	20.00	40.00	80.00

STARDAY

❏ SLP-284 [M]	Back Again with the Songs That Made Them Famous	1964	7.50	15.00	30.00

KING, PEGGY

COLUMBIA

❏ CL 2549 [10]	Wish Upon a Star	1955	12.50	25.00	50.00

IMPERIAL

❏ LP-9078 [M]	Lazy Afternoon	1959	5.00	10.00	20.00
❏ LP-12026 [S]	Lazy Afternoon	1959	7.50	15.00	30.00

KING, REV. MARTIN LUTHER
The 1968 releases are posthumous tributes.

BUDDAH

❏ BDS-2002	Man of Love	1968	5.00	10.00	20.00

CREED

❏ 3201 [M]	I Have a Dream	1968	5.00	10.00	20.00

DOOTO

❏ DTL-831 [M]	Martin Luther King at Zion Hill	1962	7.50	15.00	30.00
❏ DTL-841	The American Dream	1968	5.00	10.00	20.00

GORDY

❏ G-906 [M]	The Great March to Freedom	1963	10.00	20.00	40.00
—"Gordy" in script at top of label					
❏ G-906 [M]	The Great March to Freedom	1968	3.75	7.50	15.00
—Later pressings					
❏ G-908 [M]	The Great March on Washington	1963	10.00	20.00	40.00
—"Gordy" in script at top of label					
❏ G-908 [M]	The Great March on Washington	1968	3.75	7.50	15.00
—Later pressings					
❏ G-929	...Free at Last	1968	7.50	15.00	30.00
—Original with gatefold cover					

MERCURY

❏ SR-61170	In Search of Freedom	1968	5.00	10.00	20.00

MR. MAESTRO

❏ 1000 [M]	The March on Washington	1963	7.50	15.00	30.00

SUNSET

❏ 21033	The Struggle for Freedom	1968	3.75	7.50	15.00

20TH CENTURY

❏ TCF-3110 [M]	Freedom March on Washington	1963	7.50	15.00	30.00
❏ S-3201	The Rev. Dr. Martin Luther King, Jr.	1968	5.00	10.00	20.00

UNART

❏ S 21033	In the Struggle for Freedom and Human Dignity	1968	5.00	10.00	20.00

KING, TEDDI

CORAL

❏ CRL 57278 [M]	All the King's Songs	1959	15.00	30.00	60.00
❏ CRL 757278 [S]	All the King's Songs	1959	20.00	40.00	80.00

RCA VICTOR

❏ LPM-1147 [M]	Bidin' My Time	1956	20.00	40.00	80.00
❏ LPM-1313 [M]	To You from Teddi King	1957	20.00	40.00	80.00
❏ LPM-1454 [M]	A Girl and Her Songs	1957	20.00	40.00	80.00

STORYVILLE

❏ STLP-302 [10]	'Round Midnight	1954	50.00	100.00	200.00
❏ STLP-314 [10]	Storyville Presents Teddi King	1954	50.00	100.00	200.00
❏ STLP-903 [M]	Now In Vogue	1956	30.00	60.00	120.00

KING CRIMSON

ATLANTIC

❏ SD 7212	Islands	1972	5.00	10.00	20.00
❏ SD 7263	Larks' Tongues in Aspic	1973	5.00	10.00	20.00
❏ SD 7298	Starless and Bible Black	1974	5.00	10.00	20.00
❏ 8245 [M]	In the Court of the Crimson King — An Observation by King Crimson	1969	12.50	25.00	50.00
—Mono is white label promo only; comes in stereo cover with "DJ Copy Monaural" sticker on front					
❏ SD 8245	In the Court of the Crimson King — An Observation by King Crimson	1969	5.00	10.00	20.00
❏ SD 8266	In the Wake of Poseidon	1970	5.00	10.00	20.00
❏ SD 8278	Lizard	1971	5.00	10.00	20.00
❏ SD 18110	Red	1974	3.75	7.50	15.00
❏ SD 18136	USA	1975	3.75	7.50	15.00
❏ SD 19155	In the Court of the Crimson King — An Observation by King Crimson	1978	3.00	6.00	12.00
—Reissue of Atlantic 8245					

EDITIONS EG

❏ EGKC-1	In the Court of the Crimson King — An Observation by King Crimson	1985	2.50	5.00	10.00
—Reissue of Atlantic 19155					
❏ EGKC-2	In the Wake of Poseidon	1985	2.50	5.00	10.00
—Reissue of Atlantic 8266					
❏ EGKC-3	Lizard	1985	2.50	5.00	10.00
—Reissue of Atlantic 8278					
❏ EGKC-4	Islands	1985	2.50	5.00	10.00
—Reissue of Atlantic 7212					
❏ EGKC-6	Lark's Tongue in Aspic	1985	2.50	5.00	10.00
—Reissue of Atlantic 7263					
❏ EGKC-7	Starless and Bible Black	1985	2.50	5.00	10.00
—Reissue of Atlantic 7298					
❏ EGKC-8	Red	1985	2.50	5.00	10.00
—Reissue of Atlantic 18110					
❏ EGKC-9	USA	1985	2.50	5.00	10.00
—Reissue of Atlantic 18135					
❏ EGKC-10 [(2)]	The Young Person's Guide to King Crimson	1985	3.75	7.50	15.00

MOBILE FIDELITY

❏ 1-075	In the Court of the Crimson King — An Observation by King Crimson	1981	20.00	40.00	80.00
—Audiophile vinyl					

WARNER BROS.

❏ WBMS-119 [DJ]	The Return of King Crimson	1981	15.00	30.00	60.00
—Promo-only interview and music show					
❏ BSK 3629	Discipline	1981	2.50	5.00	10.00
❏ 23692	Beat	1982	2.50	5.00	10.00
❏ 25071	Three of a Perfect Pair	1984	2.50	5.00	10.00

KING CURTIS

ATCO

❏ 33-113 [M]	Have Tenor Sax, Will Blow	1959	10.00	20.00	40.00
❏ SD 33-113 [S]	Have Tenor Sax, Will Blow	1959	15.00	30.00	60.00
❏ 33-189 [M]	That Lovin' Feeling	1966	5.00	10.00	20.00
❏ SD 33-189 [S]	That Lovin' Feeling	1966	6.25	12.50	25.00
❏ 33-198 [M]	Live at Small's Paradise	1966	5.00	10.00	20.00
❏ SD 33-198 [S]	Live at Small's Paradise	1966	6.25	12.50	25.00
❏ 33-211 [M]	The Great Memphis Hits	1967	5.00	10.00	20.00
❏ SD 33-211 [S]	The Great Memphis Hits	1967	6.25	12.50	25.00
❏ 33-231 [M]	King Size Soul	1967	6.25	12.50	25.00
❏ SD 33-231 [S]	King Size Soul	1967	5.00	10.00	20.00
❏ 33-247 [M]	Sweet Soul	1968	7.50	15.00	30.00
❏ SD 33-247 [S]	Sweet Soul	1968	5.00	10.00	20.00
❏ SD 33-266	The Best of King Curtis	1968	5.00	10.00	20.00
❏ SD 33-293	Instant Groove	1969	5.00	10.00	20.00
❏ SD 33-338	Get Ready	1970	5.00	10.00	20.00
❏ SD 33-359	Live at Fillmore West	1971	5.00	10.00	20.00
❏ SD 33-385	Everybody's Talkin'	1972	5.00	10.00	20.00

ATLANTIC

❏ SD 1637	Blues Montreux	1973	3.00	6.00	12.00

CAPITOL

❏ ST 1756 [S]	Country Soul	1963	10.00	20.00	40.00
❏ T 1756 [M]	Country Soul	1963	7.50	15.00	30.00
❏ ST 2095 [S]	Soul Serenade	1964	7.50	15.00	30.00
❏ T 2095 [M]	Soul Serenade	1964	6.25	12.50	25.00
❏ ST 2341 [S]	King Curtis Plays the Hits Made Famous by Sam Cooke	1965	7.50	15.00	30.00
❏ T 2341 [M]	King Curtis Plays the Hits Made Famous by Sam Cooke	1965	6.25	12.50	25.00
❏ ST 2858 [S]	The Best of King Curtis	1968	6.25	12.50	25.00

Number	Title (A Side/B Side)	Yr	VG	VG+	NM
❏ T 2858 [M]	The Best of King Curtis	1968	12.50	25.00	50.00
—Red and white "Starline" label; may be promo only					
❏ SM-11798	Soul Serenade	1978	2.50	5.00	10.00
—Reissue					
❏ SM-11963	The Best of King Curtis	1979	2.50	5.00	10.00
—Reissue					
CLARION					
❏ 615 [M]	The Great "K" Curtis	1966	5.00	10.00	20.00
❏ SD 615 [S]	The Great "K" Curtis	1966	6.25	12.50	25.00
COLLECTABLES					
❏ COL-5119	Soul Twist	198?	2.50	5.00	10.00
❏ COL-5156	Golden Classics: Enjoy…The Best of King Curtis	198?	2.50	5.00	10.00
ENJOY					
❏ ENLP-2001 [M]	Soul Twist	1962	12.50	25.00	50.00
EVEREST					
❏ SDBR-1121 [S]	Azure	1961	18.75	37.50	75.00
❏ LPBR-5121 [M]	Azure	1961	12.50	25.00	50.00
FANTASY					
❏ OJC-198	The New Scene of King Curtis	1985	2.50	5.00	10.00
—Reissue of New Jazz 8237					
❏ OBC-512	Trouble in Mind	1988	2.50	5.00	10.00
—Reissue of Tru-Sound 15001					
NEW JAZZ					
❏ NJLP-8237 [M]	The New Scene of King Curtis	1960	15.00	30.00	60.00
—Purple label					
❏ NJLP-8237 [M]	The New Scene of King Curtis	1965	7.50	15.00	30.00
—Blue label with trident logo on right					
PRESTIGE					
❏ PRLP-7222 [M]	Soul Meeting	1962	12.50	25.00	50.00
❏ PRST-7222 [S]	Soul Meeting	1962	18.75	37.50	75.00
❏ PRST-7709	The Best of King Curtis	1969	3.75	7.50	15.00
❏ PRST-7775	The Best of King Curtis — One More Time	1970	3.75	7.50	15.00
❏ PRST-7789	King Soul	1970	3.75	7.50	15.00
❏ PRST-7833	Soul Meeting	1971	3.75	7.50	15.00
—Reissue of 7222					
❏ 24033 [(2)]	Jazz Groove	198?	3.75	7.50	15.00
RCA CAMDEN					
❏ CAS-2242	Sax in Motion	1968	3.75	7.50	15.00
RCA VICTOR					
❏ LPM-2492 [M]	Arthur Murray's Music for Dancing: The Twist!	1962	6.25	12.50	25.00
❏ LSP-2492 [S]	Arthur Murray's Music for Dancing: The Twist!	1962	7.50	15.00	30.00
TRU-SOUND					
❏ TS-15001 [M]	Trouble in Mind	1961	12.50	25.00	50.00
❏ TS-15008 [M]	It's Party Time	1962	12.50	25.00	50.00
❏ TS-15009 [M]	Doin' the Dixie Twist	1962	12.50	25.00	50.00

KING PINS, THE (1)
KING

Number	Title (A Side/B Side)	Yr	VG	VG+	NM
❏ 865 [M]	It Won't Be This Way Always	1963	75.00	150.00	300.00

KING PLEASURE
HIFI

Number	Title (A Side/B Side)	Yr	VG	VG+	NM
❏ R-425 [M]	Golden Days	1960	10.00	20.00	40.00
❏ RS-425 [S]	Golden Days	1960	12.50	25.00	50.00
PRESTIGE					
❏ PRLP-208 [10]	King Pleasure Sings	1955	50.00	100.00	200.00
UNITED ARTISTS					
❏ UAJ-14031 [M]	Mr. Jazz	1962	10.00	20.00	40.00
❏ UAJS-15031 [S]	Mr. Jazz	1962	12.50	25.00	50.00

KING PLEASURE/ANNIE ROSS
PRESTIGE

Number	Title (A Side/B Side)	Yr	VG	VG+	NM
❏ PRLP-7128 [M]	King Pleasure Sings/Annie Ross Sings	1957	25.00	50.00	100.00

KING SISTERS, THE
CAPITOL

Number	Title (A Side/B Side)	Yr	VG	VG+	NM
❏ T 808 [M]	Aloha	1957	6.25	12.50	25.00
—Turquoise or gray label					
❏ T 919 [M]	Imagination	1958	6.25	12.50	25.00
—Turquoise or gray label					
❏ ST 1205 [S]	Warm and Wonderful	1959	7.50	15.00	30.00
—Black colorband label, logo at left					
❏ T 1205 [M]	Warm and Wonderful	1959	5.00	10.00	20.00
—Black colorband label, logo at left					

KING'S MEN FIVE, THE
CUCA

Number	Title (A Side/B Side)	Yr	VG	VG+	NM
❏ 1130 [M]	The King's Men Five	1965	5.00	10.00	20.00

KINGDOM
SPECIALTY

Number	Title (A Side/B Side)	Yr	VG	VG+	NM
❏ SPS-2135	Kingdom	1970	15.00	30.00	60.00

KINGFISH
With Bob Weir of THE GRATEFUL DEAD.
ROUND

Number	Title (A Side/B Side)	Yr	VG	VG+	NM
❏ RX-108	Kingfish	1976	6.25	12.50	25.00

KINGS, THE
ELEKTRA

Number	Title (A Side/B Side)	Yr	VG	VG+	NM
❏ 6E-277	The Kings Are Here	1980	7.50	15.00	30.00
❏ 5E-543	Amazon Beach	1981	3.00	6.00	12.00

KINGSLEY, GERSHON
Also see PERREY-KINGSLEY.
AUDIO FIDELITY

Number	Title (A Side/B Side)	Yr	VG	VG+	NM
❏ AFSD-6222	Music to Moog By	1969	10.00	20.00	40.00

KINGSMEN, THE (1)
RHINO

Number	Title (A Side/B Side)	Yr	VG	VG+	NM
❏ RNLP-126	The Best of the Kingsmen	1985	2.50	5.00	10.00
SCEPTER					
❏ CTN-18002	The Best of the Kingsmen	1972	2.50	5.00	10.00
WAND					
❏ WDM-657 [M]	The Kingsmen In Person	1964	7.50	15.00	30.00
❏ WDS-657 [P]	The Kingsmen In Person	1964	10.00	20.00	40.00
❏ WDM-659 [M]	The Kingsmen, Volume II	1964	7.50	15.00	30.00
—With "Death of an Angel"					
❏ WDM-659 [M]	The Kingsmen, Volume II	1964	10.00	20.00	40.00
—Without "Death of an Angel" (replaced by untitled instrumental)					
❏ WDS-659 [S]	The Kingsmen, Volume II	1964	10.00	20.00	40.00
—With "Death of an Angel"					
❏ WDS-659 [S]	The Kingsmen, Volume II	1964	12.50	25.00	50.00
—Without "Death of an Angel" (replaced by untitled instrumental)					
❏ WDM-662 [M]	The Kingsmen, Volume 3	1965	6.25	12.50	25.00
❏ WDS-662 [S]	The Kingsmen, Volume 3	1965	7.50	15.00	30.00
❏ WDM-670 [M]	The Kingsmen On Campus	1965	6.25	12.50	25.00
❏ WDS-670 [S]	The Kingsmen On Campus	1965	7.50	15.00	30.00
❏ WDM-674 [M]	15 Great Hits	1966	5.00	10.00	20.00
❏ WDS-674 [P]	15 Great Hits	1966	6.25	12.50	25.00
❏ WDM-675 [M]	Up and Away	1966	5.00	10.00	20.00
❏ WDS-675 [S]	Up and Away	1966	6.25	12.50	25.00
❏ WDM-681 [M]	The Kingsmen's Greatest Hits	1967	3.75	7.50	15.00
❏ WDS-681 [S]	The Kingsmen's Greatest Hits	1967	5.00	10.00	20.00
❏ ST-91011 [S]	Up and Away	1966	7.50	15.00	30.00
—Capitol Record Club edition					

KINGSTON TRIO, THE
Also see DAVE GUARD AND THE WHISKEYHILL SINGERS; JOHN STEWART.
CAPITOL

Number	Title (A Side/B Side)	Yr	VG	VG+	NM
❏ STBB-513 [(2)]	Tom Dooley/Scarlet Ribbons	1970	5.00	10.00	20.00
❏ DT 996 [R]	The Kingston Trio	196?	3.00	6.00	12.00
❏ T 996 [M]	The Kingston Trio	1958	10.00	20.00	40.00
—Black label with colorband, Capitol logo at left					
❏ T 996 [M]	The Kingston Trio	1958	12.50	25.00	50.00
—Turquoise label					
❏ T 996 [M]	The Kingston Trio	1962	5.00	10.00	20.00
—Black label with colorband, Capitol logo at top					
❏ T 1107 [M]	From the Hungry I	1959	10.00	20.00	40.00
—Black label with colorband, Capitol logo at left					
❏ T 1107 [M]	From the Hungry I	1962	5.00	10.00	20.00
—Black label with colorband, Capitol logo at top					
❏ ST 1183 [S]	Stereo Concert	1959	12.50	25.00	50.00
—Black label with colorband, Capitol logo at left					
❏ ST 1183 [S]	Stereo Concert	1962	6.25	12.50	25.00
—Black label with colorband, Capitol logo at top					
❏ ST 1199 [S]	The Kingston Trio at Large	1959	10.00	20.00	40.00
—Black label with colorband, Capitol logo at left					
❏ ST 1199 [S]	The Kingston Trio at Large	1962	5.00	10.00	20.00
—Black label with colorband, Capitol logo at top					
❏ T 1199 [M]	The Kingston Trio at Large	1959	7.50	15.00	30.00
—Black label with colorband, Capitol logo at left, "Long Playing High-Fidelity"					
❏ T 1199 [M]	The Kingston Trio at Large	1960	6.25	12.50	25.00
—Black label with colorband, Capitol logo at left, white line replaces "Long Playing High-Fidelity"					
❏ T 1199 [M]	The Kingston Trio at Large	1962	3.75	7.50	15.00
—Black label with colorband, Capitol logo at top					
❏ ST 1258 [S]	Here We Go Again!	1959	10.00	20.00	40.00
—Black label with colorband, Capitol logo at left					
❏ ST 1258 [S]	Here We Go Again!	1962	5.00	10.00	20.00
—Black label with colorband, Capitol logo at top					
❏ T 1258 [M]	Here We Go Again!	1959	7.50	15.00	30.00
—Black label with colorband, Capitol logo at left					
❏ T 1258 [M]	Here We Go Again!	1962	3.75	7.50	15.00
—Black label with colorband, Capitol logo at top					
❏ ST 1352 [S]	Sold Out	1960	10.00	20.00	40.00
—Black label with colorband, Capitol logo at left					
❏ ST 1352 [S]	Sold Out	1962	5.00	10.00	20.00
—Black label with colorband, Capitol logo at top					
❏ T 1352 [M]	Sold Out	1960	7.50	15.00	30.00
—Black label with colorband, Capitol logo at left					
❏ T 1352 [M]	Sold Out	1962	3.75	7.50	15.00
—Black label with colorband, Capitol logo at top					
❏ ST 1407 [S]	String Along	1960	10.00	20.00	40.00
—Black label with colorband, Capitol logo at left					
❏ ST 1407 [S]	String Along	1962	5.00	10.00	20.00
—Black label with colorband, Capitol logo at top					
❏ T 1407 [M]	String Along	1960	7.50	15.00	30.00
—Black label with colorband, Capitol logo at left					
❏ T 1407 [M]	String Along	1962	3.75	7.50	15.00
—Black label with colorband, Capitol logo at top					
❏ ST 1446 [S]	The Last Month of the Year	1960	10.00	20.00	40.00
—Same as above, but in stereo					
❏ T 1446 [M]	The Last Month of the Year	1960	7.50	15.00	30.00
❏ ST 1474 [S]	Make Way!	1961	10.00	20.00	40.00
—Black label with colorband, Capitol logo at left					
❏ ST 1474 [S]	Make Way!	1962	5.00	10.00	20.00
—Black label with colorband, Capitol logo at top					
❏ T 1474 [M]	Make Way!	1961	7.50	15.00	30.00
—Black label with colorband, Capitol logo at left					
❏ T 1474 [M]	Make Way!	1962	3.75	7.50	15.00
—Black label with colorband, Capitol logo at top					
❏ ST 1564 [S]	Goin' Places	1961	10.00	20.00	40.00
—Black label with colorband, Capitol logo at left					
❏ ST 1564 [S]	Goin' Places	1962	5.00	10.00	20.00
—Black label with colorband, Capitol logo at top					
❏ T 1564 [M]	Goin' Places	1961	7.50	15.00	30.00
—Black label with colorband, Capitol logo at left					
❏ T 1564 [M]	Goin' Places	1962	3.75	7.50	15.00
—Black label with colorband, Capitol logo at top					

Number	Title (A Side/B Side)	Yr	VG	VG+	NM
❏ DT 1612 [R]	Encores	1961	5.00	10.00	20.00
—Black label with colorband, Capitol logo at left					
❏ DT 1612 [R]	Encores	1962	2.50	5.00	10.00
—Black label with colorband, Capitol logo at top					
❏ T 1612 [M]	Encores	1961	7.50	15.00	30.00
—Black label with colorband, Capitol logo at left					
❏ T 1612 [M]	Encores	1962	3.75	7.50	15.00
—Black label with colorband, Capitol logo at top					
❏ ST 1642 [S]	Close-Up	1961	10.00	20.00	40.00
—Black label with colorband, Capitol logo at left					
❏ ST 1642 [S]	Close-Up	1962	5.00	10.00	20.00
—Black label with colorband, Capitol logo at top					
❏ T 1642 [M]	Close-Up	1961	7.50	15.00	30.00
—Black label with colorband, Capitol logo at left					
❏ T 1642 [M]	Close-Up	1962	3.75	7.50	15.00
—Black label with colorband, Capitol logo at top					
❏ ST 1658 [S]	College Concert	1962	6.25	12.50	25.00
❏ T 1658 [M]	College Concert	1962	5.00	10.00	20.00
❏ SM-1705	The Best of the Kingston Trio	197?	2.50	5.00	10.00
❏ ST 1705 [P]	The Best of the Kingston Trio	1962	5.00	10.00	20.00
❏ T 1705 [M]	The Best of the Kingston Trio	1962	5.00	10.00	20.00
❏ ST 1747 [S]	Something Special	1962	6.25	12.50	25.00
❏ T 1747 [M]	Something Special	1962	5.00	10.00	20.00
❏ ST 1809 [S]	New Frontier	1962	6.25	12.50	25.00
❏ T 1809 [M]	New Frontier	1962	5.00	10.00	20.00
❏ ST 1871 [S]	The Kingston Trio #16	1963	6.25	12.50	25.00
❏ T 1871 [M]	The Kingston Trio #16	1963	5.00	10.00	20.00
❏ ST 1935 [S]	Sunny Side!	1963	6.25	12.50	25.00
❏ T 1935 [M]	Sunny Side!	1963	5.00	10.00	20.00
❏ KAO 2005 [M]	Sing a Song with the Kingston Trio	1963	6.25	12.50	25.00
❏ SKAO 2005 [S]	Sing a Song with the Kingston Trio	1963	7.50	15.00	30.00
❏ ST 2011 [S]	Time to Think	1964	5.00	10.00	20.00
❏ T 2011 [M]	Time to Think	1964	3.75	7.50	15.00
❏ ST 2081 [S]	Back in Town	1964	5.00	10.00	20.00
❏ T 2081 [M]	Back in Town	1964	3.75	7.50	15.00
❏ STCL 2180 [(3)S]	The Folk Era	1964	12.50	25.00	50.00
—Box set with booklet					
❏ TCL 2180 [(3)M]	The Folk Era	1964	10.00	20.00	40.00
—Box set with booklet					
❏ SM-2280	The Best of the Kingston Trio, Volume 2	197?	2.50	5.00	10.00
❏ ST 2280 [S]	The Best of the Kingston Trio, Volume 2	1965	5.00	10.00	20.00
❏ T 2280 [M]	The Best of the Kingston Trio, Volume 2	1965	3.75	7.50	15.00
❏ SM-2614	The Best of the Kingston Trio, Volume 3	197?	2.50	5.00	10.00
❏ ST 2614 [S]	The Best of the Kingston Trio, Volume 3	1966	5.00	10.00	20.00
❏ T 2614 [M]	The Best of the Kingston Trio, Volume 3	1966	3.75	7.50	15.00
❏ M-11577	The Kingston Trio	1976	2.50	5.00	10.00
❏ M-11968	From the Hungry I	1979	2.50	5.00	10.00
❏ SN-16183	The Best of the Kingston Trio	1981	2.00	4.00	8.00
—Budget-line reissue					
❏ SN-16184	The Best of the Kingston Trio, Volume 2	1981	2.00	4.00	8.00
—Budget-line reissue					
❏ N-16185	Tom Dooley	1981	2.00	4.00	8.00
❏ SN-16186	Scarlet Ribbons	1981	2.00	4.00	8.00
DECCA					
❏ DL 4613 [M]	The Kingston Trio (Nick-Bob-John)	1965	6.25	12.50	25.00
❏ DL 4656 [M]	Stay Awhile	1965	6.25	12.50	25.00
❏ DL 4694 [M]	Somethin' Else	1965	6.25	12.50	25.00
❏ DL 4758 [M]	Children of the Morning	1966	6.25	12.50	25.00
❏ DL 74613 [S]	The Kingston Trio (Nick-Bob-John)	1965	7.50	15.00	30.00
❏ DL 74656 [S]	Stay Awhile	1965	7.50	15.00	30.00
❏ DL 74694 [S]	Somethin' Else	1965	7.50	15.00	30.00
❏ DL 74758 [S]	Children of the Morning	1966	7.50	15.00	30.00
FOLK ERA					
❏ FE-2001	Rediscover the Kingston Trio	198?	2.50	5.00	10.00
❏ FE-2036	Hidden Treasures	198?	2.50	5.00	10.00
NAUTILUS					
❏ NR-2	Aspen Gold	1979	10.00	20.00	40.00
—Audiophile vinyl					
PAIR					
❏ PDL2-1067 [(2)]	Early American Heroes	1986	3.00	6.00	12.00
PICKWICK					
❏ SPC-3260	Tom Dooley	196?	3.00	6.00	12.00
TETRAGRAMMATON					
❏ T-5101 [(2)]	Once Upon a Time	1969	6.25	12.50	25.00

KINKS, THE

ARISTA

Number	Title (A Side/B Side)	Yr	VG	VG+	NM
❏ SP-69 [DJ]	Low Budget Radio Interview	1979	10.00	20.00	40.00
—Promo-only radio show featuring Ray Davies					
❏ SP-85 [EP]	A Fistful of Kinks	1980	6.25	12.50	25.00
—Promo-only four-song sampler from "One for the Road"					
❏ AL 4106	Sleepwalker	1977	2.50	5.00	10.00
❏ AL 4106 [DJ]	Sleepwalker	1977	7.50	15.00	30.00
—White label promo					
❏ AL 4167	Misfits	1978	2.50	5.00	10.00
❏ AL 4167 [DJ]	Misfits	1978	7.50	15.00	30.00
—White label promo					
❏ AB 4240	Low Budget	1979	2.50	5.00	10.00
❏ AL 8-8018	State of Confusion	1983	2.50	5.00	10.00
❏ AL13 8041 [(2)]	One for the Road	1983	2.50	5.00	10.00
—Reissue of 8609					
❏ AL 8264	Word of Mouth	1984	2.50	5.00	10.00
❏ ALB6 8300	Low Budget	1985	2.00	4.00	8.00
—Budget-line reissue					
❏ ALB6 8328	Give the People What They Want	1985	2.00	4.00	8.00
—Budget-line reissue					
❏ ALB6 8375	Sleepwalker	1985	2.00	4.00	8.00
—Budget-line reissue					
❏ ALB6 8377	Misfits	1985	2.00	4.00	8.00
—Budget-line reissue					
❏ A2L 8401 [(2)]	One for the Road	1980	3.75	7.50	15.00
—Original edition has this number					
❏ AL11 8428 [(2)]	Come Dancing with the Kinks	1986	3.00	6.00	12.00
❏ A2L 8609 [(2)]	One for the Road	198?	3.00	6.00	12.00
—Second edition of 8401					
❏ AL 9567	Give the People What They Want	1981	2.50	5.00	10.00
COMPLEAT					
❏ CPL2-2001 [(2)]	A Compleat Collection	1984	3.00	6.00	12.00
❏ CPL2-2003 [(2)]	20th Anniversary Edition	1984	3.00	6.00	12.00
MCA					
❏ 5822	Think Visual	1987	2.50	5.00	10.00
❏ 6337	UK Jive	1989	3.00	6.00	12.00
❏ L33-17281 [DJ]	A Look at "Think Visual"	1987	12.50	25.00	50.00
—Promo only in white jacket					
❏ 42107	Live: The Road	1988	2.50	5.00	10.00
MOBILE FIDELITY					
❏ 1-070	Misfits	1981	5.00	10.00	20.00
—Audiophile vinyl					
PICKWICK					
❏ ACL-7072	Preservation Act 1	197?	3.00	6.00	12.00
—Reissue of RCA Victor LPL1-5002					
PYE					
❏ 505	The Kinks	1975	3.00	6.00	12.00
❏ 509	The Kinks, Vol. 2	1976	3.00	6.00	12.00
RCA VICTOR					
❏ APL1-1743	Celluloid Heroes (The Kinks' Greatest)	1976	2.50	5.00	10.00
❏ APL1-3520	Second Time Around	1980	2.50	5.00	10.00
❏ AYL1-3749	Schoolboys in Disgrace	1980	2.00	4.00	8.00
—Budget-line reissue					
❏ AYL1-3750	Soap Opera	1980	2.00	4.00	8.00
—Budget-line reissue					
❏ AYL1-3869	Celluloid Heroes (The Kinks' Greatest)	1981	2.00	4.00	8.00
—Budget-line reissue					
❏ AYL1-4558	Muswell Hillbillies	1982	2.00	4.00	8.00
—Budget-line reissue					
❏ LSP-4644	Muswell Hillbillies	1971	7.50	15.00	30.00
❏ AYL1-4719	Second Time Around	1983	2.00	4.00	8.00
—Budget-line reissue					
❏ LPL1-5002	Preservation Act 1	1973	3.75	7.50	15.00
❏ CPL2-5040 [(2)]	Preservation Act 2	1974	5.00	10.00	20.00
❏ LPL1-5081	Soap Opera	1975	2.50	5.00	10.00
—Brown label					
❏ LPL1-5081	Soap Opera	1975	3.75	7.50	15.00
—Orange label					
❏ LPL1-5102	Schoolboys in Disgrace	1975	2.50	5.00	10.00
❏ VPS-6065 [(2)]	Everybody's in Showbiz	1972	5.00	10.00	20.00
—Orange label					
❏ VPS-6065 [(2)]	Everybody's in Showbiz	1975	3.00	6.00	12.00
—Brown label					
REPRISE					
❏ PRO 328 [P]	Then Now and In Between	1969	12.50	25.00	50.00
—Album that came with above box is sometimes found by itself without all the other goodies.					
❏ PRO 328 [P]	God Save the Kinks	1969	125.00	250.00	500.00
—Mail-order box with decal, postcard, bag of grass, two pins, letter, Kinks consumer guide and "Then Now and In Between" LP. Price is for complete package.					
❏ MS-2127	The Great Lost Kinks Album	1973	12.50	25.00	50.00
❏ R-6143 [M]	You Really Got Me	1965	15.00	30.00	60.00
❏ R-6143 [M]	You Really Got Me	1965	100.00	200.00	400.00
—White label promo					
❏ RS-6143 [P]	You Really Got Me	1965	20.00	40.00	80.00
—Pink, gold and green label					
❏ RS-6143 [P]	You Really Got Me	1971	2.50	5.00	10.00
—Orange label with "r:" and steamboat at top					
❏ R-6158 [M]	Kinks-Size	1965	12.50	25.00	50.00
❏ R-6158 [M]	Kinks-Size	1965	50.00	100.00	200.00
—White label promo					
❏ RS-6158 [R]	Kinks-Size	1965	7.50	15.00	30.00
❏ R-6173 [M]	Kinda Kinks	1965	12.50	25.00	50.00
❏ R-6173 [M]	Kinda Kinks	1965	50.00	100.00	200.00
—White label promo					
❏ RS-6173 [R]	Kinda Kinks	1965	7.50	15.00	30.00
❏ R-6184 [M]	Kinks Kinkdom	1965	12.50	25.00	50.00
❏ R-6184 [M]	Kinks Kinkdom	1965	50.00	100.00	200.00
—White label promo					
❏ RS-6184 [R]	Kinks Kinkdom	1965	7.50	15.00	30.00
❏ R-6197 [M]	The Kink Kontroversy	1966	12.50	25.00	50.00
❏ R-6197 [M]	The Kink Kontroversy	1966	50.00	100.00	200.00
—White label promo					
❏ RS-6197 [R]	The Kink Kontroversy	1966	7.50	15.00	30.00
❏ R-6217 [M]	The Kinks Greatest Hits!	1966	10.00	20.00	40.00
❏ RS-6217 [R]	The Kinks Greatest Hits!	1966	6.25	12.50	25.00
—Pink, gold and green label					
❏ RS-6217 [R]	The Kinks Greatest Hits!	1971	2.50	5.00	10.00
—Orange label with "r:" and steamboat at top					
❏ R-6228 [M]	Face to Face	1967	10.00	20.00	40.00
❏ RS-6228 [P]	Face to Face	1967	7.50	15.00	30.00
—Pink, gold and green label					
❏ RS-6228 [P]	Face to Face	1971	2.50	5.00	10.00
—Orange label with "r:" and steamboat at top					
❏ R-6260 [M]	The Live Kinks	1967	8.75	17.50	35.00
❏ RS-6260 [S]	The Live Kinks	1967	6.25	12.50	25.00
—Pink, gold and green label					
❏ RS-6260 [S]	The Live Kinks	1971	2.50	5.00	10.00
—Orange label with "r:" and steamboat at top					
❏ R-6279 [M]	Something Else by the Kinks	1968	75.00	150.00	300.00
—White label promo; no stock copies were issued in mono					
❏ RS-6279 [S]	Something Else by the Kinks	1968	5.00	10.00	20.00
—Two-tone orange label with "r: and "W7" logos with steamboat					
❏ RS-6279 [S]	Something Else by the Kinks	1968	7.50	15.00	30.00
—Pink, gold and green label					

Number	Title (A Side/B Side)	Yr	VG	VG+	NM
❑ RS-6279 [S]	Something Else by the Kinks	1971	2.50	5.00	10.00
—Orange label with "r:" and steamboat at top					
❑ RS-6327	The Kinks Are the Village Green Preservation Society	1969	7.50	15.00	30.00
—Two-tone orange label with "r: and "W7" logos with steamboat					
❑ RS-6327	The Kinks Are the Village Green Preservation Society	1971	2.50	5.00	10.00
—Orange label with "r:" and steamboat at top					
❑ RS-6366	Arthur (Or The Decline and Fall of the British Empire)	1969	6.25	12.50	25.00
—Two-tone orange label with "r: and "W7" logos with steamboat					
❑ RS-6366	Arthur (Or The Decline and Fall of the British Empire)	1971	2.50	5.00	10.00
—Orange label with "r:" and steamboat at top					
❑ RS-6423	Lola Versus Powerman and the Moneygoround, Part One	1970	3.75	7.50	15.00
—Original pressings have blue printing on a white cover					
❑ RS-6423	Lola Versus Powerman and the Moneygoround, Part One	1971	2.50	5.00	10.00
—Later pressings have black printing on a white cover					
❑ 2XS-6454 [(2)]	The Kink Kronicles	1972	3.75	7.50	15.00
❑ SMAS-93034	Arthur (Or The Decline and Fall of the British Empire)	1970	10.00	20.00	40.00
—Capitol Record Club edition					

RHINO

Number	Title (A Side/B Side)	Yr	VG	VG+	NM
❑ R1 70086	The Kinks Greatest Hits! Vol. 1	1989	3.00	6.00	12.00
❑ R1 70315	You Really Got Me	1988	3.00	6.00	12.00
❑ R1 70316	Kinda Kinks	1988	3.00	6.00	12.00
❑ R1 70317	Kinks-Size	1988	3.00	6.00	12.00
❑ R1 70318	Kinks Kinkdom	1988	3.00	6.00	12.00

KINSEY, TONY
LONDON

Number	Title	Yr	VG	VG+	NM
❑ LL 1672 [M]	Kinsey Come On	1957	12.50	25.00	50.00

KIRBY, JOHN
COLUMBIA

Number	Title	Yr	VG	VG+	NM
❑ CL 502 [M]	John Kirby and His Orchestra	1953	10.00	20.00	40.00
—Maroon label, gold print					
❑ GL 502 [M]	John Kirby and His Orchestra	1951	12.50	25.00	50.00
—Black label, silver print					

COLUMBIA MASTERWORKS

Number	Title	Yr	VG	VG+	NM
❑ ML 4801 [10]	John Kirby and His Orchestra	195?	15.00	30.00	60.00

HARMONY

Number	Title	Yr	VG	VG+	NM
❑ HL 7124 [M]	Intimate Swing	1958	5.00	10.00	20.00

KIRK, ANDY
CORAL

Number	Title	Yr	VG	VG+	NM
❑ CRL 56019 [10]	Andy Kirk Souvenir Album — Vol. 1	1951	25.00	50.00	100.00

RCA VICTOR

Number	Title	Yr	VG	VG+	NM
❑ LPM-1302 [M]	A Mellow Bit of Rhythm	1956	10.00	20.00	40.00

KIRK, RAHSAAN ROLAND
ARGO

Number	Title	Yr	VG	VG+	NM
❑ LP-669 [M]	Introducing Roland Kirk	1960	7.50	15.00	30.00
❑ LPS-669 [S]	Introducing Roland Kirk	1960	10.00	20.00	40.00

ATLANTIC

Number	Title	Yr	VG	VG+	NM
❑ SD 2-303 [(2)]	The Art of Rahsaan Roland Kirk	1973	5.00	10.00	20.00
❑ SD 2-907 [(2)]	Bright Moments	1974	5.00	10.00	20.00
❑ 1502 [M]	The Inflated Tear	1968	6.25	12.50	25.00
❑ 3007 [M]	Here Comes the Whistle Man	1967	6.25	12.50	25.00

BETHLEHEM

Number	Title	Yr	VG	VG+	NM
❑ BCP-6064 [M]	Third Dimension	1962	37.50	75.00	150.00

KING

Number	Title	Yr	VG	VG+	NM
❑ 539 [M]	Triple Threat	1956	62.50	125.00	250.00

PRESTIGE

Number	Title	Yr	VG	VG+	NM
❑ PRLP-7210 [M]	Kirk's Work	1961	10.00	20.00	40.00
❑ PRLP-7450 [M]	Funk Underneath	1967	6.25	12.50	25.00

VERVE

Number	Title	Yr	VG	VG+	NM
❑ V-8709 [M]	Now Please Don't You Cry, Beautiful Edith	1967	6.25	12.50	25.00
❑ V6-8709 [S]	Now Please Don't You Cry, Beautiful Edith	1967	5.00	10.00	20.00

KIRKLAND, LEROY
IMPERIAL

Number	Title	Yr	VG	VG+	NM
❑ LP-12198 [S]	Twistin', Mashin' and All That Jazz	1962	5.00	10.00	20.00

KISS
Also see PETER CRISS; ACE FREHLEY; GENE SIMMONS; PAUL STANLEY.

CASABLANCA

Number	Title	Yr	VG	VG+	NM
❑ Kiss '76 [DJ]	Special Kiss Tour Album	1976	20.00	40.00	80.00
—Special four-track sampler					
❑ NBLP 737 [DJ]	Rock and Roll Over Special Edition	1977	30.00	60.00	120.00
—Five-track sampler from the LP					
❑ NBLP 7001	Kiss	1974	7.50	15.00	30.00
—All renumbered versions have "Kissin' Time"; dark blue label					
❑ NBLP 7001	Kiss	1976	3.75	7.50	15.00
—Tan label with desert scene, "Casablanca" label					
❑ NBLP 7001	Kiss	1977	3.00	6.00	12.00
—Tan label with desert scene, "Casablanca Record and FilmWorks" label					
❑ NBLP 7006	Hotter Than Hell	1974	7.50	15.00	30.00
—Dark blue label					
❑ NBLP 7006	Hotter Than Hell	1976	3.75	7.50	15.00
—Tan label with desert scene, "Casablanca" label					
❑ NBLP 7006	Hotter Than Hell	1977	3.00	6.00	12.00
—Tan label with desert scene, "Casablanca Record and FilmWorks" label					
❑ NBLP 7016	Dressed to Kill	1975	7.50	15.00	30.00
—Dark blue label					
❑ NBLP 7016	Dressed to Kill	1976	3.75	7.50	15.00
—Tan label with desert scene, "Casablanca" label					
❑ NBLP 7016	Dressed to Kill	1977	3.00	6.00	12.00
—Tan label with desert scene, "Casablanca Record and FilmWorks" label					

Number	Title (A Side/B Side)	Yr	VG	VG+	NM
❑ NBLP 7020 [(2)]	Alive!	1975	10.00	20.00	40.00
—Dark blue labels; with booklet					
❑ NBLP 7020 [(2)]	Alive!	1976	5.00	10.00	20.00
—Tan labels with desert scene, "Casablanca" label					
❑ NBLP 7020 [(2)]	Alive!	1977	3.75	7.50	15.00
—Tan labels with desert scene, "Casablanca Record and FilmWorks" label					
❑ NBLP 7025	Destroyer	1976	3.75	7.50	15.00
—Tan label with desert scene, "Casablanca" label					
❑ NBLP 7025	Destroyer	1976	7.50	15.00	30.00
—Dark blue label					
❑ NBLP 7025	Destroyer	1977	3.00	6.00	12.00
—Tan label with desert scene, "Casablanca Record and FilmWorks" label					
❑ NBLP 7032 [(3)]	The Originals	1976	25.00	50.00	100.00
—Tan label with desert scene, "Casablanca" label; without extras					
❑ NBLP 7032 [(3)]	The Originals	1976	37.50	75.00	150.00
—Tan label with desert scene, "Casablanca" label; with booklet, six Kiss cards, a Kiss Army sticker					
❑ NBLP 7032 [(3)]	The Originals	1977	12.50	25.00	50.00
—Tan label with desert scene, "Casablanca Record and FilmWorks" label; "Second Printing" on cover; without extras					
❑ NBLP 7032 [(3)]	The Originals	1977	25.00	50.00	100.00
—Tan label with desert scene, "Casablanca Record and FilmWorks" label; "Second Printing" on cover; with extras listed above					
❑ NBLP 7037	Rock and Roll Over	1976	5.00	10.00	20.00
—Tan label with desert scene, "Casablanca" label; comes with sticker and Kiss Army paraphenalia order form					
❑ NBLP 7037	Rock and Roll Over	1977	3.00	6.00	12.00
—Tan label with desert scene, "Casablanca Record and FilmWorks" label, with inserts					
❑ NBLP 7057	Love Gun	1977	3.00	6.00	12.00
—Without inserts					
❑ NBLP 7057	Love Gun	1977	10.00	20.00	40.00
—with "Hot Goods from the Supply Depot" order form, unpunched-out cardboard gun and "Bang!" sticker. All items must be intact to get top dollar for this.					
❑ NBLP 7076 [(2)]	Alive II	1977	3.75	7.50	15.00
—Without inserts					
❑ NBLP 7076 [(2)]	Alive II	1977	10.00	20.00	40.00
—With 8-page booklet, tattoo insert and "Combat Gear" order form; back cover contents are correct					
❑ NBLP 7076 [(2)]	Alive II	1977	100.00	200.00	400.00
—With 8-page booklet, tattoo insert and "Combat Gear" order form; back cover lists three tracks -- "Take Me," "Hooligan" and "Do You Love Me" -- that were not included on the record; no records with these tracks were made; perhaps as few as 50 copies of this cover were made					
❑ NBLP 7100 [(2)]	Double Platinum	1978	3.75	7.50	15.00
—Without inserts					
❑ NBLP 7100 [(2)]	Double Platinum	1978	10.00	20.00	40.00
—With "platinum award" cardboard insert and "Double Platinum Kiss Gear" order form					
❑ NBLP 7152	Dynasty	1979	2.50	5.00	10.00
—With neither poster nor order form					
❑ NBLP 7152	Dynasty	1979	3.75	7.50	15.00
—With poster and merchandise order form					
❑ NBLP 7225	Kiss Unmasked	1980	2.50	5.00	10.00
—With neither poster nor order form					
❑ NBLP 7225	Kiss Unmasked	1980	3.75	7.50	15.00
—With poster and "Kiss Essential Gear" order form					
❑ NBLP 7261	Music from The Elder	1981	7.50	15.00	30.00
—Various editions have paper or plastic innersleeves, lyric sheets, even incorrect track listings on the back cover; no difference in value is noted between variations					
❑ NBLP 7270	Creatures of the Night	1982	10.00	20.00	40.00
—Original version has band with makeup					
❑ NB 9001	Kiss	1974	12.50	25.00	50.00
—Second Warner Bros.-distributed version DOES have "Kissin' Time" on Side 2 (RE-1 on label)					
❑ NB 9001	Kiss	1974	20.00	40.00	80.00
—First Warner Bros.-distributed version does NOT have "Kissin' Time"					
❑ NB 20128 [DJ]	A Taste of Platinum	1978	12.50	25.00	50.00
—Promo-only sampler from Double Platinum					
❑ NB 20137 [DJ]	Peter Criss, Ace Frehley, Gene Simmons, Paul Stanley	1978	10.00	20.00	40.00
—Promo-only sampler from the band's solo albums					
❑ 812770-1	Dynasty	1983	2.00	4.00	8.00
—Reissue					
❑ 822780-1 [(2)]	Alive!	1984	2.50	5.00	10.00
—Reissue					
❑ 822781-1 [(2)]	Alive II	1984	2.50	5.00	10.00
—Reissue					
❑ 824146-1	Kiss	1984	2.00	4.00	8.00
—Reissue					
❑ 824147-1	Hotter Than Hell	1984	2.00	4.00	8.00
—Reissue					
❑ 824148-1	Dressed to Kill	1984	2.00	4.00	8.00
—Reissue					
❑ 824149-1	Destroyer	1984	2.00	4.00	8.00
—Reissue					
❑ 824150-1	Rock and Roll Over	1984	2.00	4.00	8.00
—Reissue					
❑ 824151-1	Love Gun	1984	2.00	4.00	8.00
—Reissue					
❑ 824153-1	Music from The Elder	1984	2.00	4.00	8.00
—Reissue					
❑ 824154-1	Creatures of the Night	1984	2.00	4.00	8.00
—Reissue; features band without its makeup on cover					
❑ 824154-1	Creatures of the Night	1994	6.25	12.50	25.00
—Reissue; glow-in-the-dark vinyl; gatefold edition; makeup cover restored					
❑ 824155-1 [(2)]	Double Platinum	1984	2.50	5.00	10.00
—Reissue					
❑ 826242-1	Unmasked	1985	2.00	4.00	8.00
—Reissue					

MERCURY

Number	Title	Yr	VG	VG+	NM
❑ 792-1 [DJ]	First Kiss, Last Licks	1990	25.00	50.00	100.00
—Promo-only sampler					
❑ 522647-1 [(2)]	Alive III	1994	6.25	12.50	25.00
—Limited edition black vinyl					
❑ 522647-1 [(2)]	Alive III	1994	6.25	12.50	25.00
—Limited edition blue vinyl					
❑ 522647-1 [(2)]	Alive III	1994	6.25	12.50	25.00
—Limited edition red vinyl					

KIT KATS, THE (continued)

Number	Title (A Side/B Side)	Yr	VG	VG+	NM
❏ 522647-1 [(2)]	Alive III	1994	6.25	12.50	25.00
—Limited edition white vinyl					
❏ 528674-1 [PD]	Creatures of the Night	1995	6.25	12.50	25.00
—Reissue; picture disc of makeup cover					
❏ 528950-1 [(2)]	MTV Unplugged	1996	5.00	10.00	20.00
—First editions are on black vinyl					
❏ 528950-1 [(2)]	MTV Unplugged	1996	5.00	10.00	20.00
—Second editions are on yellow marbled vinyl					
❏ 532741-1 [(2)]	You Wanted the Best, You Got the Best!!	1996	5.00	10.00	20.00
❏ 814297-1	Lick It Up	1983	3.00	6.00	12.00
❏ 822495-1	Animalize	1984	3.00	6.00	12.00
❏ 826099-1	Asylum	1985	2.50	5.00	10.00
❏ 832632-1	Crazy Nights	1987	2.50	5.00	10.00
❏ 832903-1 [PD]	Crazy Nights	1987	6.25	12.50	25.00
❏ 836427-1	Smashes, Thrashes and Hits	1988	2.50	5.00	10.00
❏ 836887-1 [PD]	Smashes, Thrashes and Hits	1988	6.25	12.50	25.00
❏ 838913-1	Hot in the Shade	1989	2.50	5.00	10.00

KIT KATS, THE

JAMIE

Number	Title (A Side/B Side)	Yr	VG	VG+	NM
❏ LPM-3029 [M]	It's Just a Matter of Time	1966	6.25	12.50	25.00
❏ LPS-3029 [S]	It's Just a Matter of Time	1966	7.50	15.00	30.00
❏ LPM-3032 [M]	The Kit Kats Do Their Thing — Live!	1967	7.50	15.00	30.00
❏ LPS-3032 [S]	The Kit Kats Do Their Thing — Live!	1967	10.00	20.00	40.00
❏ JLPS-3034	To Understand Is to Love	1970	7.50	15.00	30.00
—As "New Hope"					

KITAEV, ANDREI, AND BILL DOUGLASS

REFERENCE RECORDINGS

Number	Title (A Side/B Side)	Yr	VG	VG+	NM
❏ RR-6	First Takes	198?	5.00	10.00	20.00

KITCHEN CINQ, THE

LHI

Number	Title (A Side/B Side)	Yr	VG	VG+	NM
❏ E-12000 [M]	Everything But the Kitchen Cinq	1967	7.50	15.00	30.00
❏ E7-12000 [S]	Everything But the Kitchen Cinq	1967	10.00	20.00	40.00

KITT, EARTHA

DECCA

Number	Title (A Side/B Side)	Yr	VG	VG+	NM
❏ DL 4635 [M]	Eartha Kitt Sings in Spanish	1965	7.50	15.00	30.00
❏ DL 74635 [S]	Eartha Kitt Sings in Spanish	1965	10.00	20.00	40.00

KAPP

❏ KL-1162 [M]	The Fabulous Eartha Kitt	1959	6.25	12.50	25.00
❏ KL-1192 [M]	Eartha Kitt Revisited	1960	6.25	12.50	25.00
❏ KS-3046 [S]	The Fabulous Eartha Kitt	1959	7.50	15.00	30.00
❏ KS-3192 [S]	Eartha Kitt Revisited	1960	7.50	15.00	30.00

MGM

| ❏ E-4009 [M] | Bad But Beautiful | 1962 | 6.25 | 12.50 | 25.00 |
| ❏ SE-4009 [S] | Bad But Beautiful | 1962 | 7.50 | 15.00 | 30.00 |

RCA VICTOR

❏ LPM-1109 [M]	Down to Eartha	1955	12.50	25.00	50.00
❏ LPM-1153 [M]	That Bad Eartha	1955	12.50	25.00	50.00
❏ LPM-1300 [M]	Thursday's Child	1956	12.50	25.00	50.00
❏ LPM-1661 [M]	St. Louis Blues	1958	10.00	20.00	40.00
❏ LSP-1661 [S]	St. Louis Blues	1958	12.50	25.00	50.00
❏ LPM-3062 [10]	Songs	1953	20.00	40.00	80.00
❏ LPM-3187 [10]	That Bad Eartha	1953	20.00	40.00	80.00

KLARK KENT

Stewart Copeland of THE POLICE in disguise.

KRYPTONE/I.R.S.

Number	Title (A Side/B Side)	Yr	VG	VG+	NM
❏ SP 70600 [EP]	Music Madness from the Kinetic Kid	1980	5.00	10.00	20.00
—Green vinyl 10" in die-cut 12" sleeve					

KLEMMER, JOHN

CADET

Number	Title (A Side/B Side)	Yr	VG	VG+	NM
❏ LP 797 [M]	Involvement	1967	7.50	15.00	30.00
❏ LPS 797 [S]	Involvement	1967	5.00	10.00	20.00
❏ LPS 808	And We Were Lovers	1968	5.00	10.00	20.00

CADET CONCEPT

❏ LPS 321	Blowin' Gold	1969	5.00	10.00	20.00
❏ LPS 326	All the Children Cried	1970	5.00	10.00	20.00
❏ LPS 330	Eruptions	1971	5.00	10.00	20.00

MOBILE FIDELITY

| ❏ 1-006 | Touch | 1979 | 7.50 | 15.00 | 30.00 |
| —Audiophile vinyl | | | | | |

NAUTILUS

❏ NR-4	Straight from the Heart	1980	20.00	40.00	80.00
—Audiophile vinyl					
❏ NR-22	Finesse	1981	20.00	40.00	80.00
—Audiophile vinyl					

KLEMMER, JOHN, AND EDDIE HARRIS

CRUSADERS

Number	Title (A Side/B Side)	Yr	VG	VG+	NM
❏ 16015	Two Tone	1982	6.25	12.50	25.00
—Part of MCA's "Audiophile Series"					

KLINK, AL/BOB ALEXANDER

GRAND AWARD

Number	Title (A Side/B Side)	Yr	VG	VG+	NM
❏ GA 33-525 [M]	Progressive Jazz	1956	7.50	15.00	30.00
—Without removable outer cover					
❏ GA 33-525 [M]	Progressive Jazz	1956	20.00	40.00	80.00
—With removable outer cover					

KLOSS, ERIC

COBBLESTONE

Number	Title (A Side/B Side)	Yr	VG	VG+	NM
❏ 9006	Doors	1972	5.00	10.00	20.00

PRESTIGE

❏ PRLP-7442 [M]	Introducing Eric Kloss	1966	5.00	10.00	20.00
❏ PRST-7442 [S]	Introducing Eric Kloss	1966	6.25	12.50	25.00
❏ PRLP-7469 [M]	Love and All That Jazz	1966	5.00	10.00	20.00
❏ PRST-7469 [S]	Love and All That Jazz	1966	6.25	12.50	25.00
❏ PRLP-7486 [M]	Grits & Gravy	1967	6.25	12.50	25.00
❏ PRST-7486 [S]	Grits & Gravy	1967	5.00	10.00	20.00

❏ PRLP-7520 [M]	First Class Kloss	1967	7.50	15.00	30.00
❏ PRST-7520 [S]	First Class Kloss	1967	5.00	10.00	20.00
❏ PRST-7535	Life Force	1968	5.00	10.00	20.00

KLUGH, EARL

MOBILE FIDELITY

Number	Title (A Side/B Side)	Yr	VG	VG+	NM
❏ 1-025	Finger Paintings	1979	7.50	15.00	30.00
—Audiophile vinyl					
❏ UHQR 1-025	Finger Paintings	1982	30.00	60.00	120.00
—"Ultra High Quality" audiophile vinyl in box					
❏ 1-076	Late Night Guitar	1981	12.50	25.00	50.00
—Audiophile vinyl					

NAUTILUS

| ❏ NR-46 | Crazy for You | 198? | 10.00 | 20.00 | 40.00 |
| —Audiophile vinyl | | | | | |

KNEPPER, JIMMY

BETHLEHEM

Number	Title (A Side/B Side)	Yr	VG	VG+	NM
❏ BCP-77 [M]	A Swinging Introduction to Jimmy Knepper	1957	15.00	30.00	60.00

KNICKERBOCKERS, THE

CHALLENGE

Number	Title (A Side/B Side)	Yr	VG	VG+	NM
❏ CH-621 [M]	Jerk and Twine Time	1965	100.00	200.00	400.00
❏ CH-622 [M]	Lies	1966	25.00	50.00	100.00
❏ CHS-622 [S]	Lies	1966	50.00	100.00	200.00
❏ LP-12664 [M]	Llyod Thaxton Presents the Knickerbockers	1965	50.00	100.00	200.00

SUNDAZED

| ❏ LP-5000 | The Great Lost Knickerbockers Album | 1990 | 3.00 | 6.00 | 12.00 |
| —Blue vinyl | | | | | |

KNIGHT, CHRIS, AND MAUREEN MCCORMICK

Also see THE BRADY BUNCH.

PARAMOUNT

Number	Title (A Side/B Side)	Yr	VG	VG+	NM
❏ PAS-6062	Chris Knight and Maureen McCormick	1973	30.00	60.00	120.00

KNIGHT, FREDERICK

STAX

Number	Title (A Side/B Side)	Yr	VG	VG+	NM
❏ STS-3011	I've Been Lonely So Long	1973	5.00	10.00	20.00

KNIGHT, GLADYS, AND THE PIPS

ACCORD

Number	Title (A Side/B Side)	Yr	VG	VG+	NM
❏ SN-7103	Every Beat of My Heart	1981	2.50	5.00	10.00
❏ SN-7105	Letter Full of Tears	1981	2.50	5.00	10.00
❏ SN-7131	I Feel a Song	1981	2.50	5.00	10.00
❏ SN-7188	It's Showtime	1982	2.50	5.00	10.00

ALLEGIANCE

| ❏ AV-5002 | Glad to Be... | 198? | 2.50 | 5.00 | 10.00 |

BELL

| ❏ 1323 | In the Beginning | 1975 | 3.00 | 6.00 | 12.00 |
| ❏ 6013 | Tastiest Hits | 1968 | 5.00 | 10.00 | 20.00 |

BUDDAH

❏ BDS-5100	Imagination	1973	3.00	6.00	12.00
❏ BDS-5602	Claudine	1974	7.50	15.00	30.00
❏ BDS-5612	I Feel a Song	1974	3.00	6.00	12.00
❏ BDS-5639	2nd Anniversary	1975	3.00	6.00	12.00
❏ BDS-5653	The Best of Gladys Knight & The Pips	1976	3.00	6.00	12.00
❏ BDS-5676	Pipe Dreams	1976	3.00	6.00	12.00
❏ BDS-5689	Still Together	1977	3.00	6.00	12.00
❏ BDS-5701	The One and Only	1978	3.00	6.00	12.00
❏ BDS-5714	Miss Gladys Knight	1978	3.00	6.00	12.00

CASABLANCA

❏ NBLP 7081	At Last...The Pips	1977	2.50	5.00	10.00
—As "The Pips"					
❏ NBLP 7113	Callin'	1978	2.50	5.00	10.00
—As "The Pips"					

COLLECTABLES

| ❏ COL-5154 | Golden Classics: Letter Full of Tears | 198? | 2.50 | 5.00 | 10.00 |

COLUMBIA

❏ JC 35704	Gladys Knight	1979	2.50	5.00	10.00
❏ PC 35704	Gladys Knight	198?	2.00	4.00	8.00
—Budget-line reissue					
❏ JC 36387	About Love	1980	2.50	5.00	10.00
❏ PC 36387	About Love	198?	2.00	4.00	8.00
—Budget-line reissue					
❏ FC 37086	Touch	1981	2.50	5.00	10.00
❏ PC 37086	Touch	198?	2.00	4.00	8.00
—Budget-line reissue					
❏ FC 38114	That Special Time of Year	1982	2.50	5.00	10.00
❏ PC 38114	That Special Time of Year	1983	2.00	4.00	8.00
—Same as above with new prefix					
❏ FC 38205	Visions	1983	2.50	5.00	10.00
❏ PC 38205	Visions	198?	2.00	4.00	8.00
—Budget-line reissue					
❏ FC 39423	Life	1985	2.50	5.00	10.00
❏ PC 39423	Life	198?	2.00	4.00	8.00
—Budget-line reissue					
❏ FC 40376	Greatest Hits	1986	2.50	5.00	10.00
❏ FC 40878	The Best of Gladys Knight and the Pips/The Columbia Years	1988	2.50	5.00	10.00

FURY

| ❏ 1003 [M] | Letter Full of Tears | 1962 | 125.00 | 250.00 | 500.00 |

LOST-NITE

| ❏ LLP-17 [10] | The Best of Gladys Knight and the Pips | 1981 | 3.00 | 6.00 | 12.00 |
| —Red vinyl | | | | | |

MAXX

| ❏ 3000 [M] | Gladys Knight and the Pips | 1964 | 37.50 | 75.00 | 150.00 |

MCA

| ❏ 10329 | Good Woman | 1991 | 3.75 | 7.50 | 15.00 |
| ❏ 42004 | All Our Love | 1987 | 2.50 | 5.00 | 10.00 |

Number	Title (A Side/B Side)	Yr	VG	VG+	NM

MOTOWN

Number	Title (A Side/B Side)	Yr	VG	VG+	NM
❏ M5-113V	Motown Superstar Series, Vol. 13	1981	2.50	5.00	10.00
❏ M5-126V1	Everybody Needs Love	1981	3.00	6.00	12.00
—Reissue of Soul 706					
❏ M5-148V1	Nitty Gritty	1981	3.00	6.00	12.00
—Reissue of Soul 713					
❏ M5-193V1	Neither One of Us	1981	3.00	6.00	12.00
—Reissue of Soul 737					
❏ M 792S2 [(2)]	Anthology	1974	3.75	7.50	15.00
❏ MOT 5303	All the Great Hits of Gladys Knight and the Pips	198?	2.00	4.00	8.00

NATURAL RESOURCES

❏ NR 4004T1	Silk N' Soul	1978	2.50	5.00	10.00
—Reissue of Soul 711					

PAIR

❏ PDL2-1198	The Best of Gladys Knight and the Pips	1987	3.00	6.00	12.00

PICKWICK

❏ SPC-3349	Every Beat of My Heart	197?	2.50	5.00	10.00

SOUL

❏ S 706 [M]	Everybody Needs Love	1967	5.00	10.00	20.00
❏ SS 706 [S]	Everybody Needs Love	1967	6.25	12.50	25.00
❏ S 707 [M]	Feelin' Bluesy	1968	10.00	20.00	40.00
—Mono copies are white label promo only; cover has "Monaural Record DJ Copy" sticker					
❏ SS 707 [S]	Feelin' Bluesy	1968	6.25	12.50	25.00
❏ SS 711	Silk N' Soul	1968	6.25	12.50	25.00
❏ SS 713	Nitty Gritty	1969	6.25	12.50	25.00
❏ SS 723	Gladys Knight and the Pips Greatest Hits	1970	3.75	7.50	15.00
❏ SS 730	All in a Knight's Work	1970	3.75	7.50	15.00
❏ SS 731	If I Were Your Woman	1971	3.75	7.50	15.00
❏ S 736L	Standing Ovation	1971	3.75	7.50	15.00
❏ S 737L	Neither One of Us	1973	3.75	7.50	15.00
❏ S 739L	All I Need Is Time	1973	3.75	7.50	15.00
❏ S 741	Knight Time	1974	3.00	6.00	12.00
❏ S 744	A Little Knight Music	1975	3.00	6.00	12.00

SPHERE SOUND

❏ SR-7006 [M]	Gladys Knight and the Pips	196?	50.00	100.00	200.00
❏ SSR-7006 [R]	Gladys Knight and the Pips	196?	30.00	60.00	120.00

SPRINGBOARD

❏ SPB-4035	Early Hits	1972	2.50	5.00	10.00
❏ SPB-4050	How Do You Say Goodbye	1973	2.50	5.00	10.00

TRIP

❏ TLP-9509	It Hurt Me So Bad	1973	2.50	5.00	10.00

UNITED ARTISTS

❏ UA-LA503-E	The Very Best of Gladys Knight and the Pips	1975	3.00	6.00	12.00

UPFRONT

❏ UPF 130	Gladys Knight and the Pips	197?	2.50	5.00	10.00
❏ UPF 185	Gladys Knight and the Pips	197?	2.50	5.00	10.00

VEE JAY

❏ D1-74796	Every Beat of My Heart: The Greatest Hits of the Early Years	1989	3.75	7.50	15.00

KNIGHT, JEAN

COTILLION

❏ SD 5230	Jean Knight and Premium	1981	3.75	7.50	15.00

MIRAGE

❏ 90282	My Toot Toot	1985	2.50	5.00	10.00

STAX

❏ STS-2045	Mr. Big Stuff	1971	10.00	20.00	40.00
❏ MPS-8554	Mr. Big Stuff	198?	2.50	5.00	10.00

KNIGHT, ROBERT

RISING SONS

❏ RSM-7000 [M]	Everlasting Love	1967	7.50	15.00	30.00
❏ RSS-17000 [S]	Everlasting Love	1967	10.00	20.00	40.00

KNIGHT, SONNY

AURA

❏ AR-3001 [M]	If You Want This Love	1964	6.25	12.50	25.00
❏ AS-3001 [S]	If You Want This Love	1964	7.50	15.00	30.00

KNIGHT, TED

RANWOOD

❏ R-8149	Hi Guys!	1976	5.00	10.00	20.00

KNIGHT, TERRY, AND THE PACK

ABKCO

❏ AB-4217 [(2)]	Mark, Don and Terry 1966-67	1972	5.00	10.00	20.00

CAMEO

❏ C 2007 [M]	Reflections	1967	5.00	10.00	20.00
—Reissue of Lucky Eleven LE-8001					
❏ CS 2007 [S]	Reflections	1967	6.25	12.50	25.00
—Reissue of Lucky Eleven LES-8001					

LUCKY ELEVEN

❏ LE-8000 [M]	Terry Knight and the Pack	1966	10.00	20.00	40.00
❏ LES-8000 [R]	Terry Knight and the Pack	1966	6.25	12.50	25.00
❏ LE-8001 [M]	Reflections	1967	6.25	12.50	25.00
❏ LES-8001 [S]	Reflections	1967	10.00	20.00	40.00

KNIGHTS, THE

At least two, and possibly three, different groups.

ACE

❏ 4763	Cold Days, Hot Knights	196?	100.00	200.00	400.00
❏ 200854	Across the Board	1966	100.00	200.00	400.00
❏ 201302	The Knights 1967	1967	100.00	200.00	400.00

CAPITOL

❏ DT 2189 [R]	Hot Rod High	1964	100.00	200.00	400.00
❏ T 2189 [M]	Hot Rod High	1964	100.00	200.00	400.00

JUSTICE

❏ JLP-156	On the Move	196?	75.00	150.00	300.00

KNOCKOUTS, THE (1)

TRIBUTE

Number	Title (A Side/B Side)	Yr	VG	VG+	NM
❏ 1202 [M]	Go Ape with the Knockouts	1964	50.00	100.00	200.00

KNOPF, PAUL

PLAYBACK

❏ PLP-500 [M]	The Outcat	1959	10.00	20.00	40.00
❏ PLP-500ST [S]	The Outcat	1959	12.50	25.00	50.00
❏ PLP-501 [M]	Enigma of a Day	1959	10.00	20.00	40.00
❏ PLP-501ST [S]	Enigma of a Day	1959	12.50	25.00	50.00
❏ PLP-502 [M]	And the Walls Came Tumbling Down	1960	10.00	20.00	40.00
❏ PLP-502ST [S]	And the Walls Came Tumbling Down	1960	12.50	25.00	50.00
❏ PLP-503 [M]	Paul Knoft Trio	1960	10.00	20.00	40.00
❏ PLP-503ST [S]	Paul Knoft Trio	1960	12.50	25.00	50.00
❏ PLP-600 [M]	Music from the Morgue	1961	10.00	20.00	40.00
❏ PLP-600ST [S]	Music from the Morgue	1961	12.50	25.00	50.00

KNOWBODY ELSE

Members were later in BLACK OAK ARKANSAS.

HIP

❏ HIS-7003	Knowbody Else	1969	10.00	20.00	40.00

KNOX, BUDDY

ACCORD

❏ SN-7218	Party Doll and Other Hits	1981	2.50	5.00	10.00

LIBERTY

❏ LRP-3251 [M]	Buddy Knox's Golden Hits	1962	7.50	15.00	30.00
❏ LST-7251 [S]	Buddy Knox's Golden Hits	1962	10.00	20.00	40.00

ROULETTE

❏ R 25003 [M]	Buddy Knox	1957	37.50	75.00	150.00
—Black label, red and silver print					
❏ R 25003 [M]	Buddy Knox	1957	50.00	100.00	200.00
—Black label, all silver print (original)					
❏ R 25003 [M]	Buddy Knox	1959	25.00	50.00	100.00
—White label with colored spokes					
❏ R 25048 [M]	Buddy Knox and Jimmy Bowen	1959	25.00	50.00	100.00
—White label with colored spokes					
❏ R 25048 [M]	Buddy Knox and Jimmy Bowen	1959	50.00	100.00	200.00
—Black label, red and silver print					

UNITED ARTISTS

❏ UAS 6689	Gypsy Man	1969	6.25	12.50	25.00

KOALA, THE

CAPITOL

❏ SKAO-176	The Koala	1969	15.00	30.00	60.00

KODAKS, THE / THE STARLITES

SPHERE SOUND

❏ SSR-7005 [M]	The Kodaks Vs. the Starlites	1965	50.00	100.00	200.00

KOERNER, SPIDER JOHN

ELEKTRA

❏ EKL-290 [M]	Spider Blues	1965	5.00	10.00	20.00
❏ EKS-7290 [S]	Spider Blues	1965	6.25	12.50	25.00

SWEET JANE

❏ SJL-1074	Some American Folksongs Like They Used To	1974	7.50	15.00	30.00
❏ SJL-5872	Music Is Just a Bunch of Notes	1972	25.00	50.00	100.00
—With Willie and the Bumblebees and BONNIE RAITT					

KOERNER, SPIDER JOHN, AND WILLIE MURPHY

ELEKTRA

❏ EKS-74041	Running, Jumping, Standing Still	1969	5.00	10.00	20.00

KOERNER, RAY AND GLOVER

AUDIOPHILE

❏ AP-78 [M]	Blues, Rags and Hollers	1963	12.50	25.00	50.00
—Includes four songs not on the Elektra reissue					

ELEKTRA

❏ EKL-240 [M]	Blues, Rags and Hollers	1963	6.25	12.50	25.00
—Not issued in stereo on Elektra					
❏ EKL-267 [M]	Lots More Blues, Rags and Hollers	1964	5.00	10.00	20.00
❏ EKL-305 [M]	The Return of Koerner, Ray and Glover	1965	5.00	10.00	20.00
❏ EKS-7267 [S]	Lots More Blues, Rags and Hollers	1964	6.25	12.50	25.00
❏ EKS-7305 [S]	The Return of Koerner, Ray and Glover	1965	6.25	12.50	25.00

KOFFMAN, MOE

ASCOT

❏ AM 13001 [M]	Moe Koffman Plays for the Teens	1962	5.00	10.00	20.00
❏ AS 16001 [S]	Moe Koffman Plays for the Teens	1962	6.25	12.50	25.00

JUBILEE

❏ JLP-1037 [M]	Cool and Hot Sax	1957	10.00	20.00	40.00
❏ JLP-1074 [M]	The Shepherd Swings Again	1958	10.00	20.00	40.00

KAMA SUTRA

❏ KSBS-2018	Moe's Curried Soul	1970	5.00	10.00	20.00

UNITED ARTISTS

❏ UAJ-14029 [M]	Tales of Koffman	1963	6.25	12.50	25.00
❏ UAJS-15029 [S]	Tales of Koffman	1963	7.50	15.00	30.00

KOHLMAN, FREDDIE

MGM

❏ E-297 [10]	New Orleans Now — New Orleans Then	1955	20.00	40.00	80.00

KOKI, SAM, AND THE PARADISE ISLANDERS

KAPP

❏ KL-1321 [M]	Surfin' at Waikiki	1963	3.75	7.50	15.00
❏ KS-3321 [S]	Surfin' at Waikiki	1963	5.00	10.00	20.00

KOKOMO (1)

FELSTED

❏ FL 7513 [M]	Asia Minor	1961	10.00	20.00	40.00
❏ FS 17513 [S]	Asia Minor	1961	12.50	25.00	50.00

Number	Title (A Side/B Side)	Yr	VG	VG+	NM

KOLE, JERRY, AND THE STRINGERS
CROWN
❏ CST-385 [S]	Hot Rod Alley	1963	10.00	20.00	40.00
❏ CLP-5385 [M]	Hot Rod Alley	1963	7.50	15.00	30.00

KOLLER, HANS
DISCOVERY
❏ DL-2005 [10]	Hans Koller	1954	20.00	40.00	80.00

VANGUARD
❏ VRS-8509 [M]	Hans Across the Sea	1956	12.50	25.00	50.00

KOLOC, BONNIE
OVATION
❏ OVQD 14-21 [Q]	After All This Time	1971	6.25	12.50	25.00
❏ OVQD 14-26 [Q]	Hold On to Me	1972	6.25	12.50	25.00
❏ OVQD 14-29 [Q]	Bonnie Koloc	1973	6.25	12.50	25.00
❏ OVQD 14-38 [Q]	You're Gonna Love Yourself in the Morning	1974	6.25	12.50	25.00

KOMACK, JAMES
RCA VICTOR
❏ LPM-1501 [M]	Inside Me	1957	7.50	15.00	30.00

KONITZ, LEE
ATLANTIC
❏ 1217 [M]	Lee Konitz with Warne Marsh	1955	20.00	40.00	80.00
—Black label					
❏ 1217 [M]	Lee Konitz with Warne Marsh	1961	6.25	12.50	25.00
—Multicolor label, white "fan" logo at right					
❏ 1258 [M]	Inside Hi-Fi	1957	15.00	30.00	60.00
—Black label					
❏ 1258 [M]	Inside Hi-Fi	1961	6.25	12.50	25.00
—Multicolor label, white "fan" logo at right					
❏ SD 1258 [S]	Inside Hi-Fi	1958	15.00	30.00	60.00
—Green label					
❏ SD 1258 [S]	Inside Hi-Fi	1961	5.00	10.00	20.00
—Multicolor label, white "fan" logo at right					
❏ 1273 [M]	The Real Lee Konitz	1958	12.50	25.00	50.00
—Black label					
❏ 1273 [M]	The Real Lee Konitz	1961	6.25	12.50	25.00
—Multicolor label, white "fan" logo at right					

GROOVE MERCHANT
❏ 3306	Chicago and All That Jazz	197?	5.00	10.00	20.00

JAZZTONE
❏ J-1275 [M]	Jazz at Storyville❏ Jazz at Storyville	1957	10.00	20.00	40.00

MILESTONE
❏ 9013	Duets	1968	5.00	10.00	20.00
❏ 9025	Peacemeal	1968	5.00	10.00	20.00
❏ 9038	Spirits	1969	5.00	10.00	20.00
❏ 9060	Satori	197?	5.00	10.00	20.00

PRESTIGE
❏ PRLP-116 [10]	Lee Konitz — The New Sounds	1951	75.00	150.00	300.00
❏ PRLP-7004 [M]	Lee Konitz Groups	1955	37.50	75.00	150.00
❏ PRLP-7250 [M]	Subconscious-Lee	1962	12.50	25.00	50.00

ROOST
❏ LP-416 [10]	Originalee	1953	50.00	100.00	200.00

STORYVILLE
❏ STLP-304 [10]	Lee Konitz at Storyville	1954	50.00	100.00	200.00
❏ STLP-313 [10]	Konitz	1954	50.00	100.00	200.00
❏ STLP-323 [10]	Lee Konitz in Harvard Square	1955	37.50	75.00	150.00
❏ STLP-901 [M]	Lee Konitz at Storyville	1956	30.00	60.00	120.00

VERVE
❏ MGVS-6035 [S]	An Image — Lee Konitz with Strings	1959	7.50	15.00	30.00
❏ MGVS-6073 [S]	Lee Konitz Meets Jimmy Giuffre	1959	7.50	15.00	30.00
❏ MGVS-6131 [S]	You and Lee	1960	7.50	15.00	30.00
❏ MGV-8209 [M]	Very Cool	1958	12.50	25.00	50.00
❏ V-8209 [M]	Very Cool	1961	6.25	12.50	25.00
❏ MGV-8281 [M]	Tranquility	1958	12.50	25.00	50.00
❏ V-8281 [M]	Tranquility	1961	6.25	12.50	25.00
❏ MGV-8286 [M]	An Image — Lee Konitz with Strings	1958	10.00	20.00	40.00
❏ V-8286 [M]	An Image — Lee Konitz with Strings	1961	6.25	12.50	25.00
❏ V6-8286 [S]	An Image — Lee Konitz with Strings	1961	5.00	10.00	20.00
❏ MGV-8335 [M]	Lee Konitz Meets Jimmy Giuffre	1959	10.00	20.00	40.00
❏ V-8335 [M]	Lee Konitz Meets Jimmy Giuffre	1961	5.00	10.00	20.00
❏ MGV-8362 [M]	You and Lee	1960	10.00	20.00	40.00
❏ V-8362 [M]	You and Lee	1961	5.00	10.00	20.00
❏ V-8399 [M]	Motion	1961	5.00	10.00	20.00
❏ V6-8399 [S]	Motion	1961	6.25	12.50	25.00

KONITZ, LEE/MILES DAVIS/TEDDY CHARLES
NEW JAZZ
❏ NJLP-8295 [M]	Ezz-Thetic	1962	12.50	25.00	50.00
—Purple label					
❏ NJLP-8295 [M]	Ezz-Thetic	1965	6.25	12.50	25.00
—Blue label, trident logo at right					

KOOL AND THE GANG
DE-LITE
❏ MK-48 [DJ]	History of Kool and the Gang	1979	3.75	7.50	15.00
❏ 2003	Kool and the Gang	1969	6.25	12.50	25.00
❏ 2008	Live at the Sex Machine	1971	3.00	6.00	12.00
❏ 2009	The Best of Kool and the Gang	1971	3.00	6.00	12.00
❏ 2010	Live at PJ's	1971	3.00	6.00	12.00
❏ 2011	Music Is the Message	1972	3.00	6.00	12.00
❏ 2012	Good Times	1973	3.00	6.00	12.00
❏ 2013	Wild and Peaceful	1973	2.50	5.00	10.00
❏ 2014	Light of Worlds	1974	2.50	5.00	10.00
❏ 2015	Kool & The Gang Greatest Hits!	1975	2.50	5.00	10.00
❏ 2016	Spirit of the Boogie	1975	2.50	5.00	10.00
❏ 2018	Love and Understanding	1976	2.50	5.00	10.00
❏ 2023	Open Sesame	1976	2.50	5.00	10.00
❏ 4001	Kool Jazz	1973	2.50	5.00	10.00
❏ 8502	Something Special	1981	2.50	5.00	10.00
❏ 8505	As One	1982	2.50	5.00	10.00
❏ 8508	In the Heart	1983	2.50	5.00	10.00
❏ 9501	The Force	1978	2.50	5.00	10.00
❏ 9507	Kool & The Gang Spin Their Top Ten Hits	1978	2.50	5.00	10.00
❏ 9509	Everybody's Dancin'	1979	2.50	5.00	10.00
❏ 9513	Ladies Night	1979	2.50	5.00	10.00
❏ 9518	Celebrate!	1980	2.50	5.00	10.00
❏ 814351-1	In the Heart	1984	2.00	4.00	8.00
—Reissue					
❏ 822534-1	Something Special	1984	2.00	4.00	8.00
—Reissue					
❏ 822535-1	As One	1984	2.00	4.00	8.00
—Reissue					
❏ 822536-1	Kool & The Gang Spin Their Top Ten Hits	1984	2.00	4.00	8.00
—Reissue					
❏ 822537-1	Ladies Night	1984	2.00	4.00	8.00
—Reissue					
❏ 822538-1	Celebrate!	1984	2.00	4.00	8.00
—Reissue					
❏ 822943-1	Emergency	1984	2.00	4.00	8.00

MERCURY
❏ 830398-1	Forever	1986	2.00	4.00	8.00
❏ 834780-1	Everything's Kool & the Gang: Greatest Hits & More	1988	2.00	4.00	8.00
❏ 838233-1	Sweat	1989	2.00	4.00	8.00

KOOPER, AL
Also see BLOOD, SWEAT AND TEARS; MIKE BLOOMFIELD; THE BLUES PROJECT.
COLUMBIA
❏ CS 9718	I Stand Alone	1969	3.75	7.50	15.00
—"360 Sound" label					
❏ CS 9718	I Stand Alone	1970	2.50	5.00	10.00
—Orange label					
❏ CS 9855	You Never Know Who Your Friends Are	1969	3.75	7.50	15.00
—"360 Sound" label					
❏ CS 9855	You Never Know Who Your Friends Are	1970	2.50	5.00	10.00
—Orange label					
❏ CS 9951	Kooper Session	1970	2.50	5.00	10.00
—With Shuggie Otis; orange label					
❏ CS 9951	Kooper Session	1970	3.75	7.50	15.00
—With Shuggie Otis; "360 Sound" label					
❏ G 30031 [(2)]	Easy Does It	1970	5.00	10.00	20.00
❏ KC 30506	New York City (You're a Woman)	1971	3.75	7.50	15.00
❏ KC 31159	A Possible Projection of the Future/ Childhood's End	1972	3.75	7.50	15.00
❏ KC 31723	Naked Songs	1973	3.75	7.50	15.00
❏ PG 33169 [(2)]	Unclaimed Freight (Al's Big Deal)	1975	3.75	7.50	15.00
❏ FC 38137	Championship Wrestling	1982	2.50	5.00	10.00

UNITED ARTISTS
❏ UA-LA702-G	Act Like Nothing's Wrong	1976	3.00	6.00	12.00

KORNER, ALEXIS
COLUMBIA
❏ PC 33427	Get Off of My Cloud	1975	3.75	7.50	15.00

JUST SUNSHINE
❏ 13	All Star Blues Incorporated	1974	3.00	6.00	12.00

MOBILE FIDELITY
❏ 1-265	Blues at the Marquee	1996	5.00	10.00	20.00
—Audiophile vinyl					

WARNER BROS.
❏ 2XS 1966 [(2)]	Bootleg Him	1972	6.25	12.50	25.00
❏ BS 2647	Accidentally Borne in New Orleans	1972	3.75	7.50	15.00

KOSTELANETZ, ANDRE
COLUMBIA
❏ AK 1 [M]	Musical Tour of the World	195?	5.00	10.00	20.00
❏ KZ 1 [M]	Meet Andre Kostelanetz	1955	5.00	10.00	20.00
—Red and black label with six "eye" logos					
❏ GP 10 [(2)]	Sounds of Love	1969	3.00	6.00	12.00
❏ C2L 11 [M]	The Romantic Music of Tchaikovsky	195?	6.25	12.50	25.00
—Red and black label with six "eye" logos					
❏ CL 704 [M]	Mood for Love	1956	5.00	10.00	20.00
—Red and black label with six "eye" logos					
❏ CL 720 [M]	Peter and the Wolf; Carnival of the Animals	1956	5.00	10.00	20.00
—Red and black label with six "eye" logos					
❏ CL 734 [M]	The Music of Victor Youmans	1956	5.00	10.00	20.00
—Red and black label with six "eye" logos					
❏ CL 765 [M]	The Music of Victor Herbert	1956	5.00	10.00	20.00
—Red and black label with six "eye" logos					
❏ CL 768 [M]	Music of Irving Berlin	1956	5.00	10.00	20.00
—Red and black label with six "eye" logos					
❏ CL 780 [M]	Lure of the Tropics	1956	5.00	10.00	20.00
—Red and black label with six "eye" logos					
❏ CL 781 [M]	Stardust	1956	5.00	10.00	20.00
—Red and black label with six "eye" logos					
❏ CL 797 [M]	La Boheme for Orchestra	1956	5.00	10.00	20.00
—Red and black label with six "eye" logos					
❏ CL 806 [M]	Show Boat/South Pacific/Slaughter on 10th Avenue	1956	5.00	10.00	20.00
—Red and black label with six "eye" logos					
❏ CL 811 [M]	Calendar Girl	1956	5.00	10.00	20.00
—Red and black label with six "eye" logos					
❏ CL 843 [M]	The Very Thought of You	1956	5.00	10.00	20.00
—Red and black label with six "eye" logos					
❏ CL 863 [M]	Café Continental	1956	5.00	10.00	20.00
—Red and black label with six "eye" logos					
❏ CL 864 [M]	Beautiful Dreamer	1956	5.00	10.00	20.00
—Red and black label with six "eye" logos					
❏ CL 1220 [M]	Romantic Music of...	1958	3.75	7.50	15.00
❏ CL 1335 [M]	The Lure of Paradise	1959	3.00	6.00	12.00
❏ CL 1354 [M]	Strauss Waltzes	1959	3.00	6.00	12.00

Number	Title (A Side/B Side)	Yr	VG	VG+	NM
❏ CL 1431 [M]	Gypsy Passion	1960	3.00	6.00	12.00
❏ CL 1495 [M]	Gershwin: Rhapsody in Blue; Previn: Concerto in F	1960	3.00	6.00	12.00
❏ CL 1528 [M]	Joy to the World: Music for Christmas	1959	3.75	7.50	15.00
❏ CL 1657 [M]	Wonderland of Sound	1961	3.00	6.00	12.00
❏ CL 1718 [M]	Star-Spangled Marches	1962	3.00	6.00	12.00
❏ CL 1827 [M]	Wonderland of Sound (Broadway's Greatest Hits)	1962	3.00	6.00	12.00
❏ CL 1898 [M]	Wonderland of Sound (Fire and Jealousy)	1962	3.00	6.00	12.00
❏ CL 1938 [M]	Wonderland of Sound (The World's Greatest Waltzes)	1963	2.50	5.00	10.00
❏ CL 1995 [M]	Wonderland of Opera	1963	2.50	5.00	10.00
❏ CL 2039 [M]	Wonderland of Golden Hits	1963	2.50	5.00	10.00
❏ CL 2068 [M]	Wonderland of Christmas	1963	3.00	6.00	12.00
❏ CL 2078 [M]	Kostelanetz in Wonderland	1964	2.50	5.00	10.00
❏ CL 2133 [M]	Gershwin Wonderland	1964	2.50	5.00	10.00
❏ CL 2138 [M]	New York Wonderland	1964	2.50	5.00	10.00
❏ CL 2185 [M]	I Wish You Love	1964	2.50	5.00	10.00
❏ CL 2250 [M]	New Orleans Wonderland	1965	2.50	5.00	10.00
❏ CL 2359 [M]	Thunder (The Spectacular Sound of John Philip Sousa)	1965	2.50	5.00	10.00
❏ CL 2467 [M]	The Shadow of Your Smile and Other Great Movie Themes	1966	2.50	5.00	10.00
❏ CL 2534 [M]	Today's Golden Hits	1966	2.50	5.00	10.00
❏ CL 2581 [M]	Exotic Nights	1966	2.50	5.00	10.00
❏ CL 2609 [M]	The Kostelanetz Sound of Today	1967	2.50	5.00	10.00
❏ CL 2688 [M]	Concert in the Park	1967	2.50	5.00	10.00
❏ CL 2756 [M]	Today's Greatest Movie Hits	1967	3.00	6.00	12.00
❏ CL 2823 [M]	Scarborough Fair	1968	3.75	7.50	15.00
❏ CL 2891 [M]	For the Young at Heart	1968	3.75	7.50	15.00
❏ CS 8144 [S]	The Lure of Paradise	1959	3.75	7.50	15.00
❏ CS 8162 [S]	Strauss Waltzes	1959	3.75	7.50	15.00
❏ CS 8228 [S]	Gypsy Passion	1960	3.75	7.50	15.00
❏ CS 8286 [S]	Gershwin: Rhapsody in Blue; Previn: Concerto in F	1960	3.75	7.50	15.00
❏ CS 8328 [S]	Joy to the World: Music for Christmas	1959	5.00	10.00	20.00
—Red and black label with six "eye" logos					
❏ CS 8457 [S]	Wonderland of Sound	1961	3.75	7.50	15.00
❏ CS 8518 [S]	Star-Spangled Marches	1962	3.75	7.50	15.00
❏ CS 8627 [S]	Wonderland of Sound (Broadway's Greatest Hits)	1962	3.75	7.50	15.00
❏ CS 8698 [S]	Wonderland of Sound (Fire and Jealousy)	1962	3.75	7.50	15.00
❏ CS 8738 [S]	Wonderland of Sound (The World's Greatest Waltzes)	1963	3.00	6.00	12.00
❏ CS 8795 [S]	Wonderland of Opera	1963	3.00	6.00	12.00
❏ CS 8839 [S]	Wonderland of Golden Hits	1963	3.00	6.00	12.00
❏ CS 8868 [S]	Wonderland of Christmas	1963	3.75	7.50	15.00
❏ CS 8878 [S]	Kostelanetz in Wonderland	1964	3.00	6.00	12.00
❏ CS 8933 [S]	Gershwin Wonderland	1964	3.00	6.00	12.00
❏ CS 8938 [S]	New York Wonderland	1964	3.00	6.00	12.00
❏ CS 8985 [S]	I Wish You Love	1964	3.00	6.00	12.00
❏ CS 9050 [S]	New Orleans Wonderland	1965	3.00	6.00	12.00
❏ CS 9159 [S]	Thunder (The Spectacular Sound of John Philip Sousa)	1965	3.00	6.00	12.00
❏ CS 9267 [S]	The Shadow of Your Smile and Other Great Movie Themes	1966	2.50	5.00	10.00
❏ CS 9334 [S]	Today's Golden Hits	1966	3.00	6.00	12.00
❏ CS 9381 [S]	Exotic Nights	1966	2.50	5.00	10.00
❏ CS 9409 [S]	The Kostelanetz Sound of Today	1967	2.50	5.00	10.00
❏ CS 9488 [S]	Concert in the Park	1967	2.50	5.00	10.00
❏ CS 9556 [S]	Today's Greatest Movie Hits	1967	2.50	5.00	10.00
❏ CS 9623 [S]	Scarborough Fair	1968	2.50	5.00	10.00
❏ CS 9691 [S]	For the Young at Heart	1968	2.50	5.00	10.00
❏ CS 9724	Hits from Funny Girl, Finian's Rainbow, and Star!	1968	2.50	5.00	10.00
❏ CS 9740	Andre Kostelanetz' Greatest Hits	1969	2.50	5.00	10.00
❏ CS 9823	Traces	1969	2.50	5.00	10.00
❏ CS 9973	Greatest Hits of the 60's	1970	2.50	5.00	10.00
❏ CS 9998	I'll Never Fall in Love Again	1970	2.50	5.00	10.00
❏ C 30037	Everything Is Beautiful	1970	2.50	5.00	10.00
❏ C 30501	Love Story	1971	2.50	5.00	10.00
❏ C 30672	For All We Know	1971	2.50	5.00	10.00
❏ C 31002	Kostelanetz Plays Chicago	1971	2.50	5.00	10.00
❏ KG 31491 [(2)]	Andre Kostelanetz Plays Cole Porter	1972	3.75	7.50	15.00
❏ KG 32002 [(2)]	The World's Greatest Love Songs	1973	3.00	6.00	12.00
❏ KC 32187	Last Tango in Paris	1973	2.50	5.00	10.00
❏ KC 32451	Kostelanetz Plays Great Hits of Today	1973	2.50	5.00	10.00
❏ KC 32580	Andre Kostelanetz Plays Legrand's Greatest Hits	1974	2.50	5.00	10.00
❏ KG 32825 [(2)]	Andre Kostelanetz Plays Gershwin	1974	3.00	6.00	12.00
❏ CQ 32856 [Q]	Quadraphonic Pop Concert	1973	3.75	7.50	15.00
❏ KC 33061	Musical Reflections of Broadway and Hollywood	1974	2.50	5.00	10.00
❏ KG 33065 [(2)]	Strike Up the Band	1974	3.00	6.00	12.00
❏ KC 33437	Orient Express	1975	2.50	5.00	10.00
❏ C 33550	Never Can Say Goodbye	1975	2.00	4.00	8.00
❏ KC 33550	Never Can Say Goodbye	1975	2.50	5.00	10.00
❏ KC 33954	Music from A Chorus Line and Treemonisha	1975	2.50	5.00	10.00
❏ KC 34157	I'm Easy and Other Themes	1976	2.50	5.00	10.00
❏ PC 34352	Dance with Me	1977	2.50	5.00	10.00
❏ PC 34660	Music of Charlie Chaplin and Duke Ellington	1977	2.50	5.00	10.00
❏ JC 35328	You Light Up My Life	1978	2.50	5.00	10.00
❏ JC 35788	Superman	1979	2.00	4.00	8.00
❏ JC 36382	Various Themes	1980	2.00	4.00	8.00
COLUMBIA LIMITED EDITION					
❏ LE 10083	Joy to the World: Music for Christmas	197?	2.50	5.00	10.00
—Reissue of CS 8328					
❏ LE 10086	Wonderland of Christmas	197?	2.50	5.00	10.00
—Reissue of CS 8868					
COLUMBIA MASTERWORKS					
❏ ML 2007 [10]	Music of Stephen Foster	195?	6.25	12.50	25.00

Number	Title (A Side/B Side)	Yr	VG	VG+	NM
❏ ML 2011 [10]	Waltzes of Johann Strauss	195?	6.25	12.50	25.00
❏ ML 2014 [10]	Songs of Cole Porter	195?	7.50	15.00	30.00
❏ ML 2022 [10]	Motion Picture Favorites	195?	6.25	12.50	25.00
❏ ML 2056 [10]	Chopin-Kostelanetz	195?	6.25	12.50	25.00
❏ ML 4065 [M]	Favorites	195?	5.00	10.00	20.00
❏ ML 4066 [M]	Clair de Lune	195?	5.00	10.00	20.00
❏ ML 4082 [M]	Carnival Tropicana	195?	5.00	10.00	20.00
❏ ML 4253 [M]	Music of Fritz Kreisler and Sigmund Romberg	195?	5.00	10.00	20.00
❏ ML 4308 [M]	Swan Lake (Highlights)	195?	5.00	10.00	20.00
❏ ML 4409 [M]	Bizet: L'arlesienne Suites 1 & 2	195?	5.00	10.00	20.00
❏ ML 4455 [M]	An American in Paris	195?	5.00	10.00	20.00
❏ ML 4822 [M]	Lure of the Tropics	1956	5.00	10.00	20.00
❏ MS 6106 [S]	Offenbach: Gaite Parisienne; Bizet: Carmen (Highlights)	195?	5.00	10.00	20.00
❏ ML 6111 [M]	Romantic Strings	1960	3.00	6.00	12.00
❏ ML 6129 [M]	Showstoppers	1960	3.00	6.00	12.00
❏ ML 6179 [M]	Wishing You a Merry Christmas	1960	3.00	6.00	12.00
❏ ML 6206 [M]	Promenade Favorites	1966	3.00	6.00	12.00
❏ ML 6216 [M]	Romantic Waltzes of Tchaikovsky	1961	3.00	6.00	12.00
❏ ML 6226 [M]	Favorite Romantic Concertos	1961	3.00	6.00	12.00
❏ MS 6711 [S]	Romantic Strings	1960	3.75	7.50	15.00
❏ MS 6729 [S]	Showstoppers	1960	3.75	7.50	15.00
❏ MS 6779 [S]	Wishing You a Merry Christmas	1960	3.75	7.50	15.00
❏ MS 6806 [S]	Promenade Favorites	1966	3.75	7.50	15.00
❏ MS 6824 [S]	Romantic Waltzes of Tchaikovsky	1961	3.75	7.50	15.00
❏ MS 6826 [S]	Favorite Romantic Concertos	1961	3.75	7.50	15.00
❏ MS 7087	Vienna, City of Dreams	1968	3.00	6.00	12.00
❏ MS 7108 [S]	Andre Kostelanetz Conducts Great Romantic Ballads	196?	2.50	5.00	10.00
❏ MS 7319	Musical Evenings	1969	2.50	5.00	10.00
❏ MS 7427	Extravaganza	1970	2.50	5.00	10.00
❏ M 30075	Music for Strings	1970	2.50	5.00	10.00
❏ M 35114	Festive Overtures	1978	2.00	4.00	8.00
COLUMBIA SPECIAL PRODUCTS					
❏ C 10975	Wishing You a Merry Christmas	1972	2.50	5.00	10.00
—Reissue of Columbia Masterworks MS 6779					
❏ P 13286	Scarborough Fair	197?	2.00	4.00	8.00
HARMONY					
❏ HL 7368 [M]	You and the Night and the Music	196?	2.50	5.00	10.00
❏ HL 7371 [M]	Broadway Theatre Party	196?	2.50	5.00	10.00
❏ HL 7395 [M]	Grand Canyon Suite	196?	2.50	5.00	10.00
❏ HL 7432 [M]	Joy to the World: Music for Christmas	1967	3.00	6.00	12.00
—Reissue of Columbia 1528					
❏ HS 11168 [S]	You and the Night and the Music	196?	2.50	5.00	10.00
❏ HS 11171 [S]	Broadway Theatre Party	196?	2.50	5.00	10.00
❏ HS 11195 [S]	Grand Canyon Suite	196?	2.50	5.00	10.00
❏ HS 11232 [S]	Joy to the World: Music for Christmas	1967	3.00	6.00	12.00
—Reissue of Columbia 8328					
❏ HS 11281	The Magic of Music	1968	2.50	5.00	10.00
❏ H 30014	Be My Love	1970	2.50	5.00	10.00
❏ KH 31414	Greatest Hits of Broadway and Hollywood	1972	2.50	5.00	10.00
❏ KH 31500	Love Theme from "The Godfather"	1972	2.50	5.00	10.00
❏ KH 31571	Andre Kostelanetz Plays Richard Rogers	1973	2.50	5.00	10.00
❏ KH 32170	Strike Up the Band	1973	2.50	5.00	10.00
READER'S DIGEST					
❏ RD-120-A [(8)]	The Best of Andre Kostelanetz	197?	7.50	15.00	30.00

KOTTKE, LEO

CAPITOL

Number	Title (A Side/B Side)	Yr	VG	VG+	NM
❏ ST-682	Mudlark	1971	3.00	6.00	12.00
❏ ST-11000	Greenhouse	1972	2.50	5.00	10.00
❏ ST-11164	My Feet Are Smiling	1973	2.50	5.00	10.00
❏ ST-11262	Ice Water	1974	2.50	5.00	10.00
❏ ST-11335	Dreams and All That Stuff	1974	2.50	5.00	10.00
❏ ST-11446	Chewing Pine	1975	2.50	5.00	10.00
❏ ST-11576	Leo Kottke 1971-1976 — Did You Hear Me?	1976	2.50	5.00	10.00
❏ SWBC-11867 [(2)]	The Best of Leo Kottke	1979	3.00	6.00	12.00
❏ SN-16063	Mudlark	1979	2.00	4.00	8.00
—Budget-line reissue					
❏ SN-16064	Ice Water	1979	2.00	4.00	8.00
—Budget-line reissue					
❏ SN-16065	Greenhouse	1979	2.00	4.00	8.00
—Budget-line reissue					
❏ SN-16187	Dreams and All That Stuff	1980	2.00	4.00	8.00
—Budget-line reissue					
❏ SN-16188	Chewing Pine	1980	2.00	4.00	8.00
—Budget-line reissue					
❏ SN-16189	Leo Kottke 1971-1976 — Did You Hear Me?	1980	2.00	4.00	8.00
—Budget-line reissue					
CHRYSALIS					
❏ CHR 1106	Leo Kottke	1977	2.50	5.00	10.00
❏ CHR 1191	Burnt Lips	1978	2.50	5.00	10.00
❏ CHR 1234	Balance	1979	2.50	5.00	10.00
❏ CHR 1328	Guitar Music	1981	2.50	5.00	10.00
❏ PV 41106	Leo Kottke	1985	2.00	4.00	8.00
—Budget-line reissue					
❏ PV 41191	Burnt Lips	1985	2.00	4.00	8.00
—Budget-line reissue					
❏ PV 41234	Balance	1985	2.00	4.00	8.00
—Budget-line reissue					
❏ PV 41328	Guitar Music	1983	2.00	4.00	8.00
—Budget-line reissue					
❏ FV 41411	Time Step	1983	2.50	5.00	10.00
❏ PV 41411	Time Step	1986	2.00	4.00	8.00
—Budget-line reissue					
OBLIVION					
❏ S-1	12-String Blues/Live at the Scholar Coffee House	1969	6.25	12.50	25.00
PRIVATE MUSIC					
❏ 2007-1-P	A Shout Toward Noon	1986	2.50	5.00	10.00
❏ 2025-1-P	Regards from Chuck Pink	1988	2.50	5.00	10.00
❏ 2050-1-P	My Father's Face	1989	2.50	5.00	10.00

Number	Title (A Side/B Side)	Yr	VG	VG+	NM
SYMPOSIUM					
❏ 2001	Circle Round the Sun	1970	3.00	6.00	12.00
TAKOMA					
❏ 1024	6 and 12 String Guitar	1969	3.00	6.00	12.00
KRAFTWERK					
CAPITOL					
❏ ST-11457	Radio-Activity	1975	4.00	8.00	16.00
❏ SW 11603	Trans-Europe Express	1977	4.00	8.00	16.00
❏ SW-11728	The Man-Machine	1978	4.00	8.00	16.00
❏ SN-16301	Trans-Europe Express	198?	2.50	5.00	10.00
—Reissue					
❏ SN-16302	The Man-Machine	198?	2.50	5.00	10.00
—Reissue					
❏ SN-16380	Radio-Activity	1986	2.50	5.00	10.00
—Reissue					
ELEKTRA					
❏ 60789	Computer World	1988	2.00	4.00	8.00
—Reissue					
❏ 60797	Autobahn	1988	2.00	4.00	8.00
—Still another reissue of this album					
❏ 60798	Electric Cafe	1988	2.00	4.00	8.00
—Reissue					
❏ 60869 [(2)]	The Mix	1991	3.00	6.00	12.00
MERCURY					
❏ SRM-1-3704	Autobahn	1977	3.75	7.50	15.00
—Reissue of Vertigo VEL-2003					
VERTIGO					
❏ VEL-2003	Autobahn	1974	5.00	10.00	20.00
❏ VEL-2006	Ralf & Florian	1976	4.00	8.00	16.00
—Recorded in 1973					
WARNER BROS.					
❏ HS 3549	Computer World	1981	2.50	5.00	10.00
❏ 25326	Autobahn	1985	3.00	6.00	12.00
—Another reissue of Vertigo VEL-2003					
❏ 25525	Electric Cafe	1986	3.00	6.00	12.00
KRAINIA CONSORT					
MERCURY LIVING PRESENCE					
❏ SR 90397 [S]	Music in Shakespeare's England	196?	5.00	10.00	20.00
—Maroon label, with "Vendor: Mercury Record Corporation"					
❏ SR 90397 [S]	Music in Shakespeare's England	196?	15.00	30.00	60.00
—Maroon label, no "Vendor: Mercury Record Corporation"					
KRAINIS, BERNARD					
MERCURY LIVING PRESENCE					
❏ SR 90443 [S]	Concertos for Recorder and Strings	1965	6.25	12.50	25.00
—Maroon label, with "Vendor: Mercury Record Corporation"					
KRAL, IRENE					
AVA					
❏ A-33 [M]	Better Than Anything	1963	10.00	20.00	40.00
❏ AS-33 [S]	Better Than Anything	1963	12.50	25.00	50.00
MAINSTREAM					
❏ S-6058 [S]	Wonderful Life	1965	10.00	20.00	40.00
❏ 56058 [M]	Wonderful Life	1965	7.50	15.00	30.00
UNITED ARTISTS					
❏ UAL-3052 [M]	Steve Irene O!	1959	30.00	60.00	120.00
❏ UAL-4016 [M]	The Band and I	1959	30.00	60.00	120.00
❏ UAS-5016 [S]	The Band and I	1959	37.50	75.00	150.00
❏ UAS-6052 [S]	Steve Irene O!	1959	37.50	75.00	150.00
KRAMER, BILLY J., AND THE DAKOTAS					
CAPITOL					
❏ SM-11897 [P]	The Best of Billy J. Kramer and the Dakotas	1979	2.50	5.00	10.00
IMPERIAL					
❏ LP 9267 [M]	Little Children	1964	7.50	15.00	30.00
—Black and pink label					
❏ LP 9267 [M]	Little Children	1964	12.50	25.00	50.00
—Black label with stars					
❏ LP 9273 [M]	I'll Keep You Satisfied/From a Window	1964	7.50	15.00	30.00
❏ LP 9291 [M]	Trains and Boats and Planes	1965	7.50	15.00	30.00
❏ LP 12267 [P]	Little Children	1964	10.00	20.00	40.00
—Black and pink label					
❏ LP 12267 [P]	Little Children	1964	20.00	40.00	80.00
—Black label with silver print					
❏ LP 12273 [P]	I'll Keep You Satisfied/From a Window	1964	10.00	20.00	40.00
❏ LP 12921 [R]	Trains and Boats and Planes	1965	6.25	12.50	25.00
KRAVITZ, LENNY					
VIRGIN					
❏ 39169	Are You Gonna Go My Way	1993	6.25	12.50	25.00
—Clear-vinyl LP plus bonus CD with 8 unreleased tracks					
❏ 91290	Let Love Rule	1989	3.00	6.00	12.00
KRAZY KATS, THE					
DAMON					
❏ 12478 [M]	Movin' Out!! With the Krazy Kats	1964	30.00	60.00	120.00
KREED					
VISION OF SOUND					
❏ 71-56	Kreed	1971	300.00	600.00	1200.
KRESS, CARL					
CAPITOL					
❏ H 368 [10]	Classics in Jazz	1953	12.50	25.00	50.00
KRISTOFFERSON, KRIS					
COLUMBIA					
❏ PZ 30679	The Silver Tongued Devil and I	1976	2.00	4.00	8.00
—Reissue					
❏ PZ 30817	Me and Bobby McGee	1976	2.00	4.00	8.00
—Reissue					

Number	Title (A Side/B Side)	Yr	VG	VG+	NM
❏ PZ 31302	Border Lord	1976	2.00	4.00	8.00
—Reissue					
❏ PZ 31909	Jesus Was a Capricorn	1976	2.00	4.00	8.00
—Reissue					
❏ PZ 32914	Spooky Lady's Sideshow	1976	2.00	4.00	8.00
—Reissue					
❏ PZ 33379	Who's to Bless…And Who's to Blame	1976	2.00	4.00	8.00
—Reissue					
❏ PZ 34687	Songs of Kristofferson	1977	3.00	6.00	12.00
❏ JZ 35310	Easter Island	1978	3.00	6.00	12.00
❏ JZ 36135	Shake Hands with the Devil	1979	3.00	6.00	12.00
❏ JZ 36885	To the Bone	1980	3.00	6.00	12.00
MERCURY					
❏ 830406-1	Repossessed	1987	2.50	5.00	10.00
MONUMENT					
❏ SLP-18139	Kristofferson	1970	6.25	12.50	25.00
—Original label is light green with a yellow ring					
❏ Z 30679	The Silver Tongued Devil and I	1971	3.00	6.00	12.00
❏ ZQ 30679 [Q]	The Silver Tongued Devil and I	1972	5.00	10.00	20.00
❏ Z 30817	Me and Bobby McGee	1971	3.00	6.00	12.00
—Reissue of 18139 with new title					
❏ KZ 31302	Border Lord	1972	3.00	6.00	12.00
❏ ZQ 31302 [Q]	Border Lord	1972	5.00	10.00	20.00
❏ KZ 31909	Jesus Was a Capricorn	1972	3.00	6.00	12.00
❏ ZQ 31909 [Q]	Jesus Was a Capricorn	1973	5.00	10.00	20.00
❏ PZ 32914	Spooky Lady's Sideshow	1974	3.00	6.00	12.00
❏ PZQ 32914 [Q]	Spooky Lady's Sideshow	1974	5.00	10.00	20.00
❏ PZ 33379	Who's to Bless…And Who's to Blame	1975	3.00	6.00	12.00
❏ PZ 34254	Surreal Thing	1976	3.00	6.00	12.00
❏ PW 38392	Songs of Kristofferson	1982	2.00	4.00	8.00
—Reissue of 34687					
PAIR					
❏ PDL2-1078 [(2)]	My Songs	1986	3.00	6.00	12.00
KRISTYL					
(NO LABEL)					
❏ (no #)	Kristyl	1975	50.00	100.00	200.00
KRONOS QUARTET					
REFERENCE RECORDINGS					
❏ RR-9	In Formation	198?	6.25	12.50	25.00
—Audiophile vinyl					
KRUPA, GENE					
AMERICAN RECORDING SOCIETY					
❏ L-411 [M]	Gene Krupa Quartet	1956	10.00	20.00	40.00
❏ L-427 [M]	Drummer Man	1957	10.00	20.00	40.00
CLEF					
❏ MGC-121 [10]	The Gene Krupa Trio Collates	1953	20.00	40.00	80.00
—With either Clef or Mercury cover					
❏ MGC-147 [10]	The Gene Krupa Sextet #1	1954	20.00	40.00	80.00
❏ MGC-152 [10]	The Gene Krupa Sextet #2	1954	20.00	40.00	80.00
❏ MGC-500 [M]	The Gene Krupa Trio at Jazz at the Philharmonic	1953	15.00	30.00	60.00
❏ MGC-514 [10]	Gene Krupa Trio	1953	20.00	40.00	80.00
❏ MGC-627 [M]	Sing, Sing, Sing — The Rocking Mr. Krupa and His Orchestra	1954	15.00	30.00	60.00
❏ MGC-631 [M]	The Gene Krupa Sextet #3	1954	15.00	30.00	60.00
❏ MGC-668 [M]	The Gene Krupa Quartet	1955	15.00	30.00	60.00
❏ MGC-684 [M]	Krupa and Rich	1955	15.00	30.00	60.00
❏ MGC-687 [M]	The Exciting Gene Krupa and His Quartet	1956	15.00	30.00	60.00
❏ MGC-703 [M]	Drum Boogie	1956	15.00	30.00	60.00
❏ MGC-728 [M]	The Driving Gene Krupa Plays with His Sextet	1956	15.00	30.00	60.00
COLUMBIA					
❏ C2L 29 [(2)M]	Drummin' Man	1962	12.50	25.00	50.00
—Red and black labels with six "eye" logos; box set with booklet; deduct 20 percent if book is missing					
❏ C2L 29 [(2)M]	Drummin' Man	1963	5.00	10.00	20.00
—Red labels, "Guaranteed High Fidelity" or "360 Sound Mono" on label					
❏ CL 641 [M]	Gene Krupa's Sidekicks	1955	7.50	15.00	30.00
—Red and black label with six "eye" logos					
❏ CL 641 [M]	Gene Krupa's Sidekicks	1955	10.00	20.00	40.00
—Maroon label, gold print					
❏ CL 735 [M]	Gene Krupa	1956	7.50	15.00	30.00
—Red and black label with six "eye" logos					
❏ CL 2515 [10]	Drummin' Man	1955	12.50	25.00	50.00
❏ CL 6017 [10]	Gene Krupa	1949	25.00	50.00	100.00
❏ CL 6066 [10]	Dance Parade	1949	25.00	50.00	100.00
MERCURY					
❏ MGC-500 [M]	The Gene Krupa Trio at Jazz at the Philharmonic	1953	20.00	40.00	80.00
❏ MGC-514 [10]	Gene Krupa Trio	1953	30.00	60.00	120.00
RCA CAMDEN					
❏ CAL-340 [M]	Mutiny in the Parlor	1958	5.00	10.00	20.00
VERVE					
❏ MGV-2008 [M]	Drummer Man — Gene Krupa in Highest-Fi	1956	15.00	30.00	60.00
—Orange label					
❏ MGV-2008 [M]	Drummer Man — Gene Krupa in Highest-Fi	1957	12.50	25.00	50.00
—Black label					
❏ V-2008 [M]	Drummer Man — Gene Krupa in Highest-Fi	1961	6.25	12.50	25.00
❏ MGVS-6008 [S]	Gene Krupa Plays Gerry Mulligan Arrangements	1959	10.00	20.00	40.00
❏ MGVS-6042 [S]	Big Noise from Winnetka — Gene Krupa at the London House	1960	10.00	20.00	40.00
❏ MGV-8031 [M]	The Gene Krupa Trio	1957	12.50	25.00	50.00
❏ V-8031 [M]	The Gene Krupa Trio	1961	6.25	12.50	25.00
❏ MGV-8069 [M]	Krupa and Rich	1957	12.50	25.00	50.00
❏ V-8069 [M]	Krupa and Rich	1961	6.25	12.50	25.00
❏ MGV-8071 [M]	The Exciting Gene Krupa and His Quartet	1957	12.50	25.00	50.00
❏ V-8071 [M]	The Exciting Gene Krupa and His Quartet	1961	6.25	12.50	25.00
❏ MGV-8087 [M]	Drum Boogie	1957	12.50	25.00	50.00
❏ V-8087 [M]	Drum Boogie	1961	6.25	12.50	25.00

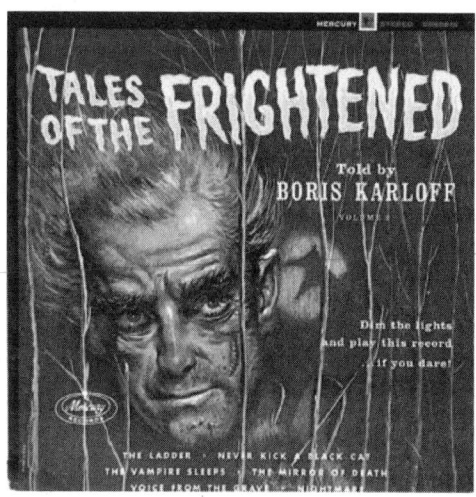

Boris Karloff recorded a number of albums reciting children's stories. This one was a far cry from those, as he played off his usual, more horrifying, reputation to narrate *Tales of the Frightened* for Mercury.

From a distance, the pairing of Beat poet Jack Kerouac and "square" pianist Steve Allen makes no sense. Yet they recorded together more than once. *Blues and Haikus* is the more "common" of their collaborations.

Look closely at this example of Kiss' debut album and you'll see a Warner Bros. promotional sticker. WB briefly distributed Casablanca in 1974.

Roots was the John Lennon album that was concocted by Morris Levy from a raw tape of sessions that became *Rock 'n' Roll*. It was sold via mail order in early 1975, but was quickly removed from the market. Authentic copies fetch a tidy sum today.

Little Eva's only album for Dimension is sought after by girl group and early 1960s pop collectors.

To capitalize on the success of "The Green Door" on Dot in 1956, Jim Lowe's prior record label, Mercury, compiled this collection of older material on LP and issued it to commercial indifference.

Number	Title (A Side/B Side)	Yr	VG	VG+	NM
❑ MGV-8107 [M]	The Driving Gene Krupa	1957	12.50	25.00	50.00
❑ V-8107 [M]	The Driving Gene Krupa	1961	6.25	12.50	25.00
❑ MGV-8190 [M]	Sing, Sing, Sing	1957	12.50	25.00	50.00
❑ V-8190 [M]	Sing, Sing, Sing	1961	6.25	12.50	25.00
❑ MGV-8204 [M]	The Jazz Rhythms of Gene Krupa	1957	12.50	25.00	50.00
❑ V-8204 [M]	The Jazz Rhythms of Gene Krupa	1961	6.25	12.50	25.00
❑ MGV-8276 [M]	Krupa Rocks	1958	12.50	25.00	50.00
❑ V-8276 [M]	Krupa Rocks	1961	6.25	12.50	25.00
❑ MGV-8292 [M]	Gene Krupa Plays Gerry Mulligan Arrangements	1958	12.50	25.00	50.00
❑ V-8292 [M]	Gene Krupa Plays Gerry Mulligan Arrangements	1961	6.25	12.50	25.00
❑ V6-8292 [S]	Gene Krupa Plays Gerry Mulligan Arrangements	1961	5.00	10.00	20.00
❑ MGV-8300 [M]	Hey! Here's Gene Krupa	1959	12.50	25.00	50.00
❑ V-8300 [M]	Hey! Here's Gene Krupa	1961	6.25	12.50	25.00
❑ MGV-8310 [M]	Big Noise from Winnetka — Gene Krupa at the London House	1959	12.50	25.00	50.00
❑ V-8310 [M]	Big Noise from Winnetka — Gene Krupa at the London House	1961	6.25	12.50	25.00
❑ V6-8310 [S]	Big Noise from Winnetka — Gene Krupa at the London House	1961	5.00	10.00	20.00
❑ MGV-8369 [M]	The Drum Battle	1960	12.50	25.00	50.00
❑ V-8400 [M]	Krupa and Rich	1961	6.25	12.50	25.00
❑ V6-8400 [S]	Krupa and Rich	1961	5.00	10.00	20.00
❑ V6-8414 [S]	Percussion King	1961	5.00	10.00	20.00
❑ V6-8450 [S]	Classics in Percussion	1962	5.00	10.00	20.00
❑ V6-8571 [S]	Let Me Off Uptown — The Essential Gene Krupa	1964	5.00	10.00	20.00
❑ V6-8584 [S]	The Great New Gene Krupa Quartet Featuring Charlie Ventura	1964	5.00	10.00	20.00

KRUPA, GENE; LIONEL HAMPTON; TEDDY WILSON
CLEF

Number	Title (A Side/B Side)	Yr	VG	VG+	NM
❑ MGC-681 [M]	Selections from "The Benny Goodman Story"	1956	20.00	40.00	80.00

VERVE

❑ MGV-8066 [M]	Gene Krupa-Lionel Hampton-Teddy Wilson with Red Callender	1957	12.50	25.00	50.00

—Reissue of Clef 681 with new title

❑ V-8066 [M]	Gene Krupa-Lionel Hampton-Teddy Wilson with Red Callender	1961	6.25	12.50	25.00

KRUPA, GENE, AND CHARLIE VENTURA
COMMODORE

❑ FL-20028 [10]	The Krupa-Ventura Trio	1950	25.00	50.00	100.00

KUBAN, BOB, AND THE IN-MEN
MUSICLAND U.S.A.

❑ LP-3500 [M]	Look Out for the Cheater	1966	7.50	15.00	30.00
❑ SLP-3500 [S]	Look Out for the Cheater	1966	10.00	20.00	40.00

KUHN, ROLF
URANIA

❑ US-1220 [M]	Sound of Jazz	1962	6.25	12.50	25.00
❑ US-41220 [S]	Sound of Jazz	1962	7.50	15.00	30.00

VANGUARD

❑ VRS-8510 [M]	Streamline	1955	10.00	20.00	40.00

KUHN, ROLF AND JOACHIM
ABC IMPULSE!

❑ AS-9150	Impressions of New York	1968	5.00	10.00	20.00

KUHN, STEVE
CONTACT

❑ CM-5 [M]	Steve Kuhn Trio Featuring Steve Swallow and Pete LaRoca	1965	5.00	10.00	20.00
❑ CS-5 [S]	Steve Kuhn Trio Featuring Steve Swallow and Pete LaRoca	1965	6.25	12.50	25.00

IMPULSE!

❑ A-9136 [M]	The October Suite	1967	6.25	12.50	25.00
❑ AS-9136 [S]	The October Suite	1967	5.00	10.00	20.00

KUHN, STEVE, AND TOSHIKO AKIYOSHI
DAUNTLESS

❑ DM-4308 [M]	The Country & Western Sound for Jazz Pianos	1963	5.00	10.00	20.00
❑ DS-6308 [S]	The Country & Western Sound for Jazz Pianos	1963	6.25	12.50	25.00

KUSTOM KINGS, THE
SMASH

❑ MGS-27051 [M]	Kustom City, U.S.A.	1964	30.00	60.00	120.00
❑ SRS-67051 [S]	Kustom City, U.S.A.	1964	50.00	100.00	200.00

KWESKIN, JIM
MOUNTAIN RAILROAD

❑ MR-52672	Jug Band Blues	198?	2.50	5.00	10.00
❑ MR-52782	Jim Kweskin Lives Again	198?	2.50	5.00	10.00
❑ MR-52790	Side by Side	198?	2.50	5.00	10.00
❑ MR-52793	Swing on a Star	198?	2.50	5.00	10.00

REPRISE

❑ R 6266 [M]	Garden of Joy	1967	5.00	10.00	20.00
❑ RS 6266 [S]	Garden of Joy	1967	3.75	7.50	15.00
❑ RS 6464	America	1971	3.75	7.50	15.00

VANGUARD

❑ VSD 13/14 [(2)]	Greatest Hits	1970	3.75	7.50	15.00
❑ VSD-2158 [S]	Jim Kweskin and the Jug Band	1963	6.25	12.50	25.00
❑ VRS-9139 [M]	Jim Kweskin and the Jug Band	1963	5.00	10.00	20.00
❑ VRS-9163 [M]	Jug Band Music	1965	5.00	10.00	20.00
❑ VRS-9188 [M]	Relax Your Mind	1966	5.00	10.00	20.00
❑ VRS-9234 [M]	See Reverse Side for Title	1967	5.00	10.00	20.00
❑ VRS-9243 [M]	Jump for Joy	1967	5.00	10.00	20.00
❑ VRS-9270 [M]	The Best of Jim Kweskin and the Jug Band	1968	10.00	20.00	40.00
❑ VSD-79163 [S]	Jug Band Music	1965	6.25	12.50	25.00
❑ VSD-79188 [S]	Relax Your Mind	1966	6.25	12.50	25.00

Number	Title (A Side/B Side)	Yr	VG	VG+	NM
❑ VSD-79234 [S]	See Reverse Side for Title	1967	6.25	12.50	25.00
❑ VSD-79243 [S]	Jump for Joy	1967	5.00	10.00	20.00
❑ VSD-79270 [S]	The Best of Jim Kweskin and the Jug Band	1968	3.75	7.50	15.00

KYNARD, CHARLES
MAINSTREAM

❑ MRL-331	Charles Kynard	1972	5.00	10.00	20.00
❑ MRL-368	Woga	1973	5.00	10.00	20.00
❑ MRL-389	Your Mama Don't Dance	1973	5.00	10.00	20.00

PACIFIC JAZZ

❑ PJ-72 [M]	Where It's At!	1963	7.50	15.00	30.00
❑ ST-72 [S]	Where It's At!	1963	10.00	20.00	40.00

PRESTIGE

❑ PRST-7599	Professor Soul	1968	5.00	10.00	20.00
❑ PRST-7630	The Soul Brotherhood	1969	5.00	10.00	20.00
❑ PRST-7688	Reelin' with the Feelin'	1969	5.00	10.00	20.00
❑ PRST-7796	Afro-disiac	1970	5.00	10.00	20.00
❑ 10008	Wa-tu-wa-zui	1971	5.00	10.00	20.00

WORLD PACIFIC

❑ ST-1823 [S]	Warm Winds	1964	7.50	15.00	30.00
❑ WP-1823 [M]	Warm Winds	1964	6.25	12.50	25.00

L

L.A. 4
CONCORD JAZZ

❑ CJ-1001	Just Friends	1980	5.00	10.00	20.00

—Direct-to-disc recording

EAST WIND

❑ 10003	Pavanne Pour Une Infante Defunte	197?	7.50	15.00	30.00

—Audiophile issue

❑ 10004	Going Home	197?	7.50	15.00	30.00

—Audiophile issue

L.A. JAZZ CHOIR, THE
MOBILE FIDELITY

❑ 1-096	Listen	1982	20.00	40.00	80.00

—Audiophile vinyl

L7
EPITAPH

❑ 86401	L7	1988	12.50	25.00	50.00

—Original press with Donita Sparks' head cut off

SLASH

❑ 45624	Hungry for Stink	1994	3.00	6.00	12.00

SUB POP

❑ 79 [EP]	Smell the Magic	1990	3.00	6.00	12.00
❑ 79 [EP]	Smell the Magic	1990	10.00	20.00	40.00

—First 1,000 on purple vinyl

LA LUPE
ROULETTE

❑ SR-42024	The Queen Does Her Thing	1969	7.50	15.00	30.00

LABEEF, SLEEPY
ROUNDER

❑ 3052	It Ain't What You Eat...	198?	2.50	5.00	10.00
❑ 3070	Electricity	198?	2.50	5.00	10.00
❑ 3072	Nothin' But the Truth	198?	2.50	5.00	10.00

SUN

❑ 130	Bull's Night Out	1974	3.00	6.00	12.00
❑ 138	Western Gold	197?	3.00	6.00	12.00
❑ 1004	Rockabilly 1977	1977	3.00	6.00	12.00
❑ 1018	Downtown Rockabilly	1978	3.00	6.00	12.00

LABELLE, PATTI, AND THE BLUE BELLES
ATLANTIC

❑ 8119 [M]	Over the Rainbow	1966	7.50	15.00	30.00
❑ SD 8119 [S]	Over the Rainbow	1966	10.00	20.00	40.00
❑ 8147 [M]	Dreamer	1967	7.50	15.00	30.00
❑ SD 8147 [S]	Dreamer	1967	10.00	20.00	40.00

MISTLETOE

❑ MLP-1204	Merry Christmas from LaBelle	1976	5.00	10.00	20.00

NEWTOWN

❑ 631 [M]	Sweethearts of the Apollo	1963	100.00	200.00	400.00
❑ 632 [M]	Sleigh Bells, Jingle Bells and Blue Bells	1963	75.00	150.00	300.00

PARKWAY

❑ P-7043 [M]	The Bluebelles On Stage	1965	30.00	60.00	120.00

—Without bonus single

❑ P-7043 [M]	The Bluebelles On Stage	1965	37.50	75.00	150.00

—With bonus single

TRIP

❑ 3508	Patti LaBelle and the Bluebelles	197?	2.50	5.00	10.00
❑ 8000	Patti LaBelle and the Bluebelles' Greatest Hits	1971	2.50	5.00	10.00
❑ 9525	Early Hits	197?	2.50	5.00	10.00

UNITED ARTISTS

❑ UA-LA504-E	The Very Best of Patti LaBelle and the Bluebelles	1975	2.50	5.00	10.00

LACEWING
MAINSTREAM

❑ S-6132	Lacewing	1971	12.50	25.00	50.00

LACY, STEVE
CANDID

❑ CD-8007 [M]	The Straight Horn of Steve Lacy	1960	10.00	20.00	40.00
❑ CS-9007 [S]	The Straight Horn of Steve Lacy	1960	12.50	25.00	50.00

Number	Title (A Side/B Side)	Yr	VG	VG+	NM
ESP-DISK'					
❏ 1060 [M]	The Forest and the Zoo	1967	7.50	15.00	30.00
❏ S-1060 [S]	The Forest and the Zoo	1967	5.00	10.00	20.00
HAT HUT					
❏ K/L [(2)]	Stamps	1978	5.00	10.00	20.00
❏ 03 [(2)]	The Way	1979	5.00	10.00	20.00
NEW JAZZ					
❏ NJLP-8206 [M]	Reflections: Steve Lacy Plays Thelonious Monk	1958	25.00	50.00	100.00
—Purple label					
❏ NJLP-8206 [M]	Reflections: Steve Lacy Plays Thelonious Monk	1965	6.25	12.50	25.00
—Blue label, trident logo at right					
❏ NJLP-8271 [M]	Evidence	1962	20.00	40.00	80.00
—Purple label					
❏ NJLP-8271 [M]	Evidence	1965	6.25	12.50	25.00
—Blue label, trident logo at right					
PRESTIGE					
❏ PRLP-7125 [M]	Steve Lacy Soprano Sax	1956	25.00	50.00	100.00
STATUS					
❏ ST-8308 [M]	Wynton Kelly with Steve Lacy	1965	10.00	20.00	40.00

LADNIER, TOMMY
RIVERSIDE

Number	Title (A Side/B Side)	Yr	VG	VG+	NM
❏ RLP-1019 [10]	Ida Cox with Tommy Ladnier	1953	25.00	50.00	100.00
❏ RLP-1026 [10]	Early Ladnier	1954	25.00	50.00	100.00
❏ RLP-1044 [10]	Tommy Ladnier Plays the Blues	1954	25.00	50.00	100.00
"X"					
❏ LVA-3027 [M]	Tommy Ladnier	1954	15.00	30.00	60.00

LAFARGE, PETER
COLUMBIA

Number	Title (A Side/B Side)	Yr	VG	VG+	NM
❏ CL 1795 [M]	Ira Hayes and Other Ballads	1962	5.00	10.00	20.00
❏ CS 8595 [S]	Ira Hayes and Other Ballads	1962	6.25	12.50	25.00
VERVE FOLKWAYS					
❏ FV-9004 [M]	Peter LaFarge Sings Women Blues	1965	5.00	10.00	20.00
❏ FVS-9004 [S]	Peter LaFarge Sings Women Blues	1965	6.25	12.50	25.00

LAFORGE, JACK
AUDIO FIDELITY

Number	Title (A Side/B Side)	Yr	VG	VG+	NM
❏ AFSD-6161 [S]	Hit the Road Jack	196?	5.00	10.00	20.00
REGINA					
❏ R-282 [M]	I Remember You	196?	5.00	10.00	20.00
❏ RS-282 [S]	I Remember You	196?	6.25	12.50	25.00
❏ R-288 [M]	Unchain My Heart	196?	5.00	10.00	20.00
❏ RS-288 [S]	Unchain My Heart	196?	6.25	12.50	25.00
❏ R-301 [M]	You Fascinate Me So	196?	5.00	10.00	20.00
❏ RS-301 [S]	You Fascinate Me So	196?	6.25	12.50	25.00
❏ R-309 [M]	Comin' Home Baby	196?	5.00	10.00	20.00
❏ RS-309 [S]	Comin' Home Baby	196?	6.25	12.50	25.00
❏ R-313 [M]	Promise Her Anything	196?	5.00	10.00	20.00
❏ RS-313 [S]	Promise Her Anything	196?	6.25	12.50	25.00
❏ R-314 [M]	Jazz Portrait of Jack LaForge	196?	5.00	10.00	20.00
❏ RS-314 [S]	Jazz Portrait of Jack LaForge	196?	6.25	12.50	25.00
❏ R-319 [M]	Goldfinger	1965	5.00	10.00	20.00
❏ RS-319 [S]	Goldfinger	1965	6.25	12.50	25.00
❏ R-327 [M]	Our Crazy Affair	196?	5.00	10.00	20.00
❏ RS-327 [S]	Our Crazy Affair	196?	6.25	12.50	25.00
❏ R-716 [M]	Hawaii and I	196?	5.00	10.00	20.00
❏ RS-716 [S]	Hawaii and I	196?	6.25	12.50	25.00

LAINE, CLEO
FONTANA

Number	Title (A Side/B Side)	Yr	VG	VG+	NM
❏ MGF-27552 [M]	Woman to Woman	1967	5.00	10.00	20.00
❏ SRF-67531 [S]	Shakespeare and All That Jazz	1966	5.00	10.00	20.00

LAINE, FRANKIE
ABC

Number	Title (A Side/B Side)	Yr	VG	VG+	NM
❏ 604 [M]	I'll Take Care of Your Cares	1967	3.00	6.00	12.00
❏ S-604 [S]	I'll Take Care of Your Cares	1967	3.75	7.50	15.00
❏ 608 [M]	I Wanted Someone to Love	1967	3.00	6.00	12.00
❏ S-608 [S]	I Wanted Someone to Love	1967	3.75	7.50	15.00
❏ 628 [M]	To Each His Own	1968	5.00	10.00	20.00
❏ S-628 [S]	To Each His Own	1968	3.75	7.50	15.00
❏ S-657	Take Me Back to Laine Country	1968	3.75	7.50	15.00
❏ S-682	You Gave Me a Mountain	1969	3.75	7.50	15.00
AMOS					
❏ 7009	Frankie Laine's Greatest Hits	1970	3.00	6.00	12.00
❏ 7013	Brand New Day	1971	3.00	6.00	12.00
BULLDOG					
❏ BDL-1035	All of Me	198?	2.50	5.00	10.00
CAPITOL					
❏ ST 2277 [S]	I Believe	1965	3.75	7.50	15.00
❏ T 2277 [M]	I Believe	1965	3.00	6.00	12.00
COLUMBIA					
❏ CL 625 [M]	Command Performance	1954	10.00	20.00	40.00
❏ CL 808 [M]	Jazz Spectacular	1956	7.50	15.00	30.00
❏ CL 975 [M]	Rockin'	1957	7.50	15.00	30.00
❏ CL 1116 [M]	Foreign Affair	1958	7.50	15.00	30.00
❏ CL 1176 [M]	Torchin'	1959	5.00	10.00	20.00
❏ CL 1231 [M]	Frankie Laine's Greatest Hits	1958	6.25	12.50	25.00
—Red and black label with six "eye" logos					
❏ CL 1231 [M]	Frankie Laine's Greatest Hits	1962	3.75	7.50	15.00
—"Guaranteed High Fidelity" or "360 Sound Mono" label					
❏ CL 1277 [M]	Reunion in Rhythm	1959	5.00	10.00	20.00
❏ CL 1317 [M]	You Are My Love	1960	5.00	10.00	20.00
❏ CL 1393 [M]	Frankie Laine, Balladeer	1960	5.00	10.00	20.00
❏ CL 1615 [M]	Hell Bent for Leather!	1961	5.00	10.00	20.00
—Red and black label with six "eye" logos					

Number	Title (A Side/B Side)	Yr	VG	VG+	NM
❏ CL 1615 [M]	Hell Bent for Leather!	1962	3.75	7.50	15.00
—"Guaranteed High Fidelity" or "360 Sound Mono" label					
❏ CL 1696 [M]	Deuces Wild	1962	3.75	7.50	15.00
—"Guaranteed High Fidelity" or "360 Sound Mono" label					
❏ CL 1696 [M]	Deuces Wild	1962	5.00	10.00	20.00
—Red and black label with six "eye" logos					
❏ CL 1829 [M]	Call of the Wild	1962	3.75	7.50	15.00
❏ CL 1962 [M]	Wanderlust	1963	3.75	7.50	15.00
❏ CL 2504 [10]	Lover's Laine	1955	10.00	20.00	40.00
❏ CL 2548 [10]	One for My Baby	1955	10.00	20.00	40.00
❏ CL 6200 [10]	One for My Baby	1952	12.50	25.00	50.00
❏ CL 6278 [10]	Mr. Rhythm	1954	12.50	25.00	50.00
❏ CS 8024 [S]	Torchin'	1959	7.50	15.00	30.00
❏ CS 8087 [S]	Reunion in Rhythm	1959	7.50	15.00	30.00
❏ CS 8119 [S]	You Are My Love	1960	6.25	12.50	25.00
❏ CS 8188 [S]	Frankie Laine, Balladeer	1960	6.25	12.50	25.00
❏ CS 8415 [S]	Hell Bent for Leather!	1961	7.50	15.00	30.00
—Red and black label with six "eye" logos					
❏ CS 8415 [S]	Hell Bent for Leather!	1962	5.00	10.00	20.00
—"360 Sound Stereo" label					
❏ CS 8496 [S]	Deuces Wild	1962	5.00	10.00	20.00
—"360 Sound Stereo" label					
❏ CS 8496 [S]	Deuces Wild	1962	6.25	12.50	25.00
—Red and black label with six "eye" logos					
❏ CS 8629 [S]	Call of the Wild	1962	5.00	10.00	20.00
❏ CS 8636 [R]	Frankie Laine's Greatest Hits	1963	3.00	6.00	12.00
❏ PC 8636	Frankie Laine's Greatest Hits	198?	2.00	4.00	8.00
—Reissue with new prefix					
❏ CS 8762 [S]	Wanderlust	1963	5.00	10.00	20.00
GALAXY SERIES					
❏ 4821 [M]	Frankie Laine Sings	195?	3.00	6.00	12.00
HARMONY					
❏ HL 7329 [M]	Roving Gambler	196?	3.00	6.00	12.00
❏ HL 7382 [M]	That's My Desire	196?	3.00	6.00	12.00
❏ HL 7425 [M]	Memories	196?	3.00	6.00	12.00
❏ HS 11129 [S]	Roving Gambler	196?	3.00	6.00	12.00
❏ HS 11182 [S]	That's My Desire	196?	3.00	6.00	12.00
❏ HS 11225 [S]	Memories	196?	3.00	6.00	12.00
❏ HS 11345	I'm Gonna Live 'Til I Die	1969	3.00	6.00	12.00
❏ H 30406	High Noon	1971	3.00	6.00	12.00
HINDSIGHT					
❏ HSR-216	Frankie Laine with Carl Fischer and His Orchestra, 1947	1985	2.50	5.00	10.00
MERCURY					
❏ PKW-2-111 [(2)]	The Great Years	1969	3.75	7.50	15.00
❏ MG-20069 [M]	Songs by Frankie Laine	1956	10.00	20.00	40.00
❏ MG-20080 [M]	That's My Desire	1957	10.00	20.00	40.00
❏ MG-20083 [M]	Frankie Laine Sings For Us	1957	10.00	20.00	40.00
❏ MG-20085 [M]	Concert Date	1957	10.00	20.00	40.00
❏ MG-20105 [M]	With All My Heart	1957	10.00	20.00	40.00
❏ MG-20587 [M]	Frankie Laine's Golden Hits	1960	6.25	12.50	25.00
❏ MG-25007 [10]	Favorites	1949	12.50	25.00	50.00
❏ MG-25024 [10]	Songs from the Heart	1950	12.50	25.00	50.00
❏ MG-25025 [10]	Frankie Laine	1950	12.50	25.00	50.00
❏ MG-25026 [10]	Frankie Laine	1950	12.50	25.00	50.00
❏ MG-25027 [10]	Frankie Laine	1950	12.50	25.00	50.00
❏ MG-25082 [10]	Christmas Favorites	1951	12.50	25.00	50.00
❏ MG-25097 [10]	Mr. Rhythm Sings	1951	12.50	25.00	50.00
❏ MG-25124 [10]	Listen to Laine	1952	12.50	25.00	50.00
❏ SR-60587 [R]	Frankie Laine's Golden Hits	196?	3.00	6.00	12.00
PICKWICK					
❏ SPC-3526	That Lucky Old Sun	197?	2.50	5.00	10.00
❏ SPC-3601	You Gave Me a Mountain	197?	2.50	5.00	10.00
TOWER					
❏ ST 5092 [S]	Memory Laine	1967	3.75	7.50	15.00
❏ T 5092 [M]	Memory Laine	1967	3.00	6.00	12.00
WING					
❏ MGW 12110 [M]	All-Time Favorites	196?	3.75	7.50	15.00
❏ MGW 12158 [M]	Singing the Blues	196?	3.75	7.50	15.00
❏ MGW 12202 [M]	That's My Desire	196?	3.75	7.50	15.00
❏ SRW 16110 [R]	All-Time Favorites	196?	3.00	6.00	12.00
❏ SRW 16158 [R]	Singing the Blues	196?	3.00	6.00	12.00
❏ SRW 16202 [R]	That's My Desire	196?	3.00	6.00	12.00

LAMARE, NAPPY, AND KID ORY
MODERN

Number	Title (A Side/B Side)	Yr	VG	VG+	NM
❏ 2010 [10]	Modern Records Volume 10	195?	15.00	30.00	60.00
—No printing on back cover					

LAMAS, FERNANDO
ROULETTE

Number	Title (A Side/B Side)	Yr	VG	VG+	NM
❏ R-25041 [M]	With Love, Fernando Lamas	1958	10.00	20.00	40.00

LAMB
FILLMORE

Number	Title (A Side/B Side)	Yr	VG	VG+	NM
❏ F 30003	Sign of Change	1970	5.00	10.00	20.00
WARNER BROS.					
❏ WS 1920	Cross Between	1971	5.00	10.00	20.00
❏ WS 1952	Bring Out the Sun	1972	5.00	10.00	20.00

LAMB, JOSEPH
FOLKWAYS

Number	Title (A Side/B Side)	Yr	VG	VG+	NM
❏ FJ-3562 [M]	Classic Ragtime	1960	5.00	10.00	20.00

LAMBERT, DAVE
UNITED ARTISTS

Number	Title (A Side/B Side)	Yr	VG	VG+	NM
❏ UAL-3084 [M]	Dave Lambert Sings and Swings Alone	1959	10.00	20.00	40.00
❏ UAS-6084 [S]	Dave Lambert Sings and Swings Alone	1959	12.50	25.00	50.00

LAMBERT, HENDRICKS AND BAVAN
RCA VICTOR

Number	Title (A Side/B Side)	Yr	VG	VG+	NM
❏ LPM-2635 [M]	Live at Basin Street East	1963	7.50	15.00	30.00

L

Number	Title (A Side/B Side)	Yr	VG	VG+	NM
❑ LSP-2635 [S]	Live at Basin Street East	1963	10.00	20.00	40.00
❑ LPM-2747 [M]	Lambert, Hendricks and Bavan at Newport	1963	7.50	15.00	30.00
❑ LSP-2747 [S]	Lambert, Hendricks and Bavan at Newport	1963	10.00	20.00	40.00
❑ LPM-2861 [M]	Lambert, Hendricks and Bavan at the Village Gate	1964	7.50	15.00	30.00
❑ LSP-2861 [S]	Lambert, Hendricks and Bavan at the Village Gate	1964	10.00	20.00	40.00

LAMBERT, HENDRICKS AND ROSS
ABC-PARAMOUNT

Number	Title (A Side/B Side)	Yr	VG	VG+	NM
❑ ABC-223 [M]	Sing a Song of Basie	1958	12.50	25.00	50.00
❑ ABCS-223 [S]	Sing a Song of Basie	1958	12.50	25.00	50.00

COLUMBIA

Number	Title (A Side/B Side)	Yr	VG	VG+	NM
❑ CL 1403 [M]	The Hottest New Group in Jazz	1959	7.50	15.00	30.00
—Black and red label with six "eye" logos					
❑ CL 1510 [M]	Lambert, Hendricks and Ross Sing Ellington	1960	7.50	15.00	30.00
—Black and red label with six "eye" logos					
❑ CL 1675 [M]	High Flying	1961	7.50	15.00	30.00
—Black and red label with six "eye" logos					
❑ CS 8198 [S]	The Hottest New Group in Jazz	1959	10.00	20.00	40.00
—Black and red label with six "eye" logos					
❑ CS 8198 [S]	The Hottest New Group in Jazz	1963	5.00	10.00	20.00
—Red label with "360 Sound Stereo" at bottom					
❑ CS 8310 [S]	Lambert, Hendricks and Ross Sing Ellington	1960	10.00	20.00	40.00
—Black and red label with six "eye" logos					
❑ CS 8310 [S]	Lambert, Hendricks and Ross Sing Ellington	1963	5.00	10.00	20.00
—Red label with "360 Sound Stereo" at bottom					
❑ CS 8475 [S]	High Flying	1961	10.00	20.00	40.00
—Black and red label with six "eye" logos					
❑ CS 8475 [S]	High Flying	1963	5.00	10.00	20.00
—Red label with "360 Sound Stereo" at bottom					

IMPULSE!

Number	Title (A Side/B Side)	Yr	VG	VG+	NM
❑ A-83 [M]	Sing a Song of Basie	1965	6.25	12.50	25.00
—Reissue of ABC-Paramount ABC-223					
❑ AS-83 [S]	Sing a Song of Basie	1965	7.50	15.00	30.00
—Reissue of ABC-Paramount ABCS-223					

ROULETTE

Number	Title (A Side/B Side)	Yr	VG	VG+	NM
❑ R-52018 [M]	Sing Along with Basie	1959	10.00	20.00	40.00
❑ SR-52018 [S]	Sing Along with Basie	1959	12.50	25.00	50.00

WORLD PACIFIC

Number	Title (A Side/B Side)	Yr	VG	VG+	NM
❑ ST-1025 [S]	The Swingers!	1959	12.50	25.00	50.00
❑ WP-1264 [M]	The Swingers!	1959	10.00	20.00	40.00

LAMEGO, DANNY, AND HIS JUMPIN' JACKS
FORGET-ME-NOT

Number	Title (A Side/B Side)	Yr	VG	VG+	NM
❑ 105 [M]	The Big Weekend	1964	25.00	50.00	100.00

LAMOND, DON
COMMAND

Number	Title (A Side/B Side)	Yr	VG	VG+	NM
❑ RS 832 SD [S]	Off Beat Percussion	1962	5.00	10.00	20.00

LAMOUR, DOROTHY
DECCA

Number	Title (A Side/B Side)	Yr	VG	VG+	NM
❑ DL 5115 [10]	Favorite Hawaiian Songs	1950	20.00	40.00	80.00

LANCASTER, BYARD
VORTEX

Number	Title (A Side/B Side)	Yr	VG	VG+	NM
❑ 2003	It's Not Up to Us	1968	7.50	15.00	30.00

LANCE, HERB
CHESS

Number	Title (A Side/B Side)	Yr	VG	VG+	NM
❑ LP-1506 [M]	The Comeback	1966	6.25	12.50	25.00
❑ LPS-1506 [S]	The Comeback	1966	7.50	15.00	30.00

LANCE, MAJOR
KAT FAMILY

Number	Title (A Side/B Side)	Yr	VG	VG+	NM
❑ FZ 38898	The Major's Back	1983	3.00	6.00	12.00

OKEH

Number	Title (A Side/B Side)	Yr	VG	VG+	NM
❑ OKM-12105 [M]	The Monkey Time	1963	10.00	20.00	40.00
❑ OKM-12106 [M]	Um, Um, Um, Um, Um, Um	1964	10.00	20.00	40.00
❑ OKM-12110 [M]	Major's Greatest Hits	1965	7.50	15.00	30.00
❑ OKS-14105 [S]	The Monkey Time	1963	12.50	25.00	50.00
❑ OKS-14106 [S]	Um, Um, Um, Um, Um, Um	1964	12.50	25.00	50.00
❑ OKS-14110 [S]	Major's Greatest Hits	1965	10.00	20.00	40.00

SOUL

Number	Title (A Side/B Side)	Yr	VG	VG+	NM
❑ S7-751	Now Arriving	1978	3.00	6.00	12.00

LANCELOT LINK AND THE EVOLUTION REVOLUTION
ABC

Number	Title (A Side/B Side)	Yr	VG	VG+	NM
❑ S-715	Lancelot Link and the Evolution Revolution	1970	10.00	20.00	40.00

LANCERS, THE
CORAL

Number	Title (A Side/B Side)	Yr	VG	VG+	NM
❑ CRL 57100 [M]	Dixieland Ball	1957	6.25	12.50	25.00

IMPERIAL

Number	Title (A Side/B Side)	Yr	VG	VG+	NM
❑ LP-9075 [M]	Concert in Contrasts	1959	7.50	15.00	30.00
❑ LP-12023 [S]	Concert in Contrasts	1959	10.00	20.00	40.00

TREND

Number	Title (A Side/B Side)	Yr	VG	VG+	NM
❑ TL-1009 [10]	The Lancers	1954	10.00	20.00	40.00

LANCHESTER, ELSA
HIFI

Number	Title (A Side/B Side)	Yr	VG	VG+	NM
❑ 405 [M]	Songs for a Smoke-Filled Room	1957	5.00	10.00	20.00
❑ 406 [M]	Songs for a Shuttered Parlor	1958	5.00	10.00	20.00

VERVE

Number	Title (A Side/B Side)	Yr	VG	VG+	NM
❑ MGV-15015 [M]	Cockney London	1960	7.50	15.00	30.00
❑ MGV-15024 [M]	Herself	1962	7.50	15.00	30.00

LAND, HAROLD
CONTEMPORARY

Number	Title (A Side/B Side)	Yr	VG	VG+	NM
❑ C-3550 [M]	Harold in the Land of Hi-Fi	1958	20.00	40.00	80.00
❑ M-3550 [M]	Grooveyard	1959	15.00	30.00	60.00
—Reissue with new title					

Number	Title (A Side/B Side)	Yr	VG	VG+	NM
❑ M-3619 [M]	The Fox	1965	5.00	10.00	20.00
❑ S-7550 [S]	Grooveyard	1959	12.50	25.00	50.00
❑ S-7619 [S]	The Fox	1965	6.25	12.50	25.00

HIFI

Number	Title (A Side/B Side)	Yr	VG	VG+	NM
❑ J-612 [M]	The Fox	1960	15.00	30.00	60.00
❑ SJ-612 [S]	The Fox	1960	20.00	40.00	80.00

IMPERIAL

Number	Title (A Side/B Side)	Yr	VG	VG+	NM
❑ LP-9247 [M]	Jazz Impressions of Folk Music	1963	6.25	12.50	25.00
❑ LP-12247 [S]	Jazz Impressions of Folk Music	1963	7.50	15.00	30.00

JAZZLAND

Number	Title (A Side/B Side)	Yr	VG	VG+	NM
❑ JLP-20 [M]	West Coast Blues!	1960	10.00	20.00	40.00
❑ JLP-33 [M]	Eastward Ho! Harold Land in New York	1961	10.00	20.00	40.00
❑ JLP-920 [S]	West Coast Blues!	1960	12.50	25.00	50.00
❑ JLP-933 [S]	Eastward Ho! Harold Land in New York	1961	12.50	25.00	50.00

LANDSLIDE
CAPITOL

Number	Title (A Side/B Side)	Yr	VG	VG+	NM
❑ ST-11006	Two-Sided Fantasy	1972	10.00	20.00	40.00

LANE, ABBE
MERCURY

Number	Title (A Side/B Side)	Yr	VG	VG+	NM
❑ MG-20643 [M]	Abbe Lane with Xavier Cugat and His Orchestra	1961	6.25	12.50	25.00
❑ MG-20930 [M]	The Many Sides of Abbe Lane	1964	5.00	10.00	20.00
❑ SR-60643 [S]	Abbe Lane with Xavier Cugat and His Orchestra	1961	7.50	15.00	30.00
❑ SR-60930 [S]	The Many Sides of Abbe Lane	1964	6.25	12.50	25.00

RCA VICTOR

Number	Title (A Side/B Side)	Yr	VG	VG+	NM
❑ LPM-1554 [M]	Be Mine Tonight	1957	7.50	15.00	30.00
❑ LSP-1554 [S]	Be Mine Tonight	1958	10.00	20.00	40.00
❑ LPM-1688 [M]	The Lady in Red	1958	7.50	15.00	30.00
❑ LSP-1688 [S]	The Lady in Red	1958	10.00	20.00	40.00

LANE, CRISTY
ARRIVAL

Number	Title (A Side/B Side)	Yr	VG	VG+	NM
❑ NU 9640	One Day at a Time: 14 Songs of Inspiration and Harmony	1983	2.50	5.00	10.00

LANE

Number	Title (A Side/B Side)	Yr	VG	VG+	NM
❑ LPS-101	Cristy Lane Salutes the G.I.'s of Vietnam	197?	6.25	12.50	25.00

LIBERTY

Number	Title (A Side/B Side)	Yr	VG	VG+	NM
❑ LT-978	Simple Little Words	1981	2.00	4.00	8.00
—Reissue of United Artists 978					
❑ LT-1023	Ask Me to Dance	1981	2.00	4.00	8.00
—Reissue of United Artists 1023					
❑ LT-1083	I Have a Dream	1981	2.00	4.00	8.00
❑ LN-10226	Christmas with Cristy	198?	2.50	5.00	10.00
❑ LN-10239	Amazing Grace	198?	—	3.00	6.00
—Budget-line reissue					
❑ LN-10306	Footprints in the Sand	1986	—	3.00	6.00
—Budget-line reissue					
❑ LN-10309	Cristy Lane At Her Best	1986	—	3.00	6.00
—Budget-line reissue					
❑ LT-51112	Fragile — Handle with Care	1981	2.00	4.00	8.00
❑ LT-51117	Amazing Grace	1982	2.00	4.00	8.00
❑ LT-51137	Here's to Us	1982	2.00	4.00	8.00
❑ LT-51148	Footprints in the Sand	1983	2.00	4.00	8.00
❑ LT-51153	Cristy Lane At Her Best	1984	2.00	4.00	8.00

LS

Number	Title (A Side/B Side)	Yr	VG	VG+	NM
❑ 1001	Easy to Love	198?	2.50	5.00	10.00
❑ 1987	Christmas Gold	1987	2.50	5.00	10.00
❑ 2002	Country Classics Vol. 2	198?	2.50	5.00	10.00
❑ 2003	Country Classics Vol. 3	198?	2.50	5.00	10.00
❑ 8027	Cristy Lane Is the Name	1978	3.00	6.00	12.00
❑ 8028	Love Lies	1979	3.00	6.00	12.00
❑ SLL-8334	The Sweetest Voice This Side of Heaven	198?	2.50	5.00	10.00
❑ SLL-8358	Christmas Is the Man from Galilee	1983	2.50	5.00	10.00
❑ SLL-8385	Greatest Hits	198?	2.50	5.00	10.00
❑ SLL-8386	One Day at a Time	198?	2.50	5.00	10.00
❑ 9227	Cristy Lane Salutes the G.I.'s of Vietnam	198?	2.50	5.00	10.00

RIVERSONG

Number	Title (A Side/B Side)	Yr	VG	VG+	NM
❑ 2413	14 Golden Hymns	198?	2.50	5.00	10.00

SUFFOLK MARKETING

Number	Title (A Side/B Side)	Yr	VG	VG+	NM
❑ SLL-8289	One Day at a Time	198?	2.50	5.00	10.00

UNITED ARTISTS

Number	Title (A Side/B Side)	Yr	VG	VG+	NM
❑ UA-LA978-H	Simple Little Words	1979	2.50	5.00	10.00
❑ LT-1023	Ask Me to Dance	1980	2.50	5.00	10.00

LANEGAN, MARK
Also see SCREAMING TREES.
SUB POP

Number	Title (A Side/B Side)	Yr	VG	VG+	NM
❑ SP 61	The Winding Sheet	1990	2.50	5.00	10.00
—Black vinyl. Among the backing musicians are Kurt Cobain and Krist Novoselic of NIRVANA.					
❑ SP 61	The Winding Sheet	1990	6.25	12.50	25.00
—First 1,000 on red vinyl					
❑ SP 132	Whisky for the Holy Ghost	1994	3.00	6.00	12.00
❑ SP 419	Scraps at Midnight	1998	3.00	6.00	12.00

LANG, K.D.
BUMSTEAD

Number	Title (A Side/B Side)	Yr	VG	VG+	NM
❑ BUM-842	A Truly Western Experience	1984	15.00	30.00	60.00
—Canadian import					
❑ BUM-862	A Truly Western Experience	1984	5.00	10.00	20.00
—Canadian import; reissue of Bumstead 842					

SIRE

Number	Title (A Side/B Side)	Yr	VG	VG+	NM
❑ PRO-A-3120 [DJ]	The Making of Shadowland	1988	6.25	12.50	25.00
❑ 25441	Angel with a Lariat	1987	2.50	5.00	10.00
❑ 25724	Shadowland	1988	2.50	5.00	10.00
❑ 25877	Absolute Torch and Twang	1989	2.50	5.00	10.00
❑ R 134567	Shadowland	1988	3.00	6.00	12.00
—BMG Direct Marketing edition					

Number	Title (A Side/B Side)	Yr	VG	VG+	NM
❏ R 160100	Angel with a Lariat	1987	3.00	6.00	12.00
—BMG Direct Marketing edition					

WARNER BROS.

Number	Title (A Side/B Side)	Yr	VG	VG+	NM
❏ 46034	All You Can Eat	1995	2.50	5.00	10.00

LANG, RONNIE
TOPS

Number	Title (A Side/B Side)	Yr	VG	VG+	NM
❏ L-1521 [M]	Modern Jazz	1958	6.25	12.50	25.00

LANGDON, DORY
VERVE

Number	Title (A Side/B Side)	Yr	VG	VG+	NM
❏ MGV-2101 [M]	Leprechauns Are Upon Me	1957	10.00	20.00	40.00

LANGDON, JIM
CUCA

Number	Title (A Side/B Side)	Yr	VG	VG+	NM
❏ 1100 [M]	Jim Langdon Trio	1965	5.00	10.00	20.00

LANGNER SISTERS, THE
STUDIO CITY

Number	Title (A Side/B Side)	Yr	VG	VG+	NM
❏ 9011	The Langner Sisters	1966	7.50	15.00	30.00
❏ 9012	It's the Country Life for Me	1967	7.50	15.00	30.00

LANIN, LESTER
AUDIO FIDELITY

Number	Title (A Side/B Side)	Yr	VG	VG+	NM
❏ AFLP-2180 [M]	Thoroughly Modern	1968	3.75	7.50	15.00
❏ AFSD-6180 [S]	Thoroughly Modern	1968	3.00	6.00	12.00

EPIC

Number	Title (A Side/B Side)	Yr	VG	VG+	NM
❏ BSN 146 [(2)S]	The Dance Album	1964	5.00	10.00	20.00
❏ BN 501 [S]	Lester Lanin Goes to College	1959	5.00	10.00	20.00
❏ BN 505 [S]	Lester Lanin at the Tiffany Ball	1959	5.00	10.00	20.00
❏ BN 516 [S]	Cocktail Dancing	1959	5.00	10.00	20.00
❏ BN 517 [S]	Have Band, Will Travel	1959	5.00	10.00	20.00
❏ BN 547 [S]	Christmas Dance Party (Volume 9)	1959	5.00	10.00	20.00
❏ BN 556 [S]	Dance to the Lester Lanin Beat	1960	5.00	10.00	20.00
❏ BN 570 [S]	High Society	1961	3.75	7.50	15.00
❏ BN 620 [S]	Twistin' in High Society!	1961	3.75	7.50	15.00
❏ BN 628 [R]	Lester Lanin and His Orchestra	1962	3.00	6.00	12.00
❏ BN 633 [R]	Dance to the Music of Lester Lanin	1962	3.00	6.00	12.00
❏ LN 3242 [M]	Lester Lanin and His Orchestra	1956	3.75	7.50	15.00
❏ LN 3340 [M]	Dance to the Music of Lester Lanin	1957	3.75	7.50	15.00
❏ LN 3410 [M]	Lester Lanin at the Tiffany Ball	1957	3.75	7.50	15.00
❏ LN 3474 [M]	Lester Lanin Goes to College	1958	3.75	7.50	15.00
❏ LN 3525 [M]	Have Band, Will Travel	1958	3.75	7.50	15.00
❏ LN 3531 [M]	Cocktail Dancing	1959	3.75	7.50	15.00
❏ LN 3617 [M]	Christmas Dance Party (Volume 9)	1959	3.75	7.50	15.00
❏ LN 3656 [M]	Dance to the Lester Lanin Beat	1960	3.75	7.50	15.00
❏ LN 3699 [M]	High Society	1961	3.00	6.00	12.00
❏ LN 3825 [M]	Twistin' in High Society!	1961	3.00	6.00	12.00
❏ SN 6046 [(2)M]	The Dance Album	1964	3.75	7.50	15.00
❏ LN 24016 [M]	Dancing Theatre Party	1962	3.00	6.00	12.00
❏ LN 24105 [M]	Richard Rogers Hits	1964	3.00	6.00	12.00
❏ LN 24317 [M]	Cole Porter's Greatest Hits	1967	3.00	6.00	12.00
❏ BN 26016 [S]	Dancing Theatre Party	1962	3.75	7.50	15.00
❏ BN 26105 [S]	Richard Rogers Hits	1964	3.75	7.50	15.00
❏ BN 26317 [S]	Cole Porter's Greatest Hits	1967	3.00	6.00	12.00

HARMONY

Number	Title (A Side/B Side)	Yr	VG	VG+	NM
❏ HS 11262	Everybody Dance	1968	2.50	5.00	10.00

HINDSIGHT

Number	Title (A Side/B Side)	Yr	VG	VG+	NM
❏ HSR-210	Dance Instrumentals: 1960-1962	198?	2.00	4.00	8.00

METROMEDIA

Number	Title (A Side/B Side)	Yr	VG	VG+	NM
❏ MD-1006	Narrowing the Generation Gap	1969	3.00	6.00	12.00

PHILIPS

Number	Title (A Side/B Side)	Yr	VG	VG+	NM
❏ PHM 200132 [M]	Lester Lanin Plays for Dancing	1964	2.50	5.00	10.00
❏ PHM 200145 [M]	Dancing at the Discotheque	1964	2.50	5.00	10.00
❏ PHM 200165 [M]	I Had a Ball	1965	2.50	5.00	10.00
❏ PHM 200181 [M]	Hits for Dancing	1965	2.50	5.00	10.00
❏ PHM 200192 [M]	Lester Lanin at the Country Club	1966	2.50	5.00	10.00
❏ PHM 200211 [M]	Forty Beatles Hits	1966	3.00	6.00	12.00
❏ PHS 600132 [S]	Lester Lanin Plays for Dancing	1964	3.00	6.00	12.00
❏ PHS 600145 [S]	Dancing at the Discotheque	1964	3.00	6.00	12.00
❏ PHS 600165 [S]	I Had a Ball	1965	3.00	6.00	12.00
❏ PHS 600181 [S]	Hits for Dancing	1965	3.00	6.00	12.00
❏ PHS 600192 [S]	Lester Lanin at the Country Club	1966	3.00	6.00	12.00
❏ PHS 600211 [S]	Forty Beatles Hits	1966	3.75	7.50	15.00

LANZA, MARIO
PAIR

Number	Title (A Side/B Side)	Yr	VG	VG+	NM
❏ PDL2-1059 [(2)]	The Voice of the Century	1986	3.00	6.00	12.00

PICKWICK

Number	Title (A Side/B Side)	Yr	VG	VG+	NM
❏ CAS-777(e) [R]	Christmas Hymns and Carols	1977	2.00	4.00	8.00
—Same contents as RCA Camden CAS-777(e)					

RCA CAMDEN

Number	Title (A Side/B Side)	Yr	VG	VG+	NM
❏ CAL-450 [M]	You Do Something to Me	195?	3.75	7.50	15.00
❏ CAS-450(e) [R]	You Do Something to Me	195?	3.00	6.00	12.00
❏ CAL-777 [M]	Christmas Hymns and Carols	196?	3.75	7.50	15.00
❏ CAS-777(e) [R]	Christmas Hymns and Carols	196?	3.00	6.00	12.00

RCA RED SEAL

Number	Title (A Side/B Side)	Yr	VG	VG+	NM
❏ ARL1-0134	Lanza Sings Caruso	1973	2.50	5.00	10.00
❏ CRL1-1750	A Legendary Performer	1976	2.50	5.00	10.00
❏ ANL1-2874	Pure Gold	1978	2.50	5.00	10.00
❏ CRM5-4158 [(5)]	The Mario Lanza Collection	1981	15.00	30.00	60.00
❏ ARL1-4405	The Great Caruso	198?	2.00	4.00	8.00
❏ VCS-6192 [(3)]	Mario Lanza's Greatest Hits	1970	6.25	12.50	25.00
❏ VCS-7073 [(2)]	Opera's Greatest Hits	1971	4.50	9.00	18.00

RCA VICTOR RED SEAL

Number	Title (A Side/B Side)	Yr	VG	VG+	NM
❏ LM-1127 [M]	The Great Caruso	195?	10.00	20.00	40.00
❏ LSC-1127(e) [R]	The Great Caruso	196?	3.00	6.00	12.00
❏ LM-1188 [M]	Love Songs and a Neapolitan Serenade	195?	10.00	20.00	40.00
❏ LSC-1188(e) [R]	Love Songs and a Neapolitan Serenade	196?	3.00	6.00	12.00
❏ LM 1837 [M]	Mario Lanza Sings the Hit Songs from "The Student Prince" and Other Great Musical Comedies	1955	10.00	20.00	40.00
❏ LSC 1837(e) [R]	Mario Lanza Sings the Hit Songs from "The Student Prince" and Other Great Musical Comedies	196?	3.00	6.00	12.00
❏ LM-1860 [M]	"A Kiss" and Other Love Songs	1955	10.00	20.00	40.00
❏ LSC-1860(e) [R]	"A Kiss" and Other Love Songs	196?	3.00	6.00	12.00
❏ LM-1927 [M]	The Touch of Your Hand	1955	10.00	20.00	40.00
❏ LSC-1927(e) [R]	The Touch of Your Hand	196?	3.00	6.00	12.00
❏ LM-1943 [M]	Magic Mario	1955	10.00	20.00	40.00
❏ LM-1996 [M]	Serenade	1956	10.00	20.00	40.00
❏ LM-2070 [M]	Lanza on Broadway	1956	7.50	15.00	30.00
❏ LSC-2070(e) [R]	Lanza on Broadway	196?	3.00	6.00	12.00
❏ LM-2090 [M]	Cavalcade of Show Tunes	1957	7.50	15.00	30.00
❏ LSC-2090(e) [R]	Cavalcade of Show Tunes	196?	3.00	6.00	12.00
❏ LM-2211 [M]	Seven Hills of Rome	1958	7.50	15.00	30.00
❏ LM-2331 [M]	Mario	1959	5.00	10.00	20.00
❏ LSC-2331 [S]	Mario!	1959	7.50	15.00	30.00
❏ LM-2333 [M]	Lanza Sings Christmas Carols	1959	3.75	7.50	15.00
❏ LSC-2333 [S]	Lanza Sings Christmas Carols	1959	5.00	10.00	20.00
—Original copies have "shaded dog" on labels					
❏ LM-2338 [M]	For the First Time	1959	3.75	7.50	15.00
❏ LSC-2338 [S]	For the First Time	1959	5.00	10.00	20.00
❏ LM-2339 [M]	The Student Prince	1959	3.75	7.50	15.00
❏ LSC-2339 [S]	The Student Prince	1959	5.00	10.00	20.00
❏ LM-2393 [M]	Mario Lanza Sings Caruso Favorites	1960	3.75	7.50	15.00
❏ LSC-2393 [S]	Mario Lanza Sings Caruso Favorites	1960	5.00	10.00	20.00
❏ LM-2422 [M]	Double Feature — Mario Lanza	1960	5.00	10.00	20.00
❏ LM-2440 [M]	The Desert Song	1960	3.75	7.50	15.00
❏ LSC-2440 [S]	The Desert Song	1960	5.00	10.00	20.00
❏ LM-2454 [M]	A Mario Lanza Program	1960	3.75	7.50	15.00
❏ LSC-2454 [S]	A Mario Lanza Program	1960	5.00	10.00	20.00
❏ LM-2509 [M]	The Vagabond King	1961	3.75	7.50	15.00
❏ LSC-2509 [S]	The Vagabond King	1961	5.00	10.00	20.00
❏ LM-2607 [M]	I'll Walk with God	1962	5.00	10.00	20.00
❏ LSC-2607(e) [R]	I'll Walk with God	1962	3.00	6.00	12.00
❏ LM-2720 [M]	I'll See You in My Dreams	1964	3.00	6.00	12.00
❏ LSC-2720 [S]	I'll See You in My Dreams	1964	3.75	7.50	15.00
❏ LM-2748 [M]	The Best of Mario Lanza	1964	3.00	6.00	12.00
❏ LSC-2748 [S]	The Best of Mario Lanza	1964	3.75	7.50	15.00
❏ LM-2790 [M]	If You Are But a Dream	196?	3.00	6.00	12.00
❏ LSC-2790 [S]	If You Are But a Dream	196?	3.75	7.50	15.00
❏ LM-2932 [M]	His Favorite Arias	196?	3.00	6.00	12.00
❏ LSC-2932 [S]	His Favorite Arias	196?	3.75	7.50	15.00
❏ LM-2998 [M]	The Best of Mario Lanza, Volume 2	1968	5.00	10.00	20.00
❏ LSC-2998 [S]	The Best of Mario Lanza, Volume 2	1968	3.75	7.50	15.00
❏ LSC-3049	Younger Than Springtime	1968	3.00	6.00	12.00
❏ LSC-3101	Mario Lanza in Opera	1969	3.75	7.50	15.00
❏ LSC-3102	Mario Lanza Memories	1969	3.75	7.50	15.00
❏ LSC-3103	Mario Lanza…Speak to Me of Love	1969	3.75	7.50	15.00
❏ LSC-3216	The Student Prince	1971	3.00	6.00	12.00
❏ LSC-3289	Be My Love	1972	3.00	6.00	12.00

LAPORTA, JOHN
DEBUT

Number	Title (A Side/B Side)	Yr	VG	VG+	NM
❏ DLP-10 [10]	The John LaPorta Quintet	1954	50.00	100.00	200.00
❏ DEB-122 [M]	Three Moods	1955	37.50	75.00	150.00

EVEREST

Number	Title (A Side/B Side)	Yr	VG	VG+	NM
❏ SDBR-1037 [S]	The Most Minor	1959	10.00	20.00	40.00
❏ LPBR-5037 [M]	The Most Minor	1959	7.50	15.00	30.00

FANTASY

Number	Title (A Side/B Side)	Yr	VG	VG+	NM
❏ 3228 [M]	Conceptions	1956	7.50	15.00	30.00
—Black vinyl					
❏ 3228 [M]	Conceptions	1956	15.00	30.00	60.00
—Red vinyl					
❏ 3237 [M]	South American Brothers	1956	7.50	15.00	30.00
—Black vinyl					
❏ 3237 [M]	South American Brothers	1956	15.00	30.00	60.00
—Red vinyl					
❏ 3248 [M]	The Clarinet Artistry of John LaPorta	1957	7.50	15.00	30.00
—Black vinyl					
❏ 3248 [M]	The Clarinet Artistry of John LaPorta	1957	15.00	30.00	60.00
—Red vinyl					

MUSIC MINUS ONE

Number	Title (A Side/B Side)	Yr	VG	VG+	NM
❏ 4003 [M]	Eight Men In Search of a Drummer	1961	6.25	12.50	25.00

LAREDO, JAIME
RCA VICTOR RED SEAL

Number	Title (A Side/B Side)	Yr	VG	VG+	NM
❏ LSC-2373 [S]	Presenting Jaime Laredo	1960	10.00	20.00	40.00
—Original with "shaded dog" label					
❏ LSC-2414 [S]	Brahms: Violin Sonata No. 3; Bach: Partita No. 3	1960	20.00	40.00	80.00
—Original with "shaded dog" label					
❏ LSC-2472 [S]	Bruch: Violin Concerto No. 1; Mozart: Violin Concerto No. 3	1961	10.00	20.00	40.00
—Original with "shaded dog" label					

LARKIN, BILLY
AURA

Number	Title (A Side/B Side)	Yr	VG	VG+	NM
❏ 23002 [S]	Pigmy	1964	6.25	12.50	25.00
—As "The Delegates"					
❏ 83002 [M]	Pigmy	1964	5.00	10.00	20.00
—As "The Delegates"					

WORLD PACIFIC

Number	Title (A Side/B Side)	Yr	VG	VG+	NM
❏ WP-1837 [M]	Hole in the Wall	1966	5.00	10.00	20.00
❏ WP-1843 [M]	Ain't That a Groove	1966	5.00	10.00	20.00
❏ WP-1850 [M]	Hold On	1967	5.00	10.00	20.00
❏ WPS-21837 [S]	Hole in the Wall	1966	6.25	12.50	25.00
❏ WPS-21843 [S]	Ain't That a Groove	1966	6.25	12.50	25.00
❏ WPS-21850 [S]	Hold On	1967	6.25	12.50	25.00

LARKINS, ELLIS
DECCA

Number	Title (A Side/B Side)	Yr	VG	VG+	NM
❏ DL 5391 [10]	Blues in the Night	1952	12.50	25.00	50.00
❏ DL 8303 [M]	Manhattan at Midnight	1956	10.00	20.00	40.00

Number	Title (A Side/B Side)	Yr	VG	VG+	NM
☐ DL 9205 [M]	The Soft Touch	1958	7.50	15.00	30.00
☐ DL 9211 [M]	Blue and Sentimental	1958	7.50	15.00	30.00
☐ DL 79205 [S]	The Soft Touch	1958	6.25	12.50	25.00
☐ DL 79211 [S]	Blue and Sentimental	1958	6.25	12.50	25.00
STORYVILLE					
☐ STLP-316 [10]	Perfume and Rain	1955	20.00	40.00	80.00
☐ STLP-913 [M]	Do Nothin' Till You Hear from Me	1956	12.50	25.00	50.00

LARKINS, ELLIS/LEE WILEY
STORYVILLE

Number	Title (A Side/B Side)	Yr	VG	VG+	NM
☐ STLP-911 [M]	Duologue	1956	15.00	30.00	60.00

LARKS, THE (1)
COLLECTABLES

Number	Title (A Side/B Side)	Yr	VG	VG+	NM
☐ COL-5176	Golden Classics: The Jerk	198?	2.50	5.00	10.00
MONEY					
☐ LP-1102 [M]	The Jerk	1965	10.00	20.00	40.00
☐ ST-1102 [S]	The Jerk	1965	12.50	25.00	50.00
☐ LP-1107 [M]	Soul Kaleidoscope	1966	10.00	20.00	40.00
☐ ST-1107 [S]	Soul Kaleidoscope	1966	12.50	25.00	50.00
☐ LP-1110 [M]	Superslick	1967	10.00	20.00	40.00
☐ ST-1110 [S]	Superslick	1967	12.50	25.00	50.00

LAROCA, PETE
BLUE NOTE

Number	Title (A Side/B Side)	Yr	VG	VG+	NM
☐ BLP-4205 [M]	Basra	1965	7.50	15.00	30.00
☐ BST-84205 [S]	Basra	1965	10.00	20.00	40.00

—With "New York, USA" address on label

LAROCCA, NICK
SOUTHLAND

Number	Title (A Side/B Side)	Yr	VG	VG+	NM
☐ 230 [M]	Nick LaRocca and His Dixieland Band	196?	5.00	10.00	20.00

LAROSA, JULIUS
AUDIOPHILE

Number	Title (A Side/B Side)	Yr	VG	VG+	NM
☐ AP-190	It's a Wrap!	1985	3.00	6.00	12.00
CADENCE					
☐ CLP 1007 [M]	Julius LaRosa (Julie's Best)	1955	10.00	20.00	40.00
FORUM					
☐ F-16012 [M]	Just Say I Love Her	1960	3.75	7.50	15.00
☐ FS-16012 [S]	Just Say I Love Her	1960	5.00	10.00	20.00
KAPP					
☐ KL-1245 [M]	The New Julie LaRosa	1961	3.75	7.50	15.00
☐ KS-3245 [S]	The New Julie LaRosa	1961	5.00	10.00	20.00
METROMEDIA					
☐ MD-1036	Words	1971	3.00	6.00	12.00
MGM					
☐ E-4398 [M]	You're Gonna Hear From Me	1966	3.00	6.00	12.00
☐ SE-4398 [S]	You're Gonna Hear From Me	1966	3.75	7.50	15.00
☐ E-4437 [M]	Hey Look Me Over	1967	3.00	6.00	12.00
☐ SE-4437 [S]	Hey Look Me Over	1967	3.75	7.50	15.00
RCA VICTOR					
☐ LPM-1299 [M]	Julius LaRosa	1956	10.00	20.00	40.00
ROULETTE					
☐ R 25054 [M]	Love Songs A LaRosa	1959	5.00	10.00	20.00
☐ SR 25054 [S]	Love Songs A LaRosa	1959	6.25	12.50	25.00
☐ R 25083 [M]	On the Sunny Side	1960	5.00	10.00	20.00
☐ SR 25083 [S]	On the Sunny Side	1960	6.25	12.50	25.00

LARRY AND HANK
PRESTIGE

Number	Title (A Side/B Side)	Yr	VG	VG+	NM
☐ PRLP-7472 [M]	The Blues/A New Generation	1965	5.00	10.00	20.00
☐ PRST-7472 [S]	The Blues/A New Generation	1965	6.25	12.50	25.00

LARRY AND LENORE
REQUEST

Number	Title (A Side/B Side)	Yr	VG	VG+	NM
☐ 10037 [M]	Traveling Guitars	1959	25.00	50.00	100.00

LASHA, PRINCE
CONTEMPORARY

Number	Title (A Side/B Side)	Yr	VG	VG+	NM
☐ M-3610 [M]	The Cry	1963	6.25	12.50	25.00
☐ S-7610 [S]	The Cry	1963	7.50	15.00	30.00
☐ S-7617	Firebirds	1968	6.25	12.50	25.00

LAST CALL OF SHILOH, THE
LAST CALL

Number	Title (A Side/B Side)	Yr	VG	VG+	NM
☐ 5136	The Last Call	196?	50.00	100.00	200.00

LAST EXIT
ENEMY

Number	Title (A Side/B Side)	Yr	VG	VG+	NM
☐ 88561-8176-1	Last Exit	1986	5.00	10.00	20.00

LAST POETS, THE
BLUE THUMB

Number	Title (A Side/B Side)	Yr	VG	VG+	NM
☐ BT-39	Chastisement	1972	7.50	15.00	30.00
☐ BT-52	At Last	1973	7.50	15.00	30.00
CASABLANCA					
☐ NBLP 7051	Delights of the Garden	1977	6.25	12.50	25.00
CELLULOID					
☐ 6101	The Last Poets	198?	2.50	5.00	10.00
☐ 6105	This Is Madness	198?	2.50	5.00	10.00
☐ 6108	Oh My People	198?	2.50	5.00	10.00
☐ 6136	Delights of the Garden	198?	2.50	5.00	10.00
COLLECTABLES					
☐ COL-6500	Right On!	198?	2.50	5.00	10.00
DOUGLAS					
☐ 3	The Last Poets	1970	12.50	25.00	50.00
☐ Z 30583	This Is Madness	1971	12.50	25.00	50.00
☐ Z 30811	The Last Poets	1971	10.00	20.00	40.00

JUGGERNAUT

Number	Title (A Side/B Side)	Yr	VG	VG+	NM
☐ 8802	Right On!	1971	12.50	25.00	50.00

—As "The Original Last Poets"

LATEEF, YUSEF
ARGO

Number	Title (A Side/B Side)	Yr	VG	VG+	NM
☐ LP-634 [M]	Live at Cranbrook	1959	7.50	15.00	30.00
CHARLIE PARKER					
☐ PLP-814 [M]	Lost in Sound	1962	6.25	12.50	25.00
☐ PLP-814S [S]	Lost in Sound	1962	7.50	15.00	30.00
DELMARK					
☐ DL-407 [M]	Yusef!	1965	5.00	10.00	20.00
☐ DS-407 [S]	Yusef!	1965	6.25	12.50	25.00
IMPULSE!					
☐ A-56 [M]	Jazz Around the World	1963	6.25	12.50	25.00
☐ AS-56 [S]	Jazz Around the World	1963	7.50	15.00	30.00
☐ A-69 [M]	Live at Pep's	1964	6.25	12.50	25.00
☐ AS-69 [S]	Live at Pep's	1964	7.50	15.00	30.00
☐ A-84 [M]	1984	1965	6.25	12.50	25.00
☐ AS-84 [S]	1984	1965	7.50	15.00	30.00
☐ A-92 [M]	Psychicemotus	1966	6.25	12.50	25.00
☐ AS-92 [S]	Psychicemotus	1966	7.50	15.00	30.00
☐ A-9117 [M]	A Flat, G Flat and C	1966	6.25	12.50	25.00
☐ AS-9117 [S]	A Flat, G Flat and C	1966	7.50	15.00	30.00
☐ A-9125 [M]	The Golden Flute	1966	6.25	12.50	25.00
☐ AS-9125 [S]	The Golden Flute	1966	7.50	15.00	30.00
MOODSVILLE					
☐ MVLP-22 [M]	Eastern Sounds	1961	10.00	20.00	40.00
—Green label, silver print					
☐ MVST-22 [S]	Eastern Sounds	1961	12.50	25.00	50.00
—Green label, silver print					
NEW JAZZ					
☐ NJLP-8218 [M]	Other Sounds	1959	12.50	25.00	50.00
—Purple label					
☐ NJLP-8218 [M]	Other Sounds	1965	6.25	12.50	25.00
—Blue label, trident logo at right					
☐ NJLP-8234 [M]	Cry! Tender	1960	12.50	25.00	50.00
—Purple label					
☐ NJLP-8234 [M]	Cry! Tender	1965	6.25	12.50	25.00
—Blue label, trident logo at right					
☐ NJLP-8261 [M]	The Sounds of Yusef	1961	12.50	25.00	50.00
—Reissue of Prestige 7122; purple label					
☐ NJLP-8261 [M]	The Sounds of Yusef	1965	6.25	12.50	25.00
—Blue label, trident logo at right					
☐ NJLP-8272 [M]	Into Something	1962	12.50	25.00	50.00
—Purple label					
☐ NJLP-8272 [M]	Into Something	1965	6.25	12.50	25.00
—Blue label, trident logo at right					
PRESTIGE					
☐ PRLP-7122 [M]	The Sounds of Yusef	1957	25.00	50.00	100.00
—Yellow label					
☐ PRLP-7319 [M]	Eastern Sounds	1964	6.25	12.50	25.00
☐ PRST-7319 [S]	Eastern Sounds	1964	6.25	12.50	25.00
—Reissue of Moodsville 22					
☐ PRLP-7398 [M]	The Sounds of Yusef Lateef	1966	5.00	10.00	20.00
☐ PRST-7398 [S]	The Sounds of Yusef Lateef	1966	6.25	12.50	25.00
☐ PRLP-7447 [M]	Yusef Lateef Plays for Lovers	1967	6.25	12.50	25.00
☐ PRST-7447 [S]	Yusef Lateef Plays for Lovers	1967	5.00	10.00	20.00
RIVERSIDE					
☐ RLP 12-325 [M]	Three Faces of Yusef Lateef	1960	10.00	20.00	40.00
☐ RLP-337 [M]	The Centaur and the Phoenix	1960	10.00	20.00	40.00
☐ RLP-1176 [S]	Three Faces of Yusef Lateef	1960	10.00	20.00	40.00
☐ RLP-9337 [S]	The Centaur and the Phoenix	1960	10.00	20.00	40.00
SAVOY					
☐ MG-12103 [M]	Jazz Mood	1957	12.50	25.00	50.00
☐ MG-12109 [M]	Jazz for the Thinker	1957	12.50	25.00	50.00
☐ MG-12117 [M]	Prayer to the East	1957	12.50	25.00	50.00
☐ MG-12120 [M]	Jazz and the Sounds of Nature	1958	12.50	25.00	50.00
☐ MG-12139 [M]	The Dreamer	1958	12.50	25.00	50.00
☐ MG-12140 [M]	The Fabric of Jazz	1958	12.50	25.00	50.00
☐ SR-13007 [S]	The Dreamer	1959	12.50	25.00	50.00
☐ SR-13008 [S]	The Fabric of Jazz	1959	12.50	25.00	50.00
VERVE					
☐ MGV-8217 [M]	Before Dawn	1958	25.00	50.00	100.00
☐ V-8217 [M]	Before Dawn	1961	6.25	12.50	25.00

LATIN ALL-STARS, THE
CROWN

Number	Title (A Side/B Side)	Yr	VG	VG+	NM
☐ CLP 5159 [M]	Jazz Heat-Bongo Beat	1959	6.25	12.50	25.00

LATIN JAZZ QUINTET, THE
NEW JAZZ

Number	Title (A Side/B Side)	Yr	VG	VG+	NM
☐ NJLP-8251 [M]	Caribe	1960	12.50	25.00	50.00
—Purple label					
☐ NJLP-8251 [M]	Caribe	1965	6.25	12.50	25.00
—Blue label, trident logo at right					
STATUS					
☐ ST-8321 [M]	Latin Soul	1965	10.00	20.00	40.00
TRU-SOUND					
☐ TRU-15003 [M]	Hot Sauce	1962	10.00	20.00	40.00
☐ TRU-15012 [M]	The Latin Jazz Quintet	1962	10.00	20.00	40.00
UNITED ARTISTS					
☐ UAL-4071 [M]	The Latin Jazz Quintet	1960	7.50	15.00	30.00
☐ UAS-5071 [S]	The Latin Jazz Quintet	1960	10.00	20.00	40.00

LATIN SOULS, THE
KAPP

Number	Title (A Side/B Side)	Yr	VG	VG+	NM
☐ KL-1524 [M]	Boo-Ga-Loo and Shing-a-Ling	1967	6.25	12.50	25.00
☐ KS-3524 [S]	Boo-Ga-Loo and Shing-a-Ling	1967	5.00	10.00	20.00
☐ KS-3553	Tigar Boo-Ga-Loo	1968	5.00	10.00	20.00

Number	Title (A Side/B Side)	Yr	VG	VG+	NM

LAUGHTON, CHARLES
CAPITOL
| ❏ STBO 1650 [(2)S] | The Story Teller | 1962 | 7.50 | 15.00 | 30.00 |
| ❏ TBO 1650 [(2)M] | The Story Teller | 1962 | 6.25 | 12.50 | 25.00 |
DECCA
| ❏ DLP 8010 [M] | A Christmas Carol/Mr. Pickwick's Christmas | 1955 | 5.00 | 10.00 | 20.00 |
—A-side read by Ronald Colman
| ❏ DL 8031 [M] | Readings from the Bible | 195? | 7.50 | 15.00 | 30.00 |
MCA
| ❏ 15010 | A Christmas Carol/Mr. Pickwick's Christmas | 1955 | 5.00 | 10.00 | 20.00 |
—A-side read by Ronald Colman; reissue of Decca LP

LAUPER, CYNDI
Also see BLUE ANGEL.
EPIC
| ❏ OE 44318 | A Night to Remember | 1989 | 3.00 | 6.00 | 12.00 |
PORTRAIT
❏ BFR 38930	She's So Unusual	1983	2.50	5.00	10.00
❏ 9R9 39610 [PD]	She's So Unusual	1984	7.50	15.00	30.00
❏ OR 40313	True Colors	1986	2.50	5.00	10.00

LAUREN, ROD
RCA VICTOR
| ❏ LPM-2176 [M] | I'm Rod Lauren | 1961 | 10.00 | 20.00 | 40.00 |
| ❏ LSP-2176 [S] | I'm Rod Lauren | 1961 | 12.50 | 25.00 | 50.00 |

LAURIE, ANNIE
AUDIO LAB
| ❏ AL-1510 [M] | It Hurts to Be in Love | 1959 | 75.00 | 150.00 | 300.00 |

LAURIE SISTERS, THE
RCA CAMDEN
| ❏ CAL-545 [M] | Hits of the Great Girl Groups | 1960 | 6.25 | 12.50 | 25.00 |
| ❏ CAS-545 [S] | Hits of the Great Girl Groups | 1960 | 7.50 | 15.00 | 30.00 |

LAWRENCE, ARNIE
EMBRYO
| ❏ SD 525 | Inside an Hour Glass | 1970 | 5.00 | 10.00 | 20.00 |
PROJECT 3
| ❏ PR-5011 | You're Gonna Hear From Me | 1967 | 5.00 | 10.00 | 20.00 |
| ❏ PR-5028 | Look Toward a Dream | 1968 | 5.00 | 10.00 | 20.00 |

LAWRENCE, BILL
TOPS
| ❏ L-1576 [M] | Bill Lawrence Sings I'm in the Mood for Love | 1957 | 5.00 | 10.00 | 20.00 |

LAWRENCE, CAROL
CAMEO
| ❏ C-1077 [M] | An Evening with Carol Lawrence | 1964 | 5.00 | 10.00 | 20.00 |
| ❏ SC-1077 [S] | An Evening with Carol Lawrence | 1964 | 6.25 | 12.50 | 25.00 |
CHANCELLOR
| ❏ CHL-5015 [M] | Tonight at 8:30 | 1960 | 5.00 | 10.00 | 20.00 |
| ❏ CHLS-5015 [S] | Tonight at 8:30 | 1960 | 7.50 | 15.00 | 30.00 |

LAWRENCE, EDDIE
CORAL
❏ CRL 57103 [M]	The Old Philosopher	1956	7.50	15.00	30.00
❏ CRL 57155 [M]	Eddie "The Old Philosopher" Lawrence	1957	7.50	15.00	30.00
❏ CRL 57203 [M]	The Kingdom of Eddie Lawrence	1958	7.50	15.00	30.00
❏ CRL 57371 [M]	The Side Splitting Personality of Eddie Lawrence	1961	7.50	15.00	30.00
❏ CRL 57411 [M]	Seven Characters In Search of Eddie Lawrence	1962	7.50	15.00	30.00
❏ CRL 757411 [S]	Seven Characters In Search of Eddie Lawrence	1962	10.00	20.00	40.00
EPIC
| ❏ LN 24149 [M] | Is That What's Bothering You Bunkie? | 1965 | 7.50 | 15.00 | 30.00 |
| ❏ BN 26149 [S] | Is That What's Bothering You Bunkie? | 1965 | 10.00 | 20.00 | 40.00 |
SIGNATURE
| ❏ SM-1003 [M] | The Garden of Eddie Lawrence | 1960 | 10.00 | 20.00 | 40.00 |

LAWRENCE, ELLIOT
DECCA
| ❏ DL 5274 [10] | College Prom | 1950 | 12.50 | 25.00 | 50.00 |
| ❏ DL 5353 [10] | Moonlight on the Campus | 1951 | 12.50 | 25.00 | 50.00 |
FANTASY
| ❏ 3206 [M] | Elliot Lawrence Plays Gerry Mulligan Arrangements | 1956 | 7.50 | 15.00 | 30.00 |
—Black vinyl, red label, non-flexible vinyl
| ❏ 3206 [M] | Elliot Lawrence Plays Gerry Mulligan Arrangements | 1956 | 12.50 | 25.00 | 50.00 |
—Red vinyl
| ❏ 3206 [M] | Elliot Lawrence Plays Gerry Mulligan Arrangements | 196? | 5.00 | 10.00 | 20.00 |
—Black vinyl, red label, flexible vinyl
| ❏ 3219 [M] | Elliot Lawrence Plays Tiny Kahn and Johnny Mandel Arrangements | 1956 | 7.50 | 15.00 | 30.00 |
—Black vinyl, red label, non-flexible vinyl
| ❏ 3219 [M] | Elliot Lawrence Plays Tiny Kahn and Johnny Mandel Arrangements | 1956 | 12.50 | 25.00 | 50.00 |
—Red vinyl
| ❏ 3219 [M] | Elliot Lawrence Plays Tiny Kahn and Johnny Mandel Arrangements | 196? | 5.00 | 10.00 | 20.00 |
—Black vinyl, red label, flexible vinyl
| ❏ 3226 [M] | Dream | 1956 | 7.50 | 15.00 | 30.00 |
—Black vinyl, red label, non-flexible vinyl
| ❏ 3226 [M] | Dream | 1956 | 12.50 | 25.00 | 50.00 |
—Red vinyl
| ❏ 3226 [M] | Dream | 196? | 5.00 | 10.00 | 20.00 |
—Black vinyl, red label, flexible vinyl
| ❏ 3236 [M] | Swinging at the Steel Pier | 1956 | 7.50 | 15.00 | 30.00 |
—Black vinyl, red label, non-flexible vinyl
| ❏ 3236 [M] | Swinging at the Steel Pier | 1956 | 12.50 | 25.00 | 50.00 |
—Red vinyl
| ❏ 3236 [M] | Swinging at the Steel Pier | 196? | 5.00 | 10.00 | 20.00 |
—Black vinyl, red label, flexible vinyl
| ❏ 3246 [M] | Elliot Lawrence Plays for Swinging Dancers | 1957 | 6.25 | 12.50 | 25.00 |
—Black vinyl, red label, non-flexible vinyl
| ❏ 3246 [M] | Elliot Lawrence Plays for Swinging Dancers | 1957 | 10.00 | 20.00 | 40.00 |
—Red vinyl
| ❏ 3261 [M] | Dream On — Dance On | 1958 | 6.25 | 12.50 | 25.00 |
—Black vinyl, red label, non-flexible vinyl
| ❏ 3261 [M] | Dream On — Dance On | 1958 | 10.00 | 20.00 | 40.00 |
—Red vinyl
| ❏ 3290 [M] | Big Band Sound | 1959 | 6.25 | 12.50 | 25.00 |
—Black vinyl, red label, non-flexible vinyl
| ❏ 3290 [M] | Big Band Sound | 1959 | 10.00 | 20.00 | 40.00 |
—Red vinyl
| ❏ 8002 [S] | Dream On — Dance On | 196? | 5.00 | 10.00 | 20.00 |
—Black vinyl, blue label, non-flexible vinyl
| ❏ 8002 [S] | Dream On — Dance On | 196? | 7.50 | 15.00 | 30.00 |
—Blue vinyl
| ❏ 8021 [S] | Elliot Lawrence Plays for Swinging Dancers | 196? | 5.00 | 10.00 | 20.00 |
—Black vinyl, blue label, non-flexible vinyl
| ❏ 8021 [S] | Elliot Lawrence Plays for Swinging Dancers | 196? | 7.50 | 15.00 | 30.00 |
—Blue vinyl
| ❏ 8031 [S] | Big Band Sound | 196? | 5.00 | 10.00 | 20.00 |
—Black vinyl, blue label, non-flexible vinyl
| ❏ 8031 [S] | Big Band Sound | 196? | 7.50 | 15.00 | 30.00 |
—Blue vinyl
JAZZTONE
| ❏ J-1279 [M] | Big Band Modern | 1958 | 10.00 | 20.00 | 40.00 |
MOBILE FIDELITY
| ❏ 2-229 [(2)] | The Music of Elliot Lawrence | 1995 | 7.50 | 15.00 | 30.00 |
—Audiophile vinyl
SESAC
| ❏ N-1153 [M] | Jump Steady | 1960 | 7.50 | 15.00 | 30.00 |
| ❏ SN-1153 [S] | Jump Steady | 1960 | 10.00 | 20.00 | 40.00 |
TOP RANK
| ❏ RM-304 [M] | Music for Trapping (Tender, That Is) | 1959 | 10.00 | 20.00 | 40.00 |
VIK
| ❏ LX-1113 [M] | Jazz Goes Broadway | 1958 | 10.00 | 20.00 | 40.00 |

LAWRENCE, GERTRUDE
DECCA
| ❏ DL 5418 [10] | Souvenir Album | 1952 | 12.50 | 25.00 | 50.00 |
| ❏ DL 8673 [M] | A Remembrance | 1958 | 7.50 | 15.00 | 30.00 |
—Black label, silver print

LAWRENCE, STEVE
ABC-PARAMOUNT
❏ 290 [M]	Swing Softly with Me	1959	6.25	12.50	25.00
❏ S-290 [S]	Swing Softly with Me	1959	7.50	15.00	30.00
❏ 392 [M]	The Best of Steve Lawrence	1960	5.00	10.00	20.00
❏ S-392 [S]	The Best of Steve Lawrence	1960	6.25	12.50	25.00
APPLAUSE
| ❏ 1001 | Take It On Home | 1981 | 2.50 | 5.00 | 10.00 |
COLUMBIA
❏ CL 1953 [M]	Winners!	1963	3.00	6.00	12.00
❏ CL 2121 [M]	Academy Award Losers	1964	3.00	6.00	12.00
❏ CL 2227 [M]	Everybody Knows	1964	3.00	6.00	12.00
❏ CL 2419 [M]	The Steve Lawrence Show	1965	3.00	6.00	12.00
❏ CL 2540 [M]	Of Love and… Sad Young Men	1966	3.00	6.00	12.00
❏ CS 8753 [S]	Winners!	1963	3.75	7.50	15.00
❏ CS 8921 [S]	Academy Award Losers	1964	3.75	7.50	15.00
❏ CS 9027 [S]	Everybody Knows	1964	3.75	7.50	15.00
❏ CS 9219 [S]	The Steve Lawrence Show	1965	3.75	7.50	15.00
❏ CS 9340 [S]	Of Love and… Sad Young Men	1966	3.75	7.50	15.00
❏ CS 9565	Greatest Hits	1968	3.00	6.00	12.00
❏ PC 9565	Greatest Hits	198?	2.00	4.00	8.00
—Reissue with new prefix
CORAL
❏ CRL 57050 [M]	About That Girl	1956	10.00	20.00	40.00
❏ CRL 57182 [M]	Songs by Steve Lawrence	1957	10.00	20.00	40.00
❏ CRL 57204 [M]	Here's Steve Lawrence	1958	10.00	20.00	40.00
❏ CRL 57268 [M]	All About Love	1959	7.50	15.00	30.00
❏ CRL 57434 [M]	Songs Everybody Knows	1963	6.25	12.50	25.00
❏ CRL 757268 [S]	All About Love	1959	10.00	20.00	40.00
❏ CRL 757434 [S]	Songs Everybody Knows	1963	7.50	15.00	30.00
HARMONY
❏ HS 11257	Moon River	196?	2.50	5.00	10.00
❏ HS 11327	Ramblin' Rose	1969	2.50	5.00	10.00
❏ HS 11397	Love Me	1970	2.50	5.00	10.00
KING
| ❏ 593 [M] | Steve Lawrence | 1959 | 20.00 | 40.00 | 80.00 |
MGM
| ❏ SE-4824 | Portrait | 1973 | 2.50 | 5.00 | 10.00 |
RCA VICTOR
| ❏ LSP-4167 | I've Gotta Be Me | 1969 | 3.00 | 6.00 | 12.00 |
| ❏ LSP-4347 | On a Clear Day | 1970 | 3.00 | 6.00 | 12.00 |
UNITED ARTISTS
❏ UAL-3098 [M]	The Steve Lawrence Sound	1960	5.00	10.00	20.00
❏ UAL-3114 [M]	Steve Lawrence Goes Latin	1960	5.00	10.00	20.00
❏ UAL-3150 [M]	Portrait of My Love	1961	5.00	10.00	20.00
❏ UAL-3190 [M]	The Very Best of Steve Lawrence	1962	5.00	10.00	20.00
❏ UAL-3265 [M]	People Will Say We're in Love	1963	5.00	10.00	20.00
❏ UAL-3368 [M]	Steve Lawrence Conquers Broadway	1964	3.75	7.50	15.00
❏ UAS-6098 [S]	The Steve Lawrence Sound	1960	6.25	12.50	25.00
❏ UAS-6114 [S]	Steve Lawrence Goes Latin	1960	6.25	12.50	25.00
❏ UAS-6150 [S]	Portrait of My Love	1961	6.25	12.50	25.00
❏ UAS-6190 [S]	The Very Best of Steve Lawrence	1962	6.25	12.50	25.00
❏ UAS-6265 [S]	People Will Say We're in Love	1963	6.25	12.50	25.00
❏ UAS-6368 [S]	Steve Lawrence Conquers Broadway	1964	5.00	10.00	20.00

L

Number	Title (A Side/B Side)	Yr	VG	VG+	NM
VOCALION					
❑ VL 3775 [M]	Here's Steve Lawrence	196?	3.00	6.00	12.00
❑ VL 73775 [R]	Here's Steve Lawrence	196?	2.50	5.00	10.00
❑ VL 73886	The More I See You	1970	2.50	5.00	10.00
LAWRENCE, STEVE, AND EYDIE GORME					
Also see each artist's individual listings.					
ABC					
❑ X-764 [(2)]	20 Golden Performances	1974	3.00	6.00	12.00
ABC-PARAMOUNT					
❑ 300 [M]	We Got Us	1960	5.00	10.00	20.00
❑ S-300 [S]	We Got Us	1960	6.25	12.50	25.00
❑ 311 [M]	Steve and Eydie Sing the Golden Hits	1960	5.00	10.00	20.00
❑ S-311 [S]	Steve and Eydie Sing the Golden Hits	1960	6.25	12.50	25.00
❑ 469 [M]	Our Best to You	1964	3.75	7.50	15.00
❑ S-469 [S]	Our Best to You	1964	5.00	10.00	20.00
CALENDAR					
❑ KOM-1001 [M]	Golden Rainbow	1968	7.50	15.00	30.00
❑ KOS-1001 [S]	Golden Rainbow	1968	10.00	20.00	40.00
COLUMBIA					
❑ CL 2021 [M]	Steve and Eydie at the Movies	1964	3.00	6.00	12.00
❑ CL 2262 [M]	That Holiday Feeling	1964	3.00	6.00	12.00
❑ CL 2636 [M]	Steve and Eydie Together On Broadway	1967	3.00	6.00	12.00
❑ CL 2730 [M]	Bonfa and Brazil	1968	3.75	7.50	15.00
❑ CS 8821 [S]	Steve and Eydie at the Movies	1964	3.75	7.50	15.00
❑ CS 9062 [S]	That Holiday Feeling	1964	3.75	7.50	15.00
❑ CS 9436 [S]	Steve and Eydie Together On Broadway	1967	3.75	7.50	15.00
❑ CS 9530 [S]	Bonfa and Brazil	1968	3.00	6.00	12.00
CORAL					
❑ CRL 57336 [M]	Steve and Eydie	1962	5.00	10.00	20.00
HARMONY					
❑ H 30292	Something's Gotta Give	1971	2.50	5.00	10.00
MATI-MOR					
❑ 8003	It's Us Again	196?	5.00	10.00	20.00
—Promotional item for Silvirkin shampoo					
MGM					
❑ SE-4803	The World of Steve Lawrence and Eydie Gorme	1972	2.50	5.00	10.00
❑ SE-4881	Feelin'	1973	2.50	5.00	10.00
RCA VICTOR					
❑ LSP-4107	Real True Lovin'	1969	3.00	6.00	12.00
❑ LSP-4115	What It Was, Was Love	1969	3.00	6.00	12.00
❑ LSP-4393	A Man and a Woman	1971	3.00	6.00	12.00
❑ VPS-6035 [(2)]	This Is Steve Lawrence and Eydie Gorme	1971	3.75	7.50	15.00
❑ VPS-6050 [(2)]	This Is Steve Lawrence and Eydie Gorme, Vol. 2	1972	3.75	7.50	15.00
STAGE 2					
❑ 712	Hallelujah	198?	2.50	5.00	10.00
UNITED ARTISTS					
❑ UAL-3191 [M]	The Very Best of Eydie and Steve	1962	5.00	10.00	20.00
❑ UAL-3268 [M]	Two on the Aisle	1963	5.00	10.00	20.00
❑ WWL-4509 [M]	Cozy	1961	5.00	10.00	20.00
❑ UAS-6191 [S]	The Very Best of Eydie and Steve	1962	6.25	12.50	25.00
❑ UAS-6268 [S]	Two on the Aisle	1963	6.25	12.50	25.00
❑ WWS-8509 [S]	Cozy	1961	6.25	12.50	25.00
VOCALION					
❑ VL 3825 [M]	Presenting Steve and Eydie	1968	3.00	6.00	12.00
❑ VL 73825 [R]	Presenting Steve and Eydie	1968	2.50	5.00	10.00
LAWS, HUBERT					
CTI					
❑ 1002	Crying Song	1970	5.00	10.00	20.00
LAWSON, DEE					
ROULETTE					
❑ R-52017 [M]	'Round Midnight	1958	7.50	15.00	30.00
❑ SR-52017 [S]	'Round Midnight	1958	10.00	20.00	40.00
LAWSON, YANK					
ABC-PARAMOUNT					
❑ ABCS-518 [S]	Big Yank Is Here	1965	5.00	10.00	20.00
❑ ABCS-567 [S]	Ole Dixie	1965	5.00	10.00	20.00
BRUNSWICK					
❑ BL 58035 [10]	Yank Lawson	1953	15.00	30.00	60.00
RIVERSIDE					
❑ RLP-2509 [10]	Yank Lawson's Dixieland Jazz	1954	20.00	40.00	80.00
LAWSON, YANK, AND BOB HAGGART					
DECCA					
❑ DL 5368 [10]	Lawson-Haggart Band Play Jelly Roll's Jazz	1952	15.00	30.00	60.00
❑ DL 5427 [10]	College Fight Songs	1952	15.00	30.00	60.00
❑ DL 5437 [10]	Lawson-Haggart Band Play King Oliver's Jazz	1952	15.00	30.00	60.00
❑ DL 5439 [10]	Lawson-Haggart Band	1952	15.00	30.00	60.00
❑ DL 5456 [10]	Blues on the River	1952	15.00	30.00	60.00
❑ DL 5502 [10]	Windy City Jazz	1953	15.00	30.00	60.00
❑ DL 5529 [10]	South of the Mason-Dixon Line	1954	15.00	30.00	60.00
❑ DL 5533 [10]	Louis' Hot Fives and Sevens	1954	15.00	30.00	60.00
❑ DL 8182 [M]	Lawson-Haggart Band Play Jelly Roll's Jazz	1955	10.00	20.00	40.00
❑ DL 8195 [M]	Lawson-Haggart Band Play King Oliver's Jazz	1955	10.00	20.00	40.00
❑ DL 8196 [M]	Blues on the River	1955	10.00	20.00	40.00
❑ DL 8197 [M]	South of the Mason-Dixon Line	1955	10.00	20.00	40.00
❑ DL 8198 [M]	Windy City Jazz	1955	10.00	20.00	40.00
❑ DL 8200 [M]	Louis' Hot Fives and Sevens	1955	10.00	20.00	40.00
❑ DL 8453 [M]	Hold That Tiger	1956	7.50	15.00	30.00
❑ DL 8801 [M]	Boppin' at the Hop	1959	7.50	15.00	30.00
❑ DL 78801 [S]	Boppin' at the Hop	1959	10.00	20.00	40.00
EVEREST					
❑ SDBR-1040 [S]	Junior Prom	1959	5.00	10.00	20.00
❑ SDBR-1084 [S]	Dixieland Goes West	1960	6.25	12.50	25.00

Number	Title (A Side/B Side)	Yr	VG	VG+	NM
❑ LPBR-5040 [M]	Junior Prom	1959	6.25	12.50	25.00
❑ LPBR-5084 [M]	Dixieland Goes West	1960	5.00	10.00	20.00
PROJECT 3					
❑ PR-5033	The World's Greatest Jazz Band	1968	5.00	10.00	20.00
❑ PR-5039	Extra	1969	5.00	10.00	20.00
STINSON					
❑ SLP-59 [10]	Lawson-Haggart with Jerry Jerome and His Orchestra	1957	6.25	12.50	25.00
LAZAR, SAM					
ARGO					
❑ LP-714 [M]	Soul Merchant	1963	6.25	12.50	25.00
❑ LPS-714 [S]	Soul Merchant	1963	7.50	15.00	30.00
❑ LP-4002 [M]	Space Flight	1961	7.50	15.00	30.00
❑ LPS-4002 [S]	Space Flight	1961	10.00	20.00	40.00
❑ LP-4015 [M]	Playback	1962	7.50	15.00	30.00
❑ LPS-4015 [S]	Playback	1962	10.00	20.00	40.00
LAZARUS					
AMAZON					
❑ 1001	Lazarus	1970	5.00	10.00	20.00
LAZY LESTER					
EXCELLO					
❑ LP-8006 [M]	True Blues	1967	100.00	200.00	400.00
❑ LPS-8006 [M]	True Blues	196?	15.00	30.00	60.00
—Says "Stereo" but plays mono					
LAZY SMOKE					
ONYX					
❑ 6003	Corridor of Faces	1967	300.00	600.00	1200.
LEA, BARBARA					
PRESTIGE					
❑ PRLP-7065 [M]	Barbara Lea	1956	37.50	75.00	150.00
❑ PRLP-7100 [M]	Lea in Love	1957	37.50	75.00	150.00
RIVERSIDE					
❑ RLP-2518 [10]	A Woman in Love	1955	50.00	100.00	200.00
LEA, TERREA					
ABC-PARAMOUNT					
❑ ABC-141 [M]	Terrea Lea and Her Singing Guitar	1956	7.50	15.00	30.00
HIFI					
❑ R-404 [M]	Folk Songs and Ballads	1957	7.50	15.00	30.00
LEACH, CURTIS					
LONGHORN					
❑ 003	Indescribable	1965	12.50	25.00	50.00
LEADBELLY					
ALLEGRO					
❑ L-4027 [10]	Sinful Songs	195?	62.50	125.00	250.00
CAPITOL					
❑ H 369 [10]	Classics in Jazz	1953	62.50	125.00	250.00
❑ T 1821 [M]	Leadbelly: Huddie Ledbetter's Best	1962	10.00	20.00	40.00
ELEKTRA					
❑ EKL-301/2 [(2)]	The Library of Congress Recordings	1966	6.25	12.50	25.00
FOLKWAYS					
❑ FP-4 [10]	Lead Belly's Legacy, Vol. 1: Take This Hammer	1950	30.00	60.00	120.00
❑ FP-14 [10]	Lead Belly's Legacy, Vol. 2: Rock Island Line	1951	30.00	60.00	120.00
❑ FP-24 [10]	Lead Belly's Legacy, Vol. 3: Early Recordings	1951	30.00	60.00	120.00
❑ FP-34 [10]	Lead Belly's Legacy, Vol. 4: Easy Rider	1951	30.00	60.00	120.00
❑ FP-241 [(2)M]	Leadbelly's Last Sessions, Vol. 1	196?	10.00	20.00	40.00
❑ FP-242 [(2)M]	Leadbelly's Last Sessions, Vol. 2	196?	10.00	20.00	40.00
❑ FA-2004 [10]	Lead Belly's Legacy, Vol. 1: Take This Hammer	195?	12.50	25.00	50.00
—Reissue of FP-4					
❑ FA-2014 [10]	Lead Belly's Legacy, Vol. 2: Rock Island Line	195?	12.50	25.00	50.00
—Reissue of FP-14					
❑ FA-2024 [10]	Lead Belly's Legacy, Vol. 3: Early Recordings	195?	12.50	25.00	50.00
—Reissue of FP-24					
❑ FA-2034 [10]	Lead Belly's Legacy, Vol. 4: Easy Rider	195?	12.50	25.00	50.00
—Reissue of FP-34					
❑ FA-2941 [M]	Leadbelly's Last Sessions, Vol. 3	196?	6.25	12.50	25.00
❑ FA-2942 [M]	Leadbelly's Last Sessions, Vol. 4	196?	6.25	12.50	25.00
❑ FA-3106 [M]	Leadbelly Sings Folk Songs	196?	6.25	12.50	25.00
RCA VICTOR					
❑ LPV-505 [M]	Midnight Special	1964	10.00	20.00	40.00
ROYALE					
❑ 18131 [10]	Blues Songs	1954	30.00	60.00	120.00
—As "The Lonesome Blues Singer"					
VERVE FOLKWAYS					
❑ FT-3019 [M]	From the Last Sessions	1967	6.25	12.50	25.00
❑ FTS-3019 [R]	From the Last Sessions	1967	3.75	7.50	15.00
❑ FV-9001 [M]	Take This Hammer	1965	6.25	12.50	25.00
❑ FVS-9001 [R]	Take This Hammer	1965	3.75	7.50	15.00
❑ FV-9021 [M]	Keep Your Hands Off Her	1965	6.25	12.50	25.00
❑ FVS-9021 [R]	Keep Your Hands Off Her	1965	3.75	7.50	15.00
LEAHY, JOE					
TOWER					
❑ ST 5014 [S]	Tabasco and Trumpets	1966	6.25	12.50	25.00
❑ T 5014 [M]	Tabasco and Trumpets	1966	5.00	10.00	20.00
❑ ST 5057 [S]	A Taste of Trumpets, A Touch of Voices	1967	6.25	12.50	25.00
❑ T 5057 [M]	A Taste of Trumpets, A Touch of Voices	1967	5.00	10.00	20.00
LEAPER, BOB					
LONDON					
❑ LL 3391 [M]	Big Band Beatle Songs	1964	3.75	7.50	15.00
❑ SP 4056 [S]	Big Band Beatle Songs	1964	5.00	10.00	20.00

Number	Title (A Side/B Side)	Yr	VG	VG+	NM

LEAPY LEE
DECCA
| DL 75076 | Little Arrows | 1968 | 5.00 | 10.00 | 20.00 |
| DL 75237 | Leapy Lee | 1970 | 3.75 | 7.50 | 15.00 |

LEARY, DR. TIMOTHY
DOUGLAS
| 1 | You Can Be Anyone This Time Around | 1969 | 25.00 | 50.00 | 100.00 |
ESP-DISK'
| 1027 [M] | Turn On, Tune In, Drop Out | 1966 | 37.50 | 75.00 | 150.00 |
MERCURY
| MG-21131 [M] | Turn On, Tune In, Drop Out | 1967 | 10.00 | 20.00 | 40.00 |
| SR-61131 [S] | Turn On, Tune In, Drop Out | 1967 | 12.50 | 25.00 | 50.00 |
PIXIE
| CA-1069 [M] | L.S.D. | 1966 | 20.00 | 40.00 | 80.00 |

LEATHERCOATED MINDS, THE
VIVA
| V-6003 [M] | Trip Down Sunset Strip | 1967 | 15.00 | 30.00 | 60.00 |
| V-36003 [S] | Trip Down Sunset Strip | 1967 | 20.00 | 40.00 | 80.00 |

LEAVES, THE
CAPITOL
| ST 2638 [S] | All the Good That's Happening | 1967 | 7.50 | 15.00 | 30.00 |
| T 2638 [M] | All the Good That's Happening | 1967 | 6.25 | 12.50 | 25.00 |
MIRA
| LP-3005 [M] | Hey Joe | 1966 | 10.00 | 20.00 | 40.00 |
| LPS-3005 [S] | Hey Joe | 1966 | 12.50 | 25.00 | 50.00 |
SURREY
| LPS-3005 | Hey Joe | 196? | 37.50 | 75.00 | 150.00 |
—Issued in Mira jackets

LED ZEPPELIN
Also see JOHN PAUL JONES; JIMMY PAGE; ROBERT PLANT.
ATLANTIC
| 7201 [M] | Led Zeppelin III | 1970 | 50.00 | 100.00 | 200.00 |
—White label promo only
| SD 7201 [DJ] | Led Zeppelin III | 1970 | 50.00 | 100.00 | 200.00 |
—Stereo white label promo
| SD 7201 [S] | Led Zeppelin III | 1970 | 3.75 | 7.50 | 15.00 |
—Die-cut cover with movable wheel; "1841 Broadway" address on label
| SD 7201 [S] | Led Zeppelin III | 1974 | 2.50 | 5.00 | 10.00 |
—"75 Rockefeller Plaza" address on label
| SD 7201 [S] | Led Zeppelin III | 2001 | 6.25 | 12.50 | 25.00 |
—Classic Records reissue on audiophile vinyl
| 7208 [M] | Led Zeppelin (IV) (Runes) | 1971 | 75.00 | 150.00 | 300.00 |
—White label promo only
| SD 7208 [DJ] | Led Zeppelin (IV) (Runes) | 1971 | 37.50 | 75.00 | 150.00 |
—Stereo white label promo
| SD 7208 [S] | Led Zeppelin (IV) (Runes) | 1971 | 3.00 | 6.00 | 12.00 |
—"1841 Broadway" address on label
| SD 7208 [S] | Led Zeppelin (IV) (Runes) | 1974 | 2.50 | 5.00 | 10.00 |
—"75 Rockefeller Plaza" address on label
| SD 7208 [S] | Led Zeppelin (IV) (Runes) | 2001 | 6.25 | 12.50 | 25.00 |
—Classic Records reissue on audiophile vinyl
| 7255 [M] | Houses of the Holy | 1973 | 250.00 | 500.00 | 1000. |
—White label promo only
| SD 7255 [S] | Houses of the Holy | 1973 | 3.00 | 6.00 | 12.00 |
—"1841 Broadway" address on label
| SD 7255 [S] | Houses of the Holy | 1974 | 2.50 | 5.00 | 10.00 |
—"75 Rockefeller Plaza" address on label
| SD 7255 [S] | Houses of the Holy | 2001 | 6.25 | 12.50 | 25.00 |
—Classic Records reissue on audiophile vinyl
| 8216 [M] | Led Zeppelin | 1969 | 100.00 | 200.00 | 400.00 |
—White label promo only
| SD 8216 [DJ] | Led Zeppelin | 1969 | 50.00 | 100.00 | 200.00 |
—Stereo white label promo
| SD 8216 [S] | Led Zeppelin | 1969 | 5.00 | 10.00 | 20.00 |
—"1841 Broadway" address on label
| SD 8216 [S] | Led Zeppelin | 1969 | 62.50 | 125.00 | 250.00 |
—Possible mispress with purple and brown labels
| SD 8216 [S] | Led Zeppelin | 1974 | 2.50 | 5.00 | 10.00 |
—"75 Rockefeller Plaza" address on label
| SD 8216 [S] | Led Zeppelin | 2000 | 6.25 | 12.50 | 25.00 |
—Classic Records reissue on audiophile vinyl
| 8236 [M] | Led Zeppelin II | 1969 | 50.00 | 100.00 | 200.00 |
—White label promo only
| SD 8236 [DJ] | Led Zeppelin II | 1969 | 75.00 | 150.00 | 300.00 |
—Stereo white label promo
| SD 8236 [S] | Led Zeppelin II | 1969 | 5.00 | 10.00 | 20.00 |
—"1841 Broadway" address on label
| SD 8236 [S] | Led Zeppelin II | 1974 | 2.50 | 5.00 | 10.00 |
—"75 Rockefeller Plaza" address on label
| SD 8236 [S] | Led Zeppelin II | 2000 | 6.25 | 12.50 | 25.00 |
—Classic Records reissue on audiophile vinyl
SD 19126	Led Zeppelin	1977	2.00	4.00	8.00
SD 19127	Led Zeppelin II	1977	2.00	4.00	8.00
SD 19128	Led Zeppelin II	1977	2.00	4.00	8.00
SD 19129	Led Zeppelin (IV) (Runes)	1977	2.00	4.00	8.00
SD 19130	Houses of the Holy	1977	2.00	4.00	8.00
82144 [(6)]	Led Zeppelin (Box Set)	1990	25.00	50.00	100.00
83061 [(4)]	BBC Sessions	2000	15.00	30.00	60.00
—Classic Records limited edition; each LP is in its own cardboard sleeve inside a box with a sheet of liner notes
83268 [(2)]	Early Days: The Best of Led Zeppelin Vol. 1	1999	3.75	7.50	15.00
83278 [(2)]	Latter Days: The Best of Led Zeppelin Vol. 2	2000	3.75	7.50	15.00
SMAS-94019	Led Zeppelin (IV) (Runes)	1972	10.00	20.00	40.00
—Capitol Record Club edition
MOBILE FIDELITY
| 1-065 | Led Zeppelin II | 1981 | 20.00 | 40.00 | 80.00 |
—Audiophile vinyl

SWAN SONG
| SS 2-200 [(2)] | Physical Graffiti | 1975 | 3.75 | 7.50 | 15.00 |
| SS 2-200 [(2)] | Physical Graffiti | 2002 | 10.00 | 20.00 | 40.00 |
—Classic Records reissue on audiophile vinyl
SS 2-201 [(2)]	The Song Remains the Same	1976	3.75	7.50	15.00
SS 8416	Presence	1976	2.50	5.00	10.00
SS 8416	Presence	2002	6.25	12.50	25.00
—Classic Records reissue on audiophile vinyl
| SS 16002 | In Through the Out Door | 1979 | 2.50 | 5.00 | 10.00 |
—Letter "B" on spine; add 50% if brown paper bag is still with jacket
| SS 16002 | In Through the Out Door | 1979 | 2.50 | 5.00 | 10.00 |
—Letter "C" on spine; add 50% if brown paper bag is still with jacket
| SS 16002 | In Through the Out Door | 1979 | 2.50 | 5.00 | 10.00 |
—Letter "D" on spine; add 50% if brown paper bag is still with jacket
| SS 16002 | In Through the Out Door | 1979 | 2.50 | 5.00 | 10.00 |
—Letter "E" on spine; add 50% if brown paper bag is still with jacket
| SS 16002 | In Through the Out Door | 1979 | 2.50 | 5.00 | 10.00 |
—Letter "F" on spine; add 50% if brown paper bag is still with jacket
| SS 16002 | In Through the Out Door | 1979 | 2.50 | 5.00 | 10.00 |
—Letter "A" on spine; add 50% if brown paper bag is still with jacket
| 90051 | Coda | 1982 | 2.50 | 5.00 | 10.00 |

LEDOUX, CHRIS
AMERICAN COWBOY SONGS
ACS 17001	Thirty Dollar Cowboy	1983	6.25	12.50	25.00
ACS 20001	Melodies and Memories	1984	7.50	15.00	30.00
ACS 23001	Chris LeDoux and the Saddle Boogie Band	198?	5.00	10.00	20.00
LUCKY MAN
NR 4249	Rodeo Songs Old and New	1973	7.50	15.00	30.00
ACS 5524	Sing Me a Song, Mr. Rodeo Man	197?	7.50	15.00	30.00
NR 7648	Songs of the American West	1976	7.50	15.00	30.00
NR 9175	Chris LeDoux Sings Western Country	1978	7.50	15.00	30.00
LM 10193	Paint Me Back Home in Wyoming	1978	7.50	15.00	30.00
LM 10194	Western Tunesmith	1980	7.50	15.00	30.00

LEE, ARTHUR
Also see LOVE.
A&M
| SP-4356 | Vindicator | 1972 | 7.50 | 15.00 | 30.00 |
RHINO
| RNLP 020 | Arthur Lee | 1981 | 2.50 | 5.00 | 10.00 |

LEE, BRENDA
DECCA
DL 4039 [M]	Brenda Lee	1960	6.25	12.50	25.00
DL 4082 [M]	This Is...Brenda	1960	6.25	12.50	25.00
DL 4104 [M]	Emotions	1961	6.25	12.50	25.00
DL 4176 [M]	All the Way	1961	6.25	12.50	25.00
DL 4216 [M]	Sincerely	1962	6.25	12.50	25.00
DL 4326 [M]	Brenda, That's All	1962	6.25	12.50	25.00
DL 4370 [M]	All Alone Am I	1963	6.25	12.50	25.00
DL 4439 [M]	Let Me Sing	1963	6.25	12.50	25.00
DL 4509 [M]	By Request	1964	5.00	10.00	20.00
DL 4583 [M]	Merry Christmas from Brenda Lee	1964	5.00	10.00	20.00
DL 4626 [M]	Top Teen Hits	1965	5.00	10.00	20.00
DL 4661 [M]	The Versatile Brenda Lee	1965	5.00	10.00	20.00
DL 4684 [M]	Too Many Rivers	1965	5.00	10.00	20.00
DL 4755 [M]	Bye Bye Blues	1966	5.00	10.00	20.00
DL 4757 [M]	10 Golden Years	196?	3.75	7.50	15.00
—With regular cover
| DL 4757 [M] | 10 Golden Years | 1966 | 6.25 | 12.50 | 25.00 |
—With gatefold cover
DL 4825 [M]	Coming On Strong	1966	3.75	7.50	15.00
DL 4941 [M]	Reflections in Blue	1967	5.00	10.00	20.00
DL 8873 [M]	Grandma, What Great Songs You Sang	1960	10.00	20.00	40.00
DL 74039 [S]	Brenda Lee	1960	7.50	15.00	30.00
DL 74082 [S]	This Is...Brenda	1960	7.50	15.00	30.00
DL 74104 [S]	Emotions	1961	7.50	15.00	30.00
DL 74176 [S]	All the Way	1961	7.50	15.00	30.00
DL 74216 [S]	Sincerely	1962	7.50	15.00	30.00
DL 74326 [S]	Brenda, That's All	1962	7.50	15.00	30.00
DL 74370 [S]	All Alone Am I	1963	7.50	15.00	30.00
DL 74439 [S]	Let Me Sing	1963	7.50	15.00	30.00
DL 74509 [S]	By Request	1964	6.25	12.50	25.00
DL 74583 [S]	Merry Christmas from Brenda Lee	1964	6.25	12.50	25.00
DL 74626 [S]	Top Teen Hits	1965	6.25	12.50	25.00
DL 74661 [S]	The Versatile Brenda Lee	1965	6.25	12.50	25.00
DL 74684 [S]	Too Many Rivers	1965	6.25	12.50	25.00
DL 74755 [S]	Bye Bye Blues	1966	6.25	12.50	25.00
DL 74757 [S]	10 Golden Years	196?	5.00	10.00	20.00
—With regular cover
| DL 74757 [S] | 10 Golden Years | 1966 | 7.50 | 15.00 | 30.00 |
—With gatefold cover
DL 74825 [S]	Coming On Strong	1966	5.00	10.00	20.00
DL 74941 [S]	Reflections in Blue	1967	3.75	7.50	15.00
DL 74955	For the First Time	1968	3.75	7.50	15.00
—With Pete Fountain
DL 75111	Johnny One Time	1969	3.75	7.50	15.00
DL 75232	Memphis Portrait	1970	3.75	7.50	15.00
DL 78873 [S]	Grandma, What Great Songs You Sang	1960	12.50	25.00	50.00
ST-92062	Johnny One Time	1969	5.00	10.00	20.00
—Capitol Record Club edition
| R 103619 [S] | Merry Christmas from Brenda Lee | 1971 | 5.00 | 10.00 | 20.00 |
—RCA Music Service edition
MCA
232 [S]	Merry Christmas from Brenda Lee	1973	3.00	6.00	12.00
305	Brenda	1973	3.75	7.50	15.00
373	New Sunrise	1973	3.00	6.00	12.00
433	Brenda Lee Now	1974	3.00	6.00	12.00
477	Sincerely, Brenda Lee	1975	2.50	5.00	10.00
758	Even Better	198?	2.00	4.00	8.00
—Reissue of 3211

L

Number	Title (A Side/B Side)	Yr	VG	VG+	NM
❏ 824	Only When I Laugh	1982	2.00	4.00	8.00
—Reissue of 5278					
❏ 2233	L.A. Sessions	1976	2.50	5.00	10.00
❏ 3211	Even Better	1979	2.50	5.00	10.00
❏ 2-4012 [(2)]	The Brenda Lee Story — Her Greatest Hits	1973	5.00	10.00	20.00
❏ 5143	Take Me Back	1980	2.50	5.00	10.00
❏ 5278	Only When I Laugh	1981	2.50	5.00	10.00
❏ 5342	Greatest Country Hits	1982	2.50	5.00	10.00
❏ 5626	Feels So Right	1985	2.50	5.00	10.00
❏ 15021 [S]	Merry Christmas from Brenda Lee	197?	2.50	5.00	10.00
❏ 15038	Rockin' Around the Christmas Tree	198?	2.50	5.00	10.00
MCA CORAL					
❏ CB-20044	Let It Be Me	197?	2.50	5.00	10.00
VOCALION					
❏ VL 3795 [M]	Here's Brenda Lee	1967	3.00	6.00	12.00
❏ VL 73795 [S]	Here's Brenda Lee	1967	3.00	6.00	12.00
❏ VL 73890	Let It Be Me	1970	3.00	6.00	12.00

LEE, BYRON, AND THE DRAGONAIRES

Number	Title (A Side/B Side)	Yr	VG	VG+	NM
ATCO					
❏ 33-182 [M]	Jump Up	1966	5.00	10.00	20.00
❏ SD 33-182 [S]	Jump Up	1966	6.25	12.50	25.00
BMN					
❏ 004	Dance the Ska	196?	5.00	10.00	20.00
JAD					
❏ JS-1004	Byron Lee and the Dragonaires	1968	5.00	10.00	20.00
TOWERS HALL					
❏ 006	The Sounds of Jamaica	196?	5.00	10.00	20.00

LEE, DICKEY

Number	Title (A Side/B Side)	Yr	VG	VG+	NM
MERCURY					
❏ SRM-1-5020	Dickey Lee	1979	2.50	5.00	10.00
❏ SRM-1-5026	Dickey Lee Again	1980	2.50	5.00	10.00
RCA VICTOR					
❏ APL1-0311	Sparklin' Brown Eyes	1974	3.00	6.00	12.00
❏ APL1-1243	Rocky	1975	3.00	6.00	12.00
❏ APL1-1725	Angels, Roses and Rain	1976	3.00	6.00	12.00
❏ LSP-4637	Never Ending Song of Love	1971	3.00	6.00	12.00
❏ LSP-4715	Ashes of Love	1972	3.00	6.00	12.00
❏ LSP-4791	Baby, Bye Bye	1972	3.00	6.00	12.00
❏ LSP-4857	Crying Over You	1973	3.00	6.00	12.00
SMASH					
❏ MGS-27020 [M]	The Tale of Patches	1962	7.50	15.00	30.00
❏ SRS-67020 [S]	The Tale of Patches	1962	10.00	20.00	40.00
TCF HALL					
❏ TCF-8001 [M]	Dickey Lee Sings "Laurie" and "The Girl from Peyton Place"	1965	5.00	10.00	20.00
❏ TCF-9001 [S]	Dickey Lee Sings "Laurie" and "The Girl from Peyton Place"	1965	6.25	12.50	25.00

LEE, EDDIE

Number	Title (A Side/B Side)	Yr	VG	VG+	NM
GEORGIAN					
❏ GR 2001 [M]	Windy City Profile	1958	10.00	20.00	40.00

LEE, JACKIE (1)

Number	Title (A Side/B Side)	Yr	VG	VG+	NM
MIRWOOD					
❏ MW-7000 [M]	The Duck	1966	5.00	10.00	20.00
❏ SW-7000 [S]	The Duck	1966	6.25	12.50	25.00

LEE, JEANNE, AND RAN BLAKE

Number	Title (A Side/B Side)	Yr	VG	VG+	NM
RCA VICTOR					
❏ LPM-2500 [M]	The Newest Sound Around	1962	7.50	15.00	30.00
❏ LSP-2500 [S]	The Newest Sound Around	1962	10.00	20.00	40.00

LEE, JULIA

Number	Title (A Side/B Side)	Yr	VG	VG+	NM
CAPITOL					
❏ H 228 [10]	Party Time	1950	30.00	60.00	120.00
❏ T 228 [M]	Party Time	195?	20.00	40.00	80.00

LEE, KATIE

Number	Title (A Side/B Side)	Yr	VG	VG+	NM
HORIZON					
❏ WP-1604 [M]	The Best of Katie Lee	1962	5.00	10.00	20.00
❏ WP-1604 Stereo [S]	The Best of Katie Lee	1962	6.25	12.50	25.00
REPRISE					
❏ R-6025 [M]	Songs of Coach and Consultation	1961	6.25	12.50	25.00
SPECIALTY					
❏ SP-5000 [M]	Spicy Songs for Cool Knights	1959	7.50	15.00	30.00

LEE, LAURA

Number	Title (A Side/B Side)	Yr	VG	VG+	NM
CHESS					
❏ CH-50031	Love More Than Pride	1972	5.00	10.00	20.00
HOT WAX					
❏ HA-708	Women's Love Rights	1971	3.75	7.50	15.00
❏ HA-714	Laura Lee	1972	3.75	7.50	15.00
❏ HA-715	The Best of Laura Lee	1973	3.75	7.50	15.00
INVICTUS					
❏ KZ 33133	Laura Lee	1974	2.50	5.00	10.00

LEE, PEGGY

Number	Title (A Side/B Side)	Yr	VG	VG+	NM
A&M					
❏ SP-4547	Mirrors	1975	3.00	6.00	12.00
ARCHIVE OF FOLK AND JAZZ					
❏ 294	Peggy Lee	197?	2.50	5.00	10.00
ATLANTIC					
❏ SD 18108	Let's Love	1974	3.00	6.00	12.00
CAPITOL					
❏ ST-105	Two Shows Nightly	1969	50.00	100.00	200.00
—Withdrawn immediately after release					
❏ H 151 [10]	Rendezvous with Peggy Lee	1952	25.00	50.00	100.00

Number	Title (A Side/B Side)	Yr	VG	VG+	NM
❏ T 151 [M]	Rendezvous with Peggy Lee	1954	12.50	25.00	50.00
—Turquoise or gray label					
❏ T 151 [M]	Rendezvous with Peggy Lee	1959	6.25	12.50	25.00
—Black label with colorband, Capitol logo at left					
❏ ST-183	A Natural Woman	1969	3.75	7.50	15.00
❏ H 204 [10]	My Best to You	1952	25.00	50.00	100.00
❏ T 204 [M]	My Best to You	1954	12.50	25.00	50.00
—Turquoise or gray label					
❏ T 204 [M]	My Best to You	1959	6.25	12.50	25.00
—Black label with colorband, Capitol logo at left					
❏ DKAO-377	Peggy Lee's Greatest	1969	3.00	6.00	12.00
❏ SM-386	Is That All There Is?	197?	2.50	5.00	10.00
—Reissue with new prefix					
❏ ST-386	Is That All There Is?	1969	3.00	6.00	12.00
❏ ST-463	Bridge Over Troubled Water	1970	3.00	6.00	12.00
❏ STBB-517 [(2)]	Folks Who Live on the Hill/Broadway Ala Lee	1970	3.75	7.50	15.00
❏ STCL-576 [(3)]	Peggy Lee	1970	6.25	12.50	25.00
❏ ST-622	Make It with You	1970	3.00	6.00	12.00
❏ ST-810	Where Did They Go	1971	3.00	6.00	12.00
❏ ST 864 [S]	The Man I Love	1959	7.50	15.00	30.00
❏ T 864 [M]	The Man I Love	1957	12.50	25.00	50.00
—Turquoise label					
❏ T 864 [M]	The Man I Love	1959	6.25	12.50	25.00
—Black label with colorband, Capitol logo at left					
❏ ST 979 [S]	Jump for Joy	1959	7.50	15.00	30.00
❏ T 979 [M]	Jump for Joy	1958	10.00	20.00	40.00
—Turquoise or gray label					
❏ T 979 [M]	Jump for Joy	1959	6.25	12.50	25.00
—Black label with colorband, Capitol logo at left					
❏ ST 1049 [S]	Things Are Swingin'	1959	7.50	15.00	30.00
❏ T 1049 [M]	Things Are Swingin'	1958	6.25	12.50	25.00
❏ ST 1131 [S]	I Like Men	1959	7.50	15.00	30.00
❏ T 1131 [M]	I Like Men	1959	6.25	12.50	25.00
❏ ST 1213 [S]	Alright, Okay, You Win	1959	7.50	15.00	30.00
❏ T 1213 [M]	Alright, Okay, You Win	1959	6.25	12.50	25.00
❏ ST 1219 [S]	Beauty and the Beat	1959	7.50	15.00	30.00
—With George Shearing; black label with colorband, Capitol logo at left					
❏ ST 1219 [S]	Beauty and the Beat	1959	5.00	10.00	20.00
—With George Shearing; black label with colorband, Capitol logo at top					
❏ T 1219 [M]	Beauty and the Beat	1959	6.25	12.50	25.00
—With George Shearing; black label with colorband, Capitol logo at left					
❏ T 1219 [M]	Beauty and the Beat	1962	3.75	7.50	15.00
—With George Shearing; black label with colorband, Capitol logo at top					
❏ SM-1290	Latin Ala Lee!	1977	2.50	5.00	10.00
—Reissue with new prefix					
❏ ST 1290 [S]	Latin Ala Lee!	1960	6.25	12.50	25.00
—Black label with colorband, Capitol logo at left					
❏ ST 1290 [S]	Latin Ala Lee!	1962	3.75	7.50	15.00
—Black label with colorband, Capitol logo at top					
❏ T 1290 [M]	Latin Ala Lee!	1960	5.00	10.00	20.00
—Black label with colorband, Capitol logo at left					
❏ T 1290 [M]	Latin Ala Lee!	1962	3.00	6.00	12.00
—Black label with colorband, Capitol logo at top					
❏ ST 1366 [S]	All Aglow Again	1960	6.25	12.50	25.00
—Black label with colorband, Capitol logo at left					
❏ ST 1366 [S]	All Aglow Again	1962	3.75	7.50	15.00
—Black label with colorband, Capitol logo at top					
❏ T 1366 [M]	All Aglow Again	1960	5.00	10.00	20.00
—Black label with colorband, Capitol logo at left					
❏ T 1366 [M]	All Aglow Again	1962	3.00	6.00	12.00
—Black label with colorband, Capitol logo at top					
❏ ST 1401 [S]	Pretty Eyes	1960	6.25	12.50	25.00
—Black label with colorband, Capitol logo at left					
❏ ST 1401 [S]	Pretty Eyes	1962	3.75	7.50	15.00
—Black label with colorband, Capitol logo at top					
❏ T 1401 [M]	Pretty Eyes	1960	5.00	10.00	20.00
—Black label with colorband, Capitol logo at left					
❏ T 1401 [M]	Pretty Eyes	1962	3.00	6.00	12.00
—Black label with colorband, Capitol logo at top					
❏ ST 1423 [S]	Christmas Carousel	1960	6.25	12.50	25.00
❏ T 1423 [M]	Christmas Carousel	1960	5.00	10.00	20.00
❏ ST 1475 [S]	Ole Ala Lee!	1961	6.25	12.50	25.00
❏ T 1475 [M]	Ole Ala Lee!	1961	5.00	10.00	20.00
❏ SM-1520	Basin Street East	1977	2.50	5.00	10.00
—Reissue with new prefix					
❏ ST 1520 [S]	Basin Street East	1961	6.25	12.50	25.00
—Black label with colorband, Capitol logo at left					
❏ ST 1520 [S]	Basin Street East	1962	3.75	7.50	15.00
—Black label with colorband, Capitol logo at top					
❏ T 1520 [M]	Basin Street East	1961	5.00	10.00	20.00
—Black label with colorband, Capitol logo at left					
❏ T 1520 [M]	Basin Street East	1962	3.00	6.00	12.00
—Black label with colorband, Capitol logo at top					
❏ ST 1630 [S]	If You Go	1962	6.25	12.50	25.00
❏ T 1630 [M]	If You Go	1962	5.00	10.00	20.00
❏ ST 1671 [S]	Blue Cross Country	1962	6.25	12.50	25.00
❏ T 1671 [M]	Blue Cross Country	1962	5.00	10.00	20.00
❏ DT 1743 [R]	Bewitching-Lee!	1962	3.75	7.50	15.00
❏ T 1743 [M]	Bewitching-Lee!	1962	6.25	12.50	25.00
—Black "The Star Line" label					
❏ ST 1772 [S]	Sugar 'n' Spice	1962	6.25	12.50	25.00
❏ T 1772 [M]	Sugar 'n' Spice	1962	5.00	10.00	20.00
❏ ST 1850 [S]	Mink Jazz	1963	6.25	12.50	25.00
❏ T 1850 [M]	Mink Jazz	1963	5.00	10.00	20.00
❏ SM-1857	I'm a Woman	1977	2.50	5.00	10.00
—Reissue with new prefix					
❏ ST 1857 [S]	I'm a Woman	1963	6.25	12.50	25.00
❏ T 1857 [M]	I'm a Woman	1963	5.00	10.00	20.00
❏ ST 1969 [S]	In Love Again	1963	6.25	12.50	25.00
❏ T 1969 [M]	In Love Again	1963	5.00	10.00	20.00
❏ ST 2096 [S]	In the Name of Love	1964	5.00	10.00	20.00
❏ T 2096 [M]	In the Name of Love	1964	3.75	7.50	15.00
❏ ST 2320 [S]	Pass Me By	1965	5.00	10.00	20.00

Number	Title (A Side/B Side)	Yr	VG	VG+	NM
❏ T 2320 [M]	Pass Me By	1965	3.75	7.50	15.00
❏ ST 2388 [S]	That Was Then, Now Is Now	1965	5.00	10.00	20.00
❏ T 2388 [M]	That Was Then, Now Is Now	1965	3.75	7.50	15.00
❏ ST 2390 [S]	Happy Holiday	1965	3.75	7.50	15.00
❏ T 2390 [M]	Happy Holiday	1965	3.00	6.00	12.00
❏ ST 2469 [S]	Guitars Ala Lee	1966	5.00	10.00	20.00
❏ T 2469 [M]	Guitars Ala Lee	1966	3.75	7.50	15.00
❏ ST 2475 [S]	Big $pender	1966	5.00	10.00	20.00
❏ T 2475 [M]	Big $pender	1966	3.75	7.50	15.00
❏ ST 2732 [S]	Extra Special	1967	3.75	7.50	15.00
❏ T 2732 [M]	Extra Special	1967	5.00	10.00	20.00
❏ ST 2781	Somethin' Groovy	1968	3.75	7.50	15.00
❏ ST 2887	The Hits of Peggy Lee	1968	3.75	7.50	15.00
❏ ST-11077	Norma Deloris Egstrom from Jamestown, North Dakota	1972	3.00	6.00	12.00
❏ SN-16140	Peggy Lee Sings Songs of Cy Coleman	198?	2.00	4.00	8.00
COLUMBIA					
❏ CL 6033 [10]	Benny Goodman and Peggy Lee	1949	15.00	30.00	60.00
DECCA					
❏ DXB 164 [(2)M]	The Best of Peggy Lee	1964	7.50	15.00	30.00
❏ DL 4458 [M]	Lover	1964	6.25	12.50	25.00
❏ DL 4461 [M]	The Fabulous Peggy Lee	1964	6.25	12.50	25.00
❏ DL 5482 [10]	Black Coffee	1953	25.00	50.00	100.00
❏ DL 5539 [10]	Songs in an Intimate Style	1953	20.00	40.00	80.00
❏ DXSB 7164 [(2)R]	The Best of Peggy Lee	1964	5.00	10.00	20.00
❏ DL 8358 [M]	Black Coffee	1956	15.00	30.00	60.00
❏ DL 8411 [M]	Dream Street	1957	15.00	30.00	60.00
❏ DL 8591 [M]	Sea Shells	1958	15.00	30.00	60.00
❏ DL 8816 [M]	Miss Wonderful	1959	15.00	30.00	60.00
❏ DL 74458 [R]	Lover	1964	3.75	7.50	15.00
❏ DL 74461 [R]	The Fabulous Peggy Lee	1964	3.75	7.50	15.00
DRG					
❏ SL-5190	Close Enough for Love	1979	3.00	6.00	12.00
GLENDALE					
❏ 6023	You Can Depend on Me	1982	2.50	5.00	10.00
HARMONY					
❏ HL 7005 [M]	Peggy Lee Sings with Benny Goodman	195?	6.25	12.50	25.00
❏ H 30024	Miss Peggy Lee	1970	2.50	5.00	10.00
HINDSIGHT					
❏ HSR-220	Peggy Lee with the David Barbour and Billy May Bands, 1948	1985	2.50	5.00	10.00
MCA					
❏ 4049 [(2)]	The Best of Peggy Lee	197?	3.00	6.00	12.00
MERCURY					
❏ SRM-1-1172	Live in London	1977	3.00	6.00	12.00
MUSICMASTERS					
❏ 5005	Peggy Sings the Blues	1988	3.00	6.00	12.00
PAUSA					
❏ PR-9043	Sugar 'n' Spice	1985	2.50	5.00	10.00
PICKWICK					
❏ SPC-3090	Once More with Feeling	196?	2.50	5.00	10.00
❏ SPC-3192	I've Got the World	1971	2.50	5.00	10.00
VOCALION					
❏ VL 3776 [M]	So Blue	1966	3.75	7.50	15.00
❏ VL 73776 [R]	So Blue	1966	2.50	5.00	10.00
❏ VL 73903	Crazy in the Heart	1969	2.50	5.00	10.00

LEE, PERRY
ROULETTE

Number	Title (A Side/B Side)	Yr	VG	VG+	NM
❏ R-52080 [M]	A Night at Count Basie's	1962	3.75	7.50	15.00
❏ SR-52080 [S]	A Night at Count Basie's	1962	5.00	10.00	20.00

LEE, PINKY
DECCA

❏ DL 8421 [M]	The Surprise Party	1957	10.00	20.00	40.00

LEE, ROBIN
DOT

❏ DLP-3661 [M]	Robin Lee	1965	6.25	12.50	25.00

LEFEVERE, KAMIEL
MERCURY LIVING PRESENCE

❏ SR 90189 [S]	The Magic of the Bells	196?	12.50	25.00	50.00

—Maroon label, no "Vendor: Mercury Record Corporation"

LEFEVRE, RAYMOND
ATLANTIC

Number	Title (A Side/B Side)	Yr	VG	VG+	NM
❏ 8044 [M]	Romantica	1961	5.00	10.00	20.00
❏ SD 8044 [S]	Romantica	1961	6.25	12.50	25.00
BUDDAH					
❏ BDS-5095	Raymond Lefevre	1971	2.50	5.00	10.00
❏ BDS-5109	Oh Happy Day	1972	2.50	5.00	10.00
4 CORNERS OF THE WORLD					
❏ FCL-4239 [M]	Love Me, Please Love Me	1967	3.00	6.00	12.00
❏ FCS-4239 [S]	Love Me, Please Love Me	1967	3.00	6.00	12.00
❏ FCS-4244	Soul Coaxing (Ame Caline)	1968	3.00	6.00	12.00
❏ FCS-4250	La La La (He Gives Me Love)	1968	3.00	6.00	12.00
❏ FCS-4257	Merry Christmas	1968	3.00	6.00	12.00
KAPP					
❏ KL-1510 [M]	You Don't Have to Stay	1967	3.75	7.50	15.00
❏ KS-3510 [S]	You Don't Have to Stay	1967	3.00	6.00	12.00
MONUMENT					
❏ MLP-8067 [M]	Paris Cancan	1967	3.75	7.50	15.00
❏ SLP-18067 [S]	Paris Cancan	1967	3.00	6.00	12.00

LEFT BANKE, THE
RHINO

❏ RNLP-123	History of the Left Banke	1985	2.50	5.00	10.00

SMASH

Number	Title (A Side/B Side)	Yr	VG	VG+	NM
❏ MGS-27088 [M]	Walk Away Renee/Pretty Ballerina	1967	10.00	20.00	40.00
❏ SRS-67088	Walk Away Renee/Pretty Ballerina	198?	2.50	5.00	10.00
—Reissue with thinner vinyl					
❏ SRS-67088 [S]	Walk Away Renee/Pretty Ballerina	1967	10.00	20.00	40.00
❏ SRS-67113	The Left Banke, Too	1968	12.50	25.00	50.00

LEGEND
Probably two different groups.
BELL

❏ 6027	Legend	1969	10.00	20.00	40.00

MEGAPHONE

❏ 101	Legend	1970	20.00	40.00	80.00

LEGENDS, THE
CAPITOL

Number	Title (A Side/B Side)	Yr	VG	VG+	NM
❏ ST 1925 [S]	The Legends Let Loose	1963	20.00	40.00	80.00
❏ T 1925 [M]	The Legends Let Loose	1963	15.00	30.00	60.00
COLUMBIA					
❏ CL 1707 [M]	Hit Sounds of Today's Smash Hit Combos	1961	7.50	15.00	30.00
❏ CS 8507 [S]	Hit Sounds of Today's Smash Hit Combos	1961	10.00	20.00	40.00
ERMINE					
❏ LP-101 [M]	The Legends Let Loose	1963	50.00	100.00	200.00

LEGGE, WADE
BLUE NOTE

❏ BLP-5031 [10]	Wade Legge Trio	1953	150.00	300.00	600.00

LEGGIO, CARMEN
GOLDEN CREST

❏ GCS-1000	Jazz	196?	5.00	10.00	20.00

LEGRAND, MICHEL
COLUMBIA

Number	Title (A Side/B Side)	Yr	VG	VG+	NM
❏ CL 555 [M]	I Love Paris	1954	10.00	20.00	40.00
❏ CL 647 [M]	Holiday in Rome	1955	6.25	12.50	25.00
❏ CL 706 [M]	Vienna Holiday	1955	6.25	12.50	25.00
❏ CL 888 [M]	Castles in Spain	1956	6.25	12.50	25.00
❏ CL 1115 [M]	Michel Legrand Plays Cole Porter	1957	6.25	12.50	25.00
❏ CL 1139 [M]	Legrand in Rio	1957	6.25	12.50	25.00
❏ CL 1250 [M]	Legrand Jazz	1958	10.00	20.00	40.00
—Miles Davis appears on this record					
❏ CL 1437 [M]	I Love Paris	1960	6.25	12.50	25.00
❏ CS 8079 [S]	Legrand Jazz	1959	10.00	20.00	40.00
—Miles Davis appears on this record					
❏ CS 8237 [S]	I Love Paris	1960	5.00	10.00	20.00
MERCURY					
❏ MG 20342 [M]	C'est Magnifique	1958	5.00	10.00	20.00
MOBILE FIDELITY					
❏ 1-504	Jazz Grand	198?	12.50	25.00	50.00
—Audiophile vinyl					
PHILIPS					
❏ PHM 200074 [M]	The Michel Legrand Big Band Plays Richard Rogers	1963	5.00	10.00	20.00
❏ PHM 200143 [M]	Michel Legrand Sings	1964	6.25	12.50	25.00
❏ PHS 600074 [S]	The Michel Legrand Big Band Plays Richard Rogers	1963	6.25	12.50	25.00
❏ PHS 600143 [S]	Michel Legrand Sings	1964	7.50	15.00	30.00

LEGS DIAMOND
CREAM

Number	Title (A Side/B Side)	Yr	VG	VG+	NM
❏ CR 1010	Firepower	1979	6.25	12.50	25.00
MERCURY					
❏ SRM-1-1136	Legs Diamond	1977	7.50	15.00	30.00
❏ SRM-1-1191	A Diamond Is a Hard Rock	1977	7.50	15.00	30.00

LEHRER, TOM
LEHRER

Number	Title (A Side/B Side)	Yr	VG	VG+	NM
❏ TLP-1 [10]	Songs by Tom Lehrer	1953	25.00	50.00	100.00
❏ TL-101 [M]	Songs by Tom Lehrer	1959	10.00	20.00	40.00
❏ TL-102 [M]	More of Tom Lehrer	1958	10.00	20.00	40.00
❏ TL-102S [S]	More of Tom Lehrer	1959	10.00	20.00	40.00
❏ TL-201 [M]	Tom Lehrer Revisited	1959	6.25	12.50	25.00
❏ TL-202 [M]	An Evening Wasted with Tom Lehrer	1959	6.25	12.50	25.00
❏ TL-202S [S]	An Evening Wasted with Tom Lehrer	1959	10.00	20.00	40.00
REPRISE					
❏ R-6179 [M]	That Was the Year That Was	1965	5.00	10.00	20.00
❏ RS-6179 [S]	That Was the Year That Was	1965	6.25	12.50	25.00
—Pink, yellow and green label					
❏ RS-6179 [S]	That Was the Year That Was	1968	3.75	7.50	15.00
—Two-tone orange label with "W7" and "r:" logos					
❏ RS-6179 [S]	That Was the Year That Was	1970	2.50	5.00	10.00
—Orange/tan label with "r:" logo					
❏ R 6199 [M]	An Evening Wasted with Tom Lehrer	1966	5.00	10.00	20.00
—Reissue of Lehrer 202					
❏ RS 6199 [S]	An Evening Wasted with Tom Lehrer	1966	6.25	12.50	25.00
—Reissue of Lehrer 202					
❏ R-6216 [M]	Songs by Tom Lehrer	1966	5.00	10.00	20.00
❏ RS-6216 [S]	Songs by Tom Lehrer	1966	6.25	12.50	25.00

LEIBER, JERRY
KAPP

❏ KL-1127 [M]	Scooby-Doo	1959	12.50	25.00	50.00

LEIBER AND STOLLER BIG BAND, THE
ATLANTIC

Number	Title (A Side/B Side)	Yr	VG	VG+	NM
❏ 8047 [M]	Yakety Yak	1960	10.00	20.00	40.00
—White "fan" logo on right side of label					
❏ 8047 [M]	Yakety Yak	1962	5.00	10.00	20.00
—Black "fan" logo on right side of label					
❏ SD 8047 [S]	Yakety Yak	1960	12.50	25.00	50.00
—White "fan" logo on right side of label					

L

Number	Title (A Side/B Side)	Yr	VG	VG+	NM
❏ SD 8047 [S]	Yakety Yak	1962	6.25	12.50	25.00

—Black "fan" logo on right side of label

LEIBERT, DICK
WESTMINSTER

Number	Title (A Side/B Side)	Yr	VG	VG+	NM
❏ WST 15006 [S]	Leibert Takes Broadway	195?	5.00	10.00	20.00
❏ WST 15009 [S]	Leibert Takes Richmond	195?	5.00	10.00	20.00
❏ WST 15020 [S]	A Merry Wurlitzer Christmas	195?	5.00	10.00	20.00
❏ WST 15034 [S]	Leibert Takes a Holiday	195?	5.00	10.00	20.00
❏ WST 15043 [S]	Leibert Takes You Dancing	195?	5.00	10.00	20.00
❏ WST 15050 [S]	Sing a Song with Leibert	195?	5.00	10.00	20.00

LEIGHTON, BERNIE
COLUMBIA

Number	Title (A Side/B Side)	Yr	VG	VG+	NM
❏ CL 6112 [10]	East Side Rendezvous	1950	20.00	40.00	80.00

LEIGHTON, BERNIE/JOHNNY GUARNIERI
EMARCY

Number	Title (A Side/B Side)	Yr	VG	VG+	NM
❏ MG-26018 [10]	Piano Stylings	1954	20.00	40.00	80.00

LEMER, PETER
ESP-DISK'

Number	Title (A Side/B Side)	Yr	VG	VG+	NM
❏ 1057	Local Colour	1968	6.25	12.50	25.00

LEMMON, JACK
CAPITOL

Number	Title (A Side/B Side)	Yr	VG	VG+	NM
❏ ST 1943 [S]	Jack Lemmon Plays Piano Selections from Irma La Douce	1963	15.00	30.00	60.00
❏ T 1943 [M]	Jack Lemmon Plays Piano Selections from Irma La Douce	1963	12.50	25.00	50.00

EPIC

Number	Title (A Side/B Side)	Yr	VG	VG+	NM
❏ BN 523 [S]	A Twist of Lemmon	1959	12.50	25.00	50.00
❏ BN 528 [S]	Jack Lemmon Sings and Plays Music from Some Like It Hot	1959	12.50	25.00	50.00
❏ LN 3491 [M]	A Twist of Lemmon	1959	10.00	20.00	40.00
❏ LN 3559 [M]	Jack Lemmon Sings and Plays Music from Some Like It Hot	1959	10.00	20.00	40.00

LEMON PIPERS, THE
BUDDAH

Number	Title (A Side/B Side)	Yr	VG	VG+	NM
❏ BD-5009 [M]	Green Tambourine	1968	6.25	12.50	25.00
❏ BDS-5009 [S]	Green Tambourine	1968	6.25	12.50	25.00
❏ BDS-5016	Jungle Marmalade	1968	6.25	12.50	25.00

LEMONHEADS, THE
ATLANTIC

Number	Title (A Side/B Side)	Yr	VG	VG+	NM
❏ 82137	Lovey	1990	3.00	6.00	12.00
❏ 82537	Come On Feel the Lemonheads	1993	5.00	10.00	20.00

—5,000 copies pressed, all on green vinyl

TAANG!

Number	Title (A Side/B Side)	Yr	VG	VG+	NM
❏ 15	Hate Your Friends	1987	2.50	5.00	10.00

—None of the above (current pressings)

❏ 15	Hate Your Friends	1987	3.00	6.00	12.00

—Fifth pressing: Yellow vinyl, yellow lettering on sleeve, yellow label

❏ 15	Hate Your Friends	1987	3.50	7.00	14.00

—Fourth pressing: Black vinyl, red lettering on sleeve, blue and green label

❏ 15	Hate Your Friends	1987	4.00	8.00	16.00

—Third pressing: Black vinyl, red lettering on sleeve, red label

❏ 15	Hate Your Friends	1987	4.50	9.00	18.00

—Second pressing: Black vinyl, red lettering on sleeve, yellow label

❏ 15	Hate Your Friends	1987	5.00	10.00	20.00

—First pressing: Black vinyl, yellow lettering on sleeve, yellow label

❏ 23	Creator	1988	2.50	5.00	10.00
❏ 32	Lick	1989	2.50	5.00	10.00

LENNON, JOHN
Includes records as "Plastic Ono Band," "John Ono Lennon," "John Lennon/Plastic Ono Band" and other records he made with Yoko Ono. Also see THE BEATLES.

ADAM VIII

Number	Title (A Side/B Side)	Yr	VG	VG+	NM
❏ A-8018	John Lennon Sings the Great Rock & Roll Hits (Roots)	1975	250.00	500.00	1000.

—Counterfeits abound. On authentic copies, cover is posterboard (not slicks); labels are normal size (not overly large); printing on cover is sharp, not blurry; the word "Greatest" does NOT appear on the spine. Authentic copies usually have ad sleeve also.

APPLE

Number	Title (A Side/B Side)	Yr	VG	VG+	NM
❏ SMAX-3361	Wedding Album	1969	37.50	75.00	150.00

—With photo strip, postcard, poster of wedding photos, poster of lithographs, "Bagism" bag, booklet, photo of slice of wedding cake. Missing inserts reduce the value.

❏ SW-3362	Live Peace in Toronto 1969	1970	3.75	7.50	15.00

—By "The Plastic Ono Band" -- without calendar

❏ SW-3362	Live Peace in Toronto 1969	1970	5.00	10.00	20.00

—By "The Plastic Ono Band"; with calendar

❏ SW-3372	John Lennon Plastic Ono Band	1970	5.00	10.00	20.00
❏ SW-3379	Imagine	1971	5.00	10.00	20.00

—With either of two postcard inserts, lyric sleeve, poster

❏ SW-3379	Imagine	1975	5.00	10.00	20.00

—"All Rights Reserved" label

❏ SVBB-3392 [(2)]	Some Time in New York City	1972	7.50	15.00	30.00

—By John and Yoko; with photo card and petition

❏ SVBB-3392 [(2)DJ]	Some Time in New York City	1972	250.00	500.00	1000.

—White label promo

❏ SW-3414	Mind Games	1973	5.00	10.00	20.00
❏ SW-3416	Walls and Bridges	1974	5.00	10.00	20.00

—With fold-open segmented front cover

❏ SK-3419	Rock 'N' Roll	1975	5.00	10.00	20.00
❏ SW-3421	Shaved Fish	1975	5.00	10.00	20.00
❏ T-5001	Two Virgins — Unfinished Music No. 1	1968	12.50	25.00	50.00

—With Yoko Ono; without brown bag

❏ T-5001	Two Virgins — Unfinished Music No. 1	1968	37.50	75.00	150.00

—With Yoko Ono; with die-cut bag

❏ T-5001	Two Virgins — Unfinished Music No. 1	1968	37.50	75.00	150.00

—With Yoko Ono; price with brown bag

❏ T-5001	Two Virgins — Unfinished Music No. 1	1985	3.75	7.50	15.00

—With Yoko Ono; reissue, flat label

Number	Title (A Side/B Side)	Yr	VG	VG+	NM
CAPITOL					
❏ SW-3372	John Lennon Plastic Ono Band	1978	3.00	6.00	12.00

—Purple label, large Capitol logo

❏ SW-3372	John Lennon Plastic Ono Band	1982	5.00	10.00	20.00

—Black label, print in colorband

❏ SW-3372	John Lennon Plastic Ono Band	1988	7.50	15.00	30.00

—Purple label, small Capitol logo

❏ SW-3379	Imagine	1978	2.50	5.00	10.00

—Purple label, large Capitol logo

❏ SW-3379	Imagine	1986	7.50	15.00	30.00

—Black label, print in colorband

❏ SW-3379	Imagine	1987	6.25	12.50	25.00

—Black label, print in colorband; "Digitally Re-Mastered" at top of front cover

❏ SW-3379	Imagine	1988	7.50	15.00	30.00

—Purple label, small Capitol logo

❏ SVBB-3392 [(2)]	Some Time in New York City	197?	6.25	12.50	25.00

—By John and Yoko; purple label, large Capitol logo

❏ SVBB-3392 [(2)]	Some Time in New York City	197?	25.00	50.00	100.00

—Both discs in single-pocket gatefold (the other pocket is glued shut)

❏ SW-3414	Mind Games	1978	10.00	20.00	40.00

—Purple label, large Capitol logo

❏ SW-3416	Walls and Bridges	1978	3.75	7.50	15.00

—Purple label, large Capitol logo; standard front cover

❏ SW-3416	Walls and Bridges	1982	7.50	15.00	30.00

—Black label, print in colorband

❏ SW-3416	Walls and Bridges	1989	7.50	15.00	30.00

—Purple label, small Capitol logo

❏ SK-3419	Rock 'N' Roll	1978	10.00	20.00	40.00

—Purple label, large Capitol logo

❏ SW-3421	Shaved Fish	1978	3.00	6.00	12.00

—Purple Capitol label with Apple logo on cover

❏ SW-3421	Shaved Fish	1978	10.00	20.00	40.00

—Purple Capitol label with Capitol logo on cover

❏ SW-3421	Shaved Fish	1983	5.00	10.00	20.00

—Black Capitol label with Apple logo on cover

❏ SW-3421	Shaved Fish	1983	10.00	20.00	40.00

—Black Capitol label with Capitol logo on cover

❏ SW-3421	Shaved Fish	1989	10.00	20.00	40.00

—Purple Capitol label (small logo) with Capitol logo on cover

❏ ST-12239	Live Peace in Toronto 1969	1982	2.50	5.00	10.00

—By "The Plastic Ono Band"; reissue, purple Capitol label

❏ ST-12239	Live Peace in Toronto 1969	1983	12.50	25.00	50.00

—By "The Plastic Ono Band"; reissue, black Capitol label

❏ SV-12451	Live in New York City	1986	3.00	6.00	12.00
❏ SJ-12533	Menlove Ave.	1986	3.75	7.50	15.00
❏ SN-16068	Mind Games	1980	3.00	6.00	12.00

—Budget-line reissue

❏ SN-16069	Rock 'N' Roll	1980	3.00	6.00	12.00

—Budget-line reissue

❏ C1-90803 [(2)]	Imagine: Music from the Motion Picture	1988	5.00	10.00	20.00
❏ C1-91425	Double Fantasy	1989	5.00	10.00	20.00

—Very briefly available reissue

❏ R 144136	Menlove Ave.	198?	12.50	25.00	50.00

—BMG Direct Marketing edition

❏ R 144136	Menlove Ave.	1986	12.50	25.00	50.00

—RCA Music Service edition

❏ R 144497	Live in New York City	1986	3.75	7.50	15.00

—RCA Music Service edition

❏ SV-512451	Live in New York City	1986	3.75	7.50	15.00

—Columbia House edition

❏ C1-591425	Double Fantasy	1989	15.00	30.00	60.00

—Columbia House edition of reissue

GEFFEN

Number	Title (A Side/B Side)	Yr	VG	VG+	NM
❏ GHS 2001	Double Fantasy	1980	2.50	5.00	10.00

—Seven tracks by John, seven by Yoko; off-white label; titles on back cover out of order

❏ GHS 2001	Double Fantasy	1981	3.00	6.00	12.00

—Columbia House edition (all have corrected back cover) without "CH" on label

❏ GHS 2001	Double Fantasy	1981	3.00	6.00	12.00

—Off-white label, titles in order on the back cover

❏ GHS 2001	Double Fantasy	1981	18.75	37.50	75.00

—Columbia House edition (all have corrected back cover) with "CH" on label

❏ GHS 2001	Double Fantasy	1986	12.50	25.00	50.00

—Same as above, but with black Geffen label

❏ GHSP 2023	The John Lennon Collection	1982	5.00	10.00	20.00
❏ GHSP 2023 [DJ]	The John Lennon Collection	1982	12.50	25.00	50.00

—Promo only on Quiex II audiophile vinyl

❏ R 104689	Double Fantasy	1981	10.00	20.00	40.00

—RCA Music Service edition

MOBILE FIDELITY

Number	Title (A Side/B Side)	Yr	VG	VG+	NM
❏ 1-153	Imagine	1984	12.50	25.00	50.00

—Audiophile vinyl

NAUTILUS

Number	Title (A Side/B Side)	Yr	VG	VG+	NM
❏ NR-47	Double Fantasy	1982	20.00	40.00	80.00

—Half-speed master

❏ NR-47	Double Fantasy	1982	500.00	1000.	2000.

—Half-speed master; alternate experimental cover with yellow and red added to black and white front

PARLOPHONE

Number	Title (A Side/B Side)	Yr	VG	VG+	NM
❏ 21954 [(2)]	Lennon Legend	1998	5.00	10.00	20.00

—"Made in U.S.A." on back cover

POLYDOR

Number	Title (A Side/B Side)	Yr	VG	VG+	NM
❏ 817160-1	Milk and Honey	1983	2.50	5.00	10.00

—Six tracks by John, six by Yoko

❏ 817160-1	Milk and Honey	1984	37.50	75.00	150.00

—Yellow or green vinyl; unauthorized "inside jobs"

❏ 817238-1	Heart Play (Unfinished Dialogue)	1983	3.00	6.00	12.00

—Interviews with John Lennon and Yoko Ono

SILHOUETTE

Number	Title (A Side/B Side)	Yr	VG	VG+	NM
❏ SM-10012 [(2)]	Reflections and Poetry	1984	6.25	12.50	25.00

ZAPPLE

Number	Title (A Side/B Side)	Yr	VG	VG+	NM
❏ ST-3357	Life with the Lions — Unfinished Music No. 2	1969	5.00	10.00	20.00

—With Yoko Ono

Number	Title (A Side/B Side)	Yr	VG	VG+	NM
LENNON, JULIAN					
ATLANTIC					
☐ PR 2693 [DJ]	Mr. Jordan According to Mr. Lennon	1989	5.00	10.00	20.00
—Promo-only interview album					
☐ 81084	Valotte	1984	2.50	5.00	10.00
☐ 81640	The Secret Value of Daydreaming	1986	2.50	5.00	10.00
☐ 81928	Mr. Jordan	1989	2.50	5.00	10.00
LENNON SISTERS, THE					
BRUNSWICK					
☐ BL 54031 [M]	Let's Get Acquainted	1957	6.25	12.50	25.00
☐ BL 54039 [M]	Lawrence Welk Presents the Lennon Sisters	1958	6.25	12.50	25.00
DOT					
☐ DLP-3250 [M]	Best-Loved Catholic Hymns	1959	3.75	7.50	15.00
☐ DLP-3292 [M]	The Lennon Sisters Sing 12 Great Hits	1960	3.75	7.50	15.00
☐ DLP 3343 [M]	Christmas with the Lennon Sisters	1961	3.75	7.50	15.00
☐ DLP-3398 [M]	Sad Movies (Make Me Cry)	1961	3.75	7.50	15.00
☐ DLP-3417 [M]	Can't Help Falling in Love	1962	3.00	6.00	12.00
☐ DLP-3481 [M]	The Lennon Sisters' Favorites	1963	3.00	6.00	12.00
☐ DLP-3557 [M]	Dominique and Other Great Folk Songs	1964	3.00	6.00	12.00
☐ DLP-3589 [M]	No. 1 Hits of the 1960s	1964	3.00	6.00	12.00
☐ DLP-3622 [M]	Twelve Great Hits, Volume 2	1965	3.00	6.00	12.00
☐ DLP-3659 [M]	Solos	1965	3.00	6.00	12.00
☐ DLP-3797 [M]	Somethin' Stupid	1967	3.75	7.50	15.00
☐ DLP-25250 [S]	Best-Loved Catholic Hymns	1959	5.00	10.00	20.00
☐ DLP-25292 [S]	The Lennon Sisters Sing 12 Great Hits	1960	5.00	10.00	20.00
☐ DLP 25343 [S]	Christmas with the Lennon Sisters	1961	5.00	10.00	20.00
☐ DLP-25398 [S]	Sad Movies (Make Me Cry)	1961	5.00	10.00	20.00
☐ DLP-25417 [S]	Can't Help Falling in Love	1962	3.75	7.50	15.00
☐ DLP-25481 [S]	The Lennon Sisters' Favorites	1963	3.75	7.50	15.00
☐ DLP-25557 [S]	Dominique and Other Great Folk Songs	1964	3.75	7.50	15.00
☐ DLP-25589 [S]	No. 1 Hits of the 1960s	1964	3.75	7.50	15.00
☐ DLP-25622 [S]	Twelve Great Hits, Volume 2	1965	3.75	7.50	15.00
☐ DLP-25659 [S]	Solos	1965	3.75	7.50	15.00
☐ DLP-25797 [S]	Somethin' Stupid	1967	3.00	6.00	12.00
HAMILTON					
☐ HLP-119 [M]	Melody of Love	196?	3.00	6.00	12.00
☐ HLP-12119 [S]	Melody of Love	196?	3.00	6.00	12.00
MERCURY					
☐ SR-61164	The Lennon Sisters Today!!	1968	3.00	6.00	12.00
☐ SR-61201	Pop Country	1969	3.00	6.00	12.00
PICKWICK					
☐ PTP-2014 [(2)]	America's Sweethearts	1973	3.00	6.00	12.00
☐ SPC-3084	Our Favorite Songs	196?	2.50	5.00	10.00
☐ SPC-3110	Goodnight Sweetheart	197?	2.50	5.00	10.00
RANWOOD					
☐ 7027 [(2)]	22 Songs of Faith and Inspiration	198?	2.50	5.00	10.00
☐ 8205	Best of the Lennon Sisters	198?	2.00	4.00	8.00
☐ 8212	How Great Thou Art	198?	2.00	4.00	8.00
VOCALION					
☐ VL 73864	Too Marvelous for Words	1969	2.50	5.00	10.00
☐ VL 73887	The Lennon Sisters with Lawrence Welk	1970	2.50	5.00	10.00
LENOIR, J.B.					
CHESS					
☐ LP-410	Natural Man	1970	10.00	20.00	40.00
☐ CH-9323	Natural Man	1990	3.00	6.00	12.00
POLYDOR					
☐ 24-4011	J.B. Lenoir	1970	3.75	7.50	15.00
LENYA, LOTTE					
COLUMBIA MASTERWORKS					
☐ ML 5056 [M]	Berlin Theater Songs by Kurt Weill	1957	7.50	15.00	30.00
☐ KL 5229 [M]	September Song	1958	7.50	15.00	30.00
LEONARD, HARLAN					
RCA VICTOR					
☐ LPV-531 [M]	Harlan Leonard and His Rockets	1965	6.25	12.50	25.00
LEONARD, HARVEY					
KEYNOTE					
☐ 1102 [M]	Jazz Ecstasy	1955	12.50	25.00	50.00
LEONARD, JACK E.					
VIK					
☐ LX-1080 [M]	Rock 'n Roll for People Over Sixteen	1957	10.00	20.00	40.00
LEOPARDS, THE					
MOON					
☐ (# unknown)	Kansas City Slickers	1977	6.25	12.50	25.00
LES JAZZ MODES					
ATLANTIC					
☐ 1280 [M]	The Most Happy Fella	1958	20.00	40.00	80.00
—Black label					
☐ 1280 [M]	The Most Happy Fella	1961	7.50	15.00	30.00
—Multicolor label, white "fan" logo at right					
☐ 1306 [M]	Les Jazz Modes	1959	15.00	30.00	60.00
—Black label					
☐ 1306 [M]	Les Jazz Modes	1961	7.50	15.00	30.00
—Multicolor label, white "fan" logo at right					
☐ SD-1306 [S]	Les Jazz Modes	1959	15.00	30.00	60.00
—Green label					
☐ SD-1306 [S]	Les Jazz Modes	1961	7.50	15.00	30.00
—Multicolor label, white "fan" logo at right					
DAWN					
☐ DLP-1101 [M]	Jazzville	1956	25.00	50.00	100.00
☐ DLP-1108 [M]	Les Jazz Modes	1956	25.00	50.00	100.00
☐ DLP-1117 [M]	Mood in Scarlet	1957	25.00	50.00	100.00
SEECO					
☐ CELP-466 [M]	Smart Jazz for the Smart Set	1960	7.50	15.00	30.00

Number	Title (A Side/B Side)	Yr	VG	VG+	NM
LESLIE, BILL					
ARGO					
☐ LP-710 [M]	Diggin' the Chicks	1962	6.25	12.50	25.00
☐ LPS-710 [S]	Diggin' the Chicks	1962	7.50	15.00	30.00
LESTER, KETTY					
AVI					
☐ 6116	A Collection of Her Best	1982	3.75	7.50	15.00
ERA					
☐ EL-108 [M]	Love Letters	1962	10.00	20.00	40.00
☐ ES-108 [S]	Love Letters	1962	15.00	30.00	60.00
PETE					
☐ 1109	Ketty Lester	1969	3.75	7.50	15.00
RCA VICTOR					
☐ LPM-2945 [M]	The Soul of Me	1964	6.25	12.50	25.00
☐ LSP-2945 [S]	The Soul of Me	1964	7.50	15.00	30.00
☐ LPM-3326 [M]	Where Is Love	1965	6.25	12.50	25.00
☐ LSP-3326 [S]	Where Is Love	1965	7.50	15.00	30.00
SHEFFIELD					
☐ 15	Ketty Lester In Concert	1977	3.75	7.50	15.00
TOWER					
☐ ST 5029 [S]	When a Woman Loves a Man	1966	6.25	12.50	25.00
☐ T 5029 [M]	When a Woman Loves a Man	1966	6.25	12.50	25.00
LETMAN, JOHN					
BETHLEHEM					
☐ BCP-6053 [M]	The Many Angles of John Letman	1961	7.50	15.00	30.00
☐ SBCP-6053 [S]	The Many Angles of John Letman	1961	10.00	20.00	40.00
LETTERMEN, THE					
APPLAUSE					
☐ 1006	Love Is...	198?	2.50	5.00	10.00
CAPITOL					
☐ SKAO-138	The Best of the Lettermen, Vol. 2	1969	3.00	6.00	12.00
☐ SM-147	Put Your Head on My Shoulder	1977	2.00	4.00	8.00
—Reissue with new prefix					
☐ ST-147	Put Your Head on My Shoulder	1968	3.75	7.50	15.00
☐ ST-202	I Have Dreamed	1969	3.00	6.00	12.00
☐ SWBB-251 [(2)]	Close-Up	1969	3.75	7.50	15.00
—Reissue of ST 2013 and ST 2083 in one package					
☐ ST 8-0269	Hurt So Bad	1969	3.75	7.50	15.00
—Capitol Record Club edition					
☐ ST-269	Hurt So Bad	1969	3.00	6.00	12.00
☐ ST-390	Traces/Memories	1970	3.00	6.00	12.00
☐ ST 8-0496	Reflections	1970	3.75	7.50	15.00
—Capitol Record Club edition					
☐ ST-496	Reflections	1970	3.00	6.00	12.00
☐ STCL-577 [(3)]	The Lettermen	1970	6.25	12.50	25.00
☐ ST-634	Everything's Good About You	1971	3.00	6.00	12.00
☐ STBB-710 [(2)]	Let It Be Me/And I Love Her	1971	3.75	7.50	15.00
☐ SW-781	Feelings	1971	3.00	6.00	12.00
☐ ST-836	Love Book	1971	3.00	6.00	12.00
☐ ST 1669 [S]	A Song for Young Love	1962	5.00	10.00	20.00
☐ T 1669 [M]	A Song for Young Love	1962	3.75	7.50	15.00
☐ ST 1711 [S]	Once Upon a Time	1962	5.00	10.00	20.00
☐ T 1711 [M]	Once Upon a Time	1962	3.75	7.50	15.00
☐ ST 1761 [S]	Jim, Tony and Bob	1962	5.00	10.00	20.00
☐ T 1761 [M]	Jim, Tony and Bob	1962	3.75	7.50	15.00
☐ ST 1829 [S]	College Standards	1963	5.00	10.00	20.00
☐ T 1829 [M]	College Standards	1963	3.75	7.50	15.00
☐ ST 1936 [S]	The Lettermen In Concert	1963	5.00	10.00	20.00
☐ T 1936 [M]	The Lettermen In Concert	1963	3.75	7.50	15.00
☐ ST 2013 [S]	A Lettermen Kind of Love	1964	3.75	7.50	15.00
☐ T 2013 [M]	A Lettermen Kind of Love	1964	3.00	6.00	12.00
☐ ST 2083 [S]	The Lettermen Look at Love	1964	3.75	7.50	15.00
☐ T 2083 [M]	The Lettermen Look at Love	1964	3.00	6.00	12.00
☐ ST 2142 [S]	She Cried	1964	3.75	7.50	15.00
☐ T 2142 [M]	She Cried	1964	3.00	6.00	12.00
☐ ST 2213 [S]	You'll Never Walk Alone	1965	3.75	7.50	15.00
☐ T 2213 [M]	You'll Never Walk Alone	1965	3.00	6.00	12.00
☐ ST 2270 [S]	Portrait of My Love	1965	3.75	7.50	15.00
☐ T 2270 [M]	Portrait of My Love	1965	3.00	6.00	12.00
☐ ST 2359 [S]	The Hit Sounds of the Lettermen	1965	3.75	7.50	15.00
☐ T 2359 [M]	The Hit Sounds of the Lettermen	1965	3.00	6.00	12.00
☐ ST 2428 [S]	More Hit Sounds of the Lettermen!	1966	3.75	7.50	15.00
☐ T 2428 [M]	More Hit Sounds of the Lettermen!	1966	3.00	6.00	12.00
☐ ST 2496 [S]	A New Song for Young Love	1966	3.75	7.50	15.00
☐ T 2496 [M]	A New Song for Young Love	1966	3.00	6.00	12.00
☐ ST 2554 [S]	The Best of the Lettermen	1966	3.75	7.50	15.00
☐ T 2554 [M]	The Best of the Lettermen	1966	3.00	6.00	12.00
☐ ST 2587 [S]	For Christmas This Year	1966	3.75	7.50	15.00
☐ ST-8-2587 [S]	For Christmas This Year	1966	5.00	10.00	20.00
—Capitol Record Club edition					
☐ T 2587 [M]	For Christmas This Year	1966	3.00	6.00	12.00
☐ ST 2633 [S]	Warm	1967	3.75	7.50	15.00
☐ T 2633 [M]	Warm	1967	3.75	7.50	15.00
☐ SM-2711	Spring!	1977	2.00	4.00	8.00
—Reissue with new prefix					
☐ ST 2711 [S]	Spring!	1967	3.75	7.50	15.00
☐ T 2711 [M]	Spring!	1967	3.75	7.50	15.00
☐ ST 2758 [S]	The Lettermen!!!... And "Live!"	1967	3.75	7.50	15.00
☐ T 2758 [M]	The Lettermen!!!... And "Live!"	1967	5.00	10.00	20.00
☐ ST 2865	Goin' Out of My Head	1968	3.75	7.50	15.00
☐ ST 2934	Special Request	1968	3.75	7.50	15.00
☐ SPRO-4798/9 [DJ]	A Collection of Their Finest Songs	1969	6.25	12.50	25.00
—Promo-only collection of excerpts of 20 songs					
☐ SW-11010	Lettermen 1	1972	2.50	5.00	10.00
☐ SW-11124	Spin Away	1972	2.50	5.00	10.00
☐ SW-11183	"Alive" Again ... Naturally	1973	2.50	5.00	10.00
☐ SW-11249	All-Time Greatest Hits	1973	2.50	5.00	10.00
☐ SW-11319	Now and Forever	1974	2.50	5.00	10.00

L

Number	Title (A Side/B Side)	Yr	VG	VG+	NM
☐ SW-11364	There Is No Greater Love	1974	2.50	5.00	10.00
☐ SW-11424	Make Time	1975	2.50	5.00	10.00
☐ SW-11470	The Time Is Right	1975	2.50	5.00	10.00
☐ SW-11508	Kind of Country	1976	2.50	5.00	10.00
☐ SM-11678	Hurt So Bad	1977	2.00	4.00	8.00
—Reissue of 269					
☐ SM-11814	The Lettermen!!! … And "Live!"	1978	2.00	4.00	8.00
—Reissue of 2758					
☐ SM-11970	Goin' Out of My Head	1979	2.00	4.00	8.00
—Reissue of 2865					
☐ SN-16071	The Best of the Lettermen	1980	2.00	4.00	8.00
—Budget-line reissue					
☐ SN-16190	Let It Be Me	1981	2.00	4.00	8.00
—Budget-line reissue					
☐ SN-16191	And I Love Her	1981	2.00	4.00	8.00
—Budget-line reissue					
☐ SN-16222	The Best of the Lettermen, Vol. 2	198?	2.00	4.00	8.00
—Budget-line reissue					
☐ SN-16312	All-Time Greatest Hits	198?	2.00	4.00	8.00
—Budget-line reissue					
LONGINES SYMPHONETTE					
☐ 220 [(5)]	A Time for Us	1972	7.50	15.00	30.00
PICKWICK					
☐ SPC-3294	Soft Hits	1972	2.50	5.00	10.00
☐ SPC-3565	With Love	1978	2.00	4.00	8.00

LEVEY, STAN
BETHLEHEM

Number	Title (A Side/B Side)	Yr	VG	VG+	NM
☐ BCP-37 [M]	This Time the Dream's On Me	1956	12.50	25.00	50.00
☐ BCP-71 [M]	Grand Stan	1957	12.50	25.00	50.00
☐ BCP-1017 [10]	Stan Levey Plays	1954	30.00	60.00	120.00
MODE					
☐ LP-101 [M]	Stan Levey Quartet	1957	20.00	40.00	80.00

LEVIATHAN
MACH

☐ XMA-12501	Leviathan	1974	10.00	20.00	40.00

LEVIN, MARC
SAVOY

☐ MG-12190 [M]	The Dragon Suite	1967	6.25	12.50	25.00
SWEET DRAGON					
☐ 1	Songs, Dances and Prayers	197?	5.00	10.00	20.00

LEVINE, HENRY
RCA CAMDEN

☐ CAL-321 [M]	Lower Basin Street	1958	6.25	12.50	25.00
RCA VICTOR					
☐ LPM-1283 [M]	Dixieland Jazz Band	1956	12.50	25.00	50.00

LEVINSON, MARK
MARK LEVINSON

☐ 7	Jazz at Long Wharf	1979	7.50	15.00	30.00
—Audiophile edition pressed at 45 rpm					

LEVISTER, ALONZO
DEBUT

☐ DEB-125 [M]	Manhattan Moondrama	1956	37.50	75.00	150.00

LEVITT, ROD
RCA VICTOR

☐ LSP-3372 [S]	Insight	1965	5.00	10.00	20.00
☐ LSP-3448 [S]	Solid Ground	1965	5.00	10.00	20.00
☐ LSP-3615 [S]	42nd Street	1966	5.00	10.00	20.00
RIVERSIDE					
☐ RS-9471 [S]	The Dynamic Sound Patterns of the Rod Levitt Orchestra	1964	5.00	10.00	20.00

LEVITTS, THE
ESP-DISK'

☐ S-1095	We Are the Levitts	1970	6.25	12.50	25.00

LEVY, LOU
JUBILEE

☐ JLP-1101 [M]	Lou Levy Plays Baby Grand Jazz	1959	10.00	20.00	40.00
☐ SDJLP-1101 [S]	Lou Levy Plays Baby Grand Jazz	1959	10.00	20.00	40.00
NOCTURNE					
☐ NLP-10 [10]	Lou Levy Trio	1954	25.00	50.00	100.00
PHILIPS					
☐ PHS 600056 [S]	The Hymn	1962	5.00	10.00	20.00
RCA VICTOR					
☐ LPM-1267 [M]	Solo Scene	1956	12.50	25.00	50.00
☐ LPM-1319 [M]	Jazz in Four Colors	1956	12.50	25.00	50.00
☐ LPM-1491 [M]	A Most Musical Fella	1957	12.50	25.00	50.00

LEVY, LOU/CONTE CANDOLI
ATLANTIC

☐ 1268 [M]	West Coast Wailers	1957	12.50	25.00	50.00
—Black label					
☐ 1268 [M]	West Coast Wailers	1961	6.25	12.50	25.00
—Multicolor label, white "fan" logo at right					

LEVY, O'DONEL
GROOVE MERCHANT

☐ 501	Black Velvet	1971	6.25	12.50	25.00
☐ 507	Breeding of Mind	1972	6.25	12.50	25.00
☐ 518	Dawn of a New Day	1973	6.25	12.50	25.00
☐ 526	Simba	1974	7.50	15.00	30.00
☐ 535	Everything I Do Gonna Be Funky	1975	7.50	15.00	30.00
☐ 3313	Windows	197?	5.00	10.00	20.00
☐ 4408 [(2)]	Hands of Fire	197?	6.25	12.50	25.00

LEWD
ICI

Number	Title (A Side/B Side)	Yr	VG	VG+	NM
☐ CF 200	American Wino	1982	10.00	20.00	40.00

LEWIS, BARBARA
ATLANTIC

☐ 8086 [M]	Hello Stranger	1963	10.00	20.00	40.00
☐ SD 8086 [S]	Hello Stranger	1963	12.50	25.00	50.00
☐ 8090 [M]	Snap Your Fingers	1964	10.00	20.00	40.00
☐ SD 8090 [S]	Snap Your Fingers	1964	12.50	25.00	50.00
☐ 8110 [M]	Baby, I'm Yours	1965	10.00	20.00	40.00
☐ SD 8110 [S]	Baby, I'm Yours	1965	12.50	25.00	50.00
☐ 8118 [M]	It's Magic	1966	7.50	15.00	30.00
☐ SD 8118 [S]	It's Magic	1966	10.00	20.00	40.00
☐ SD 8173	Workin' on a Groovy Thing	1968	6.25	12.50	25.00
☐ SD 8286	The Best of Barbara Lewis	1971	5.00	10.00	20.00
COLLECTABLES					
☐ COL-5104	Golden Classics	198?	2.50	5.00	10.00
ENTERPRISE					
☐ ENS-1006	The Many Grooves of Barbara Lewis	1970	6.25	12.50	25.00

LEWIS, BOBBY (1)
R&B singer.
BELTONE

☐ 4000 [M]	Tossin' and Turnin'	1961	50.00	100.00	200.00

LEWIS, BOBBY (2)
Country singer.
ACE OF HEARTS

☐ 1002	Too Many Memories	1974	3.75	7.50	15.00
RPA					
☐ 1002	Portrait in Love	1976	2.50	5.00	10.00
☐ 1013	Soul Full of Music	1977	2.50	5.00	10.00
UNITED ARTISTS					
☐ UAL-3582 [M]	How Long Has It Been	1967	6.25	12.50	25.00
☐ UAS-6582 [S]	How Long Has It Been	1967	6.25	12.50	25.00
☐ UAS-6616	A World of Love from Bobby Lewis	1967	5.00	10.00	20.00
☐ UAS-6629	An Ordinary Miracle	1968	5.00	10.00	20.00
☐ UAS-6673	From Heaven to Heartache	1968	5.00	10.00	20.00
☐ UAS-6717	Thanks for You and I	1969	5.00	10.00	20.00
☐ UAS-6760	The Best of Bobby Lewis, Vol. 1	1970	3.75	7.50	15.00

LEWIS, DAVE
A&M

☐ LP-105 [M]	Little Green Thing	1964	5.00	10.00	20.00
☐ SP-4105 [S]	Little Green Thing	1964	6.25	12.50	25.00
JERDEN					
☐ JRL-7006 [M]	Dave Lewis Plays Herb Alpert and the Tijuana Brass	1966	5.00	10.00	20.00
☐ JRLS-7006 [S]	Dave Lewis Plays Herb Alpert and the Tijuana Brass	1966	6.25	12.50	25.00

LEWIS, FURRY
AMPEX

☐ A-10140	Live at the Gaslight	1971	6.25	12.50	25.00
BLUESVILLE					
☐ BVLP-1036 [M]	Back on My Feet Again	1961	25.00	50.00	100.00
—Blue label, silver print					
☐ BVLP-1036 [M]	Back on My Feet Again	1964	7.50	15.00	30.00
—Blue label, trident logo at right					
☐ BVLP-1037 [M]	Done Changed My Mind	1961	25.00	50.00	100.00
—Blue label, silver print					
☐ BVLP-1037 [M]	Done Changed My Mind	1964	7.50	15.00	30.00
—Blue label, trident logo at right					

LEWIS, GARY, AND THE PLAYBOYS
LIBERTY

☐ LM-1003	This Diamond Ring	1981	2.00	4.00	8.00
—Reissue of United Artists 1008					
☐ LRP-3408 [M]	This Diamond Ring	1965	5.00	10.00	20.00
☐ LRP-3419 [M]	A Session with Gary Lewis and the Playboys	1965	5.00	10.00	20.00
☐ LRP-3428 [M]	Everybody Loves a Clown	1965	5.00	10.00	20.00
☐ LRP-3435 [M]	She's Just My Style	1966	3.75	7.50	15.00
☐ LRP-3452 [M]	Hits Again!	1966	3.75	7.50	15.00
☐ LRP-3468 [M]	Golden Greats	1966	3.75	7.50	15.00
☐ LRP-3487 [M]	(You Don't Have to) Paint Me a Picture	1967	3.75	7.50	15.00
—Side 1 plays as listed					
☐ LRP-3487 [M]	(You Don't Have to) Paint Me a Picture	1967	5.00	10.00	20.00
—Side 1, Song 4 claims to be "Tina" but plays "Ice Melts in the Sun"					
☐ LRP-3519 [M]	New Directions	1967	3.75	7.50	15.00
☐ LRP-3524 [M]	Listen	1967	3.75	7.50	15.00
☐ LST-7408 [S]	This Diamond Ring	1965	6.25	12.50	25.00
☐ LST-7419 [S]	A Session with Gary Lewis and the Playboys	1965	6.25	12.50	25.00
☐ LST-7428 [S]	Everybody Loves a Clown	1965	6.25	12.50	25.00
☐ LST-7435 [S]	She's Just My Style	1966	5.00	10.00	20.00
☐ LST-7452 [S]	Hits Again!	1966	5.00	10.00	20.00
☐ LST-7468 [S]	Golden Greats	1966	5.00	10.00	20.00
—Side 2 plays as listed					
☐ LST-7468 [S]	Golden Greats	1966	7.50	15.00	30.00
—Side 2, Song 2 claims to be "I Won't Make That Mistake Again" but it plays "You've Got to Hide Your Love Away"					
☐ LST-7487 [S]	(You Don't Have to) Paint Me a Picture	1967	5.00	10.00	20.00
—Side 1 plays as listed					
☐ LST-7487 [S]	(You Don't Have to) Paint Me a Picture	1967	6.25	12.50	25.00
—Side 1, Song 4 claims to be "Tina" but plays "Ice Melts in the Sun"					
☐ LST-7519 [S]	New Directions	1967	3.75	7.50	15.00
☐ LST-7524 [S]	Listen	1967	3.75	7.50	15.00
☐ LST-7568	Gary Lewis Now!	1968	3.75	7.50	15.00
☐ LST-7589	More Golden Greats	1968	3.75	7.50	15.00
☐ LST-7606	Close Cover Before Playing	1969	3.75	7.50	15.00
☐ LST-7623	Rhythm of the Rain	1969	3.75	7.50	15.00

Number	Title (A Side/B Side)	Yr	VG	VG+	NM
❏ LST-7633	I'm On the Right Road Now	1970	3.75	7.50	15.00
❏ LN-10241	Golden Greats	198?	2.00	4.00	8.00

—Budget-line reissue

RHINO
❏ RNLP-163	Greatest Hits (1965-1968)	1985	2.50	5.00	10.00

SUNSET
❏ SUM-1168 [M]	Gary Lewis and the Playboys	1967	3.00	6.00	12.00
❏ SUS-5168 [S]	Gary Lewis and the Playboys	1967	3.00	6.00	12.00
❏ SUS-5262	Rhythm!	1969	3.00	6.00	12.00

UNITED ARTISTS
❏ UA-LA430-E	The Very Best of Gary Lewis and the Playboys	1975	2.50	5.00	10.00
❏ LM-1003	This Diamond Ring	1980	2.50	5.00	10.00

—Edited reissue of Liberty 7408

LEWIS, GEORGE (1)
AMERICAN MUSIC
❏ 639 [10]	The George Lewis Band in the French Quarter	1951	20.00	40.00	80.00
❏ 645 [10]	George Lewis with Kid Shots Madison	1952	20.00	40.00	80.00

ATLANTIC
❏ SD 1411 [S]	The George Lewis Band	1963	5.00	10.00	20.00

BLUE NOTE
❏ BLP-1205 [M]	George Lewis and His New Orleans Stompers, Volume 1	1955	25.00	50.00	100.00

—Regular version, Lexington Ave. address on label
❏ BLP-1205 [M]	George Lewis and His New Orleans Stompers, Volume 1	1955	37.50	75.00	150.00

—"Deep groove" version (deep indentation under label on both sides)
❏ BLP-1205 [M]	George Lewis and His New Orleans Stompers, Volume 1	1963	6.25	12.50	25.00

—With "New York, USA" address on label
❏ BLP-1206 [M]	George Lewis and His New Orleans Stompers, Volume 2	1955	25.00	50.00	100.00

—Regular version, Lexington Ave. address on label
❏ BLP-1206 [M]	George Lewis and His New Orleans Stompers, Volume 2	1955	37.50	75.00	150.00

—"Deep groove" version (deep indentation under label on both sides)
❏ BLP-1206 [M]	George Lewis and His New Orleans Stompers, Volume 2	1963	6.25	12.50	25.00

—With "New York, USA" address on label
❏ BLP-1208 [M]	George Lewis Concert!	1955	25.00	50.00	100.00

—Regular version, Lexington Ave. address on label
❏ BLP-1208 [M]	George Lewis Concert!	1955	37.50	75.00	150.00

—"Deep groove" version (deep indentation under label on both sides)
❏ BLP-1208 [M]	George Lewis Concert!	1963	6.25	12.50	25.00

—With "New York, USA" address on label
❏ BLP-7010 [10]	George Lewis' New Orleans Stompers, Volume 1	1951	62.50	125.00	250.00
❏ BLP-7013 [10]	George Lewis' New Orleans Stompers, Volume 2	1951	62.50	125.00	250.00
❏ BLP-7027 [10]	George Lewis' New Orleans Stompers, Volume 3	1954	62.50	125.00	250.00
❏ BLP-7028 [10]	George Lewis' New Orleans Stompers, Volume 4	1954	62.50	125.00	250.00

CAVALIER
❏ CVLP-6004 [M]	George Lewis in Hi-Fi	1956	15.00	30.00	60.00

CIRCLE
❏ L-421 [10]	George Lewis and His New Orleans All-Stars	1951	20.00	40.00	80.00

DELMAR
❏ DL-201 [M]	Doctor Jazz	195?	12.50	25.00	50.00
❏ DL-202 [M]	On Parade	195?	12.50	25.00	50.00

DELMARK
❏ DL-202	George Lewis' New Orleans Stompers	196?	6.25	12.50	25.00
❏ DL-203	George Lewis Memorial Album	196?	5.00	10.00	20.00

DISC JOCKEY
❏ DDL-100 [(2)M]	Jazz at Ohio Union	195?	300.00	600.00	1200.

—Box set with booklet

EMPIRICAL
❏ EM-107 [10]	Spirituals in Ragtime	1956	20.00	40.00	80.00

JAZZ MAN
❏ LP-1 [10]	George Lewis' Ragtime Band	1953	20.00	40.00	80.00

—"Limited First Pressing Dec. 25, 1953" on label at left
❏ LJ-331 [10]	New Orleans Music	1954	20.00	40.00	80.00

MOSAIC
❏ M5-132 [(5)]	The Complete Blue Note Recordings of George Lewis	199?	25.00	50.00	100.00

PARADOX
❏ LP-6001 [10]	George Lewis	1951	20.00	40.00	80.00

RIVERSIDE
❏ RLP 12-207 [M]	Jazz in the Classic New Orleans Tradition	1956	12.50	25.00	50.00

—White label, blue print
❏ RLP 12-207 [M]	Jazz in the Classic New Orleans Tradition	1959	7.50	15.00	30.00

—Blue label, microphone logo at top
❏ RLP 12-230 [M]	Jazz at Vespers	1957	12.50	25.00	50.00

—White label, blue print
❏ RLP 12-230 [M]	Jazz at Vespers	1959	7.50	15.00	30.00

—Blue label, microphone logo at top
❏ RLP 12-283 [M]	George Lewis of New Orleans	1958	10.00	20.00	40.00
❏ RLP-2507 [10]	George Lewis	1954	25.00	50.00	100.00
❏ RLP-2512 [10]	George Lewis with Guest Artist Red Allen	1955	25.00	50.00	100.00

SOUTHLAND
❏ SLP-208 [10]	George Lewis	1955	20.00	40.00	80.00

VERVE
❏ MGV-1019 [M]	Blues from the Bayou	1957	12.50	25.00	50.00
❏ V-1019 [M]	Blues from the Bayou	1961	5.00	10.00	20.00
❏ MGV-1021 [M]	Doctor Jazz	1957	12.50	25.00	50.00
❏ V-1021 [M]	Doctor Jazz	1961	5.00	10.00	20.00
❏ MGV-1024 [M]	Hot Time in the Old Town Tonight	1957	12.50	25.00	50.00
❏ V-1024 [M]	Hot Time in the Old Town Tonight	1961	5.00	10.00	20.00

Number	Title (A Side/B Side)	Yr	VG	VG+	NM
❏ V6-1024 [S]	Hot Time in the Old Town Tonight	1961	5.00	10.00	20.00
❏ MGV-1027 [M]	George Lewis' Dixieland Band	1957	12.50	25.00	50.00
❏ V-1027 [M]	George Lewis' Dixieland Band	1961	5.00	10.00	20.00
❏ MGVS-6064 [S]	Oh, Didn't He Ramble	1960	10.00	20.00	40.00
❏ MGVS-6113 [S]	Blues from the Bayou	1960	10.00	20.00	40.00
❏ MGVS-6122 [S]	Doctor Jazz	1960	10.00	20.00	40.00
❏ MGV-8232 [M]	George Lewis and Turk Murphy at Newport	1958	12.50	25.00	50.00
❏ V-8232 [M]	George Lewis and Turk Murphy at Newport	1961	5.00	10.00	20.00
❏ MGV-8277 [M]	The Perennial George Lewis	1958	12.50	25.00	50.00
❏ V-8277 [M]	The Perennial George Lewis	1961	5.00	10.00	20.00
❏ MGV-8303 [M]	On Stage: George Lewis Concert, Volume 1	1959	12.50	25.00	50.00
❏ V-8303 [M]	On Stage: George Lewis Concert, Volume 1	1961	5.00	10.00	20.00
❏ MGV-8304 [M]	On Stage: George Lewis Concert, Volume 2	1959	12.50	25.00	50.00
❏ V-8304 [M]	On Stage: George Lewis Concert, Volume 2	1961	5.00	10.00	20.00
❏ MGV-8325 [M]	Oh, Didn't He Ramble	1959	12.50	25.00	50.00
❏ V-8325 [M]	Oh, Didn't He Ramble	1961	5.00	10.00	20.00

LEWIS, HUEY, AND THE NEWS
CHRYSALIS
❏ CHR 1292	Huey Lewis and the News	1980	3.00	6.00	12.00
❏ CHR 1340	Picture This	1982	2.50	5.00	10.00
❏ FV 41292	Huey Lewis and the News	1983	2.00	4.00	8.00

—Reissue of 1292
❏ PV 41292	Huey Lewis and the News	198?	—	3.00	6.00

—Reissue with new prefix
❏ FV 41340	Picture This	1983	2.00	4.00	8.00

—Reissue of 1340
❏ FV 41412	Sports	1983	2.00	4.00	8.00
❏ OV 41412	Sports	198?	—	3.00	6.00

—Reissue with new prefix
❏ OV 41534	Fore!	1986	2.00	4.00	8.00
❏ OV 41622	Small World	1988	2.00	4.00	8.00

MOBILE FIDELITY
❏ 1-181	Sports	1985	6.25	12.50	25.00

—Audiophile vinyl

LEWIS, HUGH X.
KAPP
❏ KL-1462 [M]	The Hugh X. Lewis Album	1966	5.00	10.00	20.00
❏ KL-1494 [M]	Just Before Dawn	1966	5.00	10.00	20.00
❏ KL-1522 [M]	My Kind of Country	1967	7.50	15.00	30.00
❏ KS-3462 [S]	The Hugh X. Lewis Album	1966	6.25	12.50	25.00
❏ KS-3494 [S]	Just Before Dawn	1966	6.25	12.50	25.00
❏ KS-3522 [S]	My Kind of Country	1967	6.25	12.50	25.00
❏ KS-3545	Just a Prayer Away	1968	6.25	12.50	25.00
❏ KS-3563	Country Fever	1968	6.25	12.50	25.00

LEWIS, JERRY
DECCA
❏ DL 8410 [M]	Jerry Lewis Just Sings	1956	15.00	30.00	60.00
❏ DL 8595 [M]	More Jerry Lewis	1957	15.00	30.00	60.00
❏ DL 8936 [M]	Big Songs for Little People	1959	12.50	25.00	50.00
❏ DL 78936 [S]	Big Songs for Little People	1959	15.00	30.00	60.00

DOT
❏ DLP 3664 [M]	The Jerry Lewis Singers	1964	3.75	7.50	15.00
❏ DLP 25664 [S]	The Jerry Lewis Singers	1964	5.00	10.00	20.00

LEWIS, JERRY LEE
ACCORD
❏ SN-7133	I Walk the Line	1981	2.50	5.00	10.00

DESIGN
❏ DLP-165 [M]	Rockin' with Jerry Lee Lewis	1963	6.25	12.50	25.00
❏ DST-165 [R]	Rockin' with Jerry Lee Lewis	1963	5.00	10.00	20.00

ELEKTRA
❏ 6E-184	Jerry Lee Lewis	1979	3.00	6.00	12.00
❏ 6E-254	When Two Worlds Collide	1980	3.00	6.00	12.00
❏ 6E-291	Killer Country	1980	3.00	6.00	12.00
❏ 60191	The Best of Jerry Lee Lewis Featuring 39 and Holding	1982	2.50	5.00	10.00

HILLTOP
❏ 6102	Sunday After Church	1971	2.50	5.00	10.00
❏ 6110	Roll Over Beethoven	1972	2.50	5.00	10.00
❏ 6120	Rural Route #1	1972	2.50	5.00	10.00

MCA
❏ 5387	My Fingers Do the Talkin'	1983	2.50	5.00	10.00
❏ 5478	I Am What I Am	1984	2.50	5.00	10.00

MERCURY
❏ SRM-1-637	The "Killer" Rocks On	1972	3.75	7.50	15.00
❏ SRM-1-677	Sometimes a Memory Ain't Enough	1973	3.75	7.50	15.00
❏ 690 [DJ]	A Jerry Lee Lewis Radio Special	1973	12.50	25.00	50.00
❏ SRM-1-690	Southern Roots — Back Home to Memphis	1973	3.75	7.50	15.00
❏ SRM-1-710	I-40 Country	1974	3.75	7.50	15.00
❏ SRM-2-803 [(2)]	The Session	1973	5.00	10.00	20.00
❏ SRM-1-1030	Boogie Woogie Country Man	1975	3.75	7.50	15.00
❏ SRM-1-1064	Odd Man In	1975	3.75	7.50	15.00
❏ SRM-1-1109	Country Class	1976	3.75	7.50	15.00
❏ SRM-1-5004	Country Memories	1977	3.75	7.50	15.00
❏ SRM-1-5006	The Best of Jerry Lee Lewis Volume II	1978	3.75	7.50	15.00
❏ SRM-1-5010	Jerry Lee Lewis Keeps Rockin'	1978	3.75	7.50	15.00
❏ SR-61278	Live at the International, Las Vegas	1970	3.75	7.50	15.00
❏ SR-61318	In Loving Memories	1970	7.50	15.00	30.00
❏ SR-61323	There Must Be More to Love Than This	1971	3.75	7.50	15.00
❏ SR-61343	Touching Home	1971	3.75	7.50	15.00

—With photo of Jerry Lee in front of a brick wall
❏ SR-61343	Touching Home	1971	5.00	10.00	20.00

—With drawing on cover and small photo of Jerry Lee
❏ SR-61346	Would You Take Another Chance on Me?	1971	3.75	7.50	15.00
❏ SR-61366	Who's Gonna Play This Old Piano… (Think About It Darlin')	1972	3.75	7.50	15.00
❏ 822789-1	The Best of Jerry Lee Lewis Volume II	198?	2.50	5.00	10.00
❏ 826251-1	Greatest Hits	198?	2.50	5.00	10.00

L

Number	Title (A Side/B Side)	Yr	VG	VG+	NM
❏ 830399-1	Would You Take Another Chance on Me	1987	2.50	5.00	10.00
—Reissue of 61346					
❏ 836935-1	Killer: The Mercury Years Volume One, 1963-1968	1989	3.00	6.00	12.00
❏ 836938-1	Killer: The Mercury Years Volume Two, 1969-1972	1989	3.00	6.00	12.00
❏ 836941-1	Killer: The Mercury Years Volume Three, 1973-1977	1989	3.00	6.00	12.00
PAIR					
❏ PDL2-1132 [(2)]	Solid Gold	1986	3.00	6.00	12.00
PICKWICK					
❏ PTP-2055 [(2)]	Jerry Lee Lewis	1973	3.00	6.00	12.00
❏ SPC-3224	High Heel Sneakers	1970	2.50	5.00	10.00
❏ SPC-3344	Drinking Wine Spo-Dee-O-Dee	1973	2.50	5.00	10.00
POLYDOR					
❏ 826139-1	I'm on Fire	1985	2.50	5.00	10.00
❏ 839516-1	Great Balls of Fire!	1989	3.00	6.00	12.00
POWER PAK					
❏ 247	From the Vaults of Sun	1974	2.50	5.00	10.00
RHINO					
❏ RNDF-255 [PD]	Original Sun Greatest Hits	1983	3.75	7.50	15.00
❏ RNDA-1499 [(2)]	Milestones	1985	3.75	7.50	15.00
❏ R1-70255	Original Sun Greatest Hits	1989	2.50	5.00	10.00
—Reissue of 255 on black vinyl					
❏ R1-70656	Jerry Lee Lewis	1989	3.00	6.00	12.00
—Reissue of Sun 1230					
❏ R1-70657	Jerry Lee's Greatest	1989	3.00	6.00	12.00
—Reissue of Sun 1265					
❏ R1-70899	Wild One: Rare Tracks from Jerry Lee Lewis	1989	3.00	6.00	12.00
❏ R1-71499 [(2)]	Milestones	1989	3.00	6.00	12.00
—Reissue of 1499					
SEARS					
❏ SPS-610	Hound Dog	1970	6.25	12.50	25.00
SMASH					
❏ SL-7001	Golden Hits	1980	3.00	6.00	12.00
❏ MGS-27040 [M]	The Golden Hits of Jerry Lee Lewis	1964	6.25	12.50	25.00
❏ MGS-27056 [M]	The Greatest Live Show on Earth	1964	25.00	50.00	100.00
❏ MGS-27063 [M]	The Return of Rock	1965	7.50	15.00	30.00
❏ MGS-27071 [M]	Country Songs for City Folks	1965	6.25	12.50	25.00
❏ MGS-27079 [M]	Memphis Beat	1966	6.25	12.50	25.00
❏ MGS-27086 [M]	By Request — More of the Greatest Live Show on Earth	1966	7.50	15.00	30.00
❏ MGS-27097 [M]	Soul My Way	1967	7.50	15.00	30.00
❏ SRS-67040 [S]	The Golden Hits of Jerry Lee Lewis	1964	7.50	15.00	30.00
❏ SRS-67040 [S]	The Golden Rock Hits of Jerry Lee Lewis	1969	3.75	7.50	15.00
—Retitled reissue					
❏ SRS-67056 [S]	The Greatest Live Show on Earth	1964	37.50	75.00	150.00
❏ SRS-67063 [S]	The Return of Rock	1965	10.00	20.00	40.00
❏ SRS-67071	All Country	1969	3.75	7.50	15.00
—Retitled reissue					
❏ SRS-67071 [S]	Country Songs for City Folks	1965	7.50	15.00	30.00
❏ SRS-67079 [S]	Memphis Beat	1966	7.50	15.00	30.00
❏ SRS-67086 [S]	By Request — More of the Greatest Live Show on Earth	1966	10.00	20.00	40.00
❏ SRS-67097 [S]	Soul My Way	1967	10.00	20.00	40.00
❏ SRS-67104	Another Place Another Time	1968	5.00	10.00	20.00
❏ SRS-67112	She Still Comes Around (To Love What's Left of Me)	1969	5.00	10.00	20.00
❏ SRS-67117	Jerry Lee Lewis Sings the Country Music Hall of Fame Hits, Vol. 1	1969	5.00	10.00	20.00
❏ SRS-67118	Jerry Lee Lewis Sings the Country Music Hall of Fame Hits, Vol. 2	1969	5.00	10.00	20.00
❏ SRS-67128	She Even Woke Me Up to Say Goodbye	1970	5.00	10.00	20.00
❏ SRS-67131	The Best of Jerry Lee Lewis	1970	5.00	10.00	20.00
SUN					
❏ LP-102	Original Golden Hits — Volume 1	1969	3.75	7.50	15.00
❏ LP-103	Original Golden Hits — Volume 2	1969	3.75	7.50	15.00
❏ LP-107	Rockin' Rhythm and Blues	1969	3.75	7.50	15.00
❏ SUN-108	The Golden Cream of the Country	1969	3.75	7.50	15.00
❏ SUN-108 [M]	The Golden Cream of the Country	1969	10.00	20.00	40.00
—Mono version is white label promo only; the word "MONO" appears at 9 o'clock on the label					
❏ LP-114	A Taste of Country	1970	3.75	7.50	15.00
❏ LP-121	Ole Tyme Country Music	1971	3.75	7.50	15.00
❏ LP-124	Monsters	1971	3.75	7.50	15.00
❏ LP-128	Original Golden Hits — Volume 3	1972	3.75	7.50	15.00
❏ SUN-145	Roots	1982	3.00	6.00	12.00
❏ 1005	The Original	1978	3.00	6.00	12.00
❏ SUN-1011	Duets	1978	3.75	7.50	15.00
—As "Jerry Lewis and Friends"; gold vinyl					
❏ 1018	Trio +	1979	3.00	6.00	12.00
—With Carl Perkins, Charlie Rich and (uncredited) Orion					
❏ SLP-1230 [M]	Jerry Lee Lewis	1958	50.00	100.00	200.00
❏ SLP-1265 [M]	Jerry Lee's Greatest	1961	62.50	125.00	250.00
❏ SLP-1265 [M]	Jerry Lee's Greatest	1961	200.00	400.00	800.00
—White label promo					
SUNNYVALE					
❏ 905	The Sun Story, Vol. 5	1977	2.50	5.00	10.00
WING					
❏ PKW2-125 [(2)]	The Legend of Jerry Lee Lewis	1969	6.25	12.50	25.00
❏ MGW-12340 [M]	The Return of Rock	1967	3.00	6.00	12.00
❏ SRW-16340	In Demand	1968	2.50	5.00	10.00
❏ SRW-16340 [S]	The Return of Rock	1967	3.00	6.00	12.00
❏ SRW-16406	Unlimited	1968	3.00	6.00	12.00

LEWIS, JERRY LEE, AND LINDA GAIL LEWIS
SMASH

Number	Title (A Side/B Side)	Yr	VG	VG+	NM
❏ SRS-67126	Together	1969	5.00	10.00	20.00

LEWIS, JOHN
ATLANTIC

Number	Title (A Side/B Side)	Yr	VG	VG+	NM
❏ 1272 [M]	The John Lewis Piano	1958	10.00	20.00	40.00
—Black label					
❏ 1272 [M]	The John Lewis Piano	1961	5.00	10.00	20.00
—Multicolor label, white "fan" logo at right					
❏ 1313 [M]	Improvised Meditations and Excursions	1959	10.00	20.00	40.00
—Black label					
❏ 1313 [M]	Improvised Meditations and Excursions	1961	5.00	10.00	20.00
—Multicolor label, white "fan" logo at right					
❏ SD 1313 [S]	Improvised Meditations and Excursions	1959	12.50	25.00	50.00
—Green label					
❏ SD 1313 [S]	Improvised Meditations and Excursions	1961	5.00	10.00	20.00
—Multicolor label, white "fan" logo at right					
❏ 1334 [M]	The Golden Striker	1960	6.25	12.50	25.00
—Multicolor label, white "fan" logo at right					
❏ SD 1334 [S]	The Golden Striker	1960	7.50	15.00	30.00
—Multicolor label, white "fan" logo at right					
❏ 1365 [M]	John Lewis Presents Jazz Abstractions	1961	6.25	12.50	25.00
—Multicolor label, white "fan" logo at right					
❏ SD 1365 [S]	John Lewis Presents Jazz Abstractions	1961	7.50	15.00	30.00
—Multicolor label, white "fan" logo at right					
❏ SD 1365 [S]	John Lewis Presents Jazz Abstractions	1964	5.00	10.00	20.00
—Multicolor label, black "fan" logo at right					
❏ 1370 [M]	Original Sin	1961	6.25	12.50	25.00
—Multicolor label, white "fan" logo at right					
❏ SD 1370 [S]	Original Sin	1961	7.50	15.00	30.00
—Multicolor label, white "fan" logo at right					
❏ SD 1370 [S]	Original Sin	1964	5.00	10.00	20.00
—Multicolor label, black "fan" logo at right					
❏ 1375 [M]	The Wonderful World of Jazz	1961	6.25	12.50	25.00
—Multicolor label, white "fan" logo at right					
❏ SD 1375 [S]	The Wonderful World of Jazz	1961	7.50	15.00	30.00
—Multicolor label, white "fan" logo at right					
❏ SD 1375 [S]	The Wonderful World of Jazz	1964	5.00	10.00	20.00
—Multicolor label, black "fan" logo at right					
❏ SD 1392 [S]	European Encounter	1963	5.00	10.00	20.00
❏ SD 1402 [S]	Animal Dance	1963	5.00	10.00	20.00
❏ SD 1425 [S]	Essence	1964	5.00	10.00	20.00
RCA VICTOR					
❏ LPM-1742 [M]	European Windows	1958	12.50	25.00	50.00

LEWIS, JOHN, AND SACHA DISTEL
ATLANTIC

Number	Title (A Side/B Side)	Yr	VG	VG+	NM
❏ 1267 [M]	Afternoon in Paris	1957	10.00	20.00	40.00
—Black label					
❏ 1267 [M]	Afternoon in Paris	1964	3.75	7.50	15.00
—Multicolor label, black "fan" logo at right					

LEWIS, JOHN, AND BILL PERKINS
PACIFIC JAZZ

Number	Title (A Side/B Side)	Yr	VG	VG+	NM
❏ PJ-44 [M]	Grand Encounter: 2' East, 3' West	1962	10.00	20.00	40.00
—Reissue with new number					
❏ PJ-1217 [M]	Grand Encounter: 2' East, 3' West	1956	37.50	75.00	150.00
WORLD PACIFIC					
❏ WP-1217 [M]	Grand Encounter: 2' East, 3' West	1959	25.00	50.00	100.00

LEWIS, KATHARINE HANDY
FOLKWAYS

Number	Title (A Side/B Side)	Yr	VG	VG+	NM
❏ FJ-3540 [M]	W.C. Handy Blues	1958	7.50	15.00	30.00

LEWIS, LINDA GAIL
SMASH

Number	Title (A Side/B Side)	Yr	VG	VG+	NM
❏ SRS-67119	Two Sides of Linda Gail Lewis	1969	6.25	12.50	25.00

LEWIS, MEADE LUX
ABC-PARAMOUNT

Number	Title (A Side/B Side)	Yr	VG	VG+	NM
❏ ABC-164 [M]	Out of the Roaring 20's	1956	10.00	20.00	40.00
ATLANTIC					
❏ ALS-133 [10]	Boogie-Woogie Interpretations	1952	25.00	50.00	100.00
BLUE NOTE					
❏ BLP-7018 [10]	Boogie-Woogie Classics	1952	62.50	125.00	250.00
DISC					
❏ DLP-352 [10]	Meade Lux Lewis at the Philharmonic	195?	50.00	100.00	200.00
DOWN HOME					
❏ MGD-7 [M]	Yancey's Last Ride	1956	12.50	25.00	50.00
MERCURY					
❏ MG-25158 [10]	Meade Lux Lewis	1951	37.50	75.00	150.00
PHILIPS					
❏ PHM 200044 [M]	Boogie Woogie House Party	196?	5.00	10.00	20.00
❏ PHS 600044 [S]	Boogie Woogie House Party	196?	6.25	12.50	25.00
RIVERSIDE					
❏ RLP-402 [M]	The Blues Piano Artistry of Meade Lux Lewis	1962	6.25	12.50	25.00
❏ RS-9402 [S]	The Blues Piano Artistry of Meade Lux Lewis	1962	7.50	15.00	30.00
STINSON					
❏ 25 [M]	Meade Lux Lewis	196?	5.00	10.00	20.00
TOPS					
❏ L-1533 [M]	Barrelhouse Piano	195?	7.50	15.00	30.00
—Also see ALBERT AMMONS.					
VERVE					
❏ MGV-1006 [M]	Cat House Piano	1957	12.50	25.00	50.00
❏ V-1006 [M]	Cat House Piano	1961	6.25	12.50	25.00
❏ MGV-1007 [M]	Meade Lux Lewis	1957	12.50	25.00	50.00
❏ V-1007 [M]	Meade Lux Lewis	1961	6.25	12.50	25.00

LEWIS, MEADE LUX, AND LOUIS BELLSON
CLEF

Number	Title (A Side/B Side)	Yr	VG	VG+	NM
❏ MGC-632 [M]	Boogie Woogie Piano and Drums	1954	15.00	30.00	60.00

Number	Title (A Side/B Side)	Yr	VG	VG+	NM
LEWIS, MEL					
MODE					
❑ LP-103 [M]	Mel Lewis Sextet	1957	20.00	40.00	80.00
SAN FRANCISCO					
❑ 2 [M]	Got 'Cha	1957	25.00	50.00	100.00
VEE JAY					
❑ VJS-3062	Gettin' Together	1974	5.00	10.00	20.00
LEWIS, RAMSEY					
Includes releases by "Ramsey Lewis Trio."					
ARGO					
❑ LP-611 [M]	Gentleman of Swing	1958	12.50	25.00	50.00
❑ LPS-611 [S]	Gentleman of Swing.	1959	15.00	30.00	60.00
❑ LP-627 [M]	Gentleman of Jazz.	1958	12.50	25.00	50.00
❑ LPS-627 [S]	Gentleman of Jazz.	1959	15.00	30.00	60.00
❑ LP-642 [M]	The Ramsey Lewis Trio with Lee Winchester.	1959	10.00	20.00	40.00
❑ LPS-642 [S]	The Ramsey Lewis Trio with Lee Winchester.	1959	12.50	25.00	50.00
❑ LP-645 [M]	An Hour with the Ramsey Lewis Trio.	1959	10.00	20.00	40.00
❑ LPS-645 [S]	An Hour with the Ramsey Lewis Trio.	1959	12.50	25.00	50.00
❑ LP-665 [M]	Stretching Out.	1960	10.00	20.00	40.00
❑ LPS-665 [S]	Stretching Out.	1960	12.50	25.00	50.00
❑ LP-671 [M]	The Ramsey Lewis Trio in Chicago.	1961	10.00	20.00	40.00
❑ LPS-671 [S]	The Ramsey Lewis Trio in Chicago.	1961	12.50	25.00	50.00
❑ LP-680 [M]	More Music from the Soil.	1961	10.00	20.00	40.00
❑ LPS-680 [S]	More Music from the Soil.	1961	12.50	25.00	50.00
❑ LP-687 [M]	Sound of Christmas.	1961	10.00	20.00	40.00
❑ LPS-687 [S]	Sound of Christmas.	1961	12.50	25.00	50.00
❑ LP-693 [M]	The Sound of Spring.	1962	6.25	12.50	25.00
❑ LPS-693 [S]	The Sound of Spring.	1962	7.50	15.00	30.00
❑ LP-701 [M]	Country Meets the Blues	1962	6.25	12.50	25.00
❑ LPS-701 [S]	Country Meets the Blues	1962	7.50	15.00	30.00
❑ LP-705 [M]	Bossa Nova	1962	6.25	12.50	25.00
❑ LPS-705 [S]	Bossa Nova	1962	7.50	15.00	30.00
❑ LP-715 [M]	Pot Luck	1963	6.25	12.50	25.00
❑ LPS-715 [S]	Pot Luck	1963	7.50	15.00	30.00
❑ LP-723 [M]	Barefoot Sunday Blues	1963	6.25	12.50	25.00
❑ LPS-723 [S]	Barefoot Sunday Blues	1963	7.50	15.00	30.00
❑ LP-732 [M]	Bach to the Blues	1964	6.25	12.50	25.00
❑ LPS-732 [S]	Bach to the Blues	1964	7.50	15.00	30.00
❑ LP-741 [M]	The Ramsey Lewis Trio at the Bohemian Caverns	1964	6.25	12.50	25.00
❑ LPS-741 [S]	The Ramsey Lewis Trio at the Bohemian Caverns	1964	7.50	15.00	30.00
❑ LP-745 [M]	More Sounds of Christmas	1964	6.25	12.50	25.00
❑ LPS-745 [S]	More Sounds of Christmas	1964	7.50	15.00	30.00
❑ LP-755 [M]	Choice! The Best of the Ramsey Lewis Trio	1965	7.50	15.00	30.00
❑ LPS-755 [S]	Choice! The Best of the Ramsey Lewis Trio	1965	10.00	20.00	40.00
❑ LP-757 [M]	The In Crowd	1965	6.25	12.50	25.00
❑ LPS-757 [S]	The In Crowd	1965	7.50	15.00	30.00
CADET					
❑ LP-687X [M]	Sound of Christmas	1966	5.00	10.00	20.00
—Reissue of Argo 687					
❑ LPS-687X [S]	Sound of Christmas	1966	5.00	10.00	20.00
—Reissue of Argo 687-S					
❑ LPS-745 [S]	More Sounds of Christmas	1966	5.00	10.00	20.00
❑ LPS-755 [S]	Choice! The Best of the Ramsey Lewis Trio	1965	5.00	10.00	20.00
❑ LPS-761 [S]	Hang On Ramsey!	1966	5.00	10.00	20.00
❑ LPS-771 [S]	Swingin'	1966	5.00	10.00	20.00
❑ LPS-774 [S]	Wade in the Water	1966	5.00	10.00	20.00
❑ LP-782 [M]	The Movie Album	1967	5.00	10.00	20.00
❑ LP-790 [M]	Goin' Latin	1967	5.00	10.00	20.00
❑ LP-794 [M]	Dancing in the Street	1967	5.00	10.00	20.00
COLUMBIA					
❑ HC 47687	Live at the Savoy	1982	20.00	40.00	80.00
—Half-speed mastered edition					
EMARCY					
❑ MG-36150 [M]	Down to Earth	1958	10.00	20.00	40.00
❑ SR-80029 [S]	Down to Earth	1958	12.50	25.00	50.00
MERCURY					
❑ MG-20536 [M]	Down to Earth	1965	5.00	10.00	20.00
❑ SR-60536 [S]	Down to Earth	1965	6.25	12.50	25.00
LEWIS, RAMSEY, AND JEAN DUSHON					
ARGO					
❑ 750 [M]	You Better Believe Me	1965	6.25	12.50	25.00
❑ 750S [S]	You Better Believe Me	1965	7.50	15.00	30.00
LEWIS, ROBERT Q.					
ATCO					
❑ 33-212 [M]	I'm Just Wild About Vaudeville	1963	6.25	12.50	25.00
❑ SD 33-212 [S]	I'm Just Wild About Vaudeville	1963	7.50	15.00	30.00
"X"					
❑ LXA-1033 [M]	Robert Q. Lewis and His Gang	1956	12.50	25.00	50.00
LEWIS, SHARI					
RCA CAMDEN					
❑ CAL-1052 [M]	Jack and the Beanstalk and Other Stories	1964	7.50	15.00	30.00
❑ CAS-1052 [S]	Jack and the Beanstalk and Other Stories	1964	7.50	15.00	30.00
RCA VICTOR					
❑ LBY-1006 [M]	Fun in Shariland	1954	20.00	40.00	80.00
LEWIS, SMILEY					
IMPERIAL					
❑ LP-9141 [M]	I Hear You Knocking	1961	150.00	300.00	600.00
—Black vinyl					
❑ LP-9141 [M]	I Hear You Knocking	1961	1500.	3000.	6000.
—Green vinyl (one copy known)					
LEWIS, TED					
COLUMBIA					
❑ CL 6127 [10]	Classic Jazz	1950	12.50	25.00	50.00

Number	Title (A Side/B Side)	Yr	VG	VG+	NM
DECCA					
❑ DL 4905 [M]	Ted Lewis' Greatest Hits	1967	6.25	12.50	25.00
❑ DL 8321 [M]	Is Everybody Happy?	1956	10.00	20.00	40.00
❑ DL 8322 [M]	The Medicine Man for the Blues	1956	10.00	20.00	40.00
EPIC					
❑ LN 3170 [M]	Everybody's Happy!	1955	10.00	20.00	40.00
LEWIS AND CLARKE EXPEDITION, THE					
COLGEMS					
❑ COM-105 [M]	The Lewis and Clarke Expedition	1967	6.25	12.50	25.00
❑ COS-105 [S]	The Lewis and Clarke Expedition	1967	7.50	15.00	30.00
LEWIS CONNECTION, THE					
Minneapolis group; PRINCE is featured on one track.					
(NO LABEL)					
❑ (no #)	The Lewis Connection	1979	100.00	200.00	400.00
LEWIS FAMILY, THE					
STARDAY					
❑ SLP-121 [M]	Singin' Time Down South	1960	7.50	15.00	30.00
❑ SLP-161 [M]	Anniversary Celebration	1962	7.50	15.00	30.00
❑ SLP-193 [M]	Gospel Special	1962	7.50	15.00	30.00
❑ SLP-238 [M]	Sing Me a Gospel Song	1962	7.50	15.00	30.00
❑ SLP-252 [M]	All Night Singing Convention	1963	7.50	15.00	30.00
❑ SLP-289 [M]	Singin' in My Soul	1964	7.50	15.00	30.00
❑ SLP-331 [M]	The First Family of Gospel Music	1965	7.50	15.00	30.00
❑ SLP-364 [M]	The Lewis Family Sings the Gospel with Carl Story	1965	7.50	15.00	30.00
❑ SLP-381 [M]	The Lewis Family Album	1965	7.50	15.00	30.00
❑ SLP-395 [M]	Shall We Gather at the River	1966	6.25	12.50	25.00
❑ SLP-408 [M]	Time Is Moving On	1966	6.25	12.50	25.00
❑ SLP-422	Golden Gospel Banjo	1968	5.00	10.00	20.00
❑ SLP-433	Did You Ever Go Sailing	1969	5.00	10.00	20.00
❑ SLP-450	Golden Gospel of the Lewis Family	1970	5.00	10.00	20.00
LIBBY, JERRY					
SABRINA					
❑ SA-100 [M]	Live? At Wilkins	1964	5.00	10.00	20.00
LIBERACE					
ABC					
❑ 4002	16 Great Performances	1974	3.00	6.00	12.00
AVI					
❑ 1023	Candlelight Classics	1973	3.00	6.00	12.00
❑ 1029	The World of Liberacte	1974	3.00	6.00	12.00
CBS					
❑ FM 42244	Concert Favorites	1986	2.50	5.00	10.00
COLUMBIA					
❑ CL 575 [M]	Liberace at the Piano	1954	10.00	20.00	40.00
—Maroon label, gold print					
❑ CL 589 [M]	Christmas at Liberace's	1954	12.50	25.00	50.00
—Maroon label, gold print					
❑ CL 600 [M]	Liberace at the Hollywood Bowl	1955	10.00	20.00	40.00
❑ CL 645 [M]	Hollywood Bowl Encore	1955	10.00	20.00	40.00
❑ CL 661 [M]	Liberace by Candlelight	1955	10.00	20.00	40.00
❑ CL 800 [M]	Sincerely Yours	1956	12.50	25.00	50.00
❑ CL 896 [M]	Liberace at Home	1956	12.50	25.00	50.00
❑ CL 2516 [10]	Piano Reverie	1955	15.00	30.00	60.00
❑ CL 2592 [10]	Kiddin' on the Keys	1955	15.00	30.00	60.00
❑ CL 6217 [10]	Liberace at the Piano	1952	20.00	40.00	80.00
❑ CL 6239 [10]	An Evening with Liberace	1953	20.00	40.00	80.00
❑ CL 6251 [10]	Liberace by Candlelight	1953	20.00	40.00	80.00
❑ CL 6269 [10]	Concertos for You	1953	20.00	40.00	80.00
❑ CL 6283 [10]	Concertos for You, Volume 2	1953	20.00	40.00	80.00
❑ CL 6327 [10]	Liberace Plays Chopin	1954	20.00	40.00	80.00
❑ CL 6328 [10]	Liberace Plays Chopin, Volume 2	1954	20.00	40.00	80.00
❑ CS 9845	Liberace's Greatest Hits	1969	3.00	6.00	12.00
—Red "360 Sound" label					
❑ CS 9845	Liberace's Greatest Hits	1970	2.50	5.00	10.00
—Orange label					
CORAL					
❑ 7CXB 9 [(2)S]	The Best of Liberace	1965	5.00	10.00	20.00
❑ CXB 9 [(2)M]	The Best of Liberace	1965	3.75	7.50	15.00
❑ CRL 57292 [M]	Piano Song Book — Movie Themes	1959	3.75	7.50	15.00
❑ CRL 57305 [M]	The Magic Pianos of Liberace	1960	3.00	6.00	12.00
❑ CRL 57305 [M]	The Magic Pianos of Liberace	1960	3.75	7.50	15.00
❑ CRL 57344 [M]	My Inspiration	1961	3.00	6.00	12.00
❑ CRL 57346 [M]	Liberace at the Palladium	1961	3.00	6.00	12.00
❑ CRL 57377 [M]	My Parade of Golden Favorites	1961	3.00	6.00	12.00
❑ CRL 57392 [M]	As Time Goes By	1962	3.00	6.00	12.00
❑ CRL 57395 [M]	Rhapsody by Candlelight	1962	3.00	6.00	12.00
❑ CRL 57452 [M]	Golden Themes from Hollywood	1964	3.00	6.00	12.00
❑ CRL 757292 [S]	Piano Song Book — Movie Themes	1959	5.00	10.00	20.00
❑ CRL 757305 [S]	The Magic Pianos of Liberace	1960	3.75	7.50	15.00
❑ CRL 757305 [S]	The Magic Pianos of Liberace	1960	5.00	10.00	20.00
❑ CRL 757344 [S]	My Inspiration	1961	3.75	7.50	15.00
❑ CRL 757346 [S]	Liberace at the Palladium	1961	3.75	7.50	15.00
❑ CRL 757377 [S]	My Parade of Golden Favorites	1961	3.75	7.50	15.00
❑ CRL 757392 [S]	As Time Goes By	1962	3.75	7.50	15.00
❑ CRL 757395 [S]	Rhapsody by Candlelight	1962	3.75	7.50	15.00
❑ CRL 757452 [S]	Golden Themes from Hollywood	1964	3.75	7.50	15.00
DOT					
❑ DLP-3547 [M]	Mr. Showmanship	1964	3.00	6.00	12.00
❑ DLP-3550 [M]	A Liberace Christmas	1964	3.00	6.00	12.00
❑ DLP-3563 [M]	My Most Requested	1965	3.00	6.00	12.00
❑ DLP-3595 [M]	Liberace at the Americana, Volume 1	1965	3.00	6.00	12.00
❑ DLP-3596 [M]	Liberace at the Americana, Volume 2	1965	3.00	6.00	12.00
❑ DLP-3755 [M]	New Sounds	1966	3.00	6.00	12.00
❑ DLP-3816 [M]	Liberace Now!	1967	3.75	7.50	15.00
❑ DLP-9502 [M]	Silver Anniversary	1965	3.00	6.00	12.00
❑ DLP-25547 [S]	Mr. Showmanship	1964	3.75	7.50	15.00

L

Number	Title (A Side/B Side)	Yr	VG	VG+	NM
☐ DLP-25550 [S]	A Liberace Christmas	1964	3.75	7.50	15.00
☐ DLP-25563 [S]	My Most Requested	1965	3.75	7.50	15.00
☐ DLP-25595 [S]	Liberace at the Americana, Volume 1	1965	3.75	7.50	15.00
☐ DLP-25596 [S]	Liberace at the Americana, Volume 2	1965	3.75	7.50	15.00
☐ DLP-25755 [S]	New Sounds	1966	3.75	7.50	15.00
☐ DLP-25816 [S]	Liberace Now!	1967	3.75	7.50	15.00
☐ DLP-25858	The Love Album	1968	3.00	6.00	12.00
☐ DLP-25901	Sound of Love	1969	3.00	6.00	12.00
☐ DLP-29502 [S]	Silver Anniversary	1965	3.75	7.50	15.00

HARMONY

Number	Title (A Side/B Side)	Yr	VG	VG+	NM
☐ HL 7154 [M]	The Liberace Show	1959	3.75	7.50	15.00
☐ HL 7237 [M]	Rhapsody in Blue	196?	3.00	6.00	12.00
☐ HL 7361 [M]	Concerto by Candlelight	196?	3.00	6.00	12.00
☐ HS 11054 [R]	The Liberace Show	196?	2.50	5.00	10.00
☐ HS 11161 [R]	Concerto by Candlelight	196?	3.00	6.00	12.00
☐ HL 11175 [R]	Rhapsody in Blue	196?	2.50	5.00	10.00
☐ HS 11325	Tenderly	1969	2.50	5.00	10.00
☐ HS 11391	The Very Thought of You	1970	2.50	5.00	10.00

MCA

Number	Title (A Side/B Side)	Yr	VG	VG+	NM
☐ 740	Here's Liberace	198?	2.00	4.00	8.00
—Reissue of Vocalion 73821					
☐ 4060 [(2)]	The Best of Liberace	197?	3.00	6.00	12.00
☐ 4167 [(2)]	The Artistry of Liberace	198?	3.00	6.00	12.00

MISTLETOE

Number	Title (A Side/B Side)	Yr	VG	VG+	NM
☐ MLP-1208	Twas the Night Before Christmas	1974	2.50	5.00	10.00

PARAMOUNT

Number	Title (A Side/B Side)	Yr	VG	VG+	NM
☐ PAS-1009	The Best of Liberace	1973	3.00	6.00	12.00
☐ PAS-1032 [(2)]	Liberace In Concert	1974	3.75	7.50	15.00

PICKWICK

Number	Title (A Side/B Side)	Yr	VG	VG+	NM
☐ SPC-3085	You Made Me Love You	196?	2.50	5.00	10.00
☐ SPC-3124	Strangers in the Night	196?	2.50	5.00	10.00
☐ SPC-3159	What Now My Love	1969	2.50	5.00	10.00
☐ SPC-3208	By the Time I Get to Phoenix	197?	2.50	5.00	10.00

VOCALION

Number	Title (A Side/B Side)	Yr	VG	VG+	NM
☐ VL 3821 [M]	Here's Liberace	196?	3.00	6.00	12.00
☐ VL 73821 [R]	Here's Liberace	196?	3.00	6.00	12.00

WARNER BROS.

Number	Title (A Side/B Side)	Yr	VG	VG+	NM
☐ WS 1847	A Brand New Me	1969	3.00	6.00	12.00
☐ WS 1889	Love and Music Festival "Live"	1970	3.00	6.00	12.00

LIBERACE, GEORGE

COLUMBIA

Number	Title (A Side/B Side)	Yr	VG	VG+	NM
☐ CL 587 [M]	A Musical Journey with George Liberace	1954	10.00	20.00	40.00
—Maroon label, gold print					

IMPERIAL

Number	Title (A Side/B Side)	Yr	VG	VG+	NM
☐ LP-9039 [M]	George Liberace Goes Teenage	1957	12.50	25.00	50.00

LIBERMAN, JEFFERY

LIBRAH

Number	Title (A Side/B Side)	Yr	VG	VG+	NM
☐ 1545	Jeffery Liberman	1975	20.00	40.00	80.00
☐ 6969	Solitude Within	1975	30.00	60.00	120.00
☐ 12157	Synergy	1976	30.00	60.00	120.00

LIDSTROM, JACK

WORLD PACIFIC

Number	Title (A Side/B Side)	Yr	VG	VG+	NM
☐ PJ-1235 [M]	Look, Dad! They're Comin' Down the Street in Hi-Fi	1957	10.00	20.00	40.00

LIGGINS, JOE

MERCURY

Number	Title (A Side/B Side)	Yr	VG	VG+	NM
☐ MG-20731 [M]	Honeydripper	1962	20.00	40.00	80.00
☐ SR-60731 [S]	Honeydripper	1962	25.00	50.00	100.00

LIGHT, ENOCH

ABC WESTMINSTER/GRAND AWARD

Number	Title (A Side/B Side)	Yr	VG	VG+	NM
☐ 68008	Sing Along with the Original Roaring 20's	1974	2.50	5.00	10.00
☐ 68009	The Flirty 30's	1974	2.50	5.00	10.00
☐ 68012	The Torchy Thirties	1974	2.50	5.00	10.00

COMMAND

Number	Title (A Side/B Side)	Yr	VG	VG+	NM
☐ 800 SD [S]	Persuasive Percussion	1960	3.75	7.50	15.00
—By "Terry Snyder and the All-Stars"					
☐ 33-800 [M]	Persuasive Percussion	1960	3.00	6.00	12.00
—By "Terry Snyder and the All-Stars"					
☐ 804 SD [S]	The Sound of Strings	1960	3.75	7.50	15.00
☐ 33-804 [M]	The Sound of Strings	1960	3.00	6.00	12.00
☐ 805 SD [S]	Paperback Ballet	1960	3.75	7.50	15.00
☐ 33-805 [M]	Paperback Ballet	1960	3.00	6.00	12.00
☐ 806 SD [S]	Provocative Percussion	1960	3.75	7.50	15.00
—By "The Command All-Stars"					
☐ 33-806 [M]	Provocative Percussion	1960	3.00	6.00	12.00
—By "The Command All-Stars"					
☐ 808 SD [S]	Persuasive Percussion, Volume 2	1960	3.75	7.50	15.00
—By "Terry Snyder and the All-Stars"					
☐ 33-808 [M]	Persuasive Percussion, Volume 2	1960	3.00	6.00	12.00
—By "Terry Snyder and the All-Stars"					
☐ 810 SD [S]	Provocative Percussion, Volume 2	1960	3.75	7.50	15.00
☐ 33-810 [M]	Provocative Percussion, Volume 2	1960	3.00	6.00	12.00
☐ 814 SD [S]	Pertinent Percussion Cha-Cha's	1960	3.75	7.50	15.00
☐ 33-814 [M]	Pertinent Percussion Cha-Cha's	1960	3.00	6.00	12.00
☐ 817 SD [S]	Persuasive Percussion, Volume 3	1961	3.75	7.50	15.00
—By "The Command All-Stars"					
☐ 33-817 [M]	Persuasive Percussion, Volume 3	1961	3.00	6.00	12.00
—By "The Command All-Stars"					
☐ 818 SD [S]	Big Bold and Brassy	1961	3.75	7.50	15.00
☐ 33-818 [M]	Big Bold and Brassy	1961	3.00	6.00	12.00
☐ 821 SD [S]	Provocative Percussion, Volume 3	1961	3.75	7.50	15.00
☐ 33-821 [M]	Provocative Percussion, Volume 3	1961	3.00	6.00	12.00
☐ 822 SD [S]	Far Away Places	1961	3.75	7.50	15.00
☐ 33-822 [M]	Far Away Places	1961	3.00	6.00	12.00
☐ 826 SD [S]	Stereo 35/MM	1961	3.75	7.50	15.00
☐ 830 SD [S]	Persuasive Percussion, Volume 4	1962	3.75	7.50	15.00

Number	Title (A Side/B Side)	Yr	VG	VG+	NM
☐ 33-830 [M]	Persuasive Percussion, Volume 4	1962	3.00	6.00	12.00
☐ 831 SD [S]	Stereo 35/MM, Volume Two	1962	3.75	7.50	15.00
☐ 833 SD [S]	Vibrations	1962	3.75	7.50	15.00
☐ 33-833 [M]	Vibrations	1962	3.00	6.00	12.00
☐ 834 SD [S]	Provocative Percussion, Volume 4	1962	3.75	7.50	15.00
☐ 33-834 [M]	Provocative Percussion, Volume 4	1962	3.00	6.00	12.00
☐ 835 SD [S]	Great Themes from Hit Films	1962	3.75	7.50	15.00
☐ 33-835 [M]	Great Themes from Hit Films	1962	3.00	6.00	12.00
☐ 840 SD [S]	Enoch Light and His Orchestra At Carnegie Hall Play Irving Berlin	1962	3.75	7.50	15.00
☐ 33-840 [M]	Enoch Light and His Orchestra At Carnegie Hall Play Irving Berlin	1962	3.00	6.00	12.00
☐ 844 SD [S]	Big Band Bossa Nova	1962	3.75	7.50	15.00
☐ 33-844 [M]	Big Band Bossa Nova	1962	3.00	6.00	12.00
☐ 850 SD [S]	Far Away Places, Volume 2	1963	3.75	7.50	15.00
☐ 33-850 [M]	Far Away Places, Volume 2	1963	3.00	6.00	12.00
☐ 851 SD [S]	Let's Dance the Bossa Nova	1963	3.75	7.50	15.00
☐ 33-851 [M]	Let's Dance the Bossa Nova	1963	3.00	6.00	12.00
☐ 854 SD [S]	1963 — The Year's Most Popular Themes	1963	3.75	7.50	15.00
☐ 33-854 [M]	1963 — The Year's Most Popular Themes	1963	3.00	6.00	12.00
☐ 863 SD [S]	Rome 35/MM	1964	3.75	7.50	15.00
☐ 33-863 [M]	Rome 35/MM	1964	3.00	6.00	12.00
☐ 867 SD [S]	Dimension "3"	1964	3.75	7.50	15.00
☐ 33-867 [M]	Dimension "3"	1964	3.00	6.00	12.00
☐ 868 SD [S]	Command Performances	1964	3.75	7.50	15.00
☐ 33-868 [M]	Command Performances	1964	3.00	6.00	12.00
☐ 871 SD [S]	Great Themes from Hit Films	1964	3.75	7.50	15.00
☐ 33-871 [M]	Great Themes from Hit Films	1964	3.00	6.00	12.00
☐ 873 SD [S]	Discotheque Dance...Dance...Dance	1964	3.75	7.50	15.00
☐ 33-873 [M]	Discotheque Dance...Dance...Dance	1964	3.00	6.00	12.00
☐ 879 SD [S]	Great Cole Porter Songs	1965	3.75	7.50	15.00
☐ 33-879 [M]	Great Cole Porter Songs	1965	3.00	6.00	12.00
☐ 882 SD [S]	Discotheque Dance...Dance...Dance, Volume 2	1965	3.75	7.50	15.00
☐ 33-882 [M]	Discotheque Dance...Dance...Dance, Volume 2	1965	3.00	6.00	12.00
☐ 887 SD [S]	Magnificent Movie Themes	1965	3.75	7.50	15.00
☐ 33-887 [M]	Magnificent Movie Themes	1965	3.00	6.00	12.00
☐ 895 SD [S]	Persuasive Percussion 1966	1966	3.75	7.50	15.00
☐ 33-895 [M]	Persuasive Percussion 1966	1966	3.00	6.00	12.00
☐ 915 SD	Command Performances, Volume 2	1969	3.75	7.50	15.00
☐ QD-40002 [Q]	A New Concept	1972	3.75	7.50	15.00

GRAND AWARD

Number	Title (A Side/B Side)	Yr	VG	VG+	NM
☐ GA-201 SD [S]	The Roaring Twenties	1958	6.25	12.50	25.00
☐ GA-202 SD [S]	The Flirty Thirties	1958	6.25	12.50	25.00
☐ GA-203 SD [S]	Waltzes for Dancing	1958	6.25	12.50	25.00
☐ GA-206 SD [S]	Tommy Dorsey's Song Hits	1958	6.25	12.50	25.00
☐ GA-207 SD [S]	Glenn Miller's Song Hits	1958	6.25	12.50	25.00
☐ GA-211 SD [S]	The Roaring Twenties, Volume 2	1958	6.25	12.50	25.00
☐ GA-214 SD [S]	Around the World in 80 Days	1958	6.25	12.50	25.00
☐ GA-215 SD [S]	Gigi	1958	6.25	12.50	25.00
☐ GA-216 SD [S]	My Fair Lady	1958	6.25	12.50	25.00
☐ GA-217 SD [S]	Oklahoma/South Pacific	1958	6.25	12.50	25.00
☐ GA-220 SD [S]	The Torchy Thirties	1958	6.25	12.50	25.00
☐ GA-222 SD [S]	I Want to Be Happy Cha Cha's	1959	6.25	12.50	25.00
☐ GA-224 SD [S]	New World Symphony	1958	6.25	12.50	25.00
☐ GA-225 SD [S]	The Great Themes of America's Great Bands	1958	6.25	12.50	25.00
☐ GA-227 SD [S]	Happy Cha Cha's, Vol. 2	1959	6.25	12.50	25.00
☐ GA-228 SD [S]	Show Spectacular	1959	6.25	12.50	25.00
☐ GA-229 SD [S]	The Roaring Twenties, Volume 3	1959	6.25	12.50	25.00
☐ GA-236 SD [S]	All the Things You Are	1959	6.25	12.50	25.00
☐ GA-237 SD [S]	Come to Hawaii	1959	6.25	12.50	25.00
☐ GA-238 SD [S]	With My Eyes Wide Open I'm Dreaming	1959	6.25	12.50	25.00
☐ GA-242 SD [S]	Something to Remember You By	1959	6.25	12.50	25.00
☐ GA-246 SD [S]	Just for Kicks	1959	6.25	12.50	25.00
☐ GA-251 SD [S]	Sing Along with the Original Roaring 20's	1959	6.25	12.50	25.00
☐ GA 33-327 [M]	The Roaring Twenties	1959	5.00	10.00	20.00
☐ GA 33-353 [M]	The Roaring Twenties, Volume 3	1959	5.00	10.00	20.00
☐ GA 33-371 [M]	The Flirty Thirties	1958	5.00	10.00	20.00
☐ GA 33-372 [M]	Waltzes for Dancing	1958	5.00	10.00	20.00
☐ GA 33-380 [M]	Paris Spectacular	1958	5.00	10.00	20.00
☐ GA 33-381 [M]	Glenn Miller's Song Hits	1958	5.00	10.00	20.00
☐ GA 33-382 [M]	Tommy Dorsey's Song Hits	1958	5.00	10.00	20.00
☐ GA 33-388 [M]	I Want to Be Happy Cha Cha's	1959	5.00	10.00	20.00
☐ GA 33-391 [M]	Happy Cha Cha's, Vol. 2	1959	5.00	10.00	20.00
☐ GA 33-392 [M]	The Great Themes of America's Great Bands	1958	5.00	10.00	20.00
☐ GA 33-399 [M]	All the Things You Are	1959	5.00	10.00	20.00
☐ GA 33-405 [M]	Come to Hawaii	1959	5.00	10.00	20.00
☐ GA 33-406 [M]	With My Eyes Wide Open I'm Dreaming	1959	5.00	10.00	20.00
☐ GA 33-410 [M]	Something to Remember You By	1959	5.00	10.00	20.00
☐ GA 33-419 [M]	Sing Along with the Original Roaring 20's	1959	5.00	10.00	20.00

PROJECT 3

Number	Title (A Side/B Side)	Yr	VG	VG+	NM
☐ PR-5000 SD	Spanish Strings	1967	3.00	6.00	12.00
☐ PR4C-5000 [Q]	Spanish Strings	1973	3.75	7.50	15.00
☐ PR-5004 SD	It's Happening	1967	3.00	6.00	12.00
☐ PR-5005 SD	Film on Film — Great Movie Themes	1967	3.00	6.00	12.00
☐ PR-5013 SD	Film Fame	1968	3.00	6.00	12.00
☐ PR-5021 SD	Twelve Smash Hits	1968	3.00	6.00	12.00
☐ PR-5027 SD	The Best of Hollywood '68-'69	1968	3.00	6.00	12.00
☐ PR-5030 SD	Whoever You Are, I Love You	1968	3.00	6.00	12.00
☐ PR-5036 SD	Enoch Light and the Brass Menagerie	1969	3.00	6.00	12.00
☐ PR4C-5036 [Q]	Enoch Light and the Brass Menagerie	1973	3.75	7.50	15.00
☐ PR-5038 SD	Glittering Guitars	1969	3.00	6.00	12.00
☐ PR-5042 SD	Enoch Light and the Brass Menagerie, Volume 2	1969	3.00	6.00	12.00
☐ PR4C-5042 [Q]	Enoch Light and the Brass Menagerie, Volume 2	1973	3.75	7.50	15.00
☐ PR-5043 SD	Spaced Out	1970	3.00	6.00	12.00
☐ PR4C-5043 [Q]	Spaced Out	1973	3.75	7.50	15.00
☐ PR-5046 SD	Best of the Movie Themes 1970	1970	3.00	6.00	12.00
☐ PR4C-5046 [Q]	Best of the Movie Themes 1970	1973	3.75	7.50	15.00

Number	Title (A Side/B Side)	Yr	VG	VG+	NM
❑ PR-5048 SD	Permissive Polyphonics	1970	3.00	6.00	12.00
❑ PR4C-5048 [Q]	Permissive Polyphonics	1973	3.75	7.50	15.00
❑ PR-5049 SD	Big Band Hits of the 30's	1971	3.00	6.00	12.00
❑ PR4C-5049 [Q]	Big Band Hits of the 30's	1973	3.75	7.50	15.00
❑ PR-5051 SD	Hit Movie Themes	1971	3.00	6.00	12.00
❑ PR4C-5051 [Q]	Hit Movie Themes	1973	3.75	7.50	15.00
❑ PR-5056 SD	Big Band Hits of the 30's & 40's!	1971	3.00	6.00	12.00
❑ PR4C-5056 [Q]	Big Band Hits of the 30's & 40's!	1973	3.75	7.50	15.00
❑ PR-5059 SD	Big Hits of the 20's	1971	3.00	6.00	12.00
❑ PR4C-5059 [Q]	Big Hits of the 20's	1973	3.75	7.50	15.00
❑ PR-5060 SD	Enoch Light and the Brass Menagerie 1973	1972	3.00	6.00	12.00
❑ PR4C-5060 [Q]	Enoch Light and the Brass Menagerie 1973	1973	3.75	7.50	15.00
❑ PR-5063 SD	Movie Hits!	1972	3.00	6.00	12.00
❑ PR-5063 [Q]	Movie Hits!	1973	3.75	7.50	15.00
❑ PR4C-5068 [Q]	4 Channel Dynamite!	1973	3.75	7.50	15.00
❑ PR4C-5073 [Q]	Charge!	1973	3.75	7.50	15.00
❑ PR4C-5076 [Q]	Big Band Hits of the 40's & 50's	1973	3.75	7.50	15.00
❑ PR4C-5077 [Q]	Future Sound Shock	1973	3.75	7.50	15.00
❑ PR-5084 SD	Beatles Classics	1974	3.00	6.00	12.00
❑ PR4C-5084 [Q]	Beatles Classics	1974	3.75	7.50	15.00
❑ PR-5086 SD	Great Hits from the Gatsby Era	1974	3.00	6.00	12.00
❑ PR4C-5086 [Q]	Great Hits from the Gatsby Era	1974	3.75	7.50	15.00
❑ PR-5089 SD	Big Band Hits of the 30's, Volume 2	1975	3.00	6.00	12.00
❑ PR4C-5089 [Q]	Big Band Hits of the 30's, Volume 2	1975	3.75	7.50	15.00
❑ PR-5092 SD	Disco Disque	197?	3.00	6.00	12.00
❑ PR4C-5092 [Q]	Disco Disque	197?	3.75	7.50	15.00
❑ PR-5100	Let It Be	197?	3.00	6.00	12.00
❑ PR-5109	The Most Beautiful Music in the World	1981	3.00	6.00	12.00
❑ PR-6003/4 [(2)]	Big Hits of the Seventies	1974	3.75	7.50	15.00
❑ PR4C-6003/4 [(2)Q]Big Hits of the Seventies		1974	5.00	10.00	20.00
❑ PR-6005/6 [(2)]	Big Band Hits of the 30's, 40's & 50's	1974	3.75	7.50	15.00
❑ PR4C-6005/6 [(2)Q]Big Band Hits of the 30's, 40's & 50's		1974	5.00	10.00	20.00
❑ PR-6011/12 [(2)]	Music Maestro, Please	197?	3.75	7.50	15.00
❑ PR-6013/14 [(2)]	Big Band Hits of the 30's and 40's	197?	3.75	7.50	15.00
❑ PR4C-6013/14 [(2)Q]Big Band Hits of the 30's and 40's		197?	5.00	10.00	20.00
❑ PR-6034 [(2)]	20 Great Movie Themes	1980	3.75	7.50	15.00
SEAGULL					
❑ LG-8204	Blowin' in the Wind	198?	2.50	5.00	10.00
❑ LG-8207	Music from the Movies	198?	2.50	5.00	10.00

LIGHT CRUST DOUGHBOYS, THE
AUDIO LAB

❑ AL-1525 [M]	The Light Crust Doughboys	1959	37.50	75.00	150.00

LIGHTFOOT, GORDON
LIBERTY

❑ LN-10038	The Best of Lightfoot	198?	2.00	4.00	8.00
—Budget-line reissue					
❑ LN-10039	Sunday Concert	198?	2.00	4.00	8.00
—Budget-line reissue					
❑ LN-10040	Back Here on Earth	198?	2.00	4.00	8.00
—Budget-line reissue					
❑ LN-10041	Did She Mention My Name	198?	2.00	4.00	8.00
—Budget-line reissue					
❑ LN-10043	The Way I Feel	198?	2.00	4.00	8.00
—Budget-line reissue					
❑ LN-10044	Lightfoot	198?	2.00	4.00	8.00
—Budget-line reissue					

MOBILE FIDELITY

❑ 1-018	Sundown	1979	10.00	20.00	40.00
—Audiophile vinyl					

PAIR

❑ PDL2-1081 [(2)]	Songbook	1986	3.00	6.00	12.00

REPRISE

❑ MS 2037	Summer Side of Life	1971	3.00	6.00	12.00
❑ MS 2056	Don Quixote	1972	3.00	6.00	12.00
❑ MS 2116	Old Dan's Records	1972	3.00	6.00	12.00
❑ MS 2177	Sundown	1974	3.00	6.00	12.00
❑ MS 2206	Cold on the Shoulder	1975	3.00	6.00	12.00
❑ 2RS 2237 [(2)]	Gord's Gold	1975	3.75	7.50	15.00
❑ MS 2246	Summertime Dream	1976	3.00	6.00	12.00
❑ RS 6392	Sit Down Young Stranger	1970	3.75	7.50	15.00
❑ RS 6392	If You Could Read My Mind	1971	2.50	5.00	10.00
—Retitled version					
❑ ST-93228	Sit Down Young Stranger	1970	5.00	10.00	20.00
—Capitol Record Club edition					

UNITED ARTISTS

❑ UA-LA243-G	The Very Best of Gordon Lightfoot	1974	3.00	6.00	12.00
❑ UAL-3487 [M]	Lightfoot	1966	5.00	10.00	20.00
❑ UAL-3587 [M]	The Way I Feel	1967	5.00	10.00	20.00
❑ UAS-5510	Classic Lightfoot (The Best of Lightfoot/ Volume 2)	1971	3.75	7.50	15.00
❑ UAS-6487 [S]	Lightfoot	1966	6.25	12.50	25.00
❑ UAS-6587 [S]	The Way I Feel	1967	6.25	12.50	25.00
❑ UAS-6649	Did She Mention My Name	1968	5.00	10.00	20.00
❑ UAS-6672	Back Here on Earth	1969	5.00	10.00	20.00
❑ UAS-6714	Sunday Concert	1969	3.75	7.50	15.00
❑ UAS-6754	The Best of Gordon Lightfoot	1970	3.75	7.50	15.00

WARNER BROS.

❑ BSK 3149	Endless Wire	1978	2.50	5.00	10.00
❑ HS 3426	Dream Street Rose	1980	2.50	5.00	10.00
❑ BSK 3633	Shadows	1982	2.50	5.00	10.00
❑ 23901	Salute	1983	2.50	5.00	10.00
❑ 25482	East of Midnight	1986	2.50	5.00	10.00
❑ 25784	Gord's Gold, Volume II	1989	3.00	6.00	12.00

LIGHTHOUSE
EVOLUTION

❑ 3007	One Fine Morning	1971	3.75	7.50	15.00
❑ 3010	Thoughts of Movin' On	1972	3.75	7.50	15.00
❑ 3014 [(2)]	Lighthouse Live!	1972	5.00	10.00	20.00

Number	Title (A Side/B Side)	Yr	VG	VG+	NM
❑ 3016	Sunny Days	1973	3.75	7.50	15.00
JANUS					
❑ JSX-7025	The Best of Lighthouse	1976	3.00	6.00	12.00
POLYDOR					
❑ PD-5056	Can You Feel It	1973	3.00	6.00	12.00
❑ PD-1-6028	Good Day	1974	3.00	6.00	12.00
RCA VICTOR					
❑ LSP-4173	Lighthouse	1969	3.75	7.50	15.00
❑ LSP-4241	Suite Feeling	1969	3.75	7.50	15.00
❑ LSP-4325	Peacing It All Together	1970	3.75	7.50	15.00

LIGHTNIN' SLIM
EXCELLO

❑ LP 8000 [M]	Rooster Blues	1960	200.00	400.00	800.00
❑ LPS 8000 [M]	Rooster Blues	196?	12.50	25.00	50.00
—Thogh labeled "Electronic Stereo," this record is mono					
❑ LP 8004 [M]	Lightnin' Slim's Bell Ringer	1965	75.00	150.00	300.00
❑ LPS 8004 [M]	Lightnin' Slim's Bell Ringer	196?	12.50	25.00	50.00
—Thogh labeled "Electronic Stereo," this record is mono					
❑ LPS 8018	High and Low Down	1971	3.75	7.50	15.00
❑ LPS 8023	London Gumbo	1972	3.75	7.50	15.00
INTERMEDIA					
❑ QS-5062	That's All Right	198?	2.50	5.00	10.00

LIGHTNING
P.I.P.

❑ 6807	Lightning	1971	7.50	15.00	30.00

LIL' KIM
UNDEAS

❑ 92733 [(2)]	Hard Core	1996	5.00	10.00	20.00
❑ 92840 [(2)]	The Notorious K.I.M.	2000	3.75	7.50	15.00

LILLIE, BEATRICE
DECCA

❑ DL 5453 [10]	Souvenir Album	1954	12.50	25.00	50.00

LIBERTY MUSIC SHOP

❑ 1002 [10]	Thirty Minutes with Bea Lillie	1954	12.50	25.00	50.00

LONDON

❑ LL 1373 [M]	An Evening with Bea Little	1956	7.50	15.00	30.00
❑ 5471 [M]	Auntie Bea	1959	7.50	15.00	30.00

LILLY BROTHERS, THE
FOLKLORE

❑ FL-14010 [M]	Bluegrass Breakdown	1963	5.00	10.00	20.00
❑ FLS-14010 [S]	Bluegrass Breakdown	1963	6.25	12.50	25.00
❑ FL-14035 [M]	Country Songs	1964	5.00	10.00	20.00
❑ FLS-14035 [S]	Country Songs	1964	6.25	12.50	25.00
FOLKWAYS					
❑ FA-2433 [M]	Folk Songs from the Southern Mountains	196?	5.00	10.00	20.00

LIMELITERS, THE
Also see GLENN YARBROUGH.
ELEKTRA

❑ EKM-180 [M]	The Limeliters	1960	5.00	10.00	20.00
❑ EKS-7180 [S]	The Limeliters	1960	6.25	12.50	25.00

GNP CRESCENDO

❑ GNPS-2188	Alive! In Concert, Vol. 1	1986	2.50	5.00	10.00
❑ GNPS-2190	Alive! In Concert, Vol. 2	1987	2.50	5.00	10.00

LEGACY

❑ 113	Their First Historic Album	1970	3.00	6.00	12.00

RCA CAMDEN

❑ ACL1-0602	This Train	1974	2.50	5.00	10.00

RCA VICTOR

❑ LPM-2272 [M]	Tonight: In Person	1961	5.00	10.00	20.00
❑ LSP-2272 [S]	Tonight: In Person	1961	6.25	12.50	25.00
❑ ANL1-2336	Pure Gold	1977	2.00	4.00	8.00
❑ LPM-2393 [M]	The Slightly Fabulous Limeliters	1961	5.00	10.00	20.00
❑ LSP-2393 [S]	The Slightly Fabulous Limeliters	1961	6.25	12.50	25.00
❑ LPM-2445 [M]	Sing Out!	1962	5.00	10.00	20.00
❑ LSP-2445 [S]	Sing Out!	1962	6.25	12.50	25.00
❑ LPM-2512 [M]	Through Children's Eyes	1962	5.00	10.00	20.00
❑ LSP-2512 [S]	Through Children's Eyes	1962	6.25	12.50	25.00
❑ LPM-2547 [M]	Folk Matinee	1962	5.00	10.00	20.00
❑ LSP-2547 [S]	Folk Matinee	1962	6.25	12.50	25.00
❑ LPM-2588 [M]	Makin' a Joyful Noise	1963	5.00	10.00	20.00
❑ LSP-2588 [S]	Makin' a Joyful Noise	1963	6.25	12.50	25.00
❑ LPM-2609 [M]	Our Men in San Francisco	1963	5.00	10.00	20.00
❑ LSP-2609 [S]	Our Men in San Francisco	1963	6.25	12.50	25.00
❑ LPM-2671 [M]	Fourteen 14K Folk Songs	1963	5.00	10.00	20.00
❑ LSP-2671 [S]	Fourteen 14K Folk Songs	1963	6.25	12.50	25.00
❑ LPM-2844 [M]	More of Everything!	1964	3.75	7.50	15.00
❑ LSP-2844 [S]	More of Everything!	1964	5.00	10.00	20.00
❑ LPM-2889 [M]	The Best of the Limeliters	1964	3.75	7.50	15.00
❑ LSP-2889 [S]	The Best of the Limeliters	1964	5.00	10.00	20.00
❑ LPM-2906 [M]	Leave It to the Limeliters	1964	3.75	7.50	15.00
❑ LSP-2906 [S]	Leave It to the Limeliters	1964	5.00	10.00	20.00
❑ LPM-2907 [M]	London Concert	1964	3.75	7.50	15.00
❑ LSP-2907 [S]	London Concert	1964	5.00	10.00	20.00
❑ LPM-3385 [M]	The Limeliters Look at Love… In Depth	1965	3.75	7.50	15.00
❑ LSP-3385 [S]	The Limeliters Look at Love… In Depth	1965	5.00	10.00	20.00
❑ LSP-4100	The Original "Those Were the Days"	1969	3.75	7.50	15.00

WEST KNOLL

❑ WK-1001	Alive! In Concert, Vol. 1	198?	2.50	5.00	10.00
❑ WK-1002	Alive! In Concert, Vol. 2	198?	2.50	5.00	10.00

LIMOUSINE
GSF

❑ 1002	Limousine	1972	5.00	10.00	20.00

Number	Title (A Side/B Side)	Yr	VG	VG+	NM

LINCOLN, ABBEY
CANDID
| ❏ CD-8015 [M] | Straight Ahead | 1960 | 10.00 | 20.00 | 40.00 |
| ❏ CS-9015 [S] | Straight Ahead | 1960 | 12.50 | 25.00 | 50.00 |

LIBERTY
| ❏ LRP-3025 [M] | Abbey Lincoln's Affair | 1957 | 12.50 | 25.00 | 50.00 |

RIVERSIDE
❏ RLP 12-251 [M]	That's Him!	1957	12.50	25.00	50.00
❏ RLP 12-277 [M]	It's Magic	1958	10.00	20.00	40.00
❏ RLP 12-308 [M]	Abbey Is Blue	1959	10.00	20.00	40.00
❏ RLP-1107 [S]	That's Him!	1958	10.00	20.00	40.00
❏ RLP-1153 [S]	Abbey Is Blue	1959	12.50	25.00	50.00

LINCOLN, PHILAMORE
EPIC
| ❏ BN 26497 | North Wind Blew South | 1970 | 6.25 | 12.50 | 25.00 |

LINCOLN STREET EXIT
MAINSTREAM
| ❏ S-6126 | Drive It | 1970 | 25.00 | 50.00 | 100.00 |

LIND, BOB
CAPITOL
| ❏ ST-780 | Since There Were Circles | 1971 | 3.75 | 7.50 | 15.00 |

VERVE FOLKWAYS
| ❏ FT-3005 [M] | The Elusive Bob Lind | 1966 | 6.25 | 12.50 | 25.00 |
| ❏ FTS-3005 [S] | The Elusive Bob Lind | 1966 | 7.50 | 15.00 | 30.00 |

WORLD PACIFIC
❏ WP-1841 [M]	Don't Be Concerned	1966	5.00	10.00	20.00
❏ WP-1851 [M]	Photographs of Feeling	1966	5.00	10.00	20.00
❏ ST-21841 [S]	Don't Be Concerned	1966	6.25	12.50	25.00
❏ ST-21851 [S]	Photographs of Feeling	1966	6.25	12.50	25.00

LINDBERG, NILS
CAPITOL
| ❏ ST 10363 [S] | Trisection | 196? | 6.25 | 12.50 | 25.00 |
| ❏ T 10363 [M] | Trisection | 196? | 5.00 | 10.00 | 20.00 |

LINDE, DENNIS
INTREPID
| ❏ 4004 [M] | Linde Manor | 1966 | 5.00 | 10.00 | 20.00 |
| ❏ 74004 [S] | Linde Manor | 1966 | 6.25 | 12.50 | 25.00 |

LINDEN, KATHY
FELSTED
| ❏ 7501 [M] | That Certain Boy | 1959 | 15.00 | 30.00 | 60.00 |

LINDH, JAYSON
JAS
| ❏ JAS-4000 | Second Carneval | 1975 | 5.00 | 10.00 | 20.00 |

METRONOME
❏ DIX-3000	Ramadan	1972	6.25	12.50	25.00
❏ DIX-3001	Cous-Cous	1973	6.25	12.50	25.00
❏ DIX-3002	Sissel	1974	6.25	12.50	25.00

LINDSEY, GEORGE
CAPITOL
| ❏ ST-230 | 96 Miles to Bakersfield | 1969 | 6.25 | 12.50 | 25.00 |
| ❏ ST 2965 | Goober Sings! | 1968 | 6.25 | 12.50 | 25.00 |

LINKLETTER, ART
COLUMBIA
| ❏ CL 703 [M] | Howlers, Boners and Shockers | 1956 | 10.00 | 20.00 | 40.00 |

LINN, RAY
TREND
| ❏ 515 | Chicago Jazz | 1980 | 5.00 | 10.00 | 20.00 |
—Direct-to-disc recording

LINN COUNTY
MERCURY
| ❏ SR-61181 | Proud Flesh Soothseer | 1968 | 5.00 | 10.00 | 20.00 |
| ❏ SR-61218 | Fever Shot | 1969 | 5.00 | 10.00 | 20.00 |

PHILIPS
| ❏ PHS 600326 | Till the Break of Dawn | 1970 | 3.75 | 7.50 | 15.00 |

LINTON, SHERWIN
BLACK GOLD
| ❏ 7116 | I'm Not Johnny Cash | 1972 | 6.25 | 12.50 | 25.00 |

BREAKER
| ❏ BR-4001 | Christmas Memories | 1987 | 3.00 | 6.00 | 12.00 |

RE-CAR
| ❏ 2108 | Sherwin Linton and the Cotton Kings | 1968 | 15.00 | 30.00 | 60.00 |

LIPSCOMB, MANCE
ARHOOLIE
❏ 1001 [M]	Texas Sharecropper and Songster	1960	12.50	25.00	50.00
❏ 1023 [M]	Texas Songster, Vol. 2	1963	10.00	20.00	40.00
❏ 1026 [M]	Texas Songster, Vol. 3	1965	10.00	20.00	40.00
❏ 1033 [M]	Mance Lipscomb, Vol. 4	1966	10.00	20.00	40.00
❏ 1049	Mance Lipscomb, Vol. 5	1970	6.25	12.50	25.00
❏ 1069	Mance Lipscomb, Vol. 6	1975	6.25	12.50	25.00

REPRISE
❏ R-2012 [M]	Trouble in Mind	1961	25.00	50.00	100.00
❏ R9-2012 [S]	Trouble in Mind	1961	37.50	75.00	150.00
❏ RS-6404	Trouble in Mind	1969	7.50	15.00	30.00

LIPSTIQUE
TOM N JERRY
| ❏ TJ-4701 | At the Discotheque | 1978 | 5.00 | 10.00 | 20.00 |

LIPTON, PEGGY
ODE
| ❏ Z12 44006 | Peggy Lipton | 1968 | 6.25 | 12.50 | 25.00 |

LIQUID SMOKE
AVCO EMBASSY
| ❏ AVE-33005 | Liquid Smoke | 1970 | 6.25 | 12.50 | 25.00 |

LIST, EUGENE
MERCURY LIVING PRESENCE
| ❏ SR 90290 [S] | Gershwin Favorites | 196? | 5.00 | 10.00 | 20.00 |
—Maroon label, no "Vendor: Mercury Record Corporation"

LISTENING
VANGUARD
| ❏ VSD-6504 | Listening | 1968 | 15.00 | 30.00 | 60.00 |

LISTON, MELBA
METROJAZZ
| ❏ E-1013 [M] | Melba Liston and Her Bones | 1958 | 20.00 | 40.00 | 80.00 |
| ❏ SE-1013 [S] | Melba Liston and Her Bones | 1958 | 15.00 | 30.00 | 60.00 |

LITE STORM, THE
BEVERLY HILLS
| ❏ 1135 | Lite Storm Warning | 1973 | 15.00 | 30.00 | 60.00 |

LITTER
EVA
| ❏ 12013 | Rare Tracks | 1983 | 3.75 | 7.50 | 15.00 |

HEXAGON
| ❏ 681 | $100 Fine | 1968 | 100.00 | 200.00 | 400.00 |

PROBE
| ❏ 4504 | Emerge | 1969 | 12.50 | 25.00 | 50.00 |

WARICK
| ❏ 671 | Distortions | 1967 | 125.00 | 250.00 | 500.00 |

LITTLE, BOOKER
BETHLEHEM
| ❏ BCP-6061 [M] | Booker Little and Friends | 1962 | 12.50 | 25.00 | 50.00 |

CANDID
| ❏ CD-8027 [M] | Out Front | 1961 | 10.00 | 20.00 | 40.00 |
| ❏ CS-9027 [S] | Out Front | 1961 | 12.50 | 25.00 | 50.00 |

TIME
| ❏ S-2011 [S] | Booker Little | 1960 | 20.00 | 40.00 | 80.00 |
| ❏ 52011 [M] | Booker Little | 1960 | 15.00 | 30.00 | 60.00 |

UNITED ARTISTS
| ❏ UAL-4034 [M] | The Booker Little Four | 1959 | 20.00 | 40.00 | 80.00 |
| ❏ UAS-5034 [S] | The Booker Little Four | 1959 | 15.00 | 30.00 | 60.00 |

LITTLE, BOOKER, AND BOOKER ERVIN
TCB
| ❏ 1003 | Sounds of Inner City | 197? | 10.00 | 20.00 | 40.00 |

LITTLE ANTHONY AND THE IMPERIALS
ACCORD
| ❏ SN-7216 | Tears on My Pillow | 1983 | 2.50 | 5.00 | 10.00 |

AVCO
| ❏ AV-11012 | On a New Street | 1973 | 5.00 | 10.00 | 20.00 |

DCP
❏ DCL-3801 [M]	I'm On the Outside Looking In	1964	6.25	12.50	25.00
❏ DCL-3808 [M]	Goin' Out of My Head	1965	6.25	12.50	25.00
❏ DCL-3809 [M]	The Best of Little Anthony and the Imperials	1965	5.00	10.00	20.00
❏ DCS-6801 [S]	I'm On the Outside Looking In	1964	7.50	15.00	30.00
❏ DCS-6808 [S]	Goin' Out of My Head	1965	7.50	15.00	30.00
❏ DCS-6809 [S]	The Best of Little Anthony and the Imperials	1965	6.25	12.50	25.00

END
| ❏ LP 303 [M] | We Are The Imperials Featuring Little Anthony | 1959 | 62.50 | 125.00 | 250.00 |
| ❏ LP 311 [M] | Shades of the 40's | 1960 | 50.00 | 100.00 | 200.00 |

FORUM
| ❏ F-9107 [M] | Little Anthony and the Imperials' Greatest Hits | 196? | 3.75 | 7.50 | 15.00 |
| ❏ FS-9107 [R] | Little Anthony and the Imperials' Greatest Hits | 196? | 3.00 | 6.00 | 12.00 |

LIBERTY
| ❏ LM-1017 | Out of Sight, Out of Mind | 1981 | 2.00 | 4.00 | 8.00 |
—Reissue of United Artists 1017
| ❏ LN-10133 | The Best of Little Anthony and the Imperials | 1981 | 2.00 | 4.00 | 8.00 |
—Budget-line reissue

PICKWICK
| ❏ SPC-3029 | The Hits of Little Anthony and the Imperials | 196? | 3.00 | 6.00 | 12.00 |

RHINO
| ❏ R1-70919 | The Best of Little Anthony and the Imperials | 1989 | 3.00 | 6.00 | 12.00 |

ROULETTE
❏ R-25294 [M]	Little Anthony and the Imperials' Greatest Hits	1965	6.25	12.50	25.00
❏ SR-25294 [R]	Little Anthony and the Imperials' Greatest Hits	1965	5.00	10.00	20.00
❏ SR-42007	Forever Yours	1968	3.75	7.50	15.00

SONGBIRD
| ❏ 3245 | Daylight | 1980 | 2.50 | 5.00 | 10.00 |

SUNSET
| ❏ SUS-5287 | Little Anthony and the Imperials | 1970 | 3.75 | 7.50 | 15.00 |

UNITED ARTISTS
❏ UA-LA026-G [(2)]	Legendary Masters Series	1972	6.25	12.50	25.00
❏ UA-LA255-G	The Very Best of Little Anthony and the Imperials	1974	2.50	5.00	10.00
❏ LM-1017	Out of Sight, Out of Mind	1980	2.50	5.00	10.00
—Reissue of United Artists 6720
| ❏ UAS 6720 | Out of Sight, Out of Mind | 1969 | 5.00 | 10.00 | 20.00 |

VEEP
❏ VP 13510 [M]	I'm On the Outside Looking In	1966	3.75	7.50	15.00
❏ VP 13511 [M]	Goin' Out of My Head	1966	3.75	7.50	15.00
❏ VP 13512 [M]	The Best of Little Anthony and the Imperials	1966	3.75	7.50	15.00

Number	Title (A Side/B Side)	Yr	VG	VG+	NM
❑ VP 13513 [M]	Payin' Our Dues	1966	3.75	7.50	15.00
❑ VP 13514 [M]	Reflections	1967	3.75	7.50	15.00
❑ VP 13516 [M]	Movie Grabbers	1967	3.75	7.50	15.00
❑ VPS 16510 [S]	I'm On the Outside Looking In	1966	5.00	10.00	20.00
❑ VPS 16511 [S]	Goin' Out of My Head	1966	5.00	10.00	20.00
❑ VPS 16512 [S]	The Best of Little Anthony and the Imperials	1966	5.00	10.00	20.00
❑ VPS 16513 [S]	Payin' Our Dues	1966	5.00	10.00	20.00
❑ VPS 16514 [S]	Reflections	1967	5.00	10.00	20.00
❑ VPS 16516 [S]	Movie Grabbers	1967	5.00	10.00	20.00
❑ VPS 16519	The Best of Little Anthony, Volume 2	1968	3.75	7.50	15.00

LITTLE BILL AND THE BLUENOTES
CAMELOT
❑ 102 [M]	The Fiesta Club Presents Little Bill and the Bluenotes	1960	100.00	200.00	400.00

LITTLE BOY BLUES
FONTANA
❑ SRF-67578	In the Woodland of Weir	1968	75.00	15.00	30.00

LITTLE CAESAR AND THE ROMANS
DEL-FI
❑ DFLP-1218 [M]	Memories of Those Oldies But Goodies	1961	75.00	150.00	300.00

LITTLE ESTHER
See LITTLE ESTHER PHILLIPS.

LITTLE EVA
DIMENSION
❑ DLP-6000 [M]	LLLLLoco-Motion	1962	37.50	75.00	150.00
—Without "Keep Your Hands Off My Baby"					
❑ DLP-6000 [M]	LLLLLoco-Motion	1962	50.00	100.00	200.00
—With "Keep Your Hands Off My Baby"					
❑ DLPS-6000 [R]	LLLLLoco-Motion	1962	37.50	75.00	150.00
—Without "Keep Your Hands Off My Baby"					
❑ DLPS-6000 [R]	LLLLLoco-Motion	1962	50.00	100.00	200.00
—With "Keep Your Hands Off My Baby"					

LITTLE FEAT
MOBILE FIDELITY
❑ 1-013 [(2)]	Waiting for Columbus	1979	20.00	40.00	80.00
—Audiophile vinyl					
NAUTILUS					
❑ NR-24	Time Loves a Hero	198?	12.50	25.00	50.00
—Audiophile vinyl					
WARNER BROS.					
❑ PRO-A-984 [DJ]	Hoy-Hoy!	1981	5.00	10.00	20.00
—Single-album sampler of 2-LP set					
❑ WS 1890	Little Feat	1971	3.75	7.50	15.00
—Green "WB" label; without photo on back cover					
❑ WS 1890	Little Feat	1971	5.00	10.00	20.00
—Green "WB" label; with photo on back cover					
❑ WS 1890	Little Feat	1973	2.50	5.00	10.00
—"Burbank" palm trees label					
❑ WS 1890	Little Feat	1979	2.00	4.00	8.00
—Tan or white label					
❑ BS 2600	Sailin' Shoes	1972	3.75	7.50	15.00
—Green "WB" label					
❑ BS 2600	Sailin' Shoes	1973	2.50	5.00	10.00
—"Burbank" palm trees label					
❑ BS 2600	Sailin' Shoes	1979	2.00	4.00	8.00
—Tan or white label					
❑ BS 2686	Dixie Chicken	1973	3.75	7.50	15.00
—"Burbank" palm trees label					
❑ BS 2686	Dixie Chicken	1979	2.00	4.00	8.00
—Tan or white label					
❑ BS 2748	Feats Don't Fail Me Now	1974	3.75	7.50	15.00
—"Burbank" palm trees label					
❑ BS 2748	Feats Don't Fail Me Now	1979	2.00	4.00	8.00
—Tan or white label					
❑ BS 2884	The Last Record Album	1975	3.75	7.50	15.00
—"Burbank" palm trees label					
❑ BS 2884	The Last Record Album	1979	2.00	4.00	8.00
—Tan or white label					
❑ BS 3015	Time Loves a Hero	1977	3.00	6.00	12.00
—"Burbank" palm trees label					
❑ BS 3015	Time Loves a Hero	1979	2.00	4.00	8.00
—Tan or white label					
❑ 2WS 3140 [(2)]	Waiting for Columbus	1978	3.75	7.50	15.00
—"Burbank" palm trees label					
❑ 2WS 3140 [(2)]	Waiting for Columbus	1979	2.50	5.00	10.00
—Tan or white label					
❑ HS 3345	Down on the Farm	1979	2.50	5.00	10.00
❑ 2BSK 3538 [(2)]	Hoy-Hoy!	1981	3.00	6.00	12.00
❑ 25750	Let It Roll	1988	2.50	5.00	10.00
❑ 26263	Representing the Mambo	1990	3.75	7.50	15.00
ZOO/CLASSIC					
❑ 11097 [(2)]	Ain't Had Enough Fun	1995	4.50	9.00	18.00
—150-gram vinyl					
❑ 11097 [(2)]	Ain't Had Enough Fun	1995	5.00	10.00	20.00
—180-gram vinyl					

LITTLE GIRLS
FTM ENTERPRISES
❑ (no #) [EP]	Little Girls 1985	1985	25.00	50.00	100.00
—Promo-only three-song EP, with all songs on same side, on clear vinyl in clear plastic sleeve; also contains two black & white photos of the group and three pages of biographical notes and reviews; 100 pressed					
PVC					
❑ 5904 [EP]	Thank Heaven!	1983	5.00	10.00	20.00

LITTLE JOE
BRUNSWICK
❑ BL 754135	Little Joe (Sure Can Sing)	1968	5.00	10.00	20.00

LITTLE MILTON
CHECKER
Number	Title (A Side/B Side)	Yr	VG	VG+	NM
❑ LP-2995 [M]	We're Gonna Make It	196?	6.25	12.50	25.00
—Blue, fading to white, label					
❑ LP-2995 [M]	We're Gonna Make It	1965	25.00	50.00	100.00
—Black label					
❑ LP-2995 [M]	We're Gonna Make It	1966	17.50	35.00	70.00
—Blue label with red and black checkers					
❑ LP-3002 [M]	Little Milton Sings Big Blues	1966	12.50	25.00	50.00
❑ LP-3011	Grits Ain't Groceries	1969	6.25	12.50	25.00
❑ LP-3012	If Walls Could Talk	1970	6.25	12.50	25.00
CHESS					
❑ 204 [(2)]	Little Milton	1976	3.75	7.50	15.00
❑ CH-9252	We're Gonna Make It	1986	2.50	5.00	10.00
—Reissue of Checker 2995					
❑ CH-9265	Little Milton Sings Big Blues	1987	2.50	5.00	10.00
—Reissue of Checker 3002					
❑ CH-9289	If Walls Could Talk	1989	2.50	5.00	10.00
—Reissue of Checker 3012					
❑ CH-50013	Little Milton's Greatest Hits	1972	3.75	7.50	15.00
GLADES					
❑ 7508	Friend of Mine	1976	3.00	6.00	12.00
❑ 7511	Me for You, You for Me	1977	3.00	6.00	12.00
MALACO					
❑ 7419	Playin' for Keeps	198?	3.00	6.00	12.00
❑ 7427	I Will Survive	198?	3.00	6.00	12.00
❑ 7435	Annie Mae's Café	198?	3.00	6.00	12.00
❑ 7445	Movin' to the Country	198?	3.00	6.00	12.00
❑ 7448	Back to Back	198?	3.00	6.00	12.00
❑ 7453	Too Much Pain	198?	3.00	6.00	12.00
MCA					
❑ 5414	Age Ain't Nothin' But a Number	1983	2.50	5.00	10.00
ROUNDER					
❑ SS-35	The Sun Masters	198?	3.00	6.00	12.00
STAX					
❑ STS-3012	Waiting for Little Milton	1973	5.00	10.00	20.00
❑ 4117	Waiting for Little Milton	1978	3.00	6.00	12.00
—Reissue of 3012					
❑ 5514	Blues 'n' Soul	1974	5.00	10.00	20.00
❑ MPS-8514	Walking the Back Streets	1981	2.50	5.00	10.00
❑ MPS-8518	Blues 'n' Soul	1981	2.50	5.00	10.00
—Reissue of 5514					
❑ MPS-8529	Grits Ain't Groceries	198?	2.50	5.00	10.00
—Despite the title, this is NOT a reissue of Checker 3011, but a later live recording					
❑ MPS-8550	What It Is	198?	2.50	5.00	10.00

LITTLE MISS CORNSHUCKS
CHESS
❑ LP-1453 [M]	The Loneliest Gal in Town	1961	50.00	100.00	200.00

LITTLE RICHARD
ACCORD
❑ SN-7123	Tutti Frutti	1981	2.50	5.00	10.00
AUDIO ENCORES					
❑ 1002	Little Richard	1980	6.25	12.50	25.00
BUDDAH					
❑ BDS-7501	Little Richard	1969	7.50	15.00	30.00
CORAL					
❑ CRL 57446 [M]	Coming Home	1963	10.00	20.00	40.00
❑ CRL 757446 [S]	Coming Home	1963	12.50	25.00	50.00
CROWN					
❑ CLP-5362 [M]	Little Richard Sings Freedom Songs	1963	5.00	10.00	20.00
CUSTOM					
❑ 2061 [M]	Little Richard Sings Spirituals	196?	3.00	6.00	12.00
EPIC					
❑ EG 30428 [(2)]	Cast a Long Shadow	1971	5.00	10.00	20.00
❑ PE 40389	Little Richard's Greatest Hits	1986	2.50	5.00	10.00
❑ PE 40390	The Explosive Little Richard	1986	2.50	5.00	10.00
EXACT					
❑ 206	The Best of Little Richard	1980	2.50	5.00	10.00
GNP CRESCENDO					
❑ GNP-9033	The Big Hits	1974	3.00	6.00	12.00
GRT					
❑ 2103	The Original Little Richard	1977	2.50	5.00	10.00
GUEST STAR					
❑ GS-1429 [M]	Little Richard with Sister Rosetta Tharpe	196?	3.00	6.00	12.00
❑ GSS-1429 [R]	Little Richard with Sister Rosetta Tharpe	196?	3.00	6.00	12.00
KAMA SUTRA					
❑ KSBS-2023	Little Richard	1970	6.25	12.50	25.00
MERCURY					
❑ MG-20656 [M]	It's Real	1961	12.50	25.00	50.00
❑ SR-60656 [S]	It's Real	1961	15.00	30.00	60.00
MODERN					
❑ 100 [M]	His Greatest Hits/Recorded Live	1966	5.00	10.00	20.00
❑ 103 [M]	The Explosive Little Richard	1966	5.00	10.00	20.00
❑ 1000 [S]	His Greatest Hits/Recorded Live	1966	6.25	12.50	25.00
❑ 1003 [S]	The Explosive Little Richard	1966	6.25	12.50	25.00
OKEH					
❑ OKM 12117 [M]	The Explosive Little Richard	1967	6.25	12.50	25.00
❑ OKM 12121 [M]	Little Richard's Greatest Hits	1967	6.25	12.50	25.00
❑ OKS 14117 [S]	The Explosive Little Richard	1967	5.00	10.00	20.00
❑ OKS 14121 [S]	Little Richard's Greatest Hits	1967	5.00	10.00	20.00
PICKWICK					
❑ SPC-3258	King of the Gospel Singers	197?	2.50	5.00	10.00
RCA CAMDEN					
❑ CAL-420 [M]	Little Richard	1956	50.00	100.00	200.00
❑ CAS-2430(e)	Every Hour with Little Richard	1970	3.00	6.00	12.00

Number	Title (A Side/B Side)	Yr	VG	VG+	NM
REPRISE					
❑ MS 2107	The Second Coming	1973	5.00	10.00	20.00
❑ RS 6406	The Rill Thing	1971	5.00	10.00	20.00
❑ RS 6462	King of Rock and Roll	1972	5.00	10.00	20.00
RHINO					
❑ R1-70236	Shut Up! A Collection of Rare Tracks, 1951-1964	1988	3.00	6.00	12.00
SCEPTER					
❑ CTN-18020	The Best of Little Richard	1972	3.00	6.00	12.00
SPECIALTY					
❑ 100 [M]	Here's Little Richard	1957	175.00	350.00	700.00
❑ SP-2100 [M]	Here's Little Richard	1957	50.00	100.00	200.00
—Thick vinyl					
❑ SP-2103 [M]	Little Richard	1958	37.50	75.00	150.00
—Front cover photo occupies the entire cover					
❑ SP-2103 [M]	Little Richard	196?	25.00	50.00	100.00
—Front cover photo partially obscured by a black triangle at uper right; thick vinyl					
❑ SP-2103 [M]	Little Richard	197?	5.00	10.00	20.00
—Reissue with thinner vinyl					
❑ SP-2104 [M]	The Fabulous Little Richard	1958	37.50	75.00	150.00
—Thick vinyl					
❑ SP-2104 [M]	The Fabulous Little Richard	197?	5.00	10.00	20.00
—Reissue with thinner vinyl					
❑ SP-2111 [M]	Little Richard — His Biggest Hits	1963	12.50	25.00	50.00
—Thick vinyl					
❑ SP-2111 [M]	Little Richard — His Biggest Hits	197?	5.00	10.00	20.00
—Reissue with thinner vinyl					
❑ SP-2113	Little Richard's Grooviest 17 Original Hits	1968	6.25	12.50	25.00
—Thick vinyl					
❑ SP-2136	Well Alright!	1970	5.00	10.00	20.00
❑ SP-8508 [(5)]	The Specialty Sessions	1989	10.00	20.00	40.00
SPIN-O-RAMA					
❑ 119 [M]	Clap Your Hands	196?	3.00	6.00	12.00
TRIP					
❑ 8013 [(2)]	Greatest Hits	1972	3.00	6.00	12.00
20TH FOX					
❑ FXG-5010 [M]	Little Richard Sings Gospel	1959	25.00	50.00	100.00
❑ SGM-5010 [S]	Little Richard Sings Gospel	1959	37.50	75.00	150.00
UNITED					
❑ US-7775	His Greatest Hits/Recorded Live	197?	2.50	5.00	10.00
❑ US-7777	The Wild and Frantic Little Richard	197?	2.50	5.00	10.00
UNITED ARTISTS					
❑ UA-LA497-E	The Very Best of Little Richard	1975	2.50	5.00	10.00
UPFRONT					
❑ UPF-123	The Best of Little Richard	197?	2.50	5.00	10.00
❑ UPF-197	Little Richard Sings Gospel	197?	2.50	5.00	10.00
VEE JAY					
❑ LP-1107 [M]	Little Richard Is Back!	1964	12.50	25.00	50.00
❑ LPS-1107 [S]	Little Richard Is Back!	1964	17.50	35.00	70.00
❑ VJLP-1107	Little Richard's Back	198?	2.50	5.00	10.00
—Reissue with thin vinyl					
❑ LP-1124 [M]	Little Richard's Greatest Hits	1965	6.25	12.50	25.00
❑ LPS-1124 [S]	Little Richard's Greatest Hits	1965	10.00	20.00	40.00
❑ VJLP-1124	Little Richard's Greatest Hits	198?	2.50	5.00	10.00
—Reissue with thin vinyl					
❑ DY-7304	Talkin' 'Bout Soul	198?	3.00	6.00	12.00
VEE JAY/CHAMELEON					
❑ D1-74797	Rip It Up	1989	3.00	6.00	12.00
WING					
❑ MGW-12288 [M]	King of the Gospel Singers	1964	3.75	7.50	15.00
❑ SRW-16288 [S]	King of the Gospel Singers	1964	5.00	10.00	20.00

LITTLE RIVER BAND

Number	Title (A Side/B Side)	Yr	VG	VG+	NM
CAPITOL					
❑ SOO-11954	First Under the Wire	1979	2.00	4.00	8.00
❑ SWBK-12061 [(2)]	Backstage Pass	1980	2.50	5.00	10.00
❑ ST-12163	Time Exposure	1981	2.00	4.00	8.00
❑ ST-12247	Greatest Hits	1982	2.00	4.00	8.00
❑ ST-12273	The Net	1983	2.00	4.00	8.00
❑ SJ-12365	Playing to Win	1985	2.00	4.00	8.00
—As "LRB"					
❑ ST-12480	No Reins	1986	2.00	4.00	8.00
❑ SN-16072	After Hours	1979	2.50	5.00	10.00
—First U.S. issue of their second Australian LP					
❑ SN-16141	Beginnings	1980	2.50	5.00	10.00
❑ SN-16142	Beginnings, Vol. 2	1980	2.50	5.00	10.00
❑ SN-16345	First Under the Wire	198?	—	3.00	6.00
—Budget-line reissue					
❑ SN-16346	Time Exposure	198?	—	3.00	6.00
—Budget-line reissue					
❑ SN-16454	Little River Band	1987	—	3.00	6.00
—Budget-line reissue					
❑ SN-16455	Diamantina Cocktail	1987	—	3.00	6.00
—Budget-line reissue					
❑ SN-16456	Sleeper Catcher	1987	—	3.00	6.00
—Budget-line reissue					
❑ SN-16457	Greatest Hits	1987	—	3.00	6.00
—Budget-line reissue					
HARVEST					
❑ ST-11512	Little River Band	1976	2.50	5.00	10.00
❑ SW-11645	Diamantina Cocktail	1977	2.50	5.00	10.00
❑ SW-11783	Sleeper Catcher	1978	2.50	5.00	10.00
MCA					
❑ 6269	Get Lucky	1990	3.00	6.00	12.00
❑ 42193	Monsoon	1989	2.50	5.00	10.00
MOBILE FIDELITY					
❑ 1-036	First Under the Wire	1980	6.25	12.50	25.00
—Audiophile vinyl					

Number	Title (A Side/B Side)	Yr	VG	VG+	NM
LITTLE SISTERS, THE					
MGM					
❑ E-4116 [M]	The Joys of Love	1963	6.25	12.50	25.00
❑ SE-4116 [S]	The Joys of Love	1963	7.50	15.00	30.00
LITTLE SONNY					
ENTERPRISE					
❑ ENS-1005	New King of the Blues Harmonica	1970	10.00	20.00	40.00
❑ ENS-1018	Black and Blue	1971	10.00	20.00	40.00
❑ ENS-1036	Hard Goin' Up	1973	10.00	20.00	40.00
LITTLE WALTER					
CHECKER					
❑ LP-1428 [M]	The Best of Little Walter	1957	125.00	250.00	500.00
—Black or maroon label					
❑ LP-3004 [M]	The Best of Little Walter	1967	12.50	25.00	50.00
—Reissue of 1428					
CHESS					
❑ 2ACMB-202 [(2)]	Little Walter	1976	5.00	10.00	20.00
—Reissue of 60014					
❑ CHV-416 [M]	Confessin' the Blues	1974	3.00	6.00	12.00
❑ LP-1535 [M]	Hate to See You Go	1969	6.25	12.50	25.00
❑ 2CH-60014 [(2)]	Boss Blues Harmonica	1972	5.00	10.00	20.00
LIVE					
RADIOACTIVE					
❑ RAR-10997	Throwing Copper	1994	5.00	10.00	20.00
—Issued on clear vinyl					
❑ RAR2-11590 [(2)]	Secret Samadhi	1997	3.75	7.50	15.00
—Issued on white vinyl; includes poster					
LIVELY ONES, THE					
DEL-FI					
❑ DFLP-1226 [M]	Surf Rider	1963	25.00	50.00	100.00
❑ DFST-1226 [S]	Surf Rider	1963	37.50	75.00	150.00
❑ DFLP-1231 [M]	Surf Drums	1963	12.50	25.00	50.00
❑ DFST-1231 [S]	Surf Drums	1963	17.50	35.00	70.00
❑ DLF 1231	Surf Drums	1997	3.00	6.00	12.00
❑ DFLP-1237 [M]	Surf City	1963	10.00	20.00	40.00
❑ DFST-1237 [S]	Surf City	1963	12.50	25.00	50.00
❑ DLF 1237	Surf City	1997	3.00	6.00	12.00
❑ DFLP-1240 [M]	Surfin' South of the Border	1964	10.00	20.00	40.00
❑ DFST-1240 [S]	Surfin' South of the Border	1964	12.50	25.00	50.00
MGM					
❑ E-4449 [M]	Bugalu Party	1967	5.00	10.00	20.00
❑ SE-4449 [S]	Bugalu Party	1967	6.25	12.50	25.00
LIVERPOOL BEATS, THE					
RONDO					
❑ 2026 [M]	The New Merseyside Sound	1964	7.50	15.00	30.00
LIVERPOOL FIVE, THE					
RCA VICTOR					
❑ LPM-3583 [M]	The Liverpool Five Arrive	1966	6.25	12.50	25.00
❑ LSP-3583 [S]	The Liverpool Five Arrive	1966	7.50	15.00	30.00
❑ LPM-3682 [M]	Out of Sight	1967	6.25	12.50	25.00
❑ LSP-3682 [S]	Out of Sight	1967	7.50	15.00	30.00
LIVERPOOL SCENE, THE					
EPIC					
❑ LN 24336 [M]	The Incredible New Liverpool Scene	1967	6.25	12.50	25.00
❑ BN 26336 [S]	The Incredible New Liverpool Scene	1967	7.50	15.00	30.00
LIVERPOOLS, THE					
WYNCOTE					
❑ SW-9001 [S]	Beatle Mania! In the U.S.A.	1964	6.25	12.50	25.00
❑ W-9001 [M]	Beatle Mania! In the U.S.A.	1964	5.00	10.00	20.00
❑ SW-9061 [S]	The Hit Sounds from England	1964	5.00	10.00	20.00
❑ W-9061 [M]	The Hit Sounds from England	1964	3.75	7.50	15.00
LIVIN' BLUES					
DWARF					
❑ 2003	Dutch Treat	1971	7.50	15.00	30.00
LIVING COLOUR					
EPIC					
❑ FE 44099	Vivid	1988	3.00	6.00	12.00
❑ E 46202	Time's Up	1990	5.00	10.00	20.00
—Yellow vinyl					
LLOYD, CHARLES					
ATLANTIC					
❑ SD 1459 [S]	Dream Weaver	1966	5.00	10.00	20.00
—Blue and green label					
❑ SD 1459 [S]	Dream Weaver	1969	3.00	6.00	12.00
—Red and green label, white stripe through center hole					
❑ SD 1473 [S]	Forest Flower	1967	5.00	10.00	20.00
❑ 1481 [M]	Love-In	1967	5.00	10.00	20.00
COLUMBIA					
❑ CL 2267 [M]	Discovery!	1965	6.25	12.50	25.00
❑ CL 2412 [M]	Of Course, Of Course	1966	6.25	12.50	25.00
❑ CS 9067 [S]	Discovery!	1965	7.50	15.00	30.00
❑ CS 9212 [S]	Of Course, Of Course	1966	7.50	15.00	30.00
❑ CS 9609 [M]	Nirvana	1968	10.00	20.00	40.00
—White label promo; "Special Mono Radio Station Copy" sticker on stereo cover					
❑ CS 9609 [S]	Nirvana	1968	6.25	12.50	25.00
LLOYD, DAVID					
EPIC					
❑ LN 24151 [M]	Confidential (Sounds for a Secret Agent)	1965	5.00	10.00	20.00
❑ BN 26151 [S]	Confidential (Sounds for a Secret Agent)	1965	6.25	12.50	25.00

Number	Title (A Side/B Side)	Yr	VG	VG+	NM

LLOYD, HAROLD, JR.
CORAL
| ☐ CRL 57471 [M] | The Intimate Style of Harold Lloyd, Jr. | 1963 | 3.75 | 7.50 | 15.00 |
| ☐ CRL 757471 [S] | The Intimate Style of Harold Lloyd, Jr. | 1963 | 5.00 | 10.00 | 20.00 |

LOADING ZONE, THE
RCA VICTOR
| ☐ LSP-3959 | The Loading Zone | 1968 | 6.25 | 12.50 | 25.00 |
UMBRELLA
| ☐ US-101 | One for All | 1967 | 20.00 | 40.00 | 80.00 |

LOBO (2)
Jazz guitarist and singer named Edu Lobo. No relation to the 1970s pop singer, whose real name is Kent Lavoie.
A&M
| ☐ SP-3035 | Sergio Mendes Presents Lobo | 1970 | 6.25 | 12.50 | 25.00 |

LOCKLIN, HANK
HILLTOP
☐ JM-6003	Born to Ramble	196?	3.75	7.50	15.00
☐ JM-6041 [M]	Hank Locklin Sings Hank Locklin	196?	3.75	7.50	15.00
☐ JS-6041 [R]	Hank Locklin Sings Hank Locklin	196?	3.00	6.00	12.00
☐ JM-6083	Queen of Hearts	196?	3.75	7.50	15.00
KING
| ☐ 672 [M] | The Best of Hank Locklin | 1961 | 15.00 | 30.00 | 60.00 |
| ☐ 738 [M] | Encores | 1961 | 15.00 | 30.00 | 60.00 |
METRO
| ☐ M 541 [M] | Down Texas Way | 196? | 3.75 | 7.50 | 15.00 |
| ☐ MS 541 [R] | Down Texas Way | 196? | 3.00 | 6.00 | 12.00 |
RCA CAMDEN
| ☐ CAL-912 [M] | My Kind of Country Music | 196? | 3.75 | 7.50 | 15.00 |
| ☐ CAS-912 [R] | My Kind of Country Music | 196? | 3.00 | 6.00 | 12.00 |
RCA VICTOR
☐ LPM-1673 [M]	Foreign Love	1958	15.00	30.00	60.00
☐ LPM-2291 [M]	Please Help Me, I'm Falling	1960	7.50	15.00	30.00
☐ LSP-2291 [S]	Please Help Me, I'm Falling	1960	10.00	20.00	40.00
☐ LPM-2464 [M]	Happy Journey	1962	6.25	12.50	25.00
☐ LSP-2464 [S]	Happy Journey	1962	7.50	15.00	30.00
☐ LPM-2597 [M]	A Tribute to Roy Acuff, the King of Country Music	1962	6.25	12.50	25.00
☐ LSP-2597 [S]	A Tribute to Roy Acuff, the King of Country Music	1962	7.50	15.00	30.00
☐ LPM-2680 [M]	The Ways of Life	1963	6.25	12.50	25.00
☐ LSP-2680 [S]	The Ways of Life	1963	7.50	15.00	30.00
☐ LPM-2801 [M]	Irish Songs, Country Style	1964	5.00	10.00	20.00
☐ LSP-2801 [S]	Irish Songs, Country Style	1964	6.25	12.50	25.00
☐ LPM-2997 [M]	Hank Locklin Sings Hank Williams	1964	5.00	10.00	20.00
☐ LSP-2997 [S]	Hank Locklin Sings Hank Williams	1964	6.25	12.50	25.00
☐ LPM-3391 [M]	Hank Locklin Sings Eddy Arnold	1965	5.00	10.00	20.00
☐ LSP-3391 [S]	Hank Locklin Sings Eddy Arnold	1965	6.25	12.50	25.00
☐ LPM-3465 [M]	Once Over Lightly	1965	5.00	10.00	20.00
☐ LSP-3465 [S]	Once Over Lightly	1965	6.25	12.50	25.00
☐ LPM-3559 [M]	The Best of Hank Locklin	1966	5.00	10.00	20.00
☐ LSP-3559 [S]	The Best of Hank Locklin	1966	6.25	12.50	25.00
☐ LPM-3588 [M]	The Girls Get Prettier	1966	5.00	10.00	20.00
☐ LSP-3588 [S]	The Girls Get Prettier	1966	6.25	12.50	25.00
☐ LPM-3656 [M]	The Gloryland Way	1966	5.00	10.00	20.00
☐ LSP-3656 [S]	The Gloryland Way	1966	6.25	12.50	25.00
☐ LPM-3770 [M]	Send Me the Pillow You Dream On	1967	6.25	12.50	25.00
☐ LSP-3770 [S]	Send Me the Pillow You Dream On	1967	5.00	10.00	20.00
☐ LPM-3841 [M]	Nashville Women	1967	6.25	12.50	25.00
☐ LSP-3841 [S]	Nashville Women	1967	5.00	10.00	20.00
☐ LPM-3946 [M]	Country Hall of Fame	1968	25.00	50.00	100.00
☐ LSP-3946 [S]	Country Hall of Fame	1968	5.00	10.00	20.00
☐ LSP-4030	My Love Song for You	1968	5.00	10.00	20.00
☐ LSP-4113	Softly	1969	5.00	10.00	20.00
☐ LSP-4191	Lookin' Back	1969	3.75	7.50	15.00
SEARS
| ☐ SPS-104 | Send Me the Pillow You Dream On | 196? | 6.25 | 12.50 | 25.00 |
WRANGLER
| ☐ 1004 [M] | Hank Locklin | 1962 | 6.25 | 12.50 | 25.00 |

LOCKWOOD, ROBERT, JR.
TRIX
| ☐ 3307 | Contrasts | 197? | 5.00 | 10.00 | 20.00 |

LOCO, JOE
FANTASY
☐ 3215 [M]	Invitation to the Mambo	1956	5.00	10.00	20.00
—Black vinyl, red label, non-flexible vinyl					
☐ 3215 [M]	Invitation to the Mambo	1956	7.50	15.00	30.00
—Red vinyl					
☐ 3215 [M]	Invitation to the Mambo	196?	3.75	7.50	15.00
—Black vinyl, red label, flexible vinyl					
☐ 3277 [M]	Cha-Cha-Cha	1958	5.00	10.00	20.00
—Black vinyl, red label, non-flexible vinyl					
☐ 3277 [M]	Cha-Cha-Cha	1958	7.50	15.00	30.00
—Red vinyl					
☐ 3277 [M]	Cha-Cha-Cha	196?	3.75	7.50	15.00
—Black vinyl, red label, flexible vinyl					
☐ 3280 [M]	Going Loco	1958	5.00	10.00	20.00
—Black vinyl, red label, non-flexible vinyl					
☐ 3280 [M]	Going Loco	1958	7.50	15.00	30.00
—Red vinyl					
☐ 3280 [M]	Going Loco	196?	3.75	7.50	15.00
—Black vinyl, red label, flexible vinyl					
☐ 3285 [M]	Ole, Ole, Ole	1959	5.00	10.00	20.00
—Black vinyl, red label, non-flexible vinyl					
☐ 3285 [M]	Ole, Ole, Ole	1959	7.50	15.00	30.00
—Red vinyl					
☐ 3285 [M]	Ole, Ole, Ole	196?	3.75	7.50	15.00
—Black vinyl, red label, flexible vinyl					
☐ 3294 [M]	Latin Jewels	1959	5.00	10.00	20.00
—Black vinyl, red label, non-flexible vinyl					
☐ 3294 [M]	Latin Jewels	1959	7.50	15.00	30.00
—Red vinyl					
☐ 3294 [M]	Latin Jewels	196?	3.75	7.50	15.00
—Black vinyl, red label, flexible vinyl					
☐ 3303 [M]	The Best of Joe Loco	196?	3.75	7.50	15.00
—Black vinyl, red label, flexible vinyl					
☐ 3303 [M]	The Best of Joe Loco	1960	5.00	10.00	20.00
—Black vinyl, red label, non-flexible vinyl					
☐ 3303 [M]	The Best of Joe Loco	1960	7.50	15.00	30.00
—Red vinyl					
☐ 3321 [M]	Pachanga with Joe Loco	196?	3.75	7.50	15.00
—Black vinyl, red label, flexible vinyl					
☐ 3321 [M]	Pachanga with Joe Loco	1961	5.00	10.00	20.00
—Black vinyl, red label, non-flexible vinyl					
☐ 3321 [M]	Pachanga with Joe Loco	1961	7.50	15.00	30.00
—Red vinyl					
☐ 8022 [S]	Cha-Cha-Cha	196?	3.75	7.50	15.00
—Black vinyl, blue label, flexible vinyl					
☐ 8022 [S]	Cha-Cha-Cha	1962	5.00	10.00	20.00
—Black vinyl, blue label, non-flexible vinyl					
☐ 8022 [S]	Cha-Cha-Cha	1962	7.50	15.00	30.00
—Blue vinyl					
☐ 8028 [S]	Ole, Ole, Ole	196?	3.75	7.50	15.00
—Black vinyl, blue label, flexible vinyl					
☐ 8028 [S]	Ole, Ole, Ole	1962	5.00	10.00	20.00
—Black vinyl, blue label, non-flexible vinyl					
☐ 8028 [S]	Ole, Ole, Ole	1962	7.50	15.00	30.00
—Blue vinyl					
☐ 8041 [S]	Latin Jewels	196?	3.75	7.50	15.00
—Black vinyl, blue label, flexible vinyl					
☐ 8041 [S]	Latin Jewels	1962	5.00	10.00	20.00
—Black vinyl, blue label, non-flexible vinyl					
☐ 8041 [S]	Latin Jewels	1962	7.50	15.00	30.00
—Blue vinyl					
☐ 8042 [S]	Going Loco	196?	3.75	7.50	15.00
—Black vinyl, blue label, flexible vinyl					
☐ 8042 [S]	Going Loco	1962	5.00	10.00	20.00
—Black vinyl, blue label, non-flexible vinyl					
☐ 8042 [S]	Going Loco	1962	7.50	15.00	30.00
—Blue vinyl					
☐ 8048 [S]	The Best of Joe Loco	196?	3.75	7.50	15.00
—Black vinyl, blue label, flexible vinyl					
☐ 8048 [S]	The Best of Joe Loco	1962	5.00	10.00	20.00
—Black vinyl, blue label, non-flexible vinyl					
☐ 8048 [S]	The Best of Joe Loco	1962	7.50	15.00	30.00
—Blue vinyl					
☐ 8064 [S]	Pachanga with Joe Loco	196?	3.75	7.50	15.00
—Black vinyl, blue label, flexible vinyl					
☐ 8064 [S]	Pachanga with Joe Loco	1962	5.00	10.00	20.00
—Black vinyl, blue label, non-flexible vinyl					
☐ 8064 [S]	Pachanga with Joe Loco	1962	7.50	15.00	30.00
—Blue vinyl					
IMPERIAL
☐ LP-9070 [M]	Let's Go Loco	1959	5.00	10.00	20.00
☐ LP-9073 [M]	Happy Go Loco	1959	5.00	10.00	20.00
☐ LP-9166 [M]	Pachanga Twist	1962	5.00	10.00	20.00
☐ LP-12014 [S]	Let's Go Loco	1959	6.25	12.50	25.00
☐ LP-12019 [S]	Happy Go Loco	1959	6.25	12.50	25.00
☐ LP-12079 [S]	Pachanga Twist	1962	6.25	12.50	25.00
TICO
☐ LP-109 [10]	Mambos, Vol. 1	195?	10.00	20.00	40.00
☐ LP-111 [10]	Mambos, Vol. 2	195?	10.00	20.00	40.00
☐ LP-121 [10]	Mambos, Vol. 3	195?	10.00	20.00	40.00
☐ LP-122 [10]	Mambos, Vol. 4	195?	10.00	20.00	40.00
☐ LP-123 [10]	Mambo Dance Favorites, Vol. 5	195?	10.00	20.00	40.00
☐ LP-129 [10]	Mambo U.S.A.	1954	10.00	20.00	40.00
☐ LP-132 [10]	Instrumental Mambos (Vol. 7)	1955	10.00	20.00	40.00
☐ LP-1006 [M]	Mambo Moods	1955	7.50	15.00	30.00
☐ LP-1008 [M]	Make Mine Mambo	1955	7.50	15.00	30.00
☐ LP-1012 [M]	Mambo Fantasy	1956	7.50	15.00	30.00
☐ LP-1013 [M]	Viva Mambo!	1956	7.50	15.00	30.00

LODI
MOWEST
| ☐ MW 101L | Happiness | 1972 | 6.25 | 12.50 | 25.00 |

LOFGREN, NILS
A&M
☐ SP-3145	Cry Tough	198?	2.00	4.00	8.00
—Reissue of 4573					
☐ SP-3201	The Best	1982	2.50	5.00	10.00
☐ SP-3707 [(2)]	Night After Night	1977	3.00	6.00	12.00
☐ SP-4509	Nils Lofgren	1975	2.50	5.00	10.00
☐ SP-4573	Cry Tough	1976	2.50	5.00	10.00
☐ SP-4628	I Came to Dance	1977	2.50	5.00	10.00
☐ SP-4756	Nils	1979	2.50	5.00	10.00
☐ SP-6509 [(2)]	Night After Night	198?	2.50	5.00	10.00
—Reissue of 3707					
☐ SP-8362 [DJ]	Authorized Bootleg	1976	6.25	12.50	25.00
BACKSTREET
| ☐ 5251 | Night Fades Away | 1981 | 2.50 | 5.00 | 10.00 |
| ☐ 5421 | Wonderland | 1983 | 2.50 | 5.00 | 10.00 |
COLUMBIA
| ☐ BFC 39982 | Flip | 1985 | 2.50 | 5.00 | 10.00 |

LOFTON, CLARENCE
RIVERSIDE
| ☐ RLP-1037 [10] | Honky-Tonk and Boogie-Woogie Piano | 1954 | 20.00 | 40.00 | 80.00 |

Number	Title (A Side/B Side)	Yr	VG	VG+	NM

LOFTON, TRICKY, AND CARMELL JONES
PACIFIC JAZZ

Number	Title (A Side/B Side)	Yr	VG	VG+	NM
❑ PJ-49 [M]	Brass Bag	1962	10.00	20.00	40.00
❑ ST-49 [S]	Brass Bag	1962	12.50	25.00	50.00

LOGAN, GIUSEPPI
ESP-DISK'

❑ S-1007 [S]	Giuseppi Logan Quartet	1965	5.00	10.00	20.00
❑ S-1013 [S]	More Giuseppi Logan	1965	5.00	10.00	20.00

LOGGINS, KENNY
COLUMBIA

❑ PC 34655	Celebrate Me Home	1977	2.50	5.00	10.00
—Originals have no bar code					
❑ PC 34655	Celebrate Me Home	1979	2.00	4.00	8.00
—Reissues have bar code					
❑ JC 35387	Nightwatch	1978	2.50	5.00	10.00
—Originals have no bar code					
❑ JC 36172	Keep the Fire	1979	2.50	5.00	10.00
❑ PC 36172	Keep the Fire	198?	2.00	4.00	8.00
—Budget-line reissue					
❑ C2X 36738 [(2)]	Kenny Loggins Alive	1980	3.00	6.00	12.00
❑ TC 38127	High Adventure	1982	2.50	5.00	10.00
❑ FC 39174	Vox Humana	1985	2.00	4.00	8.00
❑ OC 40535	Back to Avalon	1988	2.00	4.00	8.00
❑ HC 45387	Nightwatch	198?	17.50	35.00	70.00
—Half-speed mastered edition					

LOGGINS AND MESSINA
Also see KENNY LOGGINS; JIM MESSINA.
COLUMBIA

❑ C 31044	Kenny Loggins with Jim Messina Sittin' In	1972	2.50	5.00	10.00
❑ PC 31044	Kenny Loggins with Jim Messina Sittin' In	197?	2.00	4.00	8.00
—Reissue with new prefix					
❑ CQ 31748 [Q]	Loggins and Messina	1973	3.75	7.50	15.00
❑ KC 31748	Loggins and Messina	1972	2.50	5.00	10.00
❑ PC 31748	Loggins and Messina	197?	2.00	4.00	8.00
—Reissue with new prefix					
❑ CQ 32540 [Q]	Full Sail	1973	3.75	7.50	15.00
❑ KC 32540	Full Sail	1973	2.50	5.00	10.00
❑ PC 32540	Full Sail	197?	2.00	4.00	8.00
—Reissue with new prefix					
❑ PG 32848 [(2)]	On Stage	1974	3.00	6.00	12.00
—Original with no bar code					
❑ PG 32848 [(2)]	On Stage	198?	2.50	5.00	10.00
—With bar code					
❑ PC 33175	Mother Lode	1974	2.50	5.00	10.00
—Original with no bar code					
❑ PC 33175	Mother Lode	198?	2.00	4.00	8.00
—With bar code					
❑ PC 33578	Native Sons	1976	2.50	5.00	10.00
—Original with no bar code					
❑ PC 33578	Native Sons	198?	2.00	4.00	8.00
—With bar code					
❑ PCQ 33578 [Q]	Native Sons	1976	3.75	7.50	15.00
❑ PC 33810	So Fine	1975	2.50	5.00	10.00
—Original with no bar code					
❑ PC 33810	So Fine	198?	2.00	4.00	8.00
—With bar code					
❑ JG 34167 [(2)]	Finale	1977	3.00	6.00	12.00
❑ PC 34388	The Best of Friends	1976	2.50	5.00	10.00
—Original with no bar code					
❑ PC 34388	The Best of Friends	198?	2.00	4.00	8.00
—With bar code					
❑ HC 44388	The Best of Friends	1982	12.50	25.00	50.00
—Half-speed mastered edition					

DIRECT DISC

❑ SD 16606	Full Sail	198?	7.50	15.00	30.00
—Audiophile vinyl					

EPIC

❑ PC 34388	The Best of Friends	1976	5.00	10.00	20.00
—Mispressing with wrong label					

LOGSDON, JIMMIE
KING

❑ 843 [M]	Howdy Neighbors	1963	15.00	30.00	60.00

LOLITA
KAPP

❑ KL-1219 [M]	Sailor	1961	6.25	12.50	25.00
❑ KL-1229 [M]	Songs You Will Never Forget	1961	6.25	12.50	25.00
❑ KS-3219 [S]	Sailor	1961	7.50	15.00	30.00
❑ KS-3229 [S]	Songs You Will Never Forget	1961	7.50	15.00	30.00

LOLLIPOP SHOPPE, THE
UNI

❑ 73019	The Lollipop Shoppe	1968	20.00	40.00	80.00

LOMAX, JACKIE
APPLE

❑ ST-3354	Is This What You Want?	1969	6.25	12.50	25.00

CAPITOL

❑ ST-11558	Livin' for Lovin'	1976	2.50	5.00	10.00
❑ ST-11668	Did You Ever	1977	2.50	5.00	10.00

WARNER BROS.

❑ PRO 520 [DJ]	An Interview with Jackie Lomax	1972	10.00	20.00	40.00
❑ WS 1914	Home Is In My Head	1971	3.00	6.00	12.00
❑ BS 2591	Three	1972	3.00	6.00	12.00

LOMBARDO, GUY
CAPITOL

❑ STCL-578 [(3)]	Guy Lombardo	1970	6.25	12.50	25.00

Number	Title (A Side/B Side)	Yr	VG	VG+	NM
❑ W 738 [M]	Lombardo in Hi-Fi	1956	5.00	10.00	20.00
—Gray label					
❑ T 739 [M]	Your Guy Lombardo Medley	1956	5.00	10.00	20.00
—Turquoise label					
❑ T 788 [M]	A Decade on Broadway 1946-56	1956	5.00	10.00	20.00
—Turquoise label					
❑ T 892 [M]	Lively Guy	1957	5.00	10.00	20.00
—Turquoise label					
❑ T 916 [M]	A Decade on Broadway 1935-45	1958	5.00	10.00	20.00
—Turquoise label					
❑ ST 1019 [S]	Berlin by Lombardo	1959	6.25	12.50	25.00
—Black colorband label, logo at left					
❑ T 1019 [M]	Berlin by Lombardo	1958	5.00	10.00	20.00
—Turquoise or gray label					
❑ ST 1121 [S]	Dancing Room Only	1959	5.00	10.00	20.00
—Black colorband label, logo at left					
❑ ST 1244 [S]	Your Guy Lombardo Medley, Vol. 2	1960	5.00	10.00	20.00
—Black colorband label, logo at left					
❑ ST 1306 [S]	The Sweetest Waltzes This Side of Heaven	1960	5.00	10.00	20.00
—Black colorband label, logo at left					
❑ ST 1393 [S]	Guy Lombardo at Harrah's Club	1960	5.00	10.00	20.00
❑ T 1393 [M]	Guy Lombardo at Harrah's Club	1960	3.75	7.50	15.00
❑ SKAO 1443 [S]	Sing the Songs of Christmas	1960	5.00	10.00	20.00
—Black colorband label, logo at left					
❑ T 1461 [M]	The Best of Guy Lombardo	1961	5.00	10.00	20.00
—Black colorband label, logo at left					
❑ ST 1593 [S]	Drifting and Dreaming	1961	5.00	10.00	20.00
—Black colorband label, logo at left					
❑ ST 1598 [S]	Your Guy Lombardo Medley, Vol. 3	1961	5.00	10.00	20.00
—Black colorband label, logo at left					
❑ STDL 2181 [(4)S]	The Lombardo Years	1964	7.50	15.00	30.00
❑ TDL 2181 [(4)M]	The Lombardo Years	1964	6.25	12.50	25.00

DECCA

❑ DXB 185 [(2)M]	The Best of Guy Lombardo	1964	5.00	10.00	20.00
❑ DL 5002 [10]	The Twin Pianos — Vol. 1	195?	7.50	15.00	30.00
—Record has "DL" prefix; sleeve may or may not have "DL"					
❑ DLP 5002 [10]	The Twin Pianos — Vol. 1	1949	10.00	20.00	40.00
—Both record and sleeve have "DLP" prefix					
❑ DL 5003 [10]	The Twin Pianos — Vol. 2	195?	7.50	15.00	30.00
—Record has "DL" prefix; sleeve may or may not have "DL"					
❑ DLP 5003 [10]	The Twin Pianos — Vol. 2	1949	10.00	20.00	40.00
—Both record and sleeve have "DLP" prefix					
❑ DL 5024 [10]	Sidewalks of New York	1949	10.00	20.00	40.00
❑ DL 5041 [10]	Lombardoland	1949	10.00	20.00	40.00
❑ DL 5097 [10]	Song Hits from Broadway Shows	1949	10.00	20.00	40.00
❑ DL 5127 [10]	Latin Rhythms	195?	7.50	15.00	30.00
❑ DL 5156 [10]	Hawaiian Songs for Dancing	195?	7.50	15.00	30.00
❑ DL 5193 [10]	Waltzes	195?	7.50	15.00	30.00
❑ DL 5235 [10]	Silver Jubilee — 1925-1950	1950	7.50	15.00	30.00
❑ DL 5277 [10]	Square Dances (Without Calls)	195?	7.50	15.00	30.00
❑ DL 5322 [10]	Souvenirs	195?	7.50	15.00	30.00
❑ DL 5325 [10]	Waltzland	195?	7.50	15.00	30.00
❑ DL 5328 [10]	Lombardoland, Vol. 2	195?	7.50	15.00	30.00
❑ DL 5329 [10]	Enjoy Yourself	195?	7.50	15.00	30.00
❑ DL 5330 [10]	The Sweetest Music This Side of Heaven	195?	7.50	15.00	30.00
❑ DL 5430 [10]	Jingle Bells	195?	7.50	15.00	30.00
❑ DL 5434 [10]	Everybody Dance to the Music of Guy Lombardo	195?	7.50	15.00	30.00
❑ DL 8070 [M]	A Night at the Roosevelt	195?	5.00	10.00	20.00
—Black label, silver print					
❑ DL 8097 [M]	Lombardoland, U.S.A.	195?	5.00	10.00	20.00
—Black label, silver print					
❑ DL 8119 [M]	Twin Pianos	195?	5.00	10.00	20.00
—Black label, silver print					
❑ DL 8135 [M]	Soft and Sweet	1955	5.00	10.00	20.00
—Black label, silver print					
❑ DL 8136 [M]	Enjoy Yourself	1955	5.00	10.00	20.00
—Black label, silver print					
❑ DL 8205 [M]	Waltz Time	1955	5.00	10.00	20.00
—Black label, silver print					
❑ DL 8208 [M]	The Band Played On	1955	5.00	10.00	20.00
—Black label, silver print					
❑ DL 8249 [M]	Lombardoland	1956	5.00	10.00	20.00
—Black label, silver print					
❑ DL 8251 [M]	Twin Piano Magic	1956	5.00	10.00	20.00
—Black label, silver print					
❑ DL 8254 [M]	Everybody Dance	1956	5.00	10.00	20.00
—Black label, silver print					
❑ DL 8255 [M]	Oh! How We Danced	1956	5.00	10.00	20.00
—Black label, silver print					
❑ DL 8256 [M]	Waltzland	1956	5.00	10.00	20.00
—Black label, silver print					
❑ DL 8333 [M]	Silver Jubilee	1956	5.00	10.00	20.00
—Black label, silver print					
❑ DL 8354 [M]	Jingle Bells	1956	5.00	10.00	20.00
—Black label, silver print					
❑ DL 8843 [M]	Instrumentally Yours	1959	5.00	10.00	20.00
—Black label, silver print					
❑ DL 8894 [M]	The Sidewalks of New York	1959	5.00	10.00	20.00
—Black label, silver print					
❑ DL 78962 [S]	The Sweetest Music This Side of Heaven (A Musical Biography 1926-1932)	1960	5.00	10.00	20.00
—Black label, silver print					

LONDON, JULIE
LIBERTY

❑ MCR-1 [M]	By Myself	196?	6.25	12.50	25.00
—Columbia Record Club exclusive					
❑ SCR-1 [S]	By Myself	196?	7.50	15.00	30.00
—Columbia Record Club exclusive					
❑ LRP-3006 [M]	Julie Is Her Name	1956	12.50	25.00	50.00
—Green label					

Number	Title (A Side/B Side)	Yr	VG	VG+	NM
❑ LRP-3006 [M]	Julie Is Her Name	1960	5.00	10.00	20.00
—Black label, colorband and logo at left					
❑ LRP-3012 [M]	Lonely Girl	1956	12.50	25.00	50.00
—Green label					
❑ LRP-3012 [M]	Lonely Girl	1960	5.00	10.00	20.00
—Black label, colorband and logo at left					
❑ LRP-3043 [M]	About the Blues	1957	10.00	20.00	40.00
—Green label					
❑ LRP-3043 [M]	About the Blues	1960	5.00	10.00	20.00
—Black label, colorband and logo at left					
❑ LRP-3060 [M]	Make Love to Me	1957	10.00	20.00	40.00
—Green label					
❑ LRP-3060 [M]	Make Love to Me	1960	5.00	10.00	20.00
—Black label, colorband and logo at left					
❑ LRP-3096 [M]	Julie	1957	10.00	20.00	40.00
—Green label					
❑ LRP-3100 [M]	Julie Is Her Name, Volume 2	1958	10.00	20.00	40.00
—Green label					
❑ LRP-3100 [M]	Julie Is Her Name, Volume 2	1960	5.00	10.00	20.00
—Black label, colorband and logo at left					
❑ LRP-3105 [M]	London By Night	1958	7.50	15.00	30.00
—Green label					
❑ LRP-3119 [M]	Swing Me an Old Song	1959	7.50	15.00	30.00
—Green label					
❑ LRP-3130 [M]	Your Number Please	1959	7.50	15.00	30.00
—Green label					
❑ LRP-3130 [M]	Your Number Please	1960	5.00	10.00	20.00
—Black label, colorband and logo at left					
❑ LRP-3152 [M]	Julie…At Home	1960	7.50	15.00	30.00
❑ LRP-3164 [M]	Around Midnight	1960	7.50	15.00	30.00
❑ LRP-3171 [M]	Send for Me	1961	7.50	15.00	30.00
❑ LRP-3192 [M]	Whatever Julie Wants	1961	7.50	15.00	30.00
❑ LRP-3203 [M]	Sophisticated Lady	1962	6.25	12.50	25.00
❑ LRP-3231 [M]	Love Letters	1962	6.25	12.50	25.00
❑ LRP-3249 [M]	Love on the Rocks	1963	6.25	12.50	25.00
❑ LRP-3278 [M]	Latin in a Satin Mood	1963	6.25	12.50	25.00
❑ LRP-3291 [M]	Julie's Golden Hits	1963	6.25	12.50	25.00
—Black cover					
❑ LRP-3291 [M]	Julie's Golden Hits	1963	6.25	12.50	25.00
—White cover					
❑ LRP-3300 [M]	The End of the World	1963	6.25	12.50	25.00
❑ LRP-3324 [M]	The Wonderful World of Julie London	1963	6.25	12.50	25.00
❑ LRP-3342 [M]	Julie London	1964	6.25	12.50	25.00
❑ LRP-3375 [M]	Julie London In Person at the Americana	1964	6.25	12.50	25.00
❑ LRP-3392 [M]	Our Fair Lady	1965	6.25	12.50	25.00
❑ LRP-3416 [M]	Feeling Good	1965	6.25	12.50	25.00
❑ LRP-3434 [M]	All Through the Night	1965	6.25	12.50	25.00
❑ LRP-3478 [M]	For the Night People	1966	6.25	12.50	25.00
❑ LRP-3493 [M]	Nice Girls Don't Stay for Breakfast	1967	6.25	12.50	25.00
❑ LRP-3514 [M]	With Body and Soul	1967	7.50	15.00	30.00
❑ L-5501 [M]	The Best of Julie London	1962	7.50	15.00	30.00
❑ S-6601 [S]	The Best of Julie London	1962	10.00	20.00	40.00
❑ LST-7004 [S]	Julie	1958	17.50	35.00	70.00
—Black label, silver print					
❑ LST-7012 [S]	About the Blues	1958	17.50	35.00	70.00
—Black label, silver print					
❑ LST-7012 [S]	About the Blues	1960	6.25	12.50	25.00
—Black label, colorband and logo at left					
❑ LST-7027 [S]	Julie Is Her Name	1958	10.00	20.00	40.00
—Black label, silver print					
❑ LST-7027 [S]	Julie Is Her Name	1958	25.00	50.00	100.00
—Blue vinyl					
❑ LST-7027 [S]	Julie Is Her Name	1958	25.00	50.00	100.00
—Red vinyl					
❑ LST-7027 [S]	Julie Is Her Name	1960	6.25	12.50	25.00
—Black label, colorband and logo at left					
❑ LST-7029 [S]	Lonely Girl	1958	10.00	20.00	40.00
—Black label, silver print					
❑ LST-7029 [S]	Lonely Girl	1960	6.25	12.50	25.00
—Black label, colorband and logo at left					
❑ LST-7060 [S]	Make Love to Me	1958	10.00	20.00	40.00
—Black label, silver print					
❑ LST-7060 [S]	Make Love to Me	1960	6.25	12.50	25.00
—Black label, colorband and logo at left					
❑ LST-7100 [S]	Julie Is Her Name, Volume 2	1958	10.00	20.00	40.00
—Black label, silver print					
❑ LST-7100 [S]	Julie Is Her Name, Volume 2	1960	6.25	12.50	25.00
—Black label, colorband and logo at left					
❑ LST-7105 [S]	London By Night	1958	10.00	20.00	40.00
—Black label, silver print					
❑ LST-7119 [S]	Swing Me an Old Song	1959	10.00	20.00	40.00
—Black label, silver print					
❑ LST-7130 [S]	Your Number Please	1959	10.00	20.00	40.00
—Black label, silver print					
❑ LST-7130 [S]	Your Number Please	1960	6.25	12.50	25.00
—Black label, colorband and logo at left					
❑ LST-7152 [S]	Julie…At Home	1960	10.00	20.00	40.00
—Black vinyl					
❑ LST-7152 [S]	Julie…At Home	1960	25.00	50.00	100.00
—Blue vinyl					
❑ LST-7164 [S]	Around Midnight	1960	10.00	20.00	40.00
❑ LST-7171 [S]	Send for Me	1961	10.00	20.00	40.00
❑ LST-7192 [S]	Whatever Julie Wants	1961	10.00	20.00	40.00
❑ LST-7203 [S]	Sophisticated Lady	1962	7.50	15.00	30.00
❑ LST-7231 [S]	Love Letters	1962	7.50	15.00	30.00
❑ LST-7249 [S]	Love on the Rocks	1963	7.50	15.00	30.00
❑ LST-7278 [S]	Latin in a Satin Mood	1963	7.50	15.00	30.00
❑ LST-7291 [S]	Julie's Golden Hits	1963	7.50	15.00	30.00
—Black cover					
❑ LST-7291 [S]	Julie's Golden Hits	1963	7.50	15.00	30.00
—White cover					
❑ LST-7300 [S]	The End of the World	1963	7.50	15.00	30.00
❑ LST-7324 [S]	The Wonderful World of Julie London	1963	7.50	15.00	30.00
❑ LST-7342 [S]	Julie London	1964	7.50	15.00	30.00
❑ LST-7375 [S]	Julie London In Person at the Americana	1964	7.50	15.00	30.00
❑ LST-7392 [S]	Our Fair Lady	1965	7.50	15.00	30.00
❑ LST-7416 [S]	Feeling Good	1965	7.50	15.00	30.00
❑ LST-7434 [S]	All Through the Night	1965	7.50	15.00	30.00
❑ LST-7478 [S]	For the Night People	1966	7.50	15.00	30.00
❑ LST-7493 [S]	Nice Girls Don't Stay for Breakfast	1967	6.25	12.50	25.00
❑ LST-7514 [S]	With Body and Soul	1967	6.25	12.50	25.00
❑ LST-7546 [S]	Easy Does It	1968	5.00	10.00	20.00
❑ LST-7609 [S]	Yummy, Yummy, Yummy	1969	5.00	10.00	20.00
❑ SL-9002 [M]	Calendar Girl	1956	25.00	50.00	100.00
SUNSET					
❑ SUM-1104 [M]	Julie London	196?	3.00	6.00	12.00
❑ SUM-1161 [M]	Soft and Sweet	196?	3.00	6.00	12.00
❑ SUS-5104 [S]	Julie London	196?	3.75	7.50	15.00
❑ SUS-5161 [S]	Soft and Sweet	196?	3.75	7.50	15.00
❑ SUS-5207	Gone with the Wind	196?	3.00	6.00	12.00
UNITED ARTISTS					
❑ UA-LA437-E	The Very Best of Julie London	1975	3.00	6.00	12.00

LONDON, LAURIE

CAPITOL

Number	Title (A Side/B Side)	Yr	VG	VG+	NM
❑ T 10169 [M]	England's 14 Year Old Singing Sensation — Laurie London	1958	12.50	25.00	50.00

LONDON POPS ORCHESTRA (FREDERICK FENNELL, CONDUCTOR)

MERCURY LIVING PRESENCE

Number	Title (A Side/B Side)	Yr	VG	VG+	NM
❑ SR 90439 [S]	Coates: Three Elizabeths; London Suite; Four Ways Suite	1965	5.00	10.00	20.00
—Maroon label, with "Vendor: Mercury Record Corporation"					

LONDON PROMS SYMPHONY ORCHESTRA (RAYMOND AGOULT, CONDUCTOR)

RCA VICTOR RED SEAL

Number	Title (A Side/B Side)	Yr	VG	VG+	NM
❑ LSC-2326 [S]	Clair de Lune	1960	55.00	110.00	220.00
—Original with "shaded dog" label					
❑ LSC-2326 [S]	Clair de Lune	199?	6.25	12.50	25.00
—Classic Records reissue					

LONDON PROMS SYMPHONY ORCHESTRA (CHARLES MACKERRAS, CONDUCTOR)

RCA VICTOR RED SEAL

Number	Title (A Side/B Side)	Yr	VG	VG+	NM
❑ LSC-2336 [S]	Sibelius: Finlandia	1960	10.00	20.00	40.00
—Original with "shaded dog" label					
❑ LSC-2336 [S]	Sibelius: Finlandia	199?	6.25	12.50	25.00
—Classic Records reissue					

LONDON PROMS SYMPHONY ORCHESTRA (ROBERT SHARPLES, CONDUCTOR)

RCA VICTOR RED SEAL

Number	Title (A Side/B Side)	Yr	VG	VG+	NM
❑ LSC-2299 [S]	Lehar: Waltzes	1959	6.25	12.50	25.00
—Original with "shaded dog" label					

LONDON SOUND 70 ORCHESTRA AND CHORUS

DECCA

Number	Title (A Side/B Side)	Yr	VG	VG+	NM
❑ DEB 7-7 [(3)]	The Sounds of Christmas	1970	6.25	12.50	25.00

LONDON SYMPHONY ORCHESTRA (ARTHUR BLISS, CONDUCTOR)

RCA VICTOR RED SEAL

Number	Title (A Side/B Side)	Yr	VG	VG+	NM
❑ LSC-2257 [S]	Elgar: Pomp and Circumstance Marches 1-5	1959	25.00	50.00	100.00
—Original with "shaded dog" label					

LONDON SYMPHONY ORCHESTRA (ANTAL DORATI, CONDUCTOR)

MERCURY LIVING PRESENCE

Number	Title (A Side/B Side)	Yr	VG	VG+	NM
❑ SR 90006 [S]	Prokofiev: Love for Three Oranges Suite; Scythian Suite	195?	75.00	150.00	300.00
❑ SR 90006 [S]	Prokofiev: Love for Three Oranges Suite; Scythian Suite	199?	6.25	12.50	25.00
—Classic Records reissue					
❑ SR 90122 [S]	Borodin: Polovetsian Dances; Rimsky-Korsakov: Coq d-Or	1960	6.25	12.50	25.00
—Maroon label, no "Vendor: Mercury Record Corporation"					
❑ SR 90123 [S]	Mendelssohn: Symphony No. 3; Fingel's Cave Overture	1960	10.00	20.00	40.00
—Maroon label, no "Vendor: Mercury Record Corporation"					
❑ SR 90153 [S]	Respighi: The Birds; Brazilian Impressions	196?	12.50	25.00	50.00
—Maroon label, no "Vendor: Mercury Record Corporation"					
❑ SR 90153 [S]	Respighi: The Birds; Brazilian Impressions	196?	50.00	100.00	200.00
—Maroon label, with "Vendor: Mercury Record Corporation"					
❑ SR 90154 [S]	Brahms: Haydn Variations; Hungarian Dances	196?	7.50	15.00	30.00
—Maroon label, no "Vendor: Mercury Record Corporation"					
❑ SR 90155 [S]	Haydn: Symphonies 100 and 101	196?	25.00	50.00	100.00
—Maroon label, no "Vendor: Mercury Record Corporation"					
❑ SR 90156 [S]	Verdi: Overtures	196?	5.00	10.00	20.00
—Maroon label, no "Vendor: Mercury Record Corporation"					
❑ SR 90158 [S]	Handel-Harty: Water Music Suite; Royal Fireworks Music	196?	12.50	25.00	50.00
—Maroon label, no "Vendor: Mercury Record Corporation"					
❑ SR 90209 [S]	Khachaturian: Gayne Ballet Suite; Tchaikovsky: Romeo and Juliet	196?	7.50	15.00	30.00
—Maroon label, no "Vendor: Mercury Record Corporation"					
❑ SR 90209 [S]	Khachaturian: Gayne Ballet Suite; Tchaikovsky: Romeo and Juliet	196?	7.50	15.00	30.00
—Maroon label, with "Vendor: Mercury Record Corporation"					
❑ SR 90214 [S]	Lizst: Les Preludes; Smetana: The Moldau; Mussorgsky: Night on Bald Mountain; Sibelius: Valse Triste	196?	10.00	20.00	40.00
—Maroon label, no "Vendor: Mercury Record Corporation"					
❑ SR 90226 [S]	Stravinsky: The Firebird	196?	6.25	12.50	25.00
—Third edition: Dark red (not maroon) label					
❑ SR 90226 [S]	Stravinsky: The Firebird	196?	7.50	15.00	30.00
—Maroon label, with "Vendor: Mercury Record Corporation"					

L

LONDON SYMPHONY ORCHESTRA

Number	Title (A Side/B Side)	Yr	VG	VG+	NM
❏ SR 90226 [S]	Stravinsky: The Firebird	196?	62.50	125.00	250.00
—Maroon label, no "Vendor: Mercury Record Corporation"					
❏ SR 90226 [S]	Stravinsky: The Firebird	199?	6.25	12.50	25.00
—Classic Records reissue					
❏ SR 90234 [S]	Wagner: Tristan und Isolde Prelude and Liebestod; Tannhauser Overture; Lohengrin Prelude	196?	6.25	12.50	25.00
—Maroon label, no "Vendor: Mercury Record Corporation"					
❏ SR 90235 [S]	Liszt: Hungarian Rhapsodies No. 2 and 3; Enescu: Rumanian Rhapsodies No. 1 and 2	196?	5.00	10.00	20.00
—Third edition: Dark red (not maroon) label					
❏ SR 90235 [S]	Liszt: Hungarian Rhapsodies No. 2 and 3; Enescu: Rumanian Rhapsodies No. 1 and 2	196?	15.00	30.00	60.00
—Maroon label, no "Vendor: Mercury Record Corporation"					
❏ SR 90235 [S]	Liszt: Hungarian Rhapsodies No. 2 and 3; Enescu: Rumanian Rhapsodies No. 1 and 2	196?	15.00	30.00	60.00
—Maroon label, with "Vendor: Mercury Record Corporation"					
❏ SR 90236 [S]	Dvorak: Symphony No. 4 (8) in G; Carnaval Overture	196?	30.00	60.00	120.00
—Maroon label, no "Vendor: Mercury Record Corporation"					
❏ SR 90246 [S]	Copland: Appalachian Spring; Billy the Kid	196?	5.00	10.00	20.00
—Third edition: Dark red (not maroon) label					
❏ SR 90246 [S]	Copland: Appalachian Spring; Billy the Kid	196?	20.00	40.00	80.00
—Maroon label, no "Vendor: Mercury Record Corporation"					
❏ SR 90246 [S]	Copland: Appalachian Spring; Billy the Kid	196?	20.00	40.00	80.00
—Maroon label, with "Vendor: Mercury Record Corporation"					
❏ SR 90255 [S]	Tchaikovsky: Symphony No. 5	196?	37.50	75.00	150.00
—Maroon label, no "Vendor: Mercury Record Corporation"					
❏ SR 90265 [S]	Rimsky-Korsakov: Capriccio Espagnol; Russian Easter Overture; Borodin: Prince Igor Overture	196?	12.50	25.00	50.00
—Maroon label, no "Vendor: Mercury Record Corporation"					
❏ SR 90268 [S]	Brahms: Symphony No. 1	196?	12.50	25.00	50.00
—Maroon label, no "Vendor: Mercury Record Corporation"					
❏ SR 90278 [S]	Berg: Suites from Lulu and Wozzeck	196?	6.25	12.50	25.00
—Maroon label, with "Vendor: Mercury Record Corporation"					
❏ SR 90278 [S]	Berg: Suites from Lulu and Wozzeck	196?	15.00	30.00	60.00
—Maroon label, no "Vendor: Mercury Record Corporation"					
❏ SR 90279 [S]	Tchakiovsky: Symphony No. 4 in F	196?	75.00	150.00	300.00
—Maroon label, no "Vendor: Mercury Record Corporation"					
❏ SR 90280 [S]	Mozart: Symphony No. 40; Haydn: Symphony No. 45	196?	5.00	10.00	20.00
—Maroon label, no "Vendor: Mercury Record Corporation"					
❏ SR 90287 [S]	Wagner: Mesitersinger Prelude; Tannhauser Overture; Parsifal; Lohengrin Selections	196?	7.50	15.00	30.00
—Maroon label, with "Vendor: Mercury Record Corporation"					
❏ SR 90287 [S]	Wagner: Mesitersinger Prelude; Tannhauser Overture; Parsifal; Lohengrin Selections	196?	10.00	20.00	40.00
—Maroon label, no "Vendor: Mercury Record Corporation"					
❏ SR 90311 [S]	Bartok: Bluebeard's Castle	196?	5.00	10.00	20.00
—Maroon label, no "Vendor: Mercury Record Corporation"					
❏ SR 90312 [S]	Tchakovsky: Symphony No. 6	196?	12.50	25.00	50.00
—Maroon label, no "Vendor: Mercury Record Corporation"					
❏ SR 90312 [S]	Tchakovsky: Symphony No. 6	196?	12.50	25.00	50.00
—Maroon label, with "Vendor: Mercury Record Corporation"					
❏ SR 90316 [S]	Vienna 1908-1914	196?	30.00	60.00	120.00
—Maroon label, with "Vendor: Mercury Record Corporation"					
❏ SR 90316 [S]	Vienna 1908-1914	196?	50.00	100.00	200.00
—Maroon label, no "Vendor: Mercury Record Corporation"					
❏ SR 90317 [S]	Beethoven: Symphony No. 5; Egmont Overture; Consecration of the House Overture	196?	6.25	12.50	25.00
—Maroon label, with "Vendor: Mercury Record Corporation"					
❏ SR 90317 [S]	Beethoven: Symphony No. 5; Egmont Overture; Consecration of the House Overture	196?	20.00	40.00	80.00
—Maroon label, no "Vendor: Mercury Record Corporation"					
❏ SR 90371 [S]	Liszt: Hungarian Rhapsodies Nos. 1, 4, 5 and 6	196?	7.50	15.00	30.00
—Third edition: Dark red (not maroon) label					
❏ SR 90371 [S]	Liszt: Hungarian Rhapsodies Nos. 1, 4, 5 and 6	196?	15.00	30.00	60.00
—Maroon label, with "Vendor: Mercury Record Corporation"					
❏ SR 90371 [S]	Liszt: Hungarian Rhapsodies Nos. 1, 4, 5 and 6	196?	100.00	200.00	400.00
—Maroon label, no "Vendor: Mercury Record Corporation"					
❏ SR 90378 [S]	Bartok: Concerto for Orchestra	196?	100.00	200.00	400.00
—Maroon label, no "Vendor: Mercury Record Corporation"					
❏ SR 90387 [S]	Stravnisky: Song of the Nightingale; Fireworks; Scherzo; Four Etudes	196?	10.00	20.00	40.00
—Maroon label, with "Vendor: Mercury Record Corporation"					
❏ SR 90387 [S]	Stravnisky: Song of the Nightingale; Fireworks; Scherzo; Four Etudes	196?	25.00	50.00	100.00
—Maroon label, no "Vendor: Mercury Record Corporation"					
❏ SR 90409 [S]	Tchaikovsky: Rococo Variations; Saint-Saens: Cello Concerto No. 1	196?	10.00	20.00	40.00
—Maroon label, with "Vendor: Mercury Record Corporation"					
❏ SR 90409 [S]	Tchaikovsky: Rococo Variations; Saint-Saens: Cello Concerto No. 1	196?	25.00	50.00	100.00
—Maroon label, no "Vendor: Mercury Record Corporation"					
❏ SR 90415 [S]	Haydn: Symphony No. 100 in G; Beethoven: Symphony No. 6 in F	196?	5.00	10.00	20.00
—Maroon label, no "Vendor: Mercury Record Corporation"					
❏ SR 90426 [S]	Bartok: The Wooden Prince	196?	5.00	10.00	20.00
—Maroon label, with "Vendor: Mercury Record Corporation"					
❏ SR 90426 [S]	Bartok: The Wooden Prince	196?	10.00	20.00	40.00
—Maroon label, no "Vendor: Mercury Record Corporation"					
❏ SR 90435 [S]	Paris 1917-1938	196?	5.00	10.00	20.00
—Maroon label, oval "Mercury" logo					
❏ SR 90435 [S]	Paris 1917-1938	1965	25.00	50.00	100.00
—Maroon label, no "Vendor: Mercury Record Corporation"					
❏ SR 90437 [S]	Brahms: 16 Hungarian Dances	1965	5.00	10.00	20.00
—Maroon label, with "Vendor: Mercury Record Corporation"					

LONDON SYMPHONY ORCHESTRA (ALEXANDER GIBSON, CONDUCTOR)

RCA VICTOR RED SEAL

Number	Title (A Side/B Side)	Yr	VG	VG+	NM
❏ LSC-2405 [S]	Sibelius: Symphony No. 5	1960	55.00	110.00	220.00
—Original with "shaded dog" label					
❏ LSC-2405 [S]	Sibelius: Symphony No. 5	199?	6.25	12.50	25.00
—Classic Records reissue					

LONDON SYMPHONY ORCHESTRA (JEAN MARTINON, CONDUCTOR)

RCA VICTOR RED SEAL

Number	Title (A Side/B Side)	Yr	VG	VG+	NM
❏ LSC-2298 [S]	Borodin: Symphony No. 2; Rimsky-Korsakov: Capriccio Espagnole	1960	17.50	35.00	70.00
—Original with "shaded dog" label					
❏ LSC-2298 [S]	Borodin: Symphony No. 2; Rimsky-Korsakov: Capriccio Espagnole	199?	6.25	12.50	25.00
—Classic Records reissue					
❏ LSC-2322 [S]	Shostakovich: Symphony No. 1	1960	25.00	50.00	100.00
—Original with "shaded dog" label					
❏ LSC-2322 [S]	Shostakovich: Symphony No. 1	199?	6.25	12.50	25.00
—Classic Records reissue					
❏ LSC-2419 [S]	Dvorak: Slavonic Dances	1960	45.00	90.00	180.00
—Original with "shaded dog" label					
❏ LSC-2419 [S]	Dvorak: Slavonic Dances	199?	6.25	12.50	25.00
—Classic Records reissue					

LONDON SYMPHONY ORCHESTRA (PIERRE MONTEUX, CONDUCTOR)

RCA VICTOR RED SEAL

Number	Title (A Side/B Side)	Yr	VG	VG+	NM
❏ LSC-2177 [S]	Tchaikovsky: Sleeping Beauty (Excerpts)	1959	6.25	12.50	25.00
—Original with "shaded dog" label					
❏ LSC-2208 [S]	Rimsky-Korsakov: Scheherazade	1959	7.50	15.00	30.00
—Original with "shaded dog" label					
❏ LSC-2342 [S]	Sibelius: Symphony No. 2	1960	5.00	10.00	20.00
—Original with "shaded dog" label					
❏ LSC-2342 [S]	Sibelius: Symphony No. 2	199?	6.25	12.50	25.00
—Classic Records reissue					
❏ LSC-2418 [S]	Elgar: Enigma Variations	1960	20.00	40.00	80.00
—Original with "shaded dog" label					
❏ LSC-2418 [S]	Elgar: Enigma Variations	199?	6.25	12.50	25.00
—Classic Records reissue					
❏ LSC-2489 [S]	Dvorak: Symphony No. 2	196?	6.25	12.50	25.00
—Original with "shaded dog" label					
❏ LSC-2489 [S]	Dvorak: Symphony No. 2	199?	6.25	12.50	25.00
—Classic Records reissue					

LONDON SYMPHONY ORCHESTRA (HANS SCHMIDT-ISSERSTEDT, CONDUCTOR)

MERCURY LIVING PRESENCE

Number	Title (A Side/B Side)	Yr	VG	VG+	NM
❏ SR 90184 [S]	Mozart: Symphonies No. 39 and 41	196?	7.50	15.00	30.00
—Maroon label, with "Vendor: Mercury Record Corporation"					
❏ SR 90184 [S]	Mozart: Symphonies No. 39 and 41	196?	30.00	60.00	120.00
—Maroon label, no "Vendor: Mercury Record Corporation"					

LONDON SYMPHONY ORCHESTRA (WALTER SUSSKIND, HANS SCHMIDT-ISSERSTEDT, CONDUCTORS)

MERCURY LIVING PRESENCE

Number	Title (A Side/B Side)	Yr	VG	VG+	NM
❏ SR 90196 [S]	Schubert: Symphonies No. 4 and 6	196?	5.00	10.00	20.00
—Maroon label, no "Vendor: Mercury Record Corporation"					

LONE STAR RAMBLERS, THE

LONGHORN

Number	Title (A Side/B Side)	Yr	VG	VG+	NM
❏ LP-600 [M]	Texas Square Dancing with Red at the 60 Club	196?	6.25	12.50	25.00

LONESOME BLUES SINGER, THE

See LEADBELLY.

LONESOME PINE FIDDLERS, THE

STARDAY

Number	Title (A Side/B Side)	Yr	VG	VG+	NM
❏ SLP-155 [M]	14 Mountain Songs Featuring 5-String Banjo	1961	10.00	20.00	40.00
❏ SLP-194 [M]	Bluegrass	1962	10.00	20.00	40.00
❏ SLP-222 [M]	More Bluegrass	1963	10.00	20.00	40.00

LONESOME RHODES

RCA VICTOR

Number	Title (A Side/B Side)	Yr	VG	VG+	NM
❏ LPM-3759 [M]	Lonesome Rhodes	1967	7.50	15.00	30.00
❏ LSP-3759 [S]	Lonesome Rhodes	1967	5.00	10.00	20.00

LONESOME SUNDOWN

EXCELLO

Number	Title (A Side/B Side)	Yr	VG	VG+	NM
❏ LPS-8012	Lonesome Lonely Blues	1970	6.25	12.50	25.00

LONG, BARBARA

SAVOY

Number	Title (A Side/B Side)	Yr	VG	VG+	NM
❏ MG-12161 [M]	Soul	1961	7.50	15.00	30.00

LONG, DANNY

CAPITOL

Number	Title (A Side/B Side)	Yr	VG	VG+	NM
❏ ST 1988 [S]	Jazz Furlough	1963	5.00	10.00	20.00

LONG, SHORTY (1)

R&B singer.

SOUL

Number	Title (A Side/B Side)	Yr	VG	VG+	NM
❏ SS-709	Here Comes the Judge	1968	5.00	10.00	20.00
❏ SS-719	The Prime of Shorty Long	1969	3.75	7.50	15.00

LONG, SHORTY (2)

C&W singer.

FORD

Number	Title (A Side/B Side)	Yr	VG	VG+	NM
❏ FXM-712 [M]	Country Jamboree	1963	5.00	10.00	20.00

Number	Title (A Side/B Side)	Yr	VG	VG+	NM
LONGBRANCH PENNYWHISTLE					
AMOS					
❏ AAS-7007	Longbranch Pennywhistle	1969	12.50	25.00	50.00
LONGMIRE, WILBERT					
PACIFIC JAZZ					
❏ ST-20161	Revolution	1969	5.00	10.00	20.00
LONGO, MIKE					
GROOVE MERCHANT					
❏ 525	Funkia	1974	5.00	10.00	20.00
LONZO AND OSCAR					
COLUMBIA					
❏ CS 9587	Mountain Dew	1968	5.00	10.00	20.00
DECCA					
❏ DL 4363 [M]	Country Comedy Time	1963	5.00	10.00	20.00
STARDAY					
❏ SLP-119 [M]	America's Greatest Country Comedians	1960	10.00	20.00	40.00
❏ SLP-244 [M]	Country Music Time	1963	10.00	20.00	40.00
LOOKOFSKY, HARRY					
ATLANTIC					
❏ 1319 [M]	Stringville	1959	10.00	20.00	40.00
—Black label					
❏ 1319 [M]	Stringville	1961	5.00	10.00	20.00
—Multicolor label, white "fan" logo at right					
❏ SD 1319 [S]	Stringville	1959	10.00	20.00	40.00
—Green label					
LOOSE					
NOCTURNE					
❏ 906	Freaky Billie, The Wheelie King	1970	7.50	15.00	30.00
LOPEZ, TRINI					
CAPITOL					
❏ SK 11009	Viva	1972	2.50	5.00	10.00
GUEST STAR					
❏ GS-1499 [M]	Trini Lopez and Scott Gregory	1964	12.50	25.00	50.00
—"Scott Gregory" is said to be a pseudonym for BILL HALEY.					
HARMONY					
❏ H 30012	Bye Bye Love	1970	2.50	5.00	10.00
KING					
❏ 863 [M]	Teenage Love Songs	1963	15.00	30.00	60.00
❏ 877 [M]	More of Trini Lopez	1964	15.00	30.00	60.00
❏ 962 [M]	24 Songs by the Great Trini Lopez	1966	7.50	15.00	30.00
REPRISE					
❏ R-6093 [M]	Trini Lopez at PJ's	1963	3.00	6.00	12.00
❏ R9-6093 [S]	Trini Lopez at PJ's	1963	3.75	7.50	15.00
❏ R-6103 [M]	More Trini Lopez at PJ's	1963	3.00	6.00	12.00
❏ RS-6103 [S]	More Trini Lopez at PJ's	1963	3.75	7.50	15.00
❏ R-6112 [M]	On the Move	1964	3.00	6.00	12.00
❏ RS-6112 [S]	On the Move	1964	3.75	7.50	15.00
❏ R-6125 [M]	The Latin Album	1964	3.00	6.00	12.00
❏ RS-6125 [S]	The Latin Album	1964	3.75	7.50	15.00
❏ R-6134 [M]	Live at Basin St. East	1964	3.00	6.00	12.00
❏ RS-6134 [S]	Live at Basin St. East	1964	3.75	7.50	15.00
❏ R-6147 [M]	The Folk Album	1965	3.00	6.00	12.00
❏ RS-6147 [S]	The Folk Album	1965	3.75	7.50	15.00
❏ R-6165 [M]	The Love Album	1965	3.00	6.00	12.00
❏ RS-6165 [S]	The Love Album	1965	3.75	7.50	15.00
❏ R-6171 [M]	The Rhythm & Blues Album	1965	3.00	6.00	12.00
❏ RS-6171 [S]	The Rhythm & Blues Album	1965	3.75	7.50	15.00
❏ R-6183 [M]	The Sing-Along World of Trini Lopez	1965	3.00	6.00	12.00
❏ RS-6183 [S]	The Sing-Along World of Trini Lopez	1965	3.75	7.50	15.00
❏ R-6196 [M]	Trini	1966	3.00	6.00	12.00
❏ RS-6196 [S]	Trini	1966	3.75	7.50	15.00
❏ R-6215 [M]	The Second Latin Album	1966	3.00	6.00	12.00
❏ RS-6215 [S]	The Second Latin Album	1966	3.75	7.50	15.00
❏ R-6226 [M]	Greatest Hits!	1966	3.00	6.00	12.00
❏ RS-6226 [S]	Greatest Hits!	1966	3.75	7.50	15.00
❏ R-6238 [M]	Trini Lopez in London	1967	3.75	7.50	15.00
❏ RS-6238 [S]	Trini Lopez in London	1967	3.00	6.00	12.00
❏ R-6255 [M]	Trini Lopez — Now!	1967	3.75	7.50	15.00
❏ RS-6255 [S]	Trini Lopez — Now!	1967	3.00	6.00	12.00
❏ RS-6285	It's a Great Life	1968	3.00	6.00	12.00
❏ RS-6300	Welcome to Trini Country	1968	3.00	6.00	12.00
❏ RS-6337	The Whole Enchilada	1969	3.00	6.00	12.00
❏ RS-6361	The Trini Lopez Show	1970	3.75	7.50	15.00
ROULETTE					
❏ 3020	Transformed by Time	1978	2.50	5.00	10.00
LORD, BOBBY					
DECCA					
❏ DL 75246	Bobby Lord	1970	3.00	6.00	12.00
HARMONY					
❏ HL 7322 [M]	Bobby Lord's Best	1964	6.25	12.50	25.00
HICKORY					
❏ LP-126 [M]	The Bobby Lord Show	1965	5.00	10.00	20.00
LORD SITAR					
CAPITOL					
❏ ST 2916	Lord Sitar	1968	7.50	15.00	30.00
LOREN, DONNA					
CAPITOL					
❏ ST 2323 [S]	Beach Blanket Bingo	1965	12.50	25.00	50.00
❏ T 2323 [M]	Beach Blanket Bingo	1965	10.00	20.00	40.00
LORING, GLORIA					
ATLANTIC					
❏ 81679	Gloria Loring	1986	2.00	4.00	8.00
❏ 81852	Full Moon, No Hesitation	1988	2.00	4.00	8.00

Number	Title (A Side/B Side)	Yr	VG	VG+	NM
MGM					
❏ SE-4499	Today	1968	5.00	10.00	20.00
LOS ANGELES PHILHARMONIC (ZUBIN MEHTA, CONDUCTOR)					
MOBILE FIDELITY					
❏ 1-008	Suites from "Star Wars" and "Close Encounters of the Third Kind"	1979	12.50	25.00	50.00
—Audiophile vinyl					
LOS BRAVOS					
Also see MIKE KENNEDY.					
PARROT					
❏ PAS 71021	Bring a Little Lovin'	1968	20.00	40.00	80.00
—Among the other tracks, "Black Is Black" in in true stereo.					
PRESS					
❏ PR 73003 [M]	Black Is Black	1966	12.50	25.00	50.00
❏ PRS 83003 [R]	Black Is Black	1966	7.50	15.00	30.00
LOS INDIOS TABAJARAS					
RCA CAMDEN					
❏ CXS-9031 [(2)]	Los Indios Tabajaras	1973	3.75	7.50	15.00
RCA INTERNATIONAL					
❏ IL5-7367	Los Grandes Exitos	198?	3.00	6.00	12.00
RCA VICTOR					
❏ AFL1-0210	Favorite Movie Themes	1977	2.50	5.00	10.00
—Reissue with new prefix					
❏ APL1-0210	Favorite Movie Themes	1973	3.00	6.00	12.00
❏ FSP-296	Maria Elena	1971	3.00	6.00	12.00
❏ FSP-300	Siempre En Mi Corazon	1972	3.00	6.00	12.00
❏ FSP-310	Softly	1972	3.00	6.00	12.00
❏ AFL1-0668	Classical Guitars	1977	2.50	5.00	10.00
—Reissue with new prefix					
❏ CPL1-0668	Classical Guitars	1974	3.00	6.00	12.00
❏ AFL1-1033	Secret Love	1977	2.50	5.00	10.00
—Reissue with new prefix					
❏ APL1-1033	Secret Love	1975	3.00	6.00	12.00
❏ ANL1-1179	Maria Elena	1976	2.50	5.00	10.00
—Reissue					
❏ LPM-1788 [M]	Sweet and Savage	1958	10.00	20.00	40.00
❏ LSP-1788 [S]	Sweet and Savage	1958	12.50	25.00	50.00
❏ APL1-2082	Mellow Nostalgia	1977	3.00	6.00	12.00
❏ ANL1-2321	In a Sentimental Mood	1977	2.50	5.00	10.00
❏ AFL1-2526	Masterpieces	1978	3.00	6.00	12.00
❏ LPM-2822 [M]	Maria Elena	1963	5.00	10.00	20.00
—Reissue of LPM-1788					
❏ LSP-2822 [S]	Maria Elena	1963	6.25	12.50	25.00
—Reissue of LSP-1788					
❏ AFL1-2912	Always in My Heart	1977	2.50	5.00	10.00
—Reissue with new prefix					
❏ LPM-2912 [M]	Always in My Heart	1964	3.75	7.50	15.00
❏ LSP-2912 [S]	Always in My Heart	1964	5.00	10.00	20.00
❏ LPM-2959 [M]	Twin Guitar Moods	1964	3.75	7.50	15.00
❏ LSP-2959 [S]	Twin Guitar Moods	1964	5.00	10.00	20.00
❏ AFL1-3241	Two Guitars	1979	2.50	5.00	10.00
❏ LPM-3413 [M]	Many-Splendored Guitars	1965	3.75	7.50	15.00
❏ LSP-3413 [S]	Many-Splendored Guitars	1965	5.00	10.00	20.00
❏ AFL1-3505	Casually Classical	1977	2.50	5.00	10.00
—Reissue with new prefix					
❏ LPM-3505 [M]	Casually Classical	1966	3.75	7.50	15.00
❏ LSP-3505 [S]	Casually Classical	1966	5.00	10.00	20.00
❏ AFL1-3535	Rainbows	1980	2.50	5.00	10.00
❏ LPM-3611 [M]	Twin Guitars — In a Mood for Lovers	1966	3.75	7.50	15.00
❏ LSP-3611 [S]	Twin Guitars — In a Mood for Lovers	1966	5.00	10.00	20.00
❏ LPM-3723 [M]	Their Very Special Touch	1967	3.75	7.50	15.00
❏ LSP-3723 [S]	Their Very Special Touch	1967	5.00	10.00	20.00
❏ LPM-3909 [M]	Fascinating Rhythms of Their Brazil	1968	5.00	10.00	20.00
❏ LSP-3909 [S]	Fascinating Rhythms of Their Brazil	1968	3.75	7.50	15.00
❏ AFL1-3990	Beautiful Sounds	1981	2.50	5.00	10.00
❏ AFL1-4007	The Best of Los Indios Tabajaras	1977	2.50	5.00	10.00
—Reissue with new prefix					
❏ LSP-4007	The Best of Los Indios Tabajaras	1968	3.75	7.50	15.00
❏ LSP-4013	In a Sentimental Mood	1968	3.75	7.50	15.00
❏ LSP-4129	Song of the Islands	1969	3.75	7.50	15.00
❏ AFL1-4273	Music for Romance	1982	2.50	5.00	10.00
❏ LSP-4365	Dreams of Love	1970	3.75	7.50	15.00
❏ LSP-4496	The Very Thought of You	1971	3.75	7.50	15.00
❏ LSP-4615	What the World Needs Now	1971	3.00	6.00	12.00
❏ AFL1-4649	Guitars on the Go	1983	2.50	5.00	10.00
LOS LOBOS					
NEW VISTAS					
❏ 1001	Just Another Band from East L.A.	1978	50.00	100.00	200.00
SLASH					
❏ 23963 [EP]	And a Time to Dance	1983	3.00	6.00	12.00
❏ 25177	How Will the Wolf Survive?	1984	3.00	6.00	12.00
❏ 25523	By the Light of the Moon	1987	3.00	6.00	12.00
❏ 25790	La Pistola y El Corazon	1988	3.00	6.00	12.00
❏ 26131	The Neighborhood	1990	3.00	6.00	12.00
❏ R 144507	By the Light of the Moon	1987	3.50	7.00	14.00
—RCA Music Service edition					
LOS LOCOS DEL RITMO					
DIMSA					
❏ 8178	Rock!	196?	25.00	50.00	100.00
LOS SEVEN DAYS					
ECO					
❏ 314	Sha-La-La	196?	12.50	25.00	50.00

Number	Title (A Side/B Side)	Yr	VG	VG+	NM

LOST & FOUND
INTERNATIONAL ARTISTS
❑ IA-3	Everybody's Here	1968	25.00	50.00	100.00

—Original pressing, no "Masterfonics" in dead wax

❑ IA-3	Everybody's Here	1979	3.75	7.50	15.00

—Reissue with "Masterfonics" in trail-off wax

LOST NATION, THE
RARE EARTH
❑ RS-518	Paradise Lost	1970	5.00	10.00	20.00

LOTHAR AND THE HAND PEOPLE
CAPITOL
❑ ST-247	Space Hymn	1969	10.00	20.00	40.00
❑ SM-2997	Presenting Lothar and the Hand People	1977	2.00	4.00	8.00

—Reissue with new prefix

❑ ST 2997	Presenting Lothar and the Hand People	1968	10.00	20.00	40.00

LOUDERMILK, JOHN D.
RCA VICTOR
❑ LPM-2434 [M]	Language of Love	1961	6.25	12.50	25.00
❑ LSP-2434 [S]	Language of Love	1961	7.50	15.00	30.00
❑ LPM-2539 [M]	Twelve Sides of Loudermilk	1962	5.00	10.00	20.00
❑ LSP-2539 [S]	Twelve Sides of Loudermilk	1962	6.25	12.50	25.00
❑ LPM-3497 [M]	A Bizarre Collection of the Most Unusual Songs	1965	5.00	10.00	20.00
❑ LSP-3497 [S]	A Bizarre Collection of the Most Unusual Songs	1965	6.25	12.50	25.00
❑ LPM-3807 [M]	Suburban Attitudes in Country Music	1967	6.25	12.50	25.00
❑ LSP-3807 [S]	Suburban Attitudes in Country Music	1967	5.00	10.00	20.00
❑ LSP-4040	Country Love Songs	1968	5.00	10.00	20.00
❑ LSP-4097	The Open Mind of John D. Loudermilk	1968	5.00	10.00	20.00

WARNER BROS.
❑ WS 1922	Volume 1, Elloree	1971	3.75	7.50	15.00

LOUDON, DOROTHY
CORAL
❑ CRL 57265 [M]	At the Blue Angel	1959	5.00	10.00	20.00
❑ CRL 757265 [S]	At the Blue Angel	1959	6.25	12.50	25.00

LOUIE AND THE LOVERS
EPIC
❑ E 30026	Rise	1970	5.00	10.00	20.00

LOUISE, TINA
CONCERT HALL
❑ H-1503 [M]	Her Portrait in Hi-Fi	1958	12.50	25.00	50.00
❑ H-1521 [M]	It's Time for Tina	1958	50.00	100.00	200.00

URANIA
❑ ULM-2005 [M]	It's Time for Tina	1959	50.00	100.00	200.00
❑ USD-2005 [S]	It's Time for Tina	1959	75.00	150.00	300.00

LOUISIANA HONEY DRIPPERS, THE
PRESTIGE
❑ PR-13035 [M]	Bluegrass	1961	6.25	12.50	25.00

LOUISIANA RED
ROULETTE
❑ R-25200 [M]	The Lowdown Back Porch Blues	1963	10.00	20.00	40.00

LOUSSIER, JACQUES
LONDON
❑ PS 454/5 [(2)S]	Bach Jazz	1965	5.00	10.00	20.00

LOUVIN, CHARLIE
Also see JIM AND JESSE; THE LOUVIN BROTHERS.
CAPITOL
❑ ST-142	Hey Daddy	1969	5.00	10.00	20.00
❑ ST-8-0142	Hey Daddy	1969	6.25	12.50	25.00

—Capitol Record Club edition

❑ ST-248	The Kind of Man I Am	1969	5.00	10.00	20.00
❑ ST-416	Here's a Toast to Mama	1970	5.00	10.00	20.00
❑ ST-555	Ten Times	1970	5.00	10.00	20.00
❑ ST 2208 [S]	Less and Less and I Don't Love You Anymore	1965	6.25	12.50	25.00
❑ T 2208 [M]	Less and Less and I Don't Love You Anymore	1965	5.00	10.00	20.00
❑ ST 2437 [S]	The Many Moods of Charlie Louvin	1966	6.25	12.50	25.00
❑ T 2437 [M]	The Many Moods of Charlie Louvin	1966	5.00	10.00	20.00
❑ ST 2482 [S]	Lonesome Is Me	1966	6.25	12.50	25.00
❑ T 2482 [M]	Lonesome Is Me	1966	5.00	10.00	20.00
❑ ST 2689 [S]	I'll Remember Always	1967	5.00	10.00	20.00
❑ T 2689 [M]	I'll Remember Always	1967	6.25	12.50	25.00
❑ ST 2787 [S]	I Forgot to Cry	1967	5.00	10.00	20.00
❑ T 2787 [M]	I Forgot to Cry	1967	6.25	12.50	25.00
❑ ST 2958	Will You Visit Me on Sundays	1968	5.00	10.00	20.00

LOUVIN, CHARLIE, AND MELBA MONTGOMERY
CAPITOL
❑ ST-686	Somethin' to Brag About	1971	5.00	10.00	20.00
❑ ST-808	Baby, You've Got What It Takes	1971	5.00	10.00	20.00

LOUVIN, IRA
Also see THE LOUVIN BROTHERS.
CAPITOL
❑ ST 2413 [S]	The Unforgettable Ira Louvin	1965	7.50	15.00	30.00
❑ T 2413 [M]	The Unforgettable Ira Louvin	1965	6.25	12.50	25.00

LOUVIN BROTHERS, THE
Also see CHARLIE LOUVIN; IRA LOUVIN.
CAPITOL
❑ DT 769 [R]	Tragic Songs of Life	196?	5.00	10.00	20.00
❑ T 769 [M]	Tragic Songs of Life	1956	25.00	50.00	100.00

—Turquoise label

❑ T 769 [M]	Tragic Songs of Life	1959	10.00	20.00	40.00

—Black colorband label, logo at left

❑ T 769 [M]	Tragic Songs of Life	1962	6.25	12.50	25.00

—Black colorband label, logo at top

❑ T 825 [M]	Nearer My God to Thee	1957	25.00	50.00	100.00

—Turquoise label

❑ T 825 [M]	Nearer My God to Thee	1959	10.00	20.00	40.00

—Black colorband label, logo at left

❑ T 825 [M]	Nearer My God to Thee	1962	6.25	12.50	25.00

—Black colorband label, logo at top

❑ T 910 [M]	Ira and Charlie	1958	25.00	50.00	100.00

—Turquoise label

❑ T 910 [M]	Ira and Charlie	1959	10.00	20.00	40.00

—Black colorband label, logo at left

❑ T 910 [M]	Ira and Charlie	1962	6.25	12.50	25.00

—Black colorband label, logo at top

❑ DT 1061 [R]	The Family Who Prays	196?	5.00	10.00	20.00
❑ T 1061 [M]	The Family Who Prays	1958	20.00	40.00	80.00

—Black colorband label, logo at left

❑ T 1061 [M]	The Family Who Prays	1962	6.25	12.50	25.00

—Black colorband label, logo at top

❑ T 1106 [M]	Country Love Ballads	1959	20.00	40.00	80.00

—Black colorband label, logo at left

❑ T 1106 [M]	Country Love Ballads	1962	6.25	12.50	25.00

—Black colorband label, logo at top

❑ T 1277 [M]	Satan Is Real	1960	20.00	40.00	80.00

—Black colorband label, logo at left

❑ T 1277 [M]	Satan Is Real	1962	6.25	12.50	25.00

—Black colorband label, logo at top

❑ T 1385 [M]	My Baby's Gone	1960	20.00	40.00	80.00

—Black colorband label, logo at left

❑ T 1385 [M]	My Baby's Gone	1962	6.25	12.50	25.00

—Black colorband label, logo at top

❑ T 1449 [M]	A Tribute to the Delmore Brothers	1960	20.00	40.00	80.00

—Black colorband label, logo at left

❑ T 1449 [M]	A Tribute to the Delmore Brothers	1962	6.25	12.50	25.00

—Black colorband label, logo at top

❑ T 1547 [M]	Encore	1961	20.00	40.00	80.00

—Black colorband label, logo at left

❑ T 1547 [M]	Encore	1962	6.25	12.50	25.00

—Black colorband label, logo at top

❑ ST 1616 [S]	Country Christmas	1961	20.00	40.00	80.00

—Black rainbow label with "Capitol" at left

❑ ST 1616 [S]	Country Christmas	1962	6.25	12.50	25.00

—Black rainbow label with "Capitol" at left

❑ T 1616 [M]	Country Christmas	1961	12.50	25.00	50.00

—Black rainbow label with "Capitol" at left

❑ T 1616 [M]	Country Christmas	1962	5.00	10.00	20.00

—Black rainbow label with "Capitol" at top

❑ ST 1721 [S]	Weapon of Prayer	1962	12.50	25.00	50.00
❑ T 1721 [M]	Weapon of Prayer	1962	10.00	20.00	40.00
❑ ST 1834 [S]	Keep Your Eyes on Jesus	1963	12.50	25.00	50.00
❑ T 1834 [M]	Keep Your Eyes on Jesus	1963	10.00	20.00	40.00
❑ ST 2091 [S]	The Louvin Brothers Sing and Play Their Current Hits	1964	7.50	15.00	30.00
❑ T 2091 [M]	The Louvin Brothers Sing and Play Their Current Hits	1964	6.25	12.50	25.00
❑ ST 2331 [S]	Thank God for My Christian Home	1965	7.50	15.00	30.00
❑ T 2331 [M]	Thank God for My Christian Home	1965	6.25	12.50	25.00
❑ ST 2827 [S]	The Great Roy Acuff Songs	1967	7.50	15.00	30.00
❑ T 2827 [M]	The Great Roy Acuff Songs	1967	10.00	20.00	40.00

METRO
❑ M-598 [M]	The Louvin Brothers	1966	6.25	12.50	25.00
❑ MS-598 [R]	The Louvin Brothers	1966	5.00	10.00	20.00

MGM
❑ E-3426 [M]	The Louvin Brothers	1957	50.00	100.00	200.00

SEARS
❑ SP-119 [M]	Ira & Charles Louvin	196?	5.00	10.00	20.00
❑ SPS-119 [R]	Ira & Charles Louvin	196?	3.75	7.50	15.00

TOWER
❑ DT 5038 [R]	Two Different Worlds	1966	5.00	10.00	20.00
❑ T 5038 [M]	Two Different Worlds	1966	7.50	15.00	30.00
❑ DT 5122	Country Heart and Soul	1968	5.00	10.00	20.00

LOVE
Also see ARTHUR LEE.
BLUE THUMB
❑ BTS-8822	False Start	1970	5.00	10.00	20.00
❑ BTS-9000 [(2)]	Out Here	1969	6.25	12.50	25.00

ELEKTRA
❑ EKL-4001 [M]	Love	1966	25.00	50.00	100.00
❑ EKL-4001 [M]	Love	1966	75.00	150.00	300.00

—White label promo

❑ EKL-4005 [M]	Da Capo	1967	25.00	50.00	100.00
❑ EKL-4013 [M]	Forever Changes	1967	12.50	25.00	50.00
❑ EKL-4013 [M]	Forever Changes	1967	37.50	75.00	150.00

—White label promo

❑ EKS-74001 [S]	Love	1966	12.50	25.00	50.00

—Brown label

❑ EKS-74001 [S]	Love	1969	3.75	7.50	15.00

—Red label with large stylized "E"

❑ EKS-74001 [S]	Love	1971	3.00	6.00	12.00

—Butterfly label

❑ EKS-74005 [S]	Da Capo	1967	10.00	20.00	40.00

—Brown label

❑ EKS-74005 [S]	Da Capo	1969	3.75	7.50	15.00

—Red label with large stylized "E"

❑ EKS-74005 [S]	Da Capo	1971	3.00	6.00	12.00

—Butterfly label

❑ EKS-74013 [S]	Forever Changes	1967	7.50	15.00	30.00

—Brown label

❑ EKS-74013 [S]	Forever Changes	1969	3.75	7.50	15.00

—Red label with large stylized "E"

Number	Title (A Side/B Side)	Yr	VG	VG+	NM
❑ EKS-74013 [S]	Forever Changes	1971	3.00	6.00	12.00
—Butterfly label					
❑ EKS-74013 [S]	Forever Changes	1980	2.50	5.00	10.00
—Red label, small "E," Warner Communications logo on label					
❑ EKS-74013 [S]	Forever Changes	1984	2.00	4.00	8.00
—Red and black label					
❑ EKS-74049	Four Sail	1969	6.25	12.50	25.00
—Red label with large stylized "E"					
❑ EKS-74049	Four Sail	1971	3.00	6.00	12.00
—Butterfly label					
❑ EKS-74049 [DJ]	Four Sail	1969	20.00	40.00	80.00
—White label promo					
❑ EKS-74058	Revisited	1970	6.25	12.50	25.00
—Red label with large stylized "E"					
❑ EKS-74058	Revisited	1971	3.00	6.00	12.00
—Butterfly label					
❑ EKS-74058	Revisited	198?	2.50	5.00	10.00
—Red label, small "E," Warner Communications logo on label					
❑ EKS-74058	Revisited	1984	2.00	4.00	8.00
—Red and black label					
MCA					
❑ 27025	Studio/Live	1982	2.50	5.00	10.00
RHINO					
❑ RNDF-251 [PD]	Love Live	1981	3.75	7.50	15.00
❑ RNLP-800	Best of Love	1980	2.50	5.00	10.00
❑ RNLP-70175	The Best of Love (1966-1969) (Golden Archive Series)	1987	2.50	5.00	10.00
RSO					
❑ SO 4804	Reel to Real	1974	3.75	7.50	15.00
SUNDAZED					
❑ LP 5100	Love	2001	3.00	6.00	12.00
—Reissue on 180-gram vinyl					
❑ LP 5101	Da Capo	2001	3.00	6.00	12.00
—Reissue on 180-gram vinyl					
❑ LP 5102	Forever Changes	2001	3.00	6.00	12.00
—Reissue on 180-gram vinyl					
❑ LP 5104	Revisited	2001	3.00	6.00	12.00
—Reissue on 180-gram vinyl					

LOVE, HOLLY
ACE

Number	Title (A Side/B Side)	Yr	VG	VG+	NM
❑ LP-1022 [M]	My Love Confessions	1962	7.50	15.00	30.00

LOVE, PRESTON
KENT

Number	Title (A Side/B Side)	Yr	VG	VG+	NM
❑ KST-540	Omaha Bar-B-Q	1968	5.00	10.00	20.00

LOVE EXCHANGE, THE
TOWER

Number	Title (A Side/B Side)	Yr	VG	VG+	NM
❑ ST 5115	The Love Exchange	1968	6.25	12.50	25.00

LOVE GENERATION, THE
IMPERIAL

Number	Title (A Side/B Side)	Yr	VG	VG+	NM
❑ LP-9351 [M]	The Love Generation	1967	5.00	10.00	20.00
❑ LP-12351 [S]	The Love Generation	1967	5.00	10.00	20.00
❑ LP-12364	A Generation of Love	1968	5.00	10.00	20.00
❑ LP-12408	Montage	1968	5.00	10.00	20.00

LOVE SCULPTURE
EMI AMERICA

Number	Title (A Side/B Side)	Yr	VG	VG+	NM
❑ SQ-17208	Blues Helping	1986	3.00	6.00	12.00
—Reissue of Rare Earth LP					
PARROT					
❑ PAS 71035	Forms and Feelings	1970	6.25	12.50	25.00
RARE EARTH					
❑ RS-505	Blues Helping	1969	10.00	20.00	40.00

LOVECRAFT
See H.P. LOVECRAFT.

LOVELITES, THE
UNI

Number	Title (A Side/B Side)	Yr	VG	VG+	NM
❑ 73081	The Lovelites	1970	6.25	12.50	25.00

LOVETT, LEE
STRAND

Number	Title (A Side/B Side)	Yr	VG	VG+	NM
❑ SL-1055 [M]	Jazz Dance Party	1962	5.00	10.00	20.00
❑ SLS-1055 [S]	Jazz Dance Party	1962	6.25	12.50	25.00
❑ SL-1059 [M]	Misty	1962	5.00	10.00	20.00
❑ SLS-1059 [S]	Misty	1962	6.25	12.50	25.00
WYNNE					
❑ WLP-108 [M]	Jazz Dance Party	195?	7.50	15.00	30.00

LOVICH, LENE
STIFF/EPIC

Number	Title (A Side/B Side)	Yr	VG	VG+	NM
❑ JE 36102	Stateless	1979	3.00	6.00	12.00
❑ JE 36102	Stateless	1979	5.00	10.00	20.00
—Red vinyl					
❑ JE 36308	Flex	1980	3.00	6.00	12.00
❑ 5E 37452 [EP]	New Toy	1981	3.75	7.50	15.00
❑ ARE 38399	No Man's Land	1983	2.50	5.00	10.00

LOVIN' SPOONFUL, THE
Also see JOHN SEBASTIAN; ZALMAN YANOVSKY.
ACCORD

Number	Title (A Side/B Side)	Yr	VG	VG+	NM
❑ SN-7196	Distant Echoes	1981	2.50	5.00	10.00
BUDDAH					
❑ BDM-5706	The Best of the Lovin' Spoonful	197?	3.00	6.00	12.00
❑ BLB6-8339	The Best of the Lovin' Spoonful	198?	2.50	5.00	10.00
—Reissue of 5706					
51 WEST					
❑ Q 16023	... So Nice	1979	2.50	5.00	10.00

KAMA SUTRA

Number	Title (A Side/B Side)	Yr	VG	VG+	NM
❑ KLPS-750-2 [(2)]	24 Karat Hits	1968	5.00	10.00	20.00
❑ KSBS-2011	The John Sebastian Song Book	1970	3.75	7.50	15.00
❑ KSBS-2013	The Very Best of the Lovin' Spoonful	1970	3.75	7.50	15.00
❑ KSBS-2029	Once Upon a Time	1971	3.75	7.50	15.00
❑ KSBS-2608 [(2)]	The Best…Lovin' Spoonful	1976	5.00	10.00	20.00
❑ KLP-8050 [M]	Do You Believe in Magic	1965	5.00	10.00	20.00
❑ KLPS-8050 [S]	Do You Believe in Magic	1965	7.50	15.00	30.00
❑ KLP-8051 [M]	Daydream	1966	5.00	10.00	20.00
❑ KLPS-8051 [S]	Daydream	1966	7.50	15.00	30.00
❑ KLP-8053 [M]	What's Up, Tiger Lily?	1966	5.00	10.00	20.00
❑ KLPS-8053 [S]	What's Up, Tiger Lily?	1966	7.50	15.00	30.00
❑ KLP-8054 [M]	Hums of the Lovin' Spoonful	1966	5.00	10.00	20.00
❑ KLPS-8054 [S]	Hums of the Lovin' Spoonful	1966	7.50	15.00	30.00
❑ KLP-8056 [M]	The Best of the Lovin' Spoonful	1967	3.75	7.50	15.00
—Came with four bonus photos of the band, which are priced separately					
❑ KLP/S-8056	The Best of the Lovin' Spoonful Bonus Photos (4)	1967	2.50	5.00	10.00
❑ KLPS-8056 [S]	The Best of the Lovin' Spoonful	1967	3.75	7.50	15.00
—Came with four bonus photos of the band, which are priced separately					
❑ KLP-8058 [M]	You're a Big Boy Now	1967	5.00	10.00	20.00
❑ KLPS-8058 [S]	You're a Big Boy Now	1967	5.00	10.00	20.00
❑ KLP-8061 [M]	Everything Playing	1968	7.50	15.00	30.00
❑ KLPS-8061 [S]	Everything Playing	1968	5.00	10.00	20.00
❑ KLP-8064 [M]	The Best of the Lovin' Spoonful, Volume 2	1968	12.50	25.00	50.00
❑ KLPS-8064 [S]	The Best of the Lovin' Spoonful, Volume 2	1968	5.00	10.00	20.00
❑ KLPS-8073	Revelation: Revolution '69	1969	6.25	12.50	25.00
❑ ST-90597 [S]	Do You Believe in Magic	1965	10.00	20.00	40.00
—Capitol Record Club edition					
❑ T-90597 [M]	Do You Believe in Magic	1965	7.50	15.00	30.00
—Capitol Record Club edition					
❑ ST-90675 [S]	Daydream	1966	10.00	20.00	40.00
—Capitol Record Club edition					
❑ T-90675 [M]	Daydream	1966	6.25	12.50	25.00
—Capitol Record Club edition					
❑ KAO-91102 [M]	The Best of the Lovin' Spoonful	1967	6.25	12.50	25.00
—Capitol Record Club edition					
❑ SKAO-91102 [S]	The Best of the Lovin' Spoonful	1967	5.00	10.00	20.00
—Capitol Record Club edition					
❑ ST-91198 [S]	You're a Big Boy Now	1967	6.25	12.50	25.00
—Capitol Record Club edition					
KOALA					
❑ KO 14221	Day Dream	1979	2.50	5.00	10.00
PAIR					
❑ PDL2-1200 [(2)]	The Best of the Lovin' Spoonful	1986	3.00	6.00	12.00
RHINO					
❑ RNLP-114	The Best of the Lovin' Spoonful, Vol. 2	1985	2.50	5.00	10.00
SUNDAZED					
❑ LP 5159	Do You Believe in Magic	2002	3.75	7.50	15.00
—Reissue on 180-gram vinyl					
❑ LP 5160	Daydream	2002	3.75	7.50	15.00
—Reissue on 180-gram vinyl					

LOWE, BERNIE, ORCHESTRA
CAMEO

Number	Title (A Side/B Side)	Yr	VG	VG+	NM
❑ C-1057 [M]	Encore	1963	5.00	10.00	20.00
❑ C-4005 [M]	If the Big Bands Were Here Today	1962	5.00	10.00	20.00
❑ SC-4005 [S]	If the Big Bands Were Here Today	1962	6.25	12.50	25.00
❑ C-4007 [M]	If the Big Bands Were Here Today, Vol. 2	1962	5.00	10.00	20.00
❑ SC-4007 [S]	If the Big Bands Were Here Today, Vol. 2	1962	6.25	12.50	25.00

LOWE, FRANK
ESP-DISK'

Number	Title (A Side/B Side)	Yr	VG	VG+	NM
❑ 3013	Black Beings	197?	6.25	12.50	25.00

LOWE, JIM
DOT

Number	Title (A Side/B Side)	Yr	VG	VG+	NM
❑ DLP-3051 [M]	The Green Door	1956	37.50	75.00	150.00
❑ DLP-3114 [M]	Wicked Women	1958	25.00	50.00	100.00
❑ DLP-3681 [M]	Songs They Sing Behind the Green Door	1965	6.25	12.50	25.00
❑ DLP-25881 [S]	Songs They Sing Behind the Green Door	1965	7.50	15.00	30.00
MERCURY					
❑ MG-20246 [M]	The Door of Fame	1957	37.50	75.00	150.00

LOWE, MUNDELL
CHARLIE PARKER

Number	Title (A Side/B Side)	Yr	VG	VG+	NM
❑ PLP-822 [M]	Blues for a Stripper	1962	6.25	12.50	25.00
❑ PLP-822S [S]	Blues for a Stripper	1962	7.50	15.00	30.00
FAMOUS DOOR					
❑ HL-102	California Guitar	197?	5.00	10.00	20.00
JAZZLAND					
❑ JLP-8 [M]	Low-Down Guitar	1960	7.50	15.00	30.00
OFFBEAT					
❑ OLP-3010 [M]	Tacet for Neurotics	1960	7.50	15.00	30.00
❑ OS-93010 [S]	Tacet for Neurotics	1960	10.00	20.00	40.00
RCA CAMDEN					
❑ CAL-490 [M]	Porgy and Bess	1959	5.00	10.00	20.00
❑ CAS-490 [S]	Porgy and Bess	1959	6.25	12.50	25.00
❑ CAL-522 [M]	TV Action Jazz!	1959	6.25	12.50	25.00
❑ CAS-522 [S]	TV Action Jazz!	1959	7.50	15.00	30.00
❑ CAL-627 [M]	TV Action Jazz! — Volume 2	1960	6.25	12.50	25.00
❑ CAS-627 [S]	TV Action Jazz! — Volume 2	1960	7.50	15.00	30.00
RCA VICTOR					
❑ LJM-3002 [10]	The Mundell Lowe Quintet	1954	25.00	50.00	100.00
RIVERSIDE					
❑ RLP 12-204 [M]	The Mundell Lowe Quartet	1956	15.00	30.00	60.00
—White label, blue print					
❑ RLP 12-204 [M]	The Mundell Lowe Quartet	1959	10.00	20.00	40.00
—Blue label, microphone logo at top					

L

LOWE, NICK

Number	Title (A Side/B Side)	Yr	VG	VG+	NM
❏ RLP 12-208 [M]	Guitar Moods	1956	15.00	30.00	60.00
—White label, blue print					
❏ RLP 12-208 [M]	Guitar Moods	1959	10.00	20.00	40.00
—Blue label, microphone logo at top					
❏ RLP 12-219 [M]	New Music of Alec Wilder	1956	15.00	30.00	60.00
—White label, blue print					
❏ RLP 12-219 [M]	New Music of Alec Wilder	1959	10.00	20.00	40.00
—Blue label, microphone logo at top					
❏ RLP 12-238 [M]	A Grand Night for Swinging	1957	15.00	30.00	60.00
—White label, blue print					
❏ RLP 12-238 [M]	A Grand Night for Swinging	1959	10.00	20.00	40.00
—Blue label, microphone logo at top					

LOWE, NICK
COLUMBIA

Number	Title (A Side/B Side)	Yr	VG	VG+	NM
❏ AS 1400 [DJ]	An Interrogation of Nick Lowe	1990	6.25	12.50	25.00
—Promo-only interview album					
❏ JC 35529	Pure Pop for Now People	1978	5.00	10.00	20.00
❏ PC 35529	Pure Pop for Now People	198?	2.00	4.00	8.00
—Budget-line reissue					
❏ JC 36087	Labour of Lust	1979	2.50	5.00	10.00
❏ PC 36087	Labour of Lust	198?	2.00	4.00	8.00
—Budget-line reissue					
❏ FC 37932	Nick the Knife	1982	3.00	6.00	12.00
❏ PC 37932	Nick the Knife	198?	2.00	4.00	8.00
—Budget-line reissue					
❏ FC 38589	The Abominable Showman	1983	3.00	6.00	12.00
❏ PC 38589	The Abominable Showman	1986	2.00	4.00	8.00
—Budget-line reissue					
❏ FC 39371	Nick Lowe and His Cowboy Outfit	1984	3.00	6.00	12.00
❏ PC 39371	Nick Lowe and His Cowboy Outfit	1986	2.00	4.00	8.00
—Budget-line reissue					
❏ FC 39958	The Rose of England	1985	3.00	6.00	12.00
❏ FC 40381	Pinker and Prouder Than Previous	1988	3.50	7.00	14.00
REPRISE					
❏ 26132	Party of One	1990	3.00	6.00	12.00

LOWE, SAMMY
RCA VICTOR

Number	Title (A Side/B Side)	Yr	VG	VG+	NM
❏ LPM-2770 [M]	Hitsville U.S.A.	1963	5.00	10.00	20.00
❏ LSP-2770 [S]	Hitsville U.S.A.	1963	6.25	12.50	25.00

LRY
CONGRESS OF THE CROW

Number	Title (A Side/B Side)	Yr	VG	VG+	NM
❏ 8031002	The LRY Record	1968	50.00	100.00	200.00

LUBOFF, NORMAN, CHOIR
COLUMBIA

Number	Title (A Side/B Side)	Yr	VG	VG+	NM
❏ CL 545 [M]	Easy to Remember	1954	5.00	10.00	20.00
—Maroon label, gold print					
❏ CL 2545 [10]	Carols for Christmas	1955	7.50	15.00	30.00
—"House Party Series"					
❏ CL 6272 [10]	Christmas Carols	1953	10.00	20.00	40.00

LUCAS, BUDDY
UNITED ARTISTS

Number	Title (A Side/B Side)	Yr	VG	VG+	NM
❏ UAL-3482 [M]	Fifty Fabulous Harmonica Favorites	1966	5.00	10.00	20.00
❏ UAS-6482 [S]	Fifty Fabulous Harmonica Favorites	1966	6.25	12.50	25.00

LUCAS, NICK
DECCA

Number	Title (A Side/B Side)	Yr	VG	VG+	NM
❏ DL 8653 [M]	Painting the Clouds with Sunshine	1957	10.00	20.00	40.00

LUCEY, CHRIS
SURREY

Number	Title (A Side/B Side)	Yr	VG	VG+	NM
❏ SS-1027 [M]	Songs of Protest and Anti-Protest	197?	10.00	20.00	40.00

LUCRAFT, HOWARD
DECCA

Number	Title (A Side/B Side)	Yr	VG	VG+	NM
❏ DL 8679 [M]	Showcase for Modern Jazz	1958	7.50	15.00	30.00

LUDDEN, ALLEN
RCA VICTOR

Number	Title (A Side/B Side)	Yr	VG	VG+	NM
❏ LPM-2934 [M]	Allen Ludden Sings His Favorite Songs	1964	5.00	10.00	20.00
❏ LSP-2934 [S]	Allen Ludden Sings His Favorite Songs	1964	6.25	12.50	25.00

LULU
ALFA

Number	Title (A Side/B Side)	Yr	VG	VG+	NM
❏ 10006	Lulu	1981	3.00	6.00	12.00
ATCO					
❏ 33-310 [M]	New Routes	1970	7.50	15.00	30.00
—White label promo; no stock copies were issued in mono					
❏ SD 33-310 [S]	New Routes	1970	3.00	6.00	12.00
❏ 33-330 [M]	Melody Fair	1970	7.50	15.00	30.00
—White label promo, "DJ Copy Monaural" on cover; no stock copies were issued in mono					
❏ SD 33-330 [S]	Melody Fair	1970	3.00	6.00	12.00
CHELSEA					
❏ BCL1-0144	Lulu	1973	3.00	6.00	12.00
❏ CHL-518	Heaven and Earth and the Stars	1976	5.00	10.00	20.00
EPIC					
❏ LN 24339 [M]	To Sir with Love	1967	6.25	12.50	25.00
❏ BN 26339 [P]	To Sir with Love	1967	7.50	15.00	30.00
❏ BN 26536	It's Lulu	1970	3.00	6.00	12.00
HARMONY					
❏ H 30249	To Love Somebody	1970	5.00	10.00	20.00
PARROT					
❏ PA 61016 [M]	From Lulu with Love	1967	15.00	30.00	60.00
❏ PAS 71016 [S]	From Lulu with Love	1967	20.00	40.00	80.00
PICKWICK					
❏ SPC-3237	Lulu	1973	2.00	4.00	8.00
ROCKET					
❏ BXL1-3073	Don't Take Love for Granted	1978	3.00	6.00	12.00

LULU BELLE AND SCOTTY
STARDAY

Number	Title (A Side/B Side)	Yr	VG	VG+	NM
❏ SLP-206 [M]	The Sweethearts of Country Music	1963	10.00	20.00	40.00
❏ SLP-285 [M]	Down Memory Lane	1964	10.00	20.00	40.00
❏ SLP-351 [M]	Lulu Belle & Scotty	1965	10.00	20.00	40.00
SUPER					
❏ 6201 [M]	Lule Belle & Scotty	1963	12.50	25.00	50.00

LUMAN, BOB
EPIC

Number	Title (A Side/B Side)	Yr	VG	VG+	NM
❏ BN 26393	Ain't Got Time to Be Unhappy	1968	5.00	10.00	20.00
❏ BN 26463	Come On Home and Sing the Blues	1969	5.00	10.00	20.00
❏ BN 26541	Gettin' Back	1970	5.00	10.00	20.00
❏ E 30617	Is It Any Wonder	1971	5.00	10.00	20.00
❏ E 30923	Chain Don't Take to Me	1972	5.00	10.00	20.00
❏ KE 31375	When You Say Love	1972	5.00	10.00	20.00
❏ KE 31746	Lonely Women Make Good Lovers	1972	5.00	10.00	20.00
❏ KE 32192	Neither One of Us	1973	3.75	7.50	15.00
❏ KE 32759	Bob Luman's Greatest Hits	1974	3.75	7.50	15.00
❏ KE 33942	Satisfied Mind	1975	3.00	6.00	12.00
❏ KE 34445	Alive and Well!	1976	3.00	6.00	12.00
HARMONY					
❏ KH 32006	Bob Luman	1973	3.00	6.00	12.00
HICKORY					
❏ LPM-124 [M]	Livin' Lovin' Sounds	1965	6.25	12.50	25.00
❏ LPS-124 [S]	Livin' Lovin' Sounds	1965	7.50	15.00	30.00
HICKORY/MGM					
❏ H3G-4508	Still Loving You	1974	3.75	7.50	15.00
POLYDOR					
❏ PD-1-6135	Bob Luman	1978	3.00	6.00	12.00
WARNER BROS.					
❏ W 1396 [M]	Let's Think About Livin'	1960	12.50	25.00	50.00
❏ WS 1396 [S]	Let's Think About Livin'	1960	17.50	35.00	70.00

LUMLEY, RUFUS
RCA VICTOR

Number	Title (A Side/B Side)	Yr	VG	VG+	NM
❏ LPM-3898 [M]	Rufus Lumley	1967	12.50	25.00	50.00
❏ LSP-3898 [S]	Rufus Lumley	1967	10.00	20.00	40.00

LUNA
ARHOOLIE

Number	Title (A Side/B Side)	Yr	VG	VG+	NM
❏ ST-8001	Space Swell	1968	5.00	10.00	20.00

LUNCEFORD, JIMMIE
ALLEGRO ELITE

Number	Title (A Side/B Side)	Yr	VG	VG+	NM
❏ (# unknown) [10]	Jimmie Lunceford Plays	195?	10.00	20.00	40.00
CAPITOL					
❏ TAO 924 [M]	Jimmie Lunceford	195?	7.50	15.00	30.00
COLUMBIA					
❏ GL 104 [10]	Lunceford Special	1950	20.00	40.00	80.00
❏ CL 634 [M]	Lunceford Special	1955	12.50	25.00	50.00
—Maroon label, gold print					
❏ CL 634 [M]	Lunceford Special	1956	10.00	20.00	40.00
—Red and black label with six "eye" logos					
❏ CL 2715 [M]	Lunceford Special	1967	7.50	15.00	30.00
COLUMBIA MASTERWORKS					
❏ ML 4804 [M]	Lunceford Special	195?	15.00	30.00	60.00
DECCA					
❏ DL 5393 [10]	For Dancers Only	1952	15.00	30.00	60.00
❏ DL 8050 [M]	Jimmie Lunceford and His Orchestra	1954	10.00	20.00	40.00
❏ DL 9237 [M]	Rhythm Is Our Business	1968	10.00	20.00	40.00
❏ DL 9238 [M]	Harlem Shout	1968	10.00	20.00	40.00
❏ DL 79237 [R]	Rhythm Is Our Business	1968	5.00	10.00	20.00
❏ DL 79238 [R]	Harlem Shout	1968	5.00	10.00	20.00
"X"					
❏ LX-3002 [M]	Jimmie Lunceford and His Chickasaw Syncopators	1954	15.00	30.00	60.00

LUNCH, LYDIA
RUBY

Number	Title (A Side/B Side)	Yr	VG	VG+	NM
❏ JRR 806	13.13	1982	7.50	15.00	30.00
ZE/BUDDAH					
❏ 33006	Queen of Siam	1980	7.50	15.00	30.00

LUND, GARRETT
(NO LABEL)

Number	Title (A Side/B Side)	Yr	VG	VG+	NM
❏ (no #)	Almost Grown	1975	75.00	150.00	300.00

LUNDY, PAT
COLUMBIA

Number	Title (A Side/B Side)	Yr	VG	VG+	NM
❏ CS 9588	Soul Ain't Nothin' But the Blues	1968	5.00	10.00	20.00

LUNN, ROBERT
STARDAY

Number	Title (A Side/B Side)	Yr	VG	VG+	NM
❏ SLP-228 [M]	The Original Talking Blues Man	1962	7.50	15.00	30.00

LUTCHER, NELLIE
CAPITOL

Number	Title (A Side/B Side)	Yr	VG	VG+	NM
❏ H 232 [10]	Real Gone	1950	15.00	30.00	60.00
❏ T 232 [M]	Real Gone	1955	10.00	20.00	40.00
EPIC					
❏ LN 1108 [10]	Whee! Nellie	1955	12.50	25.00	50.00
LIBERTY					
❏ LRP-3014 [M]	Our New Nellie	1956	10.00	20.00	40.00

LYMAN, ARTHUR
GNP CRESCENDO

Number	Title (A Side/B Side)	Yr	VG	VG+	NM
❏ GNP-605 [M]	Exotic Sounds	1963	3.75	7.50	15.00
❏ GNPS-605 [S]	Exotic Sounds	1963	5.00	10.00	20.00
❏ GNP-606 [M]	Paradise	1964	3.75	7.50	15.00

Number	Title (A Side/B Side)	Yr	VG	VG+	NM
❏ GNPS-606 [S]	Paradise	1964	5.00	10.00	20.00
❏ GNP-607 [M]	Cast Your Fate to the Wind	1965	3.75	7.50	15.00
❏ GNPS-607 [S]	Cast Your Fate to the Wind	1965	5.00	10.00	20.00
❏ GNPS-2091	Puka Shells	1975	2.50	5.00	10.00
HIFI					
❏ R-607 [M]	Leis of Jazz	1958	5.00	10.00	20.00
❏ SR-607 [S]	Leis of Jazz	1958	7.50	15.00	30.00
❏ R-806 [M]	Taboo	1958	5.00	10.00	20.00
❏ SR-806 [S]	Taboo	1958	7.50	15.00	30.00
❏ R-807 [M]	Hawaiian Sunset	1959	5.00	10.00	20.00
❏ SR-807 [S]	Hawaiian Sunset	1959	7.50	15.00	30.00
❏ R-808 [M]	Bwan-A	1959	5.00	10.00	20.00
❏ SR-808 [S]	Bwan-A	1959	7.50	15.00	30.00
❏ R-813 [M]	The Legend of Pele	1959	5.00	10.00	20.00
❏ SR-813 [S]	The Legend of Pele	1959	7.50	15.00	30.00
❏ R-815 [M]	Bahia	1959	5.00	10.00	20.00
❏ SR-815 [S]	Bahia	1959	7.50	15.00	30.00
❏ R-818 [M]	Arthur Lyman On Broadway	1960	5.00	10.00	20.00
❏ SR-818 [S]	Arthur Lyman On Broadway	1960	7.50	15.00	30.00
❏ R-822 [M]	Taboo (Volume 2)	1960	5.00	10.00	20.00
❏ SR-822 [S]	Taboo (Volume 2)	1960	7.50	15.00	30.00
LIFE					
❏ L 1004 [M]	Yellow Bird	1961	5.00	10.00	20.00
—Reissue with new title reflecting the hit single					
❏ L 1004 [M]	Percussion Spectacular	1961	7.50	15.00	30.00
❏ SL 1004 [S]	Yellow Bird	1961	6.25	12.50	25.00
—Reissue with new title reflecting the hit single					
❏ SL 1004 [S]	Percussion Spectacular	1961	10.00	20.00	40.00
❏ L 1005 [M]	The Colorful Percussions of Arthur Lyman	1962	5.00	10.00	20.00
❏ SL 1005 [S]	The Colorful Percussions of Arthur Lyman	1962	6.25	12.50	25.00
❏ L 1007 [M]	The Many Moods of Arthur Lyman	1962	5.00	10.00	20.00
❏ SL 1007 [S]	The Many Moods of Arthur Lyman	1962	6.25	12.50	25.00
❏ L 1009 [M]	I Wish You Love	1963	5.00	10.00	20.00
❏ L 1009 [M]	Love for Sale!	1963	6.25	12.50	25.00
—Alternate title					
❏ SL 1009 [S]	I Wish You Love	1963	6.25	12.50	25.00
❏ SL 1009 [S]	Love for Sale!	1963	7.50	15.00	30.00
—Alternate title					
❏ L 1010 [M]	Cotton Fields	1963	5.00	10.00	20.00
❏ SL 1010 [S]	Cotton Fields	1963	6.25	12.50	25.00
❏ L 1014 [M]	Blowin' in the Wind	1963	5.00	10.00	20.00
❏ SL 1014 [S]	Blowin' in the Wind	1963	6.25	12.50	25.00
❏ L 1018 [M]	Mele Kalikimaka (Merry Christmas)	1963	5.00	10.00	20.00
❏ SL 1018 [S]	Mele Kalikimaka (Merry Christmas)	1963	6.25	12.50	25.00
❏ L 1023 [M]	Isle of Enchantment	1964	5.00	10.00	20.00
❏ SL 1023 [S]	Isle of Enchantment	1964	6.25	12.50	25.00
❏ L 1024 [M]	Call of the Midnight Sun	1964	5.00	10.00	20.00
❏ SL 1024 [S]	Call of the Midnight Sun	1964	6.25	12.50	25.00
❏ L 1025 [M]	Hawaiian Sunset, Volume 2	1965	3.75	7.50	15.00
❏ SL 1025 [S]	Hawaiian Sunset, Volume 2	1965	5.00	10.00	20.00
❏ L 1027 [M]	Polynesia	1965	3.75	7.50	15.00
❏ SL 1027 [S]	Polynesia	1965	5.00	10.00	20.00
❏ L 1030 [M]	Greatest Hits	1965	3.00	6.00	12.00
❏ SL 1030 [S]	Greatest Hits	1965	3.75	7.50	15.00
❏ L 1031 [M]	Lyman '66	1965	3.75	7.50	15.00
❏ SL 1031 [S]	Lyman '66	1965	5.00	10.00	20.00
❏ L 1033 [M]	The Shadow of Your Smile	1966	3.75	7.50	15.00
❏ SL 1033 [S]	The Shadow of Your Smile	1966	5.00	10.00	20.00
❏ L 1034 [M]	Aloha, Amigo	1966	3.75	7.50	15.00
❏ SL 1034 [S]	Aloha, Amigo	1966	5.00	10.00	20.00
❏ L 1035 [M]	Ilikai	1967	3.75	7.50	15.00
❏ SL 1035 [S]	Ilikai	1967	5.00	10.00	20.00
❏ L 1036 [M]	Arthur Lyman at the Port of L.A.	1967	3.75	7.50	15.00
❏ SL 1036 [S]	Arthur Lyman at the Port of L.A.	1967	5.00	10.00	20.00
❏ SL 1037	Latitude 20	1968	3.75	7.50	15.00
❏ SL 1038	Aphrodisia	1968	3.75	7.50	15.00
❏ SL 1039	Winner's Circle	1969	3.75	7.50	15.00
❏ SL 1040	Today's Greatest Hits	1970	3.75	7.50	15.00

LYMON, FRANKIE
GUEST STAR

Number	Title (A Side/B Side)	Yr	VG	VG+	NM
❏ GS-1406 [M]	Teen Time Tunes Starring Frankie Lymon	1959	10.00	20.00	40.00
—Various-artists compilation; color cover					
❏ GS-1406 [M]	Rock & Roll Party Starring Frankie Lymon	196?	6.25	12.50	25.00
—Various-artists compilation; retitled, black and white cover					
ROULETTE					
❏ R-25013 [M]	Frankie Lymon at the London Palladium	1958	75.00	150.00	300.00
❏ R-25036 [M]	Rock 'N' Roll	1958	75.00	150.00	300.00
❏ R-25250 [M]	Frankie Lymon's Greatest	1964	7.50	15.00	30.00
❏ SR-25250 [R]	Frankie Lymon's Greatest	1964	6.25	12.50	25.00

LYMON, FRANKIE, AND THE TEENAGERS
ACCORD

Number	Title (A Side/B Side)	Yr	VG	VG+	NM
❏ SN-7203	Why Do Fools Fall in Love	1982	2.50	5.00	10.00
GEE					
❏ GLP-701 [M]	The Teenagers Featuring Frankie Lymon	1956	125.00	250.00	500.00
—Red label					
❏ GLP-701 [M]	The Teenagers Featuring Frankie Lymon	1961	37.50	75.00	150.00
—Gray label					
❏ GLP-701 [M]	The Teenagers Featuring Frankie Lymon	197?	3.00	6.00	12.00
—White label on thinner vinyl					
MURRAY HILL					
❏ 148 [(5)]	Frankie Lymon and the Teenagers	198?	17.50	35.00	70.00
RHINO					
❏ R1-70918	The Best of Frankie Lymon and the Teenagers	1989	3.00	6.00	12.00

LYNN, BARBARA
ATLANTIC

Number	Title (A Side/B Side)	Yr	VG	VG+	NM
❏ 8171 [M]	Here Is Barbara Lynn	1968	12.50	25.00	50.00
❏ SD 8171 [S]	Here Is Barbara Lynn	1968	10.00	20.00	40.00

Number	Title (A Side/B Side)	Yr	VG	VG+	NM
JAMIE					
❏ JLP-3023 [M]	You'll Lose a Good Thing	1962	12.50	25.00	50.00
❏ JLPS-3023 [R]	You'll Lose a Good Thing	1962	12.50	25.00	50.00
❏ JLP-3026 [M]	Sister of Soul	1964	—	—	—
—Canceled					
❏ JLPS-3026 [S]	Sister of Soul	1964	—	—	—
—Canceled					

LYNN, DIANA
CAPITOL

Number	Title (A Side/B Side)	Yr	VG	VG+	NM
❏ H 180 [10]	Piano Moods	1950	15.00	30.00	60.00

LYNN, DONNA
CAPITOL

Number	Title (A Side/B Side)	Yr	VG	VG+	NM
❏ ST 2085 [S]	Java Jones/My Boyfriend Got a Beatle Haircut	1964	7.50	15.00	30.00
❏ T 2085 [M]	Java Jones/My Boyfriend Got a Beatle Haircut	1964	5.00	10.00	20.00

LYNN, JUDY
AMARET

Number	Title (A Side/B Side)	Yr	VG	VG+	NM
❏ ST-5011	Parts of Love	1971	3.75	7.50	15.00
❏ AST-5014	Naturally	197?	3.75	7.50	15.00
COLUMBIA					
❏ CS 9879	Judy Lynn Sings at Caesar's Palace	1968	3.75	7.50	15.00
MUSICOR					
❏ MM-2096 [M]	The Judy Lynn Show Plays Again	1966	3.75	7.50	15.00
❏ MM-2112 [M]	Honey Stuff	1966	3.75	7.50	15.00
❏ MM-2126 [M]	Golden Nuggets	1967	3.75	7.50	15.00
❏ MS-3096 [S]	The Judy Lynn Show Plays Again	1966	5.00	10.00	20.00
❏ MS-3112 [S]	Honey Stuff	1966	5.00	10.00	20.00
❏ MS-3126 [S]	Golden Nuggets	1967	3.75	7.50	15.00
UNART					
❏ 20009 [M]	Judy Lynn in Las Vegas	1967	3.75	7.50	15.00
❏ 21009 [S]	Judy Lynn in Las Vegas	1967	3.00	6.00	12.00
UNITED ARTISTS					
❏ UAL-3226 [M]	Judy Lynn Sings at the Golden Nugget	1962	5.00	10.00	20.00
❏ UAL-3288 [M]	Here Is Our Gal, Judy Lynn	1963	3.75	7.50	15.00
❏ UAL-3342 [M]	America's Number One Most Promising Country and Western Girl Singer	1964	3.75	7.50	15.00
❏ UAL-3390 [M]	The Judy Lynn Show	1964	3.75	7.50	15.00
❏ UAL-3443 [M]	The Judy Lynn Show Act 2	1965	3.75	7.50	15.00
❏ UAL-3461 [M]	The Best of Judy Lynn	1966	3.75	7.50	15.00
❏ UAS-6226 [S]	Judy Lynn Sings at the Golden Nugget	1962	6.25	12.50	25.00
❏ UAS-6288 [S]	Here Is Our Gal, Judy Lynn	1963	5.00	10.00	20.00
❏ UAS-6342 [S]	America's Number One Most Promising Country and Western Girl Singer	1964	5.00	10.00	20.00
❏ UAS-6390 [S]	The Judy Lynn Show	1964	5.00	10.00	20.00
❏ UAS-6443 [S]	The Judy Lynn Show Act 2	1965	5.00	10.00	20.00
❏ UAS-6461 [S]	The Best of Judy Lynn	1966	5.00	10.00	20.00

LYNN, LORETTA
DECCA

Number	Title (A Side/B Side)	Yr	VG	VG+	NM
❏ DL 4457 [M]	Loretta Lynn Sings	1963	15.00	30.00	60.00
❏ DL 4541 [M]	Before I'm Over You	1964	7.50	15.00	30.00
❏ DL 4620 [M]	Songs from My Heart	1965	7.50	15.00	30.00
❏ DL 4665 [M]	Blue Kentucky Girl	1965	7.50	15.00	30.00
❏ DL 4695 [M]	Hymns	1965	7.50	15.00	30.00
❏ DL 4744 [M]	I Like 'Em Country	1966	6.25	12.50	25.00
❏ DL 4783 [M]	You Ain't Woman Enough	1966	6.25	12.50	25.00
❏ DL 4817 [M]	Country Christmas	1966	6.25	12.50	25.00
❏ DL 4842 [M]	Don't Come Home a-Drinkin' (With Lovin' on Your Mind)	1967	7.50	15.00	30.00
❏ DL 4928 [M]	Who Says God Is Dead!	1967	10.00	20.00	40.00
❏ DL 4930 [M]	Singin' with Feelin'	1967	7.50	15.00	30.00
❏ DL 4997 [M]	Fist City	1968	12.50	25.00	50.00
—Mono version appears to exist only as a white label promo					
❏ DL 74457 [S]	Loretta Lynn Sings	1963	20.00	40.00	80.00
❏ DL 74541 [S]	Before I'm Over You	1964	10.00	20.00	40.00
❏ DL 74620 [S]	Songs from My Heart	1965	10.00	20.00	40.00
❏ DL 74665 [S]	Blue Kentucky Girl	1965	10.00	20.00	40.00
❏ DL 74695 [S]	Hymns	1965	10.00	20.00	40.00
❏ DL 74744 [S]	I Like 'Em Country	1966	7.50	15.00	30.00
❏ DL 74783 [S]	You Ain't Woman Enough	1966	7.50	15.00	30.00
❏ DL 74817 [S]	Country Christmas	1966	7.50	15.00	30.00
❏ DL 74842 [S]	Don't Come Home a-Drinkin' (With Lovin' on Your Mind)	1967	6.25	12.50	25.00
❏ DL 74928 [S]	Who Says God Is Dead!	1967	6.25	12.50	25.00
❏ DL 74930 [S]	Singin' with Feelin'	1967	6.25	12.50	25.00
❏ DL 74997 [S]	Fist City	1968	6.25	12.50	25.00
❏ DL 75000	Loretta Lynn's Greatest Hits	1968	6.25	12.50	25.00
❏ DL 75084	Your Squaw Is On the Warpath	1969	6.25	12.50	25.00
—Later editions delete the track "Barney"					
❏ DL 75084	Your Squaw Is On the Warpath	1969	10.00	20.00	40.00
—First editions had a track called "Barney"					
❏ DL 75113	Woman of the World/To Make a Man	1969	6.25	12.50	25.00
❏ DL 75163	Wings Upon Your Horns	1970	6.25	12.50	25.00
❏ DL 75198	Loretta Lynn Writes 'Em and Sings 'Em	1970	6.25	12.50	25.00
❏ DL 75253	Coal Miner's Daughter	1971	5.00	10.00	20.00
❏ DL 75282	I Wanna Be Free	1971	5.00	10.00	20.00
❏ DL 75310	You're Lookin' at Country	1971	5.00	10.00	20.00
❏ DL 75334	One's On the Way	1972	5.00	10.00	20.00
❏ DL 75351	God Bless America Again	1972	5.00	10.00	20.00
❏ DL 75381	Here I Am Again	1972	5.00	10.00	20.00
❏ ST-91604	Loretta Lynn's Greatest Hits	1968	7.50	15.00	30.00
—Capitol Record Club edition					
MCA					
❏ 1	Loretta Lynn's Greatest Hits	1973	3.75	7.50	15.00
—Reissue of Decca 75000					
❏ 5	Hymns	1973	3.75	7.50	15.00
—Reissue of Decca 74695					
❏ 6	You Ain't Woman Enough	1973	3.75	7.50	15.00
—Reissue of Decca 74783					

L

Number	Title (A Side/B Side)	Yr	VG	VG+	NM
❏ 7	Who Says God Is Dead!	1973	3.75	7.50	15.00
—Reissue of Decca 74928					
❏ 58	Here I Am Again	1973	3.75	7.50	15.00
—Reissue of Decca 75381					
❏ 113	Don't Come Home a-Drinkin' (With Lovin' on Your Mind)	1973	3.75	7.50	15.00
—Reissue of Decca 74842					
❏ 248	Country Christmas	1973	3.75	7.50	15.00
—First reissue of Decca LP					
❏ 300	Entertainer of the Year — Loretta	1973	3.75	7.50	15.00
❏ 355	Love Is the Foundation	1973	3.75	7.50	15.00
❏ 420	Loretta Lynn's Greatest Hits Vol. II	1974	3.75	7.50	15.00
❏ 444	They Don't Make 'Em Like My Daddy	1974	3.75	7.50	15.00
❏ 471	Back to the Country	1975	3.00	6.00	12.00
❏ 628	When the Tingle Becomes a Chill	198?	2.00	4.00	8.00
—Budget-line reissue					
❏ 630	Somebody Somewhere	198?	2.00	4.00	8.00
—Budget-line reissue					
❏ 721	We've Come a Long Way, Baby	198?	2.00	4.00	8.00
—Budget-line reissue					
❏ 735	Alone with You	198?	2.50	5.00	10.00
❏ L33-1934 [DJ]	Loretta Lynn	1974	10.00	20.00	40.00
—Promo-only compilation					
❏ 2146	Home	1975	3.00	6.00	12.00
❏ 2179	When the Tingle Becomes a Chill	1976	3.00	6.00	12.00
❏ 2228	Somebody Somewhere	1976	3.00	6.00	12.00
❏ 2265	I Remember Patsy	1977	3.00	6.00	12.00
❏ 2330	Out of My Head and Back in My Bed	1978	3.00	6.00	12.00
❏ 2341	Loretta Lynn's Greatest Hits	1978	3.00	6.00	12.00
—Reissue of MCA 1					
❏ 2342	Coal Miner's Daughter	1978	3.00	6.00	12.00
—Reissue					
❏ 2353	Loretta Lynn's Greatest Hits Vol. II	1978	3.00	6.00	12.00
—Reissue of MCA 420					
❏ 3073	We've Come a Long Way, Baby	1979	3.00	6.00	12.00
❏ 3217	Loretta	1980	2.50	5.00	10.00
❏ 5148	Lookin' Good	1980	2.50	5.00	10.00
❏ 5293	I Lie	1982	2.50	5.00	10.00
❏ 5426	Lyin', Cheatin', Woman Chasin', Honky Tonkin', Whiskey Drinkin' You	1983	2.50	5.00	10.00
❏ 5613	Just a Woman	1985	2.50	5.00	10.00
❏ 15022	Country Christmas	1974	3.00	6.00	12.00
—Second reissue of Decca LP; black rainbow label					
❏ 15022	Country Christmas	1980	2.50	5.00	10.00
—Blue rainbow label					
❏ 15032	Christmas Without Daddy	198?	3.00	6.00	12.00
❏ 35013	Allis-Chalmers Presents Loretta Lynn	1978	10.00	20.00	40.00
—Special products compilation					
❏ 35018	Crisco Presents Loretta Lynn's Country Classics	1979	10.00	20.00	40.00
—Special products compilation					
❏ 37080	I Remember Patsy Cline	198?	2.00	4.00	8.00
—Budget-line reissue					
❏ 37165	Loretta	198?	2.00	4.00	8.00
—Budget-line reissue					
❏ 37205	Loretta Lynn's Greatest Hits Vol. II	198?	2.00	4.00	8.00
—Budget-line reissue					
❏ 37235	Loretta Lynn's Greatest Hits	198?	2.00	4.00	8.00
—Budget-line reissue					
❏ 37236	Coal Miner's Daughter	198?	2.00	4.00	8.00
—Budget-line reissue					
❏ 42174	Who Was That Stranger	1988	2.50	5.00	10.00
VOCALION					
❏ VL 73853	Here's Loretta Lynn	1968	3.75	7.50	15.00

LYNN, LORETTA, AND ERNEST TUBB
See ERNEST TUBB AND LORETTA LYNN.

LYNN, LORETTA, AND CONWAY TWITTY
See CONWAY TWITTY AND LORETTA LYNN.

LYNN, VERA
LONDON

Number	Title (A Side/B Side)	Yr	VG	VG+	NM
❏ LL 1306 [M]	Vera Lynn Concert	195?	5.00	10.00	20.00
❏ LL 1510 [M]	If I Am Dreaming	195?	5.00	10.00	20.00

LYNNE, GLORIA
ABC IMPULSE!

Number	Title (A Side/B Side)	Yr	VG	VG+	NM
❏ ASD-9311	I Don't Know How to Love Him	1976	3.00	6.00	12.00
CANYON					
❏ 7709	Happy and In Love	1970	3.75	7.50	15.00
COLLECTABLES					
❏ COL-5138	Golden Classics	198?	2.50	5.00	10.00
DESIGN					
❏ D-177 [M]	My Funny Valentine	196?	2.50	5.00	10.00
❏ DS-177 [S]	My Funny Valentine	196?	3.00	6.00	12.00
EVEREST					
❏ ES-1001 [S]	Gloria Lynne Live! Take 1	1959	10.00	20.00	40.00
❏ SDBR-1022 [S]	Miss Gloria Lynne	1959	7.50	15.00	30.00
❏ SDBR-1063 [S]	Lonely and Sentimental	1960	7.50	15.00	30.00
❏ SDBR-1090 [S]	Try a Little Tenderness	1960	7.50	15.00	30.00
❏ SDBR-1101 [S]	Day In, Day Out	1961	7.50	15.00	30.00
❏ SDBR-1126 [S]	I'm Glad There Is You	1961	7.50	15.00	30.00
❏ SDBR-1128 [S]	He Needs Me	1961	7.50	15.00	30.00
❏ SDBR-1131 [S]	This Little Boy of Mine	1961	7.50	15.00	30.00
❏ SDBR-1132 [S]	Gloria Lynne at Basin Street East	1962	7.50	15.00	30.00
❏ SDBR-1203 [S]	Gloria Blue	1962	7.50	15.00	30.00
❏ SDBR-1208 [S]	Gloria Lynne at the Las Vegas Thunderbird	1963	7.50	15.00	30.00
❏ EV-1220 [S]	Gloria, Marty & Strings	1963	7.50	15.00	30.00
❏ EV-1226 [S]	I Wish You Love	1964	6.25	12.50	25.00
❏ EV-1228 [S]	Glorious Gloria Lynne	1964	6.25	12.50	25.00
❏ EV-1230 [S]	After Hours	1965	6.25	12.50	25.00
❏ EV-1231 [S]	The Best of Gloria Lynne	1965	5.00	10.00	20.00
❏ EV-1237 [S]	Go! Go! Go!	1965	5.00	10.00	20.00
❏ EV-1238 [S]	Gloria Lynne '66	1966	5.00	10.00	20.00
❏ E-5001 [M]	Gloria Lynne Live! Take 1	1959	7.50	15.00	30.00
❏ LPBR-5022 [M]	Miss Gloria Lynne	1959	5.00	10.00	20.00
❏ LPBR-5063 [M]	Lonely and Sentimental	1960	5.00	10.00	20.00
❏ LPBR-5090 [M]	Try a Little Tenderness	1960	5.00	10.00	20.00
❏ LPBR-5101 [M]	Day In, Day Out	1961	5.00	10.00	20.00
❏ LPBR-5126 [M]	I'm Glad There Is You	1961	5.00	10.00	20.00
❏ LPBR-5128 [M]	He Needs Me	1961	5.00	10.00	20.00
❏ LPBR-5131 [M]	This Little Boy of Mine	1961	5.00	10.00	20.00
❏ LPBR-5132 [M]	Gloria Lynne at Basin Street East	1962	5.00	10.00	20.00
❏ LPBR-5203 [M]	Gloria Blue	1962	5.00	10.00	20.00
❏ LPBR-5208 [M]	Gloria Lynne at the Las Vegas Thunderbird	1963	5.00	10.00	20.00
❏ EV-5220 [M]	Gloria, Marty & Strings	1963	5.00	10.00	20.00
❏ EV-5226 [M]	I Wish You Love	1964	5.00	10.00	20.00
❏ EV-5228 [M]	Glorious Gloria Lynne	1964	5.00	10.00	20.00
❏ EV-5230 [M]	After Hours	1965	5.00	10.00	20.00
❏ EV-5231 [M]	The Best of Gloria Lynne	1965	3.75	7.50	15.00
❏ EV-5237 [M]	Go! Go! Go!	1965	3.75	7.50	15.00
❏ EV-5238 [M]	Gloria Lynne '66	1966	3.75	7.50	15.00
FONTANA					
❏ MGF-27528 [M]	Intimate Moments	1964	3.75	7.50	15.00
❏ MGF-27541 [M]	Soul Serenade	1965	3.75	7.50	15.00
❏ MGF-27546 [M]	Love and a Woman	1965	3.75	7.50	15.00
❏ MGF-27555 [M]	Where It's At	1966	3.75	7.50	15.00
❏ MGF-27561 [M]	Gloria	1966	3.75	7.50	15.00
❏ MGF-27571 [M]	The Other Side of Gloria Lynne	1967	5.00	10.00	20.00
❏ SRF-67528 [S]	Intimate Moments	1964	5.00	10.00	20.00
❏ SRF-67541 [S]	Soul Serenade	1965	5.00	10.00	20.00
❏ SRF-67546 [S]	Love and a Woman	1965	5.00	10.00	20.00
❏ SRF-67555 [S]	Where It's At	1966	5.00	10.00	20.00
❏ SRF-67561 [S]	Gloria	1966	5.00	10.00	20.00
❏ SRF-67571 [S]	The Other Side of Gloria Lynne	1967	3.75	7.50	15.00
❏ SRF-67577	Here, There and Everywhere	1968	3.75	7.50	15.00
HIFI					
❏ L-440 [M]	The Gloria Lynne Calendar	1966	3.75	7.50	15.00
❏ SL-440 [S]	The Gloria Lynne Calendar	1966	5.00	10.00	20.00
❏ SR-441	Greatest Hits	1969	3.75	7.50	15.00
INTERMEDIA					
❏ QS-5069	Classics	198?	2.50	5.00	10.00
MERCURY					
❏ SRM-1-633	A Very Gentle Sound	1972	3.75	7.50	15.00
MUSE					
❏ MR-5381	A Time for Love	198?	2.50	5.00	10.00
SUNSET					
❏ SUM-1145 [M]	Gloria Lynne	1966	3.00	6.00	12.00
❏ SUM-1171 [M]	I Wish You Love	1967	3.00	6.00	12.00
❏ SUS-5145 [S]	Gloria Lynne	1966	3.00	6.00	12.00
❏ SUS-5171 [S]	I Wish You Love	1967	3.00	6.00	12.00
❏ SUS-5221	Golden Greats	1968	3.00	6.00	12.00
UPFRONT					
❏ 146	Gloria Lynne	197?	3.00	6.00	12.00

LYNYRD SKYNYRD
ATLANTIC

Number	Title (A Side/B Side)	Yr	VG	VG+	NM
❏ A1-82258	Lynyrd Skynyrd 1991	1991	5.00	10.00	20.00
—The only U.S. vinyl version was released through Columbia House					
MCA					
❏ 363	(pronounced leh-nerd skin-nerd)	1975	3.00	6.00	12.00
—Reissue on black rainbow label					
❏ 413	Second Helping	1975	3.00	6.00	12.00
—Reissue on black rainbow label					
❏ 1448	Best of the Rest	1985	2.00	4.00	8.00
❏ L33-1946 [(2)DJ]	One More From the Road	1976	6.25	12.50	25.00
—Promo only on black vinyl					
❏ L33-1946 [(2)DJ]	One More From the Road	1976	12.50	25.00	50.00
—Promo on blue, gold, purple or red vinyl (each has the same value)					
❏ L33-1988 [DJ]	Skynyrd's First and…Last	1978	6.25	12.50	25.00
—Promo sampler					
❏ 2137	Nuthin' Fancy	1975	3.00	6.00	12.00
❏ 2170	Gimme Back My Bullets	1976	3.00	6.00	12.00
❏ 3019	(pronounced leh-nerd skin-nerd)	1976	2.50	5.00	10.00
—Second reissue with new number on black rainbow label					
❏ 3020	Second Helping	1976	2.50	5.00	10.00
—Second reissue with new number on black rainbow label					
❏ 3021	Nuthin' Fancy	1976	2.50	5.00	10.00
—Reissue with new number on black rainbow label					
❏ 3022	Gimme Back My Bullets	1977	2.50	5.00	10.00
—Reissue with new number on black rainbow label					
❏ 3029	Street Survivors	1977	2.50	5.00	10.00
—After the band's plane crash, the "flames" photo was replaced with the back cover photo; the back cover is black with only the song titles					
❏ 3029	Street Survivors	1977	6.25	12.50	25.00
—Originals with the band in flames on the front cover and a smaller band photo on the back cover					
❏ 3047	Skynyrd's First and…Last	1978	3.00	6.00	12.00
—Originals with tan labels and gatefold cover					
❏ 5221	(pronounced leh-nerd skin-nerd)	1980	2.00	4.00	8.00
❏ 5222	Second Helping	1980	2.00	4.00	8.00
❏ 5223	Street Survivors	1980	2.00	4.00	8.00
❏ 5370	Best of the Rest	1982	2.50	5.00	10.00
—Original version					
❏ 6001 [(2)]	One More From the Road	1976	3.75	7.50	15.00
—Originals with black rainbow label and gatefold cover					
❏ 6897 [(2)]	One More From the Road	1985	2.50	5.00	10.00
—Most, if not all, of these pressings have no gatefold					
❏ 6898 [(2)]	Gold & Platinum	1985	2.50	5.00	10.00
—Most, if not all, of these pressings have no gatefold					
❏ 8027 [(2)]	Southern by the Grace of God	1988	3.00	6.00	12.00
❏ 10014 [(2)]	One More From the Road	1980	2.50	5.00	10.00
❏ 11008 [(2)]	Gold & Platinum	1979	3.00	6.00	12.00
—Originals with embossed gatefold cover					

Number	Title (A Side/B Side)	Yr	VG	VG+	NM
❑ 37069	Gimme Back My Bullets	1980	2.00	4.00	8.00
❑ 37070	Nuthin' Fancy	1980	2.00	4.00	8.00
❑ 37071	Skynyrd's First and…Last	1980	2.00	4.00	8.00
❑ 37211	(pronounced leh-nerd skin-nerd)	1985	2.00	4.00	8.00
❑ 37212	Second Helping	1985	2.00	4.00	8.00
❑ 37213	Street Survivors	1985	2.00	4.00	8.00
❑ 42084	Legend	1987	2.50	5.00	10.00
❑ 42293	Skynyrd's Innyrds	1989	3.00	6.00	12.00

SOUNDS OF THE SOUTH

❑ 363	(pronounced leh-nerd skin-nerd)	1973	5.00	10.00	20.00
❑ 413	Second Helping	1974	5.00	10.00	20.00

—Both of the above are original pressings with yellow labels

LYONS, JIMMY
HAT HUT

❑ Y/Z/Z [(3)]	Push	1979	6.25	12.50	25.00
❑ 21 [(2)]	Jump Up/What to Do About	198?	5.00	10.00	20.00

LYTLE, JOHNNY
JAZZLAND

❑ JLP-22 [M]	Blue Vibes	1960	6.25	12.50	25.00
❑ JLP-44 [M]	Happy Ground	1961	6.25	12.50	25.00
❑ JLP-67 [M]	Nice and Easy	1962	6.25	12.50	25.00
❑ JLP-81 [M]	Moon Child	1962	6.25	12.50	25.00
❑ JLP-922 [S]	Blue Vibes	1960	7.50	15.00	30.00
❑ JLP-944 [S]	Happy Ground	1961	7.50	15.00	30.00
❑ JLP-967 [S]	Nice and Easy	1962	7.50	15.00	30.00
❑ JLP-981 [S]	Moon Child	1962	7.50	15.00	30.00

RIVERSIDE

❑ RLP-456 [M]	Got That Feeling	1963	5.00	10.00	20.00
❑ RLP-470 [M]	Happy Ground	1964	5.00	10.00	20.00
❑ RLP-480 [M]	The Village Caller	1965	5.00	10.00	20.00
❑ RM-3003 [M]	A Groove	1967	7.50	15.00	30.00
❑ RS-3003 [S]	A Groove	1967	5.00	10.00	20.00
❑ RS-9456 [S]	Got That Feeling	1963	6.25	12.50	25.00
❑ RS-9470 [S]	Happy Ground	1964	6.25	12.50	25.00
❑ RS-9480 [S]	The Village Caller	1965	6.25	12.50	25.00

SOLID STATE

❑ SS-18014	A Man and a Woman	1967	5.00	10.00	20.00
❑ SS-18044	Be Proud	1969	5.00	10.00	20.00
❑ SS-18056	Close Enough	1969	5.00	10.00	20.00

LYTTELTON, HUMPHREY
ANGEL

❑ ANG.60008 [10]	Some Like It Hot	1955	15.00	30.00	60.00

BETHLEHEM

❑ BCP-6063 [M]	Humph Plays Standards	1961	7.50	15.00	30.00

LONDON

❑ PS 178 [S]	Humph Dedicates	1959	6.25	12.50	25.00
❑ LL 3101 [M]	I Play As I Please	195?	7.50	15.00	30.00
❑ LL 3132 [M]	Humph Dedicates	195?	7.50	15.00	30.00

M

MABERN, HAROLD
PRESTIGE

❑ PRST-7568	A Few Miles from Memphis	1968	5.00	10.00	20.00
❑ PRST-7624	Rakin' and Scrapin'	1969	5.00	10.00	20.00
❑ PRST-7687	Workin' and Wailin'	1969	5.00	10.00	20.00
❑ PRST-7764	Greasy Kid Stuff	1970	5.00	10.00	20.00

MABLEY, MOMS
CHESS

❑ LP-1447 [M]	Moms Mabley, Funniest Woman in the World, Onstage	1961	6.25	12.50	25.00
❑ LP-1452 [M]	Moms Mabley at the "UN"	1961	6.25	12.50	25.00
❑ LP-1460 [M]	Moms Mabley at the Playboy Club	1961	6.25	12.50	25.00
❑ LP-1463 [M]	Moms Mabley at Geneva Conference	1962	6.25	12.50	25.00
❑ LP-1472 [M]	Moms Mabley Breaks It Up	1962	6.25	12.50	25.00
❑ LP-1477 [M]	Young Men, Si — Old Men, No	1962	6.25	12.50	25.00
❑ LP-1479 [M]	I Got Somethin' to Tell You!	1963	6.25	12.50	25.00
❑ LP-1482 [M]	The Funny Sides of Moms Mabley	1963	6.25	12.50	25.00
❑ LP-1486 [M]	Moms Wows	1964	6.25	12.50	25.00
❑ LP-1487 [M]	The Best of Moms	1964	6.25	12.50	25.00
❑ LP-1497 [M]	The Man in My Life	1965	5.00	10.00	20.00
❑ LPS-1525	Moms Mabley Breaks Up the Network	1968	5.00	10.00	20.00
❑ LPS-1530	Moms Mabley Sings	1969	5.00	10.00	20.00

MERCURY

❑ MG-20889 [M]	Out on a Limb	1964	3.75	7.50	15.00
❑ MG-20907 [M]	Moms the Word	1964	3.75	7.50	15.00
❑ MG-21012 [M]	Now Hear This	1965	3.75	7.50	15.00
❑ MG-21090 [M]	Moms Mabley at the White House	1966	3.75	7.50	15.00
❑ MG-21139 [M]	The Best of Moms Mabley	1967	6.25	12.50	25.00
❑ SR-60889 [S]	Out on a Limb	1964	5.00	10.00	20.00
❑ SR-60907 [S]	Moms the Word	1964	5.00	10.00	20.00
❑ SR-61012 [S]	Now Hear This	1965	5.00	10.00	20.00
❑ SR-61090 [S]	Moms Mabley at the White House	1966	5.00	10.00	20.00
❑ SR-61139 [S]	The Best of Moms Mabley	1967	3.75	7.50	15.00
❑ SR-61205	Her Young Thing	1969	3.75	7.50	15.00
❑ SR-61229	The Youngest Teenager	1969	3.75	7.50	15.00
❑ SR-61235	Abraham, Martin and John	1969	3.75	7.50	15.00
❑ SR-61263	Live at Sing Sing	1970	3.75	7.50	15.00

MABON, WILLIE
CHESS

❑ LP-1439 [M]	Willie Mabon	1958	100.00	200.00	400.00

—Black label

MACARTHUR, DOUGLAS
ATCO

❑ 8095 [M]	The Life of General MacArthur	1964	10.00	20.00	40.00

MACDONALD, JEANETTE, AND NELSON EDDY
RCA VICTOR

❑ LPT-16 [10]	Rose Marie	1952	15.00	30.00	60.00
❑ LPV-526 [M]	Rose Marie	1965	6.25	12.50	25.00
❑ LPM-1738 [M]	Favorites in Hi-Fi	1958	10.00	20.00	40.00

MACEO AND ALL THE KING'S MEN
EXCELLO

❑ LPS-8022	Funky Music Machine	1972	7.50	15.00	30.00

HOUSE OF FOX

❑ LP-1	Doing Their Own Thing	1971	7.50	15.00	30.00

MACEO AND THE MACKS
PEOPLE

❑ PE-6601	Us	1973	7.50	15.00	30.00

MACERO, TEO
COLUMBIA

❑ CL 842 [M]	What's New?	1956	12.50	25.00	50.00

DEBUT

❑ DLP-6 [10]	Explorations by Teo Macero	1954	62.50	125.00	250.00

PRESTIGE

❑ PRLP-7104 [M]	Teo Macero with the Prestige Jazz Quartet	1957	20.00	40.00	80.00

MACHITO
CLEF

❑ MGC-505 [10]	Afro-Cuban Jazz Suite	1953	30.00	60.00	120.00
❑ MGC-511 [10]	Machito Jazz with Flip and Bird	1953	30.00	60.00	120.00
❑ MGC-689 [M]	Afro-Cuban Jazz	1956	25.00	50.00	100.00

CORAL

❑ CRL 57258 [M]	Vacation at the Concord	1959	10.00	20.00	40.00
❑ CRL 757258 [S]	Vacation at the Concord	1959	7.50	15.00	30.00

DECCA

❑ DL 5157 [10]	Machito's Afro-Cuban	1950	37.50	75.00	150.00

MERCURY

❑ MGC-505 [10]	Afro-Cuban Jazz Suite	1951	37.50	75.00	150.00
❑ MGC-511 [10]	Machito Jazz with Flip and Bird	1952	37.50	75.00	150.00
❑ MG-25009 [10]	Jungle Drums	1950	37.50	75.00	150.00
❑ MG-25020 [10]	Rhumbas	1950	37.50	75.00	150.00

RCA VICTOR

❑ LPM-3944 [M]	Machito Goes Memphis	1968	10.00	20.00	40.00
❑ LSP-3944 [S]	Machito Goes Memphis	1968	5.00	10.00	20.00

ROULETTE

❑ R-52006 [M]	Kenya	1958	10.00	20.00	40.00
❑ SR-52006 [S]	Kenya.	1958	7.50	15.00	30.00
❑ R-52026 [M]	With Flute to Boot.	1959	10.00	20.00	40.00
❑ SR-52026 [S]	With Flute to Boot.	1959	7.50	15.00	30.00

TICO

❑ LP-138 [10]	El Niche	1956	30.00	60.00	120.00
❑ LP-1002 [M]	Cha Cha Cha at the Palladium	1955	20.00	40.00	80.00
❑ LP-1029 [M]	Asia Minor Cha Cha Cha	1956	20.00	40.00	80.00
❑ LP-1033 [M]	Si Si, No No	1957	20.00	40.00	80.00
❑ LP-1045 [M]	Inspired by "The Sun Also Rises"	1957	20.00	40.00	80.00
❑ LP-1053 [M]	Mi Amigo, Machito	1959	15.00	30.00	60.00
❑ LP-1062 [M]	Irving Berlin in Latin America	1959	15.00	30.00	60.00
❑ LP-1074 [M]	A Night with Machito	1960	12.50	25.00	50.00
❑ LPS-1074 [S]	A Night with Machito	1960	15.00	30.00	60.00
❑ LP-1084 [M]	The New Sound of Machito (El Sonido Nuevo de Machito)	1962	10.00	20.00	40.00
❑ LPS-1084 [S]	The New Sound of Machito (El Sonido Nuevo de Machito)	1962	12.50	25.00	50.00
❑ LP-1090 [M]	Variedades	1963	10.00	20.00	40.00
❑ LPS-1090 [S]	Variedades	1963	12.50	25.00	50.00
❑ LP-1094 [M]	Tremendo Cumban!	1963	10.00	20.00	40.00
❑ LPS-1094 [S]	Tremendo Cumban!	1963	12.50	25.00	50.00
❑ CLP-1314	Latin Soul Plus Jazz	1973	5.00	10.00	20.00
❑ CLP-1328	Lo Mejor De Machito Y Sus AfroCubans Con Graciela	1974	5.00	10.00	20.00

VERVE

❑ VSP-19 [M]	Soul Source	1966	5.00	10.00	20.00
❑ MGV-8073 [M]	Afro-Cuban Jazz	1957	12.50	25.00	50.00
❑ V-8073 [M]	Afro-Cuban Jazz	1961	5.00	10.00	20.00

MACK, DAVID
SEREMUS

❑ SRE-1009 [M]	New Directions	1965	5.00	10.00	20.00
❑ SRS-12009 [S]	New Directions	1965	6.25	12.50	25.00

MACK, LONNIE
ALLIGATOR

❑ AL-3903	The Wham of That Memphis Man	1987	2.50	5.00	10.00

—Reissue of Fraternity LP

❑ AL-4739	Strike Like Lightning	1985	2.50	5.00	10.00
❑ AL-4750	Second Sight	1987	2.50	5.00	10.00
❑ AL-4786	Live!: Attack of the Killer V	1990	3.00	6.00	12.00

CAPITOL

❑ ST-11611	Home at Last	1976	3.00	6.00	12.00
❑ ST-11703	Lonnie Mack and Pismo	1977	3.00	6.00	12.00

ELEKTRA

❑ EKS-74040	Glad I'm In the Band	1969	6.25	12.50	25.00
❑ EKS-74050	Whatever's Right	1969	6.25	12.50	25.00
❑ EKS-74077	For Collectors Only	1970	6.25	12.50	25.00
❑ EKS-74102	The Hills of Indiana	1971	6.25	12.50	25.00

EPIC

❑ FE 44075	Roadhouses and Dance Halls	1989	3.00	6.00	12.00

MACK, WARNER (continued)

Number	Title (A Side/B Side)	Yr	VG	VG+	NM
FRATERNITY					
❑ SF-1014 [M]	The Wham of That Memphis Man	1963	30.00	60.00	120.00
❑ SSF-1014 [S]	The Wham of That Memphis Man	1963	75.00	150.00	300.00
TRIP					
❑ TLX-9522 [(2)]	The Memphis Sounds of Lonnie Mack	1975	3.00	6.00	12.00

MACK, WARNER

Number	Title (A Side/B Side)	Yr	VG	VG+	NM
DECCA					
❑ DL 4692 [M]	The Bridge Washed Out	1965	5.00	10.00	20.00
❑ DL 4766 [M]	The Country Touch	1966	5.00	10.00	20.00
❑ DL 4883 [M]	Drifting Apart	1967	6.25	12.50	25.00
❑ DL 4912 [M]	Songs We Sand in Church and Home	1967	6.25	12.50	25.00
❑ DL 74692 [S]	The Bridge Washed Out	1965	6.25	12.50	25.00
❑ DL 74766 [S]	The Country Touch	1966	6.25	12.50	25.00
❑ DL 74883 [S]	Drifting Apart	1967	5.00	10.00	20.00
❑ DL 74912 [S]	Songs We Sand in Church and Home	1967	5.00	10.00	20.00
❑ DL 74995	The Many Country Moods of Warner Mack	1968	5.00	10.00	20.00
❑ DL 75092	The Country Beat of Warner Mack	1969	5.00	10.00	20.00
❑ DL 75165	I'll Still Be Missing You	1969	5.00	10.00	20.00
KAPP					
❑ KL-1255 [M]	Golden Country Hits	1961	5.00	10.00	20.00
❑ KL-1279 [M]	Golden Country Hits, Vol. 2	1962	5.00	10.00	20.00
❑ KL-1461 [M]	Everybody's Country Favorites	196?	3.75	7.50	15.00
❑ KS-3255 [S]	Golden Country Hits	1961	6.25	12.50	25.00
❑ KS-3279 [S]	Golden Country Hits, Vol. 2	1962	6.25	12.50	25.00
❑ KS-3461 [S]	Everybody's Country Favorites	196?	5.00	10.00	20.00

MACKAY, BRUCE

Number	Title (A Side/B Side)	Yr	VG	VG+	NM
ORO					
❑ 1	Bruce Mackay	196?	5.00	10.00	20.00

MACKAY, DAVID, AND VICKI HAMILTON

Number	Title (A Side/B Side)	Yr	VG	VG+	NM
ABC IMPULSE!					
❑ AS-9184	David MacKay and Vicki Hamilton	1969	5.00	10.00	20.00

MACKENZIE, GISELE

Number	Title (A Side/B Side)	Yr	VG	VG+	NM
EVEREST					
❑ SDBR-1069 [S]	In Person at the Empire Room	1959	7.50	15.00	30.00
❑ LPBR-5069 [M]	In Person at the Empire Room	1959	6.25	12.50	25.00
GLENDALE					
❑ 6017	Gisele MacKenzie Sings	1978	3.00	6.00	12.00
RCA VICTOR					
❑ LPM-1790 [M]	Gisele	1958	7.50	15.00	30.00
❑ LSP-1790 [S]	Gisele	1958	10.00	20.00	40.00
❑ LPM-2006 [M]	Christmas with Gisele	1959	7.50	15.00	30.00
❑ LSP-2006 [S]	Christmas with Gisele	1959	10.00	20.00	40.00
SUNSET					
❑ SUM-1155 [M]	In Person at the Empire Room	196?	3.00	6.00	12.00
❑ SUS-5155 [S]	In Person at the Empire Room	196?	3.75	7.50	15.00
VIK					
❑ LX-1055 [M]	Gisele MacKenzie	1956	10.00	20.00	40.00
❑ LX-1075 [M]	Mam'selle MacKenzie	1956	10.00	20.00	40.00
❑ LX-1099 [M]	Christmas with Gisele	1957	10.00	20.00	40.00

MACON, UNCLE DAVE

Number	Title (A Side/B Side)	Yr	VG	VG+	NM
DECCA					
❑ DL 4760 [M]	Uncle Dave Macon	1966	7.50	15.00	30.00

MACRAE, GORDON

Number	Title (A Side/B Side)	Yr	VG	VG+	NM
CAPITOL					
❑ H 231 [10]	Songs	1950	10.00	20.00	40.00
❑ T 537 [M]	Romantic Ballads	1955	7.50	15.00	30.00
—Turquoise or gray label					
❑ T 681 [M]	Operetta Favorites	1956	7.50	15.00	30.00
—Turquoise or gray label					
❑ T 765 [M]	The Best Things in Life Are Free	1956	7.50	15.00	30.00
—Turquoise or gray label					
❑ T 834 [M]	Cowboy's Lament	1957	7.50	15.00	30.00
—Turquoise or gray label					
❑ T 875 [M]	Motion Picture Soundstage	1957	7.50	15.00	30.00
—Turquoise or gray label					
❑ ST 980 [S]	Gordon MacRae in Concert	1959	10.00	20.00	40.00
—Black colorband label, logo at left					
❑ T 980 [M]	Gordon MacRae in Concert	1957	7.50	15.00	30.00
—Turquoise or gray label					
❑ T 1050 [M]	This Is Gordon MacRae	1958	7.50	15.00	30.00
—Turquoise or gray label					

MACRAE, GORDON, AND JO STAFFORD
See JO STAFFORD AND GORDON MacRAE.

MACRAE, SHEILA

Number	Title (A Side/B Side)	Yr	VG	VG+	NM
ABC					
❑ ABCS-611	How Sweet She Is	1968	6.25	12.50	25.00

MAD LADS, THE

Number	Title (A Side/B Side)	Yr	VG	VG+	NM
STAX					
❑ MPS-8525	The Best of the Mad Lads	198?	2.50	5.00	10.00
VOLT					
❑ 414 [M]	The Mad Lads In Action	1966	7.50	15.00	30.00
❑ S-414 [S]	The Mad Lads In Action.	1966	10.00	20.00	40.00
❑ VOS-6005	The Mad, Mad, Mad, Mad, Mad Lads.	1969	7.50	15.00	30.00
❑ VOS-6020	A New Beginning.	1973	5.00	10.00	20.00

MAD RIVER

Number	Title (A Side/B Side)	Yr	VG	VG+	NM
CAPITOL					
❑ ST-185	Paradise Bar and Grill	1969	10.00	20.00	40.00
❑ ST 2985	Mad River	1968	12.50	25.00	50.00

MADDOX, JOHNNY

Number	Title (A Side/B Side)	Yr	VG	VG+	NM
DOT					
❑ DLP-102 [10]	Authentic Ragtime	1952	10.00	20.00	40.00
❑ DLP-3005 [M]	Johnny Maddox Plays	1955	6.25	12.50	25.00
❑ DLP-3008 [M]	Tap Dance Rhythms	1955	6.25	12.50	25.00
❑ DLP-3044 [M]	King of Ragtime	1957	5.00	10.00	20.00
❑ DLP-3063 [M]	The Thirties in Ragtime	1957	5.00	10.00	20.00
❑ DLP-3067 [M]	My Old Flames	1957	5.00	10.00	20.00

MADDOX, LESTER

Number	Title (A Side/B Side)	Yr	VG	VG+	NM
LEFEVRE					
❑ MLSP-3485	God, Family and Country	197?	10.00	20.00	40.00

MADDOX, ROSE
Also see THE MADDOX BROTHERS AND ROSE.

Number	Title (A Side/B Side)	Yr	VG	VG+	NM
CAPITOL					
❑ ST 1312 [S]	The One Rose	1960	10.00	20.00	40.00
❑ T 1312 [M]	The One Rose	1960	7.50	15.00	30.00
❑ ST 1437 [S]	Glorybound Train	1960	10.00	20.00	40.00
❑ T 1437 [M]	Glorybound Train	1960	7.50	15.00	30.00
❑ ST 1548 [S]	A Big Bouquet of Roses	1961	10.00	20.00	40.00
❑ T 1548 [M]	A Big Bouquet of Roses	1961	7.50	15.00	30.00
❑ ST 1799 [S]	Rose Maddox Sings Bluegrass	1962	12.50	25.00	50.00
❑ T 1799 [M]	Rose Maddox Sings Bluegrass	1962	10.00	20.00	40.00
❑ ST 1993 [S]	Alone with You	1963	10.00	20.00	40.00
❑ T 1993 [M]	Alone with You	1963	7.50	15.00	30.00
COLUMBIA					
❑ CL 1159 [M]	Precious Memories	1958	10.00	20.00	40.00

MADDOX BROTHERS AND ROSE
Also see ROSE MADDOX.

Number	Title (A Side/B Side)	Yr	VG	VG+	NM
KING					
❑ 669 [M]	A Collection of Standard Sacred Songs	1959	37.50	75.00	150.00
❑ 677 [M]	The Maddox Brothers and Rose	1960	30.00	60.00	120.00
❑ 752 [M]	I'll Write Your Name in the Sand	1961	30.00	60.00	120.00
WRANGLER					
❑ W-1003 [M]	The Maddox Brothers and Rose	1962	7.50	15.00	30.00
❑ WS-1003 [S]	The Maddox Brothers and Rose	1962	10.00	20.00	40.00

MADIGAN, BETTY

Number	Title (A Side/B Side)	Yr	VG	VG+	NM
MGM					
❑ E-3448 [M]	Am I Blue?	1956	10.00	20.00	40.00

MADISON, AL

Number	Title (A Side/B Side)	Yr	VG	VG+	NM
GOLDEN CREST					
❑ GC-3048 [M]	Meet Al Madison	196?	6.25	12.50	25.00

MADONNA

Number	Title (A Side/B Side)	Yr	VG	VG+	NM
MAVERICK					
❑ PRO-A-5904 [(2)DJ]	Erotica	1992	15.00	30.00	60.00
—Vinyl is promo only					
❑ PRO-A-7311 [(2)DJ]	Bedtime Stories	1994	20.00	40.00	80.00
—Promo only on pink vinyl					
❑ PRO-A-9378 [(2)DJ]	Ray of Light	1998	12.50	25.00	50.00
—Vinyl is promo only; generic cover with sticker					
❑ PRO-A-100500-A [(2)DJ]	Music	2000	7.50	15.00	30.00
—Vinyl is promo only; generic white die-cut sleeve					
❑ PRO-A-100871 [(3)DJ]	GHV2 Remixed — The Best of 1991-2001	2001	10.00	20.00	40.00
—Promo-only remixes of 12 songs from the "GHV2" CD; comes in generic black jacket with hole in center					
SIRE					
❑ PRO-A-2892	You Can Dance	1987	7.50	15.00	30.00
—Promo-only; contains single edits of the seven songs on the stock editions					
❑ 23867	Madonna	1983	2.50	5.00	10.00
—Second pressing with 3:49 version of "Burning Up"					
❑ 23867	Madonna	1983	5.00	10.00	20.00
—First pressing with 4:48 version of "Burning Up"; this version has only been found on copies with a gold promo stamp on the cover					
❑ W1-23867	Madonna	1984	3.75	7.50	15.00
—Columbia House edition					
❑ 25157	Like a Virgin	1984	12.50	25.00	50.00
—White vinyl with cream colored spine					
❑ 25157	Like a Virgin	1984	15.00	30.00	60.00
—White vinyl with silver colored spine					
❑ 25157	Like a Virgin	1984	2.50	5.00	10.00
❑ W1-25157	Like a Virgin	1985	3.75	7.50	15.00
—Columbia House edition					
❑ 25442	True Blue	1986	2.00	4.00	8.00
—Without poster					
❑ 25442	True Blue	1986	3.00	6.00	12.00
—With poster					
❑ W1-25442	True Blue	1986	3.75	7.50	15.00
—Columbia House edition; issued with poster					
❑ 25535	You Can Dance	1987	2.00	4.00	8.00
—Without gold obi					
❑ 25535	You Can Dance	1987	3.00	6.00	12.00
—With gold obi "Madonna and Dancing"					
❑ W1-25535	You Can Dance	1987	3.75	7.50	15.00
—Columbia House edition; not issued with obi					
❑ 25844	Like a Prayer	1989	2.50	5.00	10.00
❑ W1-25844	Like a Prayer	1989	3.75	7.50	15.00
—Columbia House edition					
❑ 26209	I'm Breathless	1990	2.50	5.00	10.00
❑ W1-26209	I'm Breathless	1990	3.75	7.50	15.00
—Columbia House edition					
❑ 26440 [(2)]	The Immaculate Collection	1990	3.75	7.50	15.00
❑ W1-26440 [(2)]	The Immaculate Collection	1990	5.00	10.00	20.00
—Columbia House edition					
❑ R 100572	I'm Breathless	1990	3.75	7.50	15.00
—BMG Direct Marketing edition					
❑ R 101029	Like a Prayer	1989	3.75	7.50	15.00
—BMG Direct Marketing edition					
❑ R 134536	You Can Dance	1987	3.75	7.50	15.00
—RCA Music Service edition; not issued with obi					
❑ R 143811	True Blue	1986	3.75	7.50	15.00
—RCA Music Service edition; issued with poster					

Number	Title (A Side/B Side)	Yr	VG	VG+	NM
❏ R 161153	Like a Virgin	1985	3.75	7.50	15.00
—RCA Music Service edition					
❏ R 164288	Madonna	1984	3.75	7.50	15.00
—RCA Music Service edition					
❏ R 254164 [(2)]	The Immaculate Collection	1990	5.00	10.00	20.00
—BMG Direct Marketing edition					

MADRIGAL
SSS INTERNATIONAL

Number	Title (A Side/B Side)	Yr	VG	VG+	NM
❏ 18	Madrigal	1971	7.50	15.00	30.00

MADURA
COLUMBIA

Number	Title (A Side/B Side)	Yr	VG	VG+	NM
❏ G 30794 [(2)]	Madura	1971	5.00	10.00	20.00
❏ KC 32545	Madura II	1973	3.75	7.50	15.00

MAESTRO, JOHNNY
Also see THE CRESTS.
BUDDAH

Number	Title (A Side/B Side)	Yr	VG	VG+	NM
❏ BDS-5091	The Johnny Maestro Story	1971	10.00	20.00	40.00
—With inserts; deduct 40% if missing					

MAGI, THE
UNCLE DIRTY

Number	Title (A Side/B Side)	Yr	VG	VG+	NM
❏ 6102-N13	Win or Lose	1975	75.00	150.00	300.00

MAGIC
May be two different groups.
ARMADILLO

Number	Title (A Side/B Side)	Yr	VG	VG+	NM
❏ 8031	Enclosed	1970	100.00	200.00	400.00

RARE EARTH

Number	Title (A Side/B Side)	Yr	VG	VG+	NM
❏ RS-527	Magic	1971	6.25	12.50	25.00

MAGIC FERN, THE
PANORAMA

Number	Title (A Side/B Side)	Yr	VG	VG+	NM
❏ 108	The Magic Fern	1980	37.50	75.00	150.00

MAGIC LANTERNS
ATLANTIC

Number	Title (A Side/B Side)	Yr	VG	VG+	NM
❏ SD 8217	Shame, Shame	1969	5.00	10.00	20.00

MAGIC SAM
DELMARK

Number	Title (A Side/B Side)	Yr	VG	VG+	NM
❏ DL-615	West Side Soul	1968	12.50	25.00	50.00
❏ DL-620	Black Magic	1969	12.50	25.00	50.00

MAGIC SAND
UNI

Number	Title (A Side/B Side)	Yr	VG	VG+	NM
❏ 73094	Magic Sand	1971	6.25	12.50	25.00

MAGNIFICENT MEN, THE
CAPITOL

Number	Title (A Side/B Side)	Yr	VG	VG+	NM
❏ ST 2678 [S]	The Magnificent Men	1967	3.75	7.50	15.00
❏ T 2678 [M]	The Magnificent Men	1967	5.00	10.00	20.00
❏ ST 2775 [S]	The Magnificent Men "Live!"	1967	3.75	7.50	15.00
❏ T 2775 [M]	The Magnificent Men "Live!"	1967	5.00	10.00	20.00
❏ ST 2846 [S]	World of Soul	1968	3.75	7.50	15.00
❏ T 2846 [M]	World of Soul	1968	5.00	10.00	20.00

MERCURY

Number	Title (A Side/B Side)	Yr	VG	VG+	NM
❏ SR-61252	Better Than a Ten Cent Movie	1970	3.75	7.50	15.00

MAHAL, TAJ
COLUMBIA

Number	Title (A Side/B Side)	Yr	VG	VG+	NM
❏ CG 18 [(2)]	Giant Step/De Ole Folks at Home	198?	2.50	5.00	10.00
—Reissue with new prefix					
❏ GP 18 [(2)]	Giant Step/De Ole Folks at Home	1969	5.00	10.00	20.00
—Red "360 Sound" label					
❏ GP 18 [(2)]	Giant Step/De Ole Folks at Home	1971	3.75	7.50	15.00
—Orange label					
❏ CL 2779 [M]	Taj Mahal	1967	7.50	15.00	30.00
❏ CS 9579 [S]	Taj Mahal	1967	3.75	7.50	15.00
—Red "360 Sound" label					
❏ CS 9579 [S]	Taj Mahal	1971	3.00	6.00	12.00
—Orange label					
❏ PC 9579 [S]	Taj Mahal	198?	2.00	4.00	8.00
—Reissue with new prefix					
❏ CS 9698	The Natch'l Blues	1968	3.75	7.50	15.00
—Red "360 Sound" label					
❏ CS 9698	The Natch'l Blues	1971	3.00	6.00	12.00
—Orange label					
❏ PC 9698	The Natch'l Blues	198?	2.00	4.00	8.00
—Reissue with new prefix					
❏ CG 30619 [(2)]	The Real Thing	198?	2.50	5.00	10.00
—Reissue with new prefix					
❏ G 30619 [(2)]	The Real Thing	1971	5.00	10.00	20.00
❏ C 30767	Happy to Be Like I Am	1971	3.00	6.00	12.00
❏ PC 30767	Happy to Be Like I Am	198?	2.00	4.00	8.00
—Budget-line reissue					
❏ KC 31605	Recycling the Blues & Other Related Stuff	1972	3.00	6.00	12.00
❏ PC 31605	Recycling the Blues & Other Related Stuff	198?	2.00	4.00	8.00
—Budget-line reissue					
❏ KC 32600	Oooh So Good 'N Blues	1973	3.00	6.00	12.00
❏ PC 32600	Oooh So Good 'N Blues	198?	2.00	4.00	8.00
—Budget-line reissue					
❏ KC 33051	Mo' Roots	1974	3.00	6.00	12.00
❏ PC 33051	Mo' Roots	198?	2.00	4.00	8.00
—Budget-line reissue					
❏ PC 33801	Music Keeps Me Together	1975	3.00	6.00	12.00
❏ PC 34103	Satisfied & Tickled Too	1976	3.00	6.00	12.00
❏ PC 34466	Anthology Volume 1	1977	3.00	6.00	12.00
❏ PC 36528	The Best of Taj Mahal	1981	2.50	5.00	10.00
❏ PC 36528	The Best of Taj Mahal	198?	2.00	4.00	8.00
—Budget-line reissue					

CRYSTAL CLEAR

Number	Title (A Side/B Side)	Yr	VG	VG+	NM
❏ 5011	Live and Direct	1980	6.25	12.50	25.00
—Direct-to-disc recording					

WARNER BROS.

Number	Title (A Side/B Side)	Yr	VG	VG+	NM
❏ BS 2994	Music Fuh Ya' (Musica Para Tu)	1977	2.50	5.00	10.00
❏ BS 3024	Brothers	1977	2.50	5.00	10.00
❏ BS 3094	Evolution (Recent)	1978	2.50	5.00	10.00

MAHAN, LARRY
WARNER BROS.

Number	Title (A Side/B Side)	Yr	VG	VG+	NM
❏ BS 2959	King of the Rodeo	1976	5.00	10.00	20.00

MAHAVISHNU ORCHESTRA
COLUMBIA

Number	Title (A Side/B Side)	Yr	VG	VG+	NM
❏ CQ 31996 [Q]	Birds of Fire	1973	5.00	10.00	20.00
❏ CQ 32766 [Q]	Between Nothingness and Eternity	1973	5.00	10.00	20.00

MAHOGANY RUSH
COLUMBIA

Number	Title (A Side/B Side)	Yr	VG	VG+	NM
❏ PC 34190	Mahogany Rush IV	1976	3.75	7.50	15.00
—Original with no bar code					
❏ PC 34190	Mahogany Rush IV	198?	2.00	4.00	8.00
—Reissue with bar code					
❏ PC 34677	World Anthem	1977	3.75	7.50	15.00
—Original with no bar code					
❏ PC 34677	World Anthem	198?	2.00	4.00	8.00
—Reissue with bar code					
❏ JC 35257	Frank Marino & Mahogany Rush Live	1978	3.75	7.50	15.00
❏ PC 35257	Frank Marino & Mahogany Rush Live	198?	2.00	4.00	8.00
—Budget-line reissue					
❏ JC 35753	Tales of the Unexpected	1979	3.75	7.50	15.00
❏ PC 35753	Tales of the Unexpected	198?	2.00	4.00	8.00
—Budget-line reissue					
❏ JC 36204	What's Next	1980	3.75	7.50	15.00
❏ PC 36204	What's Next	198?	2.00	4.00	8.00
—Budget-line reissue					

20TH CENTURY

Number	Title (A Side/B Side)	Yr	VG	VG+	NM
❏ T-451	Child of the Novelty	1974	6.25	12.50	25.00
❏ T-463	Maxoom	1975	6.25	12.50	25.00
❏ T-482	Strange Universe	1975	5.00	10.00	20.00

MAHONES, GILDO
PRESTIGE

Number	Title (A Side/B Side)	Yr	VG	VG+	NM
❏ PRLP-7339 [(2)M]	The Soulful Piano of Gildo Mahones	1964	7.50	15.00	30.00
❏ PRST-7339 [(2)S]	The Soulful Piano of Gildo Mahones	1964	10.00	20.00	40.00
❏ PRLP-16004 [M]	Shooting High	1964	10.00	20.00	40.00

MAIDEN, SIDNEY
BLUESVILLE

Number	Title (A Side/B Side)	Yr	VG	VG+	NM
❏ BVLP-1035 [M]	Trouble An' Blues	1961	20.00	40.00	80.00
—Blue label, silver print					
❏ BVLP-1035 [M]	Trouble An' Blues	1964	5.00	10.00	20.00
—Blue label, trident logo at right					

MAIN ATTRACTION, THE
TOWER

Number	Title (A Side/B Side)	Yr	VG	VG+	NM
❏ ST-5117 [S]	And Now...The Main Attraction	1968	6.25	12.50	25.00
❏ T-5117 [M]	And Now...The Main Attraction	1968	12.50	25.00	50.00

MAINER, J.E.
ARHOOLIE

Number	Title (A Side/B Side)	Yr	VG	VG+	NM
❏ F 5002	J.E. Mainer's Mountaineers	197?	3.00	6.00	12.00

BLUE JAY

Number	Title (A Side/B Side)	Yr	VG	VG+	NM
❏ 101	70th Happy Birthday	1968	5.00	10.00	20.00
❏ 102	Precious Memories	1968	5.00	10.00	20.00

KING

Number	Title (A Side/B Side)	Yr	VG	VG+	NM
❏ 666	Good Ole Mountain Music	197?	3.00	6.00	12.00
—Gusto reissue					
❏ 666 [M]	Good Ole Mountain Music	1960	25.00	50.00	100.00
❏ 765 [M]	Variety Album	1961	25.00	50.00	100.00

OLD HOMESTEAD

Number	Title (A Side/B Side)	Yr	VG	VG+	NM
❏ 146	J.E. Mainer at Home with Family and Friends, Vol. 1	197?	3.75	7.50	15.00

OLD TIMEY

Number	Title (A Side/B Side)	Yr	VG	VG+	NM
❏ 107	J.E. Mainer's Mountaineers, Vol. 2	197?	3.00	6.00	12.00

RURAL RHYTHM

Number	Title (A Side/B Side)	Yr	VG	VG+	NM
❏ RRJE-185	The Legendary J.E. Mainer and His Mountaineers	198?	3.00	6.00	12.00
❏ RRJE-191	More Old Time Mountain Music	198?	3.00	6.00	12.00
❏ RRJE-198	The Legendary J.E. Mainer, Vol. 3	198?	3.00	6.00	12.00
❏ RRJE-225	The Legendary J.E. Mainer, Vol. 7	198?	3.00	6.00	12.00
❏ RRJE-246	The Legendary J.E. Mainer, Vol. 16	198?	3.00	6.00	12.00
❏ RRJE-250	The Legendary J.E. Mainer, Vol. 20	198?	3.00	6.00	12.00

MAINER, WADE
KING

Number	Title (A Side/B Side)	Yr	VG	VG+	NM
❏ 769 [M]	Soulful Sacred Songs	1961	25.00	50.00	100.00

OLD HOMESTEAD

Number	Title (A Side/B Side)	Yr	VG	VG+	NM
❏ 4000 [(2)]	From the Maple to the Hill	1976	5.00	10.00	20.00
❏ 90001	Sacred Songs of Mother and Home	1971	3.75	7.50	15.00
❏ 90016	Sacred Songs Mountain Style	197?	3.75	7.50	15.00
❏ 90123	Old Time Songs	1980	3.75	7.50	15.00

MAINIERI, MIKE
ARGO

Number	Title (A Side/B Side)	Yr	VG	VG+	NM
❏ LP-706 [M]	Blues on the Other Side	1963	6.25	12.50	25.00
❏ LPS-706 [S]	Blues on the Other Side	1963	7.50	15.00	30.00

SOLID STATE

Number	Title (A Side/B Side)	Yr	VG	VG+	NM
❏ SS-18029	Insight	1968	5.00	10.00	20.00
❏ SS-18049	Journey Thru an Electric Tube	1969	5.00	10.00	20.00

Number	Title (A Side/B Side)	Yr	VG	VG+	NM

MAIZE, JOE
DECCA
DL 4555 [M]	Isle of Dreams	1965	5.00	10.00	20.00
DL 8590 [M]	Presenting Joe Maize and His Cordsmen	1958	7.50	15.00	30.00
DL 8817 [M]	Hawaiian Dreams	1959	5.00	10.00	20.00
DL 74555 [S]	Isle of Dreams	1965	6.25	12.50	25.00
DL 78817 [S]	Hawaiian Dreams	1959	6.25	12.50	25.00

MAJIC SHIP, THE
BEL AMI
| BA-711 | The Majic Ship | 1968 | 125.00 | 250.00 | 500.00 |

MAJORS, THE (1)
IMPERIAL
| LP-9222 [M] | Meet the Majors | 1963 | 37.50 | 75.00 | 150.00 |
| LP-12222 [S] | Meet the Majors | 1963 | 75.00 | 150.00 | 300.00 |

MAKEBA, MIRIAM
KAPP
| KL-1274 [M] | The Many Voices of Miriam Makeba | 1962 | 5.00 | 10.00 | 20.00 |
| KS-3274 [S] | The Many Voices of Miriam Makeba | 1962 | 6.25 | 12.50 | 25.00 |
MERCURY
MG-21082 [M]	The Magnificent Miriam Makeba	1966	3.00	6.00	12.00
MG-21095 [M]	All About Miriam	1967	3.00	6.00	12.00
SR-61082 [S]	The Magnificent Miriam Makeba	1966	3.75	7.50	15.00
SR-61095 [S]	All About Miriam	1967	3.75	7.50	15.00
MERCURY/URBAN AFRICA
| 838208-1 | Welela | 1989 | 3.00 | 6.00 | 12.00 |
RCA VICTOR
LPM-2267 [M]	Miriam Makeba	1960	5.00	10.00	20.00
LSP-2267 [S]	Miriam Makeba.	1960	6.25	12.50	25.00
LPM-2750 [M]	The World of Miriam Makeba.	1963	3.75	7.50	15.00
LSP-2750 [S]	The World of Miriam Makeba.	1963	5.00	10.00	20.00
LPM-2845 [M]	The Voice of Africa.	1964	3.75	7.50	15.00
LSP-2845 [S]	The Voice of Africa.	1964	5.00	10.00	20.00
LPM-3321 [M]	Makeba Sings.	1965	3.75	7.50	15.00
LSP-3321 [S]	Makeba Sings.	1965	5.00	10.00	20.00
LPM-3512 [M]	The Magic of Makeba.	1966	3.75	7.50	15.00
LSP-3512 [S]	The Magic of Makeba.	1966	5.00	10.00	20.00
LPM-3982 [M]	The Best of Miriam Makeba.	1968	6.25	12.50	25.00
LSP-3982 [S]	The Best of Miriam Makeba.	1968	3.00	6.00	12.00
REPRISE
R-6253 [M]	Miriam Makeba In Concert!	1967	3.75	7.50	15.00
RS-6253 [S]	Miriam Makeba In Concert!	1967	3.00	6.00	12.00
R-6274 [M]	Pata Pata	1967	3.75	7.50	15.00
RS-6274 [S]	Pata Pata	1967	3.00	6.00	12.00
RS-6310	Makeba!	1968	3.00	6.00	12.00
RS-6381	Keep Me in Mind	1970	3.00	6.00	12.00
WARNER BROS.
| 25673 | Sangoma | 1988 | 2.50 | 5.00 | 10.00 |

MAKEM, TOMMY
TRADITION
| TLP-1044 [M] | Songs of Tommy Makem | 1961 | 7.50 | 15.00 | 30.00 |
| TLPS-1044 [S] | Songs of Tommy Makem | 1961 | 10.00 | 20.00 | 40.00 |

MAKOWICZ, ADAM
SHEFFIELD LABS
| 21 | The Name Is Makowicz (ma-ko-vitch) | 1984 | 5.00 | 10.00 | 20.00 |
—Audiophile vinyl

MALACHI
VERVE
| V-5024 [M] | Holy Music | 1967 | 7.50 | 15.00 | 30.00 |
| V6-5024 [S] | Holy Music | 1967 | 10.00 | 20.00 | 40.00 |

MALCOLM X
DOUGLAS
SD 795 [M]	Malcolm X Talks to Young People	1968	7.50	15.00	30.00
SD 797	His Wit and Wisdom	196?	7.50	15.00	30.00
Z 30743 [M]	By Any Means Necessary	1971	7.50	15.00	30.00
PAUL WINLEY
| 135 | The Ballot or the Bullet | 197? | 5.00 | 10.00 | 20.00 |
RCA
| 66132 | Words from the Frontlines: Excerpts from the Great Speeches of Malcolm X | 1992 | 5.00 | 10.00 | 20.00 |
UPFRONT
| UPF-152 | Malcolm X Speaks to the People in Harlem | 197? | 3.75 | 7.50 | 15.00 |
WARNER BROS.
BS 2619	Malcolm X	1972	6.25	12.50	25.00
PRO-A-5943 [DJ]	Malcolm X Speaks	1992	5.00	10.00	20.00
PRO-A-5957 [DJ]	Music and Dialog from the Historic 1992 Documentary Film Malcolm X	1992	5.00	10.00	20.00

MALTBY, RICHARD
COLUMBIA
CL 1271 [M]	Swingin' Down the Lane	1959	5.00	10.00	20.00
CL 1341 [M]	Hello Young Lovers	1959	5.00	10.00	20.00
CS 8083 [S]	Swingin' Down the Lane	1959	6.25	12.50	25.00
CS 8151 [S]	Hello Young Lovers	1959	6.25	12.50	25.00
RCA CAMDEN
CAL-526 [M]	A Bow to the Big Name Bands	1959	5.00	10.00	20.00
CAL-600 [M]	Music from Mr. Lucky	1960	5.00	10.00	20.00
CAL-711 [M]	Most Requested	1961	5.00	10.00	20.00
ROULETTE
R-25129 [M]	Richard Maltby Swings for Dancers	1960	5.00	10.00	20.00
R-25148 [M]	Swing Folksongs	1961	5.00	10.00	20.00
SR-25148 [S]	Swing Folksongs	1961	6.25	12.50	25.00
R-25178 [M]	Brilliant Big Band Ballads and Blues	1962	5.00	10.00	20.00
SR-25178 [S]	Brilliant Big Band Ballads and Blues	1962	6.25	12.50	25.00

VIK
LX-1051 [M]	Hue-Fi Moods by Maltby	1957	7.50	15.00	30.00
LX-1068 [M]	Manhattan Bandstand	1957	7.50	15.00	30.00
LX-1071 [M]	Maltby with Strings Attached	1958	7.50	15.00	30.00
"X"
| LX-1038 [M] | Make Mine Maltby | 1956 | 7.50 | 15.00 | 30.00 |

MALVIN, ARTIE
WALDORF MUSIC HALL
| 33-149 [10] | Rock and Roll | 1955 | 30.00 | 60.00 | 120.00 |

MAMA CASS
See CASS ELLIOT.

MAMA LION
FAMILY PRODUCTIONS
| FPS-2702 | Mama Lion | 1972 | 5.00 | 10.00 | 20.00 |
| FPS-2713 | Give It Everything I've Got | 1973 | 5.00 | 10.00 | 20.00 |

MAMAS AND THE PAPAS, THE
ABC
| AC-30005 | The ABC Collection | 1976 | 3.75 | 7.50 | 15.00 |
ABC DUNHILL
DS-50006	If You Can Believe Your Eyes and Ears	1968	3.00	6.00	12.00
DS-50010	The Mamas and the Papas	1968	3.00	6.00	12.00
DS-50014	The Mamas and the Papas Deliver	1968	3.00	6.00	12.00
DS-50025	Farewell to the First Golden Era	1968	3.00	6.00	12.00
DS-50031	The Papas and the Mamas	1968	3.75	7.50	15.00
—The five LPs above are reissues of records originally without the ABC logo
DS-50038	Golden Era, Volume 2	1968	5.00	10.00	20.00
DS-50064	16 of Their Greatest Hits	1969	3.75	7.50	15.00
DS-50073 [(2)]	A Gathering of Flowers	1970	6.25	12.50	25.00
DSX-50100	Monterey International Pop Festival	1970	3.75	7.50	15.00
DSX-50106	People Like Us	1971	3.00	6.00	12.00
DSX-50145 [(2)]	20 Golden Hits	1973	5.00	10.00	20.00
DUNHILL
| D-50006 [M] | If You Can Believe Your Eyes and Ears | 1966 | 5.00 | 10.00 | 20.00 |
—With scroll over toilet
| D-50006 [M] | If You Can Believe Your Eyes and Ears | 1966 | 10.00 | 20.00 | 40.00 |
—Black cover with photo cropped to render toilet invisible
| D-50006 [M] | If You Can Believe Your Eyes and Ears | 1966 | 20.00 | 40.00 | 80.00 |
—With toilet completely visible in lower right
| DS-50006 [S] | If You Can Believe Your Eyes and Ears | 1966 | 6.25 | 12.50 | 25.00 |
—With scroll over toilet proclaiming "Includes California Dreamin' "
| DS-50006 [S] | If You Can Believe Your Eyes and Ears | 1966 | 6.25 | 12.50 | 25.00 |
—With scroll over toilet proclaiming "Includes California Dreamin'... Monday Monday... I Call Your Name"
| DS-50006 [S] | If You Can Believe Your Eyes and Ears | 1966 | 12.50 | 25.00 | 50.00 |
—Black cover with photo cropped to render toilet invisible
| DS-50006 [S] | If You Can Believe Your Eyes and Ears | 1966 | 25.00 | 50.00 | 100.00 |
—With toilet completely visible in lower right
D-50010 [M]	The Mamas and the Papas	1966	5.00	10.00	20.00
DS-50010 [S]	The Mamas and the Papas	1966	6.25	12.50	25.00
D-50014 [M]	The Mamas and the Papas Deliver	1967	5.00	10.00	20.00
DS-50014 [S]	The Mamas and the Papas Deliver	1967	6.25	12.50	25.00
D-50025 [M]	Farewell to the First Golden Era	1967	5.00	10.00	20.00
DS-50025 [S]	Farewell to the First Golden Era	1967	5.00	10.00	20.00
DS-50031	The Papas and the Mamas	1968	6.25	12.50	25.00
ST-90797 [S]	If You Can Believe Your Eyes and Ears	1966	12.50	25.00	50.00
—Capitol Record Club edition; known copies have scroll proclaiming "Includes California Dreamin'."
| T-90797 [M] | If You Can Believe Your Eyes and Ears | 1966 | 12.50 | 25.00 | 50.00 |
—Capitol Record Club edition; known copies have scroll proclaiming "Includes California Dreamin'."
| ST-90924 [S] | The Mamas and the Papas | 1966 | 10.00 | 20.00 | 40.00 |
—Capitol Record Club edition
| T-90924 [M] | The Mamas and the Papas | 1966 | 7.50 | 15.00 | 30.00 |
—Capitol Record Club edition
MCA
709	Farewell to the First Golden Era	1980	2.00	4.00	8.00
710	The Papas and the Mamas	1980	2.00	4.00	8.00
6019 [(2)]	The Best of the Mamas and the Papas	1986	3.00	6.00	12.00
37145	16 of Their Greatest Hits	1980	2.00	4.00	8.00
PICKWICK
| SPC-3352 | California Dreaming | 1972 | 3.00 | 6.00 | 12.00 |

MAN
PHILIPS
| PHS 600313 | Revelation | 1969 | 5.00 | 10.00 | 20.00 |
—As "Manpower"

MANCE, JUNIOR
ATLANTIC
| 1479 [M] | Harlem Lullaby | 1967 | 5.00 | 10.00 | 20.00 |
| 1496 [M] | I Believe to My Soul | 1968 | 6.25 | 12.50 | 25.00 |
CAPITOL
ST 2092 [S]	Get Ready, Set, Jump!	1964	6.25	12.50	25.00
T 2092 [M]	Get Ready, Set, Jump!	1964	5.00	10.00	20.00
ST 2218 [S]	Straight Ahead	1965	5.00	10.00	20.00
ST 2393 [S]	That's Where It Is	1965	5.00	10.00	20.00
JAZZLAND
JLP-30 [M]	The Soulful Piano of Junior Mance	1960	6.25	12.50	25.00
JLP-41 [M]	Junior Mance Trio at the Village Vanguard	1961	6.25	12.50	25.00
JLP-53 [M]	Big Chief!	1961	6.25	12.50	25.00
JLP-63 [M]	The Jazz Soul of Hollywood	1961	6.25	12.50	25.00
JLP-77 [M]	Happy Time	1962	6.25	12.50	25.00
JLP-930 [S]	The Soulful Piano of Junior Mance	1960	7.50	15.00	30.00
JLP-941 [S]	Junior Mance Trio at the Village Vanguard	1961	7.50	15.00	30.00
JLP-953 [S]	Big Chief!	1961	7.50	15.00	30.00
JLP-963 [S]	The Jazz Soul of Hollywood	1961	7.50	15.00	30.00
JLP-977 [S]	Happy Time	1962	7.50	15.00	30.00
RIVERSIDE
| RLP-447 [M] | Junior's Blues | 1963 | 6.25 | 12.50 | 25.00 |
| RS-9447 [S] | Junior's Blues | 1963 | 7.50 | 15.00 | 30.00 |

Number	Title (A Side/B Side)	Yr	VG	VG+	NM
VERVE					
❏ MGVS-6057 [S]	Junior	1960	7.50	15.00	30.00
❏ MGV-8319 [M]	Junior	1959	10.00	20.00	40.00
❏ V-8319 [M]	Junior	1961	5.00	10.00	20.00

MANCHESTER, MELISSA
ARISTA

Number	Title (A Side/B Side)	Yr	VG	VG+	NM
❏ AL 4006	Home to Myself	1975	2.50	5.00	10.00
—Reissue of Bell 1123					
❏ AL 4011	Bright Eyes	1975	2.50	5.00	10.00
—Reissue of Bell 1303					
❏ AL 4031	Melissa	1975	2.50	5.00	10.00
❏ AQ 4031 [Q]	Melissa	1975	3.75	7.50	15.00
❏ AL 4067	Better Days & Happy Endings	1976	2.50	5.00	10.00
❏ AQ 4067 [Q]	Better Days & Happy Endings	1976	3.75	7.50	15.00
❏ AL 4095	Help Is On the Way	1976	2.50	5.00	10.00
❏ AL 4136	Singin'	1977	2.50	5.00	10.00
❏ AB 4186	Don't Cry Out Loud	1978	2.50	5.00	10.00
❏ AL 8055	Melissa	1983	2.00	4.00	8.00
—Budget-line reissue of 4031					
❏ AL 8094	Emergency	1983	2.50	5.00	10.00
❏ AL 8293	Greatest Hits	198?	2.00	4.00	8.00
—Budget-line reissue of 9611					
❏ AL 8350	Hey Ricky	198?	2.00	4.00	8.00
—Budget-line reissue of 9574					
❏ AL 8373	Don't Cry Out Loud	198?	2.00	4.00	8.00
—Budget-line reissue of 4186					
❏ AL 9506	Melissa Manchester	1979	2.50	5.00	10.00
❏ AL 9533	For the Working Girl	1980	2.50	5.00	10.00
❏ AL 9574	Hey Ricky	1982	2.50	5.00	10.00
❏ AL 9611	Greatest Hits	1983	2.50	5.00	10.00
BELL					
❏ 1123	Home to Myself	1973	3.00	6.00	12.00
❏ 1303	Bright Eyes	1974	3.00	6.00	12.00
MCA					
❏ 5587	Mathematics	1985	2.50	5.00	10.00
MIKA					
❏ 841273-1	Tribute	1989	3.00	6.00	12.00
MOBILE FIDELITY					
❏ 1-028	Melissa	1980	5.00	10.00	20.00
—Audiophile vinyl					
NAUTILUS					
❏ NR-33	Don't Cry Out Loud	198?	10.00	20.00	40.00
—Audiophile vinyl					
PAIR					
❏ PDL2-1086 [(2)]	The Many Moods of Melissa Manchester	1986	3.00	6.00	12.00

MANCHESTERS, THE (1)
DIPLOMAT

Number	Title (A Side/B Side)	Yr	VG	VG+	NM
❏ D-2307 [M]	Beatlerama	1964	3.75	7.50	15.00
—No artist credited on label or cover					
❏ D-2307 [M]	Beatlerama	1964	3.75	7.50	15.00
—With artist credited					
❏ DS-2307 [S]	Beatlerama	1964	5.00	10.00	20.00
—No artist credited on label or cover					
❏ DS-2307 [S]	Beatlerama	1964	5.00	10.00	20.00
—With artist credited					
GUEST STAR					
❏ G-2307 [M]	Beatlerama	1964	3.75	7.50	15.00
❏ GS-2307 [S]	Beatlerama	1964	5.00	10.00	20.00

MANCINI, HENRY
AVCO EMBASSY

Number	Title (A Side/B Side)	Yr	VG	VG+	NM
❏ AVE 0110	Sunflower	1970	3.75	7.50	15.00
DECCA					
❏ DL 79185	Sometimes a Great Notion	1971	3.75	7.50	15.00
LIBERTY					
❏ LRP-3121 [M]	The Versatile Henry Mancini	1959	5.00	10.00	20.00
❏ LST-7121 [S]	The Versatile Henry Mancini	1959	7.50	15.00	30.00
❏ LT-51135	Trail of the Pink Panther	1982	2.50	5.00	10.00
MCA					
❏ 2085	The Great Waldo Pepper	1975	3.00	6.00	12.00
❏ 6222	The Glass Menagerie	1987	2.50	5.00	10.00
PAIR					
❏ PDL2-1092 [(2)]	The Mancini Collection (Film Music)	1986	3.00	6.00	12.00
PARAMOUNT					
❏ PAS-6000	The Molly Maguires	1970	5.00	10.00	20.00
RCA CAMDEN					
❏ ACL2-0293 [(2)]	Film Music	1973	3.00	6.00	12.00
❏ CAL-928 [M]	The Second Time Around and Others	1966	3.00	6.00	12.00
❏ CAS-928 [S]	The Second Time Around and Others	1966	3.00	6.00	12.00
❏ CAL-2158 [M]	Mancini Plays Mancini and Other Composers	1968	3.00	6.00	12.00
❏ CAS-2158 [S]	Mancini Plays Mancini and Other Composers	1968	2.50	5.00	10.00
❏ CAS-2510	Dream of You	1971	2.50	5.00	10.00
❏ CXS-9005 [(2)]	Mancini Magic	1971	3.00	6.00	12.00
❏ CXS-9034	Everybody's Favorite	1972	2.50	5.00	10.00
RCA VICTOR					
❏ APD1-0013 [Q]	Mancini Salutes Sousa	1973	4.50	9.00	18.00
❏ APL1-0013	Mancini Salutes Sousa	1972	3.00	6.00	12.00
❏ APD1-0098 [Q]	Brass, Ivory and Strings	1973	4.50	9.00	18.00
❏ APL1-0098	Brass, Ivory and Strings	1973	3.00	6.00	12.00
❏ PRM-175 [M]	Academy Award Songs, Volume Two	1965	3.75	7.50	15.00
—Made for the B.F. Goodrich tire company					
❏ PRS-175 [S]	Academy Award Songs, Volume Two	1965	5.00	10.00	20.00
—Made for the B.F. Goodrich tire company					
❏ ABL1-0231	Visions of Eight	1973	3.00	6.00	12.00
❏ AFL1-0270	Country Gentlemen	1977	2.50	5.00	10.00
—Reissue with new prefix					
❏ APD1-0270 [Q]	Country Gentlemen	1973	4.50	9.00	18.00

Number	Title (A Side/B Side)	Yr	VG	VG+	NM
❏ APL1-0270	Country Gentlemen	1973	3.00	6.00	12.00
❏ APL1-0271	Oklahoma Crude	1973	3.00	6.00	12.00
❏ AFL1-0672	Hangin' Out	1977	2.50	5.00	10.00
—Reissue with new prefix					
❏ APD1-0672 [Q]	Hangin' Out	1974	4.50	9.00	18.00
❏ CPL1-0672	Hangin' Out	1974	3.00	6.00	12.00
❏ ABD1-0968 [Q]	Return of the Pink Panther	1975	4.50	9.00	18.00
❏ ABL1-0968	Return of the Pink Panther	1975	3.00	6.00	12.00
❏ ANL1-0980	Pure Gold	1975	2.50	5.00	10.00
❏ AFL1-1025	Symphonic Soul	1977	2.00	4.00	8.00
—Reissue with new prefix					
❏ APD1-1025 [Q]	Symphonic Soul	1975	4.50	9.00	18.00
❏ APL1-1025	Symphonic Soul	1975	2.50	5.00	10.00
❏ APL1-1379	Concert of Film Music	1975	2.50	5.00	10.00
❏ CPL1-1843	A Legendary Performer	1976	2.50	5.00	10.00
❏ APL1-1896	Cop Show Themes	1976	2.50	5.00	10.00
❏ ANL1-1928 [S]	A Merry Mancini Christmas	1976	2.00	4.00	8.00
—Reissue with new number and new front cover					
❏ LPM-1956 [M]	The Music from Peter Gunn	1959	5.00	10.00	20.00
—Reissue cover is green/blue with huge "Peter Gunn" in center					
❏ LPM-1956 [M]	The Music from Peter Gunn	1959	10.00	20.00	40.00
—Original cover is a "block" design with "Peter Gunn" at top					
❏ LSP-1956 [S]	The Music from Peter Gunn	1959	6.25	12.50	25.00
—Reissue cover is green/blue with huge "Peter Gunn" in center					
❏ LSP-1956 [S]	The Music from Peter Gunn	1959	12.50	25.00	50.00
—Original cover is a "block" design with "Peter Gunn" at top					
❏ LPM-2040 [M]	More Music from Peter Gunn	1959	5.00	10.00	20.00
❏ LSP-2040 [S]	More Music from Peter Gunn	1959	6.25	12.50	25.00
❏ LPM-2101 [M]	The Mancini Touch	1959	5.00	10.00	20.00
❏ LSP-2101 [S]	The Mancini Touch	1959	6.25	12.50	25.00
❏ LPM-2147 [M]	The Blues and the Beat	1960	6.25	12.50	25.00
❏ LSP-2147 [S]	The Blues and the Beat	1960	7.50	15.00	30.00
❏ LPM-2198 [M]	Music from Mr. Lucky	1960	5.00	10.00	20.00
❏ LSP-2198 [S]	Music from Mr. Lucky	1960	6.25	12.50	25.00
❏ LPM-2258 [M]	Combo!	1960	5.00	10.00	20.00
❏ LSP-2258 [S]	Combo!	1960	6.25	12.50	25.00
❏ APL1-2290	Mancini's Angels	1977	2.50	5.00	10.00
❏ LPM-2360 [M]	Mr. Lucky Goes Latin	1961	5.00	10.00	20.00
❏ LSP-2360 [S]	Mr. Lucky Goes Latin	1961	6.25	12.50	25.00
❏ LPM-2362 [M]	Breakfast at Tiffany's	1961	5.00	10.00	20.00
❏ LSP-2362 [S]	Breakfast at Tiffany's	1961	6.25	12.50	25.00
❏ LPM-2442 [M]	Experiment in Terror	1962	5.00	10.00	20.00
—Reissue cover has two mannequins					
❏ LPM-2442 [M]	Experiment in Terror	1962	6.25	12.50	25.00
—Original cover has Lee Remick under attack					
❏ LSP-2442 [S]	Experiment in Terror	1962	6.25	12.50	25.00
—Reissue cover has two mannequins					
❏ LSP-2442 [S]	Experiment in Terror	1962	10.00	20.00	40.00
—Original cover has Lee Remick under attack					
❏ ANL1-2484	Mancini Plays the Theme from Love Story	1977	2.50	5.00	10.00
—Reissue of LSP-4466					
❏ LPM-2559 [M]	Hatari!	1962	5.00	10.00	20.00
❏ LSP-2559 [S]	Hatari!	1962	6.25	12.50	25.00
❏ LPM-2604 [M]	Our Man in Hollywood	1963	3.75	7.50	15.00
❏ LSP-2604 [S]	Our Man in Hollywood	1963	5.00	10.00	20.00
❏ LPM-2692 [M]	Uniquely Mancini	1963	3.75	7.50	15.00
❏ LSP-2692 [S]	Uniquely Mancini	1963	5.00	10.00	20.00
❏ AFL1-2693	The Best of Mancini	1977	2.50	5.00	10.00
—Reissue with new prefix					
❏ LPM-2693 [M]	The Best of Mancini	1964	3.00	6.00	12.00
❏ LSP-2693 [S]	The Best of Mancini	1964	3.75	7.50	15.00
❏ LPM-2755 [M]	Charade	1963	3.75	7.50	15.00
❏ LSP-2755 [S]	Charade	1963	5.00	10.00	20.00
❏ LPM-2795 [M]	The Pink Panther	1964	3.75	7.50	15.00
❏ LSP-2795 [S]	The Pink Panther	1964	5.00	10.00	20.00
❏ LPM-2897 [M]	The Concert Sound of Henry Mancini	1964	3.00	6.00	12.00
❏ LSP-2897 [S]	The Concert Sound of Henry Mancini	1964	3.75	7.50	15.00
❏ LPM-2990 [M]	Dear Heart and Other Songs About Love	1965	3.00	6.00	12.00
❏ LSP-2990 [S]	Dear Heart and Other Songs About Love	1965	3.75	7.50	15.00
❏ AQL1-3052	The Theme Scene	1978	2.50	5.00	10.00
❏ AQL1-3347	The Best of Mancini, Volume 3	1979	2.50	5.00	10.00
❏ LPM-3356 [M]	The Latin Sound of Henry Mancini	1965	3.00	6.00	12.00
❏ LSP-3356 [S]	The Latin Sound of Henry Mancini	1965	3.75	7.50	15.00
❏ LPM-3402 [M]	The Great Race	1965	3.00	6.00	12.00
❏ LSP-3402 [S]	The Great Race	1965	3.75	7.50	15.00
❏ AFL1-3557	The Best of Mancini, Volume 2	1977	2.50	5.00	10.00
—Reissue with new prefix					
❏ LPM-3557 [M]	The Best of Mancini, Volume 2	1966	3.00	6.00	12.00
❏ LSP-3557 [S]	The Best of Mancini, Volume 2	1966	3.75	7.50	15.00
❏ LPM-3612 [M]	A Merry Mancini Christmas	1966	2.50	5.00	10.00
—Original front cover has a photo of Henry Mancini and family					
❏ LSP-3612 [S]	A Merry Mancini Christmas	1966	3.00	6.00	12.00
—Same as above, but in stereo					
❏ LPM-3623 [M]	Arabesque	1966	3.00	6.00	12.00
❏ LSP-3623 [S]	Arabesque	1966	3.75	7.50	15.00
❏ LPM-3648 [M]	What Did You Do in the War, Daddy?	1966	3.00	6.00	12.00
❏ LSP-3648 [S]	What Did You Do in the War, Daddy?	1966	3.75	7.50	15.00
❏ AYL1-3667	Pure Gold	1980	2.00	4.00	8.00
—"Best Buy Series" reissue					
❏ AYL1-3668	Mancini Country	1980	2.00	4.00	8.00
—"Best Buy Series" reissue					
❏ LPM-3694 [M]	Mancini '67	1967	3.75	7.50	15.00
❏ LSP-3694 [S]	Mancini '67	1967	3.75	7.50	15.00
❏ AFL1-3713	Music of Hawaii	1977	2.50	5.00	10.00
—Reissue with new prefix					
❏ LPM-3713 [M]	Music of Hawaii	1966	3.00	6.00	12.00
❏ LSP-3713 [S]	Music of Hawaii	1966	3.75	7.50	15.00
❏ AYL1-3756	Brass on Ivory	1980	2.00	4.00	8.00
—"Best Buy Series" reissue					
❏ AYL1-3757	A Warm Shade of Ivory	1980	2.00	4.00	8.00
—"Best Buy Series" reissue					
❏ LPM-3802 [M]	Two for the Road	1967	5.00	10.00	20.00

Number	Title (A Side/B Side)	Yr	VG	VG+	NM
☐ LSP-3802 [S]	Two for the Road	1967	3.75	7.50	15.00
☐ AYL1-3822	The Best of Mancini	1981	2.00	4.00	8.00
—"Best Buy Series" reissue					
☐ LPM-3840 [M]	Gunn	1967	5.00	10.00	20.00
☐ LSP-3840 [S]	Gunn	1967	7.50	15.00	30.00
☐ AYL1-3877	Music of Hawaii	1981	2.00	4.00	8.00
—"Best Buy Series" reissue					
☐ LPM-3887 [M]	Encore! More of the Concert Sound of Henry Mancini	1967	5.00	10.00	20.00
☐ LSP-3887 [S]	Encore! More of the Concert Sound of Henry Mancini	1967	3.75	7.50	15.00
☐ LPM-3943 [M]	The Mancini Sound	1968	5.00	10.00	20.00
☐ LSP-3943 [S]	The Mancini Sound	1968	3.75	7.50	15.00
☐ AYL1-3954	Country Gentlemen	1981	2.00	4.00	8.00
—"Best Buy Series" reissue					
☐ LPM-3997 [M]	Party	1968	6.25	12.50	25.00
☐ LSP-3997 [S]	Party	1968	3.75	7.50	15.00
☐ LSP-4049	The Big Latin Band of Henry Mancini	1968	3.75	7.50	15.00
☐ AFL1-4140	A Warm Shade of Ivory	1977	2.00	4.00	8.00
—Reissue with new prefix					
☐ LSP-4140	A Warm Shade of Ivory	1969	3.75	7.50	15.00
☐ LSP-4239	Six Hours Past Sunset	1969	3.75	7.50	15.00
☐ AFL1-4307	Mancini Country	1977	2.50	5.00	10.00
—Reissue with new prefix					
☐ LSP-4307	Mancini Country	1970	3.75	7.50	15.00
☐ LSP-4350	Theme from "Z" and Other Film Music	1970	3.75	7.50	15.00
☐ LSP-4466	Mancini Plays the Theme from Love Story	1971	3.75	7.50	15.00
☐ AFL1-4542	Mancini Concert	1977	2.50	5.00	10.00
—Reissue with new prefix					
☐ LSP-4542	Mancini Concert	1971	3.75	7.50	15.00
☐ AFL1-4629	Brass on Ivory	1977	2.00	4.00	8.00
—Reissue with new prefix					
☐ LSP-4629	Brass on Ivory	1972	3.00	6.00	12.00
☐ LSP-4630	Big Screen — Little Screen	1972	3.75	7.50	15.00
☐ LSP-4689	The Mancini Generation	1972	3.00	6.00	12.00
☐ LPM-6013 [(2)M]	The Academy Award Songs	1966	3.75	7.50	15.00
☐ LSP-6013 [(2)S]	The Academy Award Songs	1966	5.00	10.00	20.00
☐ VPS-6029 [(2)]	This Is Henry Mancini	1970	5.00	10.00	20.00
☐ VPS-6053 [(2)]	This Is Henry Mancini, Volume 2	1972	5.00	10.00	20.00
SUNSET					
☐ SUM-1105 [M]	Sounds and Voices	1966	3.00	6.00	12.00
☐ SUS-5105 [S]	Sounds and Voices	1966	3.00	6.00	12.00
UNITED ARTISTS					
☐ UA-LA694-G	The Pink Panther Strikes Again	1976	3.75	7.50	15.00
☐ UAS-5210	The Hawaiians	1970	3.00	6.00	12.00
☐ SW-93297	The Hawaiians	1970	5.00	10.00	20.00
—Capitol Record Club edition					
WARNER BROS.					
☐ W 1312 [M]	March Step in Hi-Fi	1959	5.00	10.00	20.00
☐ WS 1312 [S]	March Step in Stereo	1959	7.50	15.00	30.00
☐ W 1465 [M]	Sousa's Greatest Marches	1962	3.75	7.50	15.00
☐ WS 1465 [S]	Sousa's Greatest Marches	1962	5.00	10.00	20.00
☐ W 1491 [M]	Marches	1963	3.75	7.50	15.00
☐ WS 1491 [S]	Marches	1963	5.00	10.00	20.00
☐ BS 2700	The Thief Who Came to Dinner	1973	3.75	7.50	15.00
☐ BSK 3399	10	1979	3.75	7.50	15.00

MANCUSO, GUS

FANTASY

Number	Title (A Side/B Side)	Yr	VG	VG+	NM
☐ 3223 [M]	Introducing Gus Mancuso	1956	10.00	20.00	40.00
—Black vinyl					
☐ 3223 [M]	Introducing Gus Mancuso	1956	15.00	30.00	60.00
—Red vinyl					
☐ 3282 [M]	Music from New Faces	1958	5.00	10.00	20.00
—Black vinyl					
☐ 3282 [M]	Music from New Faces	1958	10.00	20.00	40.00
—Red vinyl					
☐ 8025 [S]	Music from New Faces	1960	7.50	15.00	30.00
—Blue vinyl					

MANDEL, HARVEY

EDITIONS EG

Number	Title (A Side/B Side)	Yr	VG	VG+	NM
☐ CAROL-1535-1	Cristo Redentor	198?	2.50	5.00	10.00
—Reissue of Philips 600-281					
JANUS					
☐ JLS-3017	Baby Batter	1970	3.00	6.00	12.00
☐ JLS-3037	The Snake	1972	3.00	6.00	12.00
☐ JLS-3047	Shangrenade	1973	3.00	6.00	12.00
☐ JSX-3067	Feel the Sound of Harvey Mandel	1974	3.00	6.00	12.00
☐ JXS-7014	The Best of Harvey Mandel	1975	3.00	6.00	12.00
OVATION					
☐ OV-1415	Get Off in Chicago	1971	3.75	7.50	15.00
PHILIPS					
☐ PHS 600281	Cristo Redentor	1969	6.25	12.50	25.00
☐ PHS 600306	Righteous	1969	6.25	12.50	25.00
☐ PHS 600325	Games Guitars Play	1970	6.25	12.50	25.00

MANDO AND THE CHILI PEPPERS

GOLDEN CREST

Number	Title (A Side/B Side)	Yr	VG	VG+	NM
☐ CR-3023 [M]	On the Road with Rock and Roll	1957	125.00	250.00	500.00

MANDRAKE MEMORIAL

POPPY

Number	Title (A Side/B Side)	Yr	VG	VG+	NM
☐ PYS 40002	Mandrake Memorial	1968	10.00	20.00	40.00
☐ PYS 40003	Medium	1969	10.00	20.00	40.00
☐ PYS 40006	Puzzle	1970	10.00	20.00	40.00

MANDRELL, BARBARA

ABC

Number	Title (A Side/B Side)	Yr	VG	VG+	NM
☐ AB-1088	Moods	1978	3.00	6.00	12.00
☐ AB-1119	The Best of Barbara Mandrell	1979	3.00	6.00	12.00

ABC DOT

Number	Title (A Side/B Side)	Yr	VG	VG+	NM
☐ DOSD-2045	This Is Barbara Mandrell	1976	3.00	6.00	12.00
☐ DOSD-2067	Midnight Angel	1976	3.00	6.00	12.00
☐ DO-2076	Lovers, Friends and Strangers	1977	3.00	6.00	12.00
☐ DO-2098	Love's Ups and Downs	1977	3.00	6.00	12.00
CAPITOL					
☐ C1-90416	I'll Be Your Jukebox Tonight	1988	2.50	5.00	10.00
☐ C1-91977	Morning Sun	1990	3.00	6.00	12.00
COLUMBIA					
☐ C 30967	Treat Him Right	1971	5.00	10.00	20.00
☐ KC 32743	The Midnight Oil	1973	3.75	7.50	15.00
☐ PC 32743	The Midnight Oil	198?	2.00	4.00	8.00
—Budget-line reissue					
☐ KC 32959	This Time I Almost Made It	1974	3.75	7.50	15.00
☐ PC 34876	The Best of Barbara Mandrell	1977	3.00	6.00	12.00
—No bar code on cover					
☐ PC 34876	The Best of Barbara Mandrell	198?	2.00	4.00	8.00
—Reissue with bar code on cover					
☐ FC 37437	Looking Back	1982	2.50	5.00	10.00
☐ PC 37437	Looking Back	198?	2.00	4.00	8.00
—Budget-line reissue					
EMI AMERICA					
☐ ET-46956	Sure Feels Good	1987	2.50	5.00	10.00
MCA					
☐ 641	Midnight Angel	198?	2.00	4.00	8.00
—Reissue of ABC Dot 2067					
☐ 672	This Is Barbara Mandrell	198?	2.00	4.00	8.00
—Reissue of ABC Dot 2045					
☐ 673	Lovers, Friends and Strangers	198?	2.00	4.00	8.00
—Reissue of ABC Dot 2076					
☐ 674	Love's Ups and Downs	198?	2.00	4.00	8.00
—Reissue of ABC Dot 2098					
☐ 3165	Just for the Record	1979	2.50	5.00	10.00
☐ 3280	Moods	1980	2.00	4.00	8.00
—Reissue of ABC 1088					
☐ 5136	Love Is Fair	1980	2.50	5.00	10.00
☐ 5243	Barbara Mandrell Live	1981	2.50	5.00	10.00
☐ 5295	…In Black and White	1982	2.50	5.00	10.00
☐ 5330	He Set My Life to Music	1982	2.50	5.00	10.00
☐ 5377	Spun Gold	1983	2.50	5.00	10.00
☐ 5474	Clean Cut	1984	2.50	5.00	10.00
☐ 5519	Christmas at Our House	1984	3.00	6.00	12.00
☐ 5566	Greatest Hits	1985	2.50	5.00	10.00
☐ 5619	Get to the Heart	1985	2.50	5.00	10.00
☐ 37173	Just for the Record	198?	2.00	4.00	8.00
—Budget-line reissue					
☐ 37202	Moods	198?	—	3.00	6.00
—Budget-line reissue					
☐ 37224	Barbara Mandrell Live	198?	2.00	4.00	8.00
—Budget-line reissue					
PAIR					
☐ PDL1-1079 [(2)]	The Best of Barbara Mandrell	1986	3.00	6.00	12.00

MANGIONE, CHUCK

JAZZLAND

Number	Title (A Side/B Side)	Yr	VG	VG+	NM
☐ JLP-84 [M]	Recuerdo	1962	10.00	20.00	40.00
☐ JLP-984 [S]	Recuerdo	1962	12.50	25.00	50.00
MOBILE FIDELITY					
☐ 1-068	Feels So Good	1981	6.25	12.50	25.00
—Audiophile vinyl					

MANGIONE, GAP

GRC

Number	Title (A Side/B Side)	Yr	VG	VG+	NM
☐ 9001	Diana in the Autumn Wind	1968	6.25	12.50	25.00

MANHATTAN JAZZ ALL-STARS, THE

COLUMBIA

Number	Title (A Side/B Side)	Yr	VG	VG+	NM
☐ CL 1426 [M]	Swinging Guys and Dolls	1960	6.25	12.50	25.00
☐ CS 8223 [S]	Swinging Guys and Dolls	1960	7.50	15.00	30.00

MANHATTAN JAZZ SEPTETTE, THE

CORAL

Number	Title (A Side/B Side)	Yr	VG	VG+	NM
☐ CRL 57090 [M]	The Manhattan Jazz Septette	1956	20.00	40.00	80.00

MANHATTAN TRANSFER

MOBILE FIDELITY

Number	Title (A Side/B Side)	Yr	VG	VG+	NM
☐ 1-022	Manhattan Transfer Live	1979	5.00	10.00	20.00
—Audiophile vinyl					
☐ 1-199	Extensions	1994	6.25	12.50	25.00
—Audiophile vinyl					

MANHATTANS, THE (1)

CARNIVAL

Number	Title (A Side/B Side)	Yr	VG	VG+	NM
☐ CMLP-201 [M]	Dedicated to You	1966	62.50	125.00	250.00
☐ CSLP-201 [S]	Dedicated to You	1966	125.00	250.00	500.00
☐ CMLP-202 [M]	For You and Yours	1967	37.50	75.00	150.00
☐ CSLP-202 [S]	For You and Yours	1967	75.00	150.00	300.00
COLLECTABLES					
☐ COL-5135	Dedicated to You: Golden Carnival Classics, Part One	198?	2.50	5.00	10.00
☐ COL-5136	For You and Yours: Golden Carnival Classics, Part Two	198?	2.50	5.00	10.00
COLUMBIA					
☐ KC 32444	There's No Me Without You	1973	3.75	7.50	15.00
☐ PC 32444	There's No Me Without You	198?	2.00	4.00	8.00
—Budget-line reissue					
☐ KC 33064	That's How Much I Love You	1975	3.75	7.50	15.00
☐ PC 33820	The Manhattans	1976	3.00	6.00	12.00
—No bar code on back cover					
☐ PC 33820	The Manhattans	198?	2.00	4.00	8.00
—With bar code on back cover					

Number	Title (A Side/B Side)	Yr	VG	VG+	NM
❏ PC 34450	It Feels So Good	1977	3.00	6.00	12.00

—No bar code on back cover

Number	Title (A Side/B Side)	Yr	VG	VG+	NM
❏ PC 34450	It Feels So Good	198?	2.00	4.00	8.00

—With bar code on back cover

Number	Title (A Side/B Side)	Yr	VG	VG+	NM
❏ PCQ 34450 [Q]	It Feels So Good	1977	5.00	10.00	20.00
❏ JC 35252	There's No Good in Goodbye	1978	3.00	6.00	12.00
❏ JC 35693	Love Talk	1979	3.00	6.00	12.00
❏ PC 35693	After Midnight	198?	2.00	4.00	8.00

—Budget-line reissue

Number	Title (A Side/B Side)	Yr	VG	VG+	NM
❏ JC 36411	After Midnight	1980	3.00	6.00	12.00
❏ JC 36861	Manhattans Greatest Hits	1980	3.00	6.00	12.00
❏ FC 37156	Black Tie	1981	2.50	5.00	10.00
❏ PC 37156	Black Tie	198?	2.00	4.00	8.00

—Budget-line reissue

Number	Title (A Side/B Side)	Yr	VG	VG+	NM
❏ FC 38600	Forever By Your Side	1983	2.50	5.00	10.00
❏ FC 39277	Too Hot to Stop It	1985	2.50	5.00	10.00

DELUXE

Number	Title	Yr	VG	VG+	NM
❏ 12000	With These Hands	1971	6.25	12.50	25.00
❏ 12004	A Million to One	1972	6.25	12.50	25.00

SOLID SMOKE

Number	Title	Yr	VG	VG+	NM
❏ 8007	Follow Your Heart	1981	2.50	5.00	10.00

VALLEY VUE

Number	Title	Yr	VG	VG+	NM
❏ D1-72946	Sweet Talk	1989	3.00	6.00	12.00

MANILLA ROAD
ROADSTER

Number	Title	Yr	VG	VG+	NM
❏ MR 1001	Invasion	1980	25.00	50.00	100.00
❏ MR 1002	Metal	1982	25.00	50.00	100.00
❏ MR 1003	Crystal Logic	1983	12.50	25.00	50.00

MANILOW, BARRY
ARISTA

Number	Title	Yr	VG	VG+	NM
❏ AB 2500 [EP]	Oh, Julie!	1982	5.00	10.00	20.00
❏ AB 4007	Barry Manilow I	1977	2.00	4.00	8.00

—Reissue of AL 4007 with new prefix

Number	Title	Yr	VG	VG+	NM
❏ AL 4007	Barry Manilow I	1975	2.50	5.00	10.00

—Revised version of Bell 1129 with new cover; "Could It Be Magic" especially is noticeably different between the Bell and Arista versions

Number	Title	Yr	VG	VG+	NM
❏ AB 4016	Barry Manilow II	1977	2.00	4.00	8.00

—Reissue of AL 4016 with new prefix

Number	Title	Yr	VG	VG+	NM
❏ AL 4016	Barry Manilow II	1975	2.50	5.00	10.00

—Reissue of Bell 1314

Number	Title	Yr	VG	VG+	NM
❏ AQ 4016 [Q]	Barry Manilow II	1975	3.75	7.50	15.00
❏ AB 4060	Tryin' to Get the Feeling	1977	2.00	4.00	8.00

—Reissue of AL 4060 with new prefix

Number	Title	Yr	VG	VG+	NM
❏ AL 4060	Tryin' to Get the Feeling	1975	2.50	5.00	10.00
❏ AQ 4060 [Q]	Tryin' to Get the Feeling	1975	3.75	7.50	15.00
❏ AB 4090	This One's for You	1977	2.00	4.00	8.00

—Reissue of AL 4090 with new prefix

Number	Title	Yr	VG	VG+	NM
❏ AL 4090	This One's for You	1976	2.50	5.00	10.00
❏ AB 4164	Even Now	1978	2.00	4.00	8.00
❏ AL8-8003	Here Comes the Night	198?	—	3.00	6.00

—Reissue of 9610

Number	Title	Yr	VG	VG+	NM
❏ AL13-8039 [(2)]	Greatest Hits	1983	2.50	5.00	10.00
❏ AL5-8046	One Voice	198?	—	3.00	6.00

—Reissue of 9505

Number	Title	Yr	VG	VG+	NM
❏ AL13-8049 [(2)]	Barry Manilow/Live	1983	2.50	5.00	10.00
❏ AL5-8052	Even Now	198?	—	3.00	6.00

—Reissue of 8322

Number	Title	Yr	VG	VG+	NM
❏ AL5-8070	Tryin' to Get the Feeling	198?	—	3.00	6.00

—Reissue of 8336

Number	Title	Yr	VG	VG+	NM
❏ AL5-8085	Barry Manilow II	198?	—	3.00	6.00

—Reissue of 8370

Number	Title	Yr	VG	VG+	NM
❏ AL8-8102	Barry Manilow/Greatest Hits, Vol. II	1983	2.00	4.00	8.00
❏ AL8-8117	Barry	198?	—	3.00	6.00

—Reissue of 9537

Number	Title	Yr	VG	VG+	NM
❏ AL8-8123	If I Should Love Again	198?	—	3.00	6.00

—Reissue of 9573

Number	Title	Yr	VG	VG+	NM
❏ AL5-8153	Barry Manilow I	198?	—	3.00	6.00

—Reissue of 8372

Number	Title	Yr	VG	VG+	NM
❏ AL5-8160	This One's for You	198?	—	3.00	6.00

—Reissue of 8331

Number	Title	Yr	VG	VG+	NM
❏ AL8-8254	2:00 A.M. Paradise Café	1984	2.00	4.00	8.00
❏ AL9-8274	The Manilow Collection — 20 Classic Hits	1985	2.00	4.00	8.00
❏ AL8-8291	Barry Manilow/Greatest Hits, Vol. II	1985	—	3.00	6.00
❏ AL8-8322	Even Now	1985	—	3.00	6.00
❏ AL8-8331	This One's for You	1985	—	3.00	6.00
❏ AL8-8336	Tryin' to Get the Feeling	1985	—	3.00	6.00
❏ AL8-8370	Barry Manilow II	1985	—	3.00	6.00
❏ AL8-8372	Barry Manilow I	1985	—	3.00	6.00
❏ AL 8500 [(2)]	Barry Manilow/Live	1977	3.00	6.00	12.00
❏ AL-8527	Swing Street	1987	2.00	4.00	8.00
❏ AL-8570	Barry Manilow	1989	2.00	4.00	8.00
❏ AL-8598	Greatest Hits, Vol. 1	1989	2.50	5.00	10.00
❏ AL-8599	Greatest Hits, Vol. 2	1989	2.50	5.00	10.00
❏ AL-8600	Greatest Hits, Vol. 3	1989	2.50	5.00	10.00
❏ A2L 8601 [(2)]	Greatest Hits	1978	3.00	6.00	12.00
❏ A2L 8601 [(2)PD]	Greatest Hits	1979	10.00	20.00	40.00

—Entire contents on two picture discs (yes, it has the same number as the regular issue)

Number	Title	Yr	VG	VG+	NM
❏ AL-8638 [(2)]	Live on Broadway	1990	5.00	10.00	20.00
❏ AL-8644	Because It's Christmas	1990	3.75	7.50	15.00
❏ AL 9505	One Voice	1979	2.00	4.00	8.00
❏ AL 9537	Barry	1980	2.00	4.00	8.00
❏ AL 9573	If I Should Love Again	1981	2.00	4.00	8.00
❏ AL-9610	Here Comes the Night	1982	2.00	4.00	8.00
❏ NU 9740	Manilow Magic	1982	3.00	6.00	12.00

—Manufactured by K-Tel

BELL

Number	Title	Yr	VG	VG+	NM
❏ 1129	Barry Manilow	1973	6.25	12.50	25.00
❏ 1314	Barry Manilow II	1974	3.75	7.50	15.00

MOBILE FIDELITY

Number	Title	Yr	VG	VG+	NM
❏ 1-097	Barry Manilow I	1981	5.00	10.00	20.00

—Audiophile vinyl

RCA VICTOR

Number	Title	Yr	VG	VG+	NM
❏ AFL1-7044	Manilow	1985	2.00	4.00	8.00

MANN, BARRY
ABC-PARAMOUNT

Number	Title	Yr	VG	VG+	NM
❏ 399 [M]	Who Put the Bomp	1963	30.00	60.00	120.00
❏ S-399 [S]	Who Put the Bomp	1963	75.00	150.00	300.00

CASABLANCA

Number	Title	Yr	VG	VG+	NM
❏ NBLP 7226	Barry Mann	1980	2.50	5.00	10.00

NEW DESIGN

Number	Title	Yr	VG	VG+	NM
❏ Z 30876	Lay It All Out	1971	3.00	6.00	12.00

RCA VICTOR

Number	Title	Yr	VG	VG+	NM
❏ APL1-0860	Survivor	1975	3.00	6.00	12.00
❏ DJL1-1162 [DJ]	Flo and Eddie Interview Barry Mann	1975	12.50	25.00	50.00

MANN, CARL
PHILLIPS INT'L.

Number	Title	Yr	VG	VG+	NM
❏ PLP-1960 [M]	Like Mann	1960	150.00	300.00	600.00

MANN, HERBIE
ATLANTIC

Number	Title	Yr	VG	VG+	NM
❏ SD 1343 [S]	The Common Ground	1960	5.00	10.00	20.00
❏ SD 1371 [S]	The Family of Mann	1961	5.00	10.00	20.00
❏ SD 1380 [S]	Herbie Mann at the Village Gate	1962	5.00	10.00	20.00
❏ SD 1384 [S]	Right Now	1962	5.00	10.00	20.00
❏ SD 1397 [S]	Do the Bossa Nova with Herbie Mann	1962	5.00	10.00	20.00
❏ SD 1407 [S]	Herbie Mann Returns to the Village Gate	1963	5.00	10.00	20.00
❏ SD 1413 [S]	Herbie Mann Live at Newport	1963	5.00	10.00	20.00
❏ SD 1422 [S]	Latin Fever	1964	5.00	10.00	20.00
❏ SD 1426 [S]	Nirvana	1964	5.00	10.00	20.00
❏ SD 1433 [S]	My Kinda Groove	1965	5.00	10.00	20.00
❏ SD 1437 [S]	The Roar of the Greasepaint, The Smell of the Crowd	1965	5.00	10.00	20.00
❏ SD 1445 [S]	Standing Ovation at Newport	1965	5.00	10.00	20.00
❏ SD 1454 [S]	Herbie Mann Today	1966	5.00	10.00	20.00
❏ SD 1462 [S]	Monday Night at the Village Gate	1966	5.00	10.00	20.00
❏ SD 1464 [S]	Our Mann Flute	1966	5.00	10.00	20.00
❏ 1471 [M]	New Mann at Newport	1967	5.00	10.00	20.00
❏ 1475 [M]	Impressions of the Middle East	1967	5.00	10.00	20.00
❏ 1483 [M]	The Beat Goes On	1967	5.00	10.00	20.00
❏ 1490 [M]	The Herbie Mann String Album	1968	6.25	12.50	25.00
❏ QD 1632 [Q]	Hold On, I'm Comin'	1973	5.00	10.00	20.00
❏ 8141 [M]	Mann and a Woman	1967	5.00	10.00	20.00

BETHLEHEM

Number	Title	Yr	VG	VG+	NM
❏ BCP-24 [M]	Flamingo, My Goodness — Four Flutes, Vol. 2	1955	12.50	25.00	50.00
❏ BCP-40 [M]	The Herbie Mann-Sam Most Quintet	1956	12.50	25.00	50.00
❏ BCP-58 [M]	Herbie Mann Plays	1956	12.50	25.00	50.00
❏ BCP-63 [M]	Love and the Weather	1956	12.50	25.00	50.00
❏ BCP-1018 [10]	East Coast Jazz 4	1954	25.00	50.00	100.00
❏ BCP-6011	Early Mann	1976	2.50	5.00	10.00

—Reissue of older material; distributed by Caytronics

Number	Title	Yr	VG	VG+	NM
❏ BCP-6020 [M]	The Mann with the Most	1960	10.00	20.00	40.00
❏ BCP-6067 [M]	The Epitome of Jazz	1963	7.50	15.00	30.00

COLUMBIA

Number	Title	Yr	VG	VG+	NM
❏ CS 9188 [S]	Latin Mann	1965	5.00	10.00	20.00

EPIC

Number	Title	Yr	VG	VG+	NM
❏ LN 3395 [M]	Salute to the Flute	1957	15.00	30.00	60.00
❏ LN 3499 [M]	Herbie Mann with the Ilcken Trio	1958	15.00	30.00	60.00

JAZZLAND

Number	Title	Yr	VG	VG+	NM
❏ JLP-5 [M]	Herbie Mann Quintet	1960	7.50	15.00	30.00

—Reissue of Riverside 245

NEW JAZZ

Number	Title	Yr	VG	VG+	NM
❏ NJLP-8211 [M]	Just Walkin'	1958	12.50	25.00	50.00

—Purple label

Number	Title	Yr	VG	VG+	NM
❏ NJLP-8211 [M]	Just Walkin'	1964	6.25	12.50	25.00

—Blue label with trident logo

PRESTIGE

Number	Title	Yr	VG	VG+	NM
❏ PRLP-7101 [M]	Flute Souffle	1957	20.00	40.00	80.00
❏ PRLP-7124 [M]	Flute Flight	1957	20.00	40.00	80.00
❏ PRLP-7136 [M]	Mann in the Morning	1958	20.00	40.00	80.00

RIVERSIDE

Number	Title	Yr	VG	VG+	NM
❏ RLP 12-234 [M]	Sultry Serenade	1957	15.00	30.00	60.00

—Blue on white label

Number	Title	Yr	VG	VG+	NM
❏ RLP 12-234 [M]	Sultry Serenade	1958	10.00	20.00	40.00

—Blue label with reel and microphone logo

Number	Title	Yr	VG	VG+	NM
❏ RLP 12-245 [M]	Great Ideas of Western Mann	1957	10.00	20.00	40.00

SAVOY

Number	Title	Yr	VG	VG+	NM
❏ MG-12102 [M]	Flute Suite	1957	12.50	25.00	50.00
❏ MG-12107 [M]	Mann Alone	1957	12.50	25.00	50.00
❏ MG-12108 [M]	Yardbird Suite	1957	12.50	25.00	50.00

SURREY

Number	Title	Yr	VG	VG+	NM
❏ SS-1015 [S]	Big Band	1965	5.00	10.00	20.00

UNITED ARTISTS

Number	Title	Yr	VG	VG+	NM
❏ UAL-4042 [M]	African Suite	1959	7.50	15.00	30.00
❏ UAS-5042 [S]	African Suite	1959	10.00	20.00	40.00
❏ UAJ-14009 [M]	Brasil, Bossa Nova and Blue	1962	7.50	15.00	30.00
❏ UAJ-14022 [M]	St. Thomas	1962	7.50	15.00	30.00
❏ UAJS-15009 [S]	Brasil, Bossa Nova and Blue	1962	10.00	20.00	40.00
❏ UAJS-15022 [S]	St. Thomas	1962	10.00	20.00	40.00

VERVE

Number	Title	Yr	VG	VG+	NM
❏ MGVS-6074 [S]	Flautista! — Herbie Mann Plays Afro-Cuban Jazz	1960	7.50	15.00	30.00
❏ MGV-8247 [M]	The Magic Flute of Herbie Mann	1958	10.00	20.00	40.00
❏ V-8247 [M]	The Magic Flute of Herbie Mann	1961	5.00	10.00	20.00
❏ MGV-8336 [M]	Flautista! — Herbie Mann Plays Afro-Cuban Jazz	1959	10.00	20.00	40.00

Number	Title (A Side/B Side)	Yr	VG	VG+	NM
❑ V-8336 [M]	Flautista! — Herbie Mann Plays Afro-Cuban Jazz	1961	5.00	10.00	20.00
❑ MGV-8392 [M]	Flute, Brass, Vibes and Percussion	1960	7.50	15.00	30.00
❑ V-8392 [M]	Flute, Brass, Vibes and Percussion	1961	5.00	10.00	20.00
❑ V-8527 [M]	The Sound of Mann	1963	5.00	10.00	20.00

MANN, HERBIE, AND BUDDY COLLETTE
INTERLUDE

Number	Title (A Side/B Side)	Yr	VG	VG+	NM
❑ MO-503 [M]	Flute Fraternity	1959	10.00	20.00	40.00
—Reissue of Mode 114					
❑ ST-1103 [S]	Flute Fraternity	1959	7.50	15.00	30.00
MODE					
❑ LP-114 [M]	Flute Fraternity	1957	17.50	35.00	70.00

MANN, HERBIE, AND JOAO GILBERTO
ATLANTIC

Number	Title (A Side/B Side)	Yr	VG	VG+	NM
❑ SD 8105 [S]	Herbie Mann and Joao Gilberto with Antonio Carlos Jobim	1965	5.00	10.00	20.00

MANN, HERBIE, AND MACHITO
ROULETTE

Number	Title (A Side/B Side)	Yr	VG	VG+	NM
❑ SR-52122 [S]	Afro-Jazziac	1963	5.00	10.00	20.00

MANN, JOHNNY, SINGERS
EPIC

Number	Title (A Side/B Side)	Yr	VG	VG+	NM
❑ KE 31954	Stand Up and Cheer!	1973	3.00	6.00	12.00
LIBERTY					
❑ LRP-3134 [M]	Alma Mater	1959	3.75	7.50	15.00
❑ LRP-3149 [M]	Roar Along with the Singing Twenties	1960	3.75	7.50	15.00
❑ LRP-3156 [M]	Swing Along with the Singing Thirties	1960	3.75	7.50	15.00
❑ LRP-3198 [M]	Ballads of the King	1961	3.75	7.50	15.00
❑ LRP-3217 [M]	Ballads of the King, Volume 2	1961	3.75	7.50	15.00
❑ LRP-3253 [M]	Golden Folk Song Hits	1963	3.00	6.00	12.00
❑ LRP-3296 [M]	Golden Folk Song Hits, Volume 2	1963	3.00	6.00	12.00
❑ LRP-3355 [M]	Golden Folk Song Hits, Volume 3	1964	3.00	6.00	12.00
❑ LRP-3387 [M]	Invisible Tears	1964	3.00	6.00	12.00
❑ LRP-3391 [M]	The Ballad Sound (Beatle Songs)	1964	3.75	7.50	15.00
❑ LRP-3411 [M]	If I Loved You	1965	3.00	6.00	12.00
❑ LRP-3436 [M]	I'll Remember You	1965	3.00	6.00	12.00
❑ LRP-3447 [M]	Daydream	1966	3.00	6.00	12.00
❑ LRP-3522 [M]	We Wish You a Merry Christmas	1967	3.75	7.50	15.00
❑ LRP-3523 [M]	We Can Fly! Up-Up and Away	1967	3.00	6.00	12.00
❑ LST-7134 [S]	Alma Mater	1959	5.00	10.00	20.00
❑ LST-7149 [S]	Roar Along with the Singing Twenties	1960	5.00	10.00	20.00
❑ LST-7156 [S]	Swing Along with the Singing Thirties	1960	5.00	10.00	20.00
❑ LST-7198 [S]	Ballads of the King	1961	5.00	10.00	20.00
❑ LST-7217 [S]	Ballads of the King, Volume 2	1961	5.00	10.00	20.00
❑ LST-7253 [S]	Golden Folk Song Hits	1963	3.75	7.50	15.00
❑ LST-7296 [S]	Golden Folk Song Hits, Volume 2	1963	3.75	7.50	15.00
❑ LST-7355 [S]	Golden Folk Song Hits, Volume 3	1964	3.75	7.50	15.00
❑ LST-7387 [S]	Invisible Tears	1964	3.75	7.50	15.00
❑ LST-7391 [S]	The Ballad Sound (Beatle Songs)	1964	5.00	10.00	20.00
❑ LST-7411 [S]	If I Loved You	1965	3.75	7.50	15.00
❑ LST-7426 [S]	I'll Remember You	1965	3.75	7.50	15.00
❑ LST-7447 [S]	Daydream	1966	3.75	7.50	15.00
❑ LST-7522 [S]	We Wish You a Merry Christmas	1967	3.75	7.50	15.00
❑ LST-7523 [S]	We Can Fly! Up-Up and Away	1967	3.75	7.50	15.00
❑ LST-7629 [S]	Golden	1969	3.00	6.00	12.00
❑ LMM-13017 [M]	The Great Bands with Great Voices Swing the Great Voices of the Great Bands	1962	3.75	7.50	15.00
❑ LSS-14017 [S]	The Great Bands with Great Voices Swing the Great Voices of the Great Bands	1962	5.00	10.00	20.00
SUNSET					
❑ SUM-1115 [M]	The Flowing Voices of the Johnny Mann Singers	196?	2.50	5.00	10.00
❑ SUS-5115 [S]	The Flowing Voices of the Johnny Mann Singers	196?	3.00	6.00	12.00
❑ SUS-5196	Heart Full of Song	1968	3.00	6.00	12.00
❑ SUS-5231	Country Style	1969	3.00	6.00	12.00
❑ SUS-5288	At Our Best	1970	3.00	6.00	12.00
UNITED ARTISTS					
❑ UXS-87 [(2)]	The Johnny Mann Singers Superpak	1972	3.75	7.50	15.00

MANN, MANFRED
ASCOT

Number	Title (A Side/B Side)	Yr	VG	VG+	NM
❑ AM-13015 [M]	The Manfred Mann Album	1964	10.00	20.00	40.00
❑ AM-13018 [M]	The Five Faces of Manfred Mann	1965	10.00	20.00	40.00
❑ AM-13021 [M]	My Little Red Book of Winners	1965	10.00	20.00	40.00
❑ AM-13024 [M]	Mann Made	1966	10.00	20.00	40.00
❑ AS-16015 [P]	The Manfred Mann Album	1964	12.50	25.00	50.00
❑ AS-16018 [P]	The Five Faces of Manfred Mann	1965	12.50	25.00	50.00
❑ AS-16021 [S]	My Little Red Book of Winners	1965	12.50	25.00	50.00
❑ AS-16024 [S]	Mann Made	1966	12.50	25.00	50.00
CAPITOL					
❑ SM-11688	The Best of Manfred Mann	1977	2.50	5.00	10.00
❑ SN-16073	The Best of Manfred Mann	1980	2.00	4.00	8.00
JANUS					
❑ JXS-3064	The Best of Manfred Mann	1974	3.00	6.00	12.00
MERCURY					
❑ SR-61168	The Mighty Quinn	1968	6.25	12.50	25.00
POLYDOR					
❑ 24-4013	Chapter Three	1970	3.75	7.50	15.00
UNITED ARTISTS					
❑ 94 [DJ]	Manfred Mann Interview	1966	50.00	100.00	200.00
—Promotional album in plain white jacket					
❑ UAL 3549 [M]	Pretty Flamingo	1966	7.50	15.00	30.00
❑ UAL 3551 [M]	Manfred Mann's Greatest Hits	1966	7.50	15.00	30.00
❑ UAS 6549 [S]	Pretty Flamingo	1966	10.00	20.00	40.00
❑ UAS 6551 [P]	Manfred Mann's Greatest Hits	1966	10.00	20.00	40.00
—"Do Wah Diddy Diddy," "Sha La La," "I Got You Babe" and "Satisfaction" are rechanneled.					

MANN, REV. COLUMBUS
TAMLA

Number	Title (A Side/B Side)	Yr	VG	VG+	NM
❑ T-227 [M]	They Shall Be Mine	1962	2000.	3000.	4000.
WINGATE					
❑ 701 [M]	He Satisfies Me	196?	300.00	600.00	900.00

MANN, SHADOW
TOMORROW

Number	Title (A Side/B Side)	Yr	VG	VG+	NM
❑ TPS-69001	Come Live with Me	1974	15.00	30.00	60.00

MANNA, CHARLIE
DECCA

Number	Title (A Side/B Side)	Yr	VG	VG+	NM
❑ DL 4159 [M]	Manna Overboard!!	1961	6.25	12.50	25.00
❑ DL 4213 [M]	Manna Live!!	1962	6.25	12.50	25.00
❑ DL 74159 [R]	Manna Overboard!!	1961	3.75	7.50	15.00
❑ DL 74213 [R]	Manna Live!!	1962	3.75	7.50	15.00
VERVE					
❑ V-15051 [M]	The Rise and Fall of the Great Society	1966	3.00	6.00	12.00
❑ V6-15051 [S]	The Rise and Fall of the Great Society	1966	3.75	7.50	15.00

MANNE, SHELLY
ATLANTIC

Number	Title (A Side/B Side)	Yr	VG	VG+	NM
❑ 1487 [M]	Jazz Gunn	1967	5.00	10.00	20.00
❑ 8157 [M]	Daktari	1968	6.25	12.50	25.00
CAPITOL					
❑ ST 2173 [S]	"My Fair Lady" with Un-Original Cast	1964	5.00	10.00	20.00
❑ ST 2313 [S]	Manne, That's Gershwin	1965	5.00	10.00	20.00
CONTEMPORARY					
❑ C-2503 [10]	Shelly Manne and His Men	1953	37.50	75.00	150.00
❑ C-2511 [10]	Shelly Manne and His Men, Volume 2	1954	37.50	75.00	150.00
❑ C-2516 [10]	The Three	1954	37.50	75.00	150.00
❑ C-2518 [10]	The Two	1954	37.50	75.00	150.00
❑ C-3507 [M]	The West Coast Sound	1955	15.00	30.00	60.00
❑ C-3516 [M]	Swinging Sounds, Vol. 4	1956	15.00	30.00	60.00
❑ C-3519 [M]	More Swinging Sounds, Vol. 5	1957	15.00	30.00	60.00
❑ C-3525 [M]	Shelly Manne and His Friends	1957	12.50	25.00	50.00
❑ C-3527 [M]	Modern Jazz Performance of Songs from "My Fair Lady"	1957	12.50	25.00	50.00
❑ C-3533 [M]	Li'l Abner	1957	12.50	25.00	50.00
❑ C-3536 [M]	Concerto for Clarinet and Combo	1957	12.50	25.00	50.00
❑ C-3557 [M]	The Gambit	1958	12.50	25.00	50.00
❑ C-3559 [M]	Bells Are Ringing	1958	10.00	20.00	40.00
❑ C-3560 [M]	Shelly Manne Plays "Peter Gunn"	1958	12.50	25.00	50.00
❑ M-3566 [M]	Son of Gunn	1959	10.00	20.00	40.00
❑ M-3577 [M]	Shelly Manne and His Men at the Black Hawk, Vol. 1	1960	10.00	20.00	40.00
❑ M-3578 [M]	Shelly Manne and His Men at the Black Hawk, Vol. 2	1960	10.00	20.00	40.00
❑ M-3579 [M]	Shelly Manne and His Men at the Black Hawk, Vol. 3	1960	10.00	20.00	40.00
❑ M-3580 [M]	Shelly Manne and His Men at the Black Hawk, Vol. 4	1960	10.00	20.00	40.00
❑ M-3584 [M]	The Three and The Two	1960	7.50	15.00	30.00
❑ M-3593/4 [(2)M]	Live! Shelly Manne and His Men at the Manne-Hole	1961	10.00	20.00	40.00
❑ M-3599 [M]	Checkmate	1961	6.25	12.50	25.00
❑ M-3609 [M]	My Son, the Jazz Drummer!	1962	6.25	12.50	25.00
❑ M-3624 [M]	Outside	1966	6.25	12.50	25.00
❑ M-5006 [M]	Sounds Unheard Of	1962	7.50	15.00	30.00
❑ S-7025 [S]	Shelly Manne Plays "Peter Gunn"	1959	10.00	20.00	40.00
❑ S-7519 [S]	Swinging Sounds in Stereo	1959	12.50	25.00	50.00
❑ S-7527 [S]	Modern Jazz Performance of Songs from "My Fair Lady"	1959	10.00	20.00	40.00
❑ S-7533 [S]	Li'l Abner	1959	10.00	20.00	40.00
❑ S-7557 [S]	The Gambit	1959	10.00	20.00	40.00
❑ S-7559 [S]	Bells Are Ringing	1959	7.50	15.00	30.00
❑ S-7566 [S]	Son of Gunn	1959	7.50	15.00	30.00
❑ S-7577 [S]	Shelly Manne and His Men at the Black Hawk, Vol. 1	1960	7.50	15.00	30.00
❑ S-7578 [S]	Shelly Manne and His Men at the Black Hawk, Vol. 2	1960	7.50	15.00	30.00
❑ S-7579 [S]	Shelly Manne and His Men at the Black Hawk, Vol. 3	1960	7.50	15.00	30.00
❑ S-7580 [S]	Shelly Manne and His Men at the Black Hawk, Vol. 4	1960	7.50	15.00	30.00
❑ S-7593/4 [(2)S]	Live! Shelly Manne and His Men at the Manne-Hole	1961	12.50	25.00	50.00
❑ S-7599 [S]	Checkmate	1961	7.50	15.00	30.00
❑ S-7609 [S]	My Son, the Jazz Drummer!	1962	7.50	15.00	30.00
❑ S-7624 [S]	Outside	1966	7.50	15.00	30.00
❑ S-9006 [S]	Sounds Unheard Of	1962	10.00	20.00	40.00
DEE GEE					
❑ 1003 [10]	Here's That Manne	1952	75.00	150.00	300.00
IMPULSE!					
❑ A-20 [M]	2 3 4	1962	6.25	12.50	25.00
❑ AS-20 [S]	2 3 4	1962	7.50	15.00	30.00
STEREO RECORDS					
❑ S-7002 [S]	Modern Jazz Performance of Songs from "My Fair Lady"	1958	12.50	25.00	50.00
❑ S-7007 [S]	Swinging Sounds in Stereo	1958	15.00	30.00	60.00
❑ S-7019 [S]	Li'l Abner	1958	12.50	25.00	50.00
❑ S-7025 [S]	Shelly Manne Plays "Peter Gunn"	1958	12.50	25.00	50.00
❑ S-7030 [S]	The Gambit	1958	12.50	25.00	50.00

MANNE, SHELLY/BILL RUSSO
SAVOY

Number	Title (A Side/B Side)	Yr	VG	VG+	NM
❑ MG-12045 [M]	Deep Purple	1955	12.50	25.00	50.00

MANNING, TERRY
ENTERPRISE

Number	Title (A Side/B Side)	Yr	VG	VG+	NM
❑ ENS-1008	Home Sweet Home	1969	10.00	20.00	40.00

Number	Title (A Side/B Side)	Yr	VG	VG+	NM
MANONE, WINGY					
DECCA					
☐ DL 8473 [M]	Trumpet on the Wing	1957	10.00	20.00	40.00
IMPERIAL					
☐ LP-12190 [S]	Wingy Manone on the Jazzband Bus	1962	5.00	10.00	20.00
RCA VICTOR					
☐ LPV-563 [M]	Wingy Manone, Volume 1	1969	5.00	10.00	20.00
"X"					
☐ LVA-3014 [10]	Wingy Manone, Vol. 1	1954	12.50	25.00	50.00
MANPOWER					
See MAN.					
MANSFIELD, JAYNE					
MGM					
☐ E-4202 [M]	Shakespeare, Tchaikovsky and Me	1964	10.00	20.00	40.00
☐ SE-4202 [S]	Shakespeare, Tchaikovsky and Me	1964	15.00	30.00	60.00
20TH CENTURY					
☐ FOX-3049 [M]	Jayne Mansfield Busts Up Las Vegas	1961	50.00	100.00	200.00
MANSON, CHARLES					
AWARENESS					
☐ 08903-1056	Lie: The Love and Terror Cult	1987	5.00	10.00	20.00
☐ LP-2144	Lie: The Love and Terror Cult	197?	10.00	20.00	40.00
ESP-DISK'					
☐ 2003	Lie: The Love and Terror Cult	1970	50.00	100.00	200.00
MANTLE, MICKEY					
RCA VICTOR					
☐ LPM-1704 [M]	My Favorite Hits	1958	100.00	200.00	400.00
MANTLER, MICHAEL					
WATT					
☐ 2	No Answer	197?	5.00	10.00	20.00
☐ 3	13 & 3/4	197?	5.00	10.00	20.00
☐ 4	Hapless Child	197?	5.00	10.00	20.00
☐ 5	Silence	197?	5.00	10.00	20.00
MANTOVANI					
BAINBRIDGE					
☐ BT-6277	Mantovani's Italia	1988	2.00	4.00	8.00
☐ 8001 [(2)]	The Magic of Mantovani: Live at the Royal Festival Hall	1982	3.00	6.00	12.00
FLEETWOOD					
☐ FMS 1019	90 Minutes with Mantovani	1978	3.00	6.00	12.00
—Side 1: Great Songs of Christmas (reissue of London recordings); Side 2: Great Songs for All Seasons					
HOLIDAY					
☐ HDY 1928	Holy Night	1981	2.50	5.00	10.00
LONDON					
☐ SS 1 [S]	Mantovani Stereo Showcase	1959	5.00	10.00	20.00
☐ PS 106 [S]	Gems Forever	1959	5.00	10.00	20.00
☐ PS 112 [S]	Music from the Films	1959	3.75	7.50	15.00
☐ PS 118 [S]	Strauss Waltzes	1959	5.00	10.00	20.00
☐ PS 119 [S]	Waltz Encores	1959	5.00	10.00	20.00
☐ PS 124 [S]	Film Encores	1959	3.75	7.50	15.00
☐ PS 125 [S]	Song Hits from Theatreland	1959	3.75	7.50	15.00
☐ PS 133 [S]	Concert Encores	1959	5.00	10.00	20.00
☐ PS 142 [S]	Christmas Carols	1959	5.00	10.00	20.00
—Originals have blue back cover, "Stereophonic" on upper left front cover and dark blue "FFSS" labels					
☐ PS 142 [S]	Christmas Carols	196?	3.75	7.50	15.00
—Reissue with white back cover					
☐ PS 147 [S]	Continental Encores	1959	5.00	10.00	20.00
☐ PS 165 [S]	Film Encores, Vol. 2.	1959	5.00	10.00	20.00
☐ PS 165 [S]	The Music of Victor Herbert and Sigmund Romberg.	1959	5.00	10.00	20.00
☐ PS 165/6 [(2)S]	All-American Showcase.	1959	6.25	12.50	25.00
☐ PS 166 [S]	The Music of Irving Berlin and Rudolf Friml.	1959	5.00	10.00	20.00
☐ PS 182 [S]	The American Scene.	1960	3.75	7.50	15.00
☐ PS 193 [S]	Songs to Remember.	1960	3.75	7.50	15.00
☐ PS 202 [S]	Operetta Memories.	1960	3.75	7.50	15.00
☐ PS 224 [S]	Mantovani Plays Music from Exodus and Other Great Themes.	1960	3.75	7.50	15.00
☐ PS 232 [S]	Italia Mia.	1961	3.75	7.50	15.00
☐ PS 242 [S]	Themes from Broadway (Carnival).	1961	3.75	7.50	15.00
☐ PS 245 [S]	Songs of Praise.	1961	3.00	6.00	12.00
☐ PS 248 [S]	American Waltzes.	1962	3.00	6.00	12.00
☐ PS 249 [S]	Moon River and Other Great Film Themes.	1962	3.00	6.00	12.00
☐ PS 269 [S]	Classical Encores.	1963	3.00	6.00	12.00
☐ PS 270 [S]	Stop the World—I Want to Get Off/Oliver.	1962	3.00	6.00	12.00
☐ PS 280 [S]	The World's Great Love Songs.	1963	3.00	6.00	12.00
☐ PS 295 [S]	Latin Rendezvous.	1963	3.00	6.00	12.00
☐ PS 328 [S]	Mantovani/Manhattan.	1963	3.00	6.00	12.00
☐ PS 338 [S]	Christmas Greetings from Mantovani.	1963	3.75	7.50	15.00
☐ PS 360 [S]	Folk Songs Around the World.	1964	3.00	6.00	12.00
☐ PS 392 [S]	The Incomparable Mantovani.	1964	3.00	6.00	12.00
☐ PS 419 [S]	The Mantovani Sound — Big Hits from Broadway and Hollywood.	1965	3.00	6.00	12.00
☐ PS 422 [S]	Mantovani Ole.	1965	3.00	6.00	12.00
☐ PS 448 [S]	Mantovani Magic.	1966	3.00	6.00	12.00
☐ PS 474 [S]	Mr. Music...Mantovani.	1966	3.00	6.00	12.00
☐ PS 483 [S]	Mantovani's Golden Hits.	1967	3.00	6.00	12.00
☐ PS 516 [S]	Mantovani/Hollywood.	1967	3.00	6.00	12.00
☐ PS 526 [S]	The Mantovani Touch.	1968	3.00	6.00	12.00
☐ PS 532 [S]	Mantovani/Tango.	1968	3.00	6.00	12.00
☐ PS 542 [S]	Mantovani...Memories.	1968	3.00	6.00	12.00
☐ PS 548 [S]	The Mantovani Scene.	1969	3.00	6.00	12.00
☐ PS 565 [S]	The World of Mantovani.	1969	3.00	6.00	12.00

Number	Title (A Side/B Side)	Yr	VG	VG+	NM
☐ LL 570 [M]	Greensleeves (A Selection of Favorite Waltzes).	1952	5.00	10.00	20.00
☐ PS 570	Greensleeves	1970	3.00	6.00	12.00
☐ PS 572 [S]	Mantovani Today	1970	3.00	6.00	12.00
☐ PS 578 [S]	Mantovani In Concert	1970	3.00	6.00	12.00
☐ XPS 585/6 [(2)S]	From Monty with Love	1971	3.75	7.50	15.00
☐ XPS 598 [S]	To Lovers Everywhere U.S.A.	1971	3.00	6.00	12.00
☐ XPS 610 [S]	Annunzio Paolo Mantovani (25th Anniversary)	1972	3.00	6.00	12.00
☐ LL 685 [M]	Strauss Waltzes	1953	5.00	10.00	20.00
☐ BP 720/1 [(2)]	Christmas Favorites	19??	3.75	7.50	15.00
☐ LL 766 [M]	An Enchanted Evening with Mantovani	1953	5.00	10.00	20.00
☐ LL 768 [M]	Mantovani Plays Tangos	1953	5.00	10.00	20.00
☐ XPS 900	Gypsy Soul	1972	2.50	5.00	10.00
☐ XPS 902	An Evening with Mantovani	1973	2.50	5.00	10.00
☐ XPS 906	All-Time Greatest Hits, Volume 1	1973	2.50	5.00	10.00
☐ APS 907	Musical Moments	1974	2.50	5.00	10.00
☐ BP 910/1 [(2)]	Romantic Hits	197?	3.00	6.00	12.00
☐ LL 913 [M]	Christmas Carols	1953	3.75	7.50	15.00
—Original recordings in mono					
☐ LL 913 [M]	Christmas Carols	1959	3.00	6.00	12.00
—Mono versions of stereo re-recordings					
☐ XPS 913	The Greatest Gift Is Love	197?	2.50	5.00	10.00
☐ XPS 914	More Golden Hits	197?	2.50	5.00	10.00
☐ XPS 915	American Encores	1976	2.50	5.00	10.00
☐ XPS 917	Strictly Mantovani	1977	2.50	5.00	10.00
☐ PS 921	Favorite Melodies from Opera	1978	2.50	5.00	10.00
☐ LL 979 [M]	Romantic Melodies	1954	5.00	10.00	20.00
☐ LL 1094 [M]	Waltz Time	1954	5.00	10.00	20.00
☐ LL 1150 [M]	The Music of Rudolf Frimi	1955	5.00	10.00	20.00
☐ LL 1219 [M]	Song Hits from Theatreland	1955	5.00	10.00	20.00
☐ LL 1259 [M]	Lonely Ballerina (Musical Modes)	1956	5.00	10.00	20.00
☐ LL 1262 [M]	Gershwin: Concerto	1955	5.00	10.00	20.00
☐ LL 1262 [M]	Gershwin: Rhapsody in Blue	1955	5.00	10.00	20.00
☐ LL 1331 [M]	Operatic Arias	1955	5.00	10.00	20.00
☐ LL 1452 [M]	Waltzes of Irving Berlin	1956	5.00	10.00	20.00
☐ LL 1502 [M]	Candlelight	195?	3.75	7.50	15.00
☐ LL 1513 [M]	Music from the Films	1956	5.00	10.00	20.00
☐ LL 1525 [M]	Music from the Ballet	1956	5.00	10.00	20.00
☐ LL 1700 [M]	Film Encores	1957	5.00	10.00	20.00
☐ LL 1748 [M]	The World's Favorite Love Songs	1957	5.00	10.00	20.00
☐ LL 3004 [M]	Concert Encores	1958	3.75	7.50	15.00
☐ LL 3032 [M]	Gems Forever	1958	3.75	7.50	15.00
☐ LL 3095 [M]	Continental Encores	1959	3.75	7.50	15.00
☐ LL 3117 [M]	Film Encores, Vol. 2	1959	3.75	7.50	15.00
☐ LL 3122 [M]	The Music of Victor Herbert and Sigmund Romberg	1959	3.75	7.50	15.00
☐ LL 3122/3 [(2)M]	All-American Showcase	1959	5.00	10.00	20.00
☐ LL 3123 [M]	The Music of Irving Berlin and Rudolf Friml	1959	3.75	7.50	15.00
☐ LL 3136 [M]	The American Scene	1960	3.00	6.00	12.00
☐ LL 3149 [M]	Songs to Remember	1960	3.00	6.00	12.00
☐ LL 3181 [M]	Operetta Memories	1960	3.00	6.00	12.00
☐ LL 3231 [M]	Mantovani Plays Music from Exodus and Other Great Themes	1960	3.00	6.00	12.00
☐ LL 3239 [M]	Italia Mia	1961	3.00	6.00	12.00
☐ LL 3250 [M]	Themes from Broadway (Carnival)	1961	3.00	6.00	12.00
☐ LL 3251 [M]	Songs of Praise	1961	2.50	5.00	10.00
☐ LL 3260 [M]	American Waltzes	1962	2.50	5.00	10.00
☐ LL 3261 [M]	Moon River and Other Great Film Themes	1962	2.50	5.00	10.00
☐ LL 3269 [M]	Classical Encores	1963	2.50	5.00	10.00
☐ LL 3270 [M]	Stop the World—I Want to Get Off/Oliver	1962	2.50	5.00	10.00
☐ LL 3280 [M]	The World's Great Love Songs	1963	2.50	5.00	10.00
☐ LL 3295 [M]	Latin Rendezvous	1963	2.50	5.00	10.00
☐ LL 3328 [M]	Mantovani/Manhattan	1963	2.50	5.00	10.00
☐ LL 3338 [M]	Christmas Greetings from Mantovani	1963	3.00	6.00	12.00
☐ LL 3360 [M]	Folk Songs Around the World	1964	2.50	5.00	10.00
☐ LL 3392 [M]	The Incomparable Mantovani	1964	2.50	5.00	10.00
☐ LL 3419 [M]	The Mantovani Sound — Big Hits from Broadway and Hollywood	1965	2.50	5.00	10.00
☐ LL 3422 [M]	Mantovani Ole	1965	2.50	5.00	10.00
☐ LL 3448 [M]	Mantovani Magic	1966	2.50	5.00	10.00
☐ LL 3474 [M]	Mr. Music...Mantovani	1966	2.50	5.00	10.00
☐ LL 3483 [M]	Mantovani's Golden Hits	1967	3.00	6.00	12.00
☐ LL 3516 [M]	Mantovani/Hollywood	1967	3.00	6.00	12.00
☐ LL 3526 [M]	The Mantovani Touch	1968	3.75	7.50	15.00
☐ PM 55001 [M]	Kismet	1964	3.00	6.00	12.00
☐ 820085-1	Mantovani's Golden Hits	198?	2.00	4.00	8.00
—Reissue of 483					
☐ 820333-1	Mantovani/Tango	198?	2.00	4.00	8.00
—Reissue of 532					
☐ 820334-1	The Incomparable Mantovani	198?	2.00	4.00	8.00
—Reissue of 392					
LONDON PHASE 4					
☐ SP-44043 [S]	Kismet	1964	3.75	7.50	15.00
☐ BP 44302/3 [(2)]	Million Sellers	1978	3.00	6.00	12.00
MAPHIS, JOE					
COLUMBIA					
☐ CL 1005 [M]	Fire on the Strings	1957	25.00	50.00	100.00
HARMONY					
☐ HL 7180 [M]	Hi-Fi Holiday for Banjo	1959	6.25	12.50	25.00
☐ HS 11032 [S]	Hi-Fi Holiday for Banjo	1959	7.50	15.00	30.00
KAPP					
☐ KL-1347 [M]	Hootenanny Star	1964	5.00	10.00	20.00
☐ KS-3347 [S]	Hootenanny Star	1964	6.25	12.50	25.00
MACGREGOR					
☐ MGR-1205 [M]	King of the Strings	196?	20.00	40.00	80.00
MOSRITE					
☐ MA-400 [M]	The New Sound of Joe Maphis	1967	7.50	15.00	30.00
☐ MS-400 [S]	The New Sound of Joe Maphis	1967	7.50	15.00	30.00

Number	Title (A Side/B Side)	Yr	VG	VG+	NM
STARDAY					
❑ SLP-316 [M]	King of the Strings	1966	12.50	25.00	50.00
❑ SLP-373 [M]	Country Guitar Goes to the Jimmy Dean Show	1966	15.00	30.00	60.00
—Deduct 1/3 if instruction book is missing					
MAPHIS, JOE AND ROSE LEE					
CAPITOL					
❑ ST 1778 [S]	Rose Lee and Joe Maphis	1962	10.00	20.00	40.00
❑ T 1778 [M]	Rose Lee and Joe Maphis	1962	7.50	15.00	30.00
STARDAY					
❑ SLP-286 [M]	Mr. and Mrs. Country Music	1964	7.50	15.00	30.00
❑ SLP-322 [M]	Golden Gospel	1966	7.50	15.00	30.00
MAPHIS, ROSE LEE					
COLUMBIA					
❑ CL 1598 [M]	Rose Lee Maphis	1961	7.50	15.00	30.00
❑ CS 8398 [S]	Rose Lee Maphis	1961	10.00	20.00	40.00
MAR-KEYS					
ATLANTIC					
❑ 8055 [M]	Last Night	1961	25.00	50.00	100.00
—White "fan" logo on right					
❑ 8055 [M]	Last Night	1962	12.50	25.00	50.00
—Black "fan" logo on right					
❑ SD 8055 [R]	Last Night	1966	10.00	20.00	40.00
❑ 8062 [M]	Do the Pop-Eye with the Mar-Keys	1962	12.50	25.00	50.00
❑ SD 8062 [R]	Do the Pop-Eye with the Mar-Keys	1966	10.00	20.00	40.00
STAX					
❑ ST-707 [M]	The Great Memphis Sound	1966	12.50	25.00	50.00
❑ STS-707 [R]	The Great Memphis Sound	1966	10.00	20.00	40.00
❑ STS-2025	Damifiknew	1969	5.00	10.00	20.00
❑ STS-2036	Memphis Experience	1971	5.00	10.00	20.00
MAR-KEYS/BOOKER T. AND THE MG'S					
Also see each artist's individual listings.					
STAX					
❑ ST-720 [M]	Back to Back	1967	5.00	10.00	20.00
❑ STS-720 [S]	Back to Back	1967	6.25	12.50	25.00
MARABLE, LAWRENCE					
JAZZ WEST					
❑ LP-8 [M]	Tenor Man	1956	75.00	150.00	300.00
MARAIS, JOSEPH					
DECCA					
❑ DL 5014 [10]	South African Veld	1949	12.50	25.00	50.00
❑ DL 5083 [10]	Songs from the Veld, Vol. 2	1950	12.50	25.00	50.00
❑ DL 5106 [10]	Songs of Many Lands	1950	12.50	25.00	50.00
MARAIS, JOSEPH, AND MIRANDA					
DECCA					
❑ DL 5268 [10]	Ballads of Many Lands	1950	12.50	25.00	50.00
❑ DL 8711 [M]	Sundown Songs	1957	6.25	12.50	25.00
❑ DL 9026 [M]	Marais and Miranda In Person, Vol. 1	1955	7.50	15.00	30.00
❑ DL 9027 [M]	Marais and Miranda In Person, Vol. 2	1955	7.50	15.00	30.00
❑ DL 9030 [M]	Christmas with Joseph and Miranda	1955	7.50	15.00	30.00
❑ DL 9047 [M]	Africana Suite and Songs of Spirit and Humor	1956	7.50	15.00	30.00
MARATHONS, THE (1)					
ARVEE					
❑ A-428 [M]	Peanut Butter	1961	45.00	90.00	180.00
MARBLE PHROGG, THE					
DERRICK					
❑ 8868	The Marble Phrogg	1968	250.00	500.00	1000.
MARCEAU, MARCEL					
GONE					
❑ LP 1F	The Best of Marcel Marceau	196?	12.50	25.00	50.00
MGM					
❑ SE-4	The Best of Marcel Marceau	196?	10.00	20.00	40.00
—The above records are identical: 38 minutes of silence and 2 minutes of applause!					
MARCELS, THE					
COLPIX					
❑ CP-416 [M]	Blue Moon	1961	87.50	175.00	350.00
—Gold label					
❑ CP-416 [M]	Blue Moon	1963	30.00	60.00	120.00
—Blue label					
MARCH, HAL					
DOT					
❑ DLP-3092 [M]	The Moods of March	1958	7.50	15.00	30.00
❑ DLP-25092 [S]	The Moods of March	1958	10.00	20.00	40.00
HAMILTON					
❑ HLP-101 [M]	Hal March Conducts	1960	3.75	7.50	15.00
❑ HLP-12101 [S]	Hal March Conducts	1960	5.00	10.00	20.00
—Reissue of Dot LP					
MARCH, LITTLE PEGGY					
RCA VICTOR					
❑ LPM-2732 [M]	I Will Follow Him	1963	15.00	30.00	60.00
❑ LSP-2732 [S]	I Will Follow Him	1963	20.00	40.00	80.00
❑ LPM-3883 [M]	No Foolin'	1968	10.00	20.00	40.00
❑ LSP-3883 [S]	No Foolin'	1968	6.25	12.50	25.00
MARCH, LITTLE PEGGY/BENNIE THOMAS					
RCA VICTOR					
❑ LPM-3408 [M]	In Our Fashion	1965	10.00	20.00	40.00
❑ LSP-3408 [S]	In Our Fashion	1965	12.50	25.00	50.00
MARCHAN, BOBBY					
COLLECTABLES					
❑ COL-5113	Golden Classics	198?	2.50	5.00	10.00

Number	Title (A Side/B Side)	Yr	VG	VG+	NM
SPHERE SOUND					
❑ SSR-7004 [M]	There's Something on Your Mind	1964	75.00	150.00	300.00
MARCUS, LEW					
SAVOY					
❑ MG-15006 [10]	Back Room Piano	1951	12.50	25.00	50.00
MARCUS, STEVE					
VORTEX					
❑ 2001	Tomorrow Never Knows	1968	6.25	12.50	25.00
❑ 2009	The Count's Rock Band	1969	6.25	12.50	25.00
❑ 2013	The Lord's Prayer	1969	6.25	12.50	25.00
MARESCA, ERNIE					
SEVILLE					
❑ SV 77001 [M]	Shout! Shout! Knock Yourself Out	1962	30.00	60.00	120.00
❑ SV 87001 [S]	Shout! Shout! Knock Yourself Out	1962	50.00	100.00	200.00
MARGOLIN, STUART					
WARNER BROS.					
❑ BSK 3439	And the Angel Sings	1980	5.00	10.00	20.00
MARGULIS, CHARLIE					
CARLTON					
❑ LP 12-103 [M]	Marvelous Margulis	1958	6.25	12.50	25.00
❑ STLP 12-103 [S]	Marvelous Margulis	1959	7.50	15.00	30.00
MARIANI					
SONOBEAT					
❑ 1001	Perpetuum Mobile	197?	1000.	1750.	2500.
—Issued in generic white cover; the band and label names are stamped on the jacket, and each of the 50 copies is numbered and autographed by the members of the band					
MARIANO, CHARLIE					
BETHLEHEM					
❑ BCP-25 [M]	Alto Sax for Young Moderns	1956	25.00	50.00	100.00
❑ BCP-49 [M]	Charlie Mariano Plays Chloe	1957	25.00	50.00	100.00
❑ BCP-1022 [10]	Charlie Mariano Sextet	1955	37.50	75.00	150.00
FANTASY					
❑ 3-10 [10]	Charlie Mariano Sextet	1953	45.00	90.00	180.00
IMPERIAL					
❑ IMP-3006 [10]	Charlie Mariano Quintet Volume 1	1955	37.50	75.00	150.00
❑ IMP-3007 [10]	Charlie Mariano Quintet Volume 2	1955	37.50	75.00	150.00
PRESTIGE					
❑ PRLP-130 [10]	Charlie Mariano	1952	50.00	100.00	200.00
❑ PRLP-153 [10]	Charlie Mariano Boston All Stars	1953	50.00	100.00	200.00
REGINA					
❑ R-286 [M]	A Jazz Portrait of Charlie Mariano	1963	6.25	12.50	25.00
❑ RS-286 [S]	A Jazz Portrait of Charlie Mariano	1963	7.50	15.00	30.00
MARIANO, CHARLIE, AND JERRY DODGION					
WORLD PACIFIC					
❑ WP-1245 [M]	Beauties of 1918	1958	12.50	25.00	50.00
MARIANO, TOSHIKO					
See TOSHIKO AKIYOSHI.					
MARINERS, THE					
CADENCE					
❑ CLP-1008 [M]	The Mariners Sing Spirituals	1956	10.00	20.00	40.00
COLUMBIA					
❑ CL 609 [M]	Hymns	1955	10.00	20.00	40.00
MARINO, FRANK, AND MAHOGANY RUSH					
See MAHOGANY RUSH.					
MARKETTS, THE					
LIBERTY					
❑ LRP-3226 [M]	The Surfing Scene	196?	7.50	15.00	30.00
—Retitled version of above					
❑ LRP-3226 [M]	Surfer's Stomp	1962	10.00	20.00	40.00
—Add 20% if "Surfer's Stomp" instruction sheet is enclosed					
❑ LST-7226 [S]	The Surfing Scene	196?	10.00	20.00	40.00
—Retitled version of above					
❑ LST-7226 [S]	Surfer's Stomp	1962	12.50	25.00	50.00
—Add 20% if "Surfer's Stomp" instruction sheet is enclosed					
MERCURY					
❑ SRM-1-679	AM, FM, Etc.	1973	3.75	7.50	15.00
WARNER BROS.					
❑ W 1509 [M]	The Marketts Take to Wheels	1963	10.00	20.00	40.00
❑ WS 1509 [S]	The Marketts Take to Wheels	1963	12.50	25.00	50.00
❑ W 1537 [M]	Out of Limits!	1964	7.50	15.00	30.00
❑ WS 1537 [S]	Out of Limits!	1964	10.00	20.00	40.00
❑ W 1642 [M]	The Batman Theme	1966	10.00	20.00	40.00
❑ WS 1642 [S]	The Batman Theme	1966	12.50	25.00	50.00
WORLD PACIFIC					
❑ WP-1870 [M]	Sun Power	1967	6.25	12.50	25.00
❑ WPS-21870 [S]	Sun Power	1967	5.00	10.00	20.00
MARKEWICH, REESE					
MODERN AGE					
❑ MA-134 [M]	New Designs in Jazz	1958	12.50	25.00	50.00
MARKHAM, PIGMEAT					
CHESS					
❑ LP-1451 [M]	The Trial	1961	6.25	12.50	25.00
❑ LP-1462 [M]	Pigmeat Markham At the Party	1962	6.25	12.50	25.00
❑ LP-1467 [M]	Anything Goes	1962	6.25	12.50	25.00
❑ LP-1475 [M]	The World's Greatest Clown	1963	6.25	12.50	25.00
❑ LP-1484 [M]	Open the Door, Richard	1964	6.25	12.50	25.00
❑ LP-1493 [M]	Mr. Funny Man	1965	6.25	12.50	25.00
❑ LP-1500 [M]	This'll Kill Ya	1965	6.25	12.50	25.00
❑ LP-1505 [M]	If You Can't Be Good, Be Careful	1966	3.75	7.50	15.00

Number	Title (A Side/B Side)	Yr	VG	VG+	NM
❏ LPS-1505 [S]	If You Can't Be Good, Be Careful	1966	5.00	10.00	20.00
❏ LP-1515 [M]	Mr. Vaudeville	1967	3.75	7.50	15.00
❏ LPS-1515 [S]	Mr. Vaudeville	1967	5.00	10.00	20.00
❏ LP-1517 [M]	Save Your Soul, Baby	1967	5.00	10.00	20.00
❏ LPS-1517 [S]	Save Your Soul, Baby	1967	5.00	10.00	20.00
❏ LP-1521 [M]	Backstage	1968	5.00	10.00	20.00
❏ LPS-1521 [S]	Backstage	1968	5.00	10.00	20.00
❏ LPS-1525	Here Comes the Judge	1968	5.00	10.00	20.00
❏ LPS-1526	Tune Me In	1968	3.75	7.50	15.00
❏ LPS-1529	Hustlers	1969	3.75	7.50	15.00
❏ LPS-1534	Bag	1970	3.75	7.50	15.00
❏ CH-9166	Here Comes the Judge	1985	2.50	5.00	10.00
—Reissue of 1525					

JEWEL
| ❏ 5007 | Crap-Shootin' Rev | 1972 | 3.00 | 6.00 | 12.00 |
| ❏ 5012 | Will the Real Pigmeat Markham Please Sit Down | 1973 | 3.00 | 6.00 | 12.00 |

MARKLEY
FORWARD
| ❏ 1007 | A Group | 1969 | 7.50 | 15.00 | 30.00 |

MARKS, GUY
ABC
❏ 549 [M]	Hollywood Sings	1966	3.75	7.50	15.00
❏ S-549 [S]	Hollywood Sings	1966	3.75	7.50	15.00
❏ S-648	Loving You Has Made Me Bananas	1968	5.00	10.00	20.00

MARKS, J., AND SHIPEN LEBZELTER
COLUMBIA MASTERWORKS
| ❏ MS 7193 | Rock and Other Four-Letter Words | 1969 | 7.50 | 15.00 | 30.00 |
| ❏ M 30006 | First National Nothing | 1970 | 5.00 | 10.00 | 20.00 |

MARLEY, BOB, AND THE WAILERS
ACCORD
| ❏ SN-7211 | Jamaican Storm | 1982 | 2.50 | 5.00 | 10.00 |

CALLA
❏ CAS-1240 [(2)]	The Birth of a Legend	1976	3.75	7.50	15.00
❏ ZX 34759	The Birth of a Legend	1977	2.50	5.00	10.00
—Reissue of Record 1 of Calla 1240					
❏ ZX 34760	Early Music	1977	2.50	5.00	10.00
—Reissue of Record 2 of Calla 1240					

COLUMBIA
❏ PZ 34759	The Birth of a Legend	198?	2.00	4.00	8.00
—Budget-line reissue of Calla 34759					
❏ PZ 34760	Early Music	198?	2.00	4.00	8.00
—Budget-line reissue of Calla 34760					

COTILLION
| ❏ SD 5228 | Chances Are | 1981 | 2.50 | 5.00 | 10.00 |

ISLAND
❏ ISLD 11 [(2)]	Babylon by Bus	1978	3.75	7.50	15.00
—Island distribution					
❏ ISLD 11 [(2)]	Babylon by Bus	1979	3.00	6.00	12.00
—Warner Bros. distribution					
❏ ILPS 9241	Catch a Fire	1975	3.75	7.50	15.00
—Reissue with standard cover; Island distribution					
❏ ILPS 9241	Catch a Fire	1978	3.00	6.00	12.00
—Reissue; Warner Bros. distribution					
❏ ILPS 9256	Burnin'	1974	3.75	7.50	15.00
—Island distribution					
❏ ILPS 9256	Burnin'	1978	3.00	6.00	12.00
—Warner Bros. distribution					
❏ ILPS 9281	Natty Dread	1974	3.75	7.50	15.00
—Island distribution					
❏ ILPS 9281	Natty Dread	1978	3.00	6.00	12.00
—Warner Bros. distribution					
❏ SW-9329	Catch a Fire	1973	12.50	25.00	50.00
—"Cigarette lighter" cover with flip-open top; Capitol distribution					
❏ SMAS-9338	Burnin'	1973	5.00	10.00	20.00
—Capitol distribution					
❏ ILPS 9376	Live!	1975	3.00	6.00	12.00
—Island distribution					
❏ ILPS 9376	Live!	1978	2.50	5.00	10.00
—Warner Bros. distribution					
❏ ILPS 9383	Rastaman Vibration	1976	3.00	6.00	12.00
—Island distribution					
❏ ILPS 9383	Rastaman Vibration	1978	2.50	5.00	10.00
—Warner Bros. distribution					
❏ ILPS 9383 [DJ]	Rastaman Vibration	1976	25.00	50.00	100.00
—Promotional package with burlap box and press kit					
❏ ILPS 9498	Exodus	1977	3.00	6.00	12.00
—Island distribution (all have multicolor labels)					
❏ ILPS 9498	Exodus	1978	2.50	5.00	10.00
—Warner Bros. distribution					
❏ ILPS 9517	Kaya	1978	3.00	6.00	12.00
—Island distribution					
❏ ILPS 9517	Kaya	1979	2.50	5.00	10.00
—Warner Bros. distribution					
❏ ILPS 9542	Survival	1979	3.00	6.00	12.00
❏ ILPS 9596	Uprising	1980	3.00	6.00	12.00
❏ 90029 [(2)]	Babylon by Bus	1983	3.00	6.00	12.00
❏ 90030	Catch a Fire	1983	2.00	4.00	8.00
❏ 90031	Burnin'	1983	2.00	4.00	8.00
❏ 90032	Live!	1983	2.00	4.00	8.00
❏ 90033	Rastaman Vibration	1983	2.00	4.00	8.00
❏ 90034	Exodus	1983	2.00	4.00	8.00
❏ 90035	Kaya	1983	2.00	4.00	8.00
❏ 90036	Uprising	1983	2.00	4.00	8.00
❏ 90037	Natty Dread	1983	2.00	4.00	8.00
—90029-90037 are reissues with Atco distribution					
❏ 90085	Confrontation	1983	2.50	5.00	10.00
❏ 90169	Legend	1984	2.50	5.00	10.00
❏ 90520	Rebel Music	1986	2.50	5.00	10.00
❏ 524419-1	Dreams of Freedom	1997	3.00	6.00	12.00
❏ 546404-1	Chant Down Babylon	1999	3.00	6.00	12.00

MOBILE FIDELITY
❏ 1-221	Exodus	1995	6.25	12.50	25.00
—Audiophile vinyl					
❏ 1-236	Catch a Fire	1995	6.25	12.50	25.00
—Audiophile vinyl					

TUFF GONG
❏ 524103-1	Natural Mystic	1995	3.75	7.50	15.00
❏ 846197-1 [(2)]	Babylon by Bus	1990	3.75	7.50	15.00
❏ 846200-1	Burnin'	1990	3.00	6.00	12.00
❏ 846201-1	Catch a Fire	1990	3.00	6.00	12.00
❏ 846202-1	Survival	1990	3.00	6.00	12.00
❏ 846203-1	Live!	1990	3.00	6.00	12.00
❏ 846204-1	Natty Dread	1990	3.00	6.00	12.00
❏ 846205-1	Rastaman Vibration	1990	3.00	6.00	12.00
❏ 846206-1	Rebel Music	1990	3.00	6.00	12.00
❏ 846207-1	Confrontation	1990	3.00	6.00	12.00
❏ 846208-1	Exodus	1990	3.00	6.00	12.00
❏ 846209-1	Kaya	1990	3.00	6.00	12.00
❏ 846210-1	Legend	1990	3.00	6.00	12.00
❏ 846211-1	Uprising	1990	3.00	6.00	12.00
❏ 848243-1	Talkin' Blues	1991	3.00	6.00	12.00

MARLO, MICKI
ABC-PARAMOUNT
| ❏ 295 [M] | Married I Can Always Get | 1959 | 5.00 | 10.00 | 20.00 |
| ❏ S-295 [S] | Married I Can Always Get | 1959 | 6.25 | 12.50 | 25.00 |

MARLOWE, MARION, AND FRANK PARKER
COLUMBIA
| ❏ CL 576 [M] | Arthur Godfrey's TV Sweethearts | 1954 | 7.50 | 15.00 | 30.00 |
| —Maroon label, gold print | | | | | |

MARLOWE, MEXIE
KING
| ❏ 799 [M] | Meet Mexie Marlowe | 1962 | 25.00 | 50.00 | 100.00 |

MARMALADE, THE
EPIC
| ❏ BN 26553 | The Best of the Marmalade | 1970 | 5.00 | 10.00 | 20.00 |

LONDON
| ❏ PS 575 | Reflections of My Life | 1970 | 5.00 | 10.00 | 20.00 |

MARMAROSA, DODO
ARGO
| ❏ LP-4012 [M] | Dodo's Back | 1961 | 6.25 | 12.50 | 25.00 |
| ❏ LPS-4012 [S] | Dodo's Back | 1961 | 7.50 | 15.00 | 30.00 |

MARMAROSA, DODO/ERROLL GARNER
CONCERT HALL JAZZ
| ❏ 1001 [10] | Piano Contrasts | 1955 | 12.50 | 25.00 | 50.00 |

DIAL
| ❏ LP-208 [10] | Piano Contrasts | 1950 | 62.50 | 125.00 | 250.00 |

MARR, HANK
KING
❏ 829 [M]	Teentime Dance Steps	1963	7.50	15.00	30.00
❏ 899 [M]	Live at Club 502	1964	10.00	20.00	40.00
❏ 933 [M]	On and Off Stage	1965	7.50	15.00	30.00
❏ 1011 [M]	Hank Marr Plays 24 Originals	1966	5.00	10.00	20.00
❏ 1025 [M]	Sounds from the Marr-Ket Place	1968	5.00	10.00	20.00
❏ KSD-1061	Greasy Spoon	1969	5.00	10.00	20.00

MARS, CHRIS
Also see THE REPLACEMENTS.
SMASH
| ❏ 513198-1 [DJ] | Horseshoes and Hand Grenades | 1992 | 5.00 | 10.00 | 20.00 |
| —Vinyl is promo only | | | | | |

MARS, SYLVIA
LYRIC
| ❏ 124 | Blues Walk Right In | 196? | 15.00 | 30.00 | 60.00 |

MARSALA, JOE/BUD FREEMAN
BRUNSWICK
| ❏ BL 58037 [10] | Battle of Jazz, Vol. 1 | 1953 | 12.50 | 25.00 | 50.00 |

MARSALIS, BRANFORD
JAZZ PLANET
| ❏ JP-5004 [(2)] | The Dark Keys | 1996 | 7.50 | 15.00 | 30.00 |

MARSALIS, WYNTON
COLUMBIA
| ❏ HC 47574 | Wynton Marsalis | 198? | 7.50 | 15.00 | 30.00 |
| —Half-speed mastered edition | | | | | |

MARSH, MILTON
STRATA-EAST
| ❏ SES-19758 | Monism | 1975 | 5.00 | 10.00 | 20.00 |

MARSH, WARNE
ATLANTIC
❏ 1291 [M]	Warne Marsh	1958	12.50	25.00	50.00
—Black label					
❏ 1291 [M]	Warne Marsh	1961	6.25	12.50	25.00
—Multicolor label, white "fan" logo at right					
❏ SD 1291 [S]	Warne Marsh	1958	12.50	25.00	50.00
—Green label					
❏ SD 1291 [S]	Warne Marsh	1961	5.00	10.00	20.00
—Multicolor label, white "fan" logo at right					

IMPERIAL
| ❏ LP-9027 [M] | Jazz of Two Cities | 1957 | 20.00 | 40.00 | 80.00 |

Number	Title (A Side/B Side)	Yr	VG	VG+	NM
❏ LP-12013 [S]	The Winds of Warne Marsh	1959	15.00	30.00	60.00

—Retitled version in stereo?

MODE

Number	Title (A Side/B Side)	Yr	VG	VG+	NM
❏ LP-125 [M]	Music for Prancing	1957	20.00	40.00	80.00

REVELATION

Number	Title (A Side/B Side)	Yr	VG	VG+	NM
❏ R-12	Ne Plus Ultra	1970	5.00	10.00	20.00

MARSHALL, CHUCK
DECCA

Number	Title (A Side/B Side)	Yr	VG	VG+	NM
❏ DL 4267 [M]	Twist to Songs Everybody Knows	1962	3.75	7.50	15.00
❏ DL 74267 [S]	Twist to Songs Everybody Knows	1962	5.00	10.00	20.00

MARSHALL, JACK
CAPITOL

Number	Title (A Side/B Side)	Yr	VG	VG+	NM
❏ ST 1108 [S]	18th Century Jazz	1959	6.25	12.50	25.00
❏ T 1108 [M]	18th Century Jazz	1959	5.00	10.00	20.00
❏ ST 1194 [S]	Soundsville!	1959	6.25	12.50	25.00
❏ T 1194 [M]	Soundsville!	1959	5.00	10.00	20.00
❏ ST 1351 [S]	The Marshall Swings	1960	6.25	12.50	25.00
❏ T 1351 [M]	The Marshall Swings	1960	5.00	10.00	20.00
❏ ST 1601 [S]	Songs Without Words	1961	6.25	12.50	25.00
❏ T 1601 [M]	Songs Without Words	1961	5.00	10.00	20.00
❏ ST 1727 [S]	The Twangy, Shoutin', Fantastic Big-Band Sounds of Tuff Jack	1962	10.00	20.00	40.00
❏ T 1727 [M]	The Twangy, Shoutin', Fantastic Big-Band Sounds of Tuff Jack	1962	7.50	15.00	30.00
❏ ST 1939 [S]	My Son the Surf Nut	1963	10.00	20.00	40.00
❏ T 1939 [M]	My Son the Surf Nut	1963	7.50	15.00	30.00

MARSHALL, PENNY, AND CINDY WILLIAMS
ATLANTIC

Number	Title (A Side/B Side)	Yr	VG	VG+	NM
❏ SD 18203	Laverne and Shirley Sing	1979	6.25	12.50	25.00

MARSHALL, PETER
DOT

Number	Title (A Side/B Side)	Yr	VG	VG+	NM
❏ DLP-25930	For the Love of Pete	1969	6.25	12.50	25.00

MARSHMALLOW WAY
UNITED ARTISTS

Number	Title (A Side/B Side)	Yr	VG	VG+	NM
❏ UAS-6708	Marshmallow Way	1969	5.00	10.00	20.00

MARTHA AND THE VANDELLAS
GORDY

Number	Title (A Side/B Side)	Yr	VG	VG+	NM
❏ G-902 [M]	Come and Get These Memories	1963	100.00	200.00	400.00
❏ GS-902 [S]	Come and Get These Memories	1963	200.00	400.00	800.00
❏ G-907 [M]	Heat Wave	1963	37.50	75.00	150.00
❏ GS-907 [R]	Heat Wave	1963	37.50	75.00	150.00

—"Stereo" banner pre-printed on cover

Number	Title (A Side/B Side)	Yr	VG	VG+	NM
❏ GS-907 [S]	Heat Wave	1963	100.00	200.00	400.00

—Mono cover with "Stereo" sticker

Number	Title (A Side/B Side)	Yr	VG	VG+	NM
❏ G-915 [M]	Dance Party	1965	10.00	20.00	40.00
❏ GS-915 [S]	Dance Party	1965	15.00	30.00	60.00
❏ G-917 [M]	Greatest Hits	1966	6.25	12.50	25.00
❏ GS-917 [S]	Greatest Hits	1966	7.50	15.00	30.00
❏ G-920 [M]	Watchout!	1966	6.25	12.50	25.00
❏ GS-920 [S]	Watchout!	1966	7.50	15.00	30.00
❏ G-925 [M]	Martha and the Vandellas Live!	1967	7.50	15.00	30.00
❏ GS-925 [S]	Martha and the Vandellas Live!	1967	6.25	12.50	25.00
❏ G-926 [M]	Ridin' High	1968	10.00	20.00	40.00

—Mono is promo only

Number	Title (A Side/B Side)	Yr	VG	VG+	NM
❏ GS-926 [S]	Ridin' High	1968	5.00	10.00	20.00
❏ GS-944	Sugar 'N Spice	1969	5.00	10.00	20.00
❏ GS-952	Natural Resources	1970	5.00	10.00	20.00
❏ GS-958	Black Magic	1972	5.00	10.00	20.00

MOTOWN

Number	Title (A Side/B Side)	Yr	VG	VG+	NM
❏ M5-111V1	Motown Superstar Series, Vol. 11	1981	2.50	5.00	10.00
❏ M5-145V1	Heat Wave	1981	2.50	5.00	10.00

—Reissue of Gordy 907

Number	Title (A Side/B Side)	Yr	VG	VG+	NM
❏ M5-204V1	Greatest Hits	1981	2.50	5.00	10.00

—Reissue of Gordy 917

Number	Title (A Side/B Side)	Yr	VG	VG+	NM
❏ M7-778 [(2)]	Anthology	1974	3.75	7.50	15.00

MARTIN, ARCH
ZEPHYR

Number	Title (A Side/B Side)	Yr	VG	VG+	NM
❏ 12009 [M]	Arch Martin Quintet	1959	7.50	15.00	30.00

MARTIN, BENNY
STARDAY

Number	Title (A Side/B Side)	Yr	VG	VG+	NM
❏ SLP-131 [M]	Country Music's Sensational Entertainer	1961	12.50	25.00	50.00

MARTIN, BOBBI
BUDDAH

Number	Title (A Side/B Side)	Yr	VG	VG+	NM
❏ BDS-5090	Tomorrow	1971	3.00	6.00	12.00

CORAL

Number	Title (A Side/B Side)	Yr	VG	VG+	NM
❏ CRL 57472 [M]	Don't Forget I Still Love You	1965	3.75	7.50	15.00
❏ CRL 57478 [M]	I Love You So	1965	3.75	7.50	15.00
❏ CRL 757472 [S]	Don't Forget I Still Love You	1965	5.00	10.00	20.00
❏ CRL 757478 [S]	I Love You So	1965	5.00	10.00	20.00

SUNSET

Number	Title (A Side/B Side)	Yr	VG	VG+	NM
❏ SUS-5319	Thinking of You	197?	2.50	5.00	10.00

UNITED ARTISTS

Number	Title (A Side/B Side)	Yr	VG	VG+	NM
❏ UAS-6668	Harper Valley P.T.A.	1968	3.00	6.00	12.00
❏ UAS-6700	For the Love of Him	1969	3.00	6.00	12.00
❏ UAS-6755	With Love	1970	3.00	6.00	12.00

VOCALION

Number	Title (A Side/B Side)	Yr	VG	VG+	NM
❏ VL 73906	Have You Ever Been Lonely	196?	2.50	5.00	10.00

MARTIN, DEAN
CAPITOL

Number	Title (A Side/B Side)	Yr	VG	VG+	NM
❏ SKAO-140	The Best of Dean Martin, Vol. 2	1968	3.75	7.50	15.00
❏ H 401 [10]	Dean Martin Sings	1953	25.00	50.00	100.00
❏ T 401 [M]	Dean Martin Sings	1953	12.50	25.00	50.00

Number	Title (A Side/B Side)	Yr	VG	VG+	NM
❏ STBB-523 [(2)]	You're Nobody 'Til Somebody Loves You/ Return to Me	1970	5.00	10.00	20.00
❏ T 576 [M]	Swingin' Down Yonder	1955	7.50	15.00	30.00
❏ T 849 [M]	Pretty Baby	1957	7.50	15.00	30.00
❏ DT 1047 [R]	This Is Dean Martin	196?	3.00	6.00	12.00
❏ T 1047 [M]	This Is Dean Martin	1958	7.50	15.00	30.00
❏ ST 1150 [S]	Sleep Warm	1959	7.50	15.00	30.00
❏ T 1150 [M]	Sleep Warm	1959	6.25	12.50	25.00
❏ ST 1285 [S]	A Winter Romance	1959	7.50	15.00	30.00
❏ T 1285 [M]	A Winter Romance	1959	5.00	10.00	20.00
❏ ST 1442 [S]	This Time I'm Swingin'	1961	7.50	15.00	30.00
❏ T 1442 [M]	This Time I'm Swingin'	1961	5.00	10.00	20.00
❏ SW 1580 [S]	Dean Martin	1961	7.50	15.00	30.00
❏ W 1580 [M]	Dean Martin	1961	5.00	10.00	20.00
❏ SM-1659	Dino — Italian Love Songs	197?	2.50	5.00	10.00

—Reissue with new prefix

Number	Title (A Side/B Side)	Yr	VG	VG+	NM
❏ ST 1659 [S]	Dino — Italian Love Songs	1962	7.50	15.00	30.00
❏ T 1659 [M]	Dino — Italian Love Songs	1962	5.00	10.00	20.00
❏ ST 1702 [S]	Cha Cha De Amor	1962	7.50	15.00	30.00
❏ T 1702 [M]	Cha Cha De Amor	1962	5.00	10.00	20.00
❏ DT 2212 [R]	Hey Brother Pour the Wine	1964	3.00	6.00	12.00
❏ T 2212 [M]	Hey Brother Pour the Wine	1964	5.00	10.00	20.00
❏ ST 2297 [S]	Dean Martin Sings — Sinatra Conducts	1965	5.00	10.00	20.00
❏ T 2297 [M]	Dean Martin Sings — Sinatra Conducts	1965	3.75	7.50	15.00
❏ DT 2333 [R]	Dean Martin — Southern Style	1965	3.00	6.00	12.00
❏ T 2333 [M]	Dean Martin — Southern Style	1965	3.75	7.50	15.00
❏ STT 2343 [S]	Holiday Cheer	1965	5.00	10.00	20.00

—Some copies of this LP have labels that state the title as "Baby, It's Cold Outside."

Number	Title (A Side/B Side)	Yr	VG	VG+	NM
❏ TT 2343 [M]	Holiday Cheer	1965	3.75	7.50	15.00

—Reissue of 1285 with one fewer track

Number	Title (A Side/B Side)	Yr	VG	VG+	NM
❏ DT 2601 [R]	The Best of Dean Martin	1966	3.00	6.00	12.00
❏ SM-2601	The Best of Dean Martin	197?	2.50	5.00	10.00

—Reissue with new prefix

Number	Title (A Side/B Side)	Yr	VG	VG+	NM
❏ T 2601 [M]	The Best of Dean Martin	1966	3.75	7.50	15.00
❏ DTCL 2815 [(3)R]	The Dean Martin Deluxe Set	1967	5.00	10.00	20.00
❏ TCL 2815 [(3)M]	The Dean Martin Deluxe Set	1967	7.50	15.00	30.00

PAIR

Number	Title (A Side/B Side)	Yr	VG	VG+	NM
❏ PDL2-1029 [(2)]	Dreams and Memories	1986	3.00	6.00	12.00

PICKWICK

Number	Title (A Side/B Side)	Yr	VG	VG+	NM
❏ PTP-2051 [(2)]	Dean Martin	197?	3.00	6.00	12.00
❏ SPC-3057	You Can't Love 'Em All	196?	2.50	5.00	10.00
❏ SPC-3089	I Can't Give You Anything But Love	196?	2.50	5.00	10.00
❏ SPC-3136	Young and Foolish	196?	2.50	5.00	10.00
❏ SPC-3175	You Were Made for Love	197?	2.50	5.00	10.00
❏ SPC-3283	Deluxe	197?	2.50	5.00	10.00

REPRISE

Number	Title (A Side/B Side)	Yr	VG	VG+	NM
❏ MS 2053	Dino	1972	3.75	7.50	15.00
❏ MS 2113	Sittin' on Top of the World	1973	3.75	7.50	15.00
❏ MS 2174	You're the Best Thing That Ever Happened to Me	1973	3.75	7.50	15.00
❏ MS 2267	Once in a Lifetime	1978	3.00	6.00	12.00
❏ R-6021 [M]	French Style	1962	3.75	7.50	15.00
❏ R9-6021 [S]	French Style	1962	5.00	10.00	20.00
❏ R-6054 [M]	Dino Latino	1962	3.75	7.50	15.00
❏ R9-6054 [S]	Dino Latino	1962	5.00	10.00	20.00
❏ R-6061 [M]	Country Style	1963	3.75	7.50	15.00
❏ R9-6061 [S]	Country Style	1963	5.00	10.00	20.00
❏ R-6085 [M]	Dean "Tex" Martin Rides Again	1963	3.75	7.50	15.00
❏ R9-6085 [S]	Dean "Tex" Martin Rides Again	1963	5.00	10.00	20.00
❏ R-6123 [M]	Dream with Dean	1964	3.00	6.00	12.00
❏ RS-6123 [S]	Dream with Dean	1964	3.75	7.50	15.00
❏ R-6130 [M]	Everybody Loves Somebody	1964	3.00	6.00	12.00
❏ RS-6130 [S]	Everybody Loves Somebody	1964	3.75	7.50	15.00
❏ R-6140 [M]	The Door Is Still Open to My Heart	1964	3.00	6.00	12.00
❏ RS-6140 [S]	The Door Is Still Open to My Heart	1964	3.75	7.50	15.00
❏ R-6146 [M]	Dean Martin Hits Again	1965	3.00	6.00	12.00
❏ RS-6146 [S]	Dean Martin Hits Again	1965	3.75	7.50	15.00
❏ R-6170 [M]	(Remember Me) I'm the One Who Loves You	1965	3.00	6.00	12.00
❏ RS-6170 [S]	(Remember Me) I'm the One Who Loves You	1965	3.75	7.50	15.00
❏ R-6181 [M]	Houston	1965	3.00	6.00	12.00
❏ RS-6181 [S]	Houston	1965	3.75	7.50	15.00
❏ R-6201 [M]	Somewhere There's a Someone	1966	3.00	6.00	12.00
❏ RS-6201 [S]	Somewhere There's a Someone	1966	3.75	7.50	15.00
❏ R-6211 [M]	The Silencers	1966	5.00	10.00	20.00
❏ RS-6211 [S]	The Silencers	1966	6.25	12.50	25.00
❏ R-6213 [M]	The Hit Sound of Dean Martin	1966	3.00	6.00	12.00
❏ RS-6213 [S]	The Hit Sound of Dean Martin	1966	3.75	7.50	15.00
❏ R 6222 [M]	The Dean Martin Christmas Album	1966	3.75	7.50	15.00
❏ RS 6222 [S]	The Dean Martin Christmas Album	1966	5.00	10.00	20.00
❏ R-6233 [M]	The Dean Martin TV Show	1966	3.00	6.00	12.00
❏ RS-6233 [S]	The Dean Martin TV Show	1966	3.75	7.50	15.00
❏ R-6242 [M]	Happiness Is Dean Martin	1967	3.75	7.50	15.00
❏ RS-6242 [S]	Happiness Is Dean Martin	1967	3.75	7.50	15.00
❏ R-6250 [M]	Welcome to My World	1967	3.75	7.50	15.00
❏ RS-6250 [S]	Welcome to My World	1967	3.75	7.50	15.00
❏ RS-6301	Dean Martin's Greatest Hits! Vol. 1	1968	3.75	7.50	15.00
❏ RS-6320	Dean Martin's Greatest Hits! Vol. 2	1968	3.75	7.50	15.00
❏ RS-6330	Gentle on My Mind	1968	3.75	7.50	15.00
❏ RS-6338	I Take a Lot of Pride in What I Am	1969	3.75	7.50	15.00
❏ RS-6403	My Woman, My Woman, My Wife	1970	3.75	7.50	15.00
❏ RS-6428	For the Good Times	1971	3.75	7.50	15.00

TOWER

Number	Title (A Side/B Side)	Yr	VG	VG+	NM
❏ DT 5006 [R]	The Lush Years	1965	3.75	7.50	15.00
❏ T 5006 [M]	The Lush Years	1965	5.00	10.00	20.00
❏ DT 5018 [R]	Relaxin'	1966	3.75	7.50	15.00
❏ T 5018 [M]	Relaxin'	1966	5.00	10.00	20.00
❏ ST 5036 [S]	Happy in Love	1966	5.00	10.00	20.00
❏ T 5036 [M]	Happy in Love	1966	3.75	7.50	15.00

WARNER BROS.

Number	Title (A Side/B Side)	Yr	VG	VG+	NM
❏ 23870	The Nashville Sessions	1983	3.00	6.00	12.00

Number	Title (A Side/B Side)	Yr	VG	VG+	NM
MARTIN, DEWEY, AND MEDICINE BALL					
Dewey is a former member of BUFFALO SPRINGFIELD.					
UNI					
❏ 73088	Dewey Martin and Medicine Ball	1970	6.25	12.50	25.00
MARTIN, FREDDY					
RCA VICTOR					
❏ LPM-1414 [M]	Freddy Martin at the Cocoanut Grove	1957	5.00	10.00	20.00
MARTIN, GEORGE					
UNITED ARTISTS					
❏ UAL 3377 [M]	Off the Beatle Track	1964	20.00	40.00	80.00
❏ UAL 3383 [M]	A Hard Day's Night	1964	10.00	20.00	40.00
❏ UAL 3420 [M]	George Martin	1965	10.00	20.00	40.00
❏ UAL 3448 [M]	George Martin Plays "Help"	1965	12.50	25.00	50.00
❏ UAL 3539 [M]	George Martin Salutes the Beatle Girls	1966	12.50	25.00	50.00
❏ UAL 3647 [M]	London by George	1967	7.50	15.00	30.00
❏ UAS 6377 [S]	Off the Beatle Track	1964	25.00	50.00	100.00
❏ UAS 6383 [S]	A Hard Day's Night	1964	12.50	25.00	50.00
❏ UAS 6420 [S]	George Martin	1965	12.50	25.00	50.00
❏ UAS 6448 [S]	George Martin Plays "Help"	1965	20.00	40.00	80.00
❏ UAS 6539 [S]	George Martin Salutes the Beatle Girls	1966	20.00	40.00	80.00
❏ UAS 6647 [S]	London by George	1967	10.00	20.00	40.00
MARTIN, GRADY					
DECCA					
❏ DL 4072 [M]	Big City Lights	1960	5.00	10.00	20.00
❏ DL 4286 [M]	Swingin' Down the River	1962	3.75	7.50	15.00
❏ DL 4476 [M]	Songs Everybody Knows	1963	3.75	7.50	15.00
❏ DL 5566 [10]	Dance-O-Rama	1955	50.00	100.00	200.00
❏ DL 8181 [M]	Powerhouse Dance Party	1955	7.50	15.00	30.00
❏ DL 8292 [M]	Juke Box Jamboree	1956	7.50	15.00	30.00
❏ DL 8648 [M]	The Roaring Twenties	1957	7.50	15.00	30.00
❏ DL 8883 [M]	Hot Time Tonight	1959	5.00	10.00	20.00
❏ DL 74072 [S]	Big City Lights	1960	6.25	12.50	25.00
❏ DL 74286 [S]	Swingin' Down the River	1962	5.00	10.00	20.00
❏ DL 74476 [S]	Songs Everybody Knows	1963	5.00	10.00	20.00
❏ DL 78883 [S]	Hot Time Tonight	1959	6.25	12.50	25.00
MARTIN, JIMMY					
DECCA					
❏ DL 4016 [M]	Good 'n Country	1960	6.25	12.50	25.00
❏ DL 4285 [M]	Country Music Time	1962	6.25	12.50	25.00
❏ DL 4360 [M]	This World Is Not My Home	1963	6.25	12.50	25.00
❏ DL 4536 [M]	Widow Maker	1964	5.00	10.00	20.00
❏ DL 4643 [M]	Sunny Side of the Mountain	1965	5.00	10.00	20.00
❏ DL 4769 [M]	Mr. Good 'n Country Music	1966	5.00	10.00	20.00
❏ DL 4891 [M]	Big and Country Instrumentals	1967	5.00	10.00	20.00
❏ DL 74016 [S]	Good 'n Country	1960	7.50	15.00	30.00
❏ DL 74285 [S]	Country Music Time	1962	7.50	15.00	30.00
❏ DL 74360 [S]	This World Is Not My Home	1963	7.50	15.00	30.00
❏ DL 74536 [S]	Widow Maker	1964	6.25	12.50	25.00
❏ DL 74643 [S]	Sunny Side of the Mountain	1965	6.25	12.50	25.00
❏ DL 74769 [S]	Mr. Good 'n Country Music	1966	6.25	12.50	25.00
❏ DL 74891 [S]	Big and Country Instrumentals	1967	5.00	10.00	20.00
❏ DL 74996	Tennessee	1968	5.00	10.00	20.00
MARTIN, MARTY					
See BOXCAR WILLIE.					
MARTIN, MARY					
COLUMBIA MASTERWORKS					
❏ ML 2061 [10]	Mary Martin Sings for You	1949	12.50	25.00	50.00
DISNEYLAND					
❏ WDL-1038 [M]	Hi-Ho — Mary Martin Sings and Swings Walt Disney Favorites	1958	5.00	10.00	20.00
❏ DQ-1296 [M]	Mary Martin Songs from Rodgers and Hammerstein's The Sound of Music	1966	3.75	7.50	15.00
❏ STER-1296 [S]	Mary Martin Songs from Rodgers and Hammerstein's The Sound of Music	1966	5.00	10.00	20.00
❏ ST-2002 [M]	The Little Lame Lamb	1958	12.50	25.00	50.00
❏ STER-3031 [S]	Mary Martin Sings a Musical Love Story	1959	6.25	12.50	25.00
❏ WD-3031 [M]	Mary Martin Sings a Musical Love Story	1958	5.00	10.00	20.00
❏ STER-3038 [S]	Hi-Ho!	1959	6.25	12.50	25.00
❏ WD-3038 [M]	Hi-Ho!	1958	5.00	10.00	20.00
❏ ST-3911 [M]	The Story of Sleeping Beauty	1958	7.50	15.00	30.00
—Back cover art features Sleeping Beauty and prince					
❏ ST-3911 [M]	The Story of Sleeping Beauty	1969	5.00	10.00	20.00
—Back cover art features pictures from the booklet					
❏ ST-3936 [M]	Mary Martin Songs from Rodgers and Hammerstein's The Sound of Music	1966	3.75	7.50	15.00
❏ STER-3936 [S]	Mary Martin Songs from Rodgers and Hammerstein's The Sound of Music	1966	5.00	10.00	20.00
❏ STER-4016 [S]	Hi-Ho!	1959	7.50	15.00	30.00
❏ WD-4016 [M]	Hi-Ho!	1958	5.00	10.00	20.00
MARTIN, TONY					
DECCA					
❏ DL 8287 [M]	Our Love Affair	195?	6.25	12.50	25.00
—Black label, silver print					
❏ DL 8366 [M]	In the Spotlight	195?	6.25	12.50	25.00
—Black label, silver print					
RCA VICTOR					
❏ LPM-2146 [M]	Tony Martin at the Desert Inn	1960	5.00	10.00	20.00
❏ LSP-2146 [S]	Tony Martin at the Desert Inn	1960	6.25	12.50	25.00
MARTIN, VINCE, AND FRED NEIL					
ELEKTRA					
❏ EKL-248 [M]	Tear Down the Walls	1964	12.50	25.00	50.00
❏ EKS-7248 [S]	Tear Down the Walls	1964	15.00	30.00	60.00

Number	Title (A Side/B Side)	Yr	VG	VG+	NM
MARTINDALE, WINK					
DOT					
❏ DLP-3245 [M]	Deck of Cards	1960	5.00	10.00	20.00
❏ DLP-3293 [M]	The Bible Story	1960	3.75	7.50	15.00
❏ DLP-3403 [M]	Big Bad John	1962	3.75	7.50	15.00
❏ DLP-3571 [M]	My True Love	1964	3.75	7.50	15.00
❏ DLP-3692 [M]	Giddyup Go	1966	3.75	7.50	15.00
❏ DLP-25245 [S]	Deck of Cards	1960	6.25	12.50	25.00
❏ DLP-25293 [S]	The Bible Story	1960	5.00	10.00	20.00
❏ DLP-25403 [S]	Big Bad John	1962	5.00	10.00	20.00
❏ DLP-25571 [S]	My True Love	1964	5.00	10.00	20.00
❏ DLP-25692 [S]	Giddyup Go	1966	5.00	10.00	20.00
MARTINEZ, TONY					
DEL-FI					
❏ DFLP-1205 [M]	The Many Sides of Pepino	1959	7.50	15.00	30.00
❏ DFLP-1205S [S]	The Many Sides of Pepino	1959	10.00	20.00	40.00
MARTINO, AL					
CAPITOL					
❏ ST-180	Sausalito	1969	3.00	6.00	12.00
❏ ST-379	Jean	1969	3.00	6.00	12.00
❏ ST-405	Can't Help Falling in Love	1970	3.00	6.00	12.00
❏ ST-497	My Heart Sings	1970	3.00	6.00	12.00
❏ STBB-526 [(2)]	Here in My Heart/Yesterday	1970	3.75	7.50	15.00
❏ STCL-572 [(3)]	Al Martino	1971	6.25	12.50	25.00
❏ STBB-713 [(2)]	I Wish You Love/Losing You	1971	3.75	7.50	15.00
❏ ST-793	Summer of '42	1971	3.00	6.00	12.00
❏ ST 1774 [S]	The Exciting Voice of Al Martino	1962	5.00	10.00	20.00
❏ T 1774 [M]	The Exciting Voice of Al Martino	1962	3.75	7.50	15.00
❏ ST 1907 [S]	The Italian Voice of Al Martino	1963	5.00	10.00	20.00
❏ T 1907 [M]	The Italian Voice of Al Martino	1963	3.75	7.50	15.00
❏ ST 1914 [S]	I Love You Because	1963	3.75	7.50	15.00
❏ T 1914 [M]	I Love You Because	1963	3.00	6.00	12.00
❏ ST 1975 [S]	Painted, Tainted Rose	1963	3.75	7.50	15.00
❏ T 1975 [M]	Painted, Tainted Rose	1963	3.00	6.00	12.00
❏ ST 2040 [S]	Living a Lie	1964	3.75	7.50	15.00
❏ T 2040 [M]	Living a Lie	1964	3.00	6.00	12.00
❏ ST 2107 [S]	I Love You More and More Every Day/Tears and Roses	1964	3.75	7.50	15.00
❏ T 2107 [M]	I Love You More and More Every Day/Tears and Roses	1964	3.00	6.00	12.00
❏ ST 2165 [S]	A Merry Christmas from Al Martino	1964	3.75	7.50	15.00
❏ T 2165 [M]	A Merry Christmas from Al Martino	1964	3.00	6.00	12.00
❏ ST 2200 [S]	We Could	1964	3.75	7.50	15.00
❏ T 2200 [M]	We Could	1964	3.00	6.00	12.00
❏ ST 2312 [S]	Somebody Else Is Taking My Place	1965	3.75	7.50	15.00
❏ T 2312 [M]	Somebody Else Is Taking My Place	1965	3.00	6.00	12.00
❏ ST 2362 [S]	My Cherie	1965	3.75	7.50	15.00
❏ T 2362 [M]	My Cherie	1965	3.00	6.00	12.00
❏ ST 2435 [S]	Spanish Eyes	1966	3.75	7.50	15.00
❏ T 2435 [M]	Spanish Eyes	1966	3.00	6.00	12.00
❏ ST 2528 [S]	Think I'll Go Somewhere and Cry Myself to Sleep	1966	3.75	7.50	15.00
❏ T 2528 [M]	Think I'll Go Somewhere and Cry Myself to Sleep	1966	3.00	6.00	12.00
❏ ST 2592 [S]	This Is Love	1966	3.75	7.50	15.00
❏ T 2592 [M]	This Is Love	1966	3.00	6.00	12.00
❏ ST 2654 [S]	This Love for You	1967	3.75	7.50	15.00
❏ T 2654 [M]	This Love for You	1967	3.75	7.50	15.00
❏ ST 2733 [S]	Daddy's Little Girl	1967	3.75	7.50	15.00
❏ T 2733 [M]	Daddy's Little Girl	1967	3.75	7.50	15.00
❏ ST 2780 [S]	Mary in the Morning	1967	3.75	7.50	15.00
❏ T 2780 [M]	Mary in the Morning	1967	3.75	7.50	15.00
❏ ST 2843	This Is Al Martino	1968	3.75	7.50	15.00
❏ ST 2908	Love Is Blue	1968	3.75	7.50	15.00
❏ SKAO 2946	The Best of Al Martino	1968	3.75	7.50	15.00
❏ SM-2946	The Best of Al Martino	197?	2.50	5.00	10.00
—Reissue with new prefix					
❏ ST 2983	Wake Up to Me Gentle	1968	3.75	7.50	15.00
❏ SM-11071	Love Theme from "The Godfather"	1977	2.00	4.00	8.00
—Reissue with new prefix					
❏ ST-11071	Love Theme from "The Godfather"	1972	2.50	5.00	10.00
❏ ST-11302	I Won't Last a Day Without You	1974	2.50	5.00	10.00
❏ ST-11366	To the Door of the Sun	1975	2.50	5.00	10.00
❏ ST-11572	Sing My Love Songs	1976	2.50	5.00	10.00
❏ SM-11679	To the Door of the Sun	1977	2.00	4.00	8.00
—Reissue of 11366					
❏ ST-11741	The Next Hundred Years	1978	2.50	5.00	10.00
❏ SN-16074	The Best of Al Martino	1981	2.00	4.00	8.00
—Budget-line reissue					
❏ SQBO-91280 [(2)]	The Romantic World of Al Martino	196?	5.00	10.00	20.00
—Capitol Record Club exclusive					
MOVIETONE					
❏ MTM 2002 [M]	That Old Feeling	196?	3.75	7.50	15.00
❏ MTM 2015 [M]	All of Me	1967	5.00	10.00	20.00
❏ MTS 72002 [S]	That Old Feeling	196?	5.00	10.00	20.00
❏ MTS 72015 [S]	All of Me	1967	3.75	7.50	15.00
PICKWICK					
❏ SPC-3049	Don't Go to Strangers	196?	3.00	6.00	12.00
❏ SPC-3276	Mary in the Morning	197?	2.50	5.00	10.00
SPRINGBOARD					
❏ 4074	Time After Time	1978	2.00	4.00	8.00
20TH CENTURY FOX					
❏ SF-3025 [M]	Al Martino	1959	6.25	12.50	25.00
❏ SFX-3025 [S]	Al Martino	1959	7.50	15.00	30.00
❏ SF-3032 [M]	Sing Along with Al Martino	1959	6.25	12.50	25.00
❏ SFX-3032 [S]	Sing Along with Al Martino	1959	7.50	15.00	30.00
❏ TF-4168 [M]	Al Martino Sings	196?	5.00	10.00	20.00
❏ TFS-4168 [S]	Al Martino Sings	196?	6.25	12.50	25.00
❏ SXG-5009 [S]	When Your Lover Has Gone	1963	6.25	12.50	25.00
❏ XG-5009 [M]	When Your Lover Has Gone	1963	5.00	10.00	20.00

Number	Title (A Side/B Side)	Yr	VG	VG+	NM

MARTINO, PAT
COBBLESTONE
| ❏ 9015 | The Visit | 1972 | 5.00 | 10.00 | 20.00 |
PRESTIGE
| ❏ PRLP-7513 [M] | El Hombre | 1967 | 6.25 | 12.50 | 25.00 |
| ❏ PRLP-7547 [M] | Strings! | 1967 | 6.25 | 12.50 | 25.00 |

MARVELETTES, THE
MOTOWN
| ❏ M5-180V1 | Greatest Hits | 1981 | 2.50 | 5.00 | 10.00 |

—Reissue of Tamla 253
| ❏ M7-827 [(2)] | Anthology | 1975 | 3.75 | 7.50 | 15.00 |
| ❏ 5266 ML | Please Mr. Postman | 1982 | 2.50 | 5.00 | 10.00 |

—Reissue of Tamla 228
TAMLA
| ❏ T-228 [M] | Please Mr. Postman | 1961 | 150.00 | 300.00 | 600.00 |

—White label
| ❏ T-228 [M] | Please Mr. Postman | 1963 | 75.00 | 150.00 | 300.00 |

—Yellow label with globes logo
| ❏ T-229 [M] | The Marveletts Sing | 1962 | 125.00 | 250.00 | 500.00 |

—Title as listed on front cover (misspelled); all-black cover with white circles
| ❏ T-229 [M] | Smash Hits of 62' | 1962 | 600.00 | 900.00 | 1200. |

—Title as listed on front cover; large black "M" with song titles in circles
| ❏ T-229 [M] | The Marveletts Sing | 1963 | 62.50 | 125.00 | 250.00 |

—Yellow label with side-by-side globes logo
| ❏ T-231 [M] | Playboy | 1962 | 125.00 | 250.00 | 500.00 |

—Yellow label with overlapping record and globe logo
| ❏ T-231 [M] | Playboy | 1962 | 150.00 | 300.00 | 600.00 |

—White label
| ❏ T-231 [M] | Playboy | 1963 | 62.50 | 125.00 | 250.00 |

—Yellow label with side-by-side globes logo
❏ T-237 [M]	The Marvelous Marvelettes	1963	37.50	75.00	150.00
❏ T-243 [M]	Recorded Live on Stage	1963	20.00	40.00	80.00
❏ T-253 [M]	Greatest Hits	1966	7.50	15.00	30.00

—Yellow cover
| ❏ T-253 [M] | Greatest Hits | 1967 | 6.25 | 12.50 | 25.00 |

—Green cover
| ❏ TS-253 [S] | Greatest Hits | 1966 | 10.00 | 20.00 | 40.00 |

—Yellow cover
| ❏ TS-253 [S] | Greatest Hits | 1967 | 5.00 | 10.00 | 20.00 |

—Green cover
❏ T-274 [M]	The Marvelettes	1967	7.50	15.00	30.00
❏ TS-274 [S]	The Marvelettes	1967	5.00	10.00	20.00
❏ T-286 [M]	Sophisticated Soul	1968	10.00	20.00	40.00
❏ TS-286 [S]	Sophisticated Soul	1968	5.00	10.00	20.00
❏ TS-288	In Full Bloom	1969	3.75	7.50	15.00
❏ TS-305	Return of the Marvelettes	1970	3.75	7.50	15.00

MARVELOWS, THE
ABC
| ❏ S-643 | The Mighty Marvelows | 1968 | 7.50 | 15.00 | 30.00 |

MARVIN AND JOHNNY
CROWN
| ❏ CST-381 [R] | Marvin and Johnny | 1963 | 3.00 | 6.00 | 12.00 |
| ❏ CLP-5381 [M] | Marvin and Johnny | 1963 | 12.50 | 25.00 | 50.00 |

MARX, BILL
VEE JAY
❏ LP-3032 [M]	Jazz Kaleidoscope	1962	5.00	10.00	20.00
❏ SR-3032 [S]	Jazz Kaleidoscope	1962	6.25	12.50	25.00
❏ LP-3035 [M]	My Son, the Folk Swinger	1963	5.00	10.00	20.00
❏ SR-3035 [S]	My Son, the Folk Swinger	1963	6.25	12.50	25.00

MARX, DICK
OMEGA
| ❏ OSL-2 [S] | Marx Makes Broadway | 1959 | 7.50 | 15.00 | 30.00 |

—The front cover of the above LP spells his last name "Marks," though it is spelled correctly on the label and back cover
| ❏ OML-1002 [M] | Marx Makes Broadway | 1958 | 10.00 | 20.00 | 40.00 |

MARX, DICK, AND JOHN FRIGO
BRUNSWICK
| ❏ BL 54006 [M] | Two Much Piano | 1955 | 10.00 | 20.00 | 40.00 |

MARX, GROUCHO
DECCA
| ❏ DL 5405 [10] | Hooray for Captain Spaulding | 1954 | 62.50 | 125.00 | 250.00 |

MARX, HARPO
MERCURY
❏ MG-20232 [M]	Harpo in Hi-Fi	1957	12.50	25.00	50.00
❏ MG-20363 [M]	Harpo at Work!	1959	12.50	25.00	50.00
❏ SR-60016 [S]	Harpo at Work!	1959	20.00	40.00	80.00
RCA VICTOR
| ❏ LPM-27 [10] | Harp by Harpo | 1952 | 37.50 | 75.00 | 150.00 |
WING
| ❏ MGW-12164 [M] | Harpo | 1960 | 6.25 | 12.50 | 25.00 |

MARY BUTTERWORTH
CUSTOM FIDELITY
| ❏ 2092 | Mary Butterworth | 1969 | 75.00 | 150.00 | 300.00 |

MASEKELA, HUGH
MERCURY
| ❏ SR-60797 [S] | The Trumpet of Hugh Masekela | 1963 | 5.00 | 10.00 | 20.00 |
UNI
| ❏ 3015 [M] | Hugh Masekela Is Alive and Well at the Whisky | 1967 | 5.00 | 10.00 | 20.00 |

MASKED MARAUDERS, THE
Fictional supergroup from a Rolling Stone magazine album review, which noted the presence of Bob Dylan, Mick Jagger, John Lennon and Paul McCartney. The below, recorded using the bogus review as a guide, was actually THE CLEANLINESS AND GODLINESS SKIFFLE BAND.
DEITY
| ❏ RS 6378 | The Masked Marauders | 1969 | 5.00 | 10.00 | 20.00 |

MASON, BARBARA
ARCTIC
❏ ALP-1000 [M]	Yes, I'm Ready	1965	7.50	15.00	30.00
❏ ALPS-1000 [P]	Yes, I'm Ready	1965	12.50	25.00	50.00
❏ ALPS-1004	Oh, How It Hurts	1968	7.50	15.00	30.00
BUDDAH
❏ BDS-5117	Give Me Your Love	1972	3.00	6.00	12.00
❏ BDS-5140	Lady Love	1973	3.00	6.00	12.00
❏ BDS-5610	Transition	1974	3.00	6.00	12.00
❏ BDS-5628	Love's the Thing	1975	3.00	6.00	12.00
NATIONAL GENERAL
| ❏ 2001 | If You Knew Him Like I Do | 1970 | 7.50 | 15.00 | 30.00 |

MASON, DAVE
BLUE THUMB
| ❏ BTS-19 | Alone Together | 1970 | 5.00 | 10.00 | 20.00 |

—Originals on multicolored vinyl
| ❏ BTS-19 | All Together | 1970 | 50.00 | 100.00 | 200.00 |

—Erroneous pressing of "Alone Together"
| ❏ BTS-19 | Alone Together | 1975 | 3.00 | 6.00 | 12.00 |

—Multicolor label with "ABC" logo
❏ BTS-34	Headkeeper	1972	3.75	7.50	15.00
❏ BTS-54	Dave Mason Is Alive!	1973	3.75	7.50	15.00
❏ ABCD-880	Dave Mason At His Best	1975	2.50	5.00	10.00
❏ BT-6013	The Best of Dave Mason	1974	2.50	5.00	10.00
❏ BT-6032	Very Best of Dave Mason	1978	2.50	5.00	10.00
❏ BTS-8819	Alone Together	1971	12.50	25.00	50.00

—Capitol-distributed black vinyl reissue
CHUMLEY
| ❏ 00101 | Some Assembly Required | 1987 | 2.50 | 5.00 | 10.00 |
COLUMBIA
❏ CQ 31721 [Q]	It's Like You Never Left	1973	4.50	9.00	18.00
❏ KC 31721	It's Like You Never Left	1973	2.50	5.00	10.00
❏ PC 31721	It's Like You Never Left	197?	2.00	4.00	8.00

—Reissue with new prefix
| ❏ PC 33096 | Dave Mason | 1974 | 2.50 | 5.00 | 10.00 |

—No bar code on cover
| ❏ PC 33096 | Dave Mason | 198? | 2.00 | 4.00 | 8.00 |

—Budget-line reissue with bar code
❏ PCQ 33096 [Q]	Dave Mason	1974	4.50	9.00	18.00
❏ PC 33698	Split Coconut	1975	2.50	5.00	10.00
❏ PCQ 33698 [Q]	Split Coconut	1975	4.50	9.00	18.00
❏ PG 34174 [(2)]	Certified Live	1976	3.00	6.00	12.00
❏ PC 34680	Let It Flow	1977	2.50	5.00	10.00

—No bar code on cover
| ❏ PC 34680 | Let It Flow | 198? | 2.00 | 4.00 | 8.00 |

—Budget-line reissue with bar code
❏ JC 35285	Mariposa de Oro	1978	2.50	5.00	10.00
❏ JC 36144	Old Crest on a New Wave	1980	2.50	5.00	10.00
❏ FC 37089	The Best of Dave Mason	1981	2.50	5.00	10.00
❏ PC 37089	The Best of Dave Mason	1983	2.00	4.00	8.00

—Budget-line reissue
MCA
| ❏ 712 | Headkeeper | 198? | 2.00 | 4.00 | 8.00 |

—Reissue of Blue Thumb 34
| ❏ 713 | Dave Mason Is Alive | 198? | 2.00 | 4.00 | 8.00 |

—Reissue of Blue Thumb 54
| ❏ 714 | Dave Mason At His Best | 198? | 2.00 | 4.00 | 8.00 |

—Reissue of Blue Thumb 880
| ❏ 715 | Very Best of Dave Mason | 198? | 2.00 | 4.00 | 8.00 |

—Reissue of Blue Thumb 6032
| ❏ 800 | The Best of Dave Mason | 1981 | 2.00 | 4.00 | 8.00 |

—Reissue of Blue Thumb 6013
| ❏ 11319 | Alone Together | 1995 | 5.00 | 10.00 | 20.00 |

—"Heavy Vinyl" gatefold reissue
| ❏ 27035 | Alone Together | 198? | 2.00 | 4.00 | 8.00 |

—Reissue of Blue Thumb 19
| ❏ 42086 | Two Hearts | 1988 | 2.50 | 5.00 | 10.00 |

MASON, DAVE, AND CASS ELLIOT
Also see each artist's individual listings.
BLUE THUMB
| ❏ BTS-8825 | Dave Mason and Cass Elliot | 1971 | 5.00 | 10.00 | 20.00 |

MASON, JACKIE
VERVE
❏ V-15033 [M]	I'm the Greatest Comedian in the World Only Nobody Knows It Yet	1962	5.00	10.00	20.00
❏ V-15034 [M]	I Want to Leave You with the Words of a Great Comedian	1963	5.00	10.00	20.00
❏ V-15045 [M]	Great Moments in Comedy	1964	5.00	10.00	20.00
WARNER BROS.
| ❏ 25603 | The World According to Me! | 1987 | 2.50 | 5.00 | 10.00 |

MASTER CYLINDER
INNER CITY
| ❏ IC-1112 | Elsewhere | 198? | 7.50 | 15.00 | 30.00 |

MASTERS, JOE
COLUMBIA
| ❏ CL 2598 [M] | Jazz Mass | 1967 | 6.25 | 12.50 | 25.00 |
| ❏ CS 9398 [S] | Jazz Mass | 1967 | 5.00 | 10.00 | 20.00 |

Number	Title (A Side/B Side)	Yr	VG	VG+	NM

MASTERSOUNDS, THE
FANTASY

Number	Title (A Side/B Side)	Yr	VG	VG+	NM
❑ 3305 [M]	Swingin' with the Mastersounds	1960	10.00	20.00	40.00
—Red vinyl					
❑ 3305 [M]	Swingin' with the Mastersounds	1962	6.25	12.50	25.00
—Black vinyl					
❑ 3316 [M]	A Date with the Mastersounds	1961	10.00	20.00	40.00
—Red vinyl					
❑ 3316 [M]	A Date with the Mastersounds	1962	6.25	12.50	25.00
—Black vinyl					
❑ 3327 [M]	The Mastersounds on Tour	1961	10.00	20.00	40.00
—Red vinyl					
❑ 3327 [M]	The Mastersounds on Tour	1962	6.25	12.50	25.00
—Black vinyl					
❑ 8050 [S]	Swingin' with the Mastersounds	1961	7.50	15.00	30.00
—Blue vinyl					
❑ 8050 [S]	Swingin' with the Mastersounds	1962	5.00	10.00	20.00
—Black vinyl					
❑ 8062 [S]	A Date with the Mastersounds	1961	7.50	15.00	30.00
—Blue vinyl					
❑ 8062 [S]	A Date with the Mastersounds	1962	5.00	10.00	20.00
—Black vinyl					
❑ 8066 [S]	The Mastersounds on Tour	1961	7.50	15.00	30.00
—Blue vinyl					
❑ 8066 [S]	The Mastersounds on Tour	1962	5.00	10.00	20.00
—Black vinyl					

PACIFIC JAZZ

Number	Title (A Side/B Side)	Yr	VG	VG+	NM
❑ PJM-403 [M]	Introducing the Mastersounds	1957	12.50	25.00	50.00
❑ PJM-405 [M]	The King and I	1958	12.50	25.00	50.00

WORLD PACIFIC

Number	Title (A Side/B Side)	Yr	VG	VG+	NM
❑ ST-1010 [S]	Kismet	1958	7.50	15.00	30.00
❑ ST-1012 [S]	Flower Drum Song	1958	7.50	15.00	30.00
❑ ST-1017 [S]	The King and I	1959	7.50	15.00	30.00
❑ ST-1019 [S]	Ballads and Blues	1959	7.50	15.00	30.00
❑ ST-1026 [S]	The Mastersounds in Concert	1959	7.50	15.00	30.00
❑ ST-1030 [S]	Happy Holidays from Many Lands	1959	7.50	15.00	30.00
❑ WP-1243 [M]	Kismet	1958	10.00	20.00	40.00
❑ WP-1252 [M]	Flower Drum Song	1958	10.00	20.00	40.00
❑ WP-1260 [M]	Ballads and Blues	1959	10.00	20.00	40.00
❑ WP-1269 [M]	The Mastersounds in Concert	1959	10.00	20.00	40.00
❑ WP-1271 [M]	Jazz Showcase	1959	7.50	15.00	30.00
—Reissue of Pacific Jazz 403					
❑ WP-1272 [M]	The King and I	1959	7.50	15.00	30.00
—Reissue of Pacific Jazz 405					
❑ WP-1280 [M]	Happy Holidays from Many Lands	1959	10.00	20.00	40.00
❑ ST-1284 [S]	The Mastersounds Play Horace Silver	1960	7.50	15.00	30.00
❑ WP-1284 [M]	The Mastersounds Play Horace Silver	1960	10.00	20.00	40.00

MATHEWS, MAT
BRUNSWICK

Number	Title (A Side/B Side)	Yr	VG	VG+	NM
❑ BL 54013 [M]	Bag's Groove	1956	12.50	25.00	50.00

DAWN

Number	Title (A Side/B Side)	Yr	VG	VG+	NM
❑ DLP-1104 [M]	The Modern Art of Jazz	1956	20.00	40.00	80.00

MATHEWS, RONNIE
PRESTIGE

Number	Title (A Side/B Side)	Yr	VG	VG+	NM
❑ PRLP-7303 [M]	Doin' the Thang	1964	7.50	15.00	30.00
❑ PRST-7303 [S]	Doin' the Thang	1964	10.00	20.00	40.00

MATHIS, COUNTRY JOHNNY
The "original" Johnny Mathis, the "Country" prefix was added to his name after the "other" Johnny Mathis became far more popular.

HILLTOP GOSPEL

Number	Title (A Side/B Side)	Yr	VG	VG+	NM
❑ GS-7004	Country Johnny Mathis	1965	6.25	12.50	25.00

LITTLE DARLIN'

Number	Title (A Side/B Side)	Yr	VG	VG+	NM
❑ 8007	He Keeps Me Singin'	1967	5.00	10.00	20.00

MATHIS, JOHNNY
COLUMBIA

Number	Title (A Side/B Side)	Yr	VG	VG+	NM
❑ GP 2 [(2)]	Warm/Open Fire, Two Guitars	1969	3.75	7.50	15.00
❑ C2L 17 [(2)M]	The Rhythms and Ballads of Broadway	1960	6.25	12.50	25.00
—Red and black label with six "eye" logos					
❑ C2L 17 [(2)M]	The Rhythms and Ballads of Broadway	1962	5.00	10.00	20.00
—Red label with either "Guaranteed High Fidelity" or "360 Sound Mono"					
❑ C2L 34 [(2)M]	The Great Years	1964	3.75	7.50	15.00
❑ C2S 803 [(2)S]	The Rhythms and Ballads of Broadway	1960	7.50	15.00	30.00
—Red and black label with six "eye" logos					
❑ C2S 803 [(2)S]	The Rhythms and Ballads of Broadway	1962	6.25	12.50	25.00
—Red "360 Sound" label					
❑ C2S 834 [(2)S]	The Great Years	1964	5.00	10.00	20.00
—Red "360 Sound" label					
❑ CL 887 [M]	Johnny Mathis	1957	12.50	25.00	50.00
❑ CS 1005	Raindrops Keep Fallin' on My Head	1970	3.00	6.00	12.00
❑ CL 1028 [M]	Wonderful Wonderful	1957	7.50	15.00	30.00
—Red and black label with six "eye" logos					
❑ CL 1028 [M]	Wonderful Wonderful	1962	3.75	7.50	15.00
—Red label with either "Guaranteed High Fidelity" or "360 Sound Mono"					
❑ CL 1078 [M]	Warm	1957	7.50	15.00	30.00
—Red and black label with six "eye" logos					
❑ CL 1078 [M]	Warm	1962	3.75	7.50	15.00
—Red label with either "Guaranteed High Fidelity" or "360 Sound Mono"					
❑ CL 1119 [M]	Good Night, Dear Lord	1958	7.50	15.00	30.00
—Red and black label with six "eye" logos					
❑ CL 1119 [M]	Good Night, Dear Lord	1962	3.75	7.50	15.00
—Red label with either "Guaranteed High Fidelity" or "360 Sound Mono"					
❑ CL 1133 [M]	Johnny's Greatest Hits	1958	7.50	15.00	30.00
—Red and black label with six "eye" logos					
❑ CL 1133 [M]	Johnny's Greatest Hits	1962	3.75	7.50	15.00
—Red label with either "Guaranteed High Fidelity" or "360 Sound Mono"					
❑ CL 1165 [M]	Swing Softly	1958	7.50	15.00	30.00
—Red and black label with six "eye" logos					
❑ CL 1165 [M]	Swing Softly	1962	3.75	7.50	15.00
—Red label with either "Guaranteed High Fidelity" or "360 Sound Mono"					
❑ CL 1195 [M]	Merry Christmas	1958	10.00	20.00	40.00
—Original cover has Johnny standing, holding skis and poles					
❑ CL 1195 [M]	Merry Christmas	196?	7.50	15.00	30.00
—Second cover has Johnny sitting, with skis and poles in snow					
❑ CL 1270 [M]	Open Fire, Two Guitars	1959	7.50	15.00	30.00
—Red and black label with six "eye" logos					
❑ CL 1270 [M]	Open Fire, Two Guitars	1962	3.75	7.50	15.00
—Red label with either "Guaranteed High Fidelity" or "360 Sound Mono"					
❑ CL 1344 [M]	More Johnny's Greatest Hits	1959	6.25	12.50	25.00
—Red and black label with six "eye" logos					
❑ CL 1344 [M]	More Johnny's Greatest Hits	1962	3.75	7.50	15.00
—Red label with either "Guaranteed High Fidelity" or "360 Sound Mono"					
❑ CL 1351 [M]	Heavenly	1959	5.00	10.00	20.00
—Red and black label with six "eye" logos					
❑ CL 1351 [M]	Heavenly	1962	3.75	7.50	15.00
—Red label with either "Guaranteed High Fidelity" or "360 Sound Mono"					
❑ CL 1422 [M]	Faithfully	1959	5.00	10.00	20.00
—Red and black label with six "eye" logos					
❑ CL 1422 [M]	Faithfully	1962	3.75	7.50	15.00
—Red label with either "Guaranteed High Fidelity" or "360 Sound Mono"					
❑ CL 1526 [M]	Johnny's Mood	1960	5.00	10.00	20.00
—Red and black label with six "eye" logos					
❑ CL 1526 [M]	Johnny's Mood	1962	3.75	7.50	15.00
—Red label with either "Guaranteed High Fidelity" or "360 Sound Mono"					
❑ CL 1623 [M]	I'll Buy You a Star	1961	3.75	7.50	15.00
—Red and black label with six "eye" logos					
❑ CL 1623 [M]	I'll Buy You a Star	1962	3.00	6.00	12.00
—Red label with either "Guaranteed High Fidelity" or "360 Sound Mono"					
❑ CL 1644 [M]	Portrait of Johnny	1961	3.75	7.50	15.00
—Red and black label with six "eye" logos; add 1/3 if portrait is there					
❑ CL 1644 [M]	Portrait of Johnny	1962	3.00	6.00	12.00
—Red label with either "Guaranteed High Fidelity" or "360 Sound Mono"					
❑ CL 1711 [M]	Live It Up!	1962	3.00	6.00	12.00
—Red label with either "Guaranteed High Fidelity" or "360 Sound Mono"					
❑ CL 1711 [M]	Live It Up!	1962	3.75	7.50	15.00
—Red and black label with six "eye" logos					
❑ CL 1915 [M]	Rapture	1962	3.00	6.00	12.00
❑ CL 2016 [M]	Johnny's Newest Hits	1963	3.00	6.00	12.00
❑ CL 2044 [M]	Johnny	1963	3.00	6.00	12.00
❑ CL 2098 [M]	Romantically	1963	3.00	6.00	12.00
❑ CL 2143 [M]	I'll Search My Heart and Other Great Hits	1964	3.00	6.00	12.00
❑ CL 2223 [M]	The Ballads of Broadway	1964	3.00	6.00	12.00
❑ CL 2224 [M]	The Rhythms of Broadway	1964	3.00	6.00	12.00
❑ CL 2726 [M]	Up, Up and Away	1967	3.75	7.50	15.00
❑ CL 2837 [M]	Love Is Blue	1968	6.25	12.50	25.00
❑ CL 2905 [M]	Those Were the Days	1968	10.00	20.00	40.00
❑ CS 8012 [S]	Good Night, Dear Lord	1958	10.00	20.00	40.00
—Red and black label with six "eye" logos					
❑ CS 8012 [S]	Good Night, Dear Lord	1962	5.00	10.00	20.00
—Red "360 Sound" label					
❑ CS 8021 [S]	Merry Christmas	1959	6.25	12.50	25.00
—Original cover has Johnny standing, holding skis and poles					
❑ CS 8021 [S]	Merry Christmas	196?	5.00	10.00	20.00
—Second cover has Johnny sitting, with skis and poles in snow					
❑ CS 8039 [S]	Warm	1958	10.00	20.00	40.00
—Red and black label with six "eye" logos					
❑ CS 8039 [S]	Warm	1962	5.00	10.00	20.00
—Red "360 Sound" label					
❑ CS 8056 [S]	Open Fire, Two Guitars	1959	10.00	20.00	40.00
—Red and black label with six "eye" logos					
❑ CS 8056 [S]	Open Fire, Two Guitars	1962	5.00	10.00	20.00
—Red "360 Sound" label					
❑ CS 8150 [S]	More Johnny's Greatest Hits	1959	7.50	15.00	30.00
—Red and black label with six "eye" logos					
❑ CS 8150 [S]	More Johnny's Greatest Hits	1962	5.00	10.00	20.00
—Red "360 Sound" label					
❑ CS 8150 [S]	More Johnny's Greatest Hits	1971	2.50	5.00	10.00
—Orange label					
❑ PC 8150 [S]	More Johnny's Greatest Hits	198?	—	3.00	6.00
—Reissue with new prefix					
❑ CS 8152 [S]	Heavenly	1959	7.50	15.00	30.00
—Red and black label with six "eye" logos					
❑ CS 8152 [S]	Heavenly	1962	5.00	10.00	20.00
—Red "360 Sound" label					
❑ CS 8152 [S]	Heavenly	1971	2.50	5.00	10.00
—Orange label					
❑ PC 8152 [S]	Heavenly	198?	—	3.00	6.00
—Reissue with new prefix					
❑ CS 8219 [S]	Faithfully	1959	6.25	12.50	25.00
—Red and black label with six "eye" logos					
❑ CS 8219 [S]	Faithfully	1962	5.00	10.00	20.00
—Red "360 Sound" label					
❑ CS 8326 [S]	Johnny's Mood	1960	6.25	12.50	25.00
—Red and black label with six "eye" logos					
❑ CS 8326 [S]	Johnny's Mood	1962	5.00	10.00	20.00
—Red "360 Sound" label					
❑ CS 8423 [S]	I'll Buy You a Star	1961	5.00	10.00	20.00
—Red and black label with six "eye" logos					
❑ CS 8423 [S]	I'll Buy You a Star	1962	3.75	7.50	15.00
—Red "360 Sound" label					
❑ CS 8444 [S]	Portrait of Johnny	1961	5.00	10.00	20.00
—Red and black label with six "eye" logos; add 1/3 if portrait is there					
❑ CS 8444 [S]	Portrait of Johnny	1962	3.75	7.50	15.00
—Red "360 Sound" label					
❑ CS 8511 [S]	Live It Up!	1962	3.75	7.50	15.00
—Red "360 Sound" label					
❑ CS 8511 [S]	Live It Up!	1962	5.00	10.00	20.00
—Red and black label with six "eye" logos; add 1/3 if portrait is there					
❑ CS 8634 [R]	Johnny's Greatest Hits	1963	3.00	6.00	12.00
❑ CS 8715 [S]	Rapture	1962	3.75	7.50	15.00
—Red "360 Sound" label					

M

Number	Title (A Side/B Side)	Yr	VG	VG+	NM
❏ CS 8816 [S]	Johnny's Newest Hits	1963	3.75	7.50	15.00
—Red "360 Sound" label					
❏ CS 8844 [S]	Johnny	1963	3.75	7.50	15.00
—Red "360 Sound" label					
❏ CS 8898 [S]	Romantically	1963	3.75	7.50	15.00
—Red "360 Sound" label					
❏ CS 8943 [S]	I'll Search My Heart and Other Great Hits	1964	3.75	7.50	15.00
—Red "360 Sound" label					
❏ CS 9023 [S]	The Ballads of Broadway	1964	3.75	7.50	15.00
—Red "360 Sound" label					
❏ CS 9024 [S]	The Ballads of Broadway	1964	3.75	7.50	15.00
❏ CS 9046 [R]	Wonderful Wonderful	1964	3.00	6.00	12.00
❏ CS 9526 [S]	Up, Up and Away	1967	3.75	7.50	15.00
❏ CS 9637 [S]	Love Is Blue	1968	3.75	7.50	15.00
❏ CS 9705 [S]	Those Were the Days	1968	3.75	7.50	15.00
❏ CS 9871	People	1969	3.75	7.50	15.00
❏ CS 9872	The Impossible Dream	1969	3.75	7.50	15.00
—Red "360 Sound" label					
❏ CS 9872	The Impossible Dream	1971	2.50	5.00	10.00
—Orange label					
❏ PC 9872	The Impossible Dream	198?	—	3.00	6.00
—Reissue with new prefix					
❏ CS 9909	Love Theme from "Romeo and Juliet"	1969	3.75	7.50	15.00
—Red "360 Sound" label					
❏ CS 9909	Love Theme from "Romeo and Juliet"	1971	2.50	5.00	10.00
—Orange label					
❏ PC 9909	Love Theme from "Romeo and Juliet"	198?	—	3.00	6.00
—Reissue with new prefix					
❏ CS 9923	Give Me Your Love for Christmas	1969	3.00	6.00	12.00
❏ C 30210	Close to You	1970	3.00	6.00	12.00
❏ G 30350 [(2)]	Johnny Mathis Sings the Music of Bacharach & Kaempfert	1970	3.75	7.50	15.00
❏ C 30499	Love Story	1971	3.00	6.00	12.00
❏ PC 30499	Love Story	198?	2.00	4.00	8.00
—Budget-line reissue					
❏ C 30740	You've Got a Friend	1971	3.00	6.00	12.00
❏ CQ 30740 [Q]	You've Got a Friend	1972	5.00	10.00	20.00
❏ PC 30740	You've Got a Friend	198?	2.00	4.00	8.00
—Budget-line reissue					
❏ 2CQ 30979 [(2)Q]	Johnny Mathis In Person	1972	6.25	12.50	25.00
❏ KG 30979 [(2)]	Johnny Mathis In Person	1972	3.75	7.50	15.00
❏ CQ 31342 [Q]	The First Time Ever (I Saw Your Face)	1972	5.00	10.00	20.00
❏ KC 31342	The First Time Ever (I Saw Your Face)	1972	3.00	6.00	12.00
❏ PC 31342	The First Time Ever (I Saw Your Face)	198?	2.00	4.00	8.00
—Budget-line reissue					
❏ KG 31345 [(2)]	Johnny Mathis' All-Time Greatest Hits	1972	3.75	7.50	15.00
❏ CQ 31626 [Q]	Song Sung Blue	1972	5.00	10.00	20.00
❏ KC 31626	Song Sung Blue	1972	3.00	6.00	12.00
❏ CQ 32114 [Q]	Me and Mrs. Jones	1973	4.50	9.00	18.00
❏ KC 32114	Me and Mrs. Jones	1973	2.50	5.00	10.00
❏ KC 32258	Killing Me Softly with Her Song	1973	2.50	5.00	10.00
❏ CQ 32435 [Q]	I'm Coming Home	1973	4.50	9.00	18.00
❏ KC 32435	I'm Coming Home	1973	2.50	5.00	10.00
❏ PC 32435	I'm Coming Home	198?	2.00	4.00	8.00
—Budget-line reissue					
❏ C 32963	What'll I Do	1974	2.50	5.00	10.00
❏ KC 33251	The Heart of a Woman	1974	2.50	5.00	10.00
❏ PC 33420	When Will I See You Again	1975	2.50	5.00	10.00
❏ CG 33621 [(2)]	Heavenly/Faithfully	1975	3.00	6.00	12.00
❏ PC 33887	Feelings	1975	2.50	5.00	10.00
❏ PC 34117	I Only Have Eyes for You	1976	2.50	5.00	10.00
❏ PC 34441	Mathis Is…	1977	2.50	5.00	10.00
❏ PC 34667	Johnny Mathis' Greatest Hits	1977	2.50	5.00	10.00
❏ PC 34872	Hold Me, Thrill Me, Kiss Me	1977	2.50	5.00	10.00
❏ PC 35259	You Light Up My Life	1986	2.00	4.00	8.00
—Budget-line reissue					
❏ JC 35359	You Light Up My Life	1978	2.50	5.00	10.00
❏ C 35578	Romantically	1978	2.00	4.00	8.00
❏ JC 35649	The Best Days of My Life	1979	2.50	5.00	10.00
❏ PC 35649	The Best Days of My Life	1985	2.00	4.00	8.00
—Budget-line reissue					
❏ JC 36216	Mathis Magic	1979	2.50	5.00	10.00
❏ JC 36505	Different Kinda Different	1980	2.50	5.00	10.00
❏ JC 36871	The Best of Johnny Mathis 1975-1980	1980	2.50	5.00	10.00
❏ C2X 37440 [(2)]	The First 25 Years — The Silver Anniversary Album	1981	3.00	6.00	12.00
❏ FC 37748	Friends in Love	1982	2.50	5.00	10.00
❏ 3C 38306	Christmas with Johnny Mathis	1982	2.00	4.00	8.00
—Reissue of Columbia LE 10196 with same contents					
❏ FC 38699	Johnny Mathis Live	1983	2.50	5.00	10.00
❏ FC 38718	A Special Part of Me	1984	2.50	5.00	10.00
❏ PC 39468	For Christmas	1984	2.00	4.00	8.00
❏ FC 39601	Right from the Heart	1985	2.50	5.00	10.00
❏ FC 40372	The Hollywood Musicals	1986	2.50	5.00	10.00
—With Henry Mancini					
❏ FC 40447	Christmas Eve with Johnny Mathis	1986	2.50	5.00	10.00
❏ OC 44156	Once in a While	1988	2.50	5.00	10.00
❏ OC 44336	In the Still of the Night	1989	3.00	6.00	12.00
COLUMBIA LIMITED EDITION					
❏ LE 10196	Christmas with Johnny Mathis	1976	2.50	5.00	10.00
—Reissue of Harmony KH 30684 with same contents					
COLUMBIA MUSICAL TREASURY					
❏ 6P 6030 [(6)]	The Johnny Mathis Treasury	197?	7.50	15.00	30.00
COLUMBIA SPECIAL PRODUCTS					
❏ C 10896	Merry Christmas	1972	3.00	6.00	12.00
—Reissue					
❏ P3 11837 [(3)]	Romantically, Johnny Mathis	197?	6.25	12.50	25.00
❏ P6 14628 [(6)]	Misty Memories: The Complete Johnny Mathis Treasury	197?	7.50	15.00	30.00
—Maunfactured for Candelite Music					

Number	Title (A Side/B Side)	Yr	VG	VG+	NM
❏ P 14658	Holidays at the Fireside	197?	5.00	10.00	20.00
—Bonus album with box set 14628					
❏ P 14908	The Heart of Johnny Mathis	197?	3.75	7.50	15.00
—Bonus album with box set 14628					
❏ P4 14971 [(4)]	Johnny	197?	6.25	12.50	25.00
HARMONY					
❏ KH 30017	Johnny Mathis	1970	2.50	5.00	10.00
❏ KH 30684	Christmas with Johnny Mathis	1971	3.00	6.00	12.00
—Reissue of Mercury SR 60837 with two fewer tracks					
❏ KH 31935	Something for Everyone	1973	2.50	5.00	10.00
MERCURY					
❏ MG 20837 [M]	Sounds of Christmas	1963	3.00	6.00	12.00
❏ MG-20890 [M]	Tender Is the Night	1964	3.00	6.00	12.00
❏ MG-20913 [M]	The Wonderful World of Make Believe	1964	3.00	6.00	12.00
❏ MG-20942 [M]	This Is Love	1964	3.00	6.00	12.00
❏ MG-20988 [M]	Johnny Mathis Ole	1965	3.00	6.00	12.00
❏ MG-20991 [M]	Love Is Everything	1965	3.00	6.00	12.00
❏ MG-21041 [M]	The Sweetheart Tree	1965	3.00	6.00	12.00
❏ MG-21073 [M]	The Shadow of Your Smile	1966	3.00	6.00	12.00
❏ MG-21093 [M]	So Nice	1966	3.00	6.00	12.00
❏ MG-21107 [M]	Johnny Mathis Sings	1967	3.75	7.50	15.00
❏ SR 60837 [S]	Sounds of Christmas	1963	3.75	7.50	15.00
❏ SR-60890 [S]	Tender Is the Night	1964	3.75	7.50	15.00
❏ SR-60913 [S]	The Wonderful World of Make Believe	1964	3.75	7.50	15.00
❏ SR-60942 [S]	This Is Love	1964	3.75	7.50	15.00
❏ SR-60988 [S]	Johnny Mathis Ole	1965	3.75	7.50	15.00
❏ SR-60991 [S]	Love Is Everything	1965	3.75	7.50	15.00
❏ SR-61041 [S]	The Sweetheart Tree	1965	3.75	7.50	15.00
❏ SR-61073 [S]	The Shadow of Your Smile	1966	3.75	7.50	15.00
❏ SR-61093 [S]	So Nice	1966	3.75	7.50	15.00
❏ SR-61107 [S]	Johnny Mathis Sings	1967	3.75	7.50	15.00
MOBILE FIDELITY					
❏ 1-171	Heavenly	1985	6.25	12.50	25.00
—Audiophile vinyl					
READER'S DIGEST					
❏ RB4-097 [(6)]	His Greatest Hits and Finest Performances	198?	6.25	12.50	25.00

MATLOCK, MATTY
RCA VICTOR

Number	Title (A Side/B Side)	Yr	VG	VG+	NM
❏ LPM-1413 [M]	Pete Kelly at Home	1957	10.00	20.00	40.00
WARNER BROS.					
❏ W 1280 [M]	Four Button Dixie	1958	7.50	15.00	30.00
❏ WS 1280 [S]	Four Button Dixie	1958	10.00	20.00	40.00
"X"					
❏ LXA-3035 [10]	Sports Parade	1955	12.50	25.00	50.00

MATTEA, KATHY
MERCURY

Number	Title (A Side/B Side)	Yr	VG	VG+	NM
❏ R 110791	A Collection of Hits	1990	5.00	10.00	20.00
—Only released on vinyl by BMG Direct Marketing					
❏ 818560-1	Kathy Mattea	1984	2.50	5.00	10.00
❏ 824308-1	From My Heart	1985	2.50	5.00	10.00
❏ 830405-1	Walk the Way the Wind Blows	1986	2.50	5.00	10.00
❏ 832793-1	Untasted Honey	1987	2.50	5.00	10.00
❏ 836950-1	Willow in the Wind	1989	3.00	6.00	12.00

MATTHEWS, ONZY
CAPITOL

Number	Title (A Side/B Side)	Yr	VG	VG+	NM
❏ ST 2099 [S]	Blues with a Touch of Elegance	1964	5.00	10.00	20.00

MAUDS, THE
MERCURY

Number	Title (A Side/B Side)	Yr	VG	VG+	NM
❏ MG-21135 [M]	The Mauds Hold On	1967	5.00	10.00	20.00
❏ SR-61135 [S]	The Mauds Hold On	1967	6.25	12.50	25.00

MAULAWI
STRATA-EAST

Number	Title (A Side/B Side)	Yr	VG	VG+	NM
❏ SES 104-74	Maulawi	1974	5.00	10.00	20.00

MAURIAT, PAUL
FANTASY

Number	Title (A Side/B Side)	Yr	VG	VG+	NM
❏ 8380	Paris by Night	1968	3.00	6.00	12.00
❏ 8389	Joyeux Noel	1968	3.00	6.00	12.00
❏ 8394	Latin Style	1969	3.00	6.00	12.00
MERCURY					
❏ SRM-1-3746	Overseas	1978	2.50	5.00	10.00
MGM					
❏ SE-4838	Love Theme from "The Godfather"	1972	2.50	5.00	10.00
❏ M3G-4999	Have You Never Been Mellow	1975	2.50	5.00	10.00
PHILIPS					
❏ PHM 200197 [M]	Listen Too	1965	3.00	6.00	12.00
❏ PHM 200215 [M]	Of Vodka and Caviar	1966	3.00	6.00	12.00
❏ PHM 200226 [M]	More Mauriat	1967	3.75	7.50	15.00
❏ PHM 200248 [M]	Blooming Hits	1967	5.00	10.00	20.00
❏ PHM 200255 [M]	The Christmas Album	1967	5.00	10.00	20.00
❏ PHS 600197 [S]	Listen Too	1965	3.75	7.50	15.00
❏ PHS 600215 [S]	Of Vodka and Caviar	1966	3.75	7.50	15.00
❏ PHS 600226 [S]	More Mauriat	1967	3.75	7.50	15.00
❏ PHS 600248 [S]	Blooming Hits	1967	3.75	7.50	15.00
—Original copies have no "blurb" for "Love Is Blue" on front cover					
❏ PHS 600248 [S]	Blooming Hits	1968	3.00	6.00	12.00
—With blurb for "Love Is Blue" on front cover					
❏ PHS 600255 [S]	The Christmas Album	1967	3.75	7.50	15.00
❏ PHS 600270	Mauriat Magic	1968	3.75	7.50	15.00
❏ PHS 600280	Prevailing Airs	1968	3.75	7.50	15.00
❏ PHS 600292	Doing My Thing	1969	3.75	7.50	15.00
❏ PHS 600299	The Soul of Paul Mauriat	1969	3.75	7.50	15.00
❏ PHS 600320	L-O-V-E	1969	3.75	7.50	15.00
❏ PHS 600337	Midnight Cowboy/Let the Sunshine In	1970	3.00	6.00	12.00
❏ PHS 600345	Gone Is Love	1970	3.00	6.00	12.00
❏ PHS 600352	El Condor Pasa	1970	3.00	6.00	12.00

Number	Title (A Side/B Side)	Yr	VG	VG+	NM
VERVE					
❏ V6-5087	Theme from "A Summer Place"	1973	2.50	5.00	10.00
MAXIMILLIAN					
ABC					
❏ S-696	Maximillian	1969	10.00	20.00	40.00
MAXTED, BILLY					
BRUNSWICK					
❏ BL 58052 [10]	Honky Tonk Piano	1953	15.00	30.00	60.00
CADENCE					
❏ CLP-1005 [M]	Billy Maxted Plays Hi-Fi Keyboard	1955	10.00	20.00	40.00
❏ CLP-1012 [M]	Jazz at Nick's	1955	10.00	20.00	40.00
❏ CLP-1013 [M]	Dixieland Manhattan Style	1955	10.00	20.00	40.00
❏ CLP-3013 [M]	Dixieland Manhattan Style	1958	7.50	15.00	30.00
SEECO					
❏ CELP-438 [M]	Bourbon St. Billy and the Blues	1960	5.00	10.00	20.00
❏ CELP-458 [M]	Art of Jazz	1960	5.00	10.00	20.00
❏ CELP-4380 [S]	Bourbon St. Billy and the Blues	1960	6.25	12.50	25.00
❏ CELP-4580 [S]	Art of Jazz	1960	6.25	12.50	25.00
MAXWELL, DIANE					
CHALLENGE					
❏ CHL-607 [M]	Almost Seventeen	1959	10.00	20.00	40.00
❏ CHS-2501 [S]	Almost Seventeen	1959	12.50	25.00	50.00
MAY BLITZ					
PARAMOUNT					
❏ PAS-5020	May Blitz	1970	5.00	10.00	20.00
MAYALL, JOHN					
ABC					
❏ ABCD-926	Notice to Appear	1976	2.50	5.00	10.00
❏ D-958	A Banquet in Blues	1976	2.50	5.00	10.00
❏ D-992	Lots of People	1977	2.50	5.00	10.00
❏ D-1039	A Hard Core Package	1977	2.50	5.00	10.00
❏ D-1086	Last of the British Blues	1978	2.50	5.00	10.00
ACCORD					
❏ SN-7209	Roadshow Blues Band	1982	2.50	5.00	10.00
BLUE THUMB					
❏ BTS-6019	New Year, New Band, New Company	1975	2.50	5.00	10.00
DECAL					
❏ LIK-1	Some of My Best Friends Are Blues	1986	2.50	5.00	10.00
DJM					
❏ 23	The Bottom Line	1979	2.50	5.00	10.00
❏ 29	No More Interviews	1979	2.50	5.00	10.00
GNP CRESCENDO					
❏ 2184	Behind the Iron Curtain	1986	2.50	5.00	10.00
ISLAND					
❏ 91005	Chicago Line	1988	2.50	5.00	10.00
❏ 842795-1	A Sense of Place	1990	3.00	6.00	12.00
LONDON					
❏ PS 492 [S]	Blues Breakers with Eric Clapton	1966	10.00	20.00	40.00
❏ PS 502 [S]	A Hard Road	1967	5.00	10.00	20.00
❏ PS 529 [S]	Crusade	1967	5.00	10.00	20.00
❏ PS 534	The Blues Alone	1968	3.75	7.50	15.00
❏ PS 537	Bare Wires	1968	3.75	7.50	15.00
❏ PS 543	Raw Blues	1968	3.75	7.50	15.00
❏ PS 545	Blues from Laurel Canyon	1969	3.75	7.50	15.00
❏ PS 562	Looking Back	1969	3.75	7.50	15.00
❏ PS 570	The Diary of a Band	1970	3.00	6.00	12.00
❏ PS 589	Live in Europe	1971	3.00	6.00	12.00
❏ 2PS 600 [(2)]	Through the Years	1971	3.00	6.00	12.00
❏ 2PS 618 [(2)]	Down the Line	1973	2.50	5.00	10.00
❏ LL 3492 [M]	Blues Breakers with Eric Clapton	1966	7.50	15.00	30.00
❏ LL 3502 [M]	A Hard Road	1967	5.00	10.00	20.00
❏ LL 3529 [M]	Crusade	1967	5.00	10.00	20.00
❏ LC-50009	Blues Breakers with Eric Clapton	1977	2.50	5.00	10.00
—Reissue of London PS 492					
❏ 800086-1	Blues Breakers with Eric Clapton	1983	2.00	4.00	8.00
—Reissue of London 50009					
❏ 820320-1	Primal Solos	1985	2.00	4.00	8.00
❏ 820331-1	Looking Back	1985	2.00	4.00	8.00
—Reissue of London PS 562					
❏ 820342-1	Raw Blues	1985	2.00	4.00	8.00
—Reissue of London PS 543					
MCA					
❏ 716	Last of the British Blues	1980	2.00	4.00	8.00
—Reissue of ABC 1086					
❏ 795	Hard Core	1980	2.00	4.00	8.00
—Reissue of ABC 1039					
MOBILE FIDELITY					
❏ 1-183	Blues Breakers Featuring Eric Clapton	1985	10.00	20.00	40.00
—Audiophile vinyl					
❏ 1-246	The Blues Alone	1996	7.50	15.00	30.00
—Audiophile vinyl					
POLYDOR					
❏ 25-3002 [(2)]	Back to the Roots	1971	3.00	6.00	12.00
❏ PD2-3005 [(2)]	Ten Years Are Gone	1973	3.00	6.00	12.00
❏ PD2-3006 [(2)]	The Best of John Mayall	1973	3.00	6.00	12.00
❏ 24-4004	The Turning Point	1970	2.50	5.00	10.00
❏ 24-4010	Empty Rooms	1970	2.50	5.00	10.00
❏ 24-4022	U.S.A. Union	1970	2.50	5.00	10.00
❏ PD-5012	Memories	1971	2.50	5.00	10.00
❏ PD-5027	Jazz-Blues Fusion	1972	2.50	5.00	10.00
❏ PD-5036	Moving On	1972	2.50	5.00	10.00
❏ PD-6030	The Latest Edition	1974	3.00	6.00	12.00
❏ SKAO-93398	U.S.A. Union	1970	3.75	7.50	15.00
—Capitol Record Club edition					
❏ 823305-1	The Turning Point	1985	2.00	4.00	8.00
—Reissue of Polydor 24-4004					
❏ 837127-1	Archive to the Eighties	1988	2.00	4.00	8.00

Number	Title (A Side/B Side)	Yr	VG	VG+	NM
MAYER, NATHANIEL					
FORTUNE					
❏ 8014 [M]	Goin' Back to the Village of Love	196?	15.00	30.00	60.00
—Yellow label					
❏ 8014 [M]	Goin' Back to the Village of Love	196?	37.50	75.00	150.00
—Purple label					
❏ 8014 [M]	Goin' Back to the Village of Love	1964	75.00	150.00	300.00
—Light blue label					
❏ 8014 [M]	Goin' Back to the Village of Love	197?	3.75	7.50	15.00
—Bluish purple label, with much more flexible vinyl than earlier pressings					
MAYFIELD, CURTIS					
Also see THE IMPRESSIONS.					
BOARDWALK					
❏ NB1-33239	Love Is the Place	1981	2.50	5.00	10.00
❏ NB1-33256	Honesty	1982	2.50	5.00	10.00
CRC					
❏ 2001	We Come in Peace with a Message of Love	1985	3.00	6.00	12.00
CURTOM					
❏ CUR-2003	There's No Place Like America Today	198?	2.00	4.00	8.00
—Reissue of 5001					
❏ CUR-2005	Something to Believe In	198?	2.00	4.00	8.00
—Reissue of RSO 3077					
❏ CUR-2008	Take It to the Street	198?	2.50	5.00	10.00
❏ CUR-2901 [(2)]	Live in Europe	198?	3.00	6.00	12.00
❏ CUR-2902 [(2)]	Greatest Hits of All Time (Classic Collection)	198?	3.00	6.00	12.00
❏ CU 5001	There's No Place Like America Today	1975	3.00	6.00	12.00
❏ CU 5007	Give, Get, Take and Have	1976	3.00	6.00	12.00
❏ CU 5013	Never Say You Can't Survive	1977	3.00	6.00	12.00
❏ CUK 5022	Do It All Night	1978	3.00	6.00	12.00
❏ CRS-8005	Curtis	1970	3.75	7.50	15.00
❏ CRS-8008 [(2)]	Curtis/Live!	1971	5.00	10.00	20.00
❏ CRS-8009	Roots	1971	3.75	7.50	15.00
❏ CRS-8014	Superfly	1972	5.00	10.00	20.00
❏ CRS-8015	Back to the World	1973	3.75	7.50	15.00
❏ CRS-8018	Curtis in Chicago	1973	3.75	7.50	15.00
❏ CRS-8601	Sweet Exorcist	1974	3.00	6.00	12.00
❏ CRS-8604	Got to Find a Way	1974	3.00	6.00	12.00
RSO					
❏ RS-1-3053	Heartbeat	1979	2.50	5.00	10.00
❏ RS-1-3077	Something to Believe In	1980	2.50	5.00	10.00
MAYFIELD, PERCY					
BRUNSWICK					
❏ BL 754145	Walking on a Tightrope	1968	5.00	10.00	20.00
INTERMEDIA					
❏ QS-5010	Please Send Me Someone to Love	198?	2.50	5.00	10.00
RCA VICTOR					
❏ LSP-4269	Percy Mayfield Sings Percy Mayfield	1970	3.75	7.50	15.00
❏ LSP-4444	Weakness Is a Thing Called Man.	1970	3.75	7.50	15.00
❏ LSP-4558	Blues And Then Some.	1971	3.75	7.50	15.00
SPECIALTY					
❏ SPS-2126	The Best of Percy Mayfield	1970	5.00	10.00	20.00
❏ SP-7001	Poet of the Blues	1990	3.75	7.50	15.00
TANGERINE					
❏ TRC-1505 [M]	My Jug and I	1966	5.00	10.00	20.00
❏ TRCS-1505 [S]	My Jug and I	1966	6.25	12.50	25.00
❏ TRC-1510 [M]	Bought Blues	1967	5.00	10.00	20.00
❏ TRCS-1510 [S]	Bought Blues	1967	6.25	12.50	25.00
MAYPOLE					
COLOSSUS					
❏ CS-1007	Maypole	1971	15.00	30.00	60.00
MAZE					
MTA					
❏ 5012	Armageddon	1969	25.00	50.00	100.00
MC5					
ALIVE					
❏ 0005 [10]	Power Trip	1994	—	3.00	6.00
❏ 0008 [10]	Ice Pick Slim/Mad Like Eldridge Cleaver	1994	—	3.00	6.00
ATLANTIC					
❏ SD 8247	Back in the USA	1970	12.50	25.00	50.00
❏ SD 8285	High Time	1971	12.50	25.00	50.00
ELEKTRA					
❏ EKS-74042	Kick Out the Jams	1969	5.00	10.00	20.00
—All other editions					
❏ EKS-74042	Kick Out the Jams	1969	12.50	25.00	50.00
—Gatefold cover with John Sinclair liner notes in center spread; brownish label					
SUNDAZED					
❏ LP 5092	Kick Out the Jams	2001	3.75	7.50	15.00
—Reissue of original Elektra album, complete with uncensored liner notes					
❏ LP 5093	Back in the USA	2002	3.00	6.00	12.00
—Reissue on 180-gram vinyl					
❏ LP 5094	High Time	2002	3.00	6.00	12.00
—Reissue on 180-gram vinyl					
TOTAL ENERGY					
❏ 2001 [10]	The American Ruse	1994	—	3.00	6.00
MCAULIFFE, LEON					
ABC-PARAMOUNT					
❏ ABC-394 [M]	Cozy Inn	1961	10.00	20.00	40.00
❏ ABCS-394 [S]	Cozy Inn	1961	15.00	30.00	60.00
CAPITOL					
❏ ST 2016 [S]	The Dancin'est Band Around	1964	10.00	20.00	40.00
❏ T 2016 [M]	The Dancin'est Band Around	1964	7.50	15.00	30.00
❏ ST 2148 [S]	Everybody Dance! Everybody Swing!	1964	10.00	20.00	40.00
❏ T 2148 [M]	Everybody Dance! Everybody Swing!	1964	7.50	15.00	30.00

Number	Title (A Side/B Side)	Yr	VG	VG+	NM

CIMARRON

Number	Title (A Side/B Side)	Yr	VG	VG+	NM
❏ CLP-2002 [M]	The Swingin' Western Strings of Leon McAuliff	1960	12.50	25.00	50.00

DOT

❏ DLP-3139 [M]	Take Off	1958	15.00	30.00	60.00
❏ DLP-3689 [M]	Golden Country Hits	1966	10.00	20.00	40.00
❏ DLP-25689 [R]	Golden Country Hits	1966	6.25	12.50	25.00

SESAC

| ❏ (# unknown) [M] | Just a Minute | 1957 | 25.00 | 50.00 | 100.00 |
| ❏ 1601 [M] | Points West | 1957 | 25.00 | 50.00 | 100.00 |

STARDAY

❏ SLP-171 [M]	Mr. Western Swing	1962	12.50	25.00	50.00
❏ SLP-280 [M]	The Swingin' West with Leon McAuliff	1964	10.00	20.00	40.00
❏ SLP-309 [M]	The Swingin' Western Strings of Leon McAuliff	1964	10.00	20.00	40.00

MCBEE, CECIL
STRATA-EAST

| ❏ SES-7417 | Mutima | 1975 | 6.25 | 12.50 | 25.00 |

MCBROWNE, LENNY
PACIFIC JAZZ

| ❏ PJ-1 [M] | The Four Souls | 1960 | 7.50 | 15.00 | 30.00 |
| ❏ ST-1 [S] | The Four Souls | 1960 | 10.00 | 20.00 | 40.00 |

RIVERSIDE

| ❏ RLP-346 [M] | Eastern Lights | 1960 | 7.50 | 15.00 | 30.00 |
| ❏ RS-9346 [S] | Eastern Lights | 1960 | 10.00 | 20.00 | 40.00 |

MCCALL, DARRELL
COLUMBIA

| ❏ KC 34718 | Lily Dale | 1977 | 3.00 | 6.00 | 12.00 |

WAYSIDE

| ❏ 1030 | Meet Darrell McCall | 1969 | 5.00 | 10.00 | 20.00 |

MCCALL, MARY ANN
CORAL

| ❏ CRL 57276 [M] | Melancholy Baby | 1959 | 10.00 | 20.00 | 40.00 |
| ❏ CRL 757276 [S] | Melancholy Baby | 1959 | 12.50 | 25.00 | 50.00 |

DISCOVERY

| ❏ 3011 [10] | Mary Ann McCall Sings | 1950 | 50.00 | 100.00 | 200.00 |

JUBILEE

| ❏ JLP-1078 [M] | Detour to the Moon | 1958 | 12.50 | 25.00 | 50.00 |

REGENT

| ❏ MG-6040 [M] | Easy Living | 1957 | 10.00 | 20.00 | 40.00 |

MCCALL, TOUSSAINT
RONN

| ❏ 7527 [M] | Nothing Can Take the Place of You | 1967 | 7.50 | 15.00 | 30.00 |
| ❏ 7527S [S] | Nothing Can Take the Place of You | 1967 | 10.00 | 20.00 | 40.00 |

MCCANN, LES
LIMELIGHT

❏ LM-82043 [M]	Bucket O' Grease	1967	5.00	10.00	20.00
❏ LM-82046 [M]	Live at the Bohemian Caverns, Washington, D.C.	1967	5.00	10.00	20.00
❏ LS-86016 [S]	But Not Really	1965	5.00	10.00	20.00
❏ LS-86025 [S]	Poo Boo	1965	5.00	10.00	20.00
❏ LS-86031 [S]	Beaux J. Pooboo	1966	5.00	10.00	20.00
❏ LS-86036 [S]	Live at Shelly's Manne-Hole	1966	5.00	10.00	20.00
❏ LS-86041 [S]	Les McCann Plays the Hits	1966	5.00	10.00	20.00

PACIFIC JAZZ

❏ PJ-2 [M]	The Truth	1960	6.25	12.50	25.00
❏ ST-2 [S]	The Truth	1960	7.50	15.00	30.00
❏ PJ-7 [M]	The Shout	1960	6.25	12.50	25.00
❏ ST-7 [S]	The Shout	1960	7.50	15.00	30.00
❏ PJ-16 [M]	Les McCann in San Francisco	1961	6.25	12.50	25.00
❏ ST-16 [S]	Les McCann in San Francisco	1961	7.50	15.00	30.00
❏ PJ-25 [M]	Pretty Lady	1961	5.00	10.00	20.00
❏ ST-25 [S]	Pretty Lady	1961	6.25	12.50	25.00
❏ PJ-31 [M]	Les McCann Sings	1961	5.00	10.00	20.00
❏ ST-31 [S]	Les McCann Sings	1961	6.25	12.50	25.00
❏ PJ-45 [M]	Les McCann in New York	1962	5.00	10.00	20.00
❏ ST-45 [S]	Les McCann in New York	1962	6.25	12.50	25.00
❏ PJ-56 [M]	On Time	1962	5.00	10.00	20.00
—Black vinyl					
❏ PJ-56 [M]	On Time	1962	10.00	20.00	40.00
—Yellow vinyl					
❏ ST-56 [S]	On Time	1962	6.25	12.50	25.00
—Black vinyl					
❏ ST-56 [S]	On Time	1962	12.50	25.00	50.00
—Yellow vinyl					
❏ ST-63 [S]	Shampoo	1962	5.00	10.00	20.00
❏ ST-69 [S]	The Gospel Truth	1963	5.00	10.00	20.00
❏ ST-78 [S]	Soul Hits	1963	5.00	10.00	20.00
❏ ST-81 [S]	Jazz Waltz	1964	5.00	10.00	20.00
❏ ST-84 [S]	McCanna	1964	5.00	10.00	20.00
❏ ST-91 [S]	McCann/Wilson	1965	5.00	10.00	20.00
—With Gerald Wilson					
❏ ST-20097 [S]	Spanish Onions	1966	5.00	10.00	20.00
❏ ST-20107 [S]	A Bag of Gold	1966	5.00	10.00	20.00

MCCARTNEY, PAUL
Includes Thrillington and Wings. Also see THE BEATLES.

APPLE

❏ SMAS-3363	McCartney	197?	5.00	10.00	20.00
—New prefix on label					
❏ SMAS-3363	McCartney	1975	25.00	50.00	100.00
—With "All Rights Reserved" on label					
❏ STAO-3363	McCartney	1970	5.00	10.00	20.00
—Only "McCartney" on label; back cover does NOT say "An Abkco managed company"					
❏ STAO-3363	McCartney	1970	6.25	12.50	25.00
—"McCartney" and "Paul McCartney" on separate lines on label; New York address on back cover					

❏ STAO-3363	McCartney	1970	6.25	12.50	25.00
—Only "McCartney" on label; back cover says "An Abkco managed company"					
❏ STAO-3363	McCartney	1970	7.50	15.00	30.00
—"McCartney" and "Paul McCartney" on separate lines on label; California addess on back cover					
❏ STAO-3363	McCartney	1970	20.00	40.00	80.00
—Apple label with small Capitol logo on B-side					
❏ MAS-3375 [M]	Ram	1971	1000.	2000.	4000.
—Credited to "Paul and Linda McCartney"; mono record in stereo cover for radio station use only					
❏ SMAS-3375	Ram	1971	3.75	7.50	15.00
—Credited to "Paul and Linda McCartney"; unsliced apple on one label, sliced apple on other					
❏ SMAS-3375	Ram	1971	7.50	15.00	30.00
—Credited to "Paul and Linda McCartney"; unsliced apple on both labels					
❏ SMAS-3375	Ram	1971	12.50	25.00	50.00
—Credited to "Paul and Linda McCartney"; Apple label with small Capitol logo on B-side					
❏ SMAS-3375	Ram	1975	25.00	50.00	100.00
—Credited to "Paul and Linda McCartney"; with "All Rights Reserved" on label					
❏ SW-3386	Wild Life	1971	3.75	7.50	15.00
—Credited to "Wings"					
❏ SMAL-3409	Red Rose Speedway	1973	5.00	10.00	20.00
—Credited to "Paul McCartney and Wings"; with bound-in booklet					
❏ SO-3415	Band on the Run	1973	5.00	10.00	20.00
—Credited to "Paul McCartney and Wings"; with photo innersleeve and poster					
❏ SPRO-6210 [DJ]	Brung to Ewe By	1971	100.00	200.00	400.00
—Promo-only radio spots for "Ram"; counterfeits have uneven spacing between tracks					

CAPITOL

❏ SMAS-3363	McCartney	1976	5.00	10.00	20.00
—Black label, "Manufactured by MPL Communications Inc" at top					
❏ SMAS-3363	McCartney	1976	6.25	12.50	25.00
—Black label, "Manufactured by McCartney Music Inc" at top					
❏ SMAS-3375	Ram	197?	5.00	10.00	20.00
—Credited to "Paul and Linda McCartney"; black label, "Manufactured by MPL Communications Inc" at top					
❏ SMAS-3375	Ram	197?	10.00	20.00	40.00
—Credited to "Paul and Linda McCartney"; black label, "Manufactured by Capitol RecordsÖ" on label					
❏ SMAS-3375	Ram	1976	7.50	15.00	30.00
—Credited to "Paul and Linda McCartney"; black label, "Manufactured by McCartney Music Inc" at top					
❏ SW-3386	Wild Life	197?	5.00	10.00	20.00
—Credited to "Wings"; black label, "Manufactured by MPL Communications Inc" at top					
❏ SW-3386	Wild Life	1976	7.50	15.00	30.00
—Credited to "Wings"; black label, "Manufactured by McCartney Music Inc" at top					
❏ SMAL-3409	Red Rose Speedway	197?	6.25	12.50	25.00
—Credited to "Paul McCartney and Wings"; black label, "Manufactured by MPL Communications Inc" at top					
❏ SMAL-3409	Red Rose Speedway	1976	7.50	15.00	30.00
—Credited to "Paul McCartney and Wings"; black label, "Manufactured by McCartney Music Inc" at top					
❏ SO-3415	Band on the Run	197?	5.00	10.00	20.00
—Credited to "Paul McCartney and Wings"; black label, "Maunfactured by MPL Communications Inc." at top					
❏ SO-3415	Band on the Run	197?	12.50	25.00	50.00
—Credited to "Paul McCartney and Wings"; black label, "Manufactured by Capitol Records..."					
❏ SO-3415	Band on the Run	1975	5.00	10.00	20.00
—Credited to "Paul McCartney and Wings"; custom label with MPL logo					
❏ SMAS-11419	Venus and Mars	1975	3.75	7.50	15.00
—Credited to "Wings"; with two posters and two stickers					
❏ SW-11525	Wings at the Speed of Sound	1976	2.50	5.00	10.00
—Credited to "Wings"; custom label					
❏ SW-11525 [DJ]	Wings at the Speed of Sound	1976	75.00	150.00	300.00
—Credited to "Wings"; white label advance promo					
❏ SWCO-11593 [(3)]	Wings Over America	1976	6.25	12.50	25.00
—Credited to "Wings"; custom labels with poster					
❏ ST-11642	Thrillington	1977	25.00	50.00	100.00
—Credited to "Percy 'Thrills' Thrillington"; instrumental versions of songs from Ram LP					
❏ SW-11777	London Town	1978	3.75	7.50	15.00
—Credited to "Wings"; custom label with poster					
❏ SEAX-11901 [PD]	Band on the Run	1978	10.00	20.00	40.00
—Credited to "Paul McCartney and Wings"; picture disc					
❏ SOO-11905	Wings Greatest	1978	3.75	7.50	15.00
—Credited to "Wings"; custom label with poster					
❏ SOO-11905 [DJ]	Wings Greatest	1978	100.00	200.00	400.00
—Credited to "Wings"; white label advance promo/test pressing					
❏ PJAS-12475	Press to Play	1986	3.00	6.00	12.00
❏ CLW-48287 [(2)]	All the Best!	1987	5.00	10.00	20.00
❏ C1-56500	Flaming Pie	1997	3.75	7.50	15.00
❏ C1-91653	Flowers in the Dirt	1989	5.00	10.00	20.00
❏ C1-94778 [(3)]	Tripping the Live Fantastic	1990	15.00	30.00	60.00
❏ 99176 [(2)]	Band on the Run	1999	10.00	20.00	40.00
—Limited-edition 180-gram reissue with original LP on one record and interviews and "The Making of.." on the second					
❏ C1-595379	Tripping the Live Fantastic — Highlights!	1990	6.25	12.50	25.00
—Released on vinyl only through Columbia House; with Canada address on back cover, this was sold in the U.S. by Columbia House					
❏ C1-595379	Tripping the Live Fantastic — Highlights!	1990	6.25	12.50	25.00
—Released on vinyl only through Columbia House; with U.S. address on back cover					

COLUMBIA

❏ A2S 821 [(2)DJ]	The McCartney Interview	1980	10.00	20.00	40.00
—Promo-only set; one LP is the entire interview, the other is banded for airplay; white labels with black print; counterfeits have blank white labels					
❏ FC 36057	Back to the Egg	1979	2.50	5.00	10.00
—Credited to "Wings"; custom label					
❏ FC 36057 [DJ]	Back to the Egg	1979	10.00	20.00	40.00
—Credited to "Wings"; "Demonstration -- Not for Sale" on custom label					
❏ PC 36057	Back to the Egg	1984	7.50	15.00	30.00
—Credited to "Wings"; "PC" cover with "FC" label					
❏ PC 36057	Back to the Egg	1984	10.00	20.00	40.00
—Credited to "Wings"; "PC" cover with "PC" label					
❏ JC 36478	McCartney	1979	3.75	7.50	15.00
❏ PC 36478	McCartney	1984	3.75	7.50	15.00
—Budget-line reissue					
❏ JC 36479	Ram	1980	3.75	7.50	15.00
—Credited to "Paul and Linda McCartney"					

Number	Title (A Side/B Side)	Yr	VG	VG+	NM
❑ PC 36479	Ram	1984	3.75	7.50	15.00
—Credited to "Paul and Linda McCartney"; budget-line reissue					
❑ JC 36480	Wild Life	1980	3.75	7.50	15.00
—Credited to "Wings"					
❑ PC 36480	Wild Life	1982	3.75	7.50	15.00
—Credited to "Wings"; budget-line reissue					
❑ JC 36481	Red Rose Speedway	1980	3.75	7.50	15.00
—Credited to "Paul McCartney and Wings"; flat or glossy cover					
❑ PC 36481	Red Rose Speedway	198?	3.75	7.50	15.00
—Credited to "Paul McCartney and Wings"; not issued with booklet					
❑ JC 36482	Band on the Run	198?	25.00	50.00	100.00
—Credited to "Paul McCartney and Wings"; white "MPL" logo on lower left front cover					
❑ JC 36482	Band on the Run	1980	3.75	7.50	15.00
—Credited to "Paul McCartney and Wings"; custom label					
❑ PC 36482	Band on the Run	198?	5.00	10.00	20.00
—Credited to "Paul McCartney and Wings"; "PC" cover with "JC" label					
❑ PC 36482	Band on the Run	198?	7.50	15.00	30.00
—Credited to "Paul McCartney and Wings"; "PC" cover with "PC" label					
❑ FC 36511	McCartney II	1980	2.50	5.00	10.00
—Add 80% if bonus single of "Coming Up (Live at Glasgow)" (AE7 1204) is with package					
❑ FC 36511 [DJ]	McCartney II	1980	7.50	15.00	30.00
—White label promo					
❑ PC 36511	McCartney II	1984	6.25	12.50	25.00
—"PC" cover with "FC" label					
❑ PC 36511	McCartney II	1984	25.00	50.00	100.00
—"PC" cover with "PC" label					
❑ JC 36801	Venus and Mars	1980	3.75	7.50	15.00
—Credited to "Wings"; with one poster and two stickers					
❑ PC 36801	Venus and Mars	1982	3.75	7.50	15.00
—Credited to "Wings"; budget-line reissue, not issued with inserts					
❑ PC 36987	The McCartney Interview	1980	3.00	6.00	12.00
—Stock release of interview originally intended for promotional use only					
❑ FC 37409	Wings at the Speed of Sound	1981	3.75	7.50	15.00
—Credited to "Wings"; custom label					
❑ PC 37409	Wings at the Speed of Sound	1982	3.75	7.50	15.00
—Credited to "Wings"; regular Columbia label, budget-line reissue					
❑ PC 37462	Tug of War	1984	7.50	15.00	30.00
—Custom label; "PC" cover with "TC" label					
❑ PC 37462	Tug of War	1984	25.00	50.00	100.00
—Regular Columbia label; "PC" cover with "PC" label					
❑ TC 37462	Tug of War	1982	2.50	5.00	10.00
❑ C3X 37990 [(3)]	Wings Over America	1982	12.50	25.00	50.00
—Credited to "Wings"; custom labels, no poster					
❑ QC 39149	Pipes of Peace	1983	3.00	6.00	12.00
❑ SC 39613	Give My Regards to Broad Street	1984	3.75	7.50	15.00
❑ HC 46382	Band on the Run	1981	12.50	25.00	50.00
—Credited to "Paul McCartney and Wings"; half-speed mastered edition					
MPL/PARLOPHONE					
❑ 96413	Unplugged (The Official Bootleg)	1991	18.75	37.50	75.00
—No U.S. pressings; "American" copies were U.K. imports with liner notes in Spanish!					
NATIONAL FEATURES CORP.					
❑ 2955/6	Band on the Run Radio Interview Special	1973	375.00	750.00	1500.
—Promo-only interview disc					

MCCLINTON, DELBERT
ABC

Number	Title (A Side/B Side)	Yr	VG	VG+	NM
❑ ABCD-907	Victim of Life's Circumstances	1975	5.00	10.00	20.00
❑ ABCD-959	Genuine Cowhide	1976	5.00	10.00	20.00
❑ AB-991	Love Rustler	1977	5.00	10.00	20.00
ACCORD					
❑ SN-7145	Wake Up Baby	198?	2.50	5.00	10.00
ALLIGATOR					
❑ AL-3902	Honky Tonkin' (I Done Me Some)	1986	2.50	5.00	10.00
❑ AL-4773	Live from Austin	1989	3.00	6.00	12.00
CAPITOL/MSS					
❑ ST-12115	The Jealous Kind	1980	3.00	6.00	12.00
❑ ST-12188	Playin' from the Heart	1981	3.00	6.00	12.00
CAPRICORN					
❑ CPN-0201	Second Wind	1978	5.00	10.00	20.00
❑ CPN-0223	Keeper of the Flame	1979	3.75	7.50	15.00
INTERMEDIA					
❑ QS-5029	Feelin' Alright!	198?	2.50	5.00	10.00
MCA					
❑ 5197	The Best of Delbert McClinton	1981	2.50	5.00	10.00

MCCLINTON, O.B.
ENTERPRISE

Number	Title (A Side/B Side)	Yr	VG	VG+	NM
❑ ENS-1023	Country	1972	7.50	15.00	30.00
❑ ENS-1029	Obie from Senatobie	1973	7.50	15.00	30.00
❑ ENS-1037	Live at Randy's Rodeo	1973	7.50	15.00	30.00
❑ ENS-7506	If You Loved Her That Way	1974	6.25	12.50	25.00
EPIC					
❑ FE 40674	The Only One	1987	2.50	5.00	10.00
HOMETOWN					
❑ 104	Album No. 1	198?	3.00	6.00	12.00

MCCORMICK BROTHERS, THE
HICKORY

Number	Title (A Side/B Side)	Yr	VG	VG+	NM
❑ LP-102 [M]	Songs for Home Folks	1961	20.00	40.00	80.00
❑ LP-108 [M]	Authentic Bluegrass Hits	1962	15.00	30.00	60.00
METROMEDIA					
❑ MM-1019	Grass Meets Brass	1969	5.00	10.00	20.00

MCCOY, CLYDE
CAPITOL

Number	Title (A Side/B Side)	Yr	VG	VG+	NM
❑ H 311 [10]	Sugar Blues	195?	25.00	50.00	100.00
❑ T 311 [M]	Sugar Blues	1955	12.50	25.00	50.00
—Turquoise or gray label					
❑ T 311 [M]	Sugar Blues	1959	10.00	20.00	40.00
—Black colorband label, logo at left					
❑ T 311 [M]	Sugar Blues	1963	6.25	12.50	25.00
—Black colorband label, logo at top					
MERCURY					
❑ MG-20110 [M]	The Blues	195?	10.00	20.00	40.00
❑ SR-60677 [S]	Really McCoy	1961	5.00	10.00	20.00
❑ SR-60730 [S]	Blue Prelude	1962	5.00	10.00	20.00
TOP RANK					
❑ RM-350 [M]	Dixieland's Best Friend	1961	7.50	15.00	30.00
❑ RS-650 [S]	Dixieland's Best Friend	1961	10.00	20.00	40.00

MCCOY, FREDDIE
COBBLESTONE

Number	Title (A Side/B Side)	Yr	VG	VG+	NM
❑ 9004	Gimme Some	1972	5.00	10.00	20.00
PRESTIGE					
❑ PRLP-7395 [M]	Lonely Avenue	1965	5.00	10.00	20.00
❑ PRST-7395 [S]	Lonely Avenue	1965	6.25	12.50	25.00
❑ PRLP-7444 [M]	Spider Man	1966	5.00	10.00	20.00
❑ PRST-7444 [S]	Spider Man	1966	6.25	12.50	25.00
❑ PRLP-7470 [M]	Funk Drops	1967	6.25	12.50	25.00
❑ PRST-7470 [S]	Funk Drops	1967	6.25	12.50	25.00
❑ PRLP-7487 [M]	Peas 'N' Rice	1967	7.50	15.00	30.00
❑ PRST-7487 [S]	Peas 'N' Rice	1967	6.25	12.50	25.00
❑ PRST-7542	Beans and Greens	1968	6.25	12.50	25.00
❑ PRST-7561	Soul Yogi	1968	6.25	12.50	25.00
❑ PRST-7582	Listen Here	1968	6.25	12.50	25.00
❑ PRST-7706	The Best of Freddie McCoy	1969	5.00	10.00	20.00

MCCOY, VAN
AVCO

Number	Title (A Side/B Side)	Yr	VG	VG+	NM
❑ AV-69002	Love Is the Answer	1974	2.50	5.00	10.00
❑ AV-69006	Disco Baby	1975	2.50	5.00	10.00
❑ AV-69009	The Disco Kid	1975	2.50	5.00	10.00
BUDDAH					
❑ BDS-5103	Soul Improvisations	1971	3.75	7.50	15.00
❑ BDS-5648	From Disco to Love	1975	2.50	5.00	10.00
—Retitled reissue of 5103					
COLUMBIA					
❑ CL 2497 [M]	Night Time Is the Lonely Time	1966	5.00	10.00	20.00
❑ CS 9297 [S]	Night Time Is the Lonely Time	1966	6.25	12.50	25.00
H&L					
❑ HL-69002	Love Is the Answer	1976	2.00	4.00	8.00
—Reissue of Avco 69002					
❑ HL-69006	Disco Baby	1976	2.00	4.00	8.00
—Reissue of Avco 69006					
❑ HL-69009	The Disco Kid	1976	2.00	4.00	8.00
—Reissue of Avco 69009					
❑ HL-69012	The Real McCoy	1976	2.50	5.00	10.00
❑ HL-69014	Rhythms of the World	1976	2.50	5.00	10.00
❑ HL-69016	The Hustle and Best of Van McCoy	1976	2.50	5.00	10.00
❑ HL-69022	Van McCoy and His Magnificent Movie Machine	1977	2.50	5.00	10.00
MCA					
❑ 3036	My Favorite Fantasy	1978	2.50	5.00	10.00
❑ 3054	A Woman Called Moses	1978	2.50	5.00	10.00
❑ 3071	Lovely Dancer	1979	2.50	5.00	10.00

MCCOYS, THE
BANG

Number	Title (A Side/B Side)	Yr	VG	VG+	NM
❑ BLP-212 [M]	Hang On Sloopy	1965	7.50	15.00	30.00
❑ BLPS-212 [S]	Hang On Sloopy	1965	10.00	20.00	40.00
❑ BLP-213 [M]	You Make Me Feel So Good	1966	7.50	15.00	30.00
❑ BLPS-213 [S]	You Make Me Feel So Good	1966	10.00	20.00	40.00
MERCURY					
❑ SR-61163	Infinite McCoys	1968	6.25	12.50	25.00
❑ SR-61207	Human Ball	1969	6.25	12.50	25.00

MCCRACKLIN, JIMMY
CHESS

Number	Title (A Side/B Side)	Yr	VG	VG+	NM
❑ LP-1464 [M]	Jimmy McCracklin Sings	1961	30.00	60.00	120.00
CROWN					
❑ CLP-5244 [M]	Twist with Jimmy McCracklin	196?	3.75	7.50	15.00
—Black label, multi-color "Crown"					
❑ CLP-5244 [M]	Twist with Jimmy McCracklin	1962	6.25	12.50	25.00
—Gray label					
❑ CLP-5244 [M]	Twist with Jimmy McCracklin	1962	12.50	25.00	50.00
—Black label, silver "Crown"					
EVEJIM					
❑ EJR-4013	Same Lovin'	198?	3.00	6.00	12.00
IMPERIAL					
❑ LP-9219 [M]	I Just Gotta Know	1964	6.25	12.50	25.00
❑ LP-9285 [M]	Every Night, Every Day	1965	6.25	12.50	25.00
❑ LP-9297 [M]	Think	1965	6.25	12.50	25.00
❑ LP-9306 [M]	My Answer	1966	6.25	12.50	25.00
❑ LP-9316 [M]	The New Soul of Jimmy McCracklin	1966	6.25	12.50	25.00
❑ LP-12219 [S]	I Just Gotta Know	1964	7.50	15.00	30.00
❑ LP-12285 [S]	Every Night, Every Day	1965	7.50	15.00	30.00
❑ LP-12297 [S]	Think	1965	7.50	15.00	30.00
❑ LP-12306 [S]	My Answer	1966	7.50	15.00	30.00
❑ LP-12316 [S]	The New Soul of Jimmy McCracklin	1966	7.50	15.00	30.00
MINIT					
❑ LP-4009 [M]	The Best of Jimmy McCracklin	1967	7.50	15.00	30.00
❑ LP-24009 [S]	The Best of Jimmy McCracklin	1967	6.25	12.50	25.00
❑ LP-24011	Let's Get Together	1968	6.25	12.50	25.00
❑ LP-24017	Stinger Man	1969	6.25	12.50	25.00
STAX					
❑ STS-2047	Yesterday Is Gone	1972	5.00	10.00	20.00
❑ MPS-8506	High on the Blues	1980	2.50	5.00	10.00

MCCULLOCH, DANNY
CAPITOL

Number	Title (A Side/B Side)	Yr	VG	VG+	NM
❑ ST-174	Wings of a Man	1969	5.00	10.00	20.00

M

Number	Title (A Side/B Side)	Yr	VG	VG+	NM
MCCURDY, ED					
DAWN					
❑ DLP-1127 [M]	The Folk Singer	195?	7.50	15.00	30.00
ELEKTRA					
❑ EKL-24 [10]	Sin Songs — Pro and Con	1955	10.00	20.00	40.00
❑ EKL-108 [M]	Blood Booze 'n' Bones	1956	7.50	15.00	30.00
❑ EKL-110 [M]	When Dalliance Was In Flower 1	1956	7.50	15.00	30.00
❑ EKL-112 [M]	Songs of the Old West	1956	7.50	15.00	30.00
❑ EKL-124 [M]	Sin Songs — Pro and Con	1957	7.50	15.00	30.00
—Reissue of EKL-24 with extra tracks					
❑ EKL-140 [M]	When Dalliance Was In Flower 2	1958	7.50	15.00	30.00
❑ EKL-160 [M]	When Dalliance Was In Flower 3	1959	7.50	15.00	30.00
❑ EKL-170 [M]	Son of Dalliance	1959	7.50	15.00	30.00
❑ EKL-205 [M]	A Treasure Chest of American Folk Song	1961	6.25	12.50	25.00
❑ EKL-213 [(2)M]	The Best of Dalliance	1961	7.50	15.00	30.00
❑ EKS-7160 [S]	When Dalliance Was In Flower 3	1959	10.00	20.00	40.00
RIVERSIDE					
❑ RLP 12-601 [M]	The Ballad Record	195?	7.50	15.00	30.00
TRADITION					
❑ TLP-1003 [M]	A Ballad Singer's Choice	195?	7.50	15.00	30.00
❑ TLP-1027 [M]	Children's Songs	195?	7.50	15.00	30.00
❑ TLP-2061 [M]	Songs of the West	196?	5.00	10.00	20.00
MCCURDY, ED; JACK ELLIOTT; OSCAR BRAND					
ELEKTRA					
❑ EKL-14 [10]	Badmen and Heroes	1955	12.50	25.00	50.00
MCCURDY, ED; JACK ELLIOTT; OSCAR BRAND; DICK WILDER					
ELEKTRA					
❑ EKL-129 [M]	Badmen, Heroes and Pirate Songs	1957	7.50	15.00	30.00
MCCURN, GEORGE					
A&M					
❑ LP-102 [M]	The Country Boy Comes to Town	1963	6.25	12.50	25.00
MCDANIEL, WILLARD					
CROWN					
❑ CLP-5024 [M]	88 A La Carte	1958	25.00	50.00	100.00
MCDANIELS, GENE					
ATLANTIC					
❑ SD 8259	Outlaw	1970	3.75	7.50	15.00
❑ SD 8281	Headless Heroes	1971	3.75	7.50	15.00
LIBERTY					
❑ LRP-3146 [M]	In Times Like These	1960	7.50	15.00	30.00
❑ LRP-3175 [M]	Sometimes I'm Happy, Sometimes I'm Blue	1960	7.50	15.00	30.00
❑ LRP-3191 [M]	100 Lbs. of Clay!	1961	7.50	15.00	30.00
❑ LRP-3204 [M]	Gene McDaniels Sings Movie Memories	1962	7.50	15.00	30.00
❑ LRP-3215 [M]	Tower of Strength	1962	7.50	15.00	30.00
❑ LRP-3258 [M]	Hit After Hit	1962	7.50	15.00	30.00
❑ LRP-3275 [M]	Spanish Lace	1963	6.25	12.50	25.00
❑ LRP-3311 [M]	The Wonderful World of Gene McDaniels	1963	6.25	12.50	25.00
❑ LST-7146 [S]	In Times Like These	1960	10.00	20.00	40.00
—Black vinyl					
❑ LST-7146 [S]	In Times Like These	1960	50.00	100.00	200.00
—Blue vinyl					
❑ LST-7175 [S]	Sometimes I'm Happy, Sometimes I'm Blue	1960	10.00	20.00	40.00
❑ LST-7191 [S]	100 Lbs. of Clay!	1961	10.00	20.00	40.00
❑ LST-7204 [S]	Gene McDaniels Sings Movie Memories	1962	10.00	20.00	40.00
❑ LST-7215 [S]	Tower of Strength	1962	10.00	20.00	40.00
❑ LST-7258 [S]	Hit After Hit	1962	10.00	20.00	40.00
❑ LST-7275 [S]	Spanish Lace	1963	7.50	15.00	30.00
❑ LST-7311 [S]	The Wonderful World of Gene McDaniels	1963	7.50	15.00	30.00
ODE					
❑ SP-77028	Natural Juices	1975	3.00	6.00	12.00
SUNSET					
❑ SUM-1122 [M]	Facts of Life	1967	3.00	6.00	12.00
❑ SUS-5122 [S]	Facts of Life	1967	3.75	7.50	15.00
UNITED ARTISTS					
❑ UA-LA447-E	The Very Best of Gene McDaniels	1975	2.50	5.00	10.00
MCDONALD, COUNTRY JOE					
See COUNTRY JOE AND THE FISH.					
MCDONALD, KATHI					
CAPITOL					
❑ ST-11224	Insane Asylum	1974	7.50	15.00	30.00
MCDONALD, MARIE					
RCA VICTOR					
❑ LPM-1585 [M]	"The Body" Sings!	1957	12.50	25.00	50.00
MCDONALD, MICHAEL					
Also see THE DOOBIE BROTHERS.					
MOBILE FIDELITY					
❑ 1-149	If That's What It Takes	1985	5.00	10.00	20.00
—Audiophile vinyl					
REPRISE					
❑ 25979	Take It to Heart	1990	3.00	6.00	12.00
WARNER BROS.					
❑ 23703	If That's What It Takes	1982	2.50	5.00	10.00
❑ 25291	No Lookin' Back	1985	2.50	5.00	10.00
MCDONALD, SKEETS					
CAPITOL					
❑ T 1040 [M]	Goin' Steady with the Blues	1958	20.00	40.00	80.00
COLUMBIA					
❑ CL 2170 [M]	Call Me Skeets	1964	6.25	12.50	25.00
❑ CS 8970 [S]	Call Me Skeets	1964	7.50	15.00	30.00
FORTUNE					
❑ 3001	The Tattooed Lady and Other Songs	1969	12.50	25.00	50.00

Number	Title (A Side/B Side)	Yr	VG	VG+	NM
SEARS					
❑ SPS-116 [R]	Skeets	196?	6.25	12.50	25.00
MCDOWELL, MISSISSIPPI FRED					
ARHOOLIE					
❑ F-1021 [M]	Delta Blues	1964	12.50	25.00	50.00
❑ F-1027 [M]	Delta Blues, Volume 2	1966	12.50	25.00	50.00
❑ F-1046	Mississippi Fred McDowell and His Blues Boys	1970	7.50	15.00	30.00
❑ F-1068	Keep Your Lamp Trimmed and Burning	1973	5.00	10.00	20.00
CAPITOL					
❑ ST-403	I Do Not Play No Rock and Roll	1970	6.25	12.50	25.00
JUST SUNSHINE					
❑ JSS-4	Mississippi Fred McDowell 1904-1972	1973	3.75	7.50	15.00
MILESTONE					
❑ MLP-3003 [M]	Long Way from Home	1966	7.50	15.00	30.00
❑ MLS-93003 [S]	Long Way from Home	1966	10.00	20.00	40.00
SIRE					
❑ SES-97018	Mississippi Fred McDowell in London	1970	7.50	15.00	30.00
MCDOWELL, RONNIE					
CURB					
❑ 10602	I'm Still Missing You	1988	2.00	4.00	8.00
EPIC					
❑ JE 36142	Rockin' You Easy, Lovin' You Slow	1979	2.50	5.00	10.00
❑ PE 36142	Rockin' You Easy, Lovin' You Slow	198?	2.00	4.00	8.00
—Budget-line reissue with new prefix					
❑ JE 36336	Love So Many Ways	1980	2.50	5.00	10.00
❑ JE 36821	Going, Going ... Gone	1980	2.50	5.00	10.00
❑ PE 36821	Going, Going ... Gone	198?	2.00	4.00	8.00
—Budget-line reissue with new prefix					
❑ FE 37399	Good Time Lovin' Man	1981	2.50	5.00	10.00
❑ PE 37399	Good Time Lovin' Man	198?	2.00	4.00	8.00
—Budget-line reissue with new prefix					
❑ FE 38017	Love to Burn	1982	2.50	5.00	10.00
❑ PE 38017	Love to Burn	198?	2.00	4.00	8.00
—Budget-line reissue with new prefix					
❑ FE 38314	Greatest Hits	1983	2.50	5.00	10.00
❑ FE 38514	Personally	1983	2.50	5.00	10.00
❑ PE 38514	Personally	1985	2.00	4.00	8.00
—Budget-line reissue with new prefix					
❑ FE 38981	Country Boy's Heart	1983	2.50	5.00	10.00
❑ PE 38981	Country Boy's Heart	1985	2.00	4.00	8.00
—Budget-line reissue with new prefix					
❑ FE 39329	Willing	1984	2.50	5.00	10.00
❑ FE 39954	In a New York Minute	1985	2.50	5.00	10.00
❑ PE 40643	Older Women and Other Greatest Hits	1987	2.50	5.00	10.00
MCA CURB					
❑ 5725	All Tied Up in Love	1986	2.00	4.00	8.00
SCORPION					
❑ 0010	Live at the Fox	1978	3.75	7.50	15.00
❑ 8021	The King Is Gone	1977	5.00	10.00	20.00
❑ 8028	I Love You, I Love You, I Love You	1978	3.75	7.50	15.00
MCDUFF, JACK					
ATLANTIC					
❑ SD 1463 [S]	A Change Is Gonna Come	1966	5.00	10.00	20.00
❑ 1472 [M]	Tobacco Road	1967	5.00	10.00	20.00
PRESTIGE					
❑ PRLP-7174 [M]	Brother Jack	1960	12.50	25.00	50.00
❑ PRLP-7185 [M]	Tough 'Duff	1960	12.50	25.00	50.00
❑ PRLP-7199 [M]	The Honeydripper	1961	12.50	25.00	50.00
❑ PRLP-7220 [M]	Goodnight, It's Time to Go	1961	10.00	20.00	40.00
❑ PRST-7220 [S]	Goodnight, It's Time to Go	1961	10.00	20.00	40.00
❑ PRLP-7228 [M]	Mellow Gravy — Brother Jack Meets the Boss	1962	10.00	20.00	40.00
❑ PRST-7228 [S]	Mellow Gravy — Brother Jack Meets the Boss	1962	10.00	20.00	40.00
❑ PRLP-7259 [M]	Screamin'	1963	10.00	20.00	40.00
❑ PRST-7259 [S]	Screamin'	1963	10.00	20.00	40.00
❑ PRLP-7265 [M]	Somethin' Slick!	1963	10.00	20.00	40.00
❑ PRST-7265 [S]	Somethin' Slick!	1963	10.00	20.00	40.00
❑ PRLP-7274 [M]	Live!	1963	10.00	20.00	40.00
❑ PRST-7274 [S]	Live!	1963	10.00	20.00	40.00
❑ PRLP-7286 [M]	Live! At the Jazz Workshop	1964	10.00	20.00	40.00
❑ PRST-7286 [S]	Live! At the Jazz Workshop	1964	10.00	20.00	40.00
❑ PRLP-7323 [M]	The Dynamic Jack McDuff	1964	10.00	20.00	40.00
❑ PRST-7323 [S]	The Dynamic Jack McDuff	1964	10.00	20.00	40.00
❑ PRLP-7333 [M]	Prelude	1964	6.25	12.50	25.00
❑ PRST-7333 [S]	Prelude	1964	7.50	15.00	30.00
❑ PRLP-7362 [M]	The Concert McDuff Recorded Live!	1965	6.25	12.50	25.00
❑ PRST-7362 [S]	The Concert McDuff Recorded Live!	1965	7.50	15.00	30.00
❑ PRLP-7404 [M]	Silk and Soul	1965	6.25	12.50	25.00
❑ PRST-7404 [S]	Silk and Soul	1965	7.50	15.00	30.00
❑ PRLP-7422 [M]	Hot Barbeque	1966	5.00	10.00	20.00
❑ PRST-7422 [S]	Hot Barbeque	1966	6.25	12.50	25.00
❑ PRLP-7476 [M]	Walk On By	1967	6.25	12.50	25.00
❑ PRST-7476 [S]	Walk On By	1967	5.00	10.00	20.00
❑ PRLP-7481 [M]	Brother Jack McDuff's Greatest Hits	1967	6.25	12.50	25.00
❑ PRST-7481 [S]	Brother Jack McDuff's Greatest Hits	1967	5.00	10.00	20.00
❑ PRLP-7492 [M]	Hallelujah Time!	1967	6.25	12.50	25.00
❑ PRST-7492 [S]	Hallelujah Time!	1967	5.00	10.00	20.00
❑ PRST-7529	The Midnight Sun	1968	5.00	10.00	20.00
❑ PRST-7567	Soul Circle	1968	5.00	10.00	20.00
❑ PRST-7596	Jack McDuff Plays for Beautiful People	1969	5.00	10.00	20.00
❑ PRST-7642	I Got a Woman	1969	5.00	10.00	20.00
❑ PRST-7666	Steppin' Out	1969	5.00	10.00	20.00
❑ PRST-7703	Live! The Best of Brother Jack McDuff	1969	5.00	10.00	20.00
MCENTIRE, REBA					
MCA					
❑ 5475	Just a Little Love	1984	2.00	4.00	8.00
❑ 5516	My Kind of Country	1984	2.00	4.00	8.00
❑ 5585	Have I Got a Deal for You	1985	2.00	4.00	8.00

Number	Title (A Side/B Side)	Yr	VG	VG+	NM
❑ 5691	Whoever's in New England	1986	2.00	4.00	8.00
❑ 5807	What Am I Gonna Do About You	1986	2.00	4.00	8.00
❑ 5979	Reba McEntire's Greatest Hits	1987	2.00	4.00	8.00
❑ 6294	Sweet Sixteen	1989	2.50	5.00	10.00
❑ 1P-8162	For My Broken Heart	1991	6.25	12.50	25.00
—Only released on vinyl through Columbia House					
❑ 10016	Rumor Has It	1990	5.00	10.00	20.00
❑ 42030	The Last One to Know	1987	2.00	4.00	8.00
❑ 42031	Merry Christmas to You	1987	2.50	5.00	10.00
❑ 42134	Reba	1988	2.00	4.00	8.00
❑ R 164184	Merry Christmas to You	1987	3.00	6.00	12.00
—BMG Direct Marketing edition					
❑ R 244602 [(2)]	Reba Live	1989	6.25	12.50	25.00
—Only released on vinyl through BMG Direct Marketing					
MERCURY					
❑ SRM-1-1177	Reba McEntire	1977	25.00	50.00	100.00
❑ SRM-1-4047	Unlimited	1982	6.25	12.50	25.00
❑ SRM-1-5002	Reba McEntire	1977	10.00	20.00	40.00
—Reissue of 1177					
❑ SRM-1-5017	Out of a Dream	1979	10.00	20.00	40.00
❑ SRM-1-5029	Feel the Fire	1980	7.50	15.00	30.00
❑ SRM-1-6003	Heart to Heart	1981	7.50	15.00	30.00
❑ 812781-1	Behind the Scene	1983	5.00	10.00	20.00
❑ 822455-1	Reba Nell McEntire	1986	2.50	5.00	10.00
❑ 822882-1	Unlimited	1986	2.50	5.00	10.00
—Reissue					
❑ 822887-1	Feel the Fire	1986	2.50	5.00	10.00
—Reissue					
❑ 824342-1	The Best of Reba McEntire	1985	2.50	5.00	10.00

MCFADDEN, BOB
BRUNSWICK

Number	Title (A Side/B Side)	Yr	VG	VG+	NM
❑ BL 54056 [M]	Songs Our Mummy Taught Us	1959	50.00	100.00	200.00
❑ BL 754056 [S]	Songs Our Mummy Taught Us	1959	75.00	150.00	300.00

MCFARLAND, GARY
IMPULSE!

Number	Title (A Side/B Side)	Yr	VG	VG+	NM
❑ A-46 [M]	Points of Departure	1963	5.00	10.00	20.00
❑ AS-46 [S]	Points of Departure	1963	6.25	12.50	25.00
❑ A-9104 [M]	Tijuana Jazz	1966	5.00	10.00	20.00
❑ AS-9104 [S]	Tijuana Jazz	1966	6.25	12.50	25.00
❑ A-9112 [M]	Profiles	1966	5.00	10.00	20.00
❑ AS-9112 [S]	Profiles	1966	6.25	12.50	25.00
❑ A-9122 [M]	Simpatico	1966	5.00	10.00	20.00
❑ AS-9122 [S]	Simpatico	1966	6.25	12.50	25.00
VERVE					
❑ V6-8443 [S]	How to Succeed in Business Without Really Trying	1962	5.00	10.00	20.00
❑ V6-8518 [S]	The Gary McFarland Orchestra with Special Guest Soloist Bill Evans	1963	5.00	10.00	20.00
❑ V6-8603 [S]	Soft Samba	1964	5.00	10.00	20.00
❑ V6-8632 [S]	The "In" Sound	1965	5.00	10.00	20.00
❑ V6-8682 [S]	Soft Samba Strings	1966	5.00	10.00	20.00
❑ V-8738 [M]	Scorpio and Other Signs	1967	5.00	10.00	20.00

MCGARITY, LOU
ARGO

Number	Title (A Side/B Side)	Yr	VG	VG+	NM
❑ LP-654 [M]	Blue Lou	1960	7.50	15.00	30.00
❑ LPS-654 [S]	Blue Lou	1960	10.00	20.00	40.00
JUBILEE					
❑ JGM-1108 [M]	Some Like It Hot	1959	12.50	25.00	50.00

MCGEE, SAM AND KIRK, AND THE CROOK BROTHERS
STARDAY

Number	Title (A Side/B Side)	Yr	VG	VG+	NM
❑ SLP-182 [M]	Opry Old Timers	1962	10.00	20.00	40.00

MCGEE, BROWNIE
BLUESVILLE

Number	Title (A Side/B Side)	Yr	VG	VG+	NM
❑ BVLP-1042 [M]	Brownie's Blues	1962	20.00	40.00	80.00
—Blue label, silver print					
❑ BVLP-1042 [M]	Brownie's Blues	1964	6.25	12.50	25.00
—Blue label, trident logo at right					
FANTASY					
❑ OBC-505	Brownie's Blues	198?	3.00	6.00	12.00
FOLKWAYS					
❑ FP-30 [10]	Brownie McGhee Blues	1951	30.00	60.00	120.00
❑ FA-2030 [10]	Brownie McGhee Blues	1951	25.00	50.00	100.00
❑ 2421/2 [(2)]	Traditional Blues Vol. 1 and 2	197?	3.75	7.50	15.00
❑ 3557	Brownie McGhee Sings the Blues	197?	3.00	6.00	12.00
SAVOY JAZZ					
❑ SJL-1204	Jumpin' the Blues	1989	3.00	6.00	12.00

MCGHEE, BROWNIE, AND SONNY TERRY
See SONNY TERRY AND BROWNIE McGHEE.

MCGHEE, HOWARD
ARGO

Number	Title (A Side/B Side)	Yr	VG	VG+	NM
❑ LP-4020 [M]	House Warmin'	1963	6.25	12.50	25.00
❑ LPS-4020 [S]	House Warmin'	1963	7.50	15.00	30.00
BETHLEHEM					
❑ BCP-42 [M]	The Return of Howard McGhee	1956	20.00	40.00	80.00
❑ BCP-61 [M]	Life Is Just a Bowl of Cherries	1957	20.00	40.00	80.00
❑ BCP-6055 [M]	Dusty Blue	1961	12.50	25.00	50.00
❑ BCPS-6055 [S]	Dusty Blue	1961	15.00	30.00	60.00
BLUE NOTE					
❑ BLP-5012 [10]	Howard McGhee's All Stars/Howard McGhee-Fats Navarro Sextet	1952	75.00	150.00	300.00
❑ BLP-5024 [10]	Howard McGhee, Volume 2	1953	75.00	150.00	300.00
CONTEMPORARY					
❑ M-3596 [M]	Maggie's Back in Town	1961	10.00	20.00	40.00
❑ S-7596 [S]	Maggie's Back in Town	1961	12.50	25.00	50.00

DIAL

Number	Title (A Side/B Side)	Yr	VG	VG+	NM
❑ LP-217 [10]	Night Music	1951	75.00	150.00	300.00
HI-LO					
❑ HL-6001 [10]	Jazz Goes to the Battlefront, Vol. 1	1952	62.50	125.00	250.00
❑ HL-6002 [10]	Jazz Goes to the Battlefront, Vol. 2	1952	62.50	125.00	250.00
SAVOY					
❑ MG-12026 [M]	Howard McGhee and Milt Jackson	1955	20.00	40.00	80.00
UNITED ARTISTS					
❑ UAJ-14028 [M]	Nobody Knows You When You're Down and Out	1963	7.50	15.00	30.00
❑ UAJS-15028 [S]	Nobody Knows You When You're Down and Out	1963	10.00	20.00	40.00

MCGHEE, STICK, AND JOHN LEE HOOKER
AUDIO LAB

Number	Title (A Side/B Side)	Yr	VG	VG+	NM
❑ AL-1520 [M]	Highway of Blues	1959	87.50	175.00	350.00

MCGOVERN, PATTY, AND THOMAS TALBERT
ATLANTIC

Number	Title (A Side/B Side)	Yr	VG	VG+	NM
❑ 1245 [M]	Wednesday's Child	1956	12.50	25.00	50.00
—Black label					
❑ 1245 [M]	Wednesday's Child	1961	6.25	12.50	25.00
—Multicolor label, white "fan" logo at right					

MCGRAW, TIM
CURB

Number	Title (A Side/B Side)	Yr	VG	VG+	NM
❑ (# unknown) [DJ]	Everywhere	1997	6.25	12.50	25.00
—Promo-only picture disc					

MCGRIFF, JIMMY
SOLID STATE

Number	Title (A Side/B Side)	Yr	VG	VG+	NM
❑ SM-17006 [M]	Cherry	1967	5.00	10.00	20.00
❑ SS-18001 [S]	The Big Band of Jimmy McGriff	1966	5.00	10.00	20.00
❑ SS-18002 [S]	A Bag Full of Soul	1966	5.00	10.00	20.00
❑ SS-18006 [S]	Cherry	1967	5.00	10.00	20.00
❑ SS-18017	A Bag Full of Blues	1968	5.00	10.00	20.00
❑ SS-18030	I've Got a New Woman	1968	5.00	10.00	20.00
❑ SS-18036	Honey	1968	5.00	10.00	20.00
❑ SS-18045	The Worm	1968	5.00	10.00	20.00
❑ SS-18053	Step I	1969	5.00	10.00	20.00
❑ SS-18060	A Thing to Come By	1969	5.00	10.00	20.00
❑ SS-18063	The Way You Look Tonight	1970	5.00	10.00	20.00
SUE					
❑ LP-1012 [M]	I've Got a Woman	1962	7.50	15.00	30.00
❑ STLP-1012 [S]	I've Got a Woman	1962	10.00	20.00	40.00
❑ LP-1013 [M]	One of Mine	1963	7.50	15.00	30.00
❑ STLP-1013 [S]	One of Mine	1963	10.00	20.00	40.00
❑ LP-1017 [M]	Jimmy McGriff at the Apollo	1963	7.50	15.00	30.00
❑ STLP-1017 [S]	Jimmy McGriff at the Apollo	1963	10.00	20.00	40.00
❑ LP-1018 [M]	Christmas with McGriff	1963	7.50	15.00	30.00
❑ STLP-1018 [S]	Christmas with McGriff	1963	10.00	20.00	40.00
❑ LP-1020 [M]	Jimmy McGriff at the Organ	1963	7.50	15.00	30.00
❑ STLP-1020 [S]	Jimmy McGriff at the Organ	1963	10.00	20.00	40.00
❑ LP-1033 [M]	Topkapi	1964	7.50	15.00	30.00
❑ STLP-1033 [S]	Topkapi	1964	10.00	20.00	40.00
❑ LP-1039 [M]	Blues for Mister Jimmy	1965	7.50	15.00	30.00
❑ STLP-1039 [S]	Blues for Mister Jimmy	1965	10.00	20.00	40.00
❑ LP-1043 [M]	Toast to Greatest Hits	1966	5.00	10.00	20.00
❑ STLP-1043 [S]	Toast to Greatest Hits	1966	6.25	12.50	25.00
VEEP					
❑ VP-13515 [M]	Live Where the Action Is	1966	5.00	10.00	20.00
❑ VP-13522 [M]	Greatest Organ Hits	1967	6.25	12.50	25.00
❑ VPS-16515 [S]	Live Where the Action Is	1966	6.25	12.50	25.00
❑ VPS-16522 [S]	Greatest Organ Hits	1967	5.00	10.00	20.00

MCGUINN, ROGER
Also see THE BYRDS.
ARISTA

Number	Title (A Side/B Side)	Yr	VG	VG+	NM
❑ AL 8648	Back from Rio	1991	3.75	7.50	15.00
COLUMBIA					
❑ AS 353 [DJ]	The Roger McGuinn Airplay Anthology	1977	7.50	15.00	30.00
—Promo only; also includes Byrds tracks					
❑ KC 31946	Roger McGuinn	1973	3.00	6.00	12.00
❑ KC 32956	Peace On You	1974	3.00	6.00	12.00
❑ PC 33541	Roger McGuinn & Band	1975	3.00	6.00	12.00
❑ PC 34154	Cardiff Rose	1976	3.00	6.00	12.00
❑ PC 34656	Thunderbyrd	1977	3.00	6.00	12.00

MCGUIRE, BARRY
Also see THE NEW CHRISTY MINSTRELS.
ABC DUNHILL

Number	Title (A Side/B Side)	Yr	VG	VG+	NM
❑ DS-50033	The World's Last Private Citizen	1968	6.25	12.50	25.00
DUNHILL					
❑ D-50003 [M]	Eve of Destruction	1965	7.50	15.00	30.00
❑ DS-50003 [S]	Eve of Destruction	1965	10.00	20.00	40.00
❑ D-50005 [M]	This Precious Time	1966	6.25	12.50	25.00
❑ DS-50005 [S]	This Precious Time	1966	7.50	15.00	30.00
HORIZON					
❑ ST-1636 [S]	The Barry McGuire Album	1963	10.00	20.00	40.00
❑ WP-1636 [M]	The Barry McGuire Album	1963	7.50	15.00	30.00
MIRA					
❑ LP-3000 [M]	The Barry McGuire Album	1965	5.00	10.00	20.00
—Reissue of Horizon LP					
❑ LPS-3000 [S]	The Barry McGuire Album	1965	6.25	12.50	25.00
—Reissue of Horizon LP					
MYRRH					
❑ MSA-6519	Seeds	1974	3.00	6.00	12.00
❑ MSA-6531	Lighten Up	1975	3.00	6.00	12.00
ODE					
❑ SP-77004	Barry McGuire with the Doctor	1970	3.75	7.50	15.00

M

Number	Title (A Side/B Side)	Yr	VG	VG+	NM

MCGUIRE, BARRY, AND BARRY KANE
HORIZON
❑ SWP-1608 [S]	Barry and Barry: Here and Now!	1962	7.50	15.00	30.00
❑ WP-1608 [M]	Barry and Barry: Here and Now!	1962	6.25	12.50	25.00

MCGUIRE, PHYLLIS
Also see THE McGUIRE SISTERS.
ABC-PARAMOUNT
❑ 552 [M]	Phyllis McGuire Sings	1966	3.75	7.50	15.00
❑ S-552 [S]	Phyllis McGuire Sings	1966	5.00	10.00	20.00

MCGUIRE SISTERS, THE
Also see PHYLLIS McGUIRE.
ABC-PARAMOUNT
❑ 530 [M]	The McGuire Sisters Today	1966	3.75	7.50	15.00
❑ S-530 [S]	The McGuire Sisters Today	1966	5.00	10.00	20.00
CORAL
❑ 7CXB 6 [(2)P]	The Best of the McGuire Sisters	1965	6.25	12.50	25.00
❑ CXB 6 [(2)M]	The Best of the McGuire Sisters	1965	6.25	12.50	25.00
❑ CRL 56123 [10]	By Request	1955	12.50	25.00	50.00
❑ CRL 57026 [M]	Do You Remember When	1956	10.00	20.00	40.00
❑ CRL 57028 [M]	'S Wonderful	1956	10.00	20.00	40.00
❑ CRL 57033 [M]	He	1956	10.00	20.00	40.00
❑ CRL 57052 [M]	Sincerely	1956	10.00	20.00	40.00
❑ CRL 57097 [M]	Children's Holiday	1956	10.00	20.00	40.00
❑ CRL 57134 [M]	Teenage Party	1957	7.50	15.00	30.00
❑ CRL 57145 [M]	While the Lights Are Low	1957	7.50	15.00	30.00
❑ CRL 57180 [M]	Musical Magic	1957	7.50	15.00	30.00
❑ CRL 57217 [M]	Sugartime	1958	7.50	15.00	30.00
❑ CRL 57225 [M]	Greetings from the McGuire Sisters	1958	7.50	15.00	30.00
❑ CRL 57296 [M]	May You Always	1959	5.00	10.00	20.00
❑ CRL 57303 [M]	In Harmony with Him	1959	6.25	12.50	25.00
❑ CRL 57337 [M]	His and Hers	1960	5.00	10.00	20.00
❑ CRL 57349 [M]	Our Golden Favorites	1961	5.00	10.00	20.00
❑ CRL 57385 [M]	Just for Old Times' Sake	1961	5.00	10.00	20.00
❑ CRL 57398 [M]	Subways Are for Sleeping	1961	3.75	7.50	15.00
❑ CRL 57415 [M]	Songs Everybody Knows	1962	3.75	7.50	15.00
❑ CRL 57443 [M]	Showcase	196?	5.00	10.00	20.00
❑ CRL 757296 [S]	May You Always	1959	7.50	15.00	30.00
❑ CRL 757303 [S]	In Harmony with Him	1959	10.00	20.00	40.00
❑ CRL 757337 [S]	His and Hers	1960	7.50	15.00	30.00
❑ CRL 757349 [R]	Our Golden Favorites	196?	3.00	6.00	12.00
❑ CRL 757385 [S]	Just for Old Times' Sake	1961	7.50	15.00	30.00
❑ CRL 757398 [S]	Subways Are for Sleeping	1961	5.00	10.00	20.00
❑ CRL 757415 [S]	Songs Everybody Knows	1962	5.00	10.00	20.00
❑ CRL 757443 [R]	Showcase	196?	3.00	6.00	12.00
MCA
❑ 4119 [(2)]	The Best of the McGuire Sisters	1978	3.00	6.00	12.00

—Reissue of Coral 6
VOCALION
❑ VL 3685 [M]	Children's Holiday	1960	5.00	10.00	20.00
❑ VL 3798 [M]	The McGuire Sisters	1967	3.75	7.50	15.00
❑ VL 73798 [R]	The McGuire Sisters	1967	3.00	6.00	12.00

MCHARGUE, ROSY
JUMP
❑ JL-8 [10]	Dixie Combo	1955	12.50	25.00	50.00

MCINTYRE, HAL
COLUMBIA
❑ CL 6124 [10]	Dance Date	1950	12.50	25.00	50.00
ROULETTE
❑ R-25079 [M]	It Seems Like Only Yesterday	1959	5.00	10.00	20.00
❑ SR-25079 [S]	It Seems Like Only Yesterday	1959	6.25	12.50	25.00

MCINTYRE, KALAPARUSHA MAURICE
DELMARK
❑ DS-419	Humility	1969	5.00	10.00	20.00
❑ DS-425	Forces and Feelings	197?	5.00	10.00	20.00

MCINTYRE, KEN
NEW JAZZ
❑ NJLP-8247 [M]	Looking Ahead	1960	12.50	25.00	50.00

—Purple label
❑ NJLP-8247 [M]	Looking Ahead	1965	6.25	12.50	25.00

—Blue label, trident logo at right
❑ NJLP-8259 [M]	Stone Blues	1961	12.50	25.00	50.00

—Purple label
❑ NJLP-8259 [M]	Stone Blues	1965	6.25	12.50	25.00

—Blue label, trident logo at right
UNITED ARTISTS
❑ UAL-3336 [M]	Way Way Out	1964	6.25	12.50	25.00
❑ UAS-6336 [S]	Way Way Out	1964	7.50	15.00	30.00
❑ UAJ-14015 [M]	Year of the Iron Sheep	1962	7.50	15.00	30.00
❑ UAJS-15015 [S]	Year of the Iron Sheep	1962	10.00	20.00	40.00

MCKAY, SCOTTY
ACE
❑ LP-1017 [M]	Tonight In Person	1961	20.00	40.00	80.00

MCKAY, STUART
RCA VICTOR
❑ LJM-1021 [M]	Stuart McKay and His Woods	1955	10.00	20.00	40.00

MCKENNA, DAVE
ABC-PARAMOUNT
❑ ABC-104 [M]	Solo Piano	1956	10.00	20.00	40.00
EPIC
❑ BN 527 [S]	Dave McKenna	1959	6.25	12.50	25.00
❑ LN 3558 [M]	Dave McKenna	1959	7.50	15.00	30.00

MCKENNA, DAVE, AND HALL OVERTON
BETHLEHEM
❑ BCP-6049 [M]	Dual Piano Jazz	1960	7.50	15.00	30.00
❑ BCPS-6049 [S]	Dual Piano Jazz	1960	7.50	15.00	30.00

MCKENZIE, SCOTT
ODE
❑ Z12 44002 [S]	The Voice of Scott McKenzie	1967	6.25	12.50	25.00
❑ SP-77007	Stained Glass Morning	1970	3.75	7.50	15.00

MCKINLEY, RAY
Also see GLENN MILLER ORCHESTRA.
ALLEGRO ELITE
❑ 4015 [10]	Ray McKinley Plays Sauter and Others	195?	12.50	25.00	50.00
❑ 4129 [10]	Ray McKinley and His Famous Orchestra	195?	25.00	50.00	100.00

MCKINLEY, RAY/JOE MARSALA
DECCA
❑ DL 5262 [10]	Dixieland Jazz Battle, Vol. 2	1950	12.50	25.00	50.00

MCKINLEY, RAY, AND EDDIE SAUTER
SAVOY
❑ MG-12024 [M]	Borderline	1955	12.50	25.00	50.00

MCKINNEY, HAROLD
TRIBE
❑ 2233	Voices and Rhythms	197?	10.00	20.00	40.00

MCKINNEY'S COTTON PICKERS
RCA VICTOR
❑ LPT-24 [10]	McKinney's Cotton Pickers	1952	15.00	30.00	60.00
"X"
❑ LVA-3031 [10]	McKinney's Cotton Pickers	1954	12.50	25.00	50.00

MCKUEN, ROD
BUDDAH
❑ BDS-5138	Cycles	197?	3.00	6.00	12.00
CAPITOL
❑ ST 2079 [S]	Rod McKuen Sings Rod McKuen	1964	5.00	10.00	20.00
❑ T 2079 [M]	Rod McKuen Sings Rod McKuen	1964	3.75	7.50	15.00
❑ ST 2838 [S]	Love Movement	1968	3.75	7.50	15.00
❑ T 2838 [M]	Love Movement	1968	6.25	12.50	25.00
DECCA
❑ DL 4969 [M]	Very Warm	1968	5.00	10.00	20.00
❑ DL 8882 [M]	Anywhere I Wander	1958	5.00	10.00	20.00
❑ DL 8946 [M]	Alone After Dark	1959	5.00	10.00	20.00
❑ DL 74969 [S]	Very Warm	1968	3.75	7.50	15.00
❑ DL 78882 [S]	Anywhere I Wander	1958	7.50	15.00	30.00
❑ DL 78946 [S]	Alone After Dark	1959	7.50	15.00	30.00
EPIC
❑ BN 26370 [M]	In Search of Eros	1968	7.50	15.00	30.00

—White label promo only; in stereo cover with "Epic Mono" sticker
❑ BN 26370 [S]	In Search of Eros	1968	3.75	7.50	15.00
EVEREST
❑ 3208	Desire Has No Special Time	1968	3.75	7.50	15.00
❑ 3267	Life Is	197?	3.75	7.50	15.00
HIFI
❑ R 407 [M]	Time of Desire	1958	5.00	10.00	20.00
❑ SR 407 [S]	Time of Desire	1958	6.25	12.50	25.00
❑ R 419 [M]	Beatsville	1960	5.00	10.00	20.00
❑ SR 419 [S]	Beatsville	1960	6.25	12.50	25.00
HORIZON
❑ ST-1612 [S]	New Sounds in Folk Music	1963	6.25	12.50	25.00
❑ WP-1612 [M]	New Sounds in Folk Music	1963	5.00	10.00	20.00
❑ WPLP-1632 [M]	There's a Hoot Tonight	1963	5.00	10.00	20.00
❑ WPLP-1632 [S]	There's a Hoot Tonight	1963	6.25	12.50	25.00
IN
❑ 1003 [M]	Seasons in the Sun	1964	5.00	10.00	20.00
❑ S-1003 [S]	Seasons in the Sun	1964	6.25	12.50	25.00
JUBILEE
❑ J-5013 [M]	Mr. Oliver Twist	1962	5.00	10.00	20.00
❑ SJ-5013 [S]	Mr. Oliver Twist	1962	6.25	12.50	25.00
KAPP
❑ KL-1538 [M]	In a Lonely Place	1967	5.00	10.00	20.00
❑ KS-3538 [S]	In a Lonely Place	1967	3.75	7.50	15.00
LIBERTY
❑ LRP-3011 [M]	Lazy Afternoon	1956	10.00	20.00	40.00
RCA VICTOR
❑ LPM-3424 [M]	Rod McKuen Sings His Own	1965	3.75	7.50	15.00
❑ LSP-3424 [S]	Rod McKuen Sings His Own	1965	5.00	10.00	20.00
❑ LPM-3508 [M]	The Loner	1966	3.75	7.50	15.00
❑ LSP-3508 [S]	The Loner	1966	5.00	10.00	20.00
❑ LPM-3635 [M]	Other Kinds of Songs	1966	3.75	7.50	15.00
❑ LSP-3635 [S]	Other Kinds of Songs	1966	5.00	10.00	20.00
❑ LPM-3786 [M]	Through European Windows	1967	5.00	10.00	20.00
❑ LSP-3786 [S]	Through European Windows	1967	3.75	7.50	15.00
❑ LPM-3863 [M]	Listen to the Warm	1967	5.00	10.00	20.00
❑ LSP-3863 [S]	Listen to the Warm	1967	3.75	7.50	15.00
❑ LSP-4010	A Single Man	1968	3.75	7.50	15.00
❑ LSP-4127	The Best of Rod McKuen	1969	3.75	7.50	15.00
STANYAN
❑ STS-001	In Concert	197?	3.75	7.50	15.00

—Originals are numbered, limited editions
❑ STS-003	Seasons in the Sun	197?	3.75	7.50	15.00
❑ 1894 [(2)]	Pastorale	197?	3.00	6.00	12.00
❑ 2560	Rod McKuen's Greatest Hits 2	197?	2.50	5.00	10.00
❑ 2688	Rod McKuen's Greatest Hits, Vol. 4	197?	2.50	5.00	10.00
❑ 4010	A Single Man	197?	2.50	5.00	10.00
❑ 5004	Seasons in the Sun Vol. 2	197?	3.00	6.00	12.00
❑ 5005	Blessings in Shades of Green	1970	3.00	6.00	12.00

Number	Title (A Side/B Side)	Yr	VG	VG+	NM
5006	Folk Album	1970	3.00	6.00	12.00
5009	Love's Been Good to Me	1970	3.00	6.00	12.00
5010	A Boy Named Charlie Brown	1970	3.75	7.50	15.00
5016 [(2)]	Live in London!	1971	3.75	7.50	15.00
5020	Try Rod McKuen in Your Own Home	197?	3.00	6.00	12.00
5022	Rod McKuen Sings Jacques Brel	197?	3.00	6.00	12.00
5025	Rod	197?	3.00	6.00	12.00
5031	Rod McKuen's Greatest Hits, Vol. 3	197?	3.00	6.00	12.00
5032	Have a Nice Day	1973	3.00	6.00	12.00
5040	Evening in Vienna	1972	3.00	6.00	12.00
5042	Rod McKuen Grand Tour, Vol. 3	1972	3.00	6.00	12.00
5046 [(2)]	Seasons in the Sun Vols. 1 and 2	197?	3.75	7.50	15.00
5047	Pastures Green	197?	3.00	6.00	12.00
5048 [(2)]	Listen to the Warm	197?	3.75	7.50	15.00
5051 [(2)]	Amsterdam Concert	1972	3.75	7.50	15.00
5072	A Portrait of Rod McKuen	1972	3.00	6.00	12.00
5075	Live at the Sydney Opera House	197?	3.00	6.00	12.00
9001	Concerto No. 1 for Four Harpsichords and Orchestra	197?	3.00	6.00	12.00
9005	Symphony No. 1: "All Men Love Something"	197?	3.00	6.00	12.00
9006	Concerto No. 2 for Guitar and Orchestra; Five Pieces	197?	3.00	6.00	12.00
9008	Piano Variations	197?	3.00	6.00	12.00
9010	McKuen Conducts McKuen	1972	3.00	6.00	12.00
9012	Concerto No. 3 for Piano and Orchestra	1972	3.00	6.00	12.00
9015	Seascapes; Plains of My Country	197?	3.00	6.00	12.00
10009	Concerto No. 1; Four Statements	197?	3.00	6.00	12.00

SUNSET

Number	Title (A Side/B Side)	Yr	VG	VG+	NM
SUS-5273	In the Beginning	1970	2.50	5.00	10.00

TRADITION

Number	Title (A Side/B Side)	Yr	VG	VG+	NM
2063 [M]	A San Francisco Hippie Trip	1967	6.25	12.50	25.00

WARNER BROS.

Number	Title (A Side/B Side)	Yr	VG	VG+	NM
WS 1722	Beautiful Strangers	1968	3.75	7.50	15.00
WS 1758	Lonesome Cities	1968	3.75	7.50	15.00
WS 1772	Greatest Hits of Rod McKuen	1969	3.75	7.50	15.00
2WS 1794 [(2)]	Rod McKuen at Carnegie Hall	1969	5.00	10.00	20.00
WS 1837	New Ballads	1970	3.00	6.00	12.00
2WS 1894 [(2)]	Pastorale	1971	3.75	7.50	15.00
2WS 1947 [(2)]	Rod McKuen Grand Tour	1971	3.75	7.50	15.00
BS 2560	Rod McKuen's Greatest Hits 2	1970	3.00	6.00	12.00
BS 2638	Odyssey	1973	3.00	6.00	12.00
BS 2688	Rod McKuen's Greatest Hits, Vol. 4	1973	3.00	6.00	12.00
2WS 2731 [(2)]	Back to Carnegie Hall	1973	3.75	7.50	15.00
BS 2785	Seasons in the Sun	1974	3.00	6.00	12.00
BS 2817	Alone	1974	3.00	6.00	12.00
BS 2931	McKuen Country	1976	2.50	5.00	10.00
ST-92042	Greatest Hits of Rod McKuen	1969	5.00	10.00	20.00

—Capitol Record Club edition

MCKUEN, ROD; TAK SHINDO; JULIE MEREDITH
IMPERIAL

Number	Title (A Side/B Side)	Yr	VG	VG+	NM
LP-9092 [M]	The Yellow Unicorn	1960	10.00	20.00	40.00
LP-12036 [S]	The Yellow Unicorn	1960	12.50	25.00	50.00

MCKUSICK, HAL
BETHLEHEM

Number	Title (A Side/B Side)	Yr	VG	VG+	NM
BCP-16 [M]	East Coast Jazz/8	1955	30.00	60.00	120.00

CORAL

Number	Title (A Side/B Side)	Yr	VG	VG+	NM
CRL 57116 [M]	Jazz at the Academy	1957	20.00	40.00	80.00
CRL 57131 [M]	Hal McKusick Quintet	1957	20.00	40.00	80.00

DECCA

Number	Title (A Side/B Side)	Yr	VG	VG+	NM
DL 9209 [M]	Cross Section Saxes	1958	12.50	25.00	50.00
DL 79209 [S]	Cross Section Saxes	1958	10.00	20.00	40.00

PRESTIGE

Number	Title (A Side/B Side)	Yr	VG	VG+	NM
PRLP-7135 [M]	Triple Exposure	1957	20.00	40.00	80.00

RCA VICTOR

Number	Title (A Side/B Side)	Yr	VG	VG+	NM
LPM-1164 [M]	Hal McKusick in the 20th Century Drawing Room	1956	17.50	35.00	70.00
LPM-1366 [M]	The Jazz Workshop	1957	20.00	40.00	80.00

MCLACHLAN, SARAH
ARISTA

Number	Title (A Side/B Side)	Yr	VG	VG+	NM
RTH-2000 [(2)]	Fumbling Toward Ecstasy and The Freedom Sessions	1997	10.00	20.00	40.00

—Audiophile vinyl issue of both CDs on 2-LP set by Classic Records, with one bonus track

Number	Title (A Side/B Side)	Yr	VG	VG+	NM
RTH-2004	Touch	2002	6.25	12.50	25.00

—Audiophile vinyl reissue by Classic Records

Number	Title (A Side/B Side)	Yr	VG	VG+	NM
RTH-2005	Solace	2002	6.25	12.50	25.00

—Audiophile vinyl reissue by Classic Records

Number	Title (A Side/B Side)	Yr	VG	VG+	NM
AL 8594	Touch	1989	5.00	10.00	20.00
RTH-18970	Surfacing	1999	6.25	12.50	25.00

—Audiophile vinyl issue by Classic Records

MCLAIN, DENNY
CAPITOL

Number	Title (A Side/B Side)	Yr	VG	VG+	NM
ST-204	Denny McLain In Las Vegas	1969	6.25	12.50	25.00
ST 2881	Denny McLain at the Organ	1968	6.25	12.50	25.00

MCLAUGHLIN, JOHN
RYKO ANALOGUE

Number	Title (A Side/B Side)	Yr	VG	VG+	NM
RALP-0051	My Goals Beyond	1987	5.00	10.00	20.00

—Clear vinyl reissue

MCLAWLER, SARAH
VEE JAY

Number	Title (A Side/B Side)	Yr	VG	VG+	NM
LP-1030 [M]	At the Break of Day	1961	10.00	20.00	40.00

—With Richard Otto

MCLEAN, DON
ARISTA

Number	Title (A Side/B Side)	Yr	VG	VG+	NM
AL 4149	Prime Time	1978	2.50	5.00	10.00

CAPITOL

Number	Title (A Side/B Side)	Yr	VG	VG+	NM
C1-48080	Love Tracks	1988	2.50	5.00	10.00

CASABLANCA

Number	Title (A Side/B Side)	Yr	VG	VG+	NM
NBLP 7173	Chain Lightning	1979	—	—	—

—Canceled

EMI AMERICA

Number	Title (A Side/B Side)	Yr	VG	VG+	NM
ST-17255	Don McLean's Greatest Hits, Then and Now	1987	2.50	5.00	10.00

LIBERTY

Number	Title (A Side/B Side)	Yr	VG	VG+	NM
LN-10037	American Pie	1980	2.00	4.00	8.00

—Reissue of United Artists 5535

Number	Title (A Side/B Side)	Yr	VG	VG+	NM
LN-10157	Tapestry	1982	2.00	4.00	8.00

—Reissue of United Artists 5522

Number	Title (A Side/B Side)	Yr	VG	VG+	NM
LN-10211	Homeless Brother	198?	2.00	4.00	8.00

—Reissue of United Artists 315

MEDIARTS

Number	Title (A Side/B Side)	Yr	VG	VG+	NM
41-4	Tapestry	1970	5.00	10.00	20.00

MILLENNIUM

Number	Title (A Side/B Side)	Yr	VG	VG+	NM
BXL1-7756	Chain Lightning	1981	2.50	5.00	10.00
BXL1-7762	Believers	1981	2.50	5.00	10.00

UNITED ARTISTS

Number	Title (A Side/B Side)	Yr	VG	VG+	NM
UA-LA161-F	Playin' Favorites	1973	3.00	6.00	12.00
UA-LA315-G	Homeless Brother	1974	3.00	6.00	12.00
UA-LA652-H2 [(2)]	Solo	1976	3.75	7.50	15.00
UAS-5522	Tapestry	1971	3.00	6.00	12.00

—Reissue of Mediarts LP

Number	Title (A Side/B Side)	Yr	VG	VG+	NM
UAS-5535	American Pie	1971	3.00	6.00	12.00
UAS-5651	Don McLean	1972	3.00	6.00	12.00

MCLEAN, JACKIE
ADLIB

Number	Title (A Side/B Side)	Yr	VG	VG+	NM
ADL-6601 [M]	The Jackie McLean Quintet	1955	250.00	500.00	1000.

BLUE NOTE

Number	Title (A Side/B Side)	Yr	VG	VG+	NM
BLP-4013 [M]	New Soil	1959	37.50	75.00	150.00
—Regular version, W. 63rd St. address on label					
BLP-4013 [M]	New Soil	1959	50.00	100.00	200.00
—"Deep groove" version (deep indentation under label on both sides)					
BLP-4013 [M]	New Soil	1963	6.25	12.50	25.00
—With "New York, USA" address on label					
BST-4013 [S]	New Soil	1959	30.00	60.00	120.00
—Regular version, W. 63rd St. address on label					
BST-4013 [S]	New Soil	1959	37.50	75.00	150.00
—"Deep groove" version (deep indentation under label on both sides)					
BST-4013 [S]	New Soil	1963	5.00	10.00	20.00
—With "New York, USA" address on label					
BLP-4024 [M]	Swing, Swang, Swingin'	1959	75.00	150.00	300.00
—Regular version, W. 63rd St. address on label					
BLP-4024 [M]	Swing, Swang, Swingin'	1959	100.00	200.00	400.00
—"Deep groove" version (deep indentation under label on both sides)					
BLP-4024 [M]	Swing, Swang, Swingin'	1963	6.25	12.50	25.00
—With "New York, USA" address on label					
BLP-4038 [M]	Capuchin Swing	1960	37.50	75.00	150.00
—Regular version, W. 63rd St. address on label					
BLP-4038 [M]	Capuchin Swing	1960	50.00	100.00	200.00
—"Deep groove" version (deep indentation under label on both sides)					
BLP-4038 [M]	Capuchin Swing	1963	6.25	12.50	25.00
—With "New York, USA" address on label					
BLP-4051 [M]	Jackie's Bag	1960	25.00	50.00	100.00
—With W. 63rd St. address on label					
BLP-4051 [M]	Jackie's Bag	1963	6.25	12.50	25.00
—With "New York, USA" address on label					
BLP-4067 [M]	Bluesnik	1961	25.00	50.00	100.00
—With W. 63rd St. address on label					
BLP-4067 [M]	Bluesnik	1963	6.25	12.50	25.00
—With "New York, USA" address on label					
BLP-4089 [M]	A Fickle Sonance	1961	20.00	40.00	80.00
—With 61st St. address on label					
BLP-4089 [M]	A Fickle Sonance	1963	6.25	12.50	25.00
—With "New York, USA" address on label					
BLP-4106 [M]	Let Freedom Ring	1962	7.50	15.00	30.00
—With "New York, USA" address on label					
BLP-4137 [M]	One Step Beyond	1963	7.50	15.00	30.00
—With "New York, USA" address on label					
BLP-4165 [M]	Destination… Out!	1964	7.50	15.00	30.00
—With "New York, USA" address on label					
BLP-4179 [M]	It's Time!	1964	7.50	15.00	30.00
—With "New York, USA" address on label					
BLP-4215 [M]	Right Now!	1965	7.50	15.00	30.00
—With "New York, USA" address on label					
BLP-4218 [M]	Action Action Action	1965	7.50	15.00	30.00
—With "New York, USA" address on label					
BLP-4262 [M]	New and Old Gospel	1967	7.50	15.00	30.00
BST-84024 [S]	Swing, Swang, Swingin'	1959	50.00	100.00	200.00
—With W. 63rd St. address on label					
BST-84024 [S]	Swing, Swang, Swingin'	1963	5.00	10.00	20.00
—With "New York, USA" address on label					
BST-84038 [S]	Capuchin Swing	1960	25.00	50.00	100.00
—With W. 63rd St. address on label					
BST-84038 [S]	Capuchin Swing	1963	5.00	10.00	20.00
—With "New York, USA" address on label					
BST-84051 [S]	Jackie's Bag	1960	20.00	40.00	80.00
—With W. 63rd St. address on label					
BST-84051 [S]	Jackie's Bag	1963	5.00	10.00	20.00
—With "New York, USA" address on label					
BST-84067 [S]	Bluesnik	1961	20.00	40.00	80.00
—With W. 63rd St. address on label					
BST-84067 [S]	Bluesnik	1963	5.00	10.00	20.00
—With "New York, USA" address on label					
BST-84089 [S]	A Fickle Sonance	1961	15.00	30.00	60.00
—With 61st St. address on label					
BST-84089 [S]	A Fickle Sonance	1963	5.00	10.00	20.00
—With "New York, USA" address on label					

Number	Title (A Side/B Side)	Yr	VG	VG+	NM
❏ BST-84106 [S]	Let Freedom Ring	1962	10.00	20.00	40.00
—With "New York, USA" address on label					
❏ BST-84106 [S]	Let Freedom Ring	1967	5.00	10.00	20.00
—With "A Division of Liberty Records" on label					
❏ BST-84137 [S]	One Step Beyond	1963	10.00	20.00	40.00
—With "New York, USA" address on label					
❏ BST-84137 [S]	One Step Beyond	1967	5.00	10.00	20.00
—With "A Division of Liberty Records" on label					
❏ BST-84165 [S]	Destination… Out!	1964	10.00	20.00	40.00
—With "New York, USA" address on label					
❏ BST-84165 [S]	Destination… Out!	1967	5.00	10.00	20.00
—With "A Division of Liberty Records" on label					
❏ BST-84179 [S]	It's Time!	1964	10.00	20.00	40.00
—With "New York, USA" address on label					
❏ BST-84179 [S]	It's Time!	1967	5.00	10.00	20.00
—With "A Division of Liberty Records" on label					
❏ BST-84215 [S]	Right Now!	1965	10.00	20.00	40.00
—With "New York, USA" address on label					
❏ BST-84215 [S]	Right Now!	1967	5.00	10.00	20.00
—With "A Division of Liberty Records" on label					
❏ BST-84218 [S]	Action Action Action	1965	10.00	20.00	40.00
—With "New York, USA" address on label					
❏ BST-84218 [S]	Action Action Action	1967	5.00	10.00	20.00
—With "A Division of Liberty Records" on label					
❏ BST-84262 [S]	New and Old Gospel	1967	5.00	10.00	20.00
—With "A Division of Liberty Records" on label					
❏ BST-84284	'Bout Soul	1968	5.00	10.00	20.00
—With "A Division of Liberty Records" on label					
❏ BST-84345	Demon's Dance	1969	5.00	10.00	20.00
—With "A Division of Liberty Records" on label					
JOSIE					
❏ JLPS-3503 [S]	Jackie McLean Sextet	1963	5.00	10.00	20.00
❏ JOZ-3503 [M]	Jackie McLean Sextet	1963	7.50	15.00	30.00
❏ JLPS-3507 [S]	Jackie McLean Sextet	1963	5.00	10.00	20.00
❏ JOZ-3507 [M]	Jackie McLean Sextet	1963	7.50	15.00	30.00
JUBILEE					
❏ JLP-1064 [M]	The Jackie McLean Quintet	1958	20.00	40.00	80.00
❏ JLP-1093 [M]	Jackie McLean Plays Fat Jazz	1959	20.00	40.00	80.00
MOSAIC					
❏ MQ6-150 [(6)]	The Complete Blue Note 1964-66 Jackie McLean Sessions	199?	25.00	50.00	100.00
NEW JAZZ					
❏ NJLP-8212 [M]	McLean's Scene	1958	25.00	50.00	100.00
—Purple label					
❏ NJLP-8212 [M]	McLean's Scene	1965	6.25	12.50	25.00
—Blue label, trident logo at right					
❏ NJLP-8231 [M]	Makin' the Changes	1960	25.00	50.00	100.00
—Purple label					
❏ NJLP-8231 [M]	Makin' the Changes	1965	6.25	12.50	25.00
—Blue label, trident logo at right					
❏ NJLP-8253 [M]	A Long Drink of the Blues	1961	20.00	40.00	80.00
—Purple label					
❏ NJLP-8253 [M]	A Long Drink of the Blues	1965	6.25	12.50	25.00
—Blue label, trident logo at right					
❏ NJLP-8263 [M]	Lights Out!	1961	12.50	25.00	50.00
—Purple label					
❏ NJLP-8263 [M]	Lights Out!	1965	6.25	12.50	25.00
—Blue label, trident logo at right					
❏ NJLP-8279 [M]	4, 5 and 6	1962	12.50	25.00	50.00
—Purple label					
❏ NJLP-8279 [M]	4, 5 and 6	1965	6.25	12.50	25.00
—Blue label, trident logo at right					
❏ NJLP-8290 [M]	Steeplechase	1962	12.50	25.00	50.00
—Purple label					
❏ NJLP-8290 [M]	Steeplechase	1965	6.25	12.50	25.00
—Blue label, trident logo at right					
PRESTIGE					
❏ PRLP-7035 [M]	Lights Out!	1956	37.50	75.00	150.00
❏ PRLP-7048 [M]	4, 5 and 6	1956	37.50	75.00	150.00
❏ PRLP-7068 [M]	Jackie's Pal — Introducing Bill Hardman	1956	37.50	75.00	150.00
❏ PRLP-7087 [M]	Jackie McLean & Co.	1957	30.00	60.00	120.00
❏ PRLP-7114 [M]	Alto Madness	1957	30.00	60.00	120.00
❏ PRLP-7500 [M]	Strange Blues	1967	6.25	12.50	25.00
RCA VICTOR					
❏ AFL1-3230 [S]	Monuments	1979	3.75	7.50	15.00
—Reissue of LSP-3230?					
❏ LPM-3230 [M]	Alto Madness	1965	5.00	10.00	20.00
❏ LSP-3230 [S]	Alto Madness	1965	6.25	12.50	25.00
STATUS					
❏ ST-8312 [M]	Alto Madness	1965	10.00	20.00	40.00
❏ ST-8323 [M]	Jackie McLean & Co.	1965	10.00	20.00	40.00

MCLOLLIE, OSCAR
CROWN

❏ CLP-5016 [M]	Oscar McLollie and His Honey Jumpers	1956	100.00	200.00	400.00
—Opinions differ as to whether this LP actually exists. Value is probably conservative.					

MCLUHAN
BRUNSWICK

❏ BL 754177	Anomaly	1972	5.00	10.00	20.00

MCLUHAN, MARSHALL
COLUMBIA

❏ CL 2701 [M]	The Medium Is the Message	1967	6.25	12.50	25.00
❏ CS 9501 [S]	The Medium Is the Message	1967	6.25	12.50	25.00

MCMAHON, ED
CAMEO

❏ C-2009 [M]	And Me...I'm Ed McMahon	1964	6.25	12.50	25.00
RCA CAMDEN					
❏ CAL-1083 [M]	What Do You Want to Be When You Grow Up?	1965	5.00	10.00	20.00
❏ CAS-1083 [S]	What Do You Want to Be When You Grow Up?	1965	6.25	12.50	25.00

MCNABB, TED
EPIC

Number	Title (A Side/B Side)	Yr	VG	VG+	NM
❏ BN 558 [S]	Ted McNabb and Company	1959	10.00	20.00	40.00
❏ LN 3663 [M]	Ted McNabb and Company	1959	12.50	25.00	50.00

MCNAIR, BARBARA
AUDIO FIDELITY

❏ AFSD-6222	More Today Than Yesterday	1969	5.00	10.00	20.00
❏ ST-92074	More Today Than Yesterday	1969	6.25	12.50	25.00
—Capitol Record Club edition					
MOTOWN					
❏ 644 [M]	Here I Am	1966	12.50	25.00	50.00
❏ S-644 [S]	Here I Am	1966	15.00	30.00	60.00
❏ S-680	The Real Barbara McNair	1969	7.50	15.00	30.00
SIGNATURE					
❏ SM 1042 [M]	Love Talk	1960	10.00	20.00	40.00
❏ SS 1042 [S]	Love Talk	1960	12.50	25.00	50.00
WARNER BROS.					
❏ W 1541 [M]	I Enjoy Being a Girl	1964	6.25	12.50	25.00
❏ WS 1541 [S]	I Enjoy Being a Girl	1964	7.50	15.00	30.00
❏ W 1570 [M]	The Livin' End	1964	6.25	12.50	25.00
❏ WS 1570 [S]	The Livin' End	1964	7.50	15.00	30.00

MCNEELY, BIG JAY
COLLECTABLES

❏ COL-5133	Golden Classics	198?	2.50	5.00	10.00
FEDERAL					
❏ 295-96 [10]	Big Jay McNeely	1954	750.00	1500.	3000.
❏ 395-530 [M]	Big Jay McNeely in 3-D	1956	200.00	400.00	800.00
KING					
❏ 650 [M]	Big Jay McNeely in 3-D	1959	125.00	250.00	500.00
SAVOY					
❏ MG-15045 [10]	A Rhythm and Blues Concert	1955	1000.	1500.	2000.
WARNER BROS.					
❏ W 1533 [M]	Big Jay McNeely	1963	20.00	40.00	80.00
❏ WS 1533 [S]	Big Jay McNeely	1963	25.00	50.00	100.00

MCNEILL, DON
CORAL

❏ CRL 57288 [M]	Book, Candle, Prayer	1958	7.50	15.00	30.00
❏ CRL 57291 [M]	March Around the Breakfast Table	1958	7.50	15.00	30.00

MCNICHOL, KRISTY AND JIMMY
RCA VICTOR

❏ AFL1-2875	Kristy and Jimmy McNichol	1978	5.00	10.00	20.00

MCPARTLAND, JIMMY
BRUNSWICK

❏ BL 54018 [M]	Dixieland Band	1955	12.50	25.00	50.00
❏ BL 58049 [10]	Shades of Bix	1953	20.00	40.00	80.00
EPIC					
❏ BN 506 [S]	"The Music Man" Goes Dixieland	1958	7.50	15.00	30.00
❏ LN 3371 [M]	Jimmy McPartland's Dixieland	1956	10.00	20.00	40.00
❏ LN 3463 [M]	"The Music Man" Goes Dixieland	1958	10.00	20.00	40.00
JAZZTONE					
❏ J-1227 [M]	The Middle Road	1956	10.00	20.00	40.00
MERCURY					
❏ MG-20460 [M]	Meet Me in Chicago	1959	6.25	12.50	25.00
❏ SR-60143 [S]	Meet Me in Chicago	1959	7.50	15.00	30.00
RCA VICTOR					
❏ LPV-549 [M]	That Happy Dixieland Jazz	1966	5.00	10.00	20.00

MCPARTLAND, JIMMY/PAUL BARBARIN
JAZZTONE

❏ J-1241 [M]	Dixieland Now and Then	195?	7.50	15.00	30.00

MCPARTLAND, MARIAN
ARGO

❏ LP-640 [M]	Marion McPartland at the London House	1959	10.00	20.00	40.00
❏ LPS-640 [S]	Marion McPartland at the London House	1959	7.50	15.00	30.00
CAPITOL					
❏ T 574 [M]	Marion McPartland at the Hickory House	1955	10.00	20.00	40.00
❏ T 699 [M]	After Dark	1956	10.00	20.00	40.00
❏ T 785 [M]	Marion McPartland Trio	1957	10.00	20.00	40.00
SAVOY					
❏ MG-12004 [M]	Marion McPartland in Concert	1955	12.50	25.00	50.00
❏ MG-12005 [M]	Lullaby of Birdland	1955	12.50	25.00	50.00
❏ MG-15019 [10]	Jazz at Storyville, Volume 3	1952	20.00	40.00	80.00
❏ MG-15021 [10]	Piano Moods	1952	20.00	40.00	80.00
❏ MG-15027 [10]	Marion McPartland	1953	20.00	40.00	80.00
❏ MG-15032 [10]	Jazz at the Hickory House	1953	20.00	40.00	80.00
TIME					
❏ S-2073 [S]	Bossa Nova Plus Soul	1963	7.50	15.00	30.00
❏ S-2189 [S]	West Side Story	196?	7.50	15.00	30.00
❏ 52073 [M]	Bossa Nova Plus Soul	1963	6.25	12.50	25.00
❏ 52189 [M]	West Side Story	196?	6.25	12.50	25.00

MCPARTLAND, MARIAN, AND GEORGE SHEARING
SAVOY

❏ MG-12016 [M]	Great Britain's Marion McPartland and George Shearing	1955	10.00	20.00	40.00

MCPEAK, CURTIS
ABC-PARAMOUNT

❏ ABC-446 [M]	Bluegrass Hillbillies	1963	5.00	10.00	20.00
❏ ABCS-446 [S]	Bluegrass Hillbillies	1963	6.25	12.50	25.00

Number	Title (A Side/B Side)	Yr	VG	VG+	NM

MCPHATTER, CLYDE
Also see THE DRIFTERS.
ALLEGIANCE

Number	Title (A Side/B Side)	Yr	VG	VG+	NM
❑ AV-5029	The Pretty One	198?	2.50	5.00	10.00

ATLANTIC

❑ 8024 [M]	Love Ballads	1958	125.00	250.00	500.00
—Black label					
❑ 8024 [M]	Love Ballads	1960	50.00	100.00	200.00
—Brown and purple label					
❑ 8024 [M]	Love Ballads	1960	100.00	200.00	400.00
—White "bullseye" label					
❑ 8031 [M]	Clyde	1959	125.00	250.00	500.00
—Black label					
❑ 8031 [M]	Clyde	1960	50.00	100.00	200.00
—Brown and purple label					
❑ 8031 [M]	Clyde	1960	100.00	200.00	400.00
—White "bullseye" label					
❑ 8077 [M]	The Best of Clyde McPhatter	1963	50.00	100.00	200.00

DECCA

| ❑ DL 75231 | Welcome Home | 1970 | 6.25 | 12.50 | 25.00 |

MERCURY

❑ MG-20597 [M]	Ta Ta	1960	12.50	25.00	50.00
❑ MG-20655 [M]	Golden Blues Hits	1961	12.50	25.00	50.00
❑ MG-20711 [M]	Lover Please	1962	12.50	25.00	50.00
❑ MG-20750 [M]	Rhythm and Soul	1962	12.50	25.00	50.00
❑ MG-20783 [M]	Clyde McPhatter's Greatest Hits	1963	7.50	15.00	30.00
❑ MG-20902 [M]	Songs of the Big City	1964	7.50	15.00	30.00
❑ MG-20915 [M]	Live at the Apollo	1964	7.50	15.00	30.00
❑ SR-60262 [S]	Ta Ta	1960	17.50	35.00	70.00
❑ SR-60655 [S]	Golden Blues Hits	1961	17.50	35.00	70.00
❑ SR-60711 [S]	Lover Please	1962	17.50	35.00	70.00
❑ SR-60750 [S]	Rhythm and Soul	1962	17.50	35.00	70.00
❑ SR-60783 [S]	Clyde McPhatter's Greatest Hits	1963	10.00	20.00	40.00
❑ SR-60902 [S]	Songs of the Big City	1964	10.00	20.00	40.00
❑ SR-60915 [S]	Live at the Apollo	1964	10.00	20.00	40.00

MGM

❑ E-3775 [M]	Let's Start Over Again	1959	37.50	75.00	150.00
❑ SE-3775 [S]	Let's Start Over Again	1959	50.00	100.00	200.00
❑ E-3866 [M]	Clyde McPhatter's Greatest Hits	1960	17.50	35.00	70.00
❑ SE-3866 [S]	Clyde McPhatter's Greatest Hits	1960	20.00	40.00	80.00

WING

| ❑ MGW-12224 [M] | May I Sing for You? | 1962 | 6.25 | 12.50 | 25.00 |
| ❑ SRW-16224 [S] | May I Sing for You? | 1962 | 7.50 | 15.00 | 30.00 |

MCPHEE, JOE
CJR

❑ 2	Nation Time	197?	6.25	12.50	25.00
❑ 3	Trinity	197?	6.25	12.50	25.00
❑ 4	Pieces of Light	197?	6.25	12.50	25.00

HAT HUT

❑ A	Black Magic Man	1974	6.25	12.50	25.00
❑ C	Tenor	1976	5.00	10.00	20.00
❑ D	Rotation	1977	5.00	10.00	20.00
❑ I/J [(2)]	Graphics	1977	7.50	15.00	30.00
❑ O	Variations on a Blue Line/'Round Midnight	1978	5.00	10.00	20.00
❑ P	Glasses	1978	5.00	10.00	20.00
❑ 01	Old Eyes	1979	5.00	10.00	20.00
❑ 1987/8 [(2)]	Topology	1981	6.25	12.50	25.00

MCPHERSON, CHARLES
PRESTIGE

❑ PRLP-7359 [M]	Bebop Revisited	1965	7.50	15.00	30.00
❑ PRST-7359 [S]	Bebop Revisited	1965	10.00	20.00	40.00
❑ PRLP-7427 [M]	Con Alma!	1966	7.50	15.00	30.00
❑ PRST-7427 [S]	Con Alma!	1966	10.00	20.00	40.00
❑ PRLP-7480 [M]	The Charles McPherson Quintet Live!	1967	10.00	20.00	40.00
❑ PRST-7480 [S]	The Charles McPherson Quintet Live!	1967	7.50	15.00	30.00
❑ PRST-7559	From This Moment On	1968	7.50	15.00	30.00
❑ PRST-7603	Horizons	1969	7.50	15.00	30.00
❑ PRST-7743	McPherson's Mood	1970	5.00	10.00	20.00

MCRAE, CARMEN
ATLANTIC

| ❑ SD 2-904 [(2)] | The Great American Songbook | 1971 | 5.00 | 10.00 | 20.00 |
| ❑ 8143 [M] | For Once in My Life | 1967 | 5.00 | 10.00 | 20.00 |

BETHLEHEM

| ❑ BCP-1023 [10] | Carmen McRae | 1955 | 25.00 | 50.00 | 100.00 |

COLUMBIA

❑ CL 1730 [M]	Lover Man	1962	5.00	10.00	20.00
❑ CL 1943 [M]	Something Wonderful	1962	5.00	10.00	20.00
❑ CS 8530 [S]	Lover Man	1962	6.25	12.50	25.00
❑ CS 8743 [S]	Something Wonderful	1962	6.25	12.50	25.00

DECCA

❑ DL 8173 [M]	By Special Request	1955	12.50	25.00	50.00
—Black label, silver print					
❑ DL 8173 [M]	By Special Request	1960	5.00	10.00	20.00
—Black label with color bars					
❑ DL 8267 [M]	Torchy!	1956	12.50	25.00	50.00
—Black label, silver print					
❑ DL 8267 [M]	Torchy!	1960	5.00	10.00	20.00
—Black label with color bars					
❑ DL 8347 [M]	Blue Moon	1957	12.50	25.00	50.00
—Black label, silver print					
❑ DL 8347 [M]	Blue Moon	1960	5.00	10.00	20.00
—Black label with color bars					
❑ DL 8583 [M]	After Glow	1957	12.50	25.00	50.00
—Black label, silver print					
❑ DL 8583 [M]	After Glow	1960	5.00	10.00	20.00
—Black label with color bars					

❑ DL 8662 [M]	Mad About the Man	1958	12.50	25.00	50.00
—Black label, silver print					
❑ DL 8662 [M]	Mad About the Man	1960	5.00	10.00	20.00
—Black label with color bars					
❑ DL 8738 [M]	Carmen for Cool Ones	1958	12.50	25.00	50.00
—Black label, silver print					
❑ DL 8738 [M]	Carmen for Cool Ones	1960	5.00	10.00	20.00
—Black label with color bars					
❑ DL 8815 [M]	Birds of a Feather	1959	12.50	25.00	50.00
—Black label, silver print					
❑ DL 8815 [M]	Birds of a Feather	1960	5.00	10.00	20.00
—Black label with color bars					

FOCUS

| ❑ FS-334 [S] | Bittersweet | 1964 | 5.00 | 10.00 | 20.00 |

HARMONY

| ❑ HL 7452 [M] | Yesterdays | 1968 | 5.00 | 10.00 | 20.00 |

KAPP

❑ KL-1117 [M]	Book of Ballads	1958	6.25	12.50	25.00
❑ KL-1135 [M]	When You're Away	1959	6.25	12.50	25.00
❑ KL-1169 [M]	Something to Swing About	1960	6.25	12.50	25.00
❑ KL-1541 [M]	This Is Carmen McRae	1967	5.00	10.00	20.00
❑ KS-3000 [S]	Book of Ballads	1958	7.50	15.00	30.00
❑ KS-3018 [S]	When You're Away	1959	7.50	15.00	30.00
❑ KS-3053 [S]	Something to Swing About	1960	7.50	15.00	30.00

MAINSTREAM

❑ S-6028 [S]	Second to None	1965	5.00	10.00	20.00
❑ S-6044 [S]	Haven't We Met?	1965	5.00	10.00	20.00
❑ S-6065 [S]	Woman Talk	1966	5.00	10.00	20.00
❑ S-6084 [S]	Alfie	1966	5.00	10.00	20.00
❑ 56091 [M]	In Person/San Francisco	1967	5.00	10.00	20.00

TIME

| ❑ S-2104 [S] | Live at Sugar Hill | 1960 | 6.25 | 12.50 | 25.00 |
| ❑ 52104 [M] | Live at Sugar Hill | 1960 | 5.00 | 10.00 | 20.00 |

MCRITCHIE, GREG
CADET

| ❑ LP-4058 [M] | Fighting Back | 1967 | 6.25 | 12.50 | 25.00 |

ZEPHYR

| ❑ 12005 [M] | Easy Jazz on a Fish Beat Bass | 1959 | 12.50 | 25.00 | 250.00 |

MCSHANN, JAY
CAPITOL

| ❑ ST 2645 [S] | McShann's Piano | 1967 | 5.00 | 10.00 | 20.00 |
| ❑ T 2645 [M] | McShann's Piano | 1967 | 5.00 | 10.00 | 20.00 |

DECCA

❑ DL 5503 [10]	Kansas City Memories	1954	125.00	250.00	500.00
—CHARLIE PARKER appears on this LP					
❑ DL 9236 [M]	Kansas City Memories	1958	50.00	100.00	200.00

MCTELL, BLIND WILLIE
BLUESVILLE

❑ BVLP-1040 [M]	Last Session	1962	30.00	60.00	120.00
—Blue label, silver print					
❑ BVLP-1040 [M]	Last Session	1964	7.50	15.00	30.00
—Blue label, trident logo at right					

MELODEON

| ❑ 7323 [M] | 1940 | 1956 | 37.50 | 75.00 | 150.00 |

MCTELL, RALPH
CAPITOL

| ❑ ST-240 | Eight Frames a Second | 1969 | 5.00 | 10.00 | 20.00 |

REPRISE

| ❑ MS 2121 | Not Till Tomorrow | 1973 | 3.75 | 7.50 | 15.00 |

MCWILLIAMS, DAVID
KAPP

| ❑ KS-3547 | Days of Pearly Spencer | 1968 | 6.25 | 12.50 | 25.00 |

MEADER, VAUGHN
CADENCE

❑ CLP 3060 [M]	The First Family	1962	3.75	7.50	15.00
❑ CLP 3065 [M]	The First Family, Volume Two	1963	5.00	10.00	20.00
❑ CLP 25065 [S]	The First Family, Volume Two	1963	7.50	15.00	30.00

KAMA SUTRA

| ❑ KSBS-2038 | The Second Coming | 1971 | 3.75 | 7.50 | 15.00 |

LAURIE

| ❑ LLP-2035 [M] | Take That! | 1966 | 3.75 | 7.50 | 15.00 |

VERVE

❑ V-15042 [M]	Have Some Nuts	1964	3.75	7.50	15.00
❑ V6-15042 [S]	Have Some Nuts	1964	5.00	10.00	20.00
❑ V-15050 [M]	If the Shoe Fits	1965	3.75	7.50	15.00

MEADOW
Supposedly, Laura Branigan was in this group.
PARAMOUNT

| ❑ PAS-6066 | The Friend Ship | 1973 | 5.00 | 10.00 | 20.00 |

MEAT LOAF
Also see STONEY AND MEATLOAF.
ATLANTIC

| ❑ 81698 | Blind Before I Stop | 1986 | 2.00 | 4.00 | 8.00 |

CLEVELAND INT'L.

❑ FE 36007	Dead Ringer	1981	2.00	4.00	8.00
❑ PE 36007	Dead Ringer	198?	—	3.00	6.00
—Budget-line reissue					

EPIC

❑ E99 34974 [PD]	Bat Out of Hell	1978	5.00	10.00	20.00
❑ JE 34974	Bat Out of Hell	1979	2.00	4.00	8.00
—Dark blue label					

Number	Title (A Side/B Side)	Yr	VG	VG+	NM
❏ PE 34974	Bat Out of Hell	1977	2.50	5.00	10.00
—Orange label; originals do not have bar code on back cover					
❏ PE 34974	Bat Out of Hell	1985	—	3.00	6.00
—Dark blue label; bar code on cover					
❏ FE 38244	Midnight at the Lost and Found	1983	2.00	4.00	8.00
❏ HE 44974	Bat Out of Hell	1981	10.00	20.00	40.00
—Half-speed mastered edition					
RCA VICTOR					
❏ AFL1-5451	Bad Attitude	1985	2.00	4.00	8.00

MEAT PUPPETS
LONDON

Number	Title (A Side/B Side)	Yr	VG	VG+	NM
❏ 1109 [10]	Raw Meat	199?	5.00	10.00	20.00
—Promo-only five-song 10-inch EP					
❏ 828484-1	Too High to Die	1994	3.00	6.00	12.00
—Includes bonus 10-inch EP (double value for DJ stamp on cover)					
MERCURY					
❏ 828665-1	No Joke!	1995	2.50	5.00	10.00
SST					
❏ 009	Meat Puppets	1982	3.75	7.50	15.00
❏ 019	Meat Puppets II	1984	3.00	6.00	12.00
❏ 039	Up on the Sun	1985	3.00	6.00	12.00
❏ 049 [10]	Out My Way	1986	2.00	4.00	8.00
—10-inch EP					
❏ 100	Mirage	1986	3.00	6.00	12.00
❏ 150	Huevos	1987	2.50	5.00	10.00
❏ 253	Monsters	1989	2.50	5.00	10.00
❏ 265 [(2)]	No Strings Attached	1990	4.00	8.00	16.00

MECCA, LOU
BLUE NOTE

Number	Title (A Side/B Side)	Yr	VG	VG+	NM
❏ BLP-5067 [10]	Lou Mecca Quartet	1955	75.00	150.00	300.00

MECKI MARK MEN, THE
LIMELIGHT

Number	Title (A Side/B Side)	Yr	VG	VG+	NM
❏ LS-86054	The Mecki Mark Men	1968	6.25	12.50	25.00
❏ LS-86068	Running in the Summer Night	1969	6.25	12.50	25.00

MEDIUM
GAMMA

Number	Title (A Side/B Side)	Yr	VG	VG+	NM
❏ GS-503	Medium	196?	25.00	50.00	100.00

MEDLEY, BILL
A&M

Number	Title (A Side/B Side)	Yr	VG	VG+	NM
❏ SP-3505	A Song for You	1971	3.00	6.00	12.00
❏ SP-3517	Smile	1972	3.00	6.00	12.00
LIBERTY					
❏ LT-1097	Sweet Thunder	1981	2.00	4.00	8.00
—Reissue of United Artists 1097					
MGM					
❏ E-4583 [M]	Bill Medley 100%	1968	12.50	25.00	50.00
—Mono is yellow label promo only					
❏ SE-4583 [S]	Bill Medley 100%	1968	5.00	10.00	20.00
❏ SE-4603	Soft and Soulful	1969	5.00	10.00	20.00
❏ SE-4640	Someone Is Standing Outside	1969	5.00	10.00	20.00
❏ SE-4702	Nobody Knows	1970	3.75	7.50	15.00
❏ SE-4741	Gone	1970	3.75	7.50	15.00
RCA VICTOR					
❏ BXL1-4434	Right Here and Now	1982	2.50	5.00	10.00
❏ CPL1-5352	Still Hung Up on You	1984	2.50	5.00	10.00
❏ MHL1-8519 [EP]	I Still Do	1985	2.00	4.00	8.00
UNITED ARTISTS					
❏ UA-LA929-H	Lay a Little Lovin' on Me	1978	2.50	5.00	10.00
❏ LT-1097	Sweet Thunder	1980	2.50	5.00	10.00

MEEUWSEN, TERRY ANN
SANDY

Number	Title (A Side/B Side)	Yr	VG	VG+	NM
❏ SRS-9003	Meet Terry	1976	7.50	15.00	30.00

MEHEGAN, JOHN
EPIC

Number	Title (A Side/B Side)	Yr	VG	VG+	NM
❏ LA 16007 [M]	Act of Jazz	1960	5.00	10.00	20.00
❏ BA 17007 [S]	Act of Jazz	1960	6.25	12.50	25.00
PERSPECTIVE					
❏ PR-1 [M]	From Barrelhouse to Bop	195?	12.50	25.00	50.00
SAVOY					
❏ MG-12028 [M]	Reflections	1956	10.00	20.00	40.00
❏ MG-15054 [10]	The Last Mehegan	1955	15.00	30.00	60.00
TJ					
❏ LP-1 [M]	Casual Affair	1959	10.00	20.00	40.00

MEHEGAN, JOHN, AND EDDIE COSTA
SAVOY

Number	Title (A Side/B Side)	Yr	VG	VG+	NM
❏ MG-12049 [M]	A Pair of Pianos	1956	10.00	20.00	40.00

MEL AND TIM
BAMBOO

Number	Title (A Side/B Side)	Yr	VG	VG+	NM
❏ BMS-8001	Good Guys Only Win in the Movies	1970	6.25	12.50	25.00
STAX					
❏ STS-3007	Starting All Over Again	1972	5.00	10.00	20.00
❏ STS-5501	Mel and Tim	1974	5.00	10.00	20.00

MELACHRINO, GEORGE
RCA VICTOR

Number	Title (A Side/B Side)	Yr	VG	VG+	NM
❏ LPM-1000 [M]	Music for Dining	195?	6.25	12.50	25.00
❏ LPM-1001 [M]	Music for Relaxation	195?	6.25	12.50	25.00
❏ LPM-1002 [M]	Music for Reading	195?	6.25	12.50	25.00
❏ LPM-1005 [M]	Music for Courage and Confidence	195?	6.25	12.50	25.00
❏ LPM-1006 [M]	Music to Help You Sleep	195?	6.25	12.50	25.00
❏ LPM-1008 [M]	Show Tunes	195?	6.25	12.50	25.00
❏ LPM-1027 [M]	Music for Two People Alone	195?	6.25	12.50	25.00
❏ LPM-1028 [M]	Music for Daydreaming	195?	6.25	12.50	25.00
❏ LPM-1029 [M]	Music to Work or Study By	195?	6.25	12.50	25.00
❏ LPM-1045 [M]	Christmas in High Fidelity	1954	6.25	12.50	25.00
❏ LPM-1110 [M]	Immortal Ladies	1955	5.00	10.00	20.00
❏ LPM-1184 [M]	Masquerade	1955	5.00	10.00	20.00
❏ LPM-1261 [M]	Sounds of Paris	1956	5.00	10.00	20.00
❏ LPM-1307 [M]	Melachrino on Broadway	1956	5.00	10.00	20.00
❏ LPM-1329 [M]	I'll Walk Beside You	1956	5.00	10.00	20.00
❏ LPM-1330 [M]	Those Beautiful Strings	1956	5.00	10.00	20.00
❏ LPM-1757 [M]	Strauss Waltzes	1958	3.75	7.50	15.00
❏ LSP-1757 [S]	Strauss Waltzes	1958	5.00	10.00	20.00
❏ LPM-1762 [M]	Lisbon at Twilight	1958	3.75	7.50	15.00
❏ LSP-1762 [S]	Lisbon at Twilight	1958	5.00	10.00	20.00

MELLE, GIL
BLUE NOTE

Number	Title (A Side/B Side)	Yr	VG	VG+	NM
❏ BLP-1517 [M]	Patterns in Jazz	1956	37.50	75.00	150.00
—Regular version, Lexington Ave. address on label					
❏ BLP-1517 [M]	Patterns in Jazz	1956	50.00	100.00	200.00
—"Deep groove" version (deep indentation under label on both sides)					
❏ BLP-5020 [10]	Gil Melle Quintet/Sextet	1953	75.00	150.00	300.00
❏ BLP-5033 [10]	Gil Melle Quintet, Volume 2	1953	75.00	150.00	300.00
❏ BLP-5054 [10]	Gil Melle Quintet, Volume 3	1954	75.00	150.00	300.00
❏ BLP-5063 [10]	Gil Melle Quintet, Volume 4 — Five Impressions of Color	1954	75.00	150.00	300.00
PRESTIGE					
❏ PRLP-7040 [M]	Melle Plays Primitive Modern	1956	20.00	40.00	80.00
❏ PRLP-7063 [M]	Gil's Guests	1956	20.00	40.00	80.00
❏ PRLP-7097 [M]	Quadrama	1957	20.00	40.00	80.00
VERVE					
❏ V6-8744	Tome VI	1968	5.00	10.00	20.00

MELLENCAMP, JOHN
COLUMBIA

Number	Title (A Side/B Side)	Yr	VG	VG+	NM
❏ C 69602	John Mellencamp	1998	3.75	7.50	15.00
MCA					
❏ 2225	Chestnut Street Incident	1977	6.25	12.50	25.00
—As "Johnny Cougar"					
MERCURY					
❏ 832465-1	The Lonesome Jubilee	1987	2.00	4.00	8.00
❏ 838220-1	Big Daddy	1989	2.50	5.00	10.00
MOBILE FIDELITY					
❏ 1-222	The Lonesome Jubilee	1995	5.00	10.00	20.00
—Audiophile vinyl					
RIVA					
❏ RVL 7401	John Cougar	1979	2.50	5.00	10.00
—As "John Cougar"					
❏ RVL 7403	Nothin' Matters and What If It Did	1980	2.50	5.00	10.00
—As "John Cougar"					
❏ RVL 7501	American Fool	1982	2.00	4.00	8.00
—As "John Cougar"					
❏ RVL 7504	Uh-Huh	1983	2.00	4.00	8.00
—As "John Cougar Mellencamp"					
❏ 824865-1	Scarecrow	1985	2.00	4.00	8.00
—As "John Cougar Mellencamp"					

MELLO-KINGS, THE
COLLECTABLES

Number	Title (A Side/B Side)	Yr	VG	VG+	NM
❏ COL-5020	Greatest Hits	198?	2.50	5.00	10.00
HERALD					
❏ H-1013 [M]	Tonight-Tonight	196?	62.50	125.00	250.00
—Multi-color label					
❏ H-1013 [M]	Tonight-Tonight	1960	125.00	250.00	500.00
—Yellow label					
RELIC					
❏ LP-5035	Greatest Hits	198?	3.00	6.00	12.00

MELLO-LARKS, THE
RCA CAMDEN

Number	Title (A Side/B Side)	Yr	VG	VG+	NM
❏ CAL-530 [M]	Just for a Lark	1959	10.00	20.00	40.00

MELROSE, FRANK
ABC-PARAMOUNT

Number	Title (A Side/B Side)	Yr	VG	VG+	NM
❏ (# unknown) [M]	Kansas City Frank Melrose	1956	12.50	25.00	50.00

MELTZER, DAVID AND TINA
VANGUARD

Number	Title (A Side/B Side)	Yr	VG	VG+	NM
❏ VSD-6619	Poet Song	1969	6.25	12.50	25.00

MELVIN, HAROLD, AND THE BLUE NOTES
ABC

Number	Title (A Side/B Side)	Yr	VG	VG+	NM
❏ AB-969	Reaching for the World	1977	2.50	5.00	10.00
❏ AB-1041	Now Is the Time	1978	2.50	5.00	10.00
MCA					
❏ 5261	All Things Happen in Time	1981	2.50	5.00	10.00
PHILADELPHIA INT'L.					
❏ KZ 31648	Harold Melvin and the Blue Notes	1972	3.00	6.00	12.00
❏ KZ 32407	Black & Blue	1973	3.00	6.00	12.00
❏ ZQ 32407 [Q]	Black & Blue	1973	5.00	10.00	20.00
❏ PZ 33148	To Be True	1975	3.00	6.00	12.00
❏ PZ 33808	Wake Up Everybody	1975	3.00	6.00	12.00
❏ PZQ 33808 [Q]	Wake Up Everybody	1975	5.00	10.00	20.00
❏ PZ 34232	Collector's Item — All Their Greatest Hits!	1976	3.00	6.00	12.00
PHILLY WORLD					
❏ 90187	Talk It Up (Tell Everybody)	1985	2.50	5.00	10.00
SOURCE					
❏ 3197	The Blue Album	1980	2.50	5.00	10.00

MEMPHIS SLIM
BATTLE

Number	Title (A Side/B Side)	Yr	VG	VG+	NM
❏ BM-6118 [M]	Alone with My Friends	1963	12.50	25.00	50.00
❏ BM-6122 [M]	Baby Please Come Home	1963	12.50	25.00	50.00

The original edition of *If You Can Believe Your Eyes and Ears* by the Mamas and the Papas had a toilet visible in the right corner. Later editions covered this threat to the republic with a scroll.

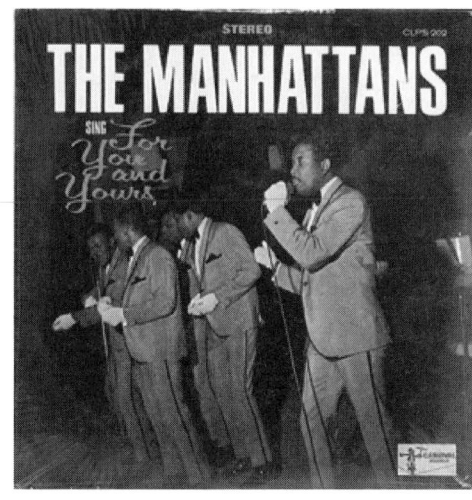

Long before "Kiss and Say Goodbye" became a big pop hit in 1976, the Manhattans were recording for the Carnival label. *For You and Yours* was the second of their two hard-to-find LPs on Carnival.

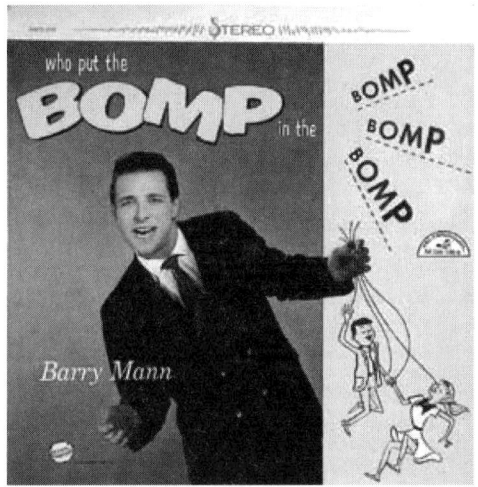

Barry Mann certainly helped put the bomp in the bomp-ba-bomp-ba-bomp. But he never again had a big hit as a singer, thus this album faded into obscurity.

Before Loggins and Messina, even before Buffalo Springfield, Jim Messina was making surf-style music for the Audio Fidelity label.

Marilyn Monroe was not known as a singer. But 20th Century Fox thought she could do well enough to sell an album – especially if her face adorned the cover and the LP contained a bonus photo. This record was reissued several times, but this is the original.

Moon Mullican had one of the biggest country hit singles of the early 1950s with "I'll Sail My Ship Alone." Years later, the Sterling label, which has a logo that looks curiously like that of Starday, released an album of him singing the song and others.

Number	Title (A Side/B Side)	Yr	VG	VG+	NM
BLUESVILLE					
❏ BVLP-1018 [M] Just Blues		1961	30.00	60.00	120.00
—Blue label, silver print					
❏ BVLP-1018 [M] Just Blues		1964	7.50	15.00	30.00
—Blue label, trident logo at right					
❏ BVLP-1031 [M] No Strain		1961	30.00	60.00	120.00
—Blue label, silver print					
❏ BVLP-1031 [M] No Strain		1964	7.50	15.00	30.00
—Blue label, trident logo at right					
❏ BVLP-1053 [M] All Kinds of Blues		1962	25.00	50.00	100.00
—Blue label, silver print					
❏ BVLP-1053 [M] All Kinds of Blues		1964	7.50	15.00	30.00
—Blue label, trident logo at right					
❏ BVLP-1075 [M] Steady Rollin' Blues		1963	25.00	50.00	100.00
—Blue label, silver print					
❏ BVLP-1075 [M] Steady Rollin' Blues		1964	7.50	15.00	30.00
—Blue label, trident logo at right					
BUDDAH					
❏ BDS-7505 Mother Earth		1969	5.00	10.00	20.00
CANDID					
❏ CM-8023 [M] Slim's Tribute to Big Bill Broonzy		1961	15.00	30.00	60.00
❏ CM-8024 [M] Memphis Slim U.S.A.		1962	15.00	30.00	60.00
❏ CS-9023 [S] Slim's Tribute to Big Bill Broonzy		1961	20.00	40.00	80.00
❏ CS-9024 [S] Memphis Slim U.S.A.		1962	20.00	40.00	80.00
CHESS					
❏ LP-1455 [M] Memphis Slim		1961	37.50	75.00	150.00
—Black label					
❏ LP-1510 [M] The Real Folk Blues		1966	20.00	40.00	80.00
DISC					
❏ D-105 [M] If the Rabbit Had a Gun		1964	10.00	20.00	40.00
FOLKWAYS					
❏ FG-3524 [M] The Real Boogie Woogie		1959	25.00	50.00	100.00
❏ FG-3535 [M] Memphis Slim…And the Real Honky Tonk		1960	25.00	50.00	100.00
❏ FG-3536 [M] Chicago Blues		1961	25.00	50.00	100.00
JUBILEE					
❏ JGM-8003 [M] Legend of the Blues		1967	6.25	12.50	25.00
❏ JGS-8003 [S] Legend of the Blues		1967	6.25	12.50	25.00
KING					
❏ 885 [M] Memphis Slim Sings Folk Blues		1964	12.50	25.00	50.00
SCEPTER					
❏ SM-535 [M] Self Portrait		1966	5.00	10.00	20.00
❏ SMS-535 [S] Self Portrait		1966	6.25	12.50	25.00
SPIN-O-RAMA					
❏ 149 [M] Lonesome Blues		196?	5.00	10.00	20.00
STRAND					
❏ SL-1046 [M] The World's Foremost Blues Singer		1962	10.00	20.00	40.00
❏ SLS-1046 [S] The World's Foremost Blues Singer		1962	12.50	25.00	50.00
UNITED ARTISTS					
❏ UAL-3137 [M] Broken Soul Blues		1961	15.00	30.00	60.00
❏ UAS-6137 [S] Broken Soul Blues		1961	20.00	40.00	80.00
VEE JAY					
❏ LP-1012 [M] Memphis Slim at the Gate of the Horn		1959	50.00	100.00	200.00
—Maroon label					
❏ LP-1012 [M] Memphis Slim at the Gate of the Horn		1961	30.00	60.00	120.00
—Black rainbow label, oval logo					

MEMPHIS WILLIE B

Number	Title (A Side/B Side)	Yr	VG	VG+	NM
BLUESVILLE					
❏ BVLP-1034 [M] Introducing Memphis Willie B		1961	25.00	50.00	100.00
—Blue label, silver print					
❏ BVLP-1034 [M] Introducing Memphis Willie B		1964	7.50	15.00	30.00
—Blue label, trident logo at right					
❏ BVLP-1048 [M] Hard Working Man Blues		1962	25.00	50.00	100.00
—Blue label, silver print					
❏ BVLP-1048 [M] Hard Working Man Blues		1964	7.50	15.00	30.00
—Blue label, trident logo at right					

MEN, THE

Number	Title (A Side/B Side)	Yr	VG	VG+	NM
SNAT-5					
❏ 2001 Hermeneutics		1981	6.25	12.50	25.00

MEN AT WORK

Number	Title (A Side/B Side)	Yr	VG	VG+	NM
COLUMBIA					
❏ A2S 1650 [(2)DJ]Cargo (World Premiere Weekend)		1983	3.75	7.50	15.00
—Promo-only two-record package of interviews and music					
❏ ARC 37978 Business as Usual		1982	2.50	5.00	10.00
❏ FC 37978 Business as Usual		1982	2.00	4.00	8.00
—New prefix to reflect list-price increase					
❏ PC 38660 Cargo		198?	2.00	4.00	8.00
—Reissue with new prefix					
❏ QC 38660 Cargo		1983	2.50	5.00	10.00
❏ FC 40078 Two Hearts		1985	2.00	4.00	8.00
❏ HC 47978 Business as Usual		1983	6.25	12.50	25.00
—Half-speed mastered edition					
❏ HC 48660 Cargo		1983	6.25	12.50	25.00
—Half-speed mastered edition					

MEN WITHOUT HATS

Number	Title (A Side/B Side)	Yr	VG	VG+	NM
BACKSTREET					
❏ 5436 Rhythm of Youth		1983	2.50	5.00	10.00
—Reissue					
❏ 39002 Rhythm of Youth		1983	3.00	6.00	12.00
MCA					
❏ 5487 Folk of the 80's, Part 3		1984	2.50	5.00	10.00
MERCURY					
❏ 842000-1 In the 21st Century		1989	2.50	5.00	10.00
STIFF					
❏ TEES-12-01 [EP]Folk of the 80's		1981	7.50	15.00	30.00
—Reissue of Trend 10-inch EP					

Number	Title (A Side/B Side)	Yr	VG	VG+	NM
TREND					
❏ HATS-001 [10] Folk of the 80's		1981	10.00	20.00	40.00
—10-inch four-song EP; possibly released only in Canada					

MENDES, SERGIO

Number	Title (A Side/B Side)	Yr	VG	VG+	NM
ATLANTIC					
❏ SD 1466 [S] Great Arrival		1966	5.00	10.00	20.00
❏ 1480 [M] The Beat of Brazil		1967	5.00	10.00	20.00
CAPITOL					
❏ ST 2294 [S] In a Brazilan Bag		1965	15.00	30.00	60.00
❏ T 2294 [M] In a Brazilan Bag		1965	12.50	25.00	50.00
MOBILE FIDELITY					
❏ 1-118 Sergio Mendes and Brasil '66		1984	12.50	25.00	50.00
—Audiophile vinyl					
PHILIPS					
❏ PHM 200263 [M] Quiet Nights		1968	5.00	10.00	20.00
TOWER					
❏ ST 5052 [S] In a Brazilan Bag		1966	12.50	25.00	50.00
—Reissue of Capitol 2294					
❏ T 5052 [M] In a Brazilan Bag		1966	10.00	20.00	40.00
—Reissue of Capitol 2294					

MENUHIN, YEHUDI

Number	Title (A Side/B Side)	Yr	VG	VG+	NM
MERCURY LIVING PRESENCE					
❏ SR 90003 [S] Bartok: Violin Concerto No. 2		1959	17.50	35.00	70.00
—With Antal Dorati/Minneapolis Symphony Orch.; maroon label, no "Vendor: Mercury Record Corporation"					
❏ SR 90003 [S] Bartok: Violin Concerto No. 2		196?	7.50	15.00	30.00
—With Antal Dorati/Minneapolis Symphony Orch.; maroon label, with "Vendor: Mercury Record Corporation"					

MEPHISTOPHELES

Number	Title (A Side/B Side)	Yr	VG	VG+	NM
REPRISE					
❏ RS 6355 In Frustration I Hear Singing		1969	10.00	20.00	40.00

MERCER, JOHNNY

Number	Title (A Side/B Side)	Yr	VG	VG+	NM
CAPITOL					
❏ H 210 [10] Music of Jerome Kern		1950	20.00	40.00	80.00
❏ H 214 [10] Johnny Mercer Sings		1950	20.00	40.00	80.00
❏ T 907 [M] Ac-Cent-Tchu-Ate the Positive		1957	12.50	25.00	50.00
JUPITER					
❏ JLP-1001 [M] Johnny Mercer Sings Just for Fun		1956	12.50	25.00	50.00

MERCER, MABEL

Number	Title (A Side/B Side)	Yr	VG	VG+	NM
ATLANTIC					
❏ ALS-402 [10] Songs by Mabel Mercer, Volume 1		1954	20.00	40.00	80.00
❏ ALS-403 [10] Songs by Mabel Mercer, Volume 2		1954	20.00	40.00	80.00
❏ 2-602 [(2)M] The Art of Mabel Mercer		1959	15.00	30.00	60.00
—Black labels					
❏ 2-602 [(2)M] The Art of Mabel Mercer		1961	7.50	15.00	30.00
—Multicolor labels, white "fan" logo at right					
❏ 2-602 [(2)M] The Art of Mabel Mercer		1963	5.00	10.00	20.00
—Multicolor labels, black "fan" logo at right					
❏ SD 2-605 [(2)] The Second Town Hall Concert		1969	5.00	10.00	20.00
❏ 1213 [M] Mabel Mercer Sings Cole Porter		1955	10.00	20.00	40.00
—Black label					
❏ 1213 [M] Mabel Mercer Sings Cole Porter		1961	5.00	10.00	20.00
—Multicolor label, white "fan" logo at right					
❏ 1244 [M] Midnight at Mabel Mercer's		1956	10.00	20.00	40.00
—Black label					
❏ 1244 [M] Midnight at Mabel Mercer's		1961	5.00	10.00	20.00
—Multicolor label, white "fan" logo at right					
❏ 1301 [M] Once in a Blue Moon		1959	10.00	20.00	40.00
—Black label					
❏ 1301 [M] Once in a Blue Moon		1961	5.00	10.00	20.00
—Multicolor label, white "fan" logo at right					
❏ SD 1301 [S] Once in a Blue Moon		1959	12.50	25.00	50.00
—Green label					
❏ SD 1301 [S] Once in a Blue Moon		1961	6.25	12.50	25.00
—Multicolor labels, white "fan" logo at right					
❏ SD 1301 [S] Once in a Blue Moon		1963	5.00	10.00	20.00
—Multicolor labels, black "fan" logo at right					
❏ 1322 [M] Merely Marvelous Mabel Mercer		1960	10.00	20.00	40.00
—Black label					
❏ 1322 [M] Merely Marvelous Mabel Mercer		1961	5.00	10.00	20.00
—Multicolor label, white "fan" logo at right					
❏ SD 1322 [S] Merely Marvelous Mabel Mercer		1960	12.50	25.00	50.00
—Green label					
❏ SD 1322 [S] Merely Marvelous Mabel Mercer		1961	6.25	12.50	25.00
—Multicolor labels, white "fan" logo at right					
❏ SD 1322 [S] Merely Marvelous Mabel Mercer		1963	5.00	10.00	20.00
—Multicolor labels, black "fan" logo at right					
DECCA					
❏ DL 74472 [S] Mabel Mercer Sings		1964	5.00	10.00	20.00

MERCER, MABEL, AND BOBBY SHORT

Number	Title (A Side/B Side)	Yr	VG	VG+	NM
ATLANTIC					
❏ SD 2-604 [(2)] Mabel Mercer and Bobby Short at Town Hall		1968	5.00	10.00	20.00

MERCHANTS OF DREAM, THE

Number	Title (A Side/B Side)	Yr	VG	VG+	NM
A&M					
❏ SP-4149 Strange Night Voyage		1969	6.25	12.50	25.00

MERCY

Number	Title (A Side/B Side)	Yr	VG	VG+	NM
SUNDI					
❏ SRLP-803 The Mercy & Love (Can Make You Happy)		1969	5.00	10.00	20.00
—Has the original version of the title song plus filler instrumentals					
WARNER BROS.					
❏ WS 1799 Love (Can Make You Happy)		1969	3.75	7.50	15.00
—"Love (Can Make You Happy)" was re-recorded for this LP					

Number	Title (A Side/B Side)	Yr	VG	VG+	NM
MERCY DEE					
ARHOOLIE					
❏ F-1007 [M]	Mercy Dee	1961	15.00	30.00	60.00
BLUESVILLE					
❏ BVLP-1039 [M]	A Pity and a Shame	1962	20.00	40.00	80.00
—Blue label, silver print					
❏ BVLP-1039 [M]	A Pity and a Shame	1964	6.25	12.50	25.00
—Blue label, trident logo at right					
MEREDITH, BUDDY					
STARDAY					
❏ SLP-225 [M]	Sing Me a Heart Song	1963	7.50	15.00	30.00
MEREDITH, BURGESS					
COLPIX					
❏ CP-452 [M]	Burgess Meredith Sings Songs from "How the West Was Won"	1964	5.00	10.00	20.00
❏ SCP-452 [S]	Burgess Meredith Sings Songs from "How the West Was Won"	1964	6.25	12.50	25.00
EPIC					
❏ BN 590 [S]	Songs and Stories of the Gold Rush	1961	7.50	15.00	30.00
❏ LN 3656 [M]	Songs and Stories of the Gold Rush	1961	6.25	12.50	25.00
MERIAN, LEON					
SEECO					
❏ CELP-4470 [S]	This Time the Swing's On Me	1960	5.00	10.00	20.00
❏ CELP-4590 [S]	Fiorello!	1960	5.00	10.00	20.00
MERIWETHER, ROY					
CAPITOL					
❏ ST-102	Soul Knight	1969	7.50	15.00	30.00
COLUMBIA					
❏ CL 2584 [M]	Stone Truth	1967	5.00	10.00	20.00
❏ CL 2744 [M]	Soul Invader	1968	7.50	15.00	30.00
❏ CS 9233 [S]	Soup and Onions (Soul Cookin')	1966	5.00	10.00	20.00
❏ CS 9298 [S]	Popcorn and Soul Groovin' at the Movies	1966	5.00	10.00	20.00
MERKIN					
WINDI					
❏ 1004/5	Music from Merkin	1972	100.00	200.00	400.00
MERMAIDS, THE					
See THE MURMAIDS.					
MERMAN, ETHEL					
DECCA					
❏ DXA 153 [(2)M]	A Musical Autobiography	195?	10.00	20.00	40.00
—Black label, silver print					
❏ DL 5053 [10]	Songs She Made Famous	1950	15.00	30.00	60.00
❏ DL 8178 [M]	A Musical Autobiography, Volume 1	195?	6.25	12.50	25.00
—Black label, silver print					
❏ DL 8179 [M]	A Musical Autobiography, Volume 2	195?	6.25	12.50	25.00
—Black label, silver print					
❏ DL 9028 [M]	Memories	1955	10.00	20.00	40.00
MERRILL, HELEN					
ATCO					
❏ 33-112 [M]	American Country Songs	1959	10.00	20.00	40.00
EMARCY					
❏ MG-36006 [M]	Helen Merrill	1955	20.00	40.00	80.00
❏ MG-36057 [M]	Helen Merrill with Strings	1955	20.00	40.00	80.00
❏ MG-36078 [M]	Dream of You	1956	15.00	30.00	60.00
❏ MG-36107 [M]	Merrill at Midnight	1957	15.00	30.00	60.00
❏ MG-36134 [M]	The Nearness of You	1958	12.50	25.00	50.00
MAINSTREAM					
❏ S-6014 [S]	The Artistry of Helen Merrill	1965	6.25	12.50	25.00
❏ 56014 [M]	The Artistry of Helen Merrill	1965	6.25	12.50	25.00
MERCURY					
❏ 826340-1 [(4)]	The Complete Helen Merrill on Mercury	1985	10.00	20.00	40.00
METROJAZZ					
❏ E-1010 [M]	You've Got a Date with the Blues	1958	10.00	20.00	40.00
❏ SE-1010 [S]	You've Got a Date with the Blues	1958	12.50	25.00	50.00
MILESTONE					
❏ MLP-1003 [M]	The Feeling Is Mutual	1967	6.25	12.50	25.00
❏ MLS-9003 [S]	The Feeling Is Mutual	1967	5.00	10.00	20.00
❏ M-9019	Shade of Difference	1969	5.00	10.00	20.00
MERRILL, TONI					
RAMA					
❏ RLP-5004 [M]	Songs from the Heart	1957	20.00	40.00	80.00
MERRY-GO-ROUND, THE					
A&M					
❏ LP-132 [M]	The Merry-Go-Round	1967	10.00	20.00	40.00
❏ SP-4132 [S]	The Merry-Go-Round	1967	7.50	15.00	30.00
RHINO					
❏ RNLP 126	The Best of the Merry-Go-Round	1985	2.50	5.00	10.00
MERRYWEATHER, NEIL					
CAPITOL					
❏ SKAO-220	Merryweather	1969	3.75	7.50	15.00
❏ STBB-278 [(2)]	Word of Mouth	1969	5.00	10.00	20.00
KENT					
❏ KST-546	Neil Merryweather and the Boers	197?	3.75	7.50	15.00
MERCURY					
❏ SRM-1-1007	Space Rangers	1974	3.00	6.00	12.00
❏ SRM-1-1024	Kryptonite	1975	3.00	6.00	12.00
MERSEYBEATS, THE					
ARC INTERNATIONAL					
❏ 834 [M]	England's Best Sellers	1964	10.00	20.00	40.00

Number	Title (A Side/B Side)	Yr	VG	VG+	NM
MERSEYBOYS, THE					
VEE JAY					
❏ VJ-1101 [DJ]	The 15 Greatest Songs of the Beatles	1964	37.50	75.00	150.00
—White label, all-blue print; without typographical error on label: "Saluting Their Return To America"					
❏ VJ-1101 [DJ]	The 15 Greatest Songs of the Beatles	1964	37.50	75.00	150.00
—White label, blue and black print; with typographical error on label: "Saluting Their Return to Amercia"					
❏ VJ-1101 [M]	The 15 Greatest Songs of the Beatles	1964	25.00	50.00	100.00
—With typographical error on label "Saluting Their Return to Amercia"; this album is not known to exist in stereo					
❏ VJ-1101 [M]	The 15 Greatest Songs of the Beatles	1964	25.00	50.00	100.00
—Without typographical error on label "Saluting Their Return To America"; this album is not known to exist in stereo					
MESHEL, BILLY					
PROBE					
❏ CPLP-4502	The Love Songs of A. Wilbur Meshel	1969	5.00	10.00	20.00
MESMERIZING EYE, THE					
SMASH					
❏ MGS-27090 [M]	Psychedelia — A Musical Light Show	1967	12.50	25.00	50.00
❏ SRS-67090 [S]	Psychedelia — A Musical Light Show	1967	15.00	30.00	60.00
MESSENGERS, THE (1)					
RARE EARTH					
❏ RS-509	The Messengers	1969	5.00	10.00	20.00
MESSINA, JIM					
Also see BUFFALO SPRINGFIELD; LOGGINS AND MESSINA; POCO.					
AUDIO FIDELITY					
❏ DFM-3037 [M]	The Dragsters	1964	20.00	40.00	80.00
❏ DFS-7037 [S]	The Dragsters	1964	25.00	50.00	100.00
COLUMBIA					
❏ JC 36141	Oasis	1979	2.50	5.00	10.00
THIMBLE					
❏ TLP-3	Jim Messina	197?	3.75	7.50	15.00
WARNER BROS.					
❏ BSK 3559	Messina	1981	2.50	5.00	10.00
❏ BSK 3559 [DJ]	Messina	1981	5.00	10.00	20.00
—Promo-only version on Quiex II vinyl					
❏ 23825	One More Mile	1983	2.50	5.00	10.00
METALLICA					
ELEKTRA					
❏ 60396	Ride the Lightning	1984	3.00	6.00	12.00
❏ 60439	Master of Puppets	1986	3.00	6.00	12.00
❏ 60757 [EP]	Garage Days Re-Revisited	1987	10.00	20.00	40.00
❏ 60766	Kill 'Em All	1987	3.00	6.00	12.00
—Reissue of Megaforce 069 with two extra tracks					
❏ 60812 [(2)]	...And Justice for All	1988	5.00	10.00	20.00
❏ 61113 [(2)]	Metallica	1991	10.00	20.00	40.00
❏ 61923 [(2)]	Load	1996	3.75	7.50	15.00
❏ 62126 [(2)]	Re-Load	1997	3.75	7.50	15.00
❏ 62299 [(3)]	Garage Inc.	1998	5.00	10.00	20.00
❏ 62504 [(3)]	S&M	1999	5.00	10.00	20.00
MEGAFORCE					
❏ MRI 069	Kill 'Em All	1983	7.50	15.00	30.00
❏ MRI 069 [PD]	Kill 'Em All	1983	10.00	20.00	40.00
—Un-numbered version					
❏ MRI 069 [PD]	Kill 'Em All	1983	20.00	40.00	80.00
—Numbered limited edition version					
❏ MRI 769	Ride the Lightning	1984	7.50	15.00	30.00
METERS, THE					
JOSIE					
❏ JOS-4010	The Meters	1969	17.50	35.00	70.00
❏ JOS-4011	Look-Ka Py Py	1970	17.50	35.00	70.00
❏ JOS-4012	Struttin'	1970	17.50	35.00	70.00
REPRISE					
❏ MS 2076	Cabbage Alley	1972	17.50	35.00	70.00
❏ MS 2200	Rejuvenation	1974	12.50	25.00	50.00
❏ MS 2228	Fire on the Bayou	1975	12.50	25.00	50.00
❏ MS 2252	Trick Bag	1976	12.50	25.00	50.00
ROUNDER					
❏ 2103	Look-Ka Py Py	1990	5.00	10.00	20.00
—Reissue of Josie 4011					
❏ 2104	Good Old Funky Music	1990	5.00	10.00	20.00
SUNDAZED					
❏ LP 5081	Kickback	2001	3.00	6.00	12.00
VIRGO					
❏ 12002	The Best of the Meters	1972	12.50	25.00	50.00
WARNER BROS.					
❏ BS 3042	New Directions	1977	12.50	25.00	50.00
METHENY, MIKE					
HEADFIRST					
❏ 9712	Blue Jay Sessions	198?	5.00	10.00	20.00
METHOD ACTOR					
The lead singer was Washington, D.C. cult favorite Eva Cassidy.					
(LABEL UNKNOWN)					
❏ (# unknown)	Method Actor	1988	125.00	250.00	500.00
METRONOMES, THE (U)					
STRAND					
❏ SL-1057 [M]	The Fabulous Metronomes Sing the Standard Hits	1962	7.50	15.00	30.00
❏ SLS-1057 [S]	The Fabulous Metronomes Sing the Standard Hits	1962	10.00	20.00	40.00
WYNNE					
❏ 106 [M]	And Now... The Metronomes	1960	30.00	60.00	120.00

M

Number	Title (A Side/B Side)	Yr	VG	VG+	NM

METROPOLITAN JAZZ OCTET
ARGO
| ☐ LP-659 [M] | The Legend of Bix | 1960 | 7.50 | 15.00 | 30.00 |

METROS, THE (1)
RCA VICTOR
| ☐ LPM-3776 [M] | Sweetest One | 1967 | 20.00 | 40.00 | 80.00 |
| ☐ LSP-3776 [S] | Sweetest One | 1967 | 25.00 | 50.00 | 100.00 |

METROTONES, THE
COLUMBIA
| ☐ CL 6341 [10] | Tops in Rock and Roll | 1955 | 62.50 | 125.00 | 250.00 |

MEYERS, AUGIE
ATLANTIC AMERICA
| ☐ 90856 | My Main Squeeze | 1988 | 2.50 | 5.00 | 10.00 |
PARAMOUNT
| ☐ PAS-6065 | You Ain't Rollin' Your Roll Rite | 1973 | 5.00 | 10.00 | 20.00 |
POLYDOR
| ☐ 24-4069 | Western Head Music Co. | 1971 | 5.00 | 10.00 | 20.00 |
TEXAS RE-CORD
| ☐ 1002 | Live at the Longneck | 197? | 7.50 | 15.00 | 30.00 |

MEZZROW, MEZZ
BLUE NOTE
| ☐ BLP-7023 [10] | Mezz Mezzrow and His Band | 1952 | 75.00 | 150.00 | 300.00 |
LONDON
| ☐ TKL-93092 [10] | A La Schola Cantorum | 195? | 15.00 | 30.00 | 60.00 |
RCA VICTOR
| ☐ LJM-1006 [M] | Mezzin' Around | 1954 | 12.50 | 25.00 | 50.00 |
"X"
| ☐ LVA-3015 [10] | Mezz Mezzrow's Swing Session | 1954 | 25.00 | 50.00 | 100.00 |
| ☐ LVA-3027 [10] | Mezz Mezzrow | 1954 | 25.00 | 50.00 | 100.00 |

MFG
HAT HUT
| ☐ S/T [(2)] | MFG in Minnesota | 1978 | 7.50 | 15.00 | 30.00 |
—Joe McPhee; Milo Fine; Steve Gnitka

MIAMI SOUND MACHINE
AUDIOFON
| ☐ AUS 5426 | Live Again — Renacer | 1977 | 25.00 | 50.00 | 100.00 |
—The rest have a cover with a blue and yellow "tropical" background
| ☐ AUS 5426 | Live Again — Renacer | 1977 | 50.00 | 100.00 | 200.00 |
—First 600 have a cover where the backdrop is clearly visible
| ☐ AUS 5427 | Miami Sound Machine | 1978 | 25.00 | 50.00 | 100.00 |
—Spanish-language version
CBS INTERNATIONAL
| ☐ DML 10306 | Imported | 1980 | 10.00 | 20.00 | 40.00 |
—Reissue of 10455
☐ DHL 10311	Miami Sound Machine	1980	12.50	25.00	50.00
☐ DIL 10320	Otra Vez	1981	12.50	25.00	50.00
☐ DIL 10330	Rio	1982	12.50	25.00	50.00
☐ DSL 10335	7Up Presenta Los Hits de Miami Sound Machine	1983	25.00	50.00	100.00
—Only available in the Miami area from 7Up dealers
| ☐ DIL 10349 | A Toda Maquina | 1984 | 10.00 | 20.00 | 40.00 |
—Spanish-language version of "Eyes of Innocence," their first all-English LP
| ☐ DKL 10455 | Imported | 1979 | 12.50 | 25.00 | 50.00 |
—Reissue of MSM album
ELECTRIC CAT
| ☐ ECS 226 | Miami Sound Machine | 1978 | 25.00 | 50.00 | 100.00 |
—Partially English-language version
EPIC
| ☐ BFE 39622 | Eyes of Innocence | 1984 | 2.50 | 5.00 | 10.00 |
| ☐ BFE 40131 | Primitive Love | 1985 | 2.00 | 4.00 | 8.00 |
—The band's breakthrough LP to non-Hispanic audiences, and the last one not to have Gloria Estefan prominently credited
MSM
| ☐ ERK 0714 | Imported | 1979 | 25.00 | 50.00 | 100.00 |
TOP HITS
| ☐ TH-AM 2185 | Live Again — Renacer | 1982 | 12.50 | 25.00 | 50.00 |
—Reissue of Audiofon LP of the same name
| ☐ TH-AM 2187 | Miami Sound Machine | 1982 | 12.50 | 25.00 | 50.00 |
—Reissue of Audiofon LP of the same name
| ☐ TH-AM 2228 | Lo Mejor De Miami Sound Machine — A Portrait of the Originals | 1983 | 12.50 | 25.00 | 50.00 |
—Compilation from first two Spanish-language LPs

MICHAELS, LEE
A&M
| ☐ SP-3158 | Lee Michaels | 198? | 2.00 | 4.00 | 8.00 |
—Budget-line reissue
☐ SP-3518	Live	1973	3.75	7.50	15.00
☐ SP-4140	Carnival of Life	1968	10.00	20.00	40.00
☐ SP-4152	Recital	1968	5.00	10.00	20.00
☐ SP-4199	Lee Michaels	1969	3.75	7.50	15.00
☐ SP-4249	Barrel	1970	3.75	7.50	15.00
☐ SP-4302	5th	1971	3.75	7.50	15.00
☐ SP-4336	Space and First Takes	1972	3.75	7.50	15.00
COLUMBIA
☐ CQ 32275 [Q]	Nice Day for Something	1973	5.00	10.00	20.00
☐ KC 32275	Nice Day for Something	1973	3.00	6.00	12.00
☐ KC 32846	Tailface	1974	3.00	6.00	12.00

MICKELSON, PAUL
RCA VICTOR
| ☐ LPM-1115 [M] | Christmas Bells | 1955 | 5.00 | 10.00 | 20.00 |
| ☐ LPM-1517 [M] | The Best of Christmas | 1957 | 5.00 | 10.00 | 20.00 |

MICKEY AND SYLVIA
Also see MICKEY BAKER; SYLVIA (1).
RCA CAMDEN
| ☐ CAL-863 [M] | Love Is Strange | 1965 | 12.50 | 25.00 | 50.00 |
| ☐ CAS-863(e) [R] | Love Is Strange | 1965 | 7.50 | 15.00 | 30.00 |
RCA VICTOR
| ☐ APM1-0327 | Do It Again | 1973 | 3.00 | 6.00 | 12.00 |
VIK
| ☐ LX-1102 [M] | New Sounds | 1957 | 100.00 | 200.00 | 400.00 |

MIDLER, BETTE
ATLANTIC
| ☐ 7238 [M] | The Divine Miss M | 1972 | 7.50 | 15.00 | 30.00 |
—Mono is promo only; white label, "dj copy monaural" sticker on stereo cover
☐ QD 7238 [Q]	The Divine Miss M	1973	4.50	9.00	18.00
☐ SD 7238	The Divine Miss M	1972	2.50	5.00	10.00
☐ SD 7270	Bette Midler	1973	2.50	5.00	10.00
☐ SD 2-9000 [(2)]	Live! At Last	1977	3.00	6.00	12.00
☐ SD 16004	Thighs and Whispers	1979	2.50	5.00	10.00
☐ SD 16010	The Rose	1979	2.50	5.00	10.00
☐ SD 16022	Divine Madness	1980	2.50	5.00	10.00
☐ SD 18155	Songs for the New Depression	1976	2.50	5.00	10.00
☐ SD 19155	Broken Blossom	1977	2.50	5.00	10.00
☐ 80070	No Frills	1983	2.50	5.00	10.00
☐ 81291	Mud Will Be Flung Tonight	1985	2.50	5.00	10.00
☐ 81933	Beaches	1988	2.50	5.00	10.00
☐ 82129	Some People's Lives	1990	3.00	6.00	12.00

MIDNIGHTERS, THE
FEDERAL
| ☐ 295-90 [10] | Their Greatest Hits | 1954 | 4000. | 6000. | 8000. |
| ☐ 541 [M] | Their Greatest Hits | 1955 | 250.00 | 500.00 | 1000. |
—Yellow cover
| ☐ 541 [M] | Their Greatest Hits | 1955 | 375.00 | 750.00 | 1500. |
—Red cover
| ☐ 581 [M] | The Midnighters, Volume 2 | 1955 | 300.00 | 600.00 | 1200. |
KING
| ☐ 541 [M] | Their Greatest Jukebox Hits | 1958 | 100.00 | 200.00 | 400.00 |
—Crownless black label, "King" is two inches wide on label
| ☐ 541 [M] | Their Greatest Jukebox Hits | 196? | 50.00 | 100.00 | 200.00 |
—Reissue with Hank Ballard on cover
| ☐ 541 [M] | Their Greatest Jukebox Hits | 196? | 75.00 | 150.00 | 300.00 |
—Crownless black label, "King" is three inches wide on label. Above two have a girl on the cover.
| ☐ 581 [M] | The Midnighters, Volume 2 | 1958 | 75.00 | 150.00 | 300.00 |
—Crownless black label, "King" is two inches wide on label
| ☐ 581 [M] | The Midnighters, Volume 2 | 196? | 50.00 | 100.00 | 200.00 |
—Crownless black label, "King" is three inches wide on label

MIGHTY BABY
HEAD
| ☐ LPS-025 | Mighty Baby | 1969 | 15.00 | 30.00 | 60.00 |

MIGHTY CLOUDS OF JOY
ABC
☐ D-899	Kickin'	1975	2.50	5.00	10.00
☐ D-986	The Truth Is the Power	1976	2.50	5.00	10.00
☐ D-1038	Live and Direct	1977	2.50	5.00	10.00
ABC DUNHILL
| ☐ DSX-50177 | It's Time | 1974 | 2.50 | 5.00 | 10.00 |
HOB
| ☐ 288 | "Live" Zion Songs | 196? | 3.75 | 7.50 | 15.00 |
KING
| ☐ SG3-1107 | Out Talking to Yourself | 1970 | 3.75 | 7.50 | 15.00 |
MCA
| ☐ 1091 [(2)] | The Very Best of Mighty Clouds of Joy | 198? | 2.50 | 5.00 | 10.00 |
| ☐ 28008 | Family Circle | 198? | 2.00 | 4.00 | 8.00 |
—Reissue of Peacock 114
| ☐ 28012 | The Bright Side | 198? | 2.00 | 4.00 | 8.00 |
—Reissue of Peacock 121
| ☐ 28017 | Mighty Clouds of Joy At the Music Hall | 198? | 2.00 | 4.00 | 8.00 |
—Reissue of Peacock 134
| ☐ 28019 | The Best of Mighty Clouds of Joy | 198? | 2.00 | 4.00 | 8.00 |
—Reissue of Peacock 136
| ☐ 28025 | The Untouchables | 198? | 2.00 | 4.00 | 8.00 |
—Reissue of Peacock 151
| ☐ 28028 | Songs of Rev. Julius Cheeks and the Nightingales | 198? | 2.00 | 4.00 | 8.00 |
—Reissue of Peacock 163
| ☐ 28030 | God Bless America | 198? | 2.00 | 4.00 | 8.00 |
—Reissue of Peacock 170
| ☐ 28032 | Live at the Apollo | 198? | 2.00 | 4.00 | 8.00 |
—Reissue of Peacock 173
| ☐ 28040 | The Best of Mighty Clouds of Joy — Volume 2 | 198? | 2.00 | 4.00 | 8.00 |
MYRRH
☐ MSB-6663	Cloudburst	1980	2.50	5.00	10.00
☐ MSB-6681	The Truth Is the Power	1981	2.50	5.00	10.00
☐ MSB-6694	Miracle Man	1982	2.50	5.00	10.00
☐ MSB-6712	Request Line	1983	2.50	5.00	10.00
☐ WR-8121	Mighty Clouds Alive	1984	2.50	5.00	10.00
☐ WR-8122	Sing and Shout	1984	2.50	5.00	10.00
PEACOCK
☐ 114	Family Circle	196?	5.00	10.00	20.00
☐ 121	The Bright Side	196?	5.00	10.00	20.00
☐ 134	Mighty Clouds of Joy At the Music Hall	196?	5.00	10.00	20.00
☐ 136	The Best of Mighty Clouds of Joy	196?	5.00	10.00	20.00
☐ 151	The Untouchables	196?	5.00	10.00	20.00
☐ 161	Out Talking to Yourself	196?	5.00	10.00	20.00
☐ 163	Songs of Rev. Julius Cheeks and the Nightingales	196?	5.00	10.00	20.00
☐ 170	God Bless America	1971	3.75	7.50	15.00
☐ 173	Live at the Apollo	1972	3.75	7.50	15.00

Number	Title (A Side/B Side)	Yr	VG	VG+	NM
PRIORITY					
❏ RV 37707	Changing Times	1982	2.50	5.00	10.00
MIGHTY FAITH INCREASERS, THE					
KING					
❏ 806 [M]	The Mighty Faith Increasers with Willa Dorsey	1962	37.50	75.00	150.00
❏ 814 [M]	A Festival of Spiritual Songs	1962	37.50	75.00	150.00
MIL-COMBO, THE					
CAPITOL					
❏ T 579 [M]	The Mil-Combo	1955	12.50	25.00	50.00
MILANOV, ZINKA					
RCA VICTOR RED SEAL					
❏ LSC-2303 [S]	Operatic Arias by Puccini	1959	10.00	20.00	40.00
—Originals on "shaded dog" label					
MILBURN, AMOS					
ALADDIN					
❏ LP-704 [10]	Rockin' the Boogie	1955	1000.	2000.	4000.
—Black vinyl					
❏ LP-704 [10]	Rockin' the Boogie	1955	200.00	4000.	8000.
—Red vinyl, blue cover					
❏ LP-810 [M]	Rockin' the Boogie	1958	—	—	—
—Canceled					
IMPERIAL					
❏ LP-9176 [M]	Million Sellers	1962	125.00	250.00	500.00
MOTOWN					
❏ 608 [M]	The Return of Amos Milburn, "The" Blues Boss	1963	225.00	450.00	900.00
SCORE					
❏ LP-4012 [M]	Let's Have a Party	1957	200.00	400.00	800.00
❏ LP-4035 [M]	Amos Milburn Sings the Blues	1958	—	—	—
—Canceled					
MILBURN, AMOS/WYNONIE HARRIS/ETC.					
ALADDIN					
❏ LP-703 [10]	Party After Hours	1955	1000.	2000.	4000.
—Black vinyl					
❏ LP-703 [10]	Party After Hours	1955	2000.	4000.	8000.
—Red vinyl, blue cover					
MILES, BARRY					
CENTURY					
❏ 1070	Fusion Is…	1979	5.00	10.00	20.00
—Audiophile edition					
CHARLIE PARKER					
❏ PLP-804 [M]	Miles of Genius	1962	6.25	12.50	25.00
❏ PLP-804S [S]	Miles of Genius	1962	7.50	15.00	30.00
POPPY					
❏ PY-40009	Barry Miles	1970	5.00	10.00	20.00
MILES, BUDDY					
ATLANTIC					
❏ SD 2-4000 [(2)]	Sneak Attack	1982	3.00	6.00	12.00
CASABLANCA					
❏ NBLP 7019	More Miles Per Gallon	1975	2.50	5.00	10.00
❏ NBLP 7024	Bicentennial Gathering of the Tribes	1976	2.50	5.00	10.00
COLUMBIA					
❏ CQ 32048 [Q]	Chapter VII	1973	5.00	10.00	20.00
❏ KC 32048	Chapter VII	1973	3.00	6.00	12.00
❏ CQ 32694 [Q]	Booger Bear	1973	5.00	10.00	20.00
❏ KC 32694	Booger Bear	1973	3.00	6.00	12.00
❏ KC 33089	All the Faces	1974	3.00	6.00	12.00
MERCURY					
❏ SRM-1-608	A Message to the People	1971	3.75	7.50	15.00
❏ SRM-2-7500 [(2)]	Buddy Miles Live	1971	3.75	7.50	15.00
❏ SR-61196	Expressway to Your Skull	1968	5.00	10.00	20.00
❏ SR-61222	Electric Church	1969	5.00	10.00	20.00
❏ SR-61280	Them Changes	1970	3.75	7.50	15.00
❏ SR-61313	We Got to Live Together	1970	3.75	7.50	15.00
MILES, LIZZIE					
COOK					
❏ 1181 [10]	Queen Mother of the Rue Royale	1955	15.00	30.00	60.00
❏ 1182 [M]	Moans and Blues	195?	12.50	25.00	50.00
❏ 1183 [M]	Hot Songs My Mother Taught Me	195?	12.50	25.00	50.00
❏ 1184 [M]	Torchy Lullabies My Mother Taught Me	195?	12.50	25.00	50.00
MILES, LUKE "LONG GONE"					
WORLD PACIFIC					
❏ ST-1820 [S]	Country Born	1964	7.50	15.00	30.00
❏ WP-1820 [M]	Country Born	1964	6.25	12.50	25.00
MILKWOOD (1)					
A&M					
❏ SP-4226	Under Milkwood	1969	75.00	150.00	300.00
MILKWOOD (2)					
PARAMOUNT					
❏ PAS-6046	How's the Weather?	1973	10.00	20.00	40.00
MILKWOOD TAPESTRY					
METROMEDIA					
❏ MD-1007	Milkwood Tapestry	1969	12.50	25.00	50.00
MILLARD & DYCE					
KAYMAR					
❏ KS-7-265	Open	1973	15.00	30.00	60.00
MILLENNIUM					
COLUMBIA					
❏ CS 9663	Begin	1968	7.50	15.00	30.00

Number	Title (A Side/B Side)	Yr	VG	VG+	NM
MILLER, CHUCK					
MERCURY					
❏ MG-20195 [M]	After Hours	1956	20.00	40.00	80.00
MILLER, CLARENCE "BIG"					
COLUMBIA					
❏ CL 1611 [M]	Revelation and the Blues	1961	6.25	12.50	25.00
❏ CL 1808 [M]	Big Miller Sings, Twists, Shouts and Preaches	1962	6.25	12.50	25.00
❏ CS 8411 [S]	Revelation and the Blues	1961	7.50	15.00	30.00
❏ CS 8608 [S]	Big Miller Sings, Twists, Shouts and Preaches	1962	7.50	15.00	30.00
UNITED ARTISTS					
❏ UAL-3047 [M]	Did You Ever Hear the Blues?	1959	10.00	20.00	40.00
❏ UAS-6047 [S]	Did You Ever Hear the Blues?	1959	15.00	30.00	60.00
MILLER, DON					
KING					
❏ 712 [M]	The Don Miller Quartet	1960	15.00	30.00	60.00
MILLER, EDDIE					
CAPITOL					
❏ T 614 [M]	Classics in Jazz	1955	12.50	25.00	50.00
MILLER, EDDIE/GEORGE VAN EPS					
JUMP					
❏ JL-5 [10]	Eddie Miller/George Van Eps	1953	12.50	25.00	50.00
MILLER, FRANKIE					
AUDIO LAB					
❏ AL-1562 [M]	The Fine Country Singing of Frankie Miller	1963	37.50	75.00	150.00
STARDAY					
❏ SLP-134 [M]	Country Music's Great New Star	1961	25.00	50.00	100.00
❏ SLP-199 [M]	The True Country Style of Frankie Miller	1962	25.00	50.00	100.00
❏ SLP-339 [M]	Blackland Farmer	1965	15.00	30.00	60.00
MILLER, GLENN					
BLUEBIRD					
❏ 9785-1-RB [(4)]	The Popular Recordings 1938-1942	1989	6.25	12.50	25.00
EPIC					
❏ LA 16002 [M]	Glenn Miller	1960	5.00	10.00	20.00
RCA VICTOR					
❏ LPT-16 [10]	Glenn Miller Concert — Volume 1	1951	15.00	30.00	60.00
❏ LPT-30 [10]	Glenn Miller Concert — Volume 2	1951	15.00	30.00	60.00
❏ LPT-31 [10]	Glenn Miller	1951	15.00	30.00	60.00
❏ PR-114 [M]	Glenn Miller Originals	1962	5.00	10.00	20.00
—Promotional item for Salada Foods Inc.					
❏ LOP-1005 [M]	The Marvelous Miller Medleys	1958	10.00	20.00	40.00
❏ LPT-1016 [M]	Juke Box Saturday Night	1955	10.00	20.00	40.00
❏ LPT-1031 [M]	The Nearness of You	1955	10.00	20.00	40.00
❏ LPM-1189 [M]	The Sound of Glenn Miller	1956	10.00	20.00	40.00
❏ LPM-1190 [M]	This Is Glenn Miller	1956	10.00	20.00	40.00
❏ LPM-1192 [M]	Selections from "The Glenn Miller Story" and Other Hits	1956	10.00	20.00	40.00
❏ LPM-1193 [M]	Glenn Miller Concert	1956	10.00	20.00	40.00
❏ LPM-1494 [M]	Marvelous Miller Moods	1957	10.00	20.00	40.00
❏ LPM-1506 [M]	The Glenn Miller Carnegie Hall Concert	1957	10.00	20.00	40.00
❏ LPM-1973 [M]	The Marvelous Miller Medleys	1959	7.50	15.00	30.00
❏ LPT-3001 [10]	Glenn Miller Concert — Volume 3	195?	15.00	30.00	60.00
❏ LPT-3002 [10]	This Is Glenn Miller	195?	15.00	30.00	60.00
❏ LPT-3036 [10]	This Is Glenn Miller — Volume 2	195?	15.00	30.00	60.00
❏ LPT-3057 [10]	Selections from the Film "The Glenn Miller Story"	1954	15.00	30.00	60.00
❏ LPT-3067 [10]	Sunrise Serenade	1954	15.00	30.00	60.00
❏ LPM-6100 [(3)M]	For the Very First Time…	195?	12.50	25.00	50.00
—Black "Long Play" labels in leatherette spiral-bound binder					
❏ LPM-6101 [(3)M]	Glenn Miller On the Air	1963	10.00	20.00	40.00
❏ LSP-6101 [(3)R]	Glenn Miller On the Air	1963	6.25	12.50	25.00
❏ LPT-6700 [(5)M]	Glenn Miller and His Orchestra Limited Edition — Second Pressing	195?	15.00	30.00	60.00
—Black "Long Play" labels in leatherette spiral-bound binder					
❏ LPT-6700 [(5)M]	Glenn Miller and His Orchestra Limited Edition	1953	37.50	75.00	150.00
—Silver labels with red print in leatherette spiral-bound binder					
❏ LPT-6701 [(5)M]	Glenn Miller and His Orchestra Limited Edition Volume Two — Second Pressing	195?	15.00	30.00	60.00
—Black "Long Play" labels in leatherette spiral-bound binder; identified as "Second Pressing" throughout					
❏ LPT-6701 [(5)M]	Glenn Miller and His Orchestra Limited Edition Volume Two	1954	30.00	60.00	120.00
—Black "Long Play" labels in leatherette spiral-bound binder					
❏ LPT-6702 [(4)M]	Glenn Miller Army Air Force Band	195?	15.00	30.00	60.00
—Same as above, but in box rather than in binder					
❏ LPT-6702 [(4)M]	Glenn Miller Army Air Force Band	1955	30.00	60.00	120.00
—Black "Long Play" labels in leatherette spiral-bound binder					
20TH FOX					
❏ TCF-100-2 [(2)M]	Glenn Miller and His Orchestra Original Film Sound Tracks	1958	7.50	15.00	30.00
❏ TCF-100-2S [(2)R]	Glenn Miller and His Orchestra Original Film Sound Tracks	1961	5.00	10.00	20.00
MILLER, GLENN, ORCHESTRA (BUDDY DEFRANCO, DIRECTOR)					
RCA VICTOR					
❏ LPM-3880 [M]	The Glenn Miller Orchestra Returns to the Glen Island Casino	1968	5.00	10.00	20.00
❏ LPM-3971 [M]	The Glenn Miller Orchestra Makes the Goin' Great	1968	10.00	20.00	40.00
MILLER, GLENN, ORCHESTRA (RAY MCKINLEY, DIRECTOR)					
EPIC					
❏ BN 26133 [S]	Glenn Miller Time — 1965	1965	5.00	10.00	20.00
❏ BN 26157 [S]	Great Songs of the 60's	1965	5.00	10.00	20.00
RCA VICTOR					
❏ LPM-1522 [M]	The New Glenn Miller Orchestra in Hi-Fi	1957	7.50	15.00	30.00
❏ LSP-1522 [S]	The New Glenn Miller Orchestra in Hi-Fi	1958	10.00	20.00	40.00

M

Number	Title (A Side/B Side)	Yr	VG	VG+	NM
❏ LPM-1678 [M]	Something Old, New, Borrowed and Blue	1958	7.50	15.00	30.00
❏ LSP-1678 [S]	Something Old, New, Borrowed and Blue	1958	10.00	20.00	40.00
❏ LPM-1852 [M]	The Miller Sound	1959	7.50	15.00	30.00
❏ LSP-1852 [S]	The Miller Sound	1959	10.00	20.00	40.00
❏ LPM-1948 [M]	On Tour with the New Glenn Miller Orchestra	1959	7.50	15.00	30.00
❏ LSP-1948 [S]	On Tour with the New Glenn Miller Orchestra	1959	10.00	20.00	40.00
❏ LPM-2080 [M]	The Great Dance Bands of the 30's and 40's	1960	6.25	12.50	25.00
❏ LSP-2080 [S]	The Great Dance Bands of the 30's and 40's	1960	7.50	15.00	30.00
❏ LPM-2193 [M]	Dance, Anyone?	1960	6.25	12.50	25.00
❏ LSP-2193 [S]	Dance, Anyone?	1960	7.50	15.00	30.00
❏ LPM-2270 [M]	The Authentic Sound of the New Glenn Miller Orchestra — Today	1961	6.25	12.50	25.00
❏ LSP-2270 [S]	The Authentic Sound of the New Glenn Miller Orchestra — Today	1961	7.50	15.00	30.00
❏ LPM-2436 [M]	Glenn Miller Time	1961	6.25	12.50	25.00
❏ LSP-2436 [S]	Glenn Miller Time	1961	7.50	15.00	30.00
❏ LPM-2519 [M]	Echoes of Glenn Miller	1962	6.25	12.50	25.00
❏ LSP-2519 [S]	Echoes of Glenn Miller	1962	7.50	15.00	30.00

MILLER, JODY
CAPITOL

Number	Title (A Side/B Side)	Yr	VG	VG+	NM
❏ ST 1913 [S]	Wednesday's Child Is Full of Woe	1963	10.00	20.00	40.00
❏ T 1913 [M]	Wednesday's Child Is Full of Woe	1963	7.50	15.00	30.00
❏ ST 2349 [S]	Queen of the House	1965	5.00	10.00	20.00
❏ T 2349 [M]	Queen of the House	1965	3.75	7.50	15.00
❏ ST 2412 [S]	Home of the Brave	1965	5.00	10.00	20.00
❏ T 2412 [M]	Home of the Brave	1965	3.75	7.50	15.00
❏ ST 2446 [S]	Jody Miller Sings the Great Hits of Buck Owens	1966	5.00	10.00	20.00
❏ T 2446 [M]	Jody Miller Sings the Great Hits of Buck Owens	1966	3.75	7.50	15.00
❏ ST 2996	The Nashville Sound of Jody Miller	1968	3.75	7.50	15.00
❏ ST-11169	The Best of Jody Miller	1973	3.00	6.00	12.00

EPIC

Number	Title (A Side/B Side)	Yr	VG	VG+	NM
❏ E 30282	Look at Mine	1971	3.00	6.00	12.00
❏ E 30659	He's So Fine	1971	3.00	6.00	12.00
❏ KE 31706	There's a Party Goin' On	1972	3.00	6.00	12.00
❏ KE 32386	Good News!	1973	3.00	6.00	12.00
❏ KE 32569	House of the Rising Sun	1974	3.00	6.00	12.00
❏ KE 33349	Country Girl	1975	3.00	6.00	12.00
❏ KE 33934	Will You Love Me Tomorrow?	1976	3.00	6.00	12.00
❏ PE 34446	Here's Jody	1977	3.00	6.00	12.00

MILLER, MICKEY
FOLKWAYS

Number	Title (A Side/B Side)	Yr	VG	VG+	NM
❏ FA-2393 [M]	American Folk Songs	1959	7.50	15.00	30.00

MILLER, MITCH
ATLANTIC

Number	Title (A Side/B Side)	Yr	VG	VG+	NM
❏ SD 8277	Peace Sing Along with Mitch	1970	3.00	6.00	12.00

COLUMBIA

Number	Title (A Side/B Side)	Yr	VG	VG+	NM
❏ CL 601 [M]	Mmmmitch!	1954	5.00	10.00	20.00
—Maroon label, gold print					
❏ CL 779 [M]	It's So Peaceful in the Country	1956	5.00	10.00	20.00
—Red and black label with 6 "eye" logos					
❏ CL 1102 [M]	Mitch's Marches	1957	3.75	7.50	15.00
❏ CL 1160 [M]	Sing Along with Mitch	1958	3.75	7.50	15.00
❏ CL 1205 [M]	Christmas Sing Along with Mitch	1958	3.75	7.50	15.00
—Originals have gatefold cover with eight detachable lyric sheets inside					
❏ CL 1243 [M]	More Sing Along with Mitch	1958	3.75	7.50	15.00
❏ CL 1283 [M]	Still More! Sing Along with Mitch	1959	3.75	7.50	15.00
❏ CL 1316 [M]	Folk Songs Sing Along with Mitch	1959	3.75	7.50	15.00
❏ CL 1331 [M]	Party Sing Along with Mitch	1959	3.75	7.50	15.00
❏ CL 1389 [M]	Fireside Sing Along with Mitch	1959	3.75	7.50	15.00
❏ CL 1414 [M]	Saturday Night Sing Along with Mitch	1960	3.00	6.00	12.00
❏ CL 1457 [M]	Sentimental Sing Along with Mitch	1960	3.00	6.00	12.00
❏ CL 1475 [M]	March Along with Mitch	1960	3.00	6.00	12.00
❏ CL 1542 [M]	Memories Sing Along with Mitch	1960	3.00	6.00	12.00
❏ CL 1544 [M]	Mitch's Greatest Hits	1961	3.00	6.00	12.00
❏ CL 1568 [M]	Happy Times! Sing Along with Mitch	1961	3.00	6.00	12.00
❏ CL 1628 [M]	TV Sing Along with Mitch	1961	3.00	6.00	12.00
❏ CL 1671 [M]	Your Request Sing Along with Mitch	1961	3.00	6.00	12.00
❏ CL 1701 [M]	Holiday Sing Along with Mitch	1961	3.00	6.00	12.00
❏ CL 1727 [M]	Rhythm Sing Along with Mitch	1962	3.00	6.00	12.00
❏ CL 1773 [M]	Family Sing Along with Mitch	1962	3.00	6.00	12.00
❏ CL 1864 [M]	Night Time Sing Along with Mitch	1963	3.00	6.00	12.00
❏ CL 2063 [M]	Hymn Sing Along with Mitch	1963	3.00	6.00	12.00
❏ CL 6222 [10]	Mitch Miller with Horns and Chorus	195?	7.50	15.00	30.00
❏ CS 8004	Sing Along with Mitch	1963	3.00	6.00	12.00
—Red label					
❏ CS 8004	Sing Along with Mitch	1970	2.00	4.00	8.00
—Orange label					
❏ CS 8004 [S]	Sing Along with Mitch	1959	5.00	10.00	20.00
—Red and black label with 6 "eye" logos					
❏ PC 8004	Sing Along with Mitch	198?	—	3.00	6.00
—Reissue with new prefix					
❏ CS 8027 [S]	Christmas Sing Along with Mitch	1959	5.00	10.00	20.00
—Originals have gatefold cover with eight detachable lyric sheets inside					
❏ CS 8043 [S]	More Sing Along with Mitch	1959	5.00	10.00	20.00
❏ CS 8099 [S]	Still More! Sing Along with Mitch	1959	5.00	10.00	20.00
❏ CS 8118 [S]	Folk Songs Sing Along with Mitch	1959	5.00	10.00	20.00
❏ CS 8138 [S]	Party Sing Along with Mitch	1959	5.00	10.00	20.00
❏ CS 8184 [S]	Fireside Sing Along with Mitch	1959	5.00	10.00	20.00
❏ CS 8211 [S]	Saturday Night Sing Along with Mitch	1960	3.75	7.50	15.00
❏ CS 8251 [S]	Sentimental Sing Along with Mitch	1960	3.75	7.50	15.00
❏ CS 8342 [S]	Memories Sing Along with Mitch	1960	3.75	7.50	15.00
❏ CS 8368 [S]	Happy Times! Sing Along with Mitch	1961	3.75	7.50	15.00
❏ CS 8428 [S]	TV Sing Along with Mitch	1961	3.75	7.50	15.00
❏ CS 8471 [S]	Your Request Sing Along with Mitch	1961	3.75	7.50	15.00
❏ CS 8501 [S]	Holiday Sing Along with Mitch	1961	3.75	7.50	15.00
❏ CS 8527 [S]	Rhythm Sing Along with Mitch	1962	3.75	7.50	15.00
❏ CS 8573 [S]	Family Sing Along with Mitch	1962	3.75	7.50	15.00
❏ CS 8638 [R]	Mitch's Greatest Hits	1963	2.50	5.00	10.00
❏ CS 8664 [S]	Night Time Sing Along with Mitch	1963	3.75	7.50	15.00
❏ CS 8863 [S]	Hymn Sing Along with Mitch	1963	3.75	7.50	15.00

Number	Title (A Side/B Side)	Yr	VG	VG+	NM
❏ G 30250 [(2)]	34 All Time Great Sing Along Selections	1970	3.00	6.00	12.00
❏ 3C 39297	Holiday Sing Along with Mitch	1984	2.00	4.00	8.00
❏ PC 39298	Christmas Sing Along with Mitch	1984	2.00	4.00	8.00

DECCA

Number	Title (A Side/B Side)	Yr	VG	VG+	NM
❏ DL 4777 [M]	Dance and Sing Along with Mitch	1966	2.50	5.00	10.00
❏ DL 74777 [S]	Dance and Sing Along with Mitch	1966	3.00	6.00	12.00

HARMONY

Number	Title (A Side/B Side)	Yr	VG	VG+	NM
❏ HL 7404 [M]	March Along with Mitch	1967	2.50	5.00	10.00
❏ HS 11204 [S]	March Along with Mitch	1967	3.00	6.00	12.00
❏ HS 11241	Fireside Sing Along with Mitch	1968	2.50	5.00	10.00
❏ HS 11242	Memories Sing Along with Mitch	1968	2.50	5.00	10.00
❏ HS 11273	Everybody Sing Along with Mitch	1968	2.50	5.00	10.00
❏ HS 11354	Night Time Sing Along with Mitch	1970	2.50	5.00	10.00

MILLER, MRS.
AMARET

Number	Title (A Side/B Side)	Yr	VG	VG+	NM
❏ 5000	Mrs. Miller Does Her Thing	1969	5.00	10.00	20.00

CAPITOL

Number	Title (A Side/B Side)	Yr	VG	VG+	NM
❏ ST 2494 [S]	Mrs. Miller's Greatest Hits	1966	7.50	15.00	30.00
❏ T 2494 [M]	Mrs. Miller's Greatest Hits	1966	6.25	12.50	25.00
❏ ST 2579 [S]	Will Success Spoil Mrs. Miller?	1966	7.50	15.00	30.00
❏ T 2579 [M]	Will Success Spoil Mrs. Miller?	1966	6.25	12.50	25.00
❏ ST 2734 [S]	The Country Soul of Mrs. Miller	1967	6.25	12.50	25.00
❏ T 2734 [M]	The Country Soul of Mrs. Miller	1967	6.25	12.50	25.00

MILLER, NED
CAPITOL

Number	Title (A Side/B Side)	Yr	VG	VG+	NM
❏ ST 2330 [S]	Ned Miller Sings the Songs of Ned Miller	1965	6.25	12.50	25.00
❏ T 2330 [M]	Ned Miller Sings the Songs of Ned Miller	1965	5.00	10.00	20.00
❏ ST 2414 [S]	The Best of Ned Miller	1966	5.00	10.00	20.00
❏ T 2414 [M]	The Best of Ned Miller	1966	3.75	7.50	15.00
❏ ST 2586 [S]	Teardrop Lane	1967	5.00	10.00	20.00
❏ T 2586 [M]	Teardrop Lane	1967	5.00	10.00	20.00
❏ ST 2914	In the Name of Love	1968	3.75	7.50	15.00

FABOR

Number	Title (A Side/B Side)	Yr	VG	VG+	NM
❏ FLP-1001 [M]	From a Jack to a King	1963	10.00	20.00	40.00
—Black vinyl					
❏ FLP-1001 [M]	From a Jack to a King	1963	25.00	50.00	100.00
—Colored vinyl					

MILLER, PUNCH
IMPERIAL

Number	Title (A Side/B Side)	Yr	VG	VG+	NM
❏ LP-9160 [M]	Hongo Fongo	1962	6.25	12.50	25.00

MILLER, ROGER
COLUMBIA

Number	Title (A Side/B Side)	Yr	VG	VG+	NM
❏ KC 32449	Dear Folks Sorry I Haven't Written Lately	1973	3.75	7.50	15.00
❏ KC 33472	Supersongs	1975	3.75	7.50	15.00

HILLTOP

Number	Title (A Side/B Side)	Yr	VG	VG+	NM
❏ 6109	King of the Road	197?	2.50	5.00	10.00
❏ 6131	Little Green Apples	197?	2.50	5.00	10.00

MCA

Number	Title (A Side/B Side)	Yr	VG	VG+	NM
❏ 5722	Roger Miller	1986	2.50	5.00	10.00

MERCURY

Number	Title (A Side/B Side)	Yr	VG	VG+	NM
❏ SR-61297	A Trip in the Country	1970	3.75	7.50	15.00
❏ SR-61361	The Best of Roger Miller	1971	3.75	7.50	15.00
❏ 826261-1	Golden Hits	198?	2.00	4.00	8.00
—Reissue of Smash 67073					

NASHVILLE

Number	Title (A Side/B Side)	Yr	VG	VG+	NM
❏ 2046	The Amazing Roger Miller	196?	3.00	6.00	12.00

PICKWICK

Number	Title (A Side/B Side)	Yr	VG	VG+	NM
❏ PTP-2057 [(2)]	King High	1973	3.00	6.00	12.00
❏ SPC-3226	Engine #9	197?	2.50	5.00	10.00

RCA CAMDEN

Number	Title (A Side/B Side)	Yr	VG	VG+	NM
❏ CAL-851 [M]	Roger Miller	1964	3.00	6.00	12.00
❏ CAS-851 [S]	Roger Miller	1964	3.75	7.50	15.00
❏ CAL-903 [M]	The One and Only Roger Miller	1965	3.00	6.00	12.00
❏ CAS-903 [S]	The One and Only Roger Miller	1965	3.75	7.50	15.00

SMASH

Number	Title (A Side/B Side)	Yr	VG	VG+	NM
❏ MGS-27049 [M]	Dang Me	196?	3.00	6.00	12.00
—Yet another retitled version of "Roger and Out"					
❏ MGS-27049 [M]	Dang Me/Chug-a-Lug	196?	3.00	6.00	12.00
—Retitled version of "Roger and Out"					
❏ MGS-27049 [M]	Roger and Out	1964	3.75	7.50	15.00
❏ MGS-27061 [M]	The Return of Roger Miller	1965	3.75	7.50	15.00
❏ MGS-27068 [M]	The 3rd Time Around	1965	3.75	7.50	15.00
❏ MGS-27073 [M]	Golden Hits	1965	3.75	7.50	15.00
❏ MGS-27075 [M]	Words and Music	1966	3.75	7.50	15.00
❏ MGS-27092 [M]	Walkin' in the Sunshine	1967	5.00	10.00	20.00
❏ MGS-27096 [M]	Waterhole #3	1967	6.25	12.50	25.00
❏ SRS-67049 [S]	Dang Me	196?	3.75	7.50	15.00
—Yet another retitled version of "Roger and Out"					
❏ SRS-67049 [S]	Dang Me/Chug-a-Lug	196?	3.75	7.50	15.00
—Retitled version of "Roger and Out"					
❏ SRS-67049 [S]	Roger and Out	1964	5.00	10.00	20.00
❏ SRS-67061 [S]	The Return of Roger Miller	1965	5.00	10.00	20.00
❏ SRS-67068 [S]	The 3rd Time Around	1965	5.00	10.00	20.00
❏ SRS-67073 [S]	Golden Hits	1965	5.00	10.00	20.00
❏ SRS-67075 [S]	Words and Music	1966	5.00	10.00	20.00
❏ SRS-67092 [S]	Walkin' in the Sunshine	1967	5.00	10.00	20.00
❏ SRS-67096 [S]	Waterhole #3	1967	5.00	10.00	20.00
❏ SRS-67103	A Tender Look at Love	1968	5.00	10.00	20.00
❏ SRS-67123	Roger Miller	1969	5.00	10.00	20.00
❏ SRS-67129	Roger Miller 1970	1970	5.00	10.00	20.00

STARDAY

Number	Title (A Side/B Side)	Yr	VG	VG+	NM
❏ SLP-318 [M]	The Country Side of Roger Miller	196?	6.25	12.50	25.00
—Retitled version of "Wild Child"					
❏ SLP-318 [M]	Wild Child Roger Miller	1965	7.50	15.00	30.00
❏ 3011	Painted Poetry	1978	2.50	5.00	10.00

Number	Title (A Side/B Side)	Yr	VG	VG+	NM

20TH CENTURY
| ❑ T-592 | Making a Name for Myself | 1979 | 3.00 | 6.00 | 12.00 |

WINDSONG
| ❑ BHL1-2337 | Off the Wall | 1977 | 3.00 | 6.00 | 12.00 |

MILLER, STEVE, BAND
CAPITOL
❑ ST-184	Brave New World	1969	5.00	10.00	20.00
—Black label with colorband					
❑ ST-184	Brave New World	1970	3.75	7.50	15.00
—Green label					
❑ ST-331	Your Saving Grace	1969	3.75	7.50	15.00
❑ SKAO-436	Number 5	1970	3.75	7.50	15.00
❑ STBB-717 [(2)]	Children of the Future/Living in the U.S.A.	1971	3.75	7.50	15.00
—Repackage of 2920 and 2984 (with new title for the latter)					
❑ SW-748	Rock Love	1971	3.75	7.50	15.00
❑ SKAO 2920	Children of the Future	1968	6.25	12.50	25.00
—Black label with colorband					
❑ SKAO 2920	Children of the Future	1970	3.75	7.50	15.00
—Green label					
❑ ST 2984	Sailor	1968	6.25	12.50	25.00
—Black label with colorband					
❑ ST 2984	Sailor	1970	3.75	7.50	15.00
—Green label					
❑ SMAS-11022	Recall the Beginning…A Journey from Eden	1972	3.75	7.50	15.00
❑ SVBB-11114 [(2)]	Anthology	1972	3.75	7.50	15.00
❑ SMAS-11235	The Joker	1973	2.50	5.00	10.00
❑ ST-11497	Fly Like an Eagle	1976	2.50	5.00	10.00
❑ SO-11630	Book of Dreams	1977	2.50	5.00	10.00
❑ SOO-11872	Greatest Hits 1974-1978	1978	2.50	5.00	10.00
❑ SOO-11872 [DJ]	Greatest Hits 1974-1978	1978	7.50	15.00	30.00
—Promo only on blue vinyl					
❑ SEAX-11903 [PD]	Book of Dreams	1978	3.75	7.50	15.00
❑ ST-12121	Circle of Love	1981	2.50	5.00	10.00
❑ ST-12216	Abracadabra	1982	2.50	5.00	10.00
❑ ST-12263	Steve Miller Live	1983	2.50	5.00	10.00
❑ SJ-12339	Italian X-Rays	1985	2.50	5.00	10.00
❑ PJ-12445	Living in the 20th Century	1987	2.50	5.00	10.00
❑ SN-16078	Brave New World	1980	2.00	4.00	8.00
❑ SN-16079	Your Saving Grace	1980	2.00	4.00	8.00
❑ SN-16262	Children of the Future	1982	2.00	4.00	8.00
❑ SN-16263	Sailor	1982	2.00	4.00	8.00
❑ SN-16321	Greatest Hits 1974-1978	1984	2.00	4.00	8.00
❑ SN-16323	Book of Dreams	1984	2.00	4.00	8.00
❑ SN-16339	Fly Like an Eagle	1984	2.00	4.00	8.00
❑ SN-16357	Circle of Love	1985	2.00	4.00	8.00
❑ 21185	Fly Like an Eagle	1999	5.00	10.00	20.00
—Limited-edition reissue on 180-gram vinyl					
❑ C1-48303	Born 2 B Blue	1988	2.50	5.00	10.00
❑ SKAO-80436	Number 5	1970	5.00	10.00	20.00
—Capitol Record Club edition					
❑ R 223186 [(2)]	Anthology	197?	3.75	7.50	15.00
—RCA Music Service edition					

DCC COMPACT CLASSICS
| ❑ LPZ-2028 | Greatest Hits 1974-1978 | 1996 | 10.00 | 20.00 | 40.00 |
| —Audiophile vinyl | | | | | |

MOBILE FIDELITY
| ❑ 1-021 | Fly Like an Eagle | 1979 | 10.00 | 20.00 | 40.00 |
| —Audiophile vinyl | | | | | |

MILLER, STEVE, BAND/QUICKSILVER MESSENGER SERVICE/THE BAND
Also see each artist's individual listings.

CAPITOL
| ❑ STCR-288 [(3)] | Sailor/Quicksilver Messenger Service/Music from Big Pink | 1969 | 10.00 | 20.00 | 40.00 |
| —Special 3-LP box set combining these three LPs, also listed separately in each group's listing, in one package | | | | | |

MILLMAN, JACK
DECCA
| ❑ DL 8156 [M] | Jazz Studio 4 | 1955 | 12.50 | 25.00 | 50.00 |

ERA
❑ EL-20005 [M]	Blowing Up a Storm	1956	10.00	20.00	40.00
—Black vinyl					
❑ EL-20005 [M]	Blowing Up a Storm	1956	15.00	30.00	60.00
—Red vinyl					

LIBERTY
| ❑ LJH-6007 [M] | Shades of Things to Come | 1956 | 12.50 | 25.00 | 50.00 |

MILLS, ALAN
FOLKWAYS
❑ FP-29 [10]	Folk Songs of French Canada	1952	12.50	25.00	50.00
❑ FP-831 [10]	Folk Songs of Newfoundland	1953	12.50	25.00	50.00
❑ FA-2313 [M]	Songs of the Sea	1957	7.50	15.00	30.00
❑ FW-3000 [(2)M]	Canada's Story in Song	1960	10.00	20.00	40.00
❑ FW-3001 [M]	O Canada: A History in Song	1956	7.50	15.00	30.00
❑ FW-6831 [M]	Folk Songs of Newfoundland	195?	7.50	15.00	30.00
❑ FW-6929 [M]	Folk Songs of French Canada	195?	7.50	15.00	30.00
❑ FC-7018 [M]	French Folk Songs for Children in English	1957	7.50	15.00	30.00
❑ FC-7208 [M]	French Folk Songs for Children	1957	7.50	15.00	30.00
❑ FC-7642 [M]	More Animals, Vol. 2	1956	7.50	15.00	30.00
❑ FC-7677 [M]	Animals, Vol. 1	1956	7.50	15.00	30.00
❑ FC-7750 [M]	Christmas Songs from Many Lands	1956	7.50	15.00	30.00
❑ FW-8771 [M]	We'll Rant and We'll Roar: Songs of Newfoundland	1958	7.50	15.00	30.00

SCHOLASTIC
| ❑ FC-7750 [M] | Christmas Songs from Many Lands | 196? | 3.75 | 7.50 | 15.00 |
| —Reissue of Folkways album with same contents | | | | | |

Number	Title (A Side/B Side)	Yr	VG	VG+	NM

MILLS, HAYLEY
BUENA VISTA
| ❑ BV-3311 [M] | Let's Get Together | 1962 | 6.25 | 12.50 | 25.00 |
| ❑ STER-3311 [S] | Let's Get Together | 1962 | 10.00 | 20.00 | 40.00 |

MILLS BROTHERS, THE
ABC
| ❑ 1027 [(2)] | The Best of the Mills Brothers, Volume 2 | 1978 | 3.00 | 6.00 | 12.00 |
| ❑ 4004 | 16 Great Performances | 1975 | 2.50 | 5.00 | 10.00 |

ABC SONGBIRD
| ❑ SBDP-255 | Inspiration | 1974 | 2.50 | 5.00 | 10.00 |

ARCHIVE OF FOLK AND JAZZ
| ❑ 300 | The Mills Brothers | 197? | 2.50 | 5.00 | 10.00 |
| ❑ 328 | The Mills Brothers, Volume 2 | 197? | 2.50 | 5.00 | 10.00 |

DECCA
❑ DXB 193 [(2)M]	The Best of the Mills Brothers	1965	5.00	10.00	20.00
❑ DL 4084 [M]	Our Golden Favorites	1960	5.00	10.00	20.00
❑ DL 5050 [10]	Barber Shop Ballads	1950	12.50	25.00	50.00
❑ DL 5051 [10]	Barber Shop Ballads	1950	12.50	25.00	50.00
❑ DL 5102 [10]	Souvenir Album	1950	12.50	25.00	50.00
❑ DL 5337 [10]	Wonderful Words	1951	12.50	25.00	50.00
❑ DL 5506 [10]	Meet the Mills Brothers	1954	12.50	25.00	50.00
❑ DL 5516 [10]	Four Boys and a Guitar	1954	12.50	25.00	50.00
❑ DXSB 7193 [(2)R]	The Best of the Mills Brothers	1965	3.75	7.50	15.00
❑ DL 8148 [M]	Souvenir Album	1955	7.50	15.00	30.00
❑ DL 8209 [M]	Singin' and Swingin'	1956	7.50	15.00	30.00
❑ DL 8219 [M]	Memory Lane	1956	7.50	15.00	30.00
❑ DL 8491 [M]	One Dozen Roses	1957	7.50	15.00	30.00
❑ DL 8664 [M]	The Mills Brothers in Hi-Fi	1958	7.50	15.00	30.00
❑ DL 8827 [M]	Glow with the Mills Brothers	1958	7.50	15.00	30.00
❑ DL 8890 [M]	Barber Shop Harmony	1959	7.50	15.00	30.00
❑ DL 8892 [M]	Harmonizin' with the Mills Brothers	1959	7.50	15.00	30.00
❑ DL 74084 [R]	Our Golden Favorites	196?	3.00	6.00	12.00
❑ DL 75174 [R]	Golden Favorites, Volume 2	1970	2.50	5.00	10.00

DOT
❑ DLP-3103 [M]	Mmmm, The Mills Brothers	1958	5.00	10.00	20.00
❑ DLP-3157 [M]	The Mills Brothers' Great Hits	1958	5.00	10.00	20.00
❑ DLP-3208 [M]	Great Barbershop Hits	1959	5.00	10.00	20.00
❑ DLP-3232 [M]	Merry Christmas	1959	5.00	10.00	20.00
❑ DLP-3237 [M]	The Mills Brothers Sing	1960	5.00	10.00	20.00
❑ DLP-3308 [M]	The Mills Brothers' Great Hits, Volume 2	1960	3.75	7.50	15.00
❑ DLP-3338 [M]	Yellow Bird	1960	3.75	7.50	15.00
❑ DLP-3363 [M]	San Antonio Rose	1961	3.75	7.50	15.00
❑ DLP-3368 [M]	Great Hawaiian Hits	1961	3.75	7.50	15.00
❑ DLP-3465 [M]	Beer Barrel Polka and Other Hits	1962	3.00	6.00	12.00
❑ DLP-3508 [M]	The End of the World	1963	3.00	6.00	12.00
❑ DLP-3565 [M]	Gems by the Mills Brothers	1964	3.00	6.00	12.00
❑ DLP-3568 [M]	Hymns We Love	1964	3.00	6.00	12.00
❑ DLP-3592 [M]	Say Si Si and Other Great Latin Hits	1964	3.00	6.00	12.00
❑ DLP-3652 [M]	Ten Years of Hits 1954-1964	1965	3.00	6.00	12.00
❑ DLP-3699 [M]	These Are the Mills Brothers	1966	3.00	6.00	12.00
❑ DLP-3744 [M]	That Country Feeling	1966	3.00	6.00	12.00
❑ DL-3766 [M]	The Mills Brothers Today	1966	3.00	6.00	12.00
❑ DLP-3783 [M]	The Mills Brothers Live	1967	3.75	7.50	15.00
❑ DLP-25103 [S]	Mmmm, The Mills Brothers	1958	7.50	15.00	30.00
❑ DLP-25157 [S]	The Mills Brothers' Great Hits	195?	15.00	30.00	60.00
—Blue vinyl					
❑ DLP-25157 [S]	The Mills Brothers' Great Hits	1958	7.50	15.00	30.00
—Black vinyl					
❑ DLP-25208 [S]	Great Barbershop Hits	1959	7.50	15.00	30.00
❑ DLP-25232 [S]	Merry Christmas	1959	7.50	15.00	30.00
—Same as above, but in stereo; with cursive "Dot" logo					
❑ DLP-25232 [S]	Merry Christmas	1968	3.00	6.00	12.00
—With "Dot"/"Paramount" logo					
❑ DLP-25237 [S]	The Mills Brothers Sing	1960	7.50	15.00	30.00
❑ DLP-25308 [S]	The Mills Brothers' Great Hits, Volume 2	1960	5.00	10.00	20.00
❑ DLP-25338 [S]	Yellow Bird	1960	5.00	10.00	20.00
❑ DLP-25363 [S]	San Antonio Rose	1961	5.00	10.00	20.00
❑ DLP-25368 [S]	Great Hawaiian Hits	1961	5.00	10.00	20.00
❑ DLP-25465 [S]	Beer Barrel Polka and Other Hits	1962	3.75	7.50	15.00
❑ DLP-25508 [S]	The End of the World	1963	3.75	7.50	15.00
❑ DLP-25565 [S]	Gems by the Mills Brothers	1964	3.75	7.50	15.00
❑ DLP-25568 [S]	Hymns We Love	1964	3.75	7.50	15.00
❑ DLP-25592 [S]	Say Si Si and Other Great Latin Hits	1964	3.75	7.50	15.00
❑ DLP-25652 [S]	Ten Years of Hits 1954-1964	1965	3.75	7.50	15.00
❑ DLP-25699 [S]	These Are the Mills Brothers	1966	3.75	7.50	15.00
❑ DLP-25744 [S]	That Country Feeling	1966	3.75	7.50	15.00
❑ DLP-25766 [S]	The Mills Brothers Today	1966	3.75	7.50	15.00
❑ DLP-25783 [S]	The Mills Brothers Live	1967	3.75	7.50	15.00
❑ DLP-25809	Fortuosity	1968	3.75	7.50	15.00
❑ DLP-25872	My Shy Violet	1968	3.75	7.50	15.00
❑ DLP-25927	Dream	1969	3.75	7.50	15.00
❑ DLP-25960	The Mills Brothers In Motion	1970	3.75	7.50	15.00

GNP CRESCENDO
| ❑ GNP-9106 | Four Boys and a Guitar | 197? | 2.50 | 5.00 | 10.00 |

HAMILTON
| ❑ HL-116 [M] | The Mills Brothers Sing for You | 1964 | 3.00 | 6.00 | 12.00 |
| ❑ HS-12116 [S] | The Mills Brothers Sing for You | 1964 | 3.00 | 6.00 | 12.00 |

MARK 56
| ❑ 709 | Original Radio Broadcasts | 197? | 2.50 | 5.00 | 10.00 |

MCA
❑ 132	Golden Favorites, Volume 2	1973	2.50	5.00	10.00
❑ 188	Old Golden Favorites	1973	2.50	5.00	10.00
❑ 717	16 Great Performances	1980	2.00	4.00	8.00
❑ 4039 [(2)]	The Best of the Mills Brothers	197?	3.00	6.00	12.00
❑ 15029	Merry Christmas	198?	2.50	5.00	10.00
❑ 27083	The Mills Brothers Great Hits	1980	2.00	4.00	8.00
❑ 28116	Were You There	198?	2.00	4.00	8.00

MCA SPECIAL MARKETS
| ❑ MSM2-35067 [(2)] | Classic Mills Brothers | 198? | 2.50 | 5.00 | 10.00 |

M

Number	Title (A Side/B Side)	Yr	VG	VG+	NM

PARAMOUNT
❏ PAS-1010	The Best of the Mills Brothers	1973	3.00	6.00	12.00
❏ PAS-1027 [(2)]	The Best of the Mills Brothers, Volume 2	1974	3.75	7.50	15.00
❏ PAS-5025	No Turnin' Back	1971	3.00	6.00	12.00
❏ PAS-6024	What a Wonderful World	1972	3.00	6.00	12.00
❏ PAS-6038	A Donut and a Dream	1973	3.00	6.00	12.00

PICKWICK
| ❏ SPC-1025 | Merry Christmas | 1979 | 2.50 | 5.00 | 10.00 |

—Reissue of Dot album with one fewer track
❏ 2008	Songs You Remember	197?	2.50	5.00	10.00
❏ 2030	The Mills Brothers	1973	2.50	5.00	10.00
❏ SPC-3076	14 Karat Gold	196?	2.50	5.00	10.00
❏ SPC-3107	Anytime	197?	2.50	5.00	10.00
❏ SPC-3137	Dream a Little Dream	197?	2.50	5.00	10.00
❏ SPC-3158	Till We Meet Again	197?	2.50	5.00	10.00
❏ SPC-3220	Cab Driver	197?	2.50	5.00	10.00
❏ SPC-3556	The Mills Brothers	1976	2.00	4.00	8.00

RANWOOD
❏ 7035 [(2)]	22 Great Hits	1985	2.50	5.00	10.00
❏ 8123	Cab Driver	197?	2.50	5.00	10.00
❏ 8133	The Mills Brothers Story	197?	2.50	5.00	10.00
❏ 8139	Country's Greatest Hits	197?	2.50	5.00	10.00
❏ 8152	50th Anniversary	197?	2.50	5.00	10.00
❏ 8198	Command Performance	198?	2.00	4.00	8.00

SUNNYVALE
| ❏ 1023 | Timeless | 1978 | 2.50 | 5.00 | 10.00 |

VOCALION
❏ VL 3607 [M]	In a Mellow Tone	196?	3.00	6.00	12.00
❏ VL 73607 [R]	In a Mellow Tone	196?	2.50	5.00	10.00
❏ VL 73859 [R]	Such Sweet Singing	1969	2.50	5.00	10.00

MILSAP, RONNIE
PAIR
| ❏ PDL2-1031 [(2)] | Believe It! | 1986 | 3.00 | 6.00 | 12.00 |
| ❏ PDL2-1105 [(2)] | Back on My Mind Again | 1986 | 3.00 | 6.00 | 12.00 |

PICKWICK
| ❏ JS-6179 | Plain and Simple | 197? | 2.50 | 5.00 | 10.00 |

RCA
| ❏ 9588-1-R | Stranger Things Have Happened | 1989 | 2.50 | 5.00 | 10.00 |
| ❏ R 183710 | Back to the Grindstone | 1991 | 5.00 | 10.00 | 20.00 |

—Only released on vinyl through BMG Direct Marketing

RCA VICTOR
❏ APL1-0338	Where My Heart Is	1973	5.00	10.00	20.00
❏ APD1-0500 [Q]	Pure Love	1974	5.00	10.00	20.00
❏ APL1-0500	Pure Love	1974	3.75	7.50	15.00
❏ APD1-0846 [Q]	A Legend in My Time	1975	5.00	10.00	20.00
❏ APL1-0846	A Legend in My Time	1975	3.75	7.50	15.00
❏ APL1-1223	Night Things	1975	3.75	7.50	15.00
❏ APL1-1666	20-20 Vision	1976	3.00	6.00	12.00
❏ APL1-2043	Ronnie Milsap Live	1976	3.00	6.00	12.00
❏ AFL1-2439	It Was Almost Like a Song	1977	3.00	6.00	12.00
❏ AFL1-2780	Only One Love in My Life	1978	3.00	6.00	12.00
❏ AHL1-3346	Images	1979	3.00	6.00	12.00
❏ AHL1-3563	Milsap Magic	1980	2.50	5.00	10.00
❏ AYL1-3760	Where My Heart Is	1980	2.00	4.00	8.00

—"Best Buy Series" reissue
| ❏ AHL1-3772 | Greatest Hits | 1980 | 2.50 | 5.00 | 10.00 |
| ❏ AYL1-3899 | Pure Love | 1981 | 2.00 | 4.00 | 8.00 |

—"Best Buy Series" reissue
❏ AAL1-3932	Out Where the Bright Lights Are Glowing	1981	2.50	5.00	10.00
❏ AHL1-4060	There's No Gettin' Over Me	1981	2.50	5.00	10.00
❏ AYL1-4171	Images	1981	2.00	4.00	8.00

—"Best Buy Series" reissue
| ❏ AYL1-4255 | Ronnie Milsap Live | 1982 | 2.00 | 4.00 | 8.00 |

—"Best Buy Series" reissue
❏ AHL1-4311	Inside Ronnie Milsap	1982	2.50	5.00	10.00
❏ AHL1-4670	Keyed Up	1983	2.50	5.00	10.00
❏ AHL1-5016	One More Try for Love	1984	2.50	5.00	10.00
❏ AYL1-5139	It Was Almost Like a Song	1984	2.00	4.00	8.00

—"Best Buy Series" reissue
| ❏ AYL1-5140 | There's No Gettin' Over Me | 1984 | 2.00 | 4.00 | 8.00 |

—"Best Buy Series" reissue
| ❏ AYL1-5142 | Inside Ronnie Milsap | 1984 | 2.00 | 4.00 | 8.00 |

—"Best Buy Series" reissue
| ❏ AHL1-5425 | Greatest Hits, Vol. 2 | 1985 | 2.50 | 5.00 | 10.00 |
| ❏ AYL1-5435 | Keyed Up | 1985 | 2.00 | 4.00 | 8.00 |

—"Best Buy Series" reissue
❏ 5624-1-R	Christmas with Ronnie Milsap	1986	2.50	5.00	10.00
❏ 6425-1-R	Heart and Soul	1987	2.50	5.00	10.00
❏ CPL1-7166	Collector's Series	1986	2.00	4.00	8.00
❏ AHL1-7194	Lost in the Fifties Tonight	1986	2.50	5.00	10.00
❏ 7618-1-R	Heart and Soul	1988	2.00	4.00	8.00

—Reissue of 6245

WARNER BROS.
| ❏ WS 1934 | Ronnie Milsap | 1971 | 5.00 | 10.00 | 20.00 |
| ❏ BS 2870 | A Rose By Any Other Name | 1975 | 3.75 | 7.50 | 15.00 |

MILTON, ROY
KENT
| ❏ KST-554 [R] | The Great Roy Milton | 196? | 7.50 | 15.00 | 30.00 |
| ❏ KLP-5054 [M] | The Great Roy Milton | 1963 | 12.50 | 25.00 | 50.00 |

MIMMS, GARNET, AND THE ENCHANTERS
ARISTA
| ❏ AL 4153 | Garnet Mimms Has It All | 1978 | 3.00 | 6.00 | 12.00 |

UNITED ARTISTS
❏ UAL 3305 [M]	Cry Baby and 11 Other Hits	1963	20.00	40.00	80.00
❏ UAL 3396 [M]	As Long As I Have You	1964	12.50	25.00	50.00
❏ UAL 3498 [M]	I'll Take Good Care of You	1966	12.50	25.00	50.00
❏ UAS 6305 [S]	Cry Baby and 11 Other Hits	1963	25.00	50.00	100.00
❏ UAS 6396 [S]	As Long As I Have You	1964	17.50	35.00	70.00
❏ UAS 6498 [S]	I'll Take Good Care of You	1966	17.50	35.00	70.00

MIND EXPANDERS, THE
DOT
| ❏ DLP-3773 [M] | What's Happening | 1967 | 25.00 | 50.00 | 100.00 |
| ❏ DLP-25773 [S] | What's Happening | 1967 | 20.00 | 40.00 | 80.00 |

MIND GARAGE, THE
RCA VICTOR
| ❏ LSP-4218 | The Mind Garage | 1969 | 5.00 | 10.00 | 20.00 |
| ❏ LSP-4319 | The Mind Garage Again! | 1970 | 5.00 | 10.00 | 20.00 |

MINDBENDERS, THE
FONTANA
| ❏ MGF-27554 [M] | A Groovy Kind of Love | 1966 | 6.25 | 12.50 | 25.00 |

—With "Ashes to Ashes"
| ❏ MGF-27554 [M] | A Groovy Kind of Love | 1966 | 7.50 | 15.00 | 30.00 |

—With "Don't Cry No More"
| ❏ SRF-67554 [R] | A Groovy Kind of Love | 1966 | 5.00 | 10.00 | 20.00 |

—With "Ashes to Ashes"
| ❏ SRF-67554 [R] | A Groovy Kind of Love | 1966 | 6.25 | 12.50 | 25.00 |

—With "Don't Cry No More"

MINEO, SAL
EPIC
| ❏ LN 3405 [M] | Sal | 1958 | 37.50 | 75.00 | 150.00 |

MINGUS, CHARLES
ABC IMPULSE!
❏ AS-35 [S]	Black Saint and Sinner Lady	1968	5.00	10.00	20.00
❏ AS-54 [S]	Mingus, Mingus, Mingus, Mingus, Mingus	1968	5.00	10.00	20.00
❏ AS-60 [S]	Charlie Mingus Plays Piano	1968	5.00	10.00	20.00

ATLANTIC
| ❏ SD 3-600 [(3)] | Passions of a Man: The Charles Mingus Anthology | 1980 | 5.00 | 10.00 | 20.00 |
| ❏ 1237 [M] | Pithecanthropus Erectus | 1956 | 20.00 | 40.00 | 80.00 |

—Black label
| ❏ 1237 [M] | Pithecanthropus Erectus | 1961 | 6.25 | 12.50 | 25.00 |

—Multicolor label, white "fan" logo at right
| ❏ 1237 [M] | Pithecanthropus Erectus | 1964 | 5.00 | 10.00 | 20.00 |

—Multicolor label, black "fan" logo at right
| ❏ 1260 [M] | The Clown | 1957 | 20.00 | 40.00 | 80.00 |

—Black label
| ❏ 1260 [M] | The Clown | 1961 | 6.25 | 12.50 | 25.00 |

—Multicolor label, white "fan" logo at right
| ❏ 1260 [M] | The Clown | 1964 | 5.00 | 10.00 | 20.00 |

—Multicolor label, black "fan" logo at right
| ❏ 1305 [M] | Blues & Roots | 1959 | 15.00 | 30.00 | 60.00 |

—White "bullseye" label
| ❏ 1305 [M] | Blues & Roots | 1961 | 6.25 | 12.50 | 25.00 |

—Multicolor label, white "fan" logo at right
| ❏ 1305 [M] | Blues & Roots | 1964 | 5.00 | 10.00 | 20.00 |

—Multicolor label, black "fan" logo at right
| ❏ SD 1305 [S] | Blues & Roots | 1959 | 15.00 | 30.00 | 60.00 |

—White "bullseye" label
| ❏ SD 1305 [S] | Blues & Roots | 1961 | 5.00 | 10.00 | 20.00 |

—Multicolor label, white "fan" logo at right
| ❏ 1377 [M] | Oh, Yeah | 1961 | 6.25 | 12.50 | 25.00 |

—Multicolor label, white "fan" logo at right
| ❏ SD 1377 [S] | Oh, Yeah | 1961 | 7.50 | 15.00 | 30.00 |

—Multicolor label, white "fan" logo at right
| ❏ SD 1377 [S] | Oh, Yeah | 1964 | 5.00 | 10.00 | 20.00 |

—Multicolor label, black "fan" logo at right
| ❏ 1417 [M] | Tonight at Noon | 1964 | 6.25 | 12.50 | 25.00 |
| ❏ SD 1417 [S] | Tonight at Noon | 1964 | 7.50 | 15.00 | 30.00 |

BETHLEHEM
❏ BCP-65 [M]	The Jazz Experiment of Charlie Mingus	1956	25.00	50.00	100.00
❏ BCP-6019 [M]	East Coasting	1957	25.00	50.00	100.00
❏ BCP-6026 [M]	A Modern Jazz Symposium of Jazz and Poetry	1958	25.00	50.00	100.00

CANDID
❏ CD-8005 [M]	Charles Mingus Presents Charles Mingus	1960	10.00	20.00	40.00
❏ CD-8021 [M]	Mingus	1960	10.00	20.00	40.00
❏ CS-9005 [S]	Charles Mingus Presents Charles Mingus	1960	12.50	25.00	50.00
❏ CS-9021 [S]	Mingus	1960	12.50	25.00	50.00

CHARLES MINGUS
| ❏ JWS-001/2 [(2)] | Mingus at Monterey | 1966 | 75.00 | 150.00 | 300.00 |

—Gatefold jacket with color photo on front; "This album can be purchased only by mail" on back cover
| ❏ JWS-001/2 [(2)] | Mingus at Monterey | 1966 | 175.00 | 350.00 | 700.00 |

—Single-pocket jacket with sepia-tone photo on front
| ❏ JWS-001/2 [(2)] | Mingus at Monterey | 1968 | 15.00 | 30.00 | 60.00 |

—Gatefold jacket with color photo on front; distributed by Fantasy
| ❏ JWS-005 | My Favorite Quintet | 1966 | 75.00 | 150.00 | 300.00 |

—"This album can be purchased only by mail" on back cover
| ❏ JWS-009 | Town Hall Concert 1964, Vol. 1 | 1966 | 75.00 | 150.00 | 300.00 |

—"This album can be purchased only by mail" on back cover
| ❏ JWS-013/14 [(2)] | Special Music Written For (But Not Heard At) Monterey | 1966 | 250.00 | 500.00 | 1000. |

—Single-pocket jacket; "This album can be purchased only by mail" on back cover

COLUMBIA
| ❏ CL 1370 [M] | Mingus Ah Um | 1959 | 10.00 | 20.00 | 40.00 |

—Red and black label with six "eye" logos
| ❏ CL 1370 [M] | Mingus Ah Um | 1963 | 6.25 | 12.50 | 25.00 |

—Red label with "Guaranteed High Fidelity" at bottom
| ❏ CL 1370 [M] | Mingus Ah Um | 1966 | 5.00 | 10.00 | 20.00 |

—Red label with "360 Sound Mono" at bottom
| ❏ CL 1440 [M] | Mingus Dynasty | 1960 | 7.50 | 15.00 | 30.00 |

—Red and black label with six "eye" logos
| ❏ CL 1440 [M] | Mingus Dynasty | 1963 | 5.00 | 10.00 | 20.00 |

—Red label with "Guaranteed High Fidelity" at bottom
| ❏ CS 8171 [S] | Mingus Ah Um | 1959 | 15.00 | 30.00 | 60.00 |

—Red and black label with six "eye" logos
| ❏ CS 8171 [S] | Mingus Ah Um | 1963 | 7.50 | 15.00 | 30.00 |

—Red label with "360 Sound Stereo" in black at bottom

Number	Title (A Side/B Side)	Yr	VG	VG+	NM
CS 8171 [S]	Mingus Ah Um	1966	6.25	12.50	25.00

—*Red label with "360 Sound Stereo" in white at bottom*

CS 8171 [S]	Mingus Ah Um	199?	6.25	12.50	25.00

—*Classic Records reissue on audiophile vinyl*

CS 8236 [S]	Mingus Dynasty	1960	10.00	20.00	40.00

—*Red and black label with six "eye" logos*

CS 8236 [S]	Mingus Dynasty	1963	6.25	12.50	25.00

—*Red label with "360 Sound Stereo" in black at bottom*

CS 8236 [S]	Mingus Dynasty	1966	5.00	10.00	20.00

—*Red label with "360 Sound Stereo" in white at bottom*

G 30628 [(2)]	Better Git It in Your Soul	1971	5.00	10.00	20.00
KG 31814 [(2)]	Charles Mingus and Friends	1973	5.00	10.00	20.00

DEBUT

DLP-1 [10]	Strings and Keys	1953	125.00	250.00	500.00
DEB-123 [M]	Mingus at the Bohemia	1956	50.00	100.00	200.00

FANTASY

JWS-001/2 [(2)]	Mingus at Monterey	1969	5.00	10.00	20.00

—*Reissue of Charles Mingus 001/2*

6002 [M]	Chazz!	1962	7.50	15.00	30.00

—*Black vinyl*

6002 [M]	Chazz!	1962	12.50	25.00	50.00

—*Red vinyl*

6009 [M]	The Charlie Mingus Quartet + Max Roach	1963	7.50	15.00	30.00
6017 [M]	Right Now — Live at the Jazz Workshop	1966	6.25	12.50	25.00
86002 [R]	Chazz!	196?	6.25	12.50	25.00

—*Blue vinyl*

86017 [S]	Right Now — Live at the Jazz Workshop	1966	7.50	15.00	30.00

GRP/IMPULSE!

217	Charlie Mingus Plays Piano	1997	5.00	10.00	20.00

—*Reissue on audiophile vinyl*

IMPULSE!

A-35 [M]	Black Saint and Sinner Lady	1963	7.50	15.00	30.00
AS-35 [S]	Black Saint and Sinner Lady	1963	10.00	20.00	40.00
A-54 [M]	Mingus, Mingus, Mingus, Mingus, Mingus	1963	7.50	15.00	30.00
AS-54 [S]	Mingus, Mingus, Mingus, Mingus, Mingus	1963	10.00	20.00	40.00
A-60 [M]	Charlie Mingus Plays Piano	1964	7.50	15.00	30.00
AS-60 [S]	Charlie Mingus Plays Piano	1964	10.00	20.00	40.00

JAZZTONE

J-1226 [M]	Jazz Experiment	1956	15.00	30.00	60.00
J-1271 [M]	The Jazz Experiments of Charlie Mingus	1957	12.50	25.00	50.00

JOSIE

JLPS-3508 [R]	Mingus Three	1963	5.00	10.00	20.00
JOZ-3508 [M]	Mingus Three	1963	7.50	15.00	30.00

JUBILEE

JLP-1054 [M]	Mingus Trio	1958	20.00	40.00	80.00

LIMELIGHT

LM-82015 [M]	Mingus Revisited	1965	6.25	12.50	25.00
LS-86105 [S]	Mingus Revisited	1965	7.50	15.00	30.00

MERCURY

MG-20627 [M]	Pre-Bird	1961	7.50	15.00	30.00
SR-60627 [S]	Pre-Bird	1961	10.00	20.00	40.00

MOSAIC

M4-111 [(4)]	The Complete Candid Recordings of Charles Mingus	199?	25.00	50.00	100.00
MQ4-143 [(4)]	The Complete 1959 CBS Charles Mingus Sessions	199?	25.00	50.00	100.00

PERIOD

SPL-1107 [10]	Jazzical Moods, Volume 1	1955	50.00	100.00	200.00
SLP-1111 [10]	Jazzical Moods, Volume 2	1955	50.00	100.00	200.00

PRESTIGE

34001 [(3)]	The Great Concert	197?	5.00	10.00	20.00

RCA VICTOR

LPM-2533 [M]	Tijuana Moods	1962	10.00	20.00	40.00
LSP-2533 [S]	Tijuana Moods	1962	12.50	25.00	50.00
LSP-2533 [S]	Tijuana Moods	199?	6.25	12.50	25.00

—*Classic Records reissue on audiophile vinyl*

SAVOY

MG-12059 [M]	Jazz Composers Workshop	1956	25.00	50.00	100.00
MG-15050 [10]	Charlie Mingus	1955	50.00	100.00	200.00

SOLID STATE

SS-18019	Wonderland	1968	5.00	10.00	20.00
SS-18024	Town Hall Concert	1968	5.00	10.00	20.00

UNITED ARTISTS

UAL-4036 [M]	Jazz Portraits	1959	10.00	20.00	40.00
UAS-5036 [S]	Jazz Portraits	1959	12.50	25.00	50.00
UAJ-14005 [M]	Wonderland	1962	10.00	20.00	40.00
UAJ-14024 [M]	Town Hall Concert	1963	10.00	20.00	40.00
UAJS-15005 [S]	Wonderland	1962	12.50	25.00	50.00
UAJS-15024 [S]	Town Hall Concert	1963	12.50	25.00	50.00

MINION, FRANK
BETHLEHEM

BCP-6033 [M]	Forward Sound	1959	10.00	20.00	40.00
BCP-6052 [M]	The Soft Land of Make Believe	1961	10.00	20.00	40.00
BCPS-6052 [S]	The Soft Land of Make Believe	1961	12.50	25.00	50.00

MINNEAPOLIS SYMPHONY ORCHESTRA (ANTAL DORATI, CONDUCTOR)
MERCURY LIVING PRESENCE

SR 90007 [S]	Albeniz-Artos: Iberia; Falla: Interlude and Dance	1959	17.50	35.00	70.00

—*Maroon label, no "Vendor: Mercury Record Corporation"*

SR 90011 [S]	Beethoven: Symphony No. 3	1959	10.00	20.00	40.00

—*Maroon label, no "Vendor: Mercury Record Corporation"*

SR 90016 [S]	Offenbach: Gaite Parisienne; Strauss, Johann: Graduation Ball	1959	5.00	10.00	20.00

—*Maroon label, no "Vendor: Mercury Record Corporation"*

SR 90098 [S]	Bartok: Suite No. 2	1959	10.00	20.00	40.00

—*Maroon label, no "Vendor: Mercury Record Corporation"*

Number	Title (A Side/B Side)	Yr	VG	VG+	NM
SR 90132 [S]	Kodaly: Hary Janos Suite; Bartok: Hungarian Sketches; Rumanian Dances	196?	7.50	15.00	30.00

—*Maroon label, with "Vendor: Mercury Record Corporation"*

SR 90132 [S]	Kodaly: Hary Janos Suite; Bartok: Hungarian Sketches; Rumanian Dances	1960	30.00	60.00	120.00

—*Maroon label, no "Vendor: Mercury Record Corporation"*

SR 90139 [S]	Rossini: Overtures	196?	6.25	12.50	25.00

—*Maroon label, no "Vendor: Mercury Record Corporation"*

SR 90139 [S]	Rossini: Overtures	196?	10.00	20.00	40.00

—*Maroon label, with "Vendor: Mercury Record Corporation" (a rare case where the second edition is more sought after than the first)*

SR 90171 [S]	Brahms: Symphony No. 2	196?	6.25	12.50	25.00

—*Maroon label, no "Vendor: Mercury Record Corporation"*

SR 90172 [S]	Copland: Rodeo; El Salon Mexico; Danzon Cubano	196?	12.50	25.00	50.00

—*Maroon label, with "Vendor: Mercury Record Corporation"*

SR 90172 [S]	Copland: Rodeo; El Salon Mexico; Danzon Cubano	196?	25.00	50.00	100.00

—*Maroon label, no "Vendor: Mercury Record Corporation"*

SR 90178 [S]	The Strauss Family Album	196?	5.00	10.00	20.00

—*Maroon label, no "Vendor: Mercury Record Corporation"*

SR 90195 [S]	Rimsky-Korsakov: Scheherazade	196?	10.00	20.00	40.00

—*Maroon label, no "Vendor: Mercury Record Corporation"*

SR 90201 [S]	Tchaikovsky: March Slave; Polonaise and Waltz; Francesca da Rimini	196?	7.50	15.00	30.00

—*Maroon label, with "Vendor: Mercury Record Corporation"*

SR 90201 [S]	Tchaikovsky: March Slave; Polonaise and Waltz; Francesca da Rimini	196?	10.00	20.00	40.00

—*Maroon label, no "Vendor: Mercury Record Corporation"*

SR 90202 [S]	Strauss, Richard: Don Juan; Death and Transfiguration	196?	20.00	40.00	80.00

—*Maroon label, no "Vendor: Mercury Record Corporation"*

SR 90216 [S]	Stravinsky: Petrouchka	196?	7.50	15.00	30.00

—*Maroon label, with "Vendor: Mercury Record Corporation"*

SR 90216 [S]	Stravinsky: Petrouchka	196?	20.00	40.00	80.00

—*Maroon label, no "Vendor: Mercury Record Corporation"*

SR 90217 [S]	Mussorgsky: Pictures at an Exhibition	196?	10.00	20.00	40.00

—*Maroon label, with "Vendor: Mercury Record Corporation"*

SR 90217 [S]	Mussorgsky: Pictures at an Exhibition	196?	55.00	110.00	220.00

—*Maroon label, no "Vendor: Mercury Record Corporation"*

SR 90248 [S]	Dorati: Symphony; Nocturne; Capriccio	196?	40.00	80.00	160.00

—*Maroon label, no "Vendor: Mercury Record Corporation"*

SR 90253 [S]	Stravinsky: Le Sacre du Printemps (The Rite of Spring)	196?	5.00	10.00	20.00

—*Maroon label, with "Vendor: Mercury Record Corporation"*

SR 90253 [S]	Stravinsky: Le Sacre du Printemps (The Rite of Spring)	196?	15.00	30.00	60.00

—*Maroon label, no "Vendor: Mercury Record Corporation"*

SR 90282 [S]	Schuller: Seven Studies on Themes of Paul Klee; Fetler: Contrasts for Orchestra	196?	12.50	25.00	50.00

—*Maroon label, with "Vendor: Mercury Record Corporation"*

SR 90282 [S]	Schuller: Seven Studies on Themes of Paul Klee; Fetler: Contrasts for Orchestra	196?	25.00	50.00	100.00

—*Maroon label, no "Vendor: Mercury Record Corporation"*

SR 90288 [S]	Bloch: Sinfonia Brave; Peterson, Wayne: Free Variations for Orchestra	196?	20.00	40.00	80.00

—*Maroon label, with "Vendor: Mercury Record Corporation"*

SR 90298 [S]	Respighi: Pines and Fountains of Rome	196?	7.50	15.00	30.00

—*Maroon label, with "Vendor: Mercury Record Corporation"*

SR 90298 [S]	Respighi: Pines and Fountains of Rome	196?	12.50	25.00	50.00

—*Maroon label, no "Vendor: Mercury Record Corporation"*

SR 90431 [S]	Offenbach: Gaite Parisienne; Gershwin: An American in Paris	1965	5.00	10.00	20.00

—*Maroon label, with "Vendor: Mercury Record Corporation"*

SR 90499 [S]	Dorati: Symphony; Nocturne and Capriccio	196?	5.00	10.00	20.00

—*Maroon label, with "Vendor: Mercury Record Corporation"*

MINNEAPOLIS SYMPHONY ORCHESTRA (STANISLAW SKROWACZEWSKI, CONDUCTOR)
MERCURY LIVING PRESENCE

SR 90060 [S]	Khachatourian: Gayne Ballet; Shostakovich: Symphony No. 5	1960	62.50	125.00	250.00

—*Maroon label, no "Vendor: Mercury Record Corporation"*

SR 90218 [S]	Schubert: Symphony in B "Unfinished"	196?	5.00	10.00	20.00

—*Maroon label, with "Vendor: Mercury Record Corporation"*

SR 90218 [S]	Schubert: Symphony in B "Unfinished"	196?	15.00	30.00	60.00

—*Maroon label, no "Vendor: Mercury Record Corporation"*

SR 90272 [S]	Schubert: Symphony No. 7 (9) in C	196?	12.50	25.00	50.00

—*Maroon label, no "Vendor: Mercury Record Corporation"*

SR 90315 [S]	Prokofiev: Romeo and Juliet Ballet Suites 1 and 2	196?	5.00	10.00	20.00

—*Maroon label, with "Vendor: Mercury Record Corporation"*

SR 90315 [S]	Prokofiev: Romeo and Juliet Ballet Suites 1 and 2	196?	12.50	25.00	50.00

—*Maroon label, no "Vendor: Mercury Record Corporation"*

SR 90356 [S]	Mendelssohn: Symphony No. 4; Schubert: Symphony No. 5	196?	6.25	12.50	25.00

—*Maroon label, no "Vendor: Mercury Record Corporation"*

MINNELLI, LIZA
A&M

SP-3524 [(2)]	Liza Minnelli Foursider	1973	3.75	7.50	15.00
SP-4141 [M]	Liza Minnelli	1968	6.25	12.50	25.00

—*Mono copies have stereo numbers, but the labels are mono white label promos*

SP-4141	Liza Minnelli	1968	3.75	7.50	15.00
SP-4164	Come Saturday Morning	1969	3.75	7.50	15.00
SP-4272	New Feelin'	1970	3.75	7.50	15.00
SP-4345	Live at the Olympia	1971	3.75	7.50	15.00
SP-6013 [(2)]	Liza Minnelli Foursider	198?	2.50	5.00	10.00

—*Reissue of 3524*

CAPITOL

ST 2174 [S]	Liza! Liza!	1964	6.25	12.50	25.00
T 2174 [M]	Liza! Liza!	1964	5.00	10.00	20.00

Number	Title (A Side/B Side)	Yr	VG	VG+	NM
❏ SM-2271	It Amazes Me	1976	2.50	5.00	10.00
—Reissue with new prefix					
❏ ST 2271 [S]	It Amazes Me	1965	6.25	12.50	25.00
❏ T 2271 [M]	It Amazes Me	1965	5.00	10.00	20.00
❏ ST 2448 [S]	There Is a Time	1966	6.25	12.50	25.00
❏ T 2448 [M]	There Is a Time	1966	5.00	10.00	20.00
❏ SM-11080	Maybe This Time	197?	2.50	5.00	10.00
—Reissue with new prefix					
❏ ST-11080	Maybe This Time	1972	3.00	6.00	12.00
❏ SM-11803	There Is a Time	1978	2.50	5.00	10.00
—Reissue of ST 2448					
COLUMBIA					
❏ KC 31762	Liza with a "Z"	1972	3.75	7.50	15.00
❏ PC 31762	Liza with a "Z"	198?	2.00	4.00	8.00
—Budget-line reissue					
❏ CQ 32149 [Q]	Liza Minnelli The Singer	1973	5.00	10.00	20.00
❏ KC 32149	Liza Minnelli The Singer	1973	3.75	7.50	15.00
❏ PC 32149	Liza Minnelli The Singer	198?	2.00	4.00	8.00
—Budget-line reissue					
❏ PC 32854	Live at the Winter Garden	1974	3.75	7.50	15.00
❏ PC 34887	Tropical Nights	1977	3.00	6.00	12.00
EPIC					
❏ OE 45098	Results	1989	3.75	7.50	15.00
TELARC					
❏ 15502 [(2)]	Liza Minnelli at Carnegie Hall	1987	3.75	7.50	15.00

MINNIE PEARL
STARDAY

Number	Title (A Side/B Side)	Yr	VG	VG+	NM
❏ SLP-224 [M]	Howdee!	1963	10.00	20.00	40.00
❏ SLP-380 [M]	America's Beloved Minnie Pearl	1965	10.00	20.00	40.00
❏ SLP-397 [M]	The Country Music Story	1966	7.50	15.00	30.00

MINOR THREAT
DISCHORD

Number	Title (A Side/B Side)	Yr	VG	VG+	NM
❏ 10	Out of Step	1983	5.00	10.00	20.00
—Second stock pressing, gray back cover with photos					
❏ 10	Out of Step	1983	12.50	25.00	50.00
—First stock pressing, black back cover with lyrics					
❏ 10 [DJ]	Out of Step	1983	125.00	250.00	500.00
—Test pressing of 50; black silkscreen cover with sheep logo; paste-on back cover; blank labels; plain innersleeve with rubber stamp					
❏ 12 [EP]	The First Two 7" On a 12"	1984	3.75	7.50	15.00

MINT TATTOO
DOT

Number	Title (A Side/B Side)	Yr	VG	VG+	NM
❏ DLP-25918	Mint Tattoo	1969	7.50	15.00	30.00

MINUTEMEN
NEW ALLIANCE

Number	Title (A Side/B Side)	Yr	VG	VG+	NM
❏ 017	The Politics of Time	1984	3.00	6.00	12.00
SST					
❏ 004	The Punch Line	1981	3.00	6.00	12.00
❏ 004	The Punch Line	1981	5.00	10.00	20.00
—Original copies have white labels					
❏ 014	What Makes a Man Start Fires?	1983	2.50	5.00	10.00
❏ 014	What Makes a Man Start Fires?	1983	3.75	7.50	15.00
—Original version has yellow labels and no UPC code					
❏ 016 [EP]	Buzz or Howl Under the Influence of Heat	1983	2.50	5.00	10.00
❏ 028 [(2)]	Double Nickels on the Dime	1984	3.00	6.00	12.00
❏ PSST E-28 [DJ]	Excerpts from Double Nickels on the Dime	1984	6.25	12.50	25.00
—One-sided promo LP with etched B-side and sticker on blank cover					
❏ 034 [EP]	Project Mersh	1985	2.50	5.00	10.00
❏ 058	3-Way Tie (For Last)	1985	3.00	6.00	12.00
❏ 068 [(2)]	Ballot Result	1987	3.00	6.00	12.00
❏ 277	The Politics of Time	198?	2.50	5.00	10.00
—Reissue of New Alliance 017					

MIRACLES, THE
COLUMBIA

Number	Title (A Side/B Side)	Yr	VG	VG+	NM
❏ PC 34460	Love Crazy	1977	3.00	6.00	12.00
❏ PCQ 34460 [Q]	Love Crazy	1977	5.00	10.00	20.00
❏ JC 34910	The Miracles	1978	3.00	6.00	12.00
MOTOWN					
❏ M5-133V1	Do It Baby	1981	2.00	4.00	8.00
—Reissue of Tamla 334					
❏ M5-136V1	Away We a Go-Go	1981	2.00	4.00	8.00
—Reissue of Tamla 271					
❏ M5-156V1	The Tears of a Clown	1981	2.00	4.00	8.00
—Reissue of Tamla 276					
❏ M5-160V1	Hi, We're the Miracles	1981	2.00	4.00	8.00
—Reissue of Tamla 220					
❏ M5-210V1	Greatest Hits, Vol. 2	1981	2.00	4.00	8.00
—Reissue of Tamla 280					
❏ M5-217V1	Doin' Mickey's Monkey	1981	2.00	4.00	8.00
—Reissue of Tamla 245					
❏ M5-220V1	Recorded Live on Stage	1981	2.00	4.00	8.00
—Reissue of Tamla 241					
❏ M8-238M2 [(2)]	Greatest Hits from the Beginning	1982	3.00	6.00	12.00
—Reissue of Tamla 254					
❏ M 793R3 [(3)]	Smokey Robinson and the Miracles Anthology	1974	5.00	10.00	20.00
❏ 5253 ML	The Season for Miracles	1982	2.00	4.00	8.00
—Reissue of Tamla 307					
❏ 5254 ML	Christmas with the Miracles	1982	2.00	4.00	8.00
—Reissue of Tamla 236					
TAMLA					
❏ T 220 [M]	Hi We're the Miracles	1961	150.00	300.00	600.00
—White label					
❏ T 223 [M]	Cookin' with the Miracles	1962	200.00	400.00	800.00
—White label					
❏ T 230 [M]	I'll Try Something New	1962	150.00	300.00	600.00
—White label					

Number	Title (A Side/B Side)	Yr	VG	VG+	NM
❏ T 236 [M]	Christmas with the Miracles	1963	75.00	150.00	300.00
—Originals have two globes on the top of the label					
❏ T 238 [M]	You've Really Got a Hold on Me	1963	50.00	100.00	200.00
—Retitled version of "The Fabulous Miracles"					
❏ T 238 [M]	The Fabulous Miracles	1963	75.00	150.00	300.00
❏ T 241 [M]	The Miracles On Stage	1963	50.00	100.00	200.00
❏ T 245 [M]	Doin' Mickey's Monkey	1963	50.00	100.00	200.00
❏ TS 245 [S]	Doin' Mickey's Monkey	1963	75.00	150.00	300.00
❏ T 254 [(2)M]	Greatest Hits from the Beginning	1965	12.50	25.00	50.00
❏ TS 254 [(2)P]	Greatest Hits from the Beginning	1965	10.00	20.00	40.00
❏ T 267 [M]	Going to a Go-Go	1966	7.50	15.00	30.00
❏ TS 267 [S]	Going to a Go-Go	1966	10.00	20.00	40.00
❏ T 271 [M]	Away We a Go-Go	1966	6.25	12.50	25.00
❏ TS 271 [S]	Away We a Go-Go	1966	7.50	15.00	30.00
❏ T 276 [M]	Make It Happen	1967	6.25	12.50	25.00
❏ TS 276 [S]	Make It Happen	1967	7.50	15.00	30.00
❏ TS 276 [S]	The Tears of a Clown	1970	3.75	7.50	15.00
—Retitled version of "Make It Happen"					
❏ TS 280	Greatest Hits, Vol. 2	1968	6.25	12.50	25.00
❏ TS 289	Live!	1969	5.00	10.00	20.00
❏ T 290 [M]	Special Occasion	1968	12.50	25.00	50.00
❏ TS 290 [S]	Special Occasion	1968	5.00	10.00	20.00
❏ TS 295	Time Out for Smokey Robinson & the Miracles	1969	5.00	10.00	20.00
❏ TS 297	Four in Blue	1969	5.00	10.00	20.00
❏ TS 301	What Love Has…Joined Together	1970	3.75	7.50	15.00
❏ TS 306	A Pocket Full of Miracles	1970	3.75	7.50	15.00
❏ TS 307	The Season for Miracles	1970	3.75	7.50	15.00
❏ TS 312	One Dozen Roses	1971	3.75	7.50	15.00
❏ TS 318	Flying High Together	1972	3.75	7.50	15.00
❏ TS 320 [(2)]	1957-1972	1972	5.00	10.00	20.00
❏ T 325F	Renaissance	1973	3.00	6.00	12.00
❏ T6-334	Do It Baby	1974	3.00	6.00	12.00
❏ T6-336	Don't Cha Love It	1975	3.00	6.00	12.00
❏ T6-339	City of Angels	1975	3.00	6.00	12.00
❏ T6-344	The Power of Music	1976	3.00	6.00	12.00
❏ T7-357	Greatest Hits	1977	3.00	6.00	12.00

MISFITS, THE
CAROLINE

Number	Title (A Side/B Side)	Yr	VG	VG+	NM
❏ 7511	Static Age	1995	—	—	—
—Canceled; finally released on 7520					
❏ 7515	Collection II	1995	7.50	15.00	30.00
—Green vinyl (3,500 made); sealed copies have bar code roughly 1/4 to 1/2 inch from bottom of back cover					
❏ 7515	Collection II	1995	10.00	20.00	40.00
—Red vinyl (6,000 made); sealed copies have bar code roughly 1 inch from the bottom of back cover					
❏ 7515	Collection II	1995	25.00	50.00	100.00
—Clear vinyl (500 made); sealed copies have bar code at upper right or not at all					
❏ 7520	Static Age	1997	7.50	15.00	30.00
—Yellow vinyl (1,000 made)					
❏ 7520	Static Age	1997	10.00	20.00	40.00
—Red vinyl (2,000 made)					
❏ 7520	Static Age	1997	25.00	50.00	100.00
—Purple vinyl (500 made)					
PLAN 9					
❏ PL9-02	Earth A.D.	1983	3.00	6.00	12.00
—At least 10,000 on black vinyl (distributed by Caroline)					
❏ PL9-02	Earth A.D.	1983	62.50	125.00	250.00
—200 on clear vinyl with red and blue swirls					
❏ PL9-02	Earth A.D.	1983	62.50	125.00	250.00
—200 on dark purple vinyl					
❏ PL9-02	Earth A.D.	1983	62.50	125.00	250.00
—500 on yellow vinyl					
❏ PL9-02	Earth A.D.	1983	100.00	200.00	400.00
—100 on green vinyl					
❏ PL9-03 [EP]	Die, Die My Darling	1984	3.00	6.00	12.00
—Common issue on black vinyl (distributed by Caroline)					
❏ PL9-03 [EP]	Die, Die My Darling	1984	30.00	60.00	120.00
—500 on white vinyl (distributed by Caroline)					
❏ PL9-03 [EP]	Die, Die My Darling	1984	37.50	75.00	150.00
—500 on purple vinyl					
❏ PL9-06	Legacy of Brutality	1986	5.00	10.00	20.00
—Black vinyl (distributed by Caroline)					
❏ PL9-06	Legacy of Brutality	1986	37.50	75.00	150.00
—500 on red vinyl					
❏ PL9-06	Legacy of Brutality	1986	50.00	100.00	200.00
—500 on white vinyl					
❏ PL9-06	Legacy of Brutality	1986	500.00	1000.	2000.
—16 (!!) on pink vinyl					
❏ PL9-08 [EP]	Evilive	1987	5.00	10.00	20.00
—Black vinyl (distributed by Caroline)					
❏ PL9-08 [EP]	Evilive	1987	15.00	30.00	60.00
—2,000 on green vinyl (distributed by Caroline)					
❏ PL9-09	Misfits	1988	3.00	6.00	12.00
RUBY/SLASH					
❏ JRR 804	Walk Among Us	1982	12.50	25.00	50.00
—Purple cover with innersleeve and insert					
❏ JRR 804	Walk Among Us	1982	25.00	50.00	100.00
—Original red cover; has custom innersleeve and insert					
SLASH					
❏ 25756	Walk Among Us	1988	5.00	10.00	20.00
—Reissue of JRR 804; some copies came with a Halloween bag, which can double or even triple the value!					

MISSOURI
PANAMA

Number	Title (A Side/B Side)	Yr	VG	VG+	NM
❏ 1022	Missouri	1977	7.50	15.00	30.00

MISSOURIANS, THE
"X"

Number	Title (A Side/B Side)	Yr	VG	VG+	NM
❏ LVA-3020 [10]	Harlem in the Twenties, Volume 1	1954	12.50	25.00	50.00

Number	Title (A Side/B Side)	Yr	VG	VG+	NM

MR. GASSER AND THE WEIRDOS
CAPITOL
❏ ST 2010 [S]	Hot Rod Hootenanny	1963	30.00	60.00	120.00
❏ T 2010 [M]	Hot Rod Hootenanny	1963	25.00	50.00	100.00
❏ ST 2057 [S]	Rods n' Ratfinks	1963	30.00	60.00	120.00
❏ T 2057 [M]	Rods n' Ratfinks	1963	25.00	50.00	100.00

—Add 25% if ratfink decal is enclosed

| ❏ ST 2114 [S] | Surfink! | 1964 | 37.50 | 75.00 | 150.00 |

—Without bonus single

| ❏ ST 2114 [S] | Surfink! | 1964 | 50.00 | 100.00 | 200.00 |

—With bonus single in pocket on cover: "Santa Barbara"/"Midnight Run" by the Super Stocks

| ❏ T 2114 [M] | Surfink! | 1964 | 25.00 | 50.00 | 100.00 |

—Without bonus single

| ❏ T 2114 [M] | Surfink! | 1964 | 37.50 | 75.00 | 150.00 |

—With bonus single in pocket on cover: "Santa Barbara"/"Midnight Run" by the Super Stocks

MR. SHORT STUFF
SPIVEY
| ❏ 1005 | Mr. Short Stuff | 196? | 5.00 | 10.00 | 20.00 |

MITCHELL, BILLY
SMASH
❏ MGS-27027 [M]	This Is Billy Mitchell	1962	6.25	12.50	25.00
❏ MGS-27042 [M]	A Little Juicy	1962	6.25	12.50	25.00
❏ SRS-67027 [S]	This Is Billy Mitchell	1962	7.50	15.00	30.00
❏ SRS-67042 [S]	A Little Juicy	1962	7.50	15.00	30.00

MITCHELL, BLUE
BLUE NOTE
❏ BLP-4178 [M]	The Thing to Do	1964	6.25	12.50	25.00
❏ BLP-4214 [M]	Down With It	1965	6.25	12.50	25.00
❏ BLP-4228 [M]	Bring It Home to Me	1966	7.50	15.00	30.00
❏ BLP-4257 [M]	Boss Horn	1967	7.50	15.00	30.00
❏ BST-84178 [S]	The Thing to Do	1964	7.50	15.00	30.00

—With "New York, USA" address on label

| ❏ BST-84214 [S] | Down With It | 1965 | 7.50 | 15.00 | 30.00 |

—With "New York, USA" address on label

| ❏ BST-84228 [S] | Bring It Home to Me | 1966 | 10.00 | 20.00 | 40.00 |

—With "New York, USA" address on label

| ❏ BST-84257 [S] | Boss Horn | 1967 | 5.00 | 10.00 | 20.00 |

—With "A Division of Liberty Records" on label

❏ BST-84272	Heads Up!	1968	5.00	10.00	20.00
❏ BST-84300	Collision in Black	1968	5.00	10.00	20.00
❏ BST-84324	Bantu Village	1969	5.00	10.00	20.00

MOSAIC
| ❏ MQ6-178 [(6)] | The Complete Blue Note Sessions | 199? | 25.00 | 50.00 | 100.00 |

RIVERSIDE
❏ RLP 12-273 [M]	The Big Six	1958	12.50	25.00	50.00
❏ RLP 12-293 [M]	Out of the Blue	1958	12.50	25.00	50.00
❏ RLP 12-309 [M]	Blue Soul	1959	12.50	25.00	50.00
❏ RLP-336 [M]	Blue's Moods	1960	10.00	20.00	40.00
❏ RLP-367 [M]	Smooth as the Wind	1961	7.50	15.00	30.00
❏ RLP-414 [M]	A Sure Thing	1962	7.50	15.00	30.00
❏ RLP-439 [M]	The Cup Bearers	1963	7.50	15.00	30.00
❏ RLP-1131 [S]	Out of the Blue	1959	10.00	20.00	40.00
❏ RLP-1155 [S]	Blue Soul	1959	10.00	20.00	40.00
❏ RS-9336 [S]	Blue's Moods	1960	10.00	20.00	40.00
❏ RS-9367 [S]	Smooth as the Wind	1961	10.00	20.00	40.00
❏ RS-9414 [S]	A Sure Thing	1962	10.00	20.00	40.00
❏ RS-9439 [S]	The Cup Bearers	1963	10.00	20.00	40.00

MITCHELL, CHAD
BELL
| ❏ 6028 | Chad | 1969 | 3.75 | 7.50 | 15.00 |

WARNER BROS.
❏ W 1667 [M]	Chad Mitchell Himself	1966	3.75	7.50	15.00
❏ WS 1667 [S]	Chad Mitchell Himself	1966	5.00	10.00	20.00
❏ W 1706 [M]	A Feeling of Love	1967	5.00	10.00	20.00
❏ WS 1706 [S]	A Feeling of Love	1967	3.75	7.50	15.00

MITCHELL, CHAD, TRIO
COLPIX
❏ CP-411 [M]	The Chad Mitchell Trio	1961	5.00	10.00	20.00
❏ SCP-411 [S]	The Chad Mitchell Trio	1961	7.50	15.00	30.00
❏ CP-463 [M]	Everybody's Listening	1964	5.00	10.00	20.00
❏ SCP-463 [S]	Everybody's Listening	1964	7.50	15.00	30.00

KAPP
| ❏ KGP-102 Bl [(3)M] | My Gift to You | 196? | 12.50 | 25.00 | 50.00 |

—Three-record boxed set containing KL-1262, KL-1281 and KL-1313 on mid-1960s reissue labels (black with white circle and "Kapp" vertical logo at top)

❏ KL-1262 [M]	Mighty Day on Campus	1962	5.00	10.00	20.00
❏ KL-1281 [M]	The Chad Mitchell Trio at the Bitter End	1962	5.00	10.00	20.00
❏ KL-1313 [M]	Chad Mitchell Trio In Action	1963	5.00	10.00	20.00
❏ KL-1334 [M]	The Best of Chad Mitchell Trio	1963	5.00	10.00	20.00
❏ KS-3262 [S]	Mighty Day on Campus	1962	6.25	12.50	25.00
❏ KS-3281 [S]	The Chad Mitchell Trio at the Bitter End	1962	6.25	12.50	25.00
❏ KS-3313 [S]	Chad Mitchell Trio In Action	1963	6.25	12.50	25.00
❏ KS-3334 [S]	The Best of Chad Mitchell Trio	1963	6.25	12.50	25.00

MERCURY
❏ MG-20838 [M]	Singin' Our Mind	1963	3.75	7.50	15.00
❏ MG-20891 [M]	Reflecting	1964	3.75	7.50	15.00
❏ SR-60838 [S]	Singin' Our Mind	1963	5.00	10.00	20.00
❏ SR-60891 [S]	Reflecting	1964	5.00	10.00	20.00

MITCHELL, FREDDIE
ALLEGRO ROYALE
| ❏ 1600 [M] | That Boogie Beat | 195? | 15.00 | 30.00 | 60.00 |

MITCHELL, GUY
COLUMBIA
| ❏ CL 1211 [M] | Guy in Love | 1958 | 10.00 | 20.00 | 40.00 |
| ❏ CL 1226 [M] | Guy's Greatest Hits | 1959 | 12.50 | 25.00 | 50.00 |

—Red and black label with six "eye" logos

| ❏ CL 1226 [M] | Guy's Greatest Hits | 1962 | 7.50 | 15.00 | 30.00 |

—"Guaranteed High Fidelity" on red label

| ❏ CL 1226 [M] | Guy's Greatest Hits | 1965 | 5.00 | 10.00 | 20.00 |

—"360 Sound Mono" on red label

❏ CL 1552 [M]	Sunshine Guitar	1960	7.50	15.00	30.00
❏ CL 6231 [10]	Open Spaces	1953	17.50	35.00	70.00
❏ CS 8011 [S]	Guy in Love	1959	12.50	25.00	50.00
❏ CS 8352 [S]	Sunshine Guitar	1960	10.00	20.00	40.00

KING
| ❏ 644 [M] | Sincerely Yours | 1959 | 75.00 | 150.00 | 300.00 |

NASHVILLE
| ❏ 2074 | Heartaches | 1970 | 3.00 | 6.00 | 12.00 |

STARDAY
| ❏ 412 | Traveling Shoes | 1968 | 5.00 | 10.00 | 20.00 |
| ❏ 432 | Singin' Up a Storm | 1969 | 5.00 | 10.00 | 20.00 |

MITCHELL, JONI
ASYLUM
❏ AB-202	Miles of Aisles	1974	2.50	5.00	10.00
❏ 5E-505	Mingus	1979	2.50	5.00	10.00
❏ BB-701 [(2)]	Don Juan's Reckless Daughter	1977	3.00	6.00	12.00
❏ BB-704 [(2)]	Shadows and Light	1980	3.00	6.00	12.00
❏ 7E-1001	Court and Spark	1974	2.50	5.00	10.00
❏ EQ-1001 [Q]	Court and Spark	1974	5.00	10.00	20.00
❏ 7E-1051	The Hissing of Summer Lawns	1975	2.50	5.00	10.00
❏ EQ-1051 [Q]	The Hissing of Summer Lawns	1975	5.00	10.00	20.00
❏ 7E-1087	Hejira	1976	2.50	5.00	10.00
❏ SD 5057	For the Roses	1972	2.50	5.00	10.00

DCC COMPACT CLASSICS
| ❏ LPZ-2044 | Court and Spark | 1997 | 30.00 | 60.00 | 120.00 |

—Audiophile vinyl

| ❏ LPZ-2069 | Blue | 2000 | — | — | — |

—Audiophile vinyl; canceled

GEFFEN
| ❏ PRO-A-1081 [DJ] | Wild Things Run Fast Sampler | 1982 | 3.00 | 6.00 | 12.00 |

—Promo-only 4-song EP

❏ GHS 2019	Wild Things Run Fast	1982	2.00	4.00	8.00
❏ GHS 24074	Dog Eat Dog	1985	2.00	4.00	8.00
❏ GHS 24172	Chalk Mark in a Rain Storm	1988	2.00	4.00	8.00
❏ GEF 24302	Night Ride Home	1991	3.75	7.50	15.00

NAUTILUS
| ❏ NR-11 | Court and Spark | 1980 | 12.50 | 25.00 | 50.00 |

—Audiophile vinyl

REPRISE
| ❏ MS 2038 | Blue | 1970 | 3.75 | 7.50 | 15.00 |
| ❏ R 6293 [M] | Joni Mitchell | 1968 | 10.00 | 20.00 | 40.00 |

—White label promo; evidently, no stock copies were issued in mono

| ❏ RS 6293 [S] | Joni Mitchell | 1968 | 5.00 | 10.00 | 20.00 |

—With "W7" and "r:" logos on two-tone orange label

| ❏ RS 6293 [S] | Joni Mitchell | 1970 | 3.00 | 6.00 | 12.00 |

—With only "r:" logo on all-orange (tan) label

| ❏ RS 6341 | Clouds | 1969 | 5.00 | 10.00 | 20.00 |

—With "W7" and "r:" logos on two-tone orange label

| ❏ RS 6341 | Clouds | 1970 | 3.00 | 6.00 | 12.00 |

—With only "r:" logo on all-orange (tan) label

| ❏ RS 6376 | Ladies of the Canyon | 1970 | 3.00 | 6.00 | 12.00 |

—With only "r:" logo on all-orange (tan) label

| ❏ RS 6376 | Ladies of the Canyon | 1970 | 5.00 | 10.00 | 20.00 |

—With "W7" and "r:" logos on two-tone orange label

MITCHELL, PAUL
VERVE
| ❏ V-8713 [M] | Live at the Atlanta Playboy Club | 1967 | 5.00 | 10.00 | 20.00 |

MITCHELL, RED
BETHLEHEM
| ❏ BCP-38 [M] | Jam for Your Bread | 1956 | 20.00 | 40.00 | 80.00 |
| ❏ BCP-1033 [10] | Happy Minors | 1955 | 100.00 | 200.00 | 400.00 |

CONTEMPORARY
| ❏ C-3538 [M] | Presenting Red Mitchell | 1957 | 20.00 | 40.00 | 80.00 |

PACIFIC JAZZ
| ❏ PJ-22 [M] | Rejoice | 1961 | 7.50 | 15.00 | 30.00 |
| ❏ ST-22 [S] | Rejoice | 1961 | 10.00 | 20.00 | 40.00 |

MITCHELL, RED, AND HAROLD LAND
ATLANTIC
| ❏ 1376 [M] | Hear Ye! | 1961 | 7.50 | 15.00 | 30.00 |

—Multicolor label, white "fan" logo at right

| ❏ 1376 [M] | Hear Ye! | 1964 | 5.00 | 10.00 | 20.00 |

—Multicolor label, black "fan" logo at right

| ❏ SD 1376 [S] | Hear Ye! | 1961 | 10.00 | 20.00 | 40.00 |

—Multicolor label, white "fan" logo at right

| ❏ SD 1376 [S] | Hear Ye! | 1964 | 6.25 | 12.50 | 25.00 |

—Multicolor label, black "fan" logo at right

MITCHELL, ROSCOE
Also see ART ENSEMBLE OF CHICAGO.
DELMARK
| ❏ D-408 [M] | Roscoe Mitchell Sextet | 1966 | 6.25 | 12.50 | 25.00 |
| ❏ DS-408 [S] | Roscoe Mitchell Sextet | 1966 | 5.00 | 10.00 | 20.00 |

NESSA
❏ N-2	Congliptious	1968	6.25	12.50	25.00
❏ N-9/10 [(2)]	Nonaah	1977	6.25	12.50	25.00
❏ N-14/15 [(2)]	L-R-G/The Maze/S II Examples	1980	5.00	10.00	20.00

MITCHELL, WHITEY
ABC-PARAMOUNT
| ❏ ABC-126 [M] | Whitey Mitchell Sextette | 1956 | 12.50 | 25.00 | 50.00 |

M

Number	Title (A Side/B Side)	Yr	VG	VG+	NM

MITCHELL, WILLIE
BEARSVILLE
| ❏ BRK 3520 | ... Listen ... Dance | 1980 | 2.50 | 5.00 | 10.00 |

HI
❏ 8002	Willie Mitchell Live	1977	2.50	5.00	10.00
❏ HL-32010 [M]	Sunrise Serenade	1963	10.00	20.00	40.00
❏ SHL-32010 [S]	Sunrise Serenade	1963	6.25	12.50	25.00
❏ HL-32021 [M]	Hold It	1964	6.25	12.50	25.00
❏ SHL-32021 [S]	Hold It	1964	7.50	15.00	30.00
❏ HL-32026 [M]	It's Dance Time	1965	6.25	12.50	25.00
❏ HL-32029 [M]	Driving Beat	1966	6.25	12.50	25.00
❏ SHL-32029 [S]	Driving Beat	1966	7.50	15.00	30.00
❏ HL-32034 [M]	The Hit Sound of Willie Mitchell	1967	7.50	15.00	30.00
❏ SHL-32034 [S]	The Hit Sound of Willie Mitchell	1967	6.25	12.50	25.00
❏ SHL-32036 [S]	It's Dance Time	1965	7.50	15.00	30.00
❏ HL-32039 [M]	Ooh Baby, You Turn Me On	1967	7.50	15.00	30.00
❏ SHL-32039 [S]	Ooh Baby, You Turn Me On	1967	6.25	12.50	25.00
❏ SHL-32042	Willie Mitchell Live	1968	6.25	12.50	25.00
❏ SHL-32045	Solid Soul	1968	6.25	12.50	25.00
❏ SHL-32048	On Top	1969	6.25	12.50	25.00
❏ SHL-32050	Soul Bag	1969	6.25	12.50	25.00
❏ SHL-32056	The Many Moods of Willie Mitchell	1970	6.25	12.50	25.00
❏ SHL-32058	Robin's Nest	1970	6.25	12.50	25.00
❏ SHL-32068/9 [(2)]	The Best of Willie Mitchell	1971	7.50	15.00	30.00

MITCHELL TRIO, THE
MERCURY
❏ MG-20944 [M]	The Slightly Irreverent Mitchell Trio	1964	3.75	7.50	15.00
❏ MG-20992 [M]	Typical American Boys	1965	3.75	7.50	15.00
❏ MG-21049 [M]	That's the Way It's Gonna Be	1965	3.75	7.50	15.00
❏ MG-21067 [M]	Violets of Dawn	1966	3.75	7.50	15.00
❏ SR-60944 [S]	The Slightly Irreverent Mitchell Trio	1964	5.00	10.00	20.00
❏ SR-60992 [S]	Typical American Boys	1965	5.00	10.00	20.00
❏ SR-61049 [S]	That's the Way It's Gonna Be	1965	5.00	10.00	20.00
❏ SR-61067 [S]	Violets of Dawn	1966	5.00	10.00	20.00

REPRISE
| ❏ R-6258 [M] | Alive | 1967 | 5.00 | 10.00 | 20.00 |
| ❏ RS-6258 [S] | Alive | 1967 | 3.75 | 7.50 | 15.00 |

MITCHELL-RUFF DUO, THE
ATLANTIC
❏ 1374 [M]	The Catbird Seat	1961	5.00	10.00	20.00
—Multicolor label, white "fan" logo at right					
❏ SD 1374 [S]	The Catbird Seat	1961	6.25	12.50	25.00
—Multicolor label, white "fan" logo at right					
❏ 1458 [M]	After This Message	1966	5.00	10.00	20.00
❏ SD 1458 [S]	After This Message	1966	6.25	12.50	25.00

EPIC
| ❏ LN 3221 [M] | The Mitchell-Ruff Duo | 1956 | 10.00 | 20.00 | 40.00 |
| ❏ LN 3318 [M] | Campus Concert | 1956 | 10.00 | 20.00 | 40.00 |

ROULETTE
❏ R-52002 [M]	Appearing Nightly	1958	10.00	20.00	40.00
❏ SR-52002 [S]	Appearing Nightly	1959	7.50	15.00	30.00
❏ R-52013 [M]	The Mitchell-Ruff Duo Plus Strings and Brass	1958	10.00	20.00	40.00
❏ SR-52013 [S]	The Mitchell-Ruff Duo Plus Strings and Brass	1959	7.50	15.00	30.00
❏ R-52025 [M]	Jazz for Juniors	1959	7.50	15.00	30.00
❏ SR-52025 [S]	Jazz for Juniors	1959	6.25	12.50	25.00
❏ R-52034 [M]	Jazz Mission to Moscow	1959	7.50	15.00	30.00
❏ SR-52034 [S]	Jazz Mission to Moscow	1959	6.25	12.50	25.00
❏ R-52037 [M]	The Sound of Music	1960	6.25	12.50	25.00
❏ SR-52037 [S]	The Sound of Music	1960	7.50	15.00	30.00

MITCHELLS, THE
METROJAZZ
| ❏ E-1012 [M] | Get Those Elephants Out'a Here | 1958 | 20.00 | 40.00 | 80.00 |
| ❏ SE-1012 [S] | Get Those Elephants Out'a Here | 1958 | 15.00 | 30.00 | 60.00 |

MITCHUM, ROBERT
CAPITOL
| ❏ T 853 [M] | Calypso — Is Like So... | 1957 | 25.00 | 50.00 | 100.00 |

MONUMENT
| ❏ MLP-8066 [M] | That Man, Robert Mitchum, Sings | 1967 | 6.25 | 12.50 | 25.00 |
| ❏ SLP-18066 [S] | That Man, Robert Mitchum, Sings | 1967 | 6.25 | 12.50 | 25.00 |

MIXTURES, THE (1)
LINDA
| ❏ 3301 [M] | Stompin' at the Rainbow | 1962 | 25.00 | 50.00 | 100.00 |

MIZE, BILLY
IMPERIAL
| ❏ LP-12441 | This Time and Place | 1969 | 5.00 | 10.00 | 20.00 |

UNITED ARTISTS
| ❏ UAS-6781 | You're Alright with Me | 1971 | 3.75 | 7.50 | 15.00 |

ZODIAC
| ❏ 5007 | Love 'n' Stuff | 1976 | 3.00 | 6.00 | 12.00 |

MJT + 3
ARGO
| ❏ LP-621 [M] | Daddy-O Presents MJT + 3 | 1957 | 10.00 | 20.00 | 40.00 |

VEE JAY
❏ LP-1013 [M]	Walter Perkins' MJT + 3	1959	7.50	15.00	30.00
❏ SR-1013 [S]	Walter Perkins' MJT + 3	1959	10.00	20.00	40.00
❏ LP-3008 [M]	Make Everybody Happy	1960	6.25	12.50	25.00
❏ SR-3008 [S]	Make Everybody Happy	1960	7.50	15.00	30.00
❏ LP-3014 [M]	MJT + 3	1961	6.25	12.50	25.00
❏ SR-3014 [S]	MJT + 3	1961	7.50	15.00	30.00

MOB, THE (1)
COLOSSUS
| ❏ CS-1006 | The Mob | 1971 | 5.00 | 10.00 | 20.00 |

MGM
| ❏ SE-4839 | The Mob | 1972 | 3.75 | 7.50 | 15.00 |

MOBLEY, HANK
BLUE NOTE
❏ BLP-1540 [M]	Hank Mobley with Donald Byrd and Lee Morgan	1957	50.00	100.00	200.00
—Regular version, Lexington Ave. address on label					
❏ BLP-1540 [M]	Hank Mobley with Donald Byrd and Lee Morgan	1957	75.00	150.00	300.00
—"Deep groove" version (deep indentation under label on both sides)					
❏ BLP-1540 [M]	Hank Mobley with Donald Byrd and Lee Morgan	1963	6.25	12.50	25.00
—With "New York, USA" address on label					
❏ BLP-1544 [M]	Hank Mobley and His All Stars	1957	37.50	75.00	150.00
—Regular version, W. 63rd St. address on label					
❏ BLP-1544 [M]	Hank Mobley and His All Stars	1957	50.00	100.00	200.00
—"Deep groove" version (deep indentation under label on both sides)					
❏ BLP-1544 [M]	Hank Mobley and His All Stars	1963	6.25	12.50	25.00
—With "New York, USA" address on label					
❏ BLP-1550 [M]	Hank Mobley	1957	37.50	75.00	150.00
—Regular version, W. 63rd St. address on label					
❏ BLP-1550 [M]	Hank Mobley	1957	50.00	100.00	200.00
—"Deep groove" version (deep indentation under label on both sides)					
❏ BLP-1550 [M]	Hank Mobley	1963	6.25	12.50	25.00
—With "New York, USA" address on label					
❏ BLP-1560 [M]	Hank	1957	37.50	75.00	150.00
—Regular version, W. 63rd St. address on label					
❏ BLP-1560 [M]	Hank	1957	50.00	100.00	200.00
—"Deep groove" version (deep indentation under label on both sides)					
❏ BLP-1560 [M]	Hank	1963	6.25	12.50	25.00
—With "New York, USA" address on label					
❏ BLP-1568 [M]	'Hank Mobley	1957	37.50	75.00	150.00
—Regular version, W. 63rd St. address on label					
❏ BLP-1568 [M]	Hank Mobley	1957	50.00	100.00	200.00
—"Deep groove" version (deep indentation under label on both sides)					
❏ BLP-1568 [M]	Hank Mobley	1963	6.25	12.50	25.00
—With "New York, USA" address on label					
❏ BST-1568 [S]	Hank Mobley	1959	25.00	50.00	100.00
—Regular version, W. 63rd St. address on label					
❏ BST-1568 [S]	Hank Mobley	1959	37.50	75.00	150.00
—"Deep groove" version (deep indentation under label on both sides)					
❏ BST-1568 [S]	Hank Mobley	1963	5.00	10.00	20.00
—With "New York, USA" address on label					
❏ BLP-1574 [M]	Peckin' Time	1958	37.50	75.00	150.00
—Regular version, W. 63rd St. address on label					
❏ BLP-1574 [M]	Peckin' Time	1958	50.00	100.00	200.00
—"Deep groove" version (deep indentation under label on both sides)					
❏ BLP-1574 [M]	Peckin' Time	1963	6.25	12.50	25.00
—With "New York, USA" address on label					
❏ BLP-4031 [M]	Soul Station	1960	20.00	40.00	80.00
—Regular version, W. 63rd St. address on label					
❏ BLP-4031 [M]	Soul Station	1960	30.00	60.00	120.00
—"Deep groove" version (deep indentation under label on both sides)					
❏ BLP-4031 [M]	Soul Station	1963	6.25	12.50	25.00
—With "New York, USA" address on label					
❏ BLP-4058 [M]	Roll Call	1961	20.00	40.00	80.00
—With W. 63rd St. address on label					
❏ BLP-4058 [M]	Roll Call	1963	6.25	12.50	25.00
—With "New York, USA" address on label					
❏ BLP-4080 [M]	Workout	1961	15.00	30.00	60.00
—With 61st St. address on label					
❏ BLP-4080 [M]	Workout	1963	6.25	12.50	25.00
—With "New York, USA" address on label					
❏ BLP-4149 [M]	No Room for Squares	1963	7.50	15.00	30.00
❏ BLP-4186 [M]	The Turnaround!	1964	7.50	15.00	30.00
❏ BLP-4209 [M]	Dippin'	1965	7.50	15.00	30.00
❏ BLP-4230 [M]	A Caddy for Daddy	1966	7.50	15.00	30.00
❏ BLP-4273 [M]	Hi Voltage	1968	30.00	60.00	120.00
❏ BLP-5066 [10]	Hank Mobley Quartet	1955	100.00	200.00	400.00
❏ BST-84031 [S]	Soul Station	1960	15.00	30.00	60.00
—With W. 63rd St. address on label					
❏ BST-84031 [S]	Soul Station	1963	5.00	10.00	20.00
—With "New York, USA" address on label					
❏ BST-84058	Roll Call	199?	6.25	12.50	25.00
—Classic Records reissue on audiophile vinyl					
❏ BST-84058 [S]	Roll Call	1961	15.00	30.00	60.00
—With W. 63rd St. address on label					
❏ BST-84058 [S]	Roll Call	1963	5.00	10.00	20.00
—With "New York, USA" address on label					
❏ BST-84080 [S]	Workout	1961	12.50	25.00	50.00
—With 61st St. address on label					
❏ BST-84080 [S]	Workout	1963	5.00	10.00	20.00
—With "New York, USA" address on label					
❏ BST-84149 [S]	No Room for Squares	1963	10.00	20.00	40.00
—With "New York, USA" address on label					
❏ BST-84149 [S]	No Room for Squares	1967	5.00	10.00	20.00
—With "A Division of Liberty Records" on label					
❏ BST-84186 [S]	The Turnaround!	1964	10.00	20.00	40.00
—With "New York, USA" address on label					
❏ BST-84186 [S]	The Turnaround!	1967	5.00	10.00	20.00
—With "A Division of Liberty Records" on label					
❏ BST-84209 [S]	Dippin'	1965	10.00	20.00	40.00
—With "New York, USA" address on label					
❏ BST-84209 [S]	Dippin'	1967	5.00	10.00	20.00
—With "A Division of Liberty Records" on label					
❏ BST-84230 [S]	A Caddy for Daddy	1966	10.00	20.00	40.00
—With "New York, USA" address on label					
❏ BST-84230 [S]	A Caddy for Daddy	1967	5.00	10.00	20.00
—With "A Division of Liberty Records" on label					
❏ BST-84273 [S]	Hi Voltage	1968	6.25	12.50	25.00
—With "A Division of Liberty Records" on label					

Number	Title (A Side/B Side)	Yr	VG	VG+	NM
❑ BST-84288	Reach Out!	1968	6.25	12.50	25.00
—With "A Division of Liberty Records" on label					
❑ BST-84329	The Flip	1969	6.25	12.50	25.00
—With "A Division of Liberty Records" on label					
PRESTIGE					
❑ PRLP-7061 [M]	Mobley's Message	1956	37.50	75.00	150.00
❑ PRLP-7082 [M]	Mobley's Second Message	1957	37.50	75.00	150.00
SAVOY					
❑ MG-12092 [M]	Jazz Message #2	1956	37.50	75.00	150.00
STATUS					
❑ ST-8311 [M]	52nd Street Theme	1965	6.25	12.50	25.00

MOBY GRAPE
Also see ALEXANDER "SKIP" SPENCE.

Number	Title (A Side/B Side)	Yr	VG	VG+	NM
COLUMBIA					
❑ MGS 1	Grape Jam	1968	5.00	10.00	20.00
❑ CXS 3 [(2)]	Wow/Grape Jam	1968	7.50	15.00	30.00
—Joint release of the two albums under one cover					
❑ CXS 3 [(2)]	Wow/Grape Jam	1971	3.75	7.50	15.00
—Orange labels					
❑ 2698/9498	Moby Grape Poster	1967	2.00	4.00	8.00
—Poster has offending finger airbrushed out					
❑ 2698/9498	Moby Grape Poster	1967	3.75	7.50	15.00
—Poster has Don Stephenson "giving the finger" on his washboard					
❑ CL 2698 [M]	Moby Grape	1967	5.00	10.00	20.00
—Cover has offending finger airbrushed out					
❑ CL 2698 [M]	Moby Grape	1967	10.00	20.00	40.00
—Cover has Don Stephenson "giving the finger" on his washboard					
❑ CS 9498	Wow	1971	3.00	6.00	12.00
—Orange label; with poster					
❑ CS 9498 [S]	Moby Grape	1967	5.00	10.00	20.00
—Cover has offending finger airbrushed out					
❑ CS 9498 [S]	Moby Grape	1967	10.00	20.00	40.00
—Cover has Don Stephenson "giving the finger" on his washboard					
❑ CS 9613	Wow	1968	5.00	10.00	20.00
❑ CS 9613 [M]	Wow	1968	10.00	20.00	40.00
—"Special Mono Radio Station Copy" with white label					
❑ CS 9696	Moby Grape '69	1969	5.00	10.00	20.00
❑ CS 9912	Truly Fine Citizen	1969	5.00	10.00	20.00
❑ C 31098	Great Grape	1972	3.75	7.50	15.00
ESCAPE					
❑ ESA 1	Live Grape	1978	3.75	7.50	15.00
HARMONY					
❑ KH 30392	Omaha	1971	3.75	7.50	15.00
REPRISE					
❑ RS 6460	20 Granite Creek	1971	5.00	10.00	20.00

MOD AND THE ROCKERS

Number	Title (A Side/B Side)	Yr	VG	VG+	NM
JUSTICE					
❑ JLP-153	Mod and the Rockers Now!	1967	100.00	200.00	400.00

MODERN FOLK QUARTET, THE

Number	Title (A Side/B Side)	Yr	VG	VG+	NM
WARNER BROS.					
❑ W 1511 [M]	The Modern Folk Quartet	1963	6.25	12.50	25.00
❑ WS 1511 [S]	The Modern Folk Quartet	1963	7.50	15.00	30.00
❑ W 1546 [M]	Changes	1964	6.25	12.50	25.00
❑ WS 1546 [S]	Changes	1964	7.50	15.00	30.00

MODERN JAZZ DISCIPLES, THE

Number	Title (A Side/B Side)	Yr	VG	VG+	NM
NEW JAZZ					
❑ NJLP-8222 [M]	Modern Jazz Disciples	1959	12.50	25.00	50.00
—Purple label					
❑ NJLP-8222 [M]	Modern Jazz Disciples	1965	6.25	12.50	25.00
—Blue label, trident logo at right					
❑ NJLP-8240 [M]	Right Down Front	1960	12.50	25.00	50.00
—Purple label					
❑ NJLP-8240 [M]	Right Down Front	1965	6.25	12.50	25.00
—Blue label, trident logo at right					

MODERN JAZZ QUARTET, THE

Number	Title (A Side/B Side)	Yr	VG	VG+	NM
APPLE					
❑ ST-3353	Under the Jasmine Tree	1969	6.25	12.50	25.00
❑ ST-5-3353	Under the Jasmine Tree	1969	10.00	20.00	40.00
—Capitol Record Club edition					
❑ STAO-3360	Space	1970	6.25	12.50	25.00
❑ STAO-5-3360	Space	1970	10.00	20.00	40.00
—Capitol Record Club edition					
ATLANTIC					
❑ 2-603 [(2)M]	The European Concert	1961	7.50	15.00	30.00
—Multicolor labels, white "fan" logo at right					
❑ 2-603 [(2)M]	The European Concert	1963	5.00	10.00	20.00
—Multicolor labels, black "fan" logo at right					
❑ SD 2-603 [(2)S]	The European Concert	1961	10.00	20.00	40.00
—Multicolor labels, white "fan" logo at right					
❑ SD 2-603 [(2)S]	The European Concert	1963	6.25	12.50	25.00
—Multicolor labels, black "fan" logo at right					
❑ SQ 2-909 [(2)Q]	The Last Concert	1975	6.25	12.50	25.00
❑ 1231 [M]	Fontessa	1956	10.00	20.00	40.00
—Black label					
❑ 1231 [M]	Fontessa	1960	5.00	10.00	20.00
—Multicolor label, white "fan" logo at right					
❑ SD 1231 [S]	Fontessa	1958	7.50	15.00	30.00
—Green label					
❑ 1247 [M]	The Modern Jazz Quartet at the Music Inn	1956	10.00	20.00	40.00
—Black label					
❑ 1247 [M]	The Modern Jazz Quartet at the Music Inn	1960	5.00	10.00	20.00
—Multicolor label, white "fan" logo at right					
❑ 1265 [M]	The Modern Jazz Quartet	1957	10.00	20.00	40.00
—Black label					
❑ 1265 [M]	The Modern Jazz Quartet	1960	5.00	10.00	20.00
—Multicolor label, white "fan" logo at right					

Number	Title (A Side/B Side)	Yr	VG	VG+	NM
❑ 1284 [M]	No Sun in Venice	1958	10.00	20.00	40.00
—Black label					
❑ 1284 [M]	No Sun in Venice	1960	5.00	10.00	20.00
—Multicolor label, white "fan" logo at right					
❑ SD 1284 [S]	No Sun in Venice	1958	7.50	15.00	30.00
—Green label					
❑ 1299 [M]	The Modern Jazz Quartet at the Music Inn, Volume 2	1958	10.00	20.00	40.00
—Black label					
❑ 1299 [M]	The Modern Jazz Quartet at the Music Inn, Volume 2	1960	5.00	10.00	20.00
—Multicolor label, white "fan" logo at right					
❑ SD 1299 [S]	The Modern Jazz Quartet at the Music Inn, Volume 2	1958	7.50	15.00	30.00
—Green label					
❑ 1325 [M]	Pyramid	1960	10.00	20.00	40.00
—Black label					
❑ 1325 [M]	Pyramid	1961	5.00	10.00	20.00
—Multicolor label, white "fan" logo at right					
❑ SD 1325 [S]	Pyramid	1960	7.50	15.00	30.00
—Green label					
❑ 1345 [M]	Third Stream Music	1960	5.00	10.00	20.00
—Multicolor label, white "fan" logo at right					
❑ SD 1345 [S]	Third Stream Music	1960	6.25	12.50	25.00
—Multicolor label, white "fan" logo at right					
❑ 1359 [M]	The Modern Jazz Quartet and Orchestra	1961	5.00	10.00	20.00
—Multicolor label, white "fan" logo at right					
❑ SD 1359 [S]	The Modern Jazz Quartet and Orchestra	1961	6.25	12.50	25.00
—Multicolor label, white "fan" logo at right					
❑ SD 1381 [S]	Lonely Woman	1962	5.00	10.00	20.00
—Multicolor label, black "fan" logo at right					
❑ SD 1385 [S]	The European Concert, Volume 1	1962	5.00	10.00	20.00
—Multicolor label, black "fan" logo at right					
❑ SD 1386 [S]	The European Concert, Volume 2	1962	5.00	10.00	20.00
—Multicolor label, black "fan" logo at right					
❑ SD 1390 [S]	The Comedy	1963	5.00	10.00	20.00
—Multicolor label, black "fan" logo at right					
❑ SD 1414 [S]	The Sheriff	1964	5.00	10.00	20.00
—Multicolor label, black "fan" logo at right					
❑ SD 1420 [S]	A Quartet Is a Quartet Is a Quartet	1964	5.00	10.00	20.00
—Multicolor label, black "fan" logo at right					
❑ 1486 [M]	Live at the Lighthouse	1967	5.00	10.00	20.00
❑ SQ 1652 [Q]	Blues on Bach	1974	5.00	10.00	20.00
MOBILE FIDELITY					
❑ 1-090	Live at the Lighthouse	1982	12.50	25.00	50.00
—Audiophile vinyl					
❑ 1-205	The Modern Jazz Quartet	1994	7.50	15.00	30.00
—Audiophile vinyl					
❑ 1-206	Blues at Carnegie Hall	1994	7.50	15.00	30.00
—Audiophile vinyl					
❑ 1-228	The Modern Jazz Quartet at the Music Inn, Volume 2	1995	15.00	30.00	60.00
—Audiophile vinyl					
PRESTIGE					
❑ PRLP-160 [10]	The Modern Jazz Quartet with Milt Jackson	1953	30.00	60.00	120.00
❑ PRLP-170 [10]	The Modern Jazz Quartet, Volume 2	1953	30.00	60.00	120.00
❑ PRLP-7005 [M]	Concorde	1955	17.50	35.00	70.00
—Yellow label originals					
❑ PRLP-7057 [M]	Django	1956	17.50	35.00	70.00
—Yellow label originals					
❑ PRLP-7059 [M]	Modern Jazz Quartet/Milt Jackson Quintet	1956	17.50	35.00	70.00
—Yellow label originals					
❑ PRLP-7421 [M]	The Modern Jazz Quartet Play for Lovers	1966	5.00	10.00	20.00
❑ PRLP-7425 [M]	The Modern Jazz Quartet Plays Jazz Classics	1966	5.00	10.00	20.00
SAVOY					
❑ MG-12046 [M]	Modern Jazz Quartet	1955	12.50	25.00	50.00
UNITED ARTISTS					
❑ UAL-4072 [M]	Patterns	1960	6.25	12.50	25.00
❑ UAS-5072 [S]	Patterns	1960	7.50	15.00	30.00

MODERN JAZZ QUINTET, THE

Number	Title (A Side/B Side)	Yr	VG	VG+	NM
SURREY					
❑ S-1030 [M]	Q.T. Hush	1966	6.25	12.50	25.00
❑ SS-1030 [S]	Q.T. Hush	1966	7.50	15.00	30.00

MODERN JAZZ SEXTET, THE

Number	Title (A Side/B Side)	Yr	VG	VG+	NM
AMERICAN RECORDING SOCIETY					
❑ G-429 [M]	The Modern Jazz Sextet	1957	10.00	20.00	40.00
NORGRAN					
❑ MGN-1076 [M]	The Modern Jazz Sextet	1956	25.00	50.00	100.00
VERVE					
❑ MGV-8166 [M]	The Modern Jazz Sextet	1957	15.00	30.00	60.00
❑ V-8166 [M]	The Modern Jazz Sextet	1961	6.25	12.50	25.00

MODERN JAZZ SOCIETY, THE

Number	Title (A Side/B Side)	Yr	VG	VG+	NM
AMERICAN RECORDING SOCIETY					
❑ G-432 [M]	A Concert of Contemporary Music	1957	10.00	20.00	40.00
NORGRAN					
❑ MGN-1040 [M]	A Concert of Contemporary Music	1955	25.00	50.00	100.00
VERVE					
❑ VSP-18 [M]	Little David's Fugue	1966	5.00	10.00	20.00
—As "The Modern Jazz Ensemble"					
❑ MGV-8131 [M]	A Concert of Contemporary Music	1957	15.00	30.00	60.00
❑ V-8131 [M]	A Concert of Contemporary Music	1961	6.25	12.50	25.00

Number	Title (A Side/B Side)	Yr	VG	VG+	NM

MODERN JAZZ TRIO
See MJT + 3.

MODERN LOVERS, THE
See JONATHAN RICHMAN AND THE MODERN LOVERS.

MODUGNO, DOMENICO
DECCA
❑ DL 4133 [M]	Viva Italia	1961	7.50	15.00	30.00
❑ DL 8808 [M]	Nel Blu Dipinto Di Blu (Volare) and Other Italian Favorites	1958	12.50	25.00	50.00
❑ DL 8853 [M]	Encore	1959	10.00	20.00	40.00

MOER, PAUL
DEL-FI
❑ DFLP-1212 [M]	Contemporary Jazz Classics	1961	5.00	10.00	20.00
❑ DFST-1212 [S]	Contemporary Jazz Classics	1961	6.25	12.50	25.00

MOFFETT, CHARLES
SAVOY
❑ MG-12194	The Gift	1969	5.00	10.00	20.00

MOJO MEN, THE
GRT
❑ 10003	Mojo Magic	1969	6.25	12.50	25.00

MOLE, MIFF/EDMUND HALL
BRUNSWICK
❑ BL 58042 [10]	Battle of Jazz, Volume 4	1953	15.00	30.00	60.00

MOLLY HATCHET
CAPITOL
❑ C1-92114	Lightning Strikes Twice	1989	3.00	6.00	12.00

EPIC
❑ AS99 694 [DJ]	Flirtin' with Disaster	1979	10.00	20.00	40.00
—Promo-only picture disc					
❑ AS99 844 [DJ]	Beatin' the Odds	1980	10.00	20.00	40.00
—Promo-only picture disc					
❑ AS99 1320 [DJ]	Take No Prisoners	1981	6.25	12.50	25.00
—Promo-only picture disc					
❑ JE 35347	Molly Hatchet	1978	3.00	6.00	12.00
—Orange label					
❑ JE 35347	Molly Hatchet	1979	2.50	5.00	10.00
—Dark blue label					
❑ PE 35347	Molly Hatchet	198?	2.00	4.00	8.00
—Budget-line reissue with new prefix					
❑ JE 36110	Flirtin' with Disaster	1979	2.50	5.00	10.00
❑ FE 36572	Beatin' the Odds	1980	2.50	5.00	10.00
❑ FE 37480	Take No Prisoners	1981	2.50	5.00	10.00
❑ PE 37480	Take No Prisoners	198?	2.00	4.00	8.00
—Budget-line reissue with new prefix					
❑ FE 38429	No Guts... No Glory	1983	2.50	5.00	10.00
❑ PE 38429	No Guts... No Glory	198?	2.00	4.00	8.00
—Budget-line reissue with new prefix					
❑ FE 39621	The Deed Is Done	1984	2.50	5.00	10.00
❑ E2 40137 [(2)]	Double Trouble Live	1985	3.75	7.50	15.00

MOLOCH
ENTERPRISE
❑ ENS-1002	Moloch	1969	5.00	10.00	20.00

MOM'S APPLE PIE
BROWN BAG
❑ BB-LA073-F	Mom's Apple Pie #2	1973	3.75	7.50	15.00
❑ 14200	Mom's Apple Pie	1972	5.00	10.00	20.00
—With barbed wire wall covering the former opening. This is much rarer than the first version, though less sought-after					
❑ 14200	Mom's Apple Pie	1972	5.00	10.00	20.00
—With vulva showing in the apple pie					

MOMENTS, THE
R&B trio. For legal reasons, their albums on Polydor were issued under the name "Ray, Goodman and Brown."
CHESS
❑ CH2-92517 [(2)]	Greatest Hits	198?	3.00	6.00	12.00

POLYDOR
❑ PD-1-6240	Ray, Goodman & Brown	1979	2.50	5.00	10.00
❑ PD-1-6299	Ray, Goodman & Brown II	1980	2.50	5.00	10.00
❑ PD-1-6341	Stay	1981	2.50	5.00	10.00

STANG
❑ ST-1000	Not On the Outside, But On the Inside Strong	1969	7.50	15.00	30.00
❑ ST-1002	The Moments On Top	1970	7.50	15.00	30.00
❑ ST-1003	A Moment with the Moments	1970	7.50	15.00	30.00
❑ ST-1004	Moments Greatest Hits	1971	5.00	10.00	20.00
❑ ST-1006	The Moments Live at the New York State Womans Prison	1971	6.25	12.50	25.00
❑ ST-1009	The Other Side of the Moments	1972	6.25	12.50	25.00
❑ ST-1015	Live at the Miss Black America Pageant	1972	5.00	10.00	20.00
❑ ST-1019	The Best of the Moments	1975	3.75	7.50	15.00
❑ ST-1022	My Thing	1973	3.75	7.50	15.00
❑ ST-1023	The Sexy Moments	1974	3.75	7.50	15.00
❑ ST-1026	Look at Me	1975	3.75	7.50	15.00
❑ ST-1030	Moments With You	1976	3.75	7.50	15.00
❑ 2ST-1033 [(2)]	Greatest Hits	1977	5.00	10.00	20.00
❑ ST-1034	Sharp	1978	3.75	7.50	15.00

MONCUR, GRACHAN, III
BLUE NOTE
❑ BLP-4153 [M]	Evolution	1963	6.25	12.50	25.00
❑ BLP-4177 [M]	Some Other Stuff	1964	6.25	12.50	25.00
❑ BST-84153 [S]	Evolution	1963	7.50	15.00	30.00
—With "New York, USA" address on label					
❑ BST-84177 [S]	Some Other Stuff	1964	7.50	15.00	30.00
—With "New York, USA" address on label					

MONDAY BLUES
VAULT
❑ 133	The Phil Spector Song Book	1970	5.00	10.00	20.00

MONEY, ZOOT
EPIC
❑ LN 24241 [M]	All Happening Zoot Money's Big Roll Band at Klooks Kleek	1966	5.00	10.00	20.00

MONICA, CORBETT
DOT
❑ DLP-3303 [M]	For Laughs1	1960	7.50	15.00	30.00

MONITORS, THE (1)
SOUL
❑ SS-714	Greetings, We're the Monitors	1969	15.00	30.00	60.00

MONK, THELONIOUS
ANALOGUE PRODUCTIONS
❑ AP-37 [(7)]	The Riverside Tenor Sessions	1999	62.50	125.00	250.00

BLUE NOTE
❑ BLP-1510 [M]	Genius of Modern Music, Vol. 1	1956	37.50	75.00	150.00
—Regular edition, Lexington Ave. address on label					
❑ BLP-1510 [M]	Genius of Modern Music, Vol. 1	1956	50.00	100.00	200.00
—"Deep groove" version (deep indentation under label on both sides)					
❑ BLP-1510 [M]	Genius of Modern Music, Vol. 1	1963	6.25	12.50	25.00
—"New York, USA" address on label					
❑ BLP-1511 [M]	Genius of Modern Music, Vol. 2	1956	37.50	75.00	150.00
—Regular edition, Lexington Ave. address on label					
❑ BLP-1511 [M]	Genius of Modern Music, Vol. 2	1956	50.00	100.00	200.00
—"Deep groove" version (deep indentation under label on both sides)					
❑ BLP-1511 [M]	Genius of Modern Music, Vol. 2	1963	6.25	12.50	25.00
—"New York, USA" address on label					
❑ BLP-5002 [10]	Genius of Modern Music, Vol. 1	1952	100.00	200.00	400.00
❑ BLP-5009 [10]	Genius of Modern Music, Vol. 2	1952	100.00	200.00	400.00

COLUMBIA
❑ CL 1965 [M]	Monk's Dream	1963	5.00	10.00	20.00
❑ CL 2038 [M]	Criss-Cross	1963	5.00	10.00	20.00
❑ CL 2164 [M]	Monk Big Band and Quartet In Concert	1964	5.00	10.00	20.00
❑ CL 2184 [M]	It's Monk's Time	1964	5.00	10.00	20.00
❑ CL 2291 [M]	Monk	1965	5.00	10.00	20.00
❑ CL 2349 [M]	Solo Monk	1965	5.00	10.00	20.00
❑ CL 2416 [M]	Misterioso	1966	5.00	10.00	20.00
❑ CL 2651 [M]	Straight No Chaser	1967	7.50	15.00	50.00
❑ CS 8765 [S]	Monk's Dream	1963	6.25	12.50	25.00
❑ CS 8838 [S]	Criss-Cross	1963	6.25	12.50	25.00
❑ CS 8964 [S]	Monk Big Band and Quartet In Concert	1964	6.25	12.50	25.00
❑ CS 8984 [S]	It's Monk's Time	1964	6.25	12.50	25.00
❑ CS 9091 [S]	Monk	1965	6.25	12.50	25.00
❑ CS 9149 [S]	Solo Monk	1965	6.25	12.50	25.00
—Red "360 Sound" label					
❑ CS 9216 [S]	Misterioso	1966	6.25	12.50	25.00
❑ CS 9451 [S]	Straight No Chaser	1967	5.00	10.00	20.00
—Red "360 Sound" label					
❑ CS 9632 [M]	Underground	1968	12.50	25.00	50.00
—White label promo only with stereo number; "Special Mono Radio Station Copy" sticker on stereo cover					
❑ CS 9632 [S]	Underground	1968	5.00	10.00	20.00
—Red "360 Sound" label					
❑ CS 9806	Monk's Blues	1969	5.00	10.00	20.00
—Red "360 Sound" label					

COLUMBIA MUSICAL TREASURY
❑ DS 338	Monk's Miracles	1967	6.25	12.50	25.00
—Columbia Record Club exclusive					

MOSAIC
❑ M4-101 [(4)]	The Complete Blue Note Recordings of Thelonious Monk	198?	25.00	50.00	100.00
❑ MR4-112 [(4)]	The Complete Black Lion and Vogue Recordings	199?	20.00	40.00	80.00

PRESTIGE
❑ PRLP-142 [10]	Thelonious Monk Trio	1953	50.00	100.00	200.00
❑ PRLP-166 [10]	Thelonious Monk Quintet with Sonny Rollins and Julius Watkins	1953	50.00	100.00	200.00
❑ PRLP-180 [10]	Thelonious Monk Quintet	1954	50.00	100.00	200.00
❑ PRLP-189 [10]	Thelonious Monk Trio	1954	50.00	100.00	200.00
❑ PRLP-7027 [M]	Thelonious Monk	1956	25.00	50.00	100.00
—Reissue of 142 and 189 on one 12-inch record					
❑ PRLP-7053 [M]	Monk	1956	25.00	50.00	100.00
—Reissue of 150					
❑ PRLP-7075 [M]	Thelonious Monk/Sonny Rollins	1957	25.00	50.00	100.00
—Reissue of 166					
❑ PRLP-7159 [M]	Monk's Moods	1959	18.75	37.50	75.00
—Reissue of 7027					
❑ PRLP-7169 [M]	Work	1959	18.75	37.50	75.00
—Reissue of 7075					
❑ PRLP-7245 [M]	We See	1962	18.75	37.50	75.00
—Reissue of 7053					
❑ PRLP-7363 [M]	The Golden Monk	1965	7.50	5.00	30.00
—Reissue of 7245					
❑ PRLP-7508 [M]	The High Priest	1967	7.50	15.00	30.00
—Reissue of 7159					

RIVERSIDE
❑ R-022 [(22)]	The Complete Riverside Recordings	1987	100.00	200.00	400.00
❑ RLP 12-201 [M]	Thelonious Monk Plays Duke Ellington	1955	100.00	200.00	400.00
—White label with blue print					
❑ RLP 12-201 [M]	Thelonious Monk Plays Duke Ellington	1958	10.00	20.00	40.00
—Blue label with reel and microphone logo					
❑ RLP 12-209 [M]	The Unique Thelonious Monk	1956	25.00	50.00	100.00
—White label with blue print					
❑ RLP 12-209 [M]	The Unique Thelonious Monk	1958	10.00	20.00	40.00
—Blue label with reel and microphone logo					

Number	Title (A Side/B Side)	Yr	VG	VG+	NM
❏ RLP 12-226 [M]	Brilliant Corners	1957	25.00	50.00	100.00
—White label with blue print					
❏ RLP 12-226 [M]	Brilliant Corners	1958	10.00	20.00	40.00
—Blue label with reel and microphone logo					
❏ RLP 12-235 [M]	Thelonious Himself	1957	25.00	50.00	100.00
—White label with blue print					
❏ RLP 12-235 [M]	Thelonious Himself	1958	10.00	20.00	40.00
—Blue label with reel and microphone logo					
❏ RLP 12-242 [M]	Monk's Music	1957	25.00	50.00	100.00
—White label with blue print					
❏ RLP 12-242 [M]	Monk's Music	1958	10.00	20.00	40.00
—Blue label with reel and microphone logo					
❏ RLP 12-247 [M]	Mulligan Meets Monk	1957	25.00	50.00	100.00
—White label with blue print					
❏ RLP 12-247 [M]	Mulligan Meets Monk	1958	10.00	20.00	40.00
—Blue label with reel and microphone logo					
❏ RLP 12-262 [M]	Thelonious in Action Recorded at the Five Spot Café, New York, With Johnny Griffn	1958	10.00	20.00	40.00
❏ RLP 12-279 [M]	Misterioso	1958	10.00	20.00	40.00
❏ RLP 12-300 [M]	The Thelonious Monk Orchestra at Town Hall	1959	10.00	20.00	40.00
❏ RLP 12-305 [M]	5 By Monk By 5	1959	10.00	20.00	40.00
❏ RLP 12-312 [M]	Thelonious Alone in San Francisco	1959	10.00	20.00	40.00
❏ RLP 12-323 [M]	Thelonious Monk Quartet Plus Two at the Blackhawk	1960	10.00	20.00	40.00
❏ RLP-421 [M]	Thelonious Monk's Greatest Hits	1962	5.00	10.00	20.00
❏ RLP-443 [M]	Thelonious Monk in Italy	1963	5.00	10.00	20.00
❏ RLP-460/1 [(2)M]	April in Paris	1963	10.00	20.00	40.00
❏ RLP-483 [M]	The Thelonious Monk Story, Volume 1	1965	5.00	10.00	20.00
❏ RLP-484 [M]	The Thelonious Monk Story, Volume 2	1965	5.00	10.00	20.00
❏ RLP-491 [M]	Monk in France	1965	5.00	10.00	20.00
❏ RLP 1101 [S]	Monk's Music	1959	10.00	20.00	40.00
—Black label with reel and microphone logo					
❏ RLP 1106 [S]	Mulligan Meets Monk	1959	10.00	20.00	40.00
—Black label with reel and microphone logo					
❏ RLP 1133 [S]	Misterioso	1958	12.50	25.00	50.00
❏ RLP 1138 [S]	The Thelonious Monk Orchestra at Town Hall	1959	12.50	25.00	50.00
❏ RLP 1150 [S]	5 By Monk By 5	1959	12.50	25.00	50.00
❏ RLP 1158 [S]	Thelonious Alone in San Francisco	1959	12.50	25.00	50.00
❏ RLP 1171 [S]	Thelonious Monk Quartet Plus Two at the Blackhawk	1960	12.50	25.00	50.00
❏ RLP 1190 [S]	Thelonious in Action Recorded at the Five Spot Café, New York, With Johnny Griffn	1960	12.50	25.00	50.00
❏ RM-3000 [M]	Mighty Monk	1967	5.00	10.00	20.00
❏ RM-3004 [M]	Monk's Music	1967	5.00	10.00	20.00
❏ RS-9421 [S]	Thelonious Monk's Greatest Hits	1962	6.25	12.50	25.00
❏ RS-9443 [S]	Monk in Italy	1963	6.25	12.50	25.00
❏ RS-9460/1 [(2)S]	April in Paris	1963	12.50	25.00	250.00
❏ RS-9483 [S]	The Thelonious Monk Story, Volume 1	1965	6.25	12.50	25.00
❏ RS-9484 [S]	The Thelonious Monk Story, Volume 2	1965	6.25	12.50	25.00
❏ RS-9491 [S]	Monk in France	1965	6.25	12.50	25.00

MONK, THELONIOUS, AND JOHN COLTRANE
JAZZLAND

Number	Title (A Side/B Side)	Yr	VG	VG+	NM
❏ JLP-46 [M]	Thelonious Monk with John Coltrane	1961	10.00	20.00	40.00
❏ JLP-946 [S]	Thelonious Monk with John Coltrane	1961	12.50	25.00	50.00

RIVERSIDE

❏ RLP-490 [M]	Thelonious Monk with John Coltrane	1965	6.25	12.50	25.00
—Reissue of Jazzland 46					
❏ RS-9490 [S]	Thelonious Monk with John Coltrane	1965	7.50	15.00	30.00
—Reissue of Jazzland 946					

MONKEES, THE
Also see DAVY JONES; MIKE NESMITH.
ARISTA

❏ AL 4089	The Monkees' Greatest Hits	1976	3.00	6.00	12.00
—Reissue of Bell LP					
❏ AL8-8313	The Monkees' Greatest Hits	198?	2.00	4.00	8.00
—Reissue of Arista 4089					
❏ AL9-8432	Then & Now...The Best of the Monkees	1986	3.00	6.00	12.00
❏ AL-8524	The Monkees	1988	3.00	6.00	12.00
❏ AL-8525	More of the Monkees	1988	3.00	6.00	12.00

BELL

❏ 6081	Re-Focus	1972	7.50	15.00	30.00

COLGEMS

❏ COM-101 [M]	The Monkees	1966	5.00	10.00	20.00
—Second pressing: Side 1, Song 5 listed as "Papa Gene's Blues" (RE after number on upper right back cover)					
❏ COM-101 [M]	The Monkees	1966	6.25	12.50	25.00
—First pressing: Side 1, Song 5 listed as "Papa Jean's Blues"					
❏ COS-101 [S]	The Monkees	1966	5.00	10.00	20.00
—Second pressing: Side 1, Song 5 listed as "Papa Gene's Blues" (RE after number on upper right back cover)					
❏ COS-101 [S]	The Monkees	1966	6.25	12.50	25.00
—First pressing: Side 1, Song 5 listed as "Papa Jean's Blues"					
❏ COM-102 [M]	More of the Monkees	1966	5.00	10.00	20.00
❏ COS-102 [S]	More of the Monkees	1966	5.00	10.00	20.00
❏ COM-103 [M]	The Monkees' Headquarters	1967	5.00	10.00	20.00
—First pressing: Back cover, center bottom photo is of two of the LP's producers					
❏ COM-103 [M]	The Monkees' Headquarters	1967	7.50	15.00	30.00
—Second pressing: Back cover, center bottom photo is of producers plus the Monkees with beards; "RE" on upper right back cover					
❏ COS-103 [S]	The Monkees' Headquarters	1967	5.00	10.00	20.00
—First pressing: Back cover, center bottom photo is of two of the LP's producers					
❏ COS-103 [S]	The Monkees' Headquarters	1967	7.50	15.00	30.00
—Second pressing: Back cover, center bottom photo is of producers plus the Monkees with beards; "RE" on upper right back cover					
❏ COM-104 [M]	Pisces, Aquarius, Capricorn & Jones Ltd.	1967	10.00	20.00	40.00
❏ COS-104 [S]	Pisces, Aquarius, Capricorn & Jones Ltd.	1967	5.00	10.00	20.00
❏ COM-109 [M]	The Birds, the Bees & the Monkees	1968	25.00	50.00	100.00
❏ COS-109 [S]	The Birds, the Bees & the Monkees	1968	5.00	10.00	20.00
❏ COS-113	Instant Replay	1969	10.00	20.00	40.00
❏ COS-115	The Monkees Greatest Hits	1969	10.00	20.00	40.00

Number	Title (A Side/B Side)	Yr	VG	VG+	NM
❏ COS-117	The Monkees Present	1969	12.50	25.00	50.00
❏ COS-119	Changes	1970	20.00	40.00	80.00
❏ PRS-329	The Monkees' Golden Hits	1971	25.00	50.00	100.00
—RCA Special Products edition					
❏ SCOS-1001 [(2)]	A Barrel Full of Monkees	1971	18.75	37.50	75.00
❏ COSO-5008	Head	1968	12.50	25.00	50.00

FSH

❏ 71110	Live, 20th Anniversary Tour	1987	5.00	10.00	20.00
—Live album sold at tour stops					

LAURIE HOUSE

❏ LH-8009	The Monkees	1974	5.00	10.00	20.00
—TV mail-order offer					

PAIR

❏ ARPDL2-1109 [(2)]	Hit Factory	1986	5.00	10.00	20.00

RCA SPECIAL PRODUCTS

❏ DPL2-0188 [(2)]	The Monkees	1976	6.25	12.50	25.00
—TV mail-order offer					

RHINO

❏ RNLP-113	Monkee Flips	1984	3.00	6.00	12.00
❏ RNLP-144	The Birds, the Bees and the Monkees	1985	3.00	6.00	12.00
❏ RNLP-145	Head	1985	3.00	6.00	12.00
❏ RNLP-146	Instant Replay	1985	3.00	6.00	12.00
❏ RNLP-147	The Monkees Present	1985	3.00	6.00	12.00
❏ RNLP-701 [PD]	Monkee Business	1982	3.75	7.50	15.00
❏ RNLP-70139	Live 1967	1987	3.00	6.00	12.00
❏ RNLP-70140	The Monkees	1986	3.00	6.00	12.00
❏ RNLP-70141	Pisces, Aquarius, Capricorn & Jones Ltd.	1986	3.00	6.00	12.00
❏ RNLP-70142	More of the Monkees	1986	3.00	6.00	12.00
❏ RNLP-70143	The Monkees' Headquarters	1986	3.00	6.00	12.00
❏ RNLP-70148	Changes	1986	3.00	6.00	12.00
❏ RNLP-70150	Missing Links	1987	3.00	6.00	12.00
❏ RNIN-70706	Pool It!	1987	2.50	5.00	10.00

SILHOUETTE

❏ SM-10012 [PD]	Tails of the Monkees	1983	3.75	7.50	15.00

SILVER EAGLE

❏ SE-1048 [(2)]	The Best of the Monkees	1986	3.75	7.50	15.00
—TV mail-order offer					

SUNDAZED

❏ LP 5045	The Monkees	1996	2.50	5.00	10.00
❏ LP 5046	More of the Monkees	1996	2.50	5.00	10.00
❏ LP 5047	The Monkees Headquarters	1996	2.50	5.00	10.00
❏ LP 5048	Pisces, Aquarius, Capricorn & Jones Ltd.	1996	2.50	5.00	10.00
❏ LP 5049	The Birds, the Bees, and the Monkees	1996	2.50	5.00	10.00
—All of the above are on colored vinyl with bonus tracks and posters					

MONRO, MATT
CAPITOL

❏ SKAO-152	Best of Matt Monro	1969	2.50	5.00	10.00
❏ ST 2540 [S]	This Is the Life	1966	3.75	7.50	15.00
❏ T 2540 [M]	This Is the Life	1966	3.00	6.00	12.00
❏ ST 2608 [S]	Here's to My Lady	1966	3.75	7.50	15.00
❏ T 2608 [M]	Here's to My Lady	1966	3.00	6.00	12.00
❏ ST 2683 [S]	Invitation to Broadway	1967	3.75	7.50	15.00
❏ T 2683 [M]	Invitation to Broadway	1967	3.00	6.00	12.00
❏ ST 2730 [S]	Invitation to the Movies/Born Free	1967	3.00	6.00	12.00
❏ T 2730 [M]	Invitation to the Movies/Born Free	1967	3.75	7.50	15.00
❏ ST 2801 [S]	These Years	1968	3.00	6.00	12.00
❏ T 2801 [M]	These Years	1968	3.75	7.50	15.00

LIBERTY

❏ LRP-3240 [M]	Matt Monro	1962	3.75	7.50	15.00
❏ LRP-3256 [M]	From Hollywood With Love	1962	3.75	7.50	15.00
❏ LRP-3402 [M]	Walk Away	1965	3.00	6.00	12.00
❏ LRP-3423 [M]	All My Loving	1965	3.00	6.00	12.00
❏ LRP-3437 [M]	Yesterday	1966	3.00	6.00	12.00
❏ LRP-3459 [M]	Matt Monro's Best	1966	3.00	6.00	12.00
❏ LST-7240 [S]	Matt Monro	1962	5.00	10.00	20.00
❏ LST-7256 [S]	From Hollywood With Love	1962	5.00	10.00	20.00
❏ LST-7402 [S]	Walk Away	1965	3.75	7.50	15.00
❏ LST-7423 [S]	All My Loving	1965	3.75	7.50	15.00
❏ LST-7437 [S]	Yesterday	1966	3.75	7.50	15.00
❏ LST-7459 [S]	Matt Monro's Best	1966	3.75	7.50	15.00

LONDON

❏ LL 1611 [M]	Blue and Sentimental	1957	7.50	15.00	30.00

PICKWICK

❏ SPC-3147	This Is All I Ask	197?	2.50	5.00	10.00

WARWICK

❏ W 2045 [M]	My Kind of Girl	1961	7.50	15.00	30.00
❏ WST 2045 [S]	My Kind of Girl	1961	12.50	25.00	50.00

MONROE, BILL
COLUMBIA

❏ FC 38904	Columbia Historic Editions	1983	3.00	6.00	12.00

DECCA

❏ DL 4080 [M]	Mr. Bluegrass	1960	7.50	15.00	30.00
❏ DL 4266 [M]	Bluegrass Ramble	1962	7.50	15.00	30.00
❏ DL 4327 [M]	My All Time Country Favorites	1962	6.25	12.50	25.00
❏ DL 4382 [M]	Bluegrass Special	1963	6.25	12.50	25.00
❏ DL 4537 [M]	I'll Meet You in Chuch Sunday Morning	1964	6.25	12.50	25.00
❏ DL 4601 [M]	Bluegrass Instrumentals	1965	5.00	10.00	20.00
❏ DL 4780 [M]	The High Lonesome Sound of Bill Monroe	1966	5.00	10.00	20.00
❏ DL 4896 [M]	Bluegrass Time	1967	7.50	15.00	30.00
❏ DL 8731 [M]	Knee Deep in Bluegrass	1958	12.50	25.00	50.00
❏ DL 8769 [M]	I Saw the Light	1959	12.50	25.00	50.00
❏ DL 74080 [S]	Mr. Bluegrass	1960	10.00	20.00	40.00
❏ DL 74266 [S]	Bluegrass Ramble	1962	10.00	20.00	40.00
❏ DL 74327 [S]	My All Time Country Favorites	1962	7.50	15.00	30.00
❏ DL 74382 [S]	Bluegrass Special	1963	7.50	15.00	30.00
❏ DL 74537 [S]	I'll Meet You in Church Sunday Morning	1964	7.50	15.00	30.00
❏ DL 74601 [S]	Bluegrass Instrumentals	1965	6.25	12.50	25.00
❏ DL 74780 [S]	The High Lonesome Sound of Bill Monroe	1966	6.25	12.50	25.00

Number	Title (A Side/B Side)	Yr	VG	VG+	NM
☐ DL 74896 [S]	Bluegrass Time	1967	5.00	10.00	20.00
☐ DL 75010	Bill Monroe's Greatest Hits	1968	5.00	10.00	20.00
☐ DL 75135	A Voice from On High	1969	5.00	10.00	20.00
☐ DL 75213	Kentucky Bluegrass	1970	5.00	10.00	20.00
☐ DL 75281	Country Music Hall of Fame	1972	5.00	10.00	20.00
☐ DL 78731 [M]	Knee Deep in Bluegrass	1958	17.50	35.00	70.00
☐ DL 78769 [S]	I Saw the Light	1959	17.50	35.00	70.00

HARMONY

Number	Title (A Side/B Side)	Yr	VG	VG+	NM
☐ HL 7290 [M]	The Great Bill Monroe and His Bluegrass Boys	1961	6.25	12.50	25.00
☐ HL 7315 [M]	Bill Monroe's Best	1964	5.00	10.00	20.00
☐ HL 7338 [M]	The Original Bluegrass Sound	1965	5.00	10.00	20.00
☐ HS 11335 [R]	The Great Bill Monroe and His Bluegrass Boys	1969	3.75	7.50	15.00

MCA

Number	Title (A Side/B Side)	Yr	VG	VG+	NM
☐ 17	Bill Monroe's Greatest Hits	1973	3.00	6.00	12.00
—Reissue of Decca 75010					
☐ 82	Mr. Bluegrass	1973	3.00	6.00	12.00
—Reissue of Decca 74080					
☐ 88	Bluegrass Ramble	1973	3.00	6.00	12.00
—Reissue of Decca 74266					
☐ 97	Bluegrass Special	1973	3.00	6.00	12.00
—Reissue of Decca 74382					
☐ 104	Bluegrass Instrumentals	1973	3.00	6.00	12.00
—Reissue of Decca 74601					
☐ 110	The High Lonesome Sound of Bill Monroe	1973	3.00	6.00	12.00
—Reissue of Decca 74780					
☐ 116	Bluegrass Time	1973	3.00	6.00	12.00
—Reissue of Decca 74896					
☐ 131	A Voice from On High	1973	3.00	6.00	12.00
—Reissue of Decca 75135					
☐ 136	Kentucky Bluegrass	1973	3.00	6.00	12.00
—Reissue of Decca 75213					
☐ 140	Country Music Hall of Fame	1973	3.00	6.00	12.00
—Reissue of Decca 75281					
☐ 226	I'll Meet You in Church Sunday Morning	1973	3.00	6.00	12.00
—Reissue of Decca 74537					
☐ 426	Road of Life	1974	3.75	7.50	15.00
☐ 500	Uncle Pen	197?	3.00	6.00	12.00
☐ 527	I Saw the Light	197?	3.00	6.00	12.00
—Reissue of Decca 78769					
☐ 707	Weary Traveler	198?	2.50	5.00	10.00
—Reissue of 2173					
☐ 708	Bill Monroe Sings Bluegrass, Body and Soul	198?	2.50	5.00	10.00
—Reissue of 2251					
☐ 765	Bean Blossom '79	198?	2.50	5.00	10.00
—Reissue of 3209					
☐ 2173	Weary Traveler	1976	3.75	7.50	15.00
☐ 2251	Bill Monroe Sings Bluegrass, Body and Soul	1977	3.75	7.50	15.00
☐ 2315	Bluegrass Memories	1978	3.75	7.50	15.00
☐ 3209	Bean Blossom '79	1979	3.75	7.50	15.00
☐ 4090 [(2)]	The Best of Bill Monroe	197?	3.75	7.50	15.00
☐ 5435	Bill Monroe and Friends	1984	3.00	6.00	12.00
☐ 5625	Bill Monroe and the Stars of the Bluegrass Hall of Fame	1985	3.00	6.00	12.00
☐ 8002 [(2)]	Bean Blossom	1973	5.00	10.00	20.00

RCA CAMDEN

Number	Title (A Side/B Side)	Yr	VG	VG+	NM
☐ CAL-719 [M]	Father of Bluegrass Music	1962	6.25	12.50	25.00

MONROE, CHARLIE
STARDAY

Number	Title (A Side/B Side)	Yr	VG	VG+	NM
☐ SLP-361 [M]	Lord, Build Me a Cabin	1965	6.25	12.50	25.00
☐ SLP-372 [M]	Charlie Monroe Sings Again	1966	6.25	12.50	25.00

MONROE, MARILYN
ASCOT

Number	Title (A Side/B Side)	Yr	VG	VG+	NM
☐ AM-13008 [M]	Marilyn Monroe	1963	10.00	20.00	40.00
☐ AS-16008 [S]	Marilyn Monroe	1963	12.50	25.00	50.00

MOVIETONE

Number	Title (A Side/B Side)	Yr	VG	VG+	NM
☐ 1016 [M]	The Unforgettable Marilyn Monroe	1967	6.25	12.50	25.00
☐ 72016 [R]	The Unforgettable Marilyn Monroe	1967	5.00	10.00	20.00

SANDY HOOK

Number	Title (A Side/B Side)	Yr	VG	VG+	NM
☐ SH-2013 [PD]	Rare Recordings 1948-1962	1980	6.25	12.50	25.00

STET

Number	Title (A Side/B Side)	Yr	VG	VG+	NM
☐ DS-15005	Never Before and Never Again	1980	3.75	7.50	15.00

20TH CENTURY

Number	Title (A Side/B Side)	Yr	VG	VG+	NM
☐ T-901	Remember Marilyn	1973	6.25	12.50	25.00

20TH FOX

Number	Title (A Side/B Side)	Yr	VG	VG+	NM
☐ F/SXG-5000	Marilyn Bonus Photo	1962	12.50	25.00	50.00
☐ FXG-5000 [M]	Marilyn	1962	37.50	75.00	150.00
☐ SXG-5000 [R]	Marilyn	1962	25.00	50.00	100.00

MONROE, VAUGHN
DOT

Number	Title (A Side/B Side)	Yr	VG	VG+	NM
☐ DLP-3419 [M]	Surfer's Stomp	1962	7.50	15.00	30.00
☐ DLP-3431 [M]	His Greatest Hits	1962	3.00	6.00	12.00
☐ DLP-3470 [M]	Great Themes of Famous Bands and Famous Singers	1962	3.00	6.00	12.00
☐ DLP-3548 [M]	Great Gospels — Great Hymns	1963	3.00	6.00	12.00
☐ DLP-3584 [M]	His Greatest Hits, Volume 2	1964	3.00	6.00	12.00
☐ DLP-25419 [S]	Surfer's Stomp	1962	10.00	20.00	40.00
☐ DLP-25431 [S]	His Greatest Hits	1962	3.75	7.50	15.00
☐ DLP-25470 [S]	Great Themes of Famous Bands and Famous Singers	1962	3.75	7.50	15.00
☐ DLP-25548 [S]	Great Gospels — Great Hymns	1963	3.75	7.50	15.00
☐ DLP-25584 [S]	His Greatest Hits, Volume 2	1964	3.75	7.50	15.00

HAMILTON

Number	Title (A Side/B Side)	Yr	VG	VG+	NM
☐ HLP-137 [M]	Racing with the Moon	1965	2.50	5.00	10.00
☐ HLP-12137 [S]	Racing with the Moon	1965	3.00	6.00	12.00

RCA CAMDEN

Number	Title (A Side/B Side)	Yr	VG	VG+	NM
☐ CAL-329 [M]	Dance with Me	1956	5.00	10.00	20.00
☐ CAL-354 [M]	Dreamland Special	1956	5.00	10.00	20.00

RCA VICTOR

Number	Title (A Side/B Side)	Yr	VG	VG+	NM
☐ LPM-13 [10]	Vaughn Monroe Plays Victor Herbert for Dancing	1952	10.00	20.00	40.00
☐ ANL1-1140	The Best of Vaughn Monroe	1976	2.00	4.00	8.00
☐ LPM-1493 [M]	House Party	1957	7.50	15.00	30.00
☐ LPM-1799 [M]	There I Sing, Swing It Again	1958	5.00	10.00	20.00
☐ LSP-1799 [S]	There I Sing, Swing It Again	1958	7.50	15.00	30.00
☐ LPM-3048 [10]	Vaughn Monroe's Caravan	1952	10.00	20.00	40.00
☐ LPM-3817 [M]	The Best of Vaughn Monroe	1967	5.00	10.00	20.00
☐ LSP-3817 [R]	The Best of Vaughn Monroe	1967	3.00	6.00	12.00
☐ VPM-6073 [(2)]	This Is Vaughn Monroe	1972	3.75	7.50	15.00

MONROES, THE
ALFA

Number	Title (A Side/B Side)	Yr	VG	VG+	NM
☐ AAE-15015 [EP]	The Monroes	1982	5.00	10.00	20.00

MONTAGE
LAURIE

Number	Title (A Side/B Side)	Yr	VG	VG+	NM
☐ SLP-2049	Montage	1969	5.00	10.00	20.00

MONTANA, PATSY
SIMS

Number	Title (A Side/B Side)	Yr	VG	VG+	NM
☐ 122 [M]	The New Sound of Patsy Montana	1964	12.50	25.00	50.00

STARDAY

Number	Title (A Side/B Side)	Yr	VG	VG+	NM
☐ SLP-376 [M]	Cowboy's Sweetheart	1966	7.50	15.00	30.00

MONTANA SLIM
DECCA

Number	Title (A Side/B Side)	Yr	VG	VG+	NM
☐ DL 4092 [M]	The Dynamite Trail	1960	12.50	25.00	50.00
☐ DL 8917 [M]	I'm Ragged But I'm Right	1959	15.00	30.00	60.00
☐ DL 74092 [S]	The Dynamite Trail	1960	15.00	30.00	60.00

RCA CAMDEN

Number	Title (A Side/B Side)	Yr	VG	VG+	NM
☐ CAL-527 [M]	Wilf Carter/Montana Slim	1958	10.00	20.00	40.00
☐ CAL-668 [M]	Reminiscin' with Montana Slim	1962	6.25	12.50	25.00
☐ CAL-846 [M]	32 Wonderful Years	1965	5.00	10.00	20.00
☐ CAS-846 [R]	32 Wonderful Years	1965	3.00	6.00	12.00

STARDAY

Number	Title (A Side/B Side)	Yr	VG	VG+	NM
☐ SLP-300 [M]	Wilf Carter As Montana Slim	1964	7.50	15.00	30.00
☐ SLP-389 [M]	Wilf Carter	1966	7.50	15.00	30.00

MONTE, LOU
RCA CAMDEN

Number	Title (A Side/B Side)	Yr	VG	VG+	NM
☐ CAL-455 [M]	Here's Lou Monte	195?	3.00	6.00	12.00

RCA VICTOR

Number	Title (A Side/B Side)	Yr	VG	VG+	NM
☐ LPM-1651 [M]	Lou Monte Sings for You	1957	6.25	12.50	25.00
☐ LPM-1877 [M]	Songs for Pizza Lovers	1958	6.25	12.50	25.00
☐ LPM-1976 [M]	Italian House Party	1959	5.00	10.00	20.00
☐ LSP-1976 [S]	Italian House Party	1959	6.25	12.50	25.00
☐ LPM-3672 [M]	The Best of Lou Monte	1966	3.75	7.50	15.00
☐ LSP-3672 [S]	The Best of Lou Monte	1966	3.00	6.00	12.00
☐ LPM-3705 [M]	Good Time Songs	1967	3.75	7.50	15.00
☐ LSP-3705 [S]	Good Time Songs	1967	3.00	6.00	12.00

REPRISE

Number	Title (A Side/B Side)	Yr	VG	VG+	NM
☐ R-6005 [M]	Great Italian-American Hits	1961	5.00	10.00	20.00
☐ R9-6005 [S]	Great Italian-American Hits	1961	6.25	12.50	25.00
☐ R-6014 [M]	Live in Person	1961	5.00	10.00	20.00
☐ R9-6014 [S]	Live in Person	1961	6.25	12.50	25.00
☐ R-6058 [M]	Pepino The Italian Mouse & Other Italian Fun Songs	1962	5.00	10.00	20.00
☐ R9-6058 [S]	Pepino The Italian Mouse & Other Italian Fun Songs	1962	6.25	12.50	25.00
☐ R-6099 [M]	More Italian Fun Songs	1963	5.00	10.00	20.00
☐ R9-6099 [S]	More Italian Fun Songs	1963	6.25	12.50	25.00
☐ R-6118 [M]	The Golden Hits of Lou Monte	1964	3.75	7.50	15.00
☐ RS-6118 [S]	The Golden Hits of Lou Monte	1964	5.00	10.00	20.00

ROULETTE

Number	Title (A Side/B Side)	Yr	VG	VG+	NM
☐ R-25126 [M]	Italiano U.S.A.	1960	5.00	10.00	20.00
☐ SR-25126 [S]	Italiano U.S.A.	1960	6.25	12.50	25.00
☐ R-25257 [M]	The Magic World of Italy	1963	3.75	7.50	15.00
☐ SR-25257 [S]	The Magic World of Italy	1963	5.00	10.00	20.00

MONTEGO JOE
ESP-DISK'

Number	Title (A Side/B Side)	Yr	VG	VG+	NM
☐ S-1067	Montego Joe's HARYOU Percussion Ensemble	1968	6.25	12.50	25.00

PRESTIGE

Number	Title (A Side/B Side)	Yr	VG	VG+	NM
☐ PRLP-7336 [M]	Arriba Con Montego Joe	1964	6.25	12.50	25.00
☐ PRST-7336 [S]	Arriba Con Montego Joe	1964	7.50	15.00	30.00
☐ PRLP-7413 [M]	Wild and Warm	1966	6.25	12.50	25.00
☐ PRST-7413 [S]	Wild and Warm	1966	7.50	15.00	30.00

MONTENEGRO, HUGO
Includes some of his soundtracks; others are in the "Soundtracks" and "Television Albums" sections.

BAINBRIDGE

Number	Title (A Side/B Side)	Yr	VG	VG+	NM
☐ 1002	American Musical Theatre, Volume 1 (1924-1935)	198?	2.00	4.00	8.00
☐ 1003	American Musical Theatre, Volume 2 (1935-1945)	198?	2.00	4.00	8.00
☐ 1004	American Musical Theatre, Volume 3 (1946-1952)	198?	2.00	4.00	8.00
☐ 1005	American Musical Theatre, Volume 4 (1953-1960)	198?	2.00	4.00	8.00
☐ 1009	Big Band Boogie	198?	2.00	4.00	8.00
☐ 1021	Camelot	198?	2.00	4.00	8.00
☐ 1028	Hugo Montenegro Plays the Movies	198?	2.00	4.00	8.00

GWP

Number	Title (A Side/B Side)	Yr	VG	VG+	NM
☐ 2003	The Dawn of Dylan	1971	3.75	7.50	15.00

MAINSTREAM

Number	Title (A Side/B Side)	Yr	VG	VG+	NM
☐ S-6101 [S]	Camelot	1967	3.00	6.00	12.00
☐ 56101 [M]	Camelot	1967	3.75	7.50	15.00

Number	Title (A Side/B Side)	Yr	VG	VG+	NM
RCA CAMDEN					
❏ CAL-729 [M]	In a Sentimental Mood	196?	3.00	6.00	12.00
❏ CAS-729 [S]	In a Sentimental Mood	196?	3.00	6.00	12.00
❏ CAS-2309	Hawaiian Wedding Song	1969	2.50	5.00	10.00
RCA VICTOR					
❏ ARD1-0001	Love Theme from "The Godfather"	1972	3.00	6.00	12.00
❏ APD1-0025 [Q]	Scenes and Themes	1973	5.00	10.00	20.00
❏ APL1-0413	Hugo in Wonderland	1974	3.00	6.00	12.00
❏ APD1-1024 [Q]	Rocket Man	1975	5.00	10.00	20.00
❏ APL1-1024	Rocket Man	1975	3.00	6.00	12.00
❏ ANL1-1094	Music from A Fistful of Dollars & For a Few Dollars More & The Good, The Bad and The Ugly	1975	2.50	5.00	10.00
❏ ANL1-2348	The Neil Diamond Songbook	1977	2.50	5.00	10.00
❏ LPM-3540 [M]	Come Spy with Me	1966	3.00	6.00	12.00
❏ LSP-3540 [S]	Come Spy with Me	1966	3.75	7.50	15.00
❏ LPM-3927 [M]	Music from A Fistful of Dollars & For a Few Dollars More & The Good, The Bad and The Ugly	1968	5.00	10.00	20.00
❏ LSP-3927 [S]	Music from A Fistful of Dollars & For a Few Dollars More & The Good, The Bad and The Ugly	1968	3.75	7.50	15.00
❏ LPM-4022 [M]	Hang 'Em High	1968	10.00	20.00	40.00
❏ LSP-4022 [S]	Hang 'Em High	1968	3.75	7.50	15.00
❏ LSP-4104	Good Vibrations	1969	3.75	7.50	15.00
❏ LSP-4170	Moog Power	1969	5.00	10.00	20.00
❏ LSP-4273	Colours of Love	1970	3.00	6.00	12.00
❏ AFL1-4361	The Best of Hugo Montenegro	1977	2.50	5.00	10.00
❏ LSP-4361	The Best of Hugo Montenegro	1970	3.00	6.00	12.00
❏ LSP-4537	People…One to One	1971	3.00	6.00	12.00
❏ LSP-4631	Mammy Blue	1971	3.00	6.00	12.00
❏ VPS-6036 [(2)]	This Is Hugo Montenegro	1971	3.75	7.50	15.00
TIME					
❏ S-2018 [S]	Cha Chas for Dancing	196?	5.00	10.00	20.00
❏ S-2020 [S]	Boogie Woogie and Bongos	196?	5.00	10.00	20.00
❏ S-2030 [S]	Arriba	196?	5.00	10.00	20.00
❏ S-2035 [S]	American Musical Theatre, Volume 1 (1924-1935)	196?	3.75	7.50	15.00
❏ S-2036 [S]	American Musical Theatre, Volume 2 (1935-1945)	196?	3.75	7.50	15.00
❏ S-2037 [S]	American Musical Theatre, Volume 3 (1946-1952)	1961	3.75	7.50	15.00
❏ S-2038 [S]	American Musical Theatre, Volume 4 (1953-1960)	1961	3.75	7.50	15.00
❏ S-2044 [S]	Great Songs from Motion Pictures Vol. 1 (1927-1937)	1961	3.75	7.50	15.00
❏ S-2045 [S]	Great Songs from Motion Pictures Vol. 2 (1938-1944)	1961	3.75	7.50	15.00
❏ S-2046 [S]	Great Songs from Motion Pictures Vol. 3 (1945-1960)	1961	3.75	7.50	15.00
❏ S-2051 [S]	Montenegro in Italy	196?	3.75	7.50	15.00
❏ 52018 [M]	Cha Chas for Dancing	196?	3.75	7.50	15.00
❏ 52020 [M]	Boogie Woogie and Bongos	196?	3.75	7.50	15.00
❏ 52030 [M]	Arriba	196?	3.75	7.50	15.00
❏ 52035 [M]	American Musical Theatre, Volume 1 (1924-1935)	196?	3.00	6.00	12.00
❏ 52036 [M]	American Musical Theatre, Volume 2 (1935-1945)	196?	3.00	6.00	12.00
❏ 52037 [M]	American Musical Theatre, Volume 3 (1946-1952)	1961	3.00	6.00	12.00
❏ 52038 [M]	American Musical Theatre, Volume 4 (1953-1960)	1961	3.00	6.00	12.00
❏ 52044 [M]	Great Songs from Motion Pictures Vol. 1 (1927-1937)	1961	3.00	6.00	12.00
❏ 52045 [M]	Great Songs from Motion Pictures Vol. 2 (1938-1944)	1961	3.00	6.00	12.00
❏ 52046 [M]	Great Songs from Motion Pictures Vol. 3 (1945-1960)	1961	3.00	6.00	12.00
❏ 52051 [M]	Montenegro in Italy	196?	3.00	6.00	12.00
20TH CENTURY FOX					
❏ S-4204	Lady in Cement	1968	5.00	10.00	20.00
20TH FOX					
❏ 3018 [M]	The 20th Century Strings, Volume 1	1959	5.00	10.00	20.00
VIK					
❏ LX-1089 [M]	Loves of My Life	1957	6.25	12.50	25.00
❏ LX-1106 [M]	Ellington Fantasy	1957	6.25	12.50	25.00

MONTEROSE, J.R.

Number	Title (A Side/B Side)	Yr	VG	VG+	NM
BLUE NOTE					
❏ BLP-1536 [M]	J.R. Monterose	1956	37.50	75.00	150.00
—Regular version, Lexington Ave. address on label					
❏ BLP-1536 [M]	J.R. Monterose	1956	50.00	100.00	200.00
—"Deep groove" version (deep indentation under label on both sides)					
❏ BLP-1536 [M]	J.R. Monterose	1963	6.25	12.50	25.00
—With "New York, USA" address on label					
JARO					
❏ JAM-5004 [M]	The Message	1959	100.00	200.00	400.00
❏ JAS-8004 [S]	The Message	1959	125.00	250.00	500.00
STUDIO 4					
❏ 100 [M]	J.R. Monterose in Action	195?	150.00	300.00	600.00

MONTEZ, CHRIS

Number	Title (A Side/B Side)	Yr	VG	VG+	NM
A&M					
❏ LP-115 [M]	The More I See You/Call Me	1966	5.00	10.00	20.00
❏ LP-120 [M]	Time After Time	1966	3.75	7.50	15.00
❏ LP-128 [M]	Foolin' Around	1967	3.75	7.50	15.00
❏ LP-157 [M]	Watch What Happens	1967	3.75	7.50	15.00
❏ ST-4115 [S]	The More I See You/Call Me	1966	6.25	12.50	25.00
❏ SP-4120 [S]	Time After Time	1966	5.00	10.00	20.00
❏ SP-4128 [S]	Foolin' Around	1967	5.00	10.00	20.00
❏ SP-4157 [S]	Watch What Happens	1967	5.00	10.00	20.00

Number	Title (A Side/B Side)	Yr	VG	VG+	NM
MONOGRAM					
❏ M-100 [M]	Let's Dance and Have Some Kinda' Fun!!!	1963	100.00	200.00	400.00

MONTGOMERY, BUDDY

Number	Title (A Side/B Side)	Yr	VG	VG+	NM
ABC IMPULSE!					
❏ AS-9192	This Rather Than That	1970	5.00	10.00	20.00
MILESTONE					
❏ M-9015	Two-Sided Album	1969	5.00	10.00	20.00

MONTGOMERY, DAVID, AND CECIL LYTLE

Number	Title (A Side/B Side)	Yr	VG	VG+	NM
SONIC ARTS					
❏ 6	Ragtime Piano for Four Hands	197?	5.00	10.00	20.00
—Direct-to-disc recording					

MONTGOMERY, LITTLE BROTHER

Number	Title (A Side/B Side)	Yr	VG	VG+	NM
BLUESVILLE					
❏ BVLP-1012 [M]	Tasty Blues	1961	20.00	40.00	80.00
—Blue label, silver print					
❏ BVLP-1012 [M]	Tasty Blues	1964	7.50	15.00	30.00
—Blue label with trident logo at right					
RIVERSIDE					
❏ RLP-410 [M]	Little Brother Montgomery, Chicago Living Legend	1962	7.50	15.00	30.00
❏ RS-9410 [S]	Little Brother Montgomery, Chicago Living Legend	1962	10.00	20.00	40.00

MONTGOMERY, MARIAN

Number	Title (A Side/B Side)	Yr	VG	VG+	NM
CAPITOL					
❏ ST 1884 [S]	Marian Montgomery Swings for Winners and Losers	1963	7.50	15.00	30.00
❏ T 1884 [M]	Marian Montgomery Swings for Winners and Losers	1963	6.25	12.50	25.00
❏ ST 1962 [S]	Let There Be Love, Let There Be Swing, Let There Be Marian Montgomery	1963	7.50	15.00	30.00
❏ T 1962 [M]	Let There Be Love, Let There Be Swing, Let There Be Marian Montgomery	1963	6.25	12.50	25.00
❏ ST 2185 [S]	Lovin' Is Livin'	1964	7.50	15.00	30.00
❏ T 2185 [M]	Lovin' Is Livin'	1964	6.25	12.50	25.00
DECCA					
❏ DL 4773 [M]	What's New?	1965	5.00	10.00	20.00
❏ DL 74773 [S]	What's New?	1965	6.25	12.50	25.00

MONTGOMERY, MELBA

Also see GEORGE JONES AND MELBA MONTGOMERY.

Number	Title (A Side/B Side)	Yr	VG	VG+	NM
CAPITOL					
❏ ST-328	The Big, Wonderful Country World of Melba Montgomery	1969	3.75	7.50	15.00
—This is the title on the cover; the label calls this "The Big, Beautiful Country World of Melba Montgomery"					
❏ ST-468	Don't Keep Me Lonely Too Long	1970	3.75	7.50	15.00
ELEKTRA					
❏ CM-2	Don't Let the Good Times Fool You	1975	2.50	5.00	10.00
❏ CM-6	The Greatest Gift of All	1975	2.50	5.00	10.00
❏ EKS-75069	Melba Montgomery	1973	3.00	6.00	12.00
❏ EKS-75079	No Charge	1974	2.50	5.00	10.00
HILLTOP					
❏ JS-6031	Miss Country Music	196?	3.00	6.00	12.00
MUSICOR					
❏ MM-2074 [M]	Country Girl	1966	3.75	7.50	15.00
❏ MM-2097 [M]	The Hallelujah Road	1966	3.75	7.50	15.00
❏ MM-2113 [M]	Melba Toast	1967	5.00	10.00	20.00
❏ MM-2114 [M]	Don't Keep Me Lonely Too Long	1967	5.00	10.00	20.00
❏ MS-3074 [S]	Country Girl	1966	5.00	10.00	20.00
❏ MS-3097 [S]	The Hallelujah Road	1966	5.00	10.00	20.00
❏ MS-3113 [S]	Melba Toast	1967	5.00	10.00	20.00
❏ MS-3114 [S]	Don't Keep Me Lonely Too Long	1967	5.00	10.00	20.00
STARDAY					
❏ SLP-352 [M]	Queen of Country Music	1965	6.25	12.50	25.00
UNITED ARTISTS					
❏ UAL-3341 [M]	America's Number One Country and Western Girl Singer	1964	5.00	10.00	20.00
❏ UAL-3369 [M]	Down Home	1964	5.00	10.00	20.00
❏ UAL-3391 [M]	I Can't Get Used to Being Lonely	1965	5.00	10.00	20.00
❏ UAS-6341 [S]	America's Number One Country and Western Girl Singer	1964	6.25	12.50	25.00
❏ UAS-6369 [S]	Down Home	1964	6.25	12.50	25.00
❏ UAS-6391 [S]	I Can't Get Used to Being Lonely	1965	6.25	12.50	25.00

MONTGOMERY, MONK

Number	Title (A Side/B Side)	Yr	VG	VG+	NM
CHISA					
❏ CS-801	It's Never Too Late	1970	5.00	10.00	20.00
❏ CS-806	Bass Odyssey	1971	5.00	10.00	20.00

MONTGOMERY, WES

Number	Title (A Side/B Side)	Yr	VG	VG+	NM
A&M					
❏ LP-2001 [M]	A Day in the Life	1967	5.00	10.00	20.00
DCC COMPACT CLASSICS					
❏ LPZ-2014	Goin' Out of My Head	1996	6.25	12.50	25.00
—Audiophile vinyl					
MOBILE FIDELITY					
❏ MFSL-508	Bumpin'	198?	7.50	15.00	30.00
—Audiophile vinyl					
PACIFIC JAZZ					
❏ PJ-5 [M]	Montgomeryland	1960	7.50	15.00	30.00
❏ ST-5 [S]	Montgomeryland	1960	10.00	20.00	40.00
❏ PJ-10130 [M]	Kismet	1967	5.00	10.00	20.00
❏ ST-20104 [S]	Easy Groove	1966	5.00	10.00	20.00
RIVERSIDE					
❏ RLP 12-310 [M]	New Concepts in Jazz Guitar	1959	7.50	15.00	30.00
❏ RLP 12-320 [M]	The Incredible Jazz Guitar of Wes Montgomery	1960	7.50	15.00	30.00

Number	Title (A Side/B Side)	Yr	VG	VG+	NM
❏ RLP-342 [M]	Movin' Along	1960	6.25	12.50	25.00
❏ RLP-382 [M]	So Much Guitar!	1961	6.25	12.50	25.00
❏ RLP-434 [M]	Full House	1962	7.50	15.00	30.00
❏ RLP-459 [M]	Boss Guitar	1963	5.00	10.00	20.00
❏ RLP-472 [M]	Fusion! Wes Montgomery with Strings	1964	5.00	10.00	20.00
❏ RLP 1156 [S]	New Concepts in Jazz Guitar	1959	7.50	15.00	30.00
❏ RLP 1169 [S]	The Incredible Jazz Guitar of Wes Montgomery	1960	7.50	15.00	30.00
❏ RS-9342 [S]	Movin' Along	1960	6.25	12.50	25.00
❏ RS-9382 [S]	So Much Guitar!	1961	6.25	12.50	25.00
❏ RS-9434 [S]	Full House	1962	7.50	15.00	30.00
❏ RS-9459 [S]	Boss Guitar	1963	6.25	12.50	25.00
❏ RS-9472 [S]	Fusion! Wes Montgomery with Strings	1964	6.25	12.50	25.00
❏ RS-9492 [S]	Portrait of Wes	1965	5.00	10.00	20.00
❏ RS-9494 [S]	Guitar on the Go	1965	5.00	10.00	20.00

VERVE

Number	Title (A Side/B Side)	Yr	VG	VG+	NM
❏ V6-8610 [S]	Movin' Wes	1965	5.00	10.00	20.00
❏ V6-8625 [S]	Bumpin'	1965	5.00	10.00	20.00
❏ V6-8642 [S]	Goin' Out of My Head	1966	5.00	10.00	20.00
❏ V6-8653 [S]	Tequila	1966	5.00	10.00	20.00
❏ V-8672 [M]	California Dreaming	1967	5.00	10.00	20.00
❏ V-8714 [M]	The Best of Wes Montgomery	1967	5.00	10.00	20.00

MONTGOMERY BROTHERS, THE
FANTASY

Number	Title (A Side/B Side)	Yr	VG	VG+	NM
❏ 3308 [M]	The Montgomery Brothers	1960	7.50	15.00	30.00
—Black vinyl					
❏ 3308 [M]	The Montgomery Brothers	1960	12.50	25.00	50.00
—Red vinyl					
❏ 3323 [M]	The Montgomery Brothers in Canada	1961	7.50	15.00	30.00
—Black vinyl					
❏ 3323 [M]	The Montgomery Brothers in Canada	1961	12.50	25.00	50.00
—Red vinyl					
❏ 3376 [M]	Wes' Best	1967	5.00	10.00	20.00
❏ 8052 [S]	The Montgomery Brothers	1960	6.25	12.50	25.00
—Black vinyl					
❏ 8052 [S]	The Montgomery Brothers	1960	10.00	20.00	40.00
—Blue vinyl					
❏ 8066 [S]	The Montgomery Brothers in Canada	1961	6.25	12.50	25.00
—Black vinyl					
❏ 8066 [S]	The Montgomery Brothers in Canada	1961	10.00	20.00	40.00
—Blue vinyl					

PACIFIC JAZZ

Number	Title (A Side/B Side)	Yr	VG	VG+	NM
❏ PJ-17 [M]	Wes, Buddy and Monk Montgomery	1961	7.50	15.00	30.00

RIVERSIDE

Number	Title (A Side/B Side)	Yr	VG	VG+	NM
❏ RLP-362 [M]	Groove Yard	1961	6.25	12.50	25.00
❏ RS-9362 [S]	Groove Yard	1961	7.50	15.00	30.00

WORLD PACIFIC

Number	Title (A Side/B Side)	Yr	VG	VG+	NM
❏ PJ-1240 [M]	The Montgomery Brothers and Five Others	1957	20.00	40.00	80.00
❏ WP-1240 [M]	The Montgomery Brothers and Five Others	1958	15.00	30.00	60.00
—Reissue with new prefix					

MONTROSE, JACK
ATLANTIC

Number	Title (A Side/B Side)	Yr	VG	VG+	NM
❏ 1223 [M]	Arranged, Played, Composed by Jack Montrose with Bob Gordon	1956	20.00	40.00	80.00
—Black label					
❏ 1223 [M]	Arranged, Played, Composed by Jack Montrose with Bob Gordon	1961	6.25	12.50	25.00
—Multicolor label, white "fan" logo at right					

PACIFIC JAZZ

Number	Title (A Side/B Side)	Yr	VG	VG+	NM
❏ PJ-1208 [M]	Jack Montrose Sextet	1955	20.00	40.00	80.00
—Black vinyl					
❏ PJ-1208 [M]	Jack Montrose Sextet	1955	37.50	75.00	150.00
—Red vinyl					

RCA VICTOR

Number	Title (A Side/B Side)	Yr	VG	VG+	NM
❏ LPM-1451 [M]	Blues and Vanilla	1957	12.50	25.00	50.00
❏ LPM-1572 [M]	The Horns Full	1957	12.50	25.00	50.00

WORLD PACIFIC

Number	Title (A Side/B Side)	Yr	VG	VG+	NM
❏ WP-1208 [M]	Jack Montrose Sextet	1958	12.50	25.00	50.00

MONTY PYTHON
ARISTA

Number	Title (A Side/B Side)	Yr	VG	VG+	NM
❏ SP-101 [DJ]	Monty Python's Contractural Obligation Sampler	1980	7.50	15.00	30.00
—One side is censored, the other is uncensored					
❏ AL 4039	Matching Tie & Handkerchief	1975	5.00	10.00	20.00
—Side 2 is "trick tracked," with two different routines depending on where you place the needle at the start					
❏ AL 4050	The Album of the Soundtrack of the Trailer of the Film of "Monty Python and the Holy Grail"	1975	5.00	10.00	20.00
❏ AL 4073	Monty Python Live! At City Center	1976	5.00	10.00	20.00
❏ AL 8296	The Monty Python Instant Record Collection	198?	2.00	4.00	8.00
—Reissue					
❏ AL 8343	Monty Python's Contractual Obligation Album	198?	2.00	4.00	8.00
—Reissue					
❏ AL 8353	Monty Python Live! At City Center	198?	2.00	4.00	8.00
—Reissue					
❏ AL 8355	The Album of the Soundtrack of the Trailer of the Film of "Monty Python and the Holy Grail"	198?	2.00	4.00	8.00
—Reissue					
❏ AL 8357	Matching Tie and Handkerchief	198?	2.00	4.00	8.00
—Reissue; we don't know whether Side 2 maintains the trick groove on this issue					
❏ AB 9536	Monty Python's Contractual Obligation Album	1980	5.00	10.00	20.00
❏ AB 9580	The Monty Python Instant Record Collection	1981	3.75	7.50	15.00

BBC

Number	Title (A Side/B Side)	Yr	VG	VG+	NM
❏ 22073	Monty Python's Flying Circus	1980	5.00	10.00	20.00
—Excerpts from TV shows; pressed by Columbia, possibly for exclusive use by the record club					

BUDDAH

Number	Title (A Side/B Side)	Yr	VG	VG+	NM
❏ BDS 5656 [(2)]	The Worst of Monty Python	1976	5.00	10.00	20.00
—Repackage of the two Charisma LPs					

CHARISMA

Number	Title (A Side/B Side)	Yr	VG	VG+	NM
❏ CAS 1049	Another Monty Python Record	1972	6.25	12.50	25.00
❏ CAS 1063	Monty Python's Previous Record	1972	6.25	12.50	25.00

MCA

Number	Title (A Side/B Side)	Yr	VG	VG+	NM
❏ 6121	Monty Python and the Meaning of Life	1983	3.00	6.00	12.00

PYE

Number	Title (A Side/B Side)	Yr	VG	VG+	NM
❏ 12116	Monty Python's Flying Circus	1975	5.00	10.00	20.00

VIRGIN

Number	Title (A Side/B Side)	Yr	VG	VG+	NM
❏ 90865 [(2)]	The Final Rip Off	1988	5.00	10.00	20.00

WARNER BROS.

Number	Title (A Side/B Side)	Yr	VG	VG+	NM
❏ BSK 3396	Life of Brian	1979	3.75	7.50	15.00

MOODY, CLYDE
KING

Number	Title (A Side/B Side)	Yr	VG	VG+	NM
❏ 891 [M]	The Best of Clyde Moody	1964	20.00	40.00	80.00

OLD HOMESTEAD

Number	Title (A Side/B Side)	Yr	VG	VG+	NM
❏ 90013	Moody's Blues — Bluesy Bluegrass	197?	3.75	7.50	15.00

MOODY, JAMES
ARGO

Number	Title (A Side/B Side)	Yr	VG	VG+	NM
❏ LP-603 [M]	Flute 'n the Blues	1956	10.00	20.00	40.00
—Reissue of Creative 603					
❏ LP-613 [M]	Moody's Mood for Love	1957	10.00	20.00	40.00
❏ LP-637 [M]	Last Train from Overbrook	1959	10.00	20.00	40.00
❏ LPS-637 [S]	Last Train from Overbrook	1959	7.50	15.00	30.00
❏ LP-648 [M]	James Moody	1959	10.00	20.00	40.00
❏ LPS-648 [S]	James Moody	1959	7.50	15.00	30.00
❏ LP-666 [M]	Hey! It's James Moody	1960	7.50	15.00	30.00
❏ LPS-666 [S]	Hey! It's James Moody	1960	10.00	20.00	40.00
❏ LP-679 [M]	Moody with Strings	1961	7.50	15.00	30.00
❏ LPS-679 [S]	Moody with Strings	1961	10.00	20.00	40.00
❏ LP-695 [M]	Another Bag	1962	7.50	15.00	30.00
❏ LPS-695 [S]	Another Bag	1962	10.00	20.00	40.00
❏ LP-725 [M]	Great Day	1963	6.25	12.50	25.00
❏ LPS-725 [S]	Great Day	1963	7.50	15.00	30.00
❏ LP-740 [M]	Comin' On Strong	1964	6.25	12.50	25.00
❏ LPS-740 [S]	Comin' On Strong	1964	7.50	15.00	30.00

BLUE NOTE

Number	Title (A Side/B Side)	Yr	VG	VG+	NM
❏ BLP-5005 [10]	James Moody with Strings	1952	75.00	150.00	300.00
❏ BLP-5006 [10]	James Moody and His Modernists	1952	75.00	150.00	300.00

CADET

Number	Title (A Side/B Side)	Yr	VG	VG+	NM
❏ LP-756 [M]	Cookin' the Blues	1965	5.00	10.00	20.00
❏ LPS-756 [S]	Cookin' the Blues	1965	6.25	12.50	25.00
❏ 2CA-60010 [(2)]	Everything About Sax and Flute	1972	5.00	10.00	20.00

CREATIVE

Number	Title (A Side/B Side)	Yr	VG	VG+	NM
❏ LP-603 [M]	Flute 'n Blues	1956	37.50	75.00	150.00

DIAL

Number	Title (A Side/B Side)	Yr	VG	VG+	NM
❏ LP-209 [10]	James Moody, His Saxophone and His Band	1950	100.00	200.00	400.00

EMARCY

Number	Title (A Side/B Side)	Yr	VG	VG+	NM
❏ MG-26004 [10]	The Moody Story	1954	37.50	75.00	150.00
❏ MG-26040 [10]	Moodsville	1954	37.50	75.00	150.00
❏ MG-36031 [M]	The Moody Story	1955	25.00	50.00	100.00

MILESTONE

Number	Title (A Side/B Side)	Yr	VG	VG+	NM
❏ M-9005	Brass Figures	1968	5.00	10.00	20.00
❏ M-9023	Blues and Other Colors	1970	5.00	10.00	20.00

PRESTIGE

Number	Title (A Side/B Side)	Yr	VG	VG+	NM
❏ PRLP-110 [10]	James Moody Favorites, No. 1	1951	50.00	100.00	200.00
❏ PRLP-125 [10]	James Moody Favorites, No. 2	1952	50.00	100.00	200.00
❏ PRLP-146 [10]	James Moody Favorites, No. 3	1953	50.00	100.00	200.00
❏ PRLP-157 [10]	Moody in France	1953	37.50	75.00	150.00
❏ PRLP-192 [10]	Moody's Mood	1954	37.50	75.00	150.00
❏ PRLP-198 [10]	James Moody and His Band	1954	37.50	75.00	150.00
❏ PRLP-7011 [M]	Hi-Fi Party	1955	25.00	50.00	100.00
❏ PRLP-7036 [M]	Wail, Moody, Wail	1956	25.00	50.00	100.00
❏ PRLP-7056 [M]	James Moody's Moods	1956	25.00	50.00	100.00
❏ PRLP-7072 [M]	Moody	1956	25.00	50.00	100.00
❏ PRLP-7179 [M]	Moody's Workshop	1960	12.50	25.00	50.00
❏ PRLP-7431 [M]	James Moody's Greatest Hits	1967	6.25	12.50	25.00
❏ PRLP-7441 [M]	James Moody's Greatest Hits, Volume 2	1967	6.25	12.50	25.00

ROOST

Number	Title (A Side/B Side)	Yr	VG	VG+	NM
❏ RST-405 [10]	James Moody in France	1951	62.50	125.00	250.00

SCEPTER

Number	Title (A Side/B Side)	Yr	VG	VG+	NM
❏ SPS-525 [S]	Running the Gamut	1965	6.25	12.50	25.00
❏ SRM-525 [M]	Running the Gamut	1965	5.00	10.00	20.00

MOODY, JAMES/GEORGE WALLINGTON
BLUE NOTE

Number	Title (A Side/B Side)	Yr	VG	VG+	NM
❏ B-6503 [M]	The Beginning and End of Bop	1969	7.50	15.00	30.00

MOODY, PHIL
SOMERSET

Number	Title (A Side/B Side)	Yr	VG	VG+	NM
❏ P-10400 [M]	Intimate Jazz	1959	7.50	15.00	30.00

MOODY BLUES, THE
Also see JUSTIN HAYWARD AND JOHN LODGE; RAY THOMAS.
COMPLEAT

Number	Title (A Side/B Side)	Yr	VG	VG+	NM
❏ 672008 [(2)]	Early Blues	1985	3.75	7.50	15.00
—Reissue of London 1964-66 material					

DERAM

Number	Title (A Side/B Side)	Yr	VG	VG+	NM
❏ DE 16012 [M]	Days of Future Passed	1968	62.50	125.00	250.00
❏ DES 18012 [S]	Days of Future Passed	1968	5.00	10.00	20.00
—With large "DERAM" on top half of label					
❏ DES 18012 [S]	Days of Future Passed	1968	7.50	15.00	30.00
—With "LONDON" under "DERAM" on top half of label					
❏ DES 18017 [S]	In Search of the Lost Chord	1968	5.00	10.00	20.00
—Originals have gatefold covers					
❏ DES 18025 [S]	On the Threshold of a Dream	1969	5.00	10.00	20.00
—Originals have gatefold covers and lyric booklet					
❏ DES 18051 [R]	In the Beginning	1971	5.00	10.00	20.00

Number	Title (A Side/B Side)	Yr	VG	VG+	NM
❏ 820006-1 [S]	Days of Future Passed	1985	2.00	4.00	8.00
❏ 820168-1	In Search of the Lost Chord	1985	2.00	4.00	8.00
❏ 820170-1	On the Threshold of a Dream	1985	2.00	4.00	8.00
LONDON					
❏ PS 428 [R]	Go Now — The Moody Blues #1	1965	10.00	20.00	40.00
❏ PS 690/1 [(2)]	Caught Live + 5	1977	3.00	6.00	12.00
❏ PS 708	Octave	1978	2.50	5.00	10.00
❏ PS 708 [DJ]	Octave	1978	7.50	15.00	30.00
—Promo only on blue vinyl					
❏ LL 3428 [M]	Go Now — The Moody Blues #1	1965	12.50	25.00	50.00
❏ 820161-1 [(2)]	Caught Live + 5	1985	2.00	4.00	8.00
❏ 820329-1	Octave	1986	2.00	4.00	8.00
MOBILE FIDELITY					
❏ 1-042	Days of Future Passed	1980	15.00	30.00	60.00
—Audiophile vinyl					
❏ 1-151	Seventh Sojourn	1984	17.50	35.00	70.00
—Audiophile vinyl					
❏ 1-215	On the Threshold of a Dream	1994	6.25	12.50	25.00
—Audiophile vinyl					
❏ 1-232	Every Good Boy Deserves Favour	1995	6.25	12.50	25.00
—Audiophile vinyl					
❏ 1-253	To Our Children's Children's Children	1996	15.00	30.00	60.00
—Audiophile vinyl					
NAUTILUS					
❏ NR-21	On the Threshold of a Dream	1981	12.50	25.00	50.00
—Audiophile vinyl; DBX-encoded version					
❏ NR-21	On the Threshold of a Dream	1981	15.00	30.00	60.00
—Audiophile vinyl					
POLYDOR					
❏ 829 179-1	The Other Side of Life	1986	2.50	5.00	10.00
❏ 835 756-1	Sur La Mer	1988	3.00	6.00	12.00
❏ 840 659-1	Greatest Hits (1967-1988)	1989	3.75	7.50	15.00
THRESHOLD					
❏ THS 1	To Our Children's Children's Children	1969	3.75	7.50	15.00
—White label with purple logo; gatefold cover					
❏ THS 1	To Our Children's Children's Children	197?	2.50	5.00	10.00
—Blue label; no gatefold					
❏ THS 3	A Question of Balance	197?	2.50	5.00	10.00
—Blue label; no gatefold					
❏ THS 3	A Question of Balance	1970	3.75	7.50	15.00
—White label with purple logo; gatefold cover					
❏ THS 5	Every Good Boy Deserves Favour	197?	2.50	5.00	10.00
—Blue label; no gatefold					
❏ THS 5	Every Good Boy Deserves Favour	197?	3.00	6.00	12.00
—Blue label; gatefold cover					
❏ THS 5	Every Good Boy Deserves Favour	1971	3.75	7.50	15.00
—White label with purple logo; gatefold cover					
❏ THS 7	Seventh Sojourn	197?	2.50	5.00	10.00
—Blue label; no gatefold					
❏ THS 7	Seventh Sojourn	197?	3.00	6.00	12.00
—Blue label; gatefold cover					
❏ THS 7	Seventh Sojourn	1972	3.75	7.50	15.00
—White label with purple logo; gatefold cover					
❏ THS 12/13 [(2)]	This Is the Moody Blues	1974	3.75	7.50	15.00
❏ THX-100 [DJ]	Special Interview Kit	1971	37.50	75.00	150.00
—Includes script					
❏ TR-1-2901	Long Distance Voyager	1981	2.50	5.00	10.00
❏ TR-1-2902	The Present	1982	2.50	5.00	10.00
❏ SMAS-93329	A Question of Balance	1971	5.00	10.00	20.00
—Capitol Record Club edition					
❏ 810119-1	The Present	1983	2.00	4.00	8.00
❏ 820007-1 [(2)]	This Is the Moody Blues	1985	2.00	4.00	8.00
❏ 820105-1	Long Distance Voyager	1985	2.00	4.00	8.00
❏ 820155-1	Voices in the Sky/The Best of the Moody Blues	1985	2.50	5.00	10.00
❏ 820159-1	Seventh Sojourn	1985	2.00	4.00	8.00
❏ 820160-1	Every Good Boy Deserves Favour	1985	2.00	4.00	8.00
❏ 820211-1	A Question of Balance	1985	2.00	4.00	8.00

MOOG MACHINE, THE
COLUMBIA

Number	Title (A Side/B Side)	Yr	VG	VG+	NM
❏ CS 9921	Switched-On Rock	1969	5.00	10.00	20.00
❏ CS 9959	Christmas Becomes Electric	1969	5.00	10.00	20.00

MOON, KEITH
Also see THE WHO.
TRACK/MCA

Number	Title (A Side/B Side)	Yr	VG	VG+	NM
❏ 2136	Two Sides of the Moon	1975	10.00	20.00	40.00

MOON, THE
IMPERIAL

Number	Title (A Side/B Side)	Yr	VG	VG+	NM
❏ LP-12381	Without Earth	1968	10.00	20.00	40.00
❏ LP-12444	The Moon	1969	10.00	20.00	40.00

MOONDOG
COLUMBIA

Number	Title (A Side/B Side)	Yr	VG	VG+	NM
❏ KC 30897	Moondog II	1971	6.25	12.50	25.00
COLUMBIA MASTERWORKS					
❏ MS 7335	Moondog	1969	6.25	12.50	25.00
EPIC					
❏ LG 1002 [10]	Moondog and His Friends	1954	50.00	100.00	200.00
FANTASY					
❏ OJC-1741	Moondog	1990	3.00	6.00	12.00
MUSICAL HERITAGE SOCIETY					
❏ 3803	Moondog	198?	7.50	15.00	30.00
PRESTIGE					
❏ PRLP-7042 [M]	Moondog	1956	25.00	50.00	100.00
❏ PRLP-7069 [M]	More Moondog	1957	25.00	50.00	100.00
❏ PRLP-7099 [M]	The Story of Moondog	1957	25.00	50.00	100.00

MOONEY, JOE
ATLANTIC

Number	Title (A Side/B Side)	Yr	VG	VG+	NM
❏ 1255 [M]	Lush Life	1958	10.00	20.00	40.00
—Black label					
❏ 1255 [M]	Lush Life	1961	5.00	10.00	20.00
—Multicolor label, white "fan" logo at right					
COLUMBIA					
❏ CS 8986 [S]	The Greatness of Joe Mooney	1964	5.00	10.00	20.00
DECCA					
❏ DL 5555 [10]	You Go to My Head	1955	12.50	25.00	50.00
❏ DL 8468 [M]	On the Rocks	1957	10.00	20.00	40.00

MOONGLOWS, THE
CHESS

Number	Title (A Side/B Side)	Yr	VG	VG+	NM
❏ LP 1430 [M]	Look! It's the Moonglows	1959	125.00	250.00	500.00
❏ LP 1471 [M]	The Best of Bobby Lester & the Moonglows	1962	75.00	150.00	300.00
—Black label					
❏ LP 1471 [M]	The Best of Bobby Lester & the Moonglows	1966	12.50	25.00	50.00
—Blue, fading to white label					
❏ CH-9111	Their Greatest Sides	1986	3.00	6.00	12.00
❏ CH-9193	Look! It's the Moonglows	1987	3.00	6.00	12.00
—Reissue of 1430					
CONSTELLATION					
❏ C-2 [M]	Collectors Showcase — The Moonglows	1964	12.50	25.00	50.00
—Dark blue lettering					
❏ C-2 [M]	Collectors Showcase — The Moonglows	1964	25.00	50.00	100.00
—Light blue lettering					
LOST-NITE					
❏ LP-23 [10]	The Moonglows	1981	3.00	6.00	12.00
RCA VICTOR					
❏ LSP-4722	The Return of the Moonglows	1972	3.75	7.50	15.00

MOONLIGHTERS, THE
CENTURY

Number	Title (A Side/B Side)	Yr	VG	VG+	NM
❏ 29132	An Evening with the Moonlighters	197?	5.00	10.00	20.00

MOONRAKERS, THE
SHAMLEY

Number	Title (A Side/B Side)	Yr	VG	VG+	NM
❏ 704	Together	1968	10.00	20.00	40.00

MOONSHINERS, THE
VILLAGE GATE

Number	Title (A Side/B Side)	Yr	VG	VG+	NM
❏ 2002 [M]	Breakout!	1964	5.00	10.00	20.00

MOOR, DET
Actually producer and composer Robert Mersey.
GALLANT

Number	Title (A Side/B Side)	Yr	VG	VG+	NM
❏ GT 4001 [M]	Great Jazz from Great TV	1962	10.00	20.00	40.00

MOORE, ADA
DEBUT

Number	Title (A Side/B Side)	Yr	VG	VG+	NM
❏ DLP-15 [10]	Jazz Workshop	1955	50.00	100.00	200.00

MOORE, BOB
HICKORY

Number	Title (A Side/B Side)	Yr	VG	VG+	NM
❏ LP-131 [M]	Viva Bob Moore	1965	3.75	7.50	15.00
❏ LPS-131 [S]	Viva Bob Moore	1965	5.00	10.00	20.00
MONUMENT					
❏ MLP-4005 [M]	Mexico and Other Great Hits!	1961	5.00	10.00	20.00
❏ SLP-4005 [S]	Mexico and Other Great Hits!	1961	6.25	12.50	25.00
❏ MLP-8008 [M]	Mexico	1967	3.00	6.00	12.00
❏ SLP-18008 [S]	Mexico	1967	3.75	7.50	15.00

MOORE, BOBBY, AND THE RHYTHM ACES
CHECKER

Number	Title (A Side/B Side)	Yr	VG	VG+	NM
❏ LP-3000 [M]	Searching for My Love	1966	7.50	15.00	30.00
❏ LPS-3000 [R]	Searching for My Love	1966	5.00	10.00	20.00

MOORE, BREW
FANTASY

Number	Title (A Side/B Side)	Yr	VG	VG+	NM
❏ 3222 [M]	The Brew Moore Quintet	1956	10.00	20.00	40.00
—Black vinyl					
❏ 3222 [M]	The Brew Moore Quintet	1956	20.00	40.00	80.00
—Red vinyl					
❏ 3264 [M]	Brew Moore	1958	7.50	15.00	30.00
—Black vinyl					
❏ 3264 [M]	Brew Moore	1958	12.50	25.00	50.00
—Red vinyl					
❏ 6013 [M]	Brew Moore in Europe	1962	6.25	12.50	25.00
—Black vinyl					
❏ 6013 [M]	Brew Moore in Europe	1962	10.00	20.00	40.00
—Red vinyl					
❏ 86013 [S]	Brew Moore in Europe	1962	5.00	10.00	20.00
—Black vinyl					
❏ 86013 [S]	Brew Moore in Europe	1962	7.50	15.00	30.00
—Blue vinyl					
SAVOY					
❏ MG-9028 [10]	Tenor Sax	1953	37.50	75.00	150.00

MOORE, CHARLIE, AND BILL NAPIER
KING

Number	Title (A Side/B Side)	Yr	VG	VG+	NM
❏ 828 [M]	Folk 'n' Hill	1963	12.50	25.00	50.00
❏ 880 [M]	The Best of Charlie Moore and Bill Napier	1964	12.50	25.00	50.00
❏ 917 [M]	Country Hymnal	1964	10.00	20.00	40.00
❏ 936 [M]	Songs of the Lonesome Truck Drivers	1965	7.50	15.00	30.00
❏ KS-936 [S]	Songs of the Lonesome Truck Drivers	1965	10.00	20.00	40.00
❏ 982 [M]	Country Music Goes to Viet Nam	1966	7.50	15.00	30.00
❏ KS-982 [S]	Country Music Goes to Viet Nam	1966	10.00	20.00	40.00
❏ 992 [M]	City Folks Back on the Farm	1966	7.50	15.00	30.00
❏ KS-992 [S]	City Folks Back on the Farm	1966	10.00	20.00	40.00
❏ 1014 [M]	Spectacular Instrumentals	1967	6.25	12.50	25.00
❏ KS-1014 [S]	Spectacular Instrumentals	1967	5.00	10.00	20.00

Number	Title (A Side/B Side)	Yr	VG	VG+	NM
❑ 1017 [M]	Gospel and Sacred Songs	1967	6.25	12.50	25.00
❑ KS-1017 [S]	Gospel and Sacred Songs	1967	5.00	10.00	20.00
❑ 1021 [M]	Brand New Country & Western Songs	1967	6.25	12.50	25.00
❑ KS-1021 [S]	Brand New Country & Western Songs	1967	5.00	10.00	20.00

MOORE, DANNY
EVEREST

Number	Title (A Side/B Side)	Yr	VG	VG+	NM
❑ SDBR-1211 [S]	Folk Songs from Here and There	1963	6.25	12.50	25.00
❑ LPBR-5211 [M]	Folk Songs from Here and There	1963	5.00	10.00	20.00

MOORE, DEBBY
TOP RANK

❑ RM-12-301 [M]	My Kind of Blues	1959	10.00	20.00	40.00

MOORE, DUDLEY
ATLANTIC

❑ 1403 [M]	Beyond the Fringe and All That Jazz	1963	6.25	12.50	25.00
❑ SD 1403 [S]	Beyond the Fringe and All That Jazz	1963	7.50	15.00	30.00

LONDON

❑ PS 558	Dudley Moore Trio	1969	6.25	12.50	25.00

MOORE, GATEMOUTH
AUDIO FIDEILITY

❑ AFLP-1921 [M]	Revival!	196?	15.00	30.00	60.00
❑ AFSD-5921 [S]	Revival!	196?	20.00	40.00	80.00

BLUESWAY

❑ BLS 6074	After 21 Years	1973	5.00	10.00	20.00

KING

❑ 684 [M]	Gatemouth Moore Sings Blues	1960	1250.	2500.	5000.

MOORE, JERRY
ESP-DISK'

❑ 1061	Life Is a Constant Journey Home	1968	5.00	10.00	20.00

MOORE, LATTIE
AUDIO LAB

❑ AL-1555 [M]	The Best of Lattie Moore	1960	50.00	100.00	200.00
❑ AL-1573 [M]	Country Side	1962	37.50	75.00	150.00

DERBYTOWN

❑ 102 [M]	Lattie Moore	196?	10.00	20.00	40.00

MOORE, MARILYN
BETHLEHEM

❑ BCP-73 [M]	Moody	1957	20.00	40.00	80.00

MOORE, OSCAR
CHARLIE PARKER

❑ PLP-830 [M]	The Fabulous Oscar Moore Guitar	1962	6.25	12.50	25.00
❑ PLP-830S [S]	The Fabulous Oscar Moore Guitar	1962	7.50	15.00	30.00

SKYLARK

❑ SKLP-19 [M]	Oscar Moore Trio	1954	25.00	50.00	100.00

TAMPA

❑ TP-16 [M]	Oscar Moore Trio	1957	20.00	40.00	80.00
—Colored vinyl					
❑ TP-16 [M]	Oscar Moore Trio	1958	12.50	25.00	50.00
—Black vinyl					
❑ TP-22 [M]	Galivantin' Guitar	1957	20.00	40.00	80.00
—Colored vinyl					
❑ TP-22 [M]	Galivantin' Guitar	1958	12.50	25.00	50.00
—Black vinyl					

MOORE, PHIL
CLEF

❑ MGC-635 [M]	Music for Moderns	1954	25.00	50.00	100.00

STRAND

❑ SL-1004 [M]	Polynesian Paradise	1959	10.00	20.00	40.00
❑ SLS-1004 [S]	Polynesian Paradise	1959	12.50	25.00	50.00

MOORE, REGGIE
MAINSTREAM

❑ MRL-341	Wishbone	1971	5.00	10.00	20.00
❑ MRL-380	Furioso	1972	5.00	10.00	20.00

MOORE, SCOTTY
EPIC

❑ LN 24103 [M]	The Guitar That Changed the World	1964	20.00	40.00	80.00
❑ BN 26103 [S]	The Guitar That Changed the World	1964	25.00	50.00	100.00

GUINNESS

❑ GNS-36038	What's Left	1977	3.75	7.50	15.00

MOORE, SHELLEY
ARGO

❑ LP-4016 [M]	For the First Time	1962	7.50	15.00	30.00
❑ LPS-4016 [S]	For the First Time	1962	10.00	20.00	40.00

MOORE, TIM
A SMALL RECORD COMPANY

❑ SRS-10001	Tim Moore	1974	7.50	15.00	30.00

ABC DUNHILL

❑ DSX-50132	Of Woodstock and Other Places	1973	3.00	6.00	12.00

ASYLUM

❑ 6E-179	High Contrast	1979	2.50	5.00	10.00
❑ 7E-1019	Tim Moore	1974	2.50	5.00	10.00
❑ 7E-1042	Behind the Eyes	1975	2.50	5.00	10.00
❑ 7E-1088	White Shadows	1977	2.50	5.00	10.00

ELEKTRA

❑ 60463	Flash Forward	1985	2.50	5.00	10.00

MOORE, WILD BILL
JAZZLAND

❑ JLP-38 [M]	Wild Bill's Beat	1961	7.50	15.00	30.00
❑ JLP-54 [M]	Bottom Groove	1961	7.50	15.00	30.00

Number	Title (A Side/B Side)	Yr	VG	VG+	NM
❑ JLP-938 [S]	Wild Bill's Beat	1961	10.00	20.00	40.00
❑ JLP-954 [S]	Bottom Groove	1961	10.00	20.00	40.00

MORAN, PAT
AUDIO FIDELITY

❑ AFLP-1875 [M]	This Is Pat Moran	1958	10.00	20.00	40.00
❑ AFSD-5875 [S]	This Is Pat Moran	1958	12.50	25.00	50.00

BETHLEHEM

❑ BCP-6007 [M]	Pat Moran Quartet	1956	12.50	25.00	50.00
❑ BCP-6018 [M]	While at Birdland	1957	12.50	25.00	50.00

MORATH, MAX
EPIC

❑ BN 26066 [S]	Celebrated Maestro	1963	5.00	10.00	20.00

RCA VICTOR

❑ LSO-1159	Max Morath at the Turn of the Century	1969	6.25	12.50	25.00

SAVOY

❑ MG-12091 [M]	Introducing Max Morath	196?	5.00	10.00	20.00

MOREL, TERRY
BETHLEHEM

❑ BCP-47 [M]	Songs of a Woman in Love	1956	37.50	75.00	150.00

MORELLO, JOE
INTRO

❑ 608 [M]	Joe Morello Sextet	1957	37.50	75.00	150.00

RCA VICTOR

❑ LPM-2486 [M]	It's About Time	1961	6.25	12.50	25.00
❑ LSP-2486 [S]	It's About Time	1961	7.50	15.00	30.00

MORENO, RITA
STRAND

❑ L-1039 [M]	Rita Moreno Sings	1962	7.50	15.00	30.00
❑ SL-1039 [S]	Rita Moreno Sings	1962	10.00	20.00	40.00

WYNNE

❑ WLP-103 [M]	Warm, Wild, Wonderful	1964	5.00	10.00	20.00
❑ WLP-703 [S]	Warm, Wild, Wonderful	1964	6.25	12.50	25.00

MOREY STORE BAND, THE
SOUND MACHINE

❑ 49007	Cry for the Dreamer	197?	25.00	50.00	100.00

MORGAN, DICK
RIVERSIDE

❑ RLP 12-329 [M]	Dick Morgan at the Showboat	1960	10.00	20.00	40.00
❑ RLP-347 [M]	See What I Mean?	1960	7.50	15.00	30.00
❑ RLP-383 [M]	Settin' In	1961	7.50	15.00	30.00
❑ RLP-1183 [S]	Dick Morgan at the Showboat	1960	10.00	20.00	40.00
❑ RS-9347 [S]	See What I Mean?	1960	10.00	20.00	40.00
❑ RS-9383 [S]	Settin' In	1961	10.00	20.00	40.00

MORGAN, FRANK
GENE NORMAN

❑ GNP-12 [M]	Frank Morgan	1955	30.00	60.00	120.00
—Red vinyl					

WHIPPET

❑ WLP-704 [M]	Frank Morgan	1956	25.00	50.00	100.00

MORGAN, GEORGE
COLUMBIA

❑ CL 1044 [M]	Morgan, By George	1957	12.50	25.00	50.00
❑ CL 1631 [M]	Golden Memories	1961	6.25	12.50	25.00
❑ CL 2111 [M]	Tender Lovin' Care	1964	5.00	10.00	20.00
❑ CL 2333 [M]	Red Roses for a Blue Lady	1965	5.00	10.00	20.00
❑ CS 8431 [S]	Golden Memories	1961	7.50	15.00	30.00
❑ CS 8911 [S]	Tender Lovin' Care	1964	6.25	12.50	25.00
❑ CS 9133 [S]	Red Roses for a Blue Lady	1965	6.25	12.50	25.00
❑ PC 33894	Remembering George Morgan	1975	3.00	6.00	12.00

4 STAR

❑ 002	From This Moment On	1975	3.00	6.00	12.00

MCA

❑ 422	Red Rose from the Blue Side of Town/ Somewhere Around Midnight	1974	3.00	6.00	12.00
❑ 461	Candy Mountain Melody	1974	3.00	6.00	12.00

STARDAY

❑ SLP-400	Candy Kisses	1967	6.25	12.50	25.00
❑ SLP-410	Country Hits by Candlelight	1967	6.25	12.50	25.00
❑ SLP-413	Steal Away	1968	5.00	10.00	20.00
❑ SLP-417	Barbara	1969	5.00	10.00	20.00

STOP

❑ 10009	George Morgan Sings Like a Bird	1969	3.75	7.50	15.00

MORGAN, JANE
ABC

❑ S-638	A Jane Morgan Happening	1968	3.00	6.00	12.00

COLPIX

❑ CP 469 [M]	The Last Time I Saw Paris	1964	5.00	10.00	20.00
❑ SCP 469 [S]	The Last Time I Saw Paris	1964	6.25	12.50	25.00
❑ CP 497 [M]	The Jane Morgan Album	1966	3.75	7.50	15.00
❑ SCP 497 [S]	The Jane Morgan Album	1966	5.00	10.00	20.00

EPIC

❑ LN 24166 [M]	In My Style	1965	3.00	6.00	12.00
❑ LN 24166 [M]	Today's Hits...Tomorrow's Golden Favorites	1966	3.00	6.00	12.00
❑ LN 24211 [M]	Fresh Flavor	1966	3.00	6.00	12.00
❑ LN 24247 [M]	Kiss Tomorrow Goodbye	1967	3.75	7.50	15.00
❑ BN 26166 [S]	In My Style	1965	3.75	7.50	15.00
❑ BN 26190 [S]	Today's Hits...Tomorrow's Golden Favorites	1966	3.75	7.50	15.00
❑ BN 26211 [S]	Fresh Flavor	1966	3.75	7.50	15.00
❑ BN 26247 [S]	Kiss Tomorrow Goodbye	1967	3.00	6.00	12.00

HARMONY

❑ HS 11398	Sounds of Silence	1970	2.50	5.00	10.00

Number	Title (A Side/B Side)	Yr	VG	VG+	NM
KAPP					
❑ KJM-1 [DJ]	Radio Station Sampler	196?	6.25	12.50	25.00
—Promo only, gatefold cover					
❑ KL-1023 [M]	Jane Morgan	1956	7.50	15.00	30.00
❑ KL-1066 [M]	Fascination	1957	7.50	15.00	30.00
❑ KL-1080 [M]	All the Way	1958	7.50	15.00	30.00
❑ KL-1089 [M]	Something Old, New, Borrowed, Blue	1958	7.50	15.00	30.00
❑ KL-1089S [S]	Something Old, New, Borrowed, Blue	1958	10.00	20.00	40.00
❑ KL-1093 [M]	Jane Morgan	1958	7.50	15.00	30.00
❑ KL-1105 [M]	The Day the Rains Came	1958	7.50	15.00	30.00
❑ KL-1105S [S]	The Day the Rains Came	1958	10.00	20.00	40.00
❑ KL-1129 [M]	Jane in Spain	1959	6.25	12.50	25.00
❑ KL-1170 [M]	Jane Morgan Time	1959	5.00	10.00	20.00
❑ KL-1191 [M]	Ballads of Lady Jane	1960	3.75	7.50	15.00
❑ KL-1239 [M]	Second Time Around	1961	3.75	7.50	15.00
❑ KL-1246 [M]	The Great Golden Hits	1961	3.75	7.50	15.00
❑ KL-1247 [M]	Big Hits from Broadway	1961	3.75	7.50	15.00
❑ KL-1250 [M]	Love Makes the World Go 'Round	1961	3.75	7.50	15.00
❑ KL-1268 [M]	Jane Morgan at the Cocoanut Grove	1962	3.75	7.50	15.00
❑ KL-1275 [M]	More Golden Hits	1962	3.75	7.50	15.00
❑ KL-1296 [M]	What Now My Love	1962	3.75	7.50	15.00
❑ KL-1329 [M]	Jane Morgan's Greatest Hits	1963	3.00	6.00	12.00
❑ KS-3001 [S]	Broadway in Stereo	1959	7.50	15.00	30.00
❑ KS-3014 [S]	Jane in Spain	1959	7.50	15.00	30.00
❑ KS-3017 [S]	Fascination	1959	7.50	15.00	30.00
❑ KS-3054 [S]	Jane Morgan Time	1959	6.25	12.50	25.00
❑ KS-3066 [S]	Fascination	1962	5.00	10.00	20.00
❑ KS-3191 [S]	Ballads of Lady Jane	1960	5.00	10.00	20.00
❑ KS-3239 [S]	Second Time Around	1961	5.00	10.00	20.00
❑ KS-3246 [S]	The Great Golden Hits	1961	5.00	10.00	20.00
❑ KS-3247 [S]	Big Hits from Broadway	1961	5.00	10.00	20.00
❑ KS-3250 [S]	Love Makes the World Go 'Round	1961	5.00	10.00	20.00
❑ KS-3268 [S]	Jane Morgan at the Cocoanut Grove	1962	5.00	10.00	20.00
❑ KS-3275 [S]	More Golden Hits	1962	5.00	10.00	20.00
❑ KS-3296 [S]	What Now My Love	1962	5.00	10.00	20.00
❑ KS-3329 [S]	Jane Morgan's Greatest Hits	1963	3.75	7.50	15.00
❑ UXL-5006 [(2)M]	Great Songs from the Great Shows of the Century	195?	10.00	20.00	40.00
MCA					
❑ 537	Jane Morgan's Greatest Hits	197?	2.50	5.00	10.00
RCA VICTOR					
❑ LSP-4171	Traces of Love	1969	3.00	6.00	12.00
❑ LSP-4322	Jane Morgan in Nashville	1970	3.00	6.00	12.00
MORGAN, JAYE P.					
MGM					
❑ E-3774 [M]	Slow and Easy	1959	6.25	12.50	25.00
❑ SE-3774 [S]	Slow and Easy	1959	7.50	15.00	30.00
❑ E-3830 [M]	Up North	1960	6.25	12.50	25.00
❑ SE-3830 [S]	Up North	1960	7.50	15.00	30.00
❑ E-3867 [M]	Down South	1960	6.25	12.50	25.00
❑ SE-3867 [S]	Down South	1960	7.50	15.00	30.00
❑ E-3940 [M]	That Country Sound	1961	6.25	12.50	25.00
❑ SE-3940 [S]	That Country Sound	1961	7.50	15.00	30.00
RCA VICTOR					
❑ LPM-1155 [M]	Jaye P. Morgan	1955	12.50	25.00	50.00
RONDO-LETTE					
❑ A-13 [M]	Jaye P. Morgan Sings	1958	6.25	12.50	25.00
MORGAN, LEE					
BLUE NOTE					
❑ BLP-1538 [M]	Lee Morgan Indeed!	1957	50.00	100.00	200.00
—Regular edition, Lexington Ave. address on label					
❑ BLP-1538 [M]	Lee Morgan Indeed!	1957	62.50	125.00	250.00
—"Deep groove" version (deep indentation under label on both sides)					
❑ BLP-1538 [M]	Lee Morgan Indeed!	1963	6.25	12.50	25.00
—"New York, USA" address on label					
❑ BLP-1541 [M]	Lee Morgan, Volume 2	1957	50.00	100.00	200.00
—Regular edition, Lexington Ave. address on label					
❑ BLP-1541 [M]	Lee Morgan, Volume 2	1957	62.50	125.00	250.00
—"Deep groove" version (deep indentation under label on both sides)					
❑ BLP-1541 [M]	Lee Morgan, Volume 2	1963	6.25	12.50	25.00
—"New York, USA" address on label					
❑ BLP-1557 [M]	Lee Morgan, Volume 3	1957	25.00	50.00	100.00
—Regular edition, W. 63rd St. address on label					
❑ BLP-1557 [M]	Lee Morgan, Volume 3	1957	37.50	75.00	150.00
—"Deep groove" version (deep indentation under label on both sides)					
❑ BLP-1557 [M]	Lee Morgan, Volume 3	1963	6.25	12.50	25.00
—"New York, USA" address on label					
❑ BLP-1575 [M]	City Lights	1958	25.00	50.00	100.00
—Regular edition, W. 63rd St. address on label					
❑ BLP-1575 [M]	City Lights	1958	37.50	75.00	150.00
—"Deep groove" version (deep indentation under label on both sides)					
❑ BLP-1575 [M]	City Lights	1963	6.25	12.50	25.00
—"New York, USA" address on label					
❑ BST-1575 [S]	City Lights	1959	20.00	40.00	80.00
—Regular edition, W. 63rd St. address on label					
❑ BST-1575 [S]	City Lights	1959	25.00	50.00	100.00
—"Deep groove" version (deep indentation under label on both sides)					
❑ BST-1575 [S]	City Lights	1963	5.00	10.00	20.00
—"New York, USA" address on label					
❑ BLP-1578 [M]	The Cooker	1958	25.00	50.00	100.00
—Regular edition, W. 63rd St. address on label					
❑ BLP-1578 [M]	The Cooker	1958	37.50	75.00	150.00
—"Deep groove" version (deep indentation under label on both sides)					
❑ BLP-1578 [M]	The Cooker	1963	6.25	12.50	25.00
—"New York, USA" address on label					
❑ BST-1578 [S]	The Cooker	1959	20.00	40.00	80.00
—Regular edition, W. 63rd St. address on label					
❑ BST-1578 [S]	The Cooker	1959	25.00	50.00	100.00
—"Deep groove" version (deep indentation under label on both sides)					

Number	Title (A Side/B Side)	Yr	VG	VG+	NM
❑ BST-1578 [S]	The Cooker	1963	5.00	10.00	20.00
—"New York, USA" address on label					
❑ BLP-1590 [M]	Candy	1958	25.00	50.00	100.00
—Regular edition, W. 63rd St. address on label					
❑ BLP-1590 [M]	Candy	1958	37.50	75.00	150.00
—"Deep groove" version (deep indentation under label on both sides)					
❑ BLP-1590 [M]	Candy	1963	6.25	12.50	25.00
—"New York, USA" address on label					
❑ BST-1590 [S]	Candy	1959	20.00	40.00	80.00
—Regular edition, W. 63rd St. address on label					
❑ BST-1590 [S]	Candy	1959	25.00	50.00	100.00
—"Deep groove" version (deep indentation under label on both sides)					
❑ BST-1590 [S]	Candy	1963	5.00	10.00	20.00
—"New York, USA" address on label					
❑ BLP-4034 [M]	Lee-Way	1960	20.00	40.00	80.00
—Regular edition, W. 63rd St. address on label					
❑ BLP-4034 [M]	Lee-Way	1960	30.00	60.00	120.00
—"Deep groove" version (deep indentation under label on both sides)					
❑ BLP-4034 [M]	Lee-Way	1963	6.25	12.50	25.00
—"New York, USA" address on label					
❑ BLP-4157 [M]	The Sidewinder	1964	7.50	15.00	30.00
❑ BLP-4169 [M]	Search for the New Land	1965	7.50	15.00	30.00
❑ BLP-4199 [M]	The Rumproller	1966	7.50	15.00	30.00
❑ BLP-4212 [M]	The Gigolo	1966	7.50	15.00	30.00
❑ BLP-4222 [M]	Cornbread	1967	7.50	15.00	30.00
❑ BLP-4243 [M]	Delightfulee Morgan	1967	10.00	20.00	40.00
❑ BST-84034 [S]	Lee-Way	1960	12.50	25.00	50.00
—Regular edition, W. 63rd St. address on label					
❑ BST-84034 [S]	Lee-Way	1963	5.00	10.00	20.00
—"New York, USA" address on label					
❑ BST-84157 [S]	The Sidewinder	1964	10.00	20.00	40.00
—"New York, USA" address on label					
❑ BST-84169 [S]	Search for the New Land	1965	10.00	20.00	40.00
—"New York, USA" address on label					
❑ BST-84199 [S]	The Rumproller	1966	10.00	20.00	40.00
—"New York, USA" address on label					
❑ BST-84212 [S]	The Gigolo	1966	10.00	20.00	40.00
—"New York, USA" address on label					
❑ BST-84222 [S]	Cornbread	1967	10.00	20.00	40.00
—"New York, USA" address on label					
❑ BST-84243 [S]	Delightfulee Morgan	1967	7.50	15.00	30.00
—"New York, USA" address on label					
❑ BST-84289	Caramba!	1969	6.25	12.50	25.00
❑ BST-84312	Charisma	1969	6.25	12.50	25.00
❑ BST-84335	The Sixth Sense	1969	6.25	12.50	25.00
❑ BST-84901 [(2)]	Lee Morgan	1972	5.00	10.00	20.00
❑ BST-89906 [(2)]	Lee Morgan at the Lighthouse	1970	6.25	12.50	25.00
GNP CRESCENDO					
❑ GNP-2079 [(2)]	Lee Morgan	1973	5.00	10.00	20.00
JAZZLAND					
❑ JLP-80 [M]	Take Twelve	1962	7.50	15.00	30.00
❑ JLP-980 [S]	Take Twelve	1962	10.00	20.00	40.00
MOSAIC					
❑ MQ6-162 [(6)]	The Complete Blue Note Lee Morgan Fifties Sessions	199?	25.00	50.00	100.00
SAVOY					
❑ MG-12091 [M]	Introducing Lee Morgan	1956	50.00	100.00	200.00
VEE JAY					
❑ VJ-2508 [M]	Lee Morgan Quintet	1965	7.50	15.00	30.00
❑ VJS-2508 [S]	Lee Morgan Quintet	1965	10.00	20.00	40.00
❑ LP-3007 [M]	Here's Lee Morgan	1960	7.50	15.00	30.00
❑ SR-3007 [S]	Here's Lee Morgan	1960	10.00	20.00	40.00
❑ LP-3015 [M]	Expoobident	1960	7.50	15.00	30.00
❑ SR-3015 [S]	Expoobident	1960	10.00	20.00	40.00
MORGAN, LORRIE					
RCA					
❑ 9594-1-R	Leave the Light On	1989	3.00	6.00	12.00
❑ R 183848	Something in Red	1991	5.00	10.00	20.00
—Only available on vinyl through BMG Direct Marketing					
MORGAN, RUSS					
DECCA					
❑ DXB 196 [(2)M]	The Best of Russ Morgan	1965	5.00	10.00	20.00
❑ DL 5098 [10]	Music in the Morgan Manner	1950	7.50	15.00	30.00
❑ DL 5278 [10]	College Marching Songs	195?	7.50	15.00	30.00
❑ DL 5324 [10]	Morgan-Airs	1951	7.50	15.00	30.00
❑ DL 5406 [10]	Everybody Dance to the Music of Russ Morgan	195?	7.50	15.00	30.00
❑ DL 8332 [M]	Does Your Heart Beat for Me	1956	5.00	10.00	20.00
—Black label, silver print					
❑ DL 8336 [M]	Tap Dancing for Pleasure	1956	5.00	10.00	20.00
—Black label, silver print					
❑ DL 8337 [M]	Everybody Dance	1956	5.00	10.00	20.00
—Black label, silver print					
❑ DL 8423 [M]	A Lovely Way to Spend an Evening (Songs of Jimmy McHugh)	1957	5.00	10.00	20.00
—Black label, silver print					
❑ DL 8581 [M]	Cheerful Little Earful (Songs of Harry Warren)	195?	5.00	10.00	20.00
—Black label, silver print					
❑ DL 8642 [M]	Velvet Violins	1957	5.00	10.00	20.00
—Black label, silver print					
❑ DL 8746 [M]	Kitten on the Keys	195?	5.00	10.00	20.00
—Black label, silver print					
❑ DL 8828 [M]	Songs Everybody Knows	1958	5.00	10.00	20.00
—Black label, silver print					
❑ DL 78828 [S]	Songs Everybody Knows	1958	6.25	12.50	25.00
—Black label, silver print					
VEE JAY					
❑ VJS-1125 [S]	His Greatest Hits	1964	5.00	10.00	20.00
❑ VJS-1139 [S]	Red Roses for a Blue Lady	1965	5.00	10.00	20.00

Number	Title (A Side/B Side)	Yr	VG	VG+	NM

MORGEN
PROBE
| ❏ CPLP-4507 | Morgen | 1969 | 37.50 | 75.00 | 150.00 |

MORLY GREY
STARSHINE
| ❏ 69000 | The Only Truth | 1969 | 50.00 | 100.00 | 200.00 |

MORMON TABERNACLE CHOIR
BOOK-OF-THE-MONTH
| ❏ 71-6406 [(3)] | Christmas Celebration | 1980 | 6.25 | 12.50 | 25.00 |

—Contains 20-page lyric booklet

CBS MASTERWORKS
❏ IM 36661	The Power and the Glory	1981	2.50	5.00	10.00
❏ FM 37200	When You Wish Upon a Star	1981	2.50	5.00	10.00
❏ IM 37206	Silent Night — The Greatest Hits of Christmas	1981	3.00	6.00	12.00
❏ FM 37286	The Twenties	1982	2.50	5.00	10.00
❏ FM 37297	Gloria!	1982	2.50	5.00	10.00
❏ M 37828	Serenade	1985	2.50	5.00	10.00
❏ MG 37853 [(2)]	The Greatest Hits of Christmas	1982	3.75	7.50	15.00
❏ XM 38299	Christmas Carols Around the World	1982	2.00	4.00	8.00
❏ IM 39034	Faith of Our Fathers	1984	2.50	5.00	10.00
❏ M2X 39102 [(2)]	The Great Choruses of Bach and Handel	1984	3.00	6.00	12.00

COLUMBIA HOUSE
❏ 6P 6007 [(6)]	The Mormon Tabernacle Choir	1973	7.50	15.00	30.00
❏ 1P 6008	What Child Is This	1973	3.00	6.00	12.00
❏ 1P 6075	Christmas with the Mormon Tabernacle Choir	1973	2.50	5.00	10.00
❏ 3P 6240 [(3)]	The Mormon Tabernacle Choir's Greatest Hits (Includes Christmas with the Mormon Tabernacle Choir)	1974	4.50	9.00	18.00
❏ 2P 7437 [(2)]	The Mormon Tabernacle Choir Christmas Treasury	1982	3.75	7.50	15.00

COLUMBIA LIMITED EDITION
| ❏ LE 10091 | Christmas Carols Around the World | 1976 | 2.50 | 5.00 | 10.00 |
| ❏ LE 10461 | Hymns and Songs of Brotherhood | 197? | 2.00 | 4.00 | 8.00 |

COLUMBIA MASTERWORKS
| ❏ M2L 263 [(2)M] | Handel: Messiah | 1959 | 5.00 | 10.00 | 20.00 |

—Gray and black labels with six "eye" logos

❏ M2L 286 [(2)M]	Brahms: A German Requiem Sung in English	1963	3.75	7.50	15.00
❏ M2L 303 [(2)M]	This Is My Country	1963	3.75	7.50	15.00
❏ M2S 607 [(2)S]	Handel: Messiah	1959	6.25	12.50	25.00

—Gray and black labels with six "eye" logos

| ❏ M2S 686 [(2)S] | Brahms: A German Requiem Sung in English | 1963 | 5.00 | 10.00 | 20.00 |

—Gray label, "360 Sound Stereo" in black

| ❏ M2S 703 [(2)S] | This Is My Country | 1963 | 5.00 | 10.00 | 20.00 |

—Gray label, "360 Sound Stereo" in black; not to be confused with the single-record LP of the same name

| ❏ ML 2077 [10] | The Mormon Tabernacle Choir of Salt Lake City | 1949 | 10.00 | 20.00 | 40.00 |

—Their first album

| ❏ ML 2098 [10] | The Mormon Tabernacle Choir of Salt Lake City Volume II | 1950 | 7.50 | 15.00 | 30.00 |
| ❏ ML 4789 [M] | The Mormon Tabernacle Choir of Salt Lake City | 195? | 6.25 | 12.50 | 25.00 |

—Reissue of two 10-inch LPs onto one 12-inch LP

❏ ML 5048 [M]	Concert of Sacred Music	1955	5.00	10.00	20.00
❏ ML 5203 [M]	Songs of Faith and Devotion	1957	5.00	10.00	20.00
❏ ML 5222 [M]	The Mormon Tabernacle Choir Sings Christmas Carols	1957	5.00	10.00	20.00
❏ ML 5302 [M]	The Lord Is My Shepherd	1958	3.75	7.50	15.00

—Gray and black label with six "eye" logos

| ❏ ML 5364 [M] | The Beloved Choruses | 1958 | 3.75 | 7.50 | 15.00 |

—Gray and black label with six "eye" logos

| ❏ ML 5386 [M] | The Lord's Prayer | 1959 | 3.75 | 7.50 | 15.00 |

—Gray and black label with six "eye" logos

| ❏ ML 5423 [M] | The Spirit of Christmas | 1959 | 3.00 | 6.00 | 12.00 |
| ❏ ML 5497 [M] | A Mighty Fortress | 1960 | 3.00 | 6.00 | 12.00 |

—Gray and black label with six "eye" logos

| ❏ ML 5592 [M] | The Holly and the Ivy | 1960 | 3.00 | 6.00 | 12.00 |
| ❏ ML 5659 [M] | Songs of the North & South 1861-1865 | 1961 | 3.00 | 6.00 | 12.00 |

—Gray and black label with six "eye" logos

❏ ML 5684 [M]	Christmas Carols Around the World	1961	3.00	6.00	12.00
❏ ML 5714 [M]	Hymns and Songs of Brotherhood	1962	3.00	6.00	12.00
❏ ML 5767 [M]	The Lord's Prayer Volume II	1962	3.00	6.00	12.00
❏ ML 5819 [M]	This Is My Country	1962	3.00	6.00	12.00
❏ ML 5899 [M]	The Joy of Christmas	1963	3.00	6.00	12.00

—With the New York Philharmonic conducted by Leonard Bernstein

| ❏ ML 6019 [M] | The Mormon Tabernacle Choir at the World's Fair | 1964 | 5.00 | 10.00 | 20.00 |
| ❏ MS 6019 [S] | The Lord Is My Shepherd | 1958 | 5.00 | 10.00 | 20.00 |

—Gray and black label with six "eye" logos

| ❏ MS 6058 [S] | The Beloved Choruses | 1958 | 5.00 | 10.00 | 20.00 |

—Gray and black label with six "eye" logos

| ❏ MS 6068 [S] | The Lord's Prayer | 1959 | 5.00 | 10.00 | 20.00 |

—Gray and black label with six "eye" logos

| ❏ ML 6079 [M] | Beloved Choruses Volume Two | 1964 | 3.00 | 6.00 | 12.00 |
| ❏ MS 6100 [S] | The Spirit of Christmas | 1959 | 3.75 | 7.50 | 15.00 |

—Same as ML 5500, but in stereo

❏ ML 6121 [M]	God Bless America	1965	3.00	6.00	12.00
❏ ML 6147 [M]	This Land Is Your Land	1965	3.00	6.00	12.00
❏ MS 6162 [S]	A Mighty Fortress	1960	3.75	7.50	15.00

—Gray and black label with six "eye" logos

| ❏ ML 6177 [M] | The Mormon Tabernacle Choir Sings Christmas Carols | 1965 | 3.00 | 6.00 | 12.00 |

—A new recording of ML 5222

| ❏ MS 6192 [S] | The Holly and the Ivy | 1960 | 3.75 | 7.50 | 15.00 |

—Same as ML 5592, but in stereo

| ❏ ML 6235 [M] | Bless This House | 1966 | 2.50 | 5.00 | 10.00 |
| ❏ MS 6259 [S] | Songs of the North & South 1861-1865 | 1961 | 3.75 | 7.50 | 15.00 |

—Gray and black label with six "eye" logos

| ❏ MS 6284 [S] | Christmas Carols Around the World | 1961 | 3.75 | 7.50 | 15.00 |

—Same as ML 5684, but in stereo

❏ ML 6308 [M]	Sing Unto God	1966	2.50	5.00	10.00
❏ MS 6314 [S]	Hymns and Songs of Brotherhood	1962	3.75	7.50	15.00
❏ ML 6351 [M]	The Mormon Tabernacle Choir's Greatest Hits	1966	2.50	5.00	10.00
❏ MS 6367 [S]	The Lord's Prayer Volume II	1962	3.75	7.50	15.00
❏ ML 6412 [M]	The Old Beloved Songs	1967	3.00	6.00	12.00
❏ MS 6419 [S]	This Is My Country	1962	3.75	7.50	15.00
❏ ML 6461 [M]	Anvil Chorus: Favorite Opera Choruses	1967	3.00	6.00	12.00
❏ ML 6486 [M]	The Mormon Tabernacle Choir's Greatest Hits, Volume 2	1967	3.00	6.00	12.00
❏ MS 6499 [S]	The Joy of Christmas	1963	3.75	7.50	15.00

—Same as ML 5899, but in stereo

❏ MS 6619 [S]	The Mormon Tabernacle Choir at the World's Fair	1964	6.25	12.50	25.00
❏ MS 6679 [S]	Beloved Choruses Volume Two	1964	3.75	7.50	15.00
❏ MS 6721 [S]	God Bless America	1965	3.75	7.50	15.00
❏ MS 6747 [S]	This Land Is Your Land	1965	3.75	7.50	15.00
❏ MS 6777 [S]	The Mormon Tabernacle Choir Sings Christmas Carols	1965	3.75	7.50	15.00

—Same as ML 6177, but in stereo

❏ MS 6835 [S]	Bless This House	1966	3.00	6.00	12.00
❏ MS 6908 [S]	Sing Unto God	1966	3.00	6.00	12.00
❏ MS 6951 [S]	The Mormon Tabernacle Choir's Greatest Hits	1966	3.00	6.00	12.00

—Same as ML 6351, but in stereo

❏ MS 7012 [S]	The Old Beloved Songs	1967	3.00	6.00	12.00
❏ MS 7061 [S]	Anvil Chorus: Favorite Opera Choruses	1967	3.00	6.00	12.00
❏ MS 7086 [S]	The Mormon Tabernacle Choir's Greatest Hits, Volume 2	1967	3.00	6.00	12.00
❏ MS 7149	Beautiful Dreamer	1968	3.00	6.00	12.00

—Gray "360 Sound" label

| ❏ MS 7292 | Hallelujah Chorus: The Great Handel Choruses | 1969 | 3.00 | 6.00 | 12.00 |

—Gray "360 Sound" label

| ❏ MS 7399 | The Mormon Tabernacle Choir's Greatest Hits, Volume 3 | 1970 | 3.00 | 6.00 | 12.00 |
| ❏ MS 7405 | Jesu, Joy of Man's Desiring: The Great Bach Choruses | 1970 | 3.00 | 6.00 | 12.00 |

—Gray "360 Sound" label

❏ M 30054	God of Our Fathers	1970	3.00	6.00	12.00
❏ M 30077	Joy to the World	1970	3.00	6.00	12.00
❏ XM 30077	Joy to the World	197?	2.50	5.00	10.00

—Reissue of M 30077

❏ M 30647	Climb Every Mountain	1971	2.50	5.00	10.00
❏ MG 31081 [(2)]	The Mormon Tabernacle Choir Album	1972	3.75	7.50	15.00
❏ M 32227	Cielito Lindo — The Mormon Tabernacle Choir En Espanol	1973	3.00	6.00	12.00
❏ M 32298	Stars & Stripes Forever	1973	2.50	5.00	10.00
❏ M 32935	The Great "Messiah" Choruses	1974	2.50	5.00	10.00
❏ M 33440	Music and the Spoken Word	1975	2.50	5.00	10.00
❏ MG 33710 [(2)]	Rock of Ages	1975	3.00	6.00	12.00
❏ M 34134	A Jubilant Song	1976	2.50	5.00	10.00
❏ M 34538	Songs of Thanks	1977	2.50	5.00	10.00
❏ M 34546	White Christmas	1977	3.00	6.00	12.00

—In box with insert of Christmas recipes

❏ M 35120	Hail to the Victors!	1978	2.50	5.00	10.00
❏ M 35148	Robertson: Oratorio from the Book of Mormon	1978	2.50	5.00	10.00
❏ M 35825	Memories: Songs America Loves Best	1980	2.50	5.00	10.00
❏ M 35868	Beyond the Blue Horizon	1980	2.50	5.00	10.00

COLUMBIA SPECIAL PRODUCTS
| ❏ CSS 1667 | The Mormon Tabernacle Choir in South Carolina — Tricentennial Concert | 1970 | 5.00 | 10.00 | 20.00 |
| ❏ P 14243 | Nearer My God to Thee | 1977 | 3.00 | 6.00 | 12.00 |

—"Mfg by CBS for Covenant Recordings"

| ❏ P 14244 | Lift Thine Eyes | 1977 | 3.00 | 6.00 | 12.00 |

—"Mfg by CBS for Covenant Recordings"

| ❏ P 14245 | For All the Saints | 1977 | 3.00 | 6.00 | 12.00 |

—"Mfg by CBS for Covenant Recordings"

| ❏ P 14246 | Now the Day Is Over | 1977 | 3.00 | 6.00 | 12.00 |

—"Mfg by CBS for Covenant Recordings"

| ❏ P 14247 | I Know That My Redeemer Lives | 1977 | 3.00 | 6.00 | 12.00 |

—"Mfg by CBS for Covenant Recordings"

| ❏ P 14303 | It's Christmas! | 1977 | 3.00 | 6.00 | 12.00 |

—"Mfg by CBS for Covenant Recordings"

| ❏ P 15935 | Songs of Faith | 1983 | 2.50 | 5.00 | 10.00 |

FRANKLIN MINT
| ❏ (no #) [(2)] | The Greatest Songs of Christmas | 1980 | 6.25 | 12.50 | 25.00 |

—Maroon vinyl; the choir's first digital recording

HARMONY
❏ HS 11272	Onward Christian Soldiers	1968	2.50	5.00	10.00
❏ HS 11370	Faith of Our Fathers	1970	3.00	6.00	12.00
❏ KH 30673	The Mormon Tabernacle Choir Sings Songs of Christmas	1971	2.50	5.00	10.00

READER'S DIGEST
❏ RD4-093 [(5)]	The Mormon Tabernacle Choir Sings	1973	6.25	12.50	25.00
❏ RBA-128/A [(4)]	Climb Ev'ry Mountain: The Mormon Tabernacle Choir Sings Great Songs of Inspiration	1988	6.25	12.50	25.00
❏ RD4A-221-1	Merry Christmas from the Mormon Tabernacle Choir	1981	2.50	5.00	10.00
❏ P2 15176/7 [(2)]	50th Anniversary Album	1980	5.00	10.00	20.00

REALM
| ❏ 3V 8039 [(3)] | The Mormon Tabernacle Choir's Greatest Hits (Includes Christmas with the Mormon Tabernacle Choir) | 197? | 3.75 | 7.50 | 15.00 |

—Reissue of Columbia House 6240

TIME-LIFE
| ❏ SMT 104 [(3)] | Christmas Celebration | 1987 | 5.00 | 10.00 | 20.00 |

—Same contents as Book-of-the-Month LP. Side 1, 2 and 6 are identical; Side 3 is BOTM's Side 5, Side 4 is BOTM's Side 3, and Side 5 is BOTM's Side 4.

Number	Title (A Side/B Side)	Yr	VG	VG+	NM

MORMON TABERNACLE ORGAN AND CHIMES
COLUMBIA MASTERWORKS

Number	Title (A Side/B Side)	Yr	VG	VG+	NM
❏ ML 6037 [M]	Christmas with the Mormon Tabernacle Organ and Chimes	1964	3.00	6.00	12.00
❏ MS 6637 [S]	Christmas with the Mormon Tabernacle Organ and Chimes	1964	3.75	7.50	15.00

MORNING DEW, THE
ROULETTE

❏ SR-42049	The Morning Dew	1970	75.00	150.00	300.00

MORNING GLORY
FONTANA

❏ SRF-67573	Two Suns Worth	1968	6.25	12.50	25.00

MORNINGLORY
TOYA

❏ STLP-003	Growing	1972	10.00	20.00	40.00

MORRIS, AUDREY
BETHLEHEM

❏ BCP-6010 [M]	The Voice of Audrey Morris	1956	30.00	60.00	120.00

MORRIS, GREG
DOT

❏ DLP-25881	For You	1968	5.00	10.00	20.00

MORRIS, MARLOWE
COLUMBIA

❏ CL 1819 [M]	Play the Thing	1962	5.00	10.00	20.00
❏ CS 8619 [S]	Play the Thing	1962	6.25	12.50	25.00

MORRISON, HAROLD
DECCA

❏ DL 4680 [M]	Hoss, He's the Boss	1965	3.75	7.50	15.00
❏ DL 74680 [S]	Hoss, He's the Boss	1965	5.00	10.00	20.00

MORRISON, VAN
BANG

❏ BLB-218 [M]	Blowin' Your Mind	1968	12.50	25.00	50.00

—With the censored "Brown Eyed Girl" lyric, "Laughin' and a-runnin', hey hey, behind the stadium with you," part of which was spliced in from another part of the song. This has been confirmed to exist in mono.

❏ BLBS-218 [S]	Blowin' Your Mind	1968	10.00	20.00	40.00

—With the censored "Brown Eyed Girl" lyric, "Laughin' and a-runnin', hey hey, behind the stadium with you," part of which was spliced in from another part of the song!

❏ BLP-218 [M]	Blowin' Your Mind	1967	7.50	15.00	30.00

—With the true "Brown Eyed Girl" lyric, "Makin' love in the green grass behind the stadium with you."

❏ BLPS-218 [S]	Blowin' Your Mind	1967	10.00	20.00	40.00

—With the true "Brown Eyed Girl" lyric, "Makin' love in the green grass behind the stadium with you."

❏ BLPS-222	The Best of Van Morrison	1970	3.75	7.50	15.00
❏ BLPS-400	T.B. Sheets	1973	5.00	10.00	20.00

DIRECT DISK

❏ SD-16604	Moondance	1981	25.00	50.00	100.00

—Audiophile vinyl

MERCURY

❏ 818336-1	Live at the Grand Opera House, Belfast	1985	2.50	5.00	10.00
❏ 822895-1	A Sense of Wonder	1985	2.00	4.00	8.00
❏ 830077-1	No Guru, No Method, No Teacher	1986	2.00	4.00	8.00
❏ 832585-1	Poetic Champions Compose	1987	2.00	4.00	8.00
❏ 834496-1	Irish Heartbeat	1988	2.00	4.00	8.00

—With the Chieftains

❏ 839262-1	Avalon Sunset	1989	2.50	5.00	10.00
❏ 841970-1	The Best of Van Morrison	1990	3.75	7.50	15.00
❏ 847100-1	Enlightenment	1990	3.75	7.50	15.00

WARNER BROS.

❏ WBMS-102 [DJ]	Live at the Roxy	1978	12.50	25.00	50.00
❏ WS 1768	Astral Weeks	1968	6.25	12.50	25.00

—With "W7" logo on green label

❏ WS 1768	Astral Weeks	1970	3.00	6.00	12.00

—With "WB" logo on green label

❏ WS 1768	Astral Weeks	1973	2.50	5.00	10.00

—"Burbank" palm-tree label

❏ WS 1768	Astral Weeks	1979	2.00	4.00	8.00

—Later white or tan label

❏ WS 1835	Moondance	1969	5.00	10.00	20.00

—With "W7" logo on green label

❏ WS 1835	Moondance	1970	3.00	6.00	12.00

—With "WB" logo on green label

❏ WS 1835	Moondance	1973	2.50	5.00	10.00

—"Burbank" palm-tree label

❏ WS 1884	His Band and the Street Choir	1970	3.75	7.50	15.00

—With "WB" logo on green label

❏ WS 1884	His Band and the Street Choir	1973	2.50	5.00	10.00

—"Burbank" palm-tree label

❏ WS 1884	His Band and the Street Choir	1979	2.00	4.00	8.00

—Later white or tan label

❏ WS 1950	Tupelo Honey	1971	3.75	7.50	15.00

—With "WB" logo on green label, plus poster

❏ WS 1950	Tupelo Honey	1973	2.50	5.00	10.00

—"Burbank" palm-tree label

❏ WS 1950	Tupelo Honey	1979	2.00	4.00	8.00

—Later white or tan label

❏ WS 2633	Saint Dominic's Preview	1972	3.75	7.50	15.00

—With "WB" logo on green label

❏ WS 2633	Saint Dominic's Preview	1973	2.50	5.00	10.00

—"Burbank" palm-tree label

❏ WS 2633	Saint Dominic's Preview	1979	2.00	4.00	8.00

—Later white or tan label

❏ BS 2712	Hard Nose the Highway	1973	3.00	6.00	12.00

—"Burbank" palm-tree label

❏ BS 2712	Hard Nose the Highway	1979	2.00	4.00	8.00

—Later white or tan label

❏ 2BS 2760 [(2)]	It's Too Late to Stop Now	1974	3.75	7.50	15.00

—"Burbank" palm-tree labels

❏ 2BS 2760 [(2)]	It's Too Late to Stop Now	1979	2.00	4.00	8.00

—Later white or tan label

❏ BS 2805	Veedon Fleece	1974	3.00	6.00	12.00

—"Burbank" palm-tree labels

❏ BS 2805	Veedon Fleece	1979	2.00	4.00	8.00

—Later white or tan label

❏ BS 2987	A Period of Transition	1977	3.00	6.00	12.00

—"Burbank" palm-tree labels

❏ BS 2987	A Period of Transition	1979	2.00	4.00	8.00

—Later white or tan label

❏ BSK 3103	Moondance	1977	2.50	5.00	10.00

—Reissue with new number; "Burbank" palm-tree label

❏ BSK 3103	Moondance	1979	2.00	4.00	8.00

—Later white or tan label

❏ BSK 3212	Wavelength	1978	3.00	6.00	12.00
❏ HS 3390	Into the Music	1979	3.00	6.00	12.00
❏ BSK 3462	Common One	1980	3.00	6.00	12.00
❏ BSK 3652	Beautiful Vision	1981	3.00	6.00	12.00
❏ 23802	Inarticulate Speech of the Heart	1983	3.00	6.00	12.00

MORRISSEY, PAT
MERCURY

❏ MG-20197 [M]	I'm Pat Morrissey, I Sing	1957	25.00	50.00	100.00

MORROW, BUDDY
EPIC

❏ LN 24095 [M]	Big Band Beatlemania	1964	6.25	12.50	25.00
❏ BN 26095 [S]	Big Band Beatlemania	1964	7.50	15.00	30.00

MERCURY

❏ MG-20062 [M]	Shall We Dance?	195?	7.50	15.00	30.00
❏ MG-20204 [M]	A Salute to the Fabulous Dorseys	1957	7.50	15.00	30.00
❏ MG-20221 [M]	Golden Trombone	1956	7.50	15.00	30.00
❏ MG-20290 [M]	Tribute to Tommy Dorsey	1957	7.50	15.00	30.00
❏ MG-20372 [M]	Just We Two	195?	7.50	15.00	30.00
❏ MG-20396 [M]	Night Train	195?	7.50	15.00	30.00
❏ MG-20702 [M]	Night Train Goes to Hollywood	1962	6.25	12.50	25.00
❏ SR-60009 [S]	Night Train	1958	10.00	20.00	40.00
❏ SR-60018 [S]	Just We Two	1958	10.00	20.00	40.00
❏ SR-60702 [S]	Night Train Goes to Hollywood	1962	7.50	15.00	30.00
❏ SR-60764 [S]	A Collection of 33 All-Time Dance Favorites	1963	5.00	10.00	20.00

RCA VICTOR

❏ LPM-1427 [M]	Night Train	1956	10.00	20.00	40.00
❏ LPM-1925 [M]	Dancing Tonight To Morrow	1958	7.50	15.00	30.00
❏ LSP-1925 [S]	Dancing Tonight To Morrow	1958	10.00	20.00	40.00
❏ LPM-2018 [M]	Big Band Guitar	1959	7.50	15.00	30.00
❏ LSP-2018 [S]	Big Band Guitar	1959	10.00	20.00	40.00
❏ LPM-2042 [M]	Impact	1959	7.50	15.00	30.00
❏ LSP-2042 [S]	Impact	1959	10.00	20.00	40.00
❏ LPM-2180 [M]	Double Impact	1960	7.50	15.00	30.00
❏ LSP-2180 [S]	Double Impact	1960	10.00	20.00	40.00
❏ LPM-2208 [M]	Poe for Moderns	1960	7.50	15.00	30.00
❏ LSP-2208 [S]	Poe for Moderns	1960	10.00	20.00	40.00

MORSE, ELLA MAE
CAPITOL

❏ H 513 [10]	Barrelhouse Boogie and the Blues	1954	100.00	200.00	400.00
❏ T 513 [M]	Barrelhouse Boogie and the Blues	1955	62.50	125.00	250.00
❏ T 898 [M]	Morse Code	1957	25.00	50.00	100.00
❏ ST 1802 [S]	Hits of Ella Mae Morse and Freddie Slack	1962	12.50	25.00	50.00
❏ T 1802 [M]	Hits of Ella Mae Morse and Freddie Slack	1962	10.00	20.00	40.00

MORSE, ROBERT, AND CHARLES NELSON REILLY
CAPITOL

❏ ST 1862 [S]	A Jolly Theatrical Christmas	1963	6.25	12.50	25.00
❏ T 1862 [M]	A Jolly Theatrical Christmas	1963	5.00	10.00	20.00

MORTIMER
PHILIPS

❏ PHS 600267	Mortimer	1969	6.25	12.50	25.00

MORTON, JELLY ROLL
CIRCLE

❏ L-14001 [M]	The Saga of Mr. Jelly Lord Volume 1: Jazz Started in New Orelans	1951	30.00	60.00	120.00
❏ L-14002 [M]	The Saga of Mr. Jelly Lord Volume 2: Way Down Yonder	1951	30.00	60.00	120.00
❏ L-14003 [M]	The Saga of Mr. Jelly Lord Volume 3: Jazz Is Strictly Music	1951	30.00	60.00	120.00
❏ L-14004 [M]	The Saga of Mr. Jelly Lord Volume 4: The Spanish Tinge	1951	30.00	60.00	120.00
❏ L-14005 [M]	The Saga of Mr. Jelly Lord Volume 5: Bad Man Ballads	1951	30.00	60.00	120.00
❏ L-14006 [M]	The Saga of Mr. Jelly Lord Volume 6: Jazz Piano Soloist #1	1951	30.00	60.00	120.00
❏ L-14007 [M]	The Saga of Mr. Jelly Lord Volume 7: Everyone Had His Style	1951	30.00	60.00	120.00
❏ L-14008 [M]	The Saga of Mr. Jelly Lord Volume 8: Jelly and the Blues	1951	30.00	60.00	120.00
❏ L-14009 [M]	The Saga of Mr. Jelly Lord Volume 9: Alabama Bound	1951	30.00	60.00	120.00
❏ L-14010 [M]	The Saga of Mr. Jelly Lord Volume 10: Jazz Piano Soloist #2	1951	30.00	60.00	120.00
❏ L-14011 [M]	The Saga of Mr. Jelly Lord Volume 11: In New Orleans	1951	30.00	60.00	120.00
❏ L-14012 [M]	The Saga of Mr. Jelly Lord Volume 12: I'm the Winin' Boy	1951	30.00	60.00	120.00

COMMODORE

❏ DL-30000 [M]	New Orleans Memories	1950	25.00	50.00	100.00

JAZZ PANORAMA

❏ 1804 [10]	Peppers	1951	25.00	50.00	100.00
❏ 1810 [10]	Peppers	1951	25.00	50.00	100.00

M

Number	Title (A Side/B Side)	Yr	VG	VG+	NM
MAINSTREAM					
❑ 56020 [M]	Jelly Roll Morton	1965	6.25	12.50	25.00
RCA VICTOR					
❑ LPT-32 [10]	A Treasury of Immortal Performances	1952	25.00	50.00	100.00
❑ LPV-508 [M]	Stomps and Joys	1965	5.00	10.00	20.00
❑ LPV-524 [M]	Hot Jazz, Pop Jazz, Hokum and Hilarity	1965	5.00	10.00	20.00
❑ LPV-546 [M]	Mr. Jelly Lord	1966	5.00	10.00	20.00
❑ LPV-559 [M]	I Thought I Heard Buddy Bolden Say	1966	5.00	10.00	20.00
❑ LPM-1649 [M]	The King of New Orleans Jazz	1957	12.50	25.00	50.00
RIVERSIDE					
❑ RLP 12-102 [M]	The New Orleans Rhythm Kings with Jelly Roll Morton	1955	12.50	25.00	50.00
❑ RLP 12-111 [M]	Classic Piano Solos	1955	12.50	25.00	50.00
❑ RLP 12-128 [M]	The Incomparable Jelly Roll Morton	1956	12.50	25.00	50.00
❑ RLP 12-132 [M]	Mr. Jelly Lord	1956	12.50	25.00	50.00
❑ RLP 12-133 [M]	Jelly Roll Morton Plays and Sings	1956	12.50	25.00	50.00
❑ RLP 12-140 [M]	Rags and Blues	1956	12.50	25.00	50.00
❑ RLP-1018 [10]	Rediscovered Solos	1953	25.00	50.00	100.00
❑ RLP-1027 [10]	Jelly Roll Morton's Kings of Jazz: His Rarest Recordings	1954	25.00	50.00	100.00
❑ RLP-1038 [10]	Classic Jazz Piano, Volume 1	1954	25.00	50.00	100.00
❑ RLP-1041 [10]	Classic Jazz Piano, Volume 2	1954	25.00	50.00	100.00
❑ RLP-9001 [M]	Library of Congress Recordings Volume 1	1955	12.50	25.00	50.00
❑ RLP-9002 [M]	Library of Congress Recordings Volume 2	1955	12.50	25.00	50.00
❑ RLP-9003 [M]	Library of Congress Recordings Volume 3	1955	12.50	25.00	50.00
❑ RLP-9004 [M]	Library of Congress Recordings Volume 4	1955	12.50	25.00	50.00
❑ RLP-9005 [M]	Library of Congress Recordings Volume 5	1955	12.50	25.00	50.00
❑ RLP-9006 [M]	Library of Congress Recordings Volume 6	1955	12.50	25.00	50.00
❑ RLP-9007 [M]	Library of Congress Recordings Volume 7	1955	12.50	25.00	50.00
❑ RLP-9008 [M]	Library of Congress Recordings Volume 8	1955	12.50	25.00	50.00
❑ RLP-9009 [M]	Library of Congress Recordings Volume 9	1955	12.50	25.00	50.00
❑ RLP-9010 [M]	Library of Congress Recordings Volume 10	1955	12.50	25.00	50.00
❑ RLP-9011 [M]	Library of Congress Recordings Volume 11	1955	12.50	25.00	50.00
❑ RLP-9012 [M]	Library of Congress Recordings Volume 12	1955	12.50	25.00	50.00
"X"					
❑ LX-3008 [10]	Red Hot Peppers, Volume 1	1954	25.00	50.00	100.00
❑ LVA-3028 [10]	Red Hot Peppers, Volume 2	1954	25.00	50.00	100.00
MOSBY, JOHNNY AND JONIE					
CAPITOL					
❑ ST-170	Just Hold My Hand	1969	3.75	7.50	15.00
❑ ST-286	Hold Me	1969	3.75	7.50	15.00
❑ ST-414	I'll Never Be Free	1970	3.75	7.50	15.00
❑ ST-556	My Happiness	1970	3.75	7.50	15.00
❑ ST-737	Oh, Love of Mine	1971	3.75	7.50	15.00
❑ ST 2903	Make a Left and Then a Right	1968	3.75	7.50	15.00
COLUMBIA					
❑ CL 2297 [M]	Mr. & Mrs. Country Music	1965	3.75	7.50	15.00
❑ CS 9097 [S]	Mr. & Mrs. Country Music	1965	5.00	10.00	20.00
HARMONY					
❑ HS 11389	Mr. & Mrs. Country Music	1970	2.50	5.00	10.00
STARDAY					
❑ SLP-328 [M]	The New Sweethearts of Country Music	1965	7.50	15.00	30.00
MOSLEY, BOB					
REPRISE					
❑ MS 2068	Bob Mosley	1972	5.00	10.00	20.00
MOSS, GENE					
RCA VICTOR					
❑ LPM-2977 [M]	Dracula's Greatest Hits	1964	7.50	15.00	30.00
❑ LSP-2977 [S]	Dracula's Greatest Hits	1964	10.00	20.00	40.00
MOSSE, SANDY					
ARGO					
❑ LP-609 [M]	Chicago Scene	1957	10.00	20.00	40.00
❑ LP-639 [M]	Relaxin' with Sandy Mosse	1959	7.50	15.00	30.00
❑ LPS-639 [S]	Relaxin' with Sandy Mosse	1959	10.00	20.00	40.00
MOST, ABE					
LIBERTY					
❑ LJH-6004 [M]	Mister Clarinet	1955	12.50	25.00	50.00
MOST, SAM					
BETHLEHEM					
❑ BCP-18 [M]	I'm Nuts About the Most: East Coast Jazz, Volume 7	1955	12.50	25.00	50.00
❑ BCP-75 [M]	Sam Most Plays Bird, Bud, Monk and Miles	1957	12.50	25.00	50.00
❑ BCP-78 [M]	The Amazing Sam Most with Strings	1958	12.50	25.00	50.00
❑ BCP-6008 [M]	Musically Yours	1956	12.50	25.00	50.00
DEBUT					
❑ DLP-11 [10]	Sam Most Sextet	1954	75.00	150.00	300.00
VANGUARD					
❑ VRS-8014 [10]	Sam Most Sextet	1954	20.00	40.00	80.00
XANADU					
❑ X-3001	Flute Talk	1980	6.25	12.50	25.00
—Audiophile edition					
MOTELS, THE					
Also see MARTHA DAVIS.					
CAPITOL					
❑ ST-11996	The Motels	1979	2.50	5.00	10.00
❑ ST-12070	Careful	1980	2.50	5.00	10.00
❑ ST-12177	All Four One	1982	2.50	5.00	10.00
❑ ST-12177 [DJ]	All Four One	1982	5.00	10.00	20.00
—Promo-only high-grade vinyl pressing (different front cover)					
❑ ST-12288	Little Robbers	1983	2.50	5.00	10.00
❑ SJ-12378	Shock	1985	2.50	5.00	10.00
❑ SN-16343	The Motels	1985	2.00	4.00	8.00
—Budget-line reissue					

Number	Title (A Side/B Side)	Yr	VG	VG+	NM
❑ SN-16347	Careful	1985	2.00	4.00	8.00
—Budget-line reissue					
❑ SN-16355	Little Robbers	1985	2.00	4.00	8.00
—Budget-line reissue					
❑ SN-16420	All Four One	198?	2.00	4.00	8.00
—Budget-line reissue					
MOTEN, BENNIE					
HISTORICAL					
❑ 9	Bennie Moten's Kansas City Orchestra	1966	5.00	10.00	20.00
RCA VICTOR					
❑ LPV-514 [M]	Bennie Moten's Great Band of 1930-32	1965	5.00	10.00	20.00
"X"					
❑ LX-3004 [10]	Kansas City Jazz, Volume 1	1954	15.00	30.00	60.00
❑ LVA-3025 [10]	Kansas City Jazz, Volume 2	1954	15.00	30.00	60.00
❑ LVA-3038 [10]	Kansas City Jazz, Volume 3	1954	15.00	30.00	60.00
MOTHER EARTH					
MERCURY					
❑ SR-61194	Living with the Animals	1968	6.25	12.50	25.00
❑ SR-61226	Make a Joyful Noise	1969	5.00	10.00	20.00
❑ SR-61230	Tracy Nelson Country	1969	5.00	10.00	20.00
❑ SR-61270	Satisfied	1970	5.00	10.00	20.00
REPRISE					
❑ MS 2054	Tracy Nelson/Mother Earth	1972	3.75	7.50	15.00
❑ RS 6431	Bring Me Home	1971	3.75	7.50	15.00
MOTHER LOVE BONE					
POLYDOR					
❑ 843191-1	Apple	1990	12.50	25.00	50.00
STARDOG					
❑ 839011-1 [EP]	Shine	1989	12.50	25.00	50.00
—Four songs on side one, the same four songs on side two					
MOTHERS OF INVENTION, THE					
See FRANK ZAPPA.					
MOTIONS, THE (3)					
PHILIPS					
❑ PHS 600317	Electric Baby	1969	5.00	10.00	20.00
MOTLEY CRUE					
ELEKTRA					
❑ 60174	Too Fast for Love	1982	2.00	4.00	8.00
—Reissue of Leathur LP with slight revisions					
❑ 60289	Shout at the Devil	1982	2.00	4.00	8.00
❑ 60418	Theatre of Pain	1985	2.00	4.00	8.00
❑ 60725	Girls, Girls, Girls	1987	2.00	4.00	8.00
❑ 60829	Dr. Feelgood	1989	2.50	5.00	10.00
LEATHUR					
❑ LR-1281	Too Fast for Love	1981	37.50	75.00	150.00
—Second pressing with red lettering on cover. Both Leathur pressings contain "Stick to Your Guns," which was not on the Elektra reissue					
❑ LR-1281	Too Fast for Love	1981	75.00	150.00	300.00
—First pressing with white lettering on cover					
MOTORHEAD					
EMI AMERICA					
❑ LN-10340	On Parole	1986	2.50	5.00	10.00
—First U.S. issue of early U.K. LP					
ENIGMA					
❑ D1-73536	The Birthday Party	1990	3.00	6.00	12.00
❑ D1-75405	No Sleep at All	1988	2.00	4.00	8.00
ISLAND					
❑ 90233 [(2)]	No Remorse	1984	3.00	6.00	12.00
—Regular cover					
❑ 90236 [(2)]	No Remorse	1984	7.50	15.00	30.00
—Leather cover					
MERCURY					
❑ SRM-1-4011	Ace of Spades	1980	2.50	5.00	10.00
❑ SRM-1-4023	No Sleep 'Til Hammersmith	1981	2.50	5.00	10.00
❑ SRM-1-4042	Iron Fist	1982	2.50	5.00	10.00
❑ 811365-1	Another Perfect Day	1983	2.00	4.00	8.00
PROFILE					
❑ PAL-1223	Orgasmatron	1986	2.00	4.00	8.00
❑ PAL-1240	Rock 'N' Roll	1987	2.00	4.00	8.00
❑ PRO-3241	Overkill	1986	2.00	4.00	8.00
—First U.S. issue of early U.K. LP					
❑ PRO-3242	Bomber	1986	2.00	4.00	8.00
—First U.S. issue of early U.K. LP					
❑ PRO-3243	Ace of Spades	1986	2.00	4.00	8.00
—Reissue of Mercury 4011					
❑ PRO-3244	No Sleep 'Til Hammersmith	1986	2.00	4.00	8.00
—Reissue of Mercury 4023					
WTG					
❑ N 46858	1916	1991	3.00	6.00	12.00
MOTT THE HOOPLE					
ATLANTIC					
❑ SD 7297	Rock and Roll Queen	1974	5.00	10.00	20.00
❑ SD 8258	Mott the Hoople	1970	5.00	10.00	20.00
—With "1841 Broadway" address and no mention of Warner Communications on label					
❑ SD 8258	Mott the Hoople	198?	2.00	4.00	8.00
—With Warner Communications "W" logo on label					
❑ SD 8272	Mad Shadows	1970	5.00	10.00	20.00
❑ SD 8284	Wildlife	1971	5.00	10.00	20.00
❑ SD 8304	Brain Capers	1972	5.00	10.00	20.00
COLUMBIA					
❑ KC 31750	All the Young Dudes	1972	3.75	7.50	15.00
❑ PC 31750	All the Young Dudes	198?	2.00	4.00	8.00
—Budget-line reissue					
❑ KC 32425	Mott	1973	3.75	7.50	15.00

Number	Title (A Side/B Side)	Yr	VG	VG+	NM
❑ PC 32425	Mott	198?	2.00	4.00	8.00
—Budget-line reissue					
❑ PC 32871	The Hoople	1974	3.75	7.50	15.00
❑ PCQ 32871 [Q]	The Hoople	1974	6.25	12.50	25.00
❑ PC 33282	Mott the Hoople Live	1974	3.75	7.50	15.00
—No bar code on cover					
❑ PC 33282	Mott the Hoople Live	198?	2.00	4.00	8.00
—Reissue with bar code on cover					
❑ PC 33705	Drive On	1975	3.75	7.50	15.00
❑ PC 34236	Shouting and Pointing	1976	3.75	7.50	15.00
❑ PC 34368	Mott the Hoople's Greatest Hits	1976	3.00	6.00	12.00
—No bar code on cover					
❑ PC 34368	Mott the Hoople's Greatest Hits	198?	2.00	4.00	8.00
—Reissue with bar code on cover					

MOTTOLA, TONY
ABC

Number	Title (A Side/B Side)	Yr	VG	VG+	NM
❑ S-738	16 Great Performances	1972	2.50	5.00	10.00
❑ X-770	Mister Guitar	1973	2.50	5.00	10.00

COMMAND

Number	Title (A Side/B Side)	Yr	VG	VG+	NM
❑ 33-807 [M]	Mr. Big	1961	3.00	6.00	12.00
❑ SD 807 [S]	Mr. Big	1961	3.75	7.50	15.00
❑ 33-816 [M]	Roman Guitar	1962	3.00	6.00	12.00
❑ SD 816 [S]	Roman Guitar	1962	3.75	7.50	15.00
❑ 33-823 [M]	Country and Western Folk Songs	1962	3.00	6.00	12.00
❑ SD 823 [S]	Country and Western Folk Songs	1962	3.75	7.50	15.00
❑ 33-828 [M]	String Band Strum-Along	1962	3.00	6.00	12.00
❑ SD 828 [S]	String Band Strum-Along	1962	3.75	7.50	15.00
❑ 33-836 [M]	Roman Guitar, Volume Two	1962	3.00	6.00	12.00
❑ SD 836 [S]	Roman Guitar, Volume Two	1962	3.75	7.50	15.00
❑ 33-841 [M]	Spanish Guitar	1963	3.00	6.00	12.00
❑ SD 841 [S]	Spanish Guitar	1963	3.75	7.50	15.00
❑ 33-847 [M]	Romantic Guitar	1963	3.00	6.00	12.00
❑ SD 847 [S]	Romantic Guitar	1963	3.75	7.50	15.00
❑ 33-864 [M]	Sentimental Guitar	1964	3.00	6.00	12.00
❑ SD 864 [S]	Sentimental Guitar	1964	3.75	7.50	15.00
❑ 33-877 [M]	Guitar — Paris	1964	3.00	6.00	12.00
❑ SD 877 [S]	Guitar — Paris	1964	3.75	7.50	15.00
❑ 33-885 [M]	Command Performance	1965	3.00	6.00	12.00
❑ SD 885 [S]	Command Performance	1965	3.75	7.50	15.00
❑ 33-889 [M]	Love Songs — Mexico/S.A.	1965	3.00	6.00	12.00
❑ SD 889 [S]	Love Songs — Mexico/S.A.	1965	3.75	7.50	15.00
❑ 33-900 [M]	Amor — Mexico/S.A.	1966	3.00	6.00	12.00
❑ SD 900 [S]	Amor — Mexico/S.A.	1966	3.75	7.50	15.00
❑ 33-908 [M]	Guitar — U.S.A.	1967	3.75	7.50	15.00
❑ SD 908 [S]	Guitar — U.S.A.	1967	3.00	6.00	12.00
❑ QD-40001 [Q]	Guitar — Paris	1972	5.00	10.00	20.00

PICKWICK

Number	Title (A Side/B Side)	Yr	VG	VG+	NM
❑ SPC-3610	Spanish Guitar	1978	2.00	4.00	8.00

PROJECT 3

Number	Title (A Side/B Side)	Yr	VG	VG+	NM
❑ PR-5003	Heart and Soul	1967	3.00	6.00	12.00
❑ PR-5010	A Latin Love-In	1967	3.00	6.00	12.00
❑ PR4C-5010 [Q]	A Latin Love-In	1973	4.50	9.00	18.00
❑ PR-5020	Lush, Latin & Lovely	1968	3.00	6.00	12.00
❑ PR4C-5020 [Q]	Lush, Latin & Lovely	1973	4.50	9.00	18.00
❑ PR-5025	Warm, Wild & Wonderful	1968	3.00	6.00	12.00
❑ PR4C-5025 [Q]	Warm, Wild & Wonderful	1973	4.50	9.00	18.00
❑ PR-5032	Roma Oggi/Rome Today	1969	3.00	6.00	12.00
❑ PR4C-5032 [Q]	Roma Oggi/Rome Today	1973	4.50	9.00	18.00
❑ PR-5035	Tony Mottola Joins the Guitar Underground	1969	3.00	6.00	12.00
❑ PR-5041	The Tony Touch	1970	3.00	6.00	12.00
❑ PR4C-5041 [Q]	The Tony Touch	1973	4.50	9.00	18.00
❑ PR-5044	Tony Mottola's Guitar Factory	1970	3.00	6.00	12.00
❑ PR-5050	Close to You	1971	3.00	6.00	12.00
❑ PR-5058	Warm Feelings	1971	3.00	6.00	12.00
❑ PR-5062	Superstar Guitar	1972	3.00	6.00	12.00
❑ PR4C-5062 [Q]	Superstar Guitar	1973	3.75	7.50	15.00
❑ PR-5069	Tony and Strings	1973	3.00	6.00	12.00
❑ PR4C-5069 [Q]	Tony and Strings	1973	4.50	9.00	18.00
❑ PR-5074	Two Guitars	1974	2.50	5.00	10.00
❑ PR4C-5078 [Q]	Tony Mottola with the Quad Guitars	1974	3.75	7.50	15.00
❑ PR-5082	Tony Mottola with the Brass Menagerie	1974	3.00	6.00	12.00
❑ PR-5094	I Only Have Eyes for You	197?	2.50	5.00	10.00
❑ PR-5101	Goin' Out of My Head	197?	2.50	5.00	10.00
❑ PR-6007/8 [(2)]	Favorite Things: The Best of Tony Mottola	1975	3.75	7.50	15.00
❑ PR-6025/6 [(2)]	Feelings	198?	3.00	6.00	12.00
❑ PR-6031/2 [(2)]	The Best of Tony Mottola	198?	3.00	6.00	12.00

MOULE, KEN
LONDON

Number	Title (A Side/B Side)	Yr	VG	VG+	NM
❑ LL 1673 [M]	Ken Moule Arranges for…	1957	12.50	25.00	50.00
—Label calls this "Cool Moule"					

MOUNT ALVERNIA SEMINARY CHOIR
ABC-PARAMOUNT

Number	Title (A Side/B Side)	Yr	VG	VG+	NM
❑ 211 [M]	Christmas in a Monastery: The Sons of St. Francis Sing	1957	5.00	10.00	20.00

MOUNT RUSHMORE
DOT

Number	Title (A Side/B Side)	Yr	VG	VG+	NM
❑ DLP-25898	High on Mount Rushmore	1968	5.00	10.00	20.00
❑ DLP-25934	Mount Rushmore '69	1969	5.00	10.00	20.00

MOUNTAIN
COLUMBIA

Number	Title (A Side/B Side)	Yr	VG	VG+	NM
❑ CQ 32079 [Q]	The Best of Mountain	1973	5.00	10.00	20.00
❑ KC 32079	The Best of Mountain	1973	3.00	6.00	12.00
❑ PC 32079	The Best of Mountain	198?	2.00	4.00	8.00
—Budget-line reissue					
❑ CG 32818 [(2)]	Twin Peaks	1974	3.75	7.50	15.00
❑ PG 32818 [(2)]	Twin Peaks	198?	2.50	5.00	10.00
—Budget-line reissue					

Number	Title (A Side/B Side)	Yr	VG	VG+	NM
❑ CQ 33008 [Q]	Avalanche	1974	5.00	10.00	20.00
❑ KC 33008	Avalanche	1974	3.00	6.00	12.00
❑ PC 33008	Avalanche	197?	2.00	4.00	8.00
—Budget-line reissue					

SCOTTI BROTHERS

Number	Title (A Side/B Side)	Yr	VG	VG+	NM
❑ FZ 40006	Go for Your Life	1985	2.50	5.00	10.00

WINDFALL

Number	Title (A Side/B Side)	Yr	VG	VG+	NM
❑ 4501	Mountain Climbing!	1970	3.75	7.50	15.00
❑ 5500	Nantucket Sleighride	1971	3.75	7.50	15.00
—Deduct 20% if inserts are missing					
❑ 5501	Flowers of Evil	1971	3.75	7.50	15.00
❑ 5502	Mountain Live (The Road Goes Ever On)	1972	3.75	7.50	15.00

MOUNTAIN BUS
GOOD

Number	Title (A Side/B Side)	Yr	VG	VG+	NM
❑ 101	Sundance	1971	37.50	75.00	150.00

MOUNTAIN RAMBLERS, THE
ATLANTIC

Number	Title (A Side/B Side)	Yr	VG	VG+	NM
❑ 1347 [M]	Blue Ridge Mountain Music	1962	6.25	12.50	25.00
❑ SD 1347 [S]	Blue Ridge Mountain Music	1962	7.50	15.00	30.00

MOUZON, ALPHONSE
BLUE NOTE

Number	Title (A Side/B Side)	Yr	VG	VG+	NM
❑ BN-LA222-G	Funky Snakefoot	1974	5.00	10.00	20.00

MOVE, THE
A&M

Number	Title (A Side/B Side)	Yr	VG	VG+	NM
❑ SP-3181	Shazam	1982	2.50	5.00	10.00
—Budget-line reissue of 4259					
❑ SP-3625 [(2)]	The Best of the Move	1974	3.75	7.50	15.00
❑ SP-4259	Shazam	1969	7.50	15.00	30.00

CAPITOL

Number	Title (A Side/B Side)	Yr	VG	VG+	NM
❑ ST-658	Looking On	1971	5.00	10.00	20.00
❑ ST-811	Message from the Country	1971	5.00	10.00	20.00

UNITED ARTISTS

Number	Title (A Side/B Side)	Yr	VG	VG+	NM
❑ UAS-5666	Split Ends	1972	3.75	7.50	15.00

MOVING SIDEWALKS, THE
TANTARA

Number	Title (A Side/B Side)	Yr	VG	VG+	NM
❑ 6919	Flash	1968	75.00	150.00	300.00

MOZIAN, ROGER KING
CLEF

Number	Title (A Side/B Side)	Yr	VG	VG+	NM
❑ MGC-166 [10]	The Colorful Music of Roger King Mozian	1954	25.00	50.00	100.00

MTUME UMOJA ENSEMBLE
STRATA-EAST

Number	Title (A Side/B Side)	Yr	VG	VG+	NM
❑ SES-1972-4 [(2)]	Alkebu-Lan, Land of the Blacks	1972	12.50	25.00	50.00

MU
CAS

Number	Title (A Side/B Side)	Yr	VG	VG+	NM
❑ 300	Mu	1971	75.00	150.00	300.00

MUDHONEY
REPRISE

Number	Title (A Side/B Side)	Yr	VG	VG+	NM
❑ 45840	My Brother the Cow	1994	2.50	5.00	10.00

SUB POP

Number	Title (A Side/B Side)	Yr	VG	VG+	NM
❑ 21 [EP]	Superfuzz Bigmuff	1988	5.00	10.00	20.00
—Without poster					
❑ 21 [EP]	Superfuzz Bigmuff	1988	7.50	15.00	30.00
—With poster					
❑ 44	Mudhoney	1989	5.00	10.00	20.00
—Without gatefold and poster					
❑ 44	Mudhoney	1989	7.50	15.00	30.00
—First 3,000 have gatefold sleeve and poster					
❑ 105	Every Good Boy Deserves Fudge	1991	2.50	5.00	10.00
❑ 105 PD [PD]	Every Good Boy Deserves Fudge	1991	7.50	15.00	30.00
—Picture disc -- limited edition of 2,500					
❑ SP 500 [(3)]	March to Fuzz	2000	6.25	12.50	25.00

SUPER ELECTRO

Number	Title (A Side/B Side)	Yr	VG	VG+	NM
❑ SE 10	Tomorrow Hit Today	1998	3.00	6.00	12.00

MUGWUMPS, THE
WARNER BROS.

Number	Title (A Side/B Side)	Yr	VG	VG+	NM
❑ W 1697 [M]	The Mugwumps	1967	6.25	12.50	25.00
❑ WS 1697 [S]	The Mugwumps	1967	7.50	15.00	30.00

MUHAMMAD, IDRIS
KUDU

Number	Title (A Side/B Side)	Yr	VG	VG+	NM
❑ 17	Power of Soul	1974	6.25	12.50	25.00
❑ 27	House of the Rising Sun	1976	6.25	12.50	25.00
❑ 34	Turn This Mutha Out	1977	5.00	10.00	20.00
❑ 38	Boogie to the Top	1978	5.00	10.00	20.00

PRESTIGE

Number	Title (A Side/B Side)	Yr	VG	VG+	NM
❑ 10005	Black Rhythm Revolution	1971	10.00	20.00	40.00
❑ 10036	Peace and Rhythm	1971	7.50	15.00	30.00

MULCAY, JIMMY AND MILDRED
JUBILEE

Number	Title (A Side/B Side)	Yr	VG	VG+	NM
❑ JGM-5017 [M]	Magic Millions	1962	7.50	15.00	30.00

MULDAUR, GEOFF
FOLKLORE

Number	Title (A Side/B Side)	Yr	VG	VG+	NM
❑ FRLP-14004 [M]	Sleepy Man Blues	1964	7.50	15.00	30.00
❑ FRST-14004 [S]	Sleepy Man Blues	1964	10.00	20.00	40.00

PRESTIGE

Number	Title (A Side/B Side)	Yr	VG	VG+	NM
❑ PRST-7727	Sleepy Man Blues	1969	5.00	10.00	20.00
—Reissue of Folklore LP					

Number	Title (A Side/B Side)	Yr	VG	VG+	NM

MULLER, WERNER
DECCA
❑ DL 8388 [M]	O, Tannenbaum (Christmas on the Rhine)	1956	5.00	10.00	20.00
—Black label, silver print					

MULLICAN, MOON
AUDIO LAB
❑ AL-1568 [M]	Instrumentals	1962	37.50	75.00	150.00

CORAL
❑ CRL 57235 [M]	Moon Over Mullican	1958	125.00	250.00	500.00

HILLTOP
❑ JS-6033	Good Times Gonna Roll Again	1966	6.25	12.50	25.00

KAPP
❑ KS-3600	Showcase	1968	7.50	15.00	30.00

KING
❑ 555 [M]	Moon Mullican Sings His All-Time Greatest Hits	1958	50.00	100.00	200.00
❑ 628 [M]	Moon Mullican Plays and Sings 16 of His Favorite Tunes	1959	37.50	75.00	150.00
❑ 681 [M]	The Many Moods of Moon Mullican	1960	37.50	75.00	150.00
❑ 937 [M]	Moon Mullican Sings 24 of His Favorite Tunes	1965	12.50	25.00	50.00

NASHVILLE
❑ 2080	I'll Sail My Ship Alone	1970	5.00	10.00	20.00

SPAR
❑ SP-3005 [M]	Mister Honky Tonk Man	1965	25.00	50.00	100.00

STARDAY
❑ SLP-135 [M]	Playin' and Singin'	1963	25.00	50.00	100.00
❑ SLP-267 [M]	Mister Piano Man	1964	12.50	25.00	50.00
❑ SLP-398 [M]	The Unforgettable Moon Mullican	1967	10.00	20.00	40.00

STERLING
❑ ST-601 [M]	I'll Sail My Ship Alone	1958	50.00	100.00	200.00

MULLIGAN, GERRY
CAPITOL
❑ H 439 [10]	Gerry Mulligan and His Ten-Tette	1953	62.50	125.00	250.00

COLUMBIA
❑ CL 1307 [M]	What Is There to Say?	1959	10.00	20.00	40.00
—Red and black label with six "eye" logos					
❑ CL 1932 [M]	Jeru	1963	7.50	15.00	30.00
—Red label, "Guaranteed High Fidelity" at bottom					
❑ CL 1932 [M]	Jeru	1965	3.00	6.00	12.00
—Red label, "360 Sound Mono" at bottom					
❑ CS 8116 [S]	What Is There to Say?	1959	10.00	20.00	40.00
—Red and black label with six "eye" logos					
❑ CS 8732 [S]	Jeru	1963	7.50	15.00	30.00
—Red label, "360 Sound Stereo" in black at bottom					

EMARCY
❑ MG-36056 [M]	Presenting the Gerry Mulligan Sextet	1955	37.50	75.00	150.00
❑ MG-36101 [M]	Mainstream of Jazz	1956	37.50	75.00	150.00

FANTASY
❑ 3-6 [10]	Gerry Mulligan Quartet	1953	50.00	100.00	200.00

GENE NORMAN
❑ GNP-3 [10]	Gerry Mulligan Quartet	1952	62.50	125.00	250.00

LIMELIGHT
❑ LM-82004 [M]	Butterfly with Hiccups	1964	6.25	12.50	25.00
❑ LM-82021 [M]	If You Can't Beat 'Em, Join 'Em	1965	6.25	12.50	25.00
❑ LM-82030 [M]	Feelin' Good	1965	6.25	12.50	25.00
❑ LM-82040 [M]	Something Borrowed, Something Blue	1966	5.00	10.00	20.00
❑ LS-86004 [S]	Butterfly with Hiccups	1964	7.50	15.00	30.00
❑ LS-86021 [S]	If You Can't Beat 'Em, Join 'Em	1965	7.50	15.00	30.00
❑ LS-86030 [S]	Feelin' Good	1965	7.50	15.00	30.00
❑ LS-86040 [S]	Something Borrowed, Something Blue	1966	6.25	12.50	25.00

MERCURY
❑ MG-20453 [M]	A Profile of Gerry Mulligan	1959	15.00	30.00	60.00

MOBILE FIDELITY
❑ 1-179	At the Village Vanguard	1985	10.00	20.00	40.00
—Audiophile vinyl					
❑ 1-234	Gerry Mulligan Meets Ben Webster	1995	10.00	20.00	40.00
—Audiophile vinyl					
❑ 1-241	Blues in Time	1996	7.50	15.00	30.00
—Audiophile vinyl					

MOSAIC
❑ M5-102 [(5)]	The Complete Pacific Jazz and Capitol Recordings of the Original Gerry Mulligan Quartet and Tentette	198?	25.00	50.00	100.00

PACIFIC JAZZ
❑ PJLP-1 [10]	Gerry Mulligan Quartet	1953	75.00	150.00	300.00
❑ PJLP-2 [10]	Lee Konitz Plays with the Gerry Mulligan Quartet	1953	75.00	150.00	300.00
❑ PJLP-5 [10]	Gerry Mulligan Quartet	1953	75.00	150.00	300.00
❑ PJ-8 [M]	The Genius of Gerry Mulligan	1960	10.00	20.00	40.00
❑ PJLP-10 [10]	Lee Konitz and the Gerry Mulligan Quartet	1954	62.50	125.00	250.00
❑ PJ-38 [M]	Konitz Meets Mulligan	1962	7.50	15.00	30.00
❑ PJ-47 [M]	Reunion with Chet Baker	1962	7.50	15.00	30.00
❑ ST-47 [S]	Reunion with Chet Baker	1962	7.50	15.00	30.00
❑ PJ-50 [M]	California Concerts	1962	7.50	15.00	30.00
❑ PJ-75 [M]	Timeless	1963	7.50	15.00	30.00
❑ PJM-406 [M]	Lee Konitz with the Gerry Mulligan Quartet	1956	37.50	75.00	150.00
❑ PJ-1201 [M]	Gerry Mulligan Sextet	1955	37.50	75.00	150.00
❑ PJ-1207 [M]	The Original Mulligan Quartet	1955	37.50	75.00	150.00
❑ PJ-1210 [M]	Paris Concert	1956	37.50	75.00	150.00
❑ PJ-1228 [M]	Gerry Mulligan at Storyville	1957	37.50	75.00	150.00
❑ PJ-10102 [M]	Paris Concert	1966	5.00	10.00	20.00
❑ ST-20102 [S]	Paris Concert	1966	5.00	10.00	20.00
❑ T 90061 [M]	Reunion with Chet Baker	196?	7.50	15.00	30.00
—Capitol Record Club edition					

PHILIPS
❑ PHM 200077 [M]	Spring Is Sprung	1963	5.00	10.00	20.00
❑ PHM 200108 [M]	Night Lights	1963	5.00	10.00	20.00
❑ PHS 600077 [S]	Spring Is Sprung	1963	6.25	12.50	25.00
❑ PHS 600108 [S]	Night Lights	1963	6.25	12.50	25.00

PRESTIGE
❑ PRLP-120 [10]	Gerry Mulligan Blows	1952	75.00	150.00	300.00
❑ PRLP-141 [10]	Mulligan Too Blows	1953	75.00	150.00	300.00
❑ PRLP-7006 [M]	Mulligan Plays Mulligan	1956	25.00	50.00	100.00
—Yellow label					
❑ PRLP-7251 [M]	Historically Speaking	1963	10.00	20.00	40.00
—Yellow label					

UNITED ARTISTS
❑ UAL-4085 [M]	Nightwatch	1960	10.00	20.00	40.00
❑ UAS-5085 [S]	Nightwatch	1960	12.50	25.00	50.00

VERVE
❑ MGVS-6003 [S]	Getz Meets Mulligan in Hi-Fi	1960	10.00	20.00	40.00
❑ MGVS-6104 [S]	Gerry Mulligan Meets Ben Webster	1960	10.00	20.00	40.00
❑ MGV-8246 [M]	The Gerry Mulligan-Paul Desmond Quartet	1958	12.50	25.00	50.00
❑ V-8246 [M]	The Gerry Mulligan-Paul Desmond Quartet	1961	5.00	10.00	20.00
❑ MGV-8249 [M]	Getz Meets Mulligan in Hi-Fi	1958	10.00	20.00	40.00
❑ V-8249 [M]	Getz Meets Mulligan in Hi-Fi	1961	5.00	10.00	20.00
❑ V6-8249 [S]	Getz Meets Mulligan in Hi-Fi	1961	6.25	12.50	25.00
❑ MGV-8343 [M]	Gerry Mulligan Meets Ben Webster	1959	10.00	20.00	40.00
❑ V-8343 [M]	Gerry Mulligan Meets Ben Webster	1961	5.00	10.00	20.00
❑ MGV-8367 [M]	Gerry Mulligan Meets Johnny Hodges	1960	10.00	20.00	40.00
❑ V-8367 [M]	Gerry Mulligan Meets Johnny Hodges	1961	5.00	10.00	20.00
❑ V6-8367 [S]	Gerry Mulligan Meets Johnny Hodges	1961	6.25	12.50	25.00
❑ MGV-8388 [M]	Gerry Mulligan and the Concert Jazz Band	1960	10.00	20.00	40.00
❑ V-8388 [M]	Gerry Mulligan and the Concert Jazz Band	1961	5.00	10.00	20.00
❑ V6-8388 [S]	Gerry Mulligan and the Concert Jazz Band	1961	6.25	12.50	25.00
❑ MGV-8396 [M]	Gerry Mulligan and the Concert Jazz Band at the Village Vanguard	1960	10.00	20.00	40.00
❑ V-8396 [M]	Gerry Mulligan and the Concert Jazz Band at the Village Vanguard	1961	5.00	10.00	20.00
❑ V6-8396 [S]	Gerry Mulligan and the Concert Jazz Band at the Village Vanguard	1961	6.25	12.50	25.00
❑ V-8415 [M]	Gerry Mulligan and the Concert Jazz Band Presents a Concert in Jazz	1961	6.25	12.50	25.00
❑ V6-8415 [S]	Gerry Mulligan and the Concert Jazz Band Presents a Concert in Jazz	1961	7.50	15.00	30.00
❑ V-8438 [M]	The Gerry Mulligan Concert Jazz Band On Tour with Guest Soloist Zoot Sims	1962	6.25	12.50	25.00
❑ V6-8438 [S]	The Gerry Mulligan Concert Jazz Band On Tour with Guest Soloist Zoot Sims	1962	7.50	15.00	30.00
❑ V-8466 [M]	The Gerry Mulligan Quartet	1962	6.25	12.50	25.00
❑ V6-8466 [S]	The Gerry Mulligan Quartet	1962	7.50	15.00	30.00
❑ V-8478 [M]	Blues in Time	1962	5.00	10.00	20.00
❑ V6-8478 [S]	Blues in Time	1962	6.25	12.50	25.00
❑ V-8515 [M]	Gerry Mulligan '63 — The Concert Jazz Band	1963	5.00	10.00	20.00
❑ V6-8515 [S]	Gerry Mulligan '63 — The Concert Jazz Band	1963	6.25	12.50	25.00
❑ V6-8534 [S]	Gerry Mulligan Meets Ben Webster	1963	5.00	10.00	20.00
❑ V6-8535 [S]	Gerry Mulligan Meets Stan Getz	1963	5.00	10.00	20.00
❑ V6-8536 [S]	Gerry Mulligan Meets Johnny Hodges	1963	5.00	10.00	20.00

WORLD PACIFIC
❑ PJM-406 [M]	Lee Konitz with the Gerry Mulligan Quartet	1958	20.00	40.00	80.00
❑ ST-1001 [S]	The Gerry Mulligan Songbook	1958	25.00	50.00	100.00
❑ ST-1006 [S]	Gerry Mulligan at Storyville	1958	25.00	50.00	100.00
❑ ST-1007 [S]	Reunion with Chet Baker	1958	20.00	40.00	80.00
❑ WP-1201 [M]	California Concerts	1958	20.00	40.00	80.00
❑ WP-1207 [M]	The Original Mulligan Quartet	1958	20.00	40.00	80.00
❑ WP-1210 [M]	Paris Concert	1958	20.00	40.00	80.00
❑ WP-1228 [M]	Gerry Mulligan at Storyville	1958	20.00	40.00	80.00
❑ PJ-1237 [M]	The Gerry Mulligan Songbook	1957	30.00	60.00	120.00
❑ WP-1237 [M]	The Gerry Mulligan Songbook	1958	20.00	40.00	80.00
❑ PJ-1241 [M]	Reunion with Chet Baker	1957	30.00	60.00	120.00
❑ WP-1241 [M]	Reunion with Chet Baker	1958	20.00	40.00	80.00
❑ WP-1273 [M]	Lee Konitz Plays with the Gerry Mulligan Quartet	1959	20.00	40.00	80.00
—Reissue of 406					

MULLIGAN, GERRY, AND CHET BAKER
JAZZTONE
❑ J-1253 [M]	Mulligan and Baker!	1957	10.00	20.00	40.00

MULLIGAN, GERRY/BUDDY DEFRANCO
GENE NORMAN
❑ GNP-26 [M]	The Gerry Mulligan Quartet with Chet Baker/Buddy DeFranco Quartet	1957	20.00	40.00	80.00
—Combined reissue of two 10-inch LPs					
❑ GNP-56 [M]	The Gerry Mulligan Quartet with Chet Baker/Buddy DeFranco Quartet	196?	10.00	20.00	40.00
—Reissue of 26					

MULLIGAN, GERRY/PAUL DESMOND
FANTASY
❑ 3220 [M]	Gerry Mulligan Quartet/Paul Desmond Quintet	1956	10.00	20.00	40.00
—Black vinyl					
❑ 3220 [M]	Gerry Mulligan Quartet/Paul Desmond Quintet	1956	20.00	40.00	80.00
—Red vinyl; combined reissue of two 10-inch LPs					

MULLIGAN, GERRY/KAI WINDING/RED RODNEY
STATUS
❑ ST-8306 [M]	Broadway	1965	10.00	20.00	40.00

MULTIPLICATION ROCK (SOUNDTRACK)
CAPITOL
❑ SJA-11174	Multiplication Rock	1973	10.00	20.00	40.00

MUMY, BILL
BB
❑ 103	Bill Mumy	1980	6.25	12.50	25.00

Number	Title (A Side/B Side)	Yr	VG	VG+	NM
MUNSTERS, THE					
DECCA					
❑ DL 4588 [M]	The Munsters	1964	25.00	50.00	100.00
❑ DL 74588 [S]	The Munsters	1964	37.50	75.00	150.00
MURE, BILLY					
EVEREST					
❑ SDBR-1067 [S]	A String of Trumpets	1960	7.50	15.00	30.00
❑ SDBR-1072 [S]	Songs of Hank Williams.	1960	7.50	15.00	30.00
❑ SDBR-1120 [S]	Strictly Cha-Cha-Cha.	1961	7.50	15.00	30.00
❑ LPBR-5067 [M]	A String of Trumpets	1960	5.00	10.00	20.00
❑ LPBR-5072 [M]	Songs of Hank Williams.	1960	5.00	10.00	20.00
❑ LPBR-5120 [M]	Strictly Cha-Cha-Cha.	1961	5.00	10.00	20.00
KAPP					
❑ KL-1253 [M]	Tough Strings	1961	5.00	10.00	20.00
❑ KS-3253 [S]	Tough Strings	1961	7.50	15.00	30.00
MGM					
❑ E-3780 [M]	Supersonic Guitars	1959	7.50	15.00	30.00
❑ SE-3780 [S]	Supersonic Guitars	1959	12.50	25.00	50.00
❑ E-3807 [M]	Supersonic Guitars, Vol. 2	1959	7.50	15.00	30.00
❑ SE-3807 [S]	Supersonic Guitars, Vol. 2	1959	12.50	25.00	50.00
❑ E-4131 [M]	Teen Bossa Nova	1963	5.00	10.00	20.00
❑ SE-4131 [S]	Teen Bossa Nova	1963	7.50	15.00	30.00
❑ E-4189 [M]	Maria Elena and Other Great Songs	1964	5.00	10.00	20.00
❑ SE-4189 [S]	Maria Elena and Other Great Songs	1964	7.50	15.00	30.00
❑ E-4406 [M]	Happy Guitars	1966	5.00	10.00	20.00
❑ SE-4406 [S]	Happy Guitars	1966	6.25	12.50	25.00
RCA VICTOR					
❑ LPM-1536 [M]	Supersonic Guitars in Hi-Fi	1957	10.00	20.00	40.00
❑ LPM-1694 [M]	Fireworks	1958	7.50	15.00	30.00
❑ LSP-1694 [S]	Fireworks	1958	10.00	20.00	40.00
❑ LPM-1869 [M]	Supersonic in Flight	1959	7.50	15.00	30.00
❑ LSP-1869 [S]	Supersonic in Flight	1959	12.50	25.00	50.00
STRAND					
❑ SL-1010 [M]	Hawaiian Percussion	1961	6.25	12.50	25.00
❑ SLS-1010 [S]	Hawaiian Percussion	1961	10.00	20.00	40.00
❑ SL-1021 [M]	'Round the World in Percussion	1961	6.25	12.50	25.00
❑ SLS-1021 [S]	'Round the World in Percussion	1961	10.00	20.00	40.00
❑ SL-1070 [M]	Pink Hawaii	1962	5.00	10.00	20.00
❑ SLS-1070 [S]	Pink Hawaii	1962	7.50	15.00	30.00
UNITED ARTISTS					
❑ UAL-3031 [M]	Bandstand Record Hop	1959	10.00	20.00	40.00
❑ UAS-6031 [S]	Bandstand Record Hop	1959	15.00	30.00	60.00
MURMAIDS, THE					
CHATTAHOOCHEE					
❑ CHLP-628 [M]	The Mermaids Resurface!	1981	7.50	15.00	30.00
MURPHY, ELLIOTT					
POLYDOR					
❑ PD-5061	Aquashow	1973	5.00	10.00	20.00
—First edition with "Like a Great Gatsby" listed as a song title					
RCA VICTOR					
❑ APL1-0916	Lost Generation	1975	5.00	10.00	20.00
—Orange or tan labels					
❑ APL1-1318	Night Lights	1976	5.00	10.00	20.00
—Orange or tan labels					
MURPHY, LYLE					
GENE NORMAN					
❑ GNP-9 [10]	Four Saxophones in Twelve Tones	1954	30.00	60.00	120.00
❑ GNP-33 [M]	New Orbits in Sound	1957	12.50	25.00	50.00
❑ GNP-152 [M]	Four Saxophones in Twelve Tones	195?	12.50	25.00	50.00
MURPHY, MARK					
CAPITOL					
❑ ST 1177 [S]	This Could Be the Start of Something	1959	7.50	15.00	30.00
❑ T 1177 [M]	This Could Be the Start of Something	1959	6.25	12.50	25.00
❑ ST 1299 [S]	Hip Parade	1960	7.50	15.00	30.00
❑ T 1299 [M]	Hip Parade	1960	6.25	12.50	25.00
❑ ST 1458 [S]	Playing the Field	1960	7.50	15.00	30.00
❑ T 1458 [M]	Playing the Field	1960	6.25	12.50	25.00
DECCA					
❑ DL 8390 [M]	Meet Mark Murphy	1957	12.50	25.00	50.00
❑ DL 8632 [M]	Let Yourself Go	1958	10.00	20.00	40.00
FONTANA					
❑ MGF-27537 [M]	A Swingin' Singin' Affair	1965	5.00	10.00	20.00
❑ SRF-67537 [S]	A Swingin' Singin' Affair	1965	6.25	12.50	25.00
RIVERSIDE					
❑ RLP-395 [M]	Rah	1961	6.25	12.50	25.00
❑ RLP-441 [M]	That's How I Love the Blues!	1962	6.25	12.50	25.00
❑ RS-9395 [S]	Rah	1961	7.50	15.00	30.00
❑ RS-9441 [S]	That's How I Love the Blues!	1962	7.50	15.00	30.00
MURPHY, ROSE					
UNITED ARTISTS					
❑ UAJ-14025 [M]	Jazz, Joy and Happiness	1962	10.00	20.00	40.00
❑ UAJS-15025 [S]	Jazz, Joy and Happiness	1962	12.50	25.00	50.00
VERVE					
❑ MGV-2070 [M]	Not Cha-Cha But Chi-Chi	1957	10.00	20.00	40.00
❑ V-2070 [M]	Not Cha-Cha But Chi-Chi	1961	5.00	10.00	20.00
MURPHY, TURK					
COLUMBIA					
❑ CL 546 [M]	When the Saints Go Marching In	1953	10.00	20.00	40.00
—Maroon label, gold print					
❑ CL 546 [M]	When the Saints Go Marching In	1955	7.50	15.00	30.00
—Red and black label with six "eye" logos					
❑ CL 559 [M]	The Music of Jelly Roll Morton	1954	10.00	20.00	40.00
—Maroon label, gold print					

Number	Title (A Side/B Side)	Yr	VG	VG+	NM
❑ CL 559 [M]	The Music of Jelly Roll Morton	1955	7.50	15.00	30.00
—Red and black label with six "eye" logos					
❑ CL 595 [M]	Barrelhouse Jazz	1954	10.00	20.00	40.00
—Maroon label, gold print					
❑ CL 595 [M]	Barrelhouse Jazz	1955	7.50	15.00	30.00
—Red and black label with six "eye" logos					
❑ CL 650 [M]	Dancing Jazz	1955	7.50	15.00	30.00
—Red and black label with six "eye" logos					
❑ CL 650 [M]	Dancing Jazz	1955	10.00	20.00	40.00
—Maroon label, gold print					
❑ CL 6257 [10]	Barrelhouse Jazz	1953	12.50	25.00	50.00
GOOD TIME JAZZ					
❑ L-7 [10]	Turk Murphy with Claire Austin	1952	12.50	25.00	50.00
❑ L-12026 [M]	San Francisco Jazz, Volume 1	1955	10.00	20.00	40.00
❑ L-12027 [M]	San Francisco Jazz, Volume 2	1955	10.00	20.00	40.00
RCA VICTOR					
❑ LPM-2501 [M]	Let the Good Times Roll	1962	5.00	10.00	20.00
❑ LSP-2501 [S]	Let the Good Times Roll	1962	6.25	12.50	25.00
ROULETTE					
❑ R-25076 [M]	Turk Murphy and His Jazz Band at the Roundtable	1959	5.00	10.00	20.00
❑ SR-25076 [S]	Turk Murphy and His Jazz Band at the Roundtable	1959	6.25	12.50	25.00
❑ R-25088 [M]	Music for Wise Guys	1960	5.00	10.00	20.00
❑ SR-25088 [S]	Music for Wise Guys	1960	6.25	12.50	25.00
VERVE					
❑ MGV-1013 [M]	Music for Losers	1957	10.00	20.00	40.00
❑ V-1013 [M]	Music for Losers	1961	5.00	10.00	20.00
❑ MGV-1015 [M]	Turk Murphy on Easy Street	1957	10.00	20.00	40.00
❑ V-1015 [M]	Turk Murphy on Easy Street	1961	5.00	10.00	20.00
MURRAY, ANNE					
CAPITOL					
❑ ST-579	Snowbird	1970	3.00	6.00	12.00
❑ ST-667	Anne Murray	1971	3.00	6.00	12.00
❑ ST-821	Talk It Over in the Morning	1971	3.00	6.00	12.00
❑ ST-11024	Annie	1972	2.50	5.00	10.00
❑ ST-11172	Danny's Song	1973	2.50	5.00	10.00
❑ ST-11266	Love Song	1974	2.50	5.00	10.00
❑ ST-11324	Country	1974	2.50	5.00	10.00
❑ ST-11354	Highly Prized Possession	1974	2.50	5.00	10.00
❑ ST-11433	Together	1975	2.50	5.00	10.00
❑ ST-11559	Keeping in Touch	1976	2.50	5.00	10.00
❑ ST-11743	Let's Keep It That Way	1978	2.50	5.00	10.00
❑ SW-11849	New Kind of Feeling	1979	2.50	5.00	10.00
❑ SOO-12012	I'll Always Love You	1979	2.50	5.00	10.00
❑ ST-12039	A Country Collection	1980	2.50	5.00	10.00
❑ SOO-12064	Somebody's Waiting	1980	2.50	5.00	10.00
❑ SOO-12110	Anne Murray's Greatest Hits	1980	2.50	5.00	10.00
❑ SOO-12144	Where Do You Go When You Dream	1981	2.50	5.00	10.00
❑ ST-12225	The Hottest Night of the Year	1982	2.50	5.00	10.00
❑ ST-12301	A Little Good News	1983	2.50	5.00	10.00
❑ SJ-12363	Heart Over Mind	1984	2.50	5.00	10.00
❑ SJ-12466	Something to Talk About	1986	2.50	5.00	10.00
❑ PJ-12562	Harmony	1987	2.50	5.00	10.00
❑ SN-16080	Talk It Over in the Morning	1980	2.00	4.00	8.00
—Budget-line reissue					
❑ SN-16081	Highly Prized Possession	1980	2.00	4.00	8.00
—Budget-line reissue					
❑ SN-16082	Keeping in Touch	1980	2.00	4.00	8.00
—Budget-line reissue					
❑ SN-16211	Danny's Song	1981	2.00	4.00	8.00
—Budget-line reissue					
❑ SN-16212	Love Song	1981	2.00	4.00	8.00
—Budget-line reissue					
❑ SN-16213	Country	1981	2.00	4.00	8.00
—Budget-line reissue					
❑ SN-16232	Christmas Wishes	1981	2.50	5.00	10.00
—Original issue was on the budget-line series					
❑ SN-16233	There's a Hippo in My Tub	1981	2.50	5.00	10.00
—Original issue was on the budget-line series					
❑ SN-16282	Together	1982	2.00	4.00	8.00
—Budget-line reissue					
❑ SN-16283	New Kind of Feeling	1982	2.00	4.00	8.00
—Budget-line reissue					
❑ SN-16338	A Country Collection	198?	2.00	4.00	8.00
—Budget-line reissue					
❑ SN-16341	Let's Keep It That Way	198?	2.00	4.00	8.00
—Budget-line reissue					
❑ C1-48764	As I Am	1988	2.50	5.00	10.00
❑ C1-90886	Christmas	1987	2.00	4.00	8.00
❑ C1-92072	Greatest Hits Volume II	1989	3.00	6.00	12.00
CAPITOL NASHVILLE					
❑ R 173232	You Will	1990	5.00	10.00	20.00
—Only released on vinyl through BMG Direct Marketing					
PICKWICK					
❑ SPC-3350	What About Me	197?	2.00	4.00	8.00
MURRAY, DAVID					
HAT HUT					
❑ U/V [(2)]	The Third Family	1979	5.00	10.00	20.00
MURRAY, SUNNY					
ESP-DISK'					
❑ 1032 [M]	Sunny Murray	1966	5.00	10.00	20.00
❑ S-1032 [S]	Sunny Murray	1966	6.25	12.50	25.00
JIHAD					
❑ 663 [M]	Sunny's Time Now	1967	50.00	100.00	200.00

Number	Title (A Side/B Side)	Yr	VG	VG+	NM

MURRAY THE "K"
See VARIOUS ARTISTS COLLECTIONS.

MUSCLE SHOALS HORNS, THE
BANG

Number	Title (A Side/B Side)	Yr	VG	VG+	NM
❑ BLP-403	Born to Get Down	1975	5.00	10.00	20.00

MUSIC ASYLUM, THE
UNITED ARTISTS

❑ UAS-6778	Commit Thyself	1970	5.00	10.00	20.00

MUSIC COMPANY, THE
CRESTVIEW

❑ CRS-3057	Hard and Heavy	196?	6.25	12.50	25.00

MIRWOOD

❑ M-7002 [M]	Rubber Soul Jazz	1966	5.00	10.00	20.00
❑ MS-7002 [S]	Rubber Soul Jazz	1966	6.25	12.50	25.00

MUSIC EMPORIUM, THE
SENTINEL

❑ 69001	The Music Emporium	1969	500.00	1000.	2000.

SUNDAZED

❑ LP 5078	The Music Emporium	2001	3.75	7.50	15.00
—First legitimate reissue of the original					

MUSIC EXPLOSION, THE
LAURIE

❑ LLP-2040 [M]	Little Bit O'Soul	1967	5.00	10.00	20.00
❑ SLLP-2040 [S]	Little Bit O'Soul	1967	6.25	12.50	25.00

MUSIC MACHINE, THE
ORIGINAL SOUND

❑ 5015 [M]	(Turn On) The Music Machine	1966	10.00	20.00	40.00
❑ 8875 [S]	(Turn On) The Music Machine	1966	12.50	25.00	50.00

SUNDAZED

❑ LP 5038	Ignition	2000	3.00	6.00	12.00

WARNER BROS.

❑ W 1732 [M]	Bonniwell's Music Machine	1967	6.25	12.50	25.00
❑ WS 1732 [S]	Bonniwell's Music Machine	1967	10.00	20.00	40.00

MUSSELWHITE, CHARLIE
VANGUARD

❑ VSD-6258	Tennessee Woman	1969	5.00	10.00	20.00
❑ VRS-9232 [M]	Stand Back! Here Comes Charlie Musselwhite's South Side Band	1966	5.00	10.00	20.00
❑ VSD-79232 [S]	Stand Back! Here Comes Charlie Musselwhite's South Side Band	1966	6.25	12.50	25.00
❑ VSD-79287	Charlie Musselwhite	1968	5.00	10.00	20.00

MUSSO, VIDO
CROWN

❑ CLP-5007 [M]	The Swingin'st	1957	12.50	25.00	50.00
—Reissue of Modern LP					
❑ CLP-5029 [M]	Teenage Dance Party	1957	12.50	25.00	50.00

MODERN

❑ MLP-1207 [M]	The Swingin'st	1956	25.00	50.00	100.00

MUSSULLI, BOOTS
CAPITOL

❑ H 6506 [10]	Boots Mussulli	1955	30.00	60.00	120.00
❑ T 6506 [M]	Boots Mussulli	1955	12.50	25.00	50.00

MUSTANGS, THE
PROVIDENCE

❑ PLP-001 [M]	Dartell Stomp	1964	12.50	25.00	50.00

MUTZIE
SUSSEX

❑ SUX-7001	Light of Your Shadow	1970	6.25	12.50	25.00

MY BLOODY VALENTINE
CREATION/RELATIVITY

❑ 1006	Isn't Anything	1989	5.00	10.00	20.00

MYERS, DAVE
CAROLE

❑ 8002 [M]	Greatest Racing Themes	1967	12.50	25.00	50.00

DEL-FI

❑ DFLP-1239 [M]	Hangin' Twenty	1963	20.00	40.00	80.00
❑ DFST-1239 [S]	Hangin' Twenty	1963	45.00	90.00	180.00
❑ DLF-1239	Hangin' Twenty	1998	3.00	6.00	12.00

MYERSON, BESS
MGM

❑ E-3785 [M]	Fashions in Music	1959	7.50	15.00	30.00
❑ SE-3785 [S]	Fashions in Music	1959	10.00	20.00	40.00

MYRICK, BERL
STRATA-EAST

❑ SES-102-74	Live 'n Well	1974	7.50	15.00	30.00

MYRICK, GARY, AND THE FIGURES
EPIC

❑ AS 912 [DJ]	Talks in Stereo	1981	10.00	20.00	40.00
—Side one has studio tracks, side two has live versions of songs on side one					
❑ AS 1389 [DJ]	Live Sampler	1982	4.00	8.00	16.00
—Four live tracks, including one unreleased song					
❑ JE 36524	Gary Myrick and the Figures	1981	2.50	5.00	10.00
—Reissue with amended prefix					
❑ NJE 36524	Gary Myrick and the Figures	1980	3.00	6.00	12.00
❑ ARE 37429	Living in a Movie	1981	2.50	5.00	10.00
❑ B5E 38637 [EP]	Language	1983	2.50	5.00	10.00

GEFFEN

❑ GHS 24076	Stand for Love	1985	2.50	5.00	10.00

MYSTERIOUS FLYING ORCHESTRA, THE
RCA VICTOR

Number	Title (A Side/B Side)	Yr	VG	VG+	NM
❑ APL1-2137	The Mysterious Flying Orchestra	1977	5.00	10.00	20.00

MYSTIC ASTROLOGICAL CRYSTAL BAND, THE
CAROLE

❑ 8001 [M]	Mystic Astrological Crystal Band	1967	6.25	12.50	25.00
❑ S-8001 [S]	Mystic Astrological Crystal Band	1967	7.50	15.00	30.00
❑ S-8003	Clip Out, Put On Book	1968	7.50	15.00	30.00

MYSTIC MOODS ORCHESTRA, THE
BAINBRIDGE

❑ 6201	More Than Music	1982	—	3.00	6.00
❑ 6202	Moods for a Stormy Night	1982	—	3.00	6.00
—Reissue of Sound Bird 7504					
❑ 6203	Mexico!	1982	—	3.00	6.00
❑ 6204	Nightide	1982	—	3.00	6.00
—Reissue of Sound Bird 7502					
❑ 6205	One Stormy Night	1982	—	3.00	6.00
—Reissue of Sound Bird 7501					
❑ 6206	Emotions	1982	—	3.00	6.00
—Reissue of Sound Bird 7505					
❑ 6207	Love Token	1982	—	3.00	6.00
❑ 6208	Stormy Weekend	1982	—	3.00	6.00
—Reissue of Sound Bird 7506					
❑ 6209	Highway One	1982	—	3.00	6.00
❑ 6210	English Muffins	1982	—	3.00	6.00
❑ 6211	Country Lovin' Folk	1982	—	3.00	6.00
—Reissue of Sound Bird 8512					
❑ 6212	Extensions	1982	—	3.00	6.00
❑ 6215	Erogenous	1982	—	3.00	6.00
—Reissue of Sound Bird 7509					
❑ 6216	Another Stormy Night	1983	2.00	4.00	8.00
❑ 6219	Summer Moods	1985	2.00	4.00	8.00

MOBILE FIDELITY

❑ 1-001	Emotions	1979	6.25	12.50	25.00
—Audiophile vinyl					
❑ 1-002	Cosmic Forces	1979	6.25	12.50	25.00
—Audiophile vinyl					
❑ 1-003	Stormy Weekend	1979	6.25	12.50	25.00
—Audiophile vinyl					

PHILIPS

❑ PHM 200205 [M]	One Stormy Night	1966	3.00	6.00	12.00
❑ PHM 200213 [M]	Nightide	1966	3.00	6.00	12.00
❑ PHM 200231 [M]	More Than Music	1967	3.75	7.50	15.00
❑ PHM 200250 [M]	Mexican Trip	1967	3.75	7.50	15.00
❑ PHM 200260 [M]	The Mystic Moods of Love	1968	3.75	7.50	15.00
❑ PHS 600205 [S]	One Stormy Night	1966	3.75	7.50	15.00
❑ PHS 600213 [S]	Nightide	1966	3.75	7.50	15.00
❑ PHS 600231 [S]	More Than Music	1967	3.00	6.00	12.00
❑ PHS 600250 [S]	Mexican Trip	1967	3.00	6.00	12.00
❑ PHS 600260 [S]	The Mystic Moods of Love	1968	3.00	6.00	12.00
❑ PHS 600277	Emotions	1968	3.00	6.00	12.00
❑ PHS 600301	Extensions	1969	3.00	6.00	12.00
❑ PHS 600321	Love Token	1969	3.00	6.00	12.00
❑ PHS 600342	Stormy Weekend	1970	3.00	6.00	12.00
❑ PHS 600349	English Muffins	1970	3.00	6.00	12.00
❑ PHS 600351	Country Lovin' Folk	1971	3.00	6.00	12.00

SOUND BIRD

❑ 7501	One Stormy Night	1975	2.00	4.00	8.00
—Reissue of Warner Bros. 2594					
❑ 7502	Nightide	1975	2.00	4.00	8.00
—Reissue of Warner Bros. 2593					
❑ 7503	Man and…	1975	2.00	4.00	8.00
❑ 7504	Moods for a Stormy Night	1975	2.00	4.00	8.00
❑ 7505	Emotions	1975	2.00	4.00	8.00
❑ 7506	Stormy Weekend	1975	2.00	4.00	8.00
—Reissue of Warner Bros. 2596					
❑ 7507	Touch	1975	2.00	4.00	8.00
❑ SQ 7507 [Q]	Touch	1975	3.00	6.00	12.00
❑ 7508	Love the One You're With	1975	2.00	4.00	8.00
—Reissue of Warner Bros. 2577					
❑ SQ 7508 [Q]	Love the One You're With	1975	3.00	6.00	12.00
—Reissue of Warner Bros. BS4 2577					
❑ 7509	Erogenous	1975	2.00	4.00	8.00
—Reissue of Warner Bros. 2786					
❑ SQ 7509 [Q]	Erogenous	1975	3.00	6.00	12.00
—Reissue of Warner Bros. BS4 2786					
❑ 7510	Being with You	1976	2.50	5.00	10.00
❑ SQ 7510 [Q]	Being with You	1976	4.00	8.00	16.00
❑ 8503	Misty	1978	2.00	4.00	8.00
❑ 8505	Midnight	1978	2.00	4.00	8.00
❑ 8508	Alone Together	1978	2.00	4.00	8.00
❑ 8510	Being with You	1978	2.00	4.00	8.00
—Reissue of Sound Bird 7510					
❑ 8511	Cosmic Forces	1978	2.00	4.00	8.00
❑ 8512	Country Lovin' Folk	1978	2.00	4.00	8.00
❑ 8514	Simple	1978	2.00	4.00	8.00

WARNER BROS.

❑ BS 2577	Love the One You're With	1972	3.00	6.00	12.00
❑ BS4 2577 [Q]	Love the One You're With	1974	4.00	8.00	16.00
❑ BS 2593	Nightide	1972	2.50	5.00	10.00
—Reissue of Philips 600-213					
❑ BS 2594	One Stormy Night	1972	2.50	5.00	10.00
—Reissue of Philips 600-205					
❑ BS 2595	Love Token	1972	2.50	5.00	10.00
—Reissue of Philips 600-321					
❑ BS 2596	Stormy Weekend	1972	2.50	5.00	10.00
—Reissue of Philips 600-342					
❑ BS 2597	Emotions	1972	2.50	5.00	10.00
—Reissue of Philips 600-277					

Number	Title (A Side/B Side)	Yr	VG	VG+	NM
❑ BS 2598	The Mystic Moods of Love	1972	2.50	5.00	10.00
—Reissue of Philips 600-260					
❑ BS 2648	Highway One	1973	3.00	6.00	12.00
❑ BS4 2648 [Q]	Highway One	1974	4.00	8.00	16.00
❑ BS 2690	Awakening	1973	3.00	6.00	12.00
❑ BS4 2690 [Q]	Awakening	1974	4.00	8.00	16.00
❑ BS 2745	Clear Light	1974	3.00	6.00	12.00
❑ BS4 2745 [Q]	Clear Light	1974	4.00	8.00	16.00
❑ BS 2786	Erogenous	1974	2.50	5.00	10.00
❑ BS4 2786 [Q]	Erogenous	1974	4.00	8.00	16.00

MYSTIC NUMBER NATIONAL BANK, THE
PROBE
❑ CPLP-4501	The Mystic Number National Bank	1969	5.00	10.00	20.00

MYSTIC SIVA
VO
❑ 19713	Mystic Siva	1971	250.00	500.00	1000.

N

N.W.A.
PRIORITY
❑ SPRO 30080 [DJ]	Greatest Hits/In-Store Play	1996	5.00	10.00	20.00
—Promo-only "clean" versions for retailer use					
❑ MRC 1057	N.W.A. and the Posse	1987	6.25	12.50	25.00
❑ 7224 [EP]	100 Miles and Runnin'	1990	3.75	7.50	15.00
❑ 50561 [(2)]	Greatest Hits	1996	3.75	7.50	15.00
❑ 57102	Straight Outta Compton	1989	5.00	10.00	20.00
❑ 57119	N.W.A. and the Posse	1990	3.75	7.50	15.00
—Reissue of MRC 1057					
❑ 57126	Efil4zaggin (Niggaz4life)	1991	5.00	10.00	20.00

NABORS, JIM
CAPITOL SPECIAL MARKETS
❑ SL-8136	20 All-Time Favorites	1977	2.50	5.00	10.00
COLUMBIA
❑ CS 1020	The Jim Nabors Hour	1970	3.00	6.00	12.00
❑ CL 2368 [M]	Shazam! (Gomer Pyle, U.S.M.C.)	1965	5.00	10.00	20.00
❑ CL 2558 [M]	Jim Nabors Sings Love Me with All Your Heart	1966	3.00	6.00	12.00
❑ CL 2665 [M]	Jim Nabors By Request	1967	3.00	6.00	12.00
❑ CL 2703 [M]	The Things I Love	1967	3.00	6.00	12.00
❑ CL 2731 [M]	Jim Nabors' Christmas Album	1967	3.00	6.00	12.00
❑ CS 9168 [S]	Shazam! (Gomer Pyle, U.S.M.C.)	1965	6.25	12.50	25.00
❑ CS 9358 [S]	Jim Nabors Sings Love Me with All Your Heart	1966	3.75	7.50	15.00
❑ CS 9465 [S]	Jim Nabors By Request	1967	3.75	7.50	15.00
❑ CS 9503 [S]	The Things I Love	1967	3.75	7.50	15.00
❑ CS 9531 [S]	Jim Nabors' Christmas Album	1970	2.50	5.00	10.00
—Later editions with orange label					
❑ CS 9531 [S]	Jim Nabors' Christmas Album	1967	3.00	6.00	12.00
—Originals with "360 Sound" label					
❑ CS 9620	Kiss Me Goodbye	1968	3.00	6.00	12.00
❑ CS 9716	The Lord's Prayer and Other Sacred Songs	1968	3.00	6.00	12.00
❑ PC 9716	The Lord's Prayer	1979	2.00	4.00	8.00
—Budget-line reissue					
❑ CS 9817	Galveston	1969	3.00	6.00	12.00
❑ C 30129	Everything Is Beautiful	1970	3.00	6.00	12.00
❑ C 30449	For the Good Times/The Jim Nabors Hour	1971	3.00	6.00	12.00
❑ 3C 30671	How Great Thou Art	198?	2.00	4.00	8.00
—Budget-line reissue					
❑ C 30671	How Great Thou Art	1971	3.00	6.00	12.00
❑ C 30810	Help Me Make It Through the Night	1971	3.00	6.00	12.00
❑ KC 31336	The Way of Love	1972	3.00	6.00	12.00
❑ KG 31591 [(2)]	Great Love Songs	1972	3.75	7.50	15.00
❑ PG 31591 [(2)]	Great Love Songs	198?	2.50	5.00	10.00
—Budget-line reissue					
❑ C 31630	Merry Christmas	1972	2.50	5.00	10.00
❑ KG 31973 [(2)]	The World of Jim Nabors	1972	3.75	7.50	15.00
❑ PG 31973 [(2)]	The World of Jim Nabors	1979	2.50	5.00	10.00
—Budget-line reissue					
❑ KC 32377	The Twelfth of Never	1972	3.00	6.00	12.00
❑ KC 32909	Peace in the Valley	1973	3.00	6.00	12.00
❑ PC 32909	Peace in the Valley	1979	2.00	4.00	8.00
—Budget-line reissue					
❑ KC 32950	It's My Life	1973	3.00	6.00	12.00
❑ KC 33401	A Very Special Love Song	1974	3.00	6.00	12.00
❑ PC 33401	A Very Special Love Song	1979	2.00	4.00	8.00
—Budget-line reissue					
❑ CG 33618 [(2)]	The Lord's Prayer/How Great Thou Art	1975	3.75	7.50	15.00
COLUMBIA SPECIAL PRODUCTS
❑ P 13507	Somewhere My Love	1977	2.50	5.00	10.00
HARMONY
❑ KH 30398	More	1971	2.50	5.00	10.00
PAIR
❑ PDL2-1077 [(2)]	The Very Special Warmth of Jim Nabors	1986	3.00	6.00	12.00
❑ PDL2-1097 [(2)]	On the Country Side	1986	3.00	6.00	12.00
RANWOOD
❑ R-7017 [(2)]	22 Great Hymn and Country Favorites	1984	3.00	6.00	12.00
❑ R-8157	Old Time Religion	1976	2.50	5.00	10.00
❑ R-8164	Town & Country	1976	2.50	5.00	10.00
❑ R-8176	Sincerely	1977	2.50	5.00	10.00
❑ R-8178	I See God	1977	2.50	5.00	10.00
REALM
❑ 1V-8170	Christmas with Jim Nabors	1982	2.00	4.00	8.00

NAGLE, RON
WARNER BROS.
❑ WS 1902	Bad Rice	1970	5.00	10.00	20.00

NAKED RAYGUN
CAROLINE
❑ 1348	Jettison	1988	5.00	10.00	20.00
❑ 1371	Understand?	1989	5.00	10.00	20.00
❑ 1642	Raygun...Naked Raygun	1990	5.00	10.00	20.00
HAUNTED TOWN
❑ HTR 11	Free Shit	2001	2.50	5.00	10.00
HOMESTEAD
❑ HMS 008	Throb Throb	1984	5.00	10.00	20.00
—Second edition has lyric innersleeve					
❑ HMS 008	Throb Throb	1984	7.50	15.00	30.00
—First edition has lyric sheet					
❑ HMS 045	All Rise	1985	7.50	15.00	30.00
RUTHLESS
❑ 03 [EP]	Basement Screams	1983	20.00	40.00	80.00

NANCE, RAY
SOLID STATE
❑ SS-18062	Body and Soul	1969	5.00	10.00	20.00

NANTON, MORRIS
PRESTIGE
❑ PRLP-7345 [M]	Preface	1964	5.00	10.00	20.00
❑ PRST-7345 [S]	Preface	1964	6.25	12.50	25.00
❑ PRLP-7409 [M]	Something We've Got	1965	5.00	10.00	20.00
❑ PRST-7409 [S]	Something We've Got	1965	6.25	12.50	25.00
❑ PRLP-7467 [M]	Soul Fingers	1966	5.00	10.00	20.00
❑ PRST-7467 [S]	Soul Fingers	1966	6.25	12.50	25.00
WARNER BROS.
❑ W-1256 [M]	Flower Drum Song	1958	6.25	12.50	25.00
❑ WS-1256 [S]	Flower Drum Song	1958	7.50	15.00	30.00
❑ W-1279 [M]	The Original Jazz Performance of "Roberta"	1959	6.25	12.50	25.00
❑ WS-1279 [S]	The Original Jazz Performance of "Roberta"	1959	7.50	15.00	30.00

NAPOLEON, PHIL
CAPITOL
❑ ST 1344 [S]	Phil Napoleon and the Memphis Five	1960	5.00	10.00	20.00
❑ T 1344 [M]	Phil Napoleon and the Memphis Five	1960	6.25	12.50	25.00
COLUMBIA
❑ CL 2505 [10]	Two-Beat	1955	12.50	25.00	50.00
EMARCY
❑ MG-26008 [10]	Dixieland Classics #1	1954	15.00	30.00	60.00
❑ MG-26009 [10]	Dixieland Classics #2	1954	15.00	30.00	60.00
❑ MG-36033 [M]	Dixieland Classics	1955	12.50	25.00	50.00
JOLLY ROGER
❑ 5006 [10]	Dixieland By Phil Napoleon	1954	12.50	25.00	50.00
MERCURY
❑ MG-25079 [10]	Dixieland Classics	1953	15.00	30.00	60.00

NAPOLEON XIV
RHINO
❑ RNLP 816	They're Coming to Take Me Away, Ha-Haaa!	1985	3.00	6.00	12.00
WARNER BROS.
❑ W 1661 [M]	They're Coming to Take Me Away, Ha-Haaa!	1966	15.00	30.00	60.00
❑ WS 1661 [S]	They're Coming to Take Me Away, Ha-Haaa!	1966	25.00	50.00	100.00

NARZ, JACK
DOT
❑ DLP-3244 [M]	Sing the Folk Hits with Jack Narz	1960	6.25	12.50	25.00
❑ DLP-25244 [S]	Sing the Folk Hits with Jack Narz	1960	7.50	15.00	30.00

NASCIMENTO, MILTON
A&M
❑ LP-(# unknown) [M]	Milton Nascimento	1967	7.50	15.00	30.00
❑ SP-(# unknown) [S]	Milton Nascimento	1967	5.00	10.00	20.00
❑ SP-3019	Courage	1969	5.00	10.00	20.00

NASH, JOHNNY
ABC-PARAMOUNT
❑ 244 [M]	Johnny Nash	1958	7.50	15.00	30.00
❑ S-244 [S]	Johnny Nash	1959	10.00	20.00	40.00
❑ 276 [M]	Quiet Hour	1959	7.50	15.00	30.00
❑ S-276 [S]	Quiet Hour	1959	10.00	20.00	40.00
❑ 299 [M]	I Got Rhythm	1959	7.50	15.00	30.00
❑ S-299 [S]	I Got Rhythm	1959	10.00	20.00	40.00
❑ 344 [M]	Let's Get Lost	1960	7.50	15.00	30.00
❑ S-344 [S]	Let's Get Lost	1960	10.00	20.00	40.00
❑ 383 [M]	Studio Time	1961	7.50	15.00	30.00
❑ S-383 [S]	Studio Time	1961	10.00	20.00	40.00
ARGO
❑ LP-4038 [M]	Composer's Choice	1964	5.00	10.00	20.00
❑ LPS-4038 [S]	Composer's Choice	1964	6.25	12.50	25.00
EPIC
❑ KE 31607	I Can See Clearly Now	1972	3.75	7.50	15.00
—Yellow label					
❑ KE 31607	I Can See Clearly Now	1973	3.00	6.00	12.00
—Orange label					
❑ KE 32158	My Merry-Go-Round	1973	3.75	7.50	15.00
❑ PE 32828	Celebrate Life	1974	3.75	7.50	15.00
JAD
❑ JS-1001	Prince of Peace	1969	6.25	12.50	25.00
❑ JS-1006	Folk Soul	1970	6.25	12.50	25.00
❑ JS-1207	Hold Me Tight	1968	7.50	15.00	30.00

NASH, TED
COLUMBIA
❑ CL 989 [M]	Star Eyes	1957	10.00	20.00	40.00

Number	Title (A Side/B Side)	Yr	VG	VG+	NM

STARLITE
| ❏ LP-6001 [10] | Ted Nash | 1954 | 12.50 | 25.00 | 50.00 |

NASH, TED & DICK
LIBERTY
| ❏ LJH-6011 [M] | The Brothers Nash | 1956 | 12.50 | 25.00 | 50.00 |

NASHVILLE ALL STARS, THE
RCA VICTOR
| ❏ LPM-2302 [M] | After the Riot at Newport | 1960 | 10.00 | 20.00 | 40.00 |
| ❏ LSP-2302 [S] | After the Riot at Newport | 1960 | 12.50 | 25.00 | 50.00 |

NASHVILLE GUITARS, THE
MONUMENT
❏ MLP-8058 [M]	The Nashville Guitars	1966	3.75	7.50	15.00
❏ SLP-18058 [S]	The Nashville Guitars	1966	5.00	10.00	20.00
❏ MLP-18093	The Nashville Guitars at Home	1968	3.75	7.50	15.00

NASHVILLE TEENS, THE
LONDON
| ❏ PS 407 [R] | Tobacco Road | 1964 | 20.00 | 40.00 | 80.00 |
| ❏ LL 3407 [M] | Tobacco Road | 1964 | 25.00 | 50.00 | 100.00 |

NASTOS, NICK
STRAND
| ❏ SL-1097 [M] | Guitars on Fire | 1962 | 5.00 | 10.00 | 20.00 |
| ❏ SLS-1097 [S] | Guitars on Fire | 1962 | 6.25 | 12.50 | 25.00 |

NATIONAL GALLERY, THE
PHILIPS
| ❏ PHS 600266 | The National Gallery (Performing Musical Interpretations of the Paintings of Paul Klee) | 1968 | 7.50 | 15.00 | 30.00 |

NATIONAL JAZZ ENSEMBLE
CHIAROSCURO
| ❏ 151 [(2)] | National Jazz Ensemble, Volume 2 | 197? | 5.00 | 10.00 | 20.00 |

NATIONAL LAMPOON
BANANA
❏ BTS 38	Radio Dinner	1972	3.75	7.50	15.00
❏ BTS 6006	Lemmings	1973	3.75	7.50	15.00
❏ BTS 6008	Missing White House Tapes	1974	3.75	7.50	15.00
EPIC
❏ PE 33410	Gold Turkey	1974	3.00	6.00	12.00
—Orange label					
❏ PE 33410	Gold Turkey	1979	2.00	4.00	8.00
—Dark blue label					
❏ PE 33956	Goodbye Pop	1975	3.00	6.00	12.00
—Orange label					
❏ PE 33956	Goodbye Pop	1979	2.00	4.00	8.00
—Dark blue label					
LABEL 21
❏ IMP-2001	That's Not Funny, That's Sick!	1978	2.50	5.00	10.00
❏ PIC-2001 [PD]	That's Not Funny, That's Sick!	1978	5.00	10.00	20.00
❏ IMP-2002	The White Album	1979	2.50	5.00	10.00
MCA
| ❏ 27023 | Lemmings | 198? | 2.00 | 4.00 | 8.00 |
| ❏ 27024 | Radio Dinner | 198? | 2.00 | 4.00 | 8.00 |
PASSPORT
| ❏ PB 6018 | Sex, Drugs, Rock and Roll and the End of the World | 1982 | 2.50 | 5.00 | 10.00 |
VISA
❏ 2001	That's Not Funny, That's Sick!	198?	2.00	4.00	8.00
❏ 2002	The White Album	198?	2.00	4.00	8.00
❏ 7008	Greatest Hits of the National Lampoon	1978	3.00	6.00	12.00

NATIONAL SYMPHONY ORCHESTRA (HOWARD MITCHELL, CONDUCTOR)
RCA VICTOR RED SEAL
| ❏ LSC-2261 [S] | Shostakovich: Symphony No. 5 | 1959 | 12.50 | 25.00 | 50.00 |
| —Original with "shaded dog" label | | | | | |

NATURAL FOUR, THE
CURTOM
| ❏ CU 5004 | Heaven Right Here on Earth | 1975 | 5.00 | 10.00 | 20.00 |
| ❏ CRT-8600 | The Natural Four | 1974 | 5.00 | 10.00 | 20.00 |

NAVARRO, FATS
BLUE NOTE
❏ BLP-1531 [M]	The Fabulous Fats Navarro, Vol. 1	1956	50.00	10.00	20.00
—Regular version, Lexington Ave. address on label					
❏ BLP-1531 [M]	The Fabulous Fats Navarro, Vol. 1	1956	62.50	125.00	250.00
—"Deep groove" version (deep indentation under label on both sides)					
❏ BLP-1531 [M]	The Fabulous Fats Navarro, Vol. 1	1963	6.25	12.50	25.00
—With "New York, USA" address on label					
❏ BLP-1532 [M]	The Fabulous Fats Navarro, Vol. 2	1956	50.00	100.00	200.00
—Regular version, Lexington Ave. address on label					
❏ BLP-1532 [M]	The Fabulous Fats Navarro, Vol. 2	1956	62.50	125.00	250.00
—"Deep groove" version (deep indentation under label on both sides)					
❏ BLP-1532 [M]	The Fabulous Fats Navarro, Vol. 2	1963	6.25	12.50	25.00
—With "New York, USA" address on label					
❏ BLP-5004 [10]	Fats Navarro Memorial Album	1952	125.00	250.00	500.00
RIVERSIDE
| ❏ 3019 | Good Bait | 1968 | 5.00 | 10.00 | 20.00 |
SAVOY
❏ MG-9005 [10]	New Sounds Of Modern Music	1952	75.00	150.00	300.00
❏ MG-9019 [10]	New Trends Of Jazz	1952	75.00	150.00	300.00
❏ MG-12011 [M]	Fats Navarro Memorial	1955	37.50	75.00	150.00
❏ MG-12133 [M]	Nostalgia	1958	25.00	50.00	100.00

NAVARRO, FATS/KAI WINDING/BREW MOORE
SAVOY
| ❏ MG-12119 [M] | In the Beginning…Bebop | 1957 | 15.00 | 30.00 | 60.00 |

NAZARETH
A&M
❏ SP-3109	Close Enough for Rock 'N' Roll	1981	2.00	4.00	8.00
—Budget-line reissue					
❏ SP-3168	Exercises	1982	2.00	4.00	8.00
—Reissue of Warner Bros. 2639					
❏ SP-3169	Nazareth	1982	2.00	4.00	8.00
—Reissue of Warner Bros. 2615					
❏ SP-3225	Hair of the Dog	1984	2.00	4.00	8.00
—Budget-line reissue					
❏ SP-3226	Hot Tracks	1984	2.00	4.00	8.00
—Budget-line reissue					
❏ SP-3609	Loud 'N' Proud	1974	2.50	5.00	10.00
❏ SP-3641	Rampant	1974	2.50	5.00	10.00
❏ SP-4396	Razamanaz	1973	3.75	7.50	15.00
—First edition with brown label					
❏ SP-4396	Razamanaz	1974	2.50	5.00	10.00
❏ SP-4511	Hair of the Dog	1975	2.50	5.00	10.00
❏ SP-4562	Close Enough for Rock 'N' Roll	1976	2.50	5.00	10.00
❏ SP-4610	Play 'N' the Game	1976	2.50	5.00	10.00
❏ SP-4643	Hot Tracks	1977	2.50	5.00	10.00
❏ SP-4666	Expect No Mercy	1977	2.50	5.00	10.00
❏ SP-4741	No Mean City	1979	2.50	5.00	10.00
❏ SP-4799	Malice in Wonderland	1980	2.50	5.00	10.00
❏ SP-4844	The Fool Circle	1981	2.50	5.00	10.00
❏ SP-4901	2XS	1982	2.50	5.00	10.00
❏ SP-6703 [(2)]	'Snaz	1981	3.00	6.00	12.00
MCA
| ❏ 5458 | Sound Elixir | 1983 | 2.50 | 5.00 | 10.00 |
WARNER BROS.
| ❏ BS 2615 | Nazareth | 1972 | 5.00 | 10.00 | 20.00 |
| ❏ BS 2639 | Exercises | 1972 | 5.00 | 10.00 | 20.00 |

NAZZ (1)
Also see TODD RUNDGREN.
RHINO
❏ RNLP 109	Nazz	1984	2.50	5.00	10.00
❏ RNLP 110	Nazz Nazz	1984	2.50	5.00	10.00
❏ RNLP 111	Nazz III	1984	2.50	5.00	10.00
❏ RNLP 116	The Best of Nazz	1984	2.50	5.00	10.00
❏ R1 70116	The Best of Nazz	1987	2.00	4.00	8.00
SGC
❏ SD 5001	Nazz	1968	10.00	20.00	40.00
❏ 5002 [M]	Nazz Nazz	1969	20.00	40.00	80.00
—Promo-only mono pressing on red vinyl					
❏ SD 5002 [S]	Nazz Nazz	1969	10.00	20.00	40.00
—Red vinyl					
❏ SD 5002 [S]	Nazz Nazz	1969	20.00	40.00	80.00
—Black vinyl					
❏ SD 5004	Nazz III	1970	10.00	20.00	40.00

NBC SYMPHONY ORCHESTRA (LEOPOLD STOKOWSKI, COND.)
RCA VICTOR RED SEAL
❏ LSC-2555 [S]	The Sound of Stokowski and Wagner	1961	15.00	30.00	60.00
—Originals with "shaded dog" label					
❏ LSC-2555 [S]	The Sound of Stokowski and Wagner	1964	6.25	12.50	25.00
—Second editions with "white dog" label					

NDEGEOCELLO, ME'SHELL
MAVERICK
| ❏ PRO-A-6622 [(2)DJ] | Plantation Lullabies | 1993 | 5.00 | 10.00 | 20.00 |
| —Promo-only U.S. vinyl release | | | | | |

NECROS
RESTLESS
| ❏ 72203 | Tangled Up | 1986 | 3.00 | 6.00 | 12.00 |
TOUCH & GO
| ❏ 2 | Conquest for Death | 1983 | 17.50 | 35.00 | 70.00 |

NEELY, JIMMY
TRU-SOUND
| ❏ TRU-15002 [M] | Misirlou | 1962 | 10.00 | 20.00 | 40.00 |

NEFF, HILDEGARDE
LONDON
| ❏ PS 596 | From Here On It Gets Rough | 1971 | 5.00 | 10.00 | 20.00 |

NEGATIVLAND
SEELAND
❏ 001	Negativland	1981	3.75	7.50	15.00
—Every copy has a different cover					
❏ 002	Points	1982	3.00	6.00	12.00
—Black vinyl					
❏ 002	Points	1982	3.75	7.50	15.00
—Blue vinyl					
❏ 003	A Big 10-8 Place	1985	3.00	6.00	12.00
SST
❏ 133	Escape from Noise	1987	4.50	9.00	18.00
—With booklet					
❏ 252	Helter Stupid	1989	3.00	6.00	12.00
❏ 272 [EP]	U2	1990	25.00	50.00	100.00
—Withdrawn thanks to pressure from the record company of U2 (the band)					
❏ 292 [EP]	Guns	1992	2.00	4.00	8.00

NEIGHB'RHOOD CHILDREN
ACTA
| ❏ 8005 [M] | The Neighb'rhood Children | 1968 | 20.00 | 40.00 | 80.00 |
| ❏ 38005 [S] | The Neighb'rhood Children | 1968 | 25.00 | 50.00 | 100.00 |
SUNDAZED
| ❏ LP 5023 [(2)] | Long Years in Space | 199? | 3.75 | 7.50 | 15.00 |

Number	Title (A Side/B Side)	Yr	VG	VG+	NM
NEIL, FRED					
CAPITOL					
❑ ST-294	Everybody's Talkin'	1969	6.25	12.50	25.00
❑ ST 2665 [S]	Fred Neil	1966	10.00	20.00	40.00
—With color photo on back					
❑ ST 2665 [S]	Fred Neil	1967	7.50	15.00	30.00
—With black & white photo on back					
❑ T 2665 [M]	Fred Neil	1966	7.50	15.00	30.00
❑ ST 2862 [S]	Fred Neil Sessions	1968	7.50	15.00	30.00
❑ T 2862 [M]	Fred Neil Sessions	1968	10.00	20.00	40.00
ELEKTRA					
❑ EKL-293 [M]	Bleecker and MacDougal	1965	7.50	15.00	30.00
❑ EKS-7293 [S]	Bleecker and MacDougal	1965	10.00	20.00	40.00
❑ EKS-74073	Little Bit of Rain	1970	5.00	10.00	20.00
—Reissue of 7293					
SUNDAZED					
❑ LP 5107	Bleecker and MacDougal	2002	3.00	6.00	12.00
NELSON, OLIVER					
ABC IMPULSE!					
❑ AS-9168 [S]	Soulful Brass	1968	5.00	10.00	20.00
ARGO					
❑ LP-737 [M]	Fantabulous	1964	5.00	10.00	20.00
❑ LPS-737 [S]	Fantabulous	1964	6.25	12.50	25.00
FLYING DUTCHMAN					
❑ 116	Black, Brown and Beautiful	1970	5.00	10.00	20.00
GRP IMPULSE!					
❑ IMP-212	More Blues and the Abstract Truth	1997	5.00	10.00	20.00
—Reissue on audiophile vinyl					
IMPULSE!					
❑ A-5 [M]	The Blues and the Abstract Truth	196?	5.00	10.00	20.00
—Photo cover					
❑ A-5 [M]	The Blues and the Abstract Truth	1961	12.50	25.00	50.00
—Art cover					
❑ AS-5 [S]	The Blues and the Abstract Truth	196?	7.50	15.00	30.00
—Photo cover					
❑ AS-5 [S]	The Blues and the Abstract Truth	1961	25.00	50.00	100.00
—Art cover					
❑ A-75 [M]	More Blues and the Abstract Truth	1964	6.25	12.50	25.00
❑ AS-75 [S]	More Blues and the Abstract Truth	1964	7.50	15.00	30.00
❑ A-9113 [M]	Michelle	1966	5.00	10.00	20.00
❑ AS-9113 [S]	Michelle	1966	6.25	12.50	25.00
❑ A-9129 [M]	Sound Pieces	1966	5.00	10.00	20.00
❑ AS-9129 [S]	Sound Pieces	1966	6.25	12.50	25.00
❑ A-9132 [M]	Happenings	1967	6.25	12.50	25.00
❑ AS-9132 [S]	Happenings	1967	5.00	10.00	20.00
❑ A-9144 [M]	The Kennedy Dream	1967	6.25	12.50	25.00
❑ AS-9144 [S]	The Kennedy Dream	1967	5.00	10.00	20.00
❑ A-9147 [M]	The Spirit of '67	1967	7.50	15.00	30.00
❑ AS-9147 [S]	The Spirit of '67	1967	5.00	10.00	20.00
❑ A-9153 [M]	Live From Los Angeles	1967	10.00	20.00	40.00
❑ AS-9153 [S]	Live From Los Angeles	1967	5.00	10.00	20.00
MOODSVILLE					
❑ MVLP-13 [M]	Nocturne	1960	12.50	25.00	50.00
—Green label					
❑ MVLP-13 [M]	Nocturne	1965	6.25	12.50	25.00
—Blue label, trident logo at right					
NEW JAZZ					
❑ NJLP-8224 [M]	Meet Oliver Nelson	1959	12.50	25.00	50.00
—Purple label					
❑ NJLP-8224 [M]	Meet Oliver Nelson	1965	6.25	12.50	25.00
—Blue label, trident logo at right					
❑ NJLP-8233 [M]	Takin' Care of Business	1960	12.50	25.00	50.00
—Purple label					
❑ NJLP-8233 [M]	Takin' Care of Business	1965	6.25	12.50	25.00
—Blue label, trident logo at right					
❑ NJLP-8243 [M]	Screamin' the Blues	1960	12.50	25.00	50.00
—Purple label					
❑ NJLP-8243 [M]	Screamin' the Blues	1965	6.25	12.50	25.00
—Blue label, trident logo at right					
❑ NJLP-8255 [M]	Straight Ahead	1961	12.50	25.00	50.00
—Purple label					
❑ NJLP-8255 [M]	Straight Ahead	1965	6.25	12.50	25.00
—Blue label, trident logo at right					
PRESTIGE					
❑ PRLP-7225 [M]	Afro/American Sketches	1962	10.00	20.00	40.00
❑ PRST-7225 [S]	Afro/American Sketches	1962	12.50	25.00	50.00
❑ PRLP-7236 [M]	Main Stem	1962	10.00	20.00	40.00
❑ PRST-7236 [S]	Main Stem	1962	12.50	25.00	50.00
STATUS					
❑ ST-8324 [M]	Screamin' the Blues	1965	10.00	20.00	40.00
UNITED ARTISTS					
❑ UAJ-14019 [M]	Impressions of Phaedra	1962	7.50	15.00	30.00
❑ UAJS-15019 [S]	Impressions of Phaedra	1962	10.00	20.00	40.00
VERVE					
❑ V-8508 [M]	Full Nelson	1963	6.25	12.50	25.00
❑ V6-8508 [S]	Full Nelson	1963	7.50	15.00	30.00
❑ V6-8743 [S]	Leonard Feather Presents the Sound of Feeling and the Sound of Oliver Nelson	1968	5.00	10.00	20.00
NELSON, OLIVER; KING CURTIS; JIMMY FORREST					
PRESTIGE					
❑ PRLP-7223 [M]	Soul Battle	1962	10.00	20.00	40.00
❑ PRST-7223 [S]	Soul Battle	1962	12.50	25.00	50.00
NELSON, RICKY					
CAPITOL					
❑ SOO-12109	Playing to Win	1981	2.50	5.00	10.00
DECCA					
❑ DL 4419 [M]	For Your Sweet Love	1963	7.50	15.00	30.00

Number	Title (A Side/B Side)	Yr	VG	VG+	NM
❑ DL 4479 [M]	Rick Nelson Sings "For You"	1963	7.50	15.00	30.00
❑ DL 4559 [M]	The Very Thought of You	1964	7.50	15.00	30.00
❑ DL 4608 [M]	Spotlight on Rick	1964	7.50	15.00	30.00
❑ DL 4660 [M]	Best Always	1965	7.50	15.00	30.00
❑ DL 4678 [M]	Love and Kisses	1965	7.50	15.00	30.00
❑ DL 4779 [M]	Bright Lights and Country Music	1966	6.25	12.50	25.00
❑ DL 4827 [M]	Country Fever	1967	6.25	12.50	25.00
❑ DL 4944 [M]	Another Side of Rick	1967	6.25	12.50	25.00
❑ DL 5014 [M]	Perspective	1968	12.50	25.00	50.00
—Mono copies are promo only					
❑ DL 74419 [S]	For Your Sweet Love	1963	10.00	2.00	40.00
❑ DL 74479 [S]	Rick Nelson Sings "For You"	1963	10.00	20.00	40.00
❑ DL 74559 [S]	The Very Thought of You	1964	10.00	20.00	40.00
❑ DL 74608 [S]	Spotlight on Rick	1964	10.00	20.00	40.00
❑ DL 74660 [S]	Best Always	1965	10.00	20.00	40.00
❑ DL 74678 [S]	Love and Kisses	1965	10.00	20.00	40.00
❑ DL 74779 [S]	Bright Lights and Country Music	1966	7.50	15.00	30.00
❑ DL 74827 [S]	Country Fever	1967	7.50	15.00	30.00
❑ DL 74944 [S]	Another Side of Rick	1967	7.50	15.00	30.00
❑ DL 75014 [S]	Perspective	1968	7.50	15.00	30.00
❑ DL 75162	Rick Nelson In Concert	1970	6.25	12.50	25.00
❑ DL 75236	Rick Sings Nelson	1970	6.25	12.50	25.00
—Deduct 20 percent if poster is missing					
❑ DL 75297	Rudy the Fifth	1971	6.25	12.50	25.00
❑ DL 75391	Garden Party	1972	6.25	12.50	25.00
EMI AMERICA					
❑ SQ-17192	The Very Best of Rick Nelson	1986	2.50	5.00	10.00
—Reissue of United Artists UA-LA330					
EPIC					
❑ JE 34420	Intakes	1977	3.00	6.00	12.00
❑ FE 40388	The Memphis Sessions	1986	2.50	5.00	10.00
EPIC/NU-DISK					
❑ 3E 36868 [10]	Four You	1981	3.00	6.00	12.00
IMPERIAL					
❑ LP 9048 [M]	Ricky	1957	25.00	50.00	100.00
—Black label with stars					
❑ LP 9048 [M]	Ricky	1964	6.25	12.50	25.00
—Black label with pink and white at left					
❑ LP 9048 [M]	Ricky	1966	5.00	10.00	20.00
—Black label with green and white at left					
❑ LP 9050 [M]	Ricky Nelson	1958	25.00	50.00	100.00
—Black label with stars					
❑ LP 9050 [M]	Ricky Nelson	1964	6.25	12.50	25.00
—Black label with pink and white at left					
❑ LP 9050 [M]	Ricky Nelson	1966	5.00	10.00	20.00
—Black label with green and white at left					
❑ LP 9061 [M]	Ricky Sings Again	1959	25.00	50.00	100.00
—Black label with stars					
❑ LP 9061 [M]	Ricky Sings Again	1964	6.25	12.50	25.00
—Black label with pink and white at left					
❑ LP 9061 [M]	Ricky Sings Again	1966	5.00	10.00	20.00
—Black label with green and white at left					
❑ LP 9082 [M]	Songs by Ricky	1959	18.75	37.50	75.00
—Black label with stars					
❑ LP 9082 [M]	Songs by Ricky	1964	6.25	12.50	25.00
—Black label with pink and white at left					
❑ LP 9082 [M]	Songs by Ricky	1966	5.00	10.00	20.00
—Black label with green and white at left					
❑ LP 9122 [M]	More Songs by Ricky	1960	18.75	37.50	75.00
—Black label with stars					
❑ LP 9122 [M]	More Songs by Ricky	1964	6.25	12.50	25.00
—Black label with pink and white at left					
❑ LP 9122 [M]	More Songs by Ricky	1966	5.00	10.00	20.00
—Black label with green and white at left					
❑ LP 9152 [M]	Rick Is 21	1961	10.00	20.00	40.00
—Black label with stars					
❑ LP 9152 [M]	Rick Is 21	1964	6.25	12.50	25.00
—Black label with pink and white at left					
❑ LP 9152 [M]	Rick Is 21	1966	5.00	10.00	20.00
—Black label with green and white at left					
❑ LP 9167 [M]	Album Seven by Rick	1962	10.00	20.00	40.00
—Black label with stars					
❑ LP 9167 [M]	Album Seven by Rick	1964	6.25	12.50	25.00
—Black label with pink and white at left					
❑ LP 9167 [M]	Album Seven by Rick	1966	5.00	10.00	20.00
—Black label with green and white at left					
❑ LP 9218 [M]	Best Sellers by Rick Nelson	1963	10.00	20.00	40.00
—Black label with stars					
❑ LP 9218 [M]	Best Sellers by Rick Nelson	1964	6.25	12.50	25.00
—Black label with pink and white at left					
❑ LP 9218 [M]	Best Sellers by Rick Nelson	1966	5.00	10.00	20.00
—Black label with green and white at left					
❑ LP 9223 [M]	It's Up to You	1963	10.00	20.00	40.00
—Black label with stars					
❑ LP 9223 [M]	It's Up to You	1964	6.25	12.50	25.00
—Black label with pink and white at left					
❑ LP 9223 [M]	It's Up to You	1966	5.00	10.00	20.00
—Black label with green and white at left					
❑ LP 9232 [M]	Million Sellers	1963	10.00	20.00	40.00
—Black label with stars					
❑ LP 9232 [M]	Million Sellers	1964	6.25	12.50	25.00
—Black label with pink and white at left					
❑ LP 9232 [M]	Million Sellers	1966	5.00	10.00	20.00
—Black label with green and white at left					
❑ LP 9244 [M]	A Long Vacation	1963	10.00	20.00	40.00
—Black label with stars					
❑ LP 9244 [M]	A Long Vacation	1964	6.25	12.50	25.00
—Black label with pink and white at left					
❑ LP 9244 [M]	A Long Vacation	1966	5.00	10.00	20.00
—Black label with green and white at left					
❑ LP 9251 [M]	Rick Nelson Sings for You	1964	6.25	12.50	25.00
—Black label with pink and white at left					

Number	Title (A Side/B Side)	Yr	VG	VG+	NM
❏ LP 9251 [M]	Rick Nelson Sings for You	1964	10.00	20.00	40.00
—Black label with stars					
❏ LP 9251 [M]	Rick Nelson Sings for You	1966	5.00	10.00	20.00
—Black label with green and white at left					
❏ LP 12030 [S]	Songs by Ricky	1959	50.00	100.00	200.00
—Black label with silver print					
❏ LP 12030 [S]	Songs by Ricky	1964	10.00	20.00	40.00
—Black label with pink and white at left					
❏ LP 12030 [S]	Songs by Ricky	1966	6.25	12.50	25.00
—Black label with green and white at left					
❏ LP 12059 [DJ]	More Songs by Ricky	1960	250.00	500.00	1000.
—Promo copy on blue vinyl. Add 20 percent for enclosed poster.					
❏ LP 12059 [S]	More Songs by Ricky	1960	25.00	50.00	100.00
—Black label with silver print					
❏ LP 12059 [S]	More Songs by Ricky	1964	10.00	20.00	40.00
—Black label with pink and white at left					
❏ LP 12059 [S]	More Songs by Ricky	1966	6.25	12.50	25.00
—Black label with green and white at left					
❏ LP 12071 [S]	Rick Is 21	1961	25.00	50.00	100.00
—Black label with silver print					
❏ LP 12071 [S]	Rick Is 21	1964	10.00	20.00	40.00
—Black label with pink and white at left					
❏ LP 12071 [S]	Rick Is 21	1966	6.25	12.50	25.00
—Black label with green and white at left					
❏ LP 12082 [S]	Album Seven by Rick	1962	25.00	50.00	100.00
—Black label with silver print					
❏ LP 12082 [S]	Album Seven by Rick	1964	10.00	20.00	40.00
—Black label with pink and white at left					
❏ LP 12082 [S]	Album Seven by Rick	1966	6.25	12.50	25.00
—Black label with green and white at left					
❏ LP 12090 [S]	Ricky Sings Again	1962	37.50	75.00	150.00
—Black label with silver print					
❏ LP 12090 [S]	Ricky Sings Again	1964	10.00	20.00	40.00
—Black label with pink and white at left					
❏ LP 12090 [S]	Ricky Sings Again	1966	6.25	12.50	25.00
—Black label with green and white at left					
❏ LP 12218 [R]	Best Sellers	1964	5.00	10.00	20.00
—Black label with pink and white at left					
❏ LP 12218 [R]	Best Sellers	1966	3.75	7.50	15.00
—Black label with green and white at left					
❏ LP 12232 [R]	Million Sellers	1964	5.00	10.00	20.00
—Black label with pink and white at left					
❏ LP 12232 [R]	Million Sellers	1966	3.75	7.50	15.00
—Black label with green and white at left					
❏ LP 12244 [R]	A Long Vacation	1964	5.00	10.00	20.00
—Black label with pink and white at left					
❏ LP 12244 [R]	A Long Vacation	1966	3.75	7.50	15.00
—Black label with green and white at left					
❏ LP 12251 [R]	Rick Nelson Sings for You	1964	5.00	10.00	20.00
—Black label with pink and white at left					
❏ LP 12251 [R]	Rick Nelson Sings for You	1964	6.25	12.50	25.00
—Black label with silver print					
❏ LP 12251 [R]	Rick Nelson Sings for You	1966	3.75	7.50	15.00
—Black label with green and white at left					
❏ LP 12392 [R]	Ricky	1968	3.75	7.50	15.00
—Rechanneled reissue of 9048					
❏ LP 12393 [R]	Ricky Nelson	1968	3.75	7.50	15.00
—Rechanneled reissue of 9050					
LIBERTY					
❏ LM-1004	Ricky	1981	2.00	4.00	8.00
—Reissue of United Artists 1004					
❏ LXB-9960 [(2)]	Legendary Masters	198?	3.00	6.00	12.00
—Reissue of United Artists 9960					
❏ LN-10134	Ricky Sings Again	1982	2.50	5.00	10.00
—Reissue of Imperial 12090					
❏ LN-10205	Souvenirs	1983	2.00	4.00	8.00
❏ LN-10253	Teen Age Idol	1984	2.00	4.00	8.00
❏ LN-10304	I Need You	1986	2.00	4.00	8.00
—Reissue of Sunset 5205					
❏ LN-10305	Ricky Nelson	1986	2.00	4.00	8.00
—Another reissue					
❏ LM-51004	Ricky	1983	2.00	4.00	8.00
—Reissue of Liberty 1004					
MCA					
❏ 3	Rick Nelson In Concert	1973	3.00	6.00	12.00
—Reissue of Decca 75162					
❏ 20	Rick Sings Nelson	1973	3.00	6.00	12.00
—Reissue of Decca 75236					
❏ 37	Rudy the Fifth	1973	3.00	6.00	12.00
—Reissue of Decca 75297					
❏ 62	Garden Party	1973	3.00	6.00	12.00
—Reissue of Decca 75391					
❏ 383	Windfall	1974	3.75	7.50	15.00
❏ 1517	The Decca Years	1982	2.00	4.00	8.00
❏ 2-4004 [(2)]	Rick Nelson Country	1973	3.75	7.50	15.00
❏ 6163	All My Best	1986	2.50	5.00	10.00
❏ 25983	Rick Nelson In Concert The Troubadour, 1969	1987	2.50	5.00	10.00
—Reissue of MCA 3 with revised title					
RHINO					
❏ RNLP 215	Greatest Hits	1985	3.00	6.00	12.00
❏ RNDF 259 [PD]	Greatest Hits	1985	3.75	7.50	15.00
❏ R1-70215	Greatest Hits	1987	2.50	5.00	10.00
❏ R1-71114	Live 1983-1985	1989	3.00	6.00	12.00
SUNSET					
❏ SUM-1118 [M]	Ricky Nelson	1966	3.75	7.50	15.00
❏ SUS-5118 [P]	Ricky Nelson	1966	5.00	10.00	20.00
❏ SUS-5205	I Need You	1968	3.75	7.50	15.00
TIME-LIFE					
❏ SRNR 31 [(2)]	Rick Nelson: 1957-1972	1989	3.75	7.50	15.00
UNITED ARTISTS					
❏ UA-LA330-E	The Very Best of Rick Nelson	1974	3.00	6.00	12.00

Number	Title (A Side/B Side)	Yr	VG	VG+	NM
❏ LM-1004	Ricky	1980	2.50	5.00	10.00
—Reissue of Imperial 9048					
❏ UAS-9960 [(2)]	Legendary Masters	1971	6.25	12.50	25.00
VERVE					
❏ V 2083 [M]	Teen Time	1957	125.00	250.00	500.00
—Has three Ricky Nelson songs plus tracks by four others; usually treated as Rick's LP because of his prominence on the cover					

NELSON, SANDY

IMPERIAL

Number	Title (A Side/B Side)	Yr	VG	VG+	NM
❏ LP 9105 [M]	Sandy Nelson Plays Teen Beat	1960	7.50	15.00	30.00
❏ LP 9136 [M]	He's a Drummer Boy	1961	7.50	15.00	30.00
❏ LP 9159 [M]	Let There Be Drums	1962	7.50	15.00	30.00
❏ LP 9168 [M]	Drums Are My Beat!	1962	5.00	10.00	20.00
❏ LP 9189 [M]	Drummin' Up a Storm	1962	5.00	10.00	20.00
❏ LP 9202 [M]	Golden Hits	1962	5.00	10.00	20.00
❏ LP 9203 [M]	Country Style	1962	5.00	10.00	20.00
❏ LP 9203 [M]	On the Wild Side	1966	3.75	7.50	15.00
—Same LP as above, but new title on cover					
❏ LP 9204 [M]	Compelling Percussion	1962	5.00	10.00	20.00
❏ LP 9215 [M]	Teenage House Party	1963	5.00	10.00	20.00
❏ LP 9224 [M]	The Best of the Beats	1963	3.75	7.50	15.00
❏ LP 9237 [M]	Beat That Drum	1963	3.75	7.50	15.00
❏ LP 9249 [M]	Sandy Nelson Plays	1963	3.75	7.50	15.00
❏ LP 9258 [M]	Be True to Your School	1964	3.75	7.50	15.00
❏ LP 9272 [M]	Live! In Las Vegas	1964	5.00	10.00	20.00
❏ LP 9278 [M]	Teen Beat '65	1965	3.75	7.50	15.00
❏ LP 9283 [M]	Drum Discotheque	1965	3.75	7.50	15.00
❏ LP 9287 [M]	Drums A Go-Go	1965	3.75	7.50	15.00
❏ LP 9298 [M]	Boss Beat	1965	3.75	7.50	15.00
❏ LP 9305 [M]	"In" Beat	1966	3.75	7.50	15.00
❏ LP 9314 [M]	Super Drums	1966	3.75	7.50	15.00
❏ LP 9329 [M]	Beat That #!!@* Drum	1966	3.00	6.00	12.00
❏ LP 9340 [M]	Cheetah Beat	1967	3.00	6.00	12.00
❏ LP 9345 [M]	The Beat Goes On	1967	3.00	6.00	12.00
❏ LP 9362 [M]	Soul Drums	1967	3.75	7.50	15.00
❏ LP 12044 [S]	Sandy Nelson Plays Teen Beat	1960	10.00	20.00	40.00
❏ LP 12080 [R]	Let There Be Drums	1962	6.25	12.50	25.00
❏ LP 12083 [S]	Drums Are My Beat!	1962	6.25	12.50	25.00
❏ LP 12089 [R]	He's a Drummer Boy	1962	6.25	12.50	25.00
❏ LP 12189 [S]	Drummin' Up a Storm	1962	6.25	12.50	25.00
❏ LP 12202 [P]	Golden Hits	1962	6.25	12.50	25.00
❏ LP 12203 [S]	Country Style	1962	6.25	12.50	25.00
❏ LP 12203 [S]	On the Wild Side	1966	5.00	10.00	20.00
—Same LP as above, but new title on cover					
❏ LP 12204 [S]	Compelling Percussion	1962	6.25	12.50	25.00
❏ LP 12215 [S]	Teenage House Party	1963	6.25	12.50	25.00
❏ LP 12224 [S]	The Best of the Beats	1963	5.00	10.00	20.00
❏ LP 12237 [S]	Beat That Drum	1963	5.00	10.00	20.00
❏ LP 12249 [S]	Sandy Nelson Plays	1963	5.00	10.00	20.00
❏ LP 12258 [S]	Be True to Your School	1964	5.00	10.00	20.00
❏ LP 12272 [R]	Live! In Las Vegas	1964	3.75	7.50	15.00
❏ LP 12278 [S]	Teen Beat '65	1965	5.00	10.00	20.00
❏ LP 12283 [S]	Drum Discotheque	1965	5.00	10.00	20.00
❏ LP 12287 [S]	Drums A Go-Go	1965	5.00	10.00	20.00
❏ LP 12298 [S]	Boss Beat	1965	5.00	10.00	20.00
❏ LP 12305 [S]	"In" Beat	1966	5.00	10.00	20.00
❏ LP 12314 [S]	Super Drums	1966	5.00	10.00	20.00
❏ LP 12329 [S]	Beat That #!!@* Drum	1966	3.75	7.50	15.00
❏ LP 12340 [S]	Cheetah Beat	1967	3.75	7.50	15.00
❏ LP 12345 [S]	The Beat Goes On	1967	3.75	7.50	15.00
❏ LP 12362 [S]	Soul Drums	1967	3.00	6.00	12.00
❏ LP 12367	Boogaloo Beat	1968	3.00	6.00	12.00
❏ LP 12400	Rock and Roll Revival	1968	3.00	6.00	12.00
❏ LP 12424	Rebirth of the Beat	1969	3.00	6.00	12.00
❏ LP 12439	Manhattan Spiritual	1969	3.00	6.00	12.00
❏ LP 12451	Groovy	1970	3.00	6.00	12.00
LIBERTY					
❏ LN-10172	The Very Best of Sandy Nelson	1982	2.00	4.00	8.00
❏ LN-10209	Collectors' Gems, Vol. 2	1983	2.00	4.00	8.00
SUNSET					
❏ SUM-1114 [M]	Walking Beat	1966	2.50	5.00	10.00
❏ SUM-1166 [M]	Teen Drums	1967	2.50	5.00	10.00
❏ SUS-5114 [S]	Walking Beat	1966	3.00	6.00	12.00
❏ SUS-5166 [S]	Teen Drums	1967	3.00	6.00	12.00
❏ SUS-5224	And There Were Drums (Drums and More Drums)	1968	2.50	5.00	10.00
❏ SUS-5261	Heavy Drums	1969	2.50	5.00	10.00
❏ SUS-5291	Sandy Nelson Plays Fats Domino Hits	1970	2.50	5.00	10.00
UNITED ARTISTS					
❏ UA-LA440-E	The Very Best of Sandy Nelson	1975	3.00	6.00	12.00

NELSON, TRACY

ADELPHI

Number	Title (A Side/B Side)	Yr	VG	VG+	NM
❏ 4119	Doin' It My Way	1981	2.50	5.00	10.00
ATLANTIC					
❏ SD 7310	Tracy Nelson	1974	3.00	6.00	12.00
COLUMBIA					
❏ KC 31759	Poor Man's Paradise	1973	3.00	6.00	12.00
FLYING FISH					
❏ FF-052	Homemade Songs	1978	2.50	5.00	10.00
❏ FF-209	Come See About Me	1980	2.50	5.00	10.00
MCA					
❏ 494	Sweet Soul Music	1975	3.00	6.00	12.00
❏ 2203	Time Is On My Side	1976	3.00	6.00	12.00
PRESTIGE					
❏ PRLP 7393 [M]	Deep Are the Roots	1965	6.25	12.50	25.00
❏ PRST 7393 [S]	Deep Are the Roots	1965	7.50	15.00	30.00
❏ PRST 7726	Deep Are the Roots	1969	3.75	7.50	15.00

Number	Title (A Side/B Side)	Yr	VG	VG+	NM

NELSON, WILLIE
ALLEGIANCE
| ❑ AV-5005 | Willie or Won't He | 1983 | 2.50 | 5.00 | 10.00 |
| ❑ AV-5010 | Wild & Willie | 1983 | 2.50 | 5.00 | 10.00 |
ATLANTIC
| ❑ SD 7262 | Shotgun Willie | 1973 | 5.00 | 10.00 | 20.00 |
| ❑ SD 7291 | Phases and Stages | 1974 | 5.00 | 10.00 | 20.00 |
COLUMBIA
| ❑ PC 33482 | Red Headed Stranger | 1975 | 3.75 | 7.50 | 15.00 |
| —No bar code on back cover |
| ❑ PC 33482 | Red Headed Stranger | 1979 | 2.00 | 4.00 | 8.00 |
| —With bar code on back cover; budget-line reissue |
| ❑ PC 34092 | The Sound in Your Mind | 1976 | 3.00 | 6.00 | 12.00 |
| —No bar code on back cover |
| ❑ PC 34092 | The Sound in Your Mind | 1979 | 2.00 | 4.00 | 8.00 |
| —With bar code on back cover; budget-line reissue |
| ❑ PC 34112 | The Troublemaker | 1976 | 3.00 | 6.00 | 12.00 |
| —No bar code on back cover |
| ❑ PC 34112 | The Troublemaker | 1979 | 2.00 | 4.00 | 8.00 |
| —With bar code on back cover; budget-line reissue |
| ❑ JC 34695 | To Lefty From Willie | 1977 | 3.00 | 6.00 | 12.00 |
| ❑ PC 34695 | To Lefty From Willie | 1979 | 2.00 | 4.00 | 8.00 |
| —Budget-line reissue |
| ❑ JC 35305 | Stardust | 1978 | 2.50 | 5.00 | 10.00 |
| ❑ JC 35305 | Stardust | 2000 | 6.25 | 12.50 | 25.00 |
| —Classic Records reissue on audiophile vinyl |
❑ KC2 35642 [(2)]	Willie and Family Live	1978	3.75	7.50	15.00
❑ JC 36188	Willie Nelson Sings Kristofferson	1979	2.50	5.00	10.00
❑ PC 36188	Willie Nelson Sings Kristofferson	1980	2.00	4.00	8.00
—Budget-line reissue
❑ JC 36189	Pretty Paper	1979	2.50	5.00	10.00
❑ JS 36327	The Electric Horseman	1979	2.50	5.00	10.00
—Side 2 by Dave Grusin
❑ S2 36752 [(2)]	Honeysuckle Rose	1980	3.00	6.00	12.00
—Over half of the LP is by Willie
❑ FC 36883	Somewhere Over the Rainbow	1981	2.50	5.00	10.00
❑ KC2 37542 [(2)]	Willie Nelson's Greatest Hits (& Some That Will Be)	1981	3.00	6.00	12.00
❑ FC 37951	Always on My Mind	1982	2.50	5.00	10.00
❑ PC 37951	Always on My Mind	1984	2.00	4.00	8.00
—Budget-line reissue
❑ PC 38248	Tougher Than Leather	1984	2.00	4.00	8.00
—Budget-line reissue
❑ QC 38248	Tougher Than Leather	1983	2.50	5.00	10.00
❑ CX 38250 [(10)]	Willie Nelson	1983	30.00	60.00	120.00
❑ FC 39110	Without a Song	1983	2.50	5.00	10.00
❑ PC 39110	Without a Song	1984	2.00	4.00	8.00
—Budget-line reissue
❑ FC 39145	City of New Orleans	1984	2.50	5.00	10.00
❑ PC 39145	City of New Orleans	1985	2.00	4.00	8.00
—Budget-line reissue
❑ FC 39363	Angel Eyes	1984	2.50	5.00	10.00
❑ PC 39363	Angel Eyes	1985	2.00	4.00	8.00
—Budget-line reissue
❑ FC 39894	Partners	1986	2.50	5.00	10.00
❑ PC 39894	Partners	1987	2.00	4.00	8.00
—Budget-line reissue
❑ 9C9 39943 [PD]	Always on My Mind	1985	5.00	10.00	20.00
❑ FC 39990	Half Nelson	1985	2.50	5.00	10.00
—Duets with 10 different artists
❑ PC 39990	Half Nelson	1986	2.00	4.00	8.00
—Budget-line reissue
❑ FC 40008	Me and Paul	1985	2.50	5.00	10.00
❑ PC 40008	Me and Paul	1986	2.00	4.00	8.00
—Budget-line reissue
❑ FC 40327	The Promiseland	1986	2.50	5.00	10.00
❑ FC 40487	Island in the Sea	1987	2.50	5.00	10.00
❑ HC 43482	Red Headed Stranger	1982	10.00	20.00	40.00
—Half-speed mastered edition
❑ FC 44431	What a Wonderful World	1988	2.50	5.00	10.00
❑ FC 45046	A Horse Called Music	1989	2.50	5.00	10.00
❑ HC 45305	Stardust	1981	17.50	35.00	70.00
—Half-speed mastered edition
❑ HC 47951	Always on My Mind	1982	12.50	25.00	50.00
—Half-speed mastered edition
❑ HC 48248	Tougher Than Leather	1983	12.50	25.00	50.00
—Half-speed mastered edition
HEARTLAND
| ❑ HL 1038/9 [(2)] | The Best of Willie Nelson | 1987 | 3.75 | 7.50 | 15.00 |
LIBERTY
❑ LRP-3239 [M]	...And Then I Wrote	1962	10.00	20.00	40.00
❑ LRP-3308 [M]	Here's Willie Nelson	1963	10.00	20.00	40.00
❑ LST-7239 [S]	...And Then I Wrote	1962	12.50	25.00	50.00
❑ LST-7308 [S]	Here's Willie Nelson	1963	12.50	25.00	50.00
❑ LN-10013	Country Willie	1980	2.00	4.00	8.00
—Budget-line reissue
❑ LN-10118	The Best of Willie Nelson	1982	2.00	4.00	8.00
—Budget-line reissue
PAIR
❑ PDL2-1007 [(2)]	Country Winners	1986	3.00	6.00	12.00
❑ PDL2-1032 [(2)]	Once More with Feeling	1986	3.00	6.00	12.00
❑ PDL2-1114 [(2)]	Good Hearted Woman	1986	3.00	6.00	12.00
PICKWICK
❑ ACL1-0326	Country Winners	1976	2.00	4.00	8.00
❑ ACL1-0705	Spotlight on Willie Nelson	1976	2.00	4.00	8.00
❑ SPC-3584	Hello Walls	197?	2.50	5.00	10.00
❑ ACL1-7018	Columbus Stockade Blues	1976	2.00	4.00	8.00
PLANTATION
| ❑ PLP-24 | The Longhorn Jamboree Presents: Willie Nelson & His Friends | 1976 | 2.50 | 5.00 | 10.00 |
| —Also includes tracks by David Allan Coe, Jerry Lee Lewis and Carl Perkins |

RCA CAMDEN
❑ ACL1-0326	Country Winners	1973	3.00	6.00	12.00
❑ ACL1-0705	Spotlight on Willie Nelson	1974	3.00	6.00	12.00
❑ CAS-2444	Columbus Stockade Blues	1970	3.75	7.50	15.00
❑ ACL1-7018	Columbus Stockade Blues	1975	2.50	5.00	10.00
RCA VICTOR
❑ ANL1-1102	Yesterday's Wine	1975	2.50	5.00	10.00
❑ APL1-1234	What Can You Do to Me Now	1975	3.00	6.00	12.00
❑ APL1-1487	Willie Nelson Live	1976	3.00	6.00	12.00
❑ APL1-2210	Before His Time	1977	2.50	5.00	10.00
❑ AHL1-3243	Sweet Memories	1979	2.50	5.00	10.00
❑ LPM-3418 [M]	Country Willie — His Own Songs	1965	5.00	10.00	20.00
❑ LSP-3418 [S]	Country Willie — His Own Songs	1965	6.25	12.50	25.00
❑ LPM-3528 [M]	Country Favorites, Willie Nelson Style	1966	5.00	10.00	20.00
❑ LSP-3528 [S]	Country Favorites, Willie Nelson Style	1966	6.25	12.50	25.00
❑ AHL1-3549	Danny Davis & Willie Nelson with the Nashville Brass	1980	2.50	5.00	10.00
❑ LPM-3659 [M]	Country Music Concert	1966	5.00	10.00	20.00
❑ LSP-3659 [S]	Country Music Concert	1966	6.25	12.50	25.00
❑ AYL1-3671	Before His Time	1980	2.00	4.00	8.00
—"Best Buy Series" reissue
❑ LPM-3748 [M]	Make Way for Willie Nelson	1967	5.00	10.00	20.00
❑ LSP-3748 [S]	Make Way for Willie Nelson	1967	6.25	12.50	25.00
❑ AYL1-3800	Yesterday's Wine	1980	2.00	4.00	8.00
—"Best Buy Series" reissue
❑ LPM-3858 [M]	The Party's Over and Other Great Willie Nelson Songs	1967	6.25	12.50	25.00
❑ LSP-3858 [S]	The Party's Over and Other Great Willie Nelson Songs	1967	5.00	10.00	20.00
❑ LPM-3937 [M]	Texas in My Soul	1968	25.00	50.00	100.00
❑ LSP-3937 [S]	Texas in My Soul	1968	5.00	10.00	20.00
❑ AYL1-3958	What Can You Do to Me Now	1981	2.00	4.00	8.00
—"Best Buy Series" reissue
❑ AHL1-4045	The Minstrel Man	1981	2.50	5.00	10.00
❑ LSP-4057	Good Times	1968	5.00	10.00	20.00
❑ LSP-4111	My Own Peculiar Way	1969	5.00	10.00	20.00
❑ AYL1-4165	Willie Nelson Live	1981	2.00	4.00	8.00
—"Best Buy Series" reissue
❑ LSP-4294	Both Sides Now	1970	5.00	10.00	20.00
❑ AYL1-4300	Sweet Memories	1982	2.00	4.00	8.00
—"Best Buy Series" reissue
❑ LSP-4404	Laying My Burdens Down	1970	5.00	10.00	20.00
❑ AHL1-4420	The Best of Willie Nelson	1982	2.50	5.00	10.00
❑ LSP-4489	Willie Nelson & Family	1971	5.00	10.00	20.00
❑ LSP-4568	Yesterday's Wine	1971	5.00	10.00	20.00
❑ LSP-4653	The Picture	1972	5.00	10.00	20.00
❑ LSP-4760	The Willie Way	1972	5.00	10.00	20.00
❑ AHL1-4819	My Own Way	1983	2.50	5.00	10.00
❑ AYL1-5143	The Best of Willie Nelson	1984	2.00	4.00	8.00
—"Best Buy Series" reissue
❑ CPL1-5174	Don't You Ever Get Tired of Hurting Me	1984	2.50	5.00	10.00
❑ AYL1-5438	My Own Way	1985	2.00	4.00	8.00
—"Best Buy Series" reissue
❑ AHL1-5470	Collector's Series	1985	2.50	5.00	10.00
❑ CPL1-7158	Willie	1986	2.50	5.00	10.00
SONGBIRD
| ❑ 3258 | Family Bible | 1980 | 2.50 | 5.00 | 10.00 |
SUNSET
| ❑ SUM-1138 [M] | Hello Walls | 1966 | 3.75 | 7.50 | 15.00 |
| ❑ SUS-5138 [S] | Hello Walls | 1966 | 5.00 | 10.00 | 20.00 |
TAKOMA
| ❑ TAK-7104 | The Legend Begins | 1983 | 2.50 | 5.00 | 10.00 |
TIME-LIFE
| ❑ P 16946 [(3)] | Country and Western Classics | 1983 | 5.00 | 10.00 | 20.00 |
UNITED ARTISTS
| ❑ UA-LA086-E | The Best of Willie Nelson | 1973 | 3.75 | 7.50 | 15.00 |
| —Reissue of Liberty tracks |
❑ UA-LA410-G	Country Willie	1975	3.75	7.50	15.00
❑ UA-LA574-H2 [(2)]	Texas Country	1975	4.50	9.00	18.00
❑ UA-LA930-G	There'll Be No Teardrops Tonight	1978	3.75	7.50	15.00

NEON PHILHARMONIC, THE
Also see TUPPER SAUSSY.
WARNER BROS.
| ❑ WS 1769 | The Moth Confesses | 1968 | 6.25 | 12.50 | 25.00 |
| ❑ WS 1804 | The Neon Philharmonic | 1969 | 3.75 | 7.50 | 15.00 |

NEP-TUNES, THE
FAMILY
| ❑ FLP-152 [M] | Surfer's Holiday | 1963 | 50.00 | 100.00 | 200.00 |
| ❑ SFLP-152 [S] | Surfer's Holiday | 1963 | 75.00 | 150.00 | 300.00 |

NERO, PAUL
SUNSET
| ❑ LP-303 [M] | Play the Music of Paul Nero and His Hi-Fiddles | 1956 | 15.00 | 30.00 | 60.00 |

NERO, PETER
ARISTA
| ❑ AL 4034 | Disco, Dance and Love Themes | 1976 | 2.50 | 5.00 | 10.00 |
BAINBRIDGE
| ❑ BT-6268 | The Sounds of Love | 1987 | 2.50 | 5.00 | 10.00 |
COLUMBIA
❑ CS 1009	I'll Never Fall in Love Again	1970	2.50	5.00	10.00
❑ CS 9800	I've Gotta Be Me	1969	3.00	6.00	12.00
❑ C 30586	Love Story	1971	2.50	5.00	10.00
❑ KC 31105	Summer of '42	1971	2.50	5.00	10.00
❑ KC 31335	The First Time Ever (I Saw Your Face)	1972	2.50	5.00	10.00
❑ C2 31982 [(2)]	The World of Peter Nero	1972	3.00	6.00	12.00
❑ KC 32689	Say, Has Anybody Seen My Sweet Gypsy Rose	1973	2.50	5.00	10.00
❑ PC 33136	Greatest Hits	1974	2.50	5.00	10.00

Number	Title (A Side/B Side)	Yr	VG	VG+	NM
CONCORD JAZZ					
❑ CJ-48	Now	1978	2.50	5.00	10.00
❑ CJ-48	Peter Nero Now	1978	2.50	5.00	10.00
CRYSTAL CLEAR					
❑ 6001	The Wiz	198?	5.00	10.00	20.00
—Direct-to-disc recording					
MODE					
❑ LP-117 [M]	Bernie Nerow Trio	1957	20.00	40.00	80.00
—As "Bernie Nerow"					
PREMIER					
❑ PM-2011 [M]	Just for You	1963	5.00	10.00	20.00
❑ PS-2011 [R]	Just for You	1963	3.00	6.00	12.00
RCA CAMDEN					
❑ CAL-2139 [M]	Peter Nero Plays Born Free and Others	1967	3.75	7.50	15.00
❑ CAS-2139 [S]	Peter Nero Plays Born Free and Others	1967	3.00	6.00	12.00
❑ CAL-2228 [M]	If Ever I Would Leave You	1968	3.75	7.50	15.00
❑ CAS-2228 [S]	If Ever I Would Leave You	1968	3.00	6.00	12.00
RCA VICTOR					
❑ PRM-241 [M]	Tender Is the Night	1967	3.75	7.50	15.00
❑ PRS-241 [S]	Tender Is the Night	1967	5.00	10.00	20.00
—Special-products release					
❑ ADL1-0284 [(2)]	Music Festival of Hits	1973	3.00	6.00	12.00
❑ LPM-2334 [M]	Piano Forte.	1961	3.75	7.50	15.00
❑ LSP-2334 [S]	Piano Forte.	1961	5.00	10.00	20.00
❑ LPM-2383 [M]	New Piano in Town.	1961	3.75	7.50	15.00
❑ LSP-2383 [S]	New Piano in Town.	1961	5.00	10.00	20.00
❑ LPM-2484 [M]	Young and Warm and Wonderful.	1962	3.75	7.50	15.00
❑ LSP-2484 [S]	Young and Warm and Wonderful.	1962	5.00	10.00	20.00
❑ LPM-2536 [M]	For the Nero-Minded.	1962	3.75	7.50	15.00
❑ LSP-2536 [S]	For the Nero-Minded.	1962	5.00	10.00	20.00
❑ LPM-2618 [M]	The Colorful Peter Nero.	1963	3.75	7.50	15.00
❑ LSP-2618 [S]	The Colorful Peter Nero.	1963	5.00	10.00	20.00
❑ LPM-2638 [M]	Hail the Conquering Nero.	1963	3.75	7.50	15.00
❑ LSP-2638 [S]	Hail the Conquering Nero.	1963	5.00	10.00	20.00
❑ LPM-2710 [M]	Peter Nero in Person.	1963	3.75	7.50	15.00
❑ LSP-2710 [S]	Peter Nero in Person.	1963	5.00	10.00	20.00
❑ LPM-2827 [M]	Sunday in New York.	1964	3.75	7.50	15.00
❑ LSP-2827 [S]	Sunday in New York.	1964	5.00	10.00	20.00
❑ LPM-2853 [M]	Reflections.	1964	3.75	7.50	15.00
❑ LSP-2853 [S]	Reflections.	1964	5.00	10.00	20.00
❑ LPM-2935 [M]	Songs You Won't Forget.	1964	3.75	7.50	15.00
❑ LSP-2935 [S]	Songs You Won't Forget.	1964	5.00	10.00	20.00
❑ LPM-2978 [M]	The Best of Peter Nero.	1965	3.75	7.50	15.00
❑ LSP-2978 [S]	The Best of Peter Nero.	1965	5.00	10.00	20.00
❑ LPM-3313 [M]	Career Girls.	1965	3.75	7.50	15.00
❑ LSP-3313 [S]	Career Girls.	1965	5.00	10.00	20.00
❑ LPM-3496 [M]	The Screen Scene.	1966	3.00	6.00	12.00
❑ LSP-3496 [S]	The Screen Scene.	1966	3.75	7.50	15.00
❑ LPM-3550 [M]	Peter Nero — Up Close.	1966	3.00	6.00	12.00
❑ LSP-3550 [S]	Peter Nero — Up Close.	1966	3.75	7.50	15.00
❑ LPM-3610 [M]	Peter Nero On Tour.	1966	3.00	6.00	12.00
❑ LSP-3610 [S]	Peter Nero On Tour.	1966	3.75	7.50	15.00
❑ LPM-3720 [M]	Plays a Salute to Herb Alpert and the Tijuana Brass.	1967	3.75	7.50	15.00
❑ LSP-3720 [S]	Plays a Salute to Herb Alpert and the Tijuana Brass.	1967	3.00	6.00	12.00
❑ LPM-3814 [M]	Xochimilico.	1967	3.75	7.50	15.00
❑ LSP-3814 [S]	Xochimilico.	1967	3.00	6.00	12.00
❑ LPM-3871 [M]	Nero-ing In on the Hits.	1968	3.75	7.50	15.00
❑ LSP-3871 [S]	Nero-ing In on the Hits.	1968	3.00	6.00	12.00
❑ LPM-3936 [M]	Peter Nero Plays Love Is Blue and Ten Other Great Songs.	1968	3.75	7.50	15.00
❑ LSP-3936 [S]	Peter Nero Plays Love Is Blue and Ten Other Great Songs.	1968	3.00	6.00	12.00
❑ LSP-4072	Impressions (Great Songs of Burt Bacharach and Hal David).	1968	3.00	6.00	12.00
❑ LSP-4205	Love Trip.	1969	3.00	6.00	12.00

NESBITT, JIM

Number	Title (A Side/B Side)	Yr	VG	VG+	NM
CHART					
❑ CHM-1005 [M]	Truck Drivin' Cat with Nine Wives	1968	7.50	15.00	30.00
❑ CHS-1005 [S]	Truck Drivin' Cat with Nine Wives	1968	5.00	10.00	20.00
❑ CHS-1031	Runnin' Bare	1970	5.00	10.00	20.00

NESMITH, MICHAEL
Also see THE MONKEES.

Number	Title (A Side/B Side)	Yr	VG	VG+	NM
PACIFIC ARTS					
❑ (no #) [DJ]	The Michael Nesmith Radio Special	1979	10.00	20.00	40.00
❑ 11-101A	The Prison	1975	12.50	25.00	50.00
—Boxed set with booklet					
❑ 7-101	The Prison	197?	5.00	10.00	20.00
—Standard cover					
❑ 7-106	Compilation	1976	5.00	10.00	20.00
❑ 7-107	From a Radio Engine to the Photon Wing	1977	5.00	10.00	20.00
❑ 7-116	And the Hits Just Keep On Comin'	1978	5.00	10.00	20.00
—Reissue of RCA 4695					
❑ 7-117	Pretty Much Your Standard Ranch Stash	1978	5.00	10.00	20.00
—Reissue of RCA APL1-0164					
❑ 7-118	Live at the Palais	1978	5.00	10.00	20.00
❑ 7-130	Infinite Rider on the Big Dogma	1979	5.00	10.00	20.00
RCA VICTOR					
❑ APL1-0164	Pretty Much Your Standard Ranch Stash	1973	6.25	12.50	25.00
❑ LSP-4371	Magnetic South	1970	7.50	15.00	30.00
❑ LSP-4415	Loose Salute	1970	7.50	15.00	30.00
❑ LSP-4497	Nevada Fighter	1971	6.25	12.50	25.00
❑ LSP-4563	Tantamount to Treason	1971	6.25	12.50	25.00
❑ LSP-4695	And the Hits Just Keep On Comin'	1972	6.25	12.50	25.00
RHINO					
❑ R1-70168	The Newer Stuff	1989	3.00	6.00	12.00

NESTICO, SAMMY

Number	Title (A Side/B Side)	Yr	VG	VG+	NM
MARK					
❑ 32244	Swingaphonic	1969	5.00	10.00	20.00

NETHERWORLD

Number	Title (A Side/B Side)	Yr	VG	VG+	NM
R.E.M.					
❑ 4441	Netherworld	196?	15.00	30.00	60.00

NEVILLE, AARON

Number	Title (A Side/B Side)	Yr	VG	VG+	NM
MINIT					
❑ LP 24007 [R]	Like It 'Tis	1967	7.50	15.00	30.00
❑ LP 40007 [M]	Like It 'Tis	1967	10.00	20.00	40.00
PAR-LO					
❑ 1 [M]	Tell It Like It Is	1967	20.00	40.00	80.00
❑ 1 [S]	Tell It Like It Is	1967	50.00	100.00	200.00

NEVILLE BROTHERS, THE
Also see AARON NEVILLE.

Number	Title (A Side/B Side)	Yr	VG	VG+	NM
CAPITOL					
❑ ST-11865	The Neville Brothers	1978	7.50	15.00	30.00

NEW APOCALYPSE, THE

Number	Title (A Side/B Side)	Yr	VG	VG+	NM
M.T.A.					
❑ S-5017	Stainless Soul	1970	5.00	10.00	20.00

NEW BIRTH, THE

Number	Title (A Side/B Side)	Yr	VG	VG+	NM
ARIOLA AMERICA					
❑ SW-50062	Platinum City	1979	2.50	5.00	10.00
BUDDAH					
❑ BDS-5636	Blind Baby	1975	2.50	5.00	10.00
COLLECTABLES					
❑ COL-5100	Golden Classics	1988	2.50	5.00	10.00
RCA VICTOR					
❑ APD1-0285 [Q]	It's Been a Long Time	1974	5.00	10.00	20.00
❑ APL1-0285	It's Been a Long Time	1974	2.50	5.00	10.00
❑ APL1-0494	Comin' From All Ends	1974	2.50	5.00	10.00
❑ APL1-1021	The Best of the New Birth	1975	2.50	5.00	10.00
❑ ANL1-2145	Birth Day	1977	2.50	5.00	10.00
—Reissue of 4797					
❑ AFL1-4411	I'm Back	1982	2.50	5.00	10.00
❑ LSP-4450	The New Birth	1970	3.75	7.50	15.00
❑ LSP-4526	Ain't No Big Thing, But It's Growing	1971	3.75	7.50	15.00
❑ LSP-4697	Coming Together	1972	3.75	7.50	15.00
❑ LSP-4797	Birth Day	1973	3.00	6.00	12.00
WARNER BROS.					
❑ BS 2953	Love Potion	1976	2.50	5.00	10.00
❑ BSK 3071	Behold the Mighty Army	1977	2.50	5.00	10.00

NEW BLACK EAGLE JAZZ BAND

Number	Title (A Side/B Side)	Yr	VG	VG+	NM
DIRTY SHAME					
❑ 2002	On the River	197?	5.00	10.00	20.00

NEW CHRISTY MINSTRELS, THE
At one time or another, KIM CARNES, Gene Clark of THE BYRDS, BARRY McGUIRE, KENNY ROGERS and RANDY SPARKS were members, as were most of the original FIRST EDITION.

Number	Title (A Side/B Side)	Yr	VG	VG+	NM
COLUMBIA					
❑ CL 1872 [M]	The New Christy Minstrels	1962	5.00	10.00	20.00
❑ CL 1941 [M]	The New Christy Minstrels In Person	1963	5.00	10.00	20.00
❑ CL 2017 [M]	Tall Tales! Legends & Nonsense	1963	5.00	10.00	20.00
❑ CL 2055 [M]	Ramblin' Feturing Green, Green	1963	5.00	10.00	20.00
❑ CL 2096 [M]	Merry Christmas	1963	5.00	10.00	20.00
❑ CL 2159 [M]	Today	1964	5.00	10.00	20.00
❑ CL 2187 [M]	Land of Giants	1964	5.00	10.00	20.00
❑ CL 2280 [M]	The Quiet Sides of the New Christy Minstrels	1965	5.00	10.00	20.00
❑ CL 2303 [M]	Cowboys and Indians	1965	5.00	10.00	20.00
❑ CL 2369 [M]	Chim Chim Cher-ee	1965	5.00	10.00	20.00
❑ CL 2384 [M]	The Wandering Minstrels	1965	5.00	10.00	20.00
❑ CL 2479 [M]	Greatest Hits	1966	5.00	10.00	20.00
❑ CL 2531 [M]	In Italy…In Italian	1966	5.00	10.00	20.00
❑ CL 2542 [M]	New Kick	1967	5.00	10.00	20.00
❑ CL 2556 [M]	Christmas with the Christies	1966	5.00	10.00	20.00
❑ CS 8672 [S]	The New Christy Minstrels	1962	6.25	12.50	25.00
❑ CS 8741 [S]	The New Christy Minstrels In Person	1963	6.25	12.50	25.00
❑ CS 8817 [S]	Tall Tales! Legends & Nonsense	1963	6.25	12.50	25.00
❑ CS 8855 [S]	Ramblin' Feturing Green, Green	1963	6.25	12.50	25.00
❑ CS 8896 [S]	Merry Christmas	1963	6.25	12.50	25.00
❑ CS 8959 [S]	Today	1964	6.25	12.50	25.00
❑ CS 8987 [S]	Land of Giants	1964	6.25	12.50	25.00
❑ CS 9080 [S]	The Quiet Sides of the New Christy Minstrels	1965	6.25	12.50	25.00
❑ CS 9103 [S]	Cowboys and Indians	1965	6.25	12.50	25.00
❑ CS 9169 [S]	Chim Chim Cher-ee	1965	6.25	12.50	25.00
❑ CS 9184 [S]	The Wandering Minstrels	1965	6.25	12.50	25.00
❑ CS 9279 [S]	Greatest Hits	1966	6.25	12.50	25.00
❑ CS 9331 [S]	In Italy…In Italian	1966	6.25	12.50	25.00
❑ CS 9342 [S]	New Kick	1967	6.25	12.50	25.00
❑ CS 9356 [S]	Christmas with the Christies	1966	6.25	12.50	25.00
❑ CS 9616 [M]	On Tour Through Motortown	1968	12.50	25.00	50.00
—White label promo only; "Special Mono Radio Station Copy" sticker on front					
❑ CS 9616 [S]	On Tour Through Motortown	1968	5.00	10.00	20.00
❑ CS 9709	Chitty Chitty Bang Bang	1969	5.00	10.00	20.00
GREGAR					
❑ 102	You Need Someone to Love	1970	3.75	7.50	15.00

NEW COLONY SIX, THE

Number	Title (A Side/B Side)	Yr	VG	VG+	NM
MERCURY					
❑ SR-61165	Revelations	1968	7.50	15.00	30.00
❑ SR-61228	Attacking a Straw Man	1969	7.50	15.00	30.00
SENTAR					
❑ LP-101 [M]	Breakthrough	1966	125.00	250.00	500.00
❑ SST-3001 [S]	Colonization	1967	15.00	30.00	60.00
❑ ST-3001 [M]	Colonization	1967	12.50	25.00	50.00
SUNDAZED					
❑ LP 5007	At the River's Edge	1995	2.50	5.00	10.00

Number	Title (A Side/B Side)	Yr	VG	VG+	NM

NEW DAWN, THE
HOOT
| ❑ GR 704569 | There's a New Dawn | 1970 | 250.00 | 500.00 | 1000. |

NEW DIMENSIONS, THE
SUNDAZED
| ❑ LP-5025 | The Best of the New Dimensions | 199? | 2.50 | 5.00 | 10.00 |
SUTTON
❑ SSU-331 [S]	Deuces and Eights	1963	25.00	50.00	100.00
❑ SU-331 [M]	Deuces and Eights	1963	20.00	40.00	80.00
❑ SSU-332 [S]	Surf 'N' Bongos	1963	12.50	25.00	50.00
❑ SU-332 [M]	Surf 'N' Bongos	1963	10.00	20.00	40.00
❑ SSU-336 [S]	Soul Surf	1964	12.50	25.00	50.00
❑ SU-336 [M]	Soul Surf	1964	10.00	20.00	40.00

NEW GLENN MILLER ORCHESTRA
See GLENN MILLER ORCHESTRA (in the M's).

NEW LEGION ROCK SPECTACULAR, THE
SPECTACULAR
| ❑ 7777 | Wild Ones! | 1975 | 15.00 | 30.00 | 60.00 |

NEW MIX, THE
UNITED ARTISTS
| ❑ UAS-6678 | The New Mix | 1968 | 5.00 | 10.00 | 20.00 |

NEW ORDER
FACTORY
❑ FACTUS 8 [EP]	1981-1982	1983	5.00	10.00	20.00
❑ FACTUS 12	Power, Corruption and Lies	1983	5.00	10.00	20.00
❑ FACTUS 50	Movement	1981	5.00	10.00	20.00
—Originals have no bar code					
❑ FACTUS 50	Movement	1981	12.50	25.00	50.00
—Purple vinyl (looks more black, but will appear purple when held to a light)					
QWEST
❑ 25289	Low Life	1985	2.50	5.00	10.00
❑ 25308	Power, Corruption and Lies	1985	2.50	5.00	10.00
—Reissue					
❑ 25511	Brotherhood	1986	2.50	5.00	10.00
❑ 25621 [(2)]	Substance	1987	3.75	7.50	15.00
❑ 25845	Technique	1989	3.00	6.00	12.00
❑ R 100938	Technique	1989	3.50	7.00	14.00
—BMG Music Service edition					

NEW ORLEANS RHYTHM KINGS
BRUNSWICK
| ❑ BL 58011 [10] | Dixieland Jazz | 1950 | 30.00 | 60.00 | 120.00 |

NEW ORLEANS SHUFFLERS, THE
KINGSWAY
| ❑ KL-700 [M] | The New Orleans Shufflers | 1955 | 10.00 | 20.00 | 40.00 |

NEW RENAISSANCE SOCIETY, THE
HANNA-BARBERA
| ❑ HLP-9504 [M] | Baroque n' Stones | 1966 | 5.00 | 10.00 | 20.00 |
| ❑ HST-9504 [S] | Baroque n' Stones | 1966 | 6.25 | 12.50 | 25.00 |

NEW RIDERS OF THE PURPLE SAGE
A&M
| ❑ SP-4818 | Feelin' All Right | 1981 | 2.50 | 5.00 | 10.00 |
COLUMBIA
❑ KC 30888	New Riders of the Purple Sage	1971	3.75	7.50	15.00
❑ PC 30888	New Riders of the Purple Sage	1979	2.00	4.00	8.00
—Budget-line reissue					
❑ KC 31284	Powerglide	1972	3.75	7.50	15.00
❑ PC 31284	Powerglide	1979	2.00	4.00	8.00
—Budget-line reissue					
❑ KC 31930	Gypsy Cowboy	1972	3.75	7.50	15.00
❑ PC 31930	Gypsy Cowboy	1979	2.00	4.00	8.00
—Budget-line reissue					
❑ CQ 32450 [Q]	The Adventures of Panama Red	1974	5.00	10.00	20.00
❑ KC 32450	The Adventures of Panama Red	1973	3.75	7.50	15.00
❑ PC 32450	The Adventures of Panama Red	1979	2.00	4.00	8.00
—Budget-line reissue					
❑ PC 32870	Home, Home on the Road	1974	3.75	7.50	15.00
—Originals have no bar code					
❑ PC 33145	Brujo	1974	3.75	7.50	15.00
—Originals have no bar code					
❑ PC 33688	Oh, What a Mighty Time	1975	3.75	7.50	15.00
—Originals have no bar code					
❑ PC 34367	The Best of New Riders of the Purple Sage	1976	3.00	6.00	12.00
—Originals have no bar code					
❑ PC 34367	The Best of New Riders of the Purple Sage	1979	2.00	4.00	8.00
—Budget-line reissue with bar code					
MCA
❑ 632	Marin County Line	1980	2.00	4.00	8.00
—Reissue of 2307					
❑ 2196	New Riders	1976	3.00	6.00	12.00
❑ 2248	Who Are These Guys	1977	3.00	6.00	12.00
❑ 2307	Marin County Line	1977	3.00	6.00	12.00
RELIX
| ❑ RRLP-2024 | Before Time Began | 1986 | 2.00 | 4.00 | 8.00 |
| ❑ RRLP-2025 | Vintage NRPS | 1987 | 2.00 | 4.00 | 8.00 |

NEW SEEKERS, THE
ELEKTRA
❑ EQ-5051 [Q]	The Best of the New Seekers	1973	5.00	10.00	20.00
❑ EKS-74088	Beautiful People	1971	3.00	6.00	12.00
❑ EKS-74108	New Colours	1971	3.00	6.00	12.00
❑ EKS-74115	We'd Like to Teach the World to Sing	1971	3.00	6.00	12.00
❑ EKS-75034	Circles	1972	3.00	6.00	12.00
❑ EKS-75051	The Best of the New Seekers	1973	3.00	6.00	12.00
MGM VERVE
❑ V 5090	Come Softly to Me	1972	2.50	5.00	10.00
❑ V 5095	The History of the New Seekers	1973	2.50	5.00	10.00
❑ V 5098	Pinball Wizards	1973	2.50	5.00	10.00

NEW STRANGERS, THE
FOLKLORE
| ❑ FRLP-14027 [M] | Meet the New Strangers | 1964 | 5.00 | 10.00 | 20.00 |
| ❑ FRST-14027 [S] | Meet the New Strangers | 1964 | 6.25 | 12.50 | 25.00 |

NEW SYMPHONY ORCHESTRA OF LONDON (RAYMOND AGOULT, CONDUCTOR)
RCA VICTOR RED SEAL
❑ LSC-2134 [S]	Overture! Overture!	1959	12.50	25.00	50.00
—Original with "shaded dog" label; issued with two different covers					
❑ LSC-2134 [S]	Overture! Overture!	199?	6.25	12.50	25.00
—Classic Records reissue					

NEW SYMPHONY ORCHESTRA OF LONDON (RONALD BINGE, CONDUCTOR)
RCA VICTOR RED SEAL
| ❑ LSC-2399 [S] | Mendelssohniana | 1960 | 75.00 | 150.00 | 300.00 |
| —Originals with "shaded dog" label | | | | | |

NEW SYMPHONY ORCHESTRA OF LONDON (ALEXANDER GIBSON, CONDUCTOR)
RCA VICTOR RED SEAL
❑ LSC-2225 [S]	Witches' Brew	1959	100.00	200.00	400.00
—Original with "shaded dog" label					
❑ LSC-2225 [S]	Witches' Brew	199?	6.25	12.50	25.00
—Classic Records reissue					

NEW TWEEDY BROTHERS, THE
RIDON
❑ 234	The New Tweedy Brothers	1968	100.00	200.00	400.00
—With plain white cover					
❑ 234	The New Tweedy Brothers	1968	500.00	1000.	2000.
—With oversized hexagonal cover designed to look like a sugar cube					

NEW WAVE, THE
CANTERBURY
| ❑ CLPS-1501 | The New Wave | 1967 | 6.25 | 12.50 | 25.00 |

NEW YORK ART QUARTET, THE
ESP-DISK'
| ❑ 1004 [M] | The New York Art Quartet | 1965 | 5.00 | 10.00 | 20.00 |
| ❑ S-1004 [S] | The New York Art Quartet | 1965 | 6.25 | 12.50 | 25.00 |

NEW YORK DOLLS
MERCURY
❑ SRM-1-675	New York Dolls	1973	10.00	20.00	40.00
❑ SRM-1-1001	In Too Much Too Soon	1974	10.00	20.00	40.00
❑ 826094-1	Night of the Living Dolls	1985	3.00	6.00	12.00

NEW YORK JAZZ QUARTET, THE (1)
CORAL
| ❑ CRL 57136 [M] | Music For Suburban Living | 1958 | 10.00 | 20.00 | 40.00 |
| ❑ CRL 757136 [S] | Music For Suburban Living | 1958 | 7.50 | 15.00 | 30.00 |
ELEKTRA
| ❑ EKL-115 [M] | The New York Jazz Quartet | 1957 | 12.50 | 25.00 | 50.00 |
| ❑ EKL-118 [M] | Gone Native | 1957 | 12.50 | 25.00 | 50.00 |
SAVOY
| ❑ MG-12172 [M] | Adam's Theme | 1960 | 7.50 | 15.00 | 30.00 |
| ❑ MG-12175 [M] | Gone Native | 1961 | 7.50 | 15.00 | 30.00 |

NEW YORK JAZZ SEXTET, THE
SCEPTER
| ❑ S-526 [M] | New York Jazz Sextet | 1964 | 5.00 | 10.00 | 20.00 |
| ❑ SS-526 [S] | New York Jazz Sextet | 1964 | 6.25 | 12.50 | 25.00 |

NEW YORK ORIGINATORS, THE
PARAMOUNT
| ❑ RS-201 [10] | The New York Style | 1952 | 15.00 | 30.00 | 60.00 |

NEW YORK PHILHARMONIC ORCHESTRA (BRUNO WALTER, CONDUCTOR)
COLUMBIA MASTERWORKS
❑ ML 4001 [M]	Mendelssohn: Violin Concerto	1948	10.00	20.00	40.00
—Violinist: Nathan Milstein; the very first modern microgroove LP!					
❑ ML 4001 [M]	Mendelssohn: Violin Concerto	1999	6.25	12.50	25.00
—Violinist: Nathan Milstein; Classic Records commemorative reissue					

NEW YORK PRO MUSICA ANTIQUA
COUNTERPOINT/ESOTERIC
| ❑ CPT 521 [M] | English Medieval Christmas Carols | 196? | 5.00 | 10.00 | 20.00 |

NEW YORK SAXOPHONE QUARTET, THE
MARK
| ❑ 32322 | The New York Saxophone Quartet | 1969 | 5.00 | 10.00 | 20.00 |
20TH CENTURY FOX
| ❑ TFM-3150 [M] | The New York Saxophone Quartet | 1964 | 5.00 | 10.00 | 20.00 |
| ❑ TFS-3150 [S] | The New York Saxophone Quartet | 1964 | 6.25 | 12.50 | 25.00 |

NEWBEATS, THE
HICKORY
❑ LPM 120 [M]	Bread and Butter	1964	12.50	25.00	50.00
❑ LPS 120 [S]	Bread and Butter	1964	37.50	75.00	150.00
❑ LPM 122 [M]	Big Beat Sounds by the Newbeats	1965	12.50	25.00	50.00
❑ LPS 122 [S]	Big Beat Sounds by the Newbeats	1965	25.00	50.00	100.00
❑ LPM 128 [M]	Run Baby Run	1965	12.50	25.00	50.00
❑ LPS 128 [S]	Run Baby Run	1965	25.00	50.00	100.00
❑ DT 90701 [R]	Bread and Butter	1965	37.50	75.00	150.00
—Capitol Record Club edition					
❑ ST 90701 [S]	Bread and Butter	1965	50.00	100.00	200.00
—Capitol Record Club edition					

Number	Title (A Side/B Side)	Yr	VG	VG+	NM
❏ T 90701 [M]	Bread and Butter	1965	37.50	75.00	150.00
—Capitol Record Club edition					

NEWBORN, PHINEAS
ATLANTIC
❏ 1235 [M]	Here Is Phineas	1956	12.50	25.00	50.00
—Black label					
❏ 1235 [M]	Here Is Phineas	1961	5.00	10.00	20.00
—Multicolor label, white "fan" logo at right					
❏ SD 1235 [S]	Here Is Phineas	1958	12.50	25.00	50.00
—Green label					

CONTEMPORARY
❏ M-3600 [M]	The World of Piano!	1961	5.00	10.00	20.00
❏ M-3611 [M]	Great Jazz Piano	1962	5.00	10.00	20.00
❏ M-3615 [M]	The Newborn Touch	1964	5.00	10.00	20.00
❏ S-7600 [S]	The World of Piano!	1961	6.25	12.50	25.00
❏ S-7611 [S]	Great Jazz Piano	1962	6.25	12.50	25.00
❏ S-7615 [S]	The Newborn Touch	1964	6.25	12.50	25.00
❏ S-7622 [S]	Please Send Me Someone to Love	1969	5.00	10.00	20.00
❏ C-7648	Back Home	198?	3.00	6.00	12.00

RCA VICTOR
❏ LPM-1421 [M]	Phineas' Rainbow	1957	12.50	25.00	50.00
❏ LPM-1474 [M]	While the Lady Sleeps	1957	12.50	25.00	50.00
❏ LPM-1589 [M]	Phineas Newborn Plays Jamaica	1957	12.50	25.00	50.00
❏ LPM-1873 [M]	Fabulous Phineas	1958	12.50	25.00	50.00
❏ LSP-1873 [S]	Fabulous Phineas	1958	10.00	20.00	40.00

ROULETTE
❏ R-52031 [M]	Piano Portraits	1959	6.25	12.50	25.00
❏ SR-52031 [S]	Piano Portraits	1959	7.50	15.00	30.00
❏ R-52043 [M]	I Love a Piano	1960	6.25	12.50	25.00
❏ SR-52043 [S]	I Love a Piano	1960	7.50	15.00	30.00

NEWBURY, MICKEY
ABC HICKORY
❏ HA-44002	Rusty Tracks	1977	2.50	5.00	10.00
❏ HA-44011	Eye on the Sparrow	1978	2.50	5.00	10.00
❏ HB-44017	The Sailor	1979	2.50	5.00	10.00

ELEKTRA
❏ 7E-1007	I Came to Hear the Music	1974	2.50	5.00	10.00
❏ 7E-1030	Lovers	1975	2.50	5.00	10.00
❏ EQ-4107 [Q]	'Frisco Mabel Joy	1974	5.00	10.00	20.00
❏ EKS-74107	'Frisco Mabel Joy	1971	2.50	5.00	10.00
❏ EKS-75055	Heaven Help the Child	1973	2.50	5.00	10.00

MCA
❏ 802	Rusty Tracks	198?	2.00	4.00	8.00
—Reissue					
❏ 803	Eye on the Sparrow	198?	2.00	4.00	8.00
—Reissue					
❏ 804	The Sailor	198?	2.00	4.00	8.00
—Reissue					
❏ 945	Sweet Memories	1985	2.50	5.00	10.00

MERCURY
❏ SR 61236	Looks Like Rain	1969	3.75	7.50	15.00

RCA VICTOR
❏ LSP-4043	Harlequin Melodies	1968	3.75	7.50	15.00

NEWHART, BOB
HARMONY
❏ HS 11344	The Very Funny Bob Newhart	196?	3.00	6.00	12.00

MURRAY HILL
❏ OP 2529 [(2)]	The Best of the Button-Down Mind	197?	5.00	10.00	20.00

WARNER BROS.
❏ W 1379 [M]	The Button-Down Mind of Bob Newhart	1960	7.50	15.00	30.00
❏ WS 1379 [S]	The Button-Down Mind of Bob Newhart	1960	6.25	12.50	25.00
❏ W 1393 [M]	The Button-Down Mind Strikes Back!	1960	7.50	15.00	30.00
❏ WS 1393 [S]	The Button-Down Mind Strikes Back!	1960	6.25	12.50	25.00
❏ 2N 1399 [(2)M]	The Bob Newhart Deluxe Edition	1961	12.50	25.00	50.00
❏ 2NS 1399 [(2)S]	The Bob Newhart Deluxe Edition	1961	10.00	20.00	40.00
❏ W 1417 [M]	Behind the Button-Down Mind of Bob Newhart	1961	6.25	12.50	25.00
❏ WS 1417 [S]	Behind the Button-Down Mind of Bob Newhart	1961	5.00	10.00	20.00
❏ W 1467 [M]	The Button-Down Mind on TV	1962	6.25	12.50	25.00
❏ WS 1467 [S]	The Button-Down Mind on TV	1962	5.00	10.00	20.00
❏ W 1517 [M]	Bob Newhart Faces Bob Newhart (Faces Bob Newhart)	1964	6.25	12.50	25.00
❏ W 1588 [M]	The Windmills Are Weakening	1965	7.50	15.00	30.00
❏ W 1672 [M]	The Best of Bob Newhart	1966	7.50	15.00	30.00
❏ WS 1672 [S]	The Best of Bob Newhart	1966	6.25	12.50	25.00
—Gold label					
❏ WS 1672 [S]	The Best of Bob Newhart	1968	5.00	10.00	20.00
—Green "W7" label					
❏ WS 1672 [S]	The Best of Bob Newhart	1970	3.75	7.50	15.00
—Green "WB" label					
❏ WS 1672 [S]	The Best of Bob Newhart	1973	3.00	6.00	12.00
—"Burbank" palm-trees label					
❏ WS 1672 [S]	The Best of Bob Newhart	1979	2.00	4.00	8.00
—White or tan label					
❏ W 1717 [M]	This Is It	1967	7.50	15.00	30.00

NEWLEY, ANTHONY
LONDON
❏ PS 244 [S]	Tony	1962	6.25	12.50	25.00
❏ PS 461 [S]	Genius	1966	3.75	7.50	15.00
❏ LL 3156 [M]	Love Is a Now and Then Thing	1960	5.00	10.00	20.00
❏ LL 3252 [M]	Tony	1962	3.75	7.50	15.00
❏ LL 3262 [M]	This Is Tony Newley	1962	3.75	7.50	15.00
❏ LL 3461 [M]	Genius	1966	3.00	6.00	12.00

RCA VICTOR
❏ LPM-2925 [M]	In My Solitude	1964	3.75	7.50	15.00
❏ LSP-2925 [S]	In My Solitude	1964	5.00	10.00	20.00
❏ LPM-3347 [M]	Who Can I Turn To	1965	3.00	6.00	12.00
❏ LSP-3347 [S]	Who Can I Turn To	1965	3.75	7.50	15.00
❏ LPM-3614 [M]	Newly Recorded	1966	3.00	6.00	12.00
❏ LSP-3614 [S]	Newly Recorded	1966	3.75	7.50	15.00
❏ LPM-3839 [M]	Doctor Dolittle	1967	3.00	6.00	12.00
❏ LSP-3839 [S]	Doctor Dolittle	1967	3.75	7.50	15.00
❏ LSP-4163	The Best of Anthony Newley	1969	3.00	6.00	12.00

NEWMAN, BOB
AUDIO LAB
❏ AL-1536 [M]	The Kentucky Colonel	1959	50.00	100.00	200.00

NEWMAN, DAVID "FATHEAD"
ATLANTIC
❏ 1304 [M]	Ray Charles Presents David "Fathead" Newman	1959	10.00	20.00	40.00
—Black label					
❏ SD 1304 [S]	Ray Charles Presents David "Fathead" Newman	1959	12.50	25.00	50.00
—Green label					
❏ SD 1304 [S]	Ray Charles Presents David "Fathead" Newman	1961	5.00	10.00	20.00
—Multicolor label with white "fan" logo					
❏ 1366 [M]	Straight Ahead	1961	7.50	15.00	30.00
—Multicolor label with white "fan" logo					
❏ SD 1366 [S]	Straight Ahead	1961	10.00	20.00	40.00
—Multicolor label with white "fan" logo					
❏ 1399 [M]	Fathead Comes On	1962	7.50	15.00	30.00
❏ SD 1399 [S]	Fathead Comes On	1962	10.00	20.00	40.00
❏ SD 1489	House of David	1968	5.00	10.00	20.00
❏ SD 1505	Bigger and Better	1968	5.00	10.00	20.00

COTILLION
❏ SD 18002	Captain Buckles	1970	5.00	10.00	20.00

NEWMAN, JIMMY
DECCA
❏ DL 4221 [M]	Jimmy Newman	1962	6.25	12.50	25.00
❏ DL 4398 [M]	Folk Songs of the Bayou Country	1963	10.00	20.00	40.00
❏ DL 4748 [M]	Artificial Rose	1966	5.00	10.00	20.00
❏ DL 4781 [M]	Jimmy Newman Sings Country Songs	1966	5.00	10.00	20.00
❏ DL 4885 [M]	The World of Country Music	1967	6.25	12.50	25.00
❏ DL 4960 [M]	The Jimmy Newman Way	1967	6.25	12.50	25.00
❏ DL 74221 [S]	Jimmy Newman	1962	7.50	15.00	30.00
❏ DL 74398 [S]	Folk Songs of the Bayou Country	1963	12.50	25.00	50.00
❏ DL 74748 [S]	Artificial Rose	1966	6.25	12.50	25.00
❏ DL 74781 [S]	Jimmy Newman Sings Country Songs	1966	6.25	12.50	25.00
❏ DL 74885 [S]	The World of Country Music	1967	5.00	10.00	20.00
❏ DL 74960 [S]	The Jimmy Newman Way	1967	5.00	10.00	20.00
❏ DL 75065	Born to Love You	1968	5.00	10.00	20.00

DOT
❏ DLP-3690 [M]	A Fallen Star	1965	7.50	15.00	30.00
❏ DLP-3736 [M]	Country Crossroads	1966	7.50	15.00	30.00
❏ DLP-25736 [R]	Country Crossroads	1966	5.00	10.00	20.00

MGM
❏ E-3777 [M]	This Is Jimmy Newman	1959	6.25	12.50	25.00
❏ SE-3777 [S]	This Is Jimmy Newman	1959	7.50	15.00	30.00
❏ E-4045 [M]	Songs by Jimmy Newman	1962	6.25	12.50	25.00
❏ SE-4045 [S]	Songs by Jimmy Newman	1962	7.50	15.00	30.00

NEWMAN, JOE
AMERICAN RECORDING SOCIETY
❏ G-447 [M]	Basically Swing	1958	10.00	20.00	40.00
❏ G-451 [M]	New Sounds In Swing	1958	10.00	20.00	40.00

CORAL
❏ CRL 57121 [M]	The Happy Cats	1957	12.50	25.00	50.00
❏ CRL 57208 [M]	Soft Swingin' Jazz	1958	12.50	25.00	50.00

JAZZTONE
❏ J-1217 [M]	New Sounds In Swing	1956	10.00	20.00	40.00
❏ J-1220 [M]	The Count's Men	1956	10.00	20.00	40.00
❏ J-1265 [M]	Swing Lightly	1957	10.00	20.00	40.00

MERCURY
❏ MG-20696 [M]	Joe Newman At Count Basie's	1962	6.25	12.50	25.00
❏ SR-60696 [S]	Joe Newman At Count Basie's	1962	7.50	15.00	30.00

RAMA
❏ LP-1003 [M]	Locking Horns	1957	30.00	60.00	120.00

RCA VICTOR
❏ LPM-1118 [M]	All I Want To Do Is Swing	1955	25.00	50.00	100.00
❏ LPM-1198 [M]	I'm Still Swinging	1956	25.00	50.00	100.00
❏ LPM-1324 [M]	Salute To Satch	1956	20.00	40.00	80.00

ROULETTE
❏ R-52009 [M]	Locking Horns	1958	10.00	20.00	40.00
❏ SR-52009 [S]	Locking Horns	1958	7.50	15.00	30.00
❏ R-52014 [M]	Joe Newman With Woodwinds	1958	10.00	20.00	40.00
❏ SR-52014 [S]	Joe Newman With Woodwinds	1958	7.50	15.00	30.00

STORYVILLE
❏ STLP-318 [10]	Joe Newman and the Boys In the Band	1955	37.50	75.00	150.00
❏ STLP-905 [M]	I Feel Like a Newman	1956	25.00	50.00	100.00

SWINGVILLE
❏ SVLP-2011 [M]	Jive At Five	1961	12.50	25.00	50.00
—Purple label					
❏ SVLP-2011 [M]	Jive At Five	1965	6.25	12.50	25.00
—Blue label, trident logo at right					
❏ SVLP-2019 [M]	Good 'N Groovy	1961	12.50	25.00	50.00
—Purple label					
❏ SVLP-2019 [M]	Good 'N Groovy	1965	6.25	12.50	25.00
—Blue label, trident logo at right					
❏ SVLP-2027 [M]	Joe's Hap'nin's	1961	12.50	25.00	50.00
—Purple label					
❏ SVLP-2027 [M]	Joe's Hap'nin's	1965	6.25	12.50	25.00
—Blue label, trident logo at right					
❏ SVST-2027 [S]	Joe's Hap'nin's	1961	12.50	25.00	50.00
—Red label					

Number	Title (A Side/B Side)	Yr	VG	VG+	NM
❑ SVST-2027 [S]	Joe's Hap'nin's	1965	6.25	12.50	25.00
—Blue label, trident logo at right					
TRIP					
❑ 5548	Live at Basie's	197?	2.50	5.00	10.00
VANGUARD					
❑ VRS-8007 [10]	Joe Newman and His Band	1954	50.00	100.00	200.00
VIK					
❑ LX-1060 [M]	Midgets	1957	20.00	40.00	80.00
WORLD PACIFIC					
❑ ST-1288 [S]	Countin'	1960	10.00	20.00	40.00
❑ WP-1288 [M]	Countin'	1960	10.00	20.00	40.00

NEWMAN, RANDY
REPRISE

Number	Title (A Side/B Side)	Yr	VG	VG+	NM
❑ MS 2064	Sail Away	1972	2.50	5.00	10.00
—With song titles listed on back					
❑ MS 2064	Sail Away	1972	3.75	7.50	15.00
—With no song titles listed on back					
❑ MS 2193	Good Old Boys	1974	2.50	5.00	10.00
❑ MS4 2193 [Q]	Good Old Boys	1974	3.75	7.50	15.00
❑ RS 6286	Randy Newman	1968	3.75	7.50	15.00
—Cover with close-up of Randy's face; "W7" and "r:" logos on two-tone orange label					
❑ RS 6286	Randy Newman	1968	5.00	10.00	20.00
—Cover with Randy standing in the clouds					
❑ RS 6286	Randy Newman	1970	3.00	6.00	12.00
—With only "r:" logo on all-orange (tan) label					
❑ RS 6373	12 Songs	1970	2.50	5.00	10.00
—With only "r:" logo on all-orange (tan) label					
❑ RS 6373	12 Songs	1970	3.75	7.50	15.00
—With "W7" and "r:" logos on two-tone orange label					
❑ RS 6459	Randy Newman/Live	1971	2.50	5.00	10.00
❑ 25773	Land of Dreams	1988	2.50	5.00	10.00

WARNER BROS.

Number	Title (A Side/B Side)	Yr	VG	VG+	NM
❑ BSK 3079	Little Criminals	1977	2.50	5.00	10.00
❑ HS 3346	Born Again	1979	2.50	5.00	10.00
❑ 23755	Trouble in Paradise	1983	2.50	5.00	10.00

NEWTON, JUICE
CAPITOL

Number	Title (A Side/B Side)	Yr	VG	VG+	NM
❑ ST-11682	Come to Me	1977	3.75	7.50	15.00
❑ ST-11811	Well-Kept Secret	1978	3.75	7.50	15.00
❑ ST-12000	Take Heart	1980	3.75	7.50	15.00
❑ ST-12136	Juice	1981	2.50	5.00	10.00
❑ ST-12210	Quiet Lies	1982	2.50	5.00	10.00
❑ ST-12294	Dirty Looks	1983	2.50	5.00	10.00
❑ SJ-12353	Greatest Hits	1984	2.50	5.00	10.00
❑ SN-16242	Come to Me	1982	2.00	4.00	8.00
—Budget-line reissue					
❑ SN-16243	Well-Kept Secret	1982	2.00	4.00	8.00
—Budget-line reissue					
❑ SN-16244	Take Heart	1982	2.00	4.00	8.00
—Budget-line reissue					
❑ SN-16313	Juice	1984	2.00	4.00	8.00
—Budget-line reissue					
❑ SN-16314	Quiet Lies	1984	2.00	4.00	8.00
—Budget-line reissue					
❑ SN-16356	Dirty Looks	1985	2.00	4.00	8.00
—Budget-line reissue					
❑ SN-16471	Greatest Hits	1987	2.00	4.00	8.00
—Budget-line reissue					

RCA

Number	Title (A Side/B Side)	Yr	VG	VG+	NM
❑ 5646-1-R	Old Flame	1986	2.50	5.00	10.00
—Reissue of 5493 with slightly different lineup					
❑ 6371-1-R	Emotion	1987	2.50	5.00	10.00
❑ 8376-1-R	Ain't Gonna Cry	1989	2.50	5.00	10.00

RCA VICTOR

Number	Title (A Side/B Side)	Yr	VG	VG+	NM
❑ APL1-1004	Juice Newton and Silver Spur	1975	5.00	10.00	20.00
❑ APL1-1722	After Dust Settled	1977	3.75	7.50	15.00
❑ AYL1-4037	Juice Newton and Silver Spur	1982	2.00	4.00	8.00
—"Best Buy Series" reissue					
❑ AYL1-4038	After Dust Settled	1982	2.00	4.00	8.00
—"Best Buy Series" reissue					
❑ AFL1-4995	Can't Wait All Night	1984	2.50	5.00	10.00
❑ AFL1-5493	Old Flame	1985	3.00	6.00	12.00

NEWTON, WAYNE
ARIES II

Number	Title (A Side/B Side)	Yr	VG	VG+	NM
❑ WY 201	Wayne Newton Christmas	1979	2.50	5.00	10.00

CAPITOL

Number	Title (A Side/B Side)	Yr	VG	VG+	NM
❑ SKAO-137	The Best of Wayne Newton, Volume 2	1968	3.75	7.50	15.00
❑ STBB-487 [(2)]	Merry Christmas to You	1970	3.75	7.50	15.00
❑ ST 1973 [S]	Danke Schoen	1963	5.00	10.00	20.00
❑ T 1973 [M]	Danke Schoen	1963	3.75	7.50	15.00
❑ ST 2029 [S]	Wayne Newton In Person	1964	5.00	10.00	20.00
❑ T 2029 [M]	Wayne Newton In Person	1964	3.75	7.50	15.00
❑ ST 2130 [S]	Wayne Newton Sings Hit Songs	1964	5.00	10.00	20.00
❑ T 2130 [M]	Wayne Newton Sings Hit Songs	1964	3.75	7.50	15.00
❑ SM-2335	Red Roses for a Blue Lady	197?	2.50	5.00	10.00
—Reissue					
❑ ST 2335 [S]	Red Roses for a Blue Lady	1965	5.00	10.00	20.00
❑ T 2335 [M]	Red Roses for a Blue Lady	1965	3.75	7.50	15.00
❑ ST 2389 [S]	Summer Wind	1965	5.00	10.00	20.00
❑ T 2389 [M]	Summer Wind	1965	3.75	7.50	15.00
❑ ST 2445 [S]	Wayne Newton — Now!	1966	5.00	10.00	20.00
❑ T 2445 [M]	Wayne Newton — Now!	1966	3.75	7.50	15.00
❑ SM-2563	The Old Rugged Cross	197?	2.50	5.00	10.00
—Reissue					
❑ ST 2563 [S]	The Old Rugged Cross	1966	5.00	10.00	20.00
❑ T 2563 [M]	The Old Rugged Cross	1966	3.75	7.50	15.00
❑ ST 2588 [S]	Songs for a Merry Christmas	1966	3.75	7.50	15.00
❑ T 2588 [M]	Songs for a Merry Christmas	1966	3.00	6.00	12.00

Number	Title (A Side/B Side)	Yr	VG	VG+	NM
❑ ST 2635 [S]	It's Only the Good Times	1967	5.00	10.00	20.00
❑ T 2635 [M]	It's Only the Good Times	1967	3.75	7.50	15.00
❑ ST 2714 [S]	Song of the Year...Wayne Newton Style	1967	3.75	7.50	15.00
❑ T 2714 [M]	Song of the Year...Wayne Newton Style	1967	5.00	10.00	20.00
❑ ST 2797 [S]	The Best of Wayne Newton	1967	3.75	7.50	15.00
❑ T 2797 [M]	The Best of Wayne Newton	1967	5.00	10.00	20.00
❑ ST 2832 [S]	God Is Alive	1968	3.75	7.50	15.00
❑ T 2832 [M]	God Is Alive	1968	5.00	10.00	20.00
❑ ST 2847 [S]	Wayne Newton — The Greatest	1968	3.75	7.50	15.00
❑ T 2847 [M]	Wayne Newton — The Greatest	1968	5.00	10.00	20.00
❑ SM-11972	Danke Schoen	1979	2.50	5.00	10.00
—Reissue					
❑ SN-16083	The Best of Wayne Newton	1980	2.00	4.00	8.00
—Budget-line reissue					

CAPITOL PICKWICK SERIES

Number	Title (A Side/B Side)	Yr	VG	VG+	NM
❑ PC-3455 [M]	Somewhere My Love	196?	2.50	5.00	10.00
❑ SPC-3455 [S]	Somewhere My Love	196?	2.50	5.00	10.00
❑ PC-3459 [M]	Everybody Loves Somebody	196?	2.50	5.00	10.00
❑ SPC-3459 [S]	Everybody Loves Somebody	196?	2.50	5.00	10.00
❑ PC-3461 [M]	Michelle	196?	2.50	5.00	10.00
❑ SPC-3461 [S]	Michelle	196?	2.50	5.00	10.00
❑ PC-3464 [M]	Wow! Wayne Newton Live	196?	2.50	5.00	10.00
❑ SPC-3464 [S]	Wow! Wayne Newton Live	196?	2.50	5.00	10.00

CHELSEA

Number	Title (A Side/B Side)	Yr	VG	VG+	NM
❑ BCL1-0367	Pour Me a Little More Wine	1973	3.00	6.00	12.00
❑ CHL-504	The Best of Wayne Newton Live	1974	2.50	5.00	10.00
❑ CHL-507	Midnight Idol	1975	2.50	5.00	10.00
❑ CHL-512	Tomorrow	1976	2.50	5.00	10.00
❑ CHL-513	Daddy Don't You Walk So Fast	1976	2.50	5.00	10.00
—Reissue of 1001					
❑ CHE 1001	Daddy Don't You Walk So Fast	1972	3.00	6.00	12.00
❑ CHE 1003	Can't You Hear the Song?	1972	3.00	6.00	12.00
❑ CHE 1006	While We're Still Young	1973	3.00	6.00	12.00

CURB

Number	Title (A Side/B Side)	Yr	VG	VG+	NM
❑ 10607	Coming Home	1989	3.00	6.00	12.00

MGM

Number	Title (A Side/B Side)	Yr	VG	VG+	NM
❑ E-4523 [M]	Walking on New Grass	1968	5.00	10.00	20.00
❑ SE-4523 [S]	Walking on New Grass	1968	3.00	6.00	12.00
❑ E-4549 [M]	One More Time	1968	5.00	10.00	20.00
❑ SE-4549 [S]	One More Time	1968	3.00	6.00	12.00
❑ SE-4593	Christmas Isn't Christmas Without You	1968	3.00	6.00	12.00
❑ SE-4594	Dreams of the Everyday Housewife/Town and Country	1969	3.00	6.00	12.00

20TH CENTURY

Number	Title (A Side/B Side)	Yr	VG	VG+	NM
❑ T-576	Change of Heart	1979	2.50	5.00	10.00

WORD

Number	Title (A Side/B Side)	Yr	VG	VG+	NM
❑ WST-8586	Only Believe	1972	3.00	6.00	12.00

NEWTON-JOHN, OLIVIA
GEFFEN

Number	Title (A Side/B Side)	Yr	VG	VG+	NM
❑ GHS 24257	Warm and Tender	1989	3.00	6.00	12.00

MCA

Number	Title (A Side/B Side)	Yr	VG	VG+	NM
❑ 389	Let Me Be There	1973	3.75	7.50	15.00
❑ 411	If You Love Me Let Me Know	1974	2.50	5.00	10.00
—With corrected song title: "I Honestly Love You"					
❑ 411	If You Love Me Let Me Know	1974	3.75	7.50	15.00
—Originals have incorrect song title: "I Love You, I Honestly Love You"					
❑ 2133	Have You Never Been Mellow	1975	2.50	5.00	10.00
❑ 2148	Clearly Love	1975	2.50	5.00	10.00
❑ 2186	Come On Over	1976	2.50	5.00	10.00
❑ 2223	Don't Stop Believin'	1976	2.50	5.00	10.00
❑ 2280	Making a Good Thing Better	1977	2.50	5.00	10.00
❑ 3012	Let Me Be There	1977	2.00	4.00	8.00
—Reissue					
❑ 3013	If You Love Me Let Me Know	1977	2.00	4.00	8.00
—Reissue					
❑ 3014	Have You Never Been Mellow	1977	2.00	4.00	8.00
—Reissue					
❑ 3015	Clearly Love	1977	2.00	4.00	8.00
—Reissue					
❑ 3016	Come On Over	1977	2.00	4.00	8.00
—Reissue					
❑ 3017	Don't Stop Believin'	1977	2.00	4.00	8.00
—Reissue					
❑ 3018	Making a Good Thing Better	1977	2.00	4.00	8.00
—Reissue					
❑ 3028	Olivia Newton-John's Greatest Hits	1977	2.50	5.00	10.00
❑ 3067	Totally Hot	1978	2.50	5.00	10.00
❑ 5229	Physical	1981	2.00	4.00	8.00
❑ 5347	Olivia's Greatest Hits, Vol. 2	1982	2.00	4.00	8.00
❑ 6151	Soul Kiss	1985	2.00	4.00	8.00
❑ 6245	The Rumour	1988	2.00	4.00	8.00
❑ 16011	Physical	1982	6.25	12.50	25.00
—Audiophile edition					
❑ 37061	Clearly Love	1980	2.00	4.00	8.00
—Reissue					
❑ 37062	Come On Over	1980	2.00	4.00	8.00
—Reissue					
❑ 37063	Don't Stop Believin'	1980	2.00	4.00	8.00
—Reissue					
❑ 37123	Totally Hot	1981	2.00	4.00	8.00
—Reissue					

MOBILE FIDELITY

Number	Title (A Side/B Side)	Yr	VG	VG+	NM
❑ 1-040	Totally Hot	1980	5.00	15.00	20.00
—Audiophile vinyl					

UNI

Number	Title (A Side/B Side)	Yr	VG	VG+	NM
❑ 73117	If Not for You	1971	20.00	40.00	80.00

NEXT MORNING, THE
CALLA

Number	Title (A Side/B Side)	Yr	VG	VG+	NM
❑ SC-2002	The Next Morning	1972	25.00	50.00	100.00

Number	Title (A Side/B Side)	Yr	VG	VG+	NM

NICE, THE
COLUMBIA SPECIAL PRODUCTS
❏ P 11633	Thoughts of Emerlist Davjack	1973	3.00	6.00	12.00
❏ P 11634	Ars Longa Vita Brevis	1973	3.00	6.00	12.00
❏ P 11635	The Nice	1973	3.00	6.00	12.00

IMMEDIATE
❏ Z12 52004	Thoughts of Emerlist Davjack	1968	5.00	10.00	20.00
❏ Z12-52020	Ars Longa Vita Brevis	1969	5.00	10.00	20.00
❏ Z12-52022	The Nice	1969	3.75	7.50	15.00

MERCURY
❏ SRM-2-6500 [(2)]	Keith Emerson with The Nice	1972	3.75	7.50	15.00
❏ SR 61295	Five Bridges	1970	3.00	6.00	12.00
❏ SR 61324	Elegy	1971	3.00	6.00	12.00

SIRE
| ❏ SASH-3710 [(2)] | The Vintage Years | 1975 | 3.75 | 7.50 | 15.00 |

NICHOLAS, ALBERT
DELMARK
| ❏ DS-209 | Albert Nicholas with Art Hodes' All-Star Stompers | 1964 | 5.00 | 10.00 | 20.00 |

NICHOLAS, ALBERT/SIDNEY BECHET
RIVERSIDE
| ❏ RLP-12-216 [M] | Creole Reeds | 1956 | 20.00 | 40.00 | 80.00 |
—White label, blue print
| ❏ RLP-12-216 [M] | Creole Reeds | 1959 | 10.00 | 20.00 | 40.00 |
—Blue label, microphone logo at top

NICHOLAS, JOSEPH "WOODEN JOE"
AMERICA MUSIC
| ❏ 640 [10] | A Nite at Artesian Hall With Wooden Joe | 1951 | 15.00 | 30.00 | 60.00 |

NICHOLAS BROTHERS, THE
MERCURY
| ❏ MG-20355 [M] | We Do Sing, Too | 1958 | 7.50 | 15.00 | 30.00 |

NICHOLS, HERBIE
BETHLEHEM
| ❏ BCP-81 [M] | Love Gloom Cash and Love | 1957 | 25.00 | 50.00 | 100.00 |

BLUE NOTE
| ❏ BLP-1519 [M] | Herbie Nichols Trio | 1956 | 25.00 | 50.00 | 100.00 |
—Regular edition, Lexington Ave. address on label
| ❏ BLP-1519 [M] | Herbie Nichols Trio | 1956 | 37.50 | 75.00 | 150.00 |
—"Deep groove" version (deep indentation under label on both sides)
| ❏ BLP-1519 [M] | Herbie Nichols Trio | 1963 | 6.25 | 12.50 | 25.00 |
—With "New York, USA" address on label
| ❏ BLP-5068 [10] | The Prophetic Herbie Nichols, Volume 1 | 1955 | 100.00 | 200.00 | 400.00 |
| ❏ BLP-5069 [10] | The Prophetic Herbie Nichols, Volume 2 | 1955 | 100.00 | 200.00 | 400.00 |

NICHOLS, MIKE, AND ELAINE MAY
MERCURY
❏ SRM-2-628 [(2)]	Retrospect	1972	5.00	10.00	20.00
❏ OCM 2200 [M]	An Evening with Mike Nichols and Elaine May	1961	7.50	15.00	30.00
❏ OCS 6200 [S]	An Evening with Mike Nichols and Elaine May	1961	10.00	20.00	40.00
❏ MG 20376 [M]	Improvisations to Music	1959	7.50	15.00	30.00
❏ MG 20680 [M]	Nichols and May Examine Doctors	1962	6.25	12.50	25.00
❏ MG 20997 [M]	The Best of Nichols and May	1965	5.00	10.00	20.00
❏ SR 60040 [S]	Improvisations to Music	1959	10.00	20.00	40.00
❏ SR 60680 [S]	Nichols and May Examine Doctors	1962	7.50	15.00	30.00
❏ SR 60997 [S]	The Best of Nichols and May	1965	6.25	12.50	25.00

NICHOLS, NAT
NAJO
| ❏ LPS-001 | Nat Nichols Trio | 1967 | 6.25 | 12.50 | 25.00 |
| ❏ LPS-002 | Spring Play | 1967 | 6.25 | 12.50 | 25.00 |

NICHOLS, NICHELLE
EPIC
| ❏ BN 26351 | Down to Earth | 1968 | 10.00 | 20.00 | 40.00 |

NICHOLS, RED, AND THE FIVE PENNIES
AUDIOPHILE
❏ AP-1 [M]	Red Nichols and Band	195?	12.50	25.00	50.00
❏ AP-7 [M]	Syncopated Chamber Music, Volume 1	195?	12.50	25.00	50.00
❏ AP-8 [M]	Syncopated Chamber Music, Volume 2	195?	12.50	25.00	50.00

BRUNSWICK
❏ BL 54008 [M]	For Collectors Only	1954	12.50	25.00	50.00
❏ BL 54047 [M]	The Red Nichols Story	1959	12.50	25.00	50.00
❏ BL 58008 [10]	Classics, Volume 1	1950	20.00	40.00	80.00
❏ BL 58009 [10]	Classics, Volume 2	1950	20.00	40.00	80.00
❏ BL 58027 [10]	Volume 3	1951	20.00	40.00	80.00

CAPITOL
❏ H 215 [10]	Jazz Time	1950	20.00	40.00	80.00
❏ T 775 [M]	Hot Pennies	1956	12.50	25.00	50.00
❏ ST 1051 [S]	Parade of the Pennies	1958	7.50	15.00	30.00
❏ T 1051 [M]	Parade of the Pennies	1958	5.00	10.00	20.00
❏ ST 1297 [S]	Dixieland Dinner Dance	1960	5.00	10.00	20.00
❏ ST 1803 [S]	The All-Time Hits of Red Nichols	1962	5.00	10.00	20.00
❏ ST 2065 [S]	Blues and Old-Time Rags	1963	5.00	10.00	20.00

MOBILE FIDELITY
| ❏ 1-093 | Red Nichols and the Five Pennies at Marineland | 1982 | 5.00 | 10.00 | 20.00 |
—Audiophile vinyl

NICKEL BAG, THE
KAMA SUTRA
| ❏ KLPS-8066 | Doing Their Love Thing | 1968 | 6.25 | 12.50 | 25.00 |

NICKS, STEVIE
ATLANTIC
| ❏ 1P-8160 | TimeSpace — The Best of Stevie Nicks | 1991 | 5.00 | 10.00 | 20.00 |
—Columbia House edition; only US vinyl version

MOBILE FIDELITY
| ❏ 1-121 | Bella Donna | 1984 | 12.50 | 25.00 | 50.00 |
—Audiophile vinyl

MODERN
| ❏ MR 38-139 | Bella Donna | 1981 | 2.50 | 5.00 | 10.00 |
| ❏ PR-2881 [DJ] | Reflections from the Other Side of the Mirror | 1989 | 10.00 | 20.00 | 40.00 |
—Promo-only interview album with script
❏ 90084	The Wild Heart	1983	2.50	5.00	10.00
❏ 90479	Rock a Little	1985	2.50	5.00	10.00
❏ 91245	The Other Side of the Mirror	1989	2.50	5.00	10.00

NICO
ELEKTRA
| ❏ EKS-74029 | The Marble Index | 1968 | 6.25 | 12.50 | 25.00 |

ISLAND
| ❏ ILPS-9311 | The End | 1975 | 3.75 | 7.50 | 15.00 |

PVC
| ❏ 8938 | Camera Obscura | 198? | 3.00 | 6.00 | 12.00 |

REPRISE
| ❏ RS 6424 | Desert Shore | 1970 | 5.00 | 10.00 | 20.00 |

VERVE
| ❏ V-5032 [M] | Chelsea Girl | 1967 | 7.50 | 15.00 | 30.00 |
| ❏ V6-5032 [S] | Chelsea Girl | 1967 | 10.00 | 20.00 | 40.00 |

NIEHAUS, LENNIE
CONTEMPORARY
❏ C-2513 [10]	Lennie Niehaus, Vol. 1: The Quintet	1954	30.00	60.00	120.00
❏ C-2517 [10]	Lennie Niehaus, Vol. 2: The Octet	1954	30.00	60.00	120.00
❏ C-3503 [M]	Lennie Niehaus, Vol. 3: The Octet No. 2	1955	20.00	40.00	80.00
❏ C-3510 [M]	Lennie Niehaus, Vol. 4: The Quintets & Strings	1956	20.00	40.00	80.00
❏ C-3518 [M]	The Lennie Niehaus Quintet	1956	20.00	40.00	80.00
❏ C-3524 [M]	Lennie Niehaus, Vol. 5: The Sextet	1956	20.00	40.00	80.00
❏ C-3540 [M]	Zounds! Lennie Niehaus, Vol. 2: The Octet	1957	20.00	40.00	80.00

EMARCY
| ❏ MG-36118 [M] | I Swing for You | 1957 | 12.50 | 25.00 | 50.00 |

MERCURY
| ❏ MG-20555 [M] | I Swing for You | 1960 | 7.50 | 15.00 | 30.00 |
| ❏ SR-60123 [S] | I Swing for You | 1960 | 6.25 | 12.50 | 25.00 |

NIELSEN, GERTRUDE
DECCA
| ❏ DL 5138 [10] | Gertrude Nielsen | 1951 | 12.50 | 25.00 | 50.00 |

NIEWOOD, GERRY
A&M
| ❏ SP-3409 | Slow, Hot Wind | 1977 | 2.50 | 5.00 | 10.00 |

HORIZON
| ❏ SP-719 | Gerry Niewood and Timepiece | 1976 | 3.00 | 6.00 | 12.00 |

NIGHT OWLS, THE
VALMOR
| ❏ 79 [M] | Twisting the Oldies | 1962 | 25.00 | 50.00 | 100.00 |

NIGHT SHADOWS, THE
HOTTRAX
| ❏ 1414 | The Square Root of Two | 1979 | 12.50 | 25.00 | 50.00 |
—Reissue of Spectrum LP
| ❏ 1430 | Live at the Spot | 1981 | 6.25 | 12.50 | 25.00 |
| ❏ 1450 | Invasion of the Acid Eaters | 1982 | 6.25 | 12.50 | 25.00 |

SPECTRUM
| ❏ 2001 | The Square Root of Two | 1968 | 250.00 | 500.00 | 1000. |
—With neither bonus 45 nor psychedelic poster
| ❏ 2001 | The Square Root of Two | 1968 | 275.00 | 550.00 | 1100. |
—With bonus 45, but no poster
| ❏ 2001 | The Square Root of Two | 1968 | 300.00 | 600.00 | 1200. |
—With poster, but no 45
| ❏ 2001 | The Square Root of Two | 1968 | 375.00 | 750.00 | 1500. |
—With both 45 and poster

NIGHTCAPS, THE
VANDAN
| ❏ VRLP-8124 | Wine, Wine, Wine | 196? | 37.50 | 75.00 | 150.00 |

NIGHTCRAWLERS, THE
KAPP
| ❏ KL-1520 [M] | The Little Black Egg | 1967 | 15.00 | 30.00 | 60.00 |
| ❏ KS-3520 [S] | The Little Black Egg | 1967 | 10.00 | 20.00 | 40.00 |

NIGHTHAWKS, THE
ALADDIN
| ❏ LP-101 | Rock and Roll | 197? | 50.00 | 100.00 | 200.00 |

NILES, JOHN JACOB
BOONE-TOLLIVER
| ❏ BTR-22 [10] | American Folk Songs to Dulcimer Accompaniment | 195? | 12.50 | 25.00 | 50.00 |
| ❏ BTR-23 [10] | Ballads | 195? | 12.50 | 25.00 | 50.00 |

RCA CAMDEN
❏ CAL-219 [M]	American Folk and Gambling Songs	195?	6.25	12.50	25.00
❏ CAL-245 [M]	American Folk Songs	195?	6.25	12.50	25.00
❏ CAL-330 [M]	50th Anniversary Album	195?	6.25	12.50	25.00

TRADITION
| ❏ TLP-1023 [M] | I Wonder As I Wander | 1957 | 7.50 | 15.00 | 30.00 |
| ❏ TLP-1036 [M] | An Evening with John Jacob Niles | 195? | 7.50 | 15.00 | 30.00 |

NILSSON
MUSICOR
| ❏ MUS-2505 [S] | Early Tymes | 1977 | 3.75 | 7.50 | 15.00 |

PICKWICK
| ❏ SPC-3321 | Rock 'N' Roll | 1977 | 2.50 | 5.00 | 10.00 |

Early 10-Inch Albums

When the LP was introduced in 1948, most non-classical LPs were 10 inches, the same width as 78s. Most of these are uncommon today, and some are outrageously rare.

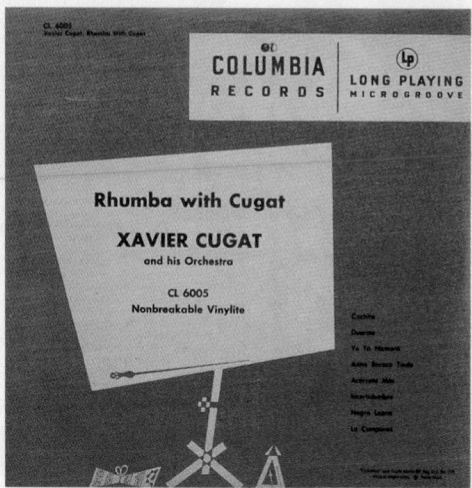

One of the very first pop LPs issued was this Xavier Cugat collection. Early Columbia LPs open from the top and have a flap that goes over the opening.

The only LP of any size ever issued on the Swing Time label was this rare Lloyd Glenn 10-incher.

A very early 10-inch LP on Decca was this Burl Ives compilation.

This compilation of recordings from 78s was the first LP release of the oeuvre of the notoriously bad aria singer Florence Foster Jenkins.

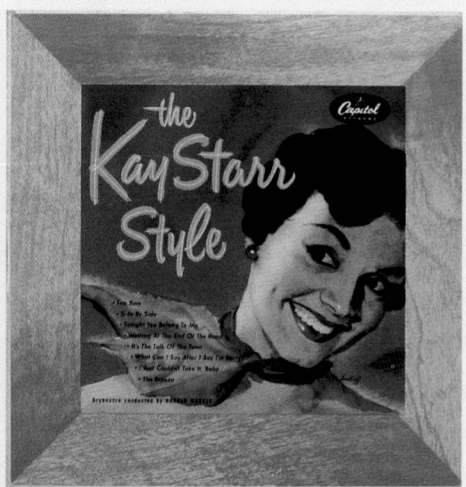

This was one of three 10-inch LPs Capitol released by Kay Starr.

One of the most valuable records of any size and genre is this Federal 10-inch LP compilation of Billy Ward and His Dominoes.

Rare 1950s Albums

Some of the most rare albums were issued in the 1950s, usually in genres that were not big sellers on long-playing records. The combined value of these six records in near-mint condition is around $10,500!

Johnny Burnette and the Rock 'n Roll Trio on the original maroon Coral label is the most sought-after rockabilly-related LP in the world.

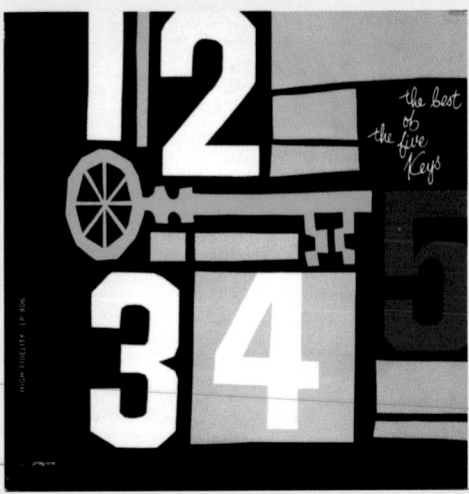

The Best of the Five Keys, a compilation on the Aladdin label, is that group's rarest LP.

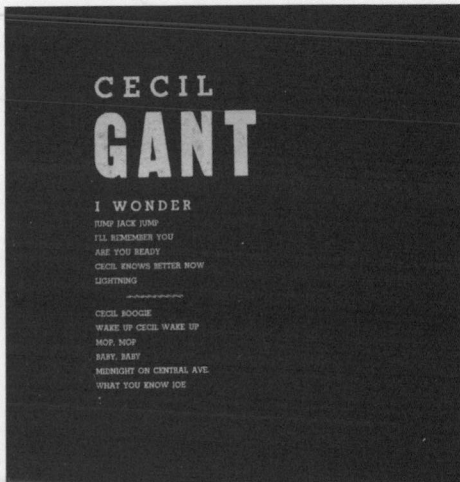

This collection of singles from the Gilt Edge label by 1940s R&B singer Cecil Gant was issued on Red Mill in the 1950s on red vinyl.

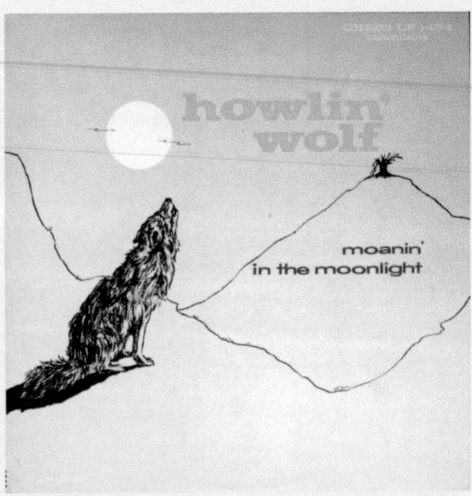

Moanin' in the Moonlight was bluesman Howlin' Wolf's first Chess LP.

The only place Mickey Mantle appears on this RCA Victor compilation is on the cover, but sports collectors have helped drive up the price of this one.

The original edition of this hits collection on DeLuxe is a major rarity; a reissue on King is also hard to find.

1950s and 1960s Pop Music

Before 1964, most of the biggest-selling albums – and all but four artists who hit the top spot on the charts – were by pop artists. Here are a few examples.

Harry Belafonte's *Jump Up Calypso,* from 1961, spent over a year on the charts and got as high as #3.

Nat King Cole's *Love Is the Thing* was originally released in mono only and hit #1 in 1957. This is a true stereo release from 1959.

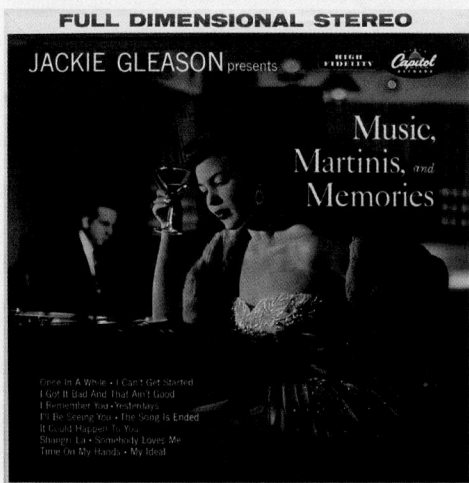

Jackie Gleason sold a lot of albums in the 1950s as the conductor of a studio orchestra that played "mood music." *Music, Martinis and Memories* was a chart-topper in 1955; this is the re-recorded stereo version from much later.

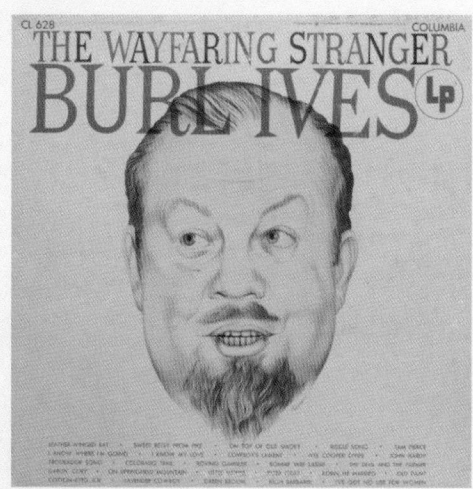

Burl Ives was a popular folk singer for years before his appearance as the narrator of *Rudolph the Red-Nosed Reindeer.* This compilation of Columbia recordings was issued in 1955.

Dean Martin had some big hits before 1964, but "Everybody Loves Somebody" became his signature song that year. This album was hastily recorded and released to coincide with that single.

Before the 12-inch LP became standard, Capitol issued two 10-inch LPs of Frank Sinatra music. The label put the two, *Swing Easy!* and *Songs for Young Lovers,* on one 12-inch disc in 1955.

Talking Freewheelin' Alteration Blues

Above are the Side 1 and Side 2 labels of one of the two known stereo copies of *The Freewheelin' Bob Dylan* that include four songs quickly removed from the LP. On Side 1, songs 2 and 3 were replaced, and on Side 2, songs 2 and 5 were replaced. Adding to the strangeness, on these discs, both sides of which have the suffix "-1A" attached to the master numbers in the trail-off wax, song 3, "Let Me Die in My Footsteps," and song 6, "A Hard Rain's A-Gonna Fall," are in the wrong order.

Mono copies of *The Freewheelin' Bob Dylan* with the "wrong" songs are known to exist, but all of them actually list the "correct" titles on the labels. Look for the "-1A" suffix in the trail-off wax, and look for track 3 on side 1 to be much wider than any other song on that side.

 COLUMBIA RECORDS RADIO STATION SERVICE NOT FOR RESALE CL 1986

Side 1			Side 2		
BLOWIN' IN THE WIND		2:46	DON'T THINK TWICE, IT'S ALL RIGHT		3:37
ROCKS AND GRAVEL		2:21	GAMBLIN' WILLIE'S DEAD MAN'S HAND		4:11
LET ME DIE IN MY FOOTSTEPS		4:05	OXFORD TOWN		1:47
DOWN THE HIGHWAY		3:10	CORRINA CORRINA		2:42
BOB DYLAN'S BLUES		2:19	TALKIN' JOHN BIRCH BLUES		3:45
A HARD RAIN'S A-GONNA FALL		6:48	HONEY, JUST ALLOW ME ONE MORE CHANCE		1:57
		21:54	I SHALL BE FREE		4:46
					23:15

COLUMBIA

THE FREEWHEELIN' BOB DYLAN

RADIO STATION COPY - NOT FOR RESALE

1. BLOWIN' IN THE WIND 2:46

CL 1986   Side 1
(x"Lp" 58717)

2. ROCKS AND GRAVEL 2:21
3. LET ME DIE IN MY FOOTSTEPS 4:05
4. DOWN THE HIGHWAY 3:10
5. BOB DYLAN'S BLUES 2:19
6. A HARD RAIN'S A-GONNA
FALL 6:48

COLUMBIA MARCAS REG. PRINTED IN U.S.A.

COLUMBIA

THE FREEWHEELIN' BOB DYLAN

RADIO STATION COPY - NOT FOR RESALE

1. DON'T THINK TWICE, IT'S ALL RIGHT 3:37
2. GAMBLIN' WILLIE'S DEAD MAN'S HAND 4:11

CL 1986   Side 2
(x"Lp" 58718)

3. OXFORD TOWN 1:47
4. CORRINA CORRINA 2:42
5. TALKIN' JOHN BIRCH BLUES 3:45
6. HONEY, JUST ALLOW ME ONE MORE
CHANCE 1:57
7. I SHALL BE FREE 4:46

COLUMBIA MARCAS REG. PRINTED IN U.S.A.

NOTICE

CL 1986/CS 8786

Please note that on Side 1, Band 3 and Band 6 are reversed.

Oddly, one known mono promo copy (pictured above) is known to exist with the "wrong" songs listed. But the record itself plays the "correct" tracks. Stranger yet, this mono promo came with a paper insert informing the listener that "Band 3 and Band 6 are reversed," but that only referred to the "wrong" edition rather than the corrected edition, so it wasn't necessary. The DJ would likely notice that some of the songs were listed wrong anyway.

Introducing the Counterfeit Beatles

Courtesy of Bruce Spizer, here's a colorful illustrated look at the difference between a real copy of *Introducing the Beatles* and a fake one. Photos of authentic editions appear on this page.

 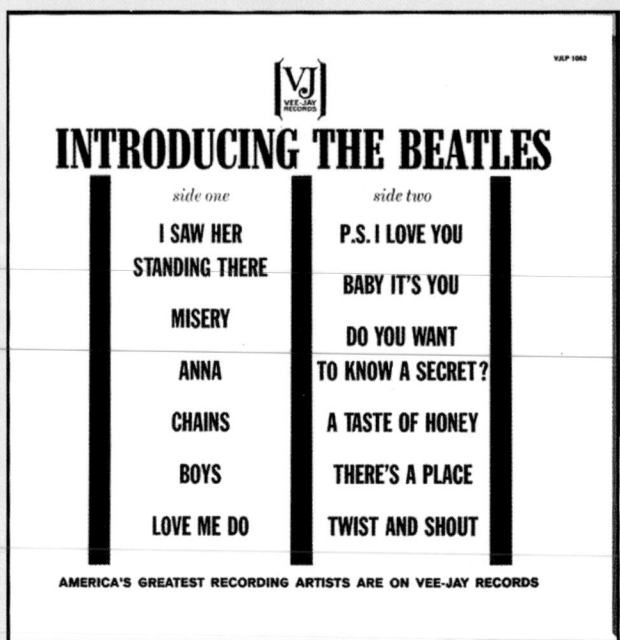

Above are authentic front and back covers in stereo with "Love Me Do" and "P.S. I Love You" included. There are two other back covers for this variation, but the only one for which questions of legitimacy exist is for the "titles" cover.

These are examples of the label variations – Side 1 of one and Side 2 of another – for stereo editions of this record. Notice that the word "STEREO" appears on both labels, though in different places. Notice, too, that the label features the "oval" Vee Jay logo. Stereo copies with "Please Please Me" and "Ask Me Why" are known on oval, brackets and plain black labels, but no known stereo copies of this version exist on other than the oval logo above.

Now, here are some counterfeit versions of *Introducing the Beatles.* We don't have space to show every counterfeit variation, but here are some of the more common ones.

If the cover has a brown border around it, it's counterfeit.

At first glance, this appears to be a legitimate label, but unlike authentic Vee Jay labels, the color green is missing.

This label looks more legitimate as it does have green in it, but it has the telltale sign of a fake: The words "INTRODUCING THE BEATLES" are above the center hole and "THE BEATLES" are below the hole. This is a 100 percent indicator that the album is fake.

Most counterfeit labels look like this – all black, again with the telltale separation of the two lines of type.

Meat – The Beatles

The original edition of the Beatles' *Yesterday and Today* LP may be the world's most common rare record. Approximately 750,000 copies of the album were pressed with the infamous "butcher cover," but most of them ended up covered up by the more innocuous "trunk cover."   Demand for this record continues to increase, especially for copies that were never "pasted over" with the trunk cover.

Here's a sealed stereo version that never had a trunk cover over it – known in collecting circles as a "first state" cover. A copy similar to this one has sold for almost $40,000! But beware of re-sealed albums; unless the seller can prove it's never been opened, stay away. Stereo "butchers," whether never pasted over or pasted over, are much harder to find than mono copies.

This is a mono version that never had a trunk cover over it – known in collecting circles as a "first state" cover.

This is a mono cover that had a trunk cover pasted over it, known to collectors as a "third state." It's not a perfect peel job, but it's better than most that aren't done by professionals. Even if it's perfect, you can tell a peeled butcher cover from a "first state" butcher by holding the cover on top of another Capitol LP of the same time period. The peeled cover will be slightly narrower than a standard Capitol LP cover.

How can you tell if your innocuous "trunk cover" might have a "butcher cover" underneath? Look for Ringo's turtleneck, which shows through the white cover fairly easily (at arrow). Today, collectors recommend *not* removing the top cover, not only because of the risk of damage, but because fewer and fewer "paste-over" jackets – known as "second state" covers – remain intact.

A regular mono "trunk cover."

A regular stereo "trunk cover." The only stereo copies of *Yesterday and Today* that can possibly have a "butcher cover" underneath will have a black Capitol label with a rainbow ring along the outside. Covers with "Gold Record Award" added to the artwork are definitely *not* butcher covers.

1960s Cover Capers

For various reasons, record labels have changed numerous album covers over the years. In almost all cases, the first cover is m ore sought after and more valuable than the reissue. Here are some examples, with the original version at the left and the revised version at the ri ght.

Simon and Garfunkel's *Sounds of Silence* from 1966. The original has no song titles on the front cover; the reissue has all the song titles on the front.

Big Hits (High Tide and Green Grass) by the Rolling Stones (1966) originally featured the title on two lines and in all lower-case print; the standard version is in all upper-case letters and has the title on five lines.

 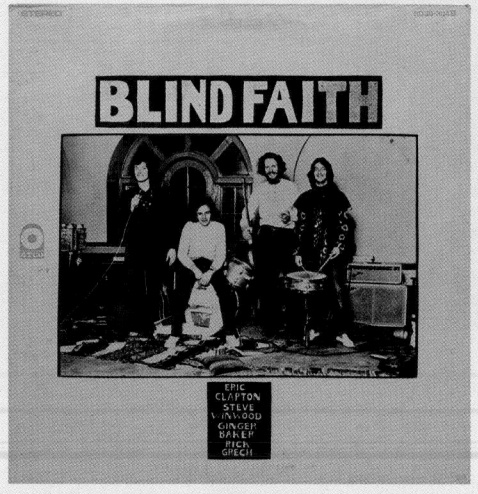

Blind Faith's only album (1969) featured a prepubescent naked girl on the front cover originally. Naturally, this didn't go over well in certain areas and stores, so the more innocuous photo of the band cover replaced it in most places.

1970s and 1980s Cover Capers

The original cover of Aerosmith's 1973 debut album had a mostly orange cover; the new version, which was on the market by the end of 1974, had changed the background to a much lighter color and gave a mention to the LP's most popular song, "Dream On."

Lynyrd Skynyrd's *Street Survivors* (1977) featured a photo of the band with flames superimposed over it. Less than a week after it was released, several members of the band died in a fiery plane crash. Within two months, the original back cover photo was blown up and moved to the front, and the original front cover photo was gone.

Guns N' Roses' 1987 album *Appetite for Destruction* was originally issued with the cover at left, known as the "rape cover." As it proved to be too much for most sellers, the vast majority of covers are the version on the right.

Columbia Records: Pop Label Guide

Columbia Records introduced the long-playing album to the marketplace in 1948 and has never stopped producing them. Here are most of the major variations of the label from pop releases (as opposed to classical or "Masterworks" releases).

1948-55: Maroon label, silver print. This appears on most 10-inch Columbia pop LPs. This label design also exists in black and silver on some very early 500-series 12-inch LPs; also, some soundtracks were issued on blue or green labels.

1955-62: Red label, black accents at left and right. This is known as the "6-eye" label because of the six Columbia "eye" logos, three at 3 o'clock and three at 9 o'clock. Some versions of this add a small "CBS" under the word "Columbia" at the top.

1958-62: Red label, black accents. This is the "Stereo Fidelity" version of the Columbia "6-eye" label. Notice the small "CBS" at the top of the label; this does not appear on all of these.

1963: Red stereo label. Notice that there are no arrows surrounding the words "360 Sound Stereo 360 Sound." This is the first version of this label.

1964-65: Red stereo label. The words "360 Sound Stereo 360 Sound" are still in black, but two arrows have been added to either side.

1966-70: Red stereo label. By this time, "360 Sound Stereo 360 Sound" is in white. The arrows remain.

1963-65: Red mono label. The words "Guaranteed High Fidelity" appear at the bottom of the otherwise all-red label.

1966: Red mono label. At the same time that the print on the stereo version changed to white, so did the mono version, with "360 Sound Mono 360 Sound" at the bottom.

1967-68: Red mono label. The last Columbia mono albums say only "Mono" in white at the bottom.

1970-83: Orange label. Except for some slight typography changes, most notably in the catalog number (early 1970s versions have bold catalog numbers), this label was the same for years. There actually are six "eye" logos along the outside of this label, but this is *not* to be confused with the original "6-eye" labels from earlier!

1984-89: Orange label. Side 1 of these LPs adds an upside-down triangle in a circle to the design.

1990-present: Mostly red label. Most people have probably never seen this label because it's been in use only since the LP disappeared from most retail shelves. Also, many Columbia LPs of the past decade or more have custom labels.

Audiophile Albums

As a response to the declining quality of U.S.-pressed records, several companies emerged that claimed to press a better record than the major labels, and they charged for them accordingly. An avid collector's market has emerged for these LPs.

Pet Sounds by the Beach Boys received the audiophile vinyl treatment from the DCC label in 1995. As with most DCC vinyl issues, the value of this has gone up significantly in the last couple years.

The best U.S. editions of the Beatles' LPs are those from Mobile Fidelity Sound Labs. This MoFi edition of *Sgt. Pepper's Lonely Hearts Club Band* was released in 1982.

Another highly collectible DCC vinyl LP is its edition of the Doors' debut LP, which now sells for more than five times its 1997 retail price.

The Nautilus Super Disc was a competitor of Mobile Fidelity for several years in the early 1980s. One of the most popular of its releases was *Dreamboat Annie* by Heart.

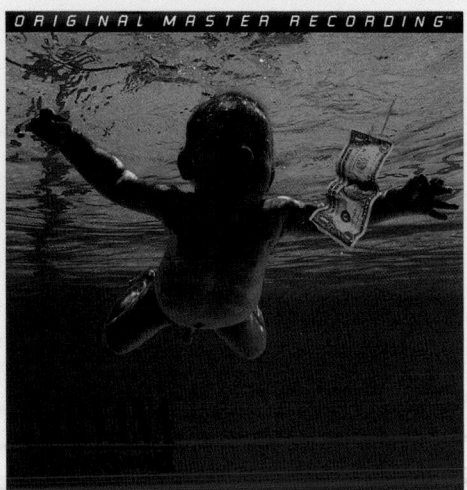

After a break in vinyl production, MoFi returned to vinyl in 1994 and stopped in 1996. One of the most highly collectible LPs from the second group of releases is Nirvana's *Nevermind*.

Against the Wind by Bob Seger and the Silver Bullet Band got the MoFi treatment in 1983.

Club Exclusives

By the end of 1990, most major retail stores were out of the vinyl business. But the music clubs continued to offer records until 1992. Often, these club editions are the *only* version of these available on vinyl.

One of the most popular albums of the 1990s, Garth Brooks' *No Fences,* exists on versions from both the BMG and Columbia House record clubs. The BMG version is more desirable because it placed the cover photo on the entire LP cover instead of on a small square with a large black background as the Columbia House version did.

Foreigner's "comeback" album, *Unusual Heat,* is shown in its Columbia House edition.

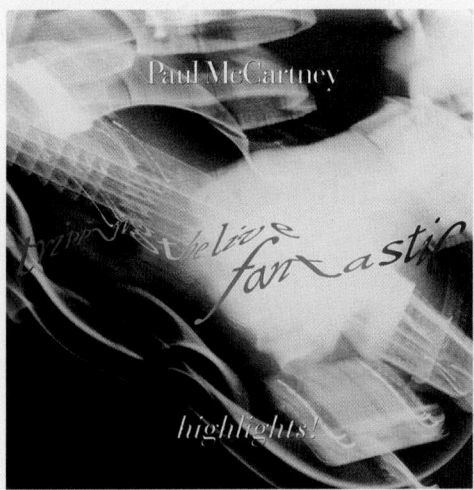

The most well known of these club exclusives is *Tripping the Live Fantastic...Highlights!* by Paul McCartney.

The Stevie Nicks greatest-hits collection *Timespace* saw a vinyl release through Columbia House.

Hank Williams Jr's *America (The Way I See It)* was one of dozens of country titles issued through the BMG club in 1990-1991 but not to retail stores.

Yes' *Union,* in which all the various feuding members reunited, appeared only on a Columbia House vinyl record in the U.S.

Vinyl Lives

In recent years, something of a vinyl revival has taken place. Many artists, both well known and otherwise, have had recent releases on record. Here are just a few.

David Bowie's *Heathen* received a small U.S. vinyl pressing in 2002, his first of new material since the Tin Machine days.

The Sundazed label has been on the forefront of new vinyl releases. Though most of their LPs are reissues of classic titles, it does sometimes create new ones, such as the four-volume *Sanctuary* series of Byrds outtakes and rarities.

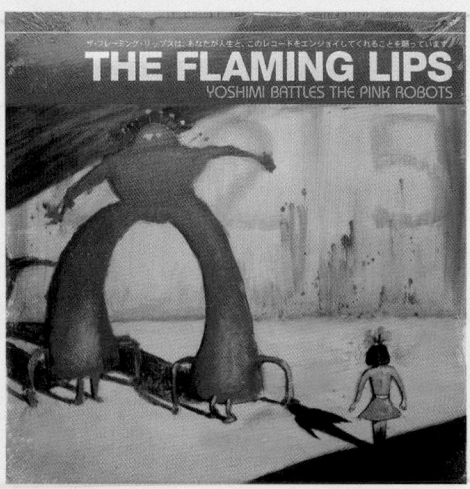

The Flaming Lips, a collectible group that began recording in the 1980s, still does limited vinyl issues, including 2002's *Yoshimi Battles the Pink Robots*.

Michael Jackson's most recent album, *Invincible* (2001), also came out on vinyl.

Lost in much of the hype surrounding the *Elv1s 30 #1 Hits* release from 2002 is that there was also a vinyl edition released on two LPs in the United States.

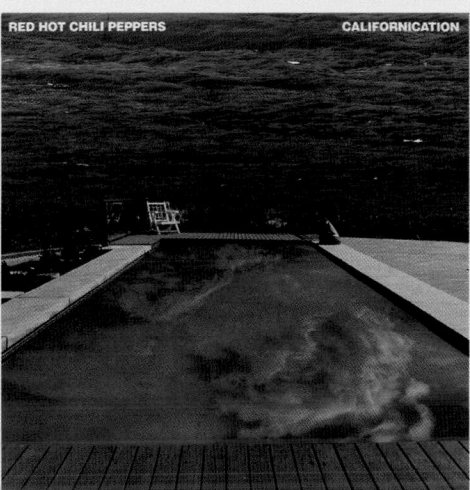

The Red Hot Chili Peppers' *Californication* (1999) was their first new material on LP since their days at the EMI label.

Number	Title (A Side/B Side)	Yr	VG	VG+	NM
RAPPLE					
❑ ABL1-0220	Son of Dracula	1974	3.00	6.00	12.00
RCA VICTOR					
❑ (no #) [M]	The True One	1967	50.00	100.00	200.00
—Boxed set with mono copy of RCA Victor 3874, two photos, button, poster, sticker, bios					
❑ APL1-0097	A Little Touch of Schmilsson in the Night	1973	3.00	6.00	12.00
❑ APL1-0203	Nilsson Sings Newman	1974	2.50	5.00	10.00
—Reissue of LSP-4289					
❑ APD1-0319 [Q]	Nilsson Schmilsson	1974	5.00	10.00	20.00
❑ SPS-33-567 [DJ]	Scatalogue	197?	25.00	50.00	100.00
❑ APD1-0570 [Q]	Pussy Cats	1974	7.50	15.00	30.00
❑ CPL1-0570	Pussy Cats	1974	5.00	10.00	20.00
❑ APD1-0817 [Q]	Duit On Mon Dei	1975	5.00	10.00	20.00
❑ APL1-0817	Duit On Mon Dei	1975	3.00	6.00	12.00
❑ LSPX-1003	The Point!	1971	3.00	6.00	12.00
❑ APD1-1031 [Q]	Sandman	1976	5.00	10.00	20.00
❑ APL1-1031	Sandman	1976	3.00	6.00	12.00
❑ APL1-1119	That's the Way It Is	1976	3.00	6.00	12.00
❑ AFL1-2276	Knnillssonn	1977	3.00	6.00	12.00
❑ AFL1-2798	Greatest Hits	1978	3.00	6.00	12.00
❑ ANL1-3464	Nilsson Schmilsson	1979	2.00	4.00	8.00
❑ AYL1-3761	A Little Touch of Schmilsson in the Night	1980	2.00	4.00	8.00
—"Best Buy Series" reissue					
❑ AYL1-3811	The Point!	1980	2.00	4.00	8.00
—"Best Buy Series" reissue					
❑ AYL1-3812	Son of Schmilsson	1980	2.00	4.00	8.00
—"Best Buy Series" reissue					
❑ LPM-3874 [M]	Pandemonium Shadow Show	1967	10.00	20.00	40.00
❑ LSP-3874 [S]	Pandemonium Shadow Show	1967	5.00	10.00	20.00
—"Stereo" on black label					
❑ LSP-3874 [S]	Pandemonium Shadow Show	1969	3.75	7.50	15.00
—Orange label					
❑ LPM-3956 [M]	Aerial Ballet	1968	12.50	25.00	50.00
❑ LSP-3956 [S]	Aerial Ballet	1968	5.00	10.00	20.00
—"Stereo" on black label					
❑ LSP-3956 [S]	Aerial Ballet	1969	3.75	7.50	15.00
—Orange label, non-flexible vinyl					
❑ LSP-4197	Harry	1969	3.75	7.50	15.00
—Orange label, non-flexible vinyl					
❑ LSP-4289	Nilsson Sings Newman	1970	3.00	6.00	12.00
—Orange label, non-flexible vinyl					
❑ LSP-4417	The Point!	1971	2.50	5.00	10.00
—Reissue of LSPX-1003					
❑ LSP-4515	Nilsson Schmilsson	1971	3.00	6.00	12.00
❑ LSP-4543	Aerial Pandemonium Ballet	1971	3.00	6.00	12.00
—Collection of tracks from 3874 and 3956, remixed with, in some cases, new vocals					
❑ LSP-4717	Son of Schmilsson	1972	3.00	6.00	12.00
—With custom black "Victor" label					
TOWER					
❑ ST 5095 [S]	Spotlight on Nilsson	1967	5.00	10.00	20.00
❑ T 5095 [M]	Spotlight on Nilsson	1967	5.00	10.00	20.00
❑ DT 5165 [R]	Spotlight on Nilsson	1969	3.75	7.50	15.00
NIMMONS, PHIL					
VERVE					
❑ MGV-8025 [M]	The Canadian Scene Via Phil Nimmons	1957	6.25	12.50	25.00
❑ V-8025 [M]	The Canadian Scene Via Phil Nimmons	1961	5.00	10.00	20.00
❑ MGV-8376 [M]	Nimmons 'n' Nine	1960	6.25	12.50	25.00
❑ V-8376 [M]	Nimmons 'n' Nine	1961	5.00	10.00	20.00
NIMOY, LEONARD					
CAEDMON					
❑ TC-1466	The Martian Chronicles	1976	7.50	15.00	30.00
❑ TC-1479	The Illustrated Man	1976	7.50	15.00	30.00
❑ TC-1520	War of the Worlds	1977	7.50	15.00	30.00
❑ TC-1526	Green Hills of Earth	1977	7.50	15.00	30.00
DOT					
❑ DLP 3794 [M]	Mr. Spock's Music from Outer Space	1967	12.50	25.00	50.00
❑ DLP 3835 [M]	Two Sides of Leonard Nimoy	1968	12.50	25.00	50.00
❑ DLP 3883 [M]	The Way I Feel	1968	20.00	40.00	80.00
—Stereo cover with "Monaural" sticker; label is black stock copy					
❑ DLP 25794 [S]	Mr. Spock's Music from Outer Space	1967	20.00	40.00	80.00
❑ DLP 25835 [S]	Two Sides of Leonard Nimoy	1968	20.00	40.00	80.00
❑ DLP 25883 [S]	The Way I Feel	1968	15.00	30.00	60.00
❑ DLP 25910	The Touch of Leonard Nimoy	1969	15.00	30.00	60.00
❑ DLP 25966	The New World of Leonard Nimoy	1969	15.00	30.00	60.00
JRT					
❑ (# unknown)	The Mysterious Golem	1982	10.00	20.00	40.00
PARAMOUNT					
❑ PAS-1030 [(2)]	Outer Space/Inner Mind	1970	12.50	25.00	50.00
PICKWICK					
❑ SPC-3199	Space Odyssey	197?	12.50	25.00	50.00
SEARS					
❑ SPS-491	Leonard Nimoy	196?	20.00	40.00	80.00
NINE INCH NAILS					
NOTHING/INTERSCOPE					
❑ 490473 [(3)]	The Fragile	1999	5.00	10.00	20.00
❑ 490744 [(2)]	Things Falling Apart	2000	3.00	6.00	12.00
NOTHING/TVT					
❑ 2610	Pretty Hate Machine	1990	3.00	6.00	12.00
NOTHING/TVT/INTERSCOPE					
❑ PR 5509 [(2)DJ]	The Downward Spiral	1994	6.25	12.50	25.00
—Prono-only U.S. vinyl					
1910 FRUITGUM COMPANY					
BUDDAH					
❑ BDM-5010 [M]	Simon Says	1968	12.50	25.00	50.00
—Appears to be promo only; "Mono" sticker on stereo cover					
❑ BDS-5010 [S]	Simon Says	1968	6.25	12.50	25.00
❑ BDS-5022	1,2,3 Red Light	1968	6.25	12.50	25.00

Number	Title (A Side/B Side)	Yr	VG	VG+	NM
❑ BDS-5027	Goody, Goody Gumdrops	1969	6.25	12.50	25.00
❑ BDS-5036	Indian Giver	1969	6.25	12.50	25.00
❑ BDS-5043	Hard Ride	1969	6.25	12.50	25.00
❑ BDS-5057	Juiciest Fruitgum	1970	6.25	12.50	25.00
94 EAST					
Early recordings by PRINCE.					
HOT PINK					
❑ HLP 3223	Minneapolis Genius — 94 East	1977	10.00	20.00	40.00
—Deduct 25% for cut-outs					
NIRVANA					
The 1990s grunge group.					
DGC					
❑ 24425	Nevermind	1991	5.00	10.00	20.00
—All copies on black vinyl					
❑ 24504	Incesticide	1992	7.50	15.00	30.00
—All copies on blue swirl vinyl					
❑ 24607	In Utero	1993	7.50	15.00	30.00
—All copies on clear vinyl					
❑ 24727	MTV Unplugged in New York	1994	5.00	10.00	20.00
—Black vinyl, issued simultaneously with white vinyl version; color of vinyl cannot be determined without opening the shrink wrap					
❑ 24727	MTV Unplugged in New York	1994	5.00	10.00	20.00
—White vinyl version					
❑ 25105 [(2)]	From the Muddy Banks of the Wishkah	1996	3.75	7.50	15.00
MOBILE FIDELITY					
❑ 1-258	Nevermind	1996	25.00	50.00	100.00
—Audiophile vinyl					
SUB POP					
❑ SP 34	Bleach	1989	5.00	10.00	20.00
—Red vinyl					
❑ SP 34	Bleach	1989	15.00	30.00	60.00
—Pink vinyl					
❑ SP 34	Bleach	1989	15.00	30.00	60.00
—Purple vinyl					
❑ SP 34	Bleach	1989	37.50	75.00	150.00
—Red and white swirl vinyl					
❑ SP 34	Bleach	1989	50.00	100.00	200.00
—First 1,000 were pressed on white vinyl					
❑ SP 34	Bleach	1989	50.00	100.00	200.00
—Second 1,000 were pressed on black vinyl and include a poster					
❑ 70034	Bleach	2000	3.00	6.00	12.00
—Reissue					
NIRVANA (1)					
The 1960s psychedelic group.					
BELL					
❑ 6015	The Story of Simon Simopath	1968	6.25	12.50	25.00
❑ 6024	All of Us	1969	6.25	12.50	25.00
METROMEDIA					
❑ MD-1018	Nirvana	1970	6.25	12.50	25.00
NISTICO, SAL					
JAZZLAND					
❑ JLP-66 [M]	Heavyweights	1962	7.50	15.00	30.00
❑ JLP-966 [S]	Heavyweights	1962	10.00	20.00	40.00
RIVERSIDE					
❑ RLP-457 [M]	Comin' On Up	1963	7.50	15.00	30.00
❑ RS-9457 [S]	Comin' On Up	1963	10.00	20.00	40.00
NITTY GRITTY DIRT BAND					
LIBERTY					
❑ LWB-184 [(2)]	Stars and Stripes Forever	1981	2.50	5.00	10.00
❑ LKCL-670 [(3)]	Dirt, Silver and Gold.	1981	3.00	6.00	12.00
❑ LO-974	An American Dream.	1981	2.00	4.00	8.00
❑ LT-1042	Make a Little Magic.	1981	2.00	4.00	8.00
❑ LRP-3501 [M]	The Nitty Gritty Dirt Band.	1967	6.25	12.50	25.00
❑ LRP-3516 [M]	Ricochet.	1967	6.25	12.50	25.00
❑ LMAS-5553	All the Good Times.	1981	2.00	4.00	8.00
❑ LST-7501 [S]	The Nitty Gritty Dirt Band.	1967	7.50	15.00	30.00
❑ LST-7516 [S]	Ricochet.	1967	7.50	15.00	30.00
❑ LST-7540	Rare Junk.	1968	6.25	12.50	25.00
❑ LST-7611	Alive.	1969	6.25	12.50	25.00
❑ LST-7642	Uncle Charlie and His Dog Teddy.	1970	6.25	12.50	25.00
—Standard issue of LP					
❑ LST-7642 [DJ]	Uncle Charlie and His Dog Teddy	1970	30.00	60.00	120.00
—Leatherette promo pack with LP, two other discs, photos, booklet					
❑ LTAO-7642	Uncle Charlie and His Dog Teddy	1981	2.00	4.00	8.00
❑ LT-51146	Let's Go	1982	2.50	5.00	10.00
❑ LWCL-51158 [(3)]	Will the Circle Be Unbroken	1986	3.75	7.50	15.00
MCA					
❑ 6407	The Rest of the Dream	1990	3.00	6.00	12.00
UNITED ARTISTS					
❑ UA-LA184-J2 [(2)]	Stars and Stripes Forever	1974	3.75	7.50	15.00
❑ UA-LA469-G	Dream	1975	3.00	6.00	12.00
❑ UA-LA670-L3 [(3)]	Dirt, Silver and Gold	1976	5.00	10.00	20.00
❑ UA-LA830-H	The Chicken Chronicles	1978	2.50	5.00	10.00
❑ UA-LA854-H	The Dirt Band	1978	2.50	5.00	10.00
❑ UA-LA974-H	An American Dream	1979	2.50	5.00	10.00
❑ LT-1042	Make a Little Magic	1980	2.50	5.00	10.00
❑ LW-1106	Jealousy	1981	2.50	5.00	10.00
❑ UAS-5553	All the Good Times	1972	3.75	7.50	15.00
❑ UAS-9801 [(3)]	Will the Circle Be Unbroken	1972	7.50	15.00	30.00
UNIVERSAL					
❑ UVL2-12500 [(2)]	Will the Circle Be Unbroken, Volume Two	1989	5.00	10.00	20.00
WARNER BROS.					
❑ 25113	Plain Dirt Fashion	1984	2.00	4.00	8.00
❑ 25304	Partners, Brothers and Friends	1985	2.00	4.00	8.00
❑ 25382	Twenty Years of Dirt: The Best of the Nitty Gritty Dirt Band	1986	2.00	4.00	8.00
❑ 25573	Hold On	1987	2.00	4.00	8.00

N

Number	Title (A Side/B Side)	Yr	VG	VG+	NM
❏ 25722	Workin' Band	1988	2.00	4.00	8.00
❏ 25830	More Great Dirt: The Best of the Nitty Gritty Dirt Band, Vol. 2	1989	2.50	5.00	10.00

NITZSCHE, JACK
REPRISE

Number	Title (A Side/B Side)	Yr	VG	VG+	NM
❏ MS 2092	St. Giles Cripplegate	1972	5.00	10.00	20.00
❏ R 6101 [M]	The Lonely Surfer	1963	25.00	50.00	100.00
❏ R9-6101 [S]	The Lonely Surfer	1963	50.00	100.00	200.00
—Pink, gold and green label					
❏ RS 6101 [S]	The Lonely Surfer	197?	5.00	10.00	20.00
—With only "r:" logo on all-orange (tan) label					
❏ R 6115 [M]	Dance to the Hits of the Beatles	1964	12.50	25.00	50.00
❏ RS 6115 [S]	Dance to the Hits of the Beatles	1964	15.00	30.00	60.00
❏ R 6200 [M]	Chopin '66	1966	6.25	12.50	25.00
❏ RS 6200 [S]	Chopin '66	1966	7.50	15.00	30.00

NKRUMAH, KWAME
COLUMBIA

Number	Title (A Side/B Side)	Yr	VG	VG+	NM
❏ CS 9863	Ninth Son	1969	6.25	12.50	25.00

NOACK, EDDIE
WIDE WORLD

Number	Title (A Side/B Side)	Yr	VG	VG+	NM
❏ 2001	Remembering Jimmie Rodgers	1970	6.25	12.50	25.00

NOBLE, NICK
COLUMBIA

Number	Title (A Side/B Side)	Yr	VG	VG+	NM
❏ CS 9810	I'm Gonna Make You Love Me	1969	3.75	7.50	15.00

LIBERTY

Number	Title (A Side/B Side)	Yr	VG	VG+	NM
❏ LRP-3302 [M]	Relax	1963	5.00	10.00	20.00
❏ LST-7302 [M]	Relax	1963	6.25	12.50	25.00

MERCURY

Number	Title (A Side/B Side)	Yr	VG	VG+	NM
❏ MG-20182 [M]	You Don't Know What Love Is	1956	6.25	12.50	25.00

WING

Number	Title (A Side/B Side)	Yr	VG	VG+	NM
❏ MGW-12184 [M]	Music for Lovers	196?	3.75	7.50	15.00

NOBLES, CLIFF
MOON SHOT

Number	Title (A Side/B Side)	Yr	VG	VG+	NM
❏ 601	Pony the Horse	1969	10.00	20.00	40.00

PHIL-L.A. OF SOUL

Number	Title (A Side/B Side)	Yr	VG	VG+	NM
❏ 4001	The Horse	1968	15.00	30.00	60.00

NOGUEZ, JACKY
JAMIE

Number	Title (A Side/B Side)	Yr	VG	VG+	NM
❏ JLP-3007 [M]	Chow Chow Bambina	1959	5.00	10.00	20.00
❏ JLPS-3007 [S]	Chow Chow Bambina	1959	7.50	15.00	30.00
❏ JLP-3012 [M]	Jacky Noguez	1960	5.00	10.00	20.00
❏ JLPS-3012 [S]	Jacky Noguez	1960	7.50	15.00	30.00
❏ JLP-3013 [M]	Dance Along with Jacky Noguez	1960	5.00	10.00	20.00
❏ JLPS-3013 [S]	Dance Along with Jacky Noguez	1960	7.50	15.00	30.00

NOLAND, TERRY
BRUNSWICK

Number	Title (A Side/B Side)	Yr	VG	VG+	NM
❏ BL 54041 [M]	Terry Noland	1958	150.00	300.00	600.00
—Buddy Holly plays guitar					

NOONE, JIMMIE
BRUNSWICK

Number	Title (A Side/B Side)	Yr	VG	VG+	NM
❏ BL 58006 [10]	The Apex Club Orchestra	1950	12.50	25.00	50.00

NORDINE, KEN
BLUE THUMB

Number	Title (A Side/B Side)	Yr	VG	VG+	NM
❏ BTS-33 [(2)]	How Are Things in Your Town?	1971	6.25	12.50	25.00
❏ BTS-35 [(2)]	Ken Nordine	1972	6.25	12.50	25.00

DECCA

Number	Title (A Side/B Side)	Yr	VG	VG+	NM
❏ DL 8550 [M]	Concert in the Sky	1957	15.00	30.00	60.00

DOT

Number	Title (A Side/B Side)	Yr	VG	VG+	NM
❏ DLP-3075 [M]	Word Jazz	1958	10.00	20.00	40.00
❏ DLP-3096 [M]	Son of Word Jazz	1958	10.00	20.00	40.00
❏ DLP-3115 [M]	Love Words	1958	10.00	20.00	40.00
❏ DLP-3142 [M]	My Baby	1959	10.00	20.00	40.00
❏ DLP-3196 [M]	Next!	1959	10.00	20.00	40.00
❏ DLP-3301 [M]	Word Jazz, Vol. 2	1960	10.00	20.00	40.00
❏ DLP-25075 [S]	Word Jazz	1959	12.50	25.00	50.00
❏ DLP-25096 [S]	Son of Word Jazz	1959	12.50	25.00	50.00
❏ DLP-25115 [S]	Love Words	1959	12.50	25.00	50.00
❏ DLP-25142 [S]	My Baby	1959	12.50	25.00	50.00
❏ DLP-25196 [S]	Next!	1959	12.50	25.00	50.00
❏ DLP-25301 [S]	Word Jazz, Vol. 2	1960	12.50	25.00	50.00
❏ DLP-25880	The Best of Word Jazz	1968	5.00	10.00	20.00

FM

Number	Title (A Side/B Side)	Yr	VG	VG+	NM
❏ 304 [M]	Passion In the Desert	1963	7.50	15.00	30.00
❏ S-304 [S]	Passion In the Desert	1963	10.00	20.00	40.00

HAMILTON

Number	Title (A Side/B Side)	Yr	VG	VG+	NM
❏ HL-102 [M]	The Voice of Love	1964	5.00	10.00	20.00
❏ HL-12102 [S]	The Voice of Love	1964	6.25	12.50	25.00

PHILIPS

Number	Title (A Side/B Side)	Yr	VG	VG+	NM
❏ PHM 200224 [M]	Colors	1966	5.00	10.00	20.00
❏ PHM 200258 [M]	Ken Nordine Does Robert Shure's "Twink"	1967	5.00	10.00	20.00
❏ PHS 600224 [S]	Colors	1966	6.25	12.50	25.00
❏ PHS 600258 [S]	Ken Nordine Does Robert Shure's "Twink"	1967	6.25	12.50	25.00

SNAIL

Number	Title (A Side/B Side)	Yr	VG	VG+	NM
❏ SR-1003	Grandson of Word Jazz	1987	5.00	10.00	20.00

NORMA JEAN
HARMONY

Number	Title (A Side/B Side)	Yr	VG	VG+	NM
❏ HL 7363 [M]	Country's Favorite	1966	5.00	10.00	20.00
❏ HS 11163 [R]	Country's Favorite	1966	3.75	7.50	15.00

RCA VICTOR

Number	Title (A Side/B Side)	Yr	VG	VG+	NM
❏ LPM-2961 [M]	Let's Go All the Way	1964	6.25	12.50	25.00
❏ LSP-2961 [S]	Let's Go All the Way	1964	7.50	15.00	30.00
❏ LPM-3449 [M]	Pretty Miss Norma Jean	1965	6.25	12.50	25.00
❏ LSP-3449 [S]	Pretty Miss Norma Jean	1965	7.50	15.00	30.00
❏ LPM-3541 [M]	Please Don't Hurt Me	1966	6.25	12.50	25.00
❏ LSP-3541 [S]	Please Don't Hurt Me	1966	7.50	15.00	30.00
❏ LPM-3664 [M]	Norma Jean Sings a Tribute to Kitty Wells	1966	6.25	12.50	25.00
❏ LSP-3664 [S]	Norma Jean Sings a Tribute to Kitty Wells	1966	7.50	15.00	30.00
❏ LPM-3700 [M]	Norma Jean Sings Porter Wagoner	1967	7.50	15.00	30.00
❏ LSP-3700 [S]	Norma Jean Sings Porter Wagoner	1967	6.25	12.50	25.00
❏ LPM-3836 [M]	Jackson Ain't a Very Big Town	1967	7.50	15.00	30.00
❏ LSP-3836 [S]	Jackson Ain't a Very Big Town	1967	6.25	12.50	25.00
❏ LPM-3910 [M]	Heaven's Just a Prayer Away	1967	12.50	25.00	50.00
❏ LSP-3910 [S]	Heaven's Just a Prayer Away	1967	6.25	12.50	25.00
❏ LSP-3977	Body and Mind	1968	6.25	12.50	25.00
❏ LSP-4060	Love's a Woman's Job	1968	6.25	12.50	25.00
❏ LSP-4146	Country Giants	1969	6.25	12.50	25.00
❏ LSP-4227	The Best of Norma Jean	1969	6.25	12.50	25.00
❏ LSP-4446	It's Time for Norma Jean	1969	6.25	12.50	25.00

NORMAN, GENE, GROUP
GNP CRESCENDO

Number	Title (A Side/B Side)	Yr	VG	VG+	NM
❏ GNP-2015 [M]	Dylan Jazz	1965	5.00	10.00	20.00
❏ GNPS-2015 [S]	Dylan Jazz	1965	6.25	12.50	25.00

NORMAN, LARRY
AB

Number	Title (A Side/B Side)	Yr	VG	VG+	NM
❏ 777	Streams of White Light Into Darkened Corners	1977	6.25	12.50	25.00

CAPITOL

Number	Title (A Side/B Side)	Yr	VG	VG+	NM
❏ ST-446	Upon This Rock	1970	7.50	15.00	30.00

IMPACT

Number	Title (A Side/B Side)	Yr	VG	VG+	NM
❏ 3121	Upon This Rock	197?	5.00	10.00	20.00

MGM

Number	Title (A Side/B Side)	Yr	VG	VG+	NM
❏ SE-4942	So Long Ago the Garden	1974	10.00	20.00	40.00

ONE WAY

Number	Title (A Side/B Side)	Yr	VG	VG+	NM
❏ 900	Bootleg	1972	7.50	15.00	30.00
—Regular cover					
❏ 4847	Bootleg	1972	10.00	20.00	40.00
—Gatefold cover					
❏ 7397	Street Level	1971	7.50	15.00	30.00

PHYDEAUX

Number	Title (A Side/B Side)	Yr	VG	VG+	NM
❏ ARF-777-6	Almost So Long Ago the Garden	1984	3.00	6.00	12.00
❏ BONE-777-6	Almost So Long Ago the Garden	1981	3.75	7.50	15.00

SOLID ROCK

Number	Title (A Side/B Side)	Yr	VG	VG+	NM
❏ 2001	In Another Land	1976	3.75	7.50	15.00
❏ 2007	Something New Under the Son	1981	3.75	7.50	15.00

STREET LEVEL

Number	Title (A Side/B Side)	Yr	VG	VG+	NM
❏ ROCK-888-5	Only Visiting This Planet	1978	3.00	6.00	12.00
—Regular cover					
❏ ROCK-888-5	Only Visiting This Planet	1978	3.75	7.50	15.00
—Gatefold cover					

VERVE

Number	Title (A Side/B Side)	Yr	VG	VG+	NM
❏ V6-5092	Only Visiting This Planet	1973	7.50	15.00	30.00
—Tri-fold cover					
❏ V6-5092	Only Visiting This Planet	1973	10.00	20.00	40.00
—Gatefold cover					

NORTH, JAY
KEM

Number	Title (A Side/B Side)	Yr	VG	VG+	NM
❏ 27	Look Who's Singing!	1960	25.00	50.00	100.00

NORTHCOTT, TOM
UNI

Number	Title (A Side/B Side)	Yr	VG	VG+	NM
❏ 73108	Upside Downside	1971	5.00	10.00	20.00

NORTHERN FRONT
KADER

Number	Title (A Side/B Side)	Yr	VG	VG+	NM
❏ (# unknown)	Furniture Store	1975	25.00	50.00	100.00

NORVO, RED
ALLEGRO

Number	Title (A Side/B Side)	Yr	VG	VG+	NM
❏ 1739 [M]	Red Norvo Jazz Trio	195?	10.00	20.00	40.00

CAPITOL

Number	Title (A Side/B Side)	Yr	VG	VG+	NM
❏ T 616 [M]	Classics in Jazz	1955	20.00	40.00	80.00

CHARLIE PARKER

Number	Title (A Side/B Side)	Yr	VG	VG+	NM
❏ PLP-833 [M]	Pretty Is the Only Way To Fly	1962	6.25	12.50	25.00
❏ PLP-833S [S]	Pretty Is the Only Way To Fly	1962	6.25	12.50	25.00

COMMODORE

Number	Title (A Side/B Side)	Yr	VG	VG+	NM
❏ FL-20023 [10]	Town Hall Concert, Volume 1	1952	37.50	75.00	150.00
❏ FL-20027 [10]	Town Hall Concert, Volume 2	1952	37.50	75.00	150.00

CONTEMPORARY

Number	Title (A Side/B Side)	Yr	VG	VG+	NM
❏ C-3534 [M]	Music To Listen To Red Norvo By	1957	12.50	25.00	50.00
❏ S-7009 [S]	Music To Listen To Red Norvo By	1959	10.00	20.00	40.00

CONTINENTAL

Number	Title (A Side/B Side)	Yr	VG	VG+	NM
❏ CS-16005 [S]	Mainstream Jazz	1962	5.00	10.00	20.00

DECCA

Number	Title (A Side/B Side)	Yr	VG	VG+	NM
❏ DL 5501 [10]	Dancing on the Ceiling	1953	30.00	60.00	120.00

DIAL

Number	Title (A Side/B Side)	Yr	VG	VG+	NM
❏ LP-903 [M]	Fabulous Jazz Session	1951	50.00	100.00	200.00

DISCOVERY

Number	Title (A Side/B Side)	Yr	VG	VG+	NM
❏ DL-3012 [10]	Red Norvo Trio	1950	37.50	75.00	150.00
❏ DL-3018 [10]	Red Norvo Trio	1952	37.50	75.00	150.00
❏ DL-4005 [M]	Red Norvo Trio, Volume 1	1951	30.00	60.00	120.00

DOT

Number	Title (A Side/B Side)	Yr	VG	VG+	NM
❏ DLP-3126 [M]	Windjammer City Style	1958	7.50	15.00	30.00
❏ DLP-25126 [S]	Windjammer City Style	1958	10.00	20.00	40.00

EMARCY

Number	Title (A Side/B Side)	Yr	VG	VG+	NM
❏ MG-26002 [10]	Improvisation	1954	37.50	75.00	150.00

EPIC

Number	Title (A Side/B Side)	Yr	VG	VG+	NM
❏ LN 3128 [M]	Red Norvo and His All Stars	1955	12.50	25.00	50.00

This is the first album by Ricky Nelson that consisted entirely of his music; it was released on the Imperial label in 1957.

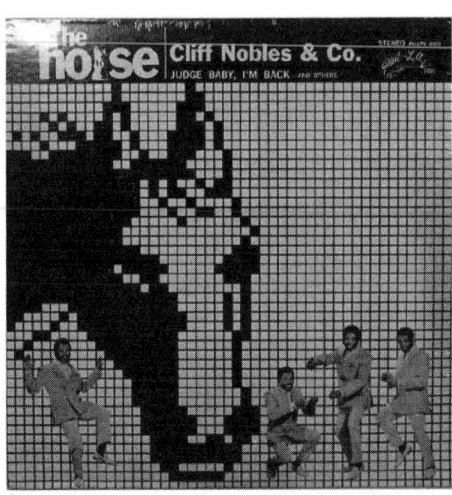

"The Horse" was a big instrumental hit for Cliff Nobles & Co. in 1968, but the album that came out in its wake is decidedly more obscure.

Terry Noland, on his Brunswick album, got some significant help from labelmate Buddy Holly on guitar.

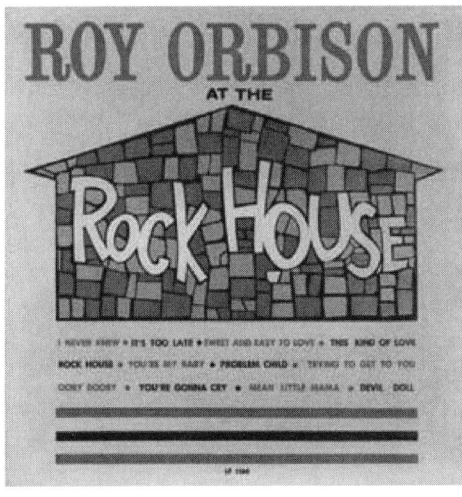

In the early 1960s, the Sun label put together this collection of mid-1950s Roy Orbison recordings in hopes of cashing in on his belated success. But the album flopped, as most of these cash-ins do, and today it's a major collectible.

In 1962, long after their heyday, the Orioles re-recorded some of their big late-1940s and early-1950s hits for the Charlie Parker label, with this album serving as a reminder.

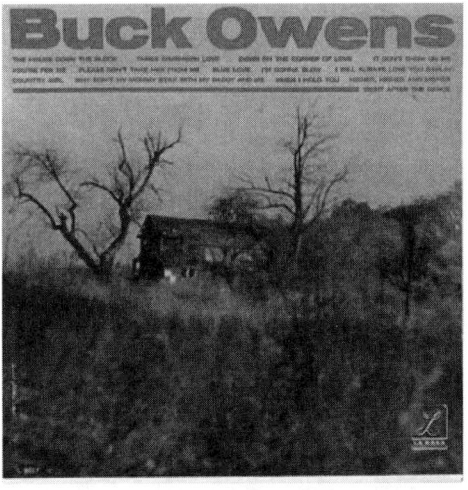

This Buck Owens album on the LaBrea label is considered his most collectible.

Number	Title (A Side/B Side)	Yr	VG	VG+	NM
FANTASY					
❏ 3-12 [10]	Red Norvo Trio	1953	25.00	50.00	100.00
—Black vinyl					
❏ 3-12 [10]	Red Norvo Trio	1953	37.50	75.00	150.00
—Colored vinyl					
❏ 3-19 [M]	Red Norvo Trio	195?	10.00	20.00	40.00
—Black vinyl					
❏ 3-19 [M]	Red Norvo Trio	1955	20.00	40.00	80.00
—Red vinyl					
❏ 3218 [M]	Red Norvo With Strings	195?	10.00	20.00	40.00
—Black vinyl					
❏ 3244 [M]	The Red Norvo Trios	195?	10.00	20.00	40.00
—Black vinyl					
❏ 3244 [M]	The Red Norvo Trios	1957	20.00	40.00	80.00
—Red vinyl					
LIBERTY					
❏ LRP-3035 [M]	Ad Lib	1957	10.00	20.00	40.00
❏ LJH-6012 [M]	Vibe-rations In Hi-Fi	1956	12.50	25.00	50.00
RAVE					
❏ 101 [M]	Red Norvo Quintet	1956	20.00	40.00	80.00
RCA VICTOR					
❏ LPM-1420 [M]	Hi Five	1957	10.00	20.00	40.00
❏ LPM-1449 [M]	Some of My Favorites	1957	10.00	20.00	40.00
❏ LSP-1711 [S]	Red Norvo In Stereo	1958	12.50	25.00	50.00
❏ LPM-1729 [M]	Red Plays the Blues	1958	10.00	20.00	40.00
❏ LSP-1729 [S]	Red Plays the Blues	1958	12.50	25.00	50.00
REFERENCE RECORDINGS					
❏ RR-8	The Forward Look	1983	5.00	10.00	20.00
❏ RR-8-UHGR	The Forward Look	1983	10.00	20.00	40.00
RONDO-LETTE					
❏ A-28 [M]	Red Norvo Trio	1958	6.25	12.50	25.00
SAVOY					
❏ MG-12088 [M]	Move!	1956	20.00	40.00	80.00
❏ MG-12093 [M]	Midnight On Cloud 69	1956	20.00	40.00	80.00
STEREO RECORDS					
❏ S-7009 [S]	Music To Listen To Red Norvo By	1958	12.50	25.00	50.00
TAMPA					
❏ TP-35 [M]	Norvo Naturally	1957	25.00	50.00	100.00
—Colored vinyl					
❏ TP-35 [M]	Norvo Naturally	1958	12.50	25.00	50.00
—Black vinyl					
"X"					
❏ LXA-3034 [M]	Red's Blue Room	1955	37.50	75.00	150.00

NORVO, RED/GEORGIE AULD

GOLDEN ERA					
❏ 15016 [M]	The Great Dance Bands, Vol. 2	195?	10.00	20.00	40.00

NORVO, RED/CAL TJADER

JAZZTONE					
❏ J-1277 [M]	Delightfully Light	195?	10.00	20.00	40.00

NOSY PARKER

(NO LABEL)					
❏ (no #)	Nosy Parker	1975	62.50	125.00	250.00

NOTES FROM THE UNDERGROUND

VANGUARD					
❏ VSD-6502	Notes from the Underground	1970	20.00	40.00	80.00

NOTHING, CHARLIE

TAKOMA					
❏ C-1015	The Psychedelic Saxophone of Charlie Nothing	1967	12.50	25.00	50.00

NOVA LOCAL, THE

DECCA					
❏ DL 74977	Nova 1	1968	17.50	35.00	70.00

NOVAC, JERRY

EMBRYO					
❏ 527	The 5th Word	1970	6.25	12.50	25.00

NOVELLS, THE

MOTHER'S					
❏ MLPS-73	A Happening	1968	12.50	25.00	50.00

NOW CREATIVE ARTS JAZZ ENSEMBLE, THE

ARHOOLIE					
❏ 8002	Now	1969	5.00	10.00	20.00

NOZERO, LARRY

STRATA					
❏ 109-75	Time	1975	5.00	10.00	20.00

NRBQ

ANNUIT COEPTIS					
❏ 1001/2 [(2)]	Scraps/Workshop	1976	5.00	10.00	20.00
—Reissue of Kama Sutra LPs					
BEARSVILLE					
❏ 23817	Grooves in Orbit	1983	2.50	5.00	10.00
COLUMBIA					
❏ CS 9858	NRBQ	1969	6.25	12.50	25.00
—"360 Sound Stereo" label					
❏ CS 9858	NRBQ	1970	3.00	6.00	12.00
—Orange label					
❏ PC 9858	NRBQ	198?	2.00	4.00	8.00
—Budget-line reissue					
KAMA SUTRA					
❏ KSBS-2045	Scraps	1972	7.50	15.00	30.00
❏ KSBS-2065	Workshop	1973	10.00	20.00	40.00

Number	Title (A Side/B Side)	Yr	VG	VG+	NM
MERCURY					
❏ SRM-1-3712	NRBQ at Yankee Stadium	1978	3.75	7.50	15.00
❏ 824462-1	NRBQ at Yankee Stadium	1984	2.50	5.00	10.00
—Reissue					
RED ROOSTER					
❏ 101	All Hopped Up	1977	3.75	7.50	15.00
ROUNDER					
❏ EP-2501 [EP]	Christmas Wish	1985	3.00	6.00	12.00
❏ 3029	All Hopped Up	1979	3.00	6.00	12.00
❏ 3030	Kick Me Hard	1979	3.00	6.00	12.00
❏ 3048	Tiddlywinks	1980	3.00	6.00	12.00
❏ 3055	Scraps	1982	2.50	5.00	10.00
❏ 3066	Tapdancin' Bats	1983	2.50	5.00	10.00
❏ 3090	RC Cola & a Moon Pie	1987	2.50	5.00	10.00
❏ 3098	Lou and the Q	1986	2.50	5.00	10.00
—With pro wrestler Captain Lou Albano					
❏ 3108	God Bless Us All	1988	2.50	5.00	10.00
❏ 3109	Live! Diggin' Uncle Q	1988	2.50	5.00	10.00
VIRGIN					
❏ 91291	Wild Weekend	1989	2.50	5.00	10.00

NUBIN, KATI BELL

VERVE					
❏ MGV-3004 [M]	Soul, Soul Searchin'	1960	20.00	40.00	80.00
❏ V-3004 [M]	Soul, Soul Searchin'	1961	10.00	20.00	40.00
❏ V6-3004 [S]	Soul, Soul Searchin'	1961	12.50	25.00	50.00

NUCLEUS

MAINSTREAM					
❏ S-6120	Nucleus	1969	12.50	25.00	50.00

NUDIE

NUDIE					
❏ 3203	Nudie and His Mandolin	196?	10.00	20.00	40.00

NUGENT, TED

Also see THE AMBOY DUKES.

ATLANTIC					
❏ SD 19365	Nugent	1982	2.50	5.00	10.00
❏ 80125	Penetrator	1984	2.50	5.00	10.00
❏ 81632	Little Miss Dangerous	1986	2.50	5.00	10.00
❏ 81812	If You Can't Lick 'Em...Lick 'Em	1988	2.50	5.00	10.00
EPIC					
❏ AS99-607 [PD]	State of Shock	1979	10.00	20.00	40.00
—Promo-only picture disc					
❏ PE 33692	Ted Nugent	1975	3.00	6.00	12.00
—Orange label					
❏ PE 33692	Ted Nugent	1979	2.00	4.00	8.00
—Reissue with dark blue label and bar code					
❏ PE 34121	Free-for-All	1976	3.00	6.00	12.00
—Orange label					
❏ PE 34121	Free-for-All	1979	2.00	4.00	8.00
—Reissue with dark blue label and bar code					
❏ PEQ 34121 [Q]	Free-for-All	1976	5.00	10.00	20.00
❏ JE 34700	Cat Scratch Fever	1977	3.00	6.00	12.00
—Orange label					
❏ PE 34700	Cat Scratch Fever	198?	2.00	4.00	8.00
—Reissue with dark blue label and bar code					
❏ KE2 35069 [(2)]	Double Live Gonzo!	1978	3.75	7.50	15.00
—Orange labels					
❏ FE 35551	Weekend Warriors	1978	3.00	6.00	12.00
—Orange label					
❏ PE 35551	Weekend Warriors	198?	2.00	4.00	8.00
—Reissue with dark blue label and bar code					
❏ FE 36000	State of Shock	1979	2.50	5.00	10.00
❏ PE 36000	State of Shock	198?	2.00	4.00	8.00
—Budget-line reissue					
❏ FE 36404	Scream Dream	1980	2.50	5.00	10.00
❏ FE 37084	Intensities in 10 Cities	1981	2.50	5.00	10.00
❏ PE 37084	Intensities in 10 Cities	198?	2.00	4.00	8.00
—Budget-line reissue					
❏ FE 37667	Great Gonzos! The Best of Ted Nugent	1981	2.50	5.00	10.00
❏ PE 37667	Great Gonzos! The Best of Ted Nugent	198?	2.00	4.00	8.00
—Budget-line reissue					

NUTTY SQUIRRELS, THE

COLUMBIA					
❏ CL 1589 [M]	Bird Watching	1961	7.50	15.00	30.00
❏ CS 8389 [S]	Bird Watching	1961	10.00	20.00	40.00
HANOVER					
❏ HML-8014 [M]	The Nutty Squirrels	1960	12.50	25.00	50.00
MGM					
❏ E-4272 [M]	A Hard Day's Night	1964	6.25	12.50	25.00
❏ SE-4272 [S]	A Hard Day's Night	1964	7.50	15.00	30.00

NYE, LOUIS

RIVERSIDE					
❏ RLP-842 [M]	Heigh-Ho, Madison Avenue	1960	6.25	12.50	25.00

NYRO, LAURA

COLUMBIA					
❏ CL 2826 [M]	Eli and the Thirteenth Confession	1968	10.00	20.00	40.00
❏ CS 9626	Eli and the Thirteenth Confession	1970	2.50	5.00	10.00
—Orange label					
❏ CS 9626 [S]	Eli and the Thirteenth Confession	1968	3.75	7.50	15.00
—"360 Sound Stereo" label					
❏ PC 9626	Eli and the Thirteenth Confession	198?	2.00	4.00	8.00
—Budget-line reissue					
❏ CS 9737	New York Tendaberry	1969	3.75	7.50	15.00
—"360 Sound Stereo" label					
❏ CS 9737	New York Tendaberry	1970	2.50	5.00	10.00
—Orange label					

Number	Title (A Side/B Side)	Yr	VG	VG+	NM
❏ PC 9737	New York Tendaberry	198?	2.00	4.00	8.00
—Budget-line reissue					
❏ KC 30259	Christmas and the Beads of Sweat	1970	2.50	5.00	10.00
—Orange label					
❏ KC 30259	Christmas and the Beads of Sweat	1970	3.75	7.50	15.00
—"360 Sound Stereo" label					
❏ PC 30259	Christmas and the Beads of Sweat	198?	2.00	4.00	8.00
—Budget-line reissue					
❏ KC 30987	Gonna Take a Miracle	1971	3.75	7.50	15.00
❏ PC 30987	Gonna Take a Miracle	197?	2.00	4.00	8.00
—Budget-line reissue					
❏ KC 31410	The First Songs	1973	3.75	7.50	15.00
—Reissue of Verve Forecast 3020					
❏ PC 31410	The First Songs	197?	2.00	4.00	8.00
—Budget-line reissue					
❏ PC 33912	Smile	1976	3.00	6.00	12.00
—No bar code on cover					
❏ PC2 34331 [(2)DJ]	Season of Lights…Laura Nyro in Concert	1977	12.50	25.00	50.00
—Promo only in plain cardboard jacket; this LP was edited to one LP for release					
❏ JC 34786	Season of Lights…Laura Nyro in Concert	1977	3.00	6.00	12.00
—Edited version of above					
❏ JC 35449	Nested	1978	3.00	6.00	12.00
❏ PC 35449	Nested	198?	2.00	4.00	8.00
—Budget-line reissue					
❏ FC 39215	Mother's Spiritual	1984	2.50	5.00	10.00
VERVE FOLKWAYS					
❏ FT-3020 [M]	Laura Nyro — More Than a New Discovery	1967	7.50	15.00	30.00
❏ FTS-3020 [S]	Laura Nyro — More Than a New Discovery	1967	7.50	15.00	30.00
VERVE FORECAST					
❏ FTS-3020 [S]	Laura Nyro — More Than a New Discovery	1967	5.00	10.00	20.00
❏ FTS-3029	Laura Nyro	1968	—	—	—
—Canceled					
❏ ST 93036	Laura Nyro — More Than a New Discovery	1968	6.25	12.50	25.00
—Capitol Record Club edition					

O

O'BRIAN, HUGH
ABC-PARAMOUNT

Number	Title (A Side/B Side)	Yr	VG	VG+	NM
❏ ABC-203 [M]	TV's Wyatt Earp Sings	1957	15.00	30.00	60.00

O'BRYANT, JOAN
FOLKWAYS

❏ FA-2134 [M]	Folksongs and Ballads of Kansas	1957	7.50	15.00	30.00
❏ FA-2338 [M]	American Ballads and Folksongs	1958	7.50	15.00	30.00

O'CONNELL, HELEN
MARK 56

❏ 711	Christmas with Helen O'Connell	19??	3.00	6.00	12.00

VIK

❏ LX-1093 [M]	Green Eyes	1957	10.00	20.00	40.00

O'CONNOR, CARROLL
A&M

❏ SP-4340	Remembering You	1972	6.25	12.50	25.00

AUDIO FIDELITY

❏ AFSD-6727	Carroll O'Connor Sings for Old P.F.A.R.T.S.	1976	6.25	12.50	25.00

O'DAY, ANITA
ADVANCE

❏ LSP-8 [10]	Anita O'Day Specials	1951	62.50	125.00	250.00

AMERICAN RECORDING SOCIETY

❏ G-426 [M]	For Oscar	1957	10.00	20.00	40.00

BASF

❏ MB 20750	Recorded Live at the Berlin Jazz Festival	1973	5.00	10.00	20.00

CLEF

❏ MGC-130 [10]	Anita O'Day Collates	1953	37.50	75.00	150.00

CORAL

❏ CRL-56073 [10]	Singin' and Swingin'	1953	37.50	75.00	150.00

NORGRAN

❏ MGN-30 [10]	Songs By Anita O'Day	1954	37.50	75.00	150.00
❏ MGN-1049 [M]	Anita O'Day	1955	30.00	60.00	120.00
❏ MGN-1057 [M]	An Evening With Anita O'Day	1956	25.00	50.00	100.00

VERVE

❏ MGV-2000 [M]	Anita	1956	20.00	40.00	80.00
❏ V-2000 [M]	Anita	1961	5.00	10.00	20.00
❏ MGV-2043 [M]	Pick Yourself Up With Anita O'Day	1957	20.00	40.00	80.00
❏ V-2043 [M]	Pick Yourself Up With Anita O'Day	1961	5.00	10.00	20.00
❏ MGV-2049 [M]	The Lady Is a Tramp	1957	15.00	30.00	60.00
❏ V-2049 [M]	The Lady Is a Tramp	1961	5.00	10.00	20.00
❏ MGV-2050 [M]	An Evening With Anita O'Day	1957	15.00	30.00	60.00
❏ V-2050 [M]	An Evening With Anita O'Day	1961	5.00	10.00	20.00
❏ MGV-2113 [M]	Anita O'Day At Mr. Kelly's	1958	12.50	25.00	50.00
❏ V-2113 [M]	Anita O'Day At Mr. Kelly's	1961	5.00	10.00	20.00
❏ V6-2113 [S]	Anita O'Day At Mr. Kelly's	1961	6.25	12.50	25.00
❏ MGV-2118 [M]	Anita O'Day Swings Cole Porter	1959	12.50	25.00	50.00
❏ V-2118 [M]	Anita O'Day Swings Cole Porter	1961	5.00	10.00	20.00
❏ V6-2118 [S]	Anita O'Day Swings Cole Porter	1961	6.25	12.50	25.00
❏ MGV-2141 [M]	Anita O'Day and Billy May Swing Rodgers and Hart	1960	15.00	30.00	60.00
❏ V-2141 [M]	Anita O'Day and Billy May Swing Rodgers and Hart	1961	5.00	10.00	20.00
❏ V6-2141 [S]	Anita O'Day and Billy May Swing Rodgers and Hart	1961	6.25	12.50	25.00
❏ MGV-2145 [M]	Waiter, Make Mine Blues	1960	15.00	30.00	60.00
❏ V-2145 [M]	Waiter, Make Mine Blues	1961	5.00	10.00	20.00
❏ V6-2145 [S]	Waiter, Make Mine Blues	1961	6.25	12.50	25.00

Number	Title (A Side/B Side)	Yr	VG	VG+	NM
❏ MGV-2157 [M]	Trav'lin' Light	1960	12.50	25.00	50.00
❏ V-2157 [M]	Trav'lin' Light	1961	5.00	10.00	20.00
❏ V6-2157 [S]	Trav'lin' Light	1961	6.25	12.50	25.00
❏ MGVS-6002 [S]	Anita O'Day Sings the Winners	1960	15.00	30.00	60.00
❏ MGVS-6043 [S]	Anita O'Day At Mr. Kelly's	1960	15.00	30.00	60.00
❏ MGVS-6046 [S]	Cool Heat — Anita O'Day Sings Jimmy Giuffre Arrangements	1960	15.00	30.00	60.00
❏ MGVS-6059 [S]	Anita O'Day Swings Cole Porter	1960	15.00	30.00	60.00
❏ MGV-8259 [M]	Anita Sings the Most	1958	12.50	25.00	50.00
❏ V-8259 [M]	Anita Sings the Most	1961	5.00	10.00	20.00
❏ MGV-8283 [M]	Anita O'Day Sings the Winners	1958	12.50	25.00	50.00
❏ V-8283 [M]	Anita O'Day Sings the Winners	1961	5.00	10.00	20.00
❏ V6-8283 [S]	Anita O'Day Sings the Winners	1961	6.25	12.50	25.00
❏ MGV-8312 [M]	Cool Heat — Anita O'Day Sings Jimmy Giuffre Arrangements	1959	12.50	25.00	50.00
❏ V-8312 [M]	Cool Heat — Anita O'Day Sings Jimmy Giuffre Arrangements	1961	5.00	10.00	20.00
❏ V6-8312 [S]	Cool Heat — Anita O'Day Sings Jimmy Giuffre Arrangements	1961	6.25	12.50	25.00
❏ V-8442 [M]	All the Sad Young Men	1962	7.50	15.00	30.00
❏ V6-8442 [S]	All the Sad Young Men	1962	10.00	20.00	40.00
❏ V-8472 [M]	Time For Two	1962	7.50	15.00	30.00
❏ V6-8472 [S]	Time For Two	1962	10.00	20.00	40.00
❏ V-8483 [M]	This Is Anita	1962	7.50	15.00	30.00
❏ V-8485 [M]	Anita O'Day Sings the Winners	1962	5.00	10.00	20.00
❏ V6-8485 [S]	Anita O'Day Sings the Winners	1962	6.25	12.50	25.00
❏ V-8514 [M]	Anita O'Day and the Three Sounds	1963	6.25	12.50	25.00
❏ V6-8514 [S]	Anita O'Day and the Three Sounds	1963	7.50	15.00	30.00
❏ V-8572 [M]	Incomparable! Anita O'Day	1964	6.25	12.50	25.00
❏ V6-8572 [S]	Incomparable! Anita O'Day	1964	7.50	15.00	30.00

O'DAY, MOLLY
AUDIO LAB

❏ AL-1544 [M]	Music for the Country Folks	1960	7.50	15.00	30.00

HARMONY

❏ HL 7299 [M]	The Unforgettable Molly O'Day	1963	5.00	10.00	20.00

STARDAY

❏ SLP-367	The Living Legend of Country Music	1966	6.25	12.50	25.00

O'DELL, DOYE
ERA

❏ EL-20004 [M]	Doye	1956	7.50	15.00	30.00
—Black vinyl					
❏ EL-20004 [M]	Doye	1956	12.50	25.00	50.00
—Red vinyl					

SAGE

❏ C-36 [M]	Crossroads	195?	7.50	15.00	30.00

O'DELL, KENNY
CAPRICORN

❏ CP 0140	Kenny O'Dell	1974	3.00	6.00	12.00
❏ CP 0211	Let's Shake Hands and Come Out Lovin'	1978	3.00	6.00	12.00

VEGAS

❏ 401	Beautiful People	1968	6.25	12.50	25.00

O'FARRILL, CHICO
CLEF

❏ MGC-131 [10]	Afro-Cuban	1953	50.00	100.00	200.00
❏ MGC-132 [10]	Chico O'Farrill Jazz	1953	50.00	100.00	200.00
❏ MGC-699 [M]	Chico O'Farrill Jazz	1956	20.00	40.00	80.00

IMPULSE!

❏ A-9135 [M]	Nine Flags	1967	6.25	12.50	25.00
❏ AS-9135 [S]	Nine Flags	1967	5.00	10.00	20.00

NORGRAN

❏ MGN-9 [10]	The Second Afro-Cuban Jazz Suite	1954	37.50	75.00	150.00
❏ MGN-27 [10]	Mambo Dance Sessions	1954	20.00	40.00	80.00
❏ MGN-28 [10]	Latino Dance Sessions	1954	20.00	40.00	80.00
❏ MGN-31 [10]	Chico O'Farrill	1954	20.00	40.00	80.00

VERVE

❏ MGV-2003 [M]	Mambo/Latino Dances	1956	12.50	25.00	50.00
❏ V-2003 [M]	Mambo/Latino Dances	1961	6.25	12.50	25.00
❏ MGV-2024 [M]	Music From South America	1956	12.50	25.00	50.00
❏ V-2024 [M]	Music From South America	1961	6.25	12.50	25.00
❏ MGV-8083 [M]	Jazz North of the Border and South of the Border	1957	12.50	25.00	50.00
❏ V-8083 [M]	Jazz North of the Border and South of the Border	1961	6.25	12.50	25.00

O'GWYNN, JAMES
MERCURY

❏ MG-20727 [M]	The Best of James O'Gwynn	1962	7.50	15.00	30.00
❏ SR-60727 [S]	The Best of James O'Gwynn	1962	10.00	20.00	40.00

PLANTATION

❏ 21	Greatest Hits	197?	3.00	6.00	12.00

WING

❏ MGW-12290 [M]	Heartaches and Memories	1964	5.00	10.00	20.00
❏ SRW-16290 [S]	Heartaches and Memories	1964	6.25	12.50	25.00

O'HARA, MAUREEN
COLUMBIA

❏ CL 1750 [M]	Maureen O'Hara Sings Her Favorite Irish Songs	1962	10.00	20.00	40.00
❏ CS 8550 [S]	Maureen O'Hara Sings Her Favorite Irish Songs	1962	12.50	25.00	50.00

RCA VICTOR

❏ LPM-1953 [M]	Love Letters	1959	12.50	25.00	50.00
❏ LSP-1953 [S]	Love Letters	1959	15.00	30.00	60.00

O'JAYS, THE
BELL

❏ 6014	Back on Top	1968	5.00	10.00	20.00

Number	Title (A Side/B Side)	Yr	VG	VG+	NM
❏ 6082	The O'Jays	1973	3.00	6.00	12.00
EMI					
❏ E1-90921	Serious	1989	2.50	5.00	10.00
❏ E1-93390	Emotionally Yours	1991	3.75	7.50	15.00
❏ E1-96420	Home for Christmas	1991	3.75	7.50	15.00
IMPERIAL					
❏ LP 9290 [M]	Comin' Through	1965	10.00	20.00	40.00
❏ LP 12290 [S]	Comin' Through	1965	12.50	25.00	50.00
KORY					
❏ 1006	The O'Jays	1977	2.50	5.00	10.00
LIBERTY					
❏ LN-10119	Greatest Hits	1980	2.00	4.00	8.00
—Budget-line reissue of Imperial material					
MINIT					
❏ LP-24008 [S]	Soul Sounds	1967	12.50	25.00	50.00
❏ LP-40008 [M]	Soul Sounds	1967	10.00	20.00	40.00
NEPTUNE					
❏ 202	The O'Jays in Philadelphia	1969	7.50	15.00	30.00
PHILADELPHIA INT'L.					
❏ ASZ 140 [DJ]	Everything You Always Wanted to Hear by the O'Jays But Were Afraid to Ask For	1975	3.75	7.50	15.00
❏ KZ 31712	Back Stabbers	1972	3.00	6.00	12.00
❏ KZ 32120	The O'Jays in Philadelphia	1973	3.00	6.00	12.00
—Reissue of Neptune LP					
❏ KZ 32408	Ship Ahoy	1973	2.50	5.00	10.00
❏ PZ 32408	Ship Ahoy	198?	2.00	4.00	8.00
—Budget-line reissue					
❏ PZQ 32408 [Q]	Ship Ahoy	1974	3.75	7.50	15.00
❏ KZ 32953	The O'Jays Live in London	1974	2.50	5.00	10.00
❏ PZQ 32953 [Q]	The O'Jays Live in London	1974	3.75	7.50	15.00
❏ PZ 33150	Survival	1975	2.50	5.00	10.00
❏ PZ 33807	Family Reunion	1975	2.50	5.00	10.00
—No bar code on back cover					
❏ PZ 33807	Family Reunion	198?	2.00	4.00	8.00
—Budget-line reissue with bar code					
❏ PZQ 33807 [Q]	Family Reunion	1975	3.75	7.50	15.00
❏ PZ 34245	Message in the Music	1976	2.50	5.00	10.00
❏ PZ 34684	Travelin' at the Speed of Thought	1977	2.50	5.00	10.00
❏ PZG 35024 [(2)]	The O'Jays: Collector's Items	1978	3.00	6.00	12.00
❏ Z2 35024 [(2)]	The O'Jays: Collector's Items	198?	2.50	5.00	10.00
—Reissue					
❏ JZ 35355	So Full of Love	1978	2.50	5.00	10.00
❏ PZ 35355	So Full of Love	198?	2.00	4.00	8.00
—Budget-line reissue					
❏ FZ 36027	Identify Yourself	1979	2.50	5.00	10.00
❏ FZ 37999	My Favorite Person	1982	2.50	5.00	10.00
❏ FZ 38518	When Will I See You Again	1983	2.50	5.00	10.00
❏ PZ 38518	When Will I See You Again	1985	2.00	4.00	8.00
—Budget-line reissue					
❏ FZ 39251	Greatest Hits	1984	2.50	5.00	10.00
❏ 53015	Love Fever	1985	2.50	5.00	10.00
❏ 53036	Let Me Touch You	1987	2.50	5.00	10.00
SUNSET					
❏ SUS-5222	Full of Soul	1968	3.75	7.50	15.00
—Reissue of Imperial LP					
TSOP					
❏ FZ 36416	The Year 2000	1980	2.50	5.00	10.00
UNITED ARTISTS					
❏ UAS-5655	The O'Jays Greatest Hits	1972	3.00	6.00	12.00
VOLCANO					
❏ 31149	Love You to Tears	1997	3.75	7.50	15.00

O'KAYSIONS, THE

Number	Title (A Side/B Side)	Yr	VG	VG+	NM
ABC					
❏ S-664	Girl Watcher	1968	10.00	20.00	40.00

O'KEEFE, DANNY

Number	Title (A Side/B Side)	Yr	VG	VG+	NM
ATLANTIC					
❏ SD 7264	Breezy Stories	1973	3.00	6.00	12.00
❏ SD 18125	So Long, Harry Truman	1975	3.00	6.00	12.00
COTILLION					
❏ SD 9036	Danny O'Keefe	1971	3.75	7.50	15.00
FIRST AMERICAN					
❏ 7700	The Seattle Tapes	1977	3.00	6.00	12.00
❏ 7721	The Seattle Tapes, Volume 2	1979	3.00	6.00	12.00
PANORAMA					
❏ 105	Introducing Danny O'Keefe	1966	10.00	20.00	40.00
SIGNPOST					
❏ SD 8404	O'Keefe	1972	3.00	6.00	12.00
WARNER BROS.					
❏ PRO 760 [DJ]	The O'Keefe File	1977	3.75	7.50	15.00
❏ BS 3050	American Roulette	1977	2.50	5.00	10.00
❏ BSK 3314	Global Blues	1978	2.50	5.00	10.00

O'SHEA, MILO

Number	Title (A Side/B Side)	Yr	VG	VG+	NM
COLUMBIA					
❏ CS 9647	An Evening in Dublin	1969	5.00	10.00	20.00

OAK RIDGE BOYS, THE

Number	Title (A Side/B Side)	Yr	VG	VG+	NM
ABC					
❏ AA-1065	Room Service	1978	2.50	5.00	10.00
❏ AA-1135	Have Arrived	1979	3.00	6.00	12.00
ABC/DOT					
❏ DA-2093	Y'all Come Back Saloon	1977	2.50	5.00	10.00
ACCORD					
❏ SN-7138	Spiritual Jubilee	198?	2.50	5.00	10.00
❏ SN-7159	Spiritual Jubilee — Volume 2	198?	2.50	5.00	10.00
❏ SN-7199	Spiritual Jubilee — Volume 3	198?	2.50	5.00	10.00
CADENCE					
❏ CLP-3019 [M]	The Oak Ridge Quartet	1958	15.00	30.00	60.00
CANAAN					
❏ 9625	Together	1966	5.00	10.00	20.00
—With the Harvesters					
COLUMBIA					
❏ KC 32742	The Oak Ridge Boys	1974	3.00	6.00	12.00
❏ PC 32742	The Oak Ridge Boys	197?	2.00	4.00	8.00
—Reissue					
❏ KC 33057	Sky High	1975	3.00	6.00	12.00
❏ PC 33057	Sky High	197?	2.00	4.00	8.00
—Reissue					
❏ KC 33935	Old Fashioned, Down Home, Hand Clappin', Foot Stompin', Southern Style, Gospel Quartet Music	1976	3.00	6.00	12.00
❏ PC 35202	The Best of the Oak Ridge Boys	1978	2.50	5.00	10.00
❏ PC 37711	Old Fashoned Gospel Quartet Music	1984	2.00	4.00	8.00
❏ FC 37737	All Our Favorite Songs	1981	2.50	5.00	10.00
❏ PC 38467	Smoky Mountain Gospel	1984	2.00	4.00	8.00
HEARTWARMING					
❏ HWS 3036	Thanks	1971	3.75	7.50	15.00
❏ HWS 3091	International	1971	3.75	7.50	15.00
❏ HWS 3159	The Light	1972	3.75	7.50	15.00
INTERMEDIA					
❏ QS-5012	Glory Train	198?	2.50	5.00	10.00
LIBERTY					
❏ LN-10046	The Oak Ridge Boys at Their Best	1981	2.00	4.00	8.00
MCA					
❏ AA-1135	Have Arrived	1979	2.50	5.00	10.00
❏ L33-2-1276 [(2)DJ]	"Step On Out" World Premiere	1985	6.25	12.50	25.00
—Promo-only interview and music LP with no script or cover					
❏ 1446	Deliver	1985	2.00	4.00	8.00
—Budget-line reissue					
❏ 1447	American Made	1985	2.00	4.00	8.00
—Budget-line reissue					
❏ 3220	Together	1980	2.50	5.00	10.00
❏ 5150	Greatest Hits	1980	2.50	5.00	10.00
❏ 5209	Fancy Free	1981	2.50	5.00	10.00
❏ 5294	Bobbie Sue	1982	2.50	5.00	10.00
❏ 5365	Christmas	1982	2.50	5.00	10.00
❏ 5390	American Made	1983	2.50	5.00	10.00
❏ 5455	Deliver	1983	2.50	5.00	10.00
❏ 5496	Greatest Hits 2	1984	2.50	5.00	10.00
❏ 5555	Step On Out	1985	2.50	5.00	10.00
❏ 5714	Seasons	1986	2.50	5.00	10.00
❏ 5799	Christmas Again	1986	2.50	5.00	10.00
❏ 5945	Where the Fast Lane Ends	1987	2.50	5.00	10.00
❏ 37153	Room Service	198?	2.00	4.00	8.00
—Budget-line reissue					
❏ 37221	Have Arrived	1984	2.00	4.00	8.00
—Budget-line reissue					
❏ 37222	Y'all Come Back Saloon	1984	2.00	4.00	8.00
—Budget-line reissue					
❏ 37223	Together	1984	2.00	4.00	8.00
—Budget-line reissue					
❏ 42036	Heartbeat	1987	2.50	5.00	10.00
❏ 42205	Monongahela	1988	2.50	5.00	10.00
❏ 42311	American Dreams	1989	2.50	5.00	10.00
NASHVILLE					
❏ 2086	Higher Power	1970	3.75	7.50	15.00
POWER PAK					
❏ 716	The Oak Ridge Boys	197?	2.50	5.00	10.00
PRIORITY					
❏ PU 37711	Old Fashoned Gospel Quartet Music	1981	2.50	5.00	10.00
❏ PU 38467	Smoky Mountain Gospel	1983	2.50	5.00	10.00
RCA					
❏ R 164223	Unstoppable	1991	3.75	7.50	15.00
—Only released on vinyl through BMG Direct Marketing					
SKYLITE					
❏ RLP-6020 [M]	The Oak Ridge Boys Sing for You	1964	5.00	10.00	20.00
❏ SRLP-6020 [S]	The Oak Ridge Boys Sing for You	1964	6.25	12.50	25.00
❏ RLP-6030 [M]	I Wouldn't Take Nothing for My Journey Now	1965	5.00	10.00	20.00
❏ SRLP-6030 [S]	I Wouldn't Take Nothing for My Journey Now	1965	6.25	12.50	25.00
❏ RLP-6040 [M]	The Solid Gospel Sound of the Oak Ridge Boys	1966	5.00	10.00	20.00
❏ SRLP-6040 [S]	The Solid Gospel Sound of the Oak Ridge Boys	1966	6.25	12.50	25.00
❏ RLP-6045 [M]	River of Love	1967	5.00	10.00	20.00
❏ SRLP-6045 [S]	River of Love	1967	6.25	12.50	25.00
STARDAY					
❏ SLP-356 [M]	The Sensational Oak Ridge Boys	1965	6.25	12.50	25.00
UNITED ARTISTS					
❏ UAL 3554 [M]	The Oak Ridge Boys at Their Best	1966	5.00	10.00	20.00
❏ UAS 6554 [S]	The Oak Ridge Boys at Their Best	1966	6.25	12.50	25.00
❏ LN-10046	The Oak Ridge Boys at Their Best	1979	2.50	5.00	10.00
WARNER BROS.					
❏ W 1497 [M]	With Sounds of Nashville	1963	5.00	10.00	20.00
❏ WS 1497 [S]	With Sounds of Nashville	1963	6.25	12.50	25.00
❏ W 1521 [M]	Folk-Minded Spirituals for Spiritual-Minded Folks	1963	5.00	10.00	20.00
❏ WS 1521 [S]	Folk-Minded Spirituals for Spiritual-Minded Folks	1963	6.25	12.50	25.00

OBERNKIRCHEN CHILDREN'S CHOIR

Number	Title (A Side/B Side)	Yr	VG	VG+	NM
ANGEL					
❏ ANG.65021 [M]	Christmas Songs	1955	5.00	10.00	20.00

Number	Title (A Side/B Side)	Yr	VG	VG+	NM

OBOLER, ARCH
CAPITOL

Number	Title (A Side/B Side)	Yr	VG	VG+	NM
❏ ST 1763 [S]	Drop Dead! An Exercise in Horror	1962	7.50	15.00	30.00
❏ T 1763 [M]	Drop Dead! An Exercise in Horror	1962	6.25	12.50	25.00

OCHS, PHIL
A&M

Number	Title (A Side/B Side)	Yr	VG	VG+	NM
❏ LP-133 [M]	Pleasures of the Harbor	1967	6.25	12.50	25.00
❏ SP-3125	Phil Ochs Greatest Hits	198?	2.00	4.00	8.00
—Budget-line reissue					
❏ SP-4133 [S]	Pleasures of the Harbor	1967	5.00	10.00	20.00
❏ SP-4148	Tape from California	1968	5.00	10.00	20.00
❏ SP-4181	Rehearsals for Retirement	1969	5.00	10.00	20.00
❏ SP-4253	Phil Ochs Greatest Hits	1970	5.00	10.00	20.00
❏ SP-6511 [(2)]	Chords of Fame	1976	5.00	10.00	20.00

CARTHAGE

Number	Title (A Side/B Side)	Yr	VG	VG+	NM
❏ CGLP-4422	I Ain't Marching Anymore	198?	2.50	5.00	10.00
❏ CGLP-4427	All the News That's Fit to Sing	198?	2.50	5.00	10.00

ELEKTRA

Number	Title (A Side/B Side)	Yr	VG	VG+	NM
❏ EKL-269 [M]	All the News That's Fit to Sing	1964	7.50	15.00	30.00
—Gold label with "guitar player" logo					
❏ EKL-269 [M]	All the News That's Fit to Sing	1966	5.00	10.00	20.00
—Gold label with stylized "E" logo					
❏ EKL-287 [M]	I Ain't Marching Anymore	1965	7.50	15.00	30.00
—Gold label with "guitar player" logo					
❏ EKL-287 [M]	I Ain't Marching Anymore	1966	5.00	10.00	20.00
—Gold label with stylized "E" logo					
❏ EKL-310 [M]	Phil Ochs in Concert	1966	5.00	10.00	20.00
❏ EKS-7269 [S]	All the News That's Fit to Sing	1964	10.00	20.00	40.00
—Gold label with "guitar player" logo					
❏ EKS-7269 [S]	All the News That's Fit to Sing	1966	6.25	12.50	25.00
—Gold label with stylized "E" logo					
❏ EKS-7287 [S]	I Ain't Marching Anymore	1965	10.00	20.00	40.00
—Gold label with "guitar player" logo					
❏ EKS-7287 [S]	I Ain't Marching Anymore	1966	6.25	12.50	25.00
—Gold label with stylized "E" logo					
❏ EKS-7310 [S]	Phil Ochs in Concert	1966	6.25	12.50	25.00

FOLKWAYS

Number	Title (A Side/B Side)	Yr	VG	VG+	NM
❏ FB-5320	Phil Ochs Sings Songs for Broadside (#10)	197?	3.00	6.00	12.00
❏ FB-5321	Phil Ochs Interviews	197?	3.00	6.00	12.00
❏ FD-5362	Broadside Tapes 1 (#14)	1979	3.00	6.00	12.00

PICKWICK

Number	Title (A Side/B Side)	Yr	VG	VG+	NM
❏ SPC-3707	Rehearsals for Retirement	197?	2.50	5.00	10.00

RHINO

Number	Title (A Side/B Side)	Yr	VG	VG+	NM
❏ RNLP-70080	A Toast to Those Who Are Gone	1986	2.50	5.00	10.00

SMITHSONIAN/FOLKWAYS

Number	Title (A Side/B Side)	Yr	VG	VG+	NM
❏ SF-40008	Broadside Tapes 1 (#14)	1989	3.00	6.00	12.00

OCTOBER COUNTRY
EPIC

Number	Title (A Side/B Side)	Yr	VG	VG+	NM
❏ BN 26381	October Country	1968	5.00	10.00	20.00

ODA
LOUD

Number	Title (A Side/B Side)	Yr	VG	VG+	NM
❏ A 0011	Oda	1973	50.00	100.00	200.00

ODETTA
ALCAZAR

Number	Title (A Side/B Side)	Yr	VG	VG+	NM
❏ ALC-104	Christmas Spirituals	198?	2.50	5.00	10.00

ARCHIVE OF FOLK & JAZZ

Number	Title (A Side/B Side)	Yr	VG	VG+	NM
❏ 273	Odetta	1973	3.00	6.00	12.00

FANTASY

Number	Title (A Side/B Side)	Yr	VG	VG+	NM
❏ 3-15 [10]	Odetta and Larry	1955	12.50	25.00	50.00
❏ OBC-509	Odetta and the Blues	198?	2.50	5.00	10.00
—Reissue of Riverside LP					
❏ F-3252 [M]	Odetta and Larry	1957	12.50	25.00	50.00
—Dark red vinyl					
❏ F-3252 [M]	Odetta and Larry	1958	7.50	15.00	30.00
❏ F-8345	Odetta and Larry	1963	3.00	6.00	12.00
—Reissue of 3252					

RCA VICTOR

Number	Title (A Side/B Side)	Yr	VG	VG+	NM
❏ LPM-2573 [M]	Sometimes I Feel Like Crying	1962	5.00	10.00	20.00
❏ LSP-2573 [S]	Sometimes I Feel Like Crying	1962	6.25	12.50	25.00
❏ LPM-2643 [M]	Odetta Sings Folk Songs	1963	5.00	10.00	20.00
❏ LSP-2643 [S]	Odetta Sings Folk Songs	1963	6.25	12.50	25.00
❏ LPM-2792 [M]	It's a Mighty World	1964	3.75	7.50	15.00
❏ LSP-2792 [S]	It's a Mighty World	1964	5.00	10.00	20.00
❏ LPM-2923 [M]	Odetta Sings of Many Things	1964	3.75	7.50	15.00
❏ LSP-2923 [S]	Odetta Sings of Many Things	1964	5.00	10.00	20.00
❏ LPM-3324 [M]	Odetta Sings Dylan	1965	3.75	7.50	15.00
❏ LSP-3324 [S]	Odetta Sings Dylan	1965	5.00	10.00	20.00
❏ LPM-3457 [M]	Odetta in Japan	1965	3.75	7.50	15.00
❏ LSP-3457 [S]	Odetta in Japan	1965	5.00	10.00	20.00

RIVERSIDE

Number	Title (A Side/B Side)	Yr	VG	VG+	NM
❏ RLP-417 [M]	Odetta and the Blues	1962	6.25	12.50	25.00
❏ RS-9417 [S]	Odetta and the Blues	1962	7.50	15.00	30.00

ROSE QUARTZ

Number	Title (A Side/B Side)	Yr	VG	VG+	NM
❏ RQ-101	Movin' It On	1987	2.50	5.00	10.00

TRADITION

Number	Title (A Side/B Side)	Yr	VG	VG+	NM
❏ TRP-1010 [M]	Odetta Sings Ballads and Blues	1957	7.50	15.00	30.00
❏ TRP-1025 [M]	Odetta at the Gate of Horn	1958	7.50	15.00	30.00
❏ TRP-1052 [M]	The Best of Odetta	1967	5.00	10.00	20.00
❏ TRS-2052 [R]	The Best of Odetta	1967	3.75	7.50	15.00

VANGUARD

Number	Title (A Side/B Side)	Yr	VG	VG+	NM
❏ VSD-43/44 [(2)]	Essential Odetta	1973	3.75	7.50	15.00
❏ VSD-2046 [S]	My Eyes Have Seen	1960	6.25	12.50	25.00
❏ VSD-2057 [S]	Ballads for Americans	1960	6.25	12.50	25.00
❏ VSD-2072 [S]	Odetta at Carnegie Hall	1961	6.25	12.50	25.00
❏ VSD-2079 [S]	Christmas Spirituals	1961	6.25	12.50	25.00

Number	Title (A Side/B Side)	Yr	VG	VG+	NM
❏ VSD-2109 [S]	Odetta at Town Hall	1962	6.25	12.50	25.00
❏ VSD-2153 [S]	One Grain of Sand	1963	6.25	12.50	25.00
❏ VRS-3003 [M]	Odetta at Carnegie Hall	1967	3.75	7.50	15.00
❏ VRS-9059 [M]	My Eyes Have Seen	1960	5.00	10.00	20.00
❏ VRS-9066 [M]	Ballads for Americans	1960	5.00	10.00	20.00
❏ VRS-9076 [M]	Odetta at Carnegie Hall	1961	5.00	10.00	20.00
❏ VRS-9079 [M]	Christmas Spirituals	1961	5.00	10.00	20.00
❏ VRS-9103 [M]	Odetta at Town Hall	1962	5.00	10.00	20.00
❏ VRS-9137 [M]	One Grain of Sand	1963	5.00	10.00	20.00
❏ VSD-73003 [S]	Odetta at Carnegie Hall	1967	5.00	10.00	20.00

OFF BROADWAY USA
ATLANTIC

Number	Title (A Side/B Side)	Yr	VG	VG+	NM
❏ SD 19263	On	1980	5.00	10.00	20.00
❏ SD 19287	Quick Turns	1981	3.75	7.50	15.00

OFFSPRING, THE
COLUMBIA

Number	Title (A Side/B Side)	Yr	VG	VG+	NM
❏ C 61419	Conspiracy of One	2000	3.00	6.00	12.00
❏ C 67810	Ixnay on the Hombre	1997	3.00	6.00	12.00
❏ C 69661	Americana	1998	3.00	6.00	12.00

EPITAPH

Number	Title (A Side/B Side)	Yr	VG	VG+	NM
❏ 86424	Ignition	1992	2.50	5.00	10.00
❏ 86432	Smash	1994	2.50	5.00	10.00

NEMESIS

Number	Title (A Side/B Side)	Yr	VG	VG+	NM
❏ 6	The Offspring	1989	25.00	50.00	100.00
—Original issue, 5,000 copies pressed					

NITRO

Number	Title (A Side/B Side)	Yr	VG	VG+	NM
❏ 86460	The Offspring	1995	2.50	5.00	10.00
—Reissue of Nemesis LP					

OGERMAN, CLAUS
RCA VICTOR

Number	Title (A Side/B Side)	Yr	VG	VG+	NM
❏ LPM-3366 [M]	Soul Searchin'	1965	5.00	10.00	20.00
❏ LSP-3366 [S]	Soul Searchin'	1965	6.25	12.50	25.00
❏ LPM-3455 [M]	Watusi Trumpets	1965	5.00	10.00	20.00
❏ LSP-3455 [S]	Watusi Trumpets	1965	6.25	12.50	25.00
❏ LPM-3640 [M]	Saxes Mexicano	1966	5.00	10.00	20.00
❏ LSP-3640 [S]	Saxes Mexicano	1966	6.25	12.50	25.00

UNITED ARTISTS

Number	Title (A Side/B Side)	Yr	VG	VG+	NM
❏ UAL-3206 [M]	Sing Along in German	1962	5.00	10.00	20.00
❏ UAS-6206 [S]	Sing Along in German	1962	6.25	12.50	25.00

OHIO EXPRESS, THE
BUDDAH

Number	Title (A Side/B Side)	Yr	VG	VG+	NM
❏ BDM 1018 [M]	The Ohio Express	1968	10.00	20.00	40.00
—Stereo cover with "mono" sticker attached; white label promo					
❏ BDS 5018 [S]	The Ohio Express	1968	5.00	10.00	20.00
❏ BDS 5026	Chewy, Chewy	1969	5.00	10.00	20.00
❏ BDS 5037	Mercy	1969	5.00	10.00	20.00
❏ BDS 5058	The Very Best of the Ohio Express	1970	5.00	10.00	20.00

CAMEO

Number	Title (A Side/B Side)	Yr	VG	VG+	NM
❏ C 20000 [M]	Beg, Borrow and Steal	1967	7.50	15.00	30.00
❏ CS 20000 [S]	Beg, Borrow and Steal	1967	10.00	20.00	40.00

OHIO PLAYERS, THE
ACCORD

Number	Title (A Side/B Side)	Yr	VG	VG+	NM
❏ SN-7102	Young and Ready	1981	2.00	4.00	8.00

ARISTA

Number	Title (A Side/B Side)	Yr	VG	VG+	NM
❏ AB 4226	Everybody Up	1979	2.00	4.00	8.00

BOARDWALK

Number	Title (A Side/B Side)	Yr	VG	VG+	NM
❏ FW 37090	Tenderness	1981	2.00	4.00	8.00

CAPITOL

Number	Title (A Side/B Side)	Yr	VG	VG+	NM
❏ ST-192	Observations in Time	1969	12.50	25.00	50.00
❏ ST-11291	The Ohio Players	1974	3.00	6.00	12.00
—Reissue of 192					

MERCURY

Number	Title (A Side/B Side)	Yr	VG	VG+	NM
❏ SRM-1-705	Skin Tight	1974	2.50	5.00	10.00
—Chicago skyline label					
❏ SRM-1-705	Skin Tight	1974	3.00	6.00	12.00
—Red label					
❏ SRM-1-1013	Fire	1974	2.50	5.00	10.00
❏ SRM-1-1038	Honey	1975	2.50	5.00	10.00
❏ SRM-1-1088	Contradiction	1976	2.50	5.00	10.00
❏ SRM-1-1122	Ohio Players Gold	1976	2.50	5.00	10.00
❏ SRM-1-3701	Angel	1977	2.50	5.00	10.00
❏ SRM-1-3707	Mr. Mean	1977	2.50	5.00	10.00
❏ SRM-1-3730	Jass-Ay-Lay-Dee	1978	2.50	5.00	10.00
❏ 824461-1	Ohio Players Gold	198?	2.00	4.00	8.00
—Reissue of 1122					

TRACK

Number	Title (A Side/B Side)	Yr	VG	VG+	NM
❏ TRK 58810	Back	1988	2.50	5.00	10.00

TRIP

Number	Title (A Side/B Side)	Yr	VG	VG+	NM
❏ 8029	First Impression	1972	3.00	6.00	12.00

UNITED ARTISTS

Number	Title (A Side/B Side)	Yr	VG	VG+	NM
❏ UA-LA502-E	The Very Best of The Ohio Players	1975	3.00	6.00	12.00

WESTBOUND

Number	Title (A Side/B Side)	Yr	VG	VG+	NM
❏ 211	Rattlesnake	1975	3.00	6.00	12.00
❏ 219	Pain	1976	3.00	6.00	12.00
—Reissue of 2015					
❏ 220	Pleasure	1976	3.00	6.00	12.00
—Reissue of 2017					
❏ 222	Ecstasy	1976	3.00	6.00	12.00
—Reissue of 2021					
❏ 304	The Best of the Early Years	1977	3.75	7.50	15.00
❏ 1003	Climax	1974	3.75	7.50	15.00
❏ 1005	Ohio Players Greatest Hits	1975	3.75	7.50	15.00
❏ 2015	Pain	1972	5.00	10.00	20.00
❏ 2017	Pleasure	1973	5.00	10.00	20.00
❏ 2021	Ecstasy	1973	5.00	10.00	20.00

Number	Title (A Side/B Side)	Yr	VG	VG+	NM

OINGO BOINGO
A&M
| ❑ SP-3250 | Only a Lad | 1984 | 2.00 | 4.00 | 8.00 |

—Reissue of 4863
| ❑ SP-3251 | Nothing to Fear | 1984 | 2.00 | 4.00 | 8.00 |

—Reissue of 4930
| ❑ SP-3252 | Good for Your Soul | 1984 | 2.00 | 4.00 | 8.00 |

—Reissue of 4959
❑ SP-4863	Only a Lad	1981	2.50	5.00	10.00
❑ SP-4903	Nothing to Fear	1982	2.50	5.00	10.00
❑ SP-4959	Good for Your Soul	1983	2.50	5.00	10.00
❑ SP-5217	Skeletons in the Closet	1988	2.50	5.00	10.00

I.R.S.
| ❑ SP-70400 | Oingo Boingo | 1980 | 3.00 | 6.00 | 12.00 |

—Limited edition 12" version
| ❑ SP-70400 [10] | Oingo Boingo | 1980 | 3.00 | 6.00 | 12.00 |

—Four-song 10-inch EP

MCA
❑ 5665	Dead Man's Party	1985	2.50	5.00	10.00
❑ 5811	BOI-NGO	1987	2.50	5.00	10.00
❑ 6365	Dark at the End of the Tunnel	1990	2.50	5.00	10.00
❑ 8030 [(2)]	Boingo Alive	1988	3.00	6.00	12.00
❑ L33-18137 [DJ]	Dark at the End of the Tunnel	1990	10.00	20.00	40.00

—Promo-only picture disc

OLA AND THE JANGLERS
GNP CRESCENDO
| ❑ GNPS-2050 | Let's Dance/What a Way to Die | 1969 | 5.00 | 10.00 | 20.00 |

OLAY, RUTH
ABC
| ❑ ABC-573 [M] | Soul In the Night | 1966 | 5.00 | 10.00 | 20.00 |
| ❑ ABCS-573 [S] | Soul In the Night | 1966 | 6.25 | 12.50 | 25.00 |

EMARCY
| ❑ MG-36125 [M] | Olay! The New Sound Of Ruth Olay | 1958 | 12.50 | 25.00 | 50.00 |

EVEREST
| ❑ SDBR-1218 [S] | Olay! OK | 1963 | 7.50 | 15.00 | 30.00 |
| ❑ LPBR-5218 [M] | Olay! OK | 1963 | 6.25 | 12.50 | 25.00 |

MERCURY
| ❑ MG-20390 [M] | Easy Living | 1959 | 10.00 | 20.00 | 40.00 |
| ❑ SR-60069 [S] | Easy Living | 1959 | 12.50 | 25.00 | 50.00 |

UNITED ARTISTS
| ❑ UAL-3115 [M] | Ruth Olay In Person | 1960 | 7.50 | 15.00 | 30.00 |
| ❑ UAS-4115 [S] | Ruth Olay In Person | 1960 | 10.00 | 20.00 | 40.00 |

OLD & IN THE WAY
ROUND
| ❑ RX-103 | Old & in the Way | 1975 | 6.25 | 12.50 | 25.00 |

SUGAR HILL
| ❑ SH-3746 | Old & in the Way | 1987 | 2.50 | 5.00 | 10.00 |

—Reissue of Round LP

OLDFIELD, MIKE
VIRGIN
| ❑ QR 13-105 [Q] | Tubular Bells | 1974 | 6.25 | 12.50 | 25.00 |
| ❑ VR 13-105 | Tubular Bells | 1973 | 3.75 | 7.50 | 15.00 |

—First stereo issue of this album
| ❑ VR 13-109 | Hergest Ridge | 1974 | 3.00 | 6.00 | 12.00 |

—First issue of this album
| ❑ VR 13-109 [DJ] | Hergest Ridge | 1974 | 5.00 | 10.00 | 20.00 |

—Promo only; banded for airplay
| ❑ VR 13-115 | The Orchestral Tubular Bells | 1975 | 3.00 | 6.00 | 12.00 |
| ❑ VR 13135 | Tubular Bells | 1979 | 2.50 | 5.00 | 10.00 |

—Third stereo issue of this album
| ❑ VR 13143 [(2)] | Airborn | 1980 | 3.75 | 7.50 | 15.00 |

—U.S.-only compilation, which may make it much more valuable overseas
| ❑ PZ 33913 | Ommadawn | 1975 | 3.00 | 6.00 | 12.00 |

—Original U.S. issue of this album
| ❑ PZ 33913 [DJ] | Ommadawn | 1975 | 5.00 | 10.00 | 20.00 |

—Promo only; banded for airplay
| ❑ PZ 34116 | Tubular Bells | 1976 | 3.00 | 6.00 | 12.00 |

—Second stereo issue of this album (note the "PZ" prefix)
| ❑ 90589 | Tubular Bells | 1987 | 2.00 | 4.00 | 8.00 |

—Fifth stereo issue of this album
| ❑ 90590 | Hergest Ridge | 1987 | 2.00 | 4.00 | 8.00 |

—Reissue of Virgin International 2013
❑ 90591	The Killing Fields	1987	2.50	5.00	10.00
❑ 90645	Islands	1988	2.50	5.00	10.00
❑ 90894	The Orchestral Tubular Bells	1989	2.50	5.00	10.00

—Reissue of 13-115
| ❑ 91270 | Earth Moving | 1990 | 3.00 | 6.00 | 12.00 |

VIRGIN INTERNATIONAL
| ❑ VI-2013 | Hergest Ridge | 1979 | 2.50 | 5.00 | 10.00 |

—Reissue of 13-109; not to be confused with UK pressings that have only a "V" prefix
| ❑ VI-2043 | Ommadawn | 1979 | 2.50 | 5.00 | 10.00 |

—Reissue of 33913; not to be confused with UK pressings that have only a "V" prefix

VIRGIN/EPIC
| ❑ PE 34116 | Tubular Bells | 1982 | 2.00 | 4.00 | 8.00 |

—Fourth stereo issue of this album (note the "PE" prefix)
❑ FE 37358	QE2	1981	2.50	5.00	10.00
❑ ARE 37983	Five Miles Out	1982	2.50	5.00	10.00
❑ HE 44116	Tubular Bells	1982	7.50	15.00	30.00

—Half-speed mastered edition

OLDHAM, ANDREW
LONDON
| ❑ PS 457 [S] | The Rolling Stones Songbook | 1965 | 37.50 | 75.00 | 150.00 |
| ❑ LL 3457 [M] | The Rolling Stones Songbook | 1965 | 25.00 | 50.00 | 100.00 |

PARROT
| ❑ PA 61003 [M] | East Meets West | 1965 | 20.00 | 40.00 | 80.00 |
| ❑ PAS 71003 [S] | East Meets West | 1965 | 25.00 | 50.00 | 100.00 |

OLENN, JOHNNY
LIBERTY
| ❑ LRP-3029 [M] | Just Rollin' with Johnny Olenn | 1956 | 75.00 | 150.00 | 300.00 |

OLIPHANT, GRASELLA
ATLANTIC
| ❑ SD-1438 [S] | The Grass Roots | 1965 | 5.00 | 10.00 | 20.00 |

OLIVA, TONY
KUBANY
| ❑ SD-600 | My Favorite Music | 1966 | 7.50 | 15.00 | 30.00 |

OLIVER, JIMMY
SUE
| ❑ LP-1041 [M] | Hits A-Go-Go | 1966 | 5.00 | 10.00 | 20.00 |
| ❑ STLP-1041 [S] | Hits A-Go-Go | 1966 | 6.25 | 12.50 | 25.00 |

OLIVER, KING
BRUNSWICK
| ❑ BL 58020 [10] | King Oliver | 1950 | 30.00 | 60.00 | 120.00 |

EPIC
❑ LN 3208 [M]	King Oliver Featuring Louis Armstrong	1956	12.50	25.00	50.00
❑ LA 16003 [M]	King Oliver and His Orchestra	1960	7.50	15.00	30.00
❑ BA 17003 [R]	King Oliver and His Orchestra	1960	5.00	10.00	20.00

LONDON
| ❑ AL 3510 [10] | King Oliver Plays the Blues | 195? | 20.00 | 40.00 | 80.00 |

RCA VICTOR
| ❑ LPV-529 [M] | King Oliver In New York | 1965 | 6.25 | 12.50 | 25.00 |

RIVERSIDE
| ❑ RLP-1007 [10] | King Oliver Plays the Blues | 1953 | 20.00 | 40.00 | 80.00 |

"X"
| ❑ LVA-3018 [10] | King Oliver's Uptown Jazz | 1954 | 25.00 | 50.00 | 100.00 |

OLIVER, SY
MOBILE FIDELITY
| ❑ 1-242 [(2)] | Oliver's Twist/Easy Walkin' | 1996 | 7.50 | 15.00 | 30.00 |

—Audiophile vinyl

OLIVER AND THE TWISTERS
COLPIX
| ❑ CP-423 [M] | Look Who's Twistin' Everybody | 1961 | 10.00 | 20.00 | 40.00 |

OLLIE AND THE NIGHTINGALES
STAX
| ❑ STS-2021 | Ollie and the Nightingales | 1969 | 12.50 | 25.00 | 50.00 |

OLSEN, DOROTHY
RCA VICTOR
| ❑ LPM-1606 [M] | I Know Where I'm Going | 1957 | 7.50 | 15.00 | 30.00 |

OLSEN, GEORGE
RCA VICTOR
| ❑ LPV-549 [M] | George Olsen and His Music | 1968 | 5.00 | 10.00 | 20.00 |

OLSHER, LESLEY
VITAL
| ❑ VTL-011 | Lesley | 1993 | 5.00 | 10.00 | 20.00 |

OLSSON, NIGEL
BANG
| ❑ JZ 35792 | Nigel | 1979 | 2.50 | 5.00 | 10.00 |
| ❑ JZ 36491 | Changing Tides | 1980 | 2.50 | 5.00 | 10.00 |

ROCKET
| ❑ L33-1962 [DJ] | Drummers Can Sing Too! | 1975 | 5.00 | 10.00 | 20.00 |

—Promo-only interview album
| ❑ PIG-2158 | Nigel Olsson | 1975 | 3.00 | 6.00 | 12.00 |

UNI
| ❑ 73113 | Nigel Olsson's Drum Orchestra | 1971 | 3.75 | 7.50 | 15.00 |

OLYMPICS, THE
ARVEE
❑ A-423 [M]	Doin' the Hully Gully	1960	40.00	80.00	160.00
❑ A-424 [M]	Dance by the Light of the Moon	1961	30.00	60.00	120.00
❑ A-429 [M]	Party Time	1961	30.00	60.00	120.00

EVEREST
| ❑ 4109 | The Olympics | 1981 | 2.50 | 5.00 | 10.00 |

MIRWOOD
| ❑ MS-7003 [S] | Something Old, Something New | 1966 | 12.50 | 25.00 | 50.00 |
| ❑ MW-7003 [M] | Something Old, Something New | 1966 | 10.00 | 20.00 | 40.00 |

POST
| ❑ 8000 | The Olympics Sing | 196? | 6.25 | 12.50 | 25.00 |

RHINO
| ❑ RNDF-207 | The Official Record Album of the Olympics | 1983 | 3.00 | 6.00 | 12.00 |

TRI-DISC
| ❑ 1001 [M] | Do the Bounce | 1963 | 20.00 | 40.00 | 80.00 |

OMNIBUS
UNITED ARTISTS
| ❑ UAS-6743 | Omnibus | 1970 | 10.00 | 20.00 | 40.00 |

ONE
VILLAGE
| ❑ (# unknown) | Creation Earth | 1977 | 12.50 | 25.00 | 50.00 |

—Includes posters

ONENESS OF JUJU
BLACK FIRE
| ❑ (# unknown) | African Rhythms | 1975 | 15.00 | 30.00 | 60.00 |
| ❑ (# unknown) | Space Jungle Luv | 1976 | 15.00 | 30.00 | 60.00 |

STRATA-EAST
| ❑ SES-7420 | Chapter 2: Nia | 1974 | 25.00 | 50.00 | 100.00 |

—As "Juju"

Number	Title (A Side/B Side)	Yr	VG	VG+	NM
❏ SES-19735	A Message from Mozambique	1973	25.00	50.00	100.00

—As "Juju"

ONO, YOKO
APPLE

Number	Title (A Side/B Side)	Yr	VG	VG+	NM
❏ SW-3373	Yoko Ono Plastic Ono Band	1970	5.00	10.00	20.00
❏ SVBB-3380 [(2)]	Fly	1971	6.50	12.50	25.00
❏ SVBB-3399 [(2)]	Approximately Infinite Universe	1973	6.25	12.50	25.00
❏ SW-3412	Feeling the Space	1973	5.00	10.00	20.00

CAPITOL
Number	Title (A Side/B Side)	Yr	VG	VG+	NM
❏ SPRO-11219 [DJ]	Rising Mixes	1996	3.00	6.00	12.00

—Promo-only vinyl EP of six remixes from the CD "Rising"

GEFFEN
Number	Title (A Side/B Side)	Yr	VG	VG+	NM
❏ GHS 2004	Season of Glass	1981	3.00	6.00	12.00

POLYDOR
Number	Title (A Side/B Side)	Yr	VG	VG+	NM
❏ PD-1-6364	It's Alright (I See Rainbows)	1982	2.50	5.00	10.00
❏ 823289-1	It's Alright (I See Rainbows)	1984	2.00	4.00	8.00

—Reissue

Number	Title (A Side/B Side)	Yr	VG	VG+	NM
❏ 827530-1	Starpeace	1985	3.00	6.00	12.00

ORANG UTAN
BELL
Number	Title (A Side/B Side)	Yr	VG	VG+	NM
❏ 6054	Orang Utan	1971	10.00	20.00	40.00

ORANGE COLORED SKY
UNI
Number	Title (A Side/B Side)	Yr	VG	VG+	NM
❏ 73031	Orange Colored Sky	1968	12.50	25.00	50.00

ORANGE WEDGE
(NO LABEL)
Number	Title (A Side/B Side)	Yr	VG	VG+	NM
❏ (no #)	No One Left But Me	1975	75.00	150.00	300.00
❏ (no #)	Wedge	1975	75.00	150.00	300.00

ORBACH, JERRY
MGM
Number	Title (A Side/B Side)	Yr	VG	VG+	NM
❏ E-4056 [M]	Jerry Orbach Off Broadway	1963	5.00	10.00	20.00
❏ SE-4056 [S]	Jerry Orbach Off Broadway	1963	6.25	12.50	25.00

ORBISON, ROY
ACCORD
Number	Title (A Side/B Side)	Yr	VG	VG+	NM
❏ SN-7150	Ooby Dooby	1981	2.00	4.00	8.00

ASYLUM
Number	Title (A Side/B Side)	Yr	VG	VG+	NM
❏ 6E-198	Laminar Flow	1979	3.00	6.00	12.00

BUCKBOARD
Number	Title (A Side/B Side)	Yr	VG	VG+	NM
❏ BBS-1015	Roy Orbison's Golden Hits	197?	2.50	5.00	10.00

CANDELITE
Number	Title (A Side/B Side)	Yr	VG	VG+	NM
❏ P2 12946 [(2)]	The Living Legend of Roy Orbison	1976	3.75	7.50	15.00

DCC COMPACT CLASSICS
Number	Title (A Side/B Side)	Yr	VG	VG+	NM
❏ LPZ-2042 [(2)]	The All-Time Greatest Hits of Roy Orbison	1997	30.00	60.00	120.00

—Audiophile vinyl

DESIGN
Number	Title (A Side/B Side)	Yr	VG	VG+	NM
❏ DLP-164 [M]	Orbiting with Roy Orbison	196?	3.75	7.50	15.00
❏ DLPS-164 [R]	Orbiting with Roy Orbison	196?	2.50	5.00	10.00

HALLMARK
Number	Title (A Side/B Side)	Yr	VG	VG+	NM
❏ SHM-824	The Exciting Roy Orbison	197?	2.00	4.00	8.00

HITS UNLIMITED
Number	Title (A Side/B Side)	Yr	VG	VG+	NM
❏ 233-0	My Spell on You	1982	2.00	4.00	8.00

MERCURY
Number	Title (A Side/B Side)	Yr	VG	VG+	NM
❏ SRM-1-1045	I'm Still in Love with You	1975	3.00	6.00	12.00

MGM
Number	Title (A Side/B Side)	Yr	VG	VG+	NM
❏ E-4308 [M]	There Is Only One Roy Orbison	1965	6.25	12.50	25.00
❏ SE-4308 [S]	There Is Only One Roy Orbison	1965	8.75	17.50	35.00
❏ E-4322 [M]	The Orbison Way	1965	6.25	12.50	25.00
❏ SE-4322 [S]	The Orbison Way	1965	8.75	17.50	35.00
❏ E-4379 [M]	The Classic Roy Orbison	1966	6.25	12.50	25.00
❏ SE-4379 [S]	The Classic Roy Orbison	1966	8.75	17.50	35.00
❏ E-4424 [M]	Roy Orbison Sings Don Gibson	1967	6.25	12.50	25.00
❏ SE-4424 [S]	Roy Orbison Sings Don Gibson	1967	8.75	17.50	35.00
❏ E-4514 [M]	Cry Softly, Lonely One	1967	6.25	12.50	25.00
❏ SE-4514 [S]	Cry Softly, Lonely One	1967	8.75	17.50	35.00
❏ SE-4636	The Many Moods of Roy Orbison	1969	6.25	12.50	25.00
❏ SE-4659	The Great Songs of Roy Orbison	1970	6.25	12.50	25.00
❏ SE-4683	Hank Williams the Roy Orbison Way	1970	6.25	12.50	25.00
❏ SE-4835	Roy Orbison Sings	1972	3.75	7.50	15.00
❏ SE-4867	Memphis	1972	3.75	7.50	15.00
❏ SE-4934	Milestones	1973	3.75	7.50	15.00
❏ ST 90454 [S]	There Is Only One Roy Orbison	1965	10.00	20.00	40.00

—Capitol Record Club edition

Number	Title (A Side/B Side)	Yr	VG	VG+	NM
❏ T 90454 [M]	There Is Only One Roy Orbison	1965	10.00	20.00	40.00

—Capitol Record Club edition

Number	Title (A Side/B Side)	Yr	VG	VG+	NM
❏ ST-90631 [S]	The Orbison Way	1965	8.75	17.50	35.00

—Capitol Record Club edition

Number	Title (A Side/B Side)	Yr	VG	VG+	NM
❏ T-90631 [M]	The Orbison Way	1965	8.75	17.50	35.00

—Capitol Record Club edition

Number	Title (A Side/B Side)	Yr	VG	VG+	NM
❏ ST-90928 [S]	The Classic Roy Orbison	1966	8.75	17.50	35.00

—Capitol Record Club edition

Number	Title (A Side/B Side)	Yr	VG	VG+	NM
❏ T-90928 [M]	The Classic Roy Orbison	1966	8.75	17.50	35.00

—Capitol Record Club edition

Number	Title (A Side/B Side)	Yr	VG	VG+	NM
❏ ST-91173 [S]	Roy Orbison Sings Don Gibson	1967	8.75	17.50	35.00

—Capitol Record Club edition

Number	Title (A Side/B Side)	Yr	VG	VG+	NM
❏ T-91173 [M]	Roy Orbison Sings Don Gibson	1967	8.75	17.50	35.00

—Capitol Record Club edition

MONUMENT
Number	Title (A Side/B Side)	Yr	VG	VG+	NM
❏ M-4002 [M]	Lonely and Blue	1961	37.50	75.00	150.00
❏ M-4007 [M]	Crying	1962	30.00	60.00	120.00
❏ M-4009 [M]	Roy Orbison's Greatest Hits	1962	12.50	25.00	50.00
❏ MC-6619	Roy Orbison's Greatest Hits	1977	3.00	6.00	12.00
❏ MC-6620	In Dreams	1977	3.00	6.00	12.00
❏ MC-6621	More of Roy Orbison's Greatest Hits	1977	3.00	6.00	12.00
❏ MC-6622	The Very Best of Roy Orbison	1977	3.00	6.00	12.00

Number	Title (A Side/B Side)	Yr	VG	VG+	NM
❏ MG-7600	Regeneration	1976	3.75	7.50	15.00
❏ MLP-8000 [M]	Roy Orbison's Greatest Hits	1963	7.50	15.00	30.00
❏ MLP-8003 [M]	In Dreams	1963	12.50	25.00	50.00

—White and rainbow label

Number	Title (A Side/B Side)	Yr	VG	VG+	NM
❏ MLP-8003 [M]	In Dreams	1964	7.50	15.00	30.00

—Green and gold label

Number	Title (A Side/B Side)	Yr	VG	VG+	NM
❏ MLP-8023 [M]	Early Orbison	1964	7.50	15.00	30.00
❏ MLP-8024 [M]	More of Roy Orbison's Greatest Hits	1964	7.50	15.00	30.00
❏ MLP-8035 [M]	Orbisongs	1965	6.25	12.50	25.00
❏ MLP-8045 [M]	The Very Best of Roy Orbison	1966	6.25	12.50	25.00
❏ MP-8600 [(2)]	The All-Time Greatest Hits of Roy Orbison	1977	4.00	8.00	16.00
❏ SM-14002 [S]	Lonely and Blue	1961	150.00	300.00	600.00
❏ SM-14007 [S]	Crying	1962	150.00	300.00	600.00
❏ SM-14009 [S]	Roy Orbison's Greatest Hits	1962	20.00	40.00	80.00
❏ SLP-18000 [S]	Roy Orbison's Greatest Hits	1963	10.00	20.00	40.00
❏ SLP-18003 [S]	In Dreams	1963	25.00	50.00	100.00

—White and rainbow label

Number	Title (A Side/B Side)	Yr	VG	VG+	NM
❏ SLP-18003 [S]	In Dreams	1964	12.50	25.00	50.00

—Green and gold label

Number	Title (A Side/B Side)	Yr	VG	VG+	NM
❏ SLP-18023 [S]	Early Orbison	1964	12.50	25.00	50.00
❏ SLP-18024 [S]	More of Roy Orbison's Greatest Hits	1964	10.00	20.00	40.00
❏ SLP-18035 [S]	Orbisongs	1965	8.75	17.50	35.00
❏ SLP-18045 [P]	The Very Best of Roy Orbison	1966	8.75	17.50	35.00

—"It's Over" is rechanneled

Number	Title (A Side/B Side)	Yr	VG	VG+	NM
❏ KZG 31484 [(2)]	The All-Time Greatest Hits of Roy Orbison	1972	6.25	12.50	25.00
❏ KWG 38384 [(2)]	The All-Time Greatest Hits of Roy Orbison	1982	2.50	5.00	10.00

RHINO
Number	Title (A Side/B Side)	Yr	VG	VG+	NM
❏ R1 70711	The Classic Roy Orbison	1989	3.00	6.00	12.00
❏ R1 70916	The Sun Years	1989	3.75	7.50	15.00
❏ R1 71493 [(2)]	For the Lonely: A Roy Orbison Anthology	1988	3.00	6.00	12.00

SUN
Number	Title (A Side/B Side)	Yr	VG	VG+	NM
❏ 113	The Original Sound	1969	3.00	6.00	12.00
❏ LP-1260 [M]	Roy Orbison at the Rock House	1961	150.00	300.00	600.00

TIME-LIFE
Number	Title (A Side/B Side)	Yr	VG	VG+	NM
❏ SRNR 34 [(2)]	Roy Orbison 1960-1965	1990	5.00	10.00	20.00

—Box set in "The Rock 'n' Roll Era" series

TRIP
Number	Title (A Side/B Side)	Yr	VG	VG+	NM
❏ TLX-8505	The Best of Roy Orbison	197?	2.00	4.00	8.00

VIRGIN
Number	Title (A Side/B Side)	Yr	VG	VG+	NM
❏ 90604 [(2)]	In Dreams: The Greatest Hits	1987	3.00	6.00	12.00

—Re-recordings of his original hits

Number	Title (A Side/B Side)	Yr	VG	VG+	NM
❏ 91058	Mystery Girl	1989	2.50	5.00	10.00
❏ 91295	A Black and White Night	1990	3.75	7.50	15.00

ORCHESTRA U.S.A.
COLPIX
Number	Title (A Side/B Side)	Yr	VG	VG+	NM
❏ CP-448 [M]	Orchestra U.S.A. Debut	1964	10.00	20.00	40.00
❏ SCP-448 [S]	Orchestra U.S.A. Debut	1964	12.50	25.00	50.00

COLUMBIA
Number	Title (A Side/B Side)	Yr	VG	VG+	NM
❏ CL 2247 [M]	Jazz Journey	1963	6.25	12.50	25.00
❏ CS 9047 [S]	Jazz Journey	1963	7.50	15.00	30.00

RCA VICTOR
Number	Title (A Side/B Side)	Yr	VG	VG+	NM
❏ LPM-3498 [M]	The Sextet Of Orchestra U.S.A.	1965	5.00	10.00	20.00
❏ LSP-3498 [S]	The Sextet Of Orchestra U.S.A.	1965	6.25	12.50	25.00

ORCHIDS, THE (U)
ROULETTE
Number	Title (A Side/B Side)	Yr	VG	VG+	NM
❏ R-25169 [M]	Twistin' at the Roundtable	1962	5.00	10.00	20.00
❏ SR-25169 [S]	Twistin' at the Roundtable	1962	6.25	12.50	25.00

OREGON
MOBILE FIDELITY
Number	Title (A Side/B Side)	Yr	VG	VG+	NM
❏ 1-514	Distant Hills	198?	17.50	35.00	70.00

—Audiophile vinyl

VANGUARD
Number	Title (A Side/B Side)	Yr	VG	VG+	NM
❏ VSQ-40031 [Q]	Distant Hills	1974	6.25	12.50	25.00

ORGAN GRINDERS, THE
MERCURY
Number	Title (A Side/B Side)	Yr	VG	VG+	NM
❏ SR-61282	Out of the Egg	1970	7.50	15.00	30.00

ORIENT EXPRESS, THE
MAINSTREAN
Number	Title (A Side/B Side)	Yr	VG	VG+	NM
❏ S-6117	The Orient Express	1969	20.00	40.00	80.00

ORIGINAL DIXIELAND JAZZ BAND, THE
RCA VICTOR
Number	Title (A Side/B Side)	Yr	VG	VG+	NM
❏ LPV-547 [M]	The Original Dixieland Jazz Band	1968	5.00	10.00	20.00

"X"
Number	Title (A Side/B Side)	Yr	VG	VG+	NM
❏ LX-3007 [M]	The Original Dixieland Jazz Band	1954	12.50	25.00	50.00

ORIGINAL LAST POETS, THE
See THE LAST POETS.

ORIGINAL SURFARIS, THE
See THE SURFARIS (2).

ORIGINAL TWISTERS, THE
WING
Number	Title (A Side/B Side)	Yr	VG	VG+	NM
❏ MGW-12217 [M]	Come On and Twist	1962	5.00	10.00	20.00
❏ SRW-16217 [S]	Come On and Twist	1962	6.25	12.50	25.00

ORIGINAL WASHBOARD BAND, THE
RCA VICTOR
Number	Title (A Side/B Side)	Yr	VG	VG+	NM
❏ LPM-1958 [M]	Scrubbin' and Pickin'	1959	5.00	10.00	20.00
❏ LSP-1958 [S]	Scrubbin' and Pickin'	1959	6.25	12.50	25.00

ORIGINALS, THE (1)
FANTASY
Number	Title (A Side/B Side)	Yr	VG	VG+	NM
❏ F-9546	Another Time, Another Place	1978	2.50	5.00	10.00
❏ F-9577	Come Away with Me	1979	2.50	5.00	10.00

Number	Title (A Side/B Side)	Yr	VG	VG+	NM
MOTOWN					
❏ M5-110V	Motown Superstar Series, Vol. 10	1982	2.50	5.00	10.00
❏ M7-826	California Sunset	1975	3.75	7.50	15.00
PHASE II					
❏ JW 37075	Yesterday and Today	1981	3.00	6.00	12.00
SOUL					
❏ SS-716	Baby I'm for Real	1969	10.00	20.00	40.00
❏ SS-724	Portrait of the Originals	1970	6.25	12.50	25.00
❏ SS-729	Naturally Together	1971	6.25	12.50	25.00
❏ SS-734	Definitions	1971	5.00	10.00	20.00
❏ SS-740	The Game Called…	1973	3.75	7.50	15.00
❏ SS-743	California Sunset	1974	—	—	—
—Unreleased					
❏ S7-746	Communique	1976	3.75	7.50	15.00
❏ S7-749	Down to Love Town	1977	3.75	7.50	15.00
ORIOLES, THE					
BIG A					
❏ LP-2001	The Orioles' Greatest All-Time Hits	1969	7.50	15.00	30.00
CHARLIE PARKER					
❏ PLP-816 [M]	Modern Sounds of the Orioles	1962	20.00	40.00	80.00
❏ PLP-816S [S]	Modern Sounds of the Orioles	1962	25.00	50.00	100.00
COLLECTABLES					
❏ COL-5014	Sonny Til and the Orioles' Greatest Hits	198?	3.00	6.00	12.00
MURRAY HILL					
❏ M 61234 [(5)]	For Collectors Only	1983	10.00	20.00	40.00
ORION					
SUN					
❏ 1012	Orion Reborn	1978	2.50	5.00	10.00
—Blue cover					
❏ 1012	Orion Reborn	1978	7.50	15.00	30.00
—White cover, also known as the "coffin cover"					
❏ 1017	Sunrise	1979	2.50	5.00	10.00
❏ 1019	Orion Country	1980	2.50	5.00	10.00
❏ 1021	Rockabilly	1981	2.50	5.00	10.00
❏ 1025	Glory	1982	2.50	5.00	10.00
❏ 1028	Fresh	1983	2.50	5.00	10.00
ORION, P.J., AND THE MAGNATES					
MAGNATE					
❏ 122459	P.J. Orion and the Magnates	196?	37.50	75.00	150.00
ORION THE HUNTER					
With Barry Goudreau, formerly of BOSTON.					
PORTRAIT					
❏ BFR 39239	Orion the Hunter	1984	5.00	10.00	20.00
ORLANDO, TONY					
CASABLANCA					
❏ NBLP 7153	I Got Rhythm	1979	2.50	5.00	10.00
❏ NBLP 7209	Living for the Music	1980	2.50	5.00	10.00
EPIC					
❏ BN 611 [S]	Bless You and 11 Other Great Hits	1961	10.00	20.00	40.00
❏ LN 3808 [M]	Bless You and 11 Other Great Hits	1961	7.50	15.00	30.00
❏ BG 33785 [(2)]	Before Dawn	1975	3.75	7.50	15.00
ORLONS, THE					
CAMEO					
❏ C 1020 [M]	The Wah-Watusi	1962	15.00	30.00	60.00
❏ C 1033 [M]	All the Hits by the Orlons	1962	15.00	30.00	60.00
❏ C 1041 [M]	South Street	1963	15.00	30.00	60.00
❏ C 1054 [M]	Not Me	1963	12.50	25.00	50.00
❏ C 1061 [M]	The Orlons' Biggest Hits	1964	12.50	25.00	50.00
❏ C 1073 [M]	Down Memory Lane with the Orlons	1964	12.50	25.00	50.00
ORLONS, THE / THE DOVELLS					
Also see each artist's individual listings.					
CAMEO					
❏ C 1067 [M]	Golden Hits of the Orlons and the Dovells	1964	12.50	25.00	50.00
ORPHAN EGG					
CAROLE					
❏ CARS-8004	Orphan Egg	1968	10.00	20.00	40.00
ORPHANN					
O.M.I.					
❏ 70021	Up for Adoption	1977	25.00	50.00	100.00
ORPHEUS					
MGM					
❏ E-4524 [M]	Orpheus	1968	6.25	12.50	25.00
❏ SE-4524 [S]	Orpheus	1968	5.00	10.00	20.00
❏ E-4569 [M]	Ascending	1968	10.00	20.00	40.00
—Known copies are yellow label promos with "DJ Monaural" sticker on stereo cover					
❏ SE-4569 [S]	Ascending	1968	5.00	10.00	20.00
❏ SE-4599	Joyful	1969	5.00	10.00	20.00
ORTEGA, ANTHONY					
BETHLEHEM					
❏ BCP-79 [M]	Jazz For Young Moderns	1957	12.50	25.00	50.00
HERALD					
❏ HLP-0101 [M]	A Man and His Horn	1956	15.00	30.00	60.00
REVELATION					
❏ REV-3 [S]	New Dance	1968	5.00	10.00	20.00
❏ REV-M3 [M]	New Dance	1968	10.00	20.00	40.00
VANTAGE					
❏ VLP-2 [10]	Anthony Ortega	1954	30.00	60.00	120.00
ORTEGA, FRANKIE					
IMPERIAL					
❏ LP-9025 [M]	Piano Stylings	1956	6.25	12.50	25.00
❏ LP-12011 [S]	Piano Stylings	1959	5.00	10.00	20.00

Number	Title (A Side/B Side)	Yr	VG	VG+	NM
JUBILEE					
❏ JLP-1051 [M]	Twinkling Pinkies	1958	6.25	12.50	25.00
❏ JLP-1080 [M]	Swingin' Abroad	1958	5.00	10.00	20.00
❏ SDJLP-1080 [S]	Swingin' Abroad	1958	6.25	12.50	25.00
❏ JGS-1106 [S]	77 Sunset Strip	1959	10.00	20.00	40.00
❏ JLP-1106 [M]	77 Sunset Strip	1959	6.25	12.50	25.00
❏ JGM-1112 [M]	Frankie Ortega at the Embers	1960	5.00	10.00	20.00
❏ JGS-1112 [S]	Frankie Ortega at the Embers	1960	6.25	12.50	25.00
ORTEGA/DOMANICO/WEST/GOODWIN					
REVELATION					
❏ REV-7 [S]	Permutations	1969	6.25	12.50	25.00
ORY, KID					
COLUMBIA					
❏ CL 835 [M]	Kid Ory	1955	12.50	25.00	50.00
❏ CL 6145 [10]	Kid Ory & His Creole Dixieland Band	1950	25.00	50.00	100.00
GOOD TIME JAZZ					
❏ L-21 [10]	Kid Ory's Creole Jazz Band, 1953	1954	12.50	25.00	50.00
❏ S-10041/2 [(2)S]	Kid Ory's Favorites!	1961	15.00	30.00	60.00
❏ L-12004 [M]	Kid Ory's Creole Jazz Band, 1954	1954	10.00	20.00	40.00
❏ L-12008 [M]	Kid Ory's Creole Jazz Band, 1955	1955	10.00	20.00	40.00
❏ L-12016 [M]	Kid Ory's Creole Jazz Band, 1956	1955	10.00	20.00	40.00
❏ L-12022 [M]	Kid Ory's Creole Jazz Band, 1944-45	1955	10.00	20.00	40.00
❏ L-12041/2 [(2)M]	Kid Ory's Favorites!	1961	12.50	25.00	50.00
❏ M-12045 [M]	This Kid's the Greatest!	1962	7.50	15.00	30.00
VERVE					
❏ MGV-1014 [M]	Song of the Wanderer	1957	12.50	25.00	50.00
❏ V-1014 [M]	Song of the Wanderer	1961	5.00	10.00	20.00
❏ MGV-1016 [M]	The Kid From New Orleans	1957	12.50	25.00	50.00
❏ V-1016 [M]	The Kid From New Orleans	1961	5.00	10.00	20.00
❏ MGV-1017 [M]	Kid Ory Plays W.C. Handy	1957	12.50	25.00	50.00
❏ V-1017 [M]	Kid Ory Plays W.C. Handy	1961	5.00	10.00	20.00
❏ MGV-1022 [M]	Dance with Kid Ory or Just Listen	1957	12.50	25.00	50.00
❏ V-1022 [M]	Dance with Kid Ory or Just Listen	1961	5.00	10.00	20.00
❏ MGV-1023 [M]	The Original Jazz	1957	12.50	25.00	50.00
❏ V-1023 [M]	The Original Jazz	1961	5.00	10.00	20.00
❏ MGV-1026 [M]	Dixieland Marching Songs	1957	12.50	25.00	50.00
❏ V-1026 [M]	Dixieland Marching Songs	1961	5.00	10.00	20.00
❏ MGVS-6011 [S]	Song of the Wanderer	1960	10.00	20.00	40.00
❏ MGVS-6061 [S]	Kid Ory Plays W.C. Handy	1960	10.00	20.00	40.00
❏ MGVS-6125 [S]	Dance with Kid Ory or Just Listen	1960	10.00	20.00	40.00
❏ MGV-8254 [M]	Kid Ory In Europe	1958	12.50	25.00	50.00
❏ V-8254 [M]	Kid Ory In Europe	1961	5.00	10.00	20.00
❏ V-8456 [M]	Storyville Nights	1962	6.25	12.50	25.00
❏ V6-8456 [S]	Storyville Nights	1962	5.00	10.00	20.00
ORY, KID/JOHNNY WITTWER					
JAZZ MAN					
❏ LP-2 [10]	Kid Ory's Creole Band/Johnny Wittwer Trio	1954	12.50	25.00	50.00
OSBORNE, JIMMIE					
AUDIO LAB					
❏ AL-1527 [M]	Singing Songs He Wrote	1959	25.00	50.00	100.00
KING					
❏ 730 [M]	The Legendary Jimmy Osborne	1961	12.50	25.00	50.00
❏ 782 [M]	Golden Harvest	1963	12.50	25.00	50.00
❏ 892 [M]	The Very Best of Jimmie Osborne	1964	10.00	20.00	40.00
❏ 941 [M]	Jimmie Osborne's Golden Harvest	1965	10.00	20.00	40.00
OSBORNE, MARY					
WARWICK					
❏ W-2004 [M]	A Girl and Her Guitar	1960	25.00	50.00	100.00
❏ W-2004ST [S]	A Girl and Her Guitar	1960	30.00	60.00	120.00
OSBORNE BROTHERS, THE					
CMH					
❏ 4501	Greatest Bluegrass Hits, Vol. 1	198?	3.00	6.00	12.00
❏ 6206	#1	197?	3.00	6.00	12.00
❏ 6231	Bluegrass Concerto	197?	3.00	6.00	12.00
❏ 6244	Kentucky Calling Me	1980	3.00	6.00	12.00
❏ 6256	Bobby and His Mandolin	1981	3.00	6.00	12.00
❏ 9008 [(2)]	From Rocky Top to Muddy Bottom	1977	3.75	7.50	15.00
❏ 9011 [(2)]	Bluegrass Collection	1978	3.75	7.50	15.00
❏ 9016 [(2)]	The Essential Bluegrass Album	1979	3.75	7.50	15.00
—With MacWiseman					
DECCA					
❏ DL 4602 [M]	Voices in the Bluegrass	1965	3.75	7.50	15.00
❏ DL 4767 [M]	Up This Hill and Down	1966	3.75	7.50	15.00
❏ DL 4903 [M]	Modern Sounds of Bluegrass Music	1967	3.75	7.50	15.00
❏ DL 4993 [M]	Yesterday, Today and The Osborne Brothers	1968	6.25	12.50	25.00
❏ DL 74602 [S]	Voices in the Bluegrass	1965	5.00	10.00	20.00
❏ DL 74767 [S]	Up This Hill and Down	1966	5.00	10.00	20.00
❏ DL 74903 [S]	Modern Sounds of Bluegrass Music	1967	5.00	10.00	20.00
❏ DL 74993 [S]	Yesterday, Today and The Osborne Brothers	1968	5.00	10.00	20.00
❏ DL 75079 [S]	Favorite Hymns by the Osborne Brothers	1969	5.00	10.00	20.00
❏ DL 75128	Up to Date and Down to Earth	1969	5.00	10.00	20.00
❏ DL 75204	Ru-Beeeee	1970	5.00	10.00	20.00
❏ DL 75276	The Osborne Brothers	1971	3.75	7.50	15.00
❏ DL 75321	Country Roads	1971	3.75	7.50	15.00
❏ DL 75356	Bobby & Sonny	1972	3.75	7.50	15.00
MCA					
❏ 105	Voices in the Bluegrass	1973	3.00	6.00	12.00
—Reissue of Decca 74602					
❏ 119	Yesterday, Today and The Osborne Brothers	1973	3.00	6.00	12.00
—Reissue of Decca 74993					
❏ 125	Favorite Hymns by the Osborne Brothers	1973	3.00	6.00	12.00
—Reissue of Decca 75079					
❏ 135	Ru-Beeeee	1973	3.00	6.00	12.00
—Reissue of Decca 75204					
❏ 4086 [(2)]	The Best of the Osborne Brothers	1974	3.75	7.50	15.00

Number	Title (A Side/B Side)	Yr	VG	VG+	NM
MGM					
❑ GAS 140	The Osborne Brothers (Golden Archives Series)	1970	5.00	10.00	20.00
❑ E-3734 [M]	Country Pickin' and Hillside Singin'	1959	12.50	25.00	50.00
❑ E-4018 [M]	Bluegrass Music	1962	6.25	12.50	25.00
❑ SE-4018 [S]	Bluegrass Music	1962	7.50	15.00	30.00
❑ E-4090 [M]	Bluegrass Instrumentals	1962	6.25	12.50	25.00
❑ SE-4090 [S]	Bluegrass Instrumentals	1962	7.50	15.00	30.00
❑ E-4149 [M]	Cuttin' Grass	1963	6.25	12.50	25.00
❑ SE-4149 [S]	Cuttin' Grass	1963	7.50	15.00	30.00
RCA VICTOR					
❑ AHL1-4324	Bluegrass Spectacular	1982	2.50	5.00	10.00
❑ AYL1-5436	Bluegrass Spectacular	1985	2.00	4.00	8.00
—"Best Buy Series" reissue					
ROUNDER					
❑ SS-03	The Osborne Brothers with Red Allen	1981	3.00	6.00	12.00
❑ SS-04	The Osborne Brothers	198?	3.00	6.00	12.00
SUGAR HILL					
❑ SH-3740	Some Things I Want to Sing About	1984	2.50	5.00	10.00
❑ SH-3754	Once More, Vol. 1	1986	2.50	5.00	10.00
❑ SH-3758	Once More, Vol. 2	1987	2.50	5.00	10.00
❑ SH-3764	Singing, Shouting Praises	1988	2.50	5.00	10.00

OSBOURNE, OZZY

Number	Title (A Side/B Side)	Yr	VG	VG+	NM
CBS ASSOCIATED					
❑ AS 1828 [DJ]	Interview with Ozzy	1984	7.50	15.00	30.00
❑ FZ 38987	Bark at the Moon	1983	2.50	5.00	10.00
❑ PZ 38987	Bark at the Moon	1985	2.00	4.00	8.00
—Budget-line reissue with new prefix					
❑ FZ 40026	The Ultimate Sin	1986	2.50	5.00	10.00
❑ 9Z9 40543 [EP]	The Ultimate Live Ozzy	1986	10.00	20.00	40.00
—Picture disc with live material					
❑ ZX2 40714	Ozzy Osbourne/Randy Rhoads Tribute	1987	3.00	6.00	12.00
❑ FZ 44245	No Rest for the Wicked	1988	2.50	5.00	10.00
❑ Z 46795	No More Tears	1991	5.00	10.00	20.00
JET					
❑ AS99 1372 [PD]	Diary of a Madman	1981	10.00	20.00	40.00
—Promo-only picture disc					
❑ JZ 36812	Blizzard of Ozz	1981	2.50	5.00	10.00
❑ FZ 37492	Diary of a Madman	1981	2.50	5.00	10.00
❑ 8Z8 37640 [EP]	Mr. Crowley	1982	7.50	15.00	30.00
—Three-song picture disc with live material					
❑ ZX2 38350 [(2)]	Speak of the Devil	1982	3.75	7.50	15.00

OSIBISA

Number	Title (A Side/B Side)	Yr	VG	VG+	NM
ANTILLES					
❑ 7051	Welcome Home	1978	2.50	5.00	10.00
❑ 7058	Ojah Awake	1978	2.50	5.00	10.00
BUDDAH					
❑ BDS-5136	Super Fly T.N.T.	1973	7.50	15.00	30.00
DECCA					
❑ DL 75285	Osibisa	1971	3.75	7.50	15.00
❑ DL 75327	Woyaya	1972	3.75	7.50	15.00
❑ DL 75368	Heads	1972	3.75	7.50	15.00
ISLAND					
❑ ILPS 9355	Welcome Home	1976	2.50	5.00	10.00
❑ ILPS 9411	Ojah Awake	1977	2.50	5.00	10.00
MCA					
❑ 32	Osibisa	1973	2.50	5.00	10.00
—Reissue of Decca 75285					
❑ 43	Woyaya	1973	2.50	5.00	10.00
—Reissue of Decca 75327					
WARNER BROS.					
❑ BS 2732	Happy Children	1973	2.50	5.00	10.00
❑ BS 2802	Osibirock	1974	2.50	5.00	10.00

OSIPOV STATE RUSSIAN FOLK ORCHESTRA (VITALY GNUTOV, CONDUCTOR)

Number	Title (A Side/B Side)	Yr	VG	VG+	NM
MERCURY LIVING PRESENCE					
❑ SR 90310 [S]	Balalaika Favorites	196?	7.50	15.00	30.00
—Third edition: Dark red (not maroon) label					
❑ SR 90310 [S]	Balalaika Favorites	196?	12.50	25.00	50.00
—Maroon label, with "Vendor: Mercury Record Corporation"					
❑ SR 90310 [S]	Balalaika Favorites	196?	20.00	40.00	80.00
—Maroon label, no "Vendor: Mercury Record Corporation"					
❑ SR 90310 [S]	Balalaika Favorites	1998	6.25	12.50	25.00
—Classic Records reissue					

OSMONDS, THE

Includes records as "The Osmond Brothers."

Number	Title (A Side/B Side)	Yr	VG	VG+	NM
ELEKTRA					
❑ 60180	The Osmond Brothers	1982	2.50	5.00	10.00
MERCURY					
❑ SRM-1-3766	Steppin' Out	1979	2.50	5.00	10.00
METRO					
❑ M 543 [M]	We Sing You a Merry Christmas	1965	3.75	7.50	15.00
—Reissue of 4187 with one track missing and remaining contents rearranged					
❑ MS 543 [S]	We Sing You a Merry Christmas	1965	5.00	10.00	20.00
MGM					
❑ PM-7 [M]	The Travels of Jaimie McPheeters	1963	12.50	25.00	50.00
—Side 1: Dialogue from TV show; Side 2: Osmond Brothers tracks. AC Spark Plugs promo.					
❑ PM-9 [M]	We Sing You a Merry Christmas	1963	10.00	20.00	40.00
—Special-products issue for AC Spark Plug dealers					
❑ E-4146 [M]	Songs We Sang on the Andy Williams Show	1963	6.25	12.50	25.00
❑ SE-4146 [S]	Songs We Sang on the Andy Williams Show	1963	7.50	15.00	30.00
—As "The Osmond Brothers"					
❑ E-4187 [M]	We Sing You a Merry Christmas	1963	6.25	12.50	25.00
—As "The Osmond Brothers"					
❑ SE-4187 [S]	We Sing You a Merry Christmas	1963	7.50	15.00	30.00
❑ E-4235 [M]	The Osmond Brothers Sing the All-Time Hymn Favorites	1964	5.00	10.00	20.00

Number	Title (A Side/B Side)	Yr	VG	VG+	NM
❑ SE-4235 [S]	The Osmond Brothers Sing the All-Time Hymn Favorites	1964	6.25	12.50	25.00
❑ E-4291 [M]	The New Sound of the Osmond Brothers	1965	5.00	10.00	20.00
❑ SE-4291 [S]	The New Sound of the Osmond Brothers	1965	6.25	12.50	25.00
❑ SE-4724	Osmonds	1971	3.00	6.00	12.00
❑ SE-4770	Homemade	1971	7.50	15.00	30.00
—With tear-off poster intact; deduct 60 percent if poster is not attached					
❑ SE-4796	Phase-III	1972	3.00	6.00	12.00
❑ SE-4826 [(2)]	The Osmonds "Live"	1972	3.75	7.50	15.00
❑ SE-4851	Crazy Horses	1972	3.00	6.00	12.00
❑ SE-4902	The Plan	1973	2.50	5.00	10.00
❑ M3G-4939	Love Me for a Reason	1974	2.50	5.00	10.00
❑ M3G-4993	The Proud One	1975	2.50	5.00	10.00
❑ MG-2-5012 [(2)]	Around the World — Live in Concert	1975	3.00	6.00	12.00
❑ ST 90403 [S]	The New Sound of the Osmond Brothers	1965	10.00	20.00	40.00
—Capitol Record Club edition					
❑ T 90403 [M]	The New Sound of the Osmond Brothers	1965	10.00	20.00	40.00
—Capitol Record Club edition					
POLYDOR					
❑ PD-1-6077	Brainstorm	1976	2.50	5.00	10.00
❑ PD-2-8001 [(2)]	The Osmond Christmas Album	1976	3.75	7.50	15.00
—Includes group, solo and duet recordings					
❑ PD-2-9005	The Osmonds Greatest Hits	1977	3.00	6.00	12.00
WARNER BROS.					
❑ 25070	One Way Rider	1984	2.00	4.00	8.00

OSTERWALD, HAZY

Number	Title (A Side/B Side)	Yr	VG	VG+	NM
BALLY					
❑ BAL-12004 [M]	Swiss Jazz	1956	10.00	20.00	40.00

OSWALD, LEE HARVEY

The below are documentary records, all based on the same radio interview.

Number	Title (A Side/B Side)	Yr	VG	VG+	NM
EYEWITNESS					
❑ 1002	Lee Harvey Oswald Speaks	1967	20.00	40.00	80.00
INCA					
❑ 1001	Oswald: Self Portrait in Red	1965	25.00	50.00	100.00
KEY					
❑ 880	The President's Assassin Speaks	1964	25.00	50.00	100.00

OTHER HALF, THE (1)

Number	Title (A Side/B Side)	Yr	VG	VG+	NM
ACTA					
❑ 38004	The Other Half	1968	25.00	50.00	100.00

OTHER HALF, THE (2)

Number	Title (A Side/B Side)	Yr	VG	VG+	NM
7/2					
❑ (no #)	The Other Half	1966	375.00	750.00	1500.
—Album has been counterfeited, but those records are translucent when held to a light, originals are not					

OTIS, JOHNNY

Number	Title (A Side/B Side)	Yr	VG	VG+	NM
ALLIGATOR					
❑ AL-4726	The New Johnny Otis Show	1982	2.50	5.00	10.00
CAPITOL					
❑ T 940 [M]	The Johnny Otis Show	1958	62.50	125.00	250.00
❑ C1-92858 [(2)]	The Capitol Years	1989	3.75	7.50	15.00
DIG					
❑ 104 [M]	Rock and Roll Hit Parade, Volume 1	1957	300.00	600.00	900.00
—Gold cover with thick cardboard and thick vinyl records. Counterfeits have noticeably thinner vinyl.					
❑ 104 [M]	Rock and Roll Hit Parade, Volume 1	1958	150.00	300.00	600.00
—Yellow cover with thick cardboard and thick vinyl records. Counterfeits have noticeably thinner vinyl.					
EPIC					
❑ BN 26524	Cuttin' Up	1970	6.25	12.50	25.00
❑ EG 30473 [(2)]	The Johnny Otis Show Live at Monterey	1971	7.50	15.00	30.00
KENT					
❑ KST-534	Cold Shot	1968	6.25	12.50	25.00
SAVOY					
❑ SJL-2230 [(2)]	The Original Johnny Otis Show	1978	3.75	7.50	15.00
❑ SJL-2252 [(2)]	The Original Johnny Otis Show, Vol. 2	1980	3.75	7.50	15.00

OTIS AND CARLA

Also see OTIS REDDING; CARLA THOMAS.

Number	Title (A Side/B Side)	Yr	VG	VG+	NM
STAX					
❑ ST-716 [M]	King and Queen	1967	8.75	17.50	35.00
❑ STS-716 [S]	King and Queen	1967	12.50	25.00	50.00
SUNDAZED					
❑ LP 5069 [S]	King and Queen	2001	3.00	6.00	12.00
—Reissue on 180-gram vinyl					

OUSLEY, HAROLD

Number	Title (A Side/B Side)	Yr	VG	VG+	NM
BETHLEHEM					
❑ BCP-6059 [M]	Tenor Sax	1961	7.50	15.00	30.00
❑ SBCP-6059 [S]	Tenor Sax	1961	10.00	20.00	40.00
COBBLESTONE					
❑ 9017	The Kid!	1971	6.25	12.50	25.00

OUTLAW BLUES BAND, THE

Number	Title (A Side/B Side)	Yr	VG	VG+	NM
BLUESWAY					
❑ BLS-6020	Breakin' In	1969	6.25	12.50	25.00
❑ BLS-6021	The Outlaw Blues Band	1968	6.25	12.50	25.00

OUTLAWS

Number	Title (A Side/B Side)	Yr	VG	VG+	NM
ARISTA					
❑ SP-132 [EP]	Radio Remixes	1982	3.00	6.00	12.00
—Promo-only four-song sampler					
❑ AL 4042	Outlaws	1975	2.50	5.00	10.00
❑ AL 4070	Lady in Waiting	1976	2.50	5.00	10.00
❑ AL 4135	Hurry Sundown	1977	2.50	5.00	10.00
❑ AB 4205	Playin' to Win	1978	2.50	5.00	10.00
❑ A2L 8114 [(2)]	Bring It Back Alive	198?	2.50	5.00	10.00
—Second reissue					
❑ A2L 8300 [(2)]	Bring It Back Alive	1978	3.00	6.00	12.00

Number	Title (A Side/B Side)	Yr	VG	VG+	NM
❑ AL 8301	Outlaws	198?	2.00	4.00	8.00
—Reissue					
❑ AL 8319	Greatest Hits of the Outlaws/High Tides Forever	198?	2.00	4.00	8.00
—Reissue					
❑ AL 8369	Hurry Sundown	198?	2.00	4.00	8.00
—Reissue					
❑ A2L 8608 [(2)]	Bring It Back Alive	198?	2.50	5.00	10.00
—Reissue					
❑ AL 9507	In the Eye of the Storm	1979	2.50	5.00	10.00
❑ AL 9542	Ghost Riders	1980	2.50	5.00	10.00
❑ AL 9584	Los Hombres Malo	1982	2.50	5.00	10.00
❑ AL 9614	Greatest Hits of the Outlaws/High Tides Forever	1982	2.50	5.00	10.00
DIRECT DISC					
❑ SD 16617	Outlaws	198?	12.50	25.00	50.00
—Audiophile vinyl					
PAIR					
❑ PDL2-1050 [(2)]	The Outlaws	1986	3.00	6.00	12.00
PASHA					
❑ BFZ 40512	Soldiers of Fortune	1986	2.00	4.00	8.00

OUTSIDERS, THE
CAPITOL

Number	Title (A Side/B Side)	Yr	VG	VG+	NM
❑ ST 2501 [S]	Time Won't Let Me	1966	7.50	15.00	30.00
❑ T 2501 [M]	Time Won't Let Me	1966	6.25	12.50	25.00
❑ ST 2558 [S]	The Outsiders Album #2	1966	7.50	15.00	30.00
❑ T 2568 [M]	The Outsiders Album #2	1966	6.25	12.50	25.00
❑ ST 2636 [S]	In	1967	6.25	12.50	25.00
❑ T 2636 [M]	In	1967	7.50	15.00	30.00
❑ ST 2745 [S]	Happening "Live!"	1967	6.25	12.50	25.00
❑ T 2745 [M]	Happening "Live!"	1967	7.50	15.00	30.00
RHINO					
❑ RNLP-70132	The Best of the Outsiders (1965-1968)	1986	2.50	5.00	10.00

OVATIONS, THE (1)
MGM

Number	Title (A Side/B Side)	Yr	VG	VG+	NM
❑ SE-4945	Having a Party	1973	3.75	7.50	15.00
SOUNDS OF MEMPHIS					
❑ 7001	Hooked on a Feeling	1972	5.00	10.00	20.00

OVERSTREET, TOMMY
ABC

Number	Title (A Side/B Side)	Yr	VG	VG+	NM
❑ AB-1066	Better Me	1978	3.00	6.00	12.00
ABC DOT					
❑ DOSD-2016	I'm a Believer	1975	3.75	7.50	15.00
❑ DOSD-2027	Greatest Hits Vol. One	1975	3.75	7.50	15.00
❑ DOSD-2038	The Tommy Overstreet Show Live from the Silver Slipper	1975	3.75	7.50	15.00
❑ DOSD-2056	Turn On to Tommy Overstreet	1976	3.75	7.50	15.00
❑ DO-2071	Vintage '77	1977	3.00	6.00	12.00
❑ DO-2086	Hangin' 'Round	1977	3.00	6.00	12.00
DOT					
❑ DLP-25992	Gwen (Congratulations)	1971	5.00	10.00	20.00
❑ DLP-25994	This Is Tommy Overstreet	1972	5.00	10.00	20.00
❑ DLP-26003	Heaven Is My Woman's Love	1972	5.00	10.00	20.00
❑ DOS-26010	My Friends Call Me T.O.	1973	5.00	10.00	20.00
❑ DOS-26021	Woman, Your Name Is My Song	1974	5.00	10.00	20.00
ELEKTRA					
❑ 6E-178	I'll Never Let You Down	1979	2.50	5.00	10.00
❑ 6E-226	The Real Tommy Overstreet	1979	2.50	5.00	10.00
❑ 6E-292	The Best of Tommy Overstreet	1980	2.50	5.00	10.00
MCA					
❑ 645	Vintage '77	198?	2.00	4.00	8.00
—Reissue					
❑ 646	Hangin' 'Round	198?	2.00	4.00	8.00
—Reissue					
❑ 797	Better Me	198?	2.00	4.00	8.00
—Reissue					

OWEN, JIM
EPIC

Number	Title (A Side/B Side)	Yr	VG	VG+	NM
❑ PEG 34852 [(2)]	A Song for Us All: A Salute to Hank Williams	1977	5.00	10.00	20.00

OWEN, REG
DECCA

Number	Title (A Side/B Side)	Yr	VG	VG+	NM
❑ DL 8859 [M]	Under Paris Skies	1959	5.00	10.00	20.00
❑ DL 78859 [S]	Under Paris Skies	1959	6.25	12.50	25.00
PALETTE					
❑ 1001 [M]	Manhattan Spiritual	1959	7.50	15.00	30.00
❑ S-1001 [S]	Manhattan Spiritual	1959	10.00	20.00	40.00
❑ PZ-1004 [M]	Get Happy	1960	5.00	10.00	20.00
❑ PZ-1018 [M]	Fiorello!	1960	5.00	10.00	20.00
❑ SPZ-31004 [S]	Get Happy	1960	6.25	12.50	25.00
❑ SPZ-31018 [S]	Fiorello!	1960	6.25	12.50	25.00
RCA VICTOR					
❑ LPM-1542 [M]	The Best of Irving Berlin	1957	6.25	12.50	25.00
❑ LPM-1580 [M]	Dreaming	1958	6.25	12.50	25.00
❑ LPM-1582 [M]	Coffee Break	1958	5.00	10.00	20.00
❑ LSP-1582 [S]	Coffee Break	1958	6.25	12.50	25.00
❑ LPM-1597 [M]	Holiday Abroad in Dublin	1958	5.00	10.00	20.00
❑ LSP-1597 [S]	Holiday Abroad in Dublin	1958	6.25	12.50	25.00
❑ LPM-1599 [M]	Holiday Abroad in London	1958	5.00	10.00	20.00
❑ LSP-1599 [S]	Holiday Abroad in London	1958	6.25	12.50	25.00
❑ LPM-1675 [M]	The British Isles	1958	5.00	10.00	20.00
❑ LSP-1675 [S]	The British Isles	1958	6.25	12.50	25.00
❑ LPM-1906 [M]	I'll Sing You 1,000 Love Songs	1959	5.00	10.00	20.00
❑ LSP-1906 [S]	I'll Sing You 1,000 Love Songs	1959	6.25	12.50	25.00
❑ LPM-1907 [M]	Deep in a Dream	1959	6.25	12.50	25.00
❑ LPM-1908 [M]	Girls Were Made to Take Care of Boys	1959	5.00	10.00	20.00
❑ LSP-1908 [S]	Girls Were Made to Take Care of Boys	1959	6.25	12.50	25.00
❑ LPM-1914 [M]	Cuddle Up a Little Closer	1959	5.00	10.00	20.00
❑ LSP-1914 [S]	Cuddle Up a Little Closer	1959	6.25	12.50	25.00
❑ LPM-1915 [M]	You Don't Know Paree	1959	6.25	12.50	25.00

OWEN-B
MUS-I-COL

Number	Title (A Side/B Side)	Yr	VG	VG+	NM
❑ 101209	Owen-B	1970	15.00	30.00	60.00

OWENS, BONNIE
CAPITOL

Number	Title (A Side/B Side)	Yr	VG	VG+	NM
❑ ST-195	Lead Me On	1969	6.25	12.50	25.00
❑ ST-341	Hi-Fi to Cry By	1969	6.25	12.50	25.00
❑ ST-557	Mother's Favorite Hymns	1970	6.25	12.50	25.00
❑ ST 2403 [S]	Don't Take Advantage of Me	1965	6.25	12.50	25.00
❑ T 2403 [M]	Don't Take Advantage of Me	1965	5.00	10.00	20.00
❑ ST 2600 [S]	All of Me Belongs to You	1967	6.25	12.50	25.00
❑ T 2600 [M]	All of Me Belongs to You	1967	6.25	12.50	25.00
❑ ST 2861	Somewhere Between	1968	6.25	12.50	25.00

OWENS, BUCK
CAPITOL

Number	Title (A Side/B Side)	Yr	VG	VG+	NM
❑ ST-131	I've Got You on My Mind Again	1969	5.00	10.00	20.00
❑ SKAO-145	The Best of Buck Owens, Volume 3	1969	5.00	10.00	20.00
❑ ST-194	Anywhere U.S.A.	1969	5.00	10.00	20.00
❑ ST-212	Tall Dark Stranger	1969	5.00	10.00	20.00
❑ ST 8-0232	Buck Owens in London	1969	6.25	12.50	25.00
—Capitol Record Club edition					
❑ ST-232	Buck Owens in London	1969	5.00	10.00	20.00
❑ SWBB-257 [(2)]	Close-Up	1969	5.00	10.00	20.00
—Reissue of "Together Again" and "No One But You"					
❑ ST-439	Your Mother's Prayer	1970	5.00	10.00	20.00
❑ ST-476	The Kansas City Song	1970	5.00	10.00	20.00
❑ STBB-486 [(2)]	A Merry "Hee Haw" Christmas	1970	6.25	12.50	25.00
❑ STCL-574 [(3)]	Buck Owens	1970	10.00	20.00	40.00
❑ ST-628	I Wouldn't Live in New York City	1970	5.00	10.00	20.00
❑ ST-685	Bridge Over Troubled Water	1971	3.75	7.50	15.00
❑ ST-830	The Best of Buck Owens, Vol. 4	1971	3.75	7.50	15.00
❑ ST 1482 [S]	Buck Owens Sings Harlan Howard	1961	12.50	25.00	50.00
❑ T 1482 [M]	Buck Owens Sings Harlan Howard	1961	10.00	20.00	40.00
❑ DT 1489 [R]	Under Your Spell Again	1968	6.25	12.50	25.00
—"Duophonic" reissue of mono original with new title					
❑ T 1489 [M]	Buck Owens	1961	10.00	20.00	40.00
—Black colorband label, Capitol logo at left					
❑ T 1489 [M]	Buck Owens	1962	7.50	15.00	30.00
—Black colorband label, Capitol logo at top					
❑ ST 1777 [S]	You're for Me	1962	12.50	25.00	50.00
❑ T 1777 [M]	You're for Me	1962	10.00	20.00	40.00
❑ ST 1879 [S]	On the Bandstand	1963	12.50	25.00	50.00
❑ T 1879 [M]	On the Bandstand	1963	10.00	20.00	40.00
❑ ST 1989 [S]	Buck Owens Sings Tommy Collins	1963	12.50	25.00	50.00
❑ T 1989 [M]	Buck Owens Sings Tommy Collins	1963	10.00	20.00	40.00
❑ ST 2105 [S]	The Best of Buck Owens	1964	7.50	15.00	30.00
❑ T 2105 [M]	The Best of Buck Owens	1964	6.25	12.50	25.00
❑ ST 2135 [S]	Together Again/My Heart Skips a Beat	1964	7.50	15.00	30.00
❑ T 2135 [M]	Together Again/My Heart Skips a Beat	1964	6.25	12.50	25.00
❑ ST 2186 [S]	I Don't Care	1964	7.50	15.00	30.00
❑ T 2186 [M]	I Don't Care	1964	6.25	12.50	25.00
❑ ST 2283 [S]	I've Got a Tiger by the Tail	1965	7.50	15.00	30.00
❑ T 2283 [M]	I've Got a Tiger by the Tail	1965	6.25	12.50	25.00
❑ ST 2353 [S]	Before You Go/No One But You	1965	7.50	15.00	30.00
❑ T 2353 [M]	Before You Go/No One But You	1965	6.25	12.50	25.00
❑ ST 2367 [S]	The Instrumental Hits of Buck Owens & the Buckaroos	1965	7.50	15.00	30.00
❑ T 2367 [M]	The Instrumental Hits of Buck Owens & the Buckaroos	1965	6.25	12.50	25.00
❑ ST 2396 [S]	Christmas with Buck Owens and His Buckaroos	1965	7.50	15.00	30.00
❑ T 2396 [M]	Christmas with Buck Owens and His Buckaroos	1965	5.00	10.00	20.00
❑ ST 2443 [S]	Roll Out the Red Carpet for Buck Owens & The Buckaroos	1966	6.25	12.50	25.00
❑ T 2443 [M]	Roll Out the Red Carpet for Buck Owens & The Buckaroos	1966	5.00	10.00	20.00
❑ ST 2497 [S]	Dust on Mother's Bible	1966	6.25	12.50	25.00
❑ T 2497 [M]	Dust on Mother's Bible	1966	5.00	10.00	20.00
❑ ST 2556 [S]	Carnegie Hall Concert	1966	6.25	12.50	25.00
❑ T 2556 [M]	Carnegie Hall Concert	1966	5.00	10.00	20.00
❑ ST 2650 [S]	Open Up Your Heart	1967	6.25	12.50	25.00
❑ T 2650 [M]	Open Up Your Heart	1967	5.00	10.00	20.00
❑ ST 2715 [S]	Buck Owens and His Buckaroos in Japan	1967	6.25	12.50	25.00
❑ T 2715 [M]	Buck Owens and His Buckaroos in Japan	1967	5.00	10.00	20.00
❑ ST 2760 [S]	Your Tender Loving Care	1967	6.25	12.50	25.00
❑ T 2760 [M]	Your Tender Loving Care	1967	6.25	12.50	25.00
❑ ST 2841 [S]	It Takes People Like You to Make People Like Me	1968	6.25	12.50	25.00
❑ T 2841 [M]	It Takes People Like You to Make People Like Me	1968	10.00	20.00	40.00
❑ ST 2897	The Best of Buck Owens, Vol. 2	1968	6.25	12.50	25.00
❑ ST 2902	A Night on the Town	1968	6.25	12.50	25.00
❑ ST 2962	Sweet Rosie Jones	1968	6.25	12.50	25.00
❑ ST 2977	Christmas Shopping	1968	6.25	12.50	25.00
❑ SPRO 2980/1 [DJ]	Minute Masters	1966	12.50	25.00	50.00
—Promo-only excerpts of 24 songs					
❑ ST 2994	Buck Owens, The Guitar Player	1968	6.25	12.50	25.00
❑ ST-11105	Live at the White House	1972	3.75	7.50	15.00
❑ ST-11136	In the Palm of Your Hand	1973	3.75	7.50	15.00
❑ SMAS-11180	Ain't It Amazing, Gracie	1973	3.75	7.50	15.00
❑ ST-11222	Arms Full of Empty	1972	3.75	7.50	15.00
❑ ST-11273	The Best of Buck Owens Volume 5	1973	3.75	7.50	15.00
❑ ST-11332	Monster's Holiday	1974	3.75	7.50	15.00
❑ ST-11390	Weekend Daddy	1974	3.75	7.50	15.00
❑ ST-11471	The Best of Buck Owens, Volume 6	1976	3.75	7.50	15.00

Number	Title (A Side/B Side)	Yr	VG	VG+	NM
❑ C1-91132	Hot Dog!	1988	3.00	6.00	12.00
❑ C1-92893	Act Naturally	1989	3.75	7.50	15.00

COUNTRY MUSIC FOUNDATION

Number	Title (A Side/B Side)	Yr	VG	VG+	NM
❑ CMF-012	Live at Carnegie Hall	198?	3.00	6.00	12.00

LABREA

Number	Title (A Side/B Side)	Yr	VG	VG+	NM
❑ 1017 [M]	Buck Owens	1961	25.00	50.00	100.00
❑ 8017 [S]	Buck Owens	1961	37.50	75.00	150.00

STARDAY

Number	Title (A Side/B Side)	Yr	VG	VG+	NM
❑ SLP-172	The Fabulous Country Music Sound of Buck Owens	1962	12.50	25.00	50.00
❑ SLP-324	Coutnry Hit Maker #1	1964	6.25	12.50	25.00

WARNER BROS.

Number	Title (A Side/B Side)	Yr	VG	VG+	NM
❑ BS 2952	Buck 'Em	1976	3.00	6.00	12.00
❑ BS 3087	Our Old Mansion	1977	3.00	6.00	12.00

OWENS, BUCK, AND SUSAN RAYE
CAPITOL

Number	Title (A Side/B Side)	Yr	VG	VG+	NM
❑ ST-448	We're Gonna Get Together	1970	5.00	10.00	20.00
❑ ST-558	Great White Horse	1970	3.75	7.50	15.00
❑ ST-837	Merry Christmas from Buck Owens and Susan Raye	1971	3.75	7.50	15.00
❑ ST-11084	The Best of Buck Owens and Susan Raye	1972	3.75	7.50	15.00
❑ ST-11204	The Good Old Days (Are Here Again)	1973	3.75	7.50	15.00

OWENS, CHARLES
VAULT

Number	Title (A Side/B Side)	Yr	VG	VG+	NM
❑ LP-(# unknown)	I Stand Alone	196?	12.50	25.00	50.00

OWENS, JIMMY
ATLANTIC

Number	Title (A Side/B Side)	Yr	VG	VG+	NM
❑ SD 1491	Jimmy Owens-Kenny Barron Quintet	1968	5.00	10.00	20.00

—*Multicolor label, black "fan" logo at right*

OXFORD, VERNON
RCA VICTOR

Number	Title (A Side/B Side)	Yr	VG	VG+	NM
❑ LPM-3704 [M]	Woman, Let Me Sing You a Song	1967	10.00	20.00	40.00
❑ LSP-3704 [S]	Woman, Let Me Sing You a Song	1967	7.50	15.00	30.00

ROUNDER

Number	Title (A Side/B Side)	Yr	VG	VG+	NM
❑ 0091	If I Had My Wife to Love Over	198?	3.75	7.50	15.00
❑ 0123	His and Hers	198?	3.75	7.50	15.00
❑ 0156	Keepin' It Country	1982	3.75	7.50	15.00

OZ KNOZZ
OZONE

Number	Title (A Side/B Side)	Yr	VG	VG+	NM
❑ O2-1000	Ruff Mix	1975	125.00	250.00	500.00

OZONE, MAKOTO
COLUMBIA

Number	Title (A Side/B Side)	Yr	VG	VG+	NM
❑ FC 40676	Now You Know	1987	2.50	5.00	10.00

P

P.H. PHACTOR
PICCADILLY

Number	Title (A Side/B Side)	Yr	VG	VG+	NM
❑ PIC-3343	Merryjuana	1980	25.00	50.00	100.00

—*Cover spells the group's name "Factor" but the label has it "Phactor"*

P.M. DAWN
GEE STREET

Number	Title (A Side/B Side)	Yr	VG	VG+	NM
❑ PRLP-6768-1 [(2)DJ]	The Bliss Album...?	1993	5.00	10.00	20.00

—*Promo-only vinyl edition*

Number	Title (A Side/B Side)	Yr	VG	VG+	NM
❑ 524147-1 [(2)]	Jesus Wept	1995	5.00	10.00	20.00

PABLO CRUISE
A&M

Number	Title (A Side/B Side)	Yr	VG	VG+	NM
❑ SP-3111	Pablo Cruise	198?	2.00	4.00	8.00

—*Budget-line reissue of 4528*

Number	Title (A Side/B Side)	Yr	VG	VG+	NM
❑ SP-3198	Worlds Away	198?	2.00	4.00	8.00

—*Budget-line reissue of 4697*

Number	Title (A Side/B Side)	Yr	VG	VG+	NM
❑ SP-3236	A Place in the Sun	198?	2.00	4.00	8.00

—*Budget-line reissue of 4625*

Number	Title (A Side/B Side)	Yr	VG	VG+	NM
❑ SP-3712	Part of the Game	1979	2.50	5.00	10.00
❑ SP-3726	Reflector	1981	2.50	5.00	10.00
❑ SP-4528	Pablo Cruise	1975	2.50	5.00	10.00
❑ SP-4575	Lifeline	1976	2.50	5.00	10.00
❑ SP-4625	A Place in the Sun	1977	2.50	5.00	10.00
❑ SP-4697	Worlds Away	1978	2.50	5.00	10.00
❑ SP-4909	Out of Our Hands	1983	2.50	5.00	10.00

MOBILE FIDELITY

Number	Title (A Side/B Side)	Yr	VG	VG+	NM
❑ 1-029	A Place in the Sun	1979	5.00	10.00	20.00

—*Audiophile vinyl*

NAUTILUS

Number	Title (A Side/B Side)	Yr	VG	VG+	NM
❑ NR-6	Lifeline	1980	5.00	10.00	20.00

—*Audiophile vinyl*

Number	Title (A Side/B Side)	Yr	VG	VG+	NM
❑ NR-28	Worlds Away	1981	5.00	10.00	20.00

—*Audiophile vinyl*

PACE, JOHNNY
RIVERSIDE

Number	Title (A Side/B Side)	Yr	VG	VG+	NM
❑ RLP 12-292 [M]	Chet Baker Introduces Johnny Pace	1958	12.50	25.00	50.00
❑ RLP-1130 [S]	Chet Baker Introduces Johnny Pace	1959	12.50	25.00	50.00

PACERS, THE
RAZORBACK

Number	Title (A Side/B Side)	Yr	VG	VG+	NM
❑ 121 [M]	You Asked For It	1965	25.00	50.00	100.00

PACHECO, MIKE
INTERLUDE

Number	Title (A Side/B Side)	Yr	VG	VG+	NM
❑ MO-513 [M]	Hot Skins	1959	10.00	20.00	40.00
❑ ST-1013 [S]	Hot Skins	1959	7.50	15.00	30.00

TAMPA

Number	Title (A Side/B Side)	Yr	VG	VG+	NM
❑ TP-10 [M]	Bongo Skins	1957	25.00	50.00	100.00
—*Colored vinyl*					
❑ TP-10 [M]	Bongo Skins	1958	12.50	25.00	50.00
—*Black vinyl*					
❑ TP-21 [M]	Bongo Session	1957	25.00	50.00	100.00
—*Colored vinyl*					
❑ TP-21 [M]	Bongo Session	1958	12.50	25.00	50.00
—*Black vinyl*					
❑ TP-30 [M]	Bongo Date	1957	25.00	50.00	100.00
—*Colored vinyl*					
❑ TP-30 [M]	Bongo Date	1958	12.50	25.00	50.00
—*Black vinyl*					

PACIFIC DRIFT
DERAM

Number	Title (A Side/B Side)	Yr	VG	VG+	NM
❑ DES 18040	Feelin' Free	1970	5.00	10.00	20.00

PACIFIC GAS & ELECTRIC
ABC DUNHILL

Number	Title (A Side/B Side)	Yr	VG	VG+	NM
❑ DSX-50157	Pacific Gas and Electric Starring Charlie Allen	1974	3.00	6.00	12.00

BRIGHT ORANGE

Number	Title (A Side/B Side)	Yr	VG	VG+	NM
❑ 701	Get It On	1968	10.00	20.00	40.00

COLUMBIA

Number	Title (A Side/B Side)	Yr	VG	VG+	NM
❑ CS 1017	Are You Ready	1970	3.00	6.00	12.00
—*Orange label*					
❑ CS 1017	Are You Ready	1970	3.75	7.50	15.00
—*"360 Sound" label*					
❑ CS 9900	Pacific Gas and Electric	1969	3.75	7.50	15.00
—*"360 Sound" label*					
❑ CS 9900	Pacific Gas and Electric	1970	3.00	6.00	12.00
—*Orange label*					
❑ C 30362	PG&E	1971	3.00	6.00	12.00
❑ C 32019	The Best of Pacific Gas & Electric	1972	3.00	6.00	12.00

POWER

Number	Title (A Side/B Side)	Yr	VG	VG+	NM
❑ 701	Get It On	1969	6.25	12.50	25.00

PACIFIC OCEAN
V.M.C.

Number	Title (A Side/B Side)	Yr	VG	VG+	NM
❑ 135	Pacific Ocean	1969	5.00	10.00	20.00

PACK, MARSHALL
STARDAY

Number	Title (A Side/B Side)	Yr	VG	VG+	NM
❑ SLP-120 [M]	Marshall Pack	1960	10.00	20.00	40.00

PACKERS, THE
PURE SOUL MUSIC

Number	Title (A Side/B Side)	Yr	VG	VG+	NM
❑ 1001 [S]	Hole in the Wall	1966	5.00	10.00	20.00

PAGE, HOT LIPS
CONTINENTAL

Number	Title (A Side/B Side)	Yr	VG	VG+	NM
❑ 16007 [M]	Hot and Cozy	1962	7.50	15.00	30.00

PAGE, JIMMY
Also see LED ZEPPELIN; THE YARDBIRDS.
GEFFEN

Number	Title (A Side/B Side)	Yr	VG	VG+	NM
❑ GHS 24188	Outrider	1988	2.00	4.00	8.00

SPRINGBOARD

Number	Title (A Side/B Side)	Yr	VG	VG+	NM
❑ SPB-4038	Special Early Works	1972	6.25	12.50	25.00

PAGE, PATTI
ACCORD

Number	Title (A Side/B Side)	Yr	VG	VG+	NM
❑ SN-7206	Special Thoughts	1982	2.50	5.00	10.00

COLUMBIA

Number	Title (A Side/B Side)	Yr	VG	VG+	NM
❑ CL 2049 [M]	Say Wonderful Things	1963	3.75	7.50	15.00
❑ CL 2132 [M]	Love After Midnight	1964	3.75	7.50	15.00
❑ CL 2353 [M]	Hush, Hush, Sweet Charlotte	1965	3.75	7.50	15.00
❑ CL 2414 [M]	Christmas with Patti Page	1965	3.00	6.00	12.00
❑ CL 2505 [M]	America's Favorite Hymns	1966	3.00	6.00	12.00
❑ CL 2526 [M]	Patti Page's Greatest Hits	1966	3.00	6.00	12.00
❑ CL 2761 [M]	Today My Way	1967	5.00	10.00	20.00
❑ CS 8849 [S]	Say Wonderful Things	1963	5.00	10.00	20.00
❑ CS 8932 [S]	Love After Midnight	1964	5.00	10.00	20.00
❑ CS 9153 [S]	Hush, Hush, Sweet Charlotte	1965	5.00	10.00	20.00
❑ CS 9214 [S]	Christmas with Patti Page	1965	3.75	7.50	15.00
❑ CS 9305 [S]	America's Favorite Hymns	1966	3.75	7.50	15.00
❑ CS 9326	Patti Page's Greatest Hits	1970	2.50	5.00	10.00
—*Orange label*					
❑ CS 9326 [S]	Patti Page's Greatest Hits	1966	3.75	7.50	15.00
—*"360 Sound" label*					
❑ PC 9326	Patti Page's Greatest Hits	198?	2.00	4.00	8.00
—*Budget-line reissue*					
❑ CS 9561 [S]	Today My Way	1967	3.75	7.50	15.00
❑ CS 9666	Gentle On My Mind	1968	3.75	7.50	15.00
❑ CS 9999	Honey Come Back	1970	3.00	6.00	12.00

EMARCY

Number	Title (A Side/B Side)	Yr	VG	VG+	NM
❑ MG-36074 [M]	In the Land of Hi-Fi	1956	12.50	25.00	50.00
❑ MG-36116 [M]	The East Side	1957	12.50	25.00	50.00
❑ MG-36136 [M]	The West Side	1957	12.50	25.00	50.00
❑ SR-60013 [S]	The West Side	1959	12.50	25.00	50.00
❑ SR-60014 [S]	The East Side	1959	12.50	25.00	50.00
❑ SR-80000 [S]	In the Land of Hi-Fi	1959	12.50	25.00	50.00

HARMONY

Number	Title (A Side/B Side)	Yr	VG	VG+	NM
❑ HS 11381	Stand By Your Man	1970	2.50	5.00	10.00
❑ KH 30407	Green, Green Grass of Home	1971	2.50	5.00	10.00

MERCURY

Number	Title (A Side/B Side)	Yr	VG	VG+	NM
❑ PKW-118 [(2)]	The Most	1969	3.75	7.50	15.00
❑ MG-20076 [M]	Romance on the Range	1955	7.50	15.00	30.00
❑ MG 20093 [M]	Christmas with Patti Page	1956	7.50	15.00	30.00
❑ MG-20095 [M]	Page I	1955	7.50	15.00	30.00
❑ MG-20096 [M]	Page II	1955	7.50	15.00	30.00
❑ MG-20097 [M]	Page III	1955	7.50	15.00	30.00
❑ MG-20098 [M]	You Go to My Head	1955	7.50	15.00	30.00

Number	Title (A Side/B Side)	Yr	VG	VG+	NM
❑ MG-20099 [M]	Music for Two in Love	1955	7.50	15.00	30.00
❑ MG-20100 [M]	The Voice of Patti Page	1955	7.50	15.00	30.00
❑ MG-20101 [M]	Page IV	1955	7.50	15.00	30.00
❑ MG-20102 [M]	This Is My Song	1955	7.50	15.00	30.00
❑ MG-20226 [M]	Manhattan Tower	1956	7.50	15.00	30.00
❑ MG-20318 [M]	The Waltz Queen	1957	10.00	20.00	40.00

—With one image of Patti Page on cover; "Custom High Fidelity" and Mercury logo at upper right of front cover

❑ MG-20318 [M]	The Waltz Queen	1959	7.50	15.00	30.00

—With two images of Patti Page on cover; Mercury logo at upper left of front cover, "High Custom Fidelity" in white strip along bottom front cover

❑ MG-20387 [M]	Let's Get Away from It All	1957	7.50	15.00	30.00
❑ MG-20388 [M]	I've Heard That Song Before	1957	7.50	15.00	30.00
❑ MG-20398 [M]	Patti Page On Camera	1958	7.50	15.00	30.00
❑ MG-20405 [M]	Indiscretion	1959	7.50	15.00	30.00
❑ MG-20406 [M]	I'll Remember April	1959	7.50	15.00	30.00
❑ MG-20417 [M]	Three Little Words	1960	7.50	15.00	30.00
❑ MG-20495 [M]	Patti Page's Golden Hits	1960	7.50	15.00	30.00
❑ MG-20573 [M]	Just a Closer Walk with Thee	1960	7.50	15.00	30.00
❑ MG-20599 [M]	Patti Page Sings and Stars In "Elmer Gantry"	1960	6.25	12.50	25.00
❑ MG-20615 [M]	Country & Western Golden Hits	1961	5.00	10.00	20.00
❑ MG-20689 [M]	Go On Home	1962	5.00	10.00	20.00
❑ MG-20712 [M]	Golden Hits of the Boys	1962	5.00	10.00	20.00
❑ MG-20758 [M]	Patti Page On Stage	1963	5.00	10.00	20.00
❑ MG-20794 [M]	Patti Page's Golden Hits, Volume 2	1963	5.00	10.00	20.00
❑ MG-20819 [M]	The Singing Rage	1963	5.00	10.00	20.00
❑ MG-20909 [M]	Blue Dream Street	1964	5.00	10.00	20.00
❑ MG-20952 [M]	The Nearness of You	1965	3.75	7.50	15.00
❑ MG-25059 [10]	Songs	1950	10.00	20.00	40.00
❑ MG-25101 [10]	Folksong Favorites	1951	10.00	20.00	40.00
❑ MG-25109 [10]	Christmas	1951	10.00	20.00	40.00
❑ MG-25154 [10]	Tennessee Waltz	1952	10.00	20.00	40.00
❑ MG-25185 [10]	Patti Sings for Romance	1954	10.00	20.00	40.00
❑ MG-25187 [10]	Song Souvenirs	1954	10.00	20.00	40.00
❑ MG-25196 [10]	Just Patti	1954	10.00	20.00	40.00
❑ MG-25197 [10]	Patti's Songs	1954	10.00	20.00	40.00
❑ MG-25205 [10]	And I Thought About You	1954	10.00	20.00	40.00
❑ MG-25210 [10]	So Many Memories	1954	10.00	20.00	40.00
❑ SR-60010 [S]	Let's Get Away from It All	1959	10.00	20.00	40.00
❑ SR-60011 [S]	I've Heard That Song Before	1959	10.00	20.00	40.00
❑ SR-60025 [S]	Patti Page On Camera	1959	10.00	20.00	40.00
❑ SR-60037 [S]	Three Little Words	1960	10.00	20.00	40.00
❑ SR-60049 [S]	The Waltz Queen	1959	10.00	20.00	40.00
❑ SR-60059 [S]	Indiscretion	1959	10.00	20.00	40.00
❑ SR-60081 [S]	I'll Remember April	1959	10.00	20.00	40.00
❑ SR-60233 [S]	Just a Closer Walk with Thee	1960	10.00	20.00	40.00
❑ SR-60260 [S]	Patti Page Sings and Stars In "Elmer Gantry"	1960	7.50	15.00	30.00
❑ SR-60495 [S]	Patti Page's Golden Hits	196?	6.25	12.50	25.00
❑ SR-60615 [S]	Country & Western Golden Hits	1961	6.25	12.50	25.00
❑ SR-60689 [S]	Go On Home	1962	6.25	12.50	25.00
❑ SR-60712 [S]	Golden Hits of the Boys	1962	6.25	12.50	25.00
❑ SR-60758 [S]	Patti Page On Stage	1963	6.25	12.50	25.00
❑ SR-60794 [S]	Patti Page's Golden Hits, Volume 2	1963	6.25	12.50	25.00
❑ SR-60819 [S]	The Singing Rage	1963	6.25	12.50	25.00
❑ SR-60909 [S]	Blue Dream Street	1964	6.25	12.50	25.00
❑ SR-60952 [S]	The Nearness of You	1965	5.00	10.00	20.00
❑ SR-61344	I'd Rather Be Sorry	1971	3.00	6.00	12.00
❑ 822740-1	Christmas with Patti Page	1987	2.50	5.00	10.00

—Reissue

PLANTATION

❑ 548	Aces	1981	2.50	5.00	10.00

WING

❑ MGW 12121 [M]	The Waltz Queen	196?	3.00	6.00	12.00
❑ MGW 12174 [M]	Christmas with Patti Page	196?	5.00	10.00	20.00

—Same contents and order as Mercury 20093

❑ MGW 12250 [M]	Let's Get Away from It All	196?	3.00	6.00	12.00
❑ SRW 16121 [S]	The Waltz Queen	196?	3.75	7.50	15.00
❑ SRW 16250 [S]	Let's Get Away from It All	196?	3.75	7.50	15.00

PAICH, MARTY
BETHLEHEM

❑ BCP-44 [M]	Jazz City Workshop	1956	20.00	40.00	80.00

CADENCE

❑ CLP-3010 [M]	Marty Paich Big Band	1958	12.50	25.00	50.00

GENE NORMAN

❑ GNP-10 [10]	Marty Paich Octet	1955	30.00	60.00	120.00

—Red vinyl

❑ GNP-21 [M]	Marty Paich Octet	1956	20.00	40.00	80.00

INTERLUDE

❑ MO-509 [M]	Revel Without Pause	1959	7.50	15.00	30.00
❑ MO-514 [M]	Like Wow — Jazz 1960	1960	7.50	15.00	30.00
❑ ST-1009 [S]	Revel Without Pause	1959	6.25	12.50	25.00
❑ ST-1014 [S]	Like Wow — Jazz 1960	1960	6.25	12.50	25.00

MODE

❑ LP-105 [M]	Marty Paich Trio	1957	20.00	40.00	80.00
❑ LP-110 [M]	Jazz Band Ball	1957	20.00	40.00	80.00

RCA VICTOR

❑ LPM-2164 [M]	Piano Quartet	1960	5.00	10.00	20.00
❑ LSP-2164 [S]	Piano Quartet	1960	6.25	12.50	25.00
❑ LPM-2259 [M]	Piano Quartet	1960	5.00	10.00	20.00
❑ LSP-2259 [S]	Piano Quartet	1960	6.25	12.50	25.00

TAMPA

❑ TP-23 [M]	Jazz for Relaxation	1957	50.00	100.00	200.00

—Colored vinyl

❑ TP-23 [M]	Jazz for Relaxation	1958	25.00	50.00	100.00
❑ TP-28 [M]	Marty Paich Quintet Featuring Art Pepper	1957	150.00	300.00	600.00

—Colored vinyl

❑ TP-28 [M]	Marty Paich Quintet Featuring Art Pepper	1958	75.00	150.00	300.00

WARNER BROS.

❑ W 1296 [M]	The Broadway Bit	1959	6.25	12.50	25.00
❑ WS 1296 [S]	The Broadway Bit	1959	7.50	15.00	30.00
❑ W 1349 [M]	I Get a Boot Out of You	1959	6.25	12.50	25.00
❑ WS 1349 [S]	I Get a Boot Out of You	1959	7.50	15.00	30.00

PAIGE, JANIS
BALLY

Number	Title (A Side/B Side)	Yr	VG	VG+	NM
❑ BAL-12008 [M]	Let's Fall in Love	1957	10.00	20.00	40.00

PAIR, THE
LIBERTY

❑ LRP-3410 [M]	The Pair Live! At the Ice House	1965	5.00	10.00	20.00
❑ LRP-3440 [M]	The Pair Extraordinaire	1966	3.75	7.50	15.00
❑ LRP-3461 [M]	"In"-Citement	1966	3.75	7.50	15.00
❑ LRP-3504 [M]	It's a Wonderful World	1967	3.75	7.50	15.00
❑ LST-7410 [S]	The Pair Live! At the Ice House	1965	6.25	12.50	25.00
❑ LST-7440 [S]	The Pair Extraordinaire	1966	5.00	10.00	20.00
❑ LST-7461 [S]	"In"-Citement	1966	5.00	10.00	20.00
❑ LST-7504 [S]	It's a Wonderful World	1967	5.00	10.00	20.00

PAISLEYS, THE
AUDIO CITY

❑ 70	Cosmic Mind at Play	1970	50.00	100.00	200.00

PALANCE, JACK
WARNER BROS.

❑ WS 1865	Palance	1970	7.50	15.00	30.00

PALEY, TOM
ELEKTRA

❑ EKL-12 [M]	Folk Songs from the Southern Appalachians	195?	10.00	20.00	40.00

PALMER, BRUCE
VERVE FORECAST

❑ FTS-3086	The Cycle Is Complete	1970	5.00	10.00	20.00

PALMER, EARL
LIBERTY

❑ LRP-3201 [M]	Drumsville	1961	7.50	15.00	30.00
❑ LRP-3227 [M]	Percolator Twist	1962	7.50	15.00	30.00
❑ LST-7201 [S]	Drumsville	1961	10.00	20.00	40.00
❑ LST-7227 [S]	Percolator Twist	1962	10.00	20.00	40.00

PALMER, ROBERT
EMI MANHATTAN

❑ E1-48057	Heavy Nova	1988	2.50	5.00	10.00

ISLAND

❑ PRO-819 [DJ]	Secrets	1979	7.50	15.00	30.00

—Promo-only picture disc

❑ ILPS 9294	Sneakin' Sally Through the Alley	1975	3.00	6.00	12.00
❑ ILPS 9372	Pressure Drop	1976	3.00	6.00	12.00
❑ ILPS 9420	Some People Can Do What They Like	1977	3.00	6.00	12.00
❑ ILPS 9476	Double Fun	1978	3.00	6.00	12.00

—Original copies of the above four albums were NOT distributed by Warner Bros.

❑ ILPS 9544	Secrets	1979	2.50	5.00	10.00
❑ ILPS 9595	Clues	1980	2.50	5.00	10.00
❑ ILPS 9665	Maybe It's Live	1982	2.50	5.00	10.00
❑ 90065	Pride	1983	2.50	5.00	10.00
❑ 90086	Sneakin' Sally Through the Alley	1984	2.00	4.00	8.00
❑ 90087	Pressure Drop	1984	2.00	4.00	8.00
❑ 90089	Secrets	1984	2.00	4.00	8.00
❑ 90471	Riptide	1985	2.50	5.00	10.00
❑ 90493	Clues	1986	2.00	4.00	8.00
❑ 90494	Double Fun	1986	2.00	4.00	8.00
❑ 91318	Addictions Volume I	1989	3.00	6.00	12.00

—Original pressing available only for a short time

❑ 842301-1	Addictions Volume I	1990	2.50	5.00	10.00

WARNER BROS.

❑ WBMS-111 [DJ]	Live in Boston	1979	7.50	15.00	30.00

—Part of "The Warner Bros. Music Show"

PALMER, ROY
RIVERSIDE

❑ RLP-1020 [10]	Roy Palmer's State Street Ramblers	1953	20.00	40.00	80.00

PANDIT, KORLA
FANTASY

❑ 3272 [M]	Music of the Exotic East	1958	6.25	12.50	25.00

—Black vinyl

❑ 3272 [M]	Music of the Exotic East	1958	10.00	20.00	40.00

—Red vinyl

❑ 3284 [M]	Latin Holiday	1959	6.25	12.50	25.00

—Black vinyl

❑ 3284 [M]	Latin Holiday	1959	10.00	20.00	40.00

—Red vinyl

❑ 3286 [M]	Korla Pandit at the Pipe Organ	1959	6.25	12.50	25.00

—Black vinyl

❑ 3286 [M]	Korla Pandit at the Pipe Organ	1959	10.00	20.00	40.00

—Red vinyl

❑ 3288 [M]	Tropical Magic	1959	6.25	12.50	25.00

—Black vinyl

❑ 3288 [M]	Tropical Magic	1959	10.00	20.00	40.00

—Red vinyl

❑ 3293 [M]	Speak to Me of Love	1959	6.25	12.50	25.00

—Black vinyl

❑ 3293 [M]	Speak to Me of Love	1959	10.00	20.00	40.00

—Red vinyl

❑ 3304 [M]	Korla Pandit in Concert	1960	6.25	12.50	25.00

—Black vinyl

❑ 3304 [M]	Korla Pandit in Concert	1960	10.00	20.00	40.00

—Red vinyl

❑ 3320 [M]	Music of Mystery and Romance	1961	6.25	12.50	25.00

—Black vinyl

❑ 3320 [M]	Music of Mystery and Romance	1961	10.00	20.00	40.00

—Red vinyl

❑ 3327 [M]	Love Letters	1961	6.25	12.50	25.00

—Black vinyl

❑ 3327 [M]	Love Letters	1961	10.00	20.00	40.00

—Red vinyl

Number	Title (A Side/B Side)	Yr	VG	VG+	NM
❑ 3329 [M]	Hypnotique	1961	6.25	12.50	25.00
—Black vinyl					
❑ 3329 [M]	Hypnotique	1961	10.00	20.00	40.00
—Red vinyl					
❑ 3334 [M]	Music of Hollywood	1962	6.25	12.50	25.00
—Black vinyl					
❑ 3334 [M]	Music of Hollywood	1962	10.00	20.00	40.00
—Red vinyl					
❑ 3342 [M]	Music for Meditation	1962	6.25	12.50	25.00
—Black vinyl					
❑ 3342 [M]	Music for Meditation	1962	10.00	20.00	40.00
—Red vinyl					
❑ 3347 [M]	Korla Pandit in Paris	1962	6.25	12.50	25.00
❑ 3350 [M]	Christmas with Korla Pandit	1962	6.25	12.00	25.00
—Black vinyl					
❑ 3350 [M]	Christmas with Korla Pandit	1962	10.00	20.00	40.00
—Red vinyl					
❑ 8013 [S]	Music of the Exotic East	1960	7.50	15.00	30.00
—Black vinyl					
❑ 8013 [S]	Music of the Exotic East	1960	12.50	25.00	50.00
—Blue vinyl					
❑ 8018 [S]	Korla Pandit at the Pipe Organ	1960	7.50	15.00	30.00
—Black vinyl					
❑ 8018 [S]	Korla Pandit at the Pipe Organ	1960	12.50	25.00	50.00
—Blue vinyl					
❑ 8027 [S]	Latin Holiday	1960	7.50	15.00	30.00
—Black vinyl					
❑ 8027 [S]	Latin Holiday	1960	12.50	25.00	50.00
—Blue vinyl					
❑ 8034 [S]	Tropical Magic	1960	7.50	15.00	30.00
—Black vinyl					
❑ 8034 [S]	Tropical Magic	1960	12.50	25.00	50.00
—Blue vinyl					
❑ 8039 [S]	Speak to Me of Love	1960	7.50	15.00	30.00
—Black vinyl					
❑ 8039 [S]	Speak to Me of Love	1960	12.50	25.00	50.00
—Blue vinyl					
❑ 8049 [S]	Korla Pandit in Concert	1960	7.50	15.00	30.00
—Black vinyl					
❑ 8049 [S]	Korla Pandit in Concert	1960	12.50	25.00	50.00
—Blue vinyl					
❑ 8061 [S]	Music of Mystery and Romance	1961	7.50	15.00	30.00
—Black vinyl					
❑ 8061 [S]	Music of Mystery and Romance	1961	12.50	25.00	50.00
—Blue vinyl					
❑ 8070 [S]	Love Letters	1961	7.50	15.00	30.00
—Black vinyl					
❑ 8070 [S]	Love Letters	1961	12.50	25.00	50.00
—Blue vinyl					
❑ 8075 [S]	Hypnotique	1961	7.50	15.00	30.00
—Black vinyl					
❑ 8075 [S]	Hypnotique	1961	12.50	25.00	50.00
—Blue vinyl					
❑ 8086 [S]	Music of Hollywood	1962	7.50	15.00	30.00
—Black vinyl					
❑ 8086 [S]	Music of Hollywood	1962	12.50	25.00	50.00
—Blue vinyl					
❑ 8342 [S]	Music for Meditation	1962	7.50	15.00	30.00
—Black vinyl					
❑ 8342 [S]	Music for Meditation	1962	12.50	25.00	50.00
—Blue vinyl					
❑ 8347 [S]	Korla Pandit in Paris	1962	7.50	15.00	30.00
❑ 8350 [S]	Christmas with Korla Pandit	1962	7.50	15.00	30.00
—Black vinyl					
❑ 8350 [S]	Christmas with Korla Pandit	1962	12.50	25.00	50.00
—Blue vinyl					
NATIONAL CUSTOM					
❑ NCR 12-574	Fantastique!	196?	7.50	15.00	30.00
SYMPATHY FOR THE RECORD INDUSTRY					
❑ SFTRI 387	Exotica 2000	1996	3.00	6.00	12.00
VITA					
❑ VLP-14 [10]	Rememb'ring with Korla Pandit	195?	20.00	40.00	80.00

PANICS, THE
CHANCELLOR

Number	Title (A Side/B Side)	Yr	VG	VG+	NM
❑ CHL-5026 [M]	Panicsville	1962	7.50	15.00	30.00
❑ CHLS-5026 [S]	Panicsville	1962	10.00	20.00	40.00
PHILIPS					
❑ PHM 200159 [M]	Discotheque Dance Party	1964	3.75	7.50	15.00
❑ PHS 600159 [S]	Discotheque Dance Party	1964	5.00	10.00	20.00

PANTERA
EASTWEST

Number	Title (A Side/B Side)	Yr	VG	VG+	NM
❑ 61908	The Great Southern Trendkill	1996	3.00	6.00	12.00
❑ 62068 [(2)]	Official Live: 101 Proof	1997	3.75	7.50	15.00
❑ 92302	Far Beyond Driven	1994	3.75	7.50	15.00
ELEKTRA					
❑ 62451	Reinventing the Steel	2000	3.00	6.00	12.00
METAL MAGIC					
❑ MMR 1283	Metal Magic	1983	25.00	50.00	100.00
❑ MMR 1984	Projects in the Jungle	1984	15.00	30.00	60.00
❑ MMR 1985	I Am the Night	1985	15.00	30.00	60.00
❑ MMR 1988	Power Metal	1988	10.00	20.00	40.00

PAPER GARDEN, THE
MUSICOR

Number	Title (A Side/B Side)	Yr	VG	VG+	NM
❑ MS-(# unknown)	The Paper Garden	1968	10.00	20.00	40.00

PARAGONS, THE & THE HARPTONES
MUSICTONE

Number	Title (A Side/B Side)	Yr	VG	VG+	NM
❑ M-8001 [M]	The Paragons vs. the Harptones	1964	10.00	20.00	40.00

PARAGONS, THE & THE JESTERS
JOSIE

Number	Title (A Side/B Side)	Yr	VG	VG+	NM
❑ 4008 [M]	The Paragons Meet the Jesters	1962	50.00	100.00	200.00
JUBILEE					
❑ JLP-1098 [M]	The Paragons Meet the Jesters	1959	75.00	150.00	300.00
—Blue label, black vinyl					
❑ JLP-1098 [M]	The Paragons Meet the Jesters	1959	750.00	1125.	1500.
—Multi-color splash vinyl					
❑ JLP-1098 [M]	The Paragons Meet the Jesters	196?	15.00	30.00	60.00
—Black label with multi-color logo					
❑ JLP-1098 [M]	The Paragons Meet the Jesters	196?	37.50	75.00	150.00
—Flat black label					
WINLEY					
❑ LP-6003 [M]	War! The Jesters vs. the Paragons	195?	125.00	250.00	500.00

PARENTI, TONY
JAZZOLOGY

Number	Title (A Side/B Side)	Yr	VG	VG+	NM
❑ JCE-1 [10]	Tony Parenti and His New Orleanians	1962	5.00	10.00	20.00
RIVERSIDE					
❑ RLP 12-205 [M]	Ragtime	195?	7.50	15.00	30.00
—Blue label, microphone logo at top					
❑ RLP 12-205 [M]	Ragtime	1956	15.00	30.00	60.00
—White label, blue print					

PARENTI, TONY/THE DIXIELAND RHYTHM KINGS
JAZZTONE

Number	Title (A Side/B Side)	Yr	VG	VG+	NM
❑ J-1273 [M]	Two Beat Bash	195?	10.00	20.00	40.00

PARHAM, TINY
"X"

Number	Title (A Side/B Side)	Yr	VG	VG+	NM
❑ LVA-3039 [10]	Tiny Parham's South Side Jazz	1955	15.00	30.00	60.00

PARIS, FREDDIE
RCA VICTOR

Number	Title (A Side/B Side)	Yr	VG	VG+	NM
❑ LSP-4064	Lovin' Mood	1968	5.00	10.00	20.00

PARIS, JACKIE
ABC IMPULSE!

Number	Title (A Side/B Side)	Yr	VG	VG+	NM
❑ AS-17 [S]	The Song Is Paris	1968	5.00	10.00	20.00
BRUNSWICK					
❑ BL-54019 [M]	Skylark	1957	25.00	50.00	100.00
CORAL					
❑ CRL-56118 [10]	That Paris Mood	195?	20.00	40.00	80.00
EASTWEST					
❑ 4002 [M]	The Jackie Paris Sound	1958	20.00	40.00	80.00
EMARCY					
❑ MG-36095 [M]	Songs by Jackie Paris	1956	25.00	50.00	100.00
IMPULSE!					
❑ A-17 [M]	The Song Is Paris	1962	7.50	15.00	30.00
❑ AS-17 [S]	The Song Is Paris	1962	10.00	20.00	40.00
TIME					
❑ ST-70009 [S]	Jackie Paris Sings the Lyrics of Ira Gershwin	1959	12.50	25.00	50.00
❑ T-70009 [M]	Jackie Paris Sings the Lyrics of Ira Gershwin	1959	10.00	20.00	40.00
WING					
❑ MGW-60004 [M]	Songs by Jackie Paris	1956	20.00	40.00	80.00

PARIS, PRISCILLA
Also see THE PARIS SISTERS.
HAPPY TIGER

Number	Title (A Side/B Side)	Yr	VG	VG+	NM
❑ HT-1002	Priscilla Loves Billy	1968	10.00	20.00	40.00
YORK					
❑ 4005 [M]	Priscilla Sings Herself	1967	7.50	15.00	30.00
❑ 4005-S [S]	Priscilla Sings Herself	1967	10.00	20.00	40.00

PARIS CONSERVATOIRE ORCHESTRE
(ANATOLE FISTOULARI, CONDUCTOR)
RCA VICTOR RED SEAL

Number	Title (A Side/B Side)	Yr	VG	VG+	NM
❑ LSC-2400 [S]	Ballet Music from the Opera	1960	100.00	200.00	400.00
—Original with "shaded dog" label					
❑ LSC-2400 [S]	Ballet Music from the Opera	199?	6.25	12.50	25.00
—Classic Records reissue					

PARIS CONSERVATOIRE ORCHESTRE
(JEAN MARTINON, CONDUCTOR)
RCA VICTOR RED SEAL

Number	Title (A Side/B Side)	Yr	VG	VG+	NM
❑ LSC-2272 [S]	Prokofiev: Symphony No. 5	1959	20.00	40.00	80.00
—Original with "shaded dog" label					
❑ LSC-2288 [S]	Prokofiev: Symphony No. 7	1959	20.00	40.00	80.00
—Original with "shaded dog" label					
❑ LSC-2288 [S]	Prokofiev: Symphony No. 7	199?	6.25	12.50	25.00
—Classic Records reissue					

PARIS CONSERVATOIRE ORCHESTRE
(PIERRE MONTEUX, CONDUCTOR)
RCA VICTOR RED SEAL

Number	Title (A Side/B Side)	Yr	VG	VG+	NM
❑ LSC-2085 [S]	Stravinsky: The Rite of Spring	1958	12.50	25.00	50.00
—Original with "shaded dog" label					
❑ LSC-2085 [S]	Stravinsky: The Rite of Spring	1964	10.00	20.00	40.00
—Second issue with "white dog" label					

PARIS CONSERVATOIRE ORCHESTRE
(JEAN-PAUL MOREL, CONDUCTOR)
RCA VICTOR RED SEAL

Number	Title (A Side/B Side)	Yr	VG	VG+	NM
❑ LSC-6094 [(2)S]	Albaniz: Iberia; Ravel: Rapsodie Espagnole	196?	100.00	200.00	400.00
—Original with "shaded dog" label					

PARIS CONSERVATOIRE ORCHESTRE
(HUGH RIGNOLD, CONDUCTOR)
RCA VICTOR RED SEAL

Number	Title (A Side/B Side)	Yr	VG	VG+	NM
❑ LSC-2485 [S]	Delibes: Sylvia and Coppelia Ballet Suites	1961	20.00	40.00	80.00
—Original with "shaded dog" label					

Number	Title (A Side/B Side)	Yr	VG	VG+	NM

PARIS CONSERVATOIRE ORCHESTRE (ALBERT WOLFF, CONDUCTOR)
RCA VICTOR RED SEAL

Number	Title (A Side/B Side)	Yr	VG	VG+	NM
❏ LSC-2301 [S]	Adam: Giselle	1959	12.50	25.00	50.00

—Original with "shaded dog" label

PARIS PILOT
HIP

| ❏ 7004 | Paris Pilot | 1970 | 6.25 | 12.50 | 25.00 |

PARIS SISTERS, THE
Also see PRISCILLA PARIS.
REPRISE

| ❏ R-6259 [M] | Everything Under the Sun | 1967 | 10.00 | 20.00 | 40.00 |
| ❏ RS-6359 [S] | Everything Under the Sun | 1967 | 15.00 | 30.00 | 60.00 |

SIDEWALK

| ❏ DT 5906 [R] | Golden Hits of the Paris Sisters | 1967 | 7.50 | 15.00 | 30.00 |
| ❏ T 5906 [M] | Golden Hits of the Paris Sisters | 1967 | 12.50 | 25.00 | 50.00 |

UNIFILMS

| ❏ 505 [M] | The Paris Sisters Sing Songs from Glass House | 1966 | 10.00 | 20.00 | 40.00 |
| ❏ S-505 [S] | The Paris Sisters Sing Songs from Glass House | 1966 | 12.50 | 25.00 | 50.00 |

PARISH HALL
FANTASY

| ❏ 8398 | Parish Hall | 1969 | 5.00 | 10.00 | 20.00 |

PARKER, BILLIE JEAN
RCA VICTOR

| ❏ LPM-3967 [M] | The Truth About Bonnie and Clyde | 1968 | 10.00 | 20.00 | 40.00 |
| ❏ LSP-3967 [S] | The Truth About Bonnie and Clyde | 1968 | 3.75 | 7.50 | 15.00 |

PARKER, BILLY
STRATA-EAST

| ❏ SES-19754 | Freedom of Speech | 1975 | 6.25 | 12.50 | 25.00 |

PARKER, CHARLIE
AMERICAN RECORDING SOCIETY

| ❏ G-441 [M] | Now's the Time | 1957 | 12.50 | 25.00 | 50.00 |

BARONET

| ❏ B-105 [M] | A Handful of Modern Jazz | 1962 | 5.00 | 10.00 | 20.00 |
| ❏ B-107 [M] | The Early Bird | 1962 | 5.00 | 10.00 | 20.00 |

BIRDLAND

| ❏ 425 [10] | A Night at Carnegie Hall | 1956 | 75.00 | 150.00 | 300.00 |

BLUE RIBBON

| ❏ 8011 [M] | The Early Bird | 1962 | 5.00 | 10.00 | 20.00 |

CHARLIE PARKER

❏ PLP-401 [M]	Bird Is Free	1961	10.00	20.00	40.00
❏ PLP-404 [M]	The Happy Bird	1961	10.00	20.00	40.00
❏ PLP-406 [M]	Charlie Parker	1961	10.00	20.00	40.00
❏ PLP-407 [M]	Bird Symbols	1961	10.00	20.00	40.00
❏ PLP-408 [M]	Once There Was Bird	1961	10.00	20.00	40.00
❏ CP-2-502 [(2)M]	Live at Rockland Palace, September 26, 1952	1961	12.50	25.00	50.00
❏ CP-513 [M]	Charlie Parker Plus Strings	196?	10.00	20.00	40.00
❏ PLP-701 [(3)]	Historical Masterpieces	196?	15.00	30.00	60.00

CLEF

| ❏ MGC-157 [10] | Charlie Parker | 1954 | 100.00 | 200.00 | 400.00 |
| ❏ MGC-501 [10] | Charlie Parker with Strings | 1954 | 100.00 | 200.00 | 400.00 |

—Reissue of Mercury 501

| ❏ MGC-509 [10] | Charlie Parker with Strings, No. 2 | 1954 | 100.00 | 200.00 | 400.00 |

—Reissue of Mercury 509

| ❏ MGC-512 [10] | Bird and Diz | 1954 | 100.00 | 200.00 | 400.00 |

—Reissue of Mercury 512

| ❏ MGC-513 [10] | South of the Border | 1954 | 100.00 | 200.00 | 400.00 |

—Reissue of Mercury 513

❏ MGC-609 [M]	Charlie Parker Big Band	1954	100.00	200.00	400.00
❏ MGC-646 [M]	The Magnificent Charlie Parker	1955	100.00	200.00	400.00
❏ MGC-675 [M]	Charlie Parker with Strings	1955	100.00	200.00	400.00
❏ MGC-725 [M]	Night and Day	1956	30.00	60.00	120.00

CONCERT HALL JAZZ

| ❏ 1004 [10] | The Fabulous Bird | 1955 | 15.00 | 30.00 | 60.00 |
| ❏ 1017 [10] | The Art of Charlie Parker, Vol. 2 | 1955 | 15.00 | 30.00 | 60.00 |

CONTINENTAL

| ❏ 16004 [M] | Bird Lives | 1962 | 10.00 | 20.00 | 40.00 |

DEBUT

| ❏ DEB-611 [M] | Bird on 52nd Street | 196? | 12.50 | 25.00 | 50.00 |

DIAL

| ❏ LP-1 [M] | The Bird Blows the Blues | 1949 | 1000. | 2000. | 4000. |

—Mail-order offer

❏ LP-201 [10]	Charlie Parker Quintet	1949	200.00	400.00	800.00
❏ LP-202 [10]	Charlie Parker Quintet	1949	200.00	400.00	800.00
❏ LP-203 [10]	Charlie Parker	1949	200.00	400.00	800.00
❏ LP-207 [10]	Charlie Parker Sextet	1949	200.00	400.00	800.00
❏ LP-901 [M]	The Bird Blows the Blues	1950	150.00	300.00	600.00
❏ LP-904 [M]	Alternate Masters	1951	150.00	300.00	600.00
❏ LP-905 [M]	Alternate Masters	1951	150.00	300.00	600.00

ESP-DISK'

| ❏ ESP-BIRD-2 | Broadcast Performances 1948-1949, Vol. 2 | 1973 | 5.00 | 10.00 | 20.00 |

FANTASY

| ❏ 6011 [M] | Bird on 52nd St. | 1964 | 7.50 | 15.00 | 30.00 |
| ❏ 6012 [M] | Bird at St. Nick's | 1964 | 7.50 | 15.00 | 30.00 |

JAZZ WORKSHOP

| ❏ JWS-500 [M] | Bird at St. Nick's | 1958 | 30.00 | 60.00 | 120.00 |
| ❏ JWS-501 [M] | Bird on 52nd Street | 1958 | 30.00 | 60.00 | 120.00 |

JAZZTONE

❏ J-(# unk) [M]	The Art of Charlie Parker, Vol. 2	1955	12.50	25.00	50.00
❏ J-1204 [M]	Giants of Modern Jazz	1955	12.50	25.00	50.00
❏ J-1214 [M]	The Fabulous Bird	1955	12.50	25.00	50.00
❏ J-1240 [M]	The Saxes of Stan Getz and Charlie Parker	1957	12.50	25.00	50.00

LES JAZZ COOL

❏ 101 [M]	Les Jazz Cool, Volume 1	1960	12.50	25.00	50.00
❏ 102 [M]	Les Jazz Cool, Volume 2	1960	12.50	25.00	50.00
❏ 103 [M]	Les Jazz Cool, Volume 3	1960	12.50	25.00	50.00

MERCURY

| ❏ MGC-101 [10] | Charlie Parker with Strings | 1950 | 125.00 | 250.00 | 500.00 |

—Reissue of 35010

| ❏ MGC-109 [10] | Charlie Parker with Strings, Volume 2 | 1950 | 125.00 | 250.00 | 500.00 |
| ❏ MGC-501 [10] | Charlie Parker with Strings | 1951 | 125.00 | 250.00 | 500.00 |

—Reissue of 101 with new number

| ❏ MGC-509 [10] | Charlie Parker with Strings, Volume 2 | 1952 | 125.00 | 250.00 | 500.00 |

—Reissue of 109 with new number

❏ MGC-512 [10]	Bird and Diz	1952	125.00	250.00	500.00
❏ MGC-513 [10]	South of the Border	1952	125.00	250.00	500.00
❏ MG-35010 [10]	Charlie Parker with Strings	1950	150.00	300.00	600.00

MOSAIC

| ❏ 129 [(10)] | The Complete Dean Benedetti Recordings of Charlie Parker | 199? | 25.00 | 50.00 | 100.00 |

ROOST

| ❏ LP-2210 [M] | All Star Sextet | 1958 | 30.00 | 60.00 | 120.00 |
| ❏ LP-2257 [M] | The World of Charlie Parker | 1963 | 10.00 | 20.00 | 40.00 |

SAVOY

❏ MG-9000 [10]	Charlie Parker	1950	125.00	250.00	500.00
❏ MG-9001 [10]	Charlie Parker, Volume 2	1951	125.00	250.00	500.00
❏ MG-9010 [10]	Charlie Parker, Volume 3	1952	125.00	250.00	500.00
❏ MG-9011 [10]	Charlie Parker, Volume 4	1952	125.00	250.00	500.00
❏ MG-12000 [M]	Charlie Parker Memorial	1955	25.00	50.00	100.00
❏ MG-12001 [M]	The Immortal Charlie Parker	1955	25.00	50.00	100.00
❏ MG-12009 [M]	Charlie Parker Memorial, Volume 2	1955	25.00	50.00	100.00
❏ MG-12014 [M]	The Genius of Charlie Parker	1955	25.00	50.00	100.00
❏ MG-12079 [M]	The Charlie Parker Story	1956	25.00	50.00	100.00
❏ MG-12138 [M]	Bird's Night	1960	10.00	20.00	40.00
❏ MG-12152 [M]	An Evening at Home with the Bird	196?	10.00	20.00	40.00
❏ MG-12179 [M]	The "Bird" Returns	196?	7.50	15.00	30.00
❏ MG-12186 [M]	Newly Discovered Sides by the Immortal Charlie Parker	1966	7.50	15.00	30.00

SAVOY JAZZ

| ❏ SJL-5500 [(5)] | The Complete Savoy Studio Sessions | 197? | 7.50 | 15.00 | 30.00 |

VERVE

❏ VSP-23 [M]	Bird Wings	1966	5.00	10.00	20.00
❏ MGV-8000 [M]	The Charlie Parker Story, Volume 1	1957	20.00	40.00	80.00
❏ V-8000 [M]	The Charlie Parker Story, Volume 1	1961	6.25	12.50	25.00
❏ MGV-8001 [M]	The Charlie Parker Story, Volume 2	1957	20.00	40.00	80.00
❏ V-8001 [M]	The Charlie Parker Story, Volume 2	1961	6.25	12.50	25.00
❏ MGV-8002 [M]	The Charlie Parker Story, Volume 3	1957	20.00	40.00	80.00
❏ V-8002 [M]	The Charlie Parker Story, Volume 3	1961	6.25	12.50	25.00
❏ MGV-8003 [M]	Night and Day (The Genius of Charlie Parker #1)	1957	20.00	40.00	80.00
❏ V-8003 [M]	Night and Day (The Genius of Charlie Parker #1)	1961	6.25	12.50	25.00
❏ MGV-8004 [M]	April in Paris (The Genius of Charlie Parker #2)	1957	20.00	40.00	80.00
❏ V-8004 [M]	April in Paris (The Genius of Charlie Parker #2)	1961	6.25	12.50	25.00
❏ MGV-8005 [M]	Now's the Time (The Genius of Charlie Parker #3)	1957	20.00	40.00	80.00
❏ V-8005 [M]	Now's the Time (The Genius of Charlie Parker #3)	1961	6.25	12.50	25.00
❏ MGV-8006 [M]	Bird and Diz (The Genius of Charlie Parker #4)	1957	20.00	40.00	80.00
❏ V-8006 [M]	Bird and Diz (The Genius of Charlie Parker #4)	1961	6.25	12.50	25.00
❏ MGV-8007 [M]	Charlie Parker Plays Cole Porter (The Genius of Charlie Parker #5)	1957	20.00	40.00	80.00
❏ V-8007 [M]	Charlie Parker Plays Cole Porter (The Genius of Charlie Parker #5)	1961	6.25	12.50	25.00
❏ MGV-8008 [M]	Fiesta (The Genius of Charlie Parker #6)	1957	20.00	40.00	80.00
❏ V-8008 [M]	Fiesta (The Genius of Charlie Parker #6)	1961	6.25	12.50	25.00
❏ MGV-8009 [M]	Jazz Perennial (The Genius of Charlie Parker #7)	1957	20.00	40.00	80.00
❏ V-8009 [M]	Jazz Perennial (The Genius of Charlie Parker #7)	1961	6.25	12.50	25.00
❏ MGV-8010 [M]	Swedish Schnapps (The Genius of Charlie Parker #8)	1957	20.00	40.00	80.00
❏ V-8010 [M]	Swedish Schnapps (The Genius of Charlie Parker #8)	1961	6.25	12.50	25.00
❏ MGV-8100-3 [(3)M]	The Charlie Parker Story	1957	37.50	75.00	150.00

—Combines 8000, 8001 and 8002 in a box set

| ❏ V-8100-3 [(3)M] | The Charlie Parker Story | 1961 | 15.00 | 30.00 | 60.00 |

—Combines 8000, 8001 and 8002 in a box set

| ❏ V-8409 [M] | The Essential Charlie Parker | 1961 | 6.25 | 12.50 | 25.00 |

VOGUE

| ❏ LAE-12002 [M] | Memorial Album | 1955 | 37.50 | 75.00 | 150.00 |

WARNER BROS.

| ❏ 6BS 3159 [(6)] | The Complete Dial Recordings | 1977 | 20.00 | 40.00 | 80.00 |

—Limited edition of 4,000 box sets

| ❏ 2WB 3198 [(2)] | The Very Best of Bird | 1977 | 5.00 | 10.00 | 20.00 |

PARKER, CHARLIE/DIZZY GILLESPIE/BUD POWELL/MAX ROACH
SAVOY

| ❏ MG-9034 [10] | Bird, Diz, Bud, Max | 1953 | 150.00 | 300.00 | 600.00 |

PARKER, CHARLIE; DIZZY GILLESPIE; RED NORVO
DIAL

| ❏ LP-903 [M] | Fabulous Jam Session | 1951 | 150.00 | 300.00 | 600.00 |

PARKER, FESS
COLUMBIA

| ❏ CL 666 [M] | Walt Disney's Davy Crockett, King of the Wild Frontier | 1955 | 25.00 | 50.00 | 100.00 |

DISNEYLAND

| ❏ WDL-1007 [M] | Yarns and Songs of the West | 1959 | 7.50 | 15.00 | 30.00 |

—Reissue of 3006

| ❏ DQ-1269 [M] | Pecos Bill and Other Stories in Song | 1965 | 7.50 | 15.00 | 30.00 |

Number	Title (A Side/B Side)	Yr	VG	VG+	NM
❑ DQ-1315 [M]	Three Adventures of Davy Crockett	1968	6.25	12.50	25.00
—Another reissue, this time of 1926					
❑ DQ-1336	Cowboy and Indian Songs	1969	7.50	15.00	30.00
❑ ST-1926 [M]	Three Adventures of Davy Crockett	1963	7.50	15.00	30.00
—Reissue of 3602					
❑ WDL-3006 [M]	Yarns and Songs	1957	10.00	20.00	40.00
❑ WDL-3041 [M]	Westward Ho the Wagons	1959	7.50	15.00	30.00
—Reissue of 4008					
❑ WDA-3602 [M]	Three Adventures of Davy Crockett	1958	12.50	25.00	50.00
—Reissue of Columbia 666					
❑ WDL-4006 [M]	Westward Ho the Wagons	1956	20.00	40.00	80.00
RCA VICTOR					
❑ LPM-2973 [M]	Fess Parker Sings About Daniel Boone, Davy Crockett and Abe Lincoln	1964	6.25	12.50	25.00
❑ LSP-2973 [S]	Fess Parker Sings About Daniel Boone, Davy Crockett and Abe Lincoln	1964	7.50	15.00	30.00

PARKER, GRAHAM
ARISTA

Number	Title (A Side/B Side)	Yr	VG	VG+	NM
❑ SP-63 [DJ]	Live Sparks	1979	7.50	15.00	30.00
❑ AL 4223	Squeezing Out Sparks	1979	3.00	6.00	12.00
❑ AL8-8023	The Real Macaw	1983	2.50	5.00	10.00
❑ AL6-8352	The Real Macaw	1985	2.00	4.00	8.00
—Budget-line reissue					
❑ AL6-8356	The Up Escalator	1985	2.00	4.00	8.00
—Budget-line reissue					
❑ AL6-8363	Squeezing Out Sparks	1985	2.00	4.00	8.00
—Budget-line reissue					
❑ AL6-8374	Another Grey Area	1985	2.00	4.00	8.00
—Budget-line reissue					
❑ AL6-8391	Look Back in Anger	1985	2.50	5.00	10.00
❑ AL 9517	The Up Escalator	1980	2.50	5.00	10.00
❑ AL 9589	Another Grey Area	1982	2.50	5.00	10.00
ELEKTRA					
❑ 60388	Steady Nerves	1985	2.50	5.00	10.00
MERCURY					
❑ SRM-2-100 [(2)]	The Parkerilla	1978	4.50	9.00	18.00
—Originals have gatefold sleeves					
❑ SRM-1-1095	Howlin' Wind	1976	3.75	7.50	15.00
❑ SRM-1-1117	Heat Treatment	1976	3.75	7.50	15.00
❑ SRM-1-3706	Stick to Me	1977	3.75	7.50	15.00
❑ 824808-1	Stick to Me	1985	3.00	6.00	12.00
—Reissue with new number					
❑ 826097-1	Pourin' It All Out: The Mercury Years	1985	3.00	6.00	12.00
RCA					
❑ 8316-1-R	The Mona Lisa's Sister	1988	2.50	5.00	10.00
❑ 9876-1-R	Human Soul	1989	2.50	5.00	10.00

PARKER, JACY
VERVE

Number	Title (A Side/B Side)	Yr	VG	VG+	NM
❑ V-8424 [M]	Spotlight On Jacy Parker	1962	10.00	20.00	40.00
❑ V6-8424 [S]	Spotlight On Jacy Parker	1962	12.50	25.00	50.00

PARKER, JUNIOR
ABC

Number	Title (A Side/B Side)	Yr	VG	VG+	NM
❑ AC-30010	The ABC Collection	1976	3.75	7.50	15.00
ABC DUKE					
❑ DLP-76	Driving Wheel	1974	3.75	7.50	15.00
❑ DLP-83	The Best of Junior Parker	1974	3.75	7.50	15.00
BLUE ROCK					
❑ SRB-64004	Honey-Drippin' Blues	1969	3.75	7.50	15.00
BLUESWAY					
❑ BLS-6066	Sometime Tomorrow	1973	3.75	7.50	15.00
CAPITOL					
❑ ST-564	Outside Man	1970	3.75	7.50	15.00
DUKE					
❑ DLP-76 [M]	Driving Wheel	196?	25.00	50.00	100.00
—With Wagon Wheel on front cover					
❑ DLP-76 [M]	Driving Wheel	1962	37.50	75.00	150.00
—With Cadillac on front cover					
❑ DLP-83 [M]	The Best of Junior Parker	1967	12.50	25.00	50.00
❑ DLPS-83 [P]	The Best of Junior Parker	1967	10.00	20.00	40.00
GROOVE MERCHANT					
❑ 513	Love Ain't Nothin'	1974	3.75	7.50	15.00
MCA					
❑ 27046	The Best of Junior Parker	1980	2.50	5.00	10.00
MERCURY					
❑ MG-21101 [M]	Like It Is	1967	7.50	15.00	30.00
❑ SR-61101 [S]	Like It Is	1967	6.25	12.50	25.00
MINIT					
❑ 24024	Blues Man	1969	6.25	12.50	25.00
UNITED ARTISTS					
❑ UAS-6823	I Tell Stories Sad and True	1971	3.75	7.50	15.00

PARKER, JUNIOR, AND BOBBY BLAND
ABC DUKE

Number	Title (A Side/B Side)	Yr	VG	VG+	NM
❑ DLP-72	Blues Consolidated	1974	3.75	7.50	15.00
DUKE					
❑ DLP-72 [M]	Blues Consolidated	1961	37.50	75.00	150.00

PARKER, KNOCKY
AUDIOPHILE

Number	Title (A Side/B Side)	Yr	VG	VG+	NM
❑ AP-28 [M]	Boogie Woogie Maxine	1956	10.00	20.00	40.00
❑ AP-102/5 [(4)]	The Complete Piano Works of Jelly Roll Morton	196?	12.50	25.00	50.00
—In box with booklet; it's unknown whether the volumes also were issued individually					
PROGRESSIVE					
❑ PLP-1 [10]	New Orleans Stomps	1954	12.50	25.00	50.00

PARKER, LEO
BLUE NOTE

Number	Title (A Side/B Side)	Yr	VG	VG+	NM
❑ BLP-4087 [M]	Let Me Tell You 'Bout It	1961	15.00	30.00	60.00
—With 61st St. address on label					
❑ BLP-4087 [M]	Let Me Tell You 'Bout It	1963	5.00	10.00	20.00
—With "New York, USA" address on label					
❑ BST-84087 [S]	Let Me Tell You 'Bout It	1961	20.00	40.00	80.00
—With 61st St. address on label					
❑ BST-84087 [S]	Let Me Tell You 'Bout It	1963	6.25	12.50	25.00
—With "New York, USA" address on label					
SAVOY					
❑ MG-9009 [10]	Leo Parker	1952	62.50	125.00	250.00
❑ MG-9018 [10]	New Trends in Modern Music	1952	62.50	125.00	250.00

PARKER, MAYNARD
PRESTIGE

Number	Title (A Side/B Side)	Yr	VG	VG+	NM
❑ 10054	Midnight Rider	1973	5.00	10.00	20.00

PARKER, ROBERT
NOLA

Number	Title (A Side/B Side)	Yr	VG	VG+	NM
❑ LP-1001 [M]	Barefootin'	1966	7.50	15.00	30.00

PARKER FAMILY, THE
AUDIO LAB

Number	Title (A Side/B Side)	Yr	VG	VG+	NM
❑ AL-1548 [M]	Songs for Salvation	196?	37.50	75.00	150.00
❑ AL-1574 [M]	Songs for Salvation, Vol. 2	196?	37.50	75.00	150.00
KING					
❑ 932 [M]	Just a Real Nice Family	1965	10.00	20.00	40.00

PARKINS, LEROY
BETHLEHEM

Number	Title (A Side/B Side)	Yr	VG	VG+	NM
❑ BCP-6047 [M]	LeRoy Parkins and His Yazoo River Band	1960	7.50	15.00	30.00
❑ SBCP-6047 [S]	LeRoy Parkins and His Yazoo River Band	1960	10.00	20.00	40.00

PARKS, ANDY
CAPITOL

Number	Title (A Side/B Side)	Yr	VG	VG+	NM
❑ ST 2799 [S]	Sex, School...And Like Other Pressures	1967	5.00	10.00	20.00
❑ T 2799 [M]	Sex, School...And Like Other Pressures	1967	5.00	10.00	20.00

PARKS, VAN DYKE
WARNER BROS.

Number	Title (A Side/B Side)	Yr	VG	VG+	NM
❑ WS 1727	Song Cycle	1968	3.75	7.50	15.00
—Green label with "W7" box logo					
❑ WS 1727	Song Cycle	1968	6.25	12.50	25.00
—Gold label					
❑ WS 1727	Song Cycle	1970	3.00	6.00	12.00
—Green label with "WB" shield logo					
❑ BS 2589	Discover America	1972	3.00	6.00	12.00
❑ BS 2878	Clang of the Yankee Reaper	1975	3.00	6.00	12.00
❑ 23829	Jump!	1984	3.00	6.00	12.00
❑ 25968	Tokyo Rose	1989	3.00	6.00	12.00

PARLAN, HORACE
BLUE NOTE

Number	Title (A Side/B Side)	Yr	VG	VG+	NM
❑ BLP-4028 [M]	Movin' and Groovin'	1960	20.00	40.00	80.00
—Regular version, W. 63rd St. address on label					
❑ BLP-4028 [M]	Movin' and Groovin'	1960	25.00	50.00	100.00
—"Deep groove" version (deep indentation under label on both sides)					
❑ BLP-4028 [M]	Movin' and Groovin'	1963	5.00	10.00	20.00
—With "New York, USA" address on label					
❑ BLP-4037 [M]	Us Three	1960	20.00	40.00	80.00
—Regular version, W. 63rd St. address on label					
❑ BLP-4037 [M]	Us Three	1960	25.00	50.00	100.00
—"Deep groove" version (deep indentation under label on both sides)					
❑ BLP-4037 [M]	Us Three	1963	5.00	10.00	20.00
—With "New York, USA" address on label					
❑ BLP-4043 [M]	Speakin' My Piece	1960	20.00	40.00	80.00
—Regular version, W. 63rd St. address on label					
❑ BLP-4043 [M]	Speakin' My Piece	1960	25.00	50.00	100.00
—"Deep groove" version (deep indentation under label on both sides)					
❑ BLP-4043 [M]	Speakin' My Piece	1963	5.00	10.00	20.00
—With "New York, USA" address on label					
❑ BLP-4062 [M]	Headin' South	1961	15.00	30.00	60.00
—With W. 63rd St. address on label					
❑ BLP-4062 [M]	Headin' South	1963	5.00	10.00	20.00
—With "New York, USA" address on label					
❑ BLP-4074 [M]	On the Spur of the Moment	1961	15.00	30.00	60.00
—With 61st St. address on label					
❑ BLP-4074 [M]	On the Spur of the Moment	1961	37.50	75.00	150.00
—With W. 63rd St. address on label					
❑ BLP-4074 [M]	On the Spur of the Moment	1963	5.00	10.00	20.00
—With "New York, USA" address on label					
❑ BST-4074	On the Spur of the Moment	199?	6.25	12.50	25.00
—Classic Records reissue on audiophile vinyl					
❑ BLP-4082 [M]	Up and Down	1961	15.00	30.00	60.00
—With 61st St. address on label					
❑ BLP-4082 [M]	Up and Down	1963	5.00	10.00	20.00
—With "New York, USA" address on label					
❑ BST-84028 [S]	Movin' and Groovin'	1960	20.00	40.00	80.00
—With W. 63rd St. address on label					
❑ BST-84028 [S]	Movin' and Groovin'	1963	6.25	12.50	25.00
—With "New York, USA" address on label					
❑ BST-84037 [S]	Us Three	1960	20.00	40.00	80.00
—With W. 63rd St. address on label					
❑ BST-84037 [S]	Us Three	1963	6.25	12.50	25.00
—With "New York, USA" address on label					
❑ BST-84043 [S]	Speakin' My Piece	1960	20.00	40.00	80.00
—With W. 63rd St. address on label					
❑ BST-84043 [S]	Speakin' My Piece	1963	6.25	12.50	25.00
—With "New York, USA" address on label					
❑ BST-84062 [S]	Headin' South	1961	17.50	35.00	70.00
—With W. 63rd St. address on label					
❑ BST-84062 [S]	Headin' South	1963	6.25	12.50	25.00
—With "New York, USA" address on label					

Number	Title (A Side/B Side)	Yr	VG	VG+	NM
❑ BST-84074 [S]	On the Spur of the Moment	1961	17.50	35.00	70.00
—With 61st St. address on label					
❑ BST-84074 [S]	On the Spur of the Moment	1961	50.00	100.00	200.00
—With W. 63rd St. address on label					
❑ BST-84074 [S]	On the Spur of the Moment	1963	6.25	12.50	25.00
—With "New York, USA" address on label					
❑ BST-84082 [S]	Up and Down	1961	17.50	35.00	70.00
—With 61st St. address on label					
❑ BST-84082 [S]	Up and Down	1963	6.25	12.50	25.00
—With "New York, USA" address on label					

MOSAIC

Number	Title (A Side/B Side)	Yr	VG	VG+	NM
❑ MQ8-197 [(8)]	The Complete Horace Parlan Blue Note Sessions	2000	37.50	75.00	150.00

PARLET
CASABLANCA

Number	Title (A Side/B Side)	Yr	VG	VG+	NM
❑ NBLP 7094	Pleasure Principle	1978	5.00	10.00	20.00
❑ NBLP 7146	Invasion of the Booty Snatchers	1979	5.00	10.00	20.00

PARLIAMENT
Also see FUNKADELIC.
CASABLANCA

Number	Title (A Side/B Side)	Yr	VG	VG+	NM
❑ NBLP 7002	Up for the Down Stroke	1974	10.00	20.00	40.00
❑ NBLP 7014	Chocolate City	1975	10.00	20.00	40.00
❑ NBLP 7022	Mothership Connection	1976	7.50	15.00	30.00
❑ NBLP 7034	The Clones of Dr. Funkenstein	1976	7.50	15.00	30.00
❑ NBLP 7053 [(2)]	Parliament Live/P. Funk Earth Tour	1977	10.00	20.00	40.00
❑ NBLP 7084	Funkentelechy vs. the Placebo Syndrome	1977	7.50	15.00	30.00
❑ NBLP 7125	Motor-Booty Affair	1978	7.50	15.00	30.00
❑ NBPIX 7125 [PD]	Motor-Booty Affair	1978	10.00	20.00	40.00
❑ NBLP 7195	Gloryhallastoopid (Or Pin the Tale on the Funky)	1979	7.50	15.00	30.00
❑ NBLP 7249	Trombipulation	1980	7.50	15.00	30.00
❑ NBLP 9003	Up for the Down Stroke	1974	12.50	25.00	50.00
—Original pressing, distributed by Warner Bros.					
❑ 822637-1	Greatest Hits	1984	3.75	7.50	15.00
❑ 824501-1	Funkentelechy vs. the Placebo Syndrome	1985	3.75	7.50	15.00
❑ 824502-1	Mothership Connection	1985	3.75	7.50	15.00

INVICTUS

Number	Title (A Side/B Side)	Yr	VG	VG+	NM
❑ ST-7302	Osmium	1970	25.00	50.00	100.00

PARSONS, ALAN, PROJECT
ARISTA

Number	Title (A Side/B Side)	Yr	VG	VG+	NM
❑ SP-68 [(6)DJ]	Audio Guide to the Alan Parsons Project	1979	12.50	25.00	50.00
—Contains first four APP LPs plus a two-record set of other Parsons work					
❑ SP-140 [(8)DJ]	Complete Audio Guide to the Alan Parsons Project	1982	20.00	40.00	80.00
—Contains first six APP LPs plus a two-record set of other Parsons work					
❑ AB 4180	Pyramid	1978	2.50	5.00	10.00
❑ AL 7002	I Robot	1977	2.50	5.00	10.00
❑ AL 8040	I Robot	1983	2.00	4.00	8.00
—Reissue					
❑ AL 8193	The Best of the Alan Parsons Project	1983	2.00	4.00	8.00
❑ AL 8204	Ammonia Avenue	1984	2.50	5.00	10.00
❑ AL 8263	Vulture Culture	1985	2.00	4.00	8.00
❑ ALPD 8263 [DJ]	Vulture Culture	1985	6.25	12.50	25.00
—Promo-only picture disc					
❑ AL 8289	Ammonia Avenue	1985	2.00	4.00	8.00
—Reissue					
❑ AL 8290	Eye in the Sky	1985	2.00	4.00	8.00
—Reissue					
❑ AL 8315	The Turn of a Friendly Card	1985	2.00	4.00	8.00
—Reissue					
❑ AL 8318	Eve	1985	2.00	4.00	8.00
—Reissue					
❑ AL 8320	Pyramid	1985	2.00	4.00	8.00
—Reissue					
❑ AL 8384	Stereotomy	1986	2.00	4.00	8.00
—With regular LP jacket					
❑ AL 8384	Stereotomy	1986	3.75	7.50	15.00
—First editions came in an oversize vinyl jacket					
❑ AL 8448	Gaudi	1987	2.00	4.00	8.00
❑ AL 8486	The Best of the Alan Parsons Project, Vol. 2	1987	2.00	4.00	8.00
❑ AL 8487	The Instrumental Works of the Alan Parsons Project	1988	2.50	5.00	10.00
❑ AB 9504	Eve	1979	2.50	5.00	10.00
❑ AL 9518	The Turn of a Friendly Card	1980	2.50	5.00	10.00
❑ AL 9599	Eye in the Sky	1982	2.50	5.00	10.00

CASABLANCA

Number	Title (A Side/B Side)	Yr	VG	VG+	NM
❑ 822784-1	Tales of Mystery and Imagination - Edgar Allan Poe	1984	2.50	5.00	10.00
—Reissue of 20th Century LP					

MOBILE FIDELITY

Number	Title (A Side/B Side)	Yr	VG	VG+	NM
❑ 1-084	I Robot	1982	10.00	20.00	40.00
—Audiophile vinyl					
❑ MFQR 1-084	I Robot	1982	20.00	40.00	80.00
—Audiophile vinyl; Ultra High Quality pressing in box					
❑ 1-204	Tales of Mystery and Imagination - Edgar Allan Poe	1994	5.00	10.00	20.00
—Audiophile vinyl					

20TH CENTURY

Number	Title (A Side/B Side)	Yr	VG	VG+	NM
❑ T-508	Tales of Mystery and Imagination - Edgar Allan Poe	1976	3.75	7.50	15.00

PARTON, DOLLY
COLUMBIA

Number	Title (A Side/B Side)	Yr	VG	VG+	NM
❑ FC 40968	Rainbow	1987	2.50	5.00	10.00
❑ FC 44384	White Limozeen	1989	3.00	6.00	12.00
❑ C 46882	Eagle When She Flies	1991	5.00	10.00	20.00
—Available on vinyl only through Columbia House					

MONUMENT

Number	Title (A Side/B Side)	Yr	VG	VG+	NM
❑ 7623	In the Beginning	197?	3.00	6.00	12.00

Number	Title (A Side/B Side)	Yr	VG	VG+	NM
❑ MLP-8085 [M]	Hello, I'm Dolly	1967	7.50	15.00	30.00
❑ SLP-18085 [S]	Hello, I'm Dolly	1967	10.00	20.00	40.00
❑ SLP-18136	As Long As I Love	1970	5.00	10.00	20.00
❑ KZG 31913 [(2)]	The World of Dolly	1972	5.00	10.00	20.00
❑ KZG 33876 [(2)]	Hello, I'm Dolly	1975	5.00	10.00	20.00

PAIR

Number	Title (A Side/B Side)	Yr	VG	VG+	NM
❑ PDL2-1009 [(2)]	Just the Way I Am	1986	3.00	6.00	12.00
❑ PDL2-1116 [(2)]	Portrait	1986	3.00	6.00	12.00

RCA

Number	Title (A Side/B Side)	Yr	VG	VG+	NM
❑ 5706-1-R	The Best of Dolly Parton, Vol. 3	1987	2.50	5.00	10.00
❑ 6497-1-R	The Best There Is	1987	2.50	5.00	10.00

RCA CAMDEN

Number	Title (A Side/B Side)	Yr	VG	VG+	NM
❑ ACL1-0307	Mine	1973	2.50	5.00	10.00
❑ CAS-2583	Just the Way I Am	1972	2.50	5.00	10.00

RCA VICTOR

Number	Title (A Side/B Side)	Yr	VG	VG+	NM
❑ APD1-0033 [Q]	My Tennessee Mountain Home	1973	5.00	10.00	20.00
❑ APL1-0033	My Tennessee Mountain Home	1973	3.00	6.00	12.00
❑ APL1-0286	Bubbling Over	1973	3.00	6.00	12.00
❑ APL1-0473	Jolene	1974	3.00	6.00	12.00
❑ APL1-0712	Love Is Like a Butterfly	1974	3.00	6.00	12.00
❑ APL1-0950	The Bargain Store	1975	3.00	6.00	12.00
❑ APL1-1117	The Best of Dolly Parton	1975	3.00	6.00	12.00
❑ APL1-1221	Dolly	1975	3.00	6.00	12.00
❑ APL1-1665	All I Can Do	1976	3.00	6.00	12.00
❑ APL1-2188	New Harvest...First Gathering	1977	3.00	6.00	12.00
❑ DJL1-2314 [DJ]	Personal Music Dialogue with Dolly Parton	1976	6.25	12.50	25.00
❑ AFL1-2544	Here You Come Again	1977	3.00	6.00	12.00
❑ AFL1-2797	Heartbreaker	1978	3.00	6.00	12.00
❑ AHL1-3361	Great Balls of Fire	1979	3.00	6.00	12.00
❑ AHL1-3546	Dolly Dolly Dolly	1980	3.00	6.00	12.00
❑ AYL1-3665	Heartbreaker	1980	2.00	4.00	8.00
—"Best Buy Series" reissue					
❑ AYL1-3764	My Tennessee Mountain Home	1980	2.00	4.00	8.00
—"Best Buy Series" reissue					
❑ AHL1-3852	9 to 5 and Odd Jobs	1980	3.00	6.00	12.00
❑ AYL1-3898	Jolene	1981	2.00	4.00	8.00
—"Best Buy Series" reissue					
❑ LPM-3949 [M]	Just Because I'm a Woman	1968	25.00	50.00	100.00
❑ LSP-3949 [S]	Just Because I'm a Woman	1968	5.00	10.00	20.00
—Orange label					
❑ LSP-3949 [S]	Just Because I'm a Woman	1968	7.50	15.00	30.00
—"Stereo" on black label					
❑ AYL1-3980	New Harvest	1981	2.00	4.00	8.00
—"Best Buy Series" reissue					
❑ LSP-4099	In the Good Old Days	1969	5.00	10.00	20.00
❑ LSP-4188	My Blue Ridge Mountain Boy	1969	5.00	10.00	20.00
❑ LSP-4288	The Fairest of Them All	1970	5.00	10.00	20.00
❑ AHL1-4289	Heartbreak Express	1982	3.00	6.00	12.00
❑ LSP-4387	A Real Live Dolly	1970	6.25	12.50	25.00
—Four songs feature Porter Wagoner					
❑ LSP-4398	Golden Streets of Glory	1971	5.00	10.00	20.00
❑ AHL1-4422	Greatest Hits	1982	3.00	6.00	12.00
❑ LSP-4449	The Best of Dolly Parton	1970	5.00	10.00	20.00
❑ LSP-4507	Joshua	1971	5.00	10.00	20.00
❑ LSP-4603	Coat of Many Colors	1971	5.00	10.00	20.00
❑ LSP-4686	Touch Your Woman	1972	5.00	10.00	20.00
❑ AHL1-4691	Burlap & Satin	1983	2.50	5.00	10.00
❑ LSP-4752	My Favorite Song Writer: Porter Wagoner	1972	5.00	10.00	20.00
❑ LSP-4762	Dolly Parton Sings	1972	3.75	7.50	15.00
❑ AYL1-4829	Here You Come Again	1984	2.00	4.00	8.00
❑ AYL1-4830	9 to 5 and Odd Jobs	1984	2.00	4.00	8.00
—"Best Buy Series" reissue					
❑ AHL1-4940	The Great Pretender	1984	2.50	5.00	10.00
❑ AYL1-5146	The Best of Dolly Parton	1984	2.00	4.00	8.00
—"Best Buy Series" reissue					
❑ AHL1-5414	Real Love	1985	2.50	5.00	10.00
❑ AYL1-5437	Burlap & Satin	1985	2.00	4.00	8.00
—"Best Buy Series" reissue					
❑ AHL1-5471	Collector's Series	1985	2.50	5.00	10.00
❑ AHL1-9508	Think About Love	1986	2.50	5.00	10.00

PARTON, DOLLY/GEORGE JONES
STARDAY

Number	Title (A Side/B Side)	Yr	VG	VG+	NM
❑ LP 429 [P]	Dolly Parton and George Jones	1968	10.00	20.00	40.00
—One side of Dolly in stereo, one side of "Possum" in rechanneled stereo					

PARTON, DOLLY/FAYE TUCKER
SOMERSET

Number	Title (A Side/B Side)	Yr	VG	VG+	NM
❑ S-9700 [M]	Hits Made Famous by Country Queens	1963	6.25	12.50	25.00
❑ SF-19700 [S]	Hits Made Famous by Country Queens	1963	7.50	15.00	30.00
—Dolly Parton sings songs made famous by Kitty Wells					
❑ SF-29400	Dolly Parton Sings Country Oldies	1968	3.75	7.50	15.00

TIME

Number	Title (A Side/B Side)	Yr	VG	VG+	NM
❑ 2108	Country & Western Soul	1963	10.00	20.00	40.00

PARTON, STELLA
ELEKTRA

Number	Title (A Side/B Side)	Yr	VG	VG+	NM
❑ 6E-126	Stella Parton	1978	3.00	6.00	12.00
❑ 6E-191	Love Ya	1979	3.00	6.00	12.00
❑ 6E-229	The Best of Stella Parton	1979	3.00	6.00	12.00
❑ 7E-1111	Country Sweet	1977	3.00	6.00	12.00

SOUL, COUNTRY & BLUES

Number	Title (A Side/B Side)	Yr	VG	VG+	NM
❑ 6006	I Want to Hold You in My Dreams Tonight	1975	5.00	10.00	20.00

TOWN HOUSE

Number	Title (A Side/B Side)	Yr	VG	VG+	NM
❑ ST-7005	So Far So Good	1982	3.00	6.00	12.00

PARTRIDGE FAMILY, THE
BELL

Number	Title (A Side/B Side)	Yr	VG	VG+	NM
❑ 1107	The Partridge Family At Home with Their Greatest Hits	1972	5.00	10.00	20.00

Number	Title (A Side/B Side)	Yr	VG	VG+	NM
❏ 1111	The Partridge Family Notebook	1972	6.25	12.50	25.00
❏ 1122	Crossword Puzzle	1973	7.50	15.00	30.00
❏ 1137	Bulletin Board	1973	12.50	25.00	50.00
❏ 1319 [(2)]	The World of the Partridge Family	1974	10.00	20.00	40.00
❏ 6050	The Partridge Family Album Bonus Photo	1970	2.50	5.00	10.00
❏ 6050	The Partridge Family Album	1970	5.00	10.00	20.00
❏ 6059	Up to Date Book Cover	1971	2.50	5.00	10.00
❏ 6059	Up to Date	1971	5.00	10.00	20.00
❏ 6064	The Partridge Family Sound Magazine	1971	5.00	10.00	20.00
❏ 6066	A Partridge Family Christmas Card	1971	3.75	7.50	15.00
—Without Christmas card					
❏ 6066	A Partridge Family Christmas Card	1971	6.25	12.50	25.00
—With attached Christmas card					
❏ 6066	A Partridge Family Christmas Card	1971	10.00	20.00	40.00
—With Christmas card printed on the cover (later pressing)					
❏ 6072	The Partridge Family Shopping Bag Bonus Shopping Bag	1972	2.50	5.00	10.00
❏ 6072	The Partridge Family Shopping Bag	1972	5.00	10.00	20.00

LAURIE HOUSE

Number	Title (A Side/B Side)	Yr	VG	VG+	NM
❏ H-8014 [(2)]	The Partridge Family	197?	12.50	25.00	50.00

PASS, JOE
PACIFIC JAZZ

Number	Title (A Side/B Side)	Yr	VG	VG+	NM
❏ PJ-73 [M]	Catch Me!	1963	6.25	12.50	25.00
❏ ST-73 [S]	Catch Me!	1963	7.50	15.00	30.00
❏ PJ-85 [M]	For Django	1964	6.25	12.50	25.00
❏ ST-85 [S]	For Django	1964	7.50	15.00	30.00

WORLD PACIFIC

Number	Title (A Side/B Side)	Yr	VG	VG+	NM
❏ WP-1854 [M]	The Stones Jazz	1967	5.00	10.00	20.00
❏ WP-1865 [M]	Simplicity	1967	5.00	10.00	20.00
❏ ST-21844 [S]	A Sign of the Times	1966	5.00	10.00	20.00
❏ ST-21854 [S]	The Stones Jazz	1967	5.00	10.00	20.00

PASS, JOE, AND ARNOLD ROSS
PACIFIC JAZZ

Number	Title (A Side/B Side)	Yr	VG	VG+	NM
❏ PJ-48 [M]	Sounds of Synanon	1962	6.25	12.50	25.00
❏ ST-48 [S]	Sounds of Synanon	1962	7.50	15.00	30.00

PASTEL SIX, THE
ZEN

Number	Title (A Side/B Side)	Yr	VG	VG+	NM
❏ 1001 [M]	The Cinnamon Cinder	1963	25.00	50.00	100.00

PASTOR, TONY
EVEREST

Number	Title (A Side/B Side)	Yr	VG	VG+	NM
❏ SDBR-1031 [S]	P.S. — Plays and Sings Shaw	1959	5.00	10.00	20.00

PASTORIUS, JACO
IAI

Number	Title (A Side/B Side)	Yr	VG	VG+	NM
❏ 373846	Jaco	1975	5.00	10.00	20.00

PATCHEN, KENNETH, WITH THE CHAMBER JAZZ SEXTET
CADENCE

Number	Title (A Side/B Side)	Yr	VG	VG+	NM
❏ CLP-3004 [M]	Kenneth Patchen Reads His Poetry	1957	75.00	150.00	300.00

PATE, JOHNNY
GIG

Number	Title (A Side/B Side)	Yr	VG	VG+	NM
❏ GLP-100 [M]	Subtle Sounds	1956	25.00	50.00	100.00

KING

Number	Title (A Side/B Side)	Yr	VG	VG+	NM
❏ 561 [M]	Jazz Goes Ivy League	1958	20.00	40.00	80.00
❏ 584 [M]	Swingin' Flute	1958	20.00	40.00	80.00
❏ 611 [M]	A Date with Johnny Pate	1959	20.00	40.00	80.00

STEPHENY

Number	Title (A Side/B Side)	Yr	VG	VG+	NM
❏ 4002 [M]	Johnny Pate at the Blue Note	1957	25.00	50.00	100.00

TALISMAN

Number	Title (A Side/B Side)	Yr	VG	VG+	NM
❏ TLP-1 [10]	Johnny Pate Trio	1956	30.00	60.00	120.00

PATRON SAINTS, THE
(NO LABEL)

Number	Title (A Side/B Side)	Yr	VG	VG+	NM
❏ JT-1001	Fohhob Bohob	1969	1000.	2000.	3000.
—100 copies were pressed					

PATRON SAINT

Number	Title (A Side/B Side)	Yr	VG	VG+	NM
❏ JT-1001	Fohhob Bohob	1997	6.25	12.50	25.00
—Authorized reissue with bonus 7-inch single; numbered edition of 500					

PATTERSON, DON
CADET

Number	Title (A Side/B Side)	Yr	VG	VG+	NM
❏ LP-787 [M]	Goin' Down Home	1967	7.50	15.00	30.00
❏ LPS-787 [S]	Goin' Down Home	1967	5.00	10.00	20.00

PRESTIGE

Number	Title (A Side/B Side)	Yr	VG	VG+	NM
❏ PRLP-7331 [M]	The Exiting New Organ of Don Patterson	1964	6.25	12.50	25.00
❏ PRST-7331 [S]	The Exciting New Organ of Don Patterson	1964	7.50	15.00	30.00
❏ PRLP-7349 [M]	Hip Cake Walk	1965	6.25	12.50	25.00
❏ PRST-7349 [S]	Hip Cake Walk	1965	7.50	15.00	30.00
❏ PRLP-7381 [M]	Patterson's People	1965	6.25	12.50	25.00
❏ PRST-7381 [S]	Patterson's People	1965	7.50	15.00	30.00
❏ PRLP-7415 [M]	Holiday Soul	1966	6.25	12.50	25.00
❏ PRST-7415 [S]	Holiday Soul	1965	7.50	15.00	30.00
❏ PRLP-7430 [M]	Satisfaction	1966	6.25	12.50	25.00
❏ PRST-7430 [S]	Satisfaction	1966	7.50	15.00	30.00
❏ PRLP-7466 [M]	The Boss Men	1967	7.50	15.00	30.00
❏ PRST-7466 [S]	The Boss Men	1967	6.25	12.50	25.00
❏ PRLP-7484 [M]	Soul Happening!	1967	6.25	12.50	25.00
❏ PRST-7484 [S]	Soul Happening!	1967	5.00	10.00	20.00
❏ PRLP-7510 [M]	Mellow Soul	1967	6.25	12.50	25.00
❏ PRST-7510 [S]	Mellow Soul	1967	5.00	10.00	20.00
❏ PRLP-7533 [M]	Four Dimensions	1967	6.25	12.50	25.00
❏ PRST-7533 [S]	Four Dimensions	1967	5.00	10.00	20.00
❏ PRST-7563	Boppin' and Burnin'	1968	5.00	10.00	20.00
❏ PRST-7577	Opus De Don	1968	5.00	10.00	20.00
❏ PRST-7613	Funk You	1969	5.00	10.00	20.00
❏ PRST-7640	Oh, Happy Days!	1969	5.00	10.00	20.00

PATTERSON, KELLEE
BLACK JAZZ

Number	Title (A Side/B Side)	Yr	VG	VG+	NM
❏ QD-12	Maiden Voyage	1974	5.00	10.00	20.00

PATTERSON SINGERS, THE
ATCO

Number	Title (A Side/B Side)	Yr	VG	VG+	NM
❏ SD 33-380	The Patterson Singers	1972	5.00	10.00	20.00

KING

Number	Title (A Side/B Side)	Yr	VG	VG+	NM
❏ 763 [M]	Gospel Songs by the Patterson Singers	1962	12.50	25.00	50.00
❏ KS-1129	Jesus Knows	1971	5.00	10.00	20.00

MINIT

Number	Title (A Side/B Side)	Yr	VG	VG+	NM
❏ LP-40021	The Soul of Gospel	1969	5.00	10.00	20.00

VEE JAY

Number	Title (A Side/B Side)	Yr	VG	VG+	NM
❏ LP-5017 [M]	My Prayer	1962	6.25	12.50	25.00
❏ LP-5032 [M]	The Lord's Prayer	1963	6.25	12.50	25.00
❏ LP-5046 [M]	Songs of Faith	1963	5.00	10.00	20.00
❏ SR-5046 [S]	Songs of Faith	1963	7.50	15.00	30.00
❏ LP-5060 [M]	The Soul of the Patterson Singers	1964	5.00	10.00	20.00

PATTO
ISLAND

Number	Title (A Side/B Side)	Yr	VG	VG+	NM
❏ SW-9322	Roll 'Em, Smoke 'Em, Put Another Line Out	1972	7.50	15.00	30.00

VERTIGO

Number	Title (A Side/B Side)	Yr	VG	VG+	NM
❏ VEL-1001	Patto	1971	3.75	7.50	15.00
❏ VEL-1008	Hold Your Fire	1972	3.75	7.50	15.00

PATTON, "BIG" JOHN
BLUE NOTE

Number	Title (A Side/B Side)	Yr	VG	VG+	NM
❏ BLP-4130 [M]	Along Came John	1963	7.50	15.00	30.00
❏ BLP-4174 [M]	The Way I Feel	1964	6.25	12.50	25.00
❏ BLP-4192 [M]	Oh Baby!	1964	6.25	12.50	25.00
❏ BLP-4229 [M]	Got a Good Thing Goin'	1966	6.25	12.50	25.00
❏ BLP-4239 [M]	Let 'Em Roll	1966	6.25	12.50	25.00
❏ BST-84130 [S]	Along Came John	1963	10.00	20.00	40.00
—With "New York, USA" address on label					
❏ BST-84174 [S]	The Way I Feel	1964	7.50	15.00	30.00
—With "New York, USA" address on label					
❏ BST-84192 [S]	Oh Baby!	1964	7.50	15.00	30.00
—With "New York, USA" address on label					
❏ BST-84229 [S]	Got a Good Thing Goin'	1966	7.50	15.00	30.00
—With "New York, USA" address on label					
❏ BST-84239 [S]	Let 'Em Roll	1966	7.50	15.00	30.00
—With "New York, USA" address on label					
❏ BST-84281 [S]	That Certain Feeling	1968	6.25	12.50	25.00
—With "A Division of Liberty Records" on label					
❏ BST-84306 [S]	Understanding	1969	6.25	12.50	25.00
—With "A Division of Liberty Records" on label					
❏ BST-84340 [S]	Accent on the Blues	1970	6.25	12.50	25.00
—With "A Division of Liberty Records" on label					

PATTON, CHARLEY
ORIGIN JAZZ LIBRARY

Number	Title (A Side/B Side)	Yr	VG	VG+	NM
❏ OJL-1 [M]	The Immortal Charley Patton No. 1	1962	6.25	12.50	25.00
❏ OJL-7 [M]	The Immortal Charley Patton No. 2	1962	6.25	12.50	25.00

YAZOO

Number	Title (A Side/B Side)	Yr	VG	VG+	NM
❏ 2001 [(2)]	King of the Delta Blues	197?	7.50	15.00	30.00
❏ 2010 [(2)]	Founder of the Delta Blues	197?	7.50	15.00	30.00

PATTON, JIMMY
MOON

Number	Title (A Side/B Side)	Yr	VG	VG+	NM
❏ 101 [M]	Make Room for the Blues	1966	10.00	20.00	40.00

SIMS

Number	Title (A Side/B Side)	Yr	VG	VG+	NM
❏ 127 [M]	Blue Darlin'	1965	10.00	20.00	40.00

SOURDOUGH

Number	Title (A Side/B Side)	Yr	VG	VG+	NM
❏ 127 [M]	Blue Darlin'	1965	12.50	25.00	50.00

STEREOPHONIC

Number	Title (A Side/B Side)	Yr	VG	VG+	NM
❏ LP-1002 [S]	Take 30 Minutes with Jimmy Patton	196?	30.00	60.00	120.00

PAUL, BILLY
GAMBLE

Number	Title (A Side/B Side)	Yr	VG	VG+	NM
❏ SG-5002	Feeling Good at the Cadillac Club	1968	7.50	15.00	30.00

ICHIBAN

Number	Title (A Side/B Side)	Yr	VG	VG+	NM
❏ ICH-1025	Wide Open	198?	2.50	5.00	10.00

NEPTUNE

Number	Title (A Side/B Side)	Yr	VG	VG+	NM
❏ 201	Ebony Woman	1970	5.00	10.00	20.00

PHILADELPHIA INT'L.

Number	Title (A Side/B Side)	Yr	VG	VG+	NM
❏ Z 30580	Going East	1971	3.00	6.00	12.00
❏ KZ 31793	360 Degrees of Billy Paul	1972	3.00	6.00	12.00
❏ ZQ 31793 [Q]	360 Degrees of Billy Paul	1972	5.00	10.00	20.00
❏ KZ 32118	Ebony Woman	1973	3.00	6.00	12.00
—Reissue of Neptune LP					
❏ KZ 32119	Feeling Good at the Cadillac Club	1973	3.00	6.00	12.00
—Reissue of Gamble LP					
❏ KZ 32409	War of the Gods	1973	2.50	5.00	10.00
❏ ZQ 32409 [Q]	War of the Gods	1973	5.00	10.00	20.00
❏ KZ 32952	Live in Europe	1974	2.50	5.00	10.00
❏ ZQ 32952 [Q]	Live in Europe	1974	5.00	10.00	20.00
❏ PZ 33157	Got My Head On Straight	1975	2.50	5.00	10.00
❏ PZ 33843	When Love Is New	1975	2.50	5.00	10.00
❏ PZ 34389	Let 'Em In	1976	2.50	5.00	10.00
❏ PZ 34923	Only the Strong Survive	1977	2.50	5.00	10.00
❏ JZ 35756	First Class	1979	2.50	5.00	10.00
❏ Z2 36314 [(2)]	The Best of Billy Paul	1980	3.75	7.50	15.00

TOTAL EXPERIENCE

Number	Title (A Side/B Side)	Yr	VG	VG+	NM
❏ TEL8-5711	Lately	1985	2.50	5.00	10.00

PAUL, LES
CAPITOL

Number	Title (A Side/B Side)	Yr	VG	VG+	NM
❏ N-16286	Early Les Paul	1982	2.00	4.00	8.00

P

Number	Title (A Side/B Side)	Yr	VG	VG+	NM
DECCA					
❏ DL-5018 [10]	Hawaiian Paradise	1949	25.00	50.00	100.00
❏ DL-5376 [10]	Galloping Guitars	1952	25.00	50.00	100.00
❏ DL 8589 [M]	More of Les	1957	10.00	20.00	40.00
GLENDALE					
❏ 6014	The Les Paul Trio	198?	2.50	5.00	10.00
LONDON					
❏ 50016	Multi-Trackin'	1979	3.00	6.00	12.00
LONDON PHASE 4					
❏ SP-44101	Les Paul Now!	1968	3.75	7.50	15.00
VOCALION					
❏ VL 3849 [M]	The Guitar Artistry of Les Paul	196?	3.00	6.00	12.00
❏ VL 73849 [R]	The Guitar Artistry of Les Paul	196?	2.50	5.00	10.00

PAUL, LES, AND MARY FORD
Also see MARY FORD.

Number	Title (A Side/B Side)	Yr	VG	VG+	NM
CAPITOL					
❏ H 226 [10]	The New Sound, Volume 1	1950	20.00	40.00	80.00
❏ T 226 [M]	The New Sound, Volume 1	1955	12.50	25.00	50.00
❏ H 286 [10]	The New Sound, Volume 2	1951	20.00	40.00	80.00
❏ SM-286	The New Sound, Volume 2	197?	2.50	5.00	10.00
❏ T 286 [M]	The New Sound, Volume 2	1955	12.50	25.00	50.00
❏ H 356 [10]	Bye Bye Blues	1952	20.00	40.00	80.00
❏ T 356 [M]	Bye Bye Blues	1955	12.50	25.00	50.00
❏ H 416 [10]	The Hit Makers	1953	20.00	40.00	80.00
❏ T 416 [M]	The Hit Makers	1955	12.50	25.00	50.00
❏ H 577 [10]	Les and Mary	1955	20.00	40.00	80.00
❏ W 577 [M]	Les and Mary	1955	12.50	25.00	50.00
❏ T 802 [M]	Time to Dream	1956	12.50	25.00	50.00
❏ DT 1476 [R]	The Hits of Les and Mary	1960	5.00	10.00	20.00
❏ T 1476 [M]	The Hits of Les and Mary	1960	6.25	12.50	25.00
❏ SM-11308	The World Is Still Waiting for the Sunrise	197?	2.50	5.00	10.00
—Reissue with new prefix					
❏ ST-11308	The World Is Still Waiting for the Sunrise	1974	3.00	6.00	12.00
CAPITOL SPECIAL MARKETS					
❏ SLCR-8130 [(3)]	The All-Time Greatest Hits of Les Paul and Mary Ford	1980	5.00	10.00	20.00
—Produced for Murray Hill Records (979462)					
COLUMBIA					
❏ CL 1276 [M]	Lovers' Luau	1959	5.00	10.00	20.00
❏ CL 1688 [M]	Warm and Wonderful	1962	5.00	10.00	20.00
❏ CL 1821 [M]	Bouquet of Roses	1962	5.00	10.00	20.00
❏ CL 1928 [M]	Swingin' South	1963	3.75	7.50	15.00
❏ CS 8086 [S]	Lovers' Luau	1959	7.50	15.00	30.00
❏ CS 8488 [S]	Warm and Wonderful	1962	6.25	12.50	25.00
❏ CS 8621 [S]	Bouquet of Roses	1962	6.25	12.50	25.00
❏ CS 8728 [S]	Swingin' South	1963	5.00	10.00	20.00
HARMONY					
❏ HL 7333 [M]	The Fabulous Les Paul and Mary Ford	1965	3.00	6.00	12.00
❏ HS 11133 [S]	The Fabulous Les Paul and Mary Ford	1965	3.00	6.00	12.00
PICKWICK					
❏ SPC-3122	Brazil	197?	2.50	5.00	10.00

PAUL AND PAULA

Number	Title (A Side/B Side)	Yr	VG	VG+	NM
PHILIPS					
❏ PHM 200078 [M]	Paul and Paula Sing for Young Lovers	1963	7.50	15.00	30.00
❏ PHM 200089 [M]	We Go Together	1963	7.50	15.00	30.00
❏ PHM 200101 [M]	Holiday for Teens	1963	7.50	15.00	30.00
❏ PHS 600078 [S]	Paul and Paula Sing for Young Lovers	1963	10.00	20.00	40.00
❏ PHS 600089 [S]	We Go Together	1963	10.00	20.00	40.00
❏ PHS 600101 [S]	Holiday for Teens	1963	10.00	20.00	40.00

PAULSON, PAT

Number	Title (A Side/B Side)	Yr	VG	VG+	NM
RUBICON/MERCURY					
❏ SR 61179	Pat Paulson for President	1968	5.00	10.00	20.00
❏ SR 61251	Live at the Ice House	1970	3.75	7.50	15.00

PAUPERS, THE

Number	Title (A Side/B Side)	Yr	VG	VG+	NM
VERVE FORECAST					
❏ FT-3026 [M]	Magic People	1967	5.00	10.00	20.00
❏ FTS-3026 [S]	Magic People	1967	5.00	10.00	20.00
❏ FTS-3051	Ellis Island	1968	3.75	7.50	15.00

PAVLOV'S DOG

Number	Title (A Side/B Side)	Yr	VG	VG+	NM
ABC					
❏ D-866	Pampered Menial	1975	6.25	12.50	25.00
COLUMBIA					
❏ PC 33552	Pampered Menial	1976	3.00	6.00	12.00
—Reissue of ABC album					
❏ PC 33964	At the Sound of the Bell	1976	3.00	6.00	12.00

PAVONE, RITA

Number	Title (A Side/B Side)	Yr	VG	VG+	NM
RCA VICTOR					
❏ LPM-2900 [M]	Rita Pavone	1964	3.75	7.50	15.00
❏ LSP-2900 [S]	Rita Pavone	1964	5.00	10.00	20.00
❏ LPM-2996 [M]	Small Wonder	1965	3.75	7.50	15.00
❏ LSP-2996 [S]	Small Wonder	1965	5.00	10.00	20.00

PAXTON, TOM

Number	Title (A Side/B Side)	Yr	VG	VG+	NM
ELEKTRA					
❏ EKL-277 [M]	Ramblin' Boy	1964	5.00	10.00	20.00
❏ EKL-298 [M]	Ain't That News	1965	5.00	10.00	20.00
❏ EKL-317 [M]	Outward Bound	1966	5.00	10.00	20.00
❏ 7E-2003 [(2)]	The Compleat Tom Paxton	1971	5.00	10.00	20.00
❏ EKS-7277 [S]	Ramblin' Boy	1964	6.25	12.50	25.00
❏ EKS-7298 [S]	Ain't That News	1965	6.25	12.50	25.00
❏ EKS-7317 [S]	Outward Bound	1966	6.25	12.50	25.00
❏ EKS-74019	Morning Again	1968	5.00	10.00	20.00
❏ EKS-74043	The Things I Notice Now	1969	3.75	7.50	15.00
❏ EKS-74066	Tom Paxton 6	1970	3.75	7.50	15.00

Number	Title (A Side/B Side)	Yr	VG	VG+	NM
FLYING FISH					
❏ FF-280	Even a Gray Day	1983	2.50	5.00	10.00
❏ FF-356	One Million Lawyers...And Other Disasters	1986	2.50	5.00	10.00
❏ FF-408	The Marvellous Toy and Other Gallimaufry	1987	2.50	5.00	10.00
❏ FF-414	And Loving You	1987	2.50	5.00	10.00
❏ FF-486	Politics	199?	3.00	6.00	12.00
❏ FF-519	The Very Best of Tom Paxton	199?	3.00	6.00	12.00
GASLIGHT					
❏ GV-116 [M]	I'm the Man Who Built the Bridges	1962	20.00	40.00	80.00
HOGEYE					
❏ 004	Bulletin...We Interrupt This Record	198?	2.50	5.00	10.00
MOUNTAIN RAILROAD					
❏ 52792	Up and Up	1980	3.00	6.00	12.00
❏ 52796	The Paxton Report	198?	3.00	6.00	12.00
PRIVATE STOCK					
❏ PS-2002	Something in My Life	1975	3.00	6.00	12.00
REPRISE					
❏ MS 2096	Peace Will Come	1972	3.75	7.50	15.00
❏ MS 2144	New Songs for Old Friends	1973	3.75	7.50	15.00
❏ RS 6443	How Come the Sun	1971	3.75	7.50	15.00
VANGUARD					
❏ VSD-79395	New Songs from the Briarpatch	1977	3.00	6.00	12.00
❏ VSD-79411	Heroes	1978	3.00	6.00	12.00

PAYCHECK, JOHNNY

Number	Title (A Side/B Side)	Yr	VG	VG+	NM
ACCORD					
❏ SN-7173	Extra Special	1981	2.50	5.00	10.00
ALLEGIANCE					
❏ AV-435	I Don't Need to Know That Right Now	198?	2.00	4.00	8.00
CERTRON					
❏ 7002	Johnny Paycheck Again	1970	3.75	7.50	15.00
EPIC					
❏ E 31141	She's All I Got	1971	3.00	6.00	12.00
❏ KE 31449	Someone to Give My Love To	1972	3.00	6.00	12.00
❏ KE 31702	Somebody Loves Me	1972	3.00	6.00	12.00
❏ KE 32387	Something About You I Love	1973	3.00	6.00	12.00
❏ KE 32570	Song and Dance Man	1973	3.00	6.00	12.00
❏ KE 33091	Greatest Hits	1974	2.50	5.00	10.00
❏ PE 33091	Greatest Hits	198?	2.00	4.00	8.00
—Budget-line reissue					
❏ KE 33354	Loving You Beats All I've Ever Seen	1975	2.50	5.00	10.00
❏ KE 33943	11 Months and 29 Days	1975	2.50	5.00	10.00
❏ PE 34693	Slide Off of Your Satin Sheets	1976	2.50	5.00	10.00
❏ KE 35045	Take This Job and Shove It	1977	2.50	5.00	10.00
❏ PE 35045	Take This Job and Shove It	198?	2.00	4.00	8.00
—Budget-line reissue					
❏ KE 35444	Armed and Crazy	1978	2.50	5.00	10.00
❏ KE 35623	Greatest Hits, Volume 2	1978	2.50	5.00	10.00
❏ PE 35623	Greatest Hits, Volume 2	198?	2.00	4.00	8.00
—Budget-line reissue					
❏ JE 36200	Everybody's Got a Family — Meet Mine	1979	2.50	5.00	10.00
❏ JE 36496	New York Town	1980	2.50	5.00	10.00
❏ FE 36761	Mr. Hag Told My Story	1981	2.50	5.00	10.00
❏ PE 36761	Mr. Hag Told My Story	1981	2.00	4.00	8.00
—Budget-line reissue					
❏ FE 37345	Encore	1981	2.50	5.00	10.00
❏ PE 37345	Encore	198?	2.00	4.00	8.00
—Budget-line reissue					
❏ FE 37933	Lovers and Losers	1982	2.50	5.00	10.00
❏ FE 38322	Johnny Paycheck's Biggest Hits	1983	2.50	5.00	10.00
❏ PE 39943	John Austin Paycheck	1984	2.00	4.00	8.00
INTERMEDIA					
❏ QS-5018	Back On the Job	198?	2.00	4.00	8.00
LITTLE DARLIN'					
❏ LD-4001 [M]	Johnny Paycheck at Carnegie Hall	1966	5.00	10.00	20.00
❏ LD-4003 [M]	The Lovin' Machine	1966	5.00	10.00	20.00
❏ LD-4004 [M]	Gospeltime in My Fashion	1967	5.00	10.00	20.00
❏ LD-4006 [M]	Johnny Paycheck Sings Jukebox Charlie	1967	6.25	12.50	25.00
❏ SLD-8001 [S]	Johnny Paycheck at Carnegie Hall	1966	6.25	12.50	25.00
❏ SLD-8003 [S]	The Lovin' Machine	1966	6.25	12.50	25.00
❏ SLD-8004 [S]	Gospeltime in My Fashion	1967	6.25	12.50	25.00
❏ SLD-8006 [S]	Johnny Paycheck Sings Jukebox Charlie	1967	6.25	12.50	25.00
❏ SLD-8010	Country Soul	1968	6.25	12.50	25.00
❏ SLD-8012	Johnny Paycheck's Greatest Hits	1968	6.25	12.50	25.00
❏ SLD-8023	Wherever You Are	1969	6.25	12.50	25.00
MERCURY					
❏ 830404-1	Modern Times	1987	2.50	5.00	10.00
POWER PAK					
❏ PO-284	Johnny Paycheck At His Best	197?	2.00	4.00	8.00

PAYNE, BENNIE

Number	Title (A Side/B Side)	Yr	VG	VG+	NM
KAPP					
❏ KL-1004 [M]	Bennie Payne Plays and Sings	1955	20.00	40.00	80.00

PAYNE, CECIL

Number	Title (A Side/B Side)	Yr	VG	VG+	NM
CHARLIE PARKER					
❏ PLP-506 [M]	Shaw Nuff	1962	6.25	12.50	25.00
❏ PLP-506S [S]	Shaw Nuff	1962	7.50	15.00	30.00
❏ PLP-801 [M]	Cecil Payne Performing Charlie Parker's Music	1962	10.00	20.00	40.00
❏ PLP-801S [S]	Cecil Payne Performing Charlie Parker's Music	1962	12.50	25.00	50.00
SAVOY					
❏ MG-12147 [M]	Patterns of Jazz	1959	20.00	40.00	80.00
SIGNAL					
❏ S-1203 [M]	Cecil Payne Quintet and Quartet	1955	50.00	100.00	200.00
STRATA-EAST					
❏ SES-19734	The Zodiac	1973	6.25	12.50	25.00

Number	Title (A Side/B Side)	Yr	VG	VG+	NM

PAYNE, DENNIS, AND THE RENEGADES
RED MAN
| ❑ 1492 | We're Indian | 1969 | 37.50 | 75.00 | 150.00 |

PAYNE, FREDA
ABC
| ❑ D-901 | Out of Payne Comes Love | 1976 | 3.00 | 6.00 | 12.00 |
ABC DUNHILL
| ❑ DSX-50176 | Payne and Pleasure | 1974 | 3.75 | 7.50 | 15.00 |
ABC IMPULSE!
| ❑ AS-53 [S] | After the Lights Go Down Low…And Much More | 1968 | 3.75 | 7.50 | 15.00 |
CAPITOL
❑ ST-11700	Stares and Whispers	1977	3.00	6.00	12.00
❑ ST-11864	Supernatural	1978	3.00	6.00	12.00
❑ ST-12003	Hot	1979	3.00	6.00	12.00
IMPULSE!
| ❑ A-53 [M] | After the Lights Go Down Low…And Much More | 1964 | 7.50 | 15.00 | 30.00 |
| ❑ AS-53 [S] | After the Lights Go Down Low…And Much More | 1964 | 10.00 | 20.00 | 40.00 |
INVICTUS
❑ ST-7301	Band of Gold	1970	3.75	7.50	15.00
❑ SMAS-7307	Contact	1971	3.75	7.50	15.00
❑ ST-9804	The Best of Freda Payne	1972	3.75	7.50	15.00
❑ Z 32493	Reaching Out	1973	3.75	7.50	15.00
MGM
❑ GAS-128	Freda Payne (Golden Archive Series)	1970	3.75	7.50	15.00
❑ E-4370 [M]	How Do You Say I Don't Love You Anymore	1966	5.00	10.00	20.00
❑ SE-4370 [S]	How Do You Say I Don't Love You Anymore	1966	6.25	12.50	25.00

PAYNE, JIMMY
EPIC
| ❑ BN 26372 | Woman, Woman! What Does It Take? | 1968 | 5.00 | 10.00 | 20.00 |

PAYNE, LEON
STARDAY
| ❑ SLP-231 [M] | Leon Payne: A Living Legend of Country Music | 1963 | 20.00 | 40.00 | 80.00 |
| ❑ SLP-236 [M] | Americana | 1963 | 12.50 | 25.00 | 50.00 |

PEACE, JOE
RITE
| ❑ 29917 | Finding Peace | 1972 | 50.00 | 100.00 | 200.00 |

PEACHES AND HERB
COLUMBIA
| ❑ FC 38746 | Remember | 1983 | 2.50 | 5.00 | 10.00 |
DATE
❑ TEM 3004 [M]	Let's Fall in Love	1967	5.00	10.00	20.00
❑ TEM 3005 [M]	For Your Love	1967	6.25	12.50	25.00
❑ TEM 3007 [M]	Golden Duets	1968	7.50	15.00	30.00
❑ TES 4004 [S]	Let's Fall in Love	1967	6.25	12.50	25.00
❑ TES 4005 [S]	For Your Love	1967	5.00	10.00	20.00
❑ TES 4007 [S]	Golden Duets	1968	5.00	10.00	20.00
❑ TES 4012	Peaches and Herb's Greatest Hits	1968	5.00	10.00	20.00
EPIC
❑ E 36089	Love Is Strange	1979	2.50	5.00	10.00
—Reissue of Date material					
❑ JE 36099	Peaches and Herb's Greatest Hits	1979	2.50	5.00	10.00
—Reissue of Date 4012					
MCA
| ❑ 2261 | Peaches and Herb | 1977 | 3.00 | 6.00 | 12.00 |
POLYDOR
❑ PD-1-6172	2 Hot!	1978	2.50	5.00	10.00
❑ PD-1-6239	Twice the Fire	1979	2.50	5.00	10.00
❑ PD-1-6298	Worth the Wait	1980	2.50	5.00	10.00
❑ PD-1-6332	Sayin' Something!	1981	2.50	5.00	10.00

PEANUT BUTTER CONSPIRACY, THE
CHALLENGE
| ❑ 2000 | For Children of All Ages | 1969 | 7.50 | 15.00 | 30.00 |
COLUMBIA
❑ CL 2654 [M]	The Peanut Butter Conspiracy Is Spreading	1967	7.50	15.00	30.00
❑ CL 2790 [M]	The Great Conspiracy	1968	10.00	20.00	40.00
❑ CS 9454 [S]	The Peanut Butter Conspiracy Is Spreading	1967	7.50	15.00	30.00
❑ CS 9590 [S]	The Great Conspiracy	1968	7.50	15.00	30.00

PEARLS BEFORE SWINE
ADELPHI
| ❑ 4111 [(2)] | The Best of Pearls Before Swine | 198? | 3.75 | 7.50 | 15.00 |
ESP-DISK
❑ 1054	One Nation Under Ground Bonus Poster	1967	6.25	12.50	25.00
❑ 1054 [M]	One Nation Under Ground	1967	12.50	25.00	50.00
❑ 1054 [S]	One Nation Under Ground	1967	12.50	25.00	50.00
—Black and white cover					
❑ 1054 [S]	One Nation Under Ground	1967	12.50	25.00	50.00
—Sepia-tone cover with no border					
❑ 1054 [S]	One Nation Under Ground	1967	12.50	25.00	50.00
—Sepia-tone cover with white border					
❑ 1054 [S]	One Nation Under Ground	1968	7.50	15.00	30.00
—Full-color cover					
❑ 1075	Balaklava	1968	10.00	20.00	40.00
REPRISE
❑ RS 6364	These Things Too	1969	7.50	15.00	30.00
❑ RS 6405	Use of Ashes	1970	7.50	15.00	30.00
❑ RS 6442	City of Gold	1971	10.00	20.00	40.00
❑ RS 6467	Beautiful Lies You Could Live In	1971	10.00	20.00	40.00

PEARSON, ALBIE
VIBRANT
| ❑ 1501 | Albie Pearson | 1973 | 6.25 | 12.50 | 25.00 |

PEARSON, DUKE
BLUE NOTE
❑ BLP-4022 [M]	Profile — Duke Pearson	1959	20.00	40.00	80.00
—Regular version with W. 63rd St. address on label					
❑ BLP-4022 [M]	Profile — Duke Pearson	1959	30.00	60.00	120.00
—"Deep groove" version (deep indentation under label on both sides)					
❑ BLP-4022 [M]	Profile — Duke Pearson	1963	6.25	12.50	25.00
—With New York, USA address on label					
❑ BLP-4035 [M]	Tender Feelin's	1960	20.00	40.00	80.00
—Regular version with W. 63rd St. address on label					
❑ BLP-4035 [M]	Tender Feelin's	1960	30.00	60.00	120.00
—"Deep groove" version (deep indentation under label on both sides)					
❑ BLP-4035 [M]	Tender Feelin's	1963	6.25	12.50	25.00
—With New York, USA address on label					
❑ BLP-4191 [M]	Wahoo!	1965	7.50	15.00	30.00
❑ BLP-4252 [M]	Sweet Honey Bee	1966	7.50	15.00	30.00
❑ BST-84022 [S]	Profile — Duke Pearson	1959	15.00	30.00	60.00
—With W. 63rd St. address on label					
❑ BST-84022 [S]	Profile — Duke Pearson	1963	5.00	10.00	20.00
—With New York, USA address on label					
❑ BST-84035 [S]	Tender Feelin's	1960	15.00	30.00	60.00
—With W. 63rd St. address on label					
❑ BST-84035 [S]	Tender Feelin's	1963	5.00	10.00	20.00
—With New York, USA address on label					
❑ BST-84191 [S]	Wahoo!	1965	7.50	15.00	30.00
—With New York, USA address on label					
❑ BST-84252 [S]	Sweet Honey Bee	1966	7.50	15.00	30.00
—With New York, USA address on label					
❑ BST-84267	The Right Touch	1968	6.25	12.50	25.00
❑ BST-84276	Introducing Duke Pearson's Big Band	1968	6.25	12.50	25.00
❑ BST-84293	The Phantom	1969	6.25	12.50	25.00
❑ BST-84308	Now Hear This	1969	6.25	12.50	25.00
❑ BST-84323	Merry Ole Soul	1970	5.00	10.00	20.00
❑ BST-84344	How Insensitive	1970	5.00	10.00	20.00
JAZZTIME
| ❑ 33-02 [M] | Hush! | 1962 | 10.00 | 20.00 | 40.00 |

PEBBLES AND BAMM BAMM
HANNA-BARBERA
| ❑ HLP-2033 [M] | Pebbles and Bamm-Bamm Sing Songs of Christmas | 1965 | 30.00 | 60.00 | 120.00 |
| ❑ HLP-2040 [M] | On the Good Ship Lollipop | 1966 | 25.00 | 50.00 | 100.00 |

PECORA, SANTO
CLEF
| ❑ MGC-123 [10] | Santo Pecora Collates | 1953 | 25.00 | 50.00 | 100.00 |
| —With either Mercury or Clef cover; all labels are Clef | | | | | |
SOUTHLAND
| ❑ SLP-213 [M] | Santo Pecora | 1955 | 12.50 | 25.00 | 50.00 |
VIK
| ❑ XLA-1081 [M] | Dixieland Mardi Gras | 1957 | 12.50 | 25.00 | 50.00 |

PEDICIN, MIKE
APOLLO
| ❑ LP-484 [M] | Musical Medicine | 1957 | 37.50 | 75.00 | 150.00 |

PEEBLES, ANN
HI
❑ HLP-6002	If This Is Heaven	1977	3.00	6.00	12.00
❑ HLP-6007	The Handwriting Is On the Wall	1978	3.00	6.00	12.00
❑ HLP-8005	Part Time Love	197?	3.00	6.00	12.00
—Reissue of 32059					
❑ HLP-8009	Straight from the Heart	197?	3.00	6.00	12.00
—Reissue of 32065					
❑ SHL-32059	Part Time Love	1971	5.00	10.00	20.00
❑ SHL-32065	Straight from the Heart	1972	5.00	10.00	20.00
❑ XSHL-32079	I Can't Stand the Rain	1974	5.00	10.00	20.00
❑ SHL-32091	Tellin' It	1975	5.00	10.00	20.00

PEEL, DAVID
APPLE
| ❑ SW-3391 | The Pope Smokes Dope | 1972 | 18.75 | 37.50 | 75.00 |
ELEKTRA
| ❑ EKS-74032 | Have a Marijuana | 1968 | 10.00 | 20.00 | 40.00 |
| ❑ EKS-74069 | The American Revolution | 1970 | 7.50 | 15.00 | 30.00 |

PEELS, THE
KARATE
| ❑ 5402 [M] | Juanita Banana | 1966 | 20.00 | 40.00 | 80.00 |

PEGGY SUE
DECCA
| ❑ DL 75153 | Dynamite! | 1969 | 6.25 | 12.50 | 25.00 |
| ❑ DL 75215 | All American Husband | 1970 | 6.25 | 12.50 | 25.00 |

PEIFFER, BERNARD
DECCA
❑ DL 8626 [M]	The Astounding Bernard Peiffer	1958	12.50	25.00	50.00
❑ DL 9203 [M]	Piano Ala Mood	1958	12.50	25.00	50.00
❑ DL 9218 [M]	The Pied Peiffer of the Piano	1959	12.50	25.00	50.00
❑ DL 79203 [S]	Piano Ala Mood	1958	10.00	20.00	40.00
❑ DL 79218 [S]	The Pied Peiffer of the Piano	1959	10.00	20.00	40.00
EMARCY
| ❑ MG-26036 [10] | Le Most | 1954 | 20.00 | 40.00 | 80.00 |
| ❑ MG-36080 [M] | Bernie's Tunes | 1956 | 12.50 | 25.00 | 50.00 |
LAURIE
| ❑ LLP-1006 [M] | Modern Jazz for People Who Like Original Music | 1960 | 6.25 | 12.50 | 25.00 |
| ❑ SLP-1006 [S] | Modern Jazz for People Who Like Original Music | 1960 | 7.50 | 15.00 | 30.00 |

PELL, DAVE

Number	Title (A Side/B Side)	Yr	VG	VG+	NM
❑ LLP-1008 [M]	Cole Porter's "Can Can"	1960	6.25	12.50	25.00
❑ SLP-1008 [S]	Cole Porter's "Can Can"	1960	7.50	15.00	30.00

NORGRAN

❑ MGN-11 [10]	Bernard Peiffer Et Son Trio	1954	20.00	40.00	80.00

PELL, DAVE
ATLANTIC

❑ 1216 [M]	Jazz and Romantic Places	1955	25.00	50.00	100.00
—Black label					
❑ 1216 [M]	Jazz and Romantic Places	1961	7.50	15.00	30.00
—Multicolor label, white "fan" logo at right					
❑ 1249 [M]	Love Story	1956	20.00	40.00	80.00
—Black label					
❑ 1249 [M]	Love Story	1961	7.50	15.00	30.00
—Multicolor label, white "fan" logo at right					

CAPITOL

❑ T 925 [M]	I Had the Craziest Dream	1958	7.50	15.00	30.00
—Turquoise label					
❑ ST 1309 [S]	The Big Small Bands	1960	6.25	12.50	25.00
❑ T 1309 [M]	The Big Small Bands	1960	5.00	10.00	20.00
❑ ST 1512 [S]	Old South Wails	1961	6.25	12.50	25.00
❑ T 1512 [M]	Old South Wails	1961	5.00	10.00	20.00
❑ ST 1687 [S]	I Remember John Kirby	1962	6.25	12.50	25.00
❑ T 1687 [M]	I Remember John Kirby	1962	5.00	10.00	20.00

CORAL

❑ CRL 57248 [M]	Swingin' School Songs	1958	7.50	15.00	30.00
❑ CRL 757248 [S]	Swingin' School Songs	1958	6.25	12.50	25.00

KAPP

❑ KL-1025 [M]	Dave Pell Plays Rodgers and Hart	1956	7.50	15.00	30.00
❑ KL-1034 [M]	Dave Pell Plays Burke and Van Heusen	1956	10.00	20.00	40.00
❑ KL-1036 [M]	Dave Pell Plays Irving Berlin	1957	10.00	20.00	40.00

LIBERTY

❑ LST-7298 [S]	Today;s Hits in Jazz	1961	5.00	10.00	20.00
❑ LST-7321 [S]	Jazz Voices in Video	1963	5.00	10.00	20.00

PRI

❑ 3002 [M]	Dave Pell Plays Harry James' Big Band Sounds	196?	5.00	10.00	20.00
❑ 3003 [M]	Dave Pell Plays Artie Shaw's Big Band Sounds	196?	5.00	10.00	20.00
❑ 3004 [M]	Dave Pell Plays Benny Goodman's Big Band Sounds	196?	5.00	10.00	20.00
❑ 3005 [M]	Dave Pell Plays Lawrence Welk's Big Band Sounds	196?	5.00	10.00	20.00
❑ 3006 [M]	Dave Pell Plays Perez Prado's Big Band Sounds	196?	5.00	10.00	20.00
❑ 3007 [M]	Dave Pell Plays Duke Ellington's Big Band Sounds	196?	5.00	10.00	20.00
❑ 3009 [M]	Dave Pell Plays Mantovani's Big Band Sounds	196?	5.00	10.00	20.00
❑ 3010 [M]	Dave Pell Plays the Dorsey Brothers' Big Band Sounds	196?	5.00	10.00	20.00
❑ 3011 [M]	Dave Pell Plays the Big Band Sounds	196?	5.00	10.00	20.00

RCA VICTOR

❑ LPM-1320 [M]	Jazz Goes Dancing	1956	12.50	25.00	50.00
❑ LPM-1394 [M]	Swingin' in the Ol' Corral	1957	12.50	25.00	50.00
❑ LPM-1524 [M]	Pell of a Time	1957	12.50	25.00	50.00
❑ LPM-1662 [M]	Campus Hop	1957	12.50	25.00	50.00

TREND

❑ TL-1003 [10]	Dave Pell Plays Irving Berlin	1953	30.00	60.00	120.00
❑ TL-1501 [M]	Dave Pell Plays Rodgers and Hart	1954	25.00	50.00	100.00

PENAZZI, ANDRE
DAUNTLESS

❑ 7020 [S]	Organ Jazz Samba Percussion	1963	5.00	10.00	20.00

PENDERGRASS, TEDDY
Also see HAROLD MELVIN AND THE BLUE NOTES.

ASYLUM

❑ 60317	Love Language	1984	2.00	4.00	8.00
❑ 60447	Workin' It Back	1985	2.00	4.00	8.00

ELEKTRA

❑ 60775	Joy	1988	2.00	4.00	8.00

PHILADELPHIA INT'L.

❑ PZ 34390	Teddy Pendergrass	1977	2.50	5.00	10.00
—No bar code on back cover					
❑ PZ 34390	Teddy Pendergrass	198?	2.00	4.00	8.00
—With bar code on back cover					
❑ PZ 35095	Life Is a Song Worth Singing	1978	2.50	5.00	10.00
—No bar code on back cover					
❑ PZ 35095	Life Is a Song Worth Singing	198?	2.00	4.00	8.00
—With bar code on back cover					
❑ FZ 36003	Teddy	1979	2.50	5.00	10.00
❑ PZ 36003	Teddy	198?	2.00	4.00	8.00
—Budget-line reissue with new prefix					
❑ KZ2 36294 [(2)]	Teddy Live! Coast to Coast	1979	3.00	6.00	12.00
❑ FZ 36745	TP	1980	2.50	5.00	10.00
❑ PZ 36745	TP	198?	2.00	4.00	8.00
—Budget-line reissue with new prefix					
❑ FZ 37491	It's Time for Love	1981	2.50	5.00	10.00
❑ PZ 37491	It's Time for Love	198?	2.00	4.00	8.00
—Budget-line reissue with new prefix					
❑ FZ 38118	This One's for You	1982	2.50	5.00	10.00
❑ PZ 38118	This One's for You	198?	2.00	4.00	8.00
—Budget-line reissue with new prefix					
❑ FZ 38646	Heaven Only Knows	1983	2.50	5.00	10.00
❑ PZ 38646	Heaven Only Knows	1985	2.00	4.00	8.00
—Budget-line reissue with new prefix					
❑ FZ 39252	Greatest Hits	1984	2.50	5.00	10.00
❑ HZ 47491	It's Time for Love	198?	10.00	20.00	40.00
—Half-speed mastered edition					

PENGUINS, THE
COLLECTABLES

Number	Title (A Side/B Side)	Yr	VG	VG+	NM
❑ COL-5045	Golden Classics	198?	2.50	5.00	10.00

DOOTO

❑ DTL-204 [M]	The Best Vocal Groups…Rhythm and Blues	1959	50.00	100.00	200.00
—Reissue of Dootone 204; blue and yellow label					
❑ DTL-204 [M]	The Best Vocal Groups…Rhythm and Blues	196?	25.00	50.00	100.00
—Black label with gold/orange/blue ring. This is NOT a counterfeit.					
❑ DTL-242 [M]	The Cool, Cool Penguins	1959	175.00	350.00	700.00
—Blue and yellow label					
❑ DTL-242 [M]	The Cool, Cool Penguins	1959	175.00	350.00	700.00
—Red and yellow label					
❑ DTL-242 [M]	The Cool, Cool Penguins	196?	50.00	100.00	200.00
—Black label with gold/orange/blue ring. This is NOT a counterfeit.					

DOOTONE

❑ DTL-204 [M]	The Best Vocal Groups…Rhythm and Blues	195?	125.00	250.00	500.00
—As above; glossy maroon label					
❑ DTL-204 [M]	The Best Vocal Groups…Rhythm and Blues	1957	375.00	750.00	1500.
—Also includes tracks by the Medallions, Don Julian and the Meadowlarks, and the Dootones. Flat maroon label.					

PENNY, HANK
AUDIO LAB

❑ AL-1508 [M]	Hank Penny Sings	1959	50.00	100.00	200.00

PENNY AND JEAN
RCA VICTOR

❑ LPM-2244 [M]	Two for the Road	1961	5.00	10.00	20.00
❑ LSP-2244 [S]	Two for the Road	1961	6.25	12.50	25.00

PENTAGON
EAST WIND

❑ 10002	Pentagon	1979	5.00	10.00	20.00

PENTANGLE, THE
GREEN LINNET

❑ SIF-3048	So Early in the Spring	1990	3.00	6.00	12.00

REPRISE

❑ MS 2100	Solomon's Seal	1972	3.75	7.50	15.00
❑ RS 6315	The Pentangle	1968	5.00	10.00	20.00
—With "W7" and "r:" logos on two-tone orange label					
❑ RS 6315	The Pentangle	1970	3.75	7.50	15.00
—With only "r:" logo on all-orange (tan) label					
❑ 2RS 6334 [(2)]	Sweet Child	1969	6.25	12.50	25.00
—With "W7" and "r:" logos on two-tone orange label					
❑ 2RS 6334 [(2)]	Sweet Child	1970	4.50	9.00	18.00
—With only "r:" logo on all-orange (tan) label					
❑ RS 6372	Basket of Light	1969	5.00	10.00	20.00
—With "W7" and "r:" logos on two-tone orange label					
❑ RS 6372	Basket of Light	1970	3.75	7.50	15.00
—With only "r:" logo on all-orange (tan) label					
❑ RS 6430	Cruel Sister	1971	3.75	7.50	15.00
❑ RS 6463	Reflection	1971	3.75	7.50	15.00

SHANACHIE

❑ 79066	A Maid That's Deep in Love	198?	2.50	5.00	10.00

VARRICK

❑ VR-017	Open the Door	1985	2.50	5.00	10.00
❑ VR-026	In the Round	1986	2.50	5.00	10.00

PEOPLE
CAPITOL

❑ ST-151	Both Sides of People	1969	10.00	20.00	40.00
❑ ST 2924	I Love You	1968	10.00	20.00	40.00

PARAMOUNT

❑ PAS-5013	There Are People	1970	5.00	10.00	20.00

PEPPER, ART
ANALOGUE PRODUCTIONS

❑ AP 010	Art Pepper Meets the Rhythm Section	199?	6.25	12.50	25.00
—Reissue on audiophile vinyl					
❑ AP 012	Smack Up!	199?	6.25	12.50	25.00
—Reissue on audiophile vinyl					
❑ AP 017	Art Pepper + Eleven: Modern Jazz Classics	199?	6.25	12.50	25.00
—Reissue on audiophile vinyl					

CONTEMPORARY

❑ C-3532 [M]	Art Pepper Meets the Rhythm Section	1957	25.00	50.00	100.00
❑ M-3568 [M]	Art Pepper + Eleven: Modern Jazz Classics	1959	20.00	40.00	80.00
❑ M-3573 [M]	Gettin' Together!	1960	12.50	25.00	50.00
❑ M-3602 [M]	Smack Up!	1961	10.00	20.00	40.00
❑ M-3607 [M]	Intensity	1963	7.50	15.00	30.00
❑ M-3630 [M]	The Way It Was!	1966	6.25	12.50	25.00
❑ S-7532 [S]	Art Pepper Meets the Rhythm Section	1959	12.50	25.00	50.00
❑ S-7568 [S]	Art Pepper + Eleven: Modern Jazz Classics	1959	15.00	30.00	60.00
❑ S-7573 [S]	Gettin' Together!	1960	15.00	30.00	60.00
❑ S-7602 [S]	Smack Up!	1961	12.50	25.00	50.00
❑ S-7607 [S]	Intensity	1963	10.00	20.00	40.00
❑ S-7630 [S]	The Way It Was!	1966	7.50	15.00	30.00

DISCOVERY

❑ 3019 [10]	Art Pepper Quartet	1952	75.00	150.00	300.00
❑ 3023 [10]	Art Pepper Quintet	1954	62.50	125.00	250.00

INTERLUDE

❑ MO-512 [M]	Art Pepper Quartet	1959	12.50	25.00	50.00
❑ ST-1012 [S]	Art Pepper Quartet	1959	10.00	20.00	40.00

INTRO

❑ 606 [M]	Modern Art	1957	200.00	400.00	800.00

JAZZ WEST

❑ JLP-10 [M]	The Return of Art Pepper	1956	125.00	250.00	500.00

MOSAIC

❑ M3-105 [(3)]	The Complete Pacific Jazz Small Group Recordings of Art Pepper	198?	12.50	25.00	50.00

Number	Title (A Side/B Side)	Yr	VG	VG+	NM
PACIFIC JAZZ					
❏ PJ-60 [M]	The Artistry of Pepper	1962	10.00	20.00	40.00
SAVOY					
❏ MG-12089 [M]	Surf Ride	1956	25.00	50.00	100.00
SCORE					
❏ SLP-4030 [M]	Modern Art	1958	25.00	50.00	100.00
❏ SLP-4031 [M]	The Art Pepper-Red Norvo Sextet	1958	25.00	50.00	100.00
❏ SLP-4032 [M]	The Return of Art Pepper	1958	25.00	50.00	100.00
STEREO RECORDS					
❏ S-7018 [S]	Art Pepper Meets the Rhythm Section	1958	20.00	40.00	80.00
TAMPA					
❏ TP-20 [M]	Art Pepper Quartet	1957	50.00	100.00	200.00
—Colored vinyl					
❏ TP-20 [M]	Art Pepper Quartet	1958	25.00	50.00	100.00
—Black vinyl					
❏ TS-1001 [S]	Art Pepper Quartet	1959	20.00	40.00	80.00
PEPPER, ART/SHELLY MANNE					
CHARLIE PARKER					
❏ PLP-836 [M]	Pepper/Manne	1963	6.25	12.50	25.00
❏ PLP-836S [S]	Pepper/Manne	1963	7.50	15.00	30.00
PEPPER, ART/SONNY REDD					
REGENT					
❏ MG-6069 [M]	Two Altos	1959	12.50	25.00	50.00
SAVOY					
❏ MG-12215 [M]	Art Pepper-Sonny Redd	1969	5.00	10.00	20.00
PEPPER, JIM					
EMBRYO					
❏ SD-731 [(2)]	Pepper's Powwow	196?	10.00	20.00	40.00
PEPPERMINT, DANNY					
CARLTON					
❏ LP-20001 [M]	Twist with Danny Peppermint	1962	10.00	20.00	40.00
❏ STLP-20001 [S]	Twist with Danny Peppermint	1962	12.50	25.00	50.00
PEPPERMINT RAINBOW, THE					
DECCA					
❏ DL 75129	Will You Be Staying After Sunday	1969	5.00	10.00	20.00
PEPPERMINT TROLLEY COMPANY, THE					
ACTA					
❏ A-8007 [M]	The Peppermint Trolley Company	1968	12.50	25.00	50.00
—In stereo cover with "Monaural" sticker					
❏ A-38007 [S]	The Peppermint Trolley Company	1968	6.25	12.50	25.00
PERE UBU					
BLANK					
❏ 001	The Modern Dance	1978	10.00	20.00	40.00
CHRYSALIS					
❏ CHR 1207	Dub Housing	1979	6.25	12.50	25.00
ENIGMA					
❏ D1-73343	The Tenement Years	1988	3.00	6.00	12.00
FONTANA					
❏ 838237-1	Cloudland	1989	3.00	6.00	12.00
ROUGH TRADE					
❏ ROUGH US 4	The Art of Walking	1980	5.00	10.00	20.00
—Revised version: Vocal added on "Arabia"; "Miles" is shortened					
❏ ROUGH US 4	The Art of Walking	1980	10.00	20.00	40.00
—First 1,800 were incorrectly mastered					
❏ ROUGH US 7	The Modern Dance	1981	5.00	10.00	20.00
—Reissue of Blank 001					
❏ ROUGH US 10	390 Degrees of Simulated Stereo	1981	5.00	10.00	20.00
❏ ROUGH US 21	The Song of the Bailing Man	1982	5.00	10.00	20.00
PERHACS, LINDA					
KAPP					
❏ KS-3636	Parallelograms	1970	50.00	100.00	200.00
PERKINS, BILL					
LIBERTY					
❏ LRP-3293 [M]	Bossa Nova	1963	5.00	10.00	20.00
❏ LST-7293 [S]	Bossa Nova	1963	6.25	12.50	25.00
PACIFIC JAZZ					
❏ PJ-1221 [M]	The Bill Perkins Octet On Stage	1956	25.00	50.00	100.00
RIVERSIDE					
❏ RS-3052	Quietly There	1969	6.25	12.50	25.00
WORLD PACIFIC					
❏ WP-1221 [M]	The Bill Perkins Octet On Stage	1958	20.00	40.00	80.00
PERKINS, BILL, AND RICHIE KAMUCA					
LIBERTY					
❏ LRP-3051 [M]	Tenors Head On	1957	15.00	30.00	60.00
PERKINS, BILL; ART PEPPER; RICHIE KAMUCA					
PACIFIC JAZZ					
❏ PJM-401 [M]	Just Friends	1956	30.00	60.00	120.00
WORLD PACIFIC					
❏ PJM-401 [M]	Just Friends	1958	20.00	40.00	80.00
PERKINS, CARL					
ACCORD					
❏ SN-7169	Presenting Carl Perkins	1982	2.50	5.00	10.00
ALBUM GLOBE					
❏ 8118	Country Soul	1980	2.50	5.00	10.00
❏ 9037	Goin' Back to Memphis	1980	2.50	5.00	10.00
ALLEGIANCE					
❏ AV-5001	The Heart and Soul of Carl Perkins	198?	2.50	5.00	10.00
BULLDOG					
❏ BDL-2034	Twenty Golden Pieces	198?	2.50	5.00	10.00

Number	Title (A Side/B Side)	Yr	VG	VG+	NM
COLUMBIA					
❏ CL 1234 [DJ]	Whole Lotta Shakin'	1958	200.00	400.00	800.00
—White label promo					
❏ CL 1234 [M]	Whole Lotta Shakin'	1958	100.00	200.00	400.00
❏ CS 9833	Carl Perkins' Greatest Hits	1969	6.25	12.50	25.00
—Red "360 Sound Stereo" label					
❏ CS 9931	Carl Perkins On Top	1969	6.25	12.50	25.00
—Red "360 Sound Stereo" label					
❏ CS 9981	Boppin' the Blues	1970	3.00	6.00	12.00
—Orange label					
❏ CS 9981	Boppin' the Blues	1970	6.25	12.50	25.00
—Red "360 Sound Stereo" label					
❏ PC 9981	Boppin' the Blues	198?	2.00	4.00	8.00
—Budget-line reissue					
❏ FC 37961	The Survivors	1982	2.50	5.00	10.00
—With Johnny Cash and Jerry Lee Lewis					
❏ PC 37961	The Survivors	198?	2.00	4.00	8.00
—Budget-line reissue					
COLUMBIA LIMITED EDITION					
❏ LE 10117	Carl Perkins' Greatest Hits	1974	3.00	6.00	12.00
—"Limited Edition" brown label					
DESIGN					
❏ DLP-611 [M]	Tennessee	1963	7.50	15.00	30.00
❏ SDLP-611 [R]	Tennessee	1963	5.00	10.00	20.00
DOLLIE					
❏ 4001	Country Boy's Dream	1967	7.50	15.00	30.00
❏ ST-91428	Country Boy's Dream	1967	10.00	20.00	40.00
—Capitol Record Club edition					
HARMONY					
❏ HS 11385	Carl Perkins	1970	3.75	7.50	15.00
❏ KH 31179	Brown Eyed Handsome Man	1971	3.00	6.00	12.00
❏ KH 31792	Greatest Hits	1972	3.00	6.00	12.00
HILLTOP					
❏ 6103	Matchbox	197?	3.00	6.00	12.00
JET					
❏ JT-LA856-H	Ol' Blue Suede's Back	1978	3.75	7.50	15.00
❏ JZ 35604	Ol' Blue Suede's Back	1978	2.50	5.00	10.00
KOALA					
❏ AW 14164	Country Soul	198?	2.50	5.00	10.00
MCA DOT					
❏ 39035	Carl Perkins	1985	2.50	5.00	10.00
MERCURY					
❏ SRM-1-691	My Kind of Country	1973	3.00	6.00	12.00
RHINO					
❏ RNLP-70221	Original Sun Greatest Hits (1955-1957)	1986	3.00	6.00	12.00
ROUNDER					
❏ SS-27	Honky Tonk Gal: Rare and Unissued Sun Masters	1989	3.00	6.00	12.00
SMASH					
❏ 830002-1	Class of '55	1986	3.00	6.00	12.00
—With Jerry Lee Lewis, Roy Orbison and Johnny Cash					
SUEDE					
❏ 002	Live at Austin City Limits	1981	2.50	5.00	10.00
SUN					
❏ LP-111	Original Golden Hits	1969	3.00	6.00	12.00
❏ LP-112	Blue Suede Shoes	1969	3.00	6.00	12.00
❏ SLP-1225 [M]	The Dance Album of Carl Perkins	1957	300.00	600.00	1200.
❏ SLP-1225 [M]	Teen Beat — The Best of Carl Perkins	1961	125.00	250.00	500.00
—Reissue with new title					
SUNNYVALE					
❏ 9330803	The Sun Story, Vol. 3	1977	3.00	6.00	12.00
TRIP					
❏ TLP-8503 [(2)]	The Best of Carl Perkins	1974	3.00	6.00	12.00
UNIVERSAL					
❏ UVL-76001	Born to Rock	1989	3.75	7.50	15.00
PERKINS, CARL (2)					
Jazz pianist.					
DOOTONE					
❏ DL-211 [M]	Introducing Carl Perkins	1956	30.00	60.00	120.00
—Black vinyl					
❏ DL-211 [M]	Introducing Carl Perkins	1956	50.00	100.00	200.00
—Red vinyl					
PERREY, JEAN-JACQUES					
PICKWICK					
❏ PC-3160 [M]	The Happy Moog	196?	5.00	10.00	20.00
❏ SPC-3160 [S]	The Happy Moog	196?	6.25	12.50	25.00
—Silver label					
VANGUARD					
❏ VSD-6549	Moog Indigo	1969	10.00	20.00	40.00
❏ VSD-79286	The Amazing New Electronic Pop Sound of Jean-Jackques Perrey	1968	10.00	20.00	40.00
PERREY-KINGSLEY					
VANGUARD					
❏ VSD-71/72 [(2)]	The Essential Perrey & Kingsley	197?	7.50	15.00	30.00
❏ VSD-6525	Kaleidoscopic Vibrations	1969	7.50	15.00	30.00
❏ VRS-9222 [M]	The In Sound from Way Out!	1966	7.50	15.00	30.00
❏ VSD-79222 [S]	The In Sound from Way Out!	1966	10.00	20.00	40.00
PERRINE, PEP					
HIDEOUT					
❏ 1003 [M]	Pep Perrine Live and In Person	196?	30.00	60.00	120.00
PERSIP, CHARLIE					
BETHLEHEM					
❏ BCP-6046 [M]	Charlie Persip and the Jazz Statesmen	1960	10.00	20.00	40.00
❏ SBCP-6046 [S]	Charlie Persip and the Jazz Statesmen	1960	10.00	20.00	40.00

Number	Title (A Side/B Side)	Yr	VG	VG+	NM

PERSON, HOUSTON
PRESTIGE
❏ PRLP-7491 [M]	Underground Soul	1967	7.50	15.00	30.00
❏ PRST-7491 [S]	Underground Soul	1967	5.00	10.00	20.00
❏ PRST-7517	Chocomotive	1968	5.00	10.00	20.00
❏ PRST-7548	Trust in Me	1968	5.00	10.00	20.00
❏ PRST-7566	Blue Odyssey	1968	5.00	10.00	20.00
❏ PRST-7621	Soul Dance!	1969	5.00	10.00	20.00
❏ PRST-7678	Goodness!	1969	5.00	10.00	20.00
❏ PRST-7767	The Truth!	1970	5.00	10.00	20.00
❏ 10003	Person to Person	1971	6.25	12.50	25.00
❏ 10017	Houston Express	1971	5.00	10.00	20.00
❏ 10044	Broken Windows, Empty Hallways	1972	5.00	10.00	20.00
❏ 10055	Sweet Buns and Barbeque	1973	5.00	10.00	20.00

20TH CENTURY
❏ W-205	Houston Person	196?	6.25	12.50	25.00

PERSSON, AAKE
EMARCY
❏ MG-26039 [10]	Swedish Modern	1954	50.00	100.00	200.00

PERSSON, AAKE/ARNE DOMNERUS
PRESTIGE
❏ PRLP-173 [10]	Aake Persson Swedish All Stars	1953	62.50	125.00	250.00

PERSUADERS, THE
Soul group.
ATCO
❏ SD 7021	The Persuaders	1973	5.00	10.00	20.00
❏ SD 7046	Best Thing That Ever Happened to Me	1974	5.00	10.00	20.00

CALLA
❏ PZ 34802	It's All About Love	1977	3.75	7.50	15.00

COLLECTABLES
❏ COL-5139	Thin Line Between Love and Hate (Golden Classics)	198?	2.50	5.00	10.00

WIN OR LOSE
❏ SD 33-387	Thin Line Between Love and Hate	1972	6.25	12.50	25.00

PERSUADERS, THE (2)
Surf group.
SATURN
❏ SAT-5000 [M]	Surfer's Nightmare	1963	75.00	150.00	300.00
❏ SATS-5000 [S]	Surfer's Nightmare	1963	100.00	200.00	400.00

PERSUASIONS, THE
A&M
❏ SP-3635	More Than Before	1974	3.00	6.00	12.00
❏ SP-3656	I Just Want to Sing with My Friends	1974	3.00	6.00	12.00

CAPITOL
❏ SM-791	We Came to Play	197?	2.50	5.00	10.00
—Reissue with new prefix					
❏ ST-791	We Came to Play	1971	6.25	12.50	25.00
❏ ST-872	Street Corner Symphony	1972	6.25	12.50	25.00
❏ ST-11101	Spread the Word	1972	6.25	12.50	25.00

CATAMOUNT
❏ 905	Stardust	197?	10.00	20.00	40.00

ELEKTRA
❏ 7E-1099	Chirpin'	1977	3.00	6.00	12.00

FLYING FISH
❏ FF-093	Comin' At Ya	1979	3.00	6.00	12.00

MCA
❏ 326	We Still Ain't Got No Band	1973	3.75	7.50	15.00

REPRISE
❏ RS 6394	Acapella	1970	7.50	15.00	30.00

ROUNDER
❏ 3053	Good News	1981	2.50	5.00	10.00
❏ 3083	No Frills	1984	2.50	5.00	10.00

PET SHOP BOYS
EMI
❏ E1-28105	Disco 2	1994	3.00	6.00	12.00
❏ E1-34023 [(3)]	Alternative	1995	10.00	20.00	40.00
—Box set pressed in UK for import into the US (regular UK pressings have gatefold sleeves)					

EMI AMERICA
❏ PW-17193	Please	1986	3.00	6.00	12.00
❏ SQ-17246	Disco	1986	3.00	6.00	12.00
❏ R 164390	Please	1986	3.50	7.00	14.00
—BMG Direct Marketing edition					

EMI MANHATTAN
❏ SPRO 04233 [(3)DJ]	Special Limited Edition: Introspective Club Mixes	1988	10.00	20.00	40.00
—Promo-only set of three 12" records of remixes					
❏ ELJ-46972	Actually	1987	3.00	6.00	12.00
❏ E1-90263 [(2)]	Actually	1988	5.00	10.00	20.00
—Limited double-LP set with extra record of remixes					
❏ E1-90868	Introspective	1988	3.00	6.00	12.00
❏ R 100681	Introspective	1988	3.50	7.00	14.00
—BMG Direct Marketing edition					
❏ R 153678	Actually	1987	3.50	7.00	14.00
—BMG Direct Marketing edition					

PETER AND GORDON
CAPITOL
❏ ST 2115 [S]	A World Without Love	1964	6.25	12.50	25.00
❏ T 2115 [M]	A World Without Love	1964	5.00	10.00	20.00
❏ ST 2220 [S]	I Don't Want to See You Again	1964	6.25	12.50	25.00
❏ T 2220 [M]	I Don't Want to See You Again	1964	5.00	10.00	20.00
❏ ST 2324 [S]	I Go to Pieces	1965	6.25	12.50	25.00
❏ T 2324 [M]	I Go to Pieces	1965	5.00	10.00	20.00
❏ ST 2368 [S]	True Love Ways	1965	6.25	12.50	25.00
❏ T 2368 [M]	True Love Ways	1965	5.00	10.00	20.00

Number	Title (A Side/B Side)	Yr	VG	VG+	NM
❏ ST 2430 [S]	Peter and Gordon Sing the Hits of Nashville	1966	6.25	12.50	25.00
❏ T 2430 [M]	Peter and Gordon Sing the Hits of Nashville	1966	5.00	10.00	20.00
❏ ST 2477 [P]	Woman	1966	6.25	12.50	25.00
—"Woman" is rechanneled					
❏ T 2477 [M]	Woman	1966	5.00	10.00	20.00
❏ ST 2549 [P]	The Best of Peter and Gordon	1966	4.50	9.00	18.00
—Black label with colorband; "Woman" is rechanneled					
❏ ST 2549 [P]	The Best of Peter and Gordon	1967	3.75	7.50	15.00
—"Starline" label					
❏ T 2549 [M]	The Best of Peter and Gordon	1966	3.75	7.50	15.00
—Black label with colorband					
❏ T 2549 [M]	The Best of Peter and Gordon	1967	3.00	6.00	12.00
—"Starline" label					
❏ ST 2664 [S]	Lady Godiva	1967	5.00	10.00	20.00
❏ T 2664 [M]	Lady Godiva	1967	3.75	7.50	15.00
❏ ST 2729 [S]	Knight in Rusty Armour	1967	5.00	10.00	20.00
❏ T 2729 [M]	Knight in Rusty Armour	1967	3.75	7.50	15.00
❏ ST 2747 [S]	In London for Tea	1967	5.00	10.00	20.00
❏ T 2747 [M]	In London for Tea	1967	3.75	7.50	15.00
❏ ST 2882 [S]	Hot, Cold and Custard	1968	6.25	12.50	25.00
❏ SN-16084 [S]	The Best of Peter and Gordon	1979	2.00	4.00	8.00

PETER, PAUL AND MARY
GOLD CASTLE
❏ D1-71301	No Easy Walk to Freedom	1988	2.50	5.00	10.00
—Reissue of 171001					
❏ D1-71316	A Holiday Celebration	1988	2.50	5.00	10.00
❏ R 164086	A Holiday Celebration	1988	3.00	6.00	12.00
—Same as above, except BMG Direct Marketing edition					
❏ 171001	No Easy Walk to Freedom	1987	3.00	6.00	12.00

PETER, PAUL AND MARY
❏ 830331	Such Is Love	1983	5.00	10.00	20.00

WARNER BROS.
❏ W 1449 [M]	Peter, Paul and Mary	1962	5.00	10.00	20.00
❏ WS 1449 [S]	Peter, Paul and Mary	1962	6.25	12.50	25.00
—Gold label					
❏ WS 1449 [S]	Peter, Paul and Mary	1968	3.00	6.00	12.00
—Green "W7" label					
❏ WS 1449 [S]	Peter, Paul and Mary	1970	2.50	5.00	10.00
—Any later Warner Bros. label (green "WB", palm trees, white label)					
❏ W 1473 [M]	(Moving)	1963	5.00	10.00	20.00
❏ WS 1473 [S]	(Moving)	1963	6.25	12.50	25.00
—Gold label					
❏ WS 1473 [S]	(Moving)	1968	2.50	5.00	10.00
—Any later Warner Bros. label (green "W7", green "WB", palm trees, white label)					
❏ W 1507 [M]	In the Wind	1963	5.00	10.00	20.00
❏ WS 1507 [S]	In the Wind	1963	6.25	12.50	25.00
—Gold label					
❏ WS 1507 [S]	In the Wind	1968	2.50	5.00	10.00
—Any later Warner Bros. label					
❏ 2W 1555 [(2)M]	Peter, Paul and Mary In Concert	1964	6.25	12.50	25.00
❏ 2WS 1555 [(2)S]	Peter, Paul and Mary In Concert	1964	7.50	15.00	30.00
—Gold labels					
❏ 2WS 1555 [(2)S]	Peter, Paul and Mary In Concert	1968	3.00	6.00	12.00
—Any later Warner Bros. label					
❏ W 1589 [M]	A Song Will Rise	1965	5.00	10.00	20.00
❏ WS 1589 [S]	A Song Will Rise	1965	6.25	12.50	25.00
—Gold label					
❏ WS 1589 [S]	A Song Will Rise	1968	2.50	5.00	10.00
—Any later Warner Bros. label					
❏ W 1615 [M]	See What Tomorrow Brings	1965	5.00	10.00	20.00
❏ WS 1615 [S]	See What Tomorrow Brings	1965	6.25	12.50	25.00
—Gold label					
❏ WS 1615 [S]	See What Tomorrow Brings	1968	2.50	5.00	10.00
—Any later Warner Bros. label					
❏ W 1648 [M]	Peter, Paul and Mary Album	1966	5.00	10.00	20.00
❏ WS 1648 [S]	Peter, Paul and Mary Album	1966	6.25	12.50	25.00
—Gold label					
❏ WS 1648 [S]	Peter, Paul and Mary Album	1968	2.50	5.00	10.00
—Any later Warner Bros. label					
❏ W 1700 [M]	Album 1700	1967	6.25	12.50	25.00
❏ WS 1700 [S]	Album 1700	1967	6.25	12.50	25.00
—Gold label					
❏ WS 1700 [S]	Album 1700	1968	3.00	6.00	12.00
—Green "W7" label					
❏ WS 1700 [S]	Album 1700	1970	2.50	5.00	10.00
—Any later Warner Bros. label					
❏ WS 1751	Late Again	1968	3.75	7.50	15.00
—Green "W7" label					
❏ WS 1751	Late Again	1970	2.50	5.00	10.00
—Any later Warner Bros. label					
❏ WS 1785	Peter, Paul and Mommy	1969	3.75	7.50	15.00
—Green "W7" label					
❏ WS 1785	Peter, Paul and Mommy	1970	2.50	5.00	10.00
—Any later Warner Bros. label					
❏ BS 2552	(Ten) Years Together — The Best of Peter, Paul and Mary	1970	3.75	7.50	15.00
—Green "WB" label					
❏ BS 2552	(Ten) Years Together — The Best of Peter, Paul and Mary	1973	3.00	6.00	12.00
—"Burbank" palm-trees label					
❏ BSK 3105	(Ten) Years Together — The Best of Peter, Paul and Mary	1977	2.50	5.00	10.00
—"Burbank" palm-trees label					
❏ BSK 3105	(Ten) Years Together — The Best of Peter, Paul and Mary	1979	2.00	4.00	8.00
—White or tan label					
❏ BSK 3231	Reunion	1978	2.50	5.00	10.00

PETERS, BROCK
UNITED ARTISTS
❏ UAL-3041 [M]	Sing'a Man	1960	7.50	15.00	30.00
❏ UAL-3062 [M]	Brock Peters at the Village Gate	1961	6.25	12.50	25.00

Number	Title (A Side/B Side)	Yr	VG	VG+	NM
❑ UAL-3127 [M]	Brock Peters	1963	5.00	10.00	20.00
❑ UAS-6041 [S]	Sing'a Man	1960	10.00	20.00	40.00
❑ UAS-6062 [S]	Brock Peters at the Village Gate	1961	7.50	15.00	30.00
❑ UAS-6127 [S]	Brock Peters	1963	6.25	12.50	25.00

PETERS, RAY
JCW

❑ 1333	From the Heart	1968	6.25	12.50	25.00

PETERS, ROBERTA
RCA VICTOR RED SEAL

❑ LSC-2379 [S]	Roberta Peters in Recital	1960	5.00	10.00	20.00
—Original with "shaded dog" label					

PETERSEN, PAUL
COLPIX

❑ CP-429 [M]	Lollipops and Roses	1962	12.50	25.00	50.00
❑ SCP-429 [S]	Lollipops and Roses	1962	15.00	30.00	60.00
❑ CP-442 [M]	My Dad	1963	12.50	25.00	50.00
❑ SCP-442 [S]	My Dad	1963	15.00	30.00	60.00

PETERSON, OSCAR
AMERICAN RECORDING SOCIETY

❑ G-415 [M]	An Oscar for Peterson	1957	10.00	20.00	40.00
❑ G-438 [M]	Oscar Peterson Trio at Newport	1957	10.00	20.00	40.00

CLEF

❑ MGC-106 [10]	Oscar Peterson Piano Solos	1951	25.00	50.00	100.00
—Reissue of Mercury 25024					
❑ MGC-107 [10]	Oscar Peterson at Carnegie Hall	1951	25.00	50.00	100.00
❑ MGC-110 [10]	Oscar Peterson Collates	1952	25.00	50.00	100.00
❑ MGC-116 [10]	The Oscar Peterson Quartet	1952	25.00	50.00	100.00
❑ MGC-119 [10]	Oscar Peterson Plays Pretty	1952	25.00	50.00	100.00
❑ MGC-127 [10]	Oscar Peterson Collates No. 2	1953	20.00	40.00	80.00
❑ MGC-145 [10]	Oscar Peterson Sings	1954	20.00	40.00	80.00
❑ MGC-155 [10]	Oscar Peterson Plays Pretty No. 2	1954	20.00	40.00	80.00
❑ MGC-168 [10]	The Oscar Peterson Quartet No. 2	1954	20.00	40.00	80.00
❑ MGC-603 [M]	Oscar Peterson Plays Cole Porter	1953	15.00	30.00	60.00
❑ MGC-604 [M]	Oscar Peterson Plays Irving Berlin	1953	15.00	30.00	60.00
❑ MGC-605 [M]	Oscar Peterson Plays George Gershwin	1953	15.00	30.00	60.00
❑ MGC-606 [M]	Oscar Peterson Plays Duke Ellington	1953	15.00	30.00	60.00
❑ MGC-623 [M]	Oscar Peterson Plays Jerome Kern	1954	12.50	25.00	50.00
❑ MGC-624 [M]	Oscar Peterson Plays Richard Rodgers	1954	12.50	25.00	50.00
❑ MGC-625 [M]	Oscar Peterson Plays Vincent Youmans	1954	12.50	25.00	50.00
❑ MGC-648 [M]	Oscar Peterson Plays Harry Warren	1955	12.50	25.00	50.00
❑ MGC-649 [M]	Oscar Peterson Plays Harold Arlen	1955	12.50	25.00	50.00
❑ MGC-650 [M]	Oscar Peterson Plays Jimmy McHugh	1955	12.50	25.00	50.00
❑ MGC-688 [M]	The Oscar Peterson Quartet	1956	12.50	25.00	50.00
—Reissue of 116					
❑ MGC-694 [M]	Recital by Oscar Peterson	1956	12.50	25.00	50.00
❑ MGC-695 [M]	Nostalgic Memories by Oscar Peterson	1956	12.50	25.00	50.00
❑ MGC-696 [M]	Tenderly — Music by Oscar Peterson	1956	12.50	25.00	50.00
❑ MGC-697 [M]	Keyboard Music by Oscar Peterson	1956	12.50	25.00	50.00
❑ MGC-698 [M]	An Evening with the Oscar Peterson Duo/Quartet	1956	12.50	25.00	50.00
❑ MGC-708 [M]	Oscar Peterson Plays Count Basie	1956	12.50	25.00	50.00

DCC COMPACT CLASSICS

❑ LPZ-2021	West Side Story	1996	25.00	50.00	100.00
—Audiophile vinyl					

LIMELIGHT

❑ LM-82044 [M]	Soul Espanol	1967	5.00	10.00	20.00
❑ LS-86010 [S]	Canadiana Suite	1965	5.00	10.00	20.00
❑ LS-86023 [S]	Eloquence	1965	5.00	10.00	20.00
❑ LS-86029 [S]	With Respect to Nat	1966	5.00	10.00	20.00

MERCURY

❑ MGC-106 [10]	Oscar Peterson Piano Solos	1951	30.00	60.00	120.00
❑ MGC-107 [10]	Oscar Peterson at Carnegie Hall	1951	30.00	60.00	120.00
❑ MGC-110 [10]	Oscar Peterson Collates	1952	30.00	60.00	120.00
❑ MGC-116 [10]	The Oscar Peterson Quartet	1952	30.00	60.00	120.00
❑ MGC-119 [10]	Oscar Peterson Plays Pretty	1952	30.00	60.00	120.00
❑ MGC-603 [M]	Oscar Peterson Plays Cole Porter	1953	25.00	50.00	100.00
❑ MGC-604 [M]	Oscar Peterson Plays Irving Berlin	1953	25.00	50.00	100.00
❑ MGC-605 [M]	Oscar Peterson Plays George Gershwin	1953	25.00	50.00	100.00
❑ MGC-606 [M]	Oscar Peterson Plays Duke Ellington	1953	25.00	50.00	100.00
❑ MG-20975 [M]	Oscar Peterson Trio + One	1964	6.25	12.50	25.00
❑ MG-25024 [10]	Oscar Peterson Piano Solos	1950	37.50	75.00	150.00
❑ SR-60975 [S]	Oscar Peterson Trio + One	1964	7.50	15.00	30.00

MOBILE FIDELITY

❑ 1-243	Very Tall	1995	5.00	10.00	20.00
—Audiophile vinyl					

RCA VICTOR

❑ LPT-3006 [10]	This Is Oscar Peterson	1952	30.00	60.00	120.00

VERVE

❑ MGV-2002 [M]	In a Romantic Mood — Oscar Peterson with Strings	1956	10.00	20.00	40.00
❑ V-2002 [M]	In a Romantic Mood — Oscar Peterson with Strings	1961	5.00	10.00	20.00
❑ MGV-2004 [M]	Pastel Moods by Oscar Peterson	1956	10.00	20.00	40.00
❑ V-2004 [M]	Pastel Moods by Oscar Peterson	1961	5.00	10.00	20.00
❑ MGV-2012 [M]	Romance — The Vocal Styling of Oscar Peterson	1956	10.00	20.00	40.00
—Reissue of Clef 145					
❑ V-2012 [M]	Romance — The Vocal Styling of Oscar Peterson	1961	5.00	10.00	20.00
❑ MGV-2044 [M]	Recital by Oscar Peterson	1957	10.00	20.00	40.00
—Reissue of Clef 694					
❑ V-2044 [M]	Recital by Oscar Peterson	1961	5.00	10.00	20.00
❑ MGV-2045 [M]	Nostalgic Memories by Oscar Peterson	1957	10.00	20.00	40.00
—Reissue of Clef 695					
❑ V-2045 [M]	Nostalgic Memories by Oscar Peterson	1961	5.00	10.00	20.00
❑ MGV-2046 [M]	Tenderly — Music by Oscar Peterson	1957	10.00	20.00	40.00
—Reissue of Clef 696					

Number	Title (A Side/B Side)	Yr	VG	VG+	NM
❑ V-2046 [M]	Tenderly — Music by Oscar Peterson	1961	5.00	10.00	20.00
❑ MGV-2047 [M]	Keyboard Music by Oscar Peterson	1957	10.00	20.00	40.00
—Reissue of Clef 697					
❑ V-2047 [M]	Keyboard Music by Oscar Peterson	1961	5.00	10.00	20.00
❑ MGV-2048 [M]	An Evening with Oscar Peterson	1957	10.00	20.00	40.00
—Reissue of Clef 698					
❑ V-2048 [M]	An Evening with Oscar Peterson	1961	5.00	10.00	20.00
❑ MGV-2052 [M]	Oscar Peterson Plays the Cole Porter Songbook	1957	10.00	20.00	40.00
—Reissue of Clef 603					
❑ V-2052 [M]	Oscar Peterson Plays the Cole Porter Songbook	1961	5.00	10.00	20.00
❑ MGV-2053 [M]	Oscar Peterson Plays the Irving Berlin Songbook	1957	10.00	20.00	40.00
—Reissue of Clef 604					
❑ V-2053 [M]	Oscar Peterson Plays the Irving Berlin Songbook	1961	5.00	10.00	20.00
❑ MGV-2054 [M]	Oscar Peterson Plays the George Gershwin Songbook	1957	10.00	20.00	40.00
—Reissue of Clef 605					
❑ V-2054 [M]	Oscar Peterson Plays the George Gershwin Songbook	1961	5.00	10.00	20.00
❑ MGV-2055 [M]	Oscar Peterson Plays the Duke Ellington Songbook	1957	10.00	20.00	40.00
—Reissue of Clef 606					
❑ V-2055 [M]	Oscar Peterson Plays the Duke Ellington Songbook	1961	5.00	10.00	20.00
❑ MGV-2056 [M]	Oscar Peterson Plays the Jerome Kern Songbook	1957	10.00	20.00	40.00
—Reissue of Clef 623					
❑ V-2056 [M]	Oscar Peterson Plays the Jerome Kern Songbook	1961	5.00	10.00	20.00
❑ MGV-2057 [M]	Oscar Peterson Plays the Richard Rodgers Songbook	1957	10.00	20.00	40.00
—Reissue of Clef 624					
❑ V-2057 [M]	Oscar Peterson Plays the Richard Rodgers Songbook	1961	5.00	10.00	20.00
❑ MGV-2059 [M]	Oscar Peterson Plays the Harry Warren Songbook	1957	10.00	20.00	40.00
—Reissue of Clef 648					
❑ V-2059 [M]	Oscar Peterson Plays the Harry Warren Songbook	1961	5.00	10.00	20.00
❑ MGV-2060 [M]	Oscar Peterson Plays the Harold Arlen Songbook	1957	10.00	20.00	40.00
—Reissue of Clef 649					
❑ V-2060 [M]	Oscar Peterson Plays the Harold Arlen Songbook	1961	5.00	10.00	20.00
❑ MGV-2061 [M]	Oscar Peterson Plays the Jimmy McHugh Songbook	1957	10.00	20.00	40.00
—Reissue of Clef 650					
❑ V-2061 [M]	Oscar Peterson Plays the Jimmy McHugh Songbook	1961	5.00	10.00	20.00
❑ MGV-2079 [M]	Soft Sands	1957	10.00	20.00	40.00
❑ V-2079 [M]	Soft Sands	1961	5.00	10.00	20.00
❑ MGV-2119 [M]	Oscar Peterson Plays "My Fair Lady"	1958	10.00	20.00	40.00
❑ V-2119 [M]	Oscar Peterson Plays "My Fair Lady"	1961	5.00	10.00	20.00
❑ BOMC 70-5601 [S]	Night Train	197?	6.25	12.50	25.00
—Book-of-the-Month Club edition					
❑ MGVS-6060 [S]	Oscar Peterson Plays "My Fair Lady"	1960	7.50	15.00	30.00
❑ MGVS-6069 [S]	The Oscar Peterson Trio with the Modern Jazz Quartet at the Opera House	1960	7.50	15.00	30.00
❑ MGVS-6071 [S]	Songs for a Swingin' Affair — A Jazz Portrait of Sinatra	1960	10.00	20.00	40.00
❑ MGVS-6083 [S]	Oscar Peterson Plays the Cole Porter Songbook	1960	7.50	15.00	30.00
❑ MGVS-6084 [S]	Oscar Peterson Plays the Irving Berlin Songbook	1960	7.50	15.00	30.00
❑ MGVS-6085 [S]	Oscar Peterson Plays the George Gershwin Songbook	1960	7.50	15.00	30.00
❑ MGVS-6086 [S]	Oscar Peterson Plays the Duke Ellington Songbook	1960	7.50	15.00	30.00
❑ MGVS-6087 [S]	Oscar Peterson Plays the Jerome Kern Songbook	1960	7.50	15.00	30.00
❑ MGVS-6088 [S]	Oscar Peterson Plays the Richard Rodgers Songbook	1960	7.50	15.00	30.00
❑ MGVS-6090 [S]	Oscar Peterson Plays the Harry Warren Songbook	1960	7.50	15.00	30.00
❑ MGVS-6091 [S]	Oscar Peterson Plays the Harold Arlen Songbook	1960	7.50	15.00	30.00
❑ MGVS-6092 [S]	Oscar Peterson Plays the Jimmy McHugh Songbook	1960	7.50	15.00	30.00
❑ MGVS-6119 [S]	Swinging Brass with the Oscar Peterson Trio	1960	7.50	15.00	30.00
❑ MGV-8024 [M]	The Oscar Peterson Trio at the Stratford Shakespearean Festival	1957	10.00	20.00	40.00
❑ V-8024 [M]	The Oscar Peterson Trio at the Stratford Shakespearean Festival	1961	5.00	10.00	20.00
❑ MGV-8072 [M]	The Oscar Peterson Quartet No. 1	1957	10.00	20.00	40.00
❑ V-8072 [M]	The Oscar Peterson Quartet No. 1	1961	5.00	10.00	20.00
❑ MGV-8092 [M]	Oscar Peterson Plays Count Basie	1957	10.00	20.00	40.00
—Reissue of Clef 708					
❑ V-8092 [M]	Oscar Peterson Plays Count Basie	1961	5.00	10.00	20.00
❑ MGV-8239 [M]	The Oscar Peterson Trio with Sonny Stitt, Roy Eldredge and Jo Jones at Newport	1958	10.00	20.00	40.00
❑ V-8239 [M]	The Oscar Peterson Trio with Sonny Stitt, Roy Eldredge and Jo Jones at Newport	1961	5.00	10.00	20.00
❑ MGV-8268 [M]	The Oscar Peterson Trio at the Concertgebouw	1958	10.00	20.00	40.00
❑ V-8268 [M]	The Oscar Peterson Trio at the Concertgebouw	1961	5.00	10.00	20.00
❑ MGV-8269 [M]	The Oscar Peterson Trio with the Modern Jazz Quartet at the Opera House	1958	10.00	20.00	40.00

Number	Title (A Side/B Side)	Yr	VG	VG+	NM
❏ V-8269 [M]	The Oscar Peterson Trio with the Modern Jazz Quartet at the Opera House	1961	5.00	10.00	20.00
❏ MGV-8287 [M]	A Night on the Town	1958	10.00	20.00	40.00
❏ V-8287 [M]	A Night on the Town	1961	5.00	10.00	20.00
❏ MGV-8334 [M]	Songs for a Swingin' Affair — A Jazz Portrait of Sinatra	1959	12.50	25.00	50.00
❏ V-8334 [M]	Songs for a Swingin' Affair — A Jazz Portrait of Sinatra	1961	5.00	10.00	20.00
❏ MGV-8340 [M]	Porgy and Bess	1959	10.00	20.00	40.00
❏ V-8340 [M]	Porgy and Bess	1961	5.00	10.00	20.00
❏ MGV-8351 [M]	The Jazz Soul of Oscar Peterson	1959	10.00	20.00	40.00
❏ V-8351 [M]	The Jazz Soul of Oscar Peterson	1961	5.00	10.00	20.00
❏ MGV-8364 [M]	Swinging Brass with the Oscar Peterson Trio	1959	10.00	20.00	40.00
❏ V-8364 [M]	Swinging Brass with the Oscar Peterson Trio	1961	5.00	10.00	20.00
❏ MGV-8366 [M]	The Music from "Fiorello!"	1960	10.00	20.00	40.00
❏ V-8366 [M]	The Music from "Fiorello!"	1961	5.00	10.00	20.00
❏ MGV-8368 [M]	The Oscar Peterson Trio at J.A.T.P.	1960	10.00	20.00	40.00
❏ V-8368 [M]	The Oscar Peterson Trio at J.A.T.P.	1961	5.00	10.00	20.00
❏ V-8420 [M]	The Trio — Live from Chicago	1961	6.25	12.50	25.00
❏ V6-8420 [S]	The Trio — Live from Chicago	1961	7.50	15.00	30.00
❏ V-8429 [M]	Very Tall	1962	6.25	12.50	25.00
❏ V6-8429 [S]	Very Tall	1962	7.50	15.00	30.00
❏ V-8454 [M]	West Side Story	1962	6.25	12.50	25.00
❏ V6-8454 [S]	West Side Story	1962	7.50	15.00	30.00
❏ V-8476 [M]	Bursting Out with the All Star Big Band!	1962	6.25	12.50	25.00
❏ V6-8476 [S]	Bursting Out with the All Star Big Band!	1962	7.50	15.00	30.00
❏ V-8480 [M]	The Sound of the Trio	1962	6.25	12.50	25.00
❏ V6-8480 [S]	The Sound of the Trio	1962	7.50	15.00	30.00
❏ V-8482 [M]	The Modern Jazz Quartet and the Oscar Peterson Trio at the Opera House	1962	5.00	10.00	20.00
—Reissue of 8269					
❏ V6-8482 [S]	The Modern Jazz Quartet and the Oscar Peterson Trio at the Opera House	1962	5.00	10.00	20.00
—Reissue of 8269					
❏ V-8516 [M]	Affinity	1963	6.25	12.50	25.00
❏ V6-8516 [S]	Affinity	1963	7.50	15.00	30.00
❏ V-8538 [M]	Night Train	1963	6.25	12.50	25.00
❏ V6-8538 [S]	Night Train	1963	7.50	15.00	30.00
❏ V-8562 [M]	The Oscar Peterson Trio with Nelson Riddle	1963	6.25	12.50	25.00
❏ V6-8562 [S]	The Oscar Peterson Trio with Nelson Riddle	1963	7.50	15.00	30.00
❏ V6-8581 [S]	Oscar Peterson Plays "My Fair Lady"	1964	5.00	10.00	20.00
❏ V6-8591 [S]	The Oscar Peterson Trio Plays	1964	5.00	10.00	20.00
❏ V6-8606 [S]	We Get Requests	1965	5.00	10.00	20.00
❏ V6-8660 [S]	Put On a Happy Face	1966	5.00	10.00	20.00
❏ V6-8681 [S]	Something Warm	1966	5.00	10.00	20.00
❏ V-8740 [M]	Night Train, Volume 2	1967	5.00	10.00	20.00

PETERSON, OSCAR/GERRY MULLIGAN
VERVE

Number	Title (A Side/B Side)	Yr	VG	VG+	NM
❏ V-8559 [M]	The Oscar Peterson Trio and the Gerry Mulligan Four at Newport	1963	6.25	12.50	25.00
❏ V6-8559 [S]	The Oscar Peterson Trio and the Gerry Mulligan Four at Newport	1963	7.50	15.00	30.00

PETERSON, RAY
DECCA

Number	Title (A Side/B Side)	Yr	VG	VG+	NM
❏ DL 75307	Ray Peterson Country	1971	5.00	10.00	20.00

MGM

Number	Title (A Side/B Side)	Yr	VG	VG+	NM
❏ E-4250 [M]	The Very Best of Ray Peterson	1964	6.25	12.50	25.00
❏ SE-4250 [S]	The Very Best of Ray Peterson	1964	7.50	15.00	30.00
❏ E-4277 [M]	The Other Side of Ray Peterson	1965	6.25	12.50	25.00
❏ SE-4277 [S]	The Other Side of Ray Peterson	1965	7.50	15.00	30.00

RCA CAMDEN

Number	Title (A Side/B Side)	Yr	VG	VG+	NM
❏ CAL-2119 [M]	Goodnight My Love	1966	3.00	6.00	12.00
❏ CAS-2119 [S]	Goodnight My Love	1966	3.00	6.00	12.00

RCA VICTOR

Number	Title (A Side/B Side)	Yr	VG	VG+	NM
❏ LPM-2297 [M]	Tell Laura I Love Her	1960	25.00	50.00	100.00
❏ LSP-2297 [S]	Tell Laura I Love Her	1960	37.50	75.00	150.00

UNI

Number	Title (A Side/B Side)	Yr	VG	VG+	NM
❏ 73078	Missing You/Featuring His Greatest Hits!	1969	5.00	10.00	20.00

PETERSTEIN, SHORTY
WORLD PACIFIC

Number	Title (A Side/B Side)	Yr	VG	VG+	NM
❏ WP-1274 [M]	The Wide Weird World of Shorty Petterstein	1959	10.00	20.00	40.00

PETTIFORD, OSCAR
ABC-PARAMOUNT

Number	Title (A Side/B Side)	Yr	VG	VG+	NM
❏ ABC-135 [M]	Oscar Pettiford Orchestra in Hi-Fi	1956	25.00	50.00	100.00
❏ ABC-227 [M]	O.P.'s Jazz Men: Oscar Pettiford Orchestra in Hi-Fi, Vol. 2	1958	20.00	40.00	80.00
❏ ABCS-227 [S]	O.P.'s Jazz Men: Oscar Pettiford Orchestra in Hi-Fi, Vol. 2	1958	15.00	30.00	60.00

ATLANTIC

Number	Title (A Side/B Side)	Yr	VG	VG+	NM
❏ 8111 [M]	Live at Jilly's	1965	—	—	—
❏ SD 8111 [S]	Live at Jilly's	1965	—	—	—

BETHLEHEM

Number	Title (A Side/B Side)	Yr	VG	VG+	NM
❏ BCP-33 [M]	Oscar Pettiford Sextet	1955	25.00	50.00	100.00
❏ BCP-1003 [10]	Oscar Pettiford	1954	37.50	75.00	150.00
❏ BCP-1019 [10]	Basically Duke	1955	37.50	75.00	150.00

DEBUT

Number	Title (A Side/B Side)	Yr	VG	VG+	NM
❏ DLP-8 [10]	Oscar Pettiford Sextet	1954	75.00	150.00	300.00

FANTASY

Number	Title (A Side/B Side)	Yr	VG	VG+	NM
❏ 6010 [M]	My Little Cello	1964	7.50	15.00	30.00
❏ 6015 [M]	The Essen Jazz Festival	1964	7.50	15.00	30.00

JAZZLAND

Number	Title (A Side/B Side)	Yr	VG	VG+	NM
❏ JLP-64 [M]	Last Recordings by the Late, Great Bassist	1962	12.50	25.00	50.00
❏ JLP-964 [R]	Last Recordings by the Late, Great Bassist	1962	7.50	15.00	30.00

PETTIFORD, OSCAR/VINNIE BURKE
BETHLEHEM

Number	Title (A Side/B Side)	Yr	VG	VG+	NM
❏ BCP-6 [M]	Bass by Pettiford/Burke	1957	25.00	50.00	100.00

PETTIFORD, OSCAR/RED MITCHELL
BETHLEHEM

Number	Title (A Side/B Side)	Yr	VG	VG+	NM
❏ BCP-2 [M]	Jazz Mainstream	1957	25.00	50.00	100.00

PETTY, NORMAN, TRIO
COLUMBIA

Number	Title (A Side/B Side)	Yr	VG	VG+	NM
❏ CL 1092 [M]	Moondreams	1958	37.50	75.00	150.00

TOP RANK

Number	Title (A Side/B Side)	Yr	VG	VG+	NM
❏ R-639 [M]	Petty for Your Thoughts	1960	7.50	15.00	30.00
❏ RS-639 [S]	Petty for Your Thoughts	1960	10.00	20.00	40.00

VIK

Number	Title (A Side/B Side)	Yr	VG	VG+	NM
❏ LX-1073 [M]	Corsage	1957	17.50	35.00	70.00

PETTY, TOM, AND THE HEARTBREAKERS
BACKSTREET

Number	Title (A Side/B Side)	Yr	VG	VG+	NM
❏ BSR-5106	Damn the Torpedoes	1979	2.50	5.00	10.00
❏ BSR-5160	Hard Promises	1981	2.50	5.00	10.00
❏ BSR-5360	Long After Dark	1982	2.50	5.00	10.00

MCA

Number	Title (A Side/B Side)	Yr	VG	VG+	NM
❏ 1486	Damn the Torpedoes	1987	2.00	4.00	8.00
❏ 5486	Southern Accents	1985	2.50	5.00	10.00
❏ 5836	Let Me Up (I've Had Enough)	1987	2.50	5.00	10.00
❏ 6253	Full Moon Fever	1989	2.50	5.00	10.00
❏ 2-8021 [(2)]	Pack Up the Plantation — Live!	1985	3.00	6.00	12.00
❏ 10317	Into the Great Wide Open	1991	3.75	7.50	15.00
❏ 37116	You're Gonna Get It!	1982	2.00	4.00	8.00
❏ 37143	Tom Petty and the Heartbreakers	1982	2.00	4.00	8.00
❏ 37239	Hard Promises	1984	2.00	4.00	8.00

SHELTER

Number	Title (A Side/B Side)	Yr	VG	VG+	NM
❏ TP-12677 [DJ]	Official Live 'Leg	1977	10.00	20.00	40.00
—Promo-only live album with letter to radio (has been counterfeited)					
❏ SRL-52006	Tom Petty and the Heartbreakers	1976	3.75	7.50	15.00
—Original copies were distributed by ABC					
❏ SRL-52006	Tom Petty and the Heartbreakers	1979	3.00	6.00	12.00
—Later copies were distributed by MCA					
❏ DA-52029	You're Gonna Get It!	1978	3.75	7.50	15.00
—Original copies were distributed by ABC					
❏ DA-52029	You're Gonna Get It!	1979	3.00	6.00	12.00
—Later copies were distributed by MCA					
❏ DA-52029 [DJ]	You're Gonna Get It!	1978	6.25	12.50	25.00
—Promo only on red vinyl					

WARNER BROS.

Number	Title (A Side/B Side)	Yr	VG	VG+	NM
❏ 45759 [(2)]	Wildflowers	1994	5.00	10.00	20.00
❏ 46285	Songs and Music from the Motion Picture "She's the One"	1996	2.50	5.00	10.00
❏ 47294 [(2)]	Echo	1999	5.00	10.00	20.00
❏ 47955	The Last DJ	2002	5.00	10.00	20.00

PHANTOM, THE (1)
CAPITOL

Number	Title (A Side/B Side)	Yr	VG	VG+	NM
❏ ST-11313	The Phantom's Divine Comedy, Part One	1974	15.00	30.00	60.00

PHAPHNER
DRAGON

Number	Title (A Side/B Side)	Yr	VG	VG+	NM
❏ LP-101	Overdrive	1971	1000.	2000.	3000.

PHILBIN, REGIS
MERCURY

Number	Title (A Side/B Side)	Yr	VG	VG+	NM
❏ SR-61169	It's Time for Regis!	1968	6.25	12.50	25.00

PHILHARMONIA HUNGARICA (ANTAL DORATI, CONDUCTOR)
MERCURY LIVING PRESENCE

Number	Title (A Side/B Side)	Yr	VG	VG+	NM
❏ SR 90179 [S]	Kodaly: Dances of Galanta; Maroszek Dancves; Bartok-Weiner: Two Romanian Dances	196?	10.00	20.00	40.00
—Maroon label, no "Vendor: Mercury Record Corporation"					
❏ SR 90183 [S]	Bartok: Dance Suite; Deux Portraits; Mikrokosmos	196?	30.00	60.00	120.00
—Maroon label, no "Vendor: Mercury Record Corporation"					
❏ SR 90190 [S]	Wienerwalzer Paprika	196?	5.00	10.00	20.00
—Maroon label, no "Vendor: Mercury Record Corporation"					
❏ SR 90199 [S]	Respighi: Ancient Airs and Dances, Suites 1-3	196?	5.00	10.00	20.00
—Third edition: Dark red (not maroon) label					
❏ SR 90199 [S]	Respighi: Ancient Airs and Dances, Suites 1-3	196?	10.00	20.00	40.00
—Maroon label, with "Vendor: Mercury Record Corporation"					
❏ SR 90199 [S]	Respighi: Ancient Airs and Dances, Suites 1-3	196?	15.00	30.00	60.00
—Maroon label, no "Vendor: Mercury Record Corporation"					
❏ SR 90200 [S]	Tchaikovsky: Serenade in C; Arensky: Tchaikovsky Variations	196?	20.00	40.00	80.00
—Maroon label, no "Vendor: Mercury Record Corporation"					
❏ SR 90208 [S]	Haydn: Symphonies 94 and 103	196?	10.00	20.00	40.00
—Maroon label, no "Vendor: Mercury Record Corporation"					

PHILLIPS, BILL
DECCA

Number	Title (A Side/B Side)	Yr	VG	VG+	NM
❏ DL 4792 [M]	Put It Off Until Tomorrow	1966	7.50	15.00	30.00
❏ DL 4897 [M]	Bill Phillips' Style	1967	7.50	15.00	30.00
❏ DL 74792 [S]	Put It Off Until Tomorrow	1966	10.00	20.00	40.00
❏ DL 74897 [S]	Bill Phillips' Style	1967	6.25	12.50	25.00
❏ DL 75022	Country Action	1968	5.00	10.00	20.00
❏ DL 75182	Little Boy Sad	1970	5.00	10.00	20.00

HARMONY

Number	Title (A Side/B Side)	Yr	VG	VG+	NM
❏ HL 7309 [M]	Bill Phillips' Best	1964	5.00	10.00	20.00

PHILLIPS, ESTHER
ATLANTIC

Number	Title (A Side/B Side)	Yr	VG	VG+	NM
❏ SD 1565	Burnin'	1970	6.25	12.50	25.00
❏ SD 1680	Confessin' the Blues	1975	3.75	7.50	15.00
❏ 8102 [M]	And I Love Him	1965	12.50	25.00	50.00
—Cover has a pink Cupid on it					
❏ 8102 [M]	And I Love Him	1966	7.50	15.00	30.00
—Cover has a black photo on it					

Number	Title (A Side/B Side)	Yr	VG	VG+	NM
❑ SD 8102 [S]	And I Love Him	1965	20.00	40.00	80.00
—Cover has a pink Cupid on it					
❑ SD 8102 [S]	And I Love Him	1966	10.00	20.00	40.00
—Cover has a black photo on it					
❑ 8122 [M]	Esther	1966	7.50	15.00	30.00
❑ SD 8122 [S]	Esther	1966	10.00	20.00	40.00
❑ 8130 [M]	The Country Side of Esther Phillips	1966	7.50	15.00	30.00
—Reissue of Lenox 227					
❑ SD 8130 [S]	The Country Side of Esther Phillips	1966	10.00	20.00	40.00
—Reissue of Lenox S-227					
❑ 90670	Confessin' the Blues	1987	2.50	5.00	10.00
—Reissue of 1680					
CBS ASSOCIATED					
❑ PZ 40710	What a Diff'rence a Day Makes	1987	2.00	4.00	8.00
—Reissue of Kudu 23					
❑ PZ 40935	From a Whisper to a Scream	1988	2.00	4.00	8.00
—Reissue of Kudu 05					
KING					
❑ 622 [M]	Memory Lane	1959	1000.	2000.	4000.
KUDU					
❑ 05	From a Whisper to a Scream	1972	3.00	6.00	12.00
❑ 09	Alone Again, Naturally	1972	3.00	6.00	12.00
❑ 14	Black-Eyed Blues	1973	3.00	6.00	12.00
❑ 18	Performance	1974	3.00	6.00	12.00
❑ 23	What a Diff'rence a Day Makes	1975	3.00	6.00	12.00
❑ 28	For All We Know	1976	3.00	6.00	12.00
❑ 31	Capricorn Princess	1976	3.00	6.00	12.00
LENOX					
❑ 227 [M]	Release Me	1962	25.00	50.00	100.00
❑ S-227 [S]	Release Me	1962	50.00	100.00	200.00
MERCURY					
❑ SRM-1-1187	You've Come a Long Way, Baby	1977	2.50	5.00	10.00
❑ SRM-1-3733	All About Esther Phillips	1978	2.50	5.00	10.00
❑ SRM-1-3769	Here's Esther — Are You Ready?	1979	2.50	5.00	10.00
❑ SRM-1-4005	A Good Black Is Hard to Crack	1981	2.50	5.00	10.00
MUSE					
❑ MR-5302	A Way to Say Goodbye	1986	3.00	6.00	12.00
SAVOY JAZZ					
❑ SJL-2258	The Complete Savoy Recordings	1984	2.50	5.00	10.00

PHILLIPS, FLIP
BRUNSWICK

Number	Title (A Side/B Side)	Yr	VG	VG+	NM
❑ BL 58032 [10]	Tenor Sax Stylings	1953	37.50	75.00	150.00
CLEF					
❑ MGC-105 [10]	Flip Phillips Quartet	1953	37.50	75.00	150.00
❑ MGC-109 [10]	Flip Phillips Collates	1953	37.50	75.00	150.00
❑ MGC-133 [10]	Flip Phillips Collates No. 2	1953	50.00	100.00	200.00
❑ MGC-158 [10]	Jumping Moods with Flip Phillips	1954	37.50	75.00	150.00
❑ MGC-634 [M]	The Flip Phillips-Buddy Rich Trio	1954	30.00	60.00	120.00
❑ MGC-637 [M]	The Flip Phillips Quintet	1954	30.00	60.00	120.00
❑ MGC-691 [M]	Flip Wails	1956	25.00	50.00	100.00
❑ MGC-692 [M]	Swinging with Flip Phillips and His Orchestra	1956	25.00	50.00	100.00
❑ MGC-693 [M]	Flip	1956	25.00	50.00	100.00
❑ MGC-740 [M]	Rock with Flip	1956	25.00	50.00	100.00
MERCURY					
❑ MGC-105 [10]	Flip Phillips Quartet	1951	62.50	125.00	250.00
❑ MGC-109 [10]	Flip Phillips Collates	1952	50.00	100.00	200.00
❑ MG-25023 [10]	Flip Phillips Quartet	1950	75.00	150.00	300.00
SUE					
❑ LP-1035 [M]	Flip Phillips Revisited	1965	7.50	15.00	30.00
❑ STLP-1035 [S]	Flip Phillips Revisited	1965	10.00	20.00	40.00
VERVE					
❑ MGV-8075 [M]	Flip Wails	1957	20.00	40.00	80.00
❑ V-8075 [M]	Flip Wails	1961	6.25	12.50	25.00
❑ MGV-8076 [M]	Swingin' with Flip	1957	20.00	40.00	80.00
❑ V-8076 [M]	Swingin' with Flip	1961	6.25	12.50	25.00
❑ MGV-8077 [M]	Flip	1957	20.00	40.00	80.00
❑ V-8077 [M]	Flip	1961	6.25	12.50	25.00
❑ MGV-8116 [M]	Rock with Flip	1957	20.00	40.00	80.00
❑ V-8116 [M]	Rock with Flip	1961	6.25	12.50	25.00

PHILLIPS, GENE
CROWN

Number	Title (A Side/B Side)	Yr	VG	VG+	NM
❑ CLP-5375 [M]	Gene Phillips and the Rockers	1963	7.50	15.00	30.00

PHILLIPS, SONNY
PRESTIGE

Number	Title (A Side/B Side)	Yr	VG	VG+	NM
❑ PRST-7737	Sure 'Nuff	1970	5.00	10.00	20.00
❑ PRST-7799	Black Magic	1970	5.00	10.00	20.00
❑ 10007	Black On Black	1971	5.00	10.00	20.00

PHILLIPS, STU
CAPITOL

Number	Title (A Side/B Side)	Yr	VG	VG+	NM
❑ ST 2356 [S]	Feels Like Lovin'	1965	7.50	15.00	30.00
❑ T 2356 [M]	Feels Like Lovin'	1965	6.25	12.50	25.00
RCA VICTOR					
❑ LPM-3619 [M]	Singin' Stu Phillips	1966	5.00	10.00	20.00
❑ LSP-3619 [S]	Singin' Stu Phillips	1966	6.25	12.50	25.00
❑ LPM-3717 [M]	Grassroots Country	1967	7.50	15.00	30.00
❑ LSP-3717 [S]	Grassroots Country	1967	6.25	12.50	25.00
❑ LPM-4012 [M]	Our Last Rendezvous	1968	12.50	25.00	50.00
❑ LSP-4012 [S]	Our Last Rendezvous	1968	6.25	12.50	25.00

PHILLIPS, WARREN, AND THE ROCKETS
PARROT

Number	Title (A Side/B Side)	Yr	VG	VG+	NM
❑ PAS 71044	Rocked Out	1970	7.50	15.00	30.00

PHILLIPS, WOOLF
CORAL

Number	Title (A Side/B Side)	Yr	VG	VG+	NM
❑ CRL 56036 [10]	Woolf Phillips Plays Duke Ellington Songs	1951	12.50	25.00	50.00

PHILOSOPHERS, THE
PHILO

Number	Title (A Side/B Side)	Yr	VG	VG+	NM
❑ 1001	After Sundown	1969	37.50	75.00	150.00

PHIPPS FAMILY, THE
STARDAY

Number	Title (A Side/B Side)	Yr	VG	VG+	NM
❑ SLP-139 [M]	The Phipps Family Sings the Most Requested Sacred Songs of the Carter Family	1961	10.00	20.00	40.00
❑ SLP-195 [M]	Old Time Pickin' and Singin'	1962	7.50	15.00	30.00
❑ SLP-248 [M]	Echoes of the Carter Family	1963	7.50	15.00	30.00

PHLUPH
VERVE

Number	Title (A Side/B Side)	Yr	VG	VG+	NM
❑ V6-5054	Phluph	1968	7.50	15.00	30.00

PIAF, EDITH
CAPITOL

Number	Title (A Side/B Side)	Yr	VG	VG+	NM
❑ DTCL 2953 [(3)]	The Edith Piaf Deluxe Set	1968	7.50	15.00	30.00
❑ T 10210 [M]	Piaf	1959	6.25	12.50	25.00
❑ ST 10283 [S]	Piaf of Paris	1961	5.00	10.00	20.00
❑ T 10283 [M]	Piaf of Paris	1961	3.75	7.50	15.00
❑ ST 10295 [S]	Potpourri Par Piaf	1962	5.00	10.00	20.00
❑ T 10295 [M]	Potpourri Par Piaf	1962	3.75	7.50	15.00
❑ ST 10348 [S]	Piaf and Sarapo at the Bobido	1963	5.00	10.00	20.00
❑ T 10348 [M]	Piaf and Sarapo at the Bobido	1963	3.75	7.50	15.00
❑ ST 10368 [S]	Piaf at the Olympia	1964	5.00	10.00	20.00
❑ T 10368 [M]	Piaf at the Olympia	1964	3.75	7.50	15.00
COLUMBIA					
❑ CL 898 [M]	La Vie En Rose	1956	10.00	20.00	40.00
❑ CL 6223 [10]	Encore Parisiennes	1952	12.50	25.00	50.00
DECCA					
❑ DL 6004 [10]	Chansons de Cafes du Paris	1951	15.00	30.00	60.00
PHILIPS					
❑ PCC 208 [M]	Adieu, Edith Piaf, Little Sparrow	1964	5.00	10.00	20.00
POLYDOR VOX					
❑ PL 3050 [10]	Edith Piaf Sings	195?	20.00	40.00	80.00

PIANO CHOIR, THE
STRATA-EAST

Number	Title (A Side/B Side)	Yr	VG	VG+	NM
❑ SES-19730 [(2)]	Handscapes	1973	6.25	12.50	25.00
❑ SES-19750	Handscapes 2	1975	5.00	10.00	20.00

PIANO RED
ARHOOLIE

Number	Title (A Side/B Side)	Yr	VG	VG+	NM
❑ 1064	William Perryman (Alone with Piano)	197?	3.00	6.00	12.00
EUPHONIC					
❑ 1212	Percussive Piano	198?	2.50	5.00	10.00
GROOVE					
❑ LG-1001 [M]	Jump Man, Jump	1956	—	—	—
—The existence of this LP has not been confirmed					
❑ LG-1002 [M]	Piano Red in Concert	1956	150.00	300.00	600.00
KING					
❑ KS-1117	Happiness Is Piano Red	1970	5.00	10.00	20.00
RCA CAMDEN					
❑ ACL1-0547	Rockin' with Red	1974	3.00	6.00	12.00
SOUTHLAND					
❑ 8	Willie Perryman-Piano Red-Dr. Feelgood	1983	3.75	7.50	15.00

PIATIGORSKI, GREGOR
RCA VICTOR RED SEAL

Number	Title (A Side/B Side)	Yr	VG	VG+	NM
❑ LSC-2490 [S]	Dvorak: Cello Concerto	1961	10.00	20.00	40.00
—With Charles Munch/Boston Symphony Orch.; original with "shaded dog" label					
❑ LSC-2490 [S]	Dvorak: Cello Concerto	199?	6.25	12.50	25.00
—With Charles Munch/Boston Symphony Orch.; Classic Records reissue					

PICHON, WALTER "FATS"
DECCA

Number	Title (A Side/B Side)	Yr	VG	VG+	NM
❑ DL 8390 [M]	Appearing Nightly	1956	10.00	20.00	40.00

PICKETT, BOBBY "BORIS"
GARPAX

Number	Title (A Side/B Side)	Yr	VG	VG+	NM
❑ GPX 57001 [M]	The Original Monster Mash	1962	37.50	75.00	150.00
❑ SGP 67001 [S]	The Original Monster Mash	1962	62.50	125.00	250.00
PARROT					
❑ XPAS 71063 [R]	The Original Monster Mash	1973	6.25	12.50	25.00
—Reissue of Garpax LP with four tracks deleted and one added					

PICKETT, WILSON
ATLANTIC

Number	Title (A Side/B Side)	Yr	VG	VG+	NM
❑ SD 2-501 [(2)]	Wilson Pickett's Greatest Hits	1973	5.00	10.00	20.00
❑ 8114 [M]	In the Midnight Hour	1965	10.00	20.00	40.00
❑ SD 8114 [R]	In the Midnight Hour	1965	7.50	15.00	30.00
❑ 8129 [M]	The Exciting Wilson Pickett	1966	10.00	20.00	40.00
❑ SD 8129 [R]	The Exciting Wilson Pickett	1966	7.50	15.00	30.00
❑ 8136 [M]	The Wicked Pickett	1967	10.00	20.00	40.00
❑ SD 8136 [R]	The Wicked Pickett	1967	7.50	15.00	30.00
❑ 8145 [M]	The Sound of Wilson Pickett	1967	10.00	20.00	40.00
❑ SD 8145 [P]	The Sound of Wilson Pickett	1967	10.00	20.00	40.00
❑ 8151 [M]	The Best of Wilson Pickett	1967	10.00	20.00	40.00
❑ SD 8151 [R]	The Best of Wilson Pickett	1967	5.00	10.00	20.00
❑ SD 8175	I'm in Love	1968	6.25	12.50	25.00
❑ SD 8183	The Midnight Mover	1968	6.25	12.50	25.00
❑ SD 8215	Hey Jude	1969	5.00	10.00	20.00
❑ SD 8250	Right On	1970	5.00	10.00	20.00
❑ SD 8270	Wilson Pickett in Philadelphia	1970	5.00	10.00	20.00
❑ 8290 [M]	The Best of Wilson Pickett, Vol. II	1971	6.25	12.50	25.00
—Mono copies are promo only					
❑ SD 8290 [S]	The Best of Wilson Pickett, Vol. II	1971	3.75	7.50	15.00
❑ SD 8300	Don't Knock My Love	1971	3.75	7.50	15.00
❑ 81283	The Best of Wilson Pickett	1985	2.50	5.00	10.00
BIG TREE					
❑ SD 76011	Funky Situation	1978	3.00	6.00	12.00

Number	Title (A Side/B Side)	Yr	VG	VG+	NM
DOUBLE-L					
❏ DL-2300 [M]	It's Too Late	1963	12.50	25.00	50.00
❏ SDL-8300 [S]	It's Too Late	1963	17.50	35.00	70.00
EMI AMERICA					
❏ SW-17019	I Want You	1979	3.00	6.00	12.00
❏ SW-17043	Right Track	1981	3.00	6.00	12.00
MOTOWN					
❏ 6244 ML	American Soul Man	1987	2.50	5.00	10.00
RCA VICTOR					
❏ APL1-0312	Miz Lena's Boy	1973	3.75	7.50	15.00
❏ APL1-0495	Pickett in the Pocket	1974	3.75	7.50	15.00
❏ APL1-0856	Join Me and Let's Be Free	1975	3.75	7.50	15.00
❏ ANL1-2149	Join Me and Let's Be Free	1977	2.50	5.00	10.00
—Reissue					
❏ LSP-4858	Mr. Magic Man	1973	3.75	7.50	15.00
TRIP					
❏ 8010	Wickedness	1972	2.50	5.00	10.00
WAND					
❏ WD-672 [M]	Great Wilson Pickett Hits	1966	7.50	15.00	30.00
❏ WDS-672 [R]	Great Wilson Pickett Hits	1966	5.00	10.00	20.00
WICKED					
❏ 9001	Chocolate Mountain	1976	6.25	12.50	25.00

PIERCE, BILLIE AND DEDE

Number	Title (A Side/B Side)	Yr	VG	VG+	NM
RIVERSIDE					
❏ RLP-370 [M]	Blues in the Classic Tradition	1961	7.50	15.00	30.00
❏ RLP-394 [M]	Blues and Tonks From the Delta	1961	7.50	15.00	30.00

PIERCE, NAT

Number	Title (A Side/B Side)	Yr	VG	VG+	NM
CORAL					
❏ CRL 57091 [M]	Kansas City Memories	1957	12.50	25.00	50.00
❏ CRL 57128 [M]	Chamber Music for Moderns	1957	10.00	20.00	40.00
FANTASY					
❏ 3-14 [10]	Nat Pierce and the Herdsmen Featuring Dick Collins	1954	20.00	40.00	80.00
KEYNOTE					
❏ LP-1101 [M]	Nat Pierce Octet and Tentette	1955	20.00	40.00	80.00
RCA VICTOR					
❏ LPM-2543 [M]	Big Band at the Savoy Ballroom	1962	6.25	12.50	25.00
❏ LSP-2543 [S]	Big Band at the Savoy Ballroom	1962	7.50	15.00	30.00
VANGUARD					
❏ VRS-8017 [10]	Nat Pierce Bandstand	1955	20.00	40.00	80.00

PIERCE, NAT; DICK COLLINS; CHARLIE MARIANO

Number	Title (A Side/B Side)	Yr	VG	VG+	NM
FANTASY					
❏ 3224 [M]	Nat Pierce-Dick Collins Nonet/Charlie Mariano Sextet	195?	15.00	30.00	60.00
—Black vinyl					
❏ 3224 [M]	Nat Pierce-Dick Collins Nonet/Charlie Mariano Sextet	1956	30.00	60.00	120.00
—Red vinyl					

PIERCE, NAT; MILT HINTON; BARRY GALBRAITH; OSIE JOHNSON

Number	Title (A Side/B Side)	Yr	VG	VG+	NM
MUSIC MINUS ONE					
❏ Vol. 1 [M]	Nat Pierce and Milt Hinton and Barry Galbraith and Osie Johnson	1956	7.50	15.00	30.00
—With sheet music attached					

PIERCE, WEBB

Number	Title (A Side/B Side)	Yr	VG	VG+	NM
DECCA					
❏ DXB 181 [(2)M]	The Webb Pierce Story	1964	7.50	15.00	30.00
—Deduct 25% if booklet is missing					
❏ DL 4015 [M]	Webb with a Beat	1960	7.50	15.00	30.00
❏ DL 4079 [M]	Walking the Streets	1960	7.50	15.00	30.00
❏ DL 4110 [M]	Golden Favorites	1961	7.50	15.00	30.00
❏ DL 4144 [M]	Fallen Angel	1961	7.50	15.00	30.00
❏ DL 4218 [M]	Hideaway Heart	1962	7.50	15.00	30.00
❏ DL 4294 [M]	Cross Country	1962	7.50	15.00	30.00
❏ DL 4358 [M]	I've Got a New Heartache	1963	6.25	12.50	25.00
❏ DL 4384 [M]	Bow Thy Head	1963	6.25	12.50	25.00
❏ DL 4486 [M]	Sands of Gold	1964	6.25	12.50	25.00
❏ DL 4604 [M]	Memory #1	1965	6.25	12.50	25.00
❏ DL 4659 [M]	Country Music Time	1965	6.25	12.50	25.00
❏ DL 4739 [M]	Sweet Memories	1966	6.25	12.50	25.00
❏ DL 4782 [M]	Webb's Choice	1966	6.25	12.50	25.00
❏ DL 4844 [M]	Where'd Ya Stay Last Night	1967	7.50	15.00	30.00
❏ DL 4964 [M]	Fool, Fool, Fool	1968	12.50	25.00	50.00
❏ DL 5536 [10]	That Wondering Boy	1954	30.00	60.00	120.00
❏ DXSB 7181 [(2)S]	The Webb Pierce Story	1964	10.00	20.00	40.00
—Deduct 25% if booklet is missing					
❏ DL 8129 [M]	Webb Pierce	1955	15.00	30.00	60.00
—Black label, silver print					
❏ DL 8129 [M]	Webb Pierce	196?	7.50	15.00	30.00
—Black label with color bar					
❏ DL 8295 [M]	That Wondering Boy	1956	15.00	30.00	60.00
—Black label, silver print					
❏ DL 8295 [M]	That Wondering Boy	196?	7.50	15.00	30.00
—Black label with color bar					
❏ DL 8728 [M]	Just Imagination	1957	12.50	25.00	50.00
—Black label, silver print					
❏ DL 8728 [M]	Just Imagination	196?	7.50	15.00	30.00
—Black label with color bar					
❏ DL 8889 [M]	Bound for the Kingdom	1959	10.00	20.00	40.00
—Black label, silver print					
❏ DL 8889 [M]	Bound for the Kingdom	196?	6.25	12.50	25.00
—Black label with color bar					
❏ DL 8899 [M]	Webb!	1959	10.00	20.00	40.00
—Black label, silver print					
❏ DL 8899 [M]	Webb!	196?	6.25	12.50	25.00
—Black label with color bar					
❏ DL 74015 [S]	Webb with a Beat	1960	10.00	20.00	40.00
❏ DL 74079 [S]	Walking the Streets	1960	10.00	20.00	40.00
❏ DL 74110 [S]	Golden Favorites	1961	10.00	20.00	40.00
❏ DL 74144 [S]	Fallen Angel	1961	10.00	20.00	40.00
❏ DL 74218 [S]	Hideaway Heart	1962	10.00	20.00	40.00
❏ DL 74294 [S]	Cross Country	1962	10.00	20.00	40.00
❏ DL 74358 [S]	I've Got a New Heartache	1963	7.50	15.00	30.00
❏ DL 74384 [S]	Bow Thy Head	1963	7.50	15.00	30.00
❏ DL 74486 [S]	Sands of Gold	1964	7.50	15.00	30.00
❏ DL 74604 [S]	Memory #1	1965	7.50	15.00	30.00
❏ DL 74659 [S]	Country Music Time	1965	7.50	15.00	30.00
❏ DL 74739 [S]	Sweet Memories	1966	7.50	15.00	30.00
❏ DL 74782 [S]	Webb's Choice	1966	7.50	15.00	30.00
❏ DL 74844 [S]	Where'd Ya Stay Last Night	1967	6.25	12.50	25.00
❏ DL 74964 [S]	Fool, Fool, Fool	1968	6.25	12.50	25.00
❏ DL 74999 [S]	Webb Pierce's Greatest Hits	1968	6.25	12.50	25.00
❏ DL 75071	Saturday Night	1969	6.25	12.50	25.00
❏ DL 75132	Webb Pierce Sings This Thing	1969	6.25	12.50	25.00
❏ DL 75168	Love Ain't Never Gonna Be No Better	1970	6.25	12.50	25.00
❏ DL 75210	Merry-Go-Round World	1970	5.00	10.00	20.00
❏ DL 75280	The Webb Pierce Road Show	1971	5.00	10.00	20.00
❏ DL 75393	I'm Gonna Be a Swinger	1972	5.00	10.00	20.00
❏ DL 78889 [S]	Bound for the Kingdom	1959	12.50	25.00	50.00
—Black label, silver print					
❏ DL 78889 [S]	Bound for the Kingdom	196?	7.50	15.00	30.00
—Black label with color bar					
❏ DL 78899 [M]	Webb!	196?	7.50	15.00	30.00
—Black label with color bar					
❏ DL 78899 [S]	Webb!	1959	12.50	25.00	50.00
—Black label, silver print					
KING					
❏ 648 [M]	The One and Only Webb Pierce	1959	17.50	35.00	70.00
MCA					
❏ 130	Greatest Hits	1973	3.00	6.00	12.00
❏ 513	I'm Gonna Be a Swinger	197?	3.00	6.00	12.00
—Reissue of Decca 75393					
❏ 4087 [(2)]	The Best of Webb Pierce	1974	3.75	7.50	15.00
VOCALION					
❏ VL 73830	Country Songs	1968	3.00	6.00	12.00
❏ VL 73911	Country Favorites	1970	3.75	7.50	15.00

PIERCE, WEBB; MARVIN RAINWATER; STUART HAMBLEN

Number	Title (A Side/B Side)	Yr	VG	VG+	NM
AUDIO LAB					
❏ AL-1563 [M]	Sing for You	1960	50.00	100.00	200.00

PIKE, DAVE

Number	Title (A Side/B Side)	Yr	VG	VG+	NM
ATLANTIC					
❏ SD 1457 [S]	Jazz for the Jet Set	1966	5.00	10.00	20.00
BASF					
❏ 25112 [(2)]	Riff for Rent	1973	5.00	10.00	20.00
DECCA					
❏ DL 74568 [S]	Manhattan Latin	1965	5.00	10.00	20.00
EPIC					
❏ LA-16025 [M]	Pike's Peak	1962	7.50	15.00	30.00
❏ BA-17025 [S]	Pike's Peak	1962	6.25	12.50	25.00
MOODSVILLE					
❏ MVLP-36 [M]	Dave Pike Plays the Jazz Version of "Oliver"	1963	12.50	25.00	50.00
—Green label					
❏ MVLP-36 [M]	Dave Pike Plays the Jazz Version of "Oliver"	1965	6.25	12.50	25.00
—Blue label, trident logo at right					
NEW JAZZ					
❏ NJLP-8281 [M]	Bossa Nova Carnival	1962	12.50	25.00	50.00
—Purple label					
❏ NJLP-8281 [M]	Bossa Nova Carnival	1965	6.25	12.50	25.00
—Blue label, trident logo at right					
❏ NJLP-8284 [M]	Limbo Carnival	1962	12.50	25.00	50.00
—Purple label					
❏ NJLP-8284 [M]	Limbo Carnival	1965	6.25	12.50	25.00
—Blue label, trident logo at right					
RIVERSIDE					
❏ RLP-360 [M]	It's Time for David Pike	1961	6.25	12.50	25.00
❏ RS-9360 [S]	It's Time for David Pike	1961	7.50	15.00	30.00
VORTEX					
❏ 2007	The Doors of Perception	1970	5.00	10.00	20.00

PIKE, PETE

Number	Title (A Side/B Side)	Yr	VG	VG+	NM
AUDIO LAB					
❏ AL-1559 [M]	Pete Pike	1960	25.00	50.00	100.00

PILHOFER, HERB

Number	Title (A Side/B Side)	Yr	VG	VG+	NM
ARGO					
❏ LP-657 [M]	Jazz	1960	6.25	12.50	25.00
❏ LPS-657 [S]	Jazz	1960	7.50	15.00	30.00
ZEPHYR					
❏ ZP-12103-G [M]	Dick and Don Maw Present the Herb Pilhofer Octet — Jazz from the North Coast, Volume 2	1959	12.50	25.00	50.00

PILLOW, RAY

Number	Title (A Side/B Side)	Yr	VG	VG+	NM
ABC					
❏ ABCS-665	Ray Pillow Sings	1968	3.75	7.50	15.00
ABC DOT					
❏ DOSD-2013	Countryfied	1975	3.00	6.00	12.00
CAPITOL					
❏ ST 2417 [S]	Presenting Ray Pillow	1965	5.00	10.00	20.00
❏ T 2417 [M]	Presenting Ray Pillow	1965	3.75	7.50	15.00
❏ ST 2738 [S]	Even When It's Bad, It's Good!	1967	3.75	7.50	15.00
❏ T 2738 [M]	Even When It's Bad, It's Good!	1967	5.00	10.00	20.00
HILLTOP					
❏ JS-6164	Wonderful Day	197?	3.00	6.00	12.00
MEGA					
❏ 1017	Slippin' Around with Ray Pillow	1972	3.75	7.50	15.00
PLANTATION					
❏ PLP-6	People Music	1970	3.75	7.50	15.00

Number	Title (A Side/B Side)	Yr	VG	VG+	NM

PILOT (2)
RCA VICTOR
❏ LSP-4730	Pilot	1972	3.00	6.00	12.00
❏ LSP-4825	Point of View	1973	5.00	10.00	20.00

PINE, COURTNEY
ANTILLES
❏ 510769-1	Closer to Home	1992	5.00	10.00	20.00

PINETOPPERS, THE
CORAL
❏ CRL 56200 [10]	Square Dances	195?	10.00	20.00	40.00
❏ CRL 57048 [M]	The Pinetoppers	195?	7.50	15.00	30.00
DECCA
❏ DL 8348 [M]	Saturday Night Barn Dance	1956	7.50	15.00	30.00

PINK FLOYD
Also see SYD BARRETT; ROGER WATERS; RICHARD WRIGHT.
CAPITOL
❏ SPRO-8116/7 [DJ]	Pink Floyd Tour '75	1975	20.00	40.00	80.00
❏ SEAX-11902 [PD]	The Dark Side of the Moon	1978	7.50	15.00	30.00
❏ ST-12276	Works	1983	2.50	5.00	10.00
❏ SN-16230	More	1982	2.00	4.00	8.00
—Budget-line reissue					
❏ SN-16234	Relics	1982	2.00	4.00	8.00
—Budget-line reissue					
❏ SN-16330	Obscured by Clouds	1985	2.00	4.00	8.00
—Budget-line reissue					
❏ SN-16337	Atom Heart Mother	1985	2.00	4.00	8.00
—Budget-line reissue					
COLUMBIA
❏ AP-1 [DJ]	Animals	1977	37.50	75.00	150.00
—White cover, with the song "Pigs" edited for airplay					
❏ AS 736 [DJ]	Off the Wall	1979	37.50	75.00	150.00
—Sampler from 2-LP set					
❏ AS 1636 [DJ]	The Final Cut	1983	6.25	12.50	25.00
—White label, record banded for airplay					
❏ HC 33453	Wish You Were Here	1981	15.00	30.00	60.00
—Half-speed mastered edition (original)					
❏ PC 33453	Wish You Were Here	1975	3.00	6.00	12.00
—Standard copy (no blue wraparound) without bar code					
❏ PC 33453	Wish You Were Here	1975	6.25	12.50	25.00
—Original copies had a blue wraparound with title/artist sticker. Most buyers threw this out upon opening the LP!					
❏ PC 33453 [DJ]	Wish You Were Here	1975	62.50	125.00	250.00
—White cover, "Special DJ Copy"; banded for airplay					
❏ PC 33453 [DJ]	Wish You Were Here	1975	75.00	150.00	300.00
—Blue cover with photo and title on jacket; unbanded record					
❏ PCQ 33453 [Q]	Wish You Were Here	1975	50.00	100.00	200.00
❏ JC 33474	Animals	1977	2.50	5.00	10.00
❏ JC 33474 [DJ]	Animals	1977	25.00	50.00	100.00
—"Demonstration Not for Sale" on label; also has insert					
❏ PC2 36183 [(2)]	The Wall	1979	3.75	7.50	15.00
❏ PC 37680	A Collection of Great Dance Songs	198?	2.00	4.00	8.00
—Budget-line reissue					
❏ TC 37680	A Collection of Great Dance Songs	1981	2.50	5.00	10.00
❏ QC 38243	The Final Cut	1983	2.50	5.00	10.00
❏ OC 40599	A Momentary Lapse of Reason	1987	2.50	5.00	10.00
❏ HC 43453	Wish You Were Here	1982	10.00	20.00	40.00
—Half-speed mastered edition (reissue)					
❏ PC2 44484 [(2)]	Delicate Sound of Thunder	1988	5.00	10.00	20.00
❏ HC2 46183 [(2)]	The Wall	1983	62.50	125.00	250.00
—Half-speed mastered edition					
❏ HC 47680	A Collection of Great Dance Songs	1982	12.50	25.00	50.00
—Half-speed mastered edition					
❏ C 64200	The Division Bell	1994	5.00	10.00	20.00
—U.S. pressings on blue vinyl					
EMI
❏ 32700 [(4)]	Pulse	1995	15.00	30.00	60.00
—Pressed in U.K. for U.S. release; box set with 12x12 hardback book; identical to British pressings except for American bar code (67065) on shrink wrap					
HARVEST
❏ SKAO-382	Atom Heart Mother	197?	3.75	7.50	15.00
—With title on front cover					
❏ SKAO-382	Atom Heart Mother	1970	6.25	12.50	25.00
—Without title on front cover					
❏ SKBB-388 [(2)]	Ummagumma	1969	10.00	20.00	40.00
—With the soundtrack LP from "Gigi" leaning against wall on front cover					
❏ SKBB-388 [(2)]	Ummagumma	1970	5.00	10.00	20.00
—With white LP cover leaning against wall on front cover					
❏ SW-759	Relics	1971	3.75	7.50	15.00
❏ SMAS-832	Meddle	1971	3.75	7.50	15.00
❏ ST-11078	Obscured by Clouds	1972	3.75	7.50	15.00
❏ SMAS-11163	The Dark Side of the Moon	1973	3.00	6.00	12.00
—With no inserts					
❏ SMAS-11163	The Dark Side of the Moon	1973	6.25	12.50	25.00
—With poster and two stickers					
❏ ST-11198	More	1973	3.00	6.00	12.00
—Reissue of Tower 5169					
❏ SABB-11257 [(2)]	A Nice Pair	1973	3.75	7.50	15.00
MOBILE FIDELITY
❏ 1-017	The Dark Side of the Moon	1980	12.50	25.00	50.00
—Audiophile vinyl					
❏ MFQR-017	The Dark Side of the Moon	1982	75.00	150.00	300.00
—Audiophile vinyl; "Ultra High Quality Recording" in box					
❏ 1-190	Meddle	1987	12.50	25.00	50.00
—Audiophile vinyl					
❏ 1-202	Atom Heart Mother	1994	7.50	15.00	30.00
—Audiophile vinyl					
TOWER
❏ ST 5093 [S]	Pink Floyd (The Piper at the Gates of Dawn)	1967	20.00	40.00	80.00
—Orange label					

❏ ST 5093 [S]	Pink Floyd (The Piper at the Gates of Dawn)	1968	10.00	20.00	40.00
—Multi-color striped label					
❏ T 5093 [M]	Pink Floyd (The Piper at the Gates of Dawn)	1967	62.50	125.00	250.00
❏ ST 5131	A Saucerful of Secrets	1968	10.00	20.00	40.00
—Multi-color striped label					
❏ ST 5131	A Saucerful of Secrets	1968	20.00	40.00	80.00
—Orange label					
❏ ST 5169	More	1968	12.50	25.00	50.00

PIPKINS, THE
CAPITOL
❏ ST-483	Gimme Dat Ding	1970	6.25	12.50	25.00

PIRANHAS, THE
CUSTOM FIDELITY
❏ 1452	Somethin' Fishy	1969	37.50	75.00	150.00

PISANO, JOHNNY, AND BILLY BEAN
DECCA
❏ DL 9206 [M]	Makin' It	1958	7.50	15.00	30.00
❏ DL 9219 [M]	Take Your Pick	1958	7.50	15.00	30.00
❏ DL 79206 [S]	Makin' It	1958	6.25	12.50	25.00
❏ DL 79219 [S]	Take Your Pick	1958	6.25	12.50	25.00

PITNEY, GENE
MUSIC DISC
❏ MDS 1003	The Man Who Shot Liberty Valance	1969	3.00	6.00	12.00
❏ MDS 1005	Town Without Pity	1969	3.00	6.00	12.00
❏ MDS 1006	America's Greatest Country Songs	1969	3.00	6.00	12.00
❏ MDS 1008	Twenty Four Hours from Tulsa	1969	3.00	6.00	12.00
❏ MDS 1014	Baby, I Need Your Lovin'	1969	3.00	6.00	12.00
MUSICOR
❏ MM-2001 [M]	The Many Sides of Gene Pitney	1962	12.50	25.00	50.00
—Brown label					
❏ MM-2001 [M]	The Many Sides of Gene Pitney	1963	6.25	12.50	25.00
—Black label					
❏ MM-2003 [M]	Only Love Can Break a Heart	1962	10.00	20.00	40.00
—Brown label					
❏ MM-2003 [M]	Only Love Can Break a Heart	1963	6.25	12.50	25.00
—Black label					
❏ MM-2004 [M]	Gene Pitney Sings Just for You	1963	7.50	15.00	30.00
❏ MM-2005 [M]	World-Wide Winners	1963	7.50	15.00	30.00
❏ MM-2006 [M]	Blue Gene	1963	7.50	15.00	30.00
❏ MM-2007 [M]	Gene Pitney Meets the Fair Young Ladies of Folkland	1964	7.50	15.00	30.00
❏ MM-2008 [M]	Gene Pitney's Big Sixteen	1964	7.50	15.00	30.00
❏ MM-2015 [M]	Gene Italiano	1964	6.25	12.50	25.00
❏ MM-2019 [M]	It Hurts to Be in Love	1964	6.25	12.50	25.00
❏ MM-2043 [M]	Gene Pitney's More Big Sixteen	1965	6.25	12.50	25.00
❏ MM-2056 [M]	I Must Be Seeing Things	1965	6.25	12.50	25.00
❏ MM-2069 [M]	Looking Through the Eyes of Love	1965	6.25	12.50	25.00
❏ MM-2072 [M]	Gene Pitney En Espanol	1965	6.25	12.50	25.00
❏ MM-2085 [M]	Big Sixteen, Vol. 3	1966	5.00	10.00	20.00
❏ MM-2095 [M]	Backstage I'm Lonely	1966	5.00	10.00	20.00
❏ MM-2100 [M]	Messumo Mi Puo Giudicare	1966	5.00	10.00	20.00
❏ MM-2101 [M]	The Gene Pitney Show	1966	5.00	10.00	20.00
❏ MM-2102 [M]	Greatest Hits of All Times	1966	5.00	10.00	20.00
❏ MM-2104 [M]	The Country Side of Gene Pitney	1967	5.00	10.00	20.00
❏ MM-2108 [M]	Young and Warm and Wonderful	1967	5.00	10.00	20.00
❏ MM-2117 [M]	Just One Smile	1967	5.00	10.00	20.00
❏ MM-2134 [M]	Golden Greats	1967	6.25	12.50	25.00
❏ MS-3001 [R]	The Many Sides of Gene Pitney	1962	7.50	15.00	30.00
—Brown label					
❏ MS-3001 [R]	The Many Sides of Gene Pitney	1963	5.00	10.00	20.00
—Black label					
❏ MS-3003 [S]	Only Love Can Break a Heart	1962	12.50	25.00	50.00
—Brown label					
❏ MS-3003 [S]	Only Love Can Break a Heart	1963	7.50	15.00	30.00
—Black label					
❏ MS-3004 [S]	Gene Pitney Sings Just for You	1963	10.00	20.00	40.00
❏ MS-3005 [S]	World-Wide Winners	1963	10.00	20.00	40.00
❏ MS-3006 [S]	Blue Gene	1963	10.00	20.00	40.00
❏ MS-3007 [S]	Gene Pitney Meets the Fair Young Ladies of Folkland	1964	10.00	20.00	40.00
❏ MS-3008 [P]	Gene Pitney's Big Sixteen	1964	10.00	20.00	40.00
❏ MS-3015 [P]	Gene Italiano	1964	7.50	15.00	30.00
❏ MS-3019 [P]	It Hurts to Be in Love	1964	7.50	15.00	30.00
❏ MS-3043 [P]	Gene Pitney's More Big Sixteen	1965	7.50	15.00	30.00
❏ MS-3056 [S]	I Must Be Seeing Things	1965	7.50	15.00	30.00
❏ MS-3069 [S]	Looking Through the Eyes of Love	1965	7.50	15.00	30.00
❏ MS-3072 [S]	Gene Pitney En Espanol	1965	7.50	15.00	30.00
❏ MS-3085 [S]	Big Sixteen, Vol. 3	1966	6.25	12.50	25.00
❏ MS-3095 [S]	Backstage I'm Lonely	1966	6.25	12.50	25.00
❏ MS-3100 [S]	Messumo Mi Puo Giudicare	1966	6.25	12.50	25.00
❏ MS-3101 [S]	The Gene Pitney Show	1966	6.25	12.50	25.00
❏ MS-3102 [P]	Greatest Hits of All Times	1966	6.25	12.50	25.00
❏ MS-3104 [S]	The Country Side of Gene Pitney	1967	6.25	12.50	25.00
❏ MS-3108 [S]	Young and Warm and Wonderful	1967	6.25	12.50	25.00
❏ MS-3117 [S]	Just One Smile	1967	6.25	12.50	25.00
❏ MS-3134 [S]	Golden Greats	1967	5.00	10.00	20.00
❏ M2-3148 [(2)M]	The Gene Pitney Story	1968	10.00	20.00	40.00
—Mono is promo only					
❏ M2S-3148 [(2)S]	The Gene Pitney Story	1968	6.25	12.50	25.00
—Add 40% if bonus photo is enclosed					
❏ MS-3161	Gene Pitney Sings Burt Bacharach	1968	5.00	10.00	20.00
❏ MS-3164	She's a Heartbreaker	1968	5.00	10.00	20.00
❏ MS-3174	The Greatest Hits of Gene Pitney	1969	5.00	10.00	20.00
❏ MS-3183	Gene Pitney Sings the Platters' Golden Platters	1970	3.75	7.50	15.00
❏ MS-3193	Gene Pitney Super Star	1971	3.75	7.50	15.00
❏ MS-3206	Ten Years After	1971	3.75	7.50	15.00
❏ MS-3233	Golden Hour	1972	3.75	7.50	15.00
❏ MUX-4600 [(2)]	The Best of Gene Pitney (Double Gold Series)	1977	3.75	7.50	15.00

Number	Title (A Side/B Side)	Yr	VG	VG+	NM

RHINO
| ❑ RNDA-1102 [(2)] | Anthology (1961-1968) | 1984 | 3.00 | 6.00 | 12.00 |

SPRINGBOARD
| ❑ SPB-4057 | Gene Pitney | 1975 | 2.50 | 5.00 | 10.00 |

PITNEY, GENE, AND GEORGE JONES
MUSICOR
❑ MM-2044 [M]	For the First Time! Two Great Singers Together: George Jones and Gene Pitney	1965	6.25	12.50	25.00
❑ MM-2065 [M]	It's Country Time Again	1965	6.25	12.50	25.00
❑ MS-3044 [S]	For the First Time! Two Great Singers Together: George Jones and Gene Pitney	1965	7.50	15.00	30.00
❑ MS-3065 [S]	It's Country Time Again	1965	7.50	15.00	30.00

PITNEY, GENE, AND MELBA MONTGOMERY
MUSICOR
| ❑ MM-2077 [M] | Being Together | 1966 | 6.25 | 12.50 | 25.00 |
| ❑ MS-3077 [S] | Being Together | 1966 | 7.50 | 15.00 | 30.00 |

PIXIES
ELEKTRA
❑ PR-8127 [DJ]	Live	1989	12.50	25.00	50.00
—Promo-only seven-song live collection of mostly songs from their pre-Elektra days					
❑ 60856	Doolittle	1989	2.50	5.00	10.00
❑ 60856 [DJ]	Doolittle	1989	3.00	6.00	12.00
—Promo-only on audiophile vinyl					
❑ 60963	Bossanova	1990	2.50	5.00	10.00

ROUGH TRADE
| ❑ ROUGH US 38 | Surfer Rosa | 1988 | 5.00 | 10.00 | 20.00 |

PIXIES THREE, THE
MERCURY
| ❑ MG-20912 [M] | Party with the Pixies Three | 1964 | 37.50 | 75.00 | 150.00 |
| ❑ SR-60912 [S] | Party with the Pixies Three | 1964 | 50.00 | 100.00 | 200.00 |

PIZZARELLI, BUCKY, AND VINNIE BURKE
SAVOY
| ❑ MG-12158 [M] | Music Minus Many Men | 1960 | 7.50 | 15.00 | 30.00 |

PLAIN JANE
HOBBIT
| ❑ 5000 | Plain Jane | 1969 | 6.25 | 12.50 | 25.00 |

PLANET P
GEFFEN
| ❑ GHS 4000 | Planet P | 1983 | 3.00 | 6.00 | 12.00 |

MCA
❑ L33-1227 [EP]	Pink World	1984	3.00	6.00	12.00
—Promo-only pink vinyl EP					
❑ 8019 [(2)]	Pink World	1984	5.00	10.00	20.00
—As "Planet P Project"					

PLANT, ROBERT
Also see LED ZEPPELIN.
ES PARANZA
❑ PR 2244 [(2)DJ]	Non-Stop Go	1988	12.50	25.00	50.00
—Promo-only interview album					
❑ 90101	The Principle of Moments	1983	2.00	4.00	8.00
❑ 90265	Shaken 'n' Stirred	1985	2.00	4.00	8.00
❑ 90485 [EP]	Little by Little Collector's Edition	1985	2.00	4.00	8.00
❑ 90863	Now and Zen	1988	2.00	4.00	8.00
❑ 91336	Manic Nirvana	1990	3.75	7.50	15.00

SWAN SONG
| ❑ SS 8512 | Pictures at Eleven | 1982 | 2.50 | 5.00 | 10.00 |

PLANT & SEE
WHITE WHALE
| ❑ WWS-7120 | Plant & See | 1969 | 6.25 | 12.50 | 25.00 |

PLASMATICS
CAPITOL
| ❑ ST-12237 | Coup d'Etat | 1982 | 3.75 | 7.50 | 15.00 |

PVC
❑ 6908	Metal Priestess	1983	3.75	7.50	15.00
—Reissue of Stiff WOW-666					
❑ 8929	Beyond the Valley of 1984	1983	3.75	7.50	15.00
—Reissue of Stiff USE-11					

STIFF
❑ USE-9	New Hope for the Wretched	1980	6.25	12.50	25.00
❑ USE-11	Beyond the Valley of 1984	1981	6.25	12.50	25.00
❑ WOW-666 [EP]	Metal Priestess	1981	6.25	12.50	25.00

VICE SQUAD
| ❑ VS 105/106 [EP] | Meet the Plasmatics | 1979 | 12.50 | 25.00 | 50.00 |

PLASTER CASTERS, THE
BLUESTIME
| ❑ BTS-9001 | The Plaster Casters Blues Band | 1969 | 12.50 | 25.00 | 50.00 |

PLASTIC COW, THE
DOT
| ❑ DLP 25961 | The Plastic Cow Goes Mooooooog | 1969 | 5.00 | 10.00 | 20.00 |

PLASTIC ONO BAND
See JOHN LENNON; YOKO ONO.

PLATTERS, THE
More than one group has used this name over the years, but all are related. Also see TONY WILLIAMS.
CANDELITE MUSIC
| ❑ CMI 1000 [(5)] | The 50 Golden Hits of the Platters | 197? | 10.00 | 20.00 | 40.00 |

COLUMBIA SPECIAL PRODUCTS
| ❑ P 11834 [S] | Christmas with the Platters | 1973 | 3.75 | 7.50 | 15.00 |
| —Reissue of Mercury SR-60841 with fewer tracks | | | | | |

FEDERAL
| ❑ 549 [M] | The Platters | 1957 | 400.00 | 800.00 | 1600. |

KING
❑ 651 [M]	The Platters	1959	200.00	400.00	800.00
❑ KLP-651 [M]	The Platters	1987	2.50	5.00	10.00
—Reissue with "Highland Records" on label					
❑ 5002	19 Hits of the Platters	197?	3.00	6.00	12.00

MERCURY
❑ SRM-1-4050	Platterama	1982	2.50	5.00	10.00
❑ MG-20146 [M]	The Platters	1956	25.00	50.00	100.00
❑ MG-20216 [M]	The Platters, Volume Two	1956	25.00	50.00	100.00
❑ MG-20298 [M]	The Flying Platters	1957	25.00	50.00	100.00
❑ MG-20366 [M]	The Flying Platters Around the World	1958	7.50	15.00	30.00
❑ MG-20410 [M]	Remember When?	1959	7.50	15.00	30.00
❑ MG-20472 [M]	Encore of Golden Hits	1960	7.50	15.00	30.00
❑ MG-20481 [M]	Reflections	1960	6.25	12.50	25.00
❑ MG-20589 [M]	Life Is Just a Bowl of Cherries	1960	6.25	12.50	25.00
❑ MG-20591 [M]	More Encore of Golden Hits	1960	6.25	12.50	25.00
❑ MG-20613 [M]	Encore of Broadway Golden Hits	1961	5.00	10.00	20.00
❑ MG-20669 [M]	Song for the Lonely	1962	5.00	10.00	20.00
❑ MG-20759 [M]	Moonlight Memories	1963	5.00	10.00	20.00
❑ MG-20782 [M]	The Platters Present All-Time Movie Hits	1963	5.00	10.00	20.00
❑ MG-20808 [M]	The Platters Sing Latino	1963	5.00	10.00	20.00
❑ MG-20841 [M]	Christmas with the Platters	1963	7.50	15.00	30.00
❑ MG-20893 [M]	Encore of Golden Hits of the Groups	1964	5.00	10.00	20.00
❑ MG-20933 [M]	10th Anniversary Album	1964	5.00	10.00	20.00
❑ MG-20983 [M]	The New Soul of the Platters	1965	3.75	7.50	15.00
❑ SR-60043 [S]	The Flying Platters Around the World	1959	12.50	25.00	50.00
❑ SR-60087 [S]	Remember When?	1959	12.50	25.00	50.00
❑ SR-60160 [S]	Reflections	1960	7.50	15.00	30.00
❑ SR-60243 [P]	Encore of Golden Hits	1960	10.00	20.00	40.00
—Original: Black label, silver print; 12 songs on LP					
❑ SR-60243 [P]	Encore of Golden Hits	1965	6.25	12.50	25.00
—Second edition: Red label, "MERCURY" in white across top; may or may not have "Gold Record Award" insignia on back cover; 12 songs on LP					
❑ SR-60243 [P]	Encore of Golden Hits	1975	3.00	6.00	12.00
—Chicago skyline label; album has 10 songs					
❑ SR-60252 [S]	Life Is Just a Bowl of Cherries	1960	7.50	15.00	30.00
❑ SR-60252 [S]	More Encore of Golden Hits	1960	7.50	15.00	30.00
❑ SR-60613 [S]	Encore of Broadway Golden Hits	1961	6.25	12.50	25.00
❑ SR-60669 [S]	Song for the Lonely	1962	6.25	12.50	25.00
❑ SR-60759 [S]	Moonlight Memories	1963	6.25	12.50	25.00
❑ SR-60782 [S]	The Platters Present All-Time Movie Hits	1963	6.25	12.50	25.00
❑ SR-60808 [S]	The Platters Sing Latino	1963	6.25	12.50	25.00
❑ SR-60841 [S]	Christmas with the Platters	1963	10.00	20.00	40.00
—Same as above, but in stereo					
❑ SR-60893 [S]	Encore of Golden Hits of the Groups	1964	6.25	12.50	25.00
❑ SR-60933 [S]	10th Anniversary Album	1964	6.25	12.50	25.00
❑ SR-60983 [S]	The New Soul of the Platters	1965	5.00	10.00	20.00
❑ 828246-1	More Encore of Golden Hits	198?	2.00	4.00	8.00
—Reissue					
❑ 828254-1	Encore of Golden Hits	198?	2.00	4.00	8.00
—Reissue					

MUSIC DISC
| ❑ MDS-1002 | Only You | 1969 | 3.00 | 6.00 | 12.00 |

MUSICOR
❑ MM-2091 [M]	I Love You 1,000 Times	1966	3.75	7.50	15.00
❑ MM-2111 [M]	The Platters Have the Magic Touch	1966	3.75	7.50	15.00
❑ MM-2125 [M]	Going Back to Detroit	1967	3.75	7.50	15.00
❑ MM-2141 [M]	New Golden Hits of the Platters	1967	5.00	10.00	20.00
❑ MS-3091 [S]	I Love You 1,000 Times	1966	5.00	10.00	20.00
❑ MS-3111 [S]	The Platters Have the Magic Touch	1966	5.00	10.00	20.00
❑ MS-3125 [S]	Going Back to Detroit	1967	3.75	7.50	15.00
❑ MS-3141 [S]	New Golden Hits of the Platters	1967	3.75	7.50	15.00
❑ MS-3156	Sweet, Sweet Lovin'	1968	3.75	7.50	15.00
❑ MS-3171	I Get the Sweetest Feeling	1968	3.75	7.50	15.00
❑ MS-3185	Singing the Great Hits Our Way	1969	3.75	7.50	15.00
❑ MS-3231	Golden Hour	1973	3.00	6.00	12.00
❑ MS-3254	The Golden Hits of the Platters	1973	3.00	6.00	12.00

PICKWICK
| ❑ PTP-2083 [(2)] | Only You | 1973 | 3.00 | 6.00 | 12.00 |
| ❑ SPC-3236 | Super Hits | 197? | 2.50 | 5.00 | 10.00 |

RHINO
| ❑ RNFP-71495 [(2)] | Anthology (1955-1967) | 1986 | 3.00 | 6.00 | 12.00 |

SPRINGBOARD
| ❑ SPB-4059 | The Platters | 197? | 2.50 | 5.00 | 10.00 |

WING
❑ MGW-12112 [M]	Encores!	1959	7.50	15.00	30.00
—With liner notes on back cover					
❑ MGW-12112 [M]	Encores!	196?	3.75	7.50	15.00
—With photos of other Wing LPs on back cover					
❑ MGW-12226 [M]	Flying Platters	1963	3.00	6.00	12.00
❑ MGW-12272 [M]	Reflections	1964	3.00	6.00	12.00
❑ MGW-12346 [M]	10th Anniversary Album	196?	3.00	6.00	12.00
❑ SRW-16112 [R]	Encores!	196?	3.00	6.00	12.00
❑ SRW-16226 [S]	Flying Platters	1963	3.00	6.00	12.00
❑ SRW-16272 [S]	Reflections	1964	3.00	6.00	12.00
❑ SRW-16346 [S]	10th Anniversary Album	196?	3.00	6.00	12.00

PLAYERS, THE
MINIT
| ❑ LP-24006 [S] | He'll Be Back | 1966 | 7.50 | 15.00 | 30.00 |
| ❑ LP-40006 [M] | He'll Be Back | 1966 | 6.25 | 12.50 | 25.00 |

PLAYMATES, THE
FORUM
❑ F-9012 [M]	At Play with the Playmates	196?	3.00	6.00	12.00
❑ SF-9012 [S]	At Play with the Playmates	196?	3.75	7.50	15.00
❑ F-9021 [M]	Broadway Show Stoppers	196?	3.00	6.00	12.00
❑ SF-9021 [S]	Broadway Show Stoppers	196?	3.75	7.50	15.00
❑ F-16001 [M]	The Playmates Visit West of the Indies	1960	3.75	7.50	15.00
❑ SF-16001 [S]	The Playmates Visit West of the Indies	1960	5.00	10.00	20.00

Number	Title (A Side/B Side)	Yr	VG	VG+	NM
ROULETTE					
❏ R-25001 [M]	Calypso	1957	6.25	12.50	25.00
❏ R-25043 [M]	At Play with the Playmates	1958	6.25	12.50	25.00
❏ SR-25043 [S]	At Play with the Playmates	1958	7.50	15.00	30.00
❏ R-25059 [M]	Rock and Roll Record Hop	1959	5.00	10.00	20.00
❏ SR-25059 [S]	Rock and Roll Record Hop	1959	6.25	12.50	25.00
❏ R-25068 [M]	Cuttin' Capers	1960	5.00	10.00	20.00
❏ SR-25068 [S]	Cuttin' Capers	1960	6.25	12.50	25.00
❏ R-25084 [M]	Broadway Show Stoppers	1961	5.00	10.00	20.00
❏ SR-25084 [S]	Broadway Show Stoppers	1961	6.25	12.50	25.00

PLEASURE FAIR, THE
With Robb Royer, later of BREAD.

Number	Title (A Side/B Side)	Yr	VG	VG+	NM
UNI					
❏ 3008 [M]	The Pleasure Fair	1967	5.00	10.00	20.00
❏ 73008 [S]	The Pleasure Fair	1967	5.00	10.00	20.00

PLIMSOULS, THE

Number	Title (A Side/B Side)	Yr	VG	VG+	NM
BEAT					
❏ BE-1001 [EP]	Zero Hour	1980	6.25	12.50	25.00
GEFFEN					
❏ GHS 4002	Everywhere at Once	1983	3.00	6.00	12.00
PLANET					
❏ 13	The Plimsouls	1981	5.00	10.00	20.00

PLONSKY, JOHN

Number	Title (A Side/B Side)	Yr	VG	VG+	NM
GOLDEN CREST					
❏ GC-3014 [M]	Cool Man, Cool	1958	7.50	15.00	30.00

PLUGZ

Number	Title (A Side/B Side)	Yr	VG	VG+	NM
FATIMA					
❏ 80	Better Luck	1981	6.25	12.50	25.00
PLUG/REAL LIFE					
❏ 001	Electrify Me	1979	15.00	30.00	60.00

PLUM NELLY

Number	Title (A Side/B Side)	Yr	VG	VG+	NM
CAPITOL					
❏ ST-692	Deceptive Lines	1971	5.00	10.00	20.00

PLUMMER, BILL

Number	Title (A Side/B Side)	Yr	VG	VG+	NM
ABC IMPULSE!					
❏ A-9164 [M]	Bill Plummer and the Cosmic Brotherhood	1968	10.00	20.00	40.00
❏ AS-9164 [S]	Bill Plummer and the Cosmic Brotherhood	1968	5.00	10.00	20.00

PO' BOYS, THE

Number	Title (A Side/B Side)	Yr	VG	VG+	NM
DECCA					
❏ DL 4725 [M]	Bill Anderson Presents the Po' Boys	1966	5.00	10.00	20.00
❏ DL 4884 [M]	The Po' Boys Pick Again	1967	6.25	12.50	25.00
❏ DL 74725 [S]	Bill Anderson Presents the Po' Boys	1966	6.25	12.50	25.00
❏ DL 74884 [S]	The Po' Boys Pick Again	1967	5.00	10.00	20.00
MCA					
❏ 337	The Rich Sounds of Bill Anderson's Po' Boys	1973	3.75	7.50	15.00

POCO

Number	Title (A Side/B Side)	Yr	VG	VG+	NM
ABC					
❏ D-890	Head Over Heels	1975	2.50	5.00	10.00
❏ D-946	Rose of Cimarron	1976	2.50	5.00	10.00
❏ D-989	Indian Summer	1977	2.50	5.00	10.00
❏ AA-1099	Legend	1978	3.00	6.00	12.00
ATLANTIC					
❏ 80008	Ghost Town	1982	2.50	5.00	10.00
❏ 80148	Inamorata	1984	2.50	5.00	10.00
EPIC					
❏ BN 26460	Pickin' Up the Pieces	1969	3.75	7.50	15.00
—Yellow label					
❏ BN 26460	Pickin' Up the Pieces	1973	2.50	5.00	10.00
—Orange label					
❏ BN 26522	Poco	1970	3.75	7.50	15.00
—Yellow label					
❏ BN 26522	Poco	1973	2.50	5.00	10.00
—Orange label					
❏ EQ 30209 [Q]	Deliverin'	1972	5.00	10.00	20.00
❏ KE 30209	Deliverin'	1971	3.75	7.50	15.00
—Yellow label					
❏ KE 30209	Deliverin'	1973	2.50	5.00	10.00
—Orange label					
❏ E 30753	From the Inside	1973	2.50	5.00	10.00
—Reissue with new prefix					
❏ KE 30753	From the Inside	1971	3.75	7.50	15.00
—Yellow label					
❏ KE 30753	From the Inside	1973	2.50	5.00	10.00
—Orange label					
❏ KE 31601	A Good Feelin' to Know	1972	3.75	7.50	15.00
—Yellow label					
❏ KE 31601	A Good Feelin' to Know	1973	2.50	5.00	10.00
—Orange label					
❏ PE 31601	A Good Feelin' to Know	198?	2.00	4.00	8.00
—Budget-line reissue					
❏ EQ 32354 [Q]	Crazy Eyes	1973	5.00	10.00	20.00
❏ KE 32354	Crazy Eyes	1973	3.00	6.00	12.00
—Orange label					
❏ PE 32354	Crazy Eyes	1979	2.00	4.00	8.00
—Blue label					
❏ EQ 32895 [Q]	Seven	1974	5.00	10.00	20.00
❏ KE 32895	Seven	1974	3.00	6.00	12.00
—Orange label					
❏ PCQ 33192 [Q]	Cantamos	1974	5.00	10.00	20.00
❏ PE 33192	Cantamos	1974	3.00	6.00	12.00
—Orange label					
❏ PE 33336	Live	1976	3.00	6.00	12.00
—Orange label					

Number	Title (A Side/B Side)	Yr	VG	VG+	NM
❏ PEG 33537 [(2)]	The Very Best of Poco	1975	3.75	7.50	15.00
—Orange labels					
❏ JE 36210	The Songs of Paul Cotton	1980	2.50	5.00	10.00
❏ JE 36211	The Songs of Richie Furay	1980	2.50	5.00	10.00
MCA					
❏ AA-1099	Legend	1979	2.50	5.00	10.00
—Reissue of ABC 1099					
❏ 5132	Under the Gun	1980	2.50	5.00	10.00
❏ 5227	Blue and Gray	1981	2.50	5.00	10.00
❏ 5288	Cowboys & Englishmen	1982	2.50	5.00	10.00
❏ 5363	Backtracks	1983	2.50	5.00	10.00
❏ 37009	Head Over Heels	1980	2.00	4.00	8.00
—Budget-line reissue					
❏ 37010	Rose of Cimarron	1980	2.00	4.00	8.00
—Budget-line reissue					
❏ 37011	Indian Summer	1980	2.00	4.00	8.00
—Budget-line reissue					
❏ 37117	Legend	1981	2.00	4.00	8.00
—Budget-line reissue					
❏ 37160	Under the Gun	198?	2.00	4.00	8.00
—Budget-line reissue					
MOBILE FIDELITY					
❏ 1-020	Legend	1979	5.00	10.00	20.00
—Audiophile vinyl					
RCA					
❏ 9694-1-R	Legacy	1989	2.50	5.00	10.00

POGUES, THE

Number	Title (A Side/B Side)	Yr	VG	VG+	NM
ENIGMA					
❏ ST-73225	Red Roses for Me	1986	6.25	12.50	25.00
ISLAND					
❏ 90872	If I Should Fall from Grace With God	1988	3.00	6.00	12.00
STIFF/MCA					
❏ 5744	Rum, Sodomy and the Lash	1985	5.00	10.00	20.00
❏ 36015 [EP]	Poguetry in Motion	1986	5.00	10.00	20.00

POI DOG PONDERING

Number	Title (A Side/B Side)	Yr	VG	VG+	NM
COLUMBIA					
❏ CAS 1856 [DJ]	Interchords	1989	5.00	10.00	20.00
—Promo-only interview and music					
❏ CAS 2219 [EP]	Untitled (Fruitless)	1990	3.75	7.50	15.00
—Promo-only six-song sampler					
❏ C 45403	Wishing Like a Mountain and Thinking Like the Sea	1990	3.00	6.00	12.00
TEXAS HOTEL					
❏ 11 [EP]	Poi Dog Pondering	1988	2.00	4.00	8.00
❏ 16 [EP]	Circle Around the Sun	198?	2.00	4.00	8.00

POINDEXTER, PONY

Number	Title (A Side/B Side)	Yr	VG	VG+	NM
EPIC					
❏ LA-16035 [M]	Pony's Express	1962	15.00	30.00	60.00
❏ BA-17035 [S]	Pony's Express	1962	20.00	40.00	80.00
NEW JAZZ					
❏ NJLP-8285 [M]	Pony Poindexter Plays the Big Ones	1962	20.00	40.00	80.00
—Purple label					
❏ NJLP-8285 [M]	Pony Poindexter Plays the Big Ones	1965	6.25	12.50	25.00
—Blue label, trident logo at right					

POISON

Number	Title (A Side/B Side)	Yr	VG	VG+	NM
CAPITOL/ENIGMA					
❏ ST-12523	Look What the Cat Dragged In	1986	2.00	4.00	8.00
❏ C1-48493	Open Up and Say...Ahh!	1988	2.00	4.00	8.00
—With cropped front cover photo (woman's tongue is cut off; large black bars at top and bottom of cover)					
❏ C1-48493	Open Up and Say...Ahh!	1988	3.00	6.00	12.00
—With uncropped front cover photo (woman's tongue is fully visible)					
❏ SPRO 79319/22 [(2)]	Open Up and Say...Ahh! World Premiere Weekend	1988	6.25	12.50	25.00
—Special radio-only version to promote the LP's release					
❏ C1-91813	Flesh & Blood	1990	3.00	6.00	12.00
—With blood airbrushed out of front cover photo					
❏ C1-91813	Flesh & Blood	1990	3.00	6.00	12.00
—With blood dripping from letters "Flesh & Blood"					
❏ R 144402	Look What the Cat Dragged In	1986	2.50	5.00	10.00
—BMG Direct Marketing club edition					
❏ ST-512523	Look What the Cat Dragged In	1986	2.50	5.00	10.00
—Columbia House club edition					
❏ C1-591813	Flesh & Blood	1990	3.00	6.00	12.00
—Columbia House club edition					

POITIER, SIDNEY

Number	Title (A Side/B Side)	Yr	VG	VG+	NM
WARNER BROS.					
❏ W 1561 [M]	Poitier Meets Plato	1965	6.25	12.50	25.00
❏ WS 1561 [S]	Poitier Meets Plato	1965	7.50	15.00	30.00

POLICE, THE
Also see KLARK KENT; STING; ANDY SUMMERS.

Number	Title (A Side/B Side)	Yr	VG	VG+	NM
A&M					
❏ SP-3311	Outlandos d'Amour	198?	2.00	4.00	8.00
—Reissue					
❏ SP-3312	Reggatta da Blanc	198?	2.00	4.00	8.00
—Reissue					
❏ SP-3713 [(2)10]	Reggatta da Blanc	1979	10.00	20.00	40.00
—Two 10" records with poster					
❏ SP-3720	Zenyatta Mondatta	1980	2.50	5.00	10.00
❏ SP-3730	Ghost in the Machine	1981	2.50	5.00	10.00
❏ SP-3730 [DJ]	Ghost in the Machine	1981	250.00	500.00	1000.
—Special prototype picture disc that lights up when placed on a turntable					
❏ SP-3735	Synchronicity	1983	2.50	5.00	10.00
—With blue, yellow and red color bands; 93 versions of this cover exist, none more valuable than any other					
❏ SP-3735	Synchronicity	1983	10.00	20.00	40.00
—With gold, silver and bronze color bands on cover; used on audiophile pressings					

P

Number	Title (A Side/B Side)	Yr	VG	VG+	NM
❏ SP-3735	Synchronicity	1983	20.00	40.00	80.00
—Black & white cover					
❏ SP-3902	Every Breath You Take — The Singles	1986	2.50	5.00	10.00
❏ SP-4753	Outlandos d'Amour	1979	3.00	6.00	12.00
❏ SP-4792	Reggatta da Blanc	1979	3.00	6.00	12.00
❏ R 123571	Ghost in the Machine	1981	3.00	6.00	12.00
—RCA Music Service edition					
❏ R 124159	Outlandos d'Amour	1979	3.00	6.00	12.00
—RCA Music Service edition					
❏ R 130108	Zenyatta Mondatta	1980	3.00	6.00	12.00
—RCA Music Service edition					
❏ R 134070	Synchronicity	1983	3.00	6.00	12.00
—RCA Music Service edition					
❏ R 153349	Reggatta da Blanc	1979	3.00	6.00	12.00
—RCA Music Service edition					
❏ R 173924	Every Breath You Take — The Singles	1986	3.00	6.00	12.00
—BMG Direct Marketing edition					
NAUTILUS					
❏ NR-19	Zenyatta Mondatta	1981	10.00	20.00	40.00
—Audiophile vinyl					
❏ NR-40	Ghost in the Machine	1982	10.00	20.00	40.00
—Audiophile vinyl					

POLK, LUCY ANN
INTERLUDE

Number	Title (A Side/B Side)	Yr	VG	VG+	NM
❏ MO-504 [M]	Easy Livin'	1959	12.50	25.00	50.00
❏ ST-1004 [S]	Easy Livin'	1959	10.00	20.00	40.00
MODE					
❏ LP-115 [M]	Lucky Lucy Ann	1957	37.50	75.00	150.00
TREND					
❏ TL-1008 [10]	Lucy Ann Polk with Dave Pell	1954	25.00	50.00	100.00

POLL WINNERS, THE
CONTEMPORARY

Number	Title	Yr	VG	VG+	NM
❏ C-3535 [M]	The Poll Winners	1957	12.50	25.00	50.00
❏ C-3556 [M]	The Poll Winners Ride Again	1958	12.50	25.00	50.00
❏ M-3576 [M]	Poll Winners Three	1960	10.00	20.00	40.00
❏ M-3581 [M]	Exploring the Scene	1960	10.00	20.00	40.00
❏ S-7535 [S]	The Poll Winners	1959	10.00	20.00	40.00
❏ S-7556 [S]	The Poll Winners Ride Again	1959	10.00	20.00	40.00
❏ S-7576 [S]	Poll Winners Three	1960	7.50	15.00	30.00
❏ S-7581 [S]	Exploring the Scene	1960	7.50	15.00	30.00
STEREO RECORDS					
❏ S-7010 [S]	The Poll Winners	1958	12.50	25.00	50.00
❏ S-7029 [S]	The Poll Winners Ride Again	1958	12.50	25.00	50.00

POLLACK, BEN
BRUNSWICK

Number	Title	Yr	VG	VG+	NM
❏ BL 58025 [10]	Ben Pollack	1951	15.00	30.00	60.00
SAVOY					
❏ MG-12090 [M]	Pick a Rib Boys	1956	12.50	25.00	50.00
❏ MG-12207 [M]	Dixieland Strut	196?	5.00	10.00	20.00
"X"					
❏ LX-3003 [10]	Ben Pollack and His Orchestra Featuring Benny Goodman	1954	15.00	30.00	60.00

POLLARD, TERRY
BETHLEHEM

Number	Title	Yr	VG	VG+	NM
❏ BCP-1015 [10]	Terry Pollard	1954	25.00	50.00	100.00

POLLARD, TERRY/BOBBY SCOTT
BETHLEHEM

Number	Title	Yr	VG	VG+	NM
❏ BCP-1 [M]	Young Moderns	1957	12.50	25.00	50.00

POLLUTION
CAPITOL

Number	Title	Yr	VG	VG+	NM
❏ ST-205	Heir: Pollution	1969	5.00	10.00	20.00
PROPHECY					
❏ SD 6051	Pollution	1971	5.00	10.00	20.00
❏ SD 6067	Pollution II	1972	5.00	10.00	20.00

POMEROY, HERB
ROULETTE

Number	Title	Yr	VG	VG+	NM
❏ R-52001 [M]	Life Is A Many Splendored Gig	1958	20.00	40.00	80.00
❏ SR-52001 [S]	Life Is A Many Splendored Gig	1958	15.00	30.00	60.00
TRANSITION					
❏ TRLP-1 [M]	Jazz in a Stable	1956	50.00	100.00	200.00
—Deduct 25 percent if booklet is missing					
UNITED ARTISTS					
❏ UAL-4015 [M]	Band in Boston	1959	20.00	40.00	80.00
❏ UAS-5015 [S]	Band in Boston	1959	15.00	30.00	60.00

PONCE, PONCIE
WARNER BROS.

Number	Title	Yr	VG	VG+	NM
❏ W 1453 [M]	Poncie Ponce Sings	1962	5.00	10.00	20.00
❏ WS 1453 [S]	Poncie Ponce Sings	1962	6.25	12.50	25.00

PONTY, JEAN-LUC
DIRECT DISC

Number	Title	Yr	VG	VG+	NM
❏ SD-16603	Cosmic Messenger	1980	7.50	15.00	30.00
—Audiophile vinyl					
PACIFIC JAZZ					
❏ ST-20172	King Kong — Jean-Luc Ponty Plays the Music of Frank Zappa	1970	6.25	12.50	25.00

POOBAH
A.E.I.

Number	Title	Yr	VG	VG+	NM
❏ A-LP-1	U.S. Rock	1976	62.50	125.00	250.00
PEPPERMINT					
❏ PP-1180	Steamroller	1979	37.50	75.00	150.00
RITE					
❏ (no #)	Let Me In	1972	150.00	300.00	600.00

POOLE, BILLIE
RIVERSIDE

Number	Title (A Side/B Side)	Yr	VG	VG+	NM
❏ RLP-425 [M]	Sermonette	1962	7.50	15.00	30.00
❏ RLP-458 [M]	Confessin' the Blues	1963	7.50	15.00	30.00
❏ RS-9425 [S]	Sermonette	1962	10.00	20.00	40.00
❏ RS-9458 [S]	Confessin' the Blues	1963	10.00	20.00	40.00

POOLE, BRIAN, AND THE TREMELOES
AUDIO FIDELITY

Number	Title	Yr	VG	VG+	NM
❏ AFLP 2151 [M]	Brian Poole Is Here	1966	12.50	25.00	50.00
❏ AFSD 2151 [R]	Brian Poole Is Here	1966	10.00	20.00	40.00
❏ AFLP 2177 [M]	The Tremeloes Are Here	1967	10.00	20.00	40.00
—Reissue of above album with new title					
❏ AFSD 2177 [R]	The Tremeloes Are Here	1967	7.50	15.00	30.00
—Reissue of above album with new title					

POP WILL EAT ITSELF
NOTHING

Number	Title	Yr	VG	VG+	NM
❏ 95887	Amalgamation	1994	2.50	5.00	10.00
RCA					
❏ 9742-1-R	This Is the Day...This Is the Hour...This Is This!	1989	6.25	12.50	25.00
ROUGH TRADE					
❏ ROUGH 22	Now for a Feast	198?	6.25	12.50	25.00
❏ ROUGH 33	Box Frenzy!	1988	6.25	12.50	25.00

POPCORN BLIZZARD, THE
DE-LITE

Number	Title	Yr	VG	VG+	NM
❏ DE-2004	Explode!	1969	10.00	20.00	40.00

POPPIES, THE
EPIC

Number	Title	Yr	VG	VG+	NM
❏ LN 24200 [M]	Lullaby of Love	1966	10.00	20.00	40.00
❏ BN 26200 [S]	Lullaby of Love	1966	12.50	25.00	50.00

PORCELAIN BEARMEAT
DILL PICKLE

Number	Title	Yr	VG	VG+	NM
❏ 3468	Free Love, Free Sex, Free Music	1971	5.00	10.00	20.00

PORT OF HARLEM JAZZMEN, THE
MOSAIC

Number	Title	Yr	VG	VG+	NM
❏ M-108	The Complete Recordings of the Port of Harlem Jazzmen	198?	5.00	10.00	20.00

PORTER, DAVID
ENTERPRISE

Number	Title	Yr	VG	VG+	NM
❏ ENS-1009	Gritty, Groovy, & Gettin' It	1970	5.00	10.00	20.00
❏ ENS-1012	David Porter...Into a Real Thing	1971	5.00	10.00	20.00
❏ ENS-1019	Victim of the Joke?	1972	5.00	10.00	20.00
❏ ENS-1026	Sweat and Love	1973	5.00	10.00	20.00

PORTER, JERRY
MIRROR

Number	Title	Yr	VG	VG+	NM
❏ SWB-123 [M]	Don't Bother Me!	1966	25.00	50.00	100.00

PORTER, PEPPER
FIRST AMERICAN

Number	Title	Yr	VG	VG+	NM
❏ FA-7756	Invasion	1980	6.25	12.50	25.00

POSEY, SANDY
COLUMBIA

Number	Title	Yr	VG	VG+	NM
❏ KC 31594	Why Don't We Go Somewhere and Love	1972	3.00	6.00	12.00
MGM					
❏ GAS-125	Sandy Posey (Golden Archive Series)	1970	3.75	7.50	15.00
❏ E-4418 [M]	Born a Woman	1966	3.75	7.50	15.00
❏ SE-4418 [S]	Born a Woman	1966	5.00	10.00	20.00
❏ E-4455 [M]	Single Girl	1967	5.00	10.00	20.00
❏ SE-4455 [S]	Single Girl	1967	5.00	10.00	20.00
❏ E-4480 [M]	I Take It Back	1967	5.00	10.00	20.00
❏ SE-4480 [S]	I Take It Back	1967	5.00	10.00	20.00
❏ E-4509 [M]	The Best of Sandy Posey	1967	6.25	12.50	25.00
❏ SE-4509 [S]	The Best of Sandy Posey	1967	5.00	10.00	20.00
❏ E-4525 [M]	Looking at You	1968	6.25	12.50	25.00
❏ SE-4525 [S]	Looking at You	1968	3.75	7.50	15.00
❏ ST-91110	Single Girl	1967	6.25	12.50	25.00
—Capitol Record Club issue					

POSSUM HUNTERS, THE
TAKOMA

Number	Title	Yr	VG	VG+	NM
❏ C-1010	Death on Lee Highway	1970	5.00	10.00	20.00

POTTER, CURTIS
DOT

Number	Title	Yr	VG	VG+	NM
❏ DLP-25988	Here Comes Curtis Potter	1971	5.00	10.00	20.00
STEP ONE					
❏ 0004	Down in Texas Today	1984	5.00	10.00	20.00
❏ 0020	All I Need Is Time	1987	5.00	10.00	20.00

POTTER, TOMMY
EASTWEST

Number	Title	Yr	VG	VG+	NM
❏ 4001 [M]	Tommy Potter's Hard Funk	1958	12.50	25.00	50.00

POTTS, BILL
COLPIX

Number	Title	Yr	VG	VG+	NM
❏ CP-451 [M]	Bye Bye Birdie	1963	7.50	15.00	30.00
❏ SCP-451 [S]	Bye Bye Birdie	1963	10.00	20.00	40.00
UNITED ARTISTS					
❏ UAL-4032 [M]	The Jazz Soul of Porgy and Bess	1959	7.50	15.00	30.00
❏ UAS-5032 [S]	The Jazz Soul of Porgy and Bess	1959	10.00	20.00	40.00

POWELL, ANDREW, AND THE PHILHARMONIA ORCHESTRA
MOBILE FIDELITY

Number	Title	Yr	VG	VG+	NM
❏ 1-175	The Best of the Alan Parsons Project	1986	6.25	12.50	25.00
—Audiophile vinyl					

A few years after their biggest success with the Gregmark label, the Paris Sisters had this album on Reprise.

Carl Perkins' first album on the Columbia label, *Whole Lotta Shakin'*, is his most collectible on a label other than Sun.

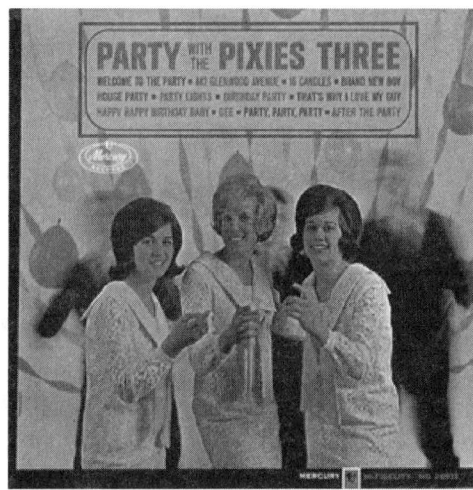

The Pixies Three never had a really big hit single. Even so, they had an album issued on Mercury, which is sought-after today, especially by girl group collectors.

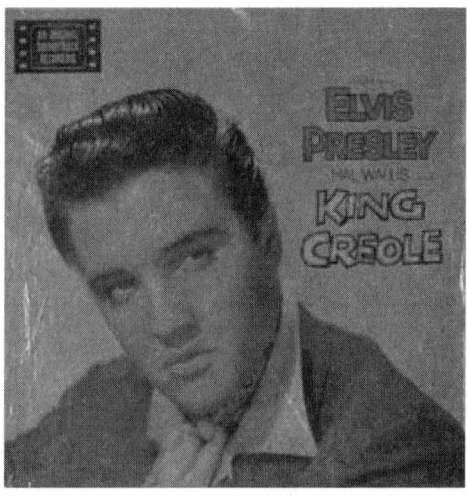

Many people consider *King Creole* to be Elvis Presley's best movie. This is the soundtrack album, from 1958.

This is the front cover of a souvenir box set that patrons of the International Hotel in Las Vegas received in 1969, when Elvis Presley had an extended stay there. These boxes are quite hard to find.

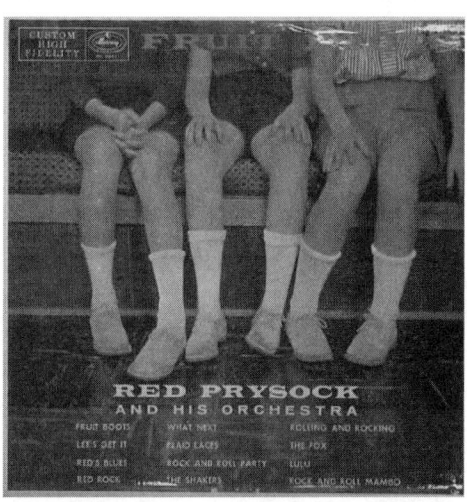

Red Prysock, a tenor saxophonist who sometimes played on his brother Arthur's records, made a few discs of his own, including this 1957 album for Mercury.

Number	Title (A Side/B Side)	Yr	VG	VG+	NM

POWELL, BADEN
BASF
| ❏ 25155 [(2)] | Canto on Guitar | 197? | 5.00 | 10.00 | 20.00 |

POWELL, BUD
BLUE NOTE
| ❏ BLP-1503 [M] | The Amazing Bud Powell, Vol. 1 | 1955 | 37.50 | 75.00 | 150.00 |
| —Regular version, Lexington Ave. address on label |
| ❏ BLP-1503 [M] | The Amazing Bud Powell, Vol. 1 | 1955 | 50.00 | 100.00 | 200.00 |
| —"Deep groove" version (deep indentation under label on both sides) |
| ❏ BLP-1503 [M] | The Amazing Bud Powell, Vol. 1 | 1963 | 6.25 | 12.50 | 25.00 |
| —With "New York, USA" address on label |
| ❏ BLP-1504 [M] | The Amazing Bud Powell, Vol. 2 | 1955 | 37.50 | 75.00 | 150.00 |
| —Regular version, Lexington Ave. address on label |
| ❏ BLP-1504 [M] | The Amazing Bud Powell, Vol. 2 | 1955 | 50.00 | 100.00 | 200.00 |
| —"Deep groove" version (deep indentation under label on both sides) |
| ❏ BLP-1504 [M] | The Amazing Bud Powell, Vol. 2 | 1963 | 6.25 | 12.50 | 25.00 |
| —With "New York, USA" address on label |
| ❏ BLP-1571 [M] | Bud! | 1957 | 30.00 | 60.00 | 120.00 |
| —Regular version, W. 63rd St. address on label |
| ❏ BLP-1571 [M] | Bud! | 1957 | 37.50 | 75.00 | 150.00 |
| —"Deep groove" version (deep indentation under label on both sides) |
| ❏ BLP-1571 [M] | Bud! | 1963 | 6.25 | 12.50 | 25.00 |
| —With "New York, USA" address on label |
| ❏ BST-1571 [S] | Bud! | 1959 | 25.00 | 50.00 | 100.00 |
| —Regular version, W. 63rd St. address on label |
| ❏ BST-1571 [S] | Bud! | 1959 | 30.00 | 60.00 | 120.00 |
| —"Deep groove" version (deep indentation under label on both sides) |
| ❏ BST-1571 [S] | Bud! | 1963 | 5.00 | 120.00 | 20.00 |
| —With "New York, USA" address on label |
| ❏ BLP-1598 [M] | The Time Waits | 1959 | 30.00 | 60.00 | 120.00 |
| —Regular version, W. 63rd St. address on label |
| ❏ BLP-1598 [M] | The Time Waits | 1959 | 37.50 | 75.00 | 150.00 |
| —"Deep groove" version (deep indentation under label on both sides) |
| ❏ BLP-1598 [M] | The Time Waits | 1963 | 6.25 | 12.50 | 25.00 |
| —With "New York, USA" address on label |
| ❏ BST-1598 [S] | The Time Waits | 1959 | 25.00 | 50.00 | 100.00 |
| —Regular version, W. 63rd St. address on label |
| ❏ BST-1598 [S] | The Time Waits | 1959 | 30.00 | 60.00 | 120.00 |
| —"Deep groove" version (deep indentation under label on both sides) |
| ❏ BST-1598 [S] | The Time Waits | 1963 | 5.00 | 10.00 | 20.00 |
| —With "New York, USA" address on label |
| ❏ BLP-4009 [M] | The Scene Changes | 1959 | 30.00 | 60.00 | 120.00 |
| —Regular version, W. 63rd St. address on label |
| ❏ BLP-4009 [M] | The Scene Changes | 1959 | 37.50 | 75.00 | 150.00 |
| —"Deep groove" version (deep indentation under label on both sides) |
| ❏ BLP-4009 [M] | The Scene Changes | 1963 | 6.25 | 12.50 | 25.00 |
| —With "New York, USA" address on label |
| ❏ BST-4009 [S] | The Scene Changes | 1959 | 25.00 | 50.00 | 100.00 |
| —Regular version, W. 63rd St. address on label |
| ❏ BST-4009 [S] | The Scene Changes | 1959 | 30.00 | 60.00 | 120.00 |
| —"Deep groove" version (deep indentation under label on both sides) |
| ❏ BST-4009 [S] | The Scene Changes | 1963 | 5.00 | 10.00 | 20.00 |
| —With "New York, USA" address on label |
| ❏ BLP-5003 [10] | The Amazing Bud Powell, Vol. 1 | 1951 | 100.00 | 200.00 | 400.00 |
| ❏ BLP-5041 [10] | The Amazing Bud Powell, Vol. 2 | 1954 | 100.00 | 200.00 | 400.00 |
CLEF
❏ MGC-502 [10]	Bud Powell Piano Solos	1954	50.00	100.00	200.00
❏ MGC-507 [10]	Bud Powell Piano Solos, No. 2	1954	50.00	100.00	200.00
❏ MGC-610 [M]	Bud Powell's Moods	1954	37.50	75.00	150.00
❏ MGC-739 [M]	The Genius of Bud Powell	1956	30.00	60.00	120.00
COLUMBIA
| ❏ CL 2292 [M] | A Portrait of Thelonious | 1965 | 6.25 | 12.50 | 25.00 |
| ❏ CS 9092 [S] | A Portrait of Thelonious | 1965 | 7.50 | 15.00 | 30.00 |
DEBUT
| ❏ DLP-3 [10] | Jazz at Massey Hall, Volume 2 | 1953 | 100.00 | 200.00 | 400.00 |
DELMARK
| ❏ DL-406 [M] | Bouncing with Bud | 1966 | 6.25 | 12.50 | 25.00 |
| ❏ DS-9406 [S] | Bouncing with Bud | 1966 | 7.50 | 15.00 | 30.00 |
ESP-DISK'
| ❏ 1066 [S] | Bud Powell at the Blue Note Café, Paris | 1968 | 6.25 | 12.50 | 25.00 |
FANTASY
| ❏ 6006 [M] | Bud Powell Trio | 1962 | 7.50 | 15.00 | 30.00 |
| —Black vinyl |
| ❏ 6006 [M] | Bud Powell Trio | 1962 | 12.50 | 25.00 | 50.00 |
| —Red vinyl |
| ❏ 86006 [R] | Bud Powell Trio | 1962 | 5.00 | 10.00 | 20.00 |
| —Blue vinyl |
| ❏ 86006 [R] | Bud Powell Trio | 1962 | 7.50 | 15.00 | 30.00 |
| —Black vinyl |
MERCURY
❏ MGC-102 [10]	Bud Powell Piano	1950	62.50	125.00	250.00
❏ MGC-502 [10]	Bud Powell Piano Solos	1951	62.50	125.00	250.00
❏ MGC-507 [10]	Bud Powell Piano Solos, No. 2	1951	62.50	125.00	250.00
❏ MGC-610 [M]	Bud Powell's Moods	1953	50.00	100.00	200.00
❏ MG-35012 [10]	Bud Powell Piano	1950	75.00	150.00	300.00
MOSAIC
| ❏ M5-116 [(5)] | The Complete Bud Powell Blue Note Recordings (1949-1958) | 199? | 20.00 | 40.00 | 80.00 |
NORGRAN
❏ MGN-23 [10]	Bud Powell Trio	1954	62.50	125.00	250.00
❏ MGN-1017 [M]	Jazz Original	1955	25.00	50.00	100.00
❏ MGN-1063 [M]	Jazz Giant	1956	25.00	50.00	100.00
❏ MGN-1064 [M]	Bud Powell's Moods	1956	25.00	50.00	100.00
❏ MGN-1077 [M]	Piano Interpretations by Bud Powell	1956	25.00	50.00	100.00
❏ MGN-1098 [M]	Bud Powell '57	1957	25.00	50.00	100.00
RCA VICTOR
| ❏ LPM-1423 [M] | Strictly Powell | 1957 | 25.00 | 50.00 | 100.00 |
| ❏ LPM-1507 [M] | Swingin' with Bud | 1957 | 25.00 | 50.00 | 100.00 |

REPRISE
| ❏ R-6098 [M] | Bud Powell in Paris | 1964 | 7.50 | 15.00 | 30.00 |
| ❏ RS-6098 [S] | Bud Powell in Paris | 1964 | 10.00 | 20.00 | 40.00 |
ROOST
❏ LP-401 [10]	Bud Powell Trio	1950	100.00	200.00	400.00
❏ LP-412 [10]	Bud Powell Trio	1953	75.00	150.00	300.00
❏ LP-2224 [M]	Bud Powell Trio	1957	25.00	50.00	100.00
ROULETTE
| ❏ R-52115 [M] | The Return of Bud Powell — His First New Recordings Since 1958 | 1965 | 6.25 | 12.50 | 25.00 |
| ❏ SR-52115 [S] | The Return of Bud Powell — His First New Recordings Since 1958 | 1965 | 7.50 | 15.00 | 30.00 |
VERVE
❏ VSP-34 [M]	The Jazz Legacy of Bud Powell	1966	5.00	10.00	20.00
❏ VSP-37 [M]	This Was Bud Powell	1966	5.00	10.00	20.00
❏ MGV-8115 [M]	The Genius of Bud Powell	1957	12.50	25.00	50.00
❏ V-8115 [M]	The Genius of Bud Powell	1961	6.25	12.50	25.00
❏ MGV-8153 [M]	Jazz Giant	1957	15.00	30.00	60.00
❏ V-8153 [M]	Jazz Giant	1961	6.25	12.50	25.00
❏ MGV-8154 [M]	Bud Powell's Moods	1957	15.00	30.00	60.00
❏ V-8154 [M]	Bud Powell's Moods	1961	6.25	12.50	25.00
❏ MGV-8167 [M]	Piano Interpretations by Bud Powell	1957	15.00	30.00	60.00
❏ V-8167 [M]	Piano Interpretations by Bud Powell	1961	6.25	12.50	25.00
❏ MGV-8185 [M]	Bud Powell '57	1957	12.50	25.00	50.00
❏ V-8185 [M]	Bud Powell '57	1961	6.25	12.50	25.00
❏ MGV-8218 [M]	Blues in the Closet	1958	12.50	25.00	50.00
❏ V-8218 [M]	Blues in the Closet	1961	6.25	12.50	25.00
❏ MGV-8301 [M]	The Lonely One…	1959	12.50	25.00	50.00
❏ V-8301 [M]	The Lonely One…	1961	6.25	12.50	25.00

POWELL, DICK
DECCA
| ❏ DL 8837 [M] | Song Book | 1959 | 10.00 | 20.00 | 40.00 |
RPC
| ❏ 105 [M] | The Wonderful Teens | 1962 | 6.25 | 12.50 | 25.00 |

POWELL, JANE
COLUMBIA MASTERWORKS
| ❏ ML 2034 [10] | Romance | 1949 | 20.00 | 40.00 | 80.00 |
| ❏ ML 2045 [10] | A Date with Jane Powell | 1949 | 20.00 | 40.00 | 80.00 |
LION
| ❏ L-70111 [M] | Jane Powell Sings | 1960 | 5.00 | 10.00 | 20.00 |
MGM
| ❏ E-3451 [M] | Something Wonderful | 1957 | 10.00 | 20.00 | 40.00 |
VERVE
| ❏ MGV-2023 [M] | Can't We Be Friends? | 1957 | 10.00 | 20.00 | 40.00 |

POWELL, LOVEY
TRANSITION
| ❏ TRLP-1 [M] | Lovelady | 1956 | 25.00 | 50.00 | 100.00 |
| —Deduct 25 percent if booklet is missing |

POWELL, MEL
CAPITOL
| ❏ T 615 [M] | Classics in Jazz | 1955 | 10.00 | 20.00 | 40.00 |
METRO
| ❏ M-577 [M] | Mickey Most Presents English In-Groups | 1966 | 5.00 | 10.00 | 20.00 |
VANGUARD
❏ VRS-8004 [10]	Mel Powell Septet	1953	20.00	40.00	80.00
❏ VRS-8015 [10]	Bandstand	1954	20.00	40.00	80.00
❏ VRS-8501 [M]	Borderline	1954	12.50	25.00	50.00
❏ VRS-8502 [M]	Thigamagig	1954	12.50	25.00	50.00
❏ VRS-8506 [M]	Out on a Limb	1955	12.50	25.00	50.00
❏ VRS-8519 [M]	Easy Swing	1955	12.50	25.00	50.00

POWELL, SELDON
ROOST
| ❏ LP-2205 [M] | Seldon Powell Plays | 1956 | 12.50 | 25.00 | 50.00 |
| ❏ LP-2220 [M] | Seldon Powell Sextet | 1956 | 12.50 | 25.00 | 50.00 |

POWELL, SPECS
ROULETTE
| ❏ R-52004 [M] | Movin' In | 1958 | 7.50 | 15.00 | 30.00 |
| ❏ SR-52004 [S] | Movin' In | 1958 | 6.25 | 12.50 | 25.00 |
STRAND
| ❏ SL-1027 [M] | Specs Powell Presents Big Band Jazz | 1961 | 5.00 | 10.00 | 20.00 |
| ❏ SLS-1027 [S] | Specs Powell Presents Big Band Jazz | 1961 | 6.25 | 12.50 | 25.00 |

POWERS, JOEY
AMY
| ❏ 8001 [M] | Midnight Mary | 1964 | 7.50 | 15.00 | 30.00 |

POWERS OF BLUE, THE
MTA
| ❏ 1002 [M] | Flipout | 1967 | 7.50 | 15.00 | 30.00 |
| ❏ 5002 [S] | Flipout | 1967 | 7.50 | 15.00 | 30.00 |

POZAR, ROBERT
SAVOY
| ❏ MG-12189 [M] | Good Golly, Miss Nancy | 1967 | 5.00 | 10.00 | 20.00 |

POZO-SECO SINGERS, THE
DON WILLIAMS was in this group.
CERTRON
| ❏ CS-7007 | Spend Some Time with Me | 1970 | 3.75 | 7.50 | 15.00 |
COLUMBIA
❏ CL 2515 [M]	Time/I'll Be Gone	1966	3.75	7.50	15.00
❏ CL 2600 [M]	I Can Make It with You	1967	5.00	10.00	20.00
❏ CS 9315 [S]	Time/I'll Be Gone	1966	5.00	10.00	20.00
❏ CS 9400 [S]	I Can Make It with You	1967	3.75	7.50	15.00
❏ CS 9656	Shades of Time	1968	3.75	7.50	15.00

Number	Title (A Side/B Side)	Yr	VG	VG+	NM
POWER PAK					
❏ 285	The Pozo-Seco Singers with Don Williams	198?	2.50	5.00	10.00
PRADO, PEREZ					
RCA CAMDEN					
❏ CAL-409 [M]	Mambo Happy!	1957	5.00	10.00	20.00
❏ CAL-547 [M]	Latino!	1960	5.00	10.00	20.00
RCA VICTOR					
❏ LPM-21 [10]	Perez Prado Plays Mucho Mambo for Dancing	1951	15.00	30.00	60.00
❏ LPM-1075 [M]	Mambo Mania	1955	10.00	20.00	40.00
❏ LPM-1101 [M]	Voodoo Suite (and Six All-Time Greats)	1955	10.00	20.00	40.00
❏ LPM-1196 [M]	Mambo by the King	1956	10.00	20.00	40.00
❏ LPM-1257 [M]	Havana 3 A.M.	1956	10.00	20.00	40.00
❏ LPM-1459 [M]	Latin Satin	1957	10.00	20.00	40.00
❏ LPM-1556 [M]	"Prez"	1958	7.50	15.00	30.00
❏ LSP-1556 [S]	"Prez"	1959	10.00	20.00	40.00
❏ LPM-1883 [M]	Dilo (Ugh!)	1958	7.50	15.00	30.00
❏ LSP-1883 [S]	Dilo (Ugh!)	1959	10.00	20.00	40.00
❏ ANL1-1941	Pure Gold	1975	2.50	5.00	10.00
❏ LPM-2028 [M]	Pops and Prado	1959	7.50	15.00	30.00
❏ LSP-2028 [S]	Pops and Prado	1959	10.00	20.00	40.00
❏ LPM-2104 [M]	Big Hits by Prado	1959	7.50	15.00	30.00
❏ LSP-2104 [S]	Big Hits by Prado	1959	10.00	20.00	40.00
❏ LPM-2133 [M]	A Touch of Tabasco	1960	5.00	10.00	20.00
❏ LSP-2133 [S]	A Touch of Tabasco	1960	7.50	15.00	30.00
❏ LPM-2308 [M]	Rockambo	1961	5.00	10.00	20.00
❏ LSP-2308 [S]	Rockambo	1961	7.50	15.00	30.00
❏ LPM-2379 [M]	The New Dance La Chunga	1961	5.00	10.00	20.00
❏ LSP-2379 [S]	The New Dance La Chunga	1961	7.50	15.00	30.00
❏ LPM-2524 [M]	The Twist Goes Latin	1962	5.00	10.00	20.00
❏ LSP-2524 [S]	The Twist Goes Latin	1962	7.50	15.00	30.00
❏ LPM-2571 [M]	Exotic Suite	1962	5.00	10.00	20.00
❏ LSP-2571 [S]	Exotic Suite	1962	7.50	15.00	30.00
❏ LPM-2610 [M]	Our Man in Latin America	1963	5.00	10.00	20.00
❏ LSP-2610 [S]	Our Man in Latin America	1963	7.50	15.00	30.00
❏ LPM-3108 [10]	Mambo by the King	1953	15.00	30.00	60.00
❏ LPM-3330 [M]	Dance Latino	1965	3.75	7.50	15.00
❏ LSP-3330 [S]	Dance Latino	1965	5.00	10.00	20.00
❏ LPM-3732 [M]	The Best of Perez Prado	1967	5.00	10.00	20.00
❏ LSP-3732 [S]	The Best of Perez Prado	1967	3.75	7.50	15.00
❏ VPS-6066 [(2)]	This Is Perez Prado	1972	3.75	7.50	15.00
UNITED ARTISTS					
❏ LS-61032	Estas Si Viven (The Living End)	196?	3.75	7.50	15.00
PREACHER ROLLO					
KING					
❏ 295-101 [10]	Dixieland	195?	30.00	60.00	120.00
MGM					
❏ E-95 [10]	Preacher Rollo and the Five Saints	1951	20.00	40.00	80.00
❏ E-217 [10]	Preacher Rollo at the Jazz Band Ball	1953	20.00	40.00	80.00
❏ E-3259 [M]	Dixieland Favorites	1955	12.50	25.00	50.00
❏ E-3403 [M]	Swanee River Jazz	1956	12.50	25.00	50.00
PREMIERS, THE (1)					
WARNER BROS.					
❏ W 1565 [M]	Farmer John	1964	10.00	20.00	40.00
❏ WS 1565 [S]	Farmer John	1964	12.50	25.00	50.00
PRESIDENTS, THE (1)					
SUSSEX					
❏ SXBX-7005	5-10-15-20 (25-30 Years of Love)	1970	6.25	12.50	25.00
PRESLEY, ELVIS					
BOXCAR					
❏ (no #)	Having Fun with Elvis on Stage	1974	37.50	75.00	150.00
—All-talking record sold at Elvis concerts in 1974					
DCC COMPACT CLASSICS					
❏ LPZ-2037 [S]	Elvis Is Back!	1997	30.00	60.00	120.00
—Audiophile vinyl					
❏ LPZ-2040 [(2)]	24 Karat Hits!	1997	30.00	60.00	120.00
—Audiophile vinyl					
FOTOPLAY					
❏ FSP-1001 [PD]	To Elvis: Love Still Burning	1978	3.75	7.50	15.00
—In black cardboard cover with white printing					
❏ FSP-1001 [PD]	To Elvis: Love Still Burning	1978	6.25	12.50	25.00
—Tribute-song picture disc of Elvis; in plastic bag with 11x11 insert					
❏ FSP-1001 [PD]	To Elvis: Love Still Burning	1978	7.50	15.00	30.00
—In white cardboard cover with black printing					
GOLDEN EDITIONS					
❏ KING-1	The First Year (Elvis, Scotty and Bill)	1979	3.75	7.50	15.00
❏ GEL-101	The First Year (Elvis, Scotty and Bill)	1979	5.00	10.00	20.00
GREAT NORTHWEST					
❏ GV-2004	The King Speaks (February 1961, Memphis, Tennessee)	1977	2.50	5.00	10.00
—Label says this is on "Green Valley" while sleeve says "Great Northwest"					
❏ GNW-4005	The Elvis Tapes	1977	3.00	6.00	12.00
❏ GNW-4006	The King Speaks (February 1961, Memphis, Tennessee)	1977	2.00	4.00	8.00
—Both label and sleeve say this is on "Great Northwest"					
GREEN VALLEY					
❏ GV-2001	Elvis Exclusive Live Press Conference (Memphis, Tennessee, February 1961)	1977	10.00	20.00	40.00
—Issued with two slightly different covers					
❏ GV-2001/3 [(2)]	Elvis (Speaks to You)	1978	7.50	15.00	30.00
—Elvis interviews plus tracks by the Jordanaires					
GUSTO					
❏ SD-995	Interviews with Elvis (Canada 1957)	1978	10.00	20.00	40.00
—Reissue of Great Northwest album					
HALW					
❏ HALW-0001	The First Years	1978	5.00	10.00	20.00
—Without limited edition number					

Number	Title (A Side/B Side)	Yr	VG	VG+	NM
❏ HALW-0001	The First Years	1978	7.50	15.00	30.00
—With stamped, limited edition number					
K-TEL					
❏ NU 9900	Love Songs	1981	5.00	10.00	20.00
LOUISIANA HAYRIDE					
❏ LH-3061	Beginning Years	1984	5.00	10.00	20.00
—With booklet and facsimile contract					
MARVENCO					
❏ 101	Beginning (1954-1955)	1988	3.75	7.50	15.00
—Pink vinyl with booklet and facsimile contract					
MOBILE FIDELITY					
❏ 1-059	From Elvis in Memphis	1982	12.50	25.00	50.00
—Audiophile vinyl					
MUSIC WORKS					
❏ PB-3601	The First Live Recordings	1984	3.75	7.50	15.00
❏ PB-3602	The Hillbilly Cat	1984	3.75	7.50	15.00
OAK					
❏ 1003	Vintage 1955 Elvis	1990	15.00	30.00	60.00
PAIR					
❏ PDL2-1010 [(2)]	Double Dynamite	1982	5.00	10.00	20.00
❏ PDL2-1037 [(2)]	Remembering	1983	7.50	15.00	30.00
❏ PDL2-1185 [(2)]	Elvis Aron Presley Forever	1988	5.00	10.00	20.00
PICKWICK					
❏ (no #) [(7)]	The Pickwick Pack (unofficial title)	1978	15.00	30.00	60.00
—Seven Pickwick albums in special package and cardboard wrapper; one of the LPs is Elvis' Christmas Album					
❏ (no #) [(7)]	The Pickwick Pack (unofficial title)	1979	15.00	30.00	60.00
—Seven Pickwick albums in special package and cardboard wrapper; one of the LPs is Frankie and Johnny					
❏ CAS-2304	Elvis Sings Flaming Star	1976	2.50	5.00	10.00
❏ CAS-2408	Let's Be Friends	1975	2.50	5.00	10.00
❏ CAL-2428 [M]	Elvis' Christmas Album	1975	3.00	6.00	12.00
—Same contents as RCA Camden LP; no Christmas trim on border					
❏ CAL-2428 [M]	Elvis' Christmas Album	1976	2.50	5.00	10.00
—Same as above, but with Christmas trim on cover border					
❏ CAS-2440	Almost in Love	1975	2.50	5.00	10.00
❏ CAL-2472	You'll Never Walk Alone	1975	2.50	5.00	10.00
❏ CAL-2518	C'mon Everybody	1975	2.50	5.00	10.00
❏ CAS-2533	I Got Lucky	1975	2.50	5.00	10.00
❏ CAS-2567	Elvis Sings Hits from His Movies, Volume 1	1975	2.50	5.00	10.00
❏ CAS-2595	Burning Love And Hits from His Movies, Vol. 2	1975	3.00	6.00	12.00
—First cover contains a notice about the upcoming "Aloha from Hawaii" show					
❏ CAS-2595	Burning Love And Hits from His Movies, Vol. 2	1976	2.00	4.00	8.00
—Reissue deletes the "Aloha from Hawaii" notice					
❏ CAS-2611	Separate Ways	1975	2.50	5.00	10.00
❏ DL2-5001 [(2)]	Double Dynamite	1975	6.25	12.50	25.00
❏ ACL-7007	Frankie and Johnny	1976	2.50	5.00	10.00
❏ ACL-7064	Mahalo from Elvis	1978	5.00	10.00	20.00
PREMORE					
❏ PL-589	Early Elvis (1954-1956 Live at the Louisiana Hayride)	1989	7.50	15.00	30.00
RCA					
❏ 2023-1-R	The Million Dollar Quartet	1990	3.00	6.00	12.00
—With Jerry Lee Lewis, Carl Perkins, and perhaps Johnny Cash					
❏ 2227-1-R	The Great Performances	1990	10.00	20.00	40.00
❏ 3114-1-R [(3)]	Collectors Gold	1991	50.00	100.00	200.00
❏ 5600-1-R	Return of the Rocker	1986	5.00	10.00	20.00
❏ 6221-1-R [(2)]	The Memphis Record	1987	7.50	15.00	30.00
❏ 6313-1-R	Elvis Talks!	1987	7.50	15.00	30.00
❏ 6382-1-R	The Number One Hits	1987	7.50	15.00	30.00
❏ 6383-1-R [(2)]	The Top Ten Hits	1987	7.50	15.00	30.00
❏ 6414-1-R [(2)]	The Complete Sun Sessions	1987	7.50	15.00	30.00
❏ 6738-1-R	Essential Elvis: The First Movies	1988	6.25	12.50	25.00
❏ 6985-1-R	The Alternate Aloha	1988	5.00	10.00	20.00
❏ 8468-1-R	Elvis in Nashville (1956-1971)	1988	10.00	20.00	40.00
❏ 9586-1-R	Elvis Gospel 1957-1971 (Known Only to Him)	1989	10.00	20.00	40.00
❏ 9589-1-R	Essential Elvis, Vol. 2 (Stereo '57)	1989	6.25	12.50	25.00
❏ 07863-67642-1	Elvis' Golden Records	1997	7.50	15.00	30.00
—Reissue for the Tower Records chain with 6 bonus tracks					
❏ 07863-67643-1	Elvis' Gold Records Volume 2 — 50,000,000 Elvis Fans Can't Be Wrong	1997	7.50	15.00	30.00
—Reissue for the Tower Records chain with 10 bonus tracks					
❏ 07863-68079-1 [(2)]	30 #1 Hits	2002	5.00	10.00	20.00
RCA CAMDEN					
❏ CAS-2304	Elvis Sings Flaming Star	1969	7.50	15.00	30.00
❏ CAS-2408	Let's Be Friends	1970	7.50	15.00	30.00
❏ CAL-2428 [M]	Elvis' Christmas Album	1970	7.50	15.00	30.00
—Blue label, non-flexible vinyl					
❏ CAL-2428 [M]	Elvis' Christmas Album	1971	3.00	6.00	12.00
—Blue label, flexible vinyl					
❏ CAS-2440	Almost in Love	1970	10.00	20.00	40.00
—Last song on Side 2 is "Stay Away, Joe"					
❏ CAS-2440	Almost in Love	1973	6.25	12.50	25.00
—Last song on Side 2 is "Stay Away"					
❏ CAL-2472	You'll Never Walk Alone	1974	7.50	15.00	30.00
❏ CALX-2472	You'll Never Walk Alone	1971	3.75	7.50	15.00
❏ CAL-2518	C'mon Everybody	1971	5.00	10.00	20.00
❏ CAL-2533	I Got Lucky	1971	6.25	12.50	25.00
❏ CAS-2567	Elvis Sings Hits from His Movies, Volume 1	1972	5.00	10.00	20.00
❏ CAS-2595	Burning Love And Hits from His Movies, Vol. 2	1972	2.50	5.00	10.00
—No star on cover, no bonus photo					
❏ CAS-2595	Burning Love And Hits from His Movies, Vol. 2	1972	6.25	12.50	25.00
—With star on front cover advertising a bonus photo, the presence of which doubles the value of this LP					
❏ CAS-2611	Separate Ways	1973	7.50	15.00	30.00
RCA SPECIAL PRODUCTS					
❏ DPL2-0056(e) [(2)]	Elvis	1973	6.25	12.50	25.00
—Blue labels					
❏ DPL2-0056(e) [(2)]	Elvis	1973	12.50	25.00	50.00
—Mustard labels					

Number	Title (A Side/B Side)	Yr	VG	VG+	NM

❏ DPL2-0056(e) [(2)] Elvis Commemorative Album — 1978 — 20.00 — 40.00 — 80.00
—*Reissue of "Elvis" (same number) with new title and gold vinyl*
❏ DPL2-0168 [(2)] Elvis in Hollywood — 1976 — 15.00 — 30.00 — 60.00
—*Blue labels; with 20-page booklet*
❏ DML5-0263 [(5)] The Elvis Story — 1977 — 15.00 — 30.00 — 60.00
—*Available through Candelite Music via mail order*
❏ DML1-0264 His Songs of Inspiration — 1977 — 3.75 — 7.50 — 15.00
❏ DPL5-0347 [(5)] Memories of Elvis (A Lasting Tribute to the King of Rock 'N' Roll) — 1978 — 20.00 — 40.00 — 80.00
❏ DML1-0348 The Greatest Show on Earth — 1978 — 3.75 — 7.50 — 15.00
❏ DML6-0412 [(6)] The Legendary Recordings of Elvis Presley — 1979 — 25.00 — 50.00 — 100.00
❏ DML1-0413 The Greatest Moments in Music — 1980 — 3.75 — 7.50 — 15.00
❏ DML1-0437 Rock 'N Roll Forever — 1981 — 3.75 — 7.50 — 15.00
❏ DVL1-0461 The Legendary Magic of Elvis Presley — 1980 — 3.75 — 7.50 — 15.00
❏ DML3-0632 [(3)] The Elvis Presley Collection — 1984 — 20.00 — 40.00 — 80.00
—*Available through Candelite Music via mail order*
❏ DPL1-0647 Elvis Country — 1984 — 7.50 — 15.00 — 30.00
❏ DVM1-0704 Elvis (One Night with You) — 1984 — 15.00 — 30.00 — 60.00
—*With poster (deduct 25% if missing)*
❏ SVL3-0710 [(3)] 50 Years — 50 Hits — 1985 — 7.50 — 15.00 — 30.00
❏ DVL2-0728 [(2)] His Songs of Faith and Inspiration — 1986 — 12.50 — 25.00 — 50.00
❏ SVL2-0824 [(2)] Good Rockin' Tonight — 1988 — 5.00 — 10.00 — 20.00
❏ CAL-2428 [M] Elvis' Christmas Album — 1986 — 7.50 — 15.00 — 30.00
—*Reissue for The Special Music Company*

RCA VICTOR

❏ (no #) International Hotel, Las Vegas Nevada, Presents Elvis, 1969 — 1969 — 1250. — 1875. — 2500.
—*Gift box to guests at Elvis' July 31-Aug, 1, 1969 shows. Includes LPM-4088 and LSP-4155; press release; 1969 catalog; three photos; and thank-you note from Elvis and the Colonel. Most of the value is for the box.*
❏ (no #) International Hotel, Las Vegas Nevada, Presents Elvis, 1970 — 1970 — 1250. — 1875. — 2500.
—*Gift box to guests at Elvis' Jan. 28, 1970 show. Includes LSP-6020 and 47-9791; press release; 1970 catalog; photo; booklet; and dinner menu. Most of the value is for the box.*
❏ PRS-279 Singer Presents Elvis Singing Flaming Star and Others — 1968 — 25.00 — 50.00 — 100.00
—*Sold only at Singer sewing machine dealers; reissued on RCA Camden 2304*
❏ APL1-0283 Elvis — 1973 — 12.50 — 25.00 — 50.00
❏ CPL1-0341 A Legendary Performer, Volume 1 — 1974 — 6.25 — 12.50 — 25.00
—*Includes booklet (deduct 40% if missing); with die-cut hole in front cover*
❏ CPL1-0341 A Legendary Performer, Volume 1 — 1986 — 3.75 — 7.50 — 15.00
—*No die-cut hole in cover and no booklet*
❏ APL1-0388 Raised on Rock/For Ol' Times Sake — 1973 — 7.50 — 15.00 — 30.00
—*Orange label*
❏ APL1-0388 Raised on Rock/For Ol' Times Sake — 1975 — 7.50 — 15.00 — 30.00
—*Tan label*
❏ APL1-0388 Raised on Rock/For Ol' Times Sake — 1977 — 3.00 — 6.00 — 12.00
—*Black label, dog near top*
❏ SP-33-461 [DJ] Special Palm Sunday Programming — 1967 — 175.00 — 350.00 — 700.00
—*White label promo. Add 25% for cue sheet.*
❏ AFL1-0475 Good Times — 1977 — 3.00 — 6.00 — 12.00
—*Black label, dog near top; includes copies with sticker wrapped around spine with new number*
❏ CPL1-0475 Good Times — 1974 — 12.50 — 25.00 — 50.00
—*Orange label*
❏ CPL1-0475 Good Times — 1976 — 3.00 — 6.00 — 12.00
—*Black label, dog near top*
❏ SPS-33-571 [DJ] Elvis As Recorded at Madison Square Garden — 1972 — 75.00 — 150.00 — 300.00
—*"Radio Station Banded Special Version"; came in plain white cover with stickers*
❏ AFL1-0606 Elvis Recorded Live on Stage in Memphis — 1977 — 3.00 — 6.00 — 12.00
—*Black label, dog near top; includes copies with sticker wrapped around spine with new number*
❏ APD1-0606 [Q] Elvis Recorded Live on Stage in Memphis — 1974 — 50.00 — 100.00 — 200.00
—*"RCA QuadraDisc" labels*
❏ CPL1-0606 Elvis Recorded Live on Stage in Memphis — 1974 — 6.25 — 12.50 — 25.00
—*Orange label*
❏ CPL1-0606 Elvis Recorded Live on Stage in Memphis — 1975 — 6.25 — 12.50 — 25.00
—*Tan label*
❏ DJL1-0606 [DJ] Elvis Recorded Live on Stage in Memphis — 1974 — 75.00 — 150.00 — 300.00
—*Special banded version for radio airplay*
❏ AFM1-0818 Having Fun with Elvis on Stage — 1977 — 6.25 — 12.50 — 25.00
—*Black label, dog near top*
❏ CPM1-0818 Having Fun with Elvis on Stage — 1974 — 7.50 — 15.00 — 30.00
—*Commercial issue of Boxcar LP; orange label*
❏ CPM1-0818 Having Fun with Elvis on Stage — 1975 — 5.00 — 10.00 — 20.00
—*Tan label*
❏ DJM1-0835 [DJ] Elvis Presley Interview Record: An Audio Self-Portrait — 1984 — 20.00 — 40.00 — 80.00
—*Promotional item for "50th Anniversary" series; later issued as RCA 6313-1-R*
❏ AFL1-0873 Promised Land — 1977 — 3.75 — 7.50 — 15.00
—*Black label, dog near top*
❏ APD1-0873 [Q] Promised Land — 1975 — 50.00 — 100.00 — 200.00
—*"RCA QuadraDisc" label*
❏ APD1-0873 [Q] Promised Land — 1977 — 30.00 — 60.00 — 120.00
—*Black label, dog near top; quadraphonic reissue*
❏ APL1-0873 Promised Land — 1975 — 5.00 — 10.00 — 20.00
—*Tan label*
❏ APL1-0873 Promised Land — 1975 — 15.00 — 30.00 — 60.00
—*Orange label*
❏ ANL1-0971(e) Pure Gold — 1975 — 3.75 — 7.50 — 15.00
—*Orange label*
❏ ANL1-0971(e) Pure Gold — 1976 — 3.00 — 6.00 — 12.00
—*Yellow label*
❏ LOC-1035 [M] Elvis' Christmas Album Sticker — 1957 — 37.50 — 75.00 — 150.00
—*Gold sticker with "To_____" and "From_____" blanks*
❏ LOC-1035 [M] Elvis' Christmas Album — 1957 — 125.00 — 250.00 — 500.00
—*Gatefold cover; title printed in gold on LP spine; includes bound-in booklet but not sticker*
❏ LOC-1035 [M] Elvis' Christmas Album — 1957 — 125.00 — 250.00 — 500.00
—*Gatefold cover; title printed in silver on LP spine; includes bound-in booklet but not sticker*
❏ LOC-1035 [M] Elvis' Christmas Album — 1957 — 7500. — 11250. — 15000.
—*Red vinyl; unique*
❏ AFL1-1039 Elvis Today — 1977 — 3.00 — 6.00 — 12.00
—*Black label, dog near top; includes copies with sticker wrapped around spine with new number*
❏ APD1-1039 [Q] Elvis Today — 1975 — 50.00 — 100.00 — 200.00
—*"RCA QuadraDisc" labels*

❏ APD1-1039 [Q] Elvis Today — 1977 — 37.50 — 75.00 — 150.00
—*Black label, dog near top; quadraphonic reissue*
❏ APL1-1039 Elvis Today — 1975 — 7.50 — 15.00 — 30.00
—*Tan label*
❏ APL1-1039 Elvis Today — 1975 — 15.00 — 30.00 — 60.00
—*Orange label*
❏ AFL1-1254(e) [R] Elvis Presley — 1977 — 3.00 — 6.00 — 12.00
—*Black label, dog near top; includes copies with sticker wrapped around spine with new number*
❏ LPM-1254 [M] Elvis Presley — 1956 — 62.50 — 125.00 — 250.00
—*Version 3: "Long Play" on label; "Elvis" in pale pink, "Presley" in neon green on cover; black logo box in upper right front cover*
❏ LPM-1254 [M] Elvis Presley — 1956 — 100.00 — 200.00 — 400.00
—*Version 2: "Long Play" on label; "Elvis" in pale pink, "Presley" in neon green on cover; neon green logo box in upper right front cover*
❏ LPM-1254 [M] Elvis Presley — 1956 — 125.00 — 250.00 — 500.00
—*Version 1: "Long Play" on label; "Elvis" in pale pink, "Presley" in pale green on cover; pale green logo box in upper right front cover*
❏ LPM-1254 [M] Elvis Presley — 1958 — 50.00 — 100.00 — 200.00
—*Version 4: "Long Play" on label; "Elvis" in neon pink, almost red, "Presley" in neon green on cover; black logo box in upper right front cover*
❏ LPM-1254 [M] Elvis Presley — 1963 — 30.00 — 60.00 — 120.00
—*"Mono" on label; cover photo is slightly left of center, otherwise same as Version 4 above*
❏ LPM-1254 [M] Elvis Presley — 1964 — 15.00 — 30.00 — 60.00
—*"Monaural" on label*
❏ LSP-1254(e) [R] Elvis Presley — 1962 — 50.00 — 100.00 — 200.00
—*"Stereo Electronically Reprocessed" and silver "RCA Victor" on label*
❏ LSP-1254(e) [R] Elvis Presley — 1965 — 10.00 — 20.00 — 40.00
—*"Stereo Electronically Reprocessed" and white "RCA Victor" on label*
❏ LSP-1254(e) [R] Elvis Presley — 1968 — 7.50 — 15.00 — 30.00
—*Orange label, non-flexible vinyl*
❏ LSP-1254(e) [R] Elvis Presley — 1975 — 3.75 — 7.50 — 15.00
—*Tan label*
❏ LSP-1254(e) [R] Elvis Presley — 1976 — 3.00 — 6.00 — 12.00
—*Black label, dog near top*
❏ ANL1-1319 [S] His Hand in Mine — 1976 — 3.75 — 7.50 — 15.00
—*Reissue with more tightly cropped photo of Elvis on front cover*
❏ CPL1-1349 A Legendary Performer, Volume 2 — 1976 — 7.50 — 15.00 — 30.00
—*Includes booklet (deduct 40% if missing); with die-cut hole in front cover*
❏ CPL1-1349 A Legendary Performer, Volume 2 — 1976 — 15.00 — 30.00 — 60.00
—*Without false starts and outtakes of "Such a Night" and "Cane and a High Starched Collar," which are supposed to be there. End of matrix number may be "31."*
❏ CPL1-1349 A Legendary Performer, Volume 2 — 1986 — 3.75 — 7.50 — 15.00
—*No die-cut hole in cover and no booklet*
❏ AFL1-1382(e) [R] Elvis — 1977 — 3.00 — 6.00 — 12.00
—*Black label, dog near top; includes copies with sticker wrapped around spine with new number*
❏ LPM-1382 [M] Elvis — 1956 — 75.00 — 150.00 — 300.00
—*Back cover has ads for other albums. At least 11 different variations of this are known, all of equal value.*
❏ LPM-1382 [M] Elvis — 1956 — 75.00 — 150.00 — 300.00
—*Back cover has no ads for other albums. "Long Play" on label.*
❏ LPM-1382 [M] Elvis — 1956 — 100.00 — 200.00 — 400.00
—*With tracks listed on labels as "Band 1" through "Band 6"*
❏ LPM-1382 [M] Elvis — 1956 — 200.00 — 400.00 — 800.00
—*With alternate take of "Old Shep" on side 2. Matrix number on the "Old Shep" side ends in "15S," "17S" or "19S," but should be played for positive ID. On alternate take, Elvis sings "he grew old AND his eyes were growing dim" (no AND on standard press)*
❏ LPM-1382 [M] Elvis — 1963 — 20.00 — 40.00 — 80.00
—*"Mono" on label*
❏ LPM-1382 [M] Elvis — 1965 — 15.00 — 30.00 — 60.00
—*"Monaural" on label*
❏ LSP-1382(e) [R] Elvis — 1962 — 50.00 — 100.00 — 200.00
—*"Stereo Electronically Reprocessed" and silver "RCA Victor" on label*
❏ LSP-1382(e) [R] Elvis — 1964 — 12.50 — 25.00 — 50.00
—*"Stereo Electronically Reprocessed" and white "RCA Victor" on label*
❏ LSP-1382(e) [R] Elvis — 1968 — 7.50 — 15.00 — 30.00
—*Orange label, non-flexible vinyl*
❏ LSP-1382(e) [R] Elvis — 1971 — 5.00 — 10.00 — 20.00
—*Orange label, flexible vinyl*
❏ LSP-1382(e) [R] Elvis — 1975 — 3.75 — 7.50 — 15.00
—*Tan label*
❏ LSP-1382(e) [R] Elvis — 1976 — 3.00 — 6.00 — 12.00
—*Black label, dog near top*
❏ AFL1-1506 From Elvis Presley Boulevard, Memphis, Tennessee — 1977 — 2.50 — 5.00 — 10.00
—*Black label, dog near top; new number is on cover and label*
❏ AFL1-1506 From Elvis Presley Boulevard, Memphis, Tennessee — 1977 — 3.00 — 6.00 — 12.00
—*Black label, dog near top; with sticker wrapped around spine with new number (old number still on label)*
❏ APL1-1506 From Elvis Presley Boulevard, Memphis, Tennessee — 1976 — 7.50 — 15.00 — 30.00
—*Tan label*
❏ AFL1-1515(e) [R] Loving You — 1977 — 3.00 — 6.00 — 12.00
—*Black label, dog near top; includes copies with sticker wrapped around spine with new number*
❏ LPM-1515 [M] Loving You — 1957 — 75.00 — 150.00 — 300.00
—*"Long Play" on label*
❏ LPM-1515 [M] Loving You — 1963 — 25.00 — 50.00 — 100.00
—*"Mono" on label*
❏ LPM-1515 [M] Loving You — 1964 — 12.50 — 25.00 — 50.00
—*"Monaural" on label*
❏ LSP-1515(e) [R] Loving You — 1962 — 37.50 — 75.00 — 150.00
—*"Stereo Electronically Reprocessed" and silver "RCA Victor" on label*
❏ LSP-1515(e) [R] Loving You — 1964 — 12.50 — 25.00 — 50.00
—*"Stereo Electronically Reprocessed" and white "RCA Victor" on label*
❏ LSP-1515(e) [R] Loving You — 1968 — 10.00 — 20.00 — 40.00
—*Orange label, non-flexible vinyl*
❏ LSP-1515(e) [R] Loving You — 1971 — 5.00 — 10.00 — 20.00
—*Orange label, flexible vinyl*
❏ LSP-1515(e) [R] Loving You — 1975 — 5.00 — 10.00 — 20.00
—*Tan label*
❏ LSP-1515(e) [R] Loving You — 1976 — 3.00 — 6.00 — 12.00
—*Black label, dog near top*
❏ AFM1-1675 The Sun Sessions — 1977 — 3.75 — 7.50 — 15.00
—*Black label, dog near top; includes copies with sticker wrapped around spine with new number*

Number	Title (A Side/B Side)	Yr	VG	VG+	NM
❑ APM1-1675	The Sun Sessions	1976	3.00	6.00	12.00

—*Black label, dog near top*

❑ APM1-1675	The Sun Sessions	1976	5.00	10.00	20.00

—*Tan label*

❑ AFL1-1707(e) [R]	Elvis' Golden Records	1977	3.00	6.00	12.00

—*Black label, dog near top; includes copies with sticker wrapped around spine with new number*

❑ AQL1-1707(e) [R]	Elvis' Golden Records	1979	2.50	5.00	10.00

—*Another reissue with new prefix*

❑ LPM-1707 [M]	Elvis' Golden Records	1958	37.50	75.00	150.00

—*Title on cover in light blue letters; no song titles listed on front cover; "RE" on back cover*

❑ LPM-1707 [M]	Elvis' Golden Records	1958	62.50	125.00	250.00

—*Title on cover in light blue letters; no song titles listed on front cover*

❑ LPM-1707 [M]	Elvis' Golden Records	1963	15.00	30.00	60.00

—*"Mono" on label; title on cover in white letters; song titles added to front cover*

❑ LPM-1707 [M]	Elvis' Golden Records	1964	10.00	20.00	40.00

—*"Monaural" on label; "RE2" on back cover*

❑ LSP-1707(e) [R]	Elvis' Golden Records	1962	50.00	100.00	200.00

—*"Stereo Electronically Reprocessed" and silver "RCA Victor" on label*

❑ LSP-1707(e) [R]	Elvis' Golden Records	1964	12.50	25.00	50.00

—*"Stereo Electronically Reprocessed" and white "RCA Victor" on label*

❑ LSP-1707(e) [R]	Elvis' Golden Records	1968	7.50	15.00	30.00

—*Orange label, non-flexible vinyl*

❑ LSP-1707(e) [R]	Elvis' Golden Records	1971	5.00	10.00	20.00

—*Orange label, flexible vinyl*

❑ LSP-1707(e) [R]	Elvis' Golden Records	1975	5.00	10.00	20.00

—*Tan label*

❑ LSP-1707(e) [R]	Elvis' Golden Records	1976	3.00	6.00	12.00

—*Black label, dog near top*

❑ AFL1-1884(e) [R]	King Creole	1977	3.00	6.00	12.00

—*Black label, dog near top; includes copies with sticker wrapped around spine with new number*

❑ LPM-1884 [M]	King Creole	1958	50.00	100.00	200.00

—*"Long Play" on label; contrary to some other sources, this was NOT issued with a bonus photo*

❑ LPM-1884 [M]	King Creole	1963	20.00	40.00	80.00

—*"Mono" on label*

❑ LPM-1884 [M]	King Creole	1964	15.00	30.00	60.00

—*"Monaural" on label*

❑ LSP-1884(e) [R]	King Creole	1962	37.50	75.00	150.00

—*"Stereo Electronically Reprocessed" and silver "RCA Victor" on label*

❑ LSP-1884(e) [R]	King Creole	1964	15.00	30.00	60.00

—*"Stereo Electronically Reprocessed" and white "RCA Victor" on label*

❑ LSP-1884(e) [R]	King Creole	1968	10.00	20.00	40.00

—*Orange label, non-flexible vinyl*

❑ LSP-1884(e) [R]	King Creole	1971	5.00	10.00	20.00

—*Orange label, flexible vinyl*

❑ LSP-1884(e) [R]	King Creole	1975	5.00	10.00	20.00

—*Tan label*

❑ LSP-1884(e) [R]	King Creole	1976	3.00	6.00	12.00

—*Black label, dog near top*

❑ ANL1-1936	Elvis Sings the Wonderful World of Christmas	1975	3.75	7.50	15.00

—*New number; same contents as LSP-4579. Orange label.*

❑ ANL1-1936	Elvis Sings the Wonderful World of Christmas	1976	3.00	6.00	12.00

—*Tan label*

❑ ANL1-1936	Elvis Sings the Wonderful World of Christmas	1977	2.50	5.00	10.00

—*Black label, dog near top*

❑ LPM-1951 [M]	Elvis' Christmas Album	1958	37.50	75.00	150.00

—*Same contents as LOC-1035, but with non-gatefold blue cover; "Long Play" at bottom of label*

❑ LPM-1951 [M]	Elvis' Christmas Album	1963	17.50	35.00	70.00

—*"Mono" at bottom of label; "RE" on lower left front cover (photos on back were altered)*

❑ LPM-1951 [M]	Elvis' Christmas Album	1964	10.00	20.00	40.00

—*"Monaural" at bottom of label; "RE" on lower left front cover*

❑ LSP-1951(e) [R]	Elvis' Christmas Album	1964	12.50	25.00	50.00

—*Black label, dog on top; "Stereo Electronically Reprocessed" at bottom of label*

❑ LSP-1951(e) [R]	Elvis' Christmas Album	1968	15.00	30.00	60.00

—*Orange label, non-flexible vinyl*

❑ AFL1-1990(e) [R]	For LP Fans Only	1977	3.00	6.00	12.00

—*Black label, dog near top; includes copies with sticker wrapped around spine with new number*

❑ LPM-1990 [M]	For LP Fans Only	1959	62.50	125.00	250.00

—*"Long Play" on label*

❑ LPM-1990 [M]	For LP Fans Only	1963	20.00	40.00	80.00

—*"Mono" on label*

❑ LPM-1990 [M]	For LP Fans Only	1964	12.50	25.00	50.00

—*"Monaural" on label*

❑ LSP-1990(e) [R]	For LP Fans Only	1965	12.50	25.00	50.00

—*"Stereo Electronically Reprocessed" on label; normal cover with different front and back cover photos*

❑ LSP-1990(e) [R]	For LP Fans Only	1965	75.00	150.00	300.00

—*"Stereo Electronically Reprocessed" on label; error cover with same photo on both front and back*

❑ LSP-1990(e) [R]	For LP Fans Only	1968	7.50	15.00	30.00

—*Orange label, non-flexible vinyl*

❑ LSP-1990(e) [R]	For LP Fans Only	1975	5.00	10.00	20.00

—*Tan label*

❑ LSP-1990(e) [R]	For LP Fans Only	1976	3.00	6.00	12.00

—*Black label, dog near top*

❑ AFL1-2011(e) [R]	A Date with Elvis	1977	3.00	6.00	12.00

—*Black label, dog near top; includes copies with sticker wrapped around spine with new number*

❑ LPM-2011 [M]	A Date with Elvis	1959	100.00	200.00	400.00

—*"Long Play" on label; gatefold cover, no sticker on cover*

❑ LPM-2011 [M]	A Date with Elvis	1959	125.00	250.00	500.00

—*"Long Play" on label; gatefold cover, with sticker on cover*

❑ LPM-2011 [M]	A Date with Elvis	1963	25.00	50.00	100.00

—*"Mono" on label; no gatefold cover*

❑ LPM-2011 [M]	A Date with Elvis	1965	12.50	25.00	50.00

—*"Monaural" on label*

❑ LSP-2011(e) [R]	A Date with Elvis	1965	12.50	25.00	50.00

—*"Stereo Electronically Reprocessed" on label*

❑ LSP-2011(e) [R]	A Date with Elvis	1968	7.50	15.00	30.00

—*Orange label, non-flexible vinyl*

❑ LSP-2011(e) [R]	A Date with Elvis	1971	5.00	10.00	20.00

—*Orange label, flexible vinyl*

❑ LSP-2011(e) [R]	A Date with Elvis	1975	5.00	10.00	20.00

—*Tan label*

❑ LSP-2011(e) [R]	A Date with Elvis	1977	3.00	6.00	12.00

—*Black label, dog near top*

❑ AFL1-2075(e) [R]	Elvis' Gold Records Volume 2 — 50,000,000 Elvis Fans Can't Be Wrong	1977	3.00	6.00	12.00

—*Black label, dog near top; includes copies with sticker wrapped around spine with new number*

❑ LPM-2075 [M]	Elvis' Gold Records Volume 2 — 50,000,000 Elvis Fans Can't Be Wrong	1960	50.00	100.00	200.00

—*"Long Play" on label; "Magic Millions" on upper right front cover with RCA Victor logo*

❑ LPM-2075 [M]	Elvis' Gold Records Volume 2 — 50,000,000 Elvis Fans Can't Be Wrong	1963	20.00	40.00	80.00

—*"Mono" on label; "RE" on lower right front cover*

❑ LPM-2075 [M]	Elvis' Gold Records Volume 2 — 50,000,000 Elvis Fans Can't Be Wrong	1964	12.50	25.00	50.00

—*"Monaural" on label; label has words "50,000,000 Elvis Presley Fans Can't Be Wrong"*

❑ LPM-2075 [M]	Elvis' Gold Records Volume 2 — 50,000,000 Elvis Fans Can't Be Wrong	1964	12.50	25.00	50.00

—*"Monaural" on label; label only has "Elvis' Gold Records - Vol. 2"*

❑ LSP-2075(e) [R]	Elvis' Gold Records Volume 2 — 50,000,000 Elvis Fans Can't Be Wrong	1962	37.50	75.00	150.00

—*"Stereo Electronically Reprocessed" on label; label has words "50,000,000 Elvis Presley Fans Can't Be Wrong"*

❑ LSP-2075(e) [R]	Elvis' Gold Records Volume 2 — 50,000,000 Elvis Fans Can't Be Wrong	1964	12.50	25.00	50.00

—*"Stereo Electronically Reprocessed" and white "RCA Victor" on label*

❑ LSP-2075(e) [R]	Elvis' Gold Records Volume 2 — 50,000,000 Elvis Fans Can't Be Wrong	1968	7.50	15.00	30.00

—*Orange label, non-flexible vinyl*

❑ LSP-2075(e) [R]	Elvis' Gold Records Volume 2 — 50,000,000 Elvis Fans Can't Be Wrong	1971	5.00	10.00	20.00

—*Orange label, flexible vinyl*

❑ LSP-2075(e) [R]	Elvis' Gold Records Volume 2 — 50,000,000 Elvis Fans Can't Be Wrong	1975	5.00	10.00	20.00

—*Tan label*

❑ LSP-2075(e) [R]	Elvis' Gold Records Volume 2 — 50,000,000 Elvis Fans Can't Be Wrong	1976	3.00	6.00	12.00

—*Black label, dog near top*

❑ AFL1-2231 [S]	Elvis Is Back!	1977	3.00	6.00	12.00

—*Black label, dog near top; includes copies with sticker wrapped around spine with new number*

❑ LPM-2231 [M]	Elvis Is Back!	1960	37.50	75.00	150.00

—*With sticker attached to front cover. Side 2, Song 4 is listed as "The Girl Next Door Went a-Walking."*

❑ LPM-2231 [M]	Elvis Is Back!	1960	37.50	75.00	150.00

—*With sticker attached to front cover. Side 2, Song 4 is listed as "The Girl Next Door."*

❑ LPM-2231 [M]	Elvis Is Back!	1960	50.00	100.00	200.00

—*With no sticker attached to front cover. Side 2, Song 4 is listed as "The Girl Next Door Went a-Walking."*

❑ LPM-2231 [M]	Elvis Is Back!	1960	50.00	100.00	200.00

—*With no sticker attached to front cover. Side 2, Song 4 is listed as "The Girl Next Door."*

❑ LPM-2231 [M]	Elvis Is Back!	1963	15.00	30.00	60.00

—*"Mono" on label; song titles printed on front cover*

❑ LPM-2231 [M]	Elvis Is Back!	1964	15.00	30.00	60.00

—*"Monaural" on label*

❑ LSP-2231 [S]	Elvis Is Back!	1960	75.00	150.00	300.00

—*"Living Stereo" on label; with no sticker attached to front cover. Side 2, Song 4 is listed as "The Girl Next Door Went a-Walking."*

❑ LSP-2231 [S]	Elvis Is Back!	1960	75.00	150.00	300.00

—*"Living Stereo" on label; with no sticker attached to front cover. Side 2, Song 4 is listed as "The Girl Next Door."*

❑ LSP-2231 [S]	Elvis Is Back!	1960	75.00	150.00	300.00

—*"Living Stereo" on label; with sticker attached to front cover. Side 2, Song 4 is listed as "The Girl Next Door Went a-Walking."*

❑ LSP-2231 [S]	Elvis Is Back!	1960	75.00	150.00	300.00

—*"Living Stereo" on label; with sticker attached to front cover. Side 2, Song 4 is listed as "The Girl Next Door."*

❑ LSP-2231 [S]	Elvis Is Back!	1964	15.00	30.00	60.00

—*"Stereo" on label; song titles printed on front cover*

❑ LSP-2231 [S]	Elvis Is Back!	1968	10.00	20.00	40.00

—*Orange label, non-flexible vinyl*

❑ LSP-2231 [S]	Elvis Is Back!	1975	5.00	10.00	20.00

—*Tan label*

❑ LSP-2231 [S]	Elvis Is Back!	1976	3.75	7.50	15.00

—*Black label, dog on top*

❑ AFL1-2256 [S]	G.I. Blues	1977	3.00	6.00	12.00

—*Black label, dog near top; includes copies with sticker wrapped around spine with new number*

❑ LPM-2256 [M]	G.I. Blues	1960	30.00	60.00	120.00

—*"Long Play" on label; with no sticker on front cover*

❑ LPM-2256 [M]	G.I. Blues	1960	125.00	250.00	500.00

—*"Long Play" on label; with sticker on front cover advertising the presence of "Wooden Heart"*

❑ LPM-2256 [M]	G.I. Blues	1963	25.00	50.00	100.00

—*"Mono" on label*

❑ LPM-2256 [M]	G.I. Blues	1964	12.50	25.00	50.00

—*"Monaural" on label*

❑ LSP-2256 [S]	G.I. Blues	1960	25.00	50.00	100.00

—*"Living Stereo" on label; with no sticker on front cover*

❑ LSP-2256 [S]	G.I. Blues	1960	150.00	300.00	600.00

—*"Living Stereo" on label; with sticker on front cover advertising the presence of "Wooden Heart"*

❑ LSP-2256 [S]	G.I. Blues	1964	12.50	25.00	50.00

—*"Stereo" on black label*

❑ LSP-2256 [S]	G.I. Blues	1968	10.00	20.00	40.00

—*Orange label, non-flexible vinyl*

❑ LSP-2256 [S]	G.I. Blues	1971	5.00	10.00	20.00

—*Orange label, flexible vinyl*

❑ LSP-2256 [S]	G.I. Blues	1975	6.25	12.50	25.00

—*Tan label*

❑ LSP-2256 [S]	G.I. Blues	1976	3.00	6.00	12.00

—*Black label, dog near top*

❑ AFL1-2274	Welcome to My World	1977	3.00	6.00	12.00

—*Black label, dog near top; includes copies with sticker wrapped around spine with new number*

❑ APL1-2274	Welcome to My World	1977	5.00	10.00	20.00

—*Black label, dog near top*

❑ AQL1-2274	Welcome to My World	1979	2.50	5.00	10.00

—*Black label, dog near top; includes copies with sticker wrapped around spine with new number*

❑ LPM-2328 [M]	His Hand in Mine	1960	30.00	60.00	120.00

—*"Long Play" on label*

P

Number	Title (A Side/B Side)	Yr	VG	VG+	NM
❑ LPM-2328 [M]	His Hand in Mine	1963	15.00	30.00	60.00
—"Mono" on label					
❑ LPM-2328 [M]	His Hand in Mine	1964	12.50	25.00	50.00
—"Monaural" on label					
❑ LSP-2328 [S]	His Hand in Mine	1960	50.00	100.00	200.00
—"Living Stereo" on label					
❑ LSP-2328 [S]	His Hand in Mine	1964	25.00	50.00	100.00
—"Stereo" and white "RCA Victor" on black label					
❑ LSP-2328 [S]	His Hand in Mine	1964	150.00	300.00	600.00
—"Stereo" and silver "RCA Victor" on black label					
❑ LSP-2328 [S]	His Hand in Mine	1968	12.50	25.00	50.00
—Orange label, non-flexible vinyl					
❑ LSP-2328 [S]	His Hand in Mine	197?	5.00	10.00	20.00
—Orange label, flexible vinyl					
❑ LSP-2328 [S]	His Hand in Mine	1975	5.00	10.00	20.00
—Tan label					
❑ AHL1-2347	Greatest Hits, Volume One	1981	6.25	12.50	25.00
—With embossed cover					
❑ AHL1-2347	Greatest Hits, Volume One	1983	3.75	7.50	15.00
—Without embossed cover					
❑ AFL1-2370 [S]	Something for Everybody	1977	3.00	6.00	12.00
—Black label, dog near top; includes copies with sticker wrapped around spine with new number					
❑ LPM-2370 [M]	Something for Everybody	1961	30.00	60.00	120.00
—"Long Play" on label; back cover advertises RCA Compact 33 singles and doubles					
❑ LPM-2370 [M]	Something for Everybody	1963	20.00	40.00	80.00
—"Mono" on label; back cover advertises "Viva Las Vegas" EP					
❑ LPM-2370 [M]	Something for Everybody	1964	12.50	25.00	50.00
—"Monaural" on label; back cover advertises "Viva Las Vegas" EP					
❑ LSP-2370 [S]	Something for Everybody	1961	50.00	100.00	200.00
—"Living Stereo" on label; back cover advertises RCA Compact 33 singles and doubles					
❑ LSP-2370 [S]	Something for Everybody	1963	25.00	50.00	100.00
—"Stereo" and silver "RCA Victor" on black label; back cover advertises Elvis' Christmas Album and His Hand in Mine LPs and "Viva Las Vegas" EP					
❑ LSP-2370 [S]	Something for Everybody	1964	12.50	25.00	50.00
—"Stereo" and white "RCA Victor" on black label; back cover advertises "Viva Las Vegas" EP					
❑ LSP-2370 [S]	Something for Everybody	1968	10.00	20.00	40.00
—Orange label, non-flexible vinyl; final back cover change advertises Elvis (NBC-TV Special), Elvis' Christmas Album and His Hand in Mine LPs					
❑ LSP-2370 [S]	Something for Everybody	1971	5.00	10.00	20.00
—Orange label, flexible vinyl					
❑ LSP-2370 [S]	Something for Everybody	1975	5.00	10.00	20.00
—Tan label					
❑ LSP-2370 [S]	Something for Everybody	1976	3.00	6.00	12.00
—Black label, dog near top					
❑ AFL1-2426 [S]	Blue Hawaii	1977	3.00	6.00	12.00
—Black label, dog near top; with sticker wrapped around spine with new number					
❑ LPM-2426 [M]	Blue Hawaii	1961	25.00	50.00	100.00
—"Long Play" on label; with sticker on cover advertising the presence of "Can't Help Falling in Love" and "Rock-a-Hula Baby"					
❑ LPM-2426 [M]	Blue Hawaii	1962	15.00	30.00	60.00
—"Long Play" on label; no sticker on front cover					
❑ LPM-2426 [M]	Blue Hawaii	1963	12.50	25.00	50.00
—"Mono" on label					
❑ LPM-2426 [M]	Blue Hawaii	1964	10.00	20.00	40.00
—"Monaural" on label					
❑ LSP-2426 [S]	Blue Hawaii	1961	37.50	75.00	150.00
—"Living Stereo" on label and upper right front cover; with sticker on cover advertising the presence of "Can't Help Falling in Love" and "Rock-a-Hula Baby"					
❑ LSP-2426 [S]	Blue Hawaii	1962	20.00	40.00	80.00
—"Living Stereo" on label and upper right front cover; no sticker on front cover					
❑ LSP-2426 [S]	Blue Hawaii	1964	12.50	25.00	50.00
—"Stereo" on label; "Victor Stereo" on upper right front cover					
❑ LSP-2426 [S]	Blue Hawaii	1968	10.00	20.00	40.00
—Orange label, non-flexible vinyl					
❑ LSP-2426 [S]	Blue Hawaii	197?	250.00	500.00	1000.
—One-of-a-kind blue vinyl pressing with black label, dog near top					
❑ LSP-2426 [S]	Blue Hawaii	1971	50.00	10.00	20.00
—Orange label, flexible vinyl					
❑ LSP-2426 [S]	Blue Hawaii	1975	50.00	10.00	20.00
—Tan label					
❑ LSP-2426 [S]	Blue Hawaii	1977	3.00	6.00	12.00
—Black label, dog near top					
❑ AFK1-2428	Moody Blue	1977	1500.	2250.	3000.
—Alternate cover slick (never put on an actual cover), with the words "Moody Blue" inside the large word "Elvis." See any late-1970s Elvis inner sleeve for a black and white photo of the scrapped cover.					
❑ AFL1-2428	Moody Blue	1977	2.50	5.00	10.00
—Blue vinyl					
❑ AFL1-2428	Moody Blue	1977	50.00	100.00	200.00
—Black vinyl					
❑ AFL1-2428 [DJ]	Moody Blue	1977	500.00	1000.	2000.
—Experimental colored vinyl pressings (with no cover), any color or combination except blue or black					
❑ AQL1-2428	Moody Blue	1979	6.25	12.50	25.00
—Reissue with new prefix					
❑ AFL1-2523 [S]	Pot Luck with Elvis	1977	3.00	6.00	12.00
—Black label, dog near top; includes copies with sticker wrapped around spine with new number					
❑ LPM-2523 [M]	Pot Luck with Elvis	1962	25.00	50.00	100.00
—"Long Play" on label					
❑ LPM-2523 [M]	Pot Luck with Elvis	1964	30.00	60.00	120.00
—"Monaural" on label					
❑ LSP-2523 [S]	Pot Luck with Elvis	1962	37.50	75.00	150.00
—"Living Stereo" on label					
❑ LSP-2523 [S]	Pot Luck with Elvis	1964	15.00	30.00	60.00
—"Stereo" on black label					
❑ LSP-2523 [S]	Pot Luck with Elvis	1968	10.00	20.00	40.00
—Orange label, non-flexible vinyl					
❑ LSP-2523 [S]	Pot Luck with Elvis	1975	5.00	10.00	20.00
—Tan label					
❑ LSP-2523 [S]	Pot Luck with Elvis	1976	3.00	6.00	12.00
—Black label, dog near top					
❑ APL1-2558 [S]	Harum Scarum	1977	3.00	6.00	12.00
—Black label, dog near top					
❑ APL1-2560 [S]	Spinout	1977	3.00	6.00	12.00
—Black label, dog near top					

Number	Title (A Side/B Side)	Yr	VG	VG+	NM
❑ APL1-2564 [S]	Double Trouble	1977	3.00	6.00	12.00
—Black label, dog near top; includes copies with sticker wrapped around spine with new number					
❑ APL1-2565	Clambake	1977	3.00	6.00	12.00
❑ APL1-2568 [S]	It Happened at the World's Fair	1977	3.00	6.00	12.00
❑ AFL2-2587 [(2)]	Elvis in Concert	1977	250.00	500.00	1000.
—Both records on translucent blue vinyl; possibly an in-house demo at the RCA Indianapolis pressing plant					
❑ APL2-2587 [(2)]	Elvis in Concert	1977	6.25	12.50	25.00
❑ CPL2-2587 [(2)]	Elvis in Concert	1982	10.00	20.00	40.00
❑ AFL1-2621 [S]	Girls! Girls! Girls!	1977	3.00	6.00	12.00
—Black label, dog near top; includes copies with sticker wrapped around spine with new number					
❑ LPM-2621 [M]	Girls! Girls! Girls!	1962	20.00	40.00	80.00
—"Long Play" on label					
❑ LPM-2621 [M]	Girls! Girls! Girls!	1963	15.00	30.00	60.00
—"Mono" on label					
❑ LPM-2621 [M]	Girls! Girls! Girls!	1964	10.00	20.00	40.00
—"Monaural" on label					
❑ LPM/LSP-2621	Girls! Girls! Girls! Bonus 1963 Calendar	1962	37.50	75.00	150.00
—With listing of other Elvis records on back					
❑ LSP-2621 [S]	Girls! Girls! Girls!	1962	37.50	75.00	150.00
—"Living Stereo" on label					
❑ LSP-2621 [S]	Girls! Girls! Girls!	1964	15.00	30.00	60.00
—"Stereo" on black label					
❑ LSP-2621 [S]	Girls! Girls! Girls!	1968	10.00	20.00	40.00
—Orange label, non-flexible vinyl					
❑ LSP-2621 [S]	Girls! Girls! Girls!	1971	5.00	10.00	20.00
—Orange label, flexible vinyl					
❑ LSP-2621 [S]	Girls! Girls! Girls!	1975	6.25	12.50	25.00
—Tan label					
❑ LSP-2621 [S]	Girls! Girls! Girls!	1976	3.00	6.00	12.00
—Black label, dog near top					
❑ CPD2-2642 [(2)Q]	Aloha from Hawaii Via Satellite	1975	7.50	15.00	30.00
—Orange labels					
❑ CPD2-2642 [(2)Q]	Aloha from Hawaii Via Satellite	1977	20.00	40.00	80.00
—Black labels, dog near top					
❑ CPL2-2642 [(2)Q]	Aloha from Hawaii Via Satellite	1984	3.00	6.00	12.00
—New prefix; single-pocket instead of gatefold jacket					
❑ LPM-2697 [M]	It Happened at the World's Fair	1963	30.00	60.00	120.00
❑ LPM/LSP-2697	It Happened at the World's Fair Photo	1963	62.50	125.00	250.00
❑ LSP-2697 [S]	It Happened at the World's Fair	1963	50.00	100.00	200.00
—"Living Stereo" and silver "RCA Victor" on black label					
❑ LSP-2697 [S]	It Happened at the World's Fair	1964	20.00	40.00	80.00
—"Stereo" and white "RCA Victor" on black label					
❑ AFL1-2756 [S]	Fun in Acapulco	1977	3.00	6.00	12.00
—Black label, dog near top; includes copies with sticker wrapped around spine with new number					
❑ LPM-2756 [M]	Fun in Acapulco	1963	20.00	40.00	80.00
—"Mono" on label					
❑ LPM-2756 [M]	Fun in Acapulco	1964	12.50	25.00	50.00
—"Monaural" on label					
❑ LSP-2756 [S]	Fun in Acapulco	1963	25.00	50.00	100.00
—"Stereo" and silver "RCA Victor" on black label					
❑ LSP-2756 [S]	Fun in Acapulco	1964	15.00	30.00	60.00
—"Stereo" and white "RCA Victor" on black label					
❑ LSP-2756 [S]	Fun in Acapulco	1968	10.00	20.00	40.00
—Orange label, non-flexible vinyl					
❑ LSP-2756 [S]	Fun in Acapulco	1975	6.25	12.50	25.00
—Tan label					
❑ LSP-2756 [S]	Fun in Acapulco	1976	3.00	6.00	12.00
—Black label, dog near top					
❑ AFL1-2765 [S]	Elvis' Golden Records, Volume 3	1977	3.00	6.00	12.00
—Black label, dog near top; includes copies with sticker wrapped around spine with new number					
❑ LPM-2765 [M]	Elvis' Golden Records, Volume 3	1963	25.00	50.00	100.00
—"Mono" on label					
❑ LPM-2765 [M]	Elvis' Golden Records, Volume 3	1964	15.00	30.00	60.00
—"Monaural" on label					
❑ LSP-2765 [S]	Elvis' Golden Records, Volume 3	1963	37.50	75.00	150.00
—"Stereo" and silver "RCA Victor" on black label					
❑ LSP-2765 [S]	Elvis' Golden Records, Volume 3	1964	12.50	25.00	50.00
—"Stereo" and white "RCA Victor" on black label					
❑ LSP-2765 [S]	Elvis' Golden Records, Volume 3	1968	10.00	20.00	40.00
—Orange label, non-flexible vinyl					
❑ LSP-2765 [S]	Elvis' Golden Records, Volume 3	1975	5.00	10.00	20.00
—Tan label					
❑ LSP-2765 [S]	Elvis' Golden Records, Volume 3	1976	3.00	6.00	12.00
—Black label, dog near top					
❑ AFL1-2772	He Walks Beside Me	1978	6.25	12.50	25.00
—Includes 20-page photo booklet					
❑ AFL1-2894 [S]	Kissin' Cousins	1977	3.00	6.00	12.00
—Black label, dog near top; includes copies with sticker wrapped around spine with new number					
❑ LPM-2894 [M]	Kissin' Cousins	1964	20.00	40.00	80.00
—"Mono" on label; front cover has a small black and white photo of six cast members in lower right					
❑ LPM-2894 [M]	Kissin' Cousins	1964	25.00	50.00	100.00
—"Monaural" on label; front cover has a small black and white photo of six cast members in lower right					
❑ LPM-2894 [M]	Kissin' Cousins	1964	50.00	100.00	200.00
—"Monaural" on label; front cover does NOT have black and white photo in lower right					
❑ LPM-2894 [M]	Kissin' Cousins	1964	50.00	100.00	200.00
—"Mono" on label; front cover does NOT have black and white photo in lower right					
❑ LSP-2894 [S]	Kissin' Cousins	1964	15.00	30.00	60.00
—"Stereo" and white "RCA Victor" on black label; all front covers have the cast photo in lower right					
❑ LSP-2894 [S]	Kissin' Cousins	1964	30.00	60.00	120.00
—"Stereo" and silver "RCA Victor" on black label; front cover has a small black and white photo of six cast members in lower right					
❑ LSP-2894 [S]	Kissin' Cousins	1964	50.00	100.00	200.00
—"Stereo" and silver "RCA Victor" on black label; front cover does NOT have black and white photo in lower right					
❑ LSP-2894 [S]	Kissin' Cousins	1968	10.00	20.00	40.00
—Orange label, non-flexible vinyl					
❑ LSP-2894 [S]	Kissin' Cousins	1971	5.00	10.00	20.00
—Orange label, flexible vinyl					
❑ LSP-2894 [S]	Kissin' Cousins	1975	6.25	12.50	25.00
—Tan label					
❑ LSP-2894 [S]	Kissin' Cousins	1976	3.00	6.00	12.00
—Black label, dog near top					

Number	Title (A Side/B Side)	Yr	VG	VG+	NM
❏ LSP-2894 [S]	Kissin' Cousins	1976	375.00	750.00	1500.
—Black label, dog near top; blue vinyl					
❏ CPL1-2901	Elvis Sings for Children and Grownups Too!	1978	2.50	5.00	10.00
—With greeting card graphic printed on back cover, and no slits on back cover					
❏ CPL1-2901	Elvis Sings for Children and Grownups Too!	1978	5.00	10.00	20.00
—With two slits for removable greeting card on back cover (card should be with package)					
❏ AFL1-2999 [S]	Roustabout	1977	3.00	6.00	12.00
—Black label, dog near top; includes copies with sticker wrapped around spine with new number					
❏ LPM-2999 [M]	Roustabout	1964	25.00	50.00	100.00
—"Mono" on label					
❏ LPM-2999 [M]	Roustabout	1965	15.00	30.00	60.00
—"Monaural" on label					
❏ LSP-2999 [S]	Roustabout	1964	15.00	30.00	60.00
—"Stereo" and white "RCA Victor" on black label					
❏ LSP-2999 [S]	Roustabout	1964	150.00	300.00	600.00
—"Stereo" and silver "RCA Victor" on black label					
❏ LSP-2999 [S]	Roustabout	1968	10.00	20.00	40.00
—Orange label, non-flexible vinyl					
❏ LSP-2999 [S]	Roustabout	1971	5.00	10.00	20.00
—Orange label, flexible vinyl					
❏ LSP-2999 [S]	Roustabout	1975	5.00	10.00	20.00
—Tan label					
❏ LSP-2999 [S]	Roustabout	1976	3.00	6.00	12.00
—Black label, dog near top					
❏ CPL1-3078 [PD]	A Legendary Performer, Volume 3	1978	6.25	12.50	25.00
—Picture disc applied to blue vinyl LP; with booklet (deduct 40% if missing)					
❏ CPL1-3082	A Legendary Performer, Volume 3	1978	6.25	12.50	25.00
—Includes booklet (deduct 40% if missing); with die-cut hole in front cover					
❏ CPL1-3082	A Legendary Performer, Volume 3	1986	2.00	4.00	8.00
—No die-cut hole in cover and no booklet					
❏ AQL1-3279	Our Memories of Elvis	1979	5.00	10.00	20.00
❏ AFL1-3338 [S]	Girl Happy	1977	3.00	6.00	12.00
—Black label, dog near top; includes copies with sticker wrapped around spine with new number					
❏ LPM-3338 [M]	Girl Happy	1965	15.00	30.00	60.00
❏ LSP-3338 [S]	Girl Happy	1965	15.00	30.00	60.00
—"Stereo" on black label					
❏ LSP-3338 [S]	Girl Happy	1968	10.00	20.00	40.00
—Orange label, non-flexible vinyl					
❏ LSP-3338 [S]	Girl Happy	1971	5.00	10.00	20.00
—Orange label, flexible vinyl					
❏ LSP-3338 [S]	Girl Happy	1975	6.25	12.50	25.00
—Tan label					
❏ LSP-3338 [S]	Girl Happy	1976	3.00	6.00	12.00
—Black label, dog near top					
❏ AQL1-3448	Our Memories of Elvis, Volume 2	1979	5.00	10.00	20.00
❏ AAL1-3450 [P]	Elvis for Everyone	1977	3.00	6.00	12.00
—Black label, dog near top; includes copies with sticker wrapped around spine with new number					
❏ LPM-3450 [M]	Elvis for Everyone	1965	15.00	30.00	60.00
❏ LSP-3450 [P]	Elvis for Everyone	1965	15.00	30.00	60.00
—Black label, "Stereo" on label					
❏ LSP-3450 [P]	Elvis for Everyone	1968	10.00	20.00	40.00
—Orange label, non-flexible vinyl					
❏ LSP-3450 [P]	Elvis for Everyone	1971	5.00	10.00	20.00
—Orange label, flexible vinyl					
❏ LSP-3450 [P]	Elvis for Everyone	1975	5.00	10.00	20.00
—Tan label					
❏ LSP-3450 [P]	Elvis for Everyone	1976	3.00	6.00	12.00
—Black label, dog near top					
❏ DJL1-3455 [DJ]	Pure Elvis	1979	150.00	300.00	600.00
—Promo-only item for Our Memories of Elvis, Volume 2; contains original version of five songs on one side, "unsweetened" versions of same songs on the other					
❏ LPM-3468 [M]	Harum Scarum	1965	15.00	30.00	60.00
❏ LPM/LSP-3468	Harum Scarum Bonus Photo	1965	15.00	30.00	60.00
❏ LSP-3468 [S]	Harum Scarum	1965	15.00	30.00	60.00
—"Stereo" on black label					
❏ LPM-3553 [M]	Frankie and Johnny	1966	15.00	30.00	60.00
❏ LPM/LSP-3553	Frankie and Johnny Bonus Print	1966	15.00	30.00	60.00
❏ LSP-3553 [S]	Frankie and Johnny	1966	15.00	30.00	60.00
—"Stereo" on black label					
❏ AFL1-3643 [S]	Paradise, Hawaiian Style	1977	3.00	6.00	12.00
—Black label, dog near top; includes copies with sticker wrapped around spine with new number					
❏ LPM-3643 [M]	Paradise, Hawaiian Style	1966	15.00	30.00	60.00
❏ LSP-3643 [S]	Paradise, Hawaiian Style	1966	15.00	30.00	60.00
—"Stereo" on black label					
❏ LSP-3643 [S]	Paradise, Hawaiian Style	1968	10.00	20.00	40.00
—Orange label, non-flexible vinyl					
❏ LSP-3643 [S]	Paradise, Hawaiian Style	1971	5.00	10.00	20.00
—Orange label, flexible vinyl					
❏ LSP-3643 [S]	Paradise, Hawaiian Style	1975	3.75	7.50	15.00
—Tan label					
❏ LSP-3643 [S]	Paradise, Hawaiian Style	1976	3.00	6.00	12.00
—Black label, dog near top					
❏ AYL1-3683 [S]	Blue Hawaii	1980	2.50	5.00	10.00
—"Best Buy Series" reissue					
❏ AYL1-3684 [S]	Spinout	1980	2.00	4.00	8.00
—"Best Buy Series" reissue					
❏ CPL8-3699 [(8)]	Elvis Aron Presley	1980	25.00	50.00	100.00
—Box set; regular issue with booklet					
❏ CPL8-3699 [(8)]	Elvis Aron Presley	1980	62.50	125.00	250.00
—Box set; "Reviewer Series" edition (will be identified as such on the cover)					
❏ LPM-3702 [M]	Spinout	1966	15.00	30.00	60.00
❏ LPM/LSP-3702	Spinout Bonus Photo	1966	15.00	30.00	60.00
❏ LSP-3702 [S]	Spinout	1966	15.00	30.00	60.00
—"Stereo" on black label					
❏ DJL1-3729 [DJ]	Elvis Aron Presley (Excerpts)	1980	30.00	60.00	120.00
—Promo-only excerpts of songs from box set					
❏ AYL1-3732	Pure Gold	1980	2.00	4.00	8.00
—"Best Buy Series" reissue					
❏ AYL1-3733 [R]	King Creole	1980	2.00	4.00	8.00
—"Best Buy Series" reissue; includes copies with sticker wrapped around spine with new number					
❏ AYL1-3734 [S]	Harum Scarum	1980	2.00	4.00	8.00
—"Best Buy Series" reissue					

Number	Title (A Side/B Side)	Yr	VG	VG+	NM
❏ AYL1-3735 [S]	G.I. Blues	1980	2.00	4.00	8.00
—"Best Buy Series" reissue					
❏ AFL1-3758 [S]	How Great Thou Art	1977	3.00	6.00	12.00
—Black label, dog near top; includes copies with sticker wrapped around spine with new number					
❏ AQL1-3758 [S]	How Great Thou Art	1979	2.50	5.00	10.00
—Reissue with new prefix					
❏ LPM-3758 [M]	How Great Thou Art	1967	15.00	30.00	60.00
—"Mono Dynagroove" on label					
❏ LSP-3758 [S]	How Great Thou Art	1967	15.00	30.00	60.00
—"Stereo Dynagroove" on black label					
❏ LSP-3758 [S]	How Great Thou Art	1968	10.00	20.00	40.00
—Orange label, non-flexible vinyl					
❏ LSP-3758 [S]	How Great Thou Art	1971	6.25	12.50	25.00
—Orange label, flexible vinyl					
❏ LSP-3758 [S]	How Great Thou Art	1975	5.00	10.00	20.00
—Tan label					
❏ LSP-3758 [S]	How Great Thou Art	1976	3.00	6.00	12.00
—Black label, dog near top					
❏ DJL1-3781 [DJ]	Elvis Aron Presley (Selections)	1980	30.00	60.00	120.00
—Promo-only complete versions of songs from box set					
❏ LPM-3787 [M]	Double Trouble	1967	15.00	30.00	60.00
—With bonus photo announcement on cover					
❏ LPM-3787 [M]	Double Trouble	1967	20.00	40.00	80.00
—With no bonus photo announcement on cover					
❏ LPM/LSP-3787	Double Trouble Bonus Photo	1967	12.50	25.00	50.00
❏ LSP-3787 [S]	Double Trouble	1967	15.00	30.00	60.00
—With bonus photo announcement on cover					
❏ LSP-3787 [S]	Double Trouble	1967	17.50	35.00	70.00
—With no bonus photo announcement on cover; black label "Stereo"					
❏ LSP-3787 [S]	Double Trouble	1968	10.00	20.00	40.00
—Orange label, non-flexible vinyl					
❏ LSP-3787 [S]	Double Trouble	1975	5.00	10.00	20.00
—Tan label					
❏ LSP-3787 [S]	Double Trouble	1977	3.00	6.00	12.00
—Black label, dog near top					
❏ AYL1-3892	Elvis in Person at the International Hotel, Las Vegas, Nevada	1981	2.00	4.00	8.00
—"Best Buy Series" reissue					
❏ AYM1-3893	The Sun Sessions	1981	2.00	4.00	8.00
—"Best Buy Series" reissue; includes copies with sticker wrapped around spine with new number					
❏ LPM-3893 [M]	Clambake	1967	62.50	125.00	250.00
❏ LPM/LSP-3893	Clambake Bonus Photo	1967	12.50	25.00	50.00
❏ LSP-3893 [S]	Clambake	1967	15.00	30.00	60.00
❏ AYM1-3894	Elvis (NBC-TV Special)	1981	2.00	4.00	8.00
—"Best Buy Series" reissue					
❏ AAL1-3917	Guitar Man	1981	7.50	15.00	30.00
❏ AFL1-3921 [P]	Elvis' Gold Records, Volume 4	1976	3.75	7.50	15.00
—Tan label with new prefix					
❏ AFL1-3921 [P]	Elvis' Gold Records, Volume 4	1977	3.00	6.00	12.00
—Black label, dog near top; includes copies with sticker wrapped around spine with new number					
❏ LPM-3921 [M]	Elvis' Gold Records, Volume 4	1968	500.00	1000.	2000.
—"Monaural" on label					
❏ LSP-3921 [P]	Elvis' Gold Records, Volume 4	1968	10.00	20.00	40.00
—Orange label, non-flexible vinyl					
❏ LSP-3921 [P]	Elvis' Gold Records, Volume 4	1968	12.50	25.00	50.00
—"Stereo" and white "RCA Victor" on black label					
❏ LSP-3921 [P]	Elvis' Gold Records, Volume 4	197?	5.00	10.00	20.00
—Orange label, flexible vinyl					
❏ LSP-3921 [P]	Elvis' Gold Records, Volume 4	1975	6.25	12.50	25.00
—Tan label					
❏ LSP-3921 [P]	Elvis' Gold Records, Volume 4	1976	3.00	6.00	12.00
—Black label, dog near top					
❏ AYL1-3935 [S]	His Hand in Mine	1981	2.00	4.00	8.00
—"Best Buy Series" reissue; includes copies with sticker wrapped around spine with new number					
❏ AYL1-3956	Elvis Country ("I'm 10,000 Years Old")	1981	2.00	4.00	8.00
—"Best Buy Series" reissue					
❏ AFL1-3989 [S]	Speedway	1977	3.00	6.00	12.00
—Black label, dog near top; includes copies with sticker wrapped around spine with new number					
❏ LPM-3989 [M]	Speedway	1968	500.00	1000.	2000.
❏ LPM/LSP-3989	Speedway Bonus Photo	1968	12.50	25.00	50.00
❏ LSP-3989 [S]	Speedway	1968	10.00	20.00	40.00
—Orange label, non-flexible vinyl					
❏ LSP-3989 [S]	Speedway	1968	15.00	30.00	60.00
—"Stereo" on black label					
❏ LSP-3989 [S]	Speedway	1971	5.00	10.00	20.00
—Orange label, flexible vinyl					
❏ LSP-3989 [S]	Speedway	1975	5.00	10.00	20.00
—Tan label					
❏ LSP-3989 [S]	Speedway	1976	3.00	6.00	12.00
—Black label, dog near top					
❏ CPL2-4031 [(2)]	This Is Elvis	1980	3.75	7.50	15.00
❏ AFM1-4088	Elvis (NBC-TV Special)	1977	3.00	6.00	12.00
—Black label, dog near top; includes copies with sticker wrapped around spine with new number					
❏ LPM-4088	Elvis (NBC-TV Special)	1968	10.00	20.00	40.00
—Orange label, non-flexible vinyl					
❏ LPM-4088	Elvis (NBC-TV Special)	1971	7.50	15.00	30.00
—Orange label, flexible vinyl					
❏ LPM-4088	Elvis (NBC-TV Special)	1975	5.00	10.00	20.00
—Tan label					
❏ LPM-4088	Elvis (NBC-TV Special)	1976	3.75	7.50	15.00
—Black label, dog near top					
❏ AYL1-4114	That's the Way It Is	1981	2.00	4.00	8.00
—"Best Buy Series" reissue; includes copies with sticker wrapped around spine with new number					
❏ AYL1-4115 [S]	Kissin' Cousins	1981	2.00	4.00	8.00
—"Best Buy Series" reissue; includes copies with sticker wrapped around spine with new number					
❏ AYL1-4116 [S]	Something for Everybody	1981	2.00	4.00	8.00
—"Best Buy Series" reissue; includes copies with sticker wrapped around spine with new number					
❏ AFL1-4155	From Elvis in Memphis	1977	3.00	6.00	12.00
—Black label, dog near top; includes copies with sticker wrapped around spine with new number					
❏ LSP-4155	From Elvis in Memphis	1969	10.00	20.00	40.00
—Orange label, non-flexible vinyl					
❏ LSP-4155	From Elvis in Memphis Bonus Photo	1969	10.00	20.00	40.00

Number	Title (A Side/B Side)	Yr	VG	VG+	NM
LSP-4155	From Elvis in Memphis	1971	7.50	15.00	30.00
—Orange label, flexible vinyl					
LSP-4155	From Elvis in Memphis	1975	6.25	12.50	25.00
—Tan label					
LSP-4155	From Elvis in Memphis	1976	3.75	7.50	15.00
—Black label, dog near top					
AYL1-4232 [P]	Elvis for Everyone	1982	2.00	4.00	8.00
—"Best Buy Series" reissue					
AFL1-4362	On Stage February, 1970	1977	3.00	6.00	12.00
—Black label, dog near top; includes copies with sticker wrapped around spine with new number					
AQL1-4362	On Stage February, 1970	1983	2.00	4.00	8.00
—Reissue with some cover changes					
LSP-4362	On Stage February, 1970	1970	10.00	20.00	40.00
—Orange label, non-flexible vinyl					
LSP-4362	On Stage February, 1970	1971	6.25	12.50	25.00
—Orange label, flexible vinyl					
LSP-4362	On Stage February, 1970	1975	6.25	12.50	25.00
—Tan label					
LSP-4362	On Stage February, 1970	1976	7.50	15.00	30.00
—Black label, dog near top					
CPL1-4395	Memories of Christmas	1982	3.75	7.50	15.00
—With greeting card (deduct 1/3 if missing)					
AFL1-4428	Elvis in Person at the International Hotel, Las Vegas, Nevada	1977	3.00	6.00	12.00
—Black label, dog near top; includes copies with sticker wrapped around spine with new number					
LSP-4428	Elvis in Person at the International Hotel, Las Vegas, Nevada	1970	12.50	25.00	50.00
—Orange label, non-flexible vinyl					
LSP-4428	Elvis in Person at the International Hotel, Las Vegas, Nevada	1971	10.00	20.00	40.00
—Orange label, flexible vinyl					
LSP-4428	Elvis in Person at the International Hotel, Las Vegas, Nevada	1975	6.25	12.50	25.00
—Tan label					
LSP-4428	Elvis in Person at the International Hotel, Las Vegas, Nevada	1976	3.75	7.50	15.00
—Black label, dog near top					
AFL1-4429	Back in Memphis	1977	3.00	6.00	12.00
—Black label, dog near top; with sticker wrapped around spine with new number					
LSP-4429	Back in Memphis	1970	10.00	20.00	40.00
—Orange label, non-flexible vinyl					
LSP-4429	Back in Memphis	1971	7.50	15.00	30.00
—Orange label, flexible vinyl					
LSP-4429	Back in Memphis	1975	6.25	12.50	25.00
—Tan label					
LSP-4429	Back in Memphis	1977	3.75	7.50	15.00
—Black label, dog near top					
AFL1-4445	That's the Way It Is	1977	3.00	6.00	12.00
—Black label, dog near top; includes copies with sticker wrapped around spine with new number					
LSP-4445	That's the Way It Is	1970	20.00	40.00	80.00
—Orange label, non-flexible vinyl					
LSP-4445	That's the Way It Is	1971	6.25	12.50	25.00
—Orange label, flexible vinyl					
LSP-4445	That's the Way It Is	1975	5.00	10.00	20.00
—Tan label					
LSP-4445	That's the Way It Is	1976	3.75	7.50	15.00
—Black label, dog near top					
AFL1-4460	Elvis Country ("I'm 10,000 Years Old")	1977	3.00	6.00	12.00
—Black label, dog near top; includes copies with sticker wrapped around spine with new number					
LSP-4460	Elvis Country ("I'm 10,000 Years Old")	197?	500.00	1000.	2000.
—Green vinyl; black label, dog near top					
LSP-4460	Elvis Country ("I'm 10,000 Years Old") Bonus Photo	1971	3.75	7.50	15.00
—Available in either orange-label pressing					
LSP-4460	Elvis Country ("I'm 10,000 Years Old")	1971	6.25	12.50	25.00
—Orange label, flexible vinyl					
LSP-4460	Elvis Country ("I'm 10,000 Years Old")	1971	10.00	20.00	40.00
—Orange label, non-flexible vinyl					
LSP-4460	Elvis Country ("I'm 10,000 Years Old")	1975	6.25	12.50	25.00
—Tan label					
LSP-4460	Elvis Country ("I'm 10,000 Years Old")	1976	3.75	7.50	15.00
—Black label, dog near top					
AFL1-4530	Love Letters from Elvis	1977	3.00	6.00	12.00
—Black label, dog near top; includes copies with sticker wrapped around spine with new number					
AHL1-4530	The Elvis Medley	1982	3.00	6.00	12.00
LSP-4530	Love Letters from Elvis	1971	7.50	15.00	30.00
—Orange label; "Love Letters" on one line of cover; "from" on a second line, "Elvis" on a third line					
LSP-4530	Love Letters from Elvis	1971	10.00	20.00	40.00
—Orange label; "Love Letters from" on one line of cover, "Elvis" on a second line					
LSP-4530	Love Letters from Elvis	1975	6.25	12.50	25.00
—Tan label; "Love Letters" on one line of cover; "from" on a second line, "Elvis" on a third line					
LSP-4530	Love Letters from Elvis	1975	7.50	15.00	30.00
—Tan label; "Love Letters from" on one line of cover, "Elvis" on a second line					
LSP-4530	Love Letters from Elvis	1976	5.00	10.00	20.00
—Black label, dog near top					
LSP-4579	Elvis Sings the Wonderful World of Christmas Postcard	1971	5.00	10.00	20.00
LSP-4579	Elvis Sings the Wonderful World of Christmas	1971	7.50	15.00	30.00
—Orange label. Bonus postcard is priced separately					
AFL1-4671	Elvis Now	1977	3.00	6.00	12.00
—Black label, dog near top; includes copies with sticker wrapped around spine with new number					
LSP-4671	Elvis Now	1972	7.50	15.00	30.00
—Orange label					
LSP-4671	Elvis Now	1975	6.25	12.50	25.00
—Tan label					
LSP-4671	Elvis Now	1976	3.75	7.50	15.00
—Black label, dog near top					
LSP-4671 [DJ]	Elvis Now	1972	25.00	50.00	100.00
—Orange label; with white timing sticker on front cover					
AHL1-4678	I Was the One	1983	2.50	5.00	10.00
AFL1-4690	He Touched Me	1977	3.00	6.00	12.00
—Black label, dog near top; includes copies with sticker wrapped around spine with new number					
LSP-4690	He Touched Me	1972	10.00	20.00	40.00
—Orange label					
LSP-4690	He Touched Me	1975	5.00	10.00	20.00
—Tan label					
LSP-4690	He Touched Me	1976	3.75	7.50	15.00
—Black label, dog near top					
LSP-4690 [DJ]	He Touched Me	1972	25.00	50.00	100.00
—Orange label; with white timing sticker on front cover					
AFL1-4776	Elvis As Recorded at Madison Square Garden	1977	3.00	6.00	12.00
—Black label, dog near top; includes copies with sticker wrapped around spine with new number					
AQL1-4776	Elvis As Recorded at Madison Square Garden	1980	2.00	4.00	8.00
—Another reissue with new prefix					
LSP-4776	Elvis As Recorded at Madison Square Garden	1972	7.50	15.00	30.00
—Orange label					
LSP-4776	Elvis As Recorded at Madison Square Garden	1975	5.00	10.00	20.00
—Tan label					
LSP-4776	Elvis As Recorded at Madison Square Garden	1976	3.75	7.50	15.00
—Black label, dog near top					
LSP-4776 [DJ]	Elvis As Recorded at Madison Square Garden	1972	25.00	50.00	100.00
—Orange label; with white timing sticker on front cover					
CPL1-4848	A Legendary Performer, Volume 4	1983	7.50	15.00	30.00
—Includes booklet (deduct 40% if missing); with die-cut hole in front cover					
CPL1-4848	A Legendary Performer, Volume 4	1986	5.00	10.00	20.00
—No die-cut hole in cover					
AFL1-4941	Elvis' Gold Records, Volume 5	1984	2.50	5.00	10.00
CPM6-5172 [(6)]	A Golden Celebration	1984	25.00	50.00	100.00
AFM1-5182	Rocker	1984	5.00	10.00	20.00
AFM1-5196 [M]	Elvis' Golden Records	1984	5.00	10.00	20.00
—50th Anniversary reissue in mono with banner					
AFM1-5197 [M]	Elvis' Gold Records Volume 2 — 50,000,000 Elvis Fans Can't Be Wrong	1984	5.00	10.00	20.00
—50th Anniversary reissue in mono with banner					
AFM1-5198 [M]	Elvis Presley	1984	5.00	10.00	20.00
—50th Anniversary reissue in mono with banner					
AFM1-5199 [M]	Elvis	1984	5.00	10.00	20.00
—50th Anniversary reissue in mono with banner					
AFL1-5353	A Valentine Gift for You	1985	2.50	5.00	10.00
—Black vinyl					
AFL1-5353	A Valentine Gift for You	1985	5.00	10.00	20.00
—Red vinyl					
AFL1-5418	Reconsider Baby	1985	5.00	10.00	20.00
—All copies on blue vinyl					
AFL1-5430	Always on My Mind	1985	5.00	10.00	20.00
—All copies on purple vinyl					
AFM1-5486 [M]	Elvis' Christmas Album	1985	3.75	7.50	15.00
—Same as LOC-1035; black vinyl with booklet					
AFM1-5486 [M]	Elvis' Christmas Album	1985	5.00	10.00	20.00
—Same as LOC-1035; green vinyl with booklet					
UNRM-5697/8 [DJ]	Special Christmas Programming	1967	300.00	600.00	1200.
—White label promo. Add 25% for script.					
LSP-6020	From Memphis to Vegas/From Vegas to Memphis Bonus Photos	1969	12.50	25.00	50.00
—Four different photos came with LP, but no more than two per set. Value is for any two different of the four photos.					
LSP-6020 [(2)]	From Memphis to Vegas/From Vegas to Memphis	1969	25.00	50.00	100.00
—Orange labels, non-flexible vinyl; with composers of "Words" correctly listed as Barry, Robin and Maurice Gibb					
LSP-6020 [(2)]	From Memphis to Vegas/From Vegas to Memphis	1969	37.50	75.00	150.00
—Orange labels, non-flexible vinyl; with composers of "Words" incorrectly listed as Tommy Boyce and Bobby Hart					
LSP-6020 [(2)]	From Memphis to Vegas/From Vegas to Memphis	1971	10.00	20.00	40.00
—Orange labels, flexible vinyl					
LSP-6020 [(2)]	From Memphis to Vegas/From Vegas to Memphis Bonus Photos	1975	7.50	15.00	30.00
LSP-6020 [(2)]	From Memphis to Vegas/From Vegas to Memphis Bonus Photos	1976	5.00	10.00	20.00
—Black label, dog near top					
VPSX-6089 [(2)DJ]	Aloha from Hawaii Via Satellite	1973	500.00	1000.	2000.
—Orange or dark orange label; with white timing sticker on front cover					
VPSX-6089 [(2)Q]	Aloha from Hawaii Via Satellite	1973	10.00	20.00	40.00
—Lighter orange labels, "RCA" on side					
VPSX-6089 [(2)Q]	Aloha from Hawaii Via Satellite	1973	25.00	50.00	100.00
—Dark orange labels, "QuadraDisc" on top, "RCA" on bottom					
VPSX-6089 [(2)Q]	Aloha from Hawaii Via Satellite	1973	2500.	3750.	5000.
—Stokely-Van Camp employee version with Saturn-shaped sticker on front cover with "Chicken of the Sea" and mermaid					
LPM-6401	Worldwide 50 Gold Award Hits, Vol. 1 Photo Book	1970	10.00	20.00	40.00
—Two different books have been found in this LP box; price is for either					
LPM-6401 [(4)]	Worldwide 50 Gold Award Hits, Vol. 1	1970	20.00	40.00	80.00
—Orange labels, non-flexible vinyl; with blurb for photo book on cover					
LPM-6401 [(4)]	Worldwide 50 Gold Award Hits, Vol. 1	1970	20.00	40.00	80.00
—Orange labels, flexible vinyl; with blurb for photo book on cover					
LPM-6401 [(4)]	Worldwide 50 Gold Award Hits, Vol. 1	1975	10.00	20.00	40.00
—Tan labels					
LPM-6401 [(4)]	Worldwide 50 Gold Award Hits, Vol. 1	1977	7.50	15.00	30.00
—Black labels, dog near top					
LPM-6402	The Other Sides: Worldwide 50 Gold Award Hits, Vol. 2 Poster	1971	6.25	12.50	25.00
LPM-6402	The Other Sides: Worldwide 50 Gold Award Hits, Vol. 2 Swatch and Envelope	1971	6.25	12.50	25.00
LPM-6402 [(4)]	The Other Sides: Worldwide 50 Gold Award Hits, Vol. 2	1971	17.50	35.00	70.00
—Orange labels, flexible vinyl; with blurb for inserts on cover					
LPM-6402 [(4)]	The Other Sides: Worldwide 50 Gold Award Hits, Vol. 2	1975	7.50	15.00	30.00
—Tan labels					
LPM-6402 [(4)]	The Other Sides: Worldwide 50 Gold Award Hits, Vol. 2	1977	5.00	10.00	20.00
—Black labels, dog near top					

Number	Title (A Side/B Side)	Yr	VG	VG+	NM
❑ KKL1-7065	A Canadian Tribute	1978	5.00	10.00	20.00
—Gold vinyl, embossed cover					
❑ R 213690 [(2)]	Worldwide Gold Award Hits, Parts 1 & 2	1974	10.00	20.00	40.00
—RCA Record Club version; tan labels					
❑ R 213690 [(2)]	Worldwide Gold Award Hits, Parts 1 & 2	1974	30.00	60.00	120.00
—RCA Record Club version; one label is orange, the other is tan (orange label on both records is unknown)					
❑ R 213690 [(2)]	Worldwide Gold Award Hits, Parts 1 & 2	1977	6.25	12.50	25.00
—RCA Record Club version; black labels, dog near top					
❑ R 213736 [(2)S]	Aloha from Hawaii Via Satellite	1973	17.50	35.00	70.00
—RCA Record Club edition in stereo instead of quadrophonic; orange labels					
❑ R 213736 [(2)S]	Aloha from Hawaii Via Satellite	1975	15.00	30.00	60.00
—RCA Record Club edition in stereo instead of quadrophonic; tan labels					
❑ R 213736 [(2)S]	Aloha from Hawaii Via Satellite	1977	7.50	5.00	30.00
—RCA Record Club edition in stereo instead of quadrophonic; black labels, dog near top					
❑ R 214657 [(2)]	Worldwide Gold Award Hits, Parts 3 & 4	1978	5.00	10.00	20.00
—RCA Music Service version; black labels, dog near top					
❑ R 233299(e) [(2)]	Country Classics	1980	10.00	20.00	40.00
—RCA Music Service exclusive					
❑ R 234340 [(2)]	From Elvis with Love	1978	10.00	20.00	40.00
—RCA Music Service exclusive					
❑ R 244047 [(2)]	The Legendary Concert Performances	1978	10.00	20.00	40.00
—RCA Music Service exclusive					
❑ R 244069 [(2)]	Country Memories	1978	10.00	20.00	40.00
—RCA Music Service exclusive					
READER'S DIGEST					
❑ 010/A [(7)]	His Greatest Hits	1983	15.00	30.00	60.00
—Yellow box					
❑ 010/A [(7)]	His Greatest Hits	1990	10.00	20.00	40.00
—White box					
❑ RD-10/A [(8)]	His Greatest Hits	1979	100.00	200.00	400.00
—White box					
❑ RBA-072/D	Great Hits of 1956-57	1987	5.00	10.00	20.00
❑ RD4A-181/D	Elvis Sings Inspirational Favorites	1983	5.00	10.00	20.00
❑ RB4-191/A [(7)]	The Legend Lives On	1986	15.00	30.00	60.00
❑ RDA-242/D	Elvis Sings Country Favorites	1984	15.00	30.00	60.00
SHOW-LAND					
❑ LP-2001	The First of Elvis	1979	25.00	50.00	100.00
SILHOUETTE					
❑ 10001/2 [(2)]	Personally Elvis	1979	7.50	15.00	30.00
—Interview records; no music					
SUN					
❑ 1001	The Sun Years — Interviews and Memories	1977	2.00	4.00	8.00
—With "Nashville, U.S.A." on label; white cover with brown print					
❑ 1001	The Sun Years — Interviews and Memories	1977	3.75	7.50	15.00
—With "Nashville, U.S.A." on label; dark yellow cover with brown print					
❑ 1001	The Sun Years — Interviews and Memories	1977	6.25	12.50	25.00
—With "Memphis, Tennessee" on label					
TIME-LIFE					
❑ STL-106 [(2)]	Elvis Presley: 1954-1961	1986	7.50	15.00	30.00
❑ STW-106	Country Music	1981	5.00	10.00	20.00
❑ STL-126 [(2)]	Elvis the King: 1954-1965	1989	20.00	40.00	80.00

PRESNELL, HARVE
MGM

Number	Title (A Side/B Side)	Yr	VG	VG+	NM
❑ E-4194 [M]	The World's Greatest Love Songs	1964	5.00	10.00	20.00
❑ SE-4194 [S]	The World's Greatest Love Songs	1964	6.25	12.50	25.00
❑ E-4266 [M]	New Echoes of the Old West	1965	5.00	10.00	20.00
❑ SE-4266 [S]	New Echoes of the Old West	1965	6.25	12.50	25.00

PRESTI, IDA, AND ALEXANDRE LAGOYA
MERCURY LIVING PRESENCE

Number	Title (A Side/B Side)	Yr	VG	VG+	NM
❑ SR 90380 [S]	Four Concertos for Two Guitars by Vivaldi	196?	7.50	15.00	30.00
—Maroon label, no "Vendor: Mercury Record Corporation"					
❑ SR 90427 [S]	Spanish Music for Two Guitars	196?	7.50	15.00	30.00
—Maroon label, no "Vendor: Mercury Record Corporation"					
❑ SR 90457 [S]	Baroque Music for Two Guitars	196?	10.00	20.00	40.00
—Maroon label, with "Vendor: Mercury Record Corporation"					

PRESTIGE BLUES SWINGERS, THE
PRESTIGE

Number	Title (A Side/B Side)	Yr	VG	VG+	NM
❑ PRLP-7145 [M]	Outskirts of Town	1958	20.00	40.00	80.00
SWINGVILLE					
❑ SVLP-2013 [M]	Stasch	1960	6.25	12.50	25.00
—Blue label, trident logo at right					
❑ SVLP-2013 [M]	Stasch	1965	12.50	25.00	50.00
—Purple label					

PRESTIGE JAZZ QUARTET, THE
PRESTIGE

Number	Title (A Side/B Side)	Yr	VG	VG+	NM
❑ PRLP-7108 [M]	The Prestige Jazz Quartet	1957	12.50	25.00	50.00

PRESTON, BILLY
A&M

Number	Title (A Side/B Side)	Yr	VG	VG+	NM
❑ SP-3205	The Best of Billy Preston	1982	2.50	5.00	10.00
❑ SP-3507	I Wrote a Simple Song	1971	3.00	6.00	12.00
❑ SP-3516	Music Is My Life	1972	3.00	6.00	12.00
❑ SP-3526	Everybody Likes Some Kind of Music	1973	3.00	6.00	12.00
❑ SP-3637	Live European Tour	1974	3.00	6.00	12.00
❑ SP-3645	The Kids & Me	1974	3.00	6.00	12.00
❑ SP-4532	It's My Pleasure	1975	3.00	6.00	12.00
❑ SP-4587	Billy Preston	1976	3.00	6.00	12.00
❑ SP-4657	It's a Whole New Thing	1977	3.00	6.00	12.00
APPLE					
❑ ST-3359	That's the Way God Planned It	1969	12.50	25.00	50.00
—Cover has close-up of Billy Preston					
❑ ST-3359	That's the Way God Planned It	1972	5.00	10.00	20.00
—Cover has multiple images of Billy Preston					
❑ ST-3370	Encouraging Words	1970	5.00	10.00	20.00
BUDDAH					
❑ BDS-7502	Billy Preston	1969	3.75	7.50	15.00

Number	Title (A Side/B Side)	Yr	VG	VG+	NM
CAPITOL					
❑ ST 2532 [S]	Wildest Organ in Town!	1966	10.00	20.00	40.00
❑ T 2532 [M]	Wildest Organ in Town!	1966	7.50	15.00	30.00
❑ DT 2607 [R]	Club Meetin'	1967	—	—	—
❑ T 2607 [M]	Club Meetin'	1967	—	—	—
—The above versions of Club Meetin' may not exist					
DERBY					
❑ LPM-701 [M]	16 Year Old Soul	1963	62.50	125.00	250.00
EXODUS					
❑ 304 [M]	Early Hits of 1965	1965	6.25	12.50	25.00
GNP CRESCENDO					
❑ GNPS-2071 [(2)]	Soul'd Out	1973	3.75	7.50	15.00
MCA					
❑ 28037	Gospel Soul	198?	2.00	4.00	8.00
—Reissue of Peacock LP					
MOTOWN					
❑ M7-925	Late at Night	1980	2.50	5.00	10.00
❑ M8-941	The Way I Am	1981	2.50	5.00	10.00
❑ M7-958	Billy Preston & Syreeta	1981	2.50	5.00	10.00
❑ 6020 ML	Pressin' On	1982	2.50	5.00	10.00
MYRRH					
❑ 6605	Behold	1978	2.50	5.00	10.00
❑ 6607	Universal Love	1979	2.50	5.00	10.00
PEACOCK					
❑ 179	Gospel Soul	197?	3.00	6.00	12.00
PICKWICK					
❑ SPC-3315	Organ Transplant	197?	2.50	5.00	10.00
VEE JAY					
❑ LP-1123 [M]	The Most Exciting Organ Ever	1965	7.50	15.00	30.00
❑ LPS-1123 [S]	The Most Exciting Organ Ever	1965	12.50	25.00	50.00
❑ LP-1142 [M]	Greatest Hits	1966	7.50	15.00	30.00
❑ LPS-1142 [S]	Greatest Hits	1966	12.50	25.00	50.00

PRESTON, JOHNNY
MERCURY

Number	Title (A Side/B Side)	Yr	VG	VG+	NM
❑ MG-20592 [M]	Running Bear	1960	25.00	50.00	100.00
❑ MG-20609 [M]	Come Rock with Me	1960	25.00	50.00	100.00
❑ SR-60250 [S]	Running Bear	1960	37.50	75.00	150.00
—Black label					
❑ SR-60250 [S]	Running Bear	1981	3.00	6.00	12.00
—Reissue on Chicago skyline label					
❑ SR-60609 [S]	Come Rock with Me	1960	37.50	75.00	150.00
WING					
❑ MGW-12246 [M]	Running Bear	1963	5.00	10.00	20.00
❑ SRW-16246 [S]	Running Bear	1963	6.25	12.50	25.00

PRETENDERS
NAUTILUS

Number	Title (A Side/B Side)	Yr	VG	VG+	NM
❑ NR-38	Pretenders	1982	7.50	15.00	30.00
—Audiophile vinyl					
SIRE					
❑ MINI 3563 [EP]	Extended Play	1981	2.50	5.00	10.00
❑ SRK 3572	Pretenders II	1981	2.50	5.00	10.00
❑ SRK 6083	Pretenders	1980	2.50	5.00	10.00
❑ 23980	Learning to Crawl	1983	2.50	5.00	10.00
❑ 23980 [DJ]	Learning to Crawl	1983	3.00	6.00	12.00
—Promo-only Quiex II pressing; otherwise, same as above					
❑ 25488	Get Close	1986	2.50	5.00	10.00
❑ 25664	The Singles	1987	2.50	5.00	10.00
❑ 26219	Packed!	1990	3.00	6.00	12.00
❑ R 133248	The Singles	1987	3.00	6.00	12.00
—BMG Direct Marketing edition; otherwise, same as 25664					
❑ R 144453	Get Close	1986	3.00	6.00	12.00
—RCA Music Service edition					
WARNER BROS.					
❑ WBMS-114 [DJ]	Pretenders Live	1980	10.00	20.00	40.00
—Part of "The Warner Bros. Music Show" series; comes in red die-cut cover					
❑ WBMS-121 [DJ]	Pretenders Live (Star Fleet)	1982	10.00	20.00	40.00
—Part of "The Warner Bros. Music Show" series; comes in black cover with white sticker					
❑ WBMS-142 [DJ]	Get Close Interview	1987	5.00	10.00	20.00
—Part of "The Warner Bros. Music Show" series					

PRETTY POISON
SVENGALI

Number	Title (A Side/B Side)	Yr	VG	VG+	NM
❑ SRPP-1 [EP]	Laced	1984	5.00	10.00	20.00
VIRGIN					
❑ 90885	Catch Me I'm Falling	1987	2.50	5.00	10.00
❑ R 144099	Catch Me I'm Falling	1988	3.00	6.00	12.00
—BMG Direct Marketing edition					

PRETTY THINGS, THE
BIG BEAT

Number	Title (A Side/B Side)	Yr	VG	VG+	NM
❑ WIK-24	Live at Heartbreak Hotel	1985	2.50	5.00	10.00
FONTANA					
❑ MGF-27544 [M]	The Pretty Things	1965	20.00	40.00	80.00
❑ SRF-67544 [P]	The Pretty Things	1965	20.00	40.00	80.00
NORTON					
❑ 282	The Pretty Things	2000	3.00	6.00	12.00
❑ 283	Get the Picture?	2000	3.00	6.00	12.00
❑ 284	Midnight to Six	2000	3.00	6.00	12.00
❑ TED-1001 [10]	Defecting Grey	2000	2.00	4.00	8.00
RARE EARTH					
❑ RS 506	S.F. Sorrow	1969	5.00	10.00	20.00
—Later copies are standard in shape					
❑ RS 506	S.F. Sorrow	1969	12.50	25.00	50.00
—Original covers are rounded at top					
❑ RS 515	Parachute	1970	5.00	10.00	20.00
❑ R 549R2 [(2)]	Real Pretty	1976	3.75	7.50	15.00
—The two prior Rare Earth albums in one package					

Number	Title (A Side/B Side)	Yr	VG	VG+	NM
SIRE					
❏ SASH-3713 [(2)]	The Vintage Years	1976	3.75	7.50	15.00
SWAN SONG					
❏ SS 8411	Silk Torpedo	1975	2.50	5.00	10.00
❏ SS 8414	Savage Eye	1976	2.50	5.00	10.00
WARNER BROS.					
❏ BS 2680	Freeway Madness	1973	2.50	5.00	10.00
❏ BSK 3466	Cross Talk	1980	2.50	5.00	10.00

PREVIN, ANDRE

Number	Title (A Side/B Side)	Yr	VG	VG+	NM
COLUMBIA					
❏ CL 1530 [M]	Give My Regards to Broadway	1960	5.00	10.00	20.00
—Red and black label with six "eye" logos					
❏ CL 1569 [M]	Camelot	1961	5.00	10.00	20.00
—Red and black label with six "eye" logos					
❏ CL 1595 [M]	Thinking of You	1961	5.00	10.00	20.00
—Red and black label with six "eye" logos					
❏ CL 1649 [M]	A Touch of Elegance	1961	5.00	10.00	20.00
—Red and black label with six "eye" logos					
❏ CL 1741 [M]	Mack the Knife and Other Kurt Weill Music	1962	5.00	10.00	20.00
—Red and black label with six "eye" logos					
❏ CL 1786 [M]	Faraway Part of Town	1962	5.00	10.00	20.00
—Red and black label with six "eye" logos					
❏ CL 1888 [M]	The Light Fantastic	1962	5.00	10.00	20.00
—Red and black label with six "eye" logos					
❏ CS 8233 [S]	Like Love	1960	5.00	10.00	20.00
—Red and black label with six "eye" logos					
❏ CS 8286 [S]	Rhapsody in Blue	1960	5.00	10.00	20.00
—Red and black label with six "eye" logos					
❏ CS 8330 [S]	Give My Regards to Broadway	1960	6.25	12.50	25.00
—Red and black label with six "eye" logos					
❏ CS 8369 [S]	Camelot	1961	6.25	12.50	25.00
—Red and black label with six "eye" logos					
❏ CS 8395 [S]	Thinking of You	1961	6.25	12.50	25.00
—Red and black label with six "eye" logos					
❏ CS 8449 [S]	A Touch of Elegance	1961	6.25	12.50	25.00
—Red and black label with six "eye" logos					
❏ CS 8541 [S]	Mack the Knife and Other Kurt Weill Music	1962	6.25	12.50	25.00
—Red and black label with six "eye" logos					
❏ CS 8586 [S]	Faraway Part of Town	1962	6.25	12.50	25.00
—Red and black label with six "eye" logos					
❏ CS 8688 [S]	The Light Fantastic	1962	6.25	12.50	25.00
—Red and black label with six "eye" logos					
❏ CS 8834 [S]	Andre Previn in Hollywood	1963	5.00	10.00	20.00
—Red label with "360 Sound Stereo" in black at bottom					
❏ CS 8914 [S]	The Soft and Swinging Music of Jimmy McHugh	1964	5.00	10.00	20.00
—Red label with "360 Sound Stereo" in black at bottom					
❏ CS 8995 [S]	My Fair Lady	1964	5.00	10.00	20.00
—Red label with "360 Sound Stereo" in black at bottom					
❏ CS 9094 [S]	Popular Previn	1965	5.00	10.00	20.00
—Red label with "360 Sound Stereo" in black at bottom					
CONTEMPORARY					
❏ C-3543 [M]	Pal Joey	1957	12.50	25.00	50.00
❏ C-3548 [M]	Gigi	1958	12.50	25.00	50.00
❏ M-3558 [M]	Andre Previn Plays Vernon Duke	1959	12.50	25.00	50.00
❏ M-3567 [M]	Andre Previn Plays Jerome Kern	1959	12.50	25.00	50.00
❏ M-3570 [M]	Jazz Trio, King Size	1959	12.50	25.00	50.00
❏ M-3572 [M]	West Side Story	1960	10.00	20.00	40.00
❏ M-3575 [M]	Like Previn	1960	10.00	20.00	40.00
❏ M-3586 [M]	Andre Previn Plays Harold Arlen	1960	10.00	20.00	40.00
❏ S-7543 [S]	Pal Joey	1959	10.00	20.00	40.00
❏ S-7548 [S]	Gigi	1959	10.00	20.00	40.00
❏ S-7558 [S]	Andre Previn Plays Vernon Duke	1959	10.00	20.00	40.00
❏ S-7567 [S]	Andre Previn Plays Jerome Kern	1959	10.00	20.00	40.00
❏ S-7570 [S]	Jazz Trio, King Size	1959	10.00	20.00	40.00
❏ S-7572 [S]	West Side Story	1960	7.50	15.00	30.00
❏ S-7575 [S]	Like Previn	1960	7.50	15.00	30.00
❏ S-7586 [S]	Andre Previn Plays Harold Arlen	1960	7.50	15.00	30.00
DECCA					
❏ DL 8131 [M]	Let's Get Away from It All	1955	10.00	20.00	40.00
❏ DL 8341 [M]	Hollywood at Midnight	1957	10.00	20.00	40.00
MGM					
❏ E-3716 [M]	Secret Songs for Young Lovers	1959	5.00	10.00	20.00
❏ SE-3716 [S]	Secret Songs for Young Lovers	1959	6.25	12.50	25.00
❏ E-3811 [M]	Like Blue	1960	5.00	10.00	20.00
❏ SE-3811 [S]	Like Blue	1960	6.25	12.50	25.00
❏ SE-4186 [S]	Andre Previn — Composer, Conductor, Arranger, Pianist	1964	5.00	10.00	20.00
MOBILE FIDELITY					
❏ 1-095	West Side Story	1982	6.25	12.50	25.00
—Audiophile vinyl					
MONARCH					
❏ 203 [10]	All Star Jazz	1952	20.00	40.00	80.00
❏ 204 [10]	Andre Previn Plays Duke	1952	20.00	40.00	80.00
PRI					
❏ 3026 [S]	The World's Most Honored Pianist	1962	6.25	12.50	25.00
—Issued on yellow vinyl					
RCA VICTOR					
❏ LPM-1011 [M]	Gershwin	1955	10.00	20.00	40.00
❏ LPM-1356 [M]	Three Little Words	1957	10.00	20.00	40.00
❏ LPT-3002 [10]	Andre Previn Plays Harry Warren	1952	20.00	40.00	80.00
STEREO RECORDS					
❏ S-7004 [S]	Pal Joey	1958	12.50	25.00	50.00
❏ S-7020 [S]	Gigi	1958	12.50	25.00	50.00
STRAND					
❏ SL 1074 [M]	Andre Previn Plays	1962	3.00	6.00	12.00
❏ SLS 1074 [S]	Andre Previn Plays	1962	3.75	7.50	15.00

PREVIN, ANDRE; HERB ELLIS; SHELLY MANNE; RAY BROWN

Number	Title (A Side/B Side)	Yr	VG	VG+	NM
COLUMBIA					
❏ CS 8818 [S]	Four to Go	1963	5.00	10.00	20.00

PREVIN, ANDRE, AND RUSS FREEMAN

Number	Title (A Side/B Side)	Yr	VG	VG+	NM
CONTEMPORARY					
❏ C-3537 [M]	Double Play!	1957	12.50	25.00	50.00
❏ S-7011 [S]	Double Play!	1959	10.00	20.00	40.00
STEREO RECORDS					
❏ S-7011 [S]	Double Play!	1958	12.50	25.00	50.00

PRICE, ALAN
Also see THE ANIMALS.

Number	Title (A Side/B Side)	Yr	VG	VG+	NM
ACCORD					
❏ SJA-7904	It's Priceless	1982	2.50	5.00	10.00
JET					
❏ JT-LA809-H	Alan Price	1977	2.50	5.00	10.00
—The "H" suffix is on the label, but the front and back cover, inner sleeve and spine have a "G" prefix; it's not known if any labels have a "G" prefix					
❏ JZ 35710	Lucky Day	1979	2.50	5.00	10.00
❏ NJZ 36510	Rising Sun	1980	2.50	5.00	10.00
PARROT					
❏ PAS 71018 [P]	The Price Is Right	1968	7.50	15.00	30.00
TOWNHOUSE					
❏ SN-7126	House of the Rising Sun	1981	2.50	5.00	10.00
WARNER BROS.					
❏ BS 2710	O Lucky Man	1973	3.00	6.00	12.00
❏ BS 2783	Between Today and Yesterday	1974	3.00	6.00	12.00

PRICE, KENNY

Number	Title (A Side/B Side)	Yr	VG	VG+	NM
BOONE					
❏ 1211	One Hit Follows Another	1967	6.25	12.50	25.00
❏ 1214	Southern Bound	1968	6.25	12.50	25.00
DIMENSION					
❏ DLP-5000	The Best of Both	1980	3.00	6.00	12.00
RCA VICTOR					
❏ APL1-0208	30 California Women	1973	3.75	7.50	15.00
❏ LSP-4224	Happy Tracks	1969	5.00	10.00	20.00
❏ LSP-4225	Walking on New Grass	1969	5.00	10.00	20.00
❏ LSP-4292	The Heavyweight	1970	5.00	10.00	20.00
❏ LSP-4373	Northeast Arkansas Mississippi County Bootlegger	1970	5.00	10.00	20.00
❏ LSP-4469	The Red Foley Songbook	1971	5.00	10.00	20.00
❏ LSP-4527	The Sheriff of Boone County	1971	5.00	10.00	20.00
❏ LSP-4605	Charlotte Fever	1971	5.00	10.00	20.00
❏ LSP-4681	Supersideman	1972	5.00	10.00	20.00
❏ LSP-4763	You Almost Slipped My Mind	1972	5.00	10.00	20.00
❏ LSP-4839	Sea of Heartbreak	1973	5.00	10.00	20.00

PRICE, LEONTYNE

Number	Title (A Side/B Side)	Yr	VG	VG+	NM
LONDON					
❏ 5644 [M]	A Christmas Offering	1961	5.00	10.00	20.00
❏ OS 25280 [S]	A Christmas Offering	1961	6.25	12.50	25.00
RCA VICTOR RED SEAL					
❏ LSC-2279 [S]	A Program of Song	1959	5.00	10.00	20.00
—Original with "shaded dog" label					
❏ LSC-2600 [S]	Swing Low, Sweet Chariot	1962	6.25	12.50	25.00
—Original with "shaded dog" label					

PRICE, LLOYD

Number	Title (A Side/B Side)	Yr	VG	VG+	NM
ABC					
❏ S-297	Mr. Personality	1967	3.75	7.50	15.00
—Reissue on revised label					
❏ S-324 [R]	Mr. Personality's Big 15	1968	3.75	7.50	15.00
—Reissue on revised label					
❏ X-763	16 Greatest Hits	1972	3.75	7.50	15.00
❏ AC-30006	The ABC Collection	1976	3.75	7.50	15.00
❏ DW-94842	16 Greatest Hits	1972	5.00	10.00	20.00
—Capitol Record Club edition					
ABC-PARAMOUNT					
❏ 277 [M]	The Exciting Lloyd Price	1959	10.00	20.00	40.00
❏ S-277 [S]	The Exciting Lloyd Price	1959	20.00	40.00	80.00
❏ 297 [M]	Mr. Personality	1959	10.00	20.00	40.00
❏ S-297 [S]	Mr. Personality	1959	20.00	40.00	80.00
❏ 315 [M]	Mr. Personality Sings the Blues	1960	10.00	20.00	40.00
❏ S-315 [S]	Mr. Personality Sings the Blues	1960	20.00	40.00	80.00
❏ 324 [M]	Mr. Personality's 15 Hits	1960	10.00	20.00	40.00
—Label calls this "Mr. Personality's Big Hits"					
❏ 346 [M]	The Fantastic Lloyd Price	1960	10.00	20.00	40.00
❏ S-346 [R]	The Fantastic Lloyd Price	196?	6.25	12.50	25.00
❏ 366 [M]	Lloyd Price Sings the Million Sellers	1961	10.00	20.00	40.00
❏ S-366 [S]	Lloyd Price Sings the Million Sellers	1961	12.50	25.00	50.00
❏ 382 [M]	Cookin' with Lloyd Price	1961	10.00	20.00	40.00
❏ S-382 [S]	Cookin' with Lloyd Price	1961	12.50	25.00	50.00
DOUBLE-L					
❏ DL-2301 [M]	The Lloyd Price Orchestra	1963	6.25	12.50	25.00
❏ DL-2303 [M]	Misty	1963	6.25	12.50	25.00
❏ SDL-8301 [S]	The Lloyd Price Orchestra	1963	10.00	20.00	40.00
❏ SDL-8303 [S]	Misty	1963	10.00	20.00	40.00
GRAND PRIX					
❏ 422 [M]	Mr. Rhythm and Blues	196?	3.00	6.00	12.00
❏ S-422 [R]	Mr. Rhythm and Blues	196?	2.50	5.00	10.00
GUEST STAR					
❏ G-1910 [M]	Come to Me	196?	3.00	6.00	12.00
❏ GS-1910 [R]	Come to Me	196?	2.50	5.00	10.00
JAD					
❏ 1002	Lloyd Price Now	1969	6.25	12.50	25.00
LPG					
❏ 001	Music...Music	1976	2.50	5.00	10.00

Number	Title (A Side/B Side)	Yr	VG	VG+	NM
MCA					
❏ 1503	Greatest Hits	1982	2.00	4.00	8.00
MONUMENT					
❏ MLP-8032 [M]	Lloyd Swings for Sammy	1965	6.25	12.50	25.00
❏ SLP-18032 [S]	Lloyd Swings for Sammy	1965	10.00	20.00	40.00
PICKWICK					
❏ SPC-3518	Big Hits	197?	2.00	4.00	8.00
SCEPTER					
❏ CTN-18006	The Best of Lloyd Price	1972	2.50	5.00	10.00
SPECIALTY					
❏ SP-2105	Lloyd Price	198?	3.00	6.00	12.00
—1980s reissue					
❏ SP-2105 [M]	Lloyd Price	1959	45.00	90.00	180.00
TRIP					
❏ TOP 16-5	16 Greatest Hits	1976	2.50	5.00	10.00
TURNTABLE					
❏ TTS-5001	Lloyd Price Now	197?	3.75	7.50	15.00
UPFRONT					
❏ UPF-126	Misty	197?	3.00	6.00	12.00
PRICE, RAY					
ABC DOT					
❏ DO-2037	Say I Do	1975	3.00	6.00	12.00
❏ DO-2053	Rainbows and Tears	1976	3.00	6.00	12.00
❏ DOSD-2062	Hank 'n Me	1976	3.00	6.00	12.00
❏ DO-2073	Reunited	1977	3.00	6.00	12.00
COLUMBIA					
❏ GP 28 [(2)]	The World of Ray Price	1970	3.75	7.50	15.00
❏ CL 1015 [M]	Ray Price Sings Heart Songs	1957	12.50	25.00	50.00
❏ CL 1148 [M]	Talk to Your Heart	1958	10.00	20.00	40.00
❏ CL 1494 [M]	Faith	1960	7.50	15.00	30.00
❏ CL 1566 [M]	Ray Price's Greatest Hits	1961	7.50	15.00	30.00
❏ CL 1756 [M]	San Antonio Rose	1962	5.00	10.00	20.00
❏ CL 1971 [M]	Night Life	1963	3.75	7.50	15.00
❏ CL 2189 [M]	Love Life	1964	3.75	7.50	15.00
❏ CL 2289 [M]	Burning Memories	1965	3.75	7.50	15.00
❏ CL 2339 [M]	Western Strings	1965	5.00	10.00	20.00
❏ CL 2382 [M]	The Other Woman	1965	3.75	7.50	15.00
❏ CL 2528 [M]	Another Bridge to Burn	1966	3.75	7.50	15.00
❏ CL 2606 [M]	Touch My Heart	1967	5.00	10.00	20.00
❏ CL 2670 [M]	Ray Price's Greatest Hits, Volume 2	1967	5.00	10.00	20.00
❏ CL 2677 [M]	Danny Boy	1967	5.00	10.00	20.00
❏ CL 2806 [M]	Take Me As I Am	1968	7.50	15.00	30.00
❏ CS 8285 [S]	Faith	1960	10.00	20.00	40.00
❏ CS 8556 [S]	San Antonio Rose	1962	7.50	15.00	30.00
❏ CS 8771 [S]	Night Life	1963	5.00	10.00	20.00
❏ CS 8866 [R]	Ray Price's Greatest Hits	1964	3.00	6.00	12.00
❏ PC 8866	Ray Price's Greatest Hits	198?	2.00	4.00	8.00
—Reissue with new prefix					
❏ CS 8989 [S]	Love Life	1964	5.00	10.00	20.00
❏ CS 9089 [S]	Burning Memories	1965	5.00	10.00	20.00
❏ CS 9139 [S]	Western Strings	1965	6.25	12.50	25.00
❏ CS 9182 [S]	The Other Woman	1965	5.00	10.00	20.00
❏ CS 9328 [S]	Another Bridge to Burn	1966	5.00	10.00	20.00
❏ CS 9406 [S]	Touch My Heart	1967	3.75	7.50	15.00
❏ CS 9470 [S]	Ray Price's Greatest Hits, Volume 2	1967	3.75	7.50	15.00
❏ CS 9477 [S]	Danny Boy	1967	3.75	7.50	15.00
❏ CS 9606 [S]	Take Me As I Am	1968	3.75	7.50	15.00
❏ CS 9733	She Wears My Ring	1968	3.75	7.50	15.00
❏ CS 9822	Sweetheart of the Year	1969	3.75	7.50	15.00
❏ CS 9861	Ray Price's Christmas Album	1969	3.75	7.50	15.00
❏ CS 9918	You Wouldn't Know Love	1970	3.75	7.50	15.00
❏ C 30106	For the Good Times	1970	3.00	6.00	12.00
❏ CQ 30106 [Q]	For the Good Times	1972	5.00	10.00	20.00
❏ C 30510	I Won't Mention It Again	1971	3.00	6.00	12.00
❏ CG 30878 [(2)]	Welcome to My World	1971	3.75	7.50	15.00
❏ KG 31364 [(2)]	Ray Price's All-Time Greatest Hits	1972	3.75	7.50	15.00
❏ KC 31546	The Lonesomest Lonesome	1972	3.00	6.00	12.00
❏ KC 32033	She's Got to Be a Saint	1973	3.00	6.00	12.00
❏ PC 32033	She's Got to Be a Saint	197?	2.00	4.00	8.00
—Reissue with new prefix					
❏ KC 32777	You're the Best Thing That Ever Happened to Me	1973	3.00	6.00	12.00
❏ PC 32777	You're the Best Thing That Ever Happened to Me	197?	2.00	4.00	8.00
—Reissue with new prefix					
❏ PC 33560	If You Change Your Mind	1975	3.00	6.00	12.00
❏ CG 33633 [(2)]	For the Good Times/I Won't Mention It Again	1975	3.75	7.50	15.00
—Reissue of two LPs in one package					
❏ PC 34160	The Best of Ray Price	1976	3.00	6.00	12.00
❏ PC 34710	Help Me	1977	3.00	6.00	12.00
❏ JC 37061	A Tribute to Willie and Kris	1982	2.50	5.00	10.00
HARMONY					
❏ HL 7372 [M]	Collectors' Choice	196?	3.00	6.00	12.00
❏ HL 7440 [M]	Born to Lose	1967	3.00	6.00	12.00
❏ HS 11172 [R]	Collectors' Choice	196?	3.00	6.00	12.00
❏ HS 11240 [S]	Born to Lose	1967	3.00	6.00	12.00
❏ HS 11373	I Fall to Pieces	1969	2.50	5.00	10.00
❏ KH 30272	Make the World Go Away	1970	2.50	5.00	10.00
MONUMENT					
❏ 7633	Always Me	1979	2.50	5.00	10.00
MYRRH					
❏ 6532	This Time, Lord	1975	3.00	6.00	12.00
PAIR					
❏ PDL2-1044 [(2)]	Happens to Be the Best	1986	3.00	6.00	12.00
❏ PDL2-1044 [(2)]	Ray Price Happens to Be the Best!	1986	3.00	6.00	12.00
❏ PDL2-1096 [(2)]	Priceless	1986	3.00	6.00	12.00
ROUNDER					
❏ SS-22	The Honky Tonk Years	1986	2.50	5.00	10.00

Number	Title (A Side/B Side)	Yr	VG	VG+	NM
WORD					
❏ 8723	Precious Memories	197?	3.00	6.00	12.00
❏ 8780	How Great Thou Art	1978	3.00	6.00	12.00
PRICE, RUTH					
AVA					
❏ A-54 [M]	Live and Beautiful	1963	10.00	20.00	40.00
❏ AS-54 [S]	Live and Beautiful	1963	12.50	25.00	50.00
CONTEMPORARY					
❏ M-3590 [M]	Ruth Price with Shelly Manne at the Manne-Hole	1961	12.50	25.00	50.00
❏ S-7590 [S]	Ruth Price with Shelly Manne at the Manne-Hole	1961	15.00	30.00	60.00
KAPP					
❏ KL-1006 [M]	My Name Is Ruth Price. I Sing.	1955	25.00	50.00	100.00
❏ KL-1054 [M]	The Party's Over	1957	25.00	50.00	100.00
ROOST					
❏ LP-2217 [M]	Ruth Price Sings!	1956	25.00	50.00	100.00
PRICE, SAMMY					
CONCERT HALL JAZZ					
❏ 1008 [10]	Barrelhouse and Blues	1955	12.50	25.00	50.00
JAZZTONE					
❏ J-1207 [M]	Barrelhouse and Blues	1956	10.00	20.00	40.00
❏ J-1236 [M]	Les Jeunesses Musicales	1956	10.00	20.00	40.00
❏ J-1260 [M]	The Price Is Right	1957	10.00	20.00	40.00
PRICE, VINCENT					
CAEDMON					
❏ TC-1059 [M]	Vincent Price Reads Poems of Shelley	196?	7.50	15.00	30.00
❏ TC 1429	A Graveyard of Ghost Tales	1974	3.75	7.50	15.00
CAPITOL					
❏ SWBB-342 [(2)]	Witchcraft/Magic	1969	7.50	15.00	30.00
CAPITOL CUSTOM					
❏ SGP-6256/7 [S]	The World Tomorrow	1965	10.00	20.00	40.00
—Blue vinyl					
❏ SGP-6258/9 [S]	The World of the 21st Century	1965	10.00	20.00	40.00
—Blue vinyl					
COLUMBIA MASTERWORKS					
❏ ML 5668 [M]	America the Beautiful	1961	7.50	15.00	30.00
DOT					
❏ DLP-3195 [M]	Gallery	1962	6.25	12.50	25.00
❏ DLP-25195 [S]	Gallery	1962	7.50	15.00	30.00
NELSON INDUSTRIES					
❏ (# unknown)	International Cooking Course	1977	10.00	20.00	40.00
PRICE, VITO					
ARGO					
❏ LP-631 [M]	Swingin' the Loop	1958	10.00	20.00	40.00
❏ LPS-631 [S]	Swingin' the Loop	1958	7.50	15.00	30.00
PRIDE					
WARNER BROS.					
❏ WS 1848	Pride	1970	6.25	12.50	25.00
PRIDE, CHARLEY					
PAIR					
❏ PDL2-1023 [(2)]	Country in My Soul	1986	3.00	6.00	12.00
RCA CAMDEN					
❏ CAS-2584	The Incomparable Charley Pride	1972	3.75	7.50	15.00
RCA VICTOR					
❏ APD1-0217 [Q]	Sweet Country	1973	6.25	12.50	25.00
❏ APL1-0217	Sweet Country	1973	3.75	7.50	15.00
❏ APL1-0315	Charley Pride Presents the Pridesmen	1973	3.75	7.50	15.00
❏ APD1-0397 [Q]	Amazing Love	1974	6.25	12.50	25.00
❏ APL1-0397	Amazing Love	1974	3.75	7.50	15.00
❏ APL1-0534	Country Feelin'	1974	3.75	7.50	15.00
❏ APD1-0757 [Q]	Pride of America	1974	6.25	12.50	25.00
❏ APL1-0757	Pride of America	1974	3.75	7.50	15.00
❏ ANL1-0996	Charley Pride — In Person	1975	2.50	5.00	10.00
—Reissue of LSP-4094					
❏ APD1-1038 [Q]	Charley	1975	6.25	12.50	25.00
❏ APL1-1038	Charley	1975	3.75	7.50	15.00
❏ ANL1-1214	I'm Just Me	1975	2.50	5.00	10.00
—Reissue of LSP-4560					
❏ APD1-1241 [Q]	The Happiness of Having You	1975	6.25	12.50	25.00
❏ APL1-1241	The Happiness of Having You	1975	3.75	7.50	15.00
❏ APD1-1359 [Q]	Sunday Morning with Charley Pride	1976	6.25	12.50	25.00
❏ APL1-1359	Sunday Morning with Charley Pride	1976	3.75	7.50	15.00
❏ ANL1-1934	Christmas in My Home Town	1976	2.00	4.00	8.00
—Reissue of LSP-4406					
❏ APL1-2023	The Best of Charley Pride, Vol. III	1976	3.00	6.00	12.00
❏ APL1-2261	She's Just an Old Love Turned Memory	1977	3.00	6.00	12.00
❏ AHL1-2478	Someone Loves You Honey	1978	3.00	6.00	12.00
❏ AHL1-2963	Burgers and Fries	1978	3.00	6.00	12.00
❏ AHL1-3441	You're My Jamaica	1979	3.00	6.00	12.00
❏ AHL1-3548	There's a Little Bit of Hank in Me	1980	3.00	6.00	12.00
❏ LPM-3645 [M]	Country Charley Pride	1966	6.25	12.50	25.00
❏ LSP-3645 [S]	Country Charley Pride	1966	7.50	15.00	30.00
❏ AYL1-3676	Someone Loves You Honey	1980	2.00	4.00	8.00
—"Best Buy Series" reissue					
❏ AYL1-3740	Sunday Morning with Charley Pride	1980	2.00	4.00	8.00
—"Best Buy Series" reissue					
❏ LPM-3775 [M]	The Pride of Country Music	1967	6.25	12.50	25.00
❏ LSP-3775 [S]	The Pride of Country Music	1967	5.00	10.00	20.00
❏ AYL1-3874	I'm Just Me	1981	2.00	4.00	8.00
—"Best Buy Series" reissue					
❏ LPM-3895 [M]	The Country Way	1967	6.25	12.50	25.00
❏ LSP-3895 [S]	The Country Way	1967	5.00	10.00	20.00
❏ AHL1-3905	Roll On Mississippi	1981	2.50	5.00	10.00

Number	Title (A Side/B Side)	Yr	VG	VG+	NM
❏ AYL1-3943	The Happiness of Having You	1981	2.00	4.00	8.00
—"Best Buy Series" reissue					
❏ LPM-3952 [M]	Make Mine Country	1968	15.00	30.00	60.00
❏ LSP-3952 [S]	Make Mine Country	1968	5.00	10.00	20.00
❏ LSP-4041	Songs of Pride — Charley, That Is	1968	5.00	10.00	20.00
❏ AYL1-4074	Amazing Love	1981	2.00	4.00	8.00
—"Best Buy Series" reissue					
❏ LSP-4094	Charley Pride — In Person	1969	5.00	10.00	20.00
❏ AHL1-4151	Greatest Hits	1981	2.50	5.00	10.00
❏ LSP-4153	The Sensational Charley Pride	1969	5.00	10.00	20.00
❏ AYL1-4166	She's Just an Old Love Turned Memory	1981	2.00	4.00	8.00
—"Best Buy Series" reissue					
❏ AHL1-4223	The Best of Charley Pride	198?	2.50	5.00	10.00
—Reissue of LSP-4223					
❏ LSP-4223	The Best of Charley Pride	1969	5.00	10.00	20.00
❏ AYL1-4252	Burgers and Fries	1982	2.00	4.00	8.00
—"Best Buy Series" reissue					
❏ AHL1-4287	Charley Pride Sings Everybody's Choice	1982	2.50	5.00	10.00
❏ LSP-4290	Just Plain Charley	1970	5.00	10.00	20.00
❏ LSP-4367	Charley Pride's 10th Album	1970	5.00	10.00	20.00
❏ LSP-4406	Christmas in My Home Town	1970	5.00	10.00	20.00
❏ LSP-4468	From Me to You	1971	5.00	10.00	20.00
❏ LSP-4513	Did You Think to Pray	1971	5.00	10.00	20.00
❏ AHL1-4524	Charley Pride Live	1983	2.50	5.00	10.00
❏ LSP-4560	I'm Just Me	1971	5.00	10.00	20.00
❏ LSP-4617	Charley Pride Sings Heart Songs	1971	5.00	10.00	20.00
❏ AHL1-4662	Country Classics	1983	2.50	5.00	10.00
❏ AHL1-4682	The Best of Charley Pride, Volume 2	198?	2.50	5.00	10.00
—Reissue of LSP-4682					
❏ LSP-4682	The Best of Charley Pride, Volume 2	1972	5.00	10.00	20.00
❏ LSP-4742	A Sunshiny Day with Charley Pride	1972	5.00	10.00	20.00
❏ AHL1-4822	Night Games	1983	2.50	5.00	10.00
❏ AYL1-4831	There's a Little Bit of Hank in Me	1983	2.00	4.00	8.00
—"Best Buy Series" reissue					
❏ LSP-4837	Songs of Love by Charley Pride	1973	3.75	7.50	15.00
❏ AHL1-5031	The Power of Love	1984	2.50	5.00	10.00
❏ AYL1-5147	Greatest Hits	1984	2.00	4.00	8.00
—"Best Buy Series" reissue					
❏ AYL1-5148	The Best of Charley Pride	1984	2.00	4.00	8.00
—"Best Buy Series" reissue					
❏ AHL1-5426	Greatest Hits, Volume 2	1985	2.50	5.00	10.00
❏ AHL1-5851	Back to the Country	1986	2.50	5.00	10.00
❏ CPL1-7049	Collector's Series	1985	2.50	5.00	10.00
❏ AHL1-7174	The Best There Is	1986	2.50	5.00	10.00
READER'S DIGEST					
❏ RDA-217 [(6)]	Charley Pride's Country	1979	10.00	20.00	40.00
16TH AVENUE					
❏ ST-70550	After All This Time	1987	3.00	6.00	12.00
❏ D1-70551	I'm Gonna Love Her on the Radio	1988	3.00	6.00	12.00
❏ D1-70554	Moody Woman	1989	3.00	6.00	12.00
TIME-LIFE					
❏ STW-101	Country Music	1981	3.00	6.00	12.00

PRIESTER, JULIAN
JAZZLAND

Number	Title (A Side/B Side)	Yr	VG	VG+	NM
❏ JLP-25 [M]	Spiritsville	1960	7.50	15.00	30.00
❏ JLP-925 [S]	Spiritsville	1960	10.00	20.00	40.00
RIVERSIDE					
❏ RLP 12-316 [M]	Keep Swingin'	1960	7.50	15.00	30.00
❏ RLP 1163 [S]	Keep Swingin'	1960	10.00	20.00	40.00

PRIMA, LOUIS
CAPITOL

Number	Title (A Side/B Side)	Yr	VG	VG+	NM
❏ T 755 [M]	The Wildest	1956	12.50	25.00	50.00
❏ T 836 [M]	Call of the Wildest	1957	12.50	25.00	50.00
❏ T 908 [M]	The Wildest Show at Tahoe	1957	12.50	25.00	50.00
❏ T 1010 [M]	Las Vegas Prima Style	1958	12.50	25.00	50.00
❏ T 1132 [M]	Strictly Prima	1959	7.50	15.00	30.00
❏ ST 1723 [S]	The Wildest Comes Home	1962	7.50	15.00	30.00
❏ T 1723 [M]	The Wildest Comes Home	1962	6.25	12.50	25.00
❏ ST 1797 [S]	Lake Tahoe Prima Style	1962	7.50	15.00	30.00
❏ T 1797 [M]	Lake Tahoe Prima Style	1962	6.25	12.50	25.00
COLUMBIA					
❏ CL 1206 [M]	Breakin' It Up!	1959	10.00	20.00	40.00
DOT					
❏ DLP-3262 [M]	His Greatest Hits	1960	6.25	12.50	25.00
❏ DLP-3264 [M]	Pretty Music Prima Style	1960	6.25	12.50	25.00
❏ DLP-3272 [M]	The Wildest Clan	1960	6.25	12.50	25.00
❏ DLP-3352 [M]	Wonderland by Night	1960	6.25	12.50	25.00
❏ DLP-3385 [M]	Blue Moon	1961	6.25	12.50	25.00
❏ DLP-3392 [M]	Return of the Wildest!	1961	6.25	12.50	25.00
❏ DLP-3410 [M]	Doin' the Twist	1961	6.25	12.50	25.00
❏ DLP-25262 [S]	His Greatest Hits	1960	7.50	15.00	30.00
❏ DLP-25264 [S]	Pretty Music Prima Style	1960	7.50	15.00	30.00
❏ DLP-25272 [S]	The Wildest Clan	1960	7.50	15.00	30.00
❏ DLP-25352 [S]	Wonderland by Night	1960	7.50	15.00	30.00
❏ DLP-25385 [S]	Blue Moon	1961	7.50	15.00	30.00
❏ DLP-25392 [S]	Return of the Wildest!	1961	7.50	15.00	30.00
❏ DLP-25410 [S]	Doin' the Twist	1961	7.50	15.00	30.00
MERCURY					
❏ MG-25142 [10]	Louis Prima Plays	1953	20.00	40.00	80.00
RONDO-LETTE					
❏ A-9 [M]	Louis Prima in All His Moods	1959	7.50	15.00	30.00
❏ A-25 [M]	Louis Prima Entertains	1959	7.50	15.00	30.00
SAVOY JAZZ					
❏ SJL-2264 [(2)]	Play Pretty for the People	198?	3.00	6.00	12.00
TOPS					
❏ 9759 [M]	Italian Favorites	195?	3.75	7.50	15.00

PRIMA, LOUIS, AND KEELY SMITH
CAPITOL

Number	Title (A Side/B Side)	Yr	VG	VG+	NM
❏ T 1160 [M]	Hey Boy! Hey Girl!	1959	12.50	25.00	50.00
❏ SM-1531	The Hits of Louis and Keely	197?	2.50	5.00	10.00
—Reissue with new prefix					
❏ ST 1531 [S]	The Hits of Louis and Keely	1961	7.50	15.00	30.00
❏ T 1531 [M]	The Hits of Louis and Keely	1961	6.25	12.50	25.00
CORONET					
❏ 121 [M]	Louis Prima Digs Keely Smith	196?	3.75	7.50	15.00
DOT					
❏ DLP-3210 [M]	Louis and Keely!	1959	7.50	15.00	30.00
❏ DLP-3263 [M]	Together	1960	6.25	12.50	25.00
❏ DLP-3266 [M]	Louis and Keely on Stage	1960	6.25	12.50	25.00
❏ DLP-25210 [S]	Louis and Keely!	1959	10.00	20.00	40.00
❏ DLP-25263 [S]	Together	1960	7.50	15.00	30.00
❏ DLP-25266 [S]	Louis and Keely on Stage	1960	7.50	15.00	30.00
FLEET					
❏ 101 [M]	Louis Prima Digs Keely Smith	196?	3.75	7.50	15.00
RHINO					
❏ RNLP-70225	Zooma Zooma: The Best of Louis Prima Featuring Keely Smith	1986	2.50	5.00	10.00
SPIN-O-RAMA					
❏ 74 [M]	Box of Oldies	196?	3.75	7.50	15.00

PRINCE
Also see THE LEWIS CONNECTION; 94 EAST.
ARISTA

Number	Title (A Side/B Side)	Yr	VG	VG+	NM
❏ 14624 [(2)]	Rave Un2 the Joy Fantastic	1999	3.00	6.00	12.00
NPG/BELLMARK					
❏ 71003 [EP]	The Beautiful Experience	1994	5.00	10.00	20.00
NPG/REDLINE					
❏ 70004 [(2)]	The Rainbow Children	2001	6.25	12.50	25.00
PAISLEY PARK					
❏ 25286	Around the World in a Day	1985	2.50	5.00	10.00
—Original copies have a fold-over flap (deduct 25% or more if missing)					
❏ 25395	Parade	1986	2.00	4.00	8.00
❏ 25577 [(2)]	Sign "O" The Times	1987	3.75	7.50	15.00
❏ W1-25577 [(2)]	Sign "O" The Times	1987	4.50	9.00	18.00
—Columbia House edition					
❏ 25677	The Black Album	1987	500.00	1000.	2000.
—Withdrawn prior to release, though a few copies escaped. Numerous counterfeits exist on other labels and colored vinyl.					
❏ 25677-DJ [(2)]	The Black Album	1987	750.00	1500.	3000.
—Entire album on two 12-inch records that play at 45 RPM					
❏ 25720	Lovesexy	1988	3.00	6.00	12.00
❏ 25720-DJ [DJ]	Lovesexy	1988	5.00	10.00	20.00
—Gold stamped and stickered cover (no UPC) with promo labels; tracks are banded					
❏ 27493 [(2)]	Graffiti Bridge	1990	3.75	7.50	15.00
—Also includes The Time, Tevin Campbell					
❏ R 124370	Around the World in a Day	1985	3.00	6.00	12.00
—RCA Music Service edition					
❏ R 140234	Parade	1986	3.00	6.00	12.00
—RCA Music Service edition					
❏ R 154087	Lovesexy	1988	3.50	7.00	14.00
—BMG Direct Marketing edition					
❏ R 234107 [(2)]	Graffiti Bridge	1990	4.50	9.00	18.00
—Also includes The Time, Tevin Campbell; BMG Direct Marketing edition					
❏ R 261991 [(2)]	Sign "O" The Times	1987	4.50	9.00	18.00
—BMG Direct Marketing edition					
WARNER BROS.					
❏ BSK 3150	For You	1978	3.00	6.00	12.00
—White WB label					
❏ BSK 3150	For You	1978	5.00	10.00	20.00
—First edition on Burbank "palm trees" label					
❏ BSK 3366	Prince	1979	3.00	6.00	12.00
❏ BSK 3478	Dirty Mind	1980	3.00	6.00	12.00
❏ BSK 3601	Controversy	1981	3.00	6.00	12.00
❏ PRO-A-7270 [(2)DJ]	Come	1994	7.50	15.00	30.00
—Promo-only vinyl					
❏ PRO-A-7330 [DJ]	The Black Album	1994	12.50	25.00	50.00
—Promo-only vinyl					
❏ PRO-A-7835 [(2)DJ]	The Gold Experience	1995	20.00	40.00	80.00
—Promo-only gold vinyl with numbered gold foil jacket					
❏ 23720 [(2)]	1999	1982	3.75	7.50	15.00
❏ 25110	Purple Rain	1984	2.50	5.00	10.00
—With poster					
❏ 25110	Purple Rain	1984	12.50	25.00	50.00
—Purple vinyl; comes with poster					
❏ 25936	Batman (Soundtrack)	1989	2.50	5.00	10.00
❏ 45793 [DJ]	The Black Album	1994	25.00	50.00	100.00
—Peach vinyl; 1,000 copies					
❏ 45793 [DJ]	The Black Album	1994	50.00	100.00	200.00
—White vinyl; 300 copies, numbered in gold on the label (from 051 to 350)					
❏ 45793 [DJ]	The Black Album	1994	125.00	250.00	500.00
—Gray marbled vinyl; 50 copies					
❏ R 160175	Purple Rain	1984	3.00	6.00	12.00
—RCA Music Service edition; includes poster					
❏ R 160344	Batman (Soundtrack)	1989	3.00	6.00	12.00
—BMG Direct Marketing edition					
❏ R 252483 [(2)]	1999	1982	4.50	9.00	18.00
—RCA Music Service edition					

PRINCE, BOB
RCA VICTOR

Number	Title (A Side/B Side)	Yr	VG	VG+	NM
❏ LPM-2435 [M]	Opus Jazz	1961	5.00	10.00	20.00
❏ LSP-2435 [S]	Opus Jazz	1961	6.25	12.50	25.00
WARNER BROS.					
❏ W 1240 [M]	N.Y. Export: Op. Jazz from Ballets U.S.A.; Ballet Music from Leonard Bernstein's West Side Story	1958	5.00	10.00	20.00

Number	Title (A Side/B Side)	Yr	VG	VG+	NM
❑ WS 1240 [S]	N.Y. Export: Op. Jazz from Ballets U.S.A.; Ballet Music from Leonard Bernstein's West Side Story	1958	6.25	12.50	25.00
❑ W 1276 [M]	Charleston 1970	1959	5.00	10.00	20.00
❑ WS 1276 [S]	Charleston 1970	1959	6.25	12.50	25.00

PRINCE BUSTER
RCA VICTOR
Number	Title (A Side/B Side)	Yr	VG	VG+	NM
❑ LPM-3792 [M]	Ten Commandments	1967	6.25	12.50	25.00
❑ LSP-3792 [S]	Ten Commandments	1967	7.50	15.00	30.00

PRINZ, ROSEMARY
PHAROS
❑ MN-10001 [M]	TV's Penny Sings	1966	5.00	10.00	20.00
❑ SN-30001 [S]	TV's Penny Sings	1966	6.25	12.50	25.00

PRITCHETT, GEORGE
KINNICKINNICK
❑ 101	By Request	197?	5.00	10.00	20.00

PROBY, P.J.
LIBERTY
❑ LRP-3406 [M]	Somewhere/Go Go P.J. Proby	1965	5.00	10.00	20.00
❑ LRP-3421 [M]	P.J. Proby	1965	5.00	10.00	20.00
❑ LRP-3497 [M]	Enigma	1967	5.00	10.00	20.00
❑ LRP-3515 [M]	Phenomenon	1967	5.00	10.00	20.00
❑ LST-7406 [S]	Somewhere/Go Go P.J. Proby	1965	6.25	12.50	25.00
❑ LST-7421 [S]	P.J. Proby	1965	6.25	12.50	25.00
❑ LST-7497 [S]	Enigma	1967	6.25	12.50	25.00
❑ LST-7515 [S]	Phenomenon	1967	6.25	12.50	25.00
❑ LST-7561	What's Wrong with My World?	1968	6.25	12.50	25.00

PROCESSION
SMASH
❑ SRS-67122	Procession	1969	5.00	10.00	20.00

PROCOL HARUM
A&M
❑ SP-3123	A Salty Dog	1979	2.00	4.00	8.00
—Reissue of 4179					
❑ SP-3259	The Best of Procol Harum	198?	2.00	4.00	8.00
—Reissue of 4401					
❑ SP-4151	Shine On Brightly	1968	6.25	12.50	25.00
❑ SP-4179	A Salty Dog	1969	3.75	7.50	15.00
❑ SP-4261	Home	1970	3.00	6.00	12.00
❑ SP-4294	Broken Barricades	1971	3.00	6.00	12.00
❑ SP-4335	Procol Harum Live in Concert with the Edmonton Symphony Orchestra	1972	3.00	6.00	12.00
❑ SP-4373	A Whiter Shade of Pale	1972	3.00	6.00	12.00
—Reissue of Deram 18008 with one more track					
❑ SP-4401	The Best of Procol Harum	1973	3.00	6.00	12.00
❑ SP-8503 [DJ]	Procol Harum Lives	197?	12.50	25.00	50.00
—Interview LP alone					
❑ SP-8503 [DJ]	Procol Harum Lives	197?	75.00	150.00	300.00
—Promo-only box set with press kit, photos, keychain and interview LP					

CHRYSALIS
❑ CHR 1037	Grand Hotel	1973	3.00	6.00	12.00
—Green label with "3300 Warner Blvd." address					
❑ CHR 1037	Grand Hotel	1977	2.50	5.00	10.00
—Blue label with New York address					
❑ CHR 1058	Exotic Birds and Fruit	1974	3.00	6.00	12.00
—Green label with "3300 Warner Blvd." address					
❑ CHR 1058	Exotic Birds and Fruit	1977	2.50	5.00	10.00
—Blue label with New York address					
❑ CHR 1080	Procol's Ninth	1975	3.00	6.00	12.00
—Green label with "3300 Warner Blvd." address					
❑ CHR 1080	Procol's Ninth	1977	2.50	5.00	10.00
—Blue label with New York address					
❑ CHR 1130	Something Magic	1977	2.50	5.00	10.00
❑ PV 41037	Grand Hotel	1985	2.00	4.00	8.00
❑ PV 41058	Exotic Birds and Fruit	1985	2.00	4.00	8.00
❑ PV 41080	Procol's Ninth	1985	2.00	4.00	8.00

DERAM
❑ DE 16008 [M]	Procol Harum	1967	20.00	40.00	80.00
❑ DE/S 16008/18008	Procol Harum Poster	1967	6.25	12.50	25.00
❑ DES 18008 [R]	Procol Harum	1967	10.00	20.00	40.00

PROCOPE, RUSSELL
DOT
❑ DLP 3010 [M]	The Persuasive Sax of Russell Procope	1956	10.00	20.00	40.00

PRODIGY
MAVERICK
❑ PRO-A-8929 [(2)DJ]	The Fat of the Land	1997	6.25	12.50	25.00
—Promo-only U.S. vinyl in generic white sleeve					

PROFESSOR LONGHAIR
ATLANTIC
❑ SD 7225	New Orleans Piano	1972	6.25	12.50	25.00

PROVINE, DOROTHY
WARNER BROS.
❑ W 1394 [M]	The Roaring 20's	1961	5.00	10.00	20.00
❑ WS 1394 [S]	The Roaring 20's	1961	6.25	12.50	25.00
❑ W 1419 [M]	The Vamp of the Roaring 20's	1961	5.00	10.00	20.00
❑ WS 1419 [S]	The Vamp of the Roaring 20's	1961	6.25	12.50	25.00

PRYOR, RICHARD
AUDIOFIDELITY
❑ 349 [PD]	Richard Pryor Live	198?	3.75	7.50	15.00
DOVE
| ❑ RS 6325 | Richard Pryor | 1968 | 5.00 | 10.00 | 20.00 |
LAFF
| ❑ (# unknown) | Supernigger | 198? | 2.00 | 4.00 | 8.00 |

Number	Title (A Side/B Side)	Yr	VG	VG+	NM
❑ A 146	Craps: After Hours	1971	3.00	6.00	12.00
❑ A 170	Pryor Goes Foxx Hunting	197?	3.00	6.00	12.00
❑ A 184	Down 'N' Dirty	197?	3.00	6.00	12.00
❑ A 196	Are You Serious???	1977	3.00	6.00	12.00
❑ A 198	Who Me? I'm Not Him	1977	3.00	6.00	12.00
❑ A 200	Black Ben	1978	2.50	5.00	10.00
❑ A 202	Wizard of Comedy	1978	2.50	5.00	10.00
❑ A 206	Outrageous	1979	2.50	5.00	10.00
❑ A 209	Insane	1980	2.50	5.00	10.00
❑ A 212	Holy Smoke	1980	2.50	5.00	10.00
❑ A 216	Rev. Du Rite	1981	2.50	5.00	10.00
❑ A 221	The Very Best of Richard Pryor	1982	2.50	5.00	10.00
❑ 226	Blackjack	198?	2.00	4.00	8.00
—Reissue of 146					
❑ 227	Show Biz	198?	2.00	4.00	8.00
—Reissue of 200					
❑ 279	Richard Pryor Live	198?	2.00	4.00	8.00

PARTEE
❑ PBS-2404	That Nigger's Crazy	1974	3.75	7.50	15.00
REPRISE
❑ MS 2227	Is It Something I Said?	1975	3.00	6.00	12.00
❑ MS 2241	That Nigger's Crazy	197?	3.00	6.00	12.00
—Reissue of Partee LP					
❑ MSK 2285	Is It Something I Said?	1977	2.50	5.00	10.00
—Reissue of 2227					
❑ MSK 2287	That Nigger's Crazy	1977	2.50	5.00	10.00
—Reissue of Reprise 2241					
❑ RS 6325	Richard Pryor	197?	3.00	6.00	12.00
—Reissue of Dove LP					
TIGER LILY
| ❑ TL 14023 | L.A. Jail | 1977 | 3.00 | 6.00 | 12.00 |
WARNER BROS.
❑ BS 2960	Bicentennial Nigger	1976	3.00	6.00	12.00
❑ BSK 3057	Richard Pryor's Greatest Hits	1977	2.50	5.00	10.00
❑ BSK 3114	Bicentennial Nigger	1977	2.50	5.00	10.00
—Reissue of 2960					
❑ 2BSK 3364 [(2)]	Wanted	1978	3.00	6.00	12.00
❑ BSK 3660	Richard Pryor Live on the Sunset Strip	1982	2.50	5.00	10.00
❑ 23981	Richard Pryor: Here and Now	1983	2.50	5.00	10.00

PRYSOCK, ARTHUR
DECCA
❑ DL 4581 [M]	Strictly Sentimental	1965	3.75	7.50	15.00
❑ DL 4628 [M]	Showcase	1965	3.75	7.50	15.00
❑ DL 74581 [S]	Strictly Sentimental	1965	5.00	10.00	20.00
❑ DL 74628 [S]	Showcase	1965	5.00	10.00	20.00
KING
❑ KS-1064	The Country Side of Arthur Prysock	1969	3.00	6.00	12.00
❑ KS-1066	Where the Soul Trees Go	1970	3.00	6.00	12.00
❑ KS-1067	The Lord Is My Shepherd	1970	3.00	6.00	12.00
❑ KS-1088	Fly My Love	1970	3.00	6.00	12.00
❑ KS-1134	Unforgettable	1971	3.00	6.00	12.00
MCA
| ❑ 3061 | Here's To Good Friends | 1978 | 2.50 | 5.00 | 10.00 |
MGM
| ❑ GAS-134 | Arthur Prysock (Golden Archive Series) | 1970 | 3.00 | 6.00 | 12.00 |
| ❑ SE-4694 | Arthur Prysock | 1970 | 3.00 | 6.00 | 12.00 |
MILESTONE
❑ M-9139	A Rockin' Good Way	1986	2.50	5.00	10.00
❑ M-9146	This Guy's in Love with You	1987	2.50	5.00	10.00
❑ M-9157	Today's Love Songs, Tomorrow's Blues	1988	2.50	5.00	10.00
OLD TOWN
❑ 12-001	Arthur Prysock '74	1973	3.00	6.00	12.00
❑ 12-002	Love Makes It Right	1974	3.00	6.00	12.00
❑ 12-004	All My Life	1976	3.00	6.00	12.00
❑ LP-102 [M]	I Worry About You	1962	12.50	25.00	50.00
❑ LP-2004 [M]	Arthur Prysock Sings Only for You	1962	12.50	25.00	50.00
❑ LP-2005 [M]	Coast to Coast	1963	10.00	20.00	40.00
❑ LP-2006 [M]	A Portrait of Arthur Prysock	1963	10.00	20.00	40.00
❑ LP-2007 [M]	Everlasting Songs for Everlasting Lovers	1964	10.00	20.00	40.00
❑ LP-2008 [M]	Intimately Yours	1964	10.00	20.00	40.00
❑ LP-2009 [M]	A Double Header with Arthur Prysock	1965	10.00	20.00	40.00
❑ LP-2010 [M]	In a Mood	1965	10.00	20.00	40.00
❑ OT 12005	Arthur Prysock Does It Again	1977	3.00	6.00	12.00
❑ T-90604 [M]	A Portrait of Arthur Prysock	1965	10.00	20.00	40.00
—Capitol Record Club edition					
POLYDOR
| ❑ PD-2-8901 [(2)] | Silk and Satin | 1977 | 3.75 | 7.50 | 15.00 |
VERVE
❑ V6-650 [(2)]	24 Karat Hits	1969	3.75	7.50	15.00
❑ V-5009 [M]	Art and Soul	1966	3.00	6.00	12.00
❑ V6-5009 [S]	Art and Soul	1966	3.75	7.50	15.00
❑ V-5011 [M]	The Best of Arthur Prysock	1967	3.00	6.00	12.00
❑ V6-5011 [S]	The Best of Arthur Prysock	1967	3.75	7.50	15.00
❑ V-5012 [M]	A Portrait of Arthur Prysock	1967	3.75	7.50	15.00
❑ V6-5012 [S]	A Portrait of Arthur Prysock	1967	3.75	7.50	15.00
❑ V-5014 [M]	Mister Prysock	1967	3.75	7.50	15.00
❑ V6-5014 [S]	Mister Prysock	1967	3.75	7.50	15.00
❑ V-5029 [M]	Love Me	1968	3.75	7.50	15.00
❑ V6-5029 [S]	Love Me	1968	3.00	6.00	12.00
❑ V-5038 [M]	The Best of Arthur Prysock, Number 2	1968	5.00	10.00	20.00
—All mono copies appear to be yellow label promos					
❑ V6-5038 [S]	The Best of Arthur Prysock, Number 2	1968	3.00	6.00	12.00
❑ V-5048 [M]	To Love or Not to Love	1968	7.50	15.00	30.00
—May be promo only					
❑ V6-5048 [S]	To Love or Not to Love	1968	3.00	6.00	12.00
❑ V6-5059	I Must Be Doing Something Right	1968	3.00	6.00	12.00
❑ V6-5070	This Is My Beloved	1969	3.00	6.00	12.00

Number	Title (A Side/B Side)	Yr	VG	VG+	NM

PRYSOCK, ARTHUR/COUNT BASIE
VERVE
❑ V-8646 [M]	Arthur Prysock/Count Basie	1966	3.75	7.50	15.00
❑ V6-8646 [S]	Arthur Prysock/Count Basie	1966	5.00	10.00	20.00
❑ 827011-1	Arthur Prysock/Count Basie	1985	2.00	4.00	8.00
—Reissue					

PRYSOCK, RED
MERCURY
❑ MG-20088 [M]	Rock 'n Roll	1955	50.00	100.00	200.00
❑ MG-20211 [M]	Fruit Boots	1957	30.00	60.00	120.00
❑ MG-20307 [M]	The Beat	1957	20.00	40.00	80.00
❑ MG-20512 [M]	Swing Softly Red	1958	12.50	25.00	50.00
❑ SR-60188 [S]	Swing Softly Red	1959	20.00	40.00	80.00
WING
❑ MGW-12007 [M]	Fruit Boots	1959	10.00	20.00	40.00
—Originals have liner notes on back cover					
❑ MGW-12007 [M]	Fruit Boots	196?	5.00	10.00	20.00
—Reissues have other LPs listed on back cover					
❑ SRW-16007 [R]	Fruit Boots	196?	3.00	6.00	12.00

PSYCHEDELIC FURS
COLUMBIA
❑ AS 1296 [DJ]	Interchords	1981	6.25	12.50	25.00
❑ CAS 01310 [DJ]	Interchords with Richard Butler	1988	5.00	10.00	20.00
❑ CAS 2719 [DJ]	Richard Butler Interview	1987	3.75	7.50	15.00
❑ NFC 36791	Psychedelic Furs	1980	3.00	6.00	12.00
❑ PC 36791	The Psychedelic Furs	198?	2.00	4.00	8.00
—Budget-line reissue					
❑ NFC 37339	Talk Talk Talk	1981	2.50	5.00	10.00
❑ PC 37339	Talk Talk Talk	1983	2.00	4.00	8.00
—Budget-line reissue					
❑ ARC 38261	Forever Now	1982	2.50	5.00	10.00
❑ PC 38261	Forever Now	198?	2.00	4.00	8.00
—Budget-line reissue					
❑ BFC 39278	Mirror Moves	1984	2.50	5.00	10.00
❑ PC 39278	Mirror Moves	198?	2.00	4.00	8.00
—Budget-line reissue					
❑ FC 40466	Midnight to Midnight	1987	2.50	5.00	10.00
❑ FC 44377	All of This and Nothing	1988	2.50	5.00	10.00
❑ FC 45412	Book of Days	1989	2.50	5.00	10.00

PSYCHOTIC PINEAPPLE, THE
RICHMOND
❑ 6026	Where's the Party	1980	6.25	12.50	25.00

PUCHO AND THE LATIN SOUL BROTHERS
PRESTIGE
❑ PRLP-7471 [M]	Pucho and the Latin Soul Brothers	1967	10.00	20.00	40.00
❑ PRST-7471 [S]	Pucho and the Latin Soul Brothers	1967	7.50	15.00	30.00
❑ PRLP-7502 [M]	Saffron and Soul	1967	10.00	20.00	40.00
❑ PRST-7502 [S]	Saffron and Soul	1967	7.50	15.00	30.00
❑ PRLP-7528 [M]	Shuckin' and Jivin'	1967	12.50	25.00	50.00
❑ PRST-7528 [S]	Shuckin' and Jivin'	1967	7.50	15.00	30.00
❑ PRST-7555	Big Stick	1968	7.50	15.00	30.00
❑ PRST-7572	Heat!	1968	7.50	15.00	30.00
❑ PRST-7616	Dateline	1969	7.50	15.00	30.00
❑ PRST-7679	The Best of Pucho and the Latin Soul Brothers	1969	6.25	12.50	25.00

PUCKETT, GARY, AND THE UNION GAP
COLUMBIA
❑ CS 1042	Gary Puckett and the Union Gap's Greatest Hits	1970	5.00	10.00	20.00
❑ CL 2812 [M]	Woman, Woman	1968	10.00	20.00	40.00
—As "The Union Gap Featuring Gary Puckett"					
❑ CL 2864 [M]	Young Girl	1968	12.50	25.00	50.00
—Red label stock copy with "Mono" on label; this has been confirmed to exist					
❑ CL 2915 [M]	Incredible	1968	15.00	30.00	60.00
—Red label stock copy with "Mono" on label; this has been confirmed to exist					
❑ CS 9612 [S]	Woman, Woman	1968	5.00	10.00	20.00
—As "The Union Gap Featuring Gary Puckett"					
❑ CS 9664 [S]	Young Girl	1968	5.00	10.00	20.00
❑ CS 9715 [S]	Incredible	1968	5.00	10.00	20.00
❑ CS 9935	The New Gary Puckett and the Union Gap Album	1969	5.00	10.00	20.00
❑ C 30862	The Gary Puckett Album	1971	3.75	7.50	15.00
HARMONY
❑ KH 31184	Lady Willpower	1972	2.50	5.00	10.00

PUENTE, TITO
DECCA
❑ DL 4910 [M]	Brasilia Nueve	1967	6.25	12.50	25.00
❑ DL 74910 [S]	Brasilia Nueve	1967	5.00	10.00	20.00
GNP CRESCENDO
❑ GNP-70 [M]	The Exciting Tito Puente Band in Hollywood	196?	7.50	15.00	30.00
RCA VICTOR
❑ LPM-1251 [M]	Cuban Carnival	1955	12.50	25.00	50.00
❑ LPM-1312 [M]	Puente Goes Jazz	1956	15.00	30.00	60.00
❑ LPM-1354 [M]	Mambo on Broadway	1957	10.00	20.00	40.00
❑ LPM-1392 [M]	Let's Cha-Cha with Puente	1957	10.00	20.00	40.00
❑ LPM-1447 [M]	Night Beat	1957	10.00	20.00	40.00
❑ LPM-1479 [M]	Mucho Puente	1957	10.00	20.00	40.00
❑ LPM-1617 [M]	Top Percussion	1958	7.50	15.00	30.00
❑ LSP-1617 [S]	Top Percussion	1958	10.00	20.00	40.00
❑ LPM-1692 [M]	Dance Mania	1958	7.50	15.00	30.00
❑ LSP-1692 [S]	Dance Mania	1958	10.00	20.00	40.00
❑ LPM-1874 [M]	Dancing Under Latin Skies	1958	7.50	15.00	30.00
❑ LSP-1874 [S]	Dancing Under Latin Skies	1958	10.00	20.00	40.00
❑ LPM-2113 [M]	Mucho Cha Cha Cha	1959	7.50	15.00	30.00
❑ LSP-2113 [S]	Mucho Cha Cha Cha	1959	10.00	20.00	40.00
❑ LPM-2187 [M]	Cha Cha at Grossinger's	1959	7.50	15.00	30.00
❑ LSP-2187 [S]	Cha Cha at Grossinger's	1959	10.00	20.00	40.00

Number	Title (A Side/B Side)	Yr	VG	VG+	NM
❑ LPM-2257 [M]	Tambo	1960	7.50	15.00	30.00
❑ LSP-2257 [S]	Tambo	1960	10.00	20.00	40.00
❑ LPM-2299 [M]	Revolving Bandstand	1960	7.50	15.00	30.00
❑ LSP-2299 [S]	Revolving Bandstand	1960	10.00	20.00	40.00
❑ LPM-2974 [M]	The Best of Tito Puente	1964	6.25	12.50	25.00

ROULETTE
❑ R-25193 [M]	Bossa Nova	1962	5.00	10.00	20.00
❑ SR-25193 [S]	Bossa Nova	1962	6.25	12.50	25.00
❑ R-25276 [M]	"My Fair Lady" Goes Latin	1964	5.00	10.00	20.00
❑ SR-25276 [S]	"My Fair Lady" Goes Latin	1964	6.25	12.50	25.00

TICO
❑ LP-101 [10]	Mambos, Volume 1	1951	25.00	50.00	100.00
❑ LP-103 [10]	Mambos, Volume 2	1952	20.00	40.00	80.00
❑ LP-107 [10]	Mambos, Volume 3	195?	20.00	40.00	80.00
❑ LP-114 [10]	Mambos, Volume 4	195?	20.00	40.00	80.00
❑ LP-116 [10]	Mambos, Volume 5	195?	20.00	40.00	80.00
❑ LP-120 [10]	The King of the Mambo and His Orchestra	195?	20.00	40.00	80.00
❑ LP-124 [10]	Tito Puente at the Vibes and His Rhythm Quartet	195?	20.00	40.00	80.00
❑ LP-128 [10]	Cha Cha Cha, Volume 1	195?	20.00	40.00	80.00
❑ LP-130 [10]	Cha Cha Cha, Volume 2	195?	20.00	40.00	80.00
❑ LP-131 [10]	Mambos, Volume 8	195?	20.00	40.00	80.00
❑ LP-133 [10]	Instrumental Mambos	195?	20.00	40.00	80.00
❑ LP-134 [10]	Cha Cha Cha, Volume 3	195?	20.00	40.00	80.00
❑ LP-1001 [M]	Mamborama	1955	15.00	30.00	60.00
❑ LP-1003 [M]	Mambo and Me	1955	15.00	30.00	60.00
❑ LP-1006 [M]	Mambos for Lovers	1955	15.00	30.00	60.00
❑ LP-1010 [M]	Dance the Cha Cha Cha	195?	15.00	30.00	60.00
❑ LP-1011 [M]	Puente in Percussion	1956	15.00	30.00	60.00
❑ LP-1025 [M]	Cha Cha Cha at the El Morocco	1956	15.00	30.00	60.00
❑ LP-1032 [M]	Basic Cha Cha Cha	1957	12.50	25.00	50.00
❑ LP-1049 [M]	Tito Puente Swings/Vicentico Valdes Sings	1958	12.50	25.00	50.00
❑ LP-1058 [M]	Puente in Love	1959	10.00	20.00	40.00
❑ LP-1083 [M]	Pachanga Con Puente	1961	7.50	15.00	30.00
❑ SLP-1083 [S]	Pachanga Con Puente	1961	10.00	20.00	40.00
❑ LP-1085 [M]	Vaya Puente	1962	7.50	15.00	30.00
❑ SLP-1085 [S]	Vaya Puente	1962	10.00	20.00	40.00
❑ LP-1086 [M]	El Rey Tito: Bravo Puente	1962	7.50	15.00	30.00
❑ SLP-1086 [S]	El Rey Tito: Bravo Puente	1962	10.00	20.00	40.00
—This album contains the original version of "Oye Como Va," later a hit for Santana					
❑ LP-1088 [M]	Tito Puente in Puerto Rico	1963	6.25	12.50	25.00
❑ SLP-1088 [S]	Tito Puente in Puerto Rico	1963	7.50	15.00	30.00
❑ LP-1093 [M]	Tito Puente Bailables	1963	6.25	12.50	25.00
❑ SLP-1093 [S]	Tito Puente Bailables	1963	7.50	15.00	30.00
❑ LP-1106 [M]	Excitente Ritmo	196?	6.25	12.50	25.00
❑ SLP-1106 [S]	Excitente Ritmo	196?	7.50	15.00	30.00
❑ LP-1109 [M]	El Mundo Latino de Tito Puente	196?	6.25	12.50	25.00
❑ SLP-1109 [S]	El Mundo Latino de Tito Puente	196?	7.50	15.00	30.00
❑ LP-1115 [M]	Mucho Puente	196?	6.25	12.50	25.00
❑ SLP-1115 [S]	Mucho Puente	196?	7.50	15.00	30.00
❑ LP-1116 [M]	De Mi Para Ti	196?	6.25	12.50	25.00
❑ SLP-1116 [S]	De Mi Para Ti	196?	7.50	15.00	30.00
❑ LP-1121 [M]	Tito Puente Swings/The Exciting Lupe Sings	196?	5.00	10.00	20.00
❑ SLP-1121 [S]	Tito Puente Swings/The Exciting Lupe Sings	196?	6.25	12.50	25.00
❑ LP-1125 [M]	Tu Y Yo (You 'n' Me)	196?	5.00	10.00	20.00
❑ SLP-1125 [S]	Tu Y Yo (You 'n' Me)	196?	6.25	12.50	25.00
❑ LP-1127 [M]	Carnival in Harlem	196?	5.00	10.00	20.00
❑ SLP-1127 [S]	Carnival in Harlem	196?	6.25	12.50	25.00
❑ LP-1131 [M]	Homenaje a Rafael Hernandez	196?	5.00	10.00	20.00
❑ SLP-1131 [S]	Homenaje a Rafael Hernandez	196?	6.25	12.50	25.00
❑ LP-1136 [M]	Cuba Y Puerto Ricon Son	196?	5.00	10.00	20.00
❑ SLP-1136 [S]	Cuba Y Puerto Ricon Son	196?	6.25	12.50	25.00
❑ LP-1151 [M]	20th Anniversary	1967	6.25	12.50	25.00
❑ SLP-1151 [S]	20th Anniversary	1967	5.00	10.00	20.00
❑ LP-1154 [M]	El Rey Y Yo (The King and I)	1967	6.25	12.50	25.00
❑ SLP-1154 [S]	El Rey Y Yo (The King and I)	1967	5.00	10.00	20.00
❑ SLP-1172	El Rey (The King)	1968	5.00	10.00	20.00
❑ SLP-1191	Tito Puente En El Puente (On the Bridge)	1969	5.00	10.00	20.00
❑ SLP-1203	The Best of Tito Puente	1969	5.00	10.00	20.00
❑ SLP-1214	P'alante!	1970	5.00	10.00	20.00

PUGSLEY MUNION
J&S
❑ SLP-001	Just Like You	1969	25.00	50.00	100.00

PULLEN, DON, AND MILFORD GRAVES
PULLEN-GRAVES MUSIC
❑ (# unknown)	Graves-Pullen Duo	1967	12.50	25.00	50.00
S.R.P.
❑ LP-290	Nommo	1968	10.00	20.00	40.00

PULLEN, WHITEY
CROWN
❑ CST-332 [R]	Whitey Pullen	1963	3.00	6.00	12.00
❑ CLP-5332 [M]	Whitey Pullen	1963	10.00	20.00	40.00

PULLINS, LEROY
KAPP
❑ KL-1488 [M]	I'm a Nut	1966	6.25	12.50	25.00
❑ KS-3488 [S]	I'm a Nut	1966	7.50	15.00	30.00
❑ KS-3557	Funny Bones and Hearts	1968	6.25	12.50	25.00

PULSE
POISON RING
❑ 2237	Pulse	1969	6.25	12.50	25.00

PUMA, JOE
BETHLEHEM
❑ BCP-1012 [10]	East Coast Jazz 3	1954	50.00	100.00	200.00
COLUMBIA
❑ CL 1618 [M]	Like Tweet	1961	7.50	15.00	30.00
❑ CS 8418 [S]	Like Tweet	1961	10.00	20.00	40.00

Number	Title (A Side/B Side)	Yr	VG	VG+	NM

DAWN
| ❏ DLP-1118 [M] | Wild Kitten | 1957 | 25.00 | 50.00 | 100.00 |

JUBILEE
| ❏ JLP-1070 [M] | Joe Puma Jazz | 1958 | 20.00 | 40.00 | 80.00 |

PURDIE, BERNARD
DATE
| ❏ TEM 3006 [M] | Soul Drums | 1967 | 5.00 | 10.00 | 20.00 |
| ❏ TES 4006 [S] | Soul Drums | 1967 | 5.00 | 10.00 | 20.00 |

PRESTIGE
| ❏ 10013 | Purdie Good | 1971 | 3.75 | 7.50 | 15.00 |
| ❏ 10038 | Shaft | 1972 | 5.00 | 10.00 | 20.00 |

PURE PRAIRIE LEAGUE
CASABLANCA
| ❏ NBLP-7212 | Firin' Up | 1980 | 2.50 | 5.00 | 10.00 |
| ❏ NBLP-7255 | Something in the Night | 1981 | 2.50 | 5.00 | 10.00 |

PAIR
| ❏ PDL2-1034 [(2)] | Home on the Range | 1986 | 3.00 | 6.00 | 12.00 |

RCA VICTOR
❏ APD1-0933 [Q]	Two Lane Highway	1975	5.00	10.00	20.00
❏ APL1-0933	Two Lane Highway	1975	3.00	6.00	12.00
❏ APD1-1247 [Q]	If the Shoe Fits	1976	5.00	10.00	20.00
❏ APL1-1247	If the Shoe Fits	1976	3.00	6.00	12.00
❏ APL1-1924	Dance	1976	3.00	6.00	12.00
❏ CPL2-2404 [(2)]	Live!! Takin' the Stage	1977	3.75	7.50	15.00
❏ AFL1-2590	Just Fly	1978	3.00	6.00	12.00
❏ AFL1-3335	Can't Hold Back	1979	3.00	6.00	12.00
❏ AYL1-3669	Two Lane Highway	1980	2.00	4.00	8.00
—"Best Buy Series" reissue					
❏ AYL1-3717	If the Shoe Fits	1981	2.00	4.00	8.00
—"Best Buy Series" reissue					
❏ AYL1-3718	Just Fly	1981	2.00	4.00	8.00
—"Best Buy Series" reissue					
❏ AYL1-3719	Pure Prairie League	1981	2.00	4.00	8.00
—"Best Buy Series" reissue					
❏ AYL1-3723	Dance	1981	2.00	4.00	8.00
—"Best Buy Series" reissue					
❏ AFL1-4650	Pure Prairie League	1977	2.50	5.00	10.00
—Reissue of LSP-4650					
❏ LSP-4650	Pure Prairie League	1972	3.00	6.00	12.00
❏ AYL1-4656	Bustin' Out	1984	2.00	4.00	8.00
—"Best Buy Series" reissue					
❏ AFL1-4769	Bustin' Out	1977	2.50	5.00	10.00
—Reissue of LSP-4769					
❏ LSP-4769	Bustin' Out	1972	3.00	6.00	12.00

PURIFY, JAMES AND BOBBY
BELL
❏ 6003 [M]	James and Bobby Purify	1966	6.25	12.50	25.00
❏ S-6003 [S]	James and Bobby Purify	1966	7.50	15.00	30.00
❏ 6010 [M]	The Pure Sound of the Purifys	1967	6.25	12.50	25.00
❏ S-6010 [S]	The Pure Sound of the Purifys	1967	7.50	15.00	30.00

MERCURY
| ❏ SRM-1-1134 | The Purify Brothers | 1977 | 3.00 | 6.00 | 12.00 |

PURPLE GANG, THE
SIRE
| ❏ SES 97006 | The Purple Gang Strikes | 1969 | 5.00 | 10.00 | 20.00 |

PURPLE IMAGE
MAP CITY
| ❏ 3015 | Purple Image | 1971 | 12.50 | 25.00 | 50.00 |

PURSELL, BILL
COLUMBIA
❏ CL 1992 [M]	Our Winter Love	1963	3.75	7.50	15.00
❏ CL 2077 [M]	Chasing a Dream	1964	3.75	7.50	15.00
❏ CL 2421 [M]	Remembered Love	1965	3.75	7.50	15.00
❏ CS 8792 [S]	Our Winter Love	1963	5.00	10.00	20.00
❏ CS 8877 [S]	Chasing a Dream	1964	5.00	10.00	20.00
❏ CS 9221 [S]	Remembered Love	1965	5.00	10.00	20.00

PUSSY GALORE
BUY OUR RECORDS
| ❏ 10 [EP] | Pussy Gold 5000 | 1986 | 12.50 | 25.00 | 50.00 |

CAROLINE
| ❏ CAROL 1337 | Right Now! | 1987 | 6.25 | 12.50 | 25.00 |
| ❏ CAROL 1369 | Dial "M" for Motherfucker | 1989 | 6.25 | 12.50 | 25.00 |

SHOVE
| ❏ 2 | Groovy Hate Fuck | 1986 | 12.50 | 25.00 | 50.00 |

PUTMAN, CURLY
ABC
❏ ABC-618 [M]	Lonesome	1967	6.25	12.50	25.00
❏ ABCS-618 [S]	Lonesome	1967	3.75	7.50	15.00
❏ ABCS-686	World of Country Music	1969	3.75	7.50	15.00

PUYANA, RAFAEL
MERCURY LIVING PRESENCE
❏ SR 90259 [S]	Picchi: Belli d'Arpsichordo; Frescobaldi: Music for Harpsichord	196?	5.00	10.00	20.00
—Maroon label, no "Vendor: Mercury Record Corporation"					
❏ SR 90304 [S]	The Golden Age of Harpsichord Music	196?	5.00	10.00	20.00
—Maroon label, no "Vendor: Mercury Record Corporation"					
❏ SR 90322 [S]	Bachs: Harpsichord Music	196?	5.00	10.00	20.00
—Maroon label, no "Vendor: Mercury Record Corporation"					
❏ SR 90369 [S]	Bach for Harpsichord	196?	7.50	15.00	30.00
—Maroon label, no "Vendor: Mercury Record Corporation"					
❏ SR 90369 [S]	Bach for Harpsichord	196?	7.50	15.00	30.00
—Maroon label, with "Vendor: Mercury Record Corporation"					

Number	Title (A Side/B Side)	Yr	VG	VG+	NM
❏ SR 90411 [S]	Baroque Masterpieces for the Harpsichord	196?	7.50	15.00	30.00
—Maroon label, no "Vendor: Mercury Record Corporation"					
❏ SR 90459 [S]	Soler: Harpsichord Music	196?	7.50	15.00	30.00
—Maroon label, with "Vendor: Mercury Record Corporation"					

PUZZLE
ABC
| ❏ ABCS-671 | Puzzle | 1969 | 5.00 | 10.00 | 20.00 |

PYLE, JACK
CAMEO
| ❏ C-1017 [M] | Listen Son...And Other Readings by Jack Pyle | 1963 | 5.00 | 10.00 | 20.00 |

PYRAMIDS, THE
BEST
❏ LPM-1001 [M]	The Original Penetration! And Other Favorites	1964	62.50	125.00	250.00
—Original issue with "Walkin' the Dog"					
❏ BR 16501 [M]	The Original Penetration! And Other Favorites	1964	50.00	100.00	200.00
—Reissue with "Road Runnah"					
❏ BS 36501 [R]	The Original Penetration! And Other Favorites	1964	30.00	60.00	120.00

SUNDAZED
| ❏ LP-5012 | Penetration! The Best of the Pyramids | 1995 | 2.50 | 5.00 | 10.00 |

Q

QUARTERMASS
HARVEST
| ❏ SKAO-314 | Quartermass | 1970 | 7.50 | 15.00 | 30.00 |

QUARTETTE TRES BIEN
ATLANTIC
| ❏ SD 1461 [S] | Bully! | 1966 | 3.75 | 7.50 | 15.00 |

DECCA
❏ DL 4893 [M]	Here It Is	1967	3.75	7.50	15.00
❏ DL 4958 [M]	Four of a Kind	1967	3.75	7.50	15.00
❏ DL 74547 [S]	Boss Tres Bien	1964	3.75	7.50	15.00
❏ DL 74548 [S]	Kilimanjaro	1964	3.75	7.50	15.00
❏ DL 74617 [S]	Spring Into Spring	1965	3.75	7.50	15.00
❏ DL 74675 [S]	Stepping Out	1965	3.75	7.50	15.00
❏ DL 74715 [S]	Sky High	1966	3.75	7.50	15.00
❏ DL 74791 [S]	"In" Motion	1966	3.75	7.50	15.00
❏ DL 74822 [S]	Where It's At	1966	3.75	7.50	15.00

GNP
❏ GNP-102 [M]	Quartette Tres Bien	1962	5.00	10.00	20.00
❏ GNPS-102 [S]	Quartette Tres Bien	1962	6.25	12.50	25.00
❏ GNP-107 [M]	Kilimanjaro	1963	5.00	10.00	20.00
❏ GNPS-107 [S]	Kilimanjaro	1963	6.25	12.50	25.00

QUATTLEBAUM, DOUG
BLUESVILLE
❏ BVLP-1065 [M]	Softee Man Blues	1963	15.00	30.00	60.00
—Blue label, silver print					
❏ BVLP-1065 [M]	Softee Man Blues	1964	5.00	10.00	20.00
—Blue label, trident logo at right					

QUEBEC, IKE
BLUE NOTE
❏ BLP-4093 [M]	Heavy Soul	1961	20.00	40.00	80.00
—With 61st St. address on label					
❏ BLP-4093 [M]	Heavy Soul	1962	6.25	12.50	25.00
—With "New York, USA" address on label					
❏ BLP-4098 [M]	Blue and Sentimental	1962	6.25	12.50	25.00
—With "New York, USA" address on label					
❏ BLP-4098 [M]	Blue and Sentimental	1962	20.00	40.00	80.00
—With 61st St. address on label					
❏ BLP-4105 [M]	It Might As Well Be Spring	1962	7.50	15.00	30.00
❏ BLP-4114 [M]	Bossa Nova Soul Samba	1962	7.50	15.00	30.00
❏ BST-84093 [S]	Heavy Soul	1961	5.00	10.00	20.00
—With "New York, USA" address on label					
❏ BST-84093 [S]	Heavy Soul	1961	15.00	30.00	60.00
—With 61st St. address on label					
❏ BST-84098 [S]	Blue and Sentimental	1962	5.00	10.00	20.00
—With "New York, USA" address on label					
❏ BST-84098 [S]	Blue and Sentimental	1962	15.00	30.00	60.00
—With 61st St. address on label					
❏ BST-84105 [S]	It Might As Well Be Spring	1962	10.00	20.00	40.00
—With "New York, USA" address on label					
❏ BST-84114	Soul Samba	199?	6.25	12.50	25.00
—Classic Records reissue on audiophile vinyl					
❏ BST-84114 [S]	Bossa Nova Soul Samba	1962	10.00	20.00	40.00
—With "New York, USA" address on label					

MOSAIC
| ❏ M4-107 [(4)] | The Complete Blue Note Forties Recordings of Ike Quebec and John Hardee | 199? | 17.50 | 35.00 | 70.00 |
| ❏ M3-121 [(3)] | The Complete Blue Note 45 Sessions of Ike Quebec | 199? | 15.00 | 30.00 | 60.00 |

QUEEN
CAPITOL
❏ ST-12322	The Works	1984	2.50	5.00	10.00
❏ SMAS-12476	A Kind of Magic	1986	2.50	5.00	10.00
❏ C1-92357	The Miracle	1989	3.75	7.50	15.00

DCC COMPACT CLASSICS
| ❏ LPZ-2072 | A Night at the Opera | 2000 | 6.25 | 12.50 | 25.00 |
| —Audiophile vinyl | | | | | |

ELEKTRA
| ❏ 6E-101 | A Day at the Races | 1977 | 2.50 | 5.00 | 10.00 |
| —Butterfly, red, or red/black labels | | | | | |

Q

Number	Title (A Side/B Side)	Yr	VG	VG+	NM
❏ 6E-112	News of the World	1977	2.50	5.00	10.00
❏ 6E-112 [DJ]	News of the World	1977	37.50	75.00	150.00
—White label promo with oversize cover and press kit					
❏ 6E-166	Jazz	1978	2.00	4.00	8.00
—Without poster of the nude bicycle race. Some copies had a sticker on the shrink wrap with an address at which the poster was available free.					
❏ 6E-166	Jazz	1978	3.00	6.00	12.00
—With poster of the nude bicycle race					
❏ 5E-513	The Game	1980	2.50	5.00	10.00
—With dull gray cover					
❏ 5E-513	The Game	1980	3.75	7.50	15.00
—With shiny, mirrorlike cover					
❏ 5E-564	Queen's Greatest Hits	1981	3.00	6.00	12.00
❏ BB-702 [(2)]	Live Killers	1979	3.00	6.00	12.00
❏ 7E-1026	Sheer Heart Attack	1974	2.50	5.00	10.00
—Butterfly, red, or red/black labels					
❏ 7E-1026 [DJ]	Sheer Heart Attack	1974	12.50	25.00	50.00
—White label promo					
❏ 7E-1053	A Night at the Opera	1975	2.50	5.00	10.00
—Butterfly, red, or red/black labels					
❏ EQ-5064 [Q]	Queen	1973	10.00	20.00	40.00
❏ 60128	Hot Space	1982	2.50	5.00	10.00
❏ EKS-75064	Queen	1973	2.50	5.00	10.00
—With "Queen" printed on the cover; butterfly, red, or red/black labels					
❏ EKS-75064	Queen	1973	7.50	15.00	30.00
—With "Queen" gold-embossed on the cover					
❏ EKS-75064 [DJ]	Queen	1973	12.50	25.00	50.00
—White label promo					
❏ EKS-75082	Queen II	1974	2.50	5.00	10.00
—Butterfly, red, or red/black labels					
❏ EKS-75082 [DJ]	Queen II	1974	12.50	25.00	50.00
—White label promo					
HOLLYWOOD					
❏ ED-62005 [PD]	Queen at the BBC	1995	25.00	50.00	100.00
—Promo-only picture disc (no U.S. stock vinyl)					
❏ 62017	Made in Heaven	1996	5.00	10.00	20.00
—White vinyl; imported from Europe; the only distinguishing mark to make this a U.S. version is the Hollywood bar code, which was stuck to the shrink wrap					
MOBILE FIDELITY					
❏ 1-067	A Night at the Opera	1980	20.00	40.00	80.00
—Audiophile vinyl					
❏ 1-211	The Game	1995	7.50	15.00	30.00
—Audiophile vinyl					
❏ 1-256	A Day at the Races	1996	12.50	25.00	50.00
—Audiophile vinyl					

QUEEN'S NECTORINE MACHINE, THE
ABC

Number	Title (A Side/B Side)	Yr	VG	VG+	NM
❏ S-666	The Mystical Powers of Roving Tarot Gamble	1969	10.00	20.00	40.00

QUEENSRYCHE
EMI

Number	Title (A Side/B Side)	Yr	VG	VG+	NM
❏ E1-30711	Promised Land	1994	3.75	7.50	15.00
❏ E1-92806	Empire	1990	3.75	7.50	15.00
EMI AMERICA					
❏ ST-17134	The Warning	1984	2.50	5.00	10.00
❏ ST-17134 [DJ]	The Warning	1984	10.00	20.00	40.00
—Promo-only "High Quality Vinyl" pressing					
❏ ST-17197	Rage for Order	1986	2.50	5.00	10.00
—Black circle on front cover					
❏ ST-17197	Rage for Order	1986	3.75	7.50	15.00
—Blue circle on front cover					
❏ MLP-19006 [EP]	Queensryche	1983	3.00	6.00	12.00
❏ SPRO-MLP-19006 [DJ]	Queensryche	1983	10.00	20.00	40.00
—White label version in film can					
EMI MANHATTAN					
❏ SPRO-04136/7 [PD]	Operation: Mindcrime	1988	20.00	40.00	80.00
—Promo-only picture disc					
❏ SPRO-04194 [DJ]	Speak the Word	1988	7.50	15.00	30.00
—Promo-only interview album					
❏ E1-48640	Operation: Mindcrime	1988	3.00	6.00	12.00
206 RECORDS					
❏ R-101 [EP]	Queensryche	1983	25.00	50.00	100.00

QUEERS, THE
CLEARVIEW

Number	Title (A Side/B Side)	Yr	VG	VG+	NM
❏ (no # ?)	Suck This	1995	5.00	10.00	20.00
—Picture disc					
HOPELESS					
❏ HR 636	Punk Rock Confidential	1998	2.50	5.00	10.00
❏ HR 643	Beyond the Valley of the Assfuckers	2000	2.50	5.00	10.00
LOOKOUT!					
❏ LK 090	Grow Up	1995	2.50	5.00	10.00
—Reissue of rare Shakin' Street original					
❏ LK 114	Move Back Home	1995	2.50	5.00	10.00
❏ LK 140	Don't Back Down	1996	2.50	5.00	10.00
SELFLESS					
❏ SFLS-28	Rocket to Russia	1994	5.00	10.00	20.00
—Tour edition; 300 on pink vinyl					
SHAKIN' STREET					
❏ 010	Grow Up	1990	50.00	100.00	200.00
—Only 100-150 copies exist of a planned pressing of 500 (others were destroyed at the plant)					

? (QUESTION MARK) AND THE MYSTERIANS
CAMEO

Number	Title (A Side/B Side)	Yr	VG	VG+	NM
❏ C-2004 [M]	96 Tears	1966	25.00	50.00	100.00
❏ CS-2004 [P]	96 Tears	1966	20.00	40.00	80.00
—"96 Tears," "I Need Somebody," "Up Side" and "8-Teen" are rechanneled					
❏ C-2006 [M]	Action	1967	37.50	75.00	150.00
❏ CS-2006 [P]	Action	1967	25.00	50.00	100.00
—"Don't Hold It Against Me," "Like a Rose" and "Girl (You Captivate Me)" are rechanneled					

COLLECTABLES

Number	Title (A Side/B Side)	Yr	VG	VG+	NM
❏ COL 2004	Featuring 96 Tears	1997	3.00	6.00	12.00
—Re-recorded tracks; orange vinyl					
NORTON					
❏ 262 [(2)]	Do You Feel It Baby?	1998	3.75	7.50	15.00
—Live album recorded in 1997					

QUICKSILVER MESSENGER SERVICE
CAPITOL

Number	Title (A Side/B Side)	Yr	VG	VG+	NM
❏ ST-120	Happy Trails	1969	7.50	15.00	30.00
—Black label with colorband					
❏ ST-120	Happy Trails	1973	3.00	6.00	12.00
—Orange label					
❏ SKAO-391	Shady Grove	1969	6.25	12.50	25.00
—Lime green label					
❏ SKAO-391	Shady Grove	1973	3.00	6.00	12.00
—Orange label					
❏ SM-391	Shady Grove	1976	2.50	5.00	10.00
—Reissue on yellow label and new prefix					
❏ SMAS-498	Just for Love	1970	6.25	12.50	25.00
—Lime green label					
❏ SMAS-498	Just for Love	1973	3.00	6.00	12.00
—Orange label					
❏ SMAS-630	What About Me	1970	6.25	12.50	25.00
—Lime green label					
❏ SMAS-630	What About Me	1973	3.00	6.00	12.00
—Orange label					
❏ SW-819	Quicksilver	1971	6.25	12.50	25.00
—Red label with stylized "C" at top					
❏ SW-819	Quicksilver	1973	3.00	6.00	12.00
—Orange label					
❏ ST 2904	Quicksilver Messenger Service	1968	10.00	210.00	40.00
—Black label with colorband; glossy black cover with red and silver foil-like printing					
❏ ST-2904	Quicksilver Messenger Service	1969	5.00	10.00	20.00
—Lime green or red label					
❏ ST-2904	Quicksilver Messenger Service	1973	3.00	6.00	12.00
—Orange label					
❏ SMAS-11002	Comin' Thru	1972	3.75	7.50	15.00
❏ SVBB-11165 [(2)]	Anthology	1973	5.00	10.00	20.00
❏ ST-11462	Solid Silver	1975	3.75	7.50	15.00
❏ SM-11820	Solid Silver	1978	2.50	5.00	10.00
—Reissue of 11462					
❏ ST-12496	Peace By Piece	1986	2.50	5.00	10.00
❏ SN-16089	Quicksilver Messenger Service	1980	2.00	4.00	8.00
—Budget-line reissue					
❏ SN-16090	Happy Trails	1980	2.00	4.00	8.00
—Budget-line reissue					
❏ SN-16091	Quicksilver	1980	2.00	4.00	8.00
—Budget-line reissue					
❏ SN-16092	What About Me	1980	2.00	4.00	8.00
—Budget-line reissue					
❏ SN-16093	Just for Love	1980	2.00	4.00	8.00
—Budget-line reissue					
❏ SN-16094	Shady Grove	1980	2.00	4.00	8.00
—Budget-line reissue					

QUIGLEY, JACK
SAND

Number	Title (A Side/B Side)	Yr	VG	VG+	NM
❏ C-28 [M]	Jack Quigley in Hollywood	196?	7.50	15.00	30.00
—Red vinyl; may or may not exist on black vinyl					
❏ CS-28 [S]	Jack Quigley in Hollywood	196?	5.00	10.00	20.00
❏ C-30 [M]	Class In Session	196?	7.50	15.00	30.00
—Red vinyl; may or may not exist on black vinyl					
❏ CS-30 [S]	Class In Session	196?	5.00	10.00	20.00
❏ C-32 [M]	Listen! Quigley	196?	7.50	15.00	30.00
—Red vinyl; may or may not exist on black vinyl					
❏ CS-32 [S]	Listen! Quigley	196?	5.00	10.00	20.00
❏ C-38 [M]	D'Jever	196?	5.00	10.00	20.00
❏ CS-38 [S]	D'Jever	196?	6.25	12.50	25.00

QUILL
COTILLION

Number	Title (A Side/B Side)	Yr	VG	VG+	NM
❏ SD 9017	Quill	1970	5.00	10.00	20.00

QUILL, GENE
ROOST

Number	Title (A Side/B Side)	Yr	VG	VG+	NM
❏ LP-2229 [M]	Three Bones and a Quill	1958	12.50	25.00	50.00

QUINICHETTE, PAUL
DAWN

Number	Title (A Side/B Side)	Yr	VG	VG+	NM
❏ DLP-1109 [M]	The Kid from Denver	1956	25.00	50.00	100.00
EMARCY					
❏ MG-26022 [10]	The Vice 'Pres'	1954	50.00	100.00	200.00
❏ MG-26035 [10]	Sequel	1954	50.00	100.00	200.00
❏ MG-36003 [M]	Moods	1955	25.00	50.00	100.00
❏ MG-36027 [M]	The Vice 'Pres'	1955	25.00	50.00	100.00
PRESTIGE					
❏ PRLP-7103 [M]	On the Sunny Side	1957	20.00	40.00	80.00
❏ PRLP-7127 [M]	For Basie	1957	20.00	40.00	80.00
❏ PRLP-7147 [M]	Basie Reunion	1958	15.00	30.00	60.00
STATUS					
❏ ST-2036 [M]	For Basie	1966	5.00	10.00	20.00
—Reissue of Swingville 2036					
SWINGVILLE					
❏ SVLP-2036 [M]	For Basie	1962	12.50	25.00	50.00
—Purple label					
❏ SVLP-2036 [M]	For Basie	1965	6.25	12.50	25.00
—Blue label, trident logo at right					
❏ SVLP-2037 [M]	Basie Reunion	1962	12.50	25.00	50.00
—Purple label					
❏ SVLP-2037 [M]	Basie Reunion	1965	6.25	12.50	25.00
—Blue label, trident logo at right					

Number	Title (A Side/B Side)	Yr	VG	VG+	NM
UNITED ARTISTS					
❏ UAL-4024 [M]	Like Basie	1959	12.50	25.00	50.00
❏ UAL-4054 [M]	Like Who?	1959	10.00	20.00	40.00
❏ UAL-4077 [M]	Paul Quinichette	1960	10.00	20.00	40.00
❏ UAS-5024 [S]	Like Basie	1959	10.00	20.00	40.00
❏ UAS-5054 [S]	Like Who?	1959	7.50	15.00	30.00
❏ UAS-5077 [S]	Paul Quinichette	1960	12.50	25.00	50.00

QUINICHETTE, PAUL, AND FRANK FOSTER
DECCA

Number	Title (A Side/B Side)	Yr	VG	VG+	NM
❏ DL 8058 [M]	Jazz Studio 1	1954	25.00	50.00	100.00

QUINICHETTE, PAUL/GENE ROLAND
DAWN

Number	Title (A Side/B Side)	Yr	VG	VG+	NM
❏ DLP-1112 [M]	Jazzville	1957	25.00	50.00	100.00

QUINN, ANTHONY
CAPITOL

Number	Title (A Side/B Side)	Yr	VG	VG+	NM
❏ ST-116	In My Own Way... I Love You	1969	7.50	15.00	30.00

QUINN, CARMEL
COLUMBIA

Number	Title (A Side/B Side)	Yr	VG	VG+	NM
❏ CL 629 [M]	Arthur Godfrey Presents Carmel Quinn	1955	7.50	15.00	30.00

QUINTESSENCE
ISLAND

Number	Title (A Side/B Side)	Yr	VG	VG+	NM
❏ SMAS-9301	Quintessence	1971	6.25	12.50	25.00
❏ SW-9305	Dive Deep	1971	6.25	12.50	25.00

QUINTET, THE
DEBUT

Number	Title (A Side/B Side)	Yr	VG	VG+	NM
❏ DLP-2 [10]	Jazz at Massey Hall	1953	100.00	200.00	400.00
❏ DLP-4 [10]	Jazz at Massey Hall, Volume 3	1953	100.00	200.00	400.00
❏ DEB-124 [M]	Jazz at Massey Hall	1956	75.00	150.00	300.00
FANTASY					
❏ 6006 [M]	Jazz at Massey Hall	1962	12.50	25.00	50.00
—Red vinyl					
❏ 6006 [R]	Jazz at Massey Hall	1962	7.50	15.00	30.00
—Black vinyl					
❏ 86006 [M]	Jazz at Massey Hall	1962	7.50	15.00	30.00
—Blue vinyl					
❏ 86006 [R]	Jazz at Massey Hall	1962	5.00	10.00	20.00
—Black vinyl					
UNITED ARTISTS					
❏ UAS-5514	Future Tense	1971	3.75	7.50	15.00
❏ UAS-5599	The Quintet	1972	3.75	7.50	15.00

QUINTET OF THE HOT CLUB OF FRANCE, THE
CAPITOL

Number	Title (A Side/B Side)	Yr	VG	VG+	NM
❏ DT 2045 [R]	Hot Club of France	1964	5.00	10.00	20.00
❏ T 2045 [M]	Hot Club of France	1964	7.50	15.00	30.00
DIAL					
❏ LP-214 [10]	Django Reinhardt and the Hot Club Quintet	1951	75.00	150.00	300.00
❏ LP-218 [10]	Django Reinhardt and the Quintet	1951	75.00	150.00	300.00
LONDON					
❏ LB-810 [10]	Hot Club Quintet	1954	30.00	60.00	120.00
❏ LL 1344 [M]	Swing from Paris	1956	20.00	40.00	80.00

R

R.E.M.
I.R.S.

Number	Title (A Side/B Side)	Yr	VG	VG+	NM
❏ 5592	Fables of the Reconstruction	1985	3.00	6.00	12.00
❏ 5783	Lifes Rich Pageant	1986	3.00	6.00	12.00
❏ 6262	Eponymous	1988	2.50	5.00	10.00
❏ 42059	Document	1987	2.50	5.00	10.00
❏ SP-70014	Murmur	1983	3.00	6.00	12.00
—Reissue?					
❏ SP-70044	Reckoning	1984	3.00	6.00	12.00
❏ SP-70054	Dead Letter Office	1987	3.00	6.00	12.00
❏ SP-70502 [EP]	Chronic Town	1982	—	3.00	6.00
—Later pressings have a standard I.R.S. label					
❏ SP-70502 [EP]	Chronic Town	1982	3.00	6.00	12.00
—Original pressings have a custom gargoyle label					
❏ SP-70604	Murmur	1983	3.75	7.50	15.00
—Original number?					
❏ R 100701	Eponymous	1988	3.00	6.00	12.00
—BMG Direct Marketing edition					
❏ R 163503	Document	1987	3.00	6.00	12.00
—BMG Direct Marketing edition					
❏ R 173669	Lifes Rich Pageant	1986	3.50	7.00	14.00
—RCA Music Service edition					
MOBILE FIDELITY					
❏ 1-231	Murmur	1995	5.00	10.00	20.00
—Audiophile vinyl					
❏ 1-261	Reckoning	1996	20.00	40.00	80.00
—Audiophile vinyl					
WARNER BROS.					
❏ PRO-A-3377 [(2)DJ]	Should We Talk About the Weather?	1988	10.00	20.00	40.00
—Promo-only interviews and music					
❏ 25795	Green	1988	3.00	6.00	12.00
❏ W1-25795	Green	1988	3.75	7.50	15.00
—Columbia House edition					
❏ 26496	Out of Time	1991	2.50	5.00	10.00
❏ 45055	Automatic for the People	1992	2.50	5.00	10.00
❏ 45740	Monster	1994	2.50	5.00	10.00
❏ 46320 [(2)]	New Adventures in Hi-Fi	1996	3.75	7.50	15.00
❏ 47112 [(2)]	Up	1998	3.75	7.50	15.00
❏ 47946	Reveal	2001	5.00	10.00	20.00
❏ R 100715	Green	1988	3.00	6.00	12.00
—BMG Direct Marketing edition					
❏ R 124762	Out of Time	1991	4.00	8.00	16.00
—BMG Direct Marketing edition; one of the last BMG vinyl releases					

R.P.S.
MARS

Number	Title (A Side/B Side)	Yr	VG	VG+	NM
❏ (# unknown)	R.P.S.	197?	20.00	40.00	80.00

RABBLE, THE
ROULETTE

Number	Title (A Side/B Side)	Yr	VG	VG+	NM
❏ SR-42010	The Rabble	1968	37.50	75.00	150.00

RACKET SQUAD, THE
JUBILEE

Number	Title (A Side/B Side)	Yr	VG	VG+	NM
❏ JGS-8015	The Racket Squad	1968	10.00	20.00	40.00
❏ JGS-8026	Corners of Your Mind	1969	10.00	20.00	40.00

RADHA KRISHNA TEMPLE
APPLE

Number	Title (A Side/B Side)	Yr	VG	VG+	NM
❏ SKAO-3376	The Radha Krishna Temple	1971	5.00	10.00	20.00

RADIO BIRDMAN
SIRE

Number	Title (A Side/B Side)	Yr	VG	VG+	NM
❏ SRK 6050	Radio Appears	1978	10.00	20.00	40.00

RADIO CITY MUSIC HALL ORCHESTRA
RCA VICTOR

Number	Title (A Side/B Side)	Yr	VG	VG+	NM
❏ LOP-1010 [M]	Christmas Holidays at Radio City Music Hall	1958	5.00	10.00	20.00
—With gatefold and 10-page bound-in booklet with fold-open poster of the Rockettes					
❏ LSO-1010 [S]	Christmas Holidays at Radio City Music Hall	1958	10.00	20.00	40.00
—"Living Stereo" banner on cover					

RAE, CHARLOTTE
VANGUARD

Number	Title (A Side/B Side)	Yr	VG	VG+	NM
❏ VRS-9004 [M]	Songs I Taught My Mother	1956	10.00	20.00	40.00

RAE, JOHN
SAVOY

Number	Title (A Side/B Side)	Yr	VG	VG+	NM
❏ MG-12156 [M]	Opus De Jazz, Volume 2	1960	10.00	20.00	40.00

RAEBURN, BOYD
COLUMBIA

Number	Title (A Side/B Side)	Yr	VG	VG+	NM
❏ CL 889 [M]	Dance Spectacular	1956	7.50	15.00	30.00
❏ CL 957 [M]	Fraternity Rush	1957	7.50	15.00	30.00
SAVOY					
❏ MG-12025 [M]	Man With the Horns	1955	10.00	20.00	40.00
❏ MG-12040 [M]	Boyd Meets Stravinsky	1955	10.00	20.00	40.00
❏ MG-15010 [10]	Innovations by Boyd Raeburn, Volume 1	1951	20.00	40.00	80.00
❏ MG-15011 [10]	Innovations by Boyd Raeburn, Volume 2	1951	20.00	40.00	80.00
❏ MG-15012 [10]	Innovations by Boyd Raeburn, Volume 3	1951	20.00	40.00	80.00

RAFF, RENEE
AUDIO FIDELITY

Number	Title (A Side/B Side)	Yr	VG	VG+	NM
❏ AFSD-6142 [S]	Among the Stars	1965	5.00	10.00	20.00

RAFFERTY, GERRY
ABC/BLUE THUMB

Number	Title (A Side/B Side)	Yr	VG	VG+	NM
❏ 6031	Can I Have My Money Back?	1978	3.00	6.00	12.00
BLUE THUMB					
❏ BTS-58	Can I Have My Money Back?	1973	5.00	10.00	20.00
LIBERTY					
❏ LO-840	City to City	1981	2.00	4.00	8.00
—Reissue of United Artists 840					
❏ LOO-958	Night and Day	1981	2.00	4.00	8.00
—Reissue of United Artists 958					
❏ LOO-1039	Snakes and Ladders	1981	2.00	4.00	8.00
—Reissue of United Artists 1039					
❏ LT-51132	Sleepwalking	1982	2.50	5.00	10.00
MOBILE FIDELITY					
❏ 1-058	City to City	1980	10.00	20.00	40.00
—Audiophile vinyl					
POLYDOR					
❏ 835449-1	North and South	1988	2.50	5.00	10.00
UNITED ARTISTS					
❏ UA-LA840-H	City to City	1978	2.50	5.00	10.00
❏ UA-LA958-I	Night Owl	1979	2.50	5.00	10.00
❏ LOO-1039	Snakes and Ladders	1980	2.50	5.00	10.00
VISA					
❏ 7006	Gerry Rafferty	1978	2.50	5.00	10.00
—Reissue of Blue Thumb material					

RAHIM, EMANUEL K., AND THE KAHLIQA
COBBLESTONE

Number	Title (A Side/B Side)	Yr	VG	VG+	NM
❏ 9014	Total Submission	1972	6.25	12.50	25.00

RAIDERS, THE (3)
LIBERTY

Number	Title (A Side/B Side)	Yr	VG	VG+	NM
❏ LRP-3225 [M]	Twistin' the Country Classics	1962	6.25	12.50	25.00
❏ LST-7225 [S]	Twistin' the Country Classics	1962	7.50	15.00	30.00

RAIN
PROJECT 3

Number	Title (A Side/B Side)	Yr	VG	VG+	NM
❏ PR 5072 SD	New Rock Group	1972	6.25	12.50	25.00
WHAZOO					
❏ USR-3049	Live Christmas Night	1969	37.50	75.00	150.00
—Issued with no cover					

RAINBOW (2)
GNP CRESCENDO

Number	Title (A Side/B Side)	Yr	VG	VG+	NM
❏ GNPS-2049	After the Storm	1969	6.25	12.50	25.00

R

Number	Title (A Side/B Side)	Yr	VG	VG+	NM

RAINBOW PRESS, THE
MR. G
| ❑ 9003 | There's a War On | 1968 | 7.50 | 15.00 | 30.00 |
| ❑ 9004 | Sunday Funnies | 1969 | 7.50 | 15.00 | 30.00 |

RAINBOW PROMISE, THE
NEW WINE
| ❑ LPS-251-01 | The Rainbow Promise | 1970 | 75.00 | 150.00 | 300.00 |

RAINCOATS, THE
ROUGH TRADE
| ❑ ROUGH US 13 | Odyshape | 1981 | 6.25 | 12.50 | 25.00 |
SOUNDS LIKE
| ❑ 12 [EP] | The Raincoats | 1994 | 2.00 | 4.00 | 8.00 |

RAINDROPS, THE (1)
JUBILEE
| ❑ JGM-5023 [M] | The Raindrops | 1963 | 37.50 | 75.00 | 150.00 |
| ❑ JGS-5023 [S] | The Raindrops | 1963 | 75.00 | 150.00 | 300.00 |

RAINEY, CHUCK
COBBLESTONE
| ❑ 9008 | Chuck Rainey Coalition | 1972 | 5.00 | 10.00 | 20.00 |

RAINEY, MA
BIOGRAPH
❑ LP-12001	Blues the World Forgot	1968	3.75	7.50	15.00
❑ LP-12011	Oh My Babe Blues	197?	3.00	6.00	12.00
❑ LP-12032	Queen of the Blues	197?	3.00	6.00	12.00
MILESTONE
❑ 2001	Immortal Ma Rainey	1967	3.75	7.50	15.00
❑ 2008	Blame It on the Blues	196?	3.75	7.50	15.00
❑ 2017	Down in the Basement	197?	3.00	6.00	12.00
❑ 47021 [(2)]	Ma Rainey	197?	3.75	7.50	15.00
RIVERSIDE
❑ RLP 12-108 [M]	Ma Rainey	1955	50.00	100.00	200.00
❑ RLP 12-137 [M]	Broken Hearted Blues	1956	25.00	50.00	100.00
❑ RLP-1003 [10]	Ma Rainey, Vol. 1	1953	62.50	125.00	250.00
❑ RLP-1016 [10]	Ma Rainey, Vol. 2	1953	62.50	125.00	250.00
❑ RLP-1045 [10]	Ma Rainey, Vol. 3	1954	62.50	125.00	250.00

RAINWATER, MARVIN
CROWN
| ❑ CST-307 [R] | Marvin Rainwater | 196? | 3.00 | 6.00 | 12.00 |
| ❑ CLP-5307 [M] | Marvin Rainwater | 196? | 3.00 | 6.00 | 12.00 |
GUEST STAR
| ❑ GS-1435 [M] | Country and Western Star | 196? | 3.00 | 6.00 | 12.00 |
MGM
❑ E-3534 [M]	Songs by Marvin Rainwater	1957	37.50	75.00	150.00
❑ E-3721 [M]	Marvin Rainwater Sings with a Beat	1958	30.00	60.00	120.00
❑ E-4046 [M]	Gonna Find Me a Bluebird	1962	20.00	40.00	80.00
❑ SE-4046 [R]	Gonna Find Me a Bluebird	1962	12.50	25.00	50.00
SPIN-O-RAMA
| ❑ SPM-109 [M] | Golden Country Hits | 196? | 3.00 | 6.00 | 12.00 |

RAINY DAZE, THE
UNI
| ❑ 3002 [M] | That Acapulco Gold | 1967 | 5.00 | 10.00 | 20.00 |
| ❑ 73002 [S] | That Acapulco Gold | 1967 | 6.25 | 12.50 | 25.00 |

RAITT, BONNIE
CAPITOL
| ❑ C1-91268 | Nick of Time | 1989 | 3.00 | 6.00 | 12.00 |
| ❑ C1-96111 | Luck of the Draw | 1991 | 3.75 | 7.50 | 15.00 |
DCC COMPACT CLASSICS
❑ LPZ-2025	Nick of Time	1996	20.00	40.00	80.00
—Audiophile vinyl					
❑ LPZ-2031	Luck of the Draw	1997	20.00	40.00	80.00
—Audiophile vinyl					
WARNER BROS.
❑ WS 1953	Bonnie Raitt	1971	3.75	7.50	15.00
—Green "WB" label					
❑ WS 1953	Bonnie Raitt	1973	3.00	6.00	12.00
—"Burbank" palm trees label					
❑ WS 1953	Bonnie Raitt	1979	2.00	4.00	8.00
—White or tan label					
❑ BS 2643	Give It Up	1972	3.75	7.50	15.00
—Green "WB" label					
❑ BS 2643	Give It Up	1973	3.00	6.00	12.00
—"Burbank" palm trees label					
❑ BS 2643	Give It Up	1979	2.00	4.00	8.00
—White or tan label					
❑ BS 2729	Takin' My Time	1973	3.00	6.00	12.00
—"Burbank" palm trees label					
❑ BS 2729	Takin' My Time	1979	2.00	4.00	8.00
—White or tan label					
❑ BS 2818	Streetlights	1974	3.00	6.00	12.00
—"Burbank" palm trees label					
❑ BS 2818	Streetlights	1979	2.00	4.00	8.00
—White or tan label					
❑ BS 2864	Home Plate	1975	3.00	6.00	12.00
—"Burbank" palm trees label					
❑ BS 2864	Home Plate	1979	2.00	4.00	8.00
—White or tan label					
❑ BS 2990	Sweet Forgiveness	1977	3.00	6.00	12.00
—"Burbank" palm trees label					
❑ BS 2990	Sweet Forgiveness	1979	2.00	4.00	8.00
—White or tan label					
❑ HS 3369	The Glow	1979	3.00	6.00	12.00
❑ BSK 3630	Green Light	1982	3.00	6.00	12.00
❑ 25486	Nine Lives	1986	2.50	5.00	10.00

RAITT, JOHN
CAPITOL
❑ T 583 [M]	Highlights of Broadway	1955	7.50	15.00	30.00
❑ T 714 [M]	Mediterranean Magic	1956	7.50	15.00	30.00
❑ ST 1058 [S]	Under Open Skies	1958	10.00	20.00	40.00
❑ T 1058 [M]	Under Open Skies	1958	7.50	15.00	30.00

RALKE, DON
CROWN
| ❑ CLP-5019 [M] | Bongo Madness | 1957 | 6.25 | 12.50 | 25.00 |
WARNER BROS.
❑ W 1321 [M]	Bourbon Street Beat	1959	5.00	10.00	20.00
❑ WS 1321 [S]	Bourbon Street Beat	1959	6.25	12.50	25.00
❑ W 1360 [M]	But You've Never Heard Gershwin with Bongos	1960	5.00	10.00	20.00
❑ WS 1360 [S]	But You've Never Heard Gershwin with Bongos	1960	6.25	12.50	25.00
❑ W 1398 [M]	The Savage and Sensuous Bongos	1960	6.25	12.50	25.00
❑ WS 1398 [S]	The Savage and Sensuous Bongos	1960	7.50	15.00	30.00

RAM
POLYDOR
| ❑ 24-5013 | Where (In Conclusion) | 1972 | 6.25 | 12.50 | 25.00 |

RAM, BUCK
MERCURY
| ❑ MG-20392 [M] | The Magic Touch | 1960 | 7.50 | 15.00 | 30.00 |
| ❑ SR-60067 [S] | The Magic Touch | 1960 | 10.00 | 20.00 | 40.00 |

RAMBEAU, EDDIE
DYNO VOICE
| ❑ 9001 [M] | Concrete and Clay | 1965 | 5.00 | 10.00 | 20.00 |
| ❑ DS-9001 [S] | Concrete and Clay | 1965 | 6.25 | 12.50 | 25.00 |

RAMONES, THE
RADIOACTIVE
| ❑ 10615 | Mondo Bizarro | 1992 | 2.50 | 5.00 | 10.00 |
| ❑ 11273 | Adios Amigos! | 1995 | 2.50 | 5.00 | 10.00 |
SIRE
❑ PRO-A-605 [DJ]	Rock 'n' Roll High School Radio Sampler	1979	6.25	12.50	25.00
❑ PRO-A-756 [DJ]	Road to Ruin Radio Sampler	1978	6.25	12.50	25.00
❑ PRO-A-996 [DJ]	Pleasant Dreams Radio Sampler	1980	6.25	12.50	25.00
❑ SRK 3571	Pleasant Dreams	1981	3.75	7.50	15.00
❑ SR 6020	Ramones	1978	4.50	9.00	18.00
—Reissue, distributed by Warner Bros.; originals have no bar code					
❑ SR 6031	Ramones Leave Home	1978	4.50	9.00	18.00
—Third issue, distributed by Warner Bros., tracks as on second issue; originals have no bar code					
❑ SRK 6042	Rocket to Russia	1978	3.75	7.50	15.00
❑ SRK 6063	Road to Ruin	1979	3.75	7.50	15.00
❑ SRK 6077	End of the Century	1980	3.75	7.50	15.00
❑ SASD-7520	Ramones	1976	6.25	12.50	25.00
—First issue, distributed by ABC					
❑ SA-7528	Ramones Leave Home	1977	6.25	12.50	25.00
—Second issue, distributed by ABC, with "Sheena Is a Punk Rocker" replacing "Carbona Not Glue"					
❑ SA-7528	Ramones Leave Home	1977	12.50	25.00	50.00
—First issue, distributed by ABC, with "Carbona Not Glue"					
❑ 23800	Subterranean Jungle	1983	3.75	7.50	15.00
❑ 25187	Too Tough to Die	1984	3.00	6.00	12.00
❑ 25433	Animal Boy	1986	3.00	6.00	12.00
❑ 25641	Halfway to Sanity	1987	3.00	6.00	12.00
❑ 25709 [(2)]	RamonesMania	1988	3.75	7.50	15.00
❑ 25905	Brain Drain	1989	3.00	6.00	12.00

RAMSAY, OBRAY
PRESTIGE
| ❑ PRLP-13009 [M] | Obray Ramsay Sings Jimmie Rodgers Favorites | 1960 | 7.50 | 15.00 | 30.00 |
| ❑ PRLP-13020 [M] | Folk Songs from the Three Laurels | 1961 | 7.50 | 15.00 | 30.00 |
RIVERSIDE
| ❑ RLP-12-649 [M] | Banjo Songs of the Blue Ridge and Great Smokies | 196? | 7.50 | 15.00 | 30.00 |

RANDALL, TONY
IMPERIAL
| ❑ LP-9090 [M] | Tony Randall | 1958 | 7.50 | 15.00 | 30.00 |
MERCURY
❑ MG-21108 [M]	Vo, Vo, De Oh, Doe	1967	5.00	10.00	20.00
❑ MG-21128 [M]	Warm and Wavery	1967	5.00	10.00	20.00
❑ SR-61108 [S]	Vo, Vo, De Oh, Doe	1967	6.25	12.50	25.00
❑ SR-61128 [S]	Warm and Wavery	1967	6.25	12.50	25.00

RANDALL, TONY, AND JACK KLUGMAN
LONDON
| ❑ XPS 903 | The Odd Couple Sings | 1973 | 12.50 | 25.00 | 50.00 |

RANDAZZO, TEDDY
ABC-PARAMOUNT
❑ 352 [M]	Journey to Love	1961	7.50	15.00	30.00
❑ S-352 [S]	Journey to Love	1961	10.00	20.00	40.00
❑ 421 [M]	Teddy Randazzo Twists	1962	7.50	15.00	30.00
❑ S-421 [S]	Teddy Randazzo Twists	1962	10.00	20.00	40.00
COLPIX
| ❑ CP-445 [M] | Big Wide World | 1963 | 7.50 | 15.00 | 30.00 |
| ❑ SCP-445 [S] | Big Wide World | 1963 | 10.00 | 20.00 | 40.00 |
VIK
| ❑ LX-1121 [M] | I'm Confessin' | 1958 | 50.00 | 100.00 | 200.00 |

RANDI, DON
CAPITOL
| ❑ ST-287 | Love Theme from Romeo and Juliet | 1969 | 5.00 | 10.00 | 20.00 |
PALOMAR
| ❑ 34002 [S] | Don Randi! | 1965 | 5.00 | 10.00 | 20.00 |

Number	Title (A Side/B Side)	Yr	VG	VG+	NM
REPRISE					
❏ R-6229 [M]	Revolver Jazz	1966	5.00	10.00	20.00
—Also see THE MUSIC COMPANY.					
❏ RS-6229 [S]	Revolver Jazz	1966	6.25	12.50	25.00
WORLD PACIFIC					
❏ ST-1297 [S]	Feelin' Like Blues	1960	6.25	12.50	25.00
❏ WP-1297 [M]	Feelin' Like Blues	1960	7.50	15.00	30.00
RANDOLPH, BOOTS					
MONUMENT					
❏ DS 632	King of Yakety	197?	3.75	7.50	15.00
—Manufactured by CBS Direct Marketing Services					
❏ 6600	Boots Randolph's Yakety Sax	197?	2.50	5.00	10.00
—Reissue of 18002					
❏ 6601	Hip Boots	197?	2.50	5.00	10.00
—Reissue of 18015					
❏ 6602	Boots Randolph Plays More Yakety Sax	197?	2.50	5.00	10.00
—Reissue of 18037					
❏ 6603	The Fantastic Boots Randolph	197?	2.50	5.00	10.00
—Reissue of 18042					
❏ 6604	Boots with Strings	197?	2.50	5.00	10.00
—Reissue of 18066					
❏ MC 6605	Sax-Sational	1976	2.50	5.00	10.00
—Reissue of 18079					
❏ 6606	Boots Randolph with the Knightsbridge Strings & Voices	197?	2.50	5.00	10.00
—Reissue of 18082					
❏ 6607	Sunday Sax	197?	2.50	5.00	10.00
—Reissue of 18092					
❏ 6608	The Sound of Boots	197?	2.50	5.00	10.00
—Reissue of 18099					
❏ 6609	...With Love/The Seductive Sax of Boots Randolph	197?	2.50	5.00	10.00
—Reissue of 18111					
❏ 6610	Boots and Stockings	197?	2.50	5.00	10.00
—Reissue of 18127					
❏ 6611	Yakety Revisited	197?	2.50	5.00	10.00
—Reissue of 18128					
❏ 6612	Hit Boots 1970	197?	2.50	5.00	10.00
—Reissue of 18144					
❏ 6613	Boots with Brass	197?	2.50	5.00	10.00
—Reissue of 18147					
❏ 6614	Homer Louis Randolph, III	197?	2.50	5.00	10.00
—Reissue of 30678					
❏ 6615	Boots Randolph Plays the Great Hits of Today	197?	2.50	5.00	10.00
—Reissue of 31908					
❏ 6616	Sentimental Journey	197?	2.50	5.00	10.00
—Reissue of 32292					
❏ 6617	Country Boots	197?	2.50	5.00	10.00
—Reissue of 32912					
❏ 6618	Cool Boots	197?	2.50	5.00	10.00
—Reissue of 33803					
❏ 7602	Greatest Hits	1977	2.50	5.00	10.00
❏ 7611	Sax Appeal	1977	2.50	5.00	10.00
❏ 7627	Put a Little Sax	1978	2.50	5.00	10.00
❏ MLP-8002 [M]	Boots Randolph's Yakety Sax	1963	5.00	10.00	20.00
❏ MLP-8015 [M]	Hip Boots	1964	3.75	7.50	15.00
❏ MLP-8029 [M]	12 Monstrous Sax Hits	1965	3.75	7.50	15.00
❏ MLP-8037 [M]	Boots Randolph Plays More Yakety Sax	1965	3.75	7.50	15.00
❏ MLP-8042 [M]	The Fantastic Boots Randolph	1966	3.75	7.50	15.00
❏ MLP-8066 [M]	Boots with Strings	1966	3.75	7.50	15.00
❏ MLP-8079 [M]	Sax-Sational	1967	5.00	10.00	20.00
❏ MLP-8082 [M]	Boots Randolph with the Knightsbridge Strings & Voices	1967	5.00	10.00	20.00
❏ 8604 [(2)]	Party Boots	197?	3.00	6.00	12.00
—Reissue of 34082					
❏ SLP-18002 [S]	Boots Randolph's Yakety Sax	1963	6.25	12.50	25.00
❏ SLP-18015 [S]	Hip Boots	1964	5.00	10.00	20.00
❏ SLP-18029 [S]	12 Monstrous Sax Hits	1965	5.00	10.00	20.00
❏ SLP-18037 [S]	Boots Randolph Plays More Yakety Sax	1965	5.00	10.00	20.00
❏ SLP-18042 [S]	The Fantastic Boots Randolph	1966	5.00	10.00	20.00
❏ SLP-18066 [S]	Boots with Strings	1966	5.00	10.00	20.00
❏ SLP-18079 [S]	Sax-Sational	1967	3.75	7.50	15.00
❏ SLP-18082 [S]	Boots Randolph with the Knightsbridge Strings & Voices	1967	3.75	7.50	15.00
❏ SLP-18092	Sunday Sax	1968	5.00	10.00	20.00
❏ SLP-18099	The Sound of Boots	1968	5.00	10.00	20.00
❏ SLP-18111	...With Love/The Seductive Sax of Boots Randolph	1969	3.75	7.50	15.00
❏ SLP 18127	Boots and Stockings	1969	3.75	7.50	15.00
❏ SLP-18128	Yakety Revisited	1969	3.75	7.50	15.00
❏ SLP-18144	Hit Boots 1970	1970	3.75	7.50	15.00
❏ SLP-18147	Boots with Brass	1970	3.75	7.50	15.00
❏ Z 30678	Homer Louis Randolph, III	1971	3.00	6.00	12.00
❏ Z2 30964 [(2)]	The World of Boots Randolph	1971	3.75	7.50	15.00
❏ KZ 31908	Boots Randolph Plays the Great Hits of Today	1972	3.00	6.00	12.00
❏ KZ 32292	Sentimental Journey	1973	3.00	6.00	12.00
❏ KZ 32912	Country Boots	1974	3.00	6.00	12.00
❏ KZ 33298	Boots Randolph's Yakety Sax	1974	3.00	6.00	12.00
❏ KZ 33803	Cool Boots	1975	3.00	6.00	12.00
❏ Z2 34082 [(2)]	Party Boots	1976	3.75	7.50	15.00
❏ PW 38388	Greatest Hits	1983	2.50	5.00	10.00
❏ JW 38396	Dedication	1983	2.50	5.00	10.00
RCA CAMDEN					
❏ CAL-825 [M]	Yakin' Sax Man	1964	3.75	7.50	15.00
❏ CAS-825 [S]	Yakin' Sax Man	1964	3.75	7.50	15.00
❏ CAL-865 [M]	Sweet Talk	1965	3.75	7.50	15.00
❏ CAS-865 [R]	Sweet Talk	1965	3.00	6.00	12.00
❏ ACL-9003 [(2)]	Yakety Sax	1972	3.00	6.00	12.00
RCA VICTOR					
❏ LPM-2165 [M]	Yakety Sax	1960	10.00	20.00	40.00
❏ LSP-2165 [S]	Yakety Sax	1960	12.50	25.00	50.00

Number	Title (A Side/B Side)	Yr	VG	VG+	NM
RANELIN, PHIL					
TRIBE					
❏ PRSD-2226	Message from the Tribe	197?	25.00	50.00	100.00
❏ TRCD 4006	The Time Is Now!	1974	20.00	40.00	80.00
RANEY, JIMMY					
ABC-PARAMOUNT					
❏ ABC-129 [M]	Jimmy Raney Featuring Bob Brookmeyer	1956	12.50	25.00	50.00
❏ ABC-167 [M]	Jimmy Raney in Three Attitudes	1957	10.00	20.00	40.00
DAWN					
❏ DLP-1120 [M]	Jimmy Raney Visits Paris	1958	10.00	20.00	40.00
NEW JAZZ					
❏ NJLP-1101 [10]	Jimmy Raney Quartet Featuring Hall Overton	1953	75.00	150.00	300.00
❏ NJLP-1103 [10]	Jimmy Raney Ensemble Introducing Phil Woods	1953	75.00	150.00	300.00
PRESTIGE					
❏ PRLP-156 [10]	Jimmy Raney Plays	1953	37.50	75.00	150.00
❏ PRLP-179 [10]	Jimmy Raney in Sweden	1954	37.50	75.00	150.00
❏ PRLP-199 [10]	Jimmy Raney Quintet	1954	37.50	75.00	150.00
❏ PRLP-201 [10]	Jimmy Raney Quartet	1955	37.50	75.00	150.00
❏ PRLP-203 [10]	Jimmy Raney Ensemble	1955	37.50	75.00	150.00
❏ PRLP-7089 [M]	Jimmy Raney/A	1957	20.00	40.00	80.00
RANEY, JIMMY/GEORGE WALLINGTON					
EMARCY					
❏ MG-36121 [M]	Swingin' in Sweden	1958	15.00	30.00	60.00
RANEY, SUE					
CAPITOL					
❏ ST 1335 [S]	Songs for a Raney Day	1960	6.25	12.50	25.00
❏ T 1335 [M]	Songs for a Raney Day	1960	5.00	10.00	20.00
❏ ST 2032 [S]	All By Myself	1964	5.00	10.00	20.00
IMPERIAL					
❏ LP-9355 [M]	New and Now	1967	6.25	12.50	25.00
❏ LP-9376 [M]	With a Little Help from My Friends	1968	7.50	15.00	30.00
❏ LP-12323 [S]	Alive and In Love	1966	5.00	10.00	20.00
RANEY, WAYNE					
KING					
❏ 588 [M]	Songs from the Hills	1958	25.00	50.00	100.00
NASHVILLE					
❏ NLP-2002	Radio Gospel and Sacred Favorites	196?	3.75	7.50	15.00
STARDAY					
❏ SLP-124 [M]	Wayne Raney and the Raney Family	1960	10.00	20.00	40.00
❏ SLP-279 [M]	Don't Try to Be What You Ain't	1964	10.00	20.00	40.00
RANGER, ANDY					
DOT					
❏ DLP-3028 [M]	The Song That Never Ends	1956	15.00	30.00	60.00
RARE BIRD					
ABC					
❏ X-715	As Your Mind Flies	1972	3.75	7.50	15.00
POLYDOR					
❏ PD 5530	Epic Forest	1973	3.75	7.50	15.00
❏ PD 6502	Somebody's Watching	1974	3.75	7.50	15.00
❏ PD 6506	Born Again	1974	3.75	7.50	15.00
PROBE					
❏ 4514	Rare Bird	1970	6.25	12.50	25.00
RARE EARTH					
MOTOWN					
❏ M5-116V1	Motown Superstar Series, Vol. 16	1981	2.50	5.00	10.00
❏ M5-202V1	Ecology	1981	2.00	4.00	8.00
❏ 5229 ML	Get Ready	1982	2.00	4.00	8.00
PRODIGAL					
❏ P6-10019	Rare Earth	1977	2.50	5.00	10.00
❏ P7-10025	Band Together	1978	2.50	5.00	10.00
❏ P7-10027	Grand Slam	1979	2.50	5.00	10.00
RARE EARTH					
❏ RS 507	Get Ready	1969	7.50	15.00	30.00
—Original cover has a rounded top					
❏ RS 507	Get Ready	1970	3.00	6.00	12.00
—Regular square cover					
❏ RS 510	Generation	1970	—	—	—
—Canceled					
❏ RS 514	Ecology	1970	3.75	7.50	15.00
❏ RS 520	One World	1971	3.75	7.50	15.00
❏ R 534 [(2)]	Rare Earth in Concert	1971	3.75	7.50	15.00
❏ R 543	Willie Remembers	1972	3.00	6.00	12.00
❏ R6-546	Ma	1973	3.00	6.00	12.00
❏ R6-548	Back to Earth	1975	3.00	6.00	12.00
❏ R7-550	Midnight Lady	1976	3.00	6.00	12.00
VERVE					
❏ V6-5066	Dreams/Answers	1968	12.50	25.00	50.00
RASCALS, THE					
ATLANTIC					
❏ ST-137 [DJ]	Freedom Suite Sampler	1969	12.50	25.00	50.00
❏ SD 2-901 [(2)]	Freedom Suite	1969	5.00	10.00	20.00
❏ 8123 [M]	The Young Rascals	1966	7.50	15.00	30.00
❏ SD 8123 [S]	The Young Rascals	1966	10.00	20.00	40.00
—Green and blue label					
❏ SD 8123 [S]	The Young Rascals	1966	12.50	25.00	50.00
—Purple and green label					
❏ SD 8123 [S]	The Young Rascals	1969	3.00	6.00	12.00
—Red and green label					
❏ 8134 [M]	Collections	1967	6.25	12.50	25.00
❏ SD 8134 [S]	Collections	1967	7.50	15.00	30.00
—Green and blue label					

R

Number	Title (A Side/B Side)	Yr	VG	VG+	NM
❏ SD 8134 [S]	Collections	1969	3.00	6.00	12.00
—Red and green label					
❏ 8148 [M]	Groovin'	1967	6.25	12.50	25.00
❏ SD 8148 [S]	Groovin'	1967	7.50	15.00	30.00
—Green and blue label					
❏ SD 8148 [S]	Groovin'	1969	3.00	6.00	12.00
—Red and green label					
❏ 8169 [M]	Once Upon a Dream	1968	10.00	20.00	40.00
❏ SD 8169 [S]	Once Upon a Dream	1968	6.25	12.50	25.00
—Green and blue label					
❏ SD 8169 [S]	Once Upon a Dream	1969	3.00	6.00	12.00
—Red and green label					
❏ 8190 [M]	Time Peace/The Rascals' Greatest Hits	1968	12.50	25.00	50.00
—Mono is promo only					
❏ SD 8190 [S]	Time Peace/The Rascals' Greatest Hits	1968	3.75	7.50	15.00
—Purple and gold label					
❏ SD 8190 [S]	Time Peace/The Rascals' Greatest Hits	1968	6.25	12.50	25.00
—Green and blue label					
❏ SD 8190 [S]	Time Peace/The Rascals' Greatest Hits	1969	3.00	6.00	12.00
—Red and green label					
❏ 8246 [M]	See	1969	12.50	25.00	50.00
—Mono is promo only; cover has "dj copy monaural" sticker on front					
❏ SD 8246 [S]	See	1969	3.75	7.50	15.00
❏ 8276 [M]	Search and Nearness	1970	12.50	25.00	50.00
—Mono is promo only; cover has "dj copy monaural" sticker on front					
❏ SD 8276 [S]	Search and Nearness	1970	3.75	7.50	15.00
COLUMBIA					
❏ G 30462 [(2)]	Peaceful World	1971	3.75	7.50	15.00
❏ KC 31103	The Island of Real	1972	3.00	6.00	12.00
PAIR					
❏ PDL2-1106 [(2)]	Rock and Roll Treasures	1986	3.75	7.50	15.00
RHINO					
❏ RNLP 70237	The Young Rascals	1988	2.50	5.00	10.00
❏ RNLP 70238	Collections	1988	2.50	5.00	10.00
❏ RNLP 70239	Groovin'	1988	2.50	5.00	10.00
❏ R1-70240	Once Upon a Dream	1988	2.50	5.00	10.00
❏ R1-70241	Freedom Suite	1988	2.50	5.00	10.00
❏ R1-70242	Searching for Ecstasy: The Rest of the Rascals 1969-1972	1988	2.50	5.00	10.00
SUNDAZED					
❏ LP 5116	The Young Rascals	2002	3.00	6.00	12.00
❏ LP 5117	Collections	2002	3.00	6.00	12.00
❏ LP 5118	Groovin'	2002	3.00	6.00	12.00
❏ LP 5119	Once Upon a Dream	2002	3.00	6.00	12.00
WARNER SPECIAL PRODUCTS					
❏ SP-2502 [(2)]	24 Greatest Hits	1971	5.00	10.00	20.00
WES FARRELL					
❏ PFT-1002 [DJ]	Songs from the Rascals	197?	6.25	12.50	25.00
—Promo-only publisher's demo					

RASPBERRIES

Number	Title (A Side/B Side)	Yr	VG	VG+	NM
CAPITOL					
❏ SK-11036	Raspberries	1972	7.50	15.00	30.00
—Originals have red labels and a "scratch 'n' sniff" cover, the smell of which fades over time					
❏ ST-11036	Raspberries	1973	5.00	10.00	20.00
—Orange label, "Capitol" at bottom					
❏ ST-11123	Fresh	1972	5.00	10.00	20.00
❏ SMAS-11220	Side 3	1973	5.00	10.00	20.00
—With cover cut in the shape of a basket of raspberries					
❏ ST-11329	Starting Over	1974	5.00	10.00	20.00
❏ ST-11524	Raspberries' Best Featuring Eric Carmen	1976	3.75	7.50	15.00
❏ SN-16095	Raspberries' Best Featuring Eric Carmen	1979	2.50	5.00	10.00

RATHBONE, BASIL

Number	Title (A Side/B Side)	Yr	VG	VG+	NM
CAEDMON					
❏ TC 1028 [M]	Basil Rathbone Reads Edgar Allan Poe	195?	6.25	12.50	25.00
❏ TC 1044 [M]	The Happy Prince and Other Oscar Wilde Fairy Tales	195?	6.25	12.50	25.00
❏ TC 1115 [M]	Basil Rathbone Reads Edgar Allan Poe, Vol. 2	195?	6.25	12.50	25.00
❏ TC 1120 [M]	Stories of Hawthorne	195?	6.25	12.50	25.00
❏ TC 1172 [M]	Stories of Sherlock Holmes, Vol. 1	1963	6.25	12.50	25.00
❏ TC 1195 [M]	Basil Rathbone Reads Edgar Allan Poe, Vol. 3	196?	6.25	12.50	25.00
❏ TC 1197 [M]	Stories of Hawthorne, Vol. 2	196?	6.25	12.50	25.00
❏ TC 1208 [M]	Stories of Sherlock Holmes, Vol. 2	1966	6.25	12.50	25.00
❏ TC 1220 [M]	Stories of Sherlock Holmes, Vol. 3	1967	6.25	12.50	25.00
❏ TC 1240 [M]	Stories of Sherlock Holmes, Vol. 4	1967	6.25	12.50	25.00
CO-STAR					
❏ C-107 [M]	The Brothers Karamazov	196?	5.00	10.00	20.00
❏ CS-107 [S]	The Brothers Karamazov	196?	6.25	12.50	25.00
COLUMBIA MASTERWORKS					
❏ ML 4038 [10]	Peter and the Wolf; Treasure Island	1949	12.50	25.00	50.00
❏ ML 4081 [10]	A Christmas Carol	1950	12.50	25.00	50.00
DECCA					
❏ DL 9109 [M]	Selections from The Jungle Book	1962	7.50	15.00	30.00

RATIONALS, THE

Number	Title (A Side/B Side)	Yr	VG	VG+	NM
CREWE					
❏ CR-1334	The Rationals	1969	10.00	20.00	40.00

RATTLES, THE

Number	Title (A Side/B Side)	Yr	VG	VG+	NM
MERCURY					
❏ MG 21127 [M]	The Rattles' Greatest Hits	1967	20.00	40.00	80.00
❏ SR 61127 [R]	The Rattles' Greatest Hits	1967	12.50	25.00	50.00

RAVEN

Two different groups?

Number	Title (A Side/B Side)	Yr	VG	VG+	NM
COLUMBIA					
❏ CS 9903	Raven	1969	5.00	10.00	20.00
DISCOVERY					
❏ 36133	Live at the Inferno	1967	20.00	40.00	80.00

RAVEN, EDDY

Number	Title (A Side/B Side)	Yr	VG	VG+	NM
ABC DOT					
❏ DOSD-2031	This Is Eddy Raven	1975	3.75	7.50	15.00
DIMENSION					
❏ DLP-5001	Eyes	1980	3.75	7.50	15.00
ELEKTRA					
❏ 5E-545	Desperate Dreams	1981	3.00	6.00	12.00
LA LOUISIANNE					
❏ 127	That Cajun Country Sound	197?	5.00	10.00	20.00
MCA					
❏ 910	Thank God for Kids	198?	2.00	4.00	8.00
RCA					
❏ 5728-1-R	Right Hand Man	1987	2.00	4.00	8.00
❏ 6815-1-R	The Best of Eddy Raven	1988	2.00	4.00	8.00
RCA VICTOR					
❏ AHL1-5040	I Could Use Another You	1984	2.00	4.00	8.00
❏ AHL1-5456	Love and Other Hard Times	1985	2.00	4.00	8.00
UNIVERSAL					
❏ UVL-76003	Temporary Sanity	1989	2.50	5.00	10.00
WARNER BROS.					
❏ 5E-545	Desperate Dreams	1983	2.00	4.00	8.00
—Reissue of Elektra 5E-545					

RAVENS, THE

Number	Title (A Side/B Side)	Yr	VG	VG+	NM
HARLEM HIT PARADE					
❏ 1007	The Ravens	1975	2.50	5.00	10.00
REGENT					
❏ MG-6062 [M]	Write Me a Letter	195?	37.50	75.00	150.00
—Red label					
❏ MG-6062 [M]	Write Me a Letter	1957	75.00	150.00	300.00
—Green label					
SAVOY JAZZ					
❏ SJL-2227 [(2)]	The Greatest Group of Them All	1978	3.00	6.00	12.00

RAVENSCROFT, THURL

Number	Title (A Side/B Side)	Yr	VG	VG+	NM
DOT					
❏ DLP-3430 [M]	Great Hits	1962	7.50	15.00	30.00
❏ DLP-25430 [S]	Great Hits	1962	10.00	20.00	40.00

RAW

Number	Title (A Side/B Side)	Yr	VG	VG+	NM
CORAL					
❏ CRL 757515	Raw Holly	1971	7.50	15.00	30.00

RAW SPITT

Number	Title (A Side/B Side)	Yr	VG	VG+	NM
UNITED ARTISTS					
❏ UAS-6795	Maybe You Ain't Black	1971	6.25	12.50	25.00

RAWLS, LOU

Number	Title (A Side/B Side)	Yr	VG	VG+	NM
ALLEGIANCE					
❏ AV-5016	Trying As Hard As I Can	198?	2.50	5.00	10.00
BELL					
❏ 1318	She's Gone	1974	3.00	6.00	12.00
BLUE NOTE					
❏ B1-91441	Stormy Monday	1990	3.00	6.00	12.00
—Reissue of Capitol 1714					
❏ B1-91937	At Last	1989	3.00	6.00	12.00
❏ B1-93841	It's Supposed to Be Fun	1990	3.75	7.50	15.00
CAPITOL					
❏ ST-122	The Way It Was	1969	3.75	7.50	15.00
❏ ST 8-0215	The Way It Was — The Way It Is	1969	5.00	10.00	20.00
—Capitol Record Club edition					
❏ ST-215	The Way It Was — The Way It Is	1969	3.75	7.50	15.00
❏ SWBB-261 [(2)]	Close-Up	1969	5.00	10.00	20.00
—Reissue of 1824 and 2042 in one package					
❏ ST-325	Your Good Thing	1969	3.75	7.50	15.00
❏ ST-427	You've Made Me So Very Happy	1970	3.75	7.50	15.00
❏ ST-479	Bring It on Home	1970	3.75	7.50	15.00
❏ STBB-720 [(2)]	Down Here on the Ground/I'd Rather Drink Muddy Water	1971	5.00	10.00	20.00
❏ SM-1714	Stormy Monday	197?	2.50	5.00	10.00
—Reissue with new prefix					
❏ ST 1714 [S]	Stormy Monday	1962	6.25	12.50	25.00
❏ T 1714 [M]	Stormy Monday	1962	5.00	10.00	20.00
❏ ST 1824 [S]	Black and Blue	1963	6.25	12.50	25.00
❏ T 1824 [M]	Black and Blue	1963	5.00	10.00	20.00
❏ ST 2042 [S]	Tobacco Road	1964	6.25	12.50	25.00
❏ T 2042 [M]	Tobacco Road	1964	5.00	10.00	20.00
❏ ST 2273 [S]	Nobody But Lou	1965	6.25	12.50	25.00
❏ T 2273 [M]	Nobody But Lou	1965	5.00	10.00	20.00
❏ ST 2401 [S]	Lou Rawls and Strings	1965	6.25	12.50	25.00
❏ T 2401 [M]	Lou Rawls and Strings	1965	5.00	10.00	20.00
❏ SM-2459	Lou Rawls Live!	197?	2.50	5.00	10.00
—Reissue with new prefix					
❏ ST 2459 [S]	Lou Rawls Live!	1966	5.00	10.00	20.00
❏ T 2459 [M]	Lou Rawls Live!	1966	3.75	7.50	15.00
❏ SM-2566	Lou Rawls Soulin'	197?	2.50	5.00	10.00
—Reissue with new prefix					
❏ ST 2566 [S]	Lou Rawls Soulin'	1966	5.00	10.00	20.00
❏ T 2566 [M]	Lou Rawls Soulin'	1966	3.75	7.50	15.00
❏ ST 2632 [S]	Lou Rawls Carryin' On!	1966	5.00	10.00	20.00
❏ T 2632 [M]	Lou Rawls Carryin' On!	1966	3.75	7.50	15.00
❏ ST 2713 [S]	Too Much!	1967	3.75	7.50	15.00
❏ T 2713 [M]	Too Much!	1967	5.00	10.00	20.00
❏ ST 2756 [S]	That's Lou	1967	3.75	7.50	15.00
❏ T 2756 [M]	That's Lou	1967	5.00	10.00	20.00
❏ ST 2790 [S]	Merry Christmas, Ho, Ho, Ho	1967	3.00	6.00	12.00
❏ T 2790 [M]	Merry Christmas, Ho, Ho, Ho	1967	3.75	7.50	15.00
❏ ST 2864 [S]	Feelin' Good	1968	3.75	7.50	15.00
❏ T 2864 [M]	Feelin' Good	1968	7.50	15.00	30.00
❏ ST 2927	You're Good for Me	1968	3.75	7.50	15.00

Number	Title (A Side/B Side)	Yr	VG	VG+	NM
❑ SKAO 2948	The Best of Lou Rawls	1968	3.75	7.50	15.00
❑ SM-2948	The Best of Lou Rawls	197?	2.50	5.00	10.00
—Reissue with new prefix					
❑ SKBB-11585 [(2)]	The Best of Lou Rawls	1976	3.00	6.00	12.00
❑ SN-16096	The Best of Lou Rawls	1980	2.00	4.00	8.00
—Budget-line reissue					
❑ SN-16097	Lou Rawls Live!	1980	2.00	4.00	8.00
—Budget-line reissue					
EPIC					
❑ FE 37448	Now Is the Time	1982	2.50	5.00	10.00
❑ FE 38553	When the Night Comes.	1983	2.50	5.00	10.00
❑ FE 39403	Close Company.	1984	2.50	5.00	10.00
❑ FE 40210	Love All Your Blues Away.	1986	2.50	5.00	10.00
MGM					
❑ SE-4771	Natural Man	1971	3.00	6.00	12.00
❑ SE-4809	Silk & Soul	1972	3.00	6.00	12.00
❑ SE-4861	A Man of Value	1973	3.00	6.00	12.00
❑ SE-4965	Live at the Century Plaza	1974	3.00	6.00	12.00
PHILADELPHIA INT'L.					
❑ PZ 33957	All Things in Time	1976	2.50	5.00	10.00
—No bar code on cover					
❑ PZ 33957	All Things in Time	198?	2.00	4.00	8.00
—With bar code on cover					
❑ PZ 34488	Unmistakably Lou	1977	2.50	5.00	10.00
❑ PZ 34488	Unmistakably Lou	1986	2.00	4.00	8.00
—Budget-line reissue					
❑ JZ 35036	When You Hear Lou, You've Heard It All	1977	2.50	5.00	10.00
❑ PZ2 35517 [(2)]	Lou Rawls Live	1978	3.00	6.00	12.00
❑ JZ 36006	Let Me Be Good to You	1979	2.50	5.00	10.00
❑ PZ 36006	Let Me Be Good to You	198?	2.00	4.00	8.00
—Budget-line reissue					
❑ JZ 36304	Sit Down and Talk to Me	1979	2.50	5.00	10.00
❑ PZ 36304	Sit Down and Talk to Me	198?	2.00	4.00	8.00
—Budget-line reissue					
❑ JZ 36774	Shades of Blue	1980	2.50	5.00	10.00
❑ FZ 39285	Classics	1984	2.50	5.00	10.00
PICKWICK					
❑ SPC-3156	Come On In, Mr. Blues	1971	2.50	5.00	10.00
❑ SPC-3228	Gee Baby	1972	2.50	5.00	10.00
POLYDOR					
❑ PD-1-6086	Naturally	1976	2.50	5.00	10.00
RAY, DAVE					
ELEKTRA					
❑ EKL-284 [M]	Snaker's Here	1965	5.00	10.00	20.00
❑ EKL-319 [M]	Fine Soft Land	1966	5.00	10.00	20.00
❑ EKS-7284 [S]	Snaker's Here	1965	6.25	12.50	25.00
❑ EKS-7319 [S]	Fine Soft Land	1966	6.25	12.50	25.00
RAY, DIANE					
MERCURY					
❑ MG-20903 [M]	The Exciting Years	1964	20.00	40.00	80.00
❑ SR-60903 [S]	The Exciting Years	1964	25.00	50.00	100.00
RAY, JAMES					
CAPRICE					
❑ LP-1002 [M]	James Ray	1962	20.00	40.00	80.00
❑ SLP-1002 [S]	James Ray	1962	30.00	60.00	120.00
RAY, JOHNNIE					
COLUMBIA					
❑ CL 961 [M]	The Big Beat	1957	12.50	25.00	50.00
❑ CL 1093 [M]	At the Desert Inn in Las Vegas	1957	12.50	25.00	50.00
❑ CL 1225 [M]	'Til Morning	1958	10.00	20.00	40.00
—Red and black label with six "eye" logos					
❑ CL 1225 [M]	'Til Morning	1963	5.00	10.00	20.00
—Red label with either "Guraranteed High Fidelity" or "360 Sound Mono" at bottom					
❑ CL 1227 [M]	Johnnie Ray's Greatest Hits	1958	10.00	20.00	40.00
—Red and black label with 6 "eye" logos					
❑ CL 1227 [M]	Johnnie Ray's Greatest Hits	1962	6.25	12.50	25.00
—"Guaranteed High Fidelity" on label					
❑ CL 1227 [M]	Johnnie Ray's Greatest Hits	1965	3.75	7.50	15.00
—"360 Sound" label					
❑ CL 1385 [M]	On the Trail	1959	10.00	20.00	40.00
❑ CL 2510 [10]	I Cry for You	1955	17.50	35.00	70.00
—"House Party Series" issue					
❑ CL 6199 [10]	Johnnie Ray	1951	20.00	40.00	80.00
❑ CS 8180 [S]	On the Trail	1959	12.50	25.00	50.00
COLUMBIA SPECIAL PRODUCTS					
❑ P 13086	Greatest Hits	197?	2.50	5.00	10.00
EPIC					
❑ LN 1120 [10]	Johnnie Ray	1955	20.00	40.00	80.00
HARMONY					
❑ H 30609	The Best of Johnnie Ray	1971	3.00	6.00	12.00
LIBERTY					
❑ LRP-3221 [M]	Johnnie Ray	1962	5.00	10.00	20.00
❑ LST-7221 [S]	Johnnie Ray	1962	7.50	15.00	30.00
SUNSET					
❑ SUM-1125 [M]	Mr. Cry	196?	3.00	6.00	12.00
❑ SUS-5125 [S]	Mr. Cry	196?	3.00	6.00	12.00
RAY, WADE					
ABC-PARAMOUNT					
❑ ABC-539 [M]	A Ray of Country Sun	1966	3.75	7.50	15.00
❑ ABCS-539 [S]	A Ray of Country Sun	1966	5.00	10.00	20.00
RCA CAMDEN					
❑ CAS-2107	Walk Softly	1969	3.75	7.50	15.00
RAYBURN, MARGIE					
LIBERTY					
❑ LRP-3126 [M]	Margie	1959	6.25	12.50	25.00
❑ LST-7126 [S]	Margie	1959	10.00	20.00	40.00

Number	Title (A Side/B Side)	Yr	VG	VG+	NM
RAYE, JERRY					
DEVILLE					
❑ LP-101 [M]	The Many Sides of Jerry Raye and Fenwyck	1967	150.00	300.00	600.00
RAYE, MARTHA					
EPIC					
❑ LG 3061 [M]	Here's Martha Raye	1954	10.00	20.00	40.00
RAYMOND, LEW					
TOPS					
❑ L-1583 [M]	For Men Only	1958	10.00	20.00	40.00
—Jayne Mansfield is the cover model					
❑ L-1647 [M]	Million Sellers	1960	7.50	15.00	30.00
—Mary Tyler Moore is the cover model					
RCA VICTOR SYMPHONY ORCHESTRA					
(ROBERT RUSSELL BENNETT, CONDUCTOR)					
RCA VICTOR RED SEAL					
❑ LSC-2238 [S]	It's Classic But It's Good	1959	5.00	10.00	20.00
—Original with "shaded dog" label					
RCA VICTOR SYMPHONY ORCHESTRA					
(KIRIL KONDRASHIN, CONDUCTOR)					
RCA VICTOR RED SEAL					
❑ LSC-2323 [S]	Tchaikovsky: Capriccio Italien; Rimsky-Korsakov: Capriccio Espagnole	1959	10.00	20.00	40.00
—Original with "shaded dog" label					
❑ LSC-2323 [S]	Tchaikovsky: Capriccio Italien; Rimsky-Korsakov: Capriccio Espagnole	199?	6.25	12.50	25.00
—Classic Records reissue					
❑ LSC-2398 [S]	Khachaturian: Masquerade Suite; Kabalevsky: The Comedians	1960	30.00	60.00	120.00
—Original with "shaded dog" label					
❑ LSC-2398 [S]	Khachaturian: Masquerade Suite; Kabalevsky: The Comedians	1964	25.00	50.00	100.00
—Second edition with "white dog" label					
❑ LSC-2398 [S]	Khachaturian: Masquerade Suite; Kabalevsky: The Comedians	1969	6.25	12.50	25.00
—Third edition with no dog on label					
❑ LSC-2398 [S]	Khachaturian: Masquerade Suite; Kabalevsky: The Comedians	199?	6.25	12.50	25.00
—Classic Records reissue					
RCA VICTOR SYMPHONY ORCHESTRA					
(LEOPOLD STOKOWSKI, CONDUCTOR)					
RCA VICTOR RED SEAL					
❑ LSC-2471 [S]	Rhapsodies	196?	10.00	20.00	40.00
—Original with "shaded dog" label or second edition with "white dog" label					
❑ LSC-2471 [S]	Rhapsodies	199?	6.25	12.50	25.00
—Classic Records reissue					
❑ LSC-2612 [S]	Handel: Royal Fireworks Music; Water Music	1962	6.25	12.50	25.00
—Original with "shaded dog" label					
❑ LSC-2612 [S]	Handel: Royal Fireworks Music; Water Music	1964	5.00	10.00	20.00
—Second edition with "white dog" label					
REAGAN, RONALD					
DECCA					
❑ DL 4943 [M]	Freedom's Finest Hour	1967	6.25	12.50	25.00
❑ DL 74943 [S]	Freedom's Finest Hour	1967	7.50	15.00	30.00
KEY					
❑ 690 [M]	Rendezvous with Destiny	1964	6.25	12.50	25.00
"X"					
❑ LVA-3051 [M]	Tales from the Great Book	1956	10.00	20.00	40.00
REALLY RED					
C.I.A.					
❑ 006	Teaching You the Fear	1981	20.00	40.00	80.00
REBECCA AND THE SUNNY BROOK FARMERS					
MUSICOR					
❑ MS-3176	Rebecca and the Sunny Brook Farmers	1969	10.00	20.00	40.00
REBIRTH					
AVANT GARDE					
❑ AVS-135	Rebirth	1971	12.50	25.00	50.00
REBS, THE					
FREDLO					
❑ 6830	1968 A.D. Break Through	1968	100.00	200.00	400.00
RED, SONNY					
BLUE NOTE					
❑ BLP-4032 [M]	Out of the Blue	1960	20.00	40.00	80.00
—Regular version, W. 63rd St. address on label					
❑ BLP-4032 [M]	Out of the Blue	1960	25.00	50.00	100.00
—"Deep groove" version (deep indentation under label on both sides)					
❑ BLP-4032 [M]	Out of the Blue	1963	6.25	12.50	25.00
—With "New York, USA" address on label					
❑ ST-84032 [S]	Out of the Blue	1960	15.00	30.00	60.00
—With W. 63rd St. address on label					
❑ ST-84032 [S]	Out of the Blue	1963	5.00	10.00	20.00
—With "New York, USA" address on label					
JAZZLAND					
❑ JLP-32 [M]	Breezin'	1960	7.50	15.00	30.00
❑ JLP-59 [M]	The Mode	1961	7.50	15.00	30.00
❑ JLP-74 [M]	Images	1962	7.50	15.00	30.00
❑ JLP-932 [M]	Breezin'	1960	10.00	20.00	40.00
❑ JLP-959 [S]	The Mode	1961	10.00	20.00	40.00
❑ JLP-974 [S]	Images	1962	10.00	20.00	40.00
RED CRAYOLA, THE					
INTERNATIONAL ARTISTS					
❑ 2	Parable of the Arable Land	1979	3.75	7.50	15.00
—Reissue with "Masterfonics" in trail-off wax					

R

Number	Title (A Side/B Side)	Yr	VG	VG+	NM
❑ 2 [M]	Parable of the Arable Land	1968	25.00	50.00	100.00
❑ 2 [S]	Parable of the Arable Land	1968	15.00	30.00	60.00
❑ 7	God Bless the Red Crayola	1968	15.00	30.00	60.00
❑ 7	God Bless the Red Crayola	1979	3.75	7.50	15.00
—Reissue with "Masterfonics" in trail-off wax					

RED HOT CHILI PEPPERS
EMI

Number	Title (A Side/B Side)	Yr	VG	VG+	NM
❑ E1-29665	Out in L.A.	1994	2.50	5.00	10.00
❑ E1-92152	Mother's Milk	1989	3.00	6.00	12.00

EMI AMERICA

❑ ST-17128	Red Hot Chili Peppers	1984	2.50	5.00	10.00
❑ ST-17168	Freaky Styley	1985	2.50	5.00	10.00
❑ E1-48036	The Uplift Mofo Party Plan	1987	2.50	5.00	10.00

EMI MANHATTAN

❑ E1-90869 [EP]	The Abbey Road E.P.	1988	2.00	4.00	8.00

WARNER BROS.

❑ PRO-A-5170 [(2)DJ]	Blood Sugar Sex Magik	1991	10.00	20.00	40.00
—"Radio-ready" version of LP, this is the only U.S. vinyl release of this album					
❑ 47386 [(2)]	Californication	1999	5.00	10.00	20.00
❑ 48140 [(2)]	By the Way	2002	6.25	12.50	25.00

RED ONION JAZZ BAND, THE
RIVERSIDE

❑ RLP 12-260 [M]	Dance Off Both Your Shoes In Hi-Fi	1958	10.00	20.00	40.00

RED RIVER DAVE
CONTINENTAL

❑ 1507 [M]	Red River Dave Sings	1962	6.25	12.50	25.00

VARSITY

❑ 6962 [10]	Red River Dave	1951	17.50	35.00	70.00

REDBONE
EPIC

❑ EGP 501 [(2)]	Redbone	1970	5.00	10.00	20.00
❑ E 30109	Potlatch	1970	3.75	7.50	15.00
❑ EQ 30815 [Q]	Message from a Drum	1973	5.00	10.00	20.00
❑ KE 30815	Message from a Drum	1972	3.75	7.50	15.00
❑ KE 31598	Already Here	1972	3.75	7.50	15.00
❑ KE 32462	Wovoka	1974	3.75	7.50	15.00
❑ EQ 33053 [Q]	Bearded Dreams Through Turquoise Eyes	1974	5.00	10.00	20.00
❑ KE 33053	Bearded Dreams Through Turquoise Eyes	1974	3.75	7.50	15.00
❑ KEG 33456 [(2)]	Come & Get Your Redbone	1975	5.00	10.00	20.00

RCA VICTOR

❑ AFL1-2352	Cycles	1977	3.00	6.00	12.00

REDBONE, LEON
AUGUST

❑ AS 8890	Christmas Island	1988	3.75	7.50	15.00

WARNER BROS.

❑ BS 2888	On the Track	1975	6.25	12.50	25.00
❑ BS 2971	Double Time	1977	6.25	12.50	25.00
❑ BS 3165	Champagne Charlie	1978	6.25	12.50	25.00

REDD, FREDDIE
BLUE NOTE

❑ BLP-4027 [M]	Music From "The Connection"	1960	25.00	50.00	100.00
—Regular version, W. 63rd St. address on label					
❑ BLP-4027 [M]	Music From "The Connection"	1960	30.00	60.00	120.00
—"Deep groove" version (deep indentation under label on both sides)					
❑ BLP-4027 [M]	Music From "The Connection"	1963	6.25	12.50	25.00
—With "New York, USA" address on label					
❑ BLP-4045 [M]	Shades of Redd	1960	25.00	50.00	100.00
—Regular version, W. 63rd St. address on label					
❑ BLP-4045 [M]	Shades of Redd	1960	30.00	60.00	120.00
—"Deep groove" version (deep indentation under label on both sides)					
❑ BLP-4045 [M]	Shades of Redd	1963	6.25	12.50	25.00
—With "New York, USA" address on label					
❑ BST-84027 [S]	Music From "The Connection"	1960	25.00	50.00	100.00
—With W. 63rd St. address on label					
❑ BST-84027 [S]	Music From "The Connection"	1967	3.75	7.50	15.00
—With "A Division of Liberty Records" on label					

MOSAIC

❑ M3-124 [(3)]	The Complete Blue Note Recordings of Freddie Redd	199?	10.00	20.00	30.00

PRESTIGE

❑ PRLP-197 [10]	Introducing the Freddie Redd Trio	1954	37.50	75.00	150.00

RIVERSIDE

❑ RLP 12-250 [M]	San Francisco Suite For Jazz Trio	1957	15.00	30.00	60.00

REDD, FREDDIE, AND HAMPTON HAWES
PRESTIGE

❑ PRLP-7067 [M]	Piano: East/West	1956	20.00	40.00	80.00

STATUS

❑ ST-8307 [M]	Movin'	1965	10.00	20.00	40.00

REDD, VI
ATCO

❑ 33-157 [M]	Lady Soul	1963	7.50	15.00	30.00
❑ SD 33-157 [S]	Lady Soul	1963	10.00	20.00	40.00

UNITED ARTISTS

❑ UAJ-14016 [M]	Bird Call	1962	10.00	20.00	40.00
❑ UAJS-15016 [S]	Bird Call	1962	12.50	25.00	50.00

REDDING, OTIS
ATCO

❑ 33-161 [M]	Pain in My Heart	1964	62.50	125.00	250.00
❑ SD 33-161 [R]	Pain in My Heart	1968	62.50	125.00	250.00
❑ 33-252 [M]	The Immortal Otis Redding	1968	12.50	25.00	50.00
—Mono is white label promo only					
❑ SD 33-252 [S]	The Immortal Otis Redding	1968	3.75	7.50	15.00

Number	Title (A Side/B Side)	Yr	VG	VG+	NM
❑ SD 33-261	History of Otis Redding	1968	3.75	7.50	15.00
—Reissue of Volt 418					
❑ SD 33-265	Otis Redding In Person at the Whiskey-A-Go-Go	1968	3.75	7.50	15.00
❑ SD 33-284	Otis Blue/Otis Redding Sings Soul	1969	3.75	7.50	15.00
—Reissue of Volt 412					
❑ SD 33-285	The Soul Album	1969	3.75	7.50	15.00
—Reissue of Volt 413					
❑ SD 33-286	Otis Redding Live in Europe	1969	3.75	7.50	15.00
—Reissue of Volt 416					
❑ SD 33-287	Complete & Unbelievable...The Otis Redding Dictionary of Soul	1969	3.75	7.50	15.00
—Reissue of Volt 415					
❑ SD 33-288	The Dock of the Bay	1969	3.75	7.50	15.00
—Reissue of Volt 419					
❑ SD 33-289	Love Man	1969	3.75	7.50	15.00
❑ SD 33-333	Tell the Truth	1970	3.75	7.50	15.00
❑ SD 2-801 [(2)]	The Best of Otis Redding	1972	5.00	10.00	20.00

ATLANTIC

❑ SD 19346	Recorded Live	198?	2.50	5.00	10.00
❑ 81282	The Best of Otis Redding	1985	2.50	5.00	10.00
❑ 81762 [(4)]	The Otis Redding Story	1987	7.50	15.00	30.00

PAIR

❑ PDL2-1062 [(2)]	The Legend of Otis Redding	1984	3.75	7.50	15.00

SUNDAZED

❑ LP 5063 [M]	Complete & Unbelievable ... The Otis Redding Dictionary of Soul	2001	3.00	6.00	12.00
—Reissue on 180-gram vinyl					
❑ LP 5064 [M]	Otis Blue/Otis Redding Sings Soul	2001	3.00	6.00	12.00
—Reissue on 180-gram vinyl					

VOLT

❑ 411 [M]	The Great Otis Redding Sings Soul Ballads	1965	22.50	45.00	90.00
❑ S-411 [R]	The Great Otis Redding Sings Soul Ballads	1968	27.50	55.00	110.00
❑ 412 [M]	Otis Blue/Otis Redding Sings Soul	1965	10.00	20.00	40.00
❑ S-412 [S]	Otis Blue/Otis Redding Sings Soul	1965	12.50	25.00	50.00
❑ 413 [M]	The Soul Album	1966	10.00	20.00	40.00
❑ S-413 [S]	The Soul Album	1966	12.50	25.00	50.00
❑ 415 [M]	Complete & Unbelievable...The Otis Redding Dictionary of Soul	1966	10.00	20.00	40.00
❑ S-415 [S]	Complete & Unbelievable...The Otis Redding Dictionary of Soul	1966	12.50	25.00	50.00
❑ 416 [M]	Otis Redding Live in Europe	1967	7.50	15.00	30.00
❑ S-416 [S]	Otis Redding Live in Europe	1967	10.00	20.00	40.00
❑ 418 [M]	History of Otis Redding	1967	10.00	20.00	40.00
❑ S-418 [S]	History of Otis Redding	1967	7.50	15.00	30.00
❑ S-419	The Dock of the Bay	1968	7.50	15.00	30.00

REDMAN, DON
GOLDEN CREST

❑ GC-3017 [M]	Park Avenue Patter	1958	10.00	20.00	40.00

RCA VICTOR

❑ LPV-520 [M]	Master of the Big Band	1965	5.00	10.00	20.00

ROULETTE

❑ R-25070 [M]	Dixieland in High Society	1960	5.00	10.00	20.00
❑ SR-25070 [S]	Dixieland in High Society	1960	6.25	12.50	25.00

REDMAN, GEORGE
SKYLARK

❑ SKLP-20 [10]	The George Redman Group	1954	37.50	75.00	150.00

REDMOND, EDGAR
DISQUE-PHENOMENON

❑ 2696 [10]	Edgar Redmond & the Modern String Ensemble	1965	7.50	15.00	30.00

REDNOW, EIVETS
See STEVIE WONDER.

REDPATH, JEAN
ELEKTRA

❑ EKL-214 [M]	Scottish Ballad Book	1962	6.25	12.50	25.00
❑ EKL-224 [M]	Songs of Love, Lilt and Laughter	1963	6.25	12.50	25.00
❑ EKL-274 [M]	Laddie Lie Near Me	1964	5.00	10.00	20.00
❑ EKS-7274 [S]	Laddie Lie Near Me	1964	6.25	12.50	25.00

PRESTIGE

❑ PR-13041 [M]	Skipping Barefoot Through the Heather	1962	7.50	15.00	30.00

REECE, DIZZY
BLUE NOTE

❑ BLP-4006 [M]	Blues in Trinity	1958	25.00	50.00	100.00
—Regular version, W. 63rd St. address on label					
❑ BLP-4006 [M]	Blues in Trinity	1958	37.50	75.00	150.00
—"Deep groove" version (deep indentation under label on both sides)					
❑ BLP-4006 [M]	Blues in Trinity	1963	6.25	12.50	25.00
—With "New York, USA" address on label					
❑ BST-4006 [S]	Blues in Trinity	1959	15.00	30.00	60.00
—Regular version, W. 63rd St. address on label					
❑ BST-4006 [S]	Blues in Trinity	1959	25.00	50.00	100.00
—"Deep groove" version (deep indentation under label on both sides)					
❑ BST-4006 [S]	Blues in Trinity	1963	5.00	10.00	20.00
—With "New York, USA" address on label					
❑ BLP-4023 [M]	Star Bright	1959	20.00	40.00	80.00
—Regular version, W. 63rd St. address on label					
❑ BLP-4023 [M]	Star Bright	1959	30.00	60.00	120.00
—"Deep groove" version (deep indentation under label on both sides)					
❑ BLP-4023 [M]	Star Bright	1963	6.25	12.50	25.00
—With "New York, USA" address on label					
❑ BLP-4033 [M]	Soundin' Off	1960	20.00	40.00	80.00
—Regular version, W. 63rd St. address on label					
❑ BLP-4033 [M]	Soundin' Off	1960	30.00	60.00	120.00
—"Deep groove" version (deep indentation under label on both sides)					
❑ BLP-4033 [M]	Soundin' Off	1963	6.25	12.50	25.00
—With "New York, USA" address on label					

Number	Title (A Side/B Side)	Yr	VG	VG+	NM
❏ BST-84023 [S]	Star Bright	1959	15.00	30.00	60.00
—With W. 63rd St. address on label					
❏ BST-84023 [S]	Star Bright	1963	5.00	10.00	20.00
—With "New York, USA" address on label					
❏ BST-84033 [S]	Soundin' Off	1960	15.00	30.00	60.00
—With W. 63rd St. address on label					
❏ BST-84033 [S]	Soundin' Off	1963	5.00	10.00	20.00
—With "New York, USA" address on label					
IMPERIAL					
❏ LP-9043 [M]	London Jazz	1957	20.00	40.00	80.00
NEW JAZZ					
❏ NJLP-8274 [M]	Asia Minor	1962	12.50	25.00	50.00
—Purple label					
❏ NJLP-8274 [M]	Asia Minor	1965	6.25	12.50	25.00
—Blue label, trident logo at right					

REECE, DIZZY, AND TUBBY HAYES
SAVOY

Number	Title (A Side/B Side)	Yr	VG	VG+	NM
❏ MG-12111 [M]	Changing the Jazz at Buckingham Palace	1957	25.00	50.00	100.00

REED, JERRY
CAPITOL

Number	Title (A Side/B Side)	Yr	VG	VG+	NM
❏ ST-12492	Lookin' at You	1986	2.00	4.00	8.00
HARMONY					
❏ H 30547	I'm Movin' On	1971	2.50	5.00	10.00
RCA CAMDEN					
❏ ACL1-0331	Tupelo Mississippi Flash	1973	2.50	5.00	10.00
❏ CAS-2585	Oh What a Woman!	1972	2.50	5.00	10.00
RCA VICTOR					
❏ APD1-0238 [Q]	Lord, Mr. Ford	1973	6.25	12.50	25.00
❏ APL1-0238	Lord, Mr. Ford	1973	3.00	6.00	12.00
❏ APL1-0356	The Uptown Poker Club	1973	3.00	6.00	12.00
❏ APL1-0544	A Good Woman's Love	1974	3.00	6.00	12.00
❏ APL1-0787	Mind Your Love	1974	3.00	6.00	12.00
❏ APL1-1226	Red Hot Picker	1975	3.00	6.00	12.00
❏ ANL1-1345	When You're Hot, You're Hot	1975	2.50	5.00	10.00
—Reissue of 4506					
❏ APL1-1861	Both Barrels	1976	3.00	6.00	12.00
❏ ANL1-2167	Me and Chet	1976	2.50	5.00	10.00
—Reissue of 4707					
❏ AHL1-2346	Jerry Reed Rides Again	1977	3.00	6.00	12.00
❏ AHL1-2516	East Bound and Down	1977	3.00	6.00	12.00
❏ AHL1-2764	Sweet Love Feelings	1978	3.00	6.00	12.00
❏ AHL1-3359	Half Singin' & Half Pickin'	1979	3.00	6.00	12.00
❏ AHL1-3453	Jerry Reed Live!	1979	3.00	6.00	12.00
❏ AHL1-3604	Jerry Reed Sings Jim Croce	1980	3.00	6.00	12.00
❏ AYL1-3677	East Bound and Down	1980	2.00	4.00	8.00
—"Best Buy Series" reissue					
❏ LPM-3756 [M]	The Unbelievable Guitar and Voice of Jerry Reed	1967	6.25	12.50	25.00
❏ LSP-3756 [S]	The Unbelievable Guitar and Voice of Jerry Reed	1967	5.00	10.00	20.00
❏ AHL1-3771	Texas Bound and Flyin'	1980	3.00	6.00	12.00
❏ LPM-3978 [M]	Nashville Underground	1968	12.50	25.00	50.00
❏ LSP-3978 [S]	Nashville Underground	1968	5.00	10.00	20.00
❏ AHL1-4021	Dixie Dreams	1981	3.00	6.00	12.00
❏ LSP-4069	Alabama Wild Man	1968	5.00	10.00	20.00
❏ LSP-4147	Better Things in Life	1969	5.00	10.00	20.00
❏ AYL1-4167	Jerry Reed Live!	1982	2.00	4.00	8.00
—"Best Buy Series" reissue					
❏ LSP-4204	Jerry Reed Explores Guitar Country	1969	5.00	10.00	20.00
❏ LSP-4293	Cookin'	1970	5.00	10.00	20.00
❏ AHL1-4315	The Man with the Golden Thumb	1982	2.50	5.00	10.00
❏ LSP-4391	Georgia Sunshine	1970	5.00	10.00	20.00
❏ AYL1-4394	Texas Bound and Flyin'	1982	2.00	4.00	8.00
—"Best Buy Series" reissue					
❏ LSP-4506	When You're Hot, You're Hot	1971	3.75	7.50	15.00
❏ AHL1-4529	The Bird	1982	2.50	5.00	10.00
❏ LSP-4596	Ko-Ko Joe	1971	3.75	7.50	15.00
❏ LSP-4660	Smell the Flowers	1972	3.75	7.50	15.00
❏ AHL1-4692	Ready	1983	2.50	5.00	10.00
❏ LSP-4707	Me and Chet	1972	3.75	7.50	15.00
—With Chet Atkins					
❏ LSP-4729	The Best of Jerry Reed	1972	3.75	7.50	15.00
❏ LSP-4750	Jerry Reed	1972	3.75	7.50	15.00
❏ LSP-4838	Hot A' Mighty!	1973	3.75	7.50	15.00
❏ AYL1-5151	The Bird	1984	2.00	4.00	8.00
—"Best Buy Series" reissue					
❏ AHL1-5176	Greatest Hits	1984	2.50	5.00	10.00
❏ AHL1-5472	Collector's Series	1985	2.50	5.00	10.00

REED, JIMMY
ANTILLES

Number	Title (A Side/B Side)	Yr	VG	VG+	NM
❏ 7007	Cold Chills	197?	3.75	7.50	15.00
ARCHIVE OF FOLK AND JAZZ					
❏ 234	Jimmy Reed	197?	3.00	6.00	12.00
BLUESVILLE					
❏ BLS-6054	I Ain't From Chicago	1973	3.75	7.50	15.00
❏ BLS-6067	The Ultimate Jimmy Reed	1973	3.75	7.50	15.00
❏ BLS-6073 [(2)]	Jimmy Reed at Carnegie Hall	1973	5.00	10.00	20.00
BLUESWAY					
❏ BL-6004 [M]	The New Jimmy Reed Album	1967	5.00	10.00	20.00
❏ BLS-6004 [S]	The New Jimmy Reed Album	1967	5.00	10.00	20.00
❏ BL-6009 [M]	Soulin'	1967	5.00	10.00	20.00
❏ BLS-6009 [S]	Soulin'	1967	5.00	10.00	20.00
❏ BLS-6015	Big Boss Man	1968	5.00	10.00	20.00
❏ BLS-6024	Down in Virginia	1969	5.00	10.00	20.00
BUDDAH					
❏ BDS-4003	The Very Best of Jimmy Reed	1969	3.75	7.50	15.00
—Reissue of Vee Jay 1039					

Number	Title (A Side/B Side)	Yr	VG	VG+	NM
CHAMELEON					
❏ D1-74762	Bright Lights, Big City	1988	2.50	5.00	10.00
GNP CRESCENDO					
❏ GNPS-10006 [(2)]	The Best of Jimmy Reed	1974	3.75	7.50	15.00
SUNSET					
❏ SUS-5218	Somethin' Else	1968	3.00	6.00	12.00
TRADITION					
❏ 2069	Wailin' the Blues	1969	3.00	6.00	12.00
TRIP					
❏ 8012 [(2)]	History of Jimmy Reed	1971	3.75	7.50	15.00
VEE JAY					
❏ LP-1004 [M]	I'm Jimmy Reed	1958	55.00	110.00	220.00
—Maroon label					
❏ LP-1004 [M]	I'm Jimmy Reed	1961	20.00	40.00	80.00
—Black label with colorband					
❏ VJLP-1004	I'm Jimmy Reed	198?	2.50	5.00	10.00
—Reissue with glossy labels					
❏ LP-1008 [M]	Rockin' with Reed	1959	50.00	100.00	200.00
—Maroon label					
❏ LP-1008 [M]	Rockin' with Reed	1961	20.00	40.00	80.00
—Black label with colorband					
❏ VJLP-1008	Rockin' with Reed	198?	2.50	5.00	10.00
—Reissue with glossy labels					
❏ LP-1022 [M]	Found Love	1959	50.00	100.00	200.00
—Maroon label					
❏ LP-1022 [M]	Found Love	1961	20.00	40.00	80.00
—Black label with colorband					
❏ LP-1025 [M]	Now Appearing	1960	20.00	40.00	80.00
❏ VJLP-1025	Now Appearing	198?	2.50	5.00	10.00
—Reissue with glossy labels					
❏ 2LP-1035 [(2)M]	Jimmy Reed at Carnegie Hall	1961	12.50	25.00	50.00
❏ 2SR-1035 [(2)S]	Jimmy Reed at Carnegie Hall	1961	17.50	35.00	70.00
❏ VJLP2-1035 [(2)]	Jimmy Reed at Carnegie Hall	198?	3.00	6.00	12.00
—Reissue with glossy labels					
❏ LP-1039 [M]	The Best of Jimmy Reed	1962	10.00	20.00	40.00
❏ SR-1039 [S]	The Best of Jimmy Reed	1962	15.00	30.00	60.00
❏ VJLP-1039	The Best of Jimmy Reed	198?	2.50	5.00	10.00
—Reissue with glossy labels					
❏ LP-1050 [M]	Just Jimmy Reed	1962	10.00	20.00	40.00
❏ SR-1050 [S]	Just Jimmy Reed	1962	15.00	30.00	60.00
❏ LP-1067 [M]	T'Ain't No Big Thing…But He Is Jimmy Reed	1963	10.00	20.00	40.00
❏ SR-1067 [S]	T'Ain't No Big Thing…But He Is Jimmy Reed	1963	15.00	30.00	60.00
❏ LP-1072 [M]	The Best of the Blues	1963	10.00	20.00	40.00
❏ LP-1073 [M]	The 12 String Guitar Blues	1963	10.00	20.00	40.00
❏ SR-1073 [S]	The 12 String Guitar Blues	1963	37.50	75.00	150.00
❏ LP-1080 [M]	More of the Best of Jimmy Reed	1964	10.00	20.00	40.00
❏ SR-1080 [S]	More of the Best of Jimmy Reed	1964	37.50	75.00	150.00
❏ LP-1095 [M]	Jimmy Reed at Soul City	1964	10.00	20.00	40.00
❏ VJLP-1095	Jimmy Reed at Soul City	198?	2.50	5.00	10.00
—Reissue with glossy labels					
❏ VJS-7303	Blues Is My Business	198?	2.50	5.00	10.00
❏ LP-8501 [M]	The Legend, The Man	1965	10.00	20.00	40.00
❏ VJLP-8501	The Legend, The Man	198?	2.50	5.00	10.00
—Reissue with glossy labels					
❏ VJS-8501 [S]	The Legend, The Man	1965	37.50	75.00	150.00

REED, LOU
Also see THE VELVET UNDERGROUND.
ARISTA

Number	Title (A Side/B Side)	Yr	VG	VG+	NM
❏ AL 4100	Rock and Roll Heart	1976	3.75	7.50	15.00
—Originals on light blue labels					
❏ AL 4169	Street Hassle	1978	3.75	7.50	15.00
❏ AL 4229	The Bells	1979	3.00	6.00	12.00
❏ ALB6-8390	City Lights — Classic Performances by Lou Reed	1985	2.50	5.00	10.00
❏ AL11 8434 [(2)]	Rock and Roll Diary 1967-1980	198?	4.00	8.00	16.00
—Reissue					
❏ AL 8502 [(2)]	Live! Take No Prisoners	1978	4.50	9.00	18.00
❏ A2L 8603 [(2)]	Rock and Roll Diary 1967-1980	1980	4.50	9.00	18.00
❏ AL 9522	Growing Up in Public	1980	3.00	6.00	12.00
❏ R 252506 [(2)]	Rock and Roll Diary 1967-1980	1980	4.50	9.00	18.00
—RCA Music Service edition					
DIRECT DISK					
❏ (no #) [DJ]	The Blue Mask	1982	37.50	75.00	150.00
—Only exists on test pressings; no stock copies made					
RCA VICTOR					
❏ APL1-0207	Berlin	1973	3.00	6.00	12.00
❏ AFL1-0472	Rock & Roll Animal	1977	2.00	4.00	8.00
—Reissue					
❏ APL1-0472	Rock & Roll Animal	1974	3.00	6.00	12.00
❏ AFL1-0611	Sally Can't Dance	1977	2.00	4.00	8.00
—Reissue					
❏ CPL1-0611	Sally Can't Dance	1974	5.00	10.00	20.00
❏ APL1-0915	Coney Island Baby	1976	4.00	8.00	16.00
❏ AFL1-0959	Lou Reed Live	1977	2.00	4.00	8.00
—Reissue					
❏ APL1-0959	Lou Reed Live	1975	3.75	7.50	15.00
❏ APD2-1101 [(2)Q]	Metal Machine Music	1975	37.50	75.00	150.00
❏ CPL2-1101 [(2)]	Metal Machine Music	1975	12.50	25.00	50.00
—Orange or brown label					
❏ AFL1-2001	Walk on the Wild Side	1978	2.00	4.00	8.00
—Reissue					
❏ APL1-2001	Walk on the Wild Side	1977	3.00	6.00	12.00
❏ ANL1-2480	Coney Island Baby	1977	2.00	4.00	8.00
—Reissue					
❏ AYL1-3664	Rock & Roll Animal	1980	2.00	4.00	8.00
—Best Buy Series reissue					
❏ AYL1-3752	Lou Reed Live	1980	2.00	4.00	8.00
—Best Buy Series reissue					
❏ AYL1-3753	Walk on the Wild Side	1980	2.00	4.00	8.00
—Best Buy Series reissue					

R

Number	Title (A Side/B Side)	Yr	VG	VG+	NM
❏ AYL1-3806	Transformer	1980	2.00	4.00	8.00
—Best Buy Series reissue					
❏ AYL1-3807	Coney Island Baby	1980	2.00	4.00	8.00
—Best Buy Series reissue					
❏ AFL1-4221	The Blue Mask	1982	2.50	5.00	10.00
❏ DJL1-4266 [DJ]	Special Radio Series, Vol. XVII	1980	6.25	12.50	25.00
—Promo-only with insert					
❏ DJL1-4267	The Blue Mask Interview Album	1982	10.00	20.00	40.00
❏ DJL1-4345 [DJ]	The Blue Mask Sampler	1982	3.00	6.00	12.00
—Three-song EP released to radio					
❏ AYL1-4388	Berlin	1983	2.00	4.00	8.00
—Best Buy Series reissue					
❏ AYL1-4555	Sally Can't Dance	1983	2.00	4.00	8.00
—Best Buy Series reissue					
❏ AFL1-4568	Legendary Hearts	1983	2.50	5.00	10.00
❏ LSP-4701	Lou Reed	1972	5.00	10.00	20.00
❏ AYL1-4780	The Blue Mask	1984	2.00	4.00	8.00
—Best Buy Series reissue					
❏ AFL1-4807	Transformer	1977	2.00	4.00	8.00
—Reissue					
❏ LSP-4807	Transformer	1972	5.00	10.00	20.00
❏ AFL1-4998	New Sensations	1984	2.00	4.00	8.00
❏ AFL1-7190	Mistrial	1986	3.00	6.00	12.00
SIRE					
❏ 25829	New York	1989	2.50	5.00	10.00
❏ R 101058	New York	1989	3.00	6.00	12.00
—BMG Music Service edition					

REED, LUCY
FANTASY

Number	Title (A Side/B Side)	Yr	VG	VG+	NM
❏ 3212 [M]	The Singing Reed	195?	20.00	40.00	80.00
—Black vinyl					
❏ 3212 [M]	The Singing Reed	1956	37.50	75.00	150.00
—Red vinyl					
❏ 3243 [M]	This Is Lucy Reed	195?	20.00	40.00	80.00
—Black vinyl					
❏ 3243 [M]	This Is Lucy Reed	1957	37.50	75.00	150.00
—Red vinyl					

REED, LULA
KING

Number	Title (A Side/B Side)	Yr	VG	VG+	NM
❏ 604 [M]	Blue and Moody	1958	500.00	1000.	2000.

REESE, DELLA
ABC

Number	Title (A Side/B Side)	Yr	VG	VG+	NM
❏ 569 [M]	Della Reese Live	1966	3.75	7.50	15.00
❏ S-569 [S]	Della Reese Live	1966	5.00	10.00	20.00
❏ 589 [M]	One More Time	1967	5.00	10.00	20.00
❏ S-589 [S]	One More Time	1967	3.75	7.50	15.00
❏ 612 [M]	Della on Strings of Blue	1967	5.00	10.00	20.00
❏ S-612 [S]	Della on Strings of Blue	1967	3.75	7.50	15.00
❏ S-636	I Gotta Be Me…This Trip Out	1968	3.75	7.50	15.00
❏ AC-30002	The ABC Collection	1976	3.75	7.50	15.00
ABC-PARAMOUNT					
❏ ABC-524 [M]	C'mon and Hear Della Reese	1965	3.75	7.50	15.00
❏ ABCS-524 [S]	C'mon and Hear Della Reese	1965	5.00	10.00	20.00
❏ ABC-540 [M]	I Like It Like Dat!	1966	3.75	7.50	15.00
❏ ABCS-540 [S]	I Like It Like Dat!	1966	5.00	10.00	20.00
AVCO EMBASSY					
❏ 33004	Black Is Beautiful	1969	3.75	7.50	15.00
❏ 33017	Right Now	1970	3.75	7.50	15.00
JAZZ A LA CARTE					
❏ 3	One of a Kind	1978	3.75	7.50	15.00
JUBILEE					
❏ JLP-1026 [M]	Melancholy Baby	1957	7.50	15.00	30.00
❏ JGM-1071 [M]	A Date with Della Reese at Mr. Kelly's in Chicago	196?	5.00	10.00	20.00
—Black label with all-silver print					
❏ JGM-1071 [M]	A Date with Della Reese at Mr. Kelly's in Chicago	1963	3.75	7.50	15.00
—Black label, multi-colored spokes around "jubilee"					
❏ JGS-1071 [S]	A Date with Della Reese at Mr. Kelly's in Chicago	1965	3.75	7.50	15.00
—Black label, multi-colored spokes around "jubilee," yellow spoke goes nowhere near center hole; new prefix					
❏ JLP-1071 [M]	A Date with Della Reese at Mr. Kelly's in Chicago	1959	6.25	12.50	25.00
—Originals have blue labels					
❏ SDJLP-1071 [S]	A Date with Della Reese at Mr. Kelly's in Chicago	1959	6.25	12.50	25.00
—Black label with all-silver print					
❏ SDJLP-1071 [S]	A Date with Della Reese at Mr. Kelly's in Chicago	1959	7.50	15.00	30.00
—Originals have blue labels					
❏ SDJLP-1071 [S]	A Date with Della Reese at Mr. Kelly's in Chicago	1962	5.00	10.00	20.00
—Black label, multi-colored spokes around "jubilee," yellow spoke goes almost to center hole					
❏ JLP-1083 [M]	Amen	1959	6.25	12.50	25.00
❏ SDJLP-1083 [S]	Amen	1959	7.50	15.00	30.00
❏ JGM-1095 [M]	The Story of the Blues	1962	3.75	7.50	15.00
—Black label, multi-colored spokes around "jubilee," yellow spoke goes almost to center hole; new prefix					
❏ JGS-1095 [S]	The Story of the Blues	1964	3.75	7.50	15.00
—Black label, multi-colored spokes around "jubilee," yellow spoke goes nowhere near center hole					
❏ JLP-1095 [M]	The Story of the Blues	1960	5.00	10.00	20.00
—Black label, multi-colored spokes around "jubilee," yellow spoke goes almost to center hole					
❏ JLP-1095 [M]	The Story of the Blues	1960	6.25	12.50	25.00
—Original labels are black with all-silver print					
❏ SDJLP-1095 [S]	The Story of the Blues	1960	7.50	15.00	30.00
—Original labels are black with all-silver print					
❏ SDJLP-1095 [S]	The Story of the Blues	1962	6.25	12.50	25.00
—Black label, multi-colored spokes around "jubilee," yellow spoke goes almost to center hole					

Number	Title (A Side/B Side)	Yr	VG	VG+	NM
❏ JLP-1109 [M]	What Do You Know About Love	1960	6.25	12.50	25.00
❏ JLP-1116 [M]	And That Reminds Me	1960	6.25	12.50	25.00
❏ JGM-5002 [M]	The Best of Della Reese	196?	3.75	7.50	15.00
❏ JGS-5002 [S]	The Best of Della Reese	196?	5.00	10.00	20.00
PICKWICK					
❏ SPC-3058	And That Reminds Me	196?	3.00	6.00	12.00
RCA VICTOR					
❏ LPM-2157 [M]	Della	1960	5.00	10.00	20.00
❏ LSP-2157 [S]	Della	1960	6.25	12.50	25.00
❏ LPM-2204 [M]	Della by Starlight	1960	5.00	10.00	20.00
❏ LSP-2204 [S]	Della by Starlight	1960	6.25	12.50	25.00
❏ LPM-2280 [M]	Della Della Cha-Cha-Cha	1961	5.00	10.00	20.00
❏ LSP-2280 [S]	Della Della Cha-Cha-Cha	1961	6.25	12.50	25.00
❏ LPM-2391 [M]	Special Delivery	1961	5.00	10.00	20.00
❏ LSP-2391 [S]	Special Delivery	1961	6.25	12.50	25.00
❏ LPM-2419 [M]	The Classic Della	1962	5.00	10.00	20.00
❏ LSP-2419 [S]	The Classic Della	1962	6.25	12.50	25.00
❏ LPM-2568 [M]	Della on Stage	1962	5.00	10.00	20.00
❏ LSP-2568 [S]	Della on Stage	1962	6.25	12.50	25.00
❏ LPM-2711 [M]	Waltz with Me	1963	5.00	10.00	20.00
❏ LSP-2711 [S]	Waltz with Me	1963	6.25	12.50	25.00
❏ LPM-2814 [M]	Moody	1963	5.00	10.00	20.00
❏ LSP-2814 [S]	Moody	1963	6.25	12.50	25.00
❏ LPM-2872 [M]	Della Reese at Basin Street East	1964	5.00	10.00	20.00
❏ LSP-2872 [S]	Della Reese at Basin Street East	1964	6.25	12.50	25.00
❏ LSP-4651	The Best of Della Reese	1972	3.00	6.00	12.00

REEVES, DEL
KOALA

Number	Title (A Side/B Side)	Yr	VG	VG+	NM
❏ KO 14188	Del Reeves	1980	3.00	6.00	12.00
PLAYBACK					
❏ 12002	Here's Del Reeves	1988	3.75	7.50	15.00
STARDAY					
❏ 998	Greatest Hits	197?	2.50	5.00	10.00
SUNSET					
❏ SUS-5230	Wonderful World of Country Music	1968	3.00	6.00	12.00
❏ SUS-5279	Country Concert Live!	1969	3.00	6.00	12.00
❏ SUS-5321	Out in the Country	1970	3.00	6.00	12.00
UNITED ARTISTS					
❏ UA-LA044-F	Trucker's Paradise	1973	3.75	7.50	15.00
❏ UA-LA204-G	Live at the Palomino Club.	1974	3.75	7.50	15.00
❏ UA-LA235	The Very Best of Del Reeves.	1974	3.75	7.50	15.00
❏ UA-LA364-G	Del Reeves with Strings and Things.	1975	3.75	7.50	15.00
❏ UA-LA687-G	10th Anniversary.	1977	3.00	6.00	12.00
❏ UAL-3441 [M]	Del Reeves Sings Girl on the Billboard.	1965	6.25	12.50	25.00
❏ UAL-3458 [M]	Doodle-Oo-Doo-Doo.	1965	5.00	10.00	20.00
❏ UAL-3468 [M]	Del Reeves Sings Jim Reeves.	1966	5.00	10.00	20.00
❏ UAL-3488 [M]	Special Delivery.	1966	5.00	10.00	20.00
❏ UAL-3528 [M]	Santa's Boy.	1966	5.00	10.00	20.00
❏ UAL-3530 [M]	Gettin' Any Feed for Your Chickens?	1966	5.00	10.00	20.00
❏ UAL-3571 [M]	Struttin' My Stuff.	1967	6.25	12.50	25.00
❏ UAL-3595 [M]	Six of One, Half a Dozen of the Other.	1967	6.25	12.50	25.00
❏ UAL-3612 [M]	The Little Church in the Dell.	1967	7.50	15.00	30.00
❏ UAS-6441 [S]	Del Reeves Sings Girl on the Billboard.	1965	7.50	15.00	30.00
❏ UAS-6458 [S]	Doodle-Oo-Doo-Doo.	1965	6.25	12.50	25.00
❏ UAS-6468 [S]	Del Reeves Sings Jim Reeves.	1966	6.25	12.50	25.00
❏ UAS-6488 [S]	Special Delivery.	1966	6.25	12.50	25.00
❏ UAS-6528 [S]	Santa's Boy.	1966	6.25	12.50	25.00
❏ UAS-6530 [S]	Gettin' Any Feed for Your Chickens?	1966	6.25	12.50	25.00
❏ UAS-6571 [S]	Struttin' My Stuff.	1967	5.00	10.00	20.00
❏ UAS-6595 [S]	Six of One, Half a Dozen of the Other.	1967	5.00	10.00	20.00
❏ UAS-6612 [S]	The Little Church in the Dell.	1967	6.25	12.50	25.00
❏ UAS-6635	The Best of Del Reeves.	1968	5.00	10.00	20.00
❏ UAS-6643	Running Wild.	1968	5.00	10.00	20.00
❏ UAS-6674	Looking at the World Through a Windshield.	1968	5.00	10.00	20.00
❏ UAS-6705	Down at Good Time Charlie's.	1969	5.00	10.00	20.00
❏ UAS-6733	Big Daddy Del.	1970	5.00	10.00	20.00
❏ UAS-6758	The Best of Del Reeves, Vol. 2.	1970	5.00	10.00	20.00
❏ UAS-6789	Friends and Neighbors.	1971	5.00	10.00	20.00
❏ UAS-6820	The Del Reeves Album.	1971	5.00	10.00	20.00
❏ UAS-6830	Before Goodbye.	1972	5.00	10.00	20.00

REEVES, DEL, AND BOBBY GOLDSBORO
UNITED ARTISTS

Number	Title (A Side/B Side)	Yr	VG	VG+	NM
❏ UAL 3615 [M]	Our Way of Life	1967	5.00	10.00	20.00
❏ UAS 6615 [S]	Our Way of Life	1967	5.00	10.00	20.00

REEVES, JIM
ABBOTT

Number	Title (A Side/B Side)	Yr	VG	VG+	NM
❏ LP-5001 [M]	Jim Reeves Sings	1956	1000.	1500.	2000.
COUNTRY MUSIC FOUNDATION					
❏ CMF-008	Live at the Opry	198?	2.50	5.00	10.00
PAIR					
❏ PDL2-1002 [(2)]	The Country Side of Jim Reeves	1986	3.00	6.00	12.00
RCA CAMDEN					
❏ ACL1-0123	Kimberley Jim	1973	3.75	7.50	15.00
❏ CAL-583 [M]	According to My Heart	1960	5.00	10.00	20.00
❏ CAS-583 [R]	According to My Heart	1960	5.00	10.00	20.00
❏ CAL-686 [M]	The Country Side of Jim Reeves	1962	5.00	10.00	20.00
❏ CAS-686 [S]	The Country Side of Jim Reeves	1962	5.00	10.00	20.00
❏ CAL-784 [M]	Good 'N' Country	1963	5.00	10.00	20.00
❏ CAS-784 [S]	Good 'N' Country	1963	5.00	10.00	20.00
❏ CAL-842 [M]	Have I Told You Lately That I Love You?	1964	5.00	10.00	20.00
❏ CAS-842 [S]	Have I Told You Lately That I Love You?	1964	5.00	10.00	20.00
❏ CAS-2532	Young and Country	1971	3.75	7.50	15.00
❏ CAX-9001 [(2)]	Jim Reeves	1972	5.00	10.00	20.00
RCA VICTOR					
❏ APL1-0039	Am I That Easy to Forget	1973	5.00	10.00	20.00
❏ APL1-0330	Great Moments with Jim Reeves	1973	5.00	10.00	20.00
❏ APL1-0537	I'd Fight the World	1974	5.00	10.00	20.00
❏ APL1-0793	The Best of Jim Reeves Sacred Songs	1974	5.00	10.00	20.00

Number	Title (A Side/B Side)	Yr	VG	VG+	NM
❏ APL1-1037	Songs of Love	1975	5.00	10.00	20.00
❏ APL1-1224	I Love You Because	1976	5.00	10.00	20.00
❏ LPM-1256 [M]	Singing Down the Lane	1956	50.00	100.00	200.00
❏ LPM-1410 [M]	Bimbo	1957	50.00	100.00	200.00
—Reissue of Abbott LP					
❏ LPM-1576 [M]	Jim Reeves	1957	20.00	40.00	80.00
❏ LPM-1685 [M]	Girls I Have Known	1958	15.00	30.00	60.00
❏ CPL1-1891	A Legendary Performer	1976	5.00	10.00	20.00
❏ ANL1-1927	Twelve Songs of Christmas	1976	2.00	4.00	8.00
—Reissue of LSP-2758					
❏ LPM-1950 [M]	God Be With You	1958	10.00	20.00	40.00
❏ LSP-1950 [S]	God Be With You	1958	12.50	25.00	50.00
❏ LPM-2001 [M]	Songs to Warm the Heart	1959	10.00	20.00	40.00
❏ LSP-2001 [S]	Songs to Warm the Heart	1959	12.50	25.00	50.00
❏ LPM-2216 [M]	The Intimate Jim Reeves	1960	7.50	15.00	30.00
❏ LSP-2216 [S]	The Intimate Jim Reeves	1960	10.00	20.00	40.00
❏ LPM-2223 [M]	Featuring He'll Have to Go and Other Favorites	1960	7.50	15.00	30.00
—Black and white cover (original)					
❏ LPM-2223 [M]	Featuring He'll Have to Go and Other Favorites	1962	5.00	10.00	20.00
—Color cover (reissue)					
❏ LSP-2223 [S]	Featuring He'll Have to Go and Other Favorites	1960	10.00	20.00	40.00
—Black and white cover (original)					
❏ LSP-2223 [S]	Featuring He'll Have to Go and Other Favorites	1962	6.25	12.50	25.00
—Color cover (reissue)					
❏ LPM-2284 [M]	Tall Tales and Short Tempers	1961	6.25	12.50	25.00
❏ LSP-2284 [S]	Tall Tales and Short Tempers	1961	7.50	15.00	30.00
❏ APL1-2309	It's Nothin' to Me	1977	3.75	7.50	15.00
❏ LPM-2339 [M]	Talkin' to Your Heart	1961	6.25	12.50	25.00
❏ LSP-2339 [S]	Talkin' to Your Heart	1961	7.50	15.00	30.00
❏ LPM-2487 [M]	A Touch of Velvet	1962	6.25	12.50	25.00
❏ LSP-2487 [S]	A Touch of Velvet	1962	7.50	15.00	30.00
❏ LPM-2552 [M]	We Thank Thee	1962	6.25	12.50	25.00
❏ LSP-2552 [S]	We Thank Thee	1962	7.50	15.00	30.00
❏ LPM-2605 [M]	Gentleman Jim	1963	6.25	12.50	25.00
❏ LSP-2605 [S]	Gentleman Jim	1963	7.50	15.00	30.00
❏ LPM-2704 [M]	The International Jim Reeves	1963	6.25	12.50	25.00
❏ LSP-2704 [S]	The International Jim Reeves	1963	7.50	15.00	30.00
❏ AHL1-2720	Jim Reeves	1978	3.75	7.50	15.00
❏ LPM-2758 [M]	Twelve Songs of Christmas	1963	6.25	12.50	25.00
❏ LSP-2758 [S]	Twelve Songs of Christmas	1963	7.50	15.00	30.00
❏ LPM-2780 [M]	Kimberley Jim	1964	6.25	12.50	25.00
❏ LSP-2780 [S]	Kimberley Jim	1964	7.50	15.00	30.00
❏ LPM-2854 [M]	Moonlight and Roses	1964	6.25	12.50	25.00
❏ LSP-2854 [S]	Moonlight and Roses	1964	7.50	15.00	30.00
❏ LPM-2890 [M]	The Best of Jim Reeves	1964	5.00	10.00	20.00
❏ LSP-2890 [S]	The Best of Jim Reeves	1964	6.25	12.50	25.00
❏ LPM-2968 [M]	The Jim Reeves Way	1965	5.00	10.00	20.00
❏ LSP-2968 [S]	The Jim Reeves Way	1965	6.25	12.50	25.00
❏ ANL1-3014	Pure Gold, Volume 1	1978	3.00	6.00	12.00
❏ AHL1-3271	The Best of Jim Reeves, Volume IV	1979	3.75	7.50	15.00
❏ LPM-3427 [M]	Up Through the Years	1965	5.00	10.00	20.00
❏ LSP-3427 [S]	Up Through the Years	1965	6.25	12.50	25.00
❏ AHL1-3454	Don't Let Me Cross Over	1979	3.75	7.50	15.00
❏ LPM-3482 [M]	The Best of Jim Reeves, Vol. II	1966	5.00	10.00	20.00
❏ LSP-3482(e) [P]	The Best of Jim Reeves, Vol. II	1966	6.25	12.50	25.00
—This album is at least partially, and possibly entirely, in rechanneled stereo					
❏ LPM-3542 [M]	Distant Drums	1966	5.00	10.00	20.00
❏ LSP-3542 [P]	Distant Drums	1966	6.25	12.50	25.00
—"Overnight" and "The Gods Were Angry with Me" are rechanneled					
❏ AYL1-3678	The Best of Jim Reeves	1980	3.00	6.00	12.00
—"Best Buy Series" reissue					
❏ LPM-3709 [M]	Yours Sincerely, Jim Reeves	1966	5.00	10.00	20.00
❏ LSP-3709(e) [P]	Yours Sincerely, Jim Reeves	1966	6.25	12.50	25.00
—This album is at least partially, and possibly entirely, in rechanneled stereo					
❏ AYL1-3765	The Best of Jim Reeves Sacred Songs	1980	2.50	5.00	10.00
—"Best Buy Series" reissue					
❏ LPM-3793 [M]	Blue Side of Lonesome	1967	6.25	12.50	25.00
❏ LSP-3793 [S]	Blue Side of Lonesome	1967	5.00	10.00	20.00
❏ AHL1-3827	There's Always Me	1980	3.00	6.00	12.00
❏ LPM-3903 [M]	My Cathedral	1967	7.50	15.00	30.00
❏ LSP-3903 [S]	My Cathedral	1967	6.25	12.50	25.00
❏ AYL1-3936	Pure Gold, Volume 1	1980	2.50	5.00	10.00
—"Best Buy Series" reissue					
❏ LPM-3987 [M]	A Touch of Sadness	1968	15.00	30.00	60.00
❏ LSP-3987 [S]	A Touch of Sadness	1968	5.00	10.00	20.00
❏ LSP-4062	Jim Reeves On Stage	1968	5.00	10.00	20.00
❏ AYL1-4075	The Best of Jim Reeves, Volume IV	1981	2.50	5.00	10.00
—"Best Buy Series" reissue					
❏ LSP-4112	Jim Reeves and Some Friends	1969	5.00	10.00	20.00
❏ AYL1-4168	The Best of Jim Reeves, Vol. II	1981	2.50	5.00	10.00
—"Best Buy Series" reissue					
❏ LSP-4187	The Best of Jim Reeves Volume III	1969	5.00	10.00	20.00
❏ LSP-4475	Jim Reeves Writes You a Record	1971	5.00	10.00	20.00
❏ LSP-4528	Something Special	1971	5.00	10.00	20.00
❏ AHL1-4531	The Jim Reeves Medley	1983	2.50	5.00	10.00
❏ LSP-4646	My Friend	1972	5.00	10.00	20.00
❏ LSP-4749	Missing You	1972	5.00	10.00	20.00
❏ AYL1-4833	Don't Let Me Cross Over	1983	2.50	5.00	10.00
—"Best Buy Series" reissue					
❏ AYL1-4835	I Love You Because	1983	2.50	5.00	10.00
—"Best Buy Series" reissue					
❏ AYL1-4836	Songs of Love	1983	2.50	5.00	10.00
—"Best Buy Series" reissue					
❏ AYL1-4838	The Best of Jim Reeves Vol. III	1983	2.50	5.00	10.00
—"Best Buy Series" reissue					
❏ AYL1-4839	There's Always Me	1983	2.50	5.00	10.00
—"Best Buy Series" reissue					
❏ AYL1-4840	We Thank Thee	1983	2.50	5.00	10.00
—"Best Buy Series" reissue					
❏ AHL1-4865	A Special Collection	1983	3.00	6.00	12.00
❏ CPL2-5044 [(2)]	Just for You	1984	3.75	7.50	15.00
❏ AHL1-5424	Collector's Series	1985	3.00	6.00	12.00

REFLECTIONS, THE (1)
GOLDEN WORLD

Number	Title (A Side/B Side)	Yr	VG	VG+	NM
❏ 300 [M]	(Just Like) Romeo and Juliet	1964	37.50	75.00	150.00

REGENT CONCERT ORCHESTRA, THE
REGENT

❏ 6091 [M]	Amor	1958	12.50	25.00	50.00

—Cover model is Jayne Mansfield

REGENTS, THE (1)
GEE

❏ GLP-706 [M]	Barbara Ann	1961	37.50	75.00	150.00
❏ SGLP-706	Barbara Ann	197?	6.25	12.50	25.00

—Reissue by Publishers Central Bureau (clearly marked as such on cover)

❏ SGLP-706 [S]	Barbara Ann	1961	62.50	125.00	250.00

REGENTS, THE (U)
CAPITOL

❏ KAO 2153 [M]	Live at the AM-PM Discotheque	1964	12.50	25.00	50.00
❏ SKAO 2153 [S]	Live at the AM-PM Discotheque	1964	15.00	30.00	60.00

REHAK, FRANK/ALEX SMITH
DAWN

❏ DLP-1107 [M]	Jazzville, Vol. 2	1956	25.00	50.00	100.00

REID, CLARENCE
ATCO

❏ SD 33-307	Dancin' with Nobody But You Babe	1969	7.50	15.00	30.00

REID, IRENE
MGM

❏ E-4159 [M]	It's Only the Beginning for Irene Reid	1963	5.00	10.00	20.00
❏ SE-4159 [S]	It's Only the Beginning for Irene Reid	1963	6.25	12.50	25.00

VERVE

❏ V6-8621 [S]	Room for One More	1965	5.00	10.00	20.00

REINER, CARL, AND MEL BROOKS
CAPITOL

❏ SW 1529 [S]	2000 Years	1961	5.00	10.00	20.00
❏ W 1529 [M]	2000 Years	1961	3.75	7.50	15.00
❏ SW 1618 [S]	2000 and One Years	1961	5.00	10.00	20.00
❏ W 1618 [M]	2000 and One Years	1961	3.75	7.50	15.00
❏ SW 1815 [S]	At the Cannes Film Festival	1962	5.00	10.00	20.00
❏ W 1815 [M]	At the Cannes Film Festival	1962	3.75	7.50	15.00
❏ ST 2981	The Best of the 2000 Year Old Man	1968	3.75	7.50	15.00

WARNER BROS.

❏ BS 2741	2000 and Thirteen	1973	3.75	7.50	15.00
❏ 3XX 2744 [(3)]	The Incomplete Works of Reiner and Brooks	1973	6.25	12.50	25.00

WORLD PACIFIC

❏ WP-1401 [M]	2000 Years	1960	7.50	15.00	30.00

REINHARDT, DJANGO
ANGEL

❏ ANG.60003 [10]	Le Jazz Hot	1954	37.50	75.00	150.00
❏ ANG.60011 [10]	Django's Guitar	1955	37.50	75.00	150.00

CAPITOL

❏ TBO 10226 [(2)M]	The Best of Django Reinhardt	1960	12.50	25.00	50.00

—Black colorband labels, Capitol logo at left

CLEF

❏ MGC-516 [10]	The Great Artistry of Django Reinhardt	1954	37.50	75.00	150.00

JAY

❏ 3008 [10]	Django Reinhardt	1954	45.00	90.00	180.00

MERCURY

❏ MGC-516 [10]	The Great Artistry of Django Reinhardt	1953	50.00	100.00	200.00

PERIOD

❏ SPL-1100 [10]	Django Reinhardt Memorial, Volume 1	1954	30.00	60.00	120.00
❏ SPL-1101 [10]	Django Reinhardt Memorial, Volume 2	1954	30.00	60.00	120.00
❏ SPL-1102 [10]	Django Reinhardt Memorial, Volume 3	1954	30.00	60.00	120.00
❏ SPL-1201 [M]	Django Reinhardt Memorial Album, Volume 1	1956	12.50	25.00	50.00
❏ SPL-1201 [M]	Django Reinhardt Memorial Album, Volume 2	1956	12.50	25.00	50.00
❏ SPL-1203 [M]	Django Reinhardt Memorial Album, Volume 3	1956	12.50	25.00	50.00
❏ SPL-1204 [M]	The Best of Django Reinhardt	1956	12.50	25.00	50.00
❏ SPL-2204 [R]	The Best of Django Reinhardt	196?	6.25	12.50	25.00

RCA VICTOR

❏ LPM-1100 [M]	Django Reinhardt	1955	25.00	50.00	100.00
❏ LPM-2319 [M]	Djangology	1961	10.00	20.00	40.00
❏ LSP-2319 [R]	Djangology	196?	6.25	12.50	25.00

REPRISE

❏ R-6075 [M]	The Immortal Django Reinhardt	1963	6.25	12.50	25.00

SUTTON

❏ SU-274 [M]	Django Reinhardt and His Guitar	1966	5.00	10.00	20.00

SWING

❏ SW-8420/7 [(7)]	Djangologie USA Volumes 1-7	1988	15.00	30.00	60.00

REMAINS, THE
EPIC

❏ LN 24214 [M]	The Remains	1966	50.00	100.00	200.00
❏ BN 26214 [S]	The Remains	1966	75.00	150.00	300.00

SPOONFED

❏ SFD-3205	The Remains	1978	3.75	7.50	15.00

—Red vinyl

SUNDAZED

❏ SEP 10-162 [10]	The Remains	2000	2.00	4.00	8.00
❏ LP 5015	A Session with the Remains	199?	2.50	5.00	10.00
❏ LP 5055	The Remains	1999	3.00	6.00	12.00

REMINGTON, DAVE
JUBILEE

❏ JLP-1017 [M]	Chicago Jazz Reborn	1956	10.00	20.00	40.00

TEMPUS

❏ TL-101 [M]	Danceable Dixieland Jazz	1958	10.00	20.00	40.00

R

Number	Title (A Side/B Side)	Yr	VG	VG+	NM
VEE JAY					
❏ LP-3009 [M]	Dixie on the Rocks	1960	6.25	12.50	25.00
❏ SR-3009 [S]	Dixie on the Rocks	1960	7.50	15.00	30.00
❏ LP-3030 [M]	Dixie Chicago Style	1962	5.00	10.00	20.00
❏ SR-3030 [S]	Dixie Chicago Style	1962	6.25	12.50	25.00
REMINGTON, HERB					
D					
❏ 1376	Herby Remington Plays the Steel	197?	3.00	6.00	12.00
HILLTOP					
❏ JM-6020 [M]	Herby Remington Rides Again	196?	3.75	7.50	15.00
❏ JS-6020 [S]	Herby Remington Rides Again	196?	3.00	6.00	12.00
STONEWAY					
❏ 138	Pure Remington Steel	197?	3.00	6.00	12.00
UNITED ARTISTS					
❏ UAL-3167 [M]	Steel Guitar Holiday	1961	6.25	12.50	25.00
❏ UAS-6167 [S]	Steel Guitar Holiday	1961	7.50	15.00	30.00
RENA, KID					
CIRCLE					
❏ L-409 [10]	Kid Rena Delta Jazz Band	1951	20.00	40.00	80.00
RENAISSANCE					
CAPITOL/SOVEREIGN					
❏ SMAS-11116	Prologue	1972	3.75	7.50	15.00
❏ ST-11216	Ashes Are Burning	1973	3.75	7.50	15.00
❏ SWBC-11871 [(2)]	In the Beginning	1978	3.75	7.50	15.00
—Combines 11116 and 11216 in one package					
ELEKTRA					
❏ EKS-74068	Renaissance	1969	7.50	15.00	30.00
I.R.S.					
❏ SP-70019	Camera Camera	1981	2.50	5.00	10.00
❏ SP-70033	Time Line	1983	2.50	5.00	10.00
MOBILE FIDELITY					
❏ 1-099	Scheherazade and Other Stories	1982	12.50	25.00	50.00
—Audiophile vinyl					
SIRE					
❏ SASD-3902 [(2)]	Live at Carnegie Hall	1976	3.75	7.50	15.00
❏ SR 6015	Turn of the Cards	1977	2.50	5.00	10.00
—Reissue of 7502					
❏ SR 6017	Scheherazade and Other Stories	1977	2.50	5.00	10.00
—Reissue of 7510					
❏ SR 6024	Novella	1977	2.50	5.00	10.00
—Reissue of 7526					
❏ 2XS 6029 [(2)]	Live at Carnegie Hall	1977	3.00	6.00	12.00
—Reissue of 3902					
❏ SRK 6049	A Song for All Seasons	1978	3.00	6.00	12.00
❏ SRK 6068	Azure d'Or	1979	3.00	6.00	12.00
❏ SAS-7502	Turn of the Cards	1974	3.00	6.00	12.00
❏ SASD-7510	Scheherazade and Other Stories	1975	3.00	6.00	12.00
❏ SASD-7526	Novella	1977	3.00	6.00	12.00
RENAUD, HENRI					
CONTEMPORARY					
❏ C-2502 [10]	The Henri Renaud All-Stars	1953	30.00	60.00	120.00
PERIOD					
❏ SPL-1211 [M]	The Birdlanders	1954	20.00	40.00	80.00
❏ SPL-1212 [M]	The Birdlanders	1954	20.00	40.00	80.00
RENAY, DIANE					
20TH CENTURY FOX					
❏ TF-3133 [M]	Navy Blue	1964	20.00	40.00	80.00
❏ TFS-4133 [S]	Navy Blue	1964	37.50	75.00	150.00
RENDELL, DON					
JAZZLAND					
❏ JLP-51 [M]	Roarin'	1961	7.50	15.00	30.00
❏ JLP-951 [S]	Roarin'	1961	10.00	20.00	40.00
RENE, GOOGIE					
CLASS					
❏ LP-200 [M]	Flapjacks	1963	5.00	10.00	20.00
❏ LP-5001 [M]	Beautiful Weekend	1957	6.25	12.50	25.00
❏ LP-5003 [M]	Googie Rene Presents Romesville	1959	6.25	12.50	25.00
RENDEZVOUS					
❏ M-1311 [M]	Beautiful Weekend	196?	3.75	7.50	15.00
❏ M-1313 [M]	Romseville	196?	3.75	7.50	15.00
RENE, HENRI					
IMPERIAL					
❏ LP-9074 [M]	White Heat	1959	5.00	10.00	20.00
❏ LP-9096 [M]	Swingin' 59	1960	5.00	10.00	20.00
❏ LP-12021 [S]	White Heat	1959	7.50	15.00	30.00
❏ LP-12040 [S]	Swingin' 59	1960	7.50	15.00	30.00
RCA VICTOR					
❏ LPM-1033 [M]	Passion in Paint	1955	20.00	40.00	80.00
❏ LPM-1046 [M]	Music for Bachelors	1955	30.00	60.00	120.00
—Cover model is Jayne Mansfield					
❏ LPM-1583 [M]	Music for the Weaker Sex	1957	6.25	12.50	25.00
❏ LPM-1947 [M]	Compulsion to Swing	1958	5.00	10.00	20.00
❏ LSP-1947 [S]	Compulsion to Swing	1958	7.50	15.00	30.00
❏ LPM-2002 [M]	Riot in Rhythm	1959	5.00	10.00	20.00
❏ LSP-2002 [S]	Riot in Rhythm	1959	7.50	15.00	30.00
❏ LSA-2396 [S]	Dynamic Dimensions	1961	7.50	15.00	30.00
❏ LPM-3049 [10]	Serenade to Love	1953	10.00	20.00	40.00
❏ LPM-3076 [10]	Listen to Rene	1953	10.00	20.00	40.00
RENO, DON, AND BILL HARRELL					
JALYN					
❏ JLP-108 [M]	Bluegrass Favorites	1964	6.25	12.50	25.00
❏ JLP-119 [M]	The Most Requested Songs	1966	6.25	12.50	25.00

Number	Title (A Side/B Side)	Yr	VG	VG+	NM
KING					
❏ KSD-1029	A Variety of New Sacred Gospel Songs	1968	5.00	10.00	20.00
❏ KSD-1033	All the Way to Reno	1968	5.00	10.00	20.00
❏ KSD-1068	I'm Using My Bible for a Roadmap	1969	5.00	10.00	20.00
RENO, JACK					
ATCO					
❏ SD 33-251	Meet Jack Reno	1968	6.25	12.50	25.00
DERBYTOWN					
❏ 101	Yellow Pages	197?	5.00	10.00	20.00
DOT					
❏ DLP 25921	I Want One	1968	6.25	12.50	25.00
❏ DLP 25946	I'm a Good Man in a Bad Frame of Mind	1969	6.25	12.50	25.00
TARGET					
❏ 1313	Hitchin' a Ride	1972	5.00	10.00	20.00
RENO AND SMILEY					
DOT					
❏ DLP-3490 [M]	Bluegrass Hits	1963	6.25	12.50	25.00
❏ DLP-25490 [S]	Bluegrass Hits	1963	7.50	15.00	30.00
KING					
❏ 550 [M]	Sacred Songs	1958	30.00	60.00	120.00
❏ 552 [M]	Reno and Smiley Instrumentals	1958	25.00	50.00	100.00
❏ 579 [M]	Folk Ballads and Instrumentals	1958	25.00	50.00	100.00
❏ 617 [M]	Someone Will Love Me in Heaven	1959	25.00	50.00	100.00
❏ 621 [M]	Good Old Country Ballads	1959	25.00	50.00	100.00
❏ 646 [M]	A Variety of Country Songs	1959	25.00	50.00	100.00
❏ 693 [M]	Hymns Sacred and Gospel	1959	25.00	50.00	100.00
❏ 701 [M]	Country Songs	1959	25.00	50.00	100.00
❏ 718 [M]	Wanted	1961	25.00	50.00	100.00
❏ 756 [M]	Folk Songs of the Civil War	1961	25.00	50.00	100.00
❏ 776 [M]	Country Singing and Instrumentals	1962	20.00	40.00	80.00
❏ 787 [M]	Banjo Special	1962	20.00	40.00	80.00
❏ 816 [M]	Another Day with Reno and Smiley	1962	20.00	40.00	80.00
❏ 853 [M]	The 15 Greatest Hymns of All Time	1963	20.00	40.00	80.00
❏ 861 [M]	The World's Best Five String Banjo	1963	20.00	40.00	80.00
❏ 874 [M]	The True Meaning of Christmas	1963	20.00	40.00	80.00
❏ 874 [M]	The True Meaning of Christmas	1963	25.00	50.00	100.00
❏ 911 [M]	On the Road with Reno and Smiley	1964	20.00	40.00	80.00
❏ 914 [M]	A Bluegrass Tribute to Cowboy Copas	1964	20.00	40.00	80.00
❏ KSD-1044	I Know You're Married	1969	6.25	12.50	25.00
❏ KSD-1091	The Best of Reno and Smiley	1970	6.25	12.50	25.00
REO SPEEDWAGON					
EPIC					
❏ E 31089	REO Speedwagon	1972	3.75	7.50	15.00
—Yellow label original					
❏ KE 31089	REO Speedwagon	1973	3.00	6.00	12.00
—Orange label					
❏ PE 31089	REO Speedwagon	1979	2.00	4.00	8.00
—Dark blue label					
❏ KE 31745	R.E.O./T.W.O.	1972	3.75	7.50	15.00
—Yellow label original					
❏ KE 31745	R.E.O./T.W.O.	1973	3.00	6.00	12.00
—Orange label					
❏ PE 31745	R.E.O./T.W.O.	1979	2.00	4.00	8.00
—Dark blue label					
❏ KE 32378	Ridin' the Storm Out	1973	3.00	6.00	12.00
—Orange label					
❏ PE 32378	Ridin' the Storm Out	1979	2.00	4.00	8.00
—Dark blue label					
❏ PE 32948	Lost in a Dream	1974	3.00	6.00	12.00
—Orange label					
❏ PE 32948	Lost in a Dream	1979	2.00	4.00	8.00
—Dark blue label					
❏ PE 33338	This Time We Mean It	1975	3.00	6.00	12.00
—Orange label					
❏ PE 33338	This Time We Mean It	1979	2.00	4.00	8.00
—Dark blue label					
❏ PE 34143	R.E.O.	1976	3.00	6.00	12.00
—Orange label					
❏ PE 34143	R.E.O.	1979	2.00	4.00	8.00
—Dark blue label					
❏ PEG 34494 [(2)]	REO Speedwagon Live/You Get What You Play For	1977	3.75	7.50	15.00
—Orange labels					
❏ PEG 34494 [(2)]	REO Speedwagon Live/You Get What You Play For	1979	3.00	6.00	12.00
—Dark blue labels					
❏ JE 35082	You Can Tune a Piano, But You Can't Tuna Fish	1978	2.50	5.00	10.00
—Orange label; with bar code on back cover					
❏ JE 35082	You Can Tune a Piano, But You Can't Tuna Fish	1978	3.00	6.00	12.00
—Orange label; no bar code on back cover					
❏ JE 35082	You Can Tune a Piano, But You Can't Tuna Fish	1979	2.00	4.00	8.00
—Dark blue label					
❏ PE 35082	You Can Tune a Piano, But You Can't Tuna Fish	198?	2.00	4.00	8.00
❏ FE 35988	Nine Lives	1979	2.50	5.00	10.00
❏ PE 35988	Nine Lives	198?	2.00	4.00	8.00
—Budget-line reissue					
❏ KE2 36444 [(2)]	A Decade of Rock and Roll 1970 to 1980	1980	3.00	6.00	12.00
❏ FE 36844	Hi Infidelity	1980	2.00	4.00	8.00
❏ FE 38100	Good Trouble	1982	2.50	5.00	10.00
❏ PE 38100	Good Trouble	198?	2.00	4.00	8.00
—Budget-line reissue					
❏ QE 39593	Wheels Are Turnin'	1984	2.00	4.00	8.00
❏ FE 40444	Life As We Know It	1987	2.00	4.00	8.00
❏ OE 44202	The Hits	1988	2.50	5.00	10.00

Number	Title (A Side/B Side)	Yr	VG	VG+	NM
❑ HE 45082	You Can Tune a Piano, But You Can't Tuna Fish	198?	10.00	20.00	40.00

—Half-speed mastered edition

Number	Title (A Side/B Side)	Yr	VG	VG+	NM
❑ E 45246	The Earth, a Small Man, His Dog and a Chicken	1990	3.00	6.00	12.00
❑ HE 46844	Hi Infidelity	1982	7.50	15.00	30.00

—Half-speed mastered edition

| ❑ HE 48100 | Good Trouble | 1982 | 7.50 | 15.00 | 30.00 |

—Half-speed mastered edition

REPARATA AND THE DELRONS
AVCO EMBASSY

| ❑ AVE-33008 | Rock and Roll Revolution | 1970 | 6.25 | 12.50 | 25.00 |

WORLD ARTISTS

| ❑ WAM-2006 [M] | Whenever a Teenager Cries | 1965 | 12.50 | 25.00 | 50.00 |
| ❑ WAS-3006 [S] | Whenever a Teenager Cries | 1965 | 15.00 | 30.00 | 60.00 |

REPLACEMENTS, THE
SIRE

| ❑ PRO-A-4632 [DJ] | Don't Sell Or Buy...It's Crap | 1991 | 7.50 | 15.00 | 30.00 |

—Promo-only 5-track sampler

❑ 25330	Tim	1985	2.50	5.00	10.00
❑ 25557	Pleased to Meet Me	1987	2.50	5.00	10.00
❑ 25831	Don't Tell a Soul	1989	2.50	5.00	10.00
❑ R 101024	Don't Tell a Soul	1989	3.00	6.00	12.00

—BMG Music Service edition

TWIN/TONE

❑ TTR 8123	Sorry, Ma, Forgot to Take Out the Trash	1981	3.75	7.50	15.00
❑ TTR 8228 [EP]	The Replacements Stink	1982	3.00	6.00	12.00
❑ TTR 8332	Hootenanny	1983	3.75	7.50	15.00
❑ TTR 8441	Let It Be	1984	3.75	7.50	15.00

WARNER BROS.

| ❑ WBMS-148 [DJ] | The Warner Bros. Music Show: An Interview with Paul Westerberg | 1987 | 10.00 | 20.00 | 40.00 |

REPRISE REPERTORY THEATRE, THE

Artists who were signed to Reprise Records at the time, including ROSEMARY CLOONEY, BING CROSBY, SAMMY DAVIS, JR., DEAN MARTIN, FRANK SINATRA and JO STAFFORD, perform new versions of famous musicals under this collective name.

REPRISE

| ❑ F-2015 [M] | Finian's Rainbow | 196? | 5.00 | 10.00 | 20.00 |

—Standard cover

| ❑ F-2015 [M] | Finian's Rainbow | 1964 | 7.50 | 15.00 | 30.00 |

—Gatefold cover

| ❑ FS-2015 [S] | Finian's Rainbow | 196? | 6.25 | 12.50 | 25.00 |

—Standard cover

| ❑ FS-2015 [S] | Finian's Rainbow | 1964 | 10.00 | 20.00 | 40.00 |

—Gatefold cover

| ❑ F-2016 [M] | Guys and Dolls | 196? | 5.00 | 10.00 | 20.00 |

—Standard cover

| ❑ F-2016 [M] | Guys and Dolls | 1964 | 7.50 | 15.00 | 30.00 |

—Gatefold cover

| ❑ FS-2016 [S] | Guys and Dolls | 196? | 6.25 | 12.50 | 25.00 |

—Standard cover

| ❑ FS-2016 [S] | Guys and Dolls | 1964 | 10.00 | 20.00 | 40.00 |

—Gatefold cover

| ❑ F-2017 [M] | Kiss Me, Kate | 196? | 5.00 | 10.00 | 20.00 |

—Standard cover

| ❑ F-2017 [M] | Kiss Me, Kate | 1964 | 7.50 | 15.00 | 30.00 |

—Gatefold cover

| ❑ FS-2017 [S] | Kiss Me, Kate | 196? | 6.25 | 12.50 | 25.00 |

—Standard cover

| ❑ FS-2017 [S] | Kiss Me, Kate | 1964 | 10.00 | 20.00 | 40.00 |

—Gatefold cover

| ❑ F-2018 [M] | South Pacific | 196? | 5.00 | 10.00 | 20.00 |

—Standard cover

| ❑ F-2018 [M] | South Pacific | 1964 | 7.50 | 15.00 | 30.00 |

—Gatefold cover

| ❑ FS-2018 [S] | South Pacific | 196? | 6.25 | 12.50 | 25.00 |

—Standard cover

| ❑ FS-2018 [S] | South Pacific | 1964 | 10.00 | 20.00 | 40.00 |

—Gatefold cover

| ❑ F-2019 [(4)M] | The Reprise Repertory Theatre | 1964 | 50.00 | 100.00 | 200.00 |

—Box set of all four of the above LPs in gatefold covers

| ❑ FS-2019 [(4)S] | The Reprise Repertory Theatre | 1964 | 75.00 | 150.00 | 300.00 |

—Box set of all four of the above LPs in gatefold covers

RESIDENTS, THE
CRYPTIC

| ❑ S-18335 SP-2 | For Elsie | 1987 | 25.00 | 50.00 | 100.00 |

—Green vinyl one-sided LP

ENIGMA

| ❑ 73547 | The King & Eye | 1989 | 3.75 | 7.50 | 15.00 |

EPISODE

| ❑ ED 21 | The Census Taker (Soundtrack) | 1985 | 5.00 | 10.00 | 20.00 |
| ❑ ED 21 | The Census Taker (Soundtrack) | 1985 | 20.00 | 40.00 | 80.00 |

—Red vinyl

RALPH

| ❑ Mole Show 001 | The Mole Show (The Roxy) | 1983 | 7.50 | 15.00 | 30.00 |
| ❑ C-002A | The Mole Show (The Roxy) | 1983 | 10.00 | 20.00 | 40.00 |

—Picture disc

| ❑ OP-011 [DJ] | Freak Show | 1991 | 20.00 | 40.00 | 80.00 |

—Promo-only black vinyl pressing; 400 made

| ❑ OP-011 [PD] | Freak Show | 1991 | 10.00 | 20.00 | 40.00 |

—Picture disc

| ❑ RR 0274 | Meet the Residents | 1974 | 50.00 | 100.00 | 200.00 |

—First version: "Meet the Beatles" LP parody cover and "First Edition" on back cover

| ❑ RR 0278 | Duck Stab | 1978 | 2.50 | 5.00 | 10.00 |

—Second version: Yellow titles box on back

| ❑ RR 0278 | Duck Stab | 1978 | 3.00 | 6.00 | 12.00 |

—First version: Green titles box on back

Number	Title (A Side/B Side)	Yr	VG	VG+	NM
❑ RR 0677	Meet the Residents	1977	3.00	6.00	12.00

—Fourth version: same cover as second version, modified and orange back cover

| ❑ RR 0677 | Meet the Residents | 1977 | 3.75 | 7.50 | 15.00 |

—Third version: same cover as second version, black "a" Ralph logo

| ❑ RR 0677 | Meet the Residents | 1977 | 5.00 | 10.00 | 20.00 |

—Second version: "She Loves You" picture sleeve parody cover, split "a" Ralph logo

| ❑ RR 1075 | The Third Reich 'N' Roll | 1976 | 2.50 | 5.00 | 10.00 |

—Fourth version: Gray carrot, black "a" Ralph logo

| ❑ RR 1075 | The Third Reich 'N' Roll | 1976 | 3.00 | 6.00 | 12.00 |

—Third version: Orange carrot, black "a" Ralph logo

| ❑ RR 1075 | The Third Reich 'N' Roll | 1976 | 3.75 | 7.50 | 15.00 |

—Second version: Gray carrot, split "a" Ralph logo

| ❑ RR 1075 | The Third Reich 'N' Roll | 1976 | 12.50 | 25.00 | 50.00 |

—Censored cover with swastikas obscured, pressed in U.S. for export to Germany

| ❑ RR 1075 | The Third Reich 'N' Roll | 1976 | 12.50 | 25.00 | 50.00 |

—First version of 1,000: Liner notes inside, orange carrot

| ❑ RR 1075 | The Third Reich 'N' Roll | 1976 | 375.00 | 750.00 | 1500. |

—Numbered box set on marbled vinyl, silkscreened cover and lithographs inside

| ❑ RR 1174 | Not Available | 1978 | 2.50 | 5.00 | 10.00 |

—Green label, address is "109 Minna"

| ❑ RR 1174 | Not Available | 1978 | 3.00 | 6.00 | 12.00 |

—Green label, address is "444 Grove"

| ❑ RR 1174 | Not Available | 1978 | 3.75 | 7.50 | 15.00 |

—Orange label, remastered, "Re-3" in trail-off vinyl

| ❑ RR 1174 | Not Available | 1978 | 6.25 | 12.50 | 25.00 |

—Purple label, mis-mastered, "Re-1" in trail-off vinyl

| ❑ RR 1276 | Fingerprince | 1977 | 2.50 | 5.00 | 10.00 |

—Third version: Color cover

| ❑ RR 1276 | Fingerprince | 1977 | 5.00 | 10.00 | 20.00 |

—Second version: Lighter brown cover

| ❑ RR 1276 | Fingerprince | 1977 | 20.00 | 40.00 | 80.00 |

—First version: Dark brown cover, "First Pressing" written on back cover

| ❑ RZ 7707 [PD] | Meet the Residents | 1986 | 7.50 | 15.00 | 30.00 |

—Picture disc, with original cover on one side, replacement cover on other

| ❑ DJ 7901 [DJ] | Please Do Not Steal It! | 1979 | 10.00 | 20.00 | 40.00 |

—Promo-only sampler

| ❑ ESK 7906 | Eskimo | 1979 | 2.50 | 5.00 | 10.00 |

—Third version: Black vinyl, standard cover

| ❑ ESK 7906 | Eskimo | 1979 | 3.75 | 7.50 | 15.00 |

—Second version: Black vinyl, gatefold

| ❑ ESK 7906 | Eskimo | 1979 | 6.25 | 12.50 | 25.00 |

—First version: White vinyl, gatefold cover

| ❑ RZ 7906 [PD] | Eskimo | 1979 | 7.50 | 15.00 | 30.00 |

—Picture disc

| ❑ RZ 8052 | The Residents Commercial Album | 1980 | 3.00 | 6.00 | 12.00 |

—Third version: Green vinyl

| ❑ RZ 8052 | The Residents Commercial Album | 1980 | 3.75 | 7.50 | 15.00 |

—Second version: Corrected song order, green logo

| ❑ RZ 8052 | The Residents Commercial Album | 1980 | 5.00 | 10.00 | 20.00 |

—First version: Purple Ralph logo, songs listed in wrong order

| ❑ RZ 8152 | Mark of the Mole | 1981 | 2.50 | 5.00 | 10.00 |
| ❑ RZ 8152 | Mark of the Mole | 1981 | 12.50 | 25.00 | 50.00 |

—Signed brown vinyl edition with lyrics

| ❑ RZ 8202 | The Tunes of Two Cities | 1982 | 2.50 | 5.00 | 10.00 |

—Second edition: "109 Minna Street" address

| ❑ RZ 8202 | The Tunes of Two Cities | 1982 | 3.00 | 6.00 | 12.00 |

—First edition: "444 Grove Street" address

| ❑ RZ 8252 | Intermission | 1982 | 3.00 | 6.00 | 12.00 |
| ❑ RZ 8252 | Intermission | 1982 | 3.50 | 7.00 | 14.00 |

—Red vinyl

| ❑ RZ 8302 | Residue | 1983 | 3.00 | 6.00 | 12.00 |
| ❑ RR 8315 | Title in Limbo | 1983 | 3.00 | 6.00 | 12.00 |

—With Renaldo and The Loaf

| ❑ RZ 8402 | George & James | 1984 | 2.50 | 5.00 | 10.00 |

—Second edition: Approved mix with "Re-5" in trail-off

| ❑ RZ 8402 | George & James | 1984 | 7.50 | 15.00 | 30.00 |

—First edition: Rejected mix with "Re-1" in trail-off

| ❑ RZ 8402 | George & James | 1984 | 12.50 | 25.00 | 50.00 |

—"Re-5" in trail-off, clear vinyl

| ❑ RZ 8452 | Whatever Happened to Vileness Fats? | 1984 | 3.00 | 6.00 | 12.00 |
| ❑ RZ 8452 | Whatever Happened to Vileness Fats? | 1984 | 20.00 | 40.00 | 80.00 |

—Red vinyl

| ❑ RZ 8552 | The Big Bubble | 1985 | 3.00 | 6.00 | 12.00 |
| ❑ RZ 8552 | The Big Bubble | 1985 | 20.00 | 40.00 | 80.00 |

—Pink vinyl

| ❑ RZ 8602 | The Eyeball Show (The 13th Anniversary Show) Live in Japan | 1986 | 2.50 | 5.00 | 10.00 |
| ❑ RZ 8602 | The Eyeball Show (The 13th Anniversary Show) Live in Japan | 1986 | 20.00 | 40.00 | 80.00 |

—White vinyl

| ❑ RZ 8652 | Stars & Hank Forever | 1986 | 2.50 | 5.00 | 10.00 |
| ❑ RZ 8652 | Stars & Hank Forever | 1986 | 10.00 | 20.00 | 40.00 |

—Blue vinyl

| ❑ RR 82761 | Fingerprince | 1988 | 2.50 | 5.00 | 10.00 |

—New number, black vinyl

| ❑ RR 82761 | Fingerprince | 1988 | 3.00 | 6.00 | 12.00 |

—New number, purple vinyl

| ❑ RR 87521 | Duck Stab | 1988 | 2.50 | 5.00 | 10.00 |

—New number, black vinyl

| ❑ RR 87521 | Duck Stab | 1988 | 3.00 | 6.00 | 12.00 |

—New number, red vinyl

| ❑ RR 88521 | Meet the Residents | 1988 | 3.00 | 6.00 | 12.00 |

—Original "Meet the Beatles" parody cover restored, black vinyl

| ❑ RR 88521 | Meet the Residents | 1988 | 3.75 | 7.50 | 15.00 |

—Original "Meet the Beatles" parody cover restored, white vinyl

RYKO ANALOGUE

| ❑ RALP-0044-2 [(2)] | God in Three Persons | 1988 | 5.00 | 10.00 | 20.00 |

—Clear vinyl

| ❑ RALP-0045-2 | God in Three Persons Instrumental | 1988 | 3.75 | 7.50 | 15.00 |

—Clear vinyl

UWEB

| ❑ 0011 | Stranger Than Supper | 1990 | 6.25 | 12.50 | 25.00 |

—Fan club issue

R

Number	Title (A Side/B Side)	Yr	VG	VG+	NM

RESTIVO, JOHNNY
RCA VICTOR

Number	Title (A Side/B Side)	Yr	VG	VG+	NM
❑ LPM-2149 [M]	Oh, Johnny!	1959	15.00	30.00	60.00
❑ LSP-2149 [S]	Oh, Johnny!	1959	25.00	50.00	100.00

RESTUM, WILLIE
GONE

| ❑ LP-5011 [M] | Willie Restum at the Dream Lounge | 1960 | 62.50 | 125.00 | 250.00 |

ROULETTE

| ❑ R-25152 [M] | Dream Bar | 1961 | 15.00 | 30.00 | 60.00 |

RETURN TO FOREVER
COLUMBIA

❑ PC 34076	Romantic Warrior	1976	2.50	5.00	10.00
—No bar code on cover					
❑ PC 34076	Romantic Warrior	198?	2.00	4.00	8.00
—Reissue with bar code					
❑ PC 34682	Musicmagic	1977	2.50	5.00	10.00
—No bar code on cover					
❑ PC 34682	Musicmagic	1985	2.00	4.00	8.00
—Reissue with bar code					
❑ PCQ 34682 [Q]	Musicmagic	1977	5.00	10.00	20.00
❑ JC 35281	Return to Forever Live	1979	2.50	5.00	10.00
❑ JC 36359	The Best of Return to Forever	1980	2.50	5.00	10.00
❑ PC 36359	The Best of Return to Forever	198?	2.00	4.00	8.00
—Budget-line reissue					

ECM

| ❑ 1015 | Return to Forever | 197? | 3.75 | 7.50 | 15.00 |

POLYDOR

❑ PD-5525	Light as a Feather	1973	3.00	6.00	12.00
❑ PD-5536	Hymn of the Seventh Galaxy	1973	3.00	6.00	12.00
❑ PD-6509	Where Have I Known You Before	1974	3.00	6.00	12.00
❑ PD-6512	No Mystery	1975	3.00	6.00	12.00
❑ 825336-1	Hymn of the Seventh Galaxy	198?	2.00	4.00	8.00
—Reissue					

REVELERS, THE
RONDO-LETTE

| ❑ A-50 [M] | Jazz at the Downstairs Club | 1962 | 5.00 | 10.00 | 20.00 |
| ❑ SA-50 [S] | Jazz at the Downstairs Club | 1962 | 6.25 | 12.50 | 25.00 |

REVELLS, THE
REPRISE

| ❑ R-6160 [M] | The Go Sound of the Slots | 1965 | 37.50 | 75.00 | 150.00 |
| ❑ RS-6160 [S] | The Go Sound of the Slots | 1965 | 50.00 | 100.00 | 200.00 |

REVELS, THE (2)
IMPACT

| ❑ LPM-1 [M] | Revels on a Rampage | 1964 | 125.00 | 250.00 | 500.00 |

SUNDAZED

| ❑ LP 5010 | Intoxica! The Best of the Revels | 199? | 2.50 | 5.00 | 10.00 |

REVENGERS, THE
METRO

| ❑ M-565 [M] | Batman and Other Supermen | 1966 | 7.50 | 15.00 | 30.00 |
| ❑ MS-565 [S] | Batman and Other Supermen | 1966 | 10.00 | 20.00 | 40.00 |

REVERE, PAUL, AND THE RAIDERS
COLUMBIA

❑ GP 12 [(2)]	Two All Time Great Selling LPs	1969	6.25	12.50	25.00
—Combines 9395 and 9521 in one package; red labels					
❑ GP 12	Two All Time Great Selling LPs	1971	5.00	10.00	20.00
—Combines 9395 and 9521 in one package; orange labels					
❑ CL 2307 [M]	Here They Come!	1965	5.00	10.00	20.00
—"360 Sound Mono" on label					
❑ CL 2307 [M]	Here They Come!	1965	7.50	15.00	30.00
—"Guaranteed High Fidelity" on label					
❑ CL 2451 [M]	Just Like Us!	1966	6.25	12.50	25.00
❑ CL 2508 [M]	Midnight Ride	1966	6.25	12.50	25.00
❑ CL 2595 [M]	The Spirit of '67	1966	6.25	12.50	25.00
❑ KCL 2662 [M]	Greatest Hits	1967	7.50	15.00	30.00
—Add 20% if booklet is included; at least some copies actually are stereo with the "XSS" prefix on the label's master numbers rather than "XLP," though we don't know if all of them are					
❑ CL 2721 [M]	Revolution!	1967	7.50	15.00	30.00
❑ CL 2755 [M]	A Christmas Present…And Past	1967	15.00	30.00	60.00
❑ CL 2805 [M]	Goin' to Memphis	1968	20.00	40.00	80.00
❑ CS 9107 [S]	Here They Come!	1965	6.25	12.50	25.00
—"360 Sound Stereo" in white on label					
❑ CS 9107 [S]	Here They Come!	1965	10.00	20.00	40.00
—"360 Sound Stereo" in black on label					
❑ CS 9251 [S]	Just Like Us!	1966	7.50	15.00	30.00
❑ CS 9308 [S]	Midnight Ride	1966	7.50	15.00	30.00
❑ CS 9395 [S]	The Spirit of '67	1966	7.50	15.00	30.00
❑ KCS 9462 [P]	Greatest Hits	1967	6.25	12.50	25.00
—Add 20% if booklet is included					
❑ CS 9521 [S]	Revolution!	1967	6.25	12.50	25.00
❑ CS 9555 [S]	A Christmas Present…And Past	1967	6.25	12.50	25.00
❑ CS 9605 [S]	Goin' to Memphis	1968	5.00	10.00	20.00
❑ CS 9665	Something Happening	1968	5.00	10.00	20.00
❑ CS 9753	Hard 'N' Heavy (With Marshmallow)	1969	5.00	10.00	20.00
—Black and white cover					
❑ CS 9753	Hard 'N' Heavy (With Marshmallow)	1969	7.50	15.00	30.00
—Color cover					
❑ CS 9905	Alias Pink Puzz	1969	5.00	10.00	20.00
❑ CS 9964	Collage	1970	5.00	10.00	20.00
❑ C 30386	Greatest Hits, Volume 2	1971	5.00	10.00	20.00
❑ C 30768	Indian Reservation	1971	3.75	7.50	15.00
❑ KC 31106	Country Wine	1972	3.75	7.50	15.00
❑ KG 31464 [(2)]	All-Time Greatest Hits	1972	5.00	10.00	20.00
❑ PC 35593	Greatest Hits	1978	2.50	5.00	10.00

COLUMBIA SPECIAL PRODUCTS

| ❑ P 13512 | Goin' to Memphis | 197? | 3.75 | 7.50 | 15.00 |

GARDENA

| ❑ LP-G-1000 [M] | Like, Long Hair | 1961 | 150.00 | 300.00 | 600.00 |

HARMONY

❑ H 30089	Paul Revere and the Raiders Featuring Mark Lindsay	1970	3.00	6.00	12.00
❑ KH 30975	Good Thing	1971	3.00	6.00	12.00
❑ KH 31183	Movin' On	1972	3.00	6.00	12.00

JERDEN

❑ JRL-7004 [M]	Paul Revere and the Raiders In the Beginning	1966	15.00	30.00	60.00
❑ JRS-7004 [R]	Paul Revere and the Raiders In the Beginning	1966	7.50	15.00	30.00
❑ DT-90709 [R]	Paul Revere and the Raiders In the Beginning	1966	12.50	25.00	50.00
—Capitol Record Club edition					
❑ T-90709 [M]	Paul Revere and the Raiders In the Beginning	1966	17.50	35.00	70.00
—Capitol Record Club edition					

PICKWICK

| ❑ SPC-3176 [R] | Paul Revere and the Raiders | 1969 | 2.50 | 5.00 | 10.00 |

SANDE

❑ S-1001 [M]	Paul Revere and the Raiders	1963	300.00	600.00	1200.
—Original version with "Sande" and no mention of "Etiquette" in trail-off area					
❑ S-1001 [M]	Paul Revere and the Raiders	1979	6.25	12.50	25.00
—Legitimate reissue with "Sande" and "Etiquette" in trail-off area					

SEARS

| ❑ SPS-493 | Paul Revere and the Raiders | 1969 | 6.25 | 12.50 | 25.00 |

REXROTH, KENNETH
FANTASY

❑ 7008 [M]	Poetry and Jazz at the Blackhawk	1958	25.00	50.00	100.00
—Black vinyl					
❑ 7008 [M]	Poetry and Jazz at the Blackhawk	1958	50.00	100.00	200.00
—Red vinyl					

REXROTH, KENNETH, AND LAWRENCE FERLINGHETTI
FANTASY

❑ 7002 [M]	Poetry Readings from the Cellar	1957	25.00	50.00	100.00
—Black vinyl					
❑ 7002 [M]	Poetry Readings from the Cellar	1957	50.00	100.00	200.00
—Red vinyl					

REY, ALVINO
CAPITOL

❑ T 808 [M]	Aloha	1957	7.50	15.00	30.00
❑ ST 1085 [S]	Swinging Fling	1958	7.50	15.00	30.00
❑ T 1085 [M]	Swinging Fling	1958	6.25	12.50	25.00
❑ ST 1262 [S]	Ping Pong!	1959	6.25	12.50	25.00
❑ T 1262 [M]	Ping Pong!	1959	5.00	10.00	20.00
❑ ST 1395 [S]	That Lonely Feeling	1960	6.25	12.50	25.00
❑ T 1395 [M]	That Lonely Feeling	1960	5.00	10.00	20.00

REYNOLDS, ART, SINGERS
CAPITOL

❑ ST-191	It's a Wonderful World	1969	5.00	10.00	20.00
❑ ST 2534 [S]	Tellin' It Like It Is	1966	6.25	12.50	25.00
❑ T 2534 [M]	Tellin' It Like It Is	1966	5.00	10.00	20.00
❑ ST 2811 [S]	Long Dusty Road	1967	5.00	10.00	20.00
❑ T 2811 [M]	Long Dusty Road	1967	6.25	12.50	25.00
❑ ST 2900	Soul-Gospel Sounds	1968	5.00	10.00	20.00

REYNOLDS, BURT
MERCURY

| ❑ MK-4 [DJ] | A Burt Reynolds Radio Special | 1973 | 6.25 | 12.50 | 25.00 |
| ❑ SRM-1-693 | Ask Me What I Am | 1973 | 3.75 | 7.50 | 15.00 |

REYNOLDS, DEBBIE
DOT

❑ DLP-3191 [M]	Debbie	1959	7.50	15.00	30.00
❑ DLP-3295 [M]	Am I That Easy to Forget?	1960	7.50	15.00	30.00
❑ DLP-3298 [M]	Fine and Dandy	1960	5.00	10.00	20.00
❑ DLP-3492 [M]	Tammy	1963	5.00	10.00	20.00
❑ DLP-25191 [S]	Debbie	1959	10.00	20.00	40.00
❑ DLP-25295 [S]	Am I That Easy to Forget?	1960	10.00	20.00	40.00
—Black vinyl					
❑ DLP-25295 [S]	Am I That Easy to Forget?	1960	20.00	40.00	80.00
—Blue vinyl					
❑ DLP-25298 [S]	Fine and Dandy	1960	6.25	12.50	25.00
❑ DLP-25492 [S]	Tammy	1963	6.25	12.50	25.00

MGM

| ❑ E-3806 [M] | From Debbie with Love | 1959 | 10.00 | 20.00 | 40.00 |

REYNOLDS, LAWRENCE
WARNER BROS.

| ❑ WS 1825 | Jesus Is a Soul Man | 1969 | 5.00 | 10.00 | 20.00 |

REYNOLDS, TEDDY, AND THE TWISTERS
CROWN

| ❑ CST-247 [S] | The Twist | 1962 | 10.00 | 20.00 | 40.00 |
| ❑ CLP-5247 [M] | The Twist | 1962 | 7.50 | 15.00 | 30.00 |

REYNOLDS, TOMMY
AUDIO LAB

| ❑ AL-1509 [M] | Dixieland All-Stars | 1958 | 25.00 | 50.00 | 100.00 |

KING

| ❑ 395-510 [M] | Jazz for Happy Feet | 1956 | 20.00 | 40.00 | 80.00 |

ROYALE

| ❑ 18117 [10] | Tommy Reynolds Orchestra with Bon Bon | 195? | 20.00 | 40.00 | 80.00 |

REYS, RITA
COLUMBIA

| ❑ CL 903 [M] | The Cool Voice of Rita Reys with Art Blakey and the Jazz Messengers | 1956 | 25.00 | 50.00 | 100.00 |

EPIC

| ❑ LN 3522 [M] | Her Name Is Rita Reys | 1957 | 20.00 | 40.00 | 80.00 |

Number	Title (A Side/B Side)	Yr	VG	VG+	NM
RHEIMS, ROBERT					
RHEIMS					
❑ LP-6006 [M]	Merry Christmas Carols	1958	5.00	10.00	20.00
—Red vinyl with lyric innersleeve					
❑ ST-7706 [S]	Merry Christmas Carols	1958	6.25	12.50	25.00
—Green vinyl with lyric innersleeve					
RHINOCEROS					
ELEKTRA					
❑ EKS-74030	Rhinoceros	1968	6.25	12.50	25.00
❑ EKS-74056	Satin Chickens	1969	5.00	10.00	20.00
❑ EKS-74075	Better Times Are Coming	1970	5.00	10.00	20.00
RHODES, EMITT					
A&M					
❑ SP-4254	The American Dream	1970	6.25	12.50	25.00
—Original album contains "You're a Very Lovely Woman" and has Rhodes in front of a paint-covered backdrop on cover					
❑ SP-4254	The American Dream	1971	3.75	7.50	15.00
—Reissue contains "Saturday Night" and a framed photo of Rhodes on cover					
ABC DUNHILL					
❑ DS-50089	Emitt Rhodes	1970	3.00	6.00	12.00
❑ DS-50111	Mirror	1971	3.00	6.00	12.00
❑ DS-50122	Farewell to Paradise	1972	3.00	6.00	12.00
RHODES, GEORGE					
GROOVE					
❑ LG-1005 [M]	Real George!	1956	15.00	30.00	60.00
RHODES, TODD					
KING					
❑ 295-88 [10]	Todd Rhodes Playing His Greatest Hits	1954	375.00	750.00	1500.
❑ 658 [M]	Dance Music	1960	200.00	400.00	800.00
RHYNE, MEL					
JAZZLAND					
❑ JLP-16 [M]	Organizing	1960	7.50	15.00	30.00
❑ JLP-916 [S]	Organizing	1960	10.00	20.00	40.00
RHYTHM DEVILS, THE					
PASSPORT					
❑ PB-9844	The Rhythm Devils Play River Music	1980	5.00	10.00	20.00
RHYTHM MASTERS, THE (1)					
ACE					
❑ LP-1010 [M]	Hymns and Spirituals	1961	25.00	50.00	100.00
RHYTHM ROCKERS (1)					
CHALLENGE					
❑ CHL-617 [M]	Soul Surfin'	1963	22.50	45.00	90.00
RICE, BOBBY G.					
AUDIOGRAPH					
❑ 6000	Bobby G. Rice	1982	2.50	5.00	10.00
❑ 7772	Bobby's Back	1982	2.50	5.00	10.00
DOOR KNOB					
❑ 1008	New Beginning	198?	3.00	6.00	12.00
GRT					
❑ 8001	She Sure Laid the Lonelies on Me	1974	3.00	6.00	12.00
❑ 8003	Write Me a Letter	1975	3.00	6.00	12.00
❑ 8011	Instant Rice — The Best of Bobby G.	1976	3.00	6.00	12.00
❑ 8016	With Love from Bobby G. Rice	1977	3.00	6.00	12.00
METROMEDIA COUNTRY					
❑ BML1-0186	You Lay So Easy on My Mind	1973	5.00	10.00	20.00
ROYAL AMERICAN					
❑ 1003	Hit After Hit	1972	5.00	10.00	20.00
SUNBIRD					
❑ SN-50106	Greatest Hits	1980	3.00	6.00	12.00
RICH, BUDDY					
ARGO					
❑ LP-676 [M]	Playtime	1961	7.50	15.00	30.00
❑ LPS-676 [S]	Playtime	1961	10.00	20.00	40.00
EMARCY					
❑ 66006	Driver	1967	5.00	10.00	20.00
GREAT AMERICAN					
❑ 1030	Class of '78	1978	5.00	10.00	20.00
—Direct-to-disc version of Gryphon 781					
MERCURY					
❑ MG-20451 [M]	Richcraft	1959	15.00	30.00	60.00
❑ MG-20461 [M]	The Voice Is Rich	1959	12.50	25.00	50.00
❑ SR-60136 [S]	Richcraft	1959	17.50	35.00	70.00
❑ SR-60144 [S]	The Voice Is Rich	1959	15.00	30.00	60.00
NORGRAN					
❑ MGN-26 [10]	Buddy Rich Swingin'	1954	30.00	60.00	120.00
❑ MGN-1031 [M]	Sing and Swing with Buddy Rich	1955	20.00	40.00	80.00
❑ MGN-1052 [M]	The Swingin' Buddy Rich	1955	15.00	30.00	60.00
—Reissue of 26					
❑ MGN-1078 [M]	The Wailing Buddy Rich	1956	15.00	30.00	60.00
❑ MGN-1088 [M]	This One's for Basie	1956	15.00	30.00	60.00
PACIFIC JAZZ					
❑ PJ-10113 [M]	Swingin' New Big Band	1966	6.25	12.50	25.00
❑ PJ-10117 [M]	Big Swing Face	1967	6.25	12.50	25.00
❑ ST-20113 [S]	Swingin' New Big Band	1966	5.00	10.00	20.00
❑ ST-20117 [S]	Big Swing Face	1967	5.00	10.00	20.00
❑ ST-20126	A New One	1968	5.00	10.00	20.00
VERVE					
❑ MGV-2009 [M]	Buddy Rich Sings Johnny Mercer	1956	15.00	30.00	60.00
❑ V-2009 [M]	Buddy Rich Sings Johnny Mercer	1961	5.00	10.00	20.00
❑ MGV-2075 [M]	Buddy Rich Just Sings	1957	15.00	30.00	60.00
❑ V-2075 [M]	Buddy Rich Just Sings	1961	5.00	10.00	20.00
❑ MGV-8142 [M]	The Swingin' Buddy Rich	1957	12.50	25.00	50.00
—Reissue of Norgran 1052					
❑ V-8142 [M]	The Swingin' Buddy Rich	1961	5.00	10.00	20.00
❑ MGV-8168 [M]	The Wailing Buddy Rich	1957	12.50	25.00	50.00
—Reissue of Norgran 1078					
❑ V-8168 [M]	The Wailing Buddy Rich	1961	5.00	10.00	20.00
❑ MGV-8176 [M]	This One's for Basie	1957	12.50	25.00	50.00
—Reissue of Norgran 1086					
❑ V-8176 [M]	This One's for Basie	1961	5.00	10.00	20.00
❑ MGV-8285 [M]	Buddy Rich in Miami	1958	15.00	30.00	60.00
❑ V-8285 [M]	Buddy Rich in Miami	1961	5.00	10.00	20.00
❑ V-8425 [M]	Blues Caravan	1962	6.25	12.50	25.00
❑ V6-8425 [S]	Blues Caravan	1962	7.50	15.00	30.00
❑ V-8471 [M]	Burnin' Beat	1962	6.25	12.50	25.00
❑ V6-8471 [S]	Burnin' Beat	1962	7.50	15.00	30.00
❑ V-8484 [M]	Drum Battle: Gene Krupa vs. Buddy Rich	1962	6.25	12.50	25.00
❑ V6-8484 [S]	Drum Battle: Gene Krupa vs. Buddy Rich	1962	7.50	15.00	30.00
❑ V-8712 [M]	Big Band Shout	1967	5.00	10.00	20.00
RICH, BUDDY, AND SWEETS EDISON					
NORGRAN					
❑ MGN-1038 [M]	Buddy Rich and Sweets Edison	1955	20.00	40.00	80.00
VERVE					
❑ MGV-8129 [M]	Buddy and Sweets	1957	12.50	25.00	50.00
—Reissue of Norgran 1038					
❑ V-8129 [M]	Buddy and Sweets	1961	5.00	10.00	20.00
RICH, BUDDY, AND MAX ROACH					
MERCURY					
❑ MG-20448 [M]	Rich Versus Roach	1959	15.00	30.00	60.00
❑ SR-60133 [S]	Rich Versus Roach	1959	17.50	35.00	70.00
RICH, CHARLIE					
BUCKBOARD					
❑ 1019	The Entertainer	197?	2.50	5.00	10.00
COLUMBIA SPECIAL PRODUCTS					
❑ P2 13663 [(2)]	Super Hits	197?	3.75	7.50	15.00
ELEKTRA					
❑ 6E-301	Once a Drifter	1981	2.50	5.00	10.00
EPIC					
❑ AS 50 [DJ]	Charlie Rich	1973	7.50	15.00	30.00
—Promo-only compilation					
❑ AS 139 [DJ]	Everything You Always Wanted to Hear by Charlie Rich But Were Afraid to Ask For	1976	6.25	12.50	25.00
—Promo-only sampler					
❑ BN 26376	Set Me Free	1968	5.00	10.00	20.00
❑ BN 26516	The Fabulous Charlie Rich	1970	5.00	10.00	20.00
❑ E 30214	Boss Man	1970	5.00	10.00	20.00
❑ CQ 31933 [Q]	The Best of Charlie Rich	1972	5.00	10.00	20.00
❑ KE 31933	The Best of Charlie Rich	1972	3.75	7.50	15.00
—Yellow label; add 80 percent if bonus record AE7 1065 and its special sleeve are still there					
❑ KE 31933	The Best of Charlie Rich	1973	3.00	6.00	12.00
—Orange label					
❑ CQ 32247 [Q]	Behind Closed Doors	1973	5.00	10.00	20.00
❑ KE 32247	Behind Closed Doors	1973	3.00	6.00	12.00
❑ PE 32247	Behind Closed Doors	197?	2.00	4.00	8.00
—Reissue					
❑ PE 32531	Very Special Love Songs	1974	3.00	6.00	12.00
❑ PEQ 32531 [Q]	Very Special Love Songs	1974	5.00	10.00	20.00
❑ PE 33250	The Silver Fox	1974	3.00	6.00	12.00
❑ PEQ 33250 [Q]	The Silver Fox	1974	5.00	10.00	20.00
❑ PE 33455	Every Time You Touch Me (I Get High)	1975	3.00	6.00	12.00
❑ PEQ 33455 [Q]	Every Time You Touch Me (I Get High)	1975	5.00	10.00	20.00
❑ PE 33545	Silver Linings	1976	2.50	5.00	10.00
❑ PE 34240	Greatest Hits	1976	2.50	5.00	10.00
—Without bar code on cover					
❑ PE 34240	Greatest Hits	1979	2.00	4.00	8.00
—With bar code on cover					
❑ PE 34444	Take Me	1977	2.50	5.00	10.00
❑ PE 34444	Take Me	1977	2.50	5.00	10.00
❑ PE 34891	Rollin' with the Flow	1977	2.50	5.00	10.00
❑ JE 35394	Classic Rich, Vol. 1	1978	2.50	5.00	10.00
❑ JE 35624	Classic Rich, Vol. 2	1978	2.50	5.00	10.00
GROOVE					
❑ GM-1000 [M]	Charlie Rich	1964	37.50	75.00	150.00
❑ GS-1000 [S]	Charlie Rich	1964	75.00	150.00	300.00
HARMONY					
❑ KH 32166	I Do My Swingin' at Home	1973	3.00	6.00	12.00
HI					
❑ 8006	I'm So Lonesome I Could Cry	198?	2.00	4.00	8.00
—Reissue of Hi 32084					
❑ HL 12037 [M]	Charlie Rich Sings Country and Western	1967	7.50	15.00	30.00
❑ SHL 32037 [S]	Charlie Rich Sings Country and Western	1967	5.00	10.00	20.00
❑ SHL 32084	Charlie Rich Sings the Songs of Hank Williams & Others	1974	3.00	6.00	12.00
—Reissue of 32037					
HILLTOP					
❑ 6139	Lonely Weekends	197?	2.50	5.00	10.00
❑ 6149	Songs for Beautiful Girls	1974	2.50	5.00	10.00
❑ 6160	Entertainer of the Year	197?	2.50	5.00	10.00
MERCURY					
❑ SRM-2-7505 [(2)]	Fully Realized	1974	3.75	7.50	15.00
PHILLIPS INTERNATIONAL					
❑ PLP-1970 [M]	Lonely Weekends	1960	150.00	300.00	600.00
PICKWICK					
❑ ACL-7001	Too Many Teardrops	1975	2.50	5.00	10.00
POWER PAK					
❑ PO-241	There Won't Be Anymore	197?	2.50	5.00	10.00
❑ PO-245	Arkansas Traveler	197?	2.50	5.00	10.00
❑ PO-252	The Silver Fox	197?	2.50	5.00	10.00

R

Number	Title (A Side/B Side)	Yr	VG	VG+	NM
QUICKSILVER					
❑ QS-1005	Midnight Blue	198?	3.00	6.00	12.00
RCA CAMDEN					
❑ CAS-2417	The Versatile and Talented Charlie Rich	1970	2.50	5.00	10.00
RCA VICTOR					
❑ APL1-0258	Tomorrow Night	1973	3.00	6.00	12.00
❑ APL1-0433	There Won't Be Anymore	1974	3.00	6.00	12.00
❑ APL1-0686	She Called Me Baby	1974	3.00	6.00	12.00
❑ APL1-0857	Greatest Hits	1975	3.00	6.00	12.00
❑ APL1-1242	Now Everybody Knows	1975	3.00	6.00	12.00
❑ ANL1-1542	Tomorrow Night	1976	2.50	5.00	10.00
—Reissue					
❑ APL1-2260	Big Boss Man/My Mountain Dew	1977	3.00	6.00	12.00
❑ ANL1-2424	She Called Me Baby	1977	2.50	5.00	10.00
—Reissue of APL1-0686					
❑ LPM-3352 [M]	That's Rich	1965	10.00	20.00	40.00
❑ LSP-3352 [S]	That's Rich	1965	12.50	25.00	50.00
❑ LPM-3537 [M]	Big Boss Man	1966	10.00	20.00	40.00
❑ LSP-3557 [S]	Big Boss Man	1966	12.50	25.00	50.00
❑ AHL1-5496	Collector's Series	1985	2.00	4.00	8.00
SMASH					
❑ MGS-27070 [M]	The Many New Sides of Charlie Rich	1965	7.50	15.00	30.00
❑ MGS-27078 [M]	The Best Years	1966	7.50	15.00	30.00
❑ SRS-67070 [S]	The Many New Sides of Charlie Rich	1965	10.00	20.00	40.00
❑ SRS-67070 [S]	The Best Years	1966	10.00	20.00	40.00
SUN					
❑ LP 110	Lonely Weekend	1970	3.00	6.00	12.00
❑ LP 123	A Time for Tears	1971	3.00	6.00	12.00
❑ LP 132	The Early Years	1974	3.00	6.00	12.00
❑ LP 133	The Memphis Sound of Charlie Rich	1974	3.00	6.00	12.00
❑ LP 134	Golden Treasures	1974	3.00	6.00	12.00
❑ LP 135	Sun's Best of Charlie Rich	1974	3.00	6.00	12.00
❑ 1003	20 Golden Hits	1979	2.50	5.00	10.00
—Gold vinyl					
❑ 1007	The Original Charlie Rich	1979	2.50	5.00	10.00
SUNNYVALE					
❑ 9330	The Sun Story Vol. 2	1977	2.50	5.00	10.00
TIME-LIFE					
❑ STW 115	Country Music	1981	3.00	6.00	12.00
TRIP					
❑ TLP-8502 [(2)]	The Best of Charlie Rich	1974	3.00	6.00	12.00
UNITED ARTISTS					
❑ UA-LA876-H	I Still Believe in Love	1978	3.00	6.00	12.00
❑ UA-LA925-H	The Fool Strikes Again	1978	2.50	5.00	10.00
WING					
❑ SRW-16375	A Lonely Weekend	1969	3.00	6.00	12.00
RICH, DAVE					
STOP					
❑ 10007	Soul Brother	196?	7.50	15.00	30.00
RICH, DON					
Also see THE BUCKAROOS.					
CAPITOL					
❑ ST-643	That Fiddlin' Man	1970	6.25	12.50	25.00
RICHARD, CLIFF					
ABC-PARAMOUNT					
❑ 321 [M]	Cliff Sings	1960	20.00	40.00	80.00
❑ S-321 [S]	Cliff Sings	1960	25.00	50.00	100.00
❑ 391 [M]	Listen to Cliff	1961	20.00	40.00	80.00
❑ S-391 [S]	Listen to Cliff	1961	25.00	50.00	100.00
EMI AMERICA					
❑ SN-16220	Green Light	1981	2.00	4.00	8.00
❑ SN-16221	I'm Nearly Famous	1981	2.00	4.00	8.00
❑ SN-16253	Every Face Tells a Story	1981	2.00	4.00	8.00
❑ SW-17018	We Don't Talk Anymore	1979	2.50	5.00	10.00
❑ SW-17039	I'm No Hero	1980	2.50	5.00	10.00
❑ SW-17059	Wired for Sound	1981	2.50	5.00	10.00
❑ ST-17081	Now You See Me, Now You Don't	1982	2.50	5.00	10.00
❑ ST-17105	Give a Little Bit More	1983	2.50	5.00	10.00
EPIC					
❑ LN 24063 [M]	Summer Holiday	1963	10.00	20.00	40.00
❑ LN 24089 [M]	It's All in the Game	1964	7.50	15.00	30.00
❑ LN 24115 [M]	Cliff Richard in Spain	1965	7.50	15.00	30.00
❑ BN 26063 [S]	Summer Holiday	1963	12.50	25.00	50.00
❑ BN 26089 [S]	It's All in the Game	1964	10.00	20.00	40.00
❑ BN 26115 [S]	Cliff Richard in Spain	1965	10.00	20.00	40.00
ROCKET					
❑ PIG-2210	I'm Nearly Famous	1976	3.00	6.00	12.00
❑ PIG-2268	Every Face Tells a Story	1977	3.00	6.00	12.00
❑ BXL1-2958	Green Light	1978	3.00	6.00	12.00
WORD					
❑ WR-8306	Walking in the Light	1985	3.00	6.00	12.00
RICHARD AND JIM					
CAPITOL					
❑ ST 2058 [S]	Folk Songs and Country Sounds	1964	6.25	12.50	25.00
❑ T 2058 [M]	Folk Songs and Country Sounds	1964	5.00	10.00	20.00
❑ ST 2287 [S]	Two Boys from Alabama	1965	6.25	12.50	25.00
❑ T 2287 [M]	Two Boys from Alabama	1965	5.00	10.00	20.00
RICHARDS, ANN					
ATCO					
❑ 33-136 [M]	Ann, Man!	1961	10.00	20.00	40.00
❑ SD 33-136 [S]	Ann, Man!	1961	15.00	30.00	60.00
CAPITOL					
❑ ST 1087 [S]	I'm Shooting High	1959	10.00	20.00	40.00
❑ T 1087 [M]	I'm Shooting High	1959	7.50	15.00	30.00

Number	Title (A Side/B Side)	Yr	VG	VG+	NM
❑ ST 1406 [S]	The Many Moods of Ann Richards	1960	10.00	20.00	40.00
❑ T 1406 [M]	The Many Moods of Ann Richards	1960	7.50	15.00	30.00
❑ ST 1495 [S]	Two Much!	1961	10.00	20.00	40.00
❑ T 1495 [M]	Two Much!	1961	7.50	15.00	30.00
VEE JAY					
❑ LP-1070 [M]	Live...At the Losers	1963	10.00	20.00	40.00
❑ SR-1070 [S]	Live...At the Losers	1963	12.50	25.00	50.00
RICHARDS, EMIL					
ABC IMPULSE!					
❑ AS-9182 [S]	Spirit of '76	1968	5.00	10.00	20.00
❑ AS-9188 [S]	Journey to Bliss	1969	5.00	10.00	20.00
UNI					
❑ 3003 [M]	New Time Element	1967	6.25	12.50	25.00
❑ 3008 [M]	New Sound	1967	6.25	12.50	25.00
❑ 73003 [S]	New Time Element	1967	5.00	10.00	20.00
❑ 73008 [S]	New Sound	1967	5.00	10.00	20.00
RICHARDS, JOHNNY					
BETHLEHEM					
❑ BCP-6011 [M]	Something Else by Johnny Richards	1956	12.50	25.00	50.00
CAPITOL					
❑ T 885 [M]	Wide Range	1957	10.00	20.00	40.00
❑ T 981 [M]	Experiments In Sound	1958	10.00	20.00	40.00
CORAL					
❑ CRL 757304 [S]	Walk Softly/Run Wild	1959	5.00	10.00	20.00
ROULETTE					
❑ SR-25351	Aqui Se Habla Espanol	1967	5.00	10.00	20.00
❑ R-52008 [M]	The Rites of Diablo	1958	7.50	15.00	30.00
❑ SR-52008 [S]	The Rites of Diablo	1958	6.25	12.50	25.00
❑ SR-52114 [S]	My Fair Lady	1964	5.00	10.00	20.00
RICHARDS, TRUDY					
CAPITOL					
❑ T 838 [M]	Crazy in Love	1957	7.50	15.00	30.00
RICHARDSON, JEROME					
NEW JAZZ					
❑ NJLP-8205 [M]	Jerome Richardson Sextet	1958	20.00	40.00	80.00
—Purple label					
❑ NJLP-8205 [M]	Jerome Richardson Sextet	1965	6.25	12.50	25.00
—Blue label, trident logo at right					
❑ NJLP-8226 [M]	Roamin' with Richardson	1959	20.00	40.00	80.00
—Purple label					
❑ NJLP-8226 [M]	Roamin' with Richardson	1965	6.25	12.50	25.00
—Blue label, trident logo at right					
UNITED ARTISTS					
❑ UAJ-14006 [M]	Going to the Movies	1962	7.50	15.00	30.00
❑ UAJS-15006 [S]	Going to the Movies	1962	10.00	20.00	40.00
VERVE					
❑ V-8729 [M]	Groove Merchant	1967	5.00	10.00	20.00
RICHARDSON, JIMMY					
STARDAY					
❑ SLP-126 [M]	Sweet with a Beat	1960	7.50	15.00	30.00
RICHARDSON, WALLY					
PRESTIGE					
❑ PRST-7569	Soul Guru	1969	5.00	10.00	20.00
RICHARDSON, WARREN S., JR.					
COTILLION					
❑ SD 9013	Warren S. Richardson, Jr.	1970	7.50	15.00	30.00
RICHIE, LITTLE JOE					
See LITTLE JOE.					
RICHMAN, JONATHAN, AND THE MODERN LOVERS					
BESERKLEY					
❑ BZ-0048	Jonathan Richman and the Modern Lovers	1976	7.50	15.00	30.00
—Distributed by GRT					
❑ JBZ 0048	Jonathan Richman and the Modern Lovers	1976	6.25	12.50	25.00
—Distributed by Playboy/CBS					
❑ BZ-0050	The Modern Lovers	1976	7.50	15.00	30.00
—Distributed by GRT					
❑ JBZ 0050	The Modern Lovers	1978	6.25	12.50	25.00
—Distributed by Playboy/CBS					
❑ BZ-0053	Rock 'N' Roll with the Modern Lovers	1977	4.50	9.00	18.00
—Distributed by Janus/GRT					
❑ JBZ 0055	Modern Lovers "Live"	1978	3.50	7.00	14.00
—Distributed by Playboy/CBS					
❑ JBZ 0060	Back in Your Life	1979	2.50	5.00	10.00
—Distributed by Playboy/CBS					
❑ 10060	Back in Your Life	1980	3.00	6.00	12.00
—Reissue -- change in distributing label to Elektra					
❑ PZ 34800	Rock 'N' Roll with the Modern Lovers	1977	3.50	7.00	14.00
—Distributed by Playboy/CBS					
BOMP!					
❑ 4021	The Original Modern Lovers	1981	5.00	10.00	20.00
—Same album as Mohawk releasse					
HOME OF THE HITS					
❑ HH-1910	The Modern Lovers	1975	12.50	25.00	50.00
MOHAWK					
❑ SCALP 0002	The Original Modern Lovers	1981	6.25	12.50	25.00
RHINO					
❑ RNLP 70091	The Modern Lovers	1986	3.00	6.00	12.00
—Reissue					
❑ RNLP 70092	Jonathan Richman and the Modern Lovers	1986	3.00	6.00	12.00
—Reissue					
❑ RNLP 70093	Rock 'N' Roll with the Modern Lovers	1986	3.00	6.00	12.00
—Reissue					

Number	Title (A Side/B Side)	Yr	VG	VG+	NM
❑ RNLP 70094	Modern Lovers "Live"	1986	3.00	6.00	12.00
—Reissue					
❑ RNLP 70095	Back in Your Life	1986	3.00	6.00	12.00
—Reissue					
ROUNDER					
❑ 9014	Modern Lovers '88	1988	3.00	6.00	12.00
❑ 9021	Jonathan Richman	1989	3.00	6.00	12.00
❑ 9024	Jonathan Goes Country	1990	3.00	6.00	12.00
SIRE					
❑ 23939	Jonathan Sings!	1983	3.00	6.00	12.00

RICHMOND, DANNIE
IMPULSE!
Number	Title (A Side/B Side)	Yr	VG	VG+	NM
❑ A-98 [M]	Dannie Richmond	1966	5.00	10.00	20.00
❑ AS-98 [S]	Dannie Richmond	1966	6.25	12.50	25.00

RICKS, JIMMY
Also see THE RAVENS.
JUBILEE
Number	Title (A Side/B Side)	Yr	VG	VG+	NM
❑ JGS-8021	Tell Her You Love Her	1969	12.50	25.00	50.00
MAINSTREAM					
❑ S-6050 [S]	Vibrations	1965	15.00	30.00	60.00
❑ 56050 [M]	Vibrations	1965	12.50	25.00	50.00
SIGNATURE					
❑ SM-1032 [M]	Jimmy Ricks	1961	50.00	100.00	200.00
—White label promo					
❑ SM-1032 [M]	Jimmy Ricks	1961	75.00	150.00	300.00

RIDDLE, NELSON
ALSHIRE
Number	Title (A Side/B Side)	Yr	VG	VG+	NM
❑ 5203	Bridge Over Troubled Water	197?	2.50	5.00	10.00
AVON					
❑ 10170	Avon Wishes You a Happy Holiday and a Joyous New Year	1970	3.75	7.50	15.00
—Given to Avon salespeople					
CAPITOL					
❑ T 753 [M]	The Tender Touch	1956	6.25	12.50	25.00
❑ T 813 [M]	Hey, Let Yourself Go	1957	6.25	12.50	25.00
❑ T 893 [M]	C'mon, Get Happy	1957	6.25	12.50	25.00
❑ T 915 [M]	Sea of Dreams	1958	6.25	12.50	25.00
❑ ST 1148 [S]	The Joy of Living	1959	6.25	12.50	25.00
❑ T 1148 [M]	The Joy of Living	1959	5.00	10.00	20.00
❑ STAO 1259 [S]	Sing a Song with Riddle	1960	6.25	12.50	25.00
❑ TAO 1259 [M]	Sing a Song with Riddle	1960	5.00	10.00	20.00
❑ ST 1365 [S]	Can-Can	1961	6.25	12.50	25.00
❑ T 1365 [M]	Can-Can	1961	5.00	10.00	20.00
❑ ST 1571 [S]	Love Tide	1961	6.25	12.50	25.00
❑ T 1571 [M]	Love Tide	1961	5.00	10.00	20.00
❑ ST 1670 [S]	Magic Moments from "The Gay Life"	1962	6.25	12.50	25.00
❑ T 1670 [M]	Magic Moments from "The Gay Life"	1962	5.00	10.00	20.00
❑ ST 1771 [S]	Route 66 Theme and Other Great TV Themes	1962	7.50	15.00	30.00
❑ T 1771 [M]	Route 66 Theme and Other Great TV Themes	1962	6.25	12.50	25.00
❑ ST 1817 [S]	Love Is a Game of Poker	1962	6.25	12.50	25.00
❑ T 1817 [M]	Love Is a Game of Poker	1962	5.00	10.00	20.00
❑ ST 1869 [S]	More Hit TV Themes	1963	6.25	12.50	25.00
❑ T 1869 [M]	More Hit TV Themes	1963	5.00	10.00	20.00
❑ DT 1990 [P]	The Best of Nelson Riddle	1963	3.75	7.50	15.00
❑ T 1990 [M]	The Best of Nelson Riddle	1963	3.75	7.50	15.00
❑ SM-11764	The Best of Nelson Riddle	1976	2.50	5.00	10.00
DAYBREAK					
❑ DS 2015	Viva Legrand!	197?	5.00	10.00	20.00
HARMONY					
❑ HS 11320	Nelson Riddle and His Orchestra Play the Wonderful Nat King Cole Songs	1969	3.00	6.00	12.00
LIBERTY					
❑ LRP-3508 [M]	The Bright and the Beautiful	1967	3.75	7.50	15.00
❑ LST-3532 [M]	The Riddle of Today	1967	5.00	10.00	20.00
❑ LST-7508 [S]	The Bright and the Beautiful	1967	3.75	7.50	15.00
❑ LST-7532 [S]	The Riddle of Today	1967	3.75	7.50	15.00
PICKWICK					
❑ PC 3007 [M]	Witchcraft	1965	3.75	7.50	15.00
❑ SPC 3007 [R]	Witchcraft	1965	3.00	6.00	12.00
REPRISE					
❑ R-6071 [M]	Come Blow Your Horn	1963	3.75	7.50	15.00
❑ R9-6071 [S]	Come Blow Your Horn	1963	5.00	10.00	20.00
❑ R-6120 [M]	"White on White," "Shangri-La," "Charade" and Other Hits of 1964	1964	3.75	7.50	15.00
❑ RS-6120 [S]	"White on White," "Shangri-La," "Charade" and Other Hits of 1964	1964	5.00	10.00	20.00
❑ R-6138 [M]	Great Music, Great Films, Great Sounds	1964	3.75	7.50	15.00
❑ RS-6138 [S]	Great Music, Great Films, Great Sounds	1964	5.00	10.00	20.00
❑ R-6162 [M]	Nat	1965	3.75	7.50	15.00
❑ RS-6162 [S]	Nat	1965	5.00	10.00	20.00
SEARS					
❑ SP-406 [M]	Witchcraft	196?	3.75	7.50	15.00
❑ SPS-406 [R]	Witchcraft	196?	3.00	6.00	12.00
SOLID STATE					
❑ SS-18013	Music for Wives and Lovers	1967	5.00	10.00	20.00
❑ ST-91083	Music for Wives and Lovers	1967	6.25	12.50	25.00
—Capitol Record Club edition					
SUNSET					
❑ SUS-5233	The Riddle Touch	1968	3.00	6.00	12.00
UNITED ARTISTS					
❑ UAS 6670	The Contemporary Sound of Nelson Riddle	1968	5.00	10.00	20.00
❑ ST-91566	The Contemporary Sound of Nelson Riddle	1968	6.25	12.50	25.00
—Capitol Record Club edition					

RIDERS OF THE PURPLE SAGE, THE
See FOY WILLING.

RIDLEY, LARRY
STRATA-EAST
Number	Title (A Side/B Side)	Yr	VG	VG+	NM
❑ SES-19759	Sum of the Parts	1975	6.25	12.50	25.00

RIEDEL, GEORGE
PHILIPS
Number	Title (A Side/B Side)	Yr	VG	VG+	NM
❑ PHS 600140 [S]	Jazz Ballet	1964	5.00	10.00	20.00

RIG
CAPITOL
Number	Title (A Side/B Side)	Yr	VG	VG+	NM
❑ ST-473	Rig	1970	5.00	10.00	20.00

RIGHTEOUS BROTHERS, THE
HAVEN
Number	Title (A Side/B Side)	Yr	VG	VG+	NM
❑ ST-9201	Give It to the People	1974	3.75	7.50	15.00
❑ AS-9203	Sons of Mrs. Righteous	1975	3.75	7.50	15.00
MGM					
❑ GAS-102	The Righteous Brothers (Golden Archive Series)	1970	3.75	7.50	15.00
❑ SE-4885	The History of the Righteous Brothers	1973	3.75	7.50	15.00
MOONGLOW					
❑ MLP-1001 [M]	Right Now!	1963	10.00	20.00	40.00
❑ MSP-1001 [S]	Right Now!	1963	15.00	30.00	60.00
❑ MLP-1002 [M]	Some Blue-Eyed Soul	1964	10.00	20.00	40.00
❑ MSP-1002 [S]	Some Blue-Eyed Soul	1964	15.00	30.00	60.00
❑ MLP-1003 [M]	This Is New!	1965	10.00	20.00	40.00
❑ MSP-1003 [S]	This Is New!	1965	15.00	30.00	60.00
❑ MLP-1004 [M]	The Best of the Righteous Brothers	1966	6.25	12.50	25.00
❑ MSP-1004 [S]	The Best of the Righteous Brothers	1966	7.50	15.00	30.00
PHILLES					
❑ PHLP-4007 [M]	You've Lost That Lovin' Feelin'	1964	6.25	12.50	25.00
❑ PHLPS-4007 [S]	You've Lost That Lovin' Feelin'	1964	10.00	20.00	40.00
❑ PHLP-4008 [M]	Just Once in My Life	1965	6.25	12.50	25.00
❑ PHLPS-4008 [S]	Just Once in My Life	1965	10.00	20.00	40.00
❑ PHLP-4009 [M]	Back to Back	1965	6.25	12.50	25.00
❑ PHLPS-4009 [S]	Back to Back	1965	10.00	20.00	40.00
❑ T-90677 [M]	Back to Back	1965	7.50	15.00	30.00
—Capitol Record Club edition					
❑ ST-90692 [S]	You've Lost That Lovin' Feelin'	1965	12.50	25.00	50.00
—Capitol Record Club edition					
❑ T-90692 [M]	You've Lost That Lovin' Feelin'	1965	12.50	25.00	50.00
—Capitol Record Club edition					
RHINO					
❑ R1-71488 [(2)]	Anthology	1989	3.75	7.50	15.00
VERVE					
❑ V-5001 [M]	Soul and Inspiration	1966	5.00	10.00	20.00
❑ V6-5001 [S]	Soul and Inspiration	1966	6.25	12.50	25.00
❑ V-5004 [M]	Go Ahead and Cry	1966	5.00	10.00	20.00
❑ V6-5004 [S]	Go Ahead and Cry	1966	6.25	12.50	25.00
❑ V-5010 [M]	Sayin' Somethin'	1967	5.00	10.00	20.00
❑ V6-5010 [S]	Sayin' Somethin'	1967	6.25	12.50	25.00
❑ V-5020 [M]	Greatest Hits	1967	6.25	12.50	25.00
❑ V6-5020 [S]	Greatest Hits	1967	5.00	10.00	20.00
❑ V-5031 [M]	Souled Out	1967	7.50	15.00	30.00
❑ V6-5031 [S]	Souled Out	1967	5.00	10.00	20.00
❑ V6-5051	Standards	1968	5.00	10.00	20.00
❑ V6-5058	One for the Road	1968	5.00	10.00	20.00
—Without The Blossoms credited on the back cover					
❑ V6-5058	One for the Road	1968	7.50	15.00	30.00
—With The Blossoms credited on the back cover					
❑ V6-5071	Greatest Hits, Vol. 2	1969	5.00	10.00	20.00
❑ V6-5076	Re-Birth	1970	5.00	10.00	20.00
❑ ST-90669 [S]	Soul and Inspiration	1966	7.50	15.00	30.00
—Capitol Record Club edition					
❑ ST-91057 [S]	Sayin' Somethin'	1967	6.25	12.50	25.00
—Capitol Record Club edition					
❑ T-91057 [M]	Sayin' Somethin'	1967	7.50	15.00	30.00
—Capitol Record Club edition					
❑ 823662-1	Greatest Hits	198?	2.50	5.00	10.00

RILEY, BILLY LEE
GNP CRESCENDO
Number	Title (A Side/B Side)	Yr	VG	VG+	NM
❑ GNP-2020 [M]	Billy Lee Riley	1966	3.75	7.50	15.00
❑ GNPS-2020 [S]	Billy Lee Riley	1966	5.00	10.00	20.00
MERCURY					
❑ MG-20958 [M]	The Whiskey A-Go-Go Presents Billy Lee Riley	1964	5.00	10.00	20.00
❑ MG-20965 [M]	Big Harmonica Special	1964	5.00	10.00	20.00
❑ MG-20974 [M]	Beatlemania Harmonica	1965	5.00	10.00	20.00
❑ SR-60958 [S]	The Whiskey A-Go-Go Presents Billy Lee Riley	1964	6.25	12.50	25.00
❑ SR-60965 [S]	Big Harmonica Special	1964	6.25	12.50	25.00
❑ SR-60974 [S]	Beatlemania Harmonica	1965	6.25	12.50	25.00

RILEY, JEANNIE C.
ALLEGIANCE
Number	Title (A Side/B Side)	Yr	VG	VG+	NM
❑ AV-5026	Tears, Joys and Memories	198?	2.50	5.00	10.00
CAPITOL					
❑ ST-177	The Songs of Jeannie C. Riley	1969	3.75	7.50	15.00
LITTLE DARLIN'					
❑ SLD 8011	Sock Soul	1968	5.00	10.00	20.00
MGM					
❑ SE-4805	Give Myself a Party	1972	3.00	6.00	12.00
❑ SE-4849	Down to Earth	1973	3.00	6.00	12.00
❑ SE-4891	When Love Has Gone Away	1973	3.00	6.00	12.00
❑ SE-4909	Just Jeannie C. Riley	1973	3.00	6.00	12.00
PICKWICK					
❑ 6098	The Girl Most Likely	197?	2.50	5.00	10.00
❑ 6119	The World of Country	197?	2.50	5.00	10.00
PLANTATION					
❑ PLP 1	Harper Valley P.T.A.	1968	5.00	10.00	20.00
❑ PLP 2	Yearbooks and Yesterdays	1969	3.75	7.50	15.00

R

Number	Title (A Side/B Side)	Yr	VG	VG+	NM
❏ PLP 3	Things Go Better with Love	1969	3.75	7.50	15.00
❏ PLP 8	Country Girl	1970	3.75	7.50	15.00
❏ PLP 11	The Generation Gap	1970	3.75	7.50	15.00
❏ PLP 13	Jeannie C. Riley's Greatest Hits	1971	3.75	7.50	15.00
❏ PLP 16	Jeannie	1971	3.75	7.50	15.00
❏ 508	Country Queens	197?	3.00	6.00	12.00

POWER PAK

Number	Title (A Side/B Side)	Yr	VG	VG+	NM
❏ 250	Country Gold	197?	2.50	5.00	10.00

RINCON SURFSIDE BAND, THE
DUNHILL

Number	Title (A Side/B Side)	Yr	VG	VG+	NM
❏ D 50001 [M]	Surfing Songbook	1965	50.00	100.00	200.00
❏ DS 50001 [S]	Surfing Songbook	1965	75.00	150.00	300.00

RIOPELLE, JERRY
CAPITOL

Number	Title (A Side/B Side)	Yr	VG	VG+	NM
❏ ST-732	Jerry Riopelle	1971	5.00	10.00	20.00
❏ ST-863	Second Album	1971	5.00	10.00	20.00

RIOT
FIRE-SIGN

Number	Title (A Side/B Side)	Yr	VG	VG+	NM
❏ 87001	Rock City	1977	7.50	15.00	30.00

RIP CHORDS, THE
COLUMBIA

Number	Title (A Side/B Side)	Yr	VG	VG+	NM
❏ CL 2151 [M]	Hey Little Cobra and Other Hot Rod Hits	1964	10.00	20.00	40.00
❏ CL 2216 [M]	Three Window Coupe	1964	12.50	25.00	50.00
❏ CS 8951 [S]	Hey Little Cobra and Other Hot Rod Hits	1964	12.50	25.00	50.00
❏ CS 9016 [S]	Three Window Coupe	1964	17.50	35.00	70.00

RIPERTON, MINNIE
ACCORD

Number	Title (A Side/B Side)	Yr	VG	VG+	NM
❏ SN-7205	Wistful Memories	1981	2.50	5.00	10.00

CAPITOL

Number	Title (A Side/B Side)	Yr	VG	VG+	NM
❏ SO-11936	Minnie	1979	2.50	5.00	10.00
❏ SN-12004	Perfect Angel	1979	2.50	5.00	10.00
—Reissue of Epic 32561					
❏ SN-12005	Adventures in Paradise	1979	2.50	5.00	10.00
—Reissue of Epic 33454					
❏ SN-12006	Stay in Love	1979	2.50	5.00	10.00
—Reissue of Epic 34191					
❏ SOO-12097	Love Lives Forever	1980	2.50	5.00	10.00
❏ ST-12189	The Best of Minnie Riperton	1981	2.50	5.00	10.00
❏ SN-16145	Perfect Angel	1980	2.00	4.00	8.00
—Budget-line reissue					
❏ SN-16146	Adventures in Paradise	1980	2.00	4.00	8.00
—Budget-line reissue					
❏ SN-16147	Stay in Love	1980	2.00	4.00	8.00
—Budget-line reissue					

EPIC

Number	Title (A Side/B Side)	Yr	VG	VG+	NM
❏ KE 32561	Perfect Angel	1974	3.00	6.00	12.00
❏ PE 33454	Adventures in Paradise	1975	3.00	6.00	12.00
❏ PEQ 33454 [Q]	Adventures in Paradise	1975	5.00	10.00	20.00
❏ PE 34191	Stay in Love	1977	3.00	6.00	12.00

GRT

Number	Title (A Side/B Side)	Yr	VG	VG+	NM
❏ 30001	Come To My Garden	1970	3.75	7.50	15.00

JANUS

Number	Title (A Side/B Side)	Yr	VG	VG+	NM
❏ 7011	Come To My Garden	1974	3.00	6.00	12.00
—Reissue of GRT LP					

RIPPY, RODNEY ALLEN
BELL

Number	Title (A Side/B Side)	Yr	VG	VG+	NM
❏ 1311	Take Life a Little Easier	1974	5.00	10.00	20.00

RISERS, THE
IMPERIAL

Number	Title (A Side/B Side)	Yr	VG	VG+	NM
❏ LP-9269 [M]	She's a Bad Motorcycle	1964	25.00	50.00	100.00
❏ LP-12269 [S]	She's a Bad Motorcycle	1964	37.50	75.00	150.00

RISING STORM, THE
ARF! ARF!

Number	Title (A Side/B Side)	Yr	VG	VG+	NM
❏ 007	Alive in Anover Again	1983	30.00	60.00	120.00

REMNANT

Number	Title (A Side/B Side)	Yr	VG	VG+	NM
❏ BBA-3571	Calm Before the Rising Storm	1968	600.00	900.00	1200.

STANTON PARK

Number	Title (A Side/B Side)	Yr	VG	VG+	NM
❏ 001	Calm Before the Rising Storm	1991	5.00	10.00	20.00
—Reissue of Remnant album					

RITENOUR, LEE
MOBILE FIDELITY

Number	Title (A Side/B Side)	Yr	VG	VG+	NM
❏ 1-147	Captain Fingers	1985	6.25	12.50	25.00
—Audiophile vinyl					

NAUTILUS

Number	Title (A Side/B Side)	Yr	VG	VG+	NM
❏ NR-41	Rit	198?	10.00	20.00	40.00
—Audiophile vinyl					

RITTER, TEX
Also see STAN KENTON AND TEX RITTER.

BUCKBOARD

Number	Title (A Side/B Side)	Yr	VG	VG+	NM
❏ BBS 1030	Tex Ritter	198?	2.50	5.00	10.00

CAPITOL

Number	Title (A Side/B Side)	Yr	VG	VG+	NM
❏ ST-213	Chuck Wagon Days	1969	5.00	10.00	20.00
❏ ST-467	Green Green Valley	1970	5.00	10.00	20.00
❏ T 971 [M]	Songs from the Western Screen	1958	20.00	40.00	80.00
—Turquoise or gray label					
❏ T 971 [M]	Songs from the Western Screen	1959	10.00	20.00	40.00
—Black colorband label, logo at left					
❏ T 971 [M]	Songs from the Western Screen	1962	6.25	12.50	25.00
—Black colorband label, logo at top					
❏ T 1100 [M]	Psalms	1959	12.50	25.00	50.00
—Black colorband label, logo at left					

Number	Title (A Side/B Side)	Yr	VG	VG+	NM
❏ T 1100 [M]	Psalms	1962	6.25	12.50	25.00
—Black colorband label, logo at top					
❏ ST 1292 [S]	Blood on the Saddle	1960	10.00	20.00	40.00
—Black colorband label, logo at left					
❏ ST 1292 [S]	Blood on the Saddle	1962	6.25	12.50	25.00
—Black colorband label, logo at top					
❏ T 1292 [M]	Blood on the Saddle	1960	7.50	15.00	30.00
—Black colorband label, logo at left					
❏ T 1292 [M]	Blood on the Saddle	1962	5.00	10.00	20.00
—Black colorband label, logo at top					
❏ SW 1562 [S]	The Lincoln Hymns	1961	10.00	20.00	40.00
❏ W 1562 [M]	The Lincoln Hymns	1961	7.50	15.00	30.00
❏ SM-1623	Hillbilly Heaven	1976	2.50	5.00	10.00
—Reissue with new prefix					
❏ ST 1623 [S]	Hillbilly Heaven	1961	10.00	20.00	40.00
—Black colorband label, logo at left					
❏ ST 1623 [S]	Hillbilly Heaven	1962	6.25	12.50	25.00
—Black colorband label, logo at top					
❏ T 1623 [M]	Hillbilly Heaven	1961	7.50	15.00	30.00
—Black colorband label, logo at left					
❏ T 1623 [M]	Hillbilly Heaven	1962	5.00	10.00	20.00
—Black colorband label, logo at top					
❏ ST 1910 [S]	Border Affair	1963	6.25	12.50	25.00
❏ T 1910 [M]	Border Affair.	1963	5.00	10.00	20.00
❏ ST 2402 [S]	The Friendly Voice of Tex Ritter.	1965	6.25	12.50	25.00
❏ T 2402 [M]	The Friendly Voice of Tex Ritter.	1965	5.00	10.00	20.00
❏ DT 2595 [R]	The Best of Tex Ritter.	1966	3.75	7.50	15.00
❏ T 2595 [M]	The Best of Tex Ritter.	1966	6.25	12.50	25.00
❏ ST 2743 [S]	Sweet Land of Liberty.	1967	6.25	12.50	25.00
❏ T 2743 [M]	Sweet Land of Liberty.	1967	7.50	15.00	30.00
❏ ST 2786 [S]	Just Beyond the Moon.	1967	6.25	12.50	25.00
❏ T 2786 [M]	Just Beyond the Moon.	1967	7.50	15.00	30.00
❏ ST 2890 [S]	Bum Tiddil Dee Bum Bum!	1968	6.25	12.50	25.00
❏ T 2890 [M]	Bum Tiddil Dee Bum Bum!	1968	12.50	25.00	50.00
❏ ST 2974	Tex Ritter's Wild West.	1968	6.25	12.50	25.00
❏ H 4004 [10]	Cowboy Favorites.	195?	45.00	90.00	180.00
❏ ST-11037	Supercountrylegendary.	1972	3.75	7.50	15.00
❏ SKC-11241 [(3)]	An American Legend.	1973	7.50	15.00	30.00
❏ ST-11351	Fall Away.	1974	3.75	7.50	15.00
❏ ST-11503	Comin' After Jinny.	1976	3.75	7.50	15.00

HILLTOP

Number	Title (A Side/B Side)	Yr	VG	VG+	NM
❏ PTP-2020 [(2)]	My Kinda Songs	197?	3.75	7.50	15.00
❏ JS-6043	Tex Ritter Sings His Hits	196?	3.00	6.00	12.00
❏ JS-6075	Love You As Big As Texas	196?	3.00	6.00	12.00
❏ JS-6138	High Noon	196?	3.00	6.00	12.00
❏ JS-6155	Tex	197?	3.00	6.00	12.00

LABREA

Number	Title (A Side/B Side)	Yr	VG	VG+	NM
❏ L-8036 [M]	Jamboree, Nashville Style	196?	5.00	10.00	20.00
❏ LS-8036 [S]	Jamboree, Nashville Style	196?	6.25	12.50	25.00

PREMIER

Number	Title (A Side/B Side)	Yr	VG	VG+	NM
❏ 9023	Tex Ritter and the Rio Grande River Boys	196?	3.00	6.00	12.00

RITZ, LYLE
VERVE

Number	Title (A Side/B Side)	Yr	VG	VG+	NM
❏ MGV-2087 [M]	How About Uke?	1957	10.00	20.00	40.00
❏ MGVS-6070 [S]	50th State Jazz	1960	10.00	20.00	40.00
❏ MGV-8333 [M]	50th State Jazz	1959	12.50	25.00	50.00
❏ V-8333 [M]	50th State Jazz	1961	6.25	12.50	25.00
❏ V6-8333 [S]	50th State Jazz	1961	5.00	10.00	20.00

RIVERA, HECTOR
WING

Number	Title (A Side/B Side)	Yr	VG	VG+	NM
❏ MGW-12197 [M]	Let's Cha Cha Cha	1960	5.00	10.00	20.00

RIVERA, LUIS
IMPERIAL

Number	Title (A Side/B Side)	Yr	VG	VG+	NM
❏ LP-9139 [M]	Filet of Soul	1961	7.50	15.00	30.00

RIVERA, LUIS, AND DOC BAGBY
KING

Number	Title (A Side/B Side)	Yr	VG	VG+	NM
❏ 631 [M]	Battle of the Organs	1959	25.00	50.00	100.00

RIVERS, JERRY
STARDAY

Number	Title (A Side/B Side)	Yr	VG	VG+	NM
❏ SLP-281 [M]	Fantastic Fiddlin' and Tall Tales	1964	7.50	15.00	30.00

RIVERS, JOHNNY
ATLANTIC

Number	Title (A Side/B Side)	Yr	VG	VG+	NM
❏ SD 7301	The Road	1974	3.00	6.00	12.00

BIG TREE

Number	Title (A Side/B Side)	Yr	VG	VG+	NM
❏ BT 76004	Outside Help	1977	3.00	6.00	12.00

CAPITOL

Number	Title (A Side/B Side)	Yr	VG	VG+	NM
❏ ST 2161 [S]	The Sensational Johnny Rivers	1964	6.25	12.50	25.00
❏ T 2161 [M]	The Sensational Johnny Rivers	1964	5.00	10.00	20.00

COLUMBIA

Number	Title (A Side/B Side)	Yr	VG	VG+	NM
❏ FE 38429	Not a Through Street	1983	2.50	5.00	10.00
❏ PE 38429	Not a Through Street	1985	2.00	4.00	8.00
—Budget-line reissue					

EPIC

Number	Title (A Side/B Side)	Yr	VG	VG+	NM
❏ PE 33681	New Lovers and Old Friends	1975	3.00	6.00	12.00

IMPERIAL

Number	Title (A Side/B Side)	Yr	VG	VG+	NM
❏ LP-9264 [M]	Johnny Rivers at the Whiskey A-Go-Go	1964	5.00	10.00	20.00
—Black label with pink and white at left					
❏ LP-9264 [M]	Johnny Rivers at the Whiskey A-Go-Go	1966	3.00	6.00	12.00
—Black label with green and white at left					
❏ LP-9274 [M]	Here We A-Go-Go Again!	1964	5.00	10.00	20.00
—Black label with pink and white at left					
❏ LP-9274 [M]	Here We A-Go-Go Again!	1966	3.00	6.00	12.00
—Black label with green and white at left					
❏ LP-9280 [M]	Johnny Rivers In Action!	1965	5.00	10.00	20.00
—Black label with pink and white at left					
❏ LP-9280 [M]	Johnny Rivers In Action!	1966	3.00	6.00	12.00
—Black label with green and white at left					

James Ray of "If You Gotta Make a Fool of Somebody" fame had this album of songs on the Caprice label in 1962.

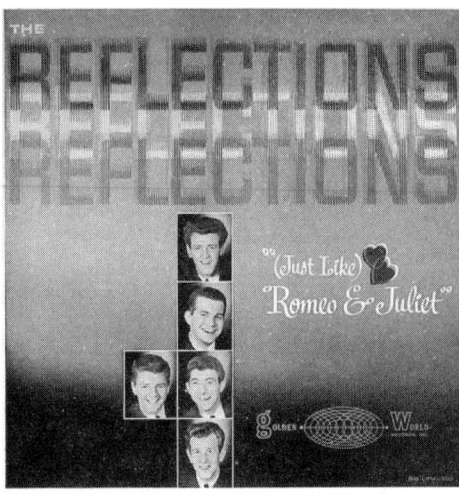

The only LP ever released on the Detroit label Golden World was the Reflections' *(Just Like) Romeo and Juliet.* Only mono copies of this 1964 release are known to exist.

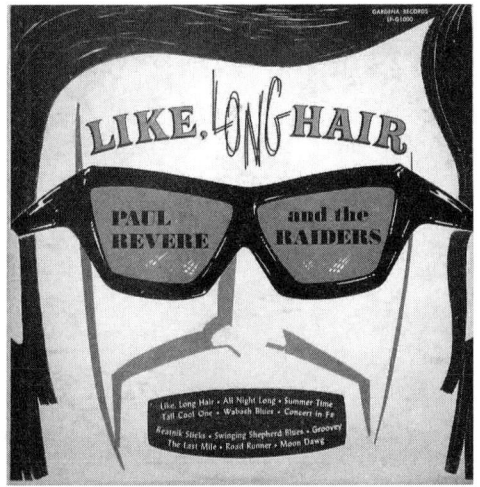

Paul Revere and the Raiders were mostly an instrumental group in their days on Gardena Records. Their only hit from that period was the title song of this hard-to-find LP, *Like, Long Hair.*

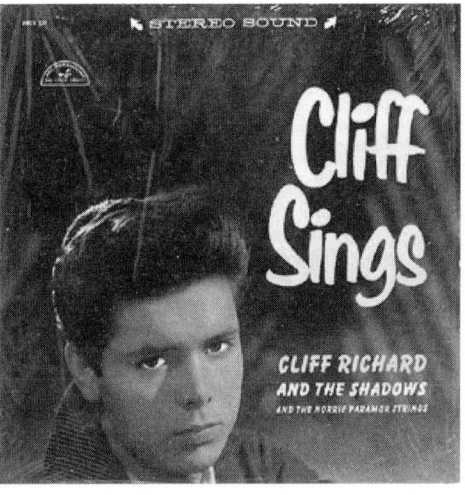

Cliff Richard was still unknown in America when ABC-Paramount released the above album. He remained a big star in England, but didn't finally have a U.S. hit until 1976, by which time this album was long gone.

In 1969, the London label compiled the above Rolling Stones promo-only LP in hopes of spurring radio play. This record, with the number RSD-1, is extremely rare.

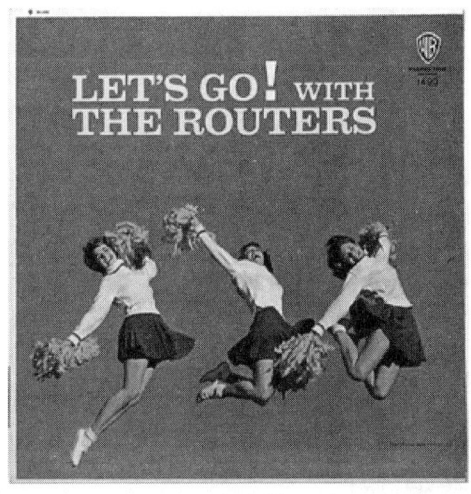

For an album that revolves around a hit song based on a cheer, why not have cheerleaders on the cover of the Routers' *Let's Go!*

Number	Title (A Side/B Side)	Yr	VG	VG+	NM
❑ LP-9284 [M]	Meanwhile Back at the Whiskey a-Go-Go	1965	5.00	10.00	20.00
—Black label with pink and white at left					
❑ LP-9284 [M]	Meanwhile Back at the Whiskey a-Go-Go	1966	3.00	6.00	12.00
—Black label with green and white at left					
❑ LP-9293 [M]	Johnny Rivers Rocks the Folk	1965	5.00	10.00	20.00
—Black label with pink and white at left					
❑ LP-9293 [M]	Johnny Rivers Rocks the Folk	1966	3.00	6.00	12.00
—Black label with green and white at left					
❑ LP-9307 [M]	...And I Know You Wanna Dance	1966	3.00	6.00	12.00
—Black label with green and white at left					
❑ LP-9307 [M]	...And I Know You Wanna Dance	1966	5.00	10.00	20.00
—Black label with pink and white at left					
❑ LP-9324 [M]	Johnny Rivers' Golden Hits	1966	3.75	7.50	15.00
❑ LP-9334 [M]	Changes	1966	3.75	7.50	15.00
❑ LP-9341 [M]	Rewind	1967	5.00	10.00	20.00
❑ LP-9372 [M]	Realization	1968	10.00	20.00	40.00
❑ LP-12264 [S]	Johnny Rivers at the Whiskey A-Go-Go	1964	6.25	12.50	25.00
—Black label with pink and white at left					
❑ LP-12264 [S]	Johnny Rivers at the Whiskey A-Go-Go	1966	3.75	7.50	15.00
—Black label with green and white at left					
❑ LP-12274 [S]	Here We A-Go-Go Again!	1964	6.25	12.50	25.00
—Black label with pink and white at left					
❑ LP-12274 [S]	Here We A-Go-Go Again!	1966	3.75	7.50	15.00
—Black label with green and white at left					
❑ LP-12280 [S]	Johnny Rivers In Action!	1965	6.25	12.50	25.00
—Black label with pink and white at left					
❑ LP-12280 [S]	Johnny Rivers In Action!	1966	3.75	7.50	15.00
—Black label with green and white at left					
❑ LP-12284 [S]	Meanwhile Back at the Whiskey a-Go-Go	1965	6.25	12.50	25.00
—Black label with pink and white at left					
❑ LP-12284 [S]	Meanwhile Back at the Whiskey a-Go-Go	1966	3.75	7.50	15.00
—Black label with green and white at left					
❑ LP-12293 [S]	Johnny Rivers Rocks the Folk	1965	6.25	12.50	25.00
—Black label with pink and white at left					
❑ LP-12293 [S]	Johnny Rivers Rocks the Folk	1966	3.75	7.50	15.00
—Black label with green and white at left					
❑ LP-12307 [S]	...And I Know You Wanna Dance	1966	3.75	7.50	15.00
—Black label with green and white at left					
❑ LP-12307 [S]	...And I Know You Wanna Dance	1966	6.25	12.50	25.00
—Black label with pink and white at left					
❑ LP-12324 [S]	Johnny Rivers' Golden Hits	1966	5.00	10.00	20.00
❑ LP-12334 [S]	Changes	1966	5.00	10.00	20.00
❑ LP-12341 [S]	Rewind	1967	5.00	10.00	20.00
❑ LP-12372 [S]	Realization	1968	5.00	10.00	20.00
❑ LP-12427	A Touch of Gold	1969	5.00	10.00	20.00
❑ LP-16001	Slim Slo Slider	1970	5.00	10.00	20.00
LIBERTY					
❑ LN-10120	The Best of Johnny Rivers	1981	2.00	4.00	8.00
❑ LN-10121	Changes	1981	2.00	4.00	8.00
—Budget-line reissue					
❑ LN-10154	Blue Suede Shoes	1981	2.00	4.00	8.00
—Budget-line reissue					
❑ LO-12324	Johnny Rivers' Golden Hits	198?	2.00	4.00	8.00
—Budget-line reissue					
❑ LW-12427	A Touch of Gold	198?	2.00	4.00	8.00
—Budget-line reissue					
MCA					
❑ 917	Greatest Hits	1985	2.50	5.00	10.00
PICKWICK					
❑ PC-3022 [M]	Johnny Rivers	196?	3.75	7.50	15.00
❑ SPC-3022 [R]	Johnny Rivers	196?	2.50	5.00	10.00
—Later covers have "electronically enhanced for STEREO" at upper right					
❑ SPC-3022 [R]	Johnny Rivers	196?	3.00	6.00	12.00
—First pressing covers have no "electronically enhanced for STEREO" at upper right					
❑ SPC-3191	If You Want It, I Got It	196?	3.00	6.00	12.00
RSO					
❑ RS-1-3082	Borrowed Time	1980	2.50	5.00	10.00
SEARS					
❑ SPS-417	Mr. Teenage	196?	6.25	12.50	25.00
❑ SPS-487	Groovin'	1968	6.25	12.50	25.00
SOUL CITY					
❑ SC 1007-1	Greatest Hits	1998	5.00	10.00	20.00
—500 copies, each autographed by Johnny Rivers					
SUNSET					
❑ SUM-1157 [M]	Whiskey A-Go-Go Revisited	1967	3.00	6.00	12.00
❑ SUS-5157 [S]	Whiskey A-Go-Go Revisited	1967	2.50	5.00	10.00
❑ SUS-5251	The Early Years	1969	2.50	5.00	10.00
UNART					
❑ M-20007 [M]	The Great Johnny Rivers	1967	3.00	6.00	12.00
❑ S-21007 [S]	The Great Johnny Rivers	1967	3.00	6.00	12.00
UNITED ARTISTS					
❑ UA-LA075-F	Blue Suede Shoes	1973	3.00	6.00	12.00
❑ USX-93 [(2)]	Johnny Rivers Superpak	1971	5.00	10.00	20.00
❑ UA-LA253-G	The Very Best of Johnny Rivers	1974	3.00	6.00	12.00
❑ UA-LA387-E	The Very Best of Johnny Rivers	1975	3.00	6.00	12.00
❑ UA-LA486-G	Wild Night	1976	3.00	6.00	12.00
❑ UAL-3386 [M]	Go, Johnny, Go	1964	5.00	10.00	20.00
❑ UAS-5532	Home Grown	1971	3.75	7.50	15.00
❑ UAS-5650	L.A. Reggae	1972	3.75	7.50	15.00
❑ UAS-6386 [S]	Go, Johnny, Go	1964	6.25	12.50	25.00
❑ ST-90813 [S]	Go, Johnny, Go	1965	7.50	15.00	30.00
—Capitol Record Club edition					
❑ T-90813 [M]	Go, Johnny, Go	1965	6.25	12.50	25.00
—Capitol Record Club edition					

RIVERS, MAVIS

CAPITOL

Number	Title (A Side/B Side)	Yr	VG	VG+	NM
❑ ST 1210 [S]	Take a Number	1959	10.00	20.00	40.00
❑ T 1210 [M]	Take a Number	1959	7.50	15.00	30.00
REPRISE					
❑ R-2002 [M]	Mavis	1961	7.50	15.00	30.00
❑ R9-2002 [S]	Mavis	1961	10.00	20.00	40.00
❑ R-6074 [M]	Mavis Rivers Meets Shorty Rogers	1963	6.25	12.50	25.00
❑ RS-6074 [S]	Mavis Rivers Meets Shorty Rogers	1963	7.50	15.00	30.00
VEE JAY					
❑ VJ-1132 [M]	We Remember Mildred Bailey	1964	6.25	12.50	25.00
❑ VJS-1132 [S]	We Remember Mildred Bailey	1964	10.00	20.00	40.00

RIVERS, SAM

BLUE NOTE

Number	Title (A Side/B Side)	Yr	VG	VG+	NM
❑ BLP-4184 [M]	Fuchsia Swing Song	1964	6.25	12.50	25.00
❑ BLP-4206 [M]	Contours	1965	6.25	12.50	25.00
❑ BLP-4249 [M]	A New Conception	1966	6.25	12.50	25.00
❑ BST-84184 [S]	Fuchsia Swing Song	1964	7.50	15.00	30.00
—With "New York, USA" address on label					
❑ BST-84184 [S]	Fuchsia Swing Song	1967	5.00	10.00	20.00
—With "A Division of Liberty Records" on label					
❑ BST-84206 [S]	Contours	1965	7.50	15.00	30.00
—With "New York, USA" address on label					
❑ BST-84206 [S]	Contours	1967	5.00	10.00	20.00
—With "A Division of Liberty Records" on label					
❑ BST-84249 [S]	A New Conception	1966	7.50	15.00	30.00
—With "New York, USA" address on label					
❑ BST-84249 [S]	A New Conception	1967	5.00	10.00	20.00
—With "A Division of Liberty Records" on label					

RIVERSIDE JAZZ STARS, THE

RIVERSIDE

Number	Title (A Side/B Side)	Yr	VG	VG+	NM
❑ RLP-397 [M]	A Jazz Version of "Kean"	1961	7.50	15.00	30.00
❑ RS-9397 [S]	A Jazz Version of "Kean"	1961	10.00	20.00	40.00

RIVIERAS, THE (1)

POST

Number	Title (A Side/B Side)	Yr	VG	VG+	NM
❑ 2000	The Rivieras Sing	196?	10.00	20.00	40.00

RIVIERAS, THE (2)

RIVIERA

Number	Title (A Side/B Side)	Yr	VG	VG+	NM
❑ 701 [M]	Campus Party	1964	62.50	125.00	250.00
U.S.A.					
❑ 102 [M]	Let's Have a Party	1964	37.50	75.00	150.00

RIVINGTONS, THE

LIBERTY

Number	Title (A Side/B Side)	Yr	VG	VG+	NM
❑ LRP-3282 [M]	Doin' the Bird	1963	25.00	50.00	100.00
❑ LST-7282 [S]	Doin' the Bird	1963	50.00	100.00	200.00

RIZZI, TONY

STARLITE

Number	Title (A Side/B Side)	Yr	VG	VG+	NM
❑ 6002 [10]	Tony Rizzi Guitar	1954	12.50	25.00	50.00

ROACH, FREDDIE

BLUE NOTE

Number	Title (A Side/B Side)	Yr	VG	VG+	NM
❑ BLP-4113 [M]	Down to Earth	1962	6.25	12.50	25.00
❑ BLP-4128 [M]	Mo' Greens, Please	1963	6.25	12.50	25.00
❑ BLP-4158 [M]	Good Move	1964	6.25	12.50	25.00
❑ BLP-4168 [M]	Brown Sugar	1964	6.25	12.50	25.00
❑ BLP-4190 [M]	All That's Good	1965	6.25	12.50	25.00
❑ BST-84113 [S]	Down to Earth	1962	7.50	15.00	30.00
—With "New York, USA" address on label					
❑ BST-84128 [S]	Mo' Greens, Please	1963	7.50	15.00	30.00
—With "New York, USA" address on label					
❑ BST-84158 [S]	Good Move	1964	7.50	15.00	30.00
—With "New York, USA" address on label					
❑ BST-84168 [S]	Brown Sugar	1964	7.50	15.00	30.00
—With "New York, USA" address on label					
❑ BST-84190 [S]	All That's Good	1965	7.50	15.00	30.00
—With "New York, USA" address on label					
PRESTIGE					
❑ PRLP-7490 [M]	The Soul Book	1967	7.50	15.00	30.00
❑ PRST-7490 [S]	The Soul Book	1967	5.00	10.00	20.00
❑ PRLP-7507 [M]	Mocha Motion	1967	7.50	15.00	30.00
❑ PRST-7507 [S]	Mocha Motion	1967	5.00	10.00	20.00
❑ PRLP-7521 [M]	My People — Soul People	1967	7.50	15.00	30.00
❑ PRST-7521 [S]	My People — Soul People	1967	5.00	10.00	20.00

ROACH, MAX

ABC IMPULSE!

Number	Title (A Side/B Side)	Yr	VG	VG+	NM
❑ AS-8 [S]	Percussion Bitter Sweet	1968	5.00	10.00	20.00
❑ AS-16 [S]	It's Time	1968	10.00	20.00	40.00
ARGO					
❑ LP-623 [M]	Max	1958	12.50	25.00	50.00
❑ LPS-623 [S]	Max	1958	10.00	20.00	40.00
ATLANTIC					
❑ 1435 [M]	Max Roach Trio Featuring the Legendary Hasaan	1965	5.00	10.00	20.00
❑ SD 1435 [S]	Max Roach Trio Featuring the Legendary Hasaan	1965	6.25	12.50	25.00
❑ 1467 [M]	Drums Unlimited	1966	5.00	10.00	20.00
❑ SD 1467 [S]	Drums Unlimited	1966	6.25	12.50	25.00
❑ SD 1510 [S]	Members Don't Get Weary	1968	5.00	10.00	20.00
CANDID					
❑ CD-8002 [M]	We Insist — Freedom Now Suite	1960	15.00	30.00	60.00
❑ CS-9002 [S]	We Insist — Freedom Now Suite	1960	15.00	30.00	60.00
DEBUT					
❑ DLP-13 [10]	Max Roach Quartet Featuring Hank Mobley	1954	75.00	150.00	300.00
EMARCY					
❑ SR-(# unk) [S]	Max Roach + 4 on the Chicago Scene	1959	12.50	25.00	50.00
❑ MG-36098 [M]	Max Roach + 4	1957	25.00	50.00	100.00
❑ MG-36108 [M]	Jazz in 3/4 Time	1957	20.00	40.00	80.00
❑ MG-36127 [M]	The Max Roach 4 Plays Charlie Parker	1958	20.00	40.00	80.00
❑ MG-36132 [M]	Max Roach + 4 on the Chicago Scene	1958	15.00	30.00	60.00
❑ MG-36140 [M]	Max Roach Plus Four At Newport	1958	15.00	30.00	60.00
❑ MG-36144 [M]	Max Roach with the Boston Percussion Ensemble	1958	15.00	30.00	60.00

Number	Title (A Side/B Side)	Yr	VG	VG+	NM
❑ SR-80000 [S]	Max Roach + 4	1959	20.00	40.00	80.00
❑ SR-80002 [S]	Jazz in 3/4 Time	1959	15.00	30.00	60.00
❑ SR-80010 [S]	Max Roach Plus Four At Newport	1959	12.50	25.00	50.00
❑ SR-80015 [S]	Max Roach with the Boston Percussion Ensemble	1959	12.50	25.00	50.00
❑ SR-80019 [S]	The Max Roach 4 Plays Charlie Parker	1959	15.00	30.00	60.00
FANTASY					
❑ 6007 [M]	Speak Brother, Speak	1963	6.25	12.50	25.00
❑ 86007 [S]	Speak Brother, Speak	1963	7.50	15.00	30.00
HAT ART					
❑ 4026 [(4)]	The Long March	1986	7.50	15.00	30.00
IMPULSE!					
❑ A-8 [M]	Percussion Bitter Sweet	1961	7.50	15.00	30.00
❑ AS-8 [S]	Percussion Bitter Sweet	1961	10.00	20.00	40.00
❑ A-16 [M]	It's Time	1962	5.00	10.00	20.00
❑ AS-16 [S]	It's Time	1962	7.50	15.00	30.00
JAZZLAND					
❑ JLP-79 [M]	Conversation	1962	7.50	15.00	30.00
❑ JLP-979 [S]	Conversation	1962	6.25	12.50	25.00
MERCURY					
❑ MG-20491 [M]	Quiet As It's Kept	1959	10.00	20.00	40.00
❑ MG-20539 [M]	Moon Faced and Starry-Eyed	1960	10.00	20.00	40.00
❑ MG-20760 [M]	Parisian Sketches	1962	7.50	15.00	30.00
❑ MG-20911 [M]	The Many Sides of Max	1964	6.25	12.50	25.00
❑ SR-60170 [S]	Quiet As It's Kept	1959	12.50	25.00	50.00
❑ SR-60215 [S]	Moon Faced and Starry-Eyed	1960	12.50	25.00	50.00
❑ SR-60760 [S]	Parisian Sketches	1962	10.00	20.00	40.00
❑ SR-60911 [S]	The Many Sides of Max	1964	7.50	15.00	30.00
RIVERSIDE					
❑ RLP 12-280 [M]	Deeds, Not Words	1958	12.50	25.00	50.00
❑ RLP-1122 [S]	Deeds, Not Words	1959	10.00	20.00	40.00
TIME					
❑ S-2087 [S]	Max Roach	1962	6.25	12.50	25.00
❑ 52087 [M]	Max Roach	1962	7.50	15.00	30.00
❑ ST-70003 [S]	Award Winning Drummer	1959	10.00	20.00	40.00
❑ T-70003 [M]	Award Winning Drummer	1959	12.50	25.00	50.00

ROACH, MAX/ART BLAKEY
BLUE NOTE

Number	Title (A Side/B Side)	Yr	VG	VG+	NM
❑ BLP-5010 [10]	Max Roach Quintet / Art Blakey and His Band	1952	150.00	300.00	600.00

ROACH, MAX, AND ANTHONY BRAXTON
HAT HUT

Number	Title (A Side/B Side)	Yr	VG	VG+	NM
❑ 06 [(2)]	One in Two — Two in One	1980	5.00	10.00	20.00

ROACH, MAX, AND CLIFFORD BROWN
See CLIFFORD BROWN.

ROACH, MAX; SONNY CLARK; GEORGE DUVIVIER
TIME

Number	Title (A Side/B Side)	Yr	VG	VG+	NM
❑ S-2101 [S]	Max Roach, Sonny Clark, George Duvivier	1962	10.00	20.00	40.00
❑ 52101 [M]	Max Roach, Sonny Clark, George Duvivier	1962	7.50	15.00	30.00

ROACH, MAX, AND STAN LEVEY
LIBERTY

Number	Title (A Side/B Side)	Yr	VG	VG+	NM
❑ LRP-3064 [M]	Drummin' the Blues	1957	20.00	40.00	80.00

ROACH, MAX, AND ARCHIE SHEPP
HAT HUT

Number	Title (A Side/B Side)	Yr	VG	VG+	NM
❑ 13 [(2)]	The Long March	1980	5.00	10.00	20.00

ROAD, THE
KAMA SUTRA

Number	Title (A Side/B Side)	Yr	VG	VG+	NM
❑ KSBS-2012	The Road	1970	3.75	7.50	15.00
—Reissue of 8075					
❑ KSBS-2032 [(2)]	Cognition	1970	5.00	10.00	20.00
❑ KLPS-8075	The Road	1969	5.00	10.00	20.00

ROAD RUNNERS, THE
LONDON

Number	Title (A Side/B Side)	Yr	VG	VG+	NM
❑ PS 381 [S]	The New Mustang (And Other Hot Rod Hits)	1964	75.00	150.00	300.00
❑ LL 3381 [M]	The New Mustang (And Other Hot Rod Hits)	1964	50.00	100.00	200.00

ROBBINS, ADELAIDE/MARIAN MCPARTLAND/BARBARA CARROLL
SAVOY

Number	Title (A Side/B Side)	Yr	VG	VG+	NM
❑ MG-12097 [M]	Lookin' for a Boy	1957	12.50	25.00	50.00

ROBBINS, HARGUS "PIG"
CHART

Number	Title (A Side/B Side)	Yr	VG	VG+	NM
❑ CHS-1011	One More Time	196?	3.75	7.50	15.00
ELEKTRA					
❑ 6E-129	Pig in a Poke	1978	3.00	6.00	12.00
❑ 6E-185	Unbreakable Hearts	1979	3.00	6.00	12.00
❑ 7E-1110	Country Instrumentalist of the Year	1977	3.00	6.00	12.00
TIME					
❑ S-2107 [S]	A Bit of Country Piano	1963	6.25	12.50	25.00
❑ 52107 [M]	A Bit of Country Piano.	1963	5.00	10.00	20.00

ROBBINS, MARTY
ARTCO

Number	Title (A Side/B Side)	Yr	VG	VG+	NM
❑ 110	The Best of Marty Robbins	1973	10.00	20.00	40.00
COLUMBIA					
❑ GP 15 [(2)]	Marty's Country	1969	6.25	12.50	25.00
❑ CL 976 [M]	The Song of Robbins	1957	25.00	50.00	100.00
—Red and black label with six "eye" logos					
❑ CL 976 [M]	The Song of Robbins	1963	5.00	10.00	20.00
—Red label with "Guaranteed High Fidelity" or "360 Sound Mono"					
❑ CL 1087 [M]	Song of the Islands	1957	30.00	60.00	120.00
—Red and black label with six "eye" logos					
❑ CL 1087 [M]	Song of the Islands	1963	5.00	10.00	20.00
—Red label with "Guaranteed High Fidelity" or "360 Sound Mono"					
❑ CL 1189 [M]	Marty Robbins	1958	20.00	40.00	80.00
—Red and black label with six "eye" logos					

Number	Title (A Side/B Side)	Yr	VG	VG+	NM
❑ CL 1189 [M]	Marty Robbins	1963	5.00	10.00	20.00
—Red label with "Guaranteed High Fidelity" or "360 Sound Mono"					
❑ CL 1325 [M]	Marty's Greatest Hits	1959	20.00	40.00	80.00
—Red and black label with six "eye" logos					
❑ CL 1325 [M]	Marty's Greatest Hits	1963	5.00	10.00	20.00
—Red label with "Guaranteed High Fidelity" or "360 Sound Mono"					
❑ CL 1349 [M]	Gunfighter Ballads and Trail Songs	1959	7.50	15.00	30.00
—Red and black label with six "eye" logos					
❑ CL 1349 [M]	Gunfighter Ballads and Trail Songs	1963	3.75	7.50	15.00
—Red label with "Guaranteed High Fidelity" or "360 Sound Mono"					
❑ CL 1481 [M]	More Gunfighter Ballads and Trail Songs	1960	7.50	15.00	30.00
—Red and black label with six "eye" logos					
❑ CL 1481 [M]	More Gunfighter Ballads and Trail Songs	1963	3.75	7.50	15.00
—Red label with "Guaranteed High Fidelity" or "360 Sound Mono"					
❑ CL 1635 [M]	More Greatest Hits	1961	6.25	12.50	25.00
—Red and black label with six "eye" logos					
❑ CL 1635 [M]	More Greatest Hits	1963	3.75	7.50	15.00
—Red label with "Guaranteed High Fidelity" or "360 Sound Mono"					
❑ CL 1666 [M]	Just a Little Sentimental	1961	6.25	12.50	25.00
—Red and black label with six "eye" logos					
❑ CL 1666 [M]	Just a Little Sentimental	1963	3.75	7.50	15.00
—Red label with "Guaranteed High Fidelity" or "360 Sound Mono"					
❑ CL 1801 [M]	Marty After Midnight	1962	5.00	10.00	20.00
—Red label with "Guaranteed High Fidelity"					
❑ CL 1801 [M]	Marty After Midnight	1962	12.50	25.00	50.00
—Red and black label with six "eye" logos					
❑ CL 1801 [M]	Marty After Midnight	1965	3.75	7.50	15.00
—Red label with "360 Sound Mono"					
❑ CL 1855 [M]	Portrait of Marty	1962	10.00	20.00	40.00
❑ CL 1855/CS 8655	Portrait of Marty Bonus Photo	1962	7.50	15.00	30.00
❑ CL 1918 [M]	Devil Woman	1962	6.25	12.50	25.00
—Red label with "Guaranteed High Fidelity"					
❑ CL 1918 [M]	Devil Woman	1965	3.75	7.50	15.00
—Red label with "360 Sound Mono"					
❑ CL 2040 [M]	Hawaii's Calling Me	1963	6.25	12.50	25.00
—Red label with "Guaranteed High Fidelity"					
❑ CL 2040 [M]	Hawaii's Calling Me	1965	3.75	7.50	15.00
—Red label with "360 Sound Mono"					
❑ CL 2072 [M]	Return of the Gunfighter	1963	5.00	10.00	20.00
—Red label with "Guaranteed High Fidelity"					
❑ CL 2072 [M]	Return of the Gunfighter	1965	3.75	7.50	15.00
—Red label with "360 Sound Mono"					
❑ CL 2176 [M]	Island Woman	1964	7.50	15.00	30.00
—Red label with "Guaranteed High Fidelity"					
❑ CL 2176 [M]	Island Woman	1965	5.00	10.00	20.00
—Red label with "360 Sound Mono"					
❑ CL 2220 [M]	R.F.D.	1964	5.00	10.00	20.00
—Red label with "Guaranteed High Fidelity"					
❑ CL 2220 [M]	R.F.D.	1965	3.75	7.50	15.00
—Red label with "360 Sound Mono"					
❑ CL 2304 [M]	Turn the Lights Down Low	1965	3.75	7.50	15.00
—Red label with "360 Sound Mono"					
❑ CL 2304 [M]	Turn the Lights Down Low	1965	6.25	12.50	25.00
—Red label with "Guaranteed High Fidelity"					
❑ CL 2448 [M]	What God Has Done	1966	3.75	7.50	15.00
❑ CL 2527 [M]	The Drifter	1966	3.75	7.50	15.00
❑ CL 2601 [10]	Rock 'N Roll 'N Robbins	1956	250.00	500.00	1000.
❑ CL 2645 [M]	My Kind of Country	1967	6.25	12.50	25.00
❑ CL 2725 [M]	Tonight Carmen	1967	7.50	15.00	30.00
❑ CL 2735 [M]	Christmas with Marty Robbins	1967	12.50	25.00	50.00
❑ CL 2817 [M]	By the Time I Get to Phoenix	1968	15.00	30.00	60.00
❑ CS 8158 [S]	Gunfighter Ballads and Trail Songs	1959	10.00	20.00	40.00
—Red and black label with six "eye" logos					
❑ CS 8158 [S]	Gunfighter Ballads and Trail Songs	1963	5.00	10.00	20.00
—Red label with "360 Sound Stereo"					
❑ CS 8158 [S]	Gunfighter Ballads and Trail Songs	1971	2.50	5.00	10.00
—Orange label					
❑ PC 8158	Gunfighter Ballads and Trail Songs	198?	2.00	4.00	8.00
—Reissue with new prefix					
❑ CS 8272 [S]	More Gunfighter Ballads and Trail Songs	1960	10.00	20.00	40.00
—Red and black label with six "eye" logos					
❑ CS 8272 [S]	More Gunfighter Ballads and Trail Songs	1963	5.00	10.00	20.00
—Red label with "360 Sound Stereo"					
❑ CS 8272 [S]	More Gunfighter Ballads and Trail Songs	1971	2.50	5.00	10.00
—Orange label					
❑ PC 8272	More Gunfighter Ballads and Trail Songs				
❑ More		198?	2.00	4.00	8.00
—Reissue with new prefix					
❑ CS 8435 [S]	More Greatest Hits	1961	7.50	15.00	30.00
—Red and black label with six "eye" logos					
❑ CS 8435 [S]	More Greatest Hits	1963	5.00	10.00	20.00
—Red label with "360 Sound Stereo"					
❑ CS 8435 [S]	More Greatest Hits	1971	2.50	5.00	10.00
—Orange label					
❑ PC 8435	More Greatest Hits	198?	2.00	4.00	8.00
—Reissue with new prefix					
❑ CS 8466 [S]	Just a Little Sentimental	1961	7.50	15.00	30.00
—Red and black label with six "eye" logos					
❑ CS 8466 [S]	Just a Little Sentimental	1963	5.00	10.00	20.00
—Red label with "360 Sound Stereo"					
❑ CS 8601 [S]	Marty After Midnight	1962	7.50	15.00	30.00
—Red label with "360 Sound Stereo" in black					
❑ CS 8601 [S]	Marty After Midnight	1962	20.00	40.00	80.00
—Red and black label with six "eye" logos					
❑ CS 8601 [S]	Marty After Midnight	1965	5.00	10.00	20.00
—Red label with "360 Sound Stereo" in white					
❑ CS 8639 [P]	Marty's Greatest Hits	1962	7.50	15.00	30.00
—Red label with "360 Sound Stereo" in black					
❑ CS 8639 [P]	Marty's Greatest Hits	1965	5.00	10.00	20.00
—Red label with "360 Sound Stereo" in white					
❑ CS 8639 [P]	Marty's Greatest Hits	1970	2.50	5.00	10.00
—Orange label					
❑ PC 8639	Marty's Greatest Hits	198?	2.00	4.00	8.00
—Reissue with new prefix					

R

Number	Title (A Side/B Side)	Yr	VG	VG+	NM
❏ CS 8655 [S]	Portrait of Marty	1962	12.50	25.00	50.00
❏ CS 8718 [S]	Devil Woman	1962	7.50	15.00	30.00
—Red label with "360 Sound Stereo" in black					
❏ CS 8718 [S]	Devil Woman	1965	5.00	10.00	20.00
—Red label with "360 Sound Stereo" in white					
❏ CS 8718 [S]	Devil Woman	1970	2.50	5.00	10.00
—Orange label					
❏ CS 8840 [S]	Hawaii's Calling Me	1963	7.50	15.00	30.00
—Red label with "360 Sound Stereo" in black					
❏ CS 8840 [S]	Hawaii's Calling Me	1965	5.00	10.00	20.00
—Red label with "360 Sound Stereo" in white					
❏ CS 8872 [S]	Return of the Gunfighter	1963	6.25	12.50	25.00
—Red label with "360 Sound Stereo" in black					
❏ CS 8872 [S]	Return of the Gunfighter	1965	5.00	10.00	20.00
—Red label with "360 Sound Stereo" in white					
❏ CS 8872 [S]	Return of the Gunfighter	1970	2.50	5.00	10.00
—Orange label					
❏ CS 8976 [S]	Island Woman	1964	10.00	20.00	40.00
—Red label with "360 Sound Stereo" in black					
❏ CS 8976 [S]	Island Woman	1965	7.50	15.00	30.00
—Red label with "360 Sound Stereo" in white					
❏ CS 9020 [S]	R.F.D.	1964	6.25	12.50	25.00
—Red label with "360 Sound Stereo" in black					
❏ CS 9020 [S]	R.F.D.	1965	5.00	10.00	20.00
—Red label with "360 Sound Stereo" in white					
❏ CS 9104 [S]	Turn the Lights Down Low	1965	5.00	10.00	20.00
—Red label with "360 Sound Stereo" in white					
❏ CS 9104 [S]	Turn the Lights Down Low	1965	7.50	15.00	30.00
—Red label with "360 Sound Stereo" in black					
❏ CS 9248 [S]	What God Has Done	1966	5.00	10.00	20.00
—Red "360 Sound" label					
❏ CS 9248 [S]	What God Has Done	1970	2.50	5.00	10.00
—Orange label					
❏ CS 9327 [S]	The Drifter	1966	5.00	10.00	20.00
—Red "360 Sound" label					
❏ CS 9327 [S]	The Drifter	1970	2.50	5.00	10.00
—Orange label					
❏ CS 9421 [R]	The Song of Robbins	1967	3.75	7.50	15.00
—Red "360 Sound" label					
❏ CS 9421 [R]	The Song of Robbins	1970	2.50	5.00	10.00
—Orange label					
❏ CS 9425 [R]	Song of the Islands	1967	3.75	7.50	15.00
❏ CS 9445 [S]	My Kind of Country	1967	5.00	10.00	20.00
❏ CS 9525 [S]	Tonight Carmen	1967	5.00	10.00	20.00
—Red "360 Sound" label					
❏ CS 9525 [S]	Tonight Carmen	1970	2.50	5.00	10.00
—Orange label					
❏ 3C 9535	Christmas with Marty Robbins	198?	2.50	5.00	10.00
—Budget-line reissue					
❏ CS 9535 [S]	Christmas with Marty Robbins	1967	7.50	15.00	30.00
❏ CS 9617 [M]	By the Time I Get to Phoenix	1968	12.50	25.00	50.00
—"Special Mono Radio Station Copy" with stereo number and "Mono" on white label					
❏ CS 9617 [M]	By the Time I Get to Phoenix	1968	10.00	20.00	—
❏ CS 9725	I Walk Alone	1968	5.00	10.00	20.00
—Red "360 Sound" label					
❏ CS 9725	I Walk Alone	1970	2.50	5.00	10.00
—Orange label					
❏ CS 9811	It's a Sin	1969	5.00	10.00	20.00
—Red "360 Sound" label					
❏ CS 9811	It's a Sin	1970	2.50	5.00	10.00
—Orange label					
❏ CS 9978	My Woman, My Woman, My Wife	1970	3.75	7.50	15.00
—Orange label					
❏ CS 9978	My Woman, My Woman, My Wife	1970	5.00	10.00	20.00
—Red "360 Sound" label					
❏ PC 30316	El Paso	198?	2.00	4.00	8.00
—Reissue of Harmony 30316					
❏ C 30571	Marty Robbins' Greatest Hits Vol. III	1971	3.75	7.50	15.00
❏ PC 30571	Marty Robbins' Greatest Hits Vol. III	198?	2.00	4.00	8.00
—Budget-line reissue					
❏ C 30816	Today	1971	3.75	7.50	15.00
❏ G 30881 [(2)]	The World of Marty Robbins	1971	5.00	10.00	20.00
❏ KC 31341	Bound for Old Mexico (Great Hits from South of the Border)	1973	3.75	7.50	15.00
❏ CG 31361 [(2)]	All Time Greatest Hits	1972	4.50	9.00	18.00
❏ KG 31361 [(2)]	Marty Robbins' All-Time Greatest Hits	1972	5.00	10.00	20.00
❏ KC 31628	I've Got a Woman's Love	1972	3.75	7.50	15.00
❏ KC 32586	Have I Told You Lately That I Love You	1974	3.75	7.50	15.00
❏ KC 33476	No Sign of Loneliness Here	1976	3.00	6.00	12.00
❏ CG 33630 [(2)]	Gunfighter Ballads and Trail Songs/My Woman, My Woman, My Wife	1976	3.75	7.50	15.00
❏ PC 34303	El Paso City	1976	3.00	6.00	12.00
—No bar code on cover					
❏ PC 34303	El Paso City	198?	2.00	4.00	8.00
—With bar code on cover					
❏ PC 34448	Adios Amigo	1977	3.00	6.00	12.00
—No bar code on cover					
❏ PC 34448	Adios Amigo	198?	2.00	4.00	8.00
—With bar code on cover					
❏ KC 35040	Don't Let Me Touch You	1977	3.00	6.00	12.00
❏ JC 35446	The Performer	1979	3.00	6.00	12.00
❏ KC 35629	Greatest Hits Vol. IV	1978	3.00	6.00	12.00
❏ JC 36085	All Around Cowboy	1979	3.00	6.00	12.00
❏ PC 36085	All Around Cowboy	198?	2.00	4.00	8.00
—Budget-line reissue					
❏ JC 36507	With Love	1980	3.00	6.00	12.00
❏ JC 36860	Everything I've Always Wanted	1981	3.00	6.00	12.00
❏ FC 37353	Encore	1981	3.00	6.00	12.00
❏ PC 37353	Encore	198?	2.00	4.00	8.00
—Budget-line reissue					
❏ FC 37541	The Legend	1982	3.00	6.00	12.00
❏ PC 37541	The Legend	1985	2.00	4.00	8.00
—Budget-line reissue					

Number	Title (A Side/B Side)	Yr	VG	VG+	NM
❏ FC 37995	Come Back to Me	1982	3.00	6.00	12.00
❏ PC 37995	Come Back to Me	198?	2.00	4.00	8.00
—Budget-line reissue					
❏ FC 38309	Biggest Hits	1982	3.00	6.00	12.00
❏ FC 38603	Some Memories Just Won't Die	1983	3.00	6.00	12.00
❏ C2 38870 [(2)]	A Lifetime of Song 1951-1982	1983	3.75	7.50	15.00
❏ KC2 39575 [(2)]	Long, Long Ago	1984	3.75	7.50	15.00
COLUMBIA MUSICAL TREASURY					
❏ P5S 5812 [(5)]	Marty	1972	10.00	20.00	40.00
COLUMBIA RECORD CLUB					
❏ DS 445	Bend in the River	1968	10.00	20.00	40.00
COLUMBIA SPECIAL PRODUCTS					
❏ C 10980 [S]	Christmas with Marty Robbins	1972	3.75	7.50	15.00
—Stereo reissue; "Distributed by Apex Rendezvous, Inc." on back cover					
❏ C 11122	Marty's Greatest Hits	1972	3.00	6.00	12.00
❏ C 11311	By the Time I Get to Phoenix	1972	3.75	7.50	15.00
❏ C 11513	By the Time I Get to Phoenix	1973	3.75	7.50	15.00
❏ P 12416	Marty Robbins' Own Favorites	1974	3.75	7.50	15.00
❏ P 13358	Christmas with Marty Robbins	1976	3.00	6.00	12.00
❏ P 14035	Legendary Music Man	1977	3.00	6.00	12.00
❏ P 14613	The Best of Marty Robbins	1978	2.50	5.00	10.00
❏ P 15594	The Number One Cowboy	1981	2.50	5.00	10.00
❏ P 15812	Marty Robbins' Best	1982	2.50	5.00	10.00
❏ P 16561	Reflections	1982	2.50	5.00	10.00
❏ 3P 16578 [(3)]	Classics	1983	5.00	10.00	20.00
❏ P 16914	Country Classics	1983	2.50	5.00	10.00
❏ P 17120	Sincerely	1983	2.50	5.00	10.00
❏ P 17136	Forever Yours	1983	2.50	5.00	10.00
❏ P 17137	That Country Feeling	1983	2.50	5.00	10.00
❏ P 17138	Banquet of Songs	1983	2.50	5.00	10.00
❏ P 17159	The Great Marty Robbins	1983	2.50	5.00	10.00
❏ P 17206	The Legendary Marty Robbins	1983	2.50	5.00	10.00
❏ P 17209	Country Cowboy	1983	2.50	5.00	10.00
❏ P 17367	Song of the Islands	1983	2.50	5.00	10.00
DECCA					
❏ DL 75389	This Much a Man	1972	3.75	7.50	15.00
HARMONY					
❏ HS 11338	Singing the Blues	1969	3.75	7.50	15.00
❏ HS 11409	The Story of My Life	1970	3.75	7.50	15.00
❏ KH 30316	El Paso	1971	3.00	6.00	12.00
❏ KH 31257	Marty Robbins Favorites	1972	3.00	6.00	12.00
❏ H 31258	Songs of the Islands	1972	5.00	10.00	20.00
❏ KH 32286	Streets of Laredo	1973	3.00	6.00	12.00
MCA					
❏ 61	This Much a Man	1973	3.00	6.00	12.00
—Reissue of Decca LP					
❏ 342	Marty Robbins	1973	3.75	7.50	15.00
❏ 421	Good'n Country	1974	3.75	7.50	15.00
ROBBINS, RONNY					
COLUMBIA					
❏ CS 9944	Columbia Records Presents Marty Robbins Jr.	1970	6.25	12.50	25.00
—As "Marty Robbins, Jr."					
ROBBS, THE					
MERCURY					
❏ MG-21130 [M]	The Robbs	1967	10.00	20.00	40.00
❏ SR-61130 [S]	The Robbs	1967	7.50	15.00	30.00
ROBERTINO					
KAPP					
❏ KL-1252 [M]	O Sole Mio	1962	3.75	7.50	15.00
❏ KL-1293 [M]	The Young Italian Singing Sensation	1962	3.75	7.50	15.00
❏ KL-1338 [M]	Italia Mia	1963	3.75	7.50	15.00
❏ KL-1471 [M]	The Best of Robertino	1966	3.00	6.00	12.00
❏ KS-3252 [S]	O Sole Mio	1962	5.00	10.00	20.00
❏ KS-3293 [S]	The Young Italian Singing Sensation	1962	5.00	10.00	20.00
❏ KS-3338 [S]	Italia Mia	1963	5.00	10.00	20.00
❏ KS-3471 [S]	The Best of Robertino	1966	3.75	7.50	15.00
ROBERTS, GEORGE					
COLUMBIA					
❏ CL 1384 [M]	Meet Mr. Roberts — George Roberts and His Big Bass Trombone	195?	20.00	40.00	80.00
ROBERTS, HOWARD					
CAPITOL					
❏ ST 1887 [S]	Color Him Funky	1963	7.50	15.00	30.00
❏ ST 1961 [S]	H.R. Is A Dirty Guitar Player	1963	5.00	10.00	20.00
❏ ST 2214 [S]	Something's Cookin'	1965	5.00	10.00	20.00
❏ ST 2400 [S]	Goodies	1965	5.00	10.00	20.00
❏ ST 2478 [S]	Whatever's Fair	1966	5.00	10.00	20.00
❏ ST 2609 [S]	All-Time Great Instrumental Hits	1966	5.00	10.00	20.00
❏ T 2716 [M]	Jaunty — Jolly	1967	6.25	12.50	25.00
❏ T 2824 [M]	Guilty	1967	5.00	10.00	20.00
VERVE					
❏ VSP-29 [M]	The Movin' Man	1966	5.00	10.00	20.00
❏ MGV-8192 [M]	Mr. Roberts Plays Guitar	1957	12.50	25.00	50.00
❏ V-8192 [M]	Mr. Roberts Plays Guitar	1961	6.25	12.50	25.00
❏ MGV-8305 [M]	Good Pickin's	1959	12.50	25.00	50.00
❏ V-8305 [M]	Good Pickin's	1961	6.25	12.50	25.00
❏ V-8662 [M]	Velvet Groove	1966	5.00	10.00	20.00
ROBERTS, KENNY					
STARDAY					
❏ SLP-336 [M]	Indian Love Call	1965	10.00	20.00	40.00
❏ SLP-406 [M]	The Incredible Kenny Roberts	1967	7.50	15.00	30.00
❏ SLP-434	Country Music Singing Sensation	1969	5.00	10.00	20.00
VOCALION					
❏ VL 73770	Kenny Roberts Sings Country Songs	196?	3.00	6.00	12.00

Number	Title (A Side/B Side)	Yr	VG	VG+	NM
ROBERTS, LUCKEY					
PERIOD					
❑ RL-1929 [M]	Happy Go Luckey	1956	10.00	20.00	40.00
ROBERTS, LUCKEY, AND WILLIE "THE LION" SMITH					
GOOD TIME JAZZ					
❑ S-10035 [S]	Harlem Piano Solos	1958	7.50	15.00	30.00
❑ L-12035 [M]	Harlem Piano Solos	1958	10.00	20.00	40.00
ROBERTS, PERNELL					
RCA VICTOR					
❑ LPM-2662 [M]	Come All Ye Fair and Tender Ladies	1963	7.50	15.00	30.00
❑ LSP-2662 [S]	Come All Ye Fair and Tender Ladies	1963	10.00	20.00	40.00
ROBERTS, ROCKY, AND THE AIREDALES					
BRUNSWICK					
❑ BL 754133	Rocky Roberts and the Airedales	1968	5.00	10.00	20.00
ROBERTSON, DALE					
RCA VICTOR					
❑ LPM-2158 [M]	Dale Robertson Presents His Album of Western Classics	1959	20.00	40.00	80.00
❑ LSP-2158 [S]	Dale Robertson Presents His Album of Western Classics	1959	25.00	50.00	100.00
ROBERTSON, DON					
RCA VICTOR					
❑ LPM-3348 [M]	Heart on My Sleeve	1965	5.00	10.00	20.00
❑ LSP-3348 [S]	Heart on My Sleeve	1965	6.25	12.50	25.00
ROBERTSON, ROBBIE					
GEFFEN					
❑ GEF-24160	Robbie Robertson	1987	2.50	5.00	10.00
❑ GEF 24303	Storyville	1991	6.25	12.50	25.00
ROBERTSON, TEXAS JIM					
DESIGN					
❑ DLP-115 [M]	Golden Hits of Country and Western Music	196?	3.00	6.00	12.00
❑ DLP-132 [M]	Sacred Country & Western Songs	196?	3.00	6.00	12.00
GRAND PRIX					
❑ 185 [M]	Texas Jim Robertson Sings the Great Hits of Country & Western	196?	3.75	7.50	15.00
MASTERSEAL					
❑ (# unknown) [10]	Eight Top Western Hits	195?	15.00	30.00	60.00
STRAND					
❑ 1016 [M]	Texas Jim Robertson	1961	10.00	20.00	40.00
ROBESON, PAUL					
COLUMBIA MASTERWORKS					
❑ ML 2038 [10]	Swing Low Sweet Chariot	1949	20.00	40.00	80.00
❑ ML 4105 [10]	Spirituals	1949	20.00	40.00	80.00
VANGUARD					
❑ VSD-57/58 [(2)]	Essential Paul Robeson	197?	5.00	10.00	20.00
❑ VRS-9037 [M]	Spirituals and Folksongs	1959	10.00	20.00	40.00
❑ VRS-9051 [M]	Paul Robeson at Carnegie Hall	1960	5.00	10.00	20.00
❑ VRS-9193 [M]	Ballad for Americans: Carnegie Hall Concert, Vol. 2	1965	5.00	10.00	20.00
❑ VSD-79193 [S]	Ballad for Americans: Carnegie Hall Concert, Vol. 2	1965	5.00	10.00	20.00
ROBINS, THE (1)					
GNP CRESCENDO					
❑ GNPS-9034	The Best of the Robins	1975	3.75	7.50	15.00
WHIPPET					
❑ WLP-703 [M]	Rock 'n' Roll with the Robins	1958	200.00	400.00	800.00
ROBINSON, FLOYD					
RCA VICTOR					
❑ LPM-2162 [M]	Floyd Robinson	1960	20.00	40.00	80.00
❑ LSP-2162 [S]	Floyd Robinson	1960	30.00	60.00	120.00
ROBINSON, JIM					
RIVERSIDE					
❑ RLP-369 [M]	Jim Robinson's New Orleans Band	1961	7.50	15.00	30.00
❑ RLP-393 [M]	Jim Robinson Plays Spirituals and Blues	1961	7.50	15.00	30.00
ROBINSON, JIM, AND BILLIE AND DEDE PIERCE					
ATLANTIC					
❑ 1409 [M]	Jim Robinson and Billie & DeDe Pierce	1963	5.00	10.00	20.00
❑ SD 1409 [S]	Jim Robinson and Billie & DeDe Pierce	1963	6.25	12.50	25.00
ROBINSON, PERRY					
SAVOY					
❑ MG-12177 [M]	Funk Dumpling	1962	6.25	12.50	25.00
ROBINSON, SMOKEY, AND THE MIRACLES					
See THE MIRACLES.					
ROBINSON, SUGAR CHILE					
CAPITOL					
❑ T 589 [M]	Boogie Woogie	1955	30.00	60.00	120.00
ROBISON, CARSON					
COLUMBIA					
❑ CL 2551 [10]	Square Dance	1955	20.00	40.00	80.00
❑ CL 6029 [10]	Square Dance	1949	20.00	40.00	80.00
MGM					
❑ E-13 [M]	Call Your Own Square Dances	195?	15.00	30.00	60.00
❑ E-557 [10]	Square Dances with Calls	1952	15.00	30.00	60.00
❑ E-3258 [M]	Square Dances	1955	7.50	15.00	30.00
❑ E-3594 [M]	Life Gets Tee-Jus, Don't It	1958	12.50	25.00	50.00
RCA VICTOR					
❑ LPM-1238 [M]	Square Dances	1956	7.50	15.00	30.00
❑ LPM-3030 [10]	Square Dances	1952	15.00	30.00	60.00
ROCCA, ANTONIO					
MGM					
❑ E-4183 [M]	In This Corner...The Musical World of Antonio Rocca	1963	5.00	10.00	20.00
❑ SE-4183 [S]	In This Corner...The Musical World of Antonio Rocca	1963	6.25	12.50	25.00
ROCHE, BETTY					
BETHLEHEM					
❑ BCP-64 [M]	Take the "A" Train	1956	20.00	40.00	80.00
PRESTIGE					
❑ PRLP-7187 [M]	Singin' and Swingin'	1961	12.50	25.00	50.00
❑ PRLP-7198 [M]	Lightly and Politely	1961	12.50	25.00	50.00
ROCHES, THE					
MCA					
❑ 10020	We Three Kings	1990	5.00	10.00	20.00
RHINO					
❑ RNEP-70616 [EP]	No Trespassing	1987	2.50	5.00	10.00
WARNER BROS.					
❑ BSK 3298	The Roches	1979	2.50	5.00	10.00
❑ BSK 3475	Nurds	1980	2.50	5.00	10.00
❑ 23735	Keep On Doing	1982	2.50	5.00	10.00
❑ 25321	Another World	1985	2.50	5.00	10.00
ROCK ISLAND					
PROJECT 3					
❑ PR-4005 SD	Rock Island	1970	7.50	15.00	30.00
ROCK-A-TEENS, THE					
ROULETTE					
❑ R-25109 [M]	Woo-Hoo	1960	37.50	75.00	150.00
❑ SR-25109 [S]	Woo-Hoo	1960	62.50	125.00	250.00
ROCKATS					
ISLAND					
❑ ILPS 9626	Live at the Ritz	1981	6.25	12.50	25.00
ROCKETS, THE (4)					
WHITE WHALE					
❑ WWS-7116	The Rockets	1968	6.25	12.50	25.00
ROCKIN' FOO					
HOBBIT					
❑ HB-5001	Rockin' Foo	1969	6.25	12.50	25.00
ROCKIN' REBELS, THE					
SWAN					
❑ SLP-509 [M]	Wild Weekend	1963	50.00	100.00	200.00
ROCKY FELLERS, THE					
SCEPTER					
❑ SP-512 [M]	Killer Joe	1964	7.50	15.00	30.00
❑ SPS-512 [S]	Killer Joe	1964	10.00	20.00	40.00
RODGERS, GENE					
EMARCY					
❑ MG-36145 [M]	Jazz Comes to the Astor	1958	10.00	20.00	40.00
RODGERS, IKE					
RIVERSIDE					
❑ RLP-1013 [10]	The Trombone of Ike Rodgers	1953	20.00	40.00	80.00
RODGERS, JIMMIE (1)					
RCA VICTOR					
❑ DPL2-0075 [(2)]	The Legendary Jimmie Rodgers, Vol. 1	1974	10.00	20.00	40.00
—Special-products issue for Country Music Magazine					
❑ ANL1-1209	My Rough and Rowdy Ways	1976	2.50	5.00	10.00
❑ LPM-1232 [M]	Never No Mo' Blues — A Memorial Album	1955	37.50	75.00	150.00
❑ LPM-1640 [M]	Train Whistle Blues	1957	37.50	75.00	150.00
❑ LPM-2112 [M]	My Rough and Rowdy Ways	1960	20.00	40.00	80.00
❑ LPM-2213 [M]	Jimmie the Kid	1961	20.00	40.00	80.00
❑ CPL1-2504	A Legendary Performer	1977	2.50	5.00	10.00
❑ LPM-2531 [M]	Country Music Hall of Fame	1962	20.00	40.00	80.00
❑ LPM-2634 [M]	The Short But Brilliant Life of Jimmie Rodgers	1963	20.00	40.00	80.00
❑ LPM-2865 [M]	My Time Ain't Long	1964	12.50	25.00	50.00
❑ LPT-3037 [10]	Yodelingly Yours Jimmie Rodgers, Volume 1	1953	100.00	200.00	400.00
❑ LPT-3038 [10]	Yodelingly Yours Jimmie Rodgers, Volume 2	1953	100.00	200.00	400.00
❑ LPT-3039 [10]	Yodelingly Yours Jimmie Rodgers, Volume 3	1953	100.00	200.00	400.00
❑ LPM-3073 [10]	Travelin' Blues	1952	100.00	200.00	400.00
❑ AHL1-3315	The Best of the Legendary Jimmie Rodgers	197?	2.00	4.00	8.00
—Reissue with new prefix					
❑ LPM-3315 [M]	The Best of the Legendary Jimmie Rodgers	1965	10.00	20.00	40.00
❑ LSP-3315 [R]	The Best of the Legendary Jimmie Rodgers	1965	5.00	10.00	20.00
❑ VPS-6091(e) [(2)]	This Is Jimmie Rodgers	1971	5.00	10.00	20.00
ROUNDER					
❑ 1056	First Sessions 1927-1928	1990	3.00	6.00	12.00
❑ 1057	The Early Years 1928-1929	1990	3.00	6.00	12.00
RODGERS, JIMMIE (2)					
A&M					
❑ SP-130 [M]	Child of Clay	1967	6.25	12.50	25.00
❑ SP-4130 [S]	Child of Clay	1967	3.75	7.50	15.00
❑ SP-4187	Windmills of Your Mind	1969	3.75	7.50	15.00
❑ SP-4242	Troubled Times	1970	3.75	7.50	15.00
ACCORD					
❑ SN-7198	Honeycomb & Other Hits	198?	2.50	5.00	10.00
DOT					
❑ DLP-3453 [M]	No One Will Ever Know	1962	3.75	7.50	15.00
❑ DLP-3496 [M]	Jimmie Rodgers Folk Concert	1963	3.75	7.50	15.00
❑ DLP-3502 [M]	My Favorite Hymns	1963	3.75	7.50	15.00
❑ DLP-3525 [M]	Honeycomb & Kisses Sweeter Than Wine	1963	3.75	7.50	15.00

R

Number	Title (A Side/B Side)	Yr	VG	VG+	NM
❑ DLP-3556 [M]	The World I Used to Know	1964	3.75	7.50	15.00
—Retitled version of above					
❑ DLP-3556 [M]	Town and Country	1964	5.00	10.00	20.00
❑ DLP-3579 [M]	12 Great Hits	1964	3.75	7.50	15.00
❑ DLP-3614 [M]	Deep Purple	1965	3.75	7.50	15.00
❑ DLP 3657 [M]	Christmas with Jimmie	1965	3.00	6.00	12.00
❑ DLP-3687 [M]	The Nashville Sound	1966	3.75	7.50	15.00
❑ DLP-3710 [M]	Country Music 1966	1966	3.75	7.50	15.00
❑ DLP-3717 [M]	It's Over	1966	3.75	7.50	15.00
❑ DLP-3780 [M]	Love Me, Please Love Me	1967	3.75	7.50	15.00
❑ DLP-3815 [M]	Golden Hits/15 Hits of Jimmie Rodgers	1967	5.00	10.00	20.00
❑ DLP-25453 [S]	No One Will Ever Know	1962	5.00	10.00	20.00
❑ DLP-25496 [S]	Jimmie Rodgers Folk Concert	1963	5.00	10.00	20.00
❑ DLP-25502 [S]	My Favorite Hymns	1963	5.00	10.00	20.00
❑ DLP-25525 [S]	Honeycomb & Kisses Sweeter Than Wine	1963	5.00	10.00	20.00
❑ DLP-25556 [S]	The World I Used to Know	1964	5.00	10.00	20.00
—Retitled version of above					
❑ DLP-25556 [S]	Town and Country	1964	6.25	12.50	25.00
❑ DLP-25579 [S]	12 Great Hits	1964	5.00	10.00	20.00
❑ DLP-25614 [S]	Deep Purple	1965	5.00	10.00	20.00
❑ DLP 25657 [S]	Christmas with Jimmie	1965	3.75	7.50	15.00
❑ DLP-25687 [S]	The Nashville Sound	1966	5.00	10.00	20.00
❑ DLP-25710 [S]	Country Music 1966	1966	5.00	10.00	20.00
❑ DLP-25717 [S]	It's Over	1966	5.00	10.00	20.00
❑ DLP-25780 [S]	Love Me, Please Love Me	1967	5.00	10.00	20.00
❑ DLP-25815 [S]	Golden Hits/15 Hits of Jimmie Rodgers	1967	3.75	7.50	15.00
FORUM					
❑ F-9025 [M]	At Home with Jimmie Rodgers: An Evening of Folk Songs	196?	3.00	6.00	12.00
❑ SF-9025 [S]	At Home with Jimmie Rodgers: An Evening of Folk Songs	196?	3.00	6.00	12.00
❑ F-9049 [M]	Just for You	196?	3.00	6.00	12.00
❑ SF-9049 [S]	Just for You	196?	3.00	6.00	12.00
❑ F-9059 [M]	Jimmie Rodgers Sings Folk Songs	196?	3.00	6.00	12.00
❑ SF-9059 [S]	Jimmie Rodgers Sings Folk Songs	196?	3.00	6.00	12.00
HAMILTON					
❑ HL-114 [M]	6 Favorite Hymns and 6 Favorite Folk Ballads	1964	3.00	6.00	12.00
❑ HL-148 [M]	12 Immortal Songs	196?	3.00	6.00	12.00
❑ HS-12114 [S]	6 Favorite Hymns and 6 Favorite Folk Ballads	1964	3.00	6.00	12.00
❑ HS-12148 [S]	12 Immortal Songs	196?	3.00	6.00	12.00
PARAMOUNT					
❑ PAS-2-1042 [(2)]	Honeycomb	1974	3.75	7.50	15.00
PICKWICK					
❑ PC-3040 [M]	Jimmie Rodgers	196?	3.00	6.00	12.00
❑ SPC-3040 [S]	Jimmie Rodgers	196?	3.00	6.00	12.00
❑ SPC-3106	Am I That Easy to Forget	196?	3.00	6.00	12.00
❑ SPC-3599	Big Hits	197?	2.50	5.00	10.00
ROULETTE					
❑ R-25020 [M]	Jimmie Rodgers	1957	12.50	25.00	50.00
—Black label					
❑ R-25020 [M]	Jimmie Rodgers	1959	6.25	12.50	25.00
—White label with colored spokes					
❑ R-25033 [M]	Number One Ballads	1958	12.50	25.00	50.00
—Black label					
❑ R-25033 [M]	Number One Ballads	1959	6.25	12.50	25.00
—White label with colored spokes					
❑ R-25042 [M]	Jimmie Rodgers Sings Folk Songs	1958	12.50	25.00	50.00
—Black label					
❑ R-25042 [M]	Jimmie Rodgers Sings Folk Songs	1959	6.25	12.50	25.00
—White label with colored spokes					
❑ R-25057 [M]	His Golden Year	1959	6.25	12.50	25.00
❑ R-25071 [M]	TV Favorites	1959	7.50	15.00	30.00
❑ SR-25071 [S]	TV Favorites	1959	12.50	25.00	50.00
❑ R-25081 [M]	Twilight on the Trail	1959	7.50	15.00	30.00
❑ SR-25081 [S]	Twilight on the Trail	1959	12.50	25.00	50.00
❑ R 25095 [M]	It's Christmas Once Again	1959	7.50	15.00	30.00
❑ SR 25095 [S]	It's Christmas Once Again	1959	12.50	25.00	50.00
❑ R-25103 [M]	When the Spirit Moves You	1960	7.50	15.00	30.00
❑ SR-25103 [S]	When the Spirit Moves You	1960	10.00	20.00	40.00
❑ R-25128 [M]	At Home with Jimmie Rodgers: An Evening of Folk Songs	1960	7.50	15.00	30.00
❑ SR-25128 [S]	At Home with Jimmie Rodgers: An Evening of Folk Songs	1960	10.00	20.00	40.00
❑ R-25150 [M]	The Folk Song World of Jimmie Rodgers	1961	7.50	15.00	30.00
❑ SR-25150 [S]	The Folk Song World of Jimmie Rodgers	1961	10.00	20.00	40.00
❑ R-25160 [M]	The Best of Jimmie Rodgers' Folk Tunes	1961	7.50	15.00	30.00
❑ SR-25160 [S]	The Best of Jimmie Rodgers' Folk Tunes	1961	10.00	20.00	40.00
—Black vinyl					
❑ SR-25160 [S]	The Best of Jimmie Rodgers' Folk Tunes	1961	62.50	125.00	250.00
—Red vinyl					
❑ R-25179 [M]	15 Million Sellers	1962	6.25	12.50	25.00
❑ SR-25179 [P]	15 Million Sellers	1962	5.00	10.00	20.00
—Orange and yellow label					
❑ SR-25179 [P]	15 Million Sellers	1962	7.50	15.00	30.00
—White label with colored spokes					
❑ R-25199 [M]	Folk Songs	1963	5.00	10.00	20.00
❑ SR-25199 [S]	Folk Songs	1963	6.25	12.50	25.00
❑ SR-42006	Yours Truly	1968	3.75	7.50	15.00
RODNEY, RED					
ARGO					
❑ LP-643 [M]	Red Rodney Returns	1959	12.50	25.00	50.00
❑ LSP-643 [S]	Red Rodney Returns	1959	10.00	20.00	40.00
FANTASY					
❑ 3208 [M]	Modern Music from Chicago	195?	20.00	40.00	80.00
—Black vinyl					
❑ 3208 [M]	Modern Music from Chicago	1956	30.00	60.00	120.00
—Red vinyl					
PRESTIGE					
❑ PRLP-122 [10]	Red Rodney	1952	50.00	100.00	200.00

Number	Title (A Side/B Side)	Yr	VG	VG+	NM
SAVOY					
❑ MG-12148 [M]	Fiery Red Rodney	1959	25.00	50.00	100.00
SIGNAL					
❑ S-1206 [M]	Red Rodney 1957	1957	150.00	300.00	600.00
❑ S-1206 [S]	Red Rodney 1957	199?	6.25	12.50	25.00
—Classic Records reissue on audiophile vinyl (in stereo)					
RODRIGUEZ, WILLIE					
RIVERSIDE					
❑ RLP-469 [M]	Flatjacks	1963	6.25	12.50	25.00
❑ RS-9469 [S]	Flatjacks	1963	7.50	15.00	30.00
ROE, TOMMY					
ABC					
❑ S-467 [R]	Something for Everybody	1968	12.50	25.00	50.00
—Issued in rechanneled stereo four years after its original release					
❑ 594 [M]	It's Now Winters Day	1967	5.00	10.00	20.00
❑ S-594 [S]	It's Now Winters Day	1967	6.25	12.50	25.00
❑ 610 [M]	Phantasy	1967	10.00	20.00	40.00
❑ S-610 [S]	Phantasy	1967	10.00	20.00	40.00
❑ S-683	Dizzy	1969	5.00	10.00	20.00
❑ S-700	12 in a Roe/A Collection of Tommy Roe's Greatest Hits	1969	5.00	10.00	20.00
❑ S-714	We Can Make Music	1970	3.75	7.50	15.00
❑ S-732	Beginnings	1971	3.75	7.50	15.00
❑ X-762	16 Greatest Hits	1972	3.75	7.50	15.00
❑ ST-90883 [S]	Sweet Pea	1966	10.00	20.00	40.00
—Capitol Record Club issue					
❑ T-90883 [M]	Sweet Pea	1966	10.00	20.00	40.00
—Capitol Record Club issue					
ABC-PARAMOUNT					
❑ 432 [M]	Sheila	1962	10.00	20.00	40.00
❑ S-432 [S]	Sheila	1962	12.50	25.00	50.00
❑ 467 [M]	Something for Everybody	1964	7.50	15.00	30.00
❑ 575 [M]	Sweet Pea	1966	7.50	51.00	30.00
❑ S-575 [S]	Sweet Pea	1966	10.00	20.00	40.00
ACCORD					
❑ SN-7155	Sheila	1981	2.50	5.00	10.00
MCA					
❑ 1519	Collectibles — Greatest Hits	1982	2.00	4.00	8.00
MONUMENT					
❑ 7604	Energy	1977	2.50	5.00	10.00
—Reissue of 34182					
❑ 7614	Full Bloom	1977	2.50	5.00	10.00
❑ PZ 34182	Energy	1976	3.00	6.00	12.00
ROGERS, BOB					
INDIGO					
❑ 1501 [M]	All That and This, Too	1961	10.00	20.00	40.00
ROGERS, DAVID					
ATLANTIC					
❑ SD 7266	Just Thank Me	1973	3.75	7.50	15.00
❑ SD 7283	Farewell to the Ryman	1973	5.00	10.00	20.00
❑ SD 7306	Hey There Girl	1974	3.75	7.50	15.00
COLUMBIA					
❑ CS 1023	A World Called You	1970	3.75	7.50	15.00
❑ C 30972	She Don't Make Me Cry	1971	3.75	7.50	15.00
❑ KC 31506	Need You	1972	3.75	7.50	15.00
REPUBLIC					
❑ 5003	Lovingly	197?	3.00	6.00	12.00
❑ 5907	I'm Gonna Love You Right Out of This World	1976	3.00	6.00	12.00
UNITED ARTISTS					
❑ UA-LA422-G	A Whole Lotta Livin' in a House	1975	3.00	6.00	12.00
ROGERS, JULIE					
MERCURY					
❑ MG-20981 [M]	Julie Rogers	1965	3.75	7.50	15.00
❑ SR-60981 [S]	Julie Rogers	1965	5.00	10.00	20.00
ROGERS, KENNY					
Also see THE BOBBY DOYLE THREE; THE FIRST EDITION; THE NEW CHRISTY MINSTRELS.					
LIBERTY					
❑ LO-607	Love Lifted Me	1981	2.00	4.00	8.00
—Reissue of United Artists 607					
❑ LO-689	Kenny Rogers	1981	2.00	4.00	8.00
—Reissue of United Artists 689					
❑ LO-754	Daytime Friends	1981	2.00	4.00	8.00
—Reissue of United Artists 754					
❑ LO-835	Ten Years of Gold	1981	2.00	4.00	8.00
—Reissue of United Artists 835					
❑ LO-903	Love Or Something Like It	1981	2.00	4.00	8.00
—Reissue of United Artists 903					
❑ LO-934	The Gambler	1981	2.00	4.00	8.00
—Reissue of United Artists 934					
❑ LOO-979	Kenny	1981	2.00	4.00	8.00
—Reissue of United Artists 979					
❑ LOO-1035	Gideon	1981	2.00	4.00	8.00
—Reissue of United Artists 1035					
❑ LOO-1072	Kenny Rogers' Greatest Hits	1980	2.00	4.00	8.00
❑ LOO-1108	Share Your Love	1981	2.00	4.00	8.00
❑ LN-10207	Love Lifted Me	1984	—	3.00	6.00
—Budget-line reissue					
❑ LN-10208	Kenny Rogers	1983	—	3.00	6.00
—Budget-line reissue					
❑ LN-10240	Christmas	198?	2.00	4.00	8.00
—Reissue of LOO 51115					
❑ LN-10243	Gideon	1984	—	3.00	6.00
—Budget-line reissue					
❑ LN-10245	We've Got Tonight	1984	—	3.00	6.00
—Budget-line reissue					

Number	Title (A Side/B Side)	Yr	VG	VG+	NM
❑ LN-10246	Love Will Turn You Around	1984	—	3.00	6.00
—Budget-line reissue					
❑ LN-10247	The Gambler	1984	—	3.00	6.00
—Budget-line reissue					
❑ LN-10248	Kenny	1984	—	3.00	6.00
—Budget-line reissue					
❑ LN-10249	Daytime Friends	1984	—	3.00	6.00
—Budget-line reissue					
❑ LN-10250	Love Or Something Like It	1984	—	3.00	6.00
—Budget-line reissue					
❑ LN-10254	Ten Years of Gold	1984	—	3.00	6.00
—Budget-line reissue					
❑ LOO-51115	Christmas	1981	2.50	5.00	10.00
❑ LO-51124	Love Will Turn You Around	1982	2.00	4.00	8.00
❑ LO-51143	We've Got Tonight	1983	2.00	4.00	8.00
❑ LV-51152	Twenty Greatest Hits	1983	2.00	4.00	8.00
❑ LO-51154	Duets	1984	2.00	4.00	8.00
❑ LO-51157	Love Is What We Make It	1985	2.00	4.00	8.00
MOBILE FIDELITY					
❑ 1-044	The Gambler	1981	5.00	10.00	20.00
—Audiophile vinyl					
❑ 1-049	Kenny Rogers' Greatest Hits	1981	5.00	10.00	20.00
—Audiophile vinyl					
RCA					
❑ 5833-1-R	They Don't Make Them Like They Used To	1986	2.00	4.00	8.00
❑ 6484-1-R	I Prefer the Moonlight	1987	2.00	4.00	8.00
❑ 8371-1-R	Greatest Hits	1988	2.00	4.00	8.00
RCA VICTOR					
❑ AFL1-4697	Eyes That See in the Dark	1983	2.00	4.00	8.00
❑ AFL1-4697	Eyes That See in the Dark	1983	50.00	100.00	200.00
—Picture disc on one side, regular RCA label on other; possibly an in-house demo at the RCA Indianapolis pressing plant					
❑ AJL1-5335	What About Me	1984	2.00	4.00	8.00
❑ AJL1-7023	The Heart of the Matter	1985	2.00	4.00	8.00
REPRISE					
❑ 25792	Something Inside So Strong	1989	2.50	5.00	10.00
❑ 25973	Christmas in America	1989	3.00	6.00	12.00
❑ R 144593	Love Is Strange	1990	5.00	10.00	20.00
—Only available on vinyl from BMG Direct Marketing					
UNITED ARTISTS					
❑ UA-LA607-G	Love Lifted Me	1976	3.75	7.50	15.00
❑ UA-LA689-G	Kenny Rogers	1976	2.50	5.00	10.00
❑ UA-LA754-G	Daytime Friends	1977	2.50	5.00	10.00
❑ UA-LA835-H	Ten Years of Gold	1978	2.50	5.00	10.00
❑ UA-LA903-H	Love Or Something Like It	1978	2.50	5.00	10.00
❑ UA-LA934-H	The Gambler	1978	2.50	5.00	10.00
❑ LWAK-979	Kenny	1979	2.50	5.00	10.00
❑ LOO-1035	Gideon	1980	2.50	5.00	10.00

ROGERS, KENNY, AND THE FIRST EDITION
See THE FIRST EDITION.

ROGERS, ROY

Number	Title (A Side/B Side)	Yr	VG	VG+	NM
CAPITOL					
❑ ST-594	The Country Side of Roy Rogers	1970	5.00	10.00	20.00
❑ ST-785	A Man from Duck Run	1971	5.00	10.00	20.00
RCA					
❑ 3024-1-RRE [PD]	Roy Rogers Tribute	1991	10.00	20.00	40.00
—Picture disc; only vinyl edition of this release					
RCA CAMDEN					
❑ CAL-1054 [M]	Pecos Bill	1964	6.25	12.50	25.00
❑ CAS-1054(e) [R]	Pecos Bill	1964	3.75	7.50	15.00
❑ CAL-1074 [M]	Lore of the West	1966	6.25	12.50	25.00
❑ CAS-1074(e) [R]	Lore of the West	1966	3.75	7.50	15.00
❑ CAL-1097 [M]	Peter Cottontail and His Friends	1968	6.25	12.50	25.00
❑ CAS-1097 [R]	Peter Cottontail and His Friends	1968	3.75	7.50	15.00
RCA VICTOR					
❑ LBY-1022 [M]	Jesus Loves Me	1959	12.50	25.00	50.00
—On the "Children's Bluebird Series"					
❑ LPM-3041 [M]	Roy Rogers Souvenir Album	1952	75.00	150.00	300.00
❑ LPM-3168 [M]	Hymns of Faith	1954	50.00	100.00	200.00
20TH CENTURY					
❑ T-487	Happy Trails to You	1975	3.75	7.50	15.00

ROGERS, ROY, AND DALE EVANS

Number	Title (A Side/B Side)	Yr	VG	VG+	NM
CAPITOL					
❑ ST 1745 [S]	The Bible Tells Me So	1962	12.50	25.00	50.00
❑ T 1745 [M]	The Bible Tells Me So	1962	10.00	20.00	40.00
❑ ST 2818 [S]	Christmas Is Always	1967	7.50	15.00	30.00
❑ T 2818 [M]	Christmas Is Always	1967	7.50	15.00	30.00
GOLDEN					
❑ A198-6 [M]	Roy Rogers' and Dale Evans' Song Wagon	1958	20.00	40.00	80.00
—Originals have black labels and "198" prefix					
❑ A198-7 [M]	16 Great Songs of the Old West	1958	20.00	40.00	80.00
—Originals have black labels and "198" prefix					
❑ LP 7 [M]	A Child's Introduction to the West (16 Great Songs of the Old West)	196?	10.00	20.00	40.00
—Yellow label, "LP" prefix					
❑ A298-81 [M]	Peter Cottontail	1962	15.00	30.00	60.00
—Originals have black labels and "298" prefix					
RCA VICTOR					
❑ LPM-1439 [M]	Sweet Hour of Prayer	1957	20.00	40.00	80.00

ROGERS, SHORTY

Number	Title (A Side/B Side)	Yr	VG	VG+	NM
ATLANTIC					
❑ 1212 [M]	The Swinging Mr. Rogers	1955	12.50	25.00	50.00
—Black label					
❑ 1212 [M]	The Swinging Mr. Rogers	1961	6.25	12.50	25.00
—Multicolor label, white "fan" logo at right					
❑ 1212 [M]	The Swinging Mr. Rogers	1963	5.00	10.00	20.00
—Multicolor label, black "fan" logo at right					

Number	Title (A Side/B Side)	Yr	VG	VG+	NM
❑ 1232 [M]	Martians, Come Back	1956	12.50	25.00	50.00
—Black label					
❑ 1232 [M]	Martians, Come Back	1961	6.25	12.50	25.00
—Multicolor label, white "fan" logo at right					
❑ 1232 [M]	Martians, Come Back	1963	5.00	10.00	20.00
—Multicolor label, black "fan" logo at right					
❑ SD 1232 [S]	Martians, Come Back	1958	12.50	25.00	50.00
—Green label					
❑ SD 1232 [S]	Martians, Come Back	1961	5.00	10.00	20.00
—Multicolor label, white "fan" logo at right					
❑ 1270 [M]	Way Up There	1957	12.50	25.00	50.00
—Black label					
❑ 1270 [M]	Way Up There	1961	6.25	12.50	25.00
—Multicolor label, white "fan" logo at right					
❑ 1270 [M]	Way Up There	1963	5.00	10.00	20.00
—Multicolor label, black "fan" logo at right					
CAPITOL					
❑ H 294 [10]	Modern Sounds	1952	50.00	100.00	200.00
❑ ST 1960 [S]	Gospel Mission	1963	5.00	10.00	20.00
❑ T 1960 [M]	Gospel Mission	1963	6.25	12.50	25.00
MGM					
❑ E-3798 [M]	Shorty Rogers Meets Tarzan	1960	7.50	15.00	30.00
❑ SE-3798 [S]	Shorty Rogers Meets Tarzan	1960	10.00	20.00	40.00
MOSAIC					
❑ M6-125 [(6)]	The Complete Atlantic and EMI Jazz Recordings of Shorty Rogers	199?	20.00	40.00	80.00
RCA VICTOR					
❑ LJM-1004 [M]	Shorty Rogers Courts the Count	1954	20.00	40.00	80.00
❑ LPM-1195 [M]	Shorty Rogers and His Giants	1956	17.50	35.00	70.00
❑ LPM-1326 [M]	Wherever the Five Winds Blow	1956	17.50	35.00	70.00
❑ LPM-1334 [M]	Collaboration	1956	15.00	30.00	60.00
❑ LPM-1350 [M]	The Big Shorty Rogers Express	1957	15.00	30.00	60.00
❑ LPM-1428 [M]	Shorty Rogers Plays Richard Rogers	1957	15.00	30.00	60.00
❑ LPM-1564 [M]	Portrait of Shorty	1957	15.00	30.00	60.00
❑ LPM-1696 [M]	Gigi Goes Jazz	1958	12.50	25.00	50.00
❑ LSP-1696 [S]	Gigi Goes Jazz	1958	15.00	30.00	60.00
❑ LPM-1763 [M]	Afro-Cuban Influence	1958	10.00	20.00	40.00
❑ LSP-1763 [S]	Afro-Cuban Influence	1958	12.50	25.00	50.00
❑ LPM-1975 [M]	Chances Are It Swings	1959	10.00	20.00	40.00
❑ LSP-1975 [S]	Chances Are It Swings	1959	12.50	25.00	50.00
❑ LPM-1997 [M]	The Wizard of Oz	1959	10.00	20.00	40.00
❑ LSP-1997 [S]	The Wizard of Oz	1959	12.50	25.00	50.00
❑ LPM-2110 [M]	The Swingin' Nutcracker	1960	10.00	20.00	40.00
❑ LSP-2110 [S]	The Swingin' Nutcracker	1960	12.50	25.00	50.00
❑ LPM-3137 [10]	Shorty Rogers' Giants	1953	50.00	100.00	200.00
❑ LPM-3138 [10]	Cool and Crazy	1953	50.00	100.00	200.00
REPRISE					
❑ R-6050 [M]	Bossa Nova	1962	5.00	10.00	20.00
❑ R9-6050 [S]	Bossa Nova	1962	6.25	12.50	25.00
❑ R-6060 [M]	Jazz Waltz	1962	5.00	10.00	20.00
❑ R9-6060 [S]	Jazz Waltz	1962	6.25	12.50	25.00
WARNER BROS.					
❑ W 1443 [M]	4th Dimension Jazz	1961	6.25	12.50	25.00
❑ WS 1443 [S]	4th Dimension Jazz	1961	7.50	15.00	30.00

ROGERS, SHORTY/GERRY MULLIGAN

Number	Title (A Side/B Side)	Yr	VG	VG+	NM
CAPITOL					
❑ T 691 [M]	Modern Sounds	1956	20.00	40.00	80.00
❑ T 2025 [M]	Modern Sounds	1963	5.00	10.00	20.00

ROGERS, SHORTY, AND ANDRE PREVIN

Number	Title (A Side/B Side)	Yr	VG	VG+	NM
RCA VICTOR					
❑ LPM-1018 [M]	Collaboration	1954	15.00	30.00	60.00

ROGERS, TIMMIE

Number	Title (A Side/B Side)	Yr	VG	VG+	NM
PHILIPS					
❑ PHM 200088 [M]	If I Were President	1963	5.00	10.00	20.00
❑ PHS 600088 [S]	If I Were President	1963	6.25	12.50	25.00

ROKES, THE

Number	Title (A Side/B Side)	Yr	VG	VG+	NM
RCA VICTOR INTERNATIONAL					
❑ FPM-185 [M]	Che Mondo Strano	1967	20.00	40.00	80.00

ROLAND, GENE

Number	Title (A Side/B Side)	Yr	VG	VG+	NM
BRUNSWICK					
❑ BL 54114 [M]	Swingin' Friends	1963	10.00	20.00	40.00
❑ BL 754114 [S]	Swingin' Friends	1963	12.50	25.00	50.00
DAWN					
❑ DLP-1122 [M]	Jazzville, Volume 4	1958	20.00	40.00	80.00

ROLAND, JOE

Number	Title (A Side/B Side)	Yr	VG	VG+	NM
BETHLEHEM					
❑ BCP-17 [M]	Joe Roland Quintet	1955	12.50	25.00	50.00
SAVOY					
❑ MG-12039 [M]	Joltin' Joe Roland	1955	12.50	25.00	50.00
❑ MG-15034 [10]	Joe Roland Quartet	1954	30.00	60.00	120.00
❑ MG-15047 [10]	Joe Roland Quartet	1954	30.00	60.00	120.00

ROLLING STONES, THE
Also see BRIAN JONES; CHARLIE WATTS; RONNIE WOOD; BILL WYMAN.

Number	Title (A Side/B Side)	Yr	VG	VG+	NM
ABKCO					
❑ ANA 1 [P]	Metamorphosis	1975	3.00	6.00	12.00
❑ MPD-1 [DJ]	Songs of the Rolling Stones	1975	175.00	350.00	700.00
—"Band in field" cover					
❑ MPD-1 [DJ]	Songs of the Rolling Stones	1975	1000.	2000.	3000.
—"Rock and Roll Circus" cover					
❑ DVL2-0268 [(2)P]	The Rolling Stones' Greatest Hits	1977	5.00	10.00	20.00
—RCA Special Products mail-order offer					
❑ 1218-1 [(4)]	Singles Collection: The London Years	1989	12.50	25.00	50.00
❑ AB-4224	Necrophilia	1973	2000.	4000.	8000.
—Canceled; covers exist. Value is for complete tri-fold cover.					

R

Number	Title (A Side/B Side)	Yr	VG	VG+	NM

LONDON

Number	Title (A Side/B Side)	Yr	VG	VG+	NM
❑ NP 1 [M]	Big Hits (High Tide and Green Grass)	1966	10.00	20.00	40.00

—With five lines of type on the front cover, all in capital letters

❑ NP 1 [M]	Big Hits (High Tide and Green Grass)	1966	2000.	4000.	8000.

—With two lines of type on the front cover, all in small letters

| ❑ NPS 1 [R] | Big Hits (High Tide and Green Grass) | 1966 | 2.50 | 5.00 | 10.00 |
| ❑ RSD-1 [DJ] | The Rolling Stones — The Promotional Album | 1969 | 1000. | 2000. | 3000. |

—Not to be confused with imports of this rare promo

| ❑ NP 2 [M] | Their Satanic Majesties Request | 1967 | 62.50 | 125.00 | 250.00 |
| ❑ NPS 2 [S] | Their Satanic Majesties Request | 1967 | 10.00 | 20.00 | 40.00 |

—With 3-D cover

| ❑ NPS 2 [S] | Their Satanic Majesties Request | 197? | 2.00 | 4.00 | 8.00 |

—Without 3-D cover

| ❑ NPS 3 [P] | Through the Past, Darkly (Big Hits Vol. 2) | 1969 | 2.50 | 5.00 | 10.00 |

—With hexagonal cover

| ❑ NPS 3 [P] | Through the Past, Darkly (Big Hits Vol. 2) | 197? | 5.00 | 10.00 | 20.00 |

—Reissue with regular square cover

| ❑ NPS 3 [PD] | Through the Past, Darkly (Big Hits Vol. 2) | 1969 | 3000. | 4500. | 6000. |

—Prototype picture discs that used the cover art from "Big Hits (High Tide and Green Grass)" either on one or both sides.

| ❑ NPS 4 [S] | Let It Bleed | 1969 | 2.50 | 5.00 | 10.00 |

—Without poster

| ❑ NPS 4 [S] | Let It Bleed | 1969 | 3.75 | 7.50 | 15.00 |

—With poster

| ❑ NPS-4 | Let It Bleed | 1970 | 5000. | 7500. | 10000. |

—One-of-a-kind red/yellow/blue/green vinyl (all on the same record!)

| ❑ NPS 5 [S] | Get Yer Ya-Ya's Out! | 1970 | 2.50 | 5.00 | 10.00 |
| ❑ PS 375 [R] | England's Newest Hit Makers — The Rolling Stones | 1964 | 75.00 | 150.00 | 300.00 |

—Dark blue label; lower left-hand corner of cover advertises a bonus photo

| ❑ PS 375 [R] | England's Newest Hit Makers — The Rolling Stones | 1965 | 6.25 | 12.50 | 25.00 |

—Dark blue label with "London" unboxed at top

| ❑ PS 375 [R] | England's Newest Hit Makers — The Rolling Stones | 1966 | 2.50 | 5.00 | 10.00 |

—Dark blue label with "London" boxed at top

| ❑ PS 402 [R] | 12 x 5 | 1964 | 6.25 | 12.50 | 25.00 |

—Dark blue label with "London" unboxed at top

| ❑ PS 402 [R] | 12 x 5 | 1965 | 2.50 | 5.00 | 10.00 |

—Dark blue label with "London" boxed at top

| ❑ PS 420 [R] | The Rolling Stones, Now! | 1965 | 6.25 | 12.50 | 25.00 |

—Dark blue label with "London" unboxed at top. Add 20% for complete liner notes (or sticker) on back cover (both columns of type about equal in length).

| ❑ PS 420 [R] | The Rolling Stones, Now! | 1966 | 2.50 | 5.00 | 10.00 |

—Dark blue label with "London" boxed at top. Add 20% for censored liner notes (or sticker) on back cover (second column an inch shorter than the first column; "offensive" notes were quietly restored in the 1970s).

| ❑ PS 429 [R] | Out of Our Heads | 1965 | 2.50 | 5.00 | 10.00 |

—Dark blue label with "London" unboxed at top

| ❑ PS 429 [R] | Out of Our Heads | 1965 | 6.25 | 12.50 | 25.00 |

—Dark blue label with "London" unboxed at top

| ❑ PS 429 [R] | Out of Our Heads | 1965 | 25.00 | 50.00 | 100.00 |

—Dark blue label with "London/ffrr" in a box at top and "Made in England by the Decca Record Co. Ltd." at top edge

| ❑ PS 451 [P] | December's Children (and Everybody's) | 1965 | 6.25 | 12.50 | 25.00 |

—Dark blue label with "London" unboxed at top

| ❑ PS 451 [P] | December's Children (and Everybody's) | 1966 | 2.50 | 5.00 | 10.00 |

—Dark blue label with "London" boxed at top. "Look What You've Done" is in true stereo; all other tracks are rechanneled.

| ❑ PS 476 [S] | Aftermath | 1966 | 2.50 | 5.00 | 10.00 |
| ❑ PS 493 [P] | Got Live If You Want It! | 1966 | 2.50 | 5.00 | 10.00 |

—"Fortune Teller" is rechanneled (it's actually an early studio recording with overdubbed crowd noise)

| ❑ PS 499 [S] | Between the Buttons | 1967 | 2.50 | 5.00 | 10.00 |
| ❑ PS 509 | Back Behind and In Front | 1967 | 1250. | 2500. | 5000. |

—Prototype cover slick for an unreleased LP; the same number was used for "Flowers"

| ❑ PS 509 [M] | Flowers | 197? | 2.00 | 4.00 | 8.00 |

—Some later "stereo" copies of this LP are actually entirely in mono

| ❑ PS 509 [P] | Flowers | 1967 | 2.50 | 5.00 | 10.00 |

—"Have You Seen Your Mother, Baby, Standing in the Shadow?" and "Mother's Little Helper" are rechanneled; all others are true stereo

| ❑ PS 539 [P] | Beggars Banquet | 1968 | 2500. | 5000. | 10000. |

—Original "toilet graffiti" cover slick (not on a cover)

| ❑ PS 539 [M] | Beggars Banquet | 1968 | 2.50 | 5.00 | 10.00 |

—With "Rev. Wilkins: credited as composer of "Prodigal Son"

| ❑ PS 539 [S] | Beggars Banquet | 1968 | 6.25 | 12.50 | 25.00 |

—With all songs credited to "Jagger-Richard"

| ❑ 2PS 606/7 [(2)P] | Hot Rocks 1964-1971 | 1971 | 5.00 | 10.00 | 20.00 |

—With regular versions of all tracks. All of Side 1 and "Mothers Little Helper" and "19th Nervous Breakdown" on Side 2 are rechanneled. All of Side 3 and 4 are stereo.

| ❑ 2PS 606/7 [(2)P] | Hot Rocks 1964-1971 | 1971 | 250.00 | 500.00 | 1000. |

—With alternate versions of "Brown Sugar" and "Wild Horses" unavailable elsewhere. The date "11-5-71" or "11-18-71" is in the Side 4 trail-off area.

| ❑ 2PS 626/7 [(2)P] | More Hot Rocks (Big Hits and Fazed Cookies) | 1972 | 5.00 | 10.00 | 20.00 |

—All of Sides 1 and 4 are rechanneled; Side 2 and 3, except "Have You Seen Your Mother, Baby, Standing in the Shadow?" are in true stereo

| ❑ LL 3375 | England's Newest Hit Makers — The Rolling Stones Bonus Photo | 1964 | 50.00 | 100.00 | 200.00 |
| ❑ LL 3375 [DJ] | England's Newest Hit Makers — The Rolling Stones | 1964 | 750.00 | 1500. | 3000. |

—White label promo

| ❑ LL 3375 [M] | England's Newest Hit Makers — The Rolling Stones | 1964 | 75.00 | 150.00 | 300.00 |

—Maroon label with "Full Frequency Range Recording" inside horizontal lines that go through the center hole; lower left-hand corner of cover advertises a bonus photo

| ❑ LL 3375 [M] | England's Newest Hit Makers — The Rolling Stones | 1965 | 15.00 | 30.00 | 60.00 |

—Maroon label with "London" unboxed at top

| ❑ LL 3375 [M] | England's Newest Hit Makers — The Rolling Stones | 1966 | 10.00 | 20.00 | 40.00 |

—Red or maroon label with "London" boxed at top

| ❑ LL 3402 [M] | 12 x 5 | 1964 | 15.00 | 30.00 | 60.00 |

—Maroon label with "London" unboxed at top

| ❑ LL 3402 [M] | 12 x 5 | 1964 | 50.00 | 100.00 | 200.00 |

—Maroon label with "London/ffrr" in a box at top

| ❑ LL 3402 [M] | 12 x 5 | 1964 | 5000. | 7500. | 10000. |

—Maroon label with "London" unboxed at top; possibly unique blue vinyl pressing

| ❑ LL 3402 [M] | 12 x 5 | 1965 | 10.00 | 20.00 | 40.00 |

—Red or maroon label with "London" boxed at top

| ❑ LL 3420 [M] | The Rolling Stones, Now! | 1965 | 15.00 | 30.00 | 60.00 |

—Maroon label with "London" unboxed at top and no lines on label. Add 20% for complete liner notes (or sticker) on back cover (both columns of type about equal in length).

| ❑ LL 3420 [M] | The Rolling Stones, Now! | 1965 | 50.00 | 100.00 | 200.00 |

—Maroon label with "London/ffrr" in a box at top. Add 20% for complete liner notes (or sticker) on back cover (both columns of type about equal in length).

| ❑ LL 3420 [M] | The Rolling Stones, Now! | 1965 | 100.00 | 200.00 | 400.00 |

—Maroon label with "London" unboxed, but with "ffrr" ear above "London" and "Full Frequency Range Recording" inside horizontal lines that go through the center hole

| ❑ LL 3420 [M] | The Rolling Stones, Now! | 1965 | 100.00 | 200.00 | 400.00 |

—Maroon label with "London" unboxed, with horizontal lines that go through the center hole, but with NO "ffrr" ear at the top and NO "Full Frequency Range Recording" between the horizonal lines

| ❑ LL 3420 [M] | The Rolling Stones, Now! | 1966 | 10.00 | 20.00 | 40.00 |

—Red or maroon label with "London" boxed at top and censored liner notes (second column an inch shorter than the first column)

| ❑ LL 3429 [M] | Out of Our Heads | 1965 | 10.00 | 20.00 | 40.00 |

—Maroon label with "London" unboxed at top

| ❑ LL 3429 [M] | Out of Our Heads | 1965 | 50.00 | 100.00 | 200.00 |

—Maroon label with "London/ffrr" in a box at top

| ❑ LL 3429 [M] | Out of Our Heads | 1966 | 6.25 | 12.50 | 25.00 |

—Red or maroon label with "London" boxed at top

| ❑ LL 3451 [M] | December's Children (and Everybody's) | 1965 | 10.00 | 20.00 | 40.00 |

—Maroon label with "London" unboxed at top

| ❑ LL 3451 [M] | December's Children (and Everybody's) | 1966 | 6.25 | 12.50 | 25.00 |

—Maroon label with "London" boxed at top

❑ LL 3476 [M]	Aftermath	1966	10.00	20.00	40.00
❑ LL 3493 [M]	Got Live If You Want It!	1966	10.00	20.00	40.00
❑ LL 3499 [M]	Between the Buttons	1967	10.00	20.00	40.00
❑ LL 3509 [M]	Flowers	1967	12.50	25.00	50.00

LONDON/ABKCO

Number	Title (A Side/B Side)	Yr	VG	VG+	NM
❑ 62671 [(2)P]	Hot Rocks 1964-1971	1986	3.75	7.50	15.00

—"Digitally Remastered from Original Master Recording" on cover; red label; same stereo content as original

| ❑ 62671 [(2)P] | More Hot Rocks (Big Hits and Fazed Cookies) | 1986 | 3.75 | 7.50 | 15.00 |

—"Digitally Remastered from Original Master Recording" on cover; red label

| ❑ 73751 [M] | England's Newest Hit Makers — The Rolling Stones | 1986 | 2.00 | 4.00 | 8.00 |

—"Digitally Remastered from Original Master Recording" on cover; red label

| ❑ 74021 [M] | 12 x 5 | 1986 | 2.00 | 4.00 | 8.00 |

—"Digitally Remastered from Original Master Recording" on cover; red label

| ❑ 74201 [P] | The Rolling Stones, Now! | 1986 | 2.00 | 4.00 | 8.00 |

—"Digitally Remastered from Original Master Recording" on cover; red label; four tracks are in true stereo

| ❑ 74291 [P] | Out of Our Heads | 1986 | 2.00 | 4.00 | 8.00 |

—"Digitally Remastered from Original Master Recording" on cover; red label

| ❑ 74511 [M] | December's Children (and Everybody's) | 1986 | 2.00 | 4.00 | 8.00 |

—"Digitally Remastered from Original Master Recording" on cover; red label

| ❑ 74761 [S] | Aftermath | 1986 | 2.00 | 4.00 | 8.00 |

—"Digitally Remastered from Original Master Recording" on cover; red label

| ❑ 74931 [S] | Got Live If You Want It! | 1986 | 2.00 | 4.00 | 8.00 |

—"Digitally Remastered from Original Master Recording" on cover; red label

| ❑ 74991 [S] | Between the Buttons | 1986 | 2.00 | 4.00 | 8.00 |

—"Digitally Remastered from Original Master Recording" on cover; red label

| ❑ 75091 [S] | Flowers | 1986 | 2.00 | 4.00 | 8.00 |

—"Digitally Remastered from Original Master Recording" on cover; red label

| ❑ 75391 [S] | Beggars Banquet | 1986 | 3.00 | 6.00 | 12.00 |

—"Digitally Remastered from Original Master Recording" on cover; red label; original banned "toilet cover" released for the first time on this reissue

| ❑ 80011 [S] | Big Hits (High Tide and Green Grass) | 1986 | 2.00 | 4.00 | 8.00 |

—"Digitally Remastered from Original Master Recording" on cover; red label

| ❑ 80021 [S] | Their Satanic Majesties Request | 1986 | 2.00 | 4.00 | 8.00 |

—"Digitally Remastered from Original Master Recording" on cover; red label

| ❑ 80031 [S] | Through the Past, Darkly (Big Hits Vol. 2) | 1986 | 2.00 | 4.00 | 8.00 |

—"Digitally Remastered from Original Master Recording" on cover; red label

| ❑ 80041 | Let It Bleed | 1986 | 2.00 | 4.00 | 8.00 |

—"Digitally Remastered from Original Master Recording" on cover; red label

| ❑ 80051 | Get Yer Ya-Ya's Out! | 1986 | 2.00 | 4.00 | 8.00 |

—"Digitally Remastered from Original Master Recording" on cover; red label

MOBILE FIDELITY

Number	Title (A Side/B Side)	Yr	VG	VG+	NM
❑ RC-1 [(11)]	The Rolling Stones	1984	125.00	250.00	500.00

—London LPs pressed on audiophile vinyl in box

| ❑ 1-060 | Sticky Fingers | 1980 | 12.50 | 25.00 | 50.00 |

—Audiophile vinyl

| ❑ 1-087 | Some Girls | 1982 | 12.50 | 25.00 | 50.00 |

—Audiophile vinyl

RADIO PULSEBEAT NEWS

Number	Title (A Side/B Side)	Yr	VG	VG+	NM
❑ 4	It's Here Luv!!	1965	45.00	90.00	180.00

—Ed Rudy interview album; this has been counterfeited, but originals can be identified thus: Charlie Watts' jacket should be completely black with no white marks; the label is very clear; the vinyl is all black

ROLLING STONES

Number	Title (A Side/B Side)	Yr	VG	VG+	NM
❑ PR 164 [DJ]	Interview with Mick Jagger by Tom Donahue	1971	50.00	100.00	200.00

—Yellow label

| ❑ COC 2-2900 [(2)] | Exile on Main St. | 1972 | 3.75 | 7.50 | 15.00 |

—Original covers have Unipak design -- cover has to be opened to remove the records. Add 33% for sheet of postcards

| ❑ COC 2-2900 [(2)] | Exile on Main St. | 1973 | 3.00 | 6.00 | 12.00 |

—Reissue covers have two pockets, one for each record

| ❑ COC 2-9001 [(2)] | Love You Live | 1977 | 3.00 | 6.00 | 12.00 |
| ❑ COC 16015 | Emotional Rescue | 1980 | 2.50 | 5.00 | 10.00 |

—Without poster

| ❑ COC 16015 | Emotional Rescue | 1980 | 3.75 | 7.50 | 15.00 |

—Originally released with a large poster wrapped around the outside of the record jacket

| ❑ COC 16028 | Sucking in the Seventies | 1981 | 2.50 | 5.00 | 10.00 |
| ❑ COC 16052 | Tattoo You | 1981 | 2.50 | 5.00 | 10.00 |

Number	Title (A Side/B Side)	Yr	VG	VG+	NM
❏ COC 39100	Jamming with Edward	1972	3.75	7.50	15.00
—Not an official Stones album, this includes Jagger, Watts and Wyman with Ry Cooder and Nicky Hopkins					
❏ COC 39100 [DJ]	Jamming with Edward	1972	43.75	87.50	175.00
—White label stereo promo					
❏ COC 39100 [M]	Jamming with Edward	1972	62.50	125.00	250.00
—White label mono promo					
❏ COC 39105	Sticky Fingers	1977	2.00	4.00	8.00
—Reissue on Atlantic with photo of zipper only					
❏ COC 39105	Sticky Fingers	1977	2.50	5.00	10.00
—Reissue on Atlantic with working zipper					
❏ COC 39106	Goats Head Soup	1977	2.00	4.00	8.00
—Reissue on Atlantic					
❏ COC 39107	Made in the Shade	1977	2.00	4.00	8.00
—Reissue on Atlantic					
❏ COC 39108	Some Girls	1978	2.50	5.00	10.00
—With "cover under reconstruction." Nine different color schemes exist for the front cover.					
❏ COC 39108	Some Girls	1978	3.75	7.50	15.00
—With all women's faces visible. Nine different color schemes exist for the front cover.					
❏ COC 39113	Still Life (American Concert 1981)	1982	2.50	5.00	10.00
❏ COC 39114 [PD]	Still Life (American Concert 1981)	1982	10.00	20.00	40.00
❏ OC 40250	Dirty Work	1986	2.00	4.00	8.00
—Originals came with red shrink wrap; add 50% if it is still with the package					
❏ FC 40488	Sticky Fingers	1986	2.00	4.00	8.00
—Reissue on CBS with photo of zipper only					
❏ CG2 40489 [(2)]	Exile on Main St.	1986	2.50	5.00	10.00
—Reissue on CBS					
❏ FC 40492	Goats Head Soup	1986	2.00	4.00	8.00
—Reissue on CBS					
❏ FC 40493	It's Only Rock 'n' Roll	1986	2.00	4.00	8.00
—Reissue on CBS					
❏ FC 40494	Made in the Shade	1986	2.00	4.00	8.00
—Reissue on CBS					
❏ FC 40495	Black and Blue	1986	2.00	4.00	8.00
—Reissue on CBS					
❏ CG2 40496 [(2)]	Love You Live	1986	2.50	5.00	10.00
—Reissue on CBS					
❏ FC 40499	Some Girls	1986	2.00	4.00	8.00
—Reissue on CBS					
❏ FC 40500	Emotional Rescue	1986	2.00	4.00	8.00
—Reissue on CBS					
❏ FC 40501	Sucking in the Seventies	1986	2.00	4.00	8.00
—Reissue on CBS					
❏ FC 40502	Tattoo You	1986	2.00	4.00	8.00
—Reissue on CBS					
❏ FC 40503	Still Life (American Concert 1981)	1986	2.00	4.00	8.00
—Reissue on CBS					
❏ FC 40504	Undercover	1986	2.00	4.00	8.00
—Reissue on CBS has no stickers on cover					
❏ FC 40505	Rewind (1971-1984)	1986	2.00	4.00	8.00
—Reissue on CBS					
❏ OC 45333	Steel Wheels	1989	2.50	5.00	10.00
❏ C 47456	Flashpoint	1991	5.00	10.00	20.00
❏ COC 59100	Sticky Fingers	1971	3.00	6.00	12.00
—With working zipper					
❏ COC 59100 [DJ]	Sticky Fingers	1971	75.00	150.00	300.00
—White label stereo promo					
❏ COC 59100 [M]	Sticky Fingers	1971	125.00	250.00	500.00
—White label mono promo					
❏ COC 59101	Goats Head Soup	1973	2.50	5.00	10.00
—Without bonus photo					
❏ COC 59101	Goats Head Soup	1973	3.75	7.50	15.00
—With bonus photo					
❏ COC 79101	It's Only Rock 'n' Roll	1974	2.50	5.00	10.00
❏ COC 79102	Made in the Shade	1975	2.50	5.00	10.00
❏ COC 79104	Black and Blue	1976	2.50	5.00	10.00
❏ 90120	Undercover	1983	2.00	4.00	8.00
—With stickers peeled off					
❏ 90120	Undercover	1983	3.00	6.00	12.00
—With stickers intact					
❏ 90176	Rewind (1971-1984)	1984	6.25	12.50	25.00
VIRGIN					
❏ V 2750 (8 39782 1) [(2)]	Voodoo Lounge	1994	5.00	10.00	20.00
—U.S. versions pressed in U.K., but have UPC code paste-over and blue sticker "Marketed by Caroline"					
❏ V 2801 (8 41040 1) [(2)]	Stripped	1995	3.75	7.50	15.00
—U.S. versions pressed in U.K., but have UPC code paste-over with "Marketed and Distributed by Caroline Records"					
❏ 8 44712 1 [(2)]	Bridges to Babylon	1997	3.75	7.50	15.00
—U.S. versions pressed in U.K., but have "Virgin Records America Inc." on back cover					
❏ 8 46740 1 [(2)]	No Security	1998	3.75	7.50	15.00
—U.S. versions pressed in U.K., but have "Virgin Records America Inc." on back cover					
❏ 47863	Sticky Fingers	1999	6.25	12.50	25.00
—Limited-edition reissue with 180-gram vinyl and original working zipper cover					
❏ 47864 [(2)]	Exile on Main St.	1999	12.50	25.00	50.00
—Limited-edition reissue with 180-gram vinyl and all original inserts					
❏ 47867	Some Girls	1999	6.25	12.50	25.00
—Limited-edition reissue with 180-gram vinyl and original inserts (except it has the "cover under reconstruction" inner sleeve)					

ROLLINI, ADRIAN
MERCURY

Number	Title (A Side/B Side)	Yr	VG	VG+	NM
❏ MG-20011 [M]	Chopsticks	1953	12.50	25.00	50.00

ROLLINS, SONNY
ANALOGUE PRODUCTIONS

Number	Title (A Side/B Side)	Yr	VG	VG+	NM
❏ AP 008	Way Out West	199?	6.25	12.50	25.00
—Audiophile vinly					

BLUE NOTE

Number	Title (A Side/B Side)	Yr	VG	VG+	NM
❏ BLP-1542 [M]	Sonny Rollins	1957	37.50	75.00	150.00
—Regular version, Lexington Ave. address on label					
❏ BLP-1542 [M]	Sonny Rollins	1957	50.00	100.00	200.00
—"Deep groove" version (deep indentation under label on both sides)					
❏ BLP-1542 [M]	Sonny Rollins	1963	6.25	12.50	25.00
—With "New York, USA" address on label					
❏ BLP-1558 [M]	Sonny Rollins, Volume 2	1957	20.00	40.00	80.00
—Regular version, W. 63rd St. address on label					
❏ BLP-1558 [M]	Sonny Rollins, Volume 2	1957	30.00	60.00	120.00
—"Deep groove" version (deep indentation under label on both sides)					
❏ BLP-1558 [M]	Sonny Rollins, Volume 2	1963	6.25	12.50	25.00
—With "New York, USA" address on label					
❏ BLP-1581 [M]	A Night at the Village Vanguard	1958	20.00	40.00	80.00
—Regular version, W. 63rd St. address on label					
❏ BLP-1581 [M]	A Night at the Village Vanguard	1958	30.00	60.00	120.00
—"Deep groove" version (deep indentation under label on both sides)					
❏ BLP-1581 [M]	A Night at the Village Vanguard	1963	6.25	12.50	25.00
—With "New York, USA" address on label					
❏ BLP-4001 [M]	Newk's Time	1958	20.00	40.00	80.00
—Regular version, W. 63rd St. address on label					
❏ BLP-4001 [M]	Newk's Time	1958	30.00	60.00	120.00
—"Deep groove" version (deep indentation under label on both sides)					
❏ BLP-4001 [M]	Newk's Time	1963	6.25	12.50	25.00
—With "New York, USA" address on label					
❏ BST-4001 [S]	Newk's Time	1959	15.00	30.00	60.00
—Regular version, W. 63rd St. address on label					
❏ BST-4001 [S]	Newk's Time	1959	20.00	40.00	80.00
—"Deep groove" version (deep indentation under label on both sides)					
❏ BST-4001 [S]	Newk's Time	1963	5.00	10.00	20.00
—With "New York, USA" address on label					

CONTEMPORARY

Number	Title (A Side/B Side)	Yr	VG	VG+	NM
❏ C-3530 [M]	Way Out West	1957	25.00	50.00	100.00
❏ M-3564 [M]	Sonny Rollins and the Contemporary Leaders	1959	20.00	40.00	80.00
❏ S-7530 [S]	Way Out West	1959	12.50	25.00	50.00
❏ S-7564 [S]	Sonny Rollins and the Contemporary Leaders	1959	12.50	25.00	50.00

DCC COMPACT CLASSICS

Number	Title (A Side/B Side)	Yr	VG	VG+	NM
❏ LPZ-2008	Saxophone Colossus	1995	12.50	25.00	50.00
—Audiophile vinyl					
❏ LPZ-2022	Tenor Madness	1996	37.50	75.00	150.00
—Audiophile vinyl					

IMPULSE!

Number	Title (A Side/B Side)	Yr	VG	VG+	NM
❏ A-91 [M]	Sonny Rollins On Impulse!	1966	6.25	12.50	25.00
❏ AS-91 [S]	Sonny Rollins On Impulse!	1966	7.50	15.00	30.00
❏ A-9121 [M]	East Broadway Run Down	1967	7.50	15.00	30.00
❏ AS-9121 [S]	East Broadway Run Down	1967	6.25	12.50	25.00

JAZZLAND

Number	Title (A Side/B Side)	Yr	VG	VG+	NM
❏ JLP-72 [M]	Sonny's Time	1962	10.00	20.00	40.00
❏ JLP-86 [M]	Shadow Waltz	1962	10.00	20.00	40.00
❏ JLP-972 [S]	Sonny's Time	1962	7.50	15.00	30.00
❏ JLP-986 [S]	Shadow Waltz	1962	7.50	15.00	30.00

METROJAZZ

Number	Title (A Side/B Side)	Yr	VG	VG+	NM
❏ E-1002 [M]	Sonny Rollins and the Big Brass	1958	15.00	30.00	60.00
❏ SE-1002 [S]	Sonny Rollins and the Big Brass	1958	12.50	25.00	50.00
❏ E-1011 [M]	Sonny Rollins at Music Inn	1958	15.00	30.00	60.00
❏ SE-1011 [S]	Sonny Rollins at Music Inn	1958	12.50	25.00	50.00

PRESTIGE

Number	Title (A Side/B Side)	Yr	VG	VG+	NM
❏ PRLP-137 [10]	Sonny Rollins Quartet	1952	75.00	150.00	300.00
❏ PRLP-186 [10]	Sonny Rollins Quartet	1954	62.50	125.00	250.00
❏ PRLP-190 [10]	Sonny Rollins	1954	62.50	125.00	250.00
❏ PRLP-7020 [M]	Work Time	1956	20.00	40.00	80.00
❏ PRLP-7029 [M]	Sonny Rollins with the Modern Jazz Quartet	1956	20.00	40.00	80.00
—Yellow cover					
❏ PRLP-7029 [M]	Sonny Rollins with the Modern Jazz Quartet	1956	25.00	50.00	100.00
—Blue cover					
❏ PRLP-7029 [M]	Sonny Rollins with the Modern Jazz Quartet	1956	25.00	50.00	100.00
—Green cover					
❏ PRLP-7038 [M]	Sonny Rollins Plus 4	1956	20.00	40.00	80.00
❏ PRLP-7047 [M]	Tenor Madness	1956	20.00	40.00	80.00
❏ PRLP-7058 [M]	Moving Out	1956	20.00	40.00	80.00
❏ PRLP-7079 [M]	Saxophone Colossus	1957	20.00	40.00	80.00
❏ PRLP-7095 [M]	Rollins Plays for Bird	1957	20.00	40.00	80.00
❏ PRLP-7126 [M]	Tour de Force	1957	20.00	40.00	80.00
❏ PRLP-7207 [M]	Sonny Boy	1961	10.00	20.00	40.00
❏ PRLP-7246 [M]	Work Time	1962	10.00	20.00	40.00
❏ PRST-7246 [R]	Work Time	1962	6.25	12.50	25.00
❏ PRLP-7269 [M]	Sonny and the Stars	1963	10.00	20.00	40.00
❏ PRST-7269 [R]	Sonny and the Stars	1963	6.25	12.50	25.00
❏ PRLP-7326 [M]	Saxophone Colossus	1964	10.00	20.00	40.00
❏ PRST-7326 [R]	Saxophone Colossus	1964	6.25	12.50	25.00
❏ PRLP-7433 [M]	Sonny Rollins Plays Jazz Classics	1967	10.00	20.00	40.00
❏ PRST-7433 [R]	Sonny Rollins Plays Jazz Classics	1967	5.00	10.00	20.00

RCA VICTOR

Number	Title (A Side/B Side)	Yr	VG	VG+	NM
❏ LPM-2527 [M]	The Bridge	1962	10.00	20.00	40.00
❏ LSP-2527 [S]	The Bridge	1962	17.50	35.00	70.00
❏ LSP-2527 [S]	The Bridge	199?	7.50	15.00	30.00
—Classic Records reissue on audiophile vinyl					
❏ LSP-2527-45 [(4)]	The Bridge	1999	10.00	20.00	40.00
—Classic Records reissue; 4 single-sided LPs that play at 45 rpm					
❏ LPM-2572 [M]	What's New?	1962	7.50	15.00	30.00
❏ LSP-2572 [S]	What's New?	1962	15.00	30.00	60.00
❏ LPM-2612 [M]	Our Man In Jazz	1962	7.50	15.00	30.00
❏ LSP-2612 [S]	Our Man In Jazz	1962	15.00	30.00	60.00
❏ LSP-2612 [S]	Our Man In Jazz	199?	6.25	12.50	25.00
—Classic Records reissue on audiophile vinyl					
❏ LPM-2712 [M]	Sonny Meets Hawk!	1963	6.25	12.50	25.00
❏ LSP-2712 [S]	Sonny Meets Hawk!	1963	15.00	30.00	60.00
❏ LSP-2712 [S]	Sonny Meets Hawk!	199?	6.25	12.50	25.00
—Classic Records reissue on audiophile vinyl					
❏ LPM-2927 [M]	Now's the Time	1964	6.25	12.50	25.00
❏ LSP-2927 [S]	Now's the Time!	1964	7.50	15.00	30.00
❏ LSP-2927 [S]	Now's the Time!	199?	6.25	12.50	25.00
—Classic Records reissue on audiophile vinyl					
❏ LPM-3355 [M]	The Standard Sonny Rollins	1965	6.25	12.50	25.00
❏ LSP-3355 [S]	The Standard Sonny Rollins	1965	7.50	15.00	30.00

R

Number	Title (A Side/B Side)	Yr	VG	VG+	NM
RIVERSIDE					
❑ RLP 12-241 [M]	The Sound of Sonny	1957	25.00	50.00	100.00
—White label, blue print					
❑ RLP 12-241 [M]	The Sound of Sonny	1959	12.50	25.00	50.00
—Blue label, microphone logo at top					
❑ RLP-258 [M]	Freedom Suite	1958	20.00	40.00	80.00
❑ RLP-1124 [S]	The Sound of Sonny	1959	12.50	25.00	50.00
STEREO RECORDS					
❑ S-7017 [S]	Way Out West	1958	20.00	40.00	80.00
VERVE					
❑ V-8430 [M]	Sonny Rollins/Brass, Sonny Rollins/Trio	1962	7.50	15.00	30.00
❑ V6-8430 [S]	Sonny Rollins/Brass, Sonny Rollins/Trio	1962	6.25	12.50	25.00
ROLLINS, SONNY; CLIFFORD BROWN; MAX ROACH					
PRESTIGE					
❑ PRLP-7291 [M]	Three Giants	1964	10.00	20.00	40.00
❑ PRST-7291 [R]	Three Giants	1964	6.25	12.50	25.00
ROLLINS, SONNY/JIMMY CLEVELAND					
PERIOD					
❑ SPL-1204 [M]	Sonny Rollins Plays/Jimmy Cleveland Plays	1956	25.00	50.00	100.00
ROMAN NEW ORLEANS JAZZ BAND, THE					
RCA VICTOR					
❑ LPT-3033 [10]	Around the World in Jazz — Italy	1953	10.00	20.00	40.00
ROMEO VOID					
COLUMBIA					
❑ PC 38178 [EP]	Never Say Never	1982	3.00	6.00	12.00
—Reissue					
❑ ARC 38182	Benefactor	1982	2.50	5.00	10.00
❑ PC 38182	Benefactor	198?	2.00	4.00	8.00
—Reissue					
❑ BFC 39155	Instincts	1984	2.50	5.00	10.00
❑ PC 39155	Instincts	1985	2.00	4.00	8.00
—Reissue					
415 RECORDS					
❑ A-0004	It's a Condition	1981	3.75	7.50	15.00
❑ A-0007 [EP]	Never Say Never	1981	6.25	12.50	25.00
ROMEOS, THE (1)					
MARK II					
❑ 1001	Precious Memories	1967	6.25	12.50	25.00
ROMERO, CELEDONIO					
MERCURY LIVING PRESENCE					
❑ SR 90296 [S]	Guitar Music from the Courts of Spain	196?	6.25	12.50	25.00
—Maroon label, no "Vendor: Mercury Record Corporation"					
ROMERO, CELEDONIO; CELIN; PEPE; AND ANGEL					
MERCURY LIVING PRESENCE					
❑ SR 90295 [S]	The Royal Family of the Spanish Guitar	196?	6.25	12.50	25.00
—Maroon label, no "Vendor: Mercury Record Corporation"					
❑ SR 90295 [S]	The Royal Family of the Spanish Guitar	196?	6.25	12.50	25.00
—Maroon label, with "Vendor: Mercury Record Corporation"					
❑ SR 90417 [S]	Spain's Royal Family of the Guitar	196?	6.25	12.50	25.00
—Maroon label, no "Vendor: Mercury Record Corporation"					
❑ SR 90434 [S]	An Evening of Flamenco Music	1965	7.50	15.00	30.00
—Maroon label, with "Vendor: Mercury Record Corporation"					
ROMERO, CESAR					
TOPS					
❑ L-1631 [M]	Songs by a Latin Lover	1958	7.50	15.00	30.00
ROMERO, PEPE					
MERCURY LIVING PRESENCE					
❑ SR 90297 [S]	Flamenco	196?	10.00	20.00	40.00
—Maroon label, no "Vendor: Mercury Record Corporation"					
ROMNEY, HUGH					
Later known as "Wavy Gravy."					
WORLD PACIFIC					
❑ ST-1805 [S]	Third Stream Humor	1962	10.00	20.00	40.00
❑ WP-1805 [M]	Third Stream Humor	1962	7.50	15.00	30.00
RONDO, DON					
JUBILEE					
❑ JLP-1052 [M]	Rondo	195?	5.00	10.00	20.00
❑ JLP-1081 [M]	Have You Met Don Rondo	195?	5.00	10.00	20.00
VOCALION					
❑ VL 73897	Two Different Worlds	1970	3.00	6.00	12.00
RONETTES, THE					
COLPIX					
❑ CP-486 [M]	The Ronettes Featuring Veronica	1965	25.00	50.00	100.00
—Blue label					
❑ CP-486 [M]	The Ronettes Featuring Veronica	1965	50.00	100.00	200.00
—Gold label					
❑ SCP-486 [S]	The Ronettes Featuring Veronica	1965	37.50	75.00	150.00
—Blue label					
❑ SCP-486 [S]	The Ronettes Featuring Veronica	1965	75.00	150.00	300.00
—Gold label					
PHILLES					
❑ PHLP-4006 [M]	Presenting the Fabulous Ronettes Featuring Veronica	1964	100.00	200.00	400.00
—Yellow and red label					
❑ PHLP-4006 [M]	Presenting the Fabulous Ronettes Featuring Veronica	1964	200.00	400.00	800.00
—Blue and black label					
❑ PHLP-ST-4006 [S]	Presenting the Fabulous Ronettes Featuring Veronica	1965	150.00	300.00	600.00
❑ ST-90721 [S]	Presenting the Fabulous Ronettes Featuring Veronica	1965	100.00	200.00	400.00
—Capitol Record Club edition					

Number	Title (A Side/B Side)	Yr	VG	VG+	NM
❑ T-90721 [M]	Presenting the Fabulous Ronettes Featuring Veronica	1965	62.50	125.00	250.00
—Capitol Record Club edition					
RONNIE AND THE DEADBEATS					
CHECK					
❑ 103 [M]	Groovin' with Ronnie and the Deadbeats	197?	5.00	10.00	20.00
RONNIE AND THE POMONA CASUALS					
DONNA					
❑ 2113 [M]	Everybody Jerk	1965	7.50	15.00	30.00
RONNY AND THE DAYTONAS					
BEAT ROCKET					
❑ BR 119	G.T.O.	199?	3.00	6.00	12.00
—Reissue of Mala 4001 with four bonus tracks					
❑ BR 120	Sandy	199?	3.00	6.00	12.00
—Reissue of Mala 4002 with three bonus tracks					
MALA					
❑ 4001 [M]	G.T.O.	1964	30.00	60.00	120.00
❑ 4002 [M]	Sandy	1966	20.00	40.00	80.00
❑ 4002S [S]	Sandy	1966	25.00	50.00	100.00
SUNDAZED					
❑ LP 5050	G.T.O. — Best of the Mala Recordings	199?	2.50	5.00	10.00
RONSTADT, LINDA					
Also see STONE PONEYS.					
ASYLUM					
❑ 6E-104	Simple Dreams	1977	2.50	5.00	10.00
❑ 6E-106	Greatest Hits	1977	2.50	5.00	10.00
❑ 6E-155	Living in the U.S.A.	1978	2.50	5.00	10.00
❑ DP-401 [PD]	Living in the U.S.A.	1978	4.50	9.00	18.00
❑ 5E-510	Mad Love	1980	2.50	5.00	10.00
❑ 5E-516	Greatest Hits, Volume 2	1980	2.50	5.00	10.00
❑ 5E-540	Keeping Out of Mischief	1981	—	—	—
—Canceled					
❑ 7E-1045	Prisoner in Disguise	1975	2.50	5.00	10.00
❑ 7E-1072	Hasten Down the Wind	1976	2.50	5.00	10.00
—"Clouds" label					
❑ 7E-1072	Hasten Down the Wind	1976	3.75	7.50	15.00
—Solid blue label with white stylized "a" at top					
❑ 7E-1092	Greatest Hits	1976	3.00	6.00	12.00
❑ SD 5064	Don't Cry Now	1973	2.50	5.00	10.00
❑ 60185	Get Closer	1982	2.50	5.00	10.00
❑ 60260	What's New	1983	2.50	5.00	10.00
❑ 60387	Lush Life	1984	2.50	5.00	10.00
❑ 60474	For Sentimental Reasons	1987	2.50	5.00	10.00
❑ 60489 [(3)]	'Round Midnight: The Nelson Riddle Sessions	1987	6.25	12.50	25.00
❑ 60765	Canciones De Mi Padre	1988	3.00	6.00	12.00
CAPITOL					
❑ ST-208	Hand Sown…Home Grown	1969	5.00	10.00	20.00
—Black label with colorband					
❑ ST-208	Hand Sown…Home Grown	1970	3.75	7.50	15.00
—Green label					
❑ ST-208	Hand Sown…Home Grown	1971	3.00	6.00	12.00
—Red label					
❑ ST-407	Silk Purse	1970	3.75	7.50	15.00
—Green label					
❑ ST-407	Silk Purse	1971	3.00	6.00	12.00
—Red label					
❑ ST-8-0407	Silk Purse	1970	5.00	10.00	20.00
—Capitol Record Club edition					
❑ SMAS-635	Linda Ronstadt	1972	3.00	6.00	12.00
❑ ST-11269	Different Drum	1974	3.00	6.00	12.00
—Also includes Stone Poneys tracks					
❑ ST-11358	Heart Like a Wheel	1974	3.00	6.00	12.00
❑ SW-11358	Heart Like a Wheel	1975	2.50	5.00	10.00
❑ SKBB-11629 [(2)]	A Retrospective	1977	3.75	7.50	15.00
—Also includes Stone Poneys tracks					
❑ SN-16130	Hand Sown…Home Grown	1980	2.00	4.00	8.00
❑ SN-16131	Silk Purse	1980	2.00	4.00	8.00
❑ SN-16132	Linda Ronstadt	1980	2.00	4.00	8.00
❑ SN-16133	Beginnings	1980	2.00	4.00	8.00
❑ SN-16299	Different Drum	198?	2.00	4.00	8.00
—Budget-line reissue					
DCC COMPACT CLASSICS					
❑ LPZ-2048	Greatest Hits	1997	20.00	40.00	80.00
—Audiophile vinyl					
❑ LPZ-2065	Greatest Hits, Volume Two	1998	10.00	20.00	40.00
—Audiophile vinyl					
ELEKTRA					
❑ 60872	Cry Like a Rainstorm, Howl Like the Wind	1989	3.00	6.00	12.00
MOBILE FIDELITY					
❑ 1-158	What's New	1984	12.50	25.00	50.00
—Audiophile vinyl					
NAUTILUS					
❑ NR-26	Simple Dreams	1982	12.50	25.00	50.00
—Audiophile vinyl					
PAIR					
❑ PDL2-1070 [(2)]	Prime of Life	1986	3.00	6.00	12.00
❑ PDL2-1125 [(2)]	Rockfile	1986	3.00	6.00	12.00
ROOFTOP SINGERS, THE					
VANGUARD					
❑ VSD-2136 [S]	Walk Right In	1963	5.00	10.00	20.00
❑ VRS-9123 [M]	Walk Right In	1963	3.75	7.50	15.00
❑ VRS-9134 [M]	Good Time	1964	3.75	7.50	15.00
❑ VRS-9190 [M]	Rainy River	1965	3.75	7.50	15.00
❑ VSD-79134 [S]	Good Time	1964	5.00	10.00	20.00
❑ VSD-79190 [S]	Rainy River	1965	5.00	10.00	20.00

Number	Title (A Side/B Side)	Yr	VG	VG+	NM
ROOMFUL OF BLUES					
ANTILLES					
❑ 7071	Let's Have a Party!	1980	5.00	10.00	20.00
BLUE FLAME					
❑ 1001	Hot Little Mama	197?	6.25	12.50	25.00
ISLAND					
❑ ILPS 9474	Roomful of Blues	1977	6.25	12.50	25.00
ROONEY, MICKEY					
RCA VICTOR					
❑ LPM-1520 [M]	Mickey Rooney Sings George M. Cohan	1957	20.00	40.00	80.00
ROSE, DAVID					
CAPITOL					
❑ ST 2853	Christmas Album	1968	3.00	6.00	12.00
INNER CITY					
❑ IC-1058	The Distance Between Dreams	197?	3.00	6.00	12.00
KAPP					
❑ K-1100-S [S]	Great Waltzes of the Fabulous Century	1958	6.25	12.50	25.00
❑ KL-1100 [M]	Great Waltzes of the Fabulous Century	1958	5.00	10.00	20.00
❑ KL-1205 [M]	Songs of the Fabulous Thirties, Vol. 1	1960	3.75	7.50	15.00
❑ KL-1206 [M]	Songs of the Fabulous Thirties, Vol. 2	1960	3.75	7.50	15.00
❑ KS-3010 [S]	Waltzes in Stereo	1959	7.50	15.00	30.00
❑ KS-3205 [S]	Songs of the Fabulous Thirties, Vol. 1	1960	5.00	10.00	20.00
❑ KS-3206 [S]	Songs of the Fabulous Thirties, Vol. 2	1960	5.00	10.00	20.00
❑ KX-5004-S [(2)S]	Songs of the Fabulous Thirties	1958	7.50	15.00	30.00
❑ KXL-5004 [(2)M]	Songs of the Fabulous Thirties	1958	6.25	12.50	25.00
MGM					
❑ E-196 [10]	Magic Music Box	195?	10.00	20.00	40.00
❑ E-3067 [M]	Beautiful Music to Love By	195?	7.50	15.00	30.00
—Yellow label					
❑ E-3101 [M]	Let's Fall in Love	195?	7.50	15.00	30.00
—Yellow label					
❑ E-3108 [M]	Fiddlin' for Fun	195?	7.50	15.00	30.00
—Yellow label					
❑ E-3123 [M]	Love Walked In — The Music of George Gershwin	195?	7.50	15.00	30.00
—Yellow label					
❑ E-3215 [M]	Holiday for Strings	195?	7.50	15.00	30.00
—Yellow label					
❑ E-3397 [M]	Music from Motion Pictures	195?	7.50	15.00	30.00
—Yellow label					
❑ E-3469 [M]	A Merry Christmas to You	1956	6.25	12.50	25.00
—Yellow label					
❑ E-3469 [M]	A Merry Christmas to You	1960	3.75	7.50	15.00
—Black label					
❑ E-3481 [M]	Hi Fiddles	195?	5.00	10.00	20.00
—Yellow label					
❑ E-3592 [M]	Autumn Leaves	195?	5.00	10.00	20.00
—Yellow label					
❑ SE-3592 [S]	Autumn Leaves	195?	7.50	15.00	30.00
—Yellow label					
❑ E-3716 [M]	Secret Songs for Young Lovers	1959	5.00	10.00	20.00
—Yellow label					
❑ SE-3716 [S]	Secret Songs for Young Lovers	1959	7.50	15.00	30.00
—Yellow label					
❑ E-3950 [M]	Exodus	1961	3.75	7.50	15.00
❑ SE-3950 [S]	Exodus	1961	5.00	10.00	20.00
❑ E-4004 [M]	21 Channel Sound	1962	3.75	7.50	15.00
❑ SE-4004 [S]	21 Channel Sound	1962	5.00	10.00	20.00
❑ E-4062 [M]	The Stripper and Other Fun Songs for the Family	1962	3.75	7.50	15.00
—Black label					
❑ SE-4062 [S]	The Stripper and Other Fun Songs for the Family	1962	5.00	10.00	20.00
—Black label					
❑ E-4099 [M]	More, More, More, Music of the Stripper	1963	3.75	7.50	15.00
❑ SE-4099 [S]	More, More, More, Music of the Stripper.	1963	5.00	10.00	20.00
❑ ST 90534 [S]	The Stripper and Other Fun Songs for the Family.	1965	5.00	10.00	20.00
—Capitol Record Club edition					
❑ T 90534 [M]	The Stripper and Other Fun Songs for the Family	1965	5.00	10.00	20.00
—Capitol Record Club edition					
ROSE, WALLY					
COLUMBIA					
❑ CL 782 [M]	Cake Walk to Lindy Hop	1956	10.00	20.00	40.00
❑ CL 2535 [10]	Honky-Tonkin'	1955	7.50	15.00	30.00
—"House Party Series" reissue					
❑ CL 6260 [10]	Wally Rose	1953	12.50	25.00	50.00
GOOD TIME JAZZ					
❑ S-10034 [S]	Ragtime Classics	1960	5.00	10.00	20.00
ROSE GARDEN, THE					
ATCO					
❑ 33-225 [M]	The Rose Garden	1968	15.00	30.00	60.00
❑ SD 33-225 [S]	The Rose Garden	1968	6.25	12.50	25.00
ROSE MARIE					
KAPP					
❑ KFL-4500 [M]	Songs for Single Girls	1964	7.50	15.00	30.00
ROSIE AND THE ORIGINALS					
BRUNSWICK					
❑ BL 54102 [M]	Lonely Blue Nights with Rosie	1961	37.50	75.00	150.00
❑ BL 754102 [S]	Lonely Blue Nights with Rosie	1961	50.00	100.00	200.00
ROSIE O'GRADY'S GOOD TIME BAND					
DIRECT DISK					
❑ DD-103	Dixieland	1979	5.00	10.00	20.00
—Audiophile recording					

Number	Title (A Side/B Side)	Yr	VG	VG+	NM
ROSOLINO, FRANK					
BETHLEHEM					
❑ BCP-26 [M]	I Play Trombone	1955	12.50	25.00	50.00
CAPITOL					
❑ H 6507 [10]	Frank Rosolino	1954	20.00	40.00	80.00
❑ T 6507 [M]	Frank Rosolino	1955	25.00	30.00	60.00
❑ T 6509 [M]	Frankly Speaking	1955	25.00	30.00	60.00
INTERLUDE					
❑ MO-500 [M]	The Legend of Frank Rosolino	1959	10.00	20.00	40.00
❑ ST-1000 [S]	The Legend of Frank Rosolino	1959	7.50	15.00	30.00
MODE					
❑ LP-107 [M]	Frank Rosolino Quintet	1957	25.00	50.00	100.00
REPRISE					
❑ R-6016 [M]	Turn Me Loose	1961	6.25	12.50	25.00
❑ R9-6016 [S]	Turn Me Loose	1961	7.50	15.00	30.00
ROSS, ANNIE					
Also see LAMBERT, HENDRICKS AND ROSS.					
DECCA					
❑ DL 4922 [M]	Fill My Heart with Song	1967	7.50	15.00	30.00
❑ DL 74922 [S]	Fill My Heart with Song	1967	5.00	10.00	20.00
KIMBERLY					
❑ 2018 [M]	Annie Ross Sings A Song With Mulligan!	1963	7.50	15.00	30.00
❑ 11018 [S]	Annie Ross Sings A Song With Mulligan!	1963	6.25	12.50	25.00
WORLD PACIFIC					
❑ ST-1020 [S]	Annie Ross Sings A Song With Mulligan!	1959	10.00	20.00	40.00
❑ ST-1028 [S]	Gypsy	1959	10.00	20.00	40.00
❑ WP-1253 [M]	Annie Ross Sings A Song With Mulligan!	1959	12.50	25.00	50.00
❑ ST-1285 [S]	A Gasser!	1960	10.00	20.00	40.00
❑ WP-1285 [M]	A Gasser!	1960	12.50	25.00	50.00
❑ WP-1808 [M]	Gypsy	1959	12.50	25.00	50.00
ROSS, ANNIE; DOROTHY DUNN; SHELBY DAVIS					
SAVOY					
❑ MG-12060 [M]	Singin' 'N Swingin'	1956	10.00	20.00	40.00
ROSS, ARNOLD					
DISCOVERY					
❑ DL-2006 [M]	Arnold Ross	1954	12.50	25.00	50.00
MERCURY					
❑ MGC-134 [10]	Arnold Ross	1952	37.50	75.00	150.00
ROSS, DIANA					
MOTOWN					
❑ M5-135V1	Diana Ross	1981	2.00	4.00	8.00
—Reissue of 711					
❑ M5-155V1	Diana!	1981	2.00	4.00	8.00
—Reissue of 719					
❑ M5-163V1	Touch Me in the Morning	1981	2.00	4.00	8.00
—Reissue of 772					
❑ M5-169V1	Diana Ross Live at Caesars Palace	1981	2.00	4.00	8.00
—Reissue of 801					
❑ M5-198V1	The Boss	1981	2.00	4.00	8.00
—Reissue of 923					
❑ M5-214V1	Duets with Diana	1981	2.50	5.00	10.00
❑ MS-711	Diana Ross	1970	3.75	7.50	15.00
❑ MS-719	Diana!	1971	3.75	7.50	15.00
❑ MS-723	Surrender	1971	3.75	7.50	15.00
❑ MS-724	Everything Is Everything	1970	3.75	7.50	15.00
❑ M-758D [(2)]	Lady Sings the Blues	1972	3.75	7.50	15.00
—With booklet; all but four tracks are by Diana Ross					
❑ M-772L	Touch Me in the Morning	1973	3.75	7.50	15.00
❑ M6-801S1	Diana Ross Live at Caesars Palace	1974	3.00	6.00	12.00
❑ M7-812V1	Last Time I Saw Him	1974	3.00	6.00	12.00
❑ M6-861S1	Diana Ross	1976	3.00	6.00	12.00
❑ M6-869S1	Diana Ross' Greatest Hits	1976	3.00	6.00	12.00
❑ M7-877R2 [(2)]	An Evening with Diana Ross	1977	3.75	7.50	15.00
❑ M7-890R1	Baby It's Me	1977	3.00	6.00	12.00
❑ M7-907R1	Ross	1978	3.00	6.00	12.00
❑ M8-923M1	The Boss	1979	2.50	5.00	10.00
❑ M8-936	Diana	1980	2.50	5.00	10.00
❑ M8-951M1	To Love Again	1981	2.50	5.00	10.00
❑ M13-960C2 [(2)]	All the Great Hits	1981	3.00	6.00	12.00
❑ 5294 ML	Diana Ross	1983	2.00	4.00	8.00
—Reissue of 861					
❑ 6049 ML2 [(2)]	Diana Ross Anthology	1983	3.75	7.50	15.00
❑ MOT-6274	Workin' Overtime	1989	2.50	5.00	10.00
❑ 37463-6377-1	The Remixes	1994	3.00	6.00	12.00
NAUTILUS					
❑ NR-37	Diana	1981	10.00	20.00	40.00
—Audiophile vinyl					
RCA VICTOR					
❑ AFL1-4153	Why Do Fools Fall in Love	1981	2.50	5.00	10.00
❑ AFL1-4384	Silk Electric	1982	2.50	5.00	10.00
❑ AFL1-4677	Ross	1983	2.00	4.00	8.00
❑ AFL1-5009	Swept Away	1984	2.00	4.00	8.00
❑ AYL1-5162	Why Do Fools Fall in Love	1985	—	3.00	6.00
—"Best Buy Series" reissue					
❑ AFL1-5422	Eaten Alive	1985	2.00	4.00	8.00
❑ 6388-1-R	Red Hot Rhythm and Blues	1987	2.00	4.00	8.00
ROSS, DIANA, AND THE SUPREMES					
See THE SUPREMES.					
ROSS, JACK					
DOT					
❑ DLP-3429 [M]	Cinderella	1962	5.00	10.00	20.00
❑ DLP-25429 [S]	Cinderella	1962	6.25	12.50	25.00

R

Number	Title (A Side/B Side)	Yr	VG	VG+	NM

ROSS, JACKIE
CHESS
❑ LP-1489 [M]	In Full Bloom	1966	7.50	15.00	30.00
❑ LPS-1489 [S]	In Full Bloom	1966	10.00	20.00	40.00

ROSS, JOE E.
ROULETTE
❑ R-25281 [M]	Love Songs from a Cop	1965	6.25	12.50	25.00
❑ SR-25281 [S]	Love Songs from a Cop	1965	7.50	15.00	30.00

ROSS, RONNIE
ATLANTIC
❑ 1333 [M]	The Jazz Makers	1960	7.50	15.00	30.00
❑ SD 1333 [S]	The Jazz Makers	1960	10.00	20.00	40.00

ROSS, SPENCER
COLUMBIA
❑ CS (# unknown) [S]	Spencer Ross and His Orchestra	1960	6.25	12.50	25.00
❑ CL 1525 [M]	Spencer Ross and His Orchestra	1960	5.00	10.00	20.00

ROSS, STAN
DEL-FI
❑ DFLP-1233 [M]	My Son the Copy Cat	1963	7.50	15.00	30.00
❑ DFST-1233 [S]	My Son the Copy Cat	1963	10.00	20.00	40.00

ROTARY CONNECTION
CADET
❑ CS-50006	Hey Love	1971	5.00	10.00	20.00
CADET CONCEPT
❑ LP-312 [M]	Rotary Connection	1968	15.00	30.00	60.00

—Mono appears to be promo only
❑ LPS-312 [S]	Rotary Connection	1968	6.25	12.50	25.00
❑ LPS-317	Aladdin	1968	6.25	12.50	25.00
❑ LPS 318	Peace	1969	5.00	10.00	20.00
❑ LPS-322	Songs	1969	6.25	12.50	25.00
❑ LSP-328	Dinner Music	1970	6.25	12.50	25.00

ROTH, LILLIAN
EPIC
❑ LN 3206 [M]	I'll Cry Tomorrow	1957	7.50	15.00	30.00
TOPS
❑ L-1567 [M]	Lillian Roth Sings	1958	6.25	12.50	25.00

ROUND, JONATHAN
WESTBOUND
❑ 2009	Jonathan Round	1971	7.50	15.00	30.00

—Round cover
❑ 2009	Jonathan Round	1972	3.75	7.50	15.00

—Square cover

ROUND ROBIN
CHALLENGE
❑ LP-620 [M]	The Land of 1,000 Dances	1965	6.25	12.50	25.00
DOMAIN
❑ 101 [M]	Greatest Dance Hits Slauson Style	1964	10.00	20.00	40.00

ROUSE, CHARLIE
BLUE NOTE
❑ BLP-4119 [M]	Bossa Nova Bacchanal	1962	7.50	15.00	30.00
❑ BST-84119 [S]	Bossa Nova Bacchanal	196?	5.00	10.00	20.00

—With "A Division of Liberty Records" on label
❑ BST-84119 [S]	Bossa Nova Bacchanal	1962	10.00	20.00	40.00

—With "New York, USA" address on label
EPIC
❑ LA 16012 [M]	Yeah!	1960	10.00	20.00	40.00
❑ LA 16018 [M]	We Paid Our Dues	1961	10.00	20.00	40.00
❑ BA 17012 [S]	Yeah!	1960	12.50	25.00	50.00
❑ BA 17012 [S]	Yeah!	199?	6.25	12.50	25.00

—Classic Records reissue on audiophile vinyl
❑ BA 17018 [S]	We Paid Our Dues	1961	12.50	25.00	50.00
JAZZLAND
❑ JLP-19 [M]	Takin' Care of Business	1960	10.00	20.00	40.00
❑ JLP-919 [S]	Takin' Care of Business	1960	12.50	25.00	50.00
STRATA-EAST
❑ SES-19746	Two Is One	1974	6.25	12.50	25.00

ROUSE, CHARLIE, AND PAUL QUINICHETTE
BETHLEHEM
❑ BCP-6021 [M]	The Chase Is On	1958	12.50	25.00	50.00

ROUTERS, THE
WARNER BROS.
❑ W 1490 [M]	Let's Go! with the Routers	1963	6.25	12.50	25.00
❑ WS 1490 [S]	Let's Go! with the Routers	1963	7.50	15.00	30.00
❑ W 1524 [M]	1963's Great Instrumental Hits	1964	7.50	15.00	30.00
❑ WS 1524 [S]	1963's Great Instrumental Hits	1964	10.00	20.00	40.00
❑ W 1559 [M]	Charge!	1964	6.25	12.50	25.00
❑ WS 1559 [S]	Charge!	1964	7.50	15.00	30.00
❑ W 1595 [M]	Go Go Go with the Chuck Berry Songbook	1965	5.00	10.00	20.00
❑ WS 1595 [S]	Go Go Go with the Chuck Berry Songbook	1965	6.25	12.50	25.00

ROVA
METALANGUAGE
❑ (# unknown)	Daredevils	1979	5.00	10.00	20.00
❑ 101	Cinema Rovate	1978	5.00	10.00	20.00
❑ 106	The Removal of Secrecy	1979	5.00	10.00	20.00

ROWLES, JIMMY
ANDEX
❑ A-3007 [M]	Weather in a Jazz Vane	1958	12.50	25.00	50.00
❑ AS-3007 [S]	Weather in a Jazz Vane	1958	10.00	20.00	40.00
CAPITOL
❑ ST 1831 [S]	Kinda Groovy!	1963	5.00	10.00	20.00

INTERLUDE
❑ MO-515 [M]	Upper Classmen	1959	10.00	20.00	40.00
❑ ST-1015 [S]	Upper Classmen	1959	7.50	15.00	30.00
LIBERTY
❑ LRP-3003 [M]	Rare, But Well Done	1955	15.00	30.00	60.00
SIGNATURE
❑ SM-6011 [M]	Fiorello Uptown, Mary Sunshine Downtown	1960	15.00	30.00	60.00
❑ SS-6011 [S]	Fiorello Uptown, Mary Sunshine Downtown	1960	20.00	40.00	80.00
TAMPA
❑ TP-8 [M]	Let's Get Acquainted with Jazz… For People Who Hate Jazz	1957	37.50	75.00	150.00

—Colored vinyl
❑ TP-8 [M]	Let's Get Acquainted with Jazz… For People Who Hate Jazz	1958	20.00	40.00	80.00
❑ TPS-8 [S]	Let's Get Acquainted with Jazz… For People Who Hate Jazz	1958	12.50	25.00	50.00

ROXETTE
CAPITOL
❑ MLP-15018 [EP]	Heartland	1984	7.50	15.00	30.00
EMI
❑ E1-91098	Look Sharp!	1989	3.75	7.50	15.00

ROXY MUSIC
ATCO
❑ SD 32-102	Flesh + Blood	1980	2.50	5.00	10.00
❑ SD 38-103	Greatest Hits	1977	2.50	5.00	10.00
❑ SD 36-106	Country Life	1975	6.25	12.50	25.00

—Original cover shows two semi-naked women on a grassy background
❑ SD 36-106A	Country Life	1975	2.50	5.00	10.00

—Revised cover deletes women, leaves only the grassy background
❑ SD 38-114	Manifesto	1979	2.50	5.00	10.00
❑ SD 38-114 [PD]	Manifesto	1979	7.50	15.00	30.00

—Picture disc
❑ SD 36-127	Siren	1975	2.50	5.00	10.00

—Originals have yellow labels
❑ SD 36-133	The First Roxy Music Album	1975	3.00	6.00	12.00

—Reissue of Reprise MS 2114; originals have yellow labels
❑ SD 36-134	For Your Pleasure	1975	3.00	6.00	12.00

—Reissue of Warner Bros. BS 2696; originals have yellow labels
❑ SD 36-139	Viva! Roxy Music (Live)	1976	2.50	5.00	10.00

—Originals have yellow labels
❑ SD 7045	Stranded	1974	3.00	6.00	12.00
❑ 90122	The Atlantic Years (1973-80)	1983	2.50	5.00	10.00
REPRISE
❑ MS 2114	Roxy Music	1972	7.50	15.00	30.00
❑ 25857 [(2)]	Street Life: 20 Greatest Hits	1989	3.75	7.50	15.00

—By "Bryan Ferry & Roxy Music"
WARNER BROS.
❑ BS 2696	For Your Pleasure	1973	6.25	12.50	25.00
❑ 23686	Avalon	1982	2.50	5.00	10.00
❑ 23808 [EP]	Musique — The High Road	1983	2.00	4.00	8.00

ROYAL, BILLY JOE
ATLANTIC AMERICA
❑ 90508	Looking Ahead	1986	2.50	5.00	10.00
❑ 90658	The Royal Treatment	1987	2.50	5.00	10.00
❑ 91064	Tell It Like It Is	1989	2.50	5.00	10.00
COLUMBIA
❑ CL 2403 [M]	Down in the Boondocks	1965	5.00	10.00	20.00
❑ CL 2781 [M]	Billy Joe Royal	1967	6.25	12.50	25.00
❑ CS 9203 [S]	Down in the Boondocks	1965	6.25	12.50	25.00
❑ CS 9581 [S]	Billy Joe Royal	1967	6.25	12.50	25.00
❑ CS 9974	Cherry Hill Park	1969	6.25	12.50	25.00
KAT FAMILY
❑ JW 37342	Billy Joe Royal	1982	2.50	5.00	10.00
MERCURY
❑ SRM-1-3837	Billy Joe Royal	1980	2.50	5.00	10.00

ROYAL, ERNIE
URANIA
❑ UJLP-1203 [M]	Accent on Trumpet	1955	12.50	25.00	50.00

ROYAL, MARSHALL
EVEREST
❑ SDBR-1087 [S]	Gordon Jenkins Presents Marshall Royal	1960	7.50	15.00	30.00
❑ LPBR-5087 [M]	Gordon Jenkins Presents Marshall Royal	1960	6.25	12.50	25.00

ROYAL CHORAL SOCIETY, THE
RCA VICTOR BLUEBIRD CLASSICS
❑ LBC-1044 [M]	Yuletide Hymns and Carols	1954	6.25	12.50	25.00

ROYAL GUARDSMEN, THE
HOLIDAY
❑ HDY 1913	Merry Snoopy's Christmas	1980	2.50	5.00	10.00

—Reissue of Laurie 2042
LAURIE
❑ LLP-2038 [M]	Snoopy vs. the Red Baron	1967	5.00	10.00	20.00
❑ SLP-2038 [S]	Snoopy vs. the Red Baron	1967	6.25	12.50	25.00
❑ LLP-2039 [M]	The Return of the Red Baron	1967	5.00	10.00	20.00
❑ SLP-2039 [S]	The Return of the Red Baron	1967	6.25	12.50	25.00
❑ LLP-2042 [M]	Snoopy and His Friends	1967	3.75	7.50	15.00

—With "Merry Snoopy's Christmas" poster missing
❑ LLP-2042 [M]	Snoopy and His Friends	1967	6.25	12.50	25.00

—With "Merry Snoopy's Christmas" poster still attached to back cover
❑ SLP 2042 [S]	Snoopy and His Friends	1967	5.00	10.00	20.00

—With "Merry Snoopy's Christmas" poster missing
❑ SLP 2042 [S]	Snoopy and His Friends	1967	7.50	15.00	30.00

—With "Merry Snoopy's Christmas" poster still attached to back cover
❑ SLP-2046	Snoopy for President	1968	6.25	12.50	25.00

Number	Title (A Side/B Side)	Yr	VG	VG+	NM

ROYAL MALE CHOIR OF HOLLAND, THE
EPIC
❑ LC 3074	Christmas Carols	195?	5.00	10.00	20.00

ROYAL OPERA HOUSE ORCHESTRA (ERNEST ANSERMET, CONDUCTOR)
RCA VICTOR RED SEAL
❑ LDS-6065 [(2)S]	The Royal Ballet Gala Performances	195?	300.00	600.00	1200.
—Original with "shaded dog" labels					
❑ LDS-6065 [(2)S]	The Royal Ballet Gala Performances	199?	10.00	20.00	40.00
—Classic Records reissue at 33 1/3 rpm					
❑ LDS-6065 [(9)S]	The Royal Ballet Gala Performances	199?	30.00	60.00	120.00
—Classic Records reissue at 45 rpm					

ROYAL OPERA HOUSE ORCHESTRA (ANATOLE FISTOULARI, CONDUCTOR)
RCA VICTOR RED SEAL
❑ LSC-2285 [S]	Walton: Facade Suite	1959	50.00	100.00	200.00
—Original with "shaded dog" label					
❑ LSC-2285 [S]	Walton: Facade Suite	199?	6.25	12.50	25.00
—Classic Records reissue					

ROYAL OPERA HOUSE ORCHESTRA (ALEXANDER GIBSON, CONDUCTOR)
RCA VICTOR RED SEAL
❑ LSC-2449 [S]	Gounod: Ballet Music of Faust; Bizet: Carmen	1960	250.00	500.00	1000.
—Original with "shaded dog" label					
❑ LSC-2449 [S]	Gounod: Ballet Music of Faust; Bizet: Carmen	199?	6.25	12.50	25.00
—Classic Records reissue					

ROYAL OPERA HOUSE ORCHESTRA (JEAN MOREL, CONDUCTOR)
RCA VICTOR RED SEAL
❑ LSC-2327 [S]	Bizet: L'Arlesienne Suites	1960	45.00	90.00	180.00
—Original with "shaded dog" label					
❑ LSC-2327 [S]	Bizet: L'Arlesienne Suites	199?	6.25	12.50	25.00
—Classic Records reissue					
❑ LSC-6094 [(2)S]	Albeniz: Iberia (Complete); Ravel: Rapsodie Espagnole	196?	100.00	200.00	400.00
—Original with "shaded dog" labels					
❑ LSC-6094 [(2)S]	Albeniz: Iberia (Complete); Ravel: Rapsodie Espagnole	199?	10.00	20.00	40.00
—Classic Records reissue					

ROYAL OPERA HOUSE ORCHESTRA (HUGO RIGNOLD, CONDUCTOR)
RCA VICTOR RED SEAL
❑ LSC-2135 [S]	Prokofiev: Cinderella	199?	6.25	12.50	25.00
—Classic Records issue; this album is not known to have been issued in stereo before this.					
❑ LSC-2450 [S]	Schumann: Carnaval; Meyerbeer: Les Patineurs	1960	15.00	30.00	60.00
—Original with "shaded dog" label					
❑ LSC-2450 [S]	Schumann: Carnaval; Meyerbeer: Les Patineurs	199?	6.25	12.50	25.00
—Classic Records reissue					

ROYAL OPERA HOUSE ORCHESTRA (SIR GEORGE SOLTI, CONDUCTOR)
RCA VICTOR RED SEAL
❑ LSC-2313 [S]	Venice	1959	25.00	50.00	100.00
—Original with "shaded dog" label					
❑ LSC-2313 [S]	Venice	199?	6.25	12.50	25.00
—Classic Records reissue					

ROYAL PHILHARMONIC ORCHESTRA (RENE LEIBOWITZ, CONDUCTOR)
RCA VICTOR RED SEAL
❑ VCS-2659 [S]	The Power of the Orchestra	1962	75.00	150.00	300.00
—Original with "shaded dog" label					

ROYAL PLAYBOYS, THE
WALDORF
❑ 33-136 [10]	Rock and Roll/New Orleans Blues	195?	125.00	250.00	500.00

ROYAL TEENS, THE
COLLECTABLES
❑ COL-5094	Short Shorts: Golden Classics	198?	2.50	5.00	10.00
MUSICOR
❑ MS-3186	Newies But Oldies	1970	5.00	10.00	20.00
TRU-GEMS
❑ 1001	Short Shorts & Others	1975	5.00	10.00	20.00

ROYALETTES, THE
MGM
❑ E-4332 [M]	It's Gonna Take a Miracle	1965	5.00	10.00	20.00
❑ SE-4332 [S]	It's Gonna Take a Miracle	1965	6.25	12.50	25.00
❑ E-4366 [M]	The Elegant Sound of the Royalettes	1966	5.00	10.00	20.00
❑ SE-4366 [S]	The Elegant Sound of the Royalettes	1966	6.25	12.50	25.00

RUBBER BAND, THE (2)
GRT
❑ 10000	Cream Songbook	1969	6.25	12.50	25.00
❑ 10007	Hendrix Songbook	1969	6.25	12.50	25.00
❑ 10015	Beatles Songbook	1969	6.25	12.50	25.00

RUBBER CITY REBELS
CAPITOL
❑ ST-12100	Rubber City Rebels	1980	10.00	20.00	40.00

RUBBER MEMORY
R.P.C.
❑ 69401	Welcome	196?	250.00	500.00	1000.

RUBENSTEIN, ARTUR
RCA VICTOR RED SEAL
❑ LSC-1831 [S]	Brahms: Piano Concerto No. 1	199?	6.25	12.50	25.00
—With the Chicago Symphony (Fritz Reiner cond.); Classic Records issue; this album is not known to have been issued in stereo before this					
❑ LSC-2068 [S]	Rachmaninoff: Piano Concerto No. 2; Lizst: Piano Conceto No. 1	1958	6.25	12.50	25.00
—Original with "shaded dog" label					
❑ LSC-2120 [S]	Beethoven: Piano Concerto No. 1	1959	6.25	12.50	25.00
—With Josef Krips/NBC "Symphony of the Air" Orchestra; original with "shaded dog" label					
❑ LSC-2121 [S]	Beethoven: Piano Concerto No. 2	1959	5.00	10.00	20.00
—With Josef Krips/NBC "Symphony of the Air" Orchestra; original with "shaded dog" label					
❑ LSC-2122 [S]	Beethoven: Piano Concerto No. 3	1959	5.00	10.00	20.00
—With Josef Krips/NBC "Symphony of the Air" Orchestra; original with "shaded dog" label					
❑ LSC-2123 [S]	Beethoven: Piano Concerto No. 4	1959	5.00	10.00	20.00
—With Josef Krips/NBC "Symphony of the Air" Orchestra; original with "shaded dog" label					
❑ LSC-2124 [S]	Beethoven: Piano Concerto No. 5	1959	5.00	10.00	20.00
—With Josef Krips/NBC "Symphony of the Air" Orchestra; original with "shaded dog" label					
❑ LSC-2234 [S]	Saint-Saens: Piano Concerto No. 2	1959	5.00	10.00	20.00
—With the Symphony of the Air Orchestra (Alfred Wallenstein, conductor); original with "shaded dog" label					
❑ LSC-2234 [S]	Saint-Saens: Piano Concerto No. 2	199?	6.25	12.50	25.00
—With the Symphony of the Air Orchestra (Alfred Wallenstein, conductor); Classic Records reissue					
❑ LSC-2256 [S]	Schubert: Piano Concerto in A	1959	5.00	10.00	20.00
—With Josef Krips/RCA Victor Symphony Orchestra; original with "shaded dog" label					
❑ LSC-2265 [S]	The Rubenstein Story	1959	7.50	15.00	30.00
—With Alfred Wallerstein/NBC Symphony Orchestra; original with "shaded dog" label and gatefold cover					
❑ LSC-2296 [S]	Brahms: Piano Concerto No. 2	1959	5.00	10.00	20.00
—With Josef Krips/RCA Victor Symphony Orchestra; original with "shaded dog" label					
❑ LSC-2368 [S]	Chopin: Scherzos 1-4	1960	5.00	10.00	20.00
—Original with "shaded dog" label					
❑ LSC-2370 [S]	Chopin: Ballades 1-4	1960	5.00	10.00	20.00
—Original with "shaded dog" label					
❑ LSC-2429 [S]	Grieg: Piano Concerto in A; Lizst: Piano Concerto No. 1	1960	7.50	15.00	30.00
—Original with "shaded dog" label					
❑ LSC-2430 [S]	Rachmaninoff: Rhapsody on a Theme of Paganini	1960	5.00	10.00	20.00
—With Fritz Reiner/Chicago Symphony Orchestra; original with "shaded dog" label					
❑ LSC-2430 [S]	Rachmaninoff: Rhapsody on a Theme of Paganini	199?	6.25	12.50	25.00
—With Fritz Reiner/Chicago Symphony Orchestra; Classic Records reissue					
❑ LSC-2459 [S]	Brahms: Piano Sonata in F; Intermezzo; Romance	1961	10.00	20.00	40.00
—Original with "shaded dog" label					
❑ LDS-2554 [S]	Chopin: Piano Sonatas No. 2 and 3	1961	6.25	12.50	25.00
—Original with "shaded dog" label					
❑ LSC-2566 [S]	Grieg: Piano Concerto	1962	5.00	10.00	20.00
—Original with "shaded dog" label					
❑ LSC-2605 [S]	Rubenstein at Carnegie Hall	1962	5.00	10.00	20.00
—Original with "shaded dog" label					
❑ LSC-2636 [S]	Mozart: Piano Concerto No. 17; Schubert: Impromptus	1962	10.00	20.00	40.00
—Original with "shaded dog" label					

RUBIN, STAN
CORAL
❑ CRL 57185 [M]	Dixieland Goes Broadway	1959	6.25	12.50	25.00
❑ CRL 757185 [S]	Dixieland Goes Broadway	1959	7.50	15.00	30.00
JUBLIEE
❑ JLP-4 [10]	The Tigertown Five, Vol. 1	1954	12.50	25.00	50.00
❑ JLP-5 [10]	The Tigertown Five, Vol. 2	1954	12.50	25.00	50.00
❑ JLP-6 [10]	The Tigertown Five, Vol. 3	1954	12.50	25.00	50.00
❑ JLP-1001 [M]	The College All Stars at Carnegie Hall	1955	10.00	20.00	40.00
❑ JLP-1003 [M]	College Jazz Comes to Carnegie Hall	1955	10.00	20.00	40.00
❑ JLP-1016 [M]	Tigertown Five	1956	10.00	20.00	40.00
❑ JLP-1024 [M]	Stan Rubin in Morocco	1956	10.00	20.00	40.00
PRINCETON
❑ LP-102 [10]	The Stan Rubin Tigertown Five	1954	15.00	30.00	60.00
RCA VICTOR
❑ LPM-1200 [M]	Dixieland Bash	1956	10.00	20.00	40.00
❑ LPM-3277 [10]	Stan Rubin's Dixieland Comes to Carnegie Hall	1955	12.50	25.00	50.00

RUBY AND THE ROMANTICS
ABC
❑ S-638	More Than Yesterday	1968	5.00	10.00	20.00
KAPP
❑ KL-1323 [M]	Our Day Will Come	1963	7.50	15.00	30.00
❑ KL-1341 [M]	Till Then	1963	6.25	12.50	25.00
❑ KL-1458 [M]	The Greatest Hits Album	1966	5.00	10.00	20.00
❑ KL-1526 [M]	Ruby and the Romantics	1967	6.25	12.50	25.00
❑ KS-3323 [S]	Our Day Will Come	1963	10.00	20.00	40.00
❑ KS-3341 [S]	Till Then	1963	7.50	15.00	30.00
❑ KS-3458 [S]	The Greatest Hits Album	1966	6.25	12.50	25.00
❑ KS-3526 [S]	Ruby and the Romantics	1967	6.25	12.50	25.00
MCA
❑ 541	The Greatest Hits Album	197?	2.50	5.00	10.00
PICKWICK
❑ SPC-3519	Makin' Out	197?	2.50	5.00	10.00

RUDD, ROSWELL
IMPULSE!
❑ A-9126 [M]	Everywhere	1967	7.50	15.00	30.00
❑ AS-9126 [S]	Everywhere	1967	6.25	12.50	25.00

RUEDEBUSCH, DICK
JUBILEE
❑ JGS-5008 [S]	Meet Mr. Trumpet	1962	5.00	10.00	20.00
❑ JGS-5015 [S]	Dick Ruedebusch Remembers the Greats	1962	5.00	10.00	20.00
❑ JGS-5021 [S]	Mr. Trumpet, Volume 2	1963	5.00	10.00	20.00

R

Number	Title (A Side/B Side)	Yr	VG	VG+	NM
RUFF, WILLIE					
COLUMBIA					
❑ CS 9603	The Smooth Side of Willie Ruff	1968	5.00	10.00	20.00
—Red "360 Sound" label					
RUFFIN, DAVID					
Also see THE TEMPTATIONS.					
MOTOWN					
❑ M5-146V1	My Whole World Ended	1981	2.00	4.00	8.00
—Reissue					
❑ M5-211V1	At His Best	1981	2.00	4.00	8.00
—Reissue					
❑ MS-685	My Whole World Ended	1969	5.00	10.00	20.00
❑ MS-696	Feelin' Good	1969	3.75	7.50	15.00
❑ M 733	David Ruffin	1971	—	—	—
—Canceled					
❑ M-762	David Ruffin	1973	3.00	6.00	12.00
❑ M6-818	Me 'N' Rock 'N' Roll Are Here to Stay	1974	3.00	6.00	12.00
❑ M6-849	Who I Am	1975	3.00	6.00	12.00
❑ M6-866	Everything's Coming Up Love	1976	3.00	6.00	12.00
❑ M6-885	In My Stride	1977	3.00	6.00	12.00
❑ M7-895	At His Best	1978	3.00	6.00	12.00
WARNER BROS.					
❑ BSK 3306	So Soon We Change	1979	2.50	5.00	10.00
❑ BSK 3416	Gentleman Ruffin	1980	2.50	5.00	10.00
RUFFIN, JIMMY					
RSO					
❑ RS-1-3078	Sunrise	1980	2.50	5.00	10.00
SOUL					
❑ 704 [M]	Top Ten	1967	6.25	12.50	25.00
—Full-color cover					
❑ 704 [M]	Top Ten	1967	12.50	25.00	50.00
—One-color cover					
❑ S-704 [S]	Top Ten	1967	6.25	12.50	25.00
❑ S-708	Ruff'n Ready	1969	6.25	12.50	25.00
❑ SS-727	The Groove Governor	1970	5.00	10.00	20.00
RUFFIN, JIMMY AND DAVID					
MOTOWN					
❑ M5-108V1	Motown Superstar Series, Vol. 8	1981	2.50	5.00	10.00
SOUL					
❑ SS-728	I Am My Brother's Keeper	1970	5.00	10.00	20.00
RUFUS					
ABC					
❑ X-783	Rufus	1973	2.50	5.00	10.00
❑ X-809	Rags to Rufus	1974	2.50	5.00	10.00
❑ D-837	Rufusized	1974	2.50	5.00	10.00
❑ D-909	Rufus Featuring Chaka Khan	1975	2.50	5.00	10.00
❑ D-975	Ask Rufus	1977	2.50	5.00	10.00
❑ AA-1049	Street Player	1978	2.50	5.00	10.00
❑ AA-1049 [PD]	Street Player	1978	6.25	12.50	25.00
—Promo-only picture disc					
❑ AA-1098	Numbers	1979	2.50	5.00	10.00
❑ AA-1098 [PD]	Numbers	1979	5.00	10.00	20.00
—Promo-only picture disc					
COMMAND					
❑ CQD-40023 [Q]	Rufusized	1974	5.00	10.00	20.00
❑ CQD-40024 [Q]	Rags to Rufus	1974	5.00	10.00	20.00
MCA					
❑ 642	Rufus	1980	—	3.00	6.00
—Reissue of ABC 783					
❑ 5103	Masterjam	1979	2.50	5.00	10.00
❑ 5159	Party 'Til You're Broke	1981	2.50	5.00	10.00
❑ 5270	Camouflage	1982	2.50	5.00	10.00
❑ 5339	The Very Best of Rufus	1983	2.50	5.00	10.00
❑ 37034	Rags to Rufus	1980	—	3.00	6.00
—Reissue of ABC 809					
❑ 37035	Rufusized	1980	—	3.00	6.00
—Reissue of ABC 837					
❑ 37036	Rufus Featuring Chaka Khan	1980	—	3.00	6.00
—Reissue of ABC 909					
❑ 37037	Ask Rufus	1980	—	3.00	6.00
—Reissue of ABC 975					
❑ 37038	Street Player	1980	—	3.00	6.00
—Reissue of ABC 1049					
❑ 37039	Numbers	1980	—	3.00	6.00
—Reissue of ABC 1098					
❑ 37157	Masterjam	198?	—	3.00	6.00
—Reissue of 5103					
WARNER BROS.					
❑ 23679 [(2)]	Live: Stompin' at the Savoy	1983	3.00	6.00	12.00
❑ 23753	Seal in Red	1984	2.50	5.00	10.00
RUGBYS, THE					
AMAZON					
❑ 1000	Hot Cargo	1970	5.00	10.00	20.00
RUGOLO, PETE					
COLUMBIA					
❑ CL 604 [M]	Adventures in Rhythm	1955	12.50	25.00	50.00
—Maroon label, gold print					
❑ CL 604 [M]	Adventures in Rhythm	1956	10.00	20.00	40.00
—Red and black label with six "eye" logos					
❑ CL 635 [M]	Introducing Pete Rugolo	1955	12.50	25.00	50.00
—Maroon label, gold print					
❑ CL 635 [M]	Introducing Pete Rugolo	1956	10.00	20.00	40.00
—Red and black label with six "eye" logos					
❑ CL 689 [M]	Rugolomania	1956	10.00	20.00	40.00
—Red and black label with six "eye" logos					
❑ CL 6289 [10]	Introducing Pete Rugolo	1954	15.00	30.00	60.00

Number	Title (A Side/B Side)	Yr	VG	VG+	NM
EMARCY					
❑ MG-36082 [M]	Music for Hi-Fi Bugs	1956	10.00	20.00	40.00
❑ MG-36115 [M]	Out on a Limb	1957	10.00	20.00	40.00
❑ MG-36122 [M]	Percussion at Work	1958	10.00	20.00	40.00
❑ MG-36143 [M]	Rugolo Plays Kenton	1958	10.00	20.00	40.00
MERCURY					
❑ MG-(# unknown) [M]	An Adventure in Sound: Reeds	1958	7.50	15.00	30.00
❑ PPS-2001 [M]	10 Trombones Like 2 Pianos	196?	5.00	10.00	20.00
❑ PPS-2016 [M]	10 Trombones and 2 Guitars.	196?	5.00	10.00	20.00
❑ PPS-2023 [M]	10 Saxophones and 2 Basses.	196?	5.00	10.00	20.00
❑ PPS-6001 [S]	10 Trombones Like 2 Pianos.	196?	6.25	12.50	25.00
❑ PPS-6016 [S]	10 Trombones and 2 Guitars.	196?	6.25	12.50	25.00
❑ PPS-6023 [S]	10 Saxophones and 2 Basses.	196?	6.25	12.50	25.00
❑ MG-20118 [M]	Music from Outer Space.	1957	12.50	25.00	50.00
❑ MG-20260 [M]	Reeds in Hi-Fi.	1958	7.50	15.00	30.00
❑ MG-20261 [M]	Brass in Hi-Fi.	1958	7.50	15.00	30.00
❑ SR-60039 [S]	An Adventure in Sound: Reeds	1959	10.00	20.00	40.00
❑ SR-60043 [S]	Reeds in Hi-Fi.	1959	10.00	20.00	40.00
❑ SR-60044 [S]	Brass in Hi-Fi.	1959	10.00	20.00	40.00
RUMBLERS, THE					
DOT					
❑ DLP-3509 [M]	Boss!	1963	12.50	25.00	50.00
❑ DLP-25509 [S]	Boss!	1963	15.00	30.00	60.00
DOWNEY					
❑ DLP-1001 [M]	Boss!	1963	45.00	90.00	180.00
❑ DLPS-1001 [S]	Boss!	1963	62.50	125.00	250.00
RUMPLESTILTSKIN					
BELL					
❑ 6047	Rumpelstiltskin	1970	5.00	10.00	20.00
RUMSEY, HOWARD					
CONTEMPORARY					
❑ C-2501 [10]	Sunday Jazz a la Lighthouse	1953	30.00	60.00	120.00
❑ C-2506 [10]	Howard Rumsey's Lighthouse All-Stars	1953	30.00	60.00	120.00
❑ C-2510 [10]	Howard Rumsey's Lighthouse All-Stars, Volume 4	1954	30.00	60.00	120.00
❑ C-2513 [10]	Howard Rumsey's Lighthouse All-Stars, Volume 1: The Quintet	1954	30.00	60.00	120.00
❑ C-2515 [10]	Howard Rumsey's Lighthouse All-Stars, Volume 2: The Octet	1954	30.00	60.00	120.00
❑ C-3501 [M]	Sunday Jazz a la Lighthouse	1955	20.00	40.00	80.00
❑ C-3504 [M]	Howard Rumsey's Lighthouse All-Stars, Vol. 6	1955	20.00	40.00	80.00
❑ C-3508 [M]	Howard Rumsey's Lighthouse All-Stars, Vol. 3	1955	20.00	40.00	80.00
❑ C-3509 [M]	Lighthouse at Laguna	1955	20.00	40.00	80.00
❑ C-3517 [M]	In the Solo Spotlight	1956	20.00	40.00	80.00
❑ C-3520 [M]	Howard Rumsey's Lighthouse All-Stars, Vol. 4: Oboe/Flute	1956	20.00	40.00	80.00
❑ C-3528 [M]	Music for Lighthousekeeping	1957	20.00	40.00	80.00
❑ S-7008 [S]	Music for Lighthousekeeping	1959	12.50	25.00	50.00
LIBERTY					
❑ LRP-3045 [M]	Double or Nothin'	1957	12.50	25.00	50.00
❑ LST-7014 [S]	Double or Nothin'	1959	10.00	20.00	40.00
LIGHTHOUSE					
❑ LP-300 [M]	Jazz Rolls-Royce	1958	10.00	20.00	40.00
❑ LP-301 [M]	Sunday Jazz a la Lighthouse	1958	10.00	20.00	40.00
—Red vinyl					
OMEGA					
❑ OML-5 [M]	Jazz Rolls-Royce	1960	7.50	15.00	30.00
❑ OSL-5 [S]	Jazz Rolls-Royce	1960	7.50	15.00	30.00
PHILIPS					
❑ PHM 200012 [M]	Jazz Structures	1961	5.00	10.00	20.00
❑ PHS 600012 [S]	Jazz Structures	1961	6.25	12.50	25.00
STEREO RECORDS					
❑ S-7008 [S]	Music for Lighthousekeeping	1958	17.50	35.00	70.00
RUNAWAYS, THE					
Also see LITA FORD; JOAN JETT.					
MARILYN					
❑ USM 1004	Born to Be Bad	1991	2.00	4.00	8.00
MERCURY					
❑ SRM-1-1090	The Runaways	1976	6.25	12.50	25.00
❑ SRM-1-1126	Queens of Noise	1977	6.25	12.50	25.00
❑ SRM-1-3705	Waiting for the Night	1977	6.25	12.50	25.00
❑ SRM-1-3740	Live in Japan	1978	12.50	25.00	50.00
RHINO					
❑ RNDF-250 [PD]	Little Lost Girls	1982	6.25	12.50	25.00
❑ RNEP-602 [EP]	Mama Weer All Crazee Now	1983	3.75	7.50	15.00
❑ RNLP-70861	Little Lost Girls	1987	3.00	6.00	12.00
—Reissue of Rhino 250 on regular vinyl					
RUNDGREN, TODD					
Also see NAZZ (1).					
AMPEX					
❑ A-10105	Runt	1970	12.50	25.00	50.00
—LP jacket and label list 10 tracks and album actually has 10					
❑ A-10105	Runt	1970	25.00	50.00	100.00
—LP jacket and label list 10 tracks, but the album has 11					
❑ A-10105	Runt	1970	37.50	75.00	150.00
—LP jacket and label list 10 tracks, but the album has 12					
BEARSVILLE					
❑ PRO 524 [DJ]	The Todd Rundgren Radio Show	1972	37.50	75.00	150.00
❑ PRO 597 [DJ]	Ikon/Todd Rundgren Interview	1974	30.00	60.00	120.00
❑ PRO-A-788 [DJ]	Todd Rundgren Radio Sampler	1978	12.50	25.00	50.00
—Highlights of "Back to the Bars" plus interview of Todd by Patti Smith					
❑ BR 2046	Runt	1972	3.75	7.50	15.00
—Another reissue, after switch from Ampex to Warner Bros. distribution					
❑ BR 2047	The Ballad of Todd Rundgren	1972	3.75	7.50	15.00
—Reissue of 10116					
❑ 2BX 2066 [(2)]	Something/Anything?	1972	6.25	12.50	25.00
—Regular copy with black vinyl					

Number	Title (A Side/B Side)	Yr	VG	VG+	NM
❏ 2BX 2066 [(2)]	Something/Anything?	1972	100.00	200.00	400.00
—White label with one record on red vinyl and the other on blue vinyl					
❏ BR 2133	A Wizard/A True Star	1973	3.00	6.00	12.00
❏ BRK 3522	Healing	1981	2.50	5.00	10.00
❏ 2BR 6952 [(2)]	Todd	1974	3.75	7.50	15.00
❏ BR 6957	Initiation	1975	2.50	5.00	10.00
❏ BR 6963	Faithful	1976	2.50	5.00	10.00
❏ BRK 6981	Hermit of Mink Hollow	1978	2.50	5.00	10.00
❏ 2BRX 6986 [(2)]	Back to the Bars	1978	3.00	6.00	12.00
❏ A-10105	Runt	1971	6.25	12.50	25.00
—Reissue with new label					
❏ A-10116	The Ballad of Todd Rundgren	1971	20.00	40.00	80.00
❏ 23732	The Ever Popular Tortured Artist Effect	1983	2.50	5.00	10.00
MOBILE FIDELITY					
❏ 2-225	Something/Anything?	1995	10.00	20.00	40.00
—Audiophile vinyl					
RHINO					
❏ RNLP 70862	Runt	1987	2.50	5.00	10.00
❏ RNLP 70863	The Ballad of Todd Rundgren	1987	2.50	5.00	10.00
❏ RNLP 70864	A Wizard/A True Star	1987	2.50	5.00	10.00
❏ RNLP 70866	Initiation	1987	2.50	5.00	10.00
❏ RNLP 70868	Faithful	1987	2.50	5.00	10.00
❏ RNLP 70871	Hermit of Mink Hollow	1988	2.50	5.00	10.00
❏ RNLP 70874	Healing	1987	2.50	5.00	10.00
❏ RNLP 70876	The Ever Popular Tortured Artist Effect	1988	2.50	5.00	10.00
❏ RNDA 71107	Something/Anything?	1987	3.00	6.00	12.00
❏ RNDA 71108	Todd	1987	3.00	6.00	12.00
❏ RNDA 71109	Back to the Bars	1987	3.00	6.00	12.00
❏ R1-71491	Anthology (1968-1985)	1989	5.00	10.00	20.00
WARNER BROS.					
❏ 25128	A Cappella	1985	2.50	5.00	10.00
❏ 25881	Nearly Human	1989	3.75	7.50	15.00

RUSH
ATLANTIC

Number	Title (A Side/B Side)	Yr	VG	VG+	NM
❏ 82040	Presto	1989	5.00	10.00	20.00
❏ 83531 [(2)]	Vapor Trails	2002	5.00	10.00	20.00
MERCURY					
❏ MK-32 [DJ]	Everything Your Listener Ever Wanted to Hear by Rush ... But You Were Afraid to Play	1977	37.50	75.00	150.00
❏ MK-185 [DJ]	Rush N Roulette	1981	30.00	60.00	120.00
—Promo-only six-track EP that has six grooves cut in it; the song it plays is based on where you place the stylus					
❏ SRM-1-1011	Rush	1974	2.50	5.00	10.00
❏ SRM-1-1023	Fly by Night	1975	2.50	5.00	10.00
❏ SRM-1-1046	Caress of Steel	1975	2.50	5.00	10.00
❏ SRM-1-1079	2112	1976	2.50	5.00	10.00
❏ SRM-1-1184	A Farewell to Kings	1977	2.50	5.00	10.00
❏ SRP-1-1300 [PD]	Hemispheres	1979	10.00	20.00	40.00
❏ SRM-1-3743	Hemispheres	1978	2.50	5.00	10.00
❏ SRM-1-4001	Permanent Waves	1980	2.50	5.00	10.00
❏ SRM-1-4013	Moving Pictures	1981	2.50	5.00	10.00
❏ SRM-1-4063	Signals	1982	2.50	5.00	10.00
❏ SRM-2-7001 [(2)]	Exit... Stage Left	1981	3.00	6.00	12.00
❏ SRM-2-7508 [(2)]	All the World's a Stage	1976	3.00	6.00	12.00
❏ SRM-3-9200 [(3)]	Archives	1978	5.00	10.00	20.00
❏ 818476-1	Grace Under Pressure	1984	2.50	5.00	10.00
❏ 822541-1	Rush	1985	2.00	4.00	8.00
—Reissue					
❏ 822542-1	Fly by Night	1985	2.00	4.00	8.00
—Reissue					
❏ 822543-1	Caress of Steel	1985	2.00	4.00	8.00
—Reissue					
❏ 822545-1	2112	1985	2.00	4.00	8.00
—Reissue					
❏ 822546-1	A Farewell to Kings	1985	2.00	4.00	8.00
—Reissue					
❏ 822547-1	Hemispheres	1985	2.00	4.00	8.00
—Reissue					
❏ 822548-1	Permanent Waves	1985	2.00	4.00	8.00
—Reissue					
❏ 822549-1	Moving Pictures	1985	2.00	4.00	8.00
—Reissue					
❏ 822550-1	Signals	1985	2.00	4.00	8.00
—Reissue					
❏ 822551-1 [(2)]	Exit...Stage Left	1985	2.50	5.00	10.00
—Reissue					
❏ 822552-1 [(2)]	All the World's a Stage	1985	2.50	5.00	10.00
—Reissue					
❏ 822553-1 [(3)]	Archives	1985	3.75	7.50	15.00
—Reissue					
❏ 826098-1	Power Windows	1985	2.50	5.00	10.00
❏ 832464-1	Hold Your Fire	1987	2.50	5.00	10.00
❏ 836346-1 [(2)]	A Show of Hands	1988	3.00	6.00	12.00

RUSH, MERRILEE
BELL

Number	Title (A Side/B Side)	Yr	VG	VG+	NM
❏ 6020	Angel of the Morning	1968	5.00	10.00	20.00
LIBERTY					
❏ LN-10166	Merilee Rush	1981	2.00	4.00	8.00
—Budget-line reissue					
UNITED ARTISTS					
❏ UA-LA735-G	Merilee Rush	1977	2.50	5.00	10.00

RUSH, OTIS
BLUE HORIZON

Number	Title (A Side/B Side)	Yr	VG	VG+	NM
❏ BH-4602	Blues Masters, Volume 2	1968	6.25	12.50	25.00
❏ BH-4805	Chicago Blues	1970	6.25	12.50	25.00
COTILLION					
❏ SD 9006	Mourning in the Morning	1969	6.25	12.50	25.00

RUSH, TOM
COLUMBIA

Number	Title (A Side/B Side)	Yr	VG	VG+	NM
❏ CS 9972	Tom Rush	1970	3.00	6.00	12.00
—Orange label					
❏ CS 9972	Tom Rush	1970	3.75	7.50	15.00
—Red "360 Sound" label					
❏ C 30402	Wrong End of the Rainbow	1970	3.00	6.00	12.00
❏ KC 31306	Merrimack County	1972	3.00	6.00	12.00
❏ KC 33054	Ladies Love Outlaws	1974	3.00	6.00	12.00
❏ PC 33907	The Best of Tom Rush	1976	3.00	6.00	12.00
ELEKTRA					
❏ EKL-288 [M]	Tom Rush	1965	3.75	7.50	15.00
❏ EKL-308 [M]	Take a Little Walk with Me	1966	3.75	7.50	15.00
❏ EKS-7288 [S]	Tom Rush	1965	3.75	7.50	15.00
❏ EKS-7308 [S]	Take a Little Walk with Me	1966	3.75	7.50	15.00
❏ EKS-74018	The Circle Game	1968	3.75	7.50	15.00
❏ EKS-74062	Classic Rush	1971	3.75	7.50	15.00
FANTASY					
❏ 24709 [(2)]	Tom Rush	1973	3.75	7.50	15.00
—Reissue of Prestige/Folklore recordings					
FOLKLORE					
❏ FRLP-14003 [M]	Got a Mind to Ramble	1964	5.00	10.00	20.00
❏ FRST-14003 [S]	Got a Mind to Ramble	1964	6.25	12.50	25.00
LY CORNU					
❏ SA-70-2	Tom Rush at the Unicorn	1962	25.00	50.00	100.00
PRESTIGE					
❏ PR-7374 [M]	Blues — Songs — Ballads	1965	5.00	10.00	20.00
❏ PRST-7374 [S]	Blues — Songs — Ballads	1965	6.25	12.50	25.00
❏ PRST-7536	Got a Mind to Ramble	1968	3.75	7.50	15.00
—Reissue of Folklore LP					

RUSHING, JIMMY
Also see CHAMPION JACK DUPREE AND JIMMY RUSHING.
AUDIO LAB

Number	Title (A Side/B Side)	Yr	VG	VG+	NM
❏ AL-1512 [M]	Two Shades of Blue	1959	30.00	60.00	120.00
BLUESWAY					
❏ BL-6005 [M]	Everyday I Have the Blues	1967	5.00	10.00	20.00
❏ BLS-6005 [S]	Everyday I Have the Blues	1967	5.00	10.00	20.00
❏ BLS-6017	Livin' the Blues	1968	5.00	10.00	20.00
❏ BLS-6057	Sent for You Yesterday	1973	3.75	7.50	15.00
COLPIX					
❏ CP-446 [M]	Five Feet of Soul	1963	10.00	20.00	40.00
❏ SCP-446 [S]	Five Feet of Soul	1963	—	—	—
—Not known to exist					
COLUMBIA					
❏ CL 963 [M]	The Jazz Odyssey of James Rushing, Esq.	1957	10.00	20.00	40.00
❏ CL 1152 [M]	Little Jimmy Rushing and the Big Brass	1958	10.00	20.00	40.00
❏ CL 1401 [M]	Rushing Lullabies	1959	10.00	20.00	40.00
❏ CL 1605 [M]	Jimmy Rushing and the Smith Girls	1961	7.50	15.00	30.00
❏ CS 8060 [S]	Little Jimmy Rushing and the Big Brass	1958	12.50	25.00	50.00
❏ CS 8196 [S]	Rushing Lullabies	1959	12.50	25.00	50.00
❏ CS 8405 [S]	Jimmy Rushing and the Smith Girls	1961	10.00	20.00	40.00
❏ C2 36419 [(2)]	Mister Five by Five	1979	3.00	6.00	12.00
JAZZTONE					
❏ J-1244 [M]	Listen to the Blues	195?	10.00	20.00	40.00
MASTER JAZZ					
❏ 8104	Gee, Baby	197?	3.75	7.50	15.00
❏ 8120	Who Was It Sang That Song?	1971	3.75	7.50	15.00
RCA VICTOR					
❏ LSP-4566	You and Me The Used to Be	1972	3.75	7.50	15.00
VANGUARD					
❏ VRS-65/66 [(2)]	Essential Jimmy Rushing	197?	3.75	7.50	15.00
❏ VSD-2008 [S]	If This Ain't the Blues	1958	15.00	30.00	60.00
❏ VRS-8011 [10]	Jimmy Rushing Sings the Blues	1955	25.00	50.00	100.00
❏ VRS-8505 [M]	Listen to the Blues	1955	12.50	25.00	50.00
❏ VRS-8513 [M]	If This Ain't the Blues	1957	12.50	25.00	50.00
❏ VRS-8518 [M]	Going to Chicago	1957	12.50	25.00	50.00
❏ VSD-73007	Listen to the Blues	1967	3.75	7.50	15.00

RUSHING, JIMMY; ADA MOORE; BUCK CLAYTON
COLUMBIA

Number	Title (A Side/B Side)	Yr	VG	VG+	NM
❏ CL 778 [M]	Cat Meets Chick	1956	15.00	30.00	60.00

RUSKIN-SPEAR, ROGER
UNITED ARTISTS

Number	Title (A Side/B Side)	Yr	VG	VG+	NM
❏ UA-LA097-F	Electric Shocks	1973	6.25	12.50	25.00

RUSSELL, ANNA
COLUMBIA MASTERWORKS

Number	Title (A Side/B Side)	Yr	VG	VG+	NM
❏ ML 4594 [M]	Anna Russell Sings?	1953	6.25	12.50	25.00
❏ ML 4733 [M]	Anna Russell Sings! Again?	1954	6.25	12.50	25.00
❏ ML 4928 [M]	Anna Russell's Guide to Concert Audiences	1955	6.25	12.50	25.00
❏ ML 5036 [M]	A Square Talk on Popular Music	1956	6.25	12.50	25.00
❏ ML 5195 [M]	In Darkest Africa	1957	7.50	15.00	30.00
❏ ML 5295 [M]	A Practical Banana Promotion	1959	12.50	25.00	50.00
❏ MG 31199 [(2)]	The Anna Russell Album?	1972	5.00	10.00	20.00

RUSSELL, BOBBY
ELF

Number	Title (A Side/B Side)	Yr	VG	VG+	NM
❏ 9500	Words, Music, Laughter & Tears	1969	5.00	10.00	20.00
❏ 9501	Unlimited	1970	3.75	7.50	15.00
UNITED ARTISTS					
❏ UAS-5548	Saturday Morning Confusion	1971	3.00	6.00	12.00

RUSSELL, GENE
BLACK JAZZ

Number	Title (A Side/B Side)	Yr	VG	VG+	NM
❏ 1	New Direction	1972	6.25	12.50	25.00
❏ QD-10	Talk to My Lady	1973	6.25	12.50	25.00

Number	Title (A Side/B Side)	Yr	VG	VG+	NM

RUSSELL, GEORGE
DECCA

Number	Title (A Side/B Side)	Yr	VG	VG+	NM
❏ DL 4183 [M]	George Russell in Kansas City	1961	7.50	15.00	30.00
❏ DL 9216 [M]	New York, N.Y.	1958	12.50	25.00	50.00
❏ DL 9219 [M]	Jazz in the Space Age	1958	12.50	25.00	50.00
❏ DL 9220 [M]	George Russell at the Five Spot	1958	12.50	25.00	50.00
❏ DL 74183 [S]	George Russell in Kansas City	1961	10.00	20.00	40.00
❏ DL 79216 [S]	New York, N.Y.	1958	10.00	20.00	40.00
❏ DL 79219 [S]	Jazz in the Space Age	1958	10.00	20.00	40.00
❏ DL 79220 [S]	George Russell at the Five Spot	1958	10.00	20.00	40.00

FLYING DUTCHMAN

Number	Title (A Side/B Side)	Yr	VG	VG+	NM
❏ FD-122	Othello Ballet Suite/Electronic Organ Sonata No. 1	1970	5.00	10.00	20.00
❏ FD-124	Electronic Sonata for Souls Loved by Nature	1970	5.00	10.00	20.00

MGM

Number	Title (A Side/B Side)	Yr	VG	VG+	NM
❏ E-3321 [M]	George Russell Octets	1955	20.00	40.00	80.00

RCA VICTOR

Number	Title (A Side/B Side)	Yr	VG	VG+	NM
❏ LPM-1372 [M]	Jazz Workshop	1957	20.00	40.00	80.00
❏ LPM-2534 [M]	Jazz Workshop	1962	7.50	15.00	30.00

RIVERSIDE

Number	Title (A Side/B Side)	Yr	VG	VG+	NM
❏ RLP-341 [M]	Stratusphunk	1960	6.25	12.50	25.00
❏ RLP-375 [M]	Ezz-thetics	1961	6.25	12.50	25.00
❏ RLP-412 [M]	The Stratus Seekers	1962	6.25	12.50	25.00
❏ RLP-440 [M]	The Outer View	1963	6.25	12.50	25.00
❏ RS-3016	The Outer View	1968	5.00	10.00	20.00
❏ RS-9341 [S]	Stratusphunk	1960	7.50	15.00	30.00
❏ RS-9375 [S]	Ezz-thetics	1961	7.50	15.00	30.00
❏ RS-9412 [S]	The Stratus Seekers	1962	7.50	15.00	30.00
❏ RS-9440 [S]	The Outer View	1963	7.50	15.00	30.00

STRATA-EAST

Number	Title (A Side/B Side)	Yr	VG	VG+	NM
❏ SES-19761	Electronic Sonata for Souls Loved by Nature	1976	5.00	10.00	20.00

RUSSELL, HAL
NESSA

Number	Title (A Side/B Side)	Yr	VG	VG+	NM
❏ N-21	NRG Ensemble	1981	5.00	10.00	20.00
❏ N-25	Generation	1982	5.00	10.00	20.00

RUSSELL, JANE
MGM

Number	Title (A Side/B Side)	Yr	VG	VG+	NM
❏ E-3715 [M]	Jane Russell	1959	12.50	25.00	50.00
❏ SE-3715 [S]	Jane Russell	1959	25.00	50.00	100.00

RUSSELL, JIMMY
CUCA

Number	Title (A Side/B Side)	Yr	VG	VG+	NM
❏ 4100 [M]	Jimmy Russell Trio	1965	6.25	12.50	25.00

RUSSELL, KURT
CAPITOL

Number	Title (A Side/B Side)	Yr	VG	VG+	NM
❏ SKAO-492	Kurt Russell	1970	7.50	15.00	30.00

RUSSELL, LEON
MCA

Number	Title (A Side/B Side)	Yr	VG	VG+	NM
❏ 682	Leon Russell	1979	2.00	4.00	8.00
—Reissue of Shelter 52007					
❏ 683	Leon Russell and the Shelter People	1979	2.00	4.00	8.00
—Reissue of Shelter 52008					
❏ 685	Carney	1979	2.00	4.00	8.00
—Reissue of Shelter 52011					
❏ 686	Will O' the Wisp	1979	2.00	4.00	8.00
—Reissue of Shelter 52020					
❏ 37114	Best of Leon	1980	2.00	4.00	8.00
—Reissue of Shelter 52004					

PARADISE

Number	Title (A Side/B Side)	Yr	VG	VG+	NM
❏ 0002	Hank Wilson Vol. II	1984	3.00	6.00	12.00
❏ PR 2943	Wedding Album	1976	3.00	6.00	12.00
—As "Leon and Mary Russell"					
❏ BSK 3066	Make Love to the Music	1977	3.00	6.00	12.00
—As "Leon and Mary Russell"					
❏ BSK 3172	Americana	1978	3.00	6.00	12.00
❏ BSK 3341	Life and Love	1979	3.00	6.00	12.00
❏ BSK 3532	The Live Album	1981	2.50	5.00	10.00

SHELTER

Number	Title (A Side/B Side)	Yr	VG	VG+	NM
❏ SHE-1001	Leon Russell	1968	5.00	10.00	20.00
❏ SR 2108	Stop All That Jazz	1974	3.75	7.50	15.00
❏ SR 2118	Leon Russell	1974	3.00	6.00	12.00
—Reissue of 8901					
❏ SR 2119	Leon Russell and the Shelter People	1974	3.00	6.00	12.00
—Reissue of 8903					
❏ SR 2121	Carney	1974	3.00	6.00	12.00
—Reissue of 8911					
❏ SR 2138	Will O' the Wisp	1975	3.75	7.50	15.00
❏ SW-8901	Leon Russell	1970	3.75	7.50	15.00
—Early reissue of 1001					
❏ SW-8903	Leon Russell and the Shelter People	1971	3.75	7.50	15.00
❏ SW-8911	Carney	1972	3.75	7.50	15.00
❏ STCO-8917 [(3)]	Leon Live	1973	5.00	10.00	20.00
❏ SW-8923	Hank Wilson's Back, Vol. 1	1973	3.75	7.50	15.00
—As "Hank Wilson"					
❏ 52004	Best of Leon	1976	2.50	5.00	10.00
❏ 52007	Leon Russell	1977	2.50	5.00	10.00
—Reissue of 2118					
❏ 52008	Leon Russell and the Shelter People	1977	2.50	5.00	10.00
—Reissue of 2119					
❏ 52011	Carney	1977	2.50	5.00	10.00
—Reissue of 2121					
❏ 52014	Hank Wilson's Back, Vol. 1	1977	2.50	5.00	10.00
—Reissue of 8923					
❏ 52016	Stop All That Jazz	1977	2.50	5.00	10.00
—Reissue of 2108					
❏ 52020	Will O' the Wisp	1977	2.50	5.00	10.00
—Reissue of 2138					

RUSSELL, LEON, AND MARC BENNO
See ASYLUM CHOIR.

RUSSELL, PEE WEE
ATLANTIC

Number	Title (A Side/B Side)	Yr	VG	VG+	NM
❏ ALS-126 [10]	Pee Wee Russell All Stars	1952	20.00	40.00	80.00

BELL

Number	Title (A Side/B Side)	Yr	VG	VG+	NM
❏ LP-42 [M]	Pee Wee Russell Plays Pee Wee	1961	6.25	12.50	25.00
❏ LPS-42 [S]	Pee Wee Russell Plays Pee Wee	1961	7.50	15.00	30.00

COLUMBIA

Number	Title (A Side/B Side)	Yr	VG	VG+	NM
❏ CS 8785 [S]	New Groove	1963	5.00	10.00	20.00

COUNTERPOINT

Number	Title (A Side/B Side)	Yr	VG	VG+	NM
❏ (# unknown) [M]	Portrait of Pee Wee	1957	15.00	30.00	60.00

DCC COMPACT CLASSICS

Number	Title (A Side/B Side)	Yr	VG	VG+	NM
❏ LPZ-2024	Portrait of Pee Wee	1996	6.25	12.50	25.00
—Audiophile vinyl					

DISC

Number	Title (A Side/B Side)	Yr	VG	VG+	NM
❏ DLP-(# unknown) [10]	Jazz Ensemble	195?	30.00	60.00	120.00

DOT

Number	Title (A Side/B Side)	Yr	VG	VG+	NM
❏ DLP-3253 [M]	Pee Wee Russell Plays	1960	6.25	12.50	25.00
❏ DLP-25253 [S]	Pee Wee Russell Plays	1960	5.00	10.00	20.00

ESOTERIC

Number	Title (A Side/B Side)	Yr	VG	VG+	NM
❏ 565 [M]	Pee Wee Russell All Stars	1959	10.00	20.00	40.00
❏ 5565 [S]	Pee Wee Russell All Stars	1959	7.50	15.00	30.00

IMPULSE!

Number	Title (A Side/B Side)	Yr	VG	VG+	NM
❏ A-96 [M]	Ask Me Now	1966	6.25	12.50	25.00
❏ AS-96 [S]	Ask Me Now	1966	7.50	15.00	30.00
❏ A-9137 [M]	College Concert of Pee Wee Russell with Henry "Red" Allen	1967	6.25	12.50	25.00
❏ AS-9137 [S]	College Concert of Pee Wee Russell with Henry "Red" Allen	1967	5.00	10.00	20.00

MAINSTREAM

Number	Title (A Side/B Side)	Yr	VG	VG+	NM
❏ S-6026 [S]	A Legend	1965	5.00	10.00	20.00

RIVERSIDE

Number	Title (A Side/B Side)	Yr	VG	VG+	NM
❏ RLP 12-141 [M]	Rhythmakers and Teagarden	1955	15.00	30.00	60.00

STEREO-CRAFT

Number	Title (A Side/B Side)	Yr	VG	VG+	NM
❏ RTN-105 [M]	Pee Wee Plays Pee Wee	196?	5.00	10.00	20.00
❏ RTS-105 [S]	Pee Wee Plays Pee Wee	196?	6.25	12.50	25.00

STORYVILLE

Number	Title (A Side/B Side)	Yr	VG	VG+	NM
❏ STLP-308 [10]	Pee Wee Russell	1954	20.00	40.00	80.00
❏ STLP-909 [M]	We're In the Money	1956	12.50	25.00	50.00

SWINGVILLE

Number	Title (A Side/B Side)	Yr	VG	VG+	NM
❏ SVLP-2008 [M]	Swingin' with Pee Wee	1960	12.50	25.00	50.00
—Purple label					
❏ SVLP-2008 [M]	Swingin' with Pee Wee	1965	6.25	12.50	25.00
—Blue label, trident logo at right					

RUSSELL, PEE WEE/BILLY BANKS
JAZZ PANORAMA

Number	Title (A Side/B Side)	Yr	VG	VG+	NM
❏ 1808 [10]	Pee Wee Russell / Billy Banks	1951	20.00	40.00	80.00

RUSSELL, PEE WEE, AND RUBY BRAFF
SAVOY

Number	Title (A Side/B Side)	Yr	VG	VG+	NM
❏ MG-12034 [M]	Jazz At Storyville, Volume 1	1955	12.50	25.00	50.00
❏ MG-12041 [M]	Jazz at Storyville, Volume 2	1955	12.50	25.00	50.00

RUSSIAN JAZZ QUARTET, THE
IMPULSE!

Number	Title (A Side/B Side)	Yr	VG	VG+	NM
❏ A-80 [M]	Happiness	1965	5.00	10.00	20.00
❏ AS-80 [S]	Happiness	1965	6.25	12.50	25.00

RUSSIN, BABE
DOT

Number	Title (A Side/B Side)	Yr	VG	VG+	NM
❏ DLP-3060 [M]	To Soothe the Savage	1956	12.50	25.00	50.00

RUSSO, BILL
ATLANTIC

Number	Title (A Side/B Side)	Yr	VG	VG+	NM
❏ 1241 [M]	The World of Alcina	1956	20.00	40.00	80.00
—Black label					
❏ 1241 [M]	The World of Alcina	1961	7.50	15.00	30.00
—Multicolor label, white "fan" logo at right					

DEE GEE

Number	Title (A Side/B Side)	Yr	VG	VG+	NM
❏ 1001 [10]	A Recital in New American Music	1952	50.00	100.00	200.00

FM

Number	Title (A Side/B Side)	Yr	VG	VG+	NM
❏ 302 [M]	Stereophony	1963	6.25	12.50	25.00
❏ S-302 [S]	Stereophony	1963	7.50	15.00	30.00

ROULETTE

Number	Title (A Side/B Side)	Yr	VG	VG+	NM
❏ R-52045 [M]	School of Rebellion	1960	6.25	12.50	25.00
❏ SR-52045 [S]	School of Rebellion	1960	7.50	15.00	30.00
❏ R-52063 [M]	Seven Deadly Sins	1960	6.25	12.50	25.00
❏ SR-52063 [S]	Seven Deadly Sins	1960	7.50	15.00	30.00

RUSTIX
RARE EARTH

Number	Title (A Side/B Side)	Yr	VG	VG+	NM
❏ RS-508	Bedlam	1969	3.75	7.50	15.00
—Regular cover					
❏ RS-508	Bedlam	1969	7.50	15.00	30.00
—Rounded-top cover					
❏ RS-513	Come On, People	1970	3.00	6.00	12.00

RUSTY AND DOUG
See RUSTY AND DOUG KERSHAW.

RUTLES, THE
WARNER BROS.

Number	Title (A Side/B Side)	Yr	VG	VG+	NM
❏ PRO-A-723 [DJ]	The Rutles	1978	6.25	12.50	25.00
—Yellow vinyl with five songs and "banana" label					
❏ HS 3151	The Rutles	1978	6.25	12.50	25.00
—With bound-in booklet					

Number	Title (A Side/B Side)	Yr	VG	VG+	NM
RYAN, BUCK, AND SMITTY IRWIN					
MONUMENT					
❑ MLP-8031 [M]	Ballads and Bluegrass	1965	5.00	10.00	20.00
❑ SLP-18031 [S]	Ballads and Bluegrass	1965	6.25	12.50	25.00
RYAN, CHARLIE					
HILLTOP					
❑ JM-6006 [M]	Hot Rod Lincoln Drags Again	1964	12.50	25.00	50.00
❑ JS-6006 [R]	Hot Rod Lincoln Drags Again	1964	6.25	12.50	25.00
KING					
❑ 751 [M]	Hot Rod Lincoln	1961	100.00	200.00	400.00
RYDELL, BOBBY					
CAMEO					
❑ C-1006 [M]	We Got Love	1959	15.00	30.00	60.00
❑ C-1007 [M]	Bobby Sings	1960	12.50	25.00	50.00
❑ C-1009 [M]	Bobby's Biggest Hits	1961	6.25	12.50	25.00
—Standard cover					
❑ C-1009 [M]	Bobby's Biggest Hits	1961	20.00	40.00	80.00
—Original with die-cut cover and textured inner sleeve					
❑ C-1010 [M]	Bobby Rydell Salutes "The Great Ones"	1961	6.25	12.50	25.00
❑ SC-1010 [S]	Bobby Rydell Salutes "The Great Ones"	1961	10.00	20.00	40.00
❑ C-1011 [M]	Rydell at the Copa	1961	6.25	12.50	25.00
❑ SC-1011 [S]	Rydell at the Copa	1961	10.00	20.00	40.00
❑ C-1019 [M]	All the Hits	1962	6.25	12.50	25.00
—Black vinyl					
❑ C-1019 [M]	All the Hits	1962	37.50	75.00	150.00
—Red vinyl					
❑ C-1028 [M]	Bobby Rydell's Biggest Hits, Volume 2	1962	6.25	12.50	25.00
❑ C-1040 [M]	All the Hits, Volume 2	1963	6.25	12.50	25.00
❑ SC-1040 [P]	All the Hits, Volume 2	1963	10.00	20.00	40.00
❑ C-1043 [M]	Bye Bye Birdie	1963	6.25	12.50	25.00
❑ C-1055 [M]	Wild (Wood) Days	1963	5.00	10.00	20.00
❑ SC-1055 [S]	Wild (Wood) Days	1963	7.50	15.00	30.00
❑ C-1070 [M]	The Top Hits of 1963	1963	5.00	10.00	20.00
—Came with bonus single, also numbered 1070					
❑ SC-1070 [S]	The Top Hits of 1963	1963	7.50	15.00	30.00
—Came with bonus single, also numbered 1070					
❑ C-1080 [M]	Forget Him	1964	5.00	10.00	20.00
❑ SC-1080 [R]	Forget Him	1964	5.00	10.00	20.00
❑ C-2001 [M]	16 Golden Hits	1965	5.00	10.00	20.00
❑ SC-2001 [R]	16 Golden Hits	1965	5.00	10.00	20.00
CAPITOL					
❑ ST 2281 [S]	Somebody Loves You	1965	5.00	10.00	20.00
❑ T 2281 [M]	Somebody Loves You	1965	3.75	7.50	15.00
P.I.P.					
❑ 6818	Born with a Smile	1976	2.50	5.00	10.00
SPIN-O-RAMA					
❑ 143 [M]	Starring Bobby Rydell	196?	3.00	6.00	12.00
❑ S-143 [S]	Starring Bobby Rydell	196?	3.00	6.00	12.00
STRAND					
❑ SL-1120 [M]	Bobby Rydell Sings	196?	6.25	12.50	25.00
❑ SLS-1120 [R]	Bobby Rydell Sings	196?	5.00	10.00	20.00
VENISE					
❑ 10035 [M]	Twistin'	1962	6.25	12.50	25.00
—Also includes tracks by Barry Norman and Stephen Garrick					
RYDELL, BOBBY/CHUBBY CHECKER					
Also see each artist's individual listings.					
CAMEO					
❑ C 1013 [M]	Bobby Rydell/Chubby Checker	1961	7.50	15.00	30.00
❑ C-1063 [M]	Chubby Checker and Bobby Rydell	1963	5.00	10.00	20.00
RYDER, MITCH					
DYNO VOICE					
❑ 1901 [M]	What Now My Love	1967	5.00	10.00	20.00
❑ 31901 [S]	What Now My Love	1967	5.00	10.00	20.00
RIVA					
❑ RV 7503	Never Kick a Sleeping Dog	1983	2.50	5.00	10.00
SEEDS & STEMS					
❑ 7801	How I Spent My Summer Vacation	1978	3.00	6.00	12.00
❑ 7804	Naked But Not Dead	1980	3.00	6.00	12.00
RYDER, MITCH, AND THE DETROIT WHEELS					
CREWE					
❑ CR-1335	All Mitch Ryder Hits!	1969	3.75	7.50	15.00
—Reissue of New Voice 2004					
NEW VOICE					
❑ 2000 [M]	Take a Ride	1966	6.25	12.50	25.00
❑ S-2000 [S]	Take a Ride	1966	7.50	15.00	30.00
❑ 2002 [M]	Breakout…!!!	1966	5.00	10.00	20.00
—With "Devil with a Blue Dress On/Good Golly Miss Molly"					
❑ 2002 [M]	Breakout…!!!	1966	6.25	12.50	25.00
—Without "Devil with a Blue Dress On/Good Golly Miss Molly"					
❑ S-2002 [S]	Breakout…!!!	1966	6.25	12.50	25.00
—With "Devil with a Blue Dress On/Good Golly Miss Molly"					
❑ S-2002 [S]	Breakout…!!!	1966	7.50	15.00	30.00
—Without "Devil with a Blue Dress On/Good Golly Miss Molly"					
❑ 2003 [M]	Sock It To Me!	1967	6.25	12.50	25.00
❑ S-2003 [S]	Sock It To Me!	1967	7.50	15.00	30.00
❑ 2004 [M]	All Mitch Ryder Hits!	1967	7.50	15.00	30.00
❑ NVS-2004 [S]	All Mitch Ryder Hits!	1967	5.00	10.00	20.00
❑ S-2005	Mitch Ryder Sings the Hits	1968	5.00	10.00	20.00
RHINO					
❑ R1-70941	Rev Up: The Best of Mitch Ryder and the Detroit Wheels	1989	3.00	6.00	12.00
SUNDAZED					
❑ LP 5083	Breakout ... !!!	2001	3.00	6.00	12.00
—Reissue on 180-gram vinyl					
VIRGO					
❑ 12001	The Best of Mitch Ryder and the Detroit Wheels	1972	3.00	6.00	12.00

Number	Title (A Side/B Side)	Yr	VG	VG+	NM
RYG, JORGEN					
EMARCY					
❑ MG-36099 [M]	Jorgen Ryg Jazz Quartet	1956	12.50	25.00	50.00
RYLES, JOHN WESLEY					
ABC					
❑ AB-1056	Shine on Me	1978	3.00	6.00	12.00
❑ AB-1112	Love's Sweet Pain	1979	3.00	6.00	12.00
ABC DOT					
❑ DO-2089	John Wesley Ryles	1977	3.00	6.00	12.00
COLUMBIA					
❑ CS 9768	Kay	1969	5.00	10.00	20.00
MCA					
❑ 643	Shine on Me	198?	2.00	4.00	8.00
—Budget-line reissue of ABC 1056					
❑ 644	John Wesley Ryles	198?	2.00	4.00	8.00
—Budget-line reissue of ABC Dot 2089					
❑ 750	Let the Night Begin	198?	2.00	4.00	8.00
—Budget-line reissue					
❑ 798	Love's Sweet Pain	198?	2.00	4.00	8.00
—Budget-line reissue of ABC 1112					
❑ 3183	Let the Night Begin	1979	3.00	6.00	12.00
PLANTATION					
❑ 517	Reconsider Me	197?	3.00	6.00	12.00

S

Number	Title (A Side/B Side)	Yr	VG	VG+	NM
SABRES, THE					
RCA VICTOR					
❑ LPM-1376 [M]	Ridin' High with the Sabres	1956	15.00	30.00	60.00
SABU					
ALEGRE					
❑ 802 [M]	Jazz Espagnole	195?	75.00	150.00	300.00
BLUE NOTE					
❑ BLP-1561 [M]	Palo Congo	1957	25.00	50.00	100.00
—Regular version, W. 63rd St. address on label					
❑ BLP-1561 [M]	Palo Congo	1957	37.50	75.00	150.00
—"Deep groove" version (deep indentation under label on both sides)					
❑ BLP-1561 [M]	Palo Congo	1963	6.25	12.50	25.00
—With "New York, USA" address on label					
SACHS, AARON					
BETHLEHEM					
❑ BCP-1008 [10]	Aaron Sachs Quintet	1954	30.00	60.00	120.00
DAWN					
❑ DLP-1114 [M]	Jazzville, Volume 3	1957	20.00	40.00	80.00
RAMA					
❑ LP-1004 [M]	Clarinet and Co.	1957	20.00	40.00	80.00
SACHS, AARON/HANK D'AMICO					
BETHLEHEM					
❑ BCP-7 [M]	We Brought Our "Axes"	1955	20.00	40.00	80.00
SACRED MUSHROOM, THE					
Members of this group were later in POCO and PURE PRAIRIE LEAGUE.					
PARALLAX					
❑ P-4001	The Sacred Mushroom	1969	37.50	75.00	150.00
SADI, FATS					
BLUE NOTE					
❑ BLP-5061 [10]	The Swinging Fats Sadi Combo	1955	75.00	150.00	300.00
SADLER, SSGT. BARRY					
RCA VICTOR					
❑ LPM-3547 [M]	Ballads of the Green Berets	1966	3.75	7.50	15.00
❑ LSP-3547 [S]	Ballads of the Green Berets	1966	5.00	10.00	20.00
❑ LPM-3605 [M]	The "A" Team	1966	3.75	7.50	15.00
❑ LSP-3605 [S]	The "A" Team	1966	5.00	10.00	20.00
❑ LPM-3691 [M]	Back Home	1967	5.00	10.00	20.00
❑ LSP-3691 [S]	Back Home	1967	3.75	7.50	15.00
SAGITTARIUS					
COLUMBIA					
❑ CS 9644	Present Tense	1968	7.50	15.00	30.00
TOGETHER					
❑ STT-1002	The Blue Marble	1969	12.50	25.00	50.00
—With two bonus photos; deduct 25 percent if missing					
SAHL, MORT					
FANTASY					
❑ 7005 [M]	Mort Sahl at Sunset	196?	7.50	15.00	30.00
—Black vinyl					
❑ 7005 [M]	Mort Sahl at Sunset	196?	10.00	20.00	40.00
—Red vinyl					
GNP CRESCENDO					
❑ GNPS-2070	Sing a Song of Watergate	1973	3.75	7.50	15.00
MERCURY					
❑ MG-21112 [M]	Anyway…Onward	1967	5.00	10.00	20.00
❑ SR-61112 [S]	Anyway…Onward	1967	5.00	10.00	20.00
REPRISE					
❑ R-5002 [M]	The New Frontier	1961	5.00	10.00	20.00
❑ R9-5002 [S]	The New Frontier	1961	6.25	12.50	25.00
❑ R-5003 [M]	Mort Sahl On Relationships	1961	10.00	20.00	40.00
❑ R9-5003 [S]	Mort Sahl On Relationships	1961	12.50	25.00	50.00
—Joan Collins appears on the cover					

S

Number	Title (A Side/B Side)	Yr	VG	VG+	NM
VERVE					
❑ MGV-15002 [M]	The Future Lies Ahead	1959	5.00	10.00	20.00
❑ MGV-15004 [M]	1960: Look Forward in Anger	1959	5.00	10.00	20.00
❑ MGV-15006 [M]	A Way of Life	1960	5.00	10.00	20.00
❑ MGV-15012 [M]	Mort Sahl at the Hungry I	1960	5.00	10.00	20.00
❑ MGVS-15012 [S]	Mort Sahl at the Hungry I	1960	6.25	12.50	25.00
❑ V-15021 [M]	The Next President	1961	5.00	10.00	20.00
❑ V6-15021 [S]	The Next President	1961	6.25	12.50	25.00
❑ V-15049 [M]	Great Moments of Comedy	1965	3.75	7.50	15.00
SAHM, DOUG					
Also see SIR DOUGLAS QUINTET.					
ABC DOT					
❑ DO-2057	Texas Rock for Country Rollers	1976	3.75	7.50	15.00
ANTONE'S					
❑ ANT-0008	Juke Box Music	1989	3.00	6.00	12.00
ATLANTIC					
❑ SD 7254	Doug Sahm and Band	1973	3.75	7.50	15.00
MERCURY					
❑ SRM-1-655	Rough Edges	1972	7.50	15.00	30.00
TAKOMA					
❑ TAK-7075	Hell of a Spell	1980	3.00	6.00	12.00
TEARDROP					
❑ TD-5000	The West Side Sound Rolls Again	1982	3.00	6.00	12.00
WARNER BROS.					
❑ BS 2810	Groovers Paradise	1974	5.00	10.00	20.00
SAIN, OLIVER					
ABAT					
❑ 404	Main Man	1973	5.00	10.00	20.00
❑ 406	Bus Stop	1974	5.00	10.00	20.00
ST. ANTHONY'S FIRE					
ZONK					
❑ (# unknown)	St. Anthony's Fire	1968	100.00	200.00	400.00
ST. CLAIRE, BETTY					
JUBILEE					
❑ JLP-15 [10]	Hal McKusick Plays — Betty St. Clair Sings	1955	30.00	60.00	120.00
❑ JLP-23 [10]	Cool and Clearer	1955	25.00	50.00	100.00
❑ JLP-1011 [M]	What Is There to Say?	1956	12.50	25.00	50.00
SEECO					
❑ SLP-456 [M]	Betty St. Claire at Basin Street	1960	10.00	20.00	40.00
❑ SLP-4560 [S]	Betty St. Claire at Basin Street	1960	10.00	20.00	40.00
ST. CLOUD, ENDLE					
INTERNATIONAL ARTISTS					
❑ IA-12	Thank You All Very Much	1970	15.00	30.00	60.00
ST. CYR, JOHNNY					
SOUTHLAND					
❑ 212	Johnny St. Cyr and His Hot Five	196?	5.00	10.00	20.00
ST. LOUIS JIMMY					
BLUESVILLE					
❑ BVLP-1028 [M]	Goin' Down Blues	1961	30.00	60.00	120.00
—Blue label, silver print					
❑ BVLP-1028 [M]	Goin' Down Blues	1964	6.25	12.50	25.00
—Blue label, trident logo at right					
ST. PETER'S CHOIR					
CORAL					
❑ CRL 56015 [10]	Hark! The Herald Angels Sing	1950	10.00	20.00	40.00
ST. PETERS, CRISPIAN					
JAMIE					
❑ JLPM-3027 [M]	The Pied Piper	1966	12.50	25.00	50.00
❑ JLPS-3027 [R]	The Pied Piper	1966	8.75	17.50	35.00
ST. SHAW, MIKE					
REPRISE					
❑ R-6128 [M]	The Mike St. Shaw Trio	1964	5.00	10.00	20.00
❑ RS-6128 [S]	The Mike St. Shaw Trio	1964	6.25	12.50	25.00
SAINT STEVEN					
PROBE					
❑ CPLP-4506	Over the Hills	1969	15.00	30.00	60.00
SAINTE-MARIE, BUFFY					
ABC					
❑ D-929	Sweet America	1976	3.00	6.00	12.00
MCA					
❑ 405	Buffy	1974	3.00	6.00	12.00
❑ 451	Changing Woman	1975	3.00	6.00	12.00
VANGUARD					
❑ VSD 3/4 [(2)]	The Best of Buffy Sainte-Marie	1970	5.00	10.00	20.00
❑ VSD 33/34 [(2)]	The Best of Buffy Sainte-Marie, Vol. 2	1974	3.75	7.50	15.00
❑ VRS 9142 [M]	It's My Way	1964	3.75	7.50	15.00
❑ VRS 9171 [M]	Many a Mile	1965	3.75	7.50	15.00
❑ VRS 9211 [M]	Little Wheel Spin and Spin	1966	3.75	7.50	15.00
❑ VRS 9250 [M]	Fire & Fire & Candlelight	1967	3.75	7.50	15.00
❑ VMS 73113	The Best of Buffy Sainte-Marie	1985	2.50	5.00	10.00
❑ VSD 79142 [S]	It's My Way	1964	5.00	10.00	20.00
❑ VSD 79171 [S]	Many a Mile	1965	5.00	10.00	20.00
❑ VSD 79211 [S]	Little Wheel Spin and Spin	1966	5.00	10.00	20.00
❑ VSD 79250 [S]	Fire & Fire & Candlelight	1967	5.00	10.00	20.00
❑ VSD 79280	I'm Gonna Be a Country Girl Again	1968	3.75	7.50	15.00
❑ VSD 79300	Illuminations	1969	3.75	7.50	15.00
❑ VSD 79311	She Used to Wanna Be a Ballerina	1971	3.75	7.50	15.00
❑ VSD 79312	Moon Shot	1972	3.75	7.50	15.00
❑ VSD 79330	Quiet Places	1973	3.00	6.00	12.00
❑ VSD 79340	Native Child: Odyssey	1974	3.00	6.00	12.00

Number	Title (A Side/B Side)	Yr	VG	VG+	NM
SAKAMOTO, KYU					
CAPITOL					
❑ DT 10349 [R]	Sukiyaki and Other Japanese Hits	1963	3.75	7.50	15.00
❑ T 10349 [M]	Sukiyaki and Other Japanese Hits	1963	6.25	12.50	25.00
SALEM MASS					
SALEM MASS					
❑ SM-101	Witch Burning	1972	62.50	125.00	250.00
SALES, SOUPY					
ABC-PARAMOUNT					
❑ 503 [M]	Spy with a Pie	1965	6.25	12.50	25.00
❑ S-503 [S]	Spy with a Pie	1965	7.50	15.00	30.00
❑ 517 [M]	Soupy Sales Sez Do the Mouse and Other Teen Hits	1965	6.25	12.50	25.00
❑ S-517 [S]	Soupy Sales Sez Do the Mouse and Other Teen Hits	1965	7.50	15.00	30.00
MCA					
❑ 5274	Still Soupy After All These Years	1981	3.00	6.00	12.00
MOTOWN					
❑ MS 686	A Bag of Soup	1969	6.25	12.50	25.00
REPRISE					
❑ R 6010 [M]	The Soupy Sales Show	1961	7.50	15.00	30.00
❑ R9 6010 [S]	The Soupy Sales Show	1961	10.00	20.00	40.00
❑ R 6052 [M]	Up in the Air	1962	7.50	15.00	30.00
❑ R9 6052 [S]	Up in the Air	1962	10.00	20.00	40.00
SALIM, A.K.					
PRESTIGE					
❑ PRLP-7379 [M]	Afro-Soul Drum Orgy	1966	6.25	12.50	25.00
❑ PRST-7379 [S]	Afro-Soul Drum Orgy	1966	7.50	15.00	30.00
SAVOY					
❑ MG-12102 [M]	The Flute Suite	1957	20.00	40.00	80.00
❑ MG-12118 [M]	Pretty for the People	1957	20.00	40.00	80.00
❑ MG-12132 [M]	Blues Suite	1958	12.50	25.00	50.00
❑ SST-13001 [S]	Blues Suite	1959	10.00	20.00	40.00
SALT CITY FIVE, THE					
JUBILEE					
❑ JLP-13 [10]	Salt City Five	1955	12.50	25.00	50.00
❑ JLP-24 [10]	Salt City Five, Volume 2	1955	12.50	25.00	50.00
❑ JLP-1012 [M]	Salt City Five	1956	10.00	20.00	40.00
SALT WATER TAFFY					
BUDDAH					
❑ BDS-5021	Finders Keepers	1968	5.00	10.00	20.00
SALVADOR, SAL					
BETHLEHEM					
❑ BCP-39 [M]	Shades of Sal Salvador	1956	12.50	25.00	50.00
❑ BCP-59 [M]	Frivolous Sal	1956	12.50	25.00	50.00
❑ BCP-74 [M]	Tribute to the Greats	1957	12.50	25.00	50.00
BLUE NOTE					
❑ BLP-5035 [10]	Sal Salvador Quintet	1954	75.00	150.00	300.00
CAPITOL					
❑ H 6505 [10]	Sal Salvador	1954	30.00	60.00	120.00
❑ T 6505 [M]	Sal Salvador	1955	20.00	40.00	80.00
DAUNTLESS					
❑ DM-4307 [M]	You Ain't Heard Nothin' Yet	1963	7.50	15.00	30.00
❑ DS-6307 [S]	You Ain't Heard Nothin' Yet	1963	10.00	20.00	40.00
DECCA					
❑ DL 4026 [M]	Beat for This Generation	1959	10.00	20.00	40.00
❑ DL 9210 [M]	Colors in Sound	1958	12.50	25.00	50.00
❑ DL 74026 [S]	Beat for This Generation	1959	12.50	25.00	50.00
❑ DL 79210 [S]	Colors in Sound	1958	10.00	20.00	40.00
GOLDEN CREST					
❑ GC-1001 [M]	Sal Salvador Quartet	1961	6.25	12.50	25.00
❑ GCS-1001 [S]	Sal Salvador Quartet	1961	7.50	15.00	30.00
ROULETTE					
❑ R-25262 [M]	Music To Stop Smoking By	1964	5.00	10.00	20.00
❑ RS-25262 [S]	Music To Stop Smoking By	1964	6.25	12.50	25.00
SALVATION					
ABC					
❑ S-623	Salvation	1968	5.00	10.00	20.00
❑ S-653	Gypsy Carnival Caravan	1968	5.00	10.00	20.00
SAM AND DAVE					
ATLANTIC					
❑ SD 8205	I Thank You	1968	6.25	12.50	25.00
❑ SD 8218	The Best of Sam and Dave	1969	5.00	10.00	20.00
❑ 81279	The Best of Sam and Dave	1985	2.50	5.00	10.00
❑ 81718	Soul Men	1987	2.50	5.00	10.00
—Reissue of Stax 725					
GUSTO					
❑ 0045	Sweet and Funky Gold	197?	2.50	5.00	10.00
ROULETTE					
❑ R-25323 [M]	Sam and Dave	1966	7.50	15.00	30.00
❑ SR-25323 [S]	Sam and Dave	1966	10.00	20.00	40.00
STAX					
❑ ST-708 [M]	Hold On, I'm Comin'	1966	10.00	20.00	40.00
❑ STS-708 [S]	Hold On, I'm Comin'	1966	12.50	25.00	50.00
❑ ST-712 [M]	Double Dynamite	1966	7.50	15.00	30.00
❑ STS-712 [S]	Double Dynamite	1966	10.00	20.00	40.00
❑ ST-725 [M]	Soul Men	1967	7.50	15.00	30.00
❑ STS-725 [S]	Soul Men	1967	10.00	20.00	40.00
UNITED ARTISTS					
❑ UA-LA524-G	Back At 'Cha!	1975	3.00	6.00	12.00

Number	Title (A Side/B Side)	Yr	VG	VG+	NM
SAM THE SHAM AND THE PHARAOHS					
ATLANTIC					
❏ SD 8271	Hard and Heavy	1971	3.75	7.50	15.00
—As "Sam Samudio"					
MGM					
❏ E-4297 [M]	Wooly Bully	1965	7.50	15.00	30.00
❏ SE-4297 [S]	Wooly Bully	1965	10.00	20.00	40.00
❏ E-4317 [M]	Their Second Album	1965	6.25	12.50	25.00
❏ SE-4317 [S]	Their Second Album	1965	7.50	15.00	30.00
❏ E-4347 [M]	On Tour	1966	6.25	12.50	25.00
❏ SE-4347 [S]	On Tour	1966	7.50	15.00	30.00
❏ E-4407 [M]	Lil' Red Riding Hood	1966	6.25	12.50	25.00
❏ SE-4407 [S]	Lil' Red Riding Hood	1966	7.50	15.00	30.00
❏ E-4422 [M]	The Best of Sam the Sham and the Pharoahs	1967	5.00	10.00	20.00
❏ SE-4422 [S]	The Best of Sam the Sham and the Pharoahs	1967	6.25	12.50	25.00
❏ E-4477 [M]	Nefertiti	1967	6.25	12.50	25.00
❏ SE-4477	The Sam The Sham Revue	1968	5.00	10.00	20.00
—Retitled reissue					
❏ SE-4477 [S]	Nefertiti	1967	6.25	12.50	25.00
❏ SE-4526	Ten of Pentacles	1968	5.00	10.00	20.00
❏ ST 90422 [S]	Wooly Bully	1965	12.50	25.00	50.00
—Capitol Record Club edition					
❏ T 90422 [M]	Wooly Bully	1965	10.00	20.00	40.00
—Capitol Record Club edition					
POLYDOR					
❏ 827917-1	The Best of Sam the Sham and the Pharoahs	1985	2.50	5.00	10.00
RHINO					
❏ RNLP-122	Pharoahization: The Best of Sam the Sham and the Pharoahs (1965-1967)	1986	2.50	5.00	10.00
SAMHAIN					
Also see THE MISFITS.					
PLAN 9					
❏ PL9-04	Initium	1984	12.50	25.00	50.00
—Black vinyl; "8-84" scrawled in trail-off wax					
❏ PL9-04	Initium	1984	25.00	50.00	100.00
—500 on red vinyl					
❏ PL9-04	Initium	1984	75.00	150.00	300.00
—100 on white vinyl					
❏ PL9-04	Initium	1984	75.00	150.00	300.00
—No more than 100 on marbled black and white vinyl					
❏ PL9-04	Initium	1984	100.00	200.00	400.00
—Pink vinyl "error" pressing					
❏ PL9-05 [EP]	Unholy Passion	1985	3.00	6.00	12.00
—Black vinyl, maroon cover					
❏ PL9-05 [EP]	Unholy Passion	1985	20.00	40.00	80.00
—Black vinyl, tan cover (original)					
❏ PL9-05 [EP]	Unholy Passion	1985	25.00	50.00	100.00
—Red vinyl, maroon cover					
❏ PL9-05 [EP]	Unholy Passion	1985	25.00	50.00	100.00
—White vinyl, tan cover					
❏ PL9-07	November Coming Fire	1986	7.50	15.00	30.00
—Regular issue on black vinyl					
❏ PL9-07	November Coming Fire	1986	37.50	75.00	150.00
—200 on orange vinyl					
SAMPLE, JOE					
CRUSADERS					
❏ 16001	Carmel	198?	5.00	10.00	20.00
—Audiophile vinyl					
MOBILE FIDELITY					
❏ 1-016	Rainbow Seeker	1979	5.00	10.00	20.00
—Audiophile vinyl					
SAMPLE, JOE; RAY BROWN; SHELLY MANNE					
EAST WIND					
❏ 10001	The Three	1976	5.00	10.00	20.00
SAMPLE, JOE, AND DAVID T. WALKER					
CRUSADERS					
❏ 16004	Swing Street Café	198?	5.00	10.00	20.00
—Audiophile vinyl					
SAMPLES, JUNIOR					
CHART					
❏ CHM-1002 [M]	The World of Junior Samples	1967	5.00	10.00	20.00
❏ CHS-1002 [S]	The World of Junior Samples	1967	5.00	10.00	20.00
❏ CHS-1007	Bull Session at Bulls Gap	1968	3.75	7.50	15.00
❏ CHS-1021	That's a Hee Haw	1969	3.75	7.50	15.00
❏ CHS-1045	Best of Junior Samples	1970	3.75	7.50	15.00
HILLTOP					
❏ JS-6113	Moonshining	197?	2.50	5.00	10.00
SAMPSON, EDGAR					
CORAL					
❏ CRL 57049 [M]	Swing Softly Sweet Sampson	1957	10.00	20.00	40.00
SAN REMO GOLDEN STRINGS					
GORDY					
❏ G-923 [M]	Hungry for Love	1967	6.25	12.50	25.00
❏ GS-923 [S]	Hungry for Love	1967	7.50	15.00	30.00
❏ GS-928	Swing	1968	5.00	10.00	20.00
RIC-TIC					
❏ 901 [M]	Hungry for Love	1966	12.50	25.00	50.00
❏ S-901 [S]	Hungry for Love	1966	15.00	30.00	60.00
SAN SEBASTIAN STRINGS, THE					
STANYAN					
❏ 10043	La Mer	1972	2.50	5.00	10.00
WARNER BROS.					
❏ W 1670 [M]	The Sea	1967	3.75	7.50	15.00
❏ WS 1670 [S]	The Sea	1967	3.00	6.00	12.00
❏ W 1705 [M]	The Earth	1967	3.75	7.50	15.00

Number	Title (A Side/B Side)	Yr	VG	VG+	NM
❏ WS 1705 [S]	The Earth	1967	3.00	6.00	12.00
❏ WS 1720	The Sky	1968	3.00	6.00	12.00
❏ 3WS 1730 [(3)]	The Sea, The Earth, The Sky	1968	5.00	10.00	20.00
❏ WS 1764	Home to the Sea	1968	3.00	6.00	12.00
❏ WS 1795	For Lovers	1969	3.00	6.00	12.00
❏ 3WS 1827 [(3)]	The Complete Sea	1969	5.00	10.00	20.00
❏ WS 1839	The Soft Sea	1970	3.00	6.00	12.00
❏ BS 2622	Winter	1972	2.50	5.00	10.00
❏ BS 2707	Summer	1973	2.50	5.00	10.00
❏ 4WS 2754 [(4)]	Seasons	1973	5.00	10.00	20.00
❏ BS 2768	Bouquet — The Best of the San Sebastian Strings	1974	2.50	5.00	10.00
❏ BS 2837	With Love	1975	2.50	5.00	10.00
SANDALS, THE					
WORLD PACIFIC					
❏ ST-1818 [S]	Scrambler	1964	25.00	50.00	100.00
—As "The Sandells"; black vinyl					
❏ ST-1818 [S]	Scrambler	1964	62.50	125.00	250.00
—As "The Sandells"; red vinyl					
❏ WP-1818 [M]	Scrambler	1964	20.00	40.00	80.00
—As "The Sandells"					
❏ ST-1832 [S]	The Endless Summer	1966	7.50	15.00	30.00
❏ WP-1832 [M]	The Endless Summer	1966	6.25	12.50	25.00
❏ ST-21884	The Last of the Ski Bums	1969	6.25	12.50	25.00
—With skiers' silhouettes on cover					
❏ ST-21884	The Last of the Ski Bums	1969	6.25	12.50	25.00
—With Volkswagon bus on cover					
SANDBERG, CARL					
COLUMBIA MASTERWORKS					
❏ ML 5539 [M]	Flat Rock Ballads	1959	5.00	10.00	20.00
DECCA					
❏ DL 5135 [10]	The People, Yes	1950	12.50	25.00	50.00
❏ DL 9105 [M]	Cowboy Songs and Negro Spirituals	1964	5.00	10.00	20.00
LYRICHORD					
❏ LL-4 [10]	American Songbag	1951	12.50	25.00	50.00
❏ LL-66 [M]	The Great Carl Sandburg	1957	7.50	15.00	30.00
SANDERS, ED					
REPRISE					
❏ MS 2105	Beer Cans on the Moon	1972	6.25	12.50	25.00
❏ RS-6374	Sanders' Truckstop	1969	6.25	12.50	25.00
SANDERS, FELICIA					
COLUMBIA					
❏ CL 654 [M]	Felicia Sanders at the Blue Angel	1955	7.50	15.00	30.00
❏ CL 713 [M]	Girl Meets Boy	1955	7.50	15.00	30.00
DECCA					
❏ DL 8762 [M]	That Certain Feeling	1958	6.25	12.50	25.00
❏ DL 78762 [S]	That Certain Feeling	1959	10.00	20.00	40.00
SANDERS, GEORGE					
ABC-PARAMOUNT					
❏ ABC-231 [M]	The George Sanders Touch	1958	7.50	15.00	30.00
SANDERS, PHAROAH					
ABC IMPULSE!					
❏ A-9138 [M]	Tauhid	1967	7.50	15.00	30.00
❏ AS-9138 [S]	Tauhid	1967	5.00	10.00	20.00
❏ AS-9181	Karma	1969	5.00	10.00	20.00
❏ AS-9190	Jewels of Thought	1970	5.00	10.00	20.00
❏ AS-9199	Summun Bukmun Umyum	1970	5.00	10.00	20.00
❏ AS-9229 [(2)]	The Best of Pharoah Sanders	1973	5.00	10.00	20.00
ESP-DISK'					
❏ 1003 [M]	Pharoah's First	1965	6.25	12.50	25.00
❏ S-1003 [S]	Pharoah's First	1965	7.50	15.00	30.00
SANDOLE, DENNIS					
FANTASY					
❏ 3251 [M]	Compositions and Arrangements for Guitar	1958	7.50	15.00	30.00
SANDOLE BROTHERS, THE					
FANTASY					
❏ 3209 [M]	Modern Music from Philadelphia	1956	12.50	25.00	50.00
—Red vinyl					
❏ 3209 [M]	Modern Music from Philadelphia	1957	7.50	15.00	30.00
—Black vinyl					
SANDS, TOMMY					
CAPITOL					
❏ T 848 [M]	Steady Date with Tommy Sands	1957	15.00	30.00	60.00
❏ T 929 [M]	Sing Boy Sing	1958	15.00	30.00	60.00
❏ T 1081 [M]	Sands Storm	1959	12.50	25.00	50.00
❏ ST 1123 [S]	This Thing Called Love	1959	10.00	20.00	40.00
❏ T 1123 [M]	This Thing Called Love	1959	7.50	15.00	30.00
❏ ST 1239 [S]	When I'm Thinking of You	1960	10.00	20.00	40.00
❏ T 1239 [M]	When I'm Thinking of You	1960	7.50	15.00	30.00
❏ ST 1364 [S]	Sands at the Sands	1960	10.00	20.00	40.00
❏ T 1364 [M]	Sands at the Sands	1960	7.50	15.00	30.00
❏ ST 1426 [S]	Dream with Me	1961	10.00	20.00	40.00
❏ T 1426 [M]	Dream with Me	1961	7.50	15.00	30.00
GREEN LINNET					
❏ SIF-3044	Singing of the Times	1989	3.00	6.00	12.00
SANTA FE					
RTV					
❏ 301	Good Earth	197?	7.50	15.00	30.00
SANTAMARIA, MONGO					
BATTLE					
❏ B-6120 [M]	Watermelon Man!	1963	5.00	10.00	20.00
❏ B-6129 [M]	Mongo at the Village Gate	1964	5.00	10.00	20.00
❏ BS-96120 [S]	Watermelon Man!	1963	6.25	12.50	25.00
❏ BS-96129 [S]	Mongo at the Village Gate	1964	6.25	12.50	25.00

S

Number	Title (A Side/B Side)	Yr	VG	VG+	NM
COLUMBIA					
❏ CL 2298 [M]	El Pussy Cat	1965	5.00	10.00	20.00
—With "Guaranteed High Fidelity" in black at bottom of red label					
❏ CS 9098 [S]	El Pussy Cat	1965	6.25	12.50	25.00
—With "360 Sound Stereo" in black at bottom of red label					
❏ CS 9175 [S]	La Bamba	1965	5.00	10.00	20.00
FANTASY					
❏ 3267 [M]	Yambu	1959	7.50	15.00	30.00
—Black vinyl					
❏ 3267 [M]	Yambu	1959	10.00	20.00	40.00
—Red vinyl					
❏ 3291 [M]	Mongo	1959	7.50	15.00	30.00
—Black vinyl					
❏ 3291 [M]	Mongo	1959	10.00	20.00	40.00
—Red vinyl					
❏ 3302 [M]	Our Man in Havana	1960	7.50	15.00	30.00
—Black vinyl					
❏ 3302 [M]	Our Man in Havana	1960	10.00	20.00	40.00
—Red vinyl					
❏ 3311 [M]	Mongo in Havana	1960	7.50	15.00	30.00
—Black vinyl					
❏ 3311 [M]	Mongo in Havana	1960	10.00	20.00	40.00
—Red vinyl					
❏ 3314 [M]	Sabroso	1960	7.50	15.00	30.00
—Black vinyl					
❏ 3314 [M]	Sabroso	1960	10.00	20.00	40.00
—Red vinyl					
❏ 3324 [M]	Arriba!	1961	7.50	15.00	30.00
—Black vinyl					
❏ 3324 [M]	Arriba!	1961	10.00	20.00	40.00
—Red vinyl					
❏ 3328 [M]	Mas Sabroso	1962	7.50	15.00	30.00
—Black vinyl					
❏ 3328 [M]	Mas Sabroso	1962	10.00	20.00	40.00
—Red vinyl					
❏ 3335 [M]	Viva Mongo!	1962	7.50	15.00	30.00
—Black vinyl					
❏ 3335 [M]	Viva Mongo!	1962	10.00	20.00	40.00
—Red vinyl					
❏ 8012 [S]	Yambu	1962	5.00	10.00	20.00
—Black vinyl					
❏ 8012 [S]	Yambu	1962	7.50	15.00	30.00
—Blue vinyl					
❏ 8032 [S]	Mongo	1962	5.00	10.00	20.00
—Black vinyl					
❏ 8032 [S]	Mongo	1962	7.50	15.00	30.00
—Blue vinyl					
❏ 8045 [S]	Our Man in Havana	1962	5.00	10.00	20.00
—Black vinyl					
❏ 8045 [S]	Our Man in Havana	1962	7.50	15.00	30.00
—Blue vinyl					
❏ 8055 [S]	Mongo in Havana	1962	5.00	10.00	20.00
—Black vinyl					
❏ 8055 [S]	Mongo in Havana	1962	7.50	15.00	30.00
—Blue vinyl					
❏ 8058 [S]	Sabroso	1962	5.00	10.00	20.00
—Black vinyl					
❏ 8058 [S]	Sabroso	1962	7.50	15.00	30.00
—Blue vinyl					
❏ 8067 [S]	Arriba!	1962	5.00	10.00	20.00
—Black vinyl					
❏ 8067 [S]	Arriba!	1962	7.50	15.00	30.00
—Blue vinyl					
❏ 8071 [S]	Mas Sabroso	1962	5.00	10.00	20.00
—Black vinyl					
❏ 8071 [S]	Mas Sabroso	1962	7.50	15.00	30.00
—Blue vinyl					
❏ 8087 [S]	Viva Mongo!	1962	5.00	10.00	20.00
—Black vinyl					
❏ 8087 [S]	Viva Mongo!	1962	7.50	15.00	30.00
—Blue vinyl					
❏ 8351 [S]	Mighty Mongo	1963	5.00	10.00	20.00
RIVERSIDE					
❏ RLP-423 [M]	Go, Mongo!	1962	6.25	12.50	25.00
❏ R-3008 [M]	Explosion	1967	6.25	12.50	25.00
❏ RM-3523 [M]	Mongo Introduces La Lupe	1963	5.00	10.00	20.00
❏ RM-3529 [M]	Mongo at the Village Gate	1963	5.00	10.00	20.00
❏ RM-3530 [M]	Mongo Santamaria Explodes!	1964	5.00	10.00	20.00
❏ RS-9423 [S]	Go, Mongo!	1962	7.50	15.00	30.00
❏ RS-93523 [S]	Mongo Introduces La Lupe	1963	6.25	12.50	25.00
❏ RS-93529 [S]	Mongo at the Village Gate	1963	6.25	12.50	25.00
❏ RS-93530 [S]	Mongo Santamaria Explodes!	1964	6.25	12.50	25.00
TICO					
❏ LP-137 [10]	Chango	1955	20.00	40.00	80.00
❏ LP-1037 [M]	Chango: Mongo Santamaria's Drums and Chants	1957	15.00	30.00	60.00
❏ LP-1149 [M]	Mongo Santamaria's Drums and Chants	1967	5.00	10.00	20.00
SANTANA					
ARISTA					
❏ 19080 [(2)]	Supernatural	2000	10.00	20.00	40.00
—Classic Records audiophile vinyl issue in gatefold cover with booklet					
CICADELIC					
❏ 1004	Santana '68	1988	3.00	6.00	12.00
COLUMBIA					
❏ CS 9781	Santana	1969	3.75	7.50	15.00
—"360 Sound" on label					
❏ CS 9781	Santana	1970	2.50	5.00	10.00
—Orange label					
❏ PC 9781	Santana	198?	2.00	4.00	8.00
❏ CQ 30130 [Q]	Abraxas	1972	5.00	10.00	20.00
❏ JC 30130	Abraxas	1977	2.00	4.00	8.00

Number	Title (A Side/B Side)	Yr	VG	VG+	NM
❏ KC 30130	Abraxas	197?	2.50	5.00	10.00
—With no poster					
❏ KC 30130	Abraxas	1970	3.75	7.50	15.00
—Original copies have a poster					
❏ PC 30130	Abraxas	1985	2.00	4.00	8.00
❏ CQ 30595 [Q]	Santana	1972	5.00	10.00	20.00
❏ KC 30595	Santana	1971	3.00	6.00	12.00
—Not the same album as CS 9781; this is often called "Santana III"					
❏ PC 30595	Santana	197?	2.00	4.00	8.00
❏ KC 31610	Caravanserai	1972	3.00	6.00	12.00
❏ PC 31610	Caravanserai	197?	2.00	4.00	8.00
❏ PCQ 31610 [Q]	Caravanserai	1974	5.00	10.00	20.00
❏ PC 32455	Welcome	1973	3.00	6.00	12.00
—No bar code on cover					
❏ PC 32455	Welcome	1979	2.00	4.00	8.00
—With bar code on cover					
❏ PCQ 32455 [Q]	Welcome	1974	5.00	10.00	20.00
❏ JC 33050	Santana's Greatest Hits	1977	2.00	4.00	8.00
❏ PC 33050	Santana's Greatest Hits	1974	3.00	6.00	12.00
—No bar code on cover					
❏ PCQ 33050 [Q]	Santana's Greatest Hits	1974	5.00	10.00	20.00
❏ PC 33135	Borboletta	1974	3.00	6.00	12.00
—No bar code on cover					
❏ PC 33135	Borboletta	1979	2.00	4.00	8.00
—With bar code on cover					
❏ PCQ 33135 [Q]	Borboletta	1974	5.00	10.00	20.00
❏ PC 33576	Amigos	1976	3.00	6.00	12.00
—No bar code on cover					
❏ PC 33576	Amigos	1979	2.00	4.00	8.00
—With bar code on cover					
❏ PCQ 33576 [Q]	Amigos	1976	5.00	10.00	20.00
❏ JC 34423	Festival	1977	3.00	6.00	12.00
❏ JCQ 34423 [Q]	Festival	1977	5.00	10.00	20.00
❏ PC 34423	Festival	198?	2.00	4.00	8.00
❏ C2 34914 [(2)]	Moonflower	1977	3.75	7.50	15.00
❏ FC 35600	Inner Secrets	1978	3.00	6.00	12.00
❏ PC 35600	Inner Secrets	198?	2.00	4.00	8.00
—Budget-line reissue					
❏ FC 36154	Marathon	1979	3.00	6.00	12.00
❏ PC 36154	Marathon	198?	2.00	4.00	8.00
—Budget-line reissue					
❏ C2 36590 [(2)]	Swing of Delight	1980	3.75	7.50	15.00
❏ FC 37158	Zebop!	1981	3.00	6.00	12.00
❏ PC 37158	Zebop!	198?	2.00	4.00	8.00
—Budget-line reissue					
❏ FC 38122	Shango	1982	3.00	6.00	12.00
❏ PC 38122	Shango	198?	2.00	4.00	8.00
—Budget-line reissue					
❏ FC 39527	Beyond Appearances	1985	2.50	5.00	10.00
❏ PC 39527	Beyond Appearances	198?	2.00	4.00	8.00
—Budget-line reissue					
❏ HC 40130	Abraxas	1981	20.00	40.00	80.00
—Half-speed mastered edition					
❏ FC 40272	Freedom	1987	2.50	5.00	10.00
❏ C3X 44344 [(3)]	Viva Santana	1988	5.00	10.00	20.00
❏ HC 47158	Zebop!	1981	10.00	20.00	40.00
—Half-speed mastered edition					
SANTO AND JOHNNY					
CANADIAN AMERICAN					
❏ CALP-1001 [M]	Santo & Johnny	1959	15.00	30.00	60.00
❏ SCALP-1001 [S]	Santo & Johnny	1959	20.00	40.00	80.00
❏ CALP-1002 [M]	Encore	1960	10.00	20.00	40.00
❏ SCALP-1002 [S]	Encore	1960	12.50	25.00	50.00
❏ CALP-1004 [M]	Hawaii	1961	10.00	20.00	40.00
❏ SCALP-1004 [S]	Hawaii	1961	12.50	25.00	50.00
❏ CALP-1006 [M]	Come On In	1962	7.50	15.00	30.00
❏ SCALP-1006 [S]	Come On In	1962	10.00	20.00	40.00
❏ CALP-1008 [M]	Around the World with Santo and Johnny	1962	7.50	15.00	30.00
❏ SCALP-1008 [S]	Around the World with Santo and Johnny	1962	10.00	20.00	40.00
❏ CALP-1011 [M]	Off Shore	1963	7.50	15.00	30.00
❏ SCALP-1011 [S]	Off Shore	1963	10.00	20.00	40.00
❏ CALP-1014 [M]	In the Still of the Night	1963	7.50	15.00	30.00
❏ SCALP-1014 [S]	In the Still of the Night	1963	10.00	20.00	40.00
❏ CALP-1016 [M]	Wish You Love	1964	7.50	15.00	30.00
❏ SCALP-1016 [S]	Wish You Love	1964	10.00	20.00	40.00
❏ CALP-1017 [M]	The Beatles' Greatest Hits	1965	10.00	20.00	40.00
❏ SCALP-1017 [S]	The Beatles' Greatest Hits	1965	12.50	25.00	50.00
❏ CALP-1018 [M]	Mucho	1965	7.50	15.00	30.00
❏ SCALP-1018 [S]	Mucho	1965	10.00	20.00	40.00
IMPERIAL					
❏ LP-9363 [M]	Brilliant Guitar Sounds	1967	3.75	7.50	15.00
❏ LP-12363 [S]	Brilliant Guitar Sounds	1967	5.00	10.00	20.00
❏ LP-12366	Golden Guitars	1968	3.75	7.50	15.00
❏ LP-12418	On the Road Again	1968	3.75	7.50	15.00
SANTOS, LARRY					
CASABLANCA					
❏ NBLP 7030	You Are Everything I Need	1976	3.00	6.00	12.00
❏ NBLP 7061	Don't Let the Music Stop	1977	3.00	6.00	12.00
EVOLUTION					
❏ 2002	Just a Man	1969	5.00	10.00	20.00
❏ 2015	Morning Sun	1971	3.75	7.50	15.00
SANTOS, MOACIR					
BLUE NOTE					
❏ BN-LA007-F	Maestro	1972	5.00	10.00	20.00
SANTOS BROTHERS, THE					
METROJAZZ					
❏ E-1015 [M]	Jazz For Two Trumpets	1958	12.50	25.00	50.00
❏ SE-1015 [S]	Jazz For Two Trumpets	1958	10.00	20.00	40.00

Number	Title (A Side/B Side)	Yr	VG	VG+	NM
SAPODILLA PUNCH					
PHILIPS					
❏ PHS 600312	Sapodilla Punch	1969	5.00	10.00	20.00
SAPPHIRE THINKERS, THE					
HOBBIT					
❏ HB-5003	From Within	1969	7.50	15.00	30.00
SAPPHIRES, THE (1)					
COLLECTABLES					
❏ COL-5007	Who Do You Love	198?	2.50	5.00	10.00
SWAN					
❏ LP-513 [M]	Who Do You Love	1964	75.00	150.00	300.00
SASH, LEON					
STORYVILLE					
❏ STLP-917 [M]	Leon Sash Quartet	1956	12.50	25.00	50.00
SATAN AND THE DISCIPLES					
GOLDBAND					
❏ 7750	Underground	1969	10.00	20.00	40.00
SATANS, THE					
(NO LABEL)					
❏ (no #) [M]	Raisin' Hell	1962	75.00	150.00	300.00
SATAN'S FOUR					
B.T. PUPPY					
❏ BTS-1010	Mixed Soul	1970	37.50	75.00	150.00
—With the Cinnamon Angels					
SAUNDERS, HERM					
VOGUE					
❏ 101 [10]	Music at the Bantam Cock	1953	50.00	100.00	200.00
SAUNDERS, MERL					
CRYSTAL CLEAR					
❏ 5006	Do I Move You	1980	5.00	10.00	20.00
—Direct-to-disc recording					
FANTASY					
❏ 9421	Fire Up	1973	5.00	10.00	20.00
—With Jerry Garcia and Tom Fogerty					
❏ 79002 [(2)]	Live at the Keystone	198?	5.00	10.00	20.00
SAUSSY, TUPPER					
Also see THE NEON PHILARMONIC.					
MONUMENT					
❏ MLP-8004 [M]	Discover Tupper Saussy	1964	5.00	10.00	20.00
❏ MLP-8027 [M]	Said I to Shostakovitch	1965	5.00	10.00	20.00
❏ MLP-8034 [M]	A Swinger's Guide to "Mary Poppins"	1965	5.00	10.00	20.00
❏ SLP-18004 [S]	Discover Tupper Saussy	1964	6.25	12.50	25.00
❏ SLP-18027 [S]	Said I to Shostakovitch	1965	6.25	12.50	25.00
❏ SLP-18034 [S]	A Swinger's Guide to "Mary Poppins"	1965	6.25	12.50	25.00
SAUTER-FINEGAN					
RCA VICTOR					
❏ LJM-1003 [M]	Inside Sauter-Finegan	1954	20.00	40.00	80.00
❏ LPM-1009 [M]	The Sound of Sauter-Finegan	1954	20.00	40.00	80.00
❏ LPM-1051 [M]	Concert Jazz	1955	15.00	30.00	60.00
❏ LPM-1104 [M]	Sons of Sauter-Finegan	1955	15.00	30.00	60.00
❏ LPM-1227 [M]	New Directions in Music	1956	15.00	30.00	60.00
❏ LPM-1240 [M]	Adventure In Time	1956	15.00	30.00	60.00
❏ LPM-1341 [M]	Under Analysis	1957	12.50	25.00	50.00
❏ LPM-1497 [M]	Straight Down the Middle	1957	12.50	25.00	50.00
❏ LPM-2473 [M]	Inside Sauter-Finegan Revisited	1961	7.50	15.00	30.00
❏ LSP-2473 [S]	Inside Sauter-Finegan Revisited	1961	10.00	20.00	40.00
❏ LPM-3115 [10]	New Directions in Music	1953	30.00	60.00	120.00
UNITED ARTISTS					
❏ WWR 3511 [M]	The Return of the Doodletown Fifers	1959	10.00	20.00	40.00
❏ WWS 7511 [S]	The Return of the Doodletown Fifers	1959	12.50	25.00	50.00
SAUTER-FINEGAN; CHICAGO SYMPHONY ORCHESTRA (FRITZ REINER, CONDUCTOR)					
RCA VICTOR RED SEAL					
❏ LM-1888 [M]	Concerto for Jazz Band and Orchestra	1954	7.50	15.00	30.00
SAVAGE RESURRECTION					
MERCURY					
❏ MG-21156 [M]	Savage Resurrection	1968	50.00	100.00	200.00
❏ SR-61156 [S]	Savage Resurrection	1968	25.00	50.00	100.00
SAVAGE ROSE					
POLYDOR					
❏ 24-6001	In the Plain	1969	5.00	10.00	20.00
—Gatefold cover					
SAVATAGE					
ATLANTIC					
❏ 81247	Power of the Night	1985	2.00	4.00	8.00
❏ 81634	Fight for the Rock	1986	2.00	4.00	8.00
❏ 81775	Hall of the Mountain King	1987	2.00	4.00	8.00
❏ 82008	Gutter Ballet	1990	3.00	6.00	12.00
COMBAT					
❏ MX 6016 [EP]	The Dungeons Are Calling	1985	3.75	7.50	15.00
❏ 8018	Sirens	1986	3.00	6.00	12.00
—Reissue of Par LP with new cover					
PAR					
❏ PAR-1050	Sirens	1983	50.00	100.00	200.00
—Black vinyl					
❏ PAR-1050	Sirens	1983	100.00	200.00	400.00
—Blue vinyl					

Number	Title (A Side/B Side)	Yr	VG	VG+	NM
SAVITT, BUDDY					
PARKWAY					
❏ P-7012 [M]	The Most Heard Sax in the World	1962	12.50	25.00	50.00
❏ SP-7012 [S]	The Most Heard Sax in the World	1962	25.00	50.00	100.00
SAVOY BROWN					
GNP CRESCENDO					
❏ GNPS-2193	Make Me Sweat	1988	2.50	5.00	10.00
❏ GNPS-2196	Kings of Boogie	1989	2.50	5.00	10.00
LONDON					
❏ APS 638	Boogie Brothers	1974	2.50	5.00	10.00
❏ PS 659	Wire Fire	1975	2.50	5.00	10.00
❏ PS 670	Skin 'n' Bone	1976	2.50	5.00	10.00
❏ PS 718	Savage Return	1978	2.50	5.00	10.00
❏ LC-50000	The Best of Savoy Brown	1977	2.50	5.00	10.00
PARROT					
❏ PAS 71024	Getting to the Point	1968	6.25	12.50	25.00
❏ PAS 71027	Blue Matter	1969	6.25	12.50	25.00
❏ PAS 71029	A Step Further	1969	3.75	7.50	15.00
❏ PAS 71036	Raw Sienna	1970	3.75	7.50	15.00
❏ PAS 71042	Looking In	1970	3.75	7.50	15.00
❏ PAS 71047	Street Corner Talking	1971	3.75	7.50	15.00
❏ XPAS 71052	Hellbound Train	1972	3.75	7.50	15.00
❏ XPAS 71057	Lion's Share	1972	3.75	7.50	15.00
❏ XPAS 71059	Jack the Toad	1973	3.75	7.50	15.00
TOWN HOUSE					
❏ ST-7002	Rock 'n' Roll Warriors	1981	3.00	6.00	12.00
❏ SKBK-7003 [(2)]	Greatest Hits Live in Concert	1982	3.75	7.50	15.00
SAWBUCK					
FILLMORE					
❏ Z 31248	Sawbuck	1972	5.00	10.00	20.00
SAXON, SKY					
Also see THE SEEDS.					
GNP CRESCENDO					
❏ GNP-2040 [M]	A Full Spoon of Seedy Blues	1967	10.00	20.00	40.00
❏ GNPS-2040 [S]	A Full Spoon of Seedy Blues	1967	7.50	15.00	30.00
SAXONS, THE					
MIRASONIC					
❏ A-1017 [M]	The Saxons	1966	10.00	20.00	40.00
❏ AS-1017 [S]	The Saxons	1966	20.00	40.00	80.00
SAYE, JOE					
EMARCY					
❏ MG-36072 [M]	Scotch on the Rocks	1956	10.00	20.00	40.00
❏ MG-36112 [M]	A Wee Bit of Jazz	1957	10.00	20.00	40.00
❏ MG-36147 [M]	A Double Shot of Saye	1958	10.00	20.00	40.00
❏ SR-80022 [S]	A Double Shot of Saye	1958	7.50	15.00	30.00
MERCURY					
❏ SR-60052 [S]	A Wee Bit of Jazz	1959	7.50	15.00	30.00
SCAFFOLD, THE					
BELL					
❏ 6018 [M]	Thank U Very Much	1968	12.50	25.00	50.00
—Mono copies are promo only					
❏ 6018 [S]	Thank U Very Much	1968	12.50	25.00	50.00
SCAGGS, BOZ					
ATLANTIC					
❏ SD 8239	Boz Scaggs	1969	3.00	6.00	12.00
❏ SD 19166	Boz Scaggs	1977	2.00	4.00	8.00
COLUMBIA					
❏ A2S 71 [(2)DJ]	KSAN Live Concert	1974	12.50	25.00	50.00
—Promo-only set released in plain cardboard jacket					
❏ AS 203 [DJ]	The Boz Scaggs Sampler	1976	5.00	10.00	20.00
❏ KC 30454	Moments	1971	2.50	5.00	10.00
❏ PC 30454	Moments	197?	2.00	4.00	8.00
❏ KC 30976	Boz Scaggs & Band	1971	2.50	5.00	10.00
❏ PC 30976	Boz Scaggs & Band	197?	2.00	4.00	8.00
❏ KC 31384	My Time	1972	2.50	5.00	10.00
❏ PC 31384	My Time	197?	2.00	4.00	8.00
❏ KC 32760	Slow Dancer	1974	2.50	5.00	10.00
—Second cover has a male dancer who is not Boz Scaggs					
❏ KC 32760	Slow Dancer	1974	3.00	6.00	12.00
—Original cover has Boz Scaggs on a beach in only a bathing suit					
❏ PC 32760	Slow Dancer	197?	2.00	4.00	8.00
❏ JC 33920	Silk Degrees	1977	2.50	5.00	10.00
—Early reissue with new prefix					
❏ PC 33920	Silk Degrees	1976	3.00	6.00	12.00
—Original edition with "PC" prefix and no bar code on back cover					
❏ PC 33920	Silk Degrees	1985	2.00	4.00	8.00
—Budget-line reissue; bar code on back cover					
❏ FC 36106	Middle Man	1980	2.50	5.00	10.00
❏ PC 36106	Middle Man	198?	2.00	4.00	8.00
—Budget-line reissue					
❏ FC 36841	Hits!	1980	2.50	5.00	10.00
❏ PC 36841	Hits!	198?	2.00	4.00	8.00
—Budget-line reissue					
❏ PC 37249	Down Two Then Left	198?	2.00	4.00	8.00
—Budget-line reissue					
❏ JC 37429	Down Two Then Left	1977	2.50	5.00	10.00
❏ FC 40463	Other Roads	1988	2.50	5.00	10.00
❏ HC 43920	Silk Degrees	1981	7.50	15.00	30.00
—Half-speed mastered edition					
SCALETTA, DON					
CAPITOL					
❏ ST 2204 [S]	Any Time, Any Groove	1965	5.00	10.00	20.00
❏ ST 2328 [S]	All in Good Time	1965	5.00	10.00	20.00
VERVE					
❏ V-5027 [M]	Sunday Afternoon at the Trident	1967	5.00	10.00	20.00

Number	Title (A Side/B Side)	Yr	VG	VG+	NM

SCAMPS, THE
PROJECT
| ❑ 8002 [M] | Teen Dance and Sing Along Party | 1962 | 10.00 | 20.00 | 40.00 |

SCANDAL
COLUMBIA
| ❑ 5C 38194 [EP] | Scandal | 1983 | 2.50 | 5.00 | 10.00 |
| ❑ PC 38194 [EP] | Scandal | 198? | — | 3.00 | 6.00 |

—*Reissue with new prefix*

| ❑ FC 39173 | Warrior | 1984 | 2.50 | 5.00 | 10.00 |
| ❑ 8C8 39905 [EP] | Scandal featuring Patty Smyth | 1985 | 5.00 | 10.00 | 20.00 |

—*Picture disc EP with four of the group's biggest hits*

SCHAEFER, HAL
RCA VICTOR
| ❑ LPM-1106 [M] | Just Too Much | 1955 | 12.50 | 25.00 | 50.00 |
| ❑ LPM-1199 [M] | The RCA Victor Jazz Workshop | 1956 | 12.50 | 25.00 | 50.00 |
UNITED ARTISTS
| ❑ UAL-4021 [M] | Ten Shades of Blue | 1959 | 10.00 | 20.00 | 40.00 |
| ❑ UAS-5021 [S] | Ten Shades of Blue | 1959 | 10.00 | 20.00 | 40.00 |

SCHAFER, KERMIT
JUBILEE
❑ BL-1 [M]	Blooperama	196?	5.00	10.00	20.00
❑ KS-1 [(2)M]	The Best of Bloopers	1959	6.25	12.50	25.00
❑ PMB-1 [M]	Pardon My Blooper! Volume 1	1958	5.00	10.00	20.00
❑ LP-2 [10]	Pardon My Blooper!	1954	10.00	20.00	40.00
❑ PMB-2 [M]	Pardon My Blooper! Volume 2	1958	5.00	10.00	20.00
❑ LP-3 [10]	Pardon My Blooper! Volume 2	1954	10.00	20.00	40.00
❑ PMB-3 [M]	Pardon My Blooper! Volume 3	1958	5.00	10.00	20.00
❑ PMB-4 [M]	Pardon My Blooper! Volume 4	1958	5.00	10.00	20.00
❑ PMB-5 [M]	Pardon My Blooper! Volume 5	1959	5.00	10.00	20.00
❑ PMB-6 [M]	Pardon My Blooper! Volume 6	1959	5.00	10.00	20.00
❑ PMB-7 [M]	Pardon My Blooper! Volume 7	1959	5.00	10.00	20.00
❑ PMB-8 [M]	Pardon My Blooper! Volume 8	1959	5.00	10.00	20.00
❑ SPMB-9 [M]	Pardon My Sports Blooper!	196?	5.00	10.00	20.00
❑ QPMB-10 [M]	Pardon My Quiz Blooper!	196?	5.00	10.00	20.00
❑ WPMB-11 [M]	Pardon My Washington Blooper!	196?	5.00	10.00	20.00
❑ LP-19 [10]	Pardon My Blooper! Volume 3	1955	10.00	20.00	40.00
❑ JLP-1000 [M]	Special Edition: Pardon My Blooper!	195?	7.50	15.00	30.00
❑ JGM-2001 [M]	Comedy of Errors	196?	5.00	10.00	20.00
❑ JGM-2002 [M]	Slipped Disks	196?	5.00	10.00	20.00
❑ JGM-2003 [M]	Prize Bloopers	196?	5.00	10.00	20.00
❑ JGM-2004 [M]	Super Bloopers	196?	5.00	10.00	20.00
❑ JGM-2005 [M]	Off the Record	196?	5.00	10.00	20.00
❑ JGM-2006 [M]	Station Breaks	196?	5.00	10.00	20.00
❑ JGM-2007 [M]	Funny Boners	196?	5.00	10.00	20.00
❑ JGM-2008 [M]	Foot 'n Mouth Club	196?	5.00	10.00	20.00

SCHIFRIN, LALO
AUDIO FIDELITY
❑ AFLP-1981 [M]	Bossa Nova — New Brazilian Jazz	1962	5.00	10.00	20.00
❑ AFLP-2117 [M]	Eso Es Latino Jazz	1963	5.00	10.00	20.00
❑ AFSD-5981 [S]	Bossa Nova — New Brazilian Jazz	1962	6.25	12.50	25.00
❑ AFSD-6117 [S]	Eso Es Latino Jazz	1963	6.25	12.50	25.00
COLGEMS
| ❑ COMO-5003 [M] | Murderer's Row | 1967 | 12.50 | 25.00 | 50.00 |
| ❑ COSO-5003 [S] | Murderer's Row | 1967 | 25.00 | 50.00 | 100.00 |
DOT
❑ DLP-3831 [M]	Music from Mission: Impossible	1967	7.50	15.00	30.00
❑ DLP-3833 [M]	Cool Hand Luke	1968	12.50	25.00	50.00
❑ DLP-25831 [S]	Music from Mission: Impossible	1967	10.00	20.00	40.00
❑ DLP-25833 [S]	Cool Hand Luke	1968	12.50	25.00	50.00
❑ DLP-25852	There's a Whole Lot of Schifrin Goin' On	1968	5.00	10.00	20.00
ENTR'ACTE
| ❑ ERS-6508 | Voyage of the Damned | 1977 | 6.25 | 12.50 | 25.00 |
MGM
❑ SE-4110 [S]	Piano, Strings and Bossa Nova	1963	5.00	10.00	20.00
❑ SE-4156 [S]	Between Broadway and Hollywood	1963	5.00	10.00	20.00
❑ E-4313 [M]	The Cincinnati Kid	1965	5.00	10.00	20.00
❑ SE-4313 [S]	The Cincinnati Kid	1965	6.25	12.50	25.00
❑ E-4413 ST [M]	Liquidator	1966	5.00	10.00	20.00
❑ SE-4413 ST [S]	Liquidator	1966	6.25	12.50	25.00
❑ SE-4742	Medical Center and Other Great Themes	1971	5.00	10.00	20.00
NAUTILUS
| ❑ NR-51 | Ins and Outs | 198? | 10.00 | 20.00 | 40.00 |

—*Audiophile vinyl*

PARAMOUNT
| ❑ PAS-5002 | More Music from Mission: Impossible | 1969 | 10.00 | 20.00 | 40.00 |
| ❑ PAS-5004 | Mannix | 1969 | 7.50 | 15.00 | 30.00 |
ROULETTE
| ❑ R 52088 [M] | Lalo Brilliance | 1962 | 5.00 | 10.00 | 20.00 |
| ❑ SR 52088 [S] | Lalo Brilliance | 1962 | 6.25 | 12.50 | 25.00 |
TETRAGRAMMATON
| ❑ T-5006 | Che! | 1969 | 7.50 | 15.00 | 30.00 |
TICO
| ❑ LP-1070 [M] | Piano Espanol | 1960 | 6.25 | 12.50 | 25.00 |
| ❑ LPS-1070 [S] | Piano Espanol | 1960 | 7.50 | 15.00 | 30.00 |
VERVE
| ❑ V6-8543 [S] | Samba Paros Dos | 1963 | 5.00 | 10.00 | 20.00 |

—*With Bob Brookmeyer*

❑ V6-8601 [S]	New Fantasy	1964	5.00	10.00	20.00
❑ V6-8624 [S]	Once a Thief and Other Themes	1965	5.00	10.00	20.00
❑ V6-8654 [S]	The Dissection and Reconstruction of Music from the Past	1966	5.00	10.00	20.00
WARNER BROS.
| ❑ WS 1777 | Bullitt | 1968 | 12.50 | 25.00 | 50.00 |
| ❑ BSK 3328 | Boulevard Nights | 1979 | 2.50 | 5.00 | 10.00 |

SCHILLER, LAWRENCE
CAPITOL
❑ TAO 2574 [M]	LSD	1966	25.00	50.00	100.00
❑ KAO 2630 [M]	Why Did Lenny Bruce Die?	1967	7.50	15.00	30.00
❑ KAO 2652 [M]	Homosexuality in the American Male	1967	7.50	15.00	30.00

SCHLAMME, MARTHA
VANGUARD
❑ VRS 497 [M]	Chansons de Noel	1956	7.50	15.00	30.00
❑ VRS-9011 [M]	Raisins and Almonds and Other Jewish Folk Songs	195?	7.50	15.00	30.00
❑ VRS-9019 [M]	Folk Songs of Many Lands	195?	7.50	15.00	30.00

SCHORY, DICK
CONCERT DISC
| ❑ SC-21 [M] | Re-Percussion | 1957 | 15.00 | 30.00 | 60.00 |
RCA VICTOR
❑ LPM-1866 [M]	Music for Bang, Barroom and Harp	1958	15.00	30.00	60.00
❑ LSP-1866 [S]	Music for Bang, Barroom and Harp	1958	50.00	100.00	200.00
❑ LPM-2125 [M]	Music to Break Any Mood	1960	7.50	15.00	30.00
❑ LSP-2125 [S]	Music to Break Any Mood	1960	25.00	50.00	100.00
❑ LPM-2289 [M]	Wild Percussion and Horns A-Plenty	1960	7.50	15.00	30.00
❑ LSP-2289 [S]	Wild Percussion and Horns A-Plenty	1960	15.00	30.00	60.00
❑ LSA-2306 [S]	Runnin' Wild	1960	10.00	20.00	40.00
❑ LSA-2382 [S]	Stereo Action Goes Broadway	1961	10.00	20.00	40.00
❑ LPM-2485 [M]	Holiday for Percussion	1962	7.50	15.00	30.00
❑ LSA-2485 [S]	Holiday for Percussion	1962	10.00	20.00	40.00
❑ LSP-2613 [S]	Supercussion	1963	10.00	20.00	40.00
❑ LPM-2738 [M]	Politely Percussive	1963	7.50	15.00	30.00
❑ LSP-2738 [S]	Politely Percussive	1963	10.00	20.00	40.00
❑ LPM-2806 [M]	Dick Schory on Tour	1964	5.00	10.00	20.00
❑ LSP-2806 [S]	Dick Schory on Tour	1964	6.25	12.50	25.00
❑ LPM-2926 [M]	The Happy Hits	1964	5.00	10.00	20.00
❑ LSP-2926 [S]	The Happy Hits	1964	6.25	12.50	25.00

SCHULLER, GUNTHER
ATLANTIC
| ❑ 1368 [M] | Jazz Abstractions | 1961 | 5.00 | 10.00 | 20.00 |

—*Multicolor label, white "fan" logo at right*

| ❑ SD 1368 [S] | Jazz Abstractions | 1961 | 6.25 | 12.50 | 25.00 |

—*Multicolor label, white "fan" logo at right*

SCHUMANN, WALTER
CAPITOL
❑ H 297 [10]	The Voices of Walter Schumann	195?	10.00	20.00	40.00
❑ T 297 [M]	The Voices of Walter Schumann	1955	6.25	12.50	25.00
❑ H 9016 [10]	Christmas in the Air!	1951	10.00	20.00	40.00

—*Original issue with purple label*

| ❑ L 9016 [10] | Christmas in the Air! | 1952? | 8.75 | 17.50 | 35.00 |

—*Reissue with red label and new prefix*

RCA VICTOR
| ❑ LPM-1025 [M] | Exploring the Unknown | 1955 | 12.50 | 25.00 | 50.00 |
| ❑ LPM-1141 [M] | The Voices of Christmas | 1955 | 5.00 | 10.00 | 20.00 |

—*Original cover has all-yellow lettering on front cover and eight LP/EP covers on back*

❑ LPM-1465 [M]	Scrapbook: The Voices of Walter Schumann	1957	5.00	10.00	20.00
❑ LPM-1477 [M]	When We Were Young	1957	5.00	10.00	20.00
❑ LSP-1558 [S]	Walter Schumann Presents the Voices	1958	5.00	10.00	20.00

SCHUUR, DIANE
MUSIC IS MEDICINE
| ❑ 9057 | Pilot of My Destiny | 1982 | 5.00 | 10.00 | 20.00 |

SCHWARTZ, THORNEL
ARGO
| ❑ LP-704 [M] | Soul Cookin' | 1962 | 6.25 | 12.50 | 25.00 |
| ❑ LPS-704 [S] | Soul Cookin' | 1962 | 7.50 | 15.00 | 30.00 |

SCIANNI, JOSEPH
SAVOY
| ❑ MG-12185 [M] | New Concepts | 1965 | 7.50 | 15.00 | 30.00 |

SCOBEY, BOB
AMERICAN RECORDING SOCIETY
| ❑ G-408 [M] | Bob Scobey's Frisco Band | 1956 | 10.00 | 20.00 | 40.00 |
DOWN HOME
| ❑ MGD-1 [M] | Bob Scobey's Frisco Band with Clancy Hayes | 1954 | 12.50 | 25.00 | 50.00 |
GOOD TIME JAZZ
❑ L-22 [10]	Bob Scobey's Frisco Band	1954	12.50	25.00	50.00
❑ L-12006 [M]	Bob Scobey's Frisco Band with Clancy Hayes	1955	10.00	20.00	40.00
❑ L-12009 [M]	Scobey and Clancy	1955	10.00	20.00	40.00
❑ L-12023 [M]	Direct from San Francisco	1955	10.00	20.00	40.00
❑ L-12032 [M]	Bob Scobey's Frisco Band, Volume 1	1957	10.00	20.00	40.00
❑ L-12033 [M]	Bob Scobey's Frisco Band, Volume 2	1957	10.00	20.00	40.00
RCA VICTOR
❑ LPM-1344 [M]	Beauty and the Beat	1957	10.00	20.00	40.00
❑ LPM-1448 [M]	Swingin' on the Golden Gate	1957	10.00	20.00	40.00
❑ LPM-1567 [M]	Between 18th and 19th on Any Street	1957	10.00	20.00	40.00
❑ LPM-1700 [M]	College Classics	1958	10.00	20.00	40.00
❑ LPM-1889 [M]	Something Is Always Happening on the River	1958	10.00	20.00	40.00
❑ LPM-2086 [M]	Rompin' and Stompin'	1959	7.50	15.00	30.00
❑ LSP-2086 [S]	Rompin' and Stompin'	1959	10.00	20.00	40.00
VERVE
❑ MGV-1001 [M]	Bob Scobey's Band	1956	10.00	20.00	40.00
❑ V-1001 [M]	Bob Scobey's Band	1961	5.00	10.00	20.00
❑ MGV-1009 [M]	Music from Bourbon Street	1956	10.00	20.00	40.00
❑ V-1009 [M]	Music from Bourbon Street	1961	5.00	10.00	20.00
❑ MGV-1011 [M]	The San Francisco Jazz of Bob Scobey	1957	10.00	20.00	40.00
❑ V-1011 [M]	The San Francisco Jazz of Bob Scobey	1961	5.00	10.00	20.00

SCOOBY DOO
ZEPHYR
| ❑ ZMP-12002 [M] | Jerry Leiber Presents Scooby Doo | 1959 | 12.50 | 25.00 | 50.00 |

Number	Title (A Side/B Side)	Yr	VG	VG+	NM

SCORPION
TOWER
| ☐ ST 5171 | Scorpion | 1969 | 12.50 | 25.00 | 50.00 |

SCORPIONS
BILLINGSGATE
| ☐ 1004 | Lonesome Crow | 1974 | 7.50 | 15.00 | 30.00 |
MERCURY
☐ SRM-1-3795	Lovedrive	1979	2.50	5.00	10.00
☐ SRM-1-3825	Animal Magnetism	1980	2.50	5.00	10.00
☐ SRM-1-4039	Blackout	1982	2.50	5.00	10.00
☐ 814981-1	Love at First Sting	1984	2.50	5.00	10.00
—With man and woman on cover					
☐ 818885-1	Blackout	198?	2.00	4.00	8.00
—Reissue of 4039					
☐ 822038-1	Love at First Sting	1984	3.00	6.00	12.00
—Reissue with band on cover					
☐ 822555-1	Lovedrive	198?	2.00	4.00	8.00
—Reissue of 3795					
☐ 822556-1	Animal Magnetism	198?	2.00	4.00	8.00
—Reissue of 3825					
☐ 824344-1 [(2)]	World Wide Live	1985	3.00	6.00	12.00
☐ 832963-1	Savage Amusement	1988	2.50	5.00	10.00
☐ 842002-1	Best of Rockers 'N' Ballads	1989	2.50	5.00	10.00
☐ 846908-1	Crazy World	1990	3.75	7.50	15.00
RCA VICTOR
☐ AFL1-2628	Taken by Force	1978	3.00	6.00	12.00
☐ CPL2-3039 [(2)]	Toyko Tapes	1978	3.75	7.50	15.00
☐ AFL1-3516	Best of Scorpions	1979	2.50	5.00	10.00
☐ AYL1-3659	Virgin Killer	1980	2.00	4.00	8.00
—"Best Buy Series" reissue					
☐ AFL1-4025	Fly to the Rainbow	1977	2.50	5.00	10.00
—Reissue with new prefix					
☐ PPL1-4025	Fly to the Rainbow	1975	3.00	6.00	12.00
☐ AFL1-4128	In Trance	1977	2.50	5.00	10.00
—Reissue with new prefix					
☐ PPL1-4128	In Trance	1976	3.00	6.00	12.00
☐ PPL1-4225	Virgin Killer	1977	3.00	6.00	12.00
☐ AYL1-4657	In Trance	1983	2.00	4.00	8.00
—"Best Buy Series" reissue					
☐ AYL1-5057	Fly to the Rainbow	1984	2.00	4.00	8.00
—"Best Buy Series" reissue					
☐ AFL1-5085	Best of Scorpions, Vol. 2	1984	2.50	5.00	10.00

SCOT, PATRICIA
ABC-PARAMOUNT
| ☐ 301 [M] | Once Around the Clock | 1959 | 5.00 | 10.00 | 20.00 |
| ☐ S-301 [S] | Once Around the Clock | 1959 | 6.25 | 12.50 | 25.00 |

SCOTT, BOBBY
ABC-PARAMOUNT
| ☐ ABC-102 [M] | Scott Free | 1956 | 12.50 | 25.00 | 50.00 |
| ☐ ABC-148 [M] | Bobby Scott and Two Horns | 1957 | 12.50 | 25.00 | 50.00 |
ATLANTIC
☐ 1341 [M]	The Compleat Musician	1960	5.00	10.00	20.00
—Multicolor label, white "fan" logo at right					
☐ SD 1341 [S]	The Compleat Musician	1960	6.25	12.50	25.00
—Multicolor label, white "fan" logo at right					
☐ 1355 [M]	A Taste of Honey	1960	5.00	10.00	20.00
—Multicolor label, white "fan" logo at right					
☐ SD 1355 [S]	A Taste of Honey	1960	6.25	12.50	25.00
—Multicolor label, white "fan" logo at right					
BETHLEHEM
☐ BCP-8 [M]	The Compositions of Bobby Scott	1957	12.50	25.00	50.00
☐ BCP-1004 [10]	Great Scott	1954	30.00	60.00	120.00
☐ BCP-1009 [10]	The Compositions of Bobby Scott, Volume 1	1954	25.00	50.00	100.00
☐ BCP-1029 [10]	The Compositions of Bobby Scott, Volume 2	1955	25.00	50.00	100.00
MERCURY
☐ MG-20701 [M]	Joyful Noises	1962	5.00	10.00	20.00
☐ MG-20767 [M]	When the Feeling Hits You	1963	5.00	10.00	20.00
☐ MG-20854 [M]	108 Pounds of Heartache	1963	5.00	10.00	20.00
☐ MG-20995 [M]	I Had a Ball	1964	5.00	10.00	20.00
☐ SR-60701 [S]	Joyful Noises	1962	6.25	12.50	25.00
☐ SR-60767 [S]	When the Feeling Hits You	1963	6.25	12.50	25.00
☐ SR-60854 [S]	108 Pounds of Heartache	1963	6.25	12.50	25.00
☐ SR-60995 [S]	I Had a Ball	1964	6.25	12.50	25.00
VERVE
☐ MGV-2106 [M]	Bobby Scott Sings the Best of Lerner and Loewe	1958	12.50	25.00	50.00
☐ V-2106 [M]	Bobby Scott Sings the Best of Lerner and Loewe	1961	6.25	12.50	25.00
☐ V6-2106 [S]	Bobby Scott Sings the Best of Lerner and Loewe	1961	5.00	10.00	20.00
☐ MGVS-6030 [S]	Bobby Scott Sings the Best of Lerner and Loewe	1960	10.00	20.00	40.00
☐ MGVS-6031 [S]	Serenate — Bobby Scott, Pianist	1960	10.00	20.00	40.00
☐ MGVS-6065 [S]	Bobby Scott Plays the Music of Leonard Bernstein	1960	10.00	20.00	40.00
☐ MGV-8297 [M]	Serenate — Bobby Scott, Pianist	1959	12.50	25.00	50.00
☐ V-8297 [M]	Serenate — Bobby Scott, Pianist	1961	6.25	12.50	25.00
☐ V6-8297 [S]	Serenate — Bobby Scott, Pianist	1961	5.00	10.00	20.00
☐ MGV-8326 [M]	Bobby Scott Plays the Music of Leonard Bernstein	1959	12.50	25.00	50.00
☐ V-8326 [M]	Bobby Scott Plays the Music of Leonard Bernstein	1961	6.25	12.50	25.00
☐ V6-8326 [S]	Bobby Scott Plays the Music of Leonard Bernstein	1961	5.00	10.00	20.00

SCOTT, CALVIN
STAX
| ☐ STS-2046 | I'm Not Blind... I Just Can't See | 1972 | 20.00 | 40.00 | 80.00 |

SCOTT, CLIFFORD
WORLD PACIFIC
☐ ST-1811 [S]	The Big Ones	1964	7.50	15.00	30.00
—Black vinyl					
☐ ST-1811 [S]	The Big Ones	1964	20.00	40.00	80.00
—Green vinyl					
☐ WP-1811 [M]	The Big Ones	1964	5.00	10.00	20.00
—Black vinyl					
☐ WP-1811 [M]	The Big Ones	1964	15.00	30.00	60.00
—Green vinyl					
☐ ST-1825 [S]	Lavender Sax	1964	10.00	20.00	40.00
☐ WP-1825 [M]	Lavender Sax	1964	7.50	15.00	30.00

SCOTT, CLIFFORD, AND LES McCANN
PACIFIC JAZZ
☐ PJ-66 [M]	Out Front	1963	5.00	10.00	20.00
—Black vinyl					
☐ PJ-66 [M]	Out Front	1963	10.00	20.00	40.00
—Colored vinyl					
☐ ST-66 [S]	Out Front	1963	6.25	12.50	25.00
—Black vinyl					
☐ ST-66 [S]	Out Front	1963	12.50	25.00	50.00
—Colored vinyl					

SCOTT, FREDDIE
COLPIX
☐ CP-461 [M]	Freddie Scott Sings and Sings and Sings	1964	15.00	30.00	60.00
—Gold label					
☐ CP-461 [M]	Freddie Scott Sings and Sings and Sings	1965	10.00	20.00	40.00
—Blue label					
☐ SCP-461 [R]	Freddie Scott Sings and Sings and Sings	1965	7.50	1.00	30.00
—Blue label					
☐ SCP-461 [S]	Freddie Scott Sings and Sings and Sings	1964	30.00	60.00	120.00
—Gold label					
COLUMBIA
☐ CL 2258 [M]	Everything I Have Is Yours	1964	5.00	10.00	20.00
☐ CL 2660 [M]	Lonely Man	1967	5.00	10.00	20.00
☐ CS 9058 [S]	Everything I Have Is Yours	1964	6.25	12.50	25.00
☐ CS 9460 [S]	Lonely Man	1967	6.25	12.50	25.00
PROBE
| ☐ CPLP-4517 | I Shall Be Released | 1970 | 6.25 | 12.50 | 25.00 |
SHOUT
| ☐ SLP-501 [M] | Are You Lonely for Me | 1967 | 5.00 | 10.00 | 20.00 |
| ☐ SLPS-501 [S] | Are You Lonely for Me | 1967 | 6.25 | 12.50 | 25.00 |

SCOTT, HAZEL
CAPITOL
| ☐ H 364 [10] | Late Show | 1953 | 20.00 | 40.00 | 80.00 |
COLUMBIA
| ☐ CL 6090 [10] | Great Scott | 1950 | 20.00 | 40.00 | 80.00 |
CORAL
| ☐ CRL 56057 [10] | Hazel Scott | 1952 | 20.00 | 40.00 | 80.00 |
DEBUT
| ☐ DLP-16 [10] | Relaxed Piano Moods | 1955 | 50.00 | 100.00 | 200.00 |
DECCA
| ☐ DL 5130 [10] | Swinging the Classics | 1950 | 20.00 | 40.00 | 80.00 |
| ☐ DL 8474 [M] | 'Round Midnight | 1957 | 10.00 | 20.00 | 40.00 |

SCOTT, JACK
CAPITOL
☐ ST 2035 [S]	Burning Bridges	1964	37.50	75.00	150.00
☐ ST-8-2035	Burning Bridges	196?	50.00	100.00	200.00
—Capitol Record Club edition					
☐ T 2035 [M]	Burning Bridges	1964	20.00	40.00	80.00
CARLTON
☐ LP-12-107 [M]	Jack Scott	1959	37.50	75.00	150.00
☐ STLP-12-107 [S]	Jack Scott	1959	50.00	100.00	200.00
—With "Stereo" printed across the top					
☐ STLP-12-107 [S]	Jack Scott	1959	75.00	150.00	300.00
—With "Stereo" in felt letters horizontally along the top of cover					
☐ STLP-12-107 [S]	Jack Scott	1959	100.00	200.00	400.00
—With "Stereo" in felt letters vertically along the left of cover					
☐ LP-12-122 [M]	What Am I Living For	1959	30.00	60.00	120.00
☐ STLP-12-122 [S]	What Am I Living For	1959	80.00	160.00	320.00
JADE
| ☐ J33-113 | Jack Is Back | 198? | 3.75 | 7.50 | 15.00 |
| ☐ J33-114 | The Way I Rock | 198? | 3.75 | 7.50 | 15.00 |
PONIE
| ☐ 563 | Jack Scott | 1974 | 3.75 | 7.50 | 15.00 |
| ☐ 7055 | Jack Scott | 1977 | 3.75 | 7.50 | 15.00 |
TOP RANK
☐ RM-319 [M]	I Remember Hank Williams	1960	37.50	75.00	150.00
☐ RM-326 [M]	What in the World's Come Over You	1960	37.50	75.00	150.00
☐ RM-348 [M]	The Spirit Moves Me	1961	37.50	75.00	150.00
☐ SM-619 [S]	I Remember Hank Williams	1960	62.50	125.00	250.00
☐ SM-626 [S]	What in the World's Come Over You	1960	62.50	125.00	250.00
☐ SM-648 [S]	The Spirit Moves Me	1961	62.50	125.00	250.00

SCOTT, JIMMY
SAVOY
☐ MG-12027 [M]	Very Truly Yours	1955	15.00	30.00	60.00
☐ MG-12150 [M]	The Fabulous Little Jimmy Scott	1959	10.00	20.00	40.00
☐ MG-12181 [M]	If You Only Knew	1963	10.00	20.00	40.00
TANGERINE
| ☐ TRCS-1501 [S] | Falling in Love Is Wonderful | 1963 | 62.50 | 125.00 | 250.00 |

SCOTT, LINDA
CANADIAN AMERICAN
| ☐ CALP-1005 [M] | Starlight, Starbright | 1961 | 25.00 | 50.00 | 100.00 |
| ☐ SCALP-1005 [S] | Starlight, Starbright | 1961 | 37.50 | 75.00 | 150.00 |

Number	Title (A Side/B Side)	Yr	VG	VG+	NM
❏ CALP-1007 [M]	Great Scott!! Her Greatest Hits	1962	25.00	50.00	100.00
❏ SCALP-1007 [S]	Great Scott!! Her Greatest Hits	1962	37.50	75.00	150.00
CONGRESS					
❏ CGL-3001 [M]	Linda	1962	10.00	20.00	40.00
❏ CGS-3001 [S]	Linda	1962	12.50	25.00	50.00
KAPP					
❏ KL-1424 [M]	Hey, Look at Me Now	1965	10.00	20.00	40.00
❏ KS-3424 [S]	Hey, Look at Me Now	1965	12.50	25.00	50.00

SCOTT, LIZABETH
VIK

❏ LX-1130 [M]	Lizabeth	1958	15.00	30.00	60.00

SCOTT, PEGGY, AND JO JO BENSON
SSS INTERNATIONAL

❏ 1	Soulshake	1968	6.25	12.50	25.00
❏ 2	Lover's Heaven	1969	6.25	12.50	25.00

SCOTT, SHIRLEY
IMPULSE!

❏ A-51 [M]	For Members Only	1963	5.00	10.00	20.00
❏ AS-51 [S]	For Members Only	1963	6.25	12.50	25.00
❏ A-67 [M]	Great Scott!	1964	5.00	10.00	20.00
❏ AS-67 [S]	Great Scott!	1964	6.25	12.50	25.00
❏ A-73 [M]	Everybody Loves a Lover	1964	5.00	10.00	20.00
❏ AS-73 [S]	Everybody Loves a Lover	1964	6.25	12.50	25.00
❏ A-81 [M]	Queen of the Organ	1965	5.00	10.00	20.00
❏ AS-81 [S]	Queen of the Organ	1965	6.25	12.50	25.00
❏ A-93 [M]	Latin Shadows	1965	5.00	10.00	20.00
❏ AS-93 [S]	Latin Shadows	1965	6.25	12.50	25.00
❏ A-9109 [M]	On a Clear Day	1967	6.25	12.50	25.00
❏ AS-9109 [S]	On a Clear Day	1967	5.00	10.00	20.00
❏ A-9119 [M]	Shirley Scott Plays the Big Bands	1966	5.00	10.00	20.00
❏ AS-9119 [S]	Shirley Scott Plays the Big Bands	1966	6.25	12.50	25.00
❏ A-9141 [M]	Girl Talk	1967	7.50	15.00	30.00
❏ AS-9141 [S]	Girl Talk	1967	5.00	10.00	20.00
MOODSVILLE					
❏ MVLP-5 [M]	Shirley Scott Trio	1960	12.50	25.00	50.00
—Green label					
❏ MVLP-5 [M]	Shirley Scott Trio	1965	6.25	12.50	25.00
—Blue label, trident logo at right					
❏ MVLP-19 [M]	Like Cozy	1961	12.50	25.00	50.00
—Green label					
❏ MVLP-19 [M]	Like Cozy	1965	6.25	12.50	25.00
—Blue label, trident logo at right					
❏ MVST-19 [S]	Like Cozy	1961	12.50	25.00	50.00
—Green label					
❏ MVST-19 [S]	Like Cozy	1965	6.25	12.50	25.00
—Blue label, trident logo at right					
PRESTIGE					
❏ PRLP-7143 [M]	Great Scott!	1958	12.50	25.00	50.00
❏ PRLP-7155 [M]	Scottie	1959	12.50	25.00	50.00
❏ PRLP-7163 [M]	Scottie Plays Duke	1959	12.50	25.00	50.00
❏ PRLP-7173 [M]	Soul Searching	1960	12.50	25.00	50.00
❏ PRLP-7182 [M]	Mucho, Mucho	1960	12.50	25.00	50.00
❏ PRLP-7195 [M]	Shirley's Sounds	1961	10.00	20.00	40.00
❏ PRST-7195 [S]	Shirley's Sounds	1961	12.50	25.00	50.00
❏ PRLP-7205 [M]	Hip Soul	1961	10.00	20.00	40.00
—Yellow label, Bergenfield, NJ address					
❏ PRLP-7205 [M]	Hip Soul	1965	5.00	10.00	20.00
—Blue label, trident logo at right					
❏ PRLP-7226 [M]	Hip Twist	1962	10.00	20.00	40.00
—Yellow label, Bergenfield, NJ address					
❏ PRLP-7226 [M]	Hip Twist	1965	5.00	10.00	20.00
—Blue label, trident logo at right					
❏ PRST-7226 [S]	Hip Twist	1962	12.50	25.00	50.00
—Silver label, Bergenfield, NJ address					
❏ PRST-7226 [S]	Hip Twist	1965	6.25	12.50	25.00
—Blue label, trident logo at right					
❏ PRLP-7240 [M]	Shirley Scott Plays Horace Silver	1962	10.00	20.00	40.00
❏ PRST-7240 [S]	Shirley Scott Plays Horace Silver	1962	12.50	25.00	50.00
❏ PRLP-7262 [M]	Happy Talk	1963	10.00	20.00	40.00
❏ PRST-7262 [S]	Happy Talk	1963	12.50	25.00	50.00
❏ PRLP-7267 [M]	The Soul Is Willing	1963	10.00	20.00	40.00
—Yellow label, Bergenfield, NJ address					
❏ PRLP-7267 [M]	The Soul Is Willing	1965	5.00	10.00	20.00
—Blue label, trident logo at right					
❏ PRST-7267 [S]	The Soul Is Willing	1963	12.50	25.00	50.00
—Silver label, Bergenfield, NJ address					
❏ PRST-7267 [S]	The Soul Is Willing	1965	6.25	12.50	25.00
—Blue label, trident logo at right					
❏ PRLP-7283 [M]	Satin Doll	1963	10.00	20.00	40.00
❏ PRST-7283 [S]	Satin Doll	1963	12.50	25.00	50.00
❏ PRLP-7305 [M]	Drag 'Em Out	1964	10.00	20.00	40.00
❏ PRST-7305 [S]	Drag 'Em Out	1964	12.50	25.00	50.00
❏ PRLP-7312 [M]	Soul Shoutin'	1964	10.00	20.00	40.00
—Yellow label, Bergenfield, NJ address					
❏ PRLP-7312 [M]	Soul Shoutin'	1965	5.00	10.00	20.00
—Blue label, trident logo at right					
❏ PRST-7312 [S]	Soul Shoutin'	1964	12.50	25.00	50.00
—Silver label, Bergenfield, NJ address					
❏ PRST-7312 [S]	Soul Shoutin'	1965	6.25	12.50	25.00
—Blue label, trident logo at right					
❏ PRLP-7328 [M]	Travelin' Light	1964	6.25	12.50	25.00
❏ PRST-7328 [S]	Travelin' Light	1964	7.50	15.00	30.00
❏ PRLP-7338 [M]	Blue Flames	1965	6.25	12.50	25.00
❏ PRST-7338 [S]	Blue Flames	1965	7.50	15.00	30.00
❏ PRLP-7360 [M]	Sweet Soul	1965	6.25	12.50	25.00
❏ PRST-7360 [S]	Sweet Soul	1965	7.50	15.00	30.00
❏ PRLP-7376 [M]	Blue Seven	1965	6.25	12.50	25.00
❏ PRST-7376 [S]	Blue Seven	1965	7.50	15.00	30.00
❏ PRLP-7392 [M]	Soul Sisters	1965	6.25	12.50	25.00
❏ PRST-7392 [S]	Soul Sisters	1965	7.50	15.00	30.00

Number	Title (A Side/B Side)	Yr	VG	VG+	NM
❏ PRLP-7424 [M]	Workin'	1966	6.25	12.50	25.00
❏ PRST-7424 [M]	Workin'	1966	7.50	15.00	30.00
❏ PRLP-7440 [M]	Now's the Time	1967	7.50	15.00	30.00
❏ PRST-7440 [S]	Now's the Time	1967	6.25	12.50	25.00
❏ PRST-7456 [S]	Stompin'	1968	6.25	12.50	25.00
❏ PRST-7707 [S]	The Best of Shirley Scott and Stanley Turrentine	1969	5.00	10.00	20.00
❏ PRST-7773	The Best for Beautiful People	1970	5.00	10.00	20.00
STRATA-EAST					
❏ SES-7430	One for Me	197?	5.00	10.00	20.00

SCOTT, SHIRLEY, AND CLARK TERRY
IMPULSE!

❏ A-9133 [M]	Soul Duo	1967	6.25	12.50	25.00
❏ AS-9133 [S]	Soul Duo	1967	5.00	10.00	20.00

SCOTT, TOM
ABC IMPULSE!

❏ A-9163 [M]	Honeysuckle Breeze	1967	10.00	20.00	40.00
❏ AS-9163 [S]	Honeysuckle Breeze	1967	6.25	12.50	25.00
❏ AS-9171	Rural Still Life	1968	6.25	12.50	25.00
FLYING DUTCHMAN					
❏ 106	Hair	1969	5.00	10.00	20.00
❏ 114	Paint Your Wagon	1970	5.00	10.00	20.00

SCOTT, TONY
ABC-PARAMOUNT

❏ ABC-235 [M]	South Pacific	1958	7.50	15.00	30.00
❏ ABCS-235 [S]	South Pacific	1958	6.25	12.50	25.00
BRUNSWICK					
❏ BL 54021 [M]	Tony Scott In Hi-Fi	1957	20.00	40.00	80.00
❏ BL 54056 [M]	Tony Scott Quartet	1957	30.00	60.00	120.00
❏ BL 58040 [10]	Music After Midnight	1953	30.00	60.00	120.00
❏ BL 58056 [10]	Tony Scott Quartet	1954	30.00	60.00	120.00
CORAL					
❏ CRL 57239 [M]	52nd Street Scene	1958	12.50	25.00	50.00
❏ CRL 757239 [S]	52nd Street Scene	1958	10.00	20.00	40.00
PERFECT					
❏ PL-12010 [M]	My Kind of Jazz	1960	10.00	20.00	40.00
❏ PL-14010 [S]	My Kind of Jazz	1960	12.50	25.00	50.00
RCA VICTOR					
❏ LJM-1022 [M]	Scott's Fling	1955	20.00	40.00	80.00
❏ LPM-1268 [M]	Both Sides of Tony Scott	1956	20.00	40.00	80.00
❏ LPM-1353 [M]	A Touch of Tony Scott	1956	20.00	40.00	80.00
❏ LPM-1452 [M]	The Complete Tony Scott	1957	20.00	40.00	80.00
SEECO					
❏ SLP-425 [M]	The Modern Art of Jazz	1959	7.50	15.00	30.00
❏ SLP-428 [M]	Hi-Fi Land of Jazz	1959	7.50	15.00	30.00
❏ SLP-4250 [S]	The Modern Art of Jazz	1959	10.00	20.00	40.00
❏ SLP-4280 [S]	Hi-Fi Land of Jazz	1959	10.00	20.00	40.00
SIGNATURE					
❏ SM-6001 [M]	Gypsy	1959	12.50	25.00	50.00
❏ SS-6001 [S]	Gypsy	1959	10.00	20.00	40.00
VERVE					
❏ V6-8634 [S]	Music for Zen Meditation	1965	5.00	10.00	20.00
❏ V-8742 [M]	Music for Yoga Meditation and Other Joys	1967	5.00	10.00	20.00

SCOTT, TONY, AND TERRY GIBBS
BRUNSWICK

❏ BL 58058 [10]	Hi-Fi Jazz	1955	30.00	60.00	120.00

SCOTT, TONY, AND JIMMY KNEPPER
CARLTON

❏ LP-12-113 [M]	Free Blown Jazz	1959	12.50	25.00	50.00
❏ ST-12-113 [S]	Free Blown Jazz	1959	12.50	25.00	50.00

SCOTT, TONY, AND MAT MATTHEWS
BRUNSWICK

❏ BL 58057 [10]	Jazz for GI's	1954	30.00	60.00	120.00

SCOTT, WALTER
MUSICLAND U.S.A.

❏ LP-3502 [M]	Great Scott	1967	5.00	10.00	20.00
❏ SLP-3502 [S]	Great Scott	1967	6.25	12.50	25.00
WHITE WHALE					
❏ WWS-7131	Walter Scott	1970	5.00	10.00	20.00

SCOTT-HERON, GIL
FLYING DUTCHMAN

❏ BLD1-0613	The Revolution Will Not Be Televised	1974	5.00	10.00	20.00
❏ FD-10143	Pieces of a Man	1971	5.00	10.00	20.00
❏ FD-10153	Free Will	1972	5.00	10.00	20.00
STRATA-EAST					
❏ SES-19742	Winter in America	1974	6.25	12.50	25.00

SCOTTSVILLE SQUIRREL BARKERS, THE
Chris Hillman, later of THE BYRDS, makes his first appearance on record here.
CROWN

❏ CST-346 [S]	Bluegrass Favorites	1963	15.00	30.00	60.00
❏ CLP-5346 [M]	Bluegrass Favorites	1963	12.50	25.00	50.00

SCRAMBLERS, THE
CROWN

❏ CST-384 [S]	Cycle Psychos	1964	6.25	12.50	25.00
❏ CLP-5384 [M]	Cycle Psychos	1964	5.00	10.00	20.00
DIPLOMAT					
❏ D-2316 [M]	Motorcycle Scramble	1964	5.00	10.00	20.00
❏ DS-2316 [S]	Motorcycle Scramble	1964	6.25	12.50	25.00
WYNCOTE					
❏ SW-9048 [S]	Little Honda	1964	6.25	12.50	25.00
❏ W-9048 [M]	Little Honda	1964	5.00	10.00	20.00

Number	Title (A Side/B Side)	Yr	VG	VG+	NM
SCREAMING GYPSY BANDITS					
BAR-B-Q					
❑ 004	The Dancer Inside You	1974	20.00	40.00	80.00
❑ 22185	In the Eye	1973	20.00	40.00	80.00
SCREAMING TREES					
Also see MARK LANEGAN.					
EPIC					
❑ E 46800	Uncle Anesthesia	1991	3.00	6.00	12.00
❑ E 48996	Sweet Oblivion	1992	3.00	6.00	12.00
SST					
❑ 105 [EP]	Other Worlds	1986	2.50	5.00	10.00
—Reissue of Velvetone cassette-only release					
❑ 132	Even If and Especially When	1987	2.50	5.00	10.00
❑ 188	Invisible Lantern	1988	2.50	5.00	10.00
❑ 248	Buzz Factory	1989	2.50	5.00	10.00
❑ 260 [(2)]	Anthology	1991	3.00	6.00	12.00
VELVETONE					
❑ 86002	Clairvoyance	1986	10.00	20.00	40.00
SEA, JOHNNY					
HILLTOP					
❑ JM-6018	Everybody's Favorite	196?	3.00	6.00	12.00
PHILIPS					
❑ PHM 200139 [M]	World of a Country Boy	1964	5.00	10.00	20.00
❑ PHM 200194 [M]	Live at the Bitter End	1965	5.00	10.00	20.00
❑ PHS 600139 [S]	World of a Country Boy	1964	6.25	12.50	25.00
❑ PHS 600194 [S]	Live at the Bitter End	1965	6.25	12.50	25.00
WARNER BROS.					
❑ W 1659 [M]	Day for Decision	1966	3.75	7.50	15.00
❑ WS 1659 [S]	Day for Decision	1966	5.00	10.00	20.00
SEALS, DAN					
CAPITOL					
❑ 1P 7999	On Arrival	1990	5.00	10.00	20.00
—Only available on vinyl from Columbia House					
❑ C1-46976	Rage On	1988	2.00	4.00	8.00
❑ CLT-48308	The Best	1988	2.00	4.00	8.00
EMI AMERICA					
❑ ST-17131	San Antone	1984	2.00	4.00	8.00
❑ ST-17166	Won't Be Blue Anymore	1985	2.00	4.00	8.00
❑ PW-17231	On the Front Line	1986	2.00	4.00	8.00
LIBERTY					
❑ LT-51149	Rebel Heart	1983	2.50	5.00	10.00
SEALS AND CROFTS					
K-TEL					
❑ NU 9610	Collection: 16 of Their Greatest Hits	1979	3.00	6.00	12.00
NAUTILUS					
❑ NR-10	Summer Breeze	1980	7.50	15.00	30.00
—Audiophile vinyl					
T-A					
❑ 5001	Seals and Crofts	1969	6.25	12.50	25.00
❑ 5004	Down Home	1970	6.25	12.50	25.00
WARNER BROS.					
❑ BS 2568	Year of Sunday	1971	3.00	6.00	12.00
—Green "WB" label					
❑ BS 2568	Year of Sunday	1973	2.50	5.00	10.00
—"Burbank" palm-tree label					
❑ BS 2629	Summer Breeze	1972	3.00	6.00	12.00
—Green "WB" label					
❑ BS 2629	Summer Breeze	1973	2.50	5.00	10.00
—"Burbank" palm-tree label					
❑ BS 2629	Summer Breeze	1979	2.00	4.00	8.00
—White or tan label					
❑ BS4 2629 [Q]	Summer Breeze	1974	5.00	10.00	20.00
❑ BS 2699	Diamond Girl	1973	3.00	6.00	12.00
—"Burbank" palm-tree label					
❑ BS 2699	Diamond Girl	1979	2.00	4.00	8.00
—White or tan label					
❑ BS4 2699 [Q]	Diamond Girl	1974	5.00	10.00	20.00
❑ BS 2761	Unborn Child	1974	3.00	6.00	12.00
❑ BS4 2761 [Q]	Unborn Child	1974	5.00	10.00	20.00
❑ 2WS 2809 [(2)]	Seals & Crofts I and II	1974	3.75	7.50	15.00
—Reissue of the two T-A LPs in one package					
❑ BS 2848	I'll Play for You	1975	2.50	5.00	10.00
❑ BS4 2848 [Q]	I'll Play for You	1975	5.00	10.00	20.00
❑ BS 2886	Greatest Hits	1975	2.50	5.00	10.00
❑ BS 2907	Get Closer	1976	2.50	5.00	10.00
❑ BS 2976	Sudan Village	1976	2.50	5.00	10.00
❑ BSK 3109	Greatest Hits	1977	2.00	4.00	8.00
—Reissue; any label variation					
❑ BSK 3165	Takin' It Easy	1978	2.50	5.00	10.00
❑ BSK 3365	The Longest Road	1980	2.50	5.00	10.00
SEARCH PARTY					
CENTURY					
❑ 32013	Montgomery Chapel	1969	500.00	1000.	2000.
SEARCHERS, THE					
KAPP					
❑ KL-1363 [M]	Meet the Searchers	1964	6.25	12.50	25.00
—With black label					
❑ KL-1363 [M]	Meet the Searchers	1964	10.00	20.00	40.00
—With black and blue label					
❑ KL-1409 [M]	This Is Us	1964	6.25	12.50	25.00
—Version 2: With sticker on front cover referring to "Love Potion No. 9"					
❑ KL-1409 [M]	This Is Us	1964	6.25	12.50	25.00
—Version 1: No sticker on front cover					
❑ KL-1412 [M]	The New Searchers LP	1965	6.25	12.50	25.00
❑ KL-1449 [M]	The Searchers No. 4	1965	6.25	12.50	25.00
❑ KL-1477 [M]	Take Me for What I'm Worth	1966	6.25	12.50	25.00

Number	Title (A Side/B Side)	Yr	VG	VG+	NM
❑ KS-3363 [S]	Meet the Searchers	1964	7.50	15.00	30.00
—With black label					
❑ KS-3363 [S]	Meet the Searchers	1964	12.50	25.00	50.00
—With black and blue label					
❑ KS-3409 [S]	This Is Us	1964	7.50	15.00	30.00
—Version 2: With sticker on front cover referring to "Love Potion No. 9"					
❑ KS-3409 [S]	This Is Us	1964	7.50	15.00	30.00
—Version 1: No sticker on front cover					
❑ KS-3412 [S]	The New Searchers LP	1965	7.50	15.00	30.00
❑ KS-3419 [S]	The Searchers No. 4	1965	7.50	15.00	30.00
❑ KS-3477 [S]	Take Me for What I'm Worth	1966	7.50	15.00	30.00
MERCURY					
❑ MG-20914 [M]	Hear! Hear!	1964	7.50	15.00	30.00
—Version 3: With "Live from the Star Club" imprinted on cover					
❑ MG-20914 [M]	Hear! Hear!	1964	10.00	20.00	40.00
—Version 2: With sticker "Live from the Star Club" on cover					
❑ MG-20914 [M]	Hear! Hear!	1964	12.50	25.00	50.00
—White label promo					
❑ MG-20914 [M]	Hear! Hear!	1964	12.50	25.00	50.00
—Version 1: With only the title on the front cover					
❑ MG-20994 [M]	The Searchers Meet the Rattles	1965	18.75	37.50	75.00
❑ SR-60914 [S]	Hear! Hear!	1964	6.25	12.50	25.00
—Version 3: With "Live from the Star Club" imprinted on cover					
❑ SR-60914 [S]	Hear! Hear!	1964	7.50	15.00	30.00
—Version 2: With sticker "Live from the Star Club" on cover					
❑ SR-60914 [S]	Hear! Hear!	1964	10.00	20.00	40.00
—Version 1: With only the title on the front cover					
❑ SR-60994 [S]	The Searchers Meet the Rattles	1965	12.50	25.00	50.00
PYE					
❑ 501	The Searchers	197?	3.75	7.50	15.00
—Reissue of Kapp hits					
❑ 508	The Searchers, Vol. 2	1976	3.75	7.50	15.00
RHINO					
❑ RNLP 162	Greatest Hits	1985	2.50	5.00	10.00
❑ R1-70162	Greatest Hits	1988	2.00	4.00	8.00
—Reissue of RNLP 162					
SIRE					
❑ SRK 3523	Love's Melodies	1981	2.50	5.00	10.00
❑ SRK 6082	The Searchers	1980	2.50	5.00	10.00
SEARS, AL					
AUDIO LAB					
❑ AL-1540 [M]	Dance Music with a Swing Beat	1959	30.00	60.00	120.00
SWINGVILLE					
❑ SVLP-2018 [M]	Swing's the Thing	1961	12.50	25.00	50.00
—Purple label					
❑ SVLP-2018 [M]	Swing's the Thing	1965	6.25	12.50	25.00
—Blue label, trident logo at right					
SEBASTIAN, JOHN					
Also see THE LOVIN' SPOONFUL.					
MGM					
❑ SE-4654	John B. Sebastian	1969	3.75	7.50	15.00
❑ SE-4720	John Sebastian Live	1970	3.75	7.50	15.00
REPRISE					
❑ MS 2036	Cheapo-Cheapo Productions Presents Real Live John Sebastian	1971	3.00	6.00	12.00
❑ MS 2041	The Four of Us	1971	3.00	6.00	12.00
❑ MS 2187	Tarzana Kid	1974	3.00	6.00	12.00
❑ MS 2249	Welcome Back	1976	3.00	6.00	12.00
❑ RS 6379	John B. Sebastian	1969	5.00	10.00	20.00
—Same album as MGM 4654, but a different mix					
RHINO					
❑ R1-70170	The Best of John Sebastian (1969-1976)	1989	3.00	6.00	12.00
SEBESKY, DON					
MOBILE FIDELITY					
❑ 1-503 [(2)]	Three Works for Jazz Soloists and Symphony Orchestra	198?	15.00	30.00	60.00
—Audiophile vinyl					
VERVE					
❑ V6-8756	Don Sebesky and the Jazz-Rock Syndrome	1968	5.00	10.00	20.00
SECOND TIME, THE					
TOWER					
❑ ST 5146	Listen to the Music	1968	5.00	10.00	20.00
SECRET OYSTER					
PETERS INT'L.					
❑ 9003	Furtive Pearl	1973	7.50	15.00	30.00
❑ 9009	Sea Son	1974	6.25	12.50	25.00
SEDAKA, NEIL					
ACCORD					
❑ SN-7152	Singer, Songwriter, Melody Maker	1981	2.50	5.00	10.00
ELEKTRA					
❑ 6E-102	A Song	1977	2.50	5.00	10.00
❑ 6E-161	All You Need Is Music	1978	2.50	5.00	10.00
❑ 6E-259	In the Pocket	1980	2.50	5.00	10.00
❑ 6E-348	Neil Sedaka Now	1981	2.50	5.00	10.00
51 WEST					
❑ Q 16003	I'm a Song	1979	3.00	6.00	12.00
INTERMEDIA					
❑ QS 5015	Superbird	1982	2.50	5.00	10.00
KIRSHNER					
❑ KES-111	Emergence	1971	3.75	7.50	15.00
❑ KES-117	Solitaire	1972	3.75	7.50	15.00
MCA					
❑ 2357	Sedaka's Back	1978	2.50	5.00	10.00
—Reissue of Rocket 463					
❑ 5466	Come See About Me	1984	2.50	5.00	10.00

S

Number	Title (A Side/B Side)	Yr	VG	VG+	NM
ORBIT					
❑ RB-17196	Bravo!	1983	2.50	5.00	10.00
PICKWICK					
❑ ACL-7006	Breaking Up Is Hard to Do	197?	2.00	4.00	8.00
POLYDOR					
❑ 831235-1	My Friend	1986	2.50	5.00	10.00
RCA CAMDEN					
❑ ACL1-7006	Breaking Up Is Hard to Do	197?	2.50	5.00	10.00
RCA SPECIAL PRODUCTS					
❑ DPL2-0149 [(2)]	Original Hits	1975	5.00	10.00	20.00
RCA VICTOR					
❑ ANL1-0879	Oh! Carol	1975	2.50	5.00	10.00
❑ AFL1-0928	Neil Sedaka Sings His Greatest Hits	1977	2.50	5.00	10.00
—Reissue with new prefix					
❑ APL1-0928	Neil Sedaka Sings His Greatest Hits	1975	3.00	6.00	12.00
—Reissue of LSP-2627					
❑ ANL1-1314	Pure Gold	1976	2.50	5.00	10.00
❑ VPL1-1540	Live in Australia	1976	3.00	6.00	12.00
❑ APL1-1789	Emergence	1976	3.00	6.00	12.00
—Reissue of Kirshner 111					
❑ APL1-1790	Solitaire	1976	3.00	6.00	12.00
—Reissue of Kirshner 117					
❑ LPM-2065 [M]	Neil Sedaka	1959	15.00	30.00	60.00
❑ LSP-2065 [S]	Neil Sedaka	1959	25.00	50.00	100.00
❑ AFL1-2254	Sedaka — The '50s and '60s	1977	2.50	5.00	10.00
❑ LPM-2317 [M]	Circulate	1960	12.50	25.00	50.00
❑ LSP-2317 [S]	Circulate	1960	15.00	30.00	60.00
❑ LPM-2421 [M]	"Little Devil" and His Other Hits	1961	12.50	25.00	50.00
❑ LSP-2421 [S]	"Little Devil" and His Other Hits	1961	15.00	30.00	60.00
❑ AFL1-2524	The Many Sides of Neil Sedaka	1978	2.50	5.00	10.00
❑ LPM-2627 [M]	Neil Sedaka Sings His Greatest Hits	1962	10.00	20.00	40.00
❑ LSP-2627 [S]	Neil Sedaka Sings His Greatest Hits	1962	12.50	25.00	50.00
—Black label, dog on top, "Living Stereo" at bottom					
❑ LSP-2627 [S]	Neil Sedaka Sings His Greatest Hits	1969	5.00	10.00	20.00
—Reissue; orange label					
❑ ANL1-3465	Neil Sedaka Sings His Greatest Hits	1979	2.00	4.00	8.00
—Reissue of AFL1-0928					
❑ R 133511	Let's Go Steady Again	1976	3.75	7.50	15.00
—RCA Record Club edition					
ROCKET					
❑ MCA-463	Sedaka's Back	1974	3.00	6.00	12.00
❑ PIG-2157	The Hungry Years	1975	3.00	6.00	12.00
❑ PIG-2195	Steppin' Out	1976	3.00	6.00	12.00
❑ PIG-2297	Neil Sedaka's Greatest Hits	1977	3.00	6.00	12.00
ROLLER SKATE					
❑ TLA-50172	Is Anybody Gonna Miss You	1982	3.75	7.50	15.00

SEDAKA, NEIL, AND THE TOKENS WITH THE COINS

Number	Title (A Side/B Side)	Yr	VG	VG+	NM
CROWN					
❑ CST-366 [R]	Neil Sedaka and the Tokens and the Coins	1963	5.00	10.00	20.00
❑ CLP-5366 [M]	Neil Sedaka and the Tokens and the Coins	1963	7.50	15.00	30.00

SEEDS, THE

Also see SKY SAXON.

Number	Title (A Side/B Side)	Yr	VG	VG+	NM
GNP CRESCENDO					
❑ GNP-2023 [M]	The Seeds	1966	15.00	30.00	60.00
❑ GNPS-2023 [S]	The Seeds	1966	10.00	20.00	40.00
❑ GNP-2033 [M]	A Web of Sound	1967	15.00	30.00	60.00
❑ GNPS-2033 [S]	A Web of Sound	1967	10.00	20.00	40.00
❑ GNP-2038 [M]	Future	1967	10.00	20.00	40.00
—Deduct 25% if two inserts are missing					
❑ GNPS-2038 [S]	Future	1967	7.50	15.00	30.00
—Deduct 25% if two inserts are missing					
❑ GNP-2040 [M]	A Full Spoon of Seedy Blues	1968	15.00	30.00	60.00
❑ GNPS-2040 [S]	A Full Spoon of Seedy Blues	1968	6.25	12.50	25.00
❑ GNPS-2043	Raw and Alive	1968	6.25	12.50	25.00
❑ GNPS-2107	Fallin' Off the Edge	1977	2.50	5.00	10.00
❑ ST-91224	A Web of Sound	1968	7.50	15.00	30.00
—Capitol Record Club edition					

SEEGER, PEGGY

Number	Title (A Side/B Side)	Yr	VG	VG+	NM
FOLK-LYRIC					
❑ FL 114 [M]	American Folksongs for Banjo	196?	7.50	15.00	30.00
❑ FL 120 [M]	Popular Ballads	196?	7.50	15.00	30.00
FOLKLORE					
❑ FRLP-14016 [M]	The Best of Peggy Seeger	196?	6.25	12.50	25.00
FOLKWAYS					
❑ FP-49 [10]	Folk Songs of Courting and Complaint	1955	25.00	50.00	100.00
❑ FP-2049 [10]	Folk Songs of Courting and Complaint	195?	20.00	40.00	80.00
❑ FC-7551 [10]	Animal Folksongs for Children	1957	25.00	50.00	100.00
❑ FW-8563 [M]	From Where I Stand	1982	2.50	5.00	10.00
PRESTIGE					
❑ PRLP-13005 [M]	The Best of Peggy Seeger	1961	7.50	15.00	30.00
❑ PRLP-13058 [M]	A Song for You and Me	1962	7.50	15.00	30.00
RIVERSIDE					
❑ RLP-12-655 [M]	Folksongs and Ballads	1958	10.00	20.00	40.00
TOPIC					
❑ 10T-9 [10]	Peggy Seeger	1956	25.00	50.00	100.00

SEEGER, PEGGY, BARBARA AND PENNY

Number	Title (A Side/B Side)	Yr	VG	VG+	NM
FOLKWAYS					
❑ FC-7553 [10]	American Folk Songs for Christmas	195?	12.50	25.00	50.00
SCHOLASTIC					
❑ SC 7553 [M]	American Folk Songs for Christmas	1966	5.00	10.00	20.00
—Reissue of Folkways material					

SEEGER, PETE

Number	Title (A Side/B Side)	Yr	VG	VG+	NM
ARAVEL					
❑ AB 1006 [M]	Live Hootenanny	1963	3.75	7.50	15.00

Number	Title (A Side/B Side)	Yr	VG	VG+	NM
ARCHIVE OF FOLK AND JAZZ					
❑ 201	Pete Seeger	1966	3.00	6.00	12.00
BROADSIDE					
❑ 502 [(2)]	Pete Seeger Sings and Answers Questions	1970	3.75	7.50	15.00
BULLDOG					
❑ BDL-2011	20 Golden Pieces of Pete Seeger	198?	2.50	5.00	10.00
CAPITOL					
❑ DW 2172 [R]	Folk Songs	1964	3.00	6.00	12.00
❑ W 2172 [M]	Folk Songs	1964	5.00	10.00	20.00
❑ DT 2718 [R]	Freight Train	1967	3.00	6.00	12.00
❑ T 2718 [M]	Freight Train	1967	5.00	10.00	20.00
COLUMBIA					
❑ CL 1668 [M]	Pete Seeger Story Songs	1961	6.25	12.50	25.00
❑ CL 1916 [M]	The Bitter and the Sweet	1962	6.25	12.50	25.00
❑ CL 1947 [M]	Children's Concert at Town Hall	1963	6.25	12.50	25.00
❑ CL 2101 [M]	We Shall Overcome	1963	3.75	7.50	15.00
❑ CL 2257 [M]	I Can See a New Day	1965	3.75	7.50	15.00
❑ CL 2334 [M]	Strangers and Cousins	1964	3.75	7.50	15.00
❑ CL 2432 [M]	God Bless the Grass	1966	3.75	7.50	15.00
❑ CL 2503 [M]	Dangerous Songs?	1966	3.75	7.50	15.00
❑ CL 2616 [M]	Pete Seeger's Greatest Hits	1967	5.00	10.00	20.00
❑ CL 2705 [M]	Waist Deep in the Big Muddy	1967	5.00	10.00	20.00
❑ CS 8468 [S]	Pete Seeger Story Songs	1961	7.50	15.00	30.00
❑ CS 8716 [S]	The Bitter and the Sweet	1962	7.50	15.00	30.00
❑ CS 8747 [S]	Children's Concert at Town Hall	1963	7.50	15.00	30.00
❑ CS 8901 [S]	We Shall Overcome	1963	5.00	10.00	20.00
❑ CS 9057 [S]	I Can See a New Day	1965	5.00	10.00	20.00
❑ CS 9134 [S]	Strangers and Cousins	1964	5.00	10.00	20.00
❑ CS 9232 [S]	God Bless the Grass	1966	5.00	10.00	20.00
❑ CS 9303 [S]	Dangerous Songs?	1966	5.00	10.00	20.00
❑ CS 9416 [S]	Pete Seeger's Greatest Hits	1967	3.75	7.50	15.00
❑ PC 9416	Pete Seeger's Greatest Hits	198?	2.00	4.00	8.00
—Reissue with new prefix					
❑ CS 9505 [S]	Waist Deep in the Big Muddy	1967	3.75	7.50	15.00
❑ CS 9717	Pete Seeger Now	1968	3.75	7.50	15.00
❑ CS 9873	Young vs. Old	1969	3.75	7.50	15.00
❑ C 30739	Rainbow Race	1971	3.00	6.00	12.00
❑ KG 31949 [(2)]	The World of Pete Seeger	1972	3.75	7.50	15.00
DISC					
❑ D-101 [M]	Sing with Seeger	1964	5.00	10.00	20.00
FOLKWAYS					
❑ FP-3 [10]	Darling Corey	1950	25.00	50.00	100.00
❑ FP-10 [10]	Lonesome Valley	195?	25.00	50.00	100.00
❑ FP-43 [10]	A Pete Seeger Sampler	195?	25.00	50.00	100.00
❑ FP-45 [10]	Goofing Off Suite	195?	25.00	50.00	100.00
❑ FP-701 [10]	American Folk Songs for Children	195?	25.00	50.00	100.00
❑ FP-710 [10]	Birds, Beasts, Bugs and Little Fishes	1954	25.00	50.00	100.00
❑ FP-911 [10]	Folk Songs of Four Continents	195?	25.00	50.00	100.00
❑ FA-2003 [10]	Darling Corey	1950	20.00	40.00	80.00
❑ FA-2010 [10]	Lonesome Valley	195?	20.00	40.00	80.00
❑ FA-2043 [10]	A Pete Seeger Sampler	1954	20.00	40.00	80.00
❑ FA-2045 [10]	Goofing Off Suite	1954	20.00	40.00	80.00
❑ FA-2175 [10]	Frontier Ballads, Volume 1	1954	20.00	40.00	80.00
❑ FA-2176 [10]	Frontier Ballads, Volume 2	1954	20.00	40.00	80.00
❑ FA-2311 [M]	Traditional Christmas Carols	1956	7.50	15.00	30.00
❑ FA-2319 [M]	American Ballads	1957	7.50	15.00	30.00
❑ FA-2320 [M]	American Favorite Ballads, Vol. 1	1957	7.50	15.00	30.00
❑ FA-2321 [M]	American Favorite Ballads, Vol. 2	1958	7.50	15.00	30.00
❑ FA-2322 [M]	American Favorite Ballads, Vol. 3	1958	7.50	15.00	30.00
❑ FA-2323 [M]	American Favorite Ballads, Vol. 4	1961	5.00	10.00	20.00
❑ FA-2412 [M]	Pete Seeger and Sonny Terry	1958	7.50	15.00	30.00
❑ FA-2439 [M]	Nonesuch	196?	5.00	10.00	20.00
❑ FA-2445 [M]	American Favorite Ballads, Vol. 5: Tunes and Songs As Sung by Pete Seeger	1962	5.00	10.00	20.00
❑ FA-2450 [M]	Highlights of Pete Seeger at the Village Gate with Memphis Slim and Willie Dixon	1960	7.50	15.00	30.00
❑ FA-2451 [M]	Pete Seeger at the Village Gate — Vol. 2	1960	7.50	15.00	30.00
❑ FA-2452 [M]	With Voices Together We Sing	1956	6.25	12.50	25.00
❑ FA-2453 [M]	Love Songs for Friends and Foes	1956	6.25	12.50	25.00
❑ FA-2454 [M]	Rainbow Quest	1960	6.25	12.50	25.00
❑ FA-2455 [M]	Sing Out with Pete!	1961	5.00	10.00	20.00
❑ FA-2456 [M]	Broadsides	1964	5.00	10.00	20.00
❑ FA-2501 [M]	Gazette, Vol. 1	1958	6.25	12.50	25.00
❑ FA-2502 [M]	Gazette, Vol. 2	1962	5.00	10.00	20.00
❑ FN-2511 [M]	Hootenanny Tonight!	195?	6.25	12.50	25.00
❑ FN-2513 [M]	Sing Out! Hootenanny	1963	5.00	10.00	20.00
❑ FS-3851 [M]	Indian Summer	1960	6.25	12.50	25.00
—With Michael Seeger					
❑ 5003 [(2)]	Frontier Ballads	1954	25.00	50.00	100.00
❑ FH-5210 [M]	Champlain Valley Songs	1960	6.25	12.50	25.00
❑ FH-5233 [M]	Songs of Struggle and Protest 1930-50	1959	6.25	12.50	25.00
❑ FH-5251 [M]	American Industrial Ballads	1956	7.50	15.00	30.00
❑ FH-5257	Fifty Sail On Newburgh Bay	1976	3.00	6.00	12.00
❑ FH-5302 [M]	Broadside Ballads, Vol. 2	1963	5.00	10.00	20.00
❑ FH-5436 [M]	Songs of the Spanish Civil War, Vol. 1	1961	5.00	10.00	20.00
❑ FH-5485 [M]	Ballads of Sacco and Vanzetti	1963	5.00	10.00	20.00
❑ FH-5595 [M]	WNEW's Story of Selma	1965	5.00	10.00	20.00
❑ FH-5702 [(2)]	Pete Seeger Sings and Answers Questions	1968	6.25	12.50	25.00
❑ FW-6843 [10]	German Folk Songs	1954	20.00	40.00	80.00
❑ FW-6911 [10]	Folk Songs of Four Continents	1955	20.00	40.00	80.00
❑ FW-6912 [10]	Bantu Choral Folk Songs	1955	20.00	40.00	80.00
❑ FC-7020 [10]	Songs to Grow On — Vol. 2	1951	20.00	40.00	80.00
❑ FC-7027 [10]	Songs to Grow On — Vol. 3	1951	20.00	40.00	80.00
❑ FC-7526 [M]	Song and Play Time	195?	12.50	25.00	50.00
❑ 7527	Zhitkov's How I Hunted the Little Fellows	1980	3.00	6.00	12.00
❑ FC-7601 [10]	American Folk Songs for Children	1953	20.00	40.00	80.00
❑ FC-7610 [10]	Birds, Beasts, Bugs and Little Fishes	1954	20.00	40.00	80.00
❑ FC-7611 [M]	Birds, Beasts, Bugs and Bigger Fishes	1954	12.50	25.00	50.00
❑ FC-7674 [M]	American Game and Activity Songs for Children	1962	5.00	10.00	20.00
❑ FI-8303 [M]	How to Play the Five String Banjo	195?	6.25	12.50	25.00

Number	Title (A Side/B Side)	Yr	VG	VG+	NM
❑ FI-8354 [M]	Folksinger's Guitar Guide Vol. 1: An Instruction Record	1955	7.50	15.00	30.00
❑ FQ-8354 [M]	The Folksinger's Guitar Gude	1955	6.25	12.50	25.00
❑ FI-8371 [M]	12-String Guitar As Played by Leadbelly	1962	5.00	10.00	20.00
❑ FTS-31002 [R]	Pete Seeger Sings Woody Guthrie	1968	3.00	6.00	12.00
❑ FTS-31017 [R]	American Favorite Ballads	1968	3.00	6.00	12.00
❑ FTS-31018 [R]	Wimoweh and Other Songs of Freedom and Protest	1968	3.00	6.00	12.00
❑ FTS-31022 [R]	Pete Seeger Sings Leadbelly	1968	3.00	6.00	12.00
❑ FTS-31040 [R]	Banks of Marble and Other Songs	1974	3.00	6.00	12.00
❑ FTS-32311 [R]	Traditional Christmas Carols	1967	3.75	7.50	15.00
❑ FT-35001 [(2)]	The Nativity: By Sholem Asch	1963	3.75	7.50	15.00
❑ FXM-36055 [(2)]	Sing Along	1980	3.75	7.50	15.00
❑ 37232	God Bless the Grass	1982	3.00	6.00	12.00
HARMONY					
❑ HS 11337	John Henry and Other Folk Favorites	1969	3.00	6.00	12.00
ODYSSEY					
❑ 32160266	3 Saints, 4 Sinners and 6 Other People	1968	3.75	7.50	15.00
OLYMPIC					
❑ 7102	America's Balladeer	1973	3.00	6.00	12.00
PAIR					
❑ PDL2-1076 [(2)]	Clearwater Classics	1986	3.00	6.00	12.00
PHILIPS					
❑ PHM 2-300 [(2)M]	The Story of the Nativity	1963	5.00	10.00	20.00
❑ PHS 2-300 [(2)S]	The Story of the Nativity	1963	6.25	12.50	25.00
SMITHSONIAN FOLKWAYS					
❑ SF-40024	Traditional Christmas Carols	1989	3.00	6.00	12.00
STINSON					
❑ SLP-52 [10]	Lincoln Brigade	1953	25.00	50.00	100.00
❑ SLP-57 [10]	A Pete Seeger Concert	1953	25.00	50.00	100.00
❑ SLP-90 [M]	Pete	1963	6.25	12.50	25.00
TRADITION					
❑ 2107	Folk Music of the World	1973	3.00	6.00	12.00
VANGUARD					
❑ VSD-97/98 [(2)]	The Essential Pete Seeger	1978	3.75	7.50	15.00
❑ VSD-73111	The Essential Pete Seeger, Vol. 1	198?	2.00	4.00	8.00
❑ VSD-73112	The Essential Pete Seeger, Vol. 2	198?	2.00	4.00	8.00
VERVE FOLKWAYS					
❑ FV-9008 [M]	Pete Seeger and Big Bill Broonzy in Concert	1965	5.00	10.00	20.00
❑ FVS-9008 [S]	Pete Seeger and Big Bill Broonzy in Concert	1965	6.25	12.50	25.00
❑ FV-9009 [M]	Pete Seeger On Campus	1965	5.00	10.00	20.00
❑ FVS-9009 [S]	Pete Seeger On Campus	1965	6.25	12.50	25.00
❑ FV-9013 [M]	Folk Music Live at the Village Gate	1965	5.00	10.00	20.00
❑ FVS-9013 [S]	Folk Music Live at the Village Gate	1965	6.25	12.50	25.00
❑ FV-9020 [M]	Little Boxes and Other Broadsides	1965	5.00	10.00	20.00
❑ FVS-9020 [S]	Little Boxes and Other Broadsides	1965	6.25	12.50	25.00
WARNER BROS.					
❑ BSK 3329	Circles and Seasons	1979	3.00	6.00	12.00

SEEGER, PETE, PENNY AND MICHAEL
PRESTIGE

Number	Title (A Side/B Side)	Yr	VG	VG+	NM
❑ PRLP-7375 [(2)M]	Pete, Penny and Michael Seeger	1965	5.00	10.00	20.00
❑ PRST-7375 [(2)S]	Pete, Penny and Michael Seeger	1965	6.25	12.50	25.00

SEELY, JEANNIE
DECCA

Number	Title (A Side/B Side)	Yr	VG	VG+	NM
❑ DL 75093	Jeannie Seely	1969	3.75	7.50	15.00
❑ DL 75228	Please Be My New Love	1970	3.75	7.50	15.00
HARMONY					
❑ KH 31029	Make the World Go Away	1972	3.00	6.00	12.00
MCA					
❑ 385	Can I Sleep in Your Arms/Lucky Ladies	1973	3.00	6.00	12.00
MONUMENT					
❑ 6640	Greatest Hits	1977	3.00	6.00	12.00
—Reissue of 31911					
❑ MLP-8057 [M]	The Seely Style	1966	3.75	7.50	15.00
—Title on label is "The Jeannie Seely Style"					
❑ MLP-8073 [M]	Thanks, Hank!	1967	6.25	12.50	25.00
❑ SLP-18057 [S]	The Seely Style	1966	5.00	10.00	20.00
—Title on label is "The Jeannie Seely Style"					
❑ SLP-18073 [S]	Thanks, Hank!	1967	5.00	10.00	20.00
❑ SLP-18091	I'll Love You More	1968	5.00	10.00	20.00
❑ SLP-18104	Little Things	1968	5.00	10.00	20.00
❑ KZ 31911	Greatest Hits	1973	3.75	7.50	15.00

SEGAL, GEORGE
PHILIPS

Number	Title (A Side/B Side)	Yr	VG	VG+	NM
❑ PHM 200242 [M]	The Yama-Yama Man	1967	5.00	10.00	20.00
❑ PHS 600242 [S]	The Yama-Yama Man	1967	5.00	10.00	20.00
SIGNATURE					
❑ BSL1-0654	A Touch of Ragtime	1976	3.75	7.50	15.00

SEGALL, RICKY
BELL

Number	Title (A Side/B Side)	Yr	VG	VG+	NM
❑ 1138	Ricky Segall and the Segalls	1973	5.00	10.00	20.00

SEGER, BOB
CAPITOL

Number	Title (A Side/B Side)	Yr	VG	VG+	NM
❑ (no #) [PD]	Night Moves	1977	10.00	20.00	40.00
—Promo-only picture disc					
❑ SM-172	Ramblin' Gamblin' Man	1977	2.00	4.00	8.00
❑ ST-172	Ramblin' Gamblin' Man	1969	7.50	15.00	30.00
—Black label with colorband					
❑ ST-236	Noah	1969	20.00	40.00	80.00
❑ SKAO-499	Mongrel	1970	6.25	12.50	25.00
❑ SM-499	Mongrel	1977	2.00	4.00	8.00
❑ ST-731	Brand New Morning	1971	25.00	50.00	100.00
❑ SPRO-8433 [DJ]	Consensus Cuts Edited for Airplay from "Live Bullet"	1976	6.25	12.50	25.00

Number	Title (A Side/B Side)	Yr	VG	VG+	NM
❑ ST-11378	Beautiful Loser	1975	2.50	5.00	10.00
—Originals have orange labels					
❑ ST-11378	Beautiful Loser	1978	2.00	4.00	8.00
—Purple label with large Capitol logo					
❑ SKBB-11523 [(2)]	Live Bullet	1976	3.75	7.50	15.00
—Originals have orange labels					
❑ SKBB-11523 [(2)]	Live Bullet	1978	3.00	6.00	12.00
—Purple label with large Capitol logo					
❑ SKBB-11523 [(2)]	Live Bullet	1983	3.00	6.00	12.00
—Black label, print in colorband					
❑ STBK-11523 [(2)]	Live Bullet	1988	3.00	6.00	12.00
—Purple label with smaller Capitol logo					
❑ ST-11557	Night Moves	1976	2.50	5.00	10.00
❑ SW-11698	Stranger in Town	1978	2.50	5.00	10.00
❑ ST-11746	Smokin' O.P.'s	1978	2.50	5.00	10.00
❑ ST-11748	Seven	1978	2.50	5.00	10.00
❑ SEAX-11904 [PD]	Stranger in Town	1978	6.25	12.50	25.00
❑ SOO-12041	Against the Wind	1980	2.50	5.00	10.00
❑ STBK-12182 [(2)]	Nine Tonight	1981	3.75	7.50	15.00
❑ ST-12254	The Distance	1983	2.50	5.00	10.00
❑ PT-12398	Like a Rock	1986	2.50	5.00	10.00
❑ SN-16105	Ramblin' Gamblin' Man	1980	2.00	4.00	8.00
❑ SN-16106	Mongrel	1980	2.00	4.00	8.00
❑ SN-16107	Smokin' O.P.'s	1980	2.00	4.00	8.00
❑ SN-16108	Seven	1980	2.00	4.00	8.00
❑ SN-16315	Beautiful Loser	1984	2.00	4.00	8.00
❑ C1-30334	Greatest Hits	1994	3.75	7.50	15.00
❑ C1-91134	The Fire Inside	1991	3.00	6.00	12.00
❑ C1-99774	It's a Mystery	1995	—	—	—
—Canceled					
MOBILE FIDELITY					
❑ 1-034	Night Moves	1980	10.00	20.00	40.00
—Audiophile vinyl					
❑ 1-127	Against the Wind	1983	10.00	20.00	40.00
—Audiophile vinyl					
PALLADIUM					
❑ P-1006	Smokin' O.P.'s	1972	6.25	12.50	25.00
REPRISE					
❑ MS 2109	Smokin' O.P.'s	1972	3.75	7.50	15.00
❑ MS 2126	Back in '72	1973	15.00	30.00	60.00
❑ MS 2184	Seven	1974	5.00	10.00	20.00

SEGO BROTHERS AND NAOMI, THE
GOSPEL TIME

Number	Title (A Side/B Side)	Yr	VG	VG+	NM
❑ 5007	From the Soul	196?	6.25	12.50	25.00
❑ 5018	Gospel Concert Special	196?	5.00	10.00	20.00
HARVEST					
❑ 1001	Keeping It Gospel	196?	6.25	12.50	25.00
HEART WARMING					
❑ 1952	With the Help of God	196?	7.50	15.00	30.00
❑ 1955	This World Has Turned Me Down	196?	7.50	15.00	30.00
❑ 3056	Happy Day	196?	6.25	12.50	25.00
❑ 3144	Meetin' Time	1972	6.25	12.50	25.00
❑ 3154	Featuring Naomi	1972	6.25	12.50	25.00
❑ 3186	Sorry I Never Knew You	1972	6.25	12.50	25.00
❑ 3206	The Dearest Friend I Ever Had	1973	6.25	12.50	25.00
❑ 3279	What a Happy Time	1974	6.25	12.50	25.00
❑ 3433	It Will Be Different the Next Time	1976	6.25	12.50	25.00
RUNA					
❑ 1941	Gospel Singing	196?	7.50	15.00	30.00
❑ 1942	Completely Gospel	196?	6.25	12.50	25.00
SCRIPTURE					
❑ 121	The Best of the Sego Brothers and Naomi	196?	7.50	15.00	30.00
❑ 122	Far Above the Starry Skies	196?	7.50	15.00	30.00
SILVER STAFF					
❑ 15003	I Pray My Way Out of Trouble	196?	6.25	12.50	25.00
SIMS					
❑ 134	With the Help of God	196?	10.00	20.00	40.00
SING					
❑ 9091M [M]	Sego Brothers and Naomi	196?	7.50	15.00	30.00
❑ 9091S [S]	Sego Brothers and Naomi	196?	10.00	20.00	40.00
❑ 9092M [M]	One Day Late	196?	7.50	15.00	30.00
❑ 9092S [S]	One Day Late	196?	10.00	20.00	40.00
SONGS OF FAITH					
❑ 103	Satisfied with Me	196?	7.50	15.00	30.00
❑ 110	The Sego Brothers and Naomi Sing the Gospel	1963	7.50	15.00	30.00
❑ 117	From the Soul	196?	7.50	15.00	30.00
❑ 121	The Award Winning Sego Brothers and Naomi	196?	7.50	15.00	30.00
❑ 126	Hem of His Garment	196?	7.50	15.00	30.00
❑ 133	He'll Walk By Your Side	196?	7.50	15.00	30.00
❑ 137	Will the Circle Be Unbroken	196?	7.50	15.00	30.00
❑ 141	Gospel Music On Stage with the Sego Brothers and Naomi	196?	7.50	15.00	30.00
❑ 143	I'm Longing for Home	196?	7.50	15.00	30.00
❑ 145	The Sego Brothers and Naomi Sing Weapon of Prayer	196?	5.00	10.00	20.00
❑ 147	Somebody Touched Me	196?	7.50	15.00	30.00
❑ 150	Daddy Sang Bass	1969	6.25	12.50	25.00
❑ 156	The Sego Brothers and Naomi Featuring W.R. Sego	1969	6.25	12.50	25.00
❑ 158	Golden Hits of the Sego Brothers and Naomi	1970	6.25	12.50	25.00
❑ 168	The Sego Brothers and Naomi at Grandfather Mountain	197?	6.25	12.50	25.00
SUPREME					
❑ 33003	I Pray My Way Out of Trouble	196?	7.50	15.00	30.00
VISTA					
❑ 1224	Old Time Singing	196?	7.50	15.00	30.00

Number	Title (A Side/B Side)	Yr	VG	VG+	NM

SELAH JUBILEE QUARTET, THE
REMINGTON
❏ 1023 [10]	Spirituals	1951	50.00	100.00	200.00

SELENA
CAPITOL/EMI LATIN
❏ H1-42144	Selena Y Los Dinos	1989	15.00	30.00	60.00
❏ H1-42299	16 Super Exitos Originales	1990	15.00	30.00	60.00
❏ H1-42359	Ven Conmingo	1990	15.00	30.00	60.00

CBS DISCOS
❏ RRL 80323	Personal Best	1990	15.00	30.00	60.00

GP
❏ LP-1002	Alpha	1986	125.00	250.00	500.00
❏ LP-1005	Menequito De Trapo	1986	75.00	150.00	300.00
❏ LP-1009	And the Winner Is…	1987	50.00	100.00	200.00

RP
❏ LP-8801	Preciosa	1988	37.50	75.00	150.00
❏ LP-8803	Dulce Amor	1988	37.50	75.00	150.00

SELLERS, BROTHER JOHN
VANGUARD
❏ VRS-8005 [10]	Brother John Sellers: Folk Songs and Blues	1954	25.00	50.00	100.00
❏ VRS-9036 [M]	Blues and Folk Songs	1957	20.00	40.00	80.00

SELLERS, PETER
ACAPELLA
❏ 1	Fool Brittania	1963	6.25	12.50	25.00

—With Joan Collins and Anthony Newley

ANGEL
❏ 35884 [M]	The Best of Sellers	1960	7.50	15.00	30.00
❏ S 35884 [S]	The Best of Sellers	1960	10.00	20.00	40.00

EMI AMERICA
❏ SN-16396	Songs for Swingin' Sellers	1986	5.00	10.00	20.00

—First American issue of 1959 U.K. LP

SELLERS, PETER, AND SOPHIA LOREN
ANGEL
❏ 35910 [M]	Peter Sellers and Sophia Loren	1961	7.50	15.00	30.00
❏ S 35910 [S]	Peter Sellers and Sophia Loren	1961	10.00	20.00	40.00

SENATOR BOBBY
PARKWAY
❏ P 7057 [M]	Boston Soul with the Hardly-Worthit Players	1967	5.00	10.00	20.00
❏ SP 7057 [S]	Boston Soul with the Hardly-Worthit Players	1967	5.00	10.00	20.00

SENOFSKY, BERL
RCA VICTOR RED SEAL
❏ LSC-2488 [S]	Debussy: Violin Sonata; Faure: Violin Sonata No. 1 in A	1961	10.00	20.00	40.00

—With Gary Graffman, piano; original with "shaded dog" label

SENSATIONS, THE
ARGO
❏ LP-4022 [M]	Let Me In/Music, Music, Music	1963	125.00	250.00	500.00

SENTINALS, THE
DEL-FI
❏ DFLP-1232 [M]	Big Surf!	1963	25.00	50.00	100.00
❏ DFST-1232 [S]	Big Surf!	1963	37.50	75.00	150.00
❏ DLF 1232	Big Surf!	1997	3.00	6.00	12.00
❏ DFLP-1241 [M]	Surfer Girl	1963	17.50	35.00	70.00
❏ DFST-1241 [S]	Surfer Girl	1963	25.00	50.00	100.00
❏ DLF 1241	Surfer Girl	1997	3.00	6.00	12.00

SUTTON
❏ SSU-338 [S]	Vegas Go-Go	1964	12.50	25.00	50.00
❏ SU-338 [M]	Vegas Go-Go	1964	10.00	20.00	40.00

SERENDIPITY SINGERS, THE
PHILIPS
❏ PHM 200115 [M]	The Serendipity Singers	1964	3.75	7.50	15.00
❏ PHM 200134 [M]	The Many Sides of the Serendipity Singers	1964	3.75	7.50	15.00
❏ PHM 200151 [M]	Take Your Shoes Off with the Serendipity Singers	1964	3.75	7.50	15.00
❏ PHM 200180 [M]	We Belong Together	1965	3.75	7.50	15.00
❏ PHM 200190 [M]	Love, Lies and Flying Festoons	1965	3.75	7.50	15.00
❏ PHS 600115 [S]	The Serendipity Singers	1964	5.00	10.00	20.00
❏ PHS 600134 [S]	The Many Sides of the Serendipity Singers	1964	5.00	10.00	20.00
❏ PHS 600151 [S]	Take Your Shoes Off with the Serendipity Singers	1964	5.00	10.00	20.00
❏ PHS 600180 [S]	We Belong Together	1965	5.00	10.00	20.00
❏ PHS 600190 [S]	Love, Lies and Flying Festoons	1965	5.00	10.00	20.00

SERPENT POWER
VANGUARD
❏ VRS-9252 [M]	Serpent Power	1967	30.00	60.00	120.00
❏ VSD-79252 [S]	Serpent Power	1967	15.00	30.00	60.00

SERRANO, PAUL
RIVERSIDE
❏ RLP-359 [M]	Blues Holiday	1961	6.25	12.50	25.00
❏ RS-9359 [S]	Blues Holiday	1961	7.50	15.00	30.00

SETE, BOLA
FANTASY
❏ 8349 [S]	Bossa Nova	1963	5.00	10.00	20.00
❏ 8364 [S]	The Incomparable Bola Sete	1965	5.00	10.00	20.00
❏ 8369 [S]	The Solo Guitar of Bola Sete	1966	5.00	10.00	20.00
❏ 8375 [S]	Autentico!	1966	5.00	10.00	20.00
❏ 8417	Shebaba	1971	3.00	6.00	12.00

VERVE
❏ V-8689 [M]	Bola Sete At the Monterey Jazz Festival	1967	5.00	10.00	20.00

SETTLE, MIKE
REPRISE
❏ R-6149 [M]	The Mike Settle Shindig	1965	5.00	10.00	20.00
❏ RS-6149 [S]	The Mike Settle Shindig	1965	6.25	12.50	25.00

SEVEN BLENDS, THE
ROULETTE
❏ R-25172 [M]	Twistin' at the Miami Beach Peppermint Lounge	1962	5.00	10.00	20.00
❏ SR-25172 [S]	Twistin' at the Miami Beach Peppermint Lounge	1962	6.25	12.50	25.00

SEVENTH WAVE, THE
JANUS
❏ 7008	Things to Come	1974	5.00	10.00	20.00
❏ 7021	Psi-Fi	1975	5.00	10.00	20.00

SEVERINSON, DOC
COMMAND
❏ RS 819 SD [S]	Tempestuous Trumpet	1961	5.00	10.00	20.00
❏ RS 837 SD [S]	The Big Band's Back in Town	1962	5.00	10.00	20.00
❏ RS 859 SD [S]	Torch Songs for Trumpet	1963	5.00	10.00	20.00
❏ RS 883 SD [S]	High, Wide and Wonderful	1965	5.00	10.00	20.00

SEVERSON, PAUL
ACADEMY
❏ MWJ-1 [M]	Midwest Jazz	1956	12.50	25.00	50.00

SEVILLA, JORGE
VERVE
❏ MGVS-6103 [S]	The Incredible Guitar of Jorge Sevilla	1960	10.00	20.00	40.00
❏ MGV-8342 [M]	The Incredible Guitar of Jorge Sevilla	1959	12.50	25.00	50.00
❏ V-8342 [M]	The Incredible Guitar of Jorge Sevilla	1961	6.25	12.50	25.00
❏ V6-8342 [S]	The Incredible Guitar of Jorge Sevilla	1961	5.00	10.00	20.00

SEVILLE, DAVID
LIBERTY
❏ LRP-3073 [M]	The Music of David Seville	1957	20.00	40.00	80.00
❏ LRP-3092 [M]	The Witch Doctor	1958	25.00	50.00	100.00

SEWARD, ALEC
BLUESVILLE
❏ BVLP-1076 [M]	Creepin' Blues	1963	20.00	40.00	80.00

—Blue label, silver print
❏ BVLP-1076 [M]	Creepin' Blues	1964	6.25	12.50	25.00

—Blue label, trident logo at right

SEX CLARK FIVE
BLOOD MONEY
❏ ERATO 59	Battle of Sex Clark Five	1989	4.50	9.00	18.00

RECORDS TO RUSSIA
❏ LP 408	Strum & Drum!	1986	30.00	60.00	120.00

—Test pressing with 24 tracks
❏ LP 408	Strum & Drum!	1987	3.75	7.50	15.00

—Second pressing: 20 tracks, no halftones, different back photo
❏ LP 408	Strum & Drum!	1987	5.00	10.00	20.00

—First pressing: 20 tracks, photos are halftones

SKYCLAD
❏ (NOT) BM 131	Antedium	1992	3.75	7.50	15.00

SEX PISTOLS
RESTLESS
❏ 72255	Better Live Than Dead	1988	3.00	6.00	12.00
❏ 72256 [EP]	The Mini-Album	1988	2.00	4.00	8.00
❏ 72257	The Ex-Pistols: The Swindle Continues	1988	3.00	6.00	12.00
❏ 72511	Live at Chelmsford Top Security Prison	1990	2.50	5.00	10.00

SKYCLAD
❏ SEX 6	We've Cum For Your Children	1988	3.00	6.00	12.00

WARNER BROS.
❏ BSK 3147	Never Mind the Bollocks Here's the Sex Pistols	1978	2.50	5.00	10.00

—With white WB label
❏ BSK 3147	Never Mind the Bollocks Here's the Sex Pistols	1978	6.25	12.50	25.00

—Any other version with custom label
❏ BSK 3147	Never Mind the Bollocks Here's the Sex Pistols	1978	7.50	15.00	30.00

—With sticker "Contains Sub-Mission"

SHA NA NA
ACCORD
❏ SN-7115	Remember Then	1981	2.50	5.00	10.00
❏ SN-7146	Sh-Boom	1981	2.50	5.00	10.00

BUDDAH
❏ BDM-5692	Rock & Roll Is Here to Stay!	1978	2.50	5.00	10.00
❏ BDM-5703	The Best of Sha Na Na	1978	2.50	5.00	10.00

EMUS
❏ ES-12037	On Stage	1978	2.50	5.00	10.00

KAMA SUTRA
❏ KSBS-2010	Rock & Roll Is Here to Stay!	1969	3.75	7.50	15.00
❏ KSBS-2034	Sha Na Na	1971	3.75	7.50	15.00
❏ KSBS-2050	The Night Is Still Young	1972	3.75	7.50	15.00
❏ KSBS-2073 [(2)]	The Golden Age of Rock 'n' Roll	1973	5.00	10.00	20.00
❏ KSBS-2075	From the Streets of New York	1973	3.75	7.50	15.00
❏ KSBS-2077	Rock & Roll Is Here to Stay!	1974	3.75	7.50	15.00
❏ KSBS-2600	Hot Sox	1974	3.75	7.50	15.00
❏ KSBS-2605	Sha Na Now	1975	3.75	7.50	15.00
❏ KSBS-2609 [(2)]	The Best…Sha Na Na	1976	3.75	7.50	15.00

NASHVILLE
❏ NR-12348-122 [(2)]	Rockin' in the 80's	1980	3.00	6.00	12.00

REALM
❏ 2V 8058 [(2)]	All-Time Greatest Rock 'n' Roll Hits	1977	3.75	7.50	15.00
❏ 1V 8059	Rock 'n' Roll Dance Party	1977	3.00	6.00	12.00

Number	Title (A Side/B Side)	Yr	VG	VG+	NM
SHACKLEFORDS, THE					
CAPITOL					
❏ ST 2450 [S]	The Shacklefords	1966	6.25	12.50	25.00
❏ T 2450 [M]	The Shacklefords	1966	5.00	10.00	20.00
MERCURY					
❏ MG-20806 [M]	Until You've Heard the Shacklefords	1963	5.00	10.00	20.00
❏ SR-60806 [S]	Until You've Heard the Shacklefords	1963	6.25	12.50	25.00
SHADES OF BLUE					
IMPACT					
❏ IM-101 [M]	Happiness Is the Shades of Blue	1966	12.50	25.00	50.00
❏ IM-1001 [S]	Happiness Is the Shades of Blue	1966	15.00	30.00	60.00
SHADES OF JOY					
FONTANA					
❏ SRF-67592	Shades of Joy	1969	5.00	10.00	20.00
SHADOWS, THE (1)					
ATLANTIC					
❏ 8084 [M]	Out of the Shadows	1962	50.00	100.00	200.00
—Canada-only release?					
❏ 8089 [M]	Surfing with the Shadows	1963	37.50	75.00	150.00
❏ SD 8089 [S]	Surfing with the Shadows	1963	75.00	150.00	300.00
❏ 8097 [M]	The Shadows Know	1964	25.00	50.00	100.00
❏ SD 8097 [S]	The Shadows Know	1964	50.00	100.00	200.00
SHADOWS OF KNIGHT, THE					
DUNWICH					
❏ 666 [M]	Gloria	1966	12.50	25.00	50.00
❏ S-666 [S]	Gloria	1966	20.00	40.00	80.00
❏ 667 [M]	Back Door Men	1966	12.50	25.00	50.00
❏ S-667 [S]	Back Door Men	1966	20.00	40.00	80.00
SUNDAZED					
❏ LP 5006	Raw and Live at the Cellar 1966	1992	2.50	5.00	10.00
❏ LP 5034	Gloria	1999	3.00	6.00	12.00
—Reissue on 180-gram vinyl					
❏ LP 5035	Back Door Men	1999	3.00	6.00	12.00
—Reissue on 180-gram vinyl					
SUPER K					
❏ SKS-6002	The Shadows of Knight	1969	12.50	25.00	50.00
SHADRACK					
IGL					
❏ 132	Chameleon	1971	75.00	150.00	300.00
SHAFRAN, DANIEL					
RCA VICTOR RED SEAL					
❏ LSC-2553 [S]	Shostakovich: Cello Sonata; Schubert: Arpeggione Sonata	1961	30.00	60.00	120.00
—Original with "shaded dog" label					
SHAGGS, THE (2)					
MGM					
❏ 1295	Wink	1967	62.50	125.00	250.00
—No number on label -- this number is found in the trail-off wax on each side					
SHAGGS, THE (3)					
ROUNDER					
❏ 3032	Philosophy of the World	1980	6.25	12.50	25.00
❏ 3056	Shaggs' Own Thing	1982	6.25	12.50	25.00
THIRD WORLD					
❏ 3001	Philosophy of the World	1969	500.00	1000.	2000.
SHAKERS, THE					
AUDIO FIDELITY					
❏ AFLP-2155 [M]	The Shakers Break It All	1966	10.00	20.00	40.00
❏ AFSD-6155 [S]	The Shakers Break It All	1966	12.50	25.00	50.00
SHAKEY JAKE					
BLUESVILLE					
❏ BVLP-1008 [M]	Good Times	1960	30.00	60.00	120.00
—Blue label, silver print					
❏ BVLP-1008 [M]	Good Times	1964	7.50	15.00	30.00
—Blue label, trident logo at right					
❏ BVLP-1027 [M]	Mouth Harp Blues	1961	30.00	60.00	120.00
—Blue label, silver print					
❏ BVLP-1027 [M]	Mouth Harp Blues	1964	7.50	15.00	30.00
—Blue label, trident logo at right					
WORLD PACIFIC					
❏ WPS-21886	Blues Makers	196?	7.50	15.00	30.00
SHAKEY VICK					
JANUS					
❏ JLS-3000	Little Woman, You're So Sweet	1970	5.00	10.00	20.00
SHANGRI-LAS, THE					
COLLECTABLES					
❏ COL-5011	Remember…Their Greatest Hits	198?	2.50	5.00	10.00
MERCURY					
❏ MG-21099 [M]	The Shangri-Las' Golden Hits	1966	10.00	20.00	40.00
❏ SR-61099 [S]	The Shangri-Las' Golden Hits	1966	12.50	25.00	50.00
POLYDOR					
❏ 824807-1	Golden Hits of the Shangri-Las	1985	2.50	5.00	10.00
POST					
❏ 4000	The Shangri-Las Sing	196?	5.00	10.00	20.00
RED BIRD					
❏ 20101 [M]	Leader of the Pack	1965	37.50	75.00	150.00
❏ 20104 [M]	Shangri-Las '65	1965	37.50	75.00	150.00
❏ 20104 [M]	I Can Never Go Home Anymore	1966	25.00	50.00	100.00
—Retitled version with title song added and "Sophisticated Boom Boom" dropped					

Number	Title (A Side/B Side)	Yr	VG	VG+	NM
SHANK, BUD					
KIMBERLY					
❏ 2025 [M]	The Talents of Bud Shank	1963	5.00	10.00	20.00
❏ 11025 [S]	The Talents of Bud Shank	1963	6.25	12.50	25.00
NOCTURNE					
❏ NLP-2 [10]	Compositions of Shorty Rogers	1953	50.00	100.00	200.00
PACIFIC JAZZ					
❏ PJ-4 [M]	Bud Shank Plays Tenor	1960	6.25	12.50	25.00
❏ ST-4 [S]	Bud Shank Plays Tenor	1960	7.50	15.00	30.00
❏ PJLP-14 [10]	Bud Shank with Three Trombones	1954	30.00	60.00	120.00
❏ PJLP-20 [10]	Bud Shank and Bob Brookmeyer	1954	30.00	60.00	120.00
❏ PJ-21 [M]	New Groove	1961	6.25	12.50	25.00
❏ ST-21 [S]	New Groove	1961	7.50	15.00	30.00
❏ PJ-58 [M]	Bossa Nova Jazz Samba	1962	6.25	12.50	25.00
❏ ST-58 [S]	Bossa Nova Jazz Samba	1962	7.50	15.00	30.00
❏ PJ-64 [M]	Brassamba Bossa Nova	1963	5.00	10.00	20.00
❏ ST-64 [S]	Brassamba Bossa Nova	1963	6.25	12.50	25.00
❏ PJ-89 [M]	Bud Shank and His Brazilian Friends	1965	5.00	10.00	20.00
❏ ST-89 [S]	Bud Shank and His Brazilian Friends	1965	6.25	12.50	25.00
❏ PJM-411 [M]	The Swing's to TV	1957	15.00	30.00	60.00
❏ PJ-1205 [M]	Bud Shank/Shorty Rogers	1955	20.00	40.00	80.00
❏ PJ-1213 [M]	Strings and Trombones	1956	20.00	40.00	80.00
❏ PJ-1215 [M]	The Bud Shank Quartet	1956	20.00	40.00	80.00
❏ PJ-1219 [M]	Jazz at Cal-Tech	1956	15.00	30.00	60.00
❏ PJ-1226 [M]	Flute 'n Oboe	1957	15.00	30.00	60.00
❏ PJ-1230 [M]	The Bud Shank Quartet	1957	15.00	30.00	60.00
❏ ST-20110 [S]	Bud Shank and the Sax Section	1966	5.00	10.00	20.00
❏ ST-20157	Windmills of Your Mind	1969	3.75	7.50	15.00
WORLD PACIFIC					
❏ PJM-411 [M]	The Swing's to TV	1958	12.50	25.00	50.00
❏ WPM-411 [M]	The Swing's to TV	1958	10.00	20.00	40.00
❏ ST-1002 [S]	The Swing's to TV	1959	7.50	15.00	30.00
❏ ST-1018 [S]	Holiday in Brazil	1959	7.50	15.00	30.00
❏ WP-1205 [M]	Bud Shank/Shorty Rogers	1958	10.00	20.00	40.00
❏ WP-1215 [M]	The Bud Shank Quartet	1958	10.00	20.00	40.00
❏ WP-1219 [M]	Jazz at Cal-Tech	1958	10.00	20.00	40.00
❏ WP-1226 [M]	Flute 'n Oboe	1958	10.00	20.00	40.00
❏ WP-1230 [M]	The Bud Shank Quartet	1958	10.00	20.00	40.00
❏ WP-1251 [M]	I'll Take Romance	1958	10.00	20.00	40.00
❏ WP-1259 [M]	Holiday in Brazil	1959	10.00	20.00	40.00
❏ ST-1281 [S]	Latin Contrasts	1959	7.50	15.00	30.00
❏ WP-1281 [M]	Latin Contrasts	1959	10.00	20.00	40.00
❏ ST-1286 [S]	Flute 'n Alto	1960	10.00	20.00	40.00
❏ WP-1286 [M]	Flute 'n Alto	1960	7.50	15.00	30.00
❏ ST-1299 [S]	Koto 'n Flute	1960	10.00	20.00	40.00
❏ WP-1299 [M]	Koto 'n Flute	1960	7.50	15.00	30.00
❏ WP-1416 [M]	Improvisations	1961	6.25	12.50	25.00
❏ WP-1424 [M]	Koto 'n Flute	1962	6.25	12.50	25.00
❏ WP-1853 [M]	Girl in Love	1967	5.00	10.00	20.00
❏ WP-1855 [M]	Brazil! Brazil! Brazil!	1967	5.00	10.00	20.00
❏ WP-1864 [M]	Bud Shank Plays Music from Today's Movies	1967	5.00	10.00	20.00
❏ ST-21819 [S]	Folk 'n Flute	1295	5.00	10.00	20.00
❏ ST-21827 [S]	Flute, Oboe and Strings	1965	5.00	10.00	20.00
❏ ST-21840 [S]	Michelle	1966	5.00	10.00	20.00
❏ ST-21845 [S]	California Dreaming	1966	5.00	10.00	20.00
SHANK, BUD/CHET BAKER					
KIMBERLY					
❏ 2016 [M]	Swinging Soundtrack	1963	5.00	10.00	20.00
❏ 11016 [S]	Swinging Soundtrack	1963	6.25	12.50	25.00
SHANKAR, ANANDA					
REPRISE					
❏ RS-6398	Ananda Shankar	1970	5.00	10.00	20.00
SHANKAR, L.					
ZAPPA					
❏ SRZ-1-1602	Touch Me There	1979	5.00	10.00	20.00
SHANKAR, RAVI					
ANGEL					
❏ 35468 [M]	Music of India	196?	6.25	12.50	25.00
❏ S 36026 [S]	West Meets East, Vol. 2	1968	3.75	7.50	15.00
❏ 36418 [M]	West Meets East	1967	6.25	12.50	25.00
—With Yahudi Menuhin					
❏ S 36418 [S]	West Meets East	1967	5.00	10.00	20.00
—With Yahudi Menuhin					
❏ S 36806	Concerto for Sitar and Orchestra	1972	3.00	6.00	12.00
❏ DS-37920	Raga Mishra Piloo	1982	2.50	5.00	10.00
❏ DS-37935	Raga-Mala (Sitar Concert No. 2)	1983	2.50	5.00	10.00
APPLE					
❏ SWAO-3384	Raga	1971	6.25	12.50	25.00
❏ SVBB-3396 [(2)]	Ravi Shankar In Concert	1973	10.00	20.00	40.00
BLUESVILLE					
❏ BVLP-1078 [M]	The Master Musician of India	1964	6.25	12.50	25.00
CAPITOL					
❏ DT 2720 [R]	Three Ragas	1967	3.75	7.50	15.00
❏ T 2720 [M]	Three Ragas	1967	5.00	10.00	20.00
❏ ST 10482 [S]	Two Raga Moods	196?	6.25	12.50	25.00
❏ T 10482 [M]	Two Raga Moods	196?	5.00	10.00	20.00
❏ ST 10497 [S]	Exotic Sitar and Sarod	196?	6.25	12.50	25.00
❏ T 10497 [M]	Exotic Sitar and Sarod	196?	5.00	10.00	20.00
❏ ST 10504	Ravi	196?	3.75	7.50	15.00
❏ SP-10561	Raga Parameshwari	1972	3.00	6.00	12.00
COLUMBIA					
❏ WL 119 [M]	The Sounds of India	196?	6.25	12.50	25.00
❏ CL 2496 [M]	Sounds of India	1966	3.75	7.50	15.00
❏ CL 2760 [M]	The Genius of Ravi Shankar	1967	5.00	10.00	20.00
❏ OS 3230	Chappaqua	1968	3.75	7.50	15.00
❏ CS 9296 [S]	Sounds of India	1966	5.00	10.00	20.00
❏ CS 9560 [S]	The Genius of Ravi Shankar	1967	3.75	7.50	15.00

S

Number	Title (A Side/B Side)	Yr	VG	VG+	NM
DARK HORSE					
❏ SP 22002	Shankar Family and Friends	1974	3.00	6.00	12.00
❏ SP 22007	Music Festival from India	1975	3.00	6.00	12.00
DEUTCHE GRAMMOPHON					
❏ 2531 216	Ragas Hameer & Gara	198?	2.50	5.00	10.00
❏ 2531 280	Raga Jogeshwari	198?	2.50	5.00	10.00
❏ 2531 356	Homage to Mahatma Gandhi; Homage to Baba Allauddin	198?	2.50	5.00	10.00
❏ 2531 381	Pad Hasapa, for Koto; etc.	198?	2.50	5.00	10.00
FANTASY					
❏ 24714 [(2)]	Ragas	1973	3.75	7.50	15.00
ORIENTAL					
❏ BGRP-108	Raga Sanjh Kalyan	198?	2.50	5.00	10.00
PRIVATE MUSIC					
❏ 2016-1-P	The Shankar Project: Tana Mana	1988	2.50	5.00	10.00
❏ 2044-1-P	Inside the Kremlin	1989	2.50	5.00	10.00
SPARK					
❏ 06	Transmigration Macabre	1973	3.00	6.00	12.00
WORLD PACIFIC					
❏ WP-1421 [M]	Ravi Shankar In Concert	1965	3.75	7.50	15.00
❏ WP-1422 [M]	India's Master Musician	1965	3.75	7.50	15.00
❏ WP-1430 [M]	Ravi Shankar In London	1966	3.75	7.50	15.00
❏ WP-1431 [M]	Ragas and Talas	1966	3.75	7.50	15.00
❏ WP-1432 [M]	Portrait of Genius	1966	3.75	7.50	15.00
❏ WP-1434 [M]	Sound of the Sitar	1967	3.75	7.50	15.00
❏ WP-1438 [M]	Three Ragas	1967	3.75	7.50	15.00
❏ WP-1441 [M]	Ravi Shankar in New York	1967	3.75	7.50	15.00
❏ WP-1442 [M]	Ravi Shankar at the Monterey International Pop Festival	1967	5.00	10.00	20.00
❏ ST-21421 [S]	Ravi Shankar In Concert	1965	5.00	10.00	20.00
❏ ST-21422 [S]	India's Master Musician	1965	5.00	10.00	20.00
❏ ST-21430 [S]	Ravi Shankar In London	1966	5.00	10.00	20.00
❏ ST-21431 [S]	Ragas and Talas	1966	5.00	10.00	20.00
❏ ST-21432 [S]	Portrait of Genius	1966	5.00	10.00	20.00
❏ ST-21434 [S]	Sound of the Sitar	1967	5.00	10.00	20.00
❏ ST-21438 [S]	Three Ragas	1967	5.00	10.00	20.00
❏ ST-21441 [S]	Ravi Shankar in New York	1967	5.00	10.00	20.00
❏ ST-21442 [S]	Ravi Shankar at the Monterey International Pop Festival	1967	5.00	10.00	20.00
❏ ST-21449	Ravi Shankar in San Francisco	1968	5.00	10.00	20.00
❏ ST-21454	Charly	1969	3.75	7.50	15.00
❏ ST-21464	Morning Raga/Evening Raga	1970	3.75	7.50	15.00
❏ ST-21467	Ravi Shankar at Woodstock	1970	3.75	7.50	15.00
❏ WPS-26201 [(2)]	His Festival from India	1968	5.00	10.00	20.00
SHANNON, DEL					
AMY					
❏ 8003 [M]	Handy Man	1964	12.50	25.00	50.00
❏ S-8003 [S]	Handy Man	1964	20.00	40.00	80.00
❏ 8004 [M]	Del Shannon Sings Hank Williams	1965	12.50	25.00	50.00
❏ S-8004 [S]	Del Shannon Sings Hank Williams	1965	20.00	40.00	80.00
❏ 8006 [M]	1,661 Seconds with Del Shannon	1965	12.50	25.00	50.00
❏ S-8006 [S]	1,661 Seconds with Del Shannon	1965	20.00	40.00	80.00
BIG TOP					
❏ 12-1303 [M]	Runaway	1961	75.00	150.00	300.00
❏ 12-1303 [S]	Runaway	1961	400.00	800.00	1600.
❏ 12-1308 [B]	Little Town Flirt	1963	250.00	500.00	1000.
—One side is mono, one side is stereo; should be played to identify					
❏ 12-1308 [M]	Little Town Flirt	1963	37.50	75.00	150.00
❏ 12-1308 [S]	Little Town Flirt	1963	375.00	750.00	1500.
—Stereo copies are not identified as such on either cover or label; some, but not all, copies have an "S" in the dead wax. Playing is the best way to identify.					
DOT					
❏ DLP 3824 [M]	The Best of Del Shannon	1967	12.50	25.00	50.00
❏ DLP 25824 [R]	The Best of Del Shannon	1967	10.00	20.00	40.00
ELEKTRA					
❏ 5E-568	Drop Down and Get Me	1981	2.50	5.00	10.00
LIBERTY					
❏ LRP-3453 [M]	This Is My Bag	1966	7.50	15.00	30.00
❏ LRP-3479 [M]	Total Commitment	1966	7.50	15.00	30.00
❏ LRP-3539 [M]	The Further Adventures of Charles Westover	1967	12.50	25.00	50.00
❏ LST-7453 [S]	This Is My Bag	1966	10.00	20.00	40.00
❏ LST-7479 [S]	Total Commitment	1966	10.00	20.00	40.00
❏ LST-7539 [S]	The Further Adventures of Charles Westover	1967	20.00	40.00	80.00
PICKWICK					
❏ SPC-3595 [R]	The Best of Del Shannon	197?	2.50	5.00	10.00
POST					
❏ 9000 [R]	Del Shannon Sings	196?	10.00	20.00	40.00
RHINO					
❏ RNLP-71056 [M]	Runaway Hits	1986	2.50	5.00	10.00
SIRE					
❏ SASH-3708 [(2)P]	The Vintage Years	1975	6.25	12.50	25.00
TWIRL					
❏ 5001 [M]	Del Shannon's Greatest Hits	196?	25.00	50.00	100.00
—LP was never issued; price is for front cover slick, which is known to exist					
UNITED ARTISTS					
❏ UA-LA151-E	Del Shannon Live in England	1973	6.25	12.50	25.00
SHANNON, HUGH					
ATLANTIC					
❏ ALS-406 [10]	Hugh Shannon Sings	195?	25.00	50.00	100.00
SHANTY BOYS, THE					
ELEKTRA					
❏ EKL-142 [M]	Off-Beat Folk Songs	1958	7.50	15.00	30.00
SHAPIRO, HELEN					
EPIC					
❏ LN 24075 [M]	A Teenager in Love	1962	6.25	12.50	25.00
❏ BN 26075 [S]	A Teenager in Love	1962	7.50	15.00	30.00

Number	Title (A Side/B Side)	Yr	VG	VG+	NM
SHARON, RALPH					
ARGO					
❏ LP-635 [M]	2:38 A.M.	1958	10.00	20.00	40.00
BETHLEHEM					
❏ BCP-13 [M]	Mr. & Mrs. Jazz	1955	10.00	20.00	40.00
❏ BCP-41 [M]	Ralph Sharon Trio	1956	10.00	20.00	40.00
COLUMBIA					
❏ CL 2321 [M]	Do I Hear a Waltz?	1965	6.25	12.50	25.00
❏ CS 9121 [S]	Do I Hear a Waltz?	1965	7.50	15.00	30.00
GORDY					
❏ G-903 [M]	Modern Innovations on Country & Western Themes	1963	50.00	100.00	200.00
LONDON					
❏ LB-733 [10]	Spring Fever	1953	12.50	25.00	50.00
❏ LB-842 [10]	Autumn Leaves	1954	12.50	25.00	50.00
❏ LL 1339 [M]	Spring Fever/Autumn Leaves	1955	10.00	20.00	40.00
❏ LL 1488 [M]	Easy Jazz	1956	10.00	20.00	40.00
RAMA					
❏ RLP-1001 [M]	Jazz Around the World	1957	12.50	25.00	50.00
SHARP, DEE DEE					
CAMEO					
❏ C-1018 [M]	It's Mashed Potato Time	1962	15.00	30.00	60.00
❏ C-1022 [M]	Songs of Faith	1962	10.00	20.00	40.00
❏ SC-1022 [S]	Songs of Faith	1962	12.50	25.00	50.00
❏ C-1027 [M]	All the Hits	1962	10.00	20.00	40.00
❏ SC-1027 [S]	All the Hits	1962	12.50	25.00	50.00
❏ C-1032 [M]	All the Hits, Vol. 2	1963	10.00	20.00	40.00
❏ SC-1032 [S]	All the Hits, Vol. 2	1963	12.50	25.00	50.00
❏ C-1050 [M]	Do the Bird	1963	10.00	20.00	40.00
❏ SC-1050 [S]	Do the Bird	1963	12.50	25.00	50.00
❏ C-1062 [M]	Biggest Hits	1963	10.00	20.00	40.00
❏ C-1074 [M]	Down Memory Lane	1963	10.00	20.00	40.00
❏ C-2002 [M]	18 Golden Hits	1964	10.00	20.00	40.00
❏ SC-2002 [S]	18 Golden Hits	1964	12.50	25.00	50.00
PHILADELPHIA INT'L.					
❏ PZ 33839	Happy 'Bout the Whole Thing	1976	2.50	5.00	10.00
❏ PZ 34437	What Color Is Love	1977	2.50	5.00	10.00
❏ JZ 36370	Dee Dee	1980	2.50	5.00	10.00
SHARP, DEE DEE, AND CHUBBY CHECKER					
CAMEO					
❏ C-1029 [M]	Down to Earth	1962	10.00	20.00	40.00
❏ SC-1029 [S]	Down to Earth	1962	12.50	25.00	50.00
SHARP, RANDY					
NAUTILUS					
❏ NR-1	First in Line	1980	10.00	20.00	40.00
—Standard cover					
❏ NR-1	First in Line	1980	12.50	25.00	50.00
—Styrofoam cover					
SHARPE, RAY					
AWARD					
❏ LMP-711 [M]	Welcome Back, Linda Lu	1964	30.00	60.00	120.00
SHARROCK, SONNY					
VORTEX					
❏ 2014	Black Woman	1970	5.00	10.00	20.00
SHATNER, WILLIAM					
DECCA					
❏ DL 5043 [M]	The Transformed Man	1969	37.50	75.00	150.00
—Mono is white label promo only; in stereo cover with "Monaural" sticker					
❏ DL 75043 [S]	The Transformed Man	1969	15.00	30.00	60.00
K-TEL					
❏ NC 494 [(2)]	Captain of the Starship	1978	12.50	25.00	50.00
—Reissue of Lemli album					
LEMLI					
❏ 9400 [(2)]	William Shatner — Live!	1977	7.50	15.00	30.00
SHAVERS, CHARLIE					
AAMCO					
❏ 310 [M]	The Most Intimate Charlie Shavers	1959	10.00	20.00	40.00
BETHLEHEM					
❏ BCP-27 [M]	Gershwin, Shavers and Strings	1955	20.00	40.00	80.00
❏ BCP-67 [M]	The Complete Charlie Shavers with Maxine Sullivan	1957	20.00	40.00	80.00
❏ BCP-1007 [10]	Horn o' Plenty	1954	25.00	50.00	100.00
❏ BCP-1021 [10]	The Most Intimate Charlie Shavers	1955	25.00	50.00	100.00
❏ BCP-5002 [M]	The Most Intimate Charlie Shavers	1958	20.00	40.00	80.00
CAPITOL					
❏ ST 1883 [S]	Excitement Unlimited	1963	6.25	12.50	25.00
❏ T 1883 [M]	Excitement Unlimited	1963	5.00	10.00	20.00
EVEREST					
❏ SDBR-1070 [S]	Girl of My Dreams	1960	6.25	12.50	25.00
❏ SDBR-1108 [S]	Here Comes Charlie	1960	6.25	12.50	25.00
❏ SDBR-1127 [S]	Like Charlie	1961	6.25	12.50	25.00
❏ LPBR-5070 [M]	Girl of My Dreams	1960	5.00	10.00	20.00
❏ LPBR-5108 [M]	Here Comes Charlie	1960	5.00	10.00	20.00
❏ LPBR-5127 [M]	Like Charlie	1961	5.00	10.00	20.00
JAZZTONE					
❏ J-1229 [M]	Flow Gently, Sweet Rhythm	1956	10.00	20.00	40.00
MGM					
❏ E-3765 [M]	Charlie Digs Paree	1959	6.25	12.50	25.00
❏ SE-3765 [S]	Charlie Digs Paree	1959	7.50	15.00	30.00
❏ E-3809 [M]	Charlie Digs Dixie	1960	6.25	12.50	25.00
❏ SE-3809 [S]	Charlie Digs Dixie	1960	7.50	15.00	30.00
PERIOD					
❏ SPL-1113 [10]	Flow Gently, Sweet Rhythm	1955	30.00	60.00	120.00

Number	Title (A Side/B Side)	Yr	VG	VG+	NM

SHAW, ARTIE
ALLEGRO
❏ 1405 [M]	An Hour with Artie Shaw	1955	10.00	20.00	40.00
❏ 1466 [M]	Artie Shaw Hour	1955	10.00	20.00	40.00

ALLEGRO EILTE
❏ 4023 [10]	Artie Shaw Plays	195?	10.00	20.00	40.00
❏ 4107 [10]	Artie Shaw Plays Cole Porter	195?	10.00	20.00	40.00

CLEF
❏ MGC-159 [10]	Artie Shaw and His Gramercy Five, Volume 1	1954	15.00	30.00	60.00
❏ MGC-160 [10]	Artie Shaw and His Gramercy Five, Volume 2	1954	15.00	30.00	60.00
❏ MGC-630 [M]	Artie Shaw and His Gramercy Five, Volume 3	1954	15.00	30.00	60.00
❏ MGC-645 [R]	Artie Shaw and His Gramercy Five, Volume 4	1955	15.00	30.00	60.00

COLUMBIA MASTERWORKS
❏ ML 4260 [M]	Modern Music for Clarinet	1950	12.50	25.00	50.00

DECCA
❏ DL 5286 [10]	Artie Shaw Dance Program	195?	12.50	25.00	50.00
❏ DL 5524 [10]	Speak to Me of Love	195?	12.50	25.00	50.00
❏ DL 8309 [M]	Did Someone Say Party?	1956	10.00	20.00	40.00
—Black label, silver print					

EPIC
❏ LG 1006 [10]	Artie Shaw with Strings	1954	12.50	25.00	50.00
❏ LG 1017 [10]	Non-Stop Flight	1954	12.50	25.00	50.00
❏ LG 1102 [10]	Artie Shaw	1955	12.50	25.00	50.00
❏ LN 3112 [M]	Artie Shaw with Strings	1955	10.00	20.00	40.00
❏ LN 3150 [M]	Artie Shaw and His Orchestra	1955	10.00	20.00	40.00

LION
❏ L-70058 [M]	Artie Shaw Plays Irving Berlin and Cole Porter	1958	6.25	12.50	25.00

MGM
❏ E-517 [10]	Artie Shaw Plays Cole Porter	1950	12.50	25.00	50.00

RCA CAMDEN
❏ CAL-465 [M]	The Great Artie Shaw	195?	5.00	10.00	20.00
❏ CAL-584 [M]	One Night Stand	1959	5.00	10.00	20.00
❏ CAL-908 [M]	September Song and Other Favorites	196?	5.00	10.00	20.00

RCA VICTOR
❏ LPT-28 [10]	Artie Shaw Favorites	195?	12.50	25.00	50.00
❏ LPM-30 [10]	Four Star Favorites	1955	12.50	25.00	50.00
❏ LPT-1020 [M]	My Concerto	195?	10.00	20.00	40.00
❏ LPM-1201 [M]	Both Feet in the Groove	1956	10.00	20.00	40.00
❏ LPM-1217 [M]	Back Bay Shuffle	1956	10.00	20.00	40.00
❏ LPM-1241 [M]	Artie Shaw and His Gramercy Five	1956	10.00	20.00	40.00
❏ LPM-1244 [M]	Moonglow	1956	10.00	20.00	40.00
❏ LPM-1570 [M]	Any Old Time	1957	10.00	20.00	40.00
❏ LPM-1648 [M]	A Man and His Dream	1957	10.00	20.00	40.00
❏ LPT-3013 [10]	This Is Artie Shaw	1952	12.50	25.00	50.00
❏ LPM-3675 [M]	The Best of Artie Shaw	1967	5.00	10.00	20.00
❏ LPT-6000 [(2)M]	In the Blue Room/In the Café Rouge	195?	12.50	25.00	50.00
—Originals are in a box; silver labels, red print					
❏ VPM-6062 [(2)]	This Is Artie Shaw, Volume 2	1976	3.00	6.00	12.00
—Black labels, dog near top					

VERVE
❏ MGV-2014 [M]	I Can't Get Started	1956	10.00	20.00	40.00
❏ V-2014 [M]	I Can't Get Started	1961	5.00	10.00	20.00
❏ MGV-2015 [M]	Sequence in Music	1956	10.00	20.00	40.00
❏ V-2015 [M]	Sequence in Music	1961	5.00	10.00	20.00

SHAW, GENE
ARGO
❏ LP-707 [M]	Breakthrough	1962	6.25	12.50	25.00
❏ LPS-707 [S]	Breakthrough	1962	7.50	15.00	30.00
❏ LP-726 [M]	Debut In Blues	1963	6.25	12.50	25.00
❏ LPS-726 [S]	Debut In Blues	1963	7.50	15.00	30.00
❏ LP-743 [M]	Carnival Sketches	1964	6.25	12.50	25.00
❏ LPS-743 [S]	Carnival Sketches	1964	7.50	15.00	30.00

SHAW, MARLENA
CADET
❏ LPS-803	Different Bags	1968	5.00	10.00	20.00
❏ LPS-833	Spice of Life	1969	5.00	10.00	20.00

SHAW, ROBERT, CHORALE
RCA VICTOR RED SEAL
❏ LM-1112 [M]	Christmas Hymns and Carols	1952	7.50	15.00	30.00
—Original has 2" brown border around all four sides of front cover					
❏ LM-1112 [M]	Christmas Hymns and Carols, Volume I	1954	5.00	10.00	20.00
—Mostly pink front cover with "Enhanced Sound" at top and under dog on label					
❏ LM-1711 [M]	Christmas Hymns and Carols Vol. 2	195?	5.00	10.00	20.00
—Pink "ornaments" cover; maroon label, large dog on top					
❏ LM-1711 [M]	Christmas Hymns and Carols Volume II	1954	6.25	12.50	25.00
—Original carolers cover; red label with outline of dog					
❏ LM-2139 [M]	Christmas Hymns and Carols, Volume 1	1957	5.00	10.00	20.00
—Original cover has "LM-2139" with "RCA Victor" in box on upper right					
❏ LM-2139 [M]	Christmas Hymns and Carols, Volume 1	1958	4.00	8.00	16.00
—Second cover has "LM-2139" in lower left corner; small "RE" is on front cover					
❏ LSC-2139 [S]	Christmas Hymns and Carols, Volume 1	1958	5.00	10.00	20.00
—Original with "shaded dog" label					
❏ LSC-2199 [S]	A Mighty Fortress	1959	5.00	10.00	20.00
—Original with "shaded dog" label					
❏ LSC-2231 [S]	On Stage	1959	5.00	10.00	20.00
—Original with "shaded dog" label					
❏ LSC-2247 [S]	Deep River and Other Spirituals	1959	5.00	10.00	20.00
—Original with "shaded dog" label					
❏ LSC-2273 [S]	Bach, J.S.: Cantata 4	1959	5.00	10.00	20.00
—Original with "shaded dog" label					
❏ LSC-2295 [S]	The Stephen Foster Song Book	1959	5.00	10.00	20.00
—Original with "shaded dog" label					
❏ LSC-2402 [S]	A Chorus of Love	1960	5.00	10.00	20.00
—Original with "shaded dog" label or second edition with "white dog" label					
❏ LSC-2403 [S]	What Wondrous Love	1960	5.00	10.00	20.00
—Original with "shaded dog" label					
❏ LSC-2416 [S]	Operatic Choruses	1960	5.00	10.00	20.00
—Original with "shaded dog" label					

❏ LSC-2551 [S]	Sea Shanties	1961	7.50	15.00	30.00
—Original with "shaded dog" label					
❏ LSC-2580 [S]	I'm Goin' to Sing	1962	10.00	20.00	40.00
—Original with "shaded dog" label					
❏ LSC-2598 [S]	23 Glee Club Favorites	1962	10.00	20.00	40.00
—Original with "shaded dog" label					
❏ LM-2684 [M]	The Many Moods of Christmas	1963	3.00	6.00	12.00
❏ LSC-2684 [S]	The Many Moods of Christmas	1963	3.75	7.50	15.00

SHAW, SANDIE
REPRISE
❏ R-6166 [M]	Sandie Shaw	1965	10.00	20.00	40.00
❏ RS-6166 [R]	Sandie Shaw	1965	12.50	25.00	50.00
❏ R-6191 [M]	Me	1966	7.50	15.00	30.00
❏ RS-6191 [S]	Me	1966	10.00	20.00	40.00

SHAW, SERENA
RAMA
❏ RLP-5001 [M]	Cry My Love	1956	100.00	200.00	400.00

SHAW, WOODY
CONTEMPORARY
❏ C-7627/8 [(2)]	Blackstone Legacy	1971	5.00	10.00	20.00

MOSAIC
❏ M4-142 [(4)]	The Complete CBS Studio Recordings of Woody Shaw	199?	20.00	40.00	80.00

SHAWN, DICK
20TH CENTURY FOX
❏ TFM-3124 [M]	Dick Shawn Sings with His Little People	1964	5.00	10.00	20.00
❏ TFS-4124 [S]	Dick Shawn Sings with His Little People	1964	6.25	12.50	25.00

SHEA, GEORGE BEVERLY
RCA VICTOR
❏ LPM-1062 [M]	Evening Vespers	1955	5.00	10.00	20.00
❏ LPM-1187 [M]	Inspirational Songs	1955	5.00	10.00	20.00
❏ LPM-1235 [M]	Sacred Songs	1956	5.00	10.00	20.00
❏ LPM-1349 [M]	Evening Prayer	1956	5.00	10.00	20.00
❏ LPM-1406 [M]	A Billy Graham Crusade in Song	1956	5.00	10.00	20.00
❏ LPM-1564 [M]	George Beverly Shea	1957	5.00	10.00	20.00
❏ LPM-1642 [M]	Through the Years	1957	5.00	10.00	20.00
❏ LSP-1949 [S]	The Love of God	1958	5.00	10.00	20.00
❏ LSP-1967 [S]	Blessed Assurance	1959	5.00	10.00	20.00
❏ LSP-2064 [S]	Christmas Hymns	1959	5.00	10.00	20.00

SHEARING, GEORGE
CAPITOL
❏ T 648 [M]	The Shearing Spell	1956	7.50	15.00	30.00
—Turquoise label					
❏ T 648 [M]	The Shearing Spell	1959	5.00	10.00	20.00
—Black label with colorband, logo on left					
❏ T 720 [M]	Velvet Carpet	1956	7.50	15.00	30.00
—Turquoise label					
❏ T 720 [M]	Velvet Carpet	1959	5.00	10.00	20.00
—Black label with colorband, logo on left					
❏ T 737 [M]	Latin Escapade	1957	7.50	15.00	30.00
—Turquoise label					
❏ T 737 [M]	Latin Escapade	1959	5.00	10.00	20.00
—Black label with colorband, logo on left					
❏ ST 858 [S]	Black Satin	1959	5.00	10.00	20.00
—Black label with colorband, logo on left					
❏ T 858 [M]	Black Satin	1957	7.50	15.00	30.00
—Turquoise label					
❏ T 858 [M]	Black Satin	1959	5.00	10.00	20.00
—Black label with colorband, logo on left					
❏ T 909 [M]	Shearing Piano	1957	7.50	15.00	30.00
—Turquoise label					
❏ T 909 [M]	Shearing Piano	1959	5.00	10.00	20.00
—Black label with colorband, logo on left					
❏ T 943 [M]	Night Mist	1957	7.50	15.00	30.00
—Turquoise label					
❏ ST 1038 [S]	Burnished Brass	1959	6.25	12.50	25.00
—Black label with colorband, logo on left					
❏ ST 1038 [S]	Burnished Brass	1962	5.00	10.00	20.00
—Black label with colorband, logo on top					
❏ T 1038 [M]	Burnished Brass	1958	5.00	10.00	20.00
—Black label with colorband, logo on left					
❏ ST 1082 [S]	Latin Lace	1958	6.25	12.50	25.00
—Black label with colorband, logo on left					
❏ ST 1082 [S]	Latin Lace	1962	5.00	10.00	20.00
—Black label with colorband, logo on top					
❏ T 1082 [M]	Latin Lace	1958	5.00	10.00	20.00
—Black label with colorband, logo on left					
❏ ST 1124 [S]	Blue Chiffon	1959	6.25	12.50	25.00
—Black label with colorband, logo on left					
❏ ST 1124 [S]	Blue Chiffon	1962	5.00	10.00	20.00
—Black label with colorband, logo on top					
❏ T 1124 [M]	Blue Chiffon	1959	5.00	10.00	20.00
—Black label with colorband, logo on left					
❏ ST 1187 [S]	George Shearing On Stage	1959	6.25	12.50	25.00
—Black label with colorband, logo on left					
❏ ST 1187 [S]	George Shearing On Stage	1962	5.00	10.00	20.00
—Black label with colorband, logo on top					
❏ T 1187 [M]	George Shearing On Stage	1959	5.00	10.00	20.00
—Black label with colorband, logo on left					
❏ ST 1275 [S]	Latin Affair	1960	6.25	12.50	25.00
—Black label with colorband, logo on left					
❏ ST 1275 [S]	Latin Affair	1962	5.00	10.00	20.00
—Black label with colorband, logo on top					
❏ T 1275 [M]	Latin Affair	1960	5.00	10.00	20.00
—Black label with colorband, logo on left					
❏ ST 1334 [S]	White Satin	1960	6.25	12.50	25.00
—Black label with colorband, logo on left					

Number	Title (A Side/B Side)	Yr	VG	VG+	NM
❑ ST 1334 [S]	White Satin	1962	5.00	10.00	20.00
—Black label with colorband, logo on top					
❑ T 1334 [M]	White Satin	1960	5.00	10.00	20.00
—Black label with colorband, logo on left					
❑ ST 1416 [S]	On the Sunny Side of the Strip	1960	6.25	12.50	25.00
—Black label with colorband, logo on left					
❑ ST 1416 [S]	On the Sunny Side of the Strip	1962	5.00	10.00	20.00
—Black label with colorband, logo on top					
❑ T 1416 [M]	On the Sunny Side of the Strip	1960	5.00	10.00	20.00
—Black label with colorband, logo on left					
❑ ST 1472 [S]	The Shearing Touch	1961	6.25	12.50	25.00
—Black label with colorband, logo on left					
❑ ST 1472 [S]	The Shearing Touch	1962	5.00	10.00	20.00
—Black label with colorband, logo on top					
❑ T 1472 [M]	The Shearing Touch	1961	5.00	10.00	20.00
—Black label with colorband, logo on left					
❑ ST 1567 [S]	Mood Latino	1961	6.25	12.50	25.00
—Black label with colorband, logo on left					
❑ ST 1567 [S]	Mood Latino	1962	5.00	10.00	20.00
—Black label with colorband, logo on top					
❑ T 1567 [M]	Mood Latino	1961	5.00	10.00	20.00
—Black label with colorband, logo on left					
❑ ST 1628 [S]	Satin Affair	1961	6.25	12.50	25.00
—Black label with colorband, logo on left					
❑ ST 1628 [S]	Satin Affair	1962	5.00	10.00	20.00
—Black label with colorband, logo on top					
❑ T 1628 [M]	Satin Affair	1961	5.00	10.00	20.00
—Black label with colorband, logo on left					
❑ ST 1715 [S]	San Francisco Scene	1962	5.00	10.00	20.00
❑ ST 1755 [S]	Concerto for My Love	1962	5.00	10.00	20.00
❑ ST 1827 [S]	Jazz Moments	1963	5.00	10.00	20.00
❑ ST 1873 [S]	Bossa Nova	1963	5.00	10.00	20.00
❑ ST 1874 [S]	Touch Me Softly	1963	5.00	10.00	20.00
DISCOVERY					
❑ DL-3002 [10]	George Shearing Quintet	1950	15.00	30.00	60.00
LONDON					
❑ LL 295 [10]	Souvenirs	1951	15.00	30.00	60.00
❑ LL 1343 [M]	By Request	1956	7.50	15.00	30.00
MGM					
❑ E-90 [10]	A Touch of Genius	1951	12.50	25.00	50.00
❑ E-155 [10]	I Hear Music	1952	12.50	25.00	50.00
❑ E-226 [10]	When Lights Are Low	1953	12.50	25.00	50.00
❑ E-252 [10]	An Evening with George Shearing	1954	12.50	25.00	50.00
❑ E-518 [10]	You're Hearing the George Shearing Quartet	1950	15.00	30.00	60.00
❑ E-3122 [M]	An Evening with Shearing	1955	7.50	15.00	30.00
❑ E-3175 [M]	Shearing Caravan	1955	7.50	15.00	30.00
❑ E-3216 [M]	You're Hearing George Shearing	1955	7.50	15.00	30.00
❑ E-3264 [M]	When Lights Are Low	1955	7.50	15.00	30.00
❑ E-3265 [M]	Touch of Genius	1955	7.50	15.00	30.00
❑ E-3266 [M]	I Hear Music	1955	7.50	15.00	30.00
❑ E-3293 [M]	Shearing in Hi-Fi	1955	7.50	15.00	30.00
MOSAIC					
❑ MQ7-157 [(7)]	The Complete Capitol Live Recordings of George Shearing	199?	30.00	60.00	120.00
SAVOY					
❑ MG-15003 [10]	Piano Solo	1951	15.00	30.00	60.00

SHEARING, GEORGE, AND THE MONTGOMERY BROTHERS

JAZZLAND

Number	Title (A Side/B Side)	Yr	VG	VG+	NM
❑ JLP-55 [M]	Love Walked In	1961	7.50	15.00	30.00
—Cover has Shearing and the brothers					
❑ JLP-55 [M]	Love Walked In	1962	6.25	12.50	25.00
—Cover has a woman					
❑ JLP-955 [S]	Love Walked In	1961	10.00	20.00	40.00
—Cover has Shearing and the brothers					
❑ JLP-955 [S]	Love Walked In	1962	7.50	15.00	30.00
—Cover has a woman					

SHEEN, MICKEY

HERALD

Number	Title (A Side/B Side)	Yr	VG	VG+	NM
❑ HLP-0105 [M]	Have Swing, Will Travel	1956	15.00	30.00	60.00

SHELDON, JACK

CAPITOL

Number	Title (A Side/B Side)	Yr	VG	VG+	NM
❑ ST 1851 [S]	Out!	1963	5.00	10.00	20.00
❑ ST 2029 [S]	Play Buddy, Play!	1966	5.00	10.00	20.00
GENE NORMAN					
❑ GNP-60 [M]	Jack's Groove	1961	10.00	20.00	40.00
JAZZ WEST					
❑ JWLP-1 [10]	Get Out of Town	1955	100.00	200.00	400.00
❑ JWLP-2 [10]	Jack Sheldon Quintet	1955	100.00	200.00	400.00
❑ JWLP-6 [M]	The Quartet and the Quintet	1956	75.00	150.00	30.00
REPRISE					
❑ R-2004 [M]	A Jazz Profile of Ray Charles	1961	6.25	12.50	25.00
❑ R9-2004 [S]	A Jazz Profile of Ray Charles	1961	7.50	15.00	30.00

SHELTON, RICKY VAN

COLUMBIA

Number	Title (A Side/B Side)	Yr	VG	VG+	NM
❑ B6C 40602	Wild-Eyed Dream	1987	2.00	4.00	8.00
❑ FC 44221	Loving Proof	1988	2.00	4.00	8.00
❑ C 45250	RVS III	1990	3.75	7.50	15.00
❑ FC 45269	Ricky Van Shelton Sings Christmas	1989	3.00	6.00	12.00
❑ C 46855	Backroads	1990	5.00	10.00	20.00
—Vinyl available only through Columbia House					

SHELTON, ROSCOE

EXCELLO

Number	Title (A Side/B Side)	Yr	VG	VG+	NM
❑ LP-8002 [M]	Roscoe Shelton Sings	1961	150.00	300.00	600.00
SOUND STAGE 7					
❑ SSS-5002 [M]	Soul in His Music, Music in His Soul	1966	10.00	20.00	40.00
❑ SSS-15002 [S]	Soul in His Music, Music in His Soul	1966	12.50	25.00	50.00

SHENANDOAH

COLUMBIA

Number	Title (A Side/B Side)	Yr	VG	VG+	NM
❑ BFC 40788	Shenandoah	1987	2.50	5.00	10.00
❑ FC 44468	The Road Not Taken	1989	3.00	6.00	12.00
❑ C 48885	Greatest Hits	1992	5.00	10.00	20.00
—Vinyl available only through Columbia House					

SHEP AND THE LIMELITES

HULL

Number	Title (A Side/B Side)	Yr	VG	VG+	NM
❑ 1001 [M]	Our Anniversary	1962	300.00	600.00	1200.
ROULETTE					
❑ R-25350 [M]	Our Anniversary	1967	20.00	40.00	80.00
❑ SR-25350 [R]	Our Anniversary	1967	12.50	25.00	50.00

SHEPARD, JEAN

CAPITOL

Number	Title (A Side/B Side)	Yr	VG	VG+	NM
❑ ST-171	I'll Fly Away	1969	3.75	7.50	15.00
❑ ST-321	Seven Lonely Days	1969	3.75	7.50	15.00
❑ ST-441	Best By Request	1970	3.75	7.50	15.00
❑ ST-559	A Woman's Hand	1970	3.75	7.50	15.00
❑ T 728 [M]	Songs of a Love Affair	1956	15.00	30.00	60.00
❑ ST-738	Here and Now	1971	3.75	7.50	15.00
❑ ST-815	Just As Soon As I Get Over Loving You	1971	3.75	7.50	15.00
❑ T 1126 [M]	Lonesome Love	1959	10.00	20.00	40.00
❑ T 1253 [M]	This Is Jean Shepard	1959	10.00	20.00	40.00
❑ ST 1525 [S]	Got You on My Mind	1961	7.50	15.00	30.00
❑ T 1525 [M]	Got You on My Mind	1961	6.25	12.50	25.00
❑ ST 1663 [S]	Heartaches and Tears	1962	7.50	15.00	30.00
❑ T 1663 [M]	Heartaches and Tears	1962	6.25	12.50	25.00
❑ DT 1922 [R]	The Best of Jean Shepherd	1963	3.75	7.50	15.00
❑ T 1922 [M]	The Best of Jean Shepherd	1963	6.25	12.50	25.00
❑ ST 2187 [S]	Lighthearted and Blue	1964	5.00	10.00	20.00
❑ T 2187 [M]	Lighthearted and Blue	1964	3.75	7.50	15.00
❑ ST 2416 [S]	It's a Man Every Time	1965	3.75	7.50	15.00
❑ T 2416 [M]	It's a Man Every Time	1965	3.00	6.00	12.00
❑ ST 2547 [S]	Many Happy Hangovers	1966	3.75	7.50	15.00
❑ T 2547 [M]	Many Happy Hangovers	1966	3.00	6.00	12.00
❑ ST 2690 [S]	Heart, We Did All That We Could	1967	3.75	7.50	15.00
❑ T 2690 [M]	Heart, We Did All That We Could	1967	3.75	7.50	15.00
❑ ST 2765 [S]	Your Forevers Don't Last Very Long	1967	3.75	7.50	15.00
❑ T 2765 [M]	Your Forevers Don't Last Very Long	1967	5.00	10.00	20.00
❑ ST 2871 [S]	Heart to Heart	1968	3.75	7.50	15.00
❑ T 2871 [M]	Heart to Heart	1968	10.00	20.00	40.00
❑ ST 2966	A Real Good Woman	1968	3.75	7.50	15.00
❑ ST-11049	Just Like Walkin' in the Sunshine	1972	3.00	6.00	12.00
❑ SM-11409	For the Good Times	1975	2.50	5.00	10.00
HILLTOP					
❑ JS-6068	Under Your Spell Again	197?	2.50	5.00	10.00
UNITED ARTISTS					
❑ UA-LA144-F	Slippin' Away	1973	3.00	6.00	12.00
❑ UA-LA307-R	I'll Do Anything It Takes	1974	3.00	6.00	12.00
❑ UA-LA363-G	Poor Sweet Baby and Ten More Bill Anderson Songs	1975	3.00	6.00	12.00
❑ UA-LA525-G	I'm a Believer	1975	3.00	6.00	12.00
❑ UA-LA609	Mercy, Ain't Love Good	1976	3.00	6.00	12.00
❑ UA-LA685-G	Jean Shepard's Greatest Hits	1976	2.50	5.00	10.00

SHEPARD, JEAN, AND RAY PILLOW

CAPITOL

Number	Title (A Side/B Side)	Yr	VG	VG+	NM
❑ ST 2537 [S]	I'll Take the Dog	1966	5.00	10.00	20.00
❑ T 2537 [M]	I'll Take the Dog	1966	3.75	7.50	15.00

SHEPARD, TOMMY

CORAL

Number	Title (A Side/B Side)	Yr	VG	VG+	NM
❑ CRL 57110 [M]	Shepard's Flock	1957	20.00	40.00	80.00

SHEPHERD, CYBILL

PARAMOUNT

Number	Title (A Side/B Side)	Yr	VG	VG+	NM
❑ PAS-1018	Cybill Does It...to Cole Porter	1974	5.00	10.00	20.00
—With poster					

SHEPHERD, JEAN

ELEKTRA

Number	Title (A Side/B Side)	Yr	VG	VG+	NM
❑ EKL-172 [M]	Jean Shepherd and Other Foibles	1959	12.50	25.00	50.00

SHEPP, ARCHIE

ABC IMPULSE!

Number	Title (A Side/B Side)	Yr	VG	VG+	NM
❑ AS-9154 [S]	The Magic of Ju Ju	1968	5.00	10.00	20.00
❑ AS-9162 [S]	Three for a Quarter, One for a Dime	1968	5.00	10.00	20.00
❑ AS-9170 [S]	The Way Ahead	1969	5.00	10.00	20.00
❑ AS-9188	For Losers	1970	5.00	10.00	20.00
DELMARK					
❑ DL-409 [M]	Archie Shepp in Europe	1968	7.50	15.00	30.00
❑ DS-9409 [S]	Archie Shepp in Europe	1968	5.00	10.00	20.00
IMPULSE!					
❑ A-71 [M]	Four for Trane	1964	6.25	12.50	25.00
❑ AS-71 [S]	Four for Trane	1964	7.50	15.00	30.00
❑ A-86 [M]	Fire Music	1965	6.25	12.50	25.00
❑ AS-86 [S]	Fire Music	1965	7.50	15.00	30.00
❑ A-97 [M]	On This Night	1966	7.50	15.00	30.00
❑ AS-97 [S]	On This Night	1966	6.25	12.50	25.00
❑ A-9118 [M]	Live In San Francisco	1967	7.50	15.00	30.00
❑ AS-9118 [S]	Live In San Francisco	1967	6.25	12.50	25.00
❑ A-9134 [M]	Mama Too Tight	1967	7.50	15.00	30.00
❑ AS-9134 [S]	Mama Too Tight	1967	6.25	12.50	25.00

SHEPP, ARCHIE, AND BILL DIXON

SAVOY

Number	Title (A Side/B Side)	Yr	VG	VG+	NM
❑ MG-12178 [M]	The Archie Shepp-Bill Dixon Quartet	1962	7.50	15.00	30.00
❑ MG-12184 [M]	Archie Shepp and the New Contemporary 5/ The Bill Dixon 7-Tette	1964	12.50	25.00	50.00
—White bordered cover					

Number	Title (A Side/B Side)	Yr	VG	VG+	NM
❏ MG-12184 [M]	Archie Shepp and the New Contemporary 5/ The Bill Dixon 7-Tette	1965	6.25	12.50	25.00
—Purple bordered cover					

SHEPPARDS, THE
COLLECTABLES
❏ COL-5078	Golden Classics	198?	2.50	5.00	10.00
CONSTELLATION					
❏ C-4 [M]	Collectors Showcase: The Sheppards	1964	20.00	40.00	80.00
❏ CS-4 [R]	Collectors Showcase: The Sheppards	1964	10.00	20.00	40.00
SOLID SMOKE					
❏ SS-8004	The Sheppards	1980	2.50	5.00	10.00
❏ SS-8028	18 Dusty Diamonds	1984	2.50	5.00	10.00

SHERMAN, ALLAN
JUBLIEE
❏ JGM 5019 [M]	More Folk Songs by Allan Sherman	1963	5.00	10.00	20.00
—Two early Allan Sherman sides plus comedy bits by others					
RCA RED SEAL					
❏ LM-2773 [M]	Peter and the Commissar	1964	5.00	10.00	20.00
❏ LSC-2773 [S]	Peter and the Commissar	1964	6.25	12.50	25.00
—With Arthur Fiedler and the Boston Pops Orchestra					
RHINO					
❏ RNLP-005	The Best of Allan Sherman	198?	2.50	5.00	10.00
❏ RNLP 70818	A Gift of Laughter	1986	2.50	5.00	10.00
WARNER BROS.					
❏ W 1475 [M]	My Son, the Folk Singer	1962	3.75	7.50	15.00
❏ WS 1475 [S]	My Son, the Folk Singer	1962	5.00	10.00	20.00
—Gold label					
❏ W 1487 [M]	My Son, the Celebrity	1963	3.75	7.50	15.00
❏ WS 1487 [S]	My Son, the Celebrity	1963	5.00	10.00	20.00
—Gold label					
❏ W 1501 [M]	My Son, the Nut	1963	3.75	7.50	15.00
❏ WS 1501 [S]	My Son, the Nut	1963	5.00	10.00	20.00
—Gold label					
❏ W 1539 [M]	Allan in Wonderland	1964	3.00	6.00	12.00
❏ WS 1539 [S]	Allan in Wonderland	1964	3.75	7.50	15.00
—Gold label					
❏ W 1569 [M]	For Swingin' Livers Only!	1964	3.00	6.00	12.00
❏ WS 1569 [S]	For Swingin' Livers Only!	1964	3.75	7.50	15.00
—Gold label					
❏ W 1604 [M]	My Name Is Allan	1965	3.00	6.00	12.00
❏ WS 1604 [S]	My Name Is Allan	1965	3.75	7.50	15.00
—Gold label					
❏ W 1649 [M]	Allan Sherman — Live	1966	3.00	6.00	12.00
❏ WS 1649 [S]	Allan Sherman — Live	1966	3.75	7.50	15.00
—Gold label					
❏ W 1684 [M]	Togetherness	1967	3.75	7.50	15.00
❏ WS 1684 [S]	Togetherness	1967	5.00	10.00	20.00
—Gold label					

SHERRILL, JOYA
COLUMBIA
❏ CL 1378 [M]	Sugar and Spice	1959	6.25	12.50	25.00
❏ CS 8178 [S]	Sugar and Spice	1960	7.50	15.00	30.00
20TH CENTURY FOX					
❏ TFL-3170 [M]	Joya Sherrill Sings Duke Ellington	196?	6.25	12.50	25.00
❏ TFS-4170 [S]	Joya Sherrill Sings Duke Ellington	196?	7.50	15.00	30.00

SHERRYS, THE
GUYDEN
| ❏ GLP 503 [M] | At the Hop with the Sherrys | 1963 | 62.50 | 125.00 | 250.00 |

SHERWOOD, BOBBY
CAPITOL
❏ H 320 [10]	Classics in Jazz	1952	15.00	30.00	60.00
❏ T 320 [M]	Classics in Jazz	1955	10.00	20.00	40.00
❏ H 463 [10]	Bobby Sherwood	1954	12.50	25.00	50.00
JUBILEE					
❏ JLP-1040 [M]	I'm an Old Cowhand	1957	7.50	15.00	30.00
❏ JLP-1061 [M]	Pal Joey	1958	7.50	15.00	30.00
❏ SDJLP-1061 [S]	Pal Joey	1959	6.25	12.50	25.00

SHIGETA, JAMES
CHOREO
| ❏ A-7 [M] | We Speak the Same Language | 1962 | 6.25 | 12.50 | 25.00 |
| ❏ AS-7 [S] | We Speak the Same Language | 1962 | 7.50 | 15.00 | 30.00 |

SHIHAB, SAHIB
ARGO
❏ LP-742 [M]	Summer Dawn	1964	6.25	12.50	25.00
❏ LPS-742 [S]	Summer Dawn	1964	7.50	15.00	30.00
SAVOY					
❏ MG-12124 [M]	Jazz Sahib	1957	12.50	25.00	50.00

SHIHAB, SAHIB/HERBIE MANN
SAVOY
| ❏ MG-12112 [M] | The Jazz We Heard Last Summer | 1957 | 12.50 | 25.00 | 50.00 |

SHILOH
AMOS
| ❏ AAS-7015 | Shiloh | 1971 | 20.00 | 40.00 | 80.00 |

SHIP, THE
ELEKTRA
| ❏ EKS-75036 | The Ship | 1972 | 5.00 | 10.00 | 20.00 |

SHIRELLES, THE
RCA VICTOR
❏ LSP-4581	Happy and In Love	1971	3.75	7.50	15.00
❏ LSP-4698	The Shirelles	1972	3.75	7.50	15.00
RHINO					
❏ RNDA-1101 [(2)]	Anthology (1959-1967)	1984	3.00	6.00	12.00

SCEPTER
❏ S-501 [M]	Tonight's the Night	1961	50.00	100.00	200.00
—"Scepter" in scroll at top of label					
❏ SPM-501 [M]	Tonight's the Night	1962	15.00	30.00	60.00
—"Scepter Records" at left of label					
❏ SPS-501 [S]	Tonight's the Night	1965	25.00	50.00	100.00
❏ S-502 [M]	The Shirelles Sing to Trumpets and Strings	1961	50.00	100.00	200.00
—"Scepter" in scroll at top of label					
❏ SPM-502 [M]	The Shirelles Sing to Trumpets and Strings	1962	15.00	30.00	60.00
—"Scepter Records" at left of label					
❏ SPS-502 [S]	The Shirelles Sing to Trumpets and Strings	1965	25.00	50.00	100.00
❏ SPM-504 [M]	Baby It's You	1962	25.00	50.00	100.00
❏ SPS-504 [S]	Baby It's You	1965	25.00	50.00	100.00
❏ SPM-505 [M]	A Twist Party	1962	20.00	40.00	80.00
❏ SPS-505 [S]	A Twist Party	1965	25.00	50.00	100.00
❏ SPM-507 [M]	The Shirelles' Greatest Hits	1962	10.00	20.00	40.00
❏ SPS-507 [S]	The Shirelles' Greatest Hits	1965	12.50	25.00	50.00
❏ SPM-511 [M]	Foolish Little Girl	1963	12.50	25.00	50.00
❏ SPS-511 [S]	Foolish Little Girl	1965	20.00	40.00	80.00
❏ SPM-514 [M]	It's a Mad, Mad, Mad, Mad World	1963	10.00	20.00	40.00
❏ SPS-514 [S]	It's a Mad, Mad, Mad, Mad World	1963	12.50	25.00	50.00
❏ SPM-516 [M]	The Shirelles Sing the Golden Oldies	1964	10.00	20.00	40.00
❏ SPS-516 [S]	The Shirelles Sing the Golden Oldies	1964	12.50	25.00	50.00
❏ SPM-560 [M]	The Shirelles' Greatest Hits, Volume 2	1967	5.00	10.00	20.00
❏ SPS-560 [S]	The Shirelles' Greatest Hits, Volume 2	1967	6.25	12.50	25.00
❏ SPM-562 [M]	Spontaneous Combustion	1967	10.00	20.00	40.00
❏ SPS-562 [S]	Spontaneous Combustion	1967	12.50	25.00	50.00
❏ SPS-569	Eternally Soul	1968	7.50	15.00	30.00
❏ SPS-2-599 [(2)]	Remember When	1972	5.00	10.00	20.00
SPRINGBOARD					
❏ 4006	The Shirelles Sing Their Very Best	1973	2.00	4.00	8.00
UNITED ARTISTS					
❏ UA-LA340-E	The Very Best of the Shirelles	1974	2.50	5.00	10.00

SHIRLEY, DON
AUDIO FIDELITY
❏ AFLP-1897 [M]	Don Shirley	1959	5.00	10.00	20.00
❏ AFSD-5897 [S]	Don Shirley	1959	7.50	15.00	30.00
CADENCE					
❏ CLP-1001 [M]	Tonal Expressions	1955	10.00	20.00	40.00
❏ CLP-1004 [M]	Piano Perspectives	1955	10.00	20.00	40.00
❏ CLP-1009 [M]	Orpheus in the Underworld	1956	10.00	20.00	40.00
❏ CLP-1015 [M]	Don Shirley Duo	1956	10.00	20.00	40.00
❏ CLP-3007 [M]	Don Shirley Solos	1958	7.50	15.00	30.00
❏ CLP-3008 [M]	Don Shirley with Two Basses	1958	7.50	15.00	30.00
❏ CLP-3032 [M]	Don Shirley Plays Gershwin	1960	6.25	12.50	25.00
❏ CLP-3033 [M]	Don Shirley Plays Standards	1960	6.25	12.50	25.00
❏ CLP-3034 [M]	Don Shirley Plays Love Songs	1960	6.25	12.50	25.00
❏ CLP-3035 [M]	Don Shirley Plays Birdland Lullabies	1960	6.25	12.50	25.00
❏ CLP-3036 [M]	Don Shirley Plays Showtunes	1960	6.25	12.50	25.00
❏ CLP-3037 [M]	Orpheus in the Underworld	1960	6.25	12.50	25.00
—Reissue of 1009					
❏ CLP-3046 [M]	Trio	1961	5.00	10.00	20.00
❏ CLP-3048 [M]	Pianist Extraordinary	1962	5.00	10.00	20.00
❏ CLP-3049 [M]	Piano Arrangements of Spirituals	1962	5.00	10.00	20.00
❏ CLP-3057 [M]	Drown in My Own Tears	1962	5.00	10.00	20.00
❏ CLP-25046 [S]	Trio	1961	7.50	15.00	30.00
❏ CLP-25048 [S]	Pianist Extraordinary	1962	7.50	15.00	30.00
❏ CLP-25049 [S]	Piano Arrangements of Spirituals	1962	7.50	15.00	30.00
❏ CLP-25057 [S]	Drown in My Own Tears	1962	7.50	15.00	30.00
COLUMBIA					
❏ CL 2396 [M]	Water Boy	1965	3.75	7.50	15.00
❏ CS 9196 [S]	Water Boy	1965	5.00	10.00	20.00

SHIRLEY AND LEE
ALADDIN
❏ 807 [M]	Let the Good Times Roll	1956	375.00	750.00	1500.
IMPERIAL					
❏ LP-9179 [M]	Let the Good Times Roll	1962	75.00	150.00	300.00
—Reissue of Aladdin LP					
SCORE					
❏ SLP-4023 [M]	Let the Good Times Roll	1957	200.00	400.00	800.00
—Reissue of Aladdin LP					
WARWICK					
❏ W-2028 [M]	Let the Good Times Roll	1961	37.50	75.00	150.00
❏ W-2028ST [S]	Let the Good Times Roll	1961	75.00	150.00	300.00

SHIVA'S HEADBAND
APE
❏ 1001	Psychedelic Yesterday	1981	5.00	10.00	20.00
ARMADILLO					
❏ (no #)	Coming to a Head	1969	62.50	125.00	250.00
CAPITOL					
❏ ST-538	Take Me to the Mountains	1970	15.00	30.00	60.00

SHOCKED, MICHELLE
MERCURY
❏ PRO 797 [DJ]	Live	1990	5.00	10.00	20.00
—Five-song mini-LP for radio stations with custom jacket					
❏ 834581-1	The Texas Campfire Tapes	1988	3.00	6.00	12.00
❏ 834924-1	Short Sharp Shocked	1988	2.50	5.00	10.00
❏ 838878-1	Captain Swing	1989	2.50	5.00	10.00

SHOCKING BLUE, THE
COLOSSUS
| ❏ CS-1000 | The Shocking Blue | 1970 | 6.25 | 12.50 | 25.00 |

SHOES
(NO LABEL)
| ❏ (no #) | One in Versailles | 1976 | 30.00 | 60.00 | 120.00 |

Number	Title (A Side/B Side)	Yr	VG	VG+	NM
BLACK VINYL					
❏ 51477	Black Vinyl Shoes	1977	20.00	40.00	80.00
ELEKTRA					
❏ 6E-244	Present Tense	1979	2.50	5.00	10.00
❏ 6E-303	Tongue Twister	1980	2.50	5.00	10.00
❏ AS 11570 [DJ]	Shoes on Ice — Live	1982	12.50	25.00	50.00
—Promo-only 7-song live record; issued in generic jacket					
❏ 60146	Boomerang	1982	2.50	5.00	10.00
PVC					
❏ 7904	Black Vinyl Shoes	1979	5.00	10.00	20.00
SHONDELL, TROY					
EVEREST					
❏ 1206 [S]	The Many Sides of Troy Shondell	1963	20.00	40.00	80.00
❏ 5206 [M]	The Many Sides of Troy Shondell	1963	12.50	25.00	50.00
SUNSET					
❏ SUM-1174 [M]	This Time	1967	3.75	7.50	15.00
❏ SUS-5174 [S]	This Time	1967	3.75	7.50	15.00
SHORE, DINAH					
BAINBRIDGE					
❏ 6232	Once Upon a Summertime	198?	2.50	5.00	10.00
CAPITOL					
❏ ST 1247 [S]	Dinah, Yes Indeed	1959	6.25	12.50	25.00
❏ T 1247 [M]	Dinah, Yes Indeed	1959	5.00	10.00	20.00
❏ ST 1296 [S]	Somebody Loves Me	1959	6.25	12.50	25.00
❏ T 1296 [M]	Somebody Loves Me	1959	5.00	10.00	20.00
❏ ST 1354 [S]	Dinah Sings Some Blues with Red	1960	7.50	15.00	30.00
❏ T 1354 [M]	Dinah Sings Some Blues with Red	1960	6.25	12.50	25.00
❏ ST 1422 [S]	Dinah Sings/Previn Plays	1960	6.25	12.50	25.00
❏ T 1422 [M]	Dinah Sings/Previn Plays	1960	5.00	10.00	20.00
❏ ST 1655 [S]	Dinah Down Home	1962	6.25	12.50	25.00
❏ T 1655 [M]	Dinah Down Home	1962	5.00	10.00	20.00
❏ ST 1704 [S]	The Fabulous Hits of Dinah Shore	1962	3.75	7.50	15.00
—Black label with colorband, logo at top					
❏ ST 1704 [S]	The Fabulous Hits of Dinah Shore	1962	6.25	12.50	25.00
—Black label with colorband, logo at left					
❏ T 1704 [M]	The Fabulous Hits of Dinah Shore	1962	3.00	6.00	12.00
—Black label with colorband, logo at top					
❏ T 1704 [M]	The Fabulous Hits of Dinah Shore	1962	5.00	10.00	20.00
—Black label with colorband, logo at left					
COLUMBIA					
❏ CL 6004 [10]	Dinah Shore Sings	1949	12.50	25.00	50.00
❏ CL 6069 [10]	Reminiscing	1949	12.50	25.00	50.00
❏ C 34395	The Best of Dinah Shore	1977	2.50	5.00	10.00
HARMONY					
❏ HL 7010 [M]	Dinah Shore Sings Cole Porter and Richard Rodgers	195?	5.00	10.00	20.00
❏ HL 7188 [M]	Buttons and Bows	195?	3.75	7.50	15.00
❏ HL 7239 [M]	Lavender Blue	1959	3.75	7.50	15.00
PICKWICK					
❏ SPC-3524	It's So Nice to Have a Man Around the House	197?	2.00	4.00	8.00
PROJECT 3					
❏ PR-5018 SD	Songs for Sometime Losers	1968	3.75	7.50	15.00
RCA VICTOR					
❏ LPM-1154 [M]	Holding Hands at Midnight	1955	7.50	15.00	30.00
❏ ANL1-1158	The Best of Dinah Shore	1976	2.50	5.00	10.00
❏ LPM-1214 [M]	Bouquet of Blues	1956	7.50	15.00	30.00
❏ LPM-1719 [M]	Moments Like These	1958	6.25	12.50	25.00
❏ LPM-3103 [10]	Dinah Shore Sings the Blues	1953	10.00	20.00	40.00
❏ LPM-3214 [10]	The Dinah Shore TV Show	1954	10.00	20.00	40.00
REPRISE					
❏ R-6150 [M]	The Lower East Side Revisited	1965	3.00	6.00	12.00
❏ RS-6150 [S]	The Lower East Side Revisited	1965	3.75	7.50	15.00
SEAGULL					
❏ LG-8203	Oh Lonesome Me	198?	2.50	5.00	10.00
STANYAN					
❏ 10071	Dinah Sings the Blues	197?	2.50	5.00	10.00
❏ 10125	Once Upon a Summertime	197?	2.50	5.00	10.00
❏ 10139	For Always	1977	2.50	5.00	10.00
SHORT, BOBBY					
ATLANTIC					
❏ SD 2-606 [(2)]	Bobby Short Loves Cole Porter	1972	5.00	10.00	20.00
❏ SD 2-607 [(2)]	Mad About Noel Coward	1972	5.00	10.00	20.00
❏ 1214 [M]	Songs by Bobby Short	1955	7.50	15.00	30.00
—Black label					
❏ 1214 [M]	Songs by Bobby Short	1961	5.00	10.00	20.00
—White "fan" logo at right of label					
❏ 1230 [M]	Bobby Short	1956	7.50	15.00	30.00
—Black label					
❏ 1230 [M]	Bobby Short	1961	5.00	10.00	20.00
—White "fan" logo at right of label					
❏ 1262 [M]	Speaking of Love	1958	7.50	15.00	30.00
—Black label					
❏ 1262 [M]	Speaking of Love	1961	5.00	10.00	20.00
—White "fan" logo at right of label					
❏ SD 1262 [S]	Speaking of Love	1959	10.00	20.00	40.00
—Green label					
❏ SD 1262 [S]	Speaking of Love	1961	6.25	12.50	25.00
—White "fan" logo at right of label					
❏ 1285 [M]	Sing Me a Swing Song	1958	7.50	15.00	30.00
—Black label					
❏ 1285 [M]	Sing Me a Swing Song	1961	5.00	10.00	20.00
—White "fan" logo at right of label					
❏ 1302 [M]	The Mad Twenties	1959	7.50	15.00	30.00
—Black label					
❏ 1302 [M]	The Mad Twenties	1961	5.00	10.00	20.00
—White "fan" logo at right of label					

Number	Title (A Side/B Side)	Yr	VG	VG+	NM
❏ SD 1302 [S]	The Mad Twenties	1959	10.00	20.00	40.00
—Green label					
❏ SD 1302 [S]	The Mad Twenties	1961	6.25	12.50	25.00
—White "fan" logo at right of label					
❏ SD 1302 [S]	The Mad Twenties	1963	5.00	10.00	20.00
—Black "fan" logo at right of label					
❏ 1321 [M]	On the East Side	1960	7.50	15.00	30.00
—Black label					
❏ 1321 [M]	On the East Side	1961	5.00	10.00	20.00
—White "fan" logo at right of label					
❏ SD 1321 [S]	On the East Side	1960	10.00	20.00	40.00
—Green label					
❏ SD 1321 [S]	On the East Side	1961	6.25	12.50	25.00
—White "fan" logo at right of label					
❏ SD 1321 [S]	On the East Side	1963	5.00	10.00	20.00
—Black "fan" logo at right of label					
❏ 81715 [(4)]	50 from Bobby Short	1987	7.50	15.00	30.00
SHORTER, ALAN					
VERVE					
❏ V6-8769	Orgasm	1969	5.00	10.00	20.00
SHORTER, WAYNE					
BLUE NOTE					
❏ BLP-4173 [M]	Night Drreamer	1964	6.25	12.50	25.00
❏ BLP-4182 [M]	Juju	1965	6.25	12.50	25.00
❏ BLP-4194 [M]	Speak No Evil	1966	6.25	12.50	25.00
❏ BLP-4219 [M]	The All Seeing Eye	1966	6.25	12.50	25.00
❏ BST-84173 [S]	Night Drreamer	1964	7.50	15.00	30.00
—With New York, USA address on label					
❏ BST-84182 [S]	Juju	1965	7.50	15.00	30.00
—With New York, USA address on label					
❏ BST-84194 [S]	Speak No Evil	1966	7.50	15.00	30.00
—With New York, USA address on label					
❏ BST-84219 [S]	The All Seeing Eye	1966	7.50	15.00	30.00
—With New York, USA address on label					
❏ BST-84232	Adam's Apple	1967	5.00	10.00	20.00
❏ BST-84297	Schizophrenia	1969	5.00	10.00	20.00
❏ BST-84332	Super Nova	1970	5.00	10.00	20.00
VEE JAY					
❏ LP-3006 [M]	Introducing Wayne Shorter	1960	10.00	20.00	40.00
❏ SR-3006 [S]	Introducing Wayne Shorter	1960	12.50	25.00	50.00
❏ LP-3029 [M]	Wayning Moments	1962	7.50	15.00	30.00
❏ SR-3029 [S]	Wayning Moments	1962	10.00	20.00	40.00
❏ LP-3057 [M]	Second Genesis	1963	7.50	15.00	30.00
❏ SR-3057 [S]	Second Genesis	1963	10.00	20.00	40.00
SHOTGUN LTD.					
PROPHESY					
❏ 6050	Shotgun Ltd.	1971	5.00	10.00	20.00
SHQ					
ESP-DISK'					
❏ 1080 [S]	The Uhu Sleeps Only During the Day	1969	7.50	15.00	30.00
SHRINER, HERB					
COLUMBIA					
❏ CL 774 [M]	Herb Shriner On Stage	1957	7.50	15.00	30.00
DOT					
❏ DLP-3149 [M]	Polka Dot Party	1959	7.50	15.00	30.00
❏ DLP-25149 [S]	Polka Dot Party	1959	10.00	20.00	40.00
SHU, EDDIE					
BETHLEHEM					
❏ BCP-1013 [10]	I Only Have Eyes For Shu	1954	25.00	50.00	100.00
SHU, EDDIE/BOB HARDAWAY					
BETHLEHEM					
❏ BCP-3 [M]	Jazz Practitioners	1957	20.00	40.00	80.00
SHU, EDDIE/JOE ROLAND/"WILD" BILL DAVIS					
MERCER					
❏ LP-1002 [10]	New Stars, New Sounds, Volume 1	1951	37.50	75.00	150.00
SHULMAN, JOEL					
JAMAL					
❏ 5162	Peninah	197?	5.00	10.00	20.00
SICKNICKS, THE					
AMY					
❏ 2 [M]	Sick #2	1961	7.50	15.00	30.00
SIDEKICKS, THE					
RCA VICTOR					
❏ LPM-3712 [M]	Fifi the Flea	1966	5.00	10.00	20.00
❏ LSP-3712 [S]	Fifi the Flea	1966	6.25	12.50	25.00
SIDEWINDERS, THE					
RCA VICTOR					
❏ LSP-4694	The Sidewinders	1972	5.00	10.00	20.00
SIDRAN, BEN					
CAPITOL					
❏ ST-825	Feel Your Groove	1971	5.00	10.00	20.00
SIEGEL-SCHWALL BAND, THE					
VANGUARD					
❏ VSD-6562	Siegel-Schwall '70	1970	5.00	10.00	20.00
❏ VRS-9235 [M]	The Siegel-Schwall Band	1966	5.00	10.00	20.00
❏ VRS-9249 [M]	Say Siegel-Schwall	1967	6.25	12.50	25.00
❏ VSD-79235 [S]	The Siegel-Schwall Band	1966	6.25	12.50	25.00
❏ VSD-79249 [S]	Say Siegel-Schwall	1967	5.00	10.00	20.00
❏ VSD-79289	Shake!	1968	5.00	10.00	20.00
WOODEN NICKEL					
❏ BWL1-0121	953 West	1973	5.00	10.00	20.00

Number	Title (A Side/B Side)	Yr	VG	VG+	NM
❑ BWL1-0288	Last Summer — Live	1974	5.00	10.00	20.00
❑ BWL1-0554	R.I.P.	1974	5.00	10.00	20.00
❑ WNS-1002	The Siegel-Schwall Band	1971	6.25	12.50	25.00
❑ WNS-1010	Sleepy Hollow	1972	6.25	12.50	25.00

SIGLER, BUNNY
GOLD MIND

Number	Title (A Side/B Side)	Yr	VG	VG+	NM
❑ 7502	Let Me Party with You	1978	3.00	6.00	12.00
❑ 9503	I've Always Wanted to Sing... Not Just Write Songs	1979	3.00	6.00	12.00

PARKWAY

Number	Title (A Side/B Side)	Yr	VG	VG+	NM
❑ P-50000 [M]	Let the Good Times Roll	1967	10.00	20.00	40.00
❑ PS-50000 [S]	Let the Good Times Roll	1967	10.00	20.00	40.00

PHILADELPHIA INT'L.

Number	Title (A Side/B Side)	Yr	VG	VG+	NM
❑ KZ 32589	That's How Long I'll Be Loving You	1974	3.75	7.50	15.00
❑ KZ 33249	Keep Smilin'	1974	3.75	7.50	15.00
❑ PZ 34267	My Music	1976	3.75	7.50	15.00

SALSOUL

Number	Title (A Side/B Side)	Yr	VG	VG+	NM
❑ SA-8531	Let It Snow	1980	3.00	6.00	12.00

SIGNATURES, THE
WARNER BROS.

Number	Title (A Side/B Side)	Yr	VG	VG+	NM
❑ W 1250 [M]	The Signatures Sing In	1958	7.50	15.00	30.00
❑ WS 1250 [S]	The Signatures Sing In	1958	10.00	20.00	40.00
❑ W 1353 [M]	Prepare to Flip!	1959	7.50	15.00	30.00
❑ WS 1353 [S]	Prepare to Flip!	1959	10.00	20.00	40.00

WHIPPET

Number	Title (A Side/B Side)	Yr	VG	VG+	NM
❑ WLP-702 [M]	The Signatures — Their Voices and Instruments	1957	15.00	30.00	60.00

SIGNORELLI, FRANK
DAVIS

Number	Title (A Side/B Side)	Yr	VG	VG+	NM
❑ JD-103 [M]	Piano Moods	1951	12.50	25.00	50.00

SILHOUETTES, THE
GOODWAY

Number	Title (A Side/B Side)	Yr	VG	VG+	NM
❑ GLP-100	The Silhouettes 1958-1968/Get a Job	1968	75.00	150.00	300.00

SILK
ABC

Number	Title (A Side/B Side)	Yr	VG	VG+	NM
❑ S-694	Smooth As Raw Silk	1969	6.25	12.50	25.00

SILKIE, THE
FONTANA

Number	Title (A Side/B Side)	Yr	VG	VG+	NM
❑ MGF 27548 [M]	You've Got to Hide Your Love Away	1965	10.00	20.00	40.00
—With purplish, black and white cover					
❑ MGF 27548 [M]	You've Got to Hide Your Love Away	1965	12.50	25.00	50.00
—With full-color cover					
❑ SRF 67548 [R]	You've Got to Hide Your Love Away	1965	7.50	15.00	30.00
—With purplish, black and white cover					
❑ SRF 67548 [R]	You've Got to Hide Your Love Away	1965	10.00	20.00	40.00
—With full-color cover					

SILLY SURFERS, THE
MERCURY

Number	Title (A Side/B Side)	Yr	VG	VG+	NM
❑ MG-20977 [M]	The Sounds of the Silly Surfers	1965	20.00	40.00	80.00
❑ SR-60977 [S]	The Sounds of the Silly Surfers	1965	25.00	50.00	100.00

SILLY SURFERS, THE / THE WEIRD-OHS
HAIRY

Number	Title (A Side/B Side)	Yr	VG	VG+	NM
❑ 101 [M]	The Sounds of the Silly Surfers/The Sounds of the Weird-Ohs	1964	37.50	75.00	150.00

SILVA, ALAN
ESP-DISK'

Number	Title (A Side/B Side)	Yr	VG	VG+	NM
❑ 1091 [S]	Alan Silva	1969	5.00	10.00	20.00

SILVER, HORACE
BLUE NOTE

Number	Title (A Side/B Side)	Yr	VG	VG+	NM
❑ BN-LA402-H2 [(2)]	Horace Silver	1975	5.00	10.00	20.00
❑ BLP-1518 [M]	Horace Silver and the Jazz Messengers	1956	37.50	75.00	150.00
—Regular edition, Lexington Ave. address on label					
❑ BLP-1518 [M]	Horace Silver and the Jazz Messengers	1956	50.00	100.00	200.00
—"Deep groove" version (deep indentation under label on both sides)					
❑ BLP-1518 [M]	Horace Silver and the Jazz Messengers	1963	6.25	12.50	25.00
—"New York, USA" address on label					
❑ BLP-1520 [M]	Spotlight on Drums	1956	37.50	75.00	150.00
—Regular edition, Lexington Ave. address on label					
❑ BLP-1520 [M]	Spotlight on Drums	1956	50.00	100.00	200.00
—"Deep groove" version (deep indentation under label on both sides)					
❑ BLP-1520 [M]	Spotlight on Drums	1963	6.25	12.50	25.00
—"New York, USA" address on label					
❑ BLP-1539 [M]	Six Pieces of Silver	1957	37.50	75.00	150.00
—Regular edition, Lexington Ave. address on label					
❑ BLP-1539 [M]	Six Pieces of Silver	1957	50.00	100.00	200.00
—"Deep groove" version (deep indentation under label on both sides)					
❑ BLP-1539 [M]	Six Pieces of Silver	1963	6.25	12.50	25.00
—"New York, USA" address on label					
❑ BLP-1562 [M]	The Stylings of Silver	1957	25.00	50.00	100.00
—Regular edition, W. 63rd St. address on label					
❑ BLP-1562 [M]	The Stylings of Silver	1957	37.50	75.00	150.00
—"Deep groove" version (deep indentation under label on both sides)					
❑ BLP-1562 [M]	The Stylings of Silver	1963	6.25	12.50	25.00
—"New York, USA" address on label					
❑ BST-1562 [S]	The Stylings of Silver	1959	20.00	40.00	80.00
—Regular edition, W. 63rd St. address on label					
❑ BST-1562 [S]	The Stylings of Silver	1959	25.00	50.00	100.00
—"Deep groove" version (deep indentation under label on both sides)					
❑ BST-1562 [S]	The Stylings of Silver	1963	5.00	10.00	20.00
—"New York, USA" address on label					
❑ BLP-1589 [M]	Further Explorations	1958	25.00	50.00	100.00
—Regular edition, W. 63rd St. address on label					
❑ BLP-1589 [M]	Further Explorations	1958	37.50	75.00	150.00
—"Deep groove" version (deep indentation under label on both sides)					

Number	Title (A Side/B Side)	Yr	VG	VG+	NM
❑ BLP-1589 [M]	Further Explorations	1963	6.25	12.50	25.00
—"New York, USA" address on label					
❑ BST-1589 [S]	Further Explorations	1959	20.00	40.00	80.00
—Regular edition, W. 63rd St. address on label					
❑ BST-1589 [S]	Further Explorations	1959	25.00	50.00	100.00
—"Deep groove" version (deep indentation under label on both sides)					
❑ BST-1589 [S]	Further Explorations	1963	5.00	10.00	20.00
—"New York, USA" address on label					
❑ BLP-4008 [M]	Finger Poppin'	1959	25.00	50.00	100.00
—Regular edition, W. 63rd St. address on label					
❑ BLP-4008 [M]	Finger Poppin'	1959	37.50	75.00	150.00
—"Deep groove" version (deep indentation under label on both sides)					
❑ BLP-4008 [M]	Finger Poppin'	1963	6.25	12.50	25.00
—"New York, USA" address on label					
❑ BST-4008 [S]	Finger Poppin'	1959	20.00	40.00	80.00
—Regular edition, W. 63rd St. address on label					
❑ BST-4008 [S]	Finger Poppin'	1959	25.00	50.00	100.00
—"Deep groove" version (deep indentation under label on both sides)					
❑ BST-4008 [S]	Finger Poppin'	1963	5.00	10.00	20.00
—"New York, USA" address on label					
❑ BLP-4017 [M]	Blowin' the Blues Away	1959	20.00	40.00	80.00
—Regular edition, W. 63rd St. address on label					
❑ BLP-4017 [M]	Blowin' the Blues Away	1959	30.00	60.00	120.00
—"Deep groove" version (deep indentation under label on both sides)					
❑ BLP-4017 [M]	Blowin' the Blues Away	1963	6.25	12.50	25.00
—"New York, USA" address on label					
❑ BLP-4042 [M]	Horace-Scope	1960	20.00	40.00	80.00
—Regular edition, W. 63rd St. address on label					
❑ BLP-4042 [M]	Horace-Scope	1960	30.00	60.00	120.00
—"Deep groove" version (deep indentation under label on both sides)					
❑ BLP-4042 [M]	Horace-Scope	1963	6.25	12.50	25.00
—"New York, USA" address on label					
❑ BLP-4076 [M]	Doin' the Thing at the Village Gate	1961	15.00	30.00	60.00
—61st St. address on label					
❑ BLP-4076 [M]	Doin' the Thing at the Village Gate	1963	5.00	10.00	20.00
—"New York, USA" address on label					
❑ BLP-4110 [M]	The Tokyo Blues	1962	7.50	15.00	30.00
❑ BLP-4131 [M]	Silver's Serenade	1963	7.50	15.00	30.00
❑ BLP-4185 [M]	Song for My Father (Cantiga Para Meu Pai)	1965	6.25	12.50	25.00
❑ BLP-4220 [M]	The Cape Verdean Blues	1965	6.25	12.50	25.00
❑ BLP-4250 [M]	The Jody Grind	1966	6.25	12.50	25.00
❑ BLP-5018 [10]	New Faces	1953	75.00	150.00	300.00
❑ BLP-5034 [10]	Horace Silver Trio, Vol. 2	1954	75.00	150.00	300.00
❑ BLP-5058 [10]	Horace Silver Quintet	1955	62.50	125.00	250.00
❑ BLP-5062 [10]	Horace Silver Quintet	1955	62.50	125.00	250.00
❑ BST-84017 [S]	Blowin' the Blues Away	1959	15.00	30.00	60.00
—W. 63rd St. address on label					
❑ BST-84017 [S]	Blowin' the Blues Away	1963	5.00	10.00	20.00
—"New York, USA" address on label					
❑ BST-84042 [S]	Horace-Scope	1960	15.00	30.00	60.00
—W. 63rd St. address on label					
❑ BST-84042 [S]	Horace-Scope	1963	5.00	10.00	20.00
—"New York, USA" address on label					
❑ BST-84076 [S]	Doin' the Thing at the Village Gate	1961	15.00	30.00	60.00
—61st St. address on label					
❑ BST-84076 [S]	Doin' the Thing at the Village Gate	1963	5.00	10.00	20.00
—"New York, USA" address on label					
❑ BST-84110 [S]	The Tokyo Blues	1962	10.00	20.00	40.00
—"New York, USA" address on label					
❑ BST-84131 [S]	Silver's Serenade	1963	10.00	20.00	40.00
—"New York, USA" address on label					
❑ BST-84185 [S]	Song for My Father (Cantiga Para Meu Pai)	1965	7.50	15.00	30.00
—"New York, USA" address on label					
❑ BST-84220 [S]	The Cape Verdean Blues	1965	7.50	15.00	30.00
—"New York, USA" address on label					
❑ BST-84250 [S]	The Jody Grind	1966	7.50	15.00	30.00
—"New York, USA" address on label					

EPIC

Number	Title (A Side/B Side)	Yr	VG	VG+	NM
❑ LN 3326 [M]	Silver's Blue	1956	20.00	40.00	80.00
❑ LA 16006 [M]	Silver's Blue	1959	10.00	20.00	40.00
❑ BA 17006 [R]	Silver's Blue	196?	5.00	10.00	20.00

SILVER APPLES
KAPP

Number	Title (A Side/B Side)	Yr	VG	VG+	NM
❑ KS-3562	Silver Apples	1968	7.50	15.00	30.00
—Add 1/3 if poster is enclosed					
❑ KS-3584	Contact	1969	7.50	15.00	30.00

SILVERS, PHIL
COLUMBIA

Number	Title (A Side/B Side)	Yr	VG	VG+	NM
❑ CL 1011 [M]	Phil Silvers and the Swinging Brass	1957	12.50	25.00	50.00

HARMONY

Number	Title (A Side/B Side)	Yr	VG	VG+	NM
❑ HL 7170 [M]	Bugle Calls for Big Band	196?	6.25	12.50	25.00

SILVERSTEIN, SHEL
ATLANTIC

Number	Title (A Side/B Side)	Yr	VG	VG+	NM
❑ 8072 [M]	Inside Folk Songs	1962	7.50	15.00	30.00
❑ SD 8072 [S]	Inside Folk Songs	1962	10.00	20.00	40.00

CADET

Number	Title (A Side/B Side)	Yr	VG	VG+	NM
❑ LP 4052 [M]	I'm So Good I Don't Have to Brag!	1965	6.25	12.50	25.00
❑ LPS 4052 [S]	I'm So Good I Don't Have to Brag!	1965	7.50	15.00	30.00
❑ LP 4054 [M]	Drain My Brain	1966	6.25	12.50	25.00
❑ LPS 4054 [S]	Drain My Brain	1966	7.50	15.00	30.00

COLUMBIA

Number	Title (A Side/B Side)	Yr	VG	VG+	NM
❑ KC 31119	Freakin' at the Freakers' Ball	1972	3.75	7.50	15.00
❑ PC 31119	Freakin' at the Freakers' Ball	1979	2.00	4.00	8.00
—Budget-line reissue					
❑ FC 39412	Where the Sidewalk Ends	1984	2.50	5.00	10.00
❑ 9C9 39611 [PD]	Where the Sidewalk Ends	1984	6.25	12.50	25.00
—Picture disc					
❑ FC 40219	A Light in the Attic	1985	2.50	5.00	10.00

Number	Title (A Side/B Side)	Yr	VG	VG+	NM
CRESTVIEW					
❏ CRV 804 [M]	Stag Party	1963	6.25	12.50	25.00
❏ CRS 7804 [S]	Stag Party	1963	7.50	15.00	30.00
ELEKTRA					
❏ EKL-176 [M]	Hairy Jazz	1961	25.00	50.00	100.00
❏ EKS-7176 [S]	Hairy Jazz	1961	37.50	75.00	150.00
FLYING FISH					
❏ FF-211	Conch Train Robbery	1980	3.00	6.00	12.00
JANUS					
❏ 2JLS 3052 [(2)]	Crouching on the Outside	1973	3.75	7.50	15.00
PARACHUTE					
❏ RRLP-9007	Songs and Stories	1978	3.00	6.00	12.00
❏ 20512 [DJ]	Selected Cuts from Songs and Stories	1978	5.00	10.00	20.00
—Promo-only EP					
RCA VICTOR					
❏ LSP-4192	A Boy Named Sue (And His Other Country Songs)	1969	5.00	10.00	20.00

SIMEON, OMER

Number	Title (A Side/B Side)	Yr	VG	VG+	NM
CONCERT HALL JAZZ					
❏ 1014 [10]	Clarinet A La Creole	195?	12.50	25.00	50.00
DISC					
❏ DLP-748 [10]	Omer Simeon Trio With James P. Johnson	195?	50.00	100.00	200.00

SIMEONE, HARRY, CHORALE

Number	Title (A Side/B Side)	Yr	VG	VG+	NM
MERCURY					
❏ SR 60820 [S]	The Wonderful Songs of Christmas	1963	5.00	10.00	20.00
20TH FOX					
❏ FOX-3002 [M]	Sing We Now of Christmas	1959	5.00	10.00	20.00
—With "The Little Drummer Boy" mentioned at bottom of front cover					
❏ FOX-3002 [M]	Sing We Now of Christmas	1959	6.25	12.50	25.00
—With no mention of "The Little Drummer Boy" at bottom of front cover					
❏ SFX-3002 [S]	Sing We Now of Christmas	1959	5.00	10.00	20.00
—Sky blue label					

SIMMONS, GENE

Also see KISS.

Number	Title (A Side/B Side)	Yr	VG	VG+	NM
CASABLANCA					
❏ NBLP 7120	Gene Simmons	1978	6.25	12.50	25.00
❏ NBPIX 7120 [PD]	Gene Simmons	1978	15.00	30.00	60.00

SIMMONS, JEFF

Number	Title (A Side/B Side)	Yr	VG	VG+	NM
REPRISE					
❏ RS-6391	Lucille Has Messed Up My Mind	1969	7.50	15.00	30.00
STRAIGHT					
❏ STS-1057	Lucille Has Messed Up My Mind	1969	20.00	40.00	80.00

SIMMONS, "JUMPIN'" GENE

Number	Title (A Side/B Side)	Yr	VG	VG+	NM
HI					
❏ HL 2018 [M]	Jumpin' Gene Simmons	1964	12.50	25.00	50.00
❏ SHL 32018 [S]	Jumpin' Gene Simmons	1964	17.50	35.00	70.00

SIMMONS, NORMAN

Number	Title (A Side/B Side)	Yr	VG	VG+	NM
ARGO					
❏ LP-607 [M]	Norman Simmons Trio	1956	10.00	20.00	40.00
CREATIVE					
❏ LP-607 [M]	Interpolations	1956	20.00	40.00	80.00

SIMMONS, SONNY

Number	Title (A Side/B Side)	Yr	VG	VG+	NM
CONTEMPORARY					
❏ M-3623 [M]	Rumasuma	1966	5.00	10.00	20.00
❏ S-7623 [S]	Rumasuma	1966	6.25	12.50	25.00
❏ S-7625/6 [(2)]	Burning Spirits	1970	5.00	10.00	20.00
ESP-DISK'					
❏ 1030 [M]	Sonny Simmons	1966	5.00	10.00	20.00
❏ S-1030 [S]	Sonny Simmons	1966	6.25	12.50	25.00
❏ 1043 [M]	Music from the Spheres	1967	6.25	12.50	25.00
❏ S-1043 [S]	Music from the Spheres	1967	5.00	10.00	20.00

SIMON, CARLY

Also see THE SIMON SISTERS.

Number	Title (A Side/B Side)	Yr	VG	VG+	NM
ARISTA					
❏ AL-8443	Coming Around Again	1987	2.00	4.00	8.00
❏ AL-8526	Greatest Hits Live	1988	2.00	4.00	8.00
❏ AL-8582	My Romance	1990	3.00	6.00	12.00
❏ AL-8650	Have You Seen Me Lately?	1990	3.00	6.00	12.00
DIRECT DISK					
❏ SD-16608	Boys in the Trees	1980	12.50	25.00	50.00
—Audiophile vinyl					
ELEKTRA					
❏ 6E-109	The Best of Carly Simon	1977	2.00	4.00	8.00
—Reissue of 7E-1048					
❏ 6E-128	Boys in the Trees	1978	2.50	5.00	10.00
❏ 5E-506	Spy	1979	2.50	5.00	10.00
❏ 7E-1002	Hotcakes	1974	2.50	5.00	10.00
❏ EQ-1002 [Q]	Hotcakes	1974	5.00	10.00	20.00
❏ 7E-1033	Playing Possum	1975	2.50	5.00	10.00
❏ EQ-1033 [Q]	Playing Possum	1975	5.00	10.00	20.00
❏ 7E-1048	The Best of Carly Simon	1975	2.50	5.00	10.00
❏ EQ-1048 [Q]	The Best of Carly Simon	1975	5.00	10.00	20.00
❏ 7E-1064	Another Passenger	1976	2.50	5.00	10.00
❏ EQ-1064 [Q]	Another Passenger	1976	5.00	10.00	20.00
❏ EQ-4082 [Q]	Carly Simon	1974	5.00	10.00	20.00
❏ EQ-5049 [Q]	No Secrets	1974	5.00	10.00	20.00
❏ EKS-74082	Carly Simon	1971	3.00	6.00	12.00
❏ EKS-75016	Anticipation	1971	3.00	6.00	12.00
❏ EKS-75049	No Secrets	1972	3.00	6.00	12.00
—With lyrics on innersleeve					
❏ EKS-75049	No Secrets	1973	2.50	5.00	10.00
—Without lyrics on innersleeve					

Number	Title (A Side/B Side)	Yr	VG	VG+	NM
EPIC					
❏ FE 39970	Spoiled Girl	1985	2.50	5.00	10.00
WARNER BROS.					
❏ BSK 3443	Come Upstairs	1980	2.50	5.00	10.00
❏ BSK 3592	Torch	1981	2.50	5.00	10.00
❏ 23886	Hello Big Man	1983	2.50	5.00	10.00

SIMON, FRANK

Number	Title (A Side/B Side)	Yr	VG	VG+	NM
AUDIO LAB					
❏ AL-1552 [M]	Four Star Hits	1960	37.50	75.00	150.00

SIMON, JOE

Number	Title (A Side/B Side)	Yr	VG	VG+	NM
BUDDAH					
❏ BDS-7512	Joe Simon	1969	6.25	12.50	25.00
COMPLEAT					
❏ 671015-1	Mr. Right	1985	3.00	6.00	12.00
POSSE					
❏ 10002	Glad You Came My Way	1981	3.00	6.00	12.00
❏ 10003	By Popular Demand	1982	3.00	6.00	12.00
SOUND STAGE 7					
❏ 5000 [(2)]	The World of Joe Simon	197?	3.00	6.00	12.00
—Reissue of 32536					
❏ SSM-5003 [M]	Pure Soul	1967	7.50	15.00	30.00
❏ SSS-15003 [S]	Pure Soul	1967	10.00	20.00	40.00
❏ SSS-15004	No Sad Songs	1968	10.00	20.00	40.00
❏ SSS-15005	Simon Sings	1968	10.00	20.00	40.00
❏ SSS-15006	The Chokin' Kind	1969	7.50	15.00	30.00
❏ SSS-15008	Joe Simon…Better Than Ever	1969	7.50	15.00	30.00
❏ SSS-15009	The Best of Joe Simon	1972	3.75	7.50	15.00
❏ KZ 31916	Greatest Hits	1972	3.00	6.00	12.00
❏ ZG 32536 [(2)]	The World of Joe Simon	1974	3.75	7.50	15.00
❏ ZG 33879 [(2)]	The Chokin' Kind/Joe Simon…Better Than Ever	1975	3.75	7.50	15.00
SPRING					
❏ SPR-4701	The Sounds of Simon	1971	6.25	12.50	25.00
❏ SPR-5702	Drowning in the Sea of Love	1972	6.25	12.50	25.00
❏ SPR-5704	The Power of Joe Simon	1973	6.25	12.50	25.00
❏ SPR-5705	Simon Country	1973	3.75	7.50	15.00
❏ SPR-6702	Mood, Heart and Soul	1974	3.75	7.50	15.00
❏ SPR-6706	Get Down	1975	3.75	7.50	15.00
❏ SPR-6710	Today	1975	3.75	7.50	15.00
❏ SPR-6713	Easy to Love	1976	3.75	7.50	15.00
❏ SPR-6716	Bad Case of Love	1977	3.75	7.50	15.00
❏ SPR-6720	Love Vibrations	1979	3.75	7.50	15.00

SIMON, PAUL

Also see SIMON AND GARFUNKEL.

Number	Title (A Side/B Side)	Yr	VG	VG+	NM
COLUMBIA					
❏ CQ 30750 [Q]	Paul Simon	1974	5.00	10.00	20.00
❏ KC 30750	Paul Simon	1972	2.50	5.00	10.00
❏ CQ 32280 [Q]	There Goes Rhymin' Simon	1974	5.00	10.00	20.00
❏ KC 32280	There Goes Rhymin' Simon	1973	2.50	5.00	10.00
❏ PC 32280	There Goes Rhymin' Simon	1980	2.00	4.00	8.00
❏ PC 32855	Paul Simon in Concert — Live Rhymin'	1974	2.50	5.00	10.00
❏ PC 33540	Still Crazy After All These Years	1975	2.50	5.00	10.00
—Original release has no bar code on cover					
❏ PC 33540	Still Crazy After All These Years	1980	2.00	4.00	8.00
—With bar code on cover					
❏ PCQ 33540 [Q]	Still Crazy After All These Years	1975	5.00	10.00	20.00
❏ JC 35032	Greatest Hits, Etc.	1977	2.50	5.00	10.00
❏ C5X 37581 [(5)]	Collected Works	1981	10.00	20.00	40.00
—Contains his first four post-S&G solo albums plus the elusive "Paul Simon Songbook," otherwise unavailable in U.S.					
❏ HC 43540	Still Crazy After All These Years	1981	10.00	20.00	40.00
—Half-speed mastered edition					
❏ HC 45032	Greatest Hits, Etc.	1981	10.00	20.00	40.00
—Half-speed mastered edition					
DCC COMPACT CLASSICS					
❏ LPZ-2060	Paul Simon	1998	7.50	15.00	30.00
—Audiophile vinyl					
❏ LPZ-2062	There Goes Rhymin' Simon	1998	7.50	15.00	30.00
—Audiophile vinyl					
WARNER BROS.					
❏ WBMS-140 [(2)DJ]	The Paul Simon Interview Show	1986	12.50	25.00	50.00
—Promo-only "Graceland"-era program in the "Warner Bros. Music Show" series					
❏ HS 3472	One-Trick Pony	1980	2.50	5.00	10.00
❏ 23942	Hearts and Bones	1983	2.50	5.00	10.00
❏ 23942 [DJ]	Hearts and Bones	1983	5.00	10.00	20.00
—Promo only on Quiex II vinyl					
❏ 25447	Graceland	1986	2.50	5.00	10.00
❏ 25588	Paul Simon	1988	3.00	6.00	12.00
❏ 25589	There Goes Rhymin' Simon	1988	3.00	6.00	12.00
❏ 25590	Paul Simon in Concert — Live Rhymin'	1988	3.00	6.00	12.00
❏ 25591	Still Crazy After All These Years	1988	3.00	6.00	12.00
❏ 25789 [(2)]	Negotiations and Love Songs	1988	3.75	7.50	15.00
❏ 26008	The Rhythm of the Saints	1990	3.75	7.50	15.00
❏ 46814	Songs from The Capeman	1997	3.75	7.50	15.00

SIMON AND GARFUNKEL

Also see ART GARFUNKEL; PAUL SIMON.

Number	Title (A Side/B Side)	Yr	VG	VG+	NM
CBS					
❏ KCS 9914	Bridge Over Troubled Water	1970	3.75	7.50	15.00
—"360 Sound Stereo" on label; pressed in U.S. for export					
COLUMBIA					
❏ CL 2249 [M]	Wednesday Morning, 3 A.M.	1964	6.25	12.50	25.00
—"Guaranteed High Fidelity" on label					
❏ CL 2249 [M]	Wednesday Morning, 3 A.M.	1965	3.75	7.50	15.00
—"Mono" on label					
❏ CL 2469 [M]	Sounds of Silence	1966	3.75	7.50	15.00
—With "Simon and Garfunkel" and "Sounds of Silence" in large upper and lowercase letters on front cover with all song titles listed; "Tiger Beat" magazines on back cover are airbrushed out					

Number	Title (A Side/B Side)	Yr	VG	VG+	NM
❑ CL 2469 [M]	Sounds of Silence	1966	5.00	10.00	20.00

—With "Simon and Garfunkel" and "Sounds of Silence" in large upper and lowercase letters on front cover with all song titles listed; "Tiger Beat" magazine is pictured twice on back cover

❑ CL 2469 [M]	Sounds of Silence	1966	7.50	15.00	30.00

—With "Simon and Garfunkel" and "Sounds of Silence" in all capital letters on front cover with no list of songs

❑ CL 2563 [M]	Parsley, Sage, Rosemary and Thyme	1966	5.00	10.00	20.00
❑ KCL 2729 [M]	Bookends	1968	25.00	50.00	100.00

—Red label, "Mono" at bottom

❑ CS 9049 [S]	Wednesday Morning, 3 A.M.	1964	6.25	12.50	25.00

—"360 Sound Stereo" in black on label

❑ CS 9049 [S]	Wednesday Morning, 3 A.M.	1965	3.75	7.50	15.00

—"360 Sound Stereo" in white on label

❑ CS 9049 [S]	Wednesday Morning, 3 A.M.	1970	2.50	5.00	10.00

—Orange label

❑ PC 9049 [S]	Wednesday Morning, 3 A.M.	197?	2.00	4.00	8.00

—Budget-line reissue

❑ CS 9269 [S]	Sounds of Silence	1966	3.00	6.00	12.00

—With "Simon and Garfunkel" and "Sounds of Silence" in large upper and lowercase letters on front cover with all song titles listed; "Tiger Beat" magazines on back cover are airbrushed out

❑ CS 9269 [S]	Sounds of Silence	1966	5.00	10.00	20.00

—With "Simon and Garfunkel" and "Sounds of Silence" in large upper and lowercase letters on front cover with all song titles listed; "Tiger Beat" magazine is pictured twice on back cover

❑ CS 9269 [S]	Sounds of Silence	1966	7.50	15.00	30.00

—With "Simon and Garfunkel" and "Sounds of Silence" in all capital letters on front cover with no list of songs

❑ CS 9269 [S]	Sounds of Silence	1970	2.50	5.00	10.00

—Orange label

❑ JC 9269	Sounds of Silence	197?	2.00	4.00	8.00

—Reissue with new prefix

❑ PC 9269	Sounds of Silence	198?	2.00	4.00	8.00

—Budget-line reissue

❑ CS 9363 [S]	Parsley, Sage, Rosemary and Thyme	1966	3.75	7.50	15.00

—"360 Sound Stereo" on label

❑ CS 9363 [S]	Parsley, Sage, Rosemary and Thyme	1970	2.50	5.00	10.00

—Orange label

❑ PC 9363 [S]	Parsley, Sage, Rosemary and Thyme	197?	2.00	4.00	8.00

—Budget-line reissue

❑ KCS 9529 [M]	Bookends	1968	7.50	15.00	30.00

—White label "Special Mono Radio Station Copy"

❑ KCS 9529 [S]	Bookends	1968	3.00	6.00	12.00

—"360 Sound Stereo" on label; add 25% for poster

❑ KCS 9529 [S]	Bookends	1970	2.50	5.00	10.00

—Orange label

❑ PC 9529 [S]	Bookends	197?	2.00	4.00	8.00

—Budget-line reissue

❑ JC 9914	Bridge Over Troubled Water	197?	2.00	4.00	8.00

—Reissue with new prefix

❑ KCS 9914	Bridge Over Troubled Water	1970	2.50	5.00	10.00

—Orange label

❑ KCS 9914	Bridge Over Troubled Water	1970	3.00	6.00	12.00

—"360 Sound Stereo" on label

❑ KCS 9914	Bridge Over Troubled Water	2000	6.25	12.50	25.00

—Classic Records reissue on audiophile vinyl

❑ PC 9914	Bridge Over Troubled Water	198?	2.00	4.00	8.00

—Budget-line reissue

❑ CQ 30995 [Q]	Bridge Over Troubled Water	1971	6.25	12.50	25.00
❑ PCQ 30995 [Q]	Bridge Over Troubled Water	1974	5.00	10.00	20.00

—Reissue with new prefix; possibly the only difference between this and the original is a sticker on the cover with the new number

❑ JC 31350	Simon and Garfunkel's Greatest Hits	197?	2.00	4.00	8.00

—Reissue with new prefix

❑ KC 31350	Simon and Garfunkel's Greatest Hits	1972	3.00	6.00	12.00

—Original covers are slightly oversized

❑ C5X 37587 [(5)]	Collected Works	1981	10.00	20.00	40.00
❑ HC 41350	Simon and Garfunkel's Greatest Hits	1982	7.50	15.00	30.00

—Half-speed mastered edition

❑ HC 49914	Bridge Over Troubled Water	1982	7.50	15.00	30.00

—Half-speed mastered edition

MOBILE FIDELITY

❑ 1-173	Bridge Over Troubled Water	198?	10.00	20.00	40.00

—Audiophile vinyl

PICKWICK

❑ PC-3059 [M]	The Hit Sounds of Simon and Garfunkel	1966	15.00	30.00	60.00
❑ SPC-3059 [R]	The Hit Sounds of Simon and Garfunkel	1966	7.50	15.00	30.00

SEARS

❑ SPS-435	Simon and Garfunkel	196?	7.50	15.00	30.00

WARNER BROS.

❑ 2BSK 3654 [(2)]	The Concert in Central Park	1982	3.00	6.00	12.00

SIMON SISTERS, THE

CARLY SIMON and her sister Lucy.

COLUMBIA

❑ CR 21525	The Lobster Quadrille	1969	3.75	7.50	15.00
❑ CR 21539	The Simon Sisters Sing for Children	1972	3.75	7.50	15.00
❑ CC 24506	The Lobster Quadrille	1969	5.00	10.00	20.00

—Special edition with booklet

KAPP

❑ KL-1359 [M]	Winkin', Blinkin' and Nod	1964	7.50	15.00	30.00
❑ KL-1397 [M]	Cuddlebug	1964	10.00	20.00	40.00
❑ KS-3359 [S]	Winkin', Blinkin' and Nod	1964	10.00	20.00	40.00
❑ KS-3397 [S]	Cuddlebug	1964	12.50	25.00	50.00

SIMONE, NINA

BETHLEHEM

❑ BCP-6028 [M]	Jazz As Played in an Exclusive Side Street Club	1959	20.00	40.00	80.00
❑ BCP-6028 [M]	The Original Nina Simone	1961	7.50	15.00	30.00

—Retitled reissue

❑ SBCP-6028 [S]	Jazz As Played in an Exclusive Side Street Club	1959	25.00	50.00	100.00
❑ SBCP-6028 [S]	The Original Nina Simone	1961	10.00	20.00	40.00

—Retitled reissue

❑ BCP-6041 [M]	Nina Simone and Her Friends	1960	10.00	20.00	40.00
❑ SBCP-6041 [S]	Nina Simone and Her Friends	1960	12.50	25.00	50.00

—With Carmen McRae and Chris Connor

COLPIX

❑ CP-407 [M]	The Amazing Nina Simone	1959	6.25	12.50	25.00
❑ SCP-407 [S]	The Amazing Nina Simone	1959	7.50	15.00	30.00
❑ CP-409 [M]	Nina at Town Hall	1960	6.25	12.50	25.00
❑ SCP-409 [S]	Nina at Town Hall	1960	7.50	15.00	30.00
❑ CP-412 [M]	Nina at Newport	1960	6.25	12.50	25.00
❑ SCP-412 [S]	Nina at Newport	1960	7.50	15.00	30.00
❑ CP-419 [M]	Forbidden Fruit	1961	6.25	12.50	25.00
❑ SCP-419 [S]	Forbidden Fruit	1961	7.50	15.00	30.00
❑ CP-421 [M]	Nina Simone at the Village Gate	1961	6.25	12.50	25.00
❑ SCP-421 [S]	Nina Simone at the Village Gate	1961	7.50	15.00	30.00
❑ CP-425 [M]	Nina Sings Ellington	1962	6.25	12.50	25.00
❑ SCP-425 [S]	Nina Sings Ellington	1962	7.50	15.00	30.00
❑ CP-443 [M]	Nina's Choice	1963	6.25	12.50	25.00
❑ SCP-443 [S]	Nina's Choice	1963	7.50	15.00	30.00
❑ CP-455 [M]	Nina Simone at Carnegie Hall	1963	6.25	12.50	25.00
❑ SCP-455 [S]	Nina Simone at Carnegie Hall	1963	7.50	15.00	30.00
❑ CP-465 [M]	Folksy Nina	1964	6.25	12.50	25.00
❑ SCP-465 [S]	Folksy Nina	1964	7.50	15.00	30.00
❑ CP-496 [M]	Nina with Strings	1966	6.25	12.50	25.00
❑ SCP-496 [S]	Nina with Strings	1966	7.50	15.00	30.00

PHILIPS

❑ PHS 600135 [S]	Nina Simone In Concert	1964	5.00	10.00	20.00
❑ PHS 600148 [S]	Broadway...Blues...Ballads	1964	5.00	10.00	20.00
❑ PHS 600172 [S]	I Put a Spell on You	1965	5.00	10.00	20.00
❑ PHS 600187 [S]	Pastel Blues	1965	5.00	10.00	20.00
❑ PHS 600202 [S]	Let It All Out	1966	5.00	10.00	20.00
❑ PHS 600207 [S]	Wild Is the Wind	1966	5.00	10.00	20.00
❑ PHS 600219 [S]	The High Priestess of Soul	1967	5.00	10.00	20.00
❑ PHS 600298	The Best of Nina Simone	1969	5.00	10.00	20.00

RCA VICTOR

❑ LPM-3789 [M]	Nina Simone Sings the Blues	1967	6.25	12.50	25.00
❑ LPM-3837 [M]	Silk and Soul	1967	6.25	12.50	25.00

SIMPLE MINDS

A&M

❑ SP-3927	Street Fighting Years	1989	2.50	5.00	10.00
❑ SP-6-4928	New Gold Dream (81-82-83-84)	1982	3.00	6.00	12.00

—Originals have gold and purple marbled vinyl

❑ SP-6-4981	Sparkle in the Rain	1984	3.00	6.00	12.00
❑ SP-5092	Once Upon a Time	1985	2.50	5.00	10.00
❑ SP-6850 [(2)]	Live in the City of Light	1987	4.50	9.00	18.00
❑ R 101142	Street Fighting Years	1989	3.75	7.50	15.00

—BMG Direct Marketing edition

❑ R 142320	Once Upon a Time	1985	3.75	7.50	15.00

—RCA Music Service edition; has front and back covers reversed

❑ R 209526 [(2)]	Live in the City of Light	1987	5.00	10.00	20.00

—BMG Direct Marketing edition

PVC

❑ 7910	Life in a Day	1979	3.75	7.50	15.00

STIFF

❑ TEES-102	Themes for Great Cities	1982	3.75	7.50	15.00

VIRGIN

❑ 90610	Sister Feelings Call	1987	2.50	5.00	10.00
❑ 90858	Life in a Day	1988	2.50	5.00	10.00

—Reissue

❑ 90859	Real to Real Cacophony	1988	2.50	5.00	10.00

SIMPLY RED

ELEKTRA

❑ ED 5236 [DJ]	Simply Red Billboard Interview	1989	10.00	20.00	40.00

—Nelson George interviews Mick Hucknall and Lamont Dozier; promo-only

❑ 60452	Picture Book	1985	2.00	4.00	8.00
❑ 60727	Men and Women	1987	2.00	4.00	8.00
❑ 60828	A New Flame	1989	2.50	5.00	10.00
❑ R 101012	A New Flame	1989	3.00	6.00	12.00

—BMG Direct Marketing edition

❑ R 152858	Men and Women	1987	2.50	5.00	10.00

—RCA Music Service edition

❑ R 153936	Picture Book	1985	2.50	5.00	10.00

—RCA Music Service edition

SIMPSON, CAROLE

CAPITOL

❑ T 878 [M]	All About Carole	1957	20.00	40.00	80.00

TOPS

❑ L-1732 [M]	Singin' and Swingin'	1960	6.25	12.50	25.00

SIMPSON, CASS

ABC-PARAMOUNT

❑ ABC-103 [M]	Cass Simpson	1956	10.00	20.00	40.00

SIMPSON, RED

CAPITOL

❑ ST-881	I'm a Truck	1972	3.75	7.50	15.00
❑ ST 2468 [S]	Roll, Truck, Roll	1966	5.00	10.00	20.00
❑ T 2468 [M]	Roll, Truck, Roll	1966	3.75	7.50	15.00
❑ ST 2569 [S]	The Man Behind the Badge	1966	5.00	10.00	20.00
❑ T 2569 [M]	The Man Behind the Badge	1966	3.75	7.50	15.00
❑ ST 2691 [S]	Truck Drivin' Fool	1967	5.00	10.00	20.00
❑ T 2691 [M]	Truck Drivin' Fool	1967	3.75	7.50	15.00
❑ ST 2829 [S]	A Bakersfield Dozen	1967	5.00	10.00	20.00
❑ T 2829 [M]	A Bakersfield Dozen	1967	6.25	12.50	25.00
❑ ST-11093	The Very Real Red Simpson	1973	3.75	7.50	15.00
❑ ST-11231	A Trucker's Christmas	1973	3.75	7.50	15.00

Number	Title (A Side/B Side)	Yr	VG	VG+	NM
PORTLAND					
❏ 1005 [M]	Hello, I'm a Truck	1965	20.00	40.00	80.00
SEA SHELL					
❏ 16253	Ramblin' Road	198?	3.00	6.00	12.00

SIMPSONS, THE
GEFFEN

Number	Title (A Side/B Side)	Yr	VG	VG+	NM
❏ GHS 24308	The Simpsons Sing the Blues	1990	6.25	12.50	25.00

SIMS, FRANKIE LEE
SPECIALTY

Number	Title (A Side/B Side)	Yr	VG	VG+	NM
❏ SPS-2124	Lucy Mae Blues	1970	10.00	20.00	40.00

SIMS, ZOOT
ABC IMPULSE!

Number	Title (A Side/B Side)	Yr	VG	VG+	NM
❏ AS-9131 [S]	The Waiting Game	1968	5.00	10.00	20.00
ABC-PARAMOUNT					
❏ ABC-155 [M]	Zoot Sims Plays Alto, Tenor and Baritone	1957	20.00	40.00	80.00
❏ ABC-198 [M]	Zoot Sims Plays Four Altos	1957	20.00	40.00	80.00
ARGO					
❏ LP-608 [M]	Zoot	1956	20.00	40.00	80.00
—Color cover					
❏ LP-608 [M]	Zoot	1957	12.50	25.00	50.00
—Black and white cover					
BETHLEHEM					
❏ BCP-6051 [M]	Down Home	1960	10.00	20.00	40.00
❏ SBCP-6051 [S]	Down Home	1960	10.00	20.00	40.00
COLPIX					
❏ CP-435 [M]	New Beat Bossa Nova	1962	10.00	20.00	40.00
❏ SCP-435 [S]	New Beat Bossa Nova	1962	12.50	25.00	50.00
❏ CP-437 [M]	New Beat Bossa Nova, Volume 2	1962	10.00	20.00	40.00
❏ SCP-437 [S]	New Beat Bossa Nova, Volume 2	1962	12.50	25.00	50.00
DAWN					
❏ DLP-1102 [M]	The Modern Age of Jazz	1956	25.00	50.00	100.00
❏ DLP-1115 [M]	Zoot Sims Goes to Jazzville	1957	25.00	50.00	100.00
DISCOVERY					
❏ DL-3015 [10]	The Zoot Sims Quartet In Paris	1951	62.50	125.00	250.00
IMPULSE!					
❏ A-9131 [M]	The Waiting Game	1967	6.25	12.50	25.00
JAZZLAND					
❏ JLP-2 [M]	Zoot Sims Quintet	1960	10.00	20.00	40.00
❏ JLP-92 [S]	Zoot Sims Quintet	1960	7.50	15.00	30.00
NEW JAZZ					
❏ NJLP-1102 [10]	Zoot Sims in Hollywood	1954	50.00	100.00	200.00
❏ NJLP-8280 [M]	Good Old Zoot	1962	12.50	25.00	50.00
PACIFIC JAZZ					
❏ PJ-20 [M]	Choice	1961	10.00	20.00	40.00
PRESTIGE					
❏ PRLP-117 [10]	Swingin' with Zoot Sims	1951	50.00	100.00	200.00
❏ PRLP-118 [10]	Tenor Sax Favorites	1951	50.00	100.00	200.00
❏ PRLP-138 [10]	Zoot Sims All Stars	1953	50.00	100.00	200.00
❏ PRLP-202 [10]	Zoot Sims Quintet	1955	37.50	75.00	150.00
❏ PRLP-7026 [M]	Zoot Sims Quartets	1956	30.00	60.00	120.00
❏ PRLP-16009 [M]	Trotting	1963	10.00	20.00	40.00
RIVERSIDE					
❏ RLP 12-228 [M]	Zoot!	1957	20.00	40.00	80.00
SEECO					
❏ CELP-452 [M]	The Modern Art of Jazz	1960	10.00	20.00	40.00
❏ CELP-4520 [S]	The Modern Art of Jazz	1960	10.00	20.00	40.00
STATUS					
❏ ST-8280 [M]	Good Old Zoot	1965	10.00	20.00	40.00
❏ ST-8309 [M]	Koo Koo	1965	10.00	20.00	40.00
UNITED ARTISTS					
❏ UAL-4040 [M]	A Night at the Half Note	1959	10.00	20.00	40.00
❏ UAS-5040 [S]	A Night at the Half Note	1959	12.50	25.00	50.00
❏ UAJ-14013 [M]	Zoot Sims in Paris	1962	10.00	20.00	40.00
❏ UAJS-15013 [S]	Zoot Sims in Paris	1962	12.50	25.00	50.00

SIMS, ZOOT; JIMMY RANEY; JIM HALL
MAINSTREAM

Number	Title (A Side/B Side)	Yr	VG	VG+	NM
❏ S-6013 [S]	Two Jims and Zoot	1965	6.25	12.50	25.00
❏ 56013 [M]	Two Jims and Zoot	1965	5.00	10.00	20.00

SIMS, ZOOT; TONY SCOTT; AL COHN
JAZZLAND

Number	Title (A Side/B Side)	Yr	VG	VG+	NM
❏ JLP-11 [M]	East Coast Sounds	1960	10.00	20.00	40.00
❏ JLP-911 [S]	East Coast Sounds	1960	10.00	20.00	40.00

SIN SAY SHUNS, THE
VENETT

Number	Title (A Side/B Side)	Yr	VG	VG+	NM
❏ V-940 [M]	I'll Be There	1966	10.00	20.00	40.00
❏ VS-940 [S]	I'll Be There	1966	12.50	25.00	50.00

SINATRA, FRANK
ARTANIS

Number	Title (A Side/B Side)	Yr	VG	VG+	NM
❏ ARZ 101 [(2)]	Sinatra '57 In Concert	1999	—	—	—
—Canceled					
BOOK-OF-THE-MONTH					
❏ (# unknown) [(6)]	Tommy Dorsey/Frank Sinatra: The Complete Sessions	1983	25.00	50.00	100.00
CAPITOL					
❏ DWBB-254 [(2)R]	Close-Up	1969	5.00	10.00	20.00
—Reissue in one package of "This Is Sinatra" and "This Is Sinatra, Volume Two"					
❏ DKAO-374 [R]	Frank Sinatra's Greatest Hits	1969	3.00	6.00	12.00
❏ H 488 [10]	Songs for Young Lovers	1954	15.00	30.00	60.00
❏ H 528 [10]	Swing Easy	1954	15.00	30.00	60.00
❏ STBB-529 [(2)]	What Is This Thing Called Love?/The Night We Called It a Day	1970	3.75	7.50	15.00
❏ DW 581 [R]	In the Wee Small Hours	196?	3.00	6.00	12.00

Number	Title (A Side/B Side)	Yr	VG	VG+	NM
❏ H1-581 [10]	In the Wee Small Hours, Part 1	1955	25.00	50.00	100.00
❏ H2-581 [10]	In the Wee Small Hours, Part 2	1955	25.00	50.00	100.00
❏ SM-581	In the Wee Small Hours	197?	2.00	4.00	8.00
❏ W 581 [M]	In the Wee Small Hours	1955	10.00	20.00	40.00
—Gray label original					
❏ W 581 [M]	In the Wee Small Hours	1959	6.25	12.50	25.00
—Black label with colorband					
❏ W 587 [M]	Swing Easy/Songs for Young Lovers	1955	10.00	20.00	40.00
—Gray label original; 12-inch version of two 10-inch LPs					
❏ W 587 [M]	Swing Easy/Songs for Young Lovers	1959	6.25	12.50	25.00
—Black label with colorband					
❏ DW 653 [R]	Songs for Swingin' Lovers!	196?	3.00	6.00	12.00
❏ SM-653	Songs for Swingin' Lovers!	197?	2.00	4.00	8.00
❏ W 653 [M]	Songs for Swingin' Lovers!	1956	10.00	20.00	40.00
—Gray label; cover has Sinatra facing toward the embracing couple					
❏ W 653 [M]	Songs for Swingin' Lovers!	1956	12.50	25.00	50.00
—Gray label; cover has Sinatra facing away from the embracing couple					
❏ W 653 [M]	Songs for Swingin' Lovers!	1959	6.25	12.50	25.00
—Black label with colorband					
❏ STBB-724 [(2)]	My One and Only Love/Sentimental Journey	1971	3.75	7.50	15.00
❏ T 735 [M]	Frank Sinatra Conducts Tone Poems of Color	1956	15.00	30.00	60.00
—Turquoise label					
❏ T 735 [M]	Frank Sinatra Conducts Tone Poems of Color	1959	10.00	20.00	40.00
—Black label with colorband					
❏ DT 768 [R]	This Is Sinatra!	196?	3.00	6.00	12.00
❏ T 768 [M]	This Is Sinatra!	1956	7.50	15.00	30.00
—Turquoise label					
❏ T 768 [M]	This Is Sinatra!	196?	3.75	7.50	15.00
—Gold "Starline" label					
❏ T 768 [M]	This Is Sinatra!	196?	5.00	10.00	20.00
—Black "Starline" label					
❏ DW 789 [R]	Close to You	196?	3.00	6.00	12.00
❏ W 789 [M]	Close to You	1957	7.50	15.00	30.00
—Gray label					
❏ W 789 [M]	Close to You	1959	5.00	10.00	20.00
—Black label with colorband					
❏ DW 803 [R]	A Swingin' Affair!	196?	3.00	6.00	12.00
❏ W 803 [M]	A Swingin' Affair!	1957	5.00	10.00	20.00
—Black label with colorband					
❏ W 803 [M]	A Swingin' Affair!	1957	7.50	15.00	30.00
—Gray label					
❏ SW 855 [S]	Where Are You?	1959	10.00	20.00	40.00
—Originals do not include "I Cover the Waterfront"					
❏ SW 855 [S]	Where Are You?	196?	7.50	15.00	30.00
—Later releases restore "I Cover the Waterfront"					
❏ W 855 [M]	Where Are You?	1957	7.50	15.00	30.00
—Gray label					
❏ W 855 [M]	Where Are You?	1959	5.00	10.00	20.00
—Black label with colorband					
❏ DT 894 [R]	The Sinatra Christmas Album	196?	2.50	5.00	10.00
—Rechanneled reissue of A Jolly Christmas with Frank Sinatra with same contents; some copies have this cover and "A Jolly Christmas" labels					
❏ SM-894 [R]	The Sinatra Christmas Album	197?	2.00	4.00	8.00
—Reissue in rechanneled stereo; any color label					
❏ T 894 [M]	The Sinatra Christmas Album	196?	5.00	10.00	20.00
—Reissue of A Jolly Christmas with Frank Sinatra with same contents; some copies have this cover and "A Jolly Christmas" labels					
❏ W 894 [M]	A Jolly Christmas from Frank Sinatra	1957	10.00	20.00	40.00
—Original mono with gray label					
❏ W 894 [M]	A Jolly Christmas from Frank Sinatra	1958	7.50	15.00	30.00
—Black colorband label, logo at left					
❏ SM-920	Come Fly with Me	197?	2.00	4.00	8.00
❏ SW 920 [S]	Come Fly with Me	1959	7.50	15.00	30.00
❏ W 920 [M]	Come Fly with Me	1958	10.00	20.00	40.00
—Gray label					
❏ W 920 [M]	Come Fly with Me	1959	5.00	10.00	20.00
—Black label with colorband					
❏ DW 982 [R]	This Is Sinatra, Volume Two	196?	3.00	6.00	12.00
❏ W 982 [M]	This Is Sinatra, Volume Two	1958	10.00	20.00	40.00
—Gray label					
❏ W 982 [M]	This Is Sinatra, Volume Two	1959	5.00	10.00	20.00
—Black label with colorband, logo at left					
❏ W 982 [M]	This Is Sinatra, Volume Two	1963	3.75	7.50	15.00
—Black label with colorband, logo at top					
❏ SW 1053 [S]	Frank Sinatra Sings for Only the Lonely	1959	7.50	15.00	30.00
—Originals do not include "It's a Lonesome Old Town" and "Spring Is Here"					
❏ SW 1053 [S]	Frank Sinatra Sings for Only the Lonely	196?	6.25	12.50	25.00
—Later releases restore "It's a Lonesome Old Town" and "Spring Is Here"					
❏ W 1053 [M]	Frank Sinatra Sings for Only the Lonely	1958	10.00	20.00	40.00
—Gray label					
❏ W 1053 [M]	Frank Sinatra Sings for Only the Lonely	1959	5.00	10.00	20.00
—Black label with colorband					
❏ SW 1069 [S]	Come Dance with Me!	1959	7.50	15.00	30.00
❏ W 1069 [M]	Come Dance with Me!	1959	5.00	10.00	20.00
❏ DW 1164 [R]	Look to Your Heart	196?	3.00	6.00	12.00
❏ W 1164 [M]	Look to Your Heart	1959	7.50	15.00	30.00
❏ SM-1221	No One Cares	197?	2.00	4.00	8.00
❏ SW 1221 [S]	No One Cares	1959	7.50	15.00	30.00
❏ W 1221 [M]	No One Cares	1959	5.00	10.00	20.00
❏ SW 1417 [S]	Nice 'N' Easy	1960	6.25	12.50	25.00
❏ W 1417 [M]	Nice 'N' Easy	1960	5.00	10.00	20.00
❏ DW 1429 [R]	Swing Easy	1960	3.00	6.00	12.00
❏ W 1429 [M]	Swing Easy	1960	5.00	10.00	20.00
❏ DW 1432 [R]	Songs for Young Lovers	1960	3.00	6.00	12.00
❏ W 1432 [M]	Songs for Young Lovers	1960	5.00	10.00	20.00
❏ SM-1491	Sinatra's Swingin' Session!!!	197?	2.00	4.00	8.00
❏ SW 1491 [S]	Sinatra's Swingin' Session!!!	1961	6.25	12.50	25.00
❏ W 1491 [M]	Sinatra's Swingin' Session!!!	1961	5.00	10.00	20.00
❏ SW 1538 [S]	All the Way	1961	6.25	12.50	25.00
❏ W 1538 [M]	All the Way	1961	5.00	10.00	20.00
❏ SW 1594 [S]	Come Swing with Me!	1961	6.25	12.50	25.00
❏ W 1594 [M]	Come Swing with Me!	1961	5.00	10.00	20.00
❏ SM-1676	Point of No Return	197?	2.00	4.00	8.00

Number	Title (A Side/B Side)	Yr	VG	VG+	NM
❏ SW 1676 [S]	Point of No Return	1962	6.25	12.50	25.00
❏ W 1676 [M]	Point of No Return	1962	5.00	10.00	20.00
❏ SW 1729 [P]	Sinatra Sings…Of Love and Things	1962	5.00	10.00	20.00
❏ W 1729 [M]	Sinatra Sings…Of Love and Things	1962	5.00	10.00	20.00
❏ SWCO 1762 [(3)P]	Sinatra, The Great Years	1962	10.00	20.00	40.00
❏ WCO 1762 [(3)M]	Sinatra, The Great Years	1962	7.50	15.00	30.00
❏ DW 1825 [R]	Sinatra Sings Rodgers and Hart	1963	3.00	6.00	12.00
❏ W 1825 [M]	Sinatra Sings Rodgers and Hart	1963	5.00	10.00	20.00
❏ DT 1919 [R]	Tell Her You Love Her	1963	3.00	6.00	12.00
❏ T 1919 [M]	Tell Her You Love Her	1963	5.00	10.00	20.00
❏ DW 1994 [R]	Sinatra Sings the Select Johnny Mercer	1963	3.00	6.00	12.00
❏ W 1994 [M]	Sinatra Sings the Select Johnny Mercer	1963	5.00	10.00	20.00
❏ DT 2036 [R]	The Greatest Hits of Frank Sinatra	1964	3.00	6.00	12.00
❏ T 2036 [M]	The Greatest Hits of Frank Sinatra	1964	5.00	10.00	20.00
❏ T 2123 [M]	Sinatra Sings the Select Harold Arlen	1964	25.00	50.00	100.00
—Only released in Canada, Australia and the UK					
❏ PRO-2163/4/5/6 [(2)DJ]	Selections from Sinatra, The Great Years	1962	10.00	20.00	40.00
❏ DW 2301 [R]	Sinatra Sings the Select Cole Porter	1965	3.00	6.00	12.00
❏ W 2301 [M]	Sinatra Sings the Select Cole Porter	1965	5.00	10.00	20.00
❏ DT 2602 [R]	Forever Frank	1966	3.00	6.00	12.00
❏ T 2602 [M]	Forever Frank	1966	5.00	10.00	20.00
❏ DT 2700 [R]	The Movie Songs	1967	3.00	6.00	12.00
❏ T 2700 [M]	The Movie Songs	1967	5.00	10.00	20.00
❏ STFL 2814 [(6)P]	The Frank Sinatra Deluxe Set	1968	15.00	30.00	60.00
❏ TFL 2814 [(6)M]	The Frank Sinatra Deluxe Set	1968	25.00	50.00	100.00
❏ DKAO 2900 [R]	The Best of Frank Sinatra	1968	3.75	7.50	15.00
❏ PRO-2974/5 [DJ]	Frank Sinatra Minute Masters	1965	10.00	20.00	40.00
—Edited version of 20 songs					
❏ DNFR 7630 [(6)P]	The Sinatra Touch	19??	15.00	30.00	60.00
❏ ST-11309	One More for the Road	1973	2.50	5.00	10.00
❏ SABB-11367 [(2)P]	Round #1	1974	3.75	7.50	15.00
❏ SM-11502	A Swingin' Affair!	1976	2.50	5.00	10.00
❏ SM-11801	Come Swing with Me	1978	2.50	5.00	10.00
❏ M-11883	This Is Sinatra!	1979	2.50	5.00	10.00
❏ SN-16109	The Best of Frank Sinatra	198?	2.00	4.00	8.00
—Budget-line reissue					
❏ DN-16110	What Is This Thing Called Love	198?	2.00	4.00	8.00
—Budget-line reissue					
❏ SN-16111	The Night We Called It a Day	198?	2.00	4.00	8.00
—Budget-line reissue					
❏ N-16112	My One and Only Love	198?	2.00	4.00	8.00
—Budget-line reissue					
❏ SN-16113	Sentimental Journey	198?	2.00	4.00	8.00
—Budget-line reissue					
❏ N-16148	Look to Your Heart	198?	2.00	4.00	8.00
—Budget-line reissue					
❏ SN-16149	Sinatra Sings…Of Love and Things	198?	2.00	4.00	8.00
—Budget-line reissue					
❏ SN-16202	Frank Sinatra Sings for Only the Lonely	198?	2.00	4.00	8.00
—Budget-line reissue					
❏ SN-16203	Come Dance with Me!	198?	2.00	4.00	8.00
—Budget-line reissue					
❏ SN-16204	Nice 'N' Easy	198?	2.00	4.00	8.00
—Budget-line reissue					
❏ SN-16205	All the Way	198?	2.00	4.00	8.00
—Budget-line reissue					
❏ SN-16267	Where Are You	198?	2.00	4.00	8.00
—Budget-line reissue					
❏ DN-16268	This Is Sinatra, Volume Two	198?	2.00	4.00	8.00
—Budget-line reissue					
❏ C1-89611	Duets	1993	5.00	10.00	20.00
❏ DW 90986 [R]	Sentimental Journey	1966	3.75	7.50	15.00
—Capitol Record Club issue					
❏ W 90986 [M]	Sentimental Journey	1966	6.25	12.50	25.00
—Capitol Record Club issue					
❏ DQBO 91261 [(2)R]	Songs for the Young at Heart	196?	7.50	15.00	30.00
❏ C1-94777 [(5)]	The Capitol Years	1990	25.00	50.00	100.00
—With book and wraparound banner. Only 5,000 were pressed					
❏ STBB-95191 [(2)]	Sinatra Sings the Great Ones	1973	5.00	10.00	20.00
—Longines Symphonette (formerly Capitol) Record Club issue					
CAPITOL PICKWICK SERIES					
❏ PC-3450 [M]	The Nearness of You	196?	3.00	6.00	12.00
❏ SPC-3450 [R]	The Nearness of You	196?	2.50	5.00	10.00
❏ PC-3452 [M]	Try a Little Tenderness	196?	3.00	6.00	12.00
❏ SPC-3452 [R]	Try a Little Tenderness	196?	2.50	5.00	10.00
❏ PC-3456 [M]	Nevertheless	196?	3.00	6.00	12.00
❏ SPC-3456 [R]	Nevertheless	196?	2.50	5.00	10.00
❏ PC-3457 [M]	Just One of Those Things	196?	3.00	6.00	12.00
❏ SPC-3457 [R]	Just One of Those Things	196?	2.50	5.00	10.00
❏ PC-3458 [M]	This Love of Mine	196?	3.00	6.00	12.00
❏ SPC-3458 [R]	This Love of Mine	196?	2.50	5.00	10.00
❏ PC-3463 [M]	My Cole Porter	196?	3.00	6.00	12.00
❏ SPC-3463 [R]	My Cole Porter	196?	2.50	5.00	10.00
COLUMBIA					
❏ C2L 6 [(2)M]	The Frank Sinatra Story	1958	7.50	15.00	30.00
❏ S3L 42 [(3)M]	The Essential Frank Sinatra	1966	25.00	50.00	100.00
❏ S3S 42 [(3)R]	The Essential Frank Sinatra	1966	12.50	25.00	50.00
❏ CL 606 [M]	Frankie	1955	6.25	12.50	25.00
—Cover has Frank with Debbie Reynolds					
❏ CL 606 [M]	Frankie	1955	7.50	15.00	30.00
—Cover has drawing of Frank Sinatra wearing a hat					
❏ CL 743 [M]	The Voice	1956	6.25	12.50	25.00
❏ CL 743 [M]	The Voice	1999	6.25	12.50	25.00
—Classic Records reissue on audiophile vinyl					
❏ CL 884 [M]	Frank Sinatra Conducts Music of Alec Wilder	1956	10.00	20.00	40.00
—Reissue of Columbia Masterworks ML 4271					
❏ CL 902 [M]	That Old Feeling	1956	6.25	12.50	25.00
❏ CL 953 [M]	Adventures of the Heart	1957	6.25	12.50	25.00
❏ CL 1032 [M]	Christmas Dreaming	1957	20.00	40.00	80.00
❏ CL 1136 [M]	Put Your Dreams Away	1958	6.25	12.50	25.00
❏ CL 1241 [M]	Love Is a Kick	1958	6.25	12.50	25.00

Number	Title (A Side/B Side)	Yr	VG	VG+	NM
❏ CL 1297 [M]	The Broadway Kick	1958	6.25	12.50	25.00
❏ CL 1359 [M]	Come Back to Sorrento	1959	6.25	12.50	25.00
❏ CL 1448 [M]	Reflections	1959	15.00	30.00	60.00
❏ CL 2474 [M]	Greatest Hits, The Early Years, Vol. 1	1966	3.75	7.50	15.00
❏ CAS 2475 [DJ]	The Voice: The Columbia Years Sampler	1986	10.00	20.00	40.00
❏ CL 2521 [10]	Get Happy	1955	15.00	30.00	60.00
—"House Party Series" release					
❏ CL 2539 [10]	I've Got a Crush on You	1955	15.00	30.00	60.00
—"House Party Series" release; different contents from CL 6290					
❏ CL 2542 [M]	Christmas with Sinatra	1955	15.00	30.00	60.00
—"House Party Series" release					
❏ CL 2572 [M]	Greatest Hits, The Early Years, Vol. 2	1966	3.75	7.50	15.00
❏ CL 2739 [M]	The Essential Frank Sinatra, Volume 1	1967	6.25	12.50	25.00
❏ CL 2740 [M]	The Essential Frank Sinatra, Volume 2	1967	6.25	12.50	25.00
❏ CL 2741 [M]	The Essential Frank Sinatra, Volume 3	1967	6.25	12.50	25.00
❏ CL 2913 [M]	Frank Sinatra in Hollywood	1968	20.00	40.00	80.00
❏ CL 6001 [10]	The Voice of Frank Sinatra	1949	17.50	35.00	70.00
—Original in pink paper cover					
❏ CL 6001 [10]	The Voice of Frank Sinatra	1950	15.00	30.00	60.00
—Blue cardboard cover					
❏ CL 6019 [10]	Christmas Songs by Sinatra	1948	25.00	50.00	100.00
—With "gingerbread man" cover					
❏ CL 6019 [10]	Christmas Songs by Sinatra	1949	20.00	40.00	80.00
—With green vinylite cover					
❏ CL 6059 [10]	Frankly Sentimental	1951	15.00	30.00	60.00
❏ CL 6087 [10]	Songs by Sinatra, Volume 1	1952	15.00	30.00	60.00
❏ CL 6096 [10]	Dedicated to You	1952	25.00	50.00	100.00
—Three of the tracks on this LP are alternate takes unavailable on vinyl anywhere else					
❏ CL 6143 [10]	Sing and Dance with Frank Sinatra	1953	15.00	30.00	60.00
❏ CL 6290 [10]	I've Got a Crush on You	1954	15.00	30.00	60.00
❏ CS 9274 [R]	Greatest Hits, The Early Years, Vol. 1	1966	2.50	5.00	10.00
❏ PC 9274	Greatest Hits, The Early Years, Vol. 1	197?	2.00	4.00	8.00
❏ CS 9372 [R]	Greatest Hits, The Early Years, Vol. 2	1966	2.50	5.00	10.00
❏ PC 9372	Greatest Hits, The Early Years, Vol. 2	197?	2.00	4.00	8.00
❏ CS 9539 [R]	The Essential Frank Sinatra, Volume 1	1967	3.00	6.00	12.00
❏ CS 9540 [R]	The Essential Frank Sinatra, Volume 2	1967	3.00	6.00	12.00
❏ CS 9541 [R]	The Essential Frank Sinatra, Volume 3	1967	3.00	6.00	12.00
❏ CS 9713 [R]	Frank Sinatra in Hollywood	1968	3.00	6.00	12.00
❏ KG 31358 [(2)]	In the Beginning	1971	10.00	20.00	40.00
—Original edition; titles of songs at left on front cover					
❏ PG 31358 [(2)]	In the Beginning	197?	3.00	6.00	12.00
—Revised version; titles of songs at right on front cover					
❏ C6X 40343 [(6)]	The Voice: The Columbia Years 1943-1952	1986	20.00	40.00	80.00
❏ PC 40707	Christmas Dreaming	1987	7.50	15.00	30.00
—Reissue of CL 1032 with an extra track					
❏ C2X 40897 [(2)]	Hello Young Lovers	1988	7.50	15.00	30.00
❏ PC 44238 [M]	Sinatra Rarities	1989	10.00	20.00	40.00
COLUMBIA MASTERWORKS					
❏ ML 4271 [M]	Frank Sinatra Conducts Music of Alec Wilder	1955	25.00	50.00	100.00
HARMONY					
❏ HL 7400 [M]	Have Yourself a Merry Little Christmas	1967	7.50	15.00	30.00
❏ HL 7405 [M]	Romantic Scenes from the Early Years	1967	7.50	15.00	30.00
❏ HS 11200 [R]	Have Yourself a Merry Little Christmas	1967	5.00	10.00	20.00
—At least two different cover designs exist					
❏ HS 11205 [R]	Romantic Scenes from the Early Years	1967	3.00	6.00	12.00
❏ HS 11277 [R]	Someone to Watch Over Me	1968	3.75	7.50	15.00
❏ HS 11390 [R]	Frank Sinatra	1969	3.75	7.50	15.00
❏ KH 30318 [R]	Greatest Hits, Early Years	1971	3.75	7.50	15.00
LONGINES SYMPHONETTE					
❏ LS-308A [(10)]	Sinatra: The Works	1972	18.75	37.50	75.00
❏ LS-309A [(6)]	Sinatra: The Works	1973	10.00	20.00	40.00
—Abridged version of LS-308A					
❏ SYS-5637	Sinatra Like Never Before	1972	6.25	12.50	25.00
—Bonus LP with purchase of LS-308A					
MOBILE FIDELITY					
❏ SC-1 [(16)]	Sinatra	1983	150.00	300.00	600.00
—Audiophile vinyl; only two of the 16 records in this box were released individually					
❏ 1-086	Nice 'N' Easy	1981	10.00	20.00	40.00
—Audiophile vinyl					
❏ 1-135 [M]	A Jolly Christmas from Frank Sinatra	1984	10.00	20.00	40.00
—Audiophile vinyl using the original title					
PAIR					
❏ PDL2-1027 [(2)]	All-Time Classics	1986	3.00	6.00	12.00
❏ PDL2-1028 [(2)]	Timeless	1986	3.00	6.00	12.00
❏ PDL2-1122 [(2)]	Classic Performances	1986	3.00	6.00	12.00
QWEST					
❏ 25145	L.A. Is My Lady	1984	3.00	6.00	12.00
RCA VICTOR					
❏ APL1-0497 [R]	What'll I Do	1974	3.00	6.00	12.00
❏ LPV-583 [M]	This Love of Mine	1971	10.00	20.00	40.00
❏ ANL1-1050 [R]	What'll I Do	1976	2.50	5.00	10.00
❏ LPM-1569 [M]	Tommy Plays, Frankie Sings	1957	10.00	20.00	40.00
—Second issue with new title					
❏ LPM-1569 [M]	Frankie and Tommy	1957	15.00	30.00	60.00
—First issue of this LP					
❏ LPM-1632 [M]	We Three	1958	10.00	20.00	40.00
—Second issue, "RE" on cover					
❏ LPM-1632 [M]	We Three	1958	15.00	30.00	60.00
—First issue					
❏ LPT-3063 [10]	Fabulous Frankie	1953	15.00	30.00	60.00
❏ CPL2-4334 [(2)]	The Sinatra/Dorsey Sessions, Vol. 1	1982	6.25	12.50	25.00
❏ CPL2-4335 [(2)]	The Sinatra/Dorsey Sessions, Vol. 2	1982	6.25	12.50	25.00
❏ CPL2-4336 [(2)]	The Sinatra/Dorsey Sessions, Vol. 3	1982	6.25	12.50	25.00
❏ AFL1-4741 [R]	Radio Years (Sinatra/Dorsey/Stordahl)	1983	3.75	7.50	15.00
REPRISE					
❏ F 1001 [M]	Ring-a-Ding-Ding!	1961	5.00	10.00	20.00
❏ R9 1001 [S]	Ring-a-Ding-Ding!	1961	6.25	12.50	25.00
❏ F 1002 [M]	Sinatra Swings	1961	5.00	10.00	20.00
—Retitled version of "Swing Along with Me"; Capitol threatened legal action because of its "Come Swing With Me!" collection					

Number	Title (A Side/B Side)	Yr	VG	VG+	NM
❏ F 1002 [M]	Swing Along with Me	1961	10.00	20.00	40.00
—Original title					
❏ R9 1002 [S]	Sinatra Swings	1961	6.25	12.50	25.00
—Retitled version of "Swing Along with Me"; Capitol threatened legal action because of its "Come Swing With Me!" collection					
❏ R9 1002 [S]	Swing Along with Me	1961	12.50	25.00	50.00
—Original title					
❏ F 1003 [M]	I Remember Tommy	1961	5.00	10.00	20.00
❏ R9 1003 [S]	I Remember Tommy	1961	6.25	12.50	25.00
❏ F 1004 [M]	Sinatra & Strings	1962	3.75	7.50	15.00
❏ R9 1004 [S]	Sinatra & Strings	1962	5.00	10.00	20.00
❏ F 1005 [M]	Sinatra and Swingin' Brass	1962	3.75	7.50	15.00
❏ R9 1005 [S]	Sinatra and Swingin' Brass	1962	5.00	10.00	20.00
❏ F 1006 [M]	Great Songs from Great Britain	1962	20.00	40.00	80.00
—Only released in the UK					
❏ R9 1006 [S]	Great Songs from Great Britain	1962	25.00	50.00	100.00
—Only released in the UK					
❏ F 1007 [M]	All Alone	1962	3.75	7.50	15.00
❏ R9 1007 [S]	All Alone	1962	5.00	10.00	20.00
❏ F 1008 [M]	Sinatra-Basie	1963	3.75	7.50	15.00
❏ R9 1008 [S]	Sinatra-Basie	1963	5.00	10.00	20.00
❏ F 1009 [M]	The Concert Sinatra	1963	3.75	7.50	15.00
❏ R9 1009 [S]	The Concert Sinatra	196?	5.00	10.00	20.00
—Without cover reference to "35mm Stereo"					
❏ R9 1009 [S]	The Concert Sinatra	1963	6.25	12.50	25.00
—Original pressings declare this was recorded in "35mm Stereo"					
❏ F 1010 [M]	Sinatra's Sinatra	1963	3.75	7.50	15.00
❏ R9 1010 [S]	Sinatra's Sinatra	1963	5.00	10.00	20.00
❏ F 1011 [M]	Days of Wine and Roses, Moon River, and Other Academy Award Winners	1964	3.75	7.50	15.00
❏ FS 1011 [S]	Days of Wine and Roses, Moon River, and Other Academy Award Winners	1964	5.00	10.00	20.00
❏ F 1012 [M]	It Might As Well Be Swing	1964	3.75	7.50	15.00
❏ FS 1012 [S]	It Might As Well Be Swing	1964	5.00	10.00	20.00
❏ F 1013 [M]	Softly, As I Leave You	1964	3.75	7.50	15.00
❏ FS 1013 [S]	Softly, As I Leave You	1964	5.00	10.00	20.00
❏ F 1014 [M]	September of My Years	1965	3.75	7.50	15.00
❏ FS 1014 [S]	September of My Years	1965	5.00	10.00	20.00
❏ F 1015 [M]	My Kind of Broadway	1965	3.75	7.50	15.00
❏ FS 1015 [S]	My Kind of Broadway	1965	5.00	10.00	20.00
❏ 2F 1016 [(2)M]	A Man and His Music	1965	5.00	10.00	20.00
❏ 2F/2FS 1016	A Man and His Music Special Box	1965	50.00	100.00	200.00
—Blue slipcase with embossed silver front, raised letters, plus 4-page booklet and a signed card (deduct 50% if card missing). Add this to LP value.					
❏ 2FS 1016 [(2)S]	A Man and His Music	1965	6.25	12.50	25.00
❏ F 1017 [M]	Strangers in the Night	1966	3.00	6.00	12.00
❏ FS 1017 [S]	Strangers in the Night	1966	3.75	7.50	15.00
❏ F 1018 [M]	Moonlight Sinatra	1966	3.75	7.50	15.00
❏ FS 1018 [S]	Moonlight Sinatra	1966	5.00	10.00	20.00
❏ 2F 1019 [(2)M]	Sinatra at the Sands	1966	5.00	10.00	20.00
❏ 2FS 1019 [(2)S]	Sinatra at the Sands	1966	6.25	12.50	25.00
❏ F 1020 [M]	That's Life	1966	3.00	6.00	12.00
❏ FS 1020 [S]	That's Life	1966	3.75	7.50	15.00
❏ F 1021 [M]	Francis Albert Sinatra & Antonio Carlos Jobim	1967	3.00	6.00	12.00
❏ FS 1021 [S]	Francis Albert Sinatra & Antonio Carlos Jobim	1967	3.75	7.50	15.00
❏ F 1022 [M]	Frank Sinatra (The World We Knew)	1967	3.75	7.50	15.00
❏ FS 1022 [S]	Frank Sinatra (The World We Knew)	1967	3.75	7.50	15.00
❏ FS 1023	The Sinatra Christmas Album	1967	25.00	50.00	100.00
—Album never released; value is for cover slick					
❏ FS 1024	Francis A. and Edward K.	1968	5.00	10.00	20.00
❏ FS 1025	Frank Sinatra's Greatest Hits	1968	3.75	7.50	15.00
❏ FS 1027	Cycles	1969	3.75	7.50	15.00
❏ FS 1028	SinatraJobim	1969	2000.	3000.	4000.
—Unreleased; test pressings exist (value is for one of these). 8-track tapes also exist and are 10% of this value					
❏ FS 1029	My Way	1969	3.75	7.50	15.00
❏ FS4 1029 [Q]	My Way	1974	6.25	12.50	25.00
❏ FS 1030	A Man Alone & Other Songs of Rod McKuen	1969	3.75	7.50	15.00
❏ FS 1030	A Man Alone & Other Songs of Rod McKuen	1969	100.00	200.00	400.00
—Signed copies with gatefold cover and hardbound book; 400 made					
❏ FS 1031	Watertown	1970	6.25	12.50	25.00
—With gatefold and poster					
❏ FS 1032	Frank Sinatra's Greatest Hits, Vol. 2	1970	—	—	—
—Canceled?					
❏ FS 1033	Sinatra and Company	1971	3.75	7.50	15.00
❏ FS 1034	Frank Sinatra's Greatest Hits, Vol. 2	1972	3.75	7.50	15.00
❏ FS 2155	Ol' Blue Eyes Is Back	1973	3.00	6.00	12.00
❏ FS4 2155 [Q]	Ol' Blue Eyes Is Back	1974	6.25	12.50	25.00
❏ FS4 2194 [Q]	Some Nice Things I've Missed	1974	6.25	12.50	25.00
❏ FS 2195	Some Nice Things I've Missed	1974	3.00	6.00	12.00
❏ FS 2207	Sinatra — The Main Event Live	1974	3.00	6.00	12.00
❏ 3FS 2300 [(3)]	Trilogy: Past, Present, Future	1980	5.00	10.00	20.00
❏ FS 2305	She Shot Me Down	1981	3.00	6.00	12.00
❏ 5004 [DJ]	A Man and His Music, Part II	1966	75.00	150.00	300.00
—Promotional album for use by Budweiser					
❏ 5230 [DJ]	Songbook, Vol. 1	1971	12.50	25.00	50.00
❏ 5267 [(2)DJ]	Songbook, Vol. 2	1972	25.00	50.00	100.00
❏ 5409 [DJ]	I Sing the Songs	1976	12.50	25.00	50.00
❏ F 6045 [M]	Sinatra Conducts Music from Pictures and Plays	1962	7.50	15.00	30.00
❏ R9 6045 [S]	Sinatra Conducts Music from Pictures and Plays	1962	10.00	2.00	40.00
❏ R 6167 [M]	Sinatra '65	1965	3.75	7.50	15.00
❏ RS 6167 [S]	Sinatra '65	1965	5.00	10.00	20.00
❏ SMAS-92081	A Man Alone & Other Songs of Rod McKuen	1969	5.00	10.00	20.00
—Capitol Record Club edition					
TIME-LIFE					
❏ SLGD-02 [(2)]	Legendary Singers	1982	6.25	12.50	25.00

Number	Title (A Side/B Side)	Yr	VG	VG+	NM
SINATRA, FRANK; DEAN MARTIN; SAMMY DAVIS, JR.					
ARTANIS					
❏ ARZ 102 [(2)]	The Summit	1999	—	—	—
—Canceled					
SINATRA, NANCY					
RCA VICTOR					
❏ LSP-4645	Nancy and Lee Again	1972	7.50	15.00	30.00
—With Lee Hazlewood					
❏ LSP-4774	Woman	1973	6.25	12.50	25.00
❏ VPS-6078 [(2)]	This Is Nancy Sinatra	1972	12.50	25.00	50.00
REPRISE					
❏ R-6202 [M]	Boots	1966	6.25	12.50	25.00
❏ RS-6202 [S]	Boots	1966	7.50	15.00	30.00
❏ R-6207 [M]	How Does That Grab You?	1966	5.00	10.00	20.00
❏ RS-6207 [S]	How Does That Grab You?	1966	6.25	12.50	25.00
❏ R-6221 [M]	Nancy in London	1966	5.00	10.00	20.00
❏ RS-6221 [S]	Nancy in London	1966	6.25	12.50	25.00
❏ R-6239 [M]	Sugar	1967	6.25	12.50	25.00
❏ RS-6239 [S]	Sugar	1967	5.00	10.00	20.00
❏ R-6251 [M]	Country, My Way	1967	6.25	12.50	25.00
❏ RS-6251 [S]	Country, My Way	1967	5.00	10.00	20.00
❏ RS-6273	Nancy and Lee	1968	5.00	10.00	20.00
—With Lee Hazlewood					
❏ R-6277 [M]	Movin' with Nancy	1967	6.25	12.50	25.00
❏ RS-6277 [S]	Movin' with Nancy	1967	5.00	10.00	20.00
❏ RS-6333	Nancy	1969	5.00	10.00	20.00
❏ RS-6409	Nancy's Greatest Hits	1970	5.00	10.00	20.00
❏ ST-91341 [S]	Boots	1967	10.00	20.00	40.00
—Capitol Record Club edition					
❏ ST-91349 [S]	Movin' with Nancy	1967	7.50	15.00	30.00
—Capitol Record Club edition					
RHINO					
❏ R1-70166	Fairy Tales and Fantasies: The Best of Nancy and Lee	1989	2.50	5.00	10.00
—With Lee Hazlewood					
❏ RNLP-70227	Boots: Nancy Sinatra's All-Time Hits (1966-1970)	1987	2.50	5.00	10.00
SING A SONG WITH THE BEATLES					
TOWER					
❏ DKAO 5000 [R]	Sing a Song with the Beatles	1965	50.00	100.00	200.00
❏ KAO 5000 [M]	Sing a Song with the Beatles	1965	37.50	75.00	150.00
—No artist listed on label					
SINGER, HAL, AND CHARLIE SHAVERS					
PRESTIGE					
❏ PRLP-7153 [M]	Blue Stompin'	1959	20.00	40.00	80.00
SWINGVILLE					
❏ SVLP-2023 [M]	Blue Stompin'	1961	12.50	25.00	50.00
—Purple label					
❏ SVLP-2023 [M]	Blue Stompin'	1965	6.25	12.50	25.00
—Blue label, trident logo at right					
SINGER ORCHESTRA, THE					
SINGER					
❏ HE-M-1 [M]	Favorite Christmas Songs from Singer	1964	3.75	7.50	15.00
—Cover photo of the cast of "The Donna Reed Show"					
❏ HE-S-1 [S]	Favorite Christmas Songs from Singer	1964	5.00	10.00	20.00
—Cover photo of the cast of "The Donna Reed Show"					
SINGLETON, CHARLIE					
RCA CAMDEN					
❏ CAL-713 [M]	Big Twist Hits	1962	5.00	10.00	20.00
❏ CAS-713 [S]	Big Twist Hits	1962	6.25	12.50	25.00
SINGLETON, MARGIE					
ASHLEY					
❏ 3003	Margie Singleton Sings Country Music with Soul	1968	3.75	7.50	15.00
PICKWICK					
❏ SPC-3133	Harper Valley P.T.A.	197?	2.50	5.00	10.00
UNITED ARTISTS					
❏ UAL-3459 [M]	Crying Time	1965	3.75	7.50	15.00
❏ UAS-6459 [S]	Crying Time	1965	5.00	10.00	20.00
SINGLETON, ZUTTY/ART TATUM					
BRUNSWICK					
❏ BL 58038 [10]	Battle of Jazz, Vol. 2	1953	12.50	25.00	50.00
SIOUXSIE AND THE BANSHEES					
GEFFEN					
❏ GHS 24030	Hyaena	1984	2.50	5.00	10.00
❏ GHS 24046	The Scream	1984	2.50	5.00	10.00
—Reissue of Polydor PD1-6207					
❏ GHS 24047	Join Hands	1984	2.50	5.00	10.00
—Apparently, this 1979 album's first U.S. release					
❏ GHS 24048	Kaleidoscope	1984	2.50	5.00	10.00
—Reissue of PVC 7921					
❏ GHS 24049	A Kiss in the Dream House	1984	2.50	5.00	10.00
—Apparently, this 1982 album's first U.S. release					
❏ GHS 24050	Juju	1984	2.50	5.00	10.00
—Reissue of PVC 8903					
❏ GHS 24051	Once Upon a Time: The Singles	1984	2.50	5.00	10.00
—Reissue of PVC 8906					
❏ GHS 24052 [(2)]	Nocturne	1984	2.50	5.00	10.00
❏ GHS 24092	Tinderbox	1986	2.50	5.00	10.00
❏ GHS 24134	Through the Looking Glass	1987	2.50	5.00	10.00
❏ GHS 24205	Peepshow	1988	2.50	5.00	10.00
❏ GEF 24387	Superstition	1991	3.00	6.00	12.00
❏ GEF 24630	The Rapture	1995	3.00	6.00	12.00
POLYDOR					
❏ PD1-6207	The Scream	1978	7.50	15.00	30.00

Number	Title (A Side/B Side)	Yr	VG	VG+	NM
PVC					
❏ 7921	Kaleidoscope	1980	6.25	12.50	25.00
❏ 8903	Ju Ju	1981	6.25	12.50	25.00
—Original copies include bonus single "Israel"/"Red Over White"					
❏ 8906	Once Upon a Time: The Singles	1981	5.00	10.00	20.00
—With poster and inner sleeve					
WARNER BROS.					
❏ WBMS-138 [DJ]	The Tinderbox Interview	1986	6.25	12.50	25.00
—Part of "The Warner Bros. Music Show"					
SIR DOUGLAS QUINTET					
Also see DOUG SAHM.					
ABC DOT					
❏ DO-2057	Texas Rock for Country Rollers	1976	3.75	7.50	15.00
—As "Sir Doug and the Texas Tornadoes"					
ATLANTIC					
❏ SD 7287	Texas Tornado	1974	3.75	7.50	15.00
—As "Sir Douglas Band"					
BEAT ROCKET					
❏ BR 123	The Best of the Sir Douglas Quintet	2000	3.00	6.00	12.00
—Reissue of Tribe LP on 180-gram vinyl					
❏ BR 124	The Sir Douglas Quintet Is Back!	2000	3.00	6.00	12.00
—New compilation of Tribe material on 180-gram vinyl					
PHILIPS					
❏ PHS 600344	1 + 1 + 1 = 4	1970	6.25	12.50	25.00
❏ PHS 600353	The Return of Doug Saldana	1971	6.25	12.50	25.00
R&M					
❏ UDL-2343	The Tracker	1981	5.00	10.00	20.00
SMASH					
❏ SRS-67108	Sir Douglas Quintet + 2 = Honkey Blues	1968	7.50	15.00	30.00
❏ SRS-67115	Mendocino	1969	6.25	12.50	25.00
❏ SRS-67130	Together After Five	1970	6.25	12.50	25.00
TAKOMA					
❏ TAK-7086	The Best of the Sir Douglas Quintet	1980	3.00	6.00	12.00
❏ TAK-7088	Border Wave	1981	3.00	6.00	12.00
❏ TAK-7095	Sir Douglas Quintet Live	1985	3.00	6.00	12.00
TRIBE					
❏ TR 37001 [M]	The Best of the Sir Douglas Quintet	1966	17.50	35.00	70.00
❏ TRS 47001 [R]	The Best of the Sir Douglas Quintet	1966	12.50	25.00	50.00
VARRICK					
❏ 004	Quintessence	1983	3.00	6.00	12.00
SIR LANCELOT					
MERCURY					
❏ MG-25159 [10]	Calypso	1952	12.50	25.00	50.00
SIR LORD BALTIMORE					
MERCURY					
❏ SRM-1-613	Sir Lord Baltimore	1971	6.25	12.50	25.00
❏ SR-61328	Kingdom Come	1970	6.25	12.50	25.00
SIRAVO, GEORGE					
AD-LIB					
❏ S-226 [S]	Out on a Limb	196?	5.00	10.00	20.00
COLUMBIA					
❏ CL 6146 [10]	Your Dance Date with George Siravo	1951	10.00	20.00	40.00
EPIC					
❏ BN 607 [S]	Everything Goes	1961	5.00	10.00	20.00
KAPP					
❏ KL-1016 [M]	Polite Jazz	1956	7.50	15.00	30.00
MERCURY					
❏ MG-20327 [M]	Darling, Please Forgive Me	1958	7.50	15.00	30.00
RCA CAMDEN					
❏ CAS-505 [S]	Siravo Swing Session	1959	5.00	10.00	20.00
RCA VICTOR					
❏ LPM-1970 [M]	Swingin' in Hi-Fi in Studio A	1959	6.25	12.50	25.00
❏ LSP-1970 [S]	Swingin' in Hi-Fi in Studio A	1959	7.50	15.00	30.00
TIME					
❏ S-2019 [S]	Seductive Strings	196?	5.00	10.00	20.00
❏ S-2115 [S]	And Then I Wrote Richard Rodgers	196?	5.00	10.00	20.00
VIK					
❏ LX-1091 [M]	Old But New	1957	7.50	15.00	30.00
❏ LX-1125 [M]	Swing Hi, Swing Fi	1958	7.50	15.00	30.00
SIREN					
ELEKTRA					
❏ EKS-74087	Strange Locomotion	1971	5.00	10.00	20.00
SISTER DOUBLE HAPPINESS					
REPRISE					
❏ PRO-A-5010 [DJ]	Heart and Mind	1991	10.00	20.00	40.00
—Vinyl is promo only					
SST					
❏ 162	Sister Double Happiness	1988	2.50	5.00	10.00
SISTER SLEDGE					
ATCO					
❏ SD 36-105	Circle of Love	1975	5.00	10.00	20.00
ATLANTIC					
❏ 81255	When the Boys Meet the Girls	1985	2.50	5.00	10.00
COTILLION					
❏ SD 5209	We Are Family	1979	2.50	5.00	10.00
❏ SD 5231	The Sisters	1982	2.50	5.00	10.00
❏ SD 9919	Together	1976	3.00	6.00	12.00
❏ SD 16012	Love Somebody Today	1980	2.50	5.00	10.00
❏ SD 16027	All American Girls	1981	2.50	5.00	10.00
❏ 90069	Bet Cha Say That to All the Girls	1983	2.50	5.00	10.00

Number	Title (A Side/B Side)	Yr	VG	VG+	NM
SIX, THE					
BETHLEHEM					
❏ BCP-28 [M]	The Six	1955	20.00	40.00	80.00
❏ BCP-57 [M]	The View From Jazzbo's Head	1956	25.00	50.00	100.00
SIX AND SEVEN-EIGHTHS STRING BAND, THE					
FOLKWAYS					
❏ FP-671 [M]	The Six and Seven-Eighths String Band	1951	12.50	25.00	50.00
❏ FP-2671 [M]	The Six and Seven-Eighths String Band	195?	10.00	20.00	40.00
SIZEMORE, ARTHUR					
DECCA					
❏ DL 4785 [M]	Mountain Ballads and Old Hymns	1966	7.50	15.00	30.00
❏ DL 74785 [S]	Mountain Ballads and Old Hymns	1966	10.00	20.00	40.00
SKAGGS, RICKY					
ATLANTIC					
❏ 82834	Solid Ground	1995	3.75	7.50	15.00
EPIC					
❏ EAS 2022 [DJ]	The Ricky Skaggs Story	1990	7.50	15.00	30.00
—Promo-only interview record					
❏ FE 37193	Waitin' for the Sun to Shine	1981	2.50	5.00	10.00
❏ FE 37996	Highways and Heartaches	1982	2.50	5.00	10.00
❏ FE 39409	Favorite Country Songs	1985	2.50	5.00	10.00
❏ FE 39410	Country Boy	1984	2.50	5.00	10.00
❏ FE 40103	Live in London	1985	2.50	5.00	10.00
❏ FE 40309	Love's Gonna Get Ya!	1986	2.00	4.00	8.00
❏ FE 40623	Comin' Home to Stay	1988	2.00	4.00	8.00
❏ FE 45027	Kentucky Thunder	1989	2.50	5.00	10.00
ROUNDER					
❏ 0151	Family and Friends	1982	3.00	6.00	12.00
SUGAR HILL					
❏ SH-3706	Sweet Temptation	1979	3.00	6.00	12.00
❏ SH-3711	Skaggs and Rice	1980	3.00	6.00	12.00
SUGAR HILL/EPIC					
❏ FE 38954	Don't Cheat in Our Hometown	1983	2.50	5.00	10.00
SKAGGS, RICKY, AND KEITH WHITLEY					
REBEL					
❏ 1504	Second Generation Bluegrass	1972	5.00	10.00	20.00
❏ 1550	That's It	1975	5.00	10.00	20.00
SKELTON, RED					
LIBERTY					
❏ LRP-3425 [M]	Red Skelton Conducts	1966	5.00	10.00	20.00
❏ LRP-3477 [M]	Music from the Heart	1966	5.00	10.00	20.00
❏ LST-7425 [S]	Red Skelton Conducts	1966	6.25	12.50	25.00
❏ LST-7477 [S]	Music from the Heart	1966	6.25	12.50	25.00
SKID ROW					
Two different groups.					
ATLANTIC					
❏ 1P-8136	Slave to the Grind	1991	5.00	10.00	20.00
—U.S. vinyl version available only from Columbia House; all copies are the censored version with "Beggars Day"					
❏ 81936	Skid Row	1989	2.50	5.00	10.00
EPIC					
❏ E 30404	Skid Row	1971	5.00	10.00	20.00
❏ E 30913	34 Hours	1971	6.25	12.50	25.00
SKIN ALLEY					
STAX					
❏ STS-3013	Two Quid Deal	1973	5.00	10.00	20.00
—With poster					
SKINNER, CORNELIA AND OTIS					
RCA CAMDEN					
❏ CAL-190 [M]	Cornelia Skinner with Otis Skinner	1955	7.50	15.00	30.00
SKINNER, JIMMIE					
DECCA					
❏ DL 4132 [M]	Country Singer	1961	10.00	20.00	40.00
MERCURY					
❏ MG-20352 [M]	Songs That Make the Jukebox Play	1957	20.00	40.00	80.00
❏ MG-20700 [M]	Jimmie Skinner Sings Jimmie Rodgers	1962	6.25	12.50	25.00
❏ SR-60700 [S]	Jimmie Skinner Sings Jimmie Rodgers	1962	7.50	15.00	30.00
STARDAY					
❏ SLP-240 [M]	Jimmie Skinner	1963	10.00	20.00	40.00
VETCO					
❏ 3001	Jimmie Skinner Sings Bluegrass	1976	3.75	7.50	15.00
WING					
❏ MGW-12277 [M]	Country Blues	1964	6.25	12.50	25.00
❏ SRW-16277 [R]	Country Blues	1964	3.75	7.50	15.00
SKIP AND THE CREATIONS					
JUSTICE					
❏ (# unknown)	Mobam	196?	100.00	200.00	400.00
SKUNKS, THE					
TEEN TOWN					
❏ TTLP-101	Getting Started	1968	12.50	25.00	50.00
SKYLINERS, THE					
CALICO					
❏ LP-3000 [M]	The Skyliners	1959	200.00	400.00	600.00
—Yellow and blue label					
❏ LP-3000 [M]	The Skyliners	196?	50.00	100.00	200.00
—Blue label					
KAMA SUTRA					
❏ KSBS-2026	Once Upon a Time	1971	6.25	12.50	25.00
ORIGINAL SOUND					
❏ OS-5010 [M]	Since I Don't Have You	1963	12.50	25.00	50.00

S

Number	Title (A Side/B Side)	Yr	VG	VG+	NM
❑ OSS-8873 [S]	Since I Don't Have You	1963	17.50	35.00	70.00
❑ OSS-8873 [S]	Since I Don't Have You	197?	3.75	7.50	15.00
—Reissue on thinner vinyl					

SLACK, FREDDIE
EMARCY
| ❑ MG-36094 [M] | Boogie-Woogie on the 88 | 1956 | 10.00 | 20.00 | 40.00 |

SLADE
CBS ASSOCIATED
❑ FZ 39336	Keep Your Hands Off My Power Supply	1984	2.50	5.00	10.00
❑ PZ 39336	Keep Your Hands Off My Power Supply	1985	2.00	4.00	8.00
—Budget-line reissue					
❑ FZ 39976	Rogues Gallery	1985	2.50	5.00	10.00
COTILLION
| ❑ SD 9035 | Play It Loud | 1970 | 5.00 | 10.00 | 20.00 |
FONTANA
❑ SRF-67598	Ballzy	1969	20.00	40.00	80.00
❑ SRF-67598 [DJ]	Ballzy	1969	12.50	25.00	50.00
—White label promo					
POLYDOR
| ❑ PD-5508 | Slade Alive! | 1972 | 3.75 | 7.50 | 15.00 |
| ❑ PD-5524 | Slayed? | 1973 | 3.75 | 7.50 | 15.00 |
REPRISE
| ❑ MS 2173 | Sladest | 1973 | 3.00 | 6.00 | 12.00 |
WARNER BROS.
❑ BS 2770	Stomp Your Hands, Clap Your Feet	1974	3.00	6.00	12.00
❑ BS 2865	Slade in Flame	1975	3.00	6.00	12.00
❑ BS 2936	Nobody's Fools	1976	3.00	6.00	12.00

SLATKIN, FELIX
LIBERTY
❑ LRP-3150 [M]	Fantastic Percussion	1960	3.75	7.50	15.00
❑ LRP-3287 [M]	Our Winter Love	1963	3.00	6.00	12.00
❑ LST-7150 [S]	Fantastic Percussion	1960	5.00	10.00	20.00
❑ LST-7287 [S]	Our Winter Love	1963	3.75	7.50	15.00
❑ LMM-13001 [M]	Paradise Found	1960	3.75	7.50	15.00
❑ LMM-13008 [M]	Street Scene	1961	3.75	7.50	15.00
❑ LMM-13011 [M]	Many Splendored Themes	1962	3.75	7.50	15.00
❑ LMM-13019 [M]	Inspired Themes from the Inspired Films	1962	3.75	7.50	15.00
❑ LMM-13021 [M]	Fantastic Strings Play Fantastic Themes	1962	3.75	7.50	15.00
❑ LMM-13024 [M]	Hoedown	1963	3.75	7.50	15.00
❑ LMM-13027 [M]	The Ballad of New Orleans	1963	3.75	7.50	15.00
❑ LSS-14001 [S]	Paradise Found	1960	4.50	9.00	18.00
❑ LSS-14008 [S]	Street Scene	1961	4.50	9.00	18.00
❑ LSS-14011 [S]	Many Splendored Themes	1962	4.50	9.00	18.00
❑ LSS-14019 [S]	Inspired Themes from the Inspired Films	1962	4.50	9.00	18.00
❑ LSS-14021 [S]	Fantastic Strings Play Fantastic Themes	1962	4.50	9.00	18.00
❑ LSS-14024 [S]	Hoedown	1963	4.50	9.00	18.00
❑ LSS-14027 [S]	The Ballad of New Orleans	1963	4.50	9.00	18.00
SUNSET
❑ SUM-1106 [M]	Love Strings	196?	3.00	6.00	12.00
❑ SUM-1141 [M]	Seasons Greetings	196?	3.00	6.00	12.00
❑ SUM-1170 [M]	Tender Strings	196?	3.00	6.00	12.00
❑ SUS-5106 [S]	Love Strings	196?	3.00	6.00	12.00
❑ SUS-5141 [S]	Seasons Greetings	196?	3.00	6.00	12.00
❑ SUS-5170 [S]	Tender Strings	196?	3.00	6.00	12.00
UNITED ARTISTS
| ❑ UAS-6818 | Classic Country | 1971 | 2.50 | 5.00 | 10.00 |

SLAUGHTER
CHRYSALIS
❑ F1-21702 [DJ]	Stick It To Ya	1990	7.50	15.00	30.00
—Black generic sleeve with hole; numbered edition of 500 with sticker that says "Limited Edition Special Vinyl Pressing Metal Radio Only"					
❑ F1-21911	The Wild Life	1992	5.00	10.00	20.00
—Vinyl version available only through Columbia House					
❑ R 120666 [EP]	Stick It Live	1990	5.00	10.00	20.00
—Vinyl version available only through BMG Direct Marketing					

SLAYER
AMERICAN
| ❑ C2 69192 [(2)] | Diabolus in Musica | 1998 | 5.00 | 10.00 | 20.00 |
COMBAT
| ❑ MX 8020 | Hell Awaits | 1985 | 3.75 | 7.50 | 15.00 |
DEF AMERICAN
| ❑ DFS 24307 | Seasons in the Abyss | 1990 | 5.00 | 10.00 | 20.00 |
DEF JAM
| ❑ GHS 24131 | Reign in Blood | 1986 | 2.00 | 4.00 | 8.00 |
| ❑ GHS 24203 | South of Heaven | 1988 | 2.00 | 4.00 | 8.00 |
METAL BLADE
❑ E 1034	Show No Mercy	1983	5.00	10.00	20.00
❑ MBR 1037 [PD]	Live Undead	1984	7.50	15.00	30.00
—Limited edition picture disc					
❑ 71034	Show No Mercy	198?	3.75	7.50	15.00
—Early reissue of 1034					
❑ 72214 [PD]	Show No Mercy	1987	6.25	12.50	25.00
—Picture disc in plastic sleeve					
❑ 72217 [EP]	Live Undead	1987	2.50	5.00	10.00
❑ 72297	Hell Awaits	1988	2.50	5.00	10.00
—Reissue of Combat LP					

SLEDGE, PERCY
ATLANTIC
❑ 8125 [M]	When a Man Loves a Woman	1966	12.50	25.00	50.00
❑ SD 8125 [R]	When a Man Loves a Woman	1966	7.50	15.00	30.00
❑ 8132 [M]	Warm and Tender Soul	1966	12.50	25.00	50.00
❑ SD 8132 [R]	Warm and Tender Soul	1966	7.50	15.00	30.00
❑ 8146 [M]	The Percy Sledge Way	1967	12.50	25.00	50.00
❑ SD 8146 [R]	The Percy Sledge Way	1967	12.50	25.00	50.00
❑ SD 8180	Take Time to Know Her	1968	12.50	25.00	50.00
❑ SD 8210	The Best of Percy Sledge	1969	6.25	12.50	25.00

Number	Title (A Side/B Side)	Yr	VG	VG+	NM
CAPRICORN					
❑ CP 0147	I'll Be Your Everything	1974	3.75	7.50	15.00
MONUMENT					
❑ FW 38532	Percy	1983	3.00	6.00	12.00

SLEET, DON
JAZZLAND
| ❑ JLP-45 [M] | All Members | 1961 | 6.25 | 12.50 | 25.00 |
| ❑ JLP-945 [S] | All Members | 1961 | 7.50 | 15.00 | 30.00 |

SLICK, GRACE
Also see THE GREAT SOCIETY; JEFFERSON AIRPLANE; JEFFERSON STARSHIP.
GRUNT
❑ BFL1-0347	Manhole	1974	3.00	6.00	12.00
❑ AYL1-3736	Manhole	1981	2.00	4.00	8.00
—"Best Buy Series" reissue					
RCA VICTOR
❑ AFL1-3544	Dreams	1980	2.50	5.00	10.00
❑ AQL1-3851	Welcome to the Wrecking Ball	1981	2.50	5.00	10.00
❑ DJL1-3922 [DJ]	Welcome to the Wrecking Ball Interview	1981	5.00	10.00	20.00
❑ DJL1-3923 [DJ]	RCA Special Radio Series	1981	5.00	10.00	20.00

SLICKEE BOYS
DACOIT
| ❑ 1001 | Separated Vegetables | 1977 | 20.00 | 40.00 | 80.00 |
| —Limited edition of 100 copies | | | | | |
GIANT
| ❑ GR 16037-1 | Live at Last | 1989 | 2.50 | 5.00 | 10.00 |
LIMP
| ❑ 1003 | Separated Vegetables | 1980 | 6.25 | 12.50 | 25.00 |
| —Limited edition of 300 copies; reissue with new cover | | | | | |
TWIN/TONE
| ❑ TTR 8337 | Cybernetic Dreams of Pi | 1983 | 3.75 | 7.50 | 15.00 |
| ❑ TTR 8544 | Uh Oh, No Breaks | 1985 | 3.00 | 6.00 | 12.00 |

SLIM JIM
SOMA
| ❑ MG 1225 [M] | Slim Jim Sings | 1958 | 10.00 | 20.00 | 40.00 |

SLITS, THE
ANTILLES
| ❑ AN-7077 | Cut | 1979 | 10.00 | 20.00 | 40.00 |

SLOAN, P.F.
ATCO
| ❑ SD 33-268 | Measure of Pleasure | 1968 | 6.25 | 12.50 | 25.00 |
DUNHILL
❑ D-50004 [M]	Songs of Our Times	1965	6.25	12.50	25.00
❑ DS-50004 [S]	Songs of Our Times	1965	7.50	15.00	30.00
❑ D-50007 [M]	Twelve More Times	1966	6.25	12.50	25.00
❑ DS-50007 [S]	Twelve More Times	1966	7.50	15.00	30.00
MUMS
| ❑ KZ 31260 | Raised on Records | 1972 | 5.00 | 10.00 | 20.00 |
RHINO
| ❑ RNLP-70133 | Precious Times: The Best of P.F. Sloan | 1986 | 2.50 | 5.00 | 10.00 |

SLOANE, CAROL
COLUMBIA
❑ CL 1766 [M]	Out of the Blue	1962	15.00	30.00	60.00
❑ CL 1923 [M]	Carol Sloane Live at 30th Street	1963	15.00	30.00	60.00
❑ CS 8566 [S]	Out of the Blue	1962	20.00	40.00	80.00
❑ CS 8723 [S]	Carol Sloane Live at 30th Street	1963	20.00	40.00	80.00

SLY AND THE FAMILY STONE
EPIC
❑ AS 264 [DJ]	Everything You Always Wanted to Hear by Sly and the Family Stone But Were Afraid to Ask For	1976	6.25	12.50	25.00
—Promo-only compilation					
❑ LN 24324 [M]	A Whole New Thing	1967	5.00	10.00	20.00
❑ LN 24371 [M]	Dance to the Music	1968	10.00	20.00	40.00
❑ BN 26324 [S]	A Whole New Thing	1967	5.00	10.00	20.00
❑ BN 26371 [S]	Dance to the Music	1968	3.75	7.50	15.00
❑ BN 26397	Life	1968	3.75	7.50	15.00
❑ BN 26456	Stand!	1969	3.75	7.50	15.00
❑ PE 26456	Stand!	1986	2.00	4.00	8.00
—Budget-line reissue					
❑ EQ 30325 [Q]	Sly and the Family Stone's Greatest Hits	1971	25.00	50.00	100.00
—Has alternate mixes of "Hot Fun in the Summertime," "Thank You" and "Everybody Is a Star," which are not rechanneled stereo as they are on other LPs					
❑ KE 30325	Sly and the Family Stone's Greatest Hits	1970	3.00	6.00	12.00
—Yellow label, gatefold cover					
❑ PE 30325	Sly and the Family Stone's Greatest Hits	1979	2.00	4.00	8.00
—Budget-line reissue					
❑ E 30333	Life	1971	3.00	6.00	12.00
—Reissue of 26397					
❑ E 30334	Dance to the Music	1971	3.00	6.00	12.00
—Reissue of 26371					
❑ E 30335	A Whole New Thing	1971	3.00	6.00	12.00
—Reissue of 26324					
❑ KE 30986	There's a Riot Goin' On	1971	3.00	6.00	12.00
—Yellow label, gatefold cover					
❑ KE 32134	Fresh	1973	2.50	5.00	10.00
—Orange label					
❑ PE 32930	Small Talk	1974	2.50	5.00	10.00
—Orange label					
❑ PEQ 32930 [Q]	Small Talk	1974	6.25	12.50	25.00
❑ PE 33835	High on You	1975	2.50	5.00	10.00
—Orange label					
❑ PEQ 33835 [Q]	High on You	1975	6.25	12.50	25.00
❑ PE 34348	Heard Ya Missed Me, Well I'm Back	1976	2.50	5.00	10.00
—Orange label					

Number	Title (A Side/B Side)	Yr	VG	VG+	NM
❑ JE 35974	Ten Years Too Soon	1979	2.50	5.00	10.00
❑ E2 37071 [(2)]	Anthology	1981	3.75	7.50	15.00
WARNER BROS.					
❑ BSK 3303	Back on the Right Track	1979	2.50	5.00	10.00
❑ 23700	Ain't But the Right Way	1983	2.50	5.00	10.00

SMACK, THE
AUDIO HOUSE

Number	Title (A Side/B Side)	Yr	VG	VG+	NM
❑ (# unknown)	The Smack	1968	500.00	1000.	2000.

SMALL, DANNY
UNITED ARTISTS

Number	Title (A Side/B Side)	Yr	VG	VG+	NM
❑ UAJ-14004 [M]	Woman She Was Born for Sorrow	1962	5.00	10.00	20.00
❑ UAJS-15004 [S]	Woman She Was Born for Sorrow	1962	6.25	12.50	25.00

SMALL, MILLIE
SMASH

Number	Title (A Side/B Side)	Yr	VG	VG+	NM
❑ MGS-27055 [M]	My Boy Lollipop	1964	12.50	25.00	50.00
❑ SRS-67055 [R]	My Boy Lollipop	1964	10.00	20.00	40.00

SMALL FACES
Also see FACES.
ACCORD

Number	Title (A Side/B Side)	Yr	VG	VG+	NM
❑ AN-7157	By Appointment	1982	2.50	5.00	10.00
ATLANTIC					
❑ SD 19113	Playmates	1977	2.50	5.00	10.00
❑ SD 19171	78 in the Shade	1978	2.50	5.00	10.00
COMPLEAT					
❑ 67-2004 [(2)]	Big Music	1985	3.00	6.00	12.00
❑ 67-5003	Ogden's Nut Gone Flake	1985	2.50	5.00	10.00
—Reissue					
IMMEDIATE					
❑ 4225	Ogden's Nut Gone Flake	1973	3.75	7.50	15.00
—Reissue has a standard square cover					
❑ Z12 52002 [S]	There Are But Four Small Faces	1967	12.50	25.00	50.00
—Color cover (counterfeits have either black and white or black and green covers)					
❑ Z12 52008 [S]	Ogden's Nut Gone Flake	1968	12.50	25.00	50.00
—Originals have a round cover					
MGM					
❑ M3F-4955	Archetypes	1974	3.00	6.00	12.00
PRIDE					
❑ PRD 0001 [R]	Early Faces	1972	3.75	7.50	15.00
❑ PRD 0014 [P]	The History of the Small Faces	1973	3.00	6.00	12.00
SIRE					
❑ SASH-3709 [(2)]	The Vintage Years	1976	3.75	7.50	15.00

SMART SET, THE
WARNER BROS.

Number	Title (A Side/B Side)	Yr	VG	VG+	NM
❑ W-1203 [M]	A New Experience in Vocal Styles	1958	7.50	15.00	30.00
❑ WS-1203 [S]	A New Experience in Vocal Styles	1958	10.00	20.00	40.00

SMASHING PUMPKINS
CAROLINE

Number	Title (A Side/B Side)	Yr	VG	VG+	NM
❑ 1705	Gish	199?	3.00	6.00	12.00
—With "Remastered" under the bar code					
❑ 1705	Gish	1991	5.00	10.00	20.00
—Originals do not have the word "Remastered" under the bar code					
❑ 1740 [(2)]	Siamese Dream	199?	3.75	7.50	15.00
—Pink marbled vinyl					
❑ 1740 [(2)]	Siamese Dream	1993	6.25	12.50	25.00
—Originals have dark red vinyl					
❑ 1767	Pisces Iscariot	1994	5.00	10.00	20.00
—Regular pressing on colored vinyl, not numbered, no bonus 7-inch single					
❑ 1767	Pisces Iscariot	1994	50.00	100.00	200.00
—First 2,000 copies, hand-numbered on back cover, came with a bonus 7-inch single					
❑ 45879 [(2)]	Adore	1998	3.75	7.50	15.00
—Different cover than CD version, and the entire LP was remixed into mono					
❑ 48936 [(2)]	Machina/The Machines of God	2000	3.75	7.50	15.00
—With bound-in booklet					
CONSTANTINOPLE					
❑ CR 01-04 [(5)]	Machina II/The Friends and Enemies of Modern Music	2000	250.00	500.00	1000.

—Exactly 25 copies were pressed as two 12-inch and three 10-inch records, with the presumption that at least some of them would be bootlegged onto CDs and into downloadable files via the Internet. (This has indeed happened, so many fans have heard the music.) It's not known whether any of the 25 copies have left the hands of their original recipients, so the price above is highly speculative and probably conservative.

SMECK, ROY
ABC-PARAMOUNT

Number	Title (A Side/B Side)	Yr	VG	VG+	NM
❑ ABC-119 [M]	South Seas Serenade	1956	10.00	20.00	40.00
❑ ABC-174 [M]	Melodies with Memories	1957	10.00	20.00	40.00
❑ ABC-234 [M]	Hi-Fi Paradise	1958	10.00	20.00	40.00
❑ ABC-279 [M]	The Magic Ukulele	1959	7.50	15.00	30.00
❑ ABCS-279 [S]	The Magic Ukulele	1959	10.00	20.00	40.00
❑ ABC-309 [M]	The Happy Banjo	1959	7.50	15.00	30.00
❑ ABCS-309 [S]	The Happy Banjo	1959	10.00	20.00	40.00
❑ ABC-329 [M]	Adventures in Paradise	1960	6.25	12.50	25.00
❑ ABCS-329 [S]	Adventures in Paradise	1960	7.50	15.00	30.00
❑ ABC-330 [M]	The Haunting Hawaiian Guitar	1960	6.25	12.50	25.00
❑ ABCS-330 [S]	The Haunting Hawaiian Guitar	1960	7.50	15.00	30.00
❑ ABC-358 [M]	Adventures in Paradise, Volume 2	1961	6.25	12.50	25.00
❑ ABCS-358 [S]	Adventures in Paradise, Volume 2	1961	7.50	15.00	30.00
❑ ABC-379 [M]	Roy Smeck, His Singing Guitar and Paradise Serenaders	1961	6.25	12.50	25.00
❑ ABCS-379 [S]	Roy Smeck, His Singing Guitar and Paradise Serenaders	1961	7.50	15.00	30.00
❑ ABC-412 [M]	Stringing Along	1962	6.25	12.50	25.00
❑ ABCS-412 [S]	Stringing Along	1962	7.50	15.00	30.00
❑ ABC-414 [M]	Adventures in Paradise, Volume 3	1962	6.25	12.50	25.00
❑ ABCS-414 [S]	Adventures in Paradise, Volume 3	1962	7.50	15.00	30.00
❑ ABC-452 [M]	The Many Guitar Moods of Roy Smeck	1963	6.25	12.50	25.00

Number	Title (A Side/B Side)	Yr	VG	VG+	NM
❑ ABCS-452 [S]	The Many Guitar Moods of Roy Smeck	1963	7.50	15.00	30.00
❑ ABC-462 [M]	Adventures in Paradise, Volume 4	1963	6.25	12.50	25.00
❑ ABCS-462 [S]	Adventures in Paradise, Volume 4	1963	7.50	15.00	30.00
❑ ABC-484 [M]	I Love to Hear a Banjo	1964	6.25	12.50	25.00
❑ ABCS-484 [S]	I Love to Hear a Banjo	1964	7.50	15.00	30.00
CORAL					
❑ CRL 56013 [10]	Drifting and Dreaming	195?	30.00	60.00	120.00
DECCA					
❑ DL 5458 [10]	Memory Lane	1953	25.00	50.00	100.00
❑ DL 5473 [10]	Songs of the Range	1953	25.00	50.00	100.00
❑ DL 8674 [M]	Memories of You	1958	10.00	20.00	40.00
—Black label, silver print					
"X"					
❑ LPX-3012 [10]	South of the Border	1954	30.00	60.00	120.00
❑ LPA-3016 [10]	Christmas in Hawaii	195?	30.00	60.00	120.00

SMILE (1)
PICKWICK

Number	Title (A Side/B Side)	Yr	VG	VG+	NM
❑ SPC-3288	Smile	1973	7.50	15.00	30.00

SMITH, AL
BLUESVILLE

Number	Title (A Side/B Side)	Yr	VG	VG+	NM
❑ BVLP-1001 [M]	Hear My Blues	1960	20.00	40.00	80.00
—Blue label, silver print					
❑ BVLP-1001 [M]	Hear My Blues	1964	6.25	12.50	25.00
—Blue label, trident logo at right					
❑ BVLP-1014 [M]	Midnight Special	1961	20.00	40.00	80.00
—Blue label, silver print					
❑ BVLP-1014 [M]	Midnight Special	1964	6.25	12.50	25.00
—Blue label, trident logo at right					
❑ BVLP-1069 [M]	Blues Shout	196?	5.00	10.00	20.00

SMITH, ARTHUR "GUITAR BOOGIE"
ABC-PARAMOUNT

Number	Title (A Side/B Side)	Yr	VG	VG+	NM
❑ ABC-441 [M]	Arthur "Guitar" Smith and Voices	1963	5.00	10.00	20.00
❑ ABCS-441 [S]	Arthur "Guitar" Smith and Voices	1963	6.25	12.50	25.00
DOT					
❑ DLP-3600 [M]	Original Guitar Boogie	1964	5.00	10.00	20.00
❑ DLP-3636 [M]	Great Country and Western Hits	1965	3.75	7.50	15.00
❑ DLP-3642 [M]	Singing on the Mountain with the Crossroads Quartet	1965	5.00	10.00	20.00
❑ DLP-3769 [M]	A Tribute to Jim Reeves	1966	3.75	7.50	15.00
❑ DLP-25600 [S]	Original Guitar Boogie	1964	6.25	12.50	25.00
❑ DLP-25636 [S]	Great Country and Western Hits	1965	5.00	10.00	20.00
❑ DLP-25642 [S]	Singing on the Mountain with the Crossroads Quartet	1965	6.25	12.50	25.00
❑ DLP-25769 [S]	A Tribute to Jim Reeves	1966	5.00	10.00	20.00
MGM					
❑ E-236 [10]	Foolish Questions	1954	30.00	60.00	120.00
❑ E-533 [10]	Fingers on Fire	1955	25.00	50.00	100.00
❑ E-3301 [M]	Specials	1955	20.00	40.00	80.00
❑ E-3525 [M]	Fingers on Fire	1957	20.00	40.00	80.00
MONUMENT					
❑ Z 32259	Battling Banjos	1973	3.00	6.00	12.00
STARDAY					
❑ SLP-173 [M]	Mister Guitar	1962	7.50	15.00	30.00
❑ SLP-186 [M]	Arthur Smith and the Crossroads Quartet	1962	10.00	20.00	40.00
❑ SLP-216 [M]	Arthur "Guitar Boogie" Smith Goes to Town	1963	7.50	15.00	30.00
❑ SLP-241 [M]	In Person	1963	7.50	15.00	30.00
❑ SLP-266 [M]	Down Home	1964	7.50	15.00	30.00

SMITH, "FIDDLIN' " ARTHUR
STARDAY

Number	Title (A Side/B Side)	Yr	VG	VG+	NM
❑ SLP-202 [M]	Rare Old Time Fiddle Tunes	1962	7.50	15.00	30.00

SMITH, BESSIE
COLUMBIA

Number	Title (A Side/B Side)	Yr	VG	VG+	NM
❑ GP 33 [(2)]	The World's Greatest Blues Singer	1970	5.00	10.00	20.00
❑ GL 503 [M]	The Bessie Smith Story, Volume 1	1951	12.50	25.00	50.00
—Maroon label, gold print					
❑ GL 504 [M]	The Bessie Smith Story, Volume 2	1951	12.50	25.00	50.00
—Maroon label, gold print					
❑ GL 505 [M]	The Bessie Smith Story, Volume 3	1951	12.50	25.00	50.00
—Maroon label, gold print					
❑ GL 506 [M]	The Bessie Smith Story, Volume 4	1951	12.50	25.00	50.00
—Maroon label, gold print					
❑ CL 855 [M]	The Bessie Smith Story, Volume 1	1956	6.25	12.50	25.00
—Red and black label with six "eye" logos					
❑ CL 856 [M]	The Bessie Smith Story, Volume 2	1956	6.25	12.50	25.00
—Red and black label with six "eye" logos					
❑ CL 857 [M]	The Bessie Smith Story, Volume 3	1956	6.25	12.50	25.00
—Red and black label with six "eye" logos					
❑ CL 858 [M]	The Bessie Smith Story, Volume 4	1956	6.25	12.50	25.00
—Red and black label with six "eye" logos					
❑ C2 47091 [(2)]	The Complete Recordings Volume 1: Empress of the Blues	1991	5.00	10.00	20.00
—Box set; none of the subsequent volumes came out on vinyl					
COLUMBIA MASTERWORKS					
❑ ML 4801 [M]	The Bessie Smith Story, Volume 1	1954	7.50	15.00	30.00
❑ ML 4802 [M]	The Bessie Smith Story, Volume 2	1954	7.50	15.00	30.00
❑ ML 4809 [M]	The Bessie Smith Story, Volume 3	1954	7.50	15.00	30.00
❑ ML 4810 [M]	The Bessie Smith Story, Volume 4	1954	7.50	15.00	30.00

SMITH, BILL
CONTEMPORARY

Number	Title (A Side/B Side)	Yr	VG	VG+	NM
❑ M-3591 [M]	Folk Jazz	1961	5.00	10.00	20.00
❑ S-7591 [S]	Folk Jazz	1961	6.25	12.50	25.00

SMITH, BOB
KENT

Number	Title (A Side/B Side)	Yr	VG	VG+	NM
❑ KST-551 [(2)]	The Visit	1970	25.00	50.00	100.00
—Deduct 25 percent if poster is missing					

S

SMITH, BUSTER

Number	Title (A Side/B Side)	Yr	VG	VG+	NM
ATLANTIC					
1323 [M]	The Legendary Buster Smith	1960	12.50	25.00	50.00
—Black label					
1323 [M]	The Legendary Buster Smith	1961	5.00	10.00	20.00
—Multi-color label, white "fan" logo					
SD 1323 [S]	The Legendary Buster Smith	1960	12.50	25.00	50.00
—Green label					
SD 1323 [S]	The Legendary Buster Smith	1961	5.00	10.00	20.00
—Multi-color label, white "fan" logo					

SMITH, CAL

Number	Title (A Side/B Side)	Yr	VG	VG+	NM
DECCA					
DL 75369	I've Found Someone of My Own	1972	3.75	7.50	15.00
KAPP					
KL-1504 [M]	All the World Is Lonely Now	1966	6.25	12.50	25.00
KL-1537 [M]	Goin' to Cal's Place	1967	6.25	12.50	25.00
KL-1544 [M]	Travelin' Man	1968	10.00	20.00	40.00
—White label promo only; in stereo cover with "Mono" sticker					
KS-3504 [S]	All the World Is Lonely Now	1966	5.00	10.00	20.00
KS-3537 [S]	Goin' to Cal's Place	1967	5.00	10.00	20.00
KS-3544 [S]	Travelin' Man	1968	5.00	10.00	20.00
KS-3585	Drinking Champagne	1968	5.00	10.00	20.00
KS-3608	Cal Smith Sings It Takes Me All Night Long	1969	5.00	10.00	20.00
KS-3642	The Best of Cal Smith	1969	3.75	7.50	15.00
MCA					
70	The Best of Cal Smith	1973	2.50	5.00	10.00
—Reissue of Kapp 3642					
344	Cal Smith	1973	2.50	5.00	10.00
—Reissue of Decca LP					
424	Country Bumpkin	1974	2.50	5.00	10.00
467	It's Time to Pay the Fiddler	1975	2.50	5.00	10.00
485	My Kind of Country	1975	2.50	5.00	10.00
2172	Jason's Farm	1976	2.50	5.00	10.00
2266	I Just Came Home to Count the Memories	1977	2.50	5.00	10.00

SMITH, CARL

Number	Title (A Side/B Side)	Yr	VG	VG+	NM
ABC HICKORY					
HB-44005	This Lady Loves Me	1977	3.00	6.00	12.00
HB-44015	The Silver-Tongued Cowboy	1978	3.00	6.00	12.00
COLUMBIA					
GP 31 [(2)]	The Carl Smith Anniversary Album/20 Years of Hits	1970	6.25	12.50	25.00
CL 959 [M]	Sunday Down South	1957	12.50	25.00	50.00
CL 1022 [M]	Smith's the Name	1957	12.50	25.00	50.00
CL 1172 [M]	Let's Live a Little	1958	12.50	25.00	50.00
CL 1532 [M]	The Carl Smith Touch	1960	6.25	12.50	25.00
CL 1740 [M]	Easy to Please	1961	6.25	12.50	25.00
CL 1937 [M]	Carl Smith's Greatest Hits	1962	5.00	10.00	20.00
CL 2091 [M]	The Tall, Tall Gentleman	1963	5.00	10.00	20.00
CL 2173 [M]	There Stands the Glass	1964	5.00	10.00	20.00
CL 2293 [M]	I Want to Live and Love	1965	5.00	10.00	20.00
CL 2358 [M]	Kisses Don't Lie	1965	5.00	10.00	20.00
CL 2501 [M]	Man with a Plan	1966	5.00	10.00	20.00
CL 2579 [10]	Carl Smith	1955	25.00	50.00	100.00
CL 2610 [M]	The Country Gentleman	1967	5.00	10.00	20.00
CL 2687 [M]	The Country Gentleman Sings His Favorites	1967	6.25	12.50	25.00
CL 2822 [M]	Deep Water	1968	7.50	15.00	30.00
CL 2888 [M]	Country on My Mind	1968	12.50	25.00	50.00
CS 8352 [S]	The Carl Smith Touch	1960	7.50	15.00	30.00
CS 8540 [S]	Easy to Please	1961	7.50	15.00	30.00
CS 8737 [S]	Carl Smith's Greatest Hits	1962	6.25	12.50	25.00
CS 8891 [S]	The Tall, Tall Gentleman	1963	6.25	12.50	25.00
CS 8973 [S]	There Stands the Glass	1964	6.25	12.50	25.00
CL 9023 [10]	Sentimental Songs	195?	25.00	50.00	100.00
CL 9026 [10]	Softly and Tenderly	195?	20.00	40.00	80.00
CS 9093 [S]	I Want to Live and Love	1965	6.25	12.50	25.00
CS 9158 [S]	Kisses Don't Lie	1965	6.25	12.50	25.00
CS 9301 [S]	Man with a Plan	1966	6.25	12.50	25.00
CS 9410 [S]	The Country Gentleman	1967	6.25	12.50	25.00
CS 9487 [S]	The Country Gentleman Sings His Favorites	1967	5.00	10.00	20.00
CS 9622 [S]	Deep Water	1968	5.00	10.00	20.00
CS 9688 [S]	Country on My Mind	1968	5.00	10.00	20.00
CS 9786	Faded Love and Winter Roses	1969	5.00	10.00	20.00
CS 9807	Carl Smith's Greatest Hits, Vol. 2	1969	5.00	10.00	20.00
CS 9870	Carl Smith Sings a Tribute to Roy Acuff	1969	5.00	10.00	20.00
CS 9898	I Love You Because	1970	5.00	10.00	20.00
C 30215	Carl Smith with the Tunesmiths	1970	5.00	10.00	20.00
C 30548	Bluegrass	1971	5.00	10.00	20.00
C 31277	Don't Say You're Mine	1972	5.00	10.00	20.00
KC 31606	If This Is Goodbye	1972	5.00	10.00	20.00
FC 38906	Carl Smith	198?	2.50	5.00	10.00
HICKORY/MGM					
H3G 4518	The Way I Lose My Mind	1975	3.00	6.00	12.00
H3G 4522	The Girl I Love	1975	3.00	6.00	12.00
ROUNDER					
SS-25	Old Lonesome Times	1988	2.50	5.00	10.00

SMITH, CARL; LEFTY FRIZZELL; MARTY ROBBINS

Number	Title (A Side/B Side)	Yr	VG	VG+	NM
COLUMBIA					
CL 2544 [10]	Carl, Lefty and Marty	1955	100.00	200.00	400.00

SMITH, CONNIE

Number	Title (A Side/B Side)	Yr	VG	VG+	NM
COLUMBIA					
KC 32185	A Lady Named Smith	1973	3.00	6.00	12.00
KC 32492	God Is Abundant	1973	3.00	6.00	12.00
KC 32581	That's the Way Love Goes	1974	3.00	6.00	12.00
KC 33055	I Never Knew (What That Song Meant Before)	1974	3.00	6.00	12.00
KC 33375	I Got a Lot of Hurtin' Done Today/I've Got My Baby on My Mind	1975	3.00	6.00	12.00
KC 33414	Connie Smith Sings Hank Williams Gospel	1975	3.00	6.00	12.00
KC 33918	The Song We Fell in Love To	1976	3.00	6.00	12.00
KC 34270	I Don't Want to Talk It Over Anymore	1976	3.00	6.00	12.00
KC 34877	The Best of Connie Smith	1977	3.00	6.00	12.00
MONUMENT					
7609	Pure Connie Smith	1977	3.00	6.00	12.00
7624	New Horizons	1978	3.00	6.00	12.00
RCA CAMDEN					
ACL1-0250	Even the Bad Times Are Good	1973	2.50	5.00	10.00
—With Nat Stuckey					
CAL-2120 [M]	Connie in the Country	1967	3.75	7.50	15.00
CAS-2120 [S]	Connie in the Country	1967	3.00	6.00	12.00
CAS-2495	My Heart Has a Mind of Its Own	1971	2.50	5.00	10.00
CAS-2550	City Lights — Country Favorites	1972	2.50	5.00	10.00
RCA VICTOR					
APL1-0188	Dream Painter	1973	3.00	6.00	12.00
APL1-0275	Connie Smith's Greatest Hits, Volume 1	1973	3.00	6.00	12.00
APL1-0607	Now	1974	3.00	6.00	12.00
LPM-3341 [M]	Connie Smith	1965	5.00	10.00	20.00
LSP-3341 [S]	Connie Smith	1965	6.25	12.50	25.00
LPM-3444 [M]	Cute 'n' Country	1965	5.00	10.00	20.00
LSP-3444 [S]	Cute 'n' Country	1965	6.25	12.50	25.00
LPM-3520 [M]	Miss Smith Goes to Nashville	1966	5.00	10.00	20.00
LSP-3520 [S]	Miss Smith Goes to Nashville	1966	6.25	12.50	25.00
LPM-3589 [M]	Connie Smith Sings Great Sacred Songs	1966	5.00	10.00	20.00
LSP-3589 [S]	Connie Smith Sings Great Sacred Songs	1966	6.25	12.50	25.00
LPM-3628 [M]	Born to Sing	1966	5.00	10.00	20.00
LSP-3628 [S]	Born to Sing	1966	6.25	12.50	25.00
LPM-3725 [M]	Downtown Country	1967	6.25	12.50	25.00
LSP-3725 [S]	Downtown Country	1967	5.00	10.00	20.00
LPM-3768 [M]	Connie Smith Sings Bill Anderson	1967	6.25	12.50	25.00
LSP-3768 [S]	Connie Smith Sings Bill Anderson	1967	5.00	10.00	20.00
LPM-3848 [M]	The Best of Connie Smith	1967	6.25	12.50	25.00
LSP-3848 [S]	The Best of Connie Smith	1967	5.00	10.00	20.00
LPM-3889 [M]	Soul of Country Music	1968	12.50	25.00	50.00
LSP-3889 [S]	Soul of Country Music	1968	5.00	10.00	20.00
LSP-4002	I Love Charley Brown	1968	5.00	10.00	20.00
LSP-4077	Sunshine and Rain	1968	5.00	10.00	20.00
LSP-4132	Connie's Country	1969	5.00	10.00	20.00
LSP-4229	Back in Baby's Arms	1969	5.00	10.00	20.00
LSP-4324	The Best of Connie Smith Volume II	1970	5.00	10.00	20.00
LSP-4394	I Never Once Stopped Loving You	1970	5.00	10.00	20.00
LSP-4474	Where's My Castle	1971	3.75	7.50	15.00
LSP-4537	Just One Time	1971	3.75	7.50	15.00
LSP-4598	Come Along and Walk with Me	1971	5.00	10.00	20.00
LSP-4694	Ain't We Having a Good Time	1972	3.75	7.50	15.00
LSP-4748	"If It Ain't Love" And Other Great Dallas Frazier Songs	1972	3.75	7.50	15.00
LSP-4840	Love Is the Look You're Looking For	1973	3.75	7.50	15.00

SMITH, CONNIE, AND NAT STUCKEY

Number	Title (A Side/B Side)	Yr	VG	VG+	NM
RCA VICTOR					
LSP-4190	Young Love	1969	5.00	10.00	20.00
LSP-4300	Sunday Morning	1970	3.75	7.50	15.00

SMITH, DARDEN

Number	Title (A Side/B Side)	Yr	VG	VG+	NM
COLUMBIA					
CAS 3034 [DJ]	Interchords	1988	3.75	7.50	15.00
—Promo-only interview record					
EPIC					
EAS 1282 [EP]	Live Tracks: Darden Smith	1988	3.75	7.50	15.00
—Promo-only three-song live EP					
E 40938	Darden Smith	1988	2.50	5.00	10.00
REDI MIX					
RM 001	Native Soil	1986	5.00	10.00	20.00

SMITH, EFFIE

Number	Title (A Side/B Side)	Yr	VG	VG+	NM
JUBILEE					
JGM-2057 [M]	Dial That Telephone	1966	6.25	12.50	25.00

SMITH, ETHEL

Number	Title (A Side/B Side)	Yr	VG	VG+	NM
DECCA					
DL 8187 [M]	Christmas Music	1955	5.00	10.00	20.00
—Black label, silver print					

SMITH, HUEY "PIANO"

Number	Title (A Side/B Side)	Yr	VG	VG+	NM
ACE					
LP-1004 [M]	Having a Good Time	1959	100.00	200.00	400.00
LP-1015 [M]	For Dancing	1961	62.50	125.00	250.00
LP-1027 [M]	'Twas the Night Before Christmas	1962	62.50	125.00	250.00
LP-1027 [M]	'Twas the Night Before Christmas	198?	3.75	7.50	15.00
—Reissue with "Dr. John Band" credited on front cover and label					
LP-2021	Rock 'N' Roll Revival	197?	7.50	15.00	30.00
2038	Good Old Rock & Roll	198?	3.75	7.50	15.00
GRAND PRIX					
K-418 [M]	Huey "Piano" Smith	196?	5.00	10.00	20.00
KS-418 [R]	Huey "Piano" Smith	196?	3.00	6.00	12.00
RHINO					
RNLP-70222	Serious Clownin': The History of Huey "Piano" Smith and the Clowns	1986	3.00	6.00	12.00

SMITH, JACK

Number	Title (A Side/B Side)	Yr	VG	VG+	NM
BEL CANTO					
BCM-37 [M]	You Asked for It: Jack Smith Sings	1959	6.25	12.50	25.00
SR-1015 [S]	You Asked for It: Jack Smith Sings	1959	7.50	15.00	30.00

SMITH, JENNIE

Number	Title (A Side/B Side)	Yr	VG	VG+	NM
CANADIAN AMERICAN					
CALP-1010 [M]	Nightly Yours on the Steve Allen Show	1963	6.25	12.50	25.00
COLUMBIA					
CL 1242 [M]	Love Among the Young	1959	7.50	15.00	30.00
CS 8028 [S]	Love Among the Young	1959	10.00	20.00	40.00

Underrated American rocker Jack Scott's original LPs on Carlton and Top Rank are in demand and have been for years. This is his second LP for Top Rank, named after the big hit "What in the World's Come Over You."

Dozens of Pete Seeger albums were released through Folkways Records. One of the earliest was this 10-inch collection called *Darling Corey.*

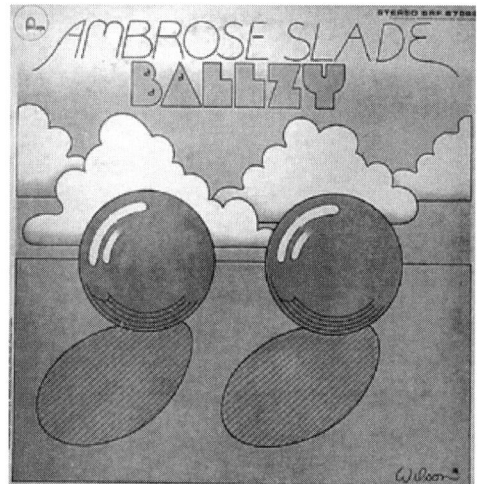

Originally, Slade was "Ambrose Slade," and under that name, their first LP was released on Fontana in the United States.

Travelin' with Ray Smith came out on the small Judd label in the wake of his top-40 hit single "Rockin' Little Angel." As is true of most rock-related albums of the early 1960s, the original LP is scarce.

Early promotional packages of Bruce Springsteen's *Born to Run* album contained this prototype cover, known to collectors as the "script cover." In addition to this unique cover, it also had a test pressing of the album, a different gatefold and promotional material.

The first edition of *Meet the Supremes* featured this cover, with the three women sitting on stools. Later, the cover was redone with a more modern, soft-focus picture of the three together.

Number	Title (A Side/B Side)	Yr	VG	VG+	NM
DOT					
❏ DLP-3586 [M]	Jennie	1964	3.75	7.50	15.00
❏ DLP-25586 [S]	Jennie	1964	5.00	10.00	20.00
RCA VICTOR					
❏ LPM-1523 [M]	Jennie	1957	10.00	20.00	40.00
SMITH, JIMMY					
BLUE NOTE					
❏ BLP-1512 [M]	Jimmy Smith at the Organ, Vol. 1	1956	25.00	50.00	100.00
—Regular edition, Lexington Ave. address on label					
❏ BLP-1512 [M]	Jimmy Smith at the Organ, Vol. 1	1956	37.50	75.00	150.00
—"Deep groove" version (deep indentation under label on both sides)					
❏ BLP-1512 [M]	Jimmy Smith at the Organ, Vol. 1	1963	6.25	12.50	25.00
—With New York, USA address on label					
❏ BLP-1514 [M]	Jimmy Smith at the Organ, Vol. 2	1956	25.00	50.00	100.00
—Regular edition, Lexington Ave. address on label					
❏ BLP-1514 [M]	Jimmy Smith at the Organ, Vol. 2	1956	37.50	75.00	150.00
—"Deep groove" version (deep indentation under label on both sides)					
❏ BLP-1514 [M]	Jimmy Smith at the Organ, Vol. 2	1963	6.25	12.50	25.00
—With New York, USA address on label					
❏ BLP-1525 [M]	The Incredible Jimmy Smith at the Organ, Vol. 3	1956	25.00	50.00	100.00
—Regular edition, Lexington Ave. address on label					
❏ BLP-1525 [M]	The Incredible Jimmy Smith at the Organ, Vol. 3	1956	37.50	75.00	150.00
—"Deep groove" version (deep indentation under label on both sides)					
❏ BLP-1525 [M]	The Incredible Jimmy Smith at the Organ, Vol. 3	1963	6.25	12.50	25.00
—With New York, USA address on label					
❏ BLP-1528 [M]	The Incredible Jimmy Smith at Club Baby Grand, Wilmington, Delaware, Vol. 1	1956	25.00	50.00	100.00
—Regular edition, Lexington Ave. address on label					
❏ BLP-1528 [M]	The Incredible Jimmy Smith at Club Baby Grand, Wilmington, Delaware, Vol. 1	1956	37.50	75.00	150.00
—"Deep groove" version (deep indentation under label on both sides)					
❏ BLP-1528 [M]	The Incredible Jimmy Smith at Club Baby Grand, Wilmington, Delaware, Vol. 1	1963	6.25	12.50	25.00
—With New York, USA address on label					
❏ BLP-1529 [M]	The Incredible Jimmy Smith at Club Baby Grand, Wilmington, Delaware, Vol. 2	1956	25.00	50.00	100.00
—Regular edition, Lexington Ave. address on label					
❏ BLP-1529 [M]	The Incredible Jimmy Smith at Club Baby Grand, Wilmington, Delaware, Vol. 2	1956	37.50	75.00	150.00
—"Deep groove" version (deep indentation under label on both sides)					
❏ BLP-1529 [M]	The Incredible Jimmy Smith at Club Baby Grand, Wilmington, Delaware, Vol. 2	1963	6.25	12.50	25.00
—With New York, USA address on label					
❏ BLP-1547 [M]	A Date with Jimmy Smith, Vol. 1	1957	20.00	40.00	80.00
—Regular edition, W. 63rd St. address on label					
❏ BLP-1547 [M]	A Date with Jimmy Smith, Vol. 1	1957	30.00	60.00	120.00
—"Deep groove" version (deep indentation under label on both sides)					
❏ BLP-1547 [M]	A Date with Jimmy Smith, Vol. 1	1963	6.25	12.50	25.00
—With New York, USA address on label					
❏ BLP-1548 [M]	A Date with Jimmy Smith, Vol. 2	1957	20.00	40.00	80.00
—Regular edition, W. 63rd St. address on label					
❏ BLP-1548 [M]	A Date with Jimmy Smith, Vol. 2	1957	30.00	60.00	120.00
—"Deep groove" version (deep indentation under label on both sides)					
❏ BLP-1548 [M]	A Date with Jimmy Smith, Vol. 2	1963	6.25	12.50	25.00
—With New York, USA address on label					
❏ BLP-1551 [M]	Jimmy Smith at the Organ, Vol. 1	1957	20.00	40.00	80.00
—Regular edition, W. 63rd St. address on label					
❏ BLP-1551 [M]	Jimmy Smith at the Organ, Vol. 1	1957	30.00	60.00	120.00
—"Deep groove" version (deep indentation under label on both sides)					
❏ BLP-1551 [M]	Jimmy Smith at the Organ, Vol. 1	1963	6.25	12.50	25.00
—With New York, USA address on label					
❏ BLP-1552 [M]	Jimmy Smith at the Organ, Vol. 2	1957	20.00	40.00	80.00
—Regular edition, W. 63rd St. address on label					
❏ BLP-1552 [M]	Jimmy Smith at the Organ, Vol. 2	1957	30.00	60.00	120.00
—"Deep groove" version (deep indentation under label on both sides)					
❏ BLP-1552 [M]	Jimmy Smith at the Organ, Vol. 2	1963	6.25	12.50	25.00
—With New York, USA address on label					
❏ BLP-1556 [M]	The Sounds of Jimmy Smith	1957	20.00	40.00	80.00
—Regular edition, W. 63rd St. address on label					
❏ BLP-1556 [M]	The Sounds of Jimmy Smith	1957	30.00	60.00	120.00
—"Deep groove" version (deep indentation under label on both sides)					
❏ BLP-1556 [M]	The Sounds of Jimmy Smith	1963	6.25	12.50	25.00
—With New York, USA address on label					
❏ BLP-1563 [M]	Jimmy Smith Plays Pretty Just for You	1957	20.00	40.00	80.00
—Regular edition, W. 63rd St. address on label					
❏ BLP-1563 [M]	Jimmy Smith Plays Pretty Just for You	1957	30.00	60.00	120.00
—"Deep groove" version (deep indentation under label on both sides)					
❏ BLP-1563 [M]	Jimmy Smith Plays Pretty Just for You	1963	6.25	12.50	25.00
—With New York, USA address on label					
❏ BST-1563 [S]	Jimmy Smith Plays Pretty Just for You	1959	12.50	25.00	50.00
—Regular edition, W. 63rd St. address on label					
❏ BST-1563 [S]	Jimmy Smith Plays Pretty Just for You	1959	20.00	40.00	80.00
—"Deep groove" version (deep indentation under label on both sides)					
❏ BST-1563 [S]	Jimmy Smith Plays Pretty Just for You	1963	5.00	10.00	20.00
—With New York, USA address on label					
❏ BLP-1585 [M]	Groovin' at Small's Paradise, Vol. 1	1958	20.00	40.00	80.00
—Regular edition, W. 63rd St. address on label					
❏ BLP-1585 [M]	Groovin' at Small's Paradise, Vol. 1	1958	30.00	60.00	120.00
—"Deep groove" version (deep indentation under label on both sides)					
❏ BLP-1585 [M]	Groovin' at Small's Paradise, Vol. 1	1963	6.25	12.50	25.00
—With New York, USA address on label					
❏ BST-1585 [S]	Groovin' at Small's Paradise, Vol. 1	1959	12.50	25.00	50.00
—Regular edition, W. 63rd St. address on label					
❏ BST-1585 [S]	Groovin' at Small's Paradise, Vol. 1	1959	20.00	40.00	80.00
—"Deep groove" version (deep indentation under label on both sides)					
❏ BST-1585 [S]	Groovin' at Small's Paradise, Vol. 1	1963	5.00	10.00	20.00
—With New York, USA address on label					
❏ BLP-1586 [M]	Groovin' at Small's Paradise, Vol. 2	1958	20.00	40.00	80.00
—Regular edition, W. 63rd St. address on label					
❏ BLP-1586 [M]	Groovin' at Small's Paradise, Vol. 2	1958	30.00	60.00	120.00
—"Deep groove" version (deep indentation under label on both sides)					
❏ BLP-1586 [M]	Groovin' at Small's Paradise, Vol. 2	1963	6.25	12.50	25.00
—With New York, USA address on label					
❏ BST-1586 [S]	Groovin' at Small's Paradise, Vol. 2	1959	12.50	25.00	50.00
—Regular edition, W. 63rd St. address on label					
❏ BST-1586 [S]	Groovin' at Small's Paradise, Vol. 2	1959	20.00	40.00	80.00
—"Deep groove" version (deep indentation under label on both sides)					
❏ BST-1586 [S]	Groovin' at Small's Paradise, Vol. 2	1963	5.00	10.00	20.00
—With New York, USA address on label					
❏ BLP-4002 [M]	House Party	1959	20.00	40.00	80.00
—Regular edition, W. 63rd St. address on label					
❏ BLP-4002 [M]	House Party	1959	30.00	60.00	120.00
—"Deep groove" version (deep indentation under label on both sides)					
❏ BLP-4002 [M]	House Party	1963	6.25	12.50	25.00
—With New York, USA address on label					
❏ BST-4002 [S]	House Party	1959	12.50	25.00	50.00
—Regular edition, W. 63rd St. address on label					
❏ BST-4002 [S]	House Party	1959	20.00	40.00	80.00
—"Deep groove" version (deep indentation under label on both sides)					
❏ BST-4002 [S]	House Party	1963	5.00	10.00	20.00
—With New York, USA address on label					
❏ BLP-4011 [M]	The Sermon	1959	20.00	40.00	80.00
—Regular edition, W. 63rd St. address on label					
❏ BLP-4011 [M]	The Sermon	1959	30.00	60.00	120.00
—"Deep groove" version (deep indentation under label on both sides)					
❏ BLP-4011 [M]	The Sermon	1963	6.25	12.50	25.00
—With New York, USA address on label					
❏ BST-4011 [S]	The Sermon	1959	12.50	25.00	50.00
—Regular edition, W. 63rd St. address on label					
❏ BST-4011 [S]	The Sermon	1959	20.00	40.00	80.00
—"Deep groove" version (deep indentation under label on both sides)					
❏ BST-4011 [S]	The Sermon	1963	5.00	10.00	20.00
—With New York, USA address on label					
❏ BLP-4030 [M]	Crazy Baby	1960	20.00	40.00	80.00
—Regular edition, W. 63rd St. address on label					
❏ BLP-4030 [M]	Crazy Baby	1960	30.00	60.00	120.00
—"Deep groove" version (deep indentation under label on both sides)					
❏ BLP-4030 [M]	Crazy Baby	1963	6.25	12.50	25.00
—With New York, USA address on label					
❏ BLP-4050 [M]	Home Cookin'	1961	12.50	25.00	50.00
—With W. 63rd St. address on label					
❏ BLP-4050 [M]	Home Cookin'	1963	5.00	10.00	20.00
—With New York, USA address on label					
❏ BLP-4078 [M]	Midnight Special	1961	12.50	25.00	50.00
—With 61st St. address on label					
❏ BLP-4078 [M]	Midnight Special	1963	5.00	10.00	20.00
—With New York, USA address on label					
❏ BLP-4100 [M]	Jimmy Smith Plays Fats Waller	1962	12.50	25.00	50.00
—With 61st St. address on label					
❏ BLP-4100 [M]	Jimmy Smith Plays Fats Waller	1963	5.00	10.00	20.00
—With New York, USA address on label					
❏ BLP-4117 [M]	Back at the Chicken Shack	1963	6.25	12.50	25.00
❏ BLP-4141 [M]	Rockin' the Boat	1963	6.25	12.50	25.00
❏ BLP-4164 [M]	Prayer Meetin'	1964	6.25	12.50	25.00
❏ BLP-4200 [M]	Softly as a Summer Breeze	1965	6.25	12.50	25.00
❏ BLP-4235 [M]	Bucket!	1966	6.25	12.50	25.00
❏ BLP-4255 [M]	I'm Movin' On	1967	7.50	15.00	30.00
❏ BST-84030 [S]	Crazy Baby	1960	12.50	25.00	50.00
—With W. 63rd St. address on label					
❏ BST-84030 [S]	Crazy Baby	1963	5.00	10.00	20.00
—With New York, USA address on label					
❏ BST-84050 [S]	Home Cookin'	1961	12.50	25.00	50.00
—With W. 63rd St. address on label					
❏ BST-84050 [S]	Home Cookin'	1963	5.00	10.00	20.00
—With New York, USA address on label					
❏ BST-84078 [S]	Midnight Special	1961	12.50	25.00	50.00
—With 61st St. address on label					
❏ BST-84078 [S]	Midnight Special	1963	5.00	10.00	20.00
—With New York, USA address on label					
❏ BST-84100 [S]	Jimmy Smith Plays Fats Waller	1962	12.50	25.00	50.00
—With 61st St. address on label					
❏ BST-84100 [S]	Jimmy Smith Plays Fats Waller	1963	5.00	10.00	20.00
—With New York, USA address on label					
❏ BST-84117 [S]	Back at the Chicken Shack	1963	7.50	15.00	30.00
—With New York, USA address on label					
❏ BST-84141 [S]	Rockin' the Boat	1963	7.50	15.00	30.00
—With New York, USA address on label					
❏ BST-84164 [S]	Prayer Meetin'	1964	7.50	15.00	30.00
—With New York, USA address on label					
❏ BST-84200 [S]	Softly as a Summer Breeze	1965	7.50	15.00	30.00
—With New York, USA address on label					
❏ BST-84235 [S]	Bucket!	1966	7.50	15.00	30.00
—With New York, USA address on label					
❏ BST-84255 [S]	I'm Movin' On	1967	5.00	10.00	20.00
❏ BST-84269	Open House	1968	5.00	10.00	20.00
❏ BST-84296	Plain Talk	1969	5.00	10.00	20.00
❏ BST-89901 [(2)]	Jimmy Smith's Greatest Hits!	1969	6.25	12.50	25.00
MOSAIC					
❏ MQ5-154 [(5)]	The Complete February 1957 Jimmy Smith Blue Note Sessions	199?	20.00	40.00	80.00
VERVE					
❏ V-8474 [M]	Bashin'	1962	5.00	10.00	20.00
❏ V6-8474 [S]	Bashin'	1962	6.25	12.50	25.00
❏ V-8544 [M]	Hobo Flats	1963	5.00	10.00	20.00
❏ V6-8544 [S]	Hobo Flats	1963	6.25	12.50	25.00
❏ V-8552 [M]	Any Number Can Win	1963	5.00	10.00	20.00
❏ V6-8552 [S]	Any Number Can Win	1963	6.25	12.50	25.00
❏ V-8583 [M]	Who's Afraid of Virginia Woolf?	1964	5.00	10.00	20.00
❏ V6-8583 [S]	Who's Afraid of Virginia Woolf?	1964	6.25	12.50	25.00
❏ V-8587 [M]	The Cat	1964	5.00	10.00	20.00
❏ V6-8587 [S]	The Cat	1964	6.25	12.50	25.00
❏ V-8604 [M]	Christmas '64	1964	5.00	10.00	20.00

Number	Title (A Side/B Side)	Yr	VG	VG+	NM
❏ V6-8604 [S]	Christmas '64	1964	6.25	12.50	25.00
❏ V6-8618 [S]	The Monster.	1965	5.00	10.00	20.00
❏ V6-8628 [S]	Organ Grinder Swing.	1965	5.00	10.00	20.00
❏ V6-8641 [S]	Got My Mojo Workin'.	1966	5.00	10.00	20.00
❏ V-8652 [M]	Peter and the Wolf.	1966	5.00	10.00	20.00
❏ V6-8652 [S]	Peter and the Wolf.	1966	6.25	12.50	25.00
❏ V-8666 [M]	Christmas Cookin'.	1966	5.00	10.00	20.00
❏ V6-8666 [S]	Christmas Cookin'.	1966	6.25	12.50	25.00
❏ V6-8667 [S]	Hoochie Coochie Man.	1966	5.00	10.00	20.00
❏ V-8705 [M]	Respect.	1967	5.00	10.00	20.00
❏ V-8721 [M]	The Best of Jimmy Smith.	1967	5.00	10.00	20.00
❏ SMAS-90643 [S]	The Monster.	1965	6.25	12.50	25.00
—Capitol Record Club edition					

SMITH, JIMMY, AND WES MONTGOMERY
VERVE

❏ V-8678 [M]	Jimmy and Wes, The Dynamic Duo	1967	5.00	10.00	20.00

SMITH, JOHNNY
LEGENDE

❏ 1401 [10]	Annotations of the Muses	1955	25.00	50.00	100.00

ROOST

❏ R-410 [10]	A Three-Dimension Sound Recording of Jazz at NBC with the Johnny Smith Quintet	1953	37.50	75.00	150.00
❏ R-413 [10]	Johnny Smith Quintet	1953	30.00	60.00	120.00
❏ R-421 [10]	In a Mellow Mood	1954	25.00	50.00	100.00
❏ R-424 [10]	In a Sentimental Mood	1954	25.00	50.00	100.00
❏ LP-2201 [M]	Johnny Smith Plays Jimmy Van Heusen	1955	20.00	40.00	80.00
❏ LP-2203 [M]	Johnny Smith Quartet	1955	20.00	40.00	80.00
❏ LP-2211 [M]	Moonlight in Vermont	1956	20.00	40.00	80.00
❏ LP-2215 [M]	Moods	1956	15.00	30.00	60.00
❏ LP-2216 [M]	New Quartet	1956	15.00	30.00	60.00
❏ LP-2223 [M]	Johnny Smith Foursome, Volume 1	1956	12.50	25.00	50.00
❏ LP-2228 [M]	Johnny Smith Foursome, Volume 2	1957	12.50	25.00	50.00
❏ LP-2231 [M]	Flower Drum Song	1958	10.00	20.00	40.00
❏ SLP-2231 [S]	Flower Drum Song	1958	7.50	15.00	30.00
❏ LP-2233 [M]	Easy Listening	1959	10.00	20.00	40.00
❏ SLP-2233 [S]	Easy Listening	1959	7.50	15.00	30.00
❏ LP-2237 [M]	Favorites	1959	10.00	20.00	40.00
❏ SLP-2237 [S]	Favorites	1959	7.50	15.00	30.00
❏ LP-2238 [M]	Designed for You	1960	7.50	15.00	30.00
❏ SLP-2238 [S]	Designed for You	1960	10.00	20.00	40.00
❏ LP-2239 [M]	Dear Little Sweetheart	1960	7.50	15.00	30.00
❏ SLP-2239 [S]	Dear Little Sweetheart	1960	10.00	20.00	40.00
❏ LP-2242 [M]	Guitar and Strings	1960	7.50	15.00	30.00
❏ SLP-2242 [S]	Guitar and Strings	1960	10.00	20.00	40.00
❏ LP-2243 [M]	Johnny Smith Plus the Trio	1960	7.50	15.00	30.00
❏ SLP-2243 [S]	Johnny Smith Plus the Trio	1960	10.00	20.00	40.00
❏ LP-2246 [M]	The Sound of the Johnny Smith Guitar	1961	7.50	15.00	30.00
❏ SLP-2246 [S]	The Sound of the Johnny Smith Guitar	1961	10.00	20.00	40.00
❏ LP-2248 [M]	Man with the Blue Guitar	1962	7.50	15.00	30.00
❏ SLP-2248 [S]	Man with the Blue Guitar	1962	10.00	20.00	40.00
❏ LP-2250 [M]	Johnny Smith Plays Jimmy Van Heusen	1963	6.25	12.50	25.00
❏ SLP-2250 [S]	Johnny Smith Plays Jimmy Van Heusen	1963	7.50	15.00	30.00
❏ LP-2254 [M]	Guitar World	1963	6.25	12.50	25.00
❏ SLP-2254 [S]	Guitar World	1963	7.50	15.00	30.00
❏ LP-2259 [M]	Reminiscing	1965	6.25	12.50	25.00
❏ SLP-2259 [S]	Reminiscing	1965	7.50	15.00	30.00

VERVE

❏ V-8692 [M]	Johnny Smith	1967	7.50	15.00	30.00
❏ V6-8692 [S]	Johnny Smith	1967	5.00	10.00	20.00
❏ V-8737 [M]	Johnny Smith's Kaleidoscope	1968	7.50	15.00	30.00
❏ V6-8737 [S]	Johnny Smith's Kaleidoscope	1968	5.00	10.00	20.00
❏ V6-8767 [S]	Phase II	1969	5.00	10.00	20.00

SMITH, JOHNNY "HAMMOND"
See JOHNNY HAMMOND.

SMITH, KEELY
Also see LOUIS PRIMA AND KEELY SMITH.
CAPITOL

❏ SW 914 [S]	I Wish You Love	1959	7.50	15.00	30.00
—Black label with colorband, Capitol logo at left					
❏ SW 914 [S]	I Wish You Love	1962	3.75	7.50	15.00
—Black label with colorband, Capitol logo at top					
❏ W 914 [M]	I Wish You Love	1957	12.50	25.00	50.00
—Turquoise label					
❏ W 914 [M]	I Wish You Love	1959	7.50	15.00	30.00
—Black label with colorband, Capitol logo at left					
❏ W 914 [M]	I Wish You Love	1962	3.75	7.50	15.00
—Black label with colorband, Capitol logo at top					
❏ ST 1073 [S]	Politely!	1959	12.50	25.00	50.00
—Black label with colorband, Capitol logo at left					
❏ ST 1073 [S]	Politely!	1962	5.00	10.00	20.00
—Black label with colorband, Capitol logo at top					
❏ T 1073 [M]	Politely!	1958	10.00	20.00	40.00
—Black label with colorband, Capitol logo at left					
❏ T 1073 [M]	Politely!	1962	3.75	7.50	15.00
—Black label with colorband, Capitol logo at top					
❏ ST 1145 [S]	Swingin' Pretty	1959	12.50	25.00	50.00
—Black label with colorband, Capitol logo at left					
❏ ST 1145 [S]	Swingin' Pretty	1962	5.00	10.00	20.00
—Black label with colorband, Capitol logo at top					
❏ T 1145 [M]	Swingin' Pretty	1959	10.00	20.00	40.00
—Black label with colorband, Capitol logo at left					
❏ T 1145 [M]	Swingin' Pretty	1962	3.75	7.50	15.00
—Black label with colorband, Capitol logo at top					

DOT

❏ DLP-3241 [M]	Be My Love	1959	6.25	12.50	25.00
❏ DLP-3265 [M]	Swing, You Lovers	1960	6.25	12.50	25.00
❏ DLP-3287 [M]	Dearly Beloved	1961	6.25	12.50	25.00
❏ DLP-3345 [M]	A Keely Christmas	1961	6.25	12.50	25.00
❏ DLP-3415 [M]	Because You're Mine	1962	6.25	12.50	25.00

Number	Title (A Side/B Side)	Yr	VG	VG+	NM
❏ DLP-3423 [M]	Twist with Keely Smith	1962	6.25	12.50	25.00
❏ DLP-3460 [M]	Cherokeely Swings	1962	6.25	12.50	25.00
❏ DLP-3461 [M]	What Kind of Fool Am I	1962	6.25	12.50	25.00
❏ DLP-25241 [S]	Be My Love	1959	7.50	15.00	30.00
❏ DLP-25265 [S]	Swing, You Lovers	1960	7.50	15.00	30.00
❏ DLP-25287 [S]	Dearly Beloved	1961	7.50	15.00	30.00
❏ DLP-25345 [S]	A Keely Christmas	1961	7.50	15.00	30.00
❏ DLP-25415 [S]	Because You're Mine	1962	7.50	15.00	30.00
❏ DLP-25423 [S]	Twist with Keely Smith	1962	7.50	15.00	30.00
❏ DLP-25460 [S]	Cherokeely Swings	1962	7.50	15.00	30.00
❏ DLP-25461 [S]	What Kind of Fool Am I	1962	7.50	15.00	30.00

HARMONY

❏ HS 11333	That Old Black Magic	1968	3.00	6.00	12.00

REPRISE

❏ R-6086 [M]	Little Girl Blue, Little Girl New	1963	5.00	10.00	20.00
❏ R9-6086 [S]	Little Girl Blue, Little Girl New	1963	6.25	12.50	25.00
❏ R-6132 [M]	The Intimate Keely Smith	1964	5.00	10.00	20.00
❏ RS-6132 [S]	The Intimate Keely Smith	1964	6.25	12.50	25.00
❏ R-6142 [M]	Keely Smith Sings the John Lennon/Paul McCartney Songbook	1964	6.25	12.50	25.00
❏ RS-6142 [S]	Keely Smith Sings the John Lennon/Paul McCartney Songbook	1964	7.50	15.00	30.00
❏ R-6175 [M]	That Old Black Magic	1965	5.00	10.00	20.00
❏ RS-6175 [S]	That Old Black Magic	1965	6.25	12.50	25.00

SMITH, LAVERGNE
COOK

❏ LP-1081 [10]	Angel in the Absinthe House	1955	37.50	75.00	150.00

SAVOY

❏ MG-12031 [M]	New Orleans Nightingale	1955	12.50	25.00	50.00

VIK

❏ LX-1056 [M]	La Vergne Smith	1956	12.50	25.00	50.00

SMITH, LONNIE
BLUE NOTE

❏ BST-84290	Think!	1968	5.00	10.00	20.00
❏ BST-84313	Turning Point	1969	5.00	10.00	20.00

COLUMBIA

❏ CL 2696 [M]	Finger-Lickin' Good Soul Organ	1967	6.25	12.50	25.00
❏ CS 9496 [S]	Finger-Lickin' Good Soul Organ	1967	5.00	10.00	20.00

SMITH, LOUIS
BLUE NOTE

❏ BLP-1584 [M]	Here Comes Louis Smith	1958	30.00	60.00	120.00
—Regular version, W. 63rd St. address on label					
❏ BLP-1584 [M]	Here Comes Louis Smith	1958	37.50	75.00	150.00
—"Deep groove" version (deep indentation under label on both sides)					
❏ BST-1584 [S]	Here Comes Louis Smith	1959	20.00	40.00	80.00
—Regular version, W. 63rd St. address on label					
❏ BST-1584 [S]	Here Comes Louis Smith	1959	25.00	50.00	100.00
—"Deep groove" version (deep indentation under label on both sides)					
❏ BLP-1594 [M]	Smithville	1958	20.00	40.00	80.00
—Regular version, W. 63rd St. address on label					
❏ BLP-1594 [M]	Smithville	1958	25.00	50.00	100.00
—"Deep groove" version (deep indentation under label on both sides)					
❏ BST-1594 [S]	Smithville	1959	15.00	30.00	60.00
—Regular version, W. 63rd St. address on label					
❏ BST-1594 [S]	Smithville	1959	20.00	40.00	80.00
—"Deep groove" version (deep indentation under label on both sides)					

SMITH, O.C.
CARIBOU

❏ PZ 34471	Together	1977	2.50	5.00	10.00

COLUMBIA

❏ CL 2714 [M]	The Dynamic O.C. Smith	1967	5.00	10.00	20.00
❏ CS 9514 [S]	The Dynamic O.C. Smith	1967	3.75	7.50	15.00
❏ CS 9680 [M]	Hickory Holler Revisited	1968	6.25	12.50	25.00
—White label promo "Special Mono Radio Station Copy" with stereo number					
❏ CS 9680 [S]	Hickory Holler Revisited	1968	3.00	6.00	12.00
❏ CS 9756	For Once in My Life	1969	3.00	6.00	12.00
❏ CS 9908	O.C. Smith at Home	1969	3.00	6.00	12.00
❏ C 30227	O.C. Smith's Greatest Hits	1970	3.00	6.00	12.00
❏ C 30664	Help Me Make It Through the Night	1971	3.00	6.00	12.00
❏ KC 33247	La La Peace Song	1974	2.50	5.00	10.00

HARMONY

❏ KH 30317	O.C. Smith	1971	2.50	5.00	10.00

MOTOWN

❏ 6019 ML	Love Changes	1982	2.50	5.00	10.00

SHADYBROOK

❏ 012	Love	1978	2.50	5.00	10.00

SMITH, OSBORNE
ARGO

❏ LP-4000 [M]	Eyes of Love	1960	7.50	15.00	30.00
❏ LPS-4000 [S]	Eyes of Love	1960	10.00	20.00	40.00

SMITH, PAUL
CAPITOL

❏ H 493 [10]	Liquid Sounds	1954	20.00	40.00	80.00
❏ T 665 [M]	Cascades	1955	10.00	20.00	40.00
❏ T 757 [M]	Cool and Sparkling	1956	10.00	20.00	40.00
❏ T 829 [M]	Softly, Baby	1957	10.00	20.00	40.00
❏ ST 1017 [S]	Delicate Jazz	1958	6.25	12.50	25.00
❏ T 1017 [M]	Delicate Jazz	1958	7.50	15.00	30.00

DISCOVERY

❏ DL-3009 [10]	Paul Smith	1950	25.00	50.00	100.00
❏ DL-3017 [10]	Paul Smith Trio	1952	20.00	40.00	80.00

MGM

❏ E-4057 [M]	Memories of Paris	1962	5.00	10.00	20.00
❏ SE-4057 [S]	Memories of Paris	1962	6.25	12.50	25.00

S

Number	Title (A Side/B Side)	Yr	VG	VG+	NM
SAVOY					
❏ MG-12094 [M]	By the Fireside	1956	12.50	25.00	50.00
SKYLARK					
❏ SKLP-13 [10]	Paul Smith Quartet	1954	30.00	60.00	120.00
TAMPA					
❏ TP-9 [M]	Fine, Sweet and Tasty	1957	25.00	50.00	100.00
—Colored vinyl					
❏ TP-9 [M]	Fine, Sweet and Tasty	1958	12.50	25.00	50.00
—Black vinyl					
VERVE					
❏ MGV-2128 [M]	The Sound of Music	1960	10.00	20.00	40.00
❏ V-2128 [M]	The Sound of Music	1961	5.00	10.00	20.00
❏ MGV-2130 [M]	The Big Men	1960	10.00	20.00	40.00
❏ V-2130 [M]	The Big Men	1961	5.00	10.00	20.00
❏ MGV-2148 [M]	Latin Keyboards and Percussion	1960	10.00	20.00	40.00
❏ V-2148 [M]	Latin Keyboards and Percussion	1961	5.00	10.00	20.00
❏ MGV-4051 [M]	Carnival! In Percussion	1961	7.50	15.00	30.00
❏ V-4051 [M]	Carnival! In Percussion	1961	5.00	10.00	20.00
❏ V6-4051 [S]	Carnival! In Percussion	1961	6.25	12.50	25.00
❏ MGVS-6128 [S]	The Sound of Music	1960	7.50	15.00	30.00
❏ MGVS-6135 [S]	The Big Men	1960	7.50	15.00	30.00
SMITH, PAUL; RAY BROWN; LOUIS BELLSON					
DISCWASHER					
❏ 001	Intensive Care	1979	5.00	10.00	20.00
SMITH, PINE TOP					
BRUNSWICK					
❏ BL 58003 [10]	Pine Top Smith	1950	30.00	60.00	120.00
SMITH, RAY					
COLUMBIA					
❏ CL 1937 [M]	Ray Smith's Greatest Hits	1963	6.25	12.50	25.00
❏ CS 8737 [S]	Ray Smith's Greatest Hits	1963	7.50	15.00	30.00
JUDD					
❏ JLPA-701 [M]	Travelin' with Ray	1960	175.00	350.00	700.00
STOMP OFF					
❏ SOS-1012	Jungle Blues	198?	3.00	6.00	12.00
"T"					
❏ 56062 [M]	The Best of Ray Smith	196?	25.00	50.00	100.00
WIX					
❏ 1000	I'm Gonna Rock Some More	197?	3.75	7.50	15.00
SMITH, ROBERT CURTIS					
BLUESVILLE					
❏ BVLP-1064 [M]	Clarksdale Blues	1963	20.00	40.00	80.00
—Blue label, silver print					
❏ BVLP-1064 [M]	Clarksdale Blues	1964	6.25	12.50	25.00
—Blue label, trident logo at right					
SMITH, ROGER					
WARNER BROS.					
❏ W 1305 [M]	Beach Romance	1960	10.00	20.00	40.00
❏ WS 1305 [S]	Beach Romance	1960	12.50	25.00	50.00
SMITH, SOMETHIN', AND THE REDHEADS					
EPIC					
❏ LN 3138 [M]	Somethin' Smith and the Redheads	1959	7.50	15.00	30.00
❏ LN 3373 [M]	Put the Blame on Mame	196?	6.25	12.50	25.00
MGM					
❏ E-3941 [M]	Ain't We Got Fun Kinda Songs	1961	5.00	10.00	20.00
❏ SE-3941 [S]	Ain't We Got Fun Kinda Songs	1961	6.25	12.50	25.00
SMITH, STUFF					
20TH FOX					
❏ FTM-3008 [M]	Sweet Singin' Stuff	1959	7.50	15.00	30.00
❏ FTS-3008 [S]	Sweet Singin' Stuff	1959	6.25	12.50	25.00
VERVE					
❏ MGVS-6097 [S]	Cat on a Hot Fiddle	1960	10.00	20.00	40.00
❏ MGV-8206 [M]	Soft Winds	1958	12.50	25.00	50.00
❏ V-8206 [M]	Soft Winds	1961	5.00	10.00	20.00
❏ MGV-8282 [M]	Have Violin, Will Swing	1958	12.50	25.00	50.00
❏ V-8282 [M]	Have Violin, Will Swing	1961	5.00	10.00	20.00
❏ MGV-8339 [M]	Cat on a Hot Fiddle	1959	12.50	25.00	50.00
❏ V-8339 [M]	Cat on a Hot Fiddle	1961	5.00	10.00	20.00
SMITH, TAB					
CHECKER					
❏ LP-2971 [M]	Tab Smith	1960	25.00	50.00	100.00
—Regular issue					
❏ LP-2971 [M]	Tab Smith	1960	150.00	300.00	600.00
—White label promo with multi-color vinyl					
UNITED					
❏ LP-001 [10]	Music Styled by Tab Smith	1955	50.00	100.00	200.00
❏ LP-003 [10]	Red, Hot and Cool Blues	1955	50.00	100.00	200.00
SMITH, WHISTLING JACK					
DERAM					
❏ DE 16006 [M]	I Was Kaiser Bill's Batman	1967	6.25	12.50	25.00
❏ DES 18006 [S]	I Was Kaiser Bill's Batman	1967	5.00	10.00	20.00
SMITH, WILLIE					
EMARCY					
❏ MG-26000 [10]	Relaxin' After Hours	1954	25.00	50.00	100.00
MERCURY					
❏ MG-25075 [10]	Alto Sax Artistry	1950	30.00	60.00	120.00
SMITH, WILLIE "THE LION"					
BLUE CIRCLE					
❏ 1500-33 [10]	Willie "The Lion" Smith	1952	20.00	40.00	80.00
COMMODORE					
❏ DL-30004 [M]	The Lion of the Piano	1951	25.00	50.00	100.00

Number	Title (A Side/B Side)	Yr	VG	VG+	NM
DIAL					
❏ LP-305 [10]	Harlem Memories	1953	62.50	125.00	250.00
DOT					
❏ DLP-3094 [M]	The Lion Roars	1958	12.50	25.00	50.00
GRAND AWARD					
❏ GA-33-368 [M]	The Legend of Willie Smith	1956	12.50	25.00	50.00
MAINSTREAM					
❏ 56027 [M]	A Legend	1965	6.25	12.50	25.00
RCA VICTOR					
❏ LSP-6016 [(2)]	Memoirs	1968	5.00	10.00	20.00
URANIA					
❏ UJLP-1207 [M]	Accent On Piano	1955	15.00	30.00	60.00
SMITH-GLAMANN QUINTET					
BETHLEHEM					
❏ BCP-22 [M]	Smith-Glamann Quintet	1955	12.50	25.00	50.00
SMITHEREENS, THE					
CAPITOL					
❏ C1-91194	11	1989	3.00	6.00	12.00
CAPITOL/ENIGMA					
❏ C1-48375	Green Thoughts	1988	2.50	5.00	10.00
❏ R 130120	Green Thoughts	1988	3.00	6.00	12.00
—BMG Direct Marketing edition					
ENIGMA					
❏ (no #) [DJ]	Live at the Roxy — Special Forces Radio Concert	1986	10.00	20.00	40.00
❏ ST-73208	Especially for You	1986	2.50	5.00	10.00
❏ 73220 [EP]	Beauty and Sadness	1988	2.00	4.00	8.00
—Remixed version of Little Ricky 103 with one track deleted					
❏ SEAX-73258 [PD]	Especially for You	1986	5.00	10.00	20.00
—Picture disc in plastic sleeve, sticker on sleeve					
❏ R 164050	Especially for You	1987	3.00	6.00	12.00
—BMG Direct Marketing edition					
LITTLE RICKY					
❏ 103 [EP]	Beauty and Sadness	1983	10.00	20.00	40.00
SMITHS, THE					
SIRE					
❏ 25065	The Smiths	1984	2.50	5.00	10.00
❏ 25269	Meat Is Murder	1985	2.50	5.00	10.00
❏ 25426	The Queen Is Dead	1986	2.50	5.00	10.00
❏ 25649	Strangeways, Here We Come	1987	2.50	5.00	10.00
❏ 25669 [(2)]	Louder Than Bombs	1987	3.75	7.50	15.00
❏ 25786	"Rank"	1988	2.50	5.00	10.00
WARNER BROS.					
❏ WBMS-130 [DJ]	Music and Interviews	1985	10.00	20.00	40.00
—Part of "The Warner Bros. Music Show" series; one side is The Smiths; the other side is The Blasters					
SMOKE, THE (1)					
California group. Jimmy Greenspoon, later a member of THREE DOG NIGHT, appears on the LP cover, but not on the record itself.					
SIDEWALK					
❏ ST 5912	The Smoke	1968	10.00	20.00	40.00
SMOKE, THE (2)					
Houston-based group.					
UNI					
❏ 73052	The Smoke	1969	6.25	12.50	25.00
❏ 73065	The Smoke at George's Coffee Shop	1970	6.25	12.50	25.00
SMOKE RISE, THE					
PARAMOUNT					
❏ PAS-9000 [(2)]	The Survival of St. Joan	1971	5.00	10.00	20.00
—With booklet					
SMOKESTACK LIGHTNIN'					
BELL					
❏ 6026	Off the Wall	1969	5.00	10.00	20.00
SMOKY BABE					
BLUESVILLE					
❏ BVLP-1063 [M]	Hottest Brand Going	1963	20.00	40.00	80.00
—Blue label, silver print					
❏ BVLP-1063 [M]	Hottest Brand Going	1964	6.25	12.50	25.00
—Blue label, trident logo at right					
FOLK-LYRIC					
❏ FL-108 [M]	Smokey Babe	196?	25.00	50.00	100.00
SMOTHERS, SMOKEY					
KING					
❏ 779 [M]	The Backporch Blues	1962	250.00	500.00	1000.
SMOTHERS BROTHERS, THE					
MERCURY					
❏ MGDJ-20 [DJ]	Best of the Smothers Brothers	1964	10.00	20.00	40.00
❏ MGDJ-25 [DJ]	It's Brothers Smothers Month	1964	10.00	20.00	40.00
❏ MG-20611 [M]	The Songs and Comedy of the Smothers Brothers!	1962	3.75	7.50	15.00
❏ MG-20675 [M]	The Two Sides of the Smothers Brothers	1962	3.75	7.50	15.00
❏ MG-20777 [M]	(Think Ethnic!)	1963	3.75	7.50	15.00
❏ MG-20862 [M]	Curb Your Tongue, Knave!	1963	3.75	7.50	15.00
❏ MG-20904 [M]	It Must Have Been Something I Said!	1964	3.75	7.50	15.00
❏ MG-20948 [M]	Tour De Farce American History and Other Unrelated Subjects	1964	3.75	7.50	15.00
❏ MG-20989 [M]	Aesop's Fables the Smothers Brothers Way	1965	3.75	7.50	15.00
❏ MG-21051 [M]	Mom Always Liked You Best!	1965	3.75	7.50	15.00
❏ MG-21064 [M]	The Smothers Brothers Play It Straight	1966	3.75	7.50	15.00
❏ MG-21089 [M]	Golden Hits of the Smothers Brothers, Vol. 2	1966	3.75	7.50	15.00
❏ SR-60611 [S]	The Songs and Comedy of the Smothers Brothers!	1962	5.00	10.00	20.00

Number	Title (A Side/B Side)	Yr	VG	VG+	NM
❏ SR-60675 [S]	The Two Sides of the Smothers Brothers	1962	5.00	10.00	20.00
❏ SR-60777 [S]	(Think Ethnic!)	1963	5.00	10.00	20.00
❏ SR-60862 [S]	Curb Your Tongue, Knave!	1963	5.00	10.00	20.00
❏ SR-60904 [S]	It Must Have Been Something I Said!	1964	5.00	10.00	20.00
❏ SR-60948 [S]	Tour De Farce American History and Other Unrelated Subjects	1964	5.00	10.00	20.00
❏ SR-60989 [S]	Aesop's Fables the Smothers Brothers Way	1965	5.00	10.00	20.00
❏ SR-61051 [S]	Mom Always Liked You Best!	1965	5.00	10.00	20.00
❏ SR-61064 [S]	The Smothers Brothers Play It Straight	1966	5.00	10.00	20.00
❏ SR-61089 [S]	Golden Hits of the Smothers Brothers, Vol. 2	1966	5.00	10.00	20.00
❏ SR-61193 [S]	Smothers Comedy Brothers Hour	1968	5.00	10.00	20.00

RHINO

❏ R1-70188	Sibling Revelry: The Best of the Smothers Brothers	1988	2.50	5.00	10.00

SNEAKY PETE
SHILO

❏ 4086	Sneaky Pete	1979	7.50	15.00	30.00

SNELL, TONY
ESP-DISK'

❏ 3004	Medieval and Latter Day Lays	197?	5.00	10.00	20.00

SNOW
EPIC

❏ BN 26435	Snow	1969	5.00	10.00	20.00

SNOW, HANK
PAIR

❏ PDL2-1004 [(2)]	I'm Movin' On	1986	3.00	6.00	12.00

RCA CAMDEN

❏ ACL1-0124	Snowbird	1973	2.50	5.00	10.00
❏ ACL2-0337 [(2)]	When My Blue Moon Turns to Gold Again	197?	3.75	7.50	15.00
❏ CAL-514 [M]	The Singing Ranger	1959	5.00	10.00	20.00
❏ CAS-514 [R]	The Singing Ranger	196?	3.00	6.00	12.00
❏ ACL1-0540	I'm Movin' On	1974	2.50	5.00	10.00
❏ CAL-680 [M]	The Southern Cannonball	1961	5.00	10.00	20.00
❏ CAS-680 [R]	The Southern Cannonball	196?	3.00	6.00	12.00
❏ CAL-722 [M]	The One and Only Hank Snow	1962	5.00	10.00	20.00
❏ CAS-722 [R]	The One and Only Hank Snow	1962	3.00	6.00	12.00
❏ CAL-782 [M]	The Last Ride	1963	5.00	10.00	20.00
❏ CAS-782 [R]	The Last Ride	1963	3.00	6.00	12.00
❏ CAL-836 [M]	Old and Great Songs	1964	3.75	7.50	15.00
❏ CAS-836 [R]	Old and Great Songs	1964	3.00	6.00	12.00
❏ CAL-910 [M]	The Highest Bidder	1965	3.00	6.00	12.00
❏ CAS-910 [S]	The Highest Bidder	1965	3.75	7.50	15.00
❏ CAL-964 [M]	Travelin' Blues	1966	3.00	6.00	12.00
❏ CAS-964 [S]	Travelin' Blues	1966	3.75	7.50	15.00
❏ CAL-2160 [M]	My Early Favorites	1967	3.75	7.50	15.00
❏ CAS-2160 [S]	My Early Favorites	1967	3.00	6.00	12.00
❏ CAS-2257	My Nova Scotia Home	1968	3.00	6.00	12.00
❏ CAS-2348	I Went to Your Wedding	1969	3.00	6.00	12.00
❏ CAS-2443	Memories Are Made of This	1970	3.00	6.00	12.00
❏ CAS-2513	Lonesome Whistle	1972	3.00	6.00	12.00
❏ CAS-2560	The Legend of Old Doc Brown	1972	3.00	6.00	12.00
❏ CXS-9009 [(2)]	The Wreck of the 97	197?	3.75	7.50	15.00

RCA VICTOR

❏ DPL2-0134 [(2)]	The Living Legend	197?	25.00	50.00	100.00
—RCA Special Products release					
❏ APL1-0162	Grand Ole Opry Favorites	1973	3.75	7.50	15.00
❏ APL1-0441	Hello Love	1974	3.75	7.50	15.00
❏ APL1-0608	That's You and Me	1974	3.75	7.50	15.00
❏ APL1-0908	You're Easy to Love	1975	3.75	7.50	15.00
❏ LPM-1113 [M]	Just Keep a-Movin'	1955	25.00	50.00	100.00
❏ LPM-1156 [M]	Old Doc Brown and Other Narrations	1955	25.00	50.00	100.00
❏ ANL1-1207	Grand Ole Opry Favorites	1975	2.50	5.00	10.00
—Reissue of APL1-0162					
❏ LPM-1233 [M]	Country Classics	1956	20.00	40.00	80.00
❏ APL1-1361	Live from Evangel Temple	1976	3.00	6.00	12.00
—With Jimmy Snow					
❏ LPM-1419 [M]	Country and Western Jamboree	1957	20.00	40.00	80.00
❏ LPM-1435 [M]	Hank Snow's Country Guitar	1957	20.00	40.00	80.00
❏ LPM-1638 [M]	Hank Snow Sings Sacred Songs	1958	15.00	30.00	60.00
❏ LPM-2043 [M]	Hank Snow Sings Jimmie Rodgers Songs	1959	12.50	25.00	50.00
❏ LSP-2043 [S]	Hank Snow Sings Jimmie Rodgers Songs	1959	20.00	40.00	80.00
❏ ANL1-2194	The Jimmie Rodgers Story	1977	2.50	5.00	10.00
—Reissue of 4708					
❏ LPM-2285 [M]	Hank Snow Souvenirs	1961	7.50	15.00	30.00
❏ LSP-2285 [S]	Hank Snow Souvenirs	1961	10.00	20.00	40.00
❏ APL1-2400	#104 — Still Movin' On	1977	3.00	6.00	12.00
❏ LPM-2458 [M]	Big Country Hits	1961	7.50	15.00	30.00
❏ LSP-2458 [S]	Big Country Hits	1961	10.00	20.00	40.00
❏ LPM-2675 [M]	I've Been Everywhere	1963	7.50	15.00	30.00
❏ LSP-2675 [S]	I've Been Everywhere	1963	10.00	20.00	40.00
❏ LPM-2705 [M]	Railroad Man	1963	7.50	15.00	30.00
❏ LSP-2705 [S]	Railroad Man	1963	10.00	20.00	40.00
❏ LPM-2812 [M]	More Hank Snow Souvenirs	1964	6.25	12.50	25.00
❏ LSP-2812 [S]	More Hank Snow Souvenirs	1964	7.50	15.00	30.00
❏ LPM-2901 [M]	Songs of Tragedy	1964	6.25	12.50	25.00
❏ LSP-2901 [S]	Songs of Tragedy	1964	7.50	15.00	30.00
❏ LPM-3026 [10]	Country Classics	1952	50.00	100.00	200.00
❏ LPM-3070 [10]	Hank Snow Sings	1952	45.00	90.00	180.00
❏ LPM-3131 [10]	Hank Snow Salutes Jimmie Rodgers	1953	45.00	90.00	180.00
❏ AHL1-3208	Mysterious Lady	1979	3.00	6.00	12.00
❏ LPM-3267 [10]	Hank Snow's Country Guitar	1954	45.00	90.00	180.00
❏ LPM-3317 [M]	Your Favorite Country Hits	1965	6.25	12.50	25.00
❏ LSP-3317 [S]	Your Favorite Country Hits	1965	7.50	15.00	30.00
❏ LPM-3378 [M]	Gloryland March	1965	6.25	12.50	25.00
❏ LSP-3378 [S]	Gloryland March	1965	7.50	15.00	30.00
❏ ANL1-3470	The Best of Hank Snow	1980	2.00	4.00	8.00
❏ LPM-3471 [M]	Heartbreak Trail - A Tribute to the Sons of the Pioneers	1966	6.25	12.50	25.00

Number	Title (A Side/B Side)	Yr	VG	VG+	NM
❏ LSP-3471 [S]	Heartbreak Trail - A Tribute to the Sons of the Pioneers	1966	7.50	15.00	30.00
❏ LPM-3478 [M]	The Best of Hank Snow	1966	5.00	10.00	20.00
❏ LSP-3478 [S]	The Best of Hank Snow	1966	6.25	12.50	25.00
❏ AHL1-3511	Instrumentally Yours	1980	3.00	6.00	12.00
❏ LPM-3548 [M]	Guitar Stylings of Hank Snow	1966	6.25	12.50	25.00
❏ LSP-3548 [S]	Guitar Stylings of Hank Snow	1966	7.50	15.00	30.00
❏ LPM-3595 [M]	Gospel Train	1966	7.50	15.00	30.00
❏ LSP-3595 [S]	Gospel Train	1966	10.00	20.00	40.00
❏ LPM-3737 [M]	Snow in Hawaii	1967	7.50	15.00	30.00
❏ LSP-3737 [S]	Snow in Hawaii	1967	6.25	12.50	25.00
❏ LPM-3826 [M]	Christmas with Hank Snow	1967	7.50	15.00	30.00
❏ LSP-3826 [S]	Christmas with Hank Snow	1967	6.25	12.50	25.00
❏ LPM-3857 [M]	Spanish Fire Ball and Other Great Hank Snow Stylings	1967	7.50	15.00	30.00
❏ LSP-3857 [S]	Spanish Fire Ball and Other Great Hank Snow Stylings	1967	6.25	12.50	25.00
❏ LPM-3965 [M]	Hits, Hits and More Hits	1968	25.00	50.00	100.00
❏ LSP-3965 [S]	Hits, Hits and More Hits	1968	6.25	12.50	25.00
❏ LSP-4032	Tales of the Yukon	1968	6.25	12.50	25.00
❏ LSP-4122	Snow in All Seasons	1969	6.25	12.50	25.00
❏ LSP-4306	Hank Snow Sings in Memory of Jimmie Rodgers	1970	5.00	10.00	20.00
❏ LSP-4379	Cure for the Blues	1970	5.00	10.00	20.00
❏ LSP-4501	Tracks and Trains	1971	5.00	10.00	20.00
❏ LSP-4601	Award Winners	1971	5.00	10.00	20.00
❏ LSP-4708	The Jimmie Rodgers Story	1972	3.75	7.50	15.00
❏ LSP-4798	The Best of Hank Snow, Vol. 2	1972	3.75	7.50	15.00
❏ AHL1-5497	Collector's Series	1986	2.50	5.00	10.00
❏ LPM-6014 [(2)M]	This Is My Story	1966	10.00	20.00	40.00
❏ LSP-6014 [(2)S]	This Is My Story	1966	12.50	25.00	50.00

READER'S DIGEST

❏ RDA-216 [(6)]	I'm Movin' On	197?	30.00	60.00	120.00

SCHOOL OF MUSIC

❏ 1149 [M]	The Guitar	1958	62.50	125.00	250.00
—Deduct 20 percent if instruction book is missing					

SNOW, HANK, AND CHET ATKINS
RCA VICTOR

❏ LPM-2952 [M]	Reminiscing	1964	6.25	12.50	25.00
❏ LSP-2952 [S]	Reminiscing	1964	7.50	15.00	30.00
❏ LSP-4254	By Special Request - C.B. Atkins and C.E. Snow	1970	5.00	10.00	20.00

SNOW, HANK, AND ANITA CARTER
RCA VICTOR

❏ LPM-2580 [M]	Together Again	1962	7.50	15.00	30.00
❏ LSP-2580 [S]	Together Again	1962	10.00	20.00	40.00

SNOW, HANK; PORTER WAGONER; HANK LOCKLIN
RCA VICTOR

❏ LPM-2723 [M]	Three Country Gentlemen	1963	7.50	15.00	30.00
❏ LSP-2723 [S]	Three Country Gentlemen	1963	10.00	20.00	40.00

SNOW, PHOEBE
COLUMBIA

❏ PC 33952	Second Childhood	1976	2.50	5.00	10.00
—Original with no bar code					
❏ PC 33952	Second Childhood	198?	2.00	4.00	8.00
—Budget-line reissue with bar code					
❏ PCQ 33952 [Q]	Second Childhood	1976	3.75	7.50	15.00
❏ PC 34387	It Looks Like Snow	1976	2.50	5.00	10.00
—Original with no bar code					
❏ PC 34387	It Looks Like Snow	198?	2.00	4.00	8.00
—Budget-line reissue with bar code					
❏ JC 34875	Never Letting Go	1977	2.50	5.00	10.00
❏ JC 35456	Against the Grain	1978	2.50	5.00	10.00
❏ JC 37091	The Best of Phoebe Snow	1981	2.50	5.00	10.00
❏ PC 37091	The Best of Phoebe Snow	1981	2.00	4.00	8.00
—Budget-line reissue					

DCC COMPACT CLASSICS

❏ LPZ-2027	Phoebe Snow	1996	7.50	15.00	30.00
—Audiophile vinyl					

ELEKTRA

❏ 60852	Something Real	1989	2.50	5.00	10.00

MCA

❏ 37119	Phoebe Snow	198?	2.00	4.00	8.00
—Budget-line reissue of Shelter LP					

MIRAGE

❏ SD 19297	Rock Away	1981	2.50	5.00	10.00

SHELTER

❏ 2109	Phoebe Snow	1974	2.50	5.00	10.00
❏ 52017	Phoebe Snow	1977	2.00	4.00	8.00
—Reissue with ABC distribution					

SNOWDEN, ELMER
RIVERSIDE

❏ RLP-348 [M]	Harlem Banjo	1960	5.00	10.00	20.00
❏ RS-9348 [S]	Harlem Banjo	1960	6.25	12.50	25.00

SNYDER, TERRY, AND THE ALL-STARS
See ENOCH LIGHT.

SOCIAL DISTORTION
EPIC

❏ E 46055	Social Distortion	1990	5.00	10.00	20.00
❏ E 47948	Somewhere Between Heaven and Hell	1992	5.00	10.00	20.00

EPIC/550 MUSIC

❏ E 64380	White Light, White Heat, White Trash	1996	3.00	6.00	12.00

RESTLESS

❏ 72251	Prison Bound	1988	5.00	10.00	20.00

Number	Title (A Side/B Side)	Yr	VG	VG+	NM
13TH FLOOR					
❏ SD 1301	Mommy's Little Monster	1983	10.00	20.00	40.00
—Standard cover with lyric sheet					
❏ SD 1301	Mommy's Little Monster	1983	15.00	30.00	60.00
—Gatefold cover					
TIME BOMB					
❏ 43500	Mommy's Little Monster	1995	2.50	5.00	10.00
❏ 43501	Prison Bound	1995	2.50	5.00	10.00
❏ 43502	Mainliner (Wreckage from the Past)	1995	2.50	5.00	10.00
❏ 43516 [(2)]	Live at the Roxy	1998	3.00	6.00	12.00
TRIPLE X					
❏ 51019	Mommy's Little Monster	1989	5.00	10.00	20.00
—Clear vinyl					
SOCIAL UNREST					
LIBERTINE					
❏ LSU 1 [EP]	Rat in a Maze	1982	6.25	12.50	25.00
❏ LSU 2461	SU-2000	1985	5.00	10.00	20.00
SOCIETY OF SEVEN					
SILVER SWORD					
❏ 7012	How Has Your Love Life Been?	1970	5.00	10.00	20.00
SOCOLOW, FRANK					
BETHLEHEM					
❏ BCP-70 [M]	Sounds By Socolow	1957	20.00	40.00	80.00
SOFT MACHINE, THE					
ACCORD					
❏ SN-7178	Memories	1981	2.50	5.00	10.00
COLUMBIA					
❏ G 30339 [(2)]	Third	1970	3.75	7.50	15.00
❏ C 30754	Fourth	1971	3.00	6.00	12.00
❏ KC 31604	5	1972	3.00	6.00	12.00
❏ KG 32260 [(2)]	Six	1973	3.75	7.50	15.00
❏ KC 32716	Seven	1974	3.00	6.00	12.00
COMMAND					
❏ 964 SD [(2)]	Soft Machine	1973	3.75	7.50	15.00
—Reissue of Probe LPs in one package					
PROBE					
❏ CPLP-4500	The Soft Machine	1968	10.00	20.00	40.00
—Cover with moving parts					
❏ CPLP-4500	The Soft Machine	1969	5.00	10.00	20.00
—Regular cover					
❏ CPLP-4505	The Soft Machine, Vol. 2	1969	6.25	12.50	25.00
SOFTWARE					
INNOVATIVE COMMUNICATION					
❏ KS 80.055 [(2)]	Electronic Universe	1987	5.00	10.00	20.00
SOLAL, MARTIAL					
CAPITOL					
❏ ST 10261 [S]	Martial Solal	1960	7.50	15.00	30.00
❏ T 10261 [M]	Martial Solal	1960	6.25	12.50	25.00
❏ ST 10354 [S]	Vive La France! Viva La Jazz! Vive Solal!	1961	6.25	12.50	25.00
❏ T 10354 [M]	Vive La France! Viva La Jazz! Vive Solal!	1961	5.00	10.00	20.00
CONTEMPORARY					
❏ C-2512 [10]	French Modern Sounds	1954	20.00	40.00	80.00
LIBERTY					
❏ LST-7335 [S]	Martial Solal in Concert	1963	5.00	10.00	20.00
MILESTONE					
❏ MLP-1001 [M]	Solal!	1967	6.25	12.50	25.00
RCA VICTOR					
❏ LSP-2777 [S]	Martial Solal at Newport '63	1963	5.00	10.00	20.00
SOMERSET STRINGS, THE					
EPIC					
❏ LN 3159 [M]	Music for Christmas at Home	1955	5.00	10.00	20.00
SOMMER, ELKE					
MGM					
❏ E-4321 [M]	Love in Any Language	1965	6.25	12.50	25.00
❏ SE-4321 [S]	Love in Any Language	1965	7.50	15.00	30.00
SOMMERS, JOANIE					
COLUMBIA					
❏ CL 2495 [M]	Come Alive	1966	5.00	10.00	20.00
❏ CS 9295 [S]	Come Alive	1966	6.25	12.50	25.00
DISCOVERY					
❏ DS-883	Dream	1983	3.00	6.00	12.00
—With Bob Florence					
WARNER BROS.					
❏ W 1346 [M]	Positively the Most	1960	7.50	15.00	30.00
❏ WS 1346 [S]	Positively the Most	1960	10.00	20.00	40.00
❏ B 1348 [M]	Behind Closed Doors at a Recording Session	1960	37.50	75.00	150.00
—Record comes in a box with a booklet included					
❏ W 1412 [M]	Joanie Sommers	1961	7.50	15.00	30.00
❏ WS 1412 [S]	Joanie Sommers	1961	10.00	20.00	40.00
❏ W 1436 [M]	For Those Who Think Young	1962	7.50	15.00	30.00
❏ WS 1436 [S]	For Those Who Think Young	1962	10.00	20.00	40.00
❏ W 1470 [M]	Johnny Get Angry	1962	10.00	20.00	40.00
❏ WS 1470 [S]	Johnny Get Angry	1962	12.50	25.00	50.00
❏ W 1474 [M]	Let's Talk About Love	1962	7.50	15.00	30.00
❏ WS 1474 [S]	Let's Talk About Love	1962	10.00	20.00	40.00
❏ W 1504 [M]	Sommers' Seasons	1963	6.25	12.50	25.00
❏ WS 1504 [S]	Sommers' Seasons	1963	7.50	15.00	30.00
❏ W 1575 [M]	Softly, The Brazilian Sound	1964	6.25	12.50	25.00
❏ WS 1575 [S]	Softly, The Brazilian Sound	1964	7.50	15.00	30.00

Number	Title (A Side/B Side)	Yr	VG	VG+	NM
SONDHEIM, ALAN					
ESP-DISK'					
❏ 1048 [S]	Ritual-All-7-70	1969	5.00	10.00	20.00
❏ 1082 [S]	T'Other Little Tune	1969	5.00	10.00	20.00
SONIC YOUTH					
DGC					
❏ 24297	Goo	1990	7.50	15.00	30.00
❏ 24485	Dirty	1992	5.00	10.00	20.00
❏ 24632	Experimental Jet Set, Trash and No Star	1994	5.00	10.00	20.00
❏ 24825 [(2)]	Washing Machine	1995	5.00	10.00	20.00
ENIGMA					
❏ 75403 [(2)]	Daydream Nation	1988	5.00	10.00	20.00
HOMESTEAD					
❏ HMS 016	Bad Moon Rising	1985	5.00	10.00	20.00
❏ HMS 021 [EP]	Death Valley '69	1985	5.00	10.00	20.00
—With Lydia Lunch					
MOBILE FIDELITY					
❏ 1-257	Goo	1996	10.00	20.00	40.00
—Audiophile vinyl					
MY SO-CALLED RECORDS					
❏ 3 [(2)]	A Thousand Leaves	1998	3.75	7.50	15.00
NEUTRAL					
❏ 001 [EP]	Sonic Youth	1982	12.50	25.00	50.00
❏ N-1 [EP]	Sonic Youth	1982	12.50	25.00	50.00
❏ 9	Confusion Is Sex	1983	10.00	20.00	40.00
RHINO					
❏ R1 71591	Made in U.S.A. (Soundtrack)	1995	3.75	7.50	15.00
—Clear vinyl record and sleeve; music recorded in 1986					
SST					
❏ 059	Evol	1986	5.00	10.00	20.00
❏ 080 [EP]	Starpower	1986	3.75	7.50	15.00
❏ 096	Confusion Is Sex	1987	5.00	10.00	20.00
—Reissue of Neutral 9					
❏ 097 [EP]	Sonic Youth	1987	3.00	6.00	12.00
❏ 134	Sister	1987	5.00	10.00	20.00
❏ 155 [EP]	Master Dik	1988	3.00	6.00	12.00
SYR					
❏ 1	Anagrama	1997	2.50	5.00	10.00
—Red vinyl					
❏ 2	Slaapkamers Met Slagroom	1997	2.50	5.00	10.00
—Teal vinyl					
❏ 3	Invito Al Cielo	1998	2.50	5.00	10.00
—With Jim O'Rourke; clear vinyl					
❏ 4 [(2)]	Goodbye 20th Century	1999	3.75	7.50	15.00
❏ 5 [(2)]	Kim Gordon - DJ Olive - Ikue Mori	2000	3.00	6.00	12.00
SONICS, THE (2)					
BEAT ROCKET					
❏ BR 114	Introducing the Sonics	199?	3.00	6.00	12.00
BOMP!					
❏ 4011	Sinderella	1980	3.75	7.50	15.00
BUCKSHOT					
❏ 001	Explosives	1973	50.00	100.00	200.00
ETIQUETTE					
❏ ETALB-024 [M]	Here Are the Sonics!!!	1965	50.00	100.00	200.00
—Purple label					
❏ ETALB-024 [M]	Here Are the Sonics!!!	1965	62.50	125.00	250.00
—Red label					
❏ ETLPS-024	Here Are the Sonics!!!	1984	2.50	5.00	10.00
—Purple label, flimsier vinyl, with date on back cover					
❏ ETLPS-024 [S]	Here Are the Sonics!!!	1965	75.00	150.00	300.00
—Purple label					
❏ ETLPS-024 [S]	Here Are the Sonics!!!	1965	100.00	200.00	400.00
—Red label					
❏ ETALB-027 [M]	The Sonics Boom	1966	75.00	150.00	300.00
❏ ETLPS-027	The Sonics Boom	1984	2.50	5.00	10.00
—Flimsier vinyl, with date on back cover					
❏ ETLPS-027 [R]	The Sonics Boom	1966	50.00	100.00	200.00
FIRST AMERICAN					
❏ FA-7715	Original Northwest Punk	1978	5.00	10.00	20.00
❏ FA-7719	Unreleased	1980	5.00	10.00	20.00
❏ FA-7779	Fire and Ice	1983	5.00	10.00	20.00
JERDEN					
❏ JRL-7007 [M]	Introducing the Sonics	1967	50.00	100.00	200.00
❏ JRS-7007 [R]	Introducing the Sonics	1967	37.50	75.00	150.00
SONICS, THE (2); THE WAILERS; THE GALAXIES					
ETIQUETTE					
❏ ETALB-025	Merry Christmas	1984	2.50	5.00	10.00
—Flimsier vinyl, with date on back cover					
❏ ETALB-025 [M]	Merry Christmas	1965	125.00	250.00	500.00
SONN, LARRY					
CORAL					
❏ CRL 57057 [M]	The Sound of Sonn	1956	10.00	20.00	40.00
DOT					
❏ DLP-9005 [M]	Jazz Band Having a Ball	1958	6.25	12.50	25.00
❏ DLP-29005 [S]	Jazz Band Having a Ball	1958	7.50	15.00	30.00
SONNY					
ATCO					
❏ 33-229 [M]	Inner Views	1967	5.00	10.00	20.00
❏ SD 33-229 [S]	Inner Views	1967	5.00	10.00	20.00
SONNY AND CHER					
ATCO					
❏ 33-177 [M]	Look At Us	1965	5.00	10.00	20.00
❏ SD 33-177 [S]	Look At Us	1965	6.25	12.50	25.00
❏ 33-183 [M]	The Wondrous World of Sonny and Cher	1966	3.75	7.50	15.00

Number	Title (A Side/B Side)	Yr	VG	VG+	NM
❑ SD 33-183 [S]	The Wondrous World of Sonny and Cher	1966	5.00	10.00	20.00
❑ 33-203 [M]	In Case You're in Love	1967	3.75	7.50	15.00
❑ SD 33-203 [S]	In Case You're in Love	1967	5.00	10.00	20.00
❑ 33-214 [M]	Good Times	1967	3.75	7.50	15.00
❑ SD 33-214 [S]	Good Times	1967	5.00	10.00	20.00
❑ 33-219 [M]	The Best of Sonny and Cher	1967	3.75	7.50	15.00
❑ SD 33-219 [P]	The Best of Sonny and Cher	1967	5.00	10.00	20.00

—"What Now My Love," "A Beautiful Story," "But You're Mine" and "Laugh at Me" are rechanneled

❑ SD 2-804 [(2)]	The Two of Us	1972	5.00	10.00	20.00

—Combines "Look at Us" and "In Case You're in Love"

❑ A2M 5177 [(2)M]	Sonny & Cher's Greatest Hits	1967	7.50	15.00	30.00

—Columbia Record Club exclusive

❑ A2S 5178 [(2)S]	Sonny & Cher's Greatest Hits	1967	7.50	15.00	30.00

—Columbia Record Club exclusive

❑ SD 11000	The Beat Goes On	1975	3.75	7.50	15.00

KAPP

❑ KS-3654	Sonny & Cher Live	1971	3.75	7.50	15.00
❑ KS-3660	All I Ever Need Is You	1972	3.75	7.50	15.00

MCA

❑ 2009	Sonny & Cher Live	1973	3.00	6.00	12.00

—Reissue of Kapp 3654

❑ 2021	All I Ever Need Is You	1973	3.00	6.00	12.00

—Reissue of Kapp 3660

❑ 2101	Mama Was a Rock & Roll Singer Papa Used to Write All Her Songs	1973	3.00	6.00	12.00
❑ 2117	Greatest Hits	1974	3.00	6.00	12.00
❑ 2-8004 [(2)]	Sonny & Cher Live in Las Vegas, Vol. 2	1973	3.75	7.50	15.00

PAIR

❑ PDL2-1140 [(2)]	Sonny & Cher At Their Best	1986	3.00	6.00	12.00

REPRISE

❑ R 6177 [M]	Baby Don't Go	1965	7.50	15.00	30.00
❑ RS 6177 [P]	Baby Don't Go	1965	7.50	15.00	30.00

—By "Sonny & Cher & Friends" (also includes The Lettermen, Bill Medley and The Blendells)

SONNY AND THE DEMONS
UNITED ARTISTS

❑ UAL-3316 [M]	Drag Kings	1964	12.50	25.00	50.00
❑ UAS-6316 [S]	Drag Kings	1964	15.00	30.00	60.00

SONS OF CHAMPLIN, THE
ARIOLA AMERICA

❑ SW-50002	The Sons of Champlin	1975	2.50	5.00	10.00
❑ ST-50007	A Circle Filled with Love	1976	2.50	5.00	10.00
❑ SW-50017	Loving Is Why	1977	2.50	5.00	10.00

CAPITOL

❑ SWBB-200 [(2)]	Loosen Up Naturally	1969	5.00	10.00	20.00

—With the F-word airbrushed off the cover artwork

❑ SWBB-200 [(2)]	Loosen Up Naturally	1969	6.25	12.50	25.00

—With the F-word scratched off the cover artwork

❑ SWBB-200 [(2)]	Loosen Up Naturally	1969	12.50	25.00	50.00

—With the F-word clearly visible as part of the cover artwork

❑ SKAO-322	The Sons	1969	6.25	12.50	25.00
❑ ST-675	Follow Your Heart	1971	5.00	10.00	20.00

COLUMBIA

❑ KC 32341	Welcome to the Dance	1973	3.75	7.50	15.00

GOLDMINE

❑ GM 94930	The Sons of Champlin	1975	5.00	10.00	20.00

SONS OF CHAMPLIN

❑ (no #)	Minus Seeds and Stems	1969	125.00	250.00	500.00

SONS OF HEROES
MCA

❑ 39010	Sons of Heroes	1983	5.00	10.00	20.00

SONS OF THE PIONEERS
COLUMBIA

❑ FC 37439	The Sons of the Pioneers: Columbia Historical Edition	1981	2.50	5.00	10.00

MCA

❑ 730	Tumbleweed Trails	198?	2.50	5.00	10.00

RCA CAMDEN

❑ CAL-413 [M]	Wagons West	1958	5.00	10.00	20.00
❑ CAS-413 [R]	Wagons West	1963	3.00	6.00	12.00
❑ CAL-587 [M]	Room Full of Roses	1960	5.00	10.00	20.00

RCA VICTOR

❑ PRM-104 [M]	Westward Ho!	1961	6.25	12.50	25.00

—Special-products issue

❑ LPM-1130 [M]	Favorite Cowboy Songs	1955	12.50	25.00	50.00
❑ LPM-1431 [M]	How Great Thou Art	1957	12.50	25.00	50.00
❑ LPM-1483 [M]	One Man's Songs	1957	12.50	25.00	50.00
❑ LPM-2118 [M]	Cool Water	1960	6.25	12.50	25.00
❑ LSP-2118 [S]	Cool Water	1960	7.50	15.00	30.00
❑ ANL1-2332	A Country-Western Songbook	1977	3.75	7.50	15.00
❑ LPM-2356 [M]	Lure of the West	1961	6.25	12.50	25.00
❑ LSP-2356 [S]	Lure of the West	1961	7.50	15.00	30.00
❑ LPM-2456 [M]	Tumbleweed Trails	1962	6.25	12.50	25.00
❑ LSP-2456 [S]	Tumbleweed Trails	1962	7.50	15.00	30.00
❑ LPM-2603 [M]	Our Men Out West	1963	5.00	10.00	20.00
❑ LSP-2603 [S]	Our Men Out West	1963	6.25	12.50	25.00
❑ LPM-2652 [M]	Hymns of the Cowboy	1963	5.00	10.00	20.00
❑ LSP-2652 [S]	Hymns of the Cowboy	1963	6.25	12.50	25.00
❑ LPM-2737 [M]	Trail Dust	1963	5.00	10.00	20.00
❑ LSP-2737 [S]	Trail Dust	1963	6.25	12.50	25.00
❑ LPM-2855 [M]	Country Fare	1964	5.00	10.00	20.00
❑ LSP-2855 [S]	Country Fare	1964	6.25	12.50	25.00
❑ LPM-2957 [M]	Down Memory Trail	1964	5.00	10.00	20.00
❑ LSP-2957 [S]	Down Memory Trail	1964	6.25	12.50	25.00
❑ LPM-3032 [10]	Cowboy Classics	1952	25.00	50.00	100.00
❑ LPM-3095 [10]	Cowboy Hymns and Spirituals	1952	25.00	50.00	100.00
❑ LPM-3162 [10]	Western Classics	1953	25.00	50.00	100.00

Number	Title (A Side/B Side)	Yr	VG	VG+	NM
❑ LPM-3351 [M]	Legends of the West	1965	3.75	7.50	15.00
❑ LSP-3351 [S]	Legends of the West	1965	5.00	10.00	20.00
❑ ANL1-3468	The Best of the Sons of the Pioneers	1980	2.50	5.00	10.00
❑ LPM-3476 [M]	The Best of Sons of the Pioneers	1966	3.75	7.50	15.00
❑ LSP-3476 [S]	The Best of Sons of the Pioneers	1966	5.00	10.00	20.00
❑ LPM-3554 [M]	The Songs of Bob Nolan	1966	3.75	7.50	15.00
❑ LSP-3554 [S]	The Songs of Bob Nolan	1966	5.00	10.00	20.00
❑ AYL1-3679	Cool Water	1980	2.50	5.00	10.00
❑ LPM-3714 [M]	Campfire Favorites	1967	6.25	12.50	25.00
❑ LSP-3714 [S]	Campfire Favorites	1967	5.00	10.00	20.00
❑ LPM-3964 [M]	South of the Border	1968	20.00	40.00	80.00
❑ LSP-3964 [S]	South of the Border	1968	5.00	10.00	20.00
❑ AYM1-4092	Let's Go West Again	1981	2.50	5.00	10.00

READER'S DIGEST

❑ RBA-135-A [(7)]	Down Memory Trail with the Sons of the Pioneers	1981	15.00	30.00	60.00

SONS OF THE PURPLE SAGE
TOPS

❑ L-1588 [M]	Western Favorites	1959	5.00	10.00	20.00

WALDORF

❑ 143 [10]	Songs of the Golden West	1955	12.50	25.00	50.00

SOPHOMORES, THE (1)
SEECO

❑ CELP-451 [M]	The Sophomores	1958	50.00	100.00	200.00

SOPWITH "CAMEL," THE
KAMA SUTRA

❑ KSBS-2063	Hello Hello	1973	5.00	10.00	20.00
❑ KLP-8060 [M]	The Sopwith Camel	1967	7.50	15.00	30.00
❑ KLPS-8060 [S]	The Sopwith Camel	1967	7.50	15.00	30.00

REPRISE

❑ MS 2108	The Miraculous Hump Returns	1973	6.25	12.50	25.00

SOTHERN, ANN
CRAFTSMAN

❑ C-8061 [M]	It's Ann Sothern Time	1961	5.00	10.00	20.00

TOPS

❑ L-1611 [M]	Sothern Exposure	1959	6.25	12.50	25.00

SOUL, JIMMY
SPQR

❑ E 16001	If You Wanna Be Happy	1963	37.50	75.00	150.00

SOUL CHILDREN, THE
EPIC

❑ PE 33902	Finders Keepers	1976	3.75	7.50	15.00
❑ PE 34455	Where Is Your Woman Tonight	1977	3.75	7.50	15.00

STAX

❑ STS-2018	Soul Children	1969	7.50	15.00	30.00
❑ STS-2043	The Best of Two Worlds	1971	7.50	15.00	30.00
❑ STS-3003	Genesis	1972	7.50	15.00	30.00
❑ STX-4105	Open Door Policy	1978	3.75	7.50	15.00
❑ STX-4120	Chronicle	1979	3.00	6.00	12.00
❑ STS-5507	Friction	1974	7.50	15.00	30.00

SOUL FINDERS, THE
RCA CAMDEN

❑ CAL-2170 [M]	Sweet Soul Music	1967	7.50	15.00	30.00
❑ CAS-2170 [S]	Sweet Soul Music	1967	7.50	15.00	30.00
❑ CAL-2239 [M]	An Explosive Album of Soul	1968	7.50	15.00	30.00
❑ CAS-2239 [S]	An Explosive Album of Soul	1968	7.50	15.00	30.00

SOUL FLUTES
A&M

❑ SP-3009	Trust in Me	1968	5.00	10.00	20.00

SOUL GENERATION, THE
EBONY SOUNDS

❑ 2000	Beyond Body and Soul	1972	5.00	10.00	20.00

SOUL SET, THE
JOHNSON

❑ 1001	The Soul Set	196?	6.25	12.50	25.00

SOUL SISTERS, THE
SUE

❑ LP-1022 [M]	I Can't Stand It	1964	50.00	100.00	200.00
❑ STLP-1022 [S]	I Can't Stand It	1964	100.00	200.00	400.00

SOUL SOCIETY, THE
DOT

❑ DLP-25842	Satisfaction	1969	6.25	12.50	25.00

SOUL STIRRERS, THE
SPECIALTY

❑ SP-2106 [M]	The Soul Stirrers Featuring Sam Cooke	1959	12.50	25.00	50.00

SOUL SURVIVORS
ATCO

❑ SD 33-277	Take Another Look	1969	6.25	12.50	25.00

CRIMSON

❑ CR-502 [M]	When the Whistle Blows Anything Goes	1967	12.50	25.00	50.00
❑ CR-502 S [S]	When the Whistle Blows Anything Goes	1967	7.50	15.00	30.00

TSOP

❑ KZ 33186	The Soul Survivors	1975	3.00	6.00	12.00

SOUND FOUNDATION
SMOBRO

❑ 9001	Sound Foundation	1971	6.25	12.50	25.00

Number	Title (A Side/B Side)	Yr	VG	VG+	NM

SOUND OF FEELING
LIMELIGHT
❏ LS-86063	Spleen	1969	5.00	10.00	20.00

SOUND SYMPOSIUM, THE
DOT
❏ DLP-3871 [M]	Paul Simon Interpreted	1968	7.50	15.00	30.00
—Stereo cover with white "Monaural" sticker; label is regular stock copy					
❏ DLP-25871 [S]	Paul Simon Interpreted	1968	5.00	10.00	20.00
❏ DLP-25952	Bob Dylan Interpreted	1969	5.00	10.00	20.00

SOUNDGARDEN
A&M
❏ 31454 0198 1 [(2)]Superunknown		1994	5.00	10.00	20.00
—Blue vinyl					
❏ 31454 0198 1 [(2)]Superunknown		1994	5.00	10.00	20.00
—Clear vinyl					
❏ 31454 0198 1 [(2)]Superunknown		1994	5.00	10.00	20.00
—Gold vinyl					
❏ SP-5252	Louder Than Love	1989	5.00	10.00	20.00
—Black vinyl					
❏ SP-5252	Louder Than Love	1989	10.00	20.00	40.00
—Red vinyl					
❏ SP-5252	Louder Than Love	1989	12.50	25.00	60.00
—Green vinyl					
❏ 75021 5374 1	Badmotorfinger	1991	6.25	12.50	25.00
—Limited edition on yellow vinyl					
❏ SP-17951 [DJ]	Louder Than Live	1990	12.50	25.00	50.00
—Promo-only live album on blue vinyl					
SST
❏ 201	Ultramega OK	1988	3.75	7.50	15.00
❏ 231 [EP]	Flower	1988	3.75	7.50	15.00
❏ 911 [10]	Flower	1988	3.75	5.00	10.00
SUB POP
❏ 12 [EP]	Screaming Life	1987	5.00	10.00	20.00
—Reissues on any color vinyl except black or orange					
❏ 12 [EP]	Screaming Life	1987	10.00	20.00	40.00
—Black vinyl					
❏ 12 [EP]	Screaming Life	1987	37.50	75.00	150.00
—First 500 copies on orange vinyl					
❏ 17 [EP]	Fopp	1988	12.50	25.00	50.00

SOUNDS OF OUR TIMES, THE
CAPITOL
❏ ST-117	Hey Jude	1969	3.00	6.00	12.00
❏ ST-8-0117	Hey Jude	1969	3.75	7.50	15.00
—Capitol Record Club edition					
❏ ST-182	Galveston	1969	3.00	6.00	12.00
❏ ST 2817 [S]	Music of the Flower Children	1968	3.00	6.00	12.00
❏ T 2817 [M]	Music of the Flower Children	1968	5.00	10.00	20.00
❏ ST 2892 [S]	The Sounds of Our Time Play "Love Is Blue"	1968	3.00	6.00	12.00
❏ T 2892 [M]	The Sounds of Our Time Play "Love Is Blue"	1968	6.25	12.50	25.00

SOUNDS ORCHESTRAL
JANUS
❏ JLS-3014	One More Time	197?	3.75	7.50	15.00
PARKWAY
❏ P 7046 [M]	Cast Your Fate to the Wind	1965	3.75	7.50	15.00
❏ SP 7046 [S]	Cast Your Fate to the Wind	1965	5.00	10.00	20.00
❏ P 7047 [M]	The Soul of Sounds Orchestral	1965	3.75	7.50	15.00
❏ SP 7047 [S]	The Soul of Sounds Orchestral	1965	5.00	10.00	20.00
❏ P 7050 [M]	Impressions of James Bond	1966	5.00	10.00	20.00
❏ SP 7050 [S]	Impressions of James Bond	1966	7.50	15.00	30.00

SOUNDSTAGE ALL-STARS, THE
DOT
❏ DLP-3204 [M]	More "Peter Gunn"	1959	6.25	12.50	25.00
❏ DLP-25204 [S]	More "Peter Gunn"	1959	7.50	15.00	30.00

SOUP
ARF ARM
❏ 1	Soup	1970	30.00	60.00	120.00
BIG TREE
❏ BTS 2007	The Album Soup	1971	6.25	12.50	25.00

SOUTH, EDDIE
MERCURY
❏ MG-20401 [M]	The Distinguished Violin of Eddie South	1959	7.50	15.00	30.00
❏ SR-60070 [S]	The Distinguished Violin of Eddie South	1959	6.25	12.50	25.00

SOUTH, JOE
ACCORD
❏ SN-7119	Party People	1981	2.50	5.00	10.00
CAPITOL
❏ ST-108	Introspect	1968	5.00	10.00	20.00
❏ ST-235	Games People Play	1969	3.75	7.50	15.00
❏ ST-392	Don't It Make You Want to Go Home	1969	3.75	7.50	15.00
❏ SM-450	Joe South's Greatest Hits	1977	2.00	4.00	8.00
—Reissue with new prefix					
❏ ST-450	Joe South's Greatest Hits	1970	3.75	7.50	15.00
❏ ST-637	So the Seeds Are Growing	1971	3.00	6.00	12.00
❏ ST-845	Joe South	1972	3.00	6.00	12.00
❏ ST-11074	A Look Inside	1972	3.00	6.00	12.00
ISLAND
❏ ILPS-9328	Midnight Rainbows	1975	2.50	5.00	10.00
MINE
❏ MSG-1100	Walkin' Shoes	1971	3.00	6.00	12.00
—Reissue with new title					
❏ MSG-1100	The Joe South Story	1971	3.75	7.50	15.00
NASHVILLE
❏ 2092	You're the Reason	1970	3.00	6.00	12.00
PICKWICK
❏ SPC-3314	Games People Play	197?	2.50	5.00	10.00

SOUTH 40
METROBEAT
❏ MBS-1000	Live at the Someplace Else	1968	6.25	12.50	25.00

SOUTH CENTRAL AVENUE MUNICIPAL BLUES BAND
BLUESWAY
❏ BL-6018	The Soul of Bonnie and Clyde	1968	6.25	12.50	25.00

SOUTHERN, HAL
SAGE & SAND
❏ 46	You Got a Man on Your Hands	1967	6.25	12.50	25.00

SOUTHERN, JERI
CAPITOL
❏ ST 1173 [S]	Jeri Southern Meets Cole Porter	1959	10.00	20.00	40.00
—Black colorband label, Capitol logo at left					
❏ ST 1173 [S]	Jeri Southern Meets Cole Porter	1963	5.00	10.00	20.00
—Black colorband label, Capitol logo at top					
❏ T 1173 [M]	Jeri Southern Meets Cole Porter	1959	7.50	15.00	30.00
—Black colorband label, Capitol logo at left					
❏ ST 1278 [S]	Jeri Southern at the Crescendo	1960	10.00	20.00	40.00
—Black colorband label, Capitol logo at left					
❏ ST 1278 [S]	Jeri Southern at the Crescendo	1963	5.00	10.00	20.00
—Black colorband label, Capitol logo at top					
❏ T 1278 [M]	Jeri Southern at the Crescendo	1960	7.50	15.00	30.00
—Black colorband label, Capitol logo at left					
DECCA
❏ DL 5531 [10]	Intimate Songs	1954	20.00	40.00	80.00
❏ DL 8055 [M]	Southern Style	1955	12.50	25.00	50.00
❏ DL 8214 [M]	You Better Go Now	1956	12.50	25.00	50.00
❏ DL 8394 [M]	When Your Heart's on Fire	1956	12.50	25.00	50.00
❏ DL 8472 [M]	Jeri Southern Gently Jumps	1957	12.50	25.00	50.00
❏ DL 8745 [M]	Prelude to a Kiss	1958	12.50	25.00	50.00
❏ DL 8761 [M]	Southern Hospitality	1958	12.50	25.00	50.00
ROULETTE
❏ R-25039 [M]	Coffee, Cigarettes and Memories	1958	10.00	20.00	40.00
❏ R-52010 [M]	Southern Breeze	1958	10.00	20.00	40.00
❏ RS-52010 [S]	Southern Breeze	1958	12.50	25.00	50.00
❏ R-52016 [M]	Jeri Southern Meets Johnny Smith	1958	10.00	20.00	40.00
❏ RS-52016 [S]	Jeri Southern Meets Johnny Smith	1958	12.50	25.00	50.00

SOUTHERN CULTURE ON THE SKIDS
LLOYD STREET
❏ SP 002	Southern Culture on the Skids	1985	6.25	12.50	25.00
SAFEHOUSE
❏ SH-2114 [PD]	Ditch Diggin'	1994	5.00	10.00	20.00
TELSTAR
❏ 20	Dirt Track Date	1995	3.00	6.00	12.00
❏ TR 30	Plastic Seat Sweat	1997	3.00	6.00	12.00
❏ 40	Liquored Up and Lacquered Down	2000	3.00	6.00	12.00

SOUTHSIDE JOHNNY AND THE ASBURY JUKES
ATLANTIC
❏ 81654	At Least We Got Shoes	1986	2.00	4.00	8.00
CYPRESS
❏ YL-0115	Slow Dance	1988	2.50	5.00	10.00
EPIC
❏ AS 275 [DJ]	Jukes Live at the Bottom Line	1976	7.50	15.00	30.00
❏ PE 34180	I Don't Want to Go Home	1976	2.50	5.00	10.00
—Orange label, no bar code					
❏ PE 34180	I Don't Want to Go Home	1979	2.00	4.00	8.00
—Dark blue label, most have bar codes on back cover					
❏ PE 34668	This Time It's for Real	1977	2.50	5.00	10.00
—Orange label, no bar code					
❏ PE 34668	This Time It's for Real	198?	2.00	4.00	8.00
—Dark blue label, bar code on back cover					
❏ JE 35488	Hearts of Stone	1978	2.50	5.00	10.00
—Orange label, no bar code					
❏ PE 35488	Hearts of Stone	198?	2.00	4.00	8.00
—Dark blue label, bar code on back cover					
❏ JE 36246	Havin' a Party with Southside Johnny	1979	2.50	5.00	10.00
❏ PE 36246	Havin' a Party with Southside Johnny	198?	2.00	4.00	8.00
—Budget-line reissue with new prefix					
MERCURY
❏ SRM-1-3793	The Jukes	1979	2.50	5.00	10.00
❏ SRM-1-3836	Love Is a Sacrifice	1980	2.50	5.00	10.00
❏ SRM-2-8602 [(2)]Live — Reach Out and Touch the Sky		1981	3.00	6.00	12.00
❏ 826285-1 [(2)]	Live — Reach Out and Touch the Sky	198?	2.50	5.00	10.00
—Reissue of 8602					
MIRAGE
❏ 90113	Trash It Up!	1983	2.50	5.00	10.00
❏ 90186	In the Heat	1984	2.50	5.00	10.00

SOUTHWEST F.O.B.
HIP
❏ 7001	Smell of Incense	1969	7.50	15.00	30.00

SOVINE, RED
CHART
❏ 1052	The Greatest Grand Ol' Opry	1972	3.75	7.50	15.00
❏ 2056	It'll Come Back	1974	3.75	7.50	15.00
DECCA
❏ DL 4445 [M]	Red Sovine	1963	7.50	15.00	30.00
❏ DL 4736 [M]	Country Music Time	1966	7.50	15.00	30.00
❏ DL 74445 [R]	Red Sovine	1963	5.00	10.00	20.00
❏ DL 74736 [R]	Country Music Time	1966	5.00	10.00	20.00
GUSTO
❏ 3010	16 All-Time Favorites	1978	3.00	6.00	12.00
MGM
❏ E-3465 [M]	Red Sovine	1957	15.00	30.00	60.00

Number	Title (A Side/B Side)	Yr	VG	VG+	NM
NASHVILLE					
❏ 2033	Giddy-Up Go	196?	3.00	6.00	12.00
❏ 2044	A Dear John Letter	196?	3.00	6.00	12.00
❏ 2056	Anytime	196?	3.00	6.00	12.00
❏ 2083	Don't Take Your Love to Town	1969	3.00	6.00	12.00
POWER PAK					
❏ 270	Phantom 309	197?	2.50	5.00	10.00
STARDAY					
❏ SLP-132 [M]	The One and Only Red Sovine	1961	10.00	20.00	40.00
❏ SLP-197 [M]	Golden Country Ballads of the 1960s	1962	10.00	20.00	40.00
❏ SLP-341 [M]	Little Rosa	1965	6.25	12.50	25.00
❏ SLP-357	That's Truckdrivin'	196?	5.00	10.00	20.00
❏ SLP-363 [M]	Giddy-Up Go	1966	5.00	10.00	20.00
❏ SLP-383 [M]	Town and Country Action	1966	5.00	10.00	20.00
❏ SLP-396 [M]	The Nashville Sound of Red Sovine	1967	5.00	10.00	20.00
❏ SLP-405 [M]	I Didn't Jump the Fence	1967	5.00	10.00	20.00
❏ SLP-414 [M]	Phantom 309	1967	5.00	10.00	20.00
❏ SLP-420	Tell Maude I Slipped	1968	5.00	10.00	20.00
❏ SLP-427	Sunday with Sovine	1968	5.00	10.00	20.00
❏ SLP-436	Classic Narrations	1968	5.00	10.00	20.00
❏ SLP-441	Closing Time 'Til Dawn	1969	5.00	10.00	20.00
❏ SLP-445	Who Am I	1969	5.00	10.00	20.00
❏ SLP-459	I Know You're Married But I Love You Still	1970	5.00	10.00	20.00
❏ 952	The Best of Red Sovine	197?	3.75	7.50	15.00
❏ 968	Teddy Bear	1976	3.75	7.50	15.00
❏ 970	Woodrow Wilson Sovine	1977	3.75	7.50	15.00
❏ 991	Red Sovine's 16 Greatest Hits	1977	3.75	7.50	15.00
VOCALION					
❏ VL 3829 [M]	The Country Way	196?	3.75	7.50	15.00
❏ VL 73829 [R]	The Country Way	196?	3.00	6.00	12.00
SPACE					
HAND					
❏ 5167	Space	1969	6.25	12.50	25.00
SPACEMEN, THE					
ROULETTE					
❏ R-25275 [M]	Rockin' in the 25th Century	1964	7.50	15.00	30.00
❏ SR-25275 [S]	Rockin' in the 25th Century	1964	10.00	20.00	40.00
❏ R-25322 [M]	Music for Batman and Robin	1966	10.00	20.00	40.00
❏ SR-25322 [S]	Music for Batman and Robin	1966	12.50	25.00	50.00
SPANDAU BALLET					
CHRYSALIS					
❏ CHR 1331	Journeys to Glory	1981	3.00	6.00	12.00
❏ CHR 1353	Diamond	1982	2.50	5.00	10.00
❏ FV 41331	Journeys to Glory	198?	2.00	4.00	8.00
—Reissue					
❏ FV 41353	Diamond	1983	2.00	4.00	8.00
—Reissue					
❏ PV 41353	Diamond	1986	2.00	4.00	8.00
—Reissue					
❏ B6V 41403	True	1983	3.00	6.00	12.00
❏ FV 41403	True	1983	2.00	4.00	8.00
—Reissue					
❏ FV 41473	Parade	1984	2.50	5.00	10.00
❏ FV 41498	The Singles Collection	1985	2.50	5.00	10.00
EPIC					
❏ FE 40642	Through the Barricades	1987	3.00	6.00	12.00
MOBILE FIDELITY					
❏ 1-152	True	1984	5.00	10.00	20.00
—Audiophile vinyl					
SPANIELS, THE					
LOST-NITE					
❏ LLP-19 [10]	The Spaniels	1981	3.00	6.00	12.00
—Red vinyl					
VEE JAY					
❏ LP-1002 [M]	Goodnite, It's Time to Go	1958	150.00	300.00	600.00
—Maroon label; group pictured on cover					
❏ LP-1002 [M]	Goodnite, It's Time to Go	1961	50.00	100.00	200.00
—Black label; dogs on cover					
❏ VJLP-1002 [M]	Goodnite, It's Time to Go	198?	3.00	6.00	12.00
—Legitimate reissue on flimsier vinyl than originals					
❏ LP-1024 [M]	The Spaniels	1960	75.00	150.00	300.00
SPANIER, MUGGSY					
COMMODORE					
❏ FL-20009 [10]	Spanier's Ragtimers	1950	25.00	50.00	100.00
❏ FL-30016 [M]	Chicago Jazz	1957	12.50	25.00	50.00
DECCA					
❏ DL 5552 [10]	Hot Horn	1955	15.00	30.00	60.00
EMARCY					
❏ MG-26011 [10]	Muggsy Spanier and His Dixieland Band	1954	25.00	50.00	100.00
LONDON					
❏ AL-3503 [S]	Muggsy, Tesch and the Chicagoans	195?	7.50	15.00	30.00
❏ LL 3528 [M]	Muggsy Spanier and the Bucktown Five	1959	10.00	20.00	40.00
MERCURY					
❏ MG-20171 [M]	Muggsy Spanier and His Dixieland Band	1956	12.50	25.00	50.00
❏ MG-25095 [10]	Muggsy Spanier and His Dixieland Band	1953	30.00	60.00	120.00
RCA VICTOR					
❏ LPM-1295 [M]	The Great 16	1956	12.50	25.00	50.00
❏ LPM-3043 [10]	Ragtime Favorites	195?	30.00	60.00	120.00
RIVERSIDE					
❏ RLP 12-107 [M]	Classic Early Recordings	1955	15.00	30.00	60.00
❏ RLP-1004 [10]	Muggsy Spanier and Frank Teschemacher	1953	30.00	60.00	120.00
❏ RLP-1035 [10]	Muggsy Spanier and His Bucktown Five	1954	30.00	60.00	120.00
STINSON					
❏ SLP 30 [M]	Muggsy Spanier's Ragtimers, Vol. 1	1962	6.25	12.50	25.00
—Black vinyl					

Number	Title (A Side/B Side)	Yr	VG	VG+	NM
❏ SLP 30 [M]	Muggsy Spanier's Ragtimers, Vol. 1	1962	12.50	25.00	50.00
—Red vinyl					
❏ SLP 31 [M]	Muggsy Spanier's Ragtimers, Vol. 2	1962	6.25	12.50	25.00
—Black vinyl					
❏ SLP 31 [M]	Muggsy Spanier's Ragtimers, Vol. 2	1962	12.50	25.00	50.00
—Red vinyl					
WEATHERS INDUSTRIES					
❏ W-5401 [M]	Dynamic Dixie	1954	15.00	30.00	60.00
ZEE GEE					
❏ 101 [10]	Muggsy Spanier's Ragtimers, Vol. 1	195?	30.00	60.00	120.00
❏ 102 [10]	Muggsy Spanier's Ragtimers, Vol. 2	195?	30.00	60.00	120.00
SPANKY AND OUR GANG					
EPIC					
❏ PE 33580	Change	1975	3.00	6.00	12.00
MERCURY					
❏ MG-21124 [M]	Spanky and Our Gang	1967	7.50	15.00	30.00
❏ SR-61124 [S]	Spanky and Our Gang	1967	5.00	10.00	20.00
❏ SR-61161	Like to Get to Know You	1968	5.00	10.00	20.00
❏ SR-61183	Anything You Choose/Without Rhyme or Reason	1969	5.00	10.00	20.00
❏ SR-61227	Spanky's Greatest Hit(s)	1969	5.00	10.00	20.00
❏ SR-61326	Live	1971	3.75	7.50	15.00
RHINO					
❏ RNLP-70131	The Best of Spanky and Our Gang (1967-1969)	1986	3.00	6.00	12.00
SPANN, LES					
JAZZLAND					
❏ JLP-35 [M]	Gemini	1961	6.25	12.50	25.00
❏ JLP-935 [S]	Gemini	1961	7.50	15.00	30.00
SPANN, LUCILLE					
BLUESWAY					
❏ BLS-6070	Cry Before I Go	1974	6.25	12.50	25.00
SPANN, OTIS					
BARNABY					
❏ Z 30246	Otis Spann Is the Blues	1970	5.00	10.00	20.00
❏ KZ 31290	Walking the Blues	1972	5.00	10.00	20.00
BLUE HORIZON					
❏ BH 4802	The Biggest Thing Since Colossus	1970	6.25	12.50	25.00
BLUES TIME					
❏ 9006	Sweet Giant of the Blues	1970	5.00	10.00	20.00
BLUESWAY					
❏ BL-6003 [M]	The Blues Is Where It's At	1967	6.25	12.50	25.00
❏ BLS-6003 [S]	The Blues Is Where It's At	1967	6.25	12.50	25.00
❏ BLS-6013	The Bottom of the Blues	1968	6.25	12.50	25.00
❏ BLS-6063	Heart Loaded with Trouble	1973	5.00	10.00	20.00
CANDID					
❏ CM-8001 [M]	Otis Spann Is the Blues	1966	37.50	75.00	150.00
❏ CS-9001 [S]	Otis Spann Is the Blues	1966	50.00	100.00	200.00
LONDON					
❏ PS 543	Raw Blues	1968	7.50	15.00	30.00
❏ PS 551	Cracked Spanner Head	1969	7.50	15.00	30.00
PRESTIGE					
❏ PRST-7719	The Blues Will Never Die	1969	5.00	10.00	20.00
TESTAMENT					
❏ T-2211	Otis Spann's Chicago Blues	1966	10.00	20.00	40.00
VANGUARD					
❏ VSD-6514	Cryin' Time	1970	5.00	10.00	20.00
SPARKS					
ANTILLES					
❏ ANT-7044	Kimono My House	198?	2.50	5.00	10.00
—Reissue of Island 9272					
ATLANTIC					
❏ SD 19347	Angst in My Pants	1982	2.50	5.00	10.00
❏ 80055	Sparks in Outer Space	1983	2.50	5.00	10.00
❏ 80160	Pulling Rabbits Out of a Hat	1984	2.50	5.00	10.00
BEARSVILLE					
❏ BV 2048	Halfnelson	1971	6.25	12.50	25.00
—Original issue of "Sparks" as "Halfnelson"					
❏ BV 2048	Sparks	1972	3.00	6.00	12.00
—Reissue under the group's new name					
❏ BR 2110	A Woofer in Tweeter's Clothing	1973	3.00	6.00	12.00
COLUMBIA					
❏ PC 34359	Big Beat	1976	2.50	5.00	10.00
—Originals have no bar code					
❏ PC 34901	Introducing Sparks	1977	2.50	5.00	10.00
—Originals have no bar code					
ELEKTRA					
❏ 6E-186	No. 1 in Heaven	1979	2.50	5.00	10.00
ISLAND					
❏ ILPS-9272	Kimono My House	1974	3.00	6.00	12.00
—Originals have multicolor island-scene label					
❏ ILPS-9312	Propaganda	1975	3.00	6.00	12.00
—Originals have multicolor island-scene label					
❏ ILPS-9345	Indiscreet	1975	3.00	6.00	12.00
—Originals have black label and no Warner Bros. distribution					
MCA CURB					
❏ 5780	Music That You Can Dance To	1986	2.50	5.00	10.00
RCA VICTOR					
❏ AFL1-4091	Whomp That Sucker	1981	2.50	5.00	10.00
RHINO					
❏ R1-70841	Interior Design	1988	2.50	5.00	10.00

S

Number	Title (A Side/B Side)	Yr	VG	VG+	NM

SPARKS, MELVIN
PRESTIGE
Number	Title (A Side/B Side)	Yr	VG	VG+	NM
❏ 10001	Sparks!	1971	5.00	10.00	20.00
❏ 10016	Spark Plug	1972	5.00	10.00	20.00
❏ 10039	Akilah!	1973	5.00	10.00	20.00

WESTBOUND
Number	Title (A Side/B Side)	Yr	VG	VG+	NM
❏ 204	Melvin Sparks '75	1975	5.00	10.00	20.00

SPARKS, RANDY
VERVE
Number	Title (A Side/B Side)	Yr	VG	VG+	NM
❏ MGV-2103 [M]	Randy Sparks	1959	7.50	15.00	30.00
❏ MGV-2126 [M]	Walkin' the Low Road	1960	7.50	15.00	30.00
❏ MGV-2143 [M]	Randy Sparks Three	1960	7.50	15.00	30.00

SPARROW, THE
COLUMBIA
Number	Title (A Side/B Side)	Yr	VG	VG+	NM
❏ CS 9758	John Kay and Sparrow	1969	10.00	20.00	40.00
—Red "360 Sound" label					

SPARROWS, THE
ELKAY
Number	Title (A Side/B Side)	Yr	VG	VG+	NM
❏ 3009 [M]	That Mersey Sound	1964	10.00	20.00	40.00

SPATS, THE
ABC-PARAMOUNT
Number	Title (A Side/B Side)	Yr	VG	VG+	NM
❏ 502 [M]	Cookin' with the Spats	1965	5.00	10.00	20.00
❏ S-502 [S]	Cookin' with the Spats	1965	7.50	15.00	30.00

SPEARS, BILLIE JO
CAPITOL
Number	Title (A Side/B Side)	Yr	VG	VG+	NM
❏ ST-114	The Voice of Billie Jo Spears	1969	5.00	10.00	20.00
❏ ST-224	Mr. Walker, It's All Over!	1969	3.75	7.50	15.00
❏ ST-397	Miss Sincerity	1969	3.75	7.50	15.00
❏ ST-454	With Love	1970	3.75	7.50	15.00
❏ ST-560	Country Girl	1970	3.75	7.50	15.00
❏ ST-688	Just Singin'	1971	3.75	7.50	15.00
❏ SM-11887	The Best of Billie Jo Spears	1979	2.50	5.00	10.00

LIBERTY
Number	Title (A Side/B Side)	Yr	VG	VG+	NM
❏ LT-1074	Only the Hits	1981	2.00	4.00	8.00
❏ LN-10018	Blanket on the Ground	1980	2.00	4.00	8.00
❏ LN-10019	Love Ain't Gonna Wait for Us	1980	2.00	4.00	8.00
❏ LN-10020	I Will Survive	1980	2.00	4.00	8.00
❏ LN-10021	If You Want Me	1980	2.00	4.00	8.00

UNITED ARTISTS
Number	Title (A Side/B Side)	Yr	VG	VG+	NM
❏ UA-LA390-G	Blanket on the Ground	1975	2.50	5.00	10.00
❏ UA-LA508-G	Billie Jo	1975	2.50	5.00	10.00
❏ UA-LA608-G	What I've Got in Mind	1976	2.50	5.00	10.00
❏ UA-LA684-G	I'm Not Easy	1976	2.50	5.00	10.00
❏ UA-LA748-G	If You Want Me	1977	2.50	5.00	10.00
❏ UA-LA859-G	Lonely Hearts Club	1977	2.50	5.00	10.00
❏ UA-LA921-H	Love Ain't Gonna Wait for Us	1978	2.50	5.00	10.00
❏ LT-983	The Singles Album	1979	2.50	5.00	10.00
❏ LT-1018	Standing Tall	1980	2.50	5.00	10.00

SPELLBINDERS, THE
COLUMBIA
Number	Title (A Side/B Side)	Yr	VG	VG+	NM
❏ CL 2514 [M]	The Magic of the Spellbinders	1966	5.00	10.00	20.00
❏ CS 9314 [S]	The Magic of the Spellbinders	1966	6.25	12.50	25.00

SPENCE, ALEXANDER "SKIP"
Also see MOBY GRAPE.
COLUMBIA
Number	Title (A Side/B Side)	Yr	VG	VG+	NM
❏ CS 9831	Oar	1969	15.00	30.00	60.00

SUNDAZED
Number	Title (A Side/B Side)	Yr	VG	VG+	NM
❏ LP 5030	Oar	2000	3.00	6.00	12.00
—Reissue on 180-gram vinyl					

SPENCER, JON, BLUES EXPLOSION
MATADOR
Number	Title (A Side/B Side)	Yr	VG	VG+	NM
❏ (# unknown) [DJ]	Controversial Negro	1997	7.50	15.00	30.00
—Promo-only vinyl issue of a Japanese live CD					
❏ OLE 52-1	Extra Width	1993	3.00	6.00	12.00
❏ OLE 105-1	Orange	1994	2.50	5.00	10.00
❏ OLE 193-1	Now I Got Worry	1996	2.50	5.00	10.00
❏ OLE 322-1	Acme	1998	2.50	5.00	10.00
❏ OLE 376-1 [(2)]	Xtra-Acme USA	1999	3.75	7.50	15.00

SPENCER, LEON, JR.
PRESTIGE
Number	Title (A Side/B Side)	Yr	VG	VG+	NM
❏ 10011	Sneak Preview!	1971	5.00	10.00	20.00
❏ 10033	Louisiana Slim	1972	5.00	10.00	20.00
❏ 10042	Bad Walking Woman	1973	5.00	10.00	20.00

SPIDER-MAN
LIFESONG
Number	Title (A Side/B Side)	Yr	VG	VG+	NM
❏ LS 6001	Rock Reflections of a Superhero	1976	6.25	12.50	25.00

SPIDERS, THE (1)
IMPERIAL
Number	Title (A Side/B Side)	Yr	VG	VG+	NM
❏ LP-9142 [M]	I Didn't Wanna Do It	1961	150.00	300.00	600.00

SPINNERS
ATLANTIC
Number	Title (A Side/B Side)	Yr	VG	VG+	NM
❏ SD 2-910 [(2)]	Spinners Live!	1975	3.75	7.50	15.00
❏ QD 7256 [Q]	Spinners	1974	5.00	10.00	20.00
❏ SD 7256	Spinners	1973	3.00	6.00	12.00
❏ SD 7296	Mighty Love	1974	3.00	6.00	12.00
❏ SD 16032	Labor of Love	1981	2.50	5.00	10.00
❏ QD 18118 [Q]	New and Improved	1974	5.00	10.00	20.00
❏ SD 18118	New and Improved	1974	3.00	6.00	12.00
❏ SD 18141	Pick of the Litter	1975	3.00	6.00	12.00
❏ SD 18181	Happiness is Being with the Spinners	1976	3.00	6.00	12.00
❏ SD 19100	Yesterday, Today & Tomorrow	1977	3.00	6.00	12.00
❏ SD 19146	Spinners/8	1977	3.00	6.00	12.00
❏ SD 19179	The Best of the Spinners	1978	3.00	6.00	12.00
❏ SD 19219	From Here to Eternally	1979	3.00	6.00	12.00
❏ SD 19256	Dancin' and Lovin'	1980	2.50	5.00	10.00
❏ SD 19270	Love Trippin'	1980	2.50	5.00	10.00
❏ SD 19318	Can't Shake This Feelin'	1981	2.50	5.00	10.00
❏ 80020	Grand Slam	1982	2.50	5.00	10.00

MIRAGE
Number	Title (A Side/B Side)	Yr	VG	VG+	NM
❏ 90456	Lovin' Feelings	1985	2.50	5.00	10.00

MOTOWN
Number	Title (A Side/B Side)	Yr	VG	VG+	NM
❏ M5-109V1	Motown Superstar Series, Vol. 9	1982	2.00	4.00	8.00
❏ M5-132V1	The Original Spinners	1981	3.00	6.00	12.00
—Reissue of Motown 639					
❏ M5-199V1	The Best of the Spinners	1981	3.00	6.00	12.00
—Reissue of Motown 769					
❏ M 639 [M]	The Original Spinners	1967	6.25	12.50	25.00
❏ MS 639 [P]	The Original Spinners	1967	7.50	15.00	30.00
❏ M 769	The Best of the Spinners	1973	3.75	7.50	15.00

V.I.P.
Number	Title (A Side/B Side)	Yr	VG	VG+	NM
❏ 405	2nd Time Around	1970	10.00	20.00	40.00

VOLT
Number	Title (A Side/B Side)	Yr	VG	VG+	NM
❏ V-3403	Down to Business	1989	3.00	6.00	12.00

SPINNERS, THE
TIME
Number	Title (A Side/B Side)	Yr	VG	VG+	NM
❏ S-2092 [S]	Party — My Pad After Surfin'	1963	7.50	15.00	30.00
❏ 52092 [M]	Party — My Pad After Surfin'	1963	6.25	12.50	25.00

SPIRAL STARECASE
COLUMBIA
Number	Title (A Side/B Side)	Yr	VG	VG+	NM
❏ CS 9852	More Today Than Yesterday	1969	6.25	12.50	25.00
—"360 Sound" label					

SPIRIT
EPIC
Number	Title (A Side/B Side)	Yr	VG	VG+	NM
❏ E 30267	Twelve Dreams of Dr. Sardonicus	1970	5.00	10.00	20.00
—Yellow label					
❏ KE 30267	Twelve Dreams of Dr. Sardonicus	1973	2.50	5.00	10.00
—Orange label					
❏ PE 30267	Twelve Dreams of Dr. Sardonicus	197?	2.00	4.00	8.00
—Orange or dark blue label, with or without bar code					
❏ KE 31175	Feedback	1972	5.00	10.00	20.00
—Yellow label					
❏ KE 31175	Feedback	1973	2.50	5.00	10.00
—Orange label					
❏ KEG 31457 [(2)]	Spirit	1972	3.75	7.50	15.00
—Reissue of Ode 44004 and 44016 in one package; yellow labels					
❏ PEG 31457 [(2)]	Spirit	197?	3.00	6.00	12.00
—Reissue with new prefix and orange labels					
❏ KE 31461	The Family That Plays Together	1972	3.00	6.00	12.00
—Reissue of Ode 44014 with slightly different cover; yellow label					
❏ KE 31461	The Family That Plays Together	1973	2.50	5.00	10.00
—Orange label					
❏ KE 32271	The Best of Spirit	1973	3.00	6.00	12.00
❏ PE 32271	The Best of Spirit	1979	2.00	4.00	8.00
—Dark blue label; bar code on cover					
❏ BG 33761 [(2)]	The Family That Plays Together/Feedback	1976	3.00	6.00	12.00

I.R.S.
Number	Title (A Side/B Side)	Yr	VG	VG+	NM
❏ 82007	Rapture in the Chambers	1989	3.00	6.00	12.00

MERCURY
Number	Title (A Side/B Side)	Yr	VG	VG+	NM
❏ SRM-2-804 [(2)]	Spirit of '76	1975	3.75	7.50	15.00
❏ SRM-1-1053	Son of Spirit	1975	3.00	6.00	12.00
❏ SRM-1-1094	Farther Along	1976	3.00	6.00	12.00
❏ SRM-1-1122	Future Games	1977	3.00	6.00	12.00
❏ 818514-1	Spirit of '84	1984	2.50	5.00	10.00

ODE
Number	Title (A Side/B Side)	Yr	VG	VG+	NM
❏ Z12 44004	Spirit	1968	6.25	12.50	25.00
❏ Z12 44014	The Family That Plays Together	1968	6.25	12.50	25.00
❏ Z12 44016	Clear Spirit	1969	6.25	12.50	25.00

POTATO
Number	Title (A Side/B Side)	Yr	VG	VG+	NM
❏ 2001	Live	1978	2.50	5.00	10.00

RHINO
Number	Title (A Side/B Side)	Yr	VG	VG+	NM
❏ RNSP-303	Potatoland	1981	2.50	5.00	10.00

SUNDAZED
Number	Title (A Side/B Side)	Yr	VG	VG+	NM
❏ LP 5067	Now or Anywhere	2000	3.00	6.00	12.00
❏ LP 5068	Eventide	2000	3.00	6.00	12.00
❏ LP 5082	Clear	2001	3.00	6.00	12.00
❏ LP 5085	The Family That Plays Together	2001	3.00	6.00	12.00

SPIRITS AND WORM
A&M
Number	Title (A Side/B Side)	Yr	VG	VG+	NM
❏ SP-4229	Spirits and Worm	1969	200.00	400.00	800.00

SPIVEY, VICTORIA
SPIVEY
Number	Title (A Side/B Side)	Yr	VG	VG+	NM
❏ LP-1001 [M]	Basket of Blues	1962	6.25	12.50	25.00
❏ LP-1002 [M]	Victoria and Her Blues	1963	6.25	12.50	25.00
❏ LP-1004 [M]	Three Kings and a Queen	196?	7.50	15.00	30.00
—"Historic Tracks, Bob Dylan Appears with Big Joe Williams" blurb on cover					
❏ LP-1004 [M]	Three Kings and a Queen	1964	12.50	25.00	50.00
—Bob Dylan plays on this LP; no blurb on cover					
❏ LP-1006 [M]	The Queen and Her Knights	1964	6.25	12.50	25.00
❏ LP-1008 [M]	The Bluesmen of the Muddy Waters Band	1964	6.25	12.50	25.00
❏ LP-1009 [M]	Encore for the Chicago Blues	1964	6.25	12.50	25.00
❏ LP-1010 [M]	The Bluesmen of the Muddy Waters Band, Volume Two	1964	6.25	12.50	25.00
❏ LP-1012 [M]	Spivey's Blues Parade	196?	6.25	12.50	25.00
❏ LP-1014 [M]	Three Kings and a Queen, Volume Two	196?	6.25	12.50	25.00
❏ LP-1015 [M]	Spivey's Blues Cavalcade	196?	6.25	12.50	25.00
❏ LP-1017 [M]	Spivey's Blues Showcase	196?	6.25	12.50	25.00
❏ LP-2001 [M]	Recorded Legacy of the Blues	196?	6.25	12.50	25.00

Number	Title (A Side/B Side)	Yr	VG	VG+	NM

SPOELSTRA, MARK
ELEKTRA
❏ EKL-283 [M]	Five and Twenty Questions	1965	5.00	10.00	20.00
❏ EKL-307 [M]	State of Mind	1966	5.00	10.00	20.00
❏ EKS-7283 [S]	Five and Twenty Questions	1965	6.25	12.50	25.00
❏ EKS-7307 [S]	State of Mind	1966	6.25	12.50	25.00
VERVE FOLKWAYS
| ❏ FV-9018 [M] | The Times I've Had | 196? | 5.00 | 10.00 | 20.00 |
| ❏ FVS-9018 [S] | The Times I've Had | 196? | 6.25 | 12.50 | 25.00 |

SPOKESMEN, THE
DECCA
| ❏ DL 4712 [M] | The Dawn of Correction | 1965 | 6.25 | 12.50 | 25.00 |
| ❏ DL 74712 [S] | The Dawn of Correction | 1965 | 7.50 | 15.00 | 30.00 |

SPONTANEOUS COMBUSTION
CAPITOL
| ❏ ST-11021 | Spontaneous Combustion | 1972 | 5.00 | 10.00 | 20.00 |
FLYING DUTCHMAN
| ❏ 102 | Spontaneous Combustion | 1969 | 6.25 | 12.50 | 25.00 |
HARVEST
| ❏ SW-11095 | Triad | 1972 | 5.00 | 10.00 | 20.00 |

SPONTANEOUS MUSIC ENSEMBLE, THE
EMANEM
| ❏ 303 | Face to Face | 1974 | 5.00 | 10.00 | 20.00 |

SPOOKY TOOTH
A&M
❏ SP-3124	Spooky Two	198?	2.00	4.00	8.00
—Budget-line reissue					
❏ SP-4194	Spooky Two	1969	3.75	7.50	15.00
❏ SP-4225	Ceremony	1970	3.75	7.50	15.00
❏ SP-4266	The Last Puff	1970	3.75	7.50	15.00
❏ SP-4300	Tobacco Road	1971	3.75	7.50	15.00
—Reissue of Bell LP					
❏ SP-4385	You Broke My Heart So I Busted Your Jaw	1973	3.75	7.50	15.00
ACCORD
| ❏ SN-7168 | Hell or High Water | 1982 | 2.50 | 5.00 | 10.00 |
BELL
❏ 6019 [M]	Spooky Tooth	1968	15.00	30.00	60.00
—Mono is white label promo only; record in stereo cover					
❏ 6019 [S]	Spooky Tooth	1968	6.25	12.50	25.00
ISLAND
❏ SW-9255	Witness	1973	3.00	6.00	12.00
❏ SW-9292	The Mirror	1974	3.00	6.00	12.00
❏ ILPS-9337	Witness	1974	2.50	5.00	10.00

SPRING
UNITED ARTISTS
❏ UAS-5571	Spring	1972	6.25	12.50	25.00
❏ UAS-5571 [DJ]	Spring	1972	25.00	50.00	100.00
—Special promo package in 12x12 folder; includes LP, press kit and a packet of seeds					

SPRING STREET STOMPERS, THE
JUBILEE
| ❏ JLP-1002 [M] | The Spring Street Stompers at Carnegie Hall | 1955 | 10.00 | 20.00 | 40.00 |
| ❏ JLP-1004 [M] | I Go, Hook, Line and Sinker | 1955 | 10.00 | 20.00 | 40.00 |

SPRINGFIELD, DUSTY
ABC DUNHILL
❏ DSX-50128	Cameo	1973	3.75	7.50	15.00
❏ DSX-50186	Longings	1974	—	—	—
—Unreleased					
ATLANTIC
❏ SD 8214	Dusty in Memphis	1969	3.75	7.50	15.00
—Second pressings have green and red labels					
❏ SD 8214	Dusty in Memphis	1969	7.50	15.00	30.00
—Originals have purple and brown labels					
❏ 8249 [DJ]	A Brand New Me	1970	10.00	20.00	40.00
—Mono white label promo					
❏ SD 8249	A Brand New Me	1970	3.75	7.50	15.00
CASABLANCA
| ❏ NBLP-7271 | White Heat | 1982 | 3.00 | 6.00 | 12.00 |
LIBERTY
❏ LN-10024	It Begins Again	1980	2.00	4.00	8.00
—Budget-line reissue of United Artists LP of same name					
❏ LN-10026	Living Without Your Love	1980	2.00	4.00	8.00
—Budget-line reissue of United Artists LP of same name					
PHILIPS
❏ PHM-200133 [M]	Stay Awhile	1964	7.50	15.00	30.00
❏ PHM-200156 [M]	Dusty	1964	7.50	15.00	30.00
❏ PHM-200174 [M]	Ooooooo Weeeee!	1965	10.00	20.00	40.00
❏ PHM-200210 [M]	You Don't Have to Say You Love Me	1966	7.50	15.00	30.00
❏ PHM-200220 [M]	Dusty Springfield's Golden Hits	1966	6.25	12.50	25.00
—With "Goin' Back"					
❏ PHM-200220 [M]	Dusty Springfield's Golden Hits	1967	5.00	10.00	20.00
—Without "Goin' Back"					
❏ PHM-200256 [M]	The Look of Love	1967	6.25	12.50	25.00
❏ PHM-200303 [M]	Everything's Coming Up Dusty	1967	6.25	12.50	25.00
❏ PHS-600133 [P]	Stay Awhile	1964	10.00	20.00	40.00
❏ PHS-600156 [P]	Dusty	1964	10.00	20.00	40.00
❏ PHS-600174 [S]	Ooooooo Weeeee!	1965	12.50	25.00	50.00
❏ PHS-600210 [P]	You Don't Have to Say You Love Me	1966	10.00	20.00	40.00
❏ PHS-600220 [P]	Dusty Springfield's Golden Hits	1966	8.75	17.50	35.00
—With "Goin' Back"					
❏ PHS-600220 [P]	Dusty Springfield's Golden Hits	1967	6.25	12.50	25.00
—Without "Goin' Back"					
❏ PHS-600256 [S]	The Look of Love	1967	7.50	15.00	30.00
❏ PHS-600303 [S]	Everything's Coming Up Dusty	1967	7.50	15.00	30.00

POLYDOR
| ❏ 824467-1 | Dusty Springfield's Golden Hits | 1985 | 2.50 | 5.00 | 10.00 |
UNITED ARTISTS
| ❏ UA-LA791 | It Begins Again | 1978 | 3.75 | 7.50 | 15.00 |
| ❏ UA-LA936 | Living Without Your Love | 1979 | 3.75 | 7.50 | 15.00 |
WING
| ❏ PKW-2-120 [(2)] | Something Special | 196? | 5.00 | 10.00 | 20.00 |
| ❏ SRW-16380 | Just Dusty | 196? | 3.00 | 6.00 | 12.00 |

SPRINGFIELD, RICK
CAPITOL
❏ SMAS-11047	Beginnings	1972	5.00	10.00	20.00
❏ SMAS-11206	Comic Book Heroes	1973	10.00	20.00	40.00
—Withdrawn and reissued on Columbia					
❏ SN-16251	Beginnings	1981	2.00	4.00	8.00
—Budget-line reissue					
CHELSEA
| ❏ 515 | Wait for Night | 1976 | 3.75 | 7.50 | 15.00 |
COLUMBIA
❏ KC 32704	Comic Book Heroes	1973	3.75	7.50	15.00
❏ PC 32704	Comic Book Heroes	1981	2.00	4.00	8.00
—Budget-line reissue					
MERCURY
| ❏ 824107-1 | Beautiful Feelings | 1984 | 2.50 | 5.00 | 10.00 |
RCA
| ❏ 6620-1-R | Rock of Life | 1988 | 2.00 | 4.00 | 8.00 |
| ❏ 9817-1-R | Rick Springfield's Greatest Hits | 1989 | 3.00 | 6.00 | 12.00 |
RCA VICTOR
❏ ARL1-3697	Working Class Dog	1981	2.50	5.00	10.00
❏ AFL1-4125	Success Hasn't Spoiled Me Yet	1982	2.50	5.00	10.00
❏ AFL1-4235	Wait for Night	1982	2.50	5.00	10.00
—Reissue of Chelsea LP					
❏ AFL1-4660	Living in Oz	1983	2.50	5.00	10.00
❏ AYL1-4766	Working Class Dog	1983	2.00	4.00	8.00
—"Best Buy Series" reissue					
❏ AYL1-4767	Success Hasn't Spoiled Me Yet	1983	2.00	4.00	8.00
—"Best Buy Series" reissue					
❏ ABL1-4935	Hard to Hold	1984	2.50	5.00	10.00
❏ AJL1-5370	Tao	1985	2.50	5.00	10.00

SPRINGFIELD RIFLE, THE
BURDETTE
| ❏ ST-5159 | The Springfield Rifle | 1969 | 6.25 | 12.50 | 25.00 |

SPRINGFIELDS, THE
PHILIPS
❏ PHM 200052 [M]	Silver Threads and Golden Needles	1962	7.50	15.00	30.00
❏ PHM 200076 [M]	Folksongs from the Hills	1963	7.50	15.00	30.00
❏ PHS 600052 [S]	Silver Threads and Golden Needles	1962	10.00	20.00	40.00
❏ PHS 600076 [S]	Folksongs from the Hills	1963	10.00	20.00	40.00

SPRINGSTEEN, BRUCE
COLUMBIA
❏ (# unknown) [PD]	Darkness on the Edge of Town	1978	37.50	75.00	150.00
—Promo-only picture disc					
❏ AS 978 [DJ]	As Requested Around the World	1981	12.50	25.00	50.00
❏ AS 1957 [DJ]	Bruce Springsteen	1985	7.50	15.00	30.00
—Five-song mini-LP with five B-sides of singles from Born in the U.S.A.					
❏ AS 1957 [DJ]	Bruce Springsteen	1987	5.00	10.00	20.00
—Five-song mini-LP with five B-sides of singles from Born in the U.S.A.; second pressings say so on the label					
❏ AS 2543 [DJ]	Bruce Springsteen and the E Street Band: Live 1975-1985	1986	7.50	15.00	30.00
—Sampler from 5-LP live set					
❏ JC 31903	Greetings from Asbury Park, N.J.	1977	2.00	4.00	8.00
—Reissue of the first PC-prefix version					
❏ KC 31903	Greetings from Asbury Park, N.J.	1973	5.00	10.00	20.00
❏ KC 31903 [DJ]	Greetings from Asbury Park, N.J.	1973	50.00	100.00	200.00
—Promotional copy with timing strip and "Bruce Springsteen Fact Sheet" attached to back cover. Authentic fact sheets are on glossy stock					
❏ PC 31903	Greetings from Asbury Park, N.J.	1975	2.50	5.00	10.00
—Without bar code on cover					
❏ PC 31903	Greetings from Asbury Park, N.J.	1979	2.00	4.00	8.00
—With bar code on cover					
❏ JC 32432	The Wild, the Innocent & the E Street Shuffle	1977	2.00	4.00	8.00
—Reissue of the first PC-prefix version					
❏ KC 32432	The Wild, the Innocent & the E Street Shuffle	1973	5.00	10.00	20.00
❏ PC 32432	The Wild, the Innocent & the E Street Shuffle	1975	2.50	5.00	10.00
—Without bar code on cover					
❏ PC 32432	The Wild, the Innocent & the E Street Shuffle	1979	2.00	4.00	8.00
—With bar code on cover					
❏ HC 33795	Born to Run	1981	12.50	25.00	50.00
—Half-speed mastered edition (original)					
❏ JC 33795	Born to Run	1977	2.00	4.00	8.00
❏ PC 33795	Born to Run	1975	2.50	5.00	10.00
—Jon Landau's name is correct on the back cover					
❏ PC 33795	Born to Run	1975	3.75	7.50	15.00
—Sticker with the correct spelling of Jon Landau is on the back cover					
❏ PC 33795	Born to Run	1975	6.25	12.50	25.00
—Jon Landau's name is misspelled "John" on the back cover					
❏ PC 33795	Born to Run	1999	6.25	12.50	25.00
—Classic Records reissue, identified as such on back cover; corrected pressing with gatefold					
❏ PC 33795	Born to Run	1999	10.00	20.00	40.00
—Classic Records reissue, identified as such on back cover; "error" first pressing with no gatefold					
❏ PC 33795 [DJ]	Born to Run	1975	25.00	50.00	100.00
—White label promo					
❏ PC 33795 [DJ]	Born to Run	1975	400.00	800.00	1200.
—Test pressing with "Bruce Springsteen -- Born to Run" in script print. Also includes mailing envelope, letter from CBS and orange patch					
❏ JC 35318	Darkness on the Edge of Town	1978	2.50	5.00	10.00
—Original pressings have thick paper innersleeves and small titles on back cover					

Number	Title (A Side/B Side)	Yr	VG	VG+	NM
❑ JC 35318	Darkness on the Edge of Town	198?	2.00	4.00	8.00
—Later pressings have thin paper innersleeves and larger titles on back cover					
❑ JC 35318 [DJ]	Darkness on the Edge of Town	1978	25.00	50.00	100.00
—White label promo					
❑ PC2 36854 [(2)]	The River	1980	3.00	6.00	12.00
❑ PC2 36854 [(2)DJ]	The River	1980	10.00	20.00	40.00
—White label promo, without letter					
❑ PC2 36854 [(2)DJ]	The River	1980	18.75	37.50	75.00
—White label promo, with photocopied letter from CBS					
❑ TC 38358	Nebraska	1982	2.50	5.00	10.00
❑ QC 38653	Born in the U.S.A.	1984	2.50	5.00	10.00
❑ C5X 40558 [(5)]	Bruce Springsteen and the E Street Band: Live 1975-1985	1986	10.00	20.00	40.00
❑ OC 40999	Tunnel of Love	1987	2.50	5.00	10.00
❑ HC 43795	Born to Run	1982	10.00	20.00	40.00
—Half-speed mastered edition (reissue)					
❑ 3C 44445 [EP]	Chimes of Freedom	1988	2.50	5.00	10.00
❑ HC 45318	Darkness on the Edge of Town	1981	10.00	20.00	40.00
—Half-speed mastered edition					
❑ C 53000	Human Touch	1992	3.00	6.00	12.00
❑ C 53001	Lucky Town	1992	3.00	6.00	12.00
❑ C2 67060 [(2)]	Greatest Hits	1995	3.75	7.50	15.00
❑ C 67484	The Ghost of Tom Joad	1995	3.00	6.00	12.00
❑ C2 69746 [(2)]	18 Tracks	1999	3.75	7.50	15.00
❑ C3 85490 [(3)]	Live in New York City	2001	5.00	10.00	20.00
—As of press date, all known copies contain "Born to Run," but the song is not listed on either the record jacket or label					
❑ C2 86600 [(2)]	The Rising	2002	3.75	7.50	15.00

SPUR
CINEMA
❑ CSLP-1500	Spur of the Moment	196?	20.00	40.00	80.00

SPYRO GYRA
MCA
❑ 16010	Catching the Sun	1982	10.00	20.00	40.00
—Audiophile vinyl					

NAUTILUS
❑ NR-9	Morning Dance	1979	10.00	20.00	40.00
—Audiophile vinyl					

SQUEEZE
A&M
❑ SP-3185	U.K. Squeeze	198?	2.00	4.00	8.00
—Reissue					
❑ SP-3231	Cool for Cats	198?	2.00	4.00	8.00
—Reissue					
❑ SP-3232	Argybargy	198?	2.00	4.00	8.00
—Reissue					
❑ SP-3253	East Side Story	198?	2.00	4.00	8.00
—Reissue					
❑ SP-3254	Sweets from a Stranger	198?	2.00	4.00	8.00
—Reissue; none of these have 2-inch flap					
❑ SP-3413 [EP]	Six Squeeze Songs Crammed Into One 10-Inch Record	1979	2.50	5.00	10.00
—10-inch EP in 12-inch "squeezed" jacket					
❑ SP-4687	U.K. Squeeze	1978	3.00	6.00	12.00
—Later pressings on black vinyl					
❑ SP-4687	U.K. Squeeze	1978	5.00	10.00	20.00
—First pressing on red vinyl					
❑ SP-4759	Cool for Cats	1979	3.00	6.00	12.00
❑ SP-4802	Argybargy	1980	3.00	6.00	12.00
❑ SP-4854	East Side Story	1981	2.50	5.00	10.00
❑ SP-4899	Sweets from a Stranger	1982	2.50	5.00	10.00
—With flap removed or never there					
❑ SP-4899	Sweets from a Stranger	1982	3.00	6.00	12.00
—Original pressings have a 2-inch flap on the right side of the front cover with critics' raves					
❑ SP-4922	Singles 45's and Under	1983	2.50	5.00	10.00
❑ SP-5085	Cosi Fan Tutti Frutti	1985	2.50	5.00	10.00
❑ SP-5161	Babylon and On	1987	2.50	5.00	10.00
❑ SP-5278	Frank	1989	2.50	5.00	10.00
❑ R 124200	Frank	1989	3.00	6.00	12.00
—BMG Music Service edition					

SRC
CAPITOL
❑ ST-134	Milestones	1969	10.00	20.00	40.00
❑ SKAO-273	Travellers Tale	1970	10.00	20.00	40.00
❑ ST 2991	SRC	1968	15.00	30.00	60.00

STACKRIDGE
DECCA
❑ DL 75317	Stackridge	1971	6.25	12.50	25.00
MCA
| ❑ 308 | Friendliness | 1973 | 2.50 | 5.00 | 10.00 |
SIRE
| ❑ SASD-7503 | Pinafore Days | 1974 | 2.50 | 5.00 | 10.00 |
| ❑ SASD-7509 | Extravaganza | 1975 | 2.50 | 5.00 | 10.00 |

STACY, JESS
ATLANTIC
❑ 1225 [M]	A Tribute to Benny Goodman	1956	12.50	25.00	50.00
—Black label					
BRUNSWICK
| ❑ BL 54017 [M] | Piano Solos | 1956 | 12.50 | 25.00 | 50.00 |
| ❑ BL 58029 [10] | Piano Solos | 1951 | 20.00 | 40.00 | 80.00 |
COLUMBIA
| ❑ CL 6147 [10] | Piano Moods | 1950 | 25.00 | 50.00 | 100.00 |
HANOVER
| ❑ HS-8010 [S] | The Return of Jess Stacy | 1964 | 5.00 | 10.00 | 20.00 |

Number	Title (A Side/B Side)	Yr	VG	VG+	NM
STAETER, TED					
ATLANTIC					
❑ 1218 [M]	Ted Staeter's New York	1955	6.25	12.50	25.00
—Multicolor label, white "fan" logo at right					
❑ 1218 [M]	Ted Staeter's New York	1961	12.50	25.00	50.00
—Black label					

STAFFORD, JO
BAINBRIDGE
❑ 6234	Look at Me Now	1982	2.50	5.00	10.00
CAPITOL
❑ H 75 [10]	American Folk Songs	1950	15.00	30.00	60.00
❑ H 197 [10]	Autumn in New York	195?	15.00	30.00	60.00
❑ T 197 [M]	Autumn in New York	1955	12.50	25.00	50.00
—Turquoise or gray label					
❑ T 197 [M]	Autumn in New York	1959	7.50	15.00	30.00
—Black colorband label, Capitol logo at left					
❑ H 247 [10]	Songs for Sunday Evening	195?	15.00	30.00	60.00
❑ T 423 [M]	Memory Songs	1955	12.50	25.00	50.00
—Turquoise or gray label					
❑ T 423 [M]	Memory Songs	1959	7.50	15.00	30.00
—Black colorband label, Capitol logo at left					
❑ H 435 [10]	Starring Jo Stafford	1953	15.00	30.00	60.00
❑ T 435 [M]	Starring Jo Stafford	1955	12.50	25.00	50.00
—Turquoise or gray label					
❑ T 435 [M]	Starring Jo Stafford	1959	7.50	15.00	30.00
—Black colorband label, Capitol logo at left					
❑ ST 1653 [S]	American Folk Songs	1962	6.25	12.50	25.00
❑ T 1653 [M]	American Folk Songs	1962	5.00	10.00	20.00
❑ SM-1696	Whispering Hope	1977	2.50	5.00	10.00
—Reissue with new prefix					
❑ ST 1921 [S]	The Hits of Jo Stafford	1963	6.25	12.50	25.00
❑ T 1921 [M]	The Hits of Jo Stafford	1963	5.00	10.00	20.00
❑ ST 2069 [S]	Sweet Hour of Prayer	1964	6.25	12.50	25.00
❑ T 2069 [M]	Sweet Hour of Prayer	1964	5.00	10.00	20.00
❑ ST 2166 [S]	The Joyful Season	1964	6.25	12.50	25.00
❑ T 2166 [M]	The Joyful Season	1964	5.00	10.00	20.00
❑ H 9014 [10]	Songs of Faith	1950	15.00	30.00	60.00
❑ SM-11889	The Hits of Jo Stafford	1979	2.50	5.00	10.00
COLUMBIA
❑ CL 578 [M]	New Orleans	1954	10.00	20.00	40.00
—Maroon label, gold print					
❑ CL 578 [M]	New Orleans	1955	7.50	15.00	30.00
—Red and black label with six "eye" logos					
❑ CL 584 [M]	Jo Stafford Sings Broadway's Best	1954	10.00	20.00	40.00
—Maroon label, gold print					
❑ CL 584 [M]	Jo Stafford Sings Broadway's Best	1955	7.50	15.00	30.00
—Red and black label with six "eye" logos					
❑ CL 691 [M]	Happy Holiday	1955	15.00	30.00	60.00
❑ CL 910 [M]	Ski Trails	1956	10.00	20.00	40.00
❑ CL 968 [M]	Once Over Lightly	1957	10.00	20.00	40.00
❑ CL 1043 [M]	Songs of Scotland	1957	10.00	20.00	40.00
❑ CL 1124 [M]	Swingin' Down Broadway	1958	10.00	20.00	40.00
❑ CL 1228 [M]	Jo Stafford's Greatest Hits	1958	10.00	20.00	40.00
—Red and black label with six "eye" logos					
❑ CL 1228 [M]	Jo Stafford's Greatest Hits	1963	5.00	10.00	20.00
—Red label with "Guaranteed High Fidelity" in black					
❑ CL 1228 [M]	Jo Stafford's Greatest Hits	1965	3.75	7.50	15.00
—Red label with "360 Sound Mono" in white					
❑ CL 1262 [M]	I'll Be Seeing You	1959	7.50	15.00	30.00
❑ CL 1339 [M]	Ballad of the Blues	1959	7.50	15.00	30.00
❑ CL 1561 [M]	Jo + Jazz	1960	10.00	20.00	40.00
❑ CL 2501 [10]	Soft and Sentimental	1955	10.00	20.00	40.00
❑ CL 2591 [10]	A Gal Named Jo	1955	10.00	20.00	40.00
❑ CL 6210 [10]	As You Desire Me	1952	12.50	25.00	50.00
❑ CL 6238 [10]	Jo Stafford Sings Broadway's Best	1953	12.50	25.00	50.00
❑ CL 6268 [10]	New Orleans	1954	12.50	25.00	50.00
❑ CL 6274 [10]	My Heart's in the Highland	1954	12.50	25.00	50.00
❑ CL 6286 [10]	Garden of Prayer	1954	12.50	25.00	50.00
❑ CS 8080 [S]	I'll Be Seeing You	1959	10.00	20.00	40.00
❑ CS 8139 [S]	Ballad of the Blues	1959	10.00	20.00	40.00
❑ CS 8361 [S]	Jo + Jazz	1960	15.00	30.00	60.00
CORINTHIAN
❑ COR-105	G.I. Jo	1977	2.50	5.00	10.00
❑ COR-106	Greatest Hits.	1977	2.50	5.00	10.00
❑ COR-108	Jo + Jazz.	197?	2.50	5.00	10.00
❑ COR-110	Jo Stafford Sings American Folk Songs.	197?	2.50	5.00	10.00
❑ COR-111	Songs of Faith, Hope and Love.	197?	2.50	5.00	10.00
❑ COR-112	Jo + Broadway.	197?	2.50	5.00	10.00
❑ COR-113	Ski Trails.	197?	2.50	5.00	10.00
❑ COR-114	Jo + Blues.	197?	2.50	5.00	10.00
❑ COR-115	International Hits.	197?	2.50	5.00	10.00
❑ COR-118	Broadway Revisited.	198?	2.50	5.00	10.00
❑ COR-119	By Request.	198?	2.50	5.00	10.00
❑ COR-123	Music of My Life.	1986	2.50	5.00	10.00
DECCA
| ❑ DL 74973 | Jo Stafford's Greatest Hits | 1968 | 3.75 | 7.50 | 15.00 |
DOT
❑ DLP-3673 [M]	Do I Hear a Waltz?	1966	3.75	7.50	15.00
❑ DLP-3745 [M]	This Is Jo Stafford	1967	3.75	7.50	15.00
❑ DLP-25673 [S]	Do I Hear a Waltz?	1966	5.00	10.00	20.00
❑ DLP-25745 [S]	This Is Jo Stafford	1967	5.00	10.00	20.00
REPRISE
| ❑ R-6090 [M] | Getting Sentimental Over Tommy Dorsey | 1963 | 5.00 | 10.00 | 20.00 |
| ❑ R9-6090 [S] | Getting Sentimental Over Tommy Dorsey | 1963 | 6.25 | 12.50 | 25.00 |
STANYAN
| ❑ 10073 | Look at Me Now | 197? | 3.00 | 6.00 | 12.00 |
VOCALION
❑ VL 73856 [R]	Happy Holidays	1968	3.00	6.00	12.00
❑ VL 73866 [R]	Sweet Singer of Songs	1969	3.00	6.00	12.00
❑ VL 73892	In the Mood for Love	1970	3.00	6.00	12.00

Number	Title (A Side/B Side)	Yr	VG	VG+	NM

STAFFORD, JO, AND GORDON MACRAE
CAPITOL
❏ T 423 [M]	Memory Songs	1955	12.50	25.00	50.00
❏ ST 1696 [S]	Whispering Hope	1962	6.25	12.50	25.00
❏ T 1696 [M]	Whispering Hope	1962	5.00	10.00	20.00
❏ ST 1916 [S]	There's Peace in the Valley	1963	6.25	12.50	25.00
❏ T 1916 [M]	There's Peace in the Valley	1963	5.00	10.00	20.00
❏ SM-11890	There's Peace in the Valley	1978	2.50	5.00	10.00
—Reissue					

STAFFORD, TERRY
ATLANTIC
❏ SD 7282	Say, Has Anybody Seen My Sweet Gypsy Rose	1974	3.00	6.00	12.00
CRUSADER
| ❏ CLP-1001 [M] | Suspicion! | 1964 | 10.00 | 20.00 | 40.00 |
| ❏ CLP-1001S [S] | Suspicion! | 1964 | 15.00 | 30.00 | 60.00 |

STAINED GLASS
CAPITOL
❏ ST-154	Crazy Horse Roads	1969	7.50	15.00	30.00
❏ ST-242	Aurora	1969	7.50	15.00	30.00

STALLINGS, MARY, AND CAL TJADER
FANTASY
❏ 3325 [M]	Cal Tjader Plays, Mary Stallings Sings	1962	7.50	15.00	30.00
—Black vinyl					
❏ 3325 [M]	Cal Tjader Plays, Mary Stallings Sings	1962	12.50	25.00	50.00
—Red vinyl					
❏ 8068 [S]	Cal Tjader Plays, Mary Stallings Sings	1962	5.00	10.00	20.00
—Black vinyl					
❏ 8068 [S]	Cal Tjader Plays, Mary Stallings Sings	1962	10.00	20.00	40.00
—Blue vinyl					

STAMM, MARVIN
VERVE
❏ V6-8759	Machinations	1968	5.00	10.00	20.00

STANDELLS, THE
LIBERTY
❏ LRP-3384 [M]	The Standells In Person at P.J.'s	1964	20.00	40.00	80.00
❏ LST-7384 [S]	The Standells In Person at P.J.'s	1964	25.00	50.00	100.00
RHINO
❏ RNLP-107	The Best of the Standells	1983	2.50	5.00	10.00
❏ RNLP-115	Rarities	1983	2.50	5.00	10.00
❏ RNLP-70176	The Best of the Standells (Golden Archive Series)	1987	2.50	5.00	10.00
SUNSET
| ❏ SUM-1136 [M] | Live and Out of Sight | 1966 | 6.25 | 12.50 | 25.00 |
| ❏ SUS-5136 [S] | Live and Out of Sight | 1966 | 7.50 | 15.00 | 30.00 |
TOWER
❏ ST 5027 [R]	Dirty Water	1966	12.50	25.00	50.00
❏ T 5027 [M]	Dirty Water	1966	15.00	30.00	60.00
❏ ST 5044 [S]	Why Pick on Me	1966	15.00	30.00	60.00
❏ T 5044 [M]	Why Pick on Me	1966	12.50	25.00	50.00
❏ ST 5049 [S]	The Hot Ones	1966	15.00	30.00	60.00
❏ T 5049 [M]	The Hot Ones	1966	12.50	25.00	50.00
❏ ST 5098 [S]	Try It	1967	15.00	30.00	60.00
❏ T 5098 [M]	Try It	1967	12.50	25.00	50.00

STANLEY, MICHAEL, BAND
ARISTA
❏ AL 4182	Cabin Fever	1978	2.50	5.00	10.00
❏ AL 4236	Greatest Hints	1979	2.50	5.00	10.00
EMI AMERICA
❏ SN-16352	Heartland	1985	2.00	4.00	8.00
—Budget-line reissue					
❏ SN-16353	You Can't Fight Fashion	1985	2.00	4.00	8.00
—Budget-line reissue					
❏ SN-16392	MSB	1986	2.00	4.00	8.00
—Budget-line reissue					
❏ SW-17040	Heartland	1980	2.50	5.00	10.00
❏ SW-17056	North Coast	1981	2.50	5.00	10.00
❏ ST-17071	MSB	1982	2.50	5.00	10.00
❏ ST-17100	You Can't Fight Fashion	1983	2.50	5.00	10.00
EPIC
❏ PE 33492	You Break It…You Bought It!	1975	3.00	6.00	12.00
—Original with orange label and no bar code					
❏ PE 33492	You Break It…You Bought It!	198?	2.00	4.00	8.00
—Reissue with dark blue label and bar code					
❏ PE 33917	Ladies' Choice	1976	3.00	6.00	12.00
—Original with orange label and no bar code					
❏ PE 33917	Ladies' Choice	198?	2.00	4.00	8.00
—Reissue with dark blue label and bar code					
❏ PEG 34661 [(2)]	Stagepass	1977	3.75	7.50	15.00
MCA
| ❏ 372 | Friends and Legends | 1973 | 3.00 | 6.00 | 12.00 |
TUMBLEWEED
| ❏ TWS 106 | Michael Stanley | 1972 | 5.00 | 10.00 | 20.00 |
| —Blue textured cover | | | | | |

STANLEY, PAUL
Also see KISS.
CASABLANCA
❏ NBLP-7123	Paul Stanley	1978	6.25	12.50	25.00
❏ NBPIX-7123 [PD]	Paul Stanley	1978	15.00	30.00	60.00

STANLEY, RALPH
JALYN
❏ JLP-118 [M]	Old Time Music	1966	6.25	12.50	25.00
❏ JLP-120 [M]	The Bluegrass Sound of Ralph Stanley	1966	6.25	12.50	25.00
❏ JLP-129 [M]	Ralph Stanley and the Clinch Mountain Boys	196?	6.25	12.50	25.00

KING
❏ KSD-1028	Brand New Country Songs by Ralph Stanley	1968	5.00	10.00	20.00
❏ KSD-1032	Over the Sunset Hill	1968	5.00	10.00	20.00
❏ KSD-1046	How Far to Little Rock?	1969	5.00	10.00	20.00
❏ KSD-1069	The Hills of Home	1969	5.00	10.00	20.00

STANLEY BROTHERS, THE
CABIN CREEK
| ❏ LP-203 [M] | Bluegrass Gospel Favorites | 1966 | 15.00 | 30.00 | 60.00 |
HARMONY
| ❏ HL 7291 [M] | The Stanley Brothers | 1961 | 6.25 | 12.50 | 25.00 |
KING
❏ 615 [M]	The Stanley Brothers	1959	25.00	50.00	100.00
❏ 645 [M]	Hymns and Sacred Songs	1960	20.00	40.00	80.00
❏ 690 [M]	Everybody's Country Favorites	1961	20.00	40.00	80.00
❏ KS-690 [S]	Everybody's Country Favorites	1961	25.00	50.00	100.00
❏ 698 [M]	For the Good People	1961	20.00	40.00	80.00
❏ 719 [M]	The Stanleys In Person	1961	20.00	40.00	80.00
❏ KS-719 [S]	The Stanleys In Person	1961	25.00	50.00	100.00
❏ 750 [M]	Old Time Camp Meeting	1962	20.00	40.00	80.00
❏ 772 [M]	The Stanley Brothers and the Clinch Mountain Boys Sing the Songs They Like Best	1962	20.00	40.00	80.00
❏ 791 [M]	Award Winners	1962	20.00	40.00	80.00
❏ KS-791 [S]	Award Winners	1962	25.00	50.00	100.00
❏ 805 [M]	Good Old Camp Meeting Songs	1963	20.00	40.00	80.00
❏ KS-805 [S]	Good Old Camp Meeting Songs	1963	25.00	50.00	100.00
❏ 834 [M]	Just Because	1964	12.50	25.00	50.00
❏ 864 [M]	Country Folk Music Spotlight	1964	12.50	25.00	50.00
❏ 872 [S]	Five String Banjo Hootenanny	1964	12.50	25.00	50.00
❏ 918 [M]	Hymns of the Cross	1964	12.50	25.00	50.00
❏ 924 [M]	The Remarkable Stanley Brothers Play and Sing Bluegrass Songs for You	1965	12.50	25.00	50.00
❏ 953 [M]	The Best of the Stanley Brothers	1966	6.25	12.50	25.00
❏ 963 [M]	A Collection of Gospel and Sacred Songs	1966	6.25	12.50	25.00
❏ 1013 [M]	The Stanley Brothers Sing the Best-Loved Sacred Songs of the Carter Family	1967	6.25	12.50	25.00
❏ KS-1013 [S]	The Stanley Brothers Sing the Best-Loved Sacred Songs of the Carter Family	1967	7.50	15.00	30.00
MERCURY
❏ MG-20349 [M]	Country Pickin' and Singin'	1958	20.00	40.00	80.00
❏ MG-20884 [M]	Hard Times	1963	6.25	12.50	25.00
❏ SR-60884 [S]	Hard Times	1963	7.50	15.00	30.00
STARDAY
❏ SLP-106 [M]	Mountain Song Favorites	1959	12.50	25.00	50.00
❏ SLP-122 [M]	Sacred Songs from the Hills	1960	12.50	25.00	50.00
❏ SLP-201 [M]	The Mountain Music Sound of the Stanley Brothers	1962	10.00	20.00	40.00
❏ SLP-384 [M]	Jacob's Vision	1966	7.50	15.00	30.00
VINTAGE
| ❏ ZK-002 [M] | The Stanley Brothers Live at Antioch College | 1961 | 17.50 | 35.00 | 70.00 |

STAPLE SINGERS, THE
ARCHIVE OF GOSPEL MUSIC
❏ 62	The Staple Singers	1968	3.00	6.00	12.00
❏ 72	The Staple Singers, Vol. 2	1969	3.00	6.00	12.00
BUDDAH
| ❏ BDS-2009 | The Best of the Staple Singers | 1969 | 5.00 | 10.00 | 20.00 |
| ❏ BDS-7508 | Will the Circle Be Unbroken | 1969 | 5.00 | 10.00 | 20.00 |
CURTOM
| ❏ CU 5005 | Let's Do It Again | 1975 | 3.00 | 6.00 | 12.00 |
EPIC
❏ LN 24132 [M]	Amen	1965	5.00	10.00	20.00
❏ LN 24163 [M]	Freedom Highway	1965	5.00	10.00	20.00
❏ LN 24196 [M]	Why	1966	5.00	10.00	20.00
❏ LN 24237 [M]	Pray On	1967	6.25	12.50	25.00
❏ LN 24332 [M]	For What It's Worth	1967	6.25	12.50	25.00
❏ BN 26132 [S]	Amen	1965	6.25	12.50	25.00
❏ BN 26163 [S]	Freedom Highway	1965	6.25	12.50	25.00
❏ BN 26196 [S]	Why	1966	6.25	12.50	25.00
❏ BN 26237 [S]	Pray On	1967	5.00	10.00	20.00
❏ BN 26332 [S]	For What It's Worth	1967	5.00	10.00	20.00
❏ BN 26373	What the World Needs Now Is Love	1968	5.00	10.00	20.00
❏ EG 30635 [(2)]	The Staple Singers Make You Happy	1971	5.00	10.00	20.00
FANTASY
| ❏ 9423 | Use What You Got | 1973 | 3.75 | 7.50 | 15.00 |
| ❏ 9442 | The 25th Day of December | 1973 | 3.75 | 7.50 | 15.00 |
HARMONY
| ❏ KH 31775 | Tell It Like It Is | 1972 | 3.00 | 6.00 | 12.00 |
MILESTONE
| ❏ 47028 [(2)] | A Great Day | 197? | 3.75 | 7.50 | 15.00 |
PICKWICK
| ❏ 7001 | The Staple Singers | 197? | 2.50 | 5.00 | 10.00 |
PRIVATE I
| ❏ FZ 39460 | The Turning Point | 1984 | 2.50 | 5.00 | 10.00 |
| ❏ BFZ 40109 | The Staple Singers | 1985 | 2.50 | 5.00 | 10.00 |
STAX
❏ STS-2004	Soul Folk in Action	1968	6.25	12.50	25.00
❏ STS-2016	We'll Get Over	1969	5.00	10.00	20.00
❏ STS-2034	The Staple Swingers	1971	5.00	10.00	20.00
❏ STS-3002	Be Altitude: Respect Yourself	1972	3.75	7.50	15.00
❏ STS-3015	Be What You Are	1973	3.75	7.50	15.00
❏ STX-4116	Be Altitude: Respect Yourself	198?	2.50	5.00	10.00
—Reissue of 3002					
❏ STX-4119	Chronicle	198?	2.50	5.00	10.00
❏ STS-5515	City in the Sky	1974	3.75	7.50	15.00
❏ STS-5523	The Best of the Staple Singers	1975	3.75	7.50	15.00
❏ MPS-8511	This Time Around	198?	2.50	5.00	10.00
❏ MPS-8532	We'll Get Over	198?	2.50	5.00	10.00
—Reissue of 2016					

S

Number	Title (A Side/B Side)	Yr	VG	VG+	NM
❏ MPS-8553	Be What You Are	1990	3.00	6.00	12.00
—Reissue of 3015					
TRIP					
❏ 7000	Uncloudy Day	197?	2.50	5.00	10.00
❏ 7014	Swing Low	197?	2.50	5.00	10.00
❏ 7019	The Best of the Staple Singers	197?	2.50	5.00	10.00
❏ 8014	The Other Side of the Staple Singers	1972	2.50	5.00	10.00
20TH CENTURY					
❏ T-636	Hold On to Your Dream	1981	2.50	5.00	10.00
VEE JAY					
❏ LP-5000 [M]	Uncloudy Day	1959	7.50	15.00	30.00
❏ LP-5008 [M]	Will the Circle Be Unbroken	1960	7.50	15.00	30.00
❏ LP-5014 [M]	Swing Low	1961	7.50	15.00	30.00
❏ LP-5019 [M]	Best of the Staple Singers	1962	7.50	15.00	30.00
❏ LP-5030 [M]	Swing Low Sweet Chariot	1963	7.50	15.00	30.00
VEE JAY/CHAMELEON					
❏ D1-74782 [(2)]	The Best of the Staple Singers	1988	3.75	7.50	15.00
WARNER BROS.					
❏ BS 2945	Pass It On	1976	3.00	6.00	12.00
—As "The Staples"					
❏ BS 3084	Family Tree	1977	3.00	6.00	12.00
—As "The Staples"					
❏ BSK 3192	Unlock Your Mind	1978	3.00	6.00	12.00
—As "The Staples"					

STAPLES, MAVIS
CURTOM

❏ CU 5019	A Piece of the Action	1977	3.00	6.00	12.00
PAISLEY PARK					
❏ 25798	Time Waits for No One	1989	3.00	6.00	12.00
STAX					
❏ STX-4118	Mavis Staples	198?	2.50	5.00	10.00
—Reissue of Volt 6007					
❏ MPS-8539	Only for the Lonely	1987	2.50	5.00	10.00
—Reissue of Volt 6010					
VOLT					
❏ VOS-6007	Mavis Staples	1969	5.00	10.00	20.00
❏ VOS-6010	Only for the Lonely	1970	5.00	10.00	20.00
WARNER BROS.					
❏ BSK 3319	Oh What a Feeling	1979	3.00	6.00	12.00

STARCASTLE
EPIC

❏ AS 296 [DJ]	Fountains of Light Banded for Airplay	1977	10.00	20.00	40.00
—White label, promo-only version with separations between tracks					
❏ PE 33914	Starcastle	1976	2.50	5.00	10.00
—Orange label					
❏ PE 34375	Fountains of Light	1977	2.50	5.00	10.00
—Orange label					
❏ 34935 [PD]	Citadel	1978	12.50	25.00	50.00
—Picture disc, possibly promo only					
❏ PE 34935	Citadel	1977	2.50	5.00	10.00
—Orange label					
❏ JE 35441	Real to Reel	1978	2.50	5.00	10.00
—Orange label					

STARCHER, BUDDY
DECCA

❏ DL 4796 [M]	History Repeats Itself	1966	5.00	10.00	20.00
❏ DL 74796 [S]	History Repeats Itself	1966	6.25	12.50	25.00
STARDAY					
❏ SLP-211 [M]	Buddy Starcher and His Mountain Guitar	1962	7.50	15.00	30.00
❏ SLP-382 [M]	History Repeats Itself	1966	7.50	15.00	30.00

STARFIRES, THE (4)
OHIO RECORDING SERVICE

❏ 34 [M]	The Starfires Play	1964	12.50	25.00	50.00

STARFIRES, THE (5)
LABREA

❏ LS-8018 [M]	Teenbeat A-Go-Go	1965	12.50	25.00	50.00

STARK NAKED
RCA VICTOR

❏ LSP-4592	Stark Naked	1971	6.25	12.50	25.00

STARKER, JANOS
MERCURY LIVING PRESENCE

❏ SR 90303 [S]	Dvorak: Cello Concerto; Bruch: Kol Nidre	196?	10.00	20.00	40.00
—With Antal Dorati/London Symphony Orchestra; third edition (dark red, not maroon, label)					
❏ SR 90303 [S]	Dvorak: Cello Concerto; Bruch: Kol Nidre	196?	17.50	35.00	70.00
—With Antal Dorati/London Symphony Orchestra; maroon label, with "Vendor: Mercury Record Corporation"					
❏ SR 90303 [S]	Dvorak: Cello Concerto; Bruch: Kol Nidre	196?	30.00	60.00	120.00
—With Antal Dorati/London Symphony Orchestra; maroon label, no "Vendor: Mercury Record Corporation"					
❏ SR 90320 [S]	Mendelssohn: Cello Sonata; Chopin: Cello Sonata in G	196?	15.00	30.00	60.00
—Maroon label, with "Vendor: Mercury Record Corporation"					
❏ SR 90320 [S]	Mendelssohn: Cello Sonata; Chopin: Cello Sonata in G	196?	25.00	50.00	100.00
—Maroon label, no "Vendor: Mercury Record Corporation"					
❏ SR 90347 [S]	Schumann: Cello Concerto; Lalo: Cello Concerto	196?	10.00	20.00	40.00
—With Stanislaw Skrowaczewski/London Symphony Orchestra; maroon label, with "Vendor: Mercury Record Corporation"					
❏ SR 90347 [S]	Schumann: Cello Concerto; Lalo: Cello Concerto	196?	30.00	60.00	120.00
—With Stanislaw Skrowaczewski/London Symphony Orchestra; maroon label, no "Vendor: Mercury Record Corporation"					
❏ SR 90370 [S]	Bach: Suites 2 and 5 for Solo Violin	196?	10.00	20.00	40.00
—Third edition: Dark red (not maroon) label					

Number	Title (A Side/B Side)	Yr	VG	VG+	NM
❏ SR 90370 [S]	Bach: Suites 2 and 5 for Solo Violin	196?	15.00	30.00	60.00
—Maroon label, with "Vendor: Mercury Record Corporation"					
❏ SR 90370 [S]	Bach: Suites 2 and 5 for Solo Violin	196?	20.00	40.00	80.00
—Maroon label, no "Vendor: Mercury Record Corporation"					
❏ SR 90392 [S]	Brahms: Cello Sonatas No. 1 and 2	196?	12.50	25.00	50.00
—Maroon label, with "Vendor: Mercury Record Corporation"					
❏ SR 90392 [S]	Brahms: Cello Sonatas No. 1 and 2	196?	37.50	75.00	150.00
—Maroon label, no "Vendor: Mercury Record Corporation"					
❏ SR 90405 [S]	Bartok: First Rhapsody; Mendelssohn: Various Concertantes; Martinu: Rossini Variations; et al.	196?	10.00	20.00	40.00
—Third edition: Dark red (not maroon) label					
❏ SR 90405 [S]	Bartok: First Rhapsody; Mendelssohn: Various Concertantes; Martinu: Rossini Variations; et al.	196?	15.00	30.00	60.00
—Maroon label, with "Vendor: Mercury Record Corporation"					
❏ SR 90405 [S]	Bartok: First Rhapsody; Mendelssohn: Various Concertantes; Martinu: Rossini Variations; et al.	196?	30.00	60.00	120.00
—Maroon label, no "Vendor: Mercury Record Corporation"					
❏ SR 90480 [S]	Bach, J.S.: Three Sonatas	196?	50.00	100.00	200.00
—Maroon label, with "Vendor: Mercury Record Corporation"					

STARR, EDWIN
GORDY

❏ GS-931	Soul Master	1968	6.25	12.50	25.00
❏ GS-940	25 Miles	1969	6.25	12.50	25.00
❏ GS-945	Just We Two	1969	5.00	10.00	20.00
—With Blinky					
❏ GS-948	War & Peace	1970	5.00	10.00	20.00
❏ GS-956	Involved	1971	5.00	10.00	20.00
GRANITE					
❏ 1005	Free to Be Myself	1975	3.00	6.00	12.00
MOTOWN					
❏ M5-103V1	Superstar Series, Vol. 3	1981	2.50	5.00	10.00
❏ M5-170V1	War & Peace	1981	2.50	5.00	10.00
PICKWICK					
❏ SPC-3387	25 Miles	197?	2.50	5.00	10.00
20TH CENTURY					
❏ T-538	Edwin Starr	1977	2.50	5.00	10.00
❏ T-559	Clean	1978	2.50	5.00	10.00
❏ T-591	Happy Radio	1979	2.50	5.00	10.00
❏ T-615	Stronger Than You	1980	2.50	5.00	10.00
❏ T-634	The Best of Edwin Starr	1981	2.50	5.00	10.00

STARR, KAY
ABC

❏ S-631	When the Lights Go On Again	1968	3.00	6.00	12.00
CAPITOL					
❏ H 211 [10]	Songs by Starr	1950	17.50	35.00	70.00
❏ T 211 [M]	Songs by Starr	1955	12.50	25.00	50.00
❏ H 363 [10]	Kay Starr Style	1953	17.50	35.00	70.00
❏ T 363 [M]	Kay Starr Style	1955	12.50	25.00	50.00
❏ DT 415 [R]	The Hits of Kay Starr	196?	3.00	6.00	12.00
❏ H 415 [10]	The Hits of Kay Starr	1953	17.50	35.00	70.00
❏ T 415 [M]	The Hits of Kay Starr	1955	12.50	25.00	50.00
—Turquoise or gray label					
❏ T 415 [M]	The Hits of Kay Starr	1958	7.50	15.00	30.00
—Black label with colorband, Capitol logo at left					
❏ T 415 [M]	The Hits of Kay Starr	1962	5.00	10.00	20.00
—Black label with colorband, Capitol logo at top					
❏ T 580 [M]	In a Blue Mood	1955	12.50	25.00	50.00
❏ ST 1254 [S]	Movin'	1959	7.50	15.00	30.00
❏ T 1254 [M]	Movin'	1959	6.25	12.50	25.00
❏ ST 1303 [S]	Losers Weepers	1960	7.50	15.00	30.00
❏ T 1303 [M]	Losers Weepers	1960	6.25	12.50	25.00
❏ ST 1358 [S]	One More Time	1960	7.50	15.00	30.00
❏ T 1358 [M]	One More Time	1960	6.25	12.50	25.00
❏ ST 1374 [S]	Movin' on Broadway	1960	7.50	15.00	30.00
❏ T 1374 [M]	Movin' on Broadway	1960	6.25	12.50	25.00
❏ ST 1438 [S]	Kay Starr, Jazz Singer	1960	10.00	20.00	40.00
❏ T 1438 [M]	Kay Starr, Jazz Singer	1960	7.50	15.00	30.00
❏ ST 1468 [S]	All Starr Hits	1961	7.50	15.00	30.00
❏ T 1468 [M]	All Starr Hits	1961	6.25	12.50	25.00
❏ ST 1681 [S]	I Cry by Night	1962	6.25	12.50	25.00
❏ T 1681 [M]	I Cry by Night	1962	5.00	10.00	20.00
❏ ST 1795 [S]	Just Plain Country	1962	6.25	12.50	25.00
❏ ST-8-1795 [S]	Just Plain Country	196?	7.50	15.00	30.00
—Capitol Record Club edition					
❏ T 1795 [M]	Just Plain Country	1962	5.00	10.00	20.00
❏ ST 2106 [S]	The Fabulous Favorites	1964	3.75	7.50	15.00
❏ T 2106 [M]	The Fabulous Favorites	1964	3.00	6.00	12.00
❏ ST 2550 [S]	Tears and Heartaches/Old Records	1966	3.75	7.50	15.00
❏ T 2550 [M]	Tears and Heartaches/Old Records	1966	3.00	6.00	12.00
❏ SM-11323	Kay Starrs Again	1977	2.00	4.00	8.00
—Reissue with new prefix					
❏ ST-11323	Kay Starrs Again	1974	2.50	5.00	10.00
❏ SM-11880	Movin'	1979	2.50	5.00	10.00
CORONET					
❏ CX-106 [M]	Kay Starr Sings	196?	3.00	6.00	12.00
❏ CXS-106 [S]	Kay Starr Sings	196?	3.00	6.00	12.00
GNP CRESCENDO					
❏ GNPS-2083	Country	1974	2.50	5.00	10.00
❏ GNPS-2090	Back to the Roots	1975	2.50	5.00	10.00
HINDSIGHT					
❏ HSR-214	Kay Starr 1947	1985	2.50	5.00	10.00
LIBERTY					
❏ LRP-3280 [M]	Swingin' with the Starr	1963	6.25	12.50	25.00
—Reissue of 9001					
❏ LRP-9001 [M]	Swingin' with the Starr	1956	12.50	25.00	50.00

Number	Title (A Side/B Side)	Yr	VG	VG+	NM
PARAMOUNT					
❏ PAS-5001	How About This	1969	3.00	6.00	12.00
RCA CAMDEN					
❏ CAL-567 [M]	Kay Starr	196?	3.00	6.00	12.00
RCA VICTOR					
❏ LPM-1149 [M]	The One and Only Kay Starr	1955	7.50	15.00	30.00
❏ ANL1-1311	Pure Gold	1976	2.00	4.00	8.00
❏ LPM-1549 [M]	Blue Starr	1957	7.50	15.00	30.00
❏ LPM-1720 [M]	Rockin' with Kay	1958	12.50	25.00	50.00
❏ LPM-2055 [M]	I Hear the Word	1959	6.25	12.50	25.00
❏ LSP-2055 [S]	I Hear the Word	1959	7.50	15.00	30.00
RONDO-LETTE					
❏ A-3 [M]	Them There Eyes	1958	6.25	12.50	25.00
SUNSET					
❏ SUM-1126 [M]	Portrait of a Starr	196?	3.75	7.50	15.00
❏ SUS-5126 [R]	Portrait of a Starr	196?	2.50	5.00	10.00
STARR, KAY/ERROLL GARNER					
CROWN					
❏ CLP-5003 [M]	Singin' Kay Starr, Swingin' Erroll Garner	1957	7.50	15.00	30.00
MODERN					
❏ LMP-1203 [M]	Singin' Kay Starr, Swingin' Erroll Garner	1956	20.00	40.00	80.00
STARR, LUCILLE					
A&M					
❏ LP-107 [M]	French Song	1966	7.50	15.00	30.00
EPIC					
❏ BN 26436	Lonely Street	1969	7.50	15.00	30.00
STARR, RINGO					
Also see THE BEATLES; GEORGE HARRISON AND FRIENDS.					
APPLE					
❏ SW-3365	Sentimental Journey	1970	5.00	10.00	20.00
❏ SMAS-3368	Beaucoups of Blues	1970	5.00	10.00	20.00
❏ SWAL-3413	Ringo	1973	5.00	10.00	20.00
—Standard issue with booklet; Side 1, Song 2 identified on cover as "Hold On"					
❏ SWAL-3413	Ringo	1973	100.00	200.00	400.00
—With a 5:26 version of "Six O'Clock." On later copies, the song is shortened to 4:05 though the label still says 5:26. All known copies have a promo punch-hole in top corner of jacket; on Side 2 record, "Six O'Clock" will be the widest track.					
❏ SWAL-3413	Ringo	1974	6.25	12.50	25.00
—Later issue with booklet; Side 1, Song 2 identified on cover as "Have You Seen My Baby"					
❏ SW-3417	Goodnight Vienna	1974	3.00	6.00	12.00
❏ SW-3422	Blast from Your Past	1975	3.75	7.50	15.00
ATLANTIC					
❏ SD 18193	Ringo's Rotogravure	1976	3.75	7.50	15.00
—Deduct 2/3 for cut-outs					
❏ SD 18193 [DJ]	Ringo's Rotogravure	1976	7.50	15.00	30.00
—With "DJ Only" scrawled into trail-off area					
❏ SD 19108	Ringo the 4th	1977	3.75	7.50	15.00
—Deduct 1/2 for cut-outs					
❏ SD 19108 [DJ]	Ringo the 4th	1977	7.50	15.00	30.00
—With "DJ Only" scrawled into trail-off area					
BOARDWALK					
❏ NB1-33246	Stop and Smell the Roses	1981	2.50	5.00	10.00
—Deduct 1/2 for cut-outs					
CAPITOL					
❏ SW-3365	Sentimental Journey	197?	10.00	20.00	40.00
—Purple label, large Capitol logo					
❏ SN-16114	Ringo	198?	3.75	7.50	15.00
—Green label budget-line reissue with all errors corrected					
❏ SN-16218	Sentimental Journey	198?	6.25	12.50	25.00
—Green label budget-line reissue					
❏ SN-16219	Goodnight Vienna	198?	6.25	12.50	25.00
—Green label budget-line reissue					
❏ SN-16235	Beaucoups of Blues	198?	5.00	10.00	20.00
—Green label budget-line reissue					
❏ SN-16236	Blast from Your Past	198?	3.75	7.50	15.00
—Green label budget-line reissue					
PORTRAIT					
❏ JR 35378	Bad Boy	1978	3.75	7.50	15.00
—Deduct 1/3 for cut-outs					
❏ JR 35378 [DJ]	Bad Boy	1978	7.50	15.00	30.00
—Regular white-label promo in standard jacket					
❏ JR 35378 [DJ]	Bad Boy	1978	25.00	50.00	100.00
—White label promo with "Advance Promotion" on label; in plain white cover					
RHINO					
❏ R1 70199	Starr Struck: Ringo's Best 1976-1983	1989	6.25	12.50	25.00
RYKODISC					
❏ RALP 0190	Ringo Starr and His All-Starr Band	1990	7.50	15.00	30.00
—With limited, numbered obi (deduct $5 if missing)					
STARR, SALLY					
ARCADE					
❏ 1001 [M]	Our Gal Sal	1960	20.00	40.00	80.00
CLYMAX					
❏ 1001 [M]	Our Gal Sal	1959	50.00	100.00	200.00
STARZ					
CAPITOL					
❏ SPRO-8657/8 [DJ]	Live at Municipal Auditorium, Louisville, March 30, 1978	1978	7.50	15.00	30.00
—Promo-only "Superstars Radio Network Presents" album					
❏ ST-11539	Starz	1976	2.50	5.00	10.00
❏ SW-11617	Violation	1977	2.50	5.00	10.00
—Black vinyl					
❏ SW-11617	Violation	1977	5.00	10.00	20.00
—Gold vinyl					
❏ ST-11730	Attention Shoppers!	1978	2.50	5.00	10.00
❏ ST-11861	Coliseum Rock	1978	2.50	5.00	10.00

Number	Title (A Side/B Side)	Yr	VG	VG+	NM
METAL BLADE					
❏ 73430	Live in Action	1989	3.00	6.00	12.00
VIOLATION					
❏ 0001	Live in America	1983	3.75	7.50	15.00
STATLER BROTHERS, THE					
COLUMBIA					
❏ CL 2449 [M]	Flowers on the Wall	1966	6.25	12.50	25.00
❏ CL 2719 [M]	The Big Hits	1967	7.50	15.00	30.00
❏ CS 9249 [S]	Flowers on the Wall	1966	7.50	15.00	30.00
❏ PC 9249	Flowers on the Wall	198?	2.00	4.00	8.00
—Reissue with new prefix					
❏ CS 9519 [S]	The Big Hits	1967	6.25	12.50	25.00
❏ PC 9519	The Big Hits	198?	2.00	4.00	8.00
—Reissue with new prefix					
❏ CS 9878	Oh Happy Day	1969	6.25	12.50	25.00
❏ PC 9878	Oh Happy Day	198?	2.00	4.00	8.00
—Reissue with new prefix					
❏ CG 31557 [(2)]	The World of the Statler Brothers	198?	3.00	6.00	12.00
—Reissue with new prefix					
❏ KG 31557 [(2)]	The World of the Statler Brothers	1972	5.00	10.00	20.00
❏ C 31560	How Great Thou Art	197?	2.50	5.00	10.00
—Reissue of Harmony 31560					
HARMONY					
❏ H 30610	Big Country Hits	1971	3.00	6.00	12.00
❏ KH 31560	How Great Thou Art	1972	3.00	6.00	12.00
❏ KH 32256	Do You Love Me Tonight	1973	3.00	6.00	12.00
MERCURY					
❏ SRM-2-101 [(2)]	Holy Bible/The Old and New Testaments	1978	5.00	10.00	20.00
—Reissue of 1051 and 1052 in one package					
❏ SRM-1-676	Carry Me Back	1973	3.75	7.50	15.00
❏ SRM-1-707	Thank You World	1974	3.75	7.50	15.00
❏ SRM-1-1019	Sons of the Motherland	1975	3.75	7.50	15.00
❏ SRM-1-1037	The Best of the Statler Brothers	1975	3.00	6.00	12.00
❏ SRM-1-1051	Holy Bible: Old Testament	1975	3.75	7.50	15.00
❏ SRM-1-1052	Holy Bible: New Testament	1975	3.75	7.50	15.00
❏ SRM-1-1077	Harold, Lew, Phil & Don	1976	3.75	7.50	15.00
❏ SRM-1-1125	The Country America Loves	1977	3.75	7.50	15.00
❏ SRM-1-4048	The Legend Goes On	1982	3.00	6.00	12.00
❏ SRM-1-5001	Short Stories	1977	3.00	6.00	12.00
❏ SRM-1-5007	Entertainers...On and Off the Record	1978	3.00	6.00	12.00
❏ SRM-1-5012	Christmas Card	1978	2.50	5.00	10.00
❏ SRM-1-5016	The Originals	1979	3.00	6.00	12.00
❏ SRM-1-5024	The Best of the Statler Brothers Rides Again, Volume II	1980	3.00	6.00	12.00
❏ SRM-1-5027	10th Anniversary	1980	3.00	6.00	12.00
❏ SRM-1-6002	Years Ago	1981	3.00	6.00	12.00
❏ SR-61317	Bed of Rose's	1970	3.75	7.50	15.00
❏ SR-61349	Pictures of Moments to Remember	1971	3.75	7.50	15.00
❏ SR-61358	Innerview	1972	3.75	7.50	15.00
❏ SR-61367	Country Music "Then and Now"	1972	3.75	7.50	15.00
❏ SR-61374	The Statler Brothers Sing Country Symphonies in E Major	1973	3.75	7.50	15.00
❏ 812184-1	Today	1983	2.50	5.00	10.00
❏ 812282-1	10th Anniversary	1983	2.00	4.00	8.00
❏ 812283-1	Entertainers...On and Off the Record	1983	2.00	4.00	8.00
❏ 812284-1	Carry Me Back	1983	2.00	4.00	8.00
❏ 818652-1	Atlanta Blue	1984	2.50	5.00	10.00
❏ 822524-1	The Best of the Statler Brothers	1984	2.00	4.00	8.00
❏ 822525-1	The Best of the Statler Brothers Rides Again, Volume II	1984	2.00	4.00	8.00
❏ 822743-1	Christmas Card	1985	2.00	4.00	8.00
❏ 824420-1	Pardners in Rhyme	1985	2.50	5.00	10.00
❏ 824785-1	Christmas Present	1985	2.50	5.00	10.00
❏ 826247-1	Bed of Rose's	1986	2.00	4.00	8.00
❏ 826259-1	Innerview	1986	2.00	4.00	8.00
❏ 826260-1	Country Music "Then and Now"	1986	2.00	4.00	8.00
❏ 826264-1 [(2)]	Holy Bible/The Old and New Testaments	1986	2.50	5.00	10.00
❏ 826267-1	Holy Bible: Old Testament	1986	2.00	4.00	8.00
❏ 826268-1	Holy Bible: New Testament	1986	2.00	4.00	8.00
❏ 826269-1	Harold, Lew, Phil & Don	1986	2.00	4.00	8.00
❏ 826275-1	The Country America Loves	1986	2.00	4.00	8.00
❏ 826278-1	The Legend Goes On	1986	2.00	4.00	8.00
❏ 826280-1	Short Stories	1986	2.00	4.00	8.00
❏ 826281-1	The Originals	1986	2.00	4.00	8.00
❏ 826710-1	Radio Gospel Favorites	1986	2.50	5.00	10.00
❏ 826782-1	Four for the Show	1986	2.50	5.00	10.00
❏ 832404-1	Maple Street Memories	1987	2.50	5.00	10.00
❏ 834626-1	The Statlers Greatest Hits	1988	2.50	5.00	10.00
❏ 838231-1	Statler Brothers Live — Sold Out	1989	3.75	7.50	15.00
PRIORITY					
❏ PU 37709	Country Gospel	1982	2.50	5.00	10.00
STATON, CANDI					
FAME					
❏ 1800	Candi Staton	1972	5.00	10.00	20.00
❏ ST-4201	I'm a Prisoner	1970	5.00	10.00	20.00
❏ ST-4202	Stand By Your Man	1971	5.00	10.00	20.00
WARNER BROS.					
❏ BS 2830	Candi	1974	3.00	6.00	12.00
❏ BS 2948	Young Hearts Run Free	1976	3.00	6.00	12.00
❏ BS 3040	Music Speaks Louder Than Words	1977	3.00	6.00	12.00
❏ BSK 3207	House of Love	1978	3.00	6.00	12.00
❏ BSK 3333	Chance	1979	3.00	6.00	12.00
❏ BSK 3428	Candi Staton	1980	3.00	6.00	12.00
STATON, DAKOTA					
CAPITOL					
❏ T 876 [M]	The Late, Late Show	1957	12.50	25.00	50.00
—Turquoise or gray label					
❏ T 876 [M]	The Late, Late Show	1959	7.50	15.00	30.00
—Black label with colorband, Capitol logo at left					

S

Number	Title (A Side/B Side)	Yr	VG	VG+	NM
❏ T 1003 [M]	In the Night	1958	12.50	25.00	50.00
—Turquoise or gray label					
❏ T 1003 [M]	In the Night	1959	7.50	15.00	30.00
—Black label with colorband, Capitol logo at left					
❏ ST 1054 [S]	Dynamic!	1959	10.00	20.00	40.00
—Black label with colorband, Capitol logo at left					
❏ ST 1054 [S]	Dynamic!	1962	5.00	10.00	20.00
—Black label with colorband, Capitol logo at top					
❏ T 1054 [M]	Dynamic!	1958	7.50	15.00	30.00
—Black label with colorband, Capitol logo at left					
❏ ST 1170 [S]	Crazy He Calls Me	1959	10.00	20.00	40.00
—Black label with colorband, Capitol logo at left					
❏ ST 1170 [S]	Crazy He Calls Me	1962	5.00	10.00	20.00
—Black label with colorband, Capitol logo at top					
❏ T 1170 [M]	Crazy He Calls Me	1959	7.50	15.00	30.00
—Black label with colorband, Capitol logo at left					
❏ ST 1241 [S]	Time to Swing	1959	10.00	20.00	40.00
—Black label with colorband, Capitol logo at left					
❏ ST 1241 [S]	Time to Swing	1962	5.00	10.00	20.00
—Black label with colorband, Capitol logo at top					
❏ T 1241 [M]	Time to Swing	1959	7.50	15.00	30.00
—Black label with colorband, Capitol logo at left					
❏ ST 1325 [S]	More Than the Most	1960	10.00	20.00	40.00
—Black label with colorband, Capitol logo at left					
❏ ST 1325 [S]	More Than the Most	1962	5.00	10.00	20.00
—Black label with colorband, Capitol logo at top					
❏ T 1325 [M]	More Than the Most	1960	7.50	15.00	30.00
—Black label with colorband, Capitol logo at left					
❏ ST 1387 [S]	Ballads and the Blues	1962	5.00	10.00	20.00
—Black label with colorband, Capitol logo at left					
❏ T 1387 [M]	Ballads and the Blues	1960	7.50	15.00	30.00
—Black label with colorband, Capitol logo at left					
❏ T 1387 [M]	Ballads and the Blues	1962	3.75	7.50	15.00
—Black label with colorband, Capitol logo at top					
❏ ST 1427 [S]	Softly	1961	10.00	20.00	40.00
—Black label with colorband, Capitol logo at left					
❏ ST 1427 [S]	Softly	1962	5.00	10.00	20.00
—Black label with colorband, Capitol logo at top					
❏ T 1427 [M]	Softly	1961	7.50	15.00	30.00
—Black label with colorband, Capitol logo at left					
❏ ST 1490 [S]	Dakota	1961	10.00	20.00	40.00
—Black label with colorband, Capitol logo at left					
❏ ST 1490 [S]	Dakota	1962	5.00	10.00	20.00
—Black label with colorband, Capitol logo at top					
❏ T 1490 [M]	Dakota	1961	7.50	15.00	30.00
—Black label with colorband, Capitol logo at left					
❏ ST 1597 [S]	'Round Midnight	1961	10.00	20.00	40.00
—Black label with colorband, Capitol logo at left					
❏ ST 1597 [S]	'Round Midnight	1962	5.00	10.00	20.00
—Black label with colorband, Capitol logo at top					
❏ T 1597 [M]	'Round Midnight	1961	7.50	15.00	30.00
—Black label with colorband, Capitol logo at left					
❏ ST 1649 [S]	Dakota at Storyville	1962	6.25	12.50	25.00
❏ T 1649 [M]	Dakota at Storyville	1962	5.00	10.00	20.00

LONDON

Number	Title (A Side/B Side)	Yr	VG	VG+	NM
❏ LL 3495 [M]	Dakota '67	1967	5.00	10.00	20.00

UNITED ARTISTS

Number	Title (A Side/B Side)	Yr	VG	VG+	NM
❏ UAL-3292 [M]	From Dakota with Love	1963	5.00	10.00	20.00
❏ UAL-3312 [M]	Live and Swinging	1963	5.00	10.00	20.00
❏ UAL-3355 [M]	Dakota Staton with Strings	1964	5.00	10.00	20.00
❏ UAS-6292 [S]	From Dakota with Love	1963	6.25	12.50	25.00
❏ UAS-6316 [S]	Live and Swinging	1963	6.25	12.50	25.00
❏ UAS-6355 [S]	Dakota Staton with Strings	1964	6.25	12.50	25.00

STATUS QUO

A&M

Number	Title (A Side/B Side)	Yr	VG	VG+	NM
❏ SP-3615	Hello!	1974	3.00	6.00	12.00
❏ SP-3649	Quo	1974	3.00	6.00	12.00
❏ SP-4381	Piledriver	1973	3.00	6.00	12.00

CADET CONCEPT

❏ LPS-315	Messages from the Status Quo	1968	12.50	25.00	50.00

CAPITOL

❏ ST-11381	On the Level	1975	2.50	5.00	10.00
❏ ST-11509	Status Quo	1976	2.50	5.00	10.00
❏ SKBB-11623 [(2)]	Status Quo Live	1977	3.00	6.00	12.00
❏ ST-11749	Rockin' All Over the World	1978	2.50	5.00	10.00

JANUS

❏ JLS-3018	Ma Kelly's Greasy Spoon	1970	3.75	7.50	15.00

MERCURY

❏ 836651-1	Status Quo	1989	3.00	6.00	12.00

PYE

❏ 3301	Dog of Two Head	1971	3.75	7.50	15.00

RIVA

❏ 7402	Now Here This	1980	2.50	5.00	10.00

STEAGALL, RED

ABC

❏ AB-1051	Hang On Feelin'	1978	3.00	6.00	12.00

ABC DOT

❏ DOSD-2055	Lone Star Beer and Bob Wills Music	1976	3.75	7.50	15.00
❏ DOSD-2068	Texas Red	1976	3.00	6.00	12.00
❏ DO-2078	For All Our Cowboy Friends	1977	3.00	6.00	12.00

CAPITOL

❏ ST-11056	Party Dolls and Wine	1972	5.00	10.00	20.00
❏ ST-11162	Somewhere My Love	1973	3.00	6.00	12.00
❏ ST-11228	If You've Got the Time, I've Got the Song	1973	3.00	6.00	12.00
❏ ST-11321	Finer Things in Life	1974	3.00	6.00	12.00

MCA

❏ 680	For All Our Cowboy Friends	198?	2.00	4.00	8.00
—Reissue of ABC Dot 2078					

Number	Title (A Side/B Side)	Yr	VG	VG+	NM
❏ 681	Hang On Feelin'	198?	2.00	4.00	8.00
—Reissue of ABC 1051					
❏ 985	Lone Star Beer and Bob Wills Music	1986	2.50	5.00	10.00
—Reissue of ABC Dot 2055					

STEAM

MERCURY

❏ SR 61254	Steam	1969	5.00	10.00	20.00

STEAMHAMMER

EPIC

❏ BN 26490	Reflection	1969	7.50	15.00	30.00
❏ BN 26552	Steamhammer	1970	7.50	15.00	30.00

STEARNS, JUNE

COLUMBIA

❏ CS 9783	River of Regret	1969	5.00	10.00	20.00

STEEL

EPIC

❏ E 30875	Steel	1971	5.00	10.00	20.00

STEELE, TOMMY

LIBERTY

❏ LRP-3426 [M]	Everything's Coming Up Broadway	1965	5.00	10.00	20.00
❏ LRP-3566 [M]	Sixpenny Millionaire	1968	7.50	15.00	30.00
—Stereo cover with "Audition Mono LP Not for Sale" sticker attached; label is stock					
❏ LST-7426 [S]	Everything's Coming Up Broadway	1965	6.25	12.50	25.00
❏ LST-7566 [S]	Sixpenny Millionaire	1968	3.75	7.50	15.00

LONDON

❏ LL 1770 [M]	Rock Around the World	195?	12.50	25.00	50.00

STEELEYE SPAN

BIG TREE

❏ BTS 2004	Please to See the King	1971	7.50	15.00	30.00

CHRYSALIS

❏ CHR 1008	Below the Salt	1972	3.75	7.50	15.00
—Green label, "3300 Warner Blvd." address					
❏ CHR 1008	Below the Salt	1977	3.00	6.00	12.00
—Blue label, New York address					
❏ CHR 1046	Parcel of Rogues	1973	3.75	7.50	15.00
—Green label, "3300 Warner Blvd." address					
❏ CHR 1046	Parcel of Rogues	1977	3.00	6.00	12.00
—Blue label, New York address					
❏ CHR 1053	Now We Are Six	1974	3.75	7.50	15.00
—Green label, "3300 Warner Blvd." address					
❏ CHR 1053	Now We Are Six	1977	3.00	6.00	12.00
—Blue label, New York address					
❏ CHR 1071	Commoners Crown	1975	3.75	7.50	15.00
—Green label, "3300 Warner Blvd." address					
❏ CHR 1071	Commoners Crown	1977	3.00	6.00	12.00
—Blue label, New York address					
❏ CHR 1091	All Around My Hat	1975	3.75	7.50	15.00
—Green label, "3300 Warner Blvd." address					
❏ CHR 1091	All Around My Hat	1977	3.00	6.00	12.00
—Blue label, New York address					
❏ CHR 1119	Please to See the King	1976	3.75	7.50	15.00
—Reissue of Big Tree LP; green label, "3300 Warner Blvd." address					
❏ CHR 1119	Please to See the King	1977	3.00	6.00	12.00
—Blue label, New York address					
❏ CHR 1120	Hark the Village Wait	1976	3.75	7.50	15.00
—First US issue of debut LP; green label, "3300 Warner Blvd." address					
❏ CHR 1120	Hark the Village Wait	1977	3.00	6.00	12.00
—Blue label, New York address					
❏ CHR 1121	Ten Man Mop	1976	3.75	7.50	15.00
—First US issue of third UK LP; green label, "3300 Warner Blvd." address					
❏ CHR 1121	Ten Man Mop	1977	3.00	6.00	12.00
—Blue label, New York address					
❏ CHR 1123	Rocket Cottage	1976	3.75	7.50	15.00
—Green label, "3300 Warner Blvd." address					
❏ CHR 1123	Rocket Cottage	1977	3.00	6.00	12.00
—Blue label, New York address					
❏ CHR2 1136 [(2)]	The Steeleye Span Story: Original Masters	1977	3.75	7.50	15.00
❏ CHR 1151	Storm Force Ten	1978	3.00	6.00	12.00
❏ CHR 1199	Live at Last	1978	3.00	6.00	12.00
❏ V2X 41136 [(2)]	The Steeleye Span Story: Original Masters	1984	3.00	6.00	12.00
—Reissue of 1136					

MOBILE FIDELITY

❏ 1-027	All Around My Hat	1980	6.25	12.50	25.00
—Audiophile vinyl					

PAIR

❏ CRPDL-2-1021 [(2)]	Dogs and Ferrets	1983	3.75	7.50	15.00

SHANACHIE

❏ 64020	Tempted and Tried	1989	3.00	6.00	12.00
❏ 79039	Below the Salt	1989	3.00	6.00	12.00
❏ 79045	Parcel of Rogues	1989	3.00	6.00	12.00
❏ 79049	Ten Man Mop	1989	3.00	6.00	12.00
❏ 79052	Hark the Village Wait	1989	3.00	6.00	12.00
❏ 79059	All Around My Hat	1989	3.00	6.00	12.00
❏ 79060	Now We Are Six	1989	3.00	6.00	12.00
❏ 79063	Back in Line	1989	3.00	6.00	12.00
❏ 79071/2 [(2)]	Portfolio	1990	5.00	10.00	20.00

TAKOMA

❏ TAK-7097	Sails of Silver	1981	2.50	5.00	10.00

STEELY DAN

ABC

❏ 758	Can't Buy a Thrill	1972	3.00	6.00	12.00
—Black label					
❏ 758	Can't Buy a Thrill	1974	2.50	5.00	10.00
—Multicolor label					
❏ 779	Countdown to Ecstasy	1973	3.00	6.00	12.00
—Black label					

Number	Title (A Side/B Side)	Yr	VG	VG+	NM
❑ 779	Countdown to Ecstasy	1974	2.50	5.00	10.00
—Multicolor label					
❑ 806	Pretzel Logic	1974	2.50	5.00	10.00
—Multicolor label					
❑ 806	Pretzel Logic	1974	3.00	6.00	12.00
—Black label					
❑ 846	Katy Lied	1975	3.00	6.00	12.00
❑ 931	The Royal Scam	1976	3.00	6.00	12.00
❑ AA-1006	Aja	1977	3.00	6.00	12.00
❑ 2022-1107 [(2)]	Greatest Hits	1978	5.00	10.00	20.00
—Canadian import on gold vinyl, widely available in U.S.					
❑ AK-1107 [(2)]	Greatest Hits	1978	3.75	7.50	15.00
ABC DUNHILL					
❑ SMAS-94976	Can't Buy a Thrill	1973	6.25	12.50	25.00
—Capitol Record Club edition pressed on the wrong label					
COMMAND					
❑ QD-40009 [Q]	Can't Buy a Thrill	1974	5.00	10.00	20.00
❑ QD-40010 [Q]	Countdown to Ecstasy	1974	5.00	10.00	20.00
❑ QD-40015 [Q]	Pretzel Logic	1974	5.00	10.00	20.00
MCA					
❑ AA-1006	Aja	1980	2.50	5.00	10.00
❑ 1591	Can't Buy a Thrill	1987	—	3.00	6.00
❑ 1592	Countdown to Ecstasy	1987	—	3.00	6.00
❑ 1593	Pretzel Logic	1987	—	3.00	6.00
❑ 1594	Katy Lied	1987	—	3.00	6.00
❑ 1595	The Royal Scam	1987	—	3.00	6.00
❑ 1688	Aja	1987	—	3.00	6.00
❑ 1693	Gaucho	1987	—	3.00	6.00
—Many in the 1500 and 1600 series have a gold stamp with the new number on the cover					
❑ 5324	Gold	1982	2.50	5.00	10.00
❑ 2-6008 [(2)]	Greatest Hits	1980	3.00	6.00	12.00
❑ 6102	Gaucho	1980	2.50	5.00	10.00
❑ 16009	Gaucho	1981	12.50	25.00	50.00
—Audiophile pressing					
❑ 16016	Gold	1982	12.50	25.00	50.00
—Audiophile pressing					
❑ 37040	Can't Buy a Thrill	1980	2.00	4.00	8.00
❑ 37041	Countdown to Ecstasy	1980	2.00	4.00	8.00
❑ 37042	Pretzel Logic	1980	2.00	4.00	8.00
❑ 37043	Katy Lied	1980	2.00	4.00	8.00
❑ 37044	The Royal Scam	1980	2.00	4.00	8.00
❑ 37243	Gold	1984	2.00	4.00	8.00
MOBILE FIDELITY					
❑ 1-007	Katy Lied	1979	20.00	40.00	80.00
—Audiophile vinyl					
❑ 1-033	Aja	1980	12.50	25.00	50.00
—Audiophile vinyl					

STEIG, JEREMY
BLUE NOTE

❑ BST-84354	Wayfaring Stranger	1970	5.00	10.00	20.00

STEIN, HAL, AND WARREN FITZGERALD
PROGRESSIVE

❑ PLP-1002 [M]	Hal Stein-Warren Fitzgerald Quintet	1955	125.00	250.00	500.00

STEIN, LOU
BRUNSWICK

❑ BL 58053 [10]	Lou Stein	1953	12.50	25.00	50.00
EPIC					
❑ LG 3101 [M]	House Top	1955	10.00	20.00	40.00
❑ LN 3148 [M]	Three, Four and Five	1955	10.00	20.00	40.00
❑ LN 3186 [M]	From Broadway to Paris	1955	10.00	20.00	40.00
JUBILEE					
❑ JLP-8 [10]	Six for Kicks	1954	12.50	25.00	50.00
❑ JLP-1019 [M]	Eight for Kicks, Four for Laughs	1956	10.00	20.00	40.00

STEPHENS, LEIGH
PHILIPS

❑ PHS 600294	Red Weather	1969	20.00	40.00	80.00

STEPPENWOLF
ABC

❑ AC-30008	The ABC Collection	1976	3.75	7.50	15.00
ABC DUNHILL					
❑ DS-50029 [S]	Steppenwolf	1968	5.00	10.00	20.00
❑ DS-50037	The Second	1968	6.25	12.50	25.00
—With chrome border on cover					
❑ DS-50037	The Second	1968	7.50	15.00	30.00
—With white border on cover					
❑ DSX-50053	At Your Birthday Party	1969	5.00	10.00	20.00
❑ DS-50060	Early Steppenwolf	1969	5.00	10.00	20.00
—Actually a 1967 concert by Sparrow (pre-Steppenwolf)					
❑ DS-50066	Monster	1969	5.00	10.00	20.00
❑ DSD-50075 [(2)]	Steppenwolf 'Live'	1970	6.25	12.50	25.00
❑ DSX-50090	Steppenwolf 7	1970	5.00	10.00	20.00
❑ DSX-50099	Steppenwolf Gold/Their Great Hits	1971	5.00	10.00	20.00
❑ DSX-50110	For Ladies Only	1971	5.00	10.00	20.00
❑ DSX-50124	Rest in Peace	1972	5.00	10.00	20.00
❑ DSX-50135	16 Greatest Hits	1973	5.00	10.00	20.00
DUNHILL					
❑ D-50029 [M]	Steppenwolf	1968	37.50	75.00	150.00
❑ DS-50029 [S]	Steppenwolf	1968	10.00	20.00	40.00
❑ ST-91487	Steppenwolf	1968	6.25	12.50	25.00
—Capitol Record Club edition					
❑ SKAO-93083	Monster	1969	6.25	12.50	25.00
—Capitol Record Club edition on old-style Dunhill label					
EPIC					
❑ PE 33583	Hour of the Wolf	1975	3.00	6.00	12.00
❑ PE 34120	Skullduggery	1976	3.00	6.00	12.00
❑ JE 34382	Reborn to Be Wild	1977	3.00	6.00	12.00

Number	Title (A Side/B Side)	Yr	VG	VG+	NM
MCA					
❑ 1599	16 Greatest Hits	198?	2.00	4.00	8.00
—Reissue of 37049					
❑ 2-6013 [(2)]	Steppenwolf 'Live'	198?	2.50	5.00	10.00
❑ 37045	Steppenwolf	1979	2.00	4.00	8.00
❑ 37046	The Second	1979	2.00	4.00	8.00
❑ 37047	Steppenwolf 7	1979	2.00	4.00	8.00
❑ 37049	16 Greatest Hits	1979	2.00	4.00	8.00
❑ DSX-50099	Steppenwolf Gold/Their Great Hits	1980	3.00	6.00	12.00
—Columbia House edition on blue rainbow label, but retaining the original ABC Dunhill catalog number					
MUMS					
❑ KZ 33093	Slow Flux	1974	3.75	7.50	15.00
NAUTILUS					
❑ NR-53	Wolftracks	198?	12.50	25.00	50.00
—As "John Kay and Steppenwolf"; audiophile vinyl					
PICKWICK					
❑ SPC-3603	Best of Steppenwolf	1978	2.50	5.00	10.00

STEVENS, APRIL
AUDIO LAB

❑ AL-1534 [M]	Torrid Tunes	1959	50.00	100.00	200.00
IMPERIAL					
❑ LP-9118 [M]	Teach Me Tiger	1960	15.00	30.00	60.00
❑ LP-12055 [S]	Teach Me Tiger	1960	25.00	50.00	100.00

STEVENS, CAT
A&M

❑ SP-3160	Mona Bone Jakon	198?	2.00	4.00	8.00
—Reissue of 4260					
❑ SP-3285	Footsteps in the Dark — Greatest Hits, Volume Two	1986	2.00	4.00	8.00
—Reissue of 3736					
❑ SP-3623	Buddha and the Chocolate Box	1974	3.00	6.00	12.00
❑ SP-3736	Footsteps in the Dark — Greatest Hits, Volume Two	1984	2.50	5.00	10.00
❑ SP-4260	Mona Bone Jakon	1970	3.00	6.00	12.00
—Brown label					
❑ SP-4260	Mona Bone Jakon	1974	2.50	5.00	10.00
—Mostly silver label with gradually fading "A&M"					
❑ SP-4280	Tea for the Tillerman	1971	3.00	6.00	12.00
—Brown label					
❑ SP-4280	Tea for the Tillerman	1974	2.50	5.00	10.00
—Mostly silver label with gradually fading "A&M"					
❑ SP-4313	Teaser and the Firecat	1971	3.00	6.00	12.00
—Brown label					
❑ SP-4313	Teaser and the Firecat	1974	2.50	5.00	10.00
—Mostly silver label with gradually fading "A&M"					
❑ SP-4365	Catch Bull at Four	1972	3.00	6.00	12.00
❑ SP-4391	Foreigner	1973	3.00	6.00	12.00
❑ SP-4519	Greatest Hits	1975	3.00	6.00	12.00
❑ SP-4555	Numbers	1975	3.00	6.00	12.00
❑ SP-4702	Izitso	1977	3.00	6.00	12.00
❑ SP-4735	Back to Earth	1978	3.00	6.00	12.00
❑ QU-53623 [Q]	Buddha and the Chocolate Box	1974	5.00	10.00	20.00
❑ QU-54280 [Q]	Tea for the Tillerman	1974	5.00	10.00	20.00
❑ QU-54313 [Q]	Teaser and the Firecat	1974	5.00	10.00	20.00
❑ QU-54365 [Q]	Catch Bull at Four	1974	5.00	10.00	20.00
❑ QU-54391 [Q]	Foreigner	1974	5.00	10.00	20.00
❑ QU-54519 [Q]	Greatest Hits	1975	5.00	10.00	20.00
DERAM					
❑ DE 16005 [M]	Matthew and Son	1967	5.00	10.00	20.00
❑ DES 18005 [P]	Matthew and Son	1967	3.75	7.50	15.00
❑ DES 18005/10 [(2)P]	Matthew and Son/New Masters	1971	3.75	7.50	15.00
❑ DES 18010 [S]	New Masters	1968	3.75	7.50	15.00
❑ DES 18061 [P]	Very Young and Early Songs	1972	3.00	6.00	12.00
LONDON					
❑ LC-50010	Cat's Cradle	1977	3.00	6.00	12.00
❑ 820321-1	Cat's Cradle	1985	2.00	4.00	8.00
MOBILE FIDELITY					
❑ 1-035	Tea for the Tillerman	1979	10.00	20.00	40.00
—Audiophile vinyl					
❑ MFQR-035	Tea for the Tillerman	1984	30.00	60.00	120.00
—Ultra High Quality Recording in a box					
❑ 1-244	Teaser and the Firecat	1996	10.00	20.00	40.00
—Audiophile vinyl					
❑ 1-254	Izitso	1996	6.25	12.50	25.00
—Audiophile vinyl					

STEVENS, CONNIE
HARMONY

❑ HS 11312	The Hank Williams Songbook	1969	3.75	7.50	15.00
WARNER BROS.					
❑ W 1208 [M]	Conchetta	1958	12.50	25.00	50.00
❑ WS 1208 [S]	Conchetta	1958	15.00	30.00	60.00
❑ W 1382 [M]	Connie Stevens from "Hawaiian Eye"	1960	7.50	15.00	30.00
❑ WS 1382 [S]	Connie Stevens from "Hawaiian Eye"	1960	10.00	20.00	40.00
❑ W 1431 [M]	From Me to You	1962	7.50	15.00	30.00
❑ WS 1431 [S]	From Me to You	1962	10.00	20.00	40.00
❑ W 1432 [M]	Connie	1962	7.50	15.00	30.00
❑ WS 1432 [S]	Connie	1962	10.00	20.00	40.00
❑ W 1460 [M]	The Hank Williams Songbook	1962	7.50	15.00	30.00
❑ WS 1460 [S]	The Hank Williams Songbook	1962	10.00	20.00	40.00

STEVENS, DODIE
DOT

❑ DLP-3212 [M]	Dodie Stevens	1960	7.50	15.00	30.00
❑ DLP-3323 [M]	Over the Rainbow	1960	7.50	15.00	30.00
❑ DLP-3371 [M]	Pink Shoelaces	1961	7.50	15.00	30.00
❑ DLP-25212 [S]	Dodie Stevens	1960	10.00	20.00	40.00
❑ DLP-25323 [S]	Over the Rainbow	1960	10.00	20.00	40.00
❑ DLP-25371 [S]	Pink Shoelaces	1961	10.00	20.00	40.00

S

Number	Title (A Side/B Side)	Yr	VG	VG+	NM
STEVENS, LEITH					
CORAL					
❑ CRL 57283 [M]	Jazz Themes for Cops and Robbers	1958	12.50	25.00	50.00
DECCA					
❑ DL 5515 [10]	Jazz Themes in "The Wild One"	1954	20.00	40.00	80.00
STEVENS, RAY					
BARNABY					
❑ 5004	Ray Stevens' Greatest Hits	1974	2.50	5.00	10.00
—Reissue of 30770					
❑ 5005	Nashville	1974	2.50	5.00	10.00
—Reissue of 15007					
❑ 6003	Boogity Boogity	1974	3.00	6.00	12.00
❑ 6012	Misty	1975	3.00	6.00	12.00
❑ 6018	The Very Best of Ray Stevens	1975	3.00	6.00	12.00
❑ BR 15007	Nashville	1973	3.00	6.00	12.00
❑ Z 30092	Ray Stevens…Unreal!!!	1970	3.00	6.00	12.00
❑ Z 30770	Ray Stevens' Greatest Hits	1971	3.00	6.00	12.00
❑ Z 30809	Turn Your Radio On	1972	3.00	6.00	12.00
❑ KZ 32139	Losin' Streak	1972	3.00	6.00	12.00
❑ Z12 35005	Everything Is Beautiful	1970	3.75	7.50	15.00
MCA					
❑ 5517	He Thinks He's Ray Stevens	1984	2.50	5.00	10.00
❑ 5635	I Have Returned	1985	2.50	5.00	10.00
❑ 5795	Surely You Joust	1986	2.50	5.00	10.00
❑ 5918	Greatest Hits	1987	2.50	5.00	10.00
❑ 42020	Crackin' Up!	1987	2.50	5.00	10.00
❑ 42062	Greatest Hits, Volume 2	1987	2.50	5.00	10.00
❑ 42172	I Never Made a Record I Didn't Like	1988	2.50	5.00	10.00
❑ 42303	Beside Myself	1989	2.50	5.00	10.00
MERCURY					
❑ MG-20732 [M]	1,837 Seconds of Humor	1962	10.00	20.00	40.00
❑ MG-20828 [M]	This Is Ray Stevens	1963	6.25	12.50	25.00
❑ SR-60732 [S]	1,837 Seconds of Humor	1962	12.50	25.00	50.00
❑ SR-60828 [S]	This Is Ray Stevens	1963	7.50	15.00	30.00
❑ SR-61272	The Best of Ray Stevens	1968	3.75	7.50	15.00
❑ 812780-1	Me	1984	2.50	5.00	10.00
MONUMENT					
❑ SLP-18102	Even Stevens	1968	3.75	7.50	15.00
❑ SLP-18115	Gitarzan	1969	3.75	7.50	15.00
❑ SLP-18134	Have a Little Talk with Myself	1970	3.75	7.50	15.00
PICKWICK					
❑ SPC-3266	Rock and Roll Show	1971	2.50	5.00	10.00
PRIORITY					
❑ PU 38075	Turn Your Radio On	1982	2.50	5.00	10.00
—Reissue of Barnaby 30809					
RCA VICTOR					
❑ AHL1-3574	Shriner's Convention	1980	2.50	5.00	10.00
❑ AHL1-3841	One More Last Chance	1981	2.50	5.00	10.00
❑ AYL1-4253	Shriner's Convention	1982	2.00	4.00	8.00
—"Best Buy Series" reissue					
❑ AHL1-4288	Don't Laugh Now	1982	2.50	5.00	10.00
❑ AHL1-4727	Greatest Hits	1983	2.50	5.00	10.00
❑ AYL1-5153	Greatest Hits	1985	2.00	4.00	8.00
—"Best Buy Series" reissue					
❑ CPL1-7161	Collector's Series	1986	2.50	5.00	10.00
WARNER BROS.					
❑ BS 2914	Just for the Record	1976	2.50	5.00	10.00
❑ BS 2997	Feel the Music	1977	2.50	5.00	10.00
❑ BS 3098	There Is Something...	1977	2.50	5.00	10.00
❑ BS 3195	Be Your Own Best Friend	1978	2.50	5.00	10.00
❑ BSK 3332	The Feeling's Not Right Again	1979	2.50	5.00	10.00
STEVENS, TERRI					
EVEREST					
❑ SDBR-1088 [S]	It's Been a Long, Long Time	1960	6.25	12.50	25.00
❑ LPBR-5088 [M]	It's Been a Long, Long Time	1960	5.00	10.00	20.00
STEWARD, ALEC					
BLUESVILLE					
❑ BVLP-1076 [M]	Creepin' Blues	1963	20.00	40.00	80.00
—Blue label, silver print					
❑ BVLP-1076 [M]	Creepin' Blues	1964	6.25	12.50	25.00
—Blue label, trident logo at right					
STEWARD, HERB					
AVA					
❑ A-9 [M]	So Pretty	1962	6.25	12.50	25.00
❑ AS-9 [S]	So Pretty	1962	7.50	15.00	30.00
STEWART, AL					
ARISTA					
❑ AL 4190	Time Passages	1978	2.50	5.00	10.00
❑ AL6-8326	Year of the Cat	198?	2.00	4.00	8.00
—Reissue of Arista 9503					
❑ AL6-8342	Time Passages	198?	2.00	4.00	8.00
—Reissue of 4190					
❑ AL6-8359	Past, Present and Future	198?	2.00	4.00	8.00
—Reissue of Arista 9524					
❑ A2L 8607 [(2)]	Live/Indian Summer	1981	3.00	6.00	12.00
❑ AL 9503	Year of the Cat	1979	2.50	5.00	10.00
—Reissue of Janus 7022					
❑ AL 9520	24 Carrots	1980	2.50	5.00	10.00
❑ AL 9524	Past, Present and Future	1980	2.50	5.00	10.00
—Reissue of Janus 3063					
❑ AL 9525	Modern Times	1980	2.50	5.00	10.00
—Reissue of Janus 7012					
ENIGMA					
❑ D1-73316	Last Days of the Century	1988	3.00	6.00	12.00
EPIC					
❑ BN 26564	Love Chronicles	1970	5.00	10.00	20.00
JANUS					
❑ 3063	Past, Present and Future	1974	3.75	7.50	15.00
❑ 7012	Modern Times	1975	3.00	6.00	12.00
❑ 7022	Year of the Cat	1976	3.00	6.00	12.00
❑ 7026 [(2)]	The Early Years	1977	3.75	7.50	15.00
❑ 7026 [DJ]	The Early Years	1977	7.50	15.00	30.00
—Promo-only condensation of 2-LP set with rubber-stamp cover					
MOBILE FIDELITY					
❑ 1-009	Year of the Cat	1979	10.00	20.00	40.00
—Audiophile vinyl					
❑ 1-082	Time Passages	1981	7.50	15.00	30.00
—Audiophile vinyl					
NAUTILUS					
❑ NR-34	24 Carrots	198?	7.50	15.00	30.00
—Audiophile vinyl					
PASSPORT					
❑ PB-6042	Russians and Americans	1986	3.00	6.00	12.00
STEWART, ANDY					
CAPITOL					
❑ ST 10320 [S]	Andy Stewart's Scotland	196?	5.00	10.00	20.00
❑ T 10320 [M]	Andy Stewart's Scotland	196?	3.75	7.50	15.00
EPIC					
❑ LF 18027 [M]	A Scottish Soldier	196?	3.00	6.00	12.00
❑ LF 18031 [M]	Tunes of Glory	196?	3.00	6.00	12.00
❑ LF 18048 [M]	I'm Off to Bonnie Scotland	196?	3.00	6.00	12.00
❑ BF 19027 [S]	A Scottish Soldier	196?	3.75	7.50	15.00
❑ BF 19031 [S]	Tunes of Glory	196?	3.75	7.50	15.00
❑ BF 19048 [S]	I'm Off to Bonnie Scotland	196?	3.75	7.50	15.00
WARWICK					
❑ W 3043 [M]	A Scottish Soldier	1961	5.00	10.00	20.00
❑ WST 3043 [S]	A Scottish Soldier	1961	7.50	15.00	30.00
STEWART, BILLY					
CHESS					
❑ LP-1496 [M]	I Do Love You	196?	7.50	15.00	30.00
—Green "woman" cover					
❑ LP-1496 [M]	I Do Love You	1965	20.00	40.00	80.00
—Red cover, black "wheel"					
❑ LPS-1496 [S]	I Do Love You	196?	10.00	20.00	40.00
—Green "woman" cover					
❑ LPS-1496 [S]	I Do Love You	1965	25.00	50.00	100.00
—Red cover, black "wheel"					
❑ LP-1499 [M]	Unbelievable	1966	7.50	15.00	30.00
❑ LPS-1499 [S]	Unbelievable	1966	10.00	20.00	40.00
❑ LP-1513 [M]	Billy Stewart Teaches Old Standards New Tricks	1967	7.50	15.00	30.00
❑ LPS-1513 [S]	Billy Stewart Teaches Old Standards New Tricks	1967	10.00	20.00	40.00
❑ LPS-1547	Billy Stewart Remembered	1970	6.25	12.50	25.00
❑ CH-9104	The Greatest Sides	198?	2.50	5.00	10.00
❑ CH-50059	Cross My Heart	1974	3.75	7.50	15.00
STEWART, BOB					
DAWN					
❑ DLP-1103 [M]	Let's Talk About Love	1956	12.50	25.00	50.00
STEWART, HELYNE					
CONTEMPORARY					
❑ M-3601 [M]	Love Moods	1962	7.50	15.00	30.00
❑ S-7601 [S]	Love Moods	1962	10.00	20.00	40.00
STEWART, JOHN					
Also see THE KINGSTON TRIO.					
AFFORDABLE DREAMS					
❑ AD-01	Trancas	1984	2.50	5.00	10.00
ALLEGIANCE					
❑ AV-431	Blondes	1982	2.50	5.00	10.00
CAPITOL					
❑ ST-203	California Bloodlines	1969	3.75	7.50	15.00
❑ ST-540	Willard	1970	3.75	7.50	15.00
❑ SM-2975	Signals Through the Glass	1977	2.50	5.00	10.00
—Reissue with new prefix					
❑ ST 2975	Signals Through the Glass	1968	5.00	10.00	20.00
❑ SN-16150	California Bloodlines	198?	2.00	4.00	8.00
—Budget-line reissue					
❑ SN-16151	Willard	198?	2.00	4.00	8.00
—Budget-line reissue					
CYPRESS					
❑ 661117-1	Punch the Big Guy	1987	2.50	5.00	10.00
HOMECOMING					
❑ HC-0200	Centennial	1984	2.50	5.00	10.00
❑ HC-0300	The Last Campaign	1985	2.50	5.00	10.00
❑ HC-0500	The Trio Years	1986	2.50	5.00	10.00
RCA VICTOR					
❑ CPL2-0265 [(2)]	The Phoenix Concerts — Live	1974	3.75	7.50	15.00
❑ APL1-0816	Wingless Angels	1975	3.00	6.00	12.00
❑ AFL1-3513	John Stewart in Concert	1980	2.50	5.00	10.00
❑ AYL1-3731	Cannons in the Rain	1981	2.00	4.00	8.00
—"Best Buy Series" reissue					
❑ LSP-4827	Cannons in the Rain	1973	3.00	6.00	12.00
RSO					
❑ RS-1-3027	Fire in the Wind	1977	2.50	5.00	10.00
❑ RS-1-3051	Bombs Away Dream Babies	1979	2.50	5.00	10.00
❑ RS-1-3074	Dream Babies Go Hollywood	1980	2.50	5.00	10.00
WARNER BROS.					
❑ WS 1948	The Lonesome Picker Rides Again	1971	3.00	6.00	12.00
❑ BS 2611	Sunstorm	1972	3.00	6.00	12.00

Number	Title (A Side/B Side)	Yr	VG	VG+	NM
STEWART, REDD					
AUDIO LAB					
❑ AL-1528 [M]	Redd Stewart Sings Favorite Old Time Tunes	1959	50.00	100.00	200.00
HICKORY/MGM					
❑ H3G-4512	I Remember	1974	3.75	7.50	15.00
STEWART, REX					
AMERICAN RECORDING SOCIETY					
❑ G-448 [M]	The Big Challenge	1958	10.00	20.00	40.00
ATLANTIC					
❑ 1209 [M]	Big Jazz	1956	12.50	25.00	50.00
CONCERT HALL JAZZ					
❑ 1202 [M]	Dixieland On Location	1954	20.00	40.00	80.00
DIAL					
❑ LP-215 [10]	Ellingtonia	1951	62.50	125.00	250.00
FELSTED					
❑ 2001 [S]	Rendezvous with Rex	1958	7.50	15.00	30.00
❑ 7001 [M]	Rendezvous with Rex	1958	10.00	20.00	40.00
GRAND AWARD					
❑ GA 33-414 [M]	Just for Kicks	195?	10.00	20.00	40.00
JAZZTONE					
❑ J-1202 [M]	Dixieland Free-for-All	1956	10.00	20.00	40.00
❑ J-1250 [M]	Rex Stewart Plays Duke Ellington	1957	10.00	20.00	40.00
❑ J-1268 [M]	The Big Challenge	1957	10.00	20.00	40.00
❑ J-1285 [M]	The Big Reunion	1957	10.00	20.00	40.00
SWINGVILLE					
❑ SVLP-2006 [M]	The Happy Jazz of Rex Stewart	1960	12.50	25.00	50.00
—Purple label					
❑ SVLP-2006 [M]	The Happy Jazz of Rex Stewart	1965	6.25	12.50	25.00
—Blue label, trident logo at right					
UNITED ARTISTS					
❑ UAL-4009 [M]	Henderson Homecoming	1959	10.00	20.00	40.00
❑ UAS-5009 [S]	Henderson Homecoming	1959	7.50	15.00	30.00
URANIA					
❑ UJLP-2012 [M]	Cool Fever	1955	15.00	30.00	60.00
WARNER BROS.					
❑ W 1260 [M]	Porgy and Bess Revisited	1958	10.00	20.00	40.00
❑ WS 1260 [S]	Porgy and Bess Revisited	1958	7.50	15.00	30.00
"X"					
❑ LX-3001 [10]	Rex Stewart and His Orchestra	1954	25.00	50.00	100.00
STEWART, REX/ILLINOIS JACQUET					
GRAND AWARD					
❑ GA 33-315 [M]	Rex Stewart Plays Duke/Uptown Jazz	1955	10.00	20.00	40.00
STEWART, REX, AND DICKIE WELLS					
RCA VICTOR					
❑ LPM-2024 [M]	Chatter Jazz	1959	6.25	12.50	25.00
❑ LSP-2024 [S]	Chatter Jazz	1959	7.50	15.00	30.00
STEWART, ROD					
Also see JEFF BECK; FACES.					
ACCORD					
❑ SN-7142	Rod the Mod	1981	3.00	6.00	12.00
DCC COMPACT CLASSICS					
❑ LPZ-2010	Never a Dull Moment	1995	7.50	15.00	30.00
—Audiophile vinyl					
MERCURY					
❑ SRM-1-609	Every Picture Tells a Story	1971	2.50	5.00	10.00
—With poster missing; red label					
❑ SRM-1-609	Every Picture Tells a Story	1971	3.75	7.50	15.00
—Original cover has an attached, perforated poster					
❑ SRM-1-646	Never a Dull Moment	1972	3.00	6.00	12.00
—Red label					
❑ SRM-1-680	Sing It Again Rod	1973	3.00	6.00	12.00
—Red label					
❑ SRM-1-697	Rod Stewart/Faces Live: Coast to Coast Overtures and Beginners	1973	3.75	7.50	15.00
—By "Rod Stewart/Faces"					
❑ SRM-1-1017	Smiler	1974	3.00	6.00	12.00
—Chicago skyline label					
❑ SRM-2-7507 [(2)]	The Best of Rod Stewart	1976	3.75	7.50	15.00
❑ SRM-2-7509 [(2)]	The Best of Rod Stewart, Volume 2	1977	3.75	7.50	15.00
❑ SR-61237	The Rod Stewart Album	1969	6.25	12.50	25.00
—Cover is yellow with no black border					
❑ SR-61237	The Rod Stewart Album	1971	3.75	7.50	15.00
—Cover is yellow with black border; red label					
❑ SR-61264	Gasoline Alley	1970	5.00	10.00	20.00
—Cover is textured, most noticeably on the pebbles					
❑ SR-61264	Gasoline Alley	1971	3.75	7.50	15.00
—Cover is not textured; red label					
❑ 822385-1	Every Picture Tells a Story	1984	2.00	4.00	8.00
❑ 822791-1 [(2)]	The Best of Rod Stewart, Volume 2	1985	3.00	6.00	12.00
❑ 824881-1	Gasoline Alley	1985	2.00	4.00	8.00
❑ 824882-1	Sing It Again Rod	1985	2.00	4.00	8.00
❑ 826287-1 [(2)]	The Best of Rod Stewart	1985	3.00	6.00	12.00
MOBILE FIDELITY					
❑ 1-054	Blondes Have More Fun	1980	6.25	12.50	25.00
—Audiophile vinyl					
PRIVATE STOCK					
❑ PS-2021	A Shot of Rhythm and Blues	1976	3.75	7.50	15.00
SPRINGBOARD					
❑ SPB-4030	Rod Stewart and The Faces	197?	3.00	6.00	12.00
TRIP					
❑ TOP-16-31	Looking Back/16 Early Hits	1974	3.00	6.00	12.00
UNITED DISTRIBUTORS					
❑ UDL-2391	The Day Will Come	1981	5.00	10.00	20.00

Number	Title (A Side/B Side)	Yr	VG	VG+	NM
WARNER BROS.					
❑ BS 2875	Atlantic Crossing	1975	2.50	5.00	10.00
❑ BS 2938	A Night on the Town	1976	2.50	5.00	10.00
❑ BSK 3092	Foot Loose and Fancy Free	1977	2.50	5.00	10.00
❑ BSK 3108	Atlantic Crossing	1977	2.00	4.00	8.00
—Reissue of 2875					
❑ BSK 3116	A Night on the Town	1977	2.00	4.00	8.00
—Reissue of 2938					
❑ BSK 3261	Blondes Have More Fun	1978	2.50	5.00	10.00
❑ BSP 3276 [PD]	Blondes Have More Fun	1978	5.00	10.00	20.00
❑ HS 3373	Rod Stewart Greatest Hits	1979	2.50	5.00	10.00
❑ HS 3485	Foolish Behaviour	1980	2.50	5.00	10.00
❑ BSK 3602	Tonight I'm Yours	1981	2.50	5.00	10.00
❑ 23743 [(2)]	Absolutely Live	1982	3.00	6.00	12.00
❑ 23743 [(2)DJ]	Absolutely Live	1982	6.25	12.50	25.00
—Promo only on Quiex II vinyl					
❑ 23877	Body Wishes	1983	2.00	4.00	8.00
❑ 23877 [DJ]	Body Wishes	1983	3.75	7.50	15.00
—Promo only on Quiex II vinyl					
❑ 25095	Camouflage	1984	2.00	4.00	8.00
—Issued with 16 different back covers, all of equal value, that, when assembled, form a giant poster					
❑ 25446	Rod Stewart	1986	2.00	4.00	8.00
❑ 25884	Out of Order	1988	2.00	4.00	8.00
❑ 26158	Downtown Train: Selections from the Storyteller Anthology	1990	3.00	6.00	12.00
STEWART, SANDY					
AUDIOPHILE					
❑ AP-205	Sandy Stewart Sings Songs of Jerome Kern	1985	2.50	5.00	10.00
—Accompanied by Dick Hyman on piano					
COLPIX					
❑ CP-441 [M]	My Coloring Book	1963	6.25	12.50	25.00
❑ SCP-441 [S]	My Coloring Book	1963	7.50	15.00	30.00
STEWART, SLAM					
SAVOY					
❑ MG-12067 [M]	Bowin' Singin' Slam	1956	10.00	20.00	40.00
STEWART, TOM					
ABC-PARAMOUNT					
❑ ABC-117 [M]	Tom Stewart Sextette/Quintet	1956	12.50	25.00	50.00
STEWART, WYNN					
CAPITOL					
❑ ST-113	In Love	1969	5.00	10.00	20.00
❑ ST-214	Let the Whole World Sing It with Me	1969	5.00	10.00	20.00
❑ ST-324	Yours Forever	1969	5.00	10.00	20.00
❑ ST 2332 [S]	The Songs of Wynn Stewart	1965	6.25	12.50	25.00
❑ T 2332 [M]	The Songs of Wynn Stewart	1965	5.00	10.00	20.00
❑ ST 2737 [S]	It's Such a Pretty World Today	1967	6.25	12.50	25.00
❑ T 2737 [M]	It's Such a Pretty World Today	1967	5.00	10.00	20.00
❑ ST 2849 [S]	Love's Gonna Happen to Me	1968	5.00	10.00	20.00
❑ T 2849 [M]	Love's Gonna Happen to Me	1968	7.50	15.00	30.00
❑ ST 2921	Something Pretty	1968	5.00	10.00	20.00
HILLTOP					
❑ JM-6050 [M]	Above and Beyond the Call of Love	1967	3.75	7.50	15.00
❑ JS-6050 [S]	Above and Beyond the Call of Love	1967	3.00	6.00	12.00
PLAYBOY					
❑ PB 416	After the Storm	1976	2.50	5.00	10.00
WRANGLER					
❑ W-1006 [M]	Wynn Stewart	1962	7.50	15.00	30.00
❑ W-31006 [S]	Wynn Stewart	1962	10.00	20.00	40.00
STEWART, WYNN, AND JAN HOWARD					
CHALLENGE					
❑ CHL-611 [M]	Sweethearts of Country Music	1961	12.50	25.00	50.00
STARDAY					
❑ SLP-421	Wynn Stewart and Jan Howard Sing Their Hits	1968	6.25	12.50	25.00
STEWART FAMILY, THE					
KING					
❑ 687 [M]	Country Sacred Songs	1960	7.50	15.00	30.00
❑ 695 [M]	Golden Country Favorites	1960	7.50	15.00	30.00
STIDHAM, ARBEE					
BLUESVILLE					
❑ BVLP-1021 [M]	Tired of Wandering	1964	6.25	12.50	25.00
—Blue label, trident logo at right					
FOLKWAYS					
❑ F-31033	There's Always Tomorrow	1973	5.00	10.00	20.00
STIFF LITTLE FINGERS					
CAROLINE					
❑ 1377	See You Up There	1990	3.00	6.00	12.00
CHRYSALIS					
❑ CHR 1270	Nobody's Heroes	1980	5.00	10.00	20.00
❑ CHR 1300	Hanx	1980	5.00	10.00	20.00
❑ CHR 1339	Go For It	1981	5.00	10.00	20.00
ROUGH TRADE					
❑ ROUGH US 5	Inflammable Material	1980	6.25	12.50	25.00
—Released in U.K. in 1979					
STILLS, STEPHEN					
ATLANTIC					
❑ SD 2-903 [(2)]	Manassas	1972	3.75	7.50	15.00
❑ SD 7202	Stephen Stills	1970	3.00	6.00	12.00
❑ SD 7206	Stephen Stills 2	1971	3.00	6.00	12.00
❑ SD 7250	Down the Road	1973	3.00	6.00	12.00
❑ SD 18156	Stephen Stills Live	1975	3.00	6.00	12.00
❑ SD 18201	Still Stills — The Best of Stephen Stills	1976	2.50	5.00	10.00
❑ 80177	Right By You	1984	2.00	4.00	8.00

S

Number	Title (A Side/B Side)	Yr	VG	VG+	NM
COLUMBIA					
❏ PC 33575	Stills	1975	2.50	5.00	10.00
—No bar code on cover					
❏ PC 33575	Stills	198?	2.00	4.00	8.00
—Bar code on cover					
❏ PCQ 33575 [Q]	Stills	1975	5.00	10.00	20.00
❏ PC 34348	Illegal Stills	1976	2.50	5.00	10.00
❏ JC 35380	Thoroughfare Gap	1978	2.50	5.00	10.00

STING
Also see THE POLICE.

Number	Title (A Side/B Side)	Yr	VG	VG+	NM
A&M					
❏ SP-3295 [EP]	...Nada Como El Sol	1988	5.00	10.00	20.00
—Spanish versions of songs from "...Nothing Like the Sun"					
❏ SP-3750	The Dream of the Blue Turtles	1985	2.50	5.00	10.00
❏ SP-6402 [(2)]	...Nothing Like the Sun	1987	3.00	6.00	12.00
❏ 75021 6405-1	The Soul Cages	1991	3.00	6.00	12.00
❏ R 150266	The Dream of the Blue Turtles	1985	3.00	6.00	12.00
—RCA Music Service edition					
❏ R 273965 [(2)]	...Nothing Like the Sun	1987	3.50	7.00	14.00
—BMG Direct Marketing edition					
MOBILE FIDELITY					
❏ 1-185	The Dream of the Blue Turtles	1985	5.00	10.00	20.00
—Audiophile vinyl					

STINGERS, THE

Number	Title (A Side/B Side)	Yr	VG	VG+	NM
CROWN					
❏ CST-476 [S]	Guitars A Go Go	196?	10.00	20.00	40.00
❏ CLP-5476 [M]	Guitars A Go Go	196?	7.50	15.00	30.00

STINSON BROTHERS, THE

Number	Title (A Side/B Side)	Yr	VG	VG+	NM
CANADIAN AMERICAN					
❏ CALP-1012 [M]	The Stinson Brothers in Las Vegas	196?	5.00	10.00	20.00
❏ SCALP-1012 [S]	The Stinson Brothers in Las Vegas	196?	6.25	12.50	25.00

STITES, GARY

Number	Title (A Side/B Side)	Yr	VG	VG+	NM
CARLTON					
❏ LP-120 [M]	Lonely for You	1960	20.00	40.00	80.00
❏ STLP-120 [S]	Lonely for You	1960	30.00	60.00	120.00

STITT, SONNY

Number	Title (A Side/B Side)	Yr	VG	VG+	NM
ARGO					
❏ LP-629 [M]	Sonny Stitt	1958	10.00	20.00	40.00
❏ LP-661 [M]	Burnin'	1960	6.25	12.50	25.00
❏ LPS-661 [S]	Burnin'	1960	7.50	15.00	30.00
❏ LP-683 [M]	Sonny Stitt at the D.J. Lounge	1961	6.25	12.50	25.00
❏ LPS-683 [S]	Sonny Stitt at the D.J. Lounge	1961	7.50	15.00	30.00
❏ LP-709 [M]	Rearin' Back	1962	6.25	12.50	25.00
❏ LPS-709 [S]	Rearin' Back	1962	7.50	15.00	30.00
❏ LP-730 [M]	Move On Over	1964	6.25	12.50	25.00
❏ LPS-730 [S]	Move On Over	1964	7.50	15.00	30.00
❏ LP-744 [M]	My Main Man	1965	6.25	12.50	25.00
❏ LPS-744 [S]	My Main Man	1965	7.50	15.00	30.00
ATLANTIC					
❏ 1395 [M]	Sonny Stitt and the Top Brass	1962	6.25	12.50	25.00
❏ SD 1395 [S]	Sonny Stitt and the Top Brass	1962	7.50	15.00	30.00
❏ 1418 [M]	Stitt Plays Bird	1964	7.50	15.00	30.00
❏ SD 1418 [S]	Stitt Plays Bird	1964	10.00	20.00	40.00
CADET					
❏ LPS-760 [S]	Inter-Action	1966	5.00	10.00	20.00
❏ LPS-770 [S]	Soul In the Night	1966	5.00	10.00	20.00
COLPIX					
❏ CP-499 [M]	Broadway Soul	1964	7.50	15.00	30.00
❏ SCP-499 [S]	Broadway Soul	1964	7.50	15.00	30.00
IMPULSE!					
❏ A-43 [M]	Sonny Stitt Now!	1963	6.25	12.50	25.00
❏ AS-43 [S]	Sonny Stitt Now!	1963	7.50	15.00	30.00
❏ A-52 [M]	Salt and Pepper	1964	6.25	12.50	25.00
❏ AS-52 [S]	Salt and Pepper	1964	7.50	15.00	30.00
—With Paul Gonsalves					
JAZZLAND					
❏ JLP-71 [M]	Low Flame	1962	6.25	12.50	25.00
❏ JLP-971 [S]	Low Flame	1962	7.50	15.00	30.00
JAZZTONE					
❏ J-1231 [M]	Early Modern	1956	12.50	25.00	50.00
❏ J-1263 [M]	Early Modern	1957	10.00	20.00	40.00
NEW JAZZ					
❏ NJLP-103 [10]	Sonny Stitt and Bud Powell	1950	75.00	150.00	300.00
PACIFIC JAZZ					
❏ PJ-71 [M]	My Mother's Eyes	1963	5.00	10.00	20.00
❏ ST-71 [S]	My Mother's Eyes	1963	6.25	12.50	25.00
PRESTIGE					
❏ PRLP-103 [10]	Sonny Stitt Plays	1951	50.00	100.00	200.00
❏ PRLP-111 [10]	Mr. Saxophone	1951	50.00	100.00	200.00
❏ PRLP-126 [10]	Favorites, Volume 1	1952	50.00	100.00	200.00
❏ PRLP-148 [10]	Favorites, Volume 2	1953	50.00	100.00	200.00
❏ PRLP-7024 [M]	Sonny Stitt with Bud Powell and J.J. Johnson	1956	25.00	50.00	100.00
❏ PRLP-7077 [M]	Kaleidoscope	1957	25.00	50.00	100.00
❏ PRLP-7133 [M]	Stitt's Bits	1958	25.00	50.00	100.00
❏ PRLP-7244 [M]	Stitt Meets Brother Jack	1962	12.50	25.00	50.00
—Yellow label					
❏ PRLP-7244 [M]	Stitt Meets Brother Jack	1964	6.25	12.50	25.00
—Blue label with trident logo					
❏ PRST-7244 [S]	Stitt Meets Brother Jack	1962	12.50	25.00	50.00
❏ PRLP-7248 [M]	All God's Chillun Got Rhythm	1962	12.50	25.00	50.00
—Yellow label					
❏ PRLP-7248 [M]	All God's Chillun Got Rhythm	1964	6.25	12.50	25.00
—Blue label with trident logo					
❏ PRST-7248 [R]	All God's Chillun Got Rhythm	1962	7.50	15.00	30.00
❏ PRLP-7297 [M]	Soul Shack	1964	12.50	25.00	50.00
—Yellow label					

Number	Title (A Side/B Side)	Yr	VG	VG+	NM
❏ PRLP-7297 [M]	Soul Shack	1965	6.25	12.50	25.00
—Blue label with trident logo					
❏ PRST-7297 [S]	Soul Shack	1964	12.50	25.00	50.00
—Silver label					
❏ PRST-7297 [S]	Soul Shack	1965	6.25	12.50	25.00
—Blue label with trident logo					
❏ PRLP-7302 [M]	Primitive Soul!	1964	10.00	20.00	40.00
—Yellow label					
❏ PRLP-7302 [M]	Primitive Soul!	1965	6.25	12.50	25.00
—Blue label with trident logo					
❏ PRST-7302 [S]	Primitive Soul!	1964	10.00	20.00	40.00
—Silver label					
❏ PRST-7302 [S]	Primitive Soul!	1965	6.25	12.50	25.00
—Blue label with trident logo					
❏ PRLP-7332 [M]	Shangri-La	1964	5.00	10.00	20.00
❏ PRST-7332 [S]	Shangri-La	1964	6.25	12.50	25.00
❏ PRLP-7372 [M]	Soul People	1965	5.00	10.00	20.00
❏ PRST-7372 [S]	Soul People	1965	6.25	12.50	25.00
❏ PRLP-7436 [M]	Night Crawler	1966	5.00	10.00	20.00
❏ PRST-7436 [S]	Night Crawler	1966	6.25	12.50	25.00
❏ PRLP-7452 [M]	'Nuther Fu'ther	1966	5.00	10.00	20.00
❏ PRST-7452 [S]	'Nuther Fu'ther	1966	6.25	12.50	25.00
❏ PRLP-7459 [M]	Pow!	1967	6.25	12.50	25.00
❏ PRST-7459 [S]	Pow!	1967	5.00	10.00	20.00
ROOST					
❏ LP-415 [10]	Sonny Stitt Plays Arrangements from the Pen of Johnny Richards	1952	75.00	150.00	300.00
❏ LP-418 [10]	Jazz at the Hi-Hat	1954	75.00	150.00	300.00
❏ LP-1203 [M]	Battle of Birdland	1955	20.00	40.00	80.00
❏ LP-1208 [M]	Sonny Stitt	1956	20.00	40.00	80.00
❏ LP-2204 [M]	Sonny Stitt Plays Arrangements of Quincy Jones	1957	12.50	25.00	50.00
❏ LP-2208 [M]	Sonny Stitt	1957	12.50	25.00	50.00
❏ LP-2219 [M]	37 Minutes and 48 Seconds of Sonny Stitt	1957	12.50	25.00	50.00
❏ LP-2226 [M]	Sonny Stitt with the New Yorkers	1958	12.50	25.00	50.00
❏ LP-2230 [M]	The Saxophone of Sonny Stitt	1959	10.00	20.00	40.00
❏ SLP-2230 [S]	The Saxophone of Sonny Stitt	1959	7.50	15.00	30.00
❏ LP-2235 [M]	A Little Bit of Stitt	1959	10.00	20.00	40.00
❏ SLP-2235 [S]	A Little Bit of Stitt	1959	7.50	15.00	30.00
❏ LP-2240 [M]	The Sonny Side of Stitt	1960	10.00	20.00	40.00
❏ SLP-2240 [S]	The Sonny Side of Stitt	1960	7.50	15.00	30.00
❏ LP-2244 [M]	Stittsville	1960	10.00	20.00	40.00
❏ SLP-2244 [S]	Stittsville	1960	7.50	15.00	30.00
❏ LP-2245 [M]	Sonny Side Up	196?	6.25	12.50	25.00
❏ SLP-2245 [S]	Sonny Side Up	196?	6.25	12.50	25.00
❏ LP-2247 [M]	Feelin's	1962	6.25	12.50	25.00
❏ SLP-2247 [S]	Feelin's	1962	6.25	12.50	25.00
❏ LP-2252 [M]	Sonny Stitt in Orbit	1963	6.25	12.50	25.00
❏ SLP-2252 [S]	Sonny Stitt in Orbit	1963	6.25	12.50	25.00
❏ LP-2253 [M]	Sonny Stitt Goes Latin	1963	6.25	12.50	25.00
❏ SLP-2253 [S]	Sonny Stitt Goes Latin	1963	6.25	12.50	25.00
ROULETTE					
❏ R-25339 [M]	The Matadors Meet the Bull	1965	5.00	10.00	20.00
❏ SR-25339 [S]	The Matadors Meet the Bull	1965	6.25	12.50	25.00
❏ R-25343 [M]	What's New?	1966	5.00	10.00	20.00
❏ SR-25343 [S]	What's New?	1966	6.25	12.50	25.00
❏ R-25348 [M]	I Keep Comin' Back	1967	6.25	12.50	25.00
❏ SR-25348 [S]	I Keep Comin' Back	1967	5.00	10.00	20.00
SAVOY					
❏ MG-9006 [10]	All Star Series: Sonny Stitt	1953	50.00	100.00	200.00
❏ MG-9012 [10]	New Sounds in Modern Music	1953	50.00	100.00	200.00
❏ MG-9014 [10]	New Trends Of Jazz	1953	50.00	100.00	200.00
VERVE					
❏ MGVS-6038 [S]	The Hard Swing	1960	10.00	20.00	40.00
❏ MGVS-6041 [S]	Sonny Stitt Plays Jimmy Giuffre Arrangements	1960	10.00	20.00	40.00
❏ MGVS-6108 [S]	Sonny Stitt Sits In with the Oscar Peterson Trio	1960	10.00	20.00	40.00
❏ MGVS-6149 [S]	Sonny Stitt Blows the Blues	1996	10.00	20.00	40.00
—Audiophile reissue by Classic Records					
❏ MGVS-6149 [S]	Sonny Stitt Blows the Blues	1960	10.00	20.00	40.00
❏ MGVS-6149-45 [(4)]	Sonny Stitt Blows the Blues	1999	10.00	20.00	40.00
—Audiophile reissue by Classic Records; plays at 45 rpm					
❏ MGV-8219 [M]	New York Jazz	1957	12.50	25.00	50.00
❏ V-8219 [M]	New York Jazz	1961	6.25	12.50	25.00
❏ MGV-8250 [M]	Only the Blues	1958	12.50	25.00	50.00
❏ V-8250 [M]	Only the Blues	1961	6.25	12.50	25.00
❏ MGV-8262 [M]	Sonny Side Up	1958	15.00	30.00	60.00
❏ V-8262 [M]	Sonny Side Up	1961	7.50	15.00	30.00
❏ MGV-8306 [M]	The Hard Swing	1959	12.50	25.00	50.00
❏ V-8306 [M]	The Hard Swing	1961	6.25	12.50	25.00
❏ V6-8306 [S]	The Hard Swing	1961	5.00	10.00	20.00
❏ MGV-8309 [M]	Sonny Stitt Plays Jimmy Giuffre Arrangements	1959	12.50	25.00	50.00
❏ V-8309 [M]	Sonny Stitt Plays Jimmy Giuffre Arrangements	1961	6.25	12.50	25.00
❏ V6-8309 [S]	Sonny Stitt Plays Jimmy Giuffre Arrangements	1961	5.00	10.00	20.00
❏ MGV-8324 [M]	Personal Appearance	1959	12.50	25.00	50.00
❏ V-8324 [M]	Personal Appearance	1961	6.25	12.50	25.00
❏ MGV-8344 [M]	Sonny Stitt Sits In with the Oscar Peterson Trio	1959	12.50	25.00	50.00
❏ V-8344 [M]	Sonny Stitt Sits In with the Oscar Peterson Trio	1961	6.25	12.50	25.00
❏ V6-8344 [S]	Sonny Stitt Sits In with the Oscar Peterson Trio	1961	5.00	10.00	20.00
❏ MGV-8374 [M]	Sonny Stitt Blows the Blues	1960	12.50	25.00	50.00
❏ V-8374 [M]	Sonny Stitt Blows the Blues	1961	6.25	12.50	25.00
❏ V6-8374 [S]	Sonny Stitt Blows the Blues	1961	5.00	10.00	20.00
❏ MGV-8377 [M]	Saxophone Supremacy	1960	12.50	25.00	50.00
❏ V-8377 [M]	Saxophone Supremacy	1961	6.25	12.50	25.00
❏ MGV-8380 [M]	Sonny Stitt Swings the Most	1960	12.50	25.00	50.00
❏ V-8380 [M]	Sommy Stitt Swings the Most	1961	6.25	12.50	25.00
❏ V-8451 [M]	The Sensual Sound of Sonny Stitt	1962	5.00	10.00	20.00
❏ V6-8451 [S]	The Sensual Sound of Sonny Stitt	1962	6.25	12.50	25.00

STITT, SONNY, AND GENE AMMONS
Also see each artist's individual listings.

Number	Title (A Side/B Side)	Yr	VG	VG+	NM
CADET					
❏ LP-785 [M]	Jug and Sonny	1967	6.25	12.50	25.00

Number	Title (A Side/B Side)	Yr	VG	VG+	NM
PRESTIGE					
❏ PRLP-107 [10]	Battle of the Saxes: Ammons vs. Stitt	1951	62.50	125.00	250.00
❏ PRLP-7234 [M]	Soul Summit	1962	10.00	20.00	40.00
—Yellow label					
❏ PRST-7234 [S]	Soul Summit	1962	12.50	25.00	50.00
—Yellow label					
❏ PRLP-7454 [M]	Soul Summit	1966	5.00	10.00	20.00
—Blue label, trident logo at right					
❏ PRST-7454 [S]	Soul Summit	1966	6.25	12.50	25.00
—Blue label, trident logo at right					
❏ PRST-7606	We'll Be Together Again	1969	5.00	10.00	20.00
VERVE					
❏ V-8426 [M]	Boss Tenors	1962	5.00	10.00	20.00
❏ V6-8426 [S]	Boss Tenors	1962	6.25	12.50	25.00
❏ V-8468 [M]	Boss Tenors in Orbit	1962	5.00	10.00	20.00
❏ V6-8468 [S]	Boss Tenors in Orbit	1962	6.25	12.50	25.00
STOECKLEIN, VAL					
DOT					
❏ DLP-3904 [M]	Grey Life	1968	25.00	50.00	100.00
—Label is black, as if stock copy, but record is found inside stereo (25904) cover with "Monaural Promotion Not for Sale" sticker on front					
❏ DLP-25904 [S]	Grey Life	1968	10.00	20.00	40.00
STOKOWSKI, LEOPOLD					
RCA VICTOR RED SEAL					
❏ LSC-2593 [S]	Inspiration	1962	5.00	10.00	20.00
—Original with "shaded dog" label					
STOLOFF, MORRIS					
DECCA					
❏ DL 8574 [M]	This Is Kim	1957	15.00	30.00	60.00
—Black label, silver print; Kim Novak is the cover model					
STONE, CLIFFIE					
CAPITOL					
❏ T 1080 [M]	The Party's on Me	1958	10.00	20.00	40.00
❏ ST 1230 [S]	Cool Cowboy	1959	10.00	20.00	40.00
❏ T 1230 [M]	Cool Cowboy	1959	7.50	15.00	30.00
❏ ST 1286 [S]	Square Dance Promenade	1960	10.00	20.00	40.00
❏ T 1286 [M]	Square Dance Promenade	1960	7.50	15.00	30.00
❏ KAO 1555 [M]	Original Cowboy Sing-A-Long	1961	7.50	15.00	30.00
❏ SKAO 1555 [S]	Original Cowboy Sing-A-Long	1961	10.00	20.00	40.00
❏ ST 1685 [S]	It's Fun to Square Dance	1962	6.25	12.50	25.00
❏ T 1685 [M]	It's Fun to Square Dance	1962	5.00	10.00	20.00
❏ H 4009 [10]	Square Dances	195?	15.00	30.00	60.00
TOWER					
❏ ST 5073 [S]	Together Again	1967	7.50	15.00	30.00
❏ T 5073 [M]	Together Again	1967	6.25	12.50	25.00
STONE, KIRBY, FOUR					
CADENCE					
❏ CLP 1023 [M]	Man I Flipped	1958	6.25	12.50	25.00
COLUMBIA					
❏ CL 1211 [M]	Baubles, Bangles and Beads	1959	5.00	10.00	20.00
❏ CL 1290 [M]	The "Go" Sound of the Kirby Stone Four	1959	5.00	10.00	20.00
❏ CL 1356 [M]	The Kirby Stone Touch	1959	5.00	10.00	20.00
❏ CL 1646 [M]	The Kirby Stone Four at the Playboy Club	1960	5.00	10.00	20.00
❏ CL 1714 [M]	Guys and Dolls	1961	5.00	10.00	20.00
❏ CS 8014 [S]	Baubles, Bangles and Beads	1959	6.25	12.50	25.00
❏ CS 8130 [S]	The "Go" Sound of the Kirby Stone Four	1959	6.25	12.50	25.00
❏ CS 8164 [S]	The Kirby Stone Touch	1959	6.25	12.50	25.00
❏ CS 8446 [S]	The Kirby Stone Four at the Playboy Club	1960	6.25	12.50	25.00
❏ CS 8514 [S]	Guys and Dolls	1961	6.25	12.50	25.00
TOPS					
❏ L-1582 [M]	The Kirby Stone Four	1957	7.50	15.00	30.00
STONE, ROLAND					
ACE					
❏ LP-1018 [M]	Just a Moment	1961	37.50	75.00	150.00
STONE CIRCUS, THE					
MAINSTREAM					
❏ S-6119	The Stone Circus	1969	20.00	40.00	80.00
STONE COUNTRY					
RCA VICTOR					
❏ LSP-3958	Stone Country	1968	5.00	10.00	20.00
STONE HARBOUR					
STONE HARBOUR					
❏ 398	Stone Harbour Emerges	197?	125.00	250.00	500.00
STONE PONEYS					
Also see LINDA RONSTADT.					
CAPITOL					
❏ ST 2666 [S]	The Stone Poneys	1967	7.50	15.00	30.00
❏ T 2666 [M]	The Stone Poneys	1967	6.25	12.50	25.00
❏ ST 2763 [S]	Evergreen, Vol. 2	1967	7.50	15.00	30.00
❏ T 2763 [M]	Evergreen, Vol. 2	1967	10.00	20.00	40.00
❏ ST 2863	Linda Ronstadt/Stone Poneys and Friends Vol. III	1968	12.50	25.00	50.00
❏ ST-11383	The Stone Poneys Featuring Linda Ronstadt	1974	2.50	5.00	10.00
PICKWICK					
❏ SPC-3298	Stoney End	1976	3.00	6.00	12.00
STONE THE CROWS					
POLYDOR					
❏ 24-4019	Stone the Crows	1970	5.00	10.00	20.00
❏ PD-5020	Teenage Licks	1972	5.00	10.00	20.00
❏ PD-5037	Continuous Performance	1972	5.00	10.00	20.00

Number	Title (A Side/B Side)	Yr	VG	VG+	NM
STONEGROUND					
WARNER BROS.					
❏ WS 1895	Stoneground	1971	3.75	7.50	15.00
❏ 2WS 1956 [(2)]	Family Album	1971	5.00	10.00	20.00
❏ BS 2645	Stoneground 3	1972	3.75	7.50	15.00
STONEHILL, RANDY					
ONE WAY					
❏ JC-31252	Born Twice	1972	15.00	30.00	60.00
STONEMANS, THE					
MGM					
❏ GAS-124	The Stonemans (Golden Archive Series)	1970	3.75	7.50	15.00
❏ E-4363 [M]	Those Singin' Swingin' Stompin' Sensational Stonemans	1966	5.00	10.00	20.00
❏ SE-4363 [S]	Those Singin' Swingin' Stompin' Sensational Stonemans	1966	6.25	12.50	25.00
❏ E-4453 [M]	Stoneman's Country	1967	5.00	10.00	20.00
❏ SE-4453 [S]	Stoneman's Country	1967	6.25	12.50	25.00
❏ E-4511 [M]	All in the Family	1968	6.25	12.50	25.00
❏ SE-4511 [S]	All in the Family	1968	5.00	10.00	20.00
❏ SE-4578	The Great Stonemans	1968	5.00	10.00	20.00
❏ SE-4613	A Stoneman Christmas	1968	5.00	10.00	20.00
RCA VICTOR					
❏ LSP-4264	Dawn of the Stonemans' Age	1970	3.75	7.50	15.00
❏ LSP-4343	In All Honesty	1970	3.75	7.50	15.00
❏ LSP-4431	California Blues	1970	3.75	7.50	15.00
STARDAY					
❏ SLP-393 [M]	White Lightning	1965	10.00	20.00	40.00
WORLD PACIFIC					
❏ ST-1828 [S]	Big Ball in Monterey	1964	10.00	20.00	40.00
❏ WP-1828 [M]	Big Ball in Monterey	1964	7.50	15.00	30.00
STONEY AND MEATLOAF					
Also see MEAT LOAF.					
PRODIGAL					
❏ 10	Stoney and Meatloaf	1978	3.00	6.00	12.00
RARE EARTH					
❏ R 528	Stoney and Meatloaf	1971	5.00	10.00	20.00
STOOGES, THE					
See IGGY AND THE STOOGES.					
STORIES					
KAMA SUTRA					
❏ KSBS-2051	Stories	1972	3.00	6.00	12.00
❏ KSBS-2068	About Us	1973	3.00	6.00	12.00
—Regular cover; with "Brother Louie"					
❏ KSBS-2068	About Us	1973	7.50	15.00	30.00
—Gatefold; does NOT contain "Brother Louie"					
❏ KSBS-2078	Traveling Underground	1974	3.00	6.00	12.00
STORM, BILLY					
BUENA VISTA					
❏ BV-3315 [M]	Billy Storm	1963	25.00	50.00	100.00
❏ STER-3315 [S]	Billy Storm	1963	30.00	60.00	120.00
FAMOUS					
❏ F-504	This Is the Night	1969	25.00	50.00	100.00
STORM, GALE					
DOT					
❏ DLP-3011 [M]	Gale Storm	1956	12.50	25.00	50.00
❏ DLP-3017 [M]	Sentimental Me	1956	12.50	25.00	50.00
❏ DLP-3098 [M]	Gale Storm Hits	1958	10.00	20.00	40.00
❏ DLP-3197 [M]	Softly and Tenderly	1959	7.50	15.00	30.00
❏ DLP-3209 [M]	Gale Storm Sings	1959	7.50	15.00	30.00
❏ DLP-25197 [S]	Softly and Tenderly	1959	10.00	20.00	40.00
❏ DLP-25209 [S]	Gale Storm Sings	1959	10.00	20.00	40.00
HAMILTON					
❏ HLP-171 [M]	I Don't Want to Walk	1966	3.00	6.00	12.00
❏ HLP-12171 [S]	I Don't Want to Walk	1966	3.75	7.50	15.00
MCA					
❏ 1504	Gale Storm	198?	2.50	5.00	10.00
STORY, CARL					
MERCURY					
❏ MG-20323 [M]	Gospel Quartet Favorites	1958	10.00	20.00	40.00
❏ MG-20584 [M]	More Gospel Quartet Favorites	1961	7.50	15.00	30.00
❏ SR-60584 [S]	More Gospel Quartet Favorites	1961	10.00	20.00	40.00
STARDAY					
❏ SLP-107 [M]	America's Favorite Country Gospel Artist	1959	12.50	25.00	50.00
❏ SLP-127 [M]	Gospel Revival	1961	10.00	20.00	40.00
❏ SLP-137 [M]	All Day Singing with Dinner on the Ground	1961	10.00	20.00	40.00
❏ SLP-152 [M]	Get Religion	1962	10.00	20.00	40.00
❏ SLP-219 [M]	Mighty Close to Heaven	1963	10.00	20.00	40.00
❏ SLP-278 [M]	All Day Sacred Singing	1964	10.00	20.00	40.00
❏ SLP-315 [M]	Sacred Songs of Life and the Hereafter	1965	10.00	20.00	40.00
❏ SLP-348 [M]	There's Nothing on Earth (That Heaven Can't Cure)	1965	10.00	20.00	40.00
❏ SLP-411 [M]	My Lord Keeps a Record	1968	7.50	15.00	30.00
STORYVILLE STOMPERS, THE					
TROPICANA					
❏ 1204 [M]	New Orleans Jazz	195?	10.00	20.00	40.00
STOVER, SMOKEY					
ARGO					
❏ LP-652 [DJ]	Smokey Stover's Original Firemen	1960	15.00	30.00	60.00
—White label, multi-color vinyl					
❏ LP-652 [M]	Smokey Stover's Original Firemen	1960	6.25	12.50	25.00
❏ LPS-652 [S]	Smokey Stover's Original Firemen	1960	7.50	15.00	30.00

S

Number	Title (A Side/B Side)	Yr	VG	VG+	NM

STOWAWAYS, THE
JUSTICE
| ❑ JLP-148 | The Stowaways | 1968 | 125.00 | 250.00 | 500.00 |

STRADIVARI STRINGS, THE
SPIN-O-RAMA
| ❑ 590 [M] | String Along with Me | 196? | 7.50 | 15.00 | 30.00 |
| ❑ S-590 [S] | String Along with Me | 196? | 10.00 | 20.00 | 40.00 |

—Cover model on the above LP is Jayne Mansfield

STRAIT, GEORGE
HEARTLAND
| ❑ HL 1172/3 [(2)] | The Very Best of George Strait | 1991 | 3.75 | 7.50 | 15.00 |
MCA
❑ 5248	Strait Country	1981	2.50	5.00	10.00
❑ 5320	Strait from the Heart	1982	2.50	5.00	10.00
❑ 5450	Right or Wrong	1983	2.50	5.00	10.00
❑ 5518	Does Fort Worth Ever Cross Your Mind	1984	2.50	5.00	10.00
❑ 5567	Greatest Hits	1985	2.50	5.00	10.00
❑ 5605	Something Special	1985	2.50	5.00	10.00
❑ 5750	#7	1986	2.50	5.00	10.00
❑ 5800	Merry Christmas Strait to You	1986	2.50	5.00	10.00
❑ 5913	Ocean Front Property	1987	2.50	5.00	10.00
❑ 6415	Livin' It Up	1990	3.00	6.00	12.00
❑ 10450	Ten Strait Hits	1992	5.00	10.00	20.00

—Only available on vinyl through Columbia House
| ❑ 10532 | Holding My Own | 1992 | 5.00 | 10.00 | 20.00 |

—Only available on vinyl through Columbia House
| ❑ 27092 | Strait Country | 1984 | 2.00 | 4.00 | 8.00 |

—Reissue of 5248
❑ 42035	Greatest Hits, Volume Two	1987	2.00	4.00	8.00
❑ 42114	If You Ain't Lovin' You Ain't Livin'	1988	2.00	4.00	8.00
❑ 42266	Beyond the Blue Neon	1989	2.00	4.00	8.00
❑ R 134172	Merry Christmas Strait to You	1986	3.00	6.00	12.00

—BMG Direct Marketing version
| ❑ R 153641 | Chill of an Early Fall | 1991 | 5.00 | 10.00 | 20.00 |

—Only released on vinyl through BMG Direct Marketing

STRAND, LES
FANTASY
| ❑ 3231 [M] | Les Strand on the Baldwin Organ | 195? | 5.00 | 10.00 | 20.00 |

—Black vinyl
| ❑ 3231 [M] | Les Strand on the Baldwin Organ | 1956 | 12.50 | 25.00 | 50.00 |

—Red vinyl
| ❑ 3242 [M] | Jazz Classics on the Baldwin Organ | 195? | 5.00 | 10.00 | 20.00 |

—Black vinyl
| ❑ 3242 [M] | Jazz Classics on the Baldwin Organ | 1956 | 12.50 | 25.00 | 50.00 |

—Red vinyl

STRANGE
OUTER GALAXIE
| ❑ 1000 | Translucent World | 1973 | 25.00 | 50.00 | 100.00 |
| ❑ 1001 | Raw Power | 1976 | 25.00 | 50.00 | 100.00 |

STRANGE, BILLY
CHESS
| ❑ CH2-6027 [(2)] | One More Time | 1988 | 3.00 | 6.00 | 12.00 |
COLISEUM
| ❑ CM-1001 [M] | Limbo Rock | 1962 | 10.00 | 20.00 | 40.00 |
GNP CRESCENDO
❑ GNP-94 [M]	Twelve String Guitar	1963	3.00	6.00	12.00
❑ GNPS-94 [S]	Twelve String Guitar	1963	3.75	7.50	15.00
❑ GNP-97 [M]	Mr. Guitar	1963	3.00	6.00	12.00
❑ GNPS-97 [S]	Mr. Guitar	1963	3.75	7.50	15.00
❑ GNP-98 [M]	Five String Banjo	1964	3.00	6.00	12.00
❑ GNPS-98 [S]	Five String Banjo	1964	3.75	7.50	15.00
❑ GNP-2004 [M]	The James Bond Theme	1964	3.00	6.00	12.00
❑ GNPS-2004 [S]	The James Bond Theme	1964	3.75	7.50	15.00
❑ GNP-2006 [M]	Goldfinger	1965	3.00	6.00	12.00
❑ GNPS-2006 [S]	Goldfinger	1965	3.75	7.50	15.00
❑ GNP-2009 [M]	English Hits of '65	1965	3.00	6.00	12.00
❑ GNPS-2009 [S]	English Hits of '65	1965	3.75	7.50	15.00
❑ GNP-2012 [M]	Billy Strange Plays the Hits	1965	3.00	6.00	12.00
❑ GNPS-2012 [S]	Billy Strange Plays the Hits	1965	3.75	7.50	15.00
❑ GNP-2016 [M]	Folk Rock Hits	1965	3.00	6.00	12.00
❑ GNPS-2016 [S]	Folk Rock Hits	1965	3.75	7.50	15.00
❑ GNP-2019 [M]	Secret Agent File	1966	3.00	6.00	12.00
❑ GNPS-2019 [S]	Secret Agent File	1966	3.75	7.50	15.00
❑ GNP-2022 [M]	In the Mexican Bag	1966	3.00	6.00	12.00
❑ GNPS-2022 [S]	In the Mexican Bag	1966	3.75	7.50	15.00
❑ GNP-2024 [M]	Billy Strange Plays Roger Miller Hits	1966	3.00	6.00	12.00
❑ GNPS-2024 [S]	Billy Strange Plays Roger Miller Hits	1966	3.75	7.50	15.00
❑ GNP-2030 [M]	Billy Strange with the Challengers	1966	3.75	7.50	15.00
❑ GNPS-2030 [S]	Billy Strange with the Challengers	1966	5.00	10.00	20.00
❑ GNP-2037 [M]	The Best of Billy Strange	1967	3.00	6.00	12.00
❑ GNPS-2037 [S]	The Best of Billy Strange	1967	3.00	6.00	12.00
❑ GNPS-2039	A James Bond Double Feature	1967	3.00	6.00	12.00
❑ GNP-2041	Railroad Man	1968	3.00	6.00	12.00
❑ GNPS-2046	Great Western Themes	1969	3.00	6.00	12.00
❑ GNPS-2094	Dyn-o-mite Guitar	197?	2.50	5.00	10.00
SUNSET
| ❑ SUS-5209 | Mr. Guitar | 1968 | 2.50 | 5.00 | 10.00 |
SURREY
| ❑ SS-1002 | The Best of Billy Strange | 1965 | 3.75 | 7.50 | 15.00 |
TRADITION
| ❑ 2080 | Strange Country | 1969 | 2.50 | 5.00 | 10.00 |

STRANGEBREW
ABC
| ❑ ABCS-672 | Very Strangebrew | 1969 | 5.00 | 10.00 | 20.00 |

STRANGELOVES, THE
BANG
| ❑ BLP-211 [M] | I Want Candy | 1965 | 20.00 | 40.00 | 80.00 |
| ❑ BLPS-211 [S] | I Want Candy | 1965 | 25.00 | 50.00 | 100.00 |

STRANGERS, THE
CAPITOL
❑ ST-169	Instrumental Sounds of Merle Haggard's Strangers	1969	5.00	10.00	20.00
❑ ST-445	Introducing My Friends the Strangers	1970	5.00	10.00	20.00
❑ ST-590	Getting to Know Merle Haggard's Strangers	1970	5.00	10.00	20.00
❑ ST-796	Honky Tonkin'	1971	5.00	10.00	20.00
❑ ST-11141	Totally Instrumental with One Exception...	1973	3.75	7.50	15.00

STRATTON, DON
ABC-PARAMOUNT
| ❑ ABC-118 [M] | Modern Jazz with Dixieland Roots | 1956 | 10.00 | 20.00 | 40.00 |

STRAWBERRY ALARM CLOCK
UNI
❑ 3014 [M]	Incense and Peppermints	1967	12.50	25.00	50.00
❑ 73014 [S]	Incense and Peppermints	1967	10.00	20.00	40.00
❑ 73025	Wake Up It's Tomorrow	1968	10.00	20.00	40.00
❑ 73035	The World in a Sea Shell	1968	10.00	20.00	40.00
❑ 73054	Good Morning Starshine	1969	10.00	20.00	40.00
❑ 73074	The Best of the Strawberry Alarm Clock	1970	10.00	20.00	40.00
VOCALION
| ❑ VL 73915 | Changes | 1971 | 12.50 | 25.00 | 50.00 |

STRAYHORN, BILLY
FELSTED
| ❑ 2008 [S] | Billy Strayhorn Septet | 1958 | 15.00 | 30.00 | 60.00 |
| ❑ 7008 [M] | Billy Strayhorn Septet | 1958 | 20.00 | 40.00 | 80.00 |
MERCER
| ❑ LP-1001 [10] | Billy Strayhorn Trio | 1951 | 50.00 | 100.00 | 200.00 |
| ❑ LP-1005 [10] | Billy Strayhorn and All-Stars | 1951 | 50.00 | 100.00 | 200.00 |
ROULETTE
| ❑ R-52119 [M] | Live! | 1965 | 5.00 | 10.00 | 20.00 |
| ❑ SR-52119 [S] | Live! | 1965 | 6.25 | 12.50 | 25.00 |
UNITED ARTISTS
| ❑ UAJ-14010 [M] | The Peaceful Side of Billy Strayhorn | 1962 | 10.00 | 20.00 | 40.00 |
| ❑ UAJS-15010 [S] | The Peaceful Side of Billy Strayhorn | 1962 | 12.50 | 25.00 | 50.00 |

STRAZZERI, FRANK
REVELATION
| ❑ REV-10 | That's Him and This Is New | 1969 | 6.25 | 12.50 | 25.00 |

STREET NOISE
EVOLUTION
| ❑ 2010 | Street Noise | 1970 | 5.00 | 10.00 | 20.00 |

STREET PEOPLE
MUSICOR
| ❑ MS-3189 | Jennifer Tomkins | 1970 | 5.00 | 10.00 | 20.00 |

STREISAND, BARBRA
COLUMBIA
| ❑ A2S 1779 [(2)DJ] | The Legend of Barbra Streisand | 1983 | 20.00 | 40.00 | 80.00 |

—Promo-only interview LP for "Yentl"
| ❑ CL 2007 [M] | The Barbra Streisand Album | 1963 | 5.00 | 10.00 | 20.00 |

—"Guaranteed High Fidelity" on label
| ❑ CL 2007 [M] | The Barbra Streisand Album | 1966 | 3.00 | 6.00 | 12.00 |

—"360 Sound Mono" on label
| ❑ CL 2054 [M] | The Second Barbra Streisand Album | 1963 | 5.00 | 10.00 | 20.00 |

—"Guaranteed High Fidelity" on label
| ❑ CL 2054 [M] | The Second Barbra Streisand Album | 1963 | 50.00 | 100.00 | 200.00 |

—Promo only on blue vinyl (white label)
| ❑ CL 2054 [M] | The Second Barbra Streisand Album | 1966 | 3.00 | 6.00 | 12.00 |

—"360 Sound Mono" on label
| ❑ CL 2154 [M] | The Third Album | 1964 | 5.00 | 10.00 | 20.00 |

—"Guaranteed High Fidelity" on label
| ❑ CL 2154 [M] | The Third Album | 1966 | 3.00 | 6.00 | 12.00 |

—"360 Sound Mono" on label
| ❑ CL 2215 [M] | People | 1964 | 5.00 | 10.00 | 20.00 |

—"Guaranteed High Fidelity" on label
| ❑ CL 2215 [M] | People | 1966 | 3.00 | 6.00 | 12.00 |

—"360 Sound Mono" on label
| ❑ CL 2336 [M] | My Name Is Barbra | 1965 | 5.00 | 10.00 | 20.00 |

—"Guaranteed High Fidelity" on label
| ❑ CL 2336 [M] | My Name Is Barbra | 1966 | 3.00 | 6.00 | 12.00 |

—"360 Sound Mono" on label
❑ CL 2409 [M]	My Name Is Barbra, Two	1965	3.75	7.50	15.00
❑ CL 2478 [M]	Color Me Barbra	1966	3.75	7.50	15.00
❑ CL 2478 [M]	Color Me Barbra	1966	50.00	100.00	200.00

—Promo only on red vinyl (white label)
❑ CL 2547 [M]	Je M'Appelle Barbra	1966	3.75	7.50	15.00
❑ CL 2682 [M]	Simply Streisand	1967	7.50	15.00	30.00
❑ CL 2757 [M]	A Christmas Album	1967	6.25	12.50	25.00
❑ CS 8807 [S]	The Barbra Streisand Album	1963	6.25	12.50	25.00

—"360 Sound Stereo" in black on label
| ❑ CS 8807 [S] | The Barbra Streisand Album | 1966 | 3.75 | 7.50 | 15.00 |

—"360 Sound Stereo" in white on label
| ❑ CS 8807 [S] | The Barbra Streisand Album | 1970 | 2.50 | 5.00 | 10.00 |

—Orange label
| ❑ PC 8807 | The Barbra Streisand Album | 197? | 2.00 | 4.00 | 8.00 |

—Reissue with new prefix
| ❑ CS 8854 [S] | The Second Barbra Streisand Album | 1963 | 6.25 | 12.50 | 25.00 |

—"360 Sound Stereo" in black on label
| ❑ CS 8854 [S] | The Second Barbra Streisand Album | 1963 | 50.00 | 100.00 | 200.00 |

—Promo only on blue vinyl (white label)
| ❑ CS 8854 [S] | The Second Barbra Streisand Album | 1966 | 3.75 | 7.50 | 15.00 |

—"360 Sound Stereo" in white on label

Number	Title (A Side/B Side)	Yr	VG	VG+	NM
❑ CS 8854 [S]	The Second Barbra Streisand Album	1970	2.50	5.00	10.00
—Orange label					
❑ PC 8854	The Second Barbra Streisand Album	197?	2.00	4.00	8.00
—Reissue with new prefix					
❑ CS 8954 [S]	The Third Album	1964	6.25	12.50	25.00
—"360 Sound Stereo" in black on label					
❑ CS 8954 [S]	The Third Album	1966	3.75	7.50	15.00
—"360 Sound Stereo" in white on label					
❑ CS 8954 [S]	The Third Album	1970	2.50	5.00	10.00
—Orange label					
❑ PC 8954	The Third Album	197?	2.00	4.00	8.00
—Reissue with new prefix					
❑ CS 9015 [S]	People	1964	6.25	12.50	25.00
—"360 Sound Stereo" in black on label					
❑ CS 9015 [S]	People	1966	3.75	7.50	15.00
—"360 Sound Stereo" in white on label					
❑ CS 9015 [S]	People	1970	2.50	5.00	10.00
—Orange label					
❑ PC 9015	People	197?	2.00	4.00	8.00
—Reissue with new prefix					
❑ CS 9136 [S]	My Name Is Barbra	1965	6.25	12.50	25.00
—"360 Sound Stereo" in black on label					
❑ CS 9136 [S]	My Name Is Barbra	1966	3.75	7.50	15.00
—"360 Sound Stereo" in white on label					
❑ CS 9136 [S]	My Name Is Barbra	1970	2.50	5.00	10.00
—Orange label					
❑ PC 9136	My Name Is Barbra	197?	2.00	4.00	8.00
—Reissue with new prefix					
❑ CS 9209 [S]	My Name Is Barbra, Two	1965	5.00	10.00	20.00
—Red "360 Sound Stereo" label					
❑ CS 9209 [S]	My Name Is Barbra, Two	1970	2.50	5.00	10.00
—Orange label					
❑ PC 9209	My Name Is Barbra, Two	197?	2.00	4.00	8.00
—Reissue with new prefix					
❑ CS 9278 [S]	Color Me Barbra	1966	5.00	10.00	20.00
—Red "360 Sound Stereo" label					
❑ CS 9278 [S]	Color Me Barbra	1966	50.00	100.00	200.00
—Promo only on red vinyl (white label)					
❑ CS 9278 [S]	Color Me Barbra	1970	2.50	5.00	10.00
—Orange label					
❑ PC 9278	Color Me Barbra	197?	2.00	4.00	8.00
—Reissue with new prefix					
❑ CS 9347 [S]	Je M'Appelle Barbra	1966	5.00	10.00	20.00
—Red "360 Sound Stereo" label					
❑ CS 9347 [S]	Je M'Appelle Barbra	1970	2.50	5.00	10.00
—Orange label					
❑ PC 9347	Je M'Appelle Barbra	197?	2.00	4.00	8.00
—Reissue with new prefix					
❑ CS 9482 [S]	Simply Streisand	1967	5.00	10.00	20.00
—Red "360 Sound Stereo" label					
❑ CS 9482 [S]	Simply Streisand	1970	2.50	5.00	10.00
—Orange label					
❑ PC 9482	Simply Streisand	197?	2.00	4.00	8.00
—Reissue with new prefix					
❑ CS 9557 [S]	A Christmas Album	1967	5.00	10.00	20.00
—Red "360 Sound Stereo" label					
❑ CS 9557 [S]	A Christmas Album	1970	2.00	4.00	8.00
—Orange label					
❑ PC 9557	A Christmas Album	198?	—	3.00	6.00
—Reissue with new prefix and bar code					
❑ CS 9710	A Happening in Central Park	1968	3.75	7.50	15.00
—Red "360 Sound Stereo" label					
❑ CS 9710	A Happening in Central Park	1970	2.50	5.00	10.00
—Orange label					
❑ PC 9710	A Happening in Central Park	197?	2.00	4.00	8.00
—Reissue with new prefix					
❑ CS 9816	What About Today?	1969	3.75	7.50	15.00
—Red "360 Sound Stereo" label					
❑ CS 9816	What About Today?	1970	2.50	5.00	10.00
—Orange label					
❑ PC 9816	What About Today?	197?	2.00	4.00	8.00
—Reissue with new prefix					
❑ JC 9968	Barbra Streisand's Greatest Hits	197?	—	3.00	6.00
—Another reissue with a new prefix (postdates PC)					
❑ KCS 9968	Barbra Streisand's Greatest Hits	1970	2.50	5.00	10.00
—Orange label					
❑ KCS 9968	Barbra Streisand's Greatest Hits	1970	3.75	7.50	15.00
—Red "360 Sound Stereo" label					
❑ PC 9968	Barbra Streisand's Greatest Hits	197?	2.00	4.00	8.00
—Reissue with new prefix					
❑ CQ 30378 [Q]	Stoney End	1972	6.25	12.50	25.00
❑ KC 30378	Stoney End	1971	3.75	7.50	15.00
❑ PC 30378	Stoney End	197?	2.00	4.00	8.00
—Reissue with new prefix					
❑ CQ 30792 [Q]	Barbra Joan Streisand	1972	6.25	12.50	25.00
❑ KC 30792	Barbra Joan Streisand	1971	3.75	7.50	15.00
❑ PC 30792	Barbra Joan Streisand	197?	2.00	4.00	8.00
—Reissue with new prefix					
❑ CQ 31760 [Q]	Live Concert at the Forum	1972	6.25	12.50	25.00
❑ KC 31760	Live Concert at the Forum	1972	3.75	7.50	15.00
❑ PC 31760	Live Concert at the Forum	197?	2.00	4.00	8.00
—Reissue with new prefix					
❑ KC 32655	Barbra Streisand…And Other Musical Instruments	1973	3.00	6.00	12.00
❑ PC 32655	Barbra Streisand…And Other Musical Instruments	197?	2.00	4.00	8.00
—Reissue with new prefix					
❑ JC 32801	The Way We Were	197?	2.00	4.00	8.00
—Reissue with new prefix					
❑ PC 32801	The Way We Were	1974	3.00	6.00	12.00
—Revised version; has this title on spine, label and front cover					

Number	Title (A Side/B Side)	Yr	VG	VG+	NM
❑ PC 32801	Barbra Streisand Featuring The Way We Were and All In Love Is Fair	1974	5.00	10.00	20.00
—Original version with this title on spine and label, and no title on front cover					
❑ PCQ 32801 [Q]	The Way We Were	1974	6.25	12.50	25.00
❑ PC 33095	Butterfly	1974	3.00	6.00	12.00
—Original with no bar code					
❑ PC 33095	Butterfly	198?	2.00	4.00	8.00
—Reissue with bar code					
❑ PC 33815	Lazy Afternoon	1975	3.00	6.00	12.00
—Original with no bar code					
❑ PC 33815	Lazy Afternoon	198?	2.00	4.00	8.00
—Reissue with bar code					
❑ PCQ 33815 [Q]	Lazy Afternoon	1975	6.25	12.50	25.00
❑ JS 34403	A Star Is Born	1976	3.00	6.00	12.00
—With Kris Kristofferson					
❑ JC 34830	Streisand Superman	1977	3.00	6.00	12.00
❑ PC 34830	Streisand Superman	198?	2.00	4.00	8.00
—Budget-line reissue					
❑ PC 35275	Songbird	198?	2.00	4.00	8.00
—Budget-line reissue					
❑ JC 35375	Songbird	1978	3.00	6.00	12.00
❑ FC 35679	Barbra Streisand's Greatest Hits, Volume 2	1978	3.00	6.00	12.00
❑ FC 36258	Wet	1979	2.50	5.00	10.00
❑ FC 36750	Guilty	1980	2.50	5.00	10.00
❑ TC 37678	Memories	1981	2.50	5.00	10.00
❑ JS 39152	Yentl	1983	2.50	5.00	10.00
❑ QC 39480	Emotion	1984	2.50	5.00	10.00
❑ OC 40092	The Broadway Album	1985	2.50	5.00	10.00
❑ OC 40788	One Voice	1987	2.50	5.00	10.00
❑ OC 40880	Till I Loved You	1988	2.50	5.00	10.00
❑ HC 42801	The Way We Were	1982	7.50	5.00	30.00
—Half-speed mastered edition					
❑ OC 45369	A Collection: Greatest Hits.. And More	1989	3.75	7.50	15.00
❑ HC 45679	Barbra Streisand's Greatest Hits, Volume 2	1980	7.50	15.00	30.00
—Half-speed mastered edition					
❑ HC 46750	Guilty	1982	7.50	15.00	30.00
—Half-speed mastered edition					
❑ HC 47678	Memories	1982	7.50	15.00	30.00
—Half-speed mastered edition					
COLUMBIA MASTERWORKS					
❑ M 33452	Classical Barbra	1976	3.00	6.00	12.00

STRENGTH, "TEXAS" BILL
RE-CAR

Number	Title (A Side/B Side)	Yr	VG	VG+	NM
❑ 2022	Greatest Hits	1967	6.25	12.50	25.00

STRIDER
WARNER BROS.

| ❑ BS 2722 | Exposed | 1973 | 5.00 | 10.00 | 20.00 |

STRING CHEESE
WOODEN NICKEL

| ❑ WNS-1001 | String Cheese | 1971 | 5.00 | 10.00 | 20.00 |

STRING-A-LONGS, THE
ATCO

| ❑ SD 33-241 | Wide World Hits | 1969 | 6.25 | 12.50 | 25.00 |

DOT

❑ DLP-3463 [M]	Matilda	1962	6.25	12.50	25.00
❑ DLP-3723 [M]	Great Instrumental Hits	1966	5.00	10.00	20.00
❑ DLP-25463 [S]	Matilda	1962	7.50	15.00	30.00
❑ DLP-25723 [S]	Great Instrumental Hits	1966	6.25	12.50	25.00

WARWICK

| ❑ W-2036 [M] | Pick-A-Hit Featuring "Wheels" | 1961 | 12.50 | 25.00 | 50.00 |
| ❑ W-2036ST [S] | Pick-A-Hit Featuring "Wheels" | 1961 | 20.00 | 40.00 | 80.00 |

STRINGBEAN
STARDAY

❑ SLP-142 [M]	Old Time Pickin' and Singin' with Stringbean	1961	15.00	30.00	60.00
❑ SLP-179 [M]	Stringbean	1962	12.50	25.00	50.00
❑ SLP-215 [M]	A Salute to Uncle Dave Macon	1963	12.50	25.00	50.00
❑ SLP-260 [M]	Way Back in the Hills of Old Kentucky	1964	12.50	25.00	50.00

STRONG, NOLAN, AND THE DIABLOS
FORTUNE

❑ LP-8010 [M]	Fortune of Hits	196?	12.50	25.00	50.00
—Yellow label					
❑ LP-8010 [M]	Fortune of Hits	1961	55.00	110.00	220.00
—Purple label, thick vinyl					
❑ LP-8010 [M]	Fortune of Hits	197?	3.75	7.50	15.00
—Purple label, thinner, more flexible vinyl					
❑ LP-8012 [M]	Fortune of Hits, Vol. 2	196?	12.50	25.00	50.00
—Yellow label					
❑ LP-8012 [M]	Fortune of Hits, Vol. 2	1962	55.00	110.00	220.00
—Purple label, thick vinyl					
❑ LP-8012 [M]	Fortune of Hits, Vol. 2	197?	3.75	7.50	15.00
—Purple label, thinner, more flexible vinyl					
❑ LP-8015 [M]	Mind Over Matter	196?	15.00	30.00	60.00
—Yellow label					
❑ LP-8015 [M]	Mind Over Matter	1963	62.50	125.00	250.00
—Purple label, thick vinyl					
❑ LP-8015 [M]	Mind Over Matter	197?	5.00	10.00	20.00
—Purple label, thinner, more flexible vinyl					

STROZIER, FRANK
JAZZLAND

❑ JLP-56 [M]	Long Night	1961	6.25	12.50	25.00
❑ JLP-70 [M]	March of the Siamese Children	1962	6.25	12.50	25.00
❑ JLP-956 [S]	Long Night	1961	7.50	15.00	30.00
❑ JLP-970 [S]	March of the Siamese Children	1962	7.50	15.00	30.00

VEE JAY

| ❑ LP-3005 [M] | Fantastic Frank Strozier | 1960 | 7.50 | 15.00 | 30.00 |
| ❑ SR-3005 [S] | Fantastic Frank Strozier | 1960 | 10.00 | 20.00 | 40.00 |

S

Number	Title (A Side/B Side)	Yr	VG	VG+	NM

STRYPER
ENIGMA
Number	Title (A Side/B Side)	Yr	VG	VG+	NM
❑ E-1064	The Yellow and Black Attack	1984	10.00	20.00	40.00

—Original with six tracks; yellow vinyl

| ❑ 71064 | The Yellow and Black Attack | 1984 | 5.00 | 10.00 | 20.00 |

—Original with six tracks; black vinyl

| ❑ 72077 | Soldiers Under Command | 1985 | 3.00 | 6.00 | 12.00 |

—Black vinyl

| ❑ 72077 | Soldiers Under Command | 1985 | 5.00 | 10.00 | 20.00 |

—White vinyl

| ❑ ST-73207 | The Yellow and Black Attack | 1985 | 2.50 | 5.00 | 10.00 |

—Reissue with eight tracks; black vinyl, square sleeve

| ❑ ST-73207 | The Yellow and Black Attack | 1985 | 5.00 | 10.00 | 20.00 |

—Reissue with eight tracks; blue vinyl, round sleeve

| ❑ ST-73217 | Soldiers Under Command | 1985 | 2.50 | 5.00 | 10.00 |

—Reissue with new number

| ❑ PJAS-73237 | To Hell with the Devil | 1986 | 2.50 | 5.00 | 10.00 |

—Cover is black

| ❑ PJAS-73237 | To Hell with the Devil | 1986 | 5.00 | 10.00 | 20.00 |

—Cover has band as winged angels in battle

| ❑ SEAX-73277 | To Hell with the Devil | 1986 | 6.25 | 12.50 | 25.00 |

—Picture disc in plastic sleeve

| ❑ D1-73317 | In God We Trust | 1988 | 2.50 | 5.00 | 10.00 |

STUART, MARTY
COLUMBIA
| ❑ B6C 40302 | Marty Stuart | 1986 | 7.50 | 15.00 | 30.00 |

MCA
| ❑ 42312 | Hillbilly Rock | 1989 | 3.75 | 7.50 | 15.00 |
| ❑ R 170076 | Tempted | 1990 | 6.25 | 12.50 | 25.00 |

—Vinyl version available only through BMG Direct Marketing

RIDGE RUNNER
| ❑ RRR 0013 | Marty | 1978 | 7.50 | 15.00 | 30.00 |

SUGAR HILL
| ❑ 3726 | Busy Bee Café | 1981 | 7.50 | 15.00 | 30.00 |

STUART, MARY
BELL
| ❑ 1133 | Mary Stuart | 1973 | 5.00 | 10.00 | 20.00 |

COLUMBIA
| ❑ CL 6333 [10] | Joanne Sings | 1954 | 10.00 | 20.00 | 40.00 |

STUCKEY, NAT
MCA
| ❑ 2184 | Independence | 1976 | 3.00 | 6.00 | 12.00 |

PAULA
❑ LP-2192 [M]	Nat Stuckey Sings	1966	5.00	10.00	20.00
❑ LPS-2192 [S]	Nat Stuckey Sings	1966	6.25	12.50	25.00
❑ LP-2196 [M]	All My Tomorrows	1967	5.00	10.00	20.00
❑ LPS-2196 [S]	All My Tomorrows	1967	6.25	12.50	25.00
❑ LPS-2203	Country Favorites	1968	6.25	12.50	25.00

RCA CAMDEN
| ❑ ACL1-0780 | In the Ghetto | 1974 | 2.50 | 5.00 | 10.00 |

RCA VICTOR
| ❑ APD1-0080 [Q] | Take Time to Love Her/I Used It All on You | 1973 | 6.25 | 12.50 | 25.00 |

—"QuadraDisc"; may not exist in regular stereo

❑ APL1-0541	The Best of Nat Stuckey	1974	3.75	7.50	15.00
❑ LSP-4090	Nat Stuckey Sings	1968	5.00	10.00	20.00
❑ LSP-4123	Keep 'Em Country	1969	5.00	10.00	20.00
❑ LSP-4226	New Country Roads	1969	5.00	10.00	20.00
❑ LSP-4330	Old Man Willie	1970	3.75	7.50	15.00
❑ LSP-4389	Country Fever	1970	3.75	7.50	15.00
❑ LSP-4477	She Wakes Me with a Kiss Every Morning	1971	3.75	7.50	15.00
❑ LSP-4559	Only a Woman Like You	1971	3.75	7.50	15.00
❑ LSP-4635	Forgive Me for Calling You Darling	1972	3.75	7.50	15.00
❑ LSP-4743	Is It Any Wonder That I Love You	1972	3.75	7.50	15.00

STUFFY AND HIS FROZEN PARACHUTE BAND
PARAMOUNT
| ❑ PAS-6070 | Stuffy and His Frozen Parachute Band | 1974 | 6.25 | 12.50 | 25.00 |

—Reissue of Water Street 1002

WATER STREET
| ❑ WST 1002 | Stuffy and His Frozen Parachute Band | 1974 | 12.50 | 25.00 | 50.00 |

STUTTGART BAROQUE ENSEMBLE (MARCEL COURAND, CONDUCTOR)
MERCURY LIVING PRESENCE
| ❑ SR 90402 [S] | Couperin: Les Nations (selections); Rameau: Concerts en Sextuor Nos. 1, 4, 5 and 6 | 196? | 12.50 | 25.00 | 50.00 |

—Maroon label, no "Vendor: Mercury Record Corporation"

STYLISTICS, THE
AMHERST
❑ AMH-743	The Best of the Stylistics	1986	2.50	5.00	10.00
❑ AMH-744	All-Time Classics	1986	2.50	5.00	10.00
❑ AMH-745	The Best of the Stylistics, Vol. 2	1986	2.50	5.00	10.00
❑ AMH-746	Greatest Love Hits	1986	2.50	5.00	10.00

AVCO
❑ 11006	Round 2: The Stylistics	1972	5.00	10.00	20.00
❑ 11010	Rockin' Roll Baby	1973	5.00	10.00	20.00
❑ AV-33023	The Stylistics	1971	5.00	10.00	20.00
❑ AV-69001	Let's Put It All Together	1974	3.75	7.50	15.00
❑ AV-69004	Heavy	1974	3.75	7.50	15.00
❑ AV-69005	The Best of the Stylistics	1975	3.75	7.50	15.00
❑ 69008	Thank You Baby	1975	3.75	7.50	15.00
❑ 69010	You Are Beautiful	1975	3.75	7.50	15.00

H&L
| ❑ 69013 | Fabulous | 1976 | 3.00 | 6.00 | 12.00 |
| ❑ 69032 | Wonder Woman | 1978 | 3.00 | 6.00 | 12.00 |

MERCURY
| ❑ SRM-1-3727 | In Fashion | 1978 | 3.00 | 6.00 | 12.00 |
| ❑ SRM-1-3753 | Love Spell | 1979 | 3.00 | 6.00 | 12.00 |

PHILADELPHIA INT'L.
| ❑ FZ 37955 | 1982 | 1982 | 2.50 | 5.00 | 10.00 |

TSOP
| ❑ JZ 36470 | Hurry Up This Way Again | 1980 | 2.50 | 5.00 | 10.00 |
| ❑ FZ 37458 | Closer Than Close | 1981 | 2.50 | 5.00 | 10.00 |

STYX
A&M
❑ SP-3217	Equinox	1984	2.00	4.00	8.00
❑ SP-3218	Crystal Ball	1984	2.00	4.00	8.00
❑ SP-3223	The Grand Illusion	1984	2.00	4.00	8.00
❑ SP-3224	Pieces of Eight	1984	2.00	4.00	8.00
❑ SP-3239	Cornerstone	1984	2.00	4.00	8.00
❑ SP-3240	Paradise Theater	1984	2.00	4.00	8.00

—3200 series LPs are reissues

| ❑ SP-3711 | Cornerstone | 1979 | 2.50 | 5.00 | 10.00 |
| ❑ SP-3711 | Cornerstone | 1979 | 7.50 | 15.00 | 30.00 |

—Silver vinyl pressing, reportedly for fan club members

❑ SP-3719	Paradise Theater	1981	2.50	5.00	10.00
❑ SP-3734	Kilroy Was Here	1983	2.50	5.00	10.00
❑ SP-4559	Equinox	1975	2.50	5.00	10.00
❑ SP-4604	Crystal Ball	1976	2.50	5.00	10.00
❑ SP-4637	The Grand Illusion	1977	2.50	5.00	10.00
❑ PR-4724 [PD]	Pieces of Eight	1978	6.25	12.50	25.00
❑ SP-4724	Pieces of Eight	1978	2.50	5.00	10.00
❑ 75021 5327 1	Edge of the Century	1990	3.75	7.50	15.00
❑ SP-6514 [(2)]	Caught in the Act	1984	3.00	6.00	12.00
❑ SP-8431 [(2)DJ]	The Styx Radio Special	1977	6.25	12.50	25.00

—Promo only; green cover

| ❑ SP-17053 [(3)DJ] | Styx Radio Special | 1978 | 10.00 | 20.00 | 40.00 |

—Promo-only box set

| ❑ SP-17222 [(2)DJ] | Radio Sampler and Interview Album | 1983 | 6.25 | 12.50 | 25.00 |

—Promo only; with "Kilroy Was Here" album graphic on cover

MOBILE FIDELITY
| ❑ 1-026 | The Grand Illusion | 1979 | 7.50 | 15.00 | 30.00 |

—Audiophile vinyl

NAUTILUS
| ❑ NR-15 | Pieces of Eight | 1981 | 6.25 | 12.50 | 25.00 |

—Audiophile vinyl

| ❑ NR-27 | Cornerstone | 1982 | 5.00 | 10.00 | 20.00 |

—Audiophile vinyl

| ❑ NR-45 | Paradise Theater | 198? | 7.50 | 15.00 | 30.00 |

—Audiophile vinyl

RCA VICTOR
| ❑ AFL1-3593 | Styx | 1979 | 2.50 | 5.00 | 10.00 |
| ❑ AFL1-3594 | Lady | 1979 | 2.50 | 5.00 | 10.00 |

—Retitled version of "Styx II"

| ❑ AFL1-3595 | Serpent | 1979 | 2.50 | 5.00 | 10.00 |

—Retitled version of "The Serpent Is Rising"

| ❑ AFL1-3596 | Miracles | 1979 | 2.50 | 5.00 | 10.00 |

—Retitled version of "Man of Miracles"

❑ AFL1-3597	Best of Styx	1979	2.50	5.00	10.00
❑ AYL1-3888	Styx	1980	2.00	4.00	8.00
❑ AYL1-4233	Lady	1981	2.00	4.00	8.00

—Retitled version of "Styx II"

| ❑ AYL1-4756 | Best of Styx | 1982 | 2.00 | 4.00 | 8.00 |

WOODEN NICKEL
| ❑ BWL1-0287 | The Serpent Is Rising | 1974 | 5.00 | 10.00 | 20.00 |
| ❑ BWL1-0638 | Man of Miracles | 1974 | 5.00 | 10.00 | 20.00 |

—Second version contains "Best Thing"

| ❑ BWL1-0638 | Man of Miracles | 1974 | 7.50 | 15.00 | 30.00 |

—Original version contains "Lies"

❑ BWL1-1008	Styx	1975	3.75	7.50	15.00
❑ WNS-1008	Styx	1972	5.00	10.00	20.00
❑ BWL1-1012	Styx II	1975	3.75	7.50	15.00
❑ WNS-1012	Styx II	1973	5.00	10.00	20.00

—With die-cut cover

| ❑ BWL1-2250 | Best of Styx | 1977 | 3.00 | 6.00 | 12.00 |

SUB-ZERO BAND, THE
SUB-ZERO
| ❑ 1172 | The Sub-Zero Band | 197? | 50.00 | 100.00 | 200.00 |

SUBRAMANIAM, DR. L.
CRUSADERS
| ❑ 16003 | Blossom | 198? | 5.00 | 10.00 | 20.00 |

—Audiophile vinyl

SUGAR BEARS, THE
KIM CARNES was in this group.
BIG TREE
| ❑ BTS-2009 | Introducing the Sugar Bears | 1972 | 5.00 | 10.00 | 20.00 |

SUGAR CREEK
METROMEDIA
| ❑ MD 1020 | Please Tell a Friend | 1969 | 15.00 | 30.00 | 60.00 |

SUGARLOAF
BRUT
| ❑ 6006 | I Got a Song | 1973 | 3.75 | 7.50 | 15.00 |

CLARIDGE
| ❑ 1000 | Don't Call Us, We'll Call You | 1975 | 3.00 | 6.00 | 12.00 |

LIBERTY
| ❑ LST-7640 | Sugarloaf | 1970 | 5.00 | 10.00 | 20.00 |
| ❑ LST-11010 | Spaceship Earth | 1971 | 5.00 | 10.00 | 20.00 |

SUICIDE COMMANDOS
BLANK
| ❑ 002 | The Suicide Commandos Make a Record | 1977 | 6.25 | 12.50 | 25.00 |

Number	Title (A Side/B Side)	Yr	VG	VG+	NM
TWIN/TONE					
❏ TTR 7906	The Commandos Commit Suicide Dance Concert	1979	18.75	37.50	75.00
—Limited edition of 1,000 copies					
SUKMAN, HARRY					
LIBERTY					
❏ LRP-3005 [M]	Nightfall	1955	5.00	10.00	20.00
❏ LRP-3135 [M]	Command Performance	1959	5.00	10.00	20.00
❏ LRP-3151 [M]	The Franz Liszt Story	1960	5.00	10.00	20.00
❏ LST-7135 [S]	Command Performance	1959	6.25	12.50	25.00
❏ LST-7151 [S]	The Franz Liszt Story	1960	6.25	12.50	25.00
SULIEMAN, IDREES					
NEW JAZZ					
❏ NJLP-8202 [M]	Roots	1958	15.00	30.00	60.00
—Purple label					
❏ NJLP-8202 [M]	Roots	1958	25.00	50.00	100.00
—Yellow label					
❏ NJLP-8202 [M]	Roots	1965	6.25	12.50	25.00
—Blue label, trident logo at right					
SULLIVAN, IRA					
ATLANTIC					
❏ 1476 [M]	Horizons	1967	6.25	12.50	25.00
DELMARK					
❏ DL-402 [M]	Blue Stroll	1961	7.50	15.00	30.00
❏ DS-402 [S]	Blue Stroll	1961	10.00	20.00	40.00
VEE JAY					
❏ LP-3003 [M]	Bird Lives!	1960	7.50	15.00	30.00
❏ SR-3003 [S]	Bird Lives!	1960	10.00	20.00	40.00
SULLIVAN, JIM					
MERCURY					
❏ MG-21137 [M]	Sitar Beat	1967	5.00	10.00	20.00
❏ SR-61137 [S]	Sitar Beat	1967	5.00	10.00	20.00
SULLIVAN, JOE					
CAPITOL					
❏ T 636 [M]	Classics in Jazz	1955	10.00	20.00	40.00
DOWN HOME					
❏ MGD-2 [M]	Mr. Piano Man: The Music of Joe Sullivan	1956	12.50	25.00	50.00
EPIC					
❏ LG 1003 [10]	Joe Sullivan Plays Fats Waller Compositions	1954	20.00	40.00	80.00
RIVERSIDE					
❏ RLP 12-202 [M]	New Solos by an Old Master	1955	15.00	30.00	60.00
VERVE					
❏ MGV-1002 [M]	Mr. Piano Man: The Music of Joe Sullivan	1957	10.00	20.00	40.00
❏ V-1002 [M]	Mr. Piano Man: The Music of Joe Sullivan	1961	5.00	10.00	20.00
SULLIVAN, MAXINE					
PERIOD					
❏ SPL-1207 [M]	Maxine Sullivan, Volume 2	1956	12.50	25.00	50.00
❏ RL-1909 [M]	Maxine Sullivan 1956	1956	12.50	25.00	50.00
SUMAC, YMA					
CAPITOL					
❏ H 244 [10]	Voice of the Xtabay	1952	25.00	50.00	100.00
❏ L 299 [10]	Legend of the Sun Virgin	1952	30.00	60.00	120.00
❏ SM-299 [M]	Legend of the Sun Virgin	197?	3.00	6.00	12.00
❏ T 299 [M]	Legend of the Sun Virgin	1955	12.50	25.00	50.00
❏ L 423 [10]	Inca Taqui	1953	25.00	50.00	100.00
❏ H 564 [10]	Mambo!	1954	25.00	50.00	100.00
❏ T 564 [M]	Mambo!	1955	12.50	25.00	50.00
❏ DW 684 [R]	Voice of the Xtabay and Inca Taqui	1963	3.75	7.50	15.00
❏ SM-684	Voice of the Xtabay and Inca Taqui	197?	3.00	6.00	12.00
—On this reissue, Side 1 is in mono					
❏ W 684 [M]	Voice of the Xtabay and Inca Taqui	1955	12.50	25.00	50.00
—Gray label					
❏ W 684 [M]	Voice of the Xtabay and Inca Taqui	1963	5.00	10.00	20.00
—Black colorband label, "Capitol" at top					
❏ T 770 [M]	Legend of the Jivaro	1956	12.50	25.00	50.00
—Turquoise label					
❏ T 770 [M]	Legend of the Jivaro	1963	5.00	10.00	20.00
—Black colorband label, "Capitol" at top					
❏ ST 1169 [S]	Fuego del Andes	1959	12.50	25.00	50.00
❏ T 1169 [M]	Fuego del Andes	1959	10.00	20.00	40.00
❏ M-11892	Mambo!	1979	3.00	6.00	12.00
CORAL					
❏ CRL 56058 [10]	Presenting Yma Sumac	1952	30.00	60.00	120.00
LONDON					
❏ XPS 608	Miracles	1972	5.00	10.00	20.00
SUMMER, DONNA					
ATLANTIC					
❏ 81987	Another Place and Time	1989	3.00	6.00	12.00
CASABLANCA					
❏ NBLP 7038	Four Seasons of Love	1976	2.50	5.00	10.00
❏ NBLP 7056	I Remember Yesterday	1977	2.50	5.00	10.00
❏ NBLP 7078 [(2)]	Once Upon a Time...	1977	3.00	6.00	12.00
❏ NBLP 7119 [(2)]	Live and More	1978	3.00	6.00	12.00
❏ NBPIX 7119 [PD]	The Best of Live and More	1979	5.00	10.00	20.00
❏ NBLP 7150 [(2)]	Bad Girls	1979	3.00	6.00	12.00
❏ NBLP 7191 [(2)]	On the Radio — Greatest Hits Vols. 1 and 2	1979	3.00	6.00	12.00
❏ NBLP 7201	Greatest Hits, Vol. 1	1979	2.00	4.00	8.00
❏ NBLP 7202	Greatest Hits, Vol. 2	1979	2.00	4.00	8.00
❏ NBLP 7244	Walk Away — Collector's Edition (The Best of 1977-1980)	1980	2.50	5.00	10.00
❏ 811123-1 [(2)]	Live and More	1985	2.50	5.00	10.00
❏ 822557-1 [(2)]	Bad Girls	1984	2.50	5.00	10.00
❏ 822558-1 [(2)]	On the Radio — Greatest Hits Vols. 1 and 2	1984	2.50	5.00	10.00
❏ 822559-1	Greatest Hits, Vol. 2	1984	2.00	4.00	8.00
❏ 822560-1	Walk Away	1984	2.00	4.00	8.00

Number	Title (A Side/B Side)	Yr	VG	VG+	NM
EPIC					
❏ E2 69910 [(2)]	Live and More Encore	1999	3.75	7.50	15.00
GEFFEN					
❏ GHS 2000	The Wanderer	1980	2.50	5.00	10.00
❏ GHS 2005	Donna Summer	1982	2.50	5.00	10.00
❏ GHS 24040	Cats Without Claws	1984	2.50	5.00	10.00
❏ GHS 24040 [DJ]	Cats Without Claws	1984	3.75	7.50	15.00
—Promo only on Quiex II vinyl					
❏ GHS 24102	All Systems Go	1987	2.50	5.00	10.00
MERCURY					
❏ 812265-1	She Works Hard for the Money	1983	2.50	5.00	10.00
❏ 826144-1	The Summer Collection	1985	2.50	5.00	10.00
OASIS					
❏ OCLP 5003	Love to Love You Baby	1975	3.00	6.00	12.00
—Add 50% if poster is included					
❏ OCLP 5004	A Love Trilogy	1976	3.00	6.00	12.00
❏ 822792-1	Love to Love You Baby	1985	2.00	4.00	8.00
SUMMER SOUNDS, THE					
LAUREL					
❏ 90973	Up Down	196?	250.00	500.00	1000.
SUMMERHILL					
TETRAGRAMMATON					
❏ T-114	Summerhill	1969	7.50	15.00	30.00
SUMMERLIN, ED					
ECCLESIA					
❏ ER-101 [M]	Liturgical Jazz	1959	15.00	30.00	60.00
SUMMERS, ANDREW ROWAN					
FOLKWAYS					
❏ FP-21 [10]	Seeds of Love	1951	12.50	25.00	50.00
❏ FP-41 [10]	The Lady Gay	1954	12.50	25.00	50.00
❏ FP-44 [10]	The Faulse Lady	1954	12.50	25.00	50.00
❏ FA-2002 [10]	Christmas Carols	195?	12.50	25.00	50.00
❏ FA-2021 [10]	Seeds of Love	1951	12.50	25.00	50.00
❏ FA-2041 [10]	The Lady Gay	1954	12.50	25.00	50.00
❏ FA-2044 [10]	The Faulse Lady	1954	12.50	25.00	50.00
❏ FA-2348 [M]	Andrew Rowan Summers	1957	7.50	15.00	30.00
❏ FA-2361 [M]	Hymns and Carols	195?	7.50	15.00	30.00
❏ FA-2364 [M]	The Unquiet Grave and Other American Tragic Ballads	195?	7.50	15.00	30.00
❏ FC 7502 [M]	Christmas Carols	196?	3.75	7.50	15.00
SUMMERS, ANDY, AND ROBERT FRIPP					
A&M					
❏ SP-4913	I Advance Masked	1982	2.50	5.00	10.00
❏ SP9-5011	Bewitched	1984	2.50	5.00	10.00
❏ SP-17299 [DJ]	Speak Out Interview	1982	6.25	12.50	25.00
—Issued in generic cover with sticker					
SUN RA					
ABC IMPULSE!					
❏ 1974	Welcome to Saturn	1974	6.25	12.50	25.00
❏ AS-9239	Atlantis	1973	5.00	10.00	20.00
❏ AS-9242	The Nubians of Plutonia	1974	5.00	10.00	20.00
❏ AS-9243	The Magic City	1973	5.00	10.00	20.00
❏ AS-9245	Angels and Demons at Play	1974	5.00	10.00	20.00
❏ AS-9255	Astro Black	1973	5.00	10.00	20.00
❏ ASD-9265	Jazz in Silhouette	1974	5.00	10.00	20.00
❏ AS-9270	Fate in a Pleasant Mood	1974	5.00	10.00	20.00
❏ AS-9271	Super Sonic Sounds	1974	5.00	10.00	20.00
❏ AS-9276	The Bad and the Beautiful	1974	5.00	10.00	20.00
❏ ASD-9298	Pathways to Unknown Worlds	1975	5.00	10.00	20.00
AFFINITY					
❏ AFF 10	The Solar-Myth Approach Volume I	1978	6.25	12.50	25.00
❏ AFF 76	The Solar-Myth Approach Volume II	1978	6.25	12.50	25.00
BASF					
❏ 20748	It's After the End of the World	1971	5.00	10.00	20.00
BLACK LION					
❏ 106	Pictures of Infinity	197?	5.00	10.00	20.00
BLUE THUMB					
❏ BTS-41	Space Is the Place	1973	5.00	10.00	20.00
DELMARK					
❏ DL-411 [M]	Sun Song	1967	7.50	15.00	30.00
DIW					
❏ DIWP-2 [PD]	Cosmo Omnibus Imaginable Illusion: Live at Pit-Inn	1988	12.50	25.00	50.00
—Picture disc; limited to under 1,000 copies					
ESP-DISK'					
❏ 1014 [M]	The Heliocentric Worlds of Sun Ra, Volume 1	1966	7.50	15.00	30.00
❏ S-1014 [S]	The Heliocentric Worlds of Sun Ra, Volume 1	1966	10.00	20.00	40.00
❏ 1017 [M]	The Heliocentric Worlds of Sun Ra, Volume 2	1966	7.50	15.00	30.00
—Without voices overdubbed on "The Sun Myth"					
❏ S-1017 [S]	The Heliocentric Worlds of Sun Ra, Volume 2	1966	10.00	20.00	40.00
—Without voices overdubbed on "The Sun Myth"					
❏ S-1045 [S]	Nothing Is	1969	5.00	10.00	20.00
HAT HUT					
❏ 17 [(2)]	Sunrise in Different Directions	1980	5.00	10.00	20.00
HORO					
❏ HDP-19/20 [(2)]	Unity	1978	6.25	12.50	25.00
❏ HDP-23/24 [(2)]	Other Voices, Other Blues	1978	6.25	12.50	25.00
❏ HDP-25/26 [(2)]	New Steps	1978	6.25	12.50	25.00
INNER CITY					
❏ IC-1039 [(2)]	Live at Montreux	1978	5.00	10.00	20.00
JIHAD					
❏ 1968 [S]	A Black Mass	1968	25.00	50.00	100.00
—Color cover					

Number	Title (A Side/B Side)	Yr	VG	VG+	NM
❏ 1968 [S]	A Black Mass	1968	37.50	75.00	150.00
—Black and white cover					
MELTDOWN					
❏ MPA-1	John Cage Meets Sun Ra	1987	5.00	10.00	20.00
PHILLY JAZZ					
❏ PJ-666	Lanquidity	1978	6.25	12.50	25.00
❏ PJ-1007	Of Mythic Worlds	1980	6.25	12.50	25.00
PRAXIS					
❏ CM 106	Sun Ra Arkestra Meets Salah Ragab in Egypt	1983	10.00	20.00	40.00
❏ CM 108	Live at Praxis Volume 1	1984	12.50	25.00	50.00
❏ CM 109	Live at Praxis Volume 2	1985	12.50	25.00	50.00
❏ CM 110	Live at Praxis 84 Volume 3	1985	12.50	25.00	50.00
RECOMMENDED					
❏ RR-11	Nuits de la Fondation Maeght Volume I	1981	7.50	15.00	30.00
—Reissue of Shandar 10.001; plays at 45 rpm					
SATURN					
❏ CMIJ 78	Disco 3000	1978	5.00	10.00	20.00
❏ IHNY-165	Sun Ra and His Arkestra Featuring Pharoah				
	Sanders and Black Harold	1976	10.00	20.00	40.00
❏ LP-200	Universe in Blue	197?	7.50	15.00	30.00
❏ LP-202 [M]	Fate in a Pleasant Mood	196?	7.50	15.00	30.00
—Chicago address on label					
❏ LP-203 [M]	Interstellar Low Ways	1969	12.50	25.00	50.00
—Chicago address on label					
❏ LP-204 [M]	Super-Sonic Jazz	1968	12.50	25.00	50.00
—Blue or green cover; Chicago address on label					
❏ LP-205 [M]	Jazz in Silhouette	1967	12.50	25.00	50.00
—Green label					
❏ LP-205 [M]	Jazz in Silhouette	1967	12.50	25.00	50.00
—Red label					
❏ LP-206 [M]	Other Planes of There	1967	10.00	20.00	40.00
—Chicago address on label					
❏ LP-207 [M]	Sun Ra Visits Planet Earth	196?	10.00	20.00	40.00
—"El Saturn" label					
❏ LP-207 [M]	Sun Ra Visits Planet Earth	1968	12.50	25.00	50.00
—Minneapolis address on label					
❏ LP-208 [M]	Secrets of the Sun	196?	12.50	25.00	50.00
—Chicago address on label					
❏ SRLP-0216 [M]	Super-Sonic Jazz	1957	37.50	75.00	150.00
—Blank cover					
❏ SRLP-0216 [M]	Super-Sonic Jazz	1957	75.00	150.00	300.00
—Silk-screened cover					
❏ SRLP-0216 [M]	Super-Sonic Jazz	1958	37.50	75.00	150.00
—Purple "keyboard" cover					
❏ SRLP-0216 [M]	Super-Sonic Jazz	1965	12.50	25.00	50.00
—Blue or green cover					
❏ LP-402	When Sun Comes Out	196?	10.00	20.00	40.00
❏ LP-403 [M]	The Magic City	196?	7.50	15.00	30.00
—Chicago address on label					
❏ LP-404 [M]	Art Forms of Dimensions Tomorrow	1969	7.50	15.00	30.00
—Chicago address on label					
❏ LP-405	When Angels Speak of Love	196?	7.50	15.00	30.00
❏ LP-406 [M]	The Nubians of Plutonia	1969	12.50	25.00	50.00
—Chicago address on label					
❏ LP-407 [M]	Angels and Demons at Play	196?	10.00	20.00	40.00
—Chicago address on label					
❏ LP-408 [S]	Cosmic Tones for Mental Therapy	1967	50.00	100.00	200.00
—Red label; Sun Ra art on cover					
❏ LP-409 [M]	We Travel the Spaceways	196?	6.25	12.50	25.00
—"El Saturn" label					
❏ LP-485	Deep Purple	1973	10.00	20.00	40.00
❏ LP-487	Song of the Stargazers	1979	12.50	25.00	50.00
❏ LP-502 [S]	Strange Strings	1967	12.50	25.00	50.00
—Red label					
❏ ESR-507 [S]	Atlantis	1969	7.50	15.00	30.00
—"El Saturn" label					
❏ LP-509 [M]	Monorails and Satellites	1968	12.50	25.00	50.00
—"El Saturn" label					
❏ LP-512	Sound Sun Pleasure!!	1970	10.00	20.00	40.00
❏ LP-519 [S]	Monorails and Satellites, Vol. II	1969	12.50	25.00	50.00
—"El Saturn" label					
❏ ESR-520	Continuation	1969	6.25	12.50	25.00
❏ LP-520	Continuation	1970	12.50	25.00	50.00
❏ ESR-521	My Brother the Wind	1970	6.25	12.50	25.00
❏ LP-521	My Brother the Wind	197?	12.50	25.00	50.00
❏ LP-522	The Night of the Purple Moon	197?	12.50	25.00	50.00
❏ LP-523	My Brother the Wind, Volume II	1971	12.50	25.00	50.00
❏ LP-527	Space Probe	197?	12.50	25.00	50.00
❏ LP-529	The Invisible Shield	1974	15.00	30.00	60.00
—Philadelphia address on label					
❏ LP-529	The Invisible Shield	1974	20.00	40.00	80.00
—Chicago address on label					
❏ LP-530	Outer Spaceways Incorporated	1974	15.00	30.00	60.00
—Philadelphia address on label					
❏ LP-530	Outer Spaceways Incorporated	1974	20.00	40.00	80.00
—Chicago address on label					
❏ LP-538	Discipline 27-II	1973	12.50	25.00	50.00
❏ LP-539	What's New?	197?	12.50	25.00	50.00
❏ LPB-711 [M]	The Magic City	1966	20.00	40.00	80.00
—Red label					
❏ LP-747	Some Blues But Not the Kind That's Blue	1977	10.00	20.00	40.00
❏ 752	What's New?	197?	5.00	10.00	20.00
❏ LP-771	The Soul Vibrations of Man	1977	10.00	20.00	40.00
❏ LP-772	Taking a Chance on Chances	1977	15.00	30.00	60.00
❏ LP-849	Horizon	1974	10.00	20.00	40.00
❏ 1272	Live in Egypt 1	1973	6.25	12.50	25.00
❏ LP-1966 [M]	When Angels Speak of Love	1966	75.00	150.00	300.00
—Red cover with a "sideways" image of Sun Ra					
❏ ESR-1970	My Brother the Wind	1970	10.00	20.00	40.00
❏ 1978	Media Dream	1978	5.00	10.00	20.00
❏ 1981	Dance of Innocent Passion	1981	5.00	10.00	20.00
❏ IX/1983-220	Ra to the Rescue	1983	10.00	20.00	40.00

Number	Title (A Side/B Side)	Yr	VG	VG+	NM
❏ 1984A/B	Just Friends	1984	5.00	10.00	20.00
❏ A/B-1984SG-9	A Fireside Chat with Lucifer	1984	5.00	10.00	20.00
❏ C/D-1984SG-9	Celestial Love	1984	5.00	10.00	20.00
❏ SRA-2000	My Brother the Wind, Volume II	1971	10.00	20.00	40.00
❏ LP-2066 [M]	When Sun Comes Out	1963	50.00	100.00	200.00
—Blank cover					
❏ LP-2066 [M]	When Sun Comes Out	1963	75.00	150.00	300.00
—Black ameboid figure on cover					
❏ LP-2066 [M]	When Sun Comes Out	1963	75.00	150.00	300.00
—Green cover with yellow sun					
❏ LP-2066 [M]	When Sun Comes Out	1967	50.00	100.00	200.00
—Spaceman at piano cover					
❏ KH-2772 [S]	Cosmic Tones for Mental Therapy	196?	7.50	15.00	30.00
—Blue cover; Chicago address on label					
❏ ESR-5000	Universe in Blue	1972	7.50	15.00	30.00
❏ HK-5445 [M]	We Travel the Spaceways	1966	15.00	30.00	60.00
—Red label					
❏ LP-5786 [M]	Jazz in Silhouette	1958	37.50	75.00	150.00
—Yellow label					
❏ 6161	Song of the Stargazers	1979	12.50	25.00	50.00
❏ 6680	I, Pharoah	1980	5.00	10.00	20.00
—"El Saturn" label					
❏ 7771	Nidhamu	197?	5.00	10.00	20.00
❏ 7877	Somewhere Over the Rainbow	1977	5.00	10.00	20.00
❏ GH-9954-E/F [M]	Secrets of the Sun	1965	25.00	50.00	100.00
—Red label					
❏ SR-9956 [M]	Art Forms of Dimensions Tomorrow	1965	12.50	25.00	50.00
—Red label					
❏ SR-9956-11A/B [M]	Sun Ra Visits Planet Earth	1966	20.00	40.00	80.00
—Red label					
❏ SR-9956-11E/F [M]	The Lady with the Golden Stockings	1966	75.00	150.00	300.00
—Cover is generic and says "Tonal Views of Times Tomorrow"					
❏ SR-9956-2-M/N [M]	Rocket #9 Take Off For the Planet Venus	1966	75.00	150.00	300.00
—Cover has "burning candle" logo					
❏ SR-9956-2/A/B [M]	Fate in a Pleasant Mood	1965	20.00	40.00	80.00
—Red label					
❏ SR-9956-2/O/P [M]	Angels and Demons at Play	1965	20.00	40.00	80.00
—Red label; metallic gold cover					
❏ 10480	Aurora Boralis	1980	5.00	10.00	20.00
❏ 11179	Sleeping Beauty	1979	20.00	40.00	80.00
❏ 13088A/12988B	Hidden Fire 2	1988	5.00	10.00	20.00
❏ 13188III/12988II	Hidden Fire 1	1988	5.00	10.00	20.00
❏ 14200-A/B	Space Probe	197?	7.50	15.00	30.00
❏ 19782	Sound Mirror	1978	5.00	10.00	20.00
❏ 19783	Media Dream	1978	5.00	10.00	20.00
❏ 19841	A Fireside Chat with Lucifer	1984	5.00	10.00	20.00
❏ 19842	Celestial Love	1984	5.00	10.00	20.00
❏ 52375	What's New?	1975	6.25	12.50	25.00
❏ 61674	Out Beyond the Kingdom Of	1974	10.00	20.00	40.00
❏ 72579	God Is More Than Love Can Ever Be	1979	5.00	10.00	20.00
❏ IX SR 72881	Oblique Parallax	1981	15.00	30.00	60.00
❏ 77771	Nidhamu	197?	6.25	12.50	25.00
❏ 81774	The Antique Blacks	1974	10.00	20.00	40.00
❏ MS 87976 [(2)]	Live at Montreux	1976	12.50	25.00	50.00
❏ 91379	Omniverse	1979	15.00	30.00	60.00
❏ 91780	Voice of the Eternal Tomorrow	1980	5.00	10.00	20.00
❏ 92074	Sub Underground	1974	10.00	20.00	40.00
❏ KH-98766 [M]	Other Planes of There	1966	20.00	40.00	80.00
—Red label					
❏ 101185	Hiroshima	1985	5.00	10.00	20.00
❏ 101477	Some Blues But Not the Kind That's Blue	1977	5.00	10.00	20.00
❏ 101485	When Spaceships Appear	1985	5.00	10.00	20.00
❏ 101679	On Jupiter	1979	5.00	10.00	20.00
—"El Saturn" label					
❏ 123180	Beyond the Purple Star Zone	1981	5.00	10.00	20.00
❏ 1014077	Some Blues But Not the Kind That's Blue	1977	6.25	12.50	25.00
❏ 1217718	Horizon	1974	5.00	10.00	20.00
❏ 9121385	Outer Reach Intensity-Energy	1985	6.25	12.50	25.00
SATURN/RECOMMENDED					
❏ SRRD-1	Cosmo Sun Connection	1985	5.00	10.00	20.00
SAVOY					
❏ MG-12169 [M]	The Futuristic Sounds of Sun Ra	1961	20.00	40.00	80.00
SHANDAR					
❏ SR 10.001	Nuits de la Fondation Maeght Volume I	1971	10.00	20.00	40.00
❏ SR 10.003	Nuits de la Fondation Maeght Volume II	1971	10.00	20.00	40.00
SWEET EARTH					
❏ SER 1003	The Other Side of the Sun	1979	5.00	10.00	20.00
THOTH INTERGALACTIC					
❏ LPB-711 [M]	The Magic City	1969	7.50	15.00	30.00
❏ KH-1272	Live in Egypt 1	1973	7.50	15.00	30.00
❏ IR-1972	The Night of the Purple Moon	1970	7.50	15.00	30.00
❏ KH-2772 [S]	Cosmic Tones for Mental Therapy	1969	7.50	15.00	30.00
❏ KH-5472 [M]	Strange Strings	196?	10.00	20.00	40.00
❏ 7771	Nidhamu	197?	7.50	15.00	30.00
❏ KH-98766 [M]	Other Planes of There	1969	10.00	20.00	40.00
TRANSITION					
❏ TLP-10 [M]	Jazz by Sun Ra	1957	62.50	125.00	250.00
—With booklet (deduct 1/5 if missing)					

SUNDOWNERS, THE

LIBERTY

Number	Title (A Side/B Side)	Yr	VG	VG+	NM
❏ LRP-3269 [M]	Folk Songs for the Rich	1962	5.00	10.00	20.00
❏ LST-7269 [S]	Folk Songs for the Rich	1962	6.25	12.50	25.00

SUNGLOWS, THE
See SUNNY AND THE SUNLINERS.

SUNKEL, PHIL

ABC-PARAMOUNT

Number	Title (A Side/B Side)	Yr	VG	VG+	NM
❏ ABC-136 [M]	Jazz Band	1956	20.00	40.00	80.00
❏ ABC-225 [M]	Gerry Mulligan and Bob Brookmeyer Play Phil Sunkel's Jazz Concerto Grosso	1958	12.50	25.00	50.00

Number	Title (A Side/B Side)	Yr	VG	VG+	NM
❏ ABCS-225 [S]	Gerry Mulligan and Bob Brookmeyer Play Phil Sunkel's Jazz Concerto Grosso	1958	10.00	20.00	40.00

SUNNY AND THE SUNLINERS
KEY-LOC
❏ 3001 [M]	Smile Now, Cry Later	196?	6.25	12.50	25.00
❏ 3002 [M]	No Te Chifles	196?	6.25	12.50	25.00
❏ 3003 [M]	Sunny and the Sunliners Live in Hollywood	196?	6.25	12.50	25.00
❏ 3004 [M]	Canta Sunny	196?	6.25	12.50	25.00
❏ 3005 [M]	A Little Brown-Eyed Soul	196?	6.25	12.50	25.00
❏ 3006 [M]	This Is My Band	196?	6.25	12.50	25.00
❏ 3007 [M]	Versatile	196?	6.25	12.50	25.00
❏ 3008 [M]	Adelante	196?	6.25	12.50	25.00
❏ 3009 [M]	Sky High	196?	6.25	12.50	25.00
❏ 3010 [M]	The Missing Link	196?	6.25	12.50	25.00

SUNGLOW
❏ SLP-101 [M]	Sunny Ozuna and the Sunglows	1963	25.00	50.00	100.00
—As "The Sunglows"					
❏ SLP-102 [M]	The Fabulous Sunglows	1964	25.00	50.00	100.00
—As "The Sunglows"					
❏ SLP-103 [M]	The Original Peanuts	1965	20.00	40.00	80.00
—As "The Sunglows"					
❏ SLP-103S [S]	The Original Peanuts	1965	25.00	50.00	100.00
—As "The Sunglows"					

TEAR DROP
❏ LPM-2000 [M]	Talk to Me	1963	25.00	50.00	100.00
❏ LPM-2001 [M]	Las Vegas Welcomes Sunny and the Sunliners	1964	10.00	20.00	40.00
❏ LPM-2008 [M]	Teardrop Presents Sunny and the Sunliners	196?	10.00	20.00	40.00

SUNNYLAND SLIM
BLUESVILLE
❏ BVLP-1016 [M]	Slim's Shout	1961	30.00	60.00	120.00
—Blue label, silver print					
❏ BVLP-1016 [M]	Slim's Shout	1964	7.50	5.00	30.00
—Blue label, trident logo at right					

PRESTIGE
❏ PRST-7723	Slim's Shout	1969	5.00	10.00	20.00

WORLD PACIFIC
❏ WPS-21890	Slim's Got His Thing Goin' On	1969	5.00	10.00	20.00

SUNRAYS, THE
TOWER
❏ ST 5017 [S]	Andrea	1966	15.00	30.00	60.00
❏ T 5017 [M]	Andrea	1966	12.50	25.00	50.00

SUNSET DRAGSTERS, THE
PALACE
❏ M-775 [M]	Hot Rod Rally	196?	15.00	30.00	60.00
❏ PST-775 [S]	Hot Rod Rally	196?	20.00	40.00	80.00

SUNSETS, THE (1)
PALACE
❏ M-752 [M]	Surfing with the Sunsets	1963	10.00	20.00	40.00
❏ PST-752 [S]	Surfing with the Sunsets	1963	12.50	25.00	50.00

SUNSHINE BOYS, THE
DOT
❏ DLP-3189 [M]	Sing Unto Him	1959	7.50	15.00	30.00
❏ DLP-25189 [S]	Sing Unto Him	1959	10.00	20.00	40.00

STARDAY
❏ SLP-113 [M]	America's Number One Gospel Group	1960	10.00	20.00	40.00
❏ SLP-166 [M]	More Country Music Sing-Along	1962	7.50	15.00	30.00
❏ SLP-349 [M]	A Happy Home Up There	1965	7.50	15.00	30.00

SUNSHINE COMPANY, THE
IMPERIAL
❏ LP-9359 [M]	Happy Is the Sunshine Company	1967	5.00	10.00	20.00
❏ LP-9368 [M]	The Sunshine Company	1968	6.25	12.50	25.00
—Mono copies are promo only					
❏ LP-12359 [S]	Happy Is the Sunshine Company	1967	5.00	10.00	20.00
❏ LP-12368 [S]	The Sunshine Company	1968	5.00	10.00	20.00
❏ LP-12399	Sunshine and Shadows	1969	5.00	10.00	20.00

SUPER STOCKS, THE
CAPITOL
❏ ST 1997 [S]	Hot Rod Rally	1963	17.50	35.00	70.00
❏ T 1997 [M]	Hot Rod Rally	1963	12.50	25.00	50.00
❏ (S)T 2060	Thunder Road Bonus Poster	1964	12.50	25.00	50.00
❏ ST 2060 [S]	Thunder Road	1964	31.25	62.50	125.00
❏ T 2060 [M]	Thunder Road	1964	25.00	50.00	100.00
❏ ST 2113 [S]	Surf Route 101	1964	31.25	62.50	125.00
—Without bonus single					
❏ ST 2113 [S]	Surf Route 101	1964	37.50	75.00	150.00
—With bonus single, "Doin' the Surfink"/"Finksville, U.S.A." by Mr. Gasser and the Weirdos, in special pocket on front cover					
❏ T 2113 [M]	Surf Route 101	1964	25.00	50.00	100.00
—Without bonus single					
❏ T 2113 [M]	Surf Route 101	1964	31.25	62.50	125.00
—With bonus single, "Doin' the Surfink"/"Finksville, U.S.A." by Mr. Gasser and the Weirdos, in special pocket on front cover					
❏ ST 2190 [S]	School Is a Drag	1964	30.00	60.00	120.00
❏ T 2190 [M]	School Is a Drag	1964	25.00	50.00	100.00

SUPERFINE DANDELION, THE
MAINSTREAM
❏ S-6102 [S]	The Superfine Dandelion	1967	10.00	20.00	40.00
❏ 56102 [M]	The Superfine Dandelion	1967	10.00	20.00	40.00

SUPERSAX
MOBILE FIDELITY
❏ 1-511	Supersax Plays Bird	1981	10.00	20.00	40.00
—Audiophile vinyl					

SUPERSISTER
DWARF
❏ PDLP-2001	Supersister	197?	7.50	15.00	30.00

SUPERTRAMP
A&M
❏ SP-3129	Indelibly Stamped	198?	2.00	4.00	8.00
—Budget-line reissue					
❏ SP-3149	Supertramp	198?	2.00	4.00	8.00
—Budget-line reissue					
❏ SP-3214	Crisis? What Crisis?	1982	2.00	4.00	8.00
—Budget-line reissue					
❏ SP-3215	Even in the Quietest Moments	1982	2.00	4.00	8.00
—Budget-line reissue					
❏ SP-3284	…Famous Last Words…	1986	2.00	4.00	8.00
—Budget-line reissue					
❏ SP-3647	Crime of the Century	1974	3.00	6.00	12.00
❏ SP-3708	Breakfast in America	1979	2.50	5.00	10.00
❏ SP-3730 [PD]	Breakfast in America	1979	125.00	250.00	500.00
—In-house picture discs featuring A&M staff members posing with the cover model					
❏ SP-3732	…Famous Last Words…	1982	2.50	5.00	10.00
❏ SP-4274	Supertramp	197?	2.50	5.00	10.00
—Second edition with silverish label					
❏ SP-4274	Supertramp	1970	5.00	10.00	20.00
—First edition with brown label					
❏ SP-4311	Indelibly Stamped	197?	2.50	5.00	10.00
—Second edition with silverish label					
❏ SP-4311	Indelibly Stamped	1971	5.00	10.00	20.00
—First edition with brown label					
❏ SP-4560	Crisis? What Crisis?	1975	3.00	6.00	12.00
❏ SP-4634	Even in the Quietest Moments…	1977	3.00	6.00	12.00
❏ SP-4665	Supertramp	1978	3.00	6.00	12.00
❏ SP-5013	Brother Where You Bound	1985	2.50	5.00	10.00
❏ SP-5181	Free as a Bird	1987	2.50	5.00	10.00
❏ SP-6702 [(2)]	Paris	1980	3.00	6.00	12.00

MOBILE FIDELITY
❏ 1-005	Crime of the Century	1979	10.00	20.00	40.00
❏ MFQR-005	Crime of the Century	1983	30.00	60.00	120.00
—Ultra High Quality Recording; in box					
❏ 1-045	Breakfast in America	1980	12.50	25.00	50.00
—Audiophile vinyl					

SWEET THUNDER
❏ 5	Even in the Quietest Moments…	198?	10.00	20.00	40.00
—Audiophile vinyl					

SUPREMES, THE
DORAL
❏ DRL 104	Doral Presents Diana Ross and the Supremes	1971	12.50	25.00	50.00
—Available through Doral cigarettes					

MOTOWN
❏ M5-101V1	Superstar Series, Vol. 1	1981	3.00	6.00	12.00
—By "Diana Ross and the Supremes"					
❏ PR-102 [DJ]	Touch Interview	1971	6.25	12.50	25.00
❏ M5-138V1	The Supremes A' Go-Go	1981	3.00	6.00	12.00
—Reissue of Motown 649					
❏ M5-147V1	I Hear a Symphony	1981	3.00	6.00	12.00
—Reissue of Motown 643					
❏ M5-158V1	The Supremes Sing Country Western and Pop	1981	2.00	4.00	8.00
—Reissue of Motown 625					
❏ M5-162V1	The Supremes at the Copa	1981	3.00	6.00	12.00
—Reissue of Motown 636					
❏ M5-182V1	The Supremes Sing Holland-Dozier-Holland	1981	3.00	6.00	12.00
—Reissue of Motown 650					
❏ M5-203V1	Diana Ross and the Supremes Greatest Hits, Volume 3	1981	3.00	6.00	12.00
—Reissue of Motown 702					
❏ M5-223V1	Meet the Supremes	1982	2.00	4.00	8.00
—Reissue of Motown 606					
❏ M5-237V1	Greatest Hits	1982	2.50	5.00	10.00
—Reissue (unknown if it's the complete 2-record set or an edited version)					
❏ M 606 [M]	Meet the Supremes	1963	7.50	15.00	30.00
—With close-up of group's faces					
❏ M 606 [M]	Meet the Supremes	1963	225.00	450.00	900.00
—With group sitting on stools					
❏ MS 606 [M]	Meet the Supremes	1964	10.00	20.00	40.00
—With close-up of group's faces					
❏ MT/MS 610	The Supremes Sing Ballads and Blues	1963	—	—	—
—Unreleased					
❏ M 621 [M]	Where Did Our Love Go	1964	7.50	15.00	30.00
❏ MS 621 [S]	Where Did Our Love Go	1964	10.00	20.00	40.00
❏ M 623 [M]	A Bit of Liverpool	1964	10.00	20.00	40.00
❏ MS 623 [S]	A Bit of Liverpool	1964	12.50	25.00	50.00
❏ MS 625 [S]	The Supremes Sing Country, Western & Pop	1965	7.50	15.00	30.00
❏ MT-625 [M]	The Supremes Sing Country, Western & Pop	1965	6.25	12.50	25.00
❏ MT/MS 626	The Supremes Live! Live! Live!	1965	—	—	—
—Unreleased					
❏ M 627 [M]	More Hits by the Supremes	1965	6.25	12.50	25.00
❏ MS 627 [S]	More Hits by the Supremes	1965	7.50	15.00	30.00
❏ MT/MS 628	There's a Place for Us	1965	—	—	—
—Unreleased					
❏ M 629 [M]	We Remember Sam Cooke	1965	6.25	12.50	25.00
❏ MS 629 [S]	We Remember Sam Cooke	1965	7.50	15.00	30.00
—The above LP came out before Motown 627					
❏ M 636 [M]	The Supremes at the Copa	1965	6.25	12.50	25.00
❏ MS 636 [S]	The Supremes at the Copa	1965	7.50	15.00	30.00
❏ MT/MS 637	A Tribute to the Girls	1965	—	—	—
—Unreleased					
❏ MS 638 [S]	Merry Christmas	1965	10.00	20.00	40.00
—Same as above, but in stereo					
❏ MT 638 [M]	Merry Christmas	1965	7.50	15.00	30.00

S

Number	Title (A Side/B Side)	Yr	VG	VG+	NM
❏ M 643 [M]	I Hear a Symphony	1966	6.25	12.50	25.00
❏ MS 643 [S]	I Hear a Symphony	1966	7.50	15.00	30.00
❏ MTMS 648	Pure Gold	1966	—	—	—
—Unreleased					
❏ M 649 [M]	The Supremes A' Go-Go	1966	6.25	12.50	25.00
❏ MS 649 [S]	The Supremes A' Go-Go	1966	7.50	15.00	30.00
❏ M 650 [M]	The Supremes Sing Holland-Dozier-Holland	1967	6.25	12.50	25.00
❏ MS 650 [S]	The Supremes Sing Holland-Dozier-Holland	1967	7.50	15.00	30.00
❏ M 659 [M]	The Supremes Sing Rodgers & Hart	1967	6.25	12.50	25.00
❏ MS 659 [S]	The Supremes Sing Rodgers & Hart	1967	7.50	15.00	30.00
❏ M 663 [(2)M]	Diana Ross and the Supremes Greatest Hits	1967	7.50	15.00	30.00
❏ MS 663 [(2)S]	Diana Ross and the Supremes Greatest Hits	1967	10.00	20.00	40.00
❏ MT/MS 663	Diana Ross and the Supremes Greatest Hits				
	Poster	1967	2.50	5.00	10.00
❏ M 665 [M]	Reflections	1968	7.50	15.00	30.00
❏ MS 665 [S]	Reflections	1968	5.00	10.00	20.00
❏ MS 670	Love Child	1968	5.00	10.00	20.00
❏ M 672 [M]	Funny Girl	1968	7.50	15.00	30.00
—Mono appears to be promo only					
❏ MS 672 [S]	Funny Girl	1968	5.00	10.00	20.00
—The above LP came out before Motown 670					
❏ M 676 [M]	Live at London's Talk of the Town	1968	7.50	51.00	30.00
—Mono is promo only					
❏ MS 676 [S]	Live at London's Talk of the Town	1968	5.00	10.00	20.00
—The above LP came out before Motown 670 and 672					
❏ MS 689	Let the Sunshine In	1969	5.00	10.00	20.00
❏ MS 694	Cream of the Crop	1969	5.00	10.00	20.00
❏ MS 702	Diana Ross and the Supremes Greatest Hits,				
	Volume 3	1970	5.00	10.00	20.00
❏ MS 705	Right On	1970	3.75	7.50	15.00
—By "The Supremes"; the first LP after Diana Ross left					
❏ MS 708 [(2)]	Farewell	1970	6.25	12.50	25.00
—By "Diana Ross and the Supremes"					
❏ MS 720	New Ways But Love Stays	1970	3.75	7.50	15.00
❏ MS 737	Touch	1971	3.75	7.50	15.00
❏ MS 746	Promises Kept	1972	—	—	—
—Unreleased					
❏ M 751L	Floy Joy	1972	3.75	7.50	15.00
❏ M 756L	The Supremes	1972	3.75	7.50	15.00
❏ M9-794L3 [(3)]	Anthology (1962-1969)	1974	6.25	12.50	25.00
—By "Diana Ross and the Supremes"					
❏ M6-828	The Supremes	1975	3.75	7.50	15.00
❏ M6-863S1	High Energy	1976	3.75	7.50	15.00
❏ M6-873S1	Mary, Scherrie and Susaye	1976	3.75	7.50	15.00
❏ M7-904R1	The Supremes at Their Best	1978	3.75	7.50	15.00
❏ 5245 ML	Love Child	1982	2.00	4.00	8.00
—Reissue of MS 670					
❏ 5252 ML	Merry Christmas	1982	2.50	5.00	10.00
—Reissue of MS 638					
❏ 5270 ML	Where Did Our Love Go	1982	2.00	4.00	8.00
—Reissue of MS 621					
❏ 5278 ML	Captured Live on Stage	1982	2.00	4.00	8.00
—Reissue?					
❏ 5305 ML	Let the Sunshine In	1983	2.00	4.00	8.00
—Reissue of MS 689					
❏ 5313 ML	Great Songs and Performances That Inspired				
	the Motown 25th Anniversary TV Special	1983	2.50	5.00	10.00
❏ 5361 ML	Motown Legends	1985	2.50	5.00	10.00
❏ 5371 ML	Diana Ross and the Supremes Sing Motown	1985	2.50	5.00	10.00
❏ 5381 ML3 [(3)]	25th Anniversary	1986	5.00	10.00	20.00
—By "Diana Ross and the Supremes"					
NATURAL RESOURCES					
❏ NR 4006T1	Where Did Our Love Go	1978	3.00	6.00	12.00
—Reissue of Motown 621					
❏ NR 4010	Merry Christmas	1978	3.00	6.00	12.00
—Reissue of Motown 638					
PICKWICK					
❏ SPC-3383	Baby Love	197?	3.00	6.00	12.00
—Edited reissue of Motown 621					

SUPREMES, THE, AND THE FOUR TOPS
Also see each artist's individual listings.
MOTOWN

Number	Title (A Side/B Side)	Yr	VG	VG+	NM
❏ M5-123V1A	The Magnificent Seven	1981	3.00	6.00	12.00
—Reissue of Motown 717					
❏ MS 717	The Magnificent Seven	1970	3.75	7.50	15.00
❏ MS 736	The Return of the Magnificent Seven	1971	3.75	7.50	15.00
❏ MS 745	Dynamite	1971	3.75	7.50	15.00

SUPREMES, THE, DIANA ROSS AND, AND THE TEMPTATIONS
Also see each artist's individual listings.
MOTOWN

Number	Title (A Side/B Side)	Yr	VG	VG+	NM
❏ M5-139V1	Diana Ross and the Supremes Join the				
	Temptations	1981	3.00	6.00	12.00
—Reissue of Motown 679					
❏ M5-171V1	TCB	1981	3.00	6.00	12.00
—Reissue of Motown 682					
❏ M 679 [M]	Diana Ross and the Supremes Join the				
	Temptations	1968	7.50	15.00	30.00
❏ MS 679 [S]	Diana Ross and the Supremes Join the				
	Temptations	1968	5.00	10.00	20.00
❏ MS 682	TCB	1968	5.00	10.00	20.00
❏ MS 692	Together	1969	5.00	10.00	20.00
❏ MS 699	On Broadway	1969	5.00	10.00	20.00

SURF STOMPERS, THE
DEL-FI

Number	Title (A Side/B Side)	Yr	VG	VG+	NM
❏ DFLP-1236 [M]	The Original Surfer Stomp	1963	15.00	30.00	60.00
❏ DFST-1236 [S]	The Original Surfer Stomp	1963	20.00	40.00	80.00
❏ DLF-1236	The Original Surfer Stomp	1997	3.00	6.00	12.00

SURF TEENS, THE
SUTTON

Number	Title (A Side/B Side)	Yr	VG	VG+	NM
❏ SSU-339 [S]	Surf Mania	1963	15.00	30.00	60.00
❏ SU-339 [M]	Surf Mania	1963	12.50	25.00	50.00

SURFARIS, THE (1)
DECCA

Number	Title (A Side/B Side)	Yr	VG	VG+	NM
❏ DL 4470 [M]	The Surfaris Play Wipe Out	1963	6.25	12.50	25.00
❏ DL 4487 [M]	Hit City '64	1964	10.00	20.00	40.00
❏ DL 4560 [M]	Fun City, U.S.A.	1964	10.00	20.00	40.00
❏ DL 4614 [M]	Hit City '65	1965	10.00	20.00	40.00
❏ DL 4663 [M]	It Ain't Me, Babe	1965	10.00	20.00	40.00
❏ DL 74470 [S]	The Surfaris Play Wipe Out	1963	7.50	15.00	30.00
❏ DL 74487 [S]	Hit City '64	1964	12.50	25.00	50.00
❏ DL 74560 [S]	Fun City, U.S.A.	1964	12.50	25.00	50.00
❏ DL 74614 [S]	Hit City '65	1965	12.50	25.00	50.00
❏ DL 74663 [S]	It Ain't Me, Babe	1965	12.50	25.00	50.00
DOT					
❏ DLP-3535 [M]	Wipe Out	1963	7.50	15.00	30.00
—With no back cover photo of the Surfaris					
❏ DLP-3535 [M]	Wipe Out	1963	10.00	20.00	40.00
—With back cover photo featuring four Surfaris					
❏ DLP-3535 [M]	Wipe Out	1963	12.50	25.00	50.00
—With back cover photo featuring five Surfaris					
❏ DLP-25535 [S]	Wipe Out	1963	10.00	20.00	40.00
—With no back cover photo of the Surfaris					
❏ DLP-25535 [S]	Wipe Out	1963	12.50	25.00	50.00
—With back cover photo featuring four Surfaris					
❏ DLP-25535 [S]	Wipe Out	1963	20.00	40.00	80.00
—With back cover photo featuring five Surfaris					
PICKWICK					
❏ SPC-3636	Wipe Out and Surfer Joe	1978	3.75	7.50	15.00

SURFARIS, THE (2)
DIPLOMAT

Number	Title (A Side/B Side)	Yr	VG	VG+	NM
❏ D-2309 [M]	Wheels-Shorts-Hot Rods	1963	6.25	12.50	25.00
—As "The Original Surfaris"					
❏ DS-2309 [S]	Wheels-Shorts-Hot Rods	1963	7.50	15.00	30.00
—As "The Original Surfaris"					
SUNDAZED					
❏ LP-5014	Bombora!	199?	2.50	5.00	10.00
—As "The Original Surfaris"					

SURFERS, THE
HIFI

Number	Title (A Side/B Side)	Yr	VG	VG+	NM
❏ R-408 [M]	On the Rocks	1959	30.00	60.00	120.00
❏ SR-408 [S]	On the Rocks	1959	37.50	75.00	150.00

SURFRIDERS, THE
VAULT

Number	Title (A Side/B Side)	Yr	VG	VG+	NM
❏ LP-105 [M]	Surfbeat, Volume 2	1963	7.50	15.00	30.00
❏ VS-105 [S]	Surfbeat, Volume 2	1963	10.00	20.00	40.00

SURFSIDERS, THE
DESIGN

Number	Title (A Side/B Side)	Yr	VG	VG+	NM
❏ DLP-208 [M]	The Beach Boys Songbook	1965	3.75	7.50	15.00
❏ DLPS-208 [S]	The Beach Boys Songbook	1965	5.00	10.00	20.00

SURPRISE PACKAGE
LHI

Number	Title (A Side/B Side)	Yr	VG	VG+	NM
❏ S-12005	Free Up	1968	10.00	20.00	40.00

SURRATT, CECIL, AND SMITTY SMITH
AUDIO LAB

Number	Title (A Side/B Side)	Yr	VG	VG+	NM
❏ AL-1565 [M]	Songs Everybody Knows	1961	25.00	50.00	100.00
KING					
❏ 860 [M]	Country Music from the Heart of the Country	1963	12.50	25.00	50.00
❏ 966 [M]	Good Country Singin' and Pickin'	1966	10.00	20.00	40.00

SUTCH, SCREAMING LORD
COTILLION

Number	Title (A Side/B Side)	Yr	VG	VG+	NM
❏ SD 9015	Lord Sutch and Heavy Friends	1970	7.50	15.00	30.00
—With Jimmy Page, John Bonham and Jeff Beck					
❏ SD 9049	Hands of Jack the Ripper	1972	7.50	15.00	30.00

SUTTON, DICK
JAGUAR

Number	Title (A Side/B Side)	Yr	VG	VG+	NM
❏ JP-802 [10]	Jazz Idiom	1954	20.00	40.00	80.00
❏ JP-804 [10]	Progressive Dixieland	1954	20.00	40.00	80.00

SUTTON, RALPH
ANALOGUE PRODUCTIONS

Number	Title (A Side/B Side)	Yr	VG	VG+	NM
❏ AP 018	Partners in Crime	199?	6.25	12.50	25.00
—Audiophile vinyl					
CIRCLE					
❏ L-413 [10]	Ralph Sutton	1951	20.00	40.00	80.00
COLUMBIA					
❏ CL 6140 [10]	Piano Moods	1950	20.00	40.00	80.00
COMMODORE					
❏ FL-30001 [M]	Ralph Sutton	1951	20.00	40.00	80.00
DECCA					
❏ DL 5498 [10]	I Got Rhythm	1953	20.00	40.00	80.00
DOWN HOME					
❏ MGD-4 [M]	Backroom Piano: The Ragtime Piano of Ralph				
	Sutton	1955	15.00	30.00	60.00
❏ DH-1003 [10]	Ragtime Piano Solos	1953	20.00	40.00	80.00
HARMONY					
❏ HL 7109 [M]	Tribute to Fats	1958	5.00	10.00	20.00
OMEGA					
❏ OSL-51 [S]	Jazz At the Olympics	196?	5.00	10.00	20.00

Number	Title (A Side/B Side)	Yr	VG	VG+	NM
RIVERSIDE					
❑ RLP 12-212 [M]	Classic Jazz Piano	1956	15.00	30.00	60.00
ROULETTE					
❑ SR-25232 [S]	Ragtime, U.S.A.	1963	5.00	10.00	20.00
VERVE					
❑ MGV-1004 [M]	Backroom Piano: The Ragtime Piano of Ralph Sutton	1956	12.50	25.00	50.00
SUZUKI, PAT					
RCA VICTOR					
❑ LPM-1965 [M]	Broadway '59	1959	5.00	10.00	20.00
❑ LSP-1965 [S]	Broadway '59	1959	6.25	12.50	25.00
❑ LPM-2030 [M]	Pat Suzuki	1959	5.00	10.00	20.00
❑ LSP-2030 [S]	Pat Suzuki	1959	6.25	12.50	25.00
❑ LPM-2186 [M]	Looking at You	1960	5.00	10.00	20.00
❑ LSP-2186 [S]	Looking at You	1960	6.25	12.50	25.00
VIK					
❑ LX-1127 [M]	The Many Sides of Pat Suzuki	1958	7.50	15.00	30.00
❑ LX-1147 [M]	Pat Suzuki	1958	7.50	15.00	30.00
SVENSSON, REINHOLD					
PRESTIGE					
❑ PRLP-106 [10]	Reinhold Svensson Piano	1951	50.00	100.00	200.00
❑ PRLP-129 [10]	Reinhold Svensson, Volume 2: Favorites	1952	50.00	100.00	200.00
❑ PRLP-155 [10]	New Sounds from Sweden, Volume 8	1953	50.00	100.00	200.00
SVENSSON, REINHOLD/BENGT HALLBERG					
PRESTIGE					
❑ PRLP-174 [10]	Piano Moderns	1953	50.00	100.00	200.00
SWAGGART, JIMMY					
JIM					
❑ 24-141 [(2)]	Silver Jubilee Album: The Very Best of Jimmy Swaggart	1981	5.00	10.00	20.00
—One of the two records is a picture disc					
SWAGMEN, THE					
PARKWAY					
❑ P-7015 [M]	Meet the Swagmen	1962	12.50	25.00	50.00
SWAMP DOGG					
CANYON					
❑ LP-7706	Total Destruction to Your Mind	1970	7.50	15.00	30.00
ELEKTRA					
❑ EKS-74089	Rat On	1971	5.00	10.00	20.00
SWAN SILVERTONES, THE					
SPECIALTY					
❑ SPS-2122	Love Lifted Me	1970	5.00	10.00	20.00
❑ SPS-2148	My Rock	1971	5.00	10.00	20.00
UPFRONT					
❑ UPF-112	The Lord's Prayer	1968	5.00	10.00	20.00
VEE JAY					
❑ LP-5003 [M]	The Swan Silvertones	1959	10.00	20.00	40.00
❑ LP-5006 [M]	Singing in My Soul	1960	7.50	15.00	30.00
❑ LP-5013 [M]	Savior Pass Me Not	1962	7.50	15.00	30.00
❑ LP-5034 [M]	Blessed Assurance	1963	7.50	15.00	30.00
❑ LP-5052 [M]	The Best of the Swan Silvertones	1963	7.50	15.00	30.00
❑ LP-5059 [M]	Let's Go to Church Together	1964	6.25	12.50	25.00
❑ SR-5059 [S]	Let's Go to Church Together	1964	7.50	15.00	30.00
❑ VJS-18008	Pray for Me	1975	5.00	10.00	20.00
SWANN, BETTYE					
MONEY					
❑ 1103 [M]	Make Me Yours	1967	6.25	12.50	25.00
❑ S-1103 [S]	Make Me Yours	1967	6.25	12.50	25.00
SWEDES FROM JAZZVILLE					
EPIC					
❑ LN 3309 [M]	Swedes from Jazzville	195?	12.50	25.00	50.00
SWEENEY TODD					
LONDON					
❑ PS 694	If Wishes Were Horses	1977	15.00	30.00	60.00
—Possibly a Canadian import only					
SWEET, THE (1)					
BEAT ROCKET					
❑ BR 125	Hell Raisers!	2000	3.00	6.00	12.00
BELL					
❑ 1125	The Sweet	1973	6.25	12.50	25.00
CAPITOL					
❑ SPRO-8371/2 [DJ]	For A.O.R. Radio Only	1976	6.25	12.50	25.00
❑ SPRO-8849 [DJ]	Short and Sweet	1978	7.50	15.00	30.00
❑ ST-11395	Desolation Boulevard	1975	3.00	6.00	12.00
❑ ST-11496	Give Us a Wink	1976	3.00	6.00	12.00
❑ STAO-11636	Off the Record	1977	3.00	6.00	12.00
❑ SKAO-11744	Level Headed	1978	3.00	6.00	12.00
❑ PRO-11929 [DJ]	Cut Above the Rest	1979	12.50	25.00	50.00
—Special promo box contains record, cassette, 8-track, photo, bio					
❑ ST-11929	Cut Above the Rest	1979	3.00	6.00	12.00
❑ ST-12106	Sweet VI	1980	3.00	6.00	12.00
❑ SN-16115	Give Us a Wink	1980	2.00	4.00	8.00
—Budget-line reissue					
❑ SN-16116	Off the Record	1980	2.00	4.00	8.00
—Budget-line reissue					
❑ SN-16117	Level Headed	1980	2.00	4.00	8.00
—Budget-line reissue					
❑ SN-16118	Cut Above the Rest	1980	2.00	4.00	8.00
—Budget-line reissue					
❑ SN-16287	Desolation Boulevard	1981	2.00	4.00	8.00
—Budget-line reissue					

Number	Title (A Side/B Side)	Yr	VG	VG+	NM
KORY					
❑ 3009	The Sweet	1977	2.50	5.00	10.00
—Reissue of Bell LP					
SWEET INSPIRATIONS, THE					
ATLANTIC					
❑ SD 8155	The Sweet Inspirations	1968	5.00	10.00	20.00
❑ SD 8182	Songs of Faith and Inspiration	1968	5.00	10.00	20.00
❑ 8201 [M]	What the World Needs Now Is Love	1969	12.50	25.00	50.00
—Mono is white label promo only; "d/j copy monaural" sticker on stereo cover					
❑ SD 8201 [S]	What the World Needs Now Is Love	1969	5.00	10.00	20.00
❑ SD 8225	Sweets for My Sweet	1969	5.00	10.00	20.00
❑ SD 8253	Sweet, Sweet Soul	1970	5.00	10.00	20.00
RSO					
❑ RS-1-3058	Hot Butterfly	1979	2.50	5.00	10.00
STAX					
❑ STS-3017	Estelle, Myrna and Sylvia	1973	5.00	10.00	20.00
SWEET PANTS					
BARKLEY					
❑ 1141	Fat Peter Presents Sweet Pants	1969	50.00	100.00	200.00
SWEET THURSDAY					
TETRAGRAMMATON					
❑ T-112	Sweet Thursday	1969	5.00	10.00	20.00
SWEET TOOTHE					
DOMINION					
❑ NR-7360	Testing	1974	75.00	150.00	300.00
SWENSON, INGA					
LIBERTY					
❑ LRP-3379 [M]	I'm Old Fashioned	1964	6.25	12.50	25.00
❑ LST-7379 [S]	I'm Old Fashioned	1964	7.50	15.00	30.00
SWINGIN' MEDALLIONS					
SMASH					
❑ MGS-27083 [M]	Double Shot (Of My Baby's Love)	1966	7.50	15.00	30.00
—Later pressings contain a "censored" version of the title song					
❑ MGS-27083 [M]	Double Shot (Of My Baby's Love)	1966	10.00	20.00	40.00
—First pressing contains the original 45 version of the title song					
❑ SRS-67083 [S]	Double Shot (Of My Baby's Love)	1966	10.00	20.00	40.00
—Later pressings contain a "censored" version of the title song					
❑ SRS-67083 [S]	Double Shot (Of My Baby's Love)	1966	12.50	25.00	50.00
—First pressing contains the original 45 version of the title song					
SWINGING BLUE JEANS, THE					
IMPERIAL					
❑ LP-9261 [M]	Hippy Hippy Shake	1964	20.00	40.00	80.00
❑ LP-12261 [R]	Hippy Hippy Shake	1964	20.00	40.00	80.00
SWINGING SWEDES, THE					
TELEFUNKEN					
❑ LGX-66050 [M]	The Swinging Swedes	195?	12.50	25.00	50.00
SWINGING SWEDES, THE/THE COOL BRITONS					
BLUE NOTE					
❑ BLP-5019 [10]	New Sounds from the Olde World	1951	75.00	150.00	300.00
SWITTEL, JIMMY					
DECCA					
❑ DL 8618 [M]	Hymns to the Blessed Virgin Mary	1957	5.00	10.00	20.00
SYKES, ROOSEVELT					
BLUESVILLE					
❑ BVLP-1006 [M]	The Return of Roosevelt Sykes	1960	25.00	50.00	100.00
—Blue label, silver print					
❑ BVLP-1006 [M]	The Return of Roosevelt Sykes	1964	7.50	15.00	30.00
—Blue label, trident logo at right					
❑ BVLP-1014 [M]	The Honeydripper	1961	25.00	50.00	100.00
—Blue label, silver print					
❑ BVLP-1014 [M]	The Honeydripper	1964	7.50	15.00	30.00
—Blue label, trident logo at right					
CROWN					
❑ CST-287 [S]	Roosevelt Sykes Sings the Blues	1962	12.50	25.00	50.00
❑ CLP-5287 [M]	Roosevelt Sykes Sings the Blues	1962	12.50	25.00	50.00
DELMARK					
❑ DL-607	The Hard Driving Blues of Roosevelt Sykes	1963	12.50	25.00	50.00
SYLVAIN SYLVAIN					
RCA VICTOR					
❑ AFL1-3475	Sylvain Sylvain	1980	3.00	6.00	12.00
❑ AFL1-3913	Syl Sylvain and the Teardrops	1982	3.00	6.00	12.00
❑ DJL1-4062 [DJ]	RCA Special Radio Series XII	1981	5.00	10.00	20.00
—Promo-only interviews and music					
SYLVERN, HANK					
ABC-PARAMOUNT					
❑ 146 [M]	Christmas in Hi-Fi	1956	6.25	12.50	25.00
SYLVIA (1)					
STANG					
❑ 1010	Sylvia	197?	5.00	10.00	20.00
SUGAR HILL					
❑ 258	Sylvia I	1981	2.50	5.00	10.00
VIBRATION					
❑ 126	Pillow Talk	1973	3.75	7.50	15.00
❑ 131	Lay It On Me	1977	3.00	6.00	12.00
❑ 143	Brand New Funk	197?	3.00	6.00	12.00
SYLVIAN, DAVID					
VIRGIN					
❑ 2167 [DJ]	Ink in the Well — A Conversation	1987	5.00	10.00	20.00
—Promo-only interview album					

Number	Title (A Side/B Side)	Yr	VG	VG+	NM
❑ 90677	Secrets of the Beehive	1987	2.50	5.00	10.00
❑ 90904	Plight and Premonition	1988	2.50	5.00	10.00

—With Holger Czukay

SYMS, SYLVIA
ATLANTIC

Number	Title (A Side/B Side)	Yr	VG	VG+	NM
❑ ALS-137 [10]	Songs by Sylvia Syms	1952	25.00	50.00	100.00
❑ 1243 [M]	Songs by Sylvia Syms	1956	12.50	25.00	50.00

—Black label

❑ 1243 [M]	Songs by Sylvia Syms	1960	6.25	12.50	25.00

—Multicolor label, white "fan" logo at right
COLUMBIA

❑ CL 1447 [M]	Torch Song	1960	7.50	15.00	30.00

—Red and black label with six "eye" logos

❑ CS 8243 [S]	Torch Song	1960	10.00	20.00	40.00

—Red and black label with six "eye" logos
DECCA

❑ DL 8188 [M]	Sylvia Syms Sings	1955	12.50	25.00	50.00

—Black label, silver print

❑ DL 8639 [M]	Songs of Love	1958	10.00	20.00	40.00

—Black label, silver print
KAPP

❑ KL-1236 [M]	That Man — Love Songs to Frank Sinatra	1961	7.50	15.00	30.00
❑ KS-3236 [S]	That Man — Love Songs to Frank Sinatra	1961	10.00	20.00	40.00

MOVIETONE

❑ 2022 [M]	In a Sentimental Mood	1967	5.00	10.00	20.00

PRESTIGE

❑ PRLP-7439 [M]	Sylvia Is!	1965	5.00	10.00	20.00
❑ PRST-7439 [S]	Sylvia Is!	1965	6.25	12.50	25.00
❑ PRLP-7489 [M]	For Once in My Life	1967	6.25	12.50	25.00
❑ PRST-7489 [S]	For Once in My Life	1967	5.00	10.00	20.00

20TH CENTURY FOX

❑ TFM-4123 [M]	The Fabulous Sylvia Syms	1963	6.25	12.50	25.00
❑ TFS-4123 [S]	The Fabulous Sylvia Syms	1963	7.50	15.00	30.00

VERSION

❑ VLP-103 [10]	After Dark	1954	20.00	40.00	80.00

SYNDICATE OF SOUND
BELL

❑ 6001 [M]	Little Girl	1966	12.50	25.00	50.00
❑ S-6001 [S]	Little Girl	1966	20.00	40.00	80.00

SUNDAZED

❑ LP 5051	Little Girl	2001	3.00	6.00	12.00

—Reissue on 180-gram vinyl

SZABO, GABOR
IMPULSE!

❑ A-9105 [M]	Gypsy 66	1966	5.00	10.00	20.00
❑ AS-9105 [S]	Gypsy 66	1966	6.25	12.50	25.00
❑ A-9123 [M]	Spellbinder	1966	5.00	10.00	20.00
❑ AS-9123 [S]	Spellbinder	1966	6.25	12.50	25.00
❑ A-9128 [M]	Jazz Raga	1967	6.25	12.50	25.00
❑ AS-9128 [S]	Jazz Raga	1967	5.00	10.00	20.00
❑ A-9146 [M]	The Sorcerer	1967	6.25	12.50	25.00
❑ AS-9146 [S]	The Sorcerer	1967	5.00	10.00	20.00
❑ AS-9151	Wind, Sky and Diamonds	1968	6.25	12.50	25.00

—This exists on the pre-ABC Impulse! label, though theoretically it shouldn't. Other titles may exist on that label also.

SZERYNG, HENRYK
MERCURY LIVING PRESENCE

❑ SR 90308 [S]	Brahms: Violin Concerto in D	196?	7.50	15.00	30.00

—With Antal Dorati/London Symphony Orchestra; maroon label, with "Vendor: Mercury Record Corporation"

❑ SR 90308 [S]	Brahms: Violin Concerto in D	196?	20.00	40.00	80.00

—With Antal Dorati/London Symphony Orchestra; maroon label, no "Vendor: Mercury Record Corporation"

❑ SR 90348 [S]	Kreisler: Caprice Viennois and 12 Others	196?	7.50	15.00	30.00

—Maroon label, no "Vendor: Mercury Record Corporation"

❑ SR 90367 [S]	Treasures	196?	6.25	12.50	25.00

—Maroon label, no "Vendor: Mercury Record Corporation"

❑ SR 90393 [S]	Khachaturian: Violin Concerto	196?	5.00	10.00	20.00

—With Antal Dorati/London Symphony Orchestra; third edition (dark red, not maroon label)

❑ SR 90393 [S]	Khachaturian: Violin Concerto	196?	10.00	20.00	40.00

—With Antal Dorati/London Symphony Orchestra; maroon label, with "Vendor: Mercury Record Corporation"

❑ SR 90393 [S]	Khachaturian: Violin Concerto	196?	12.50	25.00	50.00

—With Antal Dorati/London Symphony Orchestra; maroon label, no "Vendor: Mercury Record Corporation"

❑ SR 90406 [S]	Mendelssohn: Violin Concerto in E; Schumann: Violin Concerto in D	196?	6.25	12.50	25.00

—With Antal Dorati/London Symphony Orchestra; maroon label, no "Vendor: Mercury Record Corporation"

❑ SR 90466 [S]	Bach: Violin Concertos in A and E; Double Concerto in D	196?	17.50	35.00	70.00

—Maroon label, with "Vendor: Mercury Record Corporation"
RCA VICTOR RED SEAL

❑ LSC-2281 [S]	Brahms: Violin Concerto	1959	37.50	75.00	150.00

—With Pierre Monteux/London Symphony Orchestra; original with "shaded dog" label

❑ LSC-2363 [S]	Tchaikovsky: Violin Concerto in D	196?	20.00	40.00	80.00

—With Charles Munch/Boston Symphony Orchestra; original with "shaded dog" label

❑ LSC-2421 [S]	In Recital	1960	12.50	25.00	50.00

—Original with "shaded dog" label

❑ LSC-2456 [S]	Lalo: Symphonie Espagnole	1961	50.00	100.00	200.00

—With Walter Hendl/Chicago Symphony Orch.; original with "shaded dog" label

SZERYNG, HENRYK / ARTUR RUBENSTEIN
RCA VICTOR RED SEAL

❑ LSC-2377 [S]	Beethoven: Kreutzer and Spring Sonatas	1960	10.00	20.00	40.00

—Original with "shaded dog" label

❑ LSC-2619 [S]	Brahms: Violin Concertos 2 and 3	1962	12.50	25.00	50.00

—Original with "shaded dog" label

❑ LSC-2620 [S]	Beethoven: Violin Sonata No. 8; Brahms: Violin Sonata No. 1	1962	12.50	25.00	50.00

—Original with "shaded dog" label

SZIGETI, JOSEF
MERCURY LIVING PRESENCE

❑ SR 90225 [S]	Brahms: Violin Concerto in D	196?	45.00	90.00	180.00

—Maroon label, no "Vendor: Mercury Record Corporation"

❑ SR 90319 [S]	Prokofiev: Violin Sonatas No. 1 and 2	196?	25.00	50.00	100.00

—Maroon label, no "Vendor: Mercury Record Corporation"

❑ SR 90358 [S]	Beethoven: Violin Concerto in D	196?	25.00	50.00	100.00

—With Antal Dorati/London Symphony Orchestra; maroon label, no "Vendor: Mercury Record Corporation"

❑ SR 90419 [S]	Prokofiev: Violin Concerto No. 1; Stravinsky: Duo Concertante	196?	7.50	15.00	30.00

—Maroon label, no "Vendor: Mercury Record Corporation"

❑ SR 90419 [S]	Prokofiev: Violin Concerto No. 1; Stravinsky: Duo Concertante	196?	12.50	25.00	50.00

—Maroon label, with "Vendor: Mercury Record Corporation" (second edition is more sought after than the first)

❑ SR 90442 [S]	Violin Sonatas	1965	12.50	25.00	50.00

—Maroon label, with "Vendor: Mercury Record Corporation"

SZIGETI, JOSEF; MIECZYSLAW HORSZOWSKI; JOHN BARROWS
MERCURY LIVING PRESENCE

❑ SR 90210 [S]	Brahms: Horn Trio; Violin Sonata No. 2	196?	17.50	35.00	70.00

—Maroon label, with "Vendor: Mercury Record Corporation"

❑ SR 90210 [S]	Brahms: Horn Trio; Violin Sonata No. 2	196?	45.00	90.00	180.00

—Maroon label, no "Vendor: Mercury Record Corporation"

T

T.C. ATLANTIC
DOVE

❑ LP-4459	T.C. Atlantic	1966	25.00	50.00	100.00

T.I.M.E.
LIBERTY

❑ LST-7558	T.I.M.E.	1968	6.25	12.50	25.00
❑ LST-7605	Smooth Ball	1969	6.25	12.50	25.00

T. REX
A&M

❑ SP-3514 [(2)]	Tyrannosaurus Rex (A Beginning)	1972	3.75	7.50	15.00

—Compilation of early LPs Prophets, Seers & Sages and My People Were Fair and Had Sky in Their Hair But Now They're Content to Wear Stars on Their Brows
BLUE THUMB

❑ BTS 7	Unicorn	1969	5.00	10.00	20.00
❑ BTS 18	A Beard of Stars	1970	5.00	10.00	20.00

—Add $5 for bonus single SP-6115/6, "Ride a White Swan"/"Is It Love." For reasons unknown, the single seems to be much more readily available than the LP
CASABLANCA

❑ NBLP 7005	Light of Love	1974	3.00	6.00	12.00

—Reissue of 9006

❑ NB 9006	Light of Love	1974	3.75	7.50	15.00

—Original, distributed by Warner Bros.
MARC ON WAX/RELATIVITY

❑ 8249	Bolan's Zip Gun	198?	2.50	5.00	10.00
❑ 8250	Zinc Alloy & The Hidden Riders of Tomorrow	198?	2.50	5.00	10.00
❑ 8251	Dandy in the Underworld	198?	2.50	5.00	10.00
❑ 8252	Futuristic Dragon	198?	2.50	5.00	10.00
❑ 8253	The Slider	198?	2.50	5.00	10.00
❑ 8254	Tanx	198?	2.50	5.00	10.00

REPRISE

❑ PRO 511 [DJ]	An Interview with Marc Bolan	1971	25.00	50.00	100.00
❑ MS 2095	The Slider	1972	3.00	6.00	12.00
❑ MS 2132	Tanx	1973	3.00	6.00	12.00
❑ RS 6440	T. Rex	1971	3.00	6.00	12.00
❑ RS 6466	Electric Warrior	1971	3.00	6.00	12.00

WARNER BROS.

❑ 25333	T. Rextasy: The Best of T. Rex, 1970-1973	1985	2.50	5.00	10.00

T2
LONDON

❑ PS 583	It'll All Work Out in Boomland	1971	20.00	40.00	80.00

T.V. AND THE TRIBESMEN
HANNA-BARBERA

❑ HLP-9507 [S]	Barefootin'	1966	6.25	12.50	25.00

T-BONES, THE
Members of this group later formed HAMILTON, JOE FRANK AND REYNOLDS.
LIBERTY

❑ LRP-3346 [M]	Boss Drag	1963	15.00	30.00	60.00
❑ LRP-3363 [M]	Boss Drag at the Beach	1964	15.00	30.00	60.00
❑ LRP-3404 [M]	Doin' the Jerk	1965	10.00	20.00	40.00
❑ LRP-3439 [M]	No Matter What Shape (Your Stomach's In)	1966	5.00	10.00	20.00
❑ LRP-3446 [M]	Sippin' and Chippin'	1966	5.00	10.00	20.00
❑ LRP-3471 [M]	Everyone's Gone to the Moon	1966	5.00	10.00	20.00
❑ LST-7346 [S]	Boss Drag	1963	25.00	50.00	100.00
❑ LST-7363 [S]	Boss Drag at the Beach	1964	25.00	50.00	100.00
❑ LST-7404 [S]	Doin' the Jerk	1965	15.00	30.00	60.00
❑ LST-7439 [S]	No Matter What Shape (Your Stomach's In)	1966	6.25	12.50	25.00
❑ LST-7446 [S]	Sippin' and Chippin'	1966	6.25	12.50	25.00
❑ LST-7471 [S]	Everyone's Gone to the Moon	1966	6.25	12.50	25.00

SUNSET

❑ SUM-1119 [M]	Shapin' Things Up	196?	3.00	6.00	12.00
❑ SUS-5119 [S]	Shapin' Things Up	196?	3.75	7.50	15.00

Number	Title (A Side/B Side)	Yr	VG	VG+	NM
TABOR, ERON					
STUDIO ONE					
❏ S-104	Eron Tabor	196?	5.00	10.00	20.00
TAD					
SUB POP					
❏ 27	God's Balls	1989	2.50	5.00	10.00
—Others in standard cover					
❏ 27	God's Balls	1989	3.75	7.50	15.00
—Next 500 with "Manzine"					
❏ 27	God's Balls	1989	5.00	10.00	20.00
—First 2,000 with gatefold cover					
❏ 49 [EP]	Salt Lick	1990	2.00	4.00	8.00
❏ 89	8-Way Santa	1991	2.50	5.00	10.00
TALBERT, THOMAS					
ATLANTIC					
❏ 1250 [M]	Bix Fats Duke Interpreted by Thomas Talbert	1957	10.00	20.00	40.00
—Black label					
❏ 1250 [M]	Bix Fats Duke Interpreted by Thomas Talbert	1961	5.00	10.00	20.00
—Multicolor label, white "fan" logo at right					
❏ SD 1250 [S]	Bix Fats Duke Interpreted by Thomas Talbert	1958	10.00	20.00	40.00
—Green label					
❏ SD 1250 [S]	Bix Fats Duke Interpreted by Thomas Talbert	1961	5.00	10.00	20.00
—Multicolor label, white "fan" logo at right					
TALISMEN, THE					
BLUE STAR					
❏ M-6323 [M]	Treasury of American Railroad Songs and Ballads	1964	5.00	10.00	20.00
❏ MS-6323 [S]	Treasury of American Railroad Songs and Ballads	1964	6.25	12.50	25.00
PRESTIGE					
❏ PRLP-7406 [M]	Folk Swingers Extraordinaire	1965	5.00	10.00	20.00
❏ PRST-7406 [S]	Folk Swingers Extraordinaire	1965	6.25	12.50	25.00
TALKING HEADS					
SIRE					
❏ PRO-A-930 [DJ]	Talking Heads	1980	3.75	7.50	15.00
—Promo-only 4-song sampler from "Remain in Light"					
❏ PRO-A-1033 [DJ]	The Name of This Band Is Talking Heads Sampler	1982	3.75	7.50	15.00
—Promo only					
❏ 2SR 3590 [(2)]	The Name of This Band Is Talking Heads	1982	5.00	10.00	20.00
❏ SR 6036	Talking Heads '77	1977	3.00	6.00	12.00
❏ SR 6058	More Songs About Buildings and Food	1978	3.00	6.00	12.00
❏ SRK 6058	More Songs About Buildings and Food	1979	2.00	4.00	8.00
—Reissue with new prefix					
❏ SRK 6076	Fear of Music	1979	2.50	5.00	10.00
❏ SRK 6095	Remain in Light	1981	2.50	5.00	10.00
❏ 23771	Speaking in Tongues	1983	5.00	10.00	20.00
—Clear vinyl in oversize plastic container with Robert Rauschenberg artwork					
❏ 23883	Speaking in Tongues	1983	2.50	5.00	10.00
—Standard issue					
❏ 25121	Stop Making Sense (Soundtrack)	1984	3.75	7.50	15.00
—First issue with booklet and black & white cover					
❏ 25186	Stop Making Sense (Soundtrack)	1984	2.50	5.00	10.00
—Second issue: No booklet, color cover					
❏ 25305	Little Creatures	1985	2.50	5.00	10.00
❏ 25512	True Stories	1986	2.50	5.00	10.00
❏ 25654	Naked	1988	2.50	5.00	10.00
❏ R 124560	Stop Making Sense	1984	3.00	6.00	12.00
—RCA Music Service edition					
❏ R 150102	Speaking in Tongues	1983	3.00	6.00	12.00
—BMG Direct Marketing edition					
❏ R 153810	Naked	1988	3.00	6.00	12.00
—BMG Direct Marketing edition					
❏ R 153839	Little Creatures	1985	3.00	6.00	12.00
—RCA Music Service edition					
WARNER BROS.					
❏ WBMS-104 [DJ]	Talking Heads Live on Tour	1979	6.25	12.50	25.00
—Part of "The Warner Bros. Music Show" series (has been counterfeited)					
TAMBA FOUR, THE					
A&M					
❏ SP-3004	We and the Sea	1968	5.00	10.00	20.00
❏ SP-3013	Samba Blim	1969	5.00	10.00	20.00
TAMPA RED					
BLUEBIRD					
❏ AXM2-5501 [(2)]	Guitar Wizard	1975	3.75	7.50	15.00
BLUES CLASSICS					
❏ 25	Guitar Wizard (1935-53)	197?	3.00	6.00	12.00
BLUESVILLE					
❏ BVLP-1030 [M]	Don't Tampa with the Blues	1961	30.00	60.00	120.00
—Blue label, silver print					
❏ BVLP-1030 [M]	Don't Tampa with the Blues	1963	7.50	15.00	30.00
—Blue label, trident logo at right					
❏ BVLP-1043 [M]	Don't Jive Me	1962	30.00	60.00	120.00
—Blue label, silver print					
❏ BVLP-1043 [M]	Don't Jive Me	1963	7.50	15.00	30.00
—Blue label, trident logo at right					
FANTASY					
❏ OBC-516	Don't Tampa with the Blues	198?	2.50	5.00	10.00
YAZOO					
❏ 1039	Bottleneck Guitar	197?	3.00	6.00	12.00
TAMS, THE					
ABC					
❏ ABCS-481 [R]	Presenting the Tams	1968	5.00	10.00	20.00
—Reissue of ABC-Paramount 481					

Number	Title (A Side/B Side)	Yr	VG	VG+	NM
❏ ABCS-499 [S]	Hey Girl, Don't Bother Me	1964	5.00	10.00	20.00
—Reissue of ABC-Paramount 499					
❏ ABC-596 [M]	Time for the Tams	1967	7.50	15.00	30.00
❏ ABCS-596 [S]	Time for the Tams	1967	7.50	15.00	30.00
❏ ABCS-627	A Little More Soul	1968	6.25	12.50	25.00
❏ ABCS-673	A Portrait of the Tams	1969	6.25	12.50	25.00
ABC-PARAMOUNT					
❏ ABC-481 [M]	Presenting the Tams	1964	12.50	25.00	50.00
❏ ABCS-481 [R]	Presenting the Tams.	1964	7.50	15.00	30.00
❏ ABC-499 [M]	Hey Girl, Don't Bother Me.	1964	7.50	15.00	30.00
❏ ABCS-499 [S]	Hey Girl, Don't Bother Me.	1964	10.00	20.00	40.00
CAPITOL					
❏ SM-11839	The Best of the Tams	1979	3.00	6.00	12.00
COMPLEAT					
❏ CMLP-5001 [EP]	Beach Music from the Tams	198?	2.00	4.00	8.00
1-2-3					
❏ ST-567	The Best of the Tams	1970	5.00	10.00	20.00
SOUNDS SOUTH					
❏ SO-16010	The Mighty, Mighty Tams	1977	3.75	7.50	15.00
TANEGA, NORMA					
NEW VOICE					
❏ NV-2001 [M]	Walkin' My Cat Named Dog	1966	10.00	20.00	40.00
❏ NVS-2001 [S]	Walkin' My Cat Named Dog	1966	20.00	40.00	80.00
TANGERINE DREAM					
CAROLINE					
❏ CAROL 1349	Livemiles	1988	3.00	6.00	12.00
ELEKTRA					
❏ 5E-521	Thief	1981	2.50	5.00	10.00
❏ 5E-557	Exit	1981	2.50	5.00	10.00
EMI AMERICA					
❏ ST-17141	Flashpoint	1984	2.50	5.00	10.00
MCA					
❏ 2277	Sorcerer	1977	3.00	6.00	12.00
❏ 6165	Legend	1986	2.00	4.00	8.00
PRIVATE MUSIC					
❏ 2042-1-P	Optical Race	1988	3.75	7.50	15.00
❏ 2047-1-P	Miracle Mile	1989	3.75	7.50	15.00
❏ 2057-1-P	Lily on the Beach	1989	3.75	7.50	15.00
RELATIVITY					
❏ EMC 8043	Le Parc	198?	3.00	6.00	12.00
❏ EMC 8045 [(2)]	Poland	198?	3.75	7.50	15.00
❏ 86561 8068	Electronic Meditation	1986	3.00	6.00	12.00
❏ 86561 8069	Alpha Centauri	1986	3.00	6.00	12.00
❏ 86561 8070 [(2)]	Zeit	1986	3.75	7.50	15.00
❏ 86561 8071	Atem	1986	3.00	6.00	12.00
❏ 86561 8072	Green Desert	1986	3.00	6.00	12.00
❏ 86561 8113	Underwater Sunlight	1986	3.00	6.00	12.00
VIRGIN					
❏ VR 13-108	Phaedra	1974	3.75	7.50	15.00
❏ VR 13-116	Rubycon	1975	3.75	7.50	15.00
❏ PZ 34427	Stratosfear	1976	3.75	7.50	15.00
❏ PZG 35014 [(2)]	Encore	1977	5.00	10.00	20.00
VIRGIN INTERNATIONAL					
❏ VI 2010	Phaedra	1979	2.50	5.00	10.00
—Reissue					
❏ VI 2025	Rubycon	1979	2.50	5.00	10.00
—Reissue					
❏ VI 2044	Ricochet	1975	3.75	7.50	15.00
❏ VI 2068	Stratosfear	1979	3.00	6.00	12.00
—Reissue of 34427					
❏ VI 2097	Cyclone	1979	2.50	5.00	10.00
—Reissue					
❏ VI 2111	Force Majeure	1979	3.00	6.00	12.00
TANGERINE ZOO, THE					
MAINSTREAM					
❏ S-6107	Tangerine Zoo	1968	12.50	25.00	50.00
❏ S-6118	Outside Looking In	1969	17.50	35.00	70.00
TAPSCOTT, HORACE					
FLYING DUTCHMAN					
❏ FDS-107	The Giant Is Awakened	1969	5.00	10.00	20.00
TARANTULA					
A&M					
❏ SP-4202	Tarantula	1969	5.00	10.00	20.00
TARRIERS, THE					
ATLANTIC					
❏ 8042 [M]	Tell the World	1960	7.50	15.00	30.00
❏ SD 8042 [S]	Tell the World	1960	10.00	20.00	40.00
DECCA					
❏ DL 4342 [M]	The Tarriers	1962	6.25	12.50	25.00
❏ DL 4538 [M]	Gather 'Round	1964	6.25	12.50	25.00
❏ DL 74342 [S]	The Tarriers	1962	7.50	15.00	30.00
❏ DL 74538 [S]	Gather 'Round	1964	7.50	15.00	30.00
GLORY					
❏ PG-1200 [M]	The Tarriers	1958	15.00	30.00	60.00
KAPP					
❏ KL 1349 [M]	The Original Tarriers	1963	6.25	12.50	25.00
❏ KS 3349 [S]	The Original Tarriers	1963	7.50	15.00	30.00
UNITED ARTISTS					
❏ UAL-4033 [M]	Hard Travelin'	1959	7.50	15.00	30.00
❏ UAS-5033 [S]	Hard Travelin'	1959	10.00	20.00	40.00
TASTE					
ATCO					
❏ SD 33-296	Taste	1969	6.25	12.50	25.00
❏ SD 33-322	On the Boards	1970	6.25	12.50	25.00

T

Number	Title (A Side/B Side)	Yr	VG	VG+	NM

TATE, BABY
BLUESVILLE
| ❏ BVLP-1072 [M] | What You Done | 1963 | 6.25 | 12.50 | 25.00 |

—*Blue label, trident logo at right*

| ❏ BVLP-1072 [M] | What You Done | 1963 | 20.00 | 40.00 | 80.00 |

—*Blue label, silver print*

TATE, BUDDY
FELSTED
| ❏ 2004 [S] | Swinging Like Tate | 1958 | 20.00 | 40.00 | 80.00 |
| ❏ 7004 [M] | Swinging Like Tate | 1958 | 20.00 | 40.00 | 80.00 |
SWINGVILLE
| ❏ SVLP-2003 [M] | Tate's Date | 1960 | 12.50 | 25.00 | 50.00 |

—*Purple label*

| ❏ SVLP-2003 [M] | Tate's Date | 1965 | 6.25 | 12.50 | 25.00 |

—*Blue label, trident logo at right*

| ❏ SVLP-2014 [M] | Tate-A-Tate | 1960 | 12.50 | 25.00 | 50.00 |

—*Purple label*

| ❏ SVLP-2014 [M] | Tate-A-Tate | 1965 | 6.25 | 12.50 | 25.00 |

—*Blue label, trident logo at right*

| ❏ SVLP-2029 [M] | Groovin' with Buddy Tate | 1961 | 12.50 | 25.00 | 50.00 |

—*Purple label*

| ❏ SVLP-2029 [M] | Groovin' with Buddy Tate | 1965 | 6.25 | 12.50 | 25.00 |

—*Blue label, trident logo at right*

TATE, GRADY
SKYE
| ❏ SK-4 | Windmills of My Mind | 1969 | 5.00 | 10.00 | 20.00 |

TATRO, DUANE
CONTEMPORARY
| ❏ C-3514 [M] | Jazz for Moderns | 1956 | 20.00 | 40.00 | 80.00 |

TATUM, ART
ASCH
| ❏ ALP-356 [10] | Art Tatum | 1950 | 37.50 | 75.00 | 150.00 |
BRUNSWICK
❏ BL 54004 [M]	Here's Art Tatum	1955	30.00	60.00	120.00
❏ BL 58013 [10]	Art Tatum Trio	1950	25.00	50.00	100.00
❏ BL 58023 [10]	Art Tatum Piano Solos	1950	25.00	50.00	100.00
CAPITOL
| ❏ H 216 [10] | Art Tatum | 1950 | 25.00 | 50.00 | 100.00 |
| ❏ T 216 [M] | Art Tatum | 1955 | 20.00 | 40.00 | 80.00 |

—*Turquoise label*

| ❏ T 216 [M] | Art Tatum | 1959 | 10.00 | 20.00 | 40.00 |

—*Black colorband label, logo at left*

| ❏ T 216 [M] | Art Tatum | 196? | 5.00 | 10.00 | 20.00 |

—*Black colorband label, logo at top*

| ❏ H 269 [10] | Art Tatum Encores | 1951 | 25.00 | 50.00 | 100.00 |
| ❏ H 408 [10] | Art Tatum Trio | 1953 | 25.00 | 50.00 | 100.00 |
CLEF
| ❏ (no #) [(4)M] | Art Tatum | 1954 | 75.00 | 150.00 | 300.00 |

—*Boxed set with volumes 2, 3, 4 and 5 of The Genius of Art Tatum*

❏ MGC-612 [M]	The Genius of Art Tatum #1	1954	20.00	40.00	80.00
❏ MGC-613 [M]	The Genius of Art Tatum #2	1954	20.00	40.00	80.00
❏ MGC-614 [M]	The Genius of Art Tatum #3	1954	20.00	40.00	80.00
❏ MGC-615 [M]	The Genius of Art Tatum #4	1954	20.00	40.00	80.00
❏ MGC-618 [M]	The Genius of Art Tatum #5	1954	20.00	40.00	80.00
❏ MGC-657 [M]	The Genius of Art Tatum #6	1955	20.00	40.00	80.00
❏ MGC-658 [M]	The Genius of Art Tatum #7	1955	20.00	40.00	80.00
❏ MGC-659 [M]	The Genius of Art Tatum #8	1955	20.00	40.00	80.00
❏ MGC-660 [M]	The Genius of Art Tatum #9	1955	20.00	40.00	80.00
❏ MGC-661 [M]	The Genius of Art Tatum #10	1955	20.00	40.00	80.00
❏ MGC-712 [M]	The Genius of Art Tatum #11	1956	20.00	40.00	80.00
COLUMBIA
❏ GL 101 [10]	Gene Norman Concert at Shrine Auditorium, May 1949	1952	37.50	75.00	150.00
❏ CL 2565 [10]	The Tatum Touch	1956	12.50	25.00	50.00
❏ CL 6301 [10]	An Art Tatum Concert	1954	20.00	40.00	80.00
❏ CS 9655 [M]	Piano Starts Here	1968	10.00	20.00	40.00

—*Mono is white label promo only with stereo number; "Special Mono Radio Station Copy" sticker on cover*

| ❏ CS 9655 [S] | Piano Starts Here | 1968 | 5.00 | 10.00 | 20.00 |

—*Red "360 Sound" label*

DECCA
| ❏ DL 5086 [10] | Art Tatum Piano Solos | 1950 | 30.00 | 60.00 | 120.00 |
| ❏ DL 8715 [M] | The Art of Tatum | 1958 | 12.50 | 25.00 | 50.00 |
DIAL
| ❏ LP-206 [10] | Art Tatum Trio | 1950 | 62.50 | 125.00 | 250.00 |
FOLKWAYS
| ❏ FL-33 [10] | Art Tatum Trio | 1951 | 20.00 | 40.00 | 80.00 |
HARMONY
| ❏ HL 7006 [M] | An Art Tatum Concert | 1957 | 6.25 | 12.50 | 25.00 |
PABLO
| ❏ 2625703 [(13)] | The Tatum Solo Masterpieces | 197? | 25.00 | 50.00 | 100.00 |

—*Box set with all 13 volumes included*

| ❏ 2625706 [(8)] | The Tatum Group Masterpieces | 197? | 15.00 | 30.00 | 60.00 |

—*Boxed set with eight volumes (except 2310 775) included*

REMINGTON
| ❏ 2 [10] | Tatum Piano | 1950 | 25.00 | 50.00 | 100.00 |
STINSON
| ❏ SLP-40 [10] | Art Tatum Trio | 1950 | 37.50 | 75.00 | 150.00 |
| ❏ SLP-40 [M] | Art Tatum Solos and Trio | 195? | 10.00 | 20.00 | 40.00 |
20TH FOX
❏ FTM-102-2 [(2)M]	Piano Discoveries	1961	7.50	15.00	30.00
❏ FTS-102-2 [(2)R]	Piano Discoveries	1961	5.00	10.00	20.00
❏ FTM-3029 [M]	Piano Discoveries Vol. I	1960	5.00	10.00	20.00
❏ FTM-3033 [M]	Piano Discoveries Vol. II	1960	5.00	10.00	20.00
VERVE
| ❏ MGV-8036 [M] | The Genius of Art Tatum #1 | 1957 | 12.50 | 25.00 | 50.00 |

❏ V-8036 [M]	The Genius of Art Tatum #1	1961	5.00	10.00	20.00
❏ MGV-8037 [M]	The Genius of Art Tatum #2	1957	12.50	25.00	50.00
❏ V-8037 [M]	The Genius of Art Tatum #2	1961	5.00	10.00	20.00
❏ MGV-8038 [M]	The Genius of Art Tatum #3	1957	12.50	25.00	50.00
❏ V-8038 [M]	The Genius of Art Tatum #3	1961	5.00	10.00	20.00
❏ MGV-8039 [M]	The Genius of Art Tatum #4	1957	12.50	25.00	50.00
❏ V-8039 [M]	The Genius of Art Tatum #4	1961	5.00	10.00	20.00
❏ MGV-8040 [M]	The Genius of Art Tatum #5	1957	12.50	25.00	50.00
❏ V-8040 [M]	The Genius of Art Tatum #5	1961	5.00	10.00	20.00
❏ MGV-8055 [M]	The Genius of Art Tatum #6	1957	12.50	25.00	50.00
❏ V-8055 [M]	The Genius of Art Tatum #6	1961	5.00	10.00	20.00
❏ MGV-8056 [M]	The Genius of Art Tatum #7	1957	12.50	25.00	50.00
❏ V-8056 [M]	The Genius of Art Tatum #7	1961	5.00	10.00	20.00
❏ MGV-8057 [M]	The Genius of Art Tatum #8	1957	12.50	25.00	50.00
❏ V-8057 [M]	The Genius of Art Tatum #8	1961	5.00	10.00	20.00
❏ MGV-8058 [M]	The Genius of Art Tatum #9	1957	12.50	25.00	50.00
❏ V-8058 [M]	The Genius of Art Tatum #9	1961	5.00	10.00	20.00
❏ MGV-8059 [M]	The Genius of Art Tatum #10	1957	12.50	25.00	50.00
❏ V-8059 [M]	The Genius of Art Tatum #10	1961	5.00	10.00	20.00
❏ MGV-8095 [M]	The Genius of Art Tatum #11	1957	12.50	25.00	50.00
❏ V-8095 [M]	The Genius of Art Tatum #11	1961	5.00	10.00	20.00
❏ MGV-8101-5 [(5)M]	Art Tatum, Volume 1	1957	50.00	100.00	200.00

—*Boxed set with volumes 1-5 of The Genius of Art Tatum*

| ❏ MGV-8102-5 [(5)M] | Art Tatum, Volume 2 | 1957 | 50.00 | 100.00 | 200.00 |

—*Boxed set with volumes 6-10 of The Genius of Art Tatum*

❏ MGV-8118 [M]	Presenting the Art Tatum Trio	1957	12.50	25.00	50.00
❏ V-8118 [M]	Presenting the Art Tatum Trio	1961	5.00	10.00	20.00
❏ MGV-8220 [M]	The Art Tatum-Ben Webster Quartet	1958	12.50	25.00	50.00
❏ V-8220 [M]	The Art Tatum-Ben Webster Quartet	1961	5.00	10.00	20.00
❏ MGV-8323 [M]	The Greatest Piano of Them All	1959	12.50	25.00	50.00
❏ V-8323 [M]	The Greatest Piano of Them All	1961	5.00	10.00	20.00
❏ MGV-8332 [M]	The Incomparable Music of Art Tatum	1959	12.50	25.00	50.00
❏ V-8332 [M]	The Incomparable Music of Art Tatum	1961	5.00	10.00	20.00
❏ MGV-8347 [M]	More of the Greatest Piano of Them All	1959	12.50	25.00	50.00
❏ V-8347 [M]	More of the Greatest Piano of Them All	1961	5.00	10.00	20.00
❏ MGV-8360 [M]	Still More of the Greatest Piano of Them All	1960	12.50	25.00	50.00
❏ V-8360 [M]	Still More of the Greatest Piano of Them All	1961	5.00	10.00	20.00
❏ V-8433 [M]	The Essential Art Tatum	1962	5.00	10.00	20.00

TATUM, ART; BENNY CARTER; LOUIS BELLSON
CLEF
| ❏ MGC-643 [M] | Tatum-Carter-Bellson | 1955 | 20.00 | 40.00 | 80.00 |
VERVE
❏ MGV-8013 [M]	The Three Giants	1957	12.50	25.00	50.00
❏ V-8013 [M]	The Three Giants	1961	5.00	10.00	20.00
❏ MGV-8227 [M]	Makin' Whoopee	1958	12.50	25.00	50.00
❏ V-8227 [M]	Makin' Whoopee	1961	5.00	10.00	20.00

TATUM, ART, AND BUDDY DEFRANCO
AMERICAN RECORDING SOCIETY
| ❏ G-412 [M] | The Art Tatum-Buddy DeFranco Quartet | 1956 | 10.00 | 20.00 | 40.00 |
VERVE
| ❏ MGV-8229 [M] | The Art Tatum-Buddy DeFranco Quartet | 1958 | 12.50 | 25.00 | 50.00 |
| ❏ V-8229 [M] | The Art Tatum-Buddy DeFranco Quartet | 1961 | 5.00 | 10.00 | 20.00 |

TATUM, ART; ROY ELDRIDGE; ALVIN STOLLER; JOHN SIMMONS
CLEF
| ❏ MGC-679 [M] | The Art Tatum-Roy Eldridge-Alvin Stoller-John Simmons Quartet | 1955 | 30.00 | 60.00 | 120.00 |
VERVE
| ❏ MGV-8064 [M] | The Art Tatum-Roy Eldridge-Alvin Stoller-John Simmons Quartet | 1957 | 20.00 | 40.00 | 80.00 |
| ❏ V-8064 [M] | The Art Tatum-Roy Eldridge-Alvin Stoller-John Simmons Quartet | 1961 | 6.25 | 12.50 | 25.00 |

TATUM, ART/ERROLL GARNER
JAZZTONE
| ❏ J-1203 [M] | Kings of the Keyboard | 1956 | 10.00 | 20.00 | 40.00 |
ROOST
| ❏ LP-2213 [M] | Giants of the Piano | 1956 | 12.50 | 25.00 | 50.00 |

TAUPIN, BERNIE
ELTON JOHN's songwriting partner.
ASYLUM
| ❏ 6E-263 | He Who Rides the Tiger | 1980 | 3.00 | 6.00 | 12.00 |
ELEKTRA
| ❏ EKS-75020 | Bernie Taupin | 1972 | 3.75 | 7.50 | 15.00 |
RCA
| ❏ 5922-1-R | Tribe | 1987 | 2.50 | 5.00 | 10.00 |
| ❏ 6420-1-RAB [(2)DJ] | Interview Album | 1987 | 5.00 | 10.00 | 20.00 |

TAVENER, JOHN
APPLE
| ❏ SMAS-3369 | The Whale | 1972 | 5.00 | 10.00 | 20.00 |

TAX FREE
POLYDOR
| ❏ 24-4053 | Tax Free | 1971 | 5.00 | 10.00 | 20.00 |

TAXXI
FANTASY
❏ F-9603	Day for Night	1980	3.75	7.50	15.00
❏ F-9617	States of Emergency	1982	5.00	10.00	20.00
❏ F-9628	Foreign Tongue	1983	3.75	7.50	15.00
MCA
| ❏ 5580 | Expose | 1985 | 2.50 | 5.00 | 10.00 |

TAYLES, THE
CINEVISTA
| ❏ US 1001 | Who Are These Guys — Live at the Nitty Gritty | 1972 | 20.00 | 40.00 | 80.00 |

Number	Title (A Side/B Side)	Yr	VG	VG+	NM
TAYLOR, ART					
BLUE NOTE					
❏ BLP-4047 [M]	A.T.'s Delight	1960	20.00	40.00	80.00
—Regular version, W. 63rd St. address on label					
❏ BLP-4047 [M]	A.T.'s Delight	1960	30.00	60.00	120.00
—"Deep groove" version (deep indentation under label on both sides)					
❏ BST-84047 [S]	A.T.'s Delight	1960	15.00	30.00	60.00
—W. 63rd St. address on label					
NEW JAZZ					
❏ NJLP-8219 [M]	Taylor's Tenors	1959	12.50	25.00	50.00
—Purple label					
❏ NJLP-8219 [M]	Taylor's Tenors	1965	6.25	12.50	25.00
—Blue label, trident logo at right					
PRESTIGE					
❏ PRLP-7117 [M]	Taylor's Wailers	1957	25.00	50.00	100.00
TAYLOR, BILLY					
ABC-PARAMOUNT					
❏ ABC-112 [M]	Evergreens	1956	12.50	25.00	50.00
❏ ABC-134 [M]	Billy Taylor At the London House	1956	12.50	25.00	50.00
❏ ABC-162 [M]	Billy Taylor Introduces Ira Sullivan	1957	12.50	25.00	50.00
❏ ABC-177 [M]	My Fair Lady Loves Jazz	1957	12.50	25.00	50.00
❏ ABC-226 [M]	The New Trio	1958	12.50	25.00	50.00
❏ ABCS-226 [S]	The New Trio	1958	10.00	20.00	40.00
ARGO					
❏ LP-650 [M]	Taylor Made Flute	1959	12.50	25.00	50.00
❏ LPS-650 [S]	Taylor Made Flute	1959	10.00	20.00	40.00
ATLANTIC					
❏ ALR-113 [10]	Piano Panorama	1951	37.50	75.00	150.00
❏ 1277 [M]	The Billy Taylor Touch	1958	12.50	25.00	50.00
—Black label					
❏ 1277 [M]	The Billy Taylor Touch	1961	6.25	12.50	25.00
—Multicolor label, white "fan" logo at right					
❏ 1329 [M]	One for Fun	1960	12.50	25.00	50.00
—Black label					
❏ SD 1329 [S]	One for Fun	1960	12.50	25.00	50.00
—Green label					
CAPITOL					
❏ ST 2039 [S]	Right Here, Right Now	1963	6.25	12.50	25.00
❏ T 2039 [M]	Right Here, Right Now	1963	5.00	10.00	20.00
❏ ST 2302 [S]	Midnight Piano	1965	6.25	12.50	25.00
❏ T 2302 [M]	Midnight Piano	1965	5.00	10.00	20.00
IMPULSE!					
❏ A-71 [M]	My Fair Lady Loves Jazz	1965	5.00	10.00	20.00
❏ AS-71 [S]	My Fair Lady Loves Jazz	1965	6.25	12.50	25.00
MERCURY					
❏ MG-20722 [M]	Impromptu	1962	5.00	10.00	20.00
❏ SR-60722 [S]	Impromptu	1962	6.25	12.50	25.00
MOODSVILLE					
❏ MVLP-16 [M]	Interlude	1961	12.50	25.00	50.00
—Green label					
❏ MVLP-16 [M]	Interlude	1965	6.25	12.50	25.00
—Blue label, trident logo at right					
PRESTIGE					
❏ PRLP-139 [10]	Billy Taylor Trio, Volume 1	1953	55.00	110.00	220.00
❏ PRLP-165 [10]	Billy Taylor Trio, Volume 2	1953	55.00	110.00	220.00
❏ PRLP-168 [10]	Billy Taylor Trio, Volume 3	1953	55.00	110.00	220.00
❏ PRLP-184 [10]	Billy Taylor Trio	1954	50.00	100.00	200.00
❏ PRLP-188 [10]	Billy Taylor Trio	1954	50.00	100.00	200.00
❏ PRLP-194 [10]	Billy Taylor Trio In Concert at Town Hall, December 17, 1954	1955	50.00	100.00	200.00
❏ PRLP-7001 [M]	A Touch of Taylor	1955	20.00	40.00	80.00
❏ PRLP-7015 [M]	Billy Taylor Trio, Volume 1	1956	20.00	40.00	80.00
❏ PRLP-7016 [M]	Billy Taylor Trio, Volume 2	1956	20.00	40.00	80.00
❏ PRLP-7051 [M]	The Billy Taylor Trio with Candido	1956	20.00	40.00	80.00
❏ PRLP-7071 [M]	Cross Section	1956	20.00	40.00	80.00
❏ PRLP-7093 [M]	Billy Taylor Trio at Town Hall	1957	20.00	40.00	80.00
RIVERSIDE					
❏ RLP 12-306 [M]	Billy Taylor with Four Flutes	1959	12.50	25.00	50.00
❏ RLP 12-319 [M]	Billy Taylor Trio Uptown	1960	12.50	25.00	50.00
❏ RLP 12-339 [M]	Warming Up	1960	12.50	25.00	50.00
❏ RLP-1151 [S]	Billy Taylor with Four Flutes	1959	10.00	20.00	40.00
❏ RLP-1168 [S]	Billy Taylor Trio Uptown	1960	10.00	20.00	40.00
❏ RLP-1195 [S]	Warming Up	1960	10.00	20.00	40.00
ROOST					
❏ R-406 [10]	Jazz at Storyville	1952	30.00	60.00	120.00
❏ R-409 [10]	Taylor Made Jazz	1952	30.00	60.00	120.00
SAVOY					
❏ MG-9035 [10]	Billy Taylor Piano	1953	30.00	60.00	120.00
SESAC					
❏ N-3001 [M]	Custom Taylored	1959	15.00	30.00	60.00
❏ SN-3001 [S]	Custom Taylored	1959	12.50	25.00	50.00
STATUS					
❏ ST-8313 [M]	Live! At Town Hall	1965	10.00	20.00	40.00
SURREY					
❏ S-1033 [M]	Easy Life	1966	6.25	12.50	25.00
❏ SS-1033 [S]	Easy Life	1966	7.50	15.00	30.00
TOWER					
❏ ST-5111 [S]	I Wish I Knew	1968	6.25	12.50	25.00
TAYLOR, BOBBY, AND THE VANCOUVERS					
GORDY					
❏ G-930 [M]	Bobby Taylor and the Vancouvers	1968	20.00	40.00	80.00
—Mono is promo only					
❏ GS-930 [S]	Bobby Taylor and the Vancouvers	1968	15.00	30.00	60.00
❏ GS-942	Taylor Made Soul	1969	15.00	30.00	60.00
TAYLOR, BUCK					
JPL					
❏ 14098	That Man from Gunsmoke	197?	10.00	20.00	40.00

Number	Title (A Side/B Side)	Yr	VG	VG+	NM
TAYLOR, CATHIE					
CAPITOL					
❏ ST 1359 [S]	A Little Bit of Sweetness	1960	6.25	12.50	25.00
❏ T 1359 [M]	A Little Bit of Sweetness	1960	5.00	10.00	20.00
❏ ST 1448 [S]	The Tree Near My House	1961	6.25	12.50	25.00
❏ T 1448 [M]	The Tree Near My House	1961	5.00	10.00	20.00
TAYLOR, CECIL					
AMERICAN RECORDING SOCIETY					
❏ G-437 [M]	Modern Jazz	195?	10.00	20.00	40.00
BLUE NOTE					
❏ BLP-4237 [M]	Unit Structures	1966	6.25	12.50	25.00
❏ BLP-4260 [M]	Conquistador	1967	7.50	15.00	30.00
❏ BST-84237 [S]	Unit Structures	1966	7.50	15.00	30.00
—With "New York, USA" on label					
❏ BST-84260 [S]	Conquistador	1967	6.25	12.50	25.00
—With "A Division of Liberty Records" on label					
❏ BST-84260 [S]	Conquistador	197?	3.75	7.50	15.00
—Reissue with newer label; with "A Division of United Artists Records" on label					
CANDID					
❏ CD-8006 [M]	The World of Cecil Taylor	1960	12.50	25.00	50.00
❏ CS-9006 [S]	The World of Cecil Taylor	1960	10.00	20.00	40.00
CONTEMPORARY					
❏ C-3562 [M]	Looking Ahead!	1959	12.50	25.00	50.00
❏ S-7562 [S]	Looking Ahead!	1959	10.00	20.00	40.00
FANTASY					
❏ 6014 [M]	Live At the Café Montmarte	1964	5.00	10.00	20.00
❏ 86014 [S]	Live At the Café Montmarte	1964	6.25	12.50	25.00
HAT ART					
❏ 3011 [(3)]	One Too Many Salty Swift & Not Goodbye	1986	5.00	10.00	20.00
—Reissue of Hat Hut 02					
HAT HUT					
❏ 02 [(3)]	One Too Many Salty Swift & Not Goodbye	197?	6.25	12.50	25.00
❏ 1993/4 [(2)]	Garden	198?	5.00	10.00	20.00
MOSAIC					
❏ M6-127 [(6)]	The Complete Candid Recordings of Cecil Taylor and Buell Neidlinger	199?	25.00	50.00	100.00
PRESTIGE					
❏ 34003 [(3)]	Great Concert	197?	5.00	10.00	20.00
TRANSITION					
❏ TRLP-19 [M]	Jazz Advance	1956	50.00	100.00	200.00
—With booklet (deduct 1/4 if missing)					
UNIT CORE					
❏ 30551	Spring of Two Blue-J's	197?	5.00	10.00	20.00
UNITED ARTISTS					
❏ UAL-4014 [M]	Hard Driving Jazz	1959	12.50	25.00	50.00
❏ UAL-4046 [M]	Love for Sale	1959	12.50	25.00	50.00
❏ UAS-5014 [S]	Stereo Drive	1959	10.00	20.00	40.00
❏ UAS-5046 [S]	Love for Sale	1959	10.00	20.00	40.00
TAYLOR, CREED					
ABC-PARAMOUNT					
❏ ABC-259 [M]	Shock Music in Hi-Fi	1958	10.00	20.00	40.00
❏ ABCS-259 [S]	Shock Music in Hi-Fi	1958	15.00	30.00	60.00
❏ ABC-308 [M]	Lonelyville "The Nervous Beat"	1960	6.25	12.50	25.00
❏ ABCS-308 [S]	Lonelyville "The Nervous Beat"	1960	7.50	15.00	30.00
❏ ABC-317 [M]	The Best of the Barracks Ballads	1960	6.25	12.50	25.00
❏ ABCS-317 [S]	The Best of the Barracks Ballads	1960	7.50	15.00	30.00
TAYLOR, DICK					
SKYLARK					
❏ SKLP-18 [10]	Blue Moon	1954	20.00	40.00	80.00
TAYLOR, EARL					
CAPITOL					
❏ ST 2090 [S]	Bluegrass Taylor-Made	1963	12.50	25.00	50.00
❏ T 2090 [M]	Bluegrass Taylor-Made	1963	10.00	20.00	40.00
UNITED ARTISTS					
❏ UAL-3049 [M]	Folk Songs from the Bluegrass	1960	6.25	12.50	25.00
❏ UAS-6049 [S]	Folk Songs from the Bluegrass	1960	7.50	15.00	30.00
TAYLOR, HOUND DOG					
ALLIGATOR					
❏ 4701	Hound Dog Taylor	1971	6.25	12.50	25.00
❏ 4704	Natural Boogie	1974	5.00	10.00	20.00
TAYLOR, JAMES					
APPLE					
❏ SKAO 3352	James Taylor	1969	6.25	12.50	25.00
—With title in black print					
❏ SKAO 3352	James Taylor	1970	5.00	10.00	20.00
—With title in orange print					
COLUMBIA					
❏ JC 34811	JT	1977	2.50	5.00	10.00
❏ PC 34811	JT	198?	2.00	4.00	8.00
❏ FC 36058	Flag	1979	2.50	5.00	10.00
❏ PC 36058	Flag	198?	2.00	4.00	8.00
❏ PC 37009	Dad Loves His Work	198?	2.00	4.00	8.00
❏ TC 37009	Dad Loves His Work	1981	2.50	5.00	10.00
❏ FC 40052	That's Why I'm Here	1985	2.50	5.00	10.00
❏ FC 40851	Never Die Young	1988	2.50	5.00	10.00
❏ HC 47009	Dad Loves His Work	1983	10.00	20.00	40.00
—Half-speed mastered edition					
EUPHORIA					
❏ EST-2	James Taylor and the Original Flying Machine 1967	1971	3.00	6.00	12.00
NAUTILUS					
❏ NR-29	Gorilla	1981	10.00	20.00	40.00
—Audiophile pressing					

T

Number	Title (A Side/B Side)	Yr	VG	VG+	NM
TRIP					
☐ TLP-9513	Rainy Day Man	197?	2.50	5.00	10.00
—Reissue of Euphoria album					
WARNER BROS.					
☐ WS 1843	Sweet Baby James	1970	2.50	5.00	10.00
—Green "WB" label with "Contains Fire and Rain and Country Road" added to front cover					
☐ WS 1843	Sweet Baby James	1970	3.75	7.50	15.00
—Green "WB" label with no reference to other songs on front cover					
☐ WS 1843	Sweet Baby James	1970	6.25	12.50	25.00
—Very early pressings have green label with "W7" logo					
☐ WS 1843	Sweet Baby James	1973	2.00	4.00	8.00
—"Burbank" label or cream label					
☐ BS 2561	Mud Slide Slim and the Blue Horizon	1971	2.50	5.00	10.00
—Green "WB" label					
☐ BS 2561	Mud Slide Slim and the Blue Horizon	1973	2.00	4.00	8.00
—"Burbank" label or cream label					
☐ BS 2660	One Man Dog	1972	2.50	5.00	10.00
—Green "WB" label					
☐ BS 2660	One Man Dog	1973	2.00	4.00	8.00
—"Burbank" label or cream label					
☐ BS4 2660 [Q]	One Man Dog	1975	3.75	7.50	15.00
☐ BS 2794	Walking Man	1973	2.50	5.00	10.00
—"Burbank" label					
☐ BS 2794	Walking Man	1979	2.00	4.00	8.00
—Cream label					
☐ BS 2866	Gorilla	1975	2.50	5.00	10.00
—"Burbank" label					
☐ BS 2866	Gorilla	1979	2.00	4.00	8.00
—Cream label					
☐ BS4 2866 [Q]	Gorilla	1975	3.75	7.50	15.00
☐ BS 2912	In the Pocket	1976	2.50	5.00	10.00
—"Burbank" label					
☐ BS 2912	In the Pocket	1979	2.00	4.00	8.00
—Cream label					
☐ BS 2979	Greatest Hits	1976	3.00	6.00	12.00
—This and other variations of this title have re-recorded versions of "Carolina in My Mind" and "Something in the Way She Moves."					
☐ BSK 3113	Greatest Hits	1977	2.50	5.00	10.00
—"Burbank" label					
☐ BSK 3113	Greatest Hits	1979	2.00	4.00	8.00
—Cream label					
☐ ST-93138	Sweet Baby James	1970	5.00	10.00	20.00
—Capitol Record Club edition					

TAYLOR, JOHNNIE

Number	Title (A Side/B Side)	Yr	VG	VG+	NM
BEVERLY GLEN					
☐ 10001	Just Ain't Good Enough	1982	3.00	6.00	12.00
COLUMBIA					
☐ PC 33951	Eargasm	1976	3.00	6.00	12.00
—Originals have no bar code					
☐ PC 33951	Eargasm	1986	2.00	4.00	8.00
—Budget-line reissue with bar code					
☐ PCQ 33951 [Q]	Eargasm	1976	5.00	10.00	20.00
☐ PC 34401	Rated Extraordinaire	1977	3.00	6.00	12.00
☐ PCQ 34401 [Q]	Rated Extraordinaire	1977	5.00	10.00	20.00
☐ JC 35340	Ever Ready	1978	3.00	6.00	12.00
☐ JC 36061	She's Killing Me	1979	3.00	6.00	12.00
☐ JC 36548	A New Day	1980	3.00	6.00	12.00
☐ JC 37127	The Best of Johnnie Taylor	1981	3.00	6.00	12.00
ICHIBAN					
☐ ICH-1022	Stuck in the Mud	198?	2.50	5.00	10.00
☐ ICH-1042	Ugly Man	198?	2.50	5.00	10.00
MALACO					
☐ MAL-7421	This Is Your Night	198?	2.50	5.00	10.00
☐ MAL-7431	Wall to Wall	198?	2.50	5.00	10.00
☐ MAL-7440	Lover Boy	198?	2.50	5.00	10.00
☐ MAL-7446	In Control	198?	2.50	5.00	10.00
☐ MAL-7452	Crazy 'Bout You	1989	2.50	5.00	10.00
☐ MAL-7460	Just Can't Do Right	1991	2.50	5.00	10.00
☐ MAL-7463	The Best of Johnnie Taylor on Malaco, Vol. 1	1992	2.50	5.00	10.00
STAX					
☐ ST-715 [M]	Wanted: One Soul Singer	1967	12.50	25.00	50.00
☐ STS-715 [S]	Wanted: One Soul Singer	1967	15.00	30.00	60.00
☐ STS-2005	Who's Making Love	1968	10.00	20.00	40.00
☐ STS-2008	Raw Blues	1969	6.25	12.50	25.00
☐ STS-2012	Rare Stamps	1969	6.25	12.50	25.00
☐ STS-2023	The Johnnie Taylor Philosophy Continues	1969	6.25	12.50	25.00
☐ STS-2030	One Step Beyond	1971	6.25	12.50	25.00
☐ STS-2032	Johnnie Taylor's Greatest Hits	1970	6.25	12.50	25.00
☐ STS-3014	Taylored in Silk	1973	5.00	10.00	20.00
☐ STX-4115	Who's Making Love	198?	2.50	5.00	10.00
—Reissue of 2005					
☐ STS-5509	Super Taylor	1974	5.00	10.00	20.00
☐ STS-5521	The Best of Johnnie Taylor	1975	5.00	10.00	20.00
☐ MPS-8508	Raw Blues	1982	2.50	5.00	10.00
☐ MPS-8520	Super Hits	1983	2.50	5.00	10.00
☐ MPS-8537	Taylored in Silk	1987	2.50	5.00	10.00
—Reissue of 3014					
☐ MPS-8558	Little Bluebird	1988	2.50	5.00	10.00
☐ 88001 [(2)]	Chronicle	1977	5.00	10.00	20.00

TAYLOR, KINGSIZE, AND THE DOMINOES

Number	Title (A Side/B Side)	Yr	VG	VG+	NM
MIDNIGHT					
☐ HLP-2101 [M]	Real Gonk Man	1965	12.50	25.00	50.00
☐ HST-2101 [S]	Real Gonk Man	1965	25.00	50.00	100.00

TAYLOR, KOKO

Number	Title (A Side/B Side)	Yr	VG	VG+	NM
ALLIGATOR					
☐ 4706	I Got What It Takes	1976	3.00	6.00	12.00
CHESS					
☐ LPS-1532	Koko Taylor	1969	7.50	15.00	30.00
☐ CH-50018	Basic Soul	1972	6.25	12.50	25.00

TAYLOR, LITTLE JOHNNY

Number	Title (A Side/B Side)	Yr	VG	VG+	NM
FANTASY					
☐ MPF-4510	Little Johnny Taylor's Greatest Hits	1982	2.50	5.00	10.00
GALAXY					
☐ 203 [M]	Little Johnny Taylor	1963	25.00	50.00	100.00
☐ 207 [M]	Little Johnny Taylor	1964	25.00	50.00	100.00
☐ 8203 [S]	Little Johnny Taylor	1963	37.50	75.00	150.00
☐ 8207 [S]	Little Johnny Taylor's Greatest Hits	1964	37.50	75.00	150.00
RONN					
☐ LPS-7530	Everybody Knows About My Good Thing	1972	6.25	12.50	25.00
☐ LSP-7532	Open House at My House	1973	6.25	12.50	25.00
☐ LSP-7535	L.J.T.	1975	5.00	10.00	20.00

TAYLOR, LITTLE JOHNNY, AND TED TAYLOR

Number	Title (A Side/B Side)	Yr	VG	VG+	NM
RONN					
☐ LSP-7533	The Super Taylors	1973	5.00	10.00	20.00

TAYLOR, LYNN

Number	Title (A Side/B Side)	Yr	VG	VG+	NM
GRAND AWARD					
☐ GA-33-(# unk) [M]	Lynn Taylor Sings	195?	75.00	150.00	300.00

TAYLOR, MEL

Number	Title (A Side/B Side)	Yr	VG	VG+	NM
WARNER BROS.					
☐ W 1624 [M]	Mel Taylor in Action	1966	7.50	15.00	30.00
☐ WS 1624 [S]	Mel Taylor in Action	1966	10.00	20.00	40.00

TAYLOR, SAM "THE MAN"

Number	Title (A Side/B Side)	Yr	VG	VG+	NM
DECCA					
☐ DL 74302 [S]	Misty Mood	1962	5.00	10.00	20.00
☐ DL 74417 [S]	It's a Blue World	1963	5.00	10.00	20.00
☐ DL 74573 [S]	Somewhere in the Night	1964	5.00	10.00	20.00
LION					
☐ L-70054 [M]	Sam "The Man" Taylor	1958	6.25	12.50	25.00
METROJAZZ					
☐ E-1008 [M]	Jazz for Commuters	1958	12.50	25.00	50.00
☐ SE-1008 [S]	Jazz for Commuters	1958	10.00	20.00	40.00
MGM					
☐ E-293 [10]	Music with the Big Beat	195?	25.00	50.00	100.00
☐ E-3292 [M]	Blue Mist	1955	15.00	30.00	60.00
—Yellow label					
☐ E-3380 [M]	Out of This World	1956	15.00	30.00	60.00
—Yellow label					
☐ E-3473 [M]	Music with the Big Beat	1956	20.00	40.00	80.00
—Yellow label					
☐ E-3482 [M]	Music for Melancholy Babies	1957	15.00	30.00	60.00
—Yellow label					
☐ E-3553 [M]	Rockin' Sax and Rollin' Organ	1957	15.00	30.00	60.00
—Yellow label					
☐ E-3573 [M]	Prelude to Blues	1957	15.00	30.00	60.00
—Yellow label					
☐ E-3783 [M]	More Blue Mist	1959	7.50	15.00	30.00
☐ SE-3783 [S]	More Blue Mist	1959	10.00	20.00	40.00
☐ E-3967 [M]	Sam "The Man" Taylor Plays Hollywood	1960	7.50	15.00	30.00
☐ SE-3967 [S]	Sam "The Man" Taylor Plays Hollywood	1960	10.00	20.00	40.00
☐ E-3973 [M]	Blue Mist	1961	7.50	15.00	30.00
☐ SE-3973 [S]	Blue Mist	1961	6.25	12.50	25.00
—Possibly a re-recording of 3292					
MOODSVILLE					
☐ MVLP-24 [M]	The Bad and the Beautiful	1962	12.50	25.00	50.00
—Green label					
☐ MVLP-24 [M]	The Bad and the Beautiful	1965	6.25	12.50	25.00
—Blue label, trident logo at right					

TAYLOR, TED

Number	Title (A Side/B Side)	Yr	VG	VG+	NM
OKEH					
☐ OKM-12104 [M]	Be Ever Wonderful	1963	7.50	15.00	30.00
☐ OKM-12109 [M]	Blues and Soul	1965	7.50	15.00	30.00
☐ OKM-12113 [M]	Ted Taylor's Greatest Hits	1966	6.25	12.50	25.00
☐ OKS-14104 [S]	Be Ever Wonderful	1963	10.00	20.00	40.00
☐ OKS-14109 [S]	Blues and Soul	1965	10.00	20.00	40.00
☐ OKS-14113 [S]	Ted Taylor's Greatest Hits	1966	7.50	15.00	30.00

TAYLOR, TUT

Number	Title (A Side/B Side)	Yr	VG	VG+	NM
WORLD PACIFIC					
☐ ST-1816 [S]	12 String Dobro	1964	7.50	15.00	30.00
—Black vinyl					
☐ ST-1816 [S]	12 String Dobro	1964	20.00	40.00	80.00
—Red vinyl					
☐ WP-1816 [M]	12 String Dobro	1964	6.25	12.50	25.00
☐ ST-1829 [S]	Dobro Country	1964	7.50	15.00	30.00
☐ WP-1829 [M]	Dobro Country	1964	6.25	12.50	25.00

TCHAIKOVSKY, ANDRE

Number	Title (A Side/B Side)	Yr	VG	VG+	NM
RCA VICTOR RED SEAL					
☐ LSC-2287 [S]	Mozart: Piano Concerto No. 25	1959	25.00	50.00	100.00
—With Fritz Reiner/Chicago Symphony Orchestra; original with "shaded dog" label					
☐ LSC-2354 [S]	Mozart: Fantasia in C; Sonata in C, K. 457; Sonata in C, K. 330	1960	17.50	35.00	70.00
—Original with "shaded dog" label					
☐ LSC-2360 [S]	Chopin: Preludes; Barcarolle: Mazurkas, Etudes, Ballade 3	1960	15.00	30.00	60.00
—Original with "shaded dog" label					

TEA COMPANY, THE

Number	Title (A Side/B Side)	Yr	VG	VG+	NM
SMASH					
☐ SRS-67105	Come and Have Some Tea	1968	12.50	25.00	50.00

TEAGARDEN, JACK

Number	Title (A Side/B Side)	Yr	VG	VG+	NM
BETHLEHEM					
☐ BCP-32 [M]	Jazz Great	1955	12.50	25.00	50.00
CAPITOL					
☐ T 721 [M]	This Is Teagarden	1956	10.00	20.00	40.00

Number	Title (A Side/B Side)	Yr	VG	VG+	NM
❏ T 820 [M]	Swing Low Sweet Spiritual	1957	10.00	20.00	40.00
❏ ST 1095 [S]	Big T's Dixieland Band	1959	6.25	12.50	25.00
❏ T 1095 [M]	Big T's Dixieland Band	1959	5.00	10.00	20.00
❏ ST 1143 [S]	Shades of Night	1959	6.25	12.50	25.00
❏ T 1143 [M]	Shades of Night	1959	5.00	10.00	20.00
COLUMBIA SPECIAL PRODUCTS					
❏ JSN 6044 [(3)M]	King of the Blues Trombone	197?	6.25	12.50	25.00
COMMODORE					
❏ 20015 [10]	Big T	195?	20.00	40.00	80.00
DECCA					
❏ DL 8304 [M]	Big T's Jazz	1956	10.00	20.00	40.00
EPIC					
❏ SN 6044 [(3)M]	King of the Blues Trombone	1963	20.00	40.00	80.00
❏ LN 24045 [M]	King of the Blues Trombone, Vol. 1	1963	6.25	12.50	25.00
❏ LN 24046 [M]	King of the Blues Trombone, Vol. 2	1963	6.25	12.50	25.00
❏ LN 24047 [M]	King of the Blues Trombone, Vol. 3	1963	6.25	12.50	25.00
JAZZTONE					
❏ J-1222 [M]	Big T	195?	7.50	15.00	30.00
—Reissue of Period material					
JOLLY ROGER					
❏ 5026 [10]	Jack Teagarden	1955	12.50	25.00	50.00
MOSAIC					
❏ MQ6-168 [(6)]	The Complete Capitol Fifties Jack Teagarden Sessions	199?	25.00	50.00	100.00
PERIOD					
❏ SLP-1106 [10]	Meet Me Where They Play the Blues	1955	20.00	40.00	80.00
❏ SLP-1110 [10]	Original Dixieland	1955	20.00	40.00	80.00
RCA VICTOR					
❏ LPV-528 [M]	Jack Teagarden	1965	5.00	10.00	20.00
RONDO-LETTE					
❏ A-18 [M]	The Blues and Dixie	1958	6.25	12.50	25.00
ROULETTE					
❏ SR-25091 [S]	Jack Teagarden at the Round Table	1960	5.00	10.00	20.00
❏ SR-25119 [S]	Jazz Maverick	1961	5.00	10.00	20.00
❏ SR-25177 [S]	Dixie Sound	1962	5.00	10.00	20.00
❏ SR-25243 [S]	Portrait of Mr. T	1963	5.00	10.00	20.00
ROYALE					
❏ 18156 [10]	The Blues	195?	20.00	40.00	80.00
URANIA					
❏ UJLP-1001 [10]	Meet the New Jack Teagarden	1954	25.00	50.00	100.00
❏ UJLP-1002 [10]	Jack Teagarden Sings and Plays	1954	25.00	50.00	100.00
VERVE					
❏ V6-8416 [S]	Mis'ry and the Blues	1961	5.00	10.00	20.00
❏ V6-8465 [S]	Think Well of Me	1962	5.00	10.00	20.00
❏ V6-8495 [S]	Jack Teagarden!!	1962	5.00	10.00	20.00

TEAGARDEN, JACK/BOBBY HACKETT
COMMODORE

❏ FL-30012 [M]	Jack Teagarden and Bobby Hackett	1959	7.50	15.00	30.00

TEAGARDEN, JACK/JONAH JONES
AAMCO

❏ ALP-309 [M]	Two Boys from Dixieland	196?	6.25	12.50	25.00
—Reissue of Bethlehem material					
BETHLEHEM					
❏ BCP-6042 [M]	Dixieland	1959	10.00	20.00	40.00

TEAGARDEN, JACK/PEE WEE RUSSELL
RIVERSIDE

❏ RLP 12-141	Jack Teagarden's Big Eight / Pee Wee Russell's Rhythmakers	1956	15.00	30.00	60.00

TEARDROPS, THE (U)
20TH CENTURY FOX

❏ FXG-5011 [M]	The Teardrops at Trinchi's	1963	6.25	12.50	25.00

TEDDY AND THE PANDAS
TOWER

❏ ST-5125	Basic Magnetism	1968	6.25	12.50	25.00

TEDDY BEARS, THE
IMPERIAL

❏ LP-9067 [M]	The Teddy Bears Sing!	1959	75.00	150.00	300.00
❏ LP-12010 [S]	The Teddy Bears Sing!	1959	300.00	600.00	1200.

TEDESCO, TOMMY
DISCOVERY

❏ 789	When Do We Start	1978	3.00	6.00	12.00
❏ 851	My Desiree	1982	2.50	5.00	10.00
❏ 928	Hollywood Gypsy	1986	2.50	5.00	10.00
IMPERIAL					
❏ LP-9263 [M]	The Electric 12 String Guitar of Tommy Tedesco	1964	3.75	7.50	15.00
❏ LP-9295 [M]	Guitars	1965	3.75	7.50	15.00
❏ LP-9321 [M]	Calypso Soul	1966	3.75	7.50	15.00
❏ LP-12263 [S]	The Electric 12 String Guitar of Tommy Tedesco	1964	5.00	10.00	20.00
❏ LP-12295 [S]	Guitars	1965	5.00	10.00	20.00
❏ LP-12321 [S]	Calypso Soul	1966	5.00	10.00	20.00
TREND					
❏ TR-514	Autumn	1978	5.00	10.00	20.00
—Direct-to-disc recording					
❏ TR-517	Alone at Last	1979	5.00	10.00	20.00
—Direct-to-disc recording					
❏ TR-534	Carnival Time	1983	3.00	6.00	12.00

TEEMATES, THE
AUDIO FIDELITY

❏ AFLP-3042 [M]	Jet Set Dance Discotheque	1964	10.00	20.00	40.00
❏ AFSD-7042 [S]	Jet Set Dance Discotheque	1964	12.50	25.00	50.00

TEEN QUEENS, THE
CROWN

❏ CST-373 [R]	The Teen Queens	1963	7.50	15.00	30.00
❏ CLP-5022 [M]	Eddie My Love	1956	62.50	125.00	250.00
—Black label, all silver print					
❏ CLP-5022 [M]	Eddie My Love	196?	25.00	50.00	100.00
—Black label, "CROWN" in alternating colored letters					
❏ CLP-5373 [M]	The Teen Queens	1963	12.50	25.00	50.00
RPM					
❏ LRP-3007 [M]	Eddie My Love	1956	—	—	—
—Canceled					

TEENAGE JESUS AND THE JERKS
MIGRANE/LUST UNLUST

❏ CC-336 [EP]	Teenage Jesus and the Jerks	1979	7.50	15.00	30.00
—Black vinyl					
❏ CC-336 [EP]	Teenage Jesus and the Jerks	1979	10.00	20.00	40.00
—Pink vinyl					

TEENAGERS, THE
See FRANKIE LYMON AND THE TEENAGERS.

TELEVISION
CAPITOL

❏ SPRO-79456 [DJ]	Television	1992	5.00	10.00	20.00
—Vinyl is promo only					
ELEKTRA					
❏ 6E-133	Adventure	1978	2.50	5.00	10.00
❏ 7E-1098	Marquee Moon	1977	3.00	7.50	15.00

TEMPEST
WARNER BROS.

❏ BS 2682	Tempest	1973	6.25	12.50	25.00

TEMPESTS, THE
SMASH

❏ MGS-27098 [M]	Would You Believe?	1966	6.25	12.50	25.00
❏ SRS-67098 [S]	Would You Believe?	1966	7.50	15.00	30.00

TEMPLE, PICK
PRESTIGE INT'L.

❏ PRLP-13008 [M]	Pick of the Crop	196?	7.50	15.00	30.00
"X"					
❏ LXA-3022 [10]	Folk Songs of the People	1954	12.50	25.00	50.00

TEMPLE, SHIRLEY
MOVIETONE

❏ MTM-71001 [M]	On the Good Ship Lollipop	1966	5.00	10.00	20.00
❏ MTM-71012 [M]	Curtain Call	1966	5.00	10.00	20.00
20TH CENTURY FOX					
❏ TFM-3102 [M]	The Best of Shirley Temple	1963	6.25	12.50	25.00
❏ TFM-3172 [M]	The Best of Shirley Temple, Vol. 2	1965	6.25	12.50	25.00
20TH FOX					
❏ TCF-103 [(2)M]	The Shirley Temple Songbook	1961	12.50	25.00	50.00
❏ FOX-3006 [M]	Little Miss Wonderful	1959	10.00	20.00	40.00
—Shirley Temple pictured as an adult on cover					
❏ FOX-3006 [M]	Little Miss Wonderful	196?	10.00	20.00	40.00
—Shirley Temple pictured as a child on cover					
❏ FOX-3045 [M]	More Little Miss Wonderful	1961	10.00	20.00	40.00

TEMPLETON, ALEC
ATLANTIC

❏ 1222 [M]	The Magic Piano	1956	10.00	20.00	40.00
—Black label					
❏ 1222 [M]	The Magic Piano	1961	5.00	10.00	20.00
—Multicolor label, white "fan" logo at right					

TEMPO, NINO
A&M

❏ SP-3629	Come See Me 'Round Midnight	1974	2.50	5.00	10.00
LIBERTY					
❏ LRP-3023 [M]	Rock 'n' Roll Beach Party	1958	30.00	60.00	120.00

TEMPO, NINO, AND APRIL STEVENS
Also see each artist's individual listings.
ATCO

❏ 33-156 [M]	Deep Purple	1963	10.00	20.00	40.00
❏ SD 33-156 [S]	Deep Purple	1963	12.50	25.00	50.00
❏ 33-162 [M]	Nino and April Sing the Great Songs	1964	7.50	15.00	30.00
❏ SD 33-162 [S]	Nino and April Sing the Great Songs	1964	10.00	20.00	40.00
❏ 33-180 [M]	Hey Baby	1966	7.50	15.00	30.00
❏ SD 33-180 [S]	Hey Baby	1966	10.00	20.00	40.00
RCA CAMDEN					
❏ CAL-824 [M]	A Nino Tempo/April Stevens Program	1964	3.00	6.00	12.00
—Actually contains solo recordings by each, packaged together to capitalize on the success of "Deep Purple"					
WHITE WHALE					
❏ WW-113 [M]	All Strung Out	1967	5.00	10.00	20.00
❏ WWS-7113 [S]	All Strung Out	1967	6.25	12.50	25.00

TEMPOS, THE
JUSTICE

❏ JLP-104	Speaking of the Tempos	1966	125.00	250.00	500.00

TEMPREES
WE PRODUCE

❏ 1901	Love Men	1972	15.00	30.00	60.00
❏ 1903	Love Maze	1973	15.00	30.00	60.00
❏ 1905	Temprees 3	1974	15.00	30.00	60.00

T

Number	Title (A Side/B Side)	Yr	VG	VG+	NM

TEMPTATIONS, THE
Also see DAVID RUFFIN.
ATLANTIC
Number	Title (A Side/B Side)	Yr	VG	VG+	NM
❑ SD 19143	Hear to Tempt You	1977	3.00	6.00	12.00
❑ SD 19188	Bare Back	1978	3.00	6.00	12.00

GORDY
Number	Title (A Side/B Side)	Yr	VG	VG+	NM
❑ G 911 [M]	Meet the Temptations	1964	7.50	15.00	30.00
❑ GS 911 [S]	Meet the Temptations	1964	10.00	20.00	40.00
—Script "Gordy" at top of label					
❑ GS 911 [S]	Meet the Temptations	1967	5.00	10.00	20.00
—Block "GORDY" inside "G" on left of label					
❑ G 912 [M]	The Temptations Sing Smokey	1965	7.50	15.00	30.00
❑ GS 912 [S]	The Temptations Sing Smokey	1965	10.00	20.00	40.00
—Script "Gordy" at top of label					
❑ GS 912 [S]	The Temptations Sing Smokey	1967	5.00	10.00	20.00
—Block "GORDY" inside "G" on left of label					
❑ G 914 [M]	Temptin' Temptations	1965	6.25	12.50	25.00
❑ GS 914 [S]	Temptin' Temptations	1965	7.50	15.00	30.00
—Script "Gordy" at top of label					
❑ GS 914 [S]	Temptin' Temptations	1967	5.00	10.00	20.00
—Block "GORDY" inside "G" on left of label					
❑ G 918 [M]	Gettin' Ready	1966	6.25	12.50	25.00
❑ GS 918 [S]	Gettin' Ready	1966	7.50	15.00	30.00
—Script "Gordy" at top of label					
❑ GS 918 [S]	Gettin' Ready	1967	5.00	10.00	20.00
—Block "GORDY" inside "G" on left of label					
❑ G 919 [M]	The Temptations' Greatest Hits	1966	6.25	12.50	25.00
❑ GS 919 [S]	The Temptations' Greatest Hits	1966	7.50	15.00	30.00
—Script "Gordy" at top of label					
❑ GS 919 [S]	The Temptations' Greatest Hits	1967	5.00	10.00	20.00
—Block "GORDY" inside "G" on left of label					
❑ G 921 [M]	Temptations Live!	1967	6.25	12.50	25.00
❑ GS 921 [S]	Temptations Live!	1967	5.00	10.00	20.00
—Block "GORDY" inside "G" on left of label					
❑ GS 921 [S]	Temptations Live!	1967	7.50	15.00	30.00
—Script "Gordy" at top of label					
❑ G 922 [M]	With a Lot o' Soul	1967	6.25	12.50	25.00
❑ GS 922 [S]	With a Lot o' Soul	1967	5.00	10.00	20.00
—Block "GORDY" inside "G" on left of label					
❑ GS 922 [S]	With a Lot o' Soul	1967	6.25	12.50	25.00
—Script "Gordy" at top of label					
❑ G 924 [M]	The Temptations in a Mellow Mood	1967	6.25	12.50	25.00
❑ GS 924 [S]	The Temptations in a Mellow Mood	1967	6.25	12.50	25.00
❑ G 927 [M]	The Temptations Wish It Would Rain	1968	10.00	20.00	40.00
—Mono is white-label promo only					
❑ GS 927 [S]	The Temptations Wish It Would Rain	1968	5.00	10.00	20.00
❑ GS 933	The Temptations Show	1969	5.00	10.00	20.00
❑ GS 938	Live at the Copa	1968	5.00	10.00	20.00
❑ GS 939	Cloud Nine	1969	5.00	10.00	20.00
❑ GS 947	Psychedelic Shack	1970	5.00	10.00	20.00
❑ GS 949	Puzzle People	1969	5.00	10.00	20.00
❑ GS 951	The Temptations' Christmas Card	1969	6.25	12.50	25.00
❑ GS 953	Live at London's Talk of the Town	1970	5.00	10.00	20.00
❑ GS 954	Temptations Greatest Hits II	1970	5.00	10.00	20.00
❑ GS 957	Sky's the Limit	1971	5.00	10.00	20.00
❑ G 961L	Solid Rock	1972	5.00	10.00	20.00
❑ G 962L	All Directions	1972	5.00	10.00	20.00
❑ G 965L	Masterpiece	1973	5.00	10.00	20.00
❑ G 966V1	1990	1973	3.75	7.50	15.00
❑ G6-969S1	A Song for You	1975	3.75	7.50	15.00
❑ G6-971S1	Wings of Love	1976	3.75	7.50	15.00
❑ G6-973S1	House Party	1975	3.75	7.50	15.00
❑ G7-975S1	The Temptations Do the Temptations	1976	3.75	7.50	15.00
❑ G8-994M1	Power	1980	3.00	6.00	12.00
❑ G8-998M1	Give Love at Christmas	1980	3.75	7.50	15.00
❑ G8-1006M1	The Temptations	1981	3.00	6.00	12.00
❑ 6008 GL	Reunion	1982	3.00	6.00	12.00
❑ 6032 GL	Surface Thrills	1983	3.00	6.00	12.00
❑ 6085 GL	Back to Basics	1984	3.00	6.00	12.00
❑ 6119 GL	Truly for You	1984	3.00	6.00	12.00
❑ 6164 GL	Touch Me	1986	3.00	6.00	12.00
❑ 6207 GL	To Be Continued	1986	3.00	6.00	12.00

MOTOWN
Number	Title (A Side/B Side)	Yr	VG	VG+	NM
❑ M5-140V1	Meet the Temptations	1981	3.00	6.00	12.00
—Reissue of Gordy 911					
❑ M5-144V1	Masterpiece	1981	3.00	6.00	12.00
—Reissue of Gordy 965					
❑ M5-159V1	Cloud Nine	1981	3.00	6.00	12.00
—Reissue of Gordy 939					
❑ M5-164V1	Psychedelic Shack	1981	3.00	6.00	12.00
—Reissue of Gordy 947					
❑ M5-172V1	Puzzle People	1981	3.00	6.00	12.00
—Reissue of Gordy 949					
❑ M5-205V1	The Temptations Sing Smokey	1981	3.00	6.00	12.00
—Reissue of Gordy 912					
❑ M5-212V1	All the Million Sellers	1982	3.00	6.00	12.00
❑ M 782 [(3)]	Anthology	1973	6.25	12.50	25.00
❑ 5251 ML	The Temptations Christmas Card	1982	2.50	5.00	10.00
—Reissue of Gordy 951					
❑ 5279 ML	Give Love at Christmas	1983	2.50	5.00	10.00
—Reissue of Gordy 998					
❑ 5389 ML [(2)]	25th Anniversary	1986	3.75	7.50	15.00
❑ 6246 ML	Together Again	1987	3.00	6.00	12.00
❑ MOT-6275	Special	1989	3.00	6.00	12.00

NATURAL RESOURCES
Number	Title (A Side/B Side)	Yr	VG	VG+	NM
❑ NR 4005T1	The Temptations in a Mellow Mood	1978	3.00	6.00	12.00
—Reissue of Gordy 924					

PICKWICK
Number	Title (A Side/B Side)	Yr	VG	VG+	NM
❑ SPC-3540	Psychedelic Shack	197?	3.00	6.00	12.00
—Reissue of Gordy 947					

10,000 MANIACS
CHRISTIAN BURIAL
Number	Title (A Side/B Side)	Yr	VG	VG+	NM
❑ P-2010 [EP]	Human Conflict #5	1983	20.00	40.00	80.00
❑ P-3001	Secrets of the I Ching	1984	30.00	60.00	120.00

ELEKTRA
Number	Title (A Side/B Side)	Yr	VG	VG+	NM
❑ ED 5270 [DJ]	Interview	1987	7.50	15.00	30.00
—Lenny Kaye interviews Natalie Merchant; promo only					
❑ 60428	The Wishing Chair	1985	3.00	6.00	12.00
❑ 60738	In My Tribe	1987	2.50	5.00	10.00
❑ 60738 [DJ]	In My Tribe	1987	3.00	6.00	12.00
—Promo-only audiophile pressing					
❑ 60815	Blind Man's Zoo	1989	3.00	6.00	12.00
❑ 60815 [DJ]	Blind Man's Zoo	1989	3.75	7.50	15.00
—Promo-only audiophile pressing (white labels)					
❑ R 100481	In My Tribe	1987	3.00	6.00	12.00
—BMG Direct Marketing edition					
❑ R 130236	Blind Man's Zoo	1989	3.75	7.50	15.00
—BMG Direct Marketing edition					

TEN YEARS AFTER
CHRYSALIS
Number	Title (A Side/B Side)	Yr	VG	VG+	NM
❑ CHS 1083	Ssssh	1975	2.50	5.00	10.00
❑ CHS 1084	Cricklewood Green	1975	2.50	5.00	10.00
❑ CHS 1085	Watt	1975	2.50	5.00	10.00
❑ F1-21001	A Space in Time	1989	2.00	4.00	8.00
❑ F1-21009	Rock and Roll Music to the World	1989	2.00	4.00	8.00
❑ F1-21083	Ssssh	1989	2.00	4.00	8.00
❑ F1-21084	Cricklewood Green	1989	2.00	4.00	8.00
❑ F1-21085	Watt	1989	2.00	4.00	8.00
❑ F1-21573	Positive Vibrations	1989	2.00	4.00	8.00
❑ F1-21580	Universal	1989	2.00	4.00	8.00
❑ F1-21722	About Time	1989	3.00	6.00	12.00
❑ PV 41001	A Space in Time	1987	2.00	4.00	8.00
❑ PV 41009	Rock and Roll Music to the World	1987	2.00	4.00	8.00
❑ FV 41049 [(2)]	Recorded Live	1987	2.50	5.00	10.00
❑ PV 41083	Ssssh	1983	2.00	4.00	8.00
❑ PV 41084	Cricklewood Green	1983	2.00	4.00	8.00
❑ PV 41085	Watt	1983	2.00	4.00	8.00
❑ PV 41573	Positive Vibrations	1987	2.00	4.00	8.00
❑ FV 41580	Universal	1988	2.50	5.00	10.00

COLUMBIA
Number	Title (A Side/B Side)	Yr	VG	VG+	NM
❑ CQ 30801 [Q]	A Space in Time	1973	4.00	8.00	16.00
❑ KC 30801	A Space in Time	1971	3.00	6.00	12.00
❑ PC 30801	A Space in Time	1979	2.00	4.00	8.00
❑ C 31779	Rock and Roll Music to the World	197?	2.50	5.00	10.00
—Reissue with new prefix					
❑ KC 31779	Rock and Roll Music to the World	1972	3.00	6.00	12.00
❑ C2X 32288 [(2)]	Recorded Live	1973	3.75	7.50	15.00
❑ PC 32851	Positive Vibrations	1974	2.50	5.00	10.00
❑ PC 34366	Classic Performances of Ten Years After	1976	2.50	5.00	10.00

DERAM
Number	Title (A Side/B Side)	Yr	VG	VG+	NM
❑ DE 16009 [M]	Ten Years After	1968	12.50	25.00	50.00
❑ DES 18009 [S]	Ten Years After	1968	5.00	10.00	20.00
❑ DES 18016	Undead	1968	3.75	7.50	15.00
❑ DES 18021	Stonedhenge	1969	3.75	7.50	15.00
❑ DES 18029	Ssssh	1969	3.75	7.50	15.00
❑ DES 18038	Cricklewood Green	1970	3.75	7.50	15.00
❑ XDES 18050	Watt	1970	3.75	7.50	15.00
—With large "DERAM" on top half of label					
❑ XDES 18050	Watt	1970	6.25	12.50	25.00
—With "LONDON" under smaller "DERAM" at top of label					
❑ XDES 18064	Alvin Lee and Company	1972	3.00	6.00	12.00
❑ DES 18072	Goin' Home! Their Greatest Hits	1975	3.00	6.00	12.00
❑ SMAS-93428	Watt	1970	5.00	10.00	20.00
—Capitol Record Club edition					

LONDON
Number	Title (A Side/B Side)	Yr	VG	VG+	NM
❑ LC 50008	Greatest Hits	1977	2.50	5.00	10.00
❑ 820324-1	Greatest Hits	1986	2.00	4.00	8.00

TERRACE, PETE
FANTASY
Number	Title (A Side/B Side)	Yr	VG	VG+	NM
❑ 3203 [M]	Going Loco	195?	6.25	12.50	25.00
❑ 3203 [M]	Going Loco	1956	15.00	30.00	60.00
—Red vinyl					
❑ 3215 [M]	Invitation to the Mambo	195?	6.25	12.50	25.00
❑ 3215 [M]	Invitation to the Mambo	1956	15.00	30.00	60.00
—Red vinyl					
❑ 3234 [M]	The Pete Terrace Quintet	195?	6.25	12.50	25.00
❑ 3234 [M]	The Pete Terrace Quintet	1957	15.00	30.00	60.00
—Red vinyl					

TICO
Number	Title (A Side/B Side)	Yr	VG	VG+	NM
❑ LP-1023 [M]	A Night in Mambo Jazzland	1956	10.00	20.00	40.00
❑ LP-1028 [M]	The Nearness of You	1956	10.00	20.00	40.00
❑ LP-1036 [M]	Cha Cha Cha in New York	1957	10.00	20.00	40.00
❑ LP-1050 [M]	Pete with a Latin Beat	1958	7.50	15.00	30.00
❑ LP-1057 [M]	My One and Only Love	1959	7.50	15.00	30.00
❑ LP-1063 [M]	Cole Porter in Latin America	1959	7.50	15.00	30.00
❑ LP-1082 [M]	Bella Pachanga	1961	6.25	12.50	25.00
❑ SLP-1082 [S]	Bella Pachanga	1961	7.50	15.00	30.00

TERRACE, RAY
TOWER
Number	Title (A Side/B Side)	Yr	VG	VG+	NM
❑ ST-5105	The Home of Boogaloo	1968	5.00	10.00	20.00

TERRELL, TAMMI
MOTOWN
Number	Title (A Side/B Side)	Yr	VG	VG+	NM
❑ M5-231V1	Irresistible Tammi	1982	2.50	5.00	10.00
❑ MS-652	Irresistible Tammi	1969	12.50	25.00	50.00

TERRY, BUDDY
PRESTIGE
Number	Title (A Side/B Side)	Yr	VG	VG+	NM
❑ PRLP-7525 [M]	Electric Soul	1967	7.50	15.00	30.00

Number	Title (A Side/B Side)	Yr	VG	VG+	NM
❏ PRST-7525 [S]	Electric Soul	1967	6.25	12.50	25.00
❏ PRLP-7541 [M]	Natural Soul	1967	7.50	15.00	30.00
❏ PRST-7541 [S]	Natural Soul	1967	6.25	12.50	25.00

TERRY, CLARK
ABC IMPULSE!

Number	Title (A Side/B Side)	Yr	VG	VG+	NM
❏ AS-9157 [S]	It's What's Happenin'	1968	5.00	10.00	20.00

ARGO

❏ LP-620 [M]	Out on a Limb	1957	12.50	25.00	50.00

CAMEO

❏ C-1064 [M]	More	1964	7.50	15.00	30.00
❏ CS-1064 [S]	More	1964	10.00	20.00	40.00
❏ C-1071 [M]	Tread Ye Lightly	1964	7.50	15.00	30.00
❏ CS-1071 [S]	Tread Ye Lightly	1964	10.00	20.00	40.00

CANDID

❏ CD-8009 [M]	Color Changes	1960	12.50	25.00	50.00
❏ CS-9009 [S]	Color Changes	1960	10.00	20.00	40.00

EMARCY

❏ MG-36007 [M]	Clark Terry	1955	20.00	40.00	80.00
❏ MG-36093 [M]	The Jazz School	1956	15.00	30.00	60.00

ETOILE

❏ CPR-1	Clark Terry's Big Bad Band	197?	5.00	10.00	20.00

IMPULSE!

❏ A-64 [M]	The Happy Horn of Clark Terry	1964	6.25	12.50	25.00
❏ AS-64 [S]	The Happy Horn of Clark Terry	1964	7.50	15.00	30.00
❏ A-9127 [M]	Spanish Rice	1966	6.25	12.50	25.00
❏ AS-9127 [S]	Spanish Rice	1966	7.50	15.00	30.00

MAINSTREAM

❏ MRL-803 [(2)]	What'd He Say	197?	5.00	10.00	20.00
❏ S-6043 [S]	Clark Terry Tonight	1965	6.25	12.50	25.00
❏ S-6054 [S]	The Power of Positive Swinging	1965	6.25	12.50	25.00
❏ S-6066 [S]	Mumbles	1966	6.25	12.50	25.00
❏ S-6086	Clark Terry with Bob Brookmeyer	196?	5.00	10.00	20.00
❏ 56043 [M]	Clark Terry Tonight	1965	5.00	10.00	20.00
❏ 56054 [M]	The Power of Positive Swinging	1965	5.00	10.00	20.00
❏ 56066 [M]	Mumbles	1966	5.00	10.00	20.00

MOODSVILLE

❏ MVLP-20 [M]	Everything's Mellow	1961	12.50	25.00	50.00
—Green label					
❏ MVLP-20 [M]	Everything's Mellow	1965	6.25	12.50	25.00
—Blue label, trident logo at right					
❏ MVLP-26 [M]	The Jazz Version of "All American"	1962	12.50	25.00	50.00
—Green label					
❏ MVLP-26 [M]	The Jazz Version of "All American"	1965	6.25	12.50	25.00
—Blue label, trident logo at right					

RIVERSIDE

❏ RLP 12-237 [M]	Serenade to a Bus Seat	1957	12.50	25.00	50.00
—Blue label, microphone logo at top					
❏ RLP 12-237 [M]	Serenade to a Bus Seat	1957	37.50	75.00	150.00
—White label, blue print					
❏ RLP 12-246 [M]	Duke with a Difference	1957	25.00	50.00	100.00
❏ RLP 12-271 [M]	In Orbit	1958	25.00	50.00	100.00
❏ RLP 12-295 [M]	Top and Bottom Brass	1959	25.00	50.00	100.00
❏ RLP-1108 [S]	Duke with a Difference	1959	20.00	40.00	80.00
❏ RLP-1137 [S]	Top and Bottom Brass	1959	20.00	40.00	80.00
❏ RM-3009 [M]	C.T. Meets Monk	1967	6.25	12.50	25.00
❏ RS-3009 [S]	C.T. Meets Monk	1967	5.00	10.00	20.00

20TH CENTURY FOX

❏ TFM-3137 [M]	What Makes Sammy Swing	1963	5.00	10.00	20.00
❏ TFS-4137 [S]	What Makes Sammy Swing	1963	6.25	12.50	25.00

WING

❏ MGW-60002 [M]	The Jazz School	1955	20.00	40.00	80.00

TERRY, CLARK/COLEMAN HAWKINS
COLPIX

❏ CP-450 [M]	Eddie Costa Memorial Concert	1963	10.00	20.00	40.00
❏ SCP-450 [S]	Eddie Costa Memorial Concert	1963	12.50	25.00	50.00

TERRY, DON
COLUMBIA

❏ CL 6288 [10]	Teen-Age Dance Session	1955	12.50	25.00	50.00

TERRY, GORDON
LIBERTY

❏ LRP-3218 [M]	Liberty Square Dance Club	1962	5.00	10.00	20.00
—With calls					
❏ LRP-3219 [M]	Liberty Square Dance Club	1962	5.00	10.00	20.00
—Without calls					

PLANTATION

❏ 514	Disco Country	1977	3.00	6.00	12.00

TERRY, RON
WING

❏ MGW-12108 [M]	Polkas and Waltzes	1959	3.75	7.50	15.00
❏ SRW-16108 [S]	Polkas and Waltzes	1959	5.00	10.00	20.00

TERRY, SONNY
ALLIGATOR

❏ AL-4734	Whoopin'	198?	3.00	6.00	12.00
—With Johnny Winter, Willie Dixon and others					

BLUE LABOR

❏ 101	Robbin' the Grave	197?	3.00	6.00	12.00

BLUESVILLE

❏ BVLP-1025 [M]	Sonny's Story	1961	20.00	40.00	80.00
—Bright blue label, no trident logo					
❏ BVLP-1025 [M]	Sonny's Story	1964	6.25	12.50	25.00
—Blue label with trident logo on right					
❏ BVLP-1069 [M]	Sonny Is King	1963	20.00	40.00	80.00
—Bright blue label, no trident logo					

Number	Title (A Side/B Side)	Yr	VG	VG+	NM
❏ BVLP-1069 [M]	Sonny Is King	1964	6.25	12.50	25.00
—Blue label with trident logo on right					

COLLECTABLES

❏ COL-5195	Chain Gang Blues	198?	2.50	5.00	10.00
❏ COL-5307	Sonny Terry	198?	2.50	5.00	10.00

ELEKTRA

❏ EKL-14 [10]	Folk Blues	1954	37.50	75.00	150.00
❏ EKL-15 [10]	City Blues	1954	37.50	75.00	150.00
—With Alec Stewart					

FANTASY

❏ OBC-521	Sonny Is King	198?	2.50	5.00	10.00

FOLKWAYS

❏ FP-35 [10]	Harmonica and Vocal Solos	1952	37.50	75.00	150.00
❏ FA-2006 [10]	Sonny Terry's Washboard Band	195?	25.00	50.00	100.00
—Black and white cover (reissue)					
❏ FP-2006 [10]	Sonny Terry's Washboard Band	1950	37.50	75.00	150.00
—Blue and white cover					
❏ FA-2035 [10]	Harmonica and Vocal Solos	1952	25.00	50.00	100.00
❏ FS-2369	On the Road	196?	3.75	7.50	15.00
❏ 3821	A New Sound	198?	3.00	6.00	12.00

PRESTIGE

❏ PRST-7802	Sonny Is King	1970	3.75	7.50	15.00

RIVERSIDE

❏ RLP-644 [M]	Sonny Terry and His Mouth Harp	195?	20.00	40.00	80.00

STINSON

❏ 55	Sonny Terry and His Mouth Harp	197?	3.00	6.00	12.00
—Reissue of 10-inch LP					
❏ SLP-55 [10]	Sonny Terry and His Mouth Harp	1950	37.50	75.00	150.00

TERRY, SONNY, AND BROWNIE MCGHEE
A&M

❏ SP-4379	Sonny & Brownie	1973	3.00	6.00	12.00

ARCHIVE OF FOLK MUSIC

❏ 242	Brownie & Sonny	198?	3.00	6.00	12.00

BLUESVILLE

❏ BVLP-1002 [M]	Down Home Blues	1960	20.00	40.00	80.00
—Bright blue label, no trident logo					
❏ BVLP-1002 [M]	Down Home Blues	1964	6.25	12.50	25.00
—Blue label with trident logo on right					
❏ BVLP-1005 [M]	Blues and Folk	1960	20.00	40.00	80.00
—Bright blue label, no trident logo					
❏ BVLP-1005 [M]	Blues and Folk	1964	6.25	12.50	25.00
—Blue label with trident logo on right					
❏ BVLP-1020 [M]	Blues All Around My Head	1961	20.00	40.00	80.00
—Bright blue label, no trident logo					
❏ BVLP-1020 [M]	Blues All Around My Head	1964	6.25	12.50	25.00
—Blue label with trident logo on right					
❏ BVLP-1033 [M]	Blues in My Soul	1961	20.00	40.00	80.00
—Bright blue label, no trident logo					
❏ BVLP-1033 [M]	Blues in My Soul	1964	6.25	12.50	25.00
—Blue label with trident logo on right					
❏ BVLP-1058 [M]	Live at the Second Fret	1962	20.00	40.00	80.00
—Bright blue label, no trident logo					
❏ BVLP-1058 [M]	Live at the Second Fret	1964	6.25	12.50	25.00
—Blue label with trident logo on right					

BLUESWAY

❏ BLS-6028	Long Way from Home	1969	3.75	7.50	15.00
❏ BLS-6059	Couldn't Believe My Eyes	1970	3.75	7.50	15.00

COLLECTABLES

❏ COL-5198	Golden Classics: Blowin' the Fuses	198?	2.50	5.00	10.00

EVEREST

❏ 206	Sonny Terry	1968	6.25	12.50	25.00
❏ 242	Brownie McGhee and Sonny Terry	1969	6.25	12.50	25.00

FANTASY

❏ OBC-503	Sonny's Story	1984	2.50	5.00	10.00
❏ OBC-505	Brownie's Blues	1984	2.50	5.00	10.00
❏ F-3254 [M]	Sonny Terry & Brownie McGhee	1961	10.00	20.00	40.00
—Black vinyl					
❏ F-3254 [M]	Sonny Terry & Brownie McGhee	1961	37.50	75.00	150.00
—Red vinyl					
❏ F-3296 [M]	Just a Closer Walk with Thee	1962	10.00	20.00	40.00
—Black vinyl					
❏ F-3296 [M]	Just a Closer Walk with Thee	1962	37.50	75.00	150.00
—Red vinyl					
❏ F-3317 [M]	Blues and Shouts	1962	10.00	20.00	40.00
—Black vinyl					
❏ F-3317 [M]	Blues and Shouts	1962	37.50	75.00	150.00
—Red vinyl					
❏ F-3340 [M]	Sonny and Brownie at Sugar Hill	1962	10.00	20.00	40.00
—Black vinyl					
❏ F-3340 [M]	Sonny and Brownie at Sugar Hill	1962	37.50	75.00	150.00
—Red vinyl					
❏ FS-8091 [S]	Sonny and Brownie at Sugar Hill	1962	10.00	20.00	40.00
—Black vinyl					
❏ FS-8091 [S]	Sonny and Brownie at Sugar Hill	1962	37.50	75.00	150.00
—Blue vinyl					
❏ 24708 [(2)]	Back to New Orleans	1972	3.75	7.50	15.00
❏ 24721 [(2)]	Midnight Special	1977	3.75	7.50	15.00
❏ 24723 [(2)]	California Blues	1981	3.75	7.50	15.00

FOLKLORE

❏ FRLP-14013 [M]	Down Home Blues	1964	10.00	20.00	40.00
❏ FRST-14013 [S]	Down Home Blues	1964	12.50	25.00	50.00

FOLKWAYS

❏ FA-2327 [M]	Blues and Folk Songs	1960	7.50	15.00	30.00
❏ F-2421 [M]	Traditional Blues, Volume 1	1961	7.50	15.00	30.00
❏ FS-2421 [S]	Traditional Blues, Volume 1	1961	10.00	20.00	40.00
❏ F-2422 [M]	Traditional Blues, Volume 2	1961	7.50	15.00	30.00
❏ FS-2422 [S]	Traditional Blues, Volume 2	1961	10.00	20.00	40.00

Number	Title (A Side/B Side)	Yr	VG	VG+	NM
FONTANA					
❑ SGF-67599	Where the Blues Begin	1969	6.25	12.50	25.00
KIMBERLEY					
❑ 2017 [M]	Southern Meetin'	1963	5.00	10.00	20.00
❑ 11017 [S]	Southern Meetin'	1963	6.25	12.50	25.00
MAINSTREAM					
❑ M-6049 [M]	Hometown Blues	1966	5.00	10.00	20.00
❑ MS-6049 [S]	Hometown Blues	1966	6.25	12.50	25.00
MOBILE FIDELITY					
❑ 1-233	Sonny and Brownie	1996	5.00	10.00	20.00
—Audiophile vinyl					
MUSE					
❑ 5117	Hootin'	198?	3.00	6.00	12.00
❑ 5131	You Hear Me Talkin'	198?	3.00	6.00	12.00
OLYMPIC					
❑ 7108	Hootin' & Hollerin'	1972	3.00	6.00	12.00
PRESTIGE					
❑ PRLP-7715	Best of Sonny Terry and Brownie McGhee	1969	3.75	7.50	15.00
❑ PRLP-7803	Live at the Second Fret	1970	3.75	7.50	15.00
ROULETTE					
❑ R-25074 [M]	The Folk Songs of Sonny & Brownie	1959	12.50	25.00	50.00
❑ RS-25074 [S]	The Folk Songs of Sonny & Brownie	1959	20.00	40.00	80.00
SAVOY					
❑ SJL-1137	Climbin' Up	1984	2.50	5.00	10.00
❑ 12218	Down Home Blues	1973	3.00	6.00	12.00
SHARP					
❑ 2003 [M]	Down Home Blues	195?	37.50	75.00	150.00
SMASH					
❑ MGS-27067 [M]	Brownie McGhee at the Bunkhouse	1965	7.50	15.00	30.00
❑ SRS-67067 [S]	Brownie McGhee at the Bunkhouse	1965	10.00	20.00	40.00
SMITHSONIAN/FOLKWAYS					
❑ SF-40011	Sing	198?	2.50	5.00	10.00
STORYVILLE					
❑ 4007	Brownie & Sonny	1972	3.00	6.00	12.00
TOPIC					
❑ T-29 [M]	Songs	1958	12.50	25.00	50.00
VEE JAY					
❑ VJLP-1138	Coffee House Blues	198?	2.50	5.00	10.00
—With Lightnin' Hopkins					
VERVE					
❑ MGV 3008 [M]	Blues Is My Companion	1961	20.00	40.00	80.00
VERVE FOLKWAYS					
❑ FV 9010 [M]	Get Together	1965	6.25	12.50	25.00
❑ FVS 9010 [S]	Get Together	1965	7.50	15.00	30.00
❑ FV 9019 [M]	Guitar Highway	1965	6.25	12.50	25.00
❑ FVS 9019 [S]	Guitar Highway	1965	7.50	15.00	30.00
WASHINGTON					
❑ W-702 [M]	Talkin' 'Bout the Blues	1961	12.50	25.00	50.00
WORLD PACIFIC					
❑ ST-1294 [S]	Blues Is a Story	1960	20.00	40.00	80.00
❑ WP-1294 [M]	Blues Is a Story	1960	12.50	25.00	50.00
❑ ST-1296 [S]	Down South Summit Meetin'	1960	20.00	40.00	80.00
❑ WP-1296 [M]	Down South Summit Meetin'	1960	12.50	25.00	50.00
TESCHEMACHER, FRANK					
BRUNSWICK					
❑ BL 58017 [10]	Tesch Plays Jazz Classics	1950	20.00	40.00	80.00
TEX, JOE					
ACCORD					
❑ SN-7174	J.T.'s Funk	1982	2.50	5.00	10.00
ATLANTIC					
❑ 8106 [M]	Hold What You've Got	1965	10.00	20.00	40.00
❑ SD 8106 [P]	Hold What You've Got	1965	12.50	25.00	50.00
❑ 8115 [M]	The New Boss	1965	10.00	20.00	40.00
❑ SD 8115 [S]	The New Boss	1965	12.50	25.00	50.00
❑ 8124 [M]	The Love You Save	1966	10.00	20.00	40.00
❑ SD 8124 [S]	The Love You Save	1966	12.50	25.00	50.00
❑ 8133 [M]	I've Got to Do a Little Better	1966	10.00	20.00	40.00
❑ SD 8133 [S]	I've Got to Do a Little Better	1966	12.50	25.00	50.00
❑ 8144 [M]	The Best of Joe Tex	1967	5.00	10.00	20.00
❑ SD 8144 [P]	The Best of Joe Tex	1967	6.25	12.50	25.00
❑ SD 8156	Live and Lively	1968	5.00	10.00	20.00
❑ SD 8187	Soul Country	1968	5.00	10.00	20.00
❑ SD 8211	Happy Soul	1969	5.00	10.00	20.00
❑ SD 8231	Buying a Book	1969	5.00	10.00	20.00
❑ SD 8254	Joe Tex Sings with Strings and Things	1970	3.75	7.50	15.00
❑ SD 8292	From the Roots Came the Rapper	1972	3.75	7.50	15.00
❑ 81278	The Best of Joe Tex	1985	2.50	5.00	10.00
CHECKER					
❑ LP-2993 [M]	Hold On	1965	37.50	75.00	150.00
DIAL					
❑ DL 6002	I Gotcha	1972	3.75	7.50	15.00
❑ DL 6004	Joe Tex Spills the Beans	1973	3.75	7.50	15.00
❑ DL 6100	He Who Is Without Funk Cast the First Stone	1979	2.50	5.00	10.00
EPIC					
❑ PE 34666	Bumps and Bruises	1977	3.00	6.00	12.00
KING					
❑ 935 [M]	The Best of Joe Tex	1965	25.00	50.00	100.00
❑ KS-935 [R]	The Best of Joe Tex	1965	18.75	37.50	75.00
LONDON					
❑ LC-50017	Super Soul	1977	2.50	5.00	10.00
PARROT					
❑ PA 61002 [M]	The Best of Joe Tex	1965	12.50	25.00	50.00
❑ PAS 71002 [R]	The Best of Joe Tex	1965	7.50	15.00	30.00

Number	Title (A Side/B Side)	Yr	VG	VG+	NM
PRIDE					
❑ PRD-0020	The History of Joe Tex	1973	2.50	5.00	10.00
RHINO					
❑ RNLP-70191	I Believe I'm Gonna Make It: The Best of Joe Tex 1964-1972	1988	2.50	5.00	10.00
TEXAS RANGERS, THE					
CUMBERLAND					
❑ MGC-29507 [M]	The Best of Western Swing	1963	5.00	10.00	20.00
❑ SRC-69505 [S]	The Best of Western Swing	1963	6.25	12.50	25.00
TEXAS RUBY					
KING					
❑ 840 [M]	Texas Ruby Sings His Favorite Songs	1963	12.50	25.00	50.00
TEXAS TROUBADOURS, THE					
DECCA					
❑ DL 4459 [M]	The Texas Troubadours	1964	6.25	12.50	25.00
❑ DL 4644 [M]	Country Dance Time	1965	5.00	10.00	20.00
❑ DL 4745 [M]	Ernest Tubb's Fabulous Texas Troubadours	1966	5.00	10.00	20.00
❑ DL 74459 [S]	The Texas Troubadours	1964	7.50	15.00	30.00
❑ DL 74644 [S]	Country Dance Time	1965	6.25	12.50	25.00
❑ DL 74745 [S]	Ernest Tubb's Fabulous Texas Troubadours	1966	6.25	12.50	25.00
❑ DL 75017	The Terrific Texas Troubadours and Guests	1968	5.00	10.00	20.00
THAXTON, LLOYD					
DECCA					
❑ DL 4594 [M]	Lloyd Thaxton Presents	1964	5.00	10.00	20.00
❑ DL 74594 [S]	Lloyd Thaxton Presents	1964	6.25	12.50	25.00
THEE MIDNITERS					
CHATTAHOOCHIE					
❑ C-1001 [M]	Thee Midniters	1965	15.00	30.00	60.00
❑ CS-1001 [S]	Thee Midniters	1965	20.00	40.00	80.00
WHITTIER					
❑ W-5000 [M]	Bring You Love Special Delivery	1966	10.00	20.00	40.00
❑ WS-5000 [S]	Bring You Love Special Delivery	1966	12.50	25.00	50.00
❑ W-5001 [M]	Unlimited	1966	10.00	20.00	40.00
❑ WS-5001 [S]	Unlimited	1966	12.50	25.00	50.00
❑ W-5002 [M]	Giants	1967	10.00	20.00	40.00
❑ WS-5002 [S]	Giants	1967	12.50	25.00	50.00
ZYANYA/RHINO					
❑ RNLP-063	The Best of Thee Midniters	1983	3.00	6.00	12.00
THEE MUFFINS					
(NO LABEL)					
❑ (no #)	Thee Muffins Pop Up!	1967	50.00	100.00	200.00
THEE PROPHETS					
KAPP					
❑ KS-3596	Playgirl	1969	5.00	10.00	20.00
THEM					
Also see VAN MORRISON.					
HAPPY TIGER					
❑ HT-1004	Them	1969	12.50	25.00	50.00
❑ HT-1012	Them In Reality	1971	30.00	60.00	120.00
LONDON					
❑ PS 639 [P]	Backtrackin'	1974	2.50	5.00	10.00
❑ LC-50001 [R]	The Story of Them	1977	2.50	5.00	10.00
❑ 820326-1	Them Featuring Van Morrison	1985	2.50	5.00	10.00
PARROT					
❑ PA 61005 [M]	Them Featuring "Here Comes the Night"	1965	20.00	40.00	80.00
❑ PA 61005 [M]	Them Featuring "Gloria"	1966	12.50	25.00	50.00
—Same album as above, but with slightly different title					
❑ PA 61008 [M]	Them Again	1966	20.00	40.00	80.00
❑ PAS 71005 [R]	Them Featuring "Here Comes the Night"	1965	17.50	35.00	70.00
❑ PAS 71005 [R]	Them Featuring "Gloria"	1966	10.00	20.00	40.00
—Same album as above, but with slightly different title					
❑ PAS 71008 [R]	Them Again	1966	12.50	25.00	50.00
❑ BP 71053 [(2)P]	Them Featuring Van Morrison	1972	3.00	6.00	12.00
—"Gloria," "Here Comes the Night," "If You and I Could Be as Two," "One More Time" and "One Two Brown Eyes" are true stereo.					
TOWER					
❑ ST 5104 [S]	Now and Them	1967	20.00	40.00	80.00
❑ T 5104 [M]	Now and Them	1967	12.50	25.00	50.00
❑ ST 5116 [S]	Time Out! Time In for Them	1968	25.00	50.00	100.00
THEODORE					
CORAL					
❑ CRL 757322 [S]	Coral Records Presents Theodore in Stereo	1959	25.00	50.00	100.00
THESE TRAILS					
SINERGIA					
❑ (# unknown)	These Trails	1973	30.00	60.00	120.00
THESELIUS, GOSTA					
BALLY					
❑ BAL-12002 [M]	Swedish Jazz	1956	12.50	25.00	50.00
THIELEMANS, TOOTS					
ABC-PARAMOUNT					
❑ ABC-482 [M]	The Whistler and His Guitar	1965	6.25	12.50	25.00
❑ ABCS-482 [S]	The Whistler and His Guitar	1965	7.50	15.00	30.00
COLUMBIA					
❑ CL 658 [M]	The Sound	1955	12.50	25.00	50.00
COMMAND					
❑ RS 33-906 [M]	Contrasts	1967	5.00	10.00	20.00
❑ RS 33-918 [S]	Guitars and Strings… And Things	1967	5.00	10.00	20.00
DECCA					
❑ DL 9204 [M]	Time Out for Toots	1958	12.50	25.00	50.00
❑ DL 79204 [S]	Time Out for Toots	1958	10.00	20.00	40.00

Number	Title (A Side/B Side)	Yr	VG	VG+	NM
RIVERSIDE					
❏ RLP 12-257 [M]	Man Bites Harmonica	1958	25.00	50.00	100.00
SIGNATURE					
❏ SM-6006 [M]	The Soul of Toots Thielmans	1960	20.00	40.00	80.00
❏ SS-6006 [S]	The Soul of Toots Thielmans	1960	15.00	30.00	60.00
THIGPEN, ED					
VERVE					
❏ V-8663 [M]	Out of the Storm	1966	5.00	10.00	20.00
❏ V6-8663 [S]	Out of the Storm	1966	6.25	12.50	25.00
THIN LIZZY					
LONDON					
❏ PS 594	Thin Lizzy	1971	10.00	20.00	40.00
❏ PS 636	Vagabonds of the Western World	1973	7.50	15.00	30.00
❏ LC-50004	The Rocker (1971-1974)	1977	3.00	6.00	12.00
MERCURY					
❏ SRM-1-1081	Jailbreak	1976	3.00	6.00	12.00
❏ SRM-1-1107	Night Life	1976	3.00	6.00	12.00
—Reissue of Vertigo 2002					
❏ SRM-1-1108	Fighting	1976	3.00	6.00	12.00
—Reissue of Vertigo 2005					
❏ SRM-1-1119	Johnny the Fox	1976	3.00	6.00	12.00
❏ SRM-1-1186	Bad Reputation	1977	3.00	6.00	12.00
VERTIGO					
❏ VEL-2002	Night Life	1974	3.75	7.50	15.00
❏ VEL-2005	Fighting	1975	3.75	7.50	15.00
WARNER BROS.					
❏ BS2 3213 [(2)]	Live and Dangerous	1978	3.00	6.00	12.00
❏ BSK 3338	Black Rose/A Rock Legend	1979	2.50	5.00	10.00
❏ BSK 3496	Chinatown	1980	2.50	5.00	10.00
❏ BSK 3622	Renegade	1982	2.50	5.00	10.00
❏ 23831	Thunder and Lightning	1983	2.50	5.00	10.00
❏ 23986 [(2)]	"Life" — Live	1984	3.00	6.00	12.00
THIRD ESTATE, THE					
THIRD ESTATE					
❏ LP-1000	Years Before the Wine	1976	50.00	100.00	200.00
THIRD POWER					
VANGUARD					
❏ VSD-6554	Believe	1970	7.50	15.00	30.00
THIRD RAIL, THE					
EPIC					
❏ LN 24327 [M]	Id Music	1967	7.50	15.00	30.00
❏ BN 26327 [S]	Id Music	1967	10.00	20.00	40.00
THIRTEENTH FLOOR ELEVATORS, THE					
INTERNATIONAL ARTISTS					
❏ 1 [M]	Psychedelic Sounds	1967	62.50	125.00	250.00
—Green and yellow label					
❏ 1 [M]	Psychedelic Sounds	1968	37.50	75.00	150.00
—All-yellow label					
❏ 1 [S]	Psychedelic Sounds	1968	37.50	75.00	150.00
—All-yellow label					
❏ 1 [S]	Psychedelic Sounds	1968	50.00	100.00	200.00
—Aqua-blue label					
❏ 1 [S]	Psychedelic Sounds	1979	7.50	15.00	30.00
—Repressing with "Masterfonics" in dead wax					
❏ 5 [M]	Easter Everywhere	1968	100.00	200.00	400.00
—Mono is promo only					
❏ 5 [S]	Easter Everywhere	1968	37.50	75.00	150.00
—With custom inner sleeve					
❏ 5 [S]	Easter Everywhere	1968	37.50	75.00	150.00
—Without custom inner sleeve					
❏ 5 [S]	Easter Everywhere	1979	7.50	15.00	30.00
—Repressing with "Masterfonics" in dead wax					
❏ 8	13th Floor Elevators Live	1968	25.00	50.00	100.00
❏ 8	13th Floor Elevators Live	1979	6.25	12.50	25.00
—Repressing with "Masterfonics" in dead wax					
❏ 9	Bull of the Woods	1968	20.00	40.00	80.00
❏ 9	Bull of the Woods	1979	6.25	12.50	25.00
—Repressing with "Masterfonics" in dead wax					
31ST OF FEBRUARY, THE					
VANGUARD					
❏ VSD-6503	The 31st of February	1969	10.00	20.00	40.00
31 FLAVORS, THE					
CROWN					
❏ CST-592	Hair	1968	12.50	25.00	50.00
THOMAS, B.J.					
ABC					
❏ ABDP-858	Reunion	1975	2.50	5.00	10.00
❏ ABCD-912	Help Me Make It to My Rockin' Chair	1976	2.50	5.00	10.00
ACCORD					
❏ SN-7106	Lovin' You	198?	2.50	5.00	10.00
BUCKBOARD					
❏ 1023	B.J. Thomas Sings Hank Williams and Other Favorites	198?	2.50	5.00	10.00
CLEVELAND INT'L.					
❏ FC 38561	New Looks	1983	2.50	5.00	10.00
❏ PC 38561	New Looks	1984	2.00	4.00	8.00
—Budget-line reissue					
❏ FC 39111	The Great American Dream	1983	2.50	5.00	10.00
❏ PC 39111	The Great American Dream	1984	2.00	4.00	8.00
—Budget-line reissue					
❏ FC 39337	Shining	1984	2.50	5.00	10.00
❏ FC 40157	Throwing Rocks at the Moon	1985	2.50	5.00	10.00

Number	Title (A Side/B Side)	Yr	VG	VG+	NM
COLUMBIA					
❏ PC 38400	Love Shines	1984	2.00	4.00	8.00
—Reissue of Priority 38400					
❏ PC 40148	All Is Calm, All Is Bright...	1985	2.50	5.00	10.00
❏ FC 40496	Night Life	1986	2.50	5.00	10.00
DORAL					
❏ (# unknown)	Doral Presents B.J. Thomas	1971	5.00	10.00	20.00
—Mail-order promotion from Doral cigarettes					
EVEREST					
❏ 4104	Golden Greats	1981	2.50	5.00	10.00
HICKORY					
❏ LPM-133 [M]	The Very Best of B.J. Thomas	1966	5.00	10.00	20.00
❏ LPS-133 [S]	The Very Best of B.J. Thomas	1966	6.25	12.50	25.00
❏ ST 90956 [S]	The Very Best of B.J. Thomas	1966	7.50	15.00	30.00
—Capitol Record Club edition					
❏ T 90956 [M]	The Very Best of B.J. Thomas	1966	6.25	12.50	25.00
—Capitol Record Club edition					
MCA					
❏ 746	Everybody Loves a Rain Song	1980	2.00	4.00	8.00
—Budget-line reissue					
❏ 2286	B.J. Thomas	1977	2.50	5.00	10.00
❏ 3035	Everybody Loves a Rain Song	1978	2.50	5.00	10.00
❏ 3231	For the Best	1979	2.50	5.00	10.00
❏ 5155	In Concert	1980	2.50	5.00	10.00
❏ 5195	Some Love Songs Never Die	1980	2.50	5.00	10.00
❏ 5296	As We Know Him	1982	2.50	5.00	10.00
❏ 27032	In Concert	198?	2.00	4.00	8.00
—Reissue of MCA 5155					
MYRRH					
❏ MSB-6574	Home Where I Belong	1978	2.50	5.00	10.00
❏ MSB-6593	A Happy Man	1979	2.50	5.00	10.00
❏ MSB-6633	You Gave Me Love	1979	2.50	5.00	10.00
❏ MSB-6653	The Best of B.J. Thomas	1980	2.50	5.00	10.00
❏ MSB-6675	Amazing Grace	1981	2.50	5.00	10.00
❏ MSB-6705	Miracle	1983	2.50	5.00	10.00
❏ MSB-6710	Peace in the Valley	1983	2.50	5.00	10.00
❏ MSB-6725	The Best of B.J. Thomas, Volume 2	1984	2.50	5.00	10.00
❏ WR-8153	Peace in the Valley	1985	2.50	5.00	10.00
—Reissue of 6710					
❏ WR-8200	Amazing Grace	1985	2.00	4.00	8.00
—Reissue of 6675					
PACEMAKER					
❏ PLP-3001 [M]	B.J. Thomas and the Triumphs	1965	50.00	100.00	200.00
PAIR					
❏ PDL2-1099 [(2)]	Greatest Hits	1986	3.00	6.00	12.00
PARAMOUNT					
❏ PAS 1020	Longhorns & Londonbridges	1974	3.00	6.00	12.00
❏ PAS-6052	B.J. Thomas Songs	1973	3.00	6.00	12.00
PICKWICK					
❏ SPC-3623	The Best of B.J. Thomas	197?	2.50	5.00	10.00
PRIORITY					
❏ JU 38400	Love Shines	1982	2.50	5.00	10.00
REPRISE					
❏ 25898	Midnight Minute	1989	3.00	6.00	12.00
SCEPTER					
❏ SPS-535 [S]	I'm So Lonesome I Could Cry	1966	6.25	12.50	25.00
❏ SRM-535 [M]	I'm So Lonesome I Could Cry	1966	5.00	10.00	20.00
❏ SPS-556 [S]	Tomorrow Never Comes	1966	5.00	10.00	20.00
❏ SRM-556 [M]	Tomorrow Never Comes	1966	3.75	7.50	15.00
❏ SPS-561 [S]	For Lovers and Losers	1967	3.75	7.50	15.00
❏ SRM-561 [M]	For Lovers and Losers	1967	5.00	10.00	20.00
❏ SPS-570 [S]	On My Way	1968	3.75	7.50	15.00
❏ SRM-570 [M]	On My Way	1968	7.50	15.00	30.00
—Mono appears to be white label promo only; in stereo cover with "Promotional DJ Copy Monaural Not for Sale" sticker on front					
❏ SPS-576	Young and In Love	1969	3.75	7.50	15.00
❏ SPS-578	Greatest Hits, Volume 1	1969	3.00	6.00	12.00
❏ SPS-580	Raindrops Keep Fallin' on My Head	1970	3.00	6.00	12.00
—Remixed version; trail-off wax number on Side 1 is "SPS-580-A-1C" or "SPS-580-A-1D" and on Side 2 is "SPS-580-B-1C"					
❏ SPS-580	Raindrops Keep Fallin' on My Head	1970	3.75	7.50	15.00
—Original "muddy mix"; trail-off wax number on Side 1 is "SPS-580-A-1B" and on Side 2 is "SPS-580-B-1A"					
❏ SPS-582	Everybody's Out of Town	1970	3.00	6.00	12.00
❏ SPS-586	Most of All	1970	3.00	6.00	12.00
❏ SPS-597	Greatest Hits, Volume Two	1971	3.00	6.00	12.00
❏ 5101	Billy Joe Thomas	1972	3.00	6.00	12.00
❏ 5108	B.J. Thomas Country	1972	3.00	6.00	12.00
❏ 5112 [(2)]	Greatest All-Time Hits	1973	3.75	7.50	15.00
STARDAY					
❏ 992	The Best of B.J. Thomas	197?	2.50	5.00	10.00
UNITED ARTISTS					
❏ UA-LA389-E	The Very Best of B.J. Thomas	1974	3.00	6.00	12.00
THOMAS, CARLA					
Also see OTIS AND CARLA; RUFUS AND CARLA.					
ATLANTIC					
❏ 8057 [M]	Gee Whiz	1961	25.00	50.00	100.00
—With white "fan" logo					
❏ 8057 [M]	Gee Whiz	1963	10.00	20.00	40.00
—With black "fan" logo					
❏ SD 8057 [S]	Gee Whiz	1961	37.50	75.00	150.00
—With white "fan" logo					
❏ SD 8057 [S]	Gee Whiz	1963	12.50	25.00	50.00
—With black "fan" logo					
❏ SD 8232	The Best of Carla Thomas	1969	6.25	12.50	25.00
STAX					
❏ 706 [M]	Comfort Me	1966	8.75	17.50	35.00
❏ 706 [P]	Comfort Me	1966	12.50	25.00	50.00

Number	Title (A Side/B Side)	Yr	VG	VG+	NM
❑ 709 [M]	Carla	1966	8.75	17.50	35.00
❑ 709 [S]	Carla	1966	12.50	25.00	50.00
❑ 718 [M]	The Queen Alone	1967	8.75	17.50	35.00
❑ 718 [S]	The Queen Alone	1967	12.50	25.00	50.00
❑ STS-2019	Memphis Queen	1969	8.75	17.50	35.00
❑ STS-2044	Love Means Carla Thomas	1971	8.75	17.50	35.00
❑ MPS-8538	Memphis Queen	1987	2.50	5.00	10.00

—Budget-line reissue

THOMAS, CARLA, AND RUFUS THOMAS
See RUFUS AND CARLA.

THOMAS, DANNY
MGM
| ❑ E-201 [10] | An Evening with Danny Thomas | 1954 | 25.00 | 50.00 | 100.00 |

THOMAS, DYLAN
CAEDMON
| ❑ TC 1002 [M] | A Child's Christmas in Wales and Five Poems (Dylan Thomas, Volume 1) | 1957 | 5.00 | 10.00 | 20.00 |

—Number stamped into dead wax; "New York, 1, New York" address on label and cover

THOMAS, IRMA
BANDY
| ❑ 70003 | Irma Thomas Sings | 197? | 7.50 | 15.00 | 30.00 |
FUNGUS
| ❑ FB-25150 | In Between Tears | 1973 | 10.00 | 20.00 | 40.00 |
IMPERIAL
❑ LP-9266 [M]	Wish Someone Would Care	1964	12.50	25.00	50.00
❑ LP-9302 [M]	Take a Look	1966	12.50	25.00	50.00
❑ LP-12266 [S]	Wish Someone Would Care	1964	15.00	30.00	60.00
❑ LP-12302 [S]	Take a Look	1966	15.00	30.00	60.00
RCS
| ❑ 1004 | Safe with Me | 1980 | 7.50 | 15.00 | 30.00 |

THOMAS, JEANNIE
STRAND
| ❑ SL-1030 [M] | Jeannie Thomas Sings for the Boys | 1961 | 10.00 | 20.00 | 40.00 |
| ❑ SLS-1030 [S] | Jeannie Thomas Sings for the Boys | 1961 | 12.50 | 25.00 | 50.00 |

THOMAS, JOE, AND BILL ELLIOTT
SUE
| ❑ LP-1025 [M] | Speak Your Piece | 1964 | 12.50 | 25.00 | 50.00 |

THOMAS, JON
ABC-PARAMOUNT
| ❑ 351 [M] | Heartbreak | 1960 | 7.50 | 15.00 | 30.00 |
| ❑ S-351 [S] | Heartbreak | 1960 | 10.00 | 20.00 | 40.00 |
WING
| ❑ MGW-12258 [M] | The Big Beat on the Organ | 1963 | 5.00 | 10.00 | 20.00 |
| ❑ SRW-16258 [R] | The Big Beat on the Organ | 1963 | 3.00 | 6.00 | 12.00 |

THOMAS, LEON
FLYING DUTCHMAN
| ❑ FD-10115 | Spirits Known and Unknown | 1969 | 5.00 | 10.00 | 20.00 |
| ❑ FD-10132 | The Leon Thomas Album | 197? | 5.00 | 10.00 | 20.00 |
MEGA
| ❑ M51-5003 | Gold Sunrise on Magic Mountain | 197? | 5.00 | 10.00 | 20.00 |

THOMAS, PAT
MGM
❑ E-4103 [M]	Desafinado	1962	3.75	7.50	15.00
❑ SE-4103 [S]	Desafinado	1962	5.00	10.00	20.00
❑ E-4206 [M]	Moody's Mood	1964	3.75	7.50	15.00
❑ SE-4206 [S]	Moody's Mood	1964	5.00	10.00	20.00
STRAND
| ❑ SL-1015 [M] | Jazz Patterns | 1961 | 10.00 | 20.00 | 40.00 |
| ❑ SLS-1015 [S] | Jazz Patterns | 1961 | 12.50 | 25.00 | 50.00 |

THOMAS, RAY
Also see THE MOODY BLUES.
THRESHOLD
❑ THS 16	From Mighty Oaks	1975	3.75	7.50	15.00
❑ THS 17	Hopes Wishes & Dreams	1976	3.75	7.50	15.00
❑ THSX-102 [DJ]	Ray Thomas Discusses The Recording of His First Solo Album From Mighty Oaks	1975	12.50	25.00	50.00

THOMAS, RENE
JAZZLAND
| ❑ JLP-27 [M] | Guitar Groove | 1960 | 7.50 | 15.00 | 30.00 |
| ❑ JLP-927 [S] | Guitar Groove | 1960 | 10.00 | 20.00 | 40.00 |

THOMAS, RUFUS
A.V.I.
| ❑ 6015 | If There Were No Music | 1977 | 3.75 | 7.50 | 15.00 |
| ❑ 6046 | I Ain't Gettin' Older, I'm Gettin' Better | 1978 | 3.75 | 7.50 | 15.00 |
ALLIGATOR
| ❑ AV-4769 | That Woman Is Poison | 1988 | 2.50 | 5.00 | 10.00 |
GUSTO
| ❑ 0064 | Rufus Thomas | 1980 | 2.50 | 5.00 | 10.00 |
STAX
❑ ST-704 [M]	Walking the Dog	1963	37.50	75.00	150.00
❑ STS-2028	Do the Funky Chicken	1970	6.25	12.50	25.00
❑ STS-2039	Rufus Thomas Live/Doing the Push and Pull at P.J.'s	1971	6.25	12.50	25.00
❑ STS-3004	Did You Hear Me	1972	6.25	12.50	25.00
❑ STS-3008	Crown Prince of Dance	1973	6.25	12.50	25.00

THOMPSON, BOB
RAINBOW
| ❑ 2010 | 7 In, 7 Out | 1986 | 5.00 | 10.00 | 20.00 |

THOMPSON, CHESTER
BLACK JAZZ
| ❑ 6 | Powerhouse | 197? | 6.25 | 12.50 | 25.00 |

THOMPSON, HANK
ABC
| ❑ AB-1095 | Brand New Hank | 1978 | 3.00 | 6.00 | 12.00 |
ABC DOT
❑ DOSD-2003	Moving On	1974	3.00	6.00	12.00
❑ DOSD-2032	Hank Thompson Sings Nat King Cole	1975	3.00	6.00	12.00
❑ DOSD-2060	Back in the Swing of Things	1976	3.00	6.00	12.00
❑ DOSD-2069	The Thompson Touch	1977	3.00	6.00	12.00
❑ DO-2091	Doin' My Thing	1977	3.00	6.00	12.00
CAPITOL
❑ H 418 [10]	Songs of the Brazos Valley	1953	30.00	60.00	120.00
❑ T 418 [M]	Songs of the Brazos Valley	1956	20.00	40.00	80.00
—Turquoise or gray label					
❑ T 418 [M]	Songs of the Brazos Valley	1959	7.50	15.00	30.00
—Black colorband label, logo at left					
❑ T 418 [M]	Songs of the Brazos Valley	1962	5.00	10.00	20.00
—Black colorband label, logo at top					
❑ H 618 [10]	North of the Rio Grande	1953	30.00	60.00	120.00
❑ T 618 [M]	North of the Rio Grande	1956	20.00	40.00	80.00
—Turquoise or gray label					
❑ H 729 [10]	New Recordings of Hank's All-Time Hits	195?	30.00	60.00	120.00
❑ T 729 [M]	New Recordings of Hank's All-Time Hits	1956	20.00	40.00	80.00
—Turquoise or gray label					
❑ T 729 [M]	New Recordings of Hank's All-Time Hits	1959	7.50	15.00	30.00
—Black colorband label, logo at left					
❑ T 729 [M]	New Recordings of Hank's All-Time Hits	1962	5.00	10.00	20.00
—Black colorband label, logo at top					
❑ T 826 [M]	Hank!	1957	20.00	40.00	80.00
—Turquoise or gray label					
❑ T 826 [M]	Hank!	1959	7.50	15.00	30.00
—Black colorband label, logo at left					
❑ T 826 [M]	Hank!	1962	5.00	10.00	20.00
—Black colorband label, logo at top					
❑ T 911 [M]	Hank Thompson Favorites	1957	20.00	40.00	80.00
—Turquoise or gray label					
❑ T 975 [M]	Hank Thompson's Dance Ranch	1958	20.00	40.00	80.00
—Turquoise or gray label					
❑ T 975 [M]	Hank Thompson's Dance Ranch	1959	7.50	15.00	30.00
—Black colorband label, logo at left					
❑ T 975 [M]	Hank Thompson's Dance Ranch	1962	5.00	10.00	20.00
—Black colorband label, logo at top					
❑ T 1111 [M]	Favorite Waltzes	1959	20.00	40.00	80.00
—Black colorband label, logo at left					
❑ T 1111 [M]	Favorite Waltzes	1962	5.00	10.00	20.00
—Black colorband label, logo at top					
❑ ST 1246 [S]	Songs for Rounders	1959	10.00	20.00	40.00
❑ T 1246 [M]	Songs for Rounders	1959	7.50	15.00	30.00
❑ ST 1360 [S]	Most of All	1960	10.00	20.00	40.00
—Black colorband label, logo at left					
❑ ST 1360 [S]	Most of All	1962	6.25	12.50	25.00
—Black colorband label, logo at top					
❑ T 1360 [M]	Most of All	1960	7.50	15.00	30.00
—Black colorband label, logo at left					
❑ T 1360 [M]	Most of All	1962	5.00	10.00	20.00
—Black colorband label, logo at top					
❑ ST 1469 [S]	This Broken Heart of Mine	1960	10.00	20.00	40.00
—Black colorband label, logo at left					
❑ ST 1469 [S]	This Broken Heart of Mine	1962	6.25	12.50	25.00
—Black colorband label, logo at top					
❑ T 1469 [M]	This Broken Heart of Mine	1960	7.50	15.00	30.00
—Black colorband label, logo at left					
❑ T 1469 [M]	This Broken Heart of Mine	1962	5.00	10.00	20.00
—Black colorband label, logo at top					
❑ ST 1544 [S]	An Old Love Affair	1961	7.50	15.00	30.00
—Black colorband label, logo at top					
❑ ST 1544 [S]	An Old Love Affair	1962	5.00	10.00	20.00
—Black colorband label, logo at top					
❑ T 1544 [M]	An Old Love Affair	1961	6.25	12.50	25.00
—Black colorband label, logo at left					
❑ T 1544 [M]	An Old Love Affair	1962	3.75	7.50	15.00
—Black colorband label, logo at top					
❑ ST 1632 [S]	Hank Thompson at the Golden Nugget	1961	7.50	15.00	30.00
—Black colorband label, logo at left					
❑ ST 1632 [S]	Hank Thompson at the Golden Nugget	1962	5.00	10.00	20.00
—Black colorband label, logo at top					
❑ T 1632 [M]	Hank Thompson at the Golden Nugget	1961	6.25	12.50	25.00
—Black colorband label, logo at left					
❑ T 1632 [M]	Hank Thompson at the Golden Nugget	1962	3.75	7.50	15.00
—Black colorband label, logo at top					
❑ DT 1741 [R]	The #1 Country and Western Band	1962	3.00	6.00	12.00
—Black colorband label, logo at top					
❑ DT 1741 [R]	The #1 Country and Western Band	1962	5.00	10.00	20.00
—Black colorband label, logo at left					
❑ T 1741 [M]	The #1 Country and Western Band	1962	5.00	10.00	20.00
—Black colorband label, logo at top					
❑ T 1741 [M]	The #1 Country and Western Band	1962	7.50	15.00	30.00
—Black colorband label, logo at left					
❑ ST 1775 [S]	Cheyenne Frontier Days	1962	6.25	12.50	25.00
❑ T 1775 [M]	Cheyenne Frontier Days	1962	5.00	10.00	20.00
❑ ST 1878 [S]	The Best of Hank Thompson	1963	6.25	12.50	25.00
❑ T 1878 [M]	The Best of Hank Thompson	1963	5.00	10.00	20.00
❑ ST 1955 [S]	Hank Thompson at the State Fair of Texas	1963	6.25	12.50	25.00
❑ T 1955 [M]	Hank Thompson at the State Fair of Texas	1963	5.00	10.00	20.00
❑ ST 2089 [S]	Golden Country Hits	1964	6.25	12.50	25.00
❑ T 2089 [M]	Golden Country Hits	1964	5.00	10.00	20.00
❑ ST 2154 [S]	It's Christmas Time	1963	6.25	12.50	25.00
❑ T 2154 [M]	It's Christmas Time	1963	5.00	10.00	20.00
❑ ST 2274 [S]	Breakin' In Another Heart	1965	6.25	12.50	25.00
❑ T 2274 [M]	Breakin' In Another Heart	1965	5.00	10.00	20.00

Number	Title (A Side/B Side)	Yr	VG	VG+	NM
❏ ST 2342 [S]	Luckiest Heartache in Town	1965	6.25	12.50	25.00
❏ T 2342 [M]	Luckiest Heartache in Town	1965	5.00	10.00	20.00
❏ ST 2460 [S]	A Six Pack to Go	1966	6.25	12.50	25.00
❏ T 2460 [M]	A Six Pack to Go	1966	5.00	10.00	20.00
❏ ST 2575 [S]	Breakin' the Rules	1966	6.25	12.50	25.00
❏ T 2575 [M]	Breakin' the Rules	1966	5.00	10.00	20.00
❏ ST 2661 [S]	The Best of Hank Thompson Vol. 2	1967	5.00	10.00	20.00
❏ T 2661 [M]	The Best of Hank Thompson Vol. 2	1967	6.25	12.50	25.00
❏ ST 2826 [S]	Just an Old Flame	1967	5.00	10.00	20.00
❏ T 2826 [M]	Just an Old Flame	1967	6.25	12.50	25.00

DOT

❏ DOS 2-2000 [(2)]	Hank Thompson's 25th Anniversary Album	1971	5.00	10.00	20.00
❏ DLP-25864	Hank Thompson Sings the Gold Standards	1968	3.75	7.50	15.00
❏ DLP-25894	On Tap, In the Can, or In the Bottle	1968	3.75	7.50	15.00
❏ DLP-25932	Smoky the Bar	1969	3.75	7.50	15.00
❏ DLP-25971	Hank Thompson Salutes Oklahoma	1969	3.75	7.50	15.00
❏ DLP-25991	Next Time I Fall in Love (I Won't)	1971	3.75	7.50	15.00
❏ DOS-25996	Cab Driver (A Salute to the Mills Brothers)	1972	3.75	7.50	15.00
❏ DOS-26004	Hank Thompson's Greatest Hits Vol. 1	1972	3.75	7.50	15.00
❏ DOS-26015	Kindly Keep It Country	1973	3.75	7.50	15.00

MCA

❏ 689	Brand New Hank	198?	2.00	4.00	8.00
❏ 3250	Take Me Back to Tulsa	1980	2.50	5.00	10.00

WARNER BROS.

❏ W 1664 [M]	Where Is the Circus and Other Heart Breakin' Hits	1966	3.75	7.50	15.00
❏ WS 1664 [S]	Where Is the Circus and Other Heart Breakin' Hits	1966	5.00	10.00	20.00
❏ W 1679 [M]	The Countrypolitan Sound of Hank Thompson	1967	3.75	7.50	15.00
❏ WS 1679 [S]	The Countrypolitan Sound of Hank Thompson	1967	5.00	10.00	20.00
❏ W 1686 [M]	The Gold Standard Collection of Hank Thompson	1967	3.75	7.50	15.00
❏ WS 1686 [S]	The Gold Standard Collection of Hank Thompson	1967	5.00	10.00	20.00

THOMPSON, HAYDEN
KAPP

❏ KL-1507 [M]	Here's Hayden Thompson	1966	7.50	15.00	30.00
❏ KS-3507 [S]	Here's Hayden Thompson	1966	10.00	20.00	40.00

THOMPSON, KAY
MGM

❏ E-3146 [M]	Kay Thompson Sings	1955	7.50	15.00	30.00

SIGNATURE

❏ SM-1017 [M]	Let's Talk About Russia	1959	6.25	12.50	25.00

THOMPSON, LES
RCA VICTOR

❏ LPT-3102 [10]	Gene Norman Presents "Just Jazz"	1952	37.50	75.00	150.00

THOMPSON, LUCKY
ABC-PARAMOUNT

❏ ABC-111 [M]	Lucky Thompson Featuring Oscar Pettiford, Volume 1	1956	20.00	40.00	80.00
❏ ABC-171 [M]	Lucky Thompson Featuring Oscar Pettiford, Volume 2	1957	20.00	40.00	80.00

DAWN

❏ DLP-1113 [M]	Lucky Thompson	1957	20.00	40.00	80.00

GROOVE MERCHANT

❏ 4411 [(2)]	Illuminations	197?	5.00	10.00	20.00

LONDON

❏ D-93098 [10]	Recorded in Paris '56	1956	20.00	40.00	80.00

MOODSVILLE

❏ MVLP-39 [M]	Lucky Thompson Plays Jerome Kern and No More	1963	10.00	20.00	40.00
—Green label					
❏ MVLP-39 [M]	Lucky Thompson Plays Jerome Kern and No More	1965	5.00	10.00	20.00
—Blue label, trident logo at right					
❏ MVST-39 [S]	Lucky Thompson Plays Jerome Kern and No More	1963	12.50	25.00	50.00
—Green label					
❏ MVST-39 [S]	Lucky Thompson Plays Jerome Kern and No More	1965	6.25	12.50	25.00
—Blue label, trident logo at right					

PRESTIGE

❏ PRLP-7365 [M]	Lucky Strikes	1965	6.25	12.50	25.00
❏ PRST-7365 [S]	Lucky Strikes	1965	7.50	15.00	30.00
❏ PRLP-7394 [M]	Happy Days Are Here Again	1965	6.25	12.50	25.00
❏ PRST-7394 [S]	Happy Days Are Here Again	1965	7.50	15.00	30.00

RIVOLI

❏ 40 [M]	Lucky Is Back!	1965	6.25	12.50	25.00
❏ S-40 [S]	Lucky Is Back!	1965	7.50	15.00	30.00
❏ 44 [M]	Kinfolk's Corner	1965	6.25	12.50	25.00
❏ S-44 [S]	Kinfolk's Corner	1965	7.50	15.00	30.00

TOPS

❏ L-928 [10]	Jazz at the Auditorium	1954	30.00	60.00	120.00

TRANSITION

❏ TRLP-21 [M]	Lucky Strikes	1956	62.50	125.00	250.00
—With booklet (deduct 1/5 if missing)					

URANIA

❏ UJLP-1206 [M]	Accent on Tenor	1955	25.00	50.00	100.00

THOMPSON, MAYO
TEXAS REVOLUTION

❏ 2270	Corky's Debt to His Father	1969	20.00	40.00	80.00

THOMPSON, RICHARD
Also see FAIRPORT CONVENTION; RICHARD AND LINDA THOMPSON.
BONG LOAD

❏ BL 44 [(2)]	Mock Tudor	1999	3.75	7.50	15.00

Number	Title (A Side/B Side)	Yr	VG	VG+	NM
❏ BL 52 [(2)]	Action Packed	2001	3.75	7.50	15.00
—1,000 copies pressed on "Coke-bottle green" vinyl					

CAPITOL

❏ C1-48845	Amnesia	1988	2.00	4.00	8.00
❏ C1-95713	Rumor & Sigh	1991	3.00	6.00	12.00

CARTHAGE

❏ CGLP-4405	Henry the Human Fly	1983	2.00	4.00	8.00
—Reissue of Reprise LP					
❏ CGLP-4409	Strict Tempo	1983	2.00	4.00	8.00
❏ CGLP-4413 [(2)]	Richard Thompson (Guitar/Vocal)	1983	2.50	5.00	10.00
—Reissue of Island 9421 with original UK title					

HANNIBAL

❏ HNLP-1313	Heart of Kindness	1983	2.50	5.00	10.00
❏ HNLP-1316	Small Town Romance	1984	2.50	5.00	10.00

POLYDOR

❏ 825421-1	Across a Crowded Room	1985	2.00	4.00	8.00
❏ 829728-1	Daring Adventures	1986	2.00	4.00	8.00

REPRISE

❏ MS 2112	Henry the Human Fly	1972	5.00	10.00	20.00

THOMPSON, RICHARD AND LINDA
CARTHAGE

❏ CGLP-4403	Sunnyvista	1983	2.50	5.00	10.00
—First U.S. issue of this LP					
❏ CGLP-4404	Pour Down Like Silver	1983	2.00	4.00	8.00
—Reissue of Island 9348					
❏ CGLP-4407	I Want to See the Bright Lights Tonight	1983	2.50	5.00	10.00
—Reissue of Island 9266 (UK)					
❏ CGLP-4408	Hokey Pokey	1983	2.00	4.00	8.00
—Reissue of Island 9305					
❏ CGLP-4412	First Light	1983	2.00	4.00	8.00
—Reissue of Chrysalis 1177					

CHRYSALIS

❏ CHR 1177	First Light	1978	3.75	7.50	15.00
❏ CHR 1247	Sunnyvista	1979	—	—	—
—Unreleased in U.S.					

HANNIBAL

❏ HNBL 1303	Shoot Out the Lights	1982	2.50	5.00	10.00

ISLAND

❏ ILPS 9266	I Want to See the Bright Lights Tonight	1974	—	—	—
—Unreleased in U.S. on this number					
❏ ILPS 9305	Hokey Pokey	1974	3.75	7.50	15.00
❏ ILPS 9348	Pour Down Like Silver	1975	3.75	7.50	15.00
❏ ISLA 9421 [(2)]	Bright Lights and Live! More or Less	1977	5.00	10.00	20.00
—First U.S. issue of "I Want to See the Bright Lights Tonight" plus an LP of unreleased material					

THOMPSON, SIR CHARLES
AMERICAN RECORDING SOCIETY

❏ G-447 [M]	Basically Swing	1957	7.50	15.00	30.00

APOLLO

❏ 103 [10]	Sir Charles Thompson and His All Stars	1951	100.00	200.00	400.00

COLUMBIA

❏ CL 1364 [M]	Sir Charles Thompson and the Swing Organ	1959	6.25	12.50	25.00
❏ CL 1663 [M]	Rockin' Rhythm	1961	6.25	12.50	25.00
❏ CS 8205 [S]	Sir Charles Thompson and the Swing Organ	1959	7.50	15.00	30.00
❏ CS 8463 [S]	Rockin' Rhythm	1961	7.50	15.00	30.00

VANGUARD

❏ VRS-8003 [10]	Sir Charles Thompson Sextet	1953	25.00	50.00	100.00
❏ VRS-8006 [10]	Sir Charles Thompson Quartet	1954	25.00	50.00	100.00
❏ VRS-8009 [10]	Sir Charles Thompson and His Band	1954	37.50	75.00	150.00
❏ VRS-8018 [10]	Sir Charles Thompson Trio	1955	25.00	50.00	100.00

THOMPSON, SONNY
KING

❏ 568 [M]	Moody Blues	1956	125.00	250.00	500.00
❏ 655 [M]	Mellow Blues	1959	62.50	125.00	250.00

THOMPSON, SUE
HICKORY

❏ LPM-104 [M]	Meet Sue Thompson	1962	12.50	25.00	50.00
❏ LPS-104 [S]	Meet Sue Thompson	1962	20.00	40.00	80.00
❏ LPM-107 [M]	Two of a Kind	1962	7.50	15.00	30.00
❏ LPS-107 [S]	Two of a Kind	1962	10.00	20.00	40.00
❏ LPM-111 [M]	Sue Thompson's Golden Hits	1963	7.50	15.00	30.00
❏ LPS-111 [S]	Sue Thompson's Golden Hits	1963	10.00	20.00	40.00
❏ LPM-121 [M]	Paper Tiger	1965	7.50	15.00	30.00
❏ LPS-121 [S]	Paper Tiger	1965	10.00	20.00	40.00
❏ LPM-130 [M]	Sue Thompson with Strings Attached	1966	7.50	15.00	30.00
❏ LPS-130 [S]	Sue Thompson with Strings Attached	1966	10.00	20.00	40.00
❏ LPS-148	This Is Sue Thompson Country	1969	5.00	10.00	20.00
❏ H3F-4511	Sweet Memories	1974	3.75	7.50	15.00
❏ H3G-4515	…And Love Me	1974	3.75	7.50	15.00

WING

❏ MGW-12317 [M]	The Country Side of Sue Thompson	1965	5.00	10.00	20.00
❏ SRW-16317 [R]	The Country Side of Sue Thompson	1965	3.75	7.50	15.00

THOMPSON TWINS
ARISTA

❏ SP-137 [EP]	Identical and Fraternal	1982	3.75	7.50	15.00
—Promo-only remixes of early tracks					
❏ AL 6601	In the Name of Love	1982	3.00	6.00	12.00
❏ AL 6607	Side Kicks	1983	3.00	6.00	12.00
❏ AL8-8200	Into the Gap	1984	2.50	5.00	10.00
❏ AL8-8276	Here's to Future Days	1985	2.50	5.00	10.00
❏ AL6-8309	Side Kicks	1985	2.00	4.00	8.00
—Reissue					
❏ AL6-8310	In the Name of Love	1985	2.00	4.00	8.00
—Reissue					
❏ AL8-8449	Close to the Bone	1987	2.50	5.00	10.00
❏ AL 8542	Best of the Thompson Twins: Greatest Mixes	1988	2.50	5.00	10.00

Number	Title (A Side/B Side)	Yr	VG	VG+	NM
❏ ADP 9586 [DJ]	Interview Sampler	1987	5.00	10.00	20.00
—One side of interviews, the other of music; promo only					
❏ R 124567	Into the Gap	1984	3.00	6.00	12.00
—RCA Music Service edition					
❏ R 144367	Here's to Future Days	1985	3.00	6.00	12.00
—RCA Music Service edition					
❏ R 154307	Close to the Bone	1987	3.00	6.00	12.00
—BMG Direct Marketing edition					
❏ R 154479	Best of the Thompson Twins: Greatest Mixes	1988	3.00	6.00	12.00
—BMG Direct Marketing edition					
WARNER BROS.					
❏ 25921	Big Trash	1989	2.50	5.00	10.00

THORINSHIELD
PHILIPS

Number	Title (A Side/B Side)	Yr	VG	VG+	NM
❏ PHS 600251	Thorinshield	1968	5.00	10.00	20.00

THORNE, FRAN
TRANSITION

Number	Title (A Side/B Side)	Yr	VG	VG+	NM
❏ TRLP-27 [M]	Piano Reflections	1956	50.00	100.00	200.00
—With booklet (deduct 1/4 if missing)					

THORNHILL, CLAUDE
COLUMBIA

Number	Title (A Side/B Side)	Yr	VG	VG+	NM
❏ CL 709 [M]	Dancing After Midnight	1955	10.00	20.00	40.00
❏ CL 6035 [10]	Piano Reflections	1949	20.00	40.00	80.00
❏ CL 6050 [10]	Dance Parade	1949	20.00	40.00	80.00
❏ CL 6164 [10]	Claude Thornhill Encores	1951	20.00	40.00	80.00
DECCA					
❏ DL 8722 [M]	Claude on a Cloud	1958	6.25	12.50	25.00
❏ DL 8878 [M]	Dance to the Sound of Claude Thornhill	1958	6.25	12.50	25.00
❏ DL 78722 [S]	Claude on a Cloud	1958	7.50	15.00	30.00
❏ DL 78878 [S]	Dance to the Sound of Claude Thornhill	1958	7.50	15.00	30.00
HARMONY					
❏ HL 7088 [M]	The Thornhill Sound	1957	6.25	12.50	25.00
KAPP					
❏ KL-1058 [M]	Two Sides of Claude Thornhill	1958	7.50	15.00	30.00
❏ KS-3058 [S]	Two Sides of Claude Thornhill	1958	6.25	12.50	25.00
RCA CAMDEN					
❏ CAL-307 [M]	Dinner for Two	1958	6.25	12.50	25.00
TREND					
❏ TL-1001 [10]	Dream Stuff	1953	20.00	40.00	80.00
❏ TL-1002 [10]	Claude Thornhill Plays the Great Jazz Arrangements of Gerry Mulligan and Ralph Aldrich	1953	20.00	40.00	80.00

THORNTON, BIG MAMA
ARHOOLIE

Number	Title (A Side/B Side)	Yr	VG	VG+	NM
❏ F-1028 [M]	Big Mama Thornton in Europe	1966	7.50	15.00	30.00
❏ F-1032 [M]	Chicago Blues: The Queen at Monterey	1967	7.50	15.00	30.00
❏ F-1039 [M]	Ball and Chain	1968	7.50	15.00	30.00
BACK BEAT					
❏ BLP-68	She's Back	1970	6.25	12.50	25.00
MERCURY					
❏ SR-61225	Stronger Than Dirt	1969	6.25	12.50	25.00
❏ SR-61249	The Way It Is	1970	6.25	12.50	25.00
PENTAGRAM					
❏ PE-10005	Saved	1971	5.00	10.00	20.00
VANGUARD					
❏ VSD-79351	Jail	1974	3.75	7.50	15.00
❏ VSD-79354	Sassy Mama	1975	3.75	7.50	15.00

THORNTON, CLIFFORD
THIRD WORLD

Number	Title (A Side/B Side)	Yr	VG	VG+	NM
❏ 9636 [S]	Freedom and Unity	1969	6.25	12.50	25.00

THORNTON, TERI
COLUMBIA

Number	Title (A Side/B Side)	Yr	VG	VG+	NM
❏ CL 2094 [M]	Open Highway	1963	7.50	15.00	30.00
❏ CS 8894 [S]	Open Highway	1963	10.00	20.00	40.00
DAUNTLESS					
❏ DM-4306 [M]	Somewhere in the Night	1963	6.25	12.50	25.00
❏ DS-6306 [S]	Somewhere in the Night	1963	7.50	15.00	30.00
RIVERSIDE					
❏ RLP-352 [M]	Devil May Care	1961	10.00	20.00	40.00
❏ RM-3525 [M]	Lullabye of the Leaves	1964	6.25	12.50	25.00
❏ RS-9352 [S]	Devil May Care	1961	7.50	15.00	30.00
❏ RS-93525 [S]	Lullabye of the Leaves	1964	7.50	15.00	30.00

THORPE, BILLY
CAPRICORN

Number	Title (A Side/B Side)	Yr	VG	VG+	NM
❏ CPN 0221	Children of the Sun	1979	5.00	10.00	20.00
ELEKTRA					
❏ 6E-294	21st Century Man	1980	2.50	5.00	10.00
PASHA					
❏ ARZ 37499	Stimulation	1981	2.50	5.00	10.00
❏ FZ 38179	East of Eden's Gate	1982	2.50	5.00	10.00
❏ BFZ 40682	Children of the Sun... Revisited	1987	2.50	5.00	10.00
POLYDOR					
❏ PD-1-6228	Children of the Sun	1979	3.00	6.00	12.00

THREE CHUCKLES, THE
VIK

Number	Title (A Side/B Side)	Yr	VG	VG+	NM
❏ LX-1067 [M]	The Three Chuckles	1956	62.50	125.00	250.00

THREE D'S, THE (2)
CAPITOL

Number	Title (A Side/B Side)	Yr	VG	VG+	NM
❏ ST 2171 [S]	New Dimensions in Folk Songs	1964	6.25	12.50	25.00
❏ T 2171 [M]	New Dimensions in Folk Songs	1964	5.00	10.00	20.00
❏ ST 2314 [S]	I Won't Be Worried Long	1965	6.25	12.50	25.00
❏ T 2314 [M]	I Won't Be Worried Long	1965	5.00	10.00	20.00

THREE DEGREES, THE
ARIOLA AMERICA

Number	Title (A Side/B Side)	Yr	VG	VG+	NM
❏ OL 1501	Three D	1980	2.50	5.00	10.00
❏ SW-50044	New Dimensions	1978	2.50	5.00	10.00
EPIC					
❏ PE 34385	Standing Up for Love	1977	3.00	6.00	12.00
ICHIBAN					
❏ ICH-1041	Three Degrees...And Holding	198?	2.50	5.00	10.00
PHILADELPHIA INT'L.					
❏ KZ 32406	The Three Degrees	1974	3.00	6.00	12.00
❏ KZ 33162	International	1975	3.00	6.00	12.00
❏ PZ 33840	The Three Degrees Live	1975	3.00	6.00	12.00
ROULETTE					
❏ 3015	So Much Love	1975	2.50	5.00	10.00
❏ SR-42050	Maybe	1970	10.00	20.00	40.00

THREE DOG NIGHT
ABC

Number	Title (A Side/B Side)	Yr	VG	VG+	NM
❏ 888	Coming Down Your Way	1975	2.50	5.00	10.00
❏ 928	American Pastime	1976	2.50	5.00	10.00
ABC DUNHILL					
❏ DS-50048	Three Dog Night	1968	3.75	7.50	15.00
❏ DS-50048	Three Dog Night "One"	1969	3.00	6.00	12.00
—Same album as above, but with revised title on cover					
❏ DS-50058	Suitable for Framing	1969	3.00	6.00	12.00
❏ DS-50068	Three Dog Night Was Captured Live at the Forum	1969	3.00	6.00	12.00
❏ DS-50078	It Ain't Easy	1970	3.00	6.00	12.00
—Regular front cover with gatefold					
❏ DS-50078	It Ain't Easy	1970	25.00	50.00	100.00
—Original cover with band members in the nude					
❏ DSX-50088	Naturally	1970	3.00	6.00	12.00
—With detachable cardboard poster intact					
❏ DSX-50098	Golden Bisquits	1971	3.00	6.00	12.00
—With detachable cardboard poster intact; interestingly, the label spells the LP title "Golden Biscuits"					
❏ DSX-50108	Harmony	1971	3.00	6.00	12.00
❏ DSD-50118	Seven Separate Fools	1972	3.00	6.00	12.00
—With seven oversize playing cards included					
❏ DSY-50138 [(2)]	Around the World with Three Dog Night	1973	3.75	7.50	15.00
❏ DSX-50158	Cyan	1973	3.00	6.00	12.00
❏ DSD-50168	Hard Labor	1974	2.50	5.00	10.00
—With huge Band-Aid as part of the LP artwork					
❏ DSD-50168	Hard Labor	1974	3.75	7.50	15.00
—With huge Band-Aid attached to jacket, covering the "childbirth"					
❏ DSD-50168	Hard Labor	1974	7.50	15.00	30.00
—With uncensored "childbirth" front cover					
❏ DSD-50178	Joy to the World: Their Greatest Hits	1974	3.00	6.00	12.00
—With gatefold cover					
❏ DSD-50178	Joy to the World: Their Greatest Hits	1975	2.50	5.00	10.00
—With standard cover					
AT EASE					
❏ MD 11109	Three Dog Night: Their Greatest Recordings	1978	5.00	10.00	20.00
—"This Album Compiled Exclusively for Military Personnel" by ABC					
COMMAND					
❏ QD-40014 [Q]	Hard Labor	1974	5.00	10.00	20.00
❏ QD-40018 [Q]	Coming Down Your Way	1975	5.00	10.00	20.00
MCA					
❏ 6018 [(2)]	The Best of Three Dog Night	1982	3.00	6.00	12.00
❏ 37120	Joy to the World: Their Greatest Hits	1980	2.00	4.00	8.00
PASSPORT					
❏ PB 5001 [EP]	It's a Jungle	1983	2.00	4.00	8.00

THREE FACES WEST
OUTPOST

Number	Title (A Side/B Side)	Yr	VG	VG+	NM
❏ 1000	Three Faces West	197?	5.00	10.00	20.00

THREE FLAMES, THE
MERCURY

Number	Title (A Side/B Side)	Yr	VG	VG+	NM
❏ MG-20239 [M]	At the Ben Soir	1957	12.50	25.00	50.00

THREE MAN ARMY, THE
KAMA SUTRA

Number	Title (A Side/B Side)	Yr	VG	VG+	NM
❏ KSBS-2044	A Third of a Lifetime	1971	7.50	15.00	30.00
—Pink label, gatefold cover					
REPRISE					
❏ MS 2150	Three Man Army	1973	5.00	10.00	20.00
❏ MS 2182	Three Man Army Two	1974	5.00	10.00	20.00

THREE SOULS, THE
ARGO

Number	Title (A Side/B Side)	Yr	VG	VG+	NM
❏ LP-4005 [M]	Almost Like Being In Love	1960	—	—	—
—Canceled					
❏ LPS-4005 [S]	Almost Like Being In Love	1960	—	—	—
—Canceled					
❏ LP-4036 [M]	Dangerous Dan Express	1964	5.00	10.00	20.00
❏ LPS-4036 [S]	Dangerous Dan Express	1964	6.25	12.50	25.00
❏ LP-4044 [M]	Soul Sounds	1965	5.00	10.00	20.00
❏ LPS-4044 [S]	Soul Sounds	1965	6.25	12.50	25.00

THREE SOUNDS, THE
BLUE NOTE

Number	Title (A Side/B Side)	Yr	VG	VG+	NM
❏ BLP-1600 [M]	Introducing the Three Sounds	1958	20.00	40.00	80.00
—Regular version, W. 63rd St. address on label					
❏ BLP-1600 [M]	Introducing the Three Sounds	1958	30.00	60.00	120.00
—"Deep groove" version (deep indentation under label on both sides)					
❏ BLP-1600 [M]	Introducing the Three Sounds	1963	6.25	12.50	25.00
—With "New York, USA" address on label					
❏ BST-1600 [S]	Introducing the Three Sounds	1959	15.00	30.00	60.00
—Regular version, W. 63rd St. address on label					
❏ BST-1600 [S]	Introducing the Three Sounds	1959	20.00	40.00	80.00
—"Deep groove" version (deep indentation under label on both sides)					

Number	Title (A Side/B Side)	Yr	VG	VG+	NM
❏ BST-1600 [S]	Introducing the Three Sounds	1963	5.00	10.00	20.00
—With "New York, USA" address on label					
❏ BLP-4014 [M]	Bottoms Up	1959	20.00	40.00	80.00
—Regular version, W. 63rd St. address on label					
❏ BLP-4014 [M]	Bottoms Up	1959	30.00	60.00	120.00
—"Deep groove" version (deep indentation under label on both sides)					
❏ BLP-4014 [M]	Bottoms Up	1963	6.25	12.50	25.00
—With "New York, USA" address on label					
❏ BST-4014 [S]	Bottoms Up	1959	15.00	30.00	60.00
—Regular version, W. 63rd St. address on label					
❏ BST-4014 [S]	Bottoms Up	1959	20.00	40.00	80.00
—"Deep groove" version (deep indentation under label on both sides)					
❏ BST-4014 [S]	Bottoms Up	1963	5.00	10.00	20.00
—With "New York, USA" address on label					
❏ BLP-4020 [M]	Good Deal	1959	20.00	40.00	80.00
—Regular version, W. 63rd St. address on label					
❏ BLP-4020 [M]	Good Deal	1959	30.00	60.00	120.00
—"Deep groove" version (deep indentation under label on both sides)					
❏ BLP-4020 [M]	Good Deal	1963	6.25	12.50	25.00
—With "New York, USA" address on label					
❏ BLP-4044 [M]	Moods	1960	20.00	40.00	80.00
—Regular version, W. 63rd St. address on label					
❏ BLP-4044 [M]	Moods	1960	30.00	60.00	120.00
—"Deep groove" version (deep indentation under label on both sides)					
❏ BLP-4044 [M]	Moods	1963	6.25	12.50	25.00
—With "New York, USA" address on label					
❏ BLP-4072 [M]	Feelin' Good	1961	20.00	40.00	80.00
—With W. 63rd St. address on label					
❏ BLP-4072 [M]	Feelin' Good	1963	6.25	12.50	25.00
—With "New York, USA" address on label					
❏ BLP-4088 [M]	Here We Come	1961	20.00	40.00	80.00
—With 61st St. address on label					
❏ BLP-4088 [M]	Here We Come	1963	6.25	12.50	25.00
—With "New York, USA" address on label					
❏ BLP-4102 [M]	Hey! There	1962	7.50	15.00	30.00
❏ BLP-4120 [M]	It Just Got To Be	1963	7.50	15.00	30.00
❏ BLP-4155 [M]	Black Orchid	1963	7.50	15.00	30.00
❏ BLP-4197 [M]	Out of This World	1965	7.50	15.00	30.00
❏ BLP-4248 [M]	Vibrations	1966	7.50	15.00	30.00
❏ BLP-4265 [M]	Live at the Lighthouse	1967	7.50	15.00	30.00
❏ BST-84020 [S]	Good Deal	1959	12.50	25.00	50.00
—With W. 63rd St. address on label					
❏ BST-84020 [M]	Good Deal	1963	5.00	10.00	20.00
—With "New York, USA" address on label					
❏ BST-84044 [S]	Moods	1960	12.50	25.00	50.00
—With W. 63rd St. address on label					
❏ BST-84044 [S]	Moods	1963	5.00	10.00	20.00
—With "New York, USA" address on label					
❏ BST-84072 [S]	Feelin' Good	1961	12.50	25.00	50.00
—With W. 63rd St. address on label					
❏ BST-84072 [S]	Feelin' Good	1963	5.00	10.00	20.00
—With "New York, USA" address on label					
❏ BST-84088 [S]	Here We Come	1961	12.50	25.00	50.00
—With 61st St. address on label					
❏ BST-84088 [S]	Here We Come	1963	5.00	10.00	20.00
—With "New York, USA" address on label					
❏ BST-84102 [S]	Hey! There	1962	7.50	15.00	30.00
—With "New York, USA" address on label					
❏ BST-84120 [S]	It Just Got To Be	1963	7.50	15.00	30.00
—With "New York, USA" address on label					
❏ BST-84155 [S]	Black Orchid	1963	7.50	15.00	30.00
—With "New York, USA" address on label					
❏ BST-84197 [S]	Out of This World	1965	7.50	15.00	30.00
—With "New York, USA" address on label					
❏ BST-84248 [S]	Vibrations	1966	7.50	15.00	30.00
—With "New York, USA" address on label					
❏ BST-84265 [S]	Live at the Lighthouse	1967	5.00	10.00	20.00
—With "A Division of Liberty Records" on label					
❏ BST-84285 [S]	Coldwater Flat	1968	5.00	10.00	20.00
—With "A Division of Liberty Records" on label					
❏ BST-84301 [S]	Elegant Soul	1968	5.00	10.00	20.00
—With "A Division of Liberty Records" on label					
❏ BST-84341 [S]	Soul Symphony	1969	5.00	10.00	20.00
—With "A Division of Liberty Records" on label					

LIMELIGHT

Number	Title (A Side/B Side)	Yr	VG	VG+	NM
❏ LM-82014 [M]	Three Moods	1965	5.00	10.00	20.00
❏ LM-82026 [M]	Beautiful Friendship	1965	5.00	10.00	20.00
❏ LS-86014 [S]	Three Moods	1965	6.25	12.50	25.00
❏ LS-86026 [S]	Beautiful Friendship	1965	6.25	12.50	25.00

MERCURY

Number	Title	Yr	VG	VG+	NM
❏ MG-20776 [M]	Jazz On Broadway	1963	6.25	12.50	25.00
❏ MG-20839 [M]	Some Like It Modern	1963	6.25	12.50	25.00
❏ MG-20921 [M]	Live at the Living Room	1963	6.25	12.50	25.00
❏ SR-60776 [S]	Jazz On Broadway	1963	7.50	15.00	30.00
❏ SR-60839 [S]	Some Like It Modern	1963	7.50	15.00	30.00
❏ SR-60921 [S]	Live at the Living Room	1963	7.50	15.00	30.00

VERVE

Number	Title	Yr	VG	VG+	NM
❏ V-8513 [M]	Blue Genes	1963	6.25	12.50	25.00
❏ V6-8513 [S]	Blue Genes	1963	7.50	15.00	30.00

THREE STOOGES, THE
CORAL

Number	Title	Yr	VG	VG+	NM
❏ CRL 57289 [M]	Nonsense Song Book	1959	20.00	40.00	80.00
❏ CRL 757289 [S]	Nonsense Song Book	1959	25.00	50.00	100.00

GOLDEN

Number	Title	Yr	VG	VG+	NM
❏ GLP-43 [M]	Madcap Musical Nonsense	1962	20.00	40.00	80.00

PETER PAN

Number	Title	Yr	VG	VG+	NM
❏ 8098	The Three Stooges	1970	6.25	12.50	25.00

VOCALION

Number	Title	Yr	VG	VG+	NM
❏ VL 3823 [M]	The Three Stooges Sing for Kids	196?	5.00	10.00	20.00
❏ VL 73823 [S]	The Three Stooges Sing for Kids	196?	6.25	12.50	25.00

THREE SUNS, THE
GOLDEN TONE

Number	Title (A Side/B Side)	Yr	VG	VG+	NM
❏ 14094	In Orbit	195?	3.00	6.00	12.00

PICKWICK

Number	Title	Yr	VG	VG+	NM
❏ SPC-3037	Twilight Time	197?	2.50	5.00	10.00

RCA CAMDEN

Number	Title	Yr	VG	VG+	NM
❏ CAL-633 [M]	The Sound of Christmas	1964	3.00	6.00	12.00
❏ CAS-633(e) [R]	The Sound of Christmas	1964	3.00	6.00	12.00

RCA VICTOR

Number	Title	Yr	VG	VG+	NM
❏ LPM-3 [10]	Three-Quarter Time	1951	12.50	25.00	50.00
❏ LPM-28 [10]	Hands Across the Table	1951	12.50	25.00	50.00
❏ LPM-52 [10]	Christmas Favorites	1951	12.50	25.00	50.00
❏ LPM-1041 [M]	Soft and Sweet	1955	7.50	15.00	30.00
❏ LPM-1132 [M]	Sounds of Christmas	1955	7.50	15.00	30.00
❏ LPM-1171 [M]	Twilight Time	1956	7.50	15.00	30.00
❏ LPM-1173 [M]	My Reverie	1956	7.50	15.00	30.00
❏ LPM-1219 [M]	Slumber Time	1956	7.50	15.00	30.00
❏ LPM-1220 [M]	Malaguena	1956	7.50	15.00	30.00
❏ LPM-1249 [M]	High Fi and Wide	1956	7.50	15.00	30.00
❏ LPM-1316 [M]	Easy Listening	1956	7.50	15.00	30.00
❏ LPM-1333 [M]	Midnight for Two	1957	7.50	15.00	30.00
❏ LPM-1543 [M]	The Things in Love in Hi-Fi	1958	5.00	10.00	20.00
❏ LSP-1543 [S]	The Things in Love in Hi-Fi	1958	7.50	15.00	30.00
❏ LPM-1578 [M]	Let's Dance with the Three Suns	1958	5.00	10.00	20.00
❏ LSP-1578 [S]	Let's Dance with the Three Suns	1958	7.50	15.00	30.00
❏ LPM-1669 [M]	Love in the Afternoon	1959	5.00	10.00	20.00
❏ LSP-1669 [S]	Love in the Afternoon	1959	7.50	15.00	30.00
❏ LPM-1734 [M]	Having a Ball with the Three Suns	1959	5.00	10.00	20.00
❏ LSP-1734 [S]	Having a Ball with the Three Suns	1959	7.50	15.00	30.00
❏ ANL1-1779(e)	Pure Gold	1974	2.50	5.00	10.00
❏ LPM-1964 [M]	Swingin' on a Star	1959	5.00	10.00	20.00
❏ LSP-1964 [S]	Swingin' on a Star	1959	7.50	15.00	30.00
❏ LPM-2054 [M]	A Ding Dong Dandy Christmas!	1959	5.00	10.00	20.00
❏ LSP-2054 [S]	A Ding Dong Dandy Christmas!	1959	7.50	15.00	30.00
❏ LPM-2120 [M]	Twilight Memories	1960	5.00	10.00	20.00
❏ LSP-2120 [S]	Twilight Memories	1960	6.25	12.50	25.00
❏ LPM-2235 [M]	On a Magic Carpet	1960	5.00	10.00	20.00
❏ LSP-2235 [S]	On a Magic Carpet	1960	6.25	12.50	25.00
❏ LPM-2307 [M]	Dancing on a Cloud	1961	5.00	10.00	20.00
❏ LSP-2307 [S]	Dancing on a Cloud	1961	6.25	12.50	25.00
❏ LPM-2310 [M]	Fever and Smoke	1961	5.00	10.00	20.00
❏ LSP-2310 [S]	Fever and Smoke	1961	6.25	12.50	25.00
❏ LPM-2437 [M]	Fun in the Sun	1961	5.00	10.00	20.00
❏ LSP-2437 [S]	Fun in the Sun	1961	6.25	12.50	25.00
❏ LPM-2532 [M]	Movin' 'N' Groovin'	1962	5.00	10.00	20.00
❏ LSP-2532 [S]	Movin' 'N' Groovin'	1962	6.25	12.50	25.00
❏ LPM-2617 [M]	Warm and Tender	1962	5.00	10.00	20.00
❏ LSP-2617 [S]	Warm and Tender	1962	6.25	12.50	25.00
❏ LPM-2715 [M]	Everything Under the Sun	1963	3.75	7.50	15.00
❏ LSP-2715 [S]	Everything Under the Sun	1963	5.00	10.00	20.00
❏ LPM-2904 [M]	One Enchanted Evening	1964	3.75	7.50	15.00
❏ LSP-2904 [S]	One Enchanted Evening	1964	5.00	10.00	20.00
❏ LPM-2963 [M]	A Swingin' Thing	1964	3.75	7.50	15.00
❏ LSP-2963 [S]	A Swingin' Thing	1964	5.00	10.00	20.00
❏ LPM-3012 [10]	Twilight Moods	1952	12.50	25.00	50.00
❏ LPM-3034 [10]	The Three Suns Present	1952	12.50	25.00	50.00
❏ LPM-3040 [10]	Busy Fingers	1952	12.50	25.00	50.00
❏ LPM-3056 [10]	Christmas Party	1952	12.50	25.00	50.00
❏ LPM-3075 [10]	Slumbertime	1953	12.50	25.00	50.00
❏ LPM-3113 [10]	Pops Concert Favorites	1953	12.50	25.00	50.00
❏ LPM-3125 [10]	Mods	1953	12.50	25.00	50.00
❏ LPM-3130 [10]	Top Pops	1953	12.50	25.00	50.00
❏ LPM-3146 [10]	Polka Time	1954	12.50	25.00	50.00
❏ LPM-3174 [10]	Sacred Hymns	1954	12.50	25.00	50.00
❏ LPM-3354 [M]	Country Music Shindig	1965	3.75	7.50	15.00
❏ LSP-3354 [S]	Country Music Shindig	1965	5.00	10.00	20.00
❏ LPM-3447 [M]	The Best of the Three Suns	1965	3.75	7.50	15.00
❏ LSP-3447 [S]	The Best of the Three Suns	1965	5.00	10.00	20.00
❏ VPS-6075 [(2)]	This Is the Three Suns	1972	3.75	7.50	15.00

ROYALE

Number	Title	Yr	VG	VG+	NM
❏ 1 [10]	Twilight Time	1951	12.50	25.00	50.00
❏ 29 [10]	Midnight Time	1951	12.50	25.00	50.00

SEARS

Number	Title	Yr	VG	VG+	NM
❏ SPS-437	Twilight Time	1969	3.00	6.00	12.00

VARSITY

Number	Title	Yr	VG	VG+	NM
❏ VLP-6001 [10]	Twilight Time	1950	12.50	25.00	50.00
❏ VLP-6048 [10]	Midnight Time	1950	12.50	25.00	50.00

THRILLINGTON, PERCY "THRILLS"
See PAUL McCARTNEY.

THUDPUCKER, JIMMY
Fictional singing star from Garry Trudeau's "Doonesbury" comic strip.
WINDSONG

Number	Title	Yr	VG	VG+	NM
❏ BXL1-2589	Greatest Hits	1977	5.00	10.00	20.00

THUNDER, JOHNNY
DIAMOND

Number	Title	Yr	VG	VG+	NM
❏ D-5001 [M]	Loop De Loop	1963	25.00	50.00	100.00
❏ DS-5001 [S]	Loop De Loop	1963	37.50	75.00	150.00

REAL

Number	Title	Yr	VG	VG+	NM
❏ RR-1	So Alone	196?	3.75	7.50	15.00

THUNDER AND ROSES
UNITED ARTISTS

Number	Title	Yr	VG	VG+	NM
❏ UAS-6709	King of the Black Sunrise	1969	7.50	15.00	30.00

THUNDERBIRDS, THE
RED FEATHER

Number	Title	Yr	VG	VG+	NM
❏ TH-1 [M]	Meet the Fabulous Thunderbirds	1964	50.00	100.00	200.00

Number	Title (A Side/B Side)	Yr	VG	VG+	NM

THUNDERCLAP NEWMAN
MCA

Number	Title (A Side/B Side)	Yr	VG	VG+	NM
❑ 354	Hollywood Dream	1974	2.50	5.00	10.00
—Reissue of Track 354					

TRACK

❑ 354	Hollywood Dream	1973	3.00	6.00	12.00
—Reissue of Track 8264					
❑ SD 8264	Hollywood Dream	1970	6.25	12.50	25.00

THUNDERPUSSY
M.R.T.

| ❑ 31748 | Documents of Captivity | 1973 | 37.50 | 75.00 | 150.00 |

THUNDERTREE
ROULETTE

| ❑ SR-42038 | Thundertree | 1970 | 7.50 | 15.00 | 30.00 |

TIDE, THE
MOUTH

| ❑ 7237 | Almost Live | 1971 | 12.50 | 25.00 | 50.00 |

TIDES, THE
MERCURY

| ❑ MG-20714 [M] | Limbo Rock | 1962 | 3.75 | 7.50 | 15.00 |
| ❑ SR-60714 [S] | Limbo Rock | 1962 | 5.00 | 10.00 | 20.00 |

WING

❑ MGW-12248 [M]	The Best of Bossa Nova	1963	3.75	7.50	15.00
❑ MGW-12265 [M]	Surf City and Other Surfin' Favorites	1963	6.25	12.50	25.00
❑ SRW-16248 [S]	The Best of Bossa Nova	1963	5.00	10.00	20.00
❑ SRW-16265 [S]	Surf City and Other Surfin' Favorites	1963	7.50	15.00	30.00

TIEKEN, FREDDIE, AND THE ROCKERS
I.T.

| ❑ 2301 [M] | By Popular Demand | 1957 | 12.50 | 25.00 | 50.00 |
| ❑ 2304 [M] | Freddie Tieken and the Rockers | 1958 | 12.50 | 25.00 | 50.00 |

TIFFANY SHADE, THE
MAINSTREAM

| ❑ S-6105 | The Tiffany Shade | 1968 | 25.00 | 50.00 | 100.00 |

TIKIS, THE
Probably two different groups.
MINARET

| ❑ TLP-7001 [M] | The Tikis | 196? | 25.00 | 50.00 | 100.00 |

PHILIPS

| ❑ PHM 200043 [M] | The Tikis | 1962 | 6.25 | 12.50 | 25.00 |
| ❑ PHS 600043 [S] | The Tikis | 1962 | 7.50 | 15.00 | 30.00 |

TIL, SONNY
Also see THE ORIOLES.
DOBRE

| ❑ 1026 | Back to the Chapel | 1978 | 3.00 | 6.00 | 12.00 |

RCA VICTOR

| ❑ LSP-4451 | Sonny Til Returns | 1970 | 5.00 | 10.00 | 20.00 |
| ❑ LSP-4538 | Old Gold/New Gold | 1971 | 3.75 | 7.50 | 15.00 |

TILLIS, MEL
COLUMBIA

❑ CL 1724 [M]	Heart Over Mind and Other Big Country Hits	1962	7.50	15.00	30.00
❑ CS 8524 [S]	Heart Over Mind and Other Big Country Hits	1962	10.00	20.00	40.00
❑ C 30253	Heart Over Mind	1970	3.00	6.00	12.00

ELEKTRA

❑ 6E-236	Me and Pepper	1979	2.50	5.00	10.00
❑ 6E-271	Your Body Is an Outlaw	1980	2.50	5.00	10.00
❑ 6E-310	Southern Rain	1980	2.50	5.00	10.00
❑ 60016	It's a Long Way to Daytona	1982	2.50	5.00	10.00
❑ 60192	Mel Tillis' Greatest Hits	1982	2.50	5.00	10.00

HARMONY

❑ HL 7370 [M]	The Great Mel Tillis Sings Walk On, Boy and Other Great Country Hits	196?	3.75		7.50	15.00
❑ HS 11170 [S]	The Great Mel Tillis Sings Walk On, Boy and Other Great Country Hits	196?	3.00	6.00	12.00
❑ KH 31952	Mel	1972	3.00	6.00	12.00

HILLTOP

| ❑ JS-6153 | Detroit City | 197? | 2.50 | 5.00 | 10.00 |

KAPP

❑ KL-1493 [M]	Stateside	1966	3.75	7.50	15.00
❑ KL-1514 [M]	Life Turned Her That Way	1967	3.75	7.50	15.00
❑ KL-1535 [M]	Mr. Mel	1967	5.00	10.00	20.00
❑ KS-3493 [S]	Stateside	1966	5.00	10.00	20.00
❑ KS-3514 [S]	Life Turned Her That Way	1967	5.00	10.00	20.00
❑ KS-3535 [S]	Mr. Mel	1967	3.75	7.50	15.00
❑ KS-3543	Let Me Talk to You	1968	3.75	7.50	15.00
❑ KS-3570	Something Special	1968	3.75	7.50	15.00
❑ KS-3589	Mel Tillis' Greatest Hits	1969	3.75	7.50	15.00
❑ KS-3594	Who's Julie	1969	3.75	7.50	15.00
❑ KS-3609	Mel Tillis Sings Old Faithful	1969	3.75	7.50	15.00
❑ KS-3630	She'll Be Hanging 'Round Somewhere	1970	3.75	7.50	15.00
❑ KS-3639	Mel Tillis In Person	1970	3.75	7.50	15.00

MCA

❑ 66	Mel Tillis' Greatest Hits	1973	3.00	6.00	12.00
—Reissue of Kapp 3589					
❑ 550	Mel Tillis In Person	197?	2.50	5.00	10.00
—Reissue of Kapp 3639					
❑ 649	Love Revival	198?	2.00	4.00	8.00
—Reissue of 2204					
❑ 650	Heart Healer	198?	2.00	4.00	8.00
—Reissue of 2252					
❑ 651	Love's Troubled Waters	198?	2.00	4.00	8.00
—Reissue of 2288					

❑ 652	I Believe in You	198?	2.00	4.00	8.00
—Reissue of 2364					
❑ 653	Are You Sincere	198?	2.00	4.00	8.00
—Reissue of 3077					
❑ 789	M-M-Mel Live	198?	2.00	4.00	8.00
—Reissue of 3208					
❑ 2204	Love Revival	1976	3.00	6.00	12.00
❑ 2252	Heart Healer	1977	3.00	6.00	12.00
❑ 2288	Love's Troubled Waters	1977	3.00	6.00	12.00
❑ 2364	I Believe in You	1978	3.00	6.00	12.00
❑ 3077	Are You Sincere	1979	3.00	6.00	12.00
❑ 3167	Mr. Entertainer	1979	3.00	6.00	12.00
❑ 3208	M-M-Mel Live	1980	3.00	6.00	12.00
❑ 3274	The Very Best of Mel Tillis	1980	2.50	5.00	10.00
❑ 4091 [(2)]	The Best of Mel Tillis	1975	3.75	7.50	15.00
❑ 5378	After All This Time	1983	2.00	4.00	8.00
❑ 5472	New Patches	1984	2.00	4.00	8.00
❑ 37121	Mr. Entertainer	198?	2.00	4.00	8.00
—Reissue of 3167					

MERCURY

| ❑ 835310-1 | Brand New Mister Me | 1988 | 2.00 | 4.00 | 8.00 |

MGM

❑ SE-4681	One More Time	1970	3.75	7.50	15.00
❑ SE-4757	The Arms of a Fool/Commercial Affection	1971	3.75	7.50	15.00
❑ SE-4788	Recorded Live at the Sam Houston Coliseum, Houston, Texas	1971	3.75	7.50	15.00
❑ SE-4806	The Very Best of Mel Tillis and the Statesiders	1972	3.75	7.50	15.00
❑ SE-4841	Would You Want the World to End	1972	3.75	7.50	15.00
❑ SE-4870	I Ain't Never/Neon Rose	1972	3.75	7.50	15.00
❑ SE-4889	Mel Tillis and the Statesiders On Stage at the Birmingham Municipal Auditorium	1973	3.75	7.50	15.00
❑ SE-4907	Sawmill	1973	3.75	7.50	15.00
❑ M3F-4960	Stomp Them Grapes	1974	3.00	6.00	12.00
❑ M3G-4970	Mel Tillis' Greatest Hits	1974	3.00	6.00	12.00
❑ M3G-4981	Mel Tillis Time	1975	—	—	—
—Canceled					
❑ M3G-4987	Mel Tillis and the Statesiders	1975	3.00	6.00	12.00
❑ MG-1-5002	M-M-Mel	1975	3.00	6.00	12.00
❑ MG-1-5021	The Best of Mel Tillis and the Statesiders	1976	3.00	6.00	12.00
❑ MG-1-5022	Welcome to Mel Tillis Country	1976	3.00	6.00	12.00
❑ MG-2-5402 [(2)]	24 Great Hits	1977	3.75	7.50	15.00
❑ MG-2-5404 [(2)]	Live at the Sam Houston Coliseum & Birmingham Municipal Auditorium	1978	3.75	7.50	15.00
—Combines 4788 and 4889 in one package					

POWER PAK

| ❑ PO-295 | Mel Tillis & Friends | 197? | 2.50 | 5.00 | 10.00 |

RCA VICTOR

| ❑ AHL1-5483 | California Road | 1985 | 2.00 | 4.00 | 8.00 |

STARDAY

| ❑ SLP-471 | Stateside | 1972 | 3.00 | 6.00 | 12.00 |

VOCALION

| ❑ VL 73914 | Big 'n' Country | 1970 | 3.00 | 6.00 | 12.00 |

TILLIS, PAM
WARNER BROS.

| ❑ 23871 | Above and Beyond the Doll of Cutey | 1983 | 6.25 | 12.50 | 25.00 |

TILLMAN, FLOYD
CIMARRON

| ❑ C-2003 [M] | Let's Make Memories | 1962 | 12.50 | 25.00 | 50.00 |

HARMONY

| ❑ HL 7316 [M] | Floyd Tillman's Best | 1964 | 6.25 | 12.50 | 25.00 |
| ❑ HS 11297 | I'll Still Be Lovin' You | 1969 | 6.25 | 12.50 | 25.00 |

HILLTOP

| ❑ JM-6017 [M] | Floyd Tillman Sings His Greatest Hits of Lovin' | 196? | 3.75 | 7.50 | 15.00 |

MUSICOR

❑ MM-2136 [M]	Floyd Tillman's Country	1967	5.00	10.00	20.00
❑ MS-3136 [S]	Floyd Tillman's Country	1967	6.25	12.50	25.00
❑ MS-3157	Dream On	1968	5.00	10.00	20.00

RCA VICTOR

| ❑ LPM-1686 [M] | Floyd Tillman's Greatest | 1958 | 15.00 | 30.00 | 60.00 |

STARDAY

| ❑ SLP-310 [M] | Let's Make Memories | 1965 | 7.50 | 15.00 | 30.00 |

TILLOTSON, JOHNNY
ACCORD

| ❑ SN-7194 | Scrapbook | 1982 | 2.50 | 5.00 | 10.00 |

AMOS

| ❑ AAS 7006 | Tears on My Pillow | 1969 | 5.00 | 10.00 | 20.00 |

BARNABY

| ❑ BR-4007 | Johnny Tillotson's Greatest | 1977 | 3.00 | 6.00 | 12.00 |

BUDDAH

| ❑ BDS-5112 | Johnny Tillotson | 1972 | 3.75 | 7.50 | 15.00 |

CADENCE

❑ CLP-3052 [M]	Johnny Tillotson's Best	1961	10.00	20.00	40.00
—Maroon and silver label					
❑ CLP-3052 [M]	Johnny Tillotson's Best	1962	6.25	12.50	25.00
—Red and black label					
❑ CLP-3058 [M]	It Keeps Right On a-Hurtin'	1962	7.50	15.00	30.00
❑ CLP-3067 [M]	You Can Never Stop Me Loving You	1963	7.50	15.00	30.00
❑ CLP-25052 [P]	Johnny Tillotson's Best	1961	12.50	25.00	50.00
—Maroon and silver label					
❑ CLP-25052 [P]	Johnny Tillotson's Best	1962	7.50	15.00	30.00
—Red and black label					
❑ CLP-25058 [S]	It Keeps Right On a-Hurtin'	1962	10.00	20.00	40.00
❑ CLP-25067 [P]	You Can Never Stop Me Loving You	1963	10.00	20.00	40.00

EVEREST

| ❑ 4113 | Johnny Tillotson's Greatest Hits | 1982 | 2.50 | 5.00 | 10.00 |

Number	Title (A Side/B Side)	Yr	VG	VG+	NM
METRO					
❏ M-561 [M]	Johnny Tillotson Sings Tillotson	1967	3.75	7.50	15.00
❏ MS-561 [S]	Johnny Tillotson Sings Tillotson	1967	5.00	10.00	20.00
MGM					
❏ E-4188 [M]	Talk Back Trembling Lips	1964	5.00	10.00	20.00
❏ SE-4188 [S]	Talk Back Trembling Lips	1964	6.25	12.50	25.00
❏ E-4224 [M]	The Tillotson Touch	1964	5.00	10.00	20.00
❏ SE-4224 [S]	The Tillotson Touch	1964	6.25	12.50	25.00
❏ E-4270 [M]	She Understands Me	1965	5.00	10.00	20.00
❏ SE-4270 [S]	She Understands Me	1965	6.25	12.50	25.00
❏ E-4302 [M]	That's My Style	1965	5.00	10.00	20.00
❏ SE-4302 [S]	That's My Style	1965	6.25	12.50	25.00
❏ E-4328 [M]	Our World	1965	5.00	10.00	20.00
❏ SE-4328 [S]	Our World	1965	6.25	12.50	25.00
❏ E-4395 [M]	No Love at All	1966	5.00	10.00	20.00
❏ SE-4395 [S]	No Love at All	1966	6.25	12.50	25.00
❏ E-4402 [M]	The Christmas Touch	1966	5.00	10.00	20.00
❏ SE-4402 [S]	The Christmas Touch	1966	6.25	12.50	25.00
❏ E-4452 [M]	Here I Am	1967	5.00	10.00	20.00
❏ SE-4452 [S]	Here I Am	1967	6.25	12.50	25.00
❏ E-4532 [M]	The Best of Johnny Tillotson	1968	7.50	15.00	30.00
—May be promo only (yellow label)					
❏ SE-4532 [S]	The Best of Johnny Tillotson	1968	5.00	10.00	20.00
❏ SE-4814	The Very Best of Johnny Tillotson	1971	3.00	6.00	12.00
❏ ST 90410 [S]	The Tillotson Touch	1965	7.50	15.00	30.00
—Capitol Record Club edition					
❏ T 90410 [M]	The Tillotson Touch	1965	7.50	15.00	30.00
—Capitol Record Club edition					
UNITED ARTISTS					
❏ UA-LA759-G	Johnny Tillotson	1977	2.50	5.00	10.00
TIMBER CREEK					
RENEGADE					
❏ 95014	Hellbound Highway	1975	37.50	75.00	150.00
TIMMENS, JIM, AND HIS JAZZ ALL-STARS					
WARNER BROS.					
❏ W 1278 [M]	Gilbert and Sullivan Revisited	1958	5.00	10.00	20.00
❏ WS 1278 [S]	Gilbert and Sullivan Revisited	1958	6.25	12.50	25.00
TIMMONS, BOBBY					
MILESTONE					
❏ MSP-9011	Got to Get It	1969	5.00	10.00	20.00
❏ MSP-9020	Do You Know the Way	1969	5.00	10.00	20.00
PRESTIGE					
❏ PRLP-7335 [M]	Little Barefoot Soul	1964	6.25	12.50	25.00
❏ PRST-7335 [S]	Little Barefoot Soul	1964	7.50	15.00	30.00
❏ PRLP-7351 [M]	Chun-King	1965	6.25	12.50	25.00
❏ PRST-7351 [S]	Chun-King	1965	7.50	15.00	30.00
❏ PRLP-7387 [M]	Workin' Out	1966	6.25	12.50	25.00
❏ PRST-7387 [S]	Workin' Out	1966	7.50	15.00	30.00
❏ PRLP-7414 [M]	Holiday Soul	1966	6.25	12.50	25.00
❏ PRST-7414 [S]	Holiday Soul	1966	7.50	15.00	30.00
❏ PRLP-7429 [M]	Chicken and Dumplin's	1966	6.25	12.50	25.00
❏ PRST-7429 [S]	Chicken and Dumplin's	1966	7.50	15.00	30.00
❏ PRLP-7465 [M]	Soul Man	1967	6.25	12.50	25.00
❏ PRST-7465 [S]	Soul Man	1967	5.00	10.00	20.00
❏ PRLP-7483 [M]	Soul Food	1967	6.25	12.50	25.00
❏ PRST-7483 [S]	Soul Food	1967	5.00	10.00	20.00
RIVERSIDE					
❏ RLP 12-317 [M]	This Here Is Bobby Timmons	1960	10.00	20.00	40.00
❏ RLP-334 [M]	Soul Time	1960	7.50	15.00	30.00
❏ RLP-363 [M]	Easy Does It	1961	6.25	12.50	25.00
❏ RLP-391 [M]	The Bobby Timmons Trio In Person — Recorded "Live" at the Village Vanguard	1961	6.25	12.50	25.00
❏ RLP-422 [M]	Sweet and Soulful Sounds	1962	6.25	12.50	25.00
❏ RLP-468 [M]	Born to Be Blue!	1963	6.25	12.50	25.00
❏ RLP-1164 [S]	This Here Is Bobby Timmons	1960	7.50	15.00	30.00
❏ RS-9334 [S]	Soul Time	1960	10.00	20.00	40.00
❏ RS-9363 [S]	Easy Does It	1961	7.50	15.00	30.00
❏ RS-9391 [S]	The Bobby Timmons Trio In Person-Recorded 'Live' At the Village Vanguard	1961	7.50	15.00	30.00
❏ RS-9422 [S]	Sweet and Soulful Sounds	1962	7.50	15.00	30.00
❏ RS-9468 [S]	Born to Be Blue!	1963	7.50	15.00	30.00
TIMMOTHY					
PEAR					
❏ (# unknown)	Strange But True	1972	50.00	100.00	200.00
TIN HOUSE					
EPIC					
❏ E 30511	Tin House	1971	5.00	10.00	20.00
TINGLING MOTHER'S CIRCUS					
MUSICOR					
❏ MS-3167	Circus of the Mind	1968	6.25	12.50	25.00
TINO AND THE REVLONS					
DEARBORN					
❏ 1004	By Request at the Sway-Zee	1966	50.00	100.00	200.00
TIPTON, CARL					
SIMS					
❏ LP-143 [M]	The Carl Tipton Show	196?	10.00	20.00	40.00
TITANS, THE					
MGM					
❏ E-3992 [M]	Today's Teen Beat	1961	7.50	15.00	30.00
❏ SE-3992 [S]	Today's Teen Beat	1961	10.00	20.00	40.00
TITUS GROAN					
JANUS					
❏ JLS-3024	Titus Groan	1971	7.50	15.00	30.00

Number	Title (A Side/B Side)	Yr	VG	VG+	NM
TITUS OATES					
LIPS					
❏ (no #)	Jungle Lady	1974	50.00	100.00	200.00
TJADER, CAL					
CRYSTAL CLEAR					
❏ 8003	Huracan	1978	6.25	12.50	25.00
—Direct-to-disc recording					
FANTASY					
❏ 3-9 [10]	The Cal Tjader Trio	1953	25.00	50.00	100.00
—Black vinyl					
❏ 3-9 [10]	The Cal Tjader Trio	1953	37.50	75.00	150.00
—Any of various non-black vinyl pressings					
❏ 3-17 [10]	Ritmo Caliente	1954	25.00	50.00	100.00
—Black vinyl					
❏ 3-17 [10]	Ritmo Caliente	1954	37.50	75.00	150.00
—Any of various non-black vinyl pressings					
❏ 3202 [M]	Mambo with Tjader	1955	25.00	50.00	100.00
—Red vinyl					
❏ 3202 [M]	Mambo with Tjader	1956	12.50	25.00	50.00
—Black vinyl, red label, non-flexible vinyl					
❏ 3202 [M]	Mambo with Tjader	196?	6.25	12.50	25.00
—Black vinyl, red label, flexible vinyl					
❏ 3211 [M]	Tjader Plays Tjazz	1956	12.50	25.00	50.00
—Black vinyl, red label, non-flexible vinyl					
❏ 3211 [M]	Tjader Plays Tjazz	1956	25.00	50.00	100.00
—Red vinyl					
❏ 3216 [M]	Ritmo Caliente	1956	12.50	25.00	50.00
—Black vinyl, red label, non-flexible vinyl					
❏ 3216 [M]	Ritmo Caliente	1956	25.00	50.00	100.00
—Red vinyl					
❏ 3216 [M]	Ritmo Caliente	196?	6.25	12.50	25.00
—Black vinyl, red label, flexible vinyl					
❏ 3221 [M]	Tjader Plays Mambo	1956	12.50	25.00	50.00
—Black vinyl, red label, non-flexible vinyl					
❏ 3221 [M]	Tjader Plays Mambo	1956	25.00	50.00	100.00
—Red vinyl					
❏ 3221 [M]	Tjader Plays Mambo	196?	6.25	12.50	25.00
—Black vinyl, red label, flexible vinyl					
❏ 3227 [M]	Cal Tjader Quartet	1956	25.00	50.00	100.00
—Red vinyl					
❏ 3232 [M]	The Cal Tjader Quintet	1956	12.50	25.00	50.00
—Black vinyl, red label, non-flexible vinyl					
❏ 3232 [M]	The Cal Tjader Quintet	1956	25.00	50.00	100.00
—Red vinyl					
❏ 3232 [M]	The Cal Tjader Quintet	196?	6.25	12.50	25.00
—Black vinyl, red label, flexible vinyl					
❏ 3241 [M]	Jazz at the Blackhawk	1957	7.50	15.00	30.00
—Black vinyl, red label, non-flexible vinyl					
❏ 3241 [M]	Jazz at the Blackhawk	1957	12.50	25.00	50.00
—Red vinyl					
❏ 3250 [M]	Latin Kick	1957	7.50	15.00	30.00
—Black vinyl, red label, non-flexible vinyl					
❏ 3250 [M]	Latin Kick	1957	12.50	25.00	50.00
—Red vinyl					
❏ 3253 [M]	Cal Tjader	1958	10.00	20.00	40.00
—Black vinyl, non-flexible vinyl					
❏ 3253 [M]	Cal Tjader	1958	15.00	30.00	60.00
—Red vinyl					
❏ 3262 [M]	Mas Ritmo Caliente	1958	7.50	15.00	30.00
—Black vinyl, red label, non-flexible vinyl					
❏ 3262 [M]	Mas Ritmo Caliente	1958	12.50	25.00	50.00
—Red vinyl					
❏ 3271 [M]	San Francisco Moods	1958	7.50	15.00	30.00
—Black vinyl, red label, non-flexible vinyl					
❏ 3271 [M]	San Francisco Moods	1958	12.50	25.00	50.00
—Red vinyl					
❏ 3275 [M]	Cal Tjader's Latin Concert	1958	7.50	15.00	30.00
—Black vinyl, red label, non-flexible vinyl					
❏ 3275 [M]	Cal Tjader's Latin Concert	1958	12.50	25.00	50.00
—Red vinyl					
❏ 3278 [M]	Tjader Plays Tjazz	1958	7.50	15.00	30.00
—Black vinyl, red label, non-flexible vinyl					
❏ 3278 [M]	Tjader Plays Tjazz	1958	12.50	25.00	50.00
—Red vinyl; reissue of 3211					
❏ 3279 [M]	Latin for Lovers	1958	7.50	15.00	30.00
—Black vinyl, red label, non-flexible vinyl					
❏ 3279 [M]	Latin for Lovers	1958	12.50	25.00	50.00
—Red vinyl					
❏ 3283 [M]	A Night at the Blackhawk	1959	7.50	15.00	30.00
—Black vinyl, red label, non-flexible vinyl					
❏ 3283 [M]	A Night at the Blackhawk	1959	12.50	25.00	50.00
—Red vinyl					
❏ 3289 [M]	Tjader Goes Latin	1959	7.50	15.00	30.00
—Black vinyl, red label, non-flexible vinyl					
❏ 3289 [M]	Tjader Goes Latin	1959	12.50	25.00	50.00
—Red vinyl					
❏ 3295 [M]	Concert by the Sea	1959	7.50	15.00	30.00
—Black vinyl, red label, non-flexible vinyl					
❏ 3295 [M]	Concert by the Sea	1959	12.50	25.00	50.00
—Red vinyl					
❏ 3299 [M]	Concert on the Campus	1960	6.25	12.50	25.00
—Black vinyl, red label, non-flexible vinyl					
❏ 3299 [M]	Concert on the Campus	1960	10.00	20.00	40.00
—Red vinyl					
❏ 3307 [M]	Cal Tjader Quartet	1960	6.25	12.50	25.00
—Black vinyl, red label, non-flexible vinyl					
❏ 3307 [M]	Cal Tjader Quartet	1960	10.00	20.00	40.00
—Red vinyl					
❏ 3309 [M]	Demasiado Caliente	1960	6.25	12.50	25.00
—Black vinyl, red label, non-flexible vinyl					
❏ 3309 [M]	Demasiado Caliente	1960	10.00	20.00	40.00
—Red vinyl					

T

Number	Title (A Side/B Side)	Yr	VG	VG+	NM
❑ 3310 [M]	West Side Story	1960	6.25	12.50	25.00
—Black vinyl, red label, non-flexible vinyl					
❑ 3310 [M]	West Side Story	1960	10.00	20.00	40.00
—Red vinyl					
❑ 3313 [M]	Cal Tjader Quintet	1961	6.25	12.50	25.00
—Black vinyl, red label, non-flexible vinyl					
❑ 3313 [M]	Cal Tjader Quintet	1961	10.00	20.00	40.00
—Red vinyl; evidently a different album than 3232					
❑ 3315 [M]	Cal Tjader Live and Direct	1961	6.25	12.50	25.00
—Black vinyl, red label, non-flexible vinyl					
❑ 3315 [M]	Cal Tjader Live and Direct	1961	10.00	20.00	40.00
—Red vinyl					
❑ 3326 [M]	Mambo	1961	6.25	12.50	25.00
—Black vinyl, red label, non-flexible vinyl					
❑ 3326 [M]	Mambo	1961	10.00	20.00	40.00
—Red vinyl					
❑ 3330 [M]	Cal Tjader Plays the Harold Arlen Songbook	1961	6.25	12.50	25.00
—Black vinyl, red label, non-flexible vinyl					
❑ 3330 [M]	Cal Tjader Plays the Harold Arlen Songbook	1961	10.00	20.00	40.00
—Red vinyl					
❑ 3339 [M]	Latino	1962	6.25	12.50	25.00
—Black vinyl, red label, non-flexible vinyl					
❑ 3339 [M]	Latino	1962	10.00	20.00	40.00
—Red vinyl					
❑ 3341 [M]	Concert by the Sea, Volume 2	1962	6.25	12.50	25.00
—Black vinyl, red label, non-flexible vinyl					
❑ 3341 [M]	Concert by the Sea, Volume 2	1962	10.00	20.00	40.00
—Red vinyl					
❑ 8003 [S]	Mas Ritmo Caliente	196?	5.00	10.00	20.00
—Black vinyl, blue label, non-flexible vinyl					
❑ 8003 [S]	Mas Ritmo Caliente	196?	7.50	15.00	30.00
—Blue vinyl					
❑ 8014 [S]	Cal Tjader's Latin Concert	196?	5.00	10.00	20.00
—Black vinyl, blue label, non-flexible vinyl					
❑ 8014 [S]	Cal Tjader's Latin Concert	196?	7.50	15.00	30.00
—Blue vinyl					
❑ 8016 [S]	Latin for Lovers	196?	5.00	10.00	20.00
—Black vinyl, blue label, non-flexible vinyl					
❑ 8016 [S]	Latin for Lovers	196?	7.50	15.00	30.00
—Blue vinyl					
❑ 8017 [S]	San Francisco Moods	196?	5.00	10.00	20.00
—Black vinyl, blue label, non-flexible vinyl					
❑ 8017 [S]	San Francisco Moods	196?	7.50	15.00	30.00
—Blue vinyl					
❑ 8019 [S]	Latin for Dancers	196?	25.00	50.00	100.00
—Blue vinyl; the existence of this has been confirmed. Black vinyl copies of 8019 are unknown.					
❑ 8019 [S]	Latin for Dancers	196?	30.00	60.00	120.00
—A red vinyl copy with this number is known to exist also, probably pressed in error					
❑ 8026 [S]	A Night at the Blackhawk	196?	5.00	10.00	20.00
—Black vinyl, blue label, non-flexible vinyl					
❑ 8026 [S]	A Night at the Blackhawk	196?	7.50	15.00	30.00
—Blue vinyl					
❑ 8030 [S]	Tjader Goes Latin	196?	5.00	10.00	20.00
—Black vinyl, blue label, non-flexible vinyl					
❑ 8030 [S]	Tjader Goes Latin	196?	7.50	15.00	30.00
—Blue vinyl					
❑ 8033 [S]	Latin Kick	196?	5.00	10.00	20.00
—Black vinyl, blue label, non-flexible vinyl					
❑ 8033 [S]	Latin Kick	196?	7.50	15.00	30.00
—Blue vinyl					
❑ 8038 [S]	Concert by the Sea	196?	5.00	10.00	20.00
—Black vinyl, blue label, non-flexible vinyl					
❑ 8038 [S]	Concert by the Sea	196?	7.50	15.00	30.00
—Blue vinyl					
❑ 8044 [S]	Concert on the Campus	196?	5.00	10.00	20.00
—Black vinyl, blue label, non-flexible vinyl					
❑ 8044 [S]	Concert on the Campus	196?	7.50	15.00	30.00
—Blue vinyl					
❑ 8053 [S]	Demasiado Caliente	196?	5.00	10.00	20.00
—Black vinyl, blue label, non-flexible vinyl					
❑ 8053 [S]	Demasiado Caliente	196?	7.50	15.00	30.00
—Blue vinyl					
❑ 8054 [S]	West Side Story	196?	5.00	10.00	20.00
—Black vinyl, blue label, non-flexible vinyl					
❑ 8054 [S]	West Side Story	196?	7.50	15.00	30.00
—Blue vinyl					
❑ 8057 [S]	Mambo	1962	5.00	10.00	20.00
—Black vinyl, blue label, non-flexible vinyl					
❑ 8057 [S]	Mambo	1962	7.50	15.00	30.00
—Blue vinyl					
❑ 8059 [S]	Cal Tjader Live and Direct	1962	5.00	10.00	20.00
—Black vinyl, blue label, non-flexible vinyl					
❑ 8059 [S]	Cal Tjader Live and Direct	1962	7.50	15.00	30.00
—Blue vinyl					
❑ 8072 [S]	Cal Tjader Plays the Harold Arlen Songbook	1962	5.00	10.00	20.00
—Black vinyl, blue label, non-flexible vinyl					
❑ 8072 [S]	Cal Tjader Plays the Harold Arlen Songbook	1962	7.50	15.00	30.00
—Blue vinyl					
❑ 8077 [R]	Ritmo Caliente	1962	5.00	10.00	20.00
—Black vinyl, blue label, non-flexible vinyl					
❑ 8077 [R]	Ritmo Caliente	1962	7.50	15.00	30.00
—Blue vinyl					
❑ 8079 [S]	Latino	1962	5.00	10.00	20.00
—Black vinyl, blue label, non-flexible vinyl					
❑ 8079 [S]	Latino	1962	7.50	15.00	30.00
—Blue vinyl					
❑ 8083 [R]	Cal Tjader Quartet	1962	5.00	10.00	20.00
—Black vinyl, blue label, non-flexible vinyl					
❑ 8083 [R]	Cal Tjader Quartet	1962	7.50	15.00	30.00
—Blue vinyl					
❑ 8084 [S]	Cal Tjader Quintet	1962	5.00	10.00	20.00
—Black vinyl, blue label, non-flexible vinyl					
❑ 8084 [S]	Cal Tjader Quintet	1962	7.50	15.00	30.00
—Blue vinyl; stereo version of 3313					

Number	Title (A Side/B Side)	Yr	VG	VG+	NM
❑ 8085 [R]	The Cal Tjader Quintet	196?	5.00	10.00	20.00
—Black vinyl, blue label, non-flexible vinyl					
❑ 8085 [R]	The Cal Tjader Quintet	196?	7.50	15.00	30.00
—Blue vinyl; stereo version of 3232					
❑ 8096 [R]	Jazz at the Blackhawk	1962	5.00	10.00	20.00
—Black vinyl, blue label, non-flexible vinyl					
❑ 8096 [R]	Jazz at the Blackhawk	1962	7.50	15.00	30.00
—Blue vinyl					
❑ 8097 [R]	Tjader Plays Tjazz	1962	5.00	10.00	20.00
—Black vinyl, blue label, non-flexible vinyl					
❑ 8097 [R]	Tjader Plays Tjazz	1962	7.50	15.00	30.00
—Blue vinyl					
❑ 8098 [S]	Concert by the Sea, Volume 2	1962	5.00	10.00	20.00
—Black vinyl, blue label, non-flexible vinyl					
❑ 8098 [S]	Concert by the Sea, Volume 2	1962	7.50	15.00	30.00
—Blue vinyl					
SAVOY					
❑ MG-9036 [10]	Cal Tjader — Vibist	1954	25.00	50.00	100.00
SKYE					
❑ SK-1	Solar Heat	1968	5.00	10.00	20.00
❑ SK-10	Cal Tjader Plugs In	1969	5.00	10.00	20.00
VERVE					
❑ V-8419 [M]	In a Latin Bag	1961	5.00	10.00	20.00
❑ V6-8419 [S]	In a Latin Bag	1961	6.25	12.50	25.00
❑ V-8459 [M]	Saturday Night…Sunday Night at the Blackhawk	1962	5.00	10.00	20.00
❑ V6-8459 [S]	Saturday Night…Sunday Night at the Blackhawk	1962	6.25	12.50	25.00
❑ V-8470 [M]	The Contemporary Music of Mexico and Brazil	1962	5.00	10.00	20.00
❑ V6-8470 [S]	The Contemporary Music of Mexico and Brazil	1962	6.25	12.50	25.00
❑ V-8507 [M]	Several Shades of Jade	1963	5.00	10.00	20.00
❑ V6-8507 [S]	Several Shades of Jade	1963	6.25	12.50	25.00
❑ V-8531 [M]	Sona Libre	1963	5.00	10.00	20.00
❑ V6-8531 [S]	Sona Libre	1963	6.25	12.50	25.00
❑ V-8575 [M]	Breeze from the East	1964	5.00	10.00	20.00
❑ V6-8575 [S]	Breeze from the East	1964	6.25	12.50	25.00
❑ V-8585 [M]	Warm Wave	1964	5.00	10.00	20.00
❑ V6-8585 [S]	Warm Wave	1964	6.25	12.50	25.00
❑ V-8614 [M]	Soul Sauce	1965	5.00	10.00	20.00
❑ V6-8614 [S]	Soul Sauce	1965	6.25	12.50	25.00
❑ V-8626 [M]	Soul Bird: Whippenpoof	1965	5.00	10.00	20.00
❑ V6-8626 [S]	Soul Bird: Whippenpoof	1965	6.25	12.50	25.00
❑ V-8637 [M]	Soul Burst	1965	5.00	10.00	20.00
❑ V6-8637 [S]	Soul Burst	1965	6.25	12.50	25.00
❑ V6-8651 [S]	El Soni Do Nuevo — The New Soul Sound	1966	5.00	10.00	20.00
❑ V6-8671 [S]	Along Comes Cal	1966	5.00	10.00	20.00
❑ V6-8725 [S]	The Best of Cal Tjader	1967	5.00	10.00	20.00
❑ V-8730 [M]	Hip Vibrations	1967	5.00	10.00	20.00

TJADER, CAL/DON ELLIOTT

SAVOY

Number	Title (A Side/B Side)	Yr	VG	VG+	NM
❑ MG-12054 [M]	Vib-Rations	1956	10.00	20.00	40.00
—Reissue of 9036 and 9033					

TJADER, CAL, AND STAN GETZ

Also see each artist's individual listings.

FANTASY

Number	Title (A Side/B Side)	Yr	VG	VG+	NM
❑ 3266 [M]	Cal Tjader-Stan Getz Sextet	1958	7.50	15.00	30.00
—Black vinyl, red label, non-flexible vinyl					
❑ 3266 [M]	Cal Tjader-Stan Getz Sextet	1958	12.50	25.00	50.00
—Red vinyl					
❑ 8005 [S]	Cal Tjader-Stan Getz Sextet	196?	5.00	10.00	20.00
—Black vinyl, blue label, non-flexible vinyl					
❑ 8005 [S]	Cal Tjader-Stan Getz Sextet	196?	7.50	15.00	30.00
—Blue vinyl					

TOAD HALL

LIBERTY

Number	Title (A Side/B Side)	Yr	VG	VG+	NM
❑ LST-7580	Toad Hall	1968	6.25	12.50	25.00

TOAD THE WET SPROCKET

COLUMBIA

Number	Title (A Side/B Side)	Yr	VG	VG+	NM
❑ FC 45326	Bread and Circus	1989	3.00	6.00	12.00
❑ C 46060	Pale	1990	7.50	15.00	30.00
—Marbled white (almost greenish) vinyl					
❑ C 47309	Fear	1991	5.00	10.00	20.00

TOADS, THE

WIGGINS

Number	Title (A Side/B Side)	Yr	VG	VG+	NM
❑ 64021 [M]	The Toads	1964	75.00	150.00	300.00

TODD, ART AND DOTTY

DART

Number	Title (A Side/B Side)	Yr	VG	VG+	NM
❑ D-444 [M]	Black Velvet Eyes	1959	10.00	20.00	40.00

DOT

Number	Title (A Side/B Side)	Yr	VG	VG+	NM
❑ DLP-3742 [M]	Chanson d'Amour (Song of Love)	1966	6.25	12.50	25.00
❑ DLP-25742 [S]	Chanson d'Amour (Song of Love)	1966	7.50	15.00	30.00

TOE FAT

RARE EARTH

Number	Title (A Side/B Side)	Yr	VG	VG+	NM
❑ RS-511	Toe Fat	1970	6.25	12.50	25.00
❑ RS-525	Toe Fat Two	1971	6.25	12.50	25.00

TOGAWA, PAUL

MODE

Number	Title (A Side/B Side)	Yr	VG	VG+	NM
❑ LP-104 [M]	Paul Togawa Quartet	1957	20.00	40.00	80.00

TOKENS, THE

B.T. PUPPY

Number	Title (A Side/B Side)	Yr	VG	VG+	NM
❑ BTP-1000 [M]	I Hear Trumpets Blow	1966	5.00	10.00	20.00
❑ BTPS-1000 [P]	I Hear Trumpets Blow	1966	6.25	12.50	25.00
❑ BTPS-1006	Tokens of Gold	1969	6.25	12.50	25.00
❑ BTPS-1012	Greatest Moments	1970	6.25	12.50	25.00

Number	Title (A Side/B Side)	Yr	VG	VG+	NM
❏ BTPS-1014	December 5th	1971	50.00	100.00	200.00
❏ BTPS-1027	Intercourse	1971	150.00	300.00	600.00

BUDDAH
| ❏ BDS-5059 | Both Sides Now | 1971 | 3.75 | 7.50 | 15.00 |

DIPLOMAT
| ❏ D-2308 [M] | Kings of the Hot Rods | 196? | 6.25 | 12.50 | 25.00 |
| ❏ DS-2308 [S] | Kings of the Hot Rods | 196? | 7.50 | 15.00 | 30.00 |

RCA
| ❏ 8534-1-R | Re-Doo-Wopp | 1988 | 2.50 | 5.00 | 10.00 |

RCA VICTOR
❏ LPM-2514 [M]	The Lion Sleeps Tonight	1961	20.00	40.00	80.00
❏ LSP-2514 [S]	The Lion Sleeps Tonight	1961	37.50	75.00	150.00
❏ LPM-2631 [M]	We, The Tokens, Sing Folk	1962	10.00	20.00	40.00
❏ LSP-2631 [S]	We, The Tokens, Sing Folk	1962	12.50	25.00	50.00
❏ LPM-2886 [M]	Wheels	1964	20.00	40.00	80.00
❏ LSP-2886 [S]	Wheels	1964	25.00	50.00	100.00
❏ LPM-3685 [M]	The Tokens Again	1966	10.00	20.00	40.00
❏ LSP-3685 [S]	The Tokens Again	1966	12.50	25.00	50.00

WARNER BROS.
| ❏ W 1685 [M] | It's a Happening World | 1967 | 6.25 | 12.50 | 25.00 |
| ❏ WS 1685 [S] | It's a Happening World | 1967 | 5.00 | 10.00 | 20.00 |

TOKENS, THE AND THE HAPPENINGS
Also see each artist's individual listings.

B.T. PUPPY
| ❏ BTP-1002 [M] | Back to Back | 1967 | 6.00 | 10.00 | 20.00 |

—Half this LP is by the Tokens, the other half by the Happenings
| ❏ BTPS-1002 [S] | Back to Back | 1967 | 6.25 | 12.50 | 25.00 |

TOLBERT, ISRAEL
WARREN/STAX
| ❏ STS-2038 | Popper Stopper | 1971 | 10.00 | 20.00 | 40.00 |

—Cover says "Warren Records Distributed by Stax," label is Stax

TOLKIEN, J.R.R.
CAEDMON
| ❏ TC 1478 | J.R.R. Tolkien Reads and Sings His "The Lord of the Rings" | 1975 | 5.00 | 10.00 | 20.00 |

TOLLIVER, CHARLES
STRATA-EAST
❏ SES-1971	Music Inc.	1971	5.00	10.00	20.00
❏ SES-1972	Live at Slugs'	1972	5.00	10.00	20.00
❏ SES-19720	Live at Slugs', Vol. 2	1972	5.00	10.00	20.00
❏ SES-19740/1 [(2)]	Live at the Loosdrecht Jazz Festival	1974	6.25	12.50	25.00
❏ SES-19745	Live in Tokyo	1974	5.00	10.00	20.00

TOM AND JERRY (2)
Tommy Tomlinson and JERRY KENNEDY, a country instrumental duo.

MERCURY
❏ MG-20626 [M]	Guitar's Greatest Hits	1961	7.50	15.00	30.00
❏ MG-20671 [M]	Guitars Play the Sound of Ray Charles	1962	7.50	15.00	30.00
❏ MG-20756 [M]	Guitar's Greatest Hits, Vol. 2	1962	7.50	15.00	30.00
❏ MG-20842 [M]	Surfin' Hootenanny	1963	10.00	20.00	40.00
❏ SR-60626 [S]	Guitar's Greatest Hits	1961	10.00	20.00	40.00
❏ SR-60671 [S]	Guitars Play the Sound of Ray Charles	1962	10.00	20.00	40.00
❏ SR-60756 [S]	Guitar's Greatest Hits, Vol. 2	1962	10.00	20.00	40.00
❏ SR-60842 [S]	Surfin' Hootenanny	1963	12.50	25.00	50.00

TOM TOM CLUB
SIRE
❏ SRK 3628	Tom Tom Club	1981	2.50	5.00	10.00
❏ 23916	Close to the Bone	1983	2.50	5.00	10.00
❏ 25888	Boom Boom Chi Boom Boom	1989	2.50	5.00	10.00

WARNER BROS.
| ❏ WBMS-120 [DJ] | Wordy Rapping with the Tom Tom Club | 1986 | 6.25 | 12.50 | 25.00 |

—Part of "The Warner Bros. Music Show"; promo only

TOMMY AND THE TWISTERS
REGENT
| ❏ MG-6104 [M] | Let's All Do the Twist | 1961 | 10.00 | 20.00 | 40.00 |

TOMORROW
SIRE
| ❏ SES-97912 | Tomorrow | 1968 | 15.00 | 30.00 | 60.00 |

TOMPALL AND THE GLASER BROTHERS
DECCA
| ❏ DL 4041 [M] | This Land Folk Songs | 1960 | 7.50 | 15.00 | 30.00 |
| ❏ DL 74041 [S] | This Land Folk Songs | 1960 | 10.00 | 20.00 | 40.00 |

ELEKTRA
| ❏ 5E-542 | Lovin' Her Was Easier | 1981 | 2.50 | 5.00 | 10.00 |
| ❏ 60148 | After All These Years | 1982 | 2.50 | 5.00 | 10.00 |

MGM
❏ E-4465 [M]	Tompall & the Glaser Brothers	1967	6.25	12.50	25.00
❏ SE-4465 [S]	Tompall & the Glaser Brothers	1967	5.00	10.00	20.00
❏ SE-4510	Through the Eyes of Love	1968	3.75	7.50	15.00
❏ SE-4620	Now Country	1969	3.75	7.50	15.00
❏ SE-4775	Award Winners	1971	3.75	7.50	15.00
❏ SE-4812	Rings and Things	1972	3.75	7.50	15.00
❏ SE-4888	Great Hits from Two Decades	1973	3.75	7.50	15.00
❏ SE-4976	Vocal Group of the Decade	1974	3.75	7.50	15.00

TONEY, OSCAR, JR.
BELL
| ❏ 6006 [M] | For Your Precious Love | 1967 | 6.25 | 12.50 | 25.00 |
| ❏ S-6006 [S] | For Your Precious Love | 1967 | 7.50 | 15.00 | 30.00 |

TONGUE
HEMISPHERE
| ❏ HIS-101 | Tongue | 1970 | 7.50 | 15.00 | 30.00 |

TONGUE AND GROOVE
FONTANA
| ❏ SRF-67593 | Tongue and Groove | 1968 | 5.00 | 10.00 | 20.00 |

TONTO'S EXPANDING HEAD BAND
EMBRYO
| ❏ SD 732 | Zero Time | 1971 | 5.00 | 10.00 | 20.00 |

TOO MUCH JOY
ALIAS
| ❏ A-003 | Son of Sam I Am | 1988 | 2.50 | 5.00 | 10.00 |

GIANT
| ❏ PRO-A-5054 [DJ] | Besides | 1991 | 3.00 | 6.00 | 12.00 |

—Promo-only collection

STONEGARDEN
| ❏ SGN-901 | Green Eggs and Crack | 1987 | 50.00 | 100.00 | 200.00 |

TOP DRAWER
WISH BONE
| ❏ 721207 | Solid Oak | 1969 | 100.00 | 200.00 | 400.00 |

TOPSIDERS, THE
JOSIE
| ❏ JOZ-4000 [M] | Rock Goes Folk | 1963 | 6.25 | 12.50 | 25.00 |

TORME, MEL
ALLEGRO ELITE
| ❏ 4117 [10] | Mel Torme Sings | 195? | 7.50 | 15.00 | 30.00 |

ATLANTIC
❏ 8066 [M]	Mel Torme at the Red Hill Inn	1962	7.50	15.00	30.00
❏ SD 8066 [S]	Mel Torme at the Red Hill Inn	1962	10.00	20.00	40.00
❏ 8069 [M]	Comin' Home Baby	1962	7.50	15.00	30.00
❏ SD 8069 [S]	Comin' Home Baby	1962	10.00	20.00	40.00
❏ 8091 [M]	Sunday in New York	1963	7.50	15.00	30.00
❏ SD 8091 [S]	Sunday in New York	1963	10.00	20.00	40.00

AUDIOPHILE
| ❏ 67 | Mel Torme Sings About Love | 198? | 5.00 | 10.00 | 20.00 |

BETHLEHEM
❏ BCP-34 [M]	It's a Blue World	1956	12.50	25.00	50.00
❏ BCP-52 [M]	Mel Torme and the Marty Paich Dektette	1956	12.50	25.00	50.00
❏ BCP 6013 [M]	Mel Torme Sings Fred Astaire	1957	12.50	25.00	50.00
❏ BCP 6016 [M]	California Suite	1957	12.50	25.00	50.00
❏ BCP 6020 [M]	Mel Torme Live at the Crescendo	1958	12.50	25.00	50.00
❏ BCP 6031 [M]	Songs for Any Taste	1959	12.50	25.00	50.00
❏ BCP 6042	The Torme Touch	1978	3.00	6.00	12.00

—Black rainbow label

CAPITOL
❏ P 200 [M]	California Suite	1950	25.00	50.00	100.00
❏ ST-313	A Time for Us	1969	3.00	6.00	12.00
❏ ST-430	Raindrops Keep Falling on My Head	1970	3.00	6.00	12.00

COLUMBIA
| ❏ CS 9118 [S] | That's All — A Lush Romantic Album | 1965 | 5.00 | 10.00 | 20.00 |

CORAL
| ❏ CRL 57012 [M] | Gene Norman Presents Mel Torme "Live" at the Crescendo | 1955 | 12.50 | 25.00 | 50.00 |
| ❏ CRL 57044 [M] | Musical Sounds Are the Best Songs | 1956 | 12.50 | 25.00 | 50.00 |

LIBERTY
| ❏ LST-7560 | A Day in the Life of Bonnie and Clyde | 1968 | 5.00 | 10.00 | 20.00 |

MGM
| ❏ E 552 [10] | Mel Torme Sings | 1952 | 25.00 | 50.00 | 100.00 |

STRAND
| ❏ SL-1076 [M] | Mel Torme Sings | 1960 | 5.00 | 10.00 | 20.00 |
| ❏ SLS-1076 [S] | Mel Torme Sings | 1960 | 6.25 | 12.50 | 25.00 |

VENISE
| ❏ 10021 [M] | The Touch of Your Lips | 196? | 5.00 | 10.00 | 20.00 |

—Yellow vinyl; reissue of Tops L-1615 without patter in between songs

VERVE
| ❏ MGV 2105 [M] | Torme | 1958 | 12.50 | 25.00 | 50.00 |
| ❏ V-2105 [M] | Torme | 1961 | 5.00 | 10.00 | 20.00 |

—Reissue
| ❏ V6-2105 [S] | Torme | 1961 | 6.25 | 12.50 | 25.00 |

—Reissue
| ❏ MGV 2117 [M] | Ole Torme! Mel Torme Goes South of the Border with Billy May | 1959 | 12.50 | 25.00 | 50.00 |
| ❏ V-2117 [M] | Ole Torme! Mel Torme Goes South of the Border with Billy May | 1961 | 5.00 | 10.00 | 20.00 |

—Reissue
| ❏ V6-2117 [S] | Ole Torme! Mel Torme Goes South of the Border with Billy May | 1961 | 6.25 | 12.50 | 25.00 |

—Reissue
| ❏ MGV 2120 [M] | Back in Town | 1959 | 12.50 | 25.00 | 50.00 |
| ❏ V-2120 [M] | Back in Town | 1961 | 5.00 | 10.00 | 20.00 |

—Reissue
| ❏ V6-2120 [S] | Back in Town | 1961 | 6.25 | 12.50 | 25.00 |

—Reissue
| ❏ MGV 2132 [M] | Mel Torme Swings Schubert Alley | 1960 | 12.50 | 25.00 | 50.00 |
| ❏ V-2132 [M] | Mel Torme Swings Shubert Alley | 1961 | 5.00 | 10.00 | 20.00 |

—Reissue
| ❏ V6-2132 [S] | Mel Torme Swings Shubert Alley | 196? | 6.25 | 12.50 | 25.00 |

—Reissue of 62132
| ❏ MGV 2144 [M] | Swingin' on the Moon | 1960 | 12.50 | 25.00 | 50.00 |
| ❏ V-2144 [M] | Swingin' on the Moon | 1961 | 5.00 | 10.00 | 20.00 |

—Reissue
| ❏ V6-2144 [S] | Swingin' on the Moon | 1961 | 6.25 | 12.50 | 25.00 |

—Reissue of 62144
| ❏ MGV 2146 [M] | Broadway, Right Now | 1961 | 12.50 | 25.00 | 50.00 |
| ❏ V-2146 [M] | Broadway, Right Now | 1961 | 5.00 | 10.00 | 20.00 |

—Reissue
| ❏ V6-2146 [S] | Broadway, Right Now | 1961 | 6.25 | 12.50 | 25.00 |
| ❏ MGVS 6015 [S] | Torme | 1960 | 12.50 | 25.00 | 50.00 |

Number	Title (A Side/B Side)	Yr	VG	VG+	NM
❏ MGVS 6058 [S]	Ole Torme! Mel Torme Goes South of the Border with Billy May	1960	12.50	25.00	50.00
❏ MGVS 6063 [S]	Back in Town	1960	12.50	25.00	50.00
❏ MGVS 6146 [S]	Mel Torme Swings Shubert Alley	1960	12.50	25.00	50.00
❏ V-8440 [M]	My Kind of Music	1962	6.25	12.50	25.00
❏ V6-8440 [S]	My Kind of Music	1962	7.50	15.00	30.00
❏ V-8491 [M]	I Dig the Duke! I Dig the Count!	1962	6.25	12.50	25.00
❏ V6-8491 [S]	I Dig the Duke! I Dig the Count!	1962	7.50	15.00	30.00
❏ MGVS 62132 [S]	Mel Torme Swings Shubert Alley	196?	10.00	20.00	40.00
—Early reissue of 6146					
❏ MGVS 62144 [S]	Swingin' on the Moon	1960	15.00	30.00	60.00

TORME, MEL, AND BUDDY RICH
CENTURY
Number	Title (A Side/B Side)	Yr	VG	VG+	NM
❏ 1100	Together Again — For the First Time	1978	6.25	12.50	25.00
—Direct-to-disc recording					

TORMENTORS, THE
ROYAL
Number	Title (A Side/B Side)	Yr	VG	VG+	NM
❏ RLP-111 [M]	Hanging Around	1967	50.00	100.00	200.00

TORNADOES, THE (1)
LONDON
Number	Title (A Side/B Side)	Yr	VG	VG+	NM
❏ LL 3279 [M]	Telstar	1963	50.00	100.00	200.00
❏ LL 3293 [M]	The Sounds of the Tornadoes	1963	50.00	100.00	200.00
—Basically the same album as above, but with a new cover, one different track and the song order shuffled.					

TORNADOES, THE (2)
JOSIE
Number	Title (A Side/B Side)	Yr	VG	VG+	NM
❏ J-4005 [M]	Bustin' Surfboards	1963	50.00	100.00	200.00
❏ JS-4005 [S]	Bustin' Surfboards	1963	75.00	150.00	300.00
SUNDAZED
| ❏ LP-5024 | Bustin' Surfboards | 199? | 2.50 | 5.00 | 10.00 |

TOROK, MITCHELL
GUYDEN
Number	Title (A Side/B Side)	Yr	VG	VG+	NM
❏ GLP-502 [M]	Caribbean	1960	10.00	20.00	40.00
❏ ST-502 [S]	Caribbean	1960	12.50	25.00	50.00
REPRISE
| ❏ R 6223 [M] | Guitar Course | 1966 | 5.00 | 10.00 | 20.00 |
| ❏ RS 6223 [S] | Guitar Course | 1966 | 6.25 | 12.50 | 25.00 |

TORQUES, THE
LEMCO
Number	Title (A Side/B Side)	Yr	VG	VG+	NM
❏ 604	The Torques Live	1966	50.00	100.00	200.00
WIGGINS
| ❏ 64010 | Zoom! | 1967 | 50.00 | 100.00 | 200.00 |

TOTO
COLUMBIA
Number	Title (A Side/B Side)	Yr	VG	VG+	NM
❏ AS 577 [DJ]	Special Radio Interview	198?	5.00	10.00	20.00
❏ JC 35317	Toto	1978	2.50	5.00	10.00
❏ PC 35317	Toto	198?	2.00	4.00	8.00
—Budget-line reissue with new prefix					
❏ FC 36229	Hydra	1979	2.50	5.00	10.00
❏ PC 36229	Hydra	198?	2.00	4.00	8.00
—Budget-line reissue with new prefix					
❏ FC 36813	Turn Back	1981	2.50	5.00	10.00
❏ PC 36813	Turn Back	1984	2.00	4.00	8.00
—Budget-line reissue with new prefix					
❏ PD 36813 [PD]	Turn Back	1981	6.25	12.50	25.00
—Promo-only picture disc					
❏ FC 37728	Toto IV	1982	2.50	5.00	10.00
❏ 8C8 38685 [PD]	Africa/Rosanna	1983	5.00	10.00	20.00
—Africa-shaped picture disc; numbered like an LP although it has only these two songs on it and is (approximately) 7 inches					
❏ QC 38962	Isolation	1984	2.50	5.00	10.00
❏ 9C9 39911 [PD]	Isolation	1984	5.00	10.00	20.00
❏ FC 40273	Fahrenheit	1986	2.50	5.00	10.00
❏ FC 40873	The Seventh One	1988	2.50	5.00	10.00
❏ C 45369	Past to Present 1977-1990	1990	6.25	12.50	25.00
—Vinyl available only from Columbia House					
❏ HC 47728	Toto IV	198?	10.00	20.00	40.00
—Half-speed mastered edition					
MOBILE FIDELITY
| ❏ 1-250 | Toto IV | 1996 | 10.00 | 20.00 | 40.00 |
| —Audiophile vinyl | | | | | |

TOUCH
MAINLINE
Number	Title (A Side/B Side)	Yr	VG	VG+	NM
❏ PS-70-116-7	Street Suite	1969	1000.	1500.	2000.

TOUCH, THE
COLISEUM
Number	Title (A Side/B Side)	Yr	VG	VG+	NM
❏ DS-51004	The Touch	1968	6.25	12.50	25.00

TOUCHSTONE
UNITED ARTISTS
Number	Title (A Side/B Side)	Yr	VG	VG+	NM
❏ UAS-5563	Tarot	1972	7.50	15.00	30.00

TOUFF, CY
ARGO
Number	Title (A Side/B Side)	Yr	VG	VG+	NM
❏ LP-606 [M]	Doorway To Dixie	1956	10.00	20.00	40.00
❏ LP-641 [M]	Touff Assignment	1959	7.50	15.00	30.00
❏ LPS-641 [S]	Touff Assignment	1959	6.25	12.50	25.00
PACIFIC JAZZ
| ❏ PJ-42 [M] | Keester Parade | 1962 | 10.00 | 20.00 | 40.00 |
| ❏ PJ-1211 [M] | Cy Touff, His Octet and Quintet | 1956 | 25.00 | 50.00 | 100.00 |
WORLD PACIFIC
| ❏ PJM-410 [M] | Havin' A Ball | 1958 | 15.00 | 30.00 | 60.00 |

TOUSSAINT, ALLEN
RCA VICTOR
Number	Title (A Side/B Side)	Yr	VG	VG+	NM
❏ LPM-1767 [M]	The Wild Sounds of New Orleans	1958	75.00	150.00	300.00
—As "Al Tousan"					
REPRISE
| ❏ MS 2062 | Life, Love and Faith | 1972 | 6.25 | 12.50 | 25.00 |
SCEPTER
| ❏ 24003 | Toussaint | 1971 | 6.25 | 12.50 | 25.00 |
WARNER BROS.
| ❏ BSK 3142 | Motion | 1978 | 3.00 | 6.00 | 12.00 |

TOWER OF POWER
COLUMBIA
Number	Title (A Side/B Side)	Yr	VG	VG+	NM
❏ PC 34302	Ain't Nothin' Stoppin' Us Now	1976	2.50	5.00	10.00
—No bar code on cover					
❏ PC 34302	Ain't Nothin' Stoppin' Us Now	198?	2.00	4.00	8.00
—Budget-line reissue with bar code					
❏ JC 34906	We Came to Play!	1978	2.50	5.00	10.00
❏ JC 35784	Back on the Streets	1979	2.50	5.00	10.00
DIRECT DISC
| ❏ SD 16601 | Back to Oakland | 1980 | 6.25 | 12.50 | 25.00 |
| —Audiophile vinyl | | | | | |
SAN FRANCISCO
| ❏ SD 204 | East Bay Grease | 1971 | 12.50 | 25.00 | 50.00 |
SHEFFIELD LABS
| ❏ 17 | Direct | 1982 | 6.25 | 12.50 | 25.00 |
| —Direct-to-disc recording | | | | | |
WARNER BROS.
❏ BS 2616	Bump City	1972	3.75	7.50	15.00
—Green "WB" label					
❏ BS 2681	Tower of Power	1973	3.00	6.00	12.00
—"Burbank" palm trees label					
❏ BS 2681	Tower of Power	1973	3.75	7.50	15.00
—Green "WB" label					
❏ BS 2681	Tower of Power	1979	2.00	4.00	8.00
—White or tan label					
❏ BS 2749	Back to Oakland	1974	3.75	7.50	15.00
—"Burbank" palm trees label					
❏ BS 2749	Back to Oakland	1979	2.00	4.00	8.00
—White or tan label					
❏ BS 2834	Urban Renewal	1975	3.75	7.50	15.00
—"Burbank" palm trees label					
❏ BS 2880	In the Slot	1975	3.75	7.50	15.00
—"Burbank" palm trees label					
❏ BS 2924	Live and In Living Color	1976	3.75	7.50	15.00
—"Burbank" palm trees label					
❏ BS 2924	Live and In Living Color	1979	2.00	4.00	8.00
—White or tan label					

TOWNSEND, ED
CAPITOL
Number	Title (A Side/B Side)	Yr	VG	VG+	NM
❏ ST 1140 [S]	New in Town	1959	7.50	15.00	30.00
❏ T 1140 [M]	New in Town	1959	6.25	12.50	25.00
❏ ST 1214 [S]	Glad to Be Here	1959	7.50	15.00	30.00
❏ T 1214 [M]	Glad to Be Here	1959	6.25	12.50	25.00
CURTOM
| ❏ 5006 | Ed Townsend Now | 1976 | 3.00 | 6.00 | 12.00 |

TOWNSEND, HENRY
BLUESVILLE
Number	Title (A Side/B Side)	Yr	VG	VG+	NM
❏ BVLP-1041 [M]	Tired Bein' Mistreated	1962	30.00	60.00	120.00
—Blue label, silver print					
❏ BVLP-1041 [M]	Tired Bein' Mistreated	1964	7.50	15.00	30.00
—Blue label, trident logo at side					

TOWNSHEND, PETE
Also see THE WHO.
ATCO
Number	Title (A Side/B Side)	Yr	VG	VG+	NM
❏ SD 32-100	Empty Glass	1980	2.50	5.00	10.00
❏ SD 38-149	All the Best Cowboys Have Chinese Eyes	1982	2.50	5.00	10.00
❏ PR 940 [EP]	Deep End Sampler	1986	5.00	10.00	20.00
—Promo-only sampler from Deep End Live					
❏ 90063 [(2)]	Scoop	1983	3.00	6.00	12.00
❏ 90473	White City — A Novel	1985	2.50	5.00	10.00
❏ 90539 [(2)]	Another Scoop	1987	3.00	6.00	12.00
❏ 90553	Pete Townshend's Deep End Live!	1986	2.50	5.00	10.00
ATLANTIC
| ❏ 81996 | The Iron Man: The Musical by Pete Townshend | 1989 | 2.50 | 5.00 | 10.00 |
| —Also includes tracks by John Lee Hooker, Simon Townshend, Nina Simone, The Who | | | | | |
DECCA
| ❏ 79189 | Who Came First | 1972 | 5.00 | 10.00 | 20.00 |
| —With poster (deduct 50% if missing). Evidently a near-simultaneous release with Track 79189 | | | | | |
EEL PIE
❏ EPR-0007 [(2)]	Another Scoop	2002	10.00	20.00	40.00
—Classic Records edition on "Quiex SV" vinyl					
❏ EPR-0013 [(3)]	Scoop 3	2001	12.50	25.00	50.00
—Classic Records edition on "Quiex SV" vinyl					
MCA
| ❏ 2026 | Who Came First | 1973 | 3.00 | 6.00 | 12.00 |
| —Reissue of 79189 | | | | | |
TRACK
❏ PR-A-160 [DJ]	Pete Townshend Talks To and About Thunderclap Newman	1970	25.00	50.00	100.00
—One-sided promo-only interview record					
❏ 79189	Who Came First	1972	5.00	10.00	20.00
—With poster (deduct 50% if missing)					

Number	Title (A Side/B Side)	Yr	VG	VG+	NM

TOYS, THE
DYNOVOICE

| ❏ 9002 [M] | The Toys Sing "A Lover's Concerto" and "Attack!" | 1966 | 10.00 | 20.00 | 40.00 |
| ❏ S-9002 [P] | The Toys Sing "A Lover's Concerto" and "Attack!" | 1966 | 12.50 | 25.00 | 50.00 |

TRACEY, STAN
LONDON

| ❏ LL 3107 [M] | Showcase | 195? | 10.00 | 20.00 | 40.00 |

TRADE WINDS, THE
KAMA SUTRA

| ❏ KLP-8057 [M] | Excursions | 1967 | 6.25 | 12.50 | 25.00 |
| ❏ KSLP-8057 [S] | Excursions | 1967 | 7.50 | 15.00 | 30.00 |

TRADER HORNE
JANUS

| ❏ JLS-3012 | Morning Way | 1970 | 7.50 | 15.00 | 30.00 |

TRAFFIC
Also see DAVE MASON; STEVE WINWOOD.
ASYLUM

| ❏ 7E-1020 | When the Eagle Flies | 1974 | 3.00 | 6.00 | 12.00 |

ISLAND

❏ ILSD 2 [(2)]	Traffic — On the Road	197?	3.75	7.50	15.00
—Reissue					
❏ ILPS 9180	The Low Spark of High Heeled Boys	197?	3.00	6.00	12.00
—Reissue					
❏ ILPS 9224	Shoot Out at the Fantasy Factory	197?	3.00	6.00	12.00
—Reissue					
❏ SW-9306	The Low Spark of High Heeled Boys	1971	3.75	7.50	15.00
❏ SW-9323	Shoot Out at the Fantasy Factory	1973	3.75	7.50	15.00
❏ SMAS-9336 [(2)]	Traffic — On the Road	1973	5.00	10.00	20.00
❏ 90026	The Low Spark of High Heeled Boys	1983	2.00	4.00	8.00
—Reissue					
❏ 90027	Shoot Out at the Fantasy Factory	1983	2.00	4.00	8.00
—Reissue					
❏ 90028 [(2)]	Traffic — On the Road	1983	3.00	6.00	12.00
—Reissue					
❏ 90058	John Barleycorn Must Die	1983	2.00	4.00	8.00
—Reissue					
❏ 90059	Traffic	1983	2.00	4.00	8.00
—Reissue					
❏ 90060	Mr. Fantasy	1983	2.00	4.00	8.00
—Reissue					

MOBILE FIDELITY

| ❏ 1-209 | The Low Spark of High Heeled Boys | 1994 | 6.25 | 12.50 | 25.00 |
| —Audiophile vinyl | | | | | |

UNITED ARTISTS

❏ UA-LA421-G	Heavy Traffic	1975	3.75	7.50	15.00
❏ UA-LA526-G	More Heavy Traffic	1975	3.75	7.50	15.00
❏ UAL-3651 [M]	Heaven Is In Your Mind	1967	15.00	30.00	60.00
❏ UAS-5500	Best of Traffic	1969	5.00	10.00	20.00
—Originals have pink and orange labels					
❏ UAS-5504	John Barleycorn Must Die	1970	5.00	10.00	20.00
—Originals have black and orange labels					
❏ UAS-5550	Welcome to the Canteen	1971	3.75	7.50	15.00
❏ UAS-6651 [S]	Heaven Is In Your Mind	1967	12.50	25.00	50.00
❏ UAS-6651 [S]	Mr. Fantasy	1968	6.25	12.50	25.00
—Retitled version of "Heaven Is In Your Mind" with green strip across top of back with song titles					
❏ UAS-6651 [S]	Mr. Fantasy	1968	8.75	17.50	35.00
—Retitled version of "Heaven Is In Your Mind" with old title still on back cover					
❏ UAS-6676	Traffic	1968	5.00	10.00	20.00
—Originals have purple and orange labels					
❏ UAS-6702	Last Exit	1969	5.00	10.00	20.00
—Originals have purple and orange labels					
❏ ST-92018	Last Exit	1969	7.50	15.00	30.00
—Capitol Record Club edition; label is the old-style black with circles at the top!					

TRAILER, REX, AND THE PLAYBOYS
CROWN

| ❏ CLP-5158 [M] | Country & Western | 1958 | 6.25 | 12.50 | 25.00 |

TRAMLINE
A&M

| ❏ SP-4208 | Somewhere Down the Line | 1969 | 5.00 | 10.00 | 20.00 |

TRAMMELL, BOBBY LEE
ATLANTA

| ❏ 1503 [M] | Arkansas Twist | 1962 | 250.00 | 500.00 | 1000. |

SOUNCOT

| ❏ SC-1102 | I Dare America to Be Great | 1971 | 5.00 | 10.00 | 20.00 |
| ❏ SC-1141 | Love Isn't Love Till You Give It Away | 1972 | 3.75 | 7.50 | 15.00 |

TRAPEZE
THRESHOLD

❏ THS 2	Trapeze	1970	10.00	20.00	40.00
❏ THS 4	Medusa	1971	20.00	40.00	80.00
❏ THS 8	You Are the Music, We're Just the Band	1972	10.00	20.00	40.00
❏ THS 11	The Final Swing	1974	10.00	20.00	40.00

WARNER BROS.

| ❏ BS 2828 | Hot Wire | 1974 | 3.00 | 6.00 | 12.00 |
| ❏ BS 2887 | Trapeze | 1975 | 3.00 | 6.00 | 12.00 |

TRAPP FAMILY SINGERS, THE
RCA CAMDEN

| ❏ CAL-209 [M] | The Trapp Family Singers Present Christmas and Folk Songs | 195? | 5.00 | 10.00 | 20.00 |

TRASHMEN, THE
BEAT ROCKET

| ❏ BR 107 | Surfin' Bird | 1999 | 3.00 | 6.00 | 12.00 |
| —Reissue on 180-gram vinyl | | | | | |

GARRETT

| ❏ GA-200 [M] | Surfin' Bird | 1964 | 55.00 | 110.00 | 220.00 |
| ❏ GAS-200 [R] | Surfin' Bird | 1964 | 87.50 | 175.00 | 350.00 |

SUNDAZED

| ❏ LP 5002 | Live Bird '65-'67 | 1991 | 2.50 | 5.00 | 10.00 |
| ❏ LP 5003 | Great Lost Album | 1991 | 2.50 | 5.00 | 10.00 |

TRASK, DIANA
ABC

| ❏ ABDP-948 | Believe Me Now or Believe Me Later | 1976 | 3.00 | 6.00 | 12.00 |
| ❏ AC-30030 | The ABC Collection | 1976 | 3.00 | 6.00 | 12.00 |

ABC DOT

| ❏ DOSD-2007 | Diana Trask's Greatest Hits | 1974 | 3.00 | 6.00 | 12.00 |
| ❏ DOSD-2024 | The Mood I'm In | 1975 | 3.00 | 6.00 | 12.00 |

COLUMBIA

❏ CL 1601 [M]	Diana Trask	1961	6.25	12.50	25.00
❏ CL 1705 [M]	Diana Trask on TV	1961	6.25	12.50	25.00
❏ CS 8401 [S]	Diana Trask	1961	7.50	15.00	30.00
❏ CS 8505 [S]	Diana Trask on TV	1961	7.50	15.00	30.00

DOT

❏ DLP-25920	Miss Country Soul	1969	3.75	7.50	15.00
❏ DLP-25957	From the Heart	1969	3.75	7.50	15.00
❏ DOS-25989	Diana's Country	1971	3.75	7.50	15.00
❏ DOS-25999	Diana Trask Sings About Loving	1972	3.75	7.50	15.00
❏ DOS-26016	It's a Man's World	1973	3.75	7.50	15.00
❏ DOS-26022	Lean It All on Me	1974	3.75	7.50	15.00

PICKWICK/HILLTOP

| ❏ 6188 | Miss Country Soul | 197? | 2.50 | 5.00 | 10.00 |

TRAVEL AGENCY, THE
VIVA

| ❏ V-36017 | The Travel Agency | 1968 | 6.25 | 12.50 | 25.00 |

TRAVELERS 3, THE
ELEKTRA

❏ EKL-216 [M]	The Travelers 3	1963	6.25	12.50	25.00
❏ EKL-226 [M]	Open House	1963	6.25	12.50	25.00
❏ EKL-236 [M]	Live! Live! Live!	1963	6.25	12.50	25.00

TRAVELING WILBURYS
Also see BOB DYLAN; GEORGE HARRISON; ROY ORBISON; TOM PETTY AND THE HEARTBREAKERS.
WILBURY

| ❏ 25796 | Traveling Wilburys (Volume One) | 1988 | 5.00 | 10.00 | 20.00 |
| ❏ 26324 | Traveling Wilburys, Vol. 3 | 1990 | 5.00 | 10.00 | 20.00 |

TRAVELLERS, THE
KAPP

| ❏ KL-1157 [M] | Journey with the Travellers | 1960 | 6.25 | 12.50 | 25.00 |
| ❏ KS-3051 [S] | Journey with the Travellers | 1960 | 7.50 | 15.00 | 30.00 |

TRAVIS, MERLE
CAPITOL

❏ T 650 [M]	The Merle Travis Guitar	1956	30.00	60.00	120.00
—Turquoise or gray label					
❏ T 650 [M]	The Merle Travis Guitar	1959	7.50	15.00	30.00
—Black colorband label, logo at left					
❏ T 650 [M]	The Merle Travis Guitar	1962	5.00	10.00	20.00
—Black colorband label, logo at top					
❏ T 891 [M]	Back Home	1957	25.00	50.00	100.00
—Turquoise or gray label					
❏ T 891 [M]	Back Home	1959	7.50	15.00	30.00
—Black colorband label, logo at left					
❏ T 891 [M]	Back Home	1962	5.00	10.00	20.00
—Black colorband label, logo at top					
❏ T 1391 [M]	Walkin' the Strings	1960	20.00	40.00	80.00
—Black colorband label, logo at left					
❏ T 1391 [M]	Walkin' the Strings	1962	5.00	10.00	20.00
—Black colorband label, logo at top					
❏ ST 1664 [S]	Travis	1962	6.25	12.50	25.00
—Black colorband label, logo at top					
❏ ST 1664 [S]	Travis	1962	12.50	25.00	50.00
—Black colorband label, logo at left					
❏ T 1664 [M]	Travis	1962	5.00	10.00	20.00
—Black colorband label, logo at top					
❏ T 1664 [M]	Travis	1962	10.00	20.00	40.00
—Black colorband label, logo at left					
❏ ST 1956 [S]	Songs of the Coal Mines	1963	12.50	25.00	50.00
❏ T 1956 [M]	Songs of the Coal Mines	1963	10.00	20.00	40.00
❏ DT 2662 [R]	The Best of Merle Travis	1967	5.00	10.00	20.00
❏ T 2662 [M]	The Best of Merle Travis	1967	7.50	15.00	30.00
❏ ST 2938	Strictly Guitar	1968	6.25	12.50	25.00

TRAVIS, MERLE, AND JOE MAPHIS
CAPITOL

| ❏ ST 2102 [S] | Merle Travis and Joe Maphis | 1964 | 12.50 | 25.00 | 50.00 |
| ❏ T 2102 [M] | Merle Travis and Joe Maphis | 1964 | 10.00 | 20.00 | 40.00 |

TRAVIS, NICK
RCA VICTOR

| ❏ LPM-1010 [M] | The Panic Is On | 1954 | 20.00 | 40.00 | 80.00 |

TRAVIS, RANDY
MUSIC VALLEY

❏ (# unknown)	Randy Ray Live at the Nashville Palace	1982	75.00	150.00	300.00
—With no "Randy Travis" sticker on front cover					
❏ (# unknown)	Randy Ray Live at the Nashville Palace	1986	50.00	100.00	200.00
—With "Randy Travis" sticker on front cover; the records are the same as the first edition					

WARNER BROS.

| ❏ 25435 | Storms of Life | 1986 | 2.50 | 5.00 | 10.00 |

Number	Title (A Side/B Side)	Yr	VG	VG+	NM
❏ 25568	Always & Forever	1987	2.50	5.00	10.00
❏ 25738	Old 8x10	1988	2.50	5.00	10.00
❏ 25972	An Old-Fashioned Christmas	1989	3.00	6.00	12.00
❏ 25988	No Holdin' Back	1989	3.00	6.00	12.00
❏ R 174597	Heroes and Friends	1990	5.00	10.00	20.00

—Only released on vinyl through BMG Direct Marketing

TREE
GOAT FARM

Number	Title (A Side/B Side)	Yr	VG	VG+	NM
❏ 580	Tree	1970	17.50	35.00	70.00

TREMELOES, THE
DJM

Number	Title (A Side/B Side)	Yr	VG	VG+	NM
❏ 2	Shiner	1974	3.00	6.00	12.00

EPIC

Number	Title (A Side/B Side)	Yr	VG	VG+	NM
❏ LN 24310 [M]	Here Comes My Baby	1967	7.50	15.00	30.00
❏ LN 24326 [M]	Even the Bad Times Are Good	1967	6.25	12.50	25.00
❏ LN 24363 [M]	Suddenly You Love Me	1968	7.50	15.00	30.00
❏ LN 24388 [M]	World Explosion '58/'68	1968	15.00	30.00	60.00

—White label promo only

Number	Title (A Side/B Side)	Yr	VG	VG+	NM
❏ BN 26310 [R]	Here Comes My Baby	1967	5.00	10.00	20.00
❏ BN 26326 [P]	Even the Bad Times Are Good	1967	7.50	15.00	30.00
❏ BN 26363 [R]	Suddenly You Love Me	1968	5.00	10.00	20.00
❏ BN 26388 [S]	World Explosion '58/'68	1968	7.50	15.00	30.00

TRENIERS, THE
DOT

Number	Title (A Side/B Side)	Yr	VG	VG+	NM
❏ DLP-3257 [M]	Souvenir Album	1960	25.00	50.00	100.00

EPIC

Number	Title (A Side/B Side)	Yr	VG	VG+	NM
❏ LG 3125 [M]	The Treniers on TV	1955	50.00	100.00	200.00

TRENT, BUCK
ABC DOT

Number	Title (A Side/B Side)	Yr	VG	VG+	NM
❏ DOSD-2058	Bionic Banjo	1976	2.50	5.00	10.00
❏ DO-2077	Oh Yeah!	1977	2.50	5.00	10.00

BOONE

Number	Title (A Side/B Side)	Yr	VG	VG+	NM
❏ 1212	Give Me Five	1967	5.00	10.00	20.00

RCA VICTOR

Number	Title (A Side/B Side)	Yr	VG	VG+	NM
❏ LSP-4705	Sounds of Now and Beyond	1972	3.00	6.00	12.00

SMASH

Number	Title (A Side/B Side)	Yr	VG	VG+	NM
❏ MGS-27002 [M]	The Sound of a Bluegrass Banjo	1962	5.00	10.00	20.00

—Smash LPs as "Charles Trent"

Number	Title (A Side/B Side)	Yr	VG	VG+	NM
❏ MGS-27017 [M]	The Sound of a Five String Banjo	1962	5.00	10.00	20.00
❏ SRS-67002 [S]	The Sound of a Bluegrass Banjo	1962	6.25	12.50	25.00
❏ SRS-67017 [S]	The Sound of a Five String Banjo	1962	6.25	12.50	25.00

TREVOR, JEANNIE
MAINSTREAM

Number	Title (A Side/B Side)	Yr	VG	VG+	NM
❏ S-6075 [S]	Jeannie Trevor Sings!!	1965	7.50	15.00	30.00
❏ 56075 [M]	Jeannie Trevor Sings!!	1965	6.25	12.50	25.00

TREVOR, VAN
BAND BOX

Number	Title (A Side/B Side)	Yr	VG	VG+	NM
❏ (# unknown)	Come On Over to Our Side	1967	5.00	10.00	20.00

DATE

Number	Title (A Side/B Side)	Yr	VG	VG+	NM
❏ DES-4008	You've Been So Good to Me	1967	3.75	7.50	15.00

ROYAL AMERICAN

Number	Title (A Side/B Side)	Yr	VG	VG+	NM
❏ 2800	Funny Familiar Forgotten Feelings	1969	3.75	7.50	15.00

TRIANGLE, THE
AMARET

Number	Title (A Side/B Side)	Yr	VG	VG+	NM
❏ 5000	How Now Brown Cow	1969	6.25	12.50	25.00

TRICHT, EVERT VAN
MERCURY LIVING PRESENCE

Number	Title (A Side/B Side)	Yr	VG	VG+	NM
❏ SR 90403 [S]	Oboe Concerti	196?	7.50	15.00	30.00

—With Kurt Redel/Vienna Symphony Orchestra and Pro Arte Orchestra of Munich; maroon label, no "Vendor: Mercury Record Corporation"

TRICYCLE
ABC

Number	Title (A Side/B Side)	Yr	VG	VG+	NM
❏ S-674	Tricycle	1969	5.00	10.00	20.00

TRIGGER, VIC
SANCTUARY

Number	Title (A Side/B Side)	Yr	VG	VG+	NM
❏ 12103	Electronic Wizard	1977	25.00	50.00	100.00

TRIMBLE, BOBB
(NO LABEL)

Number	Title (A Side/B Side)	Yr	VG	VG+	NM
❏ (no #)	Harvest of Dreams	1982	37.50	75.00	150.00

VENGEANCE

Number	Title (A Side/B Side)	Yr	VG	VG+	NM
❏ BT-8458	Iron Curtain Dream	1980	200.00	400.00	800.00

TRIO
MERCURY

Number	Title (A Side/B Side)	Yr	VG	VG+	NM
❏ MX-1-509 [EP]	Trio (Contains the Hit Da Da Da)	1982	3.75	7.50	15.00
❏ 814320-1	Trio and Error	1983	5.00	10.00	20.00

TRIO, THE
SAVOY

Number	Title (A Side/B Side)	Yr	VG	VG+	NM
❏ MG-12023 [M]	The Trio	1955	25.00	50.00	100.00

TRIPSICHORD MUSIC BOX, THE
JANUS

Number	Title (A Side/B Side)	Yr	VG	VG+	NM
❏ JLS-3016	The Tripsichord Music Box	1971	50.00	100.00	200.00

TRISTANO, LENNIE
ATLANTIC

Number	Title (A Side/B Side)	Yr	VG	VG+	NM
❏ 1224 [M]	Lennie Tristano with Lee Konitz	1955	20.00	40.00	80.00

—Black label

Number	Title (A Side/B Side)	Yr	VG	VG+	NM
❏ 1224 [M]	Lennie Tristano with Lee Konitz	1960	6.25	12.50	25.00

—Multicolor label, white "fan" logo at right

Number	Title (A Side/B Side)	Yr	VG	VG+	NM
❏ 1357 [M]	The New Tristano	1960	12.50	25.00	50.00

—Multicolor label, white "fan" logo at right

EMARCY

Number	Title (A Side/B Side)	Yr	VG	VG+	NM
❏ MG-26029 [10]	Holiday in Piano	1954	37.50	75.00	150.00

MOSAIC

Number	Title (A Side/B Side)	Yr	VG	VG+	NM
❏ MQ10-174 [(10)]	The Complete Atlantic Recordings of Lennie Tristano, Lee Konitz and Warne Marsh	199?	45.00	90.00	180.00

NEW JAZZ

Number	Title (A Side/B Side)	Yr	VG	VG+	NM
❏ NJLP-101 [10]	Lennie Tristano with Lee Konitz	1950	62.50	125.00	250.00

PRESTIGE

Number	Title (A Side/B Side)	Yr	VG	VG+	NM
❏ PRLP-101 [10]	Lennie Tristano with Lee Konitz	1951	50.00	100.00	200.00

TRISTANO, LENNIE; JO BUSHKIN; BOBBY SCOTT; MARIAN McPARTLAND
SAVOY

Number	Title (A Side/B Side)	Yr	VG	VG+	NM
❏ MG-12043 [M]	The Jazz Keyboards of Lennie Tristano, Joe Bushkin, Bobby Scott & Marian McPartland	1955	12.50	25.00	50.00

TRISTANO, LENNIE/ARNOLD ROSS
EMARCY

Number	Title (A Side/B Side)	Yr	VG	VG+	NM
❏ MG-26029 [10]	Holiday Piano	1953	30.00	60.00	120.00

TRITT, TRAVIS
WARNER BROS.

Number	Title (A Side/B Side)	Yr	VG	VG+	NM
❏ W1-26589	It's All About to Change	1991	5.00	10.00	20.00

—Vinyl available only from Columbia House

TRIZO 50
CAVERN

Number	Title (A Side/B Side)	Yr	VG	VG+	NM
❏ 740142	Trizo 50	197?	75.00	150.00	300.00

TROGGS, THE
ATCO

Number	Title (A Side/B Side)	Yr	VG	VG+	NM
❏ 33-193 [M]	Wild Thing	1966	12.50	25.00	50.00
❏ SD 33-193 [R]	Wild Thing	1966	10.00	20.00	40.00

FONTANA

Number	Title (A Side/B Side)	Yr	VG	VG+	NM
❏ MGF 27556 [M]	Wild Thing/With a Girl Like You	1966	10.00	20.00	40.00

—Contents identical to the Atco LP; two slightly different cover variations are known; record has mono number and plays mono; number "27556" in trail-off

Number	Title (A Side/B Side)	Yr	VG	VG+	NM
❏ MGF 27556 [R]	Wild Thing/With a Girl Like You	1966	7.50	15.00	30.00

—Contents identical to the Atco LP; two slightly different cover variations are known; record has mono number but plays in rechanneled stereo; number "2/67556" in trail-off

Number	Title (A Side/B Side)	Yr	VG	VG+	NM
❏ SRF 67556 [R]	Wild Thing/With a Girl Like You	1966	7.50	15.00	30.00

—Contents identical to the Atco LP; two slightly different cover variations are known

Number	Title (A Side/B Side)	Yr	VG	VG+	NM
❏ SRF 67576 [R]	Love Is All Around	1968	7.50	15.00	30.00

MKC

Number	Title (A Side/B Side)	Yr	VG	VG+	NM
❏ 214	Live at Max's Kansas City	1980	3.00	6.00	12.00

PRIVATE STOCK

Number	Title (A Side/B Side)	Yr	VG	VG+	NM
❏ PS-2008	The Troggs Tapes	1976	3.00	6.00	12.00

PYE

Number	Title (A Side/B Side)	Yr	VG	VG+	NM
❏ 12112	The Troggs	1975	3.00	6.00	12.00

RHINO

Number	Title (A Side/B Side)	Yr	VG	VG+	NM
❏ RNLP-118	The Best of the Troggs	1985	2.50	5.00	10.00
❏ R1 70118	The Best of the Troggs	1988	2.00	4.00	8.00

SIRE

Number	Title (A Side/B Side)	Yr	VG	VG+	NM
❏ SASH-3714 [(2)]	The Vintage Years	1976	3.75	7.50	15.00

TROLL, THE
SMASH

Number	Title (A Side/B Side)	Yr	VG	VG+	NM
❏ SRS-67114	Animated Music	1969	12.50	25.00	50.00

TROMBONES UNLIMITED
LIBERTY

Number	Title (A Side/B Side)	Yr	VG	VG+	NM
❏ LRP-3449 [M]	These Bones are Made for Walking	1966	3.75	7.50	15.00
❏ LRP-3472 [M]	You're Gonna Hear From Me	1966	3.75	7.50	15.00
❏ LRP-3494 [M]	Big Boss Bones	1967	5.00	10.00	20.00
❏ LRP-3527 [M]	Holiday for Trombones	1967	5.00	10.00	20.00
❏ LRP-3549 [M]	One of Those Songs	1968	6.25	12.50	25.00
❏ LST-7449 [S]	These Bones are Made for Walking	1966	5.00	10.00	20.00
❏ LST-7472 [S]	You're Gonna Hear From Me	1966	5.00	10.00	20.00
❏ LST-7494 [S]	Big Boss Bones	1967	3.75	7.50	15.00
❏ LST-7527 [S]	Holiday for Trombones	1967	3.75	7.50	15.00
❏ LST-7549 [S]	One of Those Songs	1968	3.75	7.50	15.00
❏ LST-7592	Grazing in the Grass	1968	3.75	7.50	15.00

TROUP, BOBBY
BETHLEHEM

Number	Title (A Side/B Side)	Yr	VG	VG+	NM
❏ BCP-19 [M]	Bobby Troup Sings Johnny Mercer	1955	12.50	25.00	50.00
❏ BCP-35 [M]	The Distinctive Style of Bobby Troup	1955	12.50	25.00	50.00
❏ BCP-1030 [10]	Bobby Troup	1955	15.00	30.00	60.00

CAPITOL

Number	Title (A Side/B Side)	Yr	VG	VG+	NM
❏ H 484 [10]	Bobby	1953	20.00	40.00	80.00
❏ T 484 [M]	Bobby	1955	12.50	25.00	50.00

INTERLUDE

Number	Title (A Side/B Side)	Yr	VG	VG+	NM
❏ MO-501 [M]	Cool	1959	10.00	20.00	40.00
❏ ST-1001 [S]	Cool	1959	10.00	20.00	40.00

LIBERTY

Number	Title (A Side/B Side)	Yr	VG	VG+	NM
❏ LRP-3002 [M]	Bobby Troup and His Trio	1955	12.50	25.00	50.00
❏ LRP-3026 [M]	Do Re Mi	1957	12.50	25.00	50.00
❏ LRP-3078 [M]	Here's to My Lady	1958	12.50	25.00	50.00

MODE

Number	Title (A Side/B Side)	Yr	VG	VG+	NM
❏ LP-111 [M]	Bobby Swings Tenderly	1957	25.00	50.00	100.00

RCA VICTOR

Number	Title (A Side/B Side)	Yr	VG	VG+	NM
❏ LPM-1959 [M]	Bobby Troup and His Jazz All-Stars	1959	10.00	20.00	40.00
❏ LSP-1959 [S]	Bobby Troup and His Jazz All-Stars	1959	12.50	25.00	50.00

TROY, DORIS
APPLE

Number	Title (A Side/B Side)	Yr	VG	VG+	NM
❏ ST-3371	Doris Troy	1970	6.25	12.50	25.00

ATLANTIC

Number	Title (A Side/B Side)	Yr	VG	VG+	NM
❏ 8088 [M]	Just One Look	1964	7.50	15.00	30.00
❏ SD 8088 [P]	Just One Look	1964	12.50	25.00	50.00

—The title song is rechanneled

Number	Title (A Side/B Side)	Yr	VG	VG+	NM
TROYKA					
COTILLION					
❑ SD 9020	Troyka	1970	7.50	15.00	30.00
TRUMAN, MARGARET					
RCA VICTOR					
❑ LM-57 [10]	American Songs	1951	20.00	40.00	80.00
❑ LM-145 [10]	A Margaret Truman Program	1952	20.00	40.00	80.00
TRUMPETEERS, THE					
GRAND					
❑ 7701 [M]	The Last Supper	195?	25.00	50.00	100.00
SCORE					
❑ SLP-4021 [M]	Milky White Way	1956	75.00	150.00	300.00
TUBB, ERNEST					
CACHET					
❑ 33001	Ernest Tubb: The Legend and the Legacy, Volume One	1979	3.00	6.00	12.00
DECCA					
❑ DXA 159 [(2)M]	The Ernest Tubb Story	1959	20.00	40.00	80.00
—Deduct 25 percent if book is missing					
❑ DL 4046 [M]	All Time Hits	1961	7.50	15.00	30.00
❑ DL 4064 [M]	The Ernest Tubb Record Shop	1960	10.00	20.00	40.00
❑ DL 4118 [M]	Ernest Tubb's Golden Favorites	1961	7.50	15.00	30.00
❑ DL 4321 [M]	On Tour	1962	6.25	12.50	25.00
❑ DL 4385 [M]	Just Call Me Lonesome	1962	6.25	12.50	25.00
❑ DL 4397 [M]	The Family Bible	1963	6.25	12.50	25.00
❑ DL 4514 [M]	Thanks a Lot	1964	6.25	12.50	25.00
❑ DL 4518 [M]	Blue Christmas	1963	6.25	12.50	25.00
❑ DL 4640 [M]	My Pick of the Hits	1965	6.25	12.50	25.00
❑ DL 4681 [M]	Hittin' the Road	1965	6.25	12.50	25.00
❑ DL 4746 [M]	By Request	1966	6.25	12.50	25.00
❑ DL 4772 [M]	Ernest Tubb Sings Country Hits Old & New	1966	6.25	12.50	25.00
❑ DL 4867 [M]	Another Story	1967	7.50	15.00	30.00
❑ DL 4957 [M]	Ernest Tubb Sings Hank Williams	1968	12.50	25.00	50.00
❑ DL 5006 [M]	Ernest Tubb's Greatest Hits	1968	20.00	40.00	80.00
—White label promo only					
❑ DL 5301 [10]	Ernest Tubb Favorites	1951	37.50	75.00	150.00
❑ DL 5334 [10]	The Old Rugged Cross	1951	37.50	75.00	150.00
❑ DL 5336 [10]	Jimmie Rodgers Songs Sung by Ernest Tubb	1951	37.50	75.00	150.00
❑ DL 5497 [10]	Sing a Song of Christmas	1954	37.50	75.00	150.00
❑ DXSA 7159 [(2)R]	The Ernest Tubb Story	196?	7.50	15.00	30.00
—Deduct 25 percent if book is missing					
❑ DL 8291 [M]	Ernest Tubb Favorites	1955	17.50	35.00	70.00
❑ DL 8553 [M]	The Daddy of 'Em All	1956	17.50	35.00	70.00
❑ DL 8834 [M]	The Importance of Being Ernest	1959	12.50	25.00	50.00
❑ DL 74046 [S]	All Time Hits	1961	10.00	20.00	40.00
❑ DL 74064 [S]	The Ernest Tubb Record Shop	1960	12.50	25.00	50.00
❑ DL 74118 [S]	Ernest Tubb's Golden Favorites	1961	10.00	2.00	40.00
❑ DL 74321 [S]	On Tour	1962	7.50	15.00	30.00
❑ DL 74385 [S]	Just Call Me Lonesome	1962	7.50	15.00	30.00
❑ DL 74397 [S]	The Family Bible	1963	7.50	15.00	30.00
❑ DL 74514 [S]	Thanks a Lot	1964	7.50	15.00	30.00
❑ DL 74518 [S]	Blue Christmas	1963	7.50	15.00	30.00
❑ DL 74640 [S]	My Pick of the Hits	1965	7.50	15.00	30.00
❑ DL 74681 [S]	Hittin' the Road	1965	7.50	15.00	30.00
❑ DL 74746 [S]	By Request	1966	7.50	15.00	30.00
❑ DL 74772 [S]	Ernest Tubb Sings Country Hits Old & New	1966	7.50	15.00	30.00
❑ DL 74867 [S]	Another Story	1967	6.25	12.50	25.00
❑ DL 74957 [S]	Ernest Tubb Sings Hank Williams	1968	6.25	12.50	25.00
❑ DL 75006 [S]	Ernest Tubb's Greatest Hits	1968	6.25	12.50	25.00
❑ DL 75072	Country Hit Time	1968	5.00	10.00	20.00
❑ DL 75114	Let's Turn Back the Years	1969	3.75	7.50	15.00
❑ DL 75122	Saturday Satan, Sunday Saint	1969	5.00	10.00	20.00
❑ DL 75222	A Great Year for the Wine	1970	5.00	10.00	20.00
❑ DL 75252	Ernest Tubb's Greatest Hits, Vol. 2	1970	5.00	10.00	20.00
❑ DL 75301	One Sweet Hello	1971	5.00	10.00	20.00
❑ DL 75345	Say Something Nice to Sarah	1972	5.00	10.00	20.00
❑ DL 75388	Baby, It's So Hard to Be Good	1972	5.00	10.00	20.00
❑ DL 78834 [S]	The Importance of Being Ernest	1959	15.00	30.00	60.00
FIRST GENERATION					
❑ LP-0002 [(2)]	The Legend and the Legacy	1979	10.00	20.00	40.00
—With ad for Ernest Tubb Record Shop on back cover					
❑ LP-0002 [(2)]	The Legend and the Legacy	1979	12.50	25.00	50.00
—No ads on back cover					
❑ TV-1033 [(2)]	The Legend and the Legacy	1979	6.25	12.50	25.00
—Mail-order version					
MCA					
❑ 16	Ernest Tubb's Greatest Hits	1973	3.00	6.00	12.00
—Reissue of Decca 75006					
❑ 24	Ernest Tubb's Greatest Hits, Vol. 2	1973	3.00	6.00	12.00
—Reissue of Decca 75252					
❑ 84	Ernest Tubb's Golden Favorites	1973	3.00	6.00	12.00
—Reissue of Decca 74118					
❑ 341	I've Got All the Heartaches I Can Handle	1973	3.00	6.00	12.00
❑ 496	Ernest Tubb	1975	3.00	6.00	12.00
❑ 512	Baby, It's So Hard to Be Good	197?	3.00	6.00	12.00
—Reissue of Decca 75388					
❑ 4040 [(2)]	The Ernest Tubb Story	197?	3.75	7.50	15.00
—Reissue of Decca DXSA 7159					
TUBB, ERNEST, AND LORETTA LYNN					
DECCA					
❑ DL 4639 [M]	Mr. and Mrs. Used to Be	1965	7.50	15.00	30.00
❑ DL 4872 [M]	Singin' Again	1967	7.50	15.00	30.00
❑ DL 74639 [S]	Mr. and Mrs. Used to Be	1965	10.00	20.00	40.00
❑ DL 74872 [S]	Singin' Again	1967	6.25	12.50	25.00
❑ DL 75115	If We Put Our Heads Together	1969	6.25	12.50	25.00
MCA					
❑ 4000	The Ernest Tubb/Loretta Lynn Story	1973	3.75	7.50	15.00

Number	Title (A Side/B Side)	Yr	VG	VG+	NM
TUBB, JUSTIN					
CUTLASS					
❑ 123	Travelin' Singin' Man	1972	7.50	15.00	30.00
DECCA					
❑ DL 8644 [M]	Country Boy in Love	1957	15.00	30.00	60.00
DOT					
❑ DLP-25922	Things I Still Remember Very Well	1969	3.75	7.50	15.00
FIRST GENERATION					
❑ 1	What's Wrong with the Way We're Doing It Now	1979	3.00	6.00	12.00
PHONORAMA					
❑ 5565	What's Wrong with the Way We're Doing It Now	1983	2.00	4.00	8.00
RCA VICTOR					
❑ LPM-3339 [M]	Where You're Concerned	1965	5.00	10.00	20.00
❑ LSP-3339 [S]	Where You're Concerned	1965	6.25	12.50	25.00
STARDAY					
❑ SLP-160 [M]	Star of the Grand Ole Opry	1962	10.00	20.00	40.00
❑ SLP-198 [M]	The Modern Country Sound of Justin Tubb	1962	10.00	20.00	40.00
❑ SLP-334 [M]	The Best of Justin Tubb	1965	6.25	12.50	25.00
VOCALION					
❑ VL 73802	That Country Style	196?	3.00	6.00	12.00
TUBB, JUSTIN, AND LORENE MANN					
RCA VICTOR					
❑ LPM-3591 [M]	Together and Alone	1966	7.50	15.00	30.00
❑ LSP-3591 [S]	Together and Alone	1966	10.00	20.00	40.00
TUBES, THE					
A&M					
❑ SP-3161	The Tubes	198?	2.00	4.00	8.00
—Reissue					
❑ SP-3222	Young and Rich	198?	2.00	4.00	8.00
—Reissue					
❑ SP-3242	Remote Control	198?	2.00	4.00	8.00
—Reissue					
❑ SP-3243	Now	198?	2.00	4.00	8.00
—Reissue					
❑ SP-3244	T.R.A.S.H. (Tubes Rarities And Smash Hits)	198?	2.00	4.00	8.00
—Reissue					
❑ SP-4535	The Tubes	1975	3.75	7.50	15.00
❑ SP-4580	Young and Rich	1976	3.75	7.50	15.00
❑ SP-4632	Now	1977	3.75	7.50	15.00
❑ SP-4751	Remote Control	1979	3.75	7.50	15.00
❑ SP-4870	T.R.A.S.H. (Tubes Rarities And Smash Hits)	1981	3.00	6.00	12.00
❑ SP-6003 [(2)]	What Do You Want From Live!	1978	3.75	7.50	15.00
❑ SP-17012 [DJ]	Tubes Live/Edited for Trouble-Free Airplay	1978	6.25	12.50	25.00
—Generic cover with sticker; promo only					
CAPITOL					
❑ SOO-12151	The Completion Backward Principle	1981	3.00	6.00	12.00
❑ ST-12260	Outside/Inside	1983	2.50	5.00	10.00
❑ ST-12381	Love Bomb	1985	2.50	5.00	10.00
❑ SN-16360	Outside/Inside	1985	2.00	4.00	8.00
—Reissue					
❑ SN-16378	The Completion Backward Principle	1986	2.00	4.00	8.00
—Reissue					
❑ SN-16446	Love Bomb	1987	2.00	4.00	8.00
—Reissue					
TUCKER, FAYE					
TIME					
❑ S-2018 [S]	Country & Western Soul	1963	6.25	12.50	25.00
❑ 52108 [M]	Country & Western Soul	1963	5.00	10.00	20.00
TUCKER, MAUREEN					
Also see THE VELVET UNDERGROUND.					
50 SKIDILLION WATTS					
❑ MOE 1 [EP]	Moejadkatebarry	1987	3.50	7.00	14.00
❑ MOE 7	Life in Exile After Abdication	1989	3.00	6.00	12.00
TRASH					
❑ TLP-1001	Playin' Possum	1981	7.50	15.00	30.00
TUCKER, TANYA					
ARISTA					
❑ AL 8381	Changes	1984	2.00	4.00	8.00
—Reissue of 9596					
❑ AL 9596	Changes	1982	2.50	5.00	10.00
CAPITOL					
❑ ST-12474	Girls Like Me	1986	2.50	5.00	10.00
❑ CLT-46870	Love Me Like You Used To	1987	2.50	5.00	10.00
❑ C1-48865	Strong Enough to Bend	1988	2.50	5.00	10.00
❑ C1-91814	Greatest Hits	1989	3.00	6.00	12.00
CAPITOL NASHVILLE					
❑ 1P 8140	What Do I Do with Me	1991	5.00	10.00	20.00
—Only available on vinyl through Columbia House					
COLUMBIA					
❑ KC 31742	Delta Dawn	1972	3.75	7.50	15.00
❑ PC 31742	Delta Dawn	198?	2.00	4.00	8.00
❑ KC 32272	What's Your Mama's Name	1973	3.75	7.50	15.00
❑ KC 32744	Would You Lay with Me (In a Field of Stone)	1974	3.00	6.00	12.00
❑ PC 32744	Would You Lay with Me (In a Field of Stone)	197?	2.00	4.00	8.00
❑ KC 33355	Greatest Hits	1975	3.00	6.00	12.00
—No bar code on cover					
❑ PC 33355	Greatest Hits	197?	2.00	4.00	8.00
—With bar code on cover					
❑ PC 34733	You Are So Beautiful	197?	2.00	4.00	8.00
—With bar code on cover					
❑ PC 34733	You Are So Beautiful	1977	3.00	6.00	12.00
—No bar code on cover					
COLUMBIA SPECIAL PRODUCTS					
❑ P 15770	The Best of Tanya Tucker	1981	3.00	6.00	12.00

Number	Title (A Side/B Side)	Yr	VG	VG+	NM
MCA					
❏ 654	Tanya Tucker	1980	2.00	4.00	8.00
—Reissue of 2141					
❏ 655	Lovin' and Learnin'	1980	2.00	4.00	8.00
—Reissue of 2167					
❏ 656	Here's Some Love	1980	2.00	4.00	8.00
—Reissue of 2213					
❏ 657	Ridin' Rainbows	1980	2.00	4.00	8.00
—Reissue of 2253					
❏ 2141	Tanya Tucker	1975	3.00	6.00	12.00
❏ 2167	Lovin' and Learnin'	1976	3.00	6.00	12.00
❏ 2213	Here's Some Love	1976	3.00	6.00	12.00
❏ 2253	Ridin' Rainbows	1977	3.00	6.00	12.00
❏ 3032	Tanya Tucker's Greatest Hits	1978	3.00	6.00	12.00
❏ 3066	TNT	1978	3.00	6.00	12.00
—Original gatefold cover					
❏ 5106	Tear Me Apart	1979	2.50	5.00	10.00
❏ 5140	Dreamlovers	1980	2.50	5.00	10.00
❏ 5228	Should I Do It	1981	2.50	5.00	10.00
❏ 5299	Tanya Tucker Live	1982	2.50	5.00	10.00
❏ 5357	The Best of Tanya Tucker	1983	2.50	5.00	10.00
❏ 27030	Dreamlovers	198?	2.00	4.00	8.00
—Reissue of 5140					
❏ 37075	TNT	1981	2.00	4.00	8.00
—Reissue of 3066; gatefold removed					
❏ 37158	Tear Me Apart	1981	2.00	4.00	8.00
—Reissue of 5106					
❏ 37225	Greatest Hits	1984	2.00	4.00	8.00
—Reissue of 3032					
❏ 37242	Tanya Tucker Live	1984	2.00	4.00	8.00
—Reissue of 5299					

TUCKER, TOMMY
CHECKER

Number	Title (A Side/B Side)	Yr	VG	VG+	NM
❏ LP-2990 [M]	Hi-Heel Sneakers	1964	62.50	125.00	250.00
—Black label					
❏ LP-2990 [M]	Hi-Heel Sneakers	1965	30.00	60.00	120.00
—Blue label with checkers					

TURBANS, THE
HERALD

Number	Title (A Side/B Side)	Yr	VG	VG+	NM
❏ 5009	Presenting the Turbans	197?	5.00	10.00	20.00
—No such album was released in the 1950s; this is a bootleg that has some collector value.					
LOST-NITE					
❏ LLP-25 [10]	The Turbans	1981	2.50	5.00	10.00
—Red vinyl					
RELIC					
❏ 5009	The Turbans' Greatest Hits	198?	3.00	6.00	12.00

TURNER, HANK
COLUMBIA

Number	Title (A Side/B Side)	Yr	VG	VG+	NM
❏ CL 1958 [M]	Golden Country and Western Hits	1963	5.00	10.00	20.00
❏ CS 8758 [S]	Golden Country and Western Hits	1963	6.25	12.50	25.00

TURNER, IKE
Also see IKE AND TINA TURNER.
CROWN

Number	Title (A Side/B Side)	Yr	VG	VG+	NM
❏ CST-367 [R]	Ike Turner Rocks the Blues	1963	25.00	50.00	100.00
❏ CLP-5367 [M]	Ike Turner Rocks the Blues	1963	50.00	100.00	200.00
FANTASY					
❏ F-9597	The Edge	1980	2.50	5.00	10.00
POMPEII					
❏ SD 6003	A Black Man's Soul	1969	3.75	7.50	15.00
UNITED ARTISTS					
❏ UA-LA087-F	Bad Dreams	1973	3.75	7.50	15.00
❏ UAS-5576	Blues Roots	1972	3.75	7.50	15.00

TURNER, IKE AND TINA
Also see IKE TURNER; TINA TURNER.
A&M

Number	Title (A Side/B Side)	Yr	VG	VG+	NM
❏ SP-3179	River Deep — Mountain High	1982	2.50	5.00	10.00
—Budget-line reissue					
❏ SP-4178	River Deep — Mountain High	1969	6.25	12.50	25.00
—Official release of Philles 4011					
ABC					
❏ 4014	16 Great Performances	1975	3.00	6.00	12.00
ACCORD					
❏ SN-7147	Hot and Sassy	1981	2.50	5.00	10.00
BLUE THUMB					
❏ BTS 5	Outta Season	1968	3.75	7.50	15.00
❏ BTS 11	The Hunter	1969	3.75	7.50	15.00
❏ BTS 49	The Best of Ike & Tina Turner	1973	3.00	6.00	12.00
❏ BTS-8805	Outta Season	1971	3.00	6.00	12.00
—Early reissue of Blue Thumb 5					
CAPITOL					
❏ ST-571	Her Man, His Woman	1971	3.75	7.50	15.00
COLLECTABLES					
❏ COL-5107	Golden Classics	198?	2.50	5.00	10.00
❏ COL-5137	It's Gonna Work Out Fine	198?	2.50	5.00	10.00
EMI AMERICA					
❏ ST-17212	It's Gonna Work Out Fine	1986	2.50	5.00	10.00
❏ SQ-17216	Workin' Together	1986	2.50	5.00	10.00
HARMONY					
❏ HS 11360	Ooh Poo Pah Doo	1969	3.75	7.50	15.00
❏ H 30567	Something's Got a Hold on Me	1971	3.75	7.50	15.00
KENT					
❏ KST-514 [S]	The Ike and Tina Turner Revue Live	1964	10.00	20.00	40.00
❏ KST-519 [S]	The Soul of Ike and Tina	1966	10.00	20.00	40.00
❏ KST-538	Festival of Live Performances	1969	7.50	15.00	30.00
❏ KST-550	Please Please Please	1971	7.50	15.00	30.00

Number	Title (A Side/B Side)	Yr	VG	VG+	NM
❏ K-5014 [M]	The Ike and Tina Turner Revue Live	1964	7.50	15.00	30.00
❏ K-5019 [M]	The Soul of Ike and Tina	1966	7.50	15.00	30.00
LIBERTY					
❏ LT-917	Airwaves	1981	2.00	4.00	8.00
❏ LST-7637	Come Together	1970	3.75	7.50	15.00
❏ LST-7650	Workin' Together	1970	3.75	7.50	15.00
❏ LO-51156	Get Back!	1985	2.50	5.00	10.00
LOMA					
❏ L 5904 [M]	Live! The Ike & Tina Turner Show Vol. 2	1966	6.25	12.50	25.00
❏ LS 5904 [S]	Live! The Ike & Tina Turner Show, Vol. 2	1966	7.50	15.00	30.00
—Reissue of Warner Bros. 1579?					
MINIT					
❏ 24018	In Person	1969	5.00	10.00	20.00
PHILLES					
❏ PHLP 4011 [M]	River Deep — Mountain High	1967	2000.	4000.	8000.
—Value is for record alone; covers were not printed					
PICKWICK					
❏ SPC-3284	Too Hot to Hold	197?	2.50	5.00	10.00
POMPEII					
❏ SD 6000	So Fine	1968	6.25	12.50	25.00
❏ SD 6004	Cussin', Cryin' and Carryin' On	1969	6.25	12.50	25.00
❏ SD 6006	Get It Together	1969	6.25	12.50	25.00
STRIPED HORSE					
❏ SHL-2001	Golden Empire	1986	2.50	5.00	10.00
SUE					
❏ LP 1038 [M]	The Greatest Hits of Ike and Tina Turner	1965	75.00	150.00	300.00
❏ LP 2001 [M]	The Soul of Ike and Tina Turner	1961	100.00	200.00	400.00
❏ LP 2003 [M]	Ike and Tina Turner's Kings of Rhythm Dance	1962	100.00	200.00	400.00
—Despite the title, this is an all-instrumental album (Tina's vocals do not appear)					
❏ LP 2004 [M]	Dynamite	1963	100.00	200.00	400.00
❏ LP 2005 [M]	Don't Play Me Cheap	1963	100.00	200.00	400.00
❏ LP 2007 [M]	It's Gonna Work Out Fine	1963	100.00	200.00	400.00
SUNSET					
❏ SUS-5265	The Fantastic Ike & Tina Turner	1969	3.75	7.50	15.00
❏ SUS-5286	Ike & Tima Turner's Greatest Hits	1969	3.75	7.50	15.00
UNART					
❏ S 21021	Greatest Hits	197?	2.50	5.00	10.00
UNITED ARTISTS					
❏ UA-LA064-G [(2)]	The World of Ike & Tina Live	1973	3.75	7.50	15.00
❏ UA-LA180-F	Nutbush City Limits	1973	3.00	6.00	12.00
❏ UA-LA203-G	The Gospel According to Ike & Tina Turner	1974	3.00	6.00	12.00
❏ UA-LA312-G	Sweet Rhode Island Red	1974	3.00	6.00	12.00
❏ UA-LA592-G	Greatest Hits	1976	3.00	6.00	12.00
❏ UA-LA707-G	Delilah's Power	1977	3.00	6.00	12.00
❏ UA-LA917-H	Airwaves	1978	3.00	6.00	12.00
❏ UAS-5530	'Nuff Said	1971	3.00	6.00	12.00
❏ UAS-5598	Feel Good	1972	3.00	6.00	12.00
❏ UAS-5660	Let Me Touch Your Mind	1972	3.00	6.00	12.00
❏ UAS-5667	Ike & Tina Turner's Greatest Hits	1972	3.00	6.00	12.00
❏ UAS-9953 [(2)]	Live at Carnegie Hall/What You Hear Is What You Get	1971	3.75	7.50	15.00
WARNER BROS.					
❏ W 1579 [M]	Live! The Ike & Tina Turner Show	1965	7.50	15.00	30.00
❏ WS 1579 [S]	Live! The Ike & Tina Turner Show	1965	10.00	20.00	40.00
❏ WS 1810	Ike & Tina Turner's Greatest Hits	1969	6.25	12.50	25.00

TURNER, JOE
ARHOOLIE

Number	Title (A Side/B Side)	Yr	VG	VG+	NM
❏ 2004 [M]	Jumpin' the Blues	1962	5.00	10.00	20.00
ATLANTIC					
❏ 1234 [M]	The Boss of the Blues	1956	30.00	60.00	120.00
—Black label					
❏ 1234 [M]	The Boss of the Blues	1960	25.00	50.00	100.00
—White "bullseye" label					
❏ 1234 [M]	The Boss of the Blues	1961	10.00	20.00	40.00
—White "fan" logo on label					
❏ SD 1234 [S]	The Boss of the Blues	1959	45.00	90.00	180.00
—Green label					
❏ SD 1234 [S]	The Boss of the Blues	1960	37.50	75.00	150.00
—White "bullseye" label					
❏ SD 1234 [S]	The Boss of the Blues	1961	12.50	25.00	50.00
—White "fan" logo on label					
❏ SD 1234 [S]	The Boss of the Blues	1963	5.00	10.00	20.00
—Black "fan" logo on label					
❏ 1332 [M]	Big Joe Rides Again	1959	37.50	75.00	150.00
—Black label					
❏ 1332 [M]	Big Joe Rides Again	1960	10.00	20.00	40.00
—White "fan" logo on label					
❏ SD 1332 [S]	Big Joe Rides Again	1959	50.00	100.00	200.00
—Green label					
❏ SD 1332 [S]	Big Joe Rides Again	1960	12.50	25.00	50.00
—White "fan" logo on label					
❏ SD 1332 [S]	Big Joe Rides Again	1963	5.00	10.00	20.00
—Black "fan" logo on label					
❏ 8005 [M]	Joe Turner	1957	37.50	75.00	150.00
—Black label					
❏ 8005 [M]	Joe Turner	1961	10.00	20.00	40.00
—White "fan" logo on label					
❏ 8023 [M]	Rockin' the Blues	1958	30.00	60.00	120.00
—Black label					
❏ 8023 [M]	Rockin' the Blues	1960	10.00	20.00	40.00
—White "fan" logo on label					
❏ 8033 [M]	Big Joe Is Here	1959	30.00	60.00	120.00
—Black label					
❏ 8033 [M]	Big Joe Is Here	1960	10.00	20.00	40.00
—White "fan" logo on label					
❏ 8033 [M]	Big Joe Is Here	1960	25.00	50.00	100.00
—White "bullseye" label					
❏ 8081 [M]	The Best of Joe Turner	1963	12.50	25.00	50.00

Number	Title (A Side/B Side)	Yr	VG	VG+	NM

BLUESTIME

❏ 9002 [M]	The Real Boss of the Blues	196?	10.00	20.00	40.00
❏ 29002 [S]	The Real Boss of the Blues	196?	7.50	15.00	30.00

BLUESWAY

❏ BL 6006 [M]	Singing the Blues	1967	5.00	10.00	20.00
❏ BLS-6006 [S]	Singing the Blues	1967	6.25	12.50	25.00

DECCA

❏ DL 8044 [M]	Joe Turner Sings Kansas City Jazz	1953	62.50	125.00	250.00

SAVOY

❏ MG-14012 [M]	Blues'll Make You Happy	1958	37.50	75.00	150.00
❏ MG-14106 [M]	Careless Love	1963	20.00	40.00	80.00

TURNER, JOE, AND PETE JOHNSON

EMARCY

❏ MG-36014 [M]	Joe Turner and Pete Johnson	1955	50.00	100.00	200.00

TURNER, RAY

CAPITOL

❏ H 306 [10]	Kitten on the Keys	1952	12.50	25.00	50.00

TURNER, SAMMY

BIG TOP

❏ 12-1301 [M]	Lavender Blue Moods	1959	75.00	150.00	300.00

—*May not exist in stereo*

TURNER, SPYDER

MGM

❏ E-4450 [M]	Stand By Me	1967	6.25	12.50	25.00
❏ SE-4450 [S]	Stand By Me	1967	7.50	15.00	30.00

WHITFIELD

❏ BSK 3124	Music Web	1978	2.50	5.00	10.00
❏ BSK 3397	Only Love	1979	2.50	5.00	10.00

TURNER, TINA

Also see IKE AND TINA TURNER.

CAPITOL

❏ 1P 8192 [(2)]	Simply the Best	1991	5.00	10.00	20.00
—*Columbia House edition (only US vinyl version)*					
❏ ST-12330	Private Dancer	1984	2.00	4.00	8.00
❏ PJ-12530	Break Every Rule	1986	2.00	4.00	8.00
❏ C1-90126 [(2)]	Tina Live in Europe	1988	3.00	6.00	12.00
❏ C1-91873	Foreign Affair	1989	2.00	4.00	8.00

FANTASY

❏ MFP-4520 [EP]	Mini	1984	2.00	4.00	8.00

SPRINGBOARD

❏ SPB-4033	The Queen	1972	2.50	5.00	10.00

UNITED ARTISTS

❏ UA-LA200-F	Tina Turns the Country On	1973	3.75	7.50	15.00
❏ UA-LA495-G	Acid Queen	1975	3.00	6.00	12.00
❏ UA-LA919-G	Rough	1978	3.00	6.00	12.00

WAGNER

❏ 14108	Good Hearted Woman	1979	3.00	6.00	12.00

TURNER, TITUS

JAMIE

❏ JLP-3018 [M]	Sound Off	1961	5.00	10.00	20.00
❏ JLPS-3018 [S]	Sound Off	1961	7.50	15.00	30.00

TURNER, VELVERT, GROUP

FAMILY PRODUCTIONS

❏ FPS-2704	Velvert Turner Group	1972	12.50	25.00	50.00

TURNER, ZEB

AUDIO LAB

❏ AL-1537 [M]	Country Music in the Turner Style	1959	37.50	75.00	150.00

TURNQUIST REMEDY

PENTAGRAM

❏ PE-10004	Turnquist Remedy	1970	6.25	12.50	25.00

TURRENTINE, STANLEY

BLUE NOTE

❏ BLP-4039 [M]	Look Out!	1960	20.00	40.00	80.00
—*Regular version with W. 63rd St. address on label*					
❏ BLP-4039 [M]	Look Out!	1960	30.00	60.00	120.00
—*"Deep groove" version (deep indentation under label on both sides)*					
❏ BLP-4039 [M]	Look Out!	1963	6.25	12.50	25.00
—*With New York, USA address on label*					
❏ BLP-4057 [M]	Blue Hour	1961	20.00	40.00	80.00
—*With W. 63rd St. addresss on label*					
❏ BLP-4057 [M]	Blue Hour	1963	6.25	12.50	25.00
—*With New York, USA address on label*					
❏ BLP-4069 [M]	Up at Minton's, Volume 1	1961	20.00	40.00	80.00
—*With W. 63rd St. addresss on label*					
❏ BLP-4069 [M]	Up at Minton's, Volume 1	1963	6.25	12.50	25.00
—*With New York, USA address on label*					
❏ BLP-4070 [M]	Up at Minton's, Volume 2	1961	20.00	40.00	80.00
—*With W. 63rd St. addresss on label*					
❏ BLP-4070 [M]	Up at Minton's, Volume 2	1963	6.25	12.50	25.00
—*With New York, USA address on label*					
❏ BLP-4081 [M]	Dearly Beloved	1961	18.75	37.50	75.00
—*With 61st St. address on label*					
❏ BLP-4081 [M]	Dearly Beloved	1963	6.25	12.50	25.00
—*With 61st St. address on label*					
❏ BLP-4096 [M]	That's Where It's At	1962	15.00	30.00	60.00
—*With 61st St. address on label*					
❏ BLP-4096 [M]	That's Where It's At	1963	6.25	12.50	25.00
—*With New York, USA address on label*					
❏ BLP-4129 [M]	Never Let Me Go	1963	7.50	15.00	30.00
❏ BLP-4150 [M]	A Chip Off the Old Block	1963	7.50	15.00	30.00
❏ BLP-4162 [M]	Hustlin'	1964	7.50	15.00	30.00
❏ BLP-4201 [M]	Joyride	1965	6.25	12.50	25.00
❏ BLP-4240 [M]	Rough 'n Tumble	1966	6.25	12.50	25.00
❏ BLP-4256 [M]	The Spoiler	1967	6.25	12.50	25.00
❏ BLP-4268 [M]	Easy Walker	1967	6.25	12.50	25.00
❏ BST-84039 [S]	Look Out!	1960	15.00	30.00	60.00
—*With W. 63rd St. address on label*					
❏ BST-84039 [S]	Look Out!	1963	5.00	10.00	20.00
—*With New York, USA address on label*					
❏ BST-84057 [S]	Blue Hour	1961	15.00	30.00	60.00
—*With W. 63rd St. addresss on label*					
❏ BST-84057 [S]	Blue Hour	1963	5.00	10.00	20.00
—*With New York, USA address on label*					
❏ BST-84069 [S]	Up at Minton's, Volume 1	1961	15.00	30.00	60.00
—*With W. 63rd St. addresss on label*					
❏ BST-84069 [S]	Up at Minton's, Volume 1	1963	5.00	10.00	20.00
—*With New York, USA address on label*					
❏ BST-84070 [S]	Up at Minton's, Volume 2	1961	15.00	30.00	60.00
—*With W. 63rd St. addresss on label*					
❏ BST-84070 [S]	Up at Minton's, Volume 2	1963	5.00	10.00	20.00
—*With New York, USA address on label*					
❏ BST-84081 [S]	Dearly Beloved	1961	15.00	30.00	60.00
—*With 61st St. address on label*					
❏ BST-84081 [S]	Dearly Beloved	1963	5.00	10.00	20.00
—*With New York, USA address on label*					
❏ BST-84096 [S]	That's Where It's At	1962	15.00	30.00	60.00
—*With 61st St. address on label*					
❏ BST-84096 [S]	That's Where It's At	1963	5.00	10.00	20.00
—*With New York, USA address on label*					
❏ BST-84129 [S]	Never Let Me Go	1963	7.50	15.00	30.00
—*With New York, USA address on label*					
❏ BST-84150 [S]	A Chip Off the Old Block	1963	7.50	15.00	30.00
—*With New York, USA address on label*					
❏ BST-84162 [S]	Hustlin'	1964	7.50	15.00	30.00
—*With New York, USA address on label*					
❏ BST-84201 [S]	Joyride	1964	6.25	12.50	25.00
—*With New York, USA address on label*					
❏ BST-84240 [S]	Rough 'n Tumble	1966	5.00	10.00	20.00
—*With New York, USA address on label*					
❏ BST-84256 [S]	The Spoiler	1967	5.00	10.00	20.00
❏ BST-84268 [S]	Easy Walker	1967	5.00	10.00	20.00
❏ BST-84286	The Look of Love	1968	5.00	10.00	20.00
—*With "A Division of Liberty Records" on label*					
❏ BST-84298	Always Something There	1968	5.00	10.00	20.00
❏ BST-84315	Common Touch!	1969	5.00	10.00	20.00
❏ BST-84336	Another Story	1969	5.00	10.00	20.00

FANTASY

❏ FPM-4002 [Q]	Pieces of Dreams	1974	5.00	10.00	20.00

IMPULSE!

❏ AS-9115	Let It Go	1967	6.25	12.50	25.00

MAINSTREAM

❏ S-6041 [S]	Tiger Tail	1965	6.25	12.50	25.00
❏ 56041 [M]	Tiger Tail	1965	5.00	10.00	20.00

TIME

❏ S-2086 [S]	Stan the Man	1962	10.00	20.00	40.00
❏ 52086 [M]	Stan the Man	1962	10.00	20.00	40.00

TURRENTINE, TOMMY

TIME

❏ ST-70008 [S]	Tommy Turrentine	1960	12.50	25.00	50.00
❏ T-70008 [M]	Tommy Turrentine	1960	10.00	20.00	40.00

TURTLES, THE

Also see FLO AND EDDIE.

RHINO

❏ RNLP 151	It Ain't Me Babe	1983	2.50	5.00	10.00
❏ RNLP 152	Happy Together	1983	2.50	5.00	10.00
❏ RNLP 153	You Baby	1983	2.50	5.00	10.00
❏ RNLP 154	Wooden Head	1983	2.50	5.00	10.00
❏ RNLP 160	Greatest Hits	1983	2.50	5.00	10.00
❏ RNDF 280 [EP]	Turtle-Sized	1984	3.00	6.00	12.00
—*Green vinyl turtle-shaped EP*					
❏ RNPD 900	1968	1984	2.00	4.00	8.00
❏ RNPD 901 [PD]	1968	1984	3.00	6.00	12.00
❏ RNLP 70155	Chalon Road	1986	2.50	5.00	10.00
❏ RNLP 70156	The Turtles Present the Battle of the Bands	1986	2.50	5.00	10.00
❏ RNLP 70157	Turtle Soup	1986	2.50	5.00	10.00
❏ RNLP 70158	Shell Shock	1986	2.50	5.00	10.00
❏ RNLP 70159	Turtle Wax: The Best of the Turtles, Vol. 2	1988	2.50	5.00	10.00
❏ RNLP 70177	The Best of the Turtles (Golden Archives Series)	1987	2.50	5.00	10.00

SIRE

❏ SASH-3703 [(2)]	The Turtles' Greatest Hits/Happy Together Again	1974	5.00	10.00	20.00

WHITE WHALE

❏ WW 111 [M]	It Ain't Me Babe	1965	7.50	15.00	30.00
❏ WW 112 [M]	You Baby	1966	7.50	15.00	30.00
❏ WW 114 [M]	Happy Together	1967	5.00	10.00	20.00
❏ WW 115 [M]	The Turtles! Golden Hits	1967	6.25	12.50	25.00
❏ WWS 7111 [S]	It Ain't Me Babe	1965	10.00	20.00	40.00
❏ WWS 7112 [S]	You Baby	1966	10.00	20.00	40.00
❏ WWS 7114 [S]	Happy Together	1967	6.25	12.50	25.00
❏ WWS 7115 [S]	The Turtles! Golden Hits	1967	5.00	10.00	20.00
❏ WWS 7118 [S]	The Turtles Present the Battle of the Bands	1968	6.25	12.50	25.00
❏ WW 7124	Turtle Soup	1969	6.25	12.50	25.00
❏ WW 7127	The Turtles! More Golden Hits	1970	5.00	10.00	20.00
❏ WW 7133	Wooden Head	1970	5.00	10.00	20.00

TUXEDOMOON

RALPH

❏ TX 8004-L	Half-Mute	1980	3.00	6.00	12.00
❏ TX 8104	Desire	1981	3.00	6.00	12.00
❏ TX 8354	A Thousand Lives by Picture	1983	3.00	6.00	12.00

TUXEDOMOON

❏ EP 45 [EP]	Tuxedomoon	1978	5.00	10.00	20.00
❏ EP 79 [EP]	Scream with a View	1979	5.00	10.00	20.00

T

Number	Title (A Side/B Side)	Yr	VG	VG+	NM

TWARDZIK, RICHARD
PACIFIC JAZZ
| ❏ PJ-37 [M] | The Last Set | 1962 | 15.00 | 30.00 | 60.00 |

TWENTIETH CENTURY ZOO, THE
VAULT
| ❏ LPS-122 | Thunder on a Clear Day | 1968 | 15.00 | 30.00 | 60.00 |

$27 SNAP-ON FACE
HETERODYNE
| ❏ 0001 | $27 Snap-On Face | 1977 | 25.00 | 50.00 | 100.00 |

—Blue vinyl; with lyric sheet

TWINK
SIRE
| ❏ SES-97022 | Think Pink | 1970 | 25.00 | 50.00 | 100.00 |

TWINS, THE
RCA VICTOR
| ❏ LPM-1708 [M] | Teenagers Love the Twins | 1958 | 12.50 | 25.00 | 50.00 |

TWISTERS, THE
TREASURE
| ❏ TLP-890 [M] | Doin' the Twist | 1962 | 7.50 | 15.00 | 30.00 |

TWISTIN' KINGS
MOTOWN
| ❏ M-601 [M] | Twistin' the World Around | 1961 | 75.00 | 150.00 | 300.00 |

TWITTY, CONWAY
ACCORD
| ❏ SN-7169 | Early Favorites | 1982 | 3.00 | 6.00 | 12.00 |

ALLEGIANCE
| ❏ AV-5012 | You Made Me What I Am | 1983 | 3.75 | 7.50 | 15.00 |

DECCA
❏ DL 4724 [M]	Conway Twitty Sings	1965	6.25	12.50	25.00
❏ DL 4828 [M]	Look Into My Teardrops	1966	6.25	12.50	25.00
❏ DL 4913 [M]	Conway Twitty Country	1967	7.50	15.00	30.00
❏ DL 4990 [M]	Here's Conway Twitty	1968	12.50	25.00	50.00
❏ DL 74724 [S]	Conway Twitty Sings	1965	7.50	15.00	30.00
❏ DL 74828 [S]	Look Into My Teardrops	1966	7.50	15.00	30.00
❏ DL 74913 [S]	Conway Twitty Country	1967	7.50	15.00	30.00
❏ DL 74990 [S]	Here's Conway Twitty	1968	7.50	15.00	30.00
❏ DL 75062	Next in Line	1968	6.25	12.50	25.00
❏ DL 75105	Darling, You Know I Wouldn't Lie	1968	5.00	10.00	20.00
❏ DL 75131	I Love You More Today	1969	5.00	10.00	20.00
❏ DL 75172	To See My Angel Cry	1970	5.00	10.00	20.00
❏ DL 75209	Hello Darlin'	1970	5.00	10.00	20.00
❏ DL 75248	Fifteen Years Ago	1970	5.00	10.00	20.00
❏ DL 75276	How Much More Can She Stand	1971	5.00	10.00	20.00
❏ DL 75292	I Wonder What She'll Think About Me Leaving	1971	5.00	10.00	20.00
❏ DL 75335	I Can't See Me Without You	1972	5.00	10.00	20.00
❏ DL 75352	Conway Twitty's Greatest Hits Vol. I	1972	5.00	10.00	20.00
❏ DL 75361	I Can't Stop Loving You/Last Date	1972	5.00	10.00	20.00
❏ ST-93776	How Much More Can She Stand	1971	6.25	12.50	25.00

—Capitol Record Club edition

ELEKTRA
❏ 60005	Southern Confort	1982	2.50	5.00	10.00
❏ 60115	#1 Classics, Volume 1	1982	2.50	5.00	10.00
❏ 60182	Dream Maker	1982	2.50	5.00	10.00
❏ 60209	#1 Classics, Volume 2	1982	2.50	5.00	10.00

HEARTLAND
| ❏ HL-1088/9 [(2)] | The Very Best of Conway Twitty | 1989 | 5.00 | 10.00 | 20.00 |

MCA
❏ 18	To See My Angel Cry	1973	3.00	6.00	12.00
—Reissue of Decca 75172					
❏ 19	Hello Darlin'	1973	3.00	6.00	12.00
—Reissue of Decca 75209					
❏ 52	Conway Twitty's Greatest Hits	1973	3.00	6.00	12.00
—Reissue of Decca 75352					
❏ 53	I Can't Stop Loving You/Last Date	1973	3.00	6.00	12.00
—Reissue of Decca 75361					
❏ 303	She Needs Someone to Hold Her (When She Cries)	1973	3.75	7.50	15.00
❏ 359	You've Never Been This Far Before/Baby's Gone	1973	3.75	7.50	15.00
❏ 376	Clinging to a Saving Hand	1973	15.00	30.00	60.00
❏ 406	Honky Tonk Angel	1974	3.75	7.50	15.00
❏ 441	I'm Not Through Loving You Yet	1974	3.75	7.50	15.00
❏ 469	Linda on My Mind	1975	3.75	7.50	15.00
❏ 625	High Priest of Country	197?	2.50	5.00	10.00
—Reissue of MCA 2144					
❏ 702	Conway	197?	2.50	5.00	10.00
—Reissue of MCA 3063					
❏ 2144	High Priest of Country Music	1975	3.75	7.50	15.00
❏ 2176	Twitty (This Time I've Hurt Her More Than She Loves Me)	1975	3.75	7.50	15.00
❏ 2206	Now and Then	1976	3.75	7.50	15.00
❏ 2235	Conway Twitty's Greatest Hits, Vol. 2	1976	3.75	7.50	15.00
❏ 2262	Play Guitar Play	1977	3.00	6.00	12.00
❏ 2293	I've Already Loved You in My Mind	1977	3.00	6.00	12.00
❏ 2328	Georgia Keeps Pullin' on My Ring	1978	3.00	6.00	12.00
❏ 2345	Conway Twitty's Greatest Hits, Vol. 1	1978	3.00	6.00	12.00
—Reissue of Decca 75352					
❏ 3043	The Very Best of Conway Twitty	1978	3.00	6.00	12.00
❏ 3063	Conway	1978	3.00	6.00	12.00
❏ 3086	Cross Winds	1979	3.00	6.00	12.00
❏ 3210	Heart and Soul	1980	3.00	6.00	12.00
❏ 5138	Rest Your Love on Me	1980	3.00	6.00	12.00
❏ 5204	Mr. T.	1981	3.00	6.00	12.00
❏ 5318	Number Ones	1982	3.00	6.00	12.00
❏ 5424	Classic Conway	1983	2.50	5.00	10.00
❏ 5700	Songwriter	1986	2.00	4.00	8.00
❏ 5817	A Night with Conway Twitty	1986	2.00	4.00	8.00
❏ 5969	Borderline	1987	2.00	4.00	8.00
❏ 37081	Georgia Keeps Pullin' on My Ring	198?	2.00	4.00	8.00
—Budget-line reissue					
❏ 37163	Cross Winds	198?	2.00	4.00	8.00
—Budget-line reissue					
❏ 37227	Heart and Soul	1983	2.00	4.00	8.00
—Budget-line reissue					
❏ 37228	Rest Your Love on Me	1983	2.00	4.00	8.00
—Budget-line reissue					
❏ 37229	Conway Twitty's Greatest Hits, Vol. 1	1983	2.00	4.00	8.00
—Budget-line reissue					
❏ 42115	Still in Your Dreams	1988	2.00	4.00	8.00
❏ 42297	House on Old Lonesome Road	1989	3.00	6.00	12.00

MCA CORAL
| ❏ CB-20000 | I'm So Used to Loving You | 1973 | 3.00 | 6.00 | 12.00 |

METRO
| ❏ M-512 [M] | It's Only Make Believe | 1966 | 3.75 | 7.50 | 15.00 |
| ❏ MS-512 [S] | It's Only Make Believe | 1966 | 5.00 | 10.00 | 20.00 |

MGM
❏ GAS-110	Conway Twitty (Golden Archive Series)	1970	5.00	10.00	20.00
❏ E-3744 [M]	Conway Twitty Sings	1959	25.00	50.00	100.00
—Yellow label					
❏ E-3744 [M]	Conway Twitty Sings	196?	75.00	150.00	300.00
—Reissue with orange cover and a clean-cut photo of Conway					
❏ E-3744 [M]	Conway Twitty Sings	1960	10.00	20.00	40.00
—Black label					
❏ SE-3744 [S]	Conway Twitty Sings	1959	37.50	75.00	150.00
—Yellow label					
❏ SE-3744 [S]	Conway Twitty Sings	196?	75.00	150.00	300.00
—Reissue with orange cover and a clean-cut photo of Conway					
❏ SE-3744 [S]	Conway Twitty Sings	1960	12.50	25.00	50.00
—Black label					
❏ E-3786 [M]	Saturday Night with Conway Twitty	1960	17.50	35.00	70.00
❏ SE-3786 [S]	Saturday Night with Conway Twitty	1960	25.00	50.00	100.00
❏ E-3818 [M]	Lonely Blue Boy	1960	17.50	35.00	70.00
❏ SE-3818 [S]	Lonely Blue Boy	1960	25.00	50.00	100.00
❏ E-3849 [M]	Conway Twitty's Greatest Hits	1960	10.00	20.00	40.00
—Without poster					
❏ E-3849 [M]	Conway Twitty's Greatest Hits	1960	17.50	35.00	70.00
—With poster					
❏ SE-3849 [P]	Conway Twitty's Greatest Hits	1960	12.50	25.00	50.00
—Without poster					
❏ SE-3849 [P]	Conway Twitty's Greatest Hits	1960	20.00	40.00	80.00
—With poster					
❏ E-3907 [M]	The Rock and Roll Story	1961	12.50	25.00	50.00
❏ SE-3907 [S]	The Rock and Roll Story	1961	20.00	40.00	80.00
❏ E-3943 [M]	The Conway Twitty Touch	1961	12.50	25.00	50.00
❏ SE-3943 [S]	The Conway Twitty Touch	1961	20.00	40.00	80.00
❏ E-4019 [M]	Portrait of a Fool and Others	1962	10.00	20.00	40.00
❏ SE-4019 [S]	Portrait of a Fool and Others	1962	12.50	25.00	50.00
❏ E-4089 [M]	R & B '63	1963	10.00	20.00	40.00
❏ SE-4089 [S]	R & B '63	1963	12.50	25.00	50.00
❏ E-4217 [M]	Hit the Road	1964	6.25	12.50	25.00
❏ SE-4217 [S]	Hit the Road	1964	7.50	15.00	30.00
❏ SE-4650	You Can't Take the Country Out of Conway	1969	3.75	7.50	15.00
❏ SE-4799	Conway Twitty Hits	1971	3.75	7.50	15.00
❏ SE-4837	Conway Twitty Sings the Blues	1972	3.75	7.50	15.00
❏ SES-4844 [(2)]	20 Great Hits by Conway Twitty	1973	4.50	9.00	18.00

PICKWICK
| ❏ SPC-3360 | Shake It Up | 1973 | 3.00 | 6.00 | 12.00 |

TEE VEE
| ❏ 1009 | 20 Certified #1 Hits | 1978 | 3.75 | 7.50 | 15.00 |

WARNER BROS.
❏ 23869	Lost in the Feeling	1983	2.50	5.00	10.00
❏ 23971	Merry Twismas	1983	5.00	10.00	20.00
❏ 25078	By Heart	1984	2.50	5.00	10.00
❏ 25170	Conway's Latest Greatest Hits	1984	2.50	5.00	10.00
❏ 25207	Don't Call Him a Cowboy	1985	2.50	5.00	10.00
❏ 25294	Chasin' Rainbows	1985	2.50	5.00	10.00
❏ 25406	Fallin' for You for Years	1986	2.50	5.00	10.00
❏ 25777	#1's — The Warner Bros. Years	1988	2.00	4.00	8.00
❏ 60115	#1 Classics, Volume 1	1983	2.00	4.00	8.00
—Reissue of Elektra LP					
❏ 60182	Dream Maker	1983	2.00	4.00	8.00
—Reissue of Elektra LP					
❏ 60209	#1 Classics, Volume 2	1983	2.00	4.00	8.00
—Reissue of Elektra LP					

TWITTY, CONWAY, AND LORETTA LYNN
Also see each artist's individual listings.
DECCA
| ❏ DL 75251 | We Only Make Believe | 1971 | 5.00 | 10.00 | 20.00 |
| ❏ DL 75326 | Lead Me On | 1972 | 5.00 | 10.00 | 20.00 |

HEARTLAND
| ❏ HL-1059/60 [(2)] | The Best of Conway and Loretta | 1987 | 5.00 | 10.00 | 20.00 |

MCA
❏ 8	We Only Make Believe	1973	3.00	6.00	12.00
—Reissue of Decca 75251					
❏ 9	Lead Me On	1973	3.00	6.00	12.00
—Reissue of Decca 75326					
❏ 335	Louisiana Woman, Mississippi Man	1973	3.75	7.50	15.00
❏ 427	Country Partners	1974	3.75	7.50	15.00
❏ 629	United Talent	198?	2.50	5.00	10.00
—Reissue of MCA 2209					
❏ 722	Honky Tonk Heroes	198?	2.50	5.00	10.00
—Reissue of MCA 2372					
❏ 723	Diamond Duet	198?	2.50	5.00	10.00
—Reissue of MCA 3190					
❏ 2143	Feelins'	1975	3.75	7.50	15.00

Thin Lizzy's debut album, on the London label, was basically ignored at the time and is hard to find today.

When they were together, this was the only album by the Trashmen. The original on the Garrett label still can bring a three-figure sum, even with a high-quality reissue on vinyl.

When Phil Spector returned to the music scene in 1969, the album he made with Ike & Tina Turner, *River Deep – Mountain High*, finally got an official release on A&M. Rare versions of this record on Philles were not issued with a cover.

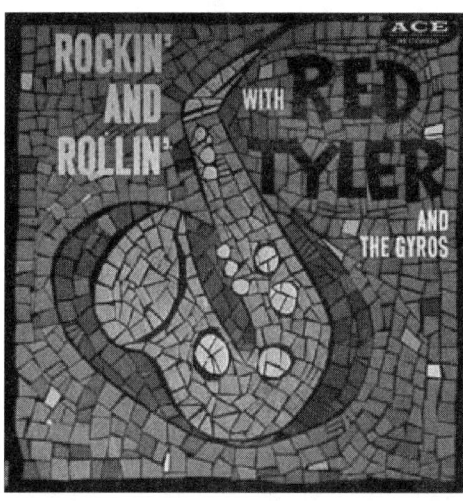

Red Tyler, another rock 'n' roll saxophone player, had two albums for New Orleans' Ace label, of which this was the first.

This Ritchie Valens album, *Ritchie,* was compiled shortly after his death.

A Gene Vincent Record Date, issued in 1958, is one of many Capitol LPs of Vincent's material that can fetch a hefty sum today.

Number	Title (A Side/B Side)	Yr	VG	VG+	NM
❏ 2209	United Talent	1976	3.75	7.50	15.00
❏ 2278	Dynamic Duo	1977	3.00	6.00	12.00
❏ 2354	Country Partners	1978	2.50	5.00	10.00
—Reissue of MCA 427					
❏ 2372	Honky Tonk Heroes	1978	3.00	6.00	12.00
❏ 3164	The Very Best of Loretta and Conway	1979	3.00	6.00	12.00
❏ 3190	Diamond Duet	1979	3.00	6.00	12.00
❏ 5178	Two's a Party	1981	3.00	6.00	12.00
❏ 37237	The Very Best of Loretta and Conway	1983	2.00	4.00	8.00
—Budget-line reissue					
❏ 42216	Making Believe	1988	2.00	4.00	8.00
MCA CORAL					
❏ CDL-8006	Never Ending Song of Love	1973	3.00	6.00	12.00

2 LIVE CREW, THE
EFFECT

Number	Title (A Side/B Side)	Yr	VG	VG+	NM
❏ E 3003	Live in Concert	1990	2.50	5.00	10.00
LIL' JOE					
❏ XR-215 [(2)]	Shake a Lil' Somethin'	1996	3.75	7.50	15.00
❏ XR-227 [(2)]	The 2 Live Crew Goes to the Movies — A Decade of Hits	1997	3.00	6.00	12.00
❏ XR-231 [(2)]	The Real One	1998	3.00	6.00	12.00
❏ XR-238 [(2)]	Greatest Hits Vol. 2	1999	3.75	7.50	15.00
❏ XR- 239 [(2)]	Greatest Hits Vol. 2/Edit	1999	3.75	7.50	15.00
❏ 264 [(2)]	Private Personal Parts	2000	3.00	6.00	12.00
❏ 286 [(2)]	Essential DJ 12" and Mega Mixes	2002	2.50	5.00	10.00
LUKE					
❏ 122 [(2)]	Greatest Hits	1992	5.00	10.00	20.00
❏ 123 [(2)]	Greatest Hits/Edit	1992	5.00	10.00	20.00
❏ 207 [(2)]	Back at Your Ass for the Nine-4	1994	5.00	10.00	20.00
—As "The New 2 Live Crew"					
❏ 208 [(2)]	Back At You for '94	1994	5.00	10.00	20.00
—As "The New 2 Live Crew"; edited version					
❏ DMD 1760 [(2)]	Sports Weekend (As Nasty As They Wanna Be Part II)	1991	3.75	7.50	15.00
—Promo-only vinyl issue in generic black cardboard sleeve					
❏ 91424	Banned in the U.S.A.	1990	3.75	7.50	15.00
—As "Luke Featuring The 2 Live Crew"					
LUKE SKYYWALKER					
❏ XR-100	The 2 Live Crew "Is What We Are"	1987	3.75	7.50	15.00
❏ XR-101	Move Somethin'	1988	3.00	6.00	12.00
❏ XR-107 [(2)]	As Nasty As They Wanna Be	1989	3.75	7.50	15.00
❏ XR- 108	As Clean As They Wanna Be	1989	3.75	7.50	15.00

2PAC
Includes records as "Makaveli."
AMARU/JIVE

Number	Title (A Side/B Side)	Yr	VG	VG+	NM
❏ 41628 [(3)]	R U Still Down? (Remember Me)	1997	6.25	12.50	25.00
DEATH ROW					
❏ 63008 [(4)]	All Eyez on Me	2001	5.00	10.00	20.00
—Reissue					
❏ 63012 [(2)]	The Don Killuminati — The 7 Day Theory	2001	3.75	7.50	15.00
—As "Makaveli"; reissue					
DEATH ROW/INTERSCOPE					
❏ INT2-90039 [(2)]	The Don Killuminati — The 7 Day Theory	1996	3.75	7.50	15.00
—As "Makaveli"					
❏ INT4-90301 [(4)]	Greatest Hits	1998	7.50	15.00	30.00
❏ 490413-1 [(2)]	Still I Rise	1999	3.75	7.50	15.00
—As "2Pac + Outlawz"					
❏ 490840-1 [(4)]	Until the End of Time	2001	7.50	15.00	30.00
❏ 524204-1 [(4)]	All Eyez on Me	1996	7.50	15.00	30.00
INTERSCOPE					
❏ 91767	2Pacalypse Now	1991	3.75	7.50	15.00
❏ 92399 [(2)]	Me Against the World	1995	5.00	10.00	20.00
RESTLESS					
❏ 72737 [(2)]	Strictly 4 My N.I.G.G.A.Z.	1998	3.75	7.50	15.00
—Vinyl reissue of 1993 album (we can't prove or disprove the existence of the original Interscope edition on vinyl)					

TYLE, TEDDY
GOLDEN CREST

Number	Title (A Side/B Side)	Yr	VG	VG+	NM
❏ GC-3060 [M]	Moon Shot	1959	10.00	20.00	40.00

TYLER, ALVIN "RED"
ACE

Number	Title (A Side/B Side)	Yr	VG	VG+	NM
❏ LP-1006 [M]	Rockin' and Rollin'	1960	37.50	75.00	150.00
❏ LP-1021 [M]	Twistin' with Mr. Sax	1962	30.00	60.00	120.00

TYLER, CHARLES
ESP-DISK'

Number	Title (A Side/B Side)	Yr	VG	VG+	NM
❏ 1029 [M]	The Charles Tyler Ensemble	1966	5.00	10.00	20.00
❏ S-1029 [S]	The Charles Tyler Ensemble	1966	6.25	12.50	25.00
❏ S-1059 [S]	Eastern Man Alone	1968	5.00	10.00	20.00

TYLER, T. TEXAS
CAPITOL

Number	Title (A Side/B Side)	Yr	VG	VG+	NM
❏ ST 1662 [S]	Salvation	1962	7.50	15.00	30.00
❏ T 1662 [M]	Salvation	1962	6.25	12.50	25.00
❏ ST 2344 [S]	The Hits of T. Texas Tyler	1965	6.25	12.50	25.00
❏ T 2344 [M]	The Hits of T. Texas Tyler	1965	5.00	10.00	20.00
KING					
❏ 664 [M]	T. Texas Tyler	1959	30.00	60.00	120.00
❏ 689 [M]	The Great Texan	1960	30.00	60.00	120.00
❏ 721 [M]	T. Texas Tyler	1961	20.00	40.00	80.00
❏ 734 [M]	Songs Along the Way	1962	20.00	40.00	80.00
SOUND					
❏ 607 [M]	Deck of Cards	1958	20.00	40.00	80.00
STARDAY					
❏ SLP-379 [M]	The Man with a Million Friends	1966	6.25	12.50	25.00
WRANGLER					
❏ W-1002 [M]	T. Texas Tyler	1962	10.00	20.00	40.00
❏ W-31002 [S]	T. Texas Tyler	1962	12.50	25.00	50.00

TYLER, WILLIE, AND LESTER
TAMLA

Number	Title (A Side/B Side)	Yr	VG	VG+	NM
❏ TM-265 [M]	Hello Dummy	1965	50.00	100.00	200.00

TYMES, THE
ABKCO

Number	Title (A Side/B Side)	Yr	VG	VG+	NM
❏ 4228	The Best of Tymes	1973	3.00	6.00	12.00
COLUMBIA					
❏ CS 9778	People	1969	3.75	7.50	15.00
PARKWAY					
❏ P 7032 [M]	So Much in Love	1963	10.00	20.00	40.00
—With group standing in front-cover photo					
❏ P 7032 [M]	So Much in Love	1963	50.00	100.00	200.00
—With head-and-shoulders group photo on front cover					
❏ P 7038 [M]	The Sound of the Wonderful Tymes	1963	10.00	20.00	40.00
❏ SP 7038 [S]	The Sound of the Wonderful Tymes	1963	12.50	25.00	50.00
❏ P 7039 [M]	Somewhere	1964	12.50	25.00	50.00
—Includes bonus single 7039 (deduct 20 percent if missing)					
❏ P 7049 [M]	18 Greatest Hits	1964	10.00	20.00	40.00
RCA VICTOR					
❏ APL1-0727	Trustmaker	1974	3.00	6.00	12.00
❏ APL1-1835	Turning Point	1976	3.00	6.00	12.00
❏ APL1-2406	Diggin' Their Roots	1977	3.00	6.00	12.00

TYNER, McCOY
BLUE NOTE

Number	Title (A Side/B Side)	Yr	VG	VG+	NM
❏ BLP-4264 [M]	The Real McCoy	1967	6.25	12.50	25.00
❏ BST-84264 [S]	The Real McCoy	1967	5.00	10.00	20.00
—With "A Division of Liberty Records" on label					
❏ BST-84275	Tender Moments	1968	5.00	10.00	20.00
—With "A Division of Liberty Records" on label					
❏ BST-84307	Time for Tyner	1969	5.00	10.00	20.00
—With "A Division of Liberty Records" on label					
❏ BST-84338	Expansions	1969	5.00	10.00	20.00
—With "A Division of Liberty Records" on label					
GRP/IMPULSE!					
❏ 216	McCoy Tyner Plays Duke Ellington	1997	5.00	10.00	20.00
—Reissue on audiophile vinyl					
❏ 220	Inception	1997	5.00	10.00	20.00
—Reissue on audiophile vinyl					
❏ 221	Nights of Ballads and Blues	1997	5.00	10.00	20.00
—Reissue on audiophile vinyl					
IMPULSE!					
❏ A-18 [M]	Inception	1962	6.25	12.50	25.00
❏ AS-18 [S]	Inception	1962	6.25	12.50	25.00
❏ A-33 [M]	Reaching Fourth	1963	6.25	12.50	25.00
❏ AS-33 [S]	Reaching Fourth	1963	6.25	12.50	25.00
❏ A-39 [M]	Nights of Ballads and Blues	1963	6.25	12.50	25.00
❏ AS-39 [S]	Nights of Ballads and Blues	1963	6.25	12.50	25.00
❏ A-48 [M]	McCoy Tyner Live at Newport	1963	6.25	12.50	25.00
❏ AS-48 [S]	McCoy Tyner Live at Newport	1963	6.25	12.50	25.00
❏ A-63 [M]	Today and Tomorrow	1964	6.25	12.50	25.00
❏ AS-63 [S]	Today and Tomorrow	1964	6.25	12.50	25.00
❏ A-79 [M]	McCoy Tyner Plays Duke Ellington	1965	6.25	12.50	25.00
❏ AS-79 [S]	McCoy Tyner Plays Duke Ellington	1965	6.25	12.50	25.00
MILESTONE					
❏ FPM-4006 [Q]	Song of the New World	197?	5.00	10.00	20.00

TYRANNOSAURUS REX
See T. REX.

U

U2
ISLAND

Number	Title (A Side/B Side)	Yr	VG	VG+	NM
❏ PR 2049 [DJ]	The Joshua Tree Interview...Their Words and Music	1987	10.00	20.00	40.00
❏ PR12 7545-1 [(2)]	PopMart Sampler	1997	12.50	25.00	50.00
—Promo-only 8-song collection of old and new U2 material					
❏ ILPS 9646	Boy	1980	3.75	7.50	15.00
❏ ILPS 9680	October	1981	3.00	6.00	12.00
—Back cover has engineering credits, etc., in upper left					
❏ ILPS 9680	October	1981	3.75	7.50	15.00
—Back cover is blank (no engineering credits, etc.) in upper left					
❏ 90040	Boy	1983	2.00	4.00	8.00
—Third pressings have black labels					
❏ 90040	Boy	1983	2.50	5.00	10.00
—Second pressings have light blue labels					
❏ 90040	Boy	1983	3.00	6.00	12.00
—Reissue; first pressings have dark purple labels					
❏ 90067	War	1983	2.00	4.00	8.00
—Third pressings have black labels					
❏ 90067	War	1983	2.50	5.00	10.00
—Second pressings have light blue labels					
❏ 90067	War	1983	3.00	6.00	12.00
—Original pressings have dark purple labels					
❏ 90092	October	1983	2.00	4.00	8.00
—Third pressings have black labels					
❏ 90092	October	1983	2.50	5.00	10.00
—Second pressings have light blue labels					
❏ 90092	October	1983	2.50	5.00	10.00
—Reissue; first pressings have dark purple labels					
❏ 90127-1-B [EP]	Under a Blood Red Sky	1983	2.50	5.00	10.00
—White labels with "Mini LP" logo; edited version of "The Electric Co."					
❏ 90127-1-B [EP]	Under a Blood Red Sky	1983	3.75	7.50	15.00
—White labels with "Mini LP" logo; with version of "The Electric Co." in which Bono sings snippets of "A-Me-Ri-Ca" from West Side Story and "Send In The Clowns" during the instrumental break.					

Number	Title (A Side/B Side)	Yr	VG	VG+	NM
❑ 90231	The Unforgettable Fire	1984	2.50	5.00	10.00
❑ 90279-1-A [EP]	Wide Awake in America	1985	2.50	5.00	10.00
❑ 90581	The Joshua Tree	1987	2.50	5.00	10.00
—With lyric sheet					
❑ 91003 [(2)]	Rattle and Hum	1988	3.75	7.50	15.00
❑ R 114632	October	1983	3.00	6.00	12.00
—RCA Music Service edition					
❑ R 124619	War	1983	3.00	6.00	12.00
—BMG Direct Marketing edition					
❑ R 140642 [EP]	Wide Awake in America	1985	3.00	6.00	12.00
—RCA Music Service edition					
❑ R 144636	Boy	1983	3.00	6.00	12.00
—RCA Music Service edition					
❑ R 153501	The Joshua Tree	1987	3.00	6.00	12.00
—RCA Music Service edition; no lyric sheet					
❑ R 153598 [EP]	Under a Blood Red Sky	1983	2.50	5.00	10.00
—BMG Direct Marketing edition					
❑ R 154515	The Unforgettable Fire	1985	3.00	6.00	12.00
—RCA Music Service edition					
❑ R 200596 [(2)]	Rattle and Hum	1988	3.75	7.50	15.00
—BMG Direct Marketing edition					
❑ 510347-1	Achtung Baby	1991	10.00	20.00	40.00
—U.S. LP covers are uncensored (Adam Clayton appears naked without any "X" or shamrock over his appendage)					
❑ 518047-1	Zooropa	1993	6.25	12.50	25.00
—All "U.S." copies actually are British imports					
❑ 524334-1 [(2)]	Pop	1997	5.00	10.00	20.00
❑ 811148-1	War	1990	2.00	4.00	8.00
—Reissue; sticker with new number placed over bar code of leftover 90067 pressings					
❑ 818008-1	Under a Blood Red Sky	1990	2.00	4.00	8.00
—Reissue; sticker with new number placed over bar code of leftover 90127 pressings					
❑ 822898-1	The Unforgettable Fire	1990	2.00	4.00	8.00
—Reissue; new sticker placed on leftover Island/Atco pressings					
❑ 842296-1	Boy	1990	2.00	4.00	8.00
—Reissue; sticker with new number placed over bar code of leftover 90040 pressings					
❑ 842297-1	October	1990	2.00	4.00	8.00
—Reissue; sticker with new number placed over bar code of leftover 90092 pressings					
❑ 842298-1	The Joshua Tree	1990	2.00	4.00	8.00
—Reissue; sticker with new number placed over bar code of leftover 90581 pressings					
❑ 842299-1 [(2)]	Rattle and Hum	1990	3.00	6.00	12.00
—Reissue; sticker with new number placed over bar code of leftover 91003 pressings					
❑ 842479-1 [EP]	Wide Awake in America	1990	2.00	4.00	8.00
—Reissue; sticker with new number placed over bar code of leftover 90279 pressings					
MOBILE FIDELITY					
❑ 1-207	The Unforgettable Fire	1994	6.25	12.50	25.00
—Audiophile vinyl					
WARNER BROS.					
❑ WBMS-117 [DJ]	Two Sides Live	1981	30.00	60.00	120.00
—Promo only, part of "The Warner Bros. Music Show"; legitimate copies are on black vinyl					

UFO

Number	Title (A Side/B Side)	Yr	VG	VG+	NM
CHRYSALIS					
❑ CHR 1059	Phenomenon	1974	3.75	7.50	15.00
—Green label					
❑ CHR 1059	Phenomenon	1977	3.00	6.00	12.00
—Fading blue label					
❑ CHR 1074	Force It	1975	3.00	6.00	12.00
❑ CHR 1103	No Heavy Petting	1976	3.00	6.00	12.00
❑ CHR 1127	Lights Out	1977	3.00	6.00	12.00
❑ CHR 1182	Obsession	1978	3.00	6.00	12.00
❑ CHR 1209 [(2)]	Strangers in the Night	1979	3.75	7.50	15.00
❑ CHR 1239	No Place to Run	1980	3.00	6.00	12.00
❑ CHR 1307	The Wild, the Willing and the Innocent	1981	3.00	6.00	12.00
❑ CHR 1360	Mechanix	1982	3.00	6.00	12.00
❑ PV 41059	Phenomenon	1983	2.00	4.00	8.00
❑ PV 41074	Force It	1983	2.00	4.00	8.00
❑ PV 41103	No Heavy Petting	1983	2.00	4.00	8.00
❑ FV 41127	Lights Out	1983	2.00	4.00	8.00
❑ PV 41127	Lights Out	1986	2.00	4.00	8.00
—Reissue of FV 41127					
❑ PV 41182	Obsession	1983	2.00	4.00	8.00
❑ V2X 41209 [(2)]	Strangers in the Night	1983	2.50	5.00	10.00
❑ PV 41239	No Place to Run	1983	2.00	4.00	8.00
❑ PV 41307	The Wild, the Willing and the Innocent	1983	2.00	4.00	8.00
❑ PV 41360	Mechanix	1983	2.00	4.00	8.00
❑ FV 41402	Making Contact	1983	2.50	5.00	10.00
❑ PV 41402	Making Contact	1986	2.00	4.00	8.00
—Reissue of FV 41402					
❑ BFV 41518	Misdemeanor	1986	2.50	5.00	10.00
❑ FV 41644	The Best of the Rest	1988	2.50	5.00	10.00
METAL BLADE/ENIGMA					
❑ 7 73404 1 [EP]	Ain't Misbehavin'	1989	3.00	6.00	12.00
RARE EARTH					
❑ RS 624	UFO 1	1971	6.25	12.50	25.00

UGGAMS, LESLIE

Number	Title (A Side/B Side)	Yr	VG	VG+	NM
ATLANTIC					
❑ 8128 [M]	Time to Love	1967	3.75	7.50	15.00
❑ SD 8128 [S]	Time to Love	1967	5.00	10.00	20.00
❑ SD 8196	What's an Uggams	1968	3.75	7.50	15.00
❑ SD 8241	Just to Satisfy You	1969	3.75	7.50	15.00
COLUMBIA					
❑ CL 1706 [M]	Leslie Uggams on TV	1962	3.75	7.50	15.00
❑ CL 1865 [M]	More Leslie Uggams on TV	1963	3.75	7.50	15.00
❑ CL 2071 [M]	So in Love	1963	3.75	7.50	15.00
❑ CS 8506 [S]	Leslie Uggams on TV	1962	5.00	10.00	20.00
❑ CS 8665 [S]	More Leslie Uggams on TV	1963	5.00	10.00	20.00
❑ CS 8871 [S]	So in Love	1963	5.00	10.00	20.00
❑ CS 9936	Leslie	1970	3.00	6.00	12.00
MOTOWN					
❑ M6-846	Leslie Uggams	1975	3.00	6.00	12.00

Number	Title (A Side/B Side)	Yr	VG	VG+	NM
SONDAY					
❑ 8000	Try to See It My Way	1972	3.00	6.00	12.00

ULANO, SAM

Number	Title (A Side/B Side)	Yr	VG	VG+	NM
LANE					
❑ LP-140 [M]	Sam Ulano	195?	12.50	25.00	50.00
❑ LP-151 [M]	Sam Ulano Is Mr. Rhythm	195?	12.50	25.00	50.00

ULMER, JAMES "BLOOD"

Number	Title (A Side/B Side)	Yr	VG	VG+	NM
ARTISTS HOUSE					
❑ 13	Are You Glad to Be in America?	1980	5.00	10.00	20.00
❑ AH 9407	Tales of Captain Black	1979	5.00	10.00	20.00
COLUMBIA					
❑ ARC 37493	Free Lancing	1981	5.00	10.00	20.00
❑ ARC 38285	Black Rock	1982	5.00	10.00	20.00

ULTIMATE SPINACH

Number	Title (A Side/B Side)	Yr	VG	VG+	NM
MGM					
❑ E-4518 [M]	Ultimate Spinach	1968	7.50	15.00	30.00
❑ SE-4518 [S]	Ultimate Spinach	1968	6.25	12.50	25.00
❑ E-4570 [M]	Behold & See	1968	12.50	25.00	50.00
—Mono is promo only (yellow label)					
❑ SE-4570 [S]	Behold & See	1968	6.25	12.50	25.00
❑ SE-4600	Ultimate Spinach	1969	6.25	12.50	25.00

ULTRA VIOLET

Number	Title (A Side/B Side)	Yr	VG	VG+	NM
CAPITOL					
❑ ST-11244	Ultra Violet	1973	6.25	12.50	25.00

UMEKI, MIYOSHI

Number	Title (A Side/B Side)	Yr	VG	VG+	NM
MERCURY					
❑ MG-20568 [M]	Miyoshi	1958	5.00	10.00	20.00
❑ SR-60228 [S]	Miyoshi	1959	6.25	12.50	25.00

UNBEATABLES, THE

Number	Title (A Side/B Side)	Yr	VG	VG+	NM
DAWN					
❑ 5050 [M]	Live at Palisades Park	1964	37.50	75.00	150.00

UNCLE JOSH AND COUSIN JAKE

Number	Title (A Side/B Side)	Yr	VG	VG+	NM
COTTON TOWN					
❑ 101 [M]	Just Joshing	1958	25.00	50.00	100.00

UNCLE LAR' AND LIL' TOMMY

Number	Title (A Side/B Side)	Yr	VG	VG+	NM
WLS					
❑ WLS-890	Animal Stories	1981	5.00	10.00	20.00
❑ WLS-947	Animal Stories Volume Three	1983	5.00	10.00	20.00
❑ WLS-1000	Animal Stories Volume Two	1982	5.00	10.00	20.00

UNDERGROUND, THE

Number	Title (A Side/B Side)	Yr	VG	VG+	NM
WING					
❑ MGW-12337 [M]	Psychedelic Visions	1967	20.00	40.00	80.00
❑ SRW-16337 [S]	Psychedelic Visions	1967	25.00	50.00	100.00

UNDERGROUND SUNSHINE

Number	Title (A Side/B Side)	Yr	VG	VG+	NM
INTREPID					
❑ IT-74003	Let There Be Light	1969	7.50	15.00	30.00

UNDISPUTED TRUTH, THE

Number	Title (A Side/B Side)	Yr	VG	VG+	NM
GORDY					
❑ G 955L	The Undisputed Truth	1971	6.25	12.50	25.00
❑ G5-959	Face to Face with the Truth	1972	5.00	10.00	20.00
❑ G5-963	Law of the Land	1973	5.00	10.00	20.00
❑ G6-968	Down to Earth	1974	5.00	10.00	20.00
❑ G6-970	Cosmic Truth	1975	5.00	10.00	20.00
❑ G6-972	Higher Than High	1975	5.00	10.00	20.00
WHITFIELD					
❑ BS 2967	Method to the Madness	1977	5.00	10.00	20.00
❑ BSK 3202	Smokin'	1979	3.75	7.50	15.00

UNFOLDING

Number	Title (A Side/B Side)	Yr	VG	VG+	NM
AUDIO FIDELITY					
❑ AFLP-2184 [M]	How to Blow Your Mind and Have a Freak-Out Party	1967	17.50	35.00	70.00
❑ AFSD-6184 [S]	How to Blow Your Mind and Have a Freak-Out Party	1967	25.00	50.00	100.00

UNIFICS, THE

Number	Title (A Side/B Side)	Yr	VG	VG+	NM
KAPP					
❑ KS-3582	Sittin' In at the Court of Love	1968	6.25	12.50	25.00

UNIQUES, THE (1)

Number	Title (A Side/B Side)	Yr	VG	VG+	NM
PAULA					
❑ LP-2190 [M]	Uniquely Yours	1966	6.25	12.50	25.00
❑ LPS-2190 [S]	Uniquely Yours	1966	7.50	15.00	30.00
❑ LP-2194 [M]	Happening Now	1967	6.25	12.50	25.00
❑ LPS-2194 [S]	Happening Now	1967	7.50	15.00	30.00
❑ LP-2199 [M]	Playtime	1968	6.25	12.50	25.00
❑ LPS-2199 [S]	Playtime	1968	6.25	12.50	25.00
❑ LPS-2204	The Uniques	1969	6.25	12.50	25.00
❑ LPS-2208	Golden Hits	1970	6.25	12.50	25.00

UNIT FOUR PLUS TWO

Number	Title (A Side/B Side)	Yr	VG	VG+	NM
LONDON					
❑ PS 427 [P]	Unit Four Plus Two #1	1965	12.50	25.00	50.00
❑ LL 3427 [M]	Unit Four Plus Two #1	1965	10.00	20.00	40.00

UNITED STATES DOUBLE QUARTET

Number	Title (A Side/B Side)	Yr	VG	VG+	NM
B.T. PUPPY					
❑ BTS-1005	Life Is Groovy	1969	12.50	25.00	50.00

UNITED STATES OF AMERICA, THE

Number	Title (A Side/B Side)	Yr	VG	VG+	NM
COLUMBIA					
❑ CL 2814 [M]	The United States of America	1968	25.00	50.00	100.00
—Mono is promo only					

Number	Title (A Side/B Side)	Yr	VG	VG+	NM
❑ CS 9614 [S]	The United States of America	1968	10.00	20.00	40.00
—Without outer bag					
❑ CS 9614 [S]	The United States of America	1968	20.00	40.00	80.00
—With outer bag					

UNSPOKEN WORD, THE
ASCOT
❑ AS 16028	Tuesday, April 19th	1968	5.00	10.00	20.00

UNUSUAL WE
PULSAR
❑ 10608	Unusual We	1969	7.50	15.00	30.00

UPCHURCH, PHIL
BLUE THUMB
❑ BTS-59	Lovin' Feelin'	1973	3.00	6.00	12.00
❑ BTS-6005 [(2)]	Darkness, Darkness	1971	5.00	10.00	20.00

BOYD
❑ B-398 [M]	You Can't Sit Down	1961	20.00	40.00	80.00
❑ BS-398 [S]	You Can't Sit Down	1961	25.00	50.00	100.00

CADET
❑ LPS-826	Upchurch	1969	3.75	7.50	15.00
❑ LPS-840	The Way I Feel	1970	3.75	7.50	15.00

JAM
❑ 007	Free and Easy	198?	3.00	6.00	12.00

KUDU
❑ 22	Phil Upchurch and Tennyson Stevens	1975	3.00	6.00	12.00

MILESTONE
❑ MSP-9010	Feeling Blue	1968	3.75	7.50	15.00

UNITED ARTISTS
❑ UAL-3162 [M]	You Can't Sit Down, Part 2	1961	7.50	15.00	30.00
❑ UAL-3175 [M]	Big Hit Dances	1962	6.25	12.50	25.00
❑ UAS-6162 [S]	You Can't Sit Down, Part 2	1961	10.00	20.00	40.00
❑ UAS-6175 [S]	Big Hit Dances	1962	7.50	15.00	30.00

URGE OVERKILL
GEFFEN
❑ GEF-24529	Saturation	1993	3.00	6.00	12.00
—All copies on orange vinyl					
❑ GEF-24818 [(2)]	Exit the Dragon	1995	3.75	7.50	15.00

TOUCH & GO
❑ 37	Jesus Urge Superstar	1989	3.00	6.00	12.00
❑ 52	Americruiser	1990	3.00	6.00	12.00
❑ 70	The Supersonic Storybook	1991	3.00	6.00	12.00
❑ 86 [10]	Stull	1992	2.50	5.00	10.00
—Black vinyl					
❑ 86 [10]	Stull	1992	10.00	20.00	40.00
—Whitish vinyl original					

URSO, PHIL
REGENT
❑ MG-6003 [M]	Sentimental Journey	1956	12.50	25.00	50.00

SAVOY
❑ MG-12056 [M]	The Philosophy of Urso	1956	12.50	25.00	50.00
❑ MG-15041 [10]	Bob Brookmeyer with Phil Urso	1954	37.50	75.00	150.00

USSELTON, BILLY
KAPP
❑ KL-1051 [M]	Bill Usselton — His First Album	1957	12.50	25.00	50.00

V

VAGABONDS, THE
UNIQUE
❑ LP-112 [M]	The Vagabonds	1957	6.25	12.50	25.00

VAGRANTS, THE
ARISTA
❑ AL-8459	The Great Lost Vagrants Album	1987	5.00	10.00	20.00

VALE, JERRY
COLUMBIA
❑ GP 16 [(2)]	With Love, Jerry Vale	1969	3.75	7.50	15.00
❑ CS 1021	Let It Be	1970	3.00	6.00	12.00
❑ CL 1114 [M]	I Remember Buddy	1958	3.75	7.50	15.00
❑ CL 1164 [M]	I Remember Russ	1958	3.75	7.50	15.00
❑ CL 1380 [M]	The Same Old Moon	1959	3.75	7.50	15.00
❑ CL 1529 [M]	Jerry Vale's Greatest Hits	1961	3.75	7.50	15.00
❑ CL 1797 [M]	I Have But One Heart	1962	3.00	6.00	12.00
❑ CL 1955 [M]	Arrivederci, Roma	1963	3.00	6.00	12.00
❑ CL 2043 [M]	The Language of Love	1963	3.00	6.00	12.00
❑ CL 2116 [M]	Till the End of Time	1964	3.00	6.00	12.00
❑ CL 2181 [M]	Be My Love	1964	3.00	6.00	12.00
❑ CL 2225 [M]	Christmas Greetings from Jerry Vale	1964	3.00	6.00	12.00
❑ CL 2273 [M]	Standing Ovation!	1965	3.00	6.00	12.00
❑ CL 2313 [M]	Have You Looked Into Your Heart	1965	3.00	6.00	12.00
❑ CL 2371 [M]	Moonlight Becomes You	1965	3.00	6.00	12.00
❑ CL 2387 [M]	There Goes My Heart	1965	3.00	6.00	12.00
❑ CL 2444 [M]	It's Magic	1966	3.00	6.00	12.00
❑ CL 2489 [M]	Great Moments on Broadway	1966	3.00	6.00	12.00
❑ CL 2530 [M]	Everybody Loves Somebody	1966	3.00	6.00	12.00
❑ CL 2583 [M]	The Impossible Dream	1967	3.00	6.00	12.00
❑ CL 2659 [M]	More Jerry Vale's Greatest Hits	1967	3.75	7.50	15.00
❑ CL 2684 [M]	Time Alone Will Tell	1967	3.00	6.00	12.00
❑ CL 2774 [M]	You Don't Have to Say You Love Me	1968	3.75	7.50	15.00
❑ CS 8016 [S]	I Remember Russ	1958	5.00	10.00	20.00
—Originals have red and black "6 eye" labels					

Number	Title (A Side/B Side)	Yr	VG	VG+	NM
❑ CS 8069 [S]	I Remember Buddy	1959	5.00	10.00	20.00
—Originals have red and black "6 eye" labels					
❑ CS 8175 [S]	The Same Old Moon	1960	3.75	7.50	15.00
❑ CS 8597 [S]	I Have But One Heart	1962	3.75	7.50	15.00
❑ CS 8755 [S]	Arrivederci, Roma	1963	3.75	7.50	15.00
❑ CS 8778 [R]	Jerry Vale's Greatest Hits	1963	3.00	6.00	12.00
❑ CS 8843 [S]	The Language of Love	1963	3.75	7.50	15.00
❑ CS 8916 [S]	Till the End of Time	1964	3.75	7.50	15.00
❑ CS 8981 [S]	Be My Love	1964	3.75	7.50	15.00
❑ CS 9025 [S]	Christmas Greetings from Jerry Vale	1964	3.75	7.50	15.00
❑ CS 9073 [S]	Standing Ovation!	1965	3.75	7.50	15.00
❑ CS 9113 [S]	Have You Looked Into Your Heart	1965	3.75	7.50	15.00
❑ CS 9171 [S]	Moonlight Becomes You	1965	3.75	7.50	15.00
❑ CS 9187 [S]	There Goes My Heart	1965	3.75	7.50	15.00
❑ CS 9244 [S]	It's Magic	1966	3.75	7.50	15.00
❑ CS 9289 [S]	Great Moments on Broadway	1966	3.75	7.50	15.00
❑ CS 9383 [S]	The Impossible Dream	1967	3.75	7.50	15.00
❑ CS 9459 [S]	More Jerry Vale's Greatest Hits	1967	3.00	6.00	12.00
❑ CS 9484 [S]	Time Alone Will Tell	1967	3.75	7.50	15.00
❑ CS 9574 [S]	You Don't Have to Say You Love Me	1968	3.75	7.50	15.00
❑ CS 9634	I Hear a Rhapsody	1968	3.75	7.50	15.00
❑ CS 9694	This Guy's in Love with You	1968	3.75	7.50	15.00
❑ CS 9757	Till	1969	3.75	7.50	15.00
❑ CS 9838	Where's the Playground Susie?	1969	3.75	7.50	15.00
❑ CS 9982	Jerry Vale Sings 16 Greatest Hits of the 60's	1970	3.00	6.00	12.00
❑ C 30104	We've Only Just Begun	1971	2.50	5.00	10.00
❑ C 30389	The Italian Album	1970	2.50	5.00	10.00
❑ C 30799	I Don't Know How to Love Her	1971	2.50	5.00	10.00
❑ C 31147	Jerry Vale Sings the Great Hits of Nat King Cole	1972	3.00	6.00	12.00
❑ KG 31543 [(2)]	All-Time Greatest Hits	1972	3.00	6.00	12.00
❑ KC 31716	Alone Again (Naturally)	1972	2.50	5.00	10.00
❑ KG 31938 [(2)]	Great Italian Hits	1973	3.00	6.00	12.00
❑ KG 32083 [(2)]	Jerry Vale Sings the Great Love Songs	1973	3.00	6.00	12.00
❑ C 32238	Love Is a Many-Splendored Thing	1973	2.50	5.00	10.00
❑ KC 32454	Jerry Vale's World	1973	2.50	5.00	10.00
❑ KC 32829	Free As the Wind	1974	2.50	5.00	10.00
❑ CG 33615 [(2)]	The Italian Album/Arrivederci, Roma	1974	3.00	6.00	12.00

COLUMBIA LIMITED EDITION
❑ LE 10058	Till	197?	2.50	5.00	10.00
—Reissue of 9757					
❑ LE 10164 [S]	Christmas Greetings from Jerry Vale	197?	2.50	5.00	10.00
—Reissue					

HARMONY
❑ HS 11298	As Long As She Needs Me	1969	2.50	5.00	10.00
❑ HS 11376	Hey Look Me Over	1970	2.50	5.00	10.00
❑ KH 30345	Born Free	1971	2.50	5.00	10.00
❑ KH 30759	More	1971	2.50	5.00	10.00
❑ KH 32478	What a Wonderful World	1973	2.50	5.00	10.00

VALE, RICKY, AND THE SURFERS
STRAND
❑ SL-1104 [M]	Everybody's Surfin'	1963	10.00	20.00	40.00
❑ SLS-1104 [S]	Everybody's Surfin'	1963	12.50	25.00	50.00

VALENS, RITCHIE
DEL-FI
❑ DFLP 1201 [M]	Ritchie Valens	1959	37.50	75.00	150.00
—Black label with "diamonds" border					
❑ DFLP 1201 [M]	Ritchie Valens	1959	62.50	125.00	250.00
—Blue label with black border					
❑ DFLP 1206 [M]	Ritchie	1959	37.50	75.00	150.00
❑ DFLP 1214 [M]	In Concert at Pacoima Jr. High	1960	62.50	125.00	250.00
❑ DFLP 1225 [M]	His Greatest Hits	1963	37.50	75.00	150.00
—White cover					
❑ DFLP 1225 [M]	His Greatest Hits	1963	87.50	175.00	350.00
—Black cover					
❑ DFLP 1247 [M]	His Greatest Hits, Volume 2	1965	37.50	75.00	150.00

GUEST STAR
❑ GS-1469 [M]	The Original Ritchie Valens	1963	7.50	15.00	30.00
❑ GSS-1469 [R]	The Original Ritchie Valens	1963	5.00	10.00	20.00
❑ GS-1484 [M]	The Original La Bamba	1963	7.50	15.00	30.00
❑ GSS-1484 [R]	The Original La Bamba	1963	5.00	10.00	20.00

MGM
❑ GAS-117	Ritchie Valens (Golden Archive Series)	1970	7.50	15.00	30.00

RHINO
❑ RNDF-200	The Best of Ritchie Valens	1981	3.00	6.00	12.00
❑ RNBC-2798 [(3)]	The History of Ritchie Valens	198?	6.25	12.50	25.00
❑ RNLP-70178	The Best of Ritchie Valens (Golden Archive Series)	1987	2.50	5.00	10.00
❑ RNLP-70231	Ritchie Valens	1987	2.50	5.00	10.00
❑ RNLP-70232	Ritchie	1987	2.50	5.00	10.00
❑ RNLP-70233	In Concert at Pacoima Jr. High	1987	2.50	5.00	10.00

VALENS, RITCHIE / JERRY KOLE
CROWN
❑ CLP-5336 [M]	Ritchie Valens and Jerry Kole	1963	7.50	15.00	30.00

VALENTE, CATERINA
DECCA
❑ DL 4035 [M]	More Schlagerparade	1959	6.25	12.50	25.00
❑ DL 4050 [M]	Caterina A La Carte	1959	6.25	12.50	25.00
❑ DL 4051 [M]	Arriba	1959	6.25	12.50	25.00
❑ DL 4052 [M]	Catarina	1959	6.25	12.50	25.00
❑ DL 4504 [M]	Golden Favorites	1964	5.00	10.00	20.00
❑ DL 8203 [M]	The Hi-Fi Nightingale	1956	6.25	12.50	25.00
❑ DL 8436 [M]	Ole Caterina	1957	6.25	12.50	25.00
❑ DL 8440 [M]	Plenty Valente!	1957	6.25	12.50	25.00
❑ DL 8755 [M]	A Toast to the Girls	1958	6.25	12.50	25.00
❑ DL 74504 [R]	Golden Favorites	1964	3.00	6.00	12.00

Number	Title (A Side/B Side)	Yr	VG	VG+	NM
RCA VICTOR					
❏ LPM-2119 [M]	Classics with a Chaser	1960	5.00	10.00	20.00
❏ LSP-2119 [S]	Classics with a Chaser	1960	6.25	12.50	25.00
❏ LPM-2241 [M]	Superfonics	1961	5.00	10.00	20.00
❏ LSP-2241 [S]	Superfonics	1961	6.25	12.50	25.00
VALENTI, DINO					
EPIC					
❏ LN 24335 [M]	Dino Valenti	1967	5.00	10.00	20.00
❏ BN 26335 [S]	Dino Valenti	1967	5.00	10.00	20.00
VALENTINE, HILTON					
Former member of THE ANIMALS.					
CAPITOL					
❏ ST-330	All in Your Head	1969	7.50	15.00	30.00
VALENTINE, JIMMIE					
JUBILEE					
❏ LP-9 [10]	Music to Beat By	1954	10.00	20.00	40.00
VALENTINO, MARK					
SWAN					
❏ SLP-508 [M]	Mark Valentino	1963	12.50	25.00	50.00
VALENTYNE, RUDY					
ROULETTE					
❏ R-25299 [M]	And Now... Rudy Valentyne	1965	5.00	10.00	20.00
❏ SR-25299 [S]	And Now... Rudy Valentyne	1965	6.25	12.50	25.00
VALHALLA					
UNITED ARTISTS					
❏ UAS-6730	Valhalla	1969	6.25	12.50	25.00
VALIDS, THE					
AMBER					
❏ 802 [M]	Accapella	1966	6.25	12.50	25.00
VALJEAN					
CARLTON					
❏ LP-142 [M]	The Theme from Ben Casey	1962	5.00	10.00	20.00
❏ STLP-142 [S]	The Theme from Ben Casey	1962	6.25	12.50	25.00
❏ LP-146 [M]	Mashin' the Classics	1963	5.00	10.00	20.00
❏ STLP-146 [S]	Mashin' the Classics	1963	6.25	12.50	25.00
VALLEE, RUDY					
RCA VICTOR					
❏ LPM-2507 [M]	Young Rudy Vallee	1961	7.50	15.00	30.00
❏ LSP-2507 [R]	Young Rudy Vallee	196?	5.00	10.00	20.00
VALLEY, JIM					
FIRST AMERICAN					
❏ 7710	Dance Inside Your Head	1977	3.75	7.50	15.00
LIGHT					
❏ LS-5564	Family	197?	3.75	7.50	15.00
PANORAMA					
❏ 104-S	Jim "Harpo" Valley	1968	10.00	20.00	40.00
VALLI, FRANKIE					
Also see THE FOUR SEASONS.					
MCA					
❏ 743	Heaven Above Me	1982	2.00	4.00	8.00
—Reissue of 5134					
❏ 756	The Very Best of Frankie Valli	1982	2.00	4.00	8.00
—Reissue of 3198					
❏ 3198	The Very Best of Frankie Valli	1980	2.50	5.00	10.00
❏ 5134	Heaven Above Me	1979	2.50	5.00	10.00
MOTOWN					
❏ M5-104V1	Motown Superstar Series, Vol. 4	1981	2.50	5.00	10.00
❏ M6-852	Inside You	1975	3.75	7.50	15.00
PHILIPS					
❏ PHM 200247 [M]	Frankie Valli — Solo	1967	10.00	20.00	40.00
❏ PHS 600247 [S]	Frankie Valli — Solo	1967	7.50	15.00	30.00
❏ PHS 600274	Timeless	1968	6.25	12.50	25.00
PRIVATE STOCK					
❏ PS-2000	Closeup	1975	3.00	6.00	12.00
❏ PS-2001	Frankie Valli Gold	1975	3.00	6.00	12.00
❏ PS-2006	Our Day Will Come	1975	3.00	6.00	12.00
❏ PS-2017	Valli	1976	3.00	6.00	12.00
❏ PS-7002	Lady Put the Light Out	1977	3.00	6.00	12.00
❏ PS-7012	Hits	1978	3.00	6.00	12.00
WARNER BROS.					
❏ BSK 3233	Frankie Valli...Is the Word	1978	2.50	5.00	10.00
VALLI, FRANKIE, AND THE FOUR SEASONS					
See THE FOUR SEASONS.					
VAMPIRES, THE					
UNITED ARTISTS					
❏ UAL-3378 [M]	The Vampires at the Monster Ball	1964	6.25	12.50	25.00
❏ UAS-6378 [S]	The Vampires at the Monster Ball	1964	7.50	15.00	30.00
VAN DAMME, ART					
BASF					
❏ 25113 [(2)]	The Many Moods of Art Van Damme	197?	5.00	10.00	20.00
❏ 25257 [(2)]	Star Spangled Rhythm	197?	5.00	10.00	20.00
CAPITOL					
❏ H 178 [10]	Cocktail Capers	1950	12.50	25.00	50.00
❏ T 178 [M]	Cocktail Capers	1954	10.00	20.00	40.00
❏ L 300 [10]	More Cocktail Capers	1952	12.50	25.00	50.00
❏ T 300 [M]	More Cocktail Capers	1954	10.00	20.00	40.00
COLUMBIA					
❏ C2L 7 [(2)M]	They're Playing Our Song	1958	10.00	20.00	40.00
❏ CL 544 [M]	The Van Damme Sound	1955	7.50	15.00	30.00

Number	Title (A Side/B Side)	Yr	VG	VG+	NM
❏ CL 630 [M]	Martini Time	1955	7.50	15.00	30.00
❏ CL 801 [M]	Manhattan Time	1956	7.50	15.00	30.00
❏ CL 876 [M]	The Art of Van Damme	1956	7.50	15.00	30.00
❏ CL 1382 [M]	Everything's Coming Up Music	1959	6.25	12.50	25.00
❏ CL 1563 [M]	Accordion A La Mode	1960	6.25	12.50	25.00
❏ CL 2585 [10]	The Art Van Damme Quintet	1956	10.00	20.00	40.00
❏ CL 6265 [10]	Martini Time	1953	10.00	20.00	40.00
❏ CS 8177 [S]	Everything's Coming Up Music	1959	7.50	15.00	30.00
❏ CS 8363 [S]	Accordion A La Mode	1960	7.50	15.00	30.00
❏ CS 8594 [S]	Art Van Damme Swings Sweetly	1962	5.00	10.00	20.00
❏ CS 8813 [S]	A Perfect Match	1963	5.00	10.00	20.00
VAN DER GRAAF GENERATOR					
ABC DUNHILL					
❏ DS 50097	H to He Who Am the Only One	1971	3.75	7.50	15.00
CHARISMA					
❏ CAS-1051	Pawn Hearts	1971	3.75	7.50	15.00
MERCURY					
❏ SRM-1-1069	Godbluff	1975	3.00	6.00	12.00
❏ SRM-1-1096	Still Life	1976	3.00	6.00	12.00
❏ SRM-1-1116	World Record	1976	3.00	6.00	12.00
❏ SR-61238	The Aerosol Grey Machine	1969	25.00	50.00	100.00
PROBE					
❏ CPLP-4515	The Least We Can Do Is Wave to Each Other	1970	7.50	5.00	30.00
PVC					
❏ 9901 [(2)]	Vital	1979	3.75	7.50	15.00
VAN DERBUR, MARILYN					
DECCA					
❏ DL 8770 [M]	Miss America	1958	10.00	20.00	40.00
VAN DYKE, DICK					
COMMAND					
❏ RS 860 SD [S]	Songs I Like	1963	7.50	15.00	30.00
❏ RS 33-860 [M]	Songs I Like	1963	6.25	12.50	25.00
VAN DYKE, EARL, AND THE SOUL BROTHERS					
MOTOWN					
❏ M-631 [M]	The Motown Sound	1965	10.00	20.00	40.00
❏ MS-631 [S]	The Motown Sound	1965	12.50	25.00	50.00
SOUL					
❏ SS-715	The Earl of Funk	1970	10.00	20.00	40.00
VAN DYKE, LEROY					
DOT					
❏ DLP 3693 [M]	Auctioneer	1966	5.00	10.00	20.00
HARMONY					
❏ HS 11308	I've Never Been Loved	196?	3.00	6.00	12.00
KAPP					
❏ KS-3571	Lonesome Is	1968	3.75	7.50	15.00
❏ KS-3605	Greatest Hits	1969	3.75	7.50	15.00
❏ KS-3607	Just a Closer Walk with Thee	1969	3.75	7.50	15.00
MCA					
❏ 145	Greatest Hits	1973	3.00	6.00	12.00
MERCURY					
❏ MG-20682 [M]	Walk On By	1962	5.00	10.00	20.00
❏ MG-20716 [M]	Movin' Van Dyke	1963	5.00	10.00	20.00
❏ MG-20802 [M]	The Great Hits of Leroy Van Dyke	1963	5.00	10.00	20.00
❏ MG-20922 [M]	Songs for Mom and Dad	1964	5.00	10.00	20.00
❏ MG-20950 [M]	Leroy Van Dyke at the Tradewinds	1964	5.00	10.00	10.00
❏ SR-60682 [S]	Walk On By	1962	6.25	12.50	25.00
❏ SR-60716 [S]	Movin' Van Dyke	1963	6.25	12.50	25.00
❏ SR-60802 [S]	The Great Hits of Leroy Van Dyke	1963	6.25	12.50	25.00
❏ SR-60922 [S]	Songs for Mom and Dad	1964	6.25	12.50	25.00
❏ SR-60950 [S]	Leroy Van Dyke at the Tradewinds	1964	6.25	12.50	25.00
PLANTATION					
❏ 516	Gospel Greats	1977	3.00	6.00	12.00
SUN					
❏ 131	Golden Hits	1974	3.00	6.00	12.00
WARNER BROS.					
❏ W 1618 [M]	The Leroy Van Dyke Show	1965	3.75	7.50	15.00
❏ WS 1618 [S]	The Leroy Van Dyke Show	1965	5.00	10.00	20.00
❏ W 1652 [M]	Country Hits	1966	3.75	7.50	15.00
❏ WS 1652 [S]	Country Hits	1966	5.00	10.00	20.00
WING					
❏ MGW-12302 [M]	Out of Love	196?	3.00	6.00	12.00
❏ MGW-12322 [M]	Movin'	196?	3.00	6.00	12.00
❏ SRW-16302 [S]	Out of Love	196?	3.75	7.50	15.00
❏ SRW-16322 [S]	Movin'	196?	3.75	7.50	15.00
VAN DYKES, THE (2)					
BELL					
❏ 6004 [M]	Tellin' It Like It Is	1967	12.50	25.00	50.00
❏ S-6004 [S]	Tellin' It Like It Is	1967	15.00	30.00	60.00
VAN EPS, GEORGE					
CAPITOL					
❏ ST 2533 [S]	My Guitar	1966	5.00	10.00	20.00
COLUMBIA					
❏ CL 929 [M]	Mellow Guitar	1956	10.00	20.00	40.00
VAN HALEN					
DCC COMPACT CLASSICS					
❏ LPZ-2066	Van Halen	1998	10.00	20.00	40.00
—Audiophile vinyl					
WARNER BROS.					
❏ PRO 705 [DJ]	Looney Tunes	1978	15.00	30.00	60.00
—Promo-only EP on red vinyl					
❏ BSK 3075	Van Halen	1978	3.00	6.00	12.00
—Early pressings have "Burbank" labels					

Number	Title (A Side/B Side)	Yr	VG	VG+	NM
❑ BSK 3075	Van Halen	1979	2.50	5.00	10.00
—White/cream labels					
❑ HS 3312	Van Halen II	1979	2.50	5.00	10.00
❑ HS 3415	Women and Children First	1980	2.50	5.00	10.00
❑ HS 3540	Fair Warning	1981	2.50	5.00	10.00
❑ BSK 3677	Diver Down	1982	2.50	5.00	10.00
❑ 23985	1984	1984	2.50	5.00	10.00
❑ 23985 [DJ]	1984	1984	6.25	12.50	25.00
—Promo on Quiex II vinyl					
❑ 25394	5150	1986	2.50	5.00	10.00
❑ 25732	OU812	1988	2.50	5.00	10.00
❑ W1-26594	For Unlawful Carnal Knowledge	1991	5.00	10.00	20.00
—The only U.S. vinyl version was released through Columbia House					
❑ 45760	Balance	1995	3.00	6.00	12.00

VAN HEUSEN, JIMMY
UNITED ARTISTS

Number	Title (A Side/B Side)	Yr	VG	VG+	NM
❑ UAL-3494 [M]	Van Heusen Plays Van Heusen	1966	5.00	10.00	20.00
❑ UAS-6494 [S]	Van Heusen Plays Van Heusen	1966	6.25	12.50	25.00

VAN RONK, DAVE
CADET

Number	Title (A Side/B Side)	Yr	VG	VG+	NM
❑ CA-50044	Songs for Aging Children	1973	5.00	10.00	20.00
FANTASY					
❑ 24710 [(2)]	Dave Van Ronk	1972	5.00	10.00	20.00
FOLKLORE					
❑ FRLP-14001 [M]	In the Tradition	1963	7.50	15.00	30.00
❑ FRST-14001 [S]	In the Tradition	1963	10.00	20.00	40.00
❑ FRLP-14012 [M]	Dave Van Ronk, Folksinger	1963	7.50	15.00	30.00
❑ FRST-14012 [S]	Dave Van Ronk, Folksinger	1963	10.00	20.00	40.00
❑ FRLP-14025 [M]	Inside Dave Van Ronk	1964	7.50	15.00	30.00
❑ FRST-14025 [S]	Inside Dave Van Ronk	1964	10.00	20.00	40.00
FOLKWAYS					
❑ FA-2383 [M]	Dave Van Ronk Sings Earthy Ballads and Blues	1961	10.00	20.00	40.00
❑ FS-3818 [M]	Dave Van Ronk Sings Ballads, Blues and Spirituals	1959	10.00	20.00	40.00
❑ FTS 31020	Black Mountain Blues	1968	6.25	12.50	25.00
MERCURY					
❑ MG-20864 [M]	Dave Van Ronk and the Ragtime Jug Stompers	1964	6.25	12.50	25.00
❑ MG-20908 [M]	Just Dave Van Ronk	1964	6.25	12.50	25.00
❑ SR-60864 [S]	Dave Van Ronk and the Ragtime Jug Stompers	1964	7.50	15.00	30.00
❑ SR-60908 [S]	Just Dave Van Ronk	1964	7.50	15.00	30.00
POLYDOR					
❑ 24-4052	Van Ronk	1972	5.00	10.00	20.00
VERVE FOLKWAYS					
❑ FV-9006 [M]	Dave Van Ronk Sings the Blues	1965	6.25	12.50	25.00
❑ FVS-9006 [S]	Dave Van Ronk Sings the Blues	1965	7.50	15.00	30.00
❑ FV-9017 [M]	Gambler's Blues	1965	6.25	12.50	25.00
❑ FVS-9017 [S]	Gambler's Blues	1965	7.50	15.00	30.00
VERVE FORECAST					
❑ FT-3009 [M]	No Dirty Names	1967	6.25	12.50	25.00
❑ FTS-3009 [S]	No Dirty Names	1967	7.50	15.00	30.00
❑ FTS-3041 [M]	Dave Van Ronk and the Hudson Dusters	1968	6.25	12.50	25.00

VAN VOOREN, MONIQUE
RCA VICTOR

Number	Title (A Side/B Side)	Yr	VG	VG+	NM
❑ LPM-1553 [M]	Mink in Hi-Fi	1958	6.25	12.50	25.00

VAN ZANDT, TOWNES
POPPY

Number	Title (A Side/B Side)	Yr	VG	VG+	NM
❑ PP-LA004-F	The Late Great Townes Van Zandt	1973	3.75	7.50	15.00
❑ PYS-5700	High, Low and In Between	1972	3.75	7.50	15.00
❑ PYS-40001	For the Sake of a Song	1968	6.25	12.50	25.00
❑ PYS-40004	Our Mother, The Mountain	1969	3.75	7.50	15.00
❑ PYS-40007	Townes Van Zandt	1969	3.75	7.50	15.00
❑ PYS-40012	Delta Momma Blues	1970	3.75	7.50	15.00
SUGAR HILL					
❑ SH-1020	At My Window	1987	2.50	5.00	10.00
❑ SH-1026	Live and Obscure	1989	2.50	5.00	10.00
TOMATO					
❑ 7001 [(2)]	Live at the Old Quarter, Houston, Texas	1977	3.75	7.50	15.00
❑ 7011	The Late Great Townes Van Zandt	1978	3.00	6.00	12.00
—Reissue of Poppy 004					
❑ 7012	High, Low and In Between	1978	3.00	6.00	12.00
—Reissue of Poppy 5700					
❑ 7013	Delta Momma Blues	1978	3.00	6.00	12.00
—Reissue of Poppy 40012					
❑ 7014	Townes Van Zandt	1978	3.00	6.00	12.00
—Reissue of Poppy 40007					
❑ 7015	Our Mother, The Mountain	1978	3.00	6.00	12.00
—Reissue of Poppy 40004					
❑ 7017	Flyin' Shoes	1978	3.00	6.00	12.00

VANDROSS, LUTHER
EPIC

Number	Title (A Side/B Side)	Yr	VG	VG+	NM
❑ FE 37451	Never Too Much	1981	2.50	5.00	10.00
❑ FE 38235	Forever, For Always, For Love.	1982	2.50	5.00	10.00
❑ FE 39196	Busy Body.	1983	2.50	5.00	10.00
❑ FE 39882	The Night I Fell in Love.	1985	2.00	4.00	8.00
❑ FE 40415	Give Me the Reason.	1986	2.00	4.00	8.00
❑ FE 44308	Any Love.	1988	2.00	4.00	8.00
❑ E2 45320 [(2)]	The Best of Luther Vandross... The Best of Love.	1989	3.00	6.00	12.00
❑ E 46789	Power of Love.	1991	3.00	6.00	12.00
❑ HE 47451	Never Too Much.	198?	7.50	15.00	30.00
—Half-speed mastered edition					
❑ E 57775	Songs	1994	3.75	7.50	15.00
❑ E 57795	This Is Christmas	1995	3.00	6.00	12.00
❑ E 67553	Your Secret Love	1996	3.00	6.00	12.00

VANILLA FUDGE
ATCO

Number	Title (A Side/B Side)	Yr	VG	VG+	NM
❑ 33-224 [M]	Vanilla Fudge	1967	6.25	12.50	25.00
❑ SD 33-224	Vanilla Fudge	197?	2.00	4.00	8.00
—Any later label					
❑ SD 33-224 [S]	Vanilla Fudge	1967	5.00	10.00	20.00
—Purple and brown label					
❑ SD 33-224 [S]	Vanilla Fudge	1969	3.00	6.00	12.00
—Yellow label					
❑ 33-237 [M]	The Beat Goes On	1968	10.00	20.00	40.00
❑ SD 33-237	The Beat Goes On	1968	5.00	10.00	20.00
—Purple and brown label					
❑ SD 33-237	The Beat Goes On	1969	3.00	6.00	12.00
—Yellow label					
❑ SD 33-244	Renaissance	1968	5.00	10.00	20.00
—Purple and brown label					
❑ SD 33-244	Renaissance	1969	3.00	6.00	12.00
—Yellow label					
❑ SD 33-278	Near the Beginning	1969	3.75	7.50	15.00
❑ SD 33-303	Rock 'N' Roll	1969	3.75	7.50	15.00
❑ 90006	The Best of Vanilla Fudge	1982	2.50	5.00	10.00
❑ 90149	Mystery	1984	3.00	6.00	12.00

VANILLA ICE
ULTRA

Number	Title (A Side/B Side)	Yr	VG	VG+	NM
❑ ULT 4019	Hooked	1990	7.50	15.00	30.00

VANITY FARE
PAGE ONE

Number	Title (A Side/B Side)	Yr	VG	VG+	NM
❑ 2502	Early in the Morning	1970	5.00	10.00	20.00

VANNELLI, GINO
A&M

Number	Title (A Side/B Side)	Yr	VG	VG+	NM
❑ SP-3112	The Gist of the Gemini	1981	2.00	4.00	8.00
—Reissue of 4596					
❑ SP-3120	Powerful People	1981	2.00	4.00	8.00
—Reissue of 3630					
❑ SP-3139	Crazy Life	1981	2.00	4.00	8.00
—Reissue of 4395					
❑ SP-3170	Brother to Brother	1981	2.00	4.00	8.00
—Reissue of 4722					
❑ SP-3260	The Best of Gino Vannelli	1982	2.00	4.00	8.00
—Reissue of 3729					
❑ SP-3630	Powerful People	1974	2.50	5.00	10.00
❑ SP-3729	The Best of Gino Vannelli	1981	2.50	5.00	10.00
❑ SP-4395	Crazy Life	1973	3.00	6.00	12.00
❑ SP-4533	Storm at Sunup	1975	2.50	5.00	10.00
❑ SP-4596	The Gist of the Gemini	1976	2.50	5.00	10.00
❑ SP-4664	A Pauper in Paradise	1977	2.50	5.00	10.00
❑ SP-4722	Brother to Brother	1978	2.50	5.00	10.00
ARISTA					
❑ AB 9539	Nightwalker	1981	2.50	5.00	10.00
CBS ASSOCIATED					
❑ BFZ 40337	Big Dreamers Never Sleep	1987	2.50	5.00	10.00
HME					
❑ FZ 40077	Black Cars	1985	2.50	5.00	10.00
MOBILE FIDELITY					
❑ 1-041	Powerful People	1980	5.00	10.00	20.00
—Audiophile vinyl					
NAUTILUS					
❑ NR-35	Brother to Brother	198?	6.25	12.50	25.00
—Audiophile vinyl					

VARIATIONS, THE
JUSTICE

Number	Title (A Side/B Side)	Yr	VG	VG+	NM
❑ JLP-212	Dig 'Em Up	196?	100.00	200.00	400.00

VAUGHAN, FRANKIE
PHILIPS

Number	Title (A Side/B Side)	Yr	VG	VG+	NM
❑ PHM 200006 [M]	Singin' Happy	1962	5.00	10.00	20.00
❑ PHS 600006 [S]	Singin' Happy	1962	6.25	12.50	25.00

VAUGHAN, SARAH
ACCORD

Number	Title (A Side/B Side)	Yr	VG	VG+	NM
❑ SN-7195	Simply Divine	1981	2.50	5.00	10.00
ALLEGRO					
❑ 1592 [M]	Sarah Vaughan	1955	12.50	25.00	50.00
❑ 1608 [M]	Sarah Vaughan	1955	12.50	25.00	50.00
❑ 3080 [10]	Early Sarah	195?	20.00	40.00	80.00
ALLEGRO ELITE					
❑ 4106 [10]	Sarah Vaughan Sings	195?	7.50	15.00	30.00
ARCHIVE OF FOLK AND JAZZ					
❑ 250	Sarah Vaughan	197?	2.50	5.00	10.00
❑ 271	Sarah Vaughan, Volume 2	197?	2.50	5.00	10.00
❑ 325	Sarah Vaughan, Volume 3	197?	2.50	5.00	10.00
ATLANTIC					
❑ SD 16037	Songs of the Beatles	1981	3.00	6.00	12.00
BRYLEN					
❑ BN 4411	Desires	198?	2.50	5.00	10.00
—Last name is misspelled "Vaughn"					
CBS MASTERWORKS					
❑ FM 37277	Gershwin Live!	1982	2.50	5.00	10.00
—With the Los Angeles Philharmonic Orchestra					
❑ FM 42519	Brazilian Romance	1987	2.50	5.00	10.00
COLUMBIA					
❑ CL 660 [M]	After Hours with Sarah Vaughan	1955	12.50	25.00	50.00
❑ CL 745 [M]	Sarah Vaughan in Hi-Fi	1956	12.50	25.00	50.00
❑ CL 914 [M]	Linger Awhile	1956	12.50	25.00	50.00
❑ CL 6133 [10]	Sarah Vaughan	1950	30.00	60.00	120.00

Number	Title (A Side/B Side)	Yr	VG	VG+	NM
COLUMBIA SPECIAL PRODUCTS					
❏ P 13084	Sarah Vaughan in Hi-Fi	1976	2.50	5.00	10.00
—Reissue of Columbia 745					
❏ P 14364	Linger Awhile	1978	2.50	5.00	10.00
—Reissue of Columbia 914					
CONCORD					
❏ 3018 [M]	Sarah Vaughan Concert	1957	7.50	15.00	30.00
CORONET					
❏ 277	Sarah Vaughan Belts the Hits	196?	3.75	7.50	15.00
EMARCY					
❏ EMS-2-412 [(2)]	Sarah Vaughan Live	197?	3.00	6.00	12.00
❏ MG-26005 [10]	Images	1954	20.00	40.00	80.00
❏ MG-36004 [M]	Sarah Vaughan	1955	20.00	40.00	80.00
❏ MG-36058 [M]	In the Land of Hi-Fi	1956	20.00	40.00	80.00
❏ MG-36089 [M]	Sassy	1956	12.50	25.00	50.00
❏ MG-36109 [M]	Swingin' Easy	1957	12.50	25.00	50.00
❏ 814187-1 [(2)]	The George Gershwin Songbook	1983	3.00	6.00	12.00
❏ 824864-1	The Rodgers & Hart Songbook	1985	2.50	5.00	10.00
❏ 826454-1	In the Land of Hi-Fi	1986	2.50	5.00	10.00
—Reissue of 36058					
FORUM					
❏ F-9034 [M]	Dreamy	196?	3.00	6.00	12.00
❏ SF-9034 [S]	Dreamy	196?	3.75	7.50	15.00
HARMONY					
❏ HL 7158 [M]	The Great Sarah Vaughan	196?	3.00	6.00	12.00
LION					
❏ L 70052 [M]	Tenderly	1958	6.25	12.50	25.00
MAINSTREAM					
❏ MRL 340	Time in My Life	1972	3.75	7.50	15.00
❏ MRL 361	Sarah Vaughan/Michel Legrand	1972	3.75	7.50	15.00
❏ MRL 379	Feelin' Good	1973	3.75	7.50	15.00
❏ MRL 404	Sarah Vaughan and the Jimmy Rowles Quintet	1974	3.75	7.50	15.00
❏ MRL 419	More Sarah Vaughan from Japan	1974	3.75	7.50	15.00
❏ MRL 2401 [(2)]	Sarah Vaughan "Live" In Japan	1973	5.00	10.00	20.00
MASTERSEAL					
❏ MS-55 [M]	Sarah Vaughan Sings	195?	6.25	12.50	25.00
MERCURY					
❏ MGP-2-100 [(2)M]	Great Songs from Hit Shows	1957	15.00	30.00	60.00
❏ MGP-2-101 [(2)M]	Sarah Vaughan Sings George Gershwin	1957	15.00	30.00	60.00
❏ MG-20094 [M]	Sarah Vaughan at the Blue Note	1956	10.00	20.00	40.00
❏ MG-20219 [M]	Wonderful Sarah	1957	10.00	20.00	40.00
❏ MG-20223 [M]	In a Romantic Mood	1957	10.00	20.00	40.00
❏ MG-20244 [M]	Great Songs from Hit Shows, Vol. 1	1958	7.50	15.00	30.00
❏ MG-20245 [M]	Great Songs from Hit Shows, Vol. 2	1958	7.50	15.00	30.00
❏ MG-20310 [M]	Sarah Vaughan Sings George Gershwin, Vol. 1	1958	7.50	15.00	30.00
❏ MG-20311 [M]	Sarah Vaughan Sings George Gershwin, Vol. 2	1958	7.50	15.00	30.00
❏ MG-20326 [M]	Sarah Vaughan and Her Trio at Mr. Kelly's	1958	10.00	20.00	40.00
❏ MG-20370 [M]	Vaughan and Violins	1958	10.00	20.00	40.00
❏ MG-20383 [M]	After Hours at the London House	1958	10.00	20.00	40.00
❏ MG-20438 [M]	The Magic of Sarah Vaughan	1959	7.50	15.00	30.00
❏ MG-20441 [M]	No 'Count Sarah	1959	7.50	15.00	30.00
❏ MG-20540 [M]	The Divine Sarah Vaughan	1960	6.25	12.50	25.00
❏ MG-20580 [M]	Close to You	1960	6.25	12.50	25.00
❏ MG-20617 [M]	My Heart Sings	1961	6.25	12.50	25.00
❏ MG-20645 [M]	Sarah Vaughan's Golden Hits	1961	5.00	10.00	20.00
❏ MG-20831 [M]	Sassy Swings the Tivoli	1962	5.00	10.00	20.00
❏ MG-20882 [M]	Vaughan with Voices	1963	5.00	10.00	20.00
❏ MG-20941 [M]	Viva Vaughan	1964	3.75	7.50	15.00
❏ MG-21009 [M]	Sarah Vaughan Sings the Mancini Songbook	1965	3.75	7.50	15.00
❏ MG-21069 [M]	Pop Artistry	1966	3.75	7.50	15.00
❏ MG-21079 [M]	The New Scene	1966	3.75	7.50	15.00
❏ MG-21116 [M]	Sassy Swings Again	1967	3.75	7.50	15.00
❏ MG-21122 [M]	It's a Man's World	1967	3.75	7.50	15.00
❏ MG-25188 [10]	Divine Sarah	1955	25.00	50.00	100.00
❏ SR-60020 [S]	After Hours at the London House	1959	10.00	20.00	40.00
❏ SR-60038 [S]	Vaughan and Violins	1959	10.00	20.00	40.00
❏ SR-60041 [S]	Great Songs from Hit Shows, Vol. 1	1959	10.00	20.00	40.00
❏ SR-60045 [S]	Sarah Vaughan Sings George Gershwin, Vol. 1	1959	10.00	20.00	40.00
❏ SR-60046 [S]	Sarah Vaughan Sings George Gershwin, Vol. 2	1959	10.00	20.00	40.00
❏ SR-60078 [S]	Great Songs from Hit Shows, Vol. 2	1959	10.00	20.00	40.00
❏ SR-60110 [S]	The Magic of Sarah Vaughan	1959	10.00	20.00	40.00
❏ SR-60116 [S]	No 'Count Sarah	1959	10.00	20.00	40.00
❏ SR-60240 [S]	Close to You	1960	7.50	15.00	30.00
❏ SR-60255 [S]	The Divine Sarah Vaughan	1960	7.50	15.00	30.00
❏ SR-60617 [S]	My Heart Sings	1961	7.50	15.00	30.00
❏ SR-60645 [S]	Sarah Vaughan's Golden Hits	1961	6.25	12.50	25.00
—Original black label version					
❏ SR-60645 [S]	Sarah Vaughan's Golden Hits	1965	3.75	7.50	15.00
—Red label version with white "MERCURY" alone at top					
❏ SR-60645 [S]	Sarah Vaughan's Golden Hits	1968	3.00	6.00	12.00
—Red label with multiple Mercury logos along the label edge					
❏ SR-60831 [S]	Sassy Swings the Tivoli	1962	6.25	12.50	25.00
❏ SR-60882 [S]	Vaughan with Voices	1963	6.25	12.50	25.00
❏ SR-60941 [S]	Viva Vaughan	1964	5.00	10.00	20.00
❏ SR-61009 [S]	Sarah Vaughan Sings the Mancini Songbook	1965	5.00	10.00	20.00
❏ SR-61069 [S]	Pop Artistry	1966	5.00	10.00	20.00
❏ SR-61079 [S]	The New Scene	1966	5.00	10.00	20.00
❏ SR-61116 [S]	Sassy Swings Again	1967	5.00	10.00	20.00
❏ SR-61122 [S]	It's a Man's World	1967	5.00	10.00	20.00
❏ 826320-1 [(6)]	The Complete Sarah Vaughan on Mercury Vol. 1: Great Jazz years (1954-56)	1986	10.00	20.00	40.00
❏ 826327-1 [(5)]	The Complete Sarah Vaughan on Mercury Vol. 2: Great American Songs (1956-57)	1986	10.00	20.00	40.00
❏ 826333-1 [(6)]	The Complete Sarah Vaughan on Mercury Vol. 3: Great Show on Stage (1954-56)	1986	10.00	20.00	40.00

Number	Title (A Side/B Side)	Yr	VG	VG+	NM
❏ 830721-1 [(4)]	The Complete Sarah Vaughan on Mercury Vol. 4 Part 1: Live in Europe (1963-64)	1987	10.00	20.00	40.00
❏ 830726-1 [(5)]	The Complete Sarah Vaughan on Mercury Vol. 4 Part 2: Sassy Swings Again	1987	10.00	20.00	40.00
METRO					
❏ M-539 [M]	Tenderly	1965	3.00	6.00	12.00
❏ MS-539 [S]	Tenderly	1965	3.75	7.50	15.00
MGM					
❏ E-165 [10]	Tenderly	1950	30.00	60.00	120.00
❏ E-544 [10]	Sarah Vaughan Sings	1951	30.00	60.00	120.00
❏ E-3274 [M]	My Kinda Love	1955	12.50	25.00	50.00
—Combination of two 10-inch LPs on one 12-inch LP					
MUSICRAFT					
❏ 504	Divine Sarah	197?	2.50	5.00	10.00
❏ MVS-2002	The Man I Love	1986	2.50	5.00	10.00
❏ MVS-2006	Lover Man	1986	2.50	5.00	10.00
PABLO					
❏ 2310821	How Long	1978	2.50	5.00	10.00
❏ 2310885	The Best of Sarah Vaughan	1983	2.50	5.00	10.00
❏ 2312101	I Love Brazil	1978	2.50	5.00	10.00
❏ 2312111	The Duke Ellington Songbook One	1979	2.50	5.00	10.00
❏ 2312116	The Duke Ellington Songbook Two	1980	2.50	5.00	10.00
❏ 2312125	Copacabana	1981	2.50	5.00	10.00
❏ 2405416	The Best of Sarah Vaughan	1990	2.50	5.00	10.00
PABLO TODAY					
❏ 2312137	Crazy and Mixed Up	1982	2.50	5.00	10.00
PALACE					
❏ 5191 [M]	Sarah Vaughan Sings	195?	6.25	12.50	25.00
PICKWICK					
❏ PCS-3035	Fabulous Sarah Vaughan	197?	2.50	5.00	10.00
REMINGTON					
❏ RLP-1024 [10]	Hot Jazz	1953	50.00	100.00	200.00
RIVERSIDE					
❏ RLP 2511 [10]	Sarah Vaughan Sings with John Kirby	1955	25.00	50.00	100.00
RONDO-LETTE					
❏ A-35 [M]	Songs of Broadway	1958	6.25	12.50	25.00
❏ A-53 [M]	Sarah Vaughan Sings	1959	6.25	12.50	25.00
ROULETTE					
❏ RE-103 [(2)]	Echoes of an Era	197?	3.00	6.00	12.00
❏ K-105 [(2)M]	The Sarah Vaughan Years	196?	5.00	10.00	20.00
❏ SK-105 [(2)S]	The Sarah Vaughan Years	196?	7.50	15.00	30.00
❏ R 52046 [M]	Dreamy	1960	7.50	15.00	30.00
❏ SR 52046 [S]	Dreamy	1960	10.00	20.00	40.00
❏ R 52060 [M]	Divine One	1960	6.25	12.50	25.00
❏ SR 52060 [S]	Divine One	1960	7.50	15.00	30.00
❏ R 52070 [M]	After Hours	1961	6.25	12.50	25.00
❏ SR 52070 [S]	After Hours	1961	7.50	15.00	30.00
❏ R 52082 [M]	You're Mine	1962	6.25	12.50	25.00
❏ SR 52082 [S]	You're Mine	1962	7.50	15.00	30.00
—Black vinyl					
❏ SR 52082 [S]	You're Mine	1962	15.00	30.00	60.00
—Red vinyl					
❏ R 52091 [M]	Snowbound	1962	5.00	10.00	20.00
❏ SR 52091 [S]	Snowbound	1962	6.25	12.50	25.00
❏ R 52092 [M]	The Explosive Side of Sarah	1962	5.00	10.00	20.00
❏ SR 52092 [S]	The Explosive Side of Sarah	1962	6.25	12.50	25.00
❏ R 52100 [M]	Star Eyes	1963	3.75	7.50	15.00
❏ SR 52100 [S]	Star Eyes	1963	5.00	10.00	20.00
❏ R 52104 [M]	Lonely Hours	1963	3.75	7.50	15.00
❏ SR 52104 [S]	Lonely Hours	1963	5.00	10.00	20.00
❏ R 52109 [M]	The World of Sarah Vaughan	1964	3.75	7.50	15.00
❏ SR 52109 [S]	The World of Sarah Vaughan	1964	5.00	10.00	20.00
❏ R 52112 [M]	Sweet 'N Sassy	1964	3.75	7.50	15.00
❏ SR 52112 [S]	Sweet 'N Sassy	1964	5.00	10.00	20.00
❏ R 52116 [M]	Sarah Sings Soulfully	1965	3.75	7.50	15.00
❏ SR 52116 [S]	Sarah Sings Soulfully	1965	5.00	10.00	20.00
❏ R 52118 [M]	Sarah Plus Two	1965	3.75	7.50	15.00
❏ SR 52118 [S]	Sarah Plus Two	1965	5.00	10.00	20.00
❏ R 52123 [M]	Sarah Slightly Classical	1966	3.75	7.50	15.00
❏ SR 52123 [S]	Sarah Slightly Classical	1966	5.00	10.00	20.00
SCEPTER					
❏ CTN-18029	The Best of Sarah Vaughan	1972	3.00	6.00	12.00
SPIN-O-RAMA					
❏ 73 [M]	Sweet, Sultry and Swinging	196?	10.00	20.00	40.00
❏ S-73 [S]	Sweet, Sultry and Swinging	196?	12.50	25.00	50.00
❏ 114 [M]	The Divine Sarah Vaughan	196?	10.00	20.00	40.00
❏ S-114 [S]	The Divine Sarah Vaughan	196?	12.50	25.00	50.00
TRIP					
❏ 5501	Sarah Vaughan	197?	2.50	5.00	10.00
❏ 5517	Sassy	197?	2.50	5.00	10.00
❏ 5523	In the Land of Hi-Fi	197?	2.50	5.00	10.00
❏ 5551	Swingin' Easy	197?	2.50	5.00	10.00
WING					
❏ MGW-12123 [M]	All Time Favorites	1963	3.00	6.00	12.00
❏ MGW-12280 [M]	The Magic of Sarah Vaughan	1964	3.00	6.00	12.00
❏ SRW-16123 [S]	All Time Favorites	1963	3.75	7.50	15.00
❏ SRW-16123 [S]	The Magic of Sarah Vaughan	1964	3.75	7.50	15.00

VAUGHAN, SARAH, AND COUNT BASIE

Also see each artist's individual listings.

Number	Title (A Side/B Side)	Yr	VG	VG+	NM
PABLO					
❏ 2312130	Send In the Clowns	1980	2.50	5.00	10.00
ROULETTE					
❏ SR 42018	Count Basie and Sarah Vaughan	1968	3.75	7.50	15.00
❏ R 52061 [M]	Count Basie and Sarah Vaughan	1960	6.25	12.50	25.00
❏ SR 52061 [S]	Count Basie and Sarah Vaughan	1960	7.50	15.00	30.00

Number	Title (A Side/B Side)	Yr	VG	VG+	NM

VAUGHAN, SARAH, AND BILLY ECKSTINE

Also see each artist's individual listings.

EMARCY

Number	Title (A Side/B Side)	Yr	VG	VG+	NM
❑ 822526-1	The Irving Berlin Songbook	1984	2.50	5.00	10.00

LION

❑ L-70088 [M]	Billy and Sarah	195?	6.25	12.50	25.00

MERCURY

❑ MG-20316 [M]	Sarah Vaughan and Billy Eckstine Sing the Best of Irving Berlin	1959	7.50	15.00	30.00
❑ SR-60002 [S]	Sarah Vaughan and Billy Eckstine Sing the Best of Irving Berlin	1959	10.00	20.00	40.00

VAUGHAN, SARAH; DINAH WASHINGTON; JOE WILLIAMS

ROULETTE

❑ R 52108 [M]	We Three	1964	3.75	7.50	15.00
❑ SR 52108 [S]	We Three	1964	5.00	10.00	20.00

VAUGHAN, STEVIE RAY

EPIC

❑ BFE 38734	Texas Flood	1983	2.50	5.00	10.00
❑ FE 39304	Couldn't Stand the Weather	1984	2.50	5.00	10.00
❑ 8E8 39609 [PD]	Couldn't Stand the Weather	1984	37.50	75.00	150.00
❑ FE 40036	Soul to Soul	1985	2.50	5.00	10.00
❑ E2 40511 [(2)]	Live Alive	1986	3.00	6.00	12.00
❑ FE 45024	In Step	1989	2.50	5.00	10.00
❑ E 47390	The Sky Is Crying	1991	6.25	12.50	25.00
❑ E 66217	Greatest Hits	1995	2.50	5.00	10.00

VAUGHAN BROTHERS, THE

CBS ASSOCIATED

❑ Z 46625	Family Style	1990	5.00	10.00	20.00

VAUGHN, BILLY

ABC

❑ 4005	16 Great Performances	1974	2.50	5.00	10.00

DOT

❑ DLP 3001 [M]	Sweet Music and Memories	1955	6.25	12.50	25.00
—Maroon label					
❑ DLP 3001 [M]	Sweet Music and Memories	1957	3.75	7.50	15.00
—Black label					
❑ DLP 3016 [M]	The Golden Instrumentals	1956	6.25	12.50	25.00
—Maroon label					
❑ DLP 3016 [M]	The Golden Instrumentals	1957	3.75	7.50	15.00
—Black label					
❑ DLP 3045 [M]	Instrumental Souvenirs	1957	3.75	7.50	15.00
❑ DLP 3064 [M]	Melodies in Gold	1957	3.75	7.50	15.00
❑ DLP 3086 [M]	Music for the Golden Hours	1958	3.75	7.50	15.00
❑ DLP 3100 [M]	Sail Along Silv'ry Moon	1958	3.75	7.50	15.00
❑ DLP 3119 [M]	Billy Vaughn Plays the Million Sellers	1958	3.75	7.50	15.00
❑ DLP 3140 [M]	La Paloma	1959	3.75	7.50	15.00
❑ DLP 3148 [M]	Christmas Carols	1958	3.75	7.50	15.00
❑ DLP 3156 [M]	Billy Vaughn Plays	1959	3.75	7.50	15.00
❑ DLP 3165 [M]	Blue Hawaii	1959	3.75	7.50	15.00
❑ DLP 3201 [M]	Golden Hits	1959	3.75	7.50	15.00
❑ DLP 3205 [M]	Golden Saxophones	1959	3.75	7.50	15.00
❑ DLP 3260 [M]	Billy Vaughn Plays Stephen Foster	1960	3.75	7.50	15.00
❑ DLP 3275 [M]	Linger Awhile	1960	3.75	7.50	15.00
❑ DLP 3276 [M]	Theme from A Summer Place	1960	3.75	7.50	15.00
❑ DLP 3280 [M]	Golden Waltzes	1961	3.75	7.50	15.00
❑ DLP 3288 [M]	Great Golden Hits	1960	3.75	7.50	15.00
❑ DLP 3322 [M]	Look for a Star	1960	3.75	7.50	15.00
❑ DLP 3349 [M]	Theme from The Sundowners	1960	3.75	7.50	15.00
❑ DLP 3366 [M]	Orange Blossom Special and Wheels	1961	3.75	7.50	15.00
❑ DLP 3396 [M]	Berlin Melody	1961	3.75	7.50	15.00
❑ DLP 3409 [M]	Greatest String Band Hits	1962	3.75	7.50	15.00
❑ DLP 3424 [M]	Chapel by the Sea	1962	3.75	7.50	15.00
❑ DLP 3442 [M]	The Shifting, Whispering Sands	1962	3.75	7.50	15.00
❑ DLP 3458 [M]	A Swingin' Safari	1962	3.75	7.50	15.00
❑ DLP 3497 [M]	1962's Greatest Hits	1963	3.00	6.00	12.00
❑ DLP 3523 [M]	Sukiyaki and 11 Hawaiian Hits	1963	3.00	6.00	12.00
❑ DLP 3540 [M]	Number One Hits, Vol. #1	1963	3.00	6.00	12.00
❑ DLP 3558 [M]	Greatest Boogie Woogie Hits	1963	3.00	6.00	12.00
❑ DLP 3559 [M]	Blue Velvet & 1963's Great Hits	1964	3.00	6.00	12.00
❑ DLP 3578 [M]	Forever	1964	3.00	6.00	12.00
❑ DLP 3593 [M]	Another Hit Album!	1964	3.00	6.00	12.00
❑ DLP 3605 [M]	Pearly Shells	1965	3.00	6.00	12.00
❑ DLP 3625 [M]	12 Golden Hits from Latin America	1965	3.00	6.00	12.00
❑ DLP 3628 [M]	Mexican Pearls	1965	3.00	6.00	12.00
❑ DLP 3654 [M]	Moon Over Naples	1965	3.00	6.00	12.00
❑ DLP 3679 [M]	Michelle	1966	3.00	6.00	12.00
❑ DLP 3698 [M]	Great Country Hits	1966	3.00	6.00	12.00
❑ DLP 3751 [M]	Alfie	1966	3.00	6.00	12.00
❑ DLP 3782 [M]	Sweet Maria	1967	3.00	6.00	12.00
❑ DLP 3788 [M]	That's Life & Pineapple Market	1967	3.00	6.00	12.00
❑ DLP 3796 [M]	Josephine	1967	3.00	6.00	12.00
❑ DLP 3800 [M]	Billy Vaughn Presents Friends from Rio Playing "Something Stupid"	1967	3.00	6.00	12.00
❑ DLP 3811 [M]	Golden Hits/The Best of Billy Vaughn	1967	3.00	6.00	12.00
❑ DLP 3813 [M]	I Love You	1967	3.00	6.00	12.00
❑ DLP 3828 [M]	Ode to Billy Joe	1967	3.00	6.00	12.00
❑ DLP 5857	Quietly Wild	1968	2.50	5.00	10.00
❑ DLP 25001 [R]	Sweet Music and Memories	196?	2.50	5.00	10.00
❑ DLP 25016 [R]	The Golden Instrumentals	196?	2.50	5.00	10.00
❑ DLP 25064 [R]	Melodies in Gold	196?	2.50	5.00	10.00
❑ DLP 25086 [R]	Music for the Golden Hours	196?	2.50	5.00	10.00
❑ DLP 25100 [S]	Sail Along Silv'ry Moon	1959	5.00	10.00	20.00
❑ DLP 25119 [S]	Billy Vaughn Plays the Million Sellers	1959	5.00	10.00	20.00
❑ DLP 25140 [S]	La Paloma	1959	5.00	10.00	20.00
❑ DLP 25156 [S]	Billy Vaughn Plays	1959	5.00	10.00	20.00
❑ DLP 25165 [S]	Blue Hawaii	1959	5.00	10.00	20.00
❑ DLP 25201 [S]	Golden Hits	1959	5.00	10.00	20.00
❑ DLP 25205 [S]	Golden Saxophones	1959	5.00	10.00	20.00
❑ DLP 25260 [S]	Billy Vaughn Plays Stephen Foster	1960	5.00	10.00	20.00
❑ DLP 25275 [S]	Linger Awhile	1960	5.00	10.00	20.00
❑ DLP 25276 [S]	Theme from A Summer Place	1960	5.00	10.00	20.00
❑ DLP 25280 [S]	Golden Waltzes	1961	5.00	10.00	20.00
❑ DLP 25288 [S]	Great Golden Hits	1960	5.00	10.00	20.00
❑ DLP 25322 [S]	Look for a Star	1960	5.00	10.00	20.00
❑ DLP 25349 [S]	Theme from The Sundowners	1960	5.00	10.00	20.00
❑ DLP 25366 [S]	Orange Blossom Special and Wheels	1961	5.00	10.00	20.00
❑ DLP 25396 [S]	Berlin Melody	1961	5.00	10.00	20.00
❑ DLP 25409 [S]	Greatest String Band Hits	1962	5.00	10.00	20.00
❑ DLP 25424 [S]	Chapel by the Sea	1962	5.00	10.00	20.00
❑ DLP 25442 [S]	The Shifting, Whispering Sands	1962	5.00	10.00	20.00
❑ DLP 25458 [S]	A Swingin' Safari	1962	5.00	10.00	20.00
❑ DLP 25497 [S]	1962's Greatest Hits	1963	3.75	7.50	15.00
❑ DLP 25523 [S]	Sukiyaki and 11 Hawaiian Hits	1963	3.75	7.50	15.00
❑ DLP 25540 [S]	Number One Hits, Vol. #1	1963	3.75	7.50	15.00
❑ DLP 25558 [S]	Greatest Boogie Woogie Hits	1963	3.75	7.50	15.00
❑ DLP 25559 [S]	Blue Velvet & 1963's Great Hits	1964	3.75	7.50	15.00
❑ DLP 25578 [S]	Forever	1964	3.75	7.50	15.00
❑ DLP 25593 [S]	Another Hit Album!	1964	3.75	7.50	15.00
❑ DLP 25605 [S]	Pearly Shells	1965	3.75	7.50	15.00
❑ DLP 25625 [S]	12 Golden Hits from Latin America	1965	3.75	7.50	15.00
❑ DLP 25628 [S]	Mexican Pearls	1965	3.75	7.50	15.00
❑ DLP 25654 [S]	Moon Over Naples	1965	3.75	7.50	15.00
❑ DLP 25679 [S]	Michelle	1966	3.75	7.50	15.00
❑ DLP 25698 [S]	Great Country Hits	1966	3.75	7.50	15.00
❑ DLP 25751 [S]	Alfie	1966	3.75	7.50	15.00
❑ DLP 25782 [S]	Sweet Maria	1967	2.50	5.00	10.00
❑ DLP 25788 [S]	That's Life & Pineapple Market	1967	2.50	5.00	10.00
❑ DLP 25796 [S]	Josephine	1967	2.50	5.00	10.00
❑ DLP 25800 [S]	Billy Vaughn Presents Friends from Rio Playing "Something Stupid"	1967	2.50	5.00	10.00
❑ DLP 25811 [S]	Golden Hits/The Best of Billy Vaughn	1967	2.50	5.00	10.00
❑ DLP 25813 [S]	I Love You	1967	2.50	5.00	10.00
❑ DLP 25828 [S]	Ode to Billy Joe	1967	2.50	5.00	10.00
❑ DLP 25837 [S]	Pretty Country	1968	2.50	5.00	10.00
❑ DLP 25841 [S]	As Requested	1968	2.50	5.00	10.00
❑ DLP 25882 [S]	A Current Set of Standards	1968	2.50	5.00	10.00
❑ DLP-25897 [S]	Alone with Today	1968	2.50	5.00	10.00
❑ DLP 25899 [S]	Have Yourself a Merry Merry Christmas	1968	3.00	6.00	12.00
❑ DLP 25911 [S]	Nashville Saxophones	1969	2.50	5.00	10.00
❑ DLP 25937 [S]	The Windmills of Your Mind	1969	2.50	5.00	10.00
❑ DLP 25969 [S]	True Grit	1969	2.50	5.00	10.00
❑ DLP 25975 [S]	Winter World of Love	1970	2.50	5.00	10.00
❑ DLP 25985 [S]	Everything Is Beautiful	1970	2.50	5.00	10.00

HAMILTON

❑ HLP 113 [M]	Golden Gems	196?	3.00	6.00	12.00
❑ HLP 147 [M]	Strauss Waltz Concert	196?	3.00	6.00	12.00
❑ HLP 162 [M]	Songs I Wrote	196?	3.00	6.00	12.00
❑ HLP 12113 [S]	Golden Gems	196?	3.00	6.00	12.00
❑ HLP 12147 [S]	Strauss Waltz Concert	196?	3.00	6.00	12.00
❑ HLP 12162 [S]	Songs I Wrote	196?	3.00	6.00	12.00

MCA

❑ 801	La Paloma	198?	2.00	4.00	8.00
—Budget-line reissue					
❑ 4164 [(2)]	The Best of Billy Vaughn	198?	3.00	6.00	12.00
❑ 27018	Blue Hawaii	198?	2.00	4.00	8.00
—Budget-line reissue					

PARAMOUNT

❑ PAS-1031 [(2)]	Billy Vaughn Plays His Greatest Hits	1974	3.00	6.00	12.00
❑ PAS-1033	Electrified	1974	2.50	5.00	10.00
❑ PAS-5032	Theme from Love Story	1971	2.50	5.00	10.00
❑ PAS-5037	I Don't Know How to Love Him	1971	2.50	5.00	10.00
❑ PAS-6025	An Old Fashioned Love Song	1972	2.50	5.00	10.00
❑ PAS-6035	Soundstage!	1972	2.50	5.00	10.00
❑ PAS-6044	Country's Greatest Hits	1973	2.50	5.00	10.00

PICKWICK

❑ SPC-3093	Embraceable You	197?	2.50	5.00	10.00
❑ SPC-3146	Up, Up and Away	197?	2.50	5.00	10.00
❑ SPC-3213	Moon River	197?	2.50	5.00	10.00

RANWOOD

❑ 7025 [(2)]	Billy Vaughn and His Orchestra Play 22 Greatest Hits	1982	3.00	6.00	12.00

VAUGHN, FATHER TOM

RCA VICTOR

❑ LSP-3577 [S]	Jazz In Concert at the Village Gate	1966	5.00	10.00	20.00
❑ LPM-3708 [M]	Cornbread (Meat Loaf, Greens and Deviled Eggs)	1967	5.00	10.00	20.00
❑ LPM-3845 [M]	Motor City Soul	1967	5.00	10.00	20.00

VAUGHN, ROBERT

MGM

❑ E-4488 [M]	Readings from Hamlet	1962	6.25	12.50	25.00
❑ SE-4488 [S]	Readings from Hamlet	1962	7.50	15.00	30.00

VAUGHT, BOB, AND THE RENEGADES

GNP CRESCENDO

❑ GNP-83 [M]	Surf Crazy	1963	7.50	15.00	30.00
❑ GNPS-83 [S]	Surf Crazy	1963	10.00	20.00	40.00

VEE, BOBBY

LIBERTY

❑ LRP-3165 [M]	Bobby Vee Sings Your Favorites	1960	12.50	25.00	50.00
❑ LRP-3181 [M]	Bobby Vee	1961	10.00	20.00	40.00
❑ LRP-3186 [M]	Bobby Vee With Strings and Things	1961	10.00	20.00	40.00
❑ LRP-3205 [M]	Bobby Vee Sings Hits of the Rockin' 50's	1961	10.00	20.00	40.00
❑ LRP-3211 [M]	Take Good Care of My Baby	1962	7.50	15.00	30.00
❑ LRP-3228 [M]	Bobby Vee Meets the Crickets	1962	10.00	20.00	40.00
❑ LRP-3232 [M]	A Bobby Vee Recording Session	1962	7.50	15.00	30.00
❑ LRP-3245 [M]	Bobby Vee's Golden Greats	1962	7.50	15.00	30.00

Number	Title (A Side/B Side)	Yr	VG	VG+	NM
❏ LRP-3267 [M]	Merry Christmas from Bobby Vee	1962	7.50	15.00	30.00
❏ LRP-3285 [M]	The Night Has a Thousand Eyes	1963	7.50	15.00	30.00
❏ LRP-3289 [M]	Bobby Vee Meets the Ventures	1963	10.00	20.00	40.00
❏ LRP-3336 [M]	I Remember Buddy Holly	1963	10.00	20.00	40.00
❏ LRP-3352 [M]	Bobby Vee Sings the New Sound from				
	England!	1964	6.25	12.50	25.00
❏ LRP-3385 [M]	30 Big Hits From the 60's	1964	6.25	12.50	25.00
❏ LRP-3393 [M]	Bobby Vee Live on Tour	1965	6.25	12.50	25.00
❏ LRP-3448 [M]	30 Big Hits From the 60's, Volume 2	1966	6.25	12.50	25.00
❏ LRP-3464 [M]	Bobby Vee's Golden Greats, Volume 2	1966	5.00	10.00	20.00
❏ LRP-3480 [M]	Look at Me Girl	1966	5.00	10.00	20.00
❏ LRP-3534 [M]	Come Back When You Grow Up	1967	5.00	10.00	20.00
❏ LRP-3554 [M]	Just Today	1968	10.00	20.00	40.00
—Cover is stereo with "Audition Mono Not for Sale" sticker, but the label is regular stock mono					
❏ LST-7165 [S]	Bobby Vee Sings Your Favorites	1960	20.00	40.00	80.00
❏ LST-7181 [S]	Bobby Vee	1961	12.50	25.00	50.00
❏ LST-7186 [S]	Bobby Vee With Strings and Things	1961	12.50	25.00	50.00
❏ LST-7205 [S]	Bobby Vee Sings Hits of the Rockin' 50's	1961	12.50	25.00	50.00
❏ LST-7211 [S]	Take Good Care of My Baby	1962	10.00	20.00	40.00
❏ LST-7228 [S]	Bobby Vee Meets the Crickets	1962	12.50	25.00	50.00
❏ LST-7232 [S]	A Bobby Vee Recording Session	1962	10.00	20.00	40.00
❏ LST-7245 [S]	Bobby Vee's Golden Greats	1962	10.00	20.00	40.00
❏ LST-7267 [S]	Merry Christmas from Bobby Vee	1962	10.00	20.00	40.00
❏ LST-7285 [S]	The Night Has a Thousand Eyes	1963	10.00	20.00	40.00
❏ LST-7289 [S]	Bobby Vee Meets the Ventures	1963	12.50	25.00	50.00
❏ LST-7336 [S]	I Remember Buddy Holly	1963	12.50	25.00	50.00
❏ LST-7352 [S]	Bobby Vee Sings the New Sound from				
	England!	1964	7.50	15.00	30.00
❏ LST-7385 [S]	30 Big Hits From the 60's	1964	7.50	15.00	30.00
❏ LST-7393 [S]	Bobby Vee Live on Tour	1965	7.50	15.00	30.00
❏ LST-7448 [S]	30 Big Hits From the 60's, Volume 2	1966	7.50	15.00	30.00
❏ LST-7464 [S]	Bobby Vee's Golden Greats, Volume 2	1966	6.25	12.50	25.00
❏ LST-7480 [S]	Look at Me Girl	1966	6.25	12.50	25.00
❏ LST-7534 [S]	Come Back When You Grow Up	1967	6.25	12.50	25.00
❏ LST-7554 [S]	Just Today	1968	6.25	12.50	25.00
❏ LST-7592	Do What You Gotta Do	1968	7.50	15.00	30.00
❏ LST-7612	Gates, Grills and Railings	1969	7.50	15.00	30.00
❏ LN-10223	I Remember Buddy Holly	198?	2.00	4.00	8.00
❏ LM-51008	Bobby Vee's Golden Greats	198?	2.00	4.00	8.00
SUNSET					
❏ SUM-1111 [M]	Bobby Vee	1966	2.50	5.00	10.00
❏ SUM-1162 [M]	A Forever Kind of Love	1967	2.50	5.00	10.00
❏ SUM-1186 [M]	The Christmas Album	1967	3.00	6.00	12.00
—Reissue of Liberty album with two fewer tracks					
❏ SUS-5111 [S]	Bobby Vee	1966	3.00	6.00	12.00
❏ SUS-5162 [S]	A Forever Kind of Love	1967	3.00	6.00	12.00
❏ SUS-5186 [S]	The Christmas Album	1967	3.00	6.00	12.00
UNITED ARTISTS					
❏ UA-LA025-G2 [(2)]	Legendary Masters Series	1973	75.00	150.00	300.00
—Withdrawn before release, but a few copies survived					
❏ UA-LA085-G	Robert Thomas Velline	1973	5.00	10.00	20.00
❏ UA-LA332-E	The Very Best of Bobby Vee	1975	3.00	6.00	12.00
❏ LT-1008	Bobby Vee's Golden Greats	1980	2.50	5.00	10.00
❏ UAS-5656	Nothin' Like a Sunny Day	1972	3.00	6.00	12.00

VEGA, AL
PRESTIGE

Number	Title (A Side/B Side)	Yr	VG	VG+	NM
❏ PRLP-152 [10]	Al Vega Piano Solos With Bongos	1953	37.50	75.00	150.00

VEGAS, PAT AND LOLLY
Also see REDBONE.
MERCURY

Number	Title (A Side/B Side)	Yr	VG	VG+	NM
❏ MG-21059 [M]	At the Haunted House	1966	7.50	15.00	30.00
❏ SR-61059 [S]	At the Haunted House	1966	10.00	20.00	40.00

VELASCO, VI
VEE JAY

Number	Title (A Side/B Side)	Yr	VG	VG+	NM
❏ VJ-1135 [M]	The Vi Velasco Album	1965	5.00	10.00	20.00

VELEZ, MARTHA
POLYDOR

Number	Title (A Side/B Side)	Yr	VG	VG+	NM
❏ PD 5034	Hypnotized	1972	3.75	7.50	15.00
SIRE					
❏ SR 6040	American Heartbeat	1977	2.50	5.00	10.00
❏ SES-7409	Matinee Weepers	1973	3.75	7.50	15.00
❏ SASD-7515	Escape from Babylon	1976	2.50	5.00	10.00
—Produced by Bob Marley					
❏ SES-97008	Fiends and Angels	1969	7.50	15.00	30.00

VELVET NIGHT
METROMEDIA

Number	Title (A Side/B Side)	Yr	VG	VG+	NM
❏ MD-1028	Velvet Night	1970	7.50	15.00	30.00

VELVET UNDERGROUND, THE
Also see JOHN CALE; LOU REED; MAUREEN TUCKER.
COTILLION

Number	Title (A Side/B Side)	Yr	VG	VG+	NM
❏ SD 9034 [DJ]	Loaded	1970	18.75	37.50	75.00
—White label promo					
❏ SD 9034	Loaded	197?	3.75	7.50	15.00
—Reissue with purplish label					
❏ SD 9034	Loaded	1970	5.00	10.00	20.00
—Original pressing has a light blue label					
❏ SD 9034	Loaded	198?	3.00	6.00	12.00
—Reissue with purplish label and bar code on back cover					
❏ SD 9500 [DJ]	Live at Max's Kansas City	1972	18.75	37.50	75.00
—White label promo					
❏ SD 9500	Live at Max's Kansas City	197?	3.75	7.50	15.00
—Reissue with purplish label					
❏ SD 9500	Live at Max's Kansas City	1972	5.00	10.00	20.00
—Original pressing has a light blue label					
❏ SD 9500	Live at Max's Kansas City	198?	3.00	6.00	12.00
—Reissue with purplish label and bar code on back cover					

Number	Title (A Side/B Side)	Yr	VG	VG+	NM
MERCURY					
❏ SRM-2-7504 [(2)]	1969 (Live)	1974	3.75	7.50	15.00
—Reissues with Chicago skyline or black labels					
❏ SRM-2-7504 [(2)]	1969 (Live)	1974	12.50	25.00	50.00
—Originals with red labels					
MGM					
❏ GAS-131	The Velvet Underground (Golden Archive				
	Series)	1970	10.00	20.00	40.00
❏ SE-4617	The Velvet Underground	1969	12.50	25.00	50.00
❏ SE-4617 [DJ]	The Velvet Underground	1969	75.00	125.00	250.00
—Yellow label promo					
❏ M3G 4950	Archetypes	1974	5.00	10.00	20.00
PRIDE					
❏ 0022	Lou Reed and the Velvet Underground	1973	3.75	7.50	15.00
VERVE					
❏ V-5008 [M]	The Velvet Underground and Nico	1967	50.00	100.00	200.00
—Version 3: With peel-off banana peel, torso is airbrushed off the cover (deduct 50% if banana sticker removed)					
❏ V-5008 [M]	The Velvet Underground and Nico	1967	75.00	150.00	300.00
—Version 1: With peel-off banana peel, photo of band framed by a male torso (deduct 50% if banana sticker is gone)					
❏ V-5008 [M]	The Velvet Underground and Nico	1967	75.00	150.00	300.00
—Version 2: With peel-off banana peel, photo of torso obscured by a sticker (deduct 50% if stickers removed)					
❏ V6-5008 [S]	The Velvet Underground and Nico	1967	37.50	75.00	150.00
—Version 3: With peel-off banana peel, torso is airbrushed off the cover (deduct 50% if banana sticker removed)					
❏ V6-5008 [S]	The Velvet Underground and Nico	1967	50.00	100.00	200.00
—Version 1: With peel-off banana peel, photo of band framed by a male torso (deduct 50% if banana sticker is gone)					
❏ V6-5008 [S]	The Velvet Underground and Nico	1967	50.00	100.00	200.00
—Version 2: With peel-off banana peel, photo of torso obscured by a sticker (deduct 50% if stickers removed)					
❏ V6-5008 [S]	The Velvet Underground and Nico	1968	25.00	50.00	100.00
—Version 4: With unpeelable banana					
❏ V-5046 [M]	White Light/White Heat	1967	15.00	30.00	60.00
—Version 2: No "skeleton" on cover					
❏ V-5046 [M]	White Light/White Heat	1967	37.50	75.00	150.00
—Version 1: "Skeleton" cover -- a black-on-black skeleton is visible when cover is viewed at an angle					
❏ V-5046 [M]	White Light/White Heat	1967	75.00	150.00	300.00
—White label promo					
❏ V6-5046 [S]	White Light/White Heat	1967	10.00	20.00	40.00
—Version 2: No "skeleton" on cover					
❏ V6-5046 [S]	White Light/White Heat	1967	20.00	40.00	80.00
—Version 1: "Skeleton" cover -- a black-on-black skeleton is visible when cover is viewed at an angle					
❏ V6-5046 [S]	White Light/White Heat	1967	62.50	125.00	250.00
—Yellow label promo					
❏ 815454-1	The Velvet Underground	1985	3.00	6.00	12.00
—Reissue of MGM SE-4617					
❏ 823290-1	The Velvet Underground and Nico	1985	3.00	6.00	12.00
—Reissue of Verve V6-5008					
❏ 823721-1	VU	1985	3.00	6.00	12.00
❏ 825119-1	White Light/White Heat	1985	3.00	6.00	12.00
—Reissue of Verve V6-5046					
❏ 826284-1 [(2)]	1969 (Live)	1985	3.00	6.00	12.00
—Reissue of Mercury SRM-2-7504					
❏ 829405-1	Another View	1986	3.00	6.00	12.00

VENTURA, CAROL
PRESTIGE

Number	Title (A Side/B Side)	Yr	VG	VG+	NM
❏ PRLP-7358 [M]	Carol!	1965	6.25	12.50	25.00
❏ PRST-7358 [S]	Carol!	1965	7.50	15.00	30.00
❏ PRLP-7405 [M]	I Love to Sing!	1965	6.25	12.50	25.00
❏ PRST-7405 [S]	I Love to Sing!	1965	7.50	15.00	30.00

VENTURA, CHARLIE
BATON

Number	Title (A Side/B Side)	Yr	VG	VG+	NM
❏ 1202 [M]	New Charlie Ventura in Hi-Fi	1957	12.50	25.00	50.00
BRUNSWICK					
❏ BL 54025 [M]	Here's Charlie	1957	20.00	40.00	80.00
CLEF					
❏ MGC-117 [10]	Charlie Ventura Collates	1953	50.00	100.00	200.00
CORAL					
❏ CRL 56067 [10]	Open House	1952	30.00	60.00	120.00
CRAFTSMAN					
❏ 8039 [M]	Charlie Ventura Plays for the People	1960	6.25	12.50	25.00
CRYSTALETTE					
❏ 5000 [10]	Stomping With the Sax	1950	37.50	75.00	150.00
DECCA					
❏ DL 8046 [M]	Charlie Ventura Concert	1954	25.00	50.00	100.00
EMARCY					
❏ MG-26028 [10]	F.Y.I. Ventura	1954	30.00	60.00	120.00
❏ MG-36015 [M]	Jumping with Ventura	1955	20.00	40.00	80.00
GENE NORMAN					
❏ GNP-1 [M]	Charlie Ventura In Concert	1954	25.00	50.00	100.00
IMPERIAL					
❏ IM-3002 [10]	Charlie Ventura and His Sextet	1953	50.00	100.00	200.00
KING					
❏ 543 [M]	Adventure with Charlie Ventura	1958	20.00	40.00	80.00
MERCURY					
❏ MGC-117 [10]	Charlie Ventura Collates	1952	55.00	110.00	220.00
MOSAIC					
❏ MQ9-182 [(9)]	The Complete Verve/Clef Charlie Ventura/Flip				
	Phillips Studio Sessions	199?	37.50	75.00	150.00
NORGRAN					
❏ MGN-8 [10]	Charlie Ventura Quartet	1953	50.00	100.00	200.00
❏ MGN-1041 [M]	Charlie Ventura's Carnegie Hall Concert	1955	30.00	60.00	120.00
❏ MGN-1073 [M]	Charlie Ventura in a Jazz Mood	1956	25.00	50.00	100.00
❏ MGN-1075 [M]	Blue Saxophone	1956	25.00	50.00	100.00
❏ MGN-1103 [M]	Charley's Parley	1956	25.00	50.00	100.00

Number	Title (A Side/B Side)	Yr	VG	VG+	NM
RCA VICTOR					
❑ LPM-1135 [M]	It's All Bop to Me	1955	30.00	60.00	120.00
REGENT					
❑ MG-6064 [M]	East of Suez	1958	12.50	25.00	50.00
TOPS					
❑ L-1528 [M]	Charlie Ventura Plays Hi-Fi Jazz	1958	6.25	12.50	25.00
VERVE					
❑ MGV-8132 [M]	Charlie Ventura's Carnegie Hall Concert	1957	20.00	40.00	80.00
❑ V-8132 [M]	Charlie Ventura'a Carnegie Hall Concert	1961	6.25	12.50	25.00
❑ MGV-8163 [M]	Charlie Ventura in a Jazz Mood	1957	15.00	30.00	60.00
❑ V-8163 [M]	Charlie Ventura in a Jazz Mood	1961	6.25	12.50	25.00
❑ MGV-8165 [M]	Blue Saxophone	1957	15.00	30.00	60.00
❑ V-8165 [M]	Blue Saxophone	1961	6.25	12.50	25.00

VENTURA, CHARLIE/CHARLIE KENNEDY

Number	Title (A Side/B Side)	Yr	VG	VG+	NM
REGENT					
❑ MG-6047 [M]	Crazy Rhythms	1957	15.00	30.00	60.00

VENTURA, CHARLIE, AND MARY ANN MCCALL

Number	Title (A Side/B Side)	Yr	VG	VG+	NM
NORGRAN					
❑ MGN-20 [10]	An Evening with Mary Ann McCall and Charlie Ventura	1954	37.50	75.00	150.00
❑ MGN-1013 [M]	Another Evening with Charlie Ventura and Mary Ann McCall	1954	30.00	60.00	120.00
❑ MGN-1053 [M]	An Evening with Mary Ann McCall and Charlie Ventura	1955	25.00	50.00	100.00
VERVE					
❑ MGV-8143 [M]	An Evening with Mary Ann McCall and Charlie Ventura	1957	20.00	40.00	80.00
❑ V-8143 [M]	An Evening with Mary Ann McCall and Charlie Ventura	1961	6.25	12.50	25.00

VENTURA, RAY

Number	Title (A Side/B Side)	Yr	VG	VG+	NM
ATLANTIC					
❑ 8011 [M]	Hi-Fi Music for Young Parisians	1956	12.50	25.00	50.00
—Black label					
DOT					
❑ DLP-3120 [M]	La Belle Bardot	1958	12.50	25.00	50.00
—Brigitte Bardot is the cover model					

VENTURAS, THE

Number	Title (A Side/B Side)	Yr	VG	VG+	NM
DRUM BOY					
❑ DBM-1003 [M]	Here They Are	1964	50.00	100.00	200.00
❑ DBS-1003 [S]	Here They Are	1964	75.00	150.00	300.00

VENTURES, THE

Number	Title (A Side/B Side)	Yr	VG	VG+	NM
COMPLEAT					
❑ 672013-1	The Best of the Ventures	1986	2.50	5.00	10.00
DOLTON					
❑ BLP 2003 [M]	Walk Don't Run	1960	12.50	25.00	50.00
—Pale blue label with dolphins on top					
❑ BLP 2003 [M]	Walk Don't Run	1963	5.00	10.00	20.00
—Dark label, logo on left					
❑ BLP 2004 [M]	The Ventures	1961	12.50	25.00	50.00
—Pale blue label with dolphins on top					
❑ BLP 2004 [M]	The Ventures	1963	5.00	10.00	20.00
—Dark label, logo on left					
❑ BLP 2006 [M]	Another Smash!!!	1961	12.50	25.00	50.00
—Pale blue label with dolphins on top					
❑ BLP 2006 [M]	Another Smash!!!	1963	5.00	10.00	20.00
—Dark label, logo on left					
❑ BLP 2008 [M]	The Colorful Ventures	1961	12.50	25.00	50.00
—Pale blue label with dolphins on top					
❑ BLP 2008 [M]	The Colorful Ventures	1963	5.00	10.00	20.00
—Dark label, logo on left					
❑ BLP 2010 [M]	Twist with the Ventures	1962	12.50	25.00	50.00
—Pale blue label with dolphins on top					
❑ BLP 2010 [M]	Dance!	1963	5.00	10.00	20.00
—Dark label, logo on left; retitled version of "Twist with the Ventures"					
❑ BLP 2014 [M]	The Ventures' Twist Party, Vol. 2	1962	12.50	25.00	50.00
—Pale blue label with dolphins on top					
❑ BLP 2014 [M]	Dance with the Ventures	1963	5.00	10.00	20.00
—Dark label, logo on left' retitled version of "The Ventures' Twist Party, Vol. 2"					
❑ BLP 2016 [M]	Mashed Potatoes and Gravy	1962	7.50	15.00	30.00
❑ BLP 2016 [M]	Beach Party	1963	5.00	10.00	20.00
—Retitled version of "Mashed Potatoes and Gravy"					
❑ BLP 2017 [M]	Going to the Ventures Dance Party!	1962	7.50	15.00	30.00
❑ BLP 2019 [M]	The Ventures Play Telstar, The Lonely Bull	1962	7.50	15.00	30.00
❑ BLP 2022 [M]	Surfing	1963	6.25	12.50	25.00
❑ BLP 2023 [M]	The Ventures Play the Country Classics	1963	6.25	12.50	25.00
❑ BLP 2024 [M]	Let's Go!	1963	6.25	12.50	25.00
❑ BLP 2027 [M]	(The) Ventures in Space	1964	10.00	20.00	40.00
❑ BLP 2029 [M]	The Fabulous Ventures	1964	6.25	12.50	25.00
❑ BLP 2031 [M]	Walk, Don't Run, Vol. 2	1964	6.25	12.50	25.00
❑ BLP 2033 [M]	The Ventures Knock Me Out!	1965	6.25	12.50	25.00
❑ BLP 2035 [M]	The Ventures on Stage	1965	6.25	12.50	25.00
❑ BLP 2037 [M]	The Ventures A-Go-Go	1965	6.25	12.50	25.00
❑ BLP-2038 [M]	The Ventures' Christmas Album	1965	7.50	15.00	30.00
❑ BLP 2040 [M]	Where the Action Is	1966	5.00	10.00	20.00
❑ BLP 2042 [M]	The Ventures/Batman Theme	1966	7.50	15.00	30.00
❑ BLP 2045 [M]	Go with the Ventures!	1966	5.00	10.00	20.00
❑ BLP 2047 [M]	Wild Things!	1966	5.00	10.00	20.00
❑ BLP 2050 [M]	Guitar Freakout	1967	5.00	10.00	20.00
❑ BST 8003 [S]	Walk Don't Run	1960	15.00	30.00	60.00
—Pale blue label with dolphins on top					
❑ BST 8003 [S]	Walk Don't Run	1963	6.25	12.50	25.00
—Dark label, logo on left					
❑ BST 8004 [S]	The Ventures	1961	15.00	30.00	60.00
—Pale blue label with dolphins on top					
❑ BST 8004 [S]	The Ventures	1963	6.25	12.50	25.00
—Dark label, logo on left					

Number	Title (A Side/B Side)	Yr	VG	VG+	NM
❑ BST 8006 [S]	Another Smash!!!	1961	15.00	30.00	60.00
—Pale blue label with dolphins on top					
❑ BST 8006 [S]	Another Smash!!!	1963	6.25	12.50	25.00
—Dark label, logo on left					
❑ BST 8008 [S]	The Colorful Ventures	1961	15.00	30.00	60.00
—Pale blue label with dolphins on top					
❑ BST 8008 [S]	The Colorful Ventures	1963	6.25	12.50	25.00
—Dark label, logo on left					
❑ BST 8010 [S]	Twist with the Ventures	1962	15.00	30.00	60.00
—Pale blue label with dolphins on top					
❑ BST 8010 [S]	Dance!	1963	6.25	12.50	25.00
—Dark label, logo on left; retitled version of "Twist with the Ventures"					
❑ BST 8014 [S]	The Ventures' Twist Party, Vol. 2	1962	15.00	30.00	60.00
—Pale blue label with dolphins on top					
❑ BST 8014 [S]	Dance with the Ventures	1963	6.25	12.50	25.00
—Dark label, logo on left' retitled version of "The Ventures' Twist Party, Vol. 2"					
❑ BST 8016 [S]	Mashed Potatoes and Gravy	1962	10.00	20.00	40.00
❑ BST 8016 [S]	Beach Party	1963	6.25	12.50	25.00
—Retitled version of "Mashed Potatoes and Gravy"					
❑ BST 8017 [S]	Going to the Ventures Dance Party!	1962	10.00	20.00	40.00
❑ BST 8019 [S]	The Ventures Play Telstar, The Lonely Bull	1962	10.00	20.00	40.00
❑ BST 8022 [S]	Surfing	1963	7.50	15.00	30.00
❑ BST 8023 [S]	The Ventures Play the Country Classics	1963	7.50	15.00	30.00
❑ BST 8024 [S]	Let's Go!	1963	7.50	15.00	30.00
❑ BST 8027 [S]	(The) Ventures in Space	1964	12.50	25.00	50.00
❑ BST 8029 [S]	The Fabulous Ventures	1964	7.50	15.00	30.00
❑ BST 8031 [S]	Walk, Don't Run, Vol. 2	1964	7.50	15.00	30.00
❑ BST 8033 [S]	The Ventures Knock Me Out!	1965	7.50	15.00	30.00
❑ BST 8035 [S]	The Ventures on Stage	1965	7.50	15.00	30.00
❑ BST 8037 [S]	The Ventures A-Go-Go	1965	7.50	15.00	30.00
❑ BST-8038 [S]	The Ventures' Christmas Album	1965	5.00	10.00	20.00
❑ BST 8040 [S]	Where the Action Is	1966	6.25	2.50	25.00
❑ BST 8042 [S]	The Ventures/Batman Theme	1966	10.00	20.00	40.00
❑ BST 8045 [S]	Go with the Ventures!	1966	6.25	12.50	25.00
❑ BST 8047 [S]	Wild Things!	1966	6.25	12.50	25.00
❑ BST 8050 [S]	Guitar Freakout	1967	6.25	12.50	25.00
❑ BLP 16501 [M]	Play Guitar with the Ventures	1965	6.25	12.50	25.00
❑ BLP 16502 [M]	Play Guitar with the Ventures, Vol. 2	196?	6.25	12.50	25.00
❑ BLP 16503 [M]	Play Guitar with the Ventures, Vol. 3	196?	6.25	12.50	25.00
❑ BLP 16504 [M]	Play Guitar with the Ventures, Vol. 4	196?	6.25	12.50	25.00
❑ BST 16504 [S]	Play Guitar with the Ventures, Vol. 4	196?	7.50	15.00	30.00
❑ BST 17501 [S]	Play Guitar with the Ventures	1965	7.50	15.00	30.00
❑ BST 17502 [S]	Play Guitar with the Ventures, Vol. 2	196?	7.50	15.00	30.00
❑ BST 17503 [S]	Play Guitar with the Ventures, Vol. 3	196?	7.50	15.00	30.00
LIBERTY					
❑ LRP-2052 [M]	Super Psychedelics	1967	5.00	10.00	20.00
❑ LRP-2053 [M]	Golden Greats by the Ventures	1967	5.00	10.00	20.00
❑ LRP-2054 [M]	$1,000,000.00 Weekend	1967	5.00	10.00	20.00
❑ LRP-2055 [M]	Flights of Fancy	1968	7.50	15.00	30.00
❑ LST-8003	Walk Don't Run	1970	3.75	7.50	15.00
—Reissue of Dolton 8003 with new front cover, original back cover					
❑ LST-8003	Walk Don't Run	1970	5.00	10.00	20.00
—Reissue of Dolton 8003 with new front and back covers					
❑ LT-8003	Walk Don't Run	1981	2.00	4.00	8.00
❑ LST-8023	I Walk the Line and Other Giant Hits	1970	5.00	10.00	20.00
—Reissue of "The Ventures Play the Country Classics"					
❑ LST-8031	Walk, Don't Run, Vol. 2	1970	6.25	12.50	25.00
—Reissue of Dolton 8031 with new cover					
❑ LST-8050	Revolving Sounds	1970	7.50	15.00	30.00
—Reissue of "Guitar Freakout"					
❑ LST-8052 [S]	Super Psychedelics	1967	6.25	12.50	25.00
❑ LST-8052 [S]	Changing Times	1970	10.00	20.00	40.00
—Reissue of "Super Psychedelics"					
❑ LST-8053 [S]	Golden Greats by the Ventures	1967	5.00	10.00	20.00
❑ LTAO-8053	Golden Greats by the Ventures	1981	2.00	4.00	8.00
❑ LST-8054 [S]	$1,000,000.00 Weekend	1967	5.00	10.00	20.00
❑ LST-8055 [S]	Flights of Fancy	1968	5.00	10.00	20.00
❑ LST-8057	The Horse	1968	5.00	10.00	20.00
❑ LST-8057	On the Scene	1970	3.75	7.50	15.00
—Reissue of "The Horse"					
❑ LST-8059	Underground Fire	1969	5.00	10.00	20.00
❑ LST-8060	More Golden Greats	1970	3.75	7.50	15.00
❑ LST-8061	Hawaii Five-O	1969	3.75	7.50	15.00
❑ LST-8062	Swamp Rock	1969	3.75	7.50	15.00
❑ LN-10122	The Very Best of the Ventures	1981	2.00	4.00	8.00
❑ LN-10155	The Ventures Play Telstar, The Lonely Bull	1981	2.00	4.00	8.00
❑ LN-10156	The Ventures Play the Country Classics	1981	2.00	4.00	8.00
❑ LN-10188	Walk, Don't Run, Vol. 2	1984	2.00	4.00	8.00
❑ LN-10190	(The) Ventures in Space	1984	2.00	4.00	8.00
❑ LN-10203	The Ventures	1984	2.00	4.00	8.00
❑ LN-10224	TV Themes	1984	2.00	4.00	8.00
❑ LST-35000 [(2)]	The Ventures 10th Anniversary Album	1970	5.00	10.00	20.00
SUNSET					
❑ SUM-1160 [M]	The Guitar Genius of the Ventures	1967	3.00	6.00	12.00
❑ SUS-5160 [S]	The Guitar Genius of the Ventures	1967	3.75	7.50	15.00
❑ SUS-5270	Super Group	1969	3.00	6.00	12.00
UNITED ARTISTS					
❑ UXS-80 [(2)]	The Ventures	1971	3.75	7.50	15.00
❑ UA-LA147-G [(2)]	Only Hits	1973	3.75	7.50	15.00
❑ UA-LA217-E	The Jim Croce Songbook	1973	3.00	6.00	12.00
❑ UA-LA331-E	The Very Best of the Ventures	1974	3.00	6.00	12.00
❑ UA-LA586-F	Rocky Road	1976	3.00	6.00	12.00
❑ UA-LA717-F	TV Themes	1977	6.25	12.50	25.00
❑ UAS-5547	Theme from Shaft	1971	3.00	6.00	12.00
❑ UAS-5575	Joy/The Ventures Play the Classics	1972	3.00	6.00	12.00
❑ UAS-5649	Rock and Roll Forever	1972	3.00	6.00	12.00
❑ UAS-6796	New Testament	1971	3.00	6.00	12.00

VENUTA, BENAY

Number	Title (A Side/B Side)	Yr	VG	VG+	NM
MERCURY					
❑ MG-25006 [10]	Old Time Favorites	1949	17.50	35.00	70.00

Number	Title (A Side/B Side)	Yr	VG	VG+	NM

VENUTI, JOE
GOLDEN CREST
| ❏ GC-3100 [M] | Joe Venuti Plays Gershwin | 1959 | 7.50 | 15.00 | 30.00 |
| ❏ GC-3101 [M] | Joe Venuti Plays Jerome Kern | 1959 | 7.50 | 15.00 | 30.00 |
GRAND AWARD
| ❏ GA-33-351 [M] | Fiddle on Fire | 1956 | 10.00 | 20.00 | 40.00 |
TOPS
| ❏ L 923 [10] | Twilight on the Trail | 195? | 7.50 | 15.00 | 30.00 |

VENUTI, JOE/EDDIE LANG
COLUMBIA
| ❏ C2L 24 [(2)M] | Swinging the Blues | 1963 | 6.25 | 12.50 | 25.00 |
—"Guaranteed High Fidelity" on labels
| ❏ C2L 24 [(2)M] | Swinging the Blues | 1965 | 5.00 | 10.00 | 20.00 |
—"360 Sound Mono" on labels
"X"
| ❏ LVA-3036 [M] | Joe Venuti and Eddie Lang | 1955 | 10.00 | 20.00 | 40.00 |

VENUTI, JOE, AND LOUIS PRIMA
DESIGN
| ❏ DLP-54 [M] | Hi-Fi Lootin' | 195? | 5.00 | 10.00 | 20.00 |

VER PLANCK, BILLY
SAVOY
| ❏ MG-12101 [M] | Dancing Jazz | 1957 | 10.00 | 20.00 | 40.00 |
| ❏ MG-12121 [M] | Jazz for Playgirls | 1957 | 10.00 | 20.00 | 40.00 |

VER PLANCK, MARLENE
SAVOY
| ❏ MG-12058 [M] | I Think of You with Every Breath I Take | 1956 | 12.50 | 25.00 | 50.00 |
—As "Marlene"

VERA, BILLY
ALFA
| ❏ 10001 | Billy and the Beaters | 1981 | 3.75 | 7.50 | 15.00 |
| ❏ 10012 | Billy Vera | 1982 | 3.00 | 6.00 | 12.00 |
ATLANTIC
| ❏ 8197 [M] | With Pen in Hand | 1968 | 10.00 | 20.00 | 40.00 |
| ❏ SD 8197 [S] | With Pen in Hand | 1968 | 6.25 | 12.50 | 25.00 |
CAPITOL
| ❏ C1-46948 | Retro Nuevo | 1988 | 2.50 | 5.00 | 10.00 |
MACOLA
| ❏ 0961 | The Billy Vera Album | 1987 | 2.50 | 5.00 | 10.00 |
—Reissue of Midsong Int'l. LP
MIDSONG INT'L.
| ❏ BKL1-2219 | Out of the Darkness | 1977 | 3.00 | 6.00 | 12.00 |
RHINO
| ❏ RNLP 70185 | The Atlantic Years | 1987 | 2.50 | 5.00 | 10.00 |
| ❏ RNLP 70858 | By Request — The Best of Billy Vera and the Beaters | 1986 | 3.00 | 6.00 | 12.00 |
THUNDER
| ❏ TVLP 0018 | The Hollywood Sessions | 1987 | 2.50 | 5.00 | 10.00 |

VERA, BILLY, AND JUDY CLAY
ATLANTIC
| ❏ 8174 [M] | Storybook Children | 1967 | 6.25 | 12.50 | 25.00 |
| ❏ SD 8174 [S] | Storybook Children | 1967 | 7.50 | 15.00 | 30.00 |

VERDON, GWEN
RCA VICTOR
| ❏ LPM-1152 [M] | The Girl I Left Home For | 1956 | 10.00 | 20.00 | 40.00 |

VERITY, JOHN, BAND
ABC DUNHILL
| ❏ DSX-50170 | The John Verity Band | 1974 | 5.00 | 10.00 | 20.00 |

VERNE, LARRY
ERA
| ❏ 104 [M] | Mister Larry Verne | 1961 | 15.00 | 30.00 | 60.00 |

VERNON, MILLIE
AUDIOPHILE
| ❏ AP-178 | Old Shoes | 1989 | 2.50 | 5.00 | 10.00 |

VERSATONES, THE
RCA VICTOR
| ❏ LPM-1538 [M] | The Versatones | 1957 | 25.00 | 50.00 | 100.00 |

VERY SPECIAL ENVOY
ROULETTE
| ❏ SR-42003 | Very Special Envoy | 1968 | 5.00 | 10.00 | 20.00 |

VETTES, THE
MGM
| ❏ E-4193 [M] | Rev-Up | 1963 | 25.00 | 50.00 | 100.00 |
| ❏ SE-4193 [S] | Rev-Up | 1963 | 30.00 | 60.00 | 120.00 |

VIBRATIONS, THE
CHECKER
| ❏ LP-2978 [M] | The Watusi | 1961 | 50.00 | 100.00 | 200.00 |
MANDALA
| ❏ 3006 | Taking a New Step | 1972 | 5.00 | 10.00 | 20.00 |
OKEH
❏ OKM-12111 [M]	Shout	1965	7.50	15.00	30.00
❏ OKM-12112 [M]	Misty	1966	7.50	15.00	30.00
❏ OKM-12114 [M]	New Vibrations	1967	7.50	15.00	30.00
❏ OKS-14111 [S]	Shout	1965	10.00	20.00	40.00
❏ OKS-14112 [S]	Misty	1966	10.00	20.00	40.00
❏ OKS-14114 [S]	New Vibrations	1967	10.00	20.00	40.00
❏ OKS-14129	The Vibrations' Greatest Hits	1969	7.50	15.00	30.00

VICEROYS, THE (3)
BOLO
| ❏ BLP-8000 [M] | The Viceroys at Granny's Pad | 1963 | 10.00 | 20.00 | 40.00 |

VICK, HAROLD
BLUE NOTE
| ❏ BLP-4138 [M] | Steppin' Out | 1963 | 10.00 | 20.00 | 40.00 |
| ❏ BST-84138 [S] | Steppin' Out | 1963 | 12.50 | 25.00 | 50.00 |
—With "New York, USA" address on label
RCA VICTOR
| ❏ LSP-3677 [S] | The Caribbean Suite | 1966 | 5.00 | 10.00 | 20.00 |
| ❏ LPM-3761 [M] | Straight Up | 1967 | 5.00 | 10.00 | 20.00 |
STRATA-EAST
| ❏ SES-7431 | Don't Look Back | 197? | 5.00 | 10.00 | 20.00 |

VICTIMS OF CHANCE, THE
CRESTVIEW
| ❏ CRS-3052 | The Victims of Chance | 197? | 15.00 | 30.00 | 60.00 |

VIDEO ALL STARS, THE
SOMERSET
| ❏ SF-8800 [M] | The Video All Stars Play TV Jazz Themes | 1956 | 30.00 | 60.00 | 120.00 |

VIENNA ART ORCHESTRA
HAT HUT
❏ 1980/1 [(2)]	Concerto Piccolo	1980	5.00	10.00	20.00
❏ 1991/2 [(2)]	Suite for the Green Eighties	1981	5.00	10.00	20.00
❏ 1999/2000 [(2)]	From No Time to Rag Time	1982	5.00	10.00	20.00

VIENNA PHILHARMONIC ORCHESTRA (WILHELM FURTWANGLER, CONDUCTOR)
URANIA
| ❏ URLP-7095 [M] | Beethoven: Symphony No. 3 | 195? | 150.00 | 300.00 | 600.00 |
—Withdrawn from the market when it was discovered that the record had been mastered slightly fast

VIENNA PHILHARMONIC ORCHESTRA (PIERRE MONTEUX, CONDUCTOR)
RCA VICTOR RED SEAL
| ❏ LSC-2316 [S] | Beethoven: Symphony No. 6 | 1959 | 12.50 | 25.00 | 50.00 |
—Original with "shaded dog" label
| ❏ LSC-2362 [S] | Berlioz: Symphonie Fantastique | 1960 | 10.00 | 20.00 | 40.00 |
—Original with "shaded dog" label
| ❏ LSC-2394 [S] | Haydn: Symphonies No. 94 and 101 | 1960 | 6.25 | 12.50 | 25.00 |
—Original with "shaded dog" label
| ❏ LSC-2491 [S] | Beethoven: Symphonies No. 1 and 8 | 1961 | 10.00 | 20.00 | 40.00 |
—Original with "shaded dog" label

VIENNA PHILHARMONIC ORCHESTRA (FRITZ REINER, CONDUCTOR)
RCA VICTOR RED SEAL
| ❏ LSC-2077 [S] | Strauss: Till Eulenspiegel | 1959 | 25.00 | 50.00 | 100.00 |
—Original with "shaded dog" label
| ❏ LSC-2077 [S] | Strauss: Till Eulenspiegel | 199? | 6.25 | 12.50 | 25.00 |
—Classic Records reissue

VIG, TOMMY
MILESTONE
| ❏ MSP-9007 | Sounds of the Seventies | 1968 | 5.00 | 10.00 | 20.00 |

VILLA, PEPE
KING
| ❏ 660 [M] | Music of Mexico | 1959 | 7.50 | 15.00 | 30.00 |

VILLAGE PEOPLE
CASABLANCA
❏ NBLP-7064	Village People	1977	2.50	5.00	10.00
❏ NBPIX-7064 [PD]	Village People	1978	5.00	10.00	20.00
❏ NBLP-7096	Macho Man	1978	2.50	5.00	10.00
❏ NBPIX-7096 [PD]	Macho Man	1978	5.00	10.00	20.00
❏ NBLP-7118	Cruisin'	1978	2.50	5.00	10.00
❏ NBPIX-7118 [PD]	Cruisin'	1978	5.00	10.00	20.00
❏ NBLP-7144	Go West	1979	2.50	5.00	10.00
❏ NBLP-7183 [(2)]	Live and Sleazy	1979	3.00	6.00	12.00
RCA VICTOR
❏ AFL1-4105	Renaissance	1981	2.50	5.00	10.00
RHINO
❏ R1-70167	Greatest Hits	1988	2.50	5.00	10.00

VILLAGE STOMPERS, THE
EPIC
❏ LN 24078 [M]	Washington Square	1963	3.75	7.50	15.00
❏ LN 24090 [M]	More Sounds of Washington Square	1964	3.75	7.50	15.00
❏ LN 24109 [M]	Around the World with the Village Stompers	1964	3.00	6.00	12.00
❏ LN 24129 [M]	New Beat on Broadway!	1964	3.00	6.00	12.00
❏ LN 24161 [M]	Some Folk, a Bit of Country and a Whole Lot of Dixie	1965	3.00	6.00	12.00
❏ LN 24180 [M]	A Taste of Honey	1965	3.00	6.00	12.00
❏ LN 24235 [M]	One More Time	1966	3.00	6.00	12.00
❏ LN 24318 [M]	The Village Stompers' Greatest Hits	1967	3.00	6.00	12.00
❏ BN 26078 [S]	Washington Square	1963	5.00	10.00	20.00
❏ BN 26090 [S]	More Sounds of Washington Square	1964	5.00	10.00	20.00
❏ BN 26109 [S]	Around the World with the Village Stompers	1964	3.75	7.50	15.00
❏ BN 26129 [S]	New Beat on Broadway!	1964	3.75	7.50	15.00
❏ BN 26161 [S]	Some Folk, a Bit of Country and a Whole Lot of Dixie	1965	3.75	7.50	15.00
❏ BN 26180 [S]	A Taste of Honey	1965	3.75	7.50	15.00
❏ BN 26235 [S]	One More Time	1966	3.75	7.50	15.00
❏ BN 26318 [S]	The Village Stompers' Greatest Hits	1967	3.75	7.50	15.00

VILLEGAS
COLUMBIA
| ❏ CL 787 [M] | Introducing Villegas | 1956 | 7.50 | 15.00 | 30.00 |
| ❏ CL 877 [M] | Very, Very Villegas | 1956 | 7.50 | 15.00 | 30.00 |

Number	Title (A Side/B Side)	Yr	VG	VG+	NM

VINCENT, GENE
CAPITOL
□ DKAO-380 [R]	Gene Vincent's Greatest	1969	12.50	25.00	50.00
□ SM-380 [R]	Gene Vincent's Greatest	197?	3.75	7.50	15.00
—Abridged reissue of DKAO-380					
□ T 764 [M]	Bluejean Bop!	1957	100.00	200.00	400.00
—Turquoise label stock copy					
□ T 764 [M]	Bluejean Bop!	1957	250.00	500.00	1000.
—Black label promo					
□ T 764 [M]	Bluejean Bop!	1957	250.00	500.00	1000.
—Yellow label promo					
□ T 811 [M]	Gene Vincent and the Blue Caps	1957	100.00	200.00	400.00
—Turquoise label stock copy					
□ T 811 [M]	Gene Vincent and the Blue Caps	1957	250.00	500.00	1000.
—Black label promo					
□ T 811 [M]	Gene Vincent and the Blue Caps	1957	250.00	500.00	1000.
—Yellow label promo					
□ T 970 [M]	Gene Vincent Rocks! And the Blue Caps Roll	1958	100.00	200.00	400.00
—Turquoise label stock copy					
□ T 970 [M]	Gene Vincent Rocks! And the Blue Caps Roll	1958	250.00	500.00	1000.
—Black label promo					
□ T 970 [M]	Gene Vincent Rocks! And the Blue Caps Roll	1958	250.00	500.00	1000.
—Yellow label promo					
□ T 1059 [M]	A Gene Vincent Record Date	1958	100.00	200.00	400.00
—Turquoise label stock copy					
□ T 1059 [M]	A Gene Vincent Record Date	1958	250.00	500.00	1000.
—Black label promo					
□ T 1059 [M]	A Gene Vincent Record Date	1958	250.00	500.00	1000.
—Yellow label promo					
□ T 1207 [M]	Sounds Like Gene Vincent	1959	75.00	150.00	300.00
—Black label with colorband, Capitol logo at left					
□ ST 1342 [S]	Crazy Times	1960	125.00	250.00	500.00
—Black label with colorband, Capitol logo at left					
□ T 1342 [M]	Crazy Times	1960	75.00	150.00	300.00
—Black label with colorband, Capitol logo at left					
□ SM-11287	The Bop That Just Won't Stop	1974	3.75	7.50	15.00
□ N-16208	Gene Vincent's Greatest	198?	3.00	6.00	12.00
—Budget-line reissue					
□ N-16209	The Bop That Just Won't Stop	198?	3.00	6.00	12.00
—Budget-line reissue					
DANDELION
| □ 9-102 | I'm Back and I'm Proud | 1970 | 12.50 | 25.00 | 50.00 |
INTERMEDIA
| □ QS-5074 | Rockabilly Fever | 198? | 3.00 | 6.00 | 12.00 |
KAMA SUTRA
| □ KSBS 2019 | Gene Vincent | 1970 | 12.50 | 25.00 | 50.00 |
| □ KSBS 2027 | The Day the World Turned Blue | 1971 | 12.50 | 25.00 | 50.00 |
ROLLIN' ROCK
| □ 022 | Forever | 1981 | 3.75 | 7.50 | 15.00 |

VINNEGAR, LEROY
CONTEMPORARY
□ C-3542 [M]	Leroy Walks!	1957	20.00	40.00	80.00
□ M-3608 [M]	Leroy Walks Again!	1962	7.50	15.00	30.00
□ S-7003 [S]	Leroy Walks!	1959	12.50	25.00	50.00
□ S-7608 [S]	Leroy Walks Again!	1962	10.00	20.00	40.00
STEREO RECORDS
| □ S-7003 [S] | Leroy Walks! | 1958 | 15.00 | 30.00 | 60.00 |
VEE JAY
| □ LP-2502 [M] | Jazz's Great Walker | 1964 | 7.50 | 15.00 | 30.00 |
| □ LPS-2502 [S] | Jazz's Great Walker | 1964 | 7.50 | 15.00 | 30.00 |

VINSON, EDDIE "CLEANHEAD"
AAMCO
| □ 312 [M] | Cleanhead's Back in Town | 196? | 10.00 | 20.00 | 40.00 |
BETHLEHEM
| □ BCP-5005 [M] | Eddie "Cleanhead" Vinson Sings | 1957 | 25.00 | 50.00 | 100.00 |
BLUESWAY
| □ BL-6007 [M] | Cherry Red | 1967 | 6.25 | 12.50 | 25.00 |
| □ BLS-6007 [S] | Cherry Red | 1967 | 6.25 | 12.50 | 25.00 |
KING
| □ KS-1087 | Cherry Red | 1969 | 6.25 | 12.50 | 25.00 |
RIVERSIDE
| □ RLP-502 [M] | Back Door Blues | 1965 | 10.00 | 20.00 | 40.00 |
| □ RLS-9502 [S] | Back Door Blues | 1965 | 10.00 | 20.00 | 40.00 |

VINSON, EDDIE "CLEANHEAD"/JIMMY WITHERSPOON
KING
| □ 634 [M] | Battle of the Blues, Volume 3 | 1960 | 375.00 | 750.00 | 1500. |

VINTON, BOBBY
ABC
□ X-851	Melodies of Love	1974	2.50	5.00	10.00
□ D-891	Heart of Hearts	1975	2.50	5.00	10.00
□ D-924	The Bobby Vinton Show	1975	2.50	5.00	10.00
□ D-957	Serenades of Love	1976	2.50	5.00	10.00
□ AB-981	The Name Is Love	1977	2.50	5.00	10.00
COLUMBIA LIMITED EDITION
| □ LE 10140 | Blue Velvet | 197? | 2.50 | 5.00 | 10.00 |
| —Reissue of Epic 26068 | | | | | |
COLUMBIA MUSICAL TREASURY
| □ 6P 6035 [(6)] | The Bobby Vinton Treasury | 197? | 7.50 | 15.00 | 30.00 |
| —"Columbia House" logo on upper right back cover | | | | | |
EPIC
□ BN 579 [S]	Dancing at the Hop	1961	12.50	25.00	50.00
□ BN 597 [S]	Young Man with a Big Band	1961	12.50	25.00	50.00
□ LN 3727 [M]	Dancing at the Hop	1961	7.50	15.00	30.00
□ LN 3780 [M]	Young Man with a Big Band	1961	7.50	15.00	30.00
□ LN 24020 [M]	Roses Are Red	1962	3.75	7.50	15.00
□ LN 24035 [M]	Bobby Vinton Sings the Big Ones	1962	3.75	7.50	15.00
□ LN 24049 [M]	The Greatest Hits of the Greatest Groups	1963	3.75	7.50	15.00
□ LN 24068 [M]	Blue Velvet	1963	3.75	7.50	15.00
—Retitled version of "Blue On Blue"					
□ LN 24068 [M]	Blue On Blue	1963	6.25	12.50	25.00
—Stock copy on black vinyl					
□ LN 24068 [M]	Blue On Blue	1963	37.50	75.00	150.00
—Promo only on blue vinyl					
□ LN 24081 [M]	There! I've Said It Again	1964	3.75	7.50	15.00
□ LN 24098 [M]	Bobby Vinton's Greatest Hits	1964	3.00	6.00	12.00
—Despite lower number, this came out after "Tell Me Why"					
□ LN 24113 [M]	Tell Me Why	1964	3.00	6.00	12.00
□ LN 24122 [M]	A Very Merry Christmas	1964	3.00	6.00	12.00
□ LN 24136 [M]	Mr. Lonely	1965	3.00	6.00	12.00
□ LN 24154 [M]	Bobby Vinton Sings for Lonely Nights	1965	3.00	6.00	12.00
□ LN 24170 [M]	Drive-In Movie Time	1965	3.00	6.00	12.00
□ LN 24182 [M]	Satin Pillows and Careless	1966	3.00	6.00	12.00
□ LN 24187 [M]	More of Bobby Vinton's Greatest Hits	1966	3.00	6.00	12.00
□ LN 24188 [M]	Country Boy	1966	3.00	6.00	12.00
□ LN 24203 [M]	Live at the Copa	1967	3.00	6.00	12.00
□ LN 24245 [M]	Bobby Vinton's Newest Hits	1967	3.00	6.00	12.00
□ LN 24341 [M]	Please Love Me Forever	1967	3.75	7.50	15.00
□ BN 26020 [S]	Roses Are Red	1962	5.00	10.00	20.00
□ BN 26035 [S]	Bobby Vinton Sings the Big Ones	1962	5.00	10.00	20.00
□ BN 26049 [S]	The Greatest Hits of the Greatest Groups	1963	5.00	10.00	20.00
□ BN 26068 [S]	Blue Velvet	1963	5.00	10.00	20.00
—Retitled version of "Blue On Blue"					
□ BN 26068 [S]	Blue On Blue	1963	7.50	15.00	30.00
□ BN 26081 [S]	There! I've Said It Again	1964	5.00	10.00	20.00
□ BN 26098 [S]	Bobby Vinton's Greatest Hits	1964	3.75	7.50	15.00
—Despite lower number, this came out after "Tell Me Why"					
□ PE 26098	Bobby Vinton's Greatest Hits	198?	2.00	4.00	8.00
—Budget-line reissue					
□ BN 26113 [S]	Tell Me Why	1964	3.75	7.50	15.00
□ BN 26122 [S]	A Very Merry Christmas	1964	3.75	7.50	15.00
□ BN 26136 [S]	Mr. Lonely	1965	3.75	7.50	15.00
□ BN 26154 [S]	Bobby Vinton Sings for Lonely Nights	1965	3.75	7.50	15.00
□ BN 26170 [S]	Drive-In Movie Time	1965	3.75	7.50	15.00
□ BN 26182 [S]	Satin Pillows and Careless	1966	3.75	7.50	15.00
□ BN 26187 [S]	More of Bobby Vinton's Greatest Hits	1966	3.75	7.50	15.00
□ BN 26188 [S]	Country Boy	1966	3.75	7.50	15.00
□ BN 26203 [S]	Live at the Copa	1967	3.75	7.50	15.00
□ BN 26245 [S]	Bobby Vinton's Newest Hits	1967	3.75	7.50	15.00
□ BN 26341 [S]	Please Love Me Forever	1967	3.75	7.50	15.00
□ BN 26382	Take Good Care of My Baby	1968	3.75	7.50	15.00
□ BN 26437	I Love How You Love Me	1968	3.75	7.50	15.00
□ BN 26471	Vinton	1969	3.75	7.50	15.00
□ BN 26517	Bobby Vinton's Greatest Hits of Love	1970	3.75	7.50	15.00
□ BN 26540	My Elusive Dreams	1970	3.75	7.50	15.00
□ KE 31286	Ev'ry Day of My Life	1972	3.00	6.00	12.00
□ KEG 31487 [(2)]	Bobby Vinton's All-Time Greatest Hits	1972	3.75	7.50	15.00
□ PEG 31487 [(2)]	Bobby Vinton's All-Time Greatest Hits	197?	3.00	6.00	12.00
—Reissue					
□ KE 31642	Sealed with a Kiss	1972	3.00	6.00	12.00
□ PE 32921	With Love	1974	2.50	5.00	10.00
□ KEG 33468 [(2)]	Bobby Vinton Sings the Golden Decade of Love	1975	3.00	6.00	12.00
□ KEG 33767 [(2)]	Greatest Hits/Greatest Hits of Love	1976	3.00	6.00	12.00
□ JE 35605	Autumn Memories	1979	2.50	5.00	10.00
□ JE 35998	Spring Sensations	1979	2.50	5.00	10.00
□ JE 35999	Summer Serenade	1979	2.50	5.00	10.00
HARMONY
| □ KH 11402 | Vinton Sings Vinton | 197? | 2.50 | 5.00 | 10.00 |
PICKWICK
| □ SPC-3353 | Melodies of Love | 197? | 2.00 | 4.00 | 8.00 |
TAPESTRY
| □ TRS-1001 [EP] | Santa Must Be Polish | 1987 | 2.50 | 5.00 | 10.00 |

VIOLA, AL
MODE
| □ LP-121 [M] | Solo Guitar | 1957 | 20.00 | 40.00 | 80.00 |

VIOLENT FEMMES
SLASH
□ 23845	Violent Femmes	1983	3.75	7.50	15.00
□ 25094	Hallowed Ground	1984	3.00	6.00	12.00
□ 25340	The Blind Leading the Naked	1986	2.50	5.00	10.00
□ 25819	3	1988	2.50	5.00	10.00
WARNER BROS.
| □ PRO-A-3519 [DJ] | 3 On 3 | 1989 | 6.25 | 12.50 | 25.00 |
| —Promo-only interviews and music | | | | | |

VIOLINAIRES, THE
CHECKER
□ LP-10011 [M]	Stand By Me	1965	6.25	12.50	25.00
□ LP-10017 [M]	The Fantastic Violinaires	1966	6.25	12.50	25.00
□ LP-10020 [M]	I'm Going to Serve the Lord	196?	5.00	10.00	20.00
□ LPS-10020 [S]	I'm Going to Serve the Lord	196?	6.25	12.50	25.00
□ LP-10030 [M]	Move On Up	196?	5.00	10.00	20.00
□ LPS-10030 [S]	Move On Up	196?	6.25	12.50	25.00
□ LP-10040 [M]	Shout!	196?	5.00	10.00	20.00
□ LPS-10040 [S]	Shout!	196?	6.25	12.50	25.00
□ LP-10045 [M]	Live the Right Way	196?	6.25	12.50	25.00
□ LPS-10045 [S]	Live the Right Way	196?	6.25	12.50	25.00
□ LPS-10053	The Violinaires in Concert	1968	5.00	10.00	20.00
□ LPS-10057	God's Creation	1969	5.00	10.00	20.00
□ LP-10060	At His Command	1970	5.00	10.00	20.00
□ 2CK-10065 [(2)]	Please Answer This Prayer	197?	6.25	12.50	25.00
□ CK-10067	Groovin' with Jesus	197?	5.00	10.00	20.00

VIRGIN INSANITY
FUNKY
| □ 71411 | Illusions of the Maintenance Man | 1970 | 50.00 | 100.00 | 200.00 |

Number	Title (A Side/B Side)	Yr	VG	VG+	NM

VIRGINIANS, THE
MONUMENT
| ❑ MLP-8031 [M] | Ballads and Bluegrass | 1965 | 5.00 | 10.00 | 20.00 |
| ❑ SLP-18031 [S] | Ballads and Bluegrass | 1965 | 6.25 | 12.50 | 25.00 |
UNITED ARTISTS
| ❑ UAL-3293 [M] | The Wonderful World of Bluegrass Music | 1963 | 5.00 | 10.00 | 20.00 |
| ❑ UAS-6293 [S] | The Wonderful World of Bluegrass Music | 1963 | 6.25 | 12.50 | 25.00 |

VIRTUES, THE
FAYETTE
❑ 1816 [M]	Frank Virtue and the Virtues	1964	10.00	20.00	40.00
—White cover					
❑ 1816 [M]	Frank Virtue and the Virtues	1964	15.00	30.00	60.00
—Blue cover					
STRAND
| ❑ L-1061 [M] | Guitar Boogie Shuffle | 1960 | 7.50 | 15.00 | 30.00 |
| ❑ SL-1061 [S] | Guitar Boogie Shuffle | 1960 | 10.00 | 20.00 | 40.00 |
WYNNE
| ❑ WLP-111 [M] | Guitar Boogie Shuffle | 1960 | 30.00 | 60.00 | 120.00 |
| ❑ WLP-711 [S] | Guitar Boogie Shuffle | 1960 | 45.00 | 90.00 | 180.00 |

VISCOUNTS, THE (1)
AMY
| ❑ 8008 [M] | Harlem Nocturne | 1965 | 10.00 | 20.00 | 40.00 |
| ❑ S-8008 [S] | Harlem Nocturne | 1965 | 12.50 | 25.00 | 50.00 |
MADISON
| ❑ 1001 [M] | The Viscounts | 1960 | 50.00 | 100.00 | 200.00 |

VISION OF SUNSHINE
AVCO EMBASSY
| ❑ 33007 | Vision of Sunshine | 1970 | 7.50 | 15.00 | 30.00 |

VISITORS, THE
COBBLESTONE
| ❑ 9010 | Neptune | 197? | 5.00 | 10.00 | 20.00 |

VOGUES, THE
CO & CE
❑ LP-1229 [M]	Meet the Vogues	1965	12.50	25.00	50.00
❑ LP-1230 [M]	Five O'Clock World	1966	12.50	25.00	50.00
—Stereo pressings of these two albums are not known to exist!					
PICKWICK
| ❑ SPC-3188 [R] | Five O'Clock World | 1971 | 2.50 | 5.00 | 10.00 |
| ❑ SPC-3214 [R] | A Lover's Concerto | 1971 | 2.50 | 5.00 | 10.00 |
REPRISE
❑ RS 6314	Turn Around, Look at Me	1968	3.75	7.50	15.00
—With "W7" and "r:" logos on two-tone orange label					
❑ RS 6326	Till	1969	3.75	7.50	15.00
—With "W7" and "r:" logos on two-tone orange label					
❑ RS 6347	Memories	1969	3.75	7.50	15.00
—With "W7" and "r:" logos on two-tone orange label					
❑ RS 6371	The Vogues' Greatest Hits	1969	3.75	7.50	15.00
—With "W7" and "r:" logos on two-tone orange label					
❑ RS 6395	The Vogues Sing the Good Old Songs	1970	3.00	6.00	12.00
❑ ST-91559	Turn Around, Look at Me	1968	5.00	10.00	20.00
—Capitol Record Club edition					
❑ SW-93040	The Vogues' Greatest Hits	1970	5.00	10.00	20.00
—Capitol Record Club edition					
SSS INTERNATIONAL
| ❑ 34 | The Vogues' Greatest Hits | 1977 | 2.50 | 5.00 | 10.00 |

VOICE OF THE BEEHIVE
LONDON
| ❑ 828100-1 | Let It Bee | 1988 | 5.00 | 10.00 | 20.00 |

VON SCHMIDT, ERIC
FOLKLORE
| ❑ FRLP-14005 [M] | Folk Blues | 1964 | 7.50 | 15.00 | 30.00 |
| ❑ FRST-14005 [S] | Folk Blues | 1964 | 10.00 | 20.00 | 40.00 |
PRESTIGE
| ❑ PRLP-7384 [M] | Eric Sings Von Schmidt | 1966 | 5.00 | 10.00 | 20.00 |
| ❑ PRST-7384 [S] | Eric Sings Von Schmidt | 1966 | 6.25 | 12.50 | 25.00 |
SMASH
| ❑ SRS-67124 | Who Knocked the Brains Out of the Sky? | 1969 | 5.00 | 10.00 | 20.00 |

VRONSKY AND BABIN
RCA VICTOR RED SEAL
| ❑ LSC-2417 [S] | 178 Keys | 1960 | 6.25 | 12.50 | 25.00 |
| —Original with "shaded dog" label | | | | | |

W

WACKER, FRED
DOLPHIN
| ❑ 9 [M] | Freddy Wacker and His Windy City Seven | 195? | 12.50 | 25.00 | 50.00 |

WADE, ADAM
COED
❑ LPC-902 [M]	And Then Came Adam	1960	12.50	25.00	50.00
❑ LPCS-902 [S]	And Then Came Adam	1960	15.00	30.00	60.00
❑ LPC-903 [M]	Adam and Evening	1961	12.50	25.00	50.00
❑ LPCS-903 [S]	Adam and Evening	1961	15.00	30.00	60.00
EPIC
❑ LN 24019 [M]	Adam Wade's Greatest Hits	1962	6.25	12.50	25.00
❑ LN 24026 [M]	One Is a Lonely Number	1962	6.25	12.50	25.00
❑ LN 24044 [M]	What Kind of Fool Am I?	1963	6.25	12.50	25.00
❑ LN 24056 [M]	A Very Good Year for Girls	1963	6.25	12.50	25.00
❑ BN 26019 [S]	Adam Wade's Greatest Hits	1962	7.50	15.00	30.00
❑ BN 26026 [S]	One Is a Lonely Number	1962	7.50	15.00	30.00
❑ BN 26044 [S]	What Kind of Fool Am I?	1963	7.50	15.00	30.00
❑ BN 26056 [S]	A Very Good Year for Girls	1963	7.50	15.00	30.00
KIRSHNER
| ❑ PZ 34919 | Adam Wade | 1977 | 3.00 | 6.00 | 12.00 |

WADSWORTH MANSION
SUSSEX
❑ SXBS-7008	Wadsworth Mansion	1971	5.00	10.00	20.00
❑ SXBS-7008	Wadsworth Manison	1971	6.25	12.50	25.00
—Some copies of this LP have the above typographical error					

WAGNER, LARRY
A44
| ❑ AP-501 [10] | Larry Wagner | 1954 | 15.00 | 30.00 | 60.00 |

WAGNER, ROGER, CHORALE
CAPITOL
❑ P 8267 [M]	Songs of Stephen Foster	195?	7.50	15.00	30.00
❑ P 8324 [M]	Folk Songs of the New World	195?	7.50	15.00	30.00
❑ P 8332 [M]	Folk Songs of the Frontier	195?	7.50	15.00	30.00
❑ PBR 8345 [(2)M]	Folk Songs of the Old World	195?	10.00	20.00	40.00
❑ SP 8353 [S]	Joy to the World!	195?	6.25	12.50	25.00
❑ P 8387 [M]	Folk Songs of the World	195?	5.00	10.00	20.00

WAGONER, PORTER
ACCORD
| ❑ SN-7179 | Down Home Country | 1982 | 3.00 | 6.00 | 12.00 |
DOT/MCA
| ❑ 39053 | Porter Wagoner | 1986 | 2.50 | 5.00 | 10.00 |
RCA CAMDEN
❑ CAL-769 [M]	A Satisfied Mind	1963	3.00	6.00	12.00
❑ CAS-769(e) [R]	A Satisfied Mind	1963	2.50	5.00	10.00
❑ CAL-861 [M]	An Old Log Cabin for Sale	1965	3.00	6.00	12.00
❑ CAS-861 [S]	An Old Log Cabin for Sale	1965	3.00	6.00	12.00
❑ CAL-942 [M]	"Your Old Love Letters" And Other Country Hits	1966	3.00	6.00	12.00
❑ CAS-942 [S]	"Your Old Love Letters" And Other Country Hits	1966	3.00	6.00	12.00
❑ CAL-2116 [M]	I'm Day Dreamin' Tonight	1967	3.00	6.00	12.00
❑ CAS-2116 [S]	I'm Day Dreamin' Tonight	1967	3.00	6.00	12.00
❑ CAL-2191 [M]	Green, Green Grass of Home	1967	3.00	6.00	12.00
❑ CAS-2191 [S]	Green, Green Grass of Home	1967	3.00	6.00	12.00
❑ CAS-2321	Country Feeling	1968	3.00	6.00	12.00
❑ CAS-2409	Howdy Neighbor	1970	3.00	6.00	12.00
❑ CAS-2478	Porter Wagoner Country	1971	3.00	6.00	12.00
❑ CAS-2588	The Silent Kind	1972	3.00	6.00	12.00
❑ CXS-9010 [(2)]	Blue Moon of Kentucky	1971	3.75	7.50	15.00
RCA VICTOR
❑ APL1-0142	I'll Keep on Lovin' You	1973	3.75	7.50	15.00
❑ APL1-0346	The Farmer	1974	3.75	7.50	15.00
❑ APL1-0496	Tore Down	1974	3.75	7.50	15.00
❑ APL1-0713	Highway Headin' South	1974	3.75	7.50	15.00
❑ APL1-1056	Sing Love	1975	3.75	7.50	15.00
❑ ANL1-1213	The Best of Porter Wagoner	1975	3.00	6.00	12.00
❑ LPM-1358 [M]	A Satisfied Mind	1956	50.00	100.00	200.00
❑ AHL1-2432	Porter	1977	3.00	6.00	12.00
❑ LPM-2447 [M]	A Slice of Life — Songs Happy 'N' Sad	1962	6.25	12.50	25.00
❑ LSP-2447 [S]	A Slice of Life — Songs Happy 'N' Sad	1962	7.50	15.00	30.00
❑ LPM-2650 [M]	The Porter Wagoner Show	1963	6.25	12.50	25.00
❑ LSP-2650 [S]	The Porter Wagoner Show	1963	7.50	15.00	30.00
❑ LPM-2706 [M]	Y'All Come	1963	6.25	12.50	25.00
❑ LSP-2706 [S]	Y'All Come	1963	7.50	15.00	30.00
❑ LPM-2840 [M]	In Person	1964	6.25	12.50	25.00
❑ LSP-2840 [S]	In Person	1964	7.50	15.00	30.00
❑ LPM-2960 [M]	The Bluegrass Story	1964	5.00	10.00	20.00
❑ LSP-2960 [S]	The Bluegrass Story	1964	6.25	12.50	25.00
❑ LPM-3389 [M]	The Thin Man from West Plains	1965	5.00	10.00	20.00
❑ LSP-3389 [S]	The Thin Man from West Plains	1965	6.25	12.50	25.00
❑ LPM-3488 [M]	Grand Old Gospel	1966	5.00	10.00	20.00
❑ LSP-3488 [S]	Grand Old Gospel	1966	6.25	12.50	25.00
❑ LPM-3509 [M]	On the Road	1966	5.00	10.00	20.00
❑ LSP-3509 [S]	On the Road	1966	6.25	12.50	25.00
❑ LPM-3560 [M]	The Best of Porter Wagoner	1966	5.00	10.00	20.00
❑ LSP-3560 [S]	The Best of Porter Wagoner	1966	6.25	12.50	25.00
❑ LPM-3593 [M]	Confessions of a Broken Man	1966	5.00	10.00	20.00
❑ LSP-3593 [S]	Confessions of a Broken Man	1966	6.25	12.50	25.00
❑ LPM-3683 [M]	Soul of a Convict	1967	6.25	12.50	25.00
❑ LSP-3683 [S]	Soul of a Convict	1967	5.00	10.00	20.00
❑ LPM-3797 [M]	The Cold Hard Facts of Life	1967	6.25	12.50	25.00
❑ LSP-3797 [S]	The Cold Hard Facts of Life	1967	5.00	10.00	20.00
❑ LPM-3855 [M]	More Grand Old Gospel	1967	6.25	12.50	25.00

Number	Title (A Side/B Side)	Yr	VG	VG+	NM
❏ LSP-3855 [S]	More Grand Old Gospel	1967	5.00	10.00	20.00
❏ LPM-3968 [M]	The Bottom of the Bottle	1968	25.00	50.00	100.00
❏ LSP-3968 [S]	The Bottom of the Bottle	1968	5.00	10.00	20.00
❏ LSP-4034	Gospel Country	1968	5.00	10.00	20.00
❏ LSP-4116	The Carroll County Accident	1969	5.00	10.00	20.00
❏ LSP-4181	Me and My Boys	1969	5.00	10.00	20.00
❏ LSP-4286	You Got-ta Have a License	1970	5.00	10.00	20.00
❏ LSP-4321	The Best of Porter Wagoner, Volume 2	1970	5.00	10.00	20.00
❏ LSP-4386	Down in the Alley	1970	5.00	10.00	20.00
❏ LSP-4508	Simple As I Am	1971	5.00	10.00	20.00
❏ LSP-4586	Porter Wagoner Sings His Own	1971	3.75	7.50	15.00
❏ LSP-4661	What Ain't to Be	1972	3.75	7.50	15.00
❏ LSP-4734	Ballads of Love	1972	3.75	7.50	15.00
❏ LSP-4810	The Porter Wagoner Experience	1973	3.75	7.50	15.00
❏ AHL1-7000	Collector's Series	1985	2.50	5.00	10.00

WARNER BROS.

Number	Title (A Side/B Side)	Yr	VG	VG+	NM
❏ 23783	Viva Porter Wagoner!	1983	2.50	5.00	10.00

WAGONER, PORTER, AND SKEETER DAVIS
Also see each artist's individual listings.

RCA VICTOR

Number	Title (A Side/B Side)	Yr	VG	VG+	NM
❏ LPM-2529 [M]	Porter Wagoner and Skeeter Davis Sing Duets	1962	6.25	12.50	25.00
❏ LSP-2529 [S]	Porter Wagoner and Skeeter Davis Sing Duets	1962	7.50	15.00	30.00

WAGONER, PORTER, AND DOLLY PARTON
Also see each artist's individual listings.

PAIR

Number	Title (A Side/B Side)	Yr	VG	VG+	NM
❏ PDL1-1013 [(2)]	Sweet Harmony	1986	3.00	6.00	12.00

RCA VICTOR

Number	Title (A Side/B Side)	Yr	VG	VG+	NM
❏ APL1-0248	Love and Music	1973	3.75	7.50	15.00
❏ APL1-0646	Porter 'N' Dolly	1974	3.75	7.50	15.00
❏ APL1-1116	Say Forever	1975	3.75	7.50	15.00
❏ AHL1-3700	Porter Wagoner and Dolly Parton	1980	3.00	6.00	12.00
❏ LPM-3926 [M]	Just Between You and Me	1968	25.00	50.00	100.00
❏ LSP-3926 [S]	Just Between You and Me	1968	5.00	10.00	20.00
❏ LSP-4039	Just the Two of Us	1968	5.00	10.00	20.00
❏ LSP-4186	Always, Always	1969	5.00	10.00	20.00
❏ AYL1-4251	Porter Wagoner and Dolly Parton	1982	2.00	4.00	8.00
—"Best Buy Series" reissue					
❏ LSP-4305	Porter Wayne and Dolly Rebecca	1970	5.00	10.00	20.00
❏ LSP-4388	Once More	1970	5.00	10.00	20.00
❏ LSP-4490	Two of a Kind	1971	5.00	10.00	20.00
❏ AHL1-4556	The Best of Porter Wagoner and Dolly Parton	1983	2.50	5.00	10.00
❏ LSP-4556	The Best of Porter Wagoner and Dolly Parton	1971	5.00	10.00	20.00
❏ LSP-4628	The Right Combination/Burning the Midnight Oil	1972	3.75	7.50	15.00
❏ LSP-4761	Together Always	1972	3.75	7.50	15.00
❏ LSP-4841	We Found It	1973	3.75	7.50	15.00

WAIKIKIS, THE
KAPP

Number	Title (A Side/B Side)	Yr	VG	VG+	NM
❏ KL-1366 [M]	Hawaii Tattoo	1964	3.75	7.50	15.00
❏ KL-1432 [M]	Hawaii Honeymoon	1965	3.75	7.50	15.00
❏ KL-1437 [M]	Beach Party	1965	3.75	7.50	15.00
❏ KL-1473 [M]	Lollipops and Roses	1966	3.75	7.50	15.00
❏ KL-1484 [M]	A Taste of Hawaii	1966	3.75	7.50	15.00
❏ KL-1555 [M]	Pearly Shells from Hawaii	1968	7.50	15.00	30.00
—White label promo in stereo cover, "Mono" sticker on front					
❏ KS-3366 [S]	Hawaii Tattoo	1964	5.00	10.00	20.00
❏ KS-3432 [S]	Hawaii Honeymoon	1965	5.00	10.00	20.00
❏ KS-3437 [S]	Beach Party	1965	5.00	10.00	20.00
❏ KS-3473 [S]	Lollipops and Roses	1966	5.00	10.00	20.00
❏ KS-3484 [S]	A Taste of Hawaii	1966	5.00	10.00	20.00
❏ KS-3555 [S]	Pearly Shells from Hawaii	1968	3.75	7.50	15.00
❏ KS-3575	Midnight Luau	1969	3.75	7.50	15.00
❏ KS-3593	Moonlight on Diamond Head	1969	3.75	7.50	15.00
❏ KS-3612	Greatest Hits	1970	3.00	6.00	12.00

MCA

Number	Title (A Side/B Side)	Yr	VG	VG+	NM
❏ 544	Pearly Shells from Hawaii	197?	2.50	5.00	10.00
❏ 547	Greatest Hits	197?	2.50	5.00	10.00

WAILERS, THE
ETIQUETTE

Number	Title (A Side/B Side)	Yr	VG	VG+	NM
❏ ALB-01 [M]	The Fabulous Wailers at the Castle	196?	25.00	50.00	100.00
❏ ALB-022 [M]	The Wailers and Company	196?	20.00	40.00	80.00
❏ ALB-023 [M]	Wailers, Wailers, Everywhere	196?	25.00	50.00	100.00
❏ ALB-026 [M]	Out of Our Tree	1966	25.00	50.00	100.00
❏ 22296/7 [(2)]	The Wailers and Their Greatest Hits	1979	6.25	12.50	25.00

GOLDEN CREST

Number	Title (A Side/B Side)	Yr	VG	VG+	NM
❏ CR-3075 [M]	Fabulous Wailers	1959	62.50	125.00	250.00
—Full-color photo on cover					
❏ CR-3075 [M]	Fabulous Wailers	196?	12.50	25.00	50.00
—Title, no photo, on cover					
❏ CR-3075 [M]	Fabulous Wailers	1962	25.00	50.00	100.00
—Black and white photo on cover					

IMPERIAL

Number	Title (A Side/B Side)	Yr	VG	VG+	NM
❏ LP-9262 [M]	Tall Cool One	1964	12.50	25.00	50.00
❏ LP-12262 [S]	Tall Cool One	1964	20.00	40.00	80.00

UNITED ARTISTS

Number	Title (A Side/B Side)	Yr	VG	VG+	NM
❏ UAL-3557 [M]	Outburst!	1966	12.50	25.00	50.00
❏ UAS-6557 [S]	Outburst!	1966	20.00	40.00	80.00

WAINWRIGHT, LOUDON, III
ARISTA

Number	Title (A Side/B Side)	Yr	VG	VG+	NM
❏ AL 4063	T Shirt	1976	3.00	6.00	12.00
❏ AB 4173	Final Exam	1978	3.00	6.00	12.00

ATLANTIC

Number	Title (A Side/B Side)	Yr	VG	VG+	NM
❏ SD 8260	Loudon Wainwright III	1970	5.00	10.00	20.00
❏ SD 8291	Album II	1971	5.00	10.00	20.00

COLUMBIA

Number	Title (A Side/B Side)	Yr	VG	VG+	NM
❏ KC 31462	Album III	1972	3.75	7.50	15.00

Number	Title (A Side/B Side)	Yr	VG	VG+	NM
❏ PC 31462	Album III	198?	2.00	4.00	8.00
—Budget-line reissue					
❏ KC 32710	Attempted Mustache	1973	3.75	7.50	15.00
❏ PC 32710	Attempted Mustache	198?	2.00	4.00	8.00
—Budget-line reissue					
❏ PC 33369	Unrequited	1975	3.00	6.00	12.00
—No bar code on cover					
❏ PC 33369	Unrequited	198?	2.00	4.00	8.00
—Budget-line reissue with bar code					

ROUNDER

Number	Title (A Side/B Side)	Yr	VG	VG+	NM
❏ 3050	A Live One	1979	3.00	6.00	12.00
❏ 3076	Fame and Wealth	1983	3.00	6.00	12.00
❏ 3096	I'm Alright	1986	2.50	5.00	10.00
❏ 3106	More Love Songs	1987	2.50	5.00	10.00

SILVERTONE

Number	Title (A Side/B Side)	Yr	VG	VG+	NM
❏ 1203-1-J	Therapy	1989	3.00	6.00	12.00

WAITE, GENEVIEVE
PARAMOUR

Number	Title (A Side/B Side)	Yr	VG	VG+	NM
❏ 5088	Romance Is on the Rise	1974	6.25	12.50	25.00

WAITRESSES, THE
POLYDOR

Number	Title (A Side/B Side)	Yr	VG	VG+	NM
❏ PX-1-507 [EP]	I Could Rule the World If I Could Only Get the Parts	1982	2.50	5.00	10.00
❏ PD1-6348	Wasn't Tomorrow Wonderful?	1982	2.50	5.00	10.00
❏ 810980-1	Bruiseology	1983	2.50	5.00	10.00
❏ 810980-1 [DJ]	Bruiseology	1983	6.25	12.50	25.00
—Promo only on purpleish vinyl					

WAKEFIELD SUN
MGM

Number	Title (A Side/B Side)	Yr	VG	VG+	NM
❏ SE-4626	Wakefield Sun	1969	6.25	12.50	25.00

WAKELY, JIMMY
CAPITOL

Number	Title (A Side/B Side)	Yr	VG	VG+	NM
❏ H 4008 [10]	Songs of the West	195?	30.00	60.00	120.00
❏ H-9004 [10]	Christmas on the Range	1950	37.50	75.00	150.00

DECCA

Number	Title (A Side/B Side)	Yr	VG	VG+	NM
❏ DL 8409 [M]	Santa Fe Trail	1956	20.00	40.00	80.00
❏ DL 8680 [M]	Enter and Rest and Pray	1957	15.00	30.00	60.00
❏ DL 75077	Heartaches	1969	3.75	7.50	15.00
❏ DL 75192	Now and Then	1970	3.75	7.50	15.00

DOT

Number	Title (A Side/B Side)	Yr	VG	VG+	NM
❏ DLP-3711 [M]	Slippin' Around	1966	5.00	10.00	20.00
❏ DLP-3754 [M]	Christmas with Jimmy Wakely	1966	5.00	10.00	20.00
❏ DLP-25711 [S]	Slippin' Around	1966	6.25	12.50	25.00
❏ DLP-25734 [S]	Christmas with Jimmy Wakely	1966	6.25	12.50	25.00

MCA CORAL

Number	Title (A Side/B Side)	Yr	VG	VG+	NM
❏ 20033	Blue Shadows	1973	2.50	5.00	10.00

MCR

Number	Title (A Side/B Side)	Yr	VG	VG+	NM
❏ 1250	Jimmy Wakely Sings a Tribute to Bob Wills	1974	3.75	7.50	15.00
❏ 1254	Jimmy Wakely Revisits Country Western Swing with the Big Band Sound	1974	3.75	7.50	15.00

SHASTA

Number	Title (A Side/B Side)	Yr	VG	VG+	NM
❏ 501	Country Million Sellers	195?	3.75	7.50	15.00
❏ 502	Merry Christmas	1959	3.75	7.50	15.00
❏ 505	Jimmy Wakely Sings	196?	3.75	7.50	15.00
❏ 512	The Jimmy Wakely Family Show	196?	3.75	7.50	15.00
❏ 528	J.W. Country	196?	3.75	7.50	15.00

TOPS

Number	Title (A Side/B Side)	Yr	VG	VG+	NM
❏ L-1601 [M]	A Cowboy Serenade	195?	6.25	12.50	25.00

VOCALION

Number	Title (A Side/B Side)	Yr	VG	VG+	NM
❏ VL 73857	Here's Jimmy Wakely	1968	3.00	6.00	12.00
❏ VL 73904	Big Country Songs	1970	3.00	6.00	12.00

WAKEMAN, RICK
Also see YES.

A&M

Number	Title (A Side/B Side)	Yr	VG	VG+	NM
❏ SP-3156	Journey to the Centre of the Earth	198?	2.00	4.00	8.00
—Budget-line reissue of 3621					
❏ SP-3229	The Six Wives of Henry VIII	1984	2.00	4.00	8.00
—Budget-line reissue of 4361					
❏ SP-3230	The Myths and Legends of King Arthur and the Knights of the Round Table	1984	2.00	4.00	8.00
—Budget-line reissue of 4515					
❏ SP-3621	Journey to the Centre of the Earth	1974	3.00	6.00	12.00
❏ SP-4361	The Six Wives of Henry VIII	1973	3.00	6.00	12.00
—Originals have brown labels					
❏ SP-4361	The Six Wives of Henry VIII	1974	2.50	5.00	10.00
—Silver label with "fading" A&M logo					
❏ SP-4515	The Myths and Legends of King Arthur and the Knights of the Round Table	1975	3.00	6.00	12.00
❏ SP-4583	No Earthly Connection	1976	3.00	6.00	12.00
❏ SP-4614	White Rock	1977	3.00	6.00	12.00
❏ SP-4660	Rick Wakeman's Criminal Record	1977	3.00	6.00	12.00
❏ SP-6501 [(2)]	Rhapsodies	1979	3.75	7.50	15.00
❏ QU-53621 [Q]	Journey to the Centre of the Earth	1974	6.25	12.50	25.00
❏ QU-54361 [Q]	The Six Wives of Henry VIII	1974	6.25	12.50	25.00
❏ QU-54515 [Q]	The Myths and Legends of King Arthur and the Knights of the Round Table	1975	6.25	12.50	25.00

MOBILE FIDELITY

Number	Title (A Side/B Side)	Yr	VG	VG+	NM
❏ 1-230	Journey to the Centre of the Earth	1995	5.00	10.00	20.00
—Audiophile vinyl					

SWEET THUNDER

Number	Title (A Side/B Side)	Yr	VG	VG+	NM
❏ 1	Journey to the Centre of the Earth	1981	12.50	25.00	50.00
—Audiophile vinyl					

WALD, JERRY
KAPP

Number	Title (A Side/B Side)	Yr	VG	VG+	NM
❏ KL-1043 [M]	Listen to the Music of Jerry Wald	1956	10.00	20.00	40.00

Number	Title (A Side/B Side)	Yr	VG	VG+	NM
LION					
❏ L-70014 [M]	Tops in Pops — Designed for Dancing	1958	6.25	12.50	25.00
WALDRON, MAL					
BETHLEHEM					
❏ BCP-6045 [M]	Left Alone	1960	10.00	20.00	40.00
❏ SBCP-6045 [S]	Left Alone	1960	10.00	20.00	40.00
MUSIC MINUS ONE					
❏ 175 [M]	Fun With Brushes	1960	5.00	10.00	20.00
❏ 1012 [M]	Moonglow and Stardust	1960	5.00	10.00	20.00
❏ 1015 [M]	Music of Duke Ellington	1960	5.00	10.00	20.00
❏ 1016 [M]	Music of McHugh	1960	5.00	10.00	20.00
❏ 1017 [M]	Mal Waldron	1960	5.00	10.00	20.00
❏ 1018 [M]	For Singers 'N Singer	1960	5.00	10.00	20.00
❏ 4005 [M]	Blue Drums	1961	5.00	10.00	20.00
❏ 4007 [M]	For Pianists Only	1961	5.00	10.00	20.00
❏ 4008 [M]	They Laughed When I Sat Down to Play	1961	5.00	10.00	20.00
NEW JAZZ					
❏ NJLP-8201 [M]	Mal/3: Sounds	1958	12.50	25.00	50.00
—Purple label					
❏ NJLP-8201 [M]	Mal/3: Sounds	1958	25.00	50.00	100.00
—Yellow label					
❏ NJLP-8201 [M]	Mal/3: Sounds	1965	6.25	12.50	25.00
—Blue label, trident logo at right					
❏ NJLP-8208 [M]	Mal/4: Trio	1958	12.50	25.00	50.00
—Purple label					
❏ NJLP-8208 [M]	Mal/4: Trio	1965	6.25	12.50	25.00
—Blue label, trident logo at right					
❏ NJLP-8242 [M]	Impressions	1960	12.50	25.00	50.00
—Purple label					
❏ NJLP-8242 [M]	Impressions	1965	6.25	12.50	25.00
—Blue label, trident logo at right					
❏ NJLP-8269 [M]	The Quest	1962	12.50	25.00	50.00
—Purple label					
❏ NJLP-8269 [M]	The Quest	1965	6.25	12.50	25.00
—Blue label, trident logo at right					
PRESTIGE					
❏ PRLP-7090 [M]	Mal/1	1957	20.00	40.00	80.00
❏ PRLP-7111 [M]	Mal/2	1957	20.00	40.00	80.00
❏ PRST-7579 [S]	The Quest	1969	5.00	10.00	20.00
STATUS					
❏ ST-8316 [M]	The Dealers	1965	10.00	20.00	40.00
WALES, HOWARD, AND JERRY GARCIA					
DOUGLAS					
❏ Z 30589	Hooteroll	1971	10.00	20.00	40.00
WALI AND THE AFRO-CARAVAN					
SOLID STATE					
❏ SS-18065	Home Lost and Found	1969	5.00	10.00	20.00
WALKER, BILLY					
COLUMBIA					
❏ CL 1624 [M]	Everybody's Hits But Mine	1961	5.00	10.00	20.00
❏ CL 1935 [M]	Billy Walker's Greatest Hits	1963	3.75	7.50	15.00
❏ CL 2206 [M]	Thank You for Calling	1964	3.75	7.50	15.00
❏ CL 2331 [M]	The Gun, the Gold and the Girl/Cross the Brazos at Waco	1965	3.75	7.50	15.00
❏ CS 8424 [S]	Everybody's Hits But Mine	1961	7.50	15.00	30.00
❏ CS 8735 [S]	Billy Walker's Greatest Hits	1963	5.00	10.00	20.00
❏ CS 9006 [S]	Thank You for Calling	1964	5.00	10.00	20.00
❏ CS 9131 [S]	The Gun, the Gold and the Girl/Cross the Brazos at Waco	1965	5.00	10.00	20.00
❏ CS 9798	Billy Walker's Greatest Hits, Volume 2	1969	3.75	7.50	15.00
❏ C 30226	Goodnight	1971	3.00	6.00	12.00
HARMONY					
❏ HL 7306 [M]	Anything Your Heart Desires	1964	3.75	7.50	15.00
❏ HL 7410 [M]	Big Country Hits	1967	3.75	7.50	15.00
❏ HS 11210 [S]	Big Country Hits	1967	3.00	6.00	12.00
❏ HS 11414	Charlie's Shoes	1970	3.00	6.00	12.00
❏ H 31177	There May Be No Tomorrow	1972	2.50	5.00	10.00
MGM					
❏ SE-4682	When a Man Loves a Woman (The Way That I Love You)	1970	3.75	7.50	15.00
❏ SE-4756	I'm Gonna Keep On Lovin' You/She Goes Walking Through My Mind	1971	3.75	7.50	15.00
❏ SE-4789	Live!	1972	3.75	7.50	15.00
❏ SE-4863	The Billy Walker Show	1973	3.00	6.00	12.00
❏ SE-4887	Billy Walker's All Time Greatest Hits	1972	3.00	6.00	12.00
❏ SE-4938	Too Many Memories	1974	3.00	6.00	12.00
MONUMENT					
❏ 6641	Billy Walker's Greatest Hits	1976	2.50	5.00	10.00
❏ MLP-8047 [M]	A Million and One	1966	3.00	6.00	12.00
❏ MLP-8072 [M]	The Walker Way	1967	5.00	10.00	20.00
❏ SLP-18047 [S]	A Million and One	1966	3.75	7.50	15.00
❏ SLP-18072 [S]	The Walker Way	1967	3.75	7.50	15.00
❏ SLP-18090	I Taught Her Everything She Knows	1968	3.75	7.50	15.00
❏ SLP-18101	Billy Walker Salutes the Country Music Hall of Fame	1969	3.75	7.50	15.00
❏ SLF-18116	Portrait of Billy	1969	3.75	7.50	15.00
❏ SLP-18143	Darling Days	1970	3.75	7.50	15.00
❏ KZ 31912	Billy Walker's Greatest Hits	1972	3.00	6.00	12.00
RCA VICTOR					
❏ APL1-1160	Lovin' and Losin'	1975	3.00	6.00	12.00
❏ APL1-1489	Alone Again	1976	3.00	6.00	12.00
WALKER, CHARLIE					
COLUMBIA					
❏ CL 1691 [M]	Charlie Walker's Greatest Hits	1961	5.00	10.00	20.00
❏ CS 8491 [S]	Charlie Walker's Greatest Hits	1961	7.50	15.00	30.00

Number	Title (A Side/B Side)	Yr	VG	VG+	NM
EPIC					
❏ LN 24137 [M]	Close All the Honky Tonks	1965	3.75	7.50	15.00
❏ LN 24153 [M]	Born to Lose	1965	3.75	7.50	15.00
❏ LN 24209 [M]	Wine, Women and Walker	1966	3.75	7.50	15.00
❏ LN 24328 [M]	Don't Squeeze My Sharmon	1967	6.25	12.50	25.00
❏ LN 24343 [M]	Charlie Walker's Greatest Hits	1968	10.00	20.00	40.00
❏ BN 26137 [S]	Close All the Honky Tonks	1965	5.00	10.00	20.00
❏ BN 26153 [S]	Born to Lose	1965	5.00	10.00	20.00
❏ BN 26209 [S]	Wine, Women and Walker	1966	5.00	10.00	20.00
❏ BN 26328 [S]	Don't Squeeze My Sharmon	1967	5.00	10.00	20.00
❏ BN 26343 [S]	Charlie Walker's Greatest Hits	1968	3.75	7.50	15.00
❏ BN 26424	He Is My Everything	1969	3.75	7.50	15.00
❏ BN 26483	Recorded Live in Dallas	1969	3.75	7.50	15.00
❏ E 30660	Honky Tonkin'	1971	3.75	7.50	15.00
HARMONY					
❏ HL 7415 [M]	Golden Hits	1967	3.75	7.50	15.00
❏ HS 11215 [S]	Golden Hits	1967	3.00	6.00	12.00
PLANTATION					
❏ 535	Golden Hits	1978	2.50	5.00	10.00
RCA VICTOR					
❏ APL1-0181	Break Out the Bottle	1973	3.00	6.00	12.00
❏ LSP-4737	Charlie Walker	1972	3.75	7.50	15.00
VOCALION					
❏ VL 73814	The Style of Charlie Walker	1968	3.00	6.00	12.00
WALKER, CINDY					
MONUMENT					
❏ MLP-8020 [M]	Words and Music by Cindy Walker	1964	5.00	10.00	20.00
❏ SLP-18020 [S]	Words and Music by Cindy Walker	1964	6.25	12.50	25.00
WALKER, CLINT					
WARNER BROS.					
❏ W 1343 [M]	Inspiration	1959	7.50	15.00	30.00
❏ WS 1343 [S]	Inspiration.	1959	10.00	20.00	40.00
WALKER, JERRY JEFF					
Also see CIRCUS MAXIMUS.					
ATCO					
❏ SD 33-259	Mr. Bojangles	1968	6.25	12.50	25.00
❏ SD 33-297	Five Years Gone	1969	7.50	15.00	30.00
❏ SD 33-336	Bein' Free	1970	5.00	10.00	20.00
BAINBRIDGE					
❏ 6222	Mr. Bojangles	198?	2.50	5.00	10.00
DECCA					
❏ DL 75384	Jerry Jeff Walker	1972	3.75	7.50	15.00
ELEKTRA					
❏ 6E-163	Jerry Jeff	1978	2.50	5.00	10.00
❏ 6E-239	Too Old to Change	1980	2.50	5.00	10.00
MCA					
❏ 382	Viva Terlingua!	1973	2.50	5.00	10.00
❏ 450	Walker's Collectibles	1974	2.50	5.00	10.00
❏ 510	Jerry Jeff Walker	1975	2.50	5.00	10.00
—Reissue of Decca LP					
❏ 2156	Ridin' High	1975	2.50	5.00	10.00
❏ 2202	It's a Good Night for Singin'	1976	2.50	5.00	10.00
❏ 2350	Viva Terlingua!	1977	2.00	4.00	8.00
—Reissue of MCA 382					
❏ 2355	Walker's Collectibles	1977	2.00	4.00	8.00
—Reissue of MCA 450					
❏ 2358	Jerry Jeff Walker	1977	2.00	4.00	8.00
—Reissue of MCA 510					
❏ 3041	Contrary to Ordinary	1978	2.50	5.00	10.00
❏ 5128	The Best of Jerry Jeff Walker	1980	2.50	5.00	10.00
❏ 5355	Cowjazz	1983	2.50	5.00	10.00
❏ 6003 [(2)]	A Man Must Carry On	198?	2.50	5.00	10.00
—Budget-line reissue					
❏ 8013 [(2)]	A Man Must Carry On	1977	3.00	6.00	12.00
❏ 27026	It's a Good Night for Singin'	198?	2.00	4.00	8.00
—Budget-line reissue					
❏ 27027	Walker's Collectibles	198?	—	3.00	6.00
—Budget-line reissue					
❏ 37004	Jerry Jeff Walker	198?	—	3.00	6.00
—Budget-line reissue					
❏ 37005	Viva Terlingua!	198?	—	3.00	6.00
—Budget-line reissue					
❏ 37006	Ridin' High	198?	2.00	4.00	8.00
—Budget-line reissue					
❏ 37162	Contrary to Ordinary	198?	2.00	4.00	8.00
—Budget-line reissue					
SOUTHCOAST					
❏ 5199	Reunion	1981	2.50	5.00	10.00
VANGUARD					
❏ VSD-6521	Driftin' Way of Life	1969	5.00	10.00	20.00
❏ VMS-73124	Driftin' Way of Life	1985	2.00	4.00	8.00
—Reissue of 6521					
WALKER, JR., AND THE ALL STARS					
MOTOWN					
❏ M5-105V1	Motown Superstar Series, Vol. 5	1981	2.50	5.00	10.00
❏ M5-141V1	Shotgun	1981	2.50	5.00	10.00
—Reissue of Soul 701					
❏ M5-208V1	Greatest Hits	1981	2.50	5.00	10.00
—Reissue of Soul 718					
❏ M7-786 [(2)]	Anthology	1974	5.00	10.00	20.00
❏ 5297 ML	All the Great Hits of Jr. Walker and the All Stars	1984	2.50	5.00	10.00
❏ 6053 ML	Blow the House Down	1983	2.50	5.00	10.00
PICKWICK					
❏ SPC-3391	Shotgun	197?	3.00	6.00	12.00
SOUL					
❏ 701 [M]	Shotgun	1965	5.00	10.00	20.00
—Purple swirl label with "Soul" at top					

Number	Title (A Side/B Side)	Yr	VG	VG+	NM
❑ 701 [M]	Shotgun	1965	15.00	30.00	60.00
—Mostly white label with vertical "Soul" at left					
❑ SS-701 [S]	Shotgun	1965	7.50	15.00	30.00
❑ 702 [M]	Soul Session	1966	5.00	10.00	20.00
—Purple swirl label with "Soul" at top					
❑ 702 [M]	Soul Session	1966	15.00	30.00	60.00
—Mostly white label with vertical "Soul" at left					
❑ SS-702 [S]	Soul Session	1966	7.50	15.00	30.00
❑ 703 [M]	Road Runner	1966	5.00	10.00	20.00
❑ SS-703 [S]	Road Runner	1966	7.50	15.00	30.00
❑ 705 [M]	"Live"	1967	5.00	10.00	20.00
❑ SS-705 [S]	"Live"	1967	7.50	15.00	30.00
❑ SS-710	Home Cookin'	1969	5.00	10.00	20.00
❑ SS-718	Greatest Hits	1969	5.00	10.00	20.00
❑ SS-721	Gotta Hold on to This Feeling	1969	6.25	12.50	25.00
❑ SS-721	What Does It Take to Win Your Love	1970	5.00	10.00	20.00
—Retitled version of above					
❑ SS-726	A Gasssss	1970	3.75	7.50	15.00
❑ SS-732	Rainbow Funk	1971	3.75	7.50	15.00
❑ SS-733	Moody Jr.	1971	3.75	7.50	15.00
❑ SS-738	Peace and Understanding Is Hard to Find	1973	3.75	7.50	15.00
❑ S6-742	Jr. Walker and the All Stars	1973	—	—	—
—Canceled					
❑ S6-745	Hot Shot	1976	3.75	7.50	15.00
❑ S6-747	Sax Appeal	1976	3.75	7.50	15.00
❑ S6-748	Whopper Bopper Show Stopper	1977	3.75	7.50	15.00
❑ S7-750	Smooth	1978	3.75	7.50	15.00
WHITFIELD					
❑ WHK 3331	Back Street Boogie	1980	3.00	6.00	12.00

WALKER, MARTIN
ABC-PARAMOUNT

Number	Title (A Side/B Side)	Yr	VG	VG+	NM
❑ ABC-483 [M]	From Scotland with Love	1964	3.75	7.50	15.00
❑ ABCS-483 [S]	From Scotland with Love	1964	5.00	10.00	20.00

WALKER, NANCY
RCA CAMDEN

❑ CAL-561 [M]	I Hate Men	1960	6.25	12.50	25.00
❑ CAS-561 [M]	I Hate Men	1960	7.50	15.00	30.00

WALKER, PETER
VANGUARD

❑ VSD-79282	Second Poem to Karmela	1968	5.00	10.00	20.00

WALKER, SCOTT
Also see THE WALKER BROTHERS.
SMASH

❑ SRS-67099	Aloner	1968	5.00	10.00	20.00
❑ SRS-67106	Scott, Volume 2	1968	5.00	10.00	20.00
❑ SRS-67121	Scott Walker 3	1969	5.00	10.00	20.00

WALKER, T-BONE
ATLANTIC

❑ 8020 [M]	T-Bone Blues	1959	55.00	110.00	220.00
—Black label					
❑ 8020 [M]	T-Bone Blues	1960	17.50	35.00	70.00
—Red and purple label					
❑ SD 8256	T-Bone Blues	1970	5.00	10.00	20.00
BLUE NOTE					
❑ BN-LA533-H2 [(2)]	Classics	1975	5.00	10.00	20.00
BLUESTIME					
❑ 29004	Everyday I Have the Blues	1968	7.50	15.00	30.00
❑ 29010	Blue Rocks	1969	7.50	15.00	30.00
BLUESWAY					
❑ BLS-6008	Stormy Monday Blues	1968	7.50	15.00	30.00
—Reissue of Wet Soul LP?					
❑ BLS-6014	Funky Town	1968	7.50	15.00	30.00
❑ BLS-6058	Dirty Mistreater	1973	3.75	7.50	15.00
BRUNSWICK					
❑ BL 754126	The Truth	1968	7.50	15.00	30.00
CAPITOL					
❑ H 370 [10]	Classics in Jazz	1953	250.00	500.00	1000.
❑ T 370 [M]	Classics in Jazz	1953	75.00	150.00	300.00
❑ T 1958 [M]	Great Blues Vocal and Guitar	1963	37.50	75.00	150.00
—Black "The Star Line" label (existence of black colorband label not confirmed)					
DELMARK					
❑ D-633 [M]	I Want a Little Girl	1967	10.00	20.00	40.00
❑ DS-633 [S]	I Want a Little Girl	1967	12.50	25.00	50.00
IMPERIAL					
❑ LP-9098 [M]	T-Bone Walker Sings the Blues	1959	75.00	150.00	300.00
❑ LP-9116 [M]	Singing the Blues	1960	62.50	125.00	250.00
❑ LP-9146 [M]	I Get So Weary	1961	75.00	150.00	300.00
MOSAIC					
❑ M9-130 [(9)]	The Complete Recordings of T-Bone Walker 1940-1954	199?	62.50	125.00	250.00
POLYDOR					
❑ 24-4502	Good Feelin'	1972	3.75	7.50	15.00
❑ PD-5521	Fly Walker Airlines	1973	3.75	7.50	15.00
REPRISE					
❑ 2RS 6483 [(2)]	Very Rare	1973	5.00	10.00	20.00
WET SOUL					
❑ 1002	Stormy Monday Blues	1967	12.50	25.00	50.00

WALKER BROTHERS, THE
SMASH

❑ MGS-27076 [M]	Introducing the Walker Brothers	1965	12.50	25.00	50.00
❑ MGS-27082 [M]	The Sun Ain't Gonna Shine (Anymore)	1966	10.00	20.00	40.00
❑ SRS-67076 [R]	Introducing the Walker Brothers	1965	10.00	20.00	40.00
❑ SRS-67082 [P]	The Sun Ain't Gonna Shine (Anymore)	1966	12.50	25.00	50.00
—"The Sun Ain't Gonna Shine (Anymore)" and "When the Lights Go Out" are rechanneled.					

TOWER

Number	Title (A Side/B Side)	Yr	VG	VG+	NM
❑ ST 5026 [S]	I Only Came to Dance with You	1966	5.00	10.00	20.00
—As "Scott Engel and John Stewart"					
❑ T 5026 [M]	I Only Came to Dance with You	1966	3.75	7.50	15.00
—As "Scott Engel and John Stewart"					

WALLACE, GEORGE, JR.
PORTRAIT

❑ JR 36579	Heroes Like You and Me	1981	6.25	12.50	25.00

WALLACE, JERRY
CHALLENGE

❑ CHL 606 [M]	Just Jerry	1959	15.00	30.00	60.00
❑ CH 612 [M]	There She Goes	1961	7.50	15.00	30.00
❑ CHS 612 [S]	There She Goes	1961	10.00	20.00	40.00
❑ CH 616 [M]	Shutters and Boards	1962	7.50	15.00	30.00
❑ CHS 616 [S]	Shutters and Boards	1962	10.00	20.00	40.00
❑ CH 619 [M]	In the Misty Moonlight	1964	5.00	10.00	20.00
❑ CHS 619 [S]	In the Misty Moonlight	1964	6.25	12.50	25.00
❑ 2002	Greatest Hits	1969	3.75	7.50	15.00
DECCA					
❑ DL 75294	This Is Jerry Wallace	1971	3.75	7.50	15.00
❑ DL 75349	To Get to You	1972	3.75	7.50	15.00
LIBERTY					
❑ LRP-3545 [M]	This One's on the House	1967	10.00	20.00	40.00
—Stock copy inside stereo cover; "Audition Mono LP Not for Sale" sticker on front					
❑ LST-7545 [S]	This One's on the House	1967	5.00	10.00	20.00
❑ LST-7564	Another Time, Another World	1968	5.00	10.00	20.00
❑ LST-7597	Sweet Child of Sunshine	1968	5.00	10.00	20.00
MCA					
❑ 301	Do You Know What It's Like to Be Lonesome?	1973	3.00	6.00	12.00
❑ 366	Primrose Lane/Don't Give Up on Me	1973	3.00	6.00	12.00
❑ 408	For Wives and Lovers	1974	3.00	6.00	12.00
❑ 462	I Wonder Whose Baby (You Are Now)/Make Hay While the Sun Shines	1975	3.00	6.00	12.00
MERCURY					
❑ MG-21072 [M]	The Best of Jerry Wallace	1966	3.75	7.50	15.00
❑ SR-61072 [S]	The Best of Jerry Wallace	1966	5.00	10.00	20.00
MGM					
❑ M3G-4990	Greatest Hits	1975	2.50	5.00	10.00
❑ M3G-4995	Comin' Home to You	1976	3.00	6.00	12.00
❑ M3G-5007	Jerry Wallace	1976	2.50	5.00	10.00
SUNSET					
❑ SUS-5294	Primrose Lane	1969	3.00	6.00	12.00
UNITED ARTISTS					
❑ UXS-95 [(2)]	Jerry Wallace Superpak	1972	5.00	10.00	20.00

WALLACE BROTHERS, THE
SIMS

❑ LP-128 [M]	Soul, Soul and More Soul	1965	50.00	100.00	200.00
❑ LPS-128 [S]	Soul, Soul and More Soul	1965	62.50	125.00	250.00

WALLER, FATS
BLUEBIRD

❑ 9983-1-RB [(4)]	The Last Years: Fats Waller and His Rhythm, 1940-1943	198?	7.50	15.00	30.00
RCA VICTOR					
❑ LPT-8 [10]	Fats Waller 1934-42	1951	37.50	75.00	150.00
❑ LPT-14 [10]	Fats Waller Favoites	1951	37.50	75.00	150.00
❑ LPV-473 [M]	The Real Fats Waller	1965	6.25	12.50	25.00
❑ LPV-516 [M]	Fats Waller '34/'35	1965	5.00	10.00	20.00
❑ LPV-525 [M]	Valentine Stomp	1966	5.00	10.00	20.00
❑ LPV-550 [M]	Smashing Thirds	1968	5.00	10.00	20.00
❑ LPV-562 [M]	African Ripples	1969	5.00	10.00	20.00
❑ LPT-1001 [M]	Fats Waller Plays and Sings	1954	20.00	40.00	80.00
❑ LPM-1246 [M]	Ain't Misbehavin'	1956	12.50	25.00	50.00
❑ LPM-1502 [M]	Handful of Keys	1957	12.50	25.00	50.00
❑ LPM-1503 [M]	One Never Knows, Do One?	1959	12.50	25.00	50.00
❑ LPT-3040 [10]	Swingin' the Organ	1953	30.00	60.00	120.00
❑ LPM-6000 [(2)M]	Fats	1960	20.00	40.00	80.00
❑ LPT-6001 [(2)M]	Fats Waller Radio Transcriptions	1954	30.00	60.00	120.00
—Boxed set with booklet					
RIVERSIDE					
❑ RLP 12-103 [M]	The Young Fats Waller	1955	15.00	30.00	60.00
❑ RLP 12-109 [M]	The Amazing Mr. Waller	1955	15.00	30.00	60.00
❑ RLP-1010 [10]	Rediscovered Fats Waller Piano Solos	1953	37.50	75.00	150.00
❑ RLP-1021 [10]	Fats Waller at the Organ	1953	37.50	75.00	150.00
❑ RLP-1022 [10]	Jiving with Fats Waller	1953	37.50	75.00	150.00
"X"					
❑ LVA-3035 [10]	The Young Fats Waller	1955	37.50	75.00	150.00

WALLER, GORDON
ABC

❑ X-749	And Gordon	1972	3.75	7.50	15.00

WALLER, JIM, AND THE DELTAS
ARVEE

❑ A-432 [M]	Surfin' Wild	1963	20.00	40.00	80.00
❑ AS-432 [S]	Surfin' Wild	1963	25.00	50.00	100.00

WALLINGTON, GEORGE
ATLANTIC

❑ 1275 [M]	Knight Music	1958	20.00	40.00	80.00
—Black label					
❑ 1275 [M]	Knight Music	1961	6.25	12.50	25.00
—Multicolor label, white "fan" logo at right					
❑ SD 1275 [S]	Knight Music	1958	20.00	40.00	80.00
—Green label					
❑ SD 1275 [M]	Knight Music	1961	5.00	10.00	20.00
—Multicolor label, white "fan" logo at right					

Number	Title (A Side/B Side)	Yr	VG	VG+	NM
BLUE NOTE					
❑ BLP-5045 [10]	George Wallington and His All-Star Band	1954	100.00	200.00	400.00
EAST-WEST					
❑ 4004 [M]	The Prestidigitator	1958	37.50	75.00	150.00
NEW JAZZ					
❑ NJLP-8207 [M]	The New York Scene	1958	37.50	75.00	150.00
—*Purple label*					
❑ NJLP-8207 [M]	The New York Scene	1965	10.00	20.00	40.00
—*Blue label, trident logo at right*					
NORGRAN					
❑ MGN-24 [10]	The Workshop of the George Wallington Trio	1954	37.50	75.00	150.00
❑ MGN-1010 [M]	George Wallington with Strings	1954	25.00	50.00	100.00
PRESTIGE					
❑ PRLP-136 [10]	The George Wallington Trio	1952	62.50	125.00	250.00
❑ PRLP-158 [10]	The George Wallington Trio, Volume 2	1953	62.50	125.00	250.00
❑ PRLP-7032 [M]	Jazz for the Carriage Trade	1956	125.00	250.00	500.00
❑ PRST-7587 [R]	The George Wallington Trios	1968	5.00	10.00	20.00
PROGRESSIVE					
❑ PLP-1001 [M]	George Wallington Quintet at the Bohemia	1955	250.00	500.00	1000.
❑ 3001 [10]	The George Wallington Trio	1952	62.50	125.00	250.00
SAVOY					
❑ MG-12081 [M]	The George Wallington Trio	1956	20.00	40.00	80.00
❑ MG-12122 [M]	Jazz at Hotchkiss	1957	20.00	40.00	80.00
❑ MG-15037 [10]	The George Wallington Trio	1954	25.00	50.00	100.00
VERVE					
❑ MGV-2017 [M]	Variations	1956	20.00	40.00	80.00
WALLIS, RUTH					
KING					
❑ 265-6 [10]	Rhumba Party	1952	30.00	60.00	120.00
❑ 265-9 [10]	House Party	1952	30.00	60.00	120.00
❑ 395-507 [M]	House Party	1956	25.00	50.00	100.00
❑ 904 [M]	Saucy Hit Parade	1964	7.50	15.00	30.00
❑ 986 [M]	Here's Looking Up Your Hatch	1966	7.50	15.00	30.00
❑ 987 [M]	Davy's Little Dinghy	1966	7.50	15.00	30.00
❑ 988 [M]	Marry Go Round	1966	7.50	15.00	30.00
❑ 989 [M]	Red Lights	1966	7.50	15.00	30.00
❑ 990 [M]	Ubangi Me	1966	7.50	15.00	30.00
❑ 991 [M]	Oil Man from Texas	1966	7.50	15.00	30.00
❑ 992 [M]	He Wants a Little…Pizza	1966	7.50	15.00	30.00
❑ 993 [M]	Bahama Mama	1966	7.50	15.00	30.00
WALLIS ORIGINAL					
❑ 2 [M]	Ruth Wallis	1957	10.00	20.00	40.00
WALSH, JOE					
Also see EAGLES; THE JAMES GANG (1).					
ABC					
❑ ABCD-932	You Can't Argue with a Sick Mind	1976	2.50	5.00	10.00
❑ AA-1083	The Best of Joe Walsh	1978	2.50	5.00	10.00
—*Also contains two James Gang tracks*					
ABC COMMAND					
❑ QD-40016 [Q]	The Smoker You Drink, the Player You Get	1974	5.00	10.00	20.00
❑ QD-40017 [Q]	So What	1975	5.00	10.00	20.00
ABC DUNHILL					
❑ DS-50130	Barnstorm	1972	2.50	5.00	10.00
—*Of the James Gang and the Eagles*					
❑ DS-50140	The Smoker You Drink, the Player You Get	1973	2.50	5.00	10.00
❑ DS-51071	So What	1974	2.50	5.00	10.00
ASYLUM					
❑ 6E-141	But Seriously, Folks…	1978	2.50	5.00	10.00
❑ 5E-523	There Goes the Neighborhood	1981	2.00	4.00	8.00
MCA					
❑ 37051	You Can't Argue with a Sick Mind	1979	2.00	4.00	8.00
—*Reissue of ABC 932*					
❑ 37052	The Best of Joe Walsh	1979	2.00	4.00	8.00
—*Reissue of ABC 1083*					
❑ 37053	Barnstorm	1979	2.00	4.00	8.00
—*Reissue of ABC Dunhill 50130*					
❑ 37054	The Smoker You Drink, the Player You Get	1979	2.00	4.00	8.00
—*Reissue of ABC Dunhill 50140*					
❑ 37055	So What	1979	2.00	4.00	8.00
—*Reissue of ABC Dunhill 50171*					
WARNER BROS.					
❑ 23884	You Bought It — You Name It	1983	2.00	4.00	8.00
❑ 25281	The Confessor	1985	2.00	4.00	8.00
❑ 25281 [DJ]	The Confessor	1985	3.75	7.50	15.00
—*Promo only on Quiex II vinyl*					
❑ 25606	Got Any Gum?	1987	2.00	4.00	8.00
WALSTON, RAY					
VEE JAY					
❑ LP-1110 [M]	My Favorite Songs from "Mary Poppins" and Other Songs to Delight	1965	6.25	12.50	25.00
❑ SR-1110 [S]	My Favorite Songs from "Mary Poppins" and Other Songs to Delight	1965	7.50	15.00	30.00
WALT, SHERMAN					
RCA VICTOR RED SEAL					
❑ LSC-2353 [S]	Vivaldi: The Four Seasons Concertos	1960	6.25	12.50	25.00
—*Original with "shaded dog" label*					
WALTER, CY					
ATLANTIC					
❑ 1236 [M]	Rodgers Revisited	1956	10.00	20.00	40.00
—*Black label*					
❑ 1236 [M]	Rodgers Revisited	1961	5.00	10.00	20.00
—*Multicolor label, white "fan" logo at right*					
WESTMINSTER					
❑ WP-6120 [M]	Dry Martini, Please	195?	6.25	12.50	25.00
❑ WST-15054 [S]	Dry Martini, Please	195?	7.50	15.00	30.00

Number	Title (A Side/B Side)	Yr	VG	VG+	NM
WALTON, CEDAR					
PRESTIGE					
❑ PRLP-7519 [M]	Cedar!	1967	6.25	12.50	25.00
❑ PRST-7519 [S]	Cedar!	1967	5.00	10.00	20.00
❑ PRST-7591	Spectrum	1968	5.00	10.00	20.00
❑ PRST-7618	The Electric Boogaloo Song	1969	5.00	10.00	20.00
❑ PRST-7693	Soul Cycle	1970	5.00	10.00	20.00
RCA VICTOR					
❑ APL1-1009	Mobius	1975	5.00	10.00	20.00
❑ APL1-1435	Beyond Mobius	1976	5.00	10.00	20.00
WALTON, MERCY DEE					
See MERCY DEE.					
WALTON, WADE					
BLUESVILLE					
❑ BVLP-1060 [M]	Shake 'Em on Down	1963	25.00	50.00	100.00
—*Blue label, silver print*					
❑ BVLP-1060 [M]	Shake 'Em on Down	1964	7.50	15.00	30.00
—*Blue label, trident logo at right*					
WALTONS, THE					
See VARIOUS ARTISTS COMPILATIONS in back.					
WANDERERS THREE, THE					
DOLTON					
❑ BLP 2021 [M]	We Sing Folk Songs	1963	5.00	10.00	20.00
❑ BST 8021 [S]	We Sing Folk Songs	1963	6.25	12.50	25.00
WANDERLEY, WALTER					
MGM LATINO SERIES					
❑ LAT 10010 [S]	Cheganca	197?	3.75	7.50	15.00
—*Reissue of Verve V6-8676*					
VERVE					
❑ V6-8658 [S]	Rain Forest	1966	5.00	10.00	20.00
❑ V6-8676 [S]	Cheganca	1966	5.00	10.00	20.00
❑ V-8706 [M]	Batucada	1967	5.00	10.00	20.00
❑ V-8739 [M]	Kee-Ka-Roo	1967	5.00	10.00	20.00
WORLD PACIFIC					
❑ WP-1856 [M]	Samba So!	1967	5.00	10.00	20.00
❑ WP-1866 [M]	Quarteto Bossamba	1967	6.25	12.50	25.00
WAR					
Also see ERIC BURDON AND WAR.					
AVENUE					
❑ R1 71706	Peace Sign	1994	3.75	7.50	15.00
BLUE NOTE					
❑ BN-LA690-G [(2)]	Platinum Jazz	1977	3.00	6.00	12.00
LAX					
❑ PW 37111	All Day Music	1981	2.50	5.00	10.00
—*Reissue of United Artists 5546*					
❑ PW 37112	The World Is a Ghetto	1981	2.50	5.00	10.00
—*Reissue of United Artists 5652*					
❑ PW 37113	Why Can't We Be Friends?	1981	2.50	5.00	10.00
—*Reissue of United Artists 441*					
MCA					
❑ 745	Galaxy	1983	2.00	4.00	8.00
—*Reissue of MCA 3030*					
❑ 747	The Music Band	1983	2.00	4.00	8.00
—*Reissue of MCA 3085*					
❑ 751	The Music Band 2	1983	2.00	4.00	8.00
—*Reissue of MCA 3193*					
❑ 3030	Galaxy	1977	2.50	5.00	10.00
❑ 3085	The Music Band.	1979	2.50	5.00	10.00
❑ 3193	The Music Band 2.	1979	2.50	5.00	10.00
❑ 5156	The Music Band Live.	1980	2.50	5.00	10.00
❑ 5362	Best of the Music Band.	1982	2.50	5.00	10.00
❑ 5411	Music Band Jazz.	1983	2.50	5.00	10.00
PRIORITY					
❑ SL 9467	The Best of War…And More	1987	2.50	5.00	10.00
RCA VICTOR					
❑ AFL1-4208	Outlaw	1982	2.50	5.00	10.00
❑ AFL1-4598	Life (Is So Strange)	1983	2.50	5.00	10.00
UNITED ARTISTS					
❑ SP-103 [DJ]	Radio Free War	1974	6.25	12.50	25.00
—*Promo only on blue vinyl*					
❑ UA-LA128-F	Deliver the Word	1973	3.00	6.00	12.00
❑ UA-LA193-J [(2)]	War Live!	1974	3.75	7.50	15.00
❑ UA-LA441-G	Why Can't We Be Friends?	1975	2.50	5.00	10.00
❑ UA-LA648-G	Greatest Hits	1976	2.50	5.00	10.00
❑ UAS-5508	War	1971	3.75	7.50	15.00
❑ UAS-5546	All Day Music	1971	3.75	7.50	15.00
❑ UAS-5652	The World Is a Ghetto	1972	3.00	6.00	12.00
WARD, ALAN					
RCA VICTOR RED SEAL					
❑ LSC-2302 [S]	Gilbert and Sullivan Overtures	1959	5.00	10.00	20.00
—*Original with "shaded dog" label*					
WARD, BILLY, AND THE DOMINOES					
DECCA					
❑ DL 8621 [M]	Billy Ward and the Dominoes	1958	50.00	100.00	200.00
FEDERAL					
❑ 295-94 [10]	Billy Ward and His Dominoes	1955	6000.	9500.	13000.
❑ 548 [M]	Billy Ward and His Dominoes	1958	375.00	750.00	1500.
❑ 559 [M]	Clyde McPhatter with Billy Ward and His Dominoes	1958	300.00	600.00	1200.
KING					
❑ 548 [M]	Billy Ward and His Dominoes	1958	—	—	—
—*Unknown*					
❑ 559 [M]	Clyde McPhatter with Billy Ward and His Dominoes	1958	150.00	300.00	600.00
—*Yellow cover*					

Number	Title (A Side/B Side)	Yr	VG	VG+	NM
❑ 559 [M]	Clyde McPhatter with Billy Ward and His Dominoes	196?	75.00	150.00	300.00
—Pink cover					
❑ 733 [M]	Billy Ward and His Dominoes Featuring Clyde McPhatter and Jackie Wilson	1961	150.00	300.00	600.00
❑ 952 [M]	24 Songs	1966	12.50	25.00	50.00
❑ 5005	14 Hits	197?	3.00	6.00	12.00
❑ 5008	21 Hits	197?	3.00	6.00	12.00

LIBERTY

Number	Title (A Side/B Side)	Yr	VG	VG+	NM
❑ LRP-3056 [M]	Sea of Glass	1957	15.00	30.00	60.00
❑ LRP-3083 [M]	Yours Forever	1958	15.00	30.00	60.00
❑ LRP-3113 [M]	Pagan Love Song	1959	15.00	30.00	60.00
❑ LST-7113 [S]	Pagan Love Song	1959	25.00	50.00	100.00

WARD, HELEN
COLUMBIA

Number	Title (A Side/B Side)	Yr	VG	VG+	NM
❑ CL-6271 [10]	It's Been So Long	1954	12.50	25.00	50.00

PAX

❑ 6004 [10]	Wild Bill Davison with Helen Ward	1954	15.00	30.00	60.00

WARD, ROBIN
DOT

Number	Title (A Side/B Side)	Yr	VG	VG+	NM
❑ DLP 3555 [M]	Wonderful Summer	1963	50.00	100.00	200.00
❑ DLP 25555 [S]	Wonderful Summer	1963	75.00	150.00	300.00

WARDELL, ROOSEVELT
RIVERSIDE

Number	Title (A Side/B Side)	Yr	VG	VG+	NM
❑ RLP-350 [M]	The Revelation	1960	6.25	12.50	25.00
❑ RS-9350 [S]	The Revelation	1960	7.50	15.00	30.00

WARE, WILBUR
RIVERSIDE

Number	Title (A Side/B Side)	Yr	VG	VG+	NM
❑ RLP 12-252 [M]	The Chicago Sound	1957	20.00	40.00	80.00

WARFIELD, WILLIAM
COLUMBIA MASTERWORKS

Number	Title (A Side/B Side)	Yr	VG	VG+	NM
❑ ML 2206 [M]	Old American Songs and Five Sea Chanties	195?	12.50	25.00	50.00

WARINER, STEVE
ARISTA

Number	Title (A Side/B Side)	Yr	VG	VG+	NM
❑ AL 8691	I Am Ready	1992	5.00	10.00	20.00
—Vinyl version available only from Columbia House					

MCA

❑ 5545	One Good Night Deserves Another	1985	2.00	4.00	8.00
❑ 5672	Life's Highway	1985	2.00	4.00	8.00
❑ 5926	It's a Crazy World	1987	2.00	4.00	8.00
❑ 42032	Greatest Hits	1987	2.00	4.00	8.00
❑ 42130	I Should Be with You	1988	2.00	4.00	8.00
❑ 42272	I Got Dreams	1989	2.50	5.00	10.00

RCA VICTOR

❑ AHL1-4154	Steve Wariner	1982	2.50	5.00	10.00
❑ AHL1-4859	Midnight Fire	1983	2.50	5.00	10.00
❑ AHL1-5326	Greatest Hits	1985	2.00	4.00	8.00
❑ AYL1-5440	Steve Wariner	1985	2.00	4.00	8.00
—"Best Buy Series" reissue					
❑ AHL1-7164	Down in Tennessee	1986	2.00	4.00	8.00

WARING, FRED, AND THE PENNSYLVANIANS
CAPITOL

Number	Title (A Side/B Side)	Yr	VG	VG+	NM
❑ STBB-347 [(2)]	Christmas Magic	1969	3.75	7.50	15.00
—Collects ST 1260 and ST 1610 in one package (abridged); green label original					
❑ STBB-347 [(2)]	Christmas Magic	1972	3.00	6.00	12.00
—Orange label reissue					
❑ ST 896 [S]	Now Is the Caroling Season	1959	3.75	7.50	15.00
—Black colorband label, logo at left					
❑ ST 896 [S]	Now Is the Caroling Season	1962	3.00	6.00	12.00
—Black colorband label, logo at top					
❑ T 896 [M]	Now Is the Caroling Season	1957	5.00	10.00	20.00
—Originals have turquoise labels					
❑ T 896 [M]	Now Is the Caroling Season	1959	3.75	7.50	15.00
—Black colorband label, logo at left					
❑ T 896 [M]	Now Is the Caroling Season	1962	3.00	6.00	12.00
—Black colorband label, logo at top					
❑ ST 936 [S]	All Through the Night	1958	5.00	10.00	20.00
❑ T 936 [M]	All Through the Night	1958	5.00	10.00	20.00
—Black colorband label, logo at left					
❑ ST 1260 [S]	The Sounds of Christmas	1959	5.00	10.00	20.00
—Originals have black label with colorband and "Capitol" logo at 9 o'clock					
❑ T 1260 [M]	The Sounds of Christmas	1959	3.75	7.50	15.00
—Black colorband label, logo at left					
❑ SM-1610	The Meaning of Christmas	197?	2.00	4.00	8.00
—Reissue of ST 1610 with same contents					
❑ ST 1610 [S]	The Meaning of Christmas	1961	5.00	10.00	20.00
❑ T 1610 [M]	The Meaning of Christmas	1961	3.75	7.50	15.00
❑ ST 2054 [S]	This I Believe	1964	3.75	7.50	15.00
❑ T 2054 [M]	This I Believe	1964	3.00	6.00	12.00
❑ ST 2625 [S]	The Best of Fred Waring and the Pennsylvanians	1967	3.75	7.50	15.00
❑ T 2625 [M]	The Best of Fred Waring and the Pennsylvanians	1967	3.00	6.00	12.00

CAPITOL CREATIVE PRODUCTS

❑ L-6550 [M]	Fred Waring and the Pennsylvanians Sing of Faith, Home and Christmas	1967	3.75	7.50	15.00
—Compiled for the E.F. MacDonald Company, Dayton, Ohio					

CAPITOL PICKWICK SERIES

❑ PC-3451 [M]	The Romantic Sound	196?	2.50	5.00	10.00
❑ SPC-3451 [S]	The Romantic Sound	196?	3.00	6.00	12.00
❑ PC-3454 [M]	Some Enchanted Evening	196?	2.50	5.00	10.00
❑ SPC-3454 [S]	Some Enchanted Evening	196?	3.00	6.00	12.00

DECCA

❑ DBX 186 [(2)M]	The Best of Fred Waring	1965	3.75	7.50	15.00
❑ DL 4158 [M]	This Is My Country	1961	3.00	6.00	12.00

Number	Title (A Side/B Side)	Yr	VG	VG+	NM
❑ DL 4234 [M]	Songs of Faith	1962	3.00	6.00	12.00
❑ DL 4345 [M]	God's Trombones	1962	3.00	6.00	12.00
❑ DL 4511 [M]	Song of Easter	1965	2.50	5.00	10.00
❑ DL 4753 [M]	Fred Waring Showcase	1966	2.50	5.00	10.00
❑ DL 4759 [M]	Magic Music	1966	2.50	5.00	10.00
❑ DL 4809 [M]	A-Caroling We Go	1966	3.00	6.00	12.00
❑ DL 4875 [M]	Barbershop Sing	1967	3.00	6.00	12.00
❑ DLP 5004 [10]	Jerome Kern Songs	1950	12.50	25.00	50.00
❑ DLP 5005 [10]	Cole Porter Songs	1950	12.50	25.00	50.00
❑ DLP 5009 [10]	Selections from Miss Liberty	1950	12.50	25.00	50.00
❑ DLP 5021 [10]	'Twas the Night Before Christmas	1950	12.50	25.00	50.00
❑ DLP 5036 [10]	Pleasure Time	1951	10.00	20.00	40.00
❑ DL 5061 [10]	Songs of Devotion, Vol. 1	1950	10.00	20.00	40.00
❑ DL 5062 [10]	Songs of Devotion, Vol. 2	1950	10.00	20.00	40.00
❑ DL 5141 [10]	This Is My Country	1950	10.00	20.00	40.00
❑ DL 5202 [10]	Columbia, the Gem of the Ocean (Patriotic and Service Songs)	1950	10.00	20.00	40.00
❑ DL 5292 [10]	Richard Rodgers and Oscar Hammerstein II Songs, Vol. 1	1950	10.00	20.00	40.00
❑ DL 5293 [10]	Richard Rodgers and Oscar Hammerstein II Songs, Vol. 2	1950	10.00	20.00	40.00
❑ DL 5295 [10]	Christmas Time	1950	10.00	20.00	40.00
❑ DXSB 7186 [(2)S]	The Best of Fred Waring	1965	3.75	7.50	15.00
❑ DL 8005 [M]	Listening Time	1950	10.00	20.00	40.00
❑ DL 8026 [M]	Program Time	1950	7.50	15.00	30.00
❑ DL 8033 [M]	Song of America	195?	10.00	20.00	40.00
❑ DL 8039 [M]	Songs of Faith, Vols. 1 and 2	195?	7.50	15.00	30.00
❑ DL 8047 [M]	God's Trombones and Other Spirituals	195?	7.50	15.00	30.00
❑ DL 8082 [M]	For Listening Only	1954	6.25	12.50	25.00
❑ DL 8084 [M]	Song of Christmas	1954	6.25	12.50	25.00
❑ DL 8110 [M]	Lullaby Time	1955	5.00	10.00	20.00
❑ DL 8111 [M]	Songs in Reverence	1955	5.00	10.00	20.00
❑ DL 8171 [M]	'Twas the Night Before Christmas	1955	5.00	10.00	20.00
❑ DL 8172 [M]	Christmas Time	1955	5.00	10.00	20.00
❑ DL 8222 [M]	College Memories	1956	3.75	7.50	15.00
❑ DL 8335 [M]	Harmonizin' the Old Songs	1956	3.75	7.50	15.00
❑ DL 8670 [M]	Songs of Devotion	1958	3.75	7.50	15.00
❑ DL 8708 [M]	Excerpts from Carousel and Oklahoma	1958	3.75	7.50	15.00
❑ DL 8709 [M]	Songs of Inspiration	1958	3.75	7.50	15.00
❑ DL 8710 [M]	Stars and Stripes Forever	1958	3.75	7.50	15.00
❑ DL 8829	Memorable Moments from Broadway Musicals	1959	3.75	7.50	15.00
❑ DL 9031 [M]	Hear, Hear	195?	3.75	7.50	15.00
❑ DL 74158 [S]	This Is My Country	1961	3.75	7.50	15.00
❑ DL 74234 [S]	Songs of Faith	1962	3.75	7.50	15.00
❑ DL 74345 [S]	God's Trombones	1962	3.75	7.50	15.00
❑ DL 74511 [S]	Song of Easter	1965	3.00	6.00	12.00
❑ DL 74753 [S]	Fred Waring Showcase	1966	3.00	6.00	12.00
❑ DL 74759 [S]	Magic Music	1966	3.00	6.00	12.00
❑ DL 74809 [S]	A-Caroling We Go	1966	3.75	7.50	15.00
❑ DL 74875 [S]	Barbershop Sing	1967	3.00	6.00	12.00
❑ DL 75007	Two Sides of Fred Waring and the Pennsylvanians	1968	3.00	6.00	12.00
❑ DL 78171 [R]	'Twas the Night Before Christmas	196?	3.00	6.00	12.00
❑ DL 78172 [R]	Christmas Time	196?	3.00	6.00	12.00

HARMONY

❑ HS 11363	In Concert	1970	2.50	5.00	10.00

MCA

❑ 193	This Is My Country	1973	2.00	4.00	8.00
—Reissue of Decca 74158					
❑ 207	God's Trombones	1973	2.00	4.00	8.00
—Reissue of Decca 74345					
❑ 4008 [(2)]	The Best of Fred Waring and the Pennsylvanians	197?	3.00	6.00	12.00
—Reissue of Decca 7186					
❑ 15009	A-Caroling We Go	1973	2.50	5.00	10.00
—Reissue of DL 74809; black label with rainbow					
❑ 15009	A-Caroling We Go	1980	2.00	4.00	8.00
—Blue label with rainbow					
❑ 15011	Christmas Time	1973	2.50	5.00	10.00
—Reissue of DL 78172; black label with rainbow					
❑ 15011	Christmas Time	1980	2.00	4.00	8.00
—Blue label with rainbow					
❑ 15016	'Twas the Night Before Christmas	1973	2.50	5.00	10.00
—Reissue of DL 78171; black label with rainbow					
❑ 15016	'Twas the Night Before Christmas	1980	2.00	4.00	8.00
—Blue label with rainbow					

MEGA

❑ 31-1005	Nashville	1971	2.50	5.00	10.00

REPRISE

❑ R 6137 [M]	To You...Forever	1964	3.00	6.00	12.00
❑ RS 6137 [S]	To You...Forever	1964	3.75	7.50	15.00
❑ R 6148 [M]	Fred Waring and the Pennsylvanians in Concert	1964	3.00	6.00	12.00
❑ RS 6148 [S]	Fred Waring and the Pennsylvanians in Concert	1964	3.75	7.50	15.00

STASH

❑ 126	Memorial Album	1985	2.50	5.00	10.00

WARNES, JENNIFER
Includes records as "Jennifer."
ARISTA

Number	Title (A Side/B Side)	Yr	VG	VG+	NM
❑ AL 4062	Jennifer Warnes	1977	2.50	5.00	10.00
❑ AB 4217	Shot Through the Heart	1979	2.50	5.00	10.00
❑ AL 9560	The Best of Jennifer Warnes	1982	2.00	4.00	8.00

CYPRESS

❑ 661111-1	Famous Blue Raincoat	1987	7.50	15.00	30.00

PARROT

❑ PAS-71020	I Can Remember Anything	1968	5.00	10.00	20.00
—As "Jennifer"					
❑ PAS-71034	See Me	1970	5.00	10.00	20.00
—As "Jennifer"					

Number	Title (A Side/B Side)	Yr	VG	VG+	NM
ROCK THE HOUSE					
❑ RTH 5052	Famous Blue Raincoat	1996	12.50	25.00	50.00
—Classic Records reissue					
WARREN, FRAN					
MGM					
❑ E-3394 [M]	Mood Indigo	1956	12.50	25.00	50.00
—Yellow label					
TOPS					
❑ L-1585 [M]	Hey There	195?	5.00	10.00	20.00
VENISE					
❑ 7019 [M]	Come Rain or Come Shine	195?	6.25	12.50	25.00
❑ 10019 [S]	Come Rain or Come Shine	195?	12.50	25.00	50.00
WARWICK					
❑ W-2012 [M]	Something's Coming	1960	6.25	12.50	25.00
WARREN, RUSTY					
GNP CRESCENDO					
❑ 2079 [(2)]	Knockers Up!/Songs for Sinners	1975	3.75	7.50	15.00
❑ 2080 [(2)]	Rusty Warren Bounces Back/Sin-Sational	1975	3.75	7.50	15.00
❑ 2081	Rusty Warren Lays It on the Line	1975	3.00	6.00	12.00
❑ 2088	Knockers Up! '76	1976	3.00	6.00	12.00
❑ 2103	Bottoms Up!	1976	3.00	6.00	12.00
❑ 2114	Sexplosion	1977	3.00	6.00	12.00
JUBILEE					
❑ JLP 2024 [M]	Songs for Sinners	1960	6.25	12.50	25.00
❑ JLP 2029 [M]	Knockers Up!	1960	6.25	12.50	25.00
❑ JLP 2034 [M]	Sin-Sational	1961	6.25	12.50	25.00
❑ JGM 2039 [M]	Rusty Warren Bounces Back	1961	6.25	12.50	25.00
❑ JGM 2044 [M]	Rusty Warren in Orbit	1962	6.25	12.50	25.00
❑ JLP 2049 [M]	Banned in Boston?	1963	6.25	12.50	25.00
❑ JLP 2054 [M]	Sex-X-Ponent	1964	6.25	12.50	25.00
❑ JLP 2059 [M]	More Knockers Up!	1965	6.25	12.50	25.00
❑ JGM 2069 [M]	Bottoms Up!	1967	5.00	10.00	20.00
❑ JGM 2074	Look What I've Got for You	1967	5.00	10.00	20.00
❑ JLP 5025 [M]	Portrait of Life	196?	5.00	10.00	20.00
❑ JLPS 5025 [S]	Portrait of Life	196?	5.00	10.00	20.00
WARWICK, DEE DEE					
ATCO					
❑ SD 33-337	Turnin' Around	1970	6.25	12.50	25.00
MERCURY					
❑ MG-21100 [M]	I Want to Be with You	1967	6.25	12.50	25.00
❑ SR-61100 [S]	I Want to Be with You	1967	6.25	12.50	25.00
❑ SR-61221	Foolish Fool	1968	6.25	12.50	25.00
WARWICK, DIONNE					
ARISTA					
❑ AB 4230	Dionne	1979	2.50	5.00	10.00
❑ AL 8104	How Many Times Can We Say Goodbye	1983	2.50	5.00	10.00
❑ A2L 8111 [(2)]	Hot! Live and Otherwise	1983	2.50	5.00	10.00
—Budget-line reissue					
❑ AL 8262	Finder of Lost Loves	1985	2.50	5.00	10.00
❑ AL 8295	Dionne	1985	2.00	4.00	8.00
—Budget-line reissue					
❑ AL 8338	Heartbreaker	1985	2.00	4.00	8.00
—Budget-line reissue					
❑ AL 8358	Friends in Love	1985	2.00	4.00	8.00
—Budget-line reissue					
❑ AL 8398	Friends	1985	2.50	5.00	10.00
❑ AL 8446	Reservations for Two	1987	2.50	5.00	10.00
❑ AL 8540	Greatest Hits 1979-1990	1989	3.00	6.00	12.00
❑ AL 8573	Dionne Warwick Sings Cole Porter	1990	3.00	6.00	12.00
❑ A2L 8605 [(2)]	Hot! Live and Otherwise	1981	3.00	6.00	12.00
❑ AL 9526	No Night So Long	1980	2.50	5.00	10.00
❑ AL 9585	Friends in Love	1982	2.50	5.00	10.00
❑ AL 9609	Heartbreaker	1982	2.50	5.00	10.00
EVEREST					
❑ 4103	Dionne Warwick	1981	2.50	5.00	10.00
MOBILE FIDELITY					
❑ 2-098 [(2)]	Hot! Live and Otherwise	1982	7.50	15.00	30.00
—Audiophile vinyl					
MUSICOR					
❑ 2501	Only Love Can Break a Heart	1977	3.00	6.00	12.00
PAIR					
❑ PDL2-1043 [(2)]	The Dynamic Dionne Warwick	1986	3.00	6.00	12.00
❑ PDL2-1098 [(2)]	Masterpieces	1986	3.00	6.00	12.00
PICKWICK					
❑ PTP-2056 [(2)]	Alfie	1973	3.00	6.00	12.00
—As "Dionne Warwicke"					
RHINO					
❑ RNDA-1100 [(2)]	Anthology 1962-1971	1985	3.75	7.50	15.00
SCEPTER					
❑ S-508 [M]	Presenting Dionne Warwick	1963	3.75	7.50	15.00
❑ SS-508 [S]	Presenting Dionne Warwick	1963	5.00	10.00	20.00
❑ S-517 [M]	Anyone Who Had a Heart	1964	3.75	7.50	15.00
❑ SS-517 [S]	Anyone Who Had a Heart	1964	5.00	10.00	20.00
❑ LP-523 [M]	Make Way for Dionne Warwick	1964	3.75	7.50	15.00
❑ SPS-523 [S]	Make Way for Dionne Warwick	1964	5.00	10.00	20.00
❑ LP-528 [M]	The Sensitive Sound of Dionne Warwick	1965	3.75	7.50	15.00
❑ SPS-528 [S]	The Sensitive Sound of Dionne Warwick	1965	5.00	10.00	20.00
❑ SPS-531 [S]	Here I Am	1965	5.00	10.00	20.00
❑ SRM-531 [M]	Here I Am	1965	3.75	7.50	15.00
❑ SPS-534 [S]	Dionne Warwick in Paris	1966	3.75	7.50	15.00
❑ SRM-534 [M]	Dionne Warwick in Paris	1966	3.00	6.00	12.00
❑ SPS-555 [S]	Here Where There Is Love	1966	3.75	7.50	15.00
❑ SRM-555 [M]	Here Where There Is Love	1966	3.00	6.00	12.00
❑ SPS-559 [S]	On Stage and in the Movies	1967	3.75	7.50	15.00
❑ SRM-559 [M]	On Stage and in the Movies	1967	3.00	6.00	12.00
❑ SPS-563 [S]	The Windows of the World	1967	3.75	7.50	15.00

Number	Title (A Side/B Side)	Yr	VG	VG+	NM
❑ SRM-563 [M]	The Windows of the World	1967	3.00	6.00	12.00
❑ SPS-565 [S]	Dionne Warwick's Golden Hits, Part One	1967	3.75	7.50	15.00
❑ SRM-565 [M]	Dionne Warwick's Golden Hits, Part One	1967	5.00	10.00	20.00
❑ SPS-567 [S]	The Magic of Believing	1968	5.00	10.00	20.00
❑ SRM-567 [M]	The Magic of Believing	1968	7.50	15.00	30.00
❑ SPS-568 [S]	Valley of the Dolls	1968	3.75	7.50	15.00
❑ SRM-568 [M]	Valley of the Dolls	1968	12.50	25.00	50.00
—May only exist as a white label promo					
❑ SPS-571	Promises, Promises	1968	3.75	7.50	15.00
❑ SPS-573	Soulful	1969	3.75	7.50	15.00
❑ SPS-575	Dionne Warwick's Greatest Motion Picture Hits	1969	3.75	7.50	15.00
❑ SPS-577	Dionne Warwick's Golden Hits, Part 2	1969	3.75	7.50	15.00
❑ SPS-581	I'll Never Fall in Love Again	1970	3.75	7.50	15.00
❑ SPS-587	Very Dionne	1970	3.75	7.50	15.00
❑ SPS 2-596 [(2)]	The Dionne Warwicke Story	1971	5.00	10.00	20.00
—As "Dionne Warwicke"					
❑ SPS-598 [(2)]	From Within	1972	5.00	10.00	20.00
—As "Dionne Warwicke"					
SPRINGBOARD					
❑ SPS-4001	The Golden Voice of Dionne Warwicke	1972	2.50	5.00	10.00
—As "Dionne Warwicke"					
❑ SPS-4002	Dionne Warwicke Sings Her Very Best	1972	2.50	5.00	10.00
—As "Dionne Warwicke"					
❑ SPS-4003	One Hit After Another	1972	2.50	5.00	10.00
—As "Dionne Warwicke"					
❑ SPS-4032	Greatest Hits, Vol. 2	197?	2.50	5.00	10.00
UNITED ARTISTS					
❑ UA-LA337-G	The Very Best of Dionne Warwicke	1974	3.00	6.00	12.00
—As "Dionne Warwicke"					
WARNER BROS.					
❑ BS 2585	Dionne	1971	3.00	6.00	12.00
—As "Dionne Warwicke"					
❑ BS 2658	Just Being Myself	1973	3.00	6.00	12.00
—As "Dionne Warwicke"					
❑ BS 2846	Then Came You	1975	3.00	6.00	12.00
—As "Dionne Warwicke"					
❑ BS4 2846 [Q]	Then Came You	1975	5.00	10.00	20.00
—As "Dionne Warwicke"					
❑ BS 2893	Track of the Cat	1975	3.00	6.00	12.00
❑ BS 3119	Love at First Sight	1976	3.00	6.00	12.00
WASHBOARD SAM					
RCA VICTOR					
❑ LPV-577 [M]	Feeling Lowdown	196?	6.25	12.50	25.00
WASHINGTON, BABY					
AVI					
❑ 6038	I Wanna Dance	1978	2.50	5.00	10.00
COLLECTABLES					
❑ COL-5040	The Best of Baby Washington	198?	2.50	5.00	10.00
❑ COL-5108	Only Those in Love	198?	2.50	5.00	10.00
❑ COL-5124	That's How Heartaches Are Made	198?	2.50	5.00	10.00
SUE					
❑ LP-1014 [M]	That's How Heartaches Are Made	1963	37.50	75.00	150.00
❑ LP-1042 [M]	Only Those in Love	1965	37.50	75.00	150.00
❑ LPS-1042 [S]	Only Those in Love	1965	75.00	150.00	300.00
TRIP					
❑ 8009	The One and Only Baby Washington	1971	3.75	7.50	15.00
VEEP					
❑ VPS-16528	With You in Mind	1968	6.25	12.50	25.00
WASHINGTON, DINAH					
ACCORD					
❑ SN-7207	Retrospective	1982	2.50	5.00	10.00
ARCHIVE OF FOLK AND JAZZ					
❑ 297	Dinah Washington	197?	3.00	6.00	12.00
COLLECTABLES					
❑ COL-5200	Golden Classics	1989	2.50	5.00	10.00
DELMARK					
❑ DL-451	Mellow Mama	1992	5.00	10.00	20.00
EMARCY					
❑ EMS-2-401 [(2)]	Jazz Sides	197?	3.75	7.50	15.00
❑ MG-26032 [10]	After Hours with Miss D	1954	30.00	60.00	120.00
❑ MG-36000 [M]	Dinah Jams	1955	12.50	25.00	50.00
❑ MG-36011 [M]	For Those in Love	1955	12.50	25.00	50.00
❑ MG-36028 [M]	After Hours with Miss D	1955	12.50	25.00	50.00
—Reissue of 26032					
❑ MG-36065 [M]	Dinah	1956	12.50	25.00	50.00
❑ MG-36073 [M]	In the Land of Hi-Fi	1956	12.50	25.00	50.00
❑ MG-36104 [M]	The Swingin' Miss "D"	1956	12.50	25.00	50.00
❑ MG-36119 [M]	Dinah Washington Sings Fats Waller	1957	12.50	25.00	50.00
❑ MG-36130 [M]	Dinah Washington Sings Bessie Smith	1957	12.50	25.00	50.00
❑ MG-36141 [M]	Newport '58	1958	10.00	20.00	40.00
❑ 814184-1 [(2)]	Slick Chick (On the Mellow Side)	1983	3.00	6.00	12.00
❑ 824883-1 [(2)]	Jazz Sides	198?	3.00	6.00	12.00
—Reissue of 401					
❑ 826453-1	In the Land of Hi-Fi	1986	2.50	5.00	10.00
GRAND AWARD					
❑ GA 33-318 [M]	Dinah Washington Sings the Blues	1955	12.50	25.00	50.00
—Add 50% if removable wrap-around cover is still there					
HARLEM HIT PARADE					
❑ 8002	Finer Dinah	197?	2.50	5.00	10.00
MERCURY					
❑ MGP-2-103 [(2)M]	This Is My Story	1963	6.25	12.50	25.00
—Combines 20788 and 20789 in one package					
❑ MGP-2-603 [(2)S]	This Is My Story	1963	7.50	15.00	30.00
—Combines 60788 and 60789 in one package					
❑ MG-20119 [M]	Music for a First Love	1957	12.50	25.00	50.00
❑ MG-20120 [M]	Music for Late Hours	1957	12.50	25.00	50.00
❑ MG-20247 [M]	The Best in Blues	1958	12.50	25.00	50.00

Number	Title (A Side/B Side)	Yr	VG	VG+	NM
❑ MG-20439 [M]	The Queen	1959	7.50	15.00	30.00
❑ MG-20479 [M]	What a Diff'rence a Day Makes!	1960	7.50	15.00	30.00
❑ MG-20523 [M]	Newport '58	1960	7.50	15.00	30.00
—Reissue of EmArcy 36141					
❑ MG-20525 [M]	Dinah Washington Sings Fats Waller	1960	7.50	15.00	30.00
—Reissue of EmArcy 36119					
❑ MG-20572 [M]	Unforgettable	1961	6.25	12.50	25.00
❑ MG-20604 [M]	I Concentrate on You	1961	6.25	12.50	25.00
❑ MG-20614 [M]	For Lonely Lovers	1961	6.25	12.50	25.00
❑ MG-20638 [M]	September in the Rain	1961	6.25	12.50	25.00
❑ MG-20661 [M]	Tears and Laughter	1962	6.25	12.50	25.00
❑ MG-20729 [M]	I Wanna Be Loved	1962	6.25	12.50	25.00
❑ MG-20788 [M]	This Is My Story — Dinah Washington's Golden Hits, Volume 1	1963	3.75	7.50	15.00
❑ MG-20789 [M]	This Is My Story — Dinah Washington's Golden Hits, Volume 2	1963	3.75	7.50	15.00
❑ MG-20829 [M]	The Good Old Days	1963	3.75	7.50	15.00
❑ MG-20928 [M]	The Queen and Quincy	1965	3.75	7.50	15.00
❑ MG-21119 [M]	Dinah Discovered	1967	5.00	10.00	20.00
❑ MG-25060 [10]	Dinah Washington	1950	30.00	60.00	120.00
❑ MG-25138 [10]	Dynamic Dinah	1952	30.00	60.00	120.00
❑ MG-25140 [10]	Blazing Ballads	1952	30.00	60.00	120.00
❑ SR-60111 [S]	The Queen	1959	10.00	20.00	40.00
❑ SR-60158 [S]	What a Diff'rence a Day Makes!	1960	10.00	20.00	40.00
❑ SR-60200 [S]	Newport '58	1960	10.00	20.00	40.00
❑ SR-60202 [S]	Dinah Washington Sings Fats Waller	1960	10.00	20.00	40.00
❑ SR-60232 [S]	Unforgettable	1961	7.50	15.00	30.00
❑ SR-60604 [S]	I Concentrate on You	1961	7.50	15.00	30.00
❑ SR-60614 [S]	For Lonely Lovers	1961	7.50	15.00	30.00
❑ SR-60638 [S]	September in the Rain	1961	7.50	15.00	30.00
❑ SR-60661 [S]	Tears and Laughter	1962	7.50	15.00	30.00
❑ SR-60729 [S]	I Wanna Be Loved	1962	7.50	15.00	30.00
❑ SR-60788 [S]	This Is My Story — Dinah Washington's Golden Hits, Volume 1	1963	5.00	10.00	20.00
❑ SR-60789 [S]	This Is My Story — Dinah Washington's Golden Hits, Volume 2	1963	5.00	10.00	20.00
❑ SR-60829 [S]	The Good Old Days	1963	5.00	10.00	20.00
❑ SR-60928 [S]	The Queen and Quincy	1965	5.00	10.00	20.00
❑ SR-61119 [S]	Dinah Discovered	1967	3.75	7.50	15.00
❑ 818815-1	What a Diff'rence a Day Makes!	198?	2.00	4.00	8.00
—Reissue					
❑ 822867-1	This Is My Story — Dinah Washington's Golden Hits, Volume 1	1985	2.00	4.00	8.00
—Reissue					

PICKWICK

❑ SPC-3043	Dinah Washington	196?	2.50	5.00	10.00
❑ SPC-3230	I Don't Hurt Anymore	197?	2.50	5.00	10.00
❑ SPC-3536	Greatest Hits	197?	2.50	5.00	10.00

ROULETTE

❑ RE 104 [(2)]	Echoes of an Era	196?	3.75	7.50	15.00
❑ RE 117 [(2)]	Queen of the Blues	1971	3.75	7.50	15.00
❑ RE 125 [(2)]	The Immortal Dinah Washington	1973	3.75	7.50	15.00
❑ R 25170 [M]	Dinah '62	1962	3.75	7.50	15.00
❑ SR 25170 [S]	Dinah '62	1962	5.00	10.00	20.00
❑ R 25180 [M]	In Love	1962	3.75	7.50	15.00
❑ SR 25180 [S]	In Love	1962	5.00	10.00	20.00
❑ R 25183 [M]	Drinking Again	1962	3.75	7.50	15.00
❑ SR 25183 [S]	Drinking Again	1962	5.00	10.00	20.00
❑ R 25189 [M]	Back to the Blues	1963	3.75	7.50	15.00
❑ SR 25189 [S]	Back to the Blues	1963	5.00	10.00	20.00
❑ R 25220 [M]	Dinah '63	1963	3.75	7.50	15.00
❑ SR 25220 [S]	Dinah '63	1963	5.00	10.00	20.00
❑ R 25244 [M]	In Tribute	1963	3.75	7.50	15.00
❑ SR 25244 [S]	In Tribute	1963	5.00	10.00	20.00
❑ R 25253 [M]	A Stranger on Earth	1964	3.75	7.50	15.00
❑ SR 25253 [S]	A Stranger on Earth	1964	5.00	10.00	20.00
❑ R 25269 [M]	Dinah Washington	1964	3.75	7.50	15.00
❑ SR 25269 [S]	Dinah Washington	1964	5.00	10.00	20.00
❑ R 25289 [M]	The Best of Dinah Washington	1965	3.75	7.50	15.00
❑ SR 25289 [S]	The Best of Dinah Washington	1965	5.00	10.00	20.00
❑ 42014	The Best of Dinah Washington	1968	3.00	6.00	12.00
—Reissue of 25289					

TRIP

❑ 5500	Dinah Jams	1973	2.50	5.00	10.00
❑ 5516	After Hours	1973	2.50	5.00	10.00
❑ 5524	Tears and Laughter	1974	2.50	5.00	10.00
❑ 5556	Dinah Washington Sings Bessie Smith	197?	2.50	5.00	10.00
❑ 5565	The Swingin' Miss D	197?	2.50	5.00	10.00
❑ TLX 9505 [(2)]	Sad Songs — Blue Songs	197?	3.00	6.00	12.00

VERVE

❑ 818930-1	The Fats Waller Songbook	1984	2.50	5.00	10.00

WING

❑ PKW-2-121 [(2)]	The Original Queen of Soul	1969	5.00	10.00	20.00
❑ MGW-12140 [M]	The Late Late Show	1963	3.00	6.00	12.00
❑ MGW-12271 [M]	Dinah Washington Sings Fats Waller	1964	3.00	6.00	12.00
❑ SRW-16140 [S]	The Late Late Show	1963	3.00	6.00	12.00
❑ SRW-16271 [S]	Dinah Washington Sings Fats Waller	1964	3.00	6.00	12.00
❑ SRW-16386	The Original Soul Sister	196?	3.00	6.00	12.00

WASHINGTON, DINAH, AND BROOK BENTON

MERCURY

❑ MG-20588 [M]	The Two of Us	1960	6.25	12.50	25.00
❑ SR-60244 [S]	The Two of Us	1960	7.50	15.00	30.00
❑ 824823-1	The Two of Us	1985	2.00	4.00	8.00
—Reissue					

WASHINGTON, EARL

JAZZ WORKSHOP

❑ JWS-202 [M]	All Star Jazz	1963	15.00	30.00	60.00
❑ JWS-213 [M]	Reflections	1963	15.00	30.00	60.00

WASHINGTON, ERNESTINE

DISC

❑ DLP-712 [10]	Ernestine Washington with Bunk Johnson	195?	50.00	100.00	200.00

WASHINGTON, GINO

ATAC

❑ 2730	Gino Washington's Golden Hits	1969	7.50	15.00	30.00

KAPP

❑ KL-1415 [M]	Gino Washington's Ram Jam Band	1967	5.00	10.00	20.00
❑ KS-3415 [S]	Gino Washington's Ram Jam Band	1967	6.25	12.50	25.00

WASHINGTON, GROVER, JR.

COLUMBIA

❑ FC 40510	Strawberry Moon	1987	2.50	5.00	10.00
❑ OC 44256	Then and Now	1988	2.50	5.00	10.00
❑ OC 45253	Time Out of Mind	1989	2.50	5.00	10.00
❑ C 48530	Next Exit	1992	5.00	10.00	20.00

ELEKTRA

❑ 6E-182	Paradise	1979	2.50	5.00	10.00
❑ 6E-305	Winelight	1980	2.50	5.00	10.00
❑ 5E-562	Come Morning	1981	2.50	5.00	10.00
❑ 60215	The Best Is Yet to Come	1982	2.50	5.00	10.00
❑ 60318	Inside Moves	1984	2.50	5.00	10.00
❑ 60415	Anthology of Grover Washington, Jr.	1985	2.50	5.00	10.00

KUDU

❑ KS-03	Inner City Blues	1971	3.00	6.00	12.00
❑ KS-07	All the King's Horses	1972	3.00	6.00	12.00
❑ KS-20	Mister Magic	1975	3.00	6.00	12.00
❑ KS-24	Feels So Good	1975	3.00	6.00	12.00
❑ KS-32	A Secret Place	1976	3.00	6.00	12.00
❑ KSQX-1213 [(2)Q]	Soul Box	1973	6.25	12.50	25.00
❑ KSX-1213 [(2)]	Soul Box	1973	3.75	7.50	15.00
❑ KSX-3637 [(2)]	Live at the Bijou	1977	3.75	7.50	15.00

MOTOWN

❑ M5-165V1	A Secret Place	1981	2.00	4.00	8.00
—Reissue of Kudu 32					
❑ M5-175V1	Mister Magic	1981	2.00	4.00	8.00
—Reissue of Kudu 20					
❑ M5-177V1	Feels So Good	1981	2.00	4.00	8.00
—Reissue of Kudu 24					
❑ M5-184V1	Soul Box Vol. 1	1981	2.00	4.00	8.00
—Reissue of half of Kudu 1213					
❑ M5-186V1	All the King's Horses	1981	2.00	4.00	8.00
—Reissue of Kudu 07					
❑ M5-187V1	Soul Box Vol. 2	1981	2.00	4.00	8.00
—Reissue of half of Kudu 1213					
❑ M5-189V1	Inner City Blues	1981	2.00	4.00	8.00
—Reissue of Kudu 03					
❑ M7-910	Reed Seed	1978	2.50	5.00	10.00
❑ M7-933	Skylarkin'	1980	2.50	5.00	10.00
❑ M9-940 [(2)]	Baddest	1980	3.00	6.00	12.00
❑ M9-961 [(2)]	Anthology	1981	3.00	6.00	12.00
❑ 5232 ML	Skylarkin'	1982	2.00	4.00	8.00
—Reissue of 933					
❑ 5236 ML	Reed Seed	1982	2.00	4.00	8.00
—Reissue of 910					
❑ 5307 ML	Greatest Performances	1983	2.50	5.00	10.00
❑ 6126 ML	Grover Washington Jr. at His Best	198?	2.50	5.00	10.00
❑ 8239 ML2 [(2)]	Live at the Bijou	198?	3.00	6.00	12.00

NAUTILUS

❑ NR-39	Winelight	1981	12.50	25.00	50.00
—Audiophile vinyl					

WASHINGTON, TYRONE

BLUE LABOR

❑ 102	Do Right	197?	5.00	10.00	20.00

BLUE NOTE

❑ BST-84274	Natural Essence	1968	6.25	12.50	25.00

WATERS, ETHEL

MERCURY

❑ MG-20051 [M]	Ethel Waters	1954	12.50	25.00	50.00

REMINGTON

❑ RLP-1025 [10]	Ethel Waters	1950	12.50	25.00	50.00

"X"

❑ LVA-1009 [M]	Ethel Waters	1955	12.50	25.00	50.00

WATERS, MUDDY

BLUE SKY

❑ PZ 34449	Hard Again	198?	2.00	4.00	8.00
—Budget-line reissue with bar code					
❑ PZ 34449	Hard Again	1977	3.00	6.00	12.00
—No bar code on cover					
❑ JZ 34928	I'm Ready	1978	3.00	6.00	12.00
❑ PZ 34928	I'm Ready	198?	2.00	4.00	8.00
—Budget-line reissue					
❑ JZ 35712	Muddy "Missisiippi" Waters Live	1980	3.00	6.00	12.00
❑ PZ 35712	Muddy "Missisiippi" Waters Live	198?	2.00	4.00	8.00
—Budget-line reissue					
❑ JZ 37064	King Bee	1981	3.00	6.00	12.00
❑ PZ 37064	King Bee	198?	2.00	4.00	8.00
—Budget-line reissue					

CADET CONCEPT

❑ CS-314	Electric Mud	1968	6.25	12.50	25.00
❑ CS-320	After the Rain	1969	6.25	12.50	25.00

CHESS

❑ 127 [(2)]	Fathers and Sons	1969	6.25	12.50	25.00
❑ LP-1427 [DJ]	The Best of Muddy Waters	1957	500.00	1000.	1500.
—White label promo					
❑ LP-1427 [M]	The Best of Muddy Waters	1957	125.00	250.00	500.00
—Black label					

Number	Title (A Side/B Side)	Yr	VG	VG+	NM
❑ LPS-1427 [R]	The Best of Muddy Waters	196?	3.00	6.00	12.00
—Black label					
❑ LP-1444 [DJ]	Muddy Waters Sings Big Bill	1960	250.00	500.00	1000.
—White label promo					
❑ LP-1444 [M]	Muddy Waters Sings Big Bill	1960	75.00	150.00	300.00
❑ LPS-1444 [R]	Muddy Waters Sings Big Bill	196?	3.75	7.50	15.00
—Rechanneled stereo reissue					
❑ LP-1449 [M]	Muddy Waters at Newport	1962	30.00	60.00	120.00
❑ LP-1483 [M]	Folk Singer	1964	30.00	60.00	120.00
❑ LP-1501 [M]	The Real Folk Blues of Muddy Waters	1965	15.00	30.00	60.00
❑ LP-1507 [M]	Muddy, Brass and Blues	1966	10.00	20.00	40.00
❑ LPS-1507 [S]	Muddy, Brass and Blues	1966	12.50	25.00	50.00
❑ LP-1511 [M]	More Real Folk Blues	1967	12.50	25.00	50.00
❑ LPS-1511 [S]	More Real Folk Blues	1967	10.00	20.00	40.00
❑ LP-1533 [M]	Blues from Big Bill's Copacabana	1968	12.50	25.00	50.00
❑ LPS-1539	Sail On	1969	6.25	12.50	25.00
❑ LPS-1553	They Call Me Muddy Waters	1971	5.00	10.00	20.00
❑ CH-9101	Rolling Stone	1985	3.00	6.00	12.00
❑ CH-9180	Rare and Unissued	1986	3.00	6.00	12.00
❑ CH-9197	Muddy Waters Sings Big Bill	1986	2.50	5.00	10.00
—Reissue of 1444					
❑ CH-9198	Muddy Waters at Newport	1986	2.50	5.00	10.00
—Reissue of 1449					
❑ CH-9255	The Best of Muddy Waters	1987	2.50	5.00	10.00
—Reissue of 1427					
❑ CH-9261	Folk Singer	1987	2.50	5.00	10.00
—Reissue of 1483					
❑ CH-9274	The Real Folk Blues of Muddy Waters	1987	2.50	5.00	10.00
—Reissue of 1501					
❑ CH-9278	More Real Folk Blues	1988	2.50	5.00	10.00
—Reissue of 1511					
❑ CH-9286	Muddy, Brass and the Blues	1989	2.50	5.00	10.00
—Reissue of 1507					
❑ CH-9291	Trouble No More: Singles 1955-1959	1989	3.00	6.00	12.00
❑ CH-9298	The London Muddy Waters Sessions	1989	2.50	5.00	10.00
—Reissue of 60013					
❑ CH-9299	They Call Me Muddy Waters	1989	2.50	5.00	10.00
—Reissue of 1553					
❑ CH-9319	Can't Get No Grindin'	1990	2.50	5.00	10.00
—Reissue of 50023					
❑ CH-50012	Muddy Waters Live	1972	5.00	10.00	20.00
❑ CH-50023	Can't Get No Grindin'	1973	5.00	10.00	20.00
❑ 2CH-50033 [(2)]	Fathers and Sons	1974	5.00	10.00	20.00
—Reissue of 127					
❑ CH-50035	The Muddy Waters Woodstock Album	1976	3.75	7.50	15.00
❑ 2CH-60006 [(2)]	McKinley Morganfield, A.K.A. Muddy Waters	1971	6.25	12.50	25.00
❑ CH-60013	The London Muddy Waters Sessions	1972	5.00	10.00	20.00
❑ CH-60026	London Revisited	1974	3.75	7.50	15.00
❑ CH-60031	"Unk" in Funk	1975	3.75	7.50	15.00
❑ CH6-80002 [(6)]	The Chess Box	1990	12.50	25.00	50.00
INTERMEDIA					
❑ QS-5071	Sweet Home Chicago	198?	2.50	5.00	10.00
MOBILE FIDELITY					
❑ 1-201	Folk Singer	1994	6.25	12.50	25.00
—Audiophile vinyl					
MUSE					
❑ MR-5008	Mud in Your Ear	198?	3.00	6.00	12.00
TESTAMENT					
❑ 2210	Stovall's Plantation	197?	3.00	6.00	12.00

WATERS, MUDDY, AND HOWLIN' WOLF
CHESS
❑ CH-9100	Muddy and The Wolf	1985	3.00	6.00	12.00

WATERS, PATTY
ESP-DISK'
❑ 1025 [M]	Patty Waters Sings	1966	6.25	12.50	25.00
❑ S-1025 [S]	Patty Waters Sings	1966	7.50	15.00	30.00
❑ 1055 [S]	Patty Waters College Tour	1968	15.00	30.00	60.00

WATERS, ROGER
Also see PINK FLOYD.
COLUMBIA
❑ FC 39290	The Pros and Cons of Hitch Hiking	1984	2.50	5.00	10.00
—Revised cover with black rectangle over woman's naked rear end					
❑ FC 39290	The Pros and Cons of Hitch Hiking	1984	5.00	10.00	20.00
—Original nude cover					
❑ PC 39290	The Pros and Cons of Hitch Hiking	1986	2.00	4.00	8.00
—Budget-line reissue with new prefix					
❑ FC 40795	Radio K.A.O.S.	1987	2.00	4.00	8.00
MERCURY					
❑ R 209833 [(2)]	The Wall — Live in Berlin	1990	5.00	10.00	20.00
—BMG Direct Marketing version					
❑ 846611-1 [(2)]	The Wall — Live in Berlin	1990	5.00	10.00	20.00

WATKINS, DOUG
NEW JAZZ
❑ NJLP-8238 [M]	Soulnik	1960	12.50	25.00	50.00
—Purple label					
❑ NJLP-8238 [M]	Soulnik	1965	6.25	12.50	25.00
—Blue label, trident logo at right					
PHILIPS					
❑ PHM 200001 [M]	French Horns for My Lady	1962	5.00	10.00	20.00
❑ PHS 600001 [S]	French Horns for My Lady	1962	6.25	12.50	25.00
TRANSITION					
❑ TRLP-20 [M]	Watkins at Large	1956	250.00	500.00	1000.
—Deduct 1/10 if booklet is missing					

WATKINS, JULIUS
BLUE NOTE
❑ BLP-5053 [10]	Julius Watkins Sextet	1954	100.00	200.00	400.00
❑ BLP-5064 [10]	Julius Watkins Sextet, Volume 2	1955	100.00	200.00	400.00

Number	Title (A Side/B Side)	Yr	VG	VG+	NM

WATKINS, LOVELACE
MGM
❑ E-3831 [M]	The Voice of Lovelace Watkins	1960	6.25	12.50	25.00
❑ SE-3831 [S]	The Voice of Lovelace Watkins	1960	10.00	20.00	40.00

WATSON, DOC
Includes records by the father-son duo of "Doc and Merle Watson."
FLYING FISH
❑ FF-252	Red Rocking Chair	1981	3.00	6.00	12.00
❑ FF-301	Guitar Album	1983	3.00	6.00	12.00
❑ FF-352	Pickin' the Blues	1985	2.50	5.00	10.00
FOLKWAYS					
❑ FA-2366 [M]	Doc Watson and Family	1963	6.25	12.50	25.00
❑ FA-31021 [S]	Doc Watson and Family	196?	3.75	7.50	15.00
INTERMEDIA					
❑ QS-5031	Out in the Country	198?	2.50	5.00	10.00
LIBERTY					
❑ LWB-423	Memories	1981	3.00	6.00	12.00
—Reissue of United Artists 423					
❑ LW-601	Doc and the Boys	1981	2.50	5.00	10.00
—Reissue of United Artists 601					
❑ LT-887	Look Away!	1981	2.50	5.00	10.00
—Reissue of United Artists 887					
❑ LT-943	Live and Pickin'	1981	2.50	5.00	10.00
—Reissue of United Artists 943					
❑ LN-10027	Lonesome Road	1981	2.00	4.00	8.00
—Budget-line reissue					
POPPY					
❑ PP-LA022-F	Then and Now	1973	3.75	7.50	15.00
❑ PP-LA210-G	Two Days in November	1974	3.75	7.50	15.00
❑ PYS-5703	The Elementary Doc Watson	1972	3.75	7.50	15.00
SMITHSONIAN/FOLKWAYS					
❑ SF-40012	The Doc Watson Family	1990	3.00	6.00	12.00
—Reissue of Folkways LP					
SUGAR HILL					
❑ SH-3742	Down South	1985	2.50	5.00	10.00
❑ SH-3752	Riding the Midnight Train	1986	2.50	5.00	10.00
❑ SH-3759	Portrait	1987	2.50	5.00	10.00
UNITED ARTISTS					
❑ UA-LA423-G [(2)]	Memories	1975	3.75	7.50	15.00
❑ UA-LA601-G	Doc and the Boys	1976	3.00	6.00	12.00
❑ UA-LA725-G	Lonesome Road	1977	3.00	6.00	12.00
❑ UA-LA887-H	Look Away!	1978	3.00	6.00	12.00
❑ UA-LA943-H	Live and Pickin'	1979	3.00	6.00	12.00
VANGUARD					
❑ VSD-9/10 [(2)]	Doc Watson on Stage	1970	5.00	10.00	20.00
❑ VSD 45/46 [(2)]	The Essential Doc Watson	1973	5.00	10.00	20.00
❑ VSD 107/8 [(2)]	Old Timey Concert	1977	5.00	10.00	20.00
❑ VSD-6576	Ballads from Deep Gap	1971	3.75	7.50	15.00
❑ VRS-9152 [M]	Doc Watson	1964	5.00	10.00	20.00
❑ VRS-9170 [M]	Doc Watson and Son	1965	5.00	10.00	20.00
❑ VRS-9213 [M]	Southbound	1966	3.75	7.50	15.00
❑ VRS-9239 [M]	Home Again	1967	3.75	7.50	15.00
❑ VMS-73108	The Essential Doc Watson, Vol. 1	1985	2.50	5.00	10.00
❑ VMS-73121	The Essential Doc Watson, Vol. 2	1985	2.50	5.00	10.00
❑ VSD-79152 [S]	Doc Watson	1964	6.25	12.50	25.00
❑ VSD-79170 [S]	Doc Watson and Son	1965	6.25	12.50	25.00
❑ VSD-79213 [S]	Southbound	1966	5.00	10.00	20.00
❑ VSD-79239 [S]	Home Again	1967	5.00	10.00	20.00
❑ VSD-79276	Good Deal	1968	3.75	7.50	15.00

WATSON, JOHNNY "GUITAR"
A&M
❑ SP-4880	That's What Time It Is	1981	2.50	5.00	10.00
CADET					
❑ LP-4056 [M]	I Cried for You	1967	6.25	12.50	25.00
❑ LPS-4056 [S]	I Cried for You	1967	7.50	15.00	30.00
CHESS					
❑ LP-1490 [M]	Blues Soul	1965	17.50	35.00	70.00
❑ LPS-1490 [S]	Blues Soul	1965	20.00	40.00	80.00
DJM					
❑ 3	Ain't That a Bitch	1976	2.50	5.00	10.00
❑ 7	A Real Mother for Ya	1977	2.50	5.00	10.00
❑ 13	Master Funk	1978	2.50	5.00	10.00
—As "Watsonian Institute"					
❑ 19	Giant	1978	2.50	5.00	10.00
❑ 24	What the Hell Is This?	1979	2.50	5.00	10.00
❑ 27	E.D.P. Extra Disco Perception	1979	2.50	5.00	10.00
—As "Watsonian Institute"					
❑ 31	Love Jones	1980	2.50	5.00	10.00
❑ 501	Johnny "Guitar" Watson and the Family Clone	1981	2.50	5.00	10.00
❑ 714	Funk Beyond the Call of Duty	1977	2.50	5.00	10.00
FANTASY					
❑ MPF-4503	Greatest Hits	1981	2.50	5.00	10.00
❑ 9437	Listen	1973	3.00	6.00	12.00
❑ 9484	I Don't Want to Be Alone Stranger	1975	3.00	6.00	12.00
KING					
❑ 857 [M]	Johnny Guitar Watson	1963	100.00	200.00	400.00
MCA					
❑ 5273	The Very Best of Johnny "Guitar" Watson	1981	2.50	5.00	10.00
OKEH					
❑ OKM 12118 [M]	Bad	1967	7.50	15.00	30.00
❑ OKM 12124 [M]	In the Fats Bag	1967	7.50	15.00	30.00
❑ OKS 14118 [S]	Bad	1967	10.00	20.00	40.00
❑ OKS 14124 [S]	In the Fats Bag	1967	10.00	20.00	40.00
POWER PAK					
❑ 306	Gangster of Love	1978	2.50	5.00	10.00

Number	Title (A Side/B Side)	Yr	VG	VG+	NM

WATSON, JOHNNY "GUITAR", AND LARRY WILLIAMS
OKEH
❏ OKM 12122 [M]	Two for the Price of One	1967	10.00	20.00	40.00
❏ OKS 14122 [S]	Two for the Price of One	1967	15.00	30.00	60.00

WATSONIAN INSTITUTE
See JOHNNY "GUITAR" WATSON.

WATT, TOMMY
BETHLEHEM
| ❏ BCP-6052 [M] | Watts Cooking | 1961 | 7.50 | 15.00 | 30.00 |

WATTERS, LU
CLEF
| ❏ MGC-503 [10] | Lu Watters Jazz | 1954 | 20.00 | 40.00 | 80.00 |
DOWN HOME
| ❏ MGD-5 [10] | Lu Watters and His Yerba Buena Jazz Band | 1955 | 15.00 | 30.00 | 60.00 |
GOOD TIME JAZZ
❏ L-A [(3)M]	San Francisco Style	195?	15.00	30.00	60.00
❏ L-8 [10]	Lu Watters and His Yerba Buena Jazz Band	1952	12.50	25.00	50.00
❏ L-12001 [M]	Dawn Club Favorites	1954	10.00	20.00	40.00
❏ L-12002 [M]	Originals and Ragtime	1954	10.00	20.00	40.00
❏ L-12003 [M]	Stomps, Etc. and the Blues	1954	10.00	20.00	40.00
❏ L-12007 [M]	1942 Series	1955	10.00	20.00	40.00
MERCURY
❏ MGC-103 [10]	Lu Watters and the Yerba Buena Jazz Band	1950	25.00	50.00	100.00
❏ MGC-503 [10]	Lu Watters Jazz	1951	25.00	50.00	100.00
❏ MGC-510 [10]	Lu Watters and His Yerba Buena Jazz Band	1952	25.00	50.00	100.00
❏ MG-35013 [10]	Lu Watters and the Yerba Buena Jazz Band	1950	30.00	60.00	120.00
RIVERSIDE
| ❏ RLP 12-213 [M] | San Francisco Style | 1956 | 15.00 | 30.00 | 60.00 |
| ❏ RLP-2513 [10] | Lu Watters 1947 | 1955 | 20.00 | 40.00 | 80.00 |
VERVE
| ❏ MGV-1005 [M] | Lu Watters and His Yerba Buena Jazz Band | 1956 | 12.50 | 25.00 | 50.00 |
| ❏ V-1005 [M] | Lu Watters and His Yerba Buena Jazz Band | 1961 | 5.00 | 10.00 | 20.00 |

WATTERS, LU/SANTO PECORA
VERVE
| ❏ MGV-1008 [M] | Dixieland Jamboree | 1956 | 12.50 | 25.00 | 50.00 |
| ❏ V-1008 [M] | Dixieland Jamboree | 1961 | 6.25 | 12.50 | 25.00 |

WATTS, ALAN
ASCENSION
| ❏ (# unknown) | Dhyana: of the Art of Meditation, Vol. 1 | 1970 | 7.50 | 15.00 | 30.00 |
| ❏ (# unknown) | Dhyana: of the Art of Meditation, Vol. 2 | 1970 | 7.50 | 15.00 | 30.00 |
MEA
❏ LP-1001 [M]	Haiku Poems	1962	12.50	25.00	50.00
❏ LP-1002 [M]	Zen and Senryu	1962	12.50	25.00	50.00
❏ LP-1007 [M]	This Is It	1962	15.00	30.00	60.00
TOGETHER
| ❏ 1025 | Why Not Now | 1970 | 6.25 | 12.50 | 25.00 |
WARNER BROS.
| ❏ W 1923 | The Sounds of Hinduism | 1968 | 6.25 | 12.50 | 25.00 |

WATTS, CHARLIE
Also see THE ROLLING STONES.
COLUMBIA
| ❏ FC 40570 | The Charlie Watts Orchestra Live Fulham Town Hall | 1986 | 3.75 | 7.50 | 15.00 |
CONTINUUM
| ❏ 19308 | From One Charlie | 1990 | 6.25 | 12.50 | 25.00 |
—Box set with LP, book ("Ode to a High Flying Bird") and photo of Charlie Parker

WATTS, ERNIE
PACIFIC JAZZ
| ❏ PJ-20155 | Planet Love | 1969 | 7.50 | 15.00 | 30.00 |
VAULT
| ❏ LP-9011 | Wonderbag | 1968 | 5.00 | 10.00 | 20.00 |

WATTS, MARZETTE
ESP-DISK'
| ❏ 1044 [S] | Marzette Watts and Company | 1971 | 5.00 | 10.00 | 20.00 |
SAVOY
| ❏ MG-12193 [M] | The Marzette Watts Ensemble | 1968 | 5.00 | 10.00 | 20.00 |

WATTS 103RD STREET RHYTHM BAND, THE
See CHARLES WRIGHT AND THE WATTS 103RD STREET RHYTHM BAND.

WAVE CRESTS, THE
VIKING
| ❏ VKL-6606 [M] | Surftime U.S.A. | 1963 | 15.00 | 30.00 | 60.00 |
| ❏ VKS-6606 [S] | Surftime U.S.A. | 1963 | 25.00 | 50.00 | 100.00 |

WAYFARERS, THE
RCA VICTOR
❏ LPM-1213 [M]	The Wayfarers	1956	12.50	25.00	50.00
❏ LPM-2666 [M]	Come Along with the Wayfarers	1963	6.25	12.50	25.00
❏ LSP-2666 [S]	Come Along with the Wayfarers	1963	7.50	15.00	30.00
❏ LPM-2735 [M]	The Wayfarers at the Hungry I	1963	6.25	12.50	25.00
❏ LSP-2735 [S]	The Wayfarers at the Hungry I	1963	7.50	15.00	30.00
❏ LPM-2946 [M]	The Wayfarers at the World's Fair	1964	7.50	15.00	30.00
❏ LSP-2946 [S]	The Wayfarers at the World's Fair	1964	10.00	20.00	40.00

WAYLON AND WILLIE
For convenience's sake, we've listed all the variations of their credits here, including "Willie Nelson and Waylon Jennings." Also see WAYLON JENNINGS; WILLIE NELSON.
COLUMBIA
| ❏ FC 38562 | Take It to the Limit | 1983 | 2.50 | 5.00 | 10.00 |
RCA VICTOR
| ❏ AAL1-2686 | Waylon and Willie | 198? | 2.00 | 4.00 | 8.00 |
—Reissue with new prefix
| ❏ AFL1-2686 | Waylon and Willie | 1978 | 2.50 | 5.00 | 10.00 |
| ❏ AFL1-2686 [DJ] | Waylon and Willie | 1978 | 6.25 | 12.50 | 25.00 |
—Promo only on gold vinyl
| ❏ AHL1-4455 | WW II | 1982 | 2.50 | 5.00 | 10.00 |
| ❏ AYL1-5134 | Waylon and Willie | 198? | 2.00 | 4.00 | 8.00 |
—"Best Buy Series" reissue
| ❏ AYL1-5138 | WW II | 198? | 2.00 | 4.00 | 8.00 |
—"Best Buy Series" reissue

WAYNE, CHUCK
FOCUS
| ❏ FL-333 [M] | Tapestry | 1964 | 6.25 | 12.50 | 25.00 |
| ❏ FS-333 [M] | Tapestry | 1964 | 7.50 | 15.00 | 30.00 |
PRESTIGE
| ❏ PRLP-7367 [M] | Morning Mist | 1965 | 5.00 | 10.00 | 20.00 |
| ❏ PRST-7367 [S] | Morning Mist | 1965 | 6.25 | 12.50 | 25.00 |
PROGRESSIVE
| ❏ 3003 [10] | The Chuck Wayne Quintet | 1953 | 50.00 | 100.00 | 200.00 |
SAVOY
| ❏ MG-12077 [M] | The Jazz Guitarist | 1956 | 12.50 | 25.00 | 50.00 |
VIK
| ❏ LX-1098 [M] | String Fever | 1957 | 12.50 | 25.00 | 50.00 |

WAYNE, FRANCES
ATLANTIC
| ❏ 1263 [M] | The Warm Sound of Frances Wayne | 1957 | 12.50 | 25.00 | 50.00 |
—Black label
| ❏ 1263 [M] | The Warm Sound of Frances Wayne | 1961 | 5.00 | 10.00 | 20.00 |
—White "fan" logo at right of label
BRUNSWICK
| ❏ BL 54022 [M] | Frances Wayne | 1958 | 10.00 | 20.00 | 40.00 |
CORAL
| ❏ CRL 56019 [10] | Salute to Ethel Waters | 195? | 15.00 | 30.00 | 60.00 |
EPIC
| ❏ LN 3222 [M] | Songs for My Man | 1956 | 12.50 | 25.00 | 50.00 |

WAYNE, JOHN
RCA VICTOR
| ❏ AFL1-3484 | America, Why I Love Her | 1979 | 2.50 | 5.00 | 10.00 |
—Reissue of 4828
| ❏ AYL1-3959 | America, Why I Love Her | 1981 | 2.00 | 4.00 | 8.00 |
—"Best Buy Series" reissue
| ❏ LSP-4828 | America, Why I Love Her | 1973 | 6.25 | 12.50 | 25.00 |

WAYNE, WEE WILLIE
IMPERIAL
| ❏ LP-9144 [M] | Travelin' Mood | 1961 | 125.00 | 250.00 | 500.00 |

WAZOO
ZIG ZAG
| ❏ 217 | Wazoo | 197? | 7.50 | 15.00 | 30.00 |

WE FIVE
A&M
❏ SP-111 [M]	You Were On My Mind	1965	3.75	7.50	15.00
❏ SP-138 [M]	Make Someone Happy	1967	5.00	10.00	20.00
❏ SP-4111 [S]	You Were On My Mind	1965	5.00	10.00	20.00
❏ SP-4138 [S]	Make Someone Happy	1967	3.75	7.50	15.00
❏ SP-4168	The Return of We Five	1969	3.75	7.50	15.00
VAULT
| ❏ 136 | Catch the Wind | 1970 | 3.75 | 7.50 | 15.00 |

WEASELS, THE
WING
| ❏ MGW-12282 [M] | The Liverpool Beat | 1964 | 6.25 | 12.50 | 25.00 |
| ❏ SRW-16282 [S] | The Liverpool Beat | 1964 | 7.50 | 15.00 | 30.00 |

WEATHER REPORT
ARC
| ❏ HC 47616 | Weather Report | 1982 | 10.00 | 20.00 | 40.00 |
—Half-speed mastered edition
COLUMBIA
❏ CQ 32494 [Q]	Mysterious Traveller	1974	5.00	10.00	20.00
❏ PCQ 33417 [Q]	Tale Spinnin'	1975	5.00	10.00	20.00
❏ HC 44418	Heavy Weather	198?	10.00	20.00	40.00
—Half-speed mastered edition

WEAVER, CHARLIE
COLUMBIA
| ❏ CL 1345 [M] | Charlie Weaver Sings for His People | 1959 | 7.50 | 15.00 | 30.00 |
STARLITE
| ❏ 6003 [10] | Charlie Weaver Sings | 1954 | 12.50 | 25.00 | 50.00 |

WEAVERS, THE
ANALOGUE PRODUCTIONS
| ❏ 005 | Reunion at Carnegie Hall, 1963 | 199? | 7.50 | 15.00 | 30.00 |
—Audiophile vinyl
DECCA
❏ DXB 173 [(2)M]	The Best of the Weavers	1965	6.25	12.50	25.00
❏ DL 4277 [M]	Weavers' Gold	1962	5.00	10.00	20.00
❏ DL 5285 [10]	Folk Songs of America and Other Lands	1951	25.00	50.00	100.00
❏ DL-5373 [10]	We Wish You a Merry Christmas	1952	25.00	50.00	100.00
❏ DXSB 7173 [(2)R]	The Best of the Weavers	1965	5.00	10.00	20.00
❏ DL 8893 [M]	The Best of the Weavers	1959	10.00	20.00	40.00
—Black label, silver print
❏ DL 8893 [M]	Folk Songs Made Famous by the Weavers	196?	5.00	10.00	20.00
❏ DL 8909 [M]	Folk Songs Around the World	1959	10.00	20.00	40.00
❏ DL 74277 [R]	Weavers' Gold	1962	3.75	7.50	15.00
❏ DL 75169 [R]	The Weavers' Greatest Hits	1971	3.00	6.00	12.00
❏ DL 78893 [R]	Folk Songs Made Famous by the Weavers	196?	3.75	7.50	15.00

Number	Title (A Side/B Side)	Yr	VG	VG+	NM
MCA					
❑ 4052 [(2)]	The Best of the Weavers	197?	3.75	7.50	15.00
—Reissue of Decca 7173; black rainbow labels					
❑ 4052 [(2)]	The Best of the Weavers	1980	3.00	6.00	12.00
—Blue rainbow labels					
VANGUARD					
❑ VSD-15/16 [(2)]	The Weavers' Greatest Hits	1971	3.75	7.50	15.00
❑ VSD 2022 [S]	Travelling on with the Weavers	1959	10.00	20.00	40.00
❑ VSD 2030 [S]	The Weavers at Home	1959	10.00	20.00	40.00
❑ VSD 2069 [S]	The Weavers at Carnegie Hall, Vol. 2	1960	10.00	20.00	40.00
❑ VSD 2101 [S]	Almanac	1961	10.00	20.00	40.00
❑ VSD 2150 [S]	Reunion at Carnegie Hall, 1963	1963	7.50	15.00	30.00
❑ SRV-3001 [(2)M]	The Weavers Song Bag	1967	5.00	10.00	20.00
❑ VRS-6533 [R]	The Weavers at Carnegie Hall	1970	3.00	6.00	12.00
❑ VRS-6537 [R]	The Weavers on Tour	1970	3.00	6.00	12.00
❑ VRS 9010 [M]	The Weavers at Carnegie Hall	1957	10.00	20.00	40.00
❑ VRS 9013 [M]	The Weavers on Tour	1957	10.00	20.00	40.00
❑ VRS 9024 [M]	The Weavers at Home	1959	7.50	15.00	30.00
❑ VRS 9043 [M]	Travelling on with the Weavers	1959	7.50	15.00	30.00
❑ VRS 9075 [M]	The Weavers at Carnegie Hall, Vol. 2	1960	7.50	15.00	30.00
❑ VRS 9100 [M]	Almanac	1961	7.50	15.00	30.00
❑ VRS 9130 [M]	Reunion at Carnegie Hall, 1963	1963	5.00	10.00	20.00
❑ VRS 9161 [M]	Reunion at Carnegie Hall, Part 2	1965	5.00	10.00	20.00
❑ SRV-73001 [(2)S]	The Weavers Song Bag	1967	6.25	12.50	25.00
❑ VMS-73101	The Weavers at Carnegie Hall	1984	2.00	4.00	8.00
—Reissue of 6533					
❑ VMS-73116	The Weavers on Tour	1985	2.00	4.00	8.00
—Reissue of 6537					
❑ VMS-73122	Classics	1985	2.50	5.00	10.00
❑ VSD 79161 [S]	Reunion at Carnegie Hall, Part 2	1965	7.50	15.00	30.00
WEB, THE					
DERAM					
❑ DES 18018	Fully Interlocking	1968	6.25	12.50	25.00
WEBB, CHICK					
COLUMBIA					
❑ CL 2639 [M]	The Immortal Chick Webb	1967	6.25	12.50	25.00
DECCA					
❑ DL 9223 [M]	Chick Webb 1937-39	1958	10.00	20.00	40.00
❑ DL 79223 [R]	Chick Webb 1937-39	1958	6.25	12.50	25.00
WEBB, JACK					
RCA VICTOR					
❑ LPM-1126 [M]	Pete Kelly's Blues	1955	12.50	25.00	50.00
—Webb narrates; jazz combo plays					
❑ LPM-2053 [M]	Pete Kelly's Blues	1959	7.50	15.00	30.00
—Reissue of 1126					
❑ LSP-2053(e) [R]	Pete Kelly's Blues	1959	5.00	10.00	20.00
❑ LPM-3199 [10]	Dragnet — The Christmas Story	1954	37.50	75.00	150.00
WARNER BROS.					
❑ W 1207 [M]	You're My Girl	1958	7.50	15.00	30.00
❑ WS 1207 [S]	You're My Girl	1958	10.00	20.00	40.00
❑ WS 1207 [S]	You're My Girl	1958	10.00	20.00	40.00
WEBB, JAY LEE					
DECCA					
❑ DL 4933 [M]	I Come Home a-Drinkin'	1967	6.25	12.50	25.00
❑ DL 74933 [S]	I Come Home a-Drinkin'	1967	5.00	10.00	20.00
❑ DL 75121	She's Looking Better by the Minute	1969	5.00	10.00	20.00
WEBB, JIMMY					
ASYLUM					
❑ SD 5070	Land's End	1974	3.75	7.50	15.00
ATLANTIC					
❑ SD 18218	El Mirage	1977	3.00	6.00	12.00
EPIC					
❑ BN 26401	Jim Webb Sings Jim Webb	1968	5.00	10.00	20.00
LORIMAR					
❑ FC 37695	Angel Heart	1982	3.00	6.00	12.00
REPRISE					
❑ MS 2055	Letters	1972	3.75	7.50	15.00
❑ RS 6421	Words and Music	1970	3.75	7.50	15.00
❑ RS 6448	And So: On	1971	3.75	7.50	15.00
WEBB, ROGER					
SWAN					
❑ SLP-516 [M]	John, Paul and All That Jazz	1964	7.50	15.00	30.00
WEBSTER, BEN					
ANALOGUE PRODUCTIONS					
❑ AP 011	Ben Webster at the Renaissance	199?	6.25	12.50	25.00
BRUNSWICK					
❑ BL 58031 [10]	Tenor Sax Stylings	1952	75.00	150.00	300.00
EMARCY					
❑ MG-26006 [10]	The Big Tenor	1954	62.50	125.00	250.00
IMPULSE!					
❑ A-65 [M]	See You at the Fair	1964	6.25	12.50	25.00
❑ AS-65 [S]	See You at the Fair	1964	7.50	15.00	30.00
NESSA					
❑ N-8	Did You Call?	197?	5.00	10.00	20.00
NORGRAN					
❑ MGN-1001 [M]	The Consummate Artistry of Ben Webster	1954	37.50	75.00	150.00
❑ MGN-1018 [M]	Music for Loving	1955	50.00	100.00	200.00
❑ MGN-1039 [M]	Ben Webster Plays Music with Feeling	1955	50.00	100.00	200.00
❑ MGN-1089 [M]	King of the Tenors	1956	30.00	60.00	120.00
REPRISE					
❑ R-2001 [M]	The Warm Moods of Ben Webster	1961	6.25	12.50	25.00
❑ R9-2001 [S]	The Warm Moods of Ben Webster	1961	7.50	15.00	30.00

Number	Title (A Side/B Side)	Yr	VG	VG+	NM
VERVE					
❑ MGV-2026 [M]	Sophisticated Lady — Ben Webster with Strings	1956	12.50	25.00	50.00
❑ V-2026 [M]	Sophisticated Lady — Ben Webster with Strings	1961	6.25	12.50	25.00
❑ MGVS-6056 [S]	Ben Webster and Associates	1959	10.00	20.00	40.00
❑ MGVS-6114 [S]	Ben Webster Meets Oscar Peterson	1960	10.00	20.00	40.00
❑ MGV-8020 [M]	King of the Tenors	1957	12.50	25.00	50.00
❑ V-8020 [M]	King of the Tenors	1961	6.25	12.50	25.00
❑ MGV-8130 [M]	Music with Feeling — Ben Webster with Strings	1957	12.50	25.00	50.00
❑ V-8130 [M]	Music with Feeling — Ben Webster with Strings	1961	6.25	12.50	25.00
❑ MGV-8274 [M]	Soulville	1958	12.50	25.00	50.00
❑ V-8274 [M]	Soulville	1961	6.25	12.50	25.00
❑ MGV-8318 [M]	Ben Webster and Associates	1959	12.50	25.00	50.00
❑ V-8318 [M]	Ben Webster and Associates	1961	6.25	12.50	25.00
❑ V6-8318 [S]	Ben Webster and Associates	1961	5.00	10.00	20.00
❑ MGV-8349 [M]	Ben Webster Meets Oscar Peterson	1959	12.50	25.00	50.00
❑ V-8349 [M]	Ben Webster Meets Oscar Peterson	1961	6.25	12.50	25.00
❑ V6-8349 [S]	Ben Webster Meets Oscar Peterson	1961	5.00	10.00	20.00
❑ MGV-8359 [M]	The Soul of Ben Webster	1960	12.50	25.00	50.00
❑ V-8359 [M]	The Soul of Ben Webster	1961	6.25	12.50	25.00
WEBSTER, BEN, AND HARRY "SWEETS" EDISON					
COLUMBIA					
❑ CL 1891 [M]	Ben Webster-Sweets Edison	1962	6.25	12.50	25.00
❑ CS 8691 [S]	Ben Webster-Sweets Edison	1962	7.50	15.00	30.00
WEBSTER, BEN, AND JOE ZAWINUL					
RIVERSIDE					
❑ RLP-476 [M]	Soulmates	1964	6.25	12.50	25.00
❑ RS-9476 [S]	Soulmates	1964	7.50	15.00	30.00
WEBSTER, MAMIE					
CUB					
❑ 8002 [M]	The Blues	1959	37.50	75.00	150.00
WECHTER, JULIUS					
JAZZ: WEST					
❑ LP-9 [M]	Linear Sketches	1956	50.00	100.00	200.00
WEDGES, THE					
TIME					
❑ S-2090 [S]	Hang Ten (For Surfers Only)	1963	17.50	35.00	70.00
❑ 52090 [M]	Hang Ten (For Surfers Only)	1963	12.50	25.00	50.00
WEED, BUDDY					
COLUMBIA					
❑ CL 6160 [10]	Piano Moods	1951	12.50	25.00	50.00
CORAL					
❑ CRL 57087 [M]	Piano Solos with Rhythm Accompaniment	1957	10.00	20.00	40.00
WEEKS, ANSON					
FANTASY					
❑ 3258 [M]	Dancin' with Anson	1958	7.50	15.00	30.00
—Red vinyl					
❑ 3269 [M]	Memories	1958	7.50	15.00	30.00
—Red vinyl					
❑ 3297 [M]	More Dancin' with Anson	1959	7.50	15.00	30.00
—Red vinyl					
❑ 3306 [M]	Cruisin' with Anson	1960	7.50	15.00	30.00
—Red vinyl					
❑ 3333 [M]	Dancin' at Anson's	1961	3.00	6.00	12.00
—Black vinyl					
❑ 3338 [M]	Old Favorites and New	1962	6.25	12.50	25.00
—Red vinyl					
❑ 8001 [S]	Dancin' with Anson	1960	6.25	12.50	25.00
—Blue vinyl					
❑ 8001 [S]	Dancin' with Anson	1960	7.50	15.00	30.00
—Red vinyl (error pressing?)					
❑ 8006 [S]	Memories	1960	6.25	12.50	25.00
—Blue vinyl					
❑ 8043 [S]	More Dancin' with Anson	1960	6.25	12.50	25.00
—Blue vinyl					
❑ 8051 [S]	Cruisin' with Anson	1960	6.25	12.50	25.00
—Blue vinyl					
❑ 8076 [S]	Dancin' at Anson's	1961	3.75	7.50	15.00
—Black vinyl					
❑ 8090 [S]	Old Favorites and New	1962	7.50	15.00	30.00
—Blue vinyl					
WEEZER					
DGC					
❑ DGC-25007	Pinkerton	1996	5.00	10.00	20.00
GEFFEN					
❑ 069-493045-1	Weezer	2001	3.00	6.00	12.00
—Black vinyl					
❑ 069-493045-1	Weezer	2001	3.75	7.50	15.00
—Green vinyl					
❑ 069-493241-1	Maladroit	2002	3.00	6.00	12.00
WEIN, GEORGE					
ATLANTIC					
❑ 1221 [M]	Wein, Women and Song	1955	12.50	25.00	50.00
—Black label					
❑ 1221 [M]	Wein, Women and Song	1961	6.25	12.50	25.00
—Multicolor label, white "fan" logo at right					
BETHLEHEM					
❑ BCP-6050 [M]	George Wein and the Storyville Sextet — Jazz at the Modern	1960	10.00	20.00	40.00
❑ SBCP-6050 [S]	George Wein and the Storyville Sextet — Jazz at the Modern	1960	10.00	20.00	40.00

Number	Title (A Side/B Side)	Yr	VG	VG+	NM

IMPULSE!

❏ A-31 [M]	George Wein and the Newport All-Stars	1963	5.00	10.00	20.00
❏ AS-31 [S]	George Wein and the Newport All-Stars	1963	6.25	12.50	25.00

RCA VICTOR

❏ LPM-1332 [M]	The Magic Horn of George Wein	1956	10.00	20.00	40.00

WEIR, BOB

Also see THE GRATEFUL DEAD.

ARISTA

❏ AL 4155	Heaven Help the Fool	1978	2.50	5.00	10.00
❏ AL 8366	Heaven Help the Fool	1985	2.00	4.00	8.00
—Budget-line reissue					
❏ AL 8367	Bobby and the Midnites	1985	2.00	4.00	8.00
—Budget-line reissue					
❏ AL 9568	Bobby and the Midnites	1981	2.50	5.00	10.00

WARNER BROS.

❏ BS 2627	Ace	1972	7.50	15.00	30.00
—Black and white photo on back cover					
❏ BS 2627	Ace	1972	10.00	20.00	40.00
—Color photo on back cover					

WEIRD-OHS, THE

MERCURY

❏ MG-20976 [M]	The Sounds of the Weird-Ohs	1964	37.50	75.00	150.00
❏ SR-60976 [S]	The Sounds of the Weird-Ohs	1964	50.00	100.00	200.00

WEIRDOS

BOMP!

❏ 4007 [EP]	Who? What? When? Where? Why?	1979	3.75	7.50	15.00

FRONTIER

❏ 4623-1-L	Condor	1990	3.00	6.00	12.00
❏ 4630-1-L	Weird World	1991	3.00	6.00	12.00

OUT OF DARKNESS

❏ OTD 001 [DJ]	Message from the Underworld	198?	10.00	20.00	40.00
—Promo-only release					

RHINO

❏ RNEP 508 [EP]	Action Design	1980	5.00	10.00	20.00

WEISBERG, TIM

NAUTILUS

❏ NR-7	Tip of the Weisberg	1980	7.50	15.00	30.00
—Audiophile vinyl					

WEISSBERG, ERIC, AND MARSHALL BRICKMAN

ELEKTRA

❏ EKL-238 [M]	New Dimensions in Banjo and Bluegrass	1963	5.00	10.00	20.00
❏ EKS-7238 [S]	New Dimensions in Banjo and Bluegrass	1963	6.25	12.50	25.00
—Mandolin-player label					
❏ EKS-7238 [S]	New Dimensions in Banjo and Bluegrass	1967	5.00	10.00	20.00
—Tan label with large stylized "E" at top					
❏ EKS-7238 [S]	New Dimensions in Banjo and Bluegrass	1969	3.75	7.50	15.00
—Red label with large stylized "E" at top					
❏ EKS-7238 [S]	New Dimensions in Banjo and Bluegrass	1971	3.00	6.00	12.00
—Butterfly label					
❏ EKS-7238 [S]	New Dimensions in Banjo and Bluegrass	1980	2.50	5.00	10.00
—Red label with Warner Communications logo in lower right					

WELCH, LENNY

CADENCE

❏ CLP 3068 [M]	Since I Fell for You	1963	7.50	15.00	30.00
❏ CLP 25068 [S]	Since I Fell for You	1963	12.50	25.00	50.00

COLUMBIA

❏ CL 2430 [M]	Since I Fell for You	1965	5.00	10.00	20.00
—Reissue of Cadence 3068					
❏ CS 9230 [S]	Since I Fell for You	1965	7.50	15.00	30.00
—Reissue of Cadence 25068					

KAPP

❏ KL-1457 [M]	Two Different Worlds	1965	3.75	7.50	15.00
❏ KL-1481 [M]	Rags to Riches	1966	3.75	7.50	15.00
❏ KL-1517 [M]	Lenny	1967	3.75	7.50	15.00
❏ KS-3457 [S]	Two Different Worlds	1965	5.00	10.00	20.00
❏ KS-3481 [S]	Rags to Riches	1966	5.00	10.00	20.00
❏ KS-3517 [S]	Lenny	1967	5.00	10.00	20.00

WELCH CHORALE, THE

VANGUARD

❏ VRS 428 [M]	A Music Box of Christmas Carols	1954	5.00	10.00	20.00
—With Music Boxes from the Bornand Collection					

WELK, LAWRENCE

CORAL

❏ 7CXSB 5 [(2)S]	The Best of Lawrence Welk	196?	3.75	7.50	15.00
❏ CXB 5 [(2)M]	The Best of Lawrence Welk	196?	5.00	10.00	20.00
❏ CRL 56088 [10]	Souvenir Album	195?	7.50	15.00	30.00
❏ CRL 56101 [10]	Nimble Fingers	195?	7.50	15.00	30.00
❏ CRL 56120 [10]	Viennese Waltzes for Dancing	1954	7.50	15.00	30.00
❏ CRL 57011 [M]	Lawrence Welk and His Sparkling Strings	1955	5.00	10.00	20.00
❏ CRL 57023 [M]	Lawrence Welk Introduces the Girl Friends	1955	6.25	12.50	25.00
❏ CRL 57025 [M]	TV Favorites	1955	5.00	10.00	20.00
❏ CRL 57036 [M]	Shamrocks and Champagne	1955	5.00	10.00	20.00
❏ CRL 57038 [M]	Bubbles in the Wine	1956	5.00	10.00	20.00
❏ CRL 57041 [M]	Say It With Music	1956	5.00	10.00	20.00
❏ CRL 57066 [M]	Lawrence Welk at Madison Square Garden	1956	5.00	10.00	20.00
❏ CRL 57067 [M]	Pick-A-Polka!	1956	5.00	10.00	20.00
❏ CRL 57068 [M]	Moments to Remember	1956	5.00	10.00	20.00
❏ CRL 57078 [M]	Champagne Pops Parade	1956	5.00	10.00	20.00
❏ CRL 57093 [M]	Merry Christmas from Lawrence Welk	1956	5.00	10.00	20.00
❏ CRL 57111 [M]	Show Time	1957	5.00	10.00	20.00
❏ CRL 57113 [M]	The World's Finest Music	1957	5.00	10.00	20.00
❏ CRL 57119 [M]	Waltz with Lawrence Welk	1957	5.00	10.00	20.00
❏ CRL 57146 [M]	Lawrence Welk Plays Dixieland	1957	5.00	10.00	20.00
❏ CRL 57178 [M]	Nimble Fingers	1957	5.00	10.00	20.00

Number	Title (A Side/B Side)	Yr	VG	VG+	NM
❏ CRL 57186 [M]	Jingle Bells	1957	5.00	10.00	20.00
❏ CRL 57191 [M]	Songs of Faith	1958	3.75	7.50	15.00
❏ CRL 57214 [M]	Lawrence Welk Presents Keyboard Kapers	1958	3.75	7.50	15.00
❏ CRL 57226 [M]	Champagne Dancing Party	1958	3.75	7.50	15.00
❏ CRL 57260 [M]	Lawrence Welk Featuring the Lennon Sisters	1959	3.75	7.50	15.00
❏ CRL 57262 [M]	Lawrence Welk Featuring Larry Hooper	1959	3.75	7.50	15.00
❏ CRL 57267 [M]	TV Western Theme Songs	1959	3.75	7.50	15.00
❏ CRL 57353 [M]	My Golden Favorites	1961	3.00	6.00	12.00
❏ CRL 57383 [M]	Lawrence Welk Showcase	1962	3.00	6.00	12.00
❏ CRL 57439 [M]	Songs Everybody Knows	1964	3.00	6.00	12.00
❏ CRL 757036 [R]	Shamrocks and Champagne	196?	3.00	6.00	12.00
❏ CRL 757041 [R]	Say It With Music	196?	3.00	6.00	12.00
❏ CRL 757067 [R]	Pick-A-Polka!	1959	3.00	6.00	12.00
❏ CRL 757093 [R]	Merry Christmas from Lawrence Welk	196?	3.00	6.00	12.00
❏ CRL 757113 [R]	The World's Finest Music	196?	3.00	6.00	12.00
❏ CRL 757186 [R]	Jingle Bells	196?	3.00	6.00	12.00
❏ CRL 757226 [S]	Champagne Dancing Party	1958	5.00	10.00	20.00
❏ CRL 757267 [S]	TV Western Theme Songs	1959	5.00	10.00	20.00
❏ CRL 757353 [S]	My Golden Favorites	1961	3.00	6.00	12.00
❏ CRL 757383 [S]	Lawrence Welk Showcase	1962	3.00	6.00	12.00
❏ CRL 757439 [S]	Songs Everybody Knows	1964	3.00	6.00	12.00

CORONET

❏ 275	Lawrence Welk and His Orchestra	196?	2.50	5.00	10.00

DECCA

❏ DL 8213 [M]	Lawrence Welk's Polka Party	1956	3.75	7.50	15.00
❏ DL 8323 [M]	Around We Go	1956	3.75	7.50	15.00
❏ DL 8324 [M]	Welktime	1956	3.75	7.50	15.00

DESIGN

❏ 200	Champagne Time	196?	2.50	5.00	10.00
❏ 912	Three of a Kind	196?	2.50	5.00	10.00

DOT

❏ DLP 3164 [M]	Mr. Music Maker	1959	3.00	6.00	12.00
❏ DLP 3200 [M]	The Voices and Strings of Lawrence Welk.	1959	3.00	6.00	12.00
❏ DLP 3218 [M]	The Lawrence Welk Glee Club.	1959	3.00	6.00	12.00
❏ DLP 3224 [M]	Dance with Lawrence Welk.	1959	3.00	6.00	12.00
❏ DLP 3238 [M]	Lawrence Welk Presents Great American Composers.	1960	2.50	5.00	10.00
❏ DLP 3247 [M]	Lawrence Welk Presents Great Overtures in Dance Time.	1960	2.50	5.00	10.00
❏ DLP 3248 [M]	I'm Forever Blowing Bubbles.	1960	2.50	5.00	10.00
❏ DLP 3251 [M]	Songs of the Islands.	1960	2.50	5.00	10.00
❏ DLP 3274 [M]	Strictly for Dancing.	1960	2.50	5.00	10.00
❏ DLP 3284 [M]	To Mother.	1960	2.50	5.00	10.00
❏ DLP 3296 [M]	Sweet and Lovely.	1960	2.50	5.00	10.00
❏ DLP 3302 [M]	Polkas.	1960	2.50	5.00	10.00
❏ DLP 3317 [M]	Lawrence in Dixieland.	1960	2.50	5.00	10.00
❏ DLP 3318 [M]	Double Shuffle.	1960	2.50	5.00	10.00
❏ DLP 3342 [M]	The Champagne Music of Lawrence Welk.	1960	2.50	5.00	10.00
❏ DLP 3350 [M]	Last Date.	1960	2.50	5.00	10.00
❏ DLP 3359 [M]	Calcutta!	1961	2.50	5.00	10.00
❏ DLP 3389 [M]	Yellow Bird.	1961	2.50	5.00	10.00
❏ DLP 3395 [M]	Diamond Jubilee.	1961	2.50	5.00	10.00
❏ DLP 3397 [M]	Silent Night and 13 Other Best-Loved Christmas Songs.	1961	3.00	6.00	12.00
❏ DLP 3412 [M]	Moon River.	1961	2.50	5.00	10.00
❏ DLP 3428 [M]	Young World.	1962	2.50	5.00	10.00
❏ DLP 3432 [M]	Sing-a-Long Party.	1962	2.50	5.00	10.00
❏ DLP 3457 [M]	Baby Elephant Walk and Theme from The Brothers Grimm.	1962	2.50	5.00	10.00
❏ DLP 3489 [M]	Bubbles in the Wine.	1962	2.50	5.00	10.00
❏ DLP 3499 [M]	Waltz Time.	1963	2.50	5.00	10.00
❏ DLP 3510 [M]	1963's Early Hits.	1963	2.50	5.00	10.00
❏ DLP 3528 [M]	Scarlett O'Hara.	1963	2.50	5.00	10.00
❏ DLP 3544 [M]	A Tribute to the All-Time Greats.	1963	2.50	5.00	10.00
❏ DLP 3552 [M]	Wonderful! Wonderful!	1963	2.50	5.00	10.00
❏ DLP 3572 [M]	Early Hits of 1964.	1964	2.50	5.00	10.00
❏ DLP 3591 [M]	The Lawrence Welk Television Show 10th Anniversary.	1964	2.50	5.00	10.00
❏ DLP 3611 [M]	The Golden Millions.	1964	2.50	5.00	10.00
❏ DLP 3616 [M]	My First of 1965.	1965	2.50	5.00	10.00
❏ DLP 3629 [M]	Apples and Bananas.	1965	2.50	5.00	10.00
❏ DLP 3653 [M]	The Happy Wanderer.	1966	2.50	5.00	10.00
❏ DLP 3663 [M]	Today's Great Hits.	1966	2.50	5.00	10.00
❏ DLP 3688 [M]	Champagne on Broadway.	1966	2.50	5.00	10.00
❏ DLP 3774 [M]	Winchester Cathedral.	1966	2.50	5.00	10.00
❏ DLP 3779 [M]	Hymns We Love.	1967	2.50	5.00	10.00
❏ DLP 3790 [M]	Lawrence Welk's "Hits of Our Time".	1967	2.50	5.00	10.00
❏ DLP 3812 [M]	Golden Hits/The Best of Lawrence Welk.	1967	3.00	6.00	12.00
❏ DLP 25164 [S]	Mr. Music Maker.	1959	3.75	7.50	15.00
❏ DLP 25200 [S]	Voices and Strings.	1959	3.75	7.50	15.00
❏ DLP 25218 [S]	The Lawrence Welk Glee Club.	1959	3.75	7.50	15.00
❏ DLP 25224 [S]	Dance with Lawrence Welk.	1959	3.75	7.50	15.00
❏ DLP 25238 [S]	Lawrence Welk Presents Great American Composers.	1960	3.00	6.00	12.00
❏ DLP 25247 [S]	Lawrence Welk Presents Great Overtures in Dance Time.	1960	3.00	6.00	12.00
❏ DLP 25248 [S]	I'm Forever Blowing Bubbles.	1960	3.00	6.00	12.00
❏ DLP 25251 [S]	Songs of the Islands.	1960	3.00	6.00	12.00
❏ DLP 25274 [S]	Strictly for Dancing.	1960	3.00	6.00	12.00
❏ DLP 25284 [S]	To Mother.	1960	3.00	6.00	12.00
❏ DLP 25296 [S]	Sweet and Lovely.	1960	3.00	6.00	12.00
❏ DLP 25302 [S]	Polkas.	1960	3.00	6.00	12.00
❏ DLP 25317 [S]	Lawrence in Dixieland.	1960	3.00	6.00	12.00
❏ DLP 25318 [S]	Double Shuffle.	1960	3.00	6.00	12.00
❏ DLP 25342 [S]	The Champagne Music of Lawrence Welk.	1960	3.00	6.00	12.00
❏ DLP 25350 [S]	Last Date.	1960	3.00	6.00	12.00
❏ DLP 25359 [S]	Calcutta!	1961	3.00	6.00	12.00
❏ DLP 25389 [S]	Yellow Bird.	1961	3.00	6.00	12.00
❏ DLP 25395 [S]	Diamond Jubilee.	1961	3.00	6.00	12.00
❏ DLP 25397 [S]	Silent Night and 13 Other Best-Loved Christmas Songs.	1961	3.75	7.50	15.00
❏ DLP 25412 [S]	Moon River.	1961	3.00	6.00	12.00
❏ DLP 25428 [S]	Young World.	1962	3.00	6.00	12.00

Number	Title (A Side/B Side)	Yr	VG	VG+	NM
❏ DLP 25432 [S]	Sing-a-Long Party	1962	3.00	6.00	12.00
❏ DLP 25457 [S]	Baby Elephant Walk and Theme from The Brothers Grimm	1962	3.00	6.00	12.00
❏ DLP 25489 [S]	Bubbles in the Wine	1962	3.00	6.00	12.00
❏ DLP 25499 [S]	Waltz Time	1963	3.00	6.00	12.00
❏ DLP 25510 [S]	1963's Early Hits	1963	3.00	6.00	12.00
❏ DLP 25528 [S]	Scarlett O'Hara	1963	3.00	6.00	12.00
❏ DLP 25544 [S]	A Tribute to the All-Time Greats	1963	3.00	6.00	12.00
❏ DLP 25552 [S]	Wonderful! Wonderful!	1963	3.00	6.00	12.00
❏ DLP 25572 [S]	Early Hits of 1964	1964	3.00	6.00	12.00
❏ DLP 25591 [S]	The Lawrence Welk Television Show 10th Anniversary	1964	3.00	6.00	12.00
❏ DLP 25611 [S]	The Golden Millions	1964	3.00	6.00	12.00
❏ DLP 25616 [S]	My First of 1965	1965	3.00	6.00	12.00
❏ DLP 25629 [S]	Apples and Bananas	1965	3.00	6.00	12.00
❏ DLP 25653 [S]	The Happy Wanderer	1966	3.00	6.00	12.00
❏ DLP 25663 [S]	Today's Great Hits	1966	3.00	6.00	12.00
❏ DLP 25688 [S]	Champagne on Broadway	1966	3.00	6.00	12.00
❏ DLP 25774 [S]	Winchester Cathedral	1966	3.00	6.00	12.00
❏ DLP 25779 [S]	Hymns We Love	1967	3.00	6.00	12.00
❏ DLP 25790 [S]	Lawrence Welk's "Hits of Our Time"	1967	3.00	6.00	12.00
❏ DLP 25812 [S]	Golden Hits/The Best of Lawrence Welk	1967	2.50	5.00	10.00

HAMILTON

❏ HLP 152 [M]	Mary Poppins	1965	2.50	5.00	10.00
❏ HLP 12152 [S]	Mary Poppins	1965	3.00	6.00	12.00

HARMONY

❏ HL 7394 [M]	Vintage Champagne	1966	3.00	6.00	12.00
❏ HS 11194 [S]	Vintage Champagne	1966	3.00	6.00	12.00
❏ HS 11301	Champagne Dance Party	1969	2.50	5.00	10.00

HEARTLAND

❏ 1006	Musical Family Reunion	198?	2.50	5.00	10.00

MCA

❏ 733	Polka and Waltz Time	197?	2.00	4.00	8.00

—Reissue of Vocalion 73670

❏ 4026 [(2)]	The Best of Lawrence Welk, Volume 2	197?	3.00	6.00	12.00
❏ 4044 [(2)]	The Best of Lawrence Welk	197?	3.00	6.00	12.00
❏ 4104 [(2)]	The Best Polkas	197?	3.00	6.00	12.00

MCA CORAL

❏ 20100	Champagne Music	197?	2.00	4.00	8.00

MERCURY

❏ MG-20092 [M]	Dance Party	1956	3.75	7.50	15.00

MISTLETOE

❏ MLP-1215	Christmas with Lawrence Welk	197?	2.50	5.00	10.00

PICKWICK

❏ SPC-1019	The Christmas Song	197?	2.50	5.00	10.00

—Reissue of Coral LP "Jingle Bells" with shuffled running order

❏ SPC-3070	Save the Last Dance for Me	196?	2.50	5.00	10.00
❏ SPC-3092	I'll See You Again	196?	2.50	5.00	10.00
❏ SPC-3116	You'll Never Walk Alone	196?	2.50	5.00	10.00
❏ SPC-3143	If You Were the Only One	196?	2.50	5.00	10.00
❏ SPC-3157	As Time Goes By	196?	2.50	5.00	10.00
❏ SPC-3196	Love Is a Many-Splendored Thing	197?	2.50	5.00	10.00
❏ SPC-3212	Blue Hawaii	197?	2.50	5.00	10.00
❏ SPC-3252	Polkas!	197?	2.50	5.00	10.00

PREMIER

❏ 9043	Lawrence Welk	196?	2.50	5.00	10.00

RANWOOD

❏ 2000	Merry Christmas	197?	2.50	5.00	10.00
❏ 2004	Polkas	197?	2.00	4.00	8.00

—With Myron Floren

❏ 2005	Moon River	197?	—	3.00	6.00

—Reissue of Ranwood 8016

❏ 2006	Yellow Bird	197?	—	3.00	6.00

—Reissue of Ranwood 8021

❏ 2007	Songs of the Islands	197?	—	3.00	6.00

—Reissue of Ranwood 8022

❏ 2008	Waltz Time	197?	—	3.00	6.00

—Reissue of Ranwood 8025

❏ 2009	Hymns We Love	197?	—	3.00	6.00

—Reissue of Ranwood 8042

❏ 2010	Memories	197?	—	3.00	6.00

—Reissue of Ranwood 8044

❏ 4100	On Tour, Volume 1	198?	2.00	4.00	8.00
❏ 4101	On Tour, Volume 2	198?	2.00	4.00	8.00
❏ 5001 [(2)]	Reminiscing	1972	3.00	6.00	12.00
❏ 5005 [(2)]	24 of the World's Greatest Polkas	197?	3.00	6.00	12.00

—With Myron Floren

❏ 6001 [(2)]	Lawrence Welk and His Musical Family in Concert	1973	3.00	6.00	12.00
❏ 6002	Lawrence Welk and His Musical Family Celebrate 50 Years in Music	1974	2.50	5.00	10.00
❏ 7002 [(2)]	200 Years of American Music	1976	3.00	6.00	12.00
❏ 7004 [(2)]	22 Great Waltzes	1977	3.00	6.00	12.00
❏ 7009 [(2)]	22 Great Songs for Dancing	1978	3.00	6.00	12.00
❏ 7016 [(2)]	22 Great Songs for Easy Listening	198?	3.00	6.00	12.00
❏ 7023 [(2)]	22 All-Time Big Band Favorites	1983	3.00	6.00	12.00
❏ 7028 [(2)]	22 All-Time Favorite Waltzes	198?	3.00	6.00	12.00
❏ 7029 [(2)]	22 Merry Christmas Favorites	198?	3.00	6.00	12.00
❏ 8003	Love Is Blue	1968	2.50	5.00	10.00
❏ 8016	Moon River	1968	2.00	4.00	8.00

—Reissue of Dot 25412

❏ 8017	Winchester Cathedral	1968	2.00	4.00	8.00

—Reissue of Dot 25774

❏ 8020	Silent Night and 13 Other Best-Loved Christmas Songs	1968	2.00	4.00	8.00

—Reissue of Dot 25397

❏ 8021	Yellow Bird	1968	2.00	4.00	8.00

—Reissue of Dot 25389

❏ 8022	Songs of the Islands	1968	2.00	4.00	8.00

—Reissue of Dot 25251

❏ 8023	The Champagne Music of Lawrence Welk	1968	2.00	4.00	8.00

—Reissue of Dot 25342

❏ 8024	Calcutta!	1968	2.00	4.00	8.00

—Reissue of Dot 25359

❏ 8025	Waltz Time	1968	2.00	4.00	8.00

—Reissue of Dot 25499

❏ 8026	The Lawrence Welk Television Show	1968	2.00	4.00	8.00

—Reissue of Dot 25591

❏ 8027	Country Music's Great Hits	1968	2.50	5.00	10.00
❏ 8028	Golden Hits/The Best of Lawrence Welk	1968	2.00	4.00	8.00

—Reissue of Dot 25812

❏ 8030	To America with Love	1968	2.50	5.00	10.00
❏ 8034	The Lawrence Welk Singers and Orchestra	1968	2.50	5.00	10.00
❏ 8042	Hymns We Love	1968	2.00	4.00	8.00

—Reissue of Dot 25779

❏ 8044	Memories	1969	2.50	5.00	10.00
❏ 8049	Galveston	1969	2.50	5.00	10.00
❏ 8053	Lawrence Welk Plays I Love You Truly and Other Songs of Love	1969	2.50	5.00	10.00
❏ 8060	Jean	1969	2.50	5.00	10.00
❏ 8068	The Golden 60's	1970	2.50	5.00	10.00
❏ 8077	The Big Band Sound	1970	2.50	5.00	10.00
❏ 8079	Champagne Strings	1970	2.50	5.00	10.00
❏ 8083	Candida	1970	2.50	5.00	10.00
❏ 8087	No, No, Nanette	1971	2.50	5.00	10.00
❏ 8091	Go Away Little Girl	1971	2.50	5.00	10.00
❏ 8109	(More of) The Big Band Sound	1972	2.50	5.00	10.00
❏ 8114	The Good Life	1973	2.50	5.00	10.00
❏ 8130	Lawrence Welk Plays From That's Entertainment	1974	2.50	5.00	10.00
❏ 8140	Most Requested TV Favorites	1974	2.50	5.00	10.00
❏ 8145	25 Years on Television	1975	2.50	5.00	10.00
❏ 8162	The Best of Lawrence Welk: 20 Great Hits	1976	2.50	5.00	10.00
❏ 8165	Nadia's Theme	1976	2.50	5.00	10.00
❏ 8183	My Personal Favorites	1978	2.50	5.00	10.00
❏ 8184	Hallelujah!	1978	2.50	5.00	10.00
❏ 8191	Remembering the Sweet and Swing Band Era, Vol. 1	1979	2.50	5.00	10.00
❏ 8192	Remembering the Sweet and Swing Band Era, Vol. 2	1979	2.50	5.00	10.00
❏ 8194	Lawrence Welk Plays Dixieland	1980	2.50	5.00	10.00
❏ 8195 [(2)]	Reminiscing, Vol. 2	1980	3.00	6.00	12.00
❏ 8201	Lawrence Welk Presents Anacani	1982	2.50	5.00	10.00
❏ 8210	Musical Memories with Lawrence Welk	1984	2.00	4.00	8.00
❏ 8211	Come Waltz with Me	1984	2.00	4.00	8.00
❏ 10001 [(2)]	Live at Lake Tahoe	1978	3.00	6.00	12.00
❏ 10002 [(2)]	The Sweet and Swing Band Era	1979	3.00	6.00	12.00

READER'S DIGEST

❏ RDA-07-A [(4)]	Merry Christmas from Lawrence Welk and His Champagne Music Makers	1970	6.25	12.50	25.00
❏ RDA 95 [(6)]	Champagne Music Varieties	196?	6.25	12.50	25.00
❏ RDA 156	Champagne Dance Time with Lawrence Welk	196?	2.50	5.00	10.00

SUNNYVALE

❏ SVL-1015	Silent Night and 13 Other Best-Loved Christmas Songs	1978	2.00	4.00	8.00

—Same contents as Dot 25397

THOMAS

❏ 20052	The Magic of Color-Glo	196?	3.00	6.00	12.00

VOCALION

❏ VL 3670 [M]	Polka and Waltz Time	196?	2.50	5.00	10.00
❏ VL 3671 [M]	Lawrence Welk and His Champagne Music	196?	2.50	5.00	10.00
❏ VL 3783 [M]	Lawrence Welk and His Champagne Music Makers Play for You	1967	3.00	6.00	12.00
❏ VL 73670 [R]	Polka and Waltz Time	196?	2.50	5.00	10.00
❏ VL 73671 [R]	Lawrence Welk and His Champagne Music	196?	2.50	5.00	10.00
❏ VL 73783 [R]	Lawrence Welk and His Champagne Music Makers Play for You	1967	2.50	5.00	10.00
❏ VL 73865	Champagne Polkas	1969	2.50	5.00	10.00
❏ VL 73888	Til the End of Time	1969	2.50	5.00	10.00
❏ VL 73921	Wonderful Music	1970	2.50	5.00	10.00

WING

❏ PKW-2-114 [(2)]	With a-One and a-Two	1969	3.75	7.50	15.00
❏ MGW-12119 [M]	Dance Party	196?	3.00	6.00	12.00
❏ MGW-12210 [M]	Music for Polka Lovers	196?	3.00	6.00	12.00
❏ MGW-12214 [M]	Aragon Trianon Memories	196?	3.00	6.00	12.00
❏ SRW-16210 [S]	Music for Polka Lovers	196?	2.50	5.00	10.00
❏ SRW-16214 [R]	Aragon Trianon Memories	196?	2.50	5.00	10.00
❏ SRW-16379	The Best of Welk	196?	2.50	5.00	10.00

WELLS, DICKY

FELSTED

❏ SJA-2006 [S]	Bones for the King	1958	10.00	20.00	40.00
❏ SJA-2009 [S]	Trombone Four in Hand	1958	10.00	20.00	40.00
❏ FAJ-7006 [M]	Bones for the King	1958	10.00	20.00	40.00
❏ FAJ-7009 [M]	Trombone Four in Hand	1958	10.00	20.00	40.00

PRESTIGE

❏ PRST-7593 [R]	Dicky Wells in Pais 1937	1968	6.25	12.50	25.00

WELLS, JUNIOR

BLUE ROCK

❏ 64002	You're Tuff Enough	1968	7.50	15.00	30.00
❏ 64003	Live at the Golden Bear	1969	7.50	15.00	30.00

DELMARK

❏ DL-612 [M]	Hoodoo Man Blues	1966	10.00	20.00	40.00
❏ DS-612 [S]	Hoodoo Man Blues	1966	12.50	25.00	50.00
❏ DS-628	Southside Blues Jam	1967	6.25	12.50	25.00
❏ DS-640	Blues Hit the Big Town	1969	6.25	12.50	25.00
❏ DS-640	Blue Hit Big Towns	1969	7.50	15.00	30.00

VANGUARD

❏ VRS-9231 [M]	It's My Life Baby	1966	7.50	15.00	30.00

Number	Title (A Side/B Side)	Yr	VG	VG+	NM
❏ VSD-79231 [S]	It's My Life Baby	1966	10.00	20.00	40.00
❏ VSD-79262	Comin' At You	1968	6.25	12.50	25.00

WELLS, KITTY
DECCA

Number	Title (A Side/B Side)	Yr	VG	VG+	NM
❏ DXB 174 [(2)M]	The Kitty Wells Story	1963	7.50	15.00	30.00
❏ DL 4075 [M]	Seasons of My Heart	1961	7.50	15.00	30.00
❏ DL 4108 [M]	Kitty Wells' Golden Favorites	1961	7.50	15.00	30.00
❏ DL 4141 [M]	Heartbreak U.S.A.	1961	7.50	15.00	30.00
❏ DL 4197 [M]	Queen of Country Music	1962	7.50	15.00	30.00
❏ DL 4270 [M]	Singing on Sunday	1962	7.50	15.00	30.00
❏ DL 4349 [M]	Christmas Day with Kitty Wells	1962	6.25	12.50	25.00
❏ DL 4493 [M]	Especially for You	1964	6.25	12.50	25.00
❏ DL 4554 [M]	Country Music Time	1964	6.25	12.50	25.00
❏ DL 4612 [M]	Burning Memories	1965	6.25	12.50	25.00
❏ DL 4658 [M]	Lonesome Sad and Blue	1965	6.25	12.50	25.00
❏ DL 4679 [M]	Family Gospel Sing	1965	6.25	12.50	25.00
❏ DL 4741 [M]	Kitty Wells Sings Songs Made Famous by Jim Reeves	1966	6.25	12.50	25.00
❏ DL 4776 [M]	Country All the Way	1966	6.25	12.50	25.00
❏ DL 4831 [M]	The Kitty Wells Show	1966	6.25	12.50	25.00
❏ DL 4857 [M]	Love Makes the World Go Around	1967	7.50	15.00	30.00
❏ DL 4929 [M]	Queen of Honky Tonk Street	1967	10.00	20.00	40.00
❏ DL 5001 [M]	Kitty Wells' Greatest Hits	1968	12.50	25.00	50.00
—White label promo only					
❏ DXSB 7174 [(2)P]	The Kitty Wells Story	1963	10.00	20.00	40.00
❏ DL 8293 [M]	Kitty Wells' Country Hit Parade	1956	15.00	30.00	60.00
—Black label, silver print					
❏ DL 8293 [M]	Kitty Wells' Country Hit Parade	1961	7.50	15.00	30.00
—Black label with color bars					
❏ DL 8552 [M]	Winner of Your Heart	1957	15.00	30.00	60.00
—Black label, silver print					
❏ DL 8552 [M]	Winner of Your Heart	1961	7.50	15.00	30.00
—Black label with color bars					
❏ DL 8732 [M]	Lonely Street	1958	15.00	30.00	60.00
—Black label, silver print					
❏ DL 8732 [M]	Lonely Street	1961	7.50	15.00	30.00
—Black label with color bars					
❏ DL 8858 [M]	Dust on the Bible	1959	15.00	30.00	60.00
—Black label, silver print					
❏ DL 8858 [M]	Dust on the Bible	1961	7.50	15.00	30.00
—Black label with color bars					
❏ DL 8888 [M]	After Dark	1959	15.00	30.00	60.00
—Black label, silver print					
❏ DL 8888 [M]	After Dark	1961	7.50	15.00	30.00
—Black label with color bars					
❏ DL 8979 [M]	Kitty's Choice	1960	12.50	25.00	50.00
—Black label, silver print					
❏ DL 8979 [M]	Kitty's Choice	1961	6.25	12.50	25.00
—Black label with color bars					
❏ DL 74075 [S]	Seasons of My Heart	1961	10.00	20.00	40.00
❏ DL 74108 [R]	Kitty Wells' Golden Favorites	196?	5.00	10.00	20.00
❏ DL 74141 [S]	Heartbreak U.S.A.	1961	10.00	20.00	40.00
❏ DL 74197 [S]	Queen of Country Music	1962	10.00	20.00	40.00
❏ DL 74270 [S]	Singing on Sunday	1962	10.00	20.00	40.00
❏ DL 74349 [S]	Christmas Day with Kitty Wells	1962	7.50	15.00	30.00
❏ DL 74493 [S]	Especially for You	1964	7.50	15.00	30.00
❏ DL 74554 [S]	Country Music Time	1964	7.50	15.00	30.00
❏ DL 74612 [S]	Burning Memories	1965	7.50	15.00	30.00
❏ DL 74658 [S]	Lonesome Sad and Blue	1965	7.50	15.00	30.00
❏ DL 74679 [S]	Family Gospel Sing	1965	7.50	15.00	30.00
❏ DL 74741 [S]	Kitty Wells Sings Songs Made Famous by Jim Reeves	1966	7.50	15.00	30.00
❏ DL 74776 [S]	Country All the Way	1966	7.50	15.00	30.00
❏ DL 74831 [S]	The Kitty Wells Show	1966	7.50	15.00	30.00
❏ DL 74857 [S]	Love Makes the World Go Around	1967	7.50	15.00	30.00
❏ DL 74929 [S]	Queen of Honky Tonk Street	1967	6.25	12.50	25.00
❏ DL 74961	Kitty Wells Showcase	1968	6.25	12.50	25.00
❏ DL 75001 [S]	Kitty Wells' Greatest Hits	1968	6.25	12.50	25.00
❏ DL 75067	Cream of Country Hits	1968	6.25	12.50	25.00
❏ DL 75098	Guilty Street	1969	6.25	12.50	25.00
❏ DL 75164	Bouquet of Country Hits	1969	5.00	10.00	20.00
❏ DL 75221	Singin' 'Em Country	1970	5.00	10.00	20.00
❏ DL 75245	Your Love Is the Way	1970	5.00	10.00	20.00
❏ DL 75277	They're Stepping All Over My Heart	1971	5.00	10.00	20.00
❏ DL 75313	Pledging My Love	1971	5.00	10.00	20.00
❏ DL 75325	Heartwarming Gospel Songs	1972	5.00	10.00	20.00
❏ DL 75350	Sincerely	1972	5.00	10.00	20.00
❏ DL 75382	I've Got Yesterday	1972	5.00	10.00	20.00
❏ DL 78293 [R]	Kitty Wells' Country Hit Parade	196?	5.00	10.00	20.00
❏ DL 78552 [R]	Winner of Your Heart	196?	5.00	10.00	20.00
❏ DL 78732 [R]	Lonely Street	196?	5.00	10.00	20.00
❏ DL 78858 [R]	Dust on the Bible	196?	5.00	10.00	20.00
❏ DL 78979 [S]	Kitty's Choice	1960	15.00	30.00	60.00
—Maroon label, silver print					
❏ DL 78979 [S]	Kitty's Choice	1961	7.50	15.00	30.00
—Black label with color bars					

WELLS, KITTY, AND RED FOLEY
Also see each artist's individual listings.
DECCA

Number	Title (A Side/B Side)	Yr	VG	VG+	NM
❏ DL 4109 [M]	Golden Favorites	1961	7.50	15.00	30.00
❏ DL 4906 [M]	Together Again	1967	7.50	15.00	30.00
❏ DL 74109 [S]	Golden Favorites	1961	10.00	20.00	40.00
❏ DL 74906 [S]	Together Again	1967	6.25	12.50	25.00

WELLS, KITTY, AND JOHNNY WRIGHT
DECCA

Number	Title (A Side/B Side)	Yr	VG	VG+	NM
❏ DL 75028	We'll Stick Together	1968	6.25	12.50	25.00

WELLS, MARY
ALLEGIANCE

Number	Title (A Side/B Side)	Yr	VG	VG+	NM
❏ AV-444	The Old, the New, and the Best of Mary Wells	1984	2.50	5.00	10.00

ATCO

Number	Title (A Side/B Side)	Yr	VG	VG+	NM
❏ 33-199 [M]	Two Sides of Mary Wells	1966	6.25	12.50	25.00
❏ SD 33-199 [S]	Two Sides of Mary Wells	1966	7.50	15.00	30.00

EPIC

Number	Title (A Side/B Side)	Yr	VG	VG+	NM
❏ ARE 37540	In and Out of Love	1981	3.75	7.50	15.00

JUBILEE

Number	Title (A Side/B Side)	Yr	VG	VG+	NM
❏ JGS-8018	Servin' Up Some Soul	1968	6.25	12.50	25.00

MOTOWN

Number	Title (A Side/B Side)	Yr	VG	VG+	NM
❏ M5-161V1	Bye Bye Baby/I Don't Want to Take a Chance	1981	2.50	5.00	10.00
❏ M5-167V1	Mary Wells Sings My Guy	1981	2.50	5.00	10.00
❏ M5-221V1	Two Lovers	1981	2.50	5.00	10.00
❏ MLP-600 [M]	Bye Bye Baby/I Don't Want to Take a Chance	1961	75.00	150.00	300.00
—White label stock copy					
❏ MLP-600 [M]	Bye Bye Baby/I Don't Want to Take a Chance	1962	62.50	125.00	250.00
—With map; label address above the center hole					
❏ M 605 [M]	The One Who Really Loves You	1964	10.00	20.00	40.00
—With map; label address around lower part of label					
❏ M 605 [M]	The One Who Really Loves You	1962	40.00	80.00	160.00
—With map; label address above the center hole					
❏ M 607 [M]	Two Lovers and Other Great Hits	1964	10.00	20.00	40.00
—With map; label address around lower part of label					
❏ M 607 [M]	Two Lovers and Other Great Hits	1963	30.00	60.00	120.00
—With map; label address above the center hole					
❏ M 611 [M]	Recorded Live on Stage	1964	10.00	20.00	40.00
—With map; label address around lower part of label					
❏ M 611 [M]	Recorded Live on Stage	1963	30.00	60.00	120.00
—With map; label address above the center hole					
❏ M 612	Second Time Around	1963	—	—	—
—Canceled					
❏ M 616 [M]	Greatest Hits	1964	10.00	20.00	40.00
❏ MS 616 [S]	Greatest Hits	1964	10.00	20.00	40.00
❏ M 617 [M]	Mary Wells Sings My Guy	1964	12.50	25.00	50.00
❏ M 653 [M]	Vintage Stock	1967	12.50	25.00	50.00
❏ MS 653 [S]	Vintage Stock	1967	12.50	25.00	50.00
❏ 5233 ML	Greatest Hits	1982	2.50	5.00	10.00

MOVIETONE

Number	Title (A Side/B Side)	Yr	VG	VG+	NM
❏ 71010 [M]	Ooh	1966	6.25	12.50	25.00
❏ 72010 [S]	Ooh	1966	7.50	15.00	30.00

20TH FOX

Number	Title (A Side/B Side)	Yr	VG	VG+	NM
❏ TFM 3171 [M]	Mary Wells	1965	10.00	20.00	40.00
❏ TFM 3178 [M]	Love Songs to the Beatles	1965	20.00	40.00	80.00
❏ TFS 4171 [S]	Mary Wells	1965	15.00	30.00	60.00
❏ TFS 4178 [S]	Love Songs to the Beatles	1965	25.00	50.00	100.00
❏ ST-90790 [S]	Love Songs to the Beatles	1965	37.50	75.00	150.00
—Capitol Record Club edition					

WELLSTOOD, DICK
RIVERSIDE

Number	Title (A Side/B Side)	Yr	VG	VG+	NM
❏ RLP-2506 [10]	Dick Wellstood	1955	25.00	50.00	100.00

WELLSTOOD, DICK, AND CLIFF JACKSON
SWINGVILLE

Number	Title (A Side/B Side)	Yr	VG	VG+	NM
❏ SVLP-2026 [M]	Uptown and Downtown	1961	12.50	25.00	50.00
—Purple label					
❏ SVLP-2026 [M]	Uptown and Downtown	1965	6.25	12.50	25.00
—Blue label, trident logo at right					

WESLEY, FRED
ATLANTIC

Number	Title (A Side/B Side)	Yr	VG	VG+	NM
❏ SD 18214	A Blow for Me, A Toot to You	1977	3.00	6.00	12.00
❏ SD 19254	Say Blow by Blow Backwards	1979	3.00	6.00	12.00

PEOPLE

Number	Title (A Side/B Side)	Yr	VG	VG+	NM
❏ PE-5601	Food for Thought	1972	20.00	40.00	80.00
❏ PE-5603	Doing It to Death	1973	20.00	40.00	80.00
❏ PE-6602	Damn Right I Am Somebody	1974	5.00	10.00	20.00
❏ PE-6604	Breakin' Bread	1974	5.00	10.00	20.00

WESS, FRANK
COMMODORE

Number	Title (A Side/B Side)	Yr	VG	VG+	NM
❏ FL-20031 [10]	Frank Wess Quintet	1952	30.00	60.00	120.00
❏ FL-20032 [10]	Frank Wess	1952	30.00	60.00	120.00

MAINSTREAM

Number	Title (A Side/B Side)	Yr	VG	VG+	NM
❏ 56033 [M]	Award Winner	1965	6.25	12.50	25.00

MOODSVILLE

Number	Title (A Side/B Side)	Yr	VG	VG+	NM
❏ MVLP-8 [M]	Frank Wess Quartet	1960	12.50	25.00	50.00
—Green label					
❏ MVLP-8 [M]	Frank Wess Quartet	1965	6.25	12.50	25.00
—Blue label, trident logo at right					

PRESTIGE

Number	Title (A Side/B Side)	Yr	VG	VG+	NM
❏ PRLP-7231 [M]	Southern Comfort	1962	10.00	20.00	40.00
❏ PRST-7231 [S]	Southern Comfort	1962	12.50	25.00	50.00
❏ PRLP-7266 [M]	Yo Ho! Poor You, Little Me	1963	10.00	20.00	40.00
❏ PRST-7266 [S]	Yo Ho! Poor You, Little Me	1963	12.50	25.00	50.00

SAVOY

Number	Title (A Side/B Side)	Yr	VG	VG+	NM
❏ MG-12022 [M]	Flutes and Reeds	1955	20.00	40.00	80.00
❏ MG-12072 [M]	North, South, East, Wess	1956	20.00	40.00	80.00
❏ MG-12095 [M]	Jazz for Playboys	1956	20.00	40.00	80.00

STATUS

Number	Title (A Side/B Side)	Yr	VG	VG+	NM
❏ ST-7266 [S]	Yo Ho! Poor You, Little Me	1965	5.00	10.00	20.00

WESS, FRANK, AND KENNY BURRELL
PRESTIGE

Number	Title (A Side/B Side)	Yr	VG	VG+	NM
❏ PRLP-7278 [M]	Steamin'	1963	10.00	20.00	40.00
❏ PRST-7278 [R]	Steamin'	1963	6.25	12.50	25.00

WESS, FRANK, AND THAD JONES
STATUS

Number	Title (A Side/B Side)	Yr	VG	VG+	NM
❏ ST-8310 [M]	Touche	1965	10.00	20.00	40.00

Number	Title (A Side/B Side)	Yr	VG	VG+	NM
WEST					
EPIC					
❑ BN 26380	West	1968	5.00	10.00	20.00
❑ BN 26433	Bridges	1969	5.00	10.00	20.00
WEST, ALVY					
COLUMBIA					
❑ CL 6062 [10]	Alvy West and His Little Band	1949	15.00	30.00	60.00
WEST, DOTTIE					
LIBERTY					
❑ LT-740	When It's Just You and Me	1981	2.00	4.00	8.00
—Reissue of United Artists 740					
❑ LT-860	Dottie	1981	2.00	4.00	8.00
—Reissue of United Artists 860					
❑ LT-1000	Special Delivery	1981	2.00	4.00	8.00
—Reissue of United Artists 1000					
❑ LT-1062	Wild West	1981	2.50	5.00	10.00
❑ LT-51114	High Times	1982	2.50	5.00	10.00
❑ LT-51129	Full Circle	1982	2.50	5.00	10.00
❑ LT-51145	New Horizons	1983	2.50	5.00	10.00
❑ LT-51155	Greatest Hits	1984	2.50	5.00	10.00
POWER PAK					
❑ 274	Country Girl Singing Sensation	197?	2.50	5.00	10.00
RCA CAMDEN					
❑ ACL1-0125	Would You Hold It Against Me	1973	2.50	5.00	10.00
❑ ACL1-0482	Loving You	1974	2.50	5.00	10.00
❑ CAL-2155 [M]	The Sound of Country Music	1967	3.75	7.50	15.00
❑ CAS-2155 [S]	The Sound of Country Music	1967	3.00	6.00	12.00
❑ CAS-2454	A Legend in My Time	1971	3.00	6.00	12.00
RCA VICTOR					
❑ APD1-0151 [Q]	If It's All Right with You/Just What I've Been Looking For	1973	5.00	10.00	20.00
❑ APL1-0151	If It's All Right with You/Just What I've Been Looking For	1973	3.00	6.00	12.00
❑ APL1-0344	Country Sunshine	1973	3.00	6.00	12.00
❑ APL1-0543	House of Love	1974	3.00	6.00	12.00
❑ APL1-1041	Carolina Cousins	1975	3.00	6.00	12.00
❑ ANL1-2327	Country Sunshine	1977	2.50	5.00	10.00
—Reissue of APL1-0344					
❑ LPM-3368 [M]	Here Comes My Baby	1965	6.25	12.50	25.00
❑ LSP-3368 [S]	Here Comes My Baby	1965	7.50	15.00	30.00
❑ LPM-3490 [M]	Dottie West Sings	1966	6.25	12.50	25.00
❑ LSP-3490 [S]	Dottie West Sings	1966	7.50	15.00	30.00
❑ LPM-3587 [M]	Suffer Time	1966	6.25	12.50	25.00
❑ LSP-3587 [S]	Suffer Time	1966	7.50	15.00	30.00
❑ LPM-3693 [M]	With All My Heart and Soul	1967	7.50	15.00	30.00
❑ LSP-3693 [S]	With All My Heart and Soul	1967	6.25	12.50	25.00
❑ LPM-3784 [M]	Dottie West Sings Sacred Ballads	1967	7.50	15.00	30.00
❑ LSP-3784 [S]	Dottie West Sings Sacred Ballads	1967	6.25	12.50	25.00
❑ LPM-3830 [M]	I'll Help You Forget Her	1967	7.50	15.00	30.00
❑ LSP-3830 [S]	I'll Help You Forget Her	1967	6.25	12.50	25.00
❑ LPM-3932 [M]	What I'm Cut Out to Be	1968	12.50	25.00	50.00
❑ LSP-3932 [S]	What I'm Cut Out to Be	1968	6.25	12.50	25.00
❑ LSP-4004	Country Girl	1968	6.25	12.50	25.00
❑ LSP-4095	Feminine Fancy	1969	5.00	10.00	20.00
❑ AHL1-4117	Once You Were Mine	1981	2.50	5.00	10.00
❑ LSP-4154	Dottie Sings Eddy	1969	5.00	10.00	20.00
❑ LSP-4276	Makin' Memories	1970	5.00	10.00	20.00
❑ AYL1-4302	Once You Were Mine	1982	2.00	4.00	8.00
❑ LSP-4332	Country and West	1970	5.00	10.00	20.00
❑ LSP-4433	Forever Yours	1970	5.00	10.00	20.00
❑ LSP-4482	Careless Hands	1971	3.75	7.50	15.00
❑ LSP-4606	Have You Heard	1971	3.75	7.50	15.00
❑ LSP-4704	I'm Only a Woman	1972	3.75	7.50	15.00
❑ LSP-4811	The Best of Dottie West	1973	3.75	7.50	15.00
❑ CPL1-7047	Collector's Series	1985	2.50	5.00	10.00
STARDAY					
❑ SLP-302 [M]	Country Girl Singing Sensation	1964	10.00	20.00	40.00
UNITED ARTISTS					
❑ UA-LA740-G	When It's Just You and Me	1977	2.50	5.00	10.00
❑ UA-LA860-G	Dottie	1978	2.50	5.00	10.00
❑ LT-1000	Special Delivery	1980	2.50	5.00	10.00
WEST, DOTTIE, AND DON GIBSON					
RCA VICTOR					
❑ LSP-4131	Dottie and Don	1969	5.00	10.00	20.00
WEST, HEDY					
VANGUARD					
❑ VSD-2124 [S]	Hedy West Accompanying Herself on the 5-String Banjo	1963	6.25	12.50	25.00
❑ VSD-2126 [S]	Hedy West, Volume 2	1963	6.25	12.50	25.00
❑ VRS-9124 [M]	Hedy West Accompanying Herself on the 5-String Banjo	1963	5.00	10.00	20.00
❑ VRS-9126 [M]	Hedy West, Volume 2	1963	5.00	10.00	20.00
WEST, LUCRETIA					
WESTMINSTER					
❑ WP-6063 [M]	Spirituals	1957	10.00	20.00	40.00
WEST, MAE					
DAGONET					
❑ DG-4 [M]	Wild Christmas	1966	7.50	15.00	30.00
❑ DGS-4 [S]	Wild Christmas	1966	10.00	20.00	40.00
DECCA					
❑ DL 9016 [M]	The Fabulous Mae West	1955	15.00	30.00	60.00
—All-black label with silver print					
❑ DL 9016 [M]	The Fabulous Mae West	1960	7.50	15.00	30.00
—Black label with colorband					
❑ DL 79016 [R]	The Fabulous Mae West	1960	3.75	7.50	15.00
❑ DL 79176	The Original Voice Tracks from Her Greatest Movies	1970	3.75	7.50	15.00
MCA					
❑ 2053	The Fabulous Mae West	1974	3.00	6.00	12.00
—Reissue of Decca LP					
MEZZOTONE					
❑ 1 [10]	Mae West Songs, Vol. 1	1952	25.00	50.00	100.00
❑ 2 [10]	Mae West Songs, Vol. 2	1952	25.00	50.00	100.00
MGM					
❑ SE-4869	Great Balls of Fire	1972	5.00	10.00	20.00
ROUND					
❑ RS-100	Under the Mistletoe with Mae West	1977	5.00	10.00	20.00
TOWER					
❑ ST 5028 [S]	Way Out West	1966	10.00	20.00	40.00
❑ T 5028 [M]	Way Out West	1966	7.50	15.00	30.00
WEST, SPEEDY					
CAPITOL					
❑ T 956 [M]	West of Hawaii	1958	20.00	40.00	80.00
❑ ST 1341 [S]	Steel Guitar	1960	15.00	30.00	60.00
❑ T 1341 [M]	Steel Guitar	1960	10.00	20.00	40.00
❑ ST 1835 [S]	Guitar Spectacular	1962	10.00	20.00	40.00
❑ T 1835 [M]	Guitar Spectacular	1962	7.50	15.00	30.00
WEST, SPEEDY, AND JIMMY BRYANT					
CAPITOL					
❑ H 520 [10]	Two Guitars Country Style	1954	50.00	100.00	200.00
❑ T 520 [M]	Two Guitars Country Style	1954	30.00	60.00	120.00
WEST, BRUCE & LAING					
WINDFALL					
❑ CQ 31929 [Q]	Why Dontcha	1972	5.00	10.00	20.00
❑ KC 31929	Why Dontcha	1972	3.00	6.00	12.00
❑ CQ 32216 [Q]	Whatever Turns You On	1973	5.00	10.00	20.00
❑ KC 32216	Whatever Turns You On	1973	3.00	6.00	12.00
❑ KC 32899	Live 'N' Kickin'	1974	3.00	6.00	12.00
WEST COAST POP ART EXPERIMENTAL BAND, THE					
AMOS					
❑ AAS-7004	Where's My Daddy	1969	12.50	25.00	50.00
FIFO					
❑ M 101	West Coast Pop Art Experimental Band	1966	125.00	250.00	500.00
—With plain cardboard cover					
❑ M 101	West Coast Pop Art Experimental Band	1966	1000.	1500.	2000.
—With regular cover					
RAZZBERRY SAWFLY					
❑ 800	West Coast Pop Art Experimental Band	1980	25.00	50.00	100.00
—Reissue of Fifo LP					
REPRISE					
❑ R 6247 [M]	The West Coast Pop Art Experimental Band, Part One	1967	20.00	40.00	80.00
❑ RS 6247 [S]	The West Coast Pop Art Experimental Band, Part One	1967	25.00	50.00	100.00
❑ R 6270 [M]	The West Coast Pop Art Experimental Band, Vol. 2	1967	20.00	40.00	80.00
❑ RS 6270 [S]	The West Coast Pop Art Experimental Band, Vol. 2	1967	25.00	50.00	100.00
❑ R 6298 [M]	Vol. 3: A Child's Guide to Good and Evil	1968	50.00	100.00	200.00
—May exist only as a white label promo					
❑ RS 6298 [S]	Vol. 3: A Child's Guide to Good and Evil	1968	25.00	50.00	100.00
SUNDAZED					
❑ LP 5036 [(2)]	West Coast Pop Art Experimental Band, Volume One	1997	3.75	7.50	15.00
WESTCHESTER WORKSHOP, THE					
UNIQUE					
❑ LP-103 [M]	Unique Jazz	1957	12.50	25.00	50.00
WESTERN, JOHNNY					
COLUMBIA					
❑ CL 1788 [M]	Have Gun, Will Travel	1962	10.00	20.00	40.00
❑ CS 8588 [S]	Have Gun, Will Travel	1962	12.50	25.00	50.00
WESTON, KIM					
MGM					
❑ E-4477 [M]	For the First Time	1967	7.50	15.00	30.00
❑ SE-4477 [S]	For the First Time	1967	10.00	20.00	40.00
❑ SE-4561	This Is America	1968	10.00	20.00	40.00
VOLT					
❑ VOS-6014	Kim, Kim, Kim	1971	6.25	12.50	25.00
WESTON, PAUL					
CAPITOL					
❑ H 222 [10]	Music for Dreaming	195?	10.00	20.00	40.00
❑ T 1153 [M]	Floatin' Like a Feather	1959	3.00	6.00	12.00
❑ ST 1154 [S]	Music for Dreaming	1959	3.75	7.50	15.00
❑ T 1154 [M]	Music for Dreaming	1959	3.00	6.00	12.00
❑ ST 1192 [S]	Music for the Fireside	1959	3.75	7.50	15.00
❑ T 1192 [M]	Music for the Fireside	1959	3.00	6.00	12.00
❑ ST 1222 [S]	Music for Memories	1959	3.75	7.50	15.00
❑ T 1222 [M]	Music for Memories	1959	3.00	6.00	12.00
❑ ST 1563 [S]	Music for My Love	1961	3.75	7.50	15.00
❑ T 1563 [M]	Music for My Love	1961	3.00	6.00	12.00
❑ ST-91212	Romantic Reflections	196?	3.75	7.50	15.00
—Capitol Record Club exclusive					
COLUMBIA					
❑ CL 572 [M]	Caribbean Cruise	1955	3.75	7.50	15.00
❑ CL 693 [M]	Mood for 12	1955	3.75	7.50	15.00
❑ CL 794 [M]	Love Music from Hollywood	1956	3.75	7.50	15.00
❑ CL 879 [M]	Solo Mood	1956	3.75	7.50	15.00
❑ CL 909 [M]	Moonlight Becomes You	1956	3.75	7.50	15.00

Number	Title (A Side/B Side)	Yr	VG	VG+	NM
❑ CL 977 [M]	Crescent City	1956	3.75	7.50	15.00
❑ CL 1112 [M]	Hollywood	1958	3.75	7.50	15.00
❑ CL 6232 [10]	Whispers in the Dark	195?	10.00	20.00	40.00

CORINTHIAN

❑ 107	Cinema Cameos	198?	2.00	4.00	8.00
❑ 109	Easy Jazz	198?	2.00	4.00	8.00
❑ 116	Crescent City	198?	2.00	4.00	8.00

HARMONY

❑ KH 31578	Paul Weston Plays Jerome Kern	1972	2.50	5.00	10.00
❑ KH 31603	Paul Weston Plays Jerome Kern, Vol. 2	1972	2.50	5.00	10.00

WESTON, RANDY

COLPIX

❑ CP-456 [M]	Highlight	1963	7.50	15.00	30.00
❑ SCP-456 [S]	Highlight	1963	15.00	30.00	60.00

DAWN

❑ DLP-1116 [M]	The Modern Art of Jazz	1957	20.00	40.00	80.00

JAZZLAND

❑ JLP-4 [M]	Zulu!	1960	10.00	20.00	40.00

JUBILEE

❑ JLP-1060 [M]	Piano A La Mode	1957	10.00	20.00	40.00

RIVERSIDE

❑ RLP 12-203 [M]	Get Happy	1956	15.00	30.00	60.00
❑ RLP 12-214 [M]	With These Hands…	1956	15.00	30.00	60.00
❑ RLP 12-227 [M]	Randy Weston Trio and Solo	1957	15.00	30.00	60.00
❑ RLP 12-232 [M]	Jazz A La Bohemia	1957	15.00	30.00	60.00
❑ RLP-2508 [10]	Cole Porter in a Modern Mood	1954	30.00	60.00	120.00
❑ RLP-2515 [10]	Randy Weston Trio	1955	30.00	60.00	120.00

ROULETTE

❑ R-65001 [M]	Uhuru Afrika	1960	7.50	15.00	30.00
❑ RS-65001 [S]	Uhuru Afrika	1960	10.00	20.00	40.00

UNITED ARTISTS

❑ UAL-4011 [M]	Little Niles	1959	10.00	20.00	40.00
❑ UAL-4045 [M]	Destry Rides Again	1959	10.00	20.00	40.00
❑ UAL-4066 [M]	Live at the Five Spot	1959	10.00	20.00	40.00
❑ UAS-5011 [S]	Little Niles	1959	12.50	25.00	50.00
❑ UAS-5045 [S]	Destry Rides Again	1959	12.50	25.00	50.00
❑ UAS-5066 [S]	Live at the Five Spot	1959	12.50	25.00	50.00

WESTON, RANDY, AND CECIL PAYNE

JAZZLAND

❑ JLP-13 [M]	Greenwich Village Jazz	1960	10.00	20.00	40.00

WESTON, RANDY/LEM WINCHESTER

METROJAZZ

❑ E-1005 [M]	New Faces at Newport	1958	12.50	25.00	50.00
❑ SE-1005 [S]	New Faces at Newport	1958	10.00	20.00	40.00

WETMORE, DICK

BETHLEHEM

❑ BCP-1035 [10]	Dick Wetmore	1955	25.00	50.00	100.00

WETTLING, GEORGE

COLUMBIA

❑ CL 2559 [10]	George Wettling's Jazz Band	1956	12.50	25.00	50.00
—"House Party Series" issue					
❑ CL 6189 [10]	George Wettling's Jazz Band	1951	20.00	40.00	80.00
—Original issue					

HARMONY

❑ HL 7080 [M]	Dixieland in Hi-Fi	1957	5.00	10.00	20.00

KAPP

❑ KL-1005 [M]	Ragtime Duo	1955	10.00	20.00	40.00
❑ KL-1028 [M]	Jazz Trios	1956	10.00	20.00	40.00

WEATHERS INDUSTRIES

❑ 5501 [M]	High Fidelity Rhythms	1955	10.00	20.00	40.00

WHALEFEATHERS, THE

NASCO

❑ 9003	The Whalefeathers Declare	1969	25.00	50.00	100.00
❑ 9005	The Whalefeathers	1970	25.00	50.00	100.00

WHAM!

COLUMBIA

❑ BFC 38911	Fantastic	1983	3.75	7.50	15.00
—Cover and label list artist as "Wham! U.K."					
❑ FC 38911	Fantastic	1985	2.50	5.00	10.00
—Reissue; cover and label list artist as "Wham!"					
❑ FC 39595	Make It Big	1984	2.50	5.00	10.00
❑ 9C9 40062 [PD]	Make It Big	1985	6.25	12.50	25.00
—Picture disc					
❑ OC 40285	Music from the Edge of Heaven	1986	2.50	5.00	10.00
—With "removable sticker" list of song titles still on front cover					

WHATNAUTS, THE

STANG

❑ 1005	The Whatnauts	1970	5.00	10.00	20.00

WHEELER, BILLY EDD

FLYING FISH

❑ FF-085	Wild Mountain Flowers	1979	3.00	6.00	12.00

FOLKWAYS

❑ 31014	When Kentucky Had No Union Men	196?	5.00	10.00	20.00

KAPP

❑ KL-1351 [M]	A New Bag of Songs Written and Sung by Billy Edd Wheeler	1964	3.75	7.50	15.00
❑ KL-1425 [M]	Memories of America/Ode to the Little Brown Shack Out Back	1965	3.75	7.50	15.00
❑ KL-1443 [M]	Wheeler Man	1965	3.75	7.50	15.00
❑ KL-1479 [M]	Goin' Town and Country	1966	3.75	7.50	15.00
❑ KL-1533 [M]	Paper Birds	1967	5.00	10.00	20.00

Number	Title (A Side/B Side)	Yr	VG	VG+	NM
❑ KS-3351 [S]	A New Bag of Songs Written and Sung by Billy Edd Wheeler	1964	5.00	10.00	20.00
❑ KS-3425 [S]	Memories of America/Ode to the Little Brown Shack Out Back	1965	5.00	10.00	20.00
❑ KS-3443 [S]	Wheeler Man	1965	5.00	10.00	20.00
❑ KS-3479 [S]	Goin' Town and Country	1966	5.00	10.00	20.00
❑ KS-3533 [S]	Paper Birds	1967	3.75	7.50	15.00
❑ KS-3567	I Ain't the Worryin' Kind	1968	3.75	7.50	15.00

MONITOR

❑ MF-354 [M]	Billy Edd U.S.A.	1961	7.50	15.00	30.00
❑ MF-367 [M]	Billy Edd and Bluegrass	1962	7.50	15.00	30.00

RCA VICTOR

❑ LSP-4491	Love	1971	3.75	7.50	15.00

UNITED ARTISTS

❑ UAS-6711	Nashville Zodiac	1969	3.75	7.50	15.00

WHEELER, CLARENCE

ATLANTIC

❑ SD 1551	Doin' What We Wanna	197?	10.00	20.00	40.00
❑ SD 1585	The Love I've Been Looking For	197?	5.00	10.00	20.00

WHEELS, BURT, AND THE SPEEDSTERS

CORONET

❑ CX-216 [M]	Sounds of the Big Racers	196?	6.25	12.50	25.00
❑ CXS-216 [S]	Sounds of the Big Racers	196?	7.50	15.00	30.00

WHEELS, THE

MONTGOMERY WARD

❑ 010	Sounds of the Hot Rods	196?	30.00	60.00	120.00

WHISPERS, THE

ACCORD

❑ SN-7100	I Can Remember	1981	2.50	5.00	10.00

ALLEGIANCE

❑ AV-5004	Excellence	1985	2.50	5.00	10.00

CAPITOL

❑ C1-92957	More of the Night	1990	3.00	6.00	12.00

DORE

❑ 338	Shhh	197?	3.00	6.00	12.00

INTERMEDIA

❑ QS-5075	Doctor Love	198?	2.50	5.00	10.00

JANUS

❑ JLS-3041	The Whispers' Love Story	1972	12.50	25.00	50.00
❑ JLS-3046	Life and Breath	1973	10.00	20.00	40.00
❑ 7006	Bingo	1974	10.00	20.00	40.00
❑ 7013	Greatest Hits	1975	7.50	15.00	30.00

SOLAR

❑ S-27	Love Is Where You Find It	1982	2.50	5.00	10.00
❑ BXL1-2270	Open Up Your Love	1978	3.00	6.00	12.00
—Reissue of Soul Train 2270					
❑ BXL1-2774	Headlights	1978	3.00	6.00	12.00
❑ BXL1-3105	Whisper in Your Ear	1979	3.00	6.00	12.00
❑ BXL1-3521	The Whispers	1979	3.00	6.00	12.00
❑ BXL1-3578	Imagination	1980	3.00	6.00	12.00
❑ AYL1-3839	Open Up Your Love	1981	2.00	4.00	8.00
—"Best Buy Series" reissue					
❑ BXL1-3976	This Kind of Lovin'	1981	3.00	6.00	12.00
❑ BXL1-4242	The Best of the Whispers	1982	3.00	6.00	12.00
❑ 60216	Love for Love	1983	2.50	5.00	10.00
❑ 60356	So Good	1984	2.50	5.00	10.00
❑ 60451	Happy Holidays to You	1985	3.00	6.00	12.00
❑ ST-72554	Just Gets Better with Time	1987	2.50	5.00	10.00
❑ PZ 75306	Vintage Whispers	1989	3.00	6.00	12.00

SOUL CLOCK

❑ 22001	Planets of Life	1969	25.00	50.00	100.00

SOUL TRAIN

❑ BVL1-1450	One for the Money	1976	3.75	7.50	15.00
❑ BVL1-2270	Open Up Your Love	1977	3.75	7.50	15.00

WHITCOMB, IAN

AUDIOPHILE

❑ AP-115	Treasures of Tin Pan Alley	197?	3.00	6.00	12.00
❑ AP-147	At the Ragtime Ball	1983	3.00	6.00	12.00

FIRST AMERICAN

❑ 7704	Crooner Tunes	1979	2.50	5.00	10.00
❑ 7725	Red Hot "Blue Heaven"	1980	2.50	5.00	10.00
❑ 7729	The Rock and Roll Years	1981	2.50	5.00	10.00
❑ 7751	Instrumentals	1981	2.50	5.00	10.00
❑ 7789	In Hollywood	1982	2.50	5.00	10.00

RHINO

❑ RNLP-127	The Best of Ian Whitcomb (1964-1968)	1986	2.00	4.00	8.00

SIERRA

❑ 8708	Pianomelt	1980	2.50	5.00	10.00

TOWER

❑ DT 5004 [R]	You Turn Me On	1965	5.00	10.00	20.00
❑ T 5004 [M]	You Turn Me On	1965	6.25	12.50	25.00
❑ ST 5042 [S]	Mod, Mod Music Hall	1966	5.00	10.00	20.00
❑ T 5042 [M]	Mod, Mod Music Hall	1966	3.75	7.50	15.00
❑ ST 5071 [S]	Yellow Underground	1967	5.00	10.00	20.00
❑ T 5071 [M]	Yellow Underground	1967	3.75	7.50	15.00
❑ ST 5100	Sock Me Some Rock	1968	5.00	10.00	20.00

UNITED ARTISTS

❑ UA-LA021-F	Under the Ragtime Moon	1972	2.50	5.00	10.00

WHITE, ANDREW
Also see THE J.F.K. QUINTET.

ANDREW'S MUSIC

❑ AM-1	Andrew Nathaniel White III	197?	5.00	10.00	20.00
❑ AM-2 [(2)]	Live at the "New Thing"	197?	6.25	12.50	25.00

Number	Title (A Side/B Side)	Yr	VG	VG+	NM
❏ AM-3	Live in Bucharest	197?	5.00	10.00	20.00
❏ AM-4	Who Got Da Funk?	197?	5.00	10.00	20.00
❏ AM-5	Passion Flower	197?	5.00	10.00	20.00
❏ AM-6	Songs for a French Lady	197?	5.00	10.00	20.00
❏ AM-7	Theme	1975	5.00	10.00	20.00

WHITE, BUKKA
ARHOOLIE
| ❏ 1019 [M] | Sky Songs, Volume 1 | 1966 | 7.50 | 15.00 | 30.00 |
| ❏ 1020 [M] | Sky Songs, Volume 2 | 1966 | 7.50 | 15.00 | 30.00 |

BLUE HORIZON
| ❏ 4604 | Blues Masters, Volume 4 | 1970 | 6.25 | 12.50 | 25.00 |

HERWIN
| ❏ 201 | Sic 'em Dogs | 196? | 6.25 | 12.50 | 25.00 |

TAKOMA
| ❏ C-1001 [M] | Mississippi Blues | 196? | 7.50 | 15.00 | 30.00 |

WHITE, DANNY
GRAND PRIX
| ❏ 101 | Danny White Sings Country | 1983 | 6.25 | 12.50 | 25.00 |

WHITE, JOSH
ABC-PARAMOUNT
❏ ABC-124 [M]	Josh White Stories, Vol. 1	1956	15.00	30.00	60.00
❏ ABC-166 [M]	Josh White Stories, Vol. 2	1957	15.00	30.00	60.00
❏ ABC-407 [M]	Josh White — Live!	1962	7.50	15.00	30.00
❏ ABCS-407 [S]	Josh White — Live!	1962	10.00	20.00	40.00

DECCA
❏ DL 5062 [10]	Ballads and Blues	1949	37.50	75.00	150.00
❏ DL 5247 [10]	Ballads and Blues, Vol. 2	195?	30.00	60.00	120.00
❏ DL 8665 [M]	Josh White	1958	10.00	20.00	40.00
—Black label, silver print

ELEKTRA
❏ EKL-102 [M]	Josh at Midnight	1956	10.00	20.00	40.00
❏ EKL-114 [M]	Josh, Ballads and Blues	1957	10.00	20.00	40.00
❏ EKL-123 [M]	25th Anniversary Album	1957	10.00	20.00	40.00
❏ EKL-158 [M]	Chain Gang Songs	1958	20.00	40.00	80.00
❏ EKL-193 [M]	Spirituals and Blues	1960	7.50	15.00	30.00
❏ EKL-203 [M]	The House I Live In	1961	7.50	15.00	30.00
❏ EKL-211 [M]	Empty Bed Blues	1962	6.25	12.50	25.00
❏ EKL-701 [(2)10]	The Story of John Henry/Ballads, Blues and Other Songs	1955	12.50	25.00	50.00
❏ EKS-7158 [S]	Chain Gang Songs	195?	25.00	50.00	100.00
❏ EKS-7193 [S]	Spirituals and Blues	1960	10.00	20.00	40.00
❏ EKS-7203 [S]	The House I Live In	1961	10.00	20.00	40.00
❏ EKS-7211 [S]	Empty Bed Blues	1962	7.50	15.00	30.00

EMARCY
| ❏ MG-26010 [10] | Strange Fruit | 1954 | 30.00 | 60.00 | 120.00 |

LONDON
❏ LPB-338 [10]	A Josh White Program	195?	30.00	60.00	120.00
❏ LPB-341 [10]	A Josh White Program, Vol. 2	195?	30.00	60.00	120.00
❏ LL 1147 [M]	A Josh White Program	1956	12.50	25.00	50.00
❏ LL 1341 [M]	A Josh White Program, Vol. 2	195?	12.50	25.00	50.00

MERCURY
❏ MG-20203 [M]	Josh White's Blues	1957	15.00	30.00	60.00
❏ MG-20821 [M]	The Beginning	1963	7.50	15.00	30.00
❏ MG-21022 [M]	I'm on My Own Way	1963	7.50	15.00	30.00
❏ MG-25014 [10]	Josh White Sings Blues	1949	37.50	75.00	150.00
❏ SR-60821 [R]	The Beginning	1963	5.00	10.00	20.00
❏ SR-61022 [R]	I'm on My Own Way	1963	5.00	10.00	20.00

PERIOD
| ❏ SLP-1115 [10] | Josh White Comes a-Visiting | 1956 | 15.00 | 30.00 | 60.00 |

STINSON
| ❏ SLP-14 [10] | Josh White Sings the Blues | 1950 | 30.00 | 60.00 | 120.00 |
| ❏ SLP-15 [10] | Josh White Sings Folk Songs | 1950 | 30.00 | 60.00 | 120.00 |

WHITE, KITTY
EMARCY
| ❏ MG-36020 [M] | A New Voice in Jazz | 1955 | 12.50 | 25.00 | 50.00 |
| ❏ MG-36068 [M] | Kitty White | 1955 | 12.50 | 25.00 | 50.00 |

PACIFICA
| ❏ PL-802 [10] | Kitty White | 1955 | 25.00 | 50.00 | 100.00 |

WHITE, MIKE
SEECO
| ❏ SLP-442 [M] | Dixieland Jazz | 1960 | 5.00 | 10.00 | 20.00 |
| ❏ SLP-4420 [S] | Dixieland Jazz | 1960 | 6.25 | 12.50 | 25.00 |

WHITE, STEVE
LIBERTY
| ❏ LJH-6006 [M] | Jazz Mad — The Unpredictable Steve White | 1955 | 12.50 | 25.00 | 50.00 |

WHITE BOY
TRADEWIND
| ❏ MM-11761 | The Average Rat Band | 1976 | 37.50 | 75.00 | 150.00 |

WHITE LIGHT
CENTURY
| ❏ 39955 | White Light | 1968 | 75.00 | 150.00 | 300.00 |

WHITE LIGHTNIN'
ABC
| ❏ S-690 | File Under Rock | 1969 | 5.00 | 10.00 | 20.00 |

WHITE TIGER
With Mark St. John, who was briefly a member of KISS.
E.M.C.
| ❏ EMC-3653 | White Tiger | 1986 | 5.00 | 10.00 | 20.00 |

WHITE WITCH
CAPRICORN
| ❏ CP 0107 | White Witch | 1973 | 6.25 | 12.50 | 25.00 |

Number	Title (A Side/B Side)	Yr	VG	VG+	NM
❏ CP 0129	A Spiritual Greeting	1974	6.25	12.50	25.00

WHITE ZOMBIE
CAROLINE
| ❏ 1350 | Soul Crusher | 1988 | 5.00 | 10.00 | 20.00 |
| ❏ 1362 | Make Them Die Slowly | 1989 | 5.00 | 10.00 | 20.00 |

GEFFEN
| ❏ GEF 24806 | Astro-Creep: 2000 | 1995 | 3.75 | 7.50 | 15.00 |

SILENT EXPLOSION
| ❏ (# unknown) [EP] | Psycho-Head Blowout | 1986 | 15.00 | 30.00 | 60.00 |
| ❏ SE 002 | Soul Crusher | 1987 | 15.00 | 30.00 | 60.00 |

WHITEMAN, PAUL
CAPITOL
| ❏ T 622 [M] | Classics in Jazz | 1955 | 12.50 | 25.00 | 50.00 |

CORAL
| ❏ CRL 57021 [M] | The Great Gershwin | 1955 | 5.00 | 10.00 | 20.00 |

GRAND AWARD
❏ GA-208 SD [S]	Hawaiian Magic	1958	7.50	15.00	30.00
❏ GA-241 SD [S]	The Night I Played at 666 Fifth Ave.	1960	7.50	15.00	30.00
❏ GA-244 SD [S]	Cavalcade of Music	1960	7.50	15.00	30.00
❏ GA-33-351	Fiddle on Fire	195?	7.50	15.00	30.00
❏ GA-33-356	Hawaiian Magic	1958	5.00	10.00	20.00
❏ GA-33-409	The Night I Played at 666 Fifth Ave.	1960	5.00	10.00	20.00
❏ GA-33-412	Cavalcade of Music	1960	5.00	10.00	20.00
❏ GA-33-502 [M]	Great Whiteman Hits	195?	7.50	15.00	30.00
❏ GA-33-503 [M]	The Greatest Stars of My Life	195?	12.50	25.00	50.00
—In red velvet jacket
| ❏ GA-33-901 [(2)M] | Paul Whiteman/50th Anniversary | 1956 | 12.50 | 25.00 | 50.00 |

"X"
| ❏ LVA-3040 [10] | Paul Whiteman's Orchestra Featuring Bix Beiderbecke | 1955 | 20.00 | 40.00 | 80.00 |

WHITING, MARGARET
AUDIOPHILE
❏ AP-152	Too Marvelous for Words	198?	2.50	5.00	10.00
❏ AP-173	Come a Little Closer	198?	2.50	5.00	10.00
❏ AP-207	This Lady's in Love with You	1986	2.50	5.00	10.00

CAPITOL
❏ H 163 [10]	South Pacific	1950	12.50	25.00	50.00
❏ H 209 [10]	Margaret Whiting Sings Rodgers and Hart	1950	12.50	25.00	50.00
❏ H 234 [10]	Songs	1950	12.50	25.00	50.00
❏ T 410 [M]	Love Songs	1954	10.00	20.00	40.00
❏ T 685 [M]	For the Starry-Eyed	1955	10.00	20.00	40.00

DOT
❏ DLP 3072 [M]	Goin' Places	1957	6.25	12.50	25.00
❏ DLP 3176 [M]	Margaret	1958	3.75	7.50	15.00
❏ DLP 3176 [M]	Margaret Whiting's Great Hits	1959	3.75	7.50	15.00
❏ DLP 3235 [M]	Ten Top Hits	1960	3.75	7.50	15.00
❏ DLP 3337 [M]	Just a Dream	1960	3.75	7.50	15.00
❏ DLP 25113 [S]	Margaret	1958	5.00	10.00	20.00
❏ DLP 25176 [S]	Margaret Whiting's Great Hits	1959	5.00	10.00	20.00
❏ DLP 25235 [S]	Ten Top Hits	1960	5.00	10.00	20.00
❏ DLP 25337 [S]	Just a Dream	1960	5.00	10.00	20.00

HAMILTON
| ❏ HLP 143 [M] | My Ideal | 196? | 3.00 | 6.00 | 12.00 |
| ❏ HLP 12143 [S] | My Ideal | 196? | 3.75 | 7.50 | 15.00 |

LONDON
❏ PS 497 [S]	The Wheel of Hurt	1967	3.75	7.50	15.00
❏ PS 510 [S]	Maggie Isn't Margaret Anymore	1967	3.75	7.50	15.00
❏ PS 527	Pop Country	1968	3.75	7.50	15.00
❏ LL 3497 [M]	The Wheel of Hurt	1967	5.00	10.00	20.00
❏ LL 3510 [M]	Maggie Isn't Margaret Anymore	1967	5.00	10.00	20.00

MGM
| ❏ E-4006 [M] | Past Midnight | 1961 | 3.75 | 7.50 | 15.00 |
| ❏ SE-4006 [S] | Past Midnight | 1961 | 5.00 | 10.00 | 20.00 |

VERVE
| ❏ V-4038 [M] | The Jerome Kern Song Book | 1960 | 3.75 | 7.50 | 15.00 |
| ❏ V6-4038 [S] | The Jerome Kern Song Book | 1960 | 5.00 | 10.00 | 20.00 |

WHITMAN, SLIM
CLEVELAND INT'L.
| ❏ AS99-875 [DJ] | Songs I Love to Sing | 1980 | 7.50 | 15.00 | 30.00 |
—Promo-only picture disc
❏ JE 36768	Songs I Love to Sing	1980	2.50	5.00	10.00
❏ JE 36847	Christmas with Slim Whitman	1980	3.00	6.00	12.00
❏ FE 37403	Mr. Songman	1982	2.50	5.00	10.00

COLUMBIA SPECIAL PRODUCTS
| ❏ P 16323 | Christmas with Slim Whitman | 1981 | 2.50 | 5.00 | 10.00 |

EPIC
| ❏ PE 36768 | Songs I Love to Sing | 198? | 2.00 | 4.00 | 8.00 |
—Reissue of Cleveland Int'l. JE 36768
| ❏ PE 36847 | Christmas with Slim Whitman | 1981 | 2.00 | 4.00 | 8.00 |
—Reissue of Cleveland Int'l. JE 36847

IMPERIAL
| ❏ LP-3004 [10] | America's Favorite Folk Artist | 1954 | 150.00 | 300.00 | 600.00 |
| ❏ LP-9003 [M] | Favorites | 1956 | 12.50 | 25.00 | 50.00 |
—Maroon label
| ❏ LP-9003 [M] | Favorites | 1958 | 7.50 | 15.00 | 30.00 |
—Black label with stars on top
| ❏ LP-9003 [M] | Favorites | 1964 | 5.00 | 10.00 | 20.00 |
—Black and pink label
| ❏ LP-9003 [M] | Favorites | 1966 | 3.75 | 7.50 | 15.00 |
—Black and green label
| ❏ LP-9026 [M] | Slim Whitman Sings | 1957 | 12.50 | 25.00 | 50.00 |
—Maroon label
| ❏ LP-9026 [M] | Slim Whitman Sings | 1958 | 7.50 | 15.00 | 30.00 |
—Black label with stars on top
| ❏ LP-9026 [M] | Slim Whitman Sings | 1964 | 5.00 | 10.00 | 20.00 |
—Black and pink label

Number	Title (A Side/B Side)	Yr	VG	VG+	NM
❏ LP-9026 [M]	Slim Whitman Sings	1966	3.75	7.50	15.00
—Black and green label					
❏ LP-9056 [M]	Slim Whitman Sings	1958	7.50	15.00	30.00
—Black label with stars on top					
❏ LP-9056 [M]	Slim Whitman Sings	1958	12.50	25.00	50.00
—Maroon label					
❏ LP-9056 [M]	Slim Whitman Sings	1964	5.00	10.00	20.00
—Black and pink label					
❏ LP-9056 [M]	Slim Whitman Sings	1966	3.75	7.50	15.00
—Black and green label					
❏ LP-9064 [M]	Slim Whitman Sings	1959	7.50	15.00	30.00
—Black label with stars on top					
❏ LP-9064 [M]	Slim Whitman Sings	1964	5.00	10.00	20.00
—Black and pink label					
❏ LP-9064 [M]	Slim Whitman Sings	1966	3.75	7.50	15.00
—Black and green label					
❏ LP-9088 [M]	I'll Walk with God	1960	7.50	15.00	30.00
—Black label with stars on top					
❏ LP-9088 [M]	I'll Walk with God	1964	5.00	10.00	20.00
—Black and pink label					
❏ LP-9088 [M]	I'll Walk with God	1966	3.75	7.50	15.00
—Black and green label					
❏ LP-9102 [M]	Million Record Hits	1960	7.50	15.00	30.00
—Black label with stars on top					
❏ LP-9102 [M]	Million Record Hits	1964	5.00	10.00	20.00
—Black and pink label					
❏ LP-9102 [M]	Million Record Hits	1966	3.75	7.50	15.00
—Black and green label					
❏ LP-9135 [M]	Slim Whitman's First Visit to Britain	1960	6.25	12.50	25.00
—Black label with stars on top					
❏ LP-9135 [M]	Slim Whitman's First Visit to Britain	1964	3.75	7.50	15.00
—Black and pink label					
❏ LP-9135 [M]	Slim Whitman's First Visit to Britain	1966	3.00	6.00	12.00
—Black and green label					
❏ LP-9137 [M]	Just Call Me Lonesome	1961	6.25	12.50	25.00
—Black label with stars on top					
❏ LP-9137 [M]	Just Call Me Lonesome	1964	3.75	7.50	15.00
—Black and pink label					
❏ LP-9137 [M]	Just Call Me Lonesome	1966	3.00	6.00	12.00
—Black and green label					
❏ LP-9156 [M]	Once in a Lifetime	1961	6.25	12.50	25.00
—Black label with stars on top					
❏ LP-9156 [M]	Once in a Lifetime	1964	3.75	7.50	15.00
—Black and pink label					
❏ LP-9156 [M]	Once in a Lifetime	1966	3.00	6.00	12.00
—Black and green label					
❏ LP-9163 [M]	Slim Whitman Sings Annie Laurie	1961	6.25	12.50	25.00
—Black label with stars on top					
❏ LP-9163 [M]	Slim Whitman Sings Annie Laurie	1964	3.75	7.50	15.00
—Black and pink label					
❏ LP-9163 [M]	Slim Whitman Sings Annie Laurie	1966	3.00	6.00	12.00
—Black and green label					
❏ LP-9171 [M]	Forever	1961	6.25	12.50	25.00
—Black label with stars on top					
❏ LP-9171 [M]	Forever	1964	3.75	7.50	15.00
—Black and pink label					
❏ LP-9171 [M]	Forever	1966	3.00	6.00	12.00
—Black and green label					
❏ LP-9194 [M]	Slim Whitman Sings	1962	6.25	12.50	25.00
—Black label with stars on top					
❏ LP-9194 [M]	Slim Whitman Sings	1964	3.75	7.50	15.00
—Black and pink label					
❏ LP-9194 [M]	Slim Whitman Sings	1966	3.00	6.00	12.00
—Black and green label					
❏ LP-9209 [M]	Heart Songs and Love Songs	1962	6.25	12.50	25.00
—Black label with stars on top					
❏ LP-9209 [M]	Heart Songs and Love Songs	1964	3.75	7.50	15.00
—Black and pink label					
❏ LP-9209 [M]	Heart Songs and Love Songs	1966	3.00	6.00	12.00
—Black and green label					
❏ LP-9226 [M]	I'm a Lonely Wanderer	1963	6.25	12.50	25.00
—Black label with stars on top					
❏ LP-9226 [M]	I'm a Lonely Wanderer	1964	3.75	7.50	15.00
—Black and pink label					
❏ LP-9226 [M]	I'm a Lonely Wanderer	1966	3.00	6.00	12.00
—Black and green label					
❏ LP-9235 [M]	Yodeling	1963	6.25	12.50	25.00
—Black label with stars on top					
❏ LP-9235 [M]	Yodeling	1964	3.75	7.50	15.00
—Black and pink label					
❏ LP-9235 [M]	Yodeling	1966	3.00	6.00	12.00
—Black and green label					
❏ LP-9245 [M]	Irish Songs The Whitman Way	1963	6.25	12.50	25.00
—Black label with stars on top					
❏ LP-9245 [M]	Irish Songs The Whitman Way	1964	3.75	7.50	15.00
—Black and pink label					
❏ LP-9245 [M]	Irish Songs The Whitman Way	1966	3.00	6.00	12.00
—Black and green label					
❏ LP-9252 [M]	All-Time Favorites	1964	3.75	7.50	15.00
—Black and pink label					
❏ LP-9252 [M]	All-Time Favorites	1964	7.50	15.00	30.00
—Black label with stars on top					
❏ LP-9252 [M]	All-Time Favorites	1966	3.00	6.00	12.00
—Black and green label					
❏ LP-9268 [M]	Country Songs/City Hits	1964	3.75	7.50	15.00
—Black and pink label					
❏ LP-9268 [M]	Country Songs/City Hits	1966	3.00	6.00	12.00
—Black and green label					
❏ LP-9277 [M]	Love Song of the Waterfall	1964	3.75	7.50	15.00
—Black and pink label					
❏ LP-9277 [M]	Love Song of the Waterfall	1966	3.00	6.00	12.00
—Black and green label					
❏ LP-9288 [M]	Reminiscing	1965	3.75	7.50	15.00
—Black and pink label					
❏ LP-9288 [M]	Reminiscing	1966	3.00	6.00	12.00
—Black and green label					
❏ LP-9303 [M]	More Than Yesterday	1965	3.75	7.50	15.00
—Black and pink label					
❏ LP-9303 [M]	More Than Yesterday	1966	3.00	6.00	12.00
—Black and green label					
❏ LP-9308 [M]	God's Hand in Mine	1966	3.00	6.00	12.00
❏ LP-9313 [M]	A Travelin' Man	1966	3.00	6.00	12.00
❏ LP-9333 [M]	A Time for Love	1966	3.00	6.00	12.00
❏ LP-9342 [M]	15th Anniversary	1967	3.75	7.50	15.00
❏ LP-9356 [M]	Country Memories	1967	3.75	7.50	15.00
❏ LP-12032 [S]	I'll Walk with God	1959	10.00	20.00	40.00
—Black label with silver top					
❏ LP-12032 [S]	I'll Walk with God	1964	6.25	12.50	25.00
—Black and pink label					
❏ LP-12032 [S]	I'll Walk with God	1966	5.00	10.00	20.00
—Black and green label					
❏ LP-12077 [S]	Slim Whitman Sings Annie Laurie	1961	7.50	15.00	30.00
—Black label with silver top					
❏ LP-12077 [S]	Slim Whitman Sings Annie Laurie	1964	5.00	10.00	20.00
—Black and pink label					
❏ LP-12077 [S]	Slim Whitman Sings Annie Laurie	1966	3.75	7.50	15.00
—Black and green label					
❏ LP-12100 [R]	Slim Whitman	1964	3.75	7.50	15.00
—Black and pink label					
❏ LP-12100 [R]	Slim Whitman	1966	3.00	6.00	12.00
—Black and green label					
❏ LP-12102 [R]	Song of the Old Waterwheel	1964	3.75	7.50	15.00
—Black and pink label					
❏ LP-12102 [R]	Song of the Old Waterwheel	1966	3.00	6.00	12.00
—Black and green label					
❏ LP-12194 [S]	Slim Whitman Sings	1962	7.50	15.00	30.00
—Black label with silver top					
❏ LP-12194 [S]	Slim Whitman Sings	1964	5.00	10.00	20.00
—Black and pink label					
❏ LP-12194 [S]	Slim Whitman Sings	1966	3.75	7.50	15.00
—Black and green label					
❏ LP-12268 [S]	Country Songs/City Hits	1964	5.00	10.00	20.00
—Black and pink label					
❏ LP-12268 [S]	Country Songs/City Hits	1966	3.75	7.50	15.00
—Black and green label					
❏ LP-12277 [S]	Love Song of the Waterfall	1964	5.00	10.00	20.00
—Black and pink label					
❏ LP-12277 [S]	Love Song of the Waterfall	1966	3.75	7.50	15.00
—Black and green label					
❏ LP-12288 [S]	Reminiscing	1965	5.00	10.00	20.00
—Black and pink label					
❏ LP-12288 [S]	Reminiscing	1966	3.75	7.50	15.00
—Black and green label					
❏ LP-12303 [S]	More Than Yesterday	1965	5.00	10.00	20.00
—Black and pink label					
❏ LP-12303 [S]	More Than Yesterday	1966	3.75	7.50	15.00
—Black and green label					
❏ LP-12313 [S]	A Travelin' Man	1966	3.75	7.50	15.00
❏ LP-12333 [S]	A Time for Love	1966	3.75	7.50	15.00
❏ LP-12342 [S]	15th Anniversary	1967	3.00	6.00	12.00
❏ LP-12356 [S]	Country Memories	1967	3.00	6.00	12.00
❏ LP-12375	In Love, The Whitman Way	1968	3.00	6.00	12.00
❏ LP-12411	Happy Street	1969	3.00	6.00	12.00
❏ LP-12436	Slim	1969	3.00	6.00	12.00
❏ LP-12448	The Slim Whitman Christmas Album	1969	3.75	7.50	15.00

LIBERTY

Number	Title (A Side/B Side)	Yr	VG	VG+	NM
❏ LM-1005	The Very Best of Slim Whitman	1981	2.00	4.00	8.00
—Reissue of United Artists 1005					
❏ LM-1067	The Slim Whitman Christmas Album	1980	2.00	4.00	8.00
—Abridged reissue of Imperial 12448					
❏ SL-8128	All My Best	1981	3.00	6.00	12.00
—Mail-order album					
❏ LN-10033	Red River Valley	1981	2.00	4.00	8.00
—Budget-line reissue					
❏ LN-10123	Till We Meet Again	1981	2.00	4.00	8.00
—Budget-line reissue					
❏ LN-10124	Ghost Riders in the Sky	1981	2.00	4.00	8.00
—Budget-line reissue					
❏ LN-10125	The Best of Slim Whitman, Vol. 2	1981	2.00	4.00	8.00
—Budget-line reissue					
❏ LN-10152	God's Hand in Mine	1981	2.00	4.00	8.00
—Budget-line reissue					
❏ LN-10153	Country Songs/City Hits	1981	2.00	4.00	8.00
—Budget-line reissue					

PAIR

Number	Title (A Side/B Side)	Yr	VG	VG+	NM
❏ PDL2-1085 [(2)]	One of a Kind	1986	3.00	6.00	12.00

PICKWICK

Number	Title (A Side/B Side)	Yr	VG	VG+	NM
❏ SPC-3590	Happy Anniversary	1978	2.50	5.00	10.00

RCA CAMDEN

Number	Title (A Side/B Side)	Yr	VG	VG+	NM
❏ CAL-954 [M]	Birmingham Jail	1966	5.00	10.00	20.00
❏ CAS-954(e) [R]	Birmingham Jail	1966	3.00	6.00	12.00

RCA VICTOR

Number	Title (A Side/B Side)	Yr	VG	VG+	NM
❏ LPM-3217 [10]	Slim Whitman Sings and Yodels	1954	75.00	150.00	300.00
❏ AYL1-3774	Birmingham Jail	1980	2.00	4.00	8.00
—"Best Buy Series" reissue					

SUNSET

Number	Title (A Side/B Side)	Yr	VG	VG+	NM
❏ SUM-1112 [M]	Unchain Your Heart	1966	3.00	6.00	12.00
❏ SUM-1167 [M]	Lonesome Heart	1967	3.00	6.00	12.00
❏ SUS-5112 [R]	Unchain Your Heart	1966	3.00	6.00	12.00
❏ SUS-5167 [R]	Lonesome Heart	1967	3.00	6.00	12.00
❏ SUS-5267	Slim Whitman	1969	3.00	6.00	12.00
❏ SUS-5320	Ramblin' Rose	1970	2.50	5.00	10.00

UNITED ARTISTS

Number	Title (A Side/B Side)	Yr	VG	VG+	NM
❏ UA-LA046-F	I'll See You When I Get There	1973	2.50	5.00	10.00
❏ UA-LA245-G	The Very Best of Slim Whitman	1974	2.50	5.00	10.00

Number	Title (A Side/B Side)	Yr	VG	VG+	NM
❑ UA-LA319-G	Happy Anniversary	1974	2.50	5.00	10.00
❑ UA-LA386-E	The Very Best of Slim Whitman	1974	2.50	5.00	10.00
❑ UA-LA513-G	Everything Leads Back to You	1975	2.50	5.00	10.00
❑ UA-LA752-G	Red River Valley	1977	2.50	5.00	10.00
❑ UA-LA787-G	Home on the Range	1978	2.50	5.00	10.00
❑ LM-1005	The Very Best of Slim Whitman	1980	2.50	5.00	10.00
❑ UAS-6763	Tomorrow Never Comes	1970	3.00	6.00	12.00
❑ UAS-6783	Guess Who	1970	3.00	6.00	12.00
❑ UAS-6819	It's a Sin to Tell a Lie	1971	3.00	6.00	12.00
❑ UAS-6832	The Best of Slim Whitman	1972	3.00	6.00	12.00

WHITNEY, MARVA
KING

Number	Title (A Side/B Side)	Yr	VG	VG+	NM
❑ KS-1053	I Sing Soul	1969	30.00	60.00	120.00
❑ KS-1062	It's My Thing	1969	30.00	60.00	120.00
❑ KS-1079	Live and Lowdown at the Apollo	1970	50.00	100.00	200.00

WHITNEY SUNDAY
DECCA

Number	Title (A Side/B Side)	Yr	VG	VG+	NM
❑ DL 75239	Whitney Sunday	1970	5.00	10.00	20.00

WHO, THE
Also see ROGER DALTREY; JOHN ENTWISTLE; KEITH MOON; PETE TOWNSHEND.
DECCA

Number	Title (A Side/B Side)	Yr	VG	VG+	NM
❑ DL 4664 [M]	The Who Sing My Generation	1966	25.00	50.00	100.00
❑ DL 4664 [M]	The Who Sing My Generation	1966	50.00	100.00	200.00
—White label promo					
❑ DL 4892 [M]	Happy Jack	1967	12.50	25.00	50.00
❑ DL 4892 [M]	Happy Jack	1967	37.50	75.00	150.00
—White label promo					
❑ DL 4950 [M]	The Who Sell Out	1967	25.00	50.00	100.00
❑ DL 4950 [M]	The Who Sell Out	1967	50.00	100.00	200.00
—White label promo with songs in the same order as the stock copy					
❑ DL 4950 [M]	The Who Sell Out	1967	75.00	150.00	300.00
—White label promo with side 1 banded for airplay and all the commercials on one side					
❑ DL 5064 [M]	Magic Bus — The Who on Tour	1968	50.00	100.00	200.00
—White label promo; no stock copies were released in mono					
❑ DXSW 7205 [(2)]	Tommy	1969	10.00	20.00	40.00
—With booklet					
❑ DXSW 7205 [(2)DJ]	Tommy	1969	50.00	100.00	200.00
—White label promo					
❑ DL 74664 [R]	The Who Sing My Generation	1966	15.00	30.00	60.00
❑ DL 74664 [R]	The Who Sing My Generation	1966	50.00	100.00	200.00
—White label promo					
❑ DL 74892 [P]	Happy Jack	1967	12.50	25.00	50.00
—All stereo except that "Happy Jack" and "Don't Look Away" are rechanneled					
❑ DL 74892 [P]	Happy Jack	1967	37.50	75.00	150.00
—White label promo					
❑ DL 74950 [S]	The Who Sell Out	1967	12.50	25.00	50.00
❑ DL 74950 [S]	The Who Sell Out	1967	62.50	125.00	250.00
—White label promo with songs in the same order as the stock copy					
❑ DL 74950 [S]	The Who Sell Out	1967	100.00	200.00	400.00
—White label promo with side 1 banded for airplay and all the commercials on one side					
❑ DL 75064 [P]	Magic Bus — The Who on Tour	1968	12.50	25.00	50.00
—All rechanneled except "Magic Bus" and "I Can't Reach You," which are true stereo.					
❑ DL 75064 [P]	Magic Bus — The Who on Tour	1968	37.50	75.00	150.00
—White label promo					
❑ DL 79175	Live at Leeds	1970	10.00	20.00	40.00
—With gatefold cover and numerous inserts					
❑ DL 79182	Who's Next	1971	6.25	12.50	25.00
❑ DL 79184	Meaty Beaty Big and Bouncy	1971	7.50	15.00	30.00
—With poster (deduct 1/3 if missing)					
❑ DL 734586	The Who/The Strawberry Alarm Clock	1969	25.00	50.00	100.00
—Special Products release for Philco. One side has Who songs, the other, Strawberry Alarm Clock songs					

DIRECT DISC

Number	Title (A Side/B Side)	Yr	VG	VG+	NM
❑ SD 16610	Who Are You	1980	7.50	15.00	30.00
—Audiophile vinyl					

LIFE

Number	Title (A Side/B Side)	Yr	VG	VG+	NM
❑ DL 74664 [R]	The Who Sing My Generation	1967	37.50	75.00	150.00

MCA

Number	Title (A Side/B Side)	Yr	VG	VG+	NM
❑ 1496	Who's Greatest Hits	1987	2.00	4.00	8.00
❑ 1577	Live at Leeds	1988	2.00	4.00	8.00
❑ 1578	Meaty Beaty Big and Bouncy	1988	2.00	4.00	8.00
❑ 1579	The Who By Numbers	1988	2.00	4.00	8.00
❑ 1580	Who Are You	1988	2.00	4.00	8.00
❑ L33-1987 [DJ]	Who Are You	1978	6.25	12.50	25.00
—White label promo with sticker "Who Are You Edited for Broadcast" on cover -- the line "Who the fuck are you?" is deleted twice.					
❑ 2022	Live at Leeds	1973	3.00	6.00	12.00
❑ 2023	Who's Next	1973	3.00	6.00	12.00
❑ 2025	Meaty Beaty Big and Bouncy	1973	3.00	6.00	12.00
❑ 2044 [R]	The Who Sing My Generation	1974	12.50	25.00	50.00
❑ 2045 [P]	Happy Jack	1974	12.50	25.00	50.00
❑ 2161	The Who By Numbers	1975	3.00	6.00	12.00
❑ 3023	Live at Leeds	1977	2.50	5.00	10.00
❑ 3024	Who's Next	1977	2.50	5.00	10.00
❑ 3025	Meaty Beaty Big and Bouncy	1977	2.50	5.00	10.00
❑ 3026	The Who By Numbers	1977	2.50	5.00	10.00
❑ 3050	Who Are You	1978	2.50	5.00	10.00
❑ 2-4067 [(2)P]	A Quick One/The Who Sell Out	1976	5.00	10.00	20.00
—Black labels with rainbow					
❑ 2-4067 [(2)P]	A Quick One/The Who Sell Out	1978	3.75	7.50	15.00
—Tan labels					
❑ 2-4067 [(2)P]	A Quick One/The Who Sell Out	1980	3.00	6.00	12.00
—Blue labels with rainbow					
❑ 2-4068 [(2)P]	Magic Bus/The Who Sing My Generation	1976	5.00	10.00	20.00
—Black labels with rainbow					
❑ 2-4068 [(2)P]	Magic Bus/The Who Sing My Generation	1978	3.75	7.50	15.00
—Tan labels					
❑ 2-4068 [(2)P]	Magic Bus/The Who Sing My Generation	1980	3.00	6.00	12.00
—Blue labels with rainbow					
❑ 5220	Who's Next	1979	2.00	4.00	8.00
❑ 5408	Who's Greatest Hits	1983	2.00	4.00	8.00
❑ 5641	Who's Missing	1986	2.50	5.00	10.00
❑ 5712	Two's Missing	1987	2.50	5.00	10.00
❑ 6895 [(2)]	Quadrophenia	1980	2.50	5.00	10.00
❑ 6899 [(2)]	The Kids Are Alright	1980	2.50	5.00	10.00
—Early versions have number stamped in gold on cover with 11005 records. No difference in value.					
❑ 8018 [(2)]	Who's Last	1984	2.50	5.00	10.00
❑ 8031 [(2)]	Who's Better, Who's Best	1989	3.75	7.50	15.00
❑ 2-10004 [(2)]	Quadrophenia	1973	3.75	7.50	15.00
—Black labels with rainbow					
❑ 2-10004 [(2)]	Quadrophenia	1978	3.00	6.00	12.00
—Tan labels					
❑ 2-10005 [(2)]	Tommy	1973	3.75	7.50	15.00
—Black labels with rainbow					
❑ 2-10005 [(2)]	Tommy	1978	3.00	6.00	12.00
—Tan labels					
❑ 2-10005 [(2)]	Tommy	1980	2.50	5.00	10.00
—Blue labels with rainbow					
❑ 2-11005 [(2)]	The Kids Are Alright	1979	3.00	6.00	12.00
❑ 11164	Who's Next	1995	6.25	12.50	25.00
—"Heavy Vinyl" reissue on 180-gram vinyl with gatefold cover					
❑ 2-12001 [(2)]	Hooligans	1981	2.50	5.00	10.00
❑ 14950 [PD]	Who Are You	1978	3.75	7.50	15.00
—Picture disc					
❑ 3-19501 [(3)]	Join Together	1990	5.00	10.00	20.00
—Box set with booklet					
❑ 25986	It's Hard	1989	2.00	4.00	8.00
❑ 25987	Face Dances	1989	2.00	4.00	8.00
❑ 37000	Live at Leeds	1979	2.00	4.00	8.00
❑ 37001	Meaty Beaty Big and Bouncy	1979	2.00	4.00	8.00
❑ 37002	The Who By Numbers	1979	2.00	4.00	8.00
❑ 37003	Who Are You	1979	2.00	4.00	8.00
❑ 37169	Odds and Sods	1980	2.00	4.00	8.00

MOBILE FIDELITY

Number	Title (A Side/B Side)	Yr	VG	VG+	NM
❑ 1-115	Face Dances	1984	6.25	12.50	25.00
—Audiophile vinyl					

TRACK

Number	Title (A Side/B Side)	Yr	VG	VG+	NM
❑ 2126	Odds and Sods	1974	6.25	12.50	25.00
❑ 2-4067 [(2)P]	A Quick One/The Who Sell Out	1974	6.25	12.50	25.00
❑ 2-4068 [(2)P]	Magic Bus/The Who Sing My Generation	1974	6.25	12.50	25.00
❑ 2-10004 [(2)]	Quadrophenia	1973	5.00	10.00	20.00

WARNER BROS.

Number	Title (A Side/B Side)	Yr	VG	VG+	NM
❑ WBMS-116 [DJ]	Filling In the Gaps	1981	12.50	25.00	50.00
—With generic "Warner Bros. Music Show" cover					
❑ WBMS-116 [DJ]	Filling In the Gaps	1981	20.00	40.00	80.00
—With drawing on cover					
❑ HS 3516	Face Dances	1981	2.00	4.00	8.00
❑ 23731	It's Hard	1982	2.00	4.00	8.00
❑ 23731 [DJ]	It's Hard	1982	7.50	15.00	30.00
—Promo version on Quiex II vinyl					

WICHITA TRAIN WHISTLE, THE
DOT

Number	Title (A Side/B Side)	Yr	VG	VG+	NM
❑ DLP-25861	Mike Nesmith Presents/The Wichita Train Whistle Sings	1968	7.50	15.00	30.00

WIGGINS, GERALD
CHALLENGE

Number	Title (A Side/B Side)	Yr	VG	VG+	NM
❑ CHP-604 [M]	The King and I	1957	15.00	30.00	60.00

CONTEMPORARY

Number	Title (A Side/B Side)	Yr	VG	VG+	NM
❑ M-3595 [M]	Relax and Enjoy It	1961	7.50	15.00	30.00
❑ S-7595 [S]	Relax and Enjoy It	1961	10.00	20.00	40.00

DIG

Number	Title (A Side/B Side)	Yr	VG	VG+	NM
❑ LP-102 [M]	Gerald Wiggins Trio	1956	15.00	30.00	60.00

DISCOVERY

Number	Title (A Side/B Side)	Yr	VG	VG+	NM
❑ DL-2003 [10]	Gerald Wiggins Trio	1953	30.00	60.00	120.00

HIFI

Number	Title (A Side/B Side)	Yr	VG	VG+	NM
❑ J-618 [M]	Wiggin' Out	1961	7.50	15.00	30.00
❑ JS-618 [S]	Wiggin' Out	1961	10.00	20.00	40.00

MOTIF

Number	Title (A Side/B Side)	Yr	VG	VG+	NM
❑ 504 [M]	Reminiscin' with Wig	1956	15.00	30.00	60.00

SPECIALTY

Number	Title (A Side/B Side)	Yr	VG	VG+	NM
❑ SP-2101 [S]	Around the World	1969	5.00	10.00	20.00

TAMPA

Number	Title (A Side/B Side)	Yr	VG	VG+	NM
❑ TP-1 [M]	The Loveliness of You	1957	25.00	50.00	100.00
—Colored vinyl					
❑ TP-1 [M]	The Loveliness of You	1958	12.50	25.00	50.00
—Black vinyl					
❑ TP-33 [M]	Gerald Wiggins Trio	1957	25.00	50.00	100.00
—Colored vinyl					
❑ TP-33 [M]	Gerald Wiggins Trio	1958	12.50	25.00	50.00
—Black vinyl					

WIGGINS, ROY
DIPLOMAT

Number	Title (A Side/B Side)	Yr	VG	VG+	NM
❑ DPL 2615 [M]	Songs I Played for Eddy Arnold	196?	3.75	7.50	15.00

STARDAY

Number	Title (A Side/B Side)	Yr	VG	VG+	NM
❑ SLP-188 [M]	Mister Steel Guitar	1962	7.50	15.00	30.00
❑ SLP-259 [M]	The Fabulous Steel Guitar Artistry of Roy Wiggins	1963	7.50	15.00	30.00
❑ SLP-392 [M]	Nashville Steel Guitar	1965	6.25	12.50	25.00

WIGGS, JOHNNY
PARAMOUNT

Number	Title (A Side/B Side)	Yr	VG	VG+	NM
❑ CJS 107 [10]	Johnny Wiggs' New Orleanians Playing Jazz Favorites and Featuring Ray Burke	195?	15.00	30.00	60.00

SOUTHLAND

Number	Title (A Side/B Side)	Yr	VG	VG+	NM
❑ LP-200 [10]	Johnny Wiggs	1954	12.50	25.00	50.00
❑ LP-200 [M]	Johnny Wiggs	195?	7.50	15.00	30.00

Number	Title (A Side/B Side)	Yr	VG	VG+	NM

WIGGS, JOHNNY, AND RAYMOND BURKE
S/D
| ❏ LP-1001 [10] | Chamber Jazz | 1955 | 12.50 | 25.00 | 50.00 |

WIGWAM
VERVE FORECAST
| ❏ FTS-3089 | Tombstone Valentine | 1970 | 5.00 | 10.00 | 20.00 |

WILBER, BOB
CIRCLE
| ❏ L-406 [10] | Bob Wilbur Jazz Band | 1951 | 12.50 | 25.00 | 50.00 |
RIVERSIDE
| ❏ RLP-2501 [10] | Young Men With Horns | 1952 | 20.00 | 40.00 | 80.00 |

WILBURN BROTHERS, THE
DECCA
❏ DL 4058 [M]	The Big Heartbreak	1960	7.50	15.00	30.00
❏ DL 4142 [M]	The Wilburn Brothers Sing	1961	7.50	15.00	30.00
❏ DL 4211 [M]	City Limits	1961	7.50	15.00	30.00
❏ DL 4225 [M]	Folk Songs	1962	5.00	10.00	20.00
❏ DL 4391 [M]	Trouble's Back in Town	1963	5.00	10.00	20.00
❏ DL 4464 [M]	Take Up Thy Cross	1964	5.00	10.00	20.00
❏ DL 4544 [M]	Never Alone	1964	5.00	10.00	20.00
❏ DL 4615 [M]	Country Gold	1965	5.00	10.00	20.00
❏ DL 4645 [M]	I'm Gonna Tie One on Tonight	1965	5.00	10.00	20.00
❏ DL 4721 [M]	The Wilburn Brothers Show	1966	15.00	30.00	60.00
—With guests Loretta Lynn, Ernest Tubb, Harold Morrison					
❏ DL 4764 [M]	Let's Go Country	1966	5.00	10.00	20.00
❏ DL 4824 [M]	Two for the Show	1967	6.25	12.50	25.00
❏ DL 4871 [M]	Cool	1967	7.50	15.00	30.00
❏ DL 4954 [M]	It's Another World	1968	10.00	20.00	40.00
❏ DL 8576 [M]	The Wilburn Brothers	1957	10.00	20.00	40.00
❏ DL 8774 [M]	Side by Side	1958	10.00	20.00	40.00
❏ DL 8959 [M]	Livin' in God's Country	1959	10.00	20.00	40.00
❏ DL 74058 [S]	The Big Heartbreak	1960	10.00	20.00	40.00
❏ DL 74142 [S]	The Wilburn Brothers Sing	1961	10.00	20.00	40.00
❏ DL 74211 [S]	City Limits	1961	10.00	20.00	40.00
❏ DL 74225 [S]	Folk Songs	1962	7.50	15.00	30.00
❏ DL 74391 [S]	Trouble's Back in Town	1963	7.50	15.00	30.00
❏ DL 74464 [S]	Take Up Thy Cross	1964	6.25	12.50	25.00
❏ DL 74544 [S]	Never Alone	1964	6.25	12.50	25.00
❏ DL 74615 [S]	Country Gold	1965	6.25	12.50	25.00
❏ DL 74645 [S]	I'm Gonna Tie One on Tonight	1965	6.25	12.50	25.00
❏ DL 74721 [S]	The Wilburn Brothers Show	1966	20.00	40.00	80.00
—With guests Loretta Lynn, Ernest Tubb, Harold Morrison					
❏ DL 74764 [S]	Let's Go Country	1966	6.25	12.50	25.00
❏ DL 74824 [S]	Two for the Show	1967	5.00	10.00	20.00
❏ DL 74871 [S]	Cool	1967	5.00	10.00	20.00
❏ DL 74954 [S]	It's Another World	1968	5.00	10.00	20.00
❏ DL 75173	Little Johnny from Down the Street	1970	5.00	10.00	20.00
❏ DL 75214	Sing Your Heart Out Country Boy	1971	5.00	10.00	20.00
❏ DL 75291	That She's Leaving Feeling	1972	5.00	10.00	20.00
❏ DL 78774 [S]	Side by Side	1959	15.00	30.00	60.00
❏ DL 78959 [S]	Livin' in God's Country	1959	15.00	30.00	60.00
KING
❏ 746 [M]	The Wonderful Wilburn Brothers	1961	25.00	50.00	100.00
MCA
❏ 4011 [(2)]	Portrait	197?	3.75	7.50	15.00
MCA CORAL
❏ 20058	That Country Feeling	1973	2.50	5.00	10.00
VOCALION
❏ VL 3691 [M]	Carefree Moments	1962	3.75	7.50	15.00
❏ VL 73691 [S]	Carefree Moments	1962	3.75	7.50	15.00
❏ VL 73876	That Country Feeling	197?	3.00	6.00	12.00
❏ VL 73889	I Walk the Line	197?	3.00	6.00	12.00

WILCOX, LARRY
COLUMBIA
| ❏ CL 2147 [M] | Hot Rod Jazz | 1964 | 7.50 | 15.00 | 30.00 |
| ❏ CS 8947 [S] | Hot Rod Jazz | 1964 | 10.00 | 20.00 | 40.00 |
COLUMBIA SPECIAL PRODUCTS
| ❏ CSRP 8947 [M] | Hot Rod Jazz | 196? | 5.00 | 10.00 | 20.00 |

WILCOX THREE, THE
RCA CAMDEN
| ❏ CAL-669 [M] | The Greatest Folk Songs Ever Sung | 1961 | 5.00 | 10.00 | 20.00 |

WILD, EARL
See BOSTON POPS ORCHESTRA (ARTHUR FIEDLER, CONDUCTOR)

WILD, JACK
BUDDAH
| ❏ BDS-5083 | Everything's Coming Up Roses | 1971 | 6.25 | 12.50 | 25.00 |
| ❏ BDS-5110 | A Beautiful World | 1972 | 6.25 | 12.50 | 25.00 |
CAPITOL
| ❏ SKAO-545 | The Jack Wild Album | 1970 | 6.25 | 12.50 | 25.00 |

WILD BUTTER
UNITED ARTISTS
| ❏ UAS-6766 | Wild Butter | 1970 | 6.25 | 12.50 | 25.00 |

WILD-CATS, THE
UNITED ARTISTS
| ❏ UAL-3031 [M] | Bandstand Record Hop | 1958 | 12.50 | 25.00 | 50.00 |

WILD COUNTRY
See ALABAMA.

WILD MAN STEVE
DEALER'S CHOICE
| ❏ 777 | Is It Good Baby | 198? | 3.75 | 7.50 | 15.00 |
| ❏ 780 | Did He Really Say That | 198? | 3.75 | 7.50 | 15.00 |

DICK-ER
| ❏ D 70 | Do Not Disturb | 1972 | 5.00 | 10.00 | 20.00 |
LAFF
| ❏ 181 | Eatin' Ain't Cheatin' | 1973 | 3.00 | 6.00 | 12.00 |
| ❏ 191 | When You're Hot You're Hot | 1976 | 3.00 | 6.00 | 12.00 |
RAW
❏ 7000	My Man! Wild Man!	1969	3.75	7.50	15.00
❏ 7001	Wild! Wild! Wild! Wild!	1970	3.75	7.50	15.00
❏ 7002	King of Them All	1971	3.75	7.50	15.00

WILD ONES, THE (1)
UNITED ARTISTS
| ❏ UAL-3450 [M] | The Arthur Sound | 1965 | 6.25 | 12.50 | 25.00 |
| ❏ UAS-6450 [S] | The Arthur Sound | 1965 | 7.50 | 15.00 | 30.00 |

WILDE, MARTY
EPIC
❏ BN 575 [S]	Wilde About Marty	1960	25.00	50.00	100.00
❏ LN 3686 [M]	Bad Boy	1960	20.00	40.00	80.00
❏ LN 3711 [M]	Wilde About Marty	1960	20.00	40.00	80.00

WILDER, ALEC
COLUMBIA
| ❏ CL 6181 [10] | Alec Wilder Octet | 1951 | 15.00 | 30.00 | 60.00 |
MERCURY
| ❏ MG 25008 [10] | Alec Wilder and His Octet | 1949 | 15.00 | 30.00 | 60.00 |

WILDER, JOE
COLUMBIA
❏ CL 1319 [M]	Jazz from "Peter Gunn"	1959	7.50	15.00	30.00
❏ CL 1372 [M]	The Pretty Sound of Joe Wilder	1959	7.50	15.00	30.00
❏ CS 8121 [S]	Jazz from "Peter Gunn"	1959	10.00	20.00	40.00
❏ CS 8173 [S]	The Pretty Sound of Joe Wilder	1959	10.00	20.00	40.00
SAVOY
❏ MG-12063 [M]	'N' Wilder....	1956	10.00	20.00	40.00

WILDERNESS ROAD
COLUMBIA
| ❏ C 31118 | Wilderness Road | 1972 | 5.00 | 10.00 | 20.00 |
REPRISE
| ❏ MS 2125 | Sold for the Prevention of Disease Only | 1973 | 5.00 | 10.00 | 20.00 |

WILDWEEDS, THE
VANGUARD
| ❏ VSD-6552 | The Wildweeds | 1970 | 6.25 | 12.50 | 25.00 |

WILEY, LEE
ALLEGRO ELITE
| ❏ 4019 [10] | Lee Wiley Sings — Lennie Tristano Plays | 195? | 25.00 | 50.00 | 100.00 |
COLUMBIA
❏ CL 656 [M]	Night in Manhattan	1955	20.00	40.00	80.00
❏ CL 6169 [10]	Night in Manhattan	1951	25.00	50.00	100.00
❏ CL 6215 [10]	Lee Wiley Sings Vincent Youmans	1952	25.00	50.00	100.00
❏ CL 6216 [10]	Lee Wiley Sings Irving Berlin	1952	25.00	50.00	100.00
JAZZTONE
❏ J-1248 [M]	The Songs of Rodgers and Hart — Intimate Jazz	1956	12.50	25.00	50.00
JJC
❏ M-2002 [M]	The One and Only Lee Wiley	195?	12.50	25.00	50.00
❏ M-2003 [M]	The Classic Interpretations of the Immortal Cole Porter	195?	12.50	25.00	50.00
LIBERTY MUSIC SHOP
❏ 1003 [10]	Cole Porter Songs by Lee Wiley	195?	75.00	150.00	300.00
❏ 1004 [10]	George Gershwin Songs by Lee Wiley	195?	75.00	150.00	300.00
RCA VICTOR
❏ LPM-1408 [M]	West of the Moon	1957	20.00	40.00	80.00
❏ LPM-1566 [M]	Touch of the Blues	1957	15.00	30.00	60.00
RIC
❏ M-2002 [M]	The One and Only Lee Wiley	1964	5.00	10.00	20.00
❏ S-2002 [S]	The One and Only Lee Wiley	1964	6.25	12.50	25.00
STORYVILLE
❏ STLP-312 [10]	Lee Wiley Sings Rodgers and Hart	1954	50.00	100.00	200.00

WILKERSON, DON
BLUE NOTE
❏ BLP-4107 [M]	Preach, Brother!	1962	7.50	15.00	30.00
❏ BLP-4121 [M]	Elder Don	1963	7.50	15.00	30.00
❏ BLP-4145 [M]	Shoutin'	1963	7.50	15.00	30.00
❏ BST-84107 [S]	Preach, Brother!	1962	10.00	20.00	40.00
—With "New York, USA" address on label					
❏ BST-84107 [S]	Preach, Brother!	1967	5.00	10.00	20.00
—With "A Division of Liberty Records" on label					
❏ BST-84121 [S]	Elder Don	1963	10.00	20.00	40.00
—With "New York, USA" address on label					
❏ BST-84121 [S]	Elder Don	1967	5.00	10.00	20.00
—With "A Division of Liberty Records" on label					
❏ BST-84145 [S]	Shoutin'	1963	10.00	20.00	40.00
—With "New York, USA" address on label					
❏ BST-84145 [S]	Shoutin'	1967	5.00	10.00	20.00
—With "A Division of Liberty Records" on label					
RIVERSIDE
❏ RLP-332 [M]	Texas Twister	1960	10.00	20.00	40.00
❏ RLP-1186 [S]	Texas Twister	1960	10.00	20.00	40.00

WILKINS, ERNIE
EVEREST
❏ SDBR-1077 [S]	Here Comes the Swingin' Mr. Wilkins	1959	7.50	15.00	30.00
❏ SDBR-1104 [S]	The Big New Band of the '60s	1960	7.50	15.00	30.00
❏ LPBR-5077 [M]	Here Comes the Swingin' Mr. Wilkins	1959	6.25	12.50	25.00
❏ LPBR-5104 [M]	The Big New Band of the '60s	1960	6.25	12.50	25.00

Number	Title (A Side/B Side)	Yr	VG	VG+	NM
SAVOY					
❏ MG-12044 [M]	Top Brass Featuring 5 Trumpets	1955	15.00	30.00	60.00
WILKINSON TRI-CYCLE					
DATE					
❏ TES 4016	Wilkinson Tri-Cycle	1969	10.00	20.00	40.00
WILLET, SLIM					
AUDIO LAB					
❏ AL-1542 [M]	Slim Willet	1959	25.00	50.00	100.00
WILLETTE, BABY FACE					
ARGO					
❏ LP-739 [M]	No Rock	1964	6.25	12.50	25.00
❏ LPS-739 [S]	No Rock	1964	7.50	15.00	30.00
❏ LP-749 [M]	Behind the 8-Ball	1965	6.25	12.50	25.00
❏ LPS-749 [S]	Behind the 8-Ball	1965	7.50	15.00	30.00
BLUE NOTE					
❏ BLP-4068 [M]	Face to Face	1961	37.50	75.00	150.00
—With W. 63rd St. address on label					
❏ BLP-4068 [M]	Face to Face	1963	6.25	12.50	25.00
—With "New York, USA" address on label					
❏ BLP-4084 [M]	Stop and Listen	1962	30.00	60.00	120.00
—With 61st St. address on label					
❏ BLP-4084 [M]	Stop and Listen	1963	6.25	12.50	25.00
—With "New York, USA" address on label					
❏ BST-84068 [S]	Face to Face	1961	30.00	60.00	120.00
—With W. 63rd St. address on label					
❏ BST-84068 [S]	Face to Face	1963	5.00	10.00	20.00
—With "New York, USA" address on label					
❏ BST-84084 [S]	Stop and Listen	1962	25.00	50.00	100.00
—With 61st St. address on label					
❏ BST-84084 [S]	Stop and Listen	1963	5.00	10.00	20.00
—With "New York, USA" address on label					
WILLIAMS, ANDY					
ATCO					
❏ 90561	Close Enough for Love	1987	2.50	5.00	10.00
CADENCE					
❏ CLP 1018 [M]	Andy Williams	1957	12.50	25.00	50.00
❏ CLP 3002 [M]	Andy Williams	1958	12.50	25.00	50.00
—Cover depicts Andy standing					
❏ CLP 3002 [M]	Andy Williams	1960	5.00	10.00	20.00
—Cover depicts Andy reclining					
❏ CLP 3005 [M]	Andy Williams Sings Rodgers and Hammerstein	1958	10.00	20.00	40.00
—Cover depicts a cafÈ scene					
❏ CLP 3005 [M]	Andy Williams Sings Rodgers and Hammerstein	1960	5.00	10.00	20.00
—Cover depicts a close-up of Andy's face					
❏ CLP 3026 [M]	Two Time Winners	1959	5.00	10.00	20.00
❏ CLP 3027 [M]	Andy Williams Sings…Steve Allen	1959	5.00	10.00	20.00
❏ CLP 3029 [M]	To You Sweetheart, Aloha	1959	5.00	10.00	20.00
❏ CLP 3030 [M]	Lonely Street	1960	5.00	10.00	20.00
❏ CLP 3038 [M]	The Village of St. Bernadette	1960	5.00	10.00	20.00
❏ CLP 3047 [M]	Under Paris Skies	1961	5.00	10.00	20.00
❏ CLP 3054 [M]	Andy Williams' Best	1962	5.00	10.00	20.00
❏ CLP 3061 [M]	Million Seller Songs	1962	5.00	10.00	20.00
❏ CLP 25026 [S]	Two Time Winners	1959	7.50	15.00	30.00
—Black vinyl					
❏ CLP 25026 [S]	Two Time Winners	1959	20.00	40.00	80.00
—Red vinyl					
❏ CLP 25027 [R]	Andy Williams Sings…Steve Allen	1959	3.75	7.50	15.00
❏ CLP 25029 [S]	To You Sweetheart, Aloha	1959	7.50	15.00	30.00
❏ CLP 25030 [S]	Lonely Street	1960	7.50	15.00	30.00
❏ CLP 25038 [S]	The Village of St. Bernadette	1960	7.50	15.00	30.00
❏ CLP 25047 [S]	Under Paris Skies	1961	7.50	15.00	30.00
❏ CLP 25054 [S]	Andy Williams' Best	1962	6.25	12.50	25.00
❏ CLP 25061 [S]	Million Seller Songs	1962	6.25	12.50	25.00
CAPITOL					
❏ ST-12387	Greatest Love Classics	1984	2.50	5.00	10.00
COLUMBIA					
❏ GP 5 [(2)]	The Andy Williams Sound of Music	1969	5.00	10.00	20.00
❏ CL 1751 [M]	Danny Boy And Other Songs I Love to Sing.	1962	3.75	7.50	15.00
❏ CL 1809 [M]	Moon River and Other Great Movie Themes.	1962	3.00	6.00	12.00
❏ CL 1879 [M]	Warm and Willing.	1962	3.00	6.00	12.00
❏ CL 2015 [M]	Days of Wine and Roses.	1963	3.00	6.00	12.00
❏ CL 2087 [M]	The Andy Williams Christmas Album.	1963	3.00	6.00	12.00
❏ CL 2137 [M]	The Wonderful World of Andy Williams.	1964	3.00	6.00	12.00
❏ CL 2171 [M]	The Academy Award Winning "Call Me Irresponsible" and Other Hits Songs from the Movies.	1964	3.00	6.00	12.00
❏ CL 2205 [M]	The Great Songs from "My Fair Lady" and Other Broadway Hits.	1964	3.00	6.00	12.00
❏ CL 2323 [M]	Hawaiian Wedding Song.	1965	3.00	6.00	12.00
—Reissue of Cadence 3029					
❏ CL 2324 [M]	Canadian Sunset	1965	3.00	6.00	12.00
—Reissue of Cadence 3054					
❏ CL 2338 [M]	Dear Heart	1965	3.00	6.00	12.00
❏ CL 2383 [M]	Andy Williams' Newest Hits	1966	3.00	6.00	12.00
❏ CL 2420 [M]	Merry Christmas	1965	3.00	6.00	12.00
❏ CL 2499 [M]	The Shadow of Your Smile	1966	3.00	6.00	12.00
❏ CL 2533 [M]	In the Arms of Love	1967	3.00	6.00	12.00
❏ CL 2680 [M]	Born Free	1967	3.00	6.00	12.00
❏ CL 2766 [M]	Love, Andy	1967	3.75	7.50	15.00
❏ CS 2862 [M]	Honey	1968	5.00	10.00	20.00
❏ CS 8551 [S]	Danny Boy And Other Songs I Love to Sing	1962	5.00	10.00	20.00
❏ CS 8609 [S]	Moon River and Other Great Movie Themes	1962	3.75	7.50	15.00
❏ CS 8679 [S]	Warm and Willing	1962	3.75	7.50	15.00
❏ CS 8815 [S]	Days of Wine and Roses	1963	3.75	7.50	15.00
❏ CS 8887 [S]	The Andy Williams Christmas Album	1963	3.00	6.00	12.00
❏ CS 8937 [S]	The Wonderful World of Andy Williams	1964	3.75	7.50	15.00

Number	Title (A Side/B Side)	Yr	VG	VG+	NM
❏ CS 8971 [S]	The Academy Award Winning "Call Me Irresponsible" and Other Hits Songs from the Movies	1964	3.75	7.50	15.00
❏ CS 9005 [S]	The Great Songs from "My Fair Lady" and Other Broadway Hits	1964	3.75	7.50	15.00
❏ CS 9123 [S]	Hawaiian Wedding Song	1965	3.75	7.50	15.00
—Reissue of Cadence 25029					
❏ CS 9124 [S]	Canadian Sunset	1965	3.75	7.50	15.00
—Reissue of Cadence 25054					
❏ CS 9138 [S]	Dear Heart	1965	3.75	7.50	15.00
❏ CS 9183 [S]	Andy Williams' Newest Hits	1966	3.75	7.50	15.00
❏ CS 9220 [S]	Merry Christmas	1965	3.00	6.00	12.00
❏ CS 9299 [S]	The Shadow of Your Smile	1966	3.75	7.50	15.00
❏ CS 9333 [S]	In the Arms of Love	1967	3.75	7.50	15.00
❏ CS 9480 [S]	Born Free	1967	3.75	7.50	15.00
❏ CS 9566 [S]	Love, Andy	1967	3.00	6.00	12.00
❏ CS 9662 [S]	Honey	1968	3.00	6.00	12.00
❏ CS 9844	Happy Heart	1969	3.00	6.00	12.00
❏ CS 9896	Raindrops Keep Fallin' on My Head	1970	3.00	6.00	12.00
❏ CS 9922	Get Together with Andy Williams	1969	3.75	7.50	15.00
—The Osmonds appear on three tracks					
❏ KCS 9979	Andy Williams' Greatest Hits	1970	3.00	6.00	12.00
❏ KC 30105	The Andy Williams Show	1970	2.50	5.00	10.00
❏ CQ 30497 [Q]	Love Story	1972	3.75	7.50	15.00
❏ KC 30497	Love Story	1971	2.50	5.00	10.00
❏ CQ 30797 [Q]	You've Got a Friend	1971	3.75	7.50	15.00
❏ KC 30797	You've Got a Friend	1971	2.50	5.00	10.00
❏ CG 31064 [(2)]	The Impossible Dream	1971	3.75	7.50	15.00
❏ CQ 31303 [Q]	Love Theme from "The Godfather"	1972	3.75	7.50	15.00
❏ KC 31303	Love Theme from "The Godfather"	1972	2.50	5.00	10.00
❏ CQ 31625 [Q]	Alone Again (Naturally)	1972	3.75	7.50	15.00
❏ KC 31625	Alone Again (Naturally)	1972	2.50	5.00	10.00
❏ KC 32383	Solitaire	1973	2.50	5.00	10.00
❏ KC 32384	Andy Williams' Greatest Hits, Vol. 2	1973	2.50	5.00	10.00
❏ KC 32949	The Way We Were	1974	2.50	5.00	10.00
❏ C 33191	Christmas Present	1974	2.50	5.00	10.00
❏ KC 33234	You Lay So Easy on My Mind	1974	2.50	5.00	10.00
❏ PC 33563	The Other Side of Me	1975	2.50	5.00	10.00
❏ CG 33597 [(2)]	Love Story/Born Free	1975	3.00	6.00	12.00
❏ CG 33600 [(2)]	Moon River/Days of Wine and Roses	1975	3.00	6.00	12.00
❏ PC 34299	Andy	1976	2.50	5.00	10.00
❏ PCQ 34299 [Q]	Andy	1976	3.75	7.50	15.00
COLUMBIA SPECIAL PRODUCTS					
❏ CSS 966	Andy… & Company	1969	3.00	6.00	12.00
—Side 1 is Andy Williams; Side 2 has tracks by the Williams Brothers, Claudine Longet and the Osmond Brothers; sold only at Woolworth's					
HARMONY					
❏ KH 30133	Andy Williams	1970	2.50	5.00	10.00
PAIR					
❏ PDL2-1103 [(2)]	The Best of Andy Williams	1986	3.00	6.00	12.00
WILLIAMS, ANN					
CHARLIE PARKER					
❏ PLP-807 [M]	First Time Out	1963	10.00	20.00	40.00
❏ PLP-807S [S]	First Time Out	1963	10.00	20.00	40.00
WILLIAMS, BETTY VAIDEN					
VANGUARD					
❏ VRS-9028 [M]	Folk Songs and Ballads of North Carolina	195?	7.50	15.00	30.00
WILLIAMS, BIG JOE					
BLUESVILLE					
❏ BVLP-1056 [M]	Blues for 9 Strings	1962	25.00	50.00	100.00
—Blue label, silver print					
❏ BVLP-1056 [M]	Blues for 9 Strings	1964	6.25	12.50	25.00
—Blue label with trident logo					
❏ BVLP-1067 [M]	Big Joe Williams at Folk City	1963	25.00	50.00	100.00
—Blue label, silver print					
❏ BVLP-1067 [M]	Big Joe Williams at Folk City	1964	6.25	12.50	25.00
—Blue label with trident logo					
❏ BVLP-1083 [M]	Studio Blues	1964	6.25	12.50	25.00
—Blue label with trident logo					
❏ BVLP-1083 [M]	Studio Blues	1964	25.00	50.00	100.00
—Blue label, silver print					
DELMARK					
❏ DL-604 [M]	Blues on Highway 49	1962	15.00	30.00	60.00
❏ DL-609 [M]	Starvin' Chain Blues	1966	6.25	12.50	25.00
FOLKWAYS					
❏ FA-3820 [M]	Mississippi's Big Joe Williams	1962	7.50	15.00	30.00
❏ FAS-3820 [R]	Mississippi's Big Joe Williams	1962	5.00	10.00	20.00
MILESTONE					
❏ 3001 [M]	Classic Delta Blues	1966	6.25	12.50	25.00
WILLIAMS, BILLY					
CORAL					
❏ CRL 57184 [M]	Billy Williams	1957	15.00	30.00	60.00
❏ CRL 57251 [M]	Half Sweet, Half Beat	1959	12.50	25.00	50.00
❏ CRL 57343 [M]	The Billy Williams Revue	1960	12.50	25.00	50.00
❏ CRL 757251 [S]	Half Sweet, Half Beat	1959	20.00	40.00	80.00
❏ CRL 757343 [S]	The Billy Williams Revue	1960	15.00	30.00	60.00
MERCURY					
❏ MG 20317 [M]	Oh Yeah!	1958	15.00	30.00	60.00
MGM					
❏ E-3400 [M]	The Billy Williams Quartet	1957	15.00	30.00	60.00
WING					
❏ MGW-12131 [M]	Vote for Billy Williams	1959	10.00	20.00	40.00
WILLIAMS, BILLY DEE					
PRESTIGE LIVELY ARTS					
❏ 30001 [M]	Let's Misbehave	1962	10.00	20.00	40.00

Number	Title (A Side/B Side)	Yr	VG	VG+	NM

WILLIAMS, CAMILLA
MGM
| ❏ E-156 [10] | Spirituals | 1952 | 25.00 | 50.00 | 100.00 |

WILLIAMS, CLARENCE
RIVERSIDE
| ❏ RLP-1033 [10] | Clarence Williams and Orchestra | 1954 | 15.00 | 30.00 | 60.00 |

WILLIAMS, COOTIE
JARO
| ❏ JAM-5001 [M] | Around Midnight | 1959 | 25.00 | 50.00 | 100.00 |
| ❏ JAS-8001 [S] | Around Midnight | 1959 | 20.00 | 40.00 | 80.00 |

MOODSVILLE
❏ MVLP-27 [M]	The Solid Trumpet of Cootie Williams	1962	12.50	25.00	50.00
—Green label					
❏ MVLP-27 [M]	The Solid Trumpet of Cootie Williams	1965	6.25	12.50	25.00
—Blue label, trident logo at right					

RCA VICTOR
| ❏ LPM-1718 [M] | Cootie Williams in Hi-Fi | 1958 | 20.00 | 40.00 | 80.00 |

WARWICK
| ❏ W-2027 [M] | Do Nothing Till You Hear From Me | 1960 | 10.00 | 20.00 | 40.00 |
| ❏ W-2027ST [S] | Do Nothing Till You Hear From Me | 1960 | 15.00 | 30.00 | 60.00 |

WILLIAMS, COOTIE/JIMMY PRESTON
ALLEGRO ELITE
| ❏ 4109 [10] | Rock 'N' Roll | 195? | 12.50 | 25.00 | 50.00 |

WILLIAMS, DANNY
UNITED ARTISTS
❏ UAL-3297 [M]	The Exciting Danny Williams	1963	3.75	7.50	15.00
❏ UAL-3359 [M]	White on White	1964	3.75	7.50	15.00
❏ UAL-3380 [M]	With You in Mind	1964	3.75	7.50	15.00
❏ UAL-3493 [M]	Magic Town	1966	3.75	7.50	15.00
❏ UAS-6297 [S]	The Exciting Danny Williams	1963	5.00	10.00	20.00
❏ UAS-6359 [S]	White on White	1964	5.00	10.00	20.00
❏ UAS-6380 [S]	With You in Mind	1964	5.00	10.00	20.00
❏ UAS-6493 [S]	Magic Town	1966	5.00	10.00	20.00

WILLIAMS, DENIECE
ARC
❏ AS 1432 [DJ]	Niecy	1982	6.25	12.50	25.00
—Promo-only picture disc					
❏ JC 35568	When Love Comes Calling	1979	2.50	5.00	10.00
❏ FC 37048	My Melody	1981	2.50	5.00	10.00
❏ PC 37048	My Melody	198?	2.00	4.00	8.00
—Budget-line reissue					
❏ FC 37952	Niecy	1982	2.50	5.00	10.00
❏ PC 37952	Niecy	198?	2.00	4.00	8.00
—Budget-line reissue					
❏ HC 47952	Niecy	1983	12.50	25.00	50.00
—Half-speed mastered edition					

COLUMBIA
❏ PC 34242	This Is Niecy	1976	2.50	5.00	10.00
—No bar code on cover					
❏ PC 34242	This Is Niecy	198?	2.00	4.00	8.00
—Reissue with bar code on cover					
❏ JC 34911	Song Bird	1977	2.50	5.00	10.00
❏ PC 34911	Song Bird	198?	2.00	4.00	8.00
—Budget-line reissue					
❏ FC 38622	I'm So Proud	1983	2.50	5.00	10.00
❏ PC 38622	I'm So Proud	198?	2.00	4.00	8.00
—Budget-line reissue					
❏ FC 39366	Let's Hear It for the Boy	1984	2.50	5.00	10.00
❏ FC 40084	Hot on the Trail	1986	2.50	5.00	10.00
❏ FC 44322	As Good As It Gets	1989	2.50	5.00	10.00

MCA
| ❏ 6338 | Special Love | 1989 | 2.50 | 5.00 | 10.00 |

SPARROW
| ❏ SPR-1256 | From the Beginning | 1990 | 3.00 | 6.00 | 12.00 |
| ❏ ST-41039 | So Glad I Know | 1986 | 3.00 | 6.00 | 12.00 |

WILLIAMS, DON
Also see THE POZO-SECO SINGERS.
ABC
| ❏ AA-1069 | Expressions | 1978 | 3.00 | 6.00 | 12.00 |

ABC/DOT
❏ DOSD-2004	Don Williams, Vol. III	1974	3.00	6.00	12.00
❏ DOSD-2014	Don Williams, Volume One	1974	3.00	6.00	12.00
—Reissue of JMI 4004					
❏ DOSD-2018	Don Williams, Vol. 2	1974	3.00	6.00	12.00
—Reissue of JMI 4006					
❏ DOSD-2021	You're My Best Friend	1975	3.00	6.00	12.00
❏ DO-2035	Greatest Hits	1975	3.00	6.00	12.00
❏ DO-2049	Harmony	1976	3.00	6.00	12.00
❏ DO-2064	Visions	1976	3.00	6.00	12.00
❏ DO-2088	I'm Just a Country Boy	1977	3.00	6.00	12.00

CAPITOL
❏ ST-12440	New Moves	1987	2.00	4.00	8.00
❏ CLT-48034	Traces	1988	2.00	4.00	8.00
❏ C1-91444	Prime Cuts	1989	2.00	4.00	8.00

JMI
| ❏ 4004 | Don Williams, Volume One | 1973 | 6.25 | 12.50 | 25.00 |
| ❏ 4006 | Don Williams, Volume 2 | 1974 | 5.00 | 10.00 | 20.00 |

MCA
❏ 1442	The Best of Don Williams, Vol. 3	1985	2.00	4.00	8.00
—Budget-line reissue					
❏ 3096	The Best of Don Williams, Vol. 2	1979	2.50	5.00	10.00
❏ 3192	Portrait	1980	2.50	5.00	10.00
❏ 3279	Expressions	1980	2.00	4.00	8.00
—Reissue of ABC 1069					
❏ 5133	I Believe in You	1980	2.50	5.00	10.00

❏ 5210	Especially for You	1981	2.50	5.00	10.00
❏ 5306	Listen to the Radio	1982	2.50	5.00	10.00
❏ 5407	Yellow Moon	1983	2.50	5.00	10.00
❏ 5465	The Best of Don Williams, Vol. 3	1984	2.50	5.00	10.00
❏ 5671	The Best of Don Williams, Vol. 4	1985	2.50	5.00	10.00
❏ 5697	Don Williams Sings Bob McDill	1986	2.50	5.00	10.00
❏ 5803	Lovers and Best Friends	1986	2.50	5.00	10.00
❏ 37135	Greatest Hits	198?	2.00	4.00	8.00
—Budget-line reissue					
❏ 37155	The Best of Don Williams, Vol. 2	198?	2.00	4.00	8.00
—Budget-line reissue					
❏ 37230	Visions	198?	2.00	4.00	8.00
—Budget-line reissue					
❏ 37231	Portrait	198?	2.00	4.00	8.00
—Budget-line reissue					
❏ 37232	I'm Just a Country Boy	198?	2.00	4.00	8.00
—Budget-line reissue					
❏ 37233	Especially for You	198?	2.00	4.00	8.00
—Budget-line reissue					
❏ 37234	I Believe in You	198?	2.00	4.00	8.00
—Budget-line reissue					

RCA
❏ 9656-1-R	One Good Well	1989	2.50	5.00	10.00
❏ R 124814	True Love	1990	3.75	7.50	15.00
—BMG Music Service pressing; only US vinyl edition					

WILLIAMS, GEORGE
BRUNSWICK
| ❏ BL 54020 [M] | The Fox | 1957 | 12.50 | 25.00 | 50.00 |

RCA VICTOR
| ❏ LPM-1205 [M] | We Could Make Such Beautiful Music | 1956 | 10.00 | 20.00 | 40.00 |
| ❏ LPM-1301 [M] | Rhythm Was His Business | 1956 | 10.00 | 20.00 | 40.00 |

WILLIAMS, HANK
COUNTRY MUSIC FOUNDATION
| ❏ CMF-006 | Just Me and My Guitar | 198? | 2.50 | 5.00 | 10.00 |
| ❏ CMF-007 | The First Recordings | 198? | 2.50 | 5.00 | 10.00 |

METRO
❏ M-509 [M]	Hank Williams	1966	5.00	10.00	20.00
❏ MS-509 [R]	Hank Williams	1966	3.00	6.00	12.00
❏ M-547 [M]	Mr. and Mrs. Hank Williams	1966	5.00	10.00	20.00
❏ MS-547 [R]	Mr. and Mrs. Hank Williams	1966	3.00	6.00	12.00
❏ M-602 [M]	The Immortal Hank Williams	1967	5.00	10.00	20.00
❏ MS-602 [R]	The Immortal Hank Williams	1967	3.00	6.00	12.00

MGM
❏ 3E-2 [(3)M]	36 of His Greatest Hits	1957	50.00	100.00	200.00
—Yellow labels					
❏ 3E-2 [(3)M]	36 of His Greatest Hits	1960	25.00	50.00	100.00
—Black labels					
❏ 3E-4 [(3)M]	Hank Williams Sings 36 More of His Greatest Hits	1958	50.00	100.00	200.00
—Yellow labels					
❏ 3E-4 [(3)M]	Hank Williams Sings 36 More of His Greatest Hits	1960	25.00	50.00	100.00
—Black labels					
❏ E-107 [10]	Hank Williams Sings	1952	100.00	200.00	400.00
❏ E-168 [10]	Moanin' the Blues	1952	100.00	200.00	400.00
❏ E-202 [10]	Memorial Album	1953	100.00	200.00	400.00
❏ E-203 [10]	Hank Williams as Luke the Drifter	1953	100.00	200.00	400.00
❏ SE 240-2 [(2)]	24 Karat Hits	1969	6.25	12.50	25.00
❏ E-242 [10]	Honky Tonkin'	1954	100.00	200.00	400.00
❏ E-243 [10]	I Saw the Light	1954	100.00	200.00	400.00
❏ E-291 [10]	Ramblin' Man	1954	100.00	200.00	400.00
❏ PRO-912 [(3)DJ]	Reflections of Those Who Loved Him	1975	62.50	125.00	250.00
—Promo-only box set					
❏ E-3219 [M]	Ramblin' Man	1955	25.00	50.00	100.00
—Yellow label					
❏ E-3219 [M]	Ramblin' Man	1960	10.00	20.00	40.00
—Black label					
❏ E-3267 [M]	Hank Williams as Luke the Drifter	1955	25.00	50.00	100.00
—Yellow label					
❏ E-3267 [M]	Hank Williams as Luke the Drifter	1960	10.00	20.00	40.00
—Black label					
❏ E-3272 [M]	Memorial Album	1955	25.00	50.00	100.00
—Yellow label					
❏ E-3272 [M]	Memorial Album	1960	10.00	20.00	40.00
—Black label					
❏ E-3272 [M]	Memorial Album	1968	5.00	10.00	20.00
—Blue and gold label					
❏ E-3330 [M]	Moanin' the Blues	1956	25.00	50.00	100.00
—Yellow label					
❏ E-3330 [M]	Moanin' the Blues	1960	10.00	20.00	40.00
—Black label					
❏ E-3331 [M]	I Saw the Light	1956	50.00	100.00	200.00
—Yellow label; green cover					
❏ E-3331 [M]	I Saw the Light	1959	25.00	50.00	100.00
—Yellow label; church on cover					
❏ E-3331 [M]	I Saw the Light	1960	10.00	20.00	40.00
—Black label					
❏ SE-3331 [R]	I Saw the Light	1968	3.00	6.00	12.00
—Blue and gold label					
❏ E-3412 [M]	Honky Tonkin'	1957	25.00	50.00	100.00
—Yellow label					
❏ E-3412 [M]	Honky Tonkin'	1960	10.00	20.00	40.00
—Black label					
❏ E-3560 [M]	Sing Me a Blue Song	1957	25.00	50.00	100.00
—Yellow label					
❏ E-3560 [M]	Sing Me a Blue Song	1960	10.00	20.00	40.00
—Black label					
❏ E-3605 [M]	The Immortal Hank Williams	1958	25.00	50.00	100.00
—Yellow label					

Number	Title (A Side/B Side)	Yr	VG	VG+	NM
❏ E-3605 [M]	The Immortal Hank Williams	1960	10.00	20.00	40.00

—Black label

Number	Title (A Side/B Side)	Yr	VG	VG+	NM
❏ E-3733 [M]	The Unforgettable Hank Williams	1959	25.00	50.00	100.00

—Yellow label

❏ E-3733 [M]	The Unforgettable Hank Williams	1960	10.00	20.00	40.00

—Black label

❏ SE-3733 [R]	The Unforgettable Hank Williams	1968	3.00	6.00	12.00

—Blue and gold label

❏ E-3803 [M]	The Lonesome Sound of Hank Williams	1960	10.00	20.00	40.00
❏ E-3850 [M]	Wait for the Light to Shine	1960	10.00	20.00	40.00
❏ SE-3850 [R]	Wait for the Light to Shine	1968	3.00	6.00	12.00

—Blue and gold label

❏ E-3918 [M]	Hank Williams' Greatest Hits	1961	10.00	20.00	40.00
❏ SE-3918 [R]	Hank Williams' Greatest Hits	1963	5.00	10.00	20.00

—Black label

❏ SE-3918 [R]	Hank Williams' Greatest Hits	1968	3.00	6.00	12.00

—Blue and gold label

❏ E-3923 [M]	Hank Williams Lives Again	1961	10.00	20.00	40.00

—Reissue of E-3272 with new title

❏ SE-3923 [R]	Hank Williams Lives Again	1968	3.00	6.00	12.00

—Blue and gold label

❏ E-3924 [M]	Let Me Sing a Blue Song	1961	10.00	20.00	40.00

—Reissue of E-3560

❏ SE-3924 [R]	Let Me Sing a Blue Song	1968	3.00	6.00	12.00

—Blue and gold label

❏ E-3925 [M]	Wanderin' Around	1961	10.00	20.00	40.00

—Reissue of E-3219

❏ SE-3925 [R]	Wanderin' Around	1968	3.00	6.00	12.00

—Blue and gold label

❏ E-3926 [M]	I'm Blue Inside	1961	10.00	20.00	40.00

—Reissue of E-3330

❏ SE-3926 [R]	I'm Blue Inside	1968	3.00	6.00	12.00

—Blue and gold label

❏ E-3927 [M]	Hank Williams as Luke the Drifter	1961	10.00	20.00	40.00

—Reissue of E-3267

❏ SE-3927 [R]	Hank Williams as Luke the Drifter	1968	3.00	6.00	12.00

—Blue and gold label

❏ E-3928 [M]	First, Last and Always	1961	10.00	20.00	40.00

—Reissue of E-3605

❏ SE-3928 [R]	First, Last and Always	1968	3.00	6.00	12.00

—Blue and gold label

❏ E-3955 [M]	The Spirit of Hank Williams	1961	10.00	20.00	40.00
❏ SE-3955 [R]	The Spirit of Hank Williams	1968	3.00	6.00	12.00
❏ E-3999 [M]	Hank Williams on Stage Recorded Live	1962	10.00	20.00	40.00

—Note revised title

❏ E-3999 [M]	On Stage! Hank Williams Recorded Live	1962	15.00	30.00	60.00
❏ SE-3999 [R]	On Stage! Hank Williams Recorded Live	196?	5.00	10.00	20.00

—Black label

❏ SE-3999 [R]	Hank Williams on Stage Recorded Live	1968	3.00	6.00	12.00

—Blue and gold label

❏ E-4040 [M]	14 More of Hank Williams' Greatest Hits — Vol. II	1962	10.00	20.00	40.00
❏ SE-4040 [R]	14 More of Hank Williams' Greatest Hits — Vol. II	1963	3.75	7.50	15.00

—Black label

❏ SE-4040 [R]	Hank Williams' Greatest Hits, Volume 2	1968	3.00	6.00	12.00

—Blue and gold label

❏ E-4109 [M]	On Stage Volume II/Hank Williams	1963	10.00	20.00	40.00
❏ SE-4109 [R]	On Stage Volume II/Hank Williams	1963	5.00	10.00	20.00

—Black label

❏ SE-4109 [R]	On Stage Volume II/Hank Williams	1968	3.00	6.00	12.00

—Blue and gold label

❏ E-4138 [M]	Beyond the Sunset	1963	7.50	15.00	30.00
❏ SE-4138 [R]	Beyond the Sunset	1963	3.75	7.50	15.00

—Black label

❏ E-4140 [M]	14 More of Hank Williams' Greatest Hits (Volume 3)	1963	7.50	15.00	30.00
❏ SE-4140 [R]	14 More of Hank Williams' Greatest Hits (Volume 3)	1963	3.75	7.50	15.00

—Black label

❏ SE-4140 [R]	14 More of Hank Williams' Greatest Hits (Volume 3)	1968	3.00	6.00	12.00

—Blue and gold label

❏ E-4168 [M]	The Very Best of Hank Williams	1963	7.50	15.00	30.00
❏ SE-4168 [R]	The Very Best of Hank Williams	1963	3.75	7.50	15.00

—Black label

❏ SE-4168 [R]	The Very Best of Hank Williams	1968	3.00	6.00	12.00

—Blue and gold label

❏ E-4227 [M]	The Very Best of Hank Williams, Volume 2	1964	7.50	15.00	30.00
❏ SE-4227 [R]	The Very Best of Hank Williams, Volume 2	1964	3.75	7.50	15.00

—Black label

❏ SE-4227 [R]	The Very Best of Hank Williams, Volume 2	1968	3.00	6.00	12.00

—Blue and gold label

❏ E-4254 [M]	Lost Highway (and Other Folk Ballads)	1964	10.00	20.00	40.00
❏ SE-4254 [R]	Lost Highway (and Other Folk Ballads)	1964	5.00	10.00	20.00

—Black label

❏ SE-4254 [R]	Lost Highway (and Other Folk Ballads)	1968	3.00	6.00	12.00

—Blue and gold label

❏ E-4267-4 [(4)M]	The Hank Williams Story	1965	15.00	30.00	60.00
❏ E-4300 [M]	Kaw-Liga and Other Humorous Songs	1965	7.50	15.00	30.00
❏ SE-4300 [R]	Kaw-Liga and Other Humorous Songs	1965	3.75	7.50	15.00

—Black label

❏ SE-4300 [R]	Kaw-Liga and Other Humorous Songs	1968	3.00	6.00	12.00

—Blue and gold label

❏ E-4377 [M]	The Legend Lives Anew — Hank Williams with Strings	1966	5.00	10.00	20.00
❏ SE-4377 [S]	The Legend Lives Anew — Hank Williams with Strings	1966	6.25	12.50	25.00

—Black label

❏ SE-4377 [S]	The Legend Lives Anew — Hank Williams with Strings	1968	3.75	7.50	15.00

—Blue and gold label

Number	Title (A Side/B Side)	Yr	VG	VG+	NM
❏ E-4380 [M]	Movin' on — Luke the Drifter	1966	7.50	15.00	30.00
❏ SE-4380 [R]	Movin' on — Luke the Drifter	1968	3.00	6.00	12.00

—Blue and gold label

❏ E-4429 [M]	More Hank Williams and Strings	1966	5.00	10.00	20.00
❏ SE-4429 [S]	More Hank Williams and Strings	1966	6.25	12.50	25.00

—Black label

❏ SE-4429 [S]	More Hank Williams and Strings	1968	3.75	7.50	15.00

—Blue and gold label

❏ E-4481 [M]	I Won't Be Home No More	1967	7.50	15.00	30.00
❏ SE-4481 [S]	I Won't Be Home No More	1967	5.00	10.00	20.00

—Blue and gold label

❏ SE-4481 [S]	I Won't Be Home No More	1968	3.75	7.50	15.00
❏ E-4529 [M]	Hank Williams and Strings, Volume 3	1968	10.00	20.00	40.00
❏ SE-4529 [S]	Hank Williams and Strings, Volume 3	1968	5.00	10.00	20.00
❏ E-4576 [M]	Hank Williams in the Beginning	1968	10.00	20.00	40.00
❏ SE-4576 [R]	Hank Williams in the Beginning	1968	3.75	7.50	15.00
❏ SE-4651	Essential Hank Williams	1969	3.00	6.00	12.00
❏ SE-4680	Life to Legend	1970	3.00	6.00	12.00
❏ SE-4755-2 [(2)]	24 Greatest Hits	1971	3.75	7.50	15.00
❏ M3G-4954	Archetypes	1974	3.00	6.00	12.00
❏ MG-1-5019	Hank Williams, Sr., Live at the Grand Old Opry	1976	3.00	6.00	12.00
❏ MG-2-5401 [(2)]	24 Greatest Hits, Volume 2	197?	3.75	7.50	15.00
❏ ST-90511 [R]	The Very Best of Hank Williams	1965	5.00	10.00	20.00

—Capitol Record Club edition

❏ T-90511 [M]	The Very Best of Hank Williams	1965	10.00	20.00	40.00

—Capitol Record Club edition

❏ ST-90884 [R]	Movin' on — Luke the Drifter	1968	3.75	7.50	15.00

—Capitol Record Club edition; blue and gold label

❏ ST-91115 [S]	The Legend Lives Anew — Hank Williams with Strings	1968	5.00	10.00	20.00

—Capitol Record Club edition; blue and gold label

POLYDOR

❏ 821233-1 [(2)]	40 Greatest Hits	1984	3.75	7.50	15.00
❏ 823291-1	Hank Williams' Greatest Hits	1984	2.00	4.00	8.00
❏ 823292-1	The Very Best of Hank Williams	1984	2.00	4.00	8.00
❏ 823293-1 [(2)]	24 Greatest Hits	1984	3.00	6.00	12.00
❏ 823294-1 [(2)]	24 Greatest Hits, Volume 2	1984	3.00	6.00	12.00
❏ 823695-1	Rare Takes and Radio Cuts	1984	2.50	5.00	10.00
❏ 825531-1	On the Air	1985	2.50	5.00	10.00
❏ 825548-1	I Ain't Got Nothin' But Time	1985	2.50	5.00	10.00
❏ 825551-1	Lovesick Blues	1985	2.50	5.00	10.00
❏ 825554-1	Lost Highway	1986	2.50	5.00	10.00
❏ 825557-1	I'm So Lonesome I Could Cry	1986	2.50	5.00	10.00
❏ 831574-1	Beyond the Sunset	1987	2.50	5.00	10.00
❏ 831633-1	Long Gone Lonesome Blues	1987	2.50	5.00	10.00
❏ 831634-1	Hey, Good Lookin'	1987	2.50	5.00	10.00
❏ 833749-1	Let's Turn Back the Years	1988	2.50	5.00	10.00
❏ 833752-1	I Won't Be Home No More	1988	2.50	5.00	10.00

TIME-LIFE

❏ 3003 [(3)]	Country and Western Classics	1981	7.50	15.00	30.00

WILLIAMS, HANK /ROY ACUFF

LAMB AND LION

❏ LL-706 [(3)]	Hank Williams, Sr./Roy Acuff "Collector's Item!"	197?	10.00	20.00	40.00

—Sides 1-4 are reissues of Hank Williams; side 5-6 are Roy Acuff

WILLIAMS, HANK, AND HANK WILLIAMS, JR.

Also see each artist's individual listings.

MGM

❏ E-4276 [M]	Father and Son	1965	5.00	10.00	20.00
❏ SE-4276 [S]	Father and Son	1965	6.25	12.50	25.00
❏ E-4378 [M]	Again	1966	5.00	10.00	20.00
❏ SE-4378 [S]	Again	1966	6.25	12.50	25.00
❏ 2SES-4865 [(2)]	Hank Williams: The Legend in Story and Song	1973	3.75	7.50	15.00
❏ M3HB 4975 [(2)]	Insights Into Hank Williams in Song and Story	1974	3.75	7.50	15.00

WILLIAMS, HANK, JR.

CAPRICORN

❏ W1-26806	Maverick	1992	5.00	10.00	20.00

—Columbia House edition (only U.S. vinyl release)

ELEKTRA

❏ 6E-194	Family Tradition	1979	3.00	6.00	12.00
❏ 6E-237	Whiskey Bent and Hell Bound	1979	2.50	5.00	10.00
❏ 6E-278	Habits Old and New	1980	2.50	5.00	10.00
❏ 6E-330	Rowdy	1981	2.50	5.00	10.00
❏ 5E-535	The Pressure Is On	1981	2.50	5.00	10.00
❏ 5E-538	One Night Stands	1982	2.50	5.00	10.00

—Reissue

❏ 5E-539	The New South	1982	2.50	5.00	10.00

—Reissue

❏ 60100	High Notes	1982	2.50	5.00	10.00
❏ 60193	Hank Williams, Jr.'s, Greatest Hits	1982	2.50	5.00	10.00
❏ 60223	Strong Stuff	1983	3.75	7.50	15.00

MGM

❏ GAS-119	Hank Williams, Jr. (Golden Archive Series)	1970	3.75	7.50	15.00
❏ E-4213 [M]	Sings the Songs of Hank Williams	1964	5.00	10.00	20.00
❏ SE-4213 [S]	Sings the Songs of Hank Williams	1964	6.25	12.50	25.00
❏ E-4260 [M]	Your Cheatin' Heart	1964	5.00	10.00	20.00
❏ SE-4260 [S]	Your Cheatin' Heart	1964	6.25	12.50	25.00
❏ E-4316 [M]	Ballads of the Hills and Plains	1965	5.00	10.00	20.00
❏ SE-4316 [S]	Ballads of the Hills and Plains	1965	6.25	12.50	25.00
❏ E-4344 [M]	Blues My Name	1966	5.00	10.00	20.00
❏ SE-4344 [S]	Blues My Name	1966	6.25	12.50	25.00
❏ E-4391 [M]	Country Shadows	1966	5.00	10.00	20.00
❏ SE-4391 [S]	Country Shadows	1966	6.25	12.50	25.00
❏ E-4428 [M]	My Own Way	1967	5.00	10.00	20.00
❏ SE-4428 [S]	My Own Way	1967	6.25	12.50	25.00
❏ E-4513 [M]	The Best of Hank Williams, Jr.	1967	5.00	10.00	20.00
❏ SE-4513 [S]	The Best of Hank Williams, Jr.	1967	6.25	12.50	25.00
❏ E-4527 [M]	My Songs	1968	10.00	20.00	40.00

Number	Title (A Side/B Side)	Yr	VG	VG+	NM
❏ SE-4527 [S]	My Songs	1968	6.25	12.50	25.00
❏ SE-4540	A Time to Sing	1968	6.25	12.50	25.00
❏ SE-4559	Luke the Drifter, Jr.	1969	5.00	10.00	20.00
❏ SE-4621	Songs My Father Left Me	1969	5.00	10.00	20.00
❏ SE-4632	Luke the Drifter, Jr. (Vol. 2)	1969	5.00	10.00	20.00
❏ SE-4644	Live at Cobo Hall, Detroit	1969	5.00	10.00	20.00
❏ SE-4656	Hank Williams, Jr.'s Greatest Hits	1970	3.75	7.50	15.00
❏ SE-4657	Sunday Morning	1970	3.75	7.50	15.00
❏ SE-4673	Luke the Drifter, Jr. (Vol. 3)	1970	3.75	7.50	15.00
❏ SE-4675	Hank Williams, Jr., Singing My Songs (Johnny Cash)	1970	3.75	7.50	15.00
❏ SE-4774	I've Got a Right to Cry/They All Used to Belong to Me	1971	3.75	7.50	15.00
❏ SE-4798	Sweet Dreams	1972	3.00	6.00	12.00
—With the Mike Curb Congregation					
❏ SE-4822	Hank Williams, Jr.'s Greatest Hits, Volume 2	1972	3.00	6.00	12.00
❏ SE-4843	Eleven Roses	1972	3.00	6.00	12.00
❏ SE-4862	After You/Pride's Not Hard to Swallow	1973	3.00	6.00	12.00
❏ SE-4906	Just Pickin' — No Singin'	1973	3.00	6.00	12.00
❏ SE-4936	The Last Love Song	1973	3.00	6.00	12.00
❏ M3G-4971	Living Proof	1974	3.00	6.00	12.00
❏ M3G-4988	Bocephus	1974	3.00	6.00	12.00
❏ MG-1-5009	Hank Williams, Jr., and Friends	1975	10.00	20.00	40.00
❏ MG-1-5020	14 Greatest Hits	1976	3.00	6.00	12.00
❏ ST-90695 [S]	Blues My Name	1966	7.50	15.00	30.00
—Capitol Record Club edition					
❏ T-90695 [M]	Blues My Name	1966	6.25	12.50	25.00
—Capitol Record Club edition					
PAIR					
❏ PDL2-1164 [(2)]	I'm Walkin'	1987	3.00	6.00	12.00
POLYDOR					
❏ 811902-1	Live at Cobo Hall, Detroit	1983	2.00	4.00	8.00
—Reissue					
❏ 811903-1	Hank Williams, Jr.'s Greatest Hits	1983	2.00	4.00	8.00
❏ 811906-1	Hank Williams, Jr.'s Greatest Hits, Volume 2	1983	2.00	4.00	8.00
❏ 825091-1	14 Greatest Hits	1985	2.00	4.00	8.00
❏ 831575-1	Hank Williams, Jr., and Friends	1987	3.00	6.00	12.00
❏ 833069-1	Blues My Name	1987	2.00	4.00	8.00
❏ 833070-1	Eleven Roses	1987	2.00	4.00	8.00
❏ 835132-1	Standing in the Shadows	1988	2.00	4.00	8.00
WARNER BROS.					
❏ 6E-194	Family Tradition	1983	2.00	4.00	8.00
❏ 6E-237	Whiskey Bent and Hell Bound	1983	2.00	4.00	8.00
❏ 6E-278	Habits Old and New	1983	2.00	4.00	8.00
❏ 6E-330	Rowdy	1983	2.00	4.00	8.00
❏ 5E-535	The Pressure Is On	1983	2.00	4.00	8.00
❏ 5E-538	One Night Stands	1983	2.00	4.00	8.00
❏ 5E-539	The New South	1983	2.00	4.00	8.00
❏ PRO-A-2092 [DJ]	The Hank Williams, Jr., Interview	1983	6.25	12.50	25.00
❏ BS 2988	One Night Stands	1977	3.00	6.00	12.00
❏ BS 3127	The New South	1977	3.00	6.00	12.00
❏ 23924	Man of Steel	1983	2.50	5.00	10.00
❏ 25088	Major Moves	1984	2.50	5.00	10.00
❏ 25267	Five-O	1985	2.50	5.00	10.00
❏ 25328	Greatest Hits — Volume 2	1985	2.00	4.00	8.00
❏ 25412	Montana Café	1986	2.00	4.00	8.00
❏ 25514 [(2)]	The Early Years	1984	3.00	6.00	12.00
❏ 25538	Hank "Live"	1987	2.00	4.00	8.00
❏ 25593	Born to Boogie	1987	2.00	4.00	8.00
❏ 25725	Wild Streak	1988	2.00	4.00	8.00
❏ 25834	Greatest Hits III	1989	2.00	4.00	8.00
❏ 26090	Lone Wolf	1990	3.00	6.00	12.00
❏ 60100	High Notes	1983	2.00	4.00	8.00
❏ 60193	Hank Williams, Jr.'s, Greatest Hits	1983	2.00	4.00	8.00
❏ 60223	Strong Stuff	1983	2.50	5.00	10.00
❏ R 120612	America (The Way I See It)	1990	5.00	10.00	20.00
—BMG Music Service edition (no regular vinyl release)					
❏ R 160351	Pure Hank	1991	5.00	10.00	20.00
—BMG Music Service edition (no regular vinyl release)					

WILLIAMS, HANK, JR., AND LOIS JOHNSON
MGM

Number	Title (A Side/B Side)	Yr	VG	VG+	NM
❏ SE-4721	Removing the Shadow	1971	3.75	7.50	15.00
—The label has the word "Shadows" instead of "Shadow"					
❏ SE-4750	All for the Love of Sunshine	1971	5.00	10.00	20.00
❏ SE-4857	Send Me Some Lovin'/Whole Lotta Lovin'	1972	5.00	10.00	20.00

WILLIAMS, HERBIE
WORKSHOP JAZZ

Number	Title (A Side/B Side)	Yr	VG	VG+	NM
❏ WSJ-216 [M]	The Soul and Sound of Herbie Williams	1963	15.00	30.00	60.00

WILLIAMS, JOE
RCA VICTOR

Number	Title (A Side/B Side)	Yr	VG	VG+	NM
❏ LPM-2713 [M]	Jump for Joy	1963	6.25	12.50	25.00
❏ LSP-2713 [S]	Jump for Joy	1963	7.50	15.00	30.00
❏ LPM-2762 [M]	Joe Williams at Newport '63	1963	6.25	12.50	25.00
❏ LSP-2762 [S]	Joe Williams at Newport '63	1963	7.50	15.00	30.00
❏ LPM-2879 [M]	Me and the Blues	1964	6.25	12.50	25.00
❏ LSP-2879 [S]	Me and the Blues	1964	7.50	15.00	30.00
❏ LPM-3433 [M]	The Song Is You	1965	5.00	10.00	20.00
❏ LSP-3433 [S]	The Song Is You	1965	6.25	12.50	25.00
❏ LPM-3461 [M]	The Exciting Joe Williams	1965	5.00	10.00	20.00
❏ LSP-3461 [S]	The Exciting Joe Williams	1965	6.25	12.50	25.00
REGENT					
❏ MG-6002 [M]	Everyday	1956	12.50	25.00	50.00
ROULETTE					
❏ R-52005 [M]	A Man Ain't Supposed to Cry	1958	7.50	15.00	30.00
❏ SR-52005 [S]	A Man Ain't Supposed to Cry	1958	10.00	20.00	40.00
❏ R-52030 [M]	Joe Williams Sings About You!	1959	7.50	15.00	30.00
❏ SR-52030 [S]	Joe Williams Sings About You!	1959	10.00	20.00	40.00
❏ R-52039 [M]	That Kind of Woman	1960	7.50	15.00	30.00
❏ SR-52039 [S]	That Kind of Woman	1960	10.00	20.00	40.00

Number	Title (A Side/B Side)	Yr	VG	VG+	NM
❏ R-52066 [M]	Sentimental and Melancholy	1961	7.50	15.00	30.00
❏ SR-52066 [S]	Sentimental and Melancholy	1961	10.00	20.00	40.00
❏ R-52069 [M]	Together	1961	7.50	15.00	30.00
❏ SR-52069 [S]	Together	1961	10.00	20.00	40.00
—With Harry "Sweets" Edison					
❏ R-52071 [M]	Have a Good Time with Joe Williams	1961	7.50	15.00	30.00
❏ SR-52071 [S]	Have a Good Time with Joe Williams	1961	10.00	20.00	40.00
❏ R-52085 [M]	Swingin' Night at Birdland	1962	6.25	12.50	25.00
❏ SR-52085 [S]	Swingin' Night at Birdland	1962	7.50	15.00	30.00
❏ R-52102 [M]	One Is a Lonesome Number	1963	6.25	12.50	25.00
❏ SR-52102 [S]	One Is a Lonesome Number	1963	7.50	15.00	30.00
❏ R-52105 [M]	New Kind of Love	1964	6.25	12.50	25.00
❏ SR-52105 [S]	New Kind of Love	1964	7.50	15.00	30.00
SOLID STATE					
❏ SM-17008 [M]	Presenting Joe Williams and the Jazz Orchestra	1967	6.25	12.50	25.00
❏ SS-18008 [S]	Presenting Joe Williams and the Jazz Orchestra	1967	5.00	10.00	20.00
❏ SS-18015 [S]	Something Old, New and Blue	1968	5.00	10.00	20.00

WILLIAMS, JOHN
EMARCY

Number	Title (A Side/B Side)	Yr	VG	VG+	NM
❏ MG-26047 [10]	John Williams	1955	25.00	50.00	100.00
❏ MG-36061 [10]	John Williams Trio	1956	12.50	25.00	50.00

WILLIAMS, JOHN TOWNER
BETHLEHEM

Number	Title (A Side/B Side)	Yr	VG	VG+	NM
❏ BCP-6025 [M]	World on a String	1958	12.50	25.00	50.00

WILLIAMS, KEITH
EDISON INTERNATIONAL

Number	Title (A Side/B Side)	Yr	VG	VG+	NM
❏ 501 [M]	Big Band Jazz Themes	1960	5.00	10.00	20.00
❏ SDP-501 [S]	Big Band Jazz Themes	1960	6.25	12.50	25.00
LIBERTY					
❏ LRP-3040 [M]	The Dazzling Sound	1957	6.25	12.50	25.00

WILLIAMS, LARRY
CHESS

Number	Title (A Side/B Side)	Yr	VG	VG+	NM
❏ LP-1457 [M]	Larry Williams	1961	50.00	100.00	200.00
OKEH					
❏ OKM-12123 [M]	Larry Williams' Greatest Hits	1967	7.50	15.00	30.00
❏ OKS-14123 [S]	Larry Williams' Greatest Hits	1967	10.00	20.00	40.00
SPECIALTY					
❏ SP-2109 [M]	Here's Larry Williams	1959	50.00	100.00	200.00
—Original pressing on thick vinyl with no copyright information on back cover					
❏ SP-2109 [M]	Here's Larry Williams	198?	2.50	5.00	10.00
—Reissue with thinner vinyl and copyright information on back					
❏ SP-7002 [(2)]	Bad Boy	1990	5.00	10.00	20.00

WILLIAMS, LAWTON
MEGA

Number	Title (A Side/B Side)	Yr	VG	VG+	NM
❏ 1004	Between Truck Stops	1971	3.00	6.00	12.00

WILLIAMS, LOIS
STARDAY

Number	Title (A Side/B Side)	Yr	VG	VG+	NM
❏ SLP-448	A Girl Named Sam	1970	5.00	10.00	20.00

WILLIAMS, LUCINDA
FOLKWAYS

Number	Title (A Side/B Side)	Yr	VG	VG+	NM
❏ 31066	Ramblin' on My Mind	1979	5.00	10.00	20.00
—As "Lucinda"					
❏ 31067	Happy Woman Blues	1980	5.00	10.00	20.00
—As "Lucinda"					
ROUGH TRADE					
❏ 66 [EP]	Passionate Kisses	1989	2.50	5.00	10.00
SMITHSONIAN/FOLKWAYS					
❏ 40003	Happy Woman Blues	1990	3.00	6.00	12.00
—Reissue					

WILLIAMS, MARY LOU
ASCH

Number	Title (A Side/B Side)	Yr	VG	VG+	NM
❏ ALP-345 [10]	Mary Lou Williams Trio	1950	50.00	100.00	200.00
ATLANTIC					
❏ ALR-114 [10]	Piano Panorama, Volume 2	1951	30.00	60.00	120.00
CIRCLE					
❏ 412 [10]	Piano Contempo	1951	30.00	60.00	120.00
CONCERT HALL JAZZ					
❏ 1007 [10]	A Keyboard History	1955	12.50	25.00	50.00
CONTEMPORARY					
❏ C-2507 [10]	Piano '53	1953	25.00	50.00	100.00
EMARCY					
❏ MG-26033 [10]	Mary Lou	1954	25.00	50.00	100.00
FOLKWAYS					
❏ FP-32 [10]	Rehearsal—Jazz Session/Footnotes to Jazz, Vol. 3	1951	25.00	50.00	100.00
JAZZTONE					
❏ J-1206 [M]	A Keyboard History	1955	10.00	20.00	40.00
KING					
❏ 295-85 [10]	Progressive Piano Stylings	1953	37.50	75.00	150.00
MARY					
❏ 32843 [M]	Black Christ of the Andes	1964	6.25	12.50	25.00
❏ 32843 [S]	Black Christ of the Andes	1964	7.50	15.00	30.00
❏ 282489 [M]	Music for Peace	1964	6.25	12.50	25.00
❏ 282489 [S]	Music for Peace	1964	7.50	15.00	30.00
STINSON					
❏ SLP-24 [10]	Mary Lou Williams	1950	37.50	75.00	150.00
❏ SLP-24 [M]	Mary Lou Williams	195?	7.50	15.00	30.00
❏ SLP-29 [10]	Jazz Variation	1950	37.50	75.00	150.00

Number	Title (A Side/B Side)	Yr	VG	VG+	NM

WILLIAMS, MARY LOU/RALPH BURNS
JAZZTONE
| J-1255 [M] | Composers — Pianists | 1956 | 10.00 | 20.00 | 40.00 |

WILLIAMS, MARY LOU, AND DON BYAS/BUCK CLAYTON AND ALIX COMBELLE
STORYVILLE
| STLP-906 [M] | Messin' 'Round in Montmarte | 1956 | 12.50 | 25.00 | 50.00 |

WILLIAMS, MASON
AMERICAN GRAMAPHONE
| AG-800 | Classical Gas | 1987 | 2.50 | 5.00 | 10.00 |

—With Mannheim Steamroller
EVEREST
| 3265 | Listening Matter | 1969 | 3.00 | 6.00 | 12.00 |
FLYING FISH
| FF-059 | Fresh Fish | 1978 | 2.50 | 5.00 | 10.00 |
VEE JAY
| VJ-1103 [M] | Them Poems and Things | 1964 | 5.00 | 10.00 | 20.00 |
| VJS-1103 [S] | Them Poems and Things | 1964 | 6.25 | 12.50 | 25.00 |
WARNER BROS.
| WS 1729 | The Mason Williams Phonograph Record | 1968 | 3.00 | 6.00 | 12.00 |

—Green label with "W7" logo
| WS 1729 | The Mason Williams Phonograph Record | 1970 | 2.50 | 5.00 | 10.00 |

—Green label with "WB" logo
| WS 1729 | The Mason Williams Phonograph Record | 1973 | 2.00 | 4.00 | 8.00 |

—"Burbank" palm trees label
| WS 1729 | The Mason Williams Phonograph Record | 1979 | — | 3.00 | 6.00 |

—White or tan label
WS 1776	The Mason Williams Ear Show	1968	3.00	6.00	12.00
WS 1788	Music by Mason Williams	1969	3.00	6.00	12.00
WS 1838	Hand Made	1970	3.00	6.00	12.00
WS 1941	Sharepickers	1971	3.00	6.00	12.00

WILLIAMS, MAURICE, AND THE ZODIACS
COLLECTABLES
| COL-5021 | The Best of Maurice Williams and the Zodiacs | 198? | 2.50 | 5.00 | 10.00 |
HERALD
| HLP-1014 [M] | Stay | 1961 | 125.00 | 250.00 | 500.00 |
RELIC
| 5017 | Greatest Hits | 197? | 3.75 | 7.50 | 15.00 |
SNYDER
| 5586 [M] | At the Beach | 196? | 25.00 | 50.00 | 100.00 |
SPHERE SOUND
| SR-7007 [M] | Stay | 1965 | 30.00 | 60.00 | 120.00 |
| SSR-7007 [R] | Stay | 1965 | 20.00 | 40.00 | 80.00 |

WILLIAMS, MEL
DIG
| LP-103 [M] | All Thru the Night | 1956 | 150.00 | 300.00 | 600.00 |

WILLIAMS, OTIS, AND HIS CHARMS
DELUXE
| 570 [M] | Their All Time Hits | 1957 | 250.00 | 500.00 | 1000. |
KING
| 570 [M] | Their All Time Hits | 1957 | 150.00 | 300.00 | 600.00 |
| 614 [M] | This Is Otis Williams and His Charms | 1959 | 100.00 | 200.00 | 400.00 |
STOP
| STLP-1022 | Otis Williams and the Midnight Cowboys | 1971 | 6.25 | 12.50 | 25.00 |

WILLIAMS, RICHARD
CANDID
| CD-8003 [M] | New Horn in Town | 1960 | 10.00 | 20.00 | 40.00 |
| CS-9003 [S] | New Horn in Town | 1960 | 12.50 | 25.00 | 50.00 |

WILLIAMS, ROBERT PETE
BLUESVILLE
| BVLP-1026 [M] | Free Again | 1961 | 25.00 | 50.00 | 100.00 |

—Blue label, silver print
| BVLP-1026 [M] | Free Again | 1964 | 7.50 | 15.00 | 30.00 |

—Blue label with trident logo
FOLK/LYRIC
| FL-109 [M] | Prison Blues | 1960 | 25.00 | 50.00 | 100.00 |

WILLIAMS, ROGER
BAINBRIDGE
| 6265 | Somewhere in Time | 1986 | 2.50 | 5.00 | 10.00 |
| 8002 [(2)] | Ivory Impact | 1982 | 3.00 | 6.00 | 12.00 |
HOLIDAY
| HDY 1927 | Golden Christmas | 1981 | 2.00 | 4.00 | 8.00 |
KAPP
| KLE-1 [(3)M] | 10th Anniversary/Limited Edition | 1964 | 5.00 | 10.00 | 20.00 |

—Reissue of Kapp 1088, 1130 and 1172 in one package
SKLE-1 [(3)S]	10th Anniversary/Limited Edition	1964	6.25	12.50	25.00
KW-900 [M]	Roger Williams Showcase	196?	3.00	6.00	12.00
SKW-900 [S]	Roger Williams Showcase	196?	3.75	7.50	15.00
KL-1003 [M]	The Boy Next Door	1955	6.25	12.50	25.00

—Maroon and silver (or blue and silver) labels
| KL-1003 [M] | The Boy Next Door | 1962 | 3.00 | 6.00 | 12.00 |

—Any later label variation
| KL-1008 [M] | It's a Big, Wide, Wonderful World | 1955 | 6.25 | 12.50 | 25.00 |

—Maroon and silver (or blue and silver) labels
| KL-1008 [M] | It's a Big, Wide, Wonderful World | 1962 | 3.00 | 6.00 | 12.00 |

—Any later label variation
| KL-1012 [M] | Autumn Leaves | 1956 | 5.00 | 10.00 | 20.00 |

—Retitled version of above; maroon and silver (or blue and silver) label
| KL-1012 [M] | Roger Williams | 1956 | 6.25 | 12.50 | 25.00 |
| KL-1012 [M] | Autumn Leaves | 1962 | 3.00 | 6.00 | 12.00 |

—Any later label variation

Number	Title (A Side/B Side)	Yr	VG	VG+	NM
KL-1031 [M]	Daydreams	1956	3.75	7.50	15.00

—Maroon and silver (or blue and silver) label
| KL-1031 [M] | Daydreams | 1962 | 3.00 | 6.00 | 12.00 |

—Any later label variation
| KL-1040 [M] | Roger Williams Plays the Wonderful Music of the Masters | 1956 | 3.75 | 7.50 | 15.00 |

—Maroon and silver (or blue and silver) label
| KL-1040 [M] | Roger Williams Plays the Wonderful Music of the Masters | 1962 | 3.00 | 6.00 | 12.00 |

—Any later label variation
| KL-1042 [M] | Roger Williams Plays Christmas Songs | 1956 | 3.75 | 7.50 | 15.00 |

—Maroon and silver label; unbanded
| KL-1062 [M] | Roger Williams Plays Beautiful Waltzes | 1957 | 3.75 | 7.50 | 15.00 |

—Maroon and silver (or blue and silver) label
| KL-1062 [M] | Roger Williams Plays Beautiful Waltzes | 1962 | 3.00 | 6.00 | 12.00 |

—Any later label variation
| KL-1063 [M] | Almost Paradise | 1957 | 3.75 | 7.50 | 15.00 |

—Maroon and silver (or blue and silver) label
| KL-1063 [M] | Almost Paradise | 1962 | 3.00 | 6.00 | 12.00 |

—Any later label variation
| K-1081-S [S] | Till | 1959 | 5.00 | 10.00 | 20.00 |

—Blue and silver labels
| KL-1081 [M] | Till | 1958 | 3.75 | 7.50 | 15.00 |

—Maroon and silver (or blue and silver) label
| KL-1081 [M] | Till | 1962 | 3.00 | 6.00 | 12.00 |

—Any later label variation
| KS-1081 [S] | Till | 1962 | 3.75 | 7.50 | 15.00 |

—Any later label variation
| KL-1088 [M] | Roger Williams Plays Gershwin | 1958 | 3.75 | 7.50 | 15.00 |

—Maroon and silver (or blue and silver) labels
| KL-1088 [M] | Roger Williams Plays Gershwin | 1962 | 3.00 | 6.00 | 12.00 |

—Any later label variation
| KL-1112 [M] | Near You | 1959 | 3.75 | 7.50 | 15.00 |

—Maroon and silver (or blue and silver) labels
| KL-1112 [M] | Near You | 1962 | 3.00 | 6.00 | 12.00 |

—Any later label variation
| KS-1112 [S] | Near You | 1959 | 5.00 | 10.00 | 20.00 |

—Maroon and silver (or blue and silver) labels
| KS-1112 [S] | Near You | 1962 | 3.75 | 7.50 | 15.00 |

—Any later label variation
| KL-1130 [M] | More Songs of the Fabulous Fifties | 1959 | 3.75 | 7.50 | 15.00 |

—Maroon and silver (or blue and silver) labels
| KL-1130 [M] | More Songs of the Fabulous Fifties | 1962 | 3.00 | 6.00 | 12.00 |

—Any later label variation
| KL-1147 [M] | With These Hands | 1959 | 3.75 | 7.50 | 15.00 |

—Maroon and silver (or blue and silver) labels
| KL-1147 [M] | With These Hands | 1962 | 3.00 | 6.00 | 12.00 |

—Any later label variation
| KL-1164 [M] | Christmas Time | 1959 | 3.75 | 7.50 | 15.00 |

—"Merry Christmas" silver, red and green label
| KL-1164 [M] | Christmas Time | 1962 | 3.00 | 6.00 | 12.00 |

—Any later label variation
| KL-1172 [M] | Always | 1960 | 3.75 | 7.50 | 15.00 |

—Maroon and silver (or blue and silver) labels
| KL-1172 [M] | Always | 1962 | 3.00 | 6.00 | 12.00 |

—Any later label variation
KL-1207 [M]	Songs of the Fabulous Forties, Volume 1	1960	3.00	6.00	12.00
KL-1208 [M]	Songs of the Fabulous Forties, Volume 2	1960	3.00	6.00	12.00
KL-1209 [M]	Songs of the Fabulous Fifties, Volume 1	1960	3.00	6.00	12.00
KL-1210 [M]	Songs of the Fabulous Fifties, Volume 2	1960	3.00	6.00	12.00
KL-1211 [M]	Songs of the Fabulous Century, Volume 1	1960	3.00	6.00	12.00
KL-1212 [M]	Songs of the Fabulous Century, Volume 2	1960	3.00	6.00	12.00
KL-1217 [M]	Temptation	1960	3.75	7.50	15.00

—Maroon and silver (or blue and silver) labels
| KL-1217 [M] | Temptation | 1962 | 3.00 | 6.00 | 12.00 |

—Any later label variation
KL-1222 [M]	Roger Williams Invites You to Dance	1961	3.75	7.50	15.00
KL-1244 [M]	Yellow Bird	1961	3.75	7.50	15.00
KL-1251 [M]	Songs of the Soaring '60s	1961	3.75	7.50	15.00
KL-1260 [M]	Greatest Hits	1962	3.00	6.00	12.00
KL-1266 [M]	Maria	1962	3.00	6.00	12.00
KL-1290 [M]	Mr. Piano	1962	3.00	6.00	12.00
KL-1305 [M]	Country Style	1963	3.00	6.00	12.00
KL-1336 [M]	For You	1963	3.00	6.00	12.00
KL-1354 [M]	The Solid Gold Steinway	1964	3.00	6.00	12.00
KL-1395 [M]	Family Album of Hymns	1964	2.50	5.00	10.00
KL-1406 [M]	Academy Award Winners	1964	2.50	5.00	10.00
KL-1414 [M]	Roger Williams Plays the Hits	1965	2.50	5.00	10.00
KL-1434 [M]	Summer Wind	1965	2.50	5.00	10.00
KL-1452 [M]	Autumn Leaves — 1965	1965	2.50	5.00	10.00
KL-1470 [M]	I'll Remember You	1966	2.50	5.00	10.00
KL-1483 [M]	Academy Award Winners, Vol. 2	1966	2.50	5.00	10.00
KL-1501 [M]	Born Free	1966	2.50	5.00	10.00
KL-1512 [M]	Roger!	1967	2.50	5.00	10.00
KL-1530 [M]	Roger Williams/Golden Hits	1967	3.00	6.00	12.00
KS-3000 [S]	Waltzes in Stereo	1959	5.00	10.00	20.00

—Maroon and silver (or blue and silver) labels
| KS-3000 [S] | Waltzes in Stereo | 1962 | 3.75 | 7.50 | 15.00 |

—Any later label variation
| KS-3013 [S] | More Songs of the Fabulous Fifties | 1959 | 5.00 | 10.00 | 20.00 |

—Maroon and silver (or blue and silver) labels
| KS-3013 [S] | More Songs of the Fabulous Fifties | 1962 | 3.75 | 7.50 | 15.00 |

—Any later label variation
| KS-3030 [S] | With These Hands | 1959 | 5.00 | 10.00 | 20.00 |

—Maroon and silver (or blue and silver) labels
| KS-3030 [S] | With These Hands | 1962 | 3.75 | 7.50 | 15.00 |

—Any later label variation
| KS-3048 [S] | Christmas Time | 1959 | 5.00 | 10.00 | 20.00 |
| KS-3056 [S] | Always | 1960 | 5.00 | 10.00 | 20.00 |

—Maroon and silver (or blue and silver) labels
| KS-3056 [S] | Always | 1962 | 3.75 | 7.50 | 15.00 |

—Any later label variation

Number	Title (A Side/B Side)	Yr	VG	VG+	NM
❏ KS-3164 [S]	Christmas Time	196?	3.00	6.00	12.00
—Reissue of KS-3048 (new cover, no gatefold)					
❏ KS-3207 [S]	Songs of the Fabulous Forties, Volume 1	1960	3.75	7.50	15.00
❏ KS-3208 [S]	Songs of the Fabulous Forties, Volume 2	1960	3.75	7.50	15.00
❏ KS-3209 [S]	Songs of the Fabulous Fifties, Volume 1	1960	3.75	7.50	15.00
❏ KS-3210 [S]	Songs of the Fabulous Fifties, Volume 2	1960	3.75	7.50	15.00
❏ KS-3211 [S]	Songs of the Fabulous Century, Volume 1	1960	3.75	7.50	15.00
❏ KS-3212 [S]	Songs of the Fabulous Century, Volume 2	1960	3.75	7.50	15.00
❏ KS-3217 [S]	Temptation	1960	5.00	10.00	20.00
❏ KS-3222 [S]	Roger Williams Invites You to Dance	1961	5.00	10.00	20.00
❏ KS-3244 [S]	Yellow Bird	1961	5.00	10.00	20.00
❏ KS-3251 [S]	Songs of the Soaring '60s	1961	5.00	10.00	20.00
❏ KS-3260 [S]	Greatest Hits	1962	3.75	7.50	15.00
❏ KS-3266 [S]	Maria	1962	3.75	7.50	15.00
❏ KS-3290 [S]	Mr. Piano	1962	3.75	7.50	15.00
❏ KS-3305 [S]	Country Style	1963	3.75	7.50	15.00
❏ KS-3336 [S]	For You.	1963	3.75	7.50	15.00
❏ KS-3354 [S]	The Solid Gold Steinway.	1964	3.75	7.50	15.00
❏ KS-3395 [S]	Family Album of Hymns.	1964	3.00	6.00	12.00
❏ KS-3406 [S]	Academy Award Winners.	1964	3.00	6.00	12.00
❏ KS-3414 [S]	Roger Williams Plays the Hits.	1965	3.00	6.00	12.00
❏ KS-3434 [S]	Summer Wind.	1965	3.00	6.00	12.00
❏ KS-3452 [S]	Autumn Leaves — 1965.	1965	3.00	6.00	12.00
❏ KS-3470 [S]	I'll Remember You.	1966	3.00	6.00	12.00
❏ KS-3483 [S]	Academy Award Winners, Vol. 2	1966	3.00	6.00	12.00
❏ KS-3501 [S]	Born Free.	1966	3.00	6.00	12.00
❏ KS-3512 [S]	Roger!	1967	3.00	6.00	12.00
❏ KS-3530 [S]	Roger Williams/Golden Hits.	1967	3.00	6.00	12.00
❏ KS-3549	Amore.	1968	3.00	6.00	12.00
❏ KS-3550	More Than a Miracle.	1968	3.00	6.00	12.00
❏ KS-3565	Only for Lovers.	1969	3.00	6.00	12.00
❏ KS-3595	Happy Heart.	1969	3.00	6.00	12.00
❏ KS-3610	Love Theme from "Romeo and Juliet".	1969	3.00	6.00	12.00
❏ KS-3629	Themes from Great Movies.	1970	3.00	6.00	12.00
❏ KS-3638	Roger Williams/Golden Hits, Volume 2.	1970	3.00	6.00	12.00
❏ KS-3645	Love Story.	1971	2.50	5.00	10.00
❏ KS-3650	Summer of '42.	1971	2.50	5.00	10.00
❏ KS-3665	Love Theme from "The Godfather".	1972	2.50	5.00	10.00
❏ KS-3671	Play Me.	1972	2.50	5.00	10.00
❏ KXL-5000 [(2)M]	Songs of the Fabulous Fifties	1957	5.00	10.00	20.00
—Maroon and silver (or blue and silver) labels					
❏ KXL-5000 [(2)M]	Songs of the Fabulous Fifties	1962	3.75	7.50	15.00
—Any later label variation					
❏ KXS-5000 [(2)S]	Songs of the Fabulous Fifties	1959	6.25	12.50	25.00
—Maroon and silver (or blue and silver) labels					
❏ KXS-5000 [(2)S]	Songs of the Fabulous Fifties	1962	5.00	10.00	20.00
—Any later label variation					
❏ KXL-5003 [(2)M]	Songs of the Fabulous Forties	1957	5.00	10.00	20.00
—Maroon and silver (or blue and silver) labels					
❏ KXL-5003 [(2)M]	Songs of the Fabulous Forties	1962	3.75	7.50	15.00
—Any later label variation					
❏ KXS-5003 [(2)S]	Songs of the Fabulous Forties	1959	6.25	12.50	25.00
—Maroon and silver (or blue and silver) labels					
❏ KXS-5003 [(2)S]	Songs of the Fabulous Forties	1962	5.00	10.00	20.00
—Any later label variation					
❏ KXL-5005 [(2)M]	Songs of the Fabulous Century	195?	5.00	10.00	20.00
—Maroon and silver (or blue and silver) labels					
❏ KXL-5005 [(2)M]	Songs of the Fabulous Century	1962	3.75	7.50	15.00
—Any later label variation					
❏ KXS-5005 [(2)S]	Songs of the Fabulous Century	1959	6.25	12.50	25.00
—Maroon and silver (or blue and silver) labels					
❏ KXS-5005 [(2)S]	Songs of the Fabulous Century	1962	5.00	10.00	20.00
—Any later label variation					
❏ KXL-5008 [(2)M]	Tonight! Roger Williams at Town Hall	196?	5.00	10.00	20.00
❏ KXS-5008 [(2)S]	Tonight! Roger Williams at Town Hall	196?	6.25	12.50	25.00
MCA					
❏ 63	Greatest Hits	1973	2.00	4.00	8.00
—Reissue of Kapp 3260					
❏ 64	Roger Williams/Golden Hits	1973	2.00	4.00	8.00
—Reissue of Kapp 3530					
❏ 68	Roger Williams/Golden Hits, Volume 2	1973	2.00	4.00	8.00
—Reissue of Kapp 3638					
❏ 71	Somewhere My Love	1973	2.00	4.00	8.00
—Retitled reissue of unknown Kapp LP					
❏ 76	Play Me	1973	2.00	4.00	8.00
—Reissue of Kapp 3671					
❏ 324	Last Tango in Paris	1973	2.50	5.00	10.00
❏ 378	Live	1973	2.50	5.00	10.00
❏ 403	The Way We Were	1974	2.50	5.00	10.00
❏ 438	I Honestly Love You	1974	2.50	5.00	10.00
❏ 539	Family Album of Hymns	1975	2.00	4.00	8.00
—Reissue of Kapp 3395					
❏ 542	Somewhere My Love	1975	—	3.00	6.00
—Reissue of MCA 71					
❏ 2175	Virtuoso	1975	2.50	5.00	10.00
❏ 2237	Nadia's Theme.	1976	2.50	5.00	10.00
❏ 2279	Evergreen.	1977	2.50	5.00	10.00
❏ 4106 [(2)]	The Best of Roger Williams.	197?	3.00	6.00	12.00
❏ 5574	To Amadeus With Love.	1985	2.50	5.00	10.00
❏ 15005	Christmas Time.	197?	2.00	4.00	8.00
—Reissue of Kapp material					
❏ 20202	Autumn Leaves	198?	2.00	4.00	8.00
—Reissue of Kapp material					
PICKWICK					
❏ PTP-2086 [(2)]	Roger Williams at the Piano	197?	3.00	6.00	12.00
❏ SPC-3367	Spanish Eyes	197?	2.00	4.00	8.00
❏ SPC-3511	Sunrise, Sunset	197?	2.00	4.00	8.00
VOCALION					
❏ VL 73918	Moments to Remember	1970	2.50	5.00	10.00

Number	Title (A Side/B Side)	Yr	VG	VG+	NM
WILLIAMS, TEX					
BOONE					
❏ LP-1210 [M]	The Two Sides of Tex Williams	1966	5.00	10.00	20.00
❏ LSP-1210 [S]	The Two Sides of Tex Williams	1966	6.25	12.50	25.00
CAPITOL					
❏ ST 1463 [S]	Smoke! Smoke! Smoke!	1960	10.00	20.00	40.00
❏ T 1463 [M]	Smoke! Smoke! Smoke!	1960	7.50	15.00	30.00
DECCA					
❏ DL 4295 [M]	Country Music Time	1962	5.00	10.00	20.00
❏ DL 5565 [10]	Dance-O-Rama #5	1955	75.00	150.00	300.00
❏ DL 74295 [S]	Country Music Time	1962	7.50	15.00	30.00
IMPERIAL					
❏ LP-9309 [M]	The Voice of Authority	1966	5.00	10.00	20.00
❏ LP-12309 [S]	The Voice of Authority	1966	6.25	12.50	25.00
LIBERTY					
❏ LRP-3304 [M]	Tex Williams in Las Vegas	1963	5.00	10.00	20.00
❏ LST-7304 [S]	Tex Williams in Las Vegas	1963	7.50	15.00	30.00
MONUMENT					
❏ Z 30909	A Man Called Tex	1971	5.00	10.00	20.00
RCA CAMDEN					
❏ CAL-363 [M]	Tex Williams' Best	1958	6.25	12.50	25.00
WILLIAMS, TONY					
Lead singer of THE PLATTERS when they were having their biggest hits in the 1950s.					
MERCURY					
❏ MG-20454 [M]	A Girl Is a Girl Is a Girl	1959	10.00	20.00	40.00
❏ SR-60138 [S]	A Girl Is a Girl Is a Girl	1959	12.50	25.00	50.00
PHILIPS					
❏ PHM 200051 [M]	The Magic Touch of Tony	1962	6.25	12.50	25.00
❏ PHS 600051 [S]	The Magic Touch of Tony	1962	7.50	15.00	30.00
REPRISE					
❏ R-6006 [M]	His Greatest Hits	1961	6.25	12.50	25.00
❏ R9-6006 [S]	His Greatest Hits	1961	7.50	15.00	30.00
WILLIAMS, TONY (2)					
Jazz drummer.					
BLUE NOTE					
❏ BLP-4180 [M]	Life Time	1964	6.25	12.50	25.00
❏ BLP-4216 [M]	Spring	1965	6.25	12.50	25.00
❏ BST-84180 [S]	Life Time	1964	7.50	15.00	30.00
—With "New York, USA" address on label					
❏ BST-84216 [S]	Spring	1965	7.50	15.00	30.00
—With "New York, USA" address on label					
COLUMBIA					
❏ HC 45705	Joy of Flying	198?	12.50	25.00	50.00
—Half-speed mastered edition					
WILLIAMS, VALDO					
SAVOY					
❏ MG-12188 [M]	New Advanced Jazz	1967	7.50	15.00	30.00
WILLIAMSON, CLAUDE					
BETHLEHEM					
❏ BCP-54 [M]	Claude Williamson	1956	10.00	20.00	40.00
❏ BCP-69 [M]	'Round Midnight	1957	10.00	20.00	40.00
CAPITOL					
❏ H 6502 [10]	Claude Williamson	1954	12.50	25.00	50.00
❏ H 6511 [10]	Keys West	1955	12.50	25.00	50.00
❏ T 6511 [10]	Keys West	1956	10.00	20.00	40.00
CONTRACT					
❏ 15001 [M]	The Fabulous Claude Williamson Trio	196?	7.50	15.00	30.00
❏ 15003 [M]	Theatre Party	196?	7.50	15.00	30.00
CRITERION					
❏ 601 [M]	Claude Williamson Mulls the Mulligan Scene	1958	10.00	20.00	40.00
WILLIAMSON, SONNY BOY (1)					
BLUES CLASSICS					
❏ 3	Blues Classics by Sonny Boy Williamson	196?	6.25	12.50	25.00
❏ 20	Blues Classics by Sonny Boy Williamson, Vol. 2	196?	6.25	12.50	25.00
❏ BC 24	Blues Classics by Sonny Boy Williamson, Volume 3	196?	6.25	12.50	25.00
WILLIAMSON, SONNY BOY (2)					
ALLIGATOR					
❏ AL-4787	Keep It To Ourselves	1990	3.00	6.00	12.00
ARHOOLIE					
❏ 2020	King Biscuit Time	197?	3.00	6.00	12.00
CHECKER					
❏ LP-1437 [M]	Down and Out Blues	1959	80.00	160.00	320.00
CHESS					
❏ 2ACMB-206 [(2)]	Sonny Boy Williamson	1976	5.00	10.00	20.00
—Reissue of 50027					
❏ CHV-417	One Way Out	1975	3.75	7.50	15.00
❏ LP-1503 [M]	The Real Folk Blues	1966	20.00	40.00	80.00
❏ LP-1509 [M]	More Real Folk Blues	1966	20.00	40.00	80.00
❏ LPS-1536	Bummer Road	1969	6.25	12.50	25.00
❏ CH-9116	One Way Out	198?	2.50	5.00	10.00
❏ CH-9257	Down and Out Blues	1988	2.50	5.00	10.00
❏ CH-9272	The Real Folk Blues	1988	2.50	5.00	10.00
❏ CH-9277	More Real Folk Blues	1988	2.50	5.00	10.00
❏ 2CH-50027 [(2)]	This Is My Story	1972	6.25	12.50	25.00
GNP CRESCENDO					
❏ GNPS-10003	Sonny Boy Williamson in Chicago	198?	2.50	5.00	10.00
STORYVILLE					
❏ 4016	A Portrait in Blues	197?	3.00	6.00	12.00
❏ 4062	The Blues of Sonny Boy Williamson	197?	3.00	6.00	12.00

Number	Title (A Side/B Side)	Yr	VG	VG+	NM

WILLIAMSON, SONNY BOY (2), AND THE YARDBIRDS
MERCURY

Number	Title (A Side/B Side)	Yr	VG	VG+	NM
❏ MG-21071 [M]	Sonny Boy Williamson and the Yardbirds	1965	20.00	40.00	80.00
❏ SR-61071 [R]	Sonny Boy Williamson and the Yardbirds.	196?	6.25	12.50	25.00
—Later cover with cartoon artwork on the cover					
❏ SR-61071 [R]	Sonny Boy Williamson and the Yardbirds	1965	12.50	25.00	50.00
—First cover with a picture of the bluesman and the band					
❏ SR-61271 [R]	Eric Clapton and the Yardbirds Live with Sonny Boy Williamson	1970	5.00	10.00	20.00
—Reissue					

WILLIAMSON, STU
BETHLEHEM

❏ BCP-31 [M]	Stu Williamson Plays	1955	20.00	40.00	80.00
❏ BCP-55 [M]	Stu Williamson	1956	20.00	40.00	80.00
❏ BCP-1024 [10]	Stu Williamson Plays	1955	30.00	60.00	120.00

WILLING, FOY, AND THE RIDERS OF THE PURPLE SAGE
CROWN

❏ CST-582	Country & Western Favorites	196?	2.50	5.00	10.00
❏ CLP-5306 [M]	Cool Water	196?	3.00	6.00	12.00

CUSTOM

❏ CS 1017	Cool, Cool Water	197?	2.50	5.00	10.00

JUBILEE

❏ JL-5028 [M]	The New Sound of American Folk	1962	5.00	10.00	20.00
❏ JLS-5028 [S]	The New Sound of American Folk	1962	6.25	12.50	25.00

ROULETTE

❏ R-25035 [M]	Cowboy	1958	10.00	20.00	40.00

ROYALE

❏ 6032 [10]	The Riders of the Purple Sage	1952	25.00	50.00	100.00

VARSITY

❏ 6032 [10]	The Riders of the Purple Sage	1950	30.00	60.00	120.00

WILLIS, CHUCK
ATLANTIC

❏ 8018 [M]	The King of the Stroll	1958	75.00	150.00	300.00
—Black label					
❏ 8018 [M]	The King of the Stroll	1960	37.50	75.00	150.00
—Purple and orange label					
❏ 8079 [M]	I Remember Chuck Willis	1963	37.50	75.00	150.00
❏ SD 8079 [P]	I Remember Chuck Willis	1963	50.00	100.00	200.00

EPIC

❏ LN 3425 [M]	Chuck Willis Wails the Blues	1958	125.00	250.00	500.00
❏ LN 3728 [M]	A Tribute to Chuck Willis	1960	75.00	150.00	300.00

WILLIS BROTHERS, THE
STARDAY

❏ SLP-163 [M]	The Willis Brothers in Action	1962	15.00	30.00	60.00
❏ SLP-229 [M]	Code of the West	1963	12.50	25.00	50.00
❏ SLP-306 [M]	Let's Hit the Road	1965	10.00	20.00	40.00
❏ SLP-323 [M]	Give Me 40 Acres	1965	10.00	20.00	40.00
❏ SLP-353 [M]	Road Stop Juke Box Hits	1966	7.50	15.00	30.00
❏ SLP-369 [M]	The Wild Side of Life	1966	7.50	15.00	30.00
❏ SLP-387 [M]	Goin' to Town	1966	7.50	15.00	30.00
❏ SLP-403 [M]	Bob	1967	6.25	12.50	25.00
❏ SLP-428	Hey, Mister Truck Driver	1968	6.25	12.50	25.00
❏ SLP-442	Bummin' Around	1969	6.25	12.50	25.00
❏ SLP-466	The Best of the Willis Brothers	1970	5.00	10.00	20.00
❏ SLP-472	For the Good Times	1971	5.00	10.00	20.00

WILLS, BOB
ANTONES

❏ 6000 [10]	Old Time Favorites	195?	125.00	250.00	500.00
—Fan club release					
❏ 6010 [10]	Old Time Favorites	195?	125.00	250.00	500.00
—Fan club release					

CAPITOL

❏ SKBB-11550 [(2)]	Bob Wills and His Texas Playboys in Concert	1976	5.00	10.00	20.00

COLUMBIA

❏ CL 9003 [10]	Bob Wills Round-Up	1949	75.00	150.00	300.00
❏ KG 32416 [(2)]	Anthology	1973	5.00	10.00	20.00

DECCA

❏ DL 5562 [10]	Dance-O-Rama #2	1955	75.00	150.00	300.00
❏ DL 8727 [M]	Bob Wills and His Texas Playboys	1957	25.00	50.00	100.00
—Black label, silver print					
❏ DL 8727 [M]	Bob Wills and His Texas Playboys	1961	10.00	20.00	40.00
—Black label with color bars					
❏ DL 78727 [R]	Bob Wills and His Texas Playboys	196?	5.00	10.00	20.00

DELTA

❏ DLP-1149	Bob Wills and His Texas Playboys On Stage	1982	2.50	5.00	10.00

HARMONY

❏ HL 7036 [M]	Bob Wills Special	1957	10.00	20.00	40.00
—Maroon label					
❏ HL 7036 [M]	Bob Wills Special	196?	5.00	10.00	20.00
—Black label					
❏ HL 7304 [M]	The Best of Bob Wills	1963	6.25	12.50	25.00
❏ HL 7345 [M]	The Great Bob Wills	1965	5.00	10.00	20.00

KAPP

❏ KL-1506 [M]	From the Heart of Texas	1966	5.00	10.00	20.00
❏ KL-1523 [M]	King of Western Swing	1967	6.25	12.50	25.00
❏ KL-1542 [M]	Here's That Man Again	1968	12.50	25.00	50.00
—Mono is white label promo only; in stereo cover with "Mono" sticker					
❏ KS-3506 [S]	From the Heart of Texas	1966	6.25	12.50	25.00
❏ KS-3523 [S]	King of Western Swing	1967	6.25	12.50	25.00
❏ KS-3542 [S]	Here's That Man Again	1968	6.25	12.50	25.00
❏ KS-3569	Time Changes Everything	1969	5.00	10.00	20.00
❏ KS-3587	The Living Legend	1969	5.00	10.00	20.00
❏ KS-3601	The Greatest String Band Hits	1969	5.00	10.00	20.00
❏ KS-3639	Bob Wills in Person	1970	5.00	10.00	20.00
❏ KS-3641	The Best of Bob Wills	1971	5.00	10.00	20.00

LIBERTY

❏ LRP-3173 [M]	Together Again	1960	7.50	15.00	30.00
❏ LRP-3182 [M]	Living Legend	1961	7.50	15.00	30.00
❏ LRP-3194 [M]	Mr. Words and Mr. Music	1961	7.50	15.00	30.00
❏ LRP-3303 [M]	Bob Wills Sings and Plays	1963	7.50	15.00	30.00
❏ LST-7173 [S]	Together Again	1960	10.00	20.00	40.00
❏ LST-7182 [S]	Living Legend	1961	10.00	20.00	40.00
❏ LST-7194 [S]	Mr. Words and Mr. Music	1961	10.00	20.00	40.00
❏ LST-7303 [S]	Bob Wills Sings and Plays	1963	10.00	20.00	40.00

LONGHORN

❏ LP-001 [M]	My Keepsake Album	1965	20.00	40.00	80.00

MGM

❏ E-91 [10]	Ranch House Favorites	1951	75.00	150.00	300.00
❏ GAS-141	A Tribute (Golden Archive Series)	1971	6.25	12.50	25.00
❏ E-3352 [M]	Ranch House Favorites	1956	37.50	75.00	150.00

STARDAY

❏ SLP-375 [M]	San Antonio Rose	1965	10.00	20.00	40.00

UNITED ARTISTS

❏ UA-LA216-J [(2)]	For the Last Time	1974	10.00	20.00	40.00
—Box set with booklet					
❏ UAS-9962 [(2)]	Legendary Masters	1971	6.25	12.50	25.00

VOCALION

❏ VL 3735 [M]	Western Swing Band	1965	5.00	10.00	20.00

WILLS, JOHNNIE LEE
FLYING FISH

❏ FF-069	Reunion	1978	3.00	6.00	12.00

ROUNDER

❏ 1027	Tulsa Swing	1978	3.00	6.00	12.00

SIMS

❏ LP-101 [M]	Where There's a Wills, There's a Way	1962	10.00	20.00	40.00
❏ LPS-101 [S]	Where There's a Wills, There's a Way	1962	15.00	30.00	60.00
❏ LP-108 [M]	Johnny Lee Wills at the Tulsa Stampede	1963	7.50	15.00	30.00
❏ LPS-108 [S]	Johnny Lee Wills at the Tulsa Stampede	1963	12.50	25.00	50.00

WILMER AND THE DUKES
APHRODISIAC

❏ 6001	Wilmer and the Dukes	1969	5.00	10.00	20.00

WILSON, AL
PLAYBOY

❏ PB 410	I've Got a Feeling	1976	3.00	6.00	12.00
❏ JZ 34744	I've Got a Feeling	1977	2.50	5.00	10.00
—Reissue of 410					

ROCKY ROAD

❏ RR-3600	Weighing In	1973	3.75	7.50	15.00
❏ RR-3601	Show and Tell	1973	3.75	7.50	15.00
❏ 3700	La La Peace Song	1974	3.75	7.50	15.00

SOUL CITY

❏ SCS-92006	Searching for the Dolphins	1969	6.25	12.50	25.00

WILSON, BRIAN
Also see THE BEACH BOYS.
SIRE

❏ PRO-A-3248 [DJ]	Words and Music	1988	6.25	12.50	25.00
—Promo-only music and interview					
❏ 25669	Brian Wilson	1988	2.50	5.00	10.00

WILSON, CARL
Also see THE BEACH BOYS.
CARIBOU

❏ NJZ 37010	Carl Wilson	1981	5.00	10.00	20.00
❏ ARZ 37970	Youngblood	1982	5.00	10.00	20.00

WILSON, DENNIS
Also see THE BEACH BOYS.
CARIBOU

❏ PZ 34354	Pacific Ocean Blue	1977	7.50	15.00	30.00

WILSON, FLIP
ATLANTIC

❏ 8149 [M]	Cowboys and Colored People	1967	6.25	12.50	25.00
❏ SD 8149 [S]	Cowboys and Colored People	1967	3.75	7.50	15.00
—Green and blue label					
❏ SD 8149 [S]	Cowboys and Colored People	1969	3.00	6.00	12.00
—Red and green label					
❏ SD 8179	You Devil You	1968	3.75	7.50	15.00
—Green and blue label					
❏ SD 8179	You Devil You	1969	3.00	6.00	12.00
—Red and green label					

IMPERIAL

❏ LP-9155 [M]	Flippin'	1961	6.25	12.50	25.00

LITTLE DAVID

❏ LD 1000	The Devil Made Me Buy This Dress	1970	3.00	6.00	12.00
❏ LD 1001 [M]	Geraldine/Don't Fight the Feeling	1972	6.25	12.50	25.00
—White label promo only; sticker on cover says "Promotional DJ Copy Monaural Not for Sale"					
❏ LD 1001 [S]	Geraldine/Don't Fight the Feeling	1972	3.00	6.00	12.00
❏ LD 2000	The Flip Wilson Show	1970	3.00	6.00	12.00

MINIT

❏ 24012	Flippin'	1968	3.75	7.50	15.00
—Reissue of Imperial LP					

SCEPTER

❏ S-520	Flip Wilson's Pot Luck	1964	5.00	10.00	20.00

SPRINGBOARD

❏ SPB-4004	Funny and Live at the Village Gate	1972	3.00	6.00	12.00
—Reissue of Scepter LP					

SUNSET

❏ SUS-5297	Flipped Out	1970	3.00	6.00	12.00
—Reissue of Minit LP					

Number	Title (A Side/B Side)	Yr	VG	VG+	NM
WILSON, GERALD					
AUDIO LAB					
❑ AL-1538 [M]	Big Band Modern	1959	37.50	75.00	150.00
FEDERAL					
❑ 295-93 [10]	Gerald Wilson	1953	75.00	150.00	300.00
PACIFIC JAZZ					
❑ PJ-34 [M]	You Better Believe It	1961	6.25	12.50	25.00
❑ ST-34 [S]	You Better Believe It	1961	7.50	15.00	30.00
❑ PJ-61 [M]	Moment of Truth	1962	6.25	12.50	25.00
❑ ST-61 [S]	Moment of Truth	1962	7.50	15.00	30.00
❑ PJ-80 [M]	Portraits	1964	6.25	12.50	25.00
❑ ST-80 [S]	Portraits	1964	7.50	15.00	30.00
❑ PJ-88 [M]	Gerald Wilson on Stage	1964	6.25	12.50	25.00
❑ ST-88 [S]	Gerald Wilson on Stage	1964	7.50	15.00	30.00
❑ PJ-10118 [M]	Live and Swinging	1967	5.00	10.00	20.00
❑ ST-20099 [S]	Feelin' Kinda Blue	1966	5.00	10.00	20.00
❑ ST-20111 [S]	Golden Sword	1966	5.00	10.00	20.00
WILSON, J. FRANK, AND THE CAVALIERS					
JOSIE					
❑ JM-4006 [M]	Last Kiss	1964	18.75	37.50	75.00
❑ JS-4006 [S]	Last Kiss	1964	25.00	50.00	100.00
WILSON, JACK					
ATLANTIC					
❑ 1406 [M]	Jack Wilson Quartet	1963	7.50	15.00	30.00
❑ SD 1406 [S]	Jack Wilson Quartet	1963	10.00	20.00	40.00
❑ 1427 [M]	The Two Sides of Jack Wilson	1964	7.50	15.00	30.00
❑ SD 1427 [S]	The Two Sides of Jack Wilson	1964	10.00	20.00	40.00
BLUE NOTE					
❑ BLP-4251 [M]	Something Personal	1967	10.00	20.00	40.00
❑ BST-84251 [S]	Something Personal	1967	5.00	10.00	20.00
—With "A Division of Liberty Records" on label					
❑ BST-84251 [S]	Something Personal	1967	7.50	15.00	30.00
—With "New York, USA" address on label					
❑ BST-84270 [S]	Easterly Winds	1968	5.00	10.00	20.00
—With "A Division of Liberty Records" on label					
❑ BST-84328 [S]	Song for My Daughter	1969	5.00	10.00	20.00
—With "A Division of Liberty Records" on label					
VAULT					
❑ LP-9001 [M]	Brazilian Mancini	1964	6.25	12.50	25.00
❑ LPS-9001 [S]	Brazilian Mancini	1964	7.50	15.00	30.00
❑ LP-9002 [M]	Ramblin'	1964	6.25	12.50	25.00
❑ LPS-9002 [S]	Ramblin'	1964	7.50	15.00	30.00
❑ LP-9008 [M]	Jazz Organs	1965	6.25	12.50	25.00
❑ LPS-9008 [S]	Jazz Organs	1965	7.50	15.00	30.00
WILSON, JACKIE					
BRUNSWICK					
❑ BL 54042 [M]	He's So Fine	1959	30.00	60.00	120.00
—All-black label					
❑ BL 54042 [M]	He's So Fine	1964	6.25	12.50	25.00
—Black label with color bars					
❑ BL 54045 [M]	Lonely Teardrops	1959	37.50	75.00	150.00
—All-black label					
❑ BL 54045 [M]	Lonely Teardrops	1964	6.25	12.50	25.00
—Black label with color bars					
❑ BL 54050 [M]	So Much	1964	5.00	10.00	20.00
—Black label with color bars					
❑ BL 54050 [M]	So Much	1960	25.00	50.00	100.00
—All-black label					
❑ BL 54055 [M]	Jackie Sings the Blues	1964	5.00	10.00	20.00
—Black label with color bars					
❑ BL 54055 [M]	Jackie Sings the Blues	1960	37.50	75.00	150.00
—All-black label					
❑ BL 54058 [M]	My Golden Favorites	1964	6.25	12.50	25.00
—Black label with color bars					
❑ BL 54058 [M]	My Golden Favorites	1960	15.00	30.00	60.00
—All-black label					
❑ BL 54059 [M]	A Woman, a Lover, a Friend	1964	5.00	10.00	20.00
—Black label with color bars					
❑ BL 54059 [M]	A Woman, a Lover, a Friend	1961	12.50	25.00	50.00
—All-black label					
❑ BL 54100 [M]	You Ain't Heard Nothin' Yet	1961	12.50	25.00	50.00
—All-black label					
❑ BL 54100 [M]	You Ain't Heard Nothin' Yet	1964	5.00	10.00	20.00
—Black label with color bars					
❑ BL 54101 [M]	By Special Request	1961	12.50	25.00	50.00
—All-black label					
❑ BL 54101 [M]	By Special Request	1964	5.00	10.00	20.00
—Black label with color bars					
❑ BL 54105 [M]	Body and Soul	1962	12.50	25.00	50.00
—All-black label					
❑ BL 54105 [M]	Body and Soul	1964	5.00	10.00	20.00
—Black label with color bars					
❑ BL 54106 [M]	The World's Greatest Melodies	1962	12.50	25.00	50.00
—All-black label					
❑ BL 54106 [M]	The World's Greatest Melodies	1964	5.00	10.00	20.00
—Black label with color bars					
❑ BL 54108 [M]	Jackie Wilson at the Copa	1962	12.50	25.00	50.00
—All-black label					
❑ BL 54108 [M]	Jackie Wilson at the Copa	1964	5.00	10.00	20.00
—Black label with color bars					
❑ BL 54110 [M]	Baby Workout	1963	5.00	10.00	20.00
—Black label with color bars					
❑ BL 54110 [M]	Baby Workout	1963	12.50	25.00	50.00
—All-black label					
❑ BL 54112 [M]	Merry Christmas from Jackie Wilson	1963	7.50	15.00	30.00
❑ BL 54113 [M]	Shake a Hand	1964	6.25	12.50	25.00
❑ BL 54115 [M]	My Golden Favorites, Volume 2	1964	6.25	12.50	25.00
❑ BL 54117 [M]	Somethin' Else	1964	6.25	12.50	25.00
❑ BL 54118 [M]	Soul Time	1965	6.25	12.50	25.00
❑ BL 54119 [M]	Spotlight on Jackie	1965	6.25	12.50	25.00
❑ BL 54120 [M]	Soul Galore	1966	6.25	12.50	25.00
❑ BL 54122 [M]	Whispers	1966	6.25	12.50	25.00
❑ BL 54130 [M]	Higher and Higher	1967	6.25	12.50	25.00
❑ BL 54134 [M]	Manufacturers of Soul	1968	12.50	25.00	50.00
—With Count Basie					
❑ BL 54138 [M]	I Get the Sweetest Feeling	1968	25.00	50.00	100.00
—Yellow label promo only; "Monaural" sticker over the word "Stereo" on cover					
❑ BL 754050 [S]	So Much	1960	37.50	75.00	150.00
—All-black label					
❑ BL 754050 [S]	So Much	1964	6.25	12.50	25.00
—Black label with color bars					
❑ BL 754055 [S]	Jackie Sings the Blues	1960	50.00	100.00	200.00
—All-black label					
❑ BL 754055 [S]	Jackie Sings the Blues	1964	6.25	12.50	25.00
—Black label with color bars					
❑ BL 754059 [S]	A Woman, a Lover, a Friend	1961	20.00	40.00	80.00
—All-black label					
❑ BL 754059 [S]	A Woman, a Lover, a Friend	1964	6.25	12.50	25.00
—Black label with color bars					
❑ BL 754100 [S]	You Ain't Heard Nothin' Yet	1961	20.00	40.00	80.00
—All-black label					
❑ BL 754100 [S]	You Ain't Heard Nothin' Yet	1964	6.25	12.50	25.00
—Black label with color bars					
❑ BL 754101 [S]	By Special Request	1961	20.00	40.00	80.00
—All-black label					
❑ BL 754101 [S]	By Special Request	1964	6.25	12.50	25.00
—Black label with color bars					
❑ BL 754105 [S]	Body and Soul	1962	20.00	40.00	80.00
—All-black label					
❑ BL 754105 [S]	Body and Soul	1964	6.25	12.50	25.00
—Black label with color bars					
❑ BL 754106 [S]	The World's Greatest Melodies	1962	20.00	40.00	80.00
—All-black label					
❑ BL 754106 [S]	The World's Greatest Melodies	1964	6.25	12.50	25.00
—Black label with color bars					
❑ BL 754108 [S]	Jackie Wilson at the Copa	1962	20.00	40.00	80.00
—All-black label					
❑ BL 754108 [S]	Jackie Wilson at the Copa	1964	6.25	12.50	25.00
—Black label with color bars					
❑ BL 754110 [S]	Baby Workout	1963	6.25	12.50	25.00
—Black label with color bars					
❑ BL 754110 [S]	Baby Workout	1963	20.00	40.00	80.00
—All-black label					
❑ BL 754112 [S]	Merry Christmas from Jackie Wilson	1963	10.00	20.00	40.00
❑ BL 754113 [S]	Shake a Hand	1964	7.50	15.00	30.00
❑ BL 754115 [S]	My Golden Favorites, Volume 2	1964	7.50	15.00	30.00
❑ BL 754117 [S]	Somethin' Else	1964	7.50	15.00	30.00
❑ BL 754118 [S]	Soul Time	1965	7.50	15.00	30.00
❑ BL 754119 [S]	Spotlight on Jackie	1965	7.50	15.00	30.00
❑ BL 754120 [S]	Soul Galore	1966	7.50	15.00	30.00
❑ BL 754122 [S]	Whispers	1966	7.50	15.00	30.00
❑ BL 754130 [S]	Higher and Higher	1967	7.50	15.00	30.00
❑ BL 754134 [S]	Manufacturers of Soul	1968	5.00	10.00	20.00
—With Count Basie					
❑ BL 754138 [S]	I Get the Sweetest Feeling	1968	5.00	10.00	20.00
❑ BL 754140	Jackie Wilson's Greatest Hits	1969	5.00	10.00	20.00
❑ BL 754154	Do Your Thing	1969	5.00	10.00	20.00
❑ BL 754158	It's All a Part of Love	1970	5.00	10.00	20.00
❑ BL 754167	This Love Is Real	1971	5.00	10.00	20.00
❑ BL 754172	You Got Me Walking	1971	5.00	10.00	20.00
❑ BL 754185	Beautiful Day	1972	3.75	7.50	15.00
❑ BL 754199	Nowstalgia	1974	3.75	7.50	15.00
❑ BL 754212	Nobody But You	1977	3.75	7.50	15.00
COLUMBIA					
❑ FC 40866	Reet Petite: The Best of Jackie Wilson	1987	3.00	6.00	12.00
EPIC					
❑ EG 38623 [(2)]	The Jackie Wilson Story	1983	5.00	10.00	20.00
❑ FE 39408	The Jackie Wilson Story, Vol. 2	1985	3.00	6.00	12.00
❑ PE 39408	The Jackie Wilson Story, Vol. 2	198?	2.00	4.00	8.00
—Budget-line reissue					
RHINO					
❑ RNLP-70230	Through the Years: A Collection of Rare Album Tracks and Single Sides	1987	3.00	6.00	12.00
WILSON, JULIE					
ARDEN					
❑ B&S-1	Julie Wilson at Brothers and Sisters, Vol. 1	1976	5.00	10.00	20.00
❑ B&S-2	Julie Wilson at Brothers and Sisters, Vol. 2	1976	5.00	10.00	20.00
CAMEO					
❑ C-1021 [M]	Meet Julie Wilson	1962	7.50	15.00	30.00
DOLPHIN					
❑ 6 [M]	Love	1956	12.50	25.00	50.00
VIK					
❑ LX-1095 [M]	My Old Flame	1957	7.50	15.00	30.00
❑ LX-1118 [M]	Julie Wilson at the St. Regis	1958	7.50	15.00	30.00
WILSON, LONNIE					
STARDAY					
❑ SLP-217 [M]	The Playboy Farmer	196?	7.50	15.00	30.00
WILSON, MARIE					
DESIGN					
❑ DLP-76 [M]	Gentlemen Prefer Marie Wilson	1959	10.00	20.00	40.00
WILSON, MARTY					
20TH CENTURY FOX					
❑ TF-3101 [M]	Young America Dances to Golden Goodies	1963	5.00	10.00	20.00
❑ TFS-4101 [S]	Young America Dances to Golden Goodies	1963	6.25	12.50	25.00

Number	Title (A Side/B Side)	Yr	VG	VG+	NM
WILSON, MURRY					

Father of Brian, Carl and Dennis Wilson of the Beach Boys.

CAPITOL

| ST 2819 [S] | The Many Moods of Murry Wilson | 1967 | 12.50 | 25.00 | 50.00 |
| T 2819 [M] | The Many Moods of Murry Wilson | 1967 | 15.00 | 30.00 | 60.00 |

WILSON, NANCY

CAPITOL

ST-148	Nancy	1969	3.75	7.50	15.00
ST-234	Son of a Preacher Man	1969	3.75	7.50	15.00
SWBB-256 [(2)]	Close-Up	1969	5.00	10.00	20.00

—Combines 1828 and 1934 into one package

ST-353	Hurt So Bad	1969	3.75	7.50	15.00
ST-429	Can't Take My Eyes Off You	1970	3.75	7.50	15.00
ST-541	Now I'm a Woman	1970	3.75	7.50	15.00
STBB-727 [(2)]	For Once in My Life/Who Can I Turn To	1971	5.00	10.00	20.00
ST-763	The Right to Love	1971	3.75	7.50	15.00

—Retitled reissue of 2757

| SM-798 | But Beautiful | 197? | 2.50 | 5.00 | 10.00 |

—Reissue

ST-798	But Beautiful	1971	3.75	7.50	15.00
ST-842	Kaleidoscope	1971	3.75	7.50	15.00
ST 1319 [S]	Like in Love	1960	5.00	10.00	20.00

—Black label with colorband, Capitol logo on top

| ST 1319 [S] | Like in Love | 1960 | 7.50 | 15.00 | 30.00 |

—Black label with colorband, Capitol logo on left

| T 1319 [M] | Like in Love | 1960 | 3.75 | 7.50 | 15.00 |

—Black label with colorband, Capitol logo on top

| T 1319 [M] | Like in Love | 1960 | 6.25 | 12.50 | 25.00 |

—Black label with colorband, Capitol logo on left

| ST 1440 [S] | Something Wonderful | 1960 | 5.00 | 10.00 | 20.00 |

—Black label with colorband, Capitol logo on top

| ST 1440 [S] | Something Wonderful | 1960 | 7.50 | 15.00 | 30.00 |

—Black label with colorband, Capitol logo on left

| T 1440 [M] | Something Wonderful | 1960 | 3.75 | 7.50 | 15.00 |

—Black label with colorband, Capitol logo on top

| T 1440 [M] | Something Wonderful | 1960 | 6.25 | 12.50 | 25.00 |

—Black label with colorband, Capitol logo on left

| ST 1524 [S] | The Swingin's Mutual | 1961 | 5.00 | 10.00 | 20.00 |

—Black label with colorband, Capitol logo on top

| ST 1524 [S] | The Swingin's Mutual | 1961 | 7.50 | 15.00 | 30.00 |

—Black label with colorband, Capitol logo on left

| T 1524 [M] | The Swingin's Mutual | 1961 | 3.75 | 7.50 | 15.00 |

—Black label with colorband, Capitol logo on top

| T 1524 [M] | The Swingin's Mutual | 1961 | 6.25 | 12.50 | 25.00 |

—Black label with colorband, Capitol logo on left

ST 1767 [S]	Hello Young Lovers	1962	6.25	12.50	25.00
T 1767 [M]	Hello Young Lovers	1962	5.00	10.00	20.00
SM-1828	Broadway My Way	197?	2.50	5.00	10.00

—Reissue

ST 1828 [S]	Broadway My Way	1963	5.00	10.00	20.00
T 1828 [M]	Broadway My Way	1963	3.75	7.50	15.00
SM-1934	Hollywood My Way	197?	2.50	5.00	10.00

—Reissue

ST 1934 [S]	Hollywood My Way	1963	5.00	10.00	20.00
T 1934 [M]	Hollywood My Way	1963	3.75	7.50	15.00
ST 2012 [S]	Yesterday's Love Songs/Today's Blues	1964	5.00	10.00	20.00
T 2012 [M]	Yesterday's Love Songs/Today's Blues	1964	3.75	7.50	15.00
ST 2082 [S]	Today, Tomorrow, Forever	1964	5.00	10.00	20.00
T 2082 [M]	Today, Tomorrow, Forever	1964	3.75	7.50	15.00
KAO 2136 [M]	The Nancy Wilson Show!	1965	3.75	7.50	15.00
SKAO 2136 [S]	The Nancy Wilson Show!	1965	5.00	10.00	20.00
ST 2155 [S]	How Glad I Am	1964	5.00	10.00	20.00
T 2155 [M]	How Glad I Am	1964	3.75	7.50	15.00
ST 2321 [S]	Today — My Way	1965	5.00	10.00	20.00
T 2321 [M]	Today — My Way	1965	3.75	7.50	15.00
ST 2351 [S]	Gentle Is My Love	1965	5.00	10.00	20.00
T 2351 [M]	Gentle Is My Love	1965	3.75	7.50	15.00
ST 2433 [S]	From Broadway with Love	1966	5.00	10.00	20.00
T 2433 [M]	From Broadway with Love	1966	3.75	7.50	15.00
SM-2495	A Touch of Today	197?	2.50	5.00	10.00

—Reissue

ST 2495 [S]	A Touch of Today	1966	5.00	10.00	20.00
T 2495 [M]	A Touch of Today	1966	3.75	7.50	15.00
ST 2555 [S]	Tender Loving Care	1966	5.00	10.00	20.00
T 2555 [M]	Tender Loving Care	1966	3.75	7.50	15.00
ST 2634 [S]	Nancy — Naturally	1967	5.00	10.00	20.00
T 2634 [M]	Nancy — Naturally	1967	3.75	7.50	15.00
ST 2712 [S]	Just for Now	1967	5.00	10.00	20.00
T 2712 [M]	Just for Now	1967	3.75	7.50	15.00
ST 2757 [S]	Lush Life	1967	3.75	7.50	15.00
T 2757 [M]	Lush Life	1967	5.00	10.00	20.00
ST 2844 [S]	Welcome to My Love	1968	3.75	7.50	15.00
T 2844 [M]	Welcome to My Love	1968	6.25	12.50	25.00
ST 2909	Easy	1968	3.75	7.50	15.00
SKAO 2947	The Best of Nancy Wilson	1968	3.75	7.50	15.00
ST 2970	The Sound of Nancy Wilson	1968	3.75	7.50	15.00
SY-4575	Broadway My Way	197?	2.50	5.00	10.00

—Odd reissue

ST-11131	I Know I Love Him	1972	3.00	6.00	12.00
ST-11317	All in Love Is Fair	1974	3.00	6.00	12.00
ST-11386	Come Get to This	1975	3.00	6.00	12.00
ST-11518	This Mother's Daughter	1976	3.00	6.00	12.00
ST-11659	I've Never Been to Me	1977	3.00	6.00	12.00
SM-11767	How Glad I Am	1978	2.50	5.00	10.00

—Reissue of 2155

| SMAS-11786 | Music on My Mind | 1978 | 3.00 | 6.00 | 12.00 |
| SM-11802 | Easy | 1978 | 2.50 | 5.00 | 10.00 |

—Reissue of 2909

| SM-11819 | Come Get to This | 1978 | 2.50 | 5.00 | 10.00 |

—Reissue of 11386

| SM-11884 | Nancy — Naturally | 1979 | 2.50 | 5.00 | 10.00 |

—Reissue of 2634

| ST-11943 | Life, Love and Happiness | 1979 | 3.00 | 6.00 | 12.00 |
| SM-12031 | Can't Take My Eyes Off You | 1980 | 2.50 | 5.00 | 10.00 |

—Reissue of 429

| ST-12055 | Take My Love | 1980 | 3.00 | 6.00 | 12.00 |
| SN-16198 | The Best of Nancy Wilson | 198? | 2.00 | 4.00 | 8.00 |

—Budget-line reissue

COLUMBIA

FC 40330	Keep You Satisfied	1986	2.50	5.00	10.00
FC 40787	Forbidden Lover	1987	2.50	5.00	10.00
FC 44464	Nancy Now!	1989	2.50	5.00	10.00

PAUSA

| PR-9041 | Nancy — Naturally | 1985 | 2.50 | 5.00 | 10.00 |

PICKWICK

| SPC-3273 | Goin' Out of My Head | 197? | 2.50 | 5.00 | 10.00 |
| SPC-3348 | The Good Life | 197? | 2.50 | 5.00 | 10.00 |

WILSON, NANCY, AND CANNONBALL ADDERLEY

CAPITOL

| SM-1657 | Nancy Wilson/Cannonball Adderley | 197? | 2.50 | 5.00 | 10.00 |

—Reissue

| ST 1657 [S] | Nancy Wilson/Cannonball Adderley | 1962 | 5.00 | 10.00 | 20.00 |

—Black label with colorband, Capitol logo on top

| ST 1657 [S] | Nancy Wilson/Cannonball Adderley | 1962 | 7.50 | 15.00 | 30.00 |

—Black label with colorband, Capitol logo on left

| T 1657 [M] | Nancy Wilson/Cannonball Adderley | 1962 | 3.75 | 7.50 | 15.00 |

—Black label with colorband, Capitol logo on top

| T 1657 [M] | Nancy Wilson/Cannonball Adderley | 1962 | 6.25 | 12.50 | 25.00 |

—Black label with colorband, Capitol logo on left

WILSON, REG

HERALD

| HLP-0104 [M] | All By Himself | 1956 | 12.50 | 25.00 | 50.00 |

WILSON, REUBEN

BLUE NOTE

| BST-84295 | On Broadway | 1968 | 6.25 | 12.50 | 25.00 |

—With "A Division of Liberty Records" on label

| BST-84317 | Love Bug | 1969 | 6.25 | 12.50 | 25.00 |

—With "A Division of Liberty Records" on label

BST-84343	Blue Mode	1970	6.25	12.50	25.00
BST-84365	Groovy Situation	1971	6.25	12.50	25.00
BST-84377	Set Us Free	1972	6.25	12.50	25.00

GROOVE MERCHANT

| 511 | Sweet Life | 1973 | 5.00 | 10.00 | 20.00 |
| 4404 [(2)] | Bad Stuff | 197? | 5.00 | 10.00 | 20.00 |

WILSON, TEDDY

ALLEGRO

| 4024 [10] | All Star Sextet | 1954 | 25.00 | 50.00 | 100.00 |
| 4031 [10] | All Star Sextet | 1954 | 25.00 | 50.00 | 100.00 |

CAMEO

| C-1059 [M] | Teddy Wilson 1964 | 1964 | 7.50 | 15.00 | 30.00 |
| SC-1059 [S] | Teddy Wilson 1964 | 1964 | 7.50 | 15.00 | 30.00 |

CLEF

| MGC-140 [10] | The Didactic Mr. Wilson | 1953 | 30.00 | 60.00 | 120.00 |
| MGC-156 [10] | Soft Moods with Teddy Wilson | 1954 | 30.00 | 60.00 | 120.00 |

COLUMBIA

CL 748 [M]	Mr. Wilson	1956	15.00	30.00	60.00
CL 1318 [M]	Mr. Wilson and Mr. Gershwin	1959	10.00	20.00	40.00
CL 1352 [M]	Gypsy	1959	7.50	15.00	30.00
CL 1442 [M]	And Then They Wrote	1960	7.50	15.00	30.00
CL 6040 [10]	Teddy Wilson Featuring Billie Holiday	1949	100.00	200.00	400.00
CL 6098 [10]	Teddy Wilson and His Piano	1950	62.50	125.00	250.00
CL 6153 [10]	Piano Moods	1950	30.00	60.00	120.00
CS 8160 [S]	Gypsy	1959	10.00	20.00	40.00
CS 8242 [S]	And Then They Wrote	1960	10.00	20.00	40.00

COMMODORE

| FL-20029 [10] | Town Hall Concert | 1952 | 50.00 | 100.00 | 200.00 |

DIAL

| LP-213 [10] | Teddy Wilson All Stars | 1950 | 75.00 | 150.00 | 300.00 |

MERCURY

| MG-25172 [10] | Piano Pastries | 1953 | 30.00 | 60.00 | 120.00 |

MGM

| E-129 [10] | Runnin' Wild | 1951 | 50.00 | 100.00 | 200.00 |

MOSAIC

| MQ8-173 [(8)] | The Complete Verve Recordings of the Teddy Wilson Trio | 199? | 37.50 | 75.00 | 150.00 |

NORGRAN

| MGN-1019 [M] | The Creative Teddy Wilson | 1955 | 25.00 | 50.00 | 100.00 |

ROYALE

| 18169 [10] | Teddy Wilson and His All Stars | 195? | 25.00 | 50.00 | 100.00 |

VERVE

MGV-2011 [M]	Intimate Listening	1956	12.50	25.00	50.00
V-2011 [M]	Intimate Listening	1961	5.00	10.00	20.00
MGV-2029 [M]	For Quiet Lovers	1956	15.00	30.00	60.00
V-2029 [M]	For Quiet Lovers	1961	6.25	12.50	25.00
MGV-2073 [M]	I Got Rhythm	1957	12.50	25.00	50.00
V-2073 [M]	I Got Rhythm	1961	5.00	10.00	20.00
MGV-8272 [M]	The Impeccable Mr. Teddy Wilson	1958	12.50	25.00	50.00
V-8272 [M]	The Impeccable Mr. Teddy Wilson	1961	5.00	10.00	20.00
MGV-8299 [M]	These Tunes Remind Me of You	1959	12.50	25.00	50.00
V-8299 [M]	These Tunes Remind Me of You	1961	5.00	10.00	20.00
MGV-8330 [M]	The Touch of Teddy Wilson	1959	12.50	25.00	50.00
V-8330 [M]	The Touch of Teddy Wilson	1961	5.00	10.00	20.00

WILSON, TEDDY/GERRY MULLIGAN

VERVE

| MGV-8235 [M] | The Teddy Wilson Trio and the Gerry Mulligan Quartet at Newport | 1958 | 12.50 | 25.00 | 50.00 |

Number	Title (A Side/B Side)	Yr	VG	VG+	NM
❑ V-8235 [M]	The Teddy Wilson Trio and the Gerry Mulligan Quartet at Newport	1961	5.00	10.00	20.00

WILSON PHILLIPS
SBK
❑ 1P-(# unk)	Shadows and Light	1992	6.25	12.50	25.00

—Only U.S. vinyl release was through Columbia House

❑ K1-93745	Wilson Phillips	1990	3.00	6.00	12.00

WINCHESTER, JESSE
AMPEX
❑ A 10104	Jesse Winchester	1970	5.00	10.00	20.00

BEARSVILLE
❑ PRO 560 [DJ]	The Jesse Winchester Radio Show	1976	10.00	20.00	40.00
❑ PRO-A-693 [(2)DJ]	Live at the Bijou Café Plus a Live Interview at Media College in Montreal	1977	10.00	20.00	40.00
❑ BR 2045	Jesse Winchester	1971	3.75	7.50	15.00

—Reissue of Ampex LP

❑ BR 2102	Third Down, 110 to Go	1972	3.75	7.50	15.00
❑ BR 6953	Learn to Love It	1974	3.00	6.00	12.00
❑ BR 6964	Let the Rough Side Drag	1976	3.00	6.00	12.00
❑ BR 6968	Nothing But a Breeze	1977	2.50	5.00	10.00
❑ BRK 6984	A Touch on the Rainy Side	1978	2.50	5.00	10.00
❑ BRK 6989	Talk Memphis	1981	2.50	5.00	10.00

RHINO
❑ R1-70085	The Best of Jesse Winchester	1989	2.50	5.00	10.00
❑ RNLP-70885	Jesse Winchester	1988	2.50	5.00	10.00
❑ RNLP-70886	Third Down, 110 to Go	1988	2.50	5.00	10.00

SUGAR HILL
❑ SH-1023	Humour Me	1988	3.00	6.00	12.00

WINCHESTER, LEM
ARGO
❑ LP-642 [M]	Lem Winchester with the Ramsey Lewis Trio	1959	12.50	25.00	50.00
❑ LPS-642 [S]	Lem Winchester with the Ramsey Lewis Trio	1959	10.00	20.00	40.00

MGM
❑ E-1005 [M]	New Faces at Newport	1960	10.00	20.00	40.00

MOODSVILLE
❑ MVLP-11 [M]	Lem Winchester with Feeling	1960	12.50	25.00	50.00

—Green label

❑ MVLP-11 [M]	Lem Winchester with Feeling	1965	6.25	12.50	25.00

—Blue label, trident logo at right

NEW JAZZ
❑ NJLP-8223 [M]	Winchester Special	1959	20.00	40.00	80.00

—Purple label

❑ NJLP-8223 [M]	Winchester Special	1965	6.25	12.50	25.00

—Blue label, trident logo at right

❑ NJLP-8239 [M]	Lem's Beat	1960	12.50	25.00	50.00

—Purple label

❑ NJLP-8239 [M]	Lem's Beat	1965	6.25	12.50	25.00

—Blue label, trident logo at right

❑ NJLP-8244 [M]	Another Opus	1960	12.50	25.00	50.00

—Purple label

❑ NJLP-8244 [M]	Another Opus	1965	6.25	12.50	25.00

—Blue label, trident logo at right

WIND
TONY ORLANDO was in this group.
LIFE
❑ LLPS-2000	Make Believe	1969	5.00	10.00	20.00

WIND HARP, THE
UNITED ARTISTS
❑ UAS-9963 [(2)]	Song from the Hill	1972	5.00	10.00	20.00

WIND IN THE WILLOWS, THE
With Debbie Harry, later of BLONDIE.
CAPITOL
❑ SKAO 2956	The Wind in the Willows	1968	12.50	25.00	50.00

WINDHURST, JOHNNY
TRANSITION
❑ TRLP-2 [M]	Jazz at Columbus Ave.	1956	50.00	100.00	200.00

—Deduct 1/4 if booklet is missing

WINDING, KAI
COLUMBIA
❑ CL 936 [M]	Trombone Sound	1956	12.50	25.00	50.00
❑ CL 999 [M]	Trombone Panorama	1957	12.50	25.00	50.00
❑ CL 1264 [M]	Swingin' State	1958	12.50	25.00	50.00
❑ CL 1329 [M]	Dance to the City Beat	1959	10.00	20.00	40.00
❑ CS 8062 [S]	Swingin' State	1958	10.00	20.00	40.00
❑ CS 8136 [S]	Dance to the City Beat	1959	7.50	15.00	30.00

IMPULSE!
❑ A 3 [M]	The Incredible Kai Winding Trombones	1960	7.50	15.00	30.00
❑ AS 3 [S]	The Incredible Kai Winding Trombones	1960	6.25	12.50	25.00

—Orange and black label

ROOST
❑ LP 408 [10]	Kai Winding All Stars	1952	30.00	60.00	120.00

SAVOY
❑ MG-9017 [10]	New Trends Of Jazz	1952	30.00	60.00	120.00

VERVE
❑ V-8427 [M]	Kai Ole	1962	6.25	12.50	25.00
❑ V6-8427 [S]	Kai Ole	1962	6.25	12.50	25.00
❑ V-8493 [M]	Suspense Themes in Jazz	1962	6.25	12.50	25.00
❑ V6-8493 [S]	Suspense Themes in Jazz	1962	6.25	12.50	25.00
❑ V-8525 [M]	Kai Winding Solo	1963	6.25	12.50	25.00
❑ V6-8525 [S]	Kai Winding Solo	1963	6.25	12.50	25.00
❑ V-8551 [M]	More!!!	1963	6.25	12.50	25.00
❑ V6-8551 [S]	More!!!	1963	6.25	12.50	25.00
❑ V-8556 [M]	The Lonely One	1963	6.25	12.50	25.00

Number	Title (A Side/B Side)	Yr	VG	VG+	NM
❑ V6-8556 [S]	The Lonely One	1963	6.25	12.50	25.00
❑ V-8573 [M]	Mondo Cane #2	1964	6.25	12.50	25.00
❑ V6-8573 [S]	Mondo Cane #2	1964	7.50	15.00	30.00
❑ V6-8602 [S]	Modern Country	1964	5.00	10.00	20.00
❑ V6-8620 [S]	Rainy Day	1965	5.00	10.00	20.00
❑ V6-8639 [S]	The "In" Instrumentals	1965	5.00	10.00	20.00

WINDOWS
(LABEL UNKNOWN)
❑ (# unknown)	Windows	1985	5.00	10.00	20.00

WINGS
See PAUL McCARTNEY.

WINNERS, THE
CROWN
❑ CST-394 [S]	Checkered Flag	1963	7.50	15.00	30.00
❑ CLP-5394 [M]	Checkered Flag	1963	6.25	12.50	25.00

WINSTONS, THE
METROMEDIA
❑ MD-1010	Color Him Father	1969	12.50	25.00	50.00

WINTER, EDGAR
BLUE SKY
❑ PZ 33483	Jasmine Nightdreams	1975	3.00	6.00	12.00
❑ PZQ 33483 [Q]	Jasmine Nightdreams	1975	5.00	10.00	20.00
❑ PZ 33798	The Edgar Winter Group with Rick Derringer	1975	3.00	6.00	12.00
❑ PZQ 33798 [Q]	The Edgar Winter Group with Rick Derringer	1975	5.00	10.00	20.00
❑ PZ 34858	Re-Cycled	1977	3.00	6.00	12.00
❑ JZ 35989	The Edgar Winter Album	1979	3.00	6.00	12.00
❑ JZ 36494	Standing on Rock	1981	3.00	6.00	12.00

EPIC
❑ BN 26503	Entrance	1970	3.75	7.50	15.00

—Yellow label

❑ BN 26503	Entrance	1973	3.00	6.00	12.00

—Orange label

❑ E 30512	Edgar Winter's White Trash	1971	3.75	7.50	15.00

—Yellow label

❑ KE 30512	Edgar Winter's White Trash	1973	3.00	6.00	12.00

—Orange label

❑ PE 30512	Edger Winter's White Trash	1985	2.00	4.00	8.00

—Budget-line reissue; dark blue label

❑ EG 31249 [(2)]	Roadwork	1987	2.50	5.00	10.00

—Budget-line reissue; dark blue labels

❑ KEG 31249 [(2)]	Roadwork	1972	5.00	10.00	20.00

—Yellow labels

❑ KEG 31249 [(2)]	Roadwork	1973	3.75	7.50	15.00

—Orange labels

❑ EQ 31584 [Q]	They Only Come Out at Night	1973	6.25	12.50	25.00
❑ KE 31584	They Only Come Out at Night	1972	3.75	7.50	15.00

—Yellow label

❑ KE 31584	They Only Come Out at Night	1973	3.00	6.00	12.00

—Orange label

❑ PE 31584	They Only Come Out at Night	197?	2.50	5.00	10.00

—Reissue with new prefix; orange label

❑ PE 31584	They Only Come Out at Night	1979	2.00	4.00	8.00

—Budget-line reissue; dark blue label

❑ PE 32461	Shock Treatment	1974	3.75	7.50	15.00

—Orange label

❑ PE 32461	Shock Treatment	1985	2.00	4.00	8.00

—Budget-line reissue; dark blue label

❑ PEQ 32461 [Q]	Shock Treatment	1974	6.25	12.50	25.00
❑ BG 33770 [(2)]	Entrance/White Trash	1975	3.75	7.50	15.00

—Combines 26503 and 30512 into one package

RHINO
❑ R1-70709	Mission Earth	1989	3.00	6.00	12.00
❑ R1-70895	The Edger Winter Collection	1989	2.50	5.00	10.00

WINTER, JOHNNY
ACCORD
❑ SN-7135	Ready for Winter	1981	2.50	5.00	10.00

ALLIGATOR
❑ 4735	Guitar Slinger	1984	2.50	5.00	10.00
❑ 4742	Serious Business	1985	2.50	5.00	10.00
❑ 4748	Third Degree	1986	2.50	5.00	10.00

BLUE SKY
❑ PZ 33292	John Dawson Winter III	1974	3.00	6.00	12.00
❑ PZQ 33292 [Q]	John Dawson Winter III	1974	5.00	10.00	20.00
❑ PZ 33944	Captured Live!	1976	3.00	6.00	12.00

—No bar code on cover

❑ PZ 33944	Captured Live	198?	2.00	4.00	8.00

—Budget-line reissue with bar code on cover

❑ PZ 34813	Nothin' But the Blues	1977	3.00	6.00	12.00

—No bar code on cover

❑ PZ 34813	Nothin' But the Blues	198?	2.00	4.00	8.00

—Budget-line reissue with bar code on cover

❑ JZ 35475	White, Hot and Blue	1978	3.00	6.00	12.00
❑ JZ 36343	Raisin' Cain	1980	3.00	6.00	12.00

BUDDAH
❑ BDS-7513	First Winter	1969	5.00	10.00	20.00

COLUMBIA
❑ CS 9826	Johnny Winter	1969	5.00	10.00	20.00

—"360 Sound" label

❑ CS 9826	Johnny Winter	1970	3.00	6.00	12.00

—Orange label

❑ PC 9826	Johnny Winter	198?	2.00	4.00	8.00

—Budget-line reissue

❑ KCS 9947 [(2)]	Second Winter	1969	6.25	12.50	25.00

—"360 Sound" labels; record 2 has music on only one side (other side is blank)

❑ KCS 9947 [(2)]	Second Winter	1970	3.75	7.50	15.00

—Orange labels

Number	Title (A Side/B Side)	Yr	VG	VG+	NM
❏ PC 9947 [(2)]	Second Winter	198?	2.50	5.00	10.00
—Budget-line reissue					
❏ C 30221	Johnny Winter And	1970	3.00	6.00	12.00
—Orange labels					
❏ C 30221	Johnny Winter And	1970	5.00	10.00	20.00
—"360 Sound" label					
❏ PC 30221	Johnny Winter And	198?	2.00	4.00	8.00
—Budget-line reissue					
❏ C 30475	Live/Johnny Winter And	1971	3.75	7.50	15.00
❏ PC 30475	Live/Johnny Winter And	198?	2.00	4.00	8.00
—Budget-line reissue					
❏ CQ 32188 [Q]	Still Alive and Well	1973	6.25	12.50	25.00
❏ KC 32188	Still Alive and Well	1973	3.75	7.50	15.00
❏ PC 32188	Still Alive and Well	198?	2.00	4.00	8.00
—Budget-line reissue					
❏ CQ 32715 [Q]	Saints and Sinners	1974	6.25	12.50	25.00
❏ KC 32715	Saints and Sinners	1974	3.75	7.50	15.00
❏ PC 32715	Saints and Sinners	197?	2.00	4.00	8.00
—Budget-line reissue					
❏ CG 33651 [(2)]	Johnny Winter And//Live/Johnny Winter And	1975	3.75	7.50	15.00
GRT					
❏ 10010	The Johnny Winter Story	1969	5.00	10.00	20.00
IMPERIAL					
❏ LP-12431	The Progressive Blues Experiment	1969	12.50	25.00	50.00
JANUS					
❏ 3008	About Blues	1970	5.00	10.00	20.00
❏ 3023	Early Times	1970	6.25	12.50	25.00
❏ 3056 [(2)]	Before the Storm	197?	5.00	10.00	20.00
LIBERTY					
❏ LN-10294	The Progressive Blues Experiment	1986	2.50	5.00	10.00
—Reissue of Imperial LP					
MCA/VOYAGER					
❏ 42241	The Winter of '88	1988	2.50	5.00	10.00
SONOBEAT					
❏ RS-1002	The Progressive Blues Experiment	1968	75.00	150.00	300.00
—Released in plain white cardboard jacket					
UNITED ARTISTS					
❏ UA-LA139-F	Austin, Tex.	1974	3.75	7.50	15.00

WINTER, JOHNNY AND EDGAR
Also see each artist's individual listings.

BLUE SKY

❏ ASZ 242 [DJ]	Johnny and Edgar Winter Discuss Together	1976	6.25	12.50	25.00
—Promo-only interview album					
❏ PZ 34033	Together	1976	3.00	6.00	12.00

WINTER, PAUL
COLUMBIA

❏ CS 8725 [S]	Jazz Meets the Bossa Nova	1962	5.00	10.00	20.00
❏ CS 8797 [S]	Jazz Premiere: Washington	1963	5.00	10.00	20.00
❏ CS 8864 [S]	New Jazz on Campus	1963	5.00	10.00	20.00
❏ CS 8955 [S]	Jazz Meets the Folk Song	1964	5.00	10.00	20.00
❏ CS 9072 [S]	The Sound of Ipanema	1965	5.00	10.00	20.00
❏ CS 9115 [S]	Rio	1965	5.00	10.00	20.00
LIVING MUSIC					
❏ LMR-1 [(2)]	Callings	1981	5.00	10.00	20.00
—With 20-page booklet					
❏ LMR-2 [(2)]	Missa Gaia/Earth Mass	1983	5.00	10.00	20.00

WINTERHALTER, HUGO
KAPP

❏ KL-1426 [M]	Semi-Classical Favorites	196?	3.00	6.00	12.00
❏ KS-3426 [S]	Semi-Classical Favorites	196?	3.75	7.50	15.00
RCA CAMDEN					
❏ CAL-449 [M]	Christmas Magic	1958	3.75	7.50	15.00
—Reissue of RCA Victor 3132 with two extra tracks					
RCA VICTOR					
❏ LPM-1020 [M]	Great Music Themes of TV	1954	6.25	12.50	25.00
❏ LPM-1179 [M]	Always	1955	5.00	10.00	20.00
❏ LPM-1185 [M]	Music by Starlight	1955	5.00	10.00	20.00
❏ LPM-1338 [M]	The Eyes of Love	1956	5.00	10.00	20.00
❏ LPM-1400 [M]	Happy Hunting	1956	5.00	10.00	20.00
❏ LPM-1677 [M]	Hugo Winterhalter Goes… Latin	1957	5.00	10.00	20.00
❏ LSP-1677 [S]	Hugo Winterhalter Goes… Latin	1958	6.25	12.50	25.00
❏ LPM-1904 [M]	Wish You Were Here	1958	5.00	10.00	20.00
❏ LSP-1904 [S]	Wish You Were Here	1958	6.25	12.50	25.00
❏ LPM-1905 [M]	Two Sides of Hugo Winterhalter	1958	5.00	10.00	20.00
❏ LSP-1905 [S]	Two Sides of Hugo Winterhalter	1958	6.25	12.50	25.00
❏ LPM-2167 [M]	Hugo Winterhalter Goes…Gypsy	1960	3.75	7.50	15.00
❏ LSP-2167 [S]	Hugo Winterhalter Goes…Gypsy	1960	5.00	10.00	20.00
❏ LPM-2271 [M]	Hugo Winterhalter Goes…South of the Border	1960	3.75	7.50	15.00
❏ LSP-2271 [S]	Hugo Winterhalter Goes…South of the Border	1960	5.00	10.00	20.00
❏ LPM-2417 [M]	Hugo Winterhalter Goes…Hawaiian	1961	3.75	7.50	15.00
❏ LSP-2417 [S]	Hugo Winterhalter Goes…Hawaiian	1961	5.00	10.00	20.00
❏ LPM-2482 [M]	Hugo Winterhalter Goes…Continental	1961	3.75	7.50	15.00
❏ LSP-2482 [S]	Hugo Winterhalter Goes…Continental	1961	5.00	10.00	20.00
❏ LPM-3100 [10]	Winterhalter Magic	195?	7.50	15.00	30.00
❏ LPM-3101 [10]	Song Hits from "Peter Pan" and "Hans Christian Andersen"	195?	7.50	15.00	30.00
❏ LPM-3132 [10]	Christmas Magic	1954	7.50	15.00	30.00

WINTERS, JERRI
BETHLEHEM

❏ BCP-76 [M]	Somebody Loves Me	1957	12.50	25.00	50.00
FRATERNITY					
❏ F-1001 [M]	Winter's Here	1955	15.00	30.00	60.00

WINTERS, JONATHAN
COLUMBIA

❏ CL 2811 [M]	Jonathan Winters Wings It!	1968	6.25	12.50	25.00
❏ CS 9611 [S]	Jonathan Winters Wings It!	1968	3.75	7.50	15.00

Number	Title (A Side/B Side)	Yr	VG	VG+	NM
❏ CS 9799	Stuff 'N' Nonsense	1969	3.75	7.50	15.00
❏ KG 31985 [(2)]	Jonathan Winters Laughs Live	1972	5.00	10.00	20.00
—Reissue of 9611 and 9799 in one package					
❏ PG 31985 [(2)]	Jonathan Winters Laughs Live	197?	3.00	6.00	12.00
—Reissue with new prefix					
VERVE					
❏ MGVS-6099 [S]	The Wonderful World of Jonathan Winters	1960	6.25	12.50	25.00
❏ MGVS-6155 [S]	Down to Earth	1960	6.25	12.50	25.00
❏ MGV-15009 [M]	The Wonderful World of Jonathan Winters	1960	6.25	12.50	25.00
❏ V-15009 [M]	The Wonderful World of Jonathan Winters	1961	5.00	10.00	20.00
❏ V6-15009 [S]	The Wonderful World of Jonathan Winters	1961	5.00	10.00	20.00
—Reissue of 6099					
❏ MGV-15011 [M]	Down to Earth	1960	6.25	12.50	25.00
❏ V-15011 [M]	Down to Earth	1961	5.00	10.00	20.00
❏ V6-15011 [S]	Down to Earth	1961	5.00	10.00	20.00
—Reissue of 6155					
❏ V-15025 [M]	Here's Jonathan	1961	6.25	12.50	25.00
❏ V6-15025 [S]	Here's Jonathan	1961	6.25	12.50	25.00
❏ V-15032 [M]	Another Day, Another World	1962	6.25	12.50	25.00
❏ V6-15032 [R]	Another Day, Another World	196?	3.00	6.00	12.00
❏ V-15035 [M]	Humor As Seen Through the Eyes of Jonathan Winters	1963	6.25	12.50	25.00
❏ V6-15035 [S]	Humor As Seen Through the Eyes of Jonathan Winters	1963	6.25	12.50	25.00
❏ V-15037 [M]	Whistle Stopping with Jonathan Winters	1964	5.00	10.00	20.00
❏ V6-15037 [R]	Whistle Stopping with Jonathan Winters	196?	3.00	6.00	12.00
❏ V-15041 [M]	Jonathan Winters' Mad, Mad, Mad, Mad World	1964	5.00	10.00	20.00
❏ V6-15041 [R]	Jonathan Winters' Mad, Mad, Mad, Mad World	196?	3.00	6.00	12.00
❏ V-15047 [M]	Great Moments in Comedy	1965	5.00	10.00	20.00
❏ V6-15047 [R]	Great Moments in Comedy	196?	3.00	6.00	12.00
❏ V-15052 [M]	The Best of Frickert and Suggins	1966	5.00	10.00	20.00
❏ V6-15052 [R]	The Best of Frickert and Suggins	196?	3.00	6.00	12.00
❏ V-15057 [M]	Movies Are Better Than Ever	1967	5.00	10.00	20.00
❏ V6-15057 [R]	Movies Are Better Than Ever	196?	3.00	6.00	12.00

WINTERS, PINKY
ARGO

❏ LP-604 [M]	Lonely One	1956	10.00	20.00	40.00
CREATIVE					
❏ LP-604 [M]	Lonely One	1956	15.00	30.00	60.00

WINTERS, SMILEY
ARHOOLIE

❏ 8004/5 [(2)]	Smiley Etc.	1969	5.00	10.00	20.00

WINWOOD, STEVE
Also see BLIND FAITH; THE SPENCER DAVIS GROUP; TRAFFIC.

ISLAND

❏ ILPS 9387	Go	1976	3.00	6.00	12.00
—With Stomo Yamahita and Michael Shrieve					
❏ ILPS 9494	Steve Winwood	1977	2.50	5.00	10.00
❏ ILPS 9576	Arc of a Diver	1981	2.50	5.00	10.00
❏ ILPS 9777	Talking Back to the Night	1982	2.50	5.00	10.00
❏ 25448	Back in the High Life	1986	2.00	4.00	8.00
❏ 25660	Chronicles	1987	2.00	4.00	8.00
UNITED ARTISTS					
❏ UAS-9950 [(2)]	Winwood	1971	3.75	7.50	15.00
—Without booklet					
❏ UAS-9950 [(2)]	Winwood	1971	6.25	12.50	25.00
—Collection of tracks Winwood recorded with the Spencer Davis Group, Traffic and Blind Faith; with booklet					
VIRGIN					
❏ 90946	Roll With It	1988	2.00	4.00	8.00
❏ 91405	Refugees of the Heart	1990	3.75	7.50	15.00

WIPERS, THE
PARK AVE.

❏ (# unknown)	Is This Real?	1980	12.50	25.00	50.00
❏ 82802	Youth of America	1981	12.50	25.00	50.00
RESTLESS					
❏ 72026	Wipers Live	1985	3.00	6.00	12.00
❏ 72094	Land of the Lost	1986	3.00	6.00	12.00
❏ 72187	Over the Edge	1987	3.00	6.00	12.00
—Reissue					
❏ 72194	Follow Blind	1987	3.00	6.00	12.00
TIM/KERR					
❏ 31	Silver Sail	1993	3.00	6.00	12.00

WISE, CHUBBY
STARDAY

❏ SLP-154 [M]	The Tennessee Fiddler	1961	12.50	25.00	50.00

WISE, CHUBBY, AND MAC WISEMAN
GILLEY'S

❏ 500	Give Me My Smokies and The Tennessee Waltz	197?	5.00	10.00	20.00

WISEMAN, MAC
ABC

❏ 4009	16 Great Performances	1974	3.00	6.00	12.00
❏ AC-30033	The ABC Collection	1976	3.00	6.00	12.00
CAPITOL					
❏ ST 1800 [S]	Bluegrass Favorites	1962	10.00	20.00	40.00
❏ T 1800 [M]	Bluegrass Favorites	1962	7.50	15.00	30.00
CMH					
❏ 4502	Greatest Bluegrass Hits	198?	2.50	5.00	10.00
❏ 6202	Country Memories	197?	3.00	6.00	12.00
❏ 6217	Mac Wiseman Sings Gordon Lightfoot	197?	3.00	6.00	12.00
❏ 9001 [(2)]	The Mac Wiseman Story	197?	3.75	7.50	15.00
❏ 9021 [(2)]	Songs That Made the Juke Box Play	197?	3.75	7.50	15.00

Number	Title (A Side/B Side)	Yr	VG	VG+	NM
DOT					
❑ DLP-3084 [M]	Tis Sweet to Be Remembered	1958	12.50	25.00	50.00
❑ DLP-3135 [M]	Beside the Still Waters	1959	7.50	15.00	30.00
❑ DLP-3213 [M]	Great Folk Ballads	1959	7.50	15.00	30.00
❑ DLP-3313 [M]	12 Great Hits	1960	7.50	15.00	30.00
❑ DLP-3336 [M]	Keep on the Sunny Side	1960	10.00	20.00	40.00
❑ DLP-3373 [M]	Best Loved Gospel Hymns	1961	7.50	15.00	30.00
❑ DLP-3408 [M]	Fireball Mail	1961	10.00	20.00	40.00
❑ DLP-3697 [M]	This Is Mac Wiseman	1966	5.00	10.00	20.00
❑ DLP-3730 [M]	A Master at Work	1966	5.00	10.00	20.00
❑ DLP-3731 [M]	Bluegrass	1966	5.00	10.00	20.00
❑ DLP-25084 [R]	Tis Sweet to Be Remembered	196?	5.00	10.00	20.00
❑ DLP-25135 [S]	Beside the Still Waters	1959	10.00	20.00	40.00
❑ DLP-25213 [S]	Great Folk Ballads	1959	10.00	20.00	40.00
❑ DLP-25313 [S]	12 Great Hits	1960	10.00	20.00	40.00
❑ DLP-25336 [R]	Keep on the Sunny Side	196?	5.00	10.00	20.00
❑ DLP-25373 [S]	Best Loved Gospel Hymns	1961	10.00	20.00	40.00
❑ DLP-25408 [R]	Fireball Mail	196?	5.00	10.00	20.00
❑ DLP-25697 [S]	This Is Mac Wiseman	1966	6.25	12.50	25.00
❑ DLP-25730 [S]	A Master at Work	1966	6.25	12.50	25.00
❑ DLP-25731 [S]	Bluegrass	1966	6.25	12.50	25.00
❑ DLP-25896	Golden Hits of Mac Wiseman	1968	5.00	10.00	20.00
HAMILTON					
❑ HLP-12130 [M]	Sincerely	1964	5.00	10.00	20.00
❑ HLP-12167 [M]	Songs of the Dear Old Days	1965	5.00	10.00	20.00
HILLTOP					
❑ JM-6047 [M]	Mac Wiseman	1967	3.75	7.50	15.00
❑ JS-6047 [R]	Mac Wiseman	1967	3.00	6.00	12.00
MCA					
❑ 4009	16 Great Performances	198?	2.00	4.00	8.00
—*Reissue of ABC 4009*					
RCA VICTOR					
❑ ANL1-1208	Concert Favorites	1975	2.50	5.00	10.00
—*Reissue of 4845*					
❑ LSP-4336	Johnny's Cash and Charley's Pride	1970	3.75	7.50	15.00
❑ LSP-4845	Concert Favorites	1972	3.75	7.50	15.00
VETCO					
❑ 508	New Traditions, Vol. 1	197?	3.75	7.50	15.00
❑ 509	New Traditions, Vol. 2	197?	3.75	7.50	15.00
WISNER, JIMMY					
CHANCELLOR					
❑ CHJ-5014 [M]	Aper-Sepshun	1960	6.25	12.50	25.00
❑ CHJS-5014 [S]	Aper-Sepshun	1960	7.50	15.00	30.00
FELSTED					
❑ FL-2509 [S]	Blues for Harvey	1962	6.25	12.50	25.00
❑ FL-7509 [M]	Blues for Harvey	1962	7.50	15.00	30.00
WITHERS, BILL					
COLUMBIA					
❑ PC 33704	Making Music	1975	2.50	5.00	10.00
❑ PC 34327	Naked and Warm	1976	2.50	5.00	10.00
❑ JC 34903	Menagerie	1977	2.50	5.00	10.00
❑ JC 35596	'Bout Love	1979	2.50	5.00	10.00
❑ JC 36877	The Best of Bill Withers	1981	—	—	—
—*Canceled?*					
❑ FC 37199	Bill Withers' Greatest Hits	1981	2.50	5.00	10.00
—*Re-release of 36877 with "Just the Two of Us" added*					
❑ FC 39887	Watching You Watching Me	1985	2.50	5.00	10.00
❑ PC 40177	Still Bill	1985	2.00	4.00	8.00
—*Reissue of Sussex 7014*					
❑ PC 40178	Just As I Am	1985	2.00	4.00	8.00
—*Reissue of Sussex 7006*					
SUSSEX					
❑ SXBS-7006	Just As I Am	1971	5.00	10.00	20.00
❑ SXBS-7014	Still Bill	1972	5.00	10.00	20.00
❑ SXBS-7025-2 [(2)]	Bill Withers Live at Carnegie Hall	1973	5.00	10.00	20.00
❑ SUX-8032	+'Justments	1974	3.75	7.50	15.00
❑ SUX-8037	The Best of Bill Withers	1975	3.75	7.50	15.00
WITHERSPOON, JIMMY					
ABC					
❑ 717	Handbags and Gladrags	1970	6.25	12.50	25.00
ANALOGUE PRODUCTIONS					
❑ APR 3008	Evenin' Blues	199?	3.75	7.50	15.00
BLUE NOTE					
❑ BN-LA534-G	Spoonful	1976	3.00	6.00	12.00
BLUESWAY					
❑ BLS-6026	Blues Singer	1969	6.25	12.50	25.00
❑ BLS-6040	Hunh	1970	6.25	12.50	25.00
❑ BLS-6051	The Best of Jimmy Witherspoon	1970	6.25	12.50	25.00
CAPITOL					
❑ ST-11360	Love Is a Five Letter Word	1975	3.00	6.00	12.00
CHESS					
❑ CH-93003	Spoon So Easy: The Chess Years	1990	3.00	6.00	12.00
CONSTELLATION					
❑ CM 1422 [M]	Take This Hammer	1964	12.50	25.00	50.00
❑ CMS 1422 [R]	Take This Hammer	1964	7.50	15.00	30.00
CROWN					
❑ CST-215 [S]	Jimmy Witherspoon Sings the Blues	1961	25.00	50.00	100.00
—*Black vinyl; this value assumes that this is in true stereo, as the red vinyl version is, but this has not been confirmed*					
❑ CST-215 [S]	Jimmy Witherspoon Sings the Blues	1961	37.50	75.00	150.00
—*Red vinyl; contrary to prior reports, this album -- at least the red vinyl version -- is in true stereo!*					
❑ CLP-5156 [M]	Jimmy Witherspoon	1959	20.00	40.00	80.00
—*Black label, silver print*					
❑ CLP-5156 [M]	Jimmy Witherspoon	1961	6.25	12.50	25.00
—*Gray label, black print*					

Number	Title (A Side/B Side)	Yr	VG	VG+	NM
❑ CLP-5192 [M]	Jimmy Witherspoon Sings the Blues	1959	20.00	40.00	80.00
—*Black label, silver print*					
❑ CLP-5192 [M]	Jimmy Witherspoon Sings the Blues	1961	6.25	12.50	25.00
—*Gray label, black print*					
FANTASY					
❑ OBC-511	Evenin' Blues	1988	3.00	6.00	12.00
—*Reissue of Prestige 7300*					
❑ OBC-527	Baby, Baby, Baby	1990	3.00	6.00	12.00
—*Reissue of Prestige 7290*					
❑ 9660	Rockin' L.A.	1989	3.00	6.00	12.00
❑ 24701 [(2)]	The 'Spoon Concerts	1972	5.00	10.00	20.00
HIFI					
❑ R-421 [M]	At the Monterey Jazz Festival	1959	25.00	50.00	100.00
❑ SR-421 [S]	At the Monterey Jazz Festival	1959	15.00	30.00	60.00
❑ R-422 [M]	Feelin' the Spirit	1959	25.00	50.00	100.00
❑ SR-422 [S]	Feelin' the Spirit	1959	15.00	30.00	60.00
❑ R-426 [M]	Jimmy Witherspoon at the Renaissance	1959	25.00	50.00	100.00
❑ SR-426 [S]	Jimmy Witherspoon at the Renaissance	1959	15.00	30.00	60.00
JAZZ MAN					
❑ 5013	Jimmy Witherspoon Sings the Blues	1980	3.00	6.00	12.00
LAX					
❑ PW 37115	Love Is a Five Letter Word	1981	2.50	5.00	10.00
—*Reissue of Capitol LP*					
MUSE					
❑ MR-5288	Jimmy Witherspoon Sings the Blues	1983	2.50	5.00	10.00
❑ MR-5327	Midnight Lady Called the Blues	1986	2.50	5.00	10.00
PRESTIGE					
❑ PRLP-7290 [M]	Baby, Baby, Baby	1963	10.00	20.00	40.00
❑ PRST-7290 [S]	Baby, Baby, Baby	1963	10.00	20.00	40.00
❑ PRLP-7300 [M]	Evenin' Blues	1964	10.00	20.00	40.00
❑ PRST-7300 [S]	Evenin' Blues	1964	10.00	20.00	40.00
❑ PRLP-7314 [M]	Blues Around the Clock	1964	10.00	20.00	40.00
❑ PRST-7314 [S]	Blues Around the Clock	1964	10.00	20.00	40.00
❑ PRLP-7327 [M]	Blue Spoon	1964	10.00	20.00	40.00
❑ PRST-7327 [S]	Blue Spoon	1964	10.00	20.00	40.00
❑ PRLP-7356 [M]	Some of My Best Friends Are the Blues	1965	6.25	12.50	25.00
❑ PRST-7356 [S]	Some of My Best Friends Are the Blues	1965	6.25	12.50	25.00
❑ PRLP-7418 [M]	Spoon in London	1966	6.25	12.50	25.00
❑ PRST-7418 [S]	Spoon in London	1966	6.25	12.50	25.00
❑ PRLP-7475 [M]	Blues for Easy Livers	1967	6.25	12.50	25.00
❑ PRST-7475 [S]	Blues for Easy Livers	1967	5.00	10.00	20.00
❑ PRST-7713	The Best of Jimmy Witherspoon	1969	5.00	10.00	20.00
❑ 7855	Mean Old Frisco	1974	3.75	7.50	15.00
RCA VICTOR					
❑ ANL1-1048	Goin' to Kansas City Blues	1976	2.50	5.00	10.00
—*Reissue*					
❑ LPM-1639 [M]	Goin' to Kansas City Blues	1957	25.00	50.00	100.00
REPRISE					
❑ R-2008 [M]	Spoon	1961	10.00	20.00	40.00
❑ R9-2008 [S]	Spoon	1961	15.00	30.00	60.00
❑ R-6012 [M]	Hey, Mrs. Jones	1961	10.00	20.00	40.00
❑ R9-6012 [S]	Hey, Mrs. Jones	1961	15.00	30.00	60.00
❑ R-6059 [M]	Roots	1962	10.00	20.00	40.00
❑ R9-6059 [S]	Roots	1962	15.00	30.00	60.00
UNITED					
❑ 7715	A Spoonful of Blues	197?	3.00	6.00	12.00
VERVE					
❑ V-5007 [M]	Blue Point of View	1966	5.00	10.00	20.00
❑ V6-5007 [S]	Blue Point of View	1966	6.25	12.50	25.00
❑ V-5030 [M]	Blues Is Now	1967	6.25	12.50	25.00
❑ V6-5030 [S]	Blues Is Now	1967	5.00	10.00	20.00
❑ V-5050 [M]	A Spoonful of Soul	1968	7.50	15.00	30.00
❑ V6-5050 [S]	A Spoonful of Soul	1968	5.00	10.00	20.00
WORLD PACIFIC					
❑ WP-1267 [M]	Singin' the Blues	1959	25.00	50.00	100.00
❑ WP-1402 [M]	There's Good Rockin' Tonight	1961	15.00	30.00	60.00
—*Reissue of 1267*					
WITHERSPOON, JIMMY, AND RICHARD "GROOVE" HOLMES					
OLYMPIC GOLD MEDAL					
❑ 7107	Groovin' and Spoonin'	1974	3.00	6.00	12.00
SURREY					
❑ S-1106 [M]	Blues for Spoon and Groove	1965	6.25	12.50	25.00
❑ SS-1106 [S]	Blues for Spoon and Groove	1965	7.50	15.00	30.00
WITHERSPOON, JIMMY, AND GERRY MULLIGAN					
ARCHIVE OF FOLK AND JAZZ					
❑ 264	Jimmy Witherspoon and Gerry Mulligan	197?	3.00	6.00	12.00
WITHERSPOON, JIMMY, AND BEN WEBSTER					
VERVE					
❑ V6-8835	Previously Unreleased Recordings	197?	3.75	7.50	15.00
WITTWER, JOHNNY					
STINSON					
❑ SLP-58	Piano Rags	195?	5.00	10.00	20.00
WIZARD					
PEON					
❑ 1069	Original Wizard	1971	50.00	100.00	200.00
WIZARDS FROM KANSAS, THE					
MERCURY					
❑ SR 61309	The Wizards from Kansas	1970	37.50	75.00	150.00
WOFFORD, MIKE					
EPIC					
❑ LN 24225 [M]	Strawberry Wine	1967	5.00	10.00	20.00
MILESTONE					
❑ MPS-9012	Summer Night	1968	5.00	10.00	20.00

Bob Weir of the Grateful Dead released his first solo album, *Ace,* in 1972.

Two Lovers and Other Hits, which focused on the hit title song, was Mary Wells' third Motown album. In its original pressing, with no address on the Motown record label, it's scarce.

I Saw the Light was a collection of some of Hank Williams' more serious songs, compiled as both a 10-inch and 12-inch LP after his death.

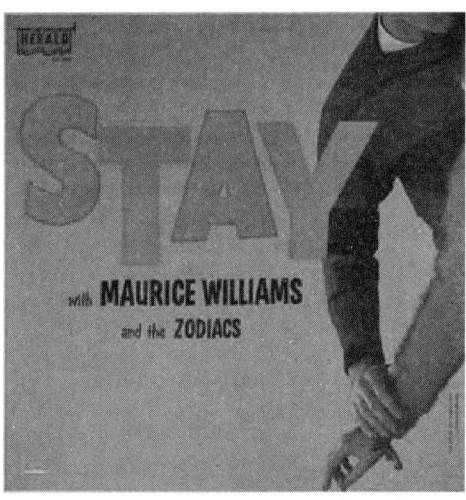

Maurice Williams and the Zodiacs had a chart-topper with "Stay" in 1960. The album that came out afterwards wasn't around very long.

Most of the Stevie Wonder albums before 1972, though not hard to find, are increasing in interest. One of these is the 1970 release *Signed, Sealed and Delivered.*

The second Frank Zappa/Mothers of Invention album was *Absolutely Free.*

Number	Title (A Side/B Side)	Yr	VG	VG+	NM
WOLFE, NEIL					
IMPERIAL					
❑ LP-12084 [S]	Neil Swings Nicely	1962	5.00	10.00	20.00
❑ LP-12192 [S]	One Order of Blues	1962	5.00	10.00	20.00
WOLFMAN JACK					
BREAD					
❑ 0170	Wolfman Jack and the Wolf Pack	1965	100.00	200.00	400.00
WOODEN NICKEL					
❑ BWS1-0119	Fun and Romance Through the Ages	1974	6.25	12.50	25.00
❑ WNS-1009	Wolfman Jack	1972	7.50	15.00	30.00
WOMACK, BOBBY					
ARISTA					
❑ AB 4222	Roads of Life	1979	2.50	5.00	10.00
BEVERLY GLEN					
❑ 10000	The Poet	1981	2.50	5.00	10.00
❑ 10003	The Poet II	1984	2.50	5.00	10.00
COLUMBIA					
❑ PC 34384	Home Is Where the Heart Is	1977	2.50	5.00	10.00
❑ JC 35083	Pieces	1978	2.50	5.00	10.00
LIBERTY					
❑ LST-7645	The Womack "Live"	1971	3.00	6.00	12.00
❑ LN-10171	Bobby Womack's Greatest Hits	198?	2.00	4.00	8.00
—Budget-line reissue of United Artists 346					
MCA					
❑ 5617	So Many Rivers	1985	2.00	4.00	8.00
MINIT					
❑ 24014	Fly Me to the Moon	1968	7.50	15.00	30.00
❑ 24027	My Prescription	1969	7.50	15.00	30.00
UNITED ARTISTS					
❑ UA-LA043-F	Facts of Life	1973	3.00	6.00	12.00
❑ UA-LA199-G	Lookin' for a Love Again	1974	3.00	6.00	12.00
❑ UA-LA346-G	Bobby Womack's Greatest Hits	1974	3.00	6.00	12.00
❑ UA-LA353-G	I Don't Know What the World Is Coming To	1975	3.00	6.00	12.00
❑ UA-LA544-G	Safety Zone	1975	3.00	6.00	12.00
❑ UA-LA638-G	B.W. Goes C and W	1976	3.00	6.00	12.00
❑ LM-1002	Understanding	1980	2.00	4.00	8.00
—Reissue of 5577					
❑ UAS-5225	Across 110th Street	1972	3.00	6.00	12.00
❑ UAS-5539	Communication	1971	3.00	6.00	12.00
❑ UAS-5577	Understanding	1972	3.00	6.00	12.00
WOMB					
DOT					
❑ DLP-25933	Womb	1969	5.00	10.00	20.00
❑ DLP-25959	Overdub	1969	5.00	10.00	20.00
WONDER, STEVIE					
GORDY					
❑ GS 932	Eivets Rednow	1968	7.50	15.00	30.00
—As "Eivets Rednow"					
JOBETE					
❑ JSA-6253 [DJ]	The Wonder of Stevie	1988	5.00	10.00	20.00
—Publisher's demo with excerpts of 105 (!) Stevie Wonder songs					
MOTOWN					
❑ M5-131V1	Recorded Live/Little Stevie Wonder/The 12 Year Old Genius	1981	3.00	6.00	12.00
—Reissue of Tamla 240					
❑ M5-150V1	With a Song in My Heart	1981	3.00	6.00	12.00
—Reissue of Tamla 250					
❑ M5-166V1	Down to Earth	1981	3.00	6.00	12.00
—Reissue of Tamla 272					
❑ M5-173V1	Tribute to Uncle Ray	1981	3.00	6.00	12.00
—Reissue of Tamla 232					
❑ M5-176V1	Signed, Sealed and Delivered	1981	3.00	6.00	12.00
—Reissue of Tamla 304					
❑ M5-179V1	My Cherie Amour	1981	3.00	6.00	12.00
—Reissue of Tamla 296					
❑ M5-183V1	Up-Tight Everything's Alright	1981	3.00	6.00	12.00
—Reissue of Tamla 268					
❑ M5-219V1	The Jazz Soul of Little Stevie	1981	3.00	6.00	12.00
—Reissue of Tamla 233					
❑ 31453 0238-1 [(2)DJ]	Conversation Peace	1995	6.25	12.50	25.00
—Vinyl is promo only; white cover with custom sticker					
❑ M9-804A3 [(3)]	Looking Back	1977	6.25	12.50	25.00
—Withdrawn after Stevie Wonder objected to its release					
❑ 5255 ML	Someday at Christmas	1982	2.50	5.00	10.00
—Reissue of Tamla 281					
❑ 6108 ML	The Woman in Red	1984	2.50	5.00	10.00
—With sticker at top proclaiming "New Stevie Wonder Album"					
❑ 6108 ML	The Woman in Red	1984	3.00	6.00	12.00
—With no sticker proclaiming "New Stevie Wonder Album"					
❑ 6248 ML	Characters	1987	2.50	5.00	10.00
❑ 6291 ML	Music from the Movie Jungle Fever	1991	5.00	10.00	20.00
TAMLA					
❑ T 232 [M]	Tribute to Uncle Ray	1962	37.50	75.00	150.00
❑ T 233 [M]	The Jazz Soul of Little Stevie	1962	37.50	75.00	150.00
❑ T 240 [M]	Recorded Live/Little Stevie Wonder/The 12 Year Old Genius	1963	30.00	60.00	120.00
—The above three LPs as "Little Stevie Wonder"					
❑ T 248 [M]	Workout Stevie, Workout	1963	250.00	500.00	1000.
—Canceled; test pressings or acetates may exist					
❑ T 250 [M]	With a Song in My Heart	1964	20.00	40.00	80.00
❑ T 255 [M]	Stevie at the Beach	1964	20.00	40.00	80.00
❑ T 268 [M]	Up-Tight Everything's Alright	1966	6.25	12.50	25.00
❑ TS 268 [S]	Up-Tight Everything's Alright	1966	7.50	15.00	30.00
❑ T 272 [M]	Down to Earth	1966	5.00	10.00	20.00
❑ TS 272 [S]	Down to Earth	1966	6.25	12.50	25.00
❑ T 279 [M]	I Was Made to Love Her	1967	5.00	10.00	20.00

Number	Title (A Side/B Side)	Yr	VG	VG+	NM
❑ TS 279 [S]	I Was Made to Love Her	1967	6.25	12.50	25.00
❑ T 281 [M]	Someday at Christmas	1967	7.50	15.00	30.00
❑ TS 281 [S]	Someday at Christmas	1967	10.00	20.00	40.00
❑ T 282 [M]	Greatest Hits	1968	7.50	15.00	30.00
❑ TS 282 [S]	Greatest Hits	1968	5.00	10.00	20.00
❑ TS 291	For Once in My Life	1968	5.00	10.00	20.00
❑ TS 296	My Cherie Amour	1969	5.00	10.00	20.00
❑ TS 298	Stevie Wonder Live	1970	5.00	10.00	20.00
❑ TS 304	Signed Sealed and Delivered	1970	5.00	10.00	20.00
❑ TS 308	Where I'm Coming From	1971	5.00	10.00	20.00
❑ T 313L	Stevie Wonder's Greatest Hits Vol. 2	1971	5.00	10.00	20.00
—Some, if not all, LP covers have the title mis-punctuated as "Stevie Wonders' Greatest Hits Vol. 2"					
❑ T 314L	Music of My Mind	1972	5.00	10.00	20.00
❑ T 319L	Talking Book	1972	3.75	7.50	15.00
—Original pressings have a braille note on cover					
❑ T 319L	Talking Book	1973	2.50	5.00	10.00
—No braille note on cover					
❑ T 326L	Innervisions	1973	3.75	7.50	15.00
❑ T6-332S1	Fulfillingness' First Finale	1974	3.75	7.50	15.00
❑ T13-340C2 [(2)]	Songs in the Key of Life	1976	5.00	10.00	20.00
—With booklet and bonus 7-inch EP (deduct 25% if missing)					
❑ T7-362R1	Someday at Christmas	1978	5.00	10.00	20.00
—Unusual reissue of 281					
❑ T13-371C2 [(2)]	Journey Through the Secret Life of Plants	1979	3.75	7.50	15.00
❑ T8-373S1	Hotter Than July	1980	3.00	6.00	12.00
❑ 6002 TL2 [(2)]	Stevie Wonder's Original Musiquarium I	1982	3.75	7.50	15.00
❑ 6134 TL	In Square Circle	1985	2.50	5.00	10.00
WOOD, BOBBY					
JOY					
❑ JL 1001 [M]	Bobby Wood	1964	10.00	20.00	40.00
WOOD, BRENTON					
BRENT					
❑ S-100 [S]	Introducing Brenton Wood! Boogaloo	1967	15.00	30.00	60.00
—Four tracks by Brenton Wood, six by other artists					
❑ 5100 [M]	Introducing Brenton Wood! Boogaloo	1967	10.00	20.00	40.00
CREAM					
❑ 1006	Come Softly	1977	3.75	7.50	15.00
DOUBLE SHOT					
❑ 1002 [M]	Oogum Boogum	1967	6.25	12.50	25.00
❑ 1003 [M]	Baby You Got It	1967	6.25	12.50	25.00
❑ 5002 [S]	Oogum Boogum	1967	7.50	15.00	30.00
❑ 5003 [S]	Baby You Got It	1967	7.50	15.00	30.00
—Black vinyl					
❑ 5003 [S]	Baby You Got It	1967	50.00	100.00	200.00
—Multi-color vinyl					
RHINO					
❑ RNLP-70223	The Best of Brenton Wood	1986	2.50	5.00	10.00
WOOD, DEL					
COLUMBIA					
❑ CL 2539 [M]	Upright, Low Down and Honky Tonk	1966	3.00	6.00	12.00
❑ CS 9339 [S]	Upright, Low Down and Honky Tonk	1966	3.75	7.50	15.00
LAMB & LION					
❑ 1009	Rag Time Glory Special	197?	3.00	6.00	12.00
MERCURY					
❑ MG-20678 [M]	Ragtime Goes South of the Border	1962	3.00	6.00	12.00
❑ MG-20713 [M]	Ragtime Goes International	1962	3.00	6.00	12.00
❑ MG-20804 [M]	Piano Roll Blues	1963	3.00	6.00	12.00
❑ MG-20978 [M]	Roll Out the Piano	1964	3.00	6.00	12.00
❑ SR-60678 [S]	Ragtime Goes South of the Border	1962	3.75	7.50	15.00
❑ SR-60713 [S]	Ragtime Goes International	1962	3.75	7.50	15.00
❑ SR-60804 [S]	Piano Roll Blues	1963	3.75	7.50	15.00
❑ SR-60978 [S]	Roll Out the Piano	1964	3.75	7.50	15.00
RCA CAMDEN					
❑ CAL-684 [M]	Honky Tonk Piano	1962	3.00	6.00	12.00
❑ CAS-684 [R]	Honky Tonk Piano	1962	2.50	5.00	10.00
❑ CAL-796 [M]	It's Honky Tonk Time	1964	3.00	6.00	12.00
❑ CAS-796 [R]	It's Honky Tonk Time	1964	2.50	5.00	10.00
RCA VICTOR					
❑ LPM-1129 [M]	Down Yonder	1955	5.00	10.00	20.00
❑ LPM-1437 [M]	Hot, Happy and Honky	1957	5.00	10.00	20.00
❑ LPM-1633 [M]	Rags to Riches	1958	3.75	7.50	15.00
❑ LSP-1633 [S]	Rags to Riches	1958	5.00	10.00	20.00
❑ LPM-2091 [M]	Mississippi Show Boat	1959	3.75	7.50	15.00
❑ LSP-2091 [S]	Mississippi Show Boat	1959	5.00	10.00	20.00
❑ LPM-2203 [M]	Flivvers, Flappers and Fox Trots	1960	3.75	7.50	15.00
❑ LSP-2203 [S]	Flivvers, Flappers and Fox Trots	1960	5.00	10.00	20.00
❑ LPM-2240 [M]	Buggies, Bustles and Barrelhouse	1960	3.75	7.50	15.00
❑ LSP-2240 [S]	Buggies, Bustles and Barrelhouse	1960	5.00	10.00	20.00
❑ LPM-3907 [M]	The Best of Del Wood	1968	6.25	12.50	25.00
❑ LSP-3907 [S]	The Best of Del Wood	1968	3.00	6.00	12.00
VOCALION					
❑ VL 3609 [M]	There's a Tavern in the Town	196?	3.00	6.00	12.00
WOOD, HALLY					
ELEKTRA					
❑ EKL-10 [10]	O Lovely Appearance of Death	1953	12.50	25.00	50.00
WOOD, RONNIE					
Also see FACES; THE ROLLING STONES.					
COLUMBIA					
❑ JC 35702	Gimme Some Neck	1979	3.75	7.50	15.00
❑ PC 35702	Gimme Some Neck	198?	2.00	4.00	8.00
—Budget-line reissue					
❑ FC 37473	1234	1981	3.75	7.50	15.00
WARNER BROS.					
❑ BS 2819	I've Got My Own Album to Do	1974	5.00	10.00	20.00
❑ BS 2872	Now Look	1975	3.75	7.50	15.00

Number	Title (A Side/B Side)	Yr	VG	VG+	NM

WOOD, ROY
Also see ELECTRIC LIGHT ORCHESTRA; THE MOVE.
TOWNHOUSE
| ❏ SN-7127 | One Man Band | 1981 | 3.00 | 6.00 | 12.00 |

UNITED ARTISTS
| ❏ (# unknown) [DJ] | Boulders Folder | 1973 | 10.00 | 20.00 | 40.00 |

—Promo version of 168 in 13x13 folder with press kit and postcards
❏ UA-LA042-F	Wizzard's Brew	1973	2.50	5.00	10.00
❏ UA-LA168-F	Boulders	1973	2.50	5.00	10.00
❏ UA-LA219-G	Introducing Eddy and the Falcons	1974	2.50	5.00	10.00
❏ UA-LA575-G	Mustard	1976	2.50	5.00	10.00

WARNER BROS.
| ❏ BS 3065 | Super Active Wizzo | 1977 | 2.50 | 5.00 | 10.00 |
| ❏ BSK 3247 | On the Road Again | 1979 | 2.50 | 5.00 | 10.00 |

WOODBURY, WOODY
STEREODDITIES
| ❏ BITOA | Booze Is the Only Answer | 1961 | 10.00 | 20.00 | 40.00 |

—With record, paperback book and smaller booklets
❏ MW 1	Woody Woodbury Looks at Love and Life	1960	6.25	12.50	25.00
❏ MW 2	Woody Woodbury's Laughing Room	1960	6.25	12.50	25.00
❏ MW 3	Woody Woodbury's Concert in Comedy	1961	6.25	12.50	25.00
❏ MW 4	Woody Woodbury's Saloonatics	1961	6.25	12.50	25.00
❏ MW 5	The Spice Is Right	1962	6.25	12.50	25.00
❏ MW 6	The Best of Woody Woodbury	1963	5.00	10.00	20.00
❏ MW 7	Through the Keyhole	1964	5.00	10.00	20.00

WOODS, BILL
COUNTRY TOWN
| ❏ CTR-24803 [M] | Bill Woods from Bakersfield | 196? | 30.00 | 60.00 | 120.00 |

WOODS, JIMMY
CAPITOL
| ❏ ST-654 | Essence | 1971 | 3.75 | 7.50 | 15.00 |

CONTEMPORARY
❏ M-3605 [M]	Awakening	1962	6.25	12.50	25.00
❏ M-3612 [M]	Conflict	1963	6.25	12.50	25.00
❏ S-7605 [S]	Awakening	1962	7.50	15.00	30.00
❏ S-7612 [S]	Conflict	1963	7.50	15.00	30.00

WOODS, MACEO
VEE JAY
| ❏ LP-5001 [M] | Amazing Grace | 1959 | 7.50 | 15.00 | 30.00 |

—Maroon label
| ❏ LP-5001 [M] | Amazing Grace | 1961 | 5.00 | 10.00 | 20.00 |

—Black colorband label
| ❏ LP-5010 [M] | The Lord Will Make a Way | 1960 | 7.50 | 15.00 | 30.00 |

—Maroon label
| ❏ LP-5010 [M] | The Lord Will Make a Way | 1961 | 5.00 | 10.00 | 20.00 |

—Black colorband label
❏ LP-5053 [M]	Garden of Prayer	1963	5.00	10.00	20.00
❏ SR-5053 [S]	Garden of Prayer	1963	7.50	15.00	30.00
❏ VJS-18002	Seeking Salvation	1975	3.75	7.50	15.00

VOLT
| ❏ VOS-6009 | Hello Sunshine | 1970 | 5.00 | 10.00 | 20.00 |
| ❏ VOS-6013 | Step to Jesus | 1971 | 5.00 | 10.00 | 20.00 |

WOODS, PHIL
CANDID
| ❏ CD-8016 [M] | Rights of Swing | 1960 | 10.00 | 20.00 | 40.00 |
| ❏ CS-9016 [S] | Rights of Swing | 1960 | 12.50 | 25.00 | 50.00 |

CENTURY
| ❏ 1050 | Songs for Sisyphus | 197? | 5.00 | 10.00 | 20.00 |

EPIC
| ❏ LN 3436 [M] | Warm Woods | 1958 | 12.50 | 25.00 | 50.00 |

IMPULSE!
| ❏ A-9143 [M] | Greek Cooking | 1967 | 7.50 | 15.00 | 30.00 |
| ❏ AS-9143 [S] | Greek Cooking | 1967 | 6.25 | 12.50 | 25.00 |

MOSAIC
| ❏ MQ7-159 [(7)] | The Phil Woods Quartet/Quintet 20th Anniversary Set | 199? | 30.00 | 60.00 | 120.00 |

NEW JAZZ
| ❏ NJLP-1104 [10] | Phil Woods New Jazz Quintet | 1954 | 75.00 | 150.00 | 300.00 |
| ❏ NJLP-8291 [M] | Pot Pie | 1962 | 20.00 | 40.00 | 80.00 |

—Purple label
| ❏ NJLP-8291 [M] | Pot Pie | 1965 | 6.25 | 12.50 | 25.00 |

—Blue label, trident logo at right
PRESTIGE
❏ PRLP-191 [10]	Phil Woods New Jazz Quartet	1954	62.50	125.00	250.00
❏ PRLP-204 [10]	Phil Woods New Jazz Quintet	1955	62.50	125.00	250.00
❏ PRLP-7018 [M]	Woodlore	1956	25.00	50.00	100.00
❏ PRLP-7046 [M]	Paring Off	1956	25.00	50.00	100.00
❏ PRLP-7080 [M]	The Young Bloods	1957	25.00	50.00	100.00

STATUS
| ❏ ST-8304 [M] | Sugan | 1965 | 10.00 | 20.00 | 40.00 |

WOODS, PHIL, AND GENE QUILL
EPIC
| ❏ BN 554 [S] | Phil Talks with Quill | 1959 | 10.00 | 20.00 | 40.00 |
| ❏ BN 554 [S] | Phil Talks with Quill | 199? | 6.25 | 12.50 | 25.00 |

—Classic Records reissue on audiophile vinyl
| ❏ LN 3521 [M] | Phil Talks with Quill | 1959 | 12.50 | 25.00 | 50.00 |

PRESTIGE
| ❏ PRLP-7115 [M] | Phil and Quill with Prestige | 1957 | 20.00 | 40.00 | 80.00 |

RCA VICTOR
| ❏ LPM-1284 [M] | The Woods-Quill Sextet | 1956 | 20.00 | 40.00 | 80.00 |

WOODS, PHIL, AND GENE QUILL/JACKIE MCLEAN AND JOHN JENKINS/HAL MCKUSICK
NEW JAZZ
| ❏ NJLP-8204 [M] | Bird Feathers | 1958 | 25.00 | 50.00 | 100.00 |

—Yellow label
| ❏ NJLP-8204 [M] | Bird Feathers | 1959 | 12.50 | 25.00 | 50.00 |

—Purple label
| ❏ NJLP-8204 [M] | Bird Feathers | 1965 | 6.25 | 12.50 | 25.00 |

—Blue label, trident logo at right
WOODY'S TRUCK STOP
SMASH
| ❏ SRS-67111 | Woody's Truck Stop | 1969 | 6.25 | 12.50 | 25.00 |

WOOFERS, THE
WYNCOTE
| ❏ SW 9011 [S] | Dragsville | 1964 | 12.50 | 25.00 | 50.00 |
| ❏ W 9011 [M] | Dragsville | 1964 | 10.00 | 20.00 | 40.00 |

WOOLEY, SHEB
Includes records by his comedic alter ego, "Ben Colder."
MGM
| ❏ GAS-139 | Ben Colder (Golden Archive Series) | 1970 | 3.75 | 7.50 | 15.00 |

—As "Ben Colder"
❏ E-3299 [M]	Sheb Wooley	1956	37.50	75.00	150.00
❏ E-3904 [M]	Songs from the Days of Rawhide	1961	10.00	20.00	40.00
❏ SE-3904 [S]	Songs from the Days of Rawhide	1961	12.50	25.00	50.00
❏ E-4026 [M]	That's My Ma and That's My Pa	1962	7.50	15.00	30.00
❏ SE-4026 [S]	That's My Ma and That's My Pa	1962	10.00	20.00	40.00
❏ E-4117 [M]	Spoofing the Big Ones	1961	10.00	20.00	40.00
❏ SE-4117 [S]	Spoofing the Big Ones	1961	12.50	25.00	50.00

—MGM 4117 as "Ben Colder"
❏ E-4136 [M]	Tales of How the West Was Won	1963	7.50	15.00	30.00
❏ SE-4136 [S]	Tales of How the West Was Won	1963	10.00	20.00	40.00
❏ E-4173 [M]	Ben Colder	1963	7.50	15.00	30.00
❏ SE-4173 [S]	Ben Colder	1963	10.00	20.00	40.00

—MGM 4173 as "Ben Colder"
❏ E-4275 [M]	The Very Best of Sheb Wooley	1965	5.00	10.00	20.00
❏ SE-4275 [S]	The Very Best of Sheb Wooley	1965	6.25	12.50	25.00
❏ E-4325 [M]	It's a Big Land	1965	5.00	10.00	20.00
❏ SE-4325 [S]	It's a Big Land	1965	6.25	12.50	25.00
❏ E-4421 [M]	Big Ben Strikes Again	1967	5.00	10.00	20.00
❏ SE-4421 [S]	Big Ben Strikes Again	1967	5.00	10.00	20.00

—MGM 4421 as "Ben Colder"
| ❏ E-4482 [M] | Wine, Women and Song | 1967 | 5.00 | 10.00 | 20.00 |
| ❏ SE-4482 [S] | Wine, Women and Song | 1967 | 5.00 | 10.00 | 20.00 |

—MGM 4482 as "Ben Colder"
| ❏ SE-4530 | The Best of Ben Colder | 1968 | 5.00 | 10.00 | 20.00 |

—As "Ben Colder"
| ❏ SE-4614 | Harper Valley P.T.A. | 1968 | 5.00 | 10.00 | 20.00 |

—As "Ben Colder"
| ❏ SE-4615 | Warm and Wooley | 1969 | 5.00 | 10.00 | 20.00 |
| ❏ SE-4629 | Have One On | 1969 | 3.75 | 7.50 | 15.00 |

—As "Ben Colder"
| ❏ SE-4674 | Wild Again | 1970 | 3.75 | 7.50 | 15.00 |

—As "Ben Colder"
| ❏ SE-4758 | Live and Loaded | 1971 | 3.75 | 7.50 | 15.00 |

—As "Ben Colder"
| ❏ SE-4807 | Warming Up to Colder | 1972 | 3.75 | 7.50 | 15.00 |

—As "Ben Colder"
| ❏ SE-4876 | The Wacky World of Ben Colder | 1973 | 3.75 | 7.50 | 15.00 |

—As "Ben Colder"
WOOLIES, THE
SPIRIT
| ❏ 9645-2001 | Basic Rock | 1971 | 10.00 | 20.00 | 40.00 |
| ❏ 9645-2005 | Live at Lizards | 1973 | 10.00 | 20.00 | 40.00 |

WORLD OF OZ, THE
DERAM
| ❏ DES 18022 | The World of Oz | 1969 | 12.50 | 25.00 | 50.00 |

WORTH, MARION
COLUMBIA
❏ CL 2011 [M]	Marion Worth's Greatest Hits	1963	5.00	10.00	20.00
❏ CL 2287 [M]	Marion Worth Sings Marty Robbins	1964	5.00	10.00	20.00
❏ CS 8811 [S]	Marion Worth's Greatest Hits	1963	6.25	12.50	25.00
❏ CS 9087 [S]	Marion Worth Sings Marty Robbins	1964	6.25	12.50	25.00

DECCA
| ❏ DL 4936 [M] | A Woman Needs Love | 1967 | 6.25 | 12.50 | 25.00 |
| ❏ DL 74936 [S] | A Woman Needs Love | 1967 | 5.00 | 10.00 | 20.00 |

WORTH, MARION, AND GEORGE MORGAN
Also see each artist's individual listings.
COLUMBIA
| ❏ CL 2197 [M] | Slippin' Around | 1964 | 5.00 | 10.00 | 20.00 |
| ❏ CS 8997 [S] | Slippin' Around | 1964 | 6.25 | 12.50 | 25.00 |

WOULD
PERCEPTION
| ❏ 24 | Would | 1972 | 7.50 | 15.00 | 30.00 |

WRAY, LINK
EPIC
| ❏ LN 3661 [M] | Link Wray and the Wraymen | 1960 | 62.50 | 125.00 | 250.00 |

NORTON
❏ 210	Hillbilly Wolf (Missing Links Vol. 1)	199?	2.50	5.00	10.00
❏ 211	Big City After Dark (Missing Links Vol. 2)	199?	2.50	5.00	10.00
❏ 212	Some Kinda Nut (Missing Links Vol. 3)	199?	2.50	5.00	10.00
❏ 253	Streets of Chicago (Missing Links Vol. 4)	1995	2.50	5.00	10.00

POLYDOR
| ❏ 24-4064 | Link Wray | 1971 | 5.00 | 10.00 | 20.00 |

Number	Title (A Side/B Side)	Yr	VG	VG+	NM
❑ PD-5047	Be What You Want To	1972	5.00	10.00	20.00
❑ PD-6025	The Link Wray Rumble	1974	5.00	10.00	20.00
RECORD FACTORY					
❑ 1929	Yesterday and Today	1969	20.00	40.00	80.00
SWAN					
❑ SLP-510 [M]	Jack the Ripper	1963	37.50	75.00	150.00
VERMILLION					
❑ 1924 [M]	Great Guitar Hits	196?	20.00	40.00	80.00
❑ 1925 [M]	Link Wray Sings and Plays Guitar	196?	20.00	40.00	80.00
VISA					
❑ 7009	Bullshot	1979	3.00	6.00	12.00
❑ 7010	Live at the Paradiso	1980	3.00	6.00	12.00

WRAY, VERNON
VERMILLION

Number	Title (A Side/B Side)	Yr	VG	VG+	NM
❑ 1972	Wasted	1972	25.00	50.00	100.00

WRICE, LARRY "WILD"
PACIFIC JAZZ

Number	Title (A Side/B Side)	Yr	VG	VG+	NM
❑ PJ-24 [M]	Wild!	1961	6.25	12.50	25.00
❑ ST-24 [S]	Wild!	1961	7.50	15.00	30.00

WRIGHT, BETTY
ALSTON

Number	Title (A Side/B Side)	Yr	VG	VG+	NM
❑ SD 33-388	I Love the Way You Love	1972	3.75	7.50	15.00
❑ 4400	Danger High Voltage	1974	3.00	6.00	12.00
❑ 4406	This Time for Real	1977	3.00	6.00	12.00
❑ 4408	Betty Wright Live	1978	3.00	6.00	12.00
❑ 4410	Betty Travelin' in the Wright Circle	1979	3.00	6.00	12.00
❑ SD 7026	Hard to Stop	1973	3.75	7.50	15.00
ATCO					
❑ SD 33-260	My First Time Around	1968	6.25	12.50	25.00
COLLECTABLES					
❑ COL-5118	Golden Classics	198?	2.50	5.00	10.00
EPIC					
❑ JE 36879	Betty Wright	1981	2.50	5.00	10.00
❑ FE 38558	Wright Back at You	1983	2.50	5.00	10.00
FANTASY					
❑ 9644	Sevens	1986	2.50	5.00	10.00
MS. B.					
❑ 3301	Mother Wit	1988	2.50	5.00	10.00
❑ 3318	Passion and Compassion	198?	3.75	7.50	15.00

WRIGHT, BOBBY
ABC

Number	Title (A Side/B Side)	Yr	VG	VG+	NM
❑ ABCD-842	Seasons of Love	1974	3.00	6.00	12.00
DECCA					
❑ DL 75319	Here I Go Again	1971	3.75	7.50	15.00

WRIGHT, CHARLES, AND THE WATTS 103RD STREET RHYTHM BAND
ABC

Number	Title (A Side/B Side)	Yr	VG	VG+	NM
❑ D-887	Lil' Encouragement	1975	3.00	6.00	12.00
ABC DUNHILL					
❑ DS-50162 [(2)]	Doin' What Comes Naturally	1973	3.75	7.50	15.00
❑ DS-50187	Ninety Day Cycle People	1974	3.00	6.00	12.00
WARNER BROS.					
❑ WS 1741	The Watts 103rd Street Rhythm Band	1968	5.00	10.00	20.00
—Green label with "W7" logo					
❑ WS 1761	Together	1969	5.00	10.00	20.00
—Green label with "W7" logo					
❑ WS 1761	Together	1970	3.75	7.50	15.00
—Green label with "WB" logo					
❑ WS 1801	In the Jungle, Babe	1969	5.00	10.00	20.00
—Green label with "W7" logo					
❑ WS 1801	In the Jungle, Babe	1970	3.75	7.50	15.00
—Green label with "WB" logo					
❑ WS 1864	Express Yourself	1970	3.75	7.50	15.00
❑ WS 1904	You're So Beautiful	1971	3.75	7.50	15.00
❑ BS 2620	Rhythm and Poetry	1972	3.75	7.50	15.00
—Green label with "WB" logo					
❑ BS 2620	Rhythm and Poetry	1973	3.00	6.00	12.00
—"Burbank" palm-trees logo					

WRIGHT, DEMPSEY
ANDEX

Number	Title (A Side/B Side)	Yr	VG	VG+	NM
❑ A-3006 [M]	The Wright Approach	1958	15.00	30.00	60.00
❑ AS-3006 [S]	The Wright Approach	1958	12.50	25.00	50.00

WRIGHT, FRANK
ESP-DISK'

Number	Title (A Side/B Side)	Yr	VG	VG+	NM
❑ 1023 [M]	Frank Wright Trio	1966	6.25	12.50	25.00
❑ S-1023 [S]	Frank Wright Trio	1966	5.00	10.00	20.00
❑ 1053 [S]	Your Prayer	1968	5.00	10.00	20.00

WRIGHT, JOHN
PRESTIGE

Number	Title (A Side/B Side)	Yr	VG	VG+	NM
❑ PRLP-7190 [M]	South Side Soul	1960	10.00	20.00	40.00
❑ PRLP-7197 [M]	Nice 'N' Nasty	1961	10.00	20.00	40.00
❑ PRLP-7212 [M]	Makin' Out	1961	10.00	20.00	40.00
❑ PRLP-7233 [M]	Mr. Soul	1962	7.50	15.00	30.00
❑ PRST-7233 [S]	Mr. Soul	1962	10.00	20.00	40.00
STATUS					
❑ ST-8322 [M]	The Last Amen	1965	10.00	20.00	40.00

WRIGHT, JOHNNY
DECCA

Number	Title (A Side/B Side)	Yr	VG	VG+	NM
❑ DL 4698 [M]	Hello Vietnam	1965	6.25	12.50	25.00
❑ DL 4770 [M]	Country Music Special	1966	6.25	12.50	25.00
❑ DL 4846 [M]	Country the Wright Way	1967	6.25	12.50	25.00
❑ DL 74698 [S]	Hello Vietnam	1965	7.50	15.00	30.00
❑ DL 74770 [S]	Country Music Special	1966	7.50	15.00	30.00
❑ DL 74846 [S]	Country the Wright Way	1967	5.00	10.00	20.00
❑ DL 75019	Johnny Wright Sings Country Favorites	1968	5.00	10.00	20.00

WRIGHT, LEO
ATLANTIC

Number	Title (A Side/B Side)	Yr	VG	VG+	NM
❑ 1358 [M]	Blues Shout	1960	6.25	12.50	25.00
—Multicolor label, white "fan" logo at right					
❑ SD 1358 [S]	Blues Shout	196?	5.00	10.00	20.00
—Multicolor label, black "fan" logo at right					
❑ SD 1358 [S]	Blues Shout	1960	7.50	15.00	30.00
—Multicolor label, white "fan" logo at right					
❑ 1393 [M]	Suddenly the Blues	1962	6.25	12.50	25.00
—Multicolor label, black "fan" logo at right					
❑ SD 1393 [S]	Suddenly the Blues	1962	7.50	15.00	30.00
—Multicolor label, black "fan" logo at right					
VORTEX					
❑ 2011	Soul Talk	197?	5.00	10.00	20.00

WRIGHT, MARVIN "LEFTY"
"X"

Number	Title (A Side/B Side)	Yr	VG	VG+	NM
❑ LXA-3028 [10]	Boogie Woogie Piano	1954	15.00	30.00	60.00

WRIGHT, NAT
WARWICK

Number	Title (A Side/B Side)	Yr	VG	VG+	NM
❑ W-2040 [M]	The Biggest Voice in Jazz	1961	12.50	25.00	50.00
❑ W-2040ST [S]	The Biggest Voice in Jazz	1961	20.00	40.00	80.00

WRIGHT, O.V.
BACK BEAT

Number	Title (A Side/B Side)	Yr	VG	VG+	NM
❑ 61 [M]	If It's Only for Tonight	1965	25.00	50.00	100.00
❑ S-61 [S]	If It's Only for Tonight	1965	37.50	75.00	150.00
❑ 66	Eight Men, Four Women	1968	15.00	30.00	60.00
❑ 67	Nucleus of Soul	1969	15.00	30.00	60.00
❑ 70	A Nickel and a Nail and Ace of Spade	1971	15.00	30.00	60.00
❑ 72	Memphis Unlimited	1973	12.50	25.00	50.00
HI					
❑ 6001	Into Something	1977	6.25	12.50	25.00
❑ 6008	Bottom Line	1978	6.25	12.50	25.00
❑ 6011	We're Still Together	1979	6.25	12.50	25.00

WRIGHT, RICHARD
Also see PINK FLOYD.
COLUMBIA

Number	Title (A Side/B Side)	Yr	VG	VG+	NM
❑ JC 35559	Wet Dream	1978	5.00	10.00	20.00

WRIGHT, SONNY
KAPP

Number	Title (A Side/B Side)	Yr	VG	VG+	NM
❑ KS-3614	I Love You, Loretta Lynn	1968	5.00	10.00	20.00

WRIGHT, WILLIE
ARGO

Number	Title (A Side/B Side)	Yr	VG	VG+	NM
❑ LP-4024 [M]	I'm on My Way	1963	5.00	10.00	20.00
❑ LPS-4024 [S]	I'm on My Way	1963	6.25	12.00	25.00
CONCERT DISC					
❑ 45 [S]	I Sing Folk Songs	1960	10.00	20.00	40.00
❑ 1045 [M]	I Sing Folk Songs	1960	7.50	15.00	30.00

WYLER, GRETCHEN
JUBILEE

Number	Title (A Side/B Side)	Yr	VG	VG+	NM
❑ JLP-1100 [M]	Wild, Wyler, Wildest	1959	6.25	12.50	25.00
❑ SDJLP-1100 [S]	Wild, Wyler, Wildest	1959	7.50	15.00	30.00

WYMAN, BILL
Also see THE ROLLING STONES.
ROLLING STONES

Number	Title (A Side/B Side)	Yr	VG	VG+	NM
❑ COC 59102	Monkey Grip	1974	3.75	7.50	15.00
❑ COC 79100	Monkey Grip	1974	3.00	6.00	12.00
—Reissue of 59102					
❑ QD 79100 [Q]	Monkey Grip	1974	5.00	10.00	20.00
❑ COC 79103	Stone Alone	1976	3.00	6.00	12.00
❑ QD 79103 [Q]	Stone Alone	1976	5.00	10.00	20.00

WYNETTE, TAMMY
Also see DAVID HOUSTON AND TAMMY WYNETTE; GEORGE JONES AND TAMMY WYNETTE
COLUMBIA LIMITED EDITION

Number	Title (A Side/B Side)	Yr	VG	VG+	NM
❑ LE 10049	The First Lady	197?	3.00	6.00	12.00
❑ LE 10193	The Ways to Love a Man	197?	3.00	6.00	12.00
❑ LE 10194	Tammy's Touch	197?	3.00	6.00	12.00
❑ LE 10195	We Sure Can Love Each Other	197?	3.00	6.00	12.00
COLUMBIA SPECIAL PRODUCTS					
❑ P 11228	Take Me to Your World	1973	3.00	6.00	12.00
❑ P 11519	Your Good Girl's Gonna Go Bad	1973	3.00	6.00	12.00
❑ P 13256	The Ways to Love a Man	1976	3.00	6.00	12.00
❑ P 13259	My Man	1976	3.00	6.00	12.00
❑ P 13261	Bedtime Story	1976	3.00	6.00	12.00
❑ P 13611	Twenty Big Hits of Tammy Wynette	197?	3.75	7.50	15.00
EPIC					
❑ EGP 503 [(2)]	The World of Tammy Wynette	1970	6.25	12.50	25.00
❑ LN 24305 [M]	Your Good Girl's Gonna Go Bad	1967	7.50	15.00	30.00
❑ LN 24353 [M]	Take Me to Your World/I Don't Wanna Play House	1968	10.00	20.00	40.00
—May exist only as a white label promo					
❑ LN 24392 [M]	D-I-V-O-R-C-E	1968	12.50	25.00	50.00
—This has been confirmed to exist on yellow label stock copies					
❑ BN 26305 [S]	Your Good Girl's Gonna Go Bad	1967	5.00	10.00	20.00
❑ BN 26353 [S]	Take Me to Your World/I Don't Wanna Play House	1968	5.00	10.00	20.00
❑ BN 26392 [S]	D-I-V-O-R-C-E	1968	5.00	10.00	20.00
❑ BN 26423	Inspiration	1969	5.00	10.00	20.00
❑ BN 26451	Stand By Your Man	1969	5.00	10.00	20.00
❑ BN 26486	Tammy's Greatest Hits	1969	5.00	10.00	20.00

Number	Title (A Side/B Side)	Yr	VG	VG+	NM
❑ PE 26486	Tammy's Greatest Hits	198?	2.00	4.00	8.00
—Budget-line reissue					
❑ BN 26519	The Ways to Love a Man	1970	5.00	10.00	20.00
❑ BN 26549	Tammy's Touch	1970	5.00	10.00	20.00
❑ E 30213	The First Lady	1970	5.00	10.00	20.00
❑ E 30343	Christmas with Tammy	1970	5.00	10.00	20.00
❑ KEG 30358 [(2)]	The First Songs of the First Lady	1970	5.00	10.00	20.00
❑ E 30658	We Sure Can Love Each Other	1971	5.00	10.00	20.00
❑ EQ 30658 [Q]	We Sure Can Love Each Other	1972	7.50	15.00	30.00
❑ E 30733	Tammy's Greatest Hits, Volume II	1971	5.00	10.00	20.00
❑ PE 30733	Tammy's Greatest Hits, Volume II	198?	2.00	4.00	8.00
—Budget-line reissue					
❑ KE 31285	Bedtime Story	1972	3.75	7.50	15.00
❑ KE 31717	My Man	1972	3.75	7.50	15.00
❑ KE 31937	Kids Say the Darndest Things	1973	3.75	7.50	15.00
❑ KE 32745	Another Lonely Song	1974	3.00	6.00	12.00
❑ KE 33246	Woman to Woman	1975	3.00	6.00	12.00
❑ KE 33396	Tammy's Greatest Hits, Volume III	1975	3.00	6.00	12.00
❑ PE 33396	Tammy's Greatest Hits, Volume III	198?	2.00	4.00	8.00
—Budget-line reissue					
❑ KE 33582	I Still Believe in Fairy Tales	1975	3.00	6.00	12.00
❑ BG 33773 [(2)]	Stand By Your Man/Bedtime Story	1976	3.75	7.50	15.00
❑ PE 34075	'Til I Can Make It on My Own	1976	3.00	6.00	12.00
❑ PE 34289	You and Me	1976	3.00	6.00	12.00
❑ PE 34694	Let's Get Together One Last Time	1977	3.00	6.00	12.00
❑ KE 35044	One of a Kind	1977	3.00	6.00	12.00
❑ KE 35442	Womanhood	1978	3.00	6.00	12.00
❑ KE 35630	Tammy's Greatest Hits, Volume IV	1978	3.00	6.00	12.00
❑ KE 36013	Just Tammy	1979	3.00	6.00	12.00
❑ JE 36485	Only Lonely Sometimes	1980	2.50	5.00	10.00
❑ FE 37104	You Brought Me Back	1981	2.50	5.00	10.00
❑ FE 37344	Encore	1981	2.50	5.00	10.00
❑ PE 37344	Encore	198?	2.00	4.00	8.00
—Budget-line reissue					
❑ FE 37980	Soft Touch	1982	2.50	5.00	10.00
❑ FE 38312	Biggest Hits	1984	2.50	5.00	10.00
❑ FE 38372	Good Love and Heartbreak	1983	2.50	5.00	10.00
❑ FE 38744	Even the Strong Get Lonely	1983	2.50	5.00	10.00
❑ FE 39971	Sometimes When We Touch	1985	2.50	5.00	10.00
❑ EG 40625 [(2)]	Anniversary: 20 Years of Hits	1987	3.75	7.50	15.00
❑ FE 40832	Higher Ground	1987	2.50	5.00	10.00
❑ FE 44498	Next to You	1989	3.00	6.00	12.00
HARMONY					
❑ KH 30096	Send Me No Roses	1970	3.00	6.00	12.00
❑ KH 30914	Just a Matter of Time	1971	3.00	6.00	12.00
PAIR					
❑ PDL2-1073 [(2)]	From the Bottom of My Heart	1986	3.00	6.00	12.00

WYNN, ALBERT
RIVERSIDE
❑ RLP-426 [M]	Albert Wynn and His Gutbucket Seven	1962	7.50	15.00	30.00
❑ RS-9426 [R]	Albert Wynn and His Gutbucket Seven	1962	5.00	10.00	20.00

WYNONNA
See WYNONNA JUDD.

WYNTERS, GAIL
HICKORY
❑ LPM-138 [M]	A Girl for All Seasons	1967	5.00	10.00	20.00
❑ LPS-138 [S]	A Girl for All Seasons	1967	3.75	7.50	15.00
RCA VICTOR
❑ APL1-2285	Let the Lady Sing	1977	5.00	10.00	20.00

X

X
ELEKTRA
❑ 60150	Under the Big Black Sun	1982	3.00	6.00	12.00
❑ 60283	More Fun in the New World	1983	2.50	5.00	10.00
❑ 60430	Ain't Love Grand	1985	2.50	5.00	10.00
❑ 60492	See How We Are	1987	2.50	5.00	10.00
❑ 60788 [(2)]	Live at the Whiskey A-Go-Go on the Fabulous Sunset Strip	1988	3.00	6.00	12.00
SLASH
❑ SR-104	Los Angeles	1980	6.25	12.50	25.00
❑ SR-107	Wild Gift	1981	5.00	10.00	20.00
❑ 23930	Los Angeles	1983	2.50	5.00	10.00
—Reissue of Slash 104					
❑ 23931	Wild Gift	1983	2.50	5.00	10.00
—Reissue of Slash 107					

XIT
CANYON
❑ 7114	Entrance	197?	12.50	25.00	50.00
❑ 7121	Relocation	197?	10.00	20.00	40.00
RARE EARTH
❑ R-536	Plight of the Redman	1972	7.50	15.00	30.00
❑ R-545	Silent Warrior	1973	7.50	15.00	30.00
WARRIOR
❑ WAR 49	Plight of the Redman	1981	3.75	7.50	15.00
—Reissue of Rare Earth 536					

XTC
GEFFEN
❑ GHS 4027	Mummer	1983	2.50	5.00	10.00
❑ GHS 4032	White Music	1984	2.50	5.00	10.00
—Reissue of Virgin/Epic 38153					

Number	Title (A Side/B Side)	Yr	VG	VG+	NM
❑ GHS 4033	Go2	1984	2.50	5.00	10.00
—Reissue of Virgin/Epic 38152					
❑ GHS 4034	Drums and Wires	1984	2.50	5.00	10.00
—Reissue of Virgin/Epic 38151					
❑ GHS 4035	Black Sea	1984	2.50	5.00	10.00
—Reissue of Virgin/Epic 38150					
❑ GHS 4036 [(2)]	English Settlement	1984	3.75	7.50	15.00
—First release of British version of this album in U.S.					
❑ GHS 4037	Waxworks (Some Singles, 1977-82)	1984	3.00	6.00	12.00
❑ GHS 24054	The Big Express	1984	2.50	5.00	10.00
❑ GHS 24117	Skylarking	1986	2.50	5.00	10.00
—Second pressing, with "Dear God" and without "Mermaid Smiled"					
❑ GHS 24117	Skylarking	1986	3.75	7.50	15.00
—First pressing, with "Mermaid Smiled" and without "Dear God"					
❑ GHS 24218 [(2)]	Oranges and Lemons	1989	3.75	7.50	15.00
❑ R 201086 [(2)]	Oranges and Lemons	1989	3.75	7.50	15.00
—BMG Direct Marketing edition					
VIRGIN					
❑ VA 13134	Drums and Wires	1979	5.00	10.00	20.00
—With bonus 7-inch record (PR 344) enclosed -- deduct 40 percent if missing					
❑ VA 13147	Black Sea	1980	7.50	15.00	30.00
—Promo only; label, jacket and innersleeve ALL must have this number					
VIRGIN INTERNATIONAL					
❑ VI-2095	White Music	1979	3.75	7.50	15.00
❑ VI-2108	Go2	1979	3.75	7.50	15.00
VIRGIN/EPIC					
❑ ARE 37943	English Settlement	1982	2.50	5.00	10.00
—Drastically edited version of U.K. original, which was a 2-record set					
❑ PE 38150	Black Sea	1982	2.50	5.00	10.00
—Reissue of Virgin/RSO 1001					
❑ PE 38151	Drums and Wires	1982	2.50	5.00	10.00
—Reissue of Virgin 13134					
❑ PE 38152	Go2	1982	2.50	5.00	10.00
—Reissue of Virgin International VI-2108					
❑ PE 38153	White Music	1982	2.50	5.00	10.00
—Reissue of Virgin International VI-2095					
VIRGIN/RSO					
❑ VR-1-1000	Black Sea	1980	3.00	6.00	12.00
—Without green outer bag; innersleeves may or may not have "VA 13147" reference					
❑ VR-1-1000	Black Sea	1980	5.00	10.00	20.00
—With green outer bag and "VA 13147" on innersleeve					
WARNER BROS.					
❑ WBMS-146 [DJ]	Skylarking Interview with Andy Partridge	1986	6.25	12.50	25.00
—Part of "The Warner Bros. Music Show" series					

Y

Y KANT TORI READ
Lead singer: Tori Amos.
ATLANTIC
❑ 81845	Y Kant Tori Read	1989	30.00	60.00	120.00
—Deduct 20% for albums with a gold promo stamp and cut-out mark					

YA HO WA 13
HIGHER KEY
❑ 3301	Kohoutek	1973	75.00	150.00	300.00
❑ 3302	Contraction	1974	125.00	250.00	500.00
❑ 3303	Expansion	1974	125.00	250.00	500.00
❑ 3304	All or Nothing at All	1974	100.00	200.00	400.00
—Above 4 as "Father Yod and the Spirit of '76"					
❑ 3305	Ya Ho Wa 13	1974	125.00	250.00	500.00
❑ 3306	The Savage Sons of Ya Ho Wa	1974	100.00	200.00	400.00
❑ 3307	Penetration: An Aquarian Symphony	1974	100.00	200.00	400.00
❑ 3308 [(2)]	I'm Gonna Take You Home	1975	200.00	400.00	800.00
❑ 3309	To the Principles for the Children	1975	200.00	400.00	800.00

YACHTSMEN, THE
BUENA VISTA
❑ BV-3310 [M]	High and Dry with the Yachtsmen	1961	6.25	12.50	25.00

YAGED, SOL
HERALD
❑ HLP-0103 [M]	It Might As Well Be Swing	1956	12.50	25.00	50.00
LANE
❑ LP-149 [M]	Live at the Gaslight Club	195?	12.50	25.00	50.00
❑ LP-154 [M]	One More Time	195?	12.50	25.00	50.00
❑ LPS-154 [S]	One More Time	195?	12.50	25.00	50.00
❑ LP-155 [M]	Sol Yaged at the Gaslight Club	195?	12.50	25.00	50.00
❑ LPS-155 [S]	Sol Yaged at the Gaslight Club	195?	12.50	25.00	50.00
PHILIPS
❑ PHS 600002 [S]	Jazz at the Metropole	1961	5.00	10.00	20.00

YALE DIXIELAND BAND, THE
COLUMBIA
❑ CL 736 [M]	Eli's Chosen Six	1955	10.00	20.00	40.00

YAMA AND THE KARMA DUSTERS
MANHOLE
❑ 1	Up from the Sewers	1970	50.00	100.00	200.00

YAMAMOTO, TSUYOSHI
THREE BLIND MICE
❑ TBM-23	Midnight Sugar	1995	7.50	15.00	30.00
—Audiophile vinyl					
❑ TBM-30	Misty	199?	7.50	15.00	30.00
—Audiophile vinyl					

Number	Title (A Side/B Side)	Yr	VG	VG+	NM

YANCEY, JIMMY
ATLANTIC
❏ ALS-103 [10]	Yancey Special	1950	25.00	50.00	100.00
❏ ALS-130 [10]	Yancey Special	1952	20.00	40.00	80.00
❏ ALS-134 [10]	Piano Solos	1952	20.00	40.00	80.00
❏ 1283 [M]	Pure Blues	1958	12.50	25.00	50.00
—Black label					
❏ 1283 [M]	Pure Blues	1961	5.00	10.00	20.00
—Multicolor label, white "fan" logo at right					
PARAMOUNT
| ❏ CJS-101 [10] | Yancey Special | 1951 | 25.00 | 50.00 | 100.00 |
PAX
| ❏ LP-6011 [10] | 1943 Mixture | 1954 | 20.00 | 40.00 | 80.00 |
| ❏ LP-6012 [10] | Evening With the Yanceys | 1954 | 20.00 | 40.00 | 80.00 |
RIVERSIDE
| ❏ RLP 12-124 [M] | Yancey's Getaway | 1956 | 15.00 | 30.00 | 60.00 |
| ❏ RLP-1028 [10] | Lost Recording Date | 1954 | 25.00 | 50.00 | 100.00 |
"X"
| ❏ LX-3000 [10] | Blues and Boogie | 1954 | 25.00 | 50.00 | 100.00 |

YANCEY, MAMA, AND ART HODES
VERVE FOLKWAYS
| ❏ FV-9015 [M] | Blues | 1965 | 5.00 | 10.00 | 20.00 |
| ❏ FVS-9015 [S] | Blues | 1965 | 6.25 | 12.50 | 25.00 |

YANCY DERRINGER
HEMISPHERE
| ❏ H-15104 | Openers | 1975 | 12.50 | 25.00 | 50.00 |

YANKEE DOLLAR, THE
DOT
| ❏ DLP-25874 | The Yankee Dollar | 1968 | 30.00 | 60.00 | 120.00 |

YANOVSKY, ZALMAN
Also see THE LOVIN' SPOONFUL.
BUDDAH
| ❏ BDS-5019 | Alive and Well in Argentina | 1968 | 10.00 | 20.00 | 40.00 |
KAMA SUTRA
| ❏ KSBS-2030 | Alive and Well in Argentina | 1971 | 5.00 | 10.00 | 20.00 |

YARBROUGH, GLENN
ELEKTRA
| ❏ EKL-135 [M] | Here We Go, Baby | 1957 | 10.00 | 20.00 | 40.00 |
FIRST AMERICAN
| ❏ 7766 | Just a Little Love | 1981 | 2.50 | 5.00 | 10.00 |
RCA VICTOR
❏ ANL1-2138	Baby the Rain Must Fall	1977	2.50	5.00	10.00
—Reissue of LSP-3422					
❏ LPM-2905 [M]	One More Round	1964	3.75	7.50	15.00
❏ LSP-2905 [S]	One More Round	1964	5.00	10.00	20.00
❏ LPM-3301 [M]	Come Share My Life	1965	3.75	7.50	15.00
❏ LSP-3301 [S]	Come Share My Life	1965	5.00	10.00	20.00
❏ LPM-3422 [M]	Baby the Rain Must Fall	1965	3.00	6.00	12.00
❏ LSP-3422 [S]	Baby the Rain Must Fall	1965	3.75	7.50	15.00
❏ LPM-3472 [M]	It's Gonna Be Fine	1965	3.00	6.00	12.00
❏ LSP-3472 [S]	It's Gonna Be Fine	1965	3.75	7.50	15.00
❏ LPM-3539 [M]	The Lonely Things	1966	3.00	6.00	12.00
❏ LSP-3539 [S]	The Lonely Things	1966	3.75	7.50	15.00
❏ LPM-3661 [M]	Live at the Hungry I	1966	3.00	6.00	12.00
❏ LSP-3661 [S]	Live at the Hungry I	1966	3.75	7.50	15.00
❏ LPM-3801 [M]	For Emily, Whenever I May Find Her	1967	3.75	7.50	15.00
❏ LSP-3801 [S]	For Emily, Whenever I May Find Her	1967	3.75	7.50	15.00
❏ LPM-3860 [M]	Honey and Wine	1967	5.00	10.00	20.00
❏ LSP-3860 [S]	Honey and Wine	1967	3.75	7.50	15.00
❏ LPM-3951 [M]	The Bitter and the Sweet	1968	7.50	15.00	30.00
❏ LSP-3951 [S]	The Bitter and the Sweet	1968	3.75	7.50	15.00
❏ LSP-4047	We Survived the Madness	1968	3.75	7.50	15.00
❏ LSP-4349	The Best of Glenn Yarbrough	1970	3.00	6.00	12.00
❏ VPS-6018 [(2)]	Glenn Yarbrough Sings the Rod McKuen Songbook	1969	3.75	7.50	15.00
STAX
| ❏ STX-5506 | My Sweet Lady | 1975 | 2.50 | 5.00 | 10.00 |
TRADITION
❏ 1019 [M]	Come Sit By My Side	195?	5.00	10.00	20.00
❏ 2054	The Best of Glenn Yarbrough	1967	3.75	7.50	15.00
❏ 2095	Looking Back	1970	3.00	6.00	12.00
WARNER BROS.
❏ WS 1736	Each of Us Alone: Glenn Yarbrough Sings the Words and Music of Rod McKuen	1968	3.00	6.00	12.00
❏ WS 1782	Somehow, Someway	1969	3.00	6.00	12.00
❏ WS 1817	Yarbrough Country	1969	3.00	6.00	12.00
❏ WS 1832	Let Me Choose Life	1969	3.00	6.00	12.00
❏ WS 1876	Jubilee	1970	3.00	6.00	12.00
❏ WS 1911	Bend Down and Touch Me	1971	3.00	6.00	12.00

YARDBIRDS, THE
Also see JEFF BECK; ERIC CLAPTON; JIMMY PAGE; KEITH RELF; SONNY BOY WILLIAMSON (2). Ex-members of the group formed LED ZEPPELIN and RENAISSANCE.
ACCORD
| ❏ SN-7143 [S] | For Your Love | 1981 | 2.00 | 4.00 | 8.00 |
| ❏ SN-7237 [R] | Having a Rave Up with the Yardbirds | 1981 | 2.00 | 4.00 | 8.00 |
COLUMBIA SPECIAL PRODUCTS
| ❏ P 13311 [S] | Live Yardbirds Featuring Jimmy Page | 1976 | 20.00 | 40.00 | 80.00 |
COMPLEAT
| ❏ CPL-2-2002 [(2)] | A Compleat Collection | 1984 | 3.00 | 6.00 | 12.00 |
EPIC
❏ LN 24167 [DJ]	For Your Love	1965	100.00	200.00	400.00
—White label promo					
❏ LN 24167 [M]	For Your Love	1965	75.00	150.00	300.00
❏ LN 24177 [DJ]	Having a Rave Up with the Yardbirds	1965	100.00	200.00	400.00
—White label promo					
❏ LN 24177 [M]	Having a Rave Up with the Yardbirds	1965	20.00	40.00	80.00
❏ LN 24210 [DJ]	Over Under Sideways Down	1966	100.00	200.00	400.00
—White label promo					
❏ LN 24210 [M]	Over Under Sideways Down	1966	15.00	30.00	60.00
❏ LN 24246 [DJ]	The Yardbirds' Greatest Hits	1966	75.00	150.00	300.00
—White label promo					
❏ LN 24246 [M]	The Yardbirds' Greatest Hits	1966	12.50	25.00	50.00
❏ LN 24313 [DJ]	Little Games	1967	75.00	150.00	300.00
❏ LN 24313 [M]	Little Games	1967	20.00	40.00	80.00
—Some copies with this number are stereo; look for the "XSB" prefix before the master number					
❏ BN 26167 [P]	For Your Love	1965	50.00	100.00	200.00
—The album is in true stereo except for "Sweet Music"					
❏ BN 26177 [R]	Having a Rave Up with the Yardbirds	1965	12.50	25.00	50.00
❏ BN 26177 [R]	Having a Rave Up with the Yardbirds	1973	7.50	15.00	30.00
—Reissue with orange label					
❏ BN 26210 [P]	Over Under Sideways Down	1966	20.00	40.00	80.00
—"Over Under Sideways Down" is rechanneled					
❏ BN 26246 [P]	The Yardbirds' Greatest Hits	1966	7.50	15.00	30.00
❏ BN 26313 [S]	Little Games	1967	12.50	25.00	50.00
❏ EG 30135 [(2)]	The Yardbirds Featuring Performances by Jeff Beck, Eric Clapton, Jimmy Page	1970	12.50	25.00	50.00
❏ E 30615 [S]	Live Yardbirds Featuring Jimmy Page	1971	20.00	40.00	80.00
❏ PE 34490 [P]	Yardbirds Favorites	1977	2.50	5.00	10.00
❏ PE 34491 [P]	Great Hits	1977	2.50	5.00	10.00
❏ FE 38455	Yardbirds (Roger the Engineer)	1982	7.50	15.00	30.00
❏ HE 48455	Yardbirds (Roger the Engineer)	1982	62.50	125.00	250.00
—"Half-Speed Mastered" edition					
PAIR
| ❏ PDL2-1151 [(2)] | Best of British Rock | 1988 | 3.00 | 6.00 | 12.00 |
RHINO
❏ RNDF 253 [PD]	Afternoon Tea	1982	3.75	7.50	15.00
❏ RNLP 70128 [M]	Greatest Hits, Volume 1: 1964-1966	1986	2.00	4.00	8.00
❏ RNLP 70189 [M]	Five Live Yardbirds	1986	2.00	4.00	8.00
SPRINGBOARD
| ❏ SPB-4036 [R] | Eric Clapton and the Yardbirds | 1972 | 2.50 | 5.00 | 10.00 |
| ❏ SPB-4039 [R] | Shapes of Things | 1972 | 2.50 | 5.00 | 10.00 |

YAZ
SIRE
❏ 23737	Upstairs at Eric's	1982	2.50	5.00	10.00
❏ 23737	Upstairs at Eric's	1982	5.00	10.00	20.00
—First pressing: Band called "Yazoo"					
❏ 23903	You and Me Both	1983	2.50	5.00	10.00

YEARWOOD, TRISHA
MCA
| ❏ 1P-8161 | Trisha Yearwood | 1991 | 6.25 | 12.50 | 25.00 |
| —Vinyl edition available only from Columbia House | | | | | |

YELL CHASERS, THE
REALTIME
| ❏ 822 | I've Got My Fingers | 197? | 5.00 | 10.00 | 20.00 |
| —Direct-to-disc recording; plays at 45 rpm | | | | | |

YELLO
ELEKTRA
| ❏ 60271 | You Gotta Say Yes to Another Excess | 1983 | 3.00 | 6.00 | 12.00 |
| ❏ 60401 | Stella | 1985 | 3.00 | 6.00 | 12.00 |
MERCURY
❏ 812166-1	You Gotta Say Yes to Another Excess	1988	2.00	4.00	8.00
—Reissue					
❏ 818339-1	Solid Pleasure	1988	2.00	4.00	8.00
—Reissue					
❏ 818340-1	Claro Que Si	1988	2.00	4.00	8.00
—Reissue					
❏ 822820-1	Stella	1988	2.00	4.00	8.00
—Reissue					
❏ 832675-1	One Second	1987	3.00	6.00	12.00
❏ 836426-1	Flag	1989	3.00	6.00	12.00
RALPH
| ❏ YL 8059-L | Solid Pleasure | 1980 | 5.00 | 10.00 | 20.00 |
| ❏ YL 8159 | Claro Que Si | 1981 | 5.00 | 10.00 | 20.00 |

YELLOW BALLOON, THE
CANTERBURY
| ❏ CLPM-1502 [M] | The Yellow Balloon | 1967 | 6.25 | 12.50 | 25.00 |
| ❏ CLPS-1502 [S] | The Yellow Balloon | 1967 | 7.50 | 15.00 | 30.00 |

YELLOW PAYGES, THE
UNI
| ❏ 73045 | The Yellow Payges, Volume 1 | 1969 | 7.50 | 15.00 | 30.00 |

YES
Also see RICK WAKEMAN.
ARISTA
| ❏ AL 8643 | Union | 1991 | 5.00 | 10.00 | 20.00 |
| —U.S. vinyl available only through Columbia House | | | | | |
ATCO
❏ 90125	90125	1984	2.00	4.00	8.00
❏ 90474	9012Live: The Solos	1985	2.00	4.00	8.00
❏ 90522	Big Generator	1987	2.00	4.00	8.00
ATLANTIC
❏ SD 3-100 [(3)]	Yessongs	1973	4.50	9.00	18.00
❏ PR 260 [DJ]	Yes Solo LP Sampler	1976	6.25	12.50	25.00
❏ PR 285 [DJ]	Yes Music: An Evening with Jon Anderson	1977	12.50	25.00	50.00
❏ SD 2-510 [(2)]	Yesshows	1980	3.00	6.00	12.00
❏ SD 2-908 [(2)]	Tales from Topographic Oceans	1974	3.75	7.50	15.00
❏ SD 2-908 [(2)DJ]	Tales from Topographic Oceans	1974	7.50	15.00	30.00
—Promo copies banded for airplay					
❏ SD 7211	Fragile	1972	3.00	6.00	12.00

Number	Title (A Side/B Side)	Yr	VG	VG+	NM
❏ 7244 [DJ]	Close to the Edge	1972	12.50	25.00	50.00
—White label mono copies banded for airplay					
❏ SD 7244	Close to the Edge	1972	3.00	6.00	12.00
❏ SD 8243	Yes	1969	3.00	6.00	12.00
❏ SD 8273	Time and a Word	1970	3.00	6.00	12.00
❏ 8283 [M]	The Yes Album	1971	10.00	20.00	40.00
—White label promo only; "DJ Copy Monaural" sticker on cover					
❏ SD 8283	The Yes Album	1971	3.00	6.00	12.00
❏ SD 16019	Drama	1980	2.50	5.00	10.00
❏ SD 18103	Yesterdays	1975	2.50	5.00	10.00
❏ SD 18122	Relayer	1975	2.50	5.00	10.00
❏ SD 18122 [DJ]	Relayer	1975	5.00	10.00	20.00
—Promo copies banded for airplay					
❏ SD 19106	Going for the One	1977	2.50	5.00	10.00
❏ SD 19131	The Yes Album	1977	2.00	4.00	8.00
❏ SD 19132	Fragile	1977	2.00	4.00	8.00
❏ SD 19133	Close to the Edge	1977	2.00	4.00	8.00
❏ SD 19134	Yesterdays	1977	2.00	4.00	8.00
❏ SD 19135	Relayer	1977	2.00	4.00	8.00
❏ SD 19202	Tormato	1978	2.50	5.00	10.00
❏ SD 19320	Classic Yes	1982	2.50	5.00	10.00
—With bonus single missing					
❏ SD 19320	Classic Yes	1982	3.75	7.50	15.00
—Original copies include a bonus 7-inch promo single					
MOBILE FIDELITY					
❏ 1-077	Close to the Edge	1982	15.00	30.00	60.00
—Audiophile vinyl					

YESTERDAY'S CHILDREN
MAP CITY
| ❏ 3012 | Yesterday's Children | 197? | 15.00 | 30.00 | 60.00 |

YESTERDAY'S FOLK
BUDDAH
| ❏ BDS-5035 | U.S. 69 | 1969 | 5.00 | 10.00 | 20.00 |

YETTI-MEN, THE / THE UPPA TRIO
KAL
| ❏ KB-4348 | The Yetti-Men/The Uppa Trio | 1967 | 200.00 | 400.00 | 600.00 |

YOAKAM, DWIGHT
OAK
| ❏ OR 2356 [EP] | Guitars, Cadillacs, Etc., Etc. | 1984 | 20.00 | 40.00 | 80.00 |
| —Six-song EP; cover is in black and white; the song "Guitars, Cadillacs" does NOT appear on this release | | | | | |
REPRISE
❏ 25372	Guitars, Cadillacs, Etc., Etc.	1986	2.50	5.00	10.00
—LP has 10 songs rather than the six on the Oak EP; front cover has color on it					
❏ W1-25372	Guitars, Cadillacs, Etc., Etc.	1986	3.00	6.00	12.00
—Columbia House edition					
❏ 25567	Hillbilly Deluxe	1987	2.50	5.00	10.00
❏ W1-25567	Hillbilly Deluxe	1987	3.00	6.00	12.00
—Columbia House edition					
❏ 25749	Buenas Noches from a Lonely Room	1988	2.50	5.00	10.00
❏ W1-25749	Buenas Noches from a Lonely Room	1988	3.00	6.00	12.00
—Columbia House edition					
❏ 25989	Just Lookin' for a Hit	1989	2.50	5.00	10.00
❏ W1-25989	Just Lookin' for a Hit	1989	3.00	6.00	12.00
—Columbia House edition					
❏ R 100009	Buenas Noches from a Lonely Room	1988	3.00	6.00	12.00
—BMG Direct Marketing edition					
❏ R 150223	Guitars, Cadillacs, Etc., Etc.	1986	3.00	6.00	12.00
—RCA Music Service edition					
❏ R 164146	Hillbilly Deluxe	1987	3.00	6.00	12.00
—BMG Direct Marketing edition					
❏ R 164310	If There Was a Way	1990	5.00	10.00	20.00
—BMG Direct Marketing edition; only U.S. vinyl version					
❏ R 174052	Just Lookin' for a Hit	1989	3.00	6.00	12.00
—BMG Direct edition					

YORK BROTHERS, THE
KING
❏ 581 [M]	The York Brothers	1958	25.00	50.00	100.00
❏ 586 [M]	The York Brothers, Volume 2	1958	25.00	50.00	100.00
❏ 820 [M]	16 Great Country and Western Hits	1963	20.00	40.00	80.00

YOST, PHIL
TAKOMA
| ❏ C-1016 | Bent City | 196? | 5.00 | 10.00 | 20.00 |
| ❏ C-1021 | Fog-Hat Ramble | 196? | 5.00 | 10.00 | 20.00 |

YOU KNOW WHO GROUP, THE
INTERNATIONAL ALLIED
| ❏ 420 [M] | The "You Know Who" Group | 1965 | 12.50 | 25.00 | 50.00 |

YOUNG, BARRY
DOT
| ❏ DLP 3672 [M] | One Has My Name | 1965 | 5.00 | 10.00 | 20.00 |
| ❏ DLP 25672 [S] | One Has My Name | 1965 | 6.25 | 12.50 | 25.00 |

YOUNG, CATHY
MAINSTREAM
| ❏ S-6121 | A Spoonful of Cathy Young | 1968 | 10.00 | 20.00 | 40.00 |

YOUNG, CECIL
AUDIO LAB
| ❏ AL-1516 [M] | Jazz on the Rocks | 1959 | 20.00 | 40.00 | 80.00 |
KING
| ❏ 295-1 [10] | A Concert of Cool Jazz | 1952 | 25.00 | 50.00 | 100.00 |

YOUNG, ELDEE
ARGO
❏ LPS-699 [S]	Just for Kicks	1962	5.00	10.00	20.00
❏ LP-1003 [M]	Eldee Young and Company	1962	5.00	10.00	20.00
❏ LPS-1003 [S]	Eldee Young and Company	1962	6.25	12.50	25.00

Number	Title (A Side/B Side)	Yr	VG	VG+	NM
YOUNG, FARON					
ALLEGIANCE					
❏ AV-5008	The Sheriff	198?	2.50	5.00	10.00
CAPITOL					
❏ T 778 [M]	Sweethearts or Strangers	1957	15.00	30.00	60.00
—Turquoise or gray label					
❏ T 778 [M]	Sweethearts or Strangers	1959	6.25	12.50	25.00
—Black colorband label, logo at left					
❏ T 1004 [M]	The Object of My Affection	1958	12.50	25.00	50.00
❏ T 1096 [M]	This Is Faron Young	1959	12.50	25.00	50.00
❏ T 1185 [M]	My Garden of Prayer	1959	10.00	20.00	40.00
❏ ST 1245 [S]	Talk About Hits	1959	10.00	20.00	40.00
❏ T 1245 [M]	Talk About Hits	1959	7.50	15.00	30.00
❏ ST 1450 [S]	The Best of Faron Young	1960	10.00	20.00	40.00
❏ T 1450 [M]	The Best of Faron Young	1960	7.50	15.00	30.00
❏ ST 1528 [S]	Hello Walls	1961	10.00	20.00	40.00
❏ T 1528 [M]	Hello Walls	1961	7.50	15.00	30.00
❏ ST 1634 [S]	The Young Approach	1961	10.00	20.00	40.00
❏ T 1634 [M]	The Young Approach	1961	7.50	15.00	30.00
❏ DT 1876 [P]	The All-Time Great Hits of Faron Young	1963	5.00	10.00	20.00
❏ T 1876 [M]	The All-Time Great Hits of Faron Young	1963	6.25	12.50	25.00
❏ DT 2037 [R]	Faron Young's Memory Lane	1964	5.00	10.00	20.00
❏ T 2037 [M]	Faron Young's Memory Lane	1964	6.25	12.50	25.00
❏ ST 2307 [S]	Falling in Love	1965	6.25	12.50	25.00
❏ T 2307 [M]	Falling in Love	1965	5.00	10.00	20.00
❏ DT 2536 [R]	If You Ain't Lovin' You Ain't Livin'	1966	5.00	10.00	20.00
❏ T 2536 [M]	If You Ain't Lovin' You Ain't Livin'	1966	6.25	12.50	25.00
HILLTOP					
❏ JM-6037 [M]	Faron Young	1966	3.75	7.50	15.00
❏ JS-6037 [S]	Faron Young	1966	3.00	6.00	12.00
❏ JS-6073	I'll Be Yours	1968	3.00	6.00	12.00
MARY CARTER					
❏ MC 1000 [M]	Faron Young Sings on Stage for Mary Carter Paints	196?	15.00	30.00	60.00
—Promotional item for sponsor of The Faron Young Show					
MCA					
❏ 757	Chapter Two	198?	2.00	4.00	8.00
—Budget-line reissue of 3092					
❏ 3092	Chapter Two	1979	3.00	6.00	12.00
❏ 3212	Free and Easy	1980	3.00	6.00	12.00
MERCURY					
❏ SRM-1-674	Just What I Had in Mind	1973	3.75	7.50	15.00
❏ SRM-1-698	Faron Young Sings "Some Kind of a Woman"	1974	3.75	7.50	15.00
❏ SRM-1-1016	A Man and His Music	1974	3.00	6.00	12.00
❏ SRM-1-1075	I'd Just Be Fool Enough	1976	3.00	6.00	12.00
❏ SRM-1-1130	The Best of Faron Young, Vol. 2	1977	3.00	6.00	12.00
❏ SRM-1-5005	Young Feelin'	1978	3.00	6.00	12.00
❏ MG 20785 [M]	This Is Faron	1963	5.00	10.00	20.00
❏ MG 20840 [M]	Faron Young Aims at the West	1963	5.00	10.00	20.00
❏ MG 20896 [M]	Story Songs for Country Folks	1964	5.00	10.00	20.00
❏ MG 20931 [M]	Country Dance Favorites	1964	5.00	10.00	20.00
❏ MG 20971 [M]	Story Songs of Mountains and Valleys	1965	5.00	10.00	20.00
❏ MG 21007 [M]	Pen and Paper	1965	5.00	10.00	20.00
❏ MG 21047 [M]	Faron Young's Greatest Hits	1965	5.00	10.00	20.00
❏ MG 21058 [M]	Faron Young Sings the Best of Jim Reeves	1966	5.00	10.00	20.00
❏ MG 21110 [M]	Unmitigated Gall	1967	6.25	12.50	25.00
❏ SR 60785 [S]	This Is Faron	1963	6.25	12.50	25.00
❏ SR 60840 [S]	Faron Young Aims at the West	1963	6.25	12.50	25.00
❏ SR 60896 [S]	Story Songs for Country Folks	1964	6.25	12.50	25.00
❏ SR 60931 [S]	Country Dance Favorites	1964	6.25	12.50	25.00
❏ SR 60971 [S]	Story Songs of Mountains and Valleys	1965	6.25	12.50	25.00
❏ SR 61007 [S]	Pen and Paper	1965	6.25	12.50	25.00
❏ SR 61047 [S]	Faron Young's Greatest Hits	1965	6.25	12.50	25.00
❏ SR 61058 [S]	Faron Young Sings the Best of Jim Reeves	1966	6.25	12.50	25.00
❏ SR 61110 [S]	Unmitigated Gall	1967	5.00	10.00	20.00
❏ SR 61143	Greatest Hits Vol. 2	1968	5.00	10.00	20.00
❏ SR 61174	Here's Faron Young	1968	5.00	10.00	20.00
❏ SR 61212	I've Got Precious Memories	1969	5.00	10.00	20.00
❏ SR 61241	Wine Me Up	1969	5.00	10.00	20.00
❏ SR 61267	The Best of Faron Young	1970	5.00	10.00	20.00
❏ SR 61275	Faron Young Sings "Occasional Wife" and "If I Ever Fall in Love with a Honky Tonk Girl"	1970	5.00	10.00	20.00
❏ SR 61337	Step Aside	1971	5.00	10.00	20.00
❏ SR 61354	Faron Young Sings "Leavin' and Sayin' Goodbye"	1971	3.75	7.50	15.00
❏ SR 61359	It's Four in the Morning	1972	3.75	7.50	15.00
—Revised title to reflect the hit?					
❏ SR 61359	Evening	1972	5.00	10.00	20.00
—Original title?					
❏ SR 61364	Faron Young Sings This Little Girl of Mine	1972	3.75	7.50	15.00
❏ SR 61376	This Time the Hurtin's on Me	1973	3.75	7.50	15.00
PICCADILLY					
❏ 3547	Hello Walls	198?	2.50	5.00	10.00
SEARS					
❏ SPS-124	Candy Kisses	1969	6.25	12.50	25.00
SESAC					
❏ (# unknown) [DJ]	Church Songs	196?	20.00	40.00	80.00
TOWER					
❏ DT 5022 [R]	It's a Great Life	1966	3.00	6.00	12.00
❏ T 5022 [M]	It's a Great Life	1966	5.00	10.00	20.00
❏ DT 5121	The World of Faron Young	1968	3.75	7.50	15.00

YOUNG, JESSE COLIN
Also see THE YOUNGBLOODS.
CAPITOL
❏ T 2070 [M]	The Soul of a City Boy	1964	12.50	25.00	50.00
❏ ST-11267	The Soul of a City Boy	1974	3.00	6.00	12.00
—Reissue of 2070					
❏ N-16129	The Soul of a City Boy	1981	2.00	4.00	8.00
—Budget-line reissue					

Number	Title (A Side/B Side)	Yr	VG	VG+	NM

CYPRESS

Number	Title (A Side/B Side)	Yr	VG	VG+	NM
❑ 0103	The Highway Is for Heroes	1987	2.50	5.00	10.00

ELEKTRA

| ❑ 6E-157 | American Dreams | 1978 | 2.50 | 5.00 | 10.00 |

MERCURY

| ❑ MG 21005 [M] | Young Blood | 1965 | 7.50 | 15.00 | 30.00 |
| ❑ SR 61005 [S] | Young Blood | 1965 | 10.00 | 20.00 | 40.00 |

RACCOON

| ❑ BS 2588 | Together | 1972 | 3.00 | 6.00 | 12.00 |

WARNER BROS.

❑ BS 2734	Song for Juli	1973	2.50	5.00	10.00
❑ BS 2790	Light Shine	1974	2.50	5.00	10.00
❑ BS 2845	Songbird	1975	2.50	5.00	10.00
❑ BS 2913	On the Road	1976	2.50	5.00	10.00
❑ BS 3033	Love on the Wing	1977	2.50	5.00	10.00

YOUNG, JOHN

ARGO

❑ LP-612 [M]	Young John Young	1957	10.00	20.00	40.00
❑ LP-692 [M]	Themes and Things	1962	6.25	12.50	25.00
❑ LPS-692 [S]	Themes and Things	1962	7.50	15.00	30.00
❑ LP-713 [M]	A Touch of Pepper	1962	6.25	12.50	25.00
❑ LPS-713 [S]	A Touch of Pepper	1962	7.50	15.00	30.00

DELMARK

| ❑ DL-403 [M] | The John Young Trio | 1961 | 7.50 | 15.00 | 30.00 |
| ❑ DS-403 [S] | The John Young Trio | 1961 | 10.00 | 20.00 | 40.00 |

VEE JAY

| ❑ VJS-3060 | Opus de Funk | 1974 | 5.00 | 10.00 | 20.00 |

YOUNG, JOHNNY

ARHOOLIE

| ❑ F-1029 | Johnny Williams and His Chicago Blues Band | 1965 | 6.25 | 12.50 | 25.00 |
| ❑ F-1037 | Chicago Blues | 1966 | 6.25 | 12.50 | 25.00 |

BLUE HORIZON

| ❑ BH-4609 | Blues Masters, Volume 9 | 1969 | 5.00 | 10.00 | 20.00 |

YOUNG, KATHY, AND THE INNOCENTS

INDIGO

| ❑ LP-504 [M] | The Sound of Kathy Young | 1961 | 75.00 | 150.00 | 300.00 |

YOUNG, LARRY

BLUE NOTE

❑ BLP-4187 [M]	Into Somethin'	1964	7.50	15.00	30.00
❑ BLP-4221 [M]	Unity	1966	7.50	15.00	30.00
❑ BLP-4242 [M]	Of Love and Peace	1966	7.50	15.00	30.00
❑ BLP-4266 [S]	Contrasts	1967	10.00	20.00	40.00
❑ BST-84187 [S]	Into Somethin'	1964	10.00	20.00	40.00
—With "New York, USA" address on label					
❑ BST-84187 [S]	Into Somethin'	1967	5.00	10.00	20.00
—With "A Division of Liberty Records" on label					
❑ BST-84221 [S]	Unity	1966	10.00	20.00	40.00
—With "New York, USA" address on label					
❑ BST-84221 [S]	Unity	1967	5.00	10.00	20.00
—With "A Division of Liberty Records" on label					
❑ BST-84242 [S]	Of Love and Peace	1966	10.00	20.00	40.00
—With "New York, USA" address on label					
❑ BST-84242 [S]	Of Love and Peace	1967	5.00	10.00	20.00
—With "A Division of Liberty Records" on label					
❑ BST-84266 [S]	Contrasts	1967	7.50	15.00	30.00
—With "A Division of Liberty Records" on label					
❑ BST-84304 [S]	Heaven on Earth	1968	7.50	15.00	30.00
—With "A Division of Liberty Records" on label					

MOSAIC

| ❑ M9-137 [(9)] | The Complete Blue Note Recordings of Larry Young | 199? | 50.00 | 100.00 | 200.00 |

NEW JAZZ

❑ NJLP-8249 [M]	Testifying	1960	12.50	25.00	50.00
—Purple label					
❑ NJLP-8249 [M]	Testifying	1965	6.25	12.50	25.00
—Blue label, trident logo at right					
❑ NJLP-8264 [M]	Young Blues	1961	12.50	25.00	50.00
—Purple label					
❑ NJLP-8264 [M]	Young Blues	1965	6.25	12.50	25.00
—Blue label, trident logo at right					

PRESTIGE

| ❑ PRLP-7237 [M] | Groove Street | 1962 | 10.00 | 20.00 | 40.00 |
| ❑ PRST-7237 [S] | Groove Street | 1962 | 10.00 | 20.00 | 40.00 |

YOUNG, LEON

ATCO

| ❑ 33-163 [M] | Liverpool Sound for Strings | 1964 | 6.25 | 12.50 | 25.00 |
| ❑ SD 33-163 [S] | Liverpool Sound for Strings | 1964 | 7.50 | 15.00 | 30.00 |

YOUNG, LESTER

ALADDIN

❑ LP-705 [10]	Lester Young Trio	1953	75.00	150.00	300.00
❑ LP-706 [10]	Easy Does It	1954	75.00	150.00	300.00
❑ LP-801 [M]	Lester Young and His Tenor Sax, Volume 1	1956	30.00	60.00	120.00
❑ LP-802 [M]	Lester Young and His Tenor Sax, Volume 2	1956	30.00	60.00	120.00

AMERICAN RECORDING SOCIETY

| ❑ G-417 [M] | Pres and Teddy | 1957 | 12.50 | 25.00 | 50.00 |

CHARLIE PARKER

| ❑ CLP-402 [M] | Pres | 1961 | 12.50 | 25.00 | 50.00 |
| ❑ CLP-405 [M] | Pres Is Blue | 1961 | 12.50 | 25.00 | 50.00 |

CLEF

❑ MGC-104 [10]	The Lester Young Trio	1953	62.50	125.00	250.00
❑ MGC-108 [10]	Lester Young Collates	1953	62.50	125.00	250.00
❑ MGC-124 [10]	Lester Young Collates No. 2	1953	62.50	125.00	250.00
—Some copies of this have Mercury covers; no difference in value					
❑ MGC-135 [10]	The Lester Young Trio No. 2	1953	62.50	125.00	250.00

COMMODORE

Number	Title (A Side/B Side)	Yr	VG	VG+	NM
❑ FL-20021 [10]	Kansas City Style	1952	75.00	150.00	300.00
❑ FL-30014 [M]	Kansas City Style	1959	25.00	50.00	100.00

CROWN

| ❑ CLP-5305 [M] | Nat "King" Cole Meets Lester Young | 196? | 6.25 | 12.50 | 25.00 |

EPIC

❑ LN 3107 [M]	Lester Leaps In	1956	25.00	50.00	100.00
❑ LN 3168 [M]	Let's Go to Pres	1956	25.00	50.00	100.00
❑ LN 3576 [M]	Lester Young Memorial Album, Volume 1	1959	12.50	25.00	50.00
❑ LN 3577 [M]	Lester Young Memorial Album, Volume 2	1959	12.50	25.00	50.00
❑ SN 6031 [(2)M]	Lester Young Memorial Album	1959	37.50	75.00	150.00

IMPERIAL

❑ LP-9181-A [M]	The Immortal Lester Young	1962	12.50	25.00	50.00
❑ LP-9187-A [M]	The Great Lester Young, Volume 2	1962	12.50	25.00	50.00
❑ LP-12181-A [R]	The Immortal Lester Young	196?	5.00	10.00	20.00
❑ LP-12187-A [R]	The Great Lester Young, Volume 2	196?	5.00	10.00	20.00

INTRO

| ❑ LP-602 [M] | Swinging Lester Young | 1957 | 25.00 | 50.00 | 100.00 |
| ❑ LP-603 [M] | The Greatest | 1957 | 25.00 | 50.00 | 100.00 |

MAINSTREAM

❑ 56002 [M]	The Influence of Five	1965	6.25	12.50	25.00
❑ 56004 [M]	Town Hall Concert	1965	6.25	12.50	25.00
❑ 56008 [M]	Chairman of the Board	1965	6.25	12.50	25.00
❑ 56009 [M]	52nd Street	1965	6.25	12.50	25.00
❑ 56012 [M]	Prez	1965	6.25	12.50	25.00

MERCURY

| ❑ MGC-104 [10] | The Lester Young Trio | 1951 | 75.00 | 150.00 | 300.00 |
| ❑ MGC-108 [10] | Lester Young Collates | 1951 | 75.00 | 150.00 | 300.00 |

NORGRAN

❑ MGN-5 [10]	Lester Young with the Oscar Peterson Trio No. 1	1954	50.00	100.00	200.00
❑ MGN-6 [10]	Lester Young with the Oscar Peterson Trio No. 2	1954	50.00	100.00	200.00
❑ MGN-1005 [M]	The President	1954	50.00	100.00	200.00
❑ MGN-1022 [M]	Lester Young	1955	50.00	100.00	200.00
❑ MGN-1043 [M]	Pres and Sweets	1955	50.00	100.00	200.00
❑ MGN-1054 [M]	The President Plays with the Oscar Peterson Trio	1955	25.00	50.00	100.00
❑ MGN-1071 [M]	Lester's Here	1956	25.00	50.00	100.00
❑ MGN-1072 [M]	Pres	1956	25.00	50.00	100.00
❑ MGN-1074 [M]	Lester Young and the Buddy Rich Trio	1956	25.00	50.00	100.00
❑ MGN-1093 [M]	Lester Swings Again	1956	25.00	50.00	100.00
❑ MGN-1100 [M]	Lester Young	1956	25.00	50.00	100.00

SAVOY

❑ MG-9002 [10]	Lester Young (All Star Be Bop)	1951	75.00	150.00	300.00
❑ MG-12068 [M]	Blue Lester	1956	20.00	40.00	80.00
❑ MG-12071 [M]	The Master's Touch	1956	20.00	40.00	80.00
❑ MG-12155 [M]	The Immortal Lester Young	1959	15.00	30.00	60.00

SCORE

❑ SLP-4019 [M]	Lester Young / The King Cole Trio	1958	20.00	40.00	80.00
❑ SLP-4028 [M]	Swinging Lester Young	1958	20.00	40.00	80.00
❑ SLP-4029 [M]	The Great Lester Young	1958	20.00	40.00	80.00

VERVE

❑ VSP-27 [M]	Pres and His Cabinet	1966	6.25	12.50	25.00
❑ VSP-30 [M]	Giants 3	1966	6.25	12.50	25.00
—With Buddy Rich and Nat King Cole					
❑ MGV-8134 [M]	Pres and Sweets	1957	15.00	30.00	60.00
❑ V-8134 [M]	Pres and Sweets	1961	6.25	12.50	25.00
❑ MGV-8144 [M]	The President Plays with the Oscar Peterson Trio	1957	15.00	30.00	60.00
❑ V-8144 [M]	The President Plays with the Oscar Peterson Trio	1961	6.25	12.50	25.00
❑ MGV-8161 [M]	Lester's Here	1957	15.00	30.00	60.00
❑ V-8161 [M]	Lester's Here	1961	6.25	12.50	25.00
❑ MGV-8162 [M]	Pres	1957	15.00	30.00	60.00
❑ V-8162 [M]	Pres	1961	6.25	12.50	25.00
❑ MGV-8164 [M]	Lester Young and the Buddy Rich Trio	1957	15.00	30.00	60.00
❑ V-8164 [M]	Lester Young and the Buddy Rich Trio	1961	6.25	12.50	25.00
❑ MGV-8181 [M]	Lester Swings Again	1957	15.00	30.00	60.00
❑ V-8181 [M]	Lester Swings Again	1961	6.25	12.50	25.00
❑ MGV-8187 [M]	It Don't Mean a Thing (If It Ain't Got That Swing)	1957	15.00	30.00	60.00
❑ V-8187 [M]	It Don't Mean a Thing (If It Ain't Got That Swing)	1961	6.25	12.50	25.00
❑ MGV-8205 [M]	Pres and Teddy	1957	15.00	30.00	60.00
❑ V-8205 [M]	Pres and Teddy	1961	6.25	12.50	25.00
❑ MGV-8308 [M]	The Lester Young Story	1959	15.00	30.00	60.00
❑ V-8308 [M]	The Lester Young Story	1961	6.25	12.50	25.00
❑ MGV-8378 [M]	Lester Young in Paris	1960	15.00	30.00	60.00
❑ V-8378 [M]	Lester Young in Paris	1961	6.25	12.50	25.00
❑ MGV-8398 [M]	The Essential Lester Young	1961	15.00	30.00	60.00
❑ V-8398 [M]	The Essential Lester Young	1961	6.25	12.50	25.00

YOUNG, LESTER/COUNT BASIE

MERCURY

| ❑ MG-25015 [10] | Lester Young Quartet/Count Basie Seven | 1950 | 62.50 | 125.00 | 250.00 |

YOUNG, LESTER/CHU BERRY

JAZZTONE

| ❑ J-1218 [M] | Tops on Tenor: Pres and Chu | 1956 | 17.50 | 35.00 | 70.00 |

YOUNG, LESTER; ROY ELDRIDGE; HARRY "SWEETS" EDISON

VERVE

❑ MGVS-6054 [S]	Laughin' to Keep from Cryin'	1960	17.50	35.00	70.00
❑ MGVS-6054 [S]	Laughin' to Keep from Cryin'	199?	6.25	12.50	25.00
—Classic Records reissue on audiophile vinyl					
❑ MGV-8298 [M]	Going for Myself	1959	15.00	30.00	60.00
❑ V-8298 [M]	Going for Myself	1961	6.25	12.50	25.00
❑ MGV-8316 [M]	Laughin' to Keep from Cryin'	1960	15.00	30.00	60.00
❑ V-8316 [M]	Laughin' to Keep from Cryin'	1961	6.25	12.50	25.00
❑ V6-8316 [S]	Laughin' to Keep from Cryin'	1961	7.50	15.00	30.00

Number	Title (A Side/B Side)	Yr	VG	VG+	NM

YOUNG, LESTER, AND ILLINOIS JACQUET
ALADDIN
| ☐ LP-701 [10] | Battle of the Saxes | 1953 | 100.00 | 200.00 | 400.00 |

YOUNG, LESTER, AND PAUL QUINICHETTE
EMARCY
| ☐ MG-26021 [10] | Pres Meets Vice-Pres | 1954 | 62.50 | 125.00 | 250.00 |

YOUNG, NEIL
Also see BUFFALO SPRINGFIELD; CROSBY, STILLS, NASH AND YOUNG.
GEFFEN
☐ GHS 2018	Trans	1982	2.50	5.00	10.00
—Later pressings have neither sticker nor title of absent song					
☐ GHS 2018	Trans	1982	3.75	7.50	15.00
—First pressings have a sticker on rear cover explaining the absence of "If You've Got Love"					
☐ GHS 2018 [DJ]	Trans	1982	5.00	10.00	20.00
—Promo on Quiex II audiophile vinyl					
☐ GHS 4013	Everybody's Rockin'	1983	2.50	5.00	10.00
☐ GHS 4013	Everybody's Rockin'	1983	5.00	10.00	20.00
—Promo on Quiex II audiophile vinyl					
☐ GHS 24068	Old Ways	1985	3.00	6.00	12.00
☐ GHS 24109	Landing on Water	1986	3.00	6.00	12.00
☐ GHS 24154	Life	1987	3.00	6.00	12.00
☐ R 134125	Landing on Water	1986	3.75	7.50	15.00
—RCA Music Service edition					
☐ R 144439	Life	1987	3.75	7.50	15.00
—BMG Direct Marketing edition					
☐ R 163233	Old Ways	1985	3.75	7.50	15.00
—RCA Music Service edition					
MOBILE FIDELITY
| ☐ 1-252 | Old Ways | 1996 | 5.00 | 10.00 | 20.00 |
| —Audiophile vinyl | | | | | |
NAUTILUS
| ☐ NR-44 | Harvest | 1982 | 37.50 | 75.00 | 150.00 |
| —Audiophile vinyl | | | | | |
REPRISE
☐ MS 2032	Harvest	1972	2.50	5.00	10.00
☐ MS 2032	Harvest	1972	3.75	7.50	15.00
—First pressings have textured cover and lyric insert					
☐ M 2151 [M]	Time Fades Away	1973	25.00	50.00	100.00
—Special mono pressing for radio stations only					
☐ MS 2151	Time Fades Away	1973	2.50	5.00	10.00
☐ MS 2151 [S]	Time Fades Away	1973	50.00	100.00	200.00
—With a cardboard inner sleeve, withdrawn after the earliest pressing					
☐ R 2180	On the Beach	1974	5.00	10.00	20.00
☐ MS 2221	Tonight's the Night	1975	2.50	5.00	10.00
☐ MS 2242	Zuma	1975	2.50	5.00	10.00
☐ 3RS 2257 [(3)]	Decade	1977	5.00	10.00	20.00
☐ 3RS 2257 [(3)DJ]	Decade	1977	125.00	250.00	500.00
—Test pressing; "Campaigner" contains extra verse deleted from the final version					
☐ MSK 2261	American Stars 'N' Bars	1977	2.50	5.00	10.00
☐ MSK 2266	Comes A Time	1978	2.50	5.00	10.00
—With "Peace of Mind" as the last song on side 1. Covers can list either "Lotta Love" or "Peace of Mind."					
☐ MSK 2266	Comes A Time	1978	18.75	37.50	75.00
—With "Lotta Love" listed and playing as the last song on side 1					
☐ MSK 2266 [DJ]	Give to the Wind	1978	250.00	500.00	1000.
—Test pressing; plain white jacket with inserts and STOCK COPY LABEL. Title changed to "Comes A Time" for commercial release.					
☐ MSK 2277	Harvest	1978	2.00	4.00	8.00
—Brown "Reprise" label; new number					
☐ MSK 2282	Everybody Knows This Is Nowhere	1978	2.00	4.00	8.00
—Brown "Reprise" label; new number					
☐ MSK 2283	After the Gold Rush	1978	10.00	20.00	40.00
—Contains remixed extended version of "When You Dance I Can Really Love." Title on cover in red, "RE 2" in trail-off vinyl					
☐ HS 2295	Rust Never Sleeps	1979	2.50	5.00	10.00
☐ 2RX 2296 [(2)]	Live Rust	1979	3.75	7.50	15.00
☐ HS 2297	Hawks and Doves	1980	2.50	5.00	10.00
☐ HS 2304	Re-Ac-Tor	1981	2.50	5.00	10.00
☐ RS 6317	Neil Young	1968	50.00	100.00	200.00
—Brown and orange "Reprise/W7" label, no name on front cover, no "RE-1" in trail-off wax					
☐ RS 6317	Neil Young	1969	15.00	30.00	60.00
—Re-release: Brown and orange "Reprise/W7" label, no name on front cover, four tracks remixed ("RE 1" in trail-off wax)					
☐ RS 6317	Neil Young	1970	3.75	7.50	15.00
—Reissue: Brown "Reprise" label, Neil Young's name is now on front cover					
☐ RS 6349	Everybody Knows This Is Nowhere	1969	7.50	15.00	30.00
—Brown and orange "Reprise/W7" label					
☐ RS 6349	Everybody Knows This Is Nowhere	1970	3.75	7.50	15.00
—Brown "Reprise" label					
☐ RS 6349 [DJ]	Everybody Knows This Is Nowhere	1969	18.75	37.50	75.00
—White label promo					
☐ RS 6383	After the Gold Rush	1970	2.50	5.00	10.00
—Brown "Reprise" label					
☐ RS 6383	After the Gold Rush	1970	3.75	7.50	15.00
—Brown and orange label; all photos correct					
☐ RS 6383	After the Gold Rush	1970	8.75	17.50	35.00
—Brown and orange label; photo of Neil Young appears erroneously printed upside down in gatefold					
☐ RS 6383	After the Gold Rush	1970	10.00	20.00	40.00
—Brown and orange label; photo of Marc Bolan (of T. Rex) appears erroneously in gatefold					
☐ 2XS 6480 [(2)]	Journey Through the Past (Soundtrack)	1972	5.00	10.00	20.00
☐ 25719	This Note's for You	1988	3.00	6.00	12.00
☐ 25899	Freedom	1989	3.75	7.50	15.00
☐ 26315	Ragged Glory	1990	5.00	10.00	20.00
☐ 45749 [(2)]	Sleeps with Angels	1994	3.75	7.50	15.00
☐ 45934 [(2)]	Mirror Ball	1995	3.75	7.50	15.00
—With Pearl Jam (uncredited)					
☐ 46291 [(2)]	Broken Arrow	1996	3.75	7.50	15.00
☐ 46652 [(2)]	Year of the Horse	1997	3.75	7.50	15.00
☐ SMAS-94285	Harvest	1972	6.25	12.50	25.00
—Capitol Record Club edition					

☐ R 113998	Harvest	1972	3.00	6.00	12.00
—RCA Music Service edition					
☐ R 154182	This Note's for You	1987	3.00	6.00	12.00
—BMG Direct Marketing edition					
VAPOR
| ☐ 46171 [(2)] | Dead Man (Soundtrack) | 1996 | 3.00 | 6.00 | 12.00 |
WARNER BROS.
| ☐ WBMS-107 [DJ] | The Warner Bros. Music Show | 1979 | 12.50 | 25.00 | 50.00 |
| —Promo-only interview album | | | | | |

YOUNG, WEBSTER
PRESTIGE
| ☐ PRLP-7106 [M] | For Lady | 1957 | 25.00 | 50.00 | 100.00 |

YOUNG HEARTS, THE
MINIT
| ☐ LP-24016 [S] | Sweet Soul Shakin'! | 1968 | 6.25 | 12.50 | 25.00 |
| ☐ LP-40016 [M] | Sweet Soul Shakin'! | 1968 | 6.25 | 12.50 | 25.00 |

YOUNG-HOLT UNLIMITED
ATLANTIC
| ☐ SD 1634 | Oh Girl | 1973 | 3.00 | 6.00 | 12.00 |
BRUNSWICK
☐ BL 54121 [M]	Wack-Wack	1966	5.00	10.00	20.00
—As "Young-Holt Trio"					
☐ BL 54125 [M]	On Stage	1967	5.00	10.00	20.00
—As "Young-Holt Trio"					
☐ BL 54128 [M]	The Beat Goes On	1967	7.50	15.00	30.00
☐ BL 754121 [S]	Wack-Wack	1966	5.00	10.00	20.00
—As "Young-Holt Trio"					
☐ BL 754125 [S]	On Stage	1967	5.00	10.00	20.00
—As "Young-Holt Trio"					
☐ BL 754128 [S]	The Beat Goes On	1967	5.00	10.00	20.00
☐ BL 754141	Funky But!	1968	5.00	10.00	20.00
☐ BL 754144	Soulful Strut	1968	3.75	7.50	15.00
☐ BL 754150	Just a Melody	1969	3.75	7.50	15.00
CADET
☐ LP-791 [M]	Feature Spot	1967	7.50	15.00	30.00
☐ LPS-791 [S]	Feature Spot	1967	5.00	10.00	20.00
—As "Eldee Young and Red Holt (of the Ramsey Lewis Trio)"					
COTILLION
| ☐ SD 18001 | Mellow Dreamin' | 1971 | 3.00 | 6.00 | 12.00 |
| ☐ SD 18004 | Born Again | 1972 | 3.00 | 6.00 | 12.00 |
PAULA
| ☐ LPS-4002 | Super Fly | 1973 | 5.00 | 10.00 | 20.00 |

YOUNG LIONS, THE
VEE JAY
| ☐ LP-3013 [M] | The Young Lions | 1960 | 10.00 | 20.00 | 40.00 |
| ☐ SR-3013 [S] | The Young Lions | 1960 | 12.50 | 25.00 | 50.00 |

YOUNG MEN FROM MEMPHIS
UNITED ARTISTS
| ☐ UAL-4029 [M] | Down Home Reunion | 1959 | 12.50 | 25.00 | 50.00 |
| ☐ UAS-5029 [S] | Down Home Reunion | 1959 | 10.00 | 20.00 | 40.00 |

YOUNG RASCALS, THE
See THE RASCALS.

YOUNG TUXEDO BRASS BAND, THE
ATLANTIC
☐ 1297 [M]	Jazz Begins	1958	10.00	20.00	40.00
—Black label					
☐ 1297 [M]	Jazz Begins	1961	5.00	10.00	20.00
—Multicolor label, white "fan" logo at right					
☐ SD-1297 [M]	Jazz Begins	1958	12.50	25.00	50.00
—Green label					

YOUNGBLOODS, THE
Also see JESSE COLIN YOUNG.
MERCURY
☐ SR-61273	Two Trips	1970	6.25	12.50	25.00
—Gold border on cover					
☐ SR-61273	Two Trips	1971	5.00	10.00	20.00
—Red border on cover					
RACCOON
☐ WS 1878	Rock Festival	1970	3.00	6.00	12.00
☐ BS 2563	Ride the Wind	1971	3.00	6.00	12.00
☐ BS 2566	Good and Dusty	1971	3.00	6.00	12.00
☐ BS 2653	High on a Ridge Top	1972	3.00	6.00	12.00
RCA VICTOR
☐ AYL1-3680	The Best of the Youngbloods	1980	2.00	4.00	8.00
—"Best Buy Series" reissue					
☐ LPM-3724 [M]	The Youngbloods	1967	10.00	20.00	40.00
☐ LSP-3724	Get Together	1969	3.75	7.50	15.00
—Retitled version of "The Youngbloods"					
☐ LSP-3724 [S]	The Youngbloods	1967	6.25	12.50	25.00
☐ LPM-3865 [M]	Earth Music	1968	12.50	25.00	50.00
☐ LSP-3865 [S]	Earth Music	1968	6.25	12.50	25.00
☐ AFL1-4150	Elephant Mountain	1977	2.50	5.00	10.00
—Reissue of LSP-4150					
☐ LSP-4150	Elephant Mountain	1969	3.75	7.50	15.00
—Orange label					
☐ LSP-4150	Elephant Mountain	1975	3.00	6.00	12.00
—Tan label					
☐ AFL1-4399	The Best of the Youngbloods	1977	2.50	5.00	10.00
—Reissue of LSP-4399					
☐ LSP-4399	The Best of the Youngbloods	1970	3.75	7.50	15.00
☐ LSP-4561	Sunlight	1971	3.00	6.00	12.00
☐ VPS-6051 [(2)]	This Is the Youngbloods	1972	3.75	7.50	15.00

Number	Title (A Side/B Side)	Yr	VG	VG+	NM

YOUNGMAN, HENNY
URANIA
Number	Title (A Side/B Side)	Yr	VG	VG+	NM
❑ UR-9014 [M]	The Horse and Auto Race Game	195?	12.50	25.00	50.00

YUM YUM KIDS, THE
MGM
| ❑ E-4396 [M] | Yummy in Your Tummy | 1966 | 3.75 | 7.50 | 15.00 |
| ❑ SE-4396 [S] | Yummy in Your Tummy | 1966 | 5.00 | 10.00 | 20.00 |

YURO, TIMI
LIBERTY
❑ LRP-3208 [M]	Hurt	1961	10.00	20.00	40.00
❑ LRP-3212 [M]	Soul	1962	3.75	7.50	15.00
❑ LRP-3234 [M]	Let Me Call You Sweetheart	1962	3.75	7.50	15.00
❑ LRP-3263 [M]	What's a Matter Baby?	1963	3.75	7.50	15.00
❑ LRP-3286 [M]	The Best of Timi Yuro	1963	3.75	7.50	15.00
❑ LRP-3319 [M]	Make the World Go Away	1963	3.75	7.50	15.00
❑ LST-7208 [S]	Hurt	1961	12.50	25.00	50.00
❑ LST-7212 [S]	Soul	1962	5.00	10.00	20.00
❑ LST-7234 [S]	Let Me Call You Sweetheart	1962	5.00	10.00	20.00
❑ LST-7263 [S]	What's a Matter Baby?	1963	5.00	10.00	20.00
❑ LST-7286 [S]	The Best of Timi Yuro	1963	5.00	10.00	20.00
❑ LST-7319 [S]	Make the World Go Away	1963	5.00	10.00	20.00
❑ LST-7594	Something Bad on My Mind	1968	3.00	6.00	12.00
MERCURY
| ❑ MG-20963 [M] | The Amazing Timi Yuro | 1964 | 3.00 | 6.00 | 12.00 |
| ❑ SR-60963 [S] | The Amazing Timi Yuro | 1964 | 3.75 | 7.50 | 15.00 |
SUNSET
| ❑ SUM-1107 [M] | Timi Yuro | 1966 | 2.50 | 5.00 | 10.00 |
| ❑ SUS-5107 [S] | Timi Yuro | 1966 | 3.00 | 6.00 | 12.00 |
UNITED ARTISTS
| ❑ UA-LA429-E | The Very Best of Timi Yuro | 1974 | 3.00 | 6.00 | 12.00 |

Z

ZABACH, FLORIAN
DECCA
❑ DL 5367 [10]	The Hot Canary	1951	12.50	25.00	50.00
❑ DL 8086 [M]	Hour of Love	195?	6.25	12.50	25.00
—Black label, silver print					
❑ DL 8158 [M]	Dream of Romance	195?	6.25	12.50	25.00
—Black label, silver print					
❑ DL 8239 [M]	Hi-Fi Fiddle	195?	6.25	12.50	25.00
—Black label, silver print					

ZACHERLE, JOHN
CRESTVIEW
| ❑ CR 803 [M] | Zacherle's Monster Gallery | 1963 | 10.00 | 20.00 | 40.00 |
| ❑ CRS 7803 [S] | Zacherle's Monster Gallery | 1963 | 12.50 | 25.00 | 50.00 |
ELEKTRA
| ❑ EKL-190 [M] | Spook Along with Zacherle | 1960 | 15.00 | 30.00 | 60.00 |
| ❑ EKS-7190 [S] | Spook Along with Zacherle | 1960 | 20.00 | 40.00 | 80.00 |
PARKWAY
| ❑ P 7018 [M] | Monster Mash | 1962 | 15.00 | 30.00 | 60.00 |
| ❑ P 7023 [M] | Scary Tales | 1963 | 15.00 | 30.00 | 60.00 |

ZACK, GEORGE
COMMODORE
| ❑ FL-20001 [10] | Party Piano of the Roaring '20s | 1950 | 12.50 | 25.00 | 50.00 |

ZAGER AND EVANS
RCA VICTOR
❑ ANL1-1077	2525 (Exordium and Terminus)	1975	2.50	5.00	10.00
—Reissue of 4214					
❑ LSP-4214	2525 (Exordium and Terminus)	1969	5.00	10.00	20.00
❑ LSP-4302	Zager and Evans	1970	5.00	10.00	20.00
VANGUARD
| ❑ VSD-6568 | Food for the Mind | 1971 | 3.75 | 7.50 | 15.00 |
WHITE WHALE
| ❑ WWS-7123 | The Early Writings of Zager and Evans (And Others) | 1969 | 5.00 | 10.00 | 20.00 |
| —Actually doesn't contain any music by Zager or Evans, but only songs they wrote; it remains here as it's usually considered a "Zager and Evans" LP | | | | | |

ZANIES, THE
DORE
| ❑ 321 | The Zanies | 1969 | 7.50 | 15.00 | 30.00 |
| ❑ 337 | The Zanies | 1979 | 3.75 | 7.50 | 15.00 |

ZAPPA, FRANK
Includes his work with The Mothers of Invention.
ANGEL
| ❑ DS-38170 | Boulez Conducts Zappa: The Perfect Stranger | 1983 | 3.00 | 6.00 | 12.00 |
BARKING PUMPKIN
❑ 7X4-1	The Old Masters Sampler	1984	6.25	12.50	25.00
❑ AS 995 [DJ]	Tinsel Town Rebellion	1981	5.00	10.00	20.00
—Promo-only sampler					
❑ BPR-1111	Shut Up 'N' Play Yer Guitar	1981	5.00	10.00	20.00
—Mail-order item only					
❑ BPR-1112	Shut Up 'N' Play Yer Guitar Some More	1981	5.00	10.00	20.00
—Mail-order item only					
❑ BPR-1113	Return of the Son of Shut Up 'N' Play Yer Guitar	1981	5.00	10.00	20.00
—Mail-order item only					
❑ BPRP-1114 [PD]	Zappa	1982	3.75	7.50	15.00
—Picture disc with two songs					
❑ BPRP-1115 [PD]	Baby Snakes	1983	3.75	7.50	15.00
—Picture disc					

Number	Title (A Side/B Side)	Yr	VG	VG+	NM
❑ AS 1294 [DJ]	You Are What You Is Special Clean Cuts Edition	1981	5.00	10.00	20.00
❑ 7777 [(8)]	The Old Masters, Box 1	1984	15.00	30.00	60.00
—Boxed set					
❑ 8888 [(8)]	The Old Masters, Box 2	1986	15.00	30.00	60.00
—Another boxed set					
❑ 8888X	The Old Masters Sampler 2	1986	6.25	12.50	25.00
❑ 9999 [(8)]	The Old Masters, Box 3	1987	15.00	30.00	60.00
—Still another boxed set					
❑ PW2 37336 [(2)]	Tinsel Town Rebellion	1981	5.00	10.00	20.00
❑ PW2 37537 [(2)]	You Are What You Is	1981	5.00	10.00	20.00
❑ FW 38066	Ship Arriving Too Late to Save a Drowning Witch	1982	3.00	6.00	12.00
❑ W3X-38289 [(3)]	Shut Up 'N' Play Yer Guitar	1982	6.25	12.50	25.00
—Box set containing all three "Shut Up 'N' Play Yer Guitar" albums					
❑ FW 38403	Man from Utopia	1983	3.00	6.00	12.00
❑ FW 38820	London Symphony Orchestra	1983	3.00	6.00	12.00
❑ SVBO-74200 [(2)]	Them Or Us	1984	3.75	7.50	15.00
❑ SWCO-74201 [(3)]	Thing-Fish	1984	5.00	10.00	20.00
❑ ST-74202	Francesco Zappa	1985	2.50	5.00	10.00
❑ ST-74203	Frank Zappa Meets the Mothers of Prevention	1985	2.50	5.00	10.00
❑ ST-74205	Jazz from Hell	1986	2.50	5.00	10.00
❑ 74206 [(3)]	Joe's Garage, Acts 1, 2 and 3	1986	12.50	25.00	50.00
—Box set, two gatefolds, with insert					
❑ SJ-74207	London Symphony Orchestra, Volume 2	1987	2.50	5.00	10.00
❑ D1-74212 [(2)]	Guitar	1988	2.50	5.00	10.00
❑ D1-74213 [(3)]	You Can't Do That on Stage Anymore Sampler	1988	2.50	5.00	10.00
❑ R1 74213	You Can't Do That on Stage Anymore Sampler	1988	3.00	6.00	12.00
❑ D1-74217 [(3)]	You Can't Do That on Stage Anymore Vol. 2	1988	2.50	5.00	10.00
❑ D1-74218	Broadway the Hard Way	1988	2.50	5.00	10.00
BIZARRE
❑ MS-2024 [(2)]	Uncle Meat	1969	8.75	17.50	35.00
—Originals come with a booklet; blue label					
❑ MS-2024 [(2)]	Uncle Meat	1973	5.00	10.00	20.00
—Reissue with brown Reprise label					
❑ MS-2028	Weasels Ripped My Flesh	1970	6.25	12.50	25.00
—Blue label original					
❑ MS-2028	Weasels Ripped My Flesh	1973	3.75	7.50	15.00
—Reissue with brown Reprise label					
❑ MS 2030 [DJ]	Chunga's Revenge	1970	12.50	25.00	50.00
—White label promo					
❑ MS-2030	Chunga's Revenge	1970	6.25	12.50	25.00
—Blue label original					
❑ MS-2030	Chunga's Revenge	1973	3.75	7.50	15.00
—Reissue with brown Reprise label					
❑ MS-2042	Fillmore East, June 1971	1971	6.25	12.50	25.00
—Blue label original					
❑ MS-2042	Fillmore East, June 1971	1973	2.75	7.50	15.00
—Reissue with brown Reprise label					
❑ MS 2075	Just Another Band from L.A.	1972	6.25	12.50	25.00
—Blue label original					
❑ MS 2075	Just Another Band from L.A.	1973	3.75	7.50	15.00
—Reissue with brown Reprise label					
❑ MS 2093	The Grand Wazoo	1972	6.25	12.50	25.00
—Blue label original					
❑ MS 2093	The Grand Wazoo	1973	3.75	7.50	15.00
—Reissue with brown Reprise label					
❑ MS 2094	Waka/Jawaka	1972	6.25	12.50	25.00
—Blue label original					
❑ MS 2094	Waka/Jawaka	1973	3.75	7.50	15.00
—Reissue with brown Reprise label					
❑ RS-6356	Hot Rats	1969	12.50	25.00	50.00
—Blue label original					
❑ RS-6356	Hot Rats	1973	3.75	7.50	15.00
—Reissue with brown Reprise label					
❑ RS-6370	Burnt Weenie Sandwich	1970	6.25	12.50	25.00
—Blue label original; with booklet					
❑ RS-6370	Burnt Weenie Sandwich	1973	3.75	7.50	15.00
—Reissue with brown Reprise label					
COLUMBIA
| ❑ (no #) [(4)DJ] | Lather | 1977 | 187.50 | 375.00 | 750.00 |
| —Test pressing only; parts of this LP are on DSK 2291, 2292 and 2294; released as a whole only after Zappa's death, with vinyl only coming out in Japan | | | | | |
DISCREET
❑ MS 2149	Over-Nite Sensation	1973	5.00	10.00	20.00
❑ MS4 2149 [Q]	Over-Nite Sensation	1973	10.00	20.00	40.00
❑ DS 2175	Apostrophe (')	1974	3.75	7.50	15.00
❑ DS 2175	Apostrophe (')	1974	12.50	25.00	50.00
—White label promo					
❑ DS4 2175 [Q]	Apostrophe (')	1974	8.75	17.50	35.00
❑ 2DS 2202 [(2)]	Roxy and Elsewhere	1974	6.25	12.50	25.00
❑ DS 2216	One Size Fits All	1975	3.75	7.50	15.00
❑ DS 2234	Bongo Fury	1975	3.75	7.50	15.00
❑ DSK 2288	Over-Nite Sensation	1977	3.00	6.00	12.00
—Reissue of DiscReet 2149 with new number					
❑ DSK 2289	Apostrophe (')	1977	3.00	6.00	12.00
—Reissue with new number					
❑ 2D 2290 [(2)]	Zappa in New York	1978	5.00	10.00	20.00
❑ 2D 2290 [(2)]	Zappa in New York	1978	62.50	125.00	250.00
—Stock copy with "Punky's Whips" erroneously listed on jacket					
❑ 2D 2290 [(2)DJ]	Zappa in New York	1978	100.00	200.00	400.00
—Test pressing with "Punky's Whips"					
❑ DSK 2291	Studio Tan	1978	3.75	7.50	15.00
❑ DSK 2292	Sleep Dirt	1978	3.75	7.50	15.00
❑ DSK 2294	Orchestral Favorites	1978	3.75	7.50	15.00
FOO-EEE
❑ R1-70372 [(11)]	Beat the Boots #2	1992	25.00	50.00	100.00
—Legitimate box-set release by Rhino of 11 bootlegged concerts					
❑ R1-70907 [(10)]	Beat the Boots	1991	25.00	50.00	100.00
—Legitimate box-set release by Rhino of eight bootlegged concerts					

Number	Title (A Side/B Side)	Yr	VG	VG+	NM
MCA					
❑ 4183 [(2)]	200 Motels (movie soundtrack)	1986	3.75	7.50	15.00
—Reissue					
MGM					
❑ GAS-112	The Mothers of Invention	1970	12.50	25.00	50.00
❑ GAS-112 [DJ]	The Mothers of Invention	1970	25.00	50.00	100.00
—Yellow label promo					
❑ SE-4754	The Worst of the Mothers	1971	12.50	25.00	50.00
❑ SE-4754 [DJ]	The Worst of the Mothers	1971	37.50	75.00	150.00
—Yellow label promo					
RHINO/DEL-FI					
❑ RNEP-604	Rare Meat: The Early Productions of Frank Zappa	1984	10.00	20.00	40.00
—With original cover					
RYKO ANALOGUE					
❑ RALP 10503	We're Only in It for the Money	1995	3.00	6.00	12.00
—Vinyl reissue; Frank Zappa/The Mothers of Invention					
❑ RALP 40500 [(2)]	Strictly Commercial: The Best of Frank Zappa	1995	5.00	10.00	20.00
—Issued with obi					
UNITED ARTISTS					
❑ UAS-9956 [(2)]	200 Motels (movie soundtrack)	1971	12.50	25.00	50.00
VERVE					
❑ V-5005-2 [(2)M]	Freak Out!	1966	37.50	75.00	150.00
—Cover version 2: Has no blurb inside on getting a map of "freak-out hot spots"					
❑ V-5005-2 [(2)M]	Freak Out!	1966	50.00	100.00	200.00
—Cover version 1: Has blurb on inside gatefold on how to get a map of "freak-out hot spots" in L.A.					
❑ V-5005-2 [(2)M]	Freak Out!	1966	100.00	200.00	400.00
—White label promo					
❑ V6-5005-2 [(2)S]	Freak Out!	1966	15.00	30.00	60.00
—Cover version 2: Has no blurb inside on getting a map of "freak-out hot spots"					
❑ V6-5005-2 [(2)S]	Freak Out!	1966	20.00	40.00	80.00
—Cover version 1: Has blurb on inside gatefold on how to get a map of "freak-out hot spots" in L.A.					
❑ V6-5005-2 [(2)S]	Freak Out!	1966	75.00	150.00	300.00
—Yellow label promo					
❑ V-5013 [M]	Absolutely Free	1967	30.00	60.00	120.00
❑ V-5013 [M]	Absolutely Free	1967	50.00	100.00	200.00
—White label promo					
❑ V6-5013 [S]	Absolutely Free	1967	15.00	30.00	60.00
❑ V-5045 [M]	We're Only in It for the Money	1968	37.50	75.00	150.00
—With sheet of cut-outs a la "Sgt. Pepper's Lonely Hearts Club Band"					
❑ V-5045 [M]	We're Only in It for the Money	1968	75.00	150.00	300.00
—White label promo					
❑ V6-5045 [S]	We're Only in It for the Money	1968	15.00	30.00	60.00
—Un-censored version, with cut-outs					
❑ V6-5045 [S]	We're Only in It for the Money	1968	37.50	75.00	150.00
—Censored version: the songs "Who Needs the Peace Corps?" and "Let's Make the Water Turn Black" have lines deleted					
❑ V6-5055	Cruising with Ruben and the Jets	1968	15.00	30.00	60.00
❑ V6-5055 [DJ]	Cruising with Ruben and the Jets	1968	37.50	75.00	150.00
—Yellow label promo					
❑ V6-5068	Mothermania — The Best of the Mothers	1969	18.75	37.50	75.00
❑ V6-5068 [DJ]	Mothermania — The Best of the Mothers	1969	37.50	75.00	150.00
—Yellow label promo					
❑ V6-5074	The XXXX of the Mothers	1969	12.50	25.00	50.00
❑ V6-5074 [DJ]	The XXXX of the Mothers	1969	37.50	75.00	150.00
—Yellow label promo					
❑ V-8741 [M]	Lumpy Gravy	1968	75.00	150.00	300.00
—Yellow label promo; no stock copies were issued in mono					
❑ V6-8741	Lumpy Gravy	1968	12.50	25.00	50.00
❑ V6-8741 [DJ]	Lumpy Gravy	1968	50.00	100.00	200.00
—Yellow label promo					
WARNER BROS.					
❑ BS-2970	Zoot Allures	1976	3.75	7.50	15.00
ZAPPA					
❑ MK-78 [DJ]	Sheik Yerbouti Clean Cuts	1979	8.75	17.50	35.00
❑ MK-129 [DJ]	Joe's Garage Acts I, II and III Sampler	1980	8.75	17.50	35.00
❑ SRZ-2-1501 [(2)]	Sheik Yerbouti	1979	5.00	10.00	20.00
❑ SRZ-2-1502 [(2)]	Joe's Garage, Acts II and III	1980	5.00	10.00	20.00
❑ SRZ-1-1603	Joe's Garage, Act I	1979	3.75	7.50	15.00
ZAWINUL, JOE					
ATLANTIC					
❑ SD 1579	Zawinul	1970	5.00	10.00	20.00
❑ 3004 [M]	Money in the Pocket	1966	5.00	10.00	20.00
❑ SD 3004 [S]	Money in the Pocket	1966	6.25	12.50	25.00
VORTEX					
❑ 2002 [S]	The Rise and Fall of the 3rd Stream	1968	5.00	10.00	20.00
ZAZU					
WOODEN NICKEL					
❑ BWL1-0791	Zazu	1975	5.00	10.00	20.00
ZEITLIN, DENNY					
COLUMBIA					
❑ CL 2182 [M]	Cathexis	1964	5.00	10.00	20.00
❑ CL 2340 [M]	Carnival	1965	5.00	10.00	20.00
❑ CS 8982 [S]	Cathexis	1964	6.25	12.50	25.00
❑ CS 9140 [S]	Carnival	1965	6.25	12.50	25.00
❑ CS 9263 [S]	My Shining Hour	1966	5.00	10.00	20.00
❑ CS 9548 [S]	Zeitgeist	1966	5.00	10.00	20.00
ZENITHS, THE					
ATLANTIC					
❑ 8043 [M]	Makin' the Scene	1960	25.00	50.00	100.00
❑ SD 8043 [S]	Makin' the Scene	1960	37.50	75.00	150.00
ZENTNER, SI					
LIBERTY					
❑ LRP-3197 [M]	Big Band Plays the Big Hits	1961	3.00	6.00	12.00
❑ LRP-3216 [M]	Up a Lazy River (Big Band Plays the Big Hits: Vol. 2)	1962	3.00	6.00	12.00
❑ LRP-3247 [M]	The Stripper and Other Big Band Hits	1962	3.00	6.00	12.00
❑ LRP-3273 [M]	Desafinado	1963	3.00	6.00	12.00
❑ LRP-3284 [M]	Waltz in Jazz Time	1963	3.00	6.00	12.00
❑ LRP-3326 [M]	More	1963	3.00	6.00	12.00
❑ LRP-3350 [M]	Big Big Band Hits	1964	3.00	6.00	12.00
❑ LRP-3353 [M]	From Russia with Love	1964	3.00	6.00	12.00
❑ LRP-3457 [M]	The Best of Si Zentner	1966	3.00	6.00	12.00
❑ LST-7197 [S]	Big Band Plays the Big Hits	1961	3.75	7.50	15.00
❑ LST-7216 [S]	Up a Lazy River (Big Band Plays the Big Hits: Vol. 2)	1962	3.75	7.50	15.00
❑ LST-7247 [S]	The Stripper and Other Big Band Hits	1962	3.75	7.50	15.00
❑ LST-7273 [S]	Desafinado	1963	3.75	7.50	15.00
❑ LST-7284 [S]	Waltz in Jazz Time	1963	3.75	7.50	15.00
❑ LST-7326 [S]	More	1963	3.75	7.50	15.00
❑ LST-7350 [S]	Big Big Band Hits	1964	3.75	7.50	15.00
❑ LST-7353 [S]	From Russia with Love	1964	3.75	7.50	15.00
❑ LST-7457 [S]	The Best of Si Zentner	1966	3.00	6.00	12.00
❑ LMM-13009 [M]	A Great Band with Great Voices	1961	3.00	6.00	12.00
❑ LMM-13017 [M]	A Great Band with Great Voices Swing the Great Voices of the Great Bands	1962	3.00	6.00	12.00
❑ LSS-14009 [S]	A Great Band with Great Voices	1961	3.75	7.50	15.00
❑ LSS-14017 [S]	A Great Band with Great Voices Swing the Great Voices of the Great Bands	1962	3.75	7.50	15.00
SMASH					
❑ MGS-27007 [M]	Presenting Si Zentner	1961	3.75	7.50	15.00
❑ MGS-27013 [M]	Swing Fever	1962	3.75	7.50	15.00
❑ SRS-67007 [S]	Presenting Si Zentner	1961	5.00	10.00	20.00
❑ SRS-67013 [S]	Swing Fever	1962	5.00	10.00	20.00
SUNSET					
❑ SUM-1110 [M]	Big Band Brilliance	196?	2.50	5.00	10.00
❑ SUS-5110 [S]	Big Band Brilliance	196?	3.00	6.00	12.00
ZENTNER, SI AND MARTIN DENNY					
LIBERTY					
❑ LMM-13020 [M]	Exotica Suite	1962	3.75	7.50	15.00
❑ LSS-14020 [S]	Exotica Suite	1962	5.00	10.00	20.00
ZEPHYR					
PROBE					
❑ 4510	Zephyr	1969	12.50	25.00	50.00
WARNER BROS.					
❑ WS 1897	Goin' Back to Colorado	1971	10.00	20.00	40.00
❑ BS 2603	Sunset Ride	1972	5.00	10.00	20.00
ZERFAS					
700 WEST					
❑ 730710	Zerfas	1973	200.00	400.00	800.00
ZERO BOYS					
NIMROD					
❑ 1	Vicious Circle	1982	25.00	50.00	100.00
TOXIC SHOCK					
❑ TXLP 11	Vicious Circle	1987	7.50	15.00	30.00
—Reissue of Nimrod release					
ZEVON, WARREN					
ASYLUM					
❑ 6E-118	Excitable Boy	1978	2.50	5.00	10.00
❑ 5E-509	Bad Luck Streak in Dancing School	1979	2.50	5.00	10.00
❑ 5E-519	Stand in the Fire	1980	2.50	5.00	10.00
❑ 7E-1060	Warren Zevon	1976	2.50	5.00	10.00
❑ 60159	The Envoy	1982	2.50	5.00	10.00
❑ 60503	A Quiet Normal Life: The Best of Warren Zevon	1987	2.50	5.00	10.00
IMPERIAL					
❑ LP-12456	Wanted Dead or Alive	1970	7.50	15.00	30.00
—As "Zevon"					
PICKWICK					
❑ SPC-3715	Wanted Dead or Alive	1979	3.75	7.50	15.00
—Reissue of Imperial album					
VIRGIN					
❑ 90603	Sentimental Hygiene	1987	2.50	5.00	10.00
❑ 91068	Transverse City	1989	2.50	5.00	10.00
ZIG ZAG PEOPLE, THE					
DECCA					
❑ DL 75110	The Zig Zag People Take Bubble Gum Music Underground	1969	6.25	12.50	25.00
ZIP CODES, THE					
LIBERTY					
❑ LRP-3367 [M]	Mustang	1964	37.50	75.00	150.00
❑ LST-7367 [S]	Mustang	1964	50.00	100.00	200.00
ZIPPERS, THE					
RHINO					
❑ RNEP 601 [EP]	Six Song Mini Album	1981	7.50	15.00	30.00
ZIRCONS, THE					
SNOWFLAKE					
❑ 1003	The Crown Kings of Acappella	196?	15.00	30.00	60.00
ZITO, PHIL					
COLUMBIA					
❑ CL 6110 [10]	International City Dixielanders	1950	12.50	25.00	50.00
ZITRO, JAMES					
ESP-DISK'					
❑ 1052 [S]	Zitro	1968	6.25	12.50	25.00
ZOLLER, ATTILA					
EMBRYO					
❑ SD 523	Gypsy Cry	1970	5.00	10.00	20.00
INNER CITY					
❑ IC-3008	Dream Bells	1976	3.75	7.50	15.00

Z

Number	Title (A Side/B Side)	Yr	VG	VG+	NM	Number	Title (A Side/B Side)	Yr	VG	VG+	NM

ZOMBIES, THE

DATE

TES-4013	Odessey and Oracle	1968	7.50	15.00	30.00
	—With no mention of "Time of the Season" on front cover				
TES-4013	Odessey and Oracle	1969	5.00	10.00	20.00
	—With "Time of the Season" mentioned on front cover				

EPIC

KEG 32861 [(2)B]	Time of the Zombies	1974	5.00	10.00	20.00
	—Record 1 is mono; Record 2 is stereo; orange labels				
PEG 32861 [(2)B]	Time of the Zombies	1979	3.75	7.50	15.00
	—Later edition with blue labels				

LONDON

| PS 557 [P] | Early Days | 1969 | 5.00 | 10.00 | 20.00 |
| | —All tracks in true stereo except "Tell Her No" | | | | |

PARROT

| PA 61001 [M] | The Zombies | 1965 | 15.00 | 30.00 | 60.00 |
| PAS 71001 [R] | The Zombies | 1965 | 10.00 | 20.00 | 40.00 |

RHINO

| RNLP-120 | Live on the BBC, 1965-67 | 1985 | 2.50 | 5.00 | 10.00 |
| RNLP 70186 [S] | Odessy and Oracle | 1986 | 2.00 | 4.00 | 8.00 |

ZOO, THE

MERCURY

| SR-61300 | The Zoo | 1970 | 5.00 | 10.00 | 20.00 |

SUNBURST

| 7500 | The Zoo Presents the Chocolate Moose | 1968 | 12.50 | 25.00 | 50.00 |

ZURKE, BOB

RCA VICTOR

| LPM-1013 [M] | The Tom Cat on the Keys | 1955 | 20.00 | 40.00 | 80.00 |

ZZ TOP

LONDON

PS 584	ZZ Top's First Album	1971	3.00	6.00	12.00
PS 612	Rio Grande Mud	1972	3.00	6.00	12.00
XPS 631	Tres Hombres	1973	3.00	6.00	12.00
PS 656	Fandango!	1975	3.00	6.00	12.00
PS 680	Tejas	1977	3.00	6.00	12.00
PS 706	The Best of ZZ Top	1977	3.00	6.00	12.00
PS-X-1001 [DJ]	Takin' Texas to the People	1976	12.50	25.00	50.00

WARNER BROS.

BSK 3268	ZZ Top's First Album	1979	2.00	4.00	8.00
BSK 3269	Rio Grande Mud	1979	2.00	4.00	8.00
BSK 3270	Tres Hombres	1979	2.00	4.00	8.00
BSK 3271	Fandango!	1979	2.00	4.00	8.00
BSK 3272	Tejas	1979	2.00	4.00	8.00
BSK 3273	The Best of ZZ Top	1979	2.00	4.00	8.00
HS 3361	Deguello	1979	2.50	5.00	10.00
BSK 3593	El Loco	1981	2.50	5.00	10.00
23774	Eliminator	1983	2.00	4.00	8.00
25342	Afterburner	1985	2.00	4.00	8.00
26265	Recycler	1990	3.75	7.50	15.00
26846	Greatest Hits	1992	5.00	10.00	20.00
	—U.S. vinyl available only through Columbia House				

Number	Title (A Side/B Side)	Yr	VG	VG+	NM

ORIGINAL CAST RECORDINGS

110 IN THE SHADE
- ❑ RCA Victor LOC-1085 [M] — 1963 — 6.25 — 12.50 — 25.00
- ❑ RCA Victor LSO-1085 [S] — 1963 — 10.00 — 20.00 — 40.00

1776
- ❑ Columbia Masterworks BOS 3310 — 1969 — 3.00 — 6.00 — 12.00
—*Revised (correct) edition has Rex Everhart shown as Ben Franklin in credits and synopsis*
- ❑ Columbia Masterworks BOS 3310 — 1969 — 7.50 — 15.00 — 30.00
—*The first edition has Howard DaSilva shown as Ben Franklin in credits and synopsis, though he does not appear on the LP*

70 GIRLS, 70
- ❑ Columbia Masterworks S 30589 — 1971 — 12.50 — 25.00 — 50.00

ALL AMERICAN
- ❑ Columbia Masterworks KOS 2160 [S] — 1962 — 7.50 — 15.00 — 30.00
- ❑ Columbia Masterworks KOL 5760 [M] — 1962 — 6.25 — 12.50 — 25.00

ANKLES AWEIGHT
- ❑ Decca DL 9025 [M] — 1955 — 10.00 — 20.00 — 40.00

ANNIE GET YOUR GUN
- ❑ Decca DL 8001 [M] — 1949 — 12.50 — 25.00 — 50.00
—*Original LP issue of the Broadway cast*
- ❑ Decca DL 9018 [M] — 1955 — 10.00 — 20.00 — 40.00
—*Early issue of DL 8001; black label with silver print*
- ❑ Decca DL 79018 [R] — 196? — 3.00 — 6.00 — 12.00
- ❑ RCA Victor LOC-1124 [M] — 1966 — 3.00 — 6.00 — 12.00
- ❑ RCA Victor LSO-1124 [S] — 1966 — 3.75 — 7.50 — 15.00
—*Revival cast; black label, dog on top, "Stereo Dynagroove" at bottom*
- ❑ RCA Victor LSO-1124 [S] — 1969 — 2.50 — 5.00 — 10.00
—*Revival cast; orange, tan or black "dog near top" label*

ANYA
- ❑ United Artists UAL-4133 [M] — 1965 — 5.00 — 10.00 — 20.00
- ❑ United Artists UAS-5133 [S] — 1965 — 12.50 — 25.00 — 50.00

APPLAUSE
- ❑ ABC ABCS-OC-11 — 1970 — 5.00 — 10.00 — 20.00

THE APPLE TREE
- ❑ Columbia Masterworks KOS 3020 [S] — 1966 — 6.25 — 12.50 — 25.00
- ❑ Columbia Masterworks KOL 6620 [M] — 1966 — 5.00 — 10.00 — 20.00

ARABIAN NIGHTS
- ❑ Decca DL 9013 [M] — 1954 — 20.00 — 40.00 — 80.00

THE ATHENIAN TOUCH
- ❑ Broadway East OCM-101 [M] — 1964 — 37.50 — 75.00 — 150.00
- ❑ Broadway East OCS-101 [S] — 1964 — 50.00 — 100.00 — 200.00

BAJOUR
- ❑ Columbia Masterworks KOS 2700 [S] — 1964 — 7.50 — 15.00 — 30.00
- ❑ Columbia Masterworks KOL 6300 [M] — 1964 — 6.25 — 12.50 — 25.00

BAKER STREET (A MUSICAL ADVENTURE OF SHERLOCK HOLMES)
- ❑ MGM E-7000 [M] — 1965 — 6.25 — 12.50 — 25.00
- ❑ MGM SE-7000 [S] — 1965 — 7.50 — 15.00 — 30.00

A BALLAD FOR BIMSHIRE
- ❑ London AM 48002 [M] — 1963 — 10.00 — 20.00 — 40.00
- ❑ London AMS 78002 [S] — 1963 — 20.00 — 40.00 — 80.00

THE BALLAD OF BABY DOE
- ❑ MGM 3GC-1 [(3)M] — 1958 — 37.50 — 75.00 — 150.00
—*Box set*

THE BAND WAGON
- ❑ "X" LVA-1001 [M] — 1955 — 17.50 — 35.00 — 70.00

BELLS ARE RINGING
- ❑ Columbia Masterworks OS 2006 [S] — 1959 — 6.25 — 12.50 — 25.00
—*Re-recording in stereo of OL 5170*
- ❑ Columbia Masterworks OL 5170 [M] — 1957 — 7.50 — 15.00 — 30.00
—*Gray and black label with six "eye" logos*

BEN FRANKLIN IN PARIS
- ❑ Capitol SVAS 2191 [S] — 1964 — 7.50 — 15.00 — 30.00
- ❑ Capitol VAS 2191 [M] — 1964 — 6.25 — 12.50 — 25.00

BEST FOOT FORWARD
- ❑ Cadence CLP-4012 [M] — 1963 — 5.00 — 10.00 — 20.00
- ❑ Cadence CLP-24012 [S] — 1963 — 7.50 — 15.00 — 30.00
—*1963 revival of 1941 play*

BEYOND THE FRINGE
- ❑ Capitol SW 1792 [S] — 1962 — 7.50 — 15.00 — 30.00
- ❑ Capitol W 1792 [M] — 1962 — 6.25 — 12.50 — 25.00

BEYOND THE FRINGE '64
- ❑ Capitol SW 2072 [S] — 1964 — 6.25 — 12.50 — 25.00
- ❑ Capitol W 2072 [M] — 1964 — 5.00 — 10.00 — 20.00

THE BOY FRIEND
- ❑ RCA Victor LOC-1018 [M] — 1954 — 7.50 — 15.00 — 30.00
—*Originals have green labels*

THE BOYS IN THE BAND
- ❑ A&M SP-6001 [(2)] — 1969 — 6.25 — 12.50 — 25.00

BRAVO, GIOVANNI
- ❑ Columbia Masterworks KOS 2200 [S] — 1962 — 5.00 — 10.00 — 20.00
- ❑ Columbia Masterworks KOL 5800 [M] — 1962 — 3.75 — 7.50 — 15.00

BRIGADOON
- ❑ RCA Victor LOC-1001 [M] — 195? — 5.00 — 10.00 — 20.00
—*Photos of kilted dancers on front cover; black "Long Play" label*
- ❑ RCA Victor LOC-1001 [M] — 1951 — 7.50 — 15.00 — 30.00
—*Green front cover; green label*
- ❑ RCA Victor LOC-1001 [M] — 1963 — 3.75 — 7.50 — 15.00
—*Drawing of kilted dancers on front cover; black "Mono" label*
- ❑ RCA Victor LSO-1001(e) [R] — 1963 — 3.00 — 6.00 — 12.00
—*Black label, dog on top*

BY JUPITER
- ❑ RCA Victor LOC-1137 [M] — 1967 — 10.00 — 20.00 — 40.00

- ❑ RCA Victor LSO-1137 [S] — 1967 — 18.75 — 37.50 — 75.00
—*Above is by a revival cast*

BY THE BEAUTIFUL SEA
- ❑ Capitol S 531 [M] — 1954 — 17.50 — 35.00 — 70.00

BYE BYE BIRDIE
- ❑ Columbia Masterworks KOS 2025 [S] — 1960 — 7.50 — 15.00 — 30.00
—*Gray and black label with six "eye" logos; with gatefold cover*
- ❑ Columbia Masterworks OS 2025 [S] — 196? — 6.25 — 12.50 — 25.00
—*Gray and black label with six "eye" logos; with regular cover*
- ❑ Columbia Masterworks KOL 5510 [M] — 1960 — 6.25 — 12.50 — 25.00
—*Gray and black label with six "eye" logos; with gatefold cover*
- ❑ Columbia Masterworks OL 5510 [M] — 196? — 5.00 — 10.00 — 20.00
—*Gray and black label with six "eye" logos; with regular cover*

CABARET
- ❑ Columbia Masterworks KOS 3040 [S] — 1966 — 5.00 — 10.00 — 20.00
- ❑ Columbia Masterworks KOL 6640 [M] — 1966 — 3.75 — 7.50 — 15.00

CABIN IN THE SKY
- ❑ Capitol SW 2073 [S] — 1964 — 12.50 — 25.00 — 50.00
—*Above is by a revival cast*
- ❑ Capitol W 2073 [M] — 1964 — 7.50 — 15.00 — 30.00

CALL ME MADAM
- ❑ RCA Victor LOC-1000 [M] — 1950 — 20.00 — 40.00 — 80.00
—*Dinah Shore sings Ethel Merman's part for contractual reasons, otherwise it's by the entire original cast*

CAMELOT
- ❑ Columbia Masterworks KOS 2031 [S] — 1960 — 6.25 — 12.50 — 25.00
—*Gray and black label with six "eye" logos; gatefold cover*
- ❑ Columbia Masterworks KOL 5620 [M] — 1960 — 5.00 — 10.00 — 20.00
—*Gray and black label with six "eye" logos*

CAN-CAN
- ❑ Capitol DW 452 [R] — 196? — 3.00 — 6.00 — 12.00
- ❑ Capitol S 452 [M] — 1953 — 6.25 — 12.50 — 25.00
—*Originals have red labels with Capitol logo at top*
- ❑ Capitol W 452 [M] — 195? — 3.75 — 7.50 — 15.00

CANTERBURY TALES
- ❑ Capitol SW-229 — 1969 — 6.25 — 12.50 — 25.00

CAPTAIN JINKS OF THE HORSE MARINES
- ❑ RCA Victor ARL2-1727 [(2)] — 1975 — 7.50 — 15.00 — 30.00
—*Box set*

CARMEN JONES
- ❑ Decca DL 8014 [M] — 1949 — 10.00 — 20.00 — 40.00
—*Black label, gold print*
- ❑ Decca DL 9021 [M] — 1955 — 5.00 — 10.00 — 20.00
—*Reissue of 8014; black label, silver print*

CARNIVAL
- ❑ MGM E-3946 [M] — 1961 — 5.00 — 10.00 — 20.00
- ❑ MGM SE-3946 [S] — 1961 — 6.25 — 12.50 — 25.00
—*Black label*
- ❑ MGM SE-3946 [S] — 1968 — 2.50 — 5.00 — 10.00
—*Blue and gold label*

CAROUSEL
- ❑ Command RS 33-843 [M] — 1962 — 3.75 — 7.50 — 15.00
—*Studio cast*
- ❑ Command RS-843 SD [M] — 1962 — 5.00 — 10.00 — 20.00
—*Studio cast witrh Alfred Drake and Roberta Peters, and Enoch Light's orchestra*
- ❑ Decca DL 8003 [M] — 1949 — 10.00 — 20.00 — 40.00
—*Original LP issue of the Broadway cast*
- ❑ Decca DL 9020 [M] — 1955 — 7.50 — 15.00 — 30.00
—*Early reissue of DL 8003; black label with silver print*
- ❑ Decca DL 79020 [R] — 196? — 2.50 — 5.00 — 10.00
- ❑ MCA 1627 [R] — 198? — 2.00 — 4.00 — 8.00
—*Reissue of MCA 37093*
- ❑ MCA 2033 [R] — 1973 — 2.00 — 4.00 — 8.00
—*Reissue of Decca 79020; black label with rainbow*
- ❑ MCA 37093 [R] — 1980 — 2.00 — 4.00 — 8.00
—*Reissue of MCA 2033*

A CHORUS LINE
- ❑ Columbia JS 33581 — 197? — 2.50 — 5.00 — 10.00
—*Second issue with new prefix; no bar code*
- ❑ Columbia JS 33581 — 1981 — 2.00 — 4.00 — 8.00
—*Third edition; bar code added to back cover*
- ❑ Columbia PS 33581 — 1975 — 3.00 — 6.00 — 12.00
—*Original edition; no bar code on back cover*
- ❑ Columbia PSQ 33581 [Q] — 1976 — 5.00 — 10.00 — 20.00

CHRISTINE
- ❑ Columbia Masterworks OS 2026 [S] — 1960 — 25.00 — 50.00 — 100.00
- ❑ Columbia Masterworks OL 5520 [M] — 1960 — 15.00 — 30.00 — 60.00

CINDY
- ❑ ABC-Paramount ABC-OC-2 [M] — 1964 — 7.50 — 15.00 — 30.00
- ❑ ABC-Paramount ABC-OCS-2 [S] — 1964 — 12.50 — 25.00 — 50.00

CLARA (BEG, BORROW OR STEAL)
- ❑ Commentary CYN-02 [M] — 1960 — 15.00 — 30.00 — 60.00

CLOWNAROUND
- ❑ RCA Victor LSP-4741 — 1972 — 62.50 — 125.00 — 250.00

CLUB 15
- ❑ Decca DL 5155 [10] — 1949 — 15.00 — 30.00 — 60.00

THE COACH WITH THE SIX INSIDES
- ❑ ESP-Disk' 1019 [M] — 1967 — 6.25 — 12.50 — 25.00

COCO
- ❑ Paramount PMS-1002 — 1969 — 6.25 — 12.50 — 25.00

THE COMMITTEE
- ❑ Reprise F-2023 [M] — 1964 — 7.50 — 15.00 — 30.00
- ❑ Reprise FS-2023 [S] — 1964 — 10.00 — 20.00 — 40.00

Number	Title (A Side/B Side)	Yr	VG	VG+	NM
COMPANY					
❑ Columbia Masterworks OS 3550		1970	3.00	6.00	12.00
❑ Columbia Masterworks SQ 30993 [Q]		1971	7.50	15.00	30.00
—Quadraphonic version has substantially different mixes than the original stereo LP					
THE CRADLE WILL ROCK					
❑ MGM E-4289-2 [(2)M]		1964	6.25	12.50	25.00
❑ MGM SE-4289-2 [(2)S]		1964	7.50	15.00	30.00
—The above is by a revival cast					
THE CRITIC					
❑ Decca DL 9154 [M]		1967	5.00	10.00	20.00
❑ Decca DL 79154 [S]		1967	5.00	10.00	20.00
CRY FOR US ALL					
❑ Project 3 TS-1000 SD		1970	10.00	20.00	40.00
DAMES AT SEA					
❑ Columbia Masterworks OS 3550		1969	5.00	10.00	20.00
DAMN YANKEES					
❑ RCA Victor LOC-1021 [M]		195?	5.00	10.00	20.00
—Orange cover					
❑ RCA Victor LOC-1021 [M]		1955	7.50	15.00	30.00
—Green cover					
❑ RCA Victor LSO-1021(e) [R]		1965	3.75	7.50	15.00
—Black label, dog on top, "Stereo Electronically Reprocessed" at bottom					
❑ RCA Victor AYL1-3948		1980	2.00	4.00	8.00
—"Best Buy Series" reissue					
THE DANCERS OF BALI					
❑ Columbia Masterworks ML 4618 [M]		1952	10.00	20.00	40.00
DARLING OF THE DAY					
❑ RCA Victor LOC-1149 [M]		1968	10.00	20.00	40.00
❑ RCA Victor LSO-1149 [S]		1968	15.00	30.00	60.00
DEAR WORLD					
❑ Columbia Masterworks BOS 3260		1969	5.00	10.00	20.00
DEATH OF A SALESMAN					
❑ Decca DX 102 [(2)M]		1951	10.00	20.00	40.00
—Two-record boxed set with contents of 9007 and 9008					
DEATH OF A SALESMAN (PART 1)					
❑ Decca DL 9006 [M]		1951	6.25	12.50	25.00
—Black label, gold print					
DEATH OF A SALESMAN (PART 2)					
❑ Decca DL 9007 [M]		1951	6.25	12.50	25.00
—Black label, gold print					
DESTRY RIDES AGAIN					
❑ Decca DL 9075 [M]		1959	7.50	15.00	30.00
❑ Decca DL 79075 [S]		1959	10.00	20.00	40.00
DO I HEAR A WALTZ?					
❑ Columbia Masterworks KOS 2770 [S]		1965	5.00	10.00	20.00
❑ Columbia Masterworks KOL 6370 [M]		1965	3.75	7.50	15.00
DO RE MI					
❑ RCA Victor LOC-1105 [M]		1965	3.75	7.50	15.00
—Reissue of 2002 with standard red cover					
❑ RCA Victor LSO-1105 [S]		1965	5.00	10.00	20.00
—Reissue of 2002 with standard red cover					
❑ RCA Victor LOCD-2002 [M]		1961	7.50	15.00	30.00
—In black box with orange sleeve					
❑ RCA Victor LSOD-2002 [S]		1961	10.00	20.00	40.00
—In black box with orange sleeve					
DOCTOR SELAVY'S MAGIC THEATRE					
❑ United Artists UA-LA196-G		1974	7.50	15.00	30.00
DONNYBROOK!					
❑ Kapp KD-8500-S [S]		1961	6.25	12.50	25.00
❑ Kapp KDL-8500 [M]		1961	5.00	10.00	20.00
DRESSED TO THE NINES					
❑ MGM E-3914 [M]		1960	6.25	12.50	25.00
❑ MGM SE-3914 [S]		1960	10.00	20.00	40.00
THE EARL OF RUSTON					
❑ Capitol ST-465		1971	10.00	20.00	40.00
ERNEST IN LOVE					
❑ Columbia Masterworks OS 2027 [S]		1960	25.00	50.00	100.00
❑ Columbia Masterworks OL 5530 [M]		1960	15.00	30.00	60.00
AN EVENING WITH RICHARD NIXON					
❑ Ode SP-77015		1972	7.50	15.00	30.00
EVITA					
❑ MCA 2-11003 [(2)]		1976	5.00	10.00	20.00
—London cast; white cover; with booklet					
❑ MCA 2-11007 [(2)]		1979	3.75	7.50	15.00
—New York cast; mostly black cover; with booklet					
FADE OUT-FADE IN					
❑ ABC-Paramount ABC-OC-3 [M]		1964	6.25	12.50	25.00
❑ ABC-Paramount ABCS-OC-3 [S]		1964	7.50	15.00	30.00
A FAMILY AFFAIR					
❑ United Artists UAL-4099 [M]		1962	7.50	15.00	30.00
❑ United Artists UAS-5099 [S]		1962	12.50	25.00	50.00
FANNY					
❑ RCA Victor LOC-1015 [M]		1954	6.25	12.50	25.00
—"Long Play" on label					
❑ RCA Victor LOC-1015 [M]		196?	3.75	7.50	15.00
—"Mono" on label					
❑ RCA Victor LSO-1015(e) [R]		196?	3.00	6.00	12.00
—"Stereo Electronically Reprocessed" on label					
THE FANTASTICKS					
❑ MGM E-3872 [M]		196?	2.50	5.00	10.00
—White gatefold cover					
❑ MGM E-3872 [M]		1963	5.00	10.00	20.00
—Original non-gatefold cover					
❑ MGM SE-3872 [S]		196?	2.50	5.00	10.00
—Black gatefold cover					
❑ MGM SE-3872 [S]		196?	3.00	6.00	12.00
—White gatefold cover					
❑ MGM SE-3872 [S]		1963	6.25	12.50	25.00
—Original non-gatefold cover					
FIDDLER ON THE ROOF					
❑ RCA Victor LOC-1093 [M]		1964	3.75	7.50	15.00
❑ RCA Victor LSO-1093 [S]		1964	5.00	10.00	20.00
—Black label, dog on top					
FINIAN'S RAINBOW					
❑ Columbia Masterworks OS 2080 [R]		1963	3.00	6.00	12.00
❑ Columbia Masterworks ML 4062 [M]		1948	7.50	15.00	30.00
—Original cover with no photo; green label					
❑ Columbia Masterworks OL 4062 [M]		196?	3.00	6.00	12.00
—Reissue cover, either pink or green; gray label					
❑ RCA Victor LOC-1057 [M]		1960	2.50	5.00	10.00
—Revival cast; cover shows co-stars hiding in the trees					
❑ RCA Victor LOC-1057 [M]		1960	3.00	6.00	12.00
—Revival cast; "pot of gold" cover					
❑ RCA Victor LSO-1057 [S]		1960	3.00	6.00	12.00
—Revival cast; cover shows co-stars hiding in the trees					
❑ RCA Victor LSO-1057 [S]		1960	3.75	7.50	15.00
—Revival cast; "pot of gold" cover					
FIORELLO!					
❑ Capitol SWAO 1321 [S]		1959	6.25	12.50	25.00
❑ Capitol WAO 1321 [M]		1959	5.00	10.00	20.00
FIRST IMPRESSIONS					
❑ Columbia Masterworks OS 2014 [S]		1959	15.00	30.00	60.00
❑ Columbia Masterworks OL 5400 [M]		1959	7.50	15.00	30.00
FLAHOOLEY					
❑ Capitol S 284 [M]		1951	37.50	75.00	150.00
❑ Capitol T-11649		1977	3.75	7.50	15.00
FLORA, THE RED MENACE					
❑ RCA Victor LOC-1111 [M]		1965	6.25	12.50	25.00
❑ RCA Victor LSO-1111 [S]		1965	7.50	15.00	30.00
FLOWER DRUM SONG					
❑ Columbia Masterworks OS 2009 [S]		1958	6.25	12.50	25.00
—Gray and black label with six "eye" logos					
❑ Columbia Masterworks OL 5350 [M]		1958	5.00	10.00	20.00
—Gray and black label with six "eye" logos					
FLY BLACKBIRD					
❑ Mercury OCM-2206 [M]		1962	7.50	15.00	30.00
❑ Mercury OCS-6206 [S]		1962	15.00	30.00	60.00
FUNNY GIRL					
❑ Capitol STAO 2059 [S]		196?	3.00	6.00	12.00
—Only Barbra Streisand is pictured on the back cover					
❑ Capitol SVAS 2059 [S]		1964	5.00	10.00	20.00
—Both Barbra Streisand and Sydney Chaplin are pictured on the back cover					
❑ Capitol VAS 2059 [M]		1964	3.75	7.50	15.00
A FUNNY THING HAPPENED ON THE WAY TO THE FORUM					
❑ Capitol SWAO 1717 [S]		1962	5.00	10.00	20.00
—Gatefold cover					
❑ Capitol WAO 1717 [M]		1962	3.75	7.50	15.00
—Gatefold cover					
THE GAY LIFE					
❑ Capitol SWAO 1560 [S]		1961	12.50	25.00	50.00
❑ Capitol WAO 1560 [M]		1961	6.25	12.50	25.00
GENTLEMEN PREFER BLONDES					
❑ Columbia Masterworks OS 2310 [R]		1963	2.50	5.00	10.00
—Gray label					
❑ Columbia Masterworks ML 4290 [M]		1949	6.25	12.50	25.00
—Original with green label					
❑ Columbia Masterworks OL 4290 [M]		196?	3.75	7.50	15.00
—Reissue with new prefix and various gray labels					
❑ Columbia Masterworks S 32610 [R]		1973	2.00	4.00	8.00
GEORGE M!					
❑ Columbia Masterworks KOS 3200 [S]		1968	5.00	10.00	20.00
❑ Columbia Masterworks KOL 6800 [M]		1968	7.50	15.00	30.00
THE GIRL IN PINK TIGHTS					
❑ Columbia Masterworks ML 4890 [M]		1954	15.00	30.00	60.00
THE GIRL WHO CAME TO SUPPER					
❑ Columbia Masterworks KOS 2420 [S]		1963	7.50	15.00	30.00
❑ Columbia Masterworks KOL 6020 [M]		1963	6.25	12.50	25.00
GIVE 'EM HELL, HARRY!					
❑ United Artists UA-LA540-H2 [(2)]		1975	5.00	10.00	20.00
THE GOLDEN APPLE					
❑ RCA Victor LOC-1014 [M]		1954	25.00	50.00	100.00
GOLDEN BOY					
❑ Capitol SVAS 2124 [S]		1964	7.50	15.00	30.00
❑ Capitol VAS 2124 [M]		1964	6.25	12.50	25.00
GOLDILOCKS					
❑ Columbia Masterworks OS 2007 [S]		1958	15.00	30.00	60.00
❑ Columbia Masterworks OL 5340 [M]		1958	6.25	12.50	25.00
GOODTIME CHARLEY					
❑ RCA Victor ARL1-1011		1975	7.50	15.00	30.00
THE GREAT WALTZ					
❑ Capitol SVAS 2426 [S]		1965	6.25	12.50	25.00
❑ Capitol VAS 2426 [M]		1965	5.00	10.00	20.00
GREENWICH VILLAGE U.S.A.					
❑ 20th Fox TCF-105-2 [(2)M]		1960	15.00	30.00	60.00
—With complete show					
❑ 20th Fox TCF-105-2S [(2)S]		1960	25.00	50.00	100.00
—With complete show					

Number	Title (A Side/B Side)	Yr	VG	VG+	NM
❑ 20th Fox FOX-4005 [M]		1960	10.00	20.00	40.00
—With excerpts from the show					
❑ 20th Fox SFX-4005 [S]		1960	12.50	25.00	50.00
—With excerpts from the show					
GREENWILLOW					
❑ RCA Victor LOC-2001 [M]		1960	5.00	10.00	20.00
❑ RCA Victor LSO-2001 [S]		1960	12.50	25.00	50.00
GUYS AND DOLLS					
❑ Decca DL 8036 [M]		1950	7.50	15.00	30.00
❑ Decca DL 9023 [M]		1955	5.00	10.00	20.00
—Reissue of 8036					
❑ Decca DL 79023 [R]		196?	3.00	6.00	12.00
❑ MCA 1628		198?	—	3.00	6.00
—Reissue of 37094					
❑ MCA 2034		1973	2.50	5.00	10.00
—Reissue of 79023					
❑ MCA 37094		198?	2.00	4.00	8.00
—Reissue of 2034					
GYPSY					
❑ Columbia Masterworks OS 2017 [S]		1959	6.25	12.50	25.00
—Original covers are white with drawings					
❑ Columbia Masterworks OS 2017 [S]		1962	3.75	7.50	15.00
—Reissue covers are brown with show photos					
❑ Columbia Masterworks OL 5420 [M]		1959	5.00	10.00	20.00
—Original covers are white with drawings					
❑ Columbia Masterworks OL 5420 [M]		1962	3.00	6.00	12.00
—Reissue covers are brown with show photos					
HAIR					
❑ Atco SD 7002		1969	6.25	12.50	25.00
—Original London cast					
❑ Philips PHS 600329		1969	6.25	12.50	25.00
—Original French cast					
❑ RCA Victor ABD1-0245 [Q]		1973	5.00	10.00	20.00
—Broadway cast; quadraphonic remix					
❑ RCA Victor ANL1-0986		1974	2.50	5.00	10.00
—Off-Broadway cast; reissue with new number					
❑ RCA Victor LOC-1143 [M]		1967	3.75	7.50	15.00
—Off-Broadway cast					
❑ RCA Victor LSO-1143 [S]		1967	3.00	6.00	12.00
—Off-Broadway cast; black label, dog at top, "Stereo" at bottom					
❑ RCA Victor LOC-1150 [M]		1968	7.50	15.00	30.00
—Broadway cast					
❑ RCA Victor LSO-1150 [S]		1968	2.50	5.00	10.00
—Broadway cast; orange label					
❑ RCA Victor LSO-1150 [S]		1968	5.00	10.00	20.00
—Broadway cast; black label, dog on top, "Stereo" at bottom					
HALF A SIXPENCE					
❑ RCA Victor LOC-1110 [M]		1965	5.00	10.00	20.00
❑ RCA Victor LSO-1110 [S]		1965	6.25	12.50	25.00
HALF PAST WEDNESDAY					
❑ Columbia CL 1917 [M]		1962	7.50	15.00	30.00
❑ Columbia CS 8717 [S]		1962	10.00	20.00	40.00
HAMLET					
❑ Columbia Masterworks DOL 302 [(4)M]		1964	6.25	12.50	25.00
—Boxed set with entire play (Broadway revival)					
❑ Columbia Masterworks DOS 702 [(4)S]		1964	6.25	12.50	25.00
—Boxed set with entire play (Broadway revival)					
❑ Columbia Masterworks OS 2620 [S]		1964	3.75	7.50	15.00
—Highlights from the box set					
❑ Columbia Masterworks OL 6220 [M]		1964	3.75	7.50	15.00
—Highlights from the box set					
THE HAPPIEST GIRL IN THE WORLD					
❑ Columbia Masterworks KOS 2050 [S]		1961	10.00	20.00	40.00
—Second covers are white					
❑ Columbia Masterworks KOS 2050 [S]		1961	15.00	30.00	60.00
—Original covers are yellow					
❑ Columbia Masterworks KOL 5650 [M]		1961	7.50	15.00	30.00
—Second covers are white					
❑ Columbia Masterworks KOL 5650 [M]		1961	10.00	20.00	40.00
—Original covers are yellow					
HAPPY HUNTING					
❑ RCA Victor LOC-1026 [M]		1956	10.00	20.00	40.00
HEAR! HEAR!					
❑ Decca DL 9031 [M]		1955	12.50	25.00	50.00
HELLO, DOLLY!					
❑ RCA Victor LOCD-1087 [M]		1964	3.75	7.50	15.00
—New back cover is in color and has a photo of Carol Channing; "RE" is on cover					
❑ RCA Victor LOCD-1087 [M]		1964	6.25	12.50	25.00
—Original cover is black and white on back and spotlights "Come and Be My Butterfly"; this song was deleted from the show, so the cover was changed					
❑ RCA Victor LSOD-1087 [S]		1964	5.00	10.00	20.00
—New back cover is in color and has a photo of Carol Channing; "RE" is on cover; black label, dog on top					
❑ RCA Victor LSOD-1087 [S]		1964	7.50	15.00	30.00
—Original cover is black and white on back and spotlights "Come and Be My Butterfly"; this song was deleted from the show, so the cover was changed					
❑ RCA Victor LSOD-1087 [S]		1969	2.50	5.00	10.00
—Orange or tan label					
HENRY, SWEET HENRY					
❑ ABC ABC-OC-4 [M]		1967	7.50	15.00	30.00
❑ ABC ABCS-OC-4 [S]		1967	12.50	25.00	50.00
HERE'S LOVE					
❑ Columbia Masterworks KOS 2400 [S]		1963	10.00	20.00	40.00
❑ Columbia Masterworks KOL 6000 [M]		1963	7.50	15.00	30.00
HIGH BUTTON SHOES					
❑ RCA Camden CAL-457 [M]		1958	7.50	15.00	30.00
❑ RCA Victor LOC-1107 [M]		1964	10.00	20.00	40.00
❑ RCA Victor LSO-1107 [R]		1964	7.50	15.00	30.00

Number	Title (A Side/B Side)	Yr	VG	VG+	NM
HIGH SPIRITS					
❑ ABC-Paramount ABC-OC-1 [M]		1964	6.25	12.50	25.00
❑ ABC-Paramount ABCS-OC-1 [S]		1964	7.50	15.00	30.00
HOUSE OF FLOWERS					
❑ Columbia Masterworks ML 4969 [M]		1954	10.00	20.00	40.00
—Blue label original					
❑ United Artists UAS-5180		1968	10.00	20.00	40.00
—Revival cast					
HOW NOW, DOW JONES					
❑ RCA Victor LOC-1142 [M]		1967	6.25	12.50	25.00
❑ RCA Victor LSO-1142 [S]		1967	7.50	15.00	30.00
HOW TO SUCCEED IN BUSINESS WITHOUT REALLY TRYING					
❑ RCA Victor LOC-1066 [M]		1961	5.00	10.00	20.00
❑ RCA Victor LSO-1066 [S]		1961	6.25	12.50	25.00
—Black label, dog on top					
❑ RCA Victor LSO-1066 [S]		1969	2.50	5.00	10.00
—Orange or tan label					
HUGHIE					
❑ Columbia Masterworks OS 2760 [S]		1965	7.50	15.00	30.00
❑ Columbia Masterworks OL 6260 [M]		1965	6.25	12.50	25.00
I CAN GET IT FOR YOU WHOLESALE					
❑ Columbia Masterworks KOS 2180 [S]		1962	7.50	15.00	30.00
❑ Columbia Masterworks KOL 5780 [M]		1962	6.25	12.50	25.00
I DO! I DO!					
❑ RCA Victor LOC-1128 [M]		1966	3.75	7.50	15.00
❑ RCA Victor LSO-1128 [S]		1966	5.00	10.00	20.00
—Black label, dog on top					
I HAD A BALL					
❑ Mercury OCM-2210 [M]		1964	5.00	10.00	20.00
❑ Mercury OCM-2210 [(2)M]		1964	10.00	20.00	40.00
—Promo-only two-record set with bonus interview record MGD-2-24					
❑ Mercury OCS-6210 [S]		1964	6.25	12.50	25.00
ICE FOLLIES					
❑ Dot DLP-3757 [M]		1967	6.25	12.50	25.00
❑ Dot DLP-25757 [S]		1967	7.50	15.00	30.00
ILLYA DARLING					
❑ United Artists UAL-8901 [M]		1967	5.00	10.00	20.00
❑ United Artists UAS-9901 [S]		1967	5.00	10.00	20.00
INTO THE WOODS					
❑ RCA 6796-1-RC		1988	5.00	10.00	20.00
IRMA LA DOUCE					
❑ Columbia Masterworks OS 2029 [S]		1960	6.25	12.50	25.00
❑ Columbia Masterworks OL 5560 [M]		1960	5.00	10.00	20.00
J.B.					
❑ RCA Victor LD-6075 [(2)M]		1959	15.00	30.00	60.00
❑ RCA Victor LDS-6075 [(2)S]		1959	17.50	35.00	70.00
JACQUES BREL IS ALIVE AND WELL AND LIVING IN PARIS					
❑ Columbia Masterworks D2S 779 [(2)]		1968	5.00	10.00	20.00
—Box set; gray "360 Sound" labels					
JENNIE					
❑ RCA Victor LOC-1083 [M]		1963	6.25	12.50	25.00
❑ RCA Victor LSO-1083 [S]		1963	12.50	25.00	50.00
JESUS CHRIST SUPERSTAR					
❑ Decca DL 71503		1971	5.00	10.00	20.00
—From the Broadway production; also see listings for this title in the VARIOUS ARTISTS COLLECTIONS sections.					
❑ MCA 5000		1973	3.00	6.00	12.00
—From the Broadway production; reissue					
JOSEPH AND THE AMAZING TECHNICOLOR DREAMCOAT					
❑ Scepter SPS-588X		1968	5.00	10.00	20.00
—With gatefold cover and libretto					
❑ Scepter SMAS-93738		197?	6.25	12.50	25.00
—Capitol Record Club edition					
JOY					
❑ RCA Victor LSO-1166		1970	5.00	10.00	20.00
JUNO					
❑ Columbia Masterworks OS 2013 [S]		1959	17.50	35.00	70.00
❑ Columbia Masterworks OL 5380 [M]		1959	10.00	20.00	40.00
KEAN					
❑ Columbia Masterworks KSO 2120 [S]		1961	10.00	20.00	40.00
❑ Columbia Masterworks KOL 5720 [M]		1961	7.50	15.00	30.00
THE KING AND I					
❑ Decca DL 9008 [M]		195?	3.00	6.00	12.00
—Drawing of Gertrude Lawrence and Yul Brynner on cover, with title on two lines					
❑ Decca DL 9008 [M]		195?	10.00	20.00	40.00
—Drawing of Gertrude Lawrence and Yul Brynner on cover, with title on three lines					
❑ Decca DL 9008 [M]		1951	6.25	12.50	25.00
—Black label, gold print					
❑ Decca DL 79008 [R]		196?	2.50	5.00	10.00
KWAMINA					
❑ Capitol SW 1645 [S]		1962	12.50	25.00	50.00
❑ Capitol W 1645 [M]		1962	7.50	15.00	30.00
THE LADY'S NOT FOR BURNING					
❑ Decca DL 9508 /9 [(2)M]		1951	12.50	25.00	50.00
—Oversize box set					
LAGINAPPE '59 PRESENTS BE MY GUEST					
❑ (no label) XCTV-10303 [M]		1959	62.50	125.00	250.00
—Custom pressing for New Trier High School, Illinois. Collectible because the future Ann-Margret sings one track on the LP!					
LEGS DIAMOND					
❑ RCA 7983-1-RC		1989	6.25	12.50	25.00

Number Title (A Side/B Side)	Yr	VG	VG+	NM
LES MISERABLES				
☐ Geffen GHS 24151 [(2)]	1987	3.75	7.50	15.00
—Original Broadway cast recording				
☐ Relativity 88561-8140-1 [(2)]	1985	5.00	10.00	20.00
—Original London cast recording				
LET IT RIDE				
☐ RCA Victor LOC-1064 [M]	1961	5.00	10.00	20.00
☐ RCA Victor LSO-1064 [S]	1961	10.00	20.00	40.00
LI'L ABNER				
☐ Columbia Masterworks OL 5150 [M]	1956	7.50	15.00	30.00
LITTLE ME				
☐ RCA Victor LOC-1078 [M]	1962	5.00	10.00	20.00
☐ RCA Victor LSO-1078 [S]	1962	6.25	12.50	25.00
LITTLE SHOP OF HORRORS				
☐ Geffen GHSP-2020	1982	6.25	12.50	25.00
LOOK MA, I'M DANCIN'!				
☐ Decca DL 5231 [M]	1950	25.00	50.00	100.00
LORELEI				
☐ MGM M3G-55	1974	7.50	15.00	30.00
—Second version, recorded with Broadway cast				
☐ Verve MV-5097-OC	1974	6.25	12.50	25.00
—First version, recorded before the show hit Broadway				
LOST IN THE STARS				
☐ Decca DL 8028 [M]	1949	12.50	25.00	50.00
☐ Decca DL 9120 [M]	1965	3.75	7.50	15.00
—Reissue of 8028				
THE MAD SHOW				
☐ Columbia Masterworks OS 2930 [S]	1965	25.00	50.00	100.00
☐ Columbia Masterworks OL 6530 [M]	1965	12.50	25.00	50.00
MAGGIE FLYNN				
☐ RCA Victor LSOD-2009	1968	5.00	10.00	20.00
☐ RCA Victor LSOD-2009	1968	6.25	12.50	25.00
THE MAGIC SHOW				
☐ Bell 9003	1974	5.00	10.00	20.00
MAKE A WISH				
☐ RCA Victor LOC-1002 [M]	1951	37.50	75.00	150.00
MAME				
☐ Columbia Masterworks KOS 3000 [S]	1966	5.00	10.00	20.00
—Gray label with "360 Sound Stereo"				
☐ Columbia Masterworks KOS 3000 [S]	1970	3.00	6.00	12.00
—Olive label with orange "Columbia" around outside				
☐ Columbia Masterworks KOL 6600 [M]	1966	3.75	7.50	15.00
MAN OF LA MANCHA				
☐ Kapp KRL-4505 [M]	1965	3.75	7.50	15.00
☐ Kapp KRS-4505 [S]	1965	5.00	10.00	20.00
MARK TWAIN TONIGHT!				
☐ Columbia Masterworks OS 2019 [S]	1959	3.75	7.50	15.00
☐ Columbia Masterworks OL 5440 [M]	1959	3.00	6.00	12.00
ME AND JULIET				
☐ RCA Victor LOC-1012 [M]	1953	17.50	35.00	70.00
MEDEA				
☐ Decca DLP 9000 [M]	1949	7.50	15.00	30.00
MEGILLA OF ITZIG MANGER				
☐ Columbia Masterworks OS 3270	1968	10.00	20.00	40.00
MERRILY WE ROLL ALONG				
☐ RCA Victor CBL1-4197	1981	7.50	15.00	30.00
THE MERRY WIDOW				
☐ RCA Victor LOC-1094 [M]	1964	5.00	10.00	20.00
☐ RCA Victor LSO-1094 [S]	1964	6.25	12.50	25.00
MEXICAN HAYRIDE				
☐ Decca DL 5232 [10]	1950	30.00	60.00	120.00
MILK AND HONEY				
☐ RCA Victor LOC-1065 [M]	1961	5.00	10.00	20.00
—With picture of Tommy Rall and two dancers on front cover				
☐ RCA Victor LOC-1065 [M]	1961	6.25	12.50	25.00
—With only credits (no picture) on front cover				
☐ RCA Victor LSO-1065 [S]	1961	6.25	12.50	25.00
—With picture of Tommy Rall and two dancers on front cover				
☐ RCA Victor LSO-1065 [S]	1961	7.50	15.00	30.00
—With only credits (no picture) on front cover				
MISS LIBERTY				
☐ Columbia Masterworks ML 4220 [M]	1949	7.50	15.00	30.00
—Originals have green labels				
MISS SAIGON				
☐ Geffen GHS 24271 [(2)]	1990	5.00	10.00	20.00
THE MOST HAPPY FELLA				
☐ Columbia Masterworks O3L 240 [(3)M]	1956	12.50	25.00	50.00
—Box set with entire show				
☐ Columbia Masterworks OS 2330 [R]	196?	3.75	7.50	15.00
☐ Columbia Masterworks OL 5118 [M]	1956	7.50	15.00	30.00
—Gray and black label with six "eye" logos				
MR. PRESIDENT				
☐ Columbia Masterworks KOS 2270 [S]	1962	7.50	15.00	30.00
—Gatefold with shiny silver cover				
☐ Columbia Masterworks KOL 5870 [M]	1962	5.00	10.00	20.00
—Gatefold with shiny silver cover				
MR. WONDERFUL				
☐ Decca DL 9032 [M]	1956	12.50	25.00	50.00
MRS. PATTERSON				
☐ RCA Victor LOC-1017 [M]	1954	37.50	75.00	150.00
THE MUSIC MAN				
☐ Capitol SW 990 [S]	196?	3.75	7.50	15.00
—Regular cover with photo of Robert Preston as Harold Hill				
☐ Capitol SWAO 990 [S]	1957	6.25	12.50	25.00
—Gatefold cover, white with credits and drawing on front; gray label				
☐ Capitol W 990 [M]	196?	3.00	6.00	12.00
—Regular cover with photo of Robert Preston as Harold Hill				
☐ Capitol WAO 990 [M]	1957	5.00	10.00	20.00
—Gatefold cover, white with credits and drawing on front; gray label				
MY FAIR LADY				
☐ Columbia Masterworks OS 2015 [S]	1959	3.00	6.00	12.00
—Gray label, "Stereo" at bottom; original London cast				
☐ Columbia Masterworks OS 2015 [S]	1959	5.00	10.00	20.00
—Gray and black label with six "eye" logos; original London cast				
☐ Columbia Masterworks PS 2015 [S]	198?	—	3.00	6.00
—Budget-line reissue with new prefix				
☐ Columbia Masterworks OL 5090 [M]	1956	2.50	5.00	10.00
—Gray label, "Mono" at bottom				
☐ Columbia Masterworks OL 5090 [M]	1956	6.25	12.50	25.00
—Gray and black label with six "eye" logos				
☐ Columbia Masterworks OL 5090 [M]	1963	3.75	7.50	15.00
—Gray label with "Guaranteed High Fidelity" at bottom				
☐ Columbia Masterworks PS 34197	1976	2.50	5.00	10.00
—Revival cast				
MY PEOPLE				
☐ Contact C-1 [M]	1966	5.00	10.00	20.00
☐ Contact CS-1 [S]	1966	6.25	12.50	25.00
THE NERVOUS SET				
☐ Columbia Masterworks OS 2018 [S]	1959	15.00	30.00	60.00
☐ Columbia Masterworks OL 5430 [M]	1959	7.50	15.00	30.00
NEW FACES OF 1952				
☐ RCA Victor LOC-1008 [M]	1952	6.25	12.50	25.00
NEW FACES OF 1956				
☐ RCA Victor LOC-1025 [M]	1956	12.50	25.00	50.00
NEW FACES OF 1968				
☐ Warner Bros. BS 2551	1968	7.50	15.00	30.00
THE NEW GIRL IN TOWN				
☐ RCA Victor LOC-1027 [M]	1957	5.00	10.00	20.00
☐ RCA Victor LSO-1027 [S]	1958	12.50	25.00	50.00
☐ RCA Victor LOC-1106 [M]	1965	5.00	10.00	20.00
☐ RCA Victor LSC-1106 [S]	1965	7.50	15.00	30.00
THE NINA, THE PINTA AND THE SANTA MARIA				
☐ Dot DLP-9009 [M]	1960	10.00	20.00	40.00
☐ Dot DLP-29009 [S]	1960	12.50	25.00	50.00
NO STRINGS				
☐ Capitol O 1695 [M]	1962	5.00	10.00	20.00
☐ Capitol SO 1695 [S]	1962	10.00	20.00	40.00
OF THEE I SING				
☐ Capitol S 350 [M]	1952	37.50	75.00	150.00
OH, KAY!				
☐ 20th Fox FOX-4003 [M]	1960	6.25	12.50	25.00
☐ 20th Fox SFX-4003 [S]	1960	12.50	25.00	50.00
OKLAHOMA!				
☐ Decca DLP 8000 [M]	1949	7.50	15.00	30.00
—Black label, gold print; the first 12-inch LP on Decca				
☐ Decca DL 9017 [M]	1955	5.00	10.00	20.00
—Reissue of 8000				
☐ Decca DL 9017 [M]	196?	5.00	10.00	20.00
—Reissue with new cover art				
☐ Decca DL 79017 [R]	196?	3.75	7.50	15.00
☐ Decca DL 79017 [R]	1968	5.00	10.00	20.00
—Special 25th Anniversary edition; cover has yellow drawing, inner sleeve has liner notes				
☐ MCA 2030	1973	2.00	4.00	8.00
—Reissue of 79017; black label with rainbow				
☐ MCA 37096	198?	2.00	4.00	8.00
—Reissue of 2030				
OLIVER!				
☐ RCA Victor LOCD-2004 [M]	1962	3.75	7.50	15.00
☐ RCA Victor LSOD-2004 [S]	1962	5.00	10.00	20.00
ON A CLEAR DAY YOU CAN SEE FOREVER				
☐ RCA Victor LOCD-2006 [M]	1965	5.00	10.00	20.00
☐ RCA Victor LSOD-2006 [S]	1965	6.25	12.50	25.00
ON YOUR TOES				
☐ Decca DL 9015 [M]	1954	18.75	37.50	75.00
ONCE UPON A MATTRESS				
☐ Kapp KDL-7004 [M]	1959	6.25	12.50	25.00
☐ Kapp KDL-7004-S [S]	1959	7.50	15.00	30.00
ONE TOUCH OF VENUS				
☐ Decca DL 9122 [M]	1965	6.25	12.50	25.00
☐ Decca DL 79122 [R]	1965	6.25	12.50	25.00
OVER HERE!				
☐ Columbia Masterworks KS 32961	1974	5.00	10.00	20.00
☐ Columbia Masterworks SQ 32961 [Q]	1974	7.50	15.00	30.00
PAINT YOUR WAGON				
☐ RCA Victor LOC-1006 [M]	1951	6.25	12.50	25.00
—Green label				
☐ RCA Victor LOC-1006 [M]	1955	5.00	10.00	20.00
—Black label, dog on top, "Long Play" at bottom				
☐ RCA Victor LOC-1006 [M]	1965	3.75	7.50	15.00
—Black label, dog on top, "Mono" at bottom				
☐ RCA Victor LSO-1006 [S]	1965	3.00	6.00	12.00
—Black label, dog on top				
☐ RCA Victor LSO-1006 [R]	1969	2.50	5.00	10.00
—Orange or tan label				
PARADE				
☐ Kapp KDL-7005 [M]	1960	50.00	100.00	200.00
☐ Kapp KDS-7005 [S]	1960	62.50	125.00	250.00

Number Title (A Side/B Side)	Yr	VG	VG+	NM
PARIS '90				
❑ Columbia Masterworks ML 4619 [M]	1952	37.50	75.00	150.00
PEACE				
❑ Metromedia MP-33001	1969	7.50	15.00	30.00
PETER PAN				
❑ RCA Victor LOC-1019 [M]	1954	10.00	20.00	40.00
❑ RCA Victor LSO-1019 [R]	196?	3.00	6.00	12.00
❑ RCA Victor AYL1-3762 [R]	1980	2.00	4.00	8.00
THE PHANTOM OF THE OPERA				
❑ Polydor 831273-1 [(2)]	1987	5.00	10.00	20.00
—With libretto				
❑ Polydor 831563-1	1987	2.50	5.00	10.00
—One-record "highlights" release				
PIPE DREAM				
❑ RCA Victor LOC-1023 [M]	1955	12.50	25.00	50.00
—Without "Special Advance Edition" sticker on cover				
❑ RCA Victor LOC-1023 [M]	1955	17.50	35.00	70.00
—With "Special Advance Edition" sticker on cover				
PLAIN AND FANCY				
❑ Capitol S 603 [M]	1955	6.25	12.50	25.00
—Red label				
PLAYGIRLS				
❑ Warner Bros. W 1530 [M]	1964	6.25	12.50	25.00
❑ Warner Bros. WS 1530 [S]	1964	7.50	15.00	30.00
PORGY AND BESS				
❑ Decca DL 7006 [10]	1950	7.50	15.00	30.00
—Reissue of material first released on 78s				
❑ Decca DL 8042 [M]	1950	7.50	15.00	30.00
❑ Decca DL 9024 [M]	1955	6.25	12.50	25.00
—Reissue of 8042; drawing of Catfish Row on cover				
❑ Decca DL 9024 [M]	196?	3.75	7.50	15.00
—Photo of cast members on cover				
❑ Decca DL 79024 [R]	196?	2.50	5.00	10.00
—Photo of cast members on cover				
❑ MCA 1631 [R]	198?	—	3.00	6.00
—Reissue of 2035				
❑ MCA 2035 [R]	1973	2.00	4.00	8.00
—Reissue of 79024; black label with rainbow				
THE PREMISE				
❑ Vanguard VRS-9092 [M]	1960	10.00	20.00	40.00
PURLIE				
❑ Ampex A-40101	1970	7.50	15.00	30.00
RASHOMON				
❑ Carlton LPX-5000 [M]	1959	6.25	12.50	25.00
❑ Carlton STLPX-5000 [S]	1959	7.50	15.00	30.00
—Not actually the original cast recording, but the play's incidental music				
REDHEAD				
❑ RCA Victor LOC-1048 [M]	1959	5.00	10.00	20.00
❑ RCA Victor LSO-1048 [S]	1959	12.50	25.00	50.00
—Without "Essie's Vision"				
❑ RCA Victor LOC-1104 [M]	1959	3.75	7.50	15.00
—Reissue of 1048				
❑ RCA Victor LSO-1104 [S]	1965	6.25	12.50	25.00
—Reissue adds "Essie's Vision" to stereo version				
THE RIVER WIND				
❑ London AM-48001 [M]	1962	10.00	20.00	40.00
❑ London AMS-78001 [S]	1962	20.00	40.00	80.00
THE ROAR OF THE GREASEPAINT — THE SMELL OF THE CROWD				
❑ RCA Victor LOC-1109 [M]	1965	3.75	7.50	15.00
❑ RCA Victor LSO-1109 [S]	1965	5.00	10.00	20.00
THE ROTHSCHILDS				
❑ Columbia Masterworks S 30337	1970	6.25	12.50	25.00
SAIL AWAY				
❑ Capitol SWAO 1643 [S]	1961	7.50	15.00	30.00
❑ Capitol WAO 1643 [M]	1961	5.00	10.00	20.00
SARATOGA				
❑ RCA Victor LOC-1051 [M]	1959	6.25	12.50	25.00
❑ RCA Victor LSO-1051 [S]	1959	12.50	25.00	50.00
SAY, DARLING				
❑ RCA Victor LOC-1045 [M]	1958	10.00	20.00	40.00
❑ RCA Victor LSO-1045 [S]	1958	15.00	30.00	60.00
SELMA				
❑ Cotillion SD 2-110 [(2)]	1976	5.00	10.00	20.00
SEVENTEEN				
❑ RCA Victor LOC-1003 [M]	1951	37.50	75.00	150.00
SEVENTH HEAVEN				
❑ Decca DL 9001 [M]	1955	37.50	75.00	150.00
SHE LOVES ME				
❑ MGM E 4118OC-2 [(2)M]	1963	10.00	20.00	40.00
❑ MGM SE 4118OC-2 [(2)S]	1963	12.50	25.00	50.00
SHOW BIZ (FROM VAUDE TO VIDEO)				
❑ RCA Victor LOC-1011 [M]	1954	10.00	20.00	40.00
SHOW BOAT				
❑ Columbia Masterworks ML 4058 [M]	1948	6.25	12.50	25.00
—From the 1946 revival; paper envelope jacket with its opening on top				
❑ Columbia Masterworks OL 4058 [M]	195?	5.00	10.00	20.00
—From the 1946 revival; reissue of ML 4058				
SHOW GIRL				
❑ Roulette R-80001 [M]	1961	5.00	10.00	20.00
❑ Roulette SR-80001 [S]	1961	6.25	12.50	25.00
SIDE BY SIDE BY SONDHEIM				
❑ RCA Victor CBL2-1851 [(2)]	1976	5.00	10.00	20.00

Number Title (A Side/B Side)	Yr	VG	VG+	NM
SILK STOCKINGS				
❑ RCA Victor LOC-1016 [M]	1955	10.00	20.00	40.00
❑ RCA Victor LOC-1102 [M]	1965	5.00	10.00	20.00
—Reissue; regular cover				
❑ RCA Victor LSO-1102 [R]	1965	5.00	10.00	20.00
SIMPLY HEAVENLY				
❑ Columbia Masterworks OL 5240 [M]	1957	6.25	12.50	25.00
SING OUT, SWEET LAND!				
❑ Decca DL 4304 [M]	1963	5.00	10.00	20.00
❑ Decca DL 8023 [M]	1950	12.50	25.00	50.00
❑ Decca DL 74304 [R]	1963	5.00	10.00	20.00
SKYSCRAPER				
❑ Capitol SVAS 2422 [S]	1965	6.25	12.50	25.00
❑ Capitol VAS 2422 [M]	1965	5.00	10.00	20.00
SNOW WHITE AND THE SEVEN DWARFS				
❑ Buena Vista STER-5009	1979	7.50	15.00	30.00
SONDHEIM: A MUSICAL TRIBUTE				
❑ Warner Bros. 2WS 2705 [(2)]	1973	5.00	10.00	20.00
SONG OF NORWAY				
❑ Columbia CL 1328 [M]	1959	5.00	10.00	20.00
—1958 revival cast				
❑ Columbia CS 8135 [S]	1959	12.50	25.00	50.00
—1958 revival cast				
❑ Decca DL 8002 [M]	1949	7.50	15.00	30.00
❑ Decca DL 9019 [M]	1955	5.00	10.00	20.00
❑ Decca DL 79019 [R]	196?	3.00	6.00	12.00
❑ MCA 2032 [R]	1973	2.50	5.00	10.00
—Reissue of 79019; black label with rainbow				
THE SOUND OF MUSIC				
❑ Columbia Masterworks KOS 2020 [S]	1959	3.00	6.00	12.00
—Gray label with "360 Sound Stereo" at bottom				
❑ Columbia Masterworks KOS 2020 [S]	1959	6.25	12.50	25.00
—Gray and black label with six "eye" logos				
❑ Columbia Masterworks KOL 5450 [M]	1959	5.00	10.00	20.00
—Gray and black label with six "eye" logos				
❑ Columbia Masterworks KOL 5450 [M]	1963	3.00	6.00	12.00
—Gray label with "Guaranteed High Fidelity" or "360 Sound Mono" on label				
❑ Columbia Masterworks S 32601 [S]	1973	2.50	5.00	10.00
—Reissue of 2020				
SOUTH PACIFIC				
❑ Columbia Masterworks OS 2040 [R]	196?	2.50	5.00	10.00
—Gray label with "360 Sound Stereo"				
❑ Columbia Masterworks ML 4180 [M]	1949	6.25	12.50	25.00
—Green or blue label; large anchor on front cover				
❑ Columbia Masterworks OL 4180 [M]	195?	3.00	6.00	12.00
—Gray and black label with six "eye" logos; glossy gatefold cover with Ezio Pinza and Mary Martin pictured				
❑ Columbia Masterworks OL 4180 [M]	195?	3.75	7.50	15.00
—Gray and black label with six "eye" logos; large anchor on front cover				
❑ Columbia Masterworks OL 4180 [M]	1963	2.50	5.00	10.00
—Gray label with "Guaranteed High Fidelity" or "360 Sound Mono"				
❑ Columbia Masterworks S 32604 [R]	1973	2.00	4.00	8.00
—Reissue of 2040				
ST. LOUIS WOMAN				
❑ Capitol L 355 [10]	1952	20.00	40.00	80.00
STOP THE WORLD-I WANT TO GET OFF				
❑ London AM 58001 [M]	1962	3.75	7.50	15.00
❑ London AMS 88001 [S]	1962	5.00	10.00	20.00
STREET SCENE				
❑ Columbia Masterworks ML 4139 [M]	1949	7.50	15.00	30.00
—Paper envelope jacket with its opening on top				
THE SUBJECT WAS ROSES				
❑ Columbia Masterworks DOL 308 [(3)M]	1964	5.00	10.00	20.00
❑ Columbia Masterworks DOS 708 [(3)S]	1964	7.50	15.00	30.00
SUBWAYS ARE FOR SLEEPING				
❑ Columbia Masterworks KOS 2130 [S]	1962	10.00	20.00	40.00
❑ Columbia Masterworks KOL 5730 [M]	1962	6.25	12.50	25.00
THE SURVIVAL OF ST. JOAN				
❑ Paramount PAS-9000 [(2)]	1971	6.25	12.50	25.00
SWEENEY TODD-THE DEMON BARBER OF FLEET STREET				
❑ RCA Victor CBL2-3379 [(2)]	1979	5.00	10.00	20.00
SWEET CHARITY				
❑ Columbia Masterworks KOS 2900 [S]	1966	5.00	10.00	20.00
❑ Columbia Masterworks KOL 6500 [M]	1966	3.75	7.50	15.00
TAKE ME ALONG				
❑ RCA Victor LOC-1050 [M]	1959	3.75	7.50	15.00
❑ RCA Victor LSO-1050 [S]	1959	5.00	10.00	20.00
—Black label				
TAMALPAIS EXCHANGE				
❑ Atlantic SD 8263	1970	7.50	15.00	30.00
TAROT				
❑ United Artists UAS-5563	1970	5.00	10.00	20.00
TENDERLOIN				
❑ Capitol SWAO 1492 [S]	1960	10.00	20.00	40.00
—With program				
❑ Capitol WAO 1492 [M]	1960	6.25	12.50	25.00
—With program				
TEVYA AND HIS DAUGHTERS				
❑ Columbia Masterworks OL 5225 [M]	1957	7.50	15.00	30.00
TEXAS, LI'L DARLIN'				
❑ Decca DL 5188 [10]	1950	20.00	40.00	80.00
THIS IS THE ARMY				
❑ Decca DL 5108 [10]	1950	25.00	50.00	100.00

Number	Title (A Side/B Side)	Yr	VG	VG+	NM

THIS WAS BURLESQUE
| ❏ Roulette R-25185 [M] | | 1962 | 6.25 | 12.50 | 25.00 |
| ❏ Roulette SR-25186 [S] | | 1962 | 7.50 | 15.00 | 30.00 |

THREE TO MAKE MUSIC
| ❏ RCA Victor LPM-2012 [M] | | 1958 | 6.25 | 12.50 | 25.00 |
| ❏ RCA Victor LSP-2012 [S] | | 1958 | 7.50 | 15.00 | 30.00 |

THREE WISHES FOR JAMIE
| ❏ Capitol S 317 [M] | | 1952 | 30.00 | 60.00 | 120.00 |

THE THREEPENNY OPERA
| ❏ Columbia Masterworks PS 34326 | | 1976 | 5.00 | 10.00 | 20.00 |
—Another revival cast
| ❏ MGM E-3121 [M] | | 1954 | 6.25 | 12.50 | 25.00 |
—Revival cast; yellow label
| ❏ MGM E-3121 [M] | | 1959 | 3.75 | 7.50 | 15.00 |
—Revival cast; black label
| ❏ MGM SE-3121 [R] | | 196? | 3.00 | 6.00 | 12.00 |
—Revival cast; rechanneled stereo
| ❏ Polydor 820260-1 | | 198? | 2.00 | 4.00 | 8.00 |
—Revival cast; reissue

TIME CHANGES
| ❏ ABC ABCS-681 | | 1969 | 7.50 | 15.00 | 30.00 |

A TIME FOR SINGING
| ❏ Warner Bros. W 1639 [M] | | 1966 | 10.00 | 20.00 | 40.00 |
| ❏ Warner Bros. WS 1639 [S] | | 1966 | 15.00 | 30.00 | 60.00 |

A TIME REMEMBERED
| ❏ Mercury MG-20380 [M] | | 1957 | 6.25 | 12.50 | 25.00 |
| ❏ Mercury SR-60023 [S] | | 1957 | 10.00 | 20.00 | 40.00 |
—Music from the dramatic play

TO BROADWAY WITH LOVE
| ❏ Columbia Masterworks OS 2630 [S] | | 1964 | 12.50 | 25.00 | 50.00 |
| ❏ Columbia Masterworks OL 6030 [M] | | 1964 | 6.25 | 12.50 | 25.00 |

TOP BANANA
| ❏ Capitol S 308 [M] | | 1952 | 25.00 | 50.00 | 100.00 |

TOVARICH
| ❏ Capitol STAO 1940 [S] | | 1963 | 7.50 | 15.00 | 30.00 |
| ❏ Capitol TAO 1940 [M] | | 1963 | 5.00 | 10.00 | 20.00 |

A TREE GROWS IN BROOKLYN
| ❏ Columbia Masterworks ML 4405 [M] | | 1951 | 7.50 | 15.00 | 30.00 |
—Blue label

TWO BY TWO
| ❏ Columbia Masterworks S 30338 | | 1970 | 5.00 | 10.00 | 20.00 |

TWO ON THE AISLE
| ❏ Decca DL 8040 [M] | | 1951 | 25.00 | 50.00 | 100.00 |
—Black label, gold print
| ❏ Decca DL 8040 [M] | | 1955 | 15.00 | 30.00 | 60.00 |
—Black label, silver print
| ❏ Decca DL 8040 [M] | | 196? | 15.00 | 30.00 | 60.00 |
—Black label with color bars

TWO'S COMPANY
| ❏ RCA Victor LOC-1009 [M] | | 1952 | 25.00 | 50.00 | 100.00 |

THE UNSINKABLE MOLLY BROWN
| ❏ Capitol SWAO 1509 [S] | | 1960 | 6.25 | 12.50 | 25.00 |
| ❏ Capitol WAO 1509 [M] | | 1960 | 5.00 | 10.00 | 20.00 |

UP IN CENTRAL PARK
| ❏ Decca DL 8016 [M] | | 1950 | 10.00 | 20.00 | 40.00 |
—Black label, gold print
| ❏ Decca DL 8016 [M] | | 1955 | 7.50 | 15.00 | 30.00 |
—Black label, silver print

WAITING FOR GODOT
| ❏ Columbia Masterworks O2L 238 [(2)M] | | 1956 | 7.50 | 15.00 | 30.00 |

WEST SIDE STORY
| ❏ Columbia Masterworks OS 2001 [S] | | 1958 | 7.50 | 15.00 | 30.00 |
—Gray and black label with six "eye" logos
| ❏ Columbia Masterworks OS 2001 [S] | | 1963 | 3.75 | 7.50 | 15.00 |
—Gray label with "360 Sound Stereo"
| ❏ Columbia Masterworks OL 5230 [M] | | 1958 | 6.25 | 12.50 | 25.00 |
—Gray and black label with six "eye" logos
| ❏ Columbia Masterworks OL 5230 [M] | | 1963 | 3.00 | 6.00 | 12.00 |
—Gray label with "Guaranteed High Fidelity" or "360 Sound Mono"
| ❏ Columbia Masterworks S 32603 [S] | | 1973 | 2.50 | 5.00 | 10.00 |
—Reissue with new number

WHAT MAKES SAMMY RUN?
| ❏ Columbia Masterworks KSO 2440 [S] | | 1964 | 10.00 | 20.00 | 40.00 |
| ❏ Columbia Masterworks KOL 6040 [M] | | 1964 | 7.50 | 15.00 | 30.00 |

WILDCAT
| ❏ RCA Victor LOC-1060 [M] | | 1961 | 6.25 | 12.50 | 25.00 |
| ❏ RCA Victor LSO-1060 [S] | | 1961 | 10.00 | 20.00 | 40.00 |

WISH YOU WERE HERE
| ❏ RCA Victor LOC-1007 [M] | | 1952 | 15.00 | 30.00 | 60.00 |

WONDERFUL TOWN
| ❏ Decca DL 9010 [M] | | 1953 | 7.50 | 15.00 | 30.00 |
—Black label, gold print

WORDS AND MUSIC
| ❏ RCA Victor LRL1-5079 | | 1974 | 5.00 | 10.00 | 20.00 |

YOU'RE A GOOD MAN, CHARLIE BROWN
| ❏ MGM 1E-9 [M] | | 1967 | 5.00 | 10.00 | 20.00 |
| ❏ MGM S1E-9 [S] | | 1967 | 5.00 | 10.00 | 20.00 |

YOUR OWN THING
| ❏ RCA Victor LOC-1148 [M] | | 1968 | 6.25 | 12.50 | 25.00 |
| ❏ RCA Victor LSO-1148 [S] | | 1968 | 5.00 | 10.00 | 20.00 |

ZORBA
| ❏ Capitol SO-118 | | 1969 | 5.00 | 10.00 | 20.00 |

SOUNDTRACKS

Number	Title (A Side/B Side)	Yr	VG	VG+	NM

101 DALMATIONS
❏ Disneyland DQ-1308 [M]		1966	5.00	10.00	20.00
❏ Disneyland ST-1908 [M]		1960	6.25	12.50	25.00
❏ Disneyland ST-3931 [M]		1965	10.00	20.00	40.00
❏ Disneyland ST-4903 [M]		1963	37.50	75.00	150.00
—Gatefold cover with pop-up scene in center

1776
| ❏ Columbia S 31741 | | 1972 | 5.00 | 10.00 | 20.00 |

40 POUNDS OF TROUBLE
| ❏ Mercury MG-20784 [M] | | 1963 | 7.50 | 15.00 | 30.00 |
| ❏ Mercury SR-60784 [S] | | 1963 | 10.00 | 20.00 | 40.00 |

55 DAYS AT PEKING
| ❏ Columbia CL 2028 [M] | | 1963 | 10.00 | 20.00 | 40.00 |
| ❏ Columbia CS 8828 [S] | | 1963 | 17.50 | 35.00 | 70.00 |

THE 633 SQUADRON
| ❏ United Artists UA-LA305-G | | 1974 | 6.25 | 12.50 | 25.00 |

THE 7TH DAWN
| ❏ United Artists UAL-4115 [M] | | 1964 | 7.50 | 15.00 | 30.00 |
| ❏ United Artists UAS-5115 [S] | | 1964 | 10.00 | 20.00 | 40.00 |

THE 7TH VOYAGE OF SINBAD
| ❏ Colpix CP-504 [M] | | 1958 | 50.00 | 100.00 | 200.00 |
| ❏ Varese Sarabande STV-81135 | | 1983 | 5.00 | 10.00 | 20.00 |

AARON SLICK FROM PUNKIN CRICK
| ❏ RCA Victor LPM-3006 [10] | | 1952 | 37.50 | 75.00 | 150.00 |

ADVENTURES IN PARADISE
| ❏ ABC-Paramount ABC-329 [M] | | 1960 | 7.50 | 15.00 | 30.00 |
| ❏ ABC-Paramount ABCS-329 [S] | | 1960 | 10.00 | 20.00 | 40.00 |

ADVISE AND CONSENT
| ❏ RCA Victor LOC-1068 [M] | | 1962 | 7.50 | 15.00 | 30.00 |
| ❏ RCA Victor LSO-1068 [S] | | 1962 | 15.00 | 30.00 | 60.00 |

AN AFFAIR TO REMEMBER
| ❏ Columbia CL 1013 [M] | | 1957 | 10.00 | 20.00 | 40.00 |

AFRICA ADDIO
| ❏ United Artists UAL-4141 [M] | | 1966 | 5.00 | 10.00 | 20.00 |
| ❏ United Artists UAS-5141 [S] | | 1966 | 6.25 | 12.50 | 25.00 |

THE AGONY AND THE ECSTASY
| ❏ Capitol MAS 2427 [M] | | 1965 | 15.00 | 30.00 | 60.00 |
| ❏ Capitol SMAS 2427 [S] | | 1965 | 20.00 | 40.00 | 80.00 |

AIRPORT
| ❏ Decca DL 79173 | | 1970 | 6.25 | 12.50 | 25.00 |

ALAKAZAM THE GREAT
| ❏ Vee Jay LP-6000 [M] | | 1961 | 20.00 | 40.00 | 80.00 |

THE ALAMO
| ❏ Columbia CL 1558 [M] | | 1960 | 5.00 | 10.00 | 20.00 |
| ❏ Columbia CS 8358 [S] | | 1960 | 6.25 | 12.50 | 25.00 |

ALBERT PECKINPAW'S REVENGE
| ❏ Sidewalk ST 5907 [S] | | 1967 | 7.50 | 15.00 | 30.00 |
| ❏ Sidewalk T 5907 [M] | | 1967 | 7.50 | 15.00 | 30.00 |

ALEXANDER THE GREAT
| ❏ Mercury MG-20148 [M] | | 1956 | 62.50 | 125.00 | 250.00 |

ALFIE
❏ ABC Impulse! AS-9111 [S]		1968	3.75	7.50	15.00
❏ Impulse! A-9111 [M]		1966	7.50	15.00	30.00
❏ Impulse! AS-9111 [S]		1966	7.50	15.00	30.00

ALIEN
| ❏ 20th Century T-593 | | 1979 | 6.25 | 12.50 | 25.00 |

ALIENS
| ❏ Varese Sarabande STV-81283 | | 1986 | 6.25 | 12.50 | 25.00 |

ALIKI, MY LOVE
| ❏ Fontana MGF-27523 [M] | | 1963 | 6.25 | 12.50 | 25.00 |
| ❏ Fontana SRF-67523 [S] | | 1963 | 7.50 | 15.00 | 30.00 |

ALL NIGHT LONG
| ❏ Epic LA 16032 [M] | | 1962 | 10.00 | 20.00 | 40.00 |
| ❏ Epic BA 17032 [S] | | 1962 | 12.50 | 25.00 | 50.00 |

ALL THE LOVING COUPLES
| ❏ GNP Crescendo GNPS-2051 | | 1969 | 10.00 | 20.00 | 40.00 |

ALL THE RIGHT NOISES
| ❏ Buddah BDS-5132 | | 1971 | 7.50 | 15.00 | 30.00 |

ALL THIS AND WORLD WAR II
| ❏ 20th Century 2T-522 [(2)] | | 1976 | 6.25 | 12.50 | 25.00 |
—Box set with booklet and flyer

THE ALLNIGHTER
| ❏ Chameleon CHPD 9601 [PD] | | 1987 | 7.50 | 15.00 | 30.00 |
—Picture disc
| ❏ Chameleon CHST 9601 | | 1987 | 3.75 | 7.50 | 15.00 |

ALMOST FAMOUS (UNTITLED)
| ❏ Dreamworks RTH-2001 [(2)] | | 2001 | 10.00 | 20.00 | 40.00 |
—Album is actually called "Untitled"; contains five songs by Stillwater not on the CD version; 180-gram vinyl; with poster

ALMOST SUMMER
| ❏ MCA 3037 | | 1978 | 6.25 | 12.50 | 25.00 |

AMERICA, AMERICA
| ❏ Warner Bros. W 1527 [M] | | 1963 | 5.00 | 10.00 | 20.00 |
| ❏ Warner Bros. WS 1527 [S] | | 1963 | 6.25 | 12.50 | 25.00 |

AMERICAN HOT WAX
| ❏ A&M SP-6500 [(2)] | | 1978 | 5.00 | 10.00 | 20.00 |

AN AMERICAN IN PARIS
| ❏ MGM E-93 [10] | | 1951 | 10.00 | 20.00 | 40.00 |

Number / Title (A Side/B Side)	Yr	VG	VG+	NM
AMERICAN POP				
❏ MCA 5201	1981	7.50	15.00	30.00
THE AMOROUS ADVENTURES OF MOLL FLANDERS				
❏ RCA Victor LOC-1113 [M]	1965	10.00	20.00	40.00
❏ RCA Victor LSO-1113 [S]	1965	20.00	40.00	80.00
ANASTASIA				
❏ Decca DL 8460 [M]	1956	7.50	15.00	30.00
ANATOMY OF A MURDER				
❏ Columbia CL 1360 [M]	1959	10.00	20.00	40.00
❏ Columbia CS 8166 [S]	1959	12.50	25.00	50.00
AND GOD CREATED WOMAN				
❏ Decca DL 8685 [M]	1957	30.00	60.00	120.00
THE ANDROMEDA STRAIN				
❏ Kapp KRS-5513	1971	10.00	20.00	40.00
—Regular cover				
❏ Kapp KRS-5513	1971	25.00	50.00	100.00
—Hexagonal cover glued onto silver cardboard				
ANGELS DIE HARD				
❏ Uni 73091	1971	7.50	15.00	30.00
ANGELS FROM HELL				
❏ Tower ST 5128	1968	15.00	30.00	60.00
THE ANONYMOUS VENETIAN				
❏ United Artists UAS-5218	1971	7.50	15.00	30.00
ANOTHER TIME, ANOTHER PLACE				
❏ Columbia CL 1180 [M]	1958	10.00	20.00	40.00
ANY WEDNESDAY				
❏ Warner Bros. W 1669 [M]	1966	6.25	12.50	25.00
❏ Warner Bros. WS 1669 [S]	1966	10.00	20.00	40.00
THE APARTMENT				
❏ United Artists UAL-3105 [M]	1960	7.50	15.00	30.00
❏ United Artists UAS-6105 [S]	1960	10.00	20.00	40.00
APOCALYPSE NOW				
❏ Elektra DP-90001 [(2)]	1979	7.50	15.00	30.00
THE APPLE				
❏ Cannon 1001	1980	17.50	35.00	70.00
APRIL LOVE				
❏ Dot DLP-9000 [M]	1957	5.00	10.00	20.00
ARMS AND THE GIRL				
❏ Decca DL 5200 [10]	1950	25.00	50.00	100.00
AROUND THE WORLD IN 80 DAYS				
❏ Decca DL 9046 [M]	1957	6.25	12.50	25.00
—Black label, silver print				
❏ Decca DL 79046 [S]	1959	10.00	20.00	40.00
—Maroon label, silver print; cover has "Full Stereo" banner				
❏ Decca DL 79046 [S]	196?	3.00	6.00	12.00
—Black label with color bars				
❏ Decca SW-94840 [S]	1972	3.75	7.50	15.00
—Capitol Record Club edition				
❏ MCA 2062 [S]	1973	2.50	5.00	10.00
—Reissue of 79046; black label with rainbow				
❏ MCA 37086 [S]	198?	2.00	4.00	8.00
—Reissue of 2062				
AROUND THE WORLD UNDER THE SEA				
❏ Monument MLP-8050 [M]	1966	7.50	15.00	30.00
❏ Monument SLP-18050 [S]	1966	12.50	25.00	50.00
ARRIVIDERCI, BABY!				
❏ RCA Victor LOC-1132 [M]	1966	5.00	10.00	20.00
❏ RCA Victor LSO-1132 [S]	1966	10.00	20.00	40.00
AT LONG LAST LOVE				
❏ RCA Victor ABL2-0967 [(2)]	1975	5.00	10.00	20.00
ATHENA				
❏ Mercury MG-25202 [10]	1954	37.50	75.00	150.00
AVIATOR				
❏ Varese Sarabande STV-81240	1985	5.00	10.00	20.00
BABES IN TOYLAND				
❏ Buena Vista BV-4022 [M]	1961	7.50	15.00	30.00
❏ Buena Vista STER-4022 [S]	1961	10.00	20.00	40.00
BABY DOLL				
❏ Columbia CL 958 [M]	195?	12.50	25.00	50.00
—No ads for LPs on back cover				
❏ Columbia CL 958 [M]	1956	15.00	30.00	60.00
—Ads for other Columbia LPs on back cover				
BABY FACE NELSON				
❏ Jubilee JLP-2021 [M]	1957	30.00	60.00	120.00
BABY, THE RAIN MUST FALL				
❏ Ava A-53 [M]	1965	10.00	20.00	40.00
❏ Ava AS-53 [S]	1965	12.50	25.00	50.00
❏ Mainstream S-6056 [S]	1965	10.00	20.00	40.00
—Reissue of Ava AS-53				
❏ Mainstream 56056 [M]	1965	7.50	15.00	30.00
—Reissue of Ava A-53				
BACK STREET				
❏ Decca DL 9097 [M]	1961	10.00	20.00	40.00
❏ Decca DL 79097 [S]	1961	20.00	40.00	80.00
THE BAD SEED				
❏ RCA Victor LPM-1395 [M]	1956	75.00	150.00	300.00
BAND OF ANGELS				
❏ RCA Victor LPM-1557 [M]	1957	25.00	50.00	100.00
THE BAND WAGON				
❏ MGM E-3051 [M]	1953	7.50	15.00	30.00
—Yellow label				
❏ MGM E-3051 [M]	1960	5.00	10.00	20.00
—Black label				
THE BANJOMAN				
❏ Sire SA-7527	1977	5.00	10.00	20.00
BARABBAS				
❏ Colpix CP 510 [M]	1962	10.00	20.00	40.00
❏ Colpix SCP 510 [S]	1962	20.00	40.00	80.00
BARBARELLA				
❏ Dyno Voice DV-31908	1968	12.50	25.00	50.00
THE BARBARIAN AND THE GEISHA				
❏ 20th Fox FOX-3004 [M]	1958	62.50	125.00	250.00
BAREFOOT ADVENTURE				
❏ Pacific Jazz PJ-35 [M]	1961	10.00	20.00	40.00
❏ Pacific Jazz ST-35 [S]	1961	15.00	30.00	60.00
BAREFOOT IN THE PARK				
❏ Dot DLP-3803 [M]	1967	5.00	10.00	20.00
❏ Dot DLP-25803 [S]	1967	7.50	15.00	30.00
THE BARKLEYS OF BROADWAY				
❏ MGM E-503 [10]	1949	20.00	40.00	80.00
BATMAN				
❏ Warner Bros. 25977	1989	5.00	10.00	20.00
—Music composed and conducted by Danny Elfman				
BATMAN FOREVER				
❏ Atlantic PR 6339 [(2)]	1995	5.00	10.00	20.00
—Promo only generic white cover with sticker				
BATTLE OF THE BULGE				
❏ Warner Bros. W 1617 [M]	1965	10.00	20.00	40.00
❏ Warner Bros. WS 1617 [S]	1965	10.00	20.00	40.00
BEACH BLANKET BINGO				
❏ Capitol ST 2323 [S]	1965	15.00	30.00	60.00
❏ Capitol T 2323 [M]	1965	7.50	15.00	30.00
BEAU JAMES				
❏ Imperial LP-9041 [M]	1957	10.00	20.00	40.00
BECKET				
❏ Decca DL 9117 [M]	1964	7.50	15.00	30.00
❏ Decca DL 79117 [S]	1964	12.50	25.00	50.00
BEDAZZLED				
❏ London MS-82009	1967	20.00	40.00	80.00
BEHOLD A PALE HORSE				
❏ Colpix CP 519 [M]	1964	12.50	25.00	50.00
❏ Colpix SCP 519 [S]	1964	17.50	35.00	70.00
THE BELIEVERS				
❏ Varese Sarabande STV-81328	1987	5.00	10.00	20.00
BELL, BOOK AND CANDLE				
❏ Colpix CP 502 [M]	1959	15.00	30.00	60.00
BELLS ARE RINGING				
❏ Capitol SW 1435 [S]	1960	7.50	15.00	30.00
❏ Capitol W 1435 [M]	1960	6.25	12.50	25.00
BEN-HUR				
❏ MGM 1E1 [M]	1959	10.00	20.00	40.00
—Boxed edition with hardcover book				
❏ MGM 1E1 [M]	196?	3.00	6.00	12.00
—Gatefold cover, no book				
❏ MGM S-1E1 [S]	1959	12.50	25.00	50.00
—Boxed edition with hardcover book				
❏ MGM S-1E1 [S]	196?	2.50	5.00	10.00
—Gatefold cover, no book; blue and gold label				
❏ MGM S-1E1 [S]	196?	3.75	7.50	15.00
—Gatefold cover, no book; black label				
BEST OF THE BEST				
❏ Relativity 88561 034 1	1989	5.00	10.00	20.00
BETRAYED				
❏ Varese Sarabande 704.700	1988	7.50	15.00	30.00
BEYOND THE GREAT WALL				
❏ Capitol T 10401 [M]	1965	12.50	25.00	50.00
BEYOND THE VALLEY OF THE DOLLS				
❏ 20th Century Fox TFS-4211	1970	50.00	100.00	200.00
THE BIBLE				
❏ 20th Century Fox TF-3184 [M]	1966	5.00	10.00	20.00
❏ 20th Century Fox TFS-4184 [S]	1966	7.50	15.00	30.00
THE BIG COUNTRY				
❏ United Artists UAL-4004 [M]	1958	6.25	12.50	25.00
❏ United Artists UAS-5004 [S]	1958	12.50	25.00	50.00
THE BIG GUNDOWN				
❏ United Artists UAS-5190	1967	10.00	20.00	40.00
THE BIGGEST BUNDLE OF THEM ALL				
❏ MGM E-4446 [M]	1967	5.00	10.00	20.00
❏ MGM SE-4446 [S]	1967	6.25	12.50	25.00
BILLIE				
❏ United Artists UAL-4131 [M]	1965	5.00	10.00	20.00
❏ United Artists UAS-5131 [S]	1965	6.25	12.50	25.00
THE BILLION DOLLAR BRAIN				
❏ United Artists UAL-4174 [M]	1967	3.75	7.50	15.00
❏ United Artists UAS-5174 [S]	1967	5.00	10.00	20.00
BILLY JACK				
❏ Warner Bros. WS 1926	1971	6.25	12.50	25.00
THE BIRD WITH THE CRYSTAL PLUMAGE				
❏ Capitol ST-642	1970	25.00	50.00	100.00
BLACK AND WHITE IN COLOR				
❏ Buddah BDS-5698	1977	10.00	20.00	40.00

Number Title (A Side/B Side)	Yr	VG	VG+	NM
BLACK GIRL				
❏ Fantasy F-9420	1973	17.50	35.00	70.00
THE BLACK HOLE				
❏ Buena Vista STER-5008	1979	12.50	25.00	50.00
THE BLACK ORCHID				
❏ Dot DLP-3178 [M]	1959	10.00	20.00	40.00
❏ Dot SLP-25178 [S]	1959	12.50	25.00	50.00
BLACK ORPHEUS				
❏ Epic LN 3672 [M]	1959	10.00	20.00	40.00
❏ Fontana MGF-27520 [M]	1963	5.00	10.00	20.00
❏ Fontana SRF-67520 [R]	1963	3.75	7.50	15.00
BLACKBIRDS OF 1928				
❏ Columbia Masterworks OL 6770 [M]	1968	3.75	7.50	15.00
❏ Revue 1 [M]	196?	7.50	15.00	30.00
❏ Sutton SSU-270 [R]	196?	3.00	6.00	12.00
❏ Sutton SU-270 [M]	196?	5.00	10.00	20.00
BLACULA				
❏ RCA Victor LSP-4806	1972	15.00	30.00	60.00
BLADE RUNNER				
❏ Full Moon/Warner Bros. 23748	1982	5.00	10.00	20.00
BLESS THE BEASTS AND CHILDREN				
❏ A&M SP-4322	1971	6.25	12.50	25.00
BLOOD AND SAND				
❏ Decca DL 5380 [10]	1952	20.00	40.00	80.00
BLOOMER GIRL				
❏ Decca DL 8015 [M]	1950	7.50	15.00	30.00
BLOW-UP				
❏ MGM E-4447 [M]	1967	10.00	20.00	40.00
❏ MGM SE-4447 [S]	1967	12.50	25.00	50.00
THE BLUE MAX				
❏ Mainstream S-6081 [S]	1966	20.00	40.00	80.00
❏ Mainstream 56081 [M]	1966	10.00	20.00	40.00
BLUE VELVET				
❏ Varese Sarabande STV-81292	1986	6.25	12.50	25.00
BOBO				
❏ Warner Bros. W 1711 [M]	1967	5.00	10.00	20.00
❏ Warner Bros. WS 1711 [S]	1967	5.00	10.00	20.00
BODY HEAT				
❏ Label X LXSE-1-002	1983	30.00	60.00	120.00
BOEING, BOEING				
❏ RCA Victor LOC-1121 [M]	1965	6.25	12.50	25.00
❏ RCA Victor LSO-1121 [S]	1965	7.50	15.00	30.00
BONNIE AND CLYDE				
❏ Warner Bros. W 1742 [M]	1968	10.00	20.00	40.00
❏ Warner Bros. WS 1742 [S]	1968	6.25	12.50	25.00
—Originals have green labels with "W7" logo in a square at top				
❏ Warner Bros. ST-91414 [S]	1968	7.50	15.00	30.00
—Capitol Record Club issue				
BORA, BORA				
❏ American Int'l. STA-1029	1970	7.50	15.00	30.00
BORN FREE				
❏ MGM E-4368 [M]	1966	3.75	7.50	15.00
❏ MGM SE-4368 [S]	1966	5.00	10.00	20.00
BORSALINO				
❏ Paramount PAS-5019	1970	7.50	15.00	30.00
THE BOY FRIEND				
❏ MGM 1SE-32	1971	5.00	10.00	20.00
A BOY NAMED CHARLIE BROWN				
❏ Columbia Masterworks OS 3500	1970	5.00	10.00	20.00
BOY ON A DOLPHIN				
❏ Decca DL 8580 [M]	1957	15.00	30.00	60.00
—Black label with silver print, or pink label with black print (promo)				
❏ Decca DL 8580 [S]	196?	5.00	10.00	20.00
—Black label with color bars				
THE BOY WHO COULD FLY				
❏ Varese Sarabande STV-81299	1986	5.00	10.00	20.00
THE BOYS FROM SYRACUSE				
❏ Capitol STAO 1933 [S]	1963	7.50	15.00	30.00
❏ Capitol TAO 1933 [M]	1963	6.25	12.50	25.00
BOYZ 'N THE HOOD				
❏ Warner Bros. PRO-A-4996 [DJ]	1991	5.00	10.00	20.00
—Promo-only vinyl release				
THE BRAVE ONE				
❏ Decca DL 8344 [M]	1956	10.00	20.00	40.00
BROTHER ON THE RUN				
❏ Perception PLP-45	1973	10.00	20.00	40.00
BUCCANEER				
❏ Columbia CL 1278 [M]	1958	6.25	12.50	25.00
❏ Columbia CS 8096 [S]	1958	10.00	20.00	40.00
BULLITT				
❏ Warner Bros. WS 1777	1968	15.00	30.00	60.00
BUNDLE OF JOY				
❏ RCA Victor LPM-1399 [M]	1956	10.00	20.00	40.00
BUNNY LAKE IS MISSING				
❏ RCA Victor LOC-1115 [M]	1965	10.00	20.00	40.00
❏ RCA Victor LSO-1115 [S]	1965	17.50	35.00	70.00
BUNNY O'HARE				
❏ American Int'l. STA-1041	1971	5.00	10.00	20.00
BUONA SERA, MRS. CAMPBELL				
❏ United Artists UAS-5192	1969	7.50	15.00	30.00

Number Title (A Side/B Side)	Yr	VG	VG+	NM
THE BURGLARS				
❏ Bell 1105	1971	10.00	20.00	40.00
BUTTERFIELD-8				
❏ MGM SE-3952 [S]	1960	6.25	12.50	25.00
BYE BYE BIRDIE				
❏ RCA Victor LOC-1081 [M]	196?	5.00	10.00	20.00
—Second cover with Ann-Margret on front, but with no credits underneath				
❏ RCA Victor LOC-1081 [M]	1963	6.25	12.50	25.00
—First cover without Ann-Margret on the front				
❏ RCA Victor LSO-1081 [S]	196?	5.00	10.00	20.00
—Third cover with Ann-Margret on front and with credits underneath				
❏ RCA Victor LSO-1081 [S]	196?	6.25	12.50	25.00
—Second cover with Ann-Margret on front, but with no credits underneath				
❏ RCA Victor LSO-1081 [S]	1963	7.50	15.00	30.00
—First cover without Ann-Margret on the front				
❏ RCA Victor AYL1-3947 [S]	1980	2.00	4.00	8.00
—"Best Buy Series" reissue				
C'MON, LET'S LIVE A LITTLE				
❏ Liberty LRP-3430 [M]	1966	6.25	12.50	25.00
❏ Liberty LST-7430 [S]	1966	7.50	15.00	30.00
CABARET				
❏ ABC ABCD-752	1972	5.00	10.00	20.00
❏ MCA 37125	198?	2.00	4.00	8.00
—Reissue; blue label with rainbow				
THE CAINE MUTINY				
❏ RCA Victor LOC-1013 [M]	1954	4000.	7000.	10000.
❏ RCA Victor LOC-1013 [M]	1993	50.00	100.00	200.00
—Very limited edition (100 copies) reproduction of the original LP				
CALL ME MADAM				
❏ Decca DL 5465 [10]	1953	12.50	25.00	50.00
CALL ME MISTER				
❏ Decca DLP 7005 [10]	1950	25.00	50.00	100.00
CAMELOT				
❏ Warner Bros. B 1712 [M]	1967	6.25	12.50	25.00
❏ Warner Bros. BS 1712 [S]	1967	5.00	10.00	20.00
—Gold label original				
❏ Warner Bros. BS 1712 [S]	1968	3.75	7.50	15.00
—Green label, "W7" box logo at top				
❏ Warner Bros. BS 1712 [S]	1970	3.00	6.00	12.00
—Green label, "WB" shield logo at top				
❏ Warner Bros. BS 1712 [S]	1973	2.50	5.00	10.00
—"Burbank" palm trees label				
❏ Warner Bros. BSK 3102 [S]	1977	2.00	4.00	8.00
—Reissue with new number				
❏ Warner Bros. SW-91347	1968	6.25	12.50	25.00
—Capitol Record Club edition				
CAN-CAN				
❏ Capitol SW 1301 [S]	1960	7.50	15.00	30.00
❏ Capitol W 1301 [M]	1960	5.00	10.00	20.00
CANDY				
❏ ABC ABCS-OC-9	1968	7.50	15.00	30.00
THE CARDINAL				
❏ RCA Victor LOC-1084 [M]	1963	10.00	20.00	40.00
❏ RCA Victor LSO-1084 [S]	1963	15.00	30.00	60.00
THE CARE BEARS MOVIE				
❏ Kid Stuff 3901	1985	5.00	10.00	20.00
THE CARETAKERS				
❏ Ava A-31 [M]	1963	5.00	10.00	20.00
❏ Ava AS-31 [S]	1963	6.25	12.50	25.00
CAROUSEL				
❏ Capitol SW 694 [S]	1962	5.00	10.00	20.00
—Black colorband label				
❏ Capitol SW 694 [S]	1969	3.75	7.50	15.00
—Lime green label				
❏ Capitol SW 694 [S]	1973	3.00	6.00	12.00
—Orange label				
❏ Capitol W 694 [M]	1956	7.50	15.00	30.00
—Gray label				
❏ Capitol W 694 [M]	1959	5.00	10.00	20.00
—Black colorband label, logo at left				
❏ Capitol W 694 [M]	1962	3.75	7.50	15.00
—Black colorband label, logo at top				
THE CARPETBAGGERS				
❏ Ava A-45 [M]	1964	7.50	15.00	30.00
❏ Ava AS-45 [S]	1964	10.00	20.00	40.00
CARRY IT ON				
❏ Vanguard VSD-79313	1971	6.25	12.50	25.00
CASINO ROYALE				
❏ Colgems COMO-5005 [M]	1967	7.50	15.00	30.00
❏ Colgems COSO-5005 [S]	1967	25.00	50.00	100.00
❏ Colgems COSO-5005 [S]	1999	6.25	12.50	25.00
—Classic Records reissue on audiophile vinyl				
❏ Colgems COSO-5005-45 [(4)]	199?	10.00	20.00	40.00
—Classic Records reissue on four 12-inch 45 rpm records				
CAT PEOPLE				
❏ Backstreet BSR 6107	1982	5.00	10.00	20.00
A CERTAIN SMILE				
❏ Columbia CL 1194 [M]	1958	10.00	20.00	40.00
❏ Columbia CS 8068 [S]	1958	20.00	40.00	80.00
THE CHAIRMAN				
❏ Tetragrammaton T-5007	1969	7.50	15.00	30.00
CHARLOTTE'S WEB				
❏ Paramount PAS-1008	1973	7.50	15.00	30.00

Number	Title (A Side/B Side)	Yr	VG	VG+	NM
THE CHASE					
❑ Columbia Masterworks OS 2960 [S]		1966	15.00	30.00	60.00
❑ Columbia Masterworks OL 6560 [M]		1966	10.00	20.00	40.00
CHINATOWN					
❑ ABC ABDP-848		1974	10.00	20.00	40.00
CHITTY CHITTY BANG BANG					
❑ United Artists UAS-5188		1968	6.25	12.50	25.00
THE CHRISTMAS THAT ALMOST WASN'T					
❑ RCA Camden CAL-1086 [M]		1966	6.25	12.50	25.00
❑ RCA Camden CAS-1086 [S]		1966	10.00	20.00	40.00
CINDERELLA					
❑ Disneyland DQ-1207 [M]		1959	10.00	20.00	40.00
—Second issue, white back cover with ads for nine other LPs					
❑ Disneyland DQ-1207 [M]		1963	7.50	15.00	30.00
—Third issue, pink back cover					
❑ Disneyland DQ-1207 [M]		1987	6.25	12.50	25.00
—Fifth issue, high gloss cover with prince putting slipper on Cinderella's foot					
❑ Disneyland 3107 [PD]		1981	7.50	15.00	30.00
—Fourth issue, picture disc					
❑ Disneyland WDL-4007 [M]		1957	50.00	100.00	200.00
—Original issue, gatefold cover					
CINDERFELLA					
❑ Dot DLP-8001 [M]		1960	15.00	30.00	60.00
❑ Dot SLP-38001 [S]		1960	25.00	50.00	100.00
—Gatefold cover with many extras including game board, spinner, booklet, music stand.					
CLEOPATRA					
❑ 20th Century Fox FXG-5008 [M]		1963	7.50	15.00	30.00
❑ 20th Century Fox SXG-5008 [S]		1963	10.00	20.00	40.00
CLEOPATRA JONES					
❑ Warner Bros. BS 2719		1973	7.50	15.00	30.00
CLOSE ENCOUNTERS OF THE THIRD KIND					
❑ Arista AL 9500 [(2)]		1977	6.25	12.50	25.00
—Includes one 12-inch record and one 7-inch record. Deduct 50 percent if the 7-inch record is missing.					
THE CLOWNS					
❑ Columbia S 30772		1971	10.00	20.00	40.00
COFFY					
❑ Polydor PD-5048		1973	25.00	50.00	100.00
THE COLLECTOR					
❑ Mainstream S-6053 [S]		1965	12.50	25.00	50.00
❑ Mainstream 56053 [M]		1965	7.50	15.00	30.00
COLLEGE CONFIDENTIAL					
❑ Chancellor CHL-5016 [M]		1960	10.00	20.00	40.00
❑ Chancellor CHLS-5016 [S]		1960	12.50	25.00	50.00
THE COLOR PURPLE					
❑ Qwest 25289 [(2)]		1985	6.25	12.50	25.00
—Box set "limited edition" on purple vinyl with booklet					
❑ Qwest 25336 [(2)]		1985	5.00	10.00	20.00
—Regular gatefold edition; records are still on purple vinyl					
COMANCHE					
❑ Coral CRL 57046 [M]		1956	100.00	200.00	400.00
COME BACK CHARLESTON BLUE					
❑ Atco SD 7010		1972	7.50	15.00	30.00
COME BLOW YOUR HORN					
❑ Reprise R-6071 [M]		1963	7.50	15.00	30.00
❑ Reprise R9-6071 [S]		1963	12.50	25.00	50.00
COMETOGETHER					
❑ Apple SW-3377		1971	5.00	10.00	20.00
THE CONNECTION					
❑ Felsted 2512 [S]		1960	75.00	150.00	300.00
❑ Felsted 7512 [M]		1960	50.00	100.00	200.00
COOL WORLD					
❑ Philips PHM 200138 [M]		1964	12.50	25.00	50.00
❑ Philips PHS 600138 [S]		1964	20.00	40.00	80.00
COOLEY HIGH					
❑ Motown M7-840 R2 [(2)]		1975	5.00	10.00	20.00
THE CORRUPT ONES					
❑ United Artists UAL-4158 [M]		1967	10.00	20.00	40.00
❑ United Artists UAS-5158 [S]		1967	10.00	20.00	40.00
COTTON COMES TO HARLEM					
❑ United Artists UAS-5211		1970	7.50	15.00	30.00
THE COURT JESTER					
❑ Decca DL 8212 [M]		1956	17.50	35.00	70.00
—Black label, silver print, or pink label, black print promo copy					
❑ Decca DL 8212 [M]		196?	7.50	15.00	30.00
—Black label with color bars					
THE COWBOY					
❑ Decca DL 8684 [M]		1958	15.00	30.00	60.00
—Black label, silver print, or pink label, black print promo copy					
❑ Decca DL 8684 [M]		196?	5.00	10.00	20.00
—Black label with color bars					
CRIME IN THE STREETS					
❑ Decca DL 8376 [M]		1956	15.00	30.00	60.00
—Black label, silver print, or pink label, black print promo copy					
❑ Decca DL 8376 [S]		196?	7.50	15.00	30.00
—Black label with color bars					
THE CROSS AND THE SWITCHBLADE					
❑ Light LS-5550		1970	7.50	15.00	30.00
CRUISING					
❑ Columbia JS 36410		1980	10.00	20.00	40.00
CUSTER OF THE WEST					
❑ ABC ABC-OC-5 [M]		1968	20.00	40.00	80.00
❑ ABC ABCS-OC-5 [S]		1968	25.00	50.00	100.00
CYCLE SAVAGES					
❑ American Int'l. STA-1033		1970	7.50	15.00	30.00
CYRANO DE BERGERAC					
❑ Capitol S 283 [M]		1951	7.50	15.00	30.00
—Originals have red labels with Capitol logo at top					
D.O.A.					
❑ Varese Sarabande 704.610		1988	10.00	20.00	40.00
DAKTARI					
❑ Leo the Lion CH-1043 [M]		1967	5.00	10.00	20.00
❑ MGM CH-1043 [M]		1967	5.00	10.00	20.00
DAMN THE DEFIANT!					
❑ Colpix CP 511 [M]		1962	7.50	15.00	30.00
❑ Colpix SCP 511 [S]		1962	15.00	30.00	60.00
DAMN YANKEES					
❑ RCA Victor LOC-1047 [M]		1958	10.00	20.00	40.00
—Original pressing with "Long Play" on label					
THE DAMNED					
❑ Warner Bros. WS 1829		1969	7.50	15.00	30.00
THE DARK OF THE SUN					
❑ MGM SE-4544		1968	10.00	20.00	40.00
DARLING LILI					
❑ RCA Victor LSPX-1000		1969	5.00	10.00	20.00
DAWN OF THE DEAD					
❑ Varese Sarabande VC-81106		1979	7.50	15.00	30.00
DAY OF ANGER					
❑ RCA Victor LSO-1165		1969	5.00	10.00	20.00
THE DAY OF THE DOLPHIN					
❑ Avco AV-11014		1973	6.25	12.50	25.00
THE DAY THE FISH CAME OUT					
❑ 20th Century Fox TF-3194 [M]		1967	7.50	15.00	30.00
❑ 20th Century Fox TFS-4194 [S]		1967	10.00	20.00	40.00
DAYDREAMER					
❑ Columbia Masterworks OS 2940 [S]		1966	10.00	20.00	40.00
❑ Columbia Masterworks OL 6540 [M]		1966	7.50	15.00	30.00
DAYS OF HEAVEN					
❑ Pacific Arts PAC8-128		1978	10.00	20.00	40.00
DAYS OF THUNDER					
❑ DGC 24294		1990	5.00	10.00	20.00
DE SADE					
❑ Tower ST-5170		1969	7.50	15.00	30.00
DEAD MAN WALKING					
❑ Columbia C3 67989 [(3)]		1997	20.00	40.00	80.00
DEADFALL					
❑ 20th Century Fox S-4203		1968	15.00	30.00	60.00
THE DEADLY AFFAIR					
❑ Verve V-8679 [M]		1966	6.25	12.50	25.00
❑ Verve V6-8679 [S]		1966	7.50	15.00	30.00
DEAR JOHN					
❑ Dunhill OCD-55001 [M]		1966	5.00	10.00	20.00
❑ Dunhill OCDS-55001 [S]		1966	6.25	12.50	25.00
THE DECLINE OF WESTERN CIVILIZATION					
❑ Slash 105		1981	5.00	10.00	20.00
DEEP IN MY HEART					
❑ MGM E-3153 [M]		1955	10.00	20.00	40.00
❑ MGM E-3153 [M]		1955	12.50	25.00	50.00
DESIRE UNDER THE ELMS					
❑ Dot DLP-3095 [M]		1958	25.00	50.00	100.00
DESTINATION MOON					
❑ Columbia CL 6151 [10]		1950	30.00	60.00	120.00
❑ Omega OL-3 [M]		1959	10.00	20.00	40.00
❑ Omega OSL-3 [S]		196?	20.00	40.00	80.00
THE DEVIL AT 4 O'CLOCK					
❑ Colpix CP 509 [M]		1962	10.00	20.00	40.00
❑ Colpix SCP 509 [S]		1962	17.50	35.00	70.00
THE DEVIL IN MISS JONES					
❑ Janus JLS-3059		1973	6.25	12.50	25.00
THE DEVIL'S BRIGADE					
❑ United Artists UAS-6654		1968	5.00	10.00	20.00
DIAMOND HEAD					
❑ Colpix CP-440 [M]		1963	7.50	15.00	30.00
❑ Colpix SCP 440 [S]		1963	15.00	30.00	60.00
DIAMONDS ARE FOREVER					
❑ United Artists UA-LA301-G		1974	3.00	6.00	12.00
—Reissue of 5520					
❑ United Artists UAS-5520		1971	5.00	10.00	20.00
THE DIARY OF ANNE FRANK					
❑ 20th Fox FOX-3012 [M]		1959	12.50	25.00	50.00
❑ 20th Fox SFX-3012 [S]		1959	20.00	40.00	80.00
DIRTY GAME					
❑ Laurie LLP-2034 [M]		1966	6.25	12.50	25.00
❑ Laurie SLP-2034 [S]		1966	7.50	15.00	30.00
DIVORCE AMERICAN STYLE					
❑ United Artists UAL-4163 [M]		1967	5.00	10.00	20.00
❑ United Artists UAS-5163 [S]		1967	5.00	10.00	20.00
DIVORCE ITALIAN STYLE					
❑ United Artists UAL-4106 [M]		1962	10.00	20.00	40.00
❑ United Artists UAS-5106 [S]		1962	12.50	25.00	50.00

Number	Title (A Side/B Side)	Yr	VG	VG+	NM
DOCTOR DOLITTLE					
❑ 20th Century Fox TCF-5101 [M]		1967	5.00	10.00	20.00
❑ 20th Century Fox TCS-5101 [S]		1967	5.00	10.00	20.00
DOCTOR GOLDFOOT AND THE GIRL BOMBS					
❑ Tower DT 5053 [R]		1966	6.25	12.50	25.00
❑ Tower T 5053 [M]		1966	5.00	10.00	20.00
DOCTOR ZHIVAGO					
❑ MCA 39042		198?	2.00	4.00	8.00
—Reissue					
❑ MGM 1E-6 [M]		1965	3.75	7.50	15.00
❑ MGM S1E-6 ST [S]		1965	5.00	10.00	20.00
❑ MGM SWAE-90620 [S]		1965	5.00	10.00	20.00
—Capitol Record Club issue					
A DOG OF FLANDERS					
❑ 20th Fox FOX-3026 [M]		1959	20.00	40.00	80.00
❑ 20th Fox SFX-3026 [S]		1959	75.00	150.00	300.00
$ (DOLLARS)					
❑ Reprise MS 2051		1971	5.00	10.00	20.00
DON'T MAKE WAVES					
❑ MGM E-4483 [M]		1967	7.50	15.00	30.00
❑ MGM SE-4483 [S]		1967	7.50	15.00	30.00
THE DOORS					
❑ Elektra E1-61047		1991	5.00	10.00	20.00
—Only vinyl edition in US released through Columbia House					
DR. NO					
❑ Liberty LT-50275		1981	2.00	4.00	8.00
—Reissue of United Artists 275					
❑ United Artists UA-LA275-G		1974	2.50	5.00	10.00
—Reissue of 5108					
❑ United Artists UAL-4108 [M]		1963	10.00	20.00	40.00
❑ United Artists UAS-5108 [S]		1963	12.50	25.00	50.00
DR. PHIBES					
❑ American Int'l. A-1040		1971	15.00	30.00	60.00
DRANGO					
❑ Liberty LRP-3036 [M]		1957	37.50	75.00	150.00
A DREAM OF KINGS					
❑ National General NG-1000		1969	7.50	15.00	30.00
DUCK, YOU SUCKER					
❑ United Artists UAS-5221		1972	10.00	20.00	40.00
DUEL AT DIABLO					
❑ United Artists UAL-4139 [M]		1966	6.25	12.50	25.00
❑ United Artists UAS-5139 [S]		1966	7.50	15.00	30.00
DUMBO					
❑ Disneyland 1204 [M]		197?	2.50	5.00	10.00
—Fourth issue, yellow rainbow label, flying Dumbo on back cover					
❑ Disneyland DQ-1204 [M]		1959	6.25	12.50	25.00
—Second issue, back cover has ads for nine other LPs					
❑ Disneyland DQ-1204 [M]		1963	3.75	7.50	15.00
—Third issue, four black & white photos on back cover					
❑ Disneyland WDL-4013 [M]		1957	50.00	100.00	200.00
—Original issue, gatefold cover					
❑ Disneyland ST-4904 [M]		1963	50.00	100.00	200.00
—Special issue with pop-up figures in gatefold					
DUNE					
❑ Polydor 823770-1		1984	7.50	15.00	30.00
THE DUNWICH HORROR					
❑ American Int'l. STA-1028		1970	10.00	20.00	40.00
E.T. THE EXTRA-TERRESTRIAL					
❑ MCA 6109		1982	2.50	5.00	10.00
❑ MCA 6113 [PD]		1982	6.25	12.50	25.00
—Picture disc in plastic envelope					
❑ MCA 16014		1982	10.00	20.00	40.00
—Audiophile edition					
❑ MCA 70000		1982	20.00	40.00	80.00
—Boxed version with booklet; story narrated by Michael Jackson					
EAST SIDE, WEST SIDE					
❑ Columbia CL 2123 [M]		1963	6.25	12.50	25.00
❑ Columbia CS 8923 [S]		1963	10.00	20.00	40.00
EASTER PARADE					
❑ MGM E-502 [10]		1950	20.00	40.00	80.00
EASY RIDER					
❑ ABC Dunhill DSX-50063		1969	6.25	12.50	25.00
ECCO					
❑ Warner Bros. W 1600 [M]		1965	6.25	12.50	25.00
❑ Warner Bros. WS 1600 [S]		1965	7.50	15.00	30.00
THE EDDY DUCHIN STORY					
❑ Decca DL 8289 [M]		1956	10.00	20.00	40.00
—Original cover with Tyrone Power and Kim Novak at a piano					
❑ Decca DL 8289 [M]		1959	5.00	10.00	20.00
—Reissue cover with Tyrone Power and Kim Novak kissing					
❑ Decca DL 9121 [M]		196?	3.00	6.00	12.00
—Reissue of 8289					
❑ Decca DL 78289 [S]		1959	6.25	12.50	25.00
—Maroon label, silver print, "Full Stereo" on front cover					
❑ Decca DL 79121 [S]		196?	3.75	7.50	15.00
—Reissue of 78289					
❑ MCA 2041		1973	2.50	5.00	10.00
—Reissue of 79121; black label with rainbow					
❑ MCA 37088		198?	2.00	4.00	8.00
—Reissue of 2041					
THE EDUCATION OF SONNY CARSON					
❑ Paramount PAS-1045		1974	5.00	10.00	20.00
THE EGYPTIAN					
❑ Decca DL 9014 [M]		1954	15.00	30.00	60.00

Number	Title (A Side/B Side)	Yr	VG	VG+	NM
❑ Decca DL 79014 [R]		196?	5.00	10.00	20.00
EIGHT MEN OUT					
❑ Varese Sarabande 704.600		1988	6.25	12.50	25.00
EL CID					
❑ MGM E-3977 [M]		1962	10.00	20.00	40.00
❑ MGM SE-3977 [S]		1962	12.50	25.00	50.00
EL DORADO					
❑ Epic FLM-13114 [M]		1967	12.50	25.00	50.00
❑ Epic LFS-15114 [S]		1967	17.50	35.00	70.00
EL TOPO					
❑ Apple SWAO-3388		1972	10.00	20.00	40.00
ELECTRA GLIDE IN BLUE					
❑ United Artists UA-LA062-H [(2)]		1973	10.00	20.00	40.00
—With booklet and two posters					
ELEPHANT STEPS					
❑ Columbia Masterworks M2X 33044 [(2)]		1975	5.00	10.00	20.00
ELMER GANTRY					
❑ United Artists UAL-4069 [M]		1960	10.00	20.00	40.00
❑ United Artists UAS-5069 [S]		1960	12.50	25.00	50.00
THE EMPIRE STRIKES BACK					
❑ RSO RS-2-4201 [(2)]		1980	5.00	10.00	20.00
—With booklet					
ENTER THE DRAGON					
❑ Warner Bros. BS 2727		1973	15.00	30.00	60.00
EVERYTHING I HAVE IS YOURS					
❑ MGM E-187 [10]		1953	10.00	20.00	40.00
EVIL DEAD					
❑ Varese Sarabande STV-81199		1984	5.00	10.00	20.00
EXODUS					
❑ RCA Victor LOC-1058 [M]		1960	5.00	10.00	20.00
—"Long Play" on label					
❑ RCA Victor LSO-1058 [S]		1960	6.25	12.50	25.00
—"Living Stereo" on label					
THE EXORCIST					
❑ Warner Bros. W 2774		1974	7.50	15.00	30.00
A FACE IN THE CROWD					
❑ Capitol W 872 [M]		1957	12.50	25.00	50.00
THE FALL OF THE ROMAN EMPIRE					
❑ Columbia Masterworks OS 2460 [S]		1964	15.00	30.00	60.00
❑ Columbia Masterworks OL 6060 [M]		1964	10.00	20.00	40.00
THE FAMILY WAY					
❑ London M 76007 [M]		1967	25.00	50.00	100.00
—No promo sticker on front cover (deduct 20 percent for promo)					
❑ London ST 82007 [S]		1967	30.00	60.00	120.00
—No promo sticker on front cover (deduct 20 percent for promo)					
FANNY					
❑ Warner Bros. W 1416 [M]		1961	6.25	12.50	25.00
❑ Warner Bros. WS 1416 [S]		1961	7.50	15.00	30.00
FANTASIA					
❑ Buena Vista 101 [(2)S]		1982	5.00	10.00	20.00
—Stereo reissue, two records, no booklet					
❑ Buena Vista STER-101 [(3)S]		1961	10.00	20.00	40.00
—First stereo issue, black and yellow rainbow labels, includes 24-page booklet					
❑ Buena Vista WDX-101 [(3)M]		1961	7.50	15.00	30.00
—Second issue, blue labels, includes 24-page booklet					
❑ Buena Vista V-104 [(2)]		1982	6.25	12.50	25.00
—Digitally re-recorded music track, Mickey Mouse as The Sorcerer on cover					
❑ Disneyland WDX-101 [(3)]		1957	15.00	30.00	60.00
—Original issue, maroon/red labels, includes 24-page booklet					
FANTASIA: NIGHT ON BALD MOUNTAIN; PASTORAL SYMPHONY; AVE MARIA					
❑ Disneyland STER-4101C [S]		1958	7.50	15.00	30.00
❑ Disneyland WDL-4101C [M]		1958	5.00	10.00	20.00
FANTASIA: RITE OF SPRING; TOCCATA AND FUGUE					
❑ Disneyland STER-4101A [S]		1959	7.50	15.00	30.00
❑ Disneyland WDL-4101A [M]		1958	5.00	10.00	20.00
FANTASIA: THE NUTCRACKER SUITE; DANCE OF THE HOURS					
❑ Disneyland STER-4101B [S]		1959	7.50	15.00	30.00
❑ Disneyland WDL-4101B [M]		1958	5.00	10.00	20.00
THE FANTASTIC PLASTIC MACHINE					
❑ Epic BN 26469		1969	6.25	12.50	25.00
FAR FROM THE MADDING CROWD					
❑ MGM 1E-11 [M]		1967	3.75	7.50	15.00
❑ MGM S1E-11 [S]		1967	6.25	12.50	25.00
A FAREWELL TO ARMS					
❑ Capitol W 918 [M]		1957	12.50	25.00	50.00
THE FASTEST GUITAR ALIVE					
❑ MGM SE-4475		1968	7.50	15.00	30.00
FATHOM					
❑ 20th Century Fox TFM-4195 [M]		1967	10.00	20.00	40.00
❑ 20th Century Fox TFS-4195 [S]		1967	12.50	25.00	50.00
FELLINI SATYRICON					
❑ United Artists UAS-5208		1969	7.50	15.00	30.00
FELLINI'S ROMA					
❑ United Artists UA-LA052-F		1972	7.50	15.00	30.00
THE FEMALE PRISONER					
❑ Columbia Masterworks OS 3320		1969	7.50	15.00	30.00
FIDDLER ON THE ROOF					
❑ United Artists UAS-10900 [(2)]		1971	5.00	10.00	20.00
—With booklet					
THE FIGHTER					
❑ Decca DL 5414 [10]		1952	20.00	40.00	80.00

Number	Title (A Side/B Side)	Yr	VG	VG+	NM
THE FINAL COUNTDOWN					
❑ Casablanca NBLP-7232		1980	10.00	20.00	40.00
FINIAN'S RAINBOW					
❑ Warner Bros. BS 2550		1968	5.00	10.00	20.00
FIRE DOWN BELOW					
❑ Decca DL 8597 [M]		1957	17.50	35.00	70.00
A FISTFUL OF DOLLARS					
❑ RCA Victor LOC-1135 [M]		1967	5.00	10.00	20.00
❑ RCA Victor LSO-1135 [S]		1967	7.50	15.00	30.00
—Black label, dog on top					
❑ RCA Victor LSO-1135 [S]		1969	3.00	6.00	12.00
—Orange label, tan label, or black label with dog at 1 o'clock					
FITZWILLY					
❑ United Artists UAL-4173 [M]		1967	5.00	10.00	20.00
❑ United Artists UAS-5173 [S]		1967	6.25	12.50	25.00
FIVE EASY PIECES					
❑ Epic KE 30456		1971	6.25	12.50	25.00
THE FIVE PENNIES					
❑ Dot DLP-9500 [M]		1959	6.25	12.50	25.00
❑ Dot DLP-29500 [S]		1959	12.50	25.00	50.00
THE FLAMINGO KID					
❑ Motown 6131ML		1984	2.50	5.00	10.00
—Commonly distributed issue					
❑ Varese Sarabande STV-81232		1984	10.00	20.00	40.00
—Original issue					
A FLEA IN HER EAR					
❑ 20th Century Fox TFS-4200		1968	7.50	15.00	30.00
FLOWER DRUM SONG					
❑ Decca DL 9098 [M]		1961	5.00	10.00	20.00
❑ Decca DL 79098 [S]		1961	6.25	12.50	25.00
❑ MCA 2069		1973	2.50	5.00	10.00
—Reissue; black label with rainbow					
THE FOG					
❑ Varese Sarabande STV-81191		1980	6.25	12.50	25.00
FOLIES BERGERE					
❑ Decca DL 8571 [M]		1958	6.25	12.50	25.00
FOLLOW ME					
❑ Uni 73056		1969	7.50	15.00	30.00
FOOTLOOSE					
❑ Columbia JS 39242		1984	2.50	5.00	10.00
❑ Columbia 9C9 39404 [PD]		1984	5.00	10.00	20.00
—Picture disc version					
FOR A FEW DOLLARS MORE					
❑ United Artists UAL-3608 [M]		1967	5.00	10.00	20.00
❑ United Artists UAS-6608 [S]		1967	6.25	12.50	25.00
FOR LOVE OF IVY					
❑ ABC SOC-7		1968	6.25	12.50	25.00
FOR THE FIRST TIME					
❑ RCA Victor Red Seal LM-2338 [M]		1959	3.75	7.50	15.00
❑ RCA Victor Red Seal LSC-2338 [S]		1959	5.00	10.00	20.00
—"Shaded dog" and smaller "RCA Victor" lettering					
❑ RCA Victor Red Seal LSC-2338 [S]		1965	3.75	7.50	15.00
—"White dog" and larger "RCA Victor" lettering					
❑ RCA Victor Red Seal LSC-2338 [S]		1969	3.00	6.00	12.00
—Red label, no dog					
FOR YOUR EYES ONLY					
❑ Liberty LOO-1109		1981	7.50	15.00	30.00
THE FOUR HORSEMEN OF THE APOCALYPSE					
❑ MGM E-3993 [M]		1962	5.00	10.00	20.00
❑ MGM SE-3993 [S]		1962	6.25	12.50	25.00
FOUR IN THE MORNING					
❑ Roulette OS 805 [M]		1966	10.00	20.00	40.00
❑ Roulette OSS 805 [S]		1966	12.50	25.00	50.00
THE FOX					
❑ Warner Bros. W 1738 [M]		1968	10.00	20.00	40.00
❑ Warner Bros. WS 1738 [S]		1968	6.25	12.50	25.00
THE FOX AND THE HOUND					
❑ Disneyland 3106 [PD]		1981	7.50	15.00	30.00
—"Disney Picture Disc" series					
❑ Disneyland ST-3823		1981	5.00	10.00	20.00
—Non-picture disc version					
FOXY BROWN					
❑ Motown M7-811		1974	5.00	10.00	20.00
FRANCIS OF ASSISI					
❑ 20th Fox FOX-3053 [M]		1961	50.00	100.00	200.00
❑ 20th Fox SFX-3053 [S]		1961	62.50	125.00	250.00
THE FRENCH LINE					
❑ Mercury MG-25182 [10]		1954	20.00	40.00	80.00
FRIENDLY PERSUASION					
❑ RKO Unique LP-110 [M]		1956	18.75	37.50	75.00
FRITZ THE CAT					
❑ Fantasy F-9406		1972	7.50	15.00	30.00
FROM RUSSIA WITH LOVE					
❑ United Artists UAL-4114 [M]		1964	5.00	10.00	20.00
❑ United Artists UAS-5114 [S]		1964	6.25	12.50	25.00
THE FUGITIVE KIND					
❑ United Artists UAL-4065 [M]		1959	12.50	25.00	50.00
❑ United Artists UAS-5065 [S]		1959	17.50	35.00	70.00
FUNERAL IN BERLIN					
❑ RCA Victor LOC-1136 [M]		1966	7.50	15.00	30.00
❑ RCA Victor LSO-1136 [S]		1966	12.50	25.00	50.00

Number	Title (A Side/B Side)	Yr	VG	VG+	NM
FUNNY GIRL					
❑ Columbia Masterworks BOS 3220		1968	3.00	6.00	12.00
—Gray "360 Sound" label; record is removed from inside the gatefold; liner notes on a tan background					
❑ Columbia Masterworks BOS 3220		1968	3.75	7.50	15.00
—Gray "360 Sound" label; record is removed from inside the gatefold; liner notes on a black background					
❑ Columbia Masterworks BOS 3220		1970	2.50	5.00	10.00
—Olive label with "Columbia" encircling the edge					
❑ Columbia Masterworks SQ 30992 [Q]		1971	10.00	20.00	40.00
A FUNNY THING HAPPENED ON THE WAY TO THE FORUM					
❑ United Artists UA-LA284-G		1974	2.50	5.00	10.00
—Reissue of 5144					
❑ United Artists UAL-4144 [M]		1966	3.00	6.00	12.00
❑ United Artists UAS-5144 [S]		1966	3.75	7.50	15.00
GAILY, GAILY					
❑ United Artists UAS 5202		1969	6.25	12.50	25.00
THE GAME IS OVER					
❑ Atco 33-205 [M]		1967	5.00	10.00	20.00
❑ Atco SD 33-205 [S]		1967	6.25	12.50	25.00
THE GAMES					
❑ Viking LPS-105		1970	50.00	100.00	200.00
GAY PURR-EE					
❑ Warner Bros. B 1479 [M]		1963	5.00	10.00	20.00
❑ Warner Bros. BS 1479 [S]		1963	7.50	15.00	30.00
GEISHA BOY					
❑ Jubilee JGS-1096 [S]		1959	20.00	40.00	80.00
❑ Jubilee JLP-1096 [M]		1958	12.50	25.00	50.00
THE GENE KRUPA STORY					
❑ Verve MGVS-6105 [S]		1959	25.00	50.00	100.00
—Original issue					
❑ Verve MGV-15010 [M]		1959	12.50	25.00	50.00
❑ Verve V-15010 [M]		1961	5.00	10.00	20.00
❑ Verve V6-15010 [S]		1963	20.00	40.00	80.00
—Early reissue					
GENGHIS KHAN					
❑ Liberty LRP-3412 [M]		1965	10.00	20.00	40.00
❑ Liberty LST-7412 [S]		1965	15.00	30.00	60.00
THE GENTLE RAIN					
❑ Mercury MG-21016 [M]		1966	5.00	10.00	20.00
❑ Mercury SR-61016 [S]		1966	6.25	12.50	25.00
GENTLEMEN MARRY BRUNETTES					
❑ Coral CRL 57013 [M]		1955	17.50	35.00	70.00
GENTLEMEN PREFER BLONDES					
❑ MGM E-208 [M]		1953	30.00	60.00	120.00
GET YOURSELF A COLLEGE GIRL					
❑ MGM E-4273 [M]		1965	5.00	10.00	20.00
❑ MGM SE-4273 [S]		1965	10.00	20.00	40.00
GETTING STRAIGHT					
❑ Colgems COSO-5010		1970	7.50	15.00	30.00
GIANT					
❑ Capitol DW 773 [R]		196?	3.00	6.00	12.00
❑ Capitol W 773 [M]		1956	10.00	20.00	40.00
—Turquoise or gray label					
❑ Capitol W 773 [M]		1959	6.25	12.50	25.00
—Black colorband label, logo at left					
❑ Capitol W 773 [M]		1962	3.75	7.50	15.00
—Black colorband label, logo at top					
GIGI					
❑ MCA 39045		1986	2.00	4.00	8.00
—Reissue					
❑ MGM E-3641 [M]		1958	5.00	10.00	20.00
—Yellow label					
❑ MGM E-3641 [M]		1960	3.00	6.00	12.00
—Black label					
❑ MGM SE-3641 [S]		1959	6.25	12.50	25.00
—Yellow label					
❑ MGM SE-3641 [S]		1960	3.75	7.50	15.00
—Black label					
❑ MGM SE-3641 [S]		1968	3.00	6.00	12.00
—Blue and gold label					
❑ MGM SW 90523 [S]		1965	3.75	7.50	15.00
❑ MGM W 90523 [M]		1965	3.00	6.00	12.00
—Capitol Record Club edition					
GIGOT					
❑ Capitol SW 1754 [S]		1962	10.00	20.00	40.00
❑ Capitol W 1754 [M]		1962	7.50	15.00	30.00
THE GIRL IN THE BIKINI					
❑ Poplar PLP 33-1002 [M]		1952	100.00	200.00	400.00
THE GIRL MOST LIKELY					
❑ Capitol W 930 [M]		1957	15.00	30.00	60.00
GIRL ON A MOTORCYCLE					
❑ Tetragrammaton T-5000		1969	7.50	15.00	30.00
THE GLENN MILLER STORY					
❑ Decca DL 5519 [10]		1954	10.00	20.00	40.00
❑ Decca DL 8226 [M]		1956	7.50	15.00	30.00
❑ Decca DL 9123 [M]		196?	5.00	10.00	20.00
—Reissue of 8226					
❑ Decca DL 79123 [R]		196?	3.75	7.50	15.00
❑ MCA 1624		198?	3.75	7.50	15.00
—This reissue is a bit more desirable because it was issued in true stereo					
❑ MCA 2036		1973	2.50	5.00	10.00
GLORY					
❑ Virgin 91329		1989	7.50	15.00	30.00

Number	Title (A Side/B Side)	Yr	VG	VG+	NM
❑ Virgin 91329		1998	5.00	10.00	20.00

—Classic Records edition; audiophile reissue; cover is noticeably less sharp than the originals

THE GLORY STOMPERS

❑ Sidewalk DT 5910 [R]		1968	12.50	25.00	50.00

GO, GO, GO WORLD

❑ Musicor MM-2059 [M]		1965	10.00	20.00	40.00
❑ Musicor MS-3059 [S]		1965	15.00	30.00	60.00

GO, JOHNNY, GO!

❑ (no label) (no number) [DJ]		1959	250.00	500.00	1000.

—Only exists as a promo

GOD'S LITTLE ACRE

❑ United Artists UAL-4002 [M]		1958	37.50	75.00	150.00

THE GODFATHER

❑ Paramount PAS-1003		1972	5.00	10.00	20.00

—Original cover with triple gatefold

THE GODFATHER PART II

❑ ABC ABDP-856		1975	5.00	10.00	20.00

THE GODFATHER PART III

❑ Columbia C 47078		1990	5.00	10.00	20.00

GOLD

❑ ABC ABCD-855		1975	7.50	15.00	30.00

GOLDEN BOY

❑ Colpix CP-478 [M]		1964	5.00	10.00	20.00
❑ Colpix SCP-478 [S]		1964	6.25	12.50	25.00

THE GOLDEN BREED

❑ Capitol ST 2886		1967	7.50	15.00	30.00

THE GOLDEN SCREW

❑ Atco 33-208 [M]		1967	7.50	15.00	30.00
❑ Atco SD 33-208 [S]		1967	10.00	20.00	40.00

GOLDFINGER

❑ United Artists UAL-4117 [M]		1964	3.75	7.50	15.00
❑ United Artists UAS-5117 [S]		1964	5.00	10.00	20.00

GOLIATH AND THE BARBARIANS

❑ American Int'l. 1001-M [M]		1960	10.00	20.00	40.00
❑ American Int'l. 1001-S [S]		1960	17.50	35.00	70.00

GONE WITH THE WAVE

❑ Colpix CP-492 [M]		1965	10.00	20.00	40.00
❑ Colpix SCP-492 [S]		1965	15.00	30.00	60.00

GONE WITH THE WIND

❑ MGM 1E-10 [M]		1967	5.00	10.00	20.00

—Gatefold edition with 32-page booklet

❑ MGM S1E-10 [S]		1967	5.00	10.00	20.00

—Gatefold edition with 32-page booklet

GOOD NEWS

❑ MGM E-504 [10]		1950	12.50	25.00	50.00

GOODBYE AGAIN

❑ United Artists UAL-4091 [M]		1961	7.50	15.00	30.00
❑ United Artists UAS-5091 [S]		1961	10.00	20.00	40.00

GOODBYE, CHARLIE

❑ 20th Century Fox TFM-3165 [M]		1964	6.25	12.50	25.00
❑ 20th Century Fox TFS-4165 [S]		1964	7.50	15.00	30.00

GOODBYE, MR. CHIPS

❑ MCA 39006		1986	2.00	4.00	8.00

—Reissue

❑ MGM 1SE-19		1969	5.00	10.00	20.00

GORDON'S WAR

❑ Buddah BDS-5137		1973	10.00	20.00	40.00

THE GOSPEL ACCORDING TO ST. MATTHEW

❑ Mainstream S-4000 [S]		1966	25.00	50.00	100.00
❑ Mainstream 54000 [M]		1966	6.25	12.50	25.00

GOTHIC

❑ Virgin 90607		1987	5.00	10.00	20.00

GOYA

❑ Decca DL 8236 [M]		1959	37.50	75.00	150.00

GRAND PRIX

❑ MGM 1E-8 [M]		1967	5.00	10.00	20.00
❑ MGM 1SE-8 [S]		1967	6.25	12.50	25.00

THE GREAT ESCAPE

❑ United Artists UAL-4107 [M]		1963	6.25	12.50	25.00
❑ United Artists UAS-5107 [S]		1963	7.50	15.00	30.00

THE GREAT GATSBY

❑ Paramount 2-3001 [(2)]		1974	5.00	10.00	20.00

THE GREATEST SHOW ON EARTH

❑ RCA Victor LPM-3018 [10]		1952	50.00	100.00	200.00

THE GREATEST STORY EVER TOLD

❑ United Artists UAL-4120 [M]		1965	6.25	12.50	25.00
❑ United Artists UAS-5120 [S]		1965	7.50	15.00	30.00

GROUNDS FOR MARRIAGE

❑ MGM E-536 [M]		1950	20.00	40.00	80.00

GUESS WHO'S COMING TO DINNER

❑ Colgems COM-108 [M]		1968	7.50	15.00	30.00
❑ Colgems COS-108 [S]		1968	7.50	15.00	30.00

GULLIVER'S TRAVELS BEYOND THE MOON

❑ Mainstream S-4001 [S]		1965	10.00	20.00	40.00
❑ Mainstream 54001 [M]		1965	7.50	15.00	30.00

GUNS FOR SAN SEBASTIAN

❑ MGM SE-4565		1968	15.00	30.00	60.00

THE GUNS OF NAVARONE

❑ Columbia CL 1655 [M]		1961	5.00	10.00	20.00
❑ Columbia CS 8455 [S]		1961	12.50	25.00	50.00

GURU

❑ RCA Victor LSO-1158		1969	5.00	10.00	20.00

GYPSY

❑ Warner Bros. B 1480 [M]		1962	5.00	10.00	20.00
❑ Warner Bros. BS 1480 [S]		1962	7.50	15.00	30.00

GYPSY GIRL

❑ Mainstream S-6090 [S]		1966	10.00	20.00	40.00
❑ Mainstream 56090 [M]		1966	7.50	15.00	30.00

HALLELUJAH THE HILLS

❑ Fontana MGF-27524 [M]		1964	6.25	12.50	25.00
❑ Fontana SRF-67524 [S]		1964	7.50	15.00	30.00

THE HALLELUJAH TRAIL

❑ United Artists UAL-4127 [M]		1965	5.00	10.00	20.00
❑ United Artists UAS-5127 [S]		1965	6.25	12.50	25.00

HAMMERHEAD

❑ Colgems COS-110		1968	10.00	20.00	40.00

HAMMERSMITH IS OUT

❑ Capitol SW-861		1972	7.50	15.00	30.00

HANG 'EM HIGH

❑ United Artists UAS-5179		1968	6.25	12.50	25.00

THE HAPPENING

❑ Colgems COMO-5006 [M]		1967	7.50	15.00	30.00
❑ Colgems COSO-5006 [S]		1967	12.50	25.00	50.00

THE HAPPIEST MILLIONAIRE

❑ Buena Vista BV-5001 [M]		1967	3.75	7.50	15.00
❑ Buena Vista STER-5001 [S]		1967	5.00	10.00	20.00

THE HARD RIDE

❑ Paramount PAS-6005		1971	7.50	15.00	30.00

HARPER

❑ Mainstream S-6078 [S]		1966	6.25	12.50	25.00
❑ Mainstream 56078 [M]		1966	5.00	10.00	20.00

THE HARRAD EXPERIMENT

❑ Capitol ST-11182		1973	6.25	12.50	25.00

HARRAD SUMMER

❑ Capitol ST-11338		1974	6.25	12.50	25.00

HAWAII

❑ United Artists UAL-4143 [M]		1966	5.00	10.00	20.00
❑ United Artists UAS-5143 [S]		1966	6.25	12.50	25.00
❑ United Artists SW-90935 [S]		1966	7.50	15.00	30.00

—Capitol Record Club issue

THE HEART IS A LONELY HUNTER

❑ Warner Bros. WS 1759		1968	7.50	15.00	30.00

HEART OF DIXIE

❑ A&M SP-3930		1989	5.00	10.00	20.00

HEAVY METAL

❑ Full Moon/Asylum DP-90004 [(2)]		1981	5.00	10.00	20.00

—Contains two LPs of pop/rock music

HEAVY METAL, THE SCORE

❑ Full Moon/Asylum 5E-547		1981	12.50	25.00	50.00

—Contains Elmer Bernstein's instrumental music

HEAVY TRAFFIC

❑ Fantasy F-9436		1973	6.25	12.50	25.00

HEIDI'S SONG

❑ K-Tel NU 5310		1982	5.00	10.00	20.00

THE HELEN MORGAN STORY

❑ RCA Victor LOC-1030 [M]		1957	15.00	30.00	60.00

HELL TO ETERNITY

❑ Warwick W 2030 [M]		1960	30.00	60.00	120.00
❑ Warwick WST 2030 [S]		1960	50.00	100.00	200.00

HELL UP IN HARLEM

❑ Motown M 802V1		1974	7.50	15.00	30.00

HELL'S ANGELS '69

❑ Capitol SKAO-303		1969	6.25	12.50	25.00

HELL'S ANGELS ON WHEELS

❑ Smash MGS-27094 [M]		1967	6.25	12.50	25.00
❑ Smash SRS-67094 [S]		1967	7.50	15.00	30.00

HELL'S BELLS

❑ Sidewalk ST 5919		1969	7.50	15.00	30.00

HELLCATS

❑ Tower ST 5124		1968	7.50	15.00	30.00

HELLO-GOODBYE

❑ 20th Century Fox S-4210		1970	10.00	20.00	40.00

HEMINGWAY'S ADVENTURES OF A YOUNG MAN

❑ RCA Victor LOC-1074 [M]		1962	10.00	20.00	40.00
❑ RCA Victor LSO-1074 [S]		1962	17.50	35.00	70.00

HERCULES

❑ Varese Sarabande STV-81187		1983	5.00	10.00	20.00

THE HERO

❑ Capitol SW-11098		1972	5.00	10.00	20.00

HEROES OF TELEMARK

❑ Mainstream S-6064 [S]		1965	7.50	15.00	30.00
❑ Mainstream 56064 [M]		1965	5.00	10.00	20.00

HEY THERE, IT'S YOGI BEAR!

❑ Colpix CP-472 [M]		1964	12.50	25.00	50.00
❑ Colpix SCP-472 [S]		1964	20.00	40.00	80.00

HIGH SOCIETY

❑ Capitol SW 750 [S]		1959	7.50	15.00	30.00

—Black colorband label, logo at left

Number	Title (A Side/B Side)	Yr	VG	VG+	NM
❏ Capitol SW 750 [S]		1962	5.00	10.00	20.00
—Black colorband label, logo at top					
❏ Capitol W 750 [M]		1956	7.50	15.00	30.00
—Gray label original					
❏ Capitol W 750 [M]		1959	5.00	10.00	20.00
—Black colorband label, logo at left					
❏ Capitol W 750 [M]		1962	3.75	7.50	15.00
—Black colorband label, logo at top					
THE HOBBIT					
❏ Buena Vista 103 [(2)]		1977	7.50	15.00	30.00
❏ Buena Vista 103A [(2)]		1977	10.00	20.00	40.00
—Special edition sold at Sears stores, with four decals and poster					
❏ Disneyland ST-3819		1978	7.50	15.00	30.00
HOLIDAY INN					
❏ Decca DL 4256		1962	6.25	12.50	25.00
❏ MCA 25205		1987	2.00	4.00	8.00
—Reissue of Decca LP					
HOMER AND EDDIE					
❏ Apache D1-71654		1989	6.25	12.50	25.00
HOOSIERS					
❏ Polydor 831475-1		1987	7.50	15.00	30.00
HOOTENANNY HOOT					
❏ MGM E-4172 [M]		1963	5.00	10.00	20.00
❏ MGM SE-4172 [S]		1963	6.25	12.50	25.00
THE HORSE SOLDIERS					
❏ United Artists UAL-4035 [M]		1959	15.00	30.00	60.00
❏ United Artists UAS-5035 [S]		1959	37.50	75.00	150.00
THE HORSEMEN					
❏ Sunflower SNF-5007		1971	10.00	20.00	40.00
THE HOT ROCK					
❏ Prophesy SD 8055		1972	5.00	10.00	20.00
HOT ROD RUMBLE					
❏ Liberty LRP-3048 [M]		1957	37.50	75.00	150.00
HOTEL PARADISO					
❏ MGM E-4419 [M]		1966	5.00	10.00	20.00
❏ MGM SE-4419 [S]		1966	6.25	12.50	25.00
THE HOUR OF THE GUN					
❏ United Artists UAL-4166 [M]		1967	10.00	20.00	40.00
❏ United Artists UAS-5166 [S]		1967	17.50	35.00	70.00
A HOUSE IS NOT A HOME					
❏ Ava A-50 [M]		1964	6.25	12.50	25.00
❏ Ava AS-50 [S]		1964	7.50	15.00	30.00
HOUSEBOAT					
❏ Columbia CL 1222 [M]		1958	12.50	25.00	50.00
HOW SWEET IT IS					
❏ RCA Victor LSP-4037		1968	5.00	10.00	20.00
HOW THE WEST WAS WON					
❏ MCA 39043		1986	2.00	4.00	8.00
—Reissue					
❏ MGM 1E-5 [M]		1963	3.75	7.50	15.00
❏ MGM 1SE-5 [S]		1963	5.00	10.00	20.00
HOW TO MURDER YOUR WIFE					
❏ United Artists UAL-4119 [M]		1965	3.75	7.50	15.00
❏ United Artists UAS-5119 [S]		1965	5.00	10.00	20.00
HOW TO SAVE A MARRIAGE AND RUIN YOUR LIFE					
❏ Columbia Masterworks OS 3140		1968	5.00	10.00	20.00
HOW TO STEAL A MILLION					
❏ 20th Century Fox TFM-3183 [M]		1966	10.00	20.00	40.00
❏ 20th Century Fox TFS-4183 [S]		1966	12.50	25.00	50.00
HOW TO STUFF A WILD BIKINI					
❏ Wand 671 [M]		1965	7.50	15.00	30.00
❏ Wand S-671 [S]		1965	10.00	20.00	40.00
HOW TO SUCCEED IN BUSINESS WITHOUT REALLY TRYING					
❏ United Artists UAL-4151 [M]		1967	5.00	10.00	20.00
❏ United Artists UAS-5151 [S]		1967	6.25	12.50	25.00
HOWARD THE DUCK					
❏ MCA 6173		1986	5.00	10.00	20.00
HUGO THE HIPPO					
❏ United Artists UA-LA637-G		1976	5.00	10.00	20.00
I LOVE MELVIN					
❏ MGM E-190 [10]		1953	12.50	25.00	50.00
I NEVER SANG FOR MY FATHER					
❏ Bell 1204		1970	10.00	20.00	40.00
I WANT TO LIVE					
❏ United Artists UXL 1 [(2)M]		1958	15.00	30.00	60.00
—Combines 4005 and 4006 into one package					
❏ United Artists UXS 51 [(2)S]		1958	20.00	40.00	80.00
—Combines 5005 and 5006 into one package					
❏ United Artists UAL-4005 [M]		1958	6.25	12.50	25.00
—Orchestral music by Johnny Mandel					
❏ United Artists UAS-4005 [S]		1958	10.00	20.00	40.00
—Orchestral music by Johnny Mandel					
❏ United Artists UAL-4006 [M]		1958	7.50	15.00	30.00
—Jazz music by Gerry Mulligan, Shelly Manne and Art Farmer					
❏ United Artists UAS-4006 [S]		1958	10.00	20.00	40.00
—Jazz music by Gerry Mulligan, Shelly Mann and Art Farmer					
I'LL NEVER FORGET WHAT'S 'IS NAME					
❏ Decca DL 9163 [M]		1967	6.25	12.50	25.00
❏ Decca DL 79163 [S]		1967	7.50	15.00	30.00
ICE STATION ZEBRA					
❏ MGM S1E-14 ST		1968	10.00	20.00	40.00

Number	Title (A Side/B Side)	Yr	VG	VG+	NM
ICEMAN					
❏ Southern Cross SCRS-1006		1983	5.00	10.00	20.00
IF HE HOLLERS, LET HIM GO					
❏ Tower ST 5152		1968	10.00	20.00	40.00
IMITATION OF LIFE					
❏ Decca DL 8879 [M]		1959	12.50	25.00	50.00
❏ Decca DL 78879 [S]		1959	20.00	40.00	80.00
IN A SHALLOW GRAVE					
❏ Varese Sarabande STV-81359		1988	10.00	20.00	40.00
IN HARM'S WAY					
❏ RCA Victor LOC-1100 [M]		1965	10.00	20.00	40.00
❏ RCA Victor LSO-1100 [S]		1965	20.00	40.00	80.00
IN LIKE FLINT					
❏ 20th Century Fox 4193 [M]		1967	10.00	20.00	40.00
❏ 20th Century Fox S-4193 [S]		1967	20.00	40.00	80.00
IN SEARCH OF THE CASTAWAYS					
❏ Disneyland ST-3916 [M]		1962	17.50	35.00	70.00
IN THE GOOD OLD SUMMERTIME					
❏ MGM E-169 [10]		1949	25.00	50.00	100.00
IN THE HEAT OF THE NIGHT					
❏ United Artists UAL-4160 [M]		1967	3.75	7.50	15.00
❏ United Artists UAS-5160 [S]		1967	5.00	10.00	20.00
INCHON					
❏ Regency RI-8502		1982	7.50	15.00	30.00
INDIANA JONES AND THE TEMPLE OF DOOM					
❏ Polydor 821592-1		1984	5.00	10.00	20.00
THE INDISCRETION OF AN AMERICAN WIFE					
❏ Columbia CL 6277 [10]		1954	20.00	40.00	80.00
THE INN OF THE SIXTH HAPPINESS					
❏ 20th Century Fox FOX-3011 [M]		1958	12.50	25.00	50.00
❏ 20th Century Fox SFX-3011 [S]		1958	17.50	35.00	70.00
INSIDE DAISY CLOVER					
❏ Warner Bros. W 1616 [M]		1965	5.00	10.00	20.00
❏ Warner Bros. WS 1616 [S]		1965	7.50	15.00	30.00
INSPECTOR CLOUSEAU					
❏ MCA 25107		1986	2.00	4.00	8.00
—Reissue					
❏ United Artists UAS-5186		1968	7.50	15.00	30.00
INTERLUDE					
❏ Colgems COSO-5007		1968	10.00	20.00	40.00
THE INTERNS					
❏ Colpix CP 427 [M]		1962	7.50	15.00	30.00
❏ Colpix SCP 427 [S]		1962	10.00	20.00	40.00
INVITATION TO THE DANCE					
❏ MGM E-3207 [M]		1956	12.50	25.00	50.00
THE IPCRESS FILE					
❏ Decca DL 9124 [M]		1965	7.50	15.00	30.00
❏ Decca DL 79124 [S]		1965	10.00	20.00	40.00
IRMA LA DOUCE					
❏ United Artists UAL-4109 [M]		1963	5.00	10.00	20.00
❏ United Artists UAS-5109 [S]		1963	6.25	12.50	25.00
IS PARIS BURNING?					
❏ Columbia Masterworks OS 3030 [S]		1966	10.00	20.00	40.00
❏ Columbia Masterworks OL 6630 [M]		1966	7.50	15.00	30.00
THE ISLAND					
❏ Varese Sarabande VC-81147		1979	5.00	10.00	20.00
THE ISLAND AT THE TOP OF THE WORLD					
❏ Disneyland ST-3814		1974	6.25	12.50	25.00
ISLAND IN THE SKY					
❏ Decca DL 7029 [10]		1953	75.00	150.00	300.00
IT STARTED IN NAPLES					
❏ Dot DLP-3324 [M]		1960	15.00	30.00	60.00
❏ Dot DLP-25324 [S]		1960	25.00	50.00	100.00
❏ Varese Sarabande STV-81122		1982	3.75	7.50	15.00
—Reissue of Dot 25324					
IT'S A MAD, MAD, MAD, MAD WORLD					
❏ MCA 39076		198?	2.00	4.00	8.00
—Reissue of United Artists 276					
❏ United Artists UA-LA276-G		1974	2.50	5.00	10.00
—Reissue of 5110					
❏ United Artists UAL-4110 [M]		1963	5.00	10.00	20.00
❏ United Artists UAS-5110 [S]		1963	6.25	12.50	25.00
IT'S ALWAYS FAIR WEATHER					
❏ MCA 25018		1986	2.50	5.00	10.00
—Reissue					
❏ MGM E-3241 [M]		1955	12.50	25.00	50.00
THE ITALIAN JOB					
❏ Paramount PAS-5007		1969	10.00	20.00	40.00
JACK THE RIPPER					
❏ RCA Victor LPM-2199 [M]		1960	7.50	15.00	30.00
❏ RCA Victor LSP-2199 [S]		1960	12.50	25.00	50.00
JAMBOREE!					
❏ Warner Bros. (no #) [M]		1957	300.00	600.00	1200.
—Album has been counterfeited. Originals have front cover slicks and back cover notes printed on the cardboard, and the records have "Jam 1" and "Jam 2" stamped (not etched) in the dead wax.					
THE JAMES DEAN STORY					
❏ Capitol W 881 [M]		1957	15.00	30.00	60.00
❏ Kimberly 2016 [M]		1960	10.00	20.00	40.00
❏ Kimberly 11016 [S]		1960	12.50	25.00	50.00
—Reissue of World Pacific 2005					
❏ World Pacific P-2005 [M]		1958	25.00	50.00	100.00

Number	Title (A Side/B Side)	Yr	VG	VG+	NM
JAWS					
❑ MCA 1660		198?	2.00	4.00	8.00
—Reissue of 2087					
❑ MCA 2087		1975	5.00	10.00	20.00
JEAN DE FLORETTE					
❑ TVT 3004		1986	5.00	10.00	20.00
JEREMIAH JOHNSON					
❑ Warner Bros. BS 2902		1972	5.00	10.00	20.00
—Green label					
JESSICA					
❑ United Artists UAL-4096 [M]		1962	5.00	10.00	20.00
❑ United Artists UAS-5096 [S]		1962	6.25	12.50	25.00
THE JOE LOUIS STORY					
❑ MGM E-221 [10]		1953	20.00	40.00	80.00
JOHN PAUL JONES					
❑ Varese Sarabande STV- 81146		1981	3.75	7.50	15.00
—Reissue of Warner Bros. WS 1293					
❑ Warner Bros. W 1293 [M]		1959	15.00	30.00	60.00
❑ Warner Bros. WS 1293 [S]		1959	30.00	60.00	120.00
JOHNNY COOL					
❑ United Artists UAL-4111 [M]		1963	5.00	10.00	20.00
❑ United Artists UAS-5111 [S]		1963	6.25	12.50	25.00
JOHNNY TREMAIN					
❑ Disneyland WDL-4014 [M]		1957	12.50	25.00	50.00
JUD					
❑ Ampex A-50101		1971	5.00	10.00	20.00
JUDGMENT AT NUREMBERG					
❑ MCA 39055		198?	2.50	5.00	10.00
—Reissue of United Artists 5095					
❑ United Artists UAL-4095 [M]		1961	5.00	10.00	20.00
❑ United Artists UAS-5095 [S]		1961	12.50	25.00	50.00
JUDITH					
❑ RCA Victor LOC-1119 [M]		1966	3.75	7.50	15.00
❑ RCA Victor LSO-1119 [S]		1966	7.50	15.00	30.00
JULIET OF THE SPIRITS					
❑ Mainstream S-6062 [S]		1965	15.00	30.00	60.00
❑ Mainstream 56062 [M]		1965	6.25	12.50	25.00
JULIUS CAESAR					
❑ MGM E-3033 [M]		1953	10.00	20.00	40.00
JUMBO (BILLY ROSE'S)					
❑ Columbia Masterworks OS 2260 [S]		1962	7.50	15.00	30.00
❑ Columbia Masterworks OL 5860 [M]		1962	5.00	10.00	20.00
THE JUNGLE BOOK					
❑ Buena Vista BV-4041 [M]		1967	3.75	7.50	15.00
❑ Buena Vista STER-4041 [S]		1967	6.25	12.50	25.00
❑ Disneyland 3105 [PD]		1981	7.50	15.00	30.00
—"Disney Picture Disc" series					
JURASSIC PARK					
❑ MCA/BMG (no #) [PD]		1993	375.00	750.00	1500.
—Custom-made picture disc; promo only					
JUSTINE					
❑ Monument SLP-18123		1969	7.50	15.00	30.00
KALEIDOSCOPE					
❑ Warner Bros. W 1663 [M]		1966	5.00	10.00	20.00
❑ Warner Bros. WS 1663 [S]		1966	6.25	12.50	25.00
KELLY'S HEROES					
❑ MGM S1E-23		1970	7.50	15.00	30.00
THE KEY					
❑ Columbia CL 1185 [M]		1958	20.00	40.00	80.00
KILLERS THREE					
❑ Tower ST-5141		1968	5.00	10.00	20.00
THE KING AND I					
❑ Capitol SW 740 [S]		1959	5.00	10.00	20.00
—Black colorband label, logo at left					
❑ Capitol SW 740 [S]		1962	3.75	7.50	15.00
—Black colorband label, logo at top					
❑ Capitol SW 740 [S]		1969	3.00	6.00	12.00
—Lime green label					
❑ Capitol SW 740 [S]		1973	2.50	5.00	10.00
—Orange label					
❑ Capitol SW 740 [S]		1978	2.00	4.00	8.00
—Purple label					
❑ Capitol W 740 [M]		1956	6.25	12.50	25.00
—Gray label					
❑ Capitol W 740 [M]		1959	3.75	7.50	15.00
—Black colorband label, logo at left					
❑ Capitol W 740 [M]		1962	3.00	6.00	12.00
—Black colorband label, logo at top					
KING KONG					
❑ Reprise MS 2260		1976	5.00	10.00	20.00
KING KONG LIVES					
❑ MCA 6203		1987	6.25	12.50	25.00
KING OF KINGS					
❑ MCA 39056		198?	2.00	4.00	8.00
—Reissue of MGM S1E-2					
❑ MGM 1E-2 [M]		1961	3.75	7.50	15.00
—Standard cover					
❑ MGM 1E-2 [M]		1961	7.50	15.00	30.00
—Boxed version with hardbound book and four 8x10 photos					
❑ MGM S1E-2 [S]		1961	5.00	10.00	20.00
—Standard cover					
❑ MGM S1E-2 [S]		1961	10.00	20.00	40.00
—Boxed version with hardbound book and four 8x10 photos					

Number	Title (A Side/B Side)	Yr	VG	VG+	NM
KING RAT					
❑ Mainstream S-6061 [S]		1965	12.50	25.00	50.00
❑ Mainstream 56061 [M]		1965	7.50	15.00	30.00
KING SOLOMON'S MINES					
❑ Restless 72106		1985	5.00	10.00	20.00
KINGS GO FORTH					
❑ Capitol W 1063 [M]		1958	37.50	75.00	150.00
KISMET					
❑ MCA 1424		198?	2.00	4.00	8.00
—Reissue of MGM 3281					
❑ Metro M-526 [M]		1965	3.00	6.00	12.00
—Reissue of MGM E-3281 with one fewer track					
❑ Metro MS-526 [R]		1955	2.50	5.00	10.00
—Rechanneled reissue of MGM E-3281 with one fewer track					
❑ MGM E-3281 [M]		1955	5.00	10.00	20.00
—Yellow label					
❑ MGM E-3281 [M]		1960	3.75	7.50	15.00
—Black label					
KISS ME, KATE					
❑ MCA 25003		1986	2.50	5.00	10.00
—Reissue of MGM 3077					
❑ Metro M-525 [M]		1965	3.00	6.00	12.00
—Reissue of MGM 3077, but with only 10 songs					
❑ Metro MS-525 [R]		1965	2.50	5.00	10.00
—Rechanneled reissue of MGM 3077, but with only 10 songs					
❑ MGM E-3077 [M]		1953	5.00	10.00	20.00
—Yellow label					
❑ MGM E-3077 [M]		1959	3.75	7.50	15.00
—Black label					
KRULL					
❑ Southern Cross SCRS-1004		1983	5.00	10.00	20.00
KWAMINA					
❑ Mercury MG-20654 [M]		1961	6.25	12.50	25.00
❑ Mercury SR-60654 [S]		1961	7.50	15.00	30.00
LADY AND THE TRAMP					
❑ Decca DL 5557 [10]		1955	15.00	30.00	60.00
❑ Decca DL 8462 [M]		1957	17.50	35.00	70.00
❑ Disneyland 3103 [PD]		1981	7.50	15.00	30.00
—"Disney Picture Disc" edition					
LADYHAWKE					
❑ Atlantic 81248		1985	5.00	10.00	20.00
THE LANDLORD					
❑ United Artists UAS-5209		1970	5.00	10.00	20.00
THE LAST AMERICAN VIRGIN					
❑ Columbia JS 38279		1982	10.00	20.00	40.00
THE LAST EMBRACE					
❑ Varese Sarabande STV-81166		1983	5.00	10.00	20.00
THE LAST OF THE SECRET AGENTS					
❑ Dot DLP-3714 [M]		1966	5.00	10.00	20.00
❑ Dot DLP-25714 [S]		1966	6.25	12.50	25.00
THE LAST RUN					
❑ MCA 25116		1986	2.00	4.00	8.00
—Reissue of MGM 1SE-30					
❑ MGM 1SE-30		1971	6.25	12.50	25.00
THE LAST STARFIGHTER					
❑ Southern Cross SCRS-1007		1984	6.25	12.50	25.00
LAST SUMMER					
❑ Warner Bros. WS 1791		1969	5.00	10.00	20.00
THE LAST VALLEY					
❑ ABC-Dunhill DSX-50102		1971	10.00	20.00	40.00
LAWRENCE OF ARABIA					
❑ Arista ABM-4009		1975	2.50	5.00	10.00
—Reissue of Bell 1205					
❑ Bell 1205		1971	2.50	5.00	10.00
—Reissue of Colgems COSO-5004					
❑ Colgems COMO-5004 [M]		1967	3.00	6.00	12.00
—Reissue of Colpix CP-514					
❑ Colgems COSO-5004 [S]		1967	3.75	7.50	15.00
—Reissue of Colpix SCP-514					
❑ Colpix CP-514 [M]		1962	5.00	10.00	20.00
❑ Colpix SCP-514 [S]		1962	7.50	15.00	30.00
LENNY					
❑ United Artists UA-LA359-H [(2)]		1974	5.00	10.00	20.00
THE LEOPARD					
❑ 20th Century Fox FXG-5015 [M]		1963	7.50	15.00	30.00
❑ 20th Century Fox SXG-5015 [S]		1963	10.00	20.00	40.00
❑ Varese Sarabande STV-81190		1982	3.75	7.50	15.00
—Reissue of 20th Century Fox SXG-5015					
LES LIAISONS DANGEREUSES					
❑ Charlie Parker PLP-813 [M]		1962	6.25	12.50	25.00
❑ Charlie Parker PLP-813S [S]		1962	7.50	15.00	30.00
❑ Epic LA 16022 [M]		1961	10.00	20.00	40.00
❑ Epic BA 17022 [S]		1961	7.50	15.00	30.00
❑ Fontana MGF-27539 [M]		1965	5.00	10.00	20.00
LET THE GOOD TIMES ROLL					
❑ Bell 9002 [(2)]		1973	6.25	12.50	25.00
LET'S MAKE LOVE					
❑ Columbia CL 1527 [M]		1960	7.50	15.00	30.00
❑ Columbia CS 8327 [S]		1960	12.50	25.00	50.00
LEVIATHAN					
❑ Varese Sarabande VS-5226		1989	5.00	10.00	20.00

Number	Title (A Side/B Side)	Yr	VG	VG+	NM

LI'L ABNER
❏ Columbia Masterworks OS 2021 [S] — 1959 — 10.00 — 20.00 — 40.00
—Credits within photo
❏ Columbia Masterworks OS 2021 [S] — 196? — 6.25 — 12.50 — 25.00
—Credits in red strip at bottom of photo
❏ Columbia Masterworks OL 5460 [M] — 1959 — 7.50 — 15.00 — 30.00
—Credits within photo
❏ Columbia Masterworks OL 5460 [M] — 196? — 5.00 — 10.00 — 20.00
—Credits in red strip at bottom of photo

THE LIFE AND TIMES OF JUDGE ROY BEAN
❏ Columbia Masterworks S 31948 — 1972 — 6.25 — 12.50 — 25.00

LIFEFORCE
❏ Varese Sarabande STV-81249 — 1985 — 6.25 — 12.50 — 25.00

LIGHT FANTASTIC
❏ 20th Century Fox FXG-5016 [M] — 1963 — 5.00 — 10.00 — 20.00
❏ 20th Century Fox SXG-5016 [S] — 1963 — 6.25 — 12.50 — 25.00

LILIES OF THE FIELD
❏ Epic LN 24094 [M] — 1964 — 5.00 — 10.00 — 20.00
❏ Epic BN 26094 [S] — 1964 — 7.50 — 15.00 — 30.00

THE LION
❏ London M-76001 [M] — 1962 — 100.00 — 200.00 — 400.00

THE LION IN WINTER
❏ Columbia Masterworks OS 3250 — 1969 — 5.00 — 10.00 — 20.00

LIONHEART
❏ Varese Sarabande STV-81304 — 1987 — 5.00 — 10.00 — 20.00

LIONHEART (MORE MUSIC FROM THE FILM)
❏ Varese Sarabande STV-81311 — 1987 — 12.50 — 25.00 — 50.00

LITTLE BIG MAN
❏ Columbia Masterworks S 30545 — 1970 — 5.00 — 10.00 — 20.00

LITTLE SHOP OF HORRORS
❏ Geffen GHS-24125 — 1986 — 5.00 — 10.00 — 20.00

LIVE AND LET DIE
❏ Liberty LMAS-100 — 1981 — 3.00 — 6.00 — 12.00
—Gray label; reissue of United Artists 100 with gatefold cover
❏ Liberty LT-50100 — 1982 — 3.00 — 6.00 — 12.00
—Gray label; reissue of Liberty 100 with standard cover
❏ United Artists LMAS-100 — 1979 — 2.50 — 5.00 — 10.00
—"Sunrise" label with this number on label (jacket still has UA-LA100-G)
❏ United Artists UA-LA100-G — 1973 — 2.50 — 5.00 — 10.00
—Tan label; cover corner is clipped
❏ United Artists UA-LA100-G — 1973 — 5.00 — 10.00 — 20.00
—Tan label; cover corner is not clipped off
❏ United Artists UA-LA100-G — 1977 — 2.50 — 5.00 — 10.00
—"Sunrise" label with this number on both jacket and label
❏ United Artists SWAO-95120 — 1973 — 7.50 — 15.00 — 30.00
—Longines (formerly Capitol) Record Club edition

LIVE FOR LIFE
❏ United Artists UAL-4165 [M] — 1967 — 5.00 — 10.00 — 20.00
❏ United Artists UAS-5165 [S] — 1967 — 5.00 — 10.00 — 20.00

THE LIVELY SET
❏ Decca DL 9119 [M] — 1964 — 7.50 — 15.00 — 30.00
❏ Decca DL 79119 [S] — 1964 — 10.00 — 20.00 — 40.00

LOGAN'S RUN
❏ MGM MG-1-5302 — 1976 — 7.50 — 15.00 — 30.00

LOLITA
❏ MCA 39067 — 198? — 2.00 — 4.00 — 8.00
—Reissue of MGM SE-4050
❏ MGM E-4050 [M] — 1962 — 5.00 — 10.00 — 20.00
❏ MGM SE-4050 [S] — 1962 — 7.50 — 15.00 — 30.00

THE LOLLIPOP COVER
❏ Mainstream S-6067 [S] — 1966 — 7.50 — 15.00 — 30.00
❏ Mainstream 56067 [M] — 1966 — 5.00 — 10.00 — 20.00

THE LONG HOT SUMMER
❏ Roulette R-25026 [M] — 1958 — 18.75 — 37.50 — 75.00

LONG JOHN SILVER
❏ RCA Victor LPM-3279 [10] — 1954 — 75.00 — 150.00 — 300.00

THE LONG SHIPS
❏ Colpix CP-517 [M] — 1964 — 12.50 — 25.00 — 50.00
❏ Colpix SCP-517 [S] — 1964 — 15.00 — 30.00 — 60.00

THE LONGEST DAY
❏ 20th Century Fox FXG-5007 [M] — 1962 — 5.00 — 10.00 — 20.00
❏ 20th Century Fox SXG-5007 [S] — 1962 — 6.25 — 12.50 — 25.00

LORD JIM
❏ Colpix CP-521 [M] — 1965 — 6.25 — 12.50 — 25.00
❏ Colpix SCP-521 [S] — 1965 — 10.00 — 20.00 — 40.00

LORD LOVE A DUCK
❏ United Artists UAL-4137 [M] — 1966 — 5.00 — 10.00 — 20.00
❏ United Artists UAS-5137 [S] — 1966 — 6.25 — 12.50 — 25.00

THE LORD OF THE RINGS
❏ Fantasy LOR-1 [(2)] — 1978 — 5.00 — 10.00 — 20.00
❏ Fantasy LOR-PD2 [(2)] — 1978 — 7.50 — 15.00 — 30.00
—Two picture discs

THE LORDS OF FLATBUSH
❏ ABC ABCD-828 — 1974 — 7.50 — 15.00 — 30.00

A LOSS OF INNOCENCE
❏ Colpix CP-508 [M] — 1961 — 10.00 — 20.00 — 40.00

THE LOST CONTINENT
❏ MGM E-3635 [M] — 1957 — 50.00 — 100.00 — 200.00

LOVE IN 4 DIMENSIONS
❏ Request RLP-8090 [M] — 1966 — 6.25 — 12.50 — 25.00
❏ Request SRLP-8090 [S] — 1966 — 7.50 — 15.00 — 30.00

LOVE LIFE
❏ Heritage 600 [M] — 195? — 15.00 — 30.00 — 60.00

LOVERS AND OTHER STRANGERS
❏ ABC ABCS-OC-15 — 1970 — 5.00 — 10.00 — 20.00
❏ ABC SW-93479 — 1971 — 6.25 — 12.50 — 25.00
—Capitol Record Club edition

M*A*S*H
❏ Columbia Masterworks OS 3520 — 1970 — 5.00 — 10.00 — 20.00
—Original copies do not have the theme song done by Ahmad Jamal
❏ Columbia Masterworks S 32753 — 1973 — 2.50 — 5.00 — 10.00
—Reissue with the movie's theme performed by Ahmad Jamal

MACARTHUR
❏ MCA 2287 — 1977 — 5.00 — 10.00 — 20.00

THE MAD ADVENTURES OF RABBI JACOB
❏ London PS 652 — 1974 — 2.50 — 5.00 — 10.00
—Cover has cut-out markings (usually a hole punch or a cut-off corner)
❏ London PS 652 — 1974 — 5.00 — 10.00 — 20.00
—Cover is intact with no cut-out markings

MADAME BOVARY
❏ MGM E-3507 [M] — 195? — 37.50 — 75.00 — 150.00

THE MAGIC CHRISTIAN
❏ Commonwealth United CU-6004 — 1970 — 6.25 — 12.50 — 25.00

MAGNIFICENT OBSESSION
❏ Decca DL 8078 [M] — 1954 — 15.00 — 30.00 — 60.00
—Black label, gold print
❏ Decca DL 8078 [M] — 1955 — 12.50 — 25.00 — 50.00
—Black label, silver print
❏ Decca DL 8078 [M] — 196? — 7.50 — 15.00 — 30.00
—Black label with color bars
❏ Varese Sarabande STV-81118 — 1981 — 3.00 — 6.00 — 12.00
—Reissue of Decca 8078

MAJOR DUNDEE
❏ Columbia Masterworks OS 2780 [S] — 1965 — 7.50 — 15.00 — 30.00
❏ Columbia Masterworks OL 6380 [M] — 1965 — 5.00 — 10.00 — 20.00

MALAMONDO
❏ Epic LN 24126 [M] — 1964 — 7.50 — 15.00 — 30.00
❏ Epic BN 26126 [S] — 1964 — 10.00 — 20.00 — 40.00

MAME
❏ Warner Bros. PRO 580 [DJ] — 1973 — 12.50 — 25.00 — 50.00
—Promo-only gatefold edition with Lucille Ball in Christmas hat on the cover
❏ Warner Bros. W 2773 — 1974 — 3.75 — 7.50 — 15.00

A MAN AND A WOMAN (UN HOMME ET UNE FEMME)
❏ United Artists UAL-4147 [M] — 1966 — 3.75 — 7.50 — 15.00
❏ United Artists UAS-5147 [S] — 1966 — 5.00 — 10.00 — 20.00

A MAN CALLED ADAM
❏ Reprise R 6180 [M] — 1966 — 3.75 — 7.50 — 15.00
❏ Reprise RS 6180 [S] — 1966 — 5.00 — 10.00 — 20.00

A MAN CALLED DAGGER
❏ MGM E-4516 [M] — 1967 — 3.75 — 7.50 — 15.00
❏ MGM SE-4516 [S] — 1967 — 5.00 — 10.00 — 20.00

A MAN COULD GET KILLED
❏ Decca DL 4750 [M] — 1966 — 3.75 — 7.50 — 15.00
❏ Decca DL 74750 [S] — 1966 — 5.00 — 10.00 — 20.00

A MAN FOR ALL SEASONS
❏ RCA Victor VDM-116 [(2)M] — 1966 — 7.50 — 15.00 — 30.00

MAN FROM SHAFT
❏ MGM SE-4836 — 1972 — 7.50 — 15.00 — 30.00

MAN IN THE MIDDLE
❏ 20th Century Fox TFM-3128 [M] — 1965 — 7.50 — 15.00 — 30.00
❏ 20th Century Fox TFS-4128 [S] — 1965 — 12.50 — 25.00 — 50.00

THE MAN OF A THOUSAND FACES
❏ Decca DL 8623 [M] — 1957 — 12.50 — 25.00 — 50.00
—Black label, silver print, or pink label, black print promos
❏ Decca DL 8623 [M] — 196? — 7.50 — 15.00 — 30.00
—Black label with color bars
❏ Varese Sarabande STV- 81121 — 1981 — 3.00 — 6.00 — 12.00
—Reissue of Decca 8623

MAN OF LA MANCHA
❏ United Artists UAS-9906 — 1972 — 2.50 — 5.00 — 10.00
—Cover has cut-out marking such as a cut-off corner
❏ United Artists UAS-9906 — 1972 — 5.00 — 10.00 — 20.00
—Cover is intact with no cut corners

THE MAN WHO WOULD BE KING
❏ Capitol SW-11474 — 1975 — 5.00 — 10.00 — 20.00

THE MAN WITH THE GOLDEN ARM
❏ Decca DL 8257 [M] — 1956 — 10.00 — 20.00 — 40.00
❏ Decca DL 78257 [R] — 196? — 5.00 — 10.00 — 20.00
❏ MCA 1528 — 198? — 2.00 — 4.00 — 8.00
—Reissue of MCA 2043
❏ MCA 2043 [R] — 1973 — 2.50 — 5.00 — 10.00
—Reissue of Decca 78257; black label with rainbow

THE MAN WITH THE GOLDEN GUN
❏ United Artists UA-LA358-G — 1974 — 5.00 — 10.00 — 20.00

MANIAC
❏ Varese Sarabande STV-81143 — 1980 — 5.00 — 10.00 — 20.00

MARACAIBO
❏ Decca DL 8756 [M] — 1958 — 10.00 — 20.00 — 40.00
—Black label, silver print, or pink label, black print promos
❏ Decca DL 8756 [M] — 196? — 5.00 — 10.00 — 20.00
—Black label with color bars

MARCO THE MAGNIFICENT
❏ Columbia Masterworks OS 2870 [S] — 1966 — 10.00 — 20.00 — 40.00
❏ Columbia Masterworks OL 6470 [M] — 1966 — 6.25 — 12.50 — 25.00

Number	Title (A Side/B Side)	Yr	VG	VG+	NM
MARIE WARD					
❏ Varese Sarabande STV-81268		1985	12.50	25.00	50.00
MARJORIE MORNINGSTAR					
❏ RCA Victor LOC-1044 [M]		1958	10.00	20.00	40.00
—"RE" next to label number					
❏ RCA Victor LOC-1044 [M]		1958	15.00	30.00	60.00
—"An Original Soundtrack Recording" on spine					
MARRY ME, MARRY ME					
❏ RCA Victor LSO-1160		1969	5.00	10.00	20.00
MARY POPPINS					
❏ Buena Vista BV-4026 [M]		1964	3.00	6.00	12.00
—Originals have gatefold covers					
❏ Buena Vista STER-4026 [S]		1964	3.75	7.50	15.00
—Originals have gatefold covers					
❏ Buena Vista STER-5005 [S]		1973	2.50	5.00	10.00
—Reissue with new number and no gatefold					
❏ RCA Victor COP-111 [M]		1964	3.75	7.50	15.00
—With gatefold; RCA Record Club edition					
❏ RCA Victor CSO-111 [M]		1964	5.00	10.00	20.00
—With gatefold; RCA Record Club edition					
MARY, QUEEN OF SCOTS					
❏ Decca DL 79186		1972	7.50	15.00	30.00
THE MASK					
❏ Chaos 6455 [DJ]		1994	5.00	10.00	20.00
—Generic cover; no other U.S. vinyl					
MASTER OF THE WORLD					
❏ Varese Sarabande VC-81070		1978	3.75	7.50	15.00
—Reissue of Vee Jay 4000					
❏ Vee Jay LP-4000 [M]		1961	6.25	12.50	25.00
❏ Vee Jay SR-4000 [S]		1961	10.00	20.00	40.00
MASTERS OF THE UNIVERSE					
❏ Varese Sarabande STV-81333		1987	5.00	10.00	20.00
MCLINTOCK!					
❏ United Artists UAL-4112 [M]		1963	15.00	30.00	60.00
❏ United Artists UAS-5112 [S]		1963	20.00	40.00	80.00
ME AND THE COLONEL					
❏ RCA Victor LOC-1046 [M]		1958	12.50	25.00	50.00
MEDITERRANEAN HOLIDAY					
❏ London M-76003 [M]		1964	12.50	25.00	50.00
❏ London MS-82003 [S]		1964	20.00	40.00	80.00
MEET ME IN ST. LOUIS					
❏ AEI 3101		1978	3.00	6.00	12.00
—Reissue of Decca LP					
❏ Decca DL 8498 [M]		1957	7.50	15.00	30.00
—LP reissue of 78 rpm album from 1944; B-side of LP is "The Harvey Girls."					
MEMORIES AUX BRUXELLES					
❏ Carlton LP-112 [M]		1959	6.25	12.50	25.00
❏ Carlton LP-12112 [S]		1959	10.00	20.00	40.00
MEN IN WAR					
❏ Imperial LP-9032 W [M]		1957	37.50	75.00	150.00
MENACE II SOCIETY					
❏ Jive 41522 [(2)DJ]		1993	5.00	10.00	20.00
—Vinyl is promo only					
MERRY ANDREW					
❏ Capitol T 1016 [M]		1958	12.50	25.00	50.00
MICKEY ONE					
❏ MGM E-4312 [M]		1965	5.00	10.00	20.00
❏ MGM SE-4312 [S]		1965	6.25	12.50	25.00
MIDNIGHT COWBOY					
❏ United Artists UAS-5198		1969	5.00	10.00	20.00
MIDNIGHT EXPRESS					
❏ Casablanca NBLP-7114		1978	5.00	10.00	20.00
A MILANESE STORY					
❏ Atlantic 1388 [M]		1962	5.00	10.00	20.00
❏ Atlantic SD 1388 [S]		1962	6.25	12.50	25.00
THE MINX					
❏ Amsterdam 12007		1970	30.00	60.00	120.00
THE MISFITS					
❏ United Artists UA-LA273-G [S]		1974	3.00	6.00	12.00
—Reissue of 5087					
❏ United Artists UAL-4087 [M]		1961	12.50	25.00	50.00
❏ United Artists UAS-5087 [S]		1961	25.00	50.00	100.00
MISS SADIE THOMPSON					
❏ Mercury MG-20123 [M]		1956	37.50	75.00	150.00
❏ Mercury MG-25181 [10]		1954	18.75	37.50	75.00
THE MISSOURI BREAKS					
❏ MCA 25113		1986	2.50	5.00	10.00
—Reissue of United Artists UA-LA623-G					
❏ United Artists UA-LA623-G		1976	7.50	15.00	30.00
MOBY DICK					
❏ RCA Victor LPM-1247 [M]		1956	30.00	60.00	120.00
MODERN TIMES					
❏ United Artists UAL-4049 [M]		1959	6.25	12.50	25.00
❏ United Artists UAS-5049 [R]		196?	5.00	10.00	20.00
MODESTY BLAISE					
❏ 20th Century Fox TFM-3182 [M]		1966	7.50	15.00	30.00
❏ 20th Century Fox TFS-4182 [S]		1966	12.50	25.00	50.00
MOHAMMAD, MESSENGER OF GOD					
❏ Namara 79001		1977	6.25	12.50	25.00
MONDO CANE					
❏ United Artists UAS-5105 [S]		1963	5.00	10.00	20.00
MONDO CANE NO. 2					
❏ 20th Century Fox TFM-3147 [M]		1964	7.50	15.00	30.00
❏ 20th Century Fox TFS-4147 [S]		1964	10.00	20.00	40.00
MOON OVER PARADOR					
❏ MCA 6249		1988	6.25	12.50	25.00
THE MOON SPINNERS					
❏ Buena Vista BV-3323 [M]		1964	10.00	20.00	40.00
MORE AMERICAN GRAFFITI					
❏ MCA MCA2-11006 [(2)]		1979	5.00	10.00	20.00
—Tan labels					
MR. BUDDWING					
❏ Verve V6-8638 [S]		1965	6.25	12.50	25.00
MR. MAGOO: 1001 ARABIAN NIGHTS					
❏ Colpix CP-410 [M]		1959	12.50	25.00	50.00
❏ Colpix SCP-410 [S]		1959	37.50	75.00	150.00
MURDER INC.					
❏ Canadian American CALP-1003 [M]		1960	25.00	50.00	100.00
MUSCLE BEACH PARTY PLUS MERLIN JONES AND THE SCRAMBLED EGGHEAD					
❏ Buena Vista BV-3314 [M]		1964	15.00	30.00	60.00
❏ Buena Vista STER-3314 [S]		1964	30.00	60.00	120.00
THE MUSIC MAN					
❏ Warner Bros. BS 1459 [S]		1962	5.00	10.00	20.00
—Gold label originals					
❏ Warner Bros. BS 1459 [S]		1968	3.00	6.00	12.00
—Green label with "W7" box logo at top					
❏ Warner Bros. BS 1459 [S]		1970	2.50	5.00	10.00
—Green label with "WB" shield logo at top					
❏ Warner Bros. BS 1459 [S]		1973	2.00	4.00	8.00
—"Burbank" palm trees label or later white label					
MUTINY ON THE BOUNTY					
❏ MCA 25007		1986	2.00	4.00	8.00
—Reissue of MGM 1SE-4					
❏ MGM 1E-4 [M]		196?	3.00	6.00	12.00
—Standard cover					
❏ MGM 1E-4 [M]		1962	7.50	15.00	30.00
—Boxed set with book and painting					
❏ MGM S1E-4 [S]		196?	3.75	7.50	15.00
—Standard cover					
❏ MGM S1E-4 [S]		1962	10.00	20.00	40.00
—Boxed set with book and painting					
MY GEISHA					
❏ RCA Victor LOC-1070 [M]		1962	12.50	25.00	50.00
❏ RCA Victor LSO-1070 [S]		1962	25.00	50.00	100.00
MY SIDE OF THE MOUNTAIN					
❏ Capitol ST-245		1969	6.25	12.50	25.00
MY WILD IRISH ROSE					
❏ RCA Victor LPM-3036 [10]		1952	10.00	20.00	40.00
NAKED ANGELS					
❏ Straight STS-1056		1969	6.25	12.50	25.00
THE NAKED MAJA					
❏ United Artists UAL-4031 [M]		1959	7.50	15.00	30.00
❏ United Artists UAS-5031 [S]		1959	10.00	20.00	40.00
NANCY GOES TO RIO					
❏ MGM E-508 [10]		1950	15.00	30.00	60.00
NASHVILLE					
❏ ABC ABCD-893		1975	5.00	10.00	20.00
NATIVE SON					
❏ MCA 6198		1986	5.00	10.00	20.00
NAVAJO JOE					
❏ United Artists UA-LA292-G		1974	6.25	12.50	25.00
NED KELLY					
❏ United Artists UA-LA300-G		1974	3.00	6.00	12.00
—Reissue of 5213					
❏ United Artists UAS-5213		1970	6.25	12.50	25.00
NEVADA SMITH					
❏ Dot DLP-3718 [M]		1966	6.25	12.50	25.00
❏ Dot DLP-25718 [S]		1966	10.00	20.00	40.00
THE NEVER ENDING STORY					
❏ EMI America ST-17139		1984	5.00	10.00	20.00
NEVER ON SUNDAY					
❏ United Artists UAL-4070 [M]		1960	3.75	7.50	15.00
❏ United Artists UAS-5070 [S]		1960	5.00	10.00	20.00
❏ United Artists SW-90834 [S]		196?	5.00	10.00	20.00
—Capitol Record Club edition					
THE NEW INTERNS					
❏ Colpix CP-473 [M]		1964	7.50	15.00	30.00
❏ Colpix SCP-473 [S]		1964	10.00	20.00	40.00
A NEW KIND OF LOVE					
❏ Mercury SR-60859 [S]		1963	5.00	10.00	20.00
THE NEW MESSIAH					
❏ Columbia KC 31713		1972	5.00	10.00	20.00
NICHOLAS AND ALEXANDRA					
❏ Bell 1103		1971	6.25	12.50	25.00
NIGHT OF THE GENERALS					
❏ Colgems COMO-5002 [M]		1967	10.00	20.00	40.00
❏ Colgems COSO-5002 [S]		1967	17.50	35.00	70.00
THE NIGHT OF THE HUNTER					
❏ RCA Victor LPM-1136 [M]		1955	62.50	125.00	250.00
NINE HOURS TO RAMA					
❏ London M-76002 [M]		1963	75.00	150.00	300.00

Number Title (A Side/B Side)	Yr	VG	VG+	NM
NO WAY TO TREAT A LADY				
❑ Dot DLP-25846	1968	6.25	12.50	25.00
NOT WITH MY WIFE, YOU DON'T				
❑ Warner Bros. W 1668 [M]	1966	3.75	7.50	15.00
❑ Warner Bros. WS 1668 [S]	1966	5.00	10.00	20.00
NOTHING BUT THE BEST				
❑ Colpix CP-477 [M]	1964	5.00	10.00	20.00
❑ Colpix SCP-477 [S]	1964	6.25	12.50	25.00
A NUN'S STORY				
❑ Warner Bros. B 1306 [M]	1959	15.00	30.00	60.00
❑ Warner Bros. BS 1306 [S]	1959	25.00	50.00	100.00
OBSESSION				
❑ London Phase 4 SPC-21160	1976	6.25	12.50	25.00
OCTOPUSSY				
❑ A&M SP-4967	1983	5.00	10.00	20.00
THE ODD COUPLE				
❑ Dot DLP-25862	1968	5.00	10.00	20.00
ODDS AGAINST TOMORROW				
❑ United Artists UAL-4061 [M]	1959	7.50	15.00	30.00
❑ United Artists UAS-5061 [S]	1959	12.50	25.00	50.00
OF LOVE AND DESIRE				
❑ 20th Century Fox FXG-5014 [M]	1963	6.25	12.50	25.00
❑ 20th Century Fox SXG-5014 [S]	1963	7.50	15.00	30.00
OH DAD, POOR DAD, MAMMA'S HUNG YOU IN THE CLOSET AND I'M FEELIN' SO SAD				
❑ RCA Victor LPM-3750 [M]	1967	5.00	10.00	20.00
❑ RCA Victor LSP-3750 [S]	1967	6.25	12.50	25.00
OH, ROSALINDA!				
❑ Mercury MG-20145 [M]	1957	12.50	25.00	50.00
OIL TOWN, U.S.A.				
❑ RCA Victor LFM-2000 [10]	1953	15.00	30.00	60.00
OKLAHOMA!				
❑ Capitol SWAO 595 [S]	1959	5.00	10.00	20.00
—Black colorband label, logo at left				
❑ Capitol SWAO 595 [S]	1962	3.75	7.50	15.00
—Black colorband label, logo at top				
❑ Capitol SWAO 595 [S]	1969	3.00	6.00	12.00
—Lime green label				
❑ Capitol SWAO 595 [S]	1973	2.50	5.00	10.00
—Orange label				
❑ Capitol WAO 595 [M]	1955	6.25	12.50	25.00
—Purple or dark red label				
❑ Capitol WAO 595 [M]	1956	5.00	10.00	20.00
—Gray label				
❑ Capitol WAO 595 [M]	1959	3.75	7.50	15.00
—Black colorband label, logo at left				
❑ Capitol WAO 595 [M]	1962	3.00	6.00	12.00
—Black colorband label, logo at top				
OLD BOYFRIENDS				
❑ Columbia Masterworks JS 36072	1979	12.50	25.00	50.00
THE OLD MAN AND THE SEA				
❑ Columbia CL 1183 [M]	1958	7.50	15.00	30.00
❑ Columbia CS 8013 [S]	1958	15.00	30.00	60.00
OLD YELLER				
❑ Disneyland 1024 [M]	1974	6.25	12.50	25.00
—Reissue with no prefix				
❑ Disneyland WDL-1024 [M]	1960	10.00	20.00	40.00
—Second edition				
❑ Disneyland WDL-3024 [M]	1957	12.50	25.00	50.00
—First edition				
OLIVER AND COMPANY				
❑ Disney 64101	1988	6.25	12.50	25.00
ON HER MAJESTY'S SECRET SERVICE				
❑ United Artists UA-LA299-G	1974	3.00	6.00	12.00
—Reissue of 5204				
❑ United Artists UAS-5204	1969	5.00	10.00	20.00
ON THE BEACH				
❑ Roulette R-25098 [M]	1959	20.00	40.00	80.00
❑ Roulette SR-25098 [S]	1959	37.50	75.00	150.00
ONCE UPON A TIME IN THE WEST				
❑ RCA Victor LSP-4736	1969	7.50	15.00	30.00
THE ONE AND ONLY, GENUINE, ORIGINAL FAMILY BAND				
❑ Buena Vista BV-5002 [M]	1968	3.75	7.50	15.00
❑ Buena Vista STER-5002 [S]	1968	5.00	10.00	20.00
ONE FLEW OVER THE CUCKOO'S NEST				
❑ Fantasy MPF-4531	198?	2.50	5.00	10.00
—Budget-line reissue of 9500				
❑ Fantasy F-9500	1975	5.00	10.00	20.00
THE ONE-EYED JACKS				
❑ Liberty LOM-16001 [M]	1961	7.50	15.00	30.00
❑ Liberty LOS-17001 [S]	1961	12.50	25.00	50.00
THE OPTIMISTS				
❑ Paramount PAS-1015	1973	7.50	15.00	30.00
ORCHESTRA WIVES				
❑ RCA Victor LPT-3065 [10]	1954	15.00	30.00	60.00
THE OSCAR				
❑ Columbia Masterworks OS 2950 [S]	1966	6.25	12.50	25.00
❑ Columbia Masterworks OL 6550 [M]	1966	5.00	10.00	20.00
OTLEY				
❑ Colgems COS-112	1969	7.50	15.00	30.00
OUR MAN FLINT				
❑ 20th Century Fox TFM-3179 [M]	1966	10.00	20.00	40.00

Number Title (A Side/B Side)	Yr	VG	VG+	NM
❑ 20th Century Fox TFS-4179 [S]	1966	15.00	30.00	60.00
OUT OF AFRICA				
❑ MCA 6158	1985	5.00	10.00	20.00
❑ MCA 11327	1995	5.00	10.00	20.00
—Limited edition on "Heavy Vinyl"				
OUT OF SIGHT				
❑ Decca DL 4751 [M]	1966	5.00	10.00	20.00
❑ Decca DL 74751 [S]	1966	6.25	12.50	25.00
OUTLAND				
❑ Warner Bros. HS 3551	1981	6.25	12.50	25.00
THE OUTLAW JOSEY WALES				
❑ Warner Bros. BS 2956	1976	6.25	12.50	25.00
THE OUTLAW RIDERS				
❑ MGM 1SE-26	1970	5.00	10.00	20.00
PAGAN LOVE SONG				
❑ MGM E-534 [M]	1950	10.00	20.00	40.00
PAINT YOUR WAGON				
❑ MCA 37099	198?	2.00	4.00	8.00
—Reissue of Paramount 1001				
❑ Paramount PMS-1001	1969	5.00	10.00	20.00
—With booklet				
THE PAJAMA GAME				
❑ Columbia Masterworks OL 5210 [M]	1957	7.50	15.00	30.00
—Gray and black label with six "eye" logos				
PAL JOEY				
❑ Capitol DW 912 [R]	196?	2.50	5.00	10.00
—Black colorband label				
❑ Capitol SM-912 [R]	1977	2.00	4.00	8.00
—Reissue with new prefix				
❑ Capitol W 912 [M]	1957	5.00	10.00	20.00
—Gray label				
❑ Capitol W 912 [M]	1959	3.75	7.50	15.00
—Black colorband label, logo at left				
❑ Capitol W 912 [M]	1962	3.00	6.00	12.00
—Black colorband label, logo on top				
PANIC BUTTON				
❑ Musicor MM-2026 [M]	1964	20.00	40.00	80.00
❑ Musicor MS-3026 [S]	1964	30.00	60.00	120.00
PAPER MOON				
❑ Paramount PAS-1012	1973	5.00	10.00	20.00
PAPER TIGER				
❑ Capitol SW-11475	1975	5.00	10.00	20.00
PAPILLON				
❑ Capitol ST-11260	1973	5.00	10.00	20.00
THE PARENT TRAP!				
❑ Buena Vista BV-3309 [M]	1961	10.00	20.00	40.00
❑ Buena Vista STER-3309 [S]	1961	15.00	30.00	60.00
—B-side of the above two: Camerata Conducts Themes from Great Motion Pictures				
PARIS BLUES				
❑ United Artists UAL-4092 [M]	1961	6.25	12.50	25.00
❑ United Artists UAS-5092 [S]	1961	7.50	15.00	30.00
PARIS HOLIDAY				
❑ United Artists UAL-4001 [M]	1958	12.50	25.00	50.00
PARIS WHEN IT SIZZLES				
❑ Reprise R 6113 [M]	1964	6.25	12.50	25.00
❑ Reprise RS 6113 [S]	1964	10.00	20.00	40.00
PARRISH				
❑ Warner Bros. W 1413 [M]	1961	7.50	15.00	30.00
❑ Warner Bros. WS 1413 [S]	1961	20.00	40.00	80.00
—B-side of the above two: Popular Piano Concertos by George Greeley				
A PATCH OF BLUE				
❑ Mainstream S-6068 [S]	1965	6.25	12.50	25.00
❑ Mainstream 56068 [M]	1965	5.00	10.00	20.00
❑ Mainstream ST-90805 [S]	1965	7.50	15.00	30.00
—Capitol Record Club edition				
PATTON				
❑ 20th Century Fox S-4208	1970	5.00	10.00	20.00
PATTY				
❑ Stang 1026	1976	5.00	10.00	20.00
PENELOPE				
❑ MGM E-4426 [M]	1966	5.00	10.00	20.00
❑ MGM SE-4426 [S]	1966	7.50	15.00	30.00
PENTHOUSE				
❑ United Artists UAL-4170 [M]	1967	5.00	10.00	20.00
❑ United Artists UAS-5170 [S]	1967	5.00	10.00	20.00
THE PEOPLE NEXT DOOR				
❑ Avco AV-11002	1970	6.25	12.50	25.00
PEPE				
❑ Colpix CP-507 [M]	1960	5.00	10.00	20.00
❑ Colpix SCP-507 [S]	1960	6.25	12.50	25.00
PERFORMANCE				
❑ Warner Bros. WS 1846	1970	375.00	750.00	1500.
—Original issue; has a completely different cover to the more common 2554				
❑ Warner Bros. BS 2554	1970	5.00	10.00	20.00
—Second issue				
PETE KELLY'S BLUES				
❑ Columbia CL 690 [M]	1955	10.00	20.00	40.00
❑ Decca DL 8166 [M]	1955	12.50	25.00	50.00
—Black label, silver print				
PETE'S DRAGON				
❑ Capitol SW-11704	1977	5.00	10.00	20.00

Number	Title (A Side/B Side)	Yr	VG	VG+	NM
PETULIA					
❑ Warner Bros. WS 1755		1968	6.25	12.50	25.00
PEYTON PLACE					
❑ RCA Victor LOC-1042 [M]		1958	7.50	15.00	30.00
—"Long Play" at bottom of label					
❑ RCA Victor LOC-1042 [M]		1965	6.25	12.50	25.00
—"Monaural" at bottom of label					
❑ RCA Victor LSO-1042 [S]		1958	25.00	50.00	100.00
—"Living Stereo" at bottom of label					
❑ RCA Victor LSO-1042 [S]		1965	15.00	30.00	60.00
—"Stereo" at bottom of label					
PHAEDRA					
❑ United Artists UAL-4102 [M]		1962	5.00	10.00	20.00
❑ United Artists UAS-5102 [S]		1962	7.50	15.00	30.00
THE PHILADELPHIA EXPERIMENT					
❑ Rhino RNSP-306		1984	6.25	12.50	25.00
PICNIC					
❑ Decca DL 8320 [M]		1956	7.50	15.00	30.00
—Black label, silver print					
❑ Decca DL 8320 [M]		196?	3.75	7.50	15.00
—Black label with color bars					
❑ Decca DL 78320 [S]		1959	7.50	15.00	30.00
—Maroon or all-black label					
❑ Decca DL 78320 [S]		196?	3.75	7.50	15.00
—Black label with color bars					
❑ MCA 1527		198?	2.00	4.00	8.00
—Reissue of 2049					
❑ MCA 2049		1973	2.50	5.00	10.00
—Reissue of Decca 78320; black label with rainbow					
A PIECE OF THE ACTION					
❑ Curtom CU 5019		1977	5.00	10.00	20.00
PINOCCHIO					
❑ Disneyland DQ-1202 [M]		1959	7.50	15.00	30.00
—Second edition					
❑ Disneyland DQ-1202MO [M]		1963	5.00	10.00	20.00
—Third edition					
❑ Disneyland 3102 [PD]		1981	7.50	15.00	30.00
—"Disney Picture Disc" edition					
❑ Disneyland WDL-4002 [M]		1956	62.50	125.00	250.00
—Original edition					
❑ Disneyland ST-4905 [M]		1963	37.50	75.00	150.00
—Gatefold cover with pop-up center graphics					
PIRANHA					
❑ Varese Sarabande STV-81126		1979	5.00	10.00	20.00
THE PIRATE					
❑ MGM E-21 [10]		1951	17.50	35.00	70.00
PLANET OF THE APES					
❑ Project 3 PR-5023 SD		1968	5.00	10.00	20.00
—Regular cover					
❑ Project 3 PR-5023 SD		1968	7.50	15.00	30.00
—Gatefold cover					
THE PLEASURE SEEKERS					
❑ RCA Victor LOC-1101 [M]		1964	12.50	25.00	50.00
❑ RCA Victor LSO-1101 [S]		1964	25.00	50.00	100.00
POLLYANNA					
❑ Disneyland DQ-1307 [M]		1967	6.25	12.50	25.00
❑ Disneyland ST-1906 [M]		1960	12.50	25.00	50.00
POLTERGEIST					
❑ MGM MG-1-5408		1982	10.00	20.00	40.00
POLTERGEIST III					
❑ Varese Sarabande 704.620		1988	20.00	40.00	80.00
PORGY AND BESS					
❑ Columbia Masterworks OS 2016 [S]		1959	5.00	10.00	20.00
❑ Columbia Masterworks OL 5410 [M]		1959	3.75	7.50	15.00
THE POWER					
❑ Cerberus CST-0211		1984	5.00	10.00	20.00
PRET-A-PORTER					
❑ Miramax CAS 6700 [DJ]		1994	6.25	12.50	25.00
—Promo only vinyl					
PRETTY BOY FLOYD					
❑ Audio Fidelity AFLP-1936 [M]		1960	15.00	30.00	60.00
❑ Audio Fidelity AFSD-5936 [S]		1960	20.00	40.00	80.00
THE PRIDE AND THE PASSION					
❑ Capitol W 873 [M]		1957	15.00	30.00	60.00
THE PRINCESS BRIDE					
❑ Warner Bros. 25610		1987	5.00	10.00	20.00
THE PRISONER OF ZENDA					
❑ United Artists UA-LA374-G		1974	5.00	10.00	20.00
PRIVATE HELL 36					
❑ Coral CRL 56122 [10]		1954	25.00	50.00	100.00
THE PRODUCERS					
❑ RCA Victor ANL1-1132		1975	2.50	5.00	10.00
—Reissue of LSP-4008					
❑ RCA Victor LPM-4008 [M]		1968	12.50	25.00	50.00
❑ RCA Victor LSP-4008 [S]		1968	7.50	15.00	30.00
THE PROFESSIONALS					
❑ Colgems COMO-5001 [M]		1966	15.00	30.00	60.00
❑ Colgems COSO-5001 [S]		1966	37.50	75.00	150.00
A PROMISE AT DAWN					
❑ Polydor 24-5502		1970	7.50	15.00	30.00
THE PROPER TIME					
❑ Contemporary M-3587 [M]		1960	7.50	15.00	30.00
❑ Contemporary S-7587 [S]		1960	10.00	20.00	40.00

Number	Title (A Side/B Side)	Yr	VG	VG+	NM
PROVIDENCE					
❑ DRG SL-9502		1977	5.00	10.00	20.00
PRUDENCE AND THE PILL					
❑ 20th Century Fox S-4199		1968	5.00	10.00	20.00
PSYCHO II					
❑ MCA 6119		1983	5.00	10.00	20.00
Q THE WINGED SERPENT					
❑ Cerberus CST-0206		1983	5.00	10.00	20.00
QUEST FOR FIRE					
❑ RCA Victor ABL1-4274		1982	5.00	10.00	20.00
THE QUIET MAN					
❑ Decca DL 5411 [10]		1952	30.00	60.00	120.00
THE QUILLER MEMORANDUM					
❑ Columbia Masterworks OS 3060 [S]		1966	15.00	30.00	60.00
❑ Columbia Masterworks OL 6660 [M]		1966	7.50	15.00	30.00
QUO VADIS?					
❑ MCA 39075		198?	2.00	4.00	8.00
—Reissue of MGM 3524					
❑ MGM E-103 [10]		1951	10.00	20.00	40.00
—Music soundtrack only					
❑ MGM E-134 [(2)10]		1951	15.00	30.00	60.00
—Box set of two discs; includes dialogue					
❑ MGM E-3524 [M]		1957	6.25	12.50	25.00
—Yellow label; has both music and dialogue					
RAGTIME					
❑ Elektra 5E-565		1981	5.00	10.00	20.00
RAIDERS OF THE LOST ARK					
❑ Columbia JS 37373		1981	3.00	6.00	12.00
—Original issue; music only					
❑ Columbia JS 37696		1981	3.00	6.00	12.00
—Music and dialogue					
❑ DCC Compact Classics LPZ 2-2009 [(2)]		1995	7.50	15.00	30.00
—Audiophile edition; includes music not on other releases of the soundtrack					
❑ Polydor 821583-1		1984	2.50	5.00	10.00
—Reissue					
THE RAILWAY CHILDREN					
❑ Capitol SW-871		1972	5.00	10.00	20.00
THE RAINMAKER					
❑ RCA Victor LPM-1434 [M]		1956	25.00	50.00	100.00
RAINTREE COUNTY					
❑ RCA Victor LOC-1038 [M]		1958	7.50	15.00	30.00
❑ RCA Victor LSO-1038 [S]		1958	12.50	25.00	50.00
❑ RCA Victor LOC-6000 [(2)M]		1957	30.00	60.00	120.00
RAN					
❑ Fantasy FSP-21004		1985	5.00	10.00	20.00
THE RAT RACE					
❑ Dot DLP-3306 [M]		1960	10.00	20.00	40.00
❑ Dot DLP-25306 [S]		1960	12.50	25.00	50.00
RED DAWN					
❑ Intrada RVF-6001		1985	10.00	20.00	40.00
RED GARTERS					
❑ Columbia CL 6282 [10]		1954	12.50	25.00	50.00
RED HEAT					
❑ Virgin Movie Music 90891		1988	6.25	12.50	25.00
THE RED PONY					
❑ Columbia Masterworks ML 5983 [M]		196?	6.25	12.50	25.00
❑ Columbia Masterworks MS 6583 [R]		196?	6.25	12.50	25.00
❑ Varese Sarabande STV-81259		1986	6.25	12.50	25.00
THE RED TENT					
❑ Paramount PAS-6019		1971	6.25	12.50	25.00
REDS					
❑ Columbia Masterworks BJS 37960		1981	5.00	10.00	20.00
RENT-A-COP					
❑ Intrada MAS-7002		1988	5.00	10.00	20.00
THE REPORTER					
❑ Columbia CL 2269 [M]		1963	7.50	15.00	30.00
❑ Columbia CS 9069 [S]		1963	10.00	20.00	40.00
THE RESCUERS					
❑ Disneyland ST-3816		1977	5.00	10.00	20.00
RETURN TO PARADISE					
❑ Decca DL 5489 [10]		1953	50.00	100.00	200.00
THE REVOLUTION					
❑ United Artists UA-LA296-G		1974	3.00	6.00	12.00
—Reissue of 5185					
❑ United Artists UAS-5185		1968	6.25	12.50	25.00
RHAPSODY OF STEEL					
❑ U.S. Steel JB-502/3		1958	25.00	50.00	100.00
RICH, YOUNG AND PRETTY					
❑ MGM E-86 [10]		1951	10.00	20.00	40.00
RIDER ON THE RAIN					
❑ Capitol ST-584		1970	6.25	12.50	25.00
RIOT ON SUNSET STRIP					
❑ Tower DT 5065 [R]		1967	6.25	12.50	25.00
❑ Tower T 5065 [M]		1967	5.00	10.00	20.00
ROAD TO HONG KONG					
❑ Liberty LOM-16002 [M]		1962	5.00	10.00	20.00
❑ Liberty LOS-17002 [S]		1962	10.00	20.00	40.00
THE ROBE					
❑ Decca DL 9012 [M]		1953	7.50	15.00	30.00
—Maroon label					

Number	Title (A Side/B Side)	Yr	VG	VG+	NM
❏ Decca DL 79012 [R]		196?	3.00	6.00	12.00
❏ MCA 1529		198?	2.00	4.00	8.00
—Reissue of MCA 2052					
❏ MCA 2052		1973	2.50	5.00	10.00
—Reissue of Decca 79012; black label with rainbow					

ROBIN AND THE SEVEN HOODS

❏ Reprise F 2021 [M]		1964	12.50	25.00	50.00
❏ Reprise FS 2021 [S]		1964	15.00	30.00	60.00

ROBIN HOOD

❏ Disneyland ST-3810		1973	6.25	12.50	25.00

ROCK ALL NIGHT

❏ Mercury MG-20293 [M]		1957	25.00	50.00	100.00

ROCK, PRETTY BABY

❏ Decca DL 8429 [M]		1957	30.00	60.00	120.00
—Black label, silver print; also includes pink label promo					
❏ Decca DL 8429 [M]		196?	7.50	15.00	30.00
—Black label with color bars					

ROCK, ROCK, ROCK

❏ (no label) (no #) [M]		1958	375.00	750.00	1500.
—Demo version, 20 tracks					
❏ Chess LP-1425 [M]		1958	50.00	100.00	200.00

ROMANCE OF A HORSETHIEF

❏ Allied Artists AAS-110-100		1971	12.50	25.00	50.00

ROME ADVENTURE

❏ Warner Bros. W 1458 [M]		1962	5.00	10.00	20.00
❏ Warner Bros. WS 1458 [S]		1962	6.25	12.50	25.00

ROMEO AND JULIET

❏ Capitol SWDR-289 [(4)]		1969	7.50	15.00	30.00
—From the 1968 Franco Zeffirelli remake; contains dialogue and music					
❏ Capitol ST-400		1970	3.75	7.50	15.00
—From the 1968 Franco Zeffirelli remake; edited version of 289					
❏ Capitol ST-2993		1968	3.00	6.00	12.00
—From the 1968 Franco Zeffirelli remake; contains the music; black label with colorband					
❏ Epic LC 3126 [M]		1954	15.00	30.00	60.00
❏ Epic FLM 13104 [M]		1966	7.50	15.00	30.00
—Reissue of 3126					
❏ Epic FLS 15104 [R]		1966	6.25	12.50	25.00

ROOTS OF HEAVEN

❏ 20th Fox FOX-3005 [M]		1958	75.00	150.00	300.00

ROSE MARIE

❏ MGM E-229 [10]		1954	10.00	20.00	40.00

THE ROSE TATTOO

❏ Columbia CL 727 [M]		1955	12.50	25.00	50.00

ROSEMARY'S BABY

❏ Dot DLP-25875		1968	5.00	10.00	20.00

THE ROYAL WEDDING

❏ MGM E-543 [10]		1951	12.50	25.00	50.00

THE RULING CLASS

❏ Avco AV-11003		1972	6.25	12.50	25.00

THE RUN OF THE ARROW

❏ Decca DL 8620 [M]		1957	15.00	30.00	60.00
—Black label, silver print, or pink label, black print promo					
❏ Decca DL 8620 [M]		196?	7.50	15.00	30.00
—Black label with color bars					

RUN WILD, RUN FREE

❏ SGC SD 5003		1969	5.00	10.00	20.00

RUN, ANGEL, RUN

❏ Epic BN 26474		1969	5.00	10.00	20.00

RYAN'S DAUGHTER

❏ MGM 1SE-27		1970	6.25	12.50	25.00

SACCO AND VANZETTI

❏ RCA Victor LSP-4612		1971	5.00	10.00	20.00

THE SACRED IDOL

❏ Capitol ST 1293 [S]		1960	7.50	15.00	30.00
❏ Capitol T 1293 [M]		1960	6.25	12.50	25.00

THE SAINT

❏ Virgin SPRO-12261 [(2)DJ]		1997	6.25	12.50	25.00

SAINT JOAN

❏ Capitol W 865 [M]		1957	7.50	15.00	30.00

SALLAH

❏ Philips PHM 200177 [M]		1965	5.00	10.00	20.00
❏ Philips PHS 600177 [S]		1965	6.25	12.50	25.00

SALOME

❏ Decca DL 6026 [10]		1953	30.00	60.00	120.00

SAMSON AND DELILAH

❏ Decca DL 6007 [10]		1952	15.00	30.00	60.00

THE SAND CASTLE

❏ Columbia CL 1455 [M]		1961	3.75	7.50	15.00
❏ Columbia CS 8249 [S]		1961	5.00	10.00	20.00

THE SAND PEBBLES

❏ 20th Century Fox 3189 [M]		1966	7.50	15.00	30.00
❏ 20th Century Fox S-4189 [S]		1966	12.50	25.00	50.00

THE SANDPIPER

❏ Mercury MG-21032 [M]		1965	6.25	12.50	25.00
❏ Mercury SR-61032 [S]		1965	7.50	15.00	30.00

SANTA AND THE 3 BEARS

❏ Mr. Pickwick SPC 1501		196?	5.00	10.00	20.00
—With "Santa" cutout intact					

SATAN IN HIGH HEELS

❏ Charlie Parker PLP-406 [M]		1962	7.50	15.00	30.00
—Standard cover					

Number	Title (A Side/B Side)	Yr	VG	VG+	NM
❏ Charlie Parker PLP-406 [M]		1962	12.50	25.00	50.00
—Gatefold cover					
❏ Charlie Parker PLP-406S [S]		1962	10.00	20.00	40.00
—Standard cover					
❏ Charlie Parker PLP-406S [S]		1962	15.00	30.00	60.00
—Gatefold cover					

SATAN'S SADISTS

❏ Smash SRS-67127		1969	7.50	15.00	30.00

SATURDAY NIGHT FEVER

❏ RSO RS-2-4001 [(2)]		1977	3.75	7.50	15.00
—First editions have the studio version of "Jive Talkin'" by the Bee Gees on side 3					
❏ RSO RS-2-4001 [(2)]		1978	3.00	6.00	12.00
—Later editions have a live version of "Jive Talkin'" by the Bee Gees on side 3 ("REV" is in the Side 3 trail-off wax)					
❏ RSO 825389-1 [(2)]		198?	2.50	5.00	10.00
—Reissue with new number					

SATURDAY NIGHT FEVER/GREASE

❏ RSO RPO 1011 [DJ]		1978	6.25	12.50	25.00
—Side 1 has "The Best of Saturday Night Fever" (side 1 of original LP); Side 2 has "The Best of Grease" (side 1 of original LP)					

THE SAVAGE SEVEN

❏ Atco 33-245 [M]		1968	7.50	15.00	30.00
❏ Atco SD 33-245 [S]		1968	7.50	15.00	30.00

SAVAGE WILD

❏ American Int'l. STA-1032		1970	5.00	10.00	20.00

SAY ONE FOR ME

❏ Columbia CL 1337 [M]		1959	10.00	20.00	40.00
❏ Columbia CS 8147 [S]		1959	20.00	40.00	80.00

SAYONARA

❏ RCA Victor LOC-1041 [M]		1957	12.50	25.00	50.00
❏ RCA Victor LSO-1041 [S]		1957	17.50	35.00	70.00

THE SCALPHUNTERS

❏ MCA 25042		1986	2.50	5.00	10.00
—Reissue of United Artists 5176					
❏ United Artists UAL-4176 [M]		1968	7.50	15.00	30.00
❏ United Artists UAS-5176 [S]		1968	10.00	20.00	40.00

SCARFACE

❏ MCA 6126		1984	5.00	10.00	20.00

THE SCARLET AND THE BLACK

❏ Cerberus CEM-0120		1983	6.25	12.50	25.00

SCENT OF MYSTERY

❏ Ramrod ST-6001 [S]		1960	25.00	50.00	100.00
❏ Ramrod T-6001 [M]		1960	12.50	25.00	50.00

SCROOGE

❏ Columbia Masterworks S 30258		1970	7.50	15.00	30.00
❏ Columbia Special Products P 14077		1977	3.00	6.00	12.00
—Special Products reissue					

SEARCH FOR PARADISE

❏ RCA Victor LOC-1034 [M]		1957	10.00	20.00	40.00

SEASIDE SWINGERS

❏ Mercury MG-21031 [M]		1965	5.00	10.00	20.00
❏ Mercury SR-61031 [S]		1965	6.25	12.50	25.00

SEBASTIAN

❏ Dot DLP-3845 [M]		1968	12.50	25.00	50.00
❏ Dot DLP-25845 [S]		1968	5.00	10.00	20.00

THE SECRET OF SANTA VITTORIA

❏ MCA 25034		1986	2.50	5.00	10.00
—Reissue of United Artists 5200					
❏ United Artists UAS-5200		1969	7.50	15.00	30.00

SERGEANTS 3

❏ Reprise R-2013 [M]		1962	7.50	15.00	30.00
❏ Reprise RS-2013 [S]		1962	12.50	25.00	50.00

THE SERPENT AND THE RAINBOW

❏ Varese Sarabande STV-81362		1988	10.00	20.00	40.00

SERPICO

❏ Paramount PAS-1016		1973	6.25	12.50	25.00

SEVEN BRIDES FOR SEVEN BROTHERS

❏ MGM E-244 [10]		1954	10.00	20.00	40.00

SEVEN GOLDEN MEN

❏ United Artists UAS-5193		1969	6.25	12.50	25.00

THE SEVEN LITTLE FOYS

❏ RCA Victor LPM-3275 [10]		1955	17.50	35.00	70.00

THE SEVENTH DAWN

❏ United Artists UAL-4115 [M]		1964	7.50	15.00	30.00
❏ United Artists UAS-5115 [S]		1964	10.00	20.00	40.00

SEX AND THE SINGLE GIRL

❏ Warner Bros. W 1572 [M]		1964	3.75	7.50	15.00
❏ Warner Bros. WS 1572 [S]		1964	5.00	10.00	20.00

SHAFT IN AFRICA

❏ ABC ABCX-793		1973	7.50	15.00	30.00

SHAFT'S BIG SCORE

❏ MGM 1SE-36		1972	7.50	15.00	30.00

SHAKE HANDS WITH THE DEVIL

❏ United Artists UAL-4043 [M]		1959	7.50	15.00	30.00
❏ United Artists UAS-5043 [S]		1959	12.50	25.00	50.00

SHALAKO

❏ Philips PHS 600286		1968	7.50	15.00	30.00

SHE-DEVIL

❏ Polydor 841583-1		1989	7.50	15.00	30.00

SHEBA BABY

❏ Buddah BDS-5634		1975	7.50	15.00	30.00

Number — Title (A Side/B Side)	Yr	VG	VG+	NM
SHENANDOAH				
Decca DL 9125 [M]	1965	7.50	15.00	30.00
Decca DL 79125 [S]	1965	10.00	20.00	40.00
THE SHINING				
Warner Bros. HS 3449	1980	5.00	10.00	20.00
THE SHOP ON MAIN STREET				
Mainstream S-6082 [S]	1966	10.00	20.00	40.00
Mainstream 56082 [M]	1966	6.25	12.50	25.00
SHORT EYES				
Curtom CU 5017	1977	6.25	12.50	25.00
SHOW BOAT				
MGM E-559 [10]	1951	7.50	15.00	30.00
THE SICILIAN CLAN				
20th Century Fox S-4209	1970	12.50	25.00	50.00
THE SIDEHACKERS				
Amaret ST-5004	1969	5.00	10.00	20.00
THE SILENCERS				
RCA Victor LOC-1120 [M]	1966	7.50	15.00	30.00
RCA Victor LSO-1120 [S]	1966	12.50	25.00	50.00
SILENT RUNNING				
Decca DL 79188	1972	10.00	20.00	40.00
Varese Sarabande STV- 81072	1980	3.75	7.50	15.00
—Reissue				
SILK STOCKINGS				
MCA 39074	198?	2.50	5.00	10.00
—Reissue				
MGM E-3542 [M]	1957	7.50	15.00	30.00
SILVERADO				
Geffen GHS 24080	1985	5.00	10.00	20.00
SINGIN' IN THE RAIN				
MCA 39044	198?	2.50	5.00	10.00
Metro M-599 [M]	1966	3.75	7.50	15.00
—Reissue of MGM LP				
Metro MS-599 [R]	1966	3.00	6.00	12.00
MGM E-113 [10]	1952	7.50	15.00	30.00
SINGLE ROOM FURNISHED				
Sidewalk ST-5917	1968	10.00	20.00	40.00
SKATEDANCER				
Mira LP-3004 [M]	1966	5.00	10.00	20.00
Mira LPS-3004 [S]	1966	6.25	12.50	25.00
SKI ON THE WILD SIDE				
MGM E-4439 [M]	1967	7.50	15.00	30.00
MGM SE-4439 [S]	1967	12.50	25.00	50.00
SLAUGHTER ON 10TH AVENUE				
Decca DL 8657 [M]	1957	6.25	12.50	25.00
—Black label, silver print				
Decca DL 8657 [M]	1960	3.00	6.00	12.00
—Black label with color bars				
Decca DL 78657 [S]	1957	7.50	15.00	30.00
—Black label, silver print				
Decca DL 78657 [S]	1960	3.75	7.50	15.00
—Black label with color bars				
SLAUGHTERHOUSE-FIVE				
Columbia Masterworks S 31333	1972	6.25	12.50	25.00
THE SLAVE TRADE IN THE WORLD TODAY				
London M-76006 [M]	1964	50.00	100.00	200.00
SLAVES				
Skye SK-11	1969	6.25	12.50	25.00
SLEEPING BEAUTY				
Disneyland STER-4018 [S]	1959	10.00	20.00	40.00
Disneyland WDL-4018 [M]	1959	7.50	15.00	30.00
Disneyland STER-4036 [S]	1970	5.00	10.00	20.00
—Reissue of STER-4018				
SLEUTH				
Columbia Masterworks S 32154	1973	5.00	10.00	20.00
SLIPPERY WHEN WET				
World Pacific WP-1265 [M]	1959	12.50	25.00	50.00
SLUMBER PARTY '57				
Mercury SRM-1-1097	1976	6.25	12.50	25.00
A SMASHING TIME				
ABC ABC-OC-6 [M]	1967	5.00	10.00	20.00
ABC ABCS-OC-6 [S]	1967	6.25	12.50	25.00
ABC SW-91399 [S]	1967	6.25	12.50	25.00
—Capitol Record Club edition				
SNOOPY COME HOME				
Columbia Masterworks S 31451	1972	5.00	10.00	20.00
THE SNOW QUEEN				
Decca DL 8977 [M]	1959	10.00	20.00	40.00
Decca DL 78977 [S]	1959	15.00	30.00	60.00
SNOW WHITE AND THE SEVEN DWARFS				
Buena Vista 102 [(3)]	1975	12.50	25.00	50.00
—Entire movie on three LPs; TV mail-order item				
Disneyland DQ-1201 [M]	1959	12.50	25.00	50.00
—Reissue of 4005; whirlpool-like designs on cover				
Disneyland DQ-1201 [M]	1968	6.25	12.50	25.00
—Reissue; with same cover as 4005, but no gatefold				
Disneyland DQ-1201 [M]	1987	7.50	15.00	30.00
—Reissue; high-gloss cover with cel photos on back				
Disneyland 3101 [PD]	1981	7.50	15.00	30.00
—"Disney Picture Disc" edition				
Disneyland WDL-4005 [M]	1956	50.00	100.00	200.00
—Gatefold cover				
SNOW WHITE AND THE THREE STOOGES				
Columbia CL 1650 [M]	1961	15.00	30.00	60.00
Columbia CS 8450 [S]	1961	25.00	50.00	100.00
SO THIS IS LOVE				
RCA Victor LOC-3000 [10]	1953	20.00	40.00	80.00
SO THIS IS PARIS				
Decca DL 5553 [10]	1955	12.50	25.00	50.00
SODOM AND GOMORRAH				
RCA Victor LOC-1076 [M]	1963	20.00	40.00	80.00
RCA Victor LSO-1076 [S]	1963	25.00	50.00	100.00
SOL MADRID				
MGM SE-4541 ST	1968	7.50	15.00	30.00
SOLOMON AND SHEBA				
MCA 1425	198?	2.00	4.00	8.00
—Reissue				
United Artists UAL-4051 [M]	1959	6.25	12.50	25.00
—Second, regular cover				
United Artists UAL-4051 [M]	1959	12.50	25.00	50.00
—First cover with silky finish				
United Artists UAS-5051 [S]	1959	15.00	30.00	60.00
—Second, regular cover				
United Artists UAS-5051 [S]	1959	30.00	60.00	120.00
—First cover with silky finish				
SOME CAME RUNNING				
Capitol SW 1109 [S]	1958	20.00	40.00	80.00
Capitol W 1109 [M]	1958	7.50	15.00	30.00
SOME LIKE IT HOT				
United Artists UA-LA272-G	1974	3.00	6.00	12.00
—Reissue of 5030				
United Artists UAL-4030 [M]	1959	12.50	25.00	50.00
United Artists UAS-5030 [S]	1959	18.75	37.50	75.00
SOMEBODY LOVES ME				
RCA Victor LPM-3097 [10]	1952	12.50	25.00	50.00
SOMEWHERE IN TIME				
MCA 5154	1980	5.00	10.00	20.00
SONG OF THE SOUTH				
Disneyland WDL-4001 [M]	1956	75.00	150.00	300.00
—Yellow label (first pressing)				
Disneyland WDL-4001 [M]	1957	50.00	100.00	200.00
—Red/maroon label (second pressing)				
SONG OF THE SOUTH (UNCLE REMUS)				
Disneyland DQ-1205 [M]	1959	6.25	12.50	25.00
SONG WITHOUT END				
Colpix CP-506 [M]	1960	5.00	10.00	20.00
Colpix SCP-506 [S]	1960	6.25	12.50	25.00
THE SONS OF KATIE ELDER				
Columbia Masterworks OS 2820 [S]	1965	25.00	50.00	100.00
Columbia Masterworks OL 6420 [M]	1965	12.50	25.00	50.00
THE SOUL OF NIGGER CHARLEY				
MGM 1SE-46	1973	5.00	10.00	20.00
THE SOUND AND THE FURY				
Decca DL 8885 [M]	1959	7.50	15.00	30.00
Decca DL 78885 [S]	1959	17.50	35.00	70.00
THE SOUND OF MUSIC				
RCA Victor LOCD-2005 [M]	1965	3.00	6.00	12.00
—With booklet; back cover lists "I Have Confidence" correctly				
RCA Victor LOCD-2005 [M]	1965	3.75	7.50	15.00
—With booklet; back cover lists "I Have Confidence" as "I Have Confidence in Me"				
RCA Victor LSOD-2005 [S]	1965	3.75	7.50	15.00
—With booklet; back cover lists "I Have Confidence" correctly				
RCA Victor LSOD-2005 [S]	1965	5.00	10.00	20.00
—With booklet; back cover lists "I Have Confidence" as "I Have Confidence in Me"				
RCA Victor LSOD-2005 [S]	1969	3.00	6.00	12.00
—No booklet; gatefold cover, record comes out from inside; orange or tan label				
RCA Victor LSOD-2005 [S]	1977	2.50	5.00	10.00
—Gatefold cover, record comes out from outside; black label with dog at 1 o'clock				
SOUTH CENTRAL				
Hollywood 61403 [DJ]	1992	5.00	10.00	20.00
—Vinyl is promo only				
SOUTH PACIFIC				
RCA Victor LOC-1032 [M]	1958	5.00	10.00	20.00
—"Long Play" on label; no "Academy Award Winner" on front cover				
RCA Victor LOC-1032 [M]	196?	3.00	6.00	12.00
—"Long Play" or "Mono" on label; with "Academy Award Winner" on front cover				
RCA Victor LSO-1032 [S]	1958	3.00	6.00	12.00
—Orange label				
RCA Victor LSO-1032 [S]	1958	6.25	12.50	25.00
—"Living Stereo" on label; no "Academy Award Winner" on front cover				
RCA Victor LSO-1032 [S]	196?	3.75	7.50	15.00
—"Living Stereo" or "Stereo" on black label; with "Academy Award Winner" on front cover				
RCA Victor LOCD-2000 [M]	1958	10.00	20.00	40.00
—Gatefold cover with photos inside				
RCA Victor AYL1-3681	1981	2.00	4.00	8.00
—"Best Buy Series" reissue				
SOUTHERN STAR				
Colgems COSO-5009	1969	15.00	30.00	60.00
SPACECAMP				
RCA Victor ABL1-5856	1986	10.00	20.00	40.00
A SPANISH AFFAIR				
Dot DLP-3078 [M]	1958	25.00	50.00	100.00
SPARKLE				
Atlantic SD 18176	1976	5.00	10.00	20.00

Number	Title (A Side/B Side)	Yr	VG	VG+	NM
SPARTACUS					
❑ Decca DL 9092 [M]		1960	5.00	10.00	20.00
—Black label, silver print					
❑ Decca DL 9092 [M]		1961	3.00	6.00	12.00
—Black label with color bars					
❑ Decca DL 79092 [S]		1960	6.25	12.50	25.00
—Maroon label, silver print					
❑ Decca DL 79092 [S]		1961	3.75	7.50	15.00
—Black label with color bars					
❑ MCA 1534		198?	2.50	5.00	10.00
—Reissue of 2068					
❑ MCA 2068		1973	3.00	6.00	12.00
—Reissue of 79092; black label with rainbow					
THE SPIRIT OF ST. LOUIS					
❑ RCA Victor LPM-1472 [M]		1957	12.50	25.00	50.00
SPLASH					
❑ Cherry Lane 00301		1984	6.25	12.50	25.00
—With poster of Daryl Hannah					
THE SPY WHO CAME IN FROM THE COLD					
❑ RCA Victor LOC-1118 [M]		1965	5.00	10.00	20.00
❑ RCA Victor LSO-1118 [S]		1965	10.00	20.00	40.00
THE SPY WITH A COLD NOSE					
❑ Columbia Masterworks OS 3070 [S]		1966	7.50	15.00	30.00
❑ Columbia Masterworks OL 6670 [M]		1966	5.00	10.00	20.00
ST. LOUIS BLUES					
❑ Capitol W 993 [M]		1958	12.50	25.00	50.00
—Turquoise or gray label					
❑ Capitol W 993 [M]		1959	6.25	12.50	25.00
—Black colorband label, logo at left					
❑ Capitol W 993 [M]		196?	5.00	10.00	20.00
—Black colorband label, logo at top					
ST. LOUIS WOMAN					
❑ Capitol L 355 [10]		1955	20.00	40.00	80.00
STAGECOACH					
❑ Mainstream S-6077 [S]		1966	7.50	15.00	30.00
❑ Mainstream 56077 [M]		1966	5.00	10.00	20.00
❑ Mainstream ST-90802 [S]		1966	7.50	15.00	30.00
—Capitol Record Club edition					
❑ Mainstream T-90802 [M]		1966	6.25	12.50	25.00
—Capitol Record Club edition					
STAR TREK — THE MOTION PICTURE					
❑ Columbia JS 36334		1979	5.00	10.00	20.00
STAR!					
❑ 20th Century Fox DTCS-5102		1968	5.00	10.00	20.00
THE STARS AND STRIPES FOREVER					
❑ MGM E-176 [10]		1952	7.50	15.00	30.00
STATE FAIR					
❑ Dot DLP-9011 [M]		1962	6.25	12.50	25.00
❑ Dot DLP-29011 [S]		1962	7.50	15.00	30.00
THE STERILE CUCKOO					
❑ Paramount PAS-5009		1970	5.00	10.00	20.00
STILETTO					
❑ Columbia Masterworks OS 3360		1969	5.00	10.00	20.00
THE STRANGE ONE					
❑ Coral CRL 57132 [M]		1957	17.50	35.00	70.00
THE STRAWBERRY STATEMENT					
❑ MGM 2SE-14 [(2)]		1970	6.25	12.50	25.00
A STREETCAR NAMED DESIRE					
❑ Capitol L 289 [10]		1951	12.50	25.00	50.00
A STUDY IN TERROR					
❑ Roulette OS-801 [M]		1965	10.00	20.00	40.00
❑ Roulette OSS-801 [S]		1965	20.00	40.00	80.00
THE STUNT MAN					
❑ 20th Century T-626		1980	6.25	12.50	25.00
THE SUBTERRANEANS					
❑ MGM E-3812 ST [M]		1960	10.00	20.00	40.00
❑ MGM SE-3812 ST [S]		1960	20.00	40.00	80.00
SUMMER AND SMOKE					
❑ RCA Victor LOC-1067 [M]		1961	12.50	25.00	50.00
❑ RCA Victor LSO-1067 [S]		1961	17.50	35.00	70.00
SUMMER HOLIDAY					
❑ Epic LN 24063 [M]		1963	6.25	12.50	25.00
❑ Epic BN 26063 [S]		1963	7.50	15.00	30.00
SUMMER LOVE					
❑ Decca DL 8714 [M]		1958	15.00	30.00	60.00
—Black label, silver print, or pink label, black print promo					
❑ Decca DL 8714 [M]		196?	7.50	15.00	30.00
—Black label with color bars					
SUMMER MAGIC					
❑ Buena Vista BV-4025 [M]		1963	10.00	20.00	40.00
❑ Buena Vista STER-4025 [S]		1963	15.00	30.00	60.00
SUMMER STOCK					
❑ MGM E-519 [10]		1950	10.00	20.00	40.00
THE SUN ALSO RISES					
❑ Kapp KDL-7001 [M]		1957	15.00	30.00	60.00
SUN VALLEY SERENADE					
❑ RCA Victor LPT-3064 [10]		1954	15.00	30.00	60.00
THE SUNNY SIDE OF THE STREET					
❑ Mercury MG-25100 [10]		1951	15.00	30.00	60.00
SURF PARTY					
❑ 20th Century Fox TFM-3131 [M]		1964	6.25	12.50	25.00
❑ 20th Century Fox TFS-4131 [S]		1964	7.50	15.00	30.00

Number	Title (A Side/B Side)	Yr	VG	VG+	NM
SURFER GIRLS					
❑ Oakwood SUS-1001		1978	25.00	50.00	100.00
THE SWAN					
❑ MCA 25086		1986	2.50	5.00	10.00
—Reissue of MGM 3399					
❑ MGM E-3399 [M]		1956	17.50	35.00	70.00
THE SWARM					
❑ Warner Bros. BSK 3208		1978	7.50	15.00	30.00
SWEDISH HEAVEN AND HELL					
❑ Ariel ARS-15000		1969	6.25	12.50	25.00
SWEET CHARITY					
❑ Decca DL 71502		1969	5.00	10.00	20.00
SWEET LOVE, BITTER					
❑ ABC Impulse! AS-9141 [S]		1968	3.75	7.50	15.00
❑ Impulse! A-9141 [M]		1967	10.00	20.00	40.00
❑ Impulse! AS-9141 [S]		1967	7.50	15.00	30.00
THE SWEET RIDE					
❑ 20th Century Fox S-4198		1968	5.00	10.00	20.00
THE SWEET SMELL OF SUCCESS					
❑ Decca DL 8610 [M]		1957	15.00	30.00	60.00
SWEET SWEETBACK'S BADASSSSSS SONG					
❑ Stax STS-3001		1971	7.50	15.00	30.00
SWEPT AWAY					
❑ Peters International PLD 1005		1957	10.00	20.00	40.00
THE SWIMMER					
❑ Columbia Masterworks OS 3210		1968	6.25	12.50	25.00
SWINGER'S PARADISE					
❑ Epic LN 24145 [M]		1965	5.00	10.00	20.00
❑ Epic BN 26145 [S]		1965	6.25	12.50	25.00
A SWINGIN' SUMMER					
❑ Hanna-Barbera HLP-8500 [M]		1966	6.25	12.50	25.00
❑ Hanna-Barbera HST-9500 [S]		1966	7.50	15.00	30.00
SYLVIA					
❑ Mercury MG-21004 [M]		1965	5.00	10.00	20.00
❑ Mercury SR-61004 [S]		1965	7.50	15.00	30.00
TARAS BULBA					
❑ United Artists UAL-4100 [M]		1962	7.50	15.00	30.00
❑ United Artists UAS-5100 [S]		1962	12.50	25.00	50.00
TAXI DRIVER					
❑ Arista AL 4079		1976	5.00	10.00	20.00
❑ Arista AL 8179		198?	3.75	7.50	15.00
—Reissue of 4079					
TEENAGE REBELLION					
❑ Sidewalk ST-5903 [S]		1967	6.25	12.50	25.00
❑ Sidewalk T-5903 [M]		1967	5.00	10.00	20.00
TELL ME THAT YOU LOVE ME, JUNIE MOON					
❑ Columbia Masterworks OS 3540		1970	5.00	10.00	20.00
THE TEN COMMANDMENTS					
❑ Dot DLP-3054 [M]		1956	10.00	20.00	40.00
❑ Dot DLP-25054 [S]		1959	6.25	12.50	25.00
—Re-recording of the original soundtrack in stereo					
❑ MCA 4159 [(2)]		198?	3.75	7.50	15.00
—Reissue of Paramount set					
❑ Paramount PAS-1006 [(2)]		1973	5.00	10.00	20.00
—Reissue of Dot 25054					
TENDER IS THE NIGHT					
❑ 20th Century Fox FOX-3054 [M]		1962	37.50	75.00	150.00
❑ 20th Century Fox SFX-3054 [S]		1962	50.00	100.00	200.00
THE TENTH VICTIM					
❑ Mainstream S-6071 [S]		1965	12.50	25.00	50.00
❑ Mainstream 56071 [M]		1965	10.00	20.00	40.00
THANK GOD IT'S FRIDAY					
❑ Casablanca NBLP-7099-3 [(3)]		1978	5.00	10.00	20.00
—Two full-length LPs plus a bonus 12-inch single by Donna Summer with blank B-side					
THAT DARN CAT					
❑ Buena Vista BV-3334 [M]		1965	5.00	10.00	20.00
❑ Buena Vista STER-3334 [S]		1965	6.25	12.50	25.00
THAT MAN IN ISTANBUL					
❑ Mainstream S-6072 [S]		1966	6.25	12.50	25.00
❑ Mainstream 56072 [M]		1966	5.00	10.00	20.00
THAT'S ENTERTAINMENT!					
❑ MCA 11002 [(2)]		1974	5.00	10.00	20.00
—Film credits in small print on back cover, and list of songs omits "That's Entertainment"					
❑ MCA 11002 [(2)]		1976	3.75	7.50	15.00
—Film credits in larger print on back cover, and list of songs includes "That's Entertainment"					
THERE'S NO BUSINESS LIKE SHOW BUSINESS					
❑ Decca DL 8091 [M]		1954	7.50	15.00	30.00
—Black label with silver print					
❑ Decca DL 8091 [M]		196?	5.00	10.00	20.00
—Black label with color bars					
THEY SHOOT HORSES, DON'T THEY?					
❑ ABC ABCS-OC-10		1969	5.00	10.00	20.00
THIEF OF HEARTS					
❑ Casablanca 822942-1		1984	5.00	10.00	20.00
THE THIN BLUE LINE					
❑ Nonesuch 79209-1		1988	5.00	10.00	20.00
THIS COULD BE THE NIGHT					
❑ MGM E-3530 [M]		1957	12.50	25.00	50.00
THIS EARTH IS MINE					
❑ Decca DL 8915 [M]		1959	20.00	40.00	80.00
❑ Decca DL 78915 [S]		1959	25.00	50.00	100.00

Number	Title (A Side/B Side)	Yr	VG	VG+	NM
❑ Varese Sarabande VC-81076		1979	3.75	7.50	15.00

—*Reissue of Decca 78915*

THIS PROPERTY IS CONDEMNED

Number	Title (A Side/B Side)	Yr	VG	VG+	NM
❑ Verve V-8664 [M]		1966	5.00	10.00	20.00
❑ Verve V6-8664 [S]		1966	7.50	15.00	30.00

THE THOMAS CROWN AFFAIR

❑ United Artists UA-LA295-G		1974	3.00	6.00	12.00

—*Reissue of 5182*

❑ United Artists UAS-5182		1968	5.00	10.00	20.00

THOROUGHLY MODERN MILLIE

❑ Decca DL 1500 [M]		1967	5.00	10.00	20.00

—*With bound-in booklet*

❑ Decca DL 71500 [S]		1967	5.00	10.00	20.00

—*With bound-in booklet*

THOSE GLORIOUS MGM MUSICALS: DEEP IN MY HEART/WORDS AND MUSIC

❑ MGM 2-SES-54-ST [(2)]		1973	5.00	10.00	20.00

THOSE GLORIOUS MGM MUSICALS: EVERYTHING I HAVE IS YOURS/SUMMER STOCK/I LOVE MELVIN

❑ MGM 2-SES-52-ST [(2)]		1973	5.00	10.00	20.00

THOSE GLORIOUS MGM MUSICALS: GOOD NEWS/IN THE GOOD OLD SUMMERTIME/TWO WEEKS WITH LOVE

❑ MGM 2-SES-49-ST [(2)]		1973	5.00	10.00	20.00

THOSE GLORIOUS MGM MUSICALS: LOVELY TO LOOK AT/BRIGADOON

❑ MGM 2-SES-50-ST [(2)]		1973	5.00	10.00	20.00

THOSE GLORIOUS MGM MUSICALS: NANCY GOES TO RIO/RICH, YOUNG AND PRETTY/ROYAL WEDDING

❑ MGM 2-SES-53-ST [(2)]		1973	5.00	10.00	20.00

THOSE GLORIOUS MGM MUSICALS: ROSE MARIE/SEVN BRIDES FOR SEVEN BROTHERS

❑ MGM 2-SES-41-ST [(2)]		1973	5.00	10.00	20.00

THOSE GLORIOUS MGM MUSICALS: SHOW BOAT/ANNIE GET YOUR GUN

❑ MGM 2-SES-42-ST [(2)]		1973	5.00	10.00	20.00

THOSE GLORIOUS MGM MUSICALS: SINGIN' IN THE RAIN/EASTER PARADE

❑ MGM 2-SES-40-ST [(2)]		1973	5.00	10.00	20.00

THOSE GLORIOUS MGM MUSICALS: THE BAND WAGON/KISS ME, KATE

❑ MGM 2-SES-44-ST [(2)]		1973	5.00	10.00	20.00

THOSE GLORIOUS MGM MUSICALS: THE BARKLEYS OF BROADWAY/LES GIRLS

❑ MGM 2-SES-51-ST [(2)]		1973	5.00	10.00	20.00

THOSE GLORIOUS MGM MUSICALS: THE PIRATE/PAGAN LOVE SONG/HIT THE DECK

❑ MGM 2-SES-43-ST [(2)]		1973	10.00	20.00	40.00

THOSE GLORIOUS MGM MUSICALS: TILL THE CLOUDS ROLL BY/THREE LITTLE WORDS

❑ MGM 2-SES-45-ST [(2)]		1973	5.00	10.00	20.00

THREE BITES OF THE APPLE

❑ MCA 25010		198?	2.00	4.00	8.00

—*Reissue of MGM SE-4444*

❑ MGM E-4444 [M]		1967	6.25	12.50	25.00
❑ MGM SE-4444 [S]		1967	5.00	10.00	20.00

THREE FOR THE SHOW

❑ Mercury MG-25204 [M]		1955	15.00	30.00	60.00

THREE IN THE ATTIC

❑ Sidewalk ST-5918		1968	7.50	15.00	30.00

THREE LITTLE WORDS

❑ MGM E-516 [10]		1959	15.00	30.00	60.00

THE THREE WORLDS OF GULLIVER

❑ Colpix CP-414 [M]		1960	15.00	30.00	60.00

THE THREEPENNY OPERA

❑ RCA Victor LOC-1086 [M]		1964	3.75	7.50	15.00

—*Reissue cover: White background, orange drawing, Sammy Davis Jr. in foreground, "RE" at bottom*

❑ RCA Victor LOC-1086 [M]		1964	37.50	75.00	150.00

—*With rare original cover: White background, pink and black drawing, characters underneath*

❑ RCA Victor LSO-1086 [S]		1964	5.00	10.00	20.00

—*Reissue cover: White background, orange drawing, Sammy Davis Jr. in foreground, "RE" at bottom*

❑ RCA Victor LSO-1086 [S]		1964	50.00	100.00	200.00

—*With rare original cover: White background, pink and black drawing, characters underneath*

THUNDER ALLEY

❑ Sidewalk ST-5902 [S]		1967	6.25	12.50	25.00
❑ Sidewalk T-5902 [M]		1967	5.00	10.00	20.00

THUNDERBALL

❑ United Artists UAL-4132 [M]		1965	5.00	10.00	20.00
❑ United Artists UAS-5132 [S]		1965	7.50	15.00	30.00
❑ United Artists SW-90820 [S]		1965	10.00	20.00	40.00

—*Capitol Record Club edition*

TICK…TICK…TICK

❑ MGM SE-4667 [M]		1970	6.25	12.50	25.00

TILL THE CLOUDS ROLL BY

❑ MCA 25000		1986	2.50	5.00	10.00
❑ Metro M-578 [M]		1966	3.00	6.00	12.00

—*Reissue of MGM 501*

❑ Metro MS-578 [R]		1966	2.50	5.00	10.00
❑ MGM E-501 [10]		1950	12.50	25.00	50.00

A TIME TO LOVE AND A TIME TO DIE

❑ Decca DL 8778 [M]		1958	25.00	50.00	100.00
❑ Varese Sarabande VC- 81075		1979	3.75	7.50	15.00

—*Reissue of Decca 8778*

TO BED… OR NOT TO BED

❑ London M-76005 [M]		1963	10.00	20.00	40.00

TO KILL A MOCKINGBIRD

❑ Ava A-20 [M]		1962	6.25	12.50	25.00
❑ Ava AS-20 [S]		1962	7.50	15.00	30.00

TOKYO OLYMPIAD

❑ Monument MLP-8046 [M]		1966	3.75	7.50	15.00
❑ Monument SLP-18046 [S]		1966	5.00	10.00	20.00

TOM JONES

❑ United Artists UAL-4113 [M]		1963	5.00	10.00	20.00
❑ United Artists UAS-5113 [S]		1963	6.25	12.50	25.00

TOM SAWYER

❑ United Artists UA-LA057-F		1973	5.00	10.00	20.00

TOMMY

❑ Polydor PD 2-9502 [(2)]		1975	5.00	10.00	20.00

TOO MUCH TOO SOON

❑ Mercury MG-20381 [M]		1958	7.50	15.00	30.00
❑ Mercury SR-60019 [S]		1958	20.00	40.00	80.00

TOPKAPI

❑ MCA 25118		1986	2.50	5.00	10.00
❑ United Artists UAL-4118 [M]		1964	5.00	10.00	20.00
❑ United Artists UAS-5118 [S]		1964	7.50	15.00	30.00

THE TOUCHABLES

❑ 20th Century Fox S-4206		1969	5.00	10.00	20.00

THE TRAIN

❑ United Artists UAL-4122 [M]		1965	5.00	10.00	20.00
❑ United Artists UAS-5122 [S]		1965	10.00	20.00	40.00

THE TRAP

❑ Atco 33-204 [M]		1966	10.00	20.00	40.00
❑ Atco SD 33-204 [S]		1966	17.50	35.00	70.00

TRAPEZE

❑ Columbia CL 870 [M]		1956	6.25	12.50	25.00

THE TRAPP FAMILY

❑ 20th Fox FOX-3044 [M]		1961	6.25	12.50	25.00
❑ 20th Fox STX-3044 [S]		1961	10.00	20.00	40.00

THE TREASURE OF SAN GENNARO

❑ Buddah BDS-5011		1968	10.00	20.00	40.00

THE TRIP

❑ Sidewalk ST-5908 [S]		1967	10.00	20.00	40.00
❑ Sidewalk T-5908 [M]		1967	7.50	15.00	30.00

TRIPLE CROSS

❑ United Artists UAL-4162 [M]		1967	5.00	10.00	20.00
❑ United Artists UAS-5162 [S]		1967	7.50	15.00	30.00

THE TROUBLE WITH ANGELS

❑ Mainstream S-6073 [S]		1966	20.00	40.00	80.00
❑ Mainstream 56073 [M]		1966	10.00	20.00	40.00

TRUE GRIT

❑ Capitol ST-263		1969	7.50	15.00	30.00
❑ Capitol ST-8-0263		1969	10.00	20.00	40.00

—*Capitol Record Club edition*

TRUE LIFE ADVENTURES

❑ Disneyland WDL-4011 [M]		1957	17.50	35.00	70.00

THE TRUE STORY OF THE CIVIL WAR

❑ Coral CRL 59100 [M]		1958	20.00	40.00	80.00

TWO MULES FOR SISTER SARA

❑ Kapp KRS-5512		1970	6.25	12.50	25.00

TWO WEEKS WITH LOVE

❑ MGM E-530 [10]		1950	10.00	20.00	40.00

ULYSSES

❑ RCA Victor LOC-1138 [M]		1967	6.25	12.50	25.00
❑ RCA Victor LSO-1138 [S]		1967	7.50	15.00	30.00

THE UMBRELLAS OF CHERBOURG (LES PARAPLUIES DE CHERBOURG)

❑ Philips PCC 216 [M]		1965	5.00	10.00	20.00
❑ Philips PCC 616 [S]		1965	7.50	15.00	30.00

THE UNBEARABLE LIGHTNESS OF BEING

❑ Fantasy FSP-21006		1988	5.00	10.00	20.00

UNCLE TOM'S CABIN

❑ Philips PHS 600272		1968	10.00	20.00	40.00

THE UNFORGIVEN

❑ United Artists UAL-4068 [M]		1960	10.00	20.00	40.00
❑ United Artists UAS-5068 [S]		1960	17.50	35.00	70.00

THE UNSINKABLE MOLLY BROWN

❑ MCA 25011		1986	2.50	5.00	10.00

—*Reissue of MGM 4232*

❑ MGM E-4232 [M]		1964	3.75	7.50	15.00
❑ MGM SE-4232 [S]		1964	5.00	10.00	20.00
❑ MGM SW-90048 [S]		1964	3.75	7.50	15.00

—*Capitol Record Club edition*

❑ MGM W-90048 [M]		1964	3.00	6.00	12.00

—*Capitol Record Club edition*

UP IN THE CELLAR

❑ American Int'l. A-1036		1970	5.00	10.00	20.00

UP THE DOWN STAIRCASE

❑ United Artists UAL-4169 [M]		1967	5.00	10.00	20.00
❑ United Artists UAS-5169 [S]		1967	10.00	20.00	40.00

UP THE JUNCTION

❑ Mercury SR-61159		1968	6.25	12.50	25.00

THE V.I.P.S

❑ MGM E-4184 [M]		1963	5.00	10.00	20.00
❑ MGM SE-4184 [S]		1963	6.25	12.50	25.00

—*Music by Bill Evans*

VALENTINO

❑ United Artists UA-LA810-H		1977	6.25	12.50	25.00

Number	Title (A Side/B Side)	Yr	VG	VG+	NM
VALLEY GIRL					
❏ Epic FE 38623		1983	20.00	40.00	80.00
❏ Roadshow RS-101		1983	30.00	60.00	120.00
VALLEY OF THE DOLLS					
❏ 20th Century Fox TF-4196 [M]		1968	7.50	15.00	30.00
❏ 20th Century Fox TFS-4196 [S]		1968	7.50	15.00	30.00
❏ 20th Century Fox SW-91374 [S]		1968	7.50	15.00	30.00
—Capitol Record Club edition					
VANILLA SKY					
❏ Reprise RTH-2002 [(2)]		2002	10.00	20.00	40.00
—Classic Records edition on 180-gram vinyl ; contains a packet with a piece of film from the movie					
THE VANISHING POINT					
❏ Amos AAS-8002		1971	5.00	10.00	20.00
THE VANISHING PRAIRIE					
❏ Columbia CL 6332 [10]		1954	20.00	40.00	80.00
VERTIGO					
❏ Mercury MG-20384 [M]		1958	37.50	75.00	150.00
VICTOR/VICTORIA					
❏ MGM MG-1-5407		1982	7.50	15.00	30.00
❏ Polydor MG-1-5407		198?	2.50	5.00	10.00
—Reissue of MGM release					
THE VICTORS					
❏ Colpix CP-516 [M]		1963	5.00	10.00	20.00
❏ Colpix SCP-516 [S]		1963	7.50	15.00	30.00
A VIEW TO A KILL					
❏ Capitol SJ-12413		1985	5.00	10.00	20.00
THE VIKINGS					
❏ United Artists UAL-4003 [M]		1958	7.50	15.00	30.00
❏ United Artists UAS-5003 [S]		1958	10.00	20.00	40.00
VILLA RIDES!					
❏ Dot DLP-25870		1968	10.00	20.00	40.00
VIVA MARIA!					
❏ United Artists UAL-4135 [M]		1965	5.00	10.00	20.00
❏ United Artists UAS-5135 [S]		1965	7.50	15.00	30.00
VIVA MAX!					
❏ RCA Victor LSP-4275		1969	5.00	10.00	20.00
THE VIXEN					
❏ Beverly Hills BHS-22		1968	12.50	25.00	50.00
VOYAGE EN BALLON					
❏ Philips PHM 200029 [M]		1960	7.50	15.00	30.00
❏ Philips PHS 600029 [S]		1960	10.00	20.00	40.00
W.W. AND THE DIXIE DANCEKINGS					
❏ 20th Century ST-103		1975	6.25	12.50	25.00
WALK DON'T RUN					
❏ Mainstream S-6080 [S]		1966	10.00	20.00	40.00
❏ Mainstream 56080 [M]		1966	5.00	10.00	20.00
WALK ON THE WILD SIDE					
❏ Ava A-4-ST [M]		1962	5.00	10.00	20.00
❏ Ava AS-4-ST [S]		1962	10.00	20.00	40.00
❏ Choreo A-4-ST [M]		1962	7.50	15.00	30.00
❏ Choreo AS-4-ST [S]		1962	12.50	25.00	50.00
A WALK WITH LOVE AND DEATH					
❏ Citadel CT-6025		1969	20.00	40.00	80.00
THE WANDERERS					
❏ Warner Bros. BSK 3359		1979	7.50	15.00	30.00
WAR AND PEACE					
❏ Columbia CL 930 [M]		1956	6.25	12.50	25.00
❏ Melodiya/Capitol SWAO 2918		1968	10.00	20.00	40.00
THE WAR LORD					
❏ Decca DL 9149 [M]		1965	6.25	12.50	25.00
❏ Decca DL 79149 [S]		1965	12.50	25.00	50.00
THE WARLOCK					
❏ Intrada MAF-7003		1990	5.00	10.00	20.00
WARNING SHOT					
❏ Liberty LRP-3498 [M]		1967	7.50	15.00	30.00
❏ Liberty LST-7498 [S]		1967	10.00	20.00	40.00
WATERLOO					
❏ Paramount PAS-6003		1971	7.50	15.00	30.00
❏ Paramount SW-93729		1971	7.50	15.00	30.00
—Capitol Record Club edition					
WATERMELON MAN					
❏ Beverly Hills BHS-26		1970	7.50	15.00	30.00
WATERSHIP DOWN					
❏ Columbia JS 35707		1978	6.25	12.50	25.00
WAY…WAY OUT					
❏ 20th Century Fox 3192 [M]		1966	7.50	15.00	30.00
❏ 20th Century Fox S-4192 [S]		1966	10.00	20.00	40.00
WEDDING IN MONACO					
❏ Mercury MG-20149 [M]		1956	62.50	125.00	250.00
WEST SIDE STORY					
❏ Columbia Masterworks OS 2070 [S]		196?	3.00	6.00	12.00
—Regular cover; gray "360 Sound Stereo" label					
❏ Columbia Masterworks OS 2070 [S]		1961	6.25	12.50	25.00
—Originals have gatefold covers and gray and black labels with six "eye" logos					
❏ Columbia Masterworks OS 2070 [S]		1963	3.75	7.50	15.00
—Gatefold cover; gray "360 Sound Stereo" label					
❏ Columbia Masterworks OS 2070 [S]		1971	2.50	5.00	10.00
—Regular cover; olive label with "Columbia" continuously around edge					
❏ Columbia Masterworks OL 5670 [M]		196?	2.50	5.00	10.00
—Regular cover; gray "360 Sound Stereo" label					
❏ Columbia Masterworks OL 5670 [M]		1961	5.00	10.00	20.00
—Originals have gatefold covers and gray and black labels with six "eye" logos					
❏ Columbia Masterworks OL 5670 [M]		1963	3.00	6.00	12.00
—Gatefold cover; gray "360 Sound Stereo" label					
WHAT A WAY TO GO!					
❏ 20th Century Fox TFM-3143 [M]		1964	5.00	10.00	20.00
❏ 20th Century Fox TFS-4143 [S]		1964	10.00	20.00	40.00
WHAT'S NEW PUSSYCAT?					
❏ United Artists UA-LA278-G		1974	3.00	6.00	12.00
—Reissue of 5128					
❏ United Artists UAL-4128 [M]		1965	5.00	10.00	20.00
❏ United Artists UAS-5128 [S]		1965	6.25	12.50	25.00
WHEN THE BOYS MEET THE GIRLS					
❏ MCA 25013		1986	2.50	5.00	10.00
—Reissue of MGM 4334					
❏ MGM E-4334 [M]		1965	3.75	7.50	15.00
❏ MGM SE-4334 [S]		1965	7.50	15.00	30.00
WHERE EAGLES DARE					
❏ MCA 25082		1986	2.50	5.00	10.00
—Reissue of MGM S1E-16					
❏ MGM S1E-16 ST		1969	7.50	15.00	30.00
WHERE'S JACK?					
❏ Paramount PAS-5005		1969	6.25	12.50	25.00
WHERE'S POPPA?					
❏ United Artists UAS-5216		1970	6.25	12.50	25.00
THE WHISPERERS					
❏ MCA 25041		1986	2.50	5.00	10.00
—Reissue of United Artists 5161					
❏ United Artists UAL-4161 [M]		1967	5.00	10.00	20.00
❏ United Artists UAS-5161 [S]		1967	7.50	15.00	30.00
WHITE CHRISTMAS					
❏ Decca DL 8083		1954	12.50	25.00	50.00
WHO FRAMED ROGER RABBIT?					
❏ Buena Vista 64100		1988	5.00	10.00	20.00
WHO'S AFRAID OF VIRGINIA WOOLF?					
❏ Warner Bros. B 1656 [M]		1966	6.25	12.50	25.00
❏ Warner Bros. BS 1656 [S]		1966	7.50	15.00	30.00
❏ Warner Bros. 2B 1657 [(2)M]		1966	10.00	20.00	40.00
—Above (1657) is the complete film, not just the music and some dialogue					
THE WILD BUNCH					
❏ Varese Sarabande STV-81145		1981	3.75	7.50	15.00
—Reissue of Warner Bros. 1814					
❏ Warner Bros. WS 1814		1969	25.00	50.00	100.00
THE WILD EYE					
❏ RCA Victor LSP-4003		1968	6.25	12.50	25.00
WILD GEESE					
❏ A&M SP-4730		1978	5.00	10.00	20.00
WILD IN THE STREETS					
❏ Tower SKAO 5099		1968	7.50	15.00	30.00
WILD IS THE WIND					
❏ Columbia CL 1090 [M]		1957	6.25	12.50	25.00
WILD ON THE BEACH					
❏ RCA Victor LPM-3441 [M]		1965	6.25	12.50	25.00
❏ RCA Victor LSP-3441 [S]		1965	10.00	20.00	40.00
THE WILD ONE					
❏ Decca DL 5515 [10]		1954	20.00	40.00	80.00
❏ Decca DL 8349 [M]		1956	10.00	20.00	40.00
THE WILD RACERS					
❏ Sidewalk ST-5914		1968	6.25	12.50	25.00
WILD WHEELS					
❏ RCA Victor LSO-1156		1969	5.00	10.00	20.00
WILD, WILD WINTER					
❏ Decca DL 4699 [M]		1966	5.00	10.00	20.00
❏ Decca DL 74699 [S]		1966	7.50	15.00	30.00
WILLIE DYNAMITE					
❏ MCA 393		1974	5.00	10.00	20.00
WILLOW					
❏ Virgin Movie Music 90939		1988	6.25	12.50	25.00
WILLY WONKA AND THE CHOCOLATE FACTORY					
❏ MCA 37124		198?	2.50	5.00	10.00
—Reissue of Paramount 6012					
❏ Paramount PAS-6012		1971	10.00	20.00	40.00
THE WITCHES OF EASTWICK					
❏ Warner Bros. 25607		1987	7.50	15.00	30.00
WITH A SONG IN MY HEART					
❏ Capitol L 309 [10]		1952	10.00	20.00	40.00
❏ Capitol T 309 [M]		195?	6.25	12.50	25.00
THE WIZARD OF OZ					
❏ MCA 39046		198?	2.50	5.00	10.00
—Reissue of MGM 3996					
❏ MGM E-3464 [M]		1956	12.50	25.00	50.00
—Yellow label					
❏ MGM E-3996 [M]		1962	3.75	7.50	15.00
—Gatefold cover, black label					
❏ MGM SE-3996 [R]		196?	3.75	7.50	15.00
—Gatefold cover, black label					
WOMEN OF THE WORLD					
❏ Decca DL 9112 [M]		1963	5.00	10.00	20.00
❏ Decca DL 79112 [S]		1963	7.50	15.00	30.00
WONDERFUL COUNTRY					
❏ United Artists UAL-4050 [M]		1959	12.50	25.00	50.00
❏ United Artists UAS-5050 [S]		1959	25.00	50.00	100.00

Number	Title (A Side/B Side)	Yr	VG	VG+	NM

WONDERFUL TO BE YOUNG
| | ❏ Dot DLP-3474 [M] | 1962 | 6.25 | 12.50 | 25.00 |
| | ❏ Dot DLP-25474 [S] | 1962 | 10.00 | 20.00 | 40.00 |

THE WONDERFUL WORLD OF THE BROTHERS GRIMM
| | ❏ MGM 1E-3 [M] | 1962 | 6.25 | 12.50 | 25.00 |
—With box and hardback book
| | ❏ MGM S1E-3 [S] | 1962 | 10.00 | 20.00 | 40.00 |
—With box and hardback book

WORDS AND MUSIC
| | ❏ MCA 25029 | 1986 | 3.00 | 6.00 | 12.00 |
—Reissue of MGM 505 with the addition of "Slaughter on Tenth Avenue," which does not appear on either the 10-inch LP or the budget-line Metro reissues
	❏ Metro M-580 [M]	1966	3.00	6.00	12.00
	❏ Metro MS-580 [R]	1966	2.50	5.00	10.00
	❏ MGM E-505 [10]	1950	12.50	25.00	50.00

THE WORLD OF SUZIE WONG
| | ❏ RCA Victor LOC-1059 [M] | 1960 | 5.00 | 10.00 | 20.00 |
| | ❏ RCA Victor LSO-1059 [S] | 1960 | 12.50 | 25.00 | 50.00 |

WRITTEN ON THE WIND
| | ❏ Decca DL 8424 [M] | 1956 | 10.00 | 20.00 | 40.00 |
—Black label, silver print, or pink label, black print promo
| | ❏ Decca DL 8424 [M] | 196? | 5.00 | 10.00 | 20.00 |
—Black label with color bars
| | ❏ Varese Sarabande VC-81074 | 1979 | 3.00 | 6.00 | 12.00 |
—Reissue of Decca 8424

THE WRONG BOX
| | ❏ Mainstream S-6088 [S] | 1966 | 37.50 | 75.00 | 150.00 |
| | ❏ Mainstream 56088 [M] | 1966 | 25.00 | 50.00 | 100.00 |

WUTHERING HEIGHTS
| | ❏ American Int'l. A-1039 | 1971 | 7.50 | 15.00 | 30.00 |

THE YELLOW CANARY
| | ❏ Verve V-8548 [M] | 1963 | 5.00 | 10.00 | 20.00 |
| | ❏ Verve V6-8548 [S] | 1963 | 6.25 | 12.50 | 25.00 |

THE YELLOW ROLLS-ROYCE
	❏ MGM E-4292 [M]	1965	5.00	10.00	20.00
	❏ MGM SE-4292 [S]	1965	7.50	15.00	30.00
	❏ MGM ST 90424 [S]	1965	3.75	7.50	15.00
—Capitol Record Club edition
| | ❏ MGM T 90424 [M] | 1965 | 3.75 | 7.50 | 15.00 |
—Capitol Record Club edition

YESTERDAY, TODAY AND TOMORROW
| | ❏ Warner Bros. W 1552 [M] | 1964 | 10.00 | 20.00 | 40.00 |
| | ❏ Warner Bros. WS 1552 [S] | 1964 | 12.50 | 25.00 | 50.00 |

YOJIMBO
| | ❏ MGM E-4096 [M] | 1962 | 25.00 | 50.00 | 100.00 |
| | ❏ MGM SE-4096 [S] | 1962 | 37.50 | 75.00 | 150.00 |

YOU ARE WHAT YOU EAT
| | ❏ Columbia Masterworks OS 3240 | 1968 | 5.00 | 10.00 | 20.00 |

YOU ONLY LIVE TWICE
| | ❏ United Artists UA-LA289-G | 1974 | 3.00 | 6.00 | 12.00 |
—Reissue of 5155
| | ❏ United Artists UAL-4155 [M] | 1967 | 5.00 | 10.00 | 20.00 |
| | ❏ United Artists UAS-5155 [S] | 1967 | 6.25 | 12.50 | 25.00 |

YOUNG BILLY YOUNG
| | ❏ MCA 25031 | 1986 | 2.50 | 5.00 | 10.00 |
—Reissue of United Artists 5199
| | ❏ United Artists UAS-5199 | 1969 | 6.25 | 12.50 | 25.00 |

YOUNG DOCTORS IN LOVE
| | ❏ Regency RI-8501 | 1982 | 5.00 | 10.00 | 20.00 |

YOUNG FRANKENSTEIN
| | ❏ ABC ABCD-870 | 1975 | 5.00 | 10.00 | 20.00 |

THE YOUNG GIRLS OF ROCHEFORT
| | ❏ Philips PCC 2-226 [(2)M] | 1968 | 5.00 | 10.00 | 20.00 |
| | ❏ Philips PCC 2-626 [(2)S] | 1968 | 7.50 | 15.00 | 30.00 |

THE YOUNG LIONS
	❏ Decca DL 8719 [M]	1958	7.50	15.00	30.00
	❏ Decca DL 78719 [S]	1958	20.00	40.00	80.00
	❏ Varese Sarabande STV-81115	1981	3.75	7.50	15.00
—Reissue of Decca 78719

YOUNG LOVERS
| | ❏ Columbia Masterworks OS 2510 [S] | 1964 | 6.25 | 12.50 | 25.00 |
| | ❏ Columbia Masterworks OL 7010 [M] | 1964 | 5.00 | 10.00 | 20.00 |

YOUNG MAN WITH A HORN
| | ❏ Columbia CL 582 [M] | 1950 | 7.50 | 15.00 | 30.00 |
| | ❏ Columbia CL 6106 [10] | 1950 | 12.50 | 25.00 | 50.00 |

THE YOUNG SAVAGES
| | ❏ Columbia CL 1672 [M] | 1961 | 7.50 | 15.00 | 30.00 |
| | ❏ Columbia CS 8472 [S] | 1961 | 25.00 | 50.00 | 100.00 |

YOUNG WINSTON
| | ❏ Angel SFO-36901 | 1972 | 6.25 | 12.50 | 25.00 |

YOURS, MINE AND OURS
| | ❏ MCA 1434 | 198? | 2.00 | 4.00 | 8.00 |
—Reissue of United Artists 5181
| | ❏ United Artists UAS-5181 | 1968 | 5.00 | 10.00 | 20.00 |

Z
| | ❏ Columbia Masterworks OS 3370 | 1970 | 5.00 | 10.00 | 20.00 |

ZABRISKIE POINT
| | ❏ MCA 25032 | 1986 | 2.50 | 5.00 | 10.00 |
—Reissue of MGM 4468
| | ❏ MGM SE-4468 | 1970 | 5.00 | 10.00 | 20.00 |

ZACHARIAH
| | ❏ ABC ABCS-OC-13 | 1970 | 6.25 | 12.50 | 25.00 |

Number	Title (A Side/B Side)	Yr	VG	VG+	NM

ZOOT SUIT
| | ❏ MCA 5267 | 1981 | 5.00 | 10.00 | 20.00 |

ZORBA THE GREEK
| | ❏ Casablanca 826245-1 | 198? | 2.00 | 4.00 | 8.00 |
—Reissue of 20th Century 903
| | ❏ 20th Century T-903 | 1973 | 3.00 | 6.00 | 12.00 |
—Reissue of 20th Century Fox 4167
| | ❏ 20th Century Fox TFM-3167 [M] | 1965 | 5.00 | 10.00 | 20.00 |
| | ❏ 20th Century Fox TFS-4167 [S] | 1965 | 6.25 | 12.50 | 25.00 |

ZULU
| | ❏ United Artists UAL-4116 [M] | 1964 | 10.00 | 20.00 | 40.00 |
| | ❏ United Artists UAS-5116 [S] | 1964 | 17.50 | 35.00 | 70.00 |

TELEVISION RECORDS

67 MELODY LANE
| | ❏ Columbia CL 724 [M] | 1955 | 7.50 | 15.00 | 30.00 |

77 SUNSET STRIP
| | ❏ Warner Bros. W 1289 [M] | 1959 | 7.50 | 15.00 | 30.00 |
| | ❏ Warner Bros. WS 1289 [S] | 1959 | 10.00 | 20.00 | 40.00 |

THE ADDAMS FAMILY
| | ❏ RCA Victor LPM-3421 [M] | 1965 | 20.00 | 40.00 | 80.00 |
| | ❏ RCA Victor LSP-3421 [S] | 1965 | 37.50 | 75.00 | 150.00 |

AFRICA
| | ❏ MGM E-4462 [M] | 1967 | 12.50 | 25.00 | 50.00 |
| | ❏ MGM SE-4462 [S] | 1967 | 15.00 | 30.00 | 60.00 |

THE AGE OF TELEVISION — A CHRONICLE OF THE FIRST 25 YEARS
| | ❏ RCA Victor LL-8 | 1972 | 5.00 | 10.00 | 20.00 |
—With booklet
| | ❏ Warner Bros. BS 2670 | 1972 | 7.50 | 15.00 | 30.00 |
—With booklet; this version seems to be much rarer than the RCA issue

ALADDIN
| | ❏ Columbia CL 1117 [M] | 1958 | 12.50 | 25.00 | 50.00 |

ALICE THROUGH THE LOOKING GLASS
| | ❏ RCA Victor LOC-1130 [M] | 1966 | 6.25 | 12.50 | 25.00 |
| | ❏ RCA Victor LSO-1130 [S] | 1966 | 7.50 | 15.00 | 30.00 |

AMAHL AND THE NIGHT VISITORS
| | ❏ RCA Red Seal LM-1701 [10] | 1952 | 12.50 | 25.00 | 50.00 |
—Soundtrack of the 1951 NBC-TV production
| | ❏ RCA Red Seal LM-1701 | 1952 | 10.00 | 20.00 | 40.00 |
—Soundtrack of the 1951 NBC-TV production; 12-inch record in box with booklet
| | ❏ RCA Red Seal LM-2762 | 1964 | 3.75 | 7.50 | 15.00 |
—Soundtrack of the 1963 NBC Opera Company TV production
| | ❏ RCA Red Seal LSC-2762 [S] | 1964 | 3.75 | 7.50 | 15.00 |
—Large "RCA Victor" and dog at top of label
| | ❏ RCA Red Seal LSC-2762 [S] | 1969 | 3.00 | 6.00 | 12.00 |
—Stereo reissue on red label without dog; no bar code on back cover
| | ❏ RCA Red Seal LSC-2762 [S] | 198? | 2.50 | 5.00 | 10.00 |
—Stereo reissue on red label without dog; with bar code on back cover

ANDROCLES AND THE LION
| | ❏ RCA Victor LOC-1141 [M] | 1967 | 6.25 | 12.50 | 25.00 |
| | ❏ RCA Victor LSO-1141 [S] | 1967 | 6.25 | 12.50 | 25.00 |

ANNIE GET YOUR GUN
| | ❏ Capitol W 913 [M] | 1957 | 7.50 | 15.00 | 30.00 |
—Los Angeles/San Francisco production aired on NBC-TV

AT HOME WITH THE MUNSTERS
| | ❏ Golden LP-139 [M] | 1964 | 50.00 | 100.00 | 200.00 |

ATOM ANT IN MUSCLE MAGIC
| | ❏ Hanna-Barbera HLP-2041 [M] | 1966 | 37.50 | 75.00 | 150.00 |

THE AVENGERS
| | ❏ Hanna-Barbera HLP-8506 [M] | 1966 | 15.00 | 30.00 | 60.00 |
| | ❏ Hanna-Barbera HST-9506 [S] | 1966 | 20.00 | 40.00 | 80.00 |

BATMAN
| | ❏ 20th Century Fox TFM-3180 [M] | 1966 | 15.00 | 30.00 | 60.00 |
| | ❏ 20th Century Fox TFS-4180 [S] | 1966 | 25.00 | 50.00 | 100.00 |

THE BEVERLY HILLBILLIES
| | ❏ Columbia CL 2402 [M] | 1965 | 10.00 | 20.00 | 40.00 |
| | ❏ Columbia CS 9202 [S] | 1965 | 15.00 | 30.00 | 60.00 |

THE BIG VALLEY
| | ❏ ABC-Paramount ABC-527 [M] | 1965 | 10.00 | 20.00 | 40.00 |
| | ❏ ABC-Paramount ABCS-527 [S] | 1965 | 12.50 | 25.00 | 50.00 |

THE BORN LOSERS
| | ❏ Tower DT 5082 [R] | 1967 | 5.00 | 10.00 | 20.00 |
| | ❏ Tower T 5082 [M] | 1967 | 6.25 | 12.50 | 25.00 |

THE BORROWERS
| | ❏ Stanyan SRQ-4014 [Q] | 1973 | 12.50 | 25.00 | 50.00 |

BOURBON STREET BEAT
| | ❏ Warner Bros. W 1321 [M] | 1960 | 6.25 | 12.50 | 25.00 |
| | ❏ Warner Bros. WS 1321 [S] | 1960 | 7.50 | 15.00 | 30.00 |

BRIGADOON
| | ❏ Columbia Special Products CSM 385 | 1968 | 5.00 | 10.00 | 20.00 |
—Sold through the mail by broadcast sponsor Armstrong

BURKE'S LAW
| | ❏ Liberty LRP-3374 [M] | 1964 | 15.00 | 30.00 | 60.00 |
| | ❏ Liberty LST-7374 [S] | 1964 | 20.00 | 40.00 | 80.00 |

CAROUSEL
| | ❏ Columbia Special Products CSM 479 | 1969 | 5.00 | 10.00 | 20.00 |
—Sold through the mail by broadcast sponsor Armstrong

A CHARLIE BROWN CHRISTMAS
| | ❏ Charlie Brown 3701 | 1977 | 5.00 | 10.00 | 20.00 |
—Complete soundtrack with dialogue, plus music by Vince Guaraldi; includes 12-page bound-in booklet with script and illustrations

Number	Title (A Side/B Side)	Yr	VG	VG+	NM
CHECKMATE					
❏ Columbia CL 1591 [M]		1960	10.00	20.00	40.00
❏ Columbia CS 8391 [S]		1960	15.00	30.00	60.00
CINDERELLA					
❏ Columbia Masterworks OS 2005 [S]		1959	10.00	20.00	40.00
—Stage presentation for TV starring Julie Andrews					
❏ Columbia Masterworks OS 2730 [S]		1965	7.50	15.00	30.00
—Stage presentation for TV starring Lesley-Ann Warren					
❏ Columbia Masterworks OL 5190 [M]		1957	7.50	15.00	30.00
❏ Columbia Masterworks OL 6330 [M]		1965	6.25	12.50	25.00
THE COMING OF CHRIST					
❏ Decca DL 9093 [M]		1960	10.00	20.00	40.00
❏ Decca DL 79093 [S]		1960	12.50	25.00	50.00
THE CRICKET ON THE HEARTH					
❏ RCA Victor LOC-1140 [M]		1967	5.00	10.00	20.00
❏ RCA Victor LSO-1140 [S]		1967	7.50	15.00	30.00
DANGER					
❏ MGM E-111 [10]		1951	30.00	60.00	120.00
THE DANGEROUS CHRISTMAS OF RED RIDING HOOD					
❏ ABC-Paramount ABC-536 [M]		1965	3.75	7.50	15.00
❏ ABC-Paramount ABCS-536 [S]		1965	6.25	12.50	25.00
DARK SHADOWS					
❏ Philips PHS 600314		1969	7.50	15.00	30.00
—With poster					
DAVID COPPERFIELD					
❏ GRT 10008		1970	37.50	75.00	150.00
DENNIS THE MENACE SONGS					
❏ Golden LP-59 [M]		1960	20.00	40.00	80.00
—Black label original					
DOGGIE DADDY TELLS AUGGY DOGGIE THE STORY OF PINOCCHIO					
❏ Hanna-Barbera HLP-2028 [M]		1965	25.00	50.00	100.00
EAST SIDE, WEST SIDE					
❏ Columbia CL 2123 [M]		1963	7.50	15.00	30.00
❏ Columbia CS 8923 [S]		1963	10.00	20.00	40.00
ELEVEN AGAINST THE ICE					
❏ RCA Victor LPM-1618 [M]		1958	15.00	30.00	60.00
ELIZABETH TAYLOR IN LONDON					
❏ Colpix CP 459 [M]		1963	7.50	15.00	30.00
❏ Colpix SCP 459 [S]		1963	12.50	25.00	50.00
THE EWOK ADVENTURE					
❏ Varese Sarabande STV-81281		198?	12.50	25.00	50.00
EXCITING HONG KONG					
❏ ABC-Paramount ABC-367 [M]		1961	10.00	20.00	40.00
❏ ABC-Paramount ABCS-367 [S]		1961	12.50	25.00	50.00
FAWLTY TOWERS					
❏ BBC 22377		1980	5.00	10.00	20.00
—Excerpts from two episodes of the series; pressed by Columbia, possibly for exclusive use by the record club					
FAWTLY TOWERS — SECOND SITTING					
❏ BBC 22405		1981	5.00	10.00	20.00
—More excerpts from the series; again, pressed by Columbia possibly for exclusive record club use					
FELIX THE CAT					
❏ Cricket CR-28 [M]		1958	25.00	50.00	100.00
FENWICK					
❏ Fenwick FLP-621		1968	5.00	10.00	20.00
—Soundtrack to TV special; packaged in oversize (13 1/2 x 13 1/2) sleeve with color cartoon booklet; made especially for Motorola					
THE FLINTSTONES					
❏ Colpix CP-302 [M]		1961	50.00	100.00	200.00
THE FLINTSTONES AND JOSE JIMENEZ IN THE TIME MACHINE					
❏ Hanna-Barbera HLP-2052 [M]		1966	20.00	40.00	80.00
THE FLINTSTONES IN S.A.S.F.A.T.P.O.G.O.B.S.O.A.L.T.					
❏ Hanna-Barbera HLP-2047 [M]		1966	25.00	50.00	100.00
THE FLINTSTONES' FLIP FABLES: GOLDI-ROCKS AND THE THREE BEAROSAURUSES					
❏ Hanna-Barbera HLP-2021 [M]		1965	25.00	50.00	100.00
THE FORD 50TH ANNIVERSARY TELEVISION SHOW					
❏ Decca DL 7027 [10]		1953	10.00	20.00	40.00
FOUR ADVENTURES OF ZORRO					
❏ Disneyland WDA-3601 [M]		1958	20.00	40.00	80.00
—Gatefold with booklet					
FRED FLINTSTONE AND BARNEY RUBBLE SING SONGS FROM MARY POPPINS					
❏ Hanna-Barbera HLP-2035 [M]		1965	25.00	50.00	100.00
FROSTY THE SNOWMAN					
❏ MGM SE-4733		1970	15.00	30.00	60.00
FROSTY'S WINTER WONDERLAND					
❏ Disneyland 1368		1976	5.00	10.00	20.00
GENERAL ELECTRIC THEATER					
❏ Columbia CL 1395 [M]		1959	10.00	20.00	40.00
❏ Columbia CS 8190 [S]		1959	12.50	25.00	50.00
GENERAL MOTORS' 50TH ANNIVERSARY SHOW					
❏ RCA Victor LOC-1037 [M]		1958	25.00	50.00	100.00
GET SMART					
❏ United Artists UAL-3533 [M]		1965	10.00	20.00	40.00
❏ United Artists UAS-6566 [S]		1965	15.00	30.00	60.00
THE GIFT OF LOVE					
❏ Columbia CL 1113 [M]		1958	7.50	15.00	30.00
THE GIFT OF THE MAGI					
❏ United Artists UAL-4013 [M]		1959	10.00	20.00	40.00
❏ United Artists UAS-5103 [S]		1959	12.50	25.00	50.00

Number	Title (A Side/B Side)	Yr	VG	VG+	NM
THE GIRL FROM U.N.C.L.E.					
❏ MGM E-4410 [M]		1966	10.00	20.00	40.00
❏ MGM SE-4410 [S]		1966	15.00	30.00	60.00
GOOFY'S TV SPECTACULAR					
❏ Disneyland DQ-1252 [M]		1964	5.00	10.00	20.00
THE GREEN HORNET					
❏ 20th Century Fox S-3186 [S]		1966	62.50	125.00	250.00
❏ 20th Century Fox TF-3186 [M]		1966	50.00	100.00	200.00
HANS BRINKER					
❏ Dot DLP-9001 [M]		1958	10.00	20.00	40.00
HANSEL AND GRETEL STARRING THE FLINTSTONES					
❏ Hanna-Barbera HLP-2038 [M]		1965	25.00	50.00	100.00
HAWAII FIVE-O					
❏ Capitol ST-410		1969	10.00	20.00	40.00
HAWAIIAN EYE					
❏ Warner Bros. W 1355 [M]		1959	7.50	15.00	30.00
❏ Warner Bros. WS 1355 [S]		1959	10.00	20.00	40.00
HECTOR, THE STOWAWAY PUP					
❏ Disneyland ST-1921 [M]		1964	7.50	15.00	30.00
HEIDI					
❏ Capitol SKAO 2995		1968	10.00	20.00	40.00
HENNESSEY					
❏ Signature 1049 [M]		1959	15.00	30.00	60.00
❏ Signature SS-1049 [S]		1959	20.00	40.00	80.00
HERE COMES HUCKLEBERRY HOUND					
❏ Colpix CP-207 [M]		1961	45.00	90.00	180.00
HERE'S JOHNNY! MAGIC MOMENTS FROM THE TONIGHT SHOW					
❏ Casablanca SPNB-1296 [(2)]		1976	5.00	10.00	20.00
—Price for intact copies with poster; cut-outs go for 50-75 percent of this					
HEY THERE, IT'S YOGI BEAR					
❏ Golden LP-124 [M]		1964	10.00	20.00	40.00
HIGH TOR					
❏ Decca DL 8272 [M]		1956	50.00	100.00	200.00
THE HILLBILLY BEARS IN HILLBILLY SHINDIG					
❏ Hanna-Barbera HLP-2044 [M]		1966	37.50	75.00	150.00
HOGAN'S HEROES SING THE BEST OF WWII					
❏ Sunset SUM-1137 [M]		1967	7.50	15.00	30.00
❏ Sunset SUS-5137 [S]		1967	10.00	20.00	40.00
HOLOCAUST					
❏ RCA Victor ARL1-2785		1978	6.25	12.50	25.00
HONEY WEST					
❏ ABC-Paramount ABC-532 [M]		1965	10.00	20.00	40.00
❏ ABC-Paramount ABCS-532 [S]		1965	12.50	25.00	50.00
HOW THE GRINCH STOLE CHRISTMAS					
❏ Leo LE-901 [M]		1966	12.50	25.00	50.00
❏ Leo LES-901 [S]		1966	17.50	35.00	70.00
❏ Mercury Nashville 528439-1		1995	5.00	10.00	20.00
—Picture disc					
HOWL ALONG WITH HUCKLEBERRY HOUND AND YOGI BEAR					
❏ Golden LP-55 [M]		1959	37.50	75.00	150.00
—Black label original					
HUCKLEBERRY HOUND AND THE GHOST SHIP					
❏ Colpix CP-210 [M]		1962	25.00	50.00	100.00
HUCKLEBERRY HOUND FOR PRESIDENT					
❏ Golden LP-60 [M]		1960	25.00	50.00	100.00
—Black label original					
HUCKLEBERRY HOUND TELLS STORIES OF UNCLE REMUS					
❏ Hanna-Barbera HLP-2022 [M]		1965	25.00	50.00	100.00
HUCKLEBERRY HOUND, THE GREAT KELLOGG'S TV SHOW					
❏ Colpix CP-202 [M]		1959	50.00	100.00	200.00
I SPY					
❏ Warner Bros. W 1637 [M]		1965	7.50	15.00	30.00
❏ Warner Bros. WS 1637 [S]		1965	10.00	20.00	40.00
I SPY, VOLUME 2					
❏ Capitol ST 2839		1968	7.50	15.00	30.00
IT'S HOWDY DOODY TIME					
❏ RCA Victor LSP-4546		1971	6.25	12.50	25.00
THE JACKSONS: AN AMERICAN DREAM					
❏ Motown 37463 6356-1 [DJ]		1992	5.00	10.00	20.00
—Promo only vinyl					
JAMES BOMB STARRING SUPER SNOOPER AND BLABBER MOUSE					
❏ Hanna-Barbera HLP-2036 [M]		1965	25.00	50.00	100.00
JANE EYRE					
❏ Capitol SW-749		1971	7.50	15.00	30.00
THE JETSONS					
❏ Colpix CP-213 [M]		1962	62.50	125.00	250.00
❏ Golden LP-98 [M]		1963	50.00	100.00	200.00
—Red cover original					
❏ Golden LP-98 [M]		1964	30.00	60.00	120.00
—Blue cover reissue					
THE JETSONS IN FIRST FAMILY ON THE MOON					
❏ Hanna-Barbera HLP-2037 [M]		1965	37.50	75.00	150.00
THE JIMMY DURANTE TV SHOW					
❏ Royale 1812 [10]		1955	25.00	50.00	100.00
JONNY QUEST IN 20,000 LEAGUES UNDER THE SEA					
❏ Hanna-Barbera HLP-2030 [M]		1965	37.50	75.00	150.00
JOURNEY BACK TO OZ					
❏ Filmation (no #)		1980	12.50	25.00	50.00

Number	Title (A Side/B Side)	Yr	VG	VG+	NM
KENT STATE					
❑ RCA Victor ABL1-3928		1981	5.00	10.00	20.00
KING KONG					
❑ Golden LP-151 [M]		1965	10.00	20.00	40.00
KISS ME, KATE					
❑ Columbia Special Products CSS 645		1968	6.25	12.50	25.00
—*Sold through the mail by broadcast sponsor Armstrong*					
A LOOK AT MONACO					
❑ Columbia CL 2019 [M]		1963	12.50	25.00	50.00
❑ Columbia CS 8819 [R]		1963	12.50	25.00	50.00
LOVE, AMERICAN STYLE					
❑ Capitol ST-11250		1973	10.00	20.00	40.00
MAGILLA GORILLA AND HIS PALS					
❑ Golden LP-120 [M]		1964	12.50	25.00	50.00
MAGILLA GORILLA TELLS OGEE THE STORY OF ALICE IN WONDERLAND					
❑ Hanna-Barbera HLP-2024 [M]		1965	25.00	50.00	100.00
THE MAN FROM INTERPOL					
❑ Top Rank RM-327 [M]		1962	12.50	25.00	50.00
❑ Top Rank RS-627 [S]		1962	15.00	30.00	60.00
THE MAN FROM U.N.C.L.E.					
❑ RCA Victor LPM-3475 [M]		1965	15.00	30.00	60.00
❑ RCA Victor LSP-3475 [S]		1965	20.00	40.00	80.00
THE MAN FROM U.N.C.L.E. VOLUME 2					
❑ RCA Victor LPM-3574 [M]		1966	10.00	20.00	40.00
❑ RCA Victor LSP-3574 [S]		1966	12.50	25.00	50.00
MARK TWAIN TONIGHT!					
❑ Columbia Masterworks OS 3080 [S]		1967	5.00	10.00	20.00
❑ Columbia Masterworks OL 6680 [M]		1967	3.75	7.50	15.00
MASADA					
❑ MCA 5168		1981	5.00	10.00	20.00
MERRY CHRISTMAS FROM KUKLA, FRAN AND OLLIE					
❑ Decca DL 8192 [M]		1955	20.00	40.00	80.00
MICKEY MOUSE CLUB — ALL NEW FROM 1977 — ORIGINAL TV CAST					
❑ Buena Vista 62501		1979	5.00	10.00	20.00
MICKEY MOUSE CLUB MOUSEKEDANCES AND OTHER MOUSEKETEER FAVORITES					
❑ Disneyland DQ-1362 [M]		1974	5.00	10.00	20.00
—*With booklet*					
❑ Disneyland STER-1362 [S]		1974	6.25	12.50	25.00
—*With booklet*					
MICKEY MOUSE CLUB SONG HITS					
❑ Disneyland ST-3815		1975	10.00	20.00	40.00
—*With 16-page photo album*					
MICKEY MOUSE CLUB: 27 NEW SONGS FROM THE MICKEY MOUSE CLUB TV SHOW					
❑ Mickey Mouse Club MM-14		1958	12.50	25.00	50.00
MICKEY MOUSE CLUB: A WALT DISNEY SONG FEST					
❑ Mickey Mouse Club MM-20		1958	10.00	20.00	40.00
MICKEY MOUSE CLUB: FUN WITH MUSIC — 30 FAVORITE DISNEY SONGS					
❑ Disneyland DQ-1209 [M]		1959	6.25	12.50	25.00
MICKEY MOUSE CLUB: HOLIDAYS WITH THE MOUSEKETEERS (A SONG FOR EVERY HOLIDAY)					
❑ Mickey Mouse Club MM-22		1958	10.00	20.00	40.00
MICKEY MOUSE CLUB: HOW TO BE A MOUSEKETEER					
❑ Disneyland ST-3918		1962	10.00	20.00	40.00
MICKEY MOUSE CLUB: MOUSEKETEERS TALENT ROUNDUP					
❑ Mickey Mouse Club MM-16		1958	10.00	20.00	40.00
MICKEY MOUSE CLUB: MUSICAL HIGHLIGHTS FROM THE MICKEY MOUSE CLUB					
❑ Disneyland DQ-1227 [M]		1962	7.50	15.00	30.00
MICKEY MOUSE CLUB: MUSICAL HIGHLIGHTS FROM THE MICKEY MOUSE CLUB TV SHOW					
❑ Mickey Mouse Club MM-12		1958	20.00	40.00	80.00
MICKEY MOUSE CLUB: SONGS FROM ANNETTE AND OTHER WALT DISNEY SERIALS					
❑ Mickey Mouse Club MM-24		1958	30.00	60.00	120.00
MICKEY MOUSE CLUB: SONGS FROM THE MICKEY MOUSE CLUB SERIALS					
❑ Disneyland DQ-1229 [M]		1962	10.00	20.00	40.00
MICKEY MOUSE CLUB: THE ALL NEW MICKEY MOUSE CLUB					
❑ Disneyland 2501		1977	5.00	10.00	20.00
MICKEY MOUSE CLUB: WE'RE THE MOUSEKETEERS					
❑ Mickey Mouse Club MM-18		1957	10.00	20.00	40.00
THE MIGHTY HERCULES					
❑ Golden LP-109 [M]		1963	50.00	100.00	200.00
MIKADO					
❑ Columbia Masterworks OS 2022 [S]		1960	25.00	50.00	100.00
❑ Columbia Masterworks OL 5480 [M]		1960	7.50	15.00	30.00
THE MISADVENTURES OF DENNIS THE MENACE					
❑ Colpix CP-204 [M]		1960	50.00	100.00	200.00
MR. BROADWAY					
❑ RCA Victor LPM-1520 [M]		1957	7.50	15.00	30.00
MR. ED, THE TALKING HORSE					
❑ Colpix CP-209 [M]		1962	75.00	150.00	300.00
MR. ED: STRAIGHT FROM THE HORSE'S MOUTH					
❑ Golden LP-88 [M]		1962	50.00	100.00	200.00
MR. JINKS, PIXIE AND DIXIE					
❑ Colpix CP-208 [M]		1961	25.00	50.00	100.00
THE MUNSTERS					
❑ Decca DL 4588 [M]		1964	15.00	30.00	60.00
❑ Decca DL 74588 [S]		1964	25.00	50.00	100.00
THE MUSIC FROM M SQUAD					
❑ RCA Victor LPM-2062 [M]		1959	7.50	15.00	30.00
❑ RCA Victor LSP-2062 [S]		1959	10.00	20.00	40.00
THE MUSIC FROM MARLBORO COUNTRY					
❑ United Artists SP-107		1967	12.50	25.00	50.00
MUSIC FROM SHUBERT ALLEY					
❑ Sinclair OSS-2250 [M]		1959	10.00	20.00	40.00
—*From the NBC TV program, November 13, 1959*					
NAKED CITY — A MUSICAL PORTRAIT					
❑ Colpix CP-505 [M]		1958	10.00	20.00	40.00
❑ Colpix SCP-505 [S]		1959	15.00	30.00	60.00
OF THEE I SING					
❑ Columbia S 31763		1972	5.00	10.00	20.00
THE OFFICIAL ALBUM OF NBC'S BAT MASTERSON					
❑ Sea Horse/Chancellor CSH-7002 [M]		1960	20.00	40.00	80.00
ON THE FLIP SIDE					
❑ Decca DL 4836		1966	6.25	12.50	25.00
❑ Decca DL 74836 [S]		1966	7.50	15.00	30.00
ONE STEP BEYOND					
❑ Decca DL 8970 [M]		1960	7.50	15.00	30.00
❑ Decca DL 78970 [S]		1960	10.00	20.00	40.00
ORIGINAL AMATEUR HOUR 25TH ANNIVERSARY ALBUM					
❑ United Artists UXL 2 [(2)M]		1960	10.00	20.00	40.00
THE ORIGINAL TV ADVENTURES OF KING KONG					
❑ Epic LN 24231 [M]		1966	6.25	12.50	25.00
❑ Epic BN 26231 [S]		1966	7.50	15.00	30.00
THE OTHER WORLD OF WINSTON CHURCHILL					
❑ Mercury MG-21033 [M]		1965	7.50	15.00	30.00
❑ Mercury SR-61033 [S]		1965	10.00	20.00	40.00
OZZIE AND HARRIET					
❑ Imperial LP-9049 [M]		1957	50.00	100.00	200.00
PEYTON PLACE					
❑ Epic LN 24147 [M]		1965	7.50	15.00	30.00
❑ Epic BN 26147 [S]		1965	10.00	20.00	40.00
THE PIED PIPER OF HAMELIN					
❑ RCA Victor LPM-1563 [M]		1957	12.50	25.00	50.00
PINOCCHIO					
❑ Columbia CL 1055 [M]		1957	10.00	20.00	40.00
PIXIE AND DIXIE WITH MR. JINKS TELL THE STORY OF CINDERELLA					
❑ Hanna-Barbera HLP-2025 [M]		1965	25.00	50.00	100.00
PRECIOUS PUPP IN HOT ROD GRANNY					
❑ Hanna-Barbera HLP-2045 [M]		1966	37.50	75.00	150.00
QUICK DRAW MCGRAW					
❑ Colpix CP-203 [M]		1960	20.00	40.00	80.00
QUICK DRAW MCGRAW AND HUCKLEBERRY HOUND					
❑ Golden LP-51 [M]		1959	37.50	75.00	150.00
—*Black label original*					
QUICK DRAW MCGRAW: THE TREASURE OF SARAH'S MATTRESS					
❑ Colpix CP-211 [M]		1962	30.00	60.00	120.00
THE REPORTER					
❑ Columbia CL 2269 [M]		1964	7.50	15.00	30.00
❑ Columbia CS 9069 [S]		1964	10.00	20.00	40.00
RICH MAN, POOR MAN					
❑ MCA 2095		1976	6.25	12.50	25.00
RICHARD DIAMOND					
❑ EmArcy MG-36162 [M]		1959	12.50	25.00	50.00
❑ EmArcy SR-80045 [S]		1959	20.00	40.00	80.00
THE RISE AND FALL OF THE THIRD REICH					
❑ MGM 1SE-12		1968	7.50	15.00	30.00
ROBIN HOOD STARRING TOP CAT					
❑ Hanna-Barbera HLP-2031 [M]		1965	25.00	50.00	100.00
ROCKY AND HIS FRIENDS					
❑ Golden LP-64 [M]		1961	50.00	100.00	200.00
—*Gold label original*					
THE ROGUES					
❑ RCA Victor LPM-2976 [M]		1964	5.00	10.00	20.00
❑ RCA Victor LSP-2976 [S]		1964	7.50	15.00	30.00
ROOTS					
❑ Warner Bros. 3WS 3048 [(3)]		1978	6.25	12.50	25.00
RUDOLPH THE RED-NOSED REINDEER					
❑ Decca DL 4815 [M]		1964	15.00	30.00	60.00
❑ Decca DL 34327 [M]		1965	10.00	20.00	40.00
—*Same as DL 4815; custom products reissue*					
❑ Decca DL 74815 [S]		1964	20.00	40.00	80.00
❑ MCA 15003		1973	5.00	10.00	20.00
—*Reissue; black rainbow label*					
❑ MCA 15003		198?	3.00	6.00	12.00
—*Reissue; blue rainbow label*					
RUFF AND READY ADVENTURES IN SPACE					
❑ Colpix CP-201 [M]		1959	50.00	100.00	200.00
RUGGLES OF RED GAP					
❑ Verve MGV-15000 [M]		1957	12.50	25.00	50.00
THE SAINT					
❑ RCA Victor LPM-3631 [M]		1966	30.00	60.00	120.00
❑ RCA Victor LSP-3631 [S]		1966	50.00	100.00	200.00
SANTA CLAUS IS COMIN' TO TOWN					
❑ MGM SE-4732		1970	15.00	30.00	60.00

Number	Title (A Side/B Side)	Yr	VG	VG+	NM
SATINS AND SPURS					
❑ Capitol L 547 [10]		1954	17.50	35.00	70.00
SECRET AGENT					
❑ RCA Victor LPM-3630 [M]		1966	62.50	125.00	250.00
❑ RCA Victor LSP-3630 [S]		1966	62.50	125.00	250.00
—With incorrect title, "Danger Man," on label					
❑ RCA Victor LSP-3630 [S]		1966	75.00	150.00	300.00
—With correct title on label					
SECRET AGENT MEETS THE SAINT					
❑ RCA Victor LPM-3467 [M]		1965	50.00	100.00	200.00
❑ RCA Victor LSP-3467 [S]		1965	55.00	110.00	220.00
—Music from both TV shows; pre-dates the individual albums					
SECRET SQUIRREL AND MOROCCO MOLE IN SUPER SPY					
❑ Hanna-Barbera HLP-2046 [M]		1966	37.50	75.00	150.00
SHOGUN					
❑ RSO RX-1-3088		1981	5.00	10.00	20.00
SHOTGUN SLADE					
❑ Mercury MG-20575 [M]		1960	10.00	20.00	40.00
❑ Mercury SR-60235 [S]		1960	15.00	30.00	60.00
SINBAD JR. IN TREASURE ISLAND					
❑ Hanna-Barbera HLP-2039 [M]		1965	30.00	60.00	120.00
SNAGGLEPUSS TELLS THE STORY OF THE WIZARD OF OZ					
❑ Hanna-Barbera HLP-2026 [M]		1965	25.00	50.00	100.00
SONGS OF THE FLINTSTONES					
❑ Golden LP-66 [M]		1961	62.50	125.00	250.00
—Gold label original					
SONGS OF YOGI BEAR AND HIS PALS					
❑ Golden LP-70 [M]		1961	20.00	40.00	80.00
—Gold label original					
THE SOUND OF JAZZ					
❑ Columbia CL 1098 [M]		1958	6.25	12.50	25.00
❑ Columbia CS 8040 [S]		1958	10.00	20.00	40.00
SPACE: 1999					
❑ RCA Victor ABL1-1422		1975	5.00	10.00	20.00
SQUIDDLEY DIDDLEY IN SURFIN' SAFARI					
❑ Hanna-Barbera HLP-2043 [M]		1966	37.50	75.00	150.00
STACCATO (MUSIC FROM JOHNNY STACCATO)					
❑ Capitol ST 1287 [S]		1959	12.50	25.00	50.00
❑ Capitol T 1287 [M]		1959	7.50	15.00	30.00
THE STINGIEST MAN IN TOWN					
❑ Columbia CL 950		1956	5.00	10.00	20.00
—Music from a television play first aired on The Alcoa Hour					
❑ Columbia Special Products P 12637		1975	2.50	5.00	10.00
—Reissue of Columbia LP; same contents					
SUPER SNOOPER AND BLABBER MOUSE IN MONSTER SHINDIG					
❑ Hanna-Barbera HLP-2020 [M]		1965	25.00	50.00	100.00
THRILLER					
❑ Time S-2034 [S]		1960	10.00	20.00	40.00
❑ Time 52034 [M]		1960	7.50	15.00	30.00
TOM SAWYER					
❑ Decca DL 8432 [M]		1957	10.00	20.00	40.00
—First aired on the U.S. Steel Hour, starring Jimmy Boyd					
TOP CAT					
❑ Colpix CP-212 [M]		1963	75.00	150.00	300.00
TOUCHE TURTLE AND DUM-DUM IN THE RELUCTANT DRAGON					
❑ Hanna-Barbera HLP-2029 [M]		1965	25.00	50.00	100.00
TWAS THE NIGHT BEFORE CHRISTMAS					
❑ Disneyland 1367		1976	5.00	10.00	20.00
THE UNTOUCHABLES					
❑ Capitol ST 1430 [S]		1960	12.50	25.00	50.00
❑ Capitol T 1430 [M]		1960	10.00	20.00	40.00
UP WITH PEOPLE!					
❑ Pace 1101		1965	5.00	10.00	20.00
—Among the many people on this LP is a young Glenn Close (first name misspelled "Gleen")					
THE VALIANT YEARS					
❑ ABC-Paramount ABC-387 [M]		1962	7.50	15.00	30.00
❑ ABC-Paramount ABCS-387 [S]		1962	10.00	20.00	40.00
VICTORY AT SEA					
❑ Mobile Fidelity 3-150 [(3)]		1984	25.00	50.00	100.00
—Audiophile vinyl					
❑ RCA Victor LM-1779 [M]		1954	6.25	12.50	25.00
—Original recording					
❑ RCA Victor LM-2335 [M]		1959	5.00	10.00	20.00
—Re-recording of 1779					
❑ RCA Victor LSC-2335 [S]		1959	5.00	10.00	20.00
—Re-recording of 1779 in stereo					
VICTORY AT SEA, VOL. 2					
❑ RCA Victor LM-2226 [M]		1958	5.00	10.00	20.00
❑ RCA Victor LSC-2226 [S]		1958	6.25	12.50	25.00
—Original with "shaded dog" label					
VICTORY AT SEA, VOL. 3					
❑ RCA Victor LM-2523 [M]		1961	5.00	10.00	20.00
❑ RCA Victor LSC-2523 [S]		1961	6.25	12.50	25.00
WAGON TRAIN					
❑ Mercury MG-20502 [M]		1959	12.50	25.00	50.00
❑ Mercury SR-60179 [S]		1959	20.00	40.00	80.00
WALT DISNEY'S WONDERFUL WORLD OF COLOR					
❑ Disneyland DQ-1245 [M]		1963	7.50	15.00	30.00
WASHINGTON: BEHIND CLOSED DOORS					
❑ ABC AB-1044		1977	6.25	12.50	25.00

Number	Title (A Side/B Side)	Yr	VG	VG+	NM
WIDE, WIDE WORLD					
❑ RCA Victor LPM-1280 [M]		1956	10.00	20.00	40.00
WILMA FLINTSTONE TELLS THE STORY OF BAMBI					
❑ Hanna-Barbera HLP-2027 [M]		1965	25.00	50.00	100.00
THE WINDS OF WAR					
❑ Varese Sarabande STV-81180		1983	5.00	10.00	20.00
WINSOME WITCH IN IT'S MAGIC					
❑ Hanna-Barbera HLP-2042 [M]		1966	37.50	75.00	150.00
WONDERFUL TOWN					
❑ Columbia Masterworks OS 2008 [S]		1958	6.25	12.50	25.00
❑ Columbia Masterworks OL 5360 [M]		1958	5.00	10.00	20.00
YOGI BEAR AND BOO-BOO					
❑ Colpix CP-205 [M]		1961	30.00	60.00	120.00
YOGI BEAR AND BOO-BOO TELL STORIES OF LITTLE RED RIDING HOOD AND JACK AND THE BEANSTALK					
❑ Hanna-Barbera HLP-2023 [M]		1965	25.00	50.00	100.00
YOGI BEAR AND THE THREE STOOGES IN THE MAD, MAD, DR. NO-NO					
❑ Hanna-Barbera HLP-2050 [M]		1966	25.00	50.00	100.00
YOGI BEAR: HOW TO BE A BETTER THAN AVERAGE CHILD					
❑ Golden LP-90 [M]		1962	20.00	40.00	80.00

VARIOUS ARTISTS COLLECTIONS

Number	Title (A Side/B Side)	Yr	VG	VG+	NM
12 + 3 = 15 HITS					
❑ End LP 310 [M]		1961	15.00	30.00	60.00
12 FLIP HITS					
❑ Flip 1001 [M]		1959	75.00	150.00	300.00
THE 12 GREATEST OLDIES IN THE WHOLE WORLD, EVER					
❑ Parkway P-7031 [M]		1963	7.50	15.00	30.00
12 MILLION SELLERS					
❑ Forum F-9057 [M]		1963	5.00	10.00	20.00
❑ Forum SF-9057 [R]		1963	3.75	7.50	15.00
12 SONGS OF CHRISTMAS					
❑ Reprise F-2022 [M]		1964	5.00	10.00	20.00
❑ Reprise FS-2022 [S]		1964	3.75	7.50	15.00
12 TOP TEEN DANCES 1961-1962					
❑ Cameo C-1016 [M]		1962	7.50	15.00	30.00
14 GOLDEN RECORDINGS FROM THE HISTORIC VAULTS OF DUKE-PEACOCK RECORDS					
❑ ABC ABCX-784		1973	5.00	10.00	20.00
14 GOLDEN RECORDINGS FROM THE HISTORIC VAULTS OF DUKE-PEACOCK RECORDS, VOLUME 2					
❑ ABC ABCX-789		1973	5.00	10.00	20.00
14 GREAT ALL TIME C&W WALTZES					
❑ King 890 [M]		1964	17.50	35.00	70.00
14 HIT FLASHBACKS FROM THE GOLDEN GROUP ERA					
❑ King 893 [M]		1964	17.50	35.00	70.00
14 MORE NEWIES BUT GOODIES					
❑ Mercury MG-20493 [M]		1960	7.50	15.00	30.00
❑ Mercury SR-60241 [S]		1960	10.00	20.00	40.00
14 NEWIES BUT GOODIES					
❑ Mercury MG-20493 [M]		1960	7.50	15.00	30.00
❑ Mercury SR-60172 [S]		1960	10.00	20.00	40.00
15 FAVORITES					
❑ Hickory LPM-105 [M]		1962	6.25	12.50	25.00
15 GOLDEN HITS					
❑ United Artists UAL-3192 [M]		1962	6.25	12.50	25.00
❑ United Artists UAS-6192 [S]		1962	7.50	15.00	30.00
15 HITS: THE ORIGINAL RECORDINGS (THE ORIGINAL HITS, VOLUME 5)					
❑ Liberty LRP-3235 [M]		1962	5.00	10.00	20.00
16 GOODIES — BLASTS FROM THE PAST					
❑ Blast BLP-6803 [M]		1964	10.00	20.00	40.00
16 ORIGINAL BIG HITS, VOLUME 2					
❑ Tamla TM 256 [M]		1964	5.00	10.00	20.00
16 ORIGINAL BIG HITS, VOLUME 3					
❑ Motown MT 624 [M]		1965	5.00	10.00	20.00
16 ORIGINAL BIG HITS, VOLUME 4					
❑ Motown M 633 [M]		1965	3.75	7.50	15.00
❑ Motown MS 633 [S]		1965	5.00	10.00	20.00
18 ALL TIME COUNTRY AND WESTERN HITS					
❑ King 1027 [M]		1968	7.50	15.00	30.00
18 ALL TIME RHYTHM 'N' BLUES HITS					
❑ King 1026 [M]		1968	7.50	15.00	30.00
18 KING-SIZE COUNTRY HITS					
❑ Columbia CL 2668 [M]		1967	5.00	10.00	20.00
❑ Columbia CS 9468 [R]		1967	5.00	10.00	20.00
18 KING-SIZE RHYTHM AND BLUES HITS					
❑ Columbia CL 2667 [M]		1967	7.50	15.00	30.00
❑ Columbia CS 9467 [R]		1967	5.00	10.00	20.00
THE 1969 WARNER/REPRISE RECORD SHOW					
❑ Warner Bros. PRO 336 [(2)]		1969	7.50	15.00	30.00
—Originals have "W7" logos on labels					
❑ Warner Bros. PRO 336 [(2)]		197?	3.75	7.50	15.00
—With "WB" logos on labels					
THE 1969 WARNER/REPRISE SONGBOOK					
❑ Warner Bros. PRO 331 [(2)]		1969	7.50	15.00	30.00
—The first of the famous Warner/Reprise "Loss Leaders" mail-order series; originals have "W7" logos on labels					

Number / Title (A Side/B Side)	Yr	VG	VG+	NM
❑ Warner Bros. PRO 331 [(2)]	197?	3.75	7.50	15.00
—With "WB" logos on labels				
20 ALL TIME NO. 1 HITS				
❑ Roulette R 25290 [M]	1965	5.00	10.00	20.00
❑ Roulette SR 25290 [R]	1965	3.00	6.00	12.00
20 BIG BOSS FAVORITES: 10 GREAT HITS OF 1964 — 10 GREAT OLDIES HITS				
❑ Roulette R 25304 [M]	1965	5.00	10.00	20.00
❑ Roulette SR 25304 [R]	1965	3.75	7.50	15.00
—Of the 20 tracks, only "Laugh, Laugh" by the Beau Brummels and "El Watusi" by Ray Barretto are true stereo				
20 GREAT COUNTRY HITS				
❑ RCA Victor CPL2-1286 [(2)]	1975	5.00	10.00	20.00
20 ORIGINAL WINNERS OF 1964				
❑ Roulette R 25293 [M]	1965	5.00	10.00	20.00
❑ Roulette SR 25293 [R]	1965	3.00	6.00	12.00
20 ORIGINAL WINNERS, VOLUME 1				
❑ Roulette R 25249 [M]	1964	5.00	10.00	20.00
20 ORIGINAL WINNERS, VOLUME 2				
❑ Roulette R 25251 [M]	1964	5.00	10.00	20.00
20 ORIGINAL WINNERS, VOLUME 3				
❑ Roulette R 25263 [M]	1965	5.00	10.00	20.00
20 ORIGINAL WINNERS, VOLUME 4				
❑ Roulette R 25264 [M]	1965	5.00	10.00	20.00
20 SOULFUL OLDIES, VOLUME 1				
❑ Vee Jay VJVS-1001 [R]	1972	5.00	10.00	20.00
20 SOULFUL OLDIES, VOLUME 2				
❑ Vee Jay VJVS-1002 [R]	1972	5.00	10.00	20.00
20 SOULFUL OLDIES, VOLUME 3				
❑ Vee Jay VJVS-1003 [R]	1972	5.00	10.00	20.00
20 SOULFUL OLDIES, VOLUME 4				
❑ Vee Jay VJVS-73-1006/7 [R]	1973	5.00	10.00	20.00
20 SOULFUL OLDIES, VOLUME 5				
❑ Vee Jay VJVS-73-1008/9 [R]	1973	5.00	10.00	20.00
20 SOULFUL OLDIES, VOLUME 6				
❑ Vee Jay VJVS-73-1010/11 [R]	1973	5.00	10.00	20.00
20 YEARS OF NO. 1 HITS (1956-1975)				
❑ Reader's Digest RBA-243A [(7)]	1986	12.50	25.00	50.00
24 KARAT GOLD FOR GROOVIN'				
❑ Verve V6-6654 [(2)]	1968	5.00	10.00	20.00
24 SACRED SONGS				
❑ King 965 [M]	1966	12.50	25.00	50.00
25 YEARS OF C&W HITS				
❑ King 1006 [M]	1966	7.50	15.00	30.00
25 YEARS OF COUNTRY AND WESTERN SACRED SONGS				
❑ King 807 [M]	1962	25.00	50.00	100.00
25 YEARS OF POPULAR MUSIC				
❑ King 1008 [M]	1966	7.50	15.00	30.00
25 YEARS OF R&B HITS				
❑ King 1004 [M]	1966	7.50	15.00	30.00
25 YEARS OF R&B HITS, VOLUME 1				
❑ King 725 [M]	1961	25.00	50.00	100.00
25 YEARS OF R&B HITS, VOLUME 2				
❑ King 749 [M]	1961	25.00	50.00	100.00
30 FAVORITE SONGS OF CHRISTMAS WITH CHIMES AND CHORUS				
❑ Disneyland DQ-1329 [M]	1963	5.00	10.00	20.00
—Performed by anonymous musicians				
30 YEARS OF NO. 1 COUNTRY HITS				
❑ Reader's Digest RBA-215-A [(7)]	1986	12.50	25.00	50.00
30X30: 30 GREAT HITS BY 30 GREAT COUNTRY ARTISTS, VOL. 1				
❑ Columbia Musical Treasuries P2S 5218 [(2)]	1968	5.00	10.00	20.00
30X30: 30 GREAT HITS BY 30 GREAT COUNTRY ARTISTS, VOL. 2				
❑ Columbia Musical Treasuries P2S 5220 [(2)]	1968	5.00	10.00	20.00
5-STRING BANJO PICKIN' AND SINGIN'				
❑ King 994 [M]	1966	10.00	20.00	40.00
50 BELOVED SONGS OF FAITH				
❑ Reader's Digest BMR3-100 [(3)]	1990	6.25	12.50	25.00
50 YEARS OF FILM				
❑ Warner Bros. 3XX 2737 [(3)]	1973	6.25	12.50	25.00
—Box set with 60-page booklet				
50 YEARS OF FILM MUSIC				
❑ Warner Bros. 3XX 2736 [(3)]	1973	6.25	12.50	25.00
—Box set with 28-page booklet				
50 YEARS OF JAZZ GREATS				
❑ Columbia Musical Treasury P3S 5932 [(3)]	197?	5.00	10.00	20.00
52ND STREET JAZZ				
❑ Waldorf Music Hall MH 33-148 [10]	195?	25.00	50.00	100.00
60 CHRISTMAS CLASSICS				
❑ Sessions DVL2-0723 [(4)]	1985	5.00	10.00	20.00
—Record 3 is numbered "P18827" and Record 4 is numbered "P18828"				
60 FLASH-BACK GREATS OF THE SIXTIES				
❑ K-Tel TU 229 [(4)]	1972	10.00	20.00	40.00
—One of the few sought-after K-Tel collections, among its contents is a Beatles track ("My Bonnie")				
60 YEARS OF COUNTRY MUSIC				
❑ RCA Victor CPL2-4351	1982	5.00	10.00	20.00
60 YEARS OF MUSIC AMERICA LOVES BEST				
❑ RCA Victor LM-6074 [(2)]	1959	7.50	15.00	30.00
60 YEARS OF MUSIC AMERICA LOVES BEST, VOLUME II				
❑ RCA Victor LM-6088 [(2)]	1960	7.50	15.00	30.00

Number / Title (A Side/B Side)	Yr	VG	VG+	NM
60 YEARS OF MUSIC AMERICA LOVES BEST, VOLUME III (POPULAR)				
❑ RCA Victor LOP-1509	1961	5.00	10.00	20.00
60 YEARS OF MUSIC AMERICA LOVES BEST, VOLUME III (RED SEAL)				
❑ RCA Victor Red Seal LM-2574	1961	5.00	10.00	20.00
$64,000 JAZZ				
❑ Columbia CL 777 [M]	1955	12.50	25.00	50.00
ACCENT ON PIANO				
❑ Urania UJLP-1207 [M]	1955	7.50	15.00	30.00
ACCENT ON TROMBONE				
❑ Urania UJLP-1205 [M]	1955	7.50	15.00	30.00
ADD-A-PART JAZZ				
❑ Columbia CL 908 [M]	1956	6.25	12.50	25.00
THE ADVANCE GUARD OF THE '40S				
❑ EmArcy MG-36016 [M]	1955	12.50	25.00	50.00
AFRO SUMMIT				
❑ BASF 20675	197?	5.00	10.00	20.00
AFRO-COOL				
❑ GNP Crescendo GNP-48 [M]	1959	5.00	10.00	20.00
AFTER HOUR JAZZ				
❑ Epic LN (# unk) [M]	1955	7.50	15.00	30.00
AFTER HOURS				
❑ King 395-528 [M]	1956	125.00	250.00	500.00
AIN'T THAT GOOD NEWS				
❑ Specialty SPS-2115	1969	5.00	10.00	20.00
ALAN FREED'S GOLDEN PICS				
❑ End LP-313 [M]	1961	15.00	30.00	60.00
ALAN FREED'S MEMORY LANE				
❑ End LP-314 [M]	1962	15.00	30.00	60.00
ALAN FREED'S TOP 15				
❑ End LP-315 [M]	1962	15.00	30.00	60.00
❑ Roulette SR 42042 [R]	1970	3.75	7.50	15.00
—Reissue of End LP-315				
ALL DAY LONG				
❑ Prestige PRLP-7081 [M]	1957	25.00	50.00	100.00
—Reissued as Prestige 7277; see KENNY BURRELL.				
ALL DAY THUMB SUCKER REVISITED				
❑ Blue Thumb BT3-7002 [(3)]	1995	5.00	10.00	20.00
—Boxed set				
ALL GIRL MILLION SELLERS				
❑ Ascot AM-13007 [M]	1964	10.00	20.00	40.00
❑ Ascot AS-16007 [P]	1964	10.00	20.00	40.00
ALL MEAT				
❑ Warner Bros. PRO 604 [(2)]	1975	5.00	10.00	20.00
ALL NIGHT LONG				
❑ Prestige PRLP-7073 [M]	1957	25.00	50.00	100.00
—Reissued as Prestige 7289; see KENNY BURRELL.				
ALL SINGING — ALL TALKING — ALL ROCKING				
❑ Warner Bros. PRO 573 [(2)]	1973	6.25	12.50	25.00
ALL STAR JAZZ				
❑ Halo 50223 [M]	195?	7.50	15.00	30.00
ALL STAR ROCK AND ROLL REVUE				
❑ King 395-513 [M]	1956	100.00	200.00	400.00
❑ King 638 [M]	1959	50.00	100.00	200.00
—Reissue of King 395-513				
ALL STAR ROCK, VOLUME 1				
❑ Original Sound Recordings OSR-1	1972	2.50	5.00	10.00
ALL STAR ROCK, VOLUME 10				
❑ Original Sound Recordings OSR-10	1972	2.50	5.00	10.00
ALL STAR ROCK, VOLUME 11				
❑ Original Sound Recordings OSR-11	1972	10.00	20.00	40.00
—This volume has an Elvis track on it, thus the higher price				
ALL STAR ROCK, VOLUME 2				
❑ Original Sound Recordings OSR-2	1972	2.50	5.00	10.00
ALL STAR ROCK, VOLUME 3				
❑ Original Sound Recordings OSR-3	1972	2.50	5.00	10.00
ALL STAR ROCK, VOLUME 4				
❑ Original Sound Recordings OSR-4	1972	2.50	5.00	10.00
ALL STAR ROCK, VOLUME 5				
❑ Original Sound Recordings OSR-5	1972	2.50	5.00	10.00
ALL STAR ROCK, VOLUME 6				
❑ Original Sound Recordings OSR-6	1972	2.50	5.00	10.00
ALL STAR ROCK, VOLUME 7				
❑ Original Sound Recordings OSR-7	1972	2.50	5.00	10.00
ALL STAR ROCK, VOLUME 8				
❑ Original Sound Recordings OSR-8	1972	2.50	5.00	10.00
ALL STAR ROCK, VOLUME 9				
❑ Original Sound Recordings OSR-9	1972	2.50	5.00	10.00
ALL STAR TRIBUTE TO TATUM				
❑ American Recording Society G-424 [M]	1957	7.50	15.00	30.00
ALL THE HITS BY ALL THE STARS				
❑ Parkway P 7013 [M]	1962	10.00	20.00	40.00
ALL THE HITS BY ALL THE STARS, VOL. 2				
❑ Parkway P 7016 [M]	1963	7.50	15.00	30.00
ALL THE STARS' BIGGEST HITS				
❑ Parkway P-7033 [M]	1963	12.50	25.00	50.00
—With "pull-off pix" still intact on cover				

And God Created Woman introduced American audiences to Brigitte Bardot. This soundtrack album, from 1957, is collectible both for its music and for its photos of the young starlet.

The Caine Mutiny soundtrack album is considered the rarest and most collectible of all movie-related albums.

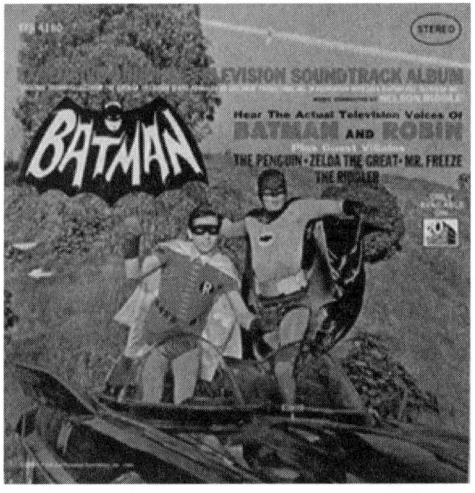

Almost everything directly related to the mid-1960s *Batman* TV series is sought after. The original soundtrack LP on the 20th Century Fox label is no exception.

In the early 1960s, the Colpix label issued a series of original soundtracks from Hanna-Barbera cartoons. These are very difficult to find in decent condition, and the album of *The Flintstones* is no exception.

This rare promotional album combined music by Stax-Volt recording artists with announcements by those artists urging inner-city youth to stay in school.

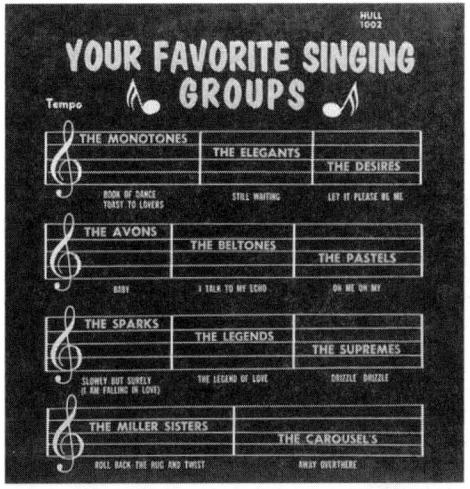

This compilation, *Your Favorite Singing Groups,* was issued by the Hull label in 1962 and is quite rare.

Number	Title (A Side/B Side)	Yr	VG	VG+	NM
ALL THE STARS' BIGGEST HITS, VOLUME 2					
❏ Parkway P-7034 [M]		1963	12.50	25.00	50.00
—With "pull-off pix" still intact on cover					
ALL THESE THINGS					
❏ Instant LP-71000		1969	7.50	15.00	30.00
ALL TIME COUNTRY AND WESTERN					
❏ Decca DL 4010 [M]		1960	7.50	15.00	30.00
❏ Decca DL 74010 [R]		196?	5.00	10.00	20.00
ALL TIME COUNTRY AND WESTERN HITS					
❏ King 537 [M]		1956	37.50	75.00	150.00
❏ King 710 [M]		1961	25.00	50.00	100.00
—Not a reissue of King 537, but a different collection					
ALL TIME COUNTRY AND WESTERN, VOL. 2					
❏ Decca DL 4090 [M]		1961	6.25	12.50	25.00
❏ Decca DL 74090 [R]		196?	3.75	7.50	15.00
ALL TIME COUNTRY AND WESTERN, VOL. 3					
❏ Decca DL 4134 [M]		1961	6.25	12.50	25.00
❏ Decca DL 74134 [R]		196?	3.75	7.50	15.00
ALL TIME COUNTRY AND WESTERN, VOL. 4					
❏ Decca DL 4359 [M]		1963	6.25	12.50	25.00
❏ Decca DL 74359 [R]		196?	3.75	7.50	15.00
ALL TIME COUNTRY AND WESTERN, VOL. 5					
❏ Decca DL 4549 [M]		1964	6.25	12.50	25.00
❏ Decca DL 74549 [R]		1964	3.75	7.50	15.00
ALL TIME COUNTRY AND WESTERN, VOL. 6					
❏ Decca DL 4657 [M]		1965	5.00	10.00	20.00
❏ Decca DL 74657 [R]		1965	3.00	6.00	12.00
ALL TIME COUNTRY AND WESTERN, VOL. 7					
❏ Decca DL 4775 [M]		1966	5.00	10.00	20.00
❏ Decca DL 74775 [R]		1966	3.00	6.00	12.00
ALL TIME COUNTRY AND WESTERN, VOL. 8					
❏ Decca DL 4881 [M]		1967	5.00	10.00	20.00
❏ Decca DL 74881 [S]		1967	5.00	10.00	20.00
ALL TIME COUNTRY AND WESTERN, VOL. 9					
❏ Decca DL 75025		1968	5.00	10.00	20.00
ALL TIME HIT SACRED AND GOSPEL SONGS					
❏ King 1023 [M]		1967	7.50	15.00	30.00
ALL-STAR DATES					
❏ RCA Victor LPT-21 [10]		1951	12.50	25.00	50.00
ALL-STAR STOMPERS					
❏ Circle L-402 [M]		1951	10.00	20.00	40.00
ALTO ALTITUDE					
❏ EmArcy MG-36018 [M]		1955	12.50	25.00	50.00
ALTO SAXES					
❏ Norgran MGN-1035 [M]		1955	20.00	40.00	80.00
❏ Verve MGV-8126 [M]		1957	7.50	15.00	30.00
❏ Verve V-8126 [M]		1961	5.00	10.00	20.00
THE AMAZING METS					
❏ Buddah 1969		1969	6.25	12.50	25.00
AMERICA'S GREATEST JAZZMEN PLAY COLE PORTER					
❏ Moodsville MVLP-34 [M]		1963	10.00	20.00	40.00
—Green label					
❏ Moodsville MVLP-34 [M]		1965	5.00	10.00	20.00
—Blue label, trident logo at right					
❏ Moodsville MVST-34 [S]		1963	10.00	20.00	40.00
—Green label					
❏ Moodsville MVST-34 [S]		1965	5.00	10.00	20.00
—Blue label, trident logo at right					
AMERICA'S GREATEST JAZZMEN PLAY GEORGE GERSHWIN					
❏ Moodsville MVLP-33 [M]		1963	10.00	20.00	40.00
—Green label					
❏ Moodsville MVLP-33 [M]		1965	5.00	10.00	20.00
—Blue label, trident logo at right					
❏ Moodsville MVST-33 [S]		1963	10.00	20.00	40.00
—Green label					
❏ Moodsville MVST-33 [S]		1965	5.00	10.00	20.00
—Blue label, trident logo at right					
AMERICA'S GREATEST JAZZMEN PLAY RICHARD RODGERS					
❏ Moodsville MVLP-35 [M]		1963	10.00	20.00	40.00
—Green label					
❏ Moodsville MVLP-35 [M]		1965	5.00	10.00	20.00
—Blue label, trident logo at right					
❏ Moodsville MVST-35 [S]		1963	10.00	20.00	40.00
—Green label					
❏ Moodsville MVST-35 [S]		1965	5.00	10.00	20.00
—Blue label, trident logo at right					
AMERICA'S GREATEST JAZZMEN PLAY THE BROADWAY SCENE					
❏ Moodsville MVLP-38 [M]		1963	10.00	20.00	40.00
—Green label					
❏ Moodsville MVLP-38 [M]		1965	5.00	10.00	20.00
—Blue label, trident logo at right					
❏ Moodsville MVST-38 [S]		1963	10.00	20.00	40.00
—Green label					
❏ Moodsville MVST-38 [S]		1965	5.00	10.00	20.00
—Blue label, trident logo at right					
AMERICAN FOLK BLUES FESTIVAL					
❏ Excello LPS-8029		1972	5.00	10.00	20.00
❏ Exodus EX-302 [M]		1966	5.00	10.00	20.00
❏ Exodus EXS-302 [S]		1966	6.25	12.50	25.00
AMERICANS ABROAD, VOL. 1					
❏ Pax LP-6009 [10]		1955	10.00	20.00	40.00
AMERICANS ABROAD, VOL. 2					
❏ Pax LP-6015 [10]		1955	10.00	20.00	40.00
AMERICANS IN EUROPE, VOL. 1					
❏ ABC Impulse! AS-36 [S]		1968	3.00	6.00	12.00
❏ Impulse! A-36 [M]		1963	5.00	10.00	20.00
❏ Impulse! AS-36 [S]		1963	6.25	12.50	25.00
AMERICANS IN EUROPE, VOL. 2					
❏ ABC Impulse! AS-37 [S]		1968	3.00	6.00	12.00
❏ Impulse! A-37 [M]		1963	5.00	10.00	20.00
❏ Impulse! AS-37 [S]		1963	6.25	12.50	25.00
THE ANATOMY OF IMPROVISATION					
❏ Verve MGV-8230 [M]		1958	7.50	15.00	30.00
❏ Verve V-8230 [M]		1961	5.00	10.00	20.00
ANOTHER MONDAY NIGHT AT BIRDLAND					
❏ Roulette R 52022 [M]		1959	7.50	15.00	30.00
❏ Roulette SR 52022 [S]		1959	7.50	15.00	30.00
AN ANTHOLOGY OF BRITISH BLUES, VOL. 1					
❏ Immediate Z12 52006		1968	7.50	15.00	30.00
AN ANTHOLOGY OF BRITISH BLUES, VOL. 2					
❏ Immediate Z12 52014		1968	7.50	15.00	30.00
AN ANTHOLOGY OF CALIFORNIA MUSIC					
❏ Jazz: West Coast JWC-500 [M]		1955	37.50	75.00	150.00
AN ANTHOLOGY OF CALIFORNIA MUSIC, VOL. 2					
❏ Jazz: West Coast JWC-501 [M]		1956	37.50	75.00	150.00
APOLLO SATURDAY NIGHT					
❏ Atco 33-159 [M]		1964	10.00	20.00	40.00
❏ Atco SD 33-159 [S]		1964	12.50	25.00	50.00
APPETIZERS					
❏ Warner Bros. PRO 569 [(2)]		1973	6.25	12.50	25.00
APPROVED BY 10,000,000					
❏ Teem LP-5004 [M]		196?	7.50	15.00	30.00
ARISTA AOR SAMPLER					
❏ Arista ALS 06 [(2)DJ]		1978	5.00	10.00	20.00
ARISTA'S GREATEST HITS: PORTRAIT OF A DECADE 1975-1985					
❏ Arista/Silver Eagle SE 10383 [(3)]		1985	5.00	10.00	20.00
THE ART OF JAZZ PIANO					
❏ Epic LN 3295 [M]		1956	7.50	15.00	30.00
THE ART OF THE JAM SESSION: MONTREUX '77					
❏ Pablo Live 2620106 [(8)]		1978	17.50	35.00	70.00
THE ARTISTS AND MUSIC THAT STARTED IT ALL					
❏ Motown PR-84 [(6)DJ]		1981	50.00	100.00	200.00
—Promo-only box set; five of the records appeared as "The Motown Story: The First Twenty-Five Years" two years later					
ASSORTED FLAVORS OF PACIFIC JAZZ					
❏ Pacific Jazz HFS-1 [M]		1956	12.50	25.00	50.00
ATLANTIC BLUES					
❏ Atlantic 81713 [(8)]		1987	12.50	25.00	50.00
—Boxed set; also available as four 2-LP sets					
ATLANTIC JAZZ					
❏ Atlantic 81712 [(15)]		1987	62.50	125.00	250.00
—Boxed set with 12 volumes in 15 records, liner notes and credits					
THE ATLANTIC NEW ORLEANS JAZZ SESSIONS					
❏ Mosaic MQ6-179 [(6)]		199?	30.00	60.00	120.00
ATLANTIC RECORDS: CLASSIC ROCK					
❏ Atlantic 81908 [(4)]		1989	7.50	15.00	30.00
—Boxed set					
ATLANTIC RECORDS: GREAT MOMENTS IN JAZZ					
❏ Atlantic 81907 [(3)]		1989	6.25	12.50	25.00
ATLANTIC RHYTHM AND BLUES					
❏ Atlantic 81620 [(14)]		1986	25.00	50.00	100.00
—Boxed set; also available as seven 2-LP sets					
AUTOBIOGRAPHY IN JAZZ					
❏ Debut DEB-198 [M]		1955	37.50	75.00	150.00
❏ Fantasy OJC-115		198?	2.50	5.00	10.00
AWARD ALBUM JAZZ VOCALS					
❏ Bethlehem BCP-6060 [M]		1961	6.25	12.50	25.00
BACKGROUNDS OF JAZZ, VOL. 1: THE JUG BANDS					
❏ "X" LX-3009 [10]		1954	20.00	40.00	80.00
BACKGROUNDS OF JAZZ, VOL. 2: COUNTRY & URBAN BLUES					
❏ "X" LVA-3016 [10]		1954	20.00	40.00	80.00
BACKGROUNDS OF JAZZ, VOL. 3: KINGS OF THE BLUES					
❏ "X" LVA-3032 [10]		1955	20.00	40.00	80.00
BACKWOOD BLUES					
❏ Riverside RLP-1039 [10]		1954	20.00	40.00	80.00
BALLADS AND BREAKDOWNS OF THE GOLDEN ERA					
❏ Columbia CS 9660		1968	5.00	10.00	20.00
BALLROOM BANDSTAND					
❏ Columbia CL 611 [M]		1955	6.25	12.50	25.00
BANG AND SHOUT SUPER HITS					
❏ Bang BLPS-220 [P]		1969	5.00	10.00	20.00
BANJO COUNTRY STYLE					
❏ Audio Lab AL-1569 [M]		1962	20.00	40.00	80.00
BARGAIN DAY					
❏ EmArcy MG-36087 [M]		1956	10.00	20.00	40.00
BARREL HOUSE PIANO					
❏ Brunswick BL 58022 [10]		1951	15.00	30.00	60.00
A BARREL OF OLDIES					
❏ Del-Fi DFLP-1219 [M]		1961	12.50	25.00	50.00

Number Title (A Side/B Side)	Yr	VG	VG+	NM
BARRY MANN AND CYNTHIA WEIL: SOLID GOLD				
❏ Screen Gems/Columbia CPL-712 [DJ]	1975	5.00	10.00	20.00
—Promo-only compilation of oldies sent to radio to spur airplay on songs owned by this publishing house				
THE BASS				
❏ ABC Impulse! AS-9284 [(3)]	197?	5.00	10.00	20.00
BATTLE OF BANDS				
❏ Capitol H 235 [10]	1950	12.50	25.00	50.00
BATTLE OF JAZZ, VOL. 3				
❏ Brunswick BL 58039 [10]	1953	12.50	25.00	50.00
BATTLE OF THE BIG BANDS				
❏ Capitol T 667 [M]	1956	7.50	15.00	30.00
BATTLE OF THE GROUPS				
❏ End LP-305 [M]	1960	15.00	30.00	60.00
BATTLE OF THE GROUPS, VOLUME 2				
❏ End LP-309 [M]	1960	15.00	30.00	60.00
BATTLE OF THE SAXES				
❏ Aladdin LP-701 [10]	1950	125.00	250.00	500.00
BATTLE OF THE SAXES-TENOR ALL STARS				
❏ EmArcy MG-36023 [M]	1955	12.50	25.00	50.00
BE OUR GUEST				
❏ Gene Norman GNP-20 [M]	1955	6.25	12.50	25.00
THE BE-BOP ERA				
❏ RCA Victor LPV-519	1965	5.00	10.00	20.00
THE BEAT: SOUND WAVE OF THE 80'S				
❏ K-Tel TU 5040	1982	5.00	10.00	20.00
THE BELLS OF CHRISTMAS				
❏ Book-of-the-Month Club 90-5677 [(3)]	1973	5.00	10.00	20.00
—Sold through Book-of-the-Month Records; secondary number is "P3 11972"				
BEST COAST JAZZ				
❏ EmArcy MG-36039 [M]	1955	20.00	40.00	80.00
BEST FROM THE WEST: MODERN SOUNDS FROM CALIFORNIA, VOL. 1				
❏ Blue Note BLP-5059 [10]	1955	50.00	100.00	200.00
BEST FROM THE WEST: MODERN SOUNDS FROM CALIFORNIA, VOL. 2				
❏ Blue Note BLP-5060 [10]	1955	50.00	100.00	200.00
THE BEST OF ARGO JAZZ				
❏ Argo ALPS-1 [M]	1961	7.50	15.00	30.00
THE BEST OF BLUE NOTE, VOL. 1				
❏ Blue Note BST-84429 [(2)]	197?	5.00	10.00	20.00
THE BEST OF BLUE NOTE, VOL. 2				
❏ Blue Note BST-84433 [(2)]	197?	5.00	10.00	20.00
THE BEST OF BOMP! VOLUME ONE				
❏ Bomp! 4002	1978	5.00	10.00	20.00
—First pressings on white vinyl.				
THE BEST OF CHRISTMAS				
❏ Capitol STBB 2979 [(2)]	1968	5.00	10.00	20.00
THE BEST OF DISNEY VOL. I				
❏ Disneyland 2502	1978	6.25	12.50	25.00
THE BEST OF DISNEY VOL. II				
❏ Disneyland 2503	1978	6.25	12.50	25.00
BEST OF DIXIELAND				
❏ RCA Victor ANL1-1431	1976	2.50	5.00	10.00
THE BEST OF DIXIELAND				
❏ RCA Victor LPM-2982 [M]	1965	5.00	10.00	20.00
❏ RCA Victor LSP-2982 [R]	1965	3.00	6.00	12.00
BEST OF LIMP, REST OF LIMP				
❏ Limp 1004	1980	10.00	20.00	40.00
—Numbered edition of 1,000				
BEST OF RALPH				
❏ Ralph RR 8251-2 [(2)]	1982	5.00	10.00	20.00
BEST OF RHYTHM AND BLUES				
❏ Jubilee JLP-1014 [M]	1956	37.50	75.00	150.00
—Blue label, black vinyl				
❏ Jubilee JLP-1014 [M]	1956	50.00	100.00	200.00
—Pink label, black vinyl				
❏ Jubilee JLP-1014 [M]	1956	125.00	250.00	500.00
—Pink label, red vinyl				
THE BEST OF RHYTHM AND BLUES				
❏ Warwick W 2026 [M]	1961	20.00	40.00	80.00
BEST OF THE BIG NAME BANDS				
❏ RCA Camden CAL-368 [M]	1958	6.25	12.50	25.00
BEST OF THE BLUES, VOLUME 1				
❏ Imperial LP-9257 [M]	1964	6.25	12.50	25.00
❏ Imperial LP-12257 [R]	1964	5.00	10.00	20.00
BEST OF THE BLUES, VOLUME 2				
❏ Imperial LP-9259 [M]	1964	6.25	12.50	25.00
❏ Imperial LP-12259 [R]	1964	5.00	10.00	20.00
THE BEST OF THE KING BISCUIT FLOWER HOUR				
❏ Silver Eagle SE 10674 [(3)]	1988	6.25	12.50	25.00
THE BEST OF THE R AND B GROUPS				
❏ Warwick W 2025 [M]	1961	25.00	50.00	100.00
BEST OF THE SOUNDTRACKS				
❏ Tower ST-5148	1969	6.25	12.50	25.00
THE BEST VOCAL GROUPS IN ROCK 'N' ROLL				
❏ Dooto DL-224 [M]	1957	25.00	50.00	100.00
—Yellow label				
❏ Dooto DL-224 [M]	196?	7.50	15.00	30.00
—Multi-color label				

Number Title (A Side/B Side)	Yr	VG	VG+	NM
BETHLEHEM'S BEST				
❏ Bethlehem EXLP-6 [(3)M]	1958	17.50	35.00	70.00
—Box set of 82, 83, and 84				
BETHLEHEM'S BEST, VOLUME 1				
❏ Bethlehem BCP-82 [M]	1958	7.50	15.00	30.00
BETHLEHEM'S BEST, VOLUME 2				
❏ Bethlehem BCP-83 [M]	1958	7.50	15.00	30.00
BETHLEHEM'S BEST, VOLUME 3				
❏ Bethlehem BCP-84 [M]	1958	7.50	15.00	30.00
BETHLEHEM'S GRAB BAG				
❏ Bethlehem EXLP-2 [M]	1958	10.00	20.00	40.00
THE BIG 18 — LIVE ECHOES OF THE SWINGING BANDS				
❏ RCA Victor LPM-1921 [M]	1959	10.00	20.00	40.00
❏ RCA Victor LSP-1921 [S]	1959	12.50	25.00	50.00
THE BIG BALL				
❏ Warner Bros. PRO 358 [(2)]	1970	6.25	12.50	25.00
—Originals have green labels				
BIG BAND CONTRAST				
❏ Bethlehem BCP-6037 [M]	1960	7.50	15.00	30.00
BIG BAND JAZZ				
❏ Brunswick BL 58050 [10]	1953	12.50	25.00	50.00
BIG BAND STEREO				
❏ Capitol SW 1055 [S]	1959	6.25	12.50	25.00
BIG BANDS				
❏ Capitol STFL-293 [(6)]	1969	7.50	15.00	30.00
—One album each by Les Brown, Glen Gray, Duke Ellington, Benny Goodman, Harry James and Woody Herman				
BIG BANDS' GREATEST HITS				
❏ Columbia CG 30009 [(2)]	197?	3.00	6.00	12.00
—"CG" prefix is a reissue of "G"				
❏ Columbia G 30009 [(2)]	1970	3.75	7.50	15.00
—Orange labels				
❏ Columbia G 30009 [(2)]	1970	5.00	10.00	20.00
—Red "360 Sound" labels				
BIG COUNTRY HITS				
❏ Pickwick JS-6166	1975	7.50	15.00	30.00
BIG COUNTRY HITS, VOL. 1				
❏ RCA Victor LPM-3606 [M]	1966	3.75	7.50	15.00
❏ RCA Victor LSP-3606 [S]	1966	5.00	10.00	20.00
THE BIG HITS				
❏ Columbia CL 1353 [M]	1959	7.50	15.00	30.00
❏ Columbia CS 8161 [S]	1959	10.00	20.00	40.00
THE BIG HITS OF MID-AMERICA				
❏ Soma MG-1245 [M]	1965	20.00	40.00	80.00
BIG HITS OF MID-AMERICA VOLUME THREE				
❏ Twin/Tone TTTR 7907/8 [(2)]	1979	5.00	10.00	20.00
THE BIG HITS OF MID-AMERICA, VOLUME 2				
❏ Soma MG-1246 [M]	1965	20.00	40.00	80.00
BIG NAME DIXIE				
❏ Score SLP-4024 [M]	1958	12.50	25.00	50.00
THE BIG ONES FROM DUKE AND PEACOCK RECORDS				
❏ Peacock PLP-2000 [M]	1967	5.00	10.00	20.00
THE BIG SOUNDS OF THE DRAGS!				
❏ Capitol ST 2001 [S]	1963	6.25	12.50	25.00
❏ Capitol T 2001 [M]	1963	5.00	10.00	20.00
BIG SUR FESTIVAL/ONE HAND CLAPPING				
❏ Columbia KC 31138	1972	5.00	10.00	20.00
BIG SURF HITS				
❏ Del-Fi DFLP-1249 [M]	1964	12.50	25.00	50.00
❏ Del-Fi DFST-1249 [S]	1964	18.75	37.50	75.00
BIRD'S NIGHT — THE MUSIC OF CHARLIE PARKER				
❏ Savoy MG-12138 [M]	1958	12.50	25.00	50.00
BIRDLAND DREAM BAND, VOL. 1				
❏ Vik LX-1070 [M]	1957	7.50	15.00	30.00
BIRDLAND DREAM BAND, VOL. 2				
❏ Vik LX-1077 [M]	1957	7.50	15.00	30.00
THE BIRDLAND STARS ON TOUR, VOL. 1				
❏ RCA Victor LPM-1327 [M]	1956	10.00	20.00	40.00
THE BIRDLAND STARS ON TOUR, VOL. 2				
❏ RCA Victor LPM-1328 [M]	1956	10.00	20.00	40.00
THE BIRDLAND STORY				
❏ Roulette RB-2 [(2)M]	1961	10.00	20.00	40.00
❏ Roulette SRB-2 [(2)S]	1961	10.00	20.00	40.00
THE BIRTH OF BOP, VOL. 1				
❏ Savoy MG-9022 [10]	1953	37.50	75.00	150.00
THE BIRTH OF BOP, VOL. 2				
❏ Savoy MG-9023 [10]	1953	37.50	75.00	150.00
THE BIRTH OF BOP, VOL. 3				
❏ Savoy MG-9024 [10]	1953	37.50	75.00	150.00
THE BIRTH OF BOP, VOL. 4				
❏ Savoy MG-9025 [10]	1953	37.50	75.00	150.00
THE BIRTH OF BOP, VOL. 5				
❏ Savoy MG-9026 [10]	1953	37.50	75.00	150.00
BLEECKER AND MACDOUGAL: THE FOLK SCENE OF THE 1960S				
❏ Elektra 60381 [(3)]	1984	5.00	10.00	20.00
BLOWIN' SESSIONS				
❏ Blue Note BN-LA521-H2 [(2)]	1975	5.00	10.00	20.00

Number	Title (A Side/B Side)	Yr	VG	VG+	NM
BLOWOUT AT MARDI GRAS					
❑ Cook LP-1084 [M]		1955	10.00	20.00	40.00
BLUE CHRISTMAS					
❑ Welk Music Group WM-3002 [DJ]		1984	20.00	40.00	80.00
—Promo only; compiled by the publisher of "Blue Christmas" and other holiday tunes for radio use					
BLUE RIBBON COUNTRY					
❑ Capitol STBB 2969 [(2)]		1968	6.25	12.50	25.00
BLUE RIBBON COUNTRY, VOL. 2					
❑ Capitol STBB-217 [(2)]		1969	6.25	12.50	25.00
BLUEGRASS OLDIES BUT GOODIES					
❑ Smash MGS-27028 [M]		1963	5.00	10.00	20.00
❑ Smash SRS-67028 [S]		1963	5.00	10.00	20.00
BLUEGRASS SPECTACULAR					
❑ Starday SLP-232 [M]		1963	6.25	12.50	25.00
THE BLUES					
❑ Vee Jay VJS-2-1007 [(2)]		1974	5.00	10.00	20.00
❑ Vee Jay LP-1020 [M]		1960	10.00	20.00	40.00
BLUES 'N' FOLK					
❑ Bethlehem BCP-6071 [M]		1963	15.00	30.00	60.00
BLUES FOR TOMORROW					
❑ Fantasy OJC-030		198?	2.50	5.00	10.00
❑ Riverside RLP 12-243 [M]		1957	10.00	20.00	40.00
BLUES FROM BIG BILL'S COPACABANA					
❑ Chess LP 1533 [M]		1969	6.25	12.50	25.00
—Possibly a reissue of "Folk Festival of the Blues," Argo 4031					
BLUES IN CONCERT					
❑ Groove Merchant 4405 [(2)]		197?	5.00	10.00	20.00
THE BLUES IN MODERN JAZZ					
❑ Atlantic 1337 [M]		1961	5.00	10.00	20.00
—Multicolor label, white "fan" logo at right					
❑ Atlantic 1337 [M]		1963	3.75	7.50	15.00
—Multicolor label, black "fan" logo at right					
❑ Atlantic SD 1337 [R]		1969	3.00	6.00	12.00
THE BLUES IN STEREO					
❑ World Pacific ST-1021 [S]		1959	7.50	15.00	30.00
BLUES LIVE IN BATON ROUGE					
❑ Excello LPS-8021		1971	6.25	12.50	25.00
THE BLUES PROJECT					
❑ Elektra EKL-264 [M]		1964	6.25	12.50	25.00
❑ Elektra EKS-7264 [S]		1964	7.50	15.00	30.00
—No relation to the band of the same name; on one track, Bob Dylan plays piano under the name "Bob Landy"					
BLUES THAT GAVE AMERICA SOUL					
❑ ABC Duke DLPX-82 [S]		1974	3.75	7.50	15.00
❑ Duke DLP-82 [M]		1966	5.00	10.00	20.00
❑ Duke DLPS-82 [S]		1966	6.25	12.50	25.00
BLUES UPTOWN: URBAN BLUES, VOLUME 1					
❑ Imperial LP-94002		1968	5.00	10.00	20.00
THE BLUES, VOL. 2					
❑ Pacific Jazz JWC-502 [M]		1956	12.50	25.00	50.00
❑ World Pacific JWC-502 [M]		1958	10.00	20.00	40.00
THE BLUES, VOL. 2: HAVE BLUES, WILL TRAVEL					
❑ World Pacific JWC-509 [M]		1958	10.00	20.00	40.00
THE BLUES, VOL. 3: BLOWIN' THE BLUES					
❑ World Pacific JWC-512 [M]		1958	10.00	20.00	40.00
❑ World Pacific ST-1029 [S]		1959	7.50	15.00	30.00
THE BLUES, VOLUME 1					
❑ Argo LP-4026 [M]		1963	6.25	12.50	25.00
THE BLUES, VOLUME 2					
❑ Argo LP-4027 [M]		1963	6.25	12.50	25.00
THE BLUES, VOLUME 3					
❑ Argo LP-4034 [M]		1964	6.25	12.50	25.00
THE BLUES, VOLUME 4					
❑ Argo LP-4042 [M]		1964	6.25	12.50	25.00
THE BLUES, VOLUME 5					
❑ Cadet LP-4051 [M]		1966	6.25	12.50	25.00
BLUESVILLE					
❑ Bethlehem BCP-6038 [M]		1960	7.50	15.00	30.00
BODY AND SOUL					
❑ RCA Victor LPV-501		1964	5.00	10.00	20.00
BONING UP ON 'BONES					
❑ EmArcy MG-36038 [M]		1955	12.50	25.00	50.00
BOOGIE WOOGIE					
❑ Decca DL 5248 [10]		1950	12.50	25.00	50.00
BOOGIE WOOGIE KINGS AND QUEENS					
❑ Decca DL 5249 [10]		1950	12.50	25.00	50.00
BOOGIE WOOGIE PIANO					
❑ Brunswick BL 58018 [10]		1950	15.00	30.00	60.00
BOPPIN'					
❑ Jubilee JGM-1118 [M]		1960	37.50	75.00	150.00
BOSS GOLDIES — SOUNDS FROM THE GROOVEYARD					
❑ Columbia CL 2559 [M]		1966	5.00	10.00	20.00
❑ Columbia CS 9339 [S]		1966	6.25	12.50	25.00
BOY MEETS GIRL					
❑ Stax STS 2-2024 [(2)]		1969	5.00	10.00	20.00
BREAKING THE RULES					
❑ Columbia A2S 881 [(2)DJ]		1980	5.00	10.00	20.00
BRIGHT LIGHTS AND HONKY TONKS					
❑ Starday SLP-239 [M]		1963	6.25	12.50	25.00
THE BRIGHTEST STARS OF CHRISTMAS					
❑ RCA Special Products DPL1-0086		1974	5.00	10.00	20.00
—Sold only at JCPenney department stores					
BRITISH FESTIVAL OF JAZZ CONCERT					
❑ Decca DL 5422 [10]		1952	12.50	25.00	50.00
BRITISH GOLD					
❑ Sire R 224095 [(2)]		1978	5.00	10.00	20.00
—RCA Music Service edition					
BRITISH JAZZ FESTIVAL					
❑ Decca DL 5424 [10]		1952	12.50	25.00	50.00
BRITISH ROCK CLASSICS					
❑ Sire R 234021 [(2)]		1978	5.00	10.00	20.00
—RCA Music Service edition					
BRITISH STERLING					
❑ Lakefront LSM 811		1981	6.25	12.50	25.00
BRUNSWICK'S GREATEST HITS					
❑ Brunswick BL 754186		1973	5.00	10.00	20.00
BUBBLE GUM MUSIC IS THE NAKED TRUTH, VOLUME 1					
❑ Buddah BDA 5032		1969	6.25	12.50	25.00
BUDDAH'S 360 DEGREE DIAL-A-HIT					
❑ Buddah BDA 5039		1969	7.50	15.00	30.00
—With rotating wheel under the front LP cover					
A BUMPER CROP OF ALL STARS					
❑ King 753 [M]		1961	25.00	50.00	100.00
BUNCH OF GOODIES					
❑ Chess LP 1441 [DJ]		1960	150.00	300.00	600.00
—Multi-color splash vinyl					
❑ Chess LP 1441 [M]		1960	30.00	60.00	120.00
—Black vinyl					
BURBANK					
❑ Warner Bros. PRO 529 [(2)]		1972	6.25	12.50	25.00
—Originals have green labels					
BURBANK'S GREATEST HITS					
❑ Warner Bros. PRO 548		1973	5.00	10.00	20.00
BUSHKIN-SAFRANSKI-WILSON GROUPS					
❑ Allegro 1590 [10]		1955	12.50	25.00	50.00
BYE BYE BIRDIE					
❑ Colpix CP-454 [M]		1963	20.00	40.00	80.00
❑ Colpix SCP-454 [S]		1963	25.00	50.00	100.00
—Studio version performed by Paul Petersen, Shelley Fabares, James Darren, the Marcels and others					
CALIFORNIA JAM 2					
❑ Columbia PC2 35389 [(2)]		1978	5.00	10.00	20.00
CAN YOU HEAR ME? MUSIC FROM THE DEAF CLUB					
❑ Optional/Walking Dead 001		1980	6.25	12.50	25.00
❑ PVC 7920		1980	5.00	10.00	20.00
CARLOAD O' HITS					
❑ Muse M-500 [M]		1959	50.00	100.00	200.00
A CARNIVAL OF SONGS					
❑ King 819 [M]		1963	25.00	50.00	100.00
THE CATS					
❑ Fantasy OJC-079		198?	2.50	5.00	10.00
❑ New Jazz NJLP-8217 [M]		1959	20.00	40.00	80.00
—Purple label					
❑ New Jazz NJLP-8217 [M]		1965	7.50	15.00	30.00
—Blue label, trident logo at right					
CATS AND JAMMER KIDS					
❑ Angel ANG-60007 [10]		1955	12.50	25.00	50.00
CATS VS. CHICKS					
❑ MGM E-255 [10]		1954	12.50	25.00	50.00
CBS TWO-FERS ARE GREAT MUSICAL VALUES!					
❑ CBS A2S 143/4 [(2)DJ]		1975	5.00	10.00	20.00
CELEBRATE THE SEASON WITH TUPPERWARE					
❑ RCA Special Products DPL1-0803		1987	5.00	10.00	20.00
—Sold only at Tupperware parties					
CHARLIE PARKER MEMORIAL CONCERT					
❑ Cadet 2CA-60002 [(2)]		1971	5.00	10.00	20.00
❑ Chess CH-92510		198?	3.00	6.00	12.00
CHART BUSTERS '62					
❑ Capitol ST 1837 [S]		1963	10.00	20.00	40.00
❑ Capitol T 1837 [M]		1963	7.50	15.00	30.00
CHARTBUSTERS, VOL. 2					
❑ Capitol ST 1945 [S]		1963	10.00	20.00	40.00
❑ Capitol T 1945 [M]		1963	7.50	15.00	30.00
CHARTBUSTERS, VOL. 3					
❑ Capitol ST 2006 [S]		1963	10.00	20.00	40.00
❑ Capitol T 2006 [M]		1963	7.50	15.00	30.00
CHARTBUSTERS, VOL. 4					
❑ Capitol ST 2094 [S]		1964	15.00	30.00	60.00
❑ Capitol T 2094 [M]		1964	10.00	20.00	40.00
CHESS IS BACK!					
❑ Chess CH-333 [DJ]		1982	5.00	10.00	20.00
—Promo only, distributed by Sugar Hill					
CHICAGO / AUSTIN HIGH SCHOOL					
❑ RCA Victor LPM-1508 [M]		1957	7.50	15.00	30.00
CHICAGO AND ALL THAT JAZZ!					
❑ Verve V-8441 [M]		1961	6.25	12.50	25.00
❑ Verve V6-8441 [S]		1962	7.50	15.00	30.00
CHICAGO BLUES ANTHOLOGY					
❑ Chess 2CH-60012 [(2)]		1972	5.00	10.00	20.00

Number / Title (A Side/B Side)	Yr	VG	VG+	NM
CHICAGO JAZZ ALBUM				
❏ Decca DL 8029 [M]	1954	10.00	20.00	40.00
CHICAGO STYLE JAZZ				
❏ Columbia CL 632 [M]	1955	6.25	12.50	25.00
CHICAGO: THE LIVING LEGENDS, VOL. 1				
❏ Riverside RLP-389 [M]	196?	5.00	10.00	20.00
❏ Riverside RS-9389 [R]	196?	3.00	6.00	12.00
CHICAGO: THE LIVING LEGENDS, VOL. 2				
❏ Riverside RLP-390 [M]	196?	5.00	10.00	20.00
❏ Riverside RS-9390 [R]	196?	3.00	6.00	12.00
A CHRISTMAS CAROL/MUSIC OF CHRISTMAS				
❏ MGM E3222 [M]	1955	7.50	15.00	30.00
—Expanded version of 10-inch LP. Also see LIONEL BARRYMORE.				
CHRISTMAS CLASSICS				
❏ WCI UN-540 [(4)]	1985	5.00	10.00	20.00
—Records individually numbered: 1. Capitol Special Markets SL-9309; 2. CBS Special Products P-18335; 3. CBS Special Products P-18334; 4. Capitol Special Markets SL-9308				
CHRISTMAS CLASSICS 1963				
❏ E.F. MacDonald EFMX-63	1963	5.00	10.00	20.00
—Special album done by the E.F. MacDonald Company, Dayton, Ohio				
CHRISTMAS DAY WITH COLONEL SANDERS				
❏ RCA Victor PRS-274	1968	5.00	10.00	20.00
—Sold only at Kentucky Fried Chicken restaurants				
CHRISTMAS EVE WITH COLONEL SANDERS				
❏ RCA Victor PRS-256	1967	5.00	10.00	20.00
—Sold only at Kentucky Fried Chicken restaurants				
CHRISTMAS GIFT 'RAP				
❏ Motown MS-725	1970	5.00	10.00	20.00
—Reissue of "Merry Christmas from Motown," MS-681				
A CHRISTMAS GIFT FOR YOU FROM PHIL SPECTOR				
❏ Phil Spector/Abkco D1-4005 [M]	1989	5.00	10.00	20.00
—Eighth edition of this group of songs				
❏ Phil Spector/Rhino RNLP 70235 [M]	1987	3.00	6.00	12.00
—Seventh edition of this group of songs; title and cover design restored to one similar to the original, with the typo on "Marshmallow World" corrected				
A CHRISTMAS GIFT FOR YOU FROM PHILLES RECORDS				
❏ Philles PHLP-4005 [M]	1963	37.50	75.00	150.00
—First edition of this group of songs; blue and black labels				
❏ Philles PHLP-4005 [M]	1964	20.00	40.00	80.00
—Second edition of this group of songs; yellow and red labels; both first and second editions have "Marshmellow [sic] World" typo on front cover; also see PHIL SPECTOR'S CHRISTMAS ALBUM				
CHRISTMAS HITS FROM WARNER BROS.				
❏ Warner Bros. 8467/8 [DJ]	1959	12.50	25.00	50.00
CHRISTMAS PROGRAMMING FROM RCA VICTOR				
❏ RCA Victor SP-33-66 [DJ]	1959	250.00	500.00	1000.
—Promo-only collection; has been counterfeited, but originals have color covers				
A CHRISTMAS RECORD				
❏ Ze/Passport PB 6020	1982	5.00	10.00	20.00
CHRISTMAS THROUGH THE YEARS				
❏ Reader's Digest RDA-143 [(5)]	1984	5.00	10.00	20.00
—Available only through Reader's Digest magazine by mail order				
CHRISTMAS WITH COLONEL SANDERS				
❏ RCA Victor PRS-291	1969	5.00	10.00	20.00
—Sold only at Kentucky Fried Chicken restaurants				
CHRISTMASTIME IN CAROL AND SONG				
❏ RCA Victor PRM-271 [M]	1968	5.00	10.00	20.00
❏ RCA Victor PRS-271 [S]	1968	3.00	6.00	12.00
CLAMBAKE ON BOURBON STREET				
❏ Cook LP-1085 [10]	1955	12.50	25.00	50.00
CLASSIC BLUES ACCOMPANISTS				
❏ Riverside RLP-1052 [10]	1955	20.00	40.00	80.00
CLASSIC CAPITOL JAZZ SESSIONS				
❏ Mosaic MQ19-170 [(19)]	199?	100.00	200.00	400.00
CLASSIC COUNTRY MUSIC				
❏ Columbia Special Products P8 15640 [(8)]	1981	12.50	25.00	50.00
—Boxed set; sold only by the Smithsonian; original version				
❏ RCA Special Products DML6-0914 [(6)]	1990	12.50	25.00	50.00
—Boxed set; sold only by the Smithsonian; revised version				
CLASSIC JAZZ PIANO STYLES				
❏ RCA Victor LPV-544 [M]	1967	5.00	10.00	20.00
CLASSICS IN JAZZ				
❏ Capitol T 320 [M]	1954	7.50	15.00	30.00
CLASSICS IN JAZZ: COOL AND QUIET				
❏ Capitol H 371 [10]	1953	12.50	25.00	50.00
CLASSICS IN JAZZ: DIXIELAND STYLISTS				
❏ Capitol H 321 [10]	1952	12.50	25.00	50.00
CLASSICS IN JAZZ: SMALL COMBOS				
❏ Capitol H 322 [10]	1952	12.50	25.00	50.00
CLAY COLE'S BIN OF ORIGINAL GOLDEN OLDIES				
❏ Jubilee JGM-5026 [M]	1964	25.00	50.00	100.00
A COLLECTION OF 16 ORIGINAL BIG HITS, VOLUME 10				
❏ Motown MS 684	1969	5.00	10.00	20.00
A COLLECTION OF 16 ORIGINAL BIG HITS, VOLUME 11				
❏ Motown MS 693	1969	5.00	10.00	20.00
A COLLECTION OF 16 ORIGINAL BIG HITS, VOLUME 3				
❏ Motown MS 624 [S]	1966	6.25	12.50	25.00
A COLLECTION OF 16 ORIGINAL BIG HITS, VOLUME 5				
❏ Motown MS 651 [S]	1966	5.00	10.00	20.00
A COLLECTION OF 16 ORIGINAL BIG HITS, VOLUME 6				
❏ Motown M 655 [M]	1967	5.00	10.00	20.00
❏ Motown MS 655 [S]	1967	5.00	10.00	20.00

Number / Title (A Side/B Side)	Yr	VG	VG+	NM
A COLLECTION OF 16 ORIGINAL BIG HITS, VOLUME 7				
❏ Motown M 661 [M]	1967	5.00	10.00	20.00
❏ Motown MS 661 [S]	1967	5.00	10.00	20.00
A COLLECTION OF 16 ORIGINAL BIG HITS, VOLUME 8				
❏ Motown M 666 [M]	1967	5.00	10.00	20.00
❏ Motown MS 666 [S]	1967	5.00	10.00	20.00
A COLLECTION OF 16 ORIGINAL BIG HITS, VOLUME 9				
❏ Motown MS 668	1968	5.00	10.00	20.00
COLLECTOR'S SERIES SAMPLER RECORD				
❏ London LCX 1004 [DJ]	1977	5.00	10.00	20.00
COLLECTORS ITEMS, VOL. 2				
❏ Riverside RLP-1040 [10]	1954	20.00	40.00	80.00
COLLECTUS INTERRUPTUS				
❏ Warner Bros. PRO 726 [(2)]	1977	5.00	10.00	20.00
COLLEGE JAZZ: DIXIELAND				
❏ Columbia CL 736 [M]	1956	5.00	10.00	20.00
COLOR ME OBG: STATION WDRC				
❏ Roulette R 25347 [M]	1967	5.00	10.00	20.00
COLORADO JAZZ PARTY				
❏ BASF 25099 [(2)]	197?	5.00	10.00	20.00
COLUMBIA JAZZ FESTIVAL				
❏ Columbia JJ-1 [M]	1959	6.25	12.50	25.00
COLUMBIA'S 24 HITS IN THE TOP 20 FOR 1982!				
❏ Columbia A2S 1588 [(2)DJ]	1982	6.25	12.50	25.00
COMBO JAZZ				
❏ Jazztone J-1221 [M]	1956	7.50	15.00	30.00
COME CLOSER TO GOD				
❏ Vee Jay LP-5061 [M]	1964	7.50	15.00	30.00
COME TOGETHER: AMERICA SALUTES THE BEATLES				
❏ Liberty 31712	1995	5.00	10.00	20.00
COMPARATIVE BLUES				
❏ Jazztone J-1258 [M]	1957	7.50	15.00	30.00
THE COMPLETE COMMODORE JAZZ RECORDINGS, VOLUME I				
❏ Mosaic M23-123 [(23)]	199?	100.00	200.00	400.00
THE COMPLETE COMMODORE JAZZ RECORDINGS, VOLUME II				
❏ Mosaic M23-128 [(23)]	199?	100.00	200.00	400.00
THE COMPLETE COMMODORE JAZZ RECORDINGS, VOLUME III				
❏ Mosaic M20-134 [(20)]	199?	75.00	150.00	300.00
THE COMPLETE KEYNOTE COLLECTION				
❏ Keynote 830121-1 [(21)]	1986	62.50	125.00	250.00
THE COMPLETE MASTER JAZZ PIANO SERIES				
❏ Mosaic M6-140 [(6)]	199?	25.00	50.00	100.00
COMPOSERS AT PLAY: HAROLD ARLEN AND COLE PORTER				
❏ "X" LVA-1003 [M]	1955	10.00	20.00	40.00
THE COMPOSITIONS OF BENNY GOLSON				
❏ Riverside RLP-3505 [M]	1962	3.75	7.50	15.00
❏ Riverside RS-93505 [S]	1962	5.00	10.00	20.00
THE COMPOSITIONS OF BOBBY TIMMONS				
❏ Riverside RLP-3512 [M]	1962	3.75	7.50	15.00
❏ Riverside RS-93512 [S]	1962	5.00	10.00	20.00
THE COMPOSITIONS OF CHARLIE PARKER				
❏ Riverside RLP-3506 [M]	1962	3.75	7.50	15.00
❏ Riverside RS-93506 [S]	1962	5.00	10.00	20.00
THE COMPOSITIONS OF COLE PORTER				
❏ Riverside RM-3515 [M]	1963	3.75	7.50	15.00
❏ Riverside RS-93515 [S]	1963	5.00	10.00	20.00
THE COMPOSITIONS OF DIZZY GILLESPIE				
❏ Riverside RLP-3508 [M]	1962	3.75	7.50	15.00
❏ Riverside RS-93508 [S]	1962	5.00	10.00	20.00
THE COMPOSITIONS OF DUKE ELLINGTON				
❏ Riverside RLP-3507 [M]	1962	3.75	7.50	15.00
❏ Riverside RS-93507 [S]	1962	5.00	10.00	20.00
THE COMPOSITIONS OF DUKE ELLINGTON, VOL. 2				
❏ Riverside RLP-3510 [M]	1962	3.75	7.50	15.00
❏ Riverside RS-93510 [S]	1962	5.00	10.00	20.00
THE COMPOSITIONS OF GEORGE GERSHWIN				
❏ Riverside RM-3517 [M]	1963	3.75	7.50	15.00
❏ Riverside RS-93517 [S]	1963	5.00	10.00	20.00
THE COMPOSITIONS OF HAROLD ARLEN				
❏ Riverside RM-3518 [M]	1963	3.75	7.50	15.00
❏ Riverside RS-93518 [S]	1963	5.00	10.00	20.00
THE COMPOSITIONS OF HORACE SILVER				
❏ Riverside RLP-3509 [M]	1962	3.75	7.50	15.00
❏ Riverside RS-93509 [S]	1962	5.00	10.00	20.00
THE COMPOSITIONS OF IRVING BERLIN				
❏ Riverside RM-3519 [M]	1963	3.75	7.50	15.00
❏ Riverside RS-93519 [S]	1963	5.00	10.00	20.00
THE COMPOSITIONS OF JEROME KERN				
❏ Riverside RM-3516 [M]	1963	3.75	7.50	15.00
❏ Riverside RS-93516 [S]	1963	5.00	10.00	20.00
COMPOSITIONS TO LIONEL HAMPTON				
❏ Crown CLP-5107 [M]	195?	6.25	12.50	25.00
THE COMPOSITIONS OF MILES DAVIS				
❏ Riverside RLP-3504 [M]	1962	3.75	7.50	15.00
❏ Riverside RS-93504 [S]	1962	5.00	10.00	20.00
THE COMPOSITIONS OF RICHARD RODGERS				
❏ Riverside RM-3514 [M]	1963	3.75	7.50	15.00
❏ Riverside RS-93514 [S]	1963	5.00	10.00	20.00

Number	Title (A Side/B Side)	Yr	VG	VG+	NM
THE COMPOSITIONS OF TADD DAMERON					
❑ Riverside RLP-3511 [M]		1962	3.75	7.50	15.00
❑ Riverside RS-93511 [S]		1962	5.00	10.00	20.00
THE COMPOSITIONS OF THELONIOUS MONK					
❑ Riverside RLP-3503 [M]		1962	3.75	7.50	15.00
❑ Riverside RS-93503 [S]		1962	5.00	10.00	20.00
CONCEPTION					
❑ Prestige PRLP-7013 [M]		1956	25.00	50.00	100.00
CONCERT IN JAZZ					
❑ Tops L-1532 [M]		1958	5.00	10.00	20.00
CONCERT JAZZ					
❑ Brunswick BL 54027 [M]		1956	7.50	15.00	30.00
CONCERTS FOR THE PEOPLE OF KAMPUCHEA					
❑ Atlantic SD 2-7005 [(2)]		1981	5.00	10.00	20.00
CONNECTED					
❑ Limp 1005		1981	5.00	10.00	20.00
COOK BOOK					
❑ Warner Bros. PRO 660 [(2)]		1976	5.00	10.00	20.00
COOL EUROPE					
❑ MGM E-3157 [M]		1955	7.50	15.00	30.00
COOL GABRIELS					
❑ Groove LG-1003 [M]		1956	15.00	30.00	60.00
COOL JAZZ					
❑ Seeco CELP-465 [M]		1960	5.00	10.00	20.00
COOL JAZZ FROM HOLLAND					
❑ Epic LN 1126 [10]		1955	10.00	20.00	40.00
COOLIN'					
❑ New Jazz NJLP-8216 [M]		1959	15.00	30.00	60.00
—Purple label					
❑ New Jazz NJLP-8216 [M]		1965	7.50	15.00	30.00
—Blue label, trident logo at right					
COUNTRY & WESTERN CLASSICS 1955					
❑ Economic Consultants 1955		1973	5.00	10.00	20.00
COUNTRY & WESTERN CLASSICS 1956					
❑ Economic Consultants 1956		1973	5.00	10.00	20.00
COUNTRY & WESTERN CLASSICS 1957					
❑ Economic Consultants 1957		1973	5.00	10.00	20.00
COUNTRY & WESTERN CLASSICS 1958					
❑ Economic Consultants 1958		1973	5.00	10.00	20.00
COUNTRY AND WESTERN AWARD WINNERS 1964					
❑ Decca DL 4622 [M]		1965	5.00	10.00	20.00
❑ Decca DL 74622 [S]		1965	6.25	12.50	25.00
COUNTRY AND WESTERN AWARD WINNERS 1966					
❑ Decca DL 4837 [M]		1967	5.00	10.00	20.00
❑ Decca DL 74837 [S]		1967	3.75	7.50	15.00
COUNTRY AND WESTERN JAMBOREE					
❑ King 697 [M]		1961	37.50	75.00	150.00
COUNTRY BOY — COUNTRY GIRL					
❑ Decca DL 4201 [M]		1962	6.25	12.50	25.00
❑ Decca DL 74201 [S]		1962	7.50	15.00	30.00
COUNTRY CHRISTMAS					
❑ King 811 [M]		1962	25.00	50.00	100.00
❑ Monument SLP-18125		1969	5.00	10.00	20.00
❑ Time-Life STL-109 [(3)]		1988	5.00	10.00	20.00
—Available from Time-Life by mail order only; boxed set					
COUNTRY CLASSICS					
❑ RCA Victor LPM-2313 [M]		1961	6.25	12.50	25.00
❑ RCA Victor LSP-2313 [S]		1961	7.50	15.00	30.00
COUNTRY EXPRESS					
❑ Starday SLP-109 [M]		1959	10.00	20.00	40.00
COUNTRY FAIR					
❑ Capitol SWBB-562 [(2)]		1970	6.25	12.50	25.00
COUNTRY GOLD					
❑ RCA Special Products DPL1-0561		1980	5.00	10.00	20.00
COUNTRY HIT PARADE					
❑ Starday SLP-110 [M]		1959	10.00	20.00	40.00
COUNTRY HITS BY COUNTRY STARS					
❑ Capitol ST 1912 [S]		1963	6.25	12.50	25.00
❑ Capitol T 1912 [M]		1963	5.00	10.00	20.00
COUNTRY JUBILEE					
❑ Decca DL 4172 [M]		1961	7.50	15.00	30.00
COUNTRY MEMORIES					
❑ Reader's Digest RBA-066-A [(7)]		1989	12.50	25.00	50.00
COUNTRY MUSIC BY THE WAYSIDE					
❑ Wayside 1013		1968	5.00	10.00	20.00
COUNTRY MUSIC HALL OF FAME					
❑ Starday SLP-164 [(2)M]		1962	7.50	15.00	30.00
COUNTRY MUSIC HALL OF FAME, VOL. 2					
❑ Starday SLP-190 [(2)M]		1963	7.50	15.00	30.00
COUNTRY MUSIC HALL OF FAME, VOL. 3					
❑ Starday SLP-256 [(2)M]		1963	7.50	15.00	30.00
COUNTRY MUSIC HALL OF FAME, VOL. 4					
❑ Starday SLP-295 [(2)M]		1964	7.50	15.00	30.00
COUNTRY MUSIC HALL OF FAME, VOL. 5					
❑ Starday SLP-360 [M]		1966	6.25	12.50	25.00
COUNTRY MUSIC HALL OF FAME, VOL. 6					
❑ Starday SLP-390		1967	6.25	12.50	25.00
COUNTRY MUSIC HALL OF FAME, VOL. 7					
❑ Starday SLP-409		1969	5.00	10.00	20.00
COUNTRY MUSIC HALL OF FAME, VOL. 8					
❑ Starday SLP-430		1969	5.00	10.00	20.00
COUNTRY MUSIC HALL OF FAME, VOL. 9					
❑ Starday SLP-449		1970	5.00	10.00	20.00
COUNTRY MUSIC HITS BY COUNTRY MUSIC STARS					
❑ RCA Camden CAL-689 [M]		1962	5.00	10.00	20.00
❑ RCA Camden CAS-689 [R]		196?	3.75	7.50	15.00
COUNTRY MUSIC HOOTENANNY					
❑ Capitol ST 2009 [S]		1963	7.50	15.00	30.00
❑ Capitol T 2009 [M]		1963	6.25	12.50	25.00
COUNTRY MUSIC JAMBOREE					
❑ Mercury MG-20350 [M]		1958	10.00	20.00	40.00
COUNTRY MUSIC SPECTACULAR					
❑ Starday SLP-117 [M]		1961	10.00	20.00	40.00
COUNTRY MUSIC STAR SPECTACULAR					
❑ Hickory LPM-116 [M]		1963	6.25	12.50	25.00
COUNTRY MUSIC WHO'S WHO					
❑ Starday SLP-304 [M]		1964	5.00	10.00	20.00
—Without booklet					
❑ Starday SLP-304 [M]		1964	7.50	15.00	30.00
—With 52-page booklet					
COUNTRY OLDIES BUT GOODIES					
❑ Smash MGS-27016 [M]		1962	5.00	10.00	20.00
❑ Smash SRS-67016 [S]		1962	5.00	10.00	20.00
A COUNTRY SALUTE TO HANK WILLIAMS					
❑ Harmony HL 7265 [M]		1960	5.00	10.00	20.00
COUNTRY SOFT AND MELLOW					
❑ Reader's Digest RB4-200 [(7)]		1989	12.50	25.00	50.00
COUNTRY SPECIAL					
❑ Capitol STBB-402 [(2)]		1969	6.25	12.50	25.00
COUNTRY SPECTACULAR					
❑ Columbia CL 894 [M]		1956	12.50	25.00	50.00
COUNTRY STARS, COUNTRY HITS					
❑ RCA Camden CAL-793 [M]		1964	5.00	10.00	20.00
❑ RCA Camden CAS-793 [S]		1964	5.00	10.00	20.00
COUNTRY USA: 1950					
❑ Time-Life CTR-23 [(2)]		1991	5.00	10.00	20.00
COUNTRY USA: 1951					
❑ Time-Life CTR-22 [(2)]		1991	5.00	10.00	20.00
COUNTRY USA: 1952					
❑ Time-Life CTR-16 [(2)]		1990	3.75	7.50	15.00
COUNTRY USA: 1953					
❑ Time-Life CTR-20 [(2)]		1990	3.75	7.50	15.00
COUNTRY USA: 1954					
❑ Time-Life CTR-15 [(2)]		1990	5.00	10.00	20.00
COUNTRY USA: 1955					
❑ Time-Life CTR-19 [(2)]		1990	5.00	10.00	20.00
COUNTRY USA: 1956					
❑ Time-Life CTR-13 [(2)]		1990	5.00	10.00	20.00
COUNTRY USA: 1957					
❑ Time-Life CTR-02 [(2)]		1988	3.75	7.50	15.00
COUNTRY USA: 1958					
❑ Time-Life CTR-07 [(2)]		1989	5.00	10.00	20.00
COUNTRY USA: 1959					
❑ Time-Life CTR-09 [(2)]		1989	3.75	7.50	15.00
COUNTRY USA: 1960					
❑ Time-Life CTR-12 [(2)]		1989	3.75	7.50	15.00
COUNTRY USA: 1961					
❑ Time-Life CTR-01 [(2)]		1988	3.75	7.50	15.00
COUNTRY USA: 1962					
❑ Time-Life CTR-03 [(2)]		1988	3.75	7.50	15.00
COUNTRY USA: 1963					
❑ Time-Life CTR-11 [(2)]		1989	3.75	7.50	15.00
COUNTRY USA: 1964					
❑ Time-Life CTR-14 [(2)]		1990	3.75	7.50	15.00
COUNTRY USA: 1965					
❑ Time-Life CTR-10 [(2)]		1989	3.75	7.50	15.00
COUNTRY USA: 1966					
❑ Time-Life CTR-21 [(2)]		1991	5.00	10.00	20.00
COUNTRY USA: 1967					
❑ Time-Life CTR-17 [(2)]		1990	3.75	7.50	15.00
COUNTRY USA: 1968					
❑ Time-Life CTR-06 [(2)]		1989	3.75	7.50	15.00
COUNTRY USA: 1969					
❑ Time-Life CTR-08 [(2)]		1989	5.00	10.00	20.00
COUNTRY USA: 1970					
❑ Time-Life CTR-04 [(2)]		1988	3.75	7.50	15.00
COUNTRY USA: 1971					
❑ Time-Life CTR-05 [(2)]		1989	3.75	7.50	15.00
COUNTRY USA: 1972					
❑ Time-Life CTR-18 [(2)]		1990	3.75	7.50	15.00
THE COUNTRY'S BEST					
❑ Capitol T 1179 [M]		1959	7.50	15.00	30.00
CRITICS' CHOICE					
❑ Dawn DLP-1123 [M]		1958	20.00	40.00	80.00

Number	Title (A Side/B Side)	Yr	VG	VG+	NM
CROSSROADS: WHITE BLUES IN THE 1960S					
❏ Elektra 60383 [(3)]		1984	5.00	10.00	20.00
CRUISIN'					
❏ Jazzland JLP-7 [M]		1960	6.25	12.50	25.00
❏ Jazzland JLP-97 [S]		1960	7.50	15.00	30.00
CURTAIN UP! AMERICAN DANCE FAVORITES					
❏ Mercury Living Presence SR 90326 [S]		196?	10.00	20.00	40.00
—*Maroon label, no "Vendor: Mercury Record Corporation"*					
CURTAIN UP! FAVORITE CONCERT OVERTURES					
❏ Mercury Living Presence SR 90323 [S]		196?	15.00	30.00	60.00
—*Maroon label, no "Vendor: Mercury Record Corporation"*					
CURTAIN UP! OPERA BALLET FAVORITES					
❏ Mercury Living Presence SR 90327 [S]		196?	7.50	15.00	30.00
—*Maroon label, no "Vendor: Mercury Record Corporation"*					
D'OES CRAZY OLDIES					
❏ Oldies 33 OL-8007 [M]		1964	6.25	12.50	25.00
THE D.I.Y. ALBUM					
❏ D.I.Y./JW Productions DIY-0001		1982	12.50	25.00	50.00
—*Band copies on black vinyl*					
❏ D.I.Y./JW Productions DIY-0001A		1982	7.50	15.00	30.00
—*Store copies on clear vinyl (3-D pressing was planned but never done)*					
DANCE BAND HITS					
❏ RCA Victor LPT-2 [10]		1951	10.00	20.00	40.00
DANCE DISCOTHEQUE					
❏ Decca DL 4556 [M]		1964	3.75	7.50	15.00
❏ Decca DL 74556 [S]		1964	5.00	10.00	20.00
DANCE ON THE WILD SIDE					
❏ Chancellor CHL-5028 [M]		1962	6.25	12.50	25.00
❏ Chancellor CHLS-5028 [S]		1962	7.50	15.00	30.00
DANCE RHYTHM 'N' ROCK NEW MUSIC SEMINAR MIXER					
❏ Warner Bros. PRO-A-2061 [DJ]		1983	20.00	40.00	80.00
DANCE THE ROCK & ROLL					
❏ Atlantic 8013 [M]		1957	20.00	40.00	80.00
DANCE TO THE BANDS					
❏ Capitol TBO 727 [(2)M]		1956	10.00	20.00	40.00
❏ Capitol T 977 [M]		1958	5.00	10.00	20.00
DANCE TUNES FROM THE VAULT, VOLUME 2					
❏ Chess LP 1476 [M]		1962	10.00	20.00	40.00
DANCE, BE HAPPY!					
❏ Columbia CL 967 [M]		1957	5.00	10.00	20.00
DANCING WITH THE STARS					
❏ Epic LN 3136 [M]		1955	7.50	15.00	30.00
DARK MUDDY BOTTOM BLUES					
❏ Specialty SPS-2149		1971	5.00	10.00	20.00
DAS IS JAZZ!					
❏ Decca DL 8229 [M]		1956	7.50	15.00	30.00
A DATE WITH GREATNESS					
❏ Imperial LP-9188A [M]		1962	12.50	25.00	50.00
—*Features Aladdin tracks by Coleman Hawkins, Howard McGhee and Lester Young*					
❏ Imperial LP-12188A [R]		1962	6.25	12.50	25.00
A DATE WITH RIVERSIDE					
❏ Riverside S-4 [M]		195?	10.00	20.00	40.00
A DAY IN THE COUNTRY					
❏ Audio Lab AL-1519 [M]		1959	20.00	40.00	80.00
DAYS OF WINE AND VINYL					
❏ Warner Bros. PRO 540 [(2)]		1973	7.50	15.00	30.00
DEEP EAR					
❏ Warner Bros. PRO 591 [(2)]		1974	6.25	12.50	25.00
DEEP SIX					
❏ C/Z CZ 001		1985	12.50	25.00	50.00
DEF JAM RECORDINGS — RETAIL TRACKS					
❏ Def Jam CAS 2715 [DJ]		1987	5.00	10.00	20.00
THE DEFINITIVE JAZZ SCENE, VOL. 1					
❏ ABC Impulse! AS-99 [S]		1968	3.00	6.00	12.00
❏ Impulse! A-99 [M]		1966	3.75	7.50	15.00
❏ Impulse! AS-99 [S]		1966	5.00	10.00	20.00
THE DEFINITIVE JAZZ SCENE, VOL. 2					
❏ ABC Impulse! AS-100 [S]		1968	3.00	6.00	12.00
❏ Impulse! A-100 [M]		1966	3.75	7.50	15.00
❏ Impulse! AS-100 [S]		1966	5.00	10.00	20.00
THE DEFINITIVE JAZZ SCENE, VOL. 3					
❏ ABC Impulse! AS-9101 [S]		1968	3.00	6.00	12.00
❏ Impulse! A-9101 [M]		1966	3.75	7.50	15.00
❏ Impulse! AS-9101 [S]		1966	5.00	10.00	20.00
DEL-FI ALBUM SAMPLER					
❏ Del-Fi (no #) [DJ]		1959	125.00	250.00	500.00
—*Green vinyl, promo only, with paper sleeve*					
DEL-FI RECORD HOP					
❏ Del-Fi DFLP-1210 [M]		1959	20.00	40.00	80.00
DEMAND PERFORMANCES					
❏ Monument MLP-8010 [M]		1963	6.25	12.50	25.00
❏ Monument SLP-18010 [S]		1963	10.00	20.00	40.00
DEMONSTRATION RECORD — DISC JOCKEYS — JAN.-FEB. 1955					
❏ Capitol PRO-213 [DJ]		1955	10.00	20.00	40.00
DESTINATION STEREO					
❏ RCA Victor Red Seal LSC-2307 [S]		1959	7.50	15.00	30.00
DIAL A HIT					
❏ Bell 6030		1969	5.00	10.00	20.00
A DIAMOND HIDDEN IN THE MOUTH OF A CORPSE					
❏ Giomo Poetry Systems 035		1985	7.50	15.00	30.00
DICK CLARK ALL TIME HITS					
❏ Click Corp. B-100/101 [Picture Sleeve]		1958	5.00	10.00	20.00
DICK CLARK: 20 YEARS OF ROCK N' ROLL					
❏ Buddah BDS 5133 [(2)]		1973	5.00	10.00	20.00
—*Gatefold cover with booklet and bonus 7-inch cardboard record*					
❏ Buddah BDS 5133 [(2)]		1974	2.50	5.00	10.00
—*With none of the extras*					
DIESEL SMOKE, DANGEROUS CURVES AND OTHER TRUCK DRIVERS FAVORITES					
❏ Starday SLP-250 [M]		1963	7.50	15.00	30.00
DISCO-TEEN '66					
❏ Columbia Record Club D 155 [M]		1966	5.00	10.00	20.00
❏ Columbia Record Club DS 155 [S]		1966	12.50	25.00	50.00
—*Sought-after for its otherwise unavailable extended stereo mix of Bob Dylan's "Positively 4th Street"*					
DISPLAY CASE #10					
❏ Warner Bros. PRO 542 [(3)]		1973	7.50	15.00	30.00
DISPLAY CASE #8					
❏ Warner Bros. PRO 532 [(2)]		1972	7.50	15.00	30.00
DISPLAY CASE #9					
❏ Warner Bros. PRO 538 [(2)]		1972	7.50	15.00	30.00
DIXIE, LONDON STYLE					
❏ London LL 1337 [M]		1956	5.00	10.00	20.00
DIXIELAND — NEW ORLEANS					
❏ Mainstream S-6003 [R]		1965	3.00	6.00	12.00
❏ Mainstream 56003 [M]		1965	6.25	2.50	25.00
DIXIELAND AT CARNEGIE HALL					
❏ Forum F-9011 [M]		196?	5.00	10.00	20.00
❏ Forum SF-9011 [S]		196?	6.25	12.50	25.00
❏ Roulette R 25038 [M]		1958	7.50	15.00	30.00
—*Originals have a black label*					
❏ Roulette R 25038 [M]		1959	5.00	10.00	20.00
—*Second pressings have a white label with colored spokes*					
DIXIELAND AT JAZZ, LTD.					
❏ Atlantic 1261 [M]		1957	10.00	20.00	40.00
—*Black label*					
❏ Atlantic 1261 [M]		1961	6.25	12.50	25.00
—*Multicolor label, white "fan" logo at right*					
DIXIELAND AT JAZZ, LTD., VOL. 1					
❏ Atlantic ALS-139 [10]		1952	15.00	30.00	60.00
DIXIELAND AT JAZZ, LTD., VOL. 2					
❏ Atlantic ALS-140 [10]		1952	15.00	30.00	60.00
DIXIELAND CLASSICS					
❏ Jazztone J-1216 [M]		1956	7.50	15.00	30.00
DIXIELAND CONTRASTS					
❏ Jazzman LJ-334 [M]		1954	7.50	15.00	30.00
DIXIELAND DETOUR					
❏ Capitol H 312 [10]		1952	12.50	25.00	50.00
DIXIELAND FESTIVAL, VOL. 1					
❏ Vik LX-1057 [M]		1956	7.50	15.00	30.00
DIXIELAND HITS					
❏ Swingville SVLP-2040 [M]		1962	10.00	20.00	40.00
—*Purple label*					
❏ Swingville SVLP-2040 [M]		1965	5.00	10.00	20.00
—*Blue label, trident logo at right*					
DIXIELAND IN OLD NEW ORLEANS					
❏ Golden Crest GC-3021 [M]		1958	5.00	10.00	20.00
DIXIELAND JAZZ					
❏ Audiophile XL-325 [M]		1954	7.50	15.00	30.00
❏ Audiophile XL-330 [M]		1954	7.50	15.00	30.00
❏ Grand Award GA 33-310 [M]		1955	6.25	12.50	25.00
—*Without wrap-around outer cover*					
❏ Grand Award GA 33-310 [M]		1955	15.00	30.00	60.00
—*With wrap-around outer cover*					
DIXIELAND JAZZ GEMS					
❏ Commodore FL-20010 [10]		1950	12.50	25.00	50.00
DIXIELAND MAIN STREAM					
❏ Savoy MG-12213 [M]		196?	5.00	10.00	20.00
DIXIELAND RHYTHM KINGS					
❏ Paradox LP-6002 [10]		1951	12.50	25.00	50.00
DIXIELAND SERIES, VOL. 1					
❏ Savoy MG-15005 [10]		1952	20.00	40.00	80.00
DIXIELAND SERIES, VOL. 2					
❏ Savoy MG-15009 [10]		1952	20.00	40.00	80.00
DIXIELAND VS. BIRDLAND					
❏ MGM E-231 [10]		1954	12.50	25.00	50.00
DIZZY ATMOSPHERE					
❏ Specialty LP-2110 [M]		1957	10.00	20.00	40.00
DOCTOR DEATH'S VOLUME 1					
❏ C'est La Mort 001		1986	7.50	15.00	30.00
DOO WOP					
❏ Specialty SPS-2114		1969	5.00	10.00	20.00
DOUBLE BARREL JAZZ					
❏ Bethlehem BCP-87 [M]		1958	7.50	15.00	30.00
DOWN BEAT JAZZ CONCERT					
❏ Dot DLP-9003 [M]		1958	7.50	15.00	30.00
❏ Dot DLP-29003 [S]		1958	6.25	12.50	25.00

Number	Title (A Side/B Side)	Yr	VG	VG+	NM
DOWN BEAT JAZZ CONCERT, VOL. 2					
❑ Dot DLP-3188 [M]		1959	7.50	15.00	30.00
❑ Dot DLP-25188 [S]		1959	6.25	12.50	25.00
DOWN BEAT'S HALL OF FAME, VOL. 1					
❑ Verve MGV-8320 [M]		1959	12.50	25.00	50.00
❑ Verve V-8320 [M]		1961	5.00	10.00	20.00
DOWN HOME STOMP: RURAL BLUES, VOLUME 3					
❑ Imperial LP-94006		1968	5.00	10.00	20.00
THE DRUMS					
❑ ABC Impulse! AS-9272 [(3)]		197?	5.00	10.00	20.00
DRUMS ON FIRE					
❑ World Pacific WP-1247 [M]		1958	10.00	20.00	40.00
THE DUTCH EXPLOSION					
❑ White Whale WWS-7130		1970	7.50	15.00	30.00
THE EARLY '60S: THESE WERE OUR SONGS					
❑ Reader's Digest RC4-100 [(7)]		1989	12.50	25.00	50.00
EARLY AND RARE: CLASSIC JAZZ "COLLECTORS ITEMS"					
❑ Riverside RLP 12-134 [M]		1957	10.00	20.00	40.00
EARLY JAZZ GREATS, VOL. 1					
❑ Jazztone J-1249 [M]		1957	7.50	15.00	30.00
EARLY JAZZ GREATS, VOL. 2					
❑ Jazztone J-1252 [M]		1957	7.50	15.00	30.00
EARTHY!					
❑ Prestige PRLP-7102 [M]		1957	25.00	50.00	100.00
THE EAST COAST JAZZ SCENE, VOL. 1					
❑ Coral CRL 57035 [M]		1956	12.50	25.00	50.00
EASY LISTENING					
❑ Audiophile AP-27 [M]		1953	7.50	15.00	30.00
❑ Audiophile AP-38 [M]		1953	7.50	15.00	30.00
❑ Audiophile XL-327 [M]		1954	7.50	15.00	30.00
EASY LISTENING HITS OF THE '60S AND '70S					
❑ Reader's Digest RBA-040A [(7)]		1989	12.50	25.00	50.00
ECLIPSE					
❑ Warner Bros. PRO-A-828 [(2)]		1978	5.00	10.00	20.00
EIGHT WAYS TO JAZZ					
❑ Riverside RLP 12-272 [M]		1958	7.50	15.00	30.00
ELEKTRA'S BEST, VOLUME 1: 1966-1968					
❑ Elektra EB-1 [(2)]		1969	6.25	12.50	25.00
—Promo only, red labels					
ELEKTROCK: THE SIXTIES					
❑ Elektra 60403 [(4)]		1985	7.50	15.00	30.00
ENCYCLOPEDIA OF JAZZ IN THE '60'S, VOL. 1					
❑ Verve V-8677 [M]		1966	3.75	7.50	15.00
❑ Verve V6-8677 [S]		1966	5.00	10.00	20.00
THE ENCYCLOPEDIA OF JAZZ ON RECORDS					
❑ Decca DXF 140 [(4)M]		1957	25.00	50.00	100.00
—Box set; individually issued as Decca 8398, 8399, 8400 and 8401					
THE ENCYCLOPEDIA OF JAZZ ON RECORDS, VOL. 1 AND 2: JAZZ OF THE TWENTIES/JAZZ OF THE THIRTIES					
❑ MCA 4061 [(2)]		197?	3.75	7.50	15.00
THE ENCYCLOPEDIA OF JAZZ ON RECORDS, VOL. 1: JAZZ OF THE TWENTIES					
❑ Decca DL 8398 [M]		1957	5.00	10.00	20.00
THE ENCYCLOPEDIA OF JAZZ ON RECORDS, VOL. 2: JAZZ OF THE THIRTIES					
❑ Decca DL 8399 [M]		1957	5.00	10.00	20.00
THE ENCYCLOPEDIA OF JAZZ ON RECORDS, VOL. 3 AND 4: JAZZ OF THE FORTIES/JAZZ OF THE FIFTIES					
❑ MCA 4062 [(2)]		197?	3.75	7.50	15.00
THE ENCYCLOPEDIA OF JAZZ ON RECORDS, VOL. 3: JAZZ OF THE FORTIES					
❑ Decca DL 8400 [M]		1957	5.00	10.00	20.00
THE ENCYCLOPEDIA OF JAZZ ON RECORDS, VOL. 4: JAZZ OF THE FIFTIES					
❑ Decca DL 8401 [M]		1957	5.00	10.00	20.00
THE ENCYCLOPEDIA OF JAZZ ON RECORDS, VOL. 5: JAZZ OF THE SIXTIES					
❑ MCA 4063 [(2)]		197?	3.75	7.50	15.00
END OF AN ERA: RHYTHM 'N' BLUES, VOLUME 1					
❑ Imperial LP-94003		1968	5.00	10.00	20.00
ENERGY ESSENTIALS					
❑ ABC Impulse! ASD-9228 [(3)]		197?	5.00	10.00	20.00
ENGLAND'S GREATEST HIT MAKERS					
❑ London PS 430 [R]		1965	5.00	10.00	20.00
❑ London LL 3430 [M]		1965	6.25	12.50	25.00
ENGLAND'S GREATEST HITS					
❑ Fontana MGF 27570 [M]		1967	10.00	20.00	40.00
—Without poster					
❑ Fontana MGF 27570 [M]		1967	12.50	25.00	50.00
—With poster					
❑ Fontana SRF 67570 [R]		1967	5.00	10.00	20.00
—Without poster					
❑ Fontana SRF 67570 [R]		1967	7.50	15.00	30.00
—With poster					
ERA OF THE CLARINET					
❑ Mainstream S-6011 [R]		1965	3.00	6.00	12.00
❑ Mainstream 56011 [M]		1965	6.25	12.50	25.00
ESCAPADE REVIEWS THE JAZZ SCENE					
❑ Liberty SL-9005 [M]		1957	7.50	15.00	30.00
ESCAPE					
❑ Gene Norman GNP-27 [M]		1958	6.25	12.50	25.00
ESQUIRE'S ALL-AMERICAN HOT JAZZ					
❑ RCA Victor LPV-544 [M]		1967	5.00	10.00	20.00
ESQUIRE'S WORLD OF JAZZ					
❑ Capitol STBO 1970 [(2)S]		1963	5.00	10.00	20.00
❑ Capitol TBO 1970 [(2)M]		1963	5.00	10.00	20.00
THE ESSENTIAL JAZZ VOCALS					
❑ Verve V-8505 [M]		1963	5.00	10.00	20.00
❑ Verve V6-8505 [S]		1963	6.25	12.50	25.00
AN EVENING OF JAZZ					
❑ Norgran MGN-1065 [M]		1956	20.00	40.00	80.00
❑ Verve MGV-8155 [M]		1957	7.50	15.00	30.00
❑ Verve V-8155 [M]		1961	5.00	10.00	20.00
EVERYBODY'S FAVORITE BLUES					
❑ King 875 [M]		1963	17.50	35.00	70.00
EVERYBODY'S GONE SURFIN'					
❑ Parkway P-7035 [M]		1963	12.50	25.00	50.00
THE EXCELLO STORY					
❑ Excello LPS-8025 [(2)]		1972	6.25	12.50	25.00
THE EXCITING NEW LIVERPOOL SOUND					
❑ Columbia CL 2172 [M]		1964	7.50	15.00	30.00
EXPLOSIVE!					
❑ Liberty MM-412 [DJ]		1962	12.50	25.00	50.00
—Promo-only release					
FABULOUS FAVORITES OF OUR TIME					
❑ Liberty LRP-3223 [M]		1962	5.00	10.00	20.00
❑ Liberty LST-7223 [S]		1962	6.25	12.50	25.00
THE FAMILY CHRISTMAS COLLECTION					
❑ Time-Life STL-131 [(5)]		1990	7.50	15.00	30.00
—Available from Time-Life by mail order only					
FAMILY PORTRAIT					
❑ A&M SP-19002		1968	5.00	10.00	20.00
FANFARE OF HITS					
❑ Argo LP-656 [M]		1960	6.25	12.50	25.00
FANTASY SAMPLER					
❑ Fantasy FS-654 [M]		195?	5.00	10.00	20.00
—Red vinyl					
FAVORITE SACRED SONGS					
❑ King 556 [M]		1956	37.50	75.00	150.00
THE FEMININE TOUCH					
❑ Decca DL 5486 [10]		1953	12.50	25.00	50.00
❑ Decca DL 8316 [M]		1956	7.50	15.00	30.00
FIDDLER'S HALL OF FAME					
❑ Starday SLP-209 [M]		1963	7.50	15.00	30.00
FIDDLIN' COUNTRY STYLE					
❑ Nashville NLP-2015 [M]		1965	5.00	10.00	20.00
❑ Power Pak PO-296		197?	2.50	5.00	10.00
❑ Starday SLP-114 [M]		1960	10.00	20.00	40.00
FIFTEEN STAR SAXOPHONES					
❑ Bethlehem BCP-6035 [M]		1959	7.50	15.00	30.00
FILLET OF SOUL					
❑ Stax STS 3021		1972	5.00	10.00	20.00
FILLMORE: THE LAST DAYS					
❑ Fillmore Z3X 31390 [(3)]		1972	12.50	25.00	50.00
—With booklet and bonus 7-inch single					
FILM MUSIC FROM FRANCE					
❑ Philips PHM 200071 [M]		1962	5.00	10.00	20.00
❑ Philips PHS 600071 [S]		1962	7.50	15.00	30.00
THE FINEST OF FOLK BLUESMEN					
❑ Bethlehem BCP-6017		197?	5.00	10.00	20.00
—Despite lower number, this is a reissue of Bethlehem 6071, distributed by RCA					
FINK ALONG WITH MAD					
❑ Big Top 12-1306 [M]		1962	25.00	50.00	100.00
FIRE ON THE STRINGS					
❑ Starday SLP-221 [M]		1963	7.50	15.00	30.00
FIRST ALBUM OF JAZZ					
❑ Folkways FP-712 [10]		1951	12.50	25.00	50.00
FIRST DECADE					
❑ WEA 10 [(3)DJ]		1981	37.50	75.00	150.00
—Only 1,000 were made paying tribute to WEA's 10th anniversary					
THE FIRST GREAT ROCK FESTIVALS OF THE SEVENTIES: ISLE OF WIGHT/ATLANTA POP FESTIVAL					
❑ Columbia G3X 30805 [(3)]		1971	6.25	12.50	25.00
FIRST OF THE FAMOUS					
❑ Capitol T 2275 [M]		1965	6.25	12.50	25.00
FIVE FEET OF SWING					
❑ Decca DL 8045 [M]		1954	10.00	20.00	40.00
FLEX YOUR HEAD					
❑ Dischord 7		1982	12.50	25.00	50.00
THE FOLK BOX					
❑ Elektra EKL-9001 [(4)]		1964	12.50	25.00	50.00
FOLK FESTIVAL					
❑ Elektra SMP 2 [M]		1956	7.50	15.00	30.00
FOLK FESTIVAL OF THE BLUES					
❑ Argo LP-4031 [M]		1964	10.00	20.00	40.00
FOLK POPS 'N JAZZ SAMPLER					
❑ Liberty SMP 3 [M]		1957	6.25	12.50	25.00
FOLK SAMPLER FIVE					
❑ Elektra SMP 5 [M]		196?	6.25	12.50	25.00
THE FOLK SCENE					
❑ Elektra SMP 6 [M]		196?	6.25	12.50	25.00

Number Title (A Side/B Side)	Yr	VG	VG+	NM
FOLKSONG '65				
❏ Elektra SMP 8 [M]	1965	5.00	10.00	20.00
❏ Elektra S 78 [S]	1965	6.25	12.50	25.00
FOOTNOTES TO JAZZ, VOL. 2: ANATOMY OF A JAZZ COMPOSITION				
❏ Folkways FP-31 [10]	1951	12.50	25.00	50.00
FOOTPRINTS IN TIME				
❏ White Whale WWS-7125	1970	6.25	12.50	25.00
FOR CHRISTMAS SEALS…A MATTER OF LIFE AND BREATH				
❏ Decca Custom Style E [DJ]	1968	5.00	10.00	20.00
—Promo-only album for Christmas Seals				
❏ Decca Custom Style F [DJ]	1968	6.25	12.50	25.00
—Promo-only album for Christmas Seals; four five-minute programs				
FOR DANCERS ONLY				
❏ Epic LN 3120 [M]	1955	7.50	15.00	30.00
FOR JAZZ LOVERS				
❏ EmArcy MG-36086 [M]	1956	10.00	20.00	40.00
FOR TWISTERS ONLY				
❏ Ace LP-1020 [M]	1962	17.50	35.00	70.00
THE FORCE				
❏ Warner Bros. PRO 593	1974	5.00	10.00	20.00
❏ Warner Bros. PRO 596 [(2)]	1974	6.25	12.50	25.00
FORD HOOTENANNY				
❏ RCA Victor PRM-152 [M]	1964	5.00	10.00	20.00
—Sold only at Ford dealers				
FOREPLAY #45				
❏ A&M SP-17162 [DJ]	1981	6.25	12.50	25.00
—Includes 20-minute collage of music from "Urgh! A Music War"				
FORGOTTEN MILLION SELLERS				
❏ King 792 [M]	1962	25.00	50.00	100.00
FORTY GOSPEL GREATS				
❏ Vee Jay VJS-2-19000 [(2)]	1975	6.25	12.50	25.00
FOUR ALTOS				
❏ Prestige PRLP-7116 [M]	1957	25.00	50.00	100.00
FOUR FRENCH HORNS				
❏ Savoy MG-12173 [M]	1961	12.50	25.00	50.00
THE FOUR MOST GUITARS				
❏ ABC-Paramount ABC-109 [M]	1956	7.50	15.00	30.00
❏ Paramount LP-109 [10]	1954	15.00	30.00	60.00
FOUR TO GO				
❏ Columbia CL 2018 [M]	1963	5.00	10.00	20.00
FRANK BULL AND GENE NORMAN PRESENT DIXIELAND JUBILEE				
❏ Decca DL 7022 [10]	1952	12.50	25.00	50.00
FRANK JOHNSON'S FAVORITES				
❏ Ralph 8110	1981	5.00	10.00	20.00
FRENCH TOAST				
❏ Angel ANG-60009 [10]	1956	12.50	25.00	50.00
FUNKY BLUES NO. 2				
❏ American Recording Society G-404 [M]	1956	7.50	15.00	30.00
THE FUTURE LOOKS BRIGHT				
❏ SST/Posh Boy PBS 120 [DJ]	1981	7.50	15.00	30.00
—Vinyl is promo only				
GALA FAVORITES				
❏ Mercury Living Presence SR 90339 [S]	196?	6.25	12.50	25.00
—Maroon label, no "Vendor: Mercury Record Corporation"				
GARDEN OF DELIGHTS				
❏ Elektra S3 10 [(3)]	1971	5.00	10.00	20.00
—Butterfly labels, possibly promo only				
GARY MOORE PRESENTS "MY KIND OF MUSIC"				
❏ Columbia CL 717 [M]	1956	6.25	12.50	25.00
GEMS OF JAZZ, VOL. 1				
❏ Decca DL 5133 [10]	1950	12.50	25.00	50.00
❏ Decca DL 8039 [M]	1954	10.00	20.00	40.00
GEMS OF JAZZ, VOL. 2				
❏ Decca DL 5134 [10]	1950	12.50	25.00	50.00
❏ Decca DL 8040 [M]	1954	10.00	20.00	40.00
GEMS OF JAZZ, VOL. 3				
❏ Decca DL 5383 [10]	1952	12.50	25.00	50.00
❏ Decca DL 8041 [M]	1954	10.00	20.00	40.00
GEMS OF JAZZ, VOL. 4				
❏ Decca DL 5384 [10]	1952	12.50	25.00	50.00
❏ Decca DL 8042 [M]	1954	10.00	20.00	40.00
GEMS OF JAZZ, VOL. 5				
❏ Decca DL 8043 [M]	1954	10.00	20.00	40.00
GENE NORMAN PRESENTS JUST JAZZ				
❏ RCA Victor LPM-3102 [10]	1953	12.50	25.00	50.00
GERRY GOFFIN AND CAROLE KING: SOLID GOLD				
❏ Screen Gems/Columbia CPL-713 [DJ]	1975	5.00	10.00	20.00
—Promo-only compilation of oldies sent to radio to spur airplay on songs owned by this publishing house				
GIANTS OF BOOGIE WOOGIE				
❏ Riverside RLP 12-106 [M]	1956	10.00	20.00	40.00
GIANTS OF JAZZ				
❏ American Recording Society G-401 [M]	1956	7.50	15.00	30.00
THE GIANTS OF JAZZ				
❏ Columbia CL 1970 [M]	1963	7.50	15.00	30.00
GIANTS OF JAZZ ORGAN				
❏ King 837 [M]	1963	30.00	60.00	120.00
GIANTS OF JAZZ VOL. 2				
❏ American Recording Society G-444 [M]	1957	7.50	15.00	30.00

Number Title (A Side/B Side)	Yr	VG	VG+	NM
GIANTS OF SMALL BAND SWING, VOL. 1				
❏ Fantasy OJC-1723	1990	2.50	5.00	10.00
❏ Riverside RLP 12-143 [M]	1957	10.00	20.00	40.00
GIANTS OF SMALL BAND SWING, VOL. 2				
❏ Fantasy OJC-1724	1990	2.50	5.00	10.00
❏ Riverside RLP 12-145 [M]	1957	10.00	20.00	40.00
THE GIRLS SING				
❏ Savoy MG-12220 [M]	196?	5.00	10.00	20.00
GOIN' UP THE COUNTRY: RURAL BLUES, VOLUME 1				
❏ Imperial LP-94000	1968	5.00	10.00	20.00
GOLD HITS				
❏ Warwick W 2008 [M]	1959	20.00	40.00	80.00
—Reissue of "Goodies But Oldies, Volume 2"; this title still appears on the label				
GOLD SOUL				
❏ Stax STS 2031	1970	5.00	10.00	20.00
GOLDEN AGE OF COUNTRY MUSIC 1940-1970				
❏ Reader's Digest RBA-005-A [(7)]	1987	10.00	20.00	40.00
THE GOLDEN AGE OF RHYTHM AND BLUES				
❏ Chess 2CH-50030 [(2)]	1972	6.25	12.50	25.00
GOLDEN COUNTRY GROUPS				
❏ Reader's Digest RBA-201-A [(7)]	1988	10.00	20.00	40.00
GOLDEN COUNTRY HITS				
❏ United Artists UAL-3327 [M]	1964	3.75	7.50	15.00
❏ United Artists UAS-6327 [S]	1964	5.00	10.00	20.00
THE GOLDEN DAYS OF BRITISH ROCK				
❏ Sire V 6046 [(4)]	1976	10.00	20.00	40.00
GOLDEN ECHOES				
❏ Arvee A-433 [M]	1962	6.25	12.50	25.00
❏ Arvee SA-433 [S]	1962	7.50	15.00	30.00
GOLDEN ENCORES				
❏ Cadence CLP-3043 [M]	1960	10.00	20.00	40.00
THE GOLDEN ERA OF JAZZ, VOL. 1				
❏ Savoy MG-15015 [10]	1952	20.00	40.00	80.00
THE GOLDEN ERA OF JAZZ, VOL. 2				
❏ Savoy MG-15018 [10]	1952	20.00	40.00	80.00
GOLDEN GASSERS				
❏ Chess LP 1458 USA [M]	1961	30.00	60.00	120.00
—National version; see listings in this section under "KYA," "Murray the K" and "WAMO" for regional releases				
GOLDEN GOODIES OF 1963, VOL. 18				
❏ Roulette R 25247 [M]	1964	5.00	10.00	20.00
GOLDEN GOODIES, VOL. 1				
❏ Roulette R 25207 [M]	1963	6.25	12.50	25.00
GOLDEN GOODIES, VOL. 10				
❏ Roulette R 25217 [M]	1963	6.25	12.50	25.00
GOLDEN GOODIES, VOL. 11				
❏ Roulette R 25219 [M]	1963	6.25	12.50	25.00
GOLDEN GOODIES, VOL. 12				
❏ Roulette R 25211 [M]	1963	6.25	12.50	25.00
GOLDEN GOODIES, VOL. 14				
❏ Roulette R 25239 [M]	1964	5.00	10.00	20.00
GOLDEN GOODIES, VOL. 15				
❏ Roulette R 25240 [M]	1964	5.00	10.00	20.00
GOLDEN GOODIES, VOL. 16				
❏ Roulette R 25241 [M]	1964	5.00	10.00	20.00
GOLDEN GOODIES, VOL. 17				
❏ Roulette R 25242 [M]	1964	5.00	10.00	20.00
GOLDEN GOODIES, VOL. 2				
❏ Roulette R 25210 [M]	1963	6.25	12.50	25.00
GOLDEN GOODIES, VOL. 3				
❏ Roulette R 25218 [M]	1963	6.25	12.50	25.00
GOLDEN GOODIES, VOL. 4: GOODIES FOR A DANCE PARTY				
❏ Roulette R 25209 [M]	1963	6.25	12.50	25.00
GOLDEN GOODIES, VOL. 5				
❏ Roulette R 25215 [M]	1963	6.25	12.50	25.00
GOLDEN GOODIES, VOL. 6				
❏ Roulette R 25216 [M]	1963	6.25	12.50	25.00
GOLDEN GOODIES, VOL. 7				
❏ Roulette R 25212 [M]	1963	6.25	12.50	25.00
GOLDEN GOODIES, VOL. 8				
❏ Roulette R 25214 [M]	1963	6.25	12.50	25.00
GOLDEN GOODIES, VOL. 9				
❏ Roulette R 25213 [M]	1963	6.25	12.50	25.00
GOLDEN GREATS				
❏ Liberty LRP-3500 [M]	1967	3.75	7.50	15.00
❏ Liberty LST-7500 [P]	1967	5.00	10.00	20.00
THE GOLDEN GROUPS				
❏ Specialty SPS-2155	1972	5.00	10.00	20.00
GOLDEN HITS FROM THE GANG AT BANG				
❏ Bang BLP-215 [M]	1967	5.00	10.00	20.00
❏ Bang BLPS-215 [P]	1967	6.25	12.50	25.00
GOLDEN INSTRUMENTALS				
❏ Dot DLP-3820 [M]	1967	6.25	12.50	25.00
❏ Dot DLP-25820 [S]	1967	6.25	12.50	25.00
GOLDEN INSTRUMENTALS COUNTRY STYLE				
❏ Wing MGW-12261 [M]	1964	5.00	10.00	20.00
❏ Wing SRW-16261 [S]	1964	5.00	10.00	20.00

Number / Title (A Side/B Side)	Yr	VG	VG+	NM
GOLDEN JAZZ INTRSUMENTALS				
❑ Bethlehem BCP-6065 [M]	1962	6.25	12.50	25.00
GOLDEN SOUVENIRS				
❑ United Artists UAL-3317 [M]	1963	6.25	12.50	25.00
❑ United Artists UAS-6317 [S]	1963	7.50	15.00	30.00
GOLDEN TEEN HITS				
❑ Liberty L-5505 [M]	1962	10.00	20.00	40.00
GOLDEN TREASURE CHEST				
❑ United Artists UAL-3314 [M]	1963	6.25	12.50	25.00
❑ United Artists UAS-6314 [S]	1963	7.50	15.00	30.00
GONE BUT NOT FORGOTTEN				
❑ Class LP-5004 [M]	1959	25.00	50.00	100.00
❑ Rendezvous M-1314 [M]	196?	10.00	20.00	40.00
—Reissue of Class 5004				
GOOD GUY JACK SPECTOR PRESENTS 22 ORIGINAL WINNERS				
❑ Roulette R 25254 [M]	1964	5.00	10.00	20.00
THE GOOD OLD 50'S				
❑ Atco 33-118 [M]	1960	15.00	30.00	60.00
GOODIES BUT OLDIES VOLUME 2				
❑ Warwick W 2008 [M]	1959	30.00	60.00	120.00
—Original title of LP appears on both cover and label; reissued as "Gold Hits" -- and there was no Volume 1!				
GOSPEL HOOTENANNY				
❑ Imperial LP-9240 [M]	1963	5.00	10.00	20.00
❑ Imperial LP-12240 [S]	1963	6.25	12.50	25.00
GOSPEL STARS IN CONCERT				
❑ Specialty SPS-2153	1971	5.00	10.00	20.00
GRAFFITI GOLD				
❑ Vee Jay VJS-2-9000 [(2)]	1974	5.00	10.00	20.00
GRAND OLE OPRY HITS				
❑ RCA Camden CAL-737 [M]	1963	5.00	10.00	20.00
❑ RCA Camden CAS-737 [R]	1966	3.75	7.50	15.00
GRAND OLE OPRY SPECTACULAR				
❑ Starday SLP-242 [(2)M]	1963	7.50	15.00	30.00
THE GREAT BANDS				
❑ Columbia Musical Treasury P2M 5267 [(2)]	1968	5.00	10.00	20.00
GREAT BLUES				
❑ Riverside RLP-1074 [10]	1955	20.00	40.00	80.00
GREAT BLUES SINGERS				
❑ Riverside RLP 12-121 [M]	1957	10.00	20.00	40.00
THE GREAT BLUES SINGERS				
❑ Riverside RLP-1032 [10]	1954	20.00	40.00	80.00
GREAT COUNTRY AND WESTERN STARS				
❑ Wing MGW-12268 [M]	1964	5.00	10.00	20.00
❑ Wing SRW-16268 [S]	1964	5.00	10.00	20.00
GREAT COUNTRY FAVORITES				
❑ MGM E-4211 [M]	1964	5.00	10.00	20.00
❑ MGM SE-4211 [S]	1964	6.25	12.50	25.00
GREAT COUNTRY HITS				
❑ United Artists UAL-3159 [M]	1961	6.25	12.50	25.00
THE GREAT GROUP GOODIES				
❑ Atco 33-143 [M]	1962	20.00	40.00	80.00
GREAT GROUP OLDIES				
❑ Oldies 33 OL-8003 [M]	1963	6.25	12.50	25.00
GREAT GROUP OLDIES, VOL. 2				
❑ Oldies 33 OL-8006 [M]	1964	6.25	12.50	25.00
GREAT GROUPS, GREAT RECORDS				
❑ Laurie LLP-2010 [M]	1961	7.50	15.00	30.00
THE GREAT HITS OF 1964 AND SOME GOLDEN OLDIES				
❑ Vee Jay LP-1112 [M]	1965	7.50	15.00	30.00
—Not known to exist in stereo				
GREAT INSTRUMENTAL R&B HITS				
❑ Imperial LP-9271 [M]	1964	6.25	12.50	25.00
❑ Imperial LP-12271 [R]	1964	5.00	10.00	20.00
GREAT JAZZ				
❑ Rondo-lette A-31 [M]	195?	6.25	12.50	25.00
GREAT JAZZ BRASS				
❑ RCA Camden CAL-383 [M]	1958	6.25	12.50	25.00
GREAT JAZZ PIANISTS				
❑ RCA Camden CAL-328 [M]	1958	6.25	12.50	25.00
GREAT JAZZ REEDS				
❑ RCA Camden CAL-339 [M]	1958	6.25	12.50	25.00
GREAT MOMENTS AT THE GRAND OLE OPRY				
❑ RCA Victor CPL2-1904 [(2)]	1977	5.00	10.00	20.00
GREAT MOTION PICTURE THEMES				
❑ United Artists UAL-3122 [M]	1960	3.75	7.50	15.00
❑ United Artists UAS-6122 [S]	1960	5.00	10.00	20.00
GREAT MOTION PICTURE THEMES (MORE ORIGINAL SOUND TRACKS AND HIT MUSIC)				
❑ United Artists UAL-3158 [M]	1961	3.75	7.50	15.00
❑ United Artists UAS-6158 [S]	1961	5.00	10.00	20.00
THE GREAT ONES				
❑ Capitol ST 1718 [S]	1962	7.50	15.00	30.00
❑ Capitol T 1718 [M]	1962	6.25	12.50	25.00
THE GREAT SOUL HITS				
❑ Brunswick BL 54129 [M]	1968	6.25	12.50	25.00
❑ Brunswick BL 754129 [S]	1968	3.75	7.50	15.00
THE GREAT SWING BANDS				
❑ Jazztone J-1245 [M]	1957	7.50	15.00	30.00
GREAT SWING BANDS OF THE FORTIES				
❑ Audio Lab AL-1530 [M]	1959	20.00	40.00	80.00
THE GREAT TENOR JAZZMEN				
❑ Allegro 1634 [M]	195?	10.00	20.00	40.00
GREAT TRUMPET ARTISTS				
❑ RCA Victor LPT-26 [10]	1951	12.50	25.00	50.00
❑ RCA Victor LPT-35 [10]	1952	12.50	25.00	50.00
THE GREATEST 15 HITS ON ACE RECORDS				
❑ Ace LP-1012 [M]	1960	17.50	35.00	70.00
GREATEST COUNTRY AND WESTERN HITS NO. 3				
❑ Columbia CL 1816 [M]	1962	5.00	10.00	20.00
❑ Columbia CS 8616 [S]	1962	6.25	12.50	25.00
GREATEST COUNTRY AND WESTERN HITS NO. 4				
❑ Columbia CL 2081 [M]	1963	5.00	10.00	20.00
❑ Columbia CS 8881 [S]	1963	6.25	12.50	25.00
THE GREATEST GOLDEN GOODIES				
❑ Laurie LLP-2014 [M]	1962	7.50	15.00	30.00
❑ Laurie SLP-2014 [R]	196?	3.75	7.50	15.00
GREATEST GOSPEL SONGS OF OUR TIMES				
❑ Vee Jay LP-5043 [M]	1963	7.50	15.00	30.00
GREATEST GOSPEL SONGS, VOLUME 1				
❑ Specialty SPS-2144	1970	5.00	10.00	20.00
GREATEST GOSPEL SONGS, VOLUME 2				
❑ Specialty SPS-2145	1970	5.00	10.00	20.00
THE GREATEST HITS FROM ENGLAND				
❑ Parrot PA 61010 [M]	1967	6.25	12.50	25.00
❑ Parrot PAS 71010 [R]	1967	5.00	10.00	20.00
THE GREATEST HITS FROM ENGLAND, VOLUME 2				
❑ Parrot PA 61017 [M]	1968	6.25	12.50	25.00
❑ Parrot PAS 71017 [R]	1968	5.00	10.00	20.00
THE GREATEST JAZZ CONCERT IN THE WORLD				
❑ Pablo 2625704 [(4)]	197?	7.50	15.00	30.00
THE GREATEST NAMES IN JAZZ				
❑ Verve PR2-3 [(3)]	196?	5.00	10.00	20.00
—Box set				
GREATEST RAP HITS, VOL. 1				
❑ Sugar Hill 9132	1984	5.00	10.00	20.00
THE GREATEST ROCK & ROLL				
❑ Atlantic 8001 [M]	1956	30.00	60.00	120.00
THE GREATEST TEENAGE HITS OF ALL TIME!				
❑ Teem LP-5003 [M]	196?	7.50	15.00	30.00
GREATEST WESTERN HITS				
❑ Columbia CL 1257 [M]	1959	7.50	15.00	30.00
❑ Columbia CS 8776 [R]	1963	5.00	10.00	20.00
GREATEST WESTERN HITS NO. 2				
❑ Columbia CL 1408 [M]	1960	7.50	15.00	30.00
❑ Columbia CS 8777 [R]	1963	5.00	10.00	20.00
GRETSCH DRUM NIGHT AT BIRDLAND				
❑ Roulette R 52049 [M]	1960	7.50	15.00	30.00
❑ Roulette SR 52049 [S]	1960	7.50	15.00	30.00
GRETSCH DRUM NIGHT, VOLUME 2				
❑ Roulette R 52067 [M]	1961	7.50	15.00	30.00
❑ Roulette SR 52067 [S]	1961	7.50	15.00	30.00
GROOVY GOODIES				
❑ Colpix CP-466 [M]	1964	20.00	40.00	80.00
❑ Colpix SCP-466 [S]	1964	25.00	50.00	100.00
GROUP OF GOODIES				
❑ Chess LP 1478 [M]	1963	12.50	25.00	50.00
❑ Chess LPS 1478 [R]	196?	5.00	10.00	20.00
GROUP OF GOODIES, VOLUME 2				
❑ Chess LP 1491 [M]	1965	12.50	25.00	50.00
GUARANTEED TO PLEASE				
❑ Teem LP-5002 [M]	196?	7.50	15.00	30.00
GUIDE TO JAZZ				
❑ RCA Victor LPM-1393 [M]	1956	7.50	15.00	30.00
HANDFUL OF COOL JAZZ				
❑ Bethlehem BCP-90 [M]	1959	7.50	15.00	30.00
HAPPY HOLIDAYS VOL. 25				
❑ RCA Special Products DPL2-0936 [(2)]	1990	6.25	12.50	25.00
—Sold only at True Value Hardware stores; the last one on vinyl LP -- and it contains an Elvis track among its 25 selections				
HAPPY JAZZ				
❑ Jazztone J-1215 [M]	1956	7.50	15.00	30.00
HARD GOODS				
❑ Warner Bros. PRO 583 [(2)]	1974	6.25	12.50	25.00
THE HARD SWING				
❑ Pacific Jazz JWC-508 [M]	1957	12.50	25.00	50.00
❑ World Pacific JWC-508 [M]	1958	10.00	20.00	40.00
HARD TO BELIEVE — A KISS COVERS COMPILATION				
❑ C/Z CZ 024	1990	7.50	15.00	30.00
HARLEM JAZZ 1930				
❑ Brunswick BL 58024 [10]	1951	12.50	25.00	50.00
HAVE YOURSELF A MERRY LITTLE CHRISTMAS				
❑ Reprise 50001 [M]	1963	6.25	12.50	25.00
—Red and green cover with ornaments at top; titled on back cover "Top Hollywood Stars Want You to..."				
❑ Reprise R 50001 [M]	1963	6.25	12.50	25.00
—Christmas tree cover; titled "Frank Sinatra and His Friends Want You to..."				
❑ Reprise R 50001 [M]	1963	6.25	12.50	25.00
—Wreath cover; titled on back cover "Top Hollywood Stars Want You to..."				

Number	Title (A Side/B Side)	Yr	VG	VG+	NM
❑ Reprise R9-50001 [S]		1963	7.50	15.00	30.00

—*Christmas tree cover; titled "Frank Sinatra and His Friends Want You to..."; stereo version of above*

HAVING A BALL

❑ End LP-302 [M]		1958	125.00	250.00	500.00

—*Original cover with groups pictured on a record*

HEAD START — BOB THIELE EMERGENCY

❑ Flying Dutchman FDS-104 [(2)]		1969	6.25	12.50	25.00

HEAVY HEADS

❑ Chess LP 1522 [M]		1967	6.25	12.50	25.00
❑ Chess LPS 1522 [P]		1967	6.25	12.50	25.00

HEAVY HEADS, VOYAGE 2

❑ Chess LP 1528 [M]		1969	5.00	10.00	20.00

HEAVY METAL (SUPERSTARS OF THE 70S, VOLUME 2)

❑ Warner Special Products SP-2001		1974	5.00	10.00	20.00

HERALD THE BEAT

❑ Herald HLP-0110 [M]		195?	37.50	75.00	150.00

—*Yellow label*

❑ Herald HLP-0110 [M]		1957	75.00	150.00	300.00

—*Black label*

HERE ARE THE HITS!

❑ Fire FLP-100 [M]		1959	100.00	200.00	400.00

—*Reissued as "Memory Lane, Hits by the Original Groups" with the same label and number*

HERE COME THE GIRLS

❑ Verve MGV-2036 [M]		1956	10.00	20.00	40.00
❑ Verve V-2036 [M]		1961	5.00	10.00	20.00

HERE COME THE SWINGING BANDS

❑ Verve MGV-8207 [M]		1957	7.50	15.00	30.00
❑ Verve V-8207 [M]		1961	5.00	10.00	20.00

HI-FI JAZZ

❑ Brunswick BL 58058 [10]		1954	12.50	25.00	50.00

HI-FI JAZZ SESSION

❑ Masterseal MSLP 5013 [M]		1957	6.25	12.50	25.00

A HI-FI SALUTE TO THE GREAT ONES

❑ MGM E-3325 [M]		1956	7.50	15.00	30.00

A HI-FI SALUTE TO THE GREAT ONES, VOL. 2

❑ MGM E-3354 [M]		1956	7.50	15.00	30.00

HILLBILLY HIT PARADE

❑ Mercury MG-20282 [M]		1957	12.50	25.00	50.00
❑ Starday SLP-102 [M]		1956	25.00	50.00	100.00

HILLBILLY HOUSE PARTY

❑ Imperial LP-9214 [M]		1963	6.25	12.50	25.00
❑ Imperial LP-12214 [R]		1963	5.00	10.00	20.00

HISTORIC JAZZ CONCERT AT MUSIC INN

❑ Atlantic 1298 [M]		1958	10.00	20.00	40.00

—*Black label*

❑ Atlantic 1298 [M]		1961	6.25	12.50	25.00

—*Multicolor label, white "fan" logo at right*

❑ Atlantic 1298 [M]		1963	5.00	10.00	20.00

—*Multicolor label, black "fan" logo at right*

HISTORY OF BRITISH BLUES, VOLUME 1

❑ Sire SASH-3701 [(2)]		1973	5.00	10.00	20.00

HISTORY OF BRITISH ROCK

❑ Sire SASH-3702 [(2)]		1974	5.00	10.00	20.00
❑ Sire 2P 6547 [(2)]		1975	5.00	10.00	20.00

—*Columbia House edition*

HISTORY OF BRITISH ROCK, VOLUME 2

❑ Sire SASH-3705 [(2)]		1974	5.00	10.00	20.00

HISTORY OF BRITISH ROCK, VOLUME 3

❑ Sire SASH-3712 [(2)]		1975	5.00	10.00	20.00

HISTORY OF CLASSIC JAZZ

❑ Riverside SDP-11 [(5)M]		1956	75.00	150.00	300.00

—*Five-record set in leatherette album with booklet; records were available separately as Riverside 112, 113, 114, 115 and 116.*

HISTORY OF CLASSIC JAZZ, VOL. 1

❑ Riverside RLP 12-112 [M]		1957	10.00	20.00	40.00

HISTORY OF CLASSIC JAZZ, VOL. 2

❑ Riverside RLP 12-113 [M]		1957	10.00	20.00	40.00

HISTORY OF CLASSIC JAZZ, VOL. 3

❑ Riverside RLP 12-114 [M]		1957	10.00	20.00	40.00

HISTORY OF CLASSIC JAZZ, VOL. 4

❑ Riverside RLP 12-115 [M]		1957	10.00	20.00	40.00

HISTORY OF CLASSIC JAZZ, VOL. 5

❑ Riverside RLP 12-116 [M]		1957	10.00	20.00	40.00

HISTORY OF JAZZ, VOL. 1: NEW ORLEANS ORIGINS

❑ Capitol T 793 [M]		1956	6.25	12.50	25.00

HISTORY OF JAZZ, VOL. 1: THE SOLID SOUTH

❑ Capitol H 239 [10]		1950	12.50	25.00	50.00

HISTORY OF JAZZ, VOL. 2: THE GOLDEN ERA

❑ Capitol H 240 [10]		1950	12.50	25.00	50.00

HISTORY OF JAZZ, VOL. 2: THE TURBULENT '20S

❑ Capitol T 794 [M]		1956	6.25	12.50	25.00

HISTORY OF JAZZ, VOL. 3: EVERYBODY SWINGS

❑ Capitol T 795 [M]		1956	6.25	12.50	25.00

HISTORY OF JAZZ, VOL. 3: THEN CAME SWING

❑ Capitol H 241 [10]		1950	12.50	25.00	50.00

HISTORY OF JAZZ, VOL. 4: ENTER THE COOL

❑ Capitol H 242 [10]		1950	12.50	25.00	50.00
❑ Capitol T 796 [M]		1956	6.25	12.50	25.00

THE HISTORY OF NEW ORLEANS ROCK 'N' ROLL VOLUME I

❑ Ace 7184		1984	5.00	10.00	20.00

—*Sold only at the Louisiana World's Fair in New Orleans, May 12-Nov. 11, 1984*

THE HISTORY OF NEW ORLEANS ROCK 'N' ROLL VOLUME II

❑ Ace 7284		1984	5.00	10.00	20.00

—*Sold only at the Louisiana World's Fair in New Orleans, May 12-Nov. 11, 1984*

THE HISTORY OF NEW ORLEANS ROCK 'N' ROLL VOLUME III

❑ Ace 7384		1984	5.00	10.00	20.00

—*Sold only at the Louisiana World's Fair in New Orleans, May 12-Nov. 11, 1984*

THE HISTORY OF NEW ORLEANS ROCK 'N' ROLL VOLUME IV

❑ Ace 7484		1984	5.00	10.00	20.00

—*Sold only at the Louisiana World's Fair in New Orleans, May 12-Nov. 11, 1984*

HISTORY OF RHYTHM & BLUES, VOLUME 1/THE ROOTS 1947-52

❑ Atlantic SD 8161		1968	5.00	10.00	20.00

HISTORY OF RHYTHM & BLUES, VOLUME 2/THE GOLDEN YEARS 1953-55

❑ Atlantic 8162 [M]		1968	10.00	20.00	40.00
❑ Atlantic SD 8162 [S]		1968	5.00	10.00	20.00

HISTORY OF RHYTHM & BLUES, VOLUME 3/ROCK & ROLL 1956-57

❑ Atlantic SD 8163		1968	5.00	10.00	20.00

HISTORY OF RHYTHM & BLUES, VOLUME 4/THE BIG BEAT 1958-60

❑ Atlantic SD 8164		1968	5.00	10.00	20.00

HISTORY OF RHYTHM & BLUES, VOLUME 5/THE BEAT GOES ON, 1961-62

❑ Atlantic 8193 [M]		1968	10.00	20.00	40.00

—*Mono is promo only; "DJ Copy Monaural" sticker on front cover*

❑ Atlantic SD 8193 [S]		1968	5.00	10.00	20.00

THE HIT MAKERS AND THEIR RECORD BREAKERS

❑ King 737 [M]		1961	25.00	50.00	100.00

HIT PARADE OF COUNTRY MUSIC

❑ Starday SLP-184 [M]		1962	7.50	15.00	30.00

HIT SOUNDS OF MERRIE MELODIES

❑ Warner Bros. PRO 550 [(2)]		1973	6.25	12.50	25.00

HITCHHIKER 2

❑ Columbia CAS 1826 [DJ]		1989	6.25	12.50	25.00

THE HITCHHIKER COLLEGE RADIO HOUR

❑ Columbia CAS 1598 [DJ]		1989	6.25	12.50	25.00

THE HITS ARE ON VERVE

❑ Verve V6-201 [S]		1964	5.00	10.00	20.00

HITS FROM THE SOUTH PRESENTED BY NICK CHARLES

❑ Stax 702 [M]		1962	25.00	50.00	100.00

—*Has the same number as "Walk Right In" by Gus Cannon, but this LP doesn't have any mention of Atlantic distribution*

HITS I FORGOT TO BUY

❑ Swan SLP-512 [M]		1963	12.50	25.00	50.00

HITS OF THE HOPS

❑ Warner Bros. W 1448 [M]		1962	7.50	15.00	30.00
❑ Warner Bros. WS 1448 [S]		1962	10.00	20.00	40.00

HITS THAT JUMPED

❑ Checker LP 2975 [M]		1959	30.00	60.00	120.00

HITSVILLE

❑ Coral CRL 57269 [M]		1959	20.00	40.00	80.00
❑ Coral CRL 757269 [S]		1959	25.00	50.00	100.00

HITSVILLE U.S.A.

❑ Imperial LP-9084 [M]		1959	10.00	20.00	40.00

HITSVILLE U.S.A., VOLUME 2

❑ Imperial LP-9099 [M]		1960	10.00	20.00	40.00

HOLIDAY IN SAX

❑ EmArcy MG-26019 [10]		1954	20.00	40.00	80.00

HOLIDAY IN TRUMPET

❑ EmArcy MG-26015 [10]		1954	20.00	40.00	80.00

HOLLAND-DOZIER-HOLLAND: YESTERDAY, TODAY AND FOREVER

❑ Jobete PRO-9 [(3)DJ]		1977	12.50	25.00	50.00

—*Promo-only publisher's demo*

HOME FOR CHRISTMAS: A JOYOUS EVENING OF YULETIDE MUSIC

❑ RCA Victor CPM-109 [M]		1964	3.75	7.50	15.00

—*Label reads "RCA Victor Club Recording Selected by the Editors of Reader's Digest Music Guide"*

❑ RCA Victor CSP-109 [S]		1964	5.00	10.00	20.00

HOME OF THE BLUES

❑ Minit LP-0001 [M]		1961	12.50	25.00	50.00

HOME OF THE BLUES, VOLUME 2

❑ Minit LP-0004 [M]		1963	12.50	25.00	50.00
❑ Minit LP-24004 [R]		1964	5.00	10.00	20.00
❑ Minit LP-40004 [M]		1964	6.25	12.50	25.00

—*Reissue of 0004*

HOMESPUN HUMOR

❑ King 726 [M]		1961	25.00	50.00	100.00

HONEST TO GOODNESS COUNTRY MUSIC HITS

❑ RCA Victor LPM-2564 [M]		1962	5.00	10.00	20.00
❑ RCA Victor LSP-2564 [S]		1962	6.25	12.50	25.00

HONEST TO GOODNESS COUNTRY MUSIC HITS, VOL. 2

❑ RCA Victor LPM-2633 [M]		1963	5.00	10.00	20.00
❑ RCA Victor LSP-2633 [S]		1963	6.25	12.50	25.00

HOT CANARIES

❑ Columbia CL 2534 [10]		1954	7.50	15.00	30.00

THE HOT ONES

❑ Columbia Special Products CSP-107 [M]		1963	5.00	10.00	20.00

—*Available only from Johnson Sea Horse boat dealers*

HOT PLATTERS

❑ Warner Bros. PRO 474 [(2)]		1971	6.25	12.50	25.00

—*Originals have green labels*

Number	Title (A Side/B Side)	Yr	VG	VG+	NM
HOT VS. COOL: A BATTLE OF JAZZ					
❏ MGM E-211 [10]		1953	12.50	25.00	50.00
HOUSE RENT PARTY					
❏ Savoy MG-12199 [M]		1961	12.50	25.00	50.00
HOW HIGH THE MOON					
❏ Clef MGC-Vol. 1 [M]		1955	12.50	25.00	50.00
—Reissue of 608					
❏ Clef MGC-608 [M]		1955	10.00	20.00	40.00
—Reissue of Mercury 608					
❏ Mercury MGC-Vol. 1 [10]		1951	15.00	30.00	60.00
—Reissue of 35001					
❏ Mercury MGC-608 [M]		1953	20.00	40.00	80.00
—Reissue of Vol. 1					
❏ Mercury MG-35001 [10]		1950	20.00	40.00	80.00
❏ Verve MGV-Vol. 1 [M]		1957	7.50	15.00	30.00
—Reissue of 12-inch Clef Vol. 1					
HYMNS OF FAITH					
❏ Colpix CP-408 [M]		1959	7.50	15.00	30.00
I DIDN'T KNOW THEY STILL MADE RECORDS LIKE THIS					
❏ Warner Bros. PRO 608 [(2)]		1975	5.00	10.00	20.00
I DIG ROCK AND ROLL					
❏ Score SLP-4002 [M]		1957	50.00	100.00	200.00
—Reissue of "Rock & Roll with Rhythm & Blues," Aladdin 710					
I LIKE JAZZ!					
❏ Columbia JZ 1 [M]		1955	7.50	15.00	30.00
IMPERIAL MOVES					
❏ Imperial MM-428 [DJ]		1966	10.00	20.00	40.00
IMPERIAL SAMPLER					
❏ Imperial DJLP-1 [10]		195?	25.00	50.00	100.00
—Promo-only item					
THE IMPOSSIBLE DREAM — THE STORY OF THE 1967 BOSTON RED SOX					
❏ Fleetwood FCLP 3024		1967	5.00	10.00	20.00
IN LOVING MEMORY					
❏ Motown M 642 [DJ]		1969	125.00	250.00	500.00
—With custom silver cover; Loucye Gordy Wakefield Scholarship Fund benefit giveaway					
❏ Motown M 642 [M]		1968	37.50	75.00	150.00
—With song titles on cover					
❏ Motown M 642 [M]		1968	62.50	125.00	250.00
—Without song titles on cover					
❏ Motown MS 642 [S]		1968	37.50	75.00	150.00
—With song titles on cover					
❏ Motown MS 642 [S]		1968	62.50	125.00	250.00
—Without song titles on cover					
INCENSE AND OLDIES					
❏ Buddah BDS 5014		1969	5.00	10.00	20.00
INFORMAL SESSION AT SQUIRREL'S BY THE SONS OF BIX					
❏ Paramount LP-104 [(2)10]		1954	20.00	40.00	80.00
INSTRUMENTAL GOLDEN GOODIES, VOL. 13					
❏ Roulette R 25238 [M]		1964	5.00	10.00	20.00
INTERCOLLEGIATE MUSIC FESTIVAL, VOL. 1					
❏ ABC Impulse! AS-9145 [S]		1968	3.00	6.00	12.00
❏ Impulse! A-9145 [M]		1967	5.00	10.00	20.00
❏ Impulse! AS-9145 [S]		1967	3.75	7.50	15.00
INTERNATIONAL JAZZ WORKSHOP					
❏ EmArcy MGE-26002 [M]		1964	6.25	12.50	25.00
❏ EmArcy SRE-66002 [S]		1964	7.50	15.00	30.00
INTERPLAY FOR TWO TRUMPETS AND TWO TENORS					
❏ Prestige PRLP-7112 [M]		1957	25.00	50.00	100.00
INTRODUCTION TO RARE EARTH RECORDS					
❏ Rare Earth RS-505 to 509 [(5)DJ]		1969	50.00	100.00	200.00
—Promo-only box set with rounded top; contains the first five LPs on the Rare Earth label					
THE ISLAND STORY					
❏ Island 90684 [(2)]		1988	4.50	9.00	18.00
❏ Island R 243395 [(2)]		1988	5.00	10.00	20.00
—BMG Direct Marketing edition					
ISLES OF JAZZ					
❏ Discovery DL-2010 [10]		1954	12.50	25.00	50.00
IT'S DANCE TIME					
❏ Cameo C-1068 [M]		1964	7.50	15.00	30.00
ITALIAN JAZZ STARS					
❏ Angel ANG-60001 [10]		1955	12.50	25.00	50.00
IVY LEAGUE JAZZ					
❏ Decca DL 8282 [M]		1956	7.50	15.00	30.00
❏ Golden Crest GC-3039 [M]		1958	5.00	10.00	20.00
JACKPOT OF HITS					
❏ Apollo LP-490 [M]		1959	37.50	75.00	150.00
JAM SESSION					
❏ Clef MGC-4001/7 [(7)M]		1953	75.00	150.00	300.00
—Boxed set containing 4001-4007					
❏ EmArcy MG-36002 [M]		1954	12.50	25.00	50.00
JAM SESSION #1					
❏ Clef MGC-601 [M]		1954	10.00	20.00	40.00
❏ Clef MGC-651 [M]		1955	10.00	20.00	40.00
—Reissue of 4001					
❏ Clef MGC-4001 [M]		1953	12.50	25.00	50.00
❏ Mercury MGC-601 [M]		1953	20.00	40.00	80.00
❏ Verve MGV-8049 [M]		1956	7.50	15.00	30.00
—Reissue of Clef 651					
JAM SESSION #2					
❏ Clef MGC-602 [M]		1954	10.00	20.00	40.00
❏ Clef MGC-652 [M]		1955	10.00	20.00	40.00
—Reissue of 4002					
❏ Clef MGC-4002 [M]		1953	12.50	25.00	50.00

Number	Title (A Side/B Side)	Yr	VG	VG+	NM
❏ Mercury MGC-602 [M]		1953	20.00	40.00	80.00
❏ Verve MGV-8050 [M]		1956	7.50	15.00	30.00
—Reissue of Clef 652					
JAM SESSION #3					
❏ Clef MGC-653 [M]		1955	10.00	20.00	40.00
—Reissue of 4003					
❏ Clef MGC-4003 [M]		1953	12.50	25.00	50.00
❏ Verve MGV-8051 [M]		1956	7.50	15.00	30.00
—Reissue of Clef 653					
JAM SESSION #4					
❏ Clef MGC-654 [M]		1955	10.00	20.00	40.00
—Reissue of 4004					
❏ Clef MGC-4004 [M]		1953	12.50	25.00	50.00
❏ Verve MGV-8052 [M]		1956	7.50	15.00	30.00
—Reissue of Clef 654					
JAM SESSION #5					
❏ Clef MGC-655 [M]		1955	10.00	20.00	40.00
—Reissue of 4005					
❏ Clef MGC-4005 [M]		1953	12.50	25.00	50.00
❏ Verve MGV-8053 [M]		1956	7.50	15.00	30.00
—Reissue of Clef 655					
JAM SESSION #6					
❏ Clef MGC-656 [M]		1955	10.00	20.00	40.00
—Reissue of 4006					
❏ Clef MGC-4006 [M]		1953	12.50	25.00	50.00
❏ Verve MGV-8054 [M]		1956	7.50	15.00	30.00
—Reissue of Clef 656					
JAM SESSION #7					
❏ Clef MGC-677 [M]		1955	10.00	20.00	40.00
❏ Verve MGV-8062 [M]		1957	7.50	15.00	30.00
—Reissue of Clef 677					
JAM SESSION #8					
❏ Clef MGC-711 [M]		1955	10.00	20.00	40.00
❏ Verve MGV-8094 [M]		1957	7.50	15.00	30.00
—Reissue of Clef 711					
JAM SESSION #9					
❏ Verve MGV-8196 [M]		1957	7.50	15.00	30.00
JAM SESSION AT CARNEGIE HALL					
❏ Columbia CL 557 [M]		1954	7.50	15.00	30.00
JAM SESSION AT COMMODORE					
❏ Commodore FL-30006 [M]		1951	10.00	20.00	40.00
JAM SESSION COAST TO COAST					
❏ Columbia CL 547 [M]		1954	7.50	1.00	30.00
JAM SESSION, VOL. 2					
❏ Skylark SKLP-12 [10]		1954	62.50	125.00	250.00
JAMES BOND — 10TH ANNIVERSARY					
❏ United Artists UXS-91 [(2)]		1972	7.50	15.00	30.00
JAMMING AT RUDI'S, VOL. 1					
❏ Circle L-407 [M]		1951	10.00	20.00	40.00
JAMMING AT RUDI'S, VOL. 2					
❏ Circle L-410 [M]		1951	10.00	20.00	40.00
THE JATP ALL-STARS AT THE OPERA HOUSE					
❏ Verve MGVS-6029 [S]		1960	7.50	15.00	30.00
❏ Verve MGV-8267 [M]		1958	10.00	20.00	40.00
❏ Verve V-8267 [M]		1961	5.00	10.00	20.00
❏ Verve V-8489 [M]		1962	6.25	12.50	25.00
❏ Verve V6-8489 [S]		1962	7.50	15.00	30.00
THE JATP ALL-STARS: FUNKY BLUES					
❏ Verve V-8486 [M]		1962	6.25	12.50	25.00
❏ Verve V6-8486 [S]		1962	7.50	15.00	30.00
JAZZ					
❏ Royale 1883 [10]		195?	7.50	15.00	30.00
JAZZ — WEST COAST VOL. III					
❏ Jazztone J-1274 [M]		195?	7.50	15.00	30.00
JAZZ A LA MIDNIGHT					
❏ Hall of Fame 608		197?	2.50	5.00	10.00
❏ Jazztone J-1282 [M]		1957	7.50	15.00	30.00
JAZZ A LA MOOD					
❏ Jazztone J-1254 [M]		1957	7.50	15.00	30.00
JAZZ AMERICANA					
❏ Tampa TP-11 [M]		1957	25.00	50.00	100.00
—Colored vinyl					
❏ Tampa TP-11 [M]		1958	10.00	20.00	40.00
—Black vinyl					
JAZZ AND POPS FROM THE SOVIET UNION					
❏ Colosseum CRLP-171 [M]		1955	7.50	15.00	30.00
JAZZ ANTHOLOGY OF WEST COAST JAZZ					
❏ Jazztone J-1243 [M]		1957	7.50	15.00	30.00
JAZZ AT CARNEGIE HALL					
❏ Arco AL-4 [10]		1950	20.00	40.00	80.00
❏ Mercury MG-35002 [10]		1950	20.00	40.00	80.00
—Reissue of Arco 4					
JAZZ AT CARNEGIE HALL, VOLUME 2					
❏ Arco AL-8 [10]		195?	20.00	40.00	80.00
JAZZ AT COLUMBIA — COLLECTORS ITEMS					
❏ Columbia CB-16 [M]		195?	5.00	10.00	20.00
—Columbia Record Club "bonus record" in generic sleeve with die-cut circle in middle					
JAZZ AT COLUMBIA — DIXIELAND					
❏ Columbia CB-8 [M]		195?	5.00	10.00	20.00
—Columbia Record Club "bonus record" in generic sleeve with die-cut circle in middle					

Number	Title (A Side/B Side)	Yr	VG	VG+	NM
JAZZ AT JAZZ LTD.					
❏ Atlantic 1338 [M]		1961	6.25	12.50	25.00
—Multicolor label, white "fan" logo at right					
JAZZ AT STORYVILLE					
❏ Paradox LP-6003 [10]		1951	12.50	25.00	50.00
❏ Savoy MG-15001 [10]		1952	20.00	40.00	80.00
❏ Savoy MG-15014 [10]		1952	20.00	40.00	80.00
❏ Storyville STLP-319 [10]		1955	20.00	40.00	80.00
JAZZ AT STORYVILLE, VOL. 2					
❏ Savoy MG-15016 [10]		1952	20.00	40.00	80.00
JAZZ AT STORYVILLE, VOL. 3					
❏ Savoy MG-15019 [10]		1953	20.00	40.00	80.00
JAZZ AT STORYVILLE, VOL. 4					
❏ Savoy MG-15020 [10]		1953	20.00	40.00	80.00
JAZZ AT THE BOSTON ARTS FESTIVAL					
❏ Storyville STLP-311 [10]		1954	20.00	40.00	80.00
JAZZ AT THE HOLLYWOOD BOWL					
❏ Verve MGV-8231-2 [(2)M]		1958	12.50	25.00	50.00
❏ Verve V-8231-2 [(2)M]		1961	6.25	12.50	25.00
JAZZ AT THE PHILHARMONIC					
❏ Stinson SLP-23 [10]		195?	20.00	40.00	80.00
—Black vinyl					
❏ Stinson SLP-23 [10]		195?	20.00	40.00	80.00
—Opaque red vinyl					
❏ Stinson SLP-23 [10]		1950	30.00	60.00	120.00
—See-through red vinyl; the first pressing of the first volume to be issued					
❏ Stinson SLP-23 [M]		195?	5.00	10.00	20.00
JAZZ AT THE PHILHARMONIC ALL STARS					
❏ American Recording Society G-416 [M]		1957	7.50	15.00	30.00
JAZZ AT THE PHILHARMONIC IN EUROPE					
❏ Verve V6-8823 [(2)]		197?	5.00	10.00	20.00
JAZZ AT THE PHILHARMONIC IN EUROPE, VOL. 1					
❏ Verve V-8539 [M]		1963	5.00	10.00	20.00
❏ Verve V6-8539 [S]		1963	6.25	12.50	25.00
JAZZ AT THE PHILHARMONIC IN EUROPE, VOL. 2					
❏ Verve V-8540 [M]		1963	5.00	10.00	20.00
❏ Verve V6-8540 [S]		1963	6.25	12.50	25.00
JAZZ AT THE PHILHARMONIC IN EUROPE, VOL. 3					
❏ Verve V-8541 [M]		1963	5.00	10.00	20.00
❏ Verve V6-8541 [S]		1963	6.25	12.50	25.00
JAZZ AT THE PHILHARMONIC IN EUROPE, VOL. 4					
❏ Verve V-8542 [M]		1963	5.00	10.00	20.00
❏ Verve V6-8542 [S]		1963	6.25	12.50	25.00
JAZZ AT THE PHILHARMONIC IN TOKYO					
❏ Pablo Live 2620104 [(3)]		198?	6.25	12.50	25.00
JAZZ AT THE PHILHARMONIC, NEW VOLUME 2					
❏ Clef MGC-Vol. 2 [M]		1955	12.50	25.00	50.00
—Side 1 is the 10-inch Vol. 2; Side 2 is the 10-inch Vol. 3					
JAZZ AT THE PHILHARMONIC, NEW VOLUME 3					
❏ Clef MGC-Vol. 3 [M]		1955	12.50	25.00	50.00
—Side 1 is the 10-inch Vol. 4; Side 2 is the 10-inch Vol. 5					
JAZZ AT THE PHILHARMONIC, NEW VOLUME 4					
❏ Clef MGC-Vol. 4 [M]		1955	12.50	25.00	50.00
—Combines the 10-inch Vol. 6 and Vol. 14 on one record					
JAZZ AT THE PHILHARMONIC, NEW VOLUME 5					
❏ Clef MGC-Vol. 5 [M]		1955	12.50	25.00	50.00
—Combines the 10-inch Vol. 7, 10 and 11 on one record					
JAZZ AT THE PHILHARMONIC, NEW VOLUME 6					
❏ Clef MGC-Vol. 6 [M]		1955	12.50	25.00	50.00
—Combines the 10-inch Vol. 8 and Vol. 9 on one record					
JAZZ AT THE PHILHARMONIC, NEW VOLUME 7					
❏ Clef MGC-Vol. 7 [M]		1955	12.50	25.00	50.00
—Combines the 10-inch Vol. 12 and 13 on one record					
JAZZ AT THE PHILHARMONIC, VOL. 10					
❏ Verve MGV-Vol. 10 [(3)M]		1957	15.00	30.00	60.00
—Reissue of Clef Vol. 17					
JAZZ AT THE PHILHARMONIC, VOL. 11					
❏ Verve MGV-Vol. 11 [(3)M]		1957	15.00	30.00	60.00
—Reissue of Clef Vol. 18					
JAZZ AT THE PHILHARMONIC, VOL. 2					
❏ Verve MGV-Vol. 2 [M]		1957	7.50	15.00	30.00
—Reissue of 12-inch Clef Vol. 2					
JAZZ AT THE PHILHARMONIC, VOL. 3					
❏ Verve MGV-Vol. 3 [M]		1957	7.50	15.00	30.00
—Reissue of 12-inch Clef Vol. 3					
JAZZ AT THE PHILHARMONIC, VOL. 4					
❏ Verve MGV-Vol. 4 [M]		1957	7.50	15.00	30.00
—Reissue of 12-inch Clef Vol. 4					
JAZZ AT THE PHILHARMONIC, VOL. 5					
❏ Verve MGV-Vol. 5 [M]		1957	7.50	15.00	30.00
—Reissue of 12-inch Clef Vol. 5					
JAZZ AT THE PHILHARMONIC, VOL. 6					
❏ Verve MGV-Vol. 6 [M]		1957	7.50	15.00	30.00
—Reissue of 12-inch Clef Vol. 6					
JAZZ AT THE PHILHARMONIC, VOL. 7					
❏ Verve MGV-Vol. 7 [M]		1957	7.50	15.00	30.00
—Reissue of 12-inch Clef Vol. 7					
JAZZ AT THE PHILHARMONIC, VOL. 8					
❏ Verve MGV-Vol. 8 [(3)M]		1957	15.00	30.00	60.00
—Reissue of Clef Vol. 15					

Number	Title (A Side/B Side)	Yr	VG	VG+	NM
JAZZ AT THE PHILHARMONIC, VOL. 9					
❏ Verve MGV-Vol. 9 [(3)M]		1957	15.00	30.00	60.00
—Reissue of Clef Vol. 16					
JAZZ AT THE PHILHARMONIC, VOLUME 10					
❏ Clef MGC-Vol. 10 [10]		1953	15.00	30.00	60.00
—Reissue of Mercury Vol. 10					
❏ Mercury MGC-Vol. 10 [10]		1951	15.00	30.00	60.00
—Reissue of 35010					
❏ Mercury MG-35010 [10]		1950	25.00	50.00	100.00
JAZZ AT THE PHILHARMONIC, VOLUME 11					
❏ Clef MGC-Vol. 11 [10]		1953	15.00	30.00	60.00
—Reissue of Mercury Vol. 11					
❏ Mercury MGC-Vol. 11 [10]		1951	15.00	30.00	60.00
—Reissue of 35011					
❏ Mercury MG-35011 [10]		1950	20.00	40.00	80.00
JAZZ AT THE PHILHARMONIC, VOLUME 12					
❏ Clef MGC-Vol. 12 [10]		1953	15.00	30.00	60.00
—Reissue of Mercury Vol. 12					
❏ Mercury MGC-Vol. 12 [10]		1951	15.00	30.00	60.00
JAZZ AT THE PHILHARMONIC, VOLUME 13					
❏ Clef MGC-Vol. 13 [10]		1953	15.00	30.00	60.00
—Reissue of Mercury Vol. 13					
❏ Mercury MGC-Vol. 13 [10]		1951	15.00	30.00	60.00
JAZZ AT THE PHILHARMONIC, VOLUME 14					
❏ Clef MGC-Vol. 14 [10]		1953	15.00	30.00	60.00
—Reissue of Mercury Vol. 14					
❏ Mercury MGC-Vol. 14 [10]		1951	15.00	30.00	60.00
JAZZ AT THE PHILHARMONIC, VOLUME 15					
❏ Clef MGC-Vol. 15 [10]		1953	15.00	30.00	60.00
—Reissue of Mercury Vol. 15					
❏ Clef MGC-Vol. 15 [(3)M]		1954	20.00	40.00	80.00
—Boxed set of new material with program					
❏ Mercury MGC-Vol. 15 [10]		1951	15.00	30.00	60.00
JAZZ AT THE PHILHARMONIC, VOLUME 16					
❏ Clef MGC-Vol. 16 [(3)M]		1954	20.00	40.00	80.00
—Boxed set of new material with program					
JAZZ AT THE PHILHARMONIC, VOLUME 17					
❏ Clef MGC-Vol. 17 [(3)M]		1955	20.00	40.00	80.00
—Boxed set of new material with photo booklet					
JAZZ AT THE PHILHARMONIC, VOLUME 18					
❏ Clef MGC-Vol. 18 [(3)M]		1955	20.00	40.00	80.00
—Boxed set of new material with booklet					
JAZZ AT THE PHILHARMONIC, VOLUME 2					
❏ Arco AL-1 [10]		1950	20.00	40.00	80.00
❏ Clef MGC-Vol. 2 [10]		1953	15.00	30.00	60.00
—Reissue of Mercury Vol. 2					
❏ Mercury MGC-Vol. 2 [10]		1951	15.00	30.00	60.00
—Reissue of 35003					
❏ Mercury MG-35003 [10]		1950	20.00	40.00	80.00
—Reissue of Arco 1					
JAZZ AT THE PHILHARMONIC, VOLUME 3					
❏ Arco AL-2 [10]		1950	20.00	40.00	80.00
❏ Clef MGC-Vol. 3 [10]		1953	15.00	30.00	60.00
—Reissue of Mercury Vol. 3					
❏ Mercury MGC-Vol. 3 [10]		1951	15.00	30.00	60.00
—Reissue of 35004					
❏ Mercury MG-35004 [10]		1950	20.00	40.00	80.00
—Reissue of Arco 2					
JAZZ AT THE PHILHARMONIC, VOLUME 4					
❏ Clef MGC-Vol. 4 [10]		1953	15.00	30.00	60.00
—Reissue of Mercury Vol. 4					
❏ Mercury MGC-Vol. 4 [10]		1951	15.00	30.00	60.00
—Reissue of 35005					
❏ Mercury MG-35005 [10]		1950	20.00	40.00	80.00
JAZZ AT THE PHILHARMONIC, VOLUME 5					
❏ Clef MGC-Vol. 5 [10]		1953	15.00	30.00	60.00
—Reissue of Mercury Vol. 5					
❏ Mercury MGC-Vol. 5 [10]		1951	15.00	30.00	60.00
—Reissue of 35006					
❏ Mercury MG-35006 [10]		1950	20.00	40.00	80.00
JAZZ AT THE PHILHARMONIC, VOLUME 6					
❏ Clef MGC-Vol. 6 [10]		1953	15.00	30.00	60.00
—Reissue of Mercury Vol. 6					
❏ Mercury MGC-Vol. 6 [10]		1951	15.00	30.00	60.00
—Reissue of 35007					
❏ Mercury MG-35007 [10]		1950	20.00	40.00	80.00
JAZZ AT THE PHILHARMONIC, VOLUME 7					
❏ Clef MGC-Vol. 7 [10]		1953	15.00	30.00	60.00
—Reissue of Mercury Vol. 7					
❏ Mercury MGC-Vol. 7 [10]		1951	15.00	30.00	60.00
—Reissue of 35008					
❏ Mercury MG-35008 [10]		1950	20.00	40.00	80.00
JAZZ AT THE PHILHARMONIC, VOLUME 8					
❏ Clef MGC-Vol. 8 [10]		1953	15.00	30.00	60.00
—Reissue of Mercury Vol. 8					
❏ Mercury MGC-Vol. 8 [10]		1951	15.00	30.00	60.00
—Reissue of 35000					
❏ Mercury MG-35000 [10]		1950	20.00	40.00	80.00
JAZZ AT THE PHILHARMONIC, VOLUME 9					
❏ Clef MGC-Vol. 9 [10]		1953	15.00	30.00	60.00
—Reissue of Mercury Vol. 9					
❏ Mercury MGC-Vol. 9 [10]		1951	15.00	30.00	60.00
—Reissue of 35009					
❏ Mercury MG-35009 [10]		1950	20.00	40.00	80.00
JAZZ AT THE PHILHARMONIC: IN TOKYO 1983					
❏ Pablo Live 2620117 [(3)]		1984	5.00	10.00	20.00

Number / Title (A Side/B Side)	Yr	VG	VG+	NM
JAZZ AT THE PHILHARMONIC: THE 1940S				
❑ Verve UMV-9070/2 [(3)]	197?	6.25	12.50	25.00
JAZZ AT THE SANTA MONICA CIVIC '72				
❑ Pablo 2625701 [(3)]	197?	6.25	12.50	25.00
JAZZ BAND BALL				
❑ Good Time Jazz L-12005 [M]	1954	5.00	10.00	20.00
JAZZ CITY PRESENTS				
❑ Bethlehem BCP-80 [M]	1957	7.50	15.00	30.00
JAZZ COMMITTEE FOR LATIN AMERICAN AFFAIRS				
❑ FM LP-303 [M]	1963	12.50	25.00	50.00
JAZZ CONCERT				
❑ Jazztone J-1219 [M]	1956	7.50	15.00	30.00
❑ Mercury MGJC-1 [(2)M]	1953	30.00	60.00	120.00
—Combines 601 and 602 in a box				
❑ Norgran MGN-3501-2 [(2)M]	1956	30.00	60.00	120.00
—Reissue of Mercury MGJC-1				
JAZZ CONCERT WEST COAST				
❑ Savoy MG-12012 [M]	1955	20.00	40.00	80.00
❑ Savoy MG-12196 [M]	1961	12.50	25.00	50.00
JAZZ CONFIDENTIAL				
❑ Crown CLP-5056 [M]	1959	5.00	10.00	20.00
JAZZ CORNUCOPIA				
❑ Coral CRL 57149 [M]	1958	7.50	15.00	30.00
JAZZ CRITICS' CHOICE: GREAT JAZZ CRITICS CHOOSE HISTORIC PERFORMANCES				
❑ Columbia CL 2126 [M]	1964	3.00	6.00	12.00
JAZZ DANCE				
❑ Jaguar JP-801 [10]	1954	12.50	25.00	50.00
JAZZ DUPLEX				
❑ Pax LP-6006 [10]	1954	7.50	15.00	30.00
JAZZ FESTIVAL				
❑ Imperial LP-9233 [M]	1963	5.00	10.00	20.00
❑ Imperial LP-12233 [S]	1963	6.25	12.50	25.00
❑ Kapp KS-1 [M]	1956	5.00	10.00	20.00
JAZZ FESTIVAL IN HI-FI: NEAR IN AND FAR OUT				
❑ Warner Bros. W 1281 [M]	1959	6.25	12.50	25.00
JAZZ FESTIVAL IN STEREO: NEAR IN AND FAR OUT				
❑ Warner Bros. WS 1281 [S]	1959	7.50	15.00	30.00
JAZZ FESTIVAL, VOLUME 2				
❑ Imperial LP-9238 [M]	1963	5.00	10.00	20.00
❑ Imperial LP-12238 [S]	1963	6.25	12.50	25.00
JAZZ FOR ART'S SAKE				
❑ Dotted Eighth 101 [M]	195?	10.00	20.00	40.00
JAZZ FOR HI-FI LOVERS				
❑ Dawn DLP-1124 [M]	1958	20.00	40.00	80.00
JAZZ FOR LOVERS				
❑ Riverside RLP 12-244 [M]	1957	10.00	20.00	40.00
JAZZ FOR PEOPLE WHO HATE JAZZ				
❑ RCA Victor LJM-1008 [M]	1954	12.50	25.00	50.00
JAZZ FOR SURF-NIKS				
❑ Bethlehem BCP-6073 [M]	1961	7.50	15.00	30.00
JAZZ FROM DOWN UNDER				
❑ Jaguar JP-803 [10]	1954	12.50	25.00	50.00
JAZZ FROM SWEDEN				
❑ Discovery DL-2002 [10]	1953	12.50	25.00	50.00
THE JAZZ GIANTS				
❑ Norgran MGN-1056 [M]	1956	20.00	40.00	80.00
JAZZ GIANTS '56				
❑ Verve UMV-2511	197?	3.00	6.00	12.00
THE JAZZ GIANTS '56				
❑ Verve MGV-8146 [M]	1957	7.50	15.00	30.00
❑ Verve V-8146 [M]	1961	5.00	10.00	20.00
JAZZ GIANTS '58				
❑ Verve MGV-8248 [M]	1958	12.50	25.00	50.00
❑ Verve V-8248 [M]	1961	6.25	12.50	25.00
JAZZ GIANTS, VOL. 1				
❑ EmArcy MG-36048 [M]	1955	10.00	20.00	40.00
JAZZ GIANTS, VOL. 2: THE PIANO PLAYERS				
❑ EmArcy MG-36049 [M]	1955	10.00	20.00	40.00
JAZZ GIANTS, VOL. 3: REEDS, PART 1				
❑ EmArcy MG-36050 [M]	1955	10.00	20.00	40.00
JAZZ GIANTS, VOL. 3: REEDS, PART 2				
❑ EmArcy MG-36051 [M]	1955	10.00	20.00	40.00
JAZZ GIANTS, VOL. 4: FOLK BLUES				
❑ EmArcy MG-36052 [M]	1955	10.00	20.00	40.00
JAZZ GIANTS, VOL. 5: BRASS				
❑ EmArcy MG-36053 [M]	1955	10.00	20.00	40.00
JAZZ GIANTS, VOL. 6: MODERN SWEDES				
❑ EmArcy MG-36054 [M]	1955	10.00	20.00	40.00
JAZZ GIANTS, VOL. 7: DIXIELAND				
❑ EmArcy MG-36055 [M]	1955	10.00	20.00	40.00
JAZZ GIANTS, VOL. 8: DRUM ROLE				
❑ EmArcy MG-36071 [M]	1956	10.00	20.00	40.00
JAZZ GOES TO BROADWAY				
❑ Kapp KL-1007 [M]	1956	5.00	10.00	20.00
JAZZ GREATS				
❑ Tops L-1508 [M]	1958	5.00	10.00	20.00
JAZZ GREATS!				
❑ Allegro 737 [M]	1958	7.50	15.00	30.00
JAZZ HALL OF FAME, VOL. 2				
❑ Design DLP-113 [M]	196?	5.00	10.00	20.00
THE JAZZ HOUR				
❑ Savoy MG-12126 [M]	1957	12.50	25.00	50.00
JAZZ IN HOLLYWOOD				
❑ Liberty LJH-6001 [M]	1955	7.50	15.00	30.00
JAZZ IN TRANSITION				
❑ Transition TRLP-30 [M]	1956	50.00	100.00	200.00
—With booklet (deduct 1/4 if missing)				
JAZZ INTERPLAY				
❑ Prestige PRLP-7341 [(2)M]	1964	10.00	20.00	40.00
❑ Prestige PRLP-7341 [(2)R]	1964	6.25	12.50	25.00
JAZZ IS BUSTING OUT ALL OVER				
❑ Savoy MG-12123 [M]	1957	12.50	25.00	50.00
❑ Savoy Jazz SJC-408	198?	2.50	5.00	10.00
JAZZ JAMBOREE				
❑ Halo 50229 [M]	1957	5.00	10.00	20.00
JAZZ LAB				
❑ Starlite ST-7003 [M]	1955	12.50	25.00	50.00
THE JAZZ LIFE				
❑ Candid CD-8019 [M]	1960	10.00	20.00	40.00
❑ Candid CS-9019 [S]	1960	7.50	15.00	30.00
JAZZ LTD.				
❑ Regal LP-11 [10]	1951	12.50	25.00	50.00
THE JAZZ MAKERS				
❑ Columbia CL 1036 [M]	1957	5.00	10.00	20.00
JAZZ MONTAGE				
❑ Liberty LRP-3292 [M]	1963	3.75	7.50	15.00
❑ Liberty LST-7292 [S]	1963	5.00	10.00	20.00
JAZZ MUSIC FOR BIRDS				
❑ Bethlehem BCP-6039 [M]	1959	7.50	15.00	30.00
JAZZ MUSIC FOR PEOPLE WHO DON'T CARE ABOUT MONEY				
❑ Bethlehem BCP-88 [M]	1958	7.50	15.00	30.00
JAZZ ODYSSEY: THE SOUND OF CHICAGO				
❑ Columbia C3L 32 [(3)M]	1964	10.00	20.00	40.00
JAZZ ODYSSEY: THE SOUND OF HARLEM				
❑ Columbia C3L 33 [(3)M]	1964	10.00	20.00	40.00
JAZZ ODYSSEY: THE SOUND OF NEW ORLEANS				
❑ Columbia C3L 30 [(3)M]	1964	10.00	20.00	40.00
JAZZ OF THE ROARING 20'S				
❑ Riverside RLP 12-801 [M]	195?	12.50	25.00	50.00
JAZZ OF THE ROARING TWENTIES: DANCE MUSIC OF THE CHARLESTON ERA				
❑ Riverside RLP 12-108 [M]	1956	10.00	20.00	40.00
JAZZ OF THE SIXTIES				
❑ Vee Jay VJS-2-1008 [(2)]	1974	5.00	10.00	20.00
JAZZ OF TWO DECADES				
❑ EmArcy DEM-2 [M]	1956	10.00	20.00	40.00
JAZZ OFF THE AIR, VOL. 1				
❑ Esoteric ESJ-2 [10]	1952	20.00	40.00	80.00
JAZZ OFF THE AIR, VOL. 2				
❑ Esoteric ESJ-3 [10]	1952	20.00	40.00	80.00
JAZZ OMNIBUS				
❑ Columbia CL 1020 [M]	1957	5.00	10.00	20.00
JAZZ ON THE AIR				
❑ Brunswick BL 58048 [10]	1953	12.50	25.00	50.00
JAZZ ON THE SCREEN				
❑ Fontana MGF-27532 [M]	1965	7.50	15.00	30.00
❑ Fontana SRF-67532 [S]	1965	10.00	20.00	40.00
JAZZ PIANISTS GALORE				
❑ Jazz: West Coast JWC-506 [M]	1956	37.50	75.00	150.00
THE JAZZ PIANO				
❑ RCA Victor LPM-3499 [M]	1966	5.00	10.00	20.00
❑ RCA Victor LSP-3499 [S]	1966	6.25	12.50	25.00
JAZZ POLL WINNERS				
❑ Columbia CL 1610 [M]	1960	5.00	10.00	20.00
JAZZ POTPOURRI				
❑ Audiophile AP-24 [M]	1953	7.50	15.00	30.00
A JAZZ SALUTE TO FREEDOM				
❑ Core 100 [(2)M]	196?	6.25	12.50	25.00
THE JAZZ SCENE				
❑ American Recording Society G-419 [M]	1957	7.50	15.00	30.00
❑ Clef MGC-674 [M]	1955	10.00	20.00	40.00
—Reissue of 4007				
❑ Clef MGC-4007 [M]	1953	12.50	25.00	50.00
❑ Clef Special Edition (no #) [(2)10]	1953	25.00	50.00	100.00
—Two 10-inch LPs in box. Buyers had the option of purchasing a collection of photos that had been used in the original 78 rpm album; add another 50 percent if these photos are included				
❑ Verve MGV-8060 [M]	1957	7.50	15.00	30.00
—Reissue of Clef 674				
❑ Verve V-8060 [M]	1961	5.00	10.00	20.00
JAZZ SOUL OF "CLEOPATRA"				
❑ New Jazz NJLP-8292 [M]	1962	10.00	20.00	40.00
—Purple label				
❑ New Jazz NJLP-8292 [M]	1965	5.00	10.00	20.00
—Blue label, trident logo at right				
JAZZ SOUTH PACIFIC				
❑ Regent MG-6001 [M]	1956	12.50	25.00	50.00
❑ Savoy MG-12205 [M]	196?	5.00	10.00	20.00

Number / Title (A Side/B Side)	Yr	VG	VG+	NM
THE JAZZ STORY				
❏ Coral CJE-100 [(3)M]	195?	25.00	50.00	100.00
—Box set; narrated by Steve Allen				
JAZZ SUPER HITS				
❏ Atlantic SD 1528	1969	6.25	12.50	25.00
JAZZ SUPER HITS, VOL. 2				
❏ Atlantic SD 1559	1970	5.00	10.00	20.00
JAZZ SURPRISE				
❏ Crown CLP-5008 [M]	1957	5.00	10.00	20.00
JAZZ SWINGS BROADWAY				
❏ Pacific Jazz PJM-404 [M]	1956	12.50	25.00	50.00
❏ World Pacific PJM-404 [M]	1958	10.00	20.00	40.00
JAZZ TIME U.S.A. — VOLUME 1				
❏ Brunswick BL 54000 [M]	1952	7.50	15.00	30.00
JAZZ TIME U.S.A. — VOLUME 2				
❏ Brunswick BL 54001 [M]	1953	7.50	15.00	30.00
JAZZ TIME U.S.A. — VOLUME 3				
❏ Brunswick BL 54002 [M]	1954	7.50	15.00	30.00
JAZZ VARIATIONS, VOL. 1				
❏ Stinson SLP-20 [10]	195?	15.00	30.00	60.00
❏ Stinson SLP-20 [M]	196?	6.25	12.50	25.00
JAZZ VARIATIONS, VOL. 2				
❏ Stinson SLP-29 [M]	196?	6.25	12.50	25.00
JAZZ VOCALS AWARD ALBUM				
❏ Bethlehem BCP-6068 [M]	1963	6.25	12.50	25.00
JAZZ WEST COAST, VOL. 1				
❏ Pacific Jazz JWC-500 [M]	1956	12.50	25.00	50.00
❏ World Pacific JWC-500 [M]	1958	10.00	20.00	40.00
JAZZ WEST COAST, VOL. 2				
❏ Pacific Jazz JWC-501 [M]	1956	12.50	25.00	50.00
❏ World Pacific JWC-501 [M]	1958	10.00	20.00	40.00
JAZZ WEST COAST, VOL. 3				
❏ Pacific Jazz JWC-507 [M]	1957	12.50	25.00	50.00
❏ World Pacific JWC-507 [M]	1958	10.00	20.00	40.00
JAZZ WEST COAST, VOL. 4				
❏ World Pacific JWC-510 [M]	1958	10.00	20.00	40.00
❏ World Pacific ST-1009 [S]	1959	7.50	15.00	30.00
JAZZ WEST COAST, VOL. 5				
❏ World Pacific JWC-511 [M]	1958	10.00	20.00	40.00
JAZZ, VOL. 1: THE SOUTH				
❏ Folkways FP-53/4 [M]	1951	6.25	12.50	25.00
JAZZ, VOL. 10: BOOGIE WOOGIE, JUMP, KANSAS CITY				
❏ Folkways FP-73/4 [M]	1951	6.25	12.50	25.00
JAZZ, VOL. 11: ADDENDA				
❏ Folkways FP-75/6 [M]	1951	6.25	12.50	25.00
JAZZ, VOL. 2: THE BLUES				
❏ Folkways FP-55/6 [M]	1951	6.25	12.50	25.00
JAZZ, VOL. 3: NEW ORLEANS				
❏ Folkways FP-57/8 [M]	1951	6.25	12.50	25.00
JAZZ, VOL. 4: JAZZ SINGERS				
❏ Folkways FP-59/60 [M]	1951	6.25	12.50	25.00
JAZZ, VOL. 5: CHICAGO				
❏ Folkways FP-63/4 [M]	1951	6.25	12.50	25.00
JAZZ, VOL. 6: CHICAGO #2				
❏ Folkways FP-65/6 [M]	1951	6.25	12.50	25.00
JAZZ, VOL. 7: NEW YORK 1922-1934				
❏ Folkways FP-67/8 [M]	1951	6.25	12.50	25.00
JAZZ, VOL. 8: BIG BANDS BEFORE 1938				
❏ Folkways FP-69/70 [M]	1951	6.25	12.50	25.00
JAZZ, VOL. 9: PIANO				
❏ Folkways FP-71/2 [M]	1951	6.25	12.50	25.00
JAZZMEN — DETROIT				
❏ Savoy MG-12083 [M]	1956	20.00	40.00	80.00
JAZZTONE SAMPLER				
❏ Jazztone J-SPEC-100 [10]	1955	12.50	25.00	50.00
—With booklet				
JAZZVILLE, VOL. 1				
❏ Dawn DLP-1101 [M]	1956	20.00	40.00	80.00
JESUS CHRIST SUPERSTAR				
❏ Decca DXA 7206 [(2)]	1970	7.50	15.00	30.00
—Box set with booklet				
❏ Decca DXSA 7206 [(2)]	1970	6.25	12.50	25.00
—Gatefold cover with booklet				
❏ Decca MCA 2-10000 [(2)]	1973	3.00	6.00	12.00
—Gatefold cover with booklet; reissue; same custom labels as Decca issue				
❏ MCA 10000 [(2)]	197?	3.00	6.00	12.00
—Gatefold cover with booklet; reissue; generic MCA labels				
JINGLE BELL JAZZ				
❏ Columbia CL 1893 [M]	1962	5.00	10.00	20.00
❏ Columbia CS 8693 [S]	1962	3.75	7.50	15.00
❏ Columbia PC 36803	1980	2.50	5.00	10.00
—Reissue of Harmony KH 32529 on the "Jazz Odyssey" series				
❏ Harmony KH 32529	1973	3.00	6.00	12.00
—Reissue of CS 8693 with one track changed				
JINGLE BELL ROCK				
❏ Time-Life SRNR-XM [(2)]	1987	5.00	10.00	20.00
—Available from Time-Life by mail order only; boxed set				
JOHN COLTRANE IN THE WINNER'S CIRCLE				
❏ Bethlehem BCP-6066 [M]	1961	6.25	12.50	25.00
—Reissue of 6024 with new title				

Number / Title (A Side/B Side)	Yr	VG	VG+	NM
JOHN HAMMOND PRESENTS "FROM SPIRITUALS TO SWING" AT CARNEGIE HALL 1938				
❏ Vanguard VRS-8523 [M]	1959	10.00	20.00	40.00
JOHN HAMMOND PRESENTS "FROM SPIRITUALS TO SWING" AT CARNEGIE HALL 1939				
❏ Vanguard VRS-8524 [M]	1959	10.00	20.00	40.00
JOY TO THE WORLD (30 CLASSIC CHRISTMAS MELODIES)				
❏ Columbia Special Products P3 14654 [(3)]	1978	5.00	10.00	20.00
—Box set; produced for Murray Hill Records				
THE JOYFUL SOUND OF CHRISTMAS				
❏ RCA Record Club CSP-0601 [(2)]	1969	5.00	10.00	20.00
—Available only through the RCA Record Club				
JOYOUS MUSIC FOR CHRISTMAS TIME				
❏ Reader's Digest RD 45-M [(4)M]	1963	5.00	10.00	20.00
❏ Reader's Digest RD 45-S [(4)S]	1963	5.00	10.00	20.00
—Available only through Reader's Digest magazine by mail order				
JOYOUS NOEL				
❏ Reader's Digest RDA-57A [(4)]	1966	5.00	10.00	20.00
—Available only through Reader's Digest magazine by mail order				
JUBILEE MONAURAL SAMPLER: VOCALS AND INSTRUMENTALS				
❏ Jubilee MSJLP-803 [M]	1959	7.50	15.00	30.00
JUBILEE STEREOSONIC VOCAL SAMPLER, VOLUME 2				
❏ Jubilee SSJLP-802 [S]	1959	10.00	20.00	40.00
JUBILEE SURPRISE PARTY				
❏ Jubilee JGM-1107 [M]	1959	37.50	75.00	150.00
❏ Jubilee JGS-1107 [S]	1959	50.00	100.00	200.00
JUST JAZZ				
❏ Imperial LP-9246 [M]	1963	5.00	10.00	20.00
❏ Imperial LP-12246 [S]	1963	6.25	12.50	25.00
K-BOX DUSTY DISCS				
❏ Roulette R 25338 [M]	1966	5.00	10.00	20.00
KANSAS CITY IN THE '30S				
❏ Capitol T 1057 [M]	1958	6.25	12.50	25.00
KANSAS CITY JAZZ				
❏ Decca DL 8044 [M]	1954	10.00	20.00	40.00
KANSAS CITY PIANO				
❏ Decca DL 9226 [M]	1967	7.50	15.00	30.00
KATS KARAVAN (OLD FAVORITES WITH JIM LOWE)				
❏ Vee Jay LP-100 [M]	1957	12.50	25.00	50.00
—Gold label, black print				
KBIG CHOICES				
❏ World Pacific KBIG-1 [S]	1964	6.25	12.50	25.00
KEATS RIDES A HARLEY				
❏ Happy Squid HS 002	1981	5.00	10.00	20.00
KEYBOARD KINGS				
❏ MGM E-100 [10]	1951	12.50	25.00	50.00
KEYBOARD KINGS OF JAZZ				
❏ RCA Victor LPT-4 [10]	1951	10.00	20.00	40.00
KGFJ SOUNDS OF SUCCESS				
❏ Roulette R 25349 [M]	1967	5.00	10.00	20.00
KINGS OF CLASSIC JAZZ				
❏ Riverside RLP 12-131 [M]	1957	10.00	20.00	40.00
KINGS OF THE KEYBOARD				
❏ American Recording Society G-406 [M]	1956	7.50	15.00	30.00
THE KINGS SING THE BLUES				
❏ Teem LP-5005 [M]	196?	7.50	15.00	30.00
KNOW YOUR JAZZ				
❏ ABC-Paramount ABC-115 [M]	1956	7.50	15.00	30.00
KPOI'S BATTLE OF THE SURFING BANDS				
❏ Del-Fi DFLP-1235 [M]	1964	15.00	30.00	60.00
❏ Del-Fi DFST-1235 [S]	1964	25.00	50.00	100.00
—Honolulu version of the above LP				
KTLA'S BATTLE OF THE SURFING BANDS				
❏ Del-Fi DFLP-1235 [M]	1964	12.50	25.00	50.00
❏ Del-Fi DFST-1235 [S]	1964	20.00	40.00	80.00
—Los Angeles version of the above LP				
KYA GOLDEN GATE GREATS				
❏ Chess LP 1458 SF [M]	1961	37.50	75.00	150.00
—San Francisco version of "Golden Gassers," Chess 1458				
KYA'S BATTLE OF THE SURFING BANDS				
❏ Del-Fi DFLP-1235 [M]	1964	12.50	25.00	50.00
❏ Del-Fi DFST-1235 [S]	1964	20.00	40.00	80.00
—San Francisco version of the above LP, with slightly different contents				
KYA'S MEMORIES OF THE COW PALACE				
❏ Autumn LP 101 [M]	1963	17.50	35.00	70.00
A LA CARTE				
❏ Warner Bros. PRO-A-794 [(2)]	1978	5.00	10.00	20.00
THE LAST RECORD ALBUM				
❏ A&M (# unknown)	1989	10.00	20.00	40.00
LATE MUSIC, VOLUME I				
❏ Columbia CL 541 [M]	1954	6.25	12.50	25.00
LATE MUSIC, VOLUME II				
❏ Columbia CL 542 [M]	1954	6.25	12.50	25.00
LATE MUSIC, VOLUME III				
❏ Columbia CL 543 [M]	1954	6.25	12.50	25.00
THE LAUGHTOUR				
❏ Sire PRO-A-3931 [EP]	1990	5.00	10.00	20.00
—Promo-only sampler				

Number	Title (A Side/B Side)	Yr	VG	VG+	NM
LAURIE GOLDEN GOODIES					
❑ Laurie LLP-2041 [M]		1967	3.75	7.50	15.00
❑ Laurie SLLP-2041 [P]		1967	6.25	12.50	25.00
LENNY TRISTANO MEMORIAL CONCERT					
❑ Jazz Records JR-3 [(5)]		198?	10.00	20.00	40.00
LEONARD FEATHER'S ENCYCLOPEDIA OF JAZZ					
❑ Vee Jay VJSP-400 [(2)]		1977	6.25	12.50	25.00
LEONARD FEATHER'S ENCYCLOPEDIA OF JAZZ OF THE '60S: BLUES BAG					
❑ Vee Jay LP-2506 [M]		1964	5.00	10.00	20.00
LEONARD FEATHER'S ENCYCLOPEDIA OF JAZZ, VOLUME ONE: GIANTS OF THE SAXOPHONE					
❑ Vee Jay LP-2501 [M]		1964	5.00	10.00	20.00
❑ Vee Jay VJS-2501 [S]		1964	6.25	12.50	25.00
LET THEM EAT JELLYBEANS					
❑ Alternative Tentacles VIRUS 4		1982	6.25	12.50	25.00
LET'S HAVE A DANCE PARTY					
❑ Ace LP-1019 [M]		1961	17.50	35.00	70.00
LET'S SING ABOUT FREEDOM					
❑ Vee Jay LP-5044 [M]		1963	7.50	15.00	30.00
LIBERTY PREMIER SERIES SPECTACULAR					
❑ Liberty L-5504 [M]		1962	5.00	10.00	20.00
❑ Liberty S-6604 [S]		1962	7.50	15.00	30.00
LIBERTY PROUDLY PRESENTS STEREO — THE VISUAL SOUND					
❑ Liberty LST-100 [S]		1959	10.00	20.00	40.00
LIFE IS BEAUTIFUL, SO WHY NOT EAT HEALTH FOOD?					
❑ New Underground 44		1981	5.00	10.00	20.00
LIFE IS UGLY, SO WHY NOT KILL YOURSELF?					
❑ New Underground 11		1981	5.00	10.00	20.00
THE LIFE TREASURY OF CHRISTMAS MUSIC					
❑ Project/Capitol TL 100 [M]		1963	5.00	10.00	20.00
—Designed as a supplement to the Life Book of Christmas; selections performed by anonymous chorus and orchestra and Boy Choristers from the Church of the Transfiguration (NY)					
LIGHTS OUT SAN FRANCISCO					
❑ Blue Thumb BT 6004		1970	6.25	12.50	25.00
LIKE 'ER RED HOT					
❑ Duke DLP-73 [M]		196?	7.50	15.00	30.00
—Green label, "Distributed by ABC-Dunhill"					
❑ Duke DLP-73 [M]		196?	12.50	25.00	50.00
—Orange label					
❑ Duke DLP-73 [M]		1960	30.00	60.00	120.00
—Purple and yellow label					
LIMO					
❑ Warner Bros. PRO 691 [(2)]		1977	5.00	10.00	20.00
LISTEN TO OUR STORY					
❑ Brunswick BL 59001 [10]		1950	15.00	30.00	60.00
A LITTLE ROCK AND ROLL FOR EVERYBODY					
❑ Audio Lab AL-1567 [M]		1960	50.00	100.00	200.00
LIVE AT CBGB'S					
❑ Atlantic SD2-508 [(2)]		1976	5.00	10.00	20.00
—Same album as CBGB/Omfug release					
❑ CBGB/Omfug 315 [(2)]		1976	7.50	15.00	30.00
LIVE AT TARGET					
❑ Subterranean 3		1980	6.25	12.50	25.00
LIVE AT THE WHISKEY A-GO-GO					
❑ Vee Jay LP-1100 [M]		1964	7.50	15.00	30.00
—Not known to exist in stereo					
THE LIVELY SOUND OF UNIVERSITY					
❑ Capitol Custom (no #) [M]		1966	5.00	10.00	20.00
—"Mustang Sweepstakes Prize Winner" on front cover					
LOADED					
❑ Savoy MG-12074 [M]		1956	12.50	25.00	50.00
LONDON BROIL					
❑ Angel ANG-60004 [10]		1955	12.50	25.00	50.00
A LOOK AT YESTERDAY					
❑ Mainstream 56025 [M]		1965	6.25	12.50	25.00
LOOK WHO'S SURFIN' NOW!					
❑ King 882 [M]		1964	37.50	75.00	150.00
LOONEY TUNES AND MERRIE MELODIES					
❑ Warner Bros. PRO 423 [(3)]		1970	25.00	50.00	100.00
—Box set with booklet of liner notes; originals have green labels					
A LOT OF YARN BUT A WELL-KNITTED JAZZ ALBUM					
❑ Bethlehem BCP-91 [M]		1958	7.50	15.00	30.00
LOVE ME TENDER					
❑ Time-Life STL-133 [(2)]		1991	6.25	12.50	25.00
LOVE THOSE GOODIES					
❑ Checker LP 2973 [DJ]		1959	125.00	250.00	500.00
—White label, multi-color splash vinyl					
❑ Checker LP 2973 [M]		1959	30.00	60.00	120.00
LULLABY OF BIRDLAND					
❑ RCA Victor LPM-1146 [M]		1955	12.50	25.00	50.00
LUSTY MOODS					
❑ Moodsville MVLP-37 [M]		1963	10.00	20.00	40.00
—Green label					
❑ Moodsville MVLP-37 [M]		1965	5.00	10.00	20.00
—Blue label, trident logo at right					
❑ Moodsville MVST-37 [S]		1963	10.00	20.00	40.00
—Green label					
❑ Moodsville MVST-37 [S]		1965	5.00	10.00	20.00
—Blue label, trident logo at right					
❑ Status ST-8319 [M]		1965	7.50	15.00	30.00

Number	Title (A Side/B Side)	Yr	VG	VG+	NM
MAD "TWISTS" ROCK 'N' ROLL					
❑ Big Top 12-1305 [M]		1962	25.00	50.00	100.00
THE MAGIC HORN					
❑ RCA Victor LPM-1332 [M]		1956	10.00	20.00	40.00
THE MAGIC OF CHRISTMAS					
❑ Columbia Musical Treasury P3S 5806 [(3)]		1972	5.00	10.00	20.00
THE MAGICAL MUSIC OF WALT DISNEY					
❑ Ovation OV-5000 [(4)]		1978	15.00	30.00	60.00
—Box set					
MAGNAVOX ALBUM OF CHRISTMAS MUSIC					
❑ Columbia Special Products CSQ 11093 [Q]		1972	5.00	10.00	20.00
—Sold only at Magnavox dealers; yes, this is in quadraphonic!					
MAMBO JAZZ					
❑ Prestige PRLP-135 [10]		1952	37.50	75.00	150.00
THE MAN WITH A HORN					
❑ Decca DL 5191 [10]		1950	12.50	25.00	50.00
THE MANY FACES OF THE BLUES					
❑ Savoy MG-12125 [M]		1957	12.50	25.00	50.00
MAX'S KANSAS CITY 1976					
❑ Ram 1213		1976	5.00	10.00	20.00
MAX'S KANSAS CITY PRESENTS NEW WAVE HITS FOR THE '80S					
❑ Max's Kansas City 19801		1981	5.00	10.00	20.00
—Compilation of first two Max's Kansas City albums plus new tracks					
MAX'S KANSAS CITY VOL. 2, 1977					
❑ Ram 2213		1977	3.00	6.00	12.00
THE MELLOW MOODS OF JAZZ					
❑ RCA Victor LPM-1365 [M]		1956	10.00	20.00	40.00
MELLOW THE MOOD/JAZZ IN A MELLOW MOOD					
❑ Blue Note BLP-5001 [10]		1951	50.00	100.00	200.00
MEMORABLE SESSIONS IN JAZZ					
❑ Blue Note BLP-5026 [10]		1953	50.00	100.00	200.00
MEMORIES ARE MADE OF HITS					
❑ Liberty LRP-3200 [M]		1961	6.25	12.50	25.00
—Reissued as "The Original Hits, Volume 4"					
MEMORY LANE, HITS BY THE ORIGINAL GROUPS					
❑ Fire FLP-100 [M]		1959	50.00	100.00	200.00
—Reissue of "Here Are the Hits!" with the same label and number					
MEMPHIS GOLD					
❑ Stax 710 [M]		1966	6.25	12.50	25.00
❑ Stax S710 [S]		1966	7.50	15.00	30.00
MEMPHIS GOLD VOLUME 2					
❑ Stax 726 [M]		1967	5.00	10.00	20.00
❑ Stax S726 [S]		1967	6.25	12.50	25.00
THE MERCURY 40TH ANNIVERSARY V.S.O.P. ALBUM					
❑ Mercury 824116-1 [(4)]		1985	10.00	20.00	40.00
MERCURY LIVING PRESENCE					
❑ Mercury Living Presence SR 90293 [S]		196?	30.00	60.00	120.00
—Maroon label, no "Vendor: Mercury Record Corporation"; contains music by groups conducted by Paul Paray, Antal Dorati and Frederick Fennell					
MERRY CHRISTMAS					
❑ Coral CRL 56080 [10]		1952	20.00	40.00	80.00
MERRY CHRISTMAS BABY (CHRISTMAS MUSIC FOR YOUNG LOVERS)					
❑ Hollywood HLP 501 [M]		1956	30.00	60.00	120.00
MERRY CHRISTMAS FROM MOTOWN					
❑ Motown MS-681		1968	7.50	15.00	30.00
MERRY CHRISTMAS FROM…					
❑ King 680 [M]		1959	50.00	100.00	200.00
❑ Reader's Digest RD4-83 [(4)]		1969	5.00	10.00	20.00
—Available only through Reader's Digest magazine by mail order					
MERRY CHRISTMAS MUSIC/CHRISTMAS FAVORITES					
❑ Plymouth P12-59 [M]		1952	5.00	10.00	20.00
—Artists not mentioned on jacket or label					
MERRY CHRISTMAS TO YOU					
❑ Capitol T 9030 [M]		1955	12.50	25.00	50.00
METRONOME ALL STARS 1956					
❑ Clef MGC-743 [M]		1956	10.00	20.00	40.00
❑ Verve MGV-8030 [M]		1957	10.00	20.00	40.00
❑ Verve V-8030 [M]		1961	5.00	10.00	20.00
METRONOME ALL-STARS					
❑ Harmony HL 7044 [M]		1957	6.25	12.50	25.00
❑ RCA Camden CAL-426 [M]		1958	6.25	12.50	25.00
THE METRONOME ALL-STARS					
❑ Columbia CL 2528 [10]		1954	7.50	15.00	30.00
MGM MILLION SELLERS: COUNTRY & WESTERN HITS, VOLUME 1					
❑ MGM E-3825 [M]		1960	6.25	12.50	25.00
MGM RECORDS PARADE OF STARS					
❑ MGM NP 90569 [M]		1965	5.00	10.00	20.00
—Capitol Record Club sampler of 12 MGM artists and soundtracks					
MICHIGAN ROCKS					
❑ Seeds and Stems 77001 [(2)]		1977	6.25	12.50	25.00
MICKEY MOST PRESENTS BRITISH GO-GO					
❑ MGM E 4306 [M]		1965	7.50	15.00	30.00
❑ MGM SE 4306 [M]		1965	7.50	15.00	30.00
MICKEY MOST PRESENTS ENGLISH IN-GROUPS					
❑ Metro M-577 [M]		1966	5.00	10.00	20.00
❑ Metro MS-577 [R]		1966	5.00	10.00	20.00
MIDDLE OF THE ROAD					
❑ Warner Bros. PRO 525 [(2)]		1972	7.50	15.00	30.00
—Originals have green labels					

Number Title (A Side/B Side)	Yr	VG	VG+	NM
MIDNIGHT JAMBOREE				
❑ Decca DL 4041 [M]	1961	6.25	12.50	25.00
❑ Decca DL 74041 [S]	1961	7.50	15.00	30.00
MIDNIGHT JAZZ AT CARNEGIE HALL				
❑ Verve MGV-8189-2 [(2)M]	1957	12.50	25.00	50.00
❑ Verve V-8189-2 [(2)M]	1961	6.25	12.50	25.00
A MILLION OR MORE				
❑ ABC-Paramount ABC-216 [M]	1959	20.00	40.00	80.00
MILLION PERFORMANCE SONGS, VOLUME 1				
❑ Jobete JSA-6251 [DJ]	1988	5.00	10.00	20.00
—Promo-only publisher's demo				
MILLION PERFORMANCE SONGS, VOLUME 2				
❑ Jobete JSA-6252 [DJ]	1988	5.00	10.00	20.00
—Promo-only publisher's demo				
MILLION SELLER DANCE HITS				
❑ Parkway P-7028 [M]	1963	7.50	15.00	30.00
THE MILLION-AIRS				
❑ Coral CRL 57310 [M]	1959	6.25	12.50	25.00
THE MODERN IDIOM				
❑ Capitol H 325 [10]	1952	12.50	25.00	50.00
MODERN JAZZ				
❑ London LL 1185 [M]	1955	5.00	10.00	20.00
❑ Tops L-1521 [M]	1958	5.00	10.00	20.00
MODERN JAZZ CONCERT				
❑ Adventures in Sound WL-127 [M]	1958	10.00	20.00	40.00
MODERN JAZZ FESTIVAL				
❑ Harmony HL 7196 [M]	1958	5.00	10.00	20.00
MODERN JAZZ GALLERY				
❑ Kapp KXL-5001 [M]	195?	5.00	10.00	20.00
MODERN JAZZ PIANO				
❑ RCA Camden CAL-384 [M]	1958	6.25	12.50	25.00
MODERN JAZZ SPECTACULAR				
❑ Jazztone J-1231 [M]	1956	7.50	15.00	30.00
MODERN JAZZ TRUMPETS				
❑ Prestige PRLP-113 [10]	1951	50.00	100.00	200.00
MODERN MOODS				
❑ Moodsville MVLP-2 [M]	1961	10.00	20.00	40.00
—Green label				
❑ Moodsville MVLP-2 [M]	1965	5.00	10.00	20.00
—Blue label, trident logo at right				
MOMENTS OF MOTOWN				
❑ Motown PR-122 [DJ]	1983	12.50	25.00	50.00
—Promo-only item with narration and song snippets				
MONARCH ALL STAR JAZZ, VOL. 1				
❑ Monarch LP-201 [10]	1952	12.50	25.00	50.00
MONARCH ALL STAR JAZZ, VOL. 2				
❑ Monarch LP-202 [10]	1952	12.50	25.00	50.00
MONARCH ALL STAR JAZZ, VOL. 3				
❑ Monarch LP-203 [10]	1952	12.50	25.00	50.00
MONARCH ALL STAR JAZZ, VOL. 4				
❑ Monarch LP-204 [10]	1952	12.50	25.00	50.00
MONARCH ALL STAR JAZZ, VOL. 5				
❑ Monarch LP-205 [10]	1952	12.50	25.00	50.00
MONDAY NIGHT AT BIRDLAND				
❑ Roulette R 52015 [M]	1958	7.50	15.00	30.00
❑ Roulette SR 52015 [S]	1959	7.50	15.00	30.00
MONSTERS				
❑ Warner Bros. PRO-A-796 [(2)]	1978	5.00	10.00	20.00
MONTAGE				
❑ Savoy MG-12029 [M]	1955	20.00	40.00	80.00
THE MONTREUX '77 COLLECTION				
❑ Pablo Live 2620107 [(8)]	1978	17.50	35.00	70.00
MONUMENTAL COUNTRY HITS				
❑ Monument SLP-18095	1968	5.00	10.00	20.00
MONUMENTAL POP HITS				
❑ Monument SLP-18096	1968	5.00	10.00	20.00
MOOD IN BLUE				
❑ Urania UJLP-1209 [M]	1955	7.50	15.00	30.00
MOOD TO BE WOOED				
❑ Cadet LP-784 [M]	1967	5.00	10.00	20.00
❑ Cadet LPS-784 [S]	1967	3.75	7.50	15.00
MORE COUNTRY CLASSICS				
❑ RCA Victor LPM-2467 [M]	1961	6.25	12.50	25.00
❑ RCA Victor LSP-2467 [S]	1961	7.50	15.00	30.00
MORE COUNTRY MUSIC SPECTACULAR				
❑ Starday SLP-140 [M]	1961	10.00	20.00	40.00
MORE DRUMS ON FIRE				
❑ World Pacific ST-1022 [S]	1960	7.50	15.00	30.00
❑ World Pacific WP-1261 [M]	1960	10.00	20.00	40.00
MORE FOR YOUR MONEY				
❑ Bell 6009	1968	5.00	10.00	20.00
MORE GOLD HITS, VOLUME 2				
❑ Warwick W 2044 [M]	1961	20.00	40.00	80.00
MORE GOLDEN GREATS				
❑ Liberty LRP-3548 [M]	1967	5.00	10.00	20.00
❑ Liberty LST-7548 [P]	1967	3.75	7.50	15.00

Number Title (A Side/B Side)	Yr	VG	VG+	NM
MORE GREAT HITS OF 1964 AND OTHER GOLDEN GOODIES				
❑ Vee Jay LP-1136 [M]	1965	7.50	15.00	30.00
—Not known to exist in stereo				
MORE LIVE ECHOES OF THE SWINGING BANDS				
❑ RCA Victor LPM-1983 [M]	1959	10.00	20.00	40.00
❑ RCA Victor LSP-1983 [S]	1959	12.50	25.00	50.00
MORE SOLID GOLD PROGRAMMING				
❑ Screen Gems/Columbia CPL-716/7 [(2)DJ]	1975	7.50	15.00	30.00
—Promo-only compilation of oldies sent to radio to spur airplay on songs owned by this publishing house; contains three Beatles recordings				
THE MOST OF THE TWIST				
❑ Roulette R 25176 [M]	1962	6.25	12.50	25.00
—Originals have a white label with colored spokes				
THE MOST, VOLUME 1				
❑ Roulette R 52050 [M]	1960	5.00	10.00	20.00
❑ Roulette SR 52050 [S]	1960	6.25	12.50	25.00
THE MOST, VOLUME 2				
❑ Roulette R 52053 [M]	1960	5.00	10.00	20.00
❑ Roulette SR 52053 [S]	1960	6.25	12.50	25.00
THE MOST, VOLUME 3				
❑ Roulette R 52057 [M]	1961	5.00	10.00	20.00
❑ Roulette SR 52057 [S]	1961	6.25	12.50	25.00
THE MOST, VOLUME 4				
❑ Roulette R 52062 [M]	1961	5.00	10.00	20.00
❑ Roulette SR 52062 [S]	1961	6.25	12.50	25.00
THE MOST, VOLUME 5				
❑ Roulette R 52075 [M]	1961	5.00	10.00	20.00
❑ Roulette SR 52075 [S]	1961	6.25	12.50	25.00
MOTOR CITY SCENE				
❑ Bethlehem BCP-6056 [M]	1961	12.50	25.00	50.00
THE MOTOR-TOWN REVIEW, VOL. 1				
❑ Motown MT 609 [M]	1963	10.00	20.00	40.00
THE MOTOR-TOWN REVIEW, VOL. 2				
❑ Motown MT 615 [M]	1964	7.50	15.00	30.00
THE MOTORTOWN REVIEW IN PARIS				
❑ Tamla T 264 [M]	1965	6.25	12.50	25.00
❑ Tamla TS 264 [S]	1965	7.50	15.00	30.00
THE MOTORTOWN REVUE LIVE!				
❑ Motown MS-688	1969	6.25	12.50	25.00
A MOTOWN CHRISTMAS				
❑ Motown M-795V2 [(2)]	1973	5.00	10.00	20.00
MOTOWN INSTRUMENTALS				
❑ Natural Resources NR 4002T1	1978	5.00	10.00	20.00
MOTOWN SHOW TUNES				
❑ Natural Resources NR 4003T1	1978	5.00	10.00	20.00
MOTOWN SPECIAL				
❑ Motown M 603 [M]	1962	20.00	40.00	80.00
THE MOTOWN STORY: THE FIRST 25 YEARS				
❑ Motown PR-121 [(7)DJ]	1983	62.50	125.00	250.00
—Promo-only box set with extra record not on the commercial release; labels are white				
THE MOTOWN STORY: THE FIRST DECADE				
❑ Motown MS-726 [(5)]	1971	7.50	15.00	30.00
THE MOTOWN STORY: THE FIRST TWENTY-FIVE YEARS				
❑ Motown 6048 ML5 [(5)]	1983	7.50	15.00	30.00
MOTOWN WINNER'S CIRCLE: #1 HITS, VOL. 1				
❑ Gordy GS-935	1969	6.25	12.50	25.00
MOTOWN WINNER'S CIRCLE: #1 HITS, VOL. 2				
❑ Gordy GS-936	1969	6.25	12.50	25.00
MOTOWN WINNER'S CIRCLE: #1 HITS, VOL. 3				
❑ Gordy GS-943	1969	6.25	12.50	25.00
MOTOWN WINNER'S CIRCLE: #1 HITS, VOL. 4				
❑ Gordy GS-946	1969	6.25	12.50	25.00
MOTOWN WINNER'S CIRCLE: #1 HITS, VOL. 5				
❑ Gordy GS-950	1970	6.25	12.50	25.00
MOTOWN'S GREAT INTERPRETATIONS				
❑ Natural Resources NR 4001T1	1978	5.00	10.00	20.00
MOUNTAIN FROLIC				
❑ Brunswick BL 59000 [10]	1950	15.00	30.00	60.00
MURRAY THE "K'S" SING ALONG WITH THE ORIGINAL GOLDEN GASSERS				
❑ Roulette R 25159 [M]	1961	7.50	15.00	30.00
MURRAY THE K — LIVE FROM THE BROOKLYN FOX				
❑ KFM 1001 [M]	1963	10.00	20.00	40.00
MURRAY THE K PRESENTS GOLDEN GASSERS FOR A DANCE PARTY				
❑ Roulette R 25192 [M]	1962	6.25	12.50	25.00
MURRAY THE K PRESENTS GOLDEN GASSERS FOR HAND HOLDERS				
❑ Roulette R 25191 [M]	1962	6.25	12.50	25.00
MURRAY THE K'S BLASTS FROM THE PAST				
❑ Chess LP 1461 [M]	1961	10.00	20.00	40.00
MURRAY THE K'S GASSERS FOR SUBMARINE RACE WATCHERS				
❑ Chess LP 1470 [M]	1962	10.00	20.00	40.00
MURRAY THE K'S GOLDEN GASSERS				
❑ Chess LP 1458 NYC [M]	1961	37.50	75.00	150.00
—New York version of "Golden Gassers," Chess 1458				
MURRAY THE K'S NINETEEN-SIXTY TWO BOSS GOLDEN GASSERS				
❑ Scepter SP-510 [M]	1963	5.00	10.00	20.00
❑ Scepter SPS-510 [P]	1963	6.25	12.50	25.00

Number Title (A Side/B Side)	Yr	VG	VG+	NM
MUSIC AND PLUNK, TINKLE, TING-A-LING				
❏ Mercury Living Presence SR 90338 [S]	196?	12.50	25.00	50.00
—Maroon label, no "Vendor: Mercury Record Corporation"				
MUSIC AND RHYTHM SAMPLER				
❏ PVC EP 2 [DJ]	1982	6.25	12.50	25.00
—Includes XTC, Peter Gabriel, David Byrne, The (English) Beat; one-LP sampler of two-record set				
MUSIC FOR FRUSTRATED CONDUCTORS				
❏ RCA Victor Red Seal LSC-2325 [S]	1959	12.50	25.00	50.00
—Original with "shaded dog" label				
MUSIC FOR THE BOY FRIEND...HE REALLY DIGS JAZZ				
❏ Decca DL 8314 [M]	1956	7.50	15.00	30.00
MUSIC FROM THE SOUTH, VOL. 1: COUNTRY BRASS BANDS				
❏ Folkways FA-2650 [M]	195?	5.00	10.00	20.00
THE MUSIC OF NEW ORLEANS, VOL. 1				
❏ Folkways FA-2461 [M]	1959	5.00	10.00	20.00
THE MUSIC OF NEW ORLEANS, VOL. 2				
❏ Folkways FA-2462 [M]	1959	5.00	10.00	20.00
THE MUSIC OF NEW ORLEANS, VOL. 3: DANCE HALLS				
❏ Folkways FA-2463 [M]	1959	5.00	10.00	20.00
THE MUSIC OF NEW ORLEANS, VOL. 4: THE BIRTH OF JAZZ				
❏ Folkways FA-2464 [M]	1959	5.00	10.00	20.00
THE MUSIC OF NEW ORLEANS, VOL. 5: NEW ORLEANS JAZZ				
❏ Folkways FA-2465 [M]	1959	5.00	10.00	20.00
THE MUSIC PEOPLE				
❏ Columbia C3X 31280 [(3)]	1972	6.25	12.50	25.00
MUSIC TO READ JAMES BOND BY				
❏ United Artists UAL-3415 [M]	1965	5.00	10.00	20.00
❏ United Artists UAS-6415 [S]	1965	6.25	12.50	25.00
MUSIC TO READ JAMES BOND BY, VOL. 2				
❏ United Artists UAL-3541 [M]	1966	5.00	10.00	20.00
❏ United Artists UAS-6541 [S]	1966	6.25	12.50	25.00
A MUSICAL HISTORY OF JAZZ				
❏ Grand Award GA 33-322 [M]	1955	5.00	10.00	20.00
MY FAIR LADY				
❏ Status ST-8315 [M]	1965	7.50	15.00	30.00
MY SON THE SURF NUT				
❏ Capitol ST 1939 [S]	1963	15.00	30.00	60.00
❏ Capitol T 1939 [M]	1963	12.50	25.00	50.00
THE NAMES OF DIXIELAND				
❏ Baronet B-108 [M]	195?	5.00	10.00	20.00
NASCAR GOES COUNTRY				
❏ MCA 474	1975	7.50	15.00	30.00
NASHVILLE BANDSTAND				
❏ King 813 [M]	1962	25.00	50.00	100.00
NASHVILLE BANDSTAND, VOLUME 2				
❏ King 847 [M]	1963	20.00	40.00	80.00
NASHVILLE SATURDAY NIGHT				
❏ Nashville NLP-2009 [M]	1965	5.00	10.00	20.00
❏ Starday SLP-128 [M]	1961	10.00	20.00	40.00
NASHVILLE STEEL GUITAR				
❏ Nashville NLP-2017 [M]	1965	5.00	10.00	20.00
❏ Starday SLP-138 [M]	1961	7.50	15.00	30.00
NATIVE NEW ORLEANS JAZZ				
❏ Dot DLP-3009 [M]	1956	7.50	15.00	30.00
NEIGHBORHOOD RHYTHMS				
❏ Freeway 213 [(2)]	1984	10.00	20.00	40.00
NEW BLUE HORNS				
❏ Riverside RLP 12-294 [M]	1958	7.50	15.00	30.00
NEW CHAMBER JAZZ				
❏ Epic LN 1124 [10]	1955	7.50	15.00	30.00
NEW FACES AT NEWPORT				
❏ Metrojazz E-1005 [M]	1959	10.00	20.00	40.00
❏ Metrojazz SE-1005 [S]	1959	7.50	15.00	30.00
NEW ORLEANS BOUNCE: URBAN BLUES, VOLUME 2				
❏ Imperial LP-94004	1968	5.00	10.00	20.00
NEW ORLEANS DIXIELAND				
❏ Southland SLP-216 [M]	1955	6.25	12.50	25.00
NEW ORLEANS ENCORE				
❏ Riverside RLP-2503 [10]	1954	20.00	40.00	80.00
NEW ORLEANS EXPRESS				
❏ EmArcy MG-36022 [M]	1955	12.50	25.00	50.00
NEW ORLEANS HORNS				
❏ Riverside RLP-1005 [10]	1953	20.00	40.00	80.00
NEW ORLEANS JAZZ				
❏ Decca DL 5483 [10]	1953	12.50	25.00	50.00
❏ Decca DL 8283 [M]	1956	7.50	15.00	30.00
NEW ORLEANS JAZZ BABIES				
❏ Southland SLP-214 [M]	1955	6.25	12.50	25.00
NEW ORLEANS JAZZ KINGS				
❏ Southland SLP-217 [M]	1955	6.25	12.50	25.00
NEW ORLEANS JAZZ STARS				
❏ Southland SLP-211 [M]	1955	6.25	12.50	25.00
NEW ORLEANS LEGENDS				
❏ Riverside RLP 12-119 [M]	1957	10.00	20.00	40.00
NEW ORLEANS REVIVAL				
❏ Riverside RLP-1047 [10]	1954	20.00	40.00	80.00

Number Title (A Side/B Side)	Yr	VG	VG+	NM
NEW ORLEANS RHYTHM KINGS				
❏ Riverside RLP 12-102 [M]	195?	15.00	30.00	60.00
—Also see NEW ORLEANS RHYTHM KINGS in the main A-Z listings.				
NEW ORLEANS STYLE				
❏ "X" LVA-3029 [10]	1954	20.00	40.00	80.00
NEW ORLEANS TO LOS ANGELES				
❏ Southland SLP-215 [M]	1955	6.25	12.50	25.00
NEW ORLEANS, OUR HOME TOWN				
❏ Imperial LP-9260 [M]	1964	6.25	12.50	25.00
❏ Imperial LP-12260 [R]	1964	5.00	10.00	20.00
NEW ORLEANS: THE LIVING LEGENDS, VOL. 1				
❏ Riverside RLP-356 [M]	196?	5.00	10.00	20.00
NEW ORLEANS: THE LIVING LEGENDS, VOL. 2				
❏ Riverside RLP-357 [M]	196?	5.00	10.00	20.00
NEW SOUNDS FROM SWEDEN, VOL. 1: THE DARING YOUNG SWEDES				
❏ Prestige PRLP-119 [10]	1951	50.00	100.00	200.00
NEW VOICES				
❏ Dawn DLP-1125 [M]	1956	20.00	40.00	80.00
THE NEW WAVE IN JAZZ				
❏ Impulse! A-90 [M]	1966	3.75	7.50	15.00
❏ Impulse! AS-90 [S]	1966	5.00	10.00	20.00
NEW YORK JAZZ OF THE TWENTIES				
❏ Riverside RLP-1048 [10]	1954	20.00	40.00	80.00
NEWPORT JAZZ FESTIVAL				
❏ RCA Victor LPM-3369 [M]	1965	3.75	7.50	15.00
❏ RCA Victor LSP-3369 [S]	1965	5.00	10.00	20.00
NEWPORT JAZZ FESTIVAL ALL STARS				
❏ Atlantic SD 1331 [S]	1961	7.50	15.00	30.00
—Multicolor label, white "fan" logo at right				
NEWPORT JAZZ FESTIVAL ALL-STARS				
❏ Atlantic 1331 [M]	1961	6.25	12.50	25.00
—Multicolor label, white "fan" logo at right				
A NIGHT AT EDDIE CONDON'S				
❏ Decca DL 8281 [M]	1956	7.50	15.00	30.00
A NIGHT AT THE BOULEVARD				
❏ Felsted FL-7503 [M]	1960	10.00	20.00	40.00
A NIGHT AT THE FIVE SPOT: A MEMORIAL CONCERT DEDICATED TO THE MUSIC OF CHARLIE PARKER				
❏ Signal S-1204 [M]	1957	30.00	60.00	120.00
THE NITTY GRITTY				
❏ Vee Jay LP-1084 [M]	1964	7.50	15.00	30.00
—Not known to exist in stereo				
NO 'COUNT				
❏ Savoy MG-12078 [M]	1956	15.00	30.00	60.00
NO ENERGY CRISIS				
❏ ABC Impulse! AS-9267 [(2)]	1974	5.00	10.00	20.00
NO NUKES: THE MUSE CONCERTS FOR A NON-NUCLEAR FUTURE				
❏ Asylum ML-801 [(3)]	1979	6.25	12.50	25.00
NO SOUR GRAPES, JUST PURE JAZZ				
❏ Bethlehem BCP-92 [M]	1958	7.50	15.00	30.00
NO WAVE				
❏ A&M PR 4738 [DJ]	1978	6.25	12.50	25.00
—White label promo on watercolor blue vinyl; numbered sticker on generic cover				
❏ A&M SP-4738	1978	2.00	4.00	8.00
—Black vinyl				
❏ A&M SP-4738	1978	3.75	7.50	15.00
—First pressing on watercolor blue vinyl				
NON DAIRY CREAMER				
❏ Warner Bros. PRO 443	1971	6.25	12.50	25.00
—Originals have green labels				
NORMAN GRANZ JAZZ CONCERT				
❏ Norgran MGN-2501 [M]	1954	20.00	40.00	80.00
❏ Norgran MGN-2502 [M]	1954	20.00	40.00	80.00
NOT SO QUIET ON THE WESTERN FRONT				
❏ Alternative Tentacles VIRUS 14 [(2)]	1982	6.25	12.50	25.00
—Includes Dead Kennedys, Flipper, lots of others				
NOTHING CHEESY ABOUT THIS JAZZ				
❏ Bethlehem BCP-85 [M]	1958	7.50	15.00	30.00
NOVA SCOTIA FOLK SONGS				
❏ Elektra EKL-23 [10]	1954	10.00	20.00	40.00
NUGGETS				
❏ Elektra 7E-2006 [(2)]	1972	10.00	20.00	40.00
O LOVE IS TEASIN': ANGLO-AMERICAN MOUNTAIN BALLADRY				
❏ Elektra 60402 [(3)]	1985	5.00	10.00	20.00
O. HENRY'S THE GIFT OF THE MAGI				
❏ E.F. MacDonald EFMX-62	1962	5.00	10.00	20.00
—Special album done by the E.F. MacDonald Company, Dayton, Ohio				
OCTOBER '61 POP SAMPLER				
❏ RCA Victor SPS-33-141 [DJ]	1961	150.00	300.00	600.00
—Promo-only collection.				
OCTOBER 1960 POPULAR STEREO SAMPLER				
❏ RCA Victor SPS-33-96 [DJ]	1960	150.00	300.00	600.00
—Promo-only collection				
OCTOBER CHRISTMAS SAMPLER 59-40-41				
❏ RCA Victor SPS-33-54 [DJ]	1959	150.00	300.00	600.00
—Promo-only collection				
THE OFFICIAL GRAMMY AWARDS ARCHIVE COLLECTION (ALBUM OF THE YEAR)				
❏ Franklin Mint GRAM-14 [(4)]	1985	15.00	30.00	60.00

Number	Title (A Side/B Side)	Yr	VG	VG+	NM
THE OFFICIAL GRAMMY AWARDS ARCHIVE COLLECTION (ALL-TIME WINNERS)					
❑ Franklin Mint GRAM-2 [(4)]		1985	15.00	30.00	60.00
THE OFFICIAL GRAMMY AWARDS ARCHIVE COLLECTION (BEST NEW ARTIST)					
❑ Franklin Mint GRAM-6 [(4)]		1985	15.00	30.00	60.00
THE OFFICIAL GRAMMY AWARDS ARCHIVE COLLECTION (FOLK PERFORMANCES)					
❑ Franklin Mint GRAM-10 [(4)]		1985	15.00	30.00	60.00
THE OFFICIAL GRAMMY AWARDS ARCHIVE COLLECTION (GREAT PERFORMANCES OF THE ROCK ERA, VOL. 1)					
❑ Franklin Mint GRAM-3 [(4)]		1985	15.00	30.00	60.00
THE OFFICIAL GRAMMY AWARDS ARCHIVE COLLECTION (JAZZ VOCALISTS)					
❑ Franklin Mint GRAM-13 [(4)]		1985	15.00	30.00	60.00
THE OFFICIAL GRAMMY AWARDS ARCHIVE COLLECTION (POP PERFORMANCES, VOL. 1)					
❑ Franklin Mint GRAM-5 [(4)]		1985	15.00	30.00	60.00
THE OFFICIAL GRAMMY AWARDS ARCHIVE COLLECTION (RECORD OF THE YEAR)					
❑ Franklin Mint GRAM-1 [(4)]		1985	15.00	30.00	60.00
THE OFFICIAL GRAMMY AWARDS ARCHIVE COLLECTION (RHYTHM AND BLUES, VOL. 1)					
❑ Franklin Mint GRAM-8 [(4)]		1985	17.50	35.00	70.00
THE OFFICIAL GRAMMY AWARDS ARCHIVE COLLECTION (SONG OF THE YEAR)					
❑ Franklin Mint GRAM-9 [(4)]		1985	15.00	30.00	60.00
THE OFFICIAL GRAMMY AWARDS ARCHIVE COLLECTION (STAGE & ORIGINAL CAST RECORDINGS)					
❑ Franklin Mint GRAM-11 [(4)]		1985	30.00	60.00	120.00
THE OFFICIAL GRAMMY AWARDS ARCHIVE COLLECTION (THE BIG BAND SOUND)					
❑ Franklin Mint GRAM-7 [(4)]		1985	15.00	30.00	60.00
THE OFFICIAL GRAMMY AWARDS ARCHIVE COLLECTION (THE GREAT SINGERS)					
❑ Franklin Mint GRAM-4 [(4)]		1985	37.50	75.00	150.00
THE OFFICIAL GRAMMY AWARDS ARCHIVE COLLECTION (THE PRODUCER'S CHOICE)					
❑ Franklin Mint GRAM-12 [(4)]		1985	15.00	30.00	60.00
OLD 'N GOLDEN					
❑ Jamie JLPS-3031		1968	5.00	10.00	20.00
OLD AND HEAVY GOLD 1955					
❑ Economic Consultants 1955		1973	5.00	10.00	20.00
OLD AND HEAVY GOLD 1956					
❑ Economic Consultants 1956		1973	7.50	15.00	30.00
OLD AND HEAVY GOLD 1957					
❑ Economic Consultants 1957		1973	7.50	15.00	30.00
OLD AND HEAVY GOLD 1958					
❑ Economic Consultants 1958		1973	7.50	15.00	30.00
OLD AND HEAVY GOLD 1959					
❑ Economic Consultants 1959		1973	5.00	10.00	20.00
OLD AND HEAVY GOLD 1960					
❑ Economic Consultants 1960		1973	7.50	15.00	30.00
OLD AND HEAVY GOLD 1961					
❑ Economic Consultants 1961		1973	7.50	15.00	30.00
OLD AND HEAVY GOLD 1962					
❑ Economic Consultants 1962		1973	7.50	15.00	30.00
OLD AND HEAVY GOLD 1963					
❑ Economic Consultants 1963		1973	5.00	10.00	20.00
OLD AND HEAVY GOLD 1964					
❑ Economic Consultants 1964		1973	5.00	10.00	20.00
—Original magazine ads claimed that six Beatles tracks would appear on this LP; they were replaced before release					
OLD AND HEAVY GOLD 1965					
❑ Economic Consultants 1965		1973	5.00	10.00	20.00
—Original magazine ads claimed that three Beatles tracks would appear on this LP; they were replaced before release					
OLD AND HEAVY GOLD 1966					
❑ Economic Consultants 1966		1973	5.00	10.00	20.00
OLD AND HEAVY GOLD 1967					
❑ Economic Consultants 1967		1973	5.00	10.00	20.00
—Original magazine ads claimed that a Beatles track would appear on this LP; it was replaced with another track before release					
OLD AND HEAVY GOLD 1968					
❑ Economic Consultants 1968		1973	5.00	10.00	20.00
—Original magazine ads claimed that a Beatles track would appear on this LP; it was replaced with another track before release					
OLD AND HEAVY GOLD 1969					
❑ Economic Consultants 1969		1973	5.00	10.00	20.00
—Original magazine ads claimed that a Beatles track would appear on this LP; it was replaced with another track before release					
OLD AND HEAVY GOLD 1970					
❑ Economic Consultants 1970		1973	5.00	10.00	20.00
—Original magazine ads claimed that a Beatles track would appear on this LP; it was replaced with another track before release					
OLD AND HEAVY GOLD 1971					
❑ Economic Consultants 1971		1973	5.00	10.00	20.00
—Original magazine ads claimed that a Paul McCartney track would appear on this LP; it was replaced with another track before release					
AN OLD FASHIONED CHRISTMAS					
❑ Reader's Digest RDA 216-A [(6)]		197?	5.00	10.00	20.00
—Available only through Reader's Digest magazine by mail order					

Number	Title (A Side/B Side)	Yr	VG	VG+	NM
OLD TIME BANJO PROJECT					
❑ Elektra EKL-276 [M]		1964	5.00	10.00	20.00
❑ Elektra EKS-7276 [S]		1964	6.25	12.50	25.00
OLDIES BUT GOODIES					
❑ Original Sound LPM-5001 [M]		1959	12.50	25.00	50.00
—Original pressing with no reference to other volumes on the back cover					
❑ Original Sound LPM-5001 [M]		1960s	3.00	6.00	12.00
—Later editions with later volumes in the series on the back cover					
OLDIES BUT GOODIES, VOL. 2					
❑ Original Sound LPM-5003 [M]		1960	10.00	20.00	40.00
—Original pressing with no reference to later volumes on the back cover					
❑ Original Sound LPM-5003 [M]		1960s	3.00	6.00	12.00
—Later editions with later volumes in the series on the back cover					
OLDIES BUT GOODIES, VOL. 3					
❑ Original Sound LPM-5004 [M]		1960s	3.00	6.00	12.00
—Later editions with later volumes in the series on the back cover					
❑ Original Sound LPM-5004 [M]		1961	7.50	15.00	30.00
—Original pressing with no reference to later volumes on the back cover					
OLDIES BUT GOODIES, VOL. 4					
❑ Original Sound LPM-5005 [M]		1960s	3.00	6.00	12.00
—Later editions with later volumes in the series on the back cover					
❑ Original Sound LPM-5005 [M]		1962	7.50	15.00	30.00
—Original pressing with no reference to later volumes on the back cover					
OLDIES BUT GOODIES, VOL. 5					
❑ Original Sound LPM-5007 [M]		1960s	3.00	6.00	12.00
—Later editions with later volumes in the series on the back cover					
❑ Original Sound LPM-5007 [M]		1963	5.00	10.00	20.00
—Original pressing with no reference to later volumes on the back cover					
OLDIES BUT GOODIES, VOL. 6					
❑ Original Sound LPM-5011 [M]		1960s	3.00	6.00	12.00
—Later editions with later volumes in the series on the back cover					
❑ Original Sound LPM-5011 [M]		1963	5.00	10.00	20.00
—Original pressing with no reference to later volumes on the back cover					
OLDIES BUT GOODIES, VOL. 7					
❑ Original Sound LPM-5012 [M]		1960s	3.00	6.00	12.00
—Later editions with later volumes in the series on the back cover					
❑ Original Sound LPM-5012 [M]		1964	5.00	10.00	20.00
—Original pressing with no reference to later volumes on the back cover					
OLDIES BY THE DOZEN					
❑ Parkway P-7035 [M]		1963	7.50	15.00	30.00
OLDIES BY THE DOZEN, VOLUME 2					
❑ Parkway P-7041 [M]		1964	12.50	25.00	50.00
—With bonus 45 of "The Twist" by Chubby Checker on on side and "Mashed Potato Time" by Dee Dee Sharp on the other; deduct 40 percent if missing					
OLDIES DANCE PARTY, VOLUME 1					
❑ Oldies 33 OL-8001 [M]		1963	5.00	10.00	20.00
OLDIES DANCE PARTY, VOLUME 2					
❑ Oldies 33 OL-8002 [M]		1963	5.00	10.00	20.00
OLDIES IN HI-FI					
❑ Chess LP 1439 [DJ]		1959	150.00	300.00	600.00
—Multi-color splash vinyl					
❑ Chess LP 1439 [M]		1959	75.00	150.00	300.00
—Black vinyl					
OLIO					
❑ Prestige PRLP-7084 [M]		1957	25.00	50.00	100.00
ON STAGE AT THE GRAND OLE OPRY					
❑ Decca DL 4393 [M]		1964	6.25	12.50	25.00
❑ Decca DL 74393 [S]		1964	7.50	15.00	30.00
ON-THE-ROAD JAZZ					
❑ Riverside RLP 12-127 [M]		1957	10.00	20.00	40.00
ONE DOZEN GOLDIES					
❑ Carlton LP 12-121 [M]		1960	12.50	25.00	50.00
ONE NIGHT STAND: A KEYBOARD EVENT					
❑ Columbia KC2 37100 [(2)]		198?	3.00	6.00	12.00
—"Half-Speed Mastered" edition					
❑ Columbia HC2 47100 [(2)]		198?	12.50	25.00	50.00
ONE NIGHT WITH BLUE NOTE PRESERVED					
❑ Blue Note BTDK-85117 [(4)]		1985	15.00	30.00	60.00
ONE WORLD JAZZ					
❑ Adventures in Sound WL-162 [M]		1959	12.50	25.00	50.00
❑ Adventures in Sound WS-314 [S]		1959	10.00	20.00	40.00
OPENING NIGHTS AT THE MET					
❑ RCA Victor Red Seal LM-6171 [(3)M]		1966	5.00	10.00	20.00
OPERA FOR PEOPLE WHO HATE OPERA					
❑ RCA Victor Red Seal LSC-2391 [S]		1960	5.00	10.00	20.00
—Original with "shaded dog" label					
OPRY OLD TIMERS					
❑ Starday SLP-182 [M]		1962	7.50	15.00	30.00
OPRY TIME IN TENNESSEE					
❑ Starday SLP-177 [M]		1962	7.50	15.00	30.00
OPUS DE BLUES					
❑ Savoy MG-12142 [M]		1959	15.00	30.00	60.00
OPUS DE JAZZ					
❑ Savoy MG-12036 [M]		1955	20.00	40.00	80.00
OPUS IN SWING					
❑ Savoy MG-12085 [M]		1956	15.00	30.00	60.00
THE ORCHESTRA "HOUSE OF SOUND"					
❑ Brunswick BL 54003 [M]		1954	7.50	15.00	30.00
THE ORGAN PLAYS MUSIC FOR A MERRY CHRISTMAS					
❑ Reader's Digest RDA 42-A [(4)]		1966	5.00	10.00	20.00
—Available only through Reader's Digest magazine by mail order					

Number	Title (A Side/B Side)	Yr	VG	VG+	NM
ORIGINAL BLUE NOTE JAZZ, VOL. 1					
❑ Blue Note B-6504		1969	5.00	10.00	20.00
ORIGINAL BLUE NOTE JAZZ, VOL. 2					
❑ Blue Note B-6506		1970	5.00	10.00	20.00
THE ORIGINAL COUNTRY HITS #1					
❑ Liberty LRP-3305 [M]		1963	5.00	10.00	20.00
THE ORIGINAL COUNTRY HITS #2					
❑ Liberty LRP-3345 [M]		1964	5.00	10.00	20.00
THE ORIGINAL COUNTRY HITS #3					
❑ Liberty LRP-3382 [M]		1964	5.00	10.00	20.00
ORIGINAL GOLDIES FROM THE FABULOUS '50S, VOLUME 1					
❑ Josie JM-4002 [M]		1963	15.00	30.00	60.00
ORIGINAL GOLDIES FROM THE FABULOUS '50S, VOLUME 2					
❑ Josie JM-4003 [M]		1963	15.00	30.00	60.00
ORIGINAL GOLDIES FROM THE FABULOUS '50S, VOLUME 3					
❑ Josie JM-4004 [M]		1963	15.00	30.00	60.00
THE ORIGINAL GREATEST HITS OF THE GREAT COUNTRY AND WESTERN STARS					
❑ Mercury MG-20825 [M]		1963	5.00	10.00	20.00
❑ Mercury SR-60825 [S]		1963	6.25	12.50	25.00
ORIGINAL HIT RECORDS					
❑ Roulette R 25106 [M]		1960	7.50	15.00	30.00
—Originals have a white label with colored spokes					
THE ORIGINAL HITS, PAST & PRESENT					
❑ Liberty LRP-3178 [M]		1960	5.00	10.00	20.00
THE ORIGINAL HITS, VOLUME 10					
❑ Liberty LRP-3344 [M]		1964	5.00	10.00	20.00
THE ORIGINAL HITS, VOLUME 11					
❑ Liberty LRP-3418 [M]		1965	5.00	10.00	20.00
❑ Liberty LST-7418 [P]		1965	5.00	10.00	20.00
THE ORIGINAL HITS, VOLUME 3: PAST & PRESENT					
❑ Liberty LRP-3187 [M]		1961	5.00	10.00	20.00
THE ORIGINAL HITS, VOLUME 4					
❑ Liberty LRP-3200 [M]		1962	5.00	10.00	20.00
—Reissue of "Memories Are Made of Hits"; for "The Original Hits, Volume 5," see "15 Hits: The Original Recordings"					
THE ORIGINAL HITS, VOLUME 6					
❑ Liberty LRP-3260 [M]		1962	5.00	10.00	20.00
THE ORIGINAL HITS, VOLUME 7: ALL-TIME HIT INSTRUMENTALS					
❑ Liberty LRP-3274 [M]		1963	5.00	10.00	20.00
THE ORIGINAL HITS, VOLUME 8					
❑ Liberty LRP-3288 [M]		1963	5.00	10.00	20.00
THE ORIGINAL HITS, VOLUME 9					
❑ Liberty LRP-3325 [M]		1963	5.00	10.00	20.00
THE ORIGINAL HITS, VOLUME TWO: PAST & PRESENT					
❑ Liberty LRP-3180 [M]		1961	5.00	10.00	20.00
THE ORIGINAL HOOTENANNY					
❑ Crestview CRV 806 [M]		1963	5.00	10.00	20.00
❑ Crestview CRS 7806 [S]		1963	6.25	12.50	25.00
ORIGINAL MEMPHIS ROCK AND ROLL, VOLUME 1					
❑ Sun 116		1970	5.00	10.00	20.00
ORIGINAL MOTION PICTURE HIT THEMES					
❑ United Artists UAL-3197 [M]		1962	3.75	7.50	15.00
❑ United Artists UAS-6197 [S]		1962	5.00	10.00	20.00
THE ORIGINAL R&B HITS, VOLUME 1					
❑ Liberty LRP-3381 [M]		1964	5.00	10.00	20.00
ORIGINAL RECORDINGS BY THE ARTISTS WHO MADE THEM HITS					
❑ Flip 1002 [M]		1960	100.00	200.00	400.00
ORIGINAL ROCK OLDIES, VOLUME 1					
❑ Specialty SPS-2129		1970	5.00	10.00	20.00
ORIGINAL ROCK OLDIES, VOLUME 2					
❑ Specialty SPS-2130		1970	5.00	10.00	20.00
THE ORIGINAL SOUND OF THE 20'S					
❑ Columbia C3L 35 [(3)]		1965	10.00	20.00	40.00
ORIGINAL SURFIN' HITS					
❑ GNP Crescendo GNP-84 [M]		1963	10.00	20.00	40.00
—With bonus photos; deduct 25-50 percent if missing					
❑ GNP Crescendo GNPS-84 [S]		1963	12.50	25.00	50.00
—With bonus photos; deduct 25-50 percent if missing					
OUR BEST					
❑ Clef MGC-639 [M]		1955	12.50	25.00	50.00
❑ Norgran MGN-1021 [M]		1955	20.00	40.00	80.00
OUR BEST TO YOU					
❑ Everlast ELP-201 [M]		1960	50.00	100.00	200.00
OUR SIGNIFICANT HITS					
❑ Specialty SP-2112 [M]		1960	30.00	60.00	120.00
—Gold and black label					
OUR SINGING HERITAGE, VOL. 1					
❑ Elektra EKL-151 [M]		1958	6.25	12.50	25.00
OUR SINGING HERITAGE, VOL. 2					
❑ Elektra EKL-152 [M]		1958	6.25	12.50	25.00
OUTSTANDING JAZZ COMPOSITIONS OF THE 20TH CENTURY					
❑ Columbia C2L 31 [(2)M]		1964	5.00	10.00	20.00
A PACKAGE OF 16 BIG HITS					
❑ Motown MS 614 [S]		1966	7.50	15.00	30.00
—No "package" on cover; contains alternate stereo versions of "Please Mr. Postman" by the Marvelettes and "Do You Love Me" by the Contours					
❑ Motown MT 614 [M]		1964	25.00	50.00	100.00
—"Package" cover					

Number	Title (A Side/B Side)	Yr	VG	VG+	NM
❑ Motown MT 614 [M]		1966	5.00	10.00	20.00
—No "package" on cover					
PAJAMA PARTY					
❑ Forum F-9006 [M]		196?	7.50	15.00	30.00
—Reissue of Roulette 25021					
❑ Forum SF-9006 [R]		196?	5.00	10.00	20.00
❑ Roulette R 25021 [M]		1958	10.00	20.00	40.00
—Originals have a black label					
❑ Roulette R 25021 [M]		1959	6.25	12.50	25.00
—Second pressings have a white label with colored spokes					
❑ Roulette SR 25021 [R]		196?	3.00	6.00	12.00
PANORAMA OF BRITISH JAZZ					
❑ Discovery DL-2001 [10]		1953	12.50	25.00	50.00
PARTY AFTER HOURS					
❑ Aladdin LP-703 [10]		1950	1000.	2000.	4000.
—Black vinyl					
❑ Aladdin LP-703 [10]		1950	2000.	4000.	8000.
—Red vinyl					
PEACHES: "PICK OF THE CROP"					
❑ Capricorn PRO 588 [(2)]		1974	6.25	12.50	25.00
THE PEOPLE'S RECORD					
❑ Warner Bros. PRO 645 [(2)]		1976	5.00	10.00	20.00
PERCUSSION UNABRIDGED					
❑ Kimberly 2022 [M]		1963	5.00	10.00	20.00
❑ Kimberly 11022 [S]		1963	6.25	12.50	25.00
PERFECT FOR DANCING: ALL TEMPOS					
❑ RCA Victor LPM-1072 [M]		1954	7.50	15.00	30.00
PERFECT FOR DANCING: FOX TROTS					
❑ RCA Victor LPM-1070		1954	7.50	15.00	30.00
PERFECT FOR DANCING: JITTERBUG OR LINDY					
❑ RCA Victor LPM-1071 [M]		1954	7.50	15.00	30.00
PERIOD'S JAZZ DIGEST					
❑ Period SPL-302 [M]		1956	12.50	25.00	50.00
PERIOD'S JAZZ DIGEST VOL. 2					
❑ Period SPL-304 [M]		1955	12.50	25.00	50.00
PETAL PUSHERS					
❑ Chess LP 1520 [M]		1967	6.25	12.50	25.00
❑ Chess LPS 1520 [S]		1967	6.25	12.50	25.00
THE PHIL SPECTOR SPECTACULAR					
❑ Philles PHLP 100 [DJ]		1972	375.00	750.00	1500.
—Not issued with cover					
PHIL SPECTOR'S CHRISTMAS ALBUM					
❑ Apple SW 3400 [M]		1972	7.50	15.00	30.00
—Reissue of A CHRISTMAS GIFT FOR YOU FROM PHILLES RECORDS; third edition of this group of songs; completely different cover with Phil Spector dressed as Santa Claus and wearing a "Back to Mono" button					
❑ Passport PB 3604 [S]		1984	3.00	6.00	12.00
—Sixth edition of this group of songs; Phil Spector-as-Santa Claus' "Back to Mono" button is airbrushed off the cover; the last version of this LP to appear in true stereo					
❑ Pavillion PZ 37686 [S]		1981	3.75	7.50	15.00
—Fifth edition of this group of songs; Phil Spector-as-Santa Claus' "Back to Mono" button is airbrushed off the cover; once again, this LP is true stereo					
❑ Warner/Spector SP 9103 [S]		1974	5.00	10.00	20.00
—Fourth edition of this group of songs; similar cover to third edition; despite the cover's "Authentic Mono" statement and Phil Spector-as-Santa Claus' "Back to Mono" button, this album is in true stereo!					
PHIL SPECTOR'S GREATEST HITS					
❑ Warner/Spector 2SP 9104 [(2)]		1977	10.00	20.00	40.00
PHIL SPECTOR: BACK TO MONO 1958-1969					
❑ Phil Spector/Abkco 7118-1 [(5)]		1991	20.00	40.00	80.00
—Box set; Sides 9 and 10 are the final vinyl reissue of A Christmas Gift for You from Phil Spector					
PIANISTS GALORE					
❑ Pacific Jazz JWC-506 [M]		1957	12.50	25.00	50.00
❑ World Pacific JWC-506 [M]		1958	10.00	20.00	40.00
PIANO ARTISTRY					
❑ Audiophile AP-28 [M]		1953	7.50	15.00	30.00
PIANO GIANTS					
❑ Prestige 24052 [(2)]		197?	3.75	7.50	15.00
PIANO IN STYLE					
❑ MCA 1332		198?	2.50	5.00	10.00
PIANO INTERPRETATIONS					
❑ Norgran MGN-1036 [M]		1955	20.00	40.00	80.00
❑ Verve MGV-8125 [M]		1957	7.50	15.00	30.00
❑ Verve V-8125 [M]		1961	5.00	10.00	20.00
PIANO JAZZ, VOLUME 1					
❑ Brunswick BL 54014 [M]		1955	7.50	15.00	30.00
PIANO JAZZ, VOLUME 2					
❑ Brunswick BL 54015 [M]		1955	7.50	15.00	30.00
PIANO MUSIC FOR PARTIES					
❑ Columbia CL 603 [M]		1955	6.25	12.50	25.00
PIANO MUSIC FOR TWO					
❑ Columbia CL 602 [M]		1955	6.25	12.50	25.00
PIANO ROLL TRANSCRIPTIONS					
❑ Riverside RLP 12-110 [M]		1956	10.00	20.00	40.00
❑ Riverside RLP 12-126 [M]		1957	10.00	20.00	40.00
PIANO STYLISTS					
❑ Capitol H 323 [10]		1952	12.50	25.00	50.00
PIANO VARIATIONS					
❑ King 540 [M]		1956	37.50	75.00	150.00
PICK HITS OF THE RADIO GOOD GUYS					
❑ Laurie LLP-2021 [M]		1963	7.50	15.00	30.00
❑ Laurie SLP-2021 [R]		196?	3.75	7.50	15.00

Number Title (A Side/B Side)	Yr	VG	VG+	NM
PICK HITS OF THE RADIO GOOD GUYS, VOLUME 2				
❏ Laurie LLP-2026 [M]	1964	6.25	12.50	25.00
❏ Laurie SLP-2026 [R]	196?	3.75	7.50	15.00
PICK OF THE COUNTRY				
❏ RCA Victor LPM-2094 [M]	1960	6.25	12.50	25.00
❏ RCA Victor LSP-2094 [S]	1960	7.50	15.00	30.00
PICK OF THE COUNTRY, VOL. 2				
❏ RCA Victor LPM-2956 [M]	1964	5.00	10.00	20.00
❏ RCA Victor LSP-2956 [S]	1964	6.25	12.50	25.00
PICK UP THE BEAT				
❏ Epic LN 3127 [M]	1955	7.50	15.00	30.00
PIONEERS OF BOOGIE WOOGIE				
❏ Riverside RLP-1009 [10]	1953	20.00	40.00	80.00
PIONEERS OF BOOGIE WOOGIE, VOL. 2				
❏ Riverside RLP-1034 [10]	1954	20.00	40.00	80.00
PITTSBURGH'S GREATEST HITS				
❏ Itzy 101 [(2)]	1966	12.50	25.00	50.00
PLAYBOY ALL STARS VOLUME 1				
❏ Playboy PB-1957 [(2)M]	1957	10.00	20.00	40.00
PLAYBOY ALL STARS VOLUME 2				
❏ Playboy PB-1958 [(2)M]	1958	10.00	20.00	40.00
PLAYBOY ALL STARS VOLUME 3				
❏ Playboy PB-1959 [(3)M]	1959	15.00	30.00	60.00
PLAYBOY MUSIC HALL OF FAME WINNERS				
❏ Playboy PB-7473 [(3)]	1978	50.00	100.00	200.00
—One of very few compilation LPs to contain both an Elvis and a Beatles track!				
POLKAS				
❏ Audio Lab AL-1543 [M]	1959	10.00	20.00	40.00
POP COUNTRY HITS				
❏ RCA Victor LPM-2949 [M]	1964	3.75	7.50	15.00
❏ RCA Victor LSP-2949 [S]	1964	5.00	10.00	20.00
POP HIT PARTY				
❏ Columbia CL 1237 [M]	195?	5.00	10.00	20.00
POP ORIGINS				
❏ Chess LP 1544 [M]	1969	6.25	12.50	25.00
POP PARADE				
❏ MGM E-194 [10]	1953	12.50	25.00	50.00
POP SHOPPER				
❏ RCA Victor SPL-12/13 [M]	1955	7.50	15.00	30.00
POPULAR FAVORITES				
❏ Columbia CL 6057 [10]	1949	10.00	20.00	40.00
THE POPULAR GOLD ALBUM				
❏ Capitol T 972 [M]	1958	7.50	15.00	30.00
PORGY AND BESS				
❏ Bethlehem EXLP-1 [(3)M]	1956	17.50	35.00	70.00
❏ Bethlehem BCP-6040 [M]	1959	7.50	15.00	30.00
A POT OF FLOWERS				
❏ Mainstream S-6100 [S]	1967	25.00	50.00	100.00
❏ Mainstream 56100 [M]	1967	20.00	40.00	80.00
POT OF GOLDEN GOODIES				
❏ Herald HLP-1015 [M]	1962	37.50	75.00	150.00
A POTPOURRI OF JAZZ				
❏ Verve MGV-2032 [M]	1956	10.00	20.00	40.00
❏ Verve V-2032 [M]	1961	5.00	10.00	20.00
THE POWER AND THE MAJESTY: RAIN 'N' TRAIN DEMONSTRATION DISC				
❏ Mobile Fidelity 1-004	1979	12.50	25.00	50.00
—Audiophile vinyl				
PRESTIGE GROOVY GOODIES, VOL. 1				
❏ Prestige PRLP-7298 [M]	1964	7.50	15.00	30.00
❏ Prestige PRST-7298 [R]	1964	5.00	10.00	20.00
PRIMITIVE PIANO				
❏ Tone 1 [M]	195?	7.50	15.00	30.00
PROGRESSIVE PIANO				
❏ RCA Victor LJM-3001 [10]	1952	12.50	25.00	50.00
PROPAGANDA				
❏ A&M SP-4786	1979	5.00	10.00	20.00
—Includes poster				
PUMPING VINYL				
❏ Warner Bros. PRO 773 [(2)]	1977	5.00	10.00	20.00
PURE MAGIC: THE SONGS OF PAM SAWYER & MARILYN MCLEOD				
❏ Jobete PRO-1A [DJ]	1978	10.00	20.00	40.00
—Promo-only publisher's demo with short excerpts of songs				
QSP PRESENTS A GIFT OF MUSIC				
❏ RCA Special Products QSP1-0034	1984	12.50	25.00	50.00
RADAR BLUES				
❏ King KLP-1050 [M]	1969	7.50	15.00	30.00
RADIO RADIO/SOUL TWIST/YOU'VE GOTTA BE CRUEL TO BE KIND				
❏ Columbia AS 443 [DJ]	1979	10.00	20.00	40.00
—Includes Elvis Costello, Mink DeVille, Nick Lowe; promo-only 3-song sampler on orange vinyl				
RADIO SMASH FLASHBACKS: DRIVE TIME				
❏ Laurie LLP-2028 [M]	1964	6.25	12.50	25.00
❏ Laurie SLP-2028 [R]	196?	3.75	7.50	15.00
RADIO SMASH FLASHBACKS: PRIME TIME				
❏ Laurie LLP-2029 [M]	1964	6.25	12.50	25.00
❏ Laurie SLP-2029 [R]	196?	3.75	7.50	15.00
RAGTIME PIANO ROLL, VOL. 1				
❏ Riverside RLP-1006 [10]	1953	25.00	50.00	100.00
RAGTIME PIANO ROLL, VOL. 2				
❏ Riverside RLP-1025 [10]	1954	20.00	40.00	80.00
RAGTIME PIANO ROLL, VOL. 3				
❏ Riverside RLP-1049 [10]	1954	20.00	40.00	80.00
RAGTIMERS' IMMORTAL PERFORMANCES				
❏ RCA Victor LPT-1000 [M]	1954	7.50	15.00	30.00
RAILROAD SONGS				
❏ King 869 [M]	1963	17.50	35.00	70.00
RAT MUSIC FOR RAT PEOPLE				
❏ Go 003	1982	5.00	10.00	20.00
THE RCA VICTOR ENCYCLOPEDIA OF RECORDED JAZZ, ALBUM 1				
❏ RCA Victor LEJ-1 [10]	1956	10.00	20.00	40.00
THE RCA VICTOR ENCYCLOPEDIA OF RECORDED JAZZ, ALBUM 10				
❏ RCA Victor LEJ-10 [10]	1956	10.00	20.00	40.00
THE RCA VICTOR ENCYCLOPEDIA OF RECORDED JAZZ, ALBUM 11				
❏ RCA Victor LEJ-11 [10]	1956	10.00	20.00	40.00
THE RCA VICTOR ENCYCLOPEDIA OF RECORDED JAZZ, ALBUM 12				
❏ RCA Victor LEJ-12 [10]	1956	10.00	20.00	40.00
THE RCA VICTOR ENCYCLOPEDIA OF RECORDED JAZZ, ALBUM 2				
❏ RCA Victor LEJ-2 [10]	1956	10.00	20.00	40.00
THE RCA VICTOR ENCYCLOPEDIA OF RECORDED JAZZ, ALBUM 3				
❏ RCA Victor LEJ-3 [10]	1956	10.00	20.00	40.00
THE RCA VICTOR ENCYCLOPEDIA OF RECORDED JAZZ, ALBUM 4				
❏ RCA Victor LEJ-4 [10]	1956	10.00	20.00	40.00
THE RCA VICTOR ENCYCLOPEDIA OF RECORDED JAZZ, ALBUM 5				
❏ RCA Victor LEJ-5 [10]	1956	10.00	20.00	40.00
THE RCA VICTOR ENCYCLOPEDIA OF RECORDED JAZZ, ALBUM 6				
❏ RCA Victor LEJ-6 [10]	1956	10.00	20.00	40.00
THE RCA VICTOR ENCYCLOPEDIA OF RECORDED JAZZ, ALBUM 7				
❏ RCA Victor LEJ-7 [10]	1956	10.00	20.00	40.00
THE RCA VICTOR ENCYCLOPEDIA OF RECORDED JAZZ, ALBUM 8				
❏ RCA Victor LEJ-8 [10]	1956	10.00	20.00	40.00
THE RCA VICTOR ENCYCLOPEDIA OF RECORDED JAZZ, ALBUM 9				
❏ RCA Victor LEJ-9 [10]	1956	10.00	20.00	40.00
REACH OUT AND TOUCH				
❏ Reader's Digest RBA-037A [(7)]	1991	12.50	25.00	50.00
THE REAL AMBASSADORS				
❏ Columbia OS 2250 [S]	1962	6.25	12.50	25.00
❏ Columbia CL 5850 [M]	1962	5.00	10.00	20.00
THE REAL BLUES				
❏ Excello LPS-8011 [R]	1969	5.00	10.00	20.00
REBIRTH OF BEALE STREET				
❏ Beale Street BS-1	1983	50.00	100.00	200.00
—Limited edition of 1,000 made for the city of Memphis				
RECORD HOP				
❏ Decca DL 8067 [M]	1955	7.50	15.00	30.00
RECORDED IN NEW ORLEANS, VOL. 1				
❏ Good Time Jazz L-12019 [M]	1955	5.00	10.00	20.00
RECORDED IN NEW ORLEANS, VOL. 2				
❏ Good Time Jazz L-12020 [M]	1955	5.00	10.00	20.00
RED BIRD GOLDIES				
❏ Red Bird LP 20-102 [M]	1965	20.00	40.00	80.00
RED HOT AND BLUE JAZZ				
❏ Waldorf Music Hall MH 33-141 [10]	195?	50.00	100.00	200.00
REGGAE CHRISTMAS BY THE JOE GIBBS FAMILY OF ARTISTS				
❏ Joe Gibbs Music 8077	1982	5.00	10.00	20.00
RELAXED SAXOPHONE MOODS				
❏ Prestige PRLP-141 [10]	1953	25.00	50.00	100.00
REMEMBER THE OLDIES				
❏ Argo LP-649 [M]	1963	10.00	20.00	40.00
❏ Argo LP-649 [M]	1963	100.00	200.00	400.00
—Multi-color splash vinyl; white label promo				
REQUESTED BY YOU				
❏ Columbia CL 607 [M]	1955	6.25	12.50	25.00
RHYTHM & BLUES				
❏ RCA Camden CAL-371 [M]	1958	6.25	12.50	25.00
RHYTHM AND BLUES				
❏ Savoy MG-15008 [10]	1952	20.00	40.00	80.00
RHYTHM PLUS ONE				
❏ Epic LN 3297 [M]	1956	7.50	15.00	30.00
THE RHYTHM SECTION				
❏ Epic LN 3271 [M]	1956	7.50	15.00	30.00
RHYTHM, BLUES AND BOOGIE-WOOGIE				
❏ Decca DL 4011 [M]	1960	7.50	15.00	30.00
RICHARD NADER/LET THE GOOD TIMES ROLL				
❏ Bell 9002 [(2)]	1973	5.00	10.00	20.00
RINGSIDE AT CONDON'S				
❏ Savoy MG-15029 [10]	1954	20.00	40.00	80.00
RINGSIDE AT CONDON'S VOL. 2				
❏ Savoy MG-15030 [10]	1954	20.00	40.00	80.00
RIVERBOAT JAZZ				
❏ Brunswick BL 58026 [10]	1951	12.50	25.00	50.00
RIVERSIDE DRIVE				
❏ Riverside RLP 12-267 [M]	1958	7.50	15.00	30.00
RIVERSIDE MODERN JAZZ SAMPLER				
❏ Riverside S-3 [M]	1956	10.00	20.00	40.00

Number	Title (A Side/B Side)	Yr	VG	VG+	NM

ROBERT W. SARNOFF — 25 YEARS OF RCA LEADERSHIP
- ❑ RCA Victor RWS-0001 [DJ] — 1973 — 1000. — 1500. — 2000.
—*Souvenir record handed out at Sarnoff's retirement party*

ROCK & ROLL FOREVER
- ❑ Atlantic 1239 [M] — 1956 — 37.50 — 75.00 — 150.00

ROCK & ROLL JAMBOREE
- ❑ End LP-302 [M] — 1959 — 30.00 — 60.00 — 120.00
—*Second cover and title with puppet and a guitar*

ROCK & ROLL WITH RHYTHM & BLUES
- ❑ Aladdin LP-710 [M] — 195? — 375.00 — 750.00 — 1500.

ROCK 'N' ROLL SOCK HOP
- ❑ Score SLP-4018 [M] — 1958 — 50.00 — 100.00 — 200.00

ROCK AND ROLL BANDSTAND
- ❑ Roulette R 25093 [M] — 1959 — 7.50 — 15.00 — 30.00
—*Originals have a white label with colored spokes*

ROCK AND ROLL DANCE PARTY
- ❑ King 536 [M] — 1956 — 75.00 — 150.00 — 300.00
- ❑ RPM LRP-3001 — 195? — 125.00 — 250.00 — 500.00

ROCK AND ROLL RECORD HOP
- ❑ Roulette R 25059 [M] — 1959 — 7.50 — 15.00 — 30.00
—*Originals have a white label with colored spokes*

ROCK AND ROLL REVUE, VOLUME 2
- ❑ King 654 [M] — 1959 — 37.50 — 75.00 — 150.00

ROCK AND ROLL VS. RHYTHM AND BLUES
- ❑ Dooto DTL-223 [M] — 1957 — 25.00 — 50.00 — 100.00

ROCK AND ROLL: THE EARLY DAYS
- ❑ RCA Victor AFM1-5463 — 1985 — 5.00 — 10.00 — 20.00

ROCK'S GREATEST HITS
- ❑ Columbia GP 11 [(2)] — 1969 — 5.00 — 10.00 — 20.00

ROCK-A-BALLADS
- ❑ Cadence CLP-3041 [M] — 1960 — 10.00 — 20.00 — 40.00

ROCK-A-HITS
- ❑ Cadence CLP-3042 [M] — 1960 — 10.00 — 20.00 — 40.00

ROCK-O-RAMA
- ❑ Abkco AB 4222 [(2)] — 1972 — 5.00 — 10.00 — 20.00

ROCK-O-RAMA, VOLUME 2
- ❑ Abkco AB 4223 [(2)] — 1972 — 5.00 — 10.00 — 20.00

ROCKIN' SLUMBER PARTY
- ❑ Famous LP-501 [M] — 1961 — 7.50 — 15.00 — 30.00

ROCKIN' TOGETHER
- ❑ Atco 33-103 [M] — 1958 — 25.00 — 50.00 — 100.00

A ROCKING CHRISTMAS STOCKING
- ❑ Capitol SPRO 9303/4/5/6 [(2)DJ] — 1984 — 5.00 — 10.00 — 20.00

RODGERS AND HART GEMS
- ❑ Pacific Jazz JWC-504 [M] — 1956 — 12.50 — 25.00 — 50.00
- ❑ World Pacific JWC-504 [M] — 1958 — 10.00 — 20.00 — 40.00

ROOST 5TH ANNIVERSARY ALBUM
- ❑ Roost RST-1201 [M] — 1955 — 12.50 — 25.00 — 50.00

ROOTS OF BRITISH ROCK
- ❑ Sire SASH-3711 [(2)] — 1975 — 5.00 — 10.00 — 20.00

ROULETTE PRESENTS A DEMONSTRATION OF THE NEW DIMENSIONAL SOUND OF DYNAMIC STEREO
- ❑ Roulette SR-100 [S] — 1958 — 7.50 — 15.00 — 30.00

RUMBLE
- ❑ Jubilee JGM-1114 [M] — 1959 — 37.50 — 75.00 — 150.00

SATURDAY NIGHT AT THE UPTOWN
- ❑ Atlantic 8101 [M] — 1964 — 6.25 — 12.50 — 25.00
- ❑ Atlantic SD 8101 [S] — 1964 — 7.50 — 15.00 — 30.00

SATURDAY NIGHT FUNCTION: RURAL BLUES, VOLUME 2
- ❑ Imperial LP-94001 — 1968 — 5.00 — 10.00 — 20.00

SATURDAY NIGHT GRAND OLE OPRY
- ❑ Decca DL 4303 [M] — 1962 — 6.25 — 12.50 — 25.00
- ❑ Decca DL 74303 [S] — 1962 — 7.50 — 15.00 — 30.00

SATURDAY NIGHT GRAND OLE OPRY, VOL. 2
- ❑ Decca DL 4539 [M] — 1964 — 5.00 — 10.00 — 20.00
- ❑ Decca DL 74539 [S] — 1964 — 6.25 — 12.50 — 25.00

SATURDAY NIGHT GRAND OLE OPRY, VOL. 3
- ❑ Decca DL 4671 [M] — 1965 — 5.00 — 10.00 — 20.00
- ❑ Decca DL 74671 [S] — 1965 — 6.25 — 12.50 — 25.00

SATURDAY NIGHT MOOD
- ❑ Columbia CL 599 [M] — 1954 — 6.25 — 12.50 — 25.00

THE SAX SECTION
- ❑ Epic LN 3278 [M] — 1956 — 10.00 — 20.00 — 40.00

SAX STYLISTS
- ❑ Capitol H 328 [10] — 1952 — 12.50 — 25.00 — 50.00

SAXOMANIAC
- ❑ Apollo LP-477 [M] — 1958 — 25.00 — 50.00 — 100.00

THE SAXOPHONE
- ❑ ABC Impulse! AS-9253 [(3)] — 197? — 5.00 — 10.00 — 20.00

SAXOPHONE REVOLT
- ❑ Riverside RLP 12-284 [M] — 1958 — 7.50 — 15.00 — 30.00

SCHLAGERS!
- ❑ Warner Bros. PRO 359 [(2)] — 1970 — 7.50 — 15.00 — 30.00
—*Originals have green labels*

A SCRAPBOOK OF BRITISH JAZZ, 1926-1956
- ❑ London LL 1444 [M] — 1956 — 5.00 — 10.00 — 20.00

SEASON'S GREETINGS FROM BARBRA STREISAND...AND FRIENDS
- ❑ Columbia Special Products CSS 1075 — 1969 — 5.00 — 10.00 — 20.00
—*Created exclusively for Maxwell House Coffee*

SEASONS GREETINGS (A CHRISTMAS FESTIVAL OF STARS)
- ❑ Columbia CL 1394 [M] — 1959 — 5.00 — 10.00 — 20.00
- ❑ Columbia CS 8189 [S] — 1959 — 6.25 — 12.50 — 25.00

SECOND SESSION AT SQUIRREL'S
- ❑ Paramount LP-108 [10] — 1954 — 15.00 — 30.00 — 60.00

SELECTIONS FROM APRIL 1956 ALBUMS FOR RADIO-TV PROGRAM USE
- ❑ Capitol PRO-252/3 [DJ] — 1956 — 10.00 — 20.00 — 40.00

SELECTIONS FROM FEBRUARY 1956 POPULAR ALBUMS FOR RADIO-TV PROGRAM USE
- ❑ Capitol PRO-240/1 [DJ] — 1956 — 10.00 — 20.00 — 40.00

SELECTIONS FROM JANUARY 1956 ALBUMS FOR RADIO-TV PROGRAM USE
- ❑ Capitol PRO-238/9 [DJ] — 1956 — 10.00 — 20.00 — 40.00

SELECTIONS FROM MARCH 1956 ALBUMS FOR RADIO-TV PROGRAM USE
- ❑ Capitol PRO-246/7 [DJ] — 1956 — 10.00 — 20.00 — 40.00

SESSION AT MIDNIGHT
- ❑ Capitol T 707 [M] — 1956 — 7.50 — 15.00 — 30.00

SESSION AT RIVERSIDE
- ❑ Capitol T 761 [M] — 1956 — 7.50 — 15.00 — 30.00

THE SEVEN AGES OF JAZZ
- ❑ Metrojazz 2-E-1009 [(2)M] — 1959 — 15.00 — 30.00 — 60.00
- ❑ Metrojazz 2-SE-1009 [(2)S] — 1959 — 12.50 — 25.00 — 50.00

SHUT DOWN
- ❑ Capitol ST 1918 [S] — 1963 — 12.50 — 25.00 — 50.00
- ❑ Capitol T 1918 [M] — 1963 — 10.00 — 20.00 — 40.00

SHUT DOWNS AND HILL CLIMBS
- ❑ Liberty LRP-3366 [M] — 1964 — 10.00 — 20.00 — 40.00
- ❑ Liberty LST-7366 [S] — 1964 — 12.50 — 25.00 — 50.00

THE SINATRA FAMILY WISH YOU A MERRY CHRISTMAS
- ❑ Reprise FS-1026 — 1969 — 12.50 — 25.00 — 50.00

SING A SONG OF SOUL
- ❑ Checker LP 2998 [M] — 1966 — 20.00 — 40.00 — 80.00
- ❑ Checker LPS 2998 [S] — 1966 — 25.00 — 50.00 — 100.00

THE SINGER-SONGWRITER PROJECT
- ❑ Elektra EKL-299 [M] — 1965 — 5.00 — 10.00 — 20.00
—*With 11 tracks, though the label and cover claim there are 13*
- ❑ Elektra EKL-299 [M] — 1965 — 6.25 — 12.50 — 25.00
—*With 13 tracks*
- ❑ Elektra EKS-7299 [S] — 1965 — 5.00 — 10.00 — 20.00
—*With 11 tracks, though the label and cover claim there are 13*
- ❑ Elektra EKS-7299 [S] — 1965 — 7.50 — 15.00 — 30.00
—*With 13 tracks*

SINGIN' AND SWINGIN'
- ❑ Savoy MG-12217 [M] — 196? — 5.00 — 10.00 — 20.00

THE SIREN
- ❑ Posh Boy PBS-103 — 1980 — 5.00 — 10.00 — 20.00

SITTIN' IN
- ❑ Verve MGV-8225 [M] — 1958 — 12.50 — 25.00 — 50.00
- ❑ Verve V-8225 [M] — 1961 — 6.25 — 12.50 — 25.00

A SLICE OF LEMON
- ❑ Columbia Special Products CSM-389 [M] — 1966 — 6.25 — 12.50 — 25.00
—*Manufactured for Dr. Pepper; contains a spoken-word introduction by Dick Clark, plus tracks by Bob Dylan, Simon & Garfunkel, the Dave Clark Five, the Brothers Four, Percy Faith, Dave Brubeck, the New Christy Minstrels, Tony Bennett and Doris Day*

SMALL COMBO HITS
- ❑ RCA Victor LPT-3 [10] — 1951 — 10.00 — 20.00 — 40.00

SMART, LUSCIOUS, BEAUTIFUL
- ❑ Bethlehem BCP-6034 [M] — 1960 — 7.50 — 15.00 — 30.00

THE SMITHSONIAN COLLECTION OF CLASSIC JAZZ
- ❑ Smithsonian/CSP P6 11891 [(6)] — 1973 — 12.50 — 25.00 — 50.00
- ❑ Smithsonian/CSP P7 19477 [(7)] — 1987 — 10.00 — 20.00 — 40.00
—*Revised version of 1973 original*

SMOKE RINGS
- ❑ RCA Victor LPT-13 [10] — 1951 — 10.00 — 20.00 — 40.00

SOFT PEDAL
- ❑ Columbia CL 2511 [10] — 1954 — 7.50 — 15.00 — 30.00

SOLID GOLD HITS
- ❑ Imperial LP-9230 [M] — 1963 — 6.25 — 12.50 — 25.00
- ❑ Imperial LP-12230 [R] — 1963 — 5.00 — 10.00 — 20.00

SOLID GOLD PROGRAMMING
- ❑ Screen Gems/Columbia CPL-711 [DJ] — 1975 — 5.00 — 10.00 — 20.00
—*Promo-only compilation of oldies sent to radio to spur airplay on songs owned by this publishing house*
- ❑ Screen Gems/Columbia CPL-715 [DJ] — 1975 — 5.00 — 10.00 — 20.00
—*Same concept as above album, but completely different contents, and mostly in stereo*

SOLID GOLD SONGS INSTRUMENTALLY
- ❑ Screen Gems/Columbia CPL-714 [DJ] — 1975 — 5.00 — 10.00 — 20.00
—*Promo-only compilation of oldies sent to radio to spur airplay on songs owned by this publishing house*

SOLID GOLD SOUL
- ❑ Atlantic 8116 [M] — 1966 — 3.75 — 7.50 — 15.00
- ❑ Atlantic SD 8116 [S] — 1966 — 5.00 — 10.00 — 20.00

SOLO FLIGHT
- ❑ Pacific Jazz JWC-505 [M] — 1956 — 12.50 — 25.00 — 50.00
- ❑ World Pacific JWC-505 [M] — 1958 — 10.00 — 20.00 — 40.00

SOLO SPOTLIGHTS
- ❑ King 745 [M] — 1961 — 25.00 — 50.00 — 100.00

SOME LIKE IT COOL
- ❑ United Artists SX-71 [S] — 1959 — 10.00 — 20.00 — 40.00
- ❑ United Artists X-71 [M] — 1959 — 10.00 — 20.00 — 40.00

Number	Title (A Side/B Side)	Yr	VG	VG+	NM
SOMETHING FOR BOTH EARS					
❑ World Pacific HFS-2 [S]		1958	10.00	20.00	40.00
—Stereo sampler					
SOMETHING NEW, SOMETHING BLUE					
❑ Columbia CL 1388 [M]		1959	5.00	10.00	20.00
SONGS BY RODGERS AND HART AND JOHNNY GREEN					
❑ Discovery DL-3014 [10]		1951	12.50	25.00	50.00
SONGS FOR A SUMMER NIGHT					
❑ Columbia PM 2 [(2)M]		1963	5.00	10.00	20.00
❑ Columbia PMS 2 [(2)S]		1963	6.25	12.50	25.00
THE SONGS OF ASHFORD AND SIMPSON					
❑ Jobete PRO-3 [DJ]		1974	10.00	20.00	40.00
—Promo-only publisher's demo with short excerpts of songs					
SONGS OF FAITH					
❑ Audio Lab AL-1504 [M]		1959	20.00	40.00	80.00
SONGS OF FAITH AND INSPIRATION					
❑ Time-Life STL-127 [(3)]		1989	6.25	12.50	25.00
SONGS OF FAITH VOLUME 2					
❑ Audio Lab AL-1523 [M]		1959	20.00	40.00	80.00
THE SONGS OF HOLLAND-DOZIER-HOLLAND					
❑ Jobete PRO-4 [DJ]		1974	10.00	20.00	40.00
—Promo-only publisher's demo with short excerpts of songs					
THE SONGS OF JOHNNY BRISTOL-FRANK WILSON-MICKEY STEVENSON AND FREDDIE PERREN					
❑ Jobete PRO-8 [DJ]		1976	10.00	20.00	40.00
—Promo-only publisher's demo with short excerpts of songs					
THE SONGS OF MARVIN GAYE					
❑ Jobete PRO-6 [DJ]		1974	10.00	20.00	40.00
—Promo-only publisher's demo with short excerpts of songs					
THE SONGS OF NORMAN WHITFIELD					
❑ Jobete PRO-7 [DJ]		1976	10.00	20.00	40.00
—Promo-only publisher's demo with short excerpts of songs					
SONGS OF RIVERS, OCEANS AND SEAS					
❑ King 871 [M]		1963	17.50	35.00	70.00
THE SONGS OF SMOKEY ROBINSON					
❑ Jobete PRO-2 [DJ]		1972	10.00	20.00	40.00
—Promo-only publisher's demo with short excerpts of songs; there are two versions of this LP, both with the same number; each is of equal value					
THE SONGS OF STEVIE WONDER					
❑ Jobete PRO-5 [DJ]		1974	10.00	20.00	40.00
—Promo-only publisher's demo with short excerpts of songs					
SONGS OF THE HILLS					
❑ Audio Lab AL-1515 [M]		1959	20.00	40.00	80.00
SOUL CHRISTMAS					
❑ Atco SD 33-269		1968	7.50	15.00	30.00
SOUL EXPLOSION					
❑ Stax STS 2-2007 [(2)]		1969	5.00	10.00	20.00
SOUL JAZZ, VOL. 1					
❑ Bluesville BVLP-1009 [M]		1960	12.50	25.00	50.00
—Blue label, silver print					
❑ Bluesville BVLP-1009 [M]		1965	6.25	12.50	25.00
—Blue label, trident logo at right					
SOUL JAZZ, VOL. 2					
❑ Bluesville BVLP-1010 [M]		1960	12.50	25.00	50.00
—Blue label, silver print					
❑ Bluesville BVLP-1010 [M]		1965	6.25	12.50	25.00
—Blue label, trident logo at right					
SOUL MEETING SATURDAY NIGHT HOOTENANNY STYLE					
❑ Vee Jay LP-1074 [M]		1963	7.50	15.00	30.00
—Not known to exist in stereo					
THE SOUL OF JAZZ					
❑ Riverside S-5 [M]		1957	10.00	20.00	40.00
❑ World Wide MGS-20002 [S]		1958	20.00	40.00	80.00
THE SOUL OF JAZZ PERCUSSION					
❑ Warwick W 5003 [M]		1961	7.50	15.00	30.00
❑ Warwick W 5003ST [S]		1961	10.00	20.00	40.00
THE SOUL OF JAZZ PIANO					
❑ Riverside 9S-7 [S]		196?	7.50	15.00	30.00
SOULED OUT					
❑ Chess LPS 1546 [S]		1969	12.50	25.00	50.00
THE SOUND OF BIG BAND JAZZ IN HI-FI					
❑ World Pacific WP-1257 [M]		1960	10.00	20.00	40.00
THE SOUND OF BIG BAND JAZZ IN STEREO					
❑ World Pacific ST-1015 [S]		1960	7.50	15.00	30.00
THE SOUND OF GENIUS					
❑ Columbia Masterworks SGM 1 [(2)M]		1963	5.00	10.00	20.00
❑ Columbia Masterworks SGS 1 [(2)S]		1963	6.25	12.50	25.00
THE SOUND OF JAZZ					
❑ Columbia CL 1098 [M]		1957	5.00	10.00	20.00
SOUNDS OF SUCCESS					
❑ Jamie JLP-3017 [M]		1961	6.25	12.50	25.00
❑ Jamie JLPS-3017 [S]		1961	7.50	15.00	30.00
SOUTHERN MEETIN'					
❑ Kimberly 2017 [M]		1963	5.00	10.00	20.00
❑ Kimberly 11017 [S]		1963	6.25	12.50	25.00
SOUVENIR/PROGRAMMING RECORD — DEALERS/DISC JOCKEYS — OCT.- NOV. 1955					
❑ Capitol PRO-232 [DJ]		1955	10.00	20.00	40.00
THE SPANISH SIDE OF JAZZ					
❑ Roulette SR-42001		1968	5.00	10.00	20.00
SPECIAL CHRISTMAS LP FOR DISC JOCKEYS					
❑ Capitol PRO-201 [DJ]		1954	12.50	25.00	50.00
SPECIAL COLLECTOR'S EDITION ALBUM FROM ROCKIN' RECORDS					
❑ Sun 1032		1986	7.50	15.00	30.00
—Limited edition of 600 copies					
SPIN TIME WITH LIBERTY					
❑ Liberty MM-417 [DJ]		1962	12.50	25.00	50.00
—Promo-only release					
SPIRITUALS					
❑ King 951 [M]		1966	12.50	25.00	50.00
—Reissue of "Spirituals, Volume 5," King 576					
SPIRITUALS, VOLUME 5					
❑ King 576 [M]		1957	37.50	75.00	150.00
STABLE MATES					
❑ Savoy MG-12115 [M]		1957	12.50	25.00	50.00
STARS					
❑ Sun 148		1982	5.00	10.00	20.00
—Includes two early Alabama tracks					
STARS FOR A SUMMER NIGHT					
❑ Columbia PM 1 [(2)M]		1961	6.25	12.50	25.00
❑ Columbia PMS 1 [(2)S]		1961	7.50	15.00	30.00
THE STARS OF CHRISTMAS					
❑ RCA Special Products DPL1-0842		1988	5.00	10.00	20.00
—Sold only through Avon dealers					
THE STARS OF HEE HAW					
❑ Capitol ST-437		1970	5.00	10.00	20.00
STARS OF JAZZ '61					
❑ Jazzland JLP-1001 [M]		1961	6.25	12.50	25.00
STARS OF THE GRAND OLE OPRY 1926-1974					
❑ RCA Victor CPL2-0466 [(2)]		1974	5.00	10.00	20.00
START SWIMMING					
❑ Stiff SINK 1		1981	5.00	10.00	20.00
THE STAX/VOLT REVUE — LIVE IN LONDON					
❑ Stax 721 [M]		1967	5.00	10.00	20.00
❑ Stax S721 [S]		1967	6.25	12.50	25.00
THE STAX/VOLT REVUE — LIVE IN LONDON, VOLUME 2					
❑ Stax 722 [M]		1967	5.00	10.00	20.00
❑ Stax S722 [S]		1967	6.25	12.50	25.00
STAX…ONCE YOU'VE BEEN THERE, YOU KNOW YOU'RE HOME					
❑ Stax STS 1 [(2)DJ]		1971	10.00	20.00	40.00
—Promo only in blank white gatefold cover					
STAY IN SCHOOL — DON'T BE A DROP OUT					
❑ Stax A-11 [DJ]		1967	125.00	250.00	500.00
STEREOSONIC JUBILEE SAMPLER, VOLUME 1					
❑ Jubilee SSJLP-801 [S]		1959	10.00	20.00	40.00
STERLING BALL 1971					
❑ Motown M 739 [DJ]		1971	62.50	125.00	250.00
—Loucye Gordy Wakefield Scholarship Fund benefit giveaway					
STILL MORE GOLD HITS, VOLUME 3					
❑ Warwick W 2048 [M]		1962	20.00	40.00	80.00
STRETCHING OUT					
❑ United Artists UAL-4023 [M]		1959	30.00	60.00	120.00
❑ United Artists UAS-5023 [S]		1959	25.00	50.00	100.00
STRICTLY FROM DIXIE					
❑ MGM E-3262 [M]		1956	7.50	15.00	30.00
THE STRING BAND PROJECT					
❑ Elektra EKL-292 [M]		1965	5.00	10.00	20.00
❑ Elektra EKS-7292 [S]		1965	6.25	12.50	25.00
A STRING OF SWINGIN' PEARLS					
❑ RCA Victor LPM-1373 [M]		1956	7.50	15.00	30.00
SUB POP 100					
❑ Sub Pop 10		1986	12.50	25.00	50.00
SUB POP 200					
❑ Sub Pop 25 [(3)EP]		1988	12.50	25.00	50.00
SUMMER FESTIVAL					
❑ RCA Victor Red Seal LM-6097 [(2)M]		1962	5.00	10.00	20.00
❑ RCA Victor Red Seal LSC-6097 [(2)S]		1962	6.25	12.50	25.00
SUMMER SOUVENIRS					
❑ Bell 6035		1969	5.00	10.00	20.00
SUMMIT MEETING					
❑ Vee Jay LP-3026 [M]		1961	5.00	10.00	20.00
❑ Vee Jay SR-3026 [S]		1961	6.25	12.50	25.00
THE SUN STORY					
❑ Rhino RNDA-71103 [(2)]		1986	5.00	10.00	20.00
SUN'S GOLD HITS					
❑ Sun LP-1250 [M]		1961	50.00	100.00	200.00
SUNDAY MORNING					
❑ Vee Jay LP-5016 [M]		1961	7.50	15.00	30.00
SUPER GOLDEN HITS					
❑ Jubilee JGS-8019		1968	25.00	50.00	100.00
—Despite the stereo prefix, this LP is mono					
SUPER GOLDEN HITS, VOLUME 2					
❑ Jubilee JGS-8023		1969	25.00	50.00	100.00
—Reissue of "Clay Cole's Bin of Original Golden Oldies," Jubilee 5026; again, despite the stereo prefix, this LP is mono					
SUPER GROUPS					
❑ Warner Bros. PRO 630 [(2)]		1976	5.00	10.00	20.00
THE SUPER GROUPS					
❑ Atco SD 33-279		1969	5.00	10.00	20.00

Number	Title (A Side/B Side)	Yr	VG	VG+	NM
THE SUPER GROUPS FROM HOLLAND					
❏ White Whale WWS-7129		1970	6.25	12.50	25.00
THE SUPER HITS					
❏ Atlantic Group 501 [M]		1967	5.00	10.00	20.00
❏ Atlantic Group SD 501 [S]		1967	5.00	10.00	20.00
THE SUPER HITS, VOL. 2					
❏ Atlantic SD 8188		1968	5.00	10.00	20.00
THE SUPER HITS, VOL. 3					
❏ Atlantic SD 8203		1968	5.00	10.00	20.00
THE SUPER HITS, VOL. 4					
❏ Atlantic SD 8224		1969	5.00	10.00	20.00
THE SUPER HITS, VOL. 5					
❏ Atlantic SD 8274		1970	5.00	10.00	20.00
SUPER OLDIES/VOL. 1					
❏ Capitol ST 2562 [S]		1966	6.25	12.50	25.00
❏ Capitol T 2562 [M]		1966	5.00	10.00	20.00
SUPER OLDIES/VOL. 2					
❏ Capitol ST 2565 [S]		1966	6.25	12.50	25.00
❏ Capitol T 2565 [M]		1966	5.00	10.00	20.00
SUPER OLDIES/VOL. 3					
❏ Capitol STBB 2910 [(2)]		1968	5.00	10.00	20.00
SUPER OLDIES/VOL. 4					
❏ Capitol STBB-149 [(2)]		1969	5.00	10.00	20.00
SUPER OLDIES/VOL. 5					
❏ Capitol STBB-216 [(2)]		1969	5.00	10.00	20.00
THE SUPER SOUL-DEES					
❏ Capitol ST 2798 [S]		1967	5.00	10.00	20.00
❏ Capitol T 2798 [M]		1967	5.00	10.00	20.00
THE SUPER SOUL-DEES, VOL. 2					
❏ Capitol STBB-2911 [(2)]		1968	5.00	10.00	20.00
THE SUPER SOUL-DEES, VOL. 3					
❏ Capitol STBB-178 [(2)]		1969	5.00	10.00	20.00
SUPERSTARS OF THE '70S					
❏ Warner Special Products SP-4000 [(4)]		1973	10.00	20.00	40.00
—Box set with booklet of liner notes					
SURF'S UP AT BANZAI PIPELINE					
❏ Northridge NM-101 [M]		1963	50.00	100.00	200.00
—Original pressing of LP reissued on Reprise					
❏ Reprise R 6094 [M]		1963	25.00	50.00	100.00
❏ Reprise RS 6094 [S]		1963	37.50	75.00	150.00
SURF'S UP! AT BANZAI PIPELINE					
❏ Northridge NM-101 [M]		1963	37.50	75.00	150.00
SURFIN' ON WAVE NINE					
❏ King 855 [M]		1963	20.00	40.00	80.00
SWAMP BLUES VOLUME 1					
❏ Excello LPS-8015 [R]		1970	5.00	10.00	20.00
SWAMP BLUES VOLUME 2					
❏ Excello LPS-8016 [R]		1970	5.00	10.00	20.00
SWEDES FROM JAZZVILLE					
❏ Epic LN 3309 [M]		1957	12.50	25.00	50.00
SWEDISH PASTRY					
❏ Discovery DL-2008 [10]		1954	12.50	25.00	50.00
SWEET 'N GREASY: RHYTHM 'N' BLUES, VOLUME 2					
❏ Imperial LP-94005		1968	5.00	10.00	20.00
SWEET ADELINES MEDALIST QUARTETS OF 1958					
❏ Cadence CLP-3018 [M]		1959	10.00	20.00	40.00
SWEET ADELINES MEDALISTS OF 1957					
❏ Cadence CLP-3009 [M]		1958	10.00	20.00	40.00
SWEET DREAMS OF COUNTRY					
❏ Reader's Digest RBA-049A [(7)]		1990	12.50	25.00	50.00
SWING AGAIN!					
❏ Capitol T 1386 [M]		1960	5.00	10.00	20.00
SWING BILLIES					
❏ Audio Lab AL-1546 [M]		1960	30.00	60.00	120.00
SWING BILLIES VOLUME 2					
❏ Audio Lab AL-1566 [M]		1960	30.00	60.00	120.00
THE SWING ERA, VOL. 1					
❏ "X" LVA-3030 [10]		1955	20.00	40.00	80.00
SWING GOES DIXIE					
❏ American Recording Society G-420 [M]		1957	7.50	15.00	30.00
SWING GUITARS					
❏ Norgran MGN-1033 [M]		1955	20.00	40.00	80.00
❏ Verve MGV-8124 [M]		1957	7.50	15.00	30.00
❏ Verve V-8124 [M]		1961	5.00	10.00	20.00
SWING HI, SWING LO					
❏ Blue Note BLP-5027 [10]		1953	50.00	100.00	200.00
❏ Blue Note B-6507 [M]		1969	3.75	7.50	15.00
SWING LIGHTLY					
❏ Jazztone J-1265 [M]		1957	7.50	15.00	30.00
SWING POTPOURRI					
❏ Audiophile AP-23 [M]		1953	7.50	15.00	30.00
SWING… NOT SPRING!					
❏ Savoy MG-12062 [M]		1956	12.50	25.00	50.00
A SWINGIN' GIG					
❏ Tampa TP-2 [M]		1957	25.00	50.00	100.00
—Colored vinyl					
❏ Tampa TP-2 [M]		1958	10.00	20.00	40.00
—Black vinyl					

Number	Title (A Side/B Side)	Yr	VG	VG+	NM
SWINGIN' LIKE SIXTY, VOL. 1					
❏ World Pacific ST-1289 [S]		1960	7.50	15.00	30.00
SWINGIN' LIKE SIXTY, VOL. 2					
❏ World Pacific ST-1290 [S]		1960	7.50	15.00	30.00
SWINGIN' LIKE SIXTY, VOL. 3					
❏ World Pacific ST-1291 [S]		1960	7.50	15.00	30.00
SWINGIN' SOUNDS					
❏ Columbia Special Products XTV 82030 [M]		1962	6.25	12.50	25.00
—Issued for the W.A. Sheaffer Pen Co.					
SWINGING BROADWAY					
❏ Kimberly 2024 [M]		1963	5.00	10.00	20.00
❏ Kimberly 11024 [S]		1963	6.25	12.50	25.00
SWINGING FOR THE KING					
❏ Mercury MG-20133 [M]		1956	12.50	25.00	50.00
SWINGING SOUNDTRACK					
❏ Kimberly 2016 [M]		1963	5.00	10.00	20.00
❏ Kimberly 11016 [S]		1963	6.25	12.50	25.00
THE SWINGVILLE ALL-STARS					
❏ Swingville SVLP-2010 [M]		1960	10.00	20.00	40.00
—Purple label					
❏ Swingville SVLP-2010 [M]		1965	5.00	10.00	20.00
—Blue label, trident logo at right					
SWITCHED ON BLUES					
❏ Soul SS-720		1969	37.50	75.00	150.00
TAKE THE LIBERTY					
❏ Liberty MM-427 [DJ]		1966	10.00	20.00	40.00
TAME YOURSELF					
❏ Rhino 90082		1991	6.25	12.50	25.00
TAMLA SPECIAL #1					
❏ Tamla TM 224 [M]		1962	37.50	75.00	150.00
—White label					
❏ Tamla TM 224 [M]		1963	17.50	35.00	70.00
—Yellow label					
TASTE TEST #1 — LIVE FROM BRAIN COOKIES					
❏ New Alliance 045 [(2)]		1990	6.25	12.50	25.00
TEEN DELIGHTS					
❏ Vee Jay LP-1021 [M]		1960	7.50	15.00	30.00
TEEN DELIGHTS, VOLUME 2					
❏ Vee Jay LP-1036 [M]		1961	7.50	15.00	30.00
TEENAGE PARTY					
❏ Gee GLP-702 [M]		1958	50.00	100.00	200.00
—Red label					
❏ Gee GLP-702 [M]		196?	15.00	30.00	60.00
—Gray label					
TEENSVILLE					
❏ Liberty L-5503 [M]		1962	10.00	20.00	40.00
TEN TUNES OF CHRISTMAS					
❏ Candee 50-50		195?	5.00	10.00	20.00
—Sold through "The 50-50 Club," a Cincinnati radio and TV show; all the artists have Cincinnati ties					
TENNESSEE					
❏ Design DLP-611 [M]		1962	5.00	10.00	20.00
TENOR CONCLAVE					
❏ Prestige PRLP-7074 [M]		1957	25.00	50.00	100.00
—Reissued as Prestige 7249; see JOHN COLTRANE.					
TENOR JAZZ					
❏ Mercury MG-20016 [10]		1950	25.00	50.00	100.00
—Issued in a paper sleeve					
TENOR SAX					
❏ Concord 3012 [M]		195?	10.00	20.00	40.00
TENOR SAX SOLOS, VOL. 1					
❏ Savoy MG-9008 [10]		1952	37.50	75.00	150.00
TENOR SAX SOLOS, VOL. 2					
❏ Savoy MG-9013 [10]		1952	37.50	75.00	150.00
TENOR SAX SOLOS, VOL. 3					
❏ Savoy MG-9021 [10]		1953	37.50	75.00	150.00
TENOR SAXES					
❏ Norgran MGN-1034 [M]		1955	20.00	40.00	80.00
❏ Verve MGV-8127 [M]		1957	7.50	15.00	30.00
❏ Verve V-8127 [M]		1961	5.00	10.00	20.00
TENORS ANYONE?					
❏ Dawn DLP-1126 [M]		1958	20.00	40.00	80.00
THEME SONGS					
❏ Columbia CL 6016 [10]		1949	10.00	20.00	40.00
❏ RCA Victor LPT-1 [10]		1951	10.00	20.00	40.00
THEMES LIKE OLD TIMES					
❏ Viva 36018 [(2)]		1969	5.00	10.00	20.00
THESAURUS OF CLASSIC JAZZ					
❏ Columbia C4L 18 [(4)]		1961	12.50	25.00	50.00
A THIRD SESSION AT SQUIRREL'S					
❏ Paramount LP-110 [10]		1954	15.00	30.00	60.00
THIS COULD LEAD TO LOVE					
❏ Riverside RLP 12-808 [M]		195?	12.50	25.00	50.00
THIS IS HOW IT ALL BEGAN: THE SPECIALTY STORY, VOLUME 1					
❏ Specialty SPS-2117		1970	5.00	10.00	20.00
THIS IS HOW IT ALL BEGAN: THE SPECIALTY STORY, VOLUME 2					
❏ Specialty SPS-2118		1970	5.00	10.00	20.00
THIS IS SOUL					
❏ Atlantic 8170 [M]		1968	10.00	20.00	40.00
❏ Atlantic SD 8170 [S]		1968	5.00	10.00	20.00

Number	Title (A Side/B Side)	Yr	VG	VG+	NM
THIS IS STEREO					
❏ Liberty LST-101 [S]		1960	10.00	20.00	40.00
—Black vinyl					
❏ Liberty LST-101 [S]		1960	30.00	60.00	120.00
—Red vinyl					
THIS IS THE BLUES					
❏ Kimberly 2020 [M]		1963	5.00	10.00	20.00
❏ Kimberly 11020 [S]		1963	6.25	12.50	25.00
THIS IS THE BLUES, VOL. 1					
❏ Pacific Jazz PJ-13 [M]		1961	7.50	15.00	30.00
THIS IS THE BLUES, VOL. 2					
❏ Pacific Jazz PJ-30 [M]		1962	6.25	12.50	25.00
❏ Pacific Jazz ST-30 [M]		1962	7.50	15.00	30.00
THREADS OF GLORY — 200 YEARS OF AMERICA IN WORDS & MUSIC					
❏ London Phase 4 6SP 14000 [(6)]		1975	7.50	15.00	30.00
THREE DECADES OF MUSIC, 1939-49, VOL. 1					
❏ Blue Note BST-89902 [(2)]		1969	6.25	12.50	25.00
THREE DECADES OF MUSIC, 1949-59, VOL. 1					
❏ Blue Note BST-89903 [(2)]		1969	6.25	12.50	25.00
THREE DECADES OF MUSIC, 1959-69, VOL. 1					
❏ Blue Note BST-89904 [(2)]		1969	6.25	12.50	25.00
THREE ROADS TO JAZZ					
❏ American Recording Society LP-100 [M]		1956	7.50	15.00	30.00
A TIME FOR PRAYER					
❏ Audio Lab AL-1518 [M]		1959	20.00	40.00	80.00
THE TIME-LIFE TREASURY OF CHRISTMAS					
❏ Time-Life STL-107 [(3)]		1986	5.00	10.00	20.00
—Available from Time-Life by mail order only; boxed set					
THE TIME-LIFE TREASURY OF CHRISTMAS, VOLUME TWO					
❏ Time-Life STL-108 [(3)]		1987	5.00	10.00	20.00
—Available from Time-Life by mail-order only; all known copies are boxed sets					
TODAY'S HITS					
❏ Philles PHLP 4004 [M]		1963	100.00	200.00	400.00
—First pressings have blue and black labels					
❏ Philles PHLP 4004 [M]		1964	50.00	100.00	200.00
—Second pressings have yellow and red labels					
TOGETHER					
❏ Warner Bros. PRO 486		1972	5.00	10.00	20.00
—Originals have green labels					
TOGETHER AT CHRISTMAS (READER'S DIGEST FAMILY ALBUM OF CHRISTMAS MUSIC)					
❏ Reader's Digest RDA 151-A [(5)]		1974	5.00	10.00	20.00
—Available only through Reader's Digest magazine by mail order					
TOMORROW'S HITS					
❏ Vee Jay LP-1042 [M]		1962	7.50	15.00	30.00
THE TOP 10 STORY IN SOUND					
❏ Jobete PRO-1 [(2)DJ]		1972	10.00	20.00	40.00
—Promo-only publisher's demo with short excerpts of songs					
TOP HITS OF '54 VOLUME II					
❏ Capitol H 9119 [10]		1954	12.50	25.00	50.00
TOP R&B ARTISTS SING COUNTRY SONGS					
❏ King 884 [M]		1964	20.00	40.00	80.00
TOWN HALL CONCERT					
❏ Mainstream S-6004 [R]		1965	3.00	6.00	12.00
❏ Mainstream 56004 [M]		1965	6.25	12.50	25.00
TRADITIONAL CHRISTMAS SONGS					
❏ Audio Lab AL-1517 [M]		1959	20.00	40.00	80.00
TRADITIONAL JAZZ					
❏ London LL 1242 [M]		1955	5.00	10.00	20.00
TRADITIONAL JAZZ AT THE ROYAL FESTIVAL HALL					
❏ London LL 1184 [M]		1955	5.00	10.00	20.00
TREASURE ALBUM					
❏ Hickory LPS-154		1970	10.00	20.00	40.00
TREASURE CHEST GOODIES					
❏ Stax 703 [M]		1963	10.00	20.00	40.00
—National version of "Hits from the South Presented by Nick Charles" with rearranged contents					
TREASURE CHEST OF HITS					
❏ Swan LP-501 [M]		1960	20.00	40.00	80.00
A TREASURE CHEST OF SONG HITS					
❏ Columbia CL 613 [M]		1955	6.25	12.50	25.00
TREASURE TUNES FROM THE VAULT (AS ADVERTISED ON WLS)					
❏ Chess LP 1474 [M]		1962	10.00	20.00	40.00
A TREASURY OF CHRISTMAS					
❏ Columbia Record Club P4S 5022 [(4)]		1965	7.50	15.00	30.00
A TREASURY OF GOLDEN CHRISTMAS SONGS					
❏ Vee Jay LP-5045 [M]		1963	7.50	15.00	30.00
TRIBUTE TO CHARLIE PARKER FROM THE NEWPORT JAZZ FESTIVAL					
❏ RCA Victor LPM-3738 [M]		1967	7.50	15.00	30.00
❏ RCA Victor LSP-3738 [S]		1967	5.00	10.00	20.00
TROMBONE BAND STAND					
❏ Bethlehem BCP-6036 [M]		1960	7.50	15.00	30.00
TROMBONE SCENE					
❏ Vik LX-1087 [M]		1957	7.50	15.00	30.00
TROMBONES					
❏ Savoy MG-12086 [M]		1956	15.00	30.00	60.00
THE TROMBONES, INC.					
❏ Warner Bros. W 1272 [M]		1959	6.25	12.50	25.00
❏ Warner Bros. WS 1272 [S]		1959	7.50	15.00	30.00
TROUBLEMAKERS					
❏ Warner Bros. PRO-A-857 [(2)DJ]		1978	5.00	10.00	20.00
TRUCK DRIVER SONGS					
❏ King 866 [M]		1963	17.50	35.00	70.00
TRUMPET INTERLUDE					
❏ EmArcy MG-36017 [M]		1955	12.50	25.00	50.00
TRUMPET STYLISTS					
❏ Capitol H 326 [10]		1952	12.50	25.00	50.00
TRUMPETER'S HOLIDAY					
❏ Epic LN 3252 [M]		1956	7.50	15.00	30.00
TRUMPETS ALL OUT					
❏ Savoy MG-12096 [M]		1957	15.00	30.00	60.00
TUNES TO BE REMEMBERED					
❏ Excello LP-8001 [M]		1960	37.50	75.00	150.00
—Original cover is green with black records that list the title and artist of each selection					
TURN BACK THE CLOCK					
❏ King 859 [M]		1963	17.50	35.00	70.00
TWISTIN' ALL NIGHT LONG					
❏ Swan LP-506 [M]		1962	30.00	60.00	120.00
TWO ROOMS: CELEBRATING THE SONGS OF ELTON JOHN & BERNIE TAUPIN					
❏ Polydor P1-47570 [(2)M]		1990	6.25	12.50	25.00
—U.S. vinyl available only through Columbia House					
THE UNAVAILABLE 16					
❏ Vee Jay LP-1051 [M]		1962	10.00	20.00	40.00
UNDER ONE ROOF					
❏ EmArcy MG-36088 [M]		1956	10.00	20.00	40.00
UNEXPURGATED JAZZ					
❏ Audiophile AP-43 [M]		1953	7.50	15.00	30.00
THE UNFORGETTABLE FIFTIES					
❏ Heartland 1072 [(4)]		1988	5.00	10.00	20.00
THE UP ANOTHER OCTAVE TRANSMISSION					
❏ Up Another Octave (no #)		1981	6.25	12.50	25.00
—Includes early Berlin					
UP SWING					
❏ RCA Victor LPT-12 [10]		1951	10.00	20.00	40.00
UPRIGHT AND LOWDOWN					
❏ Columbia CL 685 [M]		1955	5.00	10.00	20.00
A VARIETY OF COUNTRY SACRED SONGS					
❏ Audio Lab AL-1557 [M]		1960	15.00	30.00	60.00
THE VERVE COMPENDIUM OF JAZZ, NO. 1					
❏ Verve MGV-8194 [M]		1957	7.50	15.00	30.00
❏ Verve V-8194 [M]		1961	5.00	10.00	20.00
THE VERVE COMPENDIUM OF JAZZ, NO. 2					
❏ Verve MGV-8195 [M]		1957	7.50	15.00	30.00
❏ Verve V-8195 [M]		1961	5.00	10.00	20.00
A VERY MERRY CHRISTMAS					
❏ Columbia Special Products CSS 563		1967	5.00	10.00	20.00
—Sold only at Grants stores					
VERY SAXY					
❏ Fantasy OJC-458		1990	3.00	6.00	12.00
❏ Prestige PRLP-7167 [M]		1959	15.00	30.00	60.00
❏ Prestige PRST-7790		1971	5.00	10.00	20.00
—Reissue of 7167					
VICEROY CIGARETTES CAMPUS JAZZ FESTIVAL					
❏ RCA Custom KO7P-1544 [M]		1959	7.50	15.00	30.00
—Available thorugh Viceroy cigarettes					
VOICES OF HAITI					
❏ Elektra EKL-5 [10]		1953	10.00	20.00	40.00
VOLUNTEER JAM III AND IV					
❏ Epic E2 35368 [(2)]		1978	5.00	10.00	20.00
VOODOO DRUMS IN HI-FI					
❏ Atlantic 1296 [M]		1958	10.00	20.00	40.00
—Black label					
❏ Atlantic 1296 [M]		1961	6.25	12.50	25.00
—Multicolor label, white "fan" logo at right					
❏ Atlantic 1296 [M]		1963	5.00	10.00	20.00
—Multicolor label, black "fan" logo at right					
WALKIN' BY MYSELF					
❏ Chess LP 1446 [M]		1960	20.00	40.00	80.00
WAMO'S GOLDEN GASSERS					
❏ Chess LP 1458 PGH [M]		1961	37.50	75.00	150.00
—Pittsburgh version of "Golden Gassers," Chess 1458					
THE WARNER/REPRISE RADIO SHOW					
❏ Warner Bros. PRO 463		1971	6.25	12.50	25.00
—Originals have green labels					
WASHBOARD RHYTHM KINGS, VOL. 1					
❏ "X" LVA-3021 [10]		1954	20.00	40.00	80.00
WAVES					
❏ Bomp! 4003		1979	6.25	12.50	25.00
—Includes The Romantics; originals on blue vinyl					
WE CUT THIS ALBUM FOR BREAD					
❏ Bethlehem BCP-86 [M]		1958	7.50	15.00	30.00
WE LIKE BOYS/GREAT BOY OLDIES					
❏ Oldies 33 OL-8004 [M]		1964	6.25	12.50	25.00
WE SING THE BLUES					
❏ Minit LP-0003 [M]		1962	12.50	25.00	50.00
WE WISH YOU A MERRY CHRISTMAS					
❏ Warner Bros. W 1337 [M]		1960	6.25	12.50	25.00
❏ Warner Bros. WS 1337 [S]		1960	7.50	15.00	30.00

Number / Title (A Side/B Side)	Yr	VG	VG+	NM
WE'VE BUILT A JAZZ ALBUM FOR YOU				
☐ Bethlehem BCP-89 [M]	1958	7.50	15.00	30.00
WEST COAST JAZZ, VOL. 2				
☐ Jazztone J-(# unk) [M]	1957	7.50	15.00	30.00
WEST COAST VS. EAST COAST				
☐ MGM E-3390 [M]	1956	7.50	15.00	30.00
WESTERN SWING				
☐ King 876 [M]	1963	17.50	35.00	70.00
WESTERN SWING IN HI-FI				
☐ Decca DL 8730 [M]	1958	10.00	20.00	40.00
WFUN GOOD GUYS				
☐ Roulette R 25273 [M]	1965	5.00	10.00	20.00
WHAT'S NEW? ON CAPITOL STEREO, VOL. 1				
☐ Capitol SN-1 [S]	1959	6.25	12.50	25.00
WHAT'S SHAKIN'				
☐ Elektra EKL-4002 [M]	1966	10.00	20.00	40.00
—Deduct 25 percent if booklet is missing				
☐ Elektra EKS-74002 [S]	1966	12.50	25.00	50.00
—Deduct 25 percent if booklet is missing				
WHEELIN' AND DEALIN'				
☐ Prestige PRLP-7131 [M]	1957	25.00	50.00	100.00
—Reissued as Status 8327; see JOHN COLTRANE.				
WHITE MANSIONS				
☐ A&M SP 6004 [(2)]	1978	5.00	10.00	20.00
WHK GOOD GUYS				
☐ Roulette R 25295 [M]	1965	5.00	10.00	20.00
THE WHO'S WHO OF COUNTRY AND WESTERN MUSIC				
☐ Capitol ST 2538 [S]	1966	5.00	10.00	20.00
☐ Capitol T 2538 [M]	1966	5.00	10.00	20.00
THE WHOLE BURBANK CATALOG				
☐ Warner Bros. PRO 512 [(2)]	1972	5.00	10.00	20.00
—Originals have green labels				
A WHOLE LOT OF BLOWIN'				
☐ Audio Lab AL-1539 [M]	1959	15.00	30.00	60.00
WHOPPERS				
☐ Jubilee JGM-1119 [M]	1960	25.00	50.00	100.00
—Reissue of "Best of Rhythm and Blues," Jubilee 1014				
THE WIDE, WIDE WORLD OF JAZZ				
☐ RCA Victor LPM-1325 [M]	1956	7.50	15.00	30.00
WILD WILDWOOD RECORDED LIVE				
☐ Chancellor CHL-5017 [M]	1960	6.25	12.50	25.00
☐ Chancellor CHLS-5017 [S]	1960	7.50	15.00	30.00
WING LIVELY GUYS				
☐ Roulette R 25307 [M]	1965	5.00	10.00	20.00
WINNER'S CIRCLE				
☐ Bethlehem BCP-6024 [M]	1958	10.00	20.00	40.00
WINNERS ALL! THE DOWN BEAT JAZZ POLL '64				
☐ Verve V-8579 [M]	1964	5.00	10.00	20.00
☐ Verve V6-8579 [S]	1964	6.25	12.50	25.00
WINNERS CIRCLE LIMITED EDITION				
☐ Columbia GB-4 [M]	1959	6.25	12.50	25.00
WINTER WARNERLAND				
☐ Warner Bros. PRO-A-3328 [(2)]	1988	10.00	20.00	40.00
—Promo-only set; Record 1 is red vinyl, Record 2 is green vinyl				
WMAK JET SET-22 WINNERS				
☐ Roulette R 25291 [M]	1965	5.00	10.00	20.00
WOL SOUL BROTHERS				
☐ Roulette R 25337 [M]	1966	5.00	10.00	20.00
—Same LP as "WWIN Astro Jocks"				
THE WOMEN IN JAZZ				
☐ Storyville STLP-916 [M]	1956	12.50	25.00	50.00
WONDERFUL MEMORIES FROM THE FAMILY PRAYER BOOK				
☐ Vee Jay LP-5066 [M]	1964	7.50	15.00	30.00
THE WONDERFUL WORLD OF GOSPEL AND SACRED MUSIC				
☐ Starday SLP-255 [M]	1963	7.50	15.00	30.00

Number / Title (A Side/B Side)	Yr	VG	VG+	NM
WOODSTOCK				
☐ Cotillion SD 3-500 [(3)]	1970	5.00	10.00	20.00
—Pale blue labels				
☐ Cotillion SD 3-500 [(3)]	1977	3.75	7.50	15.00
—Reissue on purplish labels				
☐ Mobile Fidelity 5-200 [(5)]	1985	50.00	100.00	200.00
—Audiophile vinyl				
WOODSTOCK TWO				
☐ Cotillion SD 2-400 [(2)]	1971	5.00	10.00	20.00
THE WORKS				
☐ Warner Bros. PRO 610 [(2)]	1975	6.25	12.50	25.00
A WORLD OF BLUES				
☐ Imperial LP-9210 [M]	1963	7.50	15.00	30.00
☐ Imperial LP-12210 [R]	1963	5.00	10.00	20.00
THE WORLD OF COUNTRY MUSIC				
☐ Capitol NPB-5 [(3)]	1965	7.50	15.00	30.00
WORLD'S GREATEST MUSIC SERIES POP/JAZZ				
☐ Artia-Parliament WGM 2-A [(5)]	196?	10.00	20.00	40.00
—First of two five-record sets				
☐ Artia-Parliament WGM 2-AB [(10)]	196?	25.00	50.00	100.00
—Box set of material from the Roulette label. Also issued as two five-record boxes.				
☐ Artia-Parliament WGM 2-B [(5)]	196?	10.00	20.00	40.00
—Second of two five-record sets				
WRCA PLAYS THE HITS FOR YOUR CUSTOMERS				
☐ RCA Victor DJL1-1785 [DJ]	1976	50.00	100.00	200.00
WWIN ASTRO JOCKS				
☐ Roulette R 25337 [M]	1966	5.00	10.00	20.00
—Same LP as "WOL Soul Brothers"				
YES L.A.				
☐ Dangerhouse EW 79 [PD]	1979	20.00	40.00	80.00
—Includes X, The Germs, etc.; one-sided clear picture disc				
YOU'VE GOT TO HEAR IT TO BELIEVE IT				
☐ Solid State SS-94	1966	5.00	10.00	20.00
THE YOUNG AT BOP				
☐ EmArcy MG-26001 [10]	1954	20.00	40.00	80.00
THE YOUNG ONES OF JAZZ				
☐ EmArcy MG-36085 [M]	1956	10.00	20.00	40.00
YOUR FAVORITE GROUPS AND THEIR GOLDEN GOODIES, VOL. 19				
☐ Roulette R 25248 [M]	1964	5.00	10.00	20.00
YOUR FAVORITE SINGING GROUPS				
☐ Hull 1002 [M]	1962	375.00	750.00	1500.
YOUR INTRODUCTION TO THE SOUND OF THE 'SIXTIES				
☐ Liberty MM-403 [DJ]	1960	7.50	15.00	30.00
—Promo-only release				
YOUR MUSICAL SOUVENIR FROM QSP				
☐ RCA Special Products QSP1-0042	1986	15.00	30.00	60.00
YOUR OLD FAVORITES ON OLD TOWN				
☐ Old Town LP-101 [M]	1959	50.00	100.00	200.00
YOUR SPECIAL MUSICAL SOUVENIR FROM QSP				
☐ RCA Special Products QSP1-0047	1986	15.00	30.00	60.00
YOURS				
☐ Harmony HL 7042 [M]	1957	5.00	10.00	20.00
YULESVILLE				
☐ Warner Bros. PRO-A-2896	1987	6.25	12.50	25.00
—Promo-only on red vinyl				
ZENITH PRESENTS ALL STAR HOOTENANNY				
☐ Columbia Special Products CSP 149 [M]	1963	12.50	25.00	50.00
—With three early Bob Dylan tracks credited to "Bobby Dylan." Also has tracks by Pete Seeger (2), Orriel Smith (2) and The Clancy Brothers with Tommy Makem (3)				
ZENITH PRESENTS HOOTENANNY SPECIAL				
☐ Columbia Special Products CSP 216M [M]	1965	6.25	12.50	25.00
☐ Columbia Special Products CSP 216S [S]	1965	7.50	151.00	30.00
ZIG ZAG FESTIVAL				
☐ Mercury SRD-2-29 [DJ]	1970	6.25	12.50	25.00
ZOO'S NEXT — WMMR MORNING ZOO				
☐ Comedy Spotlight (no #) [M]	1986	5.00	10.00	20.00